2015 *Standard Catalog of* ®
WORLD COINS
2001-Date

9th Edition

George S. Cuhaj, Editor • **Thomas Michael**, Market Analyst • **Harry Miller**, U.S. Market Analyst

Deborah McCue, Database Specialist • **Kay Sanders**, Editorial Assistant

Special Contributors

Thomas Augustsson • **Hans-Henning Goehrum**

Melvyn Kassenoff • **Egon Conti Rossini**

Pabitra K. Saha • **Gerhard Schön** • **Jacek Suchan**

Bullion Value (BV) Market Valuations

Valuations for all platinum, gold, palladium and silver coins of the more common, basically bullion types, or those possessing only modest numismatic premiums are presented in this edition based on market spot prices of:

$1,450 per ounce for **platinum**   **$1,300** per ounce for **gold**

$775 per ounce for **palladium**   **$22.00** per ounce for **silver**

Published by

Krause Publications, a division of F+W Media, Inc.
700 East State Street • Iola, WI 54990-0001
715-445-2214 • 888-457-2873
www.krausebooks.com

To order books or other products call toll-free 1-800-258-0929
or visit us online at www.shopnumismaster.com

ISSN 1935-4339
ISBN-13: 978-1-4402-4040-9
ISBN-10: 1-4402-4040-X

Cover Design by Jana Tappa
Designed by Sandi Carpenter
Edited by George S. Cuhaj

Printed in the United States of America

INTRODUCTION

Welcome to the 9th edition of the 21st Century Standard Catalog of World Coins. The most recent annual version of our ever growing series of comprehensive reference catalogs is designed to meet the needs of those whose interest in coins exceeds the casual jingle of those in your pants pocket or purse. Perhaps you have traveled overseas and still have some coins that came home with you, maybe you read in the news about the Euro circulating commemoratives or issues from recently formed nations, or you are a long-term collector who wants to wade out into the most current of numismatic trends. In all cases, this book is for you.

Arranged in alphabetical order by country and with groupings for political structure, coinage type and denomination this catalog offers an easy-to-follow flow of data. You will find many illustrations, complete listings of metal content, descriptions of the designs and events depicted on the coins as well as date, mint mark varieties and values in multiple grades of preservation. In short, just about all of the information you could want on the most modern coins of the world.

With the information presented in these listings, one can marvel at the ingenuity of today's most inventive world mints, which are striking coins in a variety of shapes, sizes, colors and textures. Enjoy the practicality of coins designed for serious circulation in durable metals. Celebrate the advent of coins made of acrylic materials, those which house precious stones, display selective gold overlays or are pad-printed in colorful designs. All are here in this 21st Century edition.

The accuracy of the information offered in this volume is assured through the assistance of a vast number of contributing coin dealers, collectors, manufacturers and researchers who have lent their knowledge to the compiling of this reference by providing our staff with information on new issues, new dates to existing types, accurate mintages and expanded up-to-date pricing. To them all, we offer a heartfelt "Thank You" for their generosity and dedication to the advancement of our shared field of coin collecting.

Coins are issued throughout the year. We endeavor to keep pace with this worldwide information flow with updates to the online version of the Standard Catalog series, found at www.numismaster.com. There you will be able to see the latest issues, additional images and for a small monthly or annual subscription fee, price updates of your favorite issues. You may also find additional coin books and supplies at www.shopnumismaster.com. Thanks for using our services.

Finally, to you the reader, we extend our wishes that you may enjoy using this catalog as much as we have enjoyed its production. Look it over, put it to good use and please let us know if you have any comments or questions.

Best Wishes,

The Editorial Staff of the
Standard Catalog of World Coins

ACKNOWLEDGMENTS

Many individuals have contributed countless changes, which have been incorporated into the current edition. While all may not be acknowledged, special appreciation is extended to the following who have exhibited a special enthusiasm for this edition.

Dylan Arthur
Esko Ahlroth
Thomas Augustsson
Oksana Bandrivska
Albert Beck
Anton Belcev
Jan Bendix
Richard Benson
Shamik Biswas
Gunta Bluke
Joseph E. Boling
Richard Borek jun.
Al Boulanger
Mark A. Brown
Maruta Brûkle
Mahdi Bseiso
Chris Budesa
John T. Bucek
Adolpho Cayón
Clemente Cayón
Juan Cayón
Fred Colombo
Wilhelm R. Eglseer
Esko Ekman
Andrzej Fischer
Dagmar Flachén

Eugene Freeman
Peter Frei
Arthur Friedburg
Tom Galway
Hans-Henning Goehrum
Flemming Lyngbeck Hansen
David Harrison
Istvan Hegedus
Frans Hellendall
Emmanuel Henry
Jennifer Hird
Teréz Horváth
Serge Huard
Sadhir Humnabadkar
Nelva G. Icaza
Hector Carlos Janson
Alex Kaglyan
Melvyn Kassenoff
Craig Keplinger
Rodolphe Krempp
Alex Lazarovici
Ma Tak Wo
Ranko Mandic
Rajender Maru
Miguel Angel Pratt Mayans
Bernhard H. Mayer

Dimitar Mihov
Juozas Minikevicius
Andy Mirski
Ing. Benjamin M. Mizrachi R.
Paul Montz
Horst-Dieter Müller
Michael G. Nielsen
Bill Noyes
Alberto Paashaus
Frank Passic
Martin Peeters
Marc Pelletier
Kirsten F. Petersen
Andreas Pitsillides
Gastone Polacco
Juri Pschegorlinski
Jordi Puigdemasa
Frank Putrow
Kitty Quan
Yahya Qureshi
Dr. Dennis G. Rainey
Ivan Rakitin
William M. Rosenblum
Egon Conti Rossini
Pabitra K. Saha
Remy Said

Leon Saryan
Erwin Schäffer
Jacco Scheper
Dr. Andreas Schikora
Gerhard Schön
George Schumacher
Alexander Shapiro
Ole Sjoelund
Mira Spijker
Heimo Steriti
Jacek Suchan
Steven Tan
Mehmet Tolga Taner
Rivka Toledano
Amelia Travaglini
Anthony Tumonis
Erik J. Van Loon
Natanya van Niekerk
Neil Vance
Carmen Viciedo
Wakim Wakim
Paul Welz
J. Brix Westergaard
J. Hugh Witherow
Joseph Zaffern

AUCTION HOUSES

Dix-Noonan-Webb
Heritage World Coin Auctions
Fritz Rudolf Künker
Marudhar Arts

MPO Auctions
Münzenhandlung Harald Möller, GmbH
Noble Numismatics, Pty. Ltd.
Stack's, Bowers and Ponterio

Stephen Album Rare Coins
St. James's Auctions
World Wide Coins of California

WORLD MINTS, CENTRAL BANKS AND DISTRIBUTORS

Austrian Mint
Banco de Mexico
Banque Centrale Du
　Luxembourg
Bank du Liban
Black Mountain Coins
Casa de la Moneda de Cuba
Casa da Moeda do Brasil
Central Bank of D.P.R. Korea -
　Kumbyol Trading Corp.
Central Bank of the Russian
　Federation
CIT
Czech National Bank
Downies
East India Company
Educational Coin Company
Faude & Huguenin
Global Coins & Medals Ltd. -

Official Sales Company of
　the Bulgarian Mint
Helvetic Mint
Imprensa Nacional - Casa da
　Moeda, S.A.
Israel Coins & Medals Corp.
Istituto Poligrafico e Zecca
　dello Stato I.p.A.
Jablonex Group - Division of
　Czech Mint
Japan Mint
JVP Investment Coins
Kazakhstan Mint
KOMSCO - South Korea
Latvijas Banka
Lietuvos Bankas
Lithuanian Mint
Magyar Penzvero Zrt.
Mayer's Mint GmbH

MDM
Mennica Polska
Mincovna Kremnica
Mint of Finland, Ltd.
Mint of Norway
Monnaie de Paris
Moscow Mint
National Bank of the Republic
　of Belarus
National Bank of Ukraine
New Zealand Mint
Numiscom
Numistrade Gmbh & Co. kg.
PandaAmerica
Perth Mint
Pobjoy Mint
Real Casa de la Moneda –
　Spain
Romanian Mint

Royal Mint
Royal Australian Mint
Royal Belgian Mint
Royal Canadian Mint
Royal Dutch Mint
Royal Thai Mint
Servei D'Emissions Principat
　D'Andorra
Singapore Mint
South African Mint
Staatliche Munze Berlin
Staatliche Munze Baden-
　Wurttemberg
Talisman Coins
Thailand Treasury Department
Ufficio Filatelico e
　Numismatico - Vatican
United States Mint

COUNTRY INDEX

HOW TO USE THIS CATALOG

This catalog is designed to serve the needs of both the novice and advanced collectors. It provides a comprehensive guide to world coins struck in the 21st century (2001 to present). It is arranged so that persons with a basic knowledge of world history and a casual acquaintance with coin collecting can consult it with confidence and ease. The following explanations summarize the general practices used in preparing the catalog listings. However, because of specialized requirements, which may vary by country and political era within a country, these should not be considered ironclad.

ARRANGEMENT

Countries are arranged alphabetically. Political changes within a country are arranged chronologically. In countries where Rulers are the single most significant political entity, a chronological arrangement by Ruler has been employed. Distinctive sub-geographic regions are listed alphabetically following the country's main listings. A few exceptions to these rules may exist. If a location is in question, please refer to the Country Index.

Diverse coinage types relating to fabrication methods, revaluations and change in denomination systems have been identified, separated and arranged in a logical fashion. Chronological arrangement is employed for most circulating coinage. Monetary system reforms will flow in order of their institution. Special non-circulating types such as Essais, Piedforts, Patterns, Trial Strikes, Mint and Proof sets follow at the end of the individual county's listings.

Within a coinage type, coins will be listed by denomination, from smallest to largest. Numbered types within a denomination will be ordered by their first date of issue.

IDENTIFICATION

The most important step in the identification of a coin is the determination of the nation of origin. This is generally easily accomplished where the country name appears in easy to read characters; if in doubt, use the country index. The coins of Great Britain do not have the county name, just the name and image of the ruler.

The coins of many countries beyond the English-language realm, such as those of French, Italian or Spanish heritage, are also quite easy to identify through reference to their legends, which appear in the national languages based on Western alphabets. In many instances the name is spelled exactly the same in English as in the national language; while in other cases it varies only slightly, like Italia for Italy, Belgique or Belgie for Belgium, Brasil for Brazil and Danmark for Denmark.

This is not always the case, however, as in Soumi for Finland, Norge for Norway, Espana for Spain, Slovensko for Slovakia, Sverige for Sweden and Helvetia for Switzerland. Some other examples include: Empire Cherifin Maroc for Morocco, Estados Unidos Mexicanos for United Mexican States (Mexico) and Etat du Grand Liban - State of Great Lebanon (Lebanon).

With the introduction of the Euro Coinage, some member nations have identified their coin with only country initials, such as BE for Belgium, IR for Italy, RF for France.

Thus it can be seen there are instances in which a little effort in the rudiments of foreign languages can be most helpful. In general, colonial possessions of countries using the Western alphabet are similarly identifiable as they often carry portraits of their current rulers, the familiar lettering, sometimes in combination with a companion designation in the local language.

Collectors have the greatest difficulty with coins that do not bear legends or dates in the Western systems. These include coins bearing Cyrillic lettering attributable to Bulgaria, Russia, the Slavic states and Mongolia; the Greek script peculiar to Greece, Crete and the Ionian Islands; the Amharic characters of Ethiopia; or Hebrew in the case of Israel. Dragons and sunbursts along with the distinctive word characters attribute a coin to the Oriental countries of China, Japan, Korea, Tibet, Viet Nam and their component parts.

The most difficult coins to identify are those bearing only Persian or Arabic script and its derivatives, found on the issues of nations stretching in a wide swath across North Africa and East Asia, from Morocco to Indonesia, and the Indian subcontinent, although the task of identification on the more modern issues of these lands is often eased by the added presence of Western alphabet legends.

A predominant design feature on the coins of Nepal is the trident; while neighboring Tibet features a lotus blossom or lion on many of their issues.

To assist in identification of the more difficult coins, we have assembled the Instant Identifier Charts. They are designed to provide a point of beginning for collectors by allowing them to compare unidentified coins with photographic details from typical issues.

We also suggest reference to the comprehensive Country Index.

DENOMINATIONS

The second basic consideration to be met in the attribution of a coin is the determination of denomination. Since denominations are usually expressed in numeric rather than word form on a coin, this is usually quite easily accomplished on coins from nations which use Western numerals, except in those instances where issues are devoid of any mention of face value, and denomination must be attributed by size, metallic composition or weight. Coins illustrated in this volume are generally illustrated in actual size up to 55mm in diameter. Illustrations of coins larger than 55mm are reduced to 55mm, and the actual size is indicated in the listing of the type.

The sphere of countries stretching from North Africa through the Orient, on which numeric symbols generally unfamiliar to Westerners are employed, provide the collector with a challenge. This is particularly true on nearly all pre-20th Century issues. In many cases as the years progressed, Western-style numerals are often presented in combination with the local numeric systems on these coins.

Determination of a coin's currency system can also be valuable in attributing the issue to its country of origin. The table of Standard International Numeral Systems presents lists of the basic numeric designations found on coins of non-Western origin. Although denomination numerals are generally prominently displayed on coins, it must be remembered that these are general representations of characters, which individual coin designers may have rendered in a wide variety of engraving styles. Where numeric or script denominations designation forms peculiar to a given coin or country apply, such as the script used on some Persian (Iranian) issues, they are so indicated or illustrated in conjunction with the appropriate listings.

DATING

Coin dating is the final basic attribution consideration. Here, the problem can be more difficult because the reading of a coin date is subject not only to the vagaries of numeric styling, but to calendar variations caused by the observance of various religious eras or regal periods from country to country, or even within a country. Here again, with the exception of the sphere from North Africa through the Orient, it will be found that most countries rely on Western date numerals and Christian (AD) era reckoning, although in a few instances, coin dating has been tied to the year of a reign or government. The Vatican, for example dates its coinage according to the year of reign of the current pope, in addition to the Christian-era date.

Countries in the Arabic sphere generally date their coins to the Muslim era (AH), which commenced on July 16, 622 AD (Julian calendar), when the prophet Mohammed fled from Mecca to Medina. As their calendar is reckoned by the lunar year of 354 days, which is about three percent (precisely 2.98%) shorter than the Christian year, a formula is required to convert AH dating to its Western equivalent. To convert an AH date to the approximate AD date, subtract three percent of the AH date (round to the closest whole number) from the AH date and add 622. A chart converting all AH years from 1010 (July 2, 1601) to 1450 (May 25, 2028) may be found elsewhere in this catalog under the name Hejira Date Chart.

The Muslim calendar is not always based on the lunar year (AH), however, causing some confusion, particularly in Afghanistan and Iran, where a calendar based on the solar year (SH) was introduced around 1920. These dates can be converted to AD by simply adding 621. In 1976 the government of Iran implemented a new solar calendar based on the foundation of the Iranian monarchy in 559 BC. The first year observed on the new calendar was 2535 (MS), which commenced March 20, 1976. A reversion to the traditional SH dating standard occurred a few years later.

Several different eras of reckoning, including Christian and Muslim (AH), have been used to date coins of the Indian subcontinent. The two basic systems are the Vikrama Samvat (VS), which dates from Oct. 18, 58 BC, and the Saka era, the origin of which is reckoned from March 3, 78 AD. Dating according to both eras appears on various coins of the area.

Coins of Thailand (Siam) are found dated by three different eras. The most predominant is the Buddhist era (BE), which originated in 543 BC. Next is the Bangkok or Ratanakosindsok (RS) era, dating from 1781 AD; followed by the Chula-Sakarat (CS) era, dating from 638 AD. The latter era originated in Burma and is used on that country's coins.

Other calendars include that of the Ethiopian era (EE), which commenced seven years, eight months after AD dating; and that of the Jewish people, which commenced on Oct. 7, 3761 BC. Korea claims a legendary dating from 2333 BC, which is acknowledged in some of its coin dating. Some coin issues of the Indonesian area carry dates determined by the Javanese Aji Saka era (AS), a calendar of 354 days (100 Javanese years equal 97 Christian or Gregorian calendar years), which can be matched to AD dating by comparing it to AH dating.

The following table indicates the year dating for the various eras, which correspond to 2014 in Christian calendar reckoning, but it must be remembered that there are overlaps between the eras in some instances.

Era	Year
Christian era (AD)	2014
Muslim era (AH)	AH1435
Solar year (SH)	SH1392
Monarchic Solar era (MS)	MS2573
Vikrama Samvat (VS)	VS2071
Saka era (SE)	SE1936
Buddhist era (BE)	BE2557
Bangkok era (RS)	RS233
Chula-Sakarat era (CS)	CS1376
Ethiopian era (EE)	EE2007
Korean era	4347
Javanese Aji Saka era (AS)	AS1947
Fasli era (FE)	FE1424
Jewish era (JE)	JE5774
Roman	MMXIV

Coins of Asian origin - principally Japan, Korea, China, Turkestan and Tibet and some modern gold issues of Turkey - are generally dated to the year of the government, dynasty, reign or cyclic eras, with the dates indicated in Asian characters which usually read from right to left. In recent years, however, some dating has been according to the Christian calendar and in Western numerals. In Japan, Asian character dating was reversed to read from left to right in Showa year 23 (1948 AD).

More detailed guides to less prevalent coin dating systems, which are strictly local in nature, are presented with the appropriate listings.

Some coins carry dates according to both locally observed and Christian eras. This is particularly true in the Arabic world, where the Hejira date may be indicated in Arabic numerals and the Christian date in Western numerals, or both dates in either form.

The date actually carried on a given coin is generally cataloged here in the first column (Date). If this date is in a non-Christian dating system, such as 'AH' (Muslim), the Christian equivalent date will appear in parentheses(), for example AH1336(1917). Dates listed alone in the date column which do not actually appear on a given coin, or dates which are known, but do not appear on the coin, are generally enclosed by parentheses with 'ND' at the left, for example ND(1926).

Timing differentials between some era of reckoning, particularly the 354-day Mohammedan and 365-day Christian years, cause situations whereby coins which carry dates for both eras exist bearing two year dates from one calendar combined with a single date from another.

Counntermarked Coinage is presented with both 'Countermark Date' and 'Host Coin' date for each type. Actual date representation follows the rules outlined above.

For a more detailed information on coin dating see the *Illustrated Coin Dating Guide for the Eastern World* by Albert Galloway, Krause Publications, F+W Media, 2012.

NUMBERING SYSTEM

Some catalog numbers assigned in this volume are based on other established references. This practice has been observed for two reasons: First, when world coins are listed chronologically they are basically self-cataloging; second, there was no need to confuse collectors with totally new numeric designations where appropriate systems already existed. As time progressed we found many of these established systems incomplete and inadequate and many have now been replaced with KM numbers. If numbers have changed, appropriate cross-referencing has been provided.

Some of these references used in this catalog are (Y#) identified assigned by R.S. Yeoman, or slight adaptations thereof, in his *Modern World Coins*, and *Current Coins of the World*.

MINTAGES

Quantities minted of each date are indicated where that information is available; the uncirculated mintages numbers include those inserted into annual uncirculated sets. For combined mintage figures the abbreviation "Inc. Above" means Included Above, while "Inc. Below" means Included Below. "Est." beside a mintage figure indicates the number given is an estimate of the intended mintage or an advertised mintage limit when the final (actual) mintage figure is not known.

MINT AND PRIVY MARKS

The presence of distinctive, but frequently inconspicuously placed, mintmarks indicates the mint of issue for many of the coins listed in this catalog. An appropriate designation in the date listing note the presence, if any, of a mint mark on a particular coin type by incorporating the letter or letters of the mint mark adjoining the date, i.e., 2010D or 2005R.

The presence of mint and/or mintmaster's privy marks on a coin in non-letter form is indicated by incorporating a letter in lower case within parentheses adjoining the date; i.e. 2010(sm). The corresponding mark is illustrated or identified in the introduction of the country.

In countries where privy marks are used, such as Australia, Canada and Isle of Man, a letter in (a) may be employed or a descriptive word may be used to describe it in the listing or in reference to the chart at the beginning of that country's listings.

METALS

Each numbered type listing will contain a description of the coins metallic content. The traditional coinage metals and their symbolic chemical abbreviations are:

Platinum - (PT)	Copper - (Cu)
Gold - (Au)	Silver - (Ag)
Copper-Nickel- (CN)	Lead - (Pb)
Nickel - (Ni)	Zinc - (Zn)
Tin - (Sn)	Bronze - (Ae)
	Aluminum - (Al)

During the 18th and 19th centuries, most of the world's coins were struck of copper or bronze, silver, and gold. Commencing in the early years of the 20th century, however, numerous new coinage metals, primarily non-precious metal alloys, were introduced. Gold has not been widely used for circulation coinages since World War I, although silver remained a popular coinage metal in most parts of the world until after World War II. With the disappearance of silver for circulation coinage, numerous additional compositions were introduced to circulating coinage applications.

Most recent is the development of clad or plated planchets in order to maintain circulation life and extend the life of a set of production dies as used in the production of the copper-nickel clad copper 50 centesimos of Panama or in the latter case to reduce production costs

of the planchets and yet provide a coin quite similar in appearance to its predecessor as in the case of the copper plated zinc core United States 1983 cent.

Modern commemorative coins have employed still more unusual methods such as bimetallic coins, color applications and precious metal or gem inlays.

OFF-METAL STRIKES

Off-metal strikes previously designated by "OMS" which also included the wide range of error coinage struck in other than their officially authorized compositions have been incorporated into Pattern listings along with special issues, which were struck for presentation or other reasons.

PRECIOUS METAL WEIGHTS

Listings of weight, fineness and actual silver (ASW), gold (AGW), platinum or palladium (APW) content of most machine-struck silver, gold, platinum and palladium coins are provided in this edition. This information will be found at the start of a type description, followed by other information related to the coin.

The ASW, AGW and APW figures were determined by multiplying the gross weight of a given coin by its officially known standard or tested fineness and converting the resulting gram or grain weight into troy ounces, rounded to the nearest hundredth of an ounce. A silver coin with a 24.25-gram weight and .875 fineness for example, would have a fine weight of approximately 21.22 grams, or a .6822 ASW, a factor that can be used to accurately determine the intrinsic value for multiple examples.

The ASW, AGW or APW figure can be multiplied by the spot price of each precious metal to determine the current intrinsic value of any coin accompanied by these designations.

Coin weights are indicated in grams (abbreviated "g") along with fineness where the information is of value in differentiating between types. These weights are based on 31.103 grams per troy (scientific) ounce, as opposed to the avoirdupois (commercial) standard of 28.35 grams. Actual coin weights are generally shown in hundredths of a gram; i.e., 0.500 SILVER 2.92g.

WEIGHTS AND FINENESSES

As the silver and gold bullion markets have advanced and declined sharply over the years, the fineness and total precious metal content of coins has become especially significant where bullion coins - issues which trade on the basis of their intrinsic metallic content rather than numismatic value - are concerned. In many instances, such issues have become worth more in bullion form than their nominal collector values or denominations indicate.

Establishing the weight of a coin can also be valuable for determining its denomination. Actual weight is also necessary to ascertain the specific gravity of the coin's metallic content, an important factor in determining authenticity.

TROY WEIGHT STANDARDS

24 Grains = 1 Pennyweight
480 Grains = 1 Ounce
31.103 Grams = 1 Ounce

UNIFORM WEIGHTS

15.432 Grains = 1 Gram
0.0648 Gram = 1 Grain

AVOIRDUPOIS STANDARDS

27-11/32 Grains = 11 Dram
437-1/2 Grains = 1 Ounce
28.350 Grams = 1 Ounce

BULLION VALUE

The simplest method for determining the bullion value of a precious metal coin is to multiply the actual precious metal weight by the current spot price for that metal. Using the example above, a silver coin with a .6822 actual silver weight (ASW) would have an intrinsic value of $12.25 when the spot price of silver is $17.95. If the spot price of silver would increase to $22.50, that same coins' intrinsic value would rise to $15.35.

PHOTOGRAPHS

To assist the reader in coin identification, every effort has been made to use actual size images of each type listed. When available both sides are illustrated. When the coin has a diameter of 39mm or larger, usually the side required for identification of the type is illustrated. All coins up to 55mm are illustrated actual size, to the nearest 1/2mm up to 25mm, and to the nearest 1mm thereafter. Coins larger than 55mm diameter are illustrated in reduced size, with the actual size noted in the descriptive text of the listing. Where slight change in size is important to coin type identification, actual millimeter measurements are stated in the listing.

TRADE COINS

From approximately 1750-1940, a number of nations, particularly European colonial powers and commercial traders, minted trade coins to facilitate commerce with the local populace of Africa, the Arab countries, the Indian subcontinent, Southeast Asia and the Far East. Such coins generally circulated at a value based on the weight and fineness of their silver or gold content, rather than their stated denomination. Examples include the sovereigns of Great Britain and the gold ducat issues of Austria, Hungary and the Netherlands. These coins will be segregated into a Trade coinage section near the end of the domestic issues.

VALUATIONS

Values quoted in this catalog represent the current retail market and are compiled from recommendations provided and verified through various source documents and specialized consultants. It should be stressed, however, that this book is intended to serve only as an aid for evaluating coins, actual market conditions are constantly changing and additional influences, such as particularly strong local demand for certain coin series, fluctuation of international exchange rates, changes in spot price of precious metals and worldwide collecting patterns must also be considered. Publication of this catalog is not intended as a solicitation by the publisher, editors or contributors to buy or sell the coins listed at the prices indicated.

All valuations are stated in U.S. dollars, based on careful assessment of the varied international collector markets. Valuations for coins priced below $100.00 are generally stated in full amounts, i.e. 37.50 or 95.00, while valuations at or above that $100.00 are rounded off in even dollars - i.e. $125.00 is expressed 125. A comma is added to indicate thousands of dollars in value (12,500.)

A dash (-) to the left of given values in a specific value field indicates a lack of a collectible premium. A coin in these lower grades would be worth only its face or intrinsic value. A dash (-) to the right of given values may mean very few or no examples of that grade exist for the type.

BV in a price location stands for Bullion Value, which can be determined by multiplying the actual precious metal weight by the current spot metal price.

For the convenience of overseas collectors and for U.S. collectors doing business with overseas dealers, the exchange rate for current currencies is presented in the Foreign Exchange Table.

MEDALLIC ISSUES

Medallic issues are similar to coin-type issues and can generally be identified as commemoratives produced to the country's established coinage standards but without the usual indicator of denomination. These pieces sometimes feature designs adapted from the country's regular issue or commemorative coinage, and occasionally have been issued in conjunction with related coinage issues.

Medallic issues, though bearing these similarities to coinage issues, are not coins and therefore are not listed in this catalog but can be found in the companion catalog *Unusual World Coins*. These Medallic issues are also listed on our searchable web catalog at www.NumisMaster.com.

RESTRIKES, COUNTERFEITS

Deceptive restrike and counterfeit (both contemporary and modern) examples exist of some coin issues. Where possible, the existence of official restrikes is noted. Warnings are also incorporated in instances where particularly deceptive counterfeits are known to exist. If you are uncertain about the authenticity of a coin held in your collection, or being offered for sale, one should take the precaution of having it authenticated by one of the recognized third party grading services. Their services are reasonably priced, and their products are widely accepted by collectors and dealers alike.

NON-CIRCULATING LEGAL TENDER COINS

Coins of non-circulating legal tender (NCLT) origin are individually listed and integrated by denomination into the regular listings for each country, excepting where large, established serialized categories exist. These coins fall outside the customary definitions of coin-of-the-realm issues, but where created and sold by, or under authorization of, agencies of sovereign governments expressly for collectors. These are primarily individual coins and sets of a commemorative nature, marketed at prices substantially in excess of both face and intrinsic value, and usually do not have counterparts released for circulation. If you are only interested in coins which circulate in commerce we offer a catalog titled *Collecting World Coins*, which lists world issues since 1901. The current edition is available at www.shopnumismaster.com.

EDGE VARIETIES

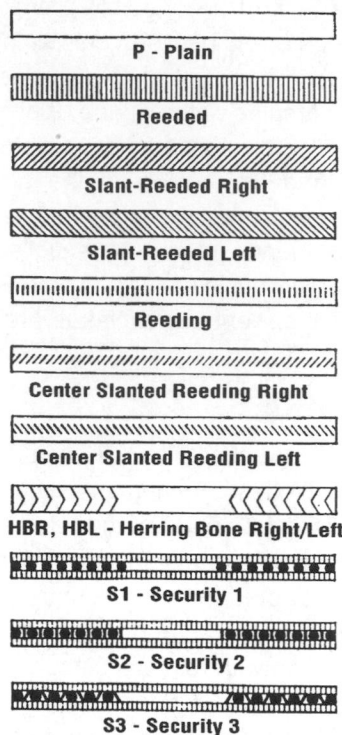

P - Plain

Reeded

Slant-Reeded Right

Slant-Reeded Left

Reeding

Center Slanted Reeding Right

Center Slanted Reeding Left

HBR, HBL - Herring Bone Right/Left

S1 - Security 1

S2 - Security 2

S3 - Security 3

NEW ISSUES

All coins dated from 2001 to present that have been physically observed by our staff or confirmed by our reliable sources have been incorporated into this edition. Exceptions exist in some countries where current date coin production lags far behind or information on current issues is less accessible. Very current listings are always available first on our web catalog at www.NumisMaster.com.

SETS

Listings in this catalog for specimen, proof and mint sets are for official, government-produced sets. In many instances privately packaged sets also exist, these are not listed.

Mint Sets / Fleur de Coin Sets: Specially prepared by worldwide mints to provide banks, collectors and government dignitaries with examples of current coinage. These coins are often subjected to rigorous inspection to insure that top quality specimens of selected business strikes are provided. One of the most popular mint set is that given out by the monarch of Great Britain each year on Maundy Thursday. This set contains four special coins in denominations of 1, 2, 3 and 4 pence, struck in silver and contained in a little pouch. They have been given away in a special ceremony for the poor for more than two centuries.

The Paris Mint introduced polyvinyl plastic cases packed within a cardboard box for homeland and colonial Fleur de Coin sets of the 1960s. British colonial sets were issued in velvet-lined metal cases similar to those used for proof sets. For its client nations, the Franklin Mint introduced a sealed composition of cardboard and specially molded hard clear plastic protective container inserted in a soft plastic wallet. Discovery that soft polyvinyl packaging has proved hazardous to coins has resulted in a change to the use of hard, inert plastics for virtually all mint sets.

Some of the highest quality mint sets ever produced were those struck by the Franklin Mint during 1972-74. In many cases matte finish dies were used to strike a polished proof planchet. Later on, from 1975, sets contained highly polished, glassy-looking coins (similar to those struck by the Bombay Mint) for collectors over a period of twelve years.

Specimen Sets: Forerunners of today's proof sets. In most cases the coins were specially struck, perhaps even double struck, to produce a very soft or matte finish on the effigies and fields, along with high, sharp, "wire" rims. The finish is rather dull to the naked eye.

The original purpose of these sets was to provide VIPs, monarchs and mintmasters around the world with samples of the highest quality workmanship of a particular mint. These were usually housed in elaborate velvet-lined leather and metal cases.

Proof-like Sets are relatively new to the field of numismatics. During the mid-1950s the Royal Canadian Mint furnished the hobby with specially selected early business strike coins that exhibited some qualities similar to proof coinage. However, the "proof-like" fields are generally flawed and the edges are rounded. These pieces are not double struck. These are commonly encountered in cardboard holders, later in soft plastic or pliofilm packaging. Of late, the Royal Canadian Mint packages such sets in rigid plastic cases.

Many worldwide officially issued proof sets would in reality fall into this category upon careful examination of the quality of the coin's finish.

Another term encountered in this category is "Special Select," used to describe the crowns of the Union of South Africa and 100-schilling coins produced for collectors in the late 1970s by the Austrian Mint.

Proof Sets: This is undoubtedly among the most misused terms in the hobby, not only by collectors and dealers, but also by many of the world mints.

A true proof set must be comprised of coins which are at least double-struck on specially prepared polished planchets and struck using dies (which are also often polished) of the highest quality under greater than normal pressure. Modern-day proof quality coins often consist of frosted portraits or design elements surrounded by absolute mirror-like fields. A reverse-proof has frosted portraits or design elements surrounded by frosted fields.

Listings for proof sets in this catalog are for officially issued proof sets so designated by the issuing authority, and depending on country of origin, may or may not possess what are considered modern proof quality standards.

It is necessary for collectors to acquire the knowledge to allow them to differentiate true proof sets from would-be proof sets and proof-like sets which are encountered.

CONDITIONS / GRADING

Wherever possible, coin valuations are presented in five grades of preservation. In this catalog we have adopted the use of the 70-point numerical grading system employed in the United States. For modern commemoratives, which do not circulate, only Mint State prices are sufficient. Proof issues are indicated by the prefix PF-60, PF-63 or PF-65 next to the valuation following the mintage. Coins which are proof in quality but not yet priced, have the notation of Proof next to the date and no price information. For very recent circulating coins and coins of limited value only one, two or three grade values are presented with lower grade fields containing a dash (-) value indicating no collector premium above face or intrinsic value.

BV indicates bullion value, which can be determined by multiplying the actual precious metal value by current spot metal prices. BV+10% indicate a coin's value at bullion value plus an additional 10%.

There are almost no grading guides for world coins. What follows is an attempt to help bridge that gap until a detailed, illustrated guide becomes available.

In grading world coins, there are two elements to look for: 1) Overall wear, and 2) loss of design details, such as strands of hair, feathers on eagles, design elements on the coat-of-arms, etc.

The age, rarity or type of a coin should not be a consideration in grading.

Grade each coin by the weaker of the two sides. This method appears to give results most nearly consistent with the American Numismatic Association standards for U.S. coins. Split grades, i.e., F/VF for obverse and reverse, respectively, are normally no more than one grade apart. If the two sides are more than one grade apart, the series of coins probably wears differently on each side and should then be graded by the weaker side alone.

Grade a coin by the amount of overall wear and loss of design detail evident on each side of the coin. On coins with a moderately small design element (which is prone to early wear) grade by that design alone. For example, the 5-ore (KM#554) of Sweden has a crown above the monogram on which the beads on the arches show wear most clearly. So, grade by the crown alone.

MS-65 (Gem Brilliant Uncirculated, GemBU) Is the condition of a coin which is often an early sharp strike from a new pair of dies. No bag marks, sharp rims and bold detail are characteristic of this grade.

For **MS-63 (Choice Brilliant Uncirculated, BU)** grade there will be no visible signs of wear or handling, even under a 10-power loop. Full mint luster will be present. Ideally no bags marks will be evident.

For **MS-60 (Uncirculated, Unc.)** grade there will be no visible signs of wear or handling, even under a 10-power loop. Bag marks may be present.

For **AU-50 (Almost Uncirculated, AU)** all details will be visible. There will be the slightest of wear only on the highest point of the coin. There will often be half or more of the original mint luster present.

On the **XF-40 (Extremely Fine, XF or EF)** coin, there will be about 95% of the original detail visible. Or, on a coin with a design with no inner detail to wear down, there will be a light wear over nearly all the coin. If a small design is used as the grading area, about 90% of the original detail will be visible. This latter rule stems from the logic that a smaller amount of detail needs to be present because a small area is being used to grade the whole coin.

The **VF-20 (Very Fine, VF)** coin will have about 75% of the original detail visible. Or, on a coin with no inner detail, there will be moderate wear over the entire coin. Corners of letters and numbers may be weak. A small grading area will have about 66% of the original detail.

For **F-12 (Fine, F)**, there will be about 50% of the original detail visible. Or, on a coin with no inner detail, there will be fairly heavy wear over all of the coin. Sides of letters will be weak. A coin which has not been cleaned will often appear as dirty or dull. A small amount of the grading area will have just about 50% of the original detail.

On the **VG-8 (Very Good, VG)** coin, there will be about 25% of the original detail visible. There will be heavy wear on all of the coin.

The **G-4 (Good, G)** coin's design will be clearly outlined but with substantial wear. Some of the larger detail may be visible. The rim may have a few weak spots of wear.

Strong or weak strikes, partially weak strikes, damage, corrosion, attractive or unattractive toning, rim bumps, dipping or cleaning should be described along with the above grades. These factors affect the quality of the coin just as do wear and loss of detail, but are easier to describe.

As the proof designation is a method of manufacture and not a grade, the price listings of PF-60, PF-63 and PF-65 are employed in these listings. At these levels, it is often the quality of strike and not actual wear, which is judged. In order to buy and sell proof coins at these designated grades, normally third-party grading and encapsulation is required. As the 21st century dawned, mints and distributors have employed special clean-room manufacturing processes which have virtually eliminated problems and imperfections in proof coins. The modern low mintage proof coin is often only available in sealed multi-coin sets, or encased within individual plastic holders within a larger fitted display case.

Coin Alignment

Medal Alignment

COIN vs MEDAL ALIGNMENT

Some coins are struck with obverse and reverse aligned at a rotation of 180° from each other. When a coin is held for vertical viewing with the obverse design aligned upright and the index finger and thumb at the top and bottom, upon rotation from left to right for viewing the reverse, the latter will be upside down. Such alignment is called "coin rotation." Other coins are struck with the obverse and reverse designs mated on an alignment of zero or 360°. If such an example is held and rotated as described, the reverse will appear upright. This is the alignment, which is generally observed in the striking of medals, and for that reason coins produced in this manner are considered struck in "medal rotation". In some instances, often through error, certain coin issues have been struck to both alignment standards, creating interesting collectible varieties, which will be found noted in some listings. In addition, some countries are now producing coins with other designated obverse to reverse alignments which are considered standard for this type.

STANDARD INTERNATIONAL GRADING TERMINOLOGY AND ABBREVIATIONS

U.S. and ENGLISH SPEAKING LANDS	UNCIRCULATED	EXTREMELY FINE	VERY FINE	FINE	VERY GOOD	GOOD	POOR
Abbreviation	UNC	EF or XF	VF	FF	VG	G	PR
BRAZIL	(1) DW	(3) S	(5) MBC	(7) BC	(8)	(9) R	UTGeG
DENMARK	O	O1	1+	1	1+	2	3
FINLAND	0	01	1+	1	1?	2	3
FRANCE	NEUF	SUP	TTB or TB	TB or TB	B	TBC	BC
GERMANY	KFR	II / VZGL	III / SS	IV / S	V / S.g.E.	VI / G.e.	G.e.s.
ITALY	FdS	SPL	BB	MB	B	M	—
JAPAN	未 使 用	極美品	美 品	並品	—	—	—
NETHERLANDS	FDC	Pr.	Z.F.	Fr.	Z.g.	G	—
NORWAY	0	01	1+	1	1+	2	3
PORTUGAL	Novo	Soberbo	Muito bo	—	—	—	—
SPAIN	Lujo	SC, IC or EBC	MBC	BC	—	RC	MC
SWEDEN	0	01	1+	1	1?	2	—

BRAZIL

FE	— Flor de Estampa
S	— Soberba
MBC	— Muito Bem Conservada
BC	— Bem Conservada
R	— Regular
UTGeG	— Um Tanto Gasto e Gasto

DENMARK

O	— Uncirkuleret
01	— Meget Paent Eksemplar
1+	— Paent Eksemplar
1	— Acceptabelt Eksemplar
1	—Noget Slidt Eksemplar
2	— Darlight Eksemplar
3	— Meget Darlight Eskemplar

FINLAND

00	— Kiiltolyönti
0	— Lyöntiveres
01	— Erittäin Hyvä
1+	— Hyvä
1?	— Heikko
2	— Huono

FRANCE

NEUF	— New
FDC	— Fleur De Coin
SPL	— Splendide
SUP	— Superbe
TTB	— Très Très Beau
TB	— Très Beau
B	— Beau
TBC	— Tres Bien Conserve
BC	— Bien Conserve

GERMANY

VZGL	— Vorzüglich
SS	— Sehr schön
S	— Schön
S.g.E.	— Sehr gut erhalten
G.e.	— Gut erhalten
G.e.S.	— Gering erhalten Schlecht

ITALY

Fds	— Fior di Stampa
SPL	— Splendid
BB	— Bellissimo
MB	— Molto Bello
B	— Bello
M	— Mediocre

JAPAN

未 使 用	— Mishiyo
極美品	— Goku Bihin
美 品	— Bihin
並品	— Futuhin

NETHERLANDS

Pr.	— Prachtig
Z.F.	— Zeer Fraai
Fr.	— Fraai
Z.g.	— Zeer Goed
G	— Goed

NORWAY

0	— Usirkuleret eks
01	— Meget pent eks
1+	— Pent eks
1	— Fullgodt eks
1-	— Ikke Fullgodt eks
2	— Darlig eks

ROMANIA

NC	— Necirculata (UNC)
FF	— Foarte Frumoasa (VF)
F	— Frumoasa (F)
FBC	— Foarte Bine Conservata (VG)
BC	— Bine Conservata (G)
M	— Mediocru Conservata (POOR)

SPAIN

EBC	— Extraordinariamente Bien Conservada
SC	— Sin Circular
IC	— Incirculante
MBC	— Muy Bien Conservada
BC	— Bien Conservada
RC	— Regular Conservada
MC	— Mala Conservada

SWEDEN

0	— Ocirkulerat
01	— Mycket Vackert
1+	— Vackert
1	— Fullgott
1?	— Ej Fullgott
2	— Dalight

STANDARD INTERNATIONAL NUMERAL SYSTEMS

Prepared especially for the *Standard Catalog of World Coins©* 2014 by Krause Publications

Western	0	½	1	2	3	4	5	6	7	8	9	10	50	100	500	1000
Roman			I	II	III	IV	V	VI	VII	VIII	IX	X	L	C	D	M
Arabic-Turkish	٠	١/٢	١	٢	٣	٤	٥	٦	٧	٨	٩	١٠	٥٠	١٠٠	٥٠٠	١٠٠٠
Malay-Persian	٠	١/٢	١	٢	۳	۴	۵	۶ or ۶	۷	۸	۹	۱۰	۵۰	۱۰۰	۵۰۰	۱۰۰۰
Eastern Arabic	٥	½	١	٢	٣	٤	٥	٦	٧	٩	٩	١٠	٤١٠	١٠٠	٤١٠٠	١٠٠٠
Hyderabad Arabic	٥	١/٢	١	٢	٣	٤	٥	٦	٧	٨	٩	١٠	٥٠	١٠٠	٥٠٠	١٠٠٠
Indian (Sanskrit)	०	½	१	२	३	४	५	६	७	८	९	१०	५०	१००	५००	१०००
Assamese	০	d/২	১	২	৩	৪	৫	৬	৭	৮	৯	১০	৫০	১০০	৫০০	১০০০
Bengali	০	১/২	১	২	৩	৪	৫	৬	৭	৮	৯	১০	৫০	১০০	৫০০	১০০০
Gujarati	૦	૧/૨	૧	૨	૩	૪	૫	૬	૭	૮	૯	૧૦	૫૦	૧૦૦	૫૦૦	૧૦૦૦
Kutch	૦	½	૧	૨	૩	૪	૫	૬	૭	૮	૯	૧૦	૪૦	૧૦૦	૪૦૦	૧૦૦૦
Devavnagri	०	½	१	२	३	४	५	६ or ६	७	८	८ or ८	१०	५०	१००	५००	१०००
Nepalese	०	½	१	२	३	४	५	६	७	८	९	१०	५०	१००	५००	१०००
Tibetan	༠	½	༡	༢	༣	༤	༥	༦	༧	༨	༩	༡༠	༥༠	༡༠༠	༥༠༠	༡༠༠༠
Mongolian	᠐	½	᠑	᠒	᠓	᠔	᠕	᠖	᠗	᠘	᠙	᠑᠐	᠕᠐	᠑᠐᠐	᠕᠐᠐	᠑᠐᠐᠐
Burmese	၀	½	၁	၂	၃	၄	၅	၆	၇	၈	၉	၁၀	၅၀	၁၀၀	၅၀၀	၁၀၀၀
Thai-Lao	๐	½	๑	๒	๓	๔	๕	๖	๗	๘	๙	๑๐	๕๐	๑๐๐	๕๐๐	๑๐๐๐
Lao-Laotian	໐		໑	ໂ	໓	໔	໕	໖	໗	໘	໙	໑໐				
Javanese	꧐		꧑	꧒	꧓	꧔	꧕	꧖	꧗	꧘	꧙	꧑꧐	꧕꧐	꧑꧐꧐	꧕꧐꧐	꧑꧐꧐꧐
Ordinary Chinese Japanese-Korean	零	半	一	二	三	四	五	六	七	八	九	十	十五	百	百五	千
Official Chinese			壹	貳	參	肆	伍	陸	柒	捌	玖	拾	拾伍	佰	佰伍	仟
Commercial Chinese			〡	〢	〣	〤	〥	〦	〧	〨	〩	十	〥十	〡百	〥百	〡千
Korean		반	일	이	삼	사	오	육	칠	팔	구	십	오십	백	오백	천
Georgian			ა	ბ	გ	დ	ე	ვ	ზ	ჱ	თ	ი	ნ	რ	ჴ	ჰ
Georgian			[11]ია	[20]კ	[30]ლ	[40]მ	[60]ჲ	[70]ო	[80]პ	[90]ჟ	[200]ს	[300]ტ	[400]ჳ	[600]ჯ	[700]ჶ	[800]ჷ
Ethiopian		◆	፩	፪	፫	፬	፭	፮	፯	፰	፱	፲	፶	፻	፭፻	፲፻
Ethiopian				[20]፳	[30]፴	[40]፵		[60]፷	[70]፸	[80]፹	[90]፺					
Hebrew			א	ב	ג	ד	ה	ו	ז	ח	ט	י	נ	ק	קת	תת
Hebrew				[20]כ	[30]ל	[40]מ		[60]ס	[70]ע	[80]פ	[90]צ	[200]ר	[300]ש	[400]ת	[700]תש	[800]תת
Greek			Α	Β	Γ	Δ	Ε	Ϛ	Ζ	Η	Θ	Ι	Ν	Ρ	Φ	͵Α
Greek			[20]Κ	[30]Λ	[40]Μ	[60]Ξ	[70]Ο	[80]Π				[200]Σ	[300]Τ	[400]Υ	[600]Χ	[800]Ω

DENOMINATION INDEX

Afghani - Afghanistan
Agorot - Israel
Angel - Isle of Man
Ariary - Madagascar
Asarphi - Nepal
Avo - Macau
Azadi - Iran
Baisa - Oman
Balboa - Panama
Ban - Moldova, Romania
Bhat - Thailand
Birr - Ethiopia
Bolivano - Bolivia
Bututs - Gambia
Cedi - Ghana
Cent - Aruba, Australia, Bahamas, Barbados, Belize, Bermuda, Canada, Cayman Islands, Cook Islands, Cyprus, East Caribbean States, Ethiopia, Fiji, Jamaica, Kenya, Kiribati, Liberia, Malta, Mauritius, Namibia, Netherlands, Netherlands Antilles, New Zealand, Niue, Pitcairn Islands, Seychelles, Singapore, Solomon Islands, South Africa, Sri Lanka, Suriname, Swaziland, Trinidad & Tobago
Centavo - Argentina, Bolivia, Brazil, Cuba ,East Timor, Ecuador, Guatemala, Honduras, Mexico, Mozambique, Nicaragua
Centesimo - Panama
Centim - Andorra
Centime - Belgium, Congo Democratic Republic, France, Morocco
Centimos - Paraguay, Peru
Centu - Lithuania
Chetrum - Bhutan
Chon - North Korea
Colon - Costa Rica
Cordoba - Nicaragua
Crown - Falkland Islands, Gibraltar, Isle of Man, Tristan da Cunha, Gough Island, Stoltenhoff Island
Dalasi - Gambia
Denar - Macedonia
Dinar - Algeria, Iran, Iraq, Jordan, Libya, Serbia, Sudan, Tunisia
Diner - Andorra
Diram - Tajikistan
Dirham - Libya, Morocco, Qatar, United Arab Emirates
Dollar - Australia, Bahamas, Barbados, Belize, Bermuda, British Virgin Islands, Brunei, Canada, Cayman Islands, Cook Islands, Creek Nation, East Caribbean States, Fiji, Guyana, Hong Kong, Jamaica, Kiribati, Liberia, Namibia, Nauru, New Zealand, Niue, Palau, Pitcairn Islands, Shawnee Tribal Nation, Sierra Leone, Singapore, Solomon Islands, Suriname, Tokelau, Trinidad & Tobago
Dram - Armenia, Nagorno-Karabakh, Tajikistan
Ducat - Netherlands

Emalangeni - Swaziland
Escudo - Cape Verde, Portugal
Euro - Austria, Belgium, Cyprus, Estonia, Finland, France, Germany, Greece, Ireland, Italy, Latvia, Luxembourg, Malta, Monaco, Netherlands, Portugal, San Marino, Slovakia, Slovenia, Spain
Fen - China
Feninga - Bosnia-Herzegovina
Fil - Bahrain, Kuwait, United Arab Emirates
Florin - Aruba
Forint - Hungary
Franc - Belgium, Burundi, Central African States, Chad, Comoros, Congo Republic, Congo Democratic Republic, Djibouti, France, French Polynesia, Gabon, Guinea, Madagascar, New Caledonia, Rwanda, Switzerland, Togo, Benin, Cameroon, Ivory Coast, Niger
Frank - Belgium
Franken - Liechtenstein
Gourde - Haiti
Gram - Mexico
Groschen - Austria
Grosz - Poland
Guarani - Paraguay
Gulden - Netherlands, Netherlands Antilles
Halala - Saudi Arabia
Haleru - Czech Republic
Halierov - Slovakia
Hryvnia - Ukraine
Jiao - China
Kilo - Mexico
Kina - Papua New Guinea
Kip - Lao
Kobo - Nigeria
Konvertible Marka - Bosnia-Herzegovina
Kopek - Russia
Kopiyka - Ukraine
Korun - Slovakia
Koruna - Czech Republic
Krona - Iceland
Krone - Denmark, Norway
Kronor - Sweden
Kroon - Estonia
Krugerrand - South Africa
Kuna - Croatia
Kune - Croatia
Kurush - Turkey
Kwacha - Malawi
Kwanza - Angola
Laari - Maldive Islands
Lari - Georgia
Lats - Latvia
Lei - Moldova, Romania
Lek - Albania

Lempiras - Honduras
Leones - Sierra Leone
Leu - Romania
Leva - Bulgaria
Licente - Lesotho
Lilangeni - Swaziland
Lipa - Croatia
Lira - Italy, Malta, Turkey
Lire - San Marino
Lita - Lithuania
Livre - Lebanon
Loti - Lesotho
Luma - Nagorno-Karabakh
Maloti - Lesotho
Mana - Azerbaijan
Mark - Germany
Markka - Finland
Meticais - Mozambique
Mil - Malta
Millim - Tunisia
Naira - Nigeria
New Kurus - Turkey
New Lira - Turkey
New Sheqel - Israel
Ngultrum - Bhutan
Noble - Isle of Man
Nuevo Sol - Peru
Omani Rial - Oman
Onza - Mexico
Ore - Denmark, Norway, Sweden
Ouguiya - Mauritania
Pa'anga - Tonga
Paisa - Nepal
Paise - India
Pataca - Macau
Pence - Alderney, Ascension Island, Cook Islands,
   Falkland Islands, Gibraltar, Great Britain, Guernsey,
   Isle of Man, Jersey, Saint Helena, Saint Helena
   & Ascension, Tristan da Cunha, Gough Island,
   Stoltenhoff Island
Penni - Finland
Penny - Falkland Islands, Gibraltar, Great Britain,
   Guernsey, Isle of Man, Jersey, Tristan da Cunha,
   Gough Island, Stoltenhoff Island
Peseta - Saharawi Arab D.R., Spain
Pesewa - Ghana
Peso - Argentina, Chile, Colombia, Cuba, Dominican
   Republic, Mexico
Pfennig - Germany
Piastre - Egypt, Sudan
Piso - Philippines
Poisha - Bangladesh
Pound - Alderney, Ascension Island, British Antarctic
   Territory, British Indian Ocean Territory, Cyprus, Egypt,
   Falkland Islands, Gibraltar, Great Britain, Guernsey,
   Isle of Man, Jersey, Saint Helena & Ascension, South

Georgia & the South Sandwich Islands, Sudan, Syria,
   Tristan da Cunha
Pula - Botswana
Qapik - Azerbaijan
Qirsh - Jordan
Quetzal - Guatemala
Rand - South Africa
Rappen - Switzerland
Reais - Brazil
Real - Brazil
Rial - Iran
Riel - Cambodia
Ringgit - Malaysia
Riyal - Qatar
Rouble - Belarus, Russia
Royal - Gibraltar
Rublei - Transnistria
Rufiyaa - Maldive Islands
Rupee - India, Mauritius, Nepal, Pakistan, Seychelles,
   Sri Lanka
Rupiah - Indonesia
Santimat - Morocco
Santims - Latvia
Satang - Thailand
Scellin - Somalia
Schilling - Austria
Scudo - San Marino
Sen - Brunei, Malaysia
Sene - Samoa
Seniti - Tonga
Sent - Estonia
Sentimo - Philippines
Sertum - Bhutan
Shilingi - Tanzania
Shilling - Kenya, Somalia, Somaliland, Uganda
Som - Kyrgyzstan
Somoni - Tajikistan
Sovereign - Gibraltar, Great Britain
Stotinka - Bulgaria
Stotinov - Slovenia
Sucre - Ecuador
Taka - Bangladesh
Tala - Samoa, Tokelau
Tambala - Malawi
Tenge - Kazakhstan
Thebe - Botswana
Thetri - Georgia
Tiyin - Kyrgyzstan
Toea - Papua New Guinea
Tolar - Slovenia
Tugrik - Mongolia
Won - North Korea, South Korea
Yen - Japan
Yuan - China, Taiwan
Zlote - Poland
Zlotych - Poland

HEJIRA DATE CONVERSION CHART

HEJIRA (Hijira, Hegira), the name of the Muslim era (A.H. = Anno Hegirae) dates back to the Christian year 622 when Mohammed "fled" from Mecca, escaping to Medina to avoid persecution from the Koreish tribemen. Based on a lunar year the Muslim year is 11 days shorter.

*=Leap Year (Christian Calendar)

AH Hejira	AD Christian Date
1010	1601, July 2
1011	1602, June 21
1012	1603, June 11
1013	1604, May 30
1014	1605, May 19
1015	1606, May 9
1016	1607, April 28
1017	1608, April 17
1018	1609, April 6
1019	1610, March 26
1020	1611, March 16
1021	1612, March 4
1022	1613, February 21
1023	1614, February 11
1024	1615, January 31
1025	1616, January 20
1026	1617, January 9
1027	1617, December 29
1028	1618, December 19
1029	1619, December 8
1030	1620, November 26
1031	1621, November 16
1032	1622, November 5
1033	1623, October 25
1034	1624, October 14
1035	1625, October 3
1036	1626, September 22
1037	1627, September 12
1038	1628, August 31
1039	1629, August 21
1040	1630, August 10
1041	1631, July 30
1042	1632, July 19
1043	1633, July 8
1044	1634, June 27
1045	1635, June 17
1046	1636, June 5
1047	1637, May 26
1048	1638, May 15
1049	1639, May 4
1050	1640, April 23
1051	1641, April 12
1052	1642, April 1
1053	1643, March 22
1054	1644, March 10
1055	1645, February 27
1056	1646, February 17
1057	1647, February 6
1058	1648, January 27
1059	1649, January 15
1060	1650, January 4
1061	1650, December 25
1062	1651, December 14
1063	1652, December 2
1064	1653, November 22
1065	1654, November 11
1066	1655, October 31
1067	1656, October 20
1068	1657, October 9
1069	1658, September 29
1070	1659, September 18
1071	1660, September 6
1072	1661, August 27
1073	1662, August 16
1074	1663, August 5
1075	1664, July 25
1076	1665, July 14
1077	1666, July 4
1078	1667, June 23
1079	1668, June 11
1080	1669, June 1
1081	1670, May 21
1082	1671, May 10
1083	1672, April 29
1084	1673, April 18
1085	1674, April 7
1086	1675, March 28
1087	1676, March 16*

AH Hejira	AD Christian Date
1088	1677, March 6
1089	1678, February 23
1090	1679, February 12
1091	1680, February 2*
1092	1681, January 21
1093	1682, January 10
1094	1682, December 31
1095	1683, December 20
1096	1684, December 8*
1097	1685, November 28
1098	1686, November 17
1099	1687, November 7
1100	1688, October 26*
1101	1689, October 15
1102	1690, October 5
1103	1691, September 24
1104	1692, September 12*
1105	1693, September 2
1106	1694, August 22
1107	1695, August 12
1108	1696, July 31*
1109	1697, July 20
1110	1698, July 10
1111	1699, June 29
1112	1700, June 18
1113	1701, June 8
1114	1702, May 28
1115	1703, May 17
1116	1704, May 6*
1117	1705, April 25
1118	1706, April 15
1119	1707, April 4
1120	1708, March 23*
1121	1709, March 13
1122	1710, March 2
1123	1711, February 19
1124	1712, February 9*
1125	1713, January 28
1126	1714, January 17
1127	1715, January 7
1128	1715, December 27
1129	1716, December 16*
1130	1717, December 5
1131	1718, November 24
1132	1719, November 14
1133	1720, November 2*
1134	1721, October 22
1135	1722, October 12
1136	1723, October 1
1137	1724, September 19
1138	1725, September 9
1139	1726, August 29
1140	1727, August 19
1141	1728, August 7*
1142	1729, July 27
1143	1730, July 17
1144	1731, July 6
1145	1732, June 24*
1146	1733, June 14
1147	1734, June 3
1148	1735, May 24
1149	1736, May 12*
1150	1737, May 1
1151	1738, April 21
1152	1739, April 10
1153	1740, March 29*
1154	1741, March 19
1155	1742, March 8
1156	1743, February 25
1157	1744, February 15*
1158	1745, February 3
1159	1746, January 24
1160	1747, January 13
1161	1748, January 2
1162	1748, December 22*
1163	1749, December 11
1164	1750, November 30
1165	1751, November 20
1166	1752, November 8*
1167	1753, October 29
1168	1754, October 18
1169	1755, October 7
1170	1756, September 26*
1171	1757, September 15
1172	1758, September 4
1173	1759, August 25
1174	1760, August 13*
1175	1761, August 2
1176	1762, July 23
1177	1763, July 12
1178	1764, July 1*

AH Hejira	AD Christian Date
1179	1765, June 20
1180	1766, June 9
1181	1767, May 30
1182	1768, May 18*
1183	1769, May 7
1184	1770, April 27
1185	1771, April 16
1186	1772, April 4*
1187	1773, March 25
1188	1774, March 14
1189	1775, March 4
1190	1776, February 21*
1191	1777, February 1
1192	1778, January 30
1193	1779, January 19
1194	1780, January 8*
1195	1780, December 28*
1196	1781, December 17
1197	1782, December 7
1198	1783, November 26
1199	1784, November 14*
1200	1785, November 4
1201	1786, October 24
1202	1787, October 13
1203	1788, October 2*
1204	1789, September 21
1205	1790, September 10
1206	1791, August 31
1207	1792, August 19*
1208	1793, August 9
1209	1794, July 29
1210	1795, July 18
1211	1796, July 7*
1212	1797, June 26
1213	1798, June 15
1214	1799, June 5
1215	1800, May 25
1216	1801, May 14
1217	1802, May 4
1218	1803, April 23
1219	1804, April 12*
1220	1805, April 1
1221	1806, March 21
1222	1807, March 11
1223	1808, February 28*
1224	1809, February 16
1225	1810, February 6
1226	1811, January 26
1227	1812, January 16*
1228	1813, January 6
1229	1813, December 24
1230	1814, December 14
1231	1815, December 3
1232	1816, November 21*
1233	1817, November 11
1234	1818, October 31
1235	1819, October 20
1236	1820, October 9*
1237	1821, September 28
1238	1822, September 18
1239	1823, September 8
1240	1824, August 26*
1241	1825, August 16
1242	1826, August 5
1243	1827, July 25
1244	1828, July 14*
1245	1829, July 3
1246	1830, June 22
1247	1831, June 12
1248	1832, May 31*
1249	1833, May 21
1250	1834, May 10
1251	1835, April 29
1252	1836, April 18*
1253	1837, April 7
1254	1838, March 27
1255	1839, March 17
1256	1840, March 5*
1257	1841, February 23
1258	1842, February 12
1259	1843, February 1
1260	1844, January 22*
1261	1845, January 10
1262	1845, December 30
1263	1846, December 20
1264	1847, December 9
1265	1848, November 27*
1266	1849, November 17
1267	1850, November 6
1268	1851, October 27
1269	1852, October 15*

AH Hejira	AD Christian Date
1270	1853, October 4
1271	1854, September 24
1272	1855, September 13
1273	1856, September 1*
1274	1857, August 22
1275	1858, August 11
1276	1859, July 31
1277	1860, July 20*
1278	1861, July 9
1279	1862, June 29
1280	1863, June 18
1281	1864, June 6*
1282	1865, May 27
1283	1866, May 16
1284	1867, May 5
1285	1868, April 24*
1286	1869, April 13
1287	1870, April 3
1288	1871, March 23
1289	1872, March 11*
1290	1873, March 1
1291	1874, February 18
1292	1875, February 7
1293	1876, January 28*
1294	1877, January 16
1295	1878, January 5
1296	1878, December 26
1297	1879, December 15
1298	1880, December 4*
1299	1881, November 23
1300	1882, November 12
1301	1883, November 2
1302	1884, October 21*
1303	1885, October 10
1304	1886, September 30
1305	1887, September 19
1306	1888, September 7*
1307	1889, August 28
1308	1890, August 17
1309	1891, August 7
1310	1892, July 26*
1311	1893, July 15
1312	1894, July 5
1313	1895, June 24
1314	1896, June 12*
1315	1897, June 2
1316	1898, May 22
1317	1899, May 12
1318	1900, May 1
1319	1901, April 20
1320	1902, April 10
1321	1903, March 30
1322	1904, March 18*
1323	1905, March 8
1324	1906, February 25
1325	1907, February 14
1326	1908, February 4*
1327	1909, January 23
1328	1910, January 13
1329	1911, January 2
1330	1911, December 22
1331	1912, December 11
1332	1913, November 30
1333	1914, November 19
1334	1915, November 9
1335	1916, October 28*
1336	1917, October 17
1337	1918, October 7
1338	1919, September 26
1339	1920, September 15*
1340	1921, September 4
1341	1922, August 24
1342	1923, August 14
1343	1924, August 2*
1344	1925, July 22
1345	1926, July 12
1346	1927, July 1
1347	1928, June 20*
1348	1929, June 9
1349	1930, May 29
1350	1931, May 19
1351	1932, May 7*
1352	1933, April 26
1353	1934, April 16
1354	1935, April 5
1355	1936, March 24*
1356	1937, March 14
1357	1938, March 3
1358	1939, February 21
1359	1940, February 10*
1360	1941, January 29

AH Hejira	AD Christian Date
1361	1942, January 19
1362	1943, January 8
1363	1943, December 28
1364	1944, December 17*
1365	1945, December 6
1366	1946, November 25
1367	1947, November 15
1368	1948, November 3*
1369	1949, October 24
1370	1950, October 13
1371	1951, October 2
1372	1952, September 21*
1373	1953, September 10
1374	1954, August 30
1375	1955, August 20
1376	1956, August 8*
1377	1957, July 29
1378	1958, July 18
1379	1959, July 7
1380	1960, June 25*
1381	1961, June 14
1382	1962, June 4
1383	1963, May 25
1384	1964, May 13*
1385	1965, May 2
1386	1966, April 22
1387	1967, April 11
1388	1968, March 31*
1389	1969, March 20
1390	1970, March 9
1391	1971, February 27
1392	1972, February 16*
1393	1973, February 4
1394	1974, January 25
1395	1975, January 14
1396	1976, January 3*
1397	1976, December 23*
1398	1977, December 12
1399	1978, December 2
1400	1979, November 21
1401	1980, November 9*
1402	1981, October 30
1403	1982, October 19
1404	1983, October 6
1405	1984, September 27*
1406	1985, September 16
1407	1986, September 6
1408	1987, August 26
1409	1988, August 14*
1410	1989, August 3
1411	1990, July 24
1412	1991, July 13
1413	1992, July 2*
1414	1993, June 21
1415	1994, June 10
1416	1995, May 31
1417	1996, May 19*
1418	1997, May 9
1419	1998, April 28
1420	1999, April 17
1421	2000, April 6*
1422	2001, March 26
1423	2002, March 15
1424	2003, March 5
1425	2004, February 22*
1426	2005, February 10
1427	2006, January 31
1428	2007, January 20
1429	2008, January 10*
1430	2008, December 29
1431	2009, December 18
1432	2010, December 8
1433	2011, November 27*
1434	2012, November 15
1435	2013, November 5
1436	2014, October 25
1437	2015, October 15*
1438	2016, October 3
1439	2017, September 22
1440	2018, September 12
1441	2019, September 1*
1442	2020, August 20
1443	2021, August 10
1444	2022, July 30
1445	2023, July 19*
1446	2024, July 8
1447	2025, June 27
1448	2026, June 17
1449	2027, June 6*
1450	2028, May25

AFGHANISTAN

The Islamic Republic of Afghanistan, which occupies a mountainous region of Southwest Asia, has an area of 251,825 sq. mi. (652,090 sq. km.) and a population of 25.59 million. Presently, about a fifth of the total population lives in exile as refugees, (mostly in Pakistan). Capital: Kabul. It is bordered by Iran, Pakistan, Turkmenistan, Uzbekistan, Tajikistan, and China's Sinkiang Province. Agriculture and herding are the principal industries; textile mills and cement factories add to the industrial sector. Cotton, wool, fruits, nuts, oil, sheepskin coats and hand-woven carpets are normally exported.

On September 11, 2001, a terrorist attack on the United States, supported by the Taliban, led to retaliatory strikes by the U.S. Military in coalition with Afghans of a Northern Alliance. The Taliban regime was deposed. During a UN-sponsored conference on Afghanistan that was held in Bonn, Germany, in early November 2001, an agreement was reached for an Interim Authority, under the leadership of Hamid Karzai, to be installed in Afghanistan on December 22, 2001 and to hold power for the following four to six months. A "loya jirga" (Grand Council) then established a Transitional Authority with Hamid Karzai as president to prepare for general elections and a new constitution.

The national symbol on most coins of the kingdom is a stylized mosque, within which is seen the *mihrab*, a niche indicating the direction of Mecca, and the *minbar*, the pulpit, with a flight of steps leading up to it.

ISLAMIC STATE
SH1373-1381 / 1994-2002AD
STANDARD COINAGE

KM# 1043 500 AFGHANIS
19.87 g., 0.999 Silver 0.6341 oz. ASW, 37.9 mm. **Subject:** World Championship of Soccer - 2006 - Germany **Obv:** State Emblem **Rev:** Soccer ball on German map **Edge:** Reeded

Date	Mintage	F12	VF20	XF40	MS60	MS63
2001	—	PF63 30.00	PF65 35.00			

KM# 1048 500 AFGHANIS
15.00 g., Silver, 35.08 mm. **Subject:** 100th Anniversary Death of Giuseppe Verdi **Obv:** National arms **Rev:** Bust of Verdi 3/4 left, music score below **Edge:** Plain

Date	Mintage	F12	VF20	XF40	MS60	MS63
SH1380(2001)	—	PF63 20.00	PF65 25.00			

REPUBLIC
SH1381- / 2002- AD
DECIMAL COINAGE
100 Pul = 1 Afghani; 20 Afghani = 1 Amani

KM# 1044 AFGHANI
3.28 g., Copper Plated Steel, 20 mm. **Obv:** Value, legend above, legend and date below **Rev:** Mosque with flags in wreath

Date	Mintage	F12	VF20	XF40	MS60	MS63
SH1383(2004)	—	—	—	—	0.25	1.00
SH1384(2005)	—	—	—	—	0.25	1.00

KM# 1045 2 AFGHANIS
4.10 g., Stainless Steel, 22 mm. **Obv:** Value, legend above, legend and date below **Rev:** Mosque with flags in wreath

Date	Mintage	F12	VF20	XF40	MS60	MS63
SH1383(2004)	—	—	—	—	0.50	1.00
SH1384(2005)	—	—	—	—	0.50	1.00

KM# 1046 5 AFGHANIS
5.08 g., Brass, 24 mm. **Obv:** Value, legend above, legend and date below **Rev:** Mosque with flags in wreath

Date	Mintage	F12	VF20	XF40	MS60	MS63
SH1383(2004)	—	—	—	—	0.50	1.00
SH1384(2005)	—	—	—	—	0.50	1.00

ALBANIA

The Republic of Albania, a Balkan republic bounded by Macedonia, Greece, Montenegro, and the Adriatic Sea, has an area of 11,100 sq. mi. (28,748 sq. km.) and a population of 3.49 million. Capital: Tirano. The country is predominantly agricultural, although recent progress has been made in the manufacturing and mining sectors. Petroleum, chrome, iron, copper, cotton textiles, tobacco and wood products are exported.

MONETARY SYSTEM
100 Qindar Leku = 1 Lek
100 Qindar Ari = 1 Frang Ar = 5 Lek

REPUBLIC
STANDARD COINAGE

KM# 75 LEK
3.00 g., Bronze, 18.1 mm. **Obv:** Dalmatian pelican **Rev:** Denomination **Edge:** Plain

Date	Mintage	F12	VF20	XF40	MS60	MS63
2008	—	—	—	0.40	1.50	2.00

KM# 76 5 LEKE
3.12 g., Nickel Plated Steel, 20 mm. **Obv:** Imperial eagle **Rev:** Olive branch, denomination

Date	Mintage	F12	VF20	XF40	MS60	MS63
2011	—	—	—	—	1.00	1.25

KM# 94 10 LEKE
3.60 g., Aluminum-Bronze, 21.25 mm. **Subject:** Culture **Obv:** Ornate vest **Obv. Legend:** SHQIPERI • ALBANIA **Rev:** Ornate value **Rev. Legend:** OBJEKTE TE TRASHEGIMISE KULTURORE **Edge:** Reeded

Date	Mintage	F12	VF20	XF40	MS60	MS63
2005	—	—	—	—	2.00	3.00

KM# 93 10 LEKE
3.60 g., Aluminum-Bronze, 21.25 mm. **Subject:** 85th Anniversary Tirana as capital **Obv:** Archaic Tomb **Obv. Legend:** SHQIPERI • ALBANIA **Rev:** Outlined bird above value **Edge:** Reeded

Date	Mintage	F12	VF20	XF40	MS60	MS63
2005	—	—	—	—	2.00	3.00

KM# 87 20 LEKE
8.54 g., Brass, 26.1 mm. **Subject:** Prehistoric art **Obv:** Horseman **Rev:** Ancient coin design with Apollo portrait **Edge:** Reeded

Date	Mintage	F12	VF20	XF40	MS60	MS63
2002	—	—	—	—	3.00	4.00

KM# 81 50 LEKE
7.50 g., Copper-Nickel, 28 mm. **Subject:** Michaelangelo's "David", 500th Anniversary **Obv:** Towered building **Rev:** Statue's head and denomination **Edge:** Plain

Date	Mintage	F12	VF20	XF40	MS60	MS63
2001	3,000	—	—	—	6.50	8.00

KM# 88 50 LEKE
12.00 g., Brass, 28 mm. **Subject:** Declaration of Independence, 90th Anniversary **Obv:** Value within circle **Rev:** Bust facing, dates below **Edge:** Reeded

Date	Mintage	F12	VF20	XF40	MS60	MS63
2002	20,000	—	—	—	3.00	4.00

KM# 86 50 LEKE
5.50 g., Copper-Nickel, 24.25 mm. **Obv:** Value and legend **Rev:** Ancient Illyrian helmet **Edge:** Reeded

Date	Mintage	F12	VF20	XF40	MS60	MS63
2003	200,000	—	—	—	6.00	7.50

KM# 89 50 LEKE
12.00 g., Brass, 28 mm. **Subject:** Jeronim de Rada, 100th Anniversary of Death **Obv:** Bust 3/4 facing, dates below, circle surrounds **Rev:** Value within box within circle **Edge:** Plain

Date	Mintage	F12	VF20	XF40	MS60	MS63
2003	—	—	—	—	3.00	4.00

KM# 90 50 LEKE
5.50 g., Copper-Nickel, 24.25 mm. **Subject:** The Beauty of

Durrës **Obv:** Wheel design **Rev:** Ancient bust above value within circle **Edge:** Reeded

Date	Mintage	F12	VF20	XF40	MS60	MS63
2004	200,000	—	—	—	3.00	4.00

KM# 91 50 LEKE
5.50 g., Copper-Nickel, 24.25 mm. **Obv:** Soldier within circle **Rev:** Value within circle **Edge:** Reeded

Date	Mintage	F12	VF20	XF40	MS60	MS63
2004	200,000	—	—	—	3.00	4.00

KM# 82 100 LEKE
15.70 g., 0.925 Silver 0.4639 oz. ASW, 32.65 mm. **Subject:** Michaelangelo's "David", 500th Anniversary **Obv:** Arch of Triumph **Rev:** Statue's upper half and denomination **Edge:** Plain

Date	Mintage	F12	VF20	XF40	MS60	MS63
2001	3,000	—	—	—	32.00	35.00

KM# 84 100 LEKE
15.00 g., 0.925 Silver 0.4432 oz. ASW, 32 mm. **Subject:** Albanian-European Integration **Obv:** Dove in flight, stars encircle **Rev:** European and Albanian maps, stars encircle **Edge:** Plain

Date	Mintage	F12	VF20	XF40	MS60	MS63
2001	3,000	—	—	—	30.00	32.50

KM# 92 100 LEKE
30.00 g., 0.925 Silver 0.8864 oz. ASW, 38 mm. **Subject:** Declaration of Independence, 90th Anniversary **Obv:** Crossed rifle and pistol on manuscript, quill pen **Obv. Legend:** SHQIPERI - ALBANIA **Rev:** Bust of Qemali 3/4 right

Date	Mintage	F12	VF20	XF40	MS60	MS63
2002	7,000			PF65 50.00		

KM# 83 200 LEKE
7.65 g., 0.900 Gold 0.2199 oz. AGW, 25.45 mm. **Subject:** Michaelangelo's "David", 500th Anniversary **Obv:** City plaza **Rev:** Statue of "David" and denomination **Edge:** Plain

Date	Mintage	F12	VF20	XF40	MS60	MS63
2001	1,000	—	—	—	400	425

KM# 85 200 LEKE
15.00 g., 0.925 Silver 0.4432 oz. ASW, 32 mm. **Subject:** Albanian-European Integration **Obv:** Dove in flight within inner circle, stars encircle **Rev:** Adult and infant hand within inner circle, stars encircle **Edge:** Plain

Date	Mintage	F12	VF20	XF40	MS60	MS63
2001	1,000	—	—	—	37.50	40.00

MINT SETS

KM#	Date	Mintage	Identification	Issue Price	Mkt Val
MS3	2002-03 (4)	—	KM86, 89 (2003), 87, 88 (2002)	—	22.50

ALDERNEY

Alderney, the northernmost and third largest of the Channel Islands, separated from the coast of France by the dangerous 8-mile-wide tidal channel, has an area of 3 sq. mi. (8 km.) and a population of 1,686. It is a dependency of the British island of Guernsey, to the southwest. Capital: St. Anne. Principal industries are agriculture and raising cattle. The Channel Islands have never been subject to the British Parliament and are self-governing units under the direct rule of the Crown acting through the Privy Council. Alderney is one of the nine Channel Islands, the only part of the Duchy of Normandy still belonging to the British Crown, and has been a British possession since the Norman Conquest of 1066. Legislation was only recently introduced for the issue of its own coinage, a right it now shares with Jersey and Guernsey.

RULER
British

MONETARY SYSTEM
100 Pence = 1 Pound Sterling

DEPENDENCY
STANDARD COINAGE

KM# 75 50 PENCE
8.00 g., 0.925 Silver 0.2364 oz. ASW **Ruler:** Elizabeth II **Subject:** 50th Anniversary of Coronation **Obv:** Crowned head right **Rev:** Royal coach **Edge:** Plain **Shape:** 7-sided

Date	Mintage	F12	VF20	XF40	MS60	MS63
2003	—		PF63 17.00	PF65 20.00		

KM# 76 50 PENCE
8.00 g., 0.925 Silver 0.2364 oz. ASW **Ruler:** Elizabeth II **Subject:** 50th Anniversary of Coronation **Obv:** Crowned head right **Rev:** St. Edward's crown **Edge:** Plain **Shape:** 7-sided

Date	Mintage	F12	VF20	XF40	MS60	MS63
2003	—		PF63 17.00	PF65 20.00		

KM# 77 50 PENCE
8.00 g., 0.925 Silver 0.2364 oz. ASW **Ruler:** Elizabeth II **Subject:** 50th Anniversay of Coronation **Obv:** Crowned head right **Rev:** Elizabeth II horseback **Edge:** Plain **Shape:** 7-sided

Date	Mintage	F12	VF20	XF40	MS60	MS63
2003	—		PF63 17.00	PF65 20.00		

KM# 78 50 PENCE
8.00 g., 0.925 Silver 0.2364 oz. ASW **Ruler:** Elizabeth II **Subject:** 50th Anniversary of Coronation **Obv:** Crowned head right **Rev:** Elizabeth II seated on throne **Edge:** Plain **Shape:** 7-sided

Date	Mintage	F12	VF20	XF40	MS60	MS63
2003	—		PF63 17.00	PF65 20.00		

KM# 73 POUND
9.50 g., 0.925 Silver 0.2807 oz. ASW **Ruler:** Elizabeth II **Subject:** Queen's 75th Birthday **Obv:** Crowned head right

Date	Mintage	F12	VF20	XF40	MS60	MS63
2001	—		PF63 17.00	PF65 20.00		

KM# 91 POUND
1.24 g., 0.999 Gold 0.0396 oz. AGW, 13.92 mm. **Ruler:** Elizabeth II **Rev:** State arms

Date	Mintage	F12	VF20	XF40	MS60	MS63
2002	—		PF63 70.00	PF65 80.00		

KM# 119 POUND
1.24 g., 0.999 Gold 0.0396 oz. AGW, 13.92 mm. **Ruler:** Elizabeth II **Subject:** Trafalgar - Horatio Nelson **Obv:** Head crowned right **Rev:** Bust right in Navy uniform

Date	Mintage	F12	VF20	XF40	MS60	MS63
2005	Est. 20000		PF63 75.00	PF65 85.00		

KM# 122 POUND
1.24 g., 0.999 Gold 0.0396 oz. AGW, 13.92 mm. **Ruler:** Elizabeth II **Rev:** Queen Elizabeth I

Date	Mintage	F12	VF20	XF40	MS60	MS63
2006	Est. 20000		PF63 75.00	PF65 85.00		

KM# 123 POUND
1.24 g., 0.999 Gold 0.0396 oz. AGW, 13.92 mm. **Ruler:** Elizabeth II **Rev:** Sir Isaac Newton

Date	Mintage	F12	VF20	XF40	MS60	MS63
2006	Est. 20000		PF63 75.00	PF65 85.00		

KM# 124 POUND
1.24 g., 0.999 Gold 0.0396 oz. AGW, 13.92 mm. **Ruler:** Elizabeth II **Rev:** William Shakespeare

Date	Mintage	F12	VF20	XF40	MS60	MS63
2006	20,000		PF63 75.00	PF65 85.00		

KM# 125 POUND
1.24 g., 0.999 Gold 0.0396 oz. AGW, 13.92 mm. **Ruler:** Elizabeth II **Rev:** Charles Dickens

Date	Mintage	F12	VF20	XF40	MS60	MS63
2006	Est. 20000		PF63 75.00	PF65 85.00		

KM# 130 POUND
1.24 g., 0.999 Gold 0.0396 oz. AGW, 13.92 mm. **Ruler:** Elizabeth II **Rev:** Sir Winston Churchill

Date	Mintage	F12	VF20	XF40	MS60	MS63
2006	—		PF63 75.00	PF65 85.00		

KM# 131 POUND
1.24 g., 0.999 Gold 0.0396 oz. AGW, 13.92 mm. **Ruler:** Elizabeth II **Rev:** Elizabeth II corronation

Date	Mintage	F12	VF20	XF40	MS60	MS63
2006	—		PF63 75.00	PF65 85.00		

KM# 154 POUND
1.24 g., 0.999 Gold 0.0396 oz. AGW, 13.92 mm. **Ruler:** Elizabeth II **Rev:** Capt. James Cook

Date	Mintage	F12	VF20	XF40	MS60	MS63
2007	Est. 20000		PF63 75.00	PF65 85.00		

KM# 155 POUND
1.24 g., 0.999 Gold 0.0396 oz. AGW, 13.92 mm. **Ruler:** Elizabeth II **Rev:** Sir Edward Elgar

Date	Mintage	F12	VF20	XF40	MS60	MS63
2007	Est. 20000		PF63 75.00	PF65 85.00		

KM# 156 POUND
1.24 g., 0.999 Gold 0.0396 oz. AGW, 13.92 mm. **Ruler:** Elizabeth II **Rev:** Sir Francis Drake

Date	Mintage	F12	VF20	XF40	MS60	MS63
2007	20,000		PF63 75.00	PF65 85.00		

KM# 157 POUND
1.24 g., 0.999 Gold 0.0396 oz. AGW, 13.92 mm. **Ruler:** Elizabeth II **Rev:** John Constable

Date	Mintage	F12	VF20	XF40	MS60	MS63
2007	Est. 20000		PF63 75.00	PF65 85.00		

KM# 174 POUND
1.24 g., 0.999 Gold 0.0396 oz. AGW, 13.92 mm. **Ruler:** Elizabeth II **Subject:** Princess Diana, 10th Anniversary of Death **Rev:** Bust 3/4 facing left

Date	Mintage	F12	VF20	XF40	MS60	MS63
2007	Est. 20000		PF63 75.00	PF65 85.00		

KM# 175a POUND
28.28 g., 0.925 Silver 0.8356 oz. ASW, 38.61 mm. **Ruler:** Elizabeth II **Rev. Designer:** Princess Diana, 10th Anniversary of Death

Date	Mintage	F12	VF20	XF40	MS60	MS63
2007	Est. 10000		PF63 50.00	PF65 55.00		

KM# 175b POUND
39.94 g., 0.916 Gold 1.1687 oz. AGW, 38.61 mm. **Ruler:** Elizabeth II **Subject:** Princess Diana, 10th Anniversary of Death

Date	Mintage	F12	VF20	XF40	MS60	MS63
2007	—	PF65 2,200				

KM# 189 POUND
1.24 g., 0.999 Gold 0.0396 oz. AGW, 13.92 mm. **Ruler:** Elizabeth II **Rev:** Concord

Date	Mintage	F12	VF20	XF40	MS60	MS63
2008	Est. 1000	PF63 75.00	PF65 85.00			

KM# 84 POUND
1.24 g., 0.999 Gold 0.0396 oz. AGW, 13.92 mm. **Ruler:** Elizabeth II **Subject:** Mini Cooper 50th Anniversary **Rev:** Mini Cooper on tiled floor **Rev. Designer:** David Cornell

Date	Mintage	F12	VF20	XF40	MS60	MS63
2009	5,000	PF63 100	PF65 120			

KM# 59 5 POUNDS
28.28 g., 0.925 Silver 0.8356 oz. ASW, 38.6 mm. **Ruler:** Elizabeth II **Subject:** Queen's 75th Birthday **Obv:** Queen's portrait right **Obv. Designer:** Raphael Maklouf **Rev:** Queen in casual dress surrounded by rose, thistle, daffodil and pimper nickel **Rev. Designer:** David Cornell

Date	Mintage	F12	VF20	XF40	MS60	MS63
2001	—	PF63 45.00	PF65 50.00			

KM# 60 5 POUNDS
28.28 g., Copper-Nickel, 38.6 mm. **Ruler:** Elizabeth II **Subject:** Queen's 75th Birrthday **Obv:** Queen's portrait right **Obv. Designer:** Raphael Maklouf **Rev:** Queen in casual dress surrounded by rose, thistle, daffodil and primper nickel **Rev. Designer:** David Cornell

Date	Mintage	F12	VF20	XF40	MS60	MS63
2001	—				13.50	15.00

KM# 24 5 POUNDS
28.28 g., Copper-Nickel, 38.6 mm. **Ruler:** Elizabeth II **Subject:** Queen Elizabeth II - 50 Years of Reigh **Obv:** Queen's head right **Rev:** Sword hilt and denomination with royal arms background **Rev. Designer:** Marcel Canioni **Edge:** Reeded

Date	Mintage	F12	VF20	XF40	MS60	MS63
2002	15,000	PF63 12.00	PF65 15.00			

KM# 24a 5 POUNDS
28.28 g., 0.925 Silver 0.8356 oz. ASW, 38.6 mm. **Ruler:** Elizabeth II **Subject:** Queen Elizabeth II - 50 Years of Reign **Obv:** Queen's head right **Rev:** Sword hilt and denomination with royal arms background **Rev. Designer:** Marcel Canioni **Edge:** Reeded

Date	Mintage	F12	VF20	XF40	MS60	MS63
2002	15,000	PF63 40.00	PF65 45.00			

KM# 25 5 POUNDS
28.28 g., 0.925 Silver 0.8356 oz. ASW, 38.6 mm. **Ruler:** Elizabeth II **Subject:** Queen's Golden Jubilee **Obv:** Queen's portrait **Rev:** Honor guard and trumpets **Rev. Designer:** Robert Lowe **Edge:** Reeded

Date	Mintage	F12	VF20	XF40	MS60	MS63
2002	15,000	PF63 40.00	PF65 45.00			

KM# 27 5 POUNDS
28.28 g., Copper-Nickel, 38.6 mm. **Ruler:** Elizabeth II **Subject:** 5th Anniversary Death of Princess Diana **Obv:** Crowned head right **Rev:** Diana accepting flowers from girl **Edge:** Reeded

Date	Mintage	F12	VF20	XF40	MS60	MS63
2002	—	—	—	—	13.50	15.00

KM# 27a 5 POUNDS
28.28 g., 0.925 Silver 0.8356 oz. ASW, 38.6 mm. **Ruler:** Elizabeth II **Subject:** 5th Anniversary Death of Princess Diana **Obv:** Crowned head right **Rev:** Diana accepting flowers from girl **Edge:** Reeded

Date	Mintage	F12	VF20	XF40	MS60	MS63
2002	20,000	PF63 40.00	PF65 45.00			

KM# 27b 5 POUNDS
39.94 g., 0.9167 Gold 1.1696 oz. AGW, 38.6 mm. **Ruler:** Elizabeth II **Subject:** 5th Anniversary Death of Princess Diana **Obv:** Crowned head right **Rev:** Diana accepting flowers from girl **Edge:** Reeded

Date	Mintage	F12	VF20	XF40	MS60	MS63
2002	100	PF65 2,250				

KM# 29 5 POUNDS
28.28 g., Copper-Nickel, 38.6 mm. **Ruler:** Elizabeth II **Subject:** 150th Anniversary Death of the Duke of Wellington **Obv:** Queen's portrait **Rev:** Coat of arms, castle and portrait **Rev. Designer:** Willem Vis **Edge:** Reeded

Date	Mintage	F12	VF20	XF40	MS60	MS63
2002	—	—	—	—	13.50	15.00

KM# 29a 5 POUNDS
28.28 g., 0.925 Silver 0.8356 oz. ASW, 38.6 mm. **Ruler:** Elizabeth II **Subject:** 150th Anniversary Death of the Duke of Wellington **Obv:** Queen's portrait **Rev:** Multicolor coat of arms, portrait and castle **Rev. Designer:** Willem Vis **Edge:** Reeded

Date	Mintage	VG8	F12	VF20	XF40	MS60
2002	15,000	PF63 50.00	PF65 55.00			

KM# 29b 5 POUNDS
39.94 g., 0.9167 Gold 1.1696 oz. AGW, 38.6 mm. **Ruler:** Elizabeth II **Subject:** 150th Anniversary Death of the Duke of Wellington **Obv:** Queen's portrait **Rev:** Coat of arms, castle and portrait **Rev. Designer:** Willem Vis **Edge:** Reeded

Date	Mintage	VG8	F12	VF20	XF40	MS60
2002	200	PF65 2,200				

KM# 44 5 POUNDS
28.28 g., Copper-Nickel, 38.6 mm. **Ruler:** Elizabeth II **Obv:** Queen's portrait **Rev:** HMS Mary Rose **Rev. Designer:** Willem Vis **Edge:** Reeded

Date	Mintage	F12	VF20	XF40	MS60	MS63
2003	—	—	—	—	12.00	13.50

KM# 45 5 POUNDS
28.28 g., Copper-Nickel, 38.6 mm. **Ruler:** Elizabeth II **Obv:** Queen's portrait **Rev:** Alfred the Great on ship **Rev. Designer:** Willem Vis **Edge:** Reeded

Date	Mintage	F12	VF20	XF40	MS60	MS63
2003	—	—	—	—	12.00	13.50

KM# 44a 5 POUNDS
28.28 g., 0.925 Silver 0.8356 oz. ASW, 38.6 mm. **Ruler:** Elizabeth II **Obv:** Queen's portrait **Rev:** HMS Mary Rose below multicolor flag **Rev. Designer:** Willem Vis **Edge:** Reeded

Date	Mintage	F12	VF20	XF40	MS60	MS63
2003	15,000	PF63 55.00	PF65 60.00			

KM# 45a 5 POUNDS
28.28 g., 0.925 Silver 0.8356 oz. ASW, 38.6 mm. **Ruler:** Elizabeth II **Obv:** Queen's portrait **Rev:** Alfred the Great on ship below multicolor flag **Rev. Designer:** Willem Vis **Edge:** Reeded

Date	Mintage	F12	VF20	XF40	MS60	MS63
2003	15,000	PF63 55.00	PF65 60.00			

KM# 45b 5 POUNDS
39.94 g., 0.9167 Gold 1.1696 oz. AGW, 38.6 mm. **Ruler:** Elizabeth II **Obv:** Queen's portrait **Rev:** Alfred the Great on ship **Rev. Designer:** Willem Vis **Edge:** Reeded

Date	Mintage	F12	VF20	XF40	MS60	MS63
2003	500	PF65 2,150				

KM# 31 5 POUNDS
28.28 g., Copper-Nickel, 38.6 mm. **Ruler:** Elizabeth II **Subject:** Prince William **Obv:** Queen's portrait **Obv. Designer:** Raphael Maklouf **Rev:** Portrait with open shirt collar **Edge:** Reeded

Date	Mintage	F12	VF20	XF40	MS60	MS63
2003	—				16.50	18.00

KM# 31a 5 POUNDS
28.28 g., 0.925 Silver 0.8356 oz. ASW, 38.6 mm. **Ruler:** Elizabeth II **Subject:** Prince William **Obv:** Queen's portrait **Obv. Designer:** Raphael Maklouf **Rev:** Portrait with open shirt collar **Edge:** Reeded

Date	Mintage	F12	VF20	XF40	MS60	MS63
2003	—	PF63 42.50	PF65 47.50			

KM# 31b 5 POUNDS
39.94 g., 0.9166 Gold 1.1694 oz. AGW, 38.6 mm. **Ruler:** Elizabeth II **Subject:** Prince Willliam **Obv:** Queen's portrait **Obv. Designer:** Raphael Maklouf **Rev:** Portrait with open shirt collar **Edge:** Reeded

Date	Mintage	F12	VF20	XF40	MS60	MS63
2003	200	PF65 2,200				

KM# 35 5 POUNDS
28.28 g., Copper-Nickel, 38.61 mm. **Ruler:** Elizabeth II **Subject:** Last Flight of the Concorde, October 24, 2003 **Obv:** Crowned bust right **Obv. Legend:** ELIZABETH II - ALDERNEY **Obv. Designer:** Raphael Maklouf **Rev:** Concorde in flight **Rev. Designer:** Emma Noble **Rev. Legend:** CONCORDE 1969 - 2003 **Edge:** Reeded

Date	Mintage	F12	VF20	XF40	MS60	MS63
2003	5,000	—	—	—	12.00	15.50

KM# 35a 5 POUNDS
28.28 g., 0.925 Silver 0.8356 oz. ASW, 38.61 mm. **Ruler:** Elizabeth II **Subject:** Last Flight of the Concorde, October 24, 2003 **Obv:** Crowned bust right **Obv. Legend:** ELIZABETH II - ALDERNEY **Obv. Designer:** Raphael Maklouf **Rev:** Concorde in flight **Rev. Designer:** Emma Noble **Rev. Legend:** CONCORDE 1969 - 2003 **Edge:** Reeded

Date	Mintage	F12	VF20	XF40	MS60	MS63
2003	5,000	PF63 45.00	PF65 50.00			

KM# 35b 5 POUNDS
39.94 g., 0.9166 Gold 1.1694 oz. AGW, 38.6 mm. **Ruler:** Elizabeth II **Obv:** Queen's portrait **Rev:** Concorde in flight, October 24, 2003 **Rev. Designer:** Emma Noble **Edge:** Reeded

Date	Mintage	F12	VF20	XF40	MS60	MS63
2003	500	PF65 2,150				

KM# 38 5 POUNDS
28.28 g., Copper-Nickel, 38.6 mm. **Ruler:** Elizabeth II **Obv:** Queen's portrait **Rev:** Battleship and transports, HMS Belfast **Rev. Designer:** Mike Guilfoyle **Edge:** Reeded **Note:** D-Day

Date	Mintage	F12	VF20	XF40	MS60	MS63
2004	—	—	—	—	15.00	17.50

KM# 38a 5 POUNDS
28.28 g., 0.925 Silver 0.8356 oz. ASW, 38.6 mm. **Ruler:** Elizabeth II **Obv:** Queen's portrait **Rev:** Battleship and transports **Rev. Designer:** Mike Guilfoyle

Date	Mintage	F12	VF20	XF40	MS60	MS63
2004	10,000	PF63 75.00	PF65 85.00			

KM# 38b 5 POUNDS
39.94 g., 0.9167 Gold 1.1696 oz. AGW, 38.6 mm. **Ruler:** Elizabeth II **Obv:** Queen's portrait **Rev:** Battleship and transports **Rev. Designer:** Mike Guilfoyle

Date	Mintage	F12	VF20	XF40	MS60	MS63
2004	500	PF65 2,150				

KM# 42 5 POUNDS
28.28 g., Copper-Nickel, 38.6 mm. **Ruler:** Elizabeth II **Obv:** Crowned head right **Rev:** Florence Nightingale **Edge:** Reeded

Date	Mintage	F12	VF20	XF40	MS60	MS63
2004	—	—	—	—	18.00	20.00

KM# 42a 5 POUNDS
28.28 g., 0.925 Silver 0.8356 oz. ASW, 38.6 mm. **Ruler:** Elizabeth II **Obv:** Queen's portrait **Rev:** Florence Nightingale **Edge:** Reeded

Date	Mintage	F12	VF20	XF40	MS60	MS63
2004	25,000	PF63 60.00	PF65 70.00			

KM# 43 5 POUNDS
28.28 g., Copper-Nickel, 38.6 mm. **Ruler:** Elizabeth II **Subject:** 150th Anniversary of the Crimean War **Obv:** Crowned head right **Rev:** Florence Nightingale head above the Battle of Inkerman scene with one multicolor soldier **Edge:** Reeded

Date	Mintage	F12	VF20	XF40	MS60	MS63
2004 plain	—	—	—	—	25.00	27.50
2004 partial color	—	—	—	—	25.00	27.50

KM# 43a 5 POUNDS
28.28 g., 0.925 Silver 0.8356 oz. ASW, 38.6 mm. **Ruler:** Elizabeth II **Subject:** 150th Anniversary Crimean War **Obv:** Crowned head right **Rev:** Florence Nightingale head above Battle of Inkerman scene with one multicolor soldier **Edge:** Reeded

Date	Mintage	F12	VF20	XF40	MS60	MS63
2004	10,000	PF63 75.00	PF65 85.00			

KM# 43b 5 POUNDS
39.94 g., 0.9166 Gold 1.1694 oz. AGW, 38.6 mm. **Ruler:** Elizabeth II **Subject:** 150th Anniversary Crimean War **Obv:** Crowned head right **Rev:** Florence Nightingale head above Battle of Inkerman scene with one multicolor soldier **Edge:** Reeded

Date	Mintage	F12	VF20	XF40	MS60	MS63
2004	500	PF65 2,150				

KM# 94 5 POUNDS
28.28 g., 0.925 Silver 0.8356 oz. ASW, 38.61 mm. **Ruler:** Elizabeth II **Subject:** David Beckham **Rev:** Soccer player and ball as background

Date	Mintage	F12	VF20	XF40	MS60	MS63
2004	—	PF63 40.00	PF65 45.00			

KM# 95 5 POUNDS
28.28 g., 0.925 Silver 0.8356 oz. ASW, 38.61 mm. **Ruler:** Elizabeth II **Subject:** Michael Owen **Rev:** Soccer player and ball as background

Date	Mintage	F12	VF20	XF40	MS60	MS63
2004	—	PF63 40.00	PF65 45.00			

KM# 47 5 POUNDS
28.28 g., Copper-Nickel, 38.6 mm. **Ruler:** Elizabeth II **Obv:** Queen's portrait **Rev:** Locomotive, The Rocket **Rev. Designer:** Robert Lowe **Edge:** Reeded

Date	Mintage	F12	VF20	XF40	MS60	MS63
2004	—	—	—	—	16.00	18.50

KM# 47a 5 POUNDS
28.28 g., 0.925 Silver 0.8356 oz. ASW, 38.6 mm. **Ruler:** Elizabeth II **Obv:** Queen's portrait **Rev:** Locomotive, The Rocket **Rev. Designer:** Robert Lowe **Edge:** Reeded

Date	Mintage	F12	VF20	XF40	MS60	MS63
2004	20,000	PF63 55.00	PF65 60.00			

KM# 47b 5 POUNDS
39.94 g., 0.9167 Gold 1.1696 oz. AGW, 38.6 mm. **Ruler:** Elizabeth II **Obv:** Queen's portrait **Rev:** Locomotive, The Rocket **Rev. Designer:** Robert Lowe **Edge:** Reeded

Date	Mintage	F12	VF20	XF40	MS60	MS63
2004	500	PF65 2,150				

KM# 48 5 POUNDS
28.28 g., Copper-Nickel, 38.6 mm. **Ruler:** Elizabeth II **Obv:** Queen's portrait **Rev:** Locomotive, The Royal Scot **Rev. Designer:** Robert Lowe **Edge:** Reeded

Date	Mintage	F12	VF20	XF40	MS60	MS63
2004	—	—	—	—	16.00	18.50

KM# 48a 5 POUNDS
28.28 g., 0.925 Silver 0.8356 oz. ASW, 38.6 mm. **Ruler:** Elizabeth II **Obv:** Queen's portrait **Rev:** Locomotive, The Royal Scot **Rev. Designer:** Robert Lowe **Edge:** Reeded

Date	Mintage	F12	VF20	XF40	MS60	MS63
2004	10,000	PF63 55.00	PF65 60.00			

KM# 49 5 POUNDS
28.28 g., Copper-Nickel, 38.6 mm. **Ruler:** Elizabeth II **Obv:** Queen's portrait **Rev:** Locomotive, The Merchant Navy 21C1 **Edge:** Reeded

Date	Mintage	F12	VF20	XF40	MS60	MS63
2004	—	—	—	—	16.00	18.50

KM# 49a 5 POUNDS
28.28 g., 0.925 Silver 0.8356 oz. ASW, 38.6 mm. **Ruler:** Elizabeth II **Obv:** Queen's portrait **Rev:** Locomotive, The Merchant Navy 21C1 **Rev. Designer:** Robert Lowe **Edge:** Reeded

Date	Mintage	F12	VF20	XF40	MS60	MS63
2004	10,000	PF63 55.00	PF65 60.00			

KM# 53a 5 POUNDS
28.28 g., 0.925 Silver 0.8356 oz. ASW, 38.6 mm. **Ruler:** Elizabeth II **Subject:** End of WWII **Obv:** Elizabeth II by Maklouf **Rev:** Flag waving crowd **Edge:** Reeded

Date	Mintage	F12	VF20	XF40	MS60	MS63
2005	5,000	PF63 75.00	PF65 85.00			

KM# 113a 5 POUNDS
28.28 g., 0.925 Silver 0.8356 oz. ASW, 38.61 mm. **Ruler:** Elizabeth II **Subject:** Prince William, 21st Birthday

Date	Mintage	F12	VF20	XF40	MS60	MS63
2005	Est. 2500	PF63 55.00	PF65 60.00			

KM# 116a 5 POUNDS
28.28 g., 0.925 Silver 0.8356 oz. ASW, 38.61 mm. **Ruler:** Elizabeth II **Subject:** British Navy - H.M.S. Warspite **Rev:** Multicolor flag

Date	Mintage	F12	VF20	XF40	MS60	MS63
2005	Est. 15000	PF63 50.00	PF65 55.00			

KM# 66a 5 POUNDS
28.28 g., 0.925 Silver 0.8356 oz. ASW, 38.6 mm. **Ruler:** Elizabeth II **Subject:** Viscount Samuel Hood on his flagship after the Battle of Saints Passage in 1782 **Obv:** Queen's portrait **Rev. Designer:** Willem Vis **Note:** Ensign is colored.

Date	Mintage	F12	VF20	XF40	MS60	MS63
2005	—	PF63 45.00	PF65 50.00			

KM# 68a 5 POUNDS
28.28 g., 0.925 Silver 0.8356 oz. ASW, 38.6 mm. **Ruler:** Elizabeth II **Obv:** Crowned head right **Rev:** HMS Revenge fighting at Azores, 1591 **Rev. Designer:** Willem Vis **Note:** Ensign is colorized.

Date	Mintage	F12	VF20	XF40	MS60	MS63
2005	—	PF63 55.00	PF65 60.00			

KM# 83a 5 POUNDS
28.28 g., 0.925 Silver 0.8356 oz. ASW, 38.61 mm. **Ruler:** Elizabeth II **Subject:** History of the Royal Navy **Obv:** Heraldic shield **Rev:** Admiral John Woodward, partially colored

Date	Mintage	F12	VF20	XF40	MS60	MS63
2005	—	PF63 40.00	PF65 45.00			

KM# 79a 5 POUNDS
28.28 g., 0.925 Silver 0.8356 oz. ASW **Ruler:** Elizabeth II **Subject:** 200th Anniversary Battle of Trafalgar **Obv:** Crowned head right

Date	Mintage	F12	VF20	XF40	MS60	MS63
2005	—	PF63 55.00	PF65 60.00			

KM# 53b 5 POUNDS
39.94 g., 0.9167 Gold 1.1696 oz. AGW, 38.6 mm. **Ruler:** Elizabeth II **Subject:** 60th Anniversary - End of WWII **Obv:** Elizabeth II by Maklouf **Rev:** Flag waving crowd **Edge:** Reeded

Date	Mintage	F12	VF20	XF40	MS60	MS63
2005	150	PF65 2,200				

KM# 54b 5 POUNDS
39.94 g., 0.9167 Gold 1.1696 oz. AGW, 38.6 mm. **Ruler:** Elizabeth II **Subject:** WWII Liberation **Obv:** Elizabeth II by Maklouf **Rev:** Churchill flashing the "V" sign **Edge:** Reeded

Date	Mintage	F12	VF20	XF40	MS60	MS63
2005	150	PF65 2,200				

KM# 53 5 POUNDS
Copper-Nickel, 38.61 mm. **Ruler:** Elizabeth II **Subject:** End of World War II, 60th Anniversary

Date	Mintage	F12	VF20	XF40	MS60	MS63
2005	—	—	—	—	—	15.00

KM# 54 5 POUNDS
28.28 g., Copper-Nickel, 38.61 mm. **Ruler:** Elizabeth II **Subject:** Winston Churchill

Date	Mintage	F12	VF20	XF40	MS60	MS63
2005	Est. 5000	—	—	—	—	15.00

KM# 54a 5 POUNDS
39.94 g., 0.916 Silver 1.1687 oz. ASW, 38.61 mm. **Ruler:** Elizabeth II **Subject:** Sir Winston Churchill

Date	Mintage	F12	VF20	XF40	MS60	MS63
2005	—	PF63 60.00	PF65 65.00			

KM# 66 5 POUNDS
28.28 g., Copper-Nickel, 38.6 mm. **Ruler:** Elizabeth II **Subject:** Viscount Samuel Hood on his flagship after the Battle of Saints Passage in 1782 **Obv:** Queen's portrait **Rev. Designer:** Willem Vis

Date	Mintage	F12	VF20	XF40	MS60	MS63
2005	—	—	—	—	13.50	15.00

KM# 68 5 POUNDS
28.28 g., Copper-Nickel, 38.6 mm. **Ruler:** Elizabeth II **Obv:** Crowned head right **Rev:** HMS Revenge fighting at Azores, 1591 **Rev. Designer:** Willem Vis

Date	Mintage	F12	VF20	XF40	MS60	MS63
2005	—	—	—	—	12.00	14.00

KM# 79 5 POUNDS
28.28 g., Copper-Nickel, 38.61 mm. **Ruler:** Elizabeth II **Subject:** 200th Anniversary Battle of Trafalgar **Obv:** Crowned head right

Date	Mintage	F12	VF20	XF40	MS60	MS63
2005	—	—	—	—	16.00	18.50

KM# 83 5 POUNDS
28.28 g., Copper-Nickel, 38.61 mm. **Ruler:** Elizabeth II **Subject:** Royal Navy - Admiral Sir John Foster Woodward

Date	Mintage	F12	VF20	XF40	MS60	MS63
2005	—	—	—	—	—	15.00

KM# 96 5 POUNDS
28.28 g., 0.925 Silver 0.8356 oz. ASW **Ruler:** Elizabeth II **Subject:** Locomotives, 200th Anniversary **Rev:** Train station on a branch line

Date	Mintage	F12	VF20	XF40	MS60	MS63
2005	Est. 10000	PF63 55.00	PF65 60.00			
2006	Est. 25000	PF63 50.00	PF65 55.00			

KM# 97 5 POUNDS
28.28 g., 0.925 Silver 0.8356 oz. ASW **Ruler:** Elizabeth II **Subject:** Locomotives, 200th Anniversary **Rev:** Locomotive Shop

Date	Mintage	F12	VF20	XF40	MS60	MS63
2005	Est. 10000	PF63 55.00	PF65 60.00			
2006 proof	—	PF63 50.00	PF65 55.00			

KM# 98 5 POUNDS
28.28 g., 0.925 Silver 0.8356 oz. ASW **Ruler:** Elizabeth II **Subject:** Locomotives, 200th Anniversary **Rev:** Viaduct

Date	Mintage	F12	VF20	XF40	MS60	MS63
2005	Est. 10000	PF63 55.00	PF65 60.00			
2006	Est. 25000	PF63 50.00	PF65 55.00			

KM# 99 5 POUNDS
28.28 g., 0.925 Silver 0.8356 oz. ASW, 38.61 mm. **Ruler:** Elizabeth II **Subject:** Wayne Rooney **Obv:** Shield **Rev:** Soccer player and ball design

Date	Mintage	F12	VF20	XF40	MS60	MS63
2005	—	PF63 40.00	PF65 45.00			

KM# 100 5 POUNDS
28.28 g., 0.925 Silver 0.8356 oz. ASW, 38.61 mm. **Ruler:** Elizabeth II **Subject:** Frank Lampard **Obv:** Shield **Rev:** Soccer player and ball design

Date	Mintage	F12	VF20	XF40	MS60	MS63
2005	—	PF63 40.00	PF65 45.00			

KM# 101 5 POUNDS
28.28 g., 0.925 Silver 0.8356 oz. ASW, 38.61 mm. **Ruler:** Elizabeth II **Obv:** Shield **Rev:** Soccer player and ball design

Date	Mintage	F12	VF20	XF40	MS60	MS63
2005	—	PF63 40.00	PF65 45.00			

KM# 102 5 POUNDS
28.28 g., 0.925 Silver 0.8356 oz. ASW, 38.61 mm. **Ruler:** Elizabeth II **Subject:** Steven Gerrard **Obv:** Shield **Rev:** Soccer player and ball design

Date	Mintage	F12	VF20	XF40	MS60	MS63
2005	—	PF63 40.00	PF65 45.00			

KM# 103 5 POUNDS
28.28 g., 0.925 Silver 0.8356 oz. ASW, 38.61 mm. **Ruler:** Elizabeth II **Obv:** Shield **Rev:** Soccer player and ball design

Date	Mintage	F12	VF20	XF40	MS60	MS63
2005	—	PF63 40.00	PF65 45.00			

KM# 104 5 POUNDS
28.28 g., 0.925 Silver 0.8356 oz. ASW, 38.61 mm. **Ruler:** Elizabeth II **Obv:** Shield **Rev:** Soccer player and ball design

Date	Mintage	F12	VF20	XF40	MS60	MS63
2005	—	PF63 40.00	PF65 45.00			

KM# 105 5 POUNDS
28.28 g., 0.925 Silver 0.8356 oz. ASW, 38.61 mm. **Ruler:** Elizabeth II **Obv:** Shield **Rev:** Soccer player and ball design

Date	Mintage	F12	VF20	XF40	MS60	MS63
2005	—	PF63 40.00	PF65 45.00			

KM# 106 5 POUNDS
28.28 g., 0.925 Silver 0.8356 oz. ASW, 38.61 mm. **Ruler:** Elizabeth II **Obv:** Shield **Rev:** Soccer player and ball design

Date	Mintage	F12	VF20	XF40	MS60	MS63
2005	—	PF63 40.00	PF65 45.00			

KM# 107 5 POUNDS
28.28 g., 0.925 Silver 0.8356 oz. ASW, 38.61 mm. **Ruler:** Elizabeth II **Obv:** Shield **Rev:** Soccer player and ball design

Date	Mintage	F12	VF20	XF40	MS60	MS63
2005	—	PF63 40.00	PF65 45.00			

KM# 108 5 POUNDS
28.25 g., 0.925 Silver 0.8347 oz. ASW, 38.61 mm. **Ruler:** Elizabeth II **Obv:** Shield **Rev:** Soccer player and ball design

Date	Mintage	F12	VF20	XF40	MS60	MS63
2005	—	PF63 40.00	PF65 45.00			

KM# 113 5 POUNDS
28.28 g., Copper-Nickel, 38.61 mm. **Ruler:** Elizabeth II **Subject:** Prince William, 21st Birthday

Date	Mintage	F12	VF20	XF40	MS60	MS63
2005	—	—	—	—	—	15.00

KM# 113b 5 POUNDS
39.94 g., 0.9167 Gold 1.1696 oz. AGW, 38.61 mm. **Ruler:** Elizabeth II **Subject:** Prince William, 21st Birthday

Date	Mintage	F12	VF20	XF40	MS60	MS63
2005	Est. 150	PF65 2,200				

KM# 116 5 POUNDS
28.28 g., Copper-Nickel, 38.61 mm. **Ruler:** Elizabeth II **Subject:** Royal Navy - H.M.S. Warspite

Date	Mintage	F12	VF20	XF40	MS60	MS63
2005	—	—	—	—	—	15.00

KM# 70 5 POUNDS
28.28 g., 0.925 Silver 0.8356 oz. ASW, 38.6 mm. **Ruler:** Elizabeth II **Subject:** Queen's 80th Birthday **Obv:** Crowned bust right - gilt **Obv. Legend:** ELIZABETH II - ALDERNEY **Rev:** 1/2 length figures of Queen mother and daughter hugging, facing

Date	Mintage	F12	VF20	XF40	MS60	MS63
2006	—	PF63 40.00	PF65 45.00			

KM# 129a 5 POUNDS
28.28 g., 0.925 Silver 0.8356 oz. ASW, 38.61 mm. **Ruler:** Elizabeth II **Rev:** Charles Dickens

Date	Mintage	F12	VF20	XF40	MS60	MS63
2006	—	PF63 50.00	PF65 55.00			

KM# 126a 5 POUNDS
28.28 g., 0.925 Silver 0.8356 oz. ASW, 38.61 mm. **Ruler:** Elizabeth II **Rev:** Queen Elizabeth I

Date	Mintage	F12	VF20	XF40	MS60	MS63
2006	Est. 25000	PF63 45.00	PF65 55.00			

KM# 127a 5 POUNDS
28.28 g., 0.925 Silver 0.8356 oz. ASW, 38.61 mm. **Ruler:** Elizabeth II **Rev:** Sir Isaac Newton

Date	Mintage	F12	VF20	XF40	MS60	MS63
2006	—	PF63 50.00	PF65 55.00			

KM# 128a 5 POUNDS
28.28 g., 0.925 Silver 0.8356 oz. ASW, 38.61 mm. **Ruler:** Elizabeth II **Rev:** William Shakespeare

Date	Mintage	F12	VF20	XF40	MS60	MS63
2006	—	PF63 50.00	PF65 55.00			

KM# 132a 5 POUNDS
28.28 g., 0.925 Silver 0.8356 oz. ASW, 38.61 mm. **Ruler:** Elizabeth II **Rev:** Elizabeth II Coronation

Date	Mintage	F12	VF20	XF40	MS60	MS63
2006	Est. 25000	PF63 50.00	PF65 55.00			

KM# 133a 5 POUNDS
28.28 g., 0.925 Silver 0.8356 oz. ASW, 38.61 mm. **Ruler:** Elizabeth II **Obv:** Head in tiara right **Obv. Designer:** Ian Rank-Broadley **Rev:** Bust in tiara right **Rev. Designer:** Raphael Maklouf

Date	Mintage	F12	VF20	XF40	MS60	MS63
2006	—	PF63 50.00	PF65 55.00			

KM# 148a 5 POUNDS
28.28 g., 0.925 Silver 0.8356 oz. ASW, 38.61 mm. **Ruler:** Elizabeth II **Subject:** Victoria Cross, 150th Anniversary **Rev:** Henry Ramage and Victoria Cross medal

Date	Mintage	F12	VF20	XF40	MS60	MS63
2006	Est. 30000	PF63 45.00	PF65 55.00			

KM# 126 5 POUNDS
28.28 g., Copper-Nickel, 38.61 mm. **Ruler:** Elizabeth II **Rev:** Elizabeth I

Date	Mintage	F12	VF20	XF40	MS60	MS63
2006	—	—	—	—	—	12.00

KM# 126b 5 POUNDS
39.94 g., 0.916 Gold 1.1687 oz. AGW, 38.61 mm. **Ruler:** Elizabeth II **Rev:** Queen Elizabeth I

Date	Mintage	F12	VF20	XF40	MS60	MS63
2006	—	PF65 2,250				

KM# 127 5 POUNDS
28.28 g., Copper-Nickel, 38.61 mm. **Ruler:** Elizabeth II **Rev:** Sir Isaac Newton

Date	Mintage	F12	VF20	XF40	MS60	MS63
2006	—	—	—	—	—	15.00

KM# 127b 5 POUNDS
39.94 g., 0.9167 Gold 1.1696 oz. AGW, 38.61 mm. **Ruler:** Elizabeth II **Rev:** Sir Isaac Newton

Date	Mintage	F12	VF20	XF40	MS60	MS63
2006	—	PF65 2,250				

KM# 128 5 POUNDS
28.28 g., Copper-Nickel, 38.61 mm. **Ruler:** Elizabeth II **Rev:** William Shakespeare

Date	Mintage	F12	VF20	XF40	MS60	MS63
2006	—	—	—	—	—	15.00

KM# 128b 5 POUNDS
39.94 g., 0.916 Gold 1.1687 oz. AGW, 38.61 mm. **Ruler:** Elizabeth II **Rev:** William Shakespeare

Date	Mintage	F12	VF20	XF40	MS60	MS63
2006	—	PF65 2,250				

KM# 129 5 POUNDS
28.28 g., Copper-Nickel, 38.61 mm. **Ruler:** Elizabeth II **Rev:** Charles Dickens

Date	Mintage	F12	VF20	XF40	MS60	MS63
2006	—	—	—	—	—	15.00

KM# 129b 5 POUNDS
39.94 g., 0.916 Gold 1.1687 oz. AGW, 38.61 mm. **Ruler:** Elizabeth II **Rev:** Charles Dickens

Date	Mintage	F12	VF20	XF40	MS60	MS63
2006	—	PF65 2,250				

KM# 132 5 POUNDS
28.28 g., Copper-Nickel, 38.61 mm. **Ruler:** Elizabeth II **Rev:** Elizabeth II Coronation

Date	Mintage	F12	VF20	XF40	MS60	MS63
2006	—	—	—	—	—	15.00

KM# 133 5 POUNDS
28.28 g., Copper-Nickel, 38.61 mm. **Ruler:** Elizabeth II **Obv:** Head in tiara right **Obv. Designer:** Ian Rank-Broadley **Rev:** Bust in tiara right **Rev. Designer:** Raphael Maklouf

Date	Mintage	F12	VF20	XF40	MS60	MS63
2006	—	—	—	—	—	15.00

KM# 133b 5 POUNDS
39.94 g., 0.9167 Gold 1.1696 oz. AGW, 38.61 mm. **Ruler:** Elizabeth II **Obv:** Head in tiara right **Obv. Designer:** Ian Rank-Broadley **Rev:** Bust in tiara right **Rev. Designer:** Raphael Maklouf

Date	Mintage	F12	VF20	XF40	MS60	MS63
2006	—				PF65	2,250

KM# 133b.1 5 POUNDS
39.94 g., 0.9167 Gold 1.1696 oz. AGW, 38.61 mm. **Ruler:** Elizabeth II **Obv:** Head in tiara right **Obv. Designer:** Ira Rank-Broadley **Rev:** Bust in tiara right **Rev. Designer:** Raphael Maklouf

Date	Mintage	F12	VF20	XF40	MS60	MS63
2006	—				PF65	2,500

KM# 138 5 POUNDS
28.28 g., 0.925 Silver 0.8356 oz. ASW, 38.61 mm. **Ruler:** Elizabeth II **Obv:** Shield **Rev:** Soccer player

Date	Mintage	F12	VF20	XF40	MS60	MS63
2006	—	PF63 45.00	PF65 55.00			

KM# 139 5 POUNDS
28.28 g., 0.925 Silver 0.8356 oz. ASW, 38.61 mm. **Ruler:** Elizabeth II **Obv:** Shield **Rev:** Soccer player

Date	Mintage	F12	VF20	XF40	MS60	MS63
2006	—	PF63 45.00	PF65 55.00			

KM# 140 5 POUNDS
28.28 g., 0.925 Silver 0.8356 oz. ASW, 38.61 mm. **Ruler:** Elizabeth II **Obv:** Shield **Rev:** Soccer player

Date	Mintage	F12	VF20	XF40	MS60	MS63
2006	—	PF63 45.00	PF65 55.00			

KM# 141 5 POUNDS
28.28 g., 0.925 Silver 0.8356 oz. ASW, 38.61 mm. **Ruler:** Elizabeth II **Obv:** Shield **Rev:** Soccer player

Date	Mintage	F12	VF20	XF40	MS60	MS63
2006	—	PF63 45.00	PF65 55.00			

KM# 142 5 POUNDS
28.28 g., 0.925 Silver 0.8356 oz. ASW, 38.61 mm. **Ruler:** Elizabeth II **Obv:** Shield **Rev:** Soccer player

Date	Mintage	F12	VF20	XF40	MS60	MS63
2006	—	PF63 45.00	PF65 55.00			

KM# 143 5 POUNDS
28.28 g., 0.925 Silver 0.8356 oz. ASW, 38.61 mm. **Ruler:** Elizabeth II **Obv:** Shield **Rev:** Soccer player

Date	Mintage	F12	VF20	XF40	MS60	MS63
2006	—	PF63 45.00	PF65 55.00			

KM# 144 5 POUNDS
28.28 g., 0.925 Silver 0.8356 oz. ASW, 38.61 mm. **Ruler:** Elizabeth II **Obv:** Shield **Rev:** Soccer player

Date	Mintage	F12	VF20	XF40	MS60	MS63
2006	—	PF63 45.00	PF65 55.00			

KM# 145 5 POUNDS
28.28 g., 0.925 Silver 0.8356 oz. ASW, 38.61 mm. **Ruler:** Elizabeth II **Obv:** Shield **Rev:** Soccer player

Date	Mintage	F12	VF20	XF40	MS60	MS63
2006	—	PF63 45.00	PF65 55.00			

KM# 146 5 POUNDS
28.28 g., 0.925 Silver 0.8356 oz. ASW, 38.61 mm. **Ruler:** Elizabeth II **Obv:** Shield **Rev:** Soccer player

Date	Mintage	F12	VF20	XF40	MS60	MS63
2006	—	PF63 45.00	PF65 55.00			

KM# 147 5 POUNDS
28.28 g., 0.925 Silver 0.8356 oz. ASW, 38.61 mm. **Ruler:** Elizabeth II **Obv:** Shield **Rev:** Soccer player

Date	Mintage	F12	VF20	XF40	MS60	MS63
2006	—	PF63 45.00	PF65 55.00			

KM# 148 5 POUNDS
28.28 g., Copper-Nickel, 38.61 mm. **Ruler:** Elizabeth II **Subject:** Victoria Cross, 150th Anniversary **Rev:** Henry Ramage and Victoria Cross medal

Date	Mintage	F12	VF20	XF40	MS60	MS63
2006	—	—	—	—	—	15.00

KM# 149 5 POUNDS
28.28 g., 0.925 Silver 0.8356 oz. ASW, 38.61 mm. **Ruler:** Elizabeth II **Subject:** Victoria Cross, 150th Anniversary **Rev:** Charles Lucas, Victoria Cross medal

Date	Mintage	F12	VF20	XF40	MS60	MS63
2006	Est. 30000	PF63 45.00	PF65 55.00			

KM# 150 5 POUNDS
28.28 g., 0.925 Silver 0.8356 oz. ASW, 38.61 mm. **Ruler:** Elizabeth II **Subject:** Victoria Cross, 150th Anniversary **Rev:** Ernest Smith, Victoria Cross medal

Date	Mintage	F12	VF20	XF40	MS60	MS63
2006	Est. 30000	PF63 45.00	PF65 55.00			

KM# 151 5 POUNDS
28.28 g., 0.925 Silver 0.8356 oz. ASW, 38.61 mm. **Ruler:** Elizabeth II **Subject:** Victoria Cross, 150th Anniversary **Rev:** Stanley Hollis, Victoria Cross medal

Date	Mintage	F12	VF20	XF40	MS60	MS63
2006	—	PF63 45.00	PF65 55.00			

KM# 152 5 POUNDS
28.28 g., 0.925 Silver 0.8356 oz. ASW, 38.61 mm. **Ruler:** Elizabeth II **Subject:** Victoria Cross, 150th Anniversary **Rev:** Geoffrey Keyes, Victoria Cross medal

Date	Mintage	F12	VF20	XF40	MS60	MS63
2006	Est. 30000	PF63 45.00	PF65 55.00			

KM# 153 5 POUNDS
28.28 g., 0.925 Silver 0.8356 oz. ASW, 38.61 mm. **Ruler:** Elizabeth II **Subject:** Victoria Cross, 150th Anniversary **Rev:** Daniel Laidlow, Victoria Cross medal

Date	Mintage	F12	VF20	XF40	MS60	MS63
2006	Est. 30000	PF63 45.00	PF65 55.00			

KM# 159a 5 POUNDS
28.28 g., 0.925 Silver 0.8356 oz. ASW, 38.61 mm. **Ruler:** Elizabeth II **Rev:** Sir Edward Elgar

Date	Mintage	F12	VF20	XF40	MS60	MS63
2007	Est. 25000	PF63 45.00	PF65 55.00			

KM# 179a 5 POUNDS
28.28 g., 0.925 Silver 0.8356 oz. ASW, 38.61 mm. **Ruler:** Elizabeth II **Subject:** Elizabeth II and Prince Philip, 60th Wedding Anniversary **Rev:** Honeymoon departure

Date	Mintage	F12	VF20	XF40	MS60	MS63
2007	—	PF63 50.00	PF65 55.00			

KM# 158a 5 POUNDS
28.28 g., 0.925 Silver 0.8356 oz. ASW, 38.61 mm. **Ruler:** Elizabeth II **Rev:** Capt. Jmes Cook

Date	Mintage	F12	VF20	XF40	MS60	MS63
2007	—	PF63 50.00	PF65 55.00			

KM# 160a 5 POUNDS
28.28 g., 0.925 Silver 0.8356 oz. ASW, 38.61 mm. **Ruler:** Elizabeth II **Rev:** Sir Francis Drake

Date	Mintage	F12	VF20	XF40	MS60	MS63
2007	Est. 25000	PF63 45.00	PF65 55.00			

KM# 161a 5 POUNDS
28.28 g., 0.925 Silver 0.8356 oz. ASW, 38.61 mm. **Ruler:** Elizabeth II **Rev:** John Constable

Date	Mintage	F12	VF20	XF40	MS60	MS63
2007	Est. 25000	PF63 45.00	PF65 55.00			

KM# 177a 5 POUNDS
28.28 g., 0.925 Silver 0.8356 oz. ASW, 38.61 mm. **Ruler:** Elizabeth II **Subject:** Elizabeth II and Prince Philip, 60th Wedding Anniversary **Rev:** 1947 Wedding Portrait

Date	Mintage	F12	VF20	XF40	MS60	MS63
2007	—	PF63 50.00	PF65 55.00			

KM# 178a 5 POUNDS
28.28 g., 0.925 Silver 0.8356 oz. ASW, 38.61 mm. **Ruler:** Elizabeth II **Subject:** Elizabeth II and Prince Philip, 60th Wedding Anniversary **Rev:** State Carriage

Date	Mintage	F12	VF20	XF40	MS60	MS63
2007	—	PF63 50.00	PF65 55.00			

KM# 180a 5 POUNDS
28.28 g., 0.925 Silver 0.8356 oz. ASW, 38.61 mm. **Ruler:** Elizabeth II **Subject:** Elizabeth II and Prince Philip, 60th Wedding Anniversary **Rev:** Elizabeth II and Philip portraits

Date	Mintage	F12	VF20	XF40	MS60	MS63
2007	—	PF63 50.00	PF65 55.00			

KM# 158 5 POUNDS
28.28 g., Copper-Nickel, 38.61 mm. **Ruler:** Elizabeth II **Rev:** Capt. James Cook

Date	Mintage	F12	VF20	XF40	MS60	MS63
2007	—	—	—	—	—	15.00

KM# 158b 5 POUNDS
39.94 g., 0.916 Gold 1.1687 oz. AGW, 38.61 mm. **Ruler:** Elizabeth II **Rev:** Capt. James Cook

Date	Mintage	F12	VF20	XF40	MS60	MS63
2007	—				PF65	2,250

KM# 159 5 POUNDS
28.28 g., Copper-Nickel, 38.61 mm. **Ruler:** Elizabeth II **Rev:** Sir Edward Elgar

Date	Mintage	F12	VF20	XF40	MS60	MS63
2007	—	—	—	—	—	15.00

KM# 159b 5 POUNDS
39.94 g., 0.9167 Gold 1.1696 oz. AGW, 38.61 mm. **Ruler:** Elizabeth II **Rev:** Sir Edward Elgar

Date	Mintage	F12	VF20	XF40	MS60	MS63
2007	—				PF65	2,250

KM# 160 5 POUNDS
28.28 g., Copper-Nickel, 38.61 mm. **Ruler:** Elizabeth II **Rev:** Sir Francis Drake

Date	Mintage	F12	VF20	XF40	MS60	MS63
2007	—	PF63 12.00	PF65 15.00			

KM# 160b 5 POUNDS
39.94 g., 0.9167 Gold 1.1696 oz. AGW, 38.61 mm. **Ruler:** Elizabeth II **Rev:** Sir Francis Drake

Date	Mintage	F12	VF20	XF40	MS60	MS63
2007	—				PF65	2,250

KM# 161 5 POUNDS
28.28 g., Copper-Nickel, 38.61 mm. **Ruler:** Elizabeth II **Rev:** John Constable

Date	Mintage	F12	VF20	XF40	MS60	MS63
2007	—	—	—	—	—	15.00

KM# 162 5 POUNDS
28.28 g., 0.925 Silver 0.8356 oz. ASW, 38.61 mm. **Ruler:** Elizabeth II **Rev:** Henry VII

Date	Mintage	F12	VF20	XF40	MS60	MS63
2007	—	PF63 45.00	PF65 55.00			

KM# 161b 5 POUNDS
39.94 g., 0.9167 Gold 1.1696 oz. AGW, 39.94 mm. **Ruler:** Elizabeth II **Rev:** John Constable

Date	Mintage	F12	VF20	XF40	MS60	MS63
2007	—				PF65	2,250

KM# 163 5 POUNDS
28.28 g., 0.925 Silver 0.8356 oz. ASW, 38.61 mm. **Ruler:** Elizabeth II **Rev:** Henry VIII

Date	Mintage	F12	VF20	XF40	MS60	MS63
2007	Est. 37500	PF63 45.00	PF65 55.00			

KM# 164 5 POUNDS
28.28 g., 0.925 Silver 0.8356 oz. ASW, 38.61 mm. **Ruler:** Elizabeth II **Rev:** Edward VI

Date	Mintage	F12	VF20	XF40	MS60	MS63
2007	Est. 37500	PF63 45.00	PF65 55.00			

KM# 165 5 POUNDS
28.28 g., 0.925 Silver 0.8356 oz. ASW, 38.61 mm. **Ruler:** Elizabeth II **Rev:** Mary I

Date	Mintage	F12	VF20	XF40	MS60	MS63
2007	Est. 37500	PF63 45.00	PF65 55.00			

KM# 166 5 POUNDS
28.28 g., 0.925 Silver 0.8356 oz. ASW, 38.61 mm. **Ruler:** Elizabeth II **Rev:** Elizabeth I

Date	Mintage	F12	VF20	XF40	MS60	MS63
2007	—	PF63 45.00	PF65 55.00			

KM# 167 5 POUNDS
28.28 g., 0.925 Silver 0.8356 oz. ASW, 38.61 mm. **Ruler:** Elizabeth II **Rev:** James I

Date	Mintage	F12	VF20	XF40	MS60	MS63
2007	Est. 37500	PF63 45.00	PF65 55.00			

KM# 168 5 POUNDS
28.28 g., 0.925 Silver 0.8356 oz. ASW, 38.61 mm. **Ruler:** Elizabeth II **Rev:** Charles I

Date	Mintage	F12	VF20	XF40	MS60	MS63
2007	Est. 37500	PF63 45.00	PF65 55.00			

KM# 169 5 POUNDS
28.28 g., 0.925 Silver 0.8356 oz. ASW, 38.61 mm. **Ruler:** Elizabeth II **Rev:** Charles II

Date	Mintage	F12	VF20	XF40	MS60	MS63
2007	Est. 37500	PF63 45.00	PF65 55.00			

KM# 170 5 POUNDS
28.28 g., 0.916 Silver 0.8275 oz. ASW, 38.61 mm. **Ruler:** Elizabeth II **Rev:** James II

Date	Mintage	F12	VF20	XF40	MS60	MS63
2007	Est. 37500	PF63 45.00	PF65 55.00			

KM# 171 5 POUNDS
28.28 g., 0.925 Silver 0.8356 oz. ASW, 38.61 mm. **Ruler:** Elizabeth II **Rev:** William and Mary

Date	Mintage	F12	VF20	XF40	MS60	MS63
2007	Est. 37500	PF63 45.00	PF65 55.00			

KM# 172 5 POUNDS
28.28 g., 0.925 Silver 0.8356 oz. ASW, 38.61 mm. **Ruler:** Elizabeth II **Rev:** William III

Date	Mintage	F12	VF20	XF40	MS60	MS63
2007	37,500	PF63 45.00	PF65 55.00			

KM# 173 5 POUNDS
28.28 g., 0.925 Silver 0.8356 oz. ASW, 38.61 mm. **Ruler:** Elizabeth II **Rev:** Anne

Date	Mintage	F12	VF20	XF40	MS60	MS63
2007	Est. 37500	PF63 45.00	PF65 55.00			

KM# 175 5 POUNDS
28.28 g., Copper-Nickel, 38.61 mm. **Ruler:** Elizabeth II **Subject:** Princess Diana, 10th Anniversary of Death

Date	Mintage	F12	VF20	XF40	MS60	MS63
2007	—	—	—	—	—	15.00

KM# 177 5 POUNDS
28.28 g., Copper-Nickel, 38.61 mm. **Ruler:** Elizabeth II **Subject:** Elizabeth II & Prince Philip, 60th Wedding Anniversary **Rev:** 1947 Wedding Portrait

Date	Mintage	F12	VF20	XF40	MS60	MS63
2007	—	—	—	—	—	15.00

KM# 178 5 POUNDS
28.28 g., Copper-Nickel, 38.61 mm. **Ruler:** Elizabeth II **Subject:** Elizabeth II and Prince Philip, 60th Wedding Anniversary **Rev:** State Carriage

Date	Mintage	F12	VF20	XF40	MS60	MS63
2007	—	—	—	—	—	15.00

KM# 179 5 POUNDS
28.28 g., Copper-Nickel, 38.61 mm. **Ruler:** Elizabeth II **Subject:** Elizabeth II and Prince Philip, 60th Wedding Anniversary **Rev:** Honeymoon departure

Date	Mintage	F12	VF20	XF40	MS60	MS63
2007	—	—	—	—	—	15.00

KM# 180 5 POUNDS
28.28 g., Copper-Nickel, 38.61 mm. **Ruler:** Elizabeth II **Subject:** Elizabeth II and Prince Philip, 60th Wedding Anniversary **Rev:** Portraits

Date	Mintage	F12	VF20	XF40	MS60	MS63
2007	—	—	—	—	—	15.00

KM# 181 5 POUNDS
28.28 g., 0.925 Silver 0.8356 oz. ASW, 38.61 mm. **Ruler:** Elizabeth II **Subject:** Elizabeth II and Prince Philip, 60th Wedding Anniversary **Rev:** Bridal couple outside Westminster Abbey

Date	Mintage	F12	VF20	XF40	MS60	MS63
2007	Est. 30000	PF63 45.00	PF65 55.00			

KM# 182 5 POUNDS
28.28 g., 0.925 Silver 0.8356 oz. ASW, 38.61 mm. **Ruler:** Elizabeth II **Subject:** Elizabeth II and Prince Philip, 60th Wedding Anniversary **Rev:** Birth of Prince Charles

Date	Mintage	F12	VF20	XF40	MS60	MS63
2007	Est. 30000	PF63 45.00	PF65 55.00			

KM# 183 5 POUNDS
28.28 g., 0.925 Silver 0.8356 oz. ASW, 38.61 mm. **Ruler:** Elizabeth II **Subject:** Elizabeth II and Prince Philip, 60th Wedding Anniversary **Rev:** Modern portrait of Elizabeth and Philip

Date	Mintage	F12	VF20	XF40	MS60	MS63
2007	Est. 30000	PF63 45.00	PF65 55.00			

KM# 222 5 POUNDS
28.28 g., 0.925 Silver 0.8356 oz. ASW, 38.61 mm. **Ruler:** Elizabeth II **Subject:** Elizabeth II 50th Wedding Anniversary **Shape:** 7-sided

Date	Mintage	F12	VF20	XF40	MS60	MS63
2007	Est. 130000	PF63 35.00	PF65 40.00			

KM# 224 5 POUNDS
28.28 g., 0.925 Silver 0.8356 oz. ASW, 38.61 mm. **Ruler:**

Subject: Birth of Prince Charles **Shape:** 7-Sided

Date	Mintage	F12	VF20	XF40	MS60	MS63
2004 (2007)	Est. 30000				PF63 35.00	PF65 40.00

KM# 184a 5 POUNDS
39.94 g., 0.9167 Gold 1.1696 oz. AGW, 38.61 mm. **Ruler:** Elizabeth II **Subject:** End of World War I, 90th Anniversary **Rev:** Soldiers and workers, flag in background

Date	Mintage	F12	VF20	XF40	MS60	MS63
2008	Est. 250	PF65 2,200				

KM# 185a 5 POUNDS
39.94 g., 0.9167 Gold 1.1696 oz. AGW, 38.61 mm. **Ruler:** Elizabeth II **Subject:** End of World War I, 90th Anniversary **Rev:** Tank and soldier

Date	Mintage	F12	VF20	XF40	MS60	MS63
2008	Est. 250	PF65 2,200				

KM# 186a 5 POUNDS
39.94 g., 0.9167 Gold 1.1696 oz. AGW, 38.61 mm. **Ruler:** Elizabeth II **Subject:** End of World War I, 90th Anniversary **Rev:** Soldiers and gravesites

Date	Mintage	F12	VF20	XF40	MS60	MS63
2008	Est. 250	PF65 2,200				

KM# 187 5 POUNDS
28.28 g., 0.925 Silver 0.8356 oz. ASW, 38.61 mm. **Ruler:** Elizabeth II **Subject:** End of World War I, 90th Anniversary **Rev:** Propaganda

Date	Mintage	F12	VF20	XF40	MS60	MS63
2008	Est. 15000	PF63 50.00	PF65 55.00			

KM# 190a 5 POUNDS
28.28 g., 0.925 Silver 0.8356 oz. ASW, 38.61 mm. **Ruler:** Elizabeth II **Rev:** Concorde

Date	Mintage	F12	VF20	XF40	MS60	MS63
2008	—	PF63 50.00	PF65 55.00			

KM# 184 5 POUNDS
28.28 g., 0.925 Silver 0.8356 oz. ASW, 38.61 mm. **Ruler:** Elizabeth II **Subject:** End of World War I, 90th Anniversary **Rev:** Soldiers and workers, flag in background

Date	Mintage	F12	VF20	XF40	MS60	MS63
2008	Est. 15000	PF63 50.00	PF65 55.00			

KM# 185 5 POUNDS
28.28 g., 0.925 Silver 0.8356 oz. ASW, 38.61 mm. **Ruler:** Elizabeth II **Subject:** End of World War I, 90th Anniversary **Rev:** Tank and soldier

Date	Mintage	F12	VF20	XF40	MS60	MS63
2008	Est. 15000	PF63 50.00	PF65 55.00			

KM# 186 5 POUNDS
28.28 g., 0.925 Silver 0.8356 oz. ASW, 38.61 mm. **Ruler:** Elizabeth II **Subject:** End of World War I, 90th Anniversary **Rev:** Soldiers and gravesites

Date	Mintage	F12	VF20	XF40	MS60	MS63
2008	Est. 15000	PF63 50.00	PF65 55.00			

KM# 190 5 POUNDS
28.28 g., Copper-Nickel, 38.61 mm. **Ruler:** Elizabeth II **Rev:** Concorde

Date	Mintage	F12	VF20	XF40	MS60	MS63
2008	—	—	—	—	—	15.00

KM# 190b 5 POUNDS
39.94 g., 0.916 Gold 1.1687 oz. AGW, 38.61 mm. **Ruler:** Elizabeth II **Rev:** Concorde

Date	Mintage	F12	VF20	XF40	MS60	MS63
2008	Est. 250	PF65 60,000				

KM# 85 5 POUNDS
28.28 g., Copper-Nickel, 38.61 mm. **Ruler:** Elizabeth II **Subject:** Mini Cooper 50th Anniversary **Rev:** 1959 Mini Cooper on tiled floor **Rev. Designer:** David Cornell

Date	Mintage	F12	VF20	XF40	MS60	MS63
2009	50,000	—	—	—	—	17.50

KM# 86 5 POUNDS
28.28 g., 0.925 Silver 0.8356 oz. ASW, 38.61 mm. **Ruler:** Elizabeth II **Subject:** Mini Cooper, 50th Anniversary **Rev:** 1959 Mini Cooper multicolor British flag on roof **Rev. Designer:** David Cornell

Date	Mintage	F12	VF20	XF40	MS60	MS63
2009	—	PF63 65.00	PF65 75.00			

KM# 87 5 POUNDS
28.28 g., 0.925 Silver 0.8356 oz. ASW, 38.61 mm. **Ruler:** Elizabeth II **Subject:** Mini Cooper, 50th Anniversary **Rev:** Mini Cooper, red and pink flowers **Rev. Designer:** David Cornell

Date	Mintage	F12	VF20	XF40	MS60	MS63
2009	2,000	PF63 65.00	PF65 75.00			

KM# 88 5 POUNDS
28.28 g., 0.925 Silver 0.8356 oz. ASW, 38.61 mm. **Ruler:** Elizabeth II **Subject:** Mini Cooper, 50th Anniversary **Rev:** Mini Cooper, 4 views **Rev. Designer:** Kerry Jones

Date	Mintage	F12	VF20	XF40	MS60	MS63
2009	2,000	PF63 65.00	PF65 75.00			

KM# 89 5 POUNDS
28.28 g., 0.925 Silver 0.8356 oz. ASW, 38.61 mm. **Ruler:** Elizabeth II **Subject:** Mini Cooper, 50th Anniversary **Rev:** Rally Minis **Rev. Designer:** Kerry Jones and David Cornell

Date	Mintage	F12	VF20	XF40	MS60	MS63
2009	2,000	PF63 65.00	PF65 75.00			

KM# 193 5 POUNDS
28.28 g., 0.925 Silver 0.8356 oz. ASW, 38.61 mm. **Ruler:** Elizabeth II **Subject:** British Automobiles **Rev:** Morris Minor

Date	Mintage	F12	VF20	XF40	MS60	MS63
2009	20,000	PF63 45.00	PF65 55.00			

KM# 194 5 POUNDS
28.28 g., 0.925 Silver 0.8356 oz. ASW, 38.61 mm. **Ruler:** Elizabeth II **Subject:** British Automobiles **Rev:** Land Rover series 1

Date	Mintage	F12	VF20	XF40	MS60	MS63
2009	Est. 20000	PF63 45.00	PF65 55.00			

KM# 195 5 POUNDS
28.28 g., 0.925 Silver 0.8356 oz. ASW, 38.61 mm. **Ruler:** Elizabeth II **Subject:** British Automobiles **Rev:** Jaguar E type series 1

Date	Mintage	F12	VF20	XF40	MS60	MS63
2009	Est. 20000	PF63 45.00	PF65 55.00			

KM# 196 5 POUNDS
28.28 g., 0.925 Silver 0.8356 oz. ASW, 38.61 mm. **Ruler:** Elizabeth II **Subject:** British Automobiles **Rev:** Rolls Royce Silver Ghost

Date	Mintage	F12	VF20	XF40	MS60	MS63
2009	Est. 20000	PF63 45.00	PF65 55.00			

KM# 197 5 POUNDS
28.28 g., 0.925 Silver 0.8356 oz. ASW, 38.61 mm. **Ruler:** Elizabeth II **Subject:** British Automobiles **Rev:** Austrin Seven "Baby Austin

Date	Mintage	F12	VF20	XF40	MS60	MS63
2009	Est. 20000	PF63 45.00	PF65 55.00			

KM# 198 5 POUNDS
28.28 g., 0.925 Silver 0.8356 oz. ASW, 38.61 mm. **Ruler:** Elizabeth II **Subject:** British Automobiles **Rev:** Triumph Herald

Date	Mintage	F12	VF20	XF40	MS60	MS63
2009	—	PF63 45.00	PF65 55.00			

KM# 199 5 POUNDS
28.28 g., 0.925 Silver 0.8356 oz. ASW **Ruler:** Elizabeth II **Subject:** British Automobiles **Rev:** Bentley R type Contiental

Date	Mintage	F12	VF20	XF40	MS60	MS63
2009	—	PF63 45.00	PF65 55.00			

KM# 200 5 POUNDS
28.28 g., 0.925 Silver 0.8356 oz. ASW, 38.61 mm. **Ruler:** Elizabeth II **Subject:** British Automobiles **Rev:** Lotus Elite (1967)

Date	Mintage	F12	VF20	XF40	MS60	MS63
2009	Est. 20000	PF63 45.00	PF65 55.00			

KM# 202 5 POUNDS
28.28 g., 0.925 Silver 0.8356 oz. ASW, 38.61 mm. **Ruler:** Elizabeth II **Subject:** British Automobiles **Rev:** Austin healey Sprint MK 1

Date	Mintage	F12	VF20	XF40	MS60	MS63
2009	Est. 20000	PF63 45.00	PF65 55.00			

KM# 203 5 POUNDS
28.28 g., 0.925 Silver 0.8356 oz. ASW, 38.61 mm. **Ruler:** Elizabeth II **Subject:** British Automobiles **Rev:** Bentley 4-1/2 Litre

Date	Mintage	F12	VF20	XF40	MS60	MS63
2009	Est. 20000	PF63 45.00	PF65 55.00			

KM# 204 5 POUNDS
28.28 g., 0.925 Silver 0.8356 oz. ASW, 38.61 mm. **Ruler:** Elizabeth II **Subject:** British Automobiles **Rev:** Hillman Imp

Date	Mintage	F12	VF20	XF40	MS60	MS63
2009	Est. 20000	PF63 45.00	PF65 55.00			

KM# 205 5 POUNDS
28.28 g., 0.925 Silver 0.8356 oz. ASW, 38.61 mm. **Ruler:** Elizabeth II **Subject:** British Automobiles **Rev:** MGB Roadster MK 1

Date	Mintage	F12	VF20	XF40	MS60	MS63
2009	Est. 20000	PF63 45.00	PF65 55.00			

KM# 206 5 POUNDS
28.28 g., 0.925 Silver 0.8356 oz. ASW, 38.61 mm. **Ruler:** Elizabeth II **Subject:** British Automobiles **Rev:** MG TC Midget

Date	Mintage	F12	VF20	XF40	MS60	MS63
2009	Est. 20000	PF63 45.00	PF65 55.00			

KM# 207 5 POUNDS
28.28 g., 0.925 Silver 0.8356 oz. ASW, 38.61 mm. **Ruler:** Elizabeth II **Subject:** British Automobiles **Rev:** BMC Mini

Date	Mintage	F12	VF20	XF40	MS60	MS63
2009	Est. 20000	PF63 45.00	PF65 55.00			

KM# 208 5 POUNDS
28.28 g., 0.925 Silver 0.8356 oz. ASW, 38.61 mm. **Ruler:** Elizabeth II **Subject:** British Automobiles **Rev:** Morgan Plus Four

Date	Mintage	F12	VF20	XF40	MS60	MS63
2009	Est. 20000	PF63 45.00	PF65 55.00			

KM# 209 5 POUNDS
28.28 g., 0.925 Silver 0.8356 oz. ASW, 38.61 mm. **Ruler:** Elizabeth II **Subject:** British Automobiles **Rev:** Rover P5B

Date	Mintage	F12	VF20	XF40	MS60	MS63
2009	Est. 20000	PF63 45.00	PF65 55.00			

KM# 210 5 POUNDS
28.28 g., 0.925 Silver 0.8356 oz. ASW, 38.61 mm. **Ruler:** Elizabeth II **Subject:** British Automobiles **Rev:** Vauhall - Prince Henry

Date	Mintage	F12	VF20	XF40	MS60	MS63
2009	Est. 20000	PF63 45.00	PF65 55.00			

KM# 201 5 POUNDS
28.28 g., 0.925 Silver 0.8356 oz. ASW, 38.61 mm. **Ruler:** Elizabeth II **Subject:** British Automobiles **Rev:** Aston Martin DB 5 (1963)

Date	Mintage	F12	VF20	XF40	MS60	MS63
2009	Est. 20000	PF63 45.00	PF65 55.00			

KM# 218 5 POUNDS
28.28 g., Copper-Nickel, 38.6 mm. **Ruler:** Elizabeth II **Subject:** Battle of Britain, 1940 **Obv:** Head in tiara right **Rev:** Fighter planes

Date	Mintage	F12	VF20	XF40	MS60	MS63
2010	—	PF63 17.00	PF65 20.00			

KM# 211 5 POUNDS
28.28 g., Copper-Nickel, 38.61 mm. **Ruler:** Elizabeth II **Subject:** Engagement - Prince William and Catherine Middleton **Obv:** Head in tiara right **Rev:** Conjoined busts left **Rev. Designer:** Matthew Bonaccorsi

Date	Mintage	F12	VF20	XF40	MS60	MS63
2010	100,000	—	—	—	—	20.00

KM# 211a 5 POUNDS
28.28 g., 0.925 Silver 0.8356 oz. ASW, 38.61 mm. **Ruler:** Elizabeth II **Subject:** Engagement - Prince William and Catherine Middleton **Obv:** Head in tiara right **Rev:** Conjoined busts left **Rev. Designer:** Matthew Bonaccorsi

Date	Mintage	F12	VF20	XF40	MS60	MS63
2010	1,500	PF63 100	PF65 120			

KM# 211b 5 POUNDS
39.94 g., 0.9167 Gold 1.1696 oz. AGW, 38.61 mm. **Ruler:** Elizabeth II **Subject:** Engagement of Prince William and Catherine Middleton **Obv:** Head in tiara right **Rev:** Conjoined busts left

Date	Mintage	F12	VF20	XF40	MS60	MS63
2010	1,000	PF65 2,300				

KM# 212 5 POUNDS
28.28 g., Copper-Nickel, 38.61 mm. **Ruler:** Elizabeth II **Subject:** Royal Wedding **Obv:** Head with tiara right **Rev:** Catherine and William busts left

Date	Mintage	F12	VF20	XF40	MS60	MS63
2011	—	—	—	—	—	17.50

KM# 212a 5 POUNDS
28.28 g., 0.925 Silver 0.8356 oz. ASW, 38.61 mm. **Ruler:** Elizabeth II **Subject:** Royal Wedding **Obv:** Head with tiara right **Rev:** Catherine and William busts left

Date	Mintage	F12	VF20	XF40	MS60	MS63
2011	—	PF63 65.00	PF65 75.00			

KM# 219 5 POUNDS
28.28 g., Copper-Nickel, 38.61 mm. **Ruler:** Elizabeth II **Subject:** Remembrance Day **Obv:** Head in tiara right **Obv. Designer:** Ian Rank-Bradley **Rev:** Large poppy in color at left, legend at right **Rev. Designer:** Emma Noble **Rev. Legend:** THE ELEVENTH HOUR OF THE ELEVENTH DAY OF THE ELEVENTH MONTH

Date	Mintage	F12	VF20	XF40	MS60	MS63
2012	—	—	—	—	—	20.00

KM# 220 5 POUNDS
28.28 g., Copper-Nickel, 38.61 mm. **Ruler:** Elizabeth II **Subject:** Titanic, 100th Anniversary **Obv:** Head with tiara right **Obv. Designer:** Ian Rank-Broadley **Rev:** Female statue from titanic memorial at top left, Ship sailing to left, at right

Date	Mintage	F12	VF20	XF40	MS60	MS63
2012	—	—	—	—	—	25.00

KM# 220a 5 POUNDS
28.28 g., 0.925 Silver 0.8356 oz. ASW, 38.61 mm. **Ruler:** Elizabeth II **Subject:** Titanic, 100th Anniversary **Obv:** Head with tiara right **Obv. Designer:** Ian Rank-Broadley **Rev:** Part of Titanic memorial at left, ship sailing left, at right **Rev. Designer:** Lee Robert Jones

Date	Mintage	F12	VF20	XF40	MS60	MS63
2012	—	PF63 65.00	PF65 75.00			

KM# 225 5 POUNDS
0.925 Silver, 38.61 mm. **Ruler:** Elizabeth II **Subject:** Royal Duties - Parliament **Obv:** Head with tiara right **Rev:** Royal standard above, outline of Parliament buildings

Date	Mintage	F12	VF20	XF40	MS60	MS63
2012	—	PF65 75.00				

KM# 227 5 POUNDS
Silver, 38.61 mm. **Ruler:** Elizabeth II **Subject:** Royal Duties - Air Force **Obv:** Jets in formation

Date	Mintage	F12	VF20	XF40	MS60	MS63
2012	—	PF65 75.00				

KM# 223 5 POUNDS
28.28 g., 0.925 Silver 0.8356 oz. ASW, 38.61 mm. **Ruler:** Elizabeth II **Subject:** Queen Elizabeth II 50th Wedding Anniversary **Shape:** 7-Sided

Date	Mintage	F12	VF20	XF40	MS60	MS63
2007 (2013)	Est. 30000	PF63 35.00	PF65 40.00			

KM# 36 10 POUNDS
155.52 g., 0.925 Silver 4.5952 oz. ASW, 65.06 mm. **Ruler:** Elizabeth II **Subject:** Last Flight of the Concorde **Obv:** Crowned bust right **Obv. Legend:** ELIIZABETH II - ALDERNEY **Obv. Designer:** Raphael Maklouf **Rev:** Concorde in flight **Rev. Designer:** Emma Noble **Rev. Legend:** CONCORDE 1969 - 2003 **Edge:** Reeded **Note:** Illustration reduced.

Date	Mintage	F12	VF20	XF40	MS60	MS63
2003	1,969	PF63 175	PF65 200			

KM# 55 10 POUNDS
155.51 g., 0.925 Silver 4.595 oz. ASW, 65 mm. **Ruler:** Elizabeth II **Subject:** WWII Liberation **Obv:** Elizabeth II by Maklouf sign **Rev:** Churchill flashing the "V **Edge:** Reeded

Date	Mintage	F12	VF20	XF40	MS60	MS63
2005	1,945	PF63 275	PF65 325			

KM# 120 10 POUNDS
155.50 g., 0.925 Silver 4.5947 oz. ASW, 65 mm. **Ruler:** Elizabeth II **Subject:** Trafalgar - England espects that every man will do his duty

Date	Mintage	F12	VF20	XF40	MS60	MS63
2005		PF65 275				

KM# 82 10 POUNDS
155.52 g., 0.925 Silver 4.5952 oz. ASW, 65 mm. **Ruler:** Elizabeth II **Obv:** Crowned bust right **Obv. Legend:** ELIZABETH II - ALDERNEY **Obv. Designer:** Raphael Maklouf **Rev:** Four small gilt coinage busts in ornate quadralobe **Rev. Designer:** Michael Guilfoyle **Rev. Legend:** + HER MAJESTY QUEEN ELIZABETH II + EIGHTIETH BIRTHDAY + **Edge:** Reeded, gilt

Date	Mintage	F12	VF20	XF40	MS60	MS63
2006	1,926	PF63 175	PF65 200			

KM# 135 10 POUNDS
155.50 g., 0.925 Silver 4.5947 oz. ASW, 65 mm. **Ruler:** Elizabeth II **Obv:** Head in tiara right **Rev:** Bust in tiara right

Date	Mintage	F12	VF20	XF40	MS60	MS63
2006	Est. 1000	PF65 250				

KM# 176 10 POUNDS
155.50 g., 0.925 Silver 4.5947 oz. ASW, 65 mm. **Ruler:** Elizabeth II **Subject:** Princess Diana, 10th Anniversary of Death

Date	Mintage	F12	VF20	XF40	MS60	MS63
2007	Est. 1500	PF63 245	PF65 275			

KM# 188 10 POUNDS
155.50 g., 0.925 Silver 4.5947 oz. ASW, 65 mm. **Ruler:** Elizabeth II **Subject:** End of World War I, 90th Anniversary

Date	Mintage	F12	VF20	XF40	MS60	MS63
2008	Est. 150	PF65 350				

KM# 191 10 POUNDS
155.50 g., 0.925 Silver 4.5947 oz. ASW, 65 mm. **Ruler:** Elizabeth II **Rev:** Corcorde

Date	Mintage	F12	VF20	XF40	MS60	MS63
2008	Est. 750	PF65 275				

KM# 213 10 POUNDS
155.50 g., 0.925 Silver 4.5947 oz. ASW, 65 mm. **Ruler:** Elizabeth II **Subject:** Royal Wedding - Prince William and Catherine Middleton **Obv:** Head in tiara right **Rev:** Conjoined busts left, rose window in background

Date	Mintage	F12	VF20	XF40	MS60	MS63
2011	500	PF65 200				

KM# 61 25 POUNDS
7.98 g., 0.9167 Gold 0.2337 oz. AGW, 22 mm. **Ruler:** Elizabeth II **Subject:** Queen's 75th Birthday **Obv:** Queen's portrait right **Obv. Designer:** Raphael Maklouf **Rev:** Queen in casual dress surrounded by rose, thistle, daffodil and pimpernel **Rev. Designer:** David Cornell

Date	Mintage	F12	VF20	XF40	MS60	MS63
2001	—	PF63 425	PF65 450			

KM# 74 25 POUNDS
7.98 g., 0.9166 Gold 0.2337 oz. AGW **Ruler:** Elizabeth II **Subject:** Queen Elizabet II - Golden Jubilee of Reign **Obv:** Crowned head right **Rev:** Honor guard and trumpets

Date	Mintage	F12	VF20	XF40	MS60	MS63
2002	—	PF63 425	PF65 450			

KM# 28 25 POUNDS
7.98 g., 0.9167 Gold 0.2337 oz. AGW, 22.05 mm. **Ruler:**
Elizabeth II **Subject:** 5th Anniversary Death of Princess Diana
Obv: Queen's portrait **Rev:** Diana's cameo portrait left above
denomination **Rev. Designer:** Avril Vaughan **Edge:** Reeded

Date	Mintage	VG8	F12	VF20	XF40	MS60
2002	2,500		PF63 425	PF65 450		

KM# 30 25 POUNDS
7.98 g., 0.9166 Gold 0.2337 oz. AGW, 22 mm. **Ruler:** Elizabeth
II **Subject:** 150th Anniversary Death of the Duke of Wellington
Obv: Queen's portrait **Rev:** Coat of arms, castle and portrait
Rev. Designer: Willem Vis **Edge:** Reeded

Date	Mintage	VG8	F12	VF20	XF40	MS60
2002	2,500		PF63 425	PF65 450		

KM# 58 25 POUNDS
7.98 g., 0.9166 Gold 0.2337 oz. AGW, 22 mm. **Ruler:** Elizabeth
II **Subject:** Queen Elizabeth II - Golden Jubilee of Reign **Obv:**
Crowned head right **Rev:** Sword hilt and denomination with
royal arms in background

Date	Mintage	F12	VF20	XF40	MS60	MS63
2002	2,500	PF63 425	PF65 450			

KM# 32 25 POUNDS
7.98 g., 0.9166 Gold 0.2337 oz. AGW, 22 mm. **Ruler:** Elizabeth
II **Subject:** Prince William **Obv:** Queen's portrait **Rev:** Portrait
with open shirt collar **Edge:** Reeded

Date	Mintage	F12	VF20	XF40	MS60	MS63
2003	1,500	PF63 425	PF65 450			

KM# 46 25 POUNDS
7.98 g., 0.9167 Gold 0.2337 oz. AGW, 22 mm. **Ruler:** Elizabeth
II **Obv:** Queen's portrait **Rev:** HMS Mary Rose **Rev. Designer:**
Willem Vis **Edge:** Reeded

Date	Mintage	F12	VF20	XF40	MS60	MS63
2003	2,500	PF63 450	PF65 475			

KM# 93 25 POUNDS
7.98 g., 0.916 Gold 0.2335 oz. AGW **Ruler:** Elizabeth II
Subject: Royal navy - Alfred the Great

Date	Mintage	F12	VF20	XF40	MS60	MS63
2003	Est. 1000	PF63 475	PF65 500			

KM# 39 25 POUNDS
7.98 g., 0.9167 Gold 0.2337 oz. AGW, 22 mm. **Ruler:** Elizabeth
II **Subject:** D-Day **Obv:** Queen's portrait **Rev:** Battleship and
transports **Edge:** Reeded

Date	Mintage	F12	VF20	XF40	MS60	MS63
2004	500	PF63 450	PF65 475			

KM# 50 25 POUNDS
7.98 g., 0.9167 Gold 0.2337 oz. AGW, 22 mm. **Ruler:** Elizabeth
II **Obv:** Queen's portrait **Rev:** Locomotive, The Rocket **Rev.
Designer:** Robert Lowe **Edge:** Reeded

Date	Mintage	F12	VF20	XF40	MS60	MS63
2004	2,500	PF63 450	PF65 475			

KM# 51 25 POUNDS
7.98 g., 0.9167 Gold 0.2337 oz. AGW, 22 mm. **Ruler:** Elizabeth
II **Obv:** Queen's portrait **Rev:** Locomotive, The Merchant Navy
21C1 **Rev. Designer:** Robert Lowe **Edge:** Reeded

Date	Mintage	F12	VF20	XF40	MS60	MS63
2004	1,500	PF63 450	PF65 475			

KM# 67 25 POUNDS
7.98 g., 0.9167 Gold 0.2337 oz. AGW, 22 mm. **Ruler:** Elizabeth
II **Subject:** Viscount Samuel Hood on his flagship after the
Battle of Saints Passage in 1782 **Obv:** Queen's portrait **Rev.
Designer:** Willem Vis

Date	Mintage	F12	VF20	XF40	MS60	MS63
2005	—	PF63 425	PF65 450			

KM# 69 25 POUNDS
7.98 g., 0.9167 Gold 0.2337 oz. AGW, 22 mm. **Ruler:** Elizabeth
II **Obv:** Queen's portrait right **Rev:** HMS Revenge fighting at
Azores, 1591 **Rev. Designer:** Willem Vis

Date	Mintage	F12	VF20	XF40	MS60	MS63
2005	—	PF63 450	PF65 475			

KM# 109 25 POUNDS
7.98 g., 0.916 Gold 0.2335 oz. AGW **Ruler:** Elizabeth II
Subject: David Beckham **Obv:** Shield **Rev:** Soccer player and
ball design

Date	Mintage	F12	VF20	XF40	MS60	MS63
2005	Est. 5000	PF63 475	PF65 500			

KM# 110 25 POUNDS
7.98 g., 0.916 Gold 0.2335 oz. AGW **Ruler:** Elizabeth II
Subject: Michael Owen **Obv:** Shield **Rev:** Soccer player and
ball design

Date	Mintage	F12	VF20	XF40	MS60	MS63
2005	Est. 5000	PF63 475	PF65 500			

KM# 111 25 POUNDS
7.98 g., 0.916 Gold 0.2335 oz. AGW **Ruler:** Elizabeth II
Subject: Lrank Lampard **Obv:** Shield **Rev:** Soccer player and
ball design

Date	Mintage	F12	VF20	XF40	MS60	MS63
2005	—	PF63 475	PF65 500			

KM# 112 25 POUNDS
7.98 g., 0.916 Gold 0.2335 oz. AGW **Ruler:** Elizabeth II
Subject: Jeremiah Campbell **Obv:** Shield **Rev:** Soccer player
and ball design.

Date	Mintage	F12	VF20	XF40	MS60	MS63
2005	Est. 5000	PF63 475	PF65 500			

KM# 117 25 POUNDS
7.98 g., 0.916 Gold 0.2335 oz. AGW **Ruler:** Elizabeth II
Subject: Royal Navy - H.M.S. Warspite

Date	Mintage	F12	VF20	XF40	MS60	MS63
2005	Est. 1500	PF63 475	PF65 500			

KM# 118 25 POUNDS
7.98 g., 0.916 Gold 0.2335 oz. AGW **Ruler:** Elizabeth II
Subject: Royal Navy - Admiral Sir John Foster Woodward

Date	Mintage	F12	VF20	XF40	MS60	MS63
2005	Est. 1500	PF63 475	PF65 500			

KM# 121 25 POUNDS
7.98 g., 0.916 Gold 0.2335 oz. AGW **Ruler:** Elizabeth II **Series:**
Trafalgar - England expects that every man will do his duty

Date	Mintage	F12	VF20	XF40	MS60	MS63
2005	—	PF63 475	PF65 500			

KM# 92 50 POUNDS
1000.00 g., Bi-Metallic, 100 mm. **Ruler:** Elizabeth II **Rev:**
Coronation at Westminster

Date	Mintage	F12	VF20	XF40	MS60	MS63
2002	Est. 2002	PF65 1,250				

KM# 62 50 POUNDS
1000.00 g., 0.925 Silver 29.548 oz. ASW, 100 mm. **Ruler:**
Elizabeth II **Subject:** 50th Anniversary of Coronation **Obv:**
Queen's portrait right **Rev:** State coach in which the Queen
travelled to and from her coronation

Date	Mintage	F12	VF20	XF40	MS60	MS63
2003	—	PF65 1,150				

KM# 33 50 POUNDS
1000.00 g., 0.925 Silver 29.548 oz. ASW, 100 mm. **Ruler:**
Elizabeth II **Subject:** Prince William **Obv:** Queen's portrait
Rev: Portrait with open shirt collar **Edge:** Reeded

Date	Mintage	F12	VF20	XF40	MS60	MS63
2003	500	PF65 1,200				

KM# 63 50 POUNDS
1000.00 g., 0.925 Silver 29.548 oz. ASW, 100 mm. **Ruler:**
Elizabeth II **Subject:** 50th Anniversary of Coronation **Obv:**
Queen's portrait right **Rev:** St. Edward's crown, royal scepter,
orb of England

Date	Mintage	F12	VF20	XF40	MS60	MS63
2003	—	PF65 1,150				

KM# 64 50 POUNDS
1000.00 g., 0.925 Silver 29.548 oz. ASW, 100 mm. **Ruler:**
Elizabeth II **Subject:** 50th Anniversary of Coronation **Obv:**
Queen's portrait right **Rev:** Queen on horseback dressed in
the ceremonial uniform of the Colonel in Chief of the Household
Brigade

Date	Mintage	F12	VF20	XF40	MS60	MS63
2003	—	PF65 1,150				

KM# 65 50 POUNDS
1000.00 g., 0.925 Silver 29.548 oz. ASW, 100 mm. **Ruler:**
Elizabeth II **Subject:** 50th Anniversary of Coronation **Obv:**
Queen's portrait right **Rev:** The Queen crowned, seated,
holding the orb and scepter

Date	Mintage	F12	VF20	XF40	MS60	MS63
2003	—	PF65 1,150				

KM# 40 50 POUNDS
1000.00 g., 0.925 Silver 29.548 oz. ASW, 100 mm. **Ruler:**
Elizabeth II **Subject:** D-Day **Obv:** Queen's portrait **Rev:** US
and British troops wading ashore **Rev. Designer:** Matthew
Bonaccorsi **Edge:** Reeded

Date	Mintage	F12	VF20	XF40	MS60	MS63
2004	600	PF65 1,200				

KM# 80 50 POUNDS
1000.00 g., 0.925 Silver 29.548 oz. ASW **Ruler:** Elizabeth II
Subject: 200th Anniversary Battle of Trafalgar **Obv:** Crowned
head right

Date	Mintage	F12	VF20	XF40	MS60	MS63
2005		PF65 1,200				

KM# 114 50 POUNDS
1000.00 g., 0.925 Silver 29.548 oz. ASW, 100 mm. **Ruler:**
Elizabeth II **Subject:** Prince William, 21st Birthday

Date	Mintage	F12	VF20	XF40	MS60	MS63
2005	Est. 100	PF65 1,200				

KM# 136 50 POUNDS
1000.00 g., 0.925 Silver 29.548 oz. ASW, 100 mm. **Ruler:**
Elizabeth II **Rev:** Portraits of Elizabeth II and cross of 8 floral
emblems

Date	Mintage	F12	VF20	XF40	MS60	MS63
2006	Est. 250	PF65 1,150				

KM# 214 50 POUNDS
1000.00 g., 0.925 Silver 29.548 oz. ASW, 100 mm. **Ruler:**
Elizabeth II **Subject:** Royal Wedding - Prince William and
Catherine Middleton **Obv:** Head in tiara right **Rev:** Conjoined
busts left, roase window in background

Date	Mintage	F12	VF20	XF40	MS60	MS63
2011	—	PF65 1,150				

KM# 34 100 POUNDS
1000.00 g., 0.9166 Gold 29.2797 oz. AGW, 100 mm. **Ruler:**
Elizabeth II **Subject:** Prince William **Obv:** Queen's portrait
Rev: Portrait with open shirt collar **Edge:** Reeded

Date	Mintage	F12	VF20	XF40	MS60	MS63
2003	—	PF65 55,000				

KM# 81 100 POUNDS
1000.00 g., 0.9166 Gold 29.2797 oz. AGW **Ruler:** Elizabeth II **Subject:** 200th Anniversary Battle of Trafalgar **Obv:** Crowned head right

Date	Mintage	F12	VF20	XF40	MS60	MS63
2005	—		PF65 55,000			

KM# 37 1000 POUNDS
1090.86 g., 0.9166 Gold 31.940 oz. AGW, 100 mm. **Ruler:** Elizabeth II **Subject:** Last Flight of the Concorde **Obv:** Queen's portrait **Rev:** Concorde in flight **Edge:** Reeded

Date	Mintage	F12	VF20	XF40	MS60	MS63
2003	34		PF65 60,000			

KM# 41 1000 POUNDS
1000.00 g., 0.9167 Gold 29.2829 oz. AGW, 100 mm. **Ruler:** Elizabeth II **Subject:** D-Day **Obv:** Queen's portrait **Rev:** US and British troops wading ashore **Rev. Designer:** Matthew Bonaccorsi **Edge:** Reeded

Date	Mintage	F12	VF20	XF40	MS60	MS63
2004	60		PF65 55,000			

KM# 216 1000 POUNDS
1090.00 g., 0.9167 Gold 31.9183 oz. AGW, 11 mm. **Ruler:** Elizabeth II **Subject:** Trafalgar, 200th Anniversary

Date	Mintage	F12	VF20	XF40	MS60	MS63
2005	—		PF65 60,000			

KM# 115 1000 POUNDS
1098.86 g., 0.916 Gold 32.1532 oz. AGW, 38.61 mm. **Ruler:** Elizabeth II **Subject:** Prince William, 21st Birthday

Date	Mintage	F12	VF20	XF40	MS60	MS63
2005	Est. 21		PF65 60,000			

KM# 137 1000 POUNDS
1090.86 g., 0.916 Gold 31.9191 oz. AGW, 100 mm. **Ruler:** Elizabeth II **Rev:** Portraits of Elizabeth II and cross of 8 floral emblems

Date	Mintage	F12	VF20	XF40	MS60	MS63
2006	—		PF65 60,000			

KM# 192 1000 POUNDS
1090.86 g., 0.916 Gold 31.9191 oz. AGW, 100 mm. **Ruler:** Elizabeth II **Subject:** Prince Charles, 60th Birthday

Date	Mintage	F12	VF20	XF40	MS60	MS63
2008	Est. 30		PF65 60,000			

KM# 215 1000 POUNDS
1000.00 g., 0.916 Gold 29.2605 oz. AGW, 100 mm. **Ruler:** Elizabeth II **Subject:** Royal Wedding - Prince William and Catherine Middleton **Obv:** Head in tiara right **Rev:** Conjoined busts left, rose window in background

Date	Mintage	F12	VF20	XF40	MS60	MS63
2011	—		PF65 57,500			

MINT SETS

KM#	Date	Mintage	Identification	Issue Price	Mkt Val
MS1	2004 (1)	—	Alderney KM#43, Guernsey KM#155, Jersey KM#126, 150th Anniversary of the Crimean War	—	95.00

ALGERIA

The People's Democratic Republic of Algeria, a North African country fronting on the Mediterranean Sea between Tunisia and Morocco, has an area of 919,595 sq. mi. (2,381,740 sq. km.) and a population of 31.6 million. Capital: Algiers (Alger). Most of the country's working population is engaged in agriculture although a recent industrial diversification, financed by oil revenues, is making steady progress. Wines, fruits, iron and zinc ores, phosphates, tobacco products, liquified natural gas, and petroleum are exported.

MONETARY SYSTEMS
100 Centimes = 1 Franc

REPUBLIC

STANDARD COINAGE

KM# 127 1/4 DINAR
1.15 g., Aluminum, 16.5 mm. **Subject:** Fennec Fox **Obv:** Value in small circle **Rev:** Head facing

Date	Mintage	F12	VF20	XF40	MS60	MS63
2003-AH1423	—	—	1.50	3.00	4.50	5.50

KM# 129 DINAR
4.24 g., Stainless Steel, 20.6 mm. **Obv:** Value on silhouette of country, within circle **Rev:** African buffalo's head 3/4 left, ancient drawings above **Edge:** Plain

Date	Mintage	F12	VF20	XF40	MS60	MS63
AH1422-2002	—	—	1.00	2.00	3.50	6.00
AH1423-2002	—	—	1.00	2.00	3.50	6.00
AH1423-2003	—	—	1.00	2.00	3.50	6.00
AH1424-2003	—	—	1.00	2.00	3.50	6.00
AH1424-2004	—	—	1.00	2.00	3.50	6.00
AH1426-2005	—	—	1.00	2.00	3.50	6.00
AH1427-2006	—	—	1.00	2.00	3.50	6.00
AH1428-2007	—	—	1.00	2.00	3.50	6.00
AH1430-2009	—	—	1.00	2.00	3.50	6.00
AH1431-2010	—	—	1.00	2.00	3.50	6.00

KM# 130 2 DINARS
5.13 g., Stainless Steel, 22.5 mm. **Obv:** Value on silhouette of country **Rev:** Dromedary camel's head right **Edge:** Plain

Date	Mintage	F12	VF20	XF40	MS60	MS63
AH1422-2001	—	—	1.00	2.00	4.00	7.00
AH1422-2002	—	—	1.00	2.00	4.00	7.00
AH1423-2002	—	—	1.00	2.00	4.00	7.00
AH1424-2003	—	—	1.00	2.00	4.00	7.00
AH1424-2004	—	—	1.00	2.00	4.00	7.00
AH1426-2005	—	—	1.00	2.00	4.00	7.00
AH1427-2006	—	—	1.00	2.00	4.00	7.00
AH1428-2007	—	—	1.00	2.00	4.00	7.00
AH1430-2009	—	—	1.00	2.00	4.00	7.00

Date	Mintage	F12	VF20	XF40	MS60	MS63
AH1431-2010	—	—	1.00	2.00	4.00	7.00

KM# 123 5 DINARS
6.20 g., Stainless Steel, 24.5 mm. **Obv:** Denomination within circle **Rev:** Forepart of African elephant right **Edge:** Plain

Date	Mintage	F12	VF20	XF40	MS60	MS63
AH1422-2003	—	—	1.50	3.50	6.50	9.50
AH1423-2003	—	—	1.00	3.50	6.50	9.50
AH1424-2003	—	—	1.00	3.50	5.50	8.00
AH1424-2004	—	—	1.00	3.50	6.50	9.50
AH1426-2005	—	—	1.00	3.00	5.50	8.00
AH1426-2006	—	—	1.00	3.50	6.50	9.50
AH1427-2006	—	—	1.00	3.00	5.50	8.00
AH1428-2007	—	—	1.00	3.00	5.50	8.00
AH1429-2008	—	—	1.00	3.00	5.50	8.00
AH1430-2009	—	—	1.00	3.00	5.50	8.00
AH1431-2010	—	—	1.00	3.00	5.50	8.00
AH1432-2011	—	—	1.00	3.00	5.50	8.00
AH1433-2012	—	—	1.00	3.00	5.50	8.00
AH1434-2013	—	—	1.00	3.00	5.50	8.00

KM# 124 10 DINARS
4.95 g., Bi-Metallic, 26.5 mm. **Obv:** Denomination **Rev:** Barbary falcon's head right **Edge:** Plain

Date	Mintage	F12	VF20	XF40	MS60	MS63
AH1422-2002	—	—	1.75	4.00	9.00	—
AH1423-2002	—	—	1.75	4.00	9.00	—
AH1424-2003	—	—	1.75	4.00	9.00	—
AH1425-2004	—	—	1.75	4.00	9.00	—
AH1426-2005	—	—	1.75	4.00	9.00	—
AH1427-2006	—	—	1.75	4.00	9.00	—
AH1428-2007	—	—	1.75	4.00	9.00	—
AH1429-2008	—	—	1.75	4.00	9.00	—
AH1430-2009	—	—	1.75	4.00	9.00	—
AH1431-2010	—	—	1.75	4.00	9.00	—
AH1432-2011	—	—	1.75	4.00	9.00	—
AH1433-2012	—	—	1.75	4.00	9.00	—
AH1434-2013	—	—	1.75	4.00	9.00	—

KM# 125 20 DINARS
8.62 g., Bi-Metallic, 27.5 mm. **Subject:** Lion **Obv:** Denomination **Rev:** Head left

Date	Mintage	F12	VF20	XF40	MS60	MS63
AH1424-2004	—	—	4.00	8.00	16.50	20.00
AH1426-2005	—	—	4.00	8.00	16.50	20.00
AH1427-2006	—	—	4.00	8.00	16.50	20.00
AH1428-2007	—	—	4.00	8.00	16.50	20.00
AH1430-2009	—	—	4.00	8.00	16.50	20.00
AH1431-2010	—	—	4.00	8.00	16.50	20.00
AH1432-2011	—	—	4.00	8.00	16.50	20.00
AM1433-2012	—	—	4.00	8.00	16.50	20.00
AM1434-2013	—	—	4.00	8.00	16.50	20.00

KM# 126 50 DINARS
9.27 g., Bi-Metallic, 28.5 mm. **Obv:** Denomination **Rev:** Dama gazelle with head left

Date	Mintage	F12	VF20	XF40	MS60	MS63
AH1424-2003	—	—	4.00	8.00	16.50	—
AH1425-2004	—	—	4.00	8.00	16.50	—
AH1428-2007	—	—	4.00	8.00	16.50	—
AH1429-2008	—	—	4.00	8.00	16.50	—
AH1430-2009	—	—	4.00	8.00	16.50	—
AH1432-2011	—	—	4.00	8.00	16.50	—
AM1434-2013	—	—	4.00	8.00	16.50	—

KM# 138 50 DINARS
9.27 g., Bi-Metallic, 28.5 mm. **Subject:** 50th Anniversary of Liberation **Obv:** Large value **Rev:** Stylized flag and two

Moudjahid (revolutionaries)

Date	Mintage	F12	VF20	XF40	MS60	MS63
AH1425-2004	3,000,000	—	—	5.00	12.50	15.00
AH1429-2008	—	—	—	5.00	12.50	15.00
AH1434-2013	—	—	—	5.00	12.50	15.00

KM# 132 100 DINARS
11.00 g., Bi-Metallic, 29.5 mm. **Obv:** Denomination stylized with reverse design **Rev:** Horse head right **Edge:** Reeded

Date	Mintage	F12	VF20	XF40	MS60	MS63
AH1422-2002	—	—	6.00	12.00	22.00	26.00
AH1423-2002	—	—	6.00	12.00	22.00	26.00
AH1423-2003	—	—	6.00	12.00	22.00	26.00
AH1425-2004	—	—	6.00	12.00	22.00	26.00
AH1428-2007	—	—	6.00	12.00	22.00	26.00
AH1430-2009	—	—	6.00	12.00	22.00	26.00
AH1431-2010	—	—	6.00	12.00	22.00	26.00
AH1432-2011	—	—	6.00	12.00	22.00	26.00
AM1434-2013	—	—	6.00	12.00	22.00	26.00

KM# 137 100 DINARS
11.00 g., Bi-Metallic, 29.5 mm. **Subject:** 40th Anniversary of Independence **Obv:** Stylized value using palm tree in doorway and two coins depicting horses' heads **Rev:** Number 40 and stylized face **Edge:** Reeded

Date	Mintage	F12	VF20	XF40	MS60	MS63
AH1422-2002	—	—	—	—	25.00	28.00

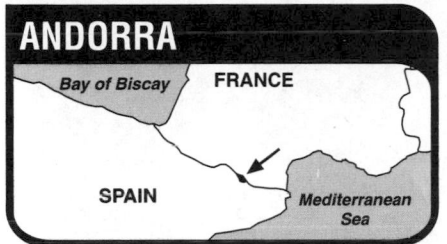

ANDORRA

Bay of Biscay — FRANCE

SPAIN — Mediterranean Sea

Principality of Andorra (Principat d'Andorra), situated on the southern slopes of the Pyrenees Mountains between France and Spain, has an area of 181 sq. mi. (453 sq. km.) and a population of 80,000. Capital: Andorra la Vella. Tourism is the chief source of income. Timber, cattle and derivatives, and furniture are exported.

RULER
Joan D.M. Bisbe D'Urgell I

MONETARY SYSTEM
100 Centims = 1 Diner
NOTE: The Diners have been struck for collectors while the Euro is used in everyday commerce. MINT MARK Crowned M = Madrid

PRINCIPALITY
DECIMAL COINAGE

KM# 176 CENTIM
2.10 g., Aluminum, 27 mm. **Subject:** Charlemagne **Obv:** National arms, date below **Rev:** Crowned head facing, denomination below **Edge:** Plain

Date	Mintage	VF20	XF40	MS60	MS63	MS65
2002	—	—	—	1.50	2.00	—

KM# 177 CENTIM
2.13 g., Aluminum, 27 mm. **Subject:** Isard **Obv:** National arms, date below **Rev:** Chamois left facing, denomination at right **Edge:** Plain

Date	Mintage	VF20	XF40	MS60	MS63	MS65
2002	—	—	—	1.50	2.00	—

KM# 178 CENTIM
2.14 g., Aluminum, 27 mm. **Subject:** Agnus Dei **Obv:** National arms **Rev:** Lamb of God **Edge:** Plain

Date	Mintage	VF20	XF40	MS60	MS63	MS65
2002	—	—	—	1.00	1.50	—

KM# 198 CENTIM
Aluminum-Magnesium, 27 mm. **Obv:** National arms **Rev:** A piece of the wall paintings belonging to the 12th century Romanesque church of St. Marti de la Cortinado

Date	Mintage	F12	VF20	XF40	MS60	MS63
2003	—	—	—	—	1.25	1.75

KM# 199 CENTIM
Aluminum-Magnesium, 27 mm. **Obv:** National arms **Rev:** Pont de la Margineda, reproduction of the bridge

Date	Mintage	F12	VF20	XF40	MS60	MS63
2003	—	—	—	—	1.25	1.75

KM# 200 CENTIM
Aluminum-Magnesium, 27 mm. **Obv:** National arms **Rev:** Image of the 12th century Romanesque church of St. Miquel d'Engolasters with its bell tower, the Romanesque apse, the small portico and the large Lombard windows

Date	Mintage	F12	VF20	XF40	MS60	MS63
2003	—	—	—	—	1.25	1.75

KM# 229 CENTIM
Aluminum **Obv:** Crowned arms **Rev:** Santa Coloma

Date	Mintage	F12	VF20	XF40	MS60	MS63
2004	—	—	—	—	0.90	1.20

KM# 230 CENTIM
Aluminum **Obv:** Crowned arms **Rev:** Sant Martí de la Cortinada

Date	Mintage	F12	VF20	XF40	MS60	MS63
2004	—	—	—	—	0.90	1.20

KM# 231 CENTIM
Aluminum **Obv:** Crowned arms **Rev:** Altar at Santa Coloma

Date	Mintage	F12	VF20	XF40	MS60	MS63
2004	—	—	—	—	0.90	1.20

KM# 236 CENTIM
2.80 g., Brass, 18 mm. **Subject:** Death of Pope John Paul II **Obv:** National arms **Rev:** Karol Wojtyla as priest **Edge:** Reeded

Date	Mintage	F12	VF20	XF40	MS60	MS63
2005	15,000	—	—	0.30	0.80	1.20

KM# 245 CENTIM
2.80 g., Brass, 18 mm. **Obv:** National arms **Rev:** Findern flower - Poet's Daffodil

Date	Mintage	F12	VF20	XF40	MS60	MS63
2005	15,000	—	—	—	0.80	1.20
2006	10,000	—	—	—	0.80	1.20
2007	10,000	—	—	—	0.80	1.20
2008	5,000	—	—	—	0.80	1.20

KM# 290 CENTIM
2.80 g., Brass, 18 mm. **Obv:** National Arms **Rev:** Portrait of Joseph Ratzinger as priest **Edge:** Reeded

Date	Mintage	F12	VF20	XF40	MS60	MS63
2006	15,000	—	—	—	—	1.20

KM# 306 CENTIM
2.80 g., Brass, 18 mm. **Subject:** Popes of the 20th Century **Obv:** National arms **Rev:** Pope Leo XIII **Edge:** Reeded

Date	Mintage	F12	VF20	XF40	MS60	MS63
2007	5,000	—	—	—	—	1.20

KM# 179 2 CENTIMS
Brass, 18 mm. **Subject:** Grandalla **Obv:** National arms **Rev:** Edelweiss flower **Edge:** Plain

Date	Mintage	VF20	XF40	MS60	MS63	MS65
2002	—	—	—	1.50	2.00	—

KM# 201 2 CENTIMS
Copper-Nickel-Zinc, 18.15 mm. **Obv:** National arms **Rev:** Clavell Deltoide, a flower found in Andorra

Date	Mintage	F12	VF20	XF40	MS60	MS63
2003	—	—	—	—	1.75	2.50

KM# 232 2 CENTIMS
Brass **Obv:** Crowned arms **Rev:** West Gothic robe

Date	Mintage	F12	VF20	XF40	MS60	MS63
2004	—	—	—	—	1.20	1.60

KM# 237 2 CENTIMS
4.00 g., Brass, 21.3 mm. **Subject:** Death of Pope John-Paul II **Obv:** National arms **Rev:** Karol Wojtyla as priest

Date	Mintage	F12	VF20	XF40	MS60	MS63
2005	15,000	—	—	0.50	1.20	1.60

KM# 246 2 CENTIMS
4.00 g., Brass, 21.3 mm. **Obv:** National arms **Rev:** Pyrenean Chamois **Edge:** Reeded

Date	Mintage	F12	VF20	XF40	MS60	MS63
2005	15,000	—	—	—	1.20	1.60
2006	10,000	—	—	—	1.20	1.60
2007	10,000	—	—	—	1.20	1.60
2008	5,000	—	—	—	1.20	1.60

KM# 291 2 CENTIMS
4.00 g., Brass, 21.3 mm. **Obv:** National Arms **Rev:** Portrait of Joseph Ratzinger as priest

Date	Mintage	F12	VF20	XF40	MS60	MS63
2006	15,000	—	—	—	—	1.60

KM# 307 2 CENTIMS
4.00 g., Brass, 21.3 mm. **Subject:** Popes of the 20th Century **Obv:** National Arms **Rev:** Pope Pius X

Date	Mintage	F12	VF20	XF40	MS60	MS63
2007	5,000	—	—	—	—	1.60

KM# 282 2 CENTIMS
0.73 g., 0.999 Gold AGW, 11 mm. **Subject:** Berlin Wall, 20th anniversary **Obv:** Shield **Rev:** Brandenburg Gate and brick wall **Edge:** Reeded

Date	Mintage	F12	VF20	XF40	MS60	MS63
2009	5,000	PF63 70.00	PF65 75.00			

KM# 180 5 CENTIMS
Brass, 21.8 mm. **Subject:** Squirrel **Obv:** National arms **Rev:** Red Squirrel on tree stump **Edge:** Plain

Date	Mintage	VF20	XF40	MS60	MS63	MS65
2002	—	—	—	2.00	2.50	—

KM# 181 5 CENTIMS
Brass, 21.8 mm. **Subject:** Gall Fer **Obv:** National arms **Rev:** Male Eurasian Capercaillie (grouse) displaying plumage **Edge:** Plain

Date	Mintage	VF20	XF40	MS60	MS63	MS65
2002	—	—	—	2.00	2.50	—

KM# 202 5 CENTIMS
Brass, 21.8 mm. **Obv:** National arms **Rev:** The cross of Seven Arms, traditional Gothic cross

Date	Mintage	F12	VF20	XF40	MS60	MS63
2003	—	—	—	—	2.25	2.75

KM# 203 5 CENTIMS
Brass, 21.8 mm. **Obv:** National arms **Rev:** Wall painting from the 11th century church of Sant Serni de Nagol showing an eagle

Date	Mintage	F12	VF20	XF40	MS60	MS63
2003	—	—	—	—	2.25	2.75

KM# 233 5 CENTIMS
Brass **Obv:** Crowned arms **Rev:** Gothic cross

Date	Mintage	F12	VF20	XF40	MS60	MS63
2004	—	—	—	—	1.80	2.40

KM# 234 5 CENTIMS
Brass **Obv:** Crowned arms **Rev:** Lady of Canolic

Date	Mintage	F12	VF20	XF40	MS60	MS63
2004	—	—	—	—	1.80	2.40

KM# 238 5 CENTIMS
5.50 g., Brass, 24.5 mm. **Subject:** Death of Pope John-Paul II **Obv:** National arms **Rev:** Karol Wojtyla as bishop **Edge:** Reeded

Date	Mintage	F12	VF20	XF40	MS60	MS63
2005	15,000	—	—	0.70	1.80	2.40

KM# 247 5 CENTIMS
5.50 g., Brass, 24.5 mm. **Obv:** National arms **Rev:** Wall painting from Santa Coloma church **Edge:** Reeded

Date	Mintage	F12	VF20	XF40	MS60	MS63
2005	15,000	—	—	—	1.80	2.40
2006	10,000	—	—	—	1.80	2.40
2007	10,000	—	—	—	1.80	2.40
2008	5,000	—	—	—	1.80	2.40

KM# 292 5 CENTIMS
5.50 g., Brass, 24.5 mm. **Obv:** National Arms **Rev:** Portrait of Joseph Ratzinger as archbishop

Date	Mintage	F12	VF20	XF40	MS60	MS63
2006	15,000	—	—	—	—	2.50

KM# 308 5 CENTIMS
5.50 g., Brass, 24.5 mm. **Subject:** Popes of the 20th Century **Obv:** National Arms **Rev:** Pope Benedict XV

Date	Mintage	F12	VF20	XF40	MS60	MS63
2007	5,000	—	—	—	—	2.40

KM# 182 10 CENTIMS
Brass **Subject:** St. Joan de Caselles **Obv:** National arms **Rev:** Tower and building **Edge:** Plain

Date	Mintage	VF20	XF40	MS60	MS63	MS65
2002	—	—	—	3.00	4.00	—

KM# 204 10 CENTIMS
Nickel Plated Steel, 27.8 mm. **Obv:** National arms **Rev:** 12th century wood carving image from Our Lady of Meritxell

Date	Mintage	F12	VF20	XF40	MS60	MS63
2003	—	—	—	—	3.50	4.50

KM# 235 10 CENTIMS
Nickel Plated Steel **Obv:** Crowned arms **Rev:** Casa de la Vall

Date	Mintage	F12	VF20	XF40	MS60	MS63
2004	—	—	—	—	3.00	4.00

KM# 239 10 CENTIMS
6.50 g., Copper-Nickel, 22.2 mm. **Subject:** Death of Pope John-Paul II **Obv:** National arms **Rev:** Karol Wojtyla as archbishop **Edge:** Reeded

Date	Mintage	F12	VF20	XF40	MS60	MS63
2005	15,000	—	—	1.00	2.40	3.20

KM# 248 10 CENTIMS
6.50 g., Copper-Nickel, 22.2 mm. **Obv:** National arms **Rev:** Saint Vicenç d'Enclar church

Date	Mintage	F12	VF20	XF40	MS60	MS63
2005	15,000	—	—	—	2.40	3.20
2006	10,000	—	—	—	2.40	3.20
2007	10,000	—	—	—	2.40	3.20
2008	5,000	—	—	—	2.40	3.20

KM# 293 10 CENTIMS
6.50 g., Copper-Nickel, 22.2 mm. **Obv:** National Arms **Rev:** Portrait of Joseph Ratzinger as archbishop

Date	Mintage	F12	VF20	XF40	MS60	MS63
2006	15,000	—	—	—	—	4.00

KM# 309 10 CENTIMS
6.50 g., Copper-Nickel, 22.2 mm. **Subject:** Popes of the 20th Century **Obv:** National Arms **Rev:** Pope Pius XI

Date	Mintage	F12	VF20	XF40	MS60	MS63
2007	5,000	—	—	—	—	3.40

KM# 240 25 CENTIMS
7.75 g., Copper-Nickel, 24.2 mm. **Subject:** Death of Pope John-Paul II **Obv:** National arms **Rev:** Karol Wojtyla as cardinal

Date	Mintage	F12	VF20	XF40	MS60	MS63
2005	15,000	—	—	1.20	3.00	4.00

KM# 249 25 CENTIMS
7.75 g., Copper-Nickel, 24.2 mm. **Obv:** National arms **Rev:** Our Lady of Meritxell sanctuary

Date	Mintage	F12	VF20	XF40	MS60	MS63
2005	15,000	—	—	—	3.00	4.00
2006	10,000	—	—	—	3.00	4.00
2007	10,000	—	—	—	3.00	4.00
2008	5,000	—	—	—	3.00	4.00

KM# 294 25 CENTIMS
7.75 g., Copper-Nickel, 24.2 mm. **Obv:** National Arms **Rev:** Portrait of Joseph Ratzinger as cardinal

Date	Mintage	F12	VF20	XF40	MS60	MS63
2006	15,000	—	—	—	—	4.00

KM# 310 25 CENTIMS
7.75 g., Copper-Nickel, 24.2 mm. **Subject:** Popes of the 20th Century **Obv:** National Arms **Rev:** Pope Pius XII

Date	Mintage	F12	VF20	XF40	MS60	MS63
2007	5,000	—	—	—	—	4.00

KM# 241 50 CENTIMS
9.00 g., Copper-Nickel, 25.9 mm. **Subject:** Death of Pope John-Paul II **Obv:** National arms **Rev:** Karol Wojtyla as cardinal

Date	Mintage	F12	VF20	XF40	MS60	MS63
2005	15,000	—	—	2.70	3.60	4.80

KM# 250 50 CENTIMS
9.00 g., Copper-Nickel, 25.9 mm. **Obv:** National arms **Rev:** Map of Andorra, 7 towns highlighted

Date	Mintage	F12	VF20	XF40	MS60	MS63
2005	15,000	—	—	—	4.00	5.00
2006	10,000	—	—	—	4.00	5.00
2007	10,000	—	—	—	4.00	5.00
2008	5,000	—	—	—	4.00	5.00

KM# 295 50 CENTIMS
9.00 g., Copper-Nickel, 25.9 mm. **Obv:** National Arms **Rev:** Portrait of Joseph Ratzinger as cardinal

Date	Mintage	F12	VF20	XF40	MS60	MS63
2006	15,000	—	—	—	—	4.80

KM# 311 50 CENTIMS
9.00 g., Copper-Nickel, 25.9 mm. **Subject:** Popes of the 20th Century **Obv:** National Arms **Rev:** Pope John XXIII

Date	Mintage	F12	VF20	XF40	MS60	MS63
2007	5,000	—	—	—	—	6.00

KM# 242 DINER
8.50 g., Bi-Metallic, 24.5 mm. **Subject:** Death of Pope John-Paul II **Obv:** National arms **Rev:** Karol Wojtyla as pope **Edge:** Reeded

Date	Mintage	F12	VF20	XF40	MS60	MS63
2005	15,000	—	—	1.60	4.00	6.00

KM# 251 DINER
8.50 g., Bi-Metallic, 24.5 mm. **Obv:** National arms **Rev:** Our Lady of Meritxell **Edge:** Reeded

Date	Mintage	F12	VF20	XF40	MS60	MS63
2005	15,000	—	—	—	4.50	6.00
2006	10,000	—	—	—	4.50	6.00
2007	10,000	—	—	—	4.50	6.00
2008	5,000	—	—	—	4.50	6.00

KM# 296 DINER
8.50 g., Bi-Metallic, 24.5 mm. **Obv:** National Arms **Rev:** Portrait of Joseph Ratzinger as Pope Benedict XVI

Date	Mintage	F12	VF20	XF40	MS60	MS63
2006	15,000	—	—	—	—	6.00

KM# 299 DINER
11.00 g., Nickel, 25x25 mm. **Subject:** Chess Set **Obv:** National Arms **Rev:** Pawn **Shape:** Square

Date	Mintage	F12	VF20	XF40	MS60	MS63
2006	40,000	—	—	—	—	6.00

KM# 299a DINER
11.00 g., Brass, 25x25 mm. **Subject:** Chess Set **Obv:** National Arms **Rev:** Pawn **Shape:** Square

Date	Mintage	F12	VF20	XF40	MS60	MS63
2006	40,000	—	—	—	—	6.00

KM# 300 DINER
11.00 g., Nickel, 25x25 mm. **Subject:** Chess Set **Obv:** National arms **Rev:** Rook **Shape:** Square

Date	Mintage	F12	VF20	XF40	MS60	MS63
2006	10,000	—	—	—	—	12.00

KM# 300a DINER
11.00 g., Brass, 25x25 mm. **Subject:** Chess Set **Obv:** National Arms **Rev:** Rook **Shape:** Square

Date	Mintage	F12	VF20	XF40	MS60	MS63
2006	10,000	—	—	—	—	12.00

KM# 301 DINER
11.00 g., Nickel, 25x25 mm. **Subject:** Chess Set **Obv:** National Arms **Rev:** Knight **Shape:** Square

Date	Mintage	F12	VF20	XF40	MS60	MS63
2006	10,000	—	—	—	—	12.00

KM# 301a DINER
11.00 g., Brass, 25x25 mm. **Subject:** Chess Set **Obv:** National Arms **Rev:** Knight **Shape:** Square

Date	Mintage	F12	VF20	XF40	MS60	MS63
2006	10,000	—	—	—	—	12.00

KM# 302 DINER
11.00 g., Nickel, 25x25 mm. **Subject:** Chess Set **Obv:** National Arms **Rev:** Bishop **Shape:** Square

Date	Mintage	F12	VF20	XF40	MS60	MS63
2006	10,000	—	—	—	—	12.00

KM# 302a DINER
11.00 g., Brass, 25x25 mm. **Subject:** Chess Set **Obv:** National Arms **Rev:** Bishop **Shape:** Square

Date	Mintage	F12	VF20	XF40	MS60	MS63
2006	10,000	—	—	—	—	12.00

KM# 303 DINER
11.00 g., Nickel, 25x25 mm. **Subject:** Chess Set **Obv:** National Arms **Rev:** Queen **Shape:** Square

Date	Mintage	F12	VF20	XF40	MS60	MS63
2006	5,000	—	—	—	—	18.00

KM# 303a DINER
11.00 g., Brass, 25x25 mm. **Subject:** Chess Set **Obv:** National Arms **Rev:** Queen **Shape:** Square

Date	Mintage	F12	VF20	XF40	MS60	MS63
2006	5,000	—	—	—	—	18.00

KM# 304 DINER
11.00 g., Nickel, 25x25 mm. **Subject:** Chess Set **Obv:** National Arms **Rev:** King **Shape:** Square

Date	Mintage	F12	VF20	XF40	MS60	MS63
2006	5,000	—	—	—	—	18.00

KM# 304a DINER
11.00 g., Brass, 25x25 mm. **Subject:** Chess Set **Obv:** National Arms **Rev:** King **Shape:** Square

Date	Mintage	F12	VF20	XF40	MS60	MS63
2006	5,000	—	—	—	—	18.00

KM# 312 DINER
8.50 g., Bi-Metallic, 24.5 mm. **Subject:** Popes of the 20th Century **Obv:** National Arms **Rev:** Pope Paul VI

Date	Mintage	F12	VF20	XF40	MS60	MS63
2007	5,000	—	—	—	—	8.00

KM# 331 DINER
1.24 g., 0.999 Gold 0.0396 oz. AGW, 13.92 mm. **Obv:** National arms **Rev:** John Paul II with cross croizer

Date	Mintage	F12	VF20	XF40	MS60	MS63
2011	—	PF63 115	PF65 125			

KM# 349 DINER
0.50 g., 0.9999 Gold AGW, 11 mm. **Subject:** Joan d'Arc

Date	Mintage	F12	VF20	XF40	MS60	MS63
2012	Est. 15000	PF63 30.00	PF65 35.00			

KM# 350 DINER
0.50 g., 0.9999 Gold AGW, 11 mm. **Subject:** Venus de Milo

Date	Mintage	F12	VF20	XF40	MS60	MS63
2012	Est. 5000	PF63 35.00	PF65 40.00			

KM# 361 DINER
0.50 g., 0.999 Gold AGW, 11 mm. **Subject:** Henry IV

Date	Mintage	F12	VF20	XF40	MS60	MS63
2013	Est. 10,000	PF63 45.00	PF65 50.00			

KM# 363 DINER
0.50 g., 0.999 Gold AGW, 11 mm. **Subject:** St. Peter's Basilica, Rome

Date	Mintage	F12	VF20	XF40	MS60	MS63
2013	Est. 5,000	PF63 45.00	PF65 50.00			

KM# 243 2 DINERS
11.25 g., Bi-Metallic, 28.4 mm. **Subject:** Death of Pope John-Paul II **Obv:** National arms **Rev:** Karol Wojtyla as pope **Edge:** Reeded

Date	Mintage	F12	VF20	XF40	MS60	MS63
2005	15,000	—	—	2.40	6.00	8.00

KM# 252 2 DINERS
11.25 g., Bi-Metallic, 28.4 mm. **Obv:** National arms **Rev:** Signing of the Umpirage between the Bishop of Urgell and Count of Foix **Edge:** Reeded

Date	Mintage	F12	VF20	XF40	MS60	MS63
2005	15,000	—	—	—	6.00	8.00
2006	10,000	—	—	—	6.00	8.00
2007	10,000	—	—	—	6.00	8.00
2008	5,000	—	—	—	6.00	8.00

KM# 297 2 DINERS
11.25 g., Bi-Metallic, 28.4 mm. **Obv:** National Arms **Rev:** Portrait of Joseph Ratzinger as Pope Benedict XVI

Date	Mintage	F12	VF20	XF40	MS60	MS63
2006	15,000	—	—	—	—	8.00

KM# 313 2 DINERS
6.00 g., Bi-Metallic, 28.4 mm. **Subject:** Popes of the 20th Century **Obv:** National Arms **Rev:** Pope John Paul I

Date	Mintage	F12	VF20	XF40	MS60	MS63
2007	5,000	—	—	—	—	10.00

KM# 269 2 DINERS
0.73 g., 0.999 Gold AGW, 11 mm. **Subject:** von Beethoven **Obv:** National arms **Rev:** Beethoven seated at desk

Date	Mintage	F12	VF20	XF40	MS60	MS63
2008	5,000	PF63 75.00			PF65 80.00	

KM# 281 2 DINERS
0.73 g., 0.999 Gold AGW, 11 mm. **Obv:** Shield **Rev:** Charlemagne **Edge:** Reeded

Date	Mintage	F12	VF20	XF40	MS60	MS63
2009	5,000	PF63 75.00			PF65 80.00	

KM# 193 5 DINERS
1.24 g., 0.999 Gold 0.0396 oz. AGW, 13.92 mm. **Obv:** National arms **Rev:** The Escorial Palace in Madrid **Edge:** Reeded

Date	Mintage	F12	VF20	XF40	MS60	MS63
2004	3,000	PF63 65.00			PF65 75.00	

KM# 194 5 DINERS
1.24 g., 0.999 Gold 0.0396 oz. AGW, 13.92 mm. **Obv:** National arms **Rev:** Eiffel Tower **Edge:** Reeded

Date	Mintage	F12	VF20	XF40	MS60	MS63
2004	3,000	PF63 65.00			PF65 75.00	

KM# 195 5 DINERS
1.24 g., 0.999 Gold 0.0396 oz. AGW, 13.92 mm. **Obv:** National arms **Rev:** Atomic model monument **Edge:** Reeded

Date	Mintage	F12	VF20	XF40	MS60	MS63
2004	3,000	PF63 65.00			PF65 75.00	

KM# 196 5 DINERS
1.24 g., 0.999 Gold 0.0396 oz. AGW, 13.92 mm. **Subject:** Andorran membership in the United Nations **Obv:** National arms **Rev:** Seated woman, world globe and UN logo **Edge:** Reeded

Date	Mintage	F12	VF20	XF40	MS60	MS63
2004	3,000	PF63 70.00			PF65 80.00	

KM# 315 5 DINERS
15.60 g., 0.999 Silver 0.4978 oz. ASW, 35 mm. **Rev:** Bear facing

Date	Mintage	F12	VF20	XF40	MS60	MS63
2010	3,000	PF63 65.00			PF65 75.00	

KM# 324 5 DINERS
20.00 g., 0.925 Silver 0.591 oz. ASW, 38.6 mm. **Subject:** Beautification of Pope John Paul II **Rev:** Hologram with image of John Paul II at left, St. Peter's facade at right

Date	Mintage	F12	VF20	XF40	MS60	MS63
2011	2,500	PF65 135				

KM# 326 5 DINERS
15.50 g., 0.925 Silver 0.458 oz. ASW, 35 mm. **Subject:** Wildlife of the Pyrenees - Golden Eagle **Obv:** National Arms **Rev:** Eagle in flight, eagle on nest

Date	Mintage	F12	VF20	XF40	MS60	MS63
2011	3,000	PF63 115	PF65 125			

KM# 329 5 DINERS
15.60 g., 0.999 Silver 0.4978 oz. ASW, 35 mm. **Subject:** Christmas **Obv:** National arms **Rev:** Star over stable with Holy Family, color

Date	Mintage	F12	VF20	XF40	MS60	MS63
2011	—	PF65 90.00				

KM# 333 5 DINERS
20.00 g., 0.925 Silver 0.591 oz. ASW, 38.6 mm. **Subject:** Birds of Andorra **Obv:** National arms **Rev:** Cappercaillie bird left, prism color

Date	Mintage	F12	VF20	XF40	MS60	MS63
2012	2,500	—	—	—	—	50.00

KM# 335 5 DINERS
20.00 g., 0.925 Silver 0.591 oz. ASW, 38.6 mm. **Subject:** Birds of Andorra **Obv:** National arms **Rev:** Robin facing left, prism color

Date	Mintage	F12	VF20	XF40	MS60	MS63
2012	2,500	—	—	—	—	50.00

KM# 337 5 DINERS
0.925 Silver **Obv:** National arms at center **Rev:** DaVinci's Last supper in color

Date	Mintage	F12	VF20	XF40	MS60	MS63
2012	—	PF63 90.00	PF65 100			

KM# 348 5 DINERS
20.00 g., 0.925 Silver 0.591 oz. ASW, 38.61 mm. **Subject:** 2014 FIFA World Cup - Brazil

Date	Mintage	F12	VF20	XF40	MS60	MS63
2012	Est. 10000	PF63 65.00	PF65 75.00			

KM# 351 5 DINERS
20.00 g., 0.999 Silver 0.6382 oz. ASW, 38.6 mm. **Subject:** Aquila Daurada

Date	Mintage	F12	VF20	XF40	MS60	MS63
2012	Est. 10000	PF63 60.00	PF65 65.00			

KM# 334 5 DINERS
20.00 g., 0.925 Silver 0.591 oz. ASW, 38.61 mm. **Subject:** Birds of Andorra **Obv:** National arms **Rev:** Northern Shoveler in flight right, prism color

Date	Mintage	F12	VF20	XF40	MS60	MS63
2012	2,500	—	—	—	—	50.00

KM# 352 5 DINERS
14.14 g., 0.925 Silver 0.4178 oz. ASW, 22.4 x 32 mm. **Subject:** Wonders of Jesus Christ **Rev:** Wedding at Canna

Date	Mintage	F12	VF20	XF40	MS60	MS63
2013	Est. 6000	PF63 55.00	PF65 60.00			

KM# 353 5 DINERS
14.14 g., 0.925 Silver 0.4178 oz. ASW, 22.4 x 32 mm. **Subject:** Wonders of Jesus Christ **Rev:** Feeding the Multitude

Date	Mintage	F12	VF20	XF40	MS60	MS63
2013	Est. 6000	PF63 55.00	PF65 60.00			

KM# 354 5 DINERS
14.14 g., 0.925 Silver 0.4178 oz. ASW, 22.4 x 32 mm. **Subject:** The Wonders of Jesus Christ **Obv:** Healing the Blind

Date	Mintage	F12	VF20	XF40	MS60	MS63
2013	Est. 6000	PF63 55.00	PF65 60.00			

KM# 355 5 DINERS
14.14 g., 0.925 Silver 0.4178 oz. ASW, 22.4 x 32 mm. **Subject:** The Wonders of Jesus Christ **Obv:** Jesus Walking on Water

Date	Mintage	F12	VF20	XF40	MS60	MS63
2013	Est. 6000	PF63 55.00	PF65 60.00			

KM# 356 5 DINERS
14.14 g., 0.925 Silver 0.4178 oz. ASW, 22.4 x 32 mm. **Subject:** The Wonders of Jesus **Obv:** The Transfiguration

Date	Mintage	F12	VF20	XF40	MS60	MS63
2013	Est. 6000	PF63 55.00	PF65 60.00			

KM# 357 5 DINERS
14.14 g., 0.925 Silver 0.4178 oz. ASW, 22.4 x 32 mm. **Subject:** The Wonders of Jesus **Obv:** Raising of Lazarus

Date	Mintage	F12	VF20	XF40	MS60	MS63
2013	Est. 6000	PF63 55.00	PF65 60.00			

KM# 358 5 DINERS
14.14 g., 0.925 Silver 0.4178 oz. ASW, 22.4 x 32 mm. **Subject:** The Wonders of Jesus **Obv:** Last Supper in color

Date	Mintage	F12	VF20	XF40	MS60	MS63
2013	Est. 6000	PF63 55.00	PF65 60.00			

KM# 359 5 DINERS
14.14 g., 0.925 Silver 0.4178 oz. ASW, 22.4 x 32 mm. **Subject:** The Wonders of Jesus Christ **Obv:** Resurrection of Christ

Date	Mintage	F12	VF20	XF40	MS60	MS63
2013	Est. 6000	PF63 55.00	PF65 60.00			

KM# 360 5 DINERS
20.00 g., 0.925 Silver 0.591 oz. ASW, 38.61 mm. **Subject:** 2016 Olympics - Badminton

Date	Mintage	F12	VF20	XF40	MS60	MS63
2013	Est. 10000	PF63 65.00	PF65 75.00			

KM# 364 5 DINERS
20.00 g., 0.999 Silver 0.6382 oz. ASW, 38.61 mm. **Subject:** Aguila Daurada

Date	Mintage	F12	VF20	XF40	MS60	MS63
2013	Est. 10,000	PF63 65.00	PF65 75.00			

KM# 172 10 DINERS
31.47 g., 0.925 Silver 0.9299 oz. ASW, 38.6 mm. **Subject:** Europa **Obv:** National arms **Rev:** Europa in chariot **Edge:** Reeded

Date	Mintage	F12	VF20	XF40	MS60	MS63
2001	15,000	PF63 40.00	PF65 45.00			

KM# 173 10 DINERS
31.47 g., 0.925 Silver 0.9299 oz. ASW, 38.6 mm. **Subject:** Concordia Europea **Obv:** National arms **Rev:** Two crowned women holding hands **Edge:** Reeded

Date	Mintage	F12	VF20	XF40	MS60	MS63
2001	15,000	PF63 40.00	PF65 45.00			

KM# 175 10 DINERS
31.47 g., 0.925 Silver 0.9299 oz. ASW, 38.6 mm. **Subject:** Olympics **Obv:** National arms **Rev:** Snowboarder **Edge:** Reeded

Date	Mintage	F12	VF20	XF40	MS60	MS63
2002	15,000	PF63 40.00	PF65 45.00			

KM# 183 10 DINERS
31.47 g., 0.925 Silver 0.9299 oz. ASW, 38.6 mm. **Subject:** Mouflon **Obv:** National arms **Rev:** Mouflon ram **Edge:** Reeded

Date	Mintage	F12	VF20	XF40	MS60	MS63
2002	15,000	PF63 45.00	PF65 50.00			

KM# 289 10 DINERS
31.47 g., 0.925 Silver 0.9299 oz. ASW, 38.61 mm. **Subject:** FIFA World Cup **Obv:** National Arms **Rev:** Soccer ball, names and years of previous World Cup host countries **Edge:** Reeded

Date	Mintage	F12	VF20	XF40	MS60	MS63
2003	50,000	PF63 75.00	PF65 85.00			

KM# 188 10 DINERS
31.10 g., 0.925 Silver 0.919 oz. ASW, 38.6 mm. **Obv:** National arms **Rev:** Pope with doves **Edge:** Reeded

Date	Mintage	F12	VF20	XF40	MS60	MS63
2004	9,999	PF63 60.00	PF65 70.00			

KM# 189 10 DINERS
31.10 g., 0.925 Silver 0.919 oz. ASW, 38.6 mm. **Obv:** National arms **Rev:** Pope holding staff with 2 hands **Edge:** Reeded

Date	Mintage	F12	VF20	XF40	MS60	MS63
2004	9,999	PF63 60.00	PF65 70.00			

KM# 190 10 DINERS
31.10 g., 0.925 Silver 0.919 oz. ASW, 38.6 mm. **Obv:** National arms **Rev:** Pope raising a chalice **Edge:** Reeded

Date	Mintage	F12	VF20	XF40	MS60	MS63
2004	9,999	PF63 60.00	PF65 70.00			

KM# 191 10 DINERS
31.10 g., 0.925 Silver 0.919 oz. ASW, 38.6 mm. **Obv:** National arms **Rev:** Pope with hammer **Edge:** Reeded

Date	Mintage	F12	VF20	XF40	MS60	MS63
2004	9,999	PF63 60.00	PF65 70.00			

KM# 192 10 DINERS
31.10 g., 0.925 Silver 0.919 oz. ASW, 38.6 mm. **Obv:** National arms **Rev:** Gold-plated Pope writing **Edge:** Reeded

Date	Mintage	F12	VF20	XF40	MS60	MS63
2004	9,999	PF63 60.00	PF65 70.00			

KM# 205 10 DINERS
31.10 g., 0.925 Silver 0.9189 oz. ASW, 38.6 mm. **Obv. Designer:** National arms **Rev:** Gold plated Pope John Paul II wearing mitre and holding crucifix staff **Edge:** Reeded

Date	Mintage	F12	VF20	XF40	MS60	MS63
2005	9,999	PF63 60.00	PF65 70.00			

KM# 206 10 DINERS
31.10 g., 0.925 Silver 0.9189 oz. ASW, 38.6 mm. **Obv:** National arms **Rev:** Pope John Paul II with the Holy Virgin in background **Edge:** Reeded

Date	Mintage	F12	VF20	XF40	MS60	MS63
2005	9,999	PF63 60.00	PF65 70.00			

KM# 207 10 DINERS
31.10 g., 0.925 Silver 0.9189 oz. ASW, 38.6 mm. **Obv:** National arms **Rev:** Pope John Paul II in prayer with crucifix at right **Edge:** Reeded

Date	Mintage	F12	VF20	XF40	MS60	MS63
2005	9,999	PF63 60.00	PF65 70.00			

KM# 208 10 DINERS
31.10 g., 0.925 Silver 0.9189 oz. ASW, 38.6 mm. **Obv:** National arms **Rev:** Pope John Paul II blessing Vatican crowd **Edge:** Reeded

Date	Mintage	F12	VF20	XF40	MS60	MS63
2005	9,999	PF63 60.00	PF65 70.00			

KM# 209 10 DINERS
31.10 g., 0.925 Silver 0.9189 oz. ASW, 38.6 mm. **Obv:** National arms **Rev:** Pope John Paul II and Mother Teresa **Edge:** Reeded

Date	Mintage	F12	VF20	XF40	MS60	MS63
2005	9,999	PF63 60.00	PF65 70.00			

KM# 210 10 DINERS
31.10 g., 0.925 Silver 0.9189 oz. ASW, 38.6 mm. **Obv:** National arms **Rev:** Bearded man above Vatican City **Edge:** Reeded

Date	Mintage	F12	VF20	XF40	MS60	MS63
2005	9,999	PF63 50.00	PF65 60.00			

KM# 211 10 DINERS
31.10 g., 0.925 Silver 0.9189 oz. ASW, 38.6 mm. **Obv:** National arms **Rev:** Sad woman above Fatima **Edge:** Reeded

Date	Mintage	F12	VF20	XF40	MS60	MS63
2005	9,999	PF63 50.00	PF65 60.00			

KM# 212 10 DINERS
31.10 g., 0.925 Silver 0.9189 oz. ASW, 38.6 mm. **Obv:** National arms **Rev:** Radiant woman above Guadalupe Cathedral **Edge:** Reeded

Date	Mintage	F12	VF20	XF40	MS60	MS63
2005	9,999	PF63 50.00	PF65 60.00			

KM# 213 10 DINERS
31.10 g., 0.925 Silver 0.9189 oz. ASW, 38.6 mm. **Obv:** National arms **Rev:** Sea shell above Santiago De Compostel-la Cathedral **Edge:** Reeded

Date	Mintage	F12	VF20	XF40	MS60	MS63
2005	9,999	PF63 50.00	PF65 60.00			

KM# 214 10 DINERS
31.10 g., 0.925 Silver 0.9189 oz. ASW, 38.6 mm. **Obv:** National arms **Rev:** Dead man's face with Church of the Holy Sepulchure in the background **Edge:** Reeded

Date	Mintage	F12	VF20	XF40	MS60	MS63
2005	9,999	PF63 50.00		PF65 60.00		

KM# 215 10 DINERS
28.80 g., 0.925 Silver 0.851 oz. ASW, 38.61 mm. **Obv:** National arms **Rev:** 2006 Olympics freestyle skier **Edge:** Reeded

Date	Mintage	F12	VF20	XF40	MS60	MS63
2005	15,000	PF63 40.00		PF65 50.00		

KM# 338 10 DINERS
28.28 g., 0.925 Silver 0.8356 oz. ASW, 38.61 mm. **Subject:** Benedict XVI election **Obv:** Naitonal arms **Rev:** Benedict XVI with hands raised, gilt; Crystal cross at right

Date	Mintage	F12	VF20	XF40	MS60	MS63
2005	—	—	—	—	—	75.00

KM# 217 10 DINERS
3.11 g., 0.9999 Gold 0.0993 oz. AGW, 20 mm. **Obv:** National arms **Rev:** Jesus carrying the cross **Edge:** Reeded

Date	Mintage	F12	VF20	XF40	MS60	MS63
2006	9,999	PF63 175		PF65 185		

KM# 218 10 DINERS
31.10 g., 0.925 Silver 0.919 oz. ASW, 38.6 mm. **Obv:** National arms **Rev:** Birth of Jesus **Edge:** Reeded

Date	Mintage	F12	VF20	XF40	MS60	MS63
2006	9,999	PF63 50.00		PF65 60.00		

KM# 219 10 DINERS
31.10 g., 0.925 Silver 0.919 oz. ASW, 38.6 mm. **Obv:** National arms **Rev:** The Last Supper **Edge:** Reeded

Date	Mintage	F12	VF20	XF40	MS60	MS63
2006	9,999	PF63 50.00		PF65 60.00		

KM# 276 10 DINERS
28.28 g., 0.925 Silver 0.8356 oz. ASW, 38.6 mm. **Subject:** Extreme Sports - Mountain Bike **Obv:** Arms **Rev:** Multicolor biker

Date	Mintage	F12	VF20	XF40	MS60	MS63
2007	5,000	PF63 60.00		PF65 65.00		

KM# 277 10 DINERS
28.28 g., 0.925 Silver 0.8356 oz. ASW, 38.6 mm. **Subject:** Extreme Sports - Snowboarding **Obv:** Arms **Rev:** Multicolor snowboarder

Date	Mintage	F12	VF20	XF40	MS60	MS63
2007	5,000	PF63 60.00		PF65 65.00		

KM# 278 10 DINERS
28.28 g., 0.925 Silver 0.8356 oz. ASW, 38.6 mm. **Subject:** Extreme Sports - Heliskiing **Obv:** Arms **Rev:** Multicolor heliskier

Date	Mintage	F12	VF20	XF40	MS60	MS63
2007	5,000	PF63 60.00		PF65 65.00		

KM# 244 10 DINERS
28.28 g., 0.925 Silver 0.8356 oz. ASW, 28x40 mm. **Subject:** Great Painters of the World **Obv:** Mona lisa, national arms at lower left, multicolor **Rev:** Head of Leonardo daVinci at lower left, study of man in background, multicolor **Edge:** Plain **Shape:** Vertical rectangular

Date	Mintage	F12	VF20	XF40	MS60	MS63
2008	15,000	—	—	—	—	60.00

KM# 271 10 DINERS
28.28 g., 0.925 Silver 0.8356 oz. ASW, 28x40 mm. **Obv:** National arms at left, color painting of ladies at a piano **Rev:** Renoir facing, female portrait in color in artist's pallet shape **Shape:** Vertical rectangle

Date	Mintage	F12	VF20	XF40	MS60	MS63
2008	20,000	PF63 60.00		PF65 65.00		

KM# 272 10 DINERS
33.00 g., 0.925 Silver 0.9751 oz. ASW, 38.6 mm. **Subject:** Vikings

Date	Mintage	F12	VF20	XF40	MS60	MS63
2008	15,000	—	—	—	—	60.00

KM# 273 10 DINERS
28.28 g., 0.925 Silver 0.8356 oz. ASW, 38.6 mm. **Subject:** Cross-country Skiing

Date	Mintage	F12	VF20	XF40	MS60	MS63
2008	10,000	PF63 35.00		PF65 45.00		

KM# 280 10 DINERS
28.28 g., 0.925 Silver 0.8356 oz. ASW, 38.61 mm. **Subject:** World Cup Football, 2010 **Obv:** Shield **Rev:** Linear and shaded player skicking ball **Edge:** Reeded

Date	Mintage	F12	VF20	XF40	MS60	MS63
2009	10,000	PF63 40.00		PF65 50.00		

KM# 316 10 DINERS
28.28 g., 0.925 Silver 0.8356 oz. ASW, 38.61 mm. **Subject:** Chopin **Rev:** Hand and autograph

Date	Mintage	F12	VF20	XF40	MS60	MS63
2009	—	PF63 35.00		PF65 45.00		

KM# 317 10 DINERS
28.28 g., 0.925 Silver 0.8356 oz. ASW **Subject:** Chopin - Vienna **Rev:** Bust at left, house at right

Date	Mintage	F12	VF20	XF40	MS60	MS63
2009	—	PF63 35.00		PF65 45.00		

KM# 318 10 DINERS
28.28 g., 0.925 Silver 0.8356 oz. ASW, 38.61 mm. **Subject:** Chopin - Paris **Rev:** Party scene, Paris

Date	Mintage	F12	VF20	XF40	MS60	MS63
2009	—	PF63 35.00		PF65 45.00		

KM# 319 10 DINERS
28.28 g., 0.925 Silver 0.8356 oz. ASW, 38.6 mm. **Subject:**
Chopin **Rev:** Bust at left, memorial stone at right

Date	Mintage	F12	VF20	XF40	MS60	MS63
2009	—	PF63 35.00	PF65 45.00			

KM# 320 10 DINERS
28.28 g., 0.925 Silver 0.8356 oz. ASW, 38.6 mm. **Subject:**
Chopin **Rev:** Portrait pair in ovals, Mallorca

Date	Mintage	F12	VF20	XF40	MS60	MS63
2009	—	PF63 35.00	PF65 45.00			

KM# 321 10 DINERS
28.28 g., 0.925 Silver 0.8356 oz. ASW, 38.61 mm. **Subject:**
Chopin **Rev:** Portrait pair in ovals, Dresden

Date	Mintage	F12	VF20	XF40	MS60	MS63
2009	—	PF63 35.00	PF65 45.00			

KM# 322 10 DINERS
28.28 g., 0.925 Silver 0.8356 oz. ASW, 38.61 mm. **Subject:**
Chopin **Rev:** Chopin at piano left, Gilt profile head at right

Date	Mintage	F12	VF20	XF40	MS60	MS63
2009	—	PF63 35.00	PF65 45.00			

KM# 323 10 DINERS
28.28 g., 0.925 Silver 0.8356 oz. ASW, 38.61 mm. **Subject:**
Chopin **Rev:** Two portraits, one in color - Wausau

Date	Mintage	F12	VF20	XF40	MS60	MS63
2009	—	PF63 35.00	PF65 45.00			

KM# 283 10 DINERS
28.28 g., 0.925 Silver 0.8356 oz. ASW, 40x28 mm. **Subject:**
Albrecht Durer **Obv:** Adama dn even engraving and shield **Rev:**
Durer's Adoration of the Holy Trinity

Date	Mintage	F12	VF20	XF40	MS60	MS63
2010	15,000	PF63 40.00	PF65 50.00			

KM# 284 10 DINERS
28.28 g., 0.925 Silver 0.8356 oz. ASW, 38.61 mm. **Obv:** Shield
Rev: St. Christopher

Date	Mintage	F12	VF20	XF40	MS60	MS63
2010	5,000	PF63 60.00	PF65 65.00			

KM# 285 10 DINERS
28.28 g., 0.925 Silver 0.8356 oz. ASW, 38.61 mm. **Obv:** Shield
Rev: St. George **Edge:** Reeded

Date	Mintage	F12	VF20	XF40	MS60	MS63
2010	5,000	PF63 60.00	PF65 65.00			

KM# 286 10 DINERS
28.28 g., 0.925 Silver 0.8356 oz. ASW, 38.61 mm. **Obv:** Shield
Rev: St. Catherine **Edge:** Reeded

Date	Mintage	F12	VF20	XF40	MS60	MS63
2010	5,000	PF63 60.00	PF65 65.00			

KM# 287 10 DINERS
28.28 g., 0.925 Silver 0.8356 oz. ASW, 38.61 mm. **Obv:** Shield
Rev: St. Barbara **Edge:** Reeded

Date	Mintage	F12	VF20	XF40	MS60	MS63
2010	5,000	PF63 60.00	PF65 65.00			

KM# 332 10 DINERS
31.10 g., 0.999 Silver 0.9926 oz. ASW, 38.6 mm. **Obv:** National
arms **Rev:** St. Margaret and dragon

Date	Mintage	F12	VF20	XF40	MS60	MS63
2011	—	PF63 90.00	PF65 100			

KM# 339 10 DINERS
31.11 g., 0.999 Silver 0.9926 oz. ASW, 30x45 mm. **Subject:**
Seven Virtures by Pierodel and Antonio Pollaiulo **Obv:** National
arms and value **Rev:** Caritas in color **Shape:** Vertical

Date	Mintage	F12	VF20	XF40	MS60	MS63
2012	4,000	PF65 120				

KM# 340 10 DINERS
31.11 g., 0.999 Silver 0.9926 oz. ASW, 30x45 mm. **Subject:**
Seven Virtures by Pierodel and Antonio Pollaiulo **Obv:** National
arms and value **Rev:** Temperantia in color **Shape:** Vertical

Date	Mintage	F12	VF20	XF40	MS60	MS63
2012	4,000	PF65 120				

KM# 341 10 DINERS
31.11 g., 0.999 Silver 0.9926 oz. ASW, 30x45 mm. **Subject:**
Seven Virtures by Pierodel and Antonio Pollaiulo **Obv:** National
arms and value **Rev:** Fides in color **Shape:** Vertical

Date	Mintage	F12	VF20	XF40	MS60	MS63
2012	4,000	PF65 120				

KM# 342 10 DINERS
31.11 g., 0.999 Silver 0.9926 oz. ASW, 30x45 mm. **Subject:**
Seven Virtures by Pierodel and Antonio Pollaiulo **Obv:** National
arms and value **Rev:** Fortitudo in color **Shape:** Vertical

Date	Mintage	F12	VF20	XF40	MS60	MS63
2012	4,000	PF65 120				

KM# 343 10 DINERS
31.11 g., 0.999 Silver 0.9926 oz. ASW, 30x45 mm. **Subject:**
Seven Virtures by Pierodel and Antonio Pollaiulo **Obv:** National
arms and value **Rev:** Iustitia in color **Shape:** Vertical

Date	Mintage	F12	VF20	XF40	MS60	MS63
2012	4,000	PF65 120				

KM# 344 10 DINERS
31.11 g., 0.999 Silver 0.9926 oz. ASW, 30x45 mm. **Subject:** Seven Virtures by Pierodel and Antonio Pollaiulo **Obv:** National arms and value **Rev:** Prudentia in color **Shape:** Vertical

Date	Mintage	F12	VF20	XF40	MS60	MS63
2012	4,000	PF65 120				

KM# 345 10 DINERS
31.11 g., 0.999 Silver 0.9926 oz. ASW, 30x45 mm. **Subject:** Seven Virtures by Pierodel and Antonio Pollaiulo **Obv:** Naitonal arms and value **Rev:** Spes in color **Shape:** Vertical

Date	Mintage	F12	VF20	XF40	MS60	MS63
2012	4,000	PF65 120				

KM# 327 15 DINERS
Silver **Subject:** Leonardo daVinci painting **Rev:** Madonna **Shape:** Vertical rectangle

Date	Mintage	F12	VF20	XF40	MS60	MS63
2011	—	PF65 150				

KM# 328 15 DINERS
Silver **Subject:** Botticelli painting **Shape:** Vertical rectangle

Date	Mintage	F12	VF20	XF40	MS60	MS63
2011	—	PF65 125				

KM# 346 15 DINERS
50.00 g., 0.999 Silver 1.5956 oz. ASW **Subject:** Painting by Lucas Cranche **Rev:** Madonna and Child in color

Date	Mintage	F12	VF20	XF40	MS60	MS63
2012	—	PF65 200				

KM# 174 25 DINERS
12.44 g., 0.999 Gold 0.397 oz. AGW, 26 mm. **Subject:** Christmas **Obv:** National arms **Rev:** Nativity scene **Edge:** Reeded

Date	Mintage	F12	VF20	XF40	MS60	MS63
2001	3,000	PF63 700	PF65 725			

KM# 184 25 DINERS
10.00 g., 0.9999 Gold 0.3194 oz. AGW, 26 mm. **Subject:** Christmas **Obv:** National arms **Rev:** Standing Christ child **Edge:** Reeded

Date	Mintage	F12	VF20	XF40	MS60	MS63
2002	2,000	PF63 600	PF65 625			

KM# 185 25 DINERS
7.78 g., 0.999 Gold 0.2481 oz. AGW, 26 mm. **Subject:** Christmas **Obv:** National arms **Rev:** Madonna-like mother and child **Edge:** Reeded

Date	Mintage	F12	VF20	XF40	MS60	MS63
2003	3,000	PF63 450	PF65 475			

KM# 197 25 DINERS
8.00 g., 0.999 Gold 0.2553 oz. AGW, 26 mm. **Subject:** Christmas **Obv:** National arms **Rev:** Nativity scene **Edge:** Reeded

Date	Mintage	F12	VF20	XF40	MS60	MS63
2004	5,000	PF63 450	PF65 475			

KM# 216 25 DINERS
6.00 g., 0.9999 Gold 0.1916 oz. AGW, 26 mm. **Obv:** National arms **Rev:** St. Joseph holding infant Jesus **Edge:** Reeded

Date	Mintage	F12	VF20	XF40	MS60	MS63
2005	9,999	PF63 365	PF65 385			

KM# 305 25 DINERS
6.00 g., 0.999 Gold 0.1915 oz. AGW, 26 mm. **Subject:** Christmas - the Holy Family **Obv:** National Arms **Rev:** St. Joseph, Mary and Jesus

Date	Mintage	F12	VF20	XF40	MS60	MS63
2006	5,000	PF63 350	PF65 400			

KM# 314 25 DINERS
6.00 g., 0.999 Gold 0.1915 oz. AGW, 26 mm. **Subject:** Christmas **Obv:** National Arms **Rev:** Angels playing musical instruments

Date	Mintage	F12	VF20	XF40	MS60	MS63
2007	2,000	PF63 525	PF65 575			

KM# 274 25 DINERS
6.00 g., 0.999 Gold 0.1915 oz. AGW, 26 mm. **Subject:** Constitution

Date	Mintage	F12	VF20	XF40	MS60	MS63
2008	2,000	PF63 400	PF65 425			

KM# 275 25 DINERS
6.00 g., 0.999 Gold 0.1915 oz. AGW, 26 mm. **Subject:** Three Kings **Rev:** Magi following star

Date	Mintage	F12	VF20	XF40	MS60	MS63
2008	2,000	PF63 375	PF65 400			

KM# 279 25 DINERS
6.00 g., 0.999 Gold 0.1915 oz. AGW, 26 mm. **Obv:** Shield **Rev:** Madonna and child, star of Bethlehem in backgorund **Edge:** Reeded

Date	Mintage	F12	VF20	XF40	MS60	MS63
2009	1,200	PF63 375	PF65 400			

KM# 288 25 DINERS
6.00 g., 0.999 Gold 0.1915 oz. AGW, 26 mm. **Subject:** Christmas **Obv:** Shield **Rev:** Archangel Gabriel telling the good news to Mary

Date	Mintage	F12	VF20	XF40	MS60	MS63
2010	1,200	PF63 375	PF65 400			

KM# 330 25 DINERS
6.00 g., 0.999 Gold 0.1915 oz. AGW, 26 mm. **Obv:** National arms **Rev:** Holy family

Date	Mintage	F12	VF20	XF40	MS60	MS63
2011	—	PF63 400	PF65 425			

KM# 186 50 DINERS
159.50 g., 0.999 Bi-Metallic 5.0899 oz., 65 mm. **Subject:** 10th Anniversary of Constitution **Obv:** National arms **Rev:** Seated allegorical woman holding scrolled constitution **Edge:** Reeded **Note:** Illustration reduced.

Date	Mintage	F12	VF20	XF40	MS60	MS63
2003	3,000	—	—	—	325	375

KM# 347 100 DINERS
1000.00 g., 0.999 Silver 31.9118 oz. ASW, 166x240 mm. **Subject:** Painting by Raffaello **Rev:** Madonna **Shape:** Vertical

Date	Mintage	F12	VF20	XF40	MS60	MS63
2012	—	PF65 1,300				

KM# 336 1000 DINERS
1000.00 g., 0.999 Gold 31.9118 oz. AGW **Subject:** Pope John Paul II Beautification **Obv:** John Paul II with arms raised, National arms at right **Rev:** Profile at right, looking left

Date	Mintage	F12	VF20	XF40	MS60	MS63
2011	—	PF65 45,000				

KM# 362 .5 DINER
0.50 g., 0.585 Gold AGW, 11 mm. **Subject:** Napoleon

Date	Mintage	F12	VF20	XF40	MS60	MS63
2013	Est. 7,500	PF63 35.00	PF65 40.00			

BULLION COINAGE

KM# 268 DINER
31.11 g., 0.999 Silver 0.9926 oz. ASW, 38.6 mm. **Obv:** Eagle with wings outstretched **Rev:** National Arms **Edge:** Reeded

Date	Mintage	F12	VF20	XF40	MS60	MS63
2008	—	—	—	—	—	37.50
2009	—	—	—	—	—	37.50
2010	—	—	—	—	—	37.50
2011	—	—	—	—	—	37.50

KM# 257 5 DINERS
1.55 g., 0.999 Gold 0.0495 oz. AGW, 13.92 mm. **Obv:** Eagle with wings outstretched **Rev:** National Arms

Date	Mintage	F12	VF20	XF40	MS60	MS63
2009	—	—	—	—	—	100
2010	—	—	—	—	—	100

KM# 258 10 DINERS
3.11 g., 0.999 Gold 0.0992 oz. AGW, 16.46 mm. **Obv:** Eagle with wings outstretched **Rev:** National Arms

Date	Mintage	F12	VF20	XF40	MS60	MS63
2009	—	—	—	—	—	200
2010	—	—	—	—	—	200

KM# 259 25 DINERS
7.77 g., 0.999 Gold 0.248 oz. AGW, 22.5 mm. **Obv:** Eagle with wings outstretched **Rev:** National Arms

Date	Mintage	F12	VF20	XF40	MS60	MS63
2009	—	—	—	—	—	450
2010	—	—	—	—	—	450

KM# 260 50 DINERS
15.55 g., 0.999 Gold 0.4962 oz. AGW, 26 mm. **Obv:** Eagle with wings outstretched **Rev:** National Arms

Date	Mintage	F12	VF20	XF40	MS60	MS63
2009	—	—	—	—	—	875
2010	—	—	—	—	—	875

KM# 254 50 DINERS
1000.00 g., 0.999 Silver 31.9118 oz. ASW, 100 mm. **Obv:** Eagle with wings outstretched **Rev:** National Arms

Date	Mintage	F12	VF20	XF40	MS60	MS63
2010	—	—	—	—	—	1,200

KM# 298 100 DINERS
31.10 g., 0.999 Gold 0.9926 oz. AGW, 35 mm. **Obv:** Eagle with open wings **Rev:** Details of National Arms **Edge:** Reeded

Date	Mintage	F12	VF20	XF40	MS60	MS63
2006	1,500	—	—	—	—	2,000

KM# 261 100 DINERS
31.11 g., 0.999 Gold 0.9926 oz. AGW, 33 mm. **Obv:** Eagle with wings outstretched **Rev:** National Arms

Date	Mintage	F12	VF20	XF40	MS60	MS63
2009	—	—	—	—	—	1,750
2010	—	—	—	—	—	1,750

KM# 255 100 DINERS
3110.50 g., 0.999 Silver 99.2618 oz. ASW, 120 mm. **Obv:** Eagle with wings outstretched **Rev:** National Arms **Note:** 29mm thick.

Date	Mintage	F12	VF20	XF40	MS60	MS63
2010	—	—	—	—	—	5,000

KM# 256 200 DINERS
6221.00 g., 0.999 Silver 198.5235 oz. ASW, 140 mm. **Obv:** Eagle with wings outstretched **Rev:** National Arms **Note:** 42mm thick

Date	Mintage	F12	VF20	XF40	MS60	MS63
2010	—	—	—	—	—	10,000

ANGOLA

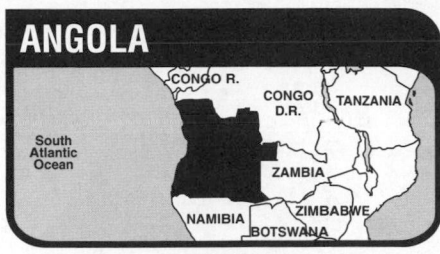

PEOPLES REPUBLIC
REFORM COINAGE
1999 -

KM# 107 50 CENTIMOS
Copper-Nickel **Obv:** BNA logo within textile pattern border **Rev:** large value within textile pattern border

Date	Mintage	F12	VF20	XF40	MS60	MS63
2012	—	—	—	—	0.75	1.00

KM# 105 KWANZA
23.00 g., Bi-Metallic, 35 mm. **Obv:** Large value **Rev:** Central Bank building

Date	Mintage	F12	VF20	XF40	MS60	MS63
2006	2,500	PF63 100				

KM# 108 KWANZA
Nickel-Brass **Obv:** BNA logo within textile border **Rev:** Value within textile border

Date	Mintage	F12	VF20	XF40	MS60	MS63
2012	—	—	—	—	1.00	1.25

KM# 109 5 KWANZAS
Bi-Metallic **Obv:** National arms within textile border **Rev:** Large value within textile border

Date	Mintage	F12	VF20	XF40	MS60	MS63
2012	—	—	—	—	1.50	2.00

KM# 110 10 KWANZAS
Bi-Metallic **Obv:** National arms within textile border **Rev:** Large value within textile border

Date	Mintage	F12	VF20	XF40	MS60	MS63
2012	—	—	—	—	5.00	7.50

KM# 106 20 KWANZAS
Silver ASW, 35 mm. **Subject:** Central Bank, 35th Anniversary **Obv:** National arms **Rev:** Linear logo

Date	Mintage	F12	VF20	XF40	MS60	MS63
2011	—	PF63 75.00				

ARGENTINA

The Argentine Republic, located in southern South America, has an area of 1,073,518 sq. mi. (3,761,274 sq. km.) and an estimated population of 37.03 million. Capital: Buenos Aires. Its varied topography ranges from the subtropical lowlands of the north to the towering Andean Mountains in the west and the wind-swept Patagonian steppe in the south. The rolling, fertile pampas of central Argentina are ideal for agriculture and grazing, and support most of the republic's population. Meatpacking, flour milling, textiles, sugar refining and dairy products are the principal industries. Oil is found in Patagonia, but most mineral requirements must be imported.

REPUBLIC
REFORM COINAGE
1992
100 Centavos = 1 Peso

KM# 109 5 CENTAVOS
2.02 g., Aluminum-Bronze, 17.2 mm. **Obv:** Radiant sunface **Rev:** Large value, date below **Edge:** Reeded **Note:** Prev. KM#84.

Date	Mintage	F12	VF20	XF40	MS60	MS63
2004	30,000,000	—	—	—	0.45	0.60
2005	76,000,000	—	—	—	0.45	0.60

KM# 109b 5 CENTAVOS
2.00 g., Brass Plated Steel, 17.2 mm. **Obv:** Radiant Sunface **Rev:** Large value, date below **Edge:** Plain

Date	Mintage	F12	VF20	XF40	MS60	MS63
2006	23,800,000	—	—	—	0.45	0.60
2007	183,000,000	—	—	—	0.45	0.60
2008	114,000,000	—	—	—	0.45	0.60
2009	—	—	—	—	0.45	0.60
2010	—	—	—	—	0.45	0.60
2011	—	—	—	—	0.45	0.60

KM# 107 10 CENTAVOS
2.25 g., Aluminum-Bronze, 18.2 mm. **Obv:** Argentine arms **Rev:** Value, date below **Edge:** Reeded **Note:** Prev. KM#82.

Date	Mintage	F12	VF20	XF40	MS60	MS63
2004	190,000,000	—	—	—	0.65	0.85
2005	114,400,000	—	—	—	0.65	0.85

KM# 107a 10 CENTAVOS
2.20 g., Brass Plated Steel, 18.2 mm. **Obv:** Argentine arms **Rev:** Large value, date below **Edge:** Plain

Date	Mintage	F12	VF20	XF40	MS60	MS63
2006	99,600,000	—	—	—	0.65	0.85
2007	204,000,000	—	—	—	0.65	0.85
2008	317,000,000	—	—	—	0.65	0.85
2009	—	—	—	—	0.65	0.85
2010	—	—	—	—	0.65	0.85
2011	—	—	—	—	0.65	0.85

KM# 110.1 25 CENTAVOS
5.40 g., Aluminum-Bronze, 24.2 mm. **Obv:** Buenos Aires City Hall, fine lettering **Rev:** Large value, date below **Edge:** Reeded **Note:** Prev. KM#85.1.

Date	Mintage	F12	VF20	XF40	MS60	MS63
2009	—	—	—	—	1.25	1.50
2010	—	—	—	—	1.25	1.50

KM# 110a 25 CENTAVOS
6.10 g., Copper-Nickel, 24.2 mm. **Obv:** Buenos Aires City Hall, bold lettering **Rev:** Large value, date below **Edge:** Reeded **Note:** Prev. KM#85a.

Date	Mintage	F12	VF20	XF40	MS60	MS63
2009	—	—	—	—	1.25	1.50

KM# 111.1 50 CENTAVOS
5.80 g., Aluminum-Bronze, 25.2 mm. **Obv:** Tucuman Province Capital Building; fine lettering **Rev:** Large value, date below **Edge:** Reeded **Note:** Prev. KM#86.1.

Date	Mintage	F12	VF20	XF40	MS60	MS63
2009	—	—	—	—	1.75	2.00
2010	—	—	—	—	1.75	2.00

KM# 111.2 50 CENTAVOS
5.80 g., Aluminum-Bronze, 25.2 mm. **Obv:** Tucuman Province Capital Building; bold lettering **Rev:** Large value, date below **Edge:** Reeded **Note:** Prev. KM#86.2.

Date	Mintage	F12	VF20	XF40	MS60	MS63
2009	—	—	—	—	1.75	2.00

KM# 112.1 PESO
6.35 g., Bi-Metallic, 23 mm. **Obv:** Argentine arms in circle **Rev:** Design of first Argentine coin in center **Edge:** Plain **Note:** Prev. KM#87.1.

Date	Mintage	F12	VF20	XF40	MS60	MS63
2006	30,000,000	—	—	0.50	1.20	1.60
2007	33,000,000	—	—	0.50	1.20	1.60
2008	89,600,000	—	—	0.50	1.20	1.60
2009 D	—	—	—	0.50	1.20	1.60
2010 E	—	—	—	0.50	1.20	1.60

KM# 132.1 PESO
6.35 g., Bi-Metallic, 23 mm. **Subject:** General Urquiza **Obv:** Stylized portrait facing **Rev:** Church tower and denomination **Edge:** Reeded

Date	Mintage	F12	VF20	XF40	MS60	MS63
2001	995,000	—	—	—	3.75	4.50

KM# 132.2 PESO
6.35 g., Bi-Metallic, 23 mm. **Subject:** General Urquiza **Obv:** Stylized portrait facing **Rev:** Church tower and denomination **Edge:** Plain

Date	Mintage	VF20	XF40	MS60	MS63	MS65
2001	5,000	—	—	7.50	8.00	—

KM# 141 PESO
25.00 g., 0.900 Silver 0.7187 oz. ASW, 37 mm. **Obv:** Maria Eva Duarte de Peron **Rev:** EVITA" audience **Edge:** Reeded

Date	Mintage	F12	VF20	XF40	MS60	MS63
ND (2004)	5,000	PF65 45.00				

KM# 140 PESO
25.00 g., 0.900 Silver 0.7187 oz. ASW, 37 mm. **Subject:** 70th Anniversary of Central Bank **Obv:** Bank building **Rev:** Liberty head in wreath **Edge:** Reeded

Date	Mintage	F12	VF20	XF40	MS60	MS63
2005	2,000	PF65 50.00				

KM# 155 PESO
25.00 g., 0.900 Silver 0.7187 oz. ASW, 37 mm. **Subject:** Jorge Luis Borges **Obv:** Stylized bust facing **Rev:** Man walking at street corner

Date	Mintage	F12	VF20	XF40	MS60	MS63
2006A	—	—	—	—	—	42.50

KM# 153 PESO
25.00 g., 0.900 Silver 0.7187 oz. ASW, 37 mm. **Subject:** 25th Anniversary Malvinas Islands Occupation - Heroes **Obv:** Soldier's bust facing **Obv. Legend:** REPUBLICA ARGENTINA -1982 - 2007 - LA NACIÓN A SUS HÉROES **Rev:** Outlined map of islands **Rev. Legend:** MALVINAS ARGENTINAS. **Rev. Inscription:** 2 DE APRIL / 1982 **Edge:** Reeded

Date	Mintage	F12	VF20	XF40	MS60	MS63
2007	3,000	PF65 75.00				

KM# 156 PESO
6.35 g., Bi-Metallic, 23 mm. **Subject:** Bicentennial - El Palmar **Obv:** Stylized radiant sun **Rev:** Palm trees

Date	Mintage	F12	VF20	XF40	MS60	MS63
2010	—	—	—	—	1.20	1.60

KM# 157 PESO
6.35 g., Bi-Metallic, 23 mm. **Subject:** Bicentennial - Aconcagua **Obv:** Stylized radiant run **Rev:** Mountains

Date	Mintage	F12	VF20	XF40	MS60	MS63
2010	—	—	—	—	1.20	1.60

KM# 158 PESO
6.35 g., Bi-Metallic, 23 mm. **Subject:** Bicentennial - Mar del Plata **Obv:** Stylized radiant sun **Rev:** Elephant seal and fishing boat

Date	Mintage	F12	VF20	XF40	MS60	MS63
2010	—	—	—	—	1.20	1.60

KM# 159 PESO
6.35 g., Bi-Metallic, 23 mm. **Subject:** Bicentennial - Pucara de Tilcara **Obv:** Stylized radiant sun **Rev:** Cactus and mountains

Date	Mintage	F12	VF20	XF40	MS60	MS63
2010	—	—	—	—	1.20	1.60

KM# 160 PESO
6.35 g., Bi-Metallic, 23 mm. **Subject:** Bicentennial - Glaciar Perito Moreno **Obv:** Stylized radiant sun **Rev:** Glaciar ice bridge and sea

Date	Mintage	F12	VF20	XF40	MS60	MS63
2010	—	—	—	—	1.20	1.60

KM# 164 PESO
6.35 g., Bi-Metallic, 23 mm. **Subject:** Revolution anniversary

Date	Mintage	F12	VF20	XF40	MS60	MS63
2010	—	—	—	—	—	—

KM# 135.1 2 PESOS
10.40 g., Copper-Nickel, 30 mm. **Subject:** Eva Peron **Obv:** Head left **Rev:** Stylized crowd scene, value **Rev. Inscription:** EVITA **Edge:** Reeded

Date	Mintage	F12	VF20	XF40	MS60	MS63
2002	1,995,000	—	—	0.85	1.85	2.50

KM# 135.2 2 PESOS
10.40 g., Copper-Nickel, 30 mm. **Subject:** Eva Peron **Obv:** Head left **Rev:** Stylized crowd scene, value **Rev. Inscription:** EVITA **Edge:** Plain

Date	Mintage	F12	VF20	XF40	MS60	MS63
2002	5,000	—	—	—	6.00	8.00

KM# 161 2 PESOS
10.47 g., Copper-Nickel, 30.35 mm. **Subject:** Declaration of Human Rights **Obv:** Legend **Rev:** Female's scarf

Date	Mintage	F12	VF20	XF40	MS60	MS63
2006	—	—	—	—	1.85	2.50

KM# 144.1 2 PESOS
10.40 g., Copper-Nickel, 30 mm. **Subject:** Malvinas Islands War, 25th Anniversary **Obv:** Soldier's bust facing **Obv. Legend:** REPUBLICA ARGENTINA - 1982 - 2007 - LA NACIÓN A SUS HÉROES **Rev:** Outlined map of islands **Rev. Legend:** MALVINAS ARGENTINAS **Rev. Inscription:** 2 DE APRIL / 1982 **Edge:** Reeded

Date	Mintage	F12	VF20	XF40	MS60	MS63
2007	1,995,000	—	—	0.85	1.85	2.50

KM# 144.2 2 PESOS
10.40 g., Copper-Nickel, 30 mm. **Subject:** Malvinas Islands War, 25th Anniversary **Obv:** Soldier's bust facing **Obv. Legend:** REPUBLICA ARGENTINA - 1982 - 2007 - LA NACIÓN A SUS HÉROES **Rev:** Outlined map of islands **Rev. Legend:** MALVINAS ARGENTINAS **Rev. Inscription:** 2 DE APRIL / 1982 **Edge:** Plain

Date	Mintage	F12	VF20	XF40	MS60	MS63
2007	5,000	—	—	—	—	9.00

KM# 145 2 PESOS
Copper-Nickel, 30.35 mm. **Subject:** 100th Anniversary First Oil Well **Obv:** Oil well **Obv. Legend:** REPÚBLICA ARGENTINA - DESCUBRIMIENTO DEL PETRÓLEO **Rev:** Modern pump **Rev. Inscription:** CHUBUT **Edge:** Reeded

Date	Mintage	F12	VF20	XF40	MS60	MS63
2007	995,000	—	—	—	6.00	8.00

KM# 165 2 PESOS
7.20 g., Bi-Metallic, 24.5 mm. **Subject:** 1810 Revolution, 200th Anniversary **Obv:** Sunburst at center of wreath **Rev:** Value at center of wreath **Edge:** Segmented reeding

Date	Mintage	F12	VF20	XF40	MS60	MS63
2010	100,000,000	—	—	—	3.00	5.00
2011	—	—	—	—	3.00	5.00

KM# 162 2 PESOS
10.47 g., Copper-Nickel, 30.35 mm. **Subject:** Central Bank, 75th Anniversary **Obv:** Head at right, facing left **Rev:** Bank's main doors

Date	Mintage	F12	VF20	XF40	MS60	MS63
2010	—	—	—	—	1.85	2.50

KM# 133 5 PESOS
8.06 g., 0.900 Gold 0.2318 oz. AGW, 22 mm. **Subject:** Gral. Justo Jose de Urquiza **Obv:** Stylized portrait facing **Rev:** Church tower and denomination **Edge:** Reeded

Date	Mintage	F12	VF20	XF40	MS60	MS63
2001	1,000	PF63 425		PF65 450		

KM# 149 5 PESOS
8.06 g., 0.900 Gold 0.2318 oz. AGW **Subject:** 100th Anniversary City of Comodoro Rivadavia

Date	Mintage	F12	VF20	XF40	MS60	MS63
2001	750	PF63 450		PF65 475		

KM# 143 5 PESOS
27.00 g., 0.925 Silver 0.7978 oz. ASW, 40 mm. **Subject:** FIFA

- XVIII World Championship Football - Germany 2006 **Obv:** Football at right on grass, chaff in background **Obv. Legend:** REPÚBLICA ARGENTINA **Rev:** Logo **Rev. Legend:** COPA MUNDIAL DE LA FIFA **Rev. Inscription:** ALEMANIA **Edge:** Reeded

Date	Mintage	F12	VF20	XF40	MS60	MS63
2003	50,000	PF63 50.00		PF65 55.00		

KM# 142 5 PESOS
8.06 g., 0.900 Gold 0.2318 oz. AGW, 22 mm. **Obv:** Maria Eva Duarte de Peron **Rev:** EVITA" and audience

Date	Mintage	F12	VF20	XF40	MS60	MS63
ND (2004)	1,000	PF63 425		PF65 450		

KM# 146 5 PESOS
27.00 g., 0.925 Silver 0.7978 oz. ASW **Subject:** FIFA - XVIII World Football Championship - Germany 2006 **Obv. Legend:** REPÚBLICA ARGENTINA **Rev:** Logo **Edge:** Reeded

Date	Mintage	F12	VF20	XF40	MS60	MS63
2004	50,000	PF63 50.00		PF65 55.00		

KM# 150 5 PESOS
27.00 g., 0.925 Silver 0.7978 oz. ASW **Subject:** FIFA - XVIII World Championship Football - Germany 2006 **Obv:** Forward player **Rev:** Logo

Date	Mintage	F12	VF20	XF40	MS60	MS63
2005	—	PF63 60.00		PF65 65.00		

KM# 154 5 PESOS
8.06 g., 0.900 Gold 0.2318 oz. AGW, 22 mm. **Subject:** 25th Anniversary Malvinas Islands Occupation - Heroes **Obv:** Soldier's bust facing **Obv. Legend:** REPUBLICA ARGENTINA - 1982 - 2007 - LA NACIÓN A SUS HÉROES **Rev:** Outlined map of islands **Rev. Legend:** MALVINAS ISLANDS **Rev. Inscription:** 2 DE APRIL / 1982 **Edge:** Reeded

Date	Mintage	F12	VF20	XF40	MS60	MS63
2007	1,000	PF63 425		PF65 450		

KM# 147 10 PESOS
6.75 g., 0.999 Gold 0.2154 oz. AGW **Subject:** FIFA - XVIII World Football Championship - Germany 2006 **Obv. Legend:** REPÚBLICA ARGENTINA **Edge:** Reeded

Date	Mintage	F12	VF20	XF40	MS60	MS63
2004	25,000	PF63 375		PF65 400		

KM# 151 10 PESOS
6.75 g., 0.999 Gold 0.2154 oz. AGW **Subject:** FIFA - XVIII World Championship Football - Germany 2006 **Obv:** Forward player **Rev:** Logo

Date	Mintage	F12	VF20	XF40	MS60	MS63
2005	—	PF63 375		PF65 400		

KM# 138 25 PESOS

27.00 g., 0.925 Silver 0.7978 oz. ASW, 40 mm. **Subject:** IBERO-AMERICA Series **Obv:** Coats of arms **Rev:** Tall ship "Presidente Sarmiento **Edge:** Reeded

Date	Mintage	F12	VF20	XF40	MS60	MS63
2002	—	PF63 60.00		PF65 65.00		

KM# 139 25 PESOS

27.00 g., 0.925 Silver 0.7978 oz. ASW, 40 mm. **Subject:** Ibero-America **Obv:** National arms in circle of arms **Rev:** Colon Theater building **Edge:** Reeded

Date	Mintage	F12	VF20	XF40	MS60	MS63
2005	15,500	PF63 50.00		PF65 55.00		

KM# 167 25 PESOS

27.00 g., 0.925 Silver 0.7978 oz. ASW, 40 mm. **Obv:** Arms within other national arms **Rev:** Arm dunking basketball

Date	Mintage	F12	VF20	XF40	MS60	MS63
2007	—	PF63 70.00		PF65 75.00		

KM# 166 25 PESOS

27.00 g., 0.925 Silver 0.7978 oz. ASW, 40 mm. **Obv:** National arms within circle of other country's arms **Rev:** 1881 Argentinian coin design at center

Date	Mintage	F12	VF20	XF40	MS60	MS63
2010	—	PF63 70.00		PF65 75.00		

PROOF SETS

KM#	Date	Mintage	Identification	Issue Price	Mkt Val
PS6	2007 (2)	300	KM#153, 154	475	525

ARMENIA

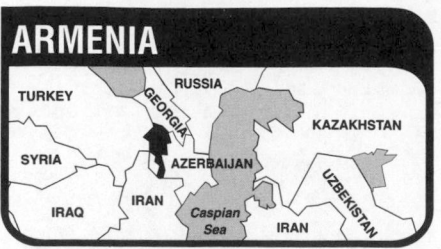

The Republic of Armenia, formerly Armenian S.S.R., is bordered to the north by Georgia, the east by Azerbaijan and the south and west by Turkey and Iran. It has an area of 11,506 sq. mi. (29,800 sq. km) and an estimated population of 3.66 million. Capital: Yerevan. Agriculture including cotton, vineyards and orchards, hydroelectricity, chemicals - primarily synthetic rubber and fertilizers, vast mineral deposits of copper, zinc and aluminum, and production of steel and paper are major industries. Fighting between Christians in Armenia and Muslim forces of Azerbaijan escalated in 1992 and continued through early 1994. Each country claimed the Nagorno-Karabakh, an Armenian ethnic enclave, in Azerbaijan. A temporary cease-fire was announced in May 1994.

MONETARY SYSTEM
100 Luma = 1 Dram

MINT NAME
Revan, (Erevan, now Yerevan)

REPUBLIC

STANDARD COINAGE

KM# 112 10 DRAM

1.30 g., Aluminum, 20 mm. **Obv:** National arms **Rev:** Value **Edge:** Plain

Date	Mintage	F12	VF20	XF40	MS60	MS63
2004	—	—	—	—	1.00	1.50

KM# 93 20 DRAM

2.75 g., Copper Plated Steel, 20.5 mm. **Obv:** National arms **Rev:** Denomination **Edge:** Plain

Date	Mintage	F12	VF20	XF40	MS60	MS63
2003	—	—	—	—	1.00	1.50

KM# 94 50 DRAM

3.50 g., Brass Plated Steel, 21.5 mm. **Obv:** National arms **Rev:** Value **Edge:** Reeded

Date	Mintage	F12	VF20	XF40	MS60	MS63
2003	—	—	—	—	1.25	1.50

KM# 212 50 DRAM

3.50 g., Brass Plated Steel, 21.5 mm. **Subject:** Aragatsotn region **Edge:** Reeded

Date	Mintage	F12	VF20	XF40	MS60	MS63
2012	60,000	—	—	—	1.50	2.50

KM# 213 50 DRAM

3.50 g., Brass Plated Steel, 21.5 mm. **Subject:** Ararat region **Edge:** Reeded

Date	Mintage	F12	VF20	XF40	MS60	MS63
2012	60,000	—	—	—	1.50	2.50

KM# 214 50 DRAM

3.50 g., Brass Plated Steel, 21.5 mm. **Subject:** Armavir region

Date	Mintage	F12	VF20	XF40	MS60	MS63
2012	—	—	—	—	1.50	2.50

KM# 215 50 DRAM

3.50 g., Brass Plated Steel, 21.5 mm. **Subject:** Gegharkunik region **Edge:** Reeded

Date	Mintage	F12	VF20	XF40	MS60	MS63
2012	60,000	—	—	—	1.50	2.50

KM# 216 50 DRAM

3.50 g., Brass Plated Steel, 21.5 mm. **Subject:** Kotayk region **Edge:** Reeded

Date	Mintage	F12	VF20	XF40	MS60	MS63
2012	60,000	—	—	—	1.50	2.50

KM# 217 50 DRAM

3.50 g., Brass Plated Steel, 21.5 mm. **Subject:** Lori region **Edge:** Reeded

Date	Mintage	F12	VF20	XF40	MS60	MS63
2012	60,000	—	—	—	1.50	2.50

KM# 218 50 DRAM

3.50 g., Brass Plated Steel, 21.5 mm. **Subject:** Shirak region **Edge:** Reeded

Date	Mintage	F12	VF20	XF40	MS60	MS63
2012	60,000	—	—	—	1.50	2.50

KM# 219 50 DRAM

3.50 g., Brass Plated Steel, 21.5 mm. **Subject:** Syunik region **Edge:** Reeded

Date	Mintage	F12	VF20	XF40	MS60	MS63
2012	60,000	—	—	—	1.50	2.50

KM# 220 50 DRAM

3.50 g., Brass Plated Steel, 21.5 mm. **Subject:** Tavush region **Edge:** Reeded

Date	Mintage	F12	VF20	XF40	MS60	MS63
2012	60,000	—	—	—	1.50	2.50

KM# 221 50 DRAM
3.50 g., Brass Plated Steel, 21.5 mm. **Subject:** Vayots Dzor region **Edge:** Reeded

Date	Mintage	F12	VF20	XF40	MS60	MS63
2012	60,000	—	—	—	1.50	2.50

KM# 222 50 DRAM
3.50 g., Brass Plated Steel, 21.5 mm. **Subject:** Yerevan region **Edge:** Reeded

Date	Mintage	F12	VF20	XF40	MS60	MS63
2012	60,000	—	—	—	1.50	2.50

KM# 86 100 DRAM
31.10 g., 0.999 Silver 0.9925 oz. ASW, 38 mm. **Obv:** National arms **Rev:** Bust of General Garegin Nzhdeh facing at right **Edge:** Plain **Edge Lettering:** Serial number

Date	Mintage	F12	VF20	XF40	MS60	MS63
2001	170	PF63 2,200	PF65 2,500			

KM# 87 100 DRAM
31.04 g., 0.999 Silver 0.9905 oz. ASW, 38 mm. **Subject:** Armenian Membership in the Council of Europe joined January 1, 2001 **Obv:** National arms **Rev:** Spiral design with star circle **Edge:** Plain **Edge Lettering:** Serial number

Date	Mintage	F12	VF20	XF40	MS60	MS63
2001	200	PF63 450	PF65 500			

KM# 86a 100 DRAM
31.10 g., 0.999 Silver Gilt 0.9925 oz., 38 mm. **Obv:** National arms **Obv. Inscription:** Bust of General Garegin Nzhdeh facing at right **Edge:** Plain **Edge Lettering:** Serial number

Date	Mintage	F12	VF20	XF40	MS60	MS63
2001	30	PF65 10,000				

KM# 98 100 DRAM
31.10 g., 0.925 Silver 0.9189 oz. ASW, 40 mm. **Obv:** National arms **Rev:** Aram Khachatryan, Birth Centennial **Edge:** Reeded

Date	Mintage	F12	VF20	XF40	MS60	MS63
2002	300	—	—	—	—	120

Note: Issued in blister pack only

KM# 99 100 DRAM
31.10 g., 0.925 Silver 0.9189 oz. ASW, 40 mm. **Obv:** The Book of Sadness **Rev:** Saint Grigor Narekatsi with book and quill millennium of his poem "The Book of Sadness **Edge:** Reeded

Date	Mintage	F12	VF20	XF40	MS60	MS63
2002	500	PF63 90.00	PF65 100			

KM# 95 100 DRAM
4.00 g., Nickel Plated Steel, 22.5 mm. **Obv:** National arms **Rev:** Value **Edge:** Reeded

Date	Mintage	F12	VF20	XF40	MS60	MS63
2003	—	—	—	—	1.50	2.00

KM# 110 100 DRAM
33.92 g., 0.925 Silver 1.0023 oz. ASW, 39 mm. **Subject:** 110th Anniversary of State Banking in Armenia and 10th Year of National Currency October 7 1893 - November 22, 1993 **Obv:** Building above value **Rev:** State Bank emblem **Edge:** Reeded

Date	Mintage	F12	VF20	XF40	MS60	MS63
2003	300	PF63 185	PF65 200			

KM# 111 100 DRAM
28.28 g., 0.925 Silver 0.8356 oz. ASW, 38.6 mm. **Subject:** FIFA World Cup Soccer Games - Germany **Obv:** National arms **Rev:** Three soccer players

Date	Mintage	F12	VF20	XF40	MS60	MS63
2004	300	PF63 130	PF65 150			

KM# 113 100 DRAM
31.10 g., 0.999 Silver 0.9925 oz. ASW, 38 mm. **Subject:** Gandzasar Monastery **Obv:** Monastery **Rev:** Folk art crucifix and denomination

Date	Mintage	F12	VF20	XF40	MS60	MS63
2004	500	PF63 90.00	PF65 100			

KM# 115 100 DRAM
31.10 g., 0.925 Silver 0.9189 oz. ASW, 40 mm. **Subject:** Anania Shirakatsi 1400 Anniversary, Scientist **Obv:** Profile of Shirakatsi, deep in thought **Rev:** Planets and stars, denomination

Date	Mintage	F12	VF20	XF40	MS60	MS63
2005	500	PF63 90.00	PF65 100			

KM# 123 100 DRAM
31.10 g., 0.925 Silver 0.9189 oz. ASW, 40.00 mm. **Subject:** Creation of the Armenian alphabet **Obv:** National arms **Rev:** King Vramshapuh standing at left, alphabet at right

Date	Mintage	F12	VF20	XF40	MS60	MS63
2005	500	PF63 130	PF65 150			

KM# 124 100 DRAM
31.10 g., 0.925 Silver 0.9189 oz. ASW, 40.00 mm. **Subject:** Creation of the Armenian alphabet **Obv:** National arms **Rev:** Sahak Partev standing at left, alphabet at right

Date	Mintage	F12	VF20	XF40	MS60	MS63
2005	500	PF63 130	PF65 150			

KM# 125 100 DRAM
31.10 g., 0.925 Silver 0.9189 oz. ASW, 40.00 mm. **Subject:** 100th Anniversary - Birth of Artem Mikoyan - Inventor of MIG Jet **Obv:** Three jet airplanes **Rev:** Bust of Mikoyan 3/4 left

Date	Mintage	F12	VF20	XF40	MS60	MS63
2005	500	PF63 125	PF65 145			

KM# 119 100 DRAM
28.28 g., 0.925 Silver 0.8356 oz. ASW, 38.61 mm. **Obv:** National arms **Rev:** Brown bear and two red lines **Edge:** Plain

Date	Mintage	F12	VF20	XF40	MS60	MS63
2006	3,000	PF63 150	PF65 165			

KM# 120 100 DRAM
28.28 g., 0.925 Silver 0.8356 oz. ASW, 38.61 mm. **Obv:** National arms **Rev:** Long-eared Hedgehog and two red lines **Edge:** Plain

Date	Mintage	F12	VF20	XF40	MS60	MS63
2006	3,000	PF63 150	PF65 165			

KM# 121 100 DRAM
28.28 g., 0.925 Silver 0.8356 oz. ASW, 38.6 mm. **Obv:** National arms, date and value **Rev:** Caucasian Forest Cat **Edge:** Plain

Date	Mintage	F12	VF20	XF40	MS60	MS63
2006	3,000	PF63 90.00	PF65 100			

KM# 122 100 DRAM
28.28 g., 0.925 Silver 0.8356 oz. ASW, 38.6 mm. **Obv:** National arms, date and value **Rev:** Armenian Tortoise **Edge:** Plain

Date	Mintage	F12	VF20	XF40	MS60	MS63
2006	3,000	PF63 110	PF65 120			

KM# 127 100 DRAM
28.28 g., 0.925 Silver 0.8356 oz. ASW, 38.61 mm. **Subject:** International Polar Year **Obv:** National arms **Obv. Legend:** REPUBLIC OF ARMENIA **Rev:** Bust of Fridtjof Nansen right at left, ship stuck in ice at lower right, multicolor emblem above

Date	Mintage	F12	VF20	XF40	MS60	MS63
2006	10,000	PF63 90.00	PF65 100			

KM# 129 100 DRAM
28.28 g., 0.925 Silver 0.8356 oz. ASW **Subject:** Hovhannes Aivazovsky **Obv:** National arms at lower left, sailing ship listing at center right multicolor **Rev:** Bust of Aivazovsky 3/4 left at lower left, sailing ships at center right **Shape:** Rectangular, 40 x 28 mm

Date	Mintage	F12	VF20	XF40	MS60	MS63
2006	5,000	PF63 350	PF65 400			

KM# 135 100 DRAM
28.24 g., 0.925 Silver 0.8344 oz. ASW, 38.53 mm. **Subject:** Caucasian Leopard **Obv:** National arms **Obv. Legend:** REPUBLIC OF ARMENIA **Rev:** Leopard walking left **Edge:** Plain

Date	Mintage	F12	VF20	XF40	MS60	MS63
2007	3,000	PF63 90.00	PF65 100			

KM# 136 100 DRAM
28.24 g., 0.925 Silver 0.8344 oz. ASW, 38.5 mm. **Subject:** Northern Shoveler duck **Obv:** National arms **Obv. Legend:** REPUBLIC OF ARMENIA **Rev:** Duck standing left **Edge:** Plain

Date	Mintage	F12	VF20	XF40	MS60	MS63
2007	3,000	PF63 75.00	PF65 85.00			

KM# 141 100 DRAM
28.28 g., 0.925 Silver 0.8356 oz. ASW, 38.5 mm. **Series:** Signs of the Zodiac **Obv:** National arms within ring of signs of the Zodiac **Obv. Legend:** REPUBLIC OF ARMENIA **Obv. Designer:** Ursula Valenazh **Rev:** Capricorn with jeweled star at left, multicolor **Edge:** Plain

Date	Mintage	F12	VF20	XF40	MS60	MS63
2007	12,000	PF63 70.00	PF65 80.00			

KM# 153 100 DRAM
28.28 g., 0.925 Silver 0.8356 oz. ASW, 38.6 mm. **Obv:** National arms **Obv. Legend:** REPUBLIC OF ARMENIA **Rev:** Lake Sevan Salmon

Date	Mintage	F12	VF20	XF40	MS60	MS63
2007	3,000	PF63 70.00	PF65 80.00			

KM# 154 100 DRAM
28.28 g., 0.925 Silver 0.8356 oz. ASW, 38.6 mm. **Obv:** National arms **Obv. Legend:** REPUBLIC OF ARMENIA **Rev:** Armenian viper

Date	Mintage	F12	VF20	XF40	MS60	MS63
2007	3,000	PF63 75.00	PF65 85.00			

KM# 157 100 DRAM
28.28 g., 0.925 Silver 0.8356 oz. ASW, 38.6 mm. **Subject:** Aquarius

Date	Mintage	F12	VF20	XF40	MS60	MS63
2007	—	PF63 70.00	PF65 80.00			

KM# 158 100 DRAM
28.28 g., 0.925 Silver 0.8356 oz. ASW, 38.6 mm. **Subject:** Pisces

Date	Mintage	F12	VF20	XF40	MS60	MS63
2007	—	PF63 70.00	PF65 80.00			

KM# 155 100 DRAM
28.28 g., 0.925 Silver 0.8356 oz. ASW, 39 mm. **Obv:** National Arms **Rev:** Caucasian owl on branch, (Aegolius Funereus Caucacious) red arcs at top and bottom **Rev. Designer:** Roussana Nowakowscy and Andrzej Nowakowscy

Date	Mintage	F12	VF20	XF40	MS60	MS63
2008	3,000	PF63 70.00	PF65 80.00			

KM# 159 100 DRAM
28.28 g., 0.925 Silver 0.8356 oz. ASW, 38.6 mm. **Subject:** Aries

Date	Mintage	F12	VF20	XF40	MS60	MS63
2008	—	PF63 70.00	PF65 80.00			

KM# 160 100 DRAM
28.28 g., 0.925 Silver 0.8356 oz. ASW, 38.6 mm. **Subject:** Taurus

Date	Mintage	F12	VF20	XF40	MS60	MS63
2008	—	PF63 70.00	PF65 80.00			

KM# 161 100 DRAM
28.28 g., 0.925 Silver 0.8356 oz. ASW, 38.6 mm. **Subject:** Gemini

Date	Mintage	F12	VF20	XF40	MS60	MS63
2008	—	PF63 70.00	PF65 80.00			

KM# 162 100 DRAM
28.28 g., 0.925 Silver 0.8356 oz. ASW **Subject:** Cancer

Date	Mintage	F12	VF20	XF40	MS60	MS63
2008	—	PF63 70.00	PF65 80.00			

KM# 163 100 DRAM
28.28 g., 0.925 Silver 0.8356 oz. ASW, 38.6 mm. **Subject:** Leo

Date	Mintage	F12	VF20	XF40	MS60	MS63
2008	—	PF63 70.00	PF65 80.00			

KM# 164 100 DRAM
28.28 g., 0.925 Silver 0.8356 oz. ASW, 38.6 mm. **Subject:** Virgo

Date	Mintage	F12	VF20	XF40	MS60	MS63
2008	—	PF63 70.00	PF65 80.00			

KM# 165 100 DRAM
28.28 g., 0.925 Silver 0.8356 oz. ASW, 38.6 mm. **Subject:** Libra

Date	Mintage	F12	VF20	XF40	MS60	MS63
2008	—	PF63 70.00	PF65 80.00			

KM# 167 100 DRAM
28.28 g., 0.925 Silver 0.8356 oz. ASW, 38.6 mm. **Subject:** Bezoar goat

Date	Mintage	F12	VF20	XF40	MS60	MS63
2008	—	PF63 70.00	PF65 80.00			

KM# 172 100 DRAM
28.28 g., 0.925 Silver 0.8356 oz. ASW, 38.6 mm. **Subject:** Scorpio

Date	Mintage	F12	VF20	XF40	MS60	MS63
2008	—	PF63 70.00	PF65 80.00			

KM# 174 100 DRAM
28.28 g., 0.925 Silver 0.8356 oz. ASW, 38.6 mm. **Subject:** Sagittarius

Date	Mintage	F12	VF20	XF40	MS60	MS63
2008	—	PF63 70.00	PF65 80.00			

KM# 177 100 DRAM
28.28 g., 0.925 Silver 0.8356 oz. ASW, 38.6 mm. **Subject:** Armenian Moufflon

Date	Mintage	F12	VF20	XF40	MS60	MS63
2008	—	PF63 65.00	PF65 75.00			

KM# 178 100 DRAM
28.28 g., 0.925 Silver 0.8356 oz. ASW, 38.6 mm. **Subject:** Toad Agama

Date	Mintage	F12	VF20	XF40	MS60	MS63
2008	—	PF63 65.00	PF65 75.00			

KM# 182 100 DRAM
28.28 g., 0.925 Silver 0.8356 oz. ASW, 38.6 mm. **Subject:** Pele

Date	Mintage	F12	VF20	XF40	MS60	MS63
2008	—	PF63 50.00	PF65 60.00			

KM# 183 100 DRAM
28.28 g., 0.925 Silver 0.8356 oz. ASW, 38.6 mm. **Subject:** Eusebio

Date	Mintage	F12	VF20	XF40	MS60	MS63
2008	—	PF63 50.00	PF65 60.00			

KM# 184 100 DRAM
28.28 g., 0.925 Silver 0.8356 oz. ASW, 38.6 mm. **Subject:** Lev Jashin

Date	Mintage	F12	VF20	XF40	MS60	MS63
2008	—	PF63 50.00		PF65 60.00		

KM# 187 100 DRAM
28.28 g., 0.925 Silver 0.8356 oz. ASW, 38.6 mm. **Subject:** Franz Beckenbauer

Date	Mintage	F12	VF20	XF40	MS60	MS63
2008	—	PF63 50.00		PF65 60.00		

KM# 156 100 DRAM
28.28 g., 0.925 Silver 0.8356 oz. ASW, 38.6 mm. **Subject:** Zbigniew Boniek **Rev:** Portrait facing, multicolor flag

Date	Mintage	F12	VF20	XF40	MS60	MS63
2009	50,000	PF63 50.00		PF65 60.00		

KM# 260 100 DRAM
28.28 g., 0.925 Silver 0.8356 oz. ASW, 28 x 40 mm. **Subject:** Vardgez Sureniants

Date	Mintage	F12	VF20	XF40	MS60	MS63
2010	Est. 500	PF63 140		PF65 150		

KM# 271 100 DRAM
28.28 g., 0.925 Silver 0.8356 oz. ASW, 40 x 28 mm. **Subject:** Teodor Axentowicz

Date	Mintage	F12	VF20	XF40	MS60	MS63
2010	Est. 4000	PF63 90.00		PF65 100		

KM# 209 100 DRAM
33.62 g., 0.925 Silver 0.9934 oz. ASW, 38.61 mm. **Obv:** Arms with lion supporters **Rev:** Michael Platini, soccer ball and flag in color

Date	Mintage	F12	VF20	XF40	MS60	MS63
2011	—	PF63 90.00		PF65 100		

KM# 223 100 DRAM
28.28 g., 0.925 Silver 0.8356 oz. ASW, 28x40 mm. **Subject:** Sergei Parajanov **Obv:** Artist in studio, painting in color **Rev:**

Self portrait **Shape:** Vertical rectangle **Designer:** Urszula Walerzak

Date	Mintage	F12	VF20	XF40	MS60	MS63
2012	Est. 5555	PF63 90.00		PF65 100		

KM# 251 100 DRAM
28.28 g., 0.925 Silver 0.8356 oz. ASW, 28 x 40 mm. **Subject:** Stephan Aghajanian

Date	Mintage	F12	VF20	XF40	MS60	MS63
2013	Est. 500	PF63 90.00		PF65 100		

KM# 254 100 DRAM
28.28 g., 0.925 Silver 0.8356 oz. ASW, 28 x 40 mm. **Series:** Ara Baqaryan

Date	Mintage	F12	VF20	XF40	MS60	MS63
2013	Est. 500	PF63 90.00		PF65 100		

KM# 96 200 DRAM
4.50 g., Brass, 24 mm. **Obv:** National arms **Rev:** Value **Edge:** Reeded

Date	Mintage	F12	VF20	XF40	MS60	MS63
2003	—				3.00	4.00

KM# 106 500 DRAM
155.50 g., 0.925 Silver 4.5947 oz. ASW, 63 mm. **Subject:** 10th Anniversary of Independence **Obv:** National arms **Rev:** Tower with flag, logo at right 9-21-91

Date	Mintage	F12	VF20	XF40	MS60	MS63
2001	200	PF63 500		PF65 550		

KM# 97 500 DRAM
5.00 g., Bi-Metallic, 22 mm. **Obv:** National arms **Rev:** Value **Edge:** Segmented reeding

Date	Mintage	F12	VF20	XF40	MS60	MS63
2003	—				6.00	8.00
2004 Requires confirmation	—				—	—

KM# 210 500 DRAM
1.24 g., 0.999 Gold 0.0396 oz. AGW, 13.92 mm. **Obv:** National arms, value below **Rev:** Pomegranate

Date	Mintage	F12	VF20	XF40	MS60	MS63
2011	—	PF63 130		PF65 150		

KM# 282 1000 DRAM
33.60 g., 0.925 Silver 0.9928 oz. ASW, 40 mm. **Subject:** National Currency, 20th Anniversary **Obv:** National arms, 20 in color

Date	Mintage	F12	VF20	XF40	MS60	MS63
2013	PF63 65.00	PF65 75.00				
2013	—	PF63 65.00		PF65 75.00		

KM# 109 1000 DRAM
15.55 g., 0.585 Gold 0.2900 oz. AGW, 20 mm. **Obv:** National arms on ancient coin design **Rev:** Tigran the Great ancient coin portrait

Date	Mintage	F12	VF20	XF40	MS60	MS63
2003	500	—	—	—	—	800

KM# 128 1000 DRAM
33.60 g., 0.925 Silver 0.9928 oz. ASW, 38 mm. **Subject:** 100th Anniversary Birth of Marshal Babajanian **Obv:** National arms **Rev:** Bust of Babajanian 3/4 right

Date	Mintage	F12	VF20	XF40	MS60	MS63
2006	500	PF63 130		PF65 150		

KM# 133 1000 DRAM
33.60 g., 0.925 Silver 0.9928 oz. ASW, 40 mm. **Subject:** Armenian grapes **Obv:** National arms **Rev:** Large bunch of grapes at left

Date	Mintage	F12	VF20	XF40	MS60	MS63
2007	5,000	PF63 115		PF65 125		

KM# 169 1000 DRAM
33.60 g., 0.925 Silver 0.9928 oz. ASW, 40 mm. **Subject:** Viktor Ambartsumian, 100th Anniversary of Birth **Edge:** Reeded

Date	Mintage	F12	VF20	XF40	MS60	MS63
2008	500	PF63 90.00		PF65 100		

KM# 171 1000 DRAM
33.60 g., 0.925 Silver 0.9928 oz. ASW, 40 mm. **Subject:** A. Spendiaryan Theater of Ballet and Opera, 75th Anniversary

Date	Mintage	F12	VF20	XF40	MS60	MS63
2008	—	PF63 90.00		PF65 100		

KM# 192 1000 DRAM
33.60 g., 0.925 Silver 0.9928 oz. ASW, 40 mm. **Subject:** Mkhitar Gosh - The Codex **Edge:** Reeded

Date	Mintage	F12	VF20	XF40	MS60	MS63
2009	500	PF63 90.00		PF65 100		

KM# 193 1000 DRAM
31.10 g., 0.999 Silver 0.9925 oz. ASW, 38 mm. **Subject:** Gladzor University, 750th Anniversary

Date	Mintage	F12	VF20	XF40	MS60	MS63
2009	—	PF63 90.00		PF65 100		

KM# 259 1000 DRAM
33.60 g., 0.925 Silver 0.9928 oz. ASW, 40 mm. **Subject:** Movses Khorenatsi

Date	Mintage	F12	VF20	XF40	MS60	MS63
2010	Est. 500	PF63 90.00		PF65 100		

KM# 262 1000 DRAM
33.60 g., 0.925 Silver 0.9928 oz. ASW, 40 mm. **Subject:** Leonid Engibarov

Date	Mintage	F12	VF20	XF40	MS60	MS63
2010	Est. 500	PF63 100		PF65 110		

KM# 264 1000 DRAM
33.60 g., 0.925 Silver 0.9928 oz. ASW, 40 mm. **Subject:** Leo

Date	Mintage	F12	VF20	XF40	MS60	MS63
2010	Est. 500	PF63 90.00		PF65 100		

KM# 266 1000 DRAM
31.10 g., 0.999 Silver 0.9925 oz. ASW, 32 x 32 mm. **Series:** Gospel Scenes in Armenian Miniatures: Annunciation

Date	Mintage	F12	VF20	XF40	MS60	MS63
2010	6,000	PF63 90.00		PF65 100		

KM# 267 1000 DRAM
31.10 g., 0.999 Silver 0.9925 oz. ASW, 32 x 32 mm. **Series:** Gospel Scenes in Armenian Miniatures: Adoration of the Magi

Date	Mintage	F12	VF20	XF40	MS60	MS63
2010	Est. 6000	PF63 90.00		PF65 100		

KM# 268 1000 DRAM
31.10 g., 0.999 Silver 0.9925 oz. ASW, 32 x 32 mm. **Subject:** Gospel Scenes in Armenian Miniatures: Entry into Jerusalem

Date	Mintage	F12	VF20	XF40	MS60	MS63
2010	Est. 6000	PF63 100		PF65 110		

KM# 269 1000 DRAM
31.10 g., 0.999 Silver 0.9925 oz. ASW, 32 x 32 mm. **Subject:** Gospel Scenes in Armenian Miniatures: Ascension

Date	Mintage	F12	VF20	XF40	MS60	MS63
2010	Est. 6000	PF63 100		PF65 110		

KM# 270 1000 DRAM
38.61 g., 0.925 Silver 1.1408 oz. ASW, 28.28 mm. **Subject:** Jazz

Date	Mintage	F12	VF20	XF40	MS60	MS63
2010	Est. 10000	PF63 65.00		PF65 75.00		

KM# 199 1000 DRAM
33.60 g., 0.925 Silver 0.9928 oz. ASW, 40 mm. **Rev:** Poppy plant and flower in color

Date	Mintage	F12	VF20	XF40	MS60	MS63
2011	—	PF63 65.00	PF65 75.00			

KM# 201 1000 DRAM
28.28 g., 0.925 Silver 0.8356 oz. ASW, 38.61 mm. **Obv:** Berries and flower in color **Rev:** Sorbus Hajastana in color **Designer:** Eduard Kurghinyan

Date	Mintage	F12	VF20	XF40	MS60	MS63
2011	10,000	PF63 65.00	PF65 75.00			

KM# 202 1000 DRAM
28.28 g., 0.925 Silver 0.8356 oz. ASW, 38.61 mm. **Obv:** Two crocus flowers in color **Rev:** Crocus flower open

Date	Mintage	F12	VF20	XF40	MS60	MS63
2011	10,000	PF63 65.00	PF65 75.00			

KM# 203 1000 DRAM
28.28 g., 0.925 Silver 0.8356 oz. ASW, 38.61 mm. **Subject:** WuSu **Obv:** Shaolin Monastery and dragons **Rev:** Three sportsmen

Date	Mintage	F12	VF20	XF40	MS60	MS63
2011	5,000	PF63 70.00	PF65 80.00			

KM# 204 1000 DRAM
28.28 g., 0.925 Silver 0.8356 oz. ASW, 38.61 mm. **Subject:** Judo **Obv:** Eishoji Tempole in Kamakura and lake reflection **Rev:** Two pair of Judo sportsmen, Mt. Fuji and cherry blossom

Date	Mintage	F12	VF20	XF40	MS60	MS63
2011	5,000	PF63 70.00	PF65 80.00			

KM# 206 1000 DRAM
33.60 g., 0.925 Silver 0.9928 oz. ASW, 40 mm. **Subject:** Treaty of Vienna, 200th Anniversary **Obv:** Two partial building façades **Rev:** Treaty with seal, building tower

Date	Mintage	F12	VF20	XF40	MS60	MS63
2011	—	PF63 90.00	PF65 100			

KM# 207 1000 DRAM
15.60 g., 0.585 Gold 0.2915 oz. AGW, 26 mm. **Subject:** Artashat, 2200th Anniversary of Founding **Obv:** Ancient coin at center, Tyche head right **Rev:** Ancient coin at center, Figure standing

Date	Mintage	F12	VF20	XF40	MS60	MS63
2011 Antique patina	1,000	—	—	—	—	600

KM# 208 1000 DRAM
Silver, 27x47 mm. **Obv:** National arms, value below **Rev:** Historic fragment and church **Shape:** Vertical rectangle

Date	Mintage	F12	VF20	XF40	MS60	MS63
2011 Antique patina	—	—	—	—	—	150

KM# 265 1000 DRAM
15.60 g., 0.585 Gold 0.2915 oz. AGW, 26 mm. **Subject:** Ani

Date	Mintage	F12	VF20	XF40	MS60	MS63
2011 Antique Patina	Est. 1000	—	—	—	—	700

KM# 272 1000 DRAM
28.28 g., 0.925 Silver 0.8356 oz. ASW, 38.61 mm. **Subject:** The Art of Fighting

Date	Mintage	F12	VF20	XF40	MS60	MS63
2011	Est. 5000	PF63 75.00	PF65 80.00			

KM# 228 1000 DRAM
33.60 g., 0.925 Silver 0.9928 oz. ASW, 40 mm. **Subject:** Army, 20th Anniversary **Rev:** Emblem of the Army and the 8-sided Order of the Motherland **Rev. Designer:** Haroution Samuelian

Date	Mintage	F12	VF20	XF40	MS60	MS63
2012	500	PF65 200				

KM# 249 1000 DRAM
0.93 g., 0.925 Silver, 40 mm. **Subject:** Hovsep Orbeli

Date	Mintage	F12	VF20	XF40	MS60	MS63
2012	—	PF63 90.00	PF65 100			

KM# 250 1000 DRAM
33.60 g., 0.925 Silver 0.9928 oz. ASW, 40 mm. **Subject:** Armenian Book Printing

Date	Mintage	F12	VF20	XF40	MS60	MS63
2012	Est. 500	PF63 90.00	PF65 100			

KM# 255 1000 DRAM
28.28 g., 0.925 Silver 0.8356 oz. ASW, 38.61 mm. **Subject:** Art of Fighting: Karate

Date	Mintage	F12	VF20	XF40	MS60	MS63
2012	Est. 5000	PF63 70.00	PF65 80.00			

KM# 256 1000 DRAM
31.10 g., 0.925 Silver 0.9189 oz. ASW, 38 mm. **Subject:** Anniversaries of the Treaty on Collective Security

Date	Mintage	F12	VF20	XF40	MS60	MS63
2012	Est. 200	PF63 90.00	PF65 100			

KM# 258 1000 DRAM
Silver, 38.61 mm. **Rev:** Tree

Date	Mintage	F12	VF20	XF40	MS60	MS63
2012	—	PF63 65.00	PF65 75.00			

KM# 277 1000 DRAM
25.00 g., 0.925 Silver 0.7387 oz. ASW, 27 x 47 mm. **Subject:** Armenian Monasteries and Churches **Obv:** Noravank Monastery **Obv. Designer:** Momik **Rev:** Coat of arms **Shape:** Rectangular

Date	Mintage	F12	VF20	XF40	MS60	MS63
2012 Proof	Est. 2500	PF63 90.00	PF65 100			

KM# 278 1000 DRAM
25.00 g., 0.925 Silver 0.7387 oz. ASW, 27 x 47 mm. **Subject:** Armenian Monasteries and Churches **Obv:** Mother Cathedral of Holy Etchmiadzin **Obv. Designer:** Momik **Shape:** Rectangular

Date	Mintage	F12	VF20	XF40	MS60	MS63
2012 Proof	Est. 2500	PF63 90.00	PF65 100			

KM# 279 1000 DRAM
28.28 g., 0.925 Silver 0.8356 oz. ASW, 38.61 mm. **Subject:** Art of Fighting **Obv:** Kokh **Obv. Designer:** Eduard Kurghinyan **Rev:** Coat of arms

Date	Mintage	F12	VF20	XF40	MS60	MS63
2012 Proof	Est. 5000	PF63 90.00	PF65 100			

KM# 281 1000 DRAM
25.00 g., 0.925 Silver 0.7387 oz. ASW, 27 x 47 mm. **Subject:** Armenian Monasteries and Churches **Obv:** Gndevank **Rev:** Coat of Arms **Shape:** Rectangular

Date	Mintage	F12	VF20	XF40	MS60	MS63
2012 Proof	Est. 2500	PF63 90.00	PF65 100			

KM# 253 1000 DRAM
33.60 g., 0.925 Silver 0.9928 oz. ASW, 40 mm. **Subject:** Beniamin Margaryan

Date	Mintage	F12	VF20	XF40	MS60	MS63
2013	Est. 500	PF63 90.00	PF65 100			

KM# 257 1000 DRAM
31.10 g., 0.999 Silver 0.9925 oz. ASW, 38 mm. **Subject:** 20th Anniversary of Armenian Dram (1933-2013)

Date	Mintage	F12	VF20	XF40	MS60	MS63
2013	Est. 500	PF63 90.00	PF65 100			

KM# 134 1957 DRAM
33.60 g., 0.925 Silver 0.9928 oz. ASW, 40 mm. **Subject:** 50th

Anniversay of Matenadaran **Obv:** Small national arms at center surrounded by intricate pattern **Rev:** Building at left center

Date	Mintage	F12	VF20	XF40	MS60	MS63
2007	500	PF63 125	PF65 145			

KM# 117 5000 DRAM
31.10 g., 0.925 Silver 0.9189 oz. ASW, 38 mm. **Subject:** Armenian Armed Forces **Obv:** Order of the Combat Cross of the Second Degree and the Emblem of the Ministry of Defense of the Republic of Armenia **Obv. Designer:** H. Samuelian **Rev:** Arms, date and denomination **Shape:** Octagonal

Date	Mintage	F12	VF20	XF40	MS60	MS63
2005	500	PF63 130	PF65 150			

KM# 126 5000 DRAM
168.10 g., 0.925 Silver 4.967 oz. ASW, 63 mm. **Subject:** 15th Anniversary of Independence **Obv:** National arms **Rev:** Building at center left, multicolor emblem above, mountains in background

Date	Mintage	F12	VF20	XF40	MS60	MS63
2006	300	PF63 350	PF65 400			

KM# 139 5000 DRAM
4.30 g., 0.900 Gold 0.1236 oz. AGW, 18 mm. **Subject:** Haik Nahapet **Obv:** Small national arms at upper left, Orion constellation at right **Rev:** 3/4 length classical Archer right

Date	Mintage	F12	VF20	XF40	MS60	MS63
2007	3,000	PF63 350	PF65 400			

KM# 179 5000 DRAM
168.10 g., 0.925 Silver 4.967 oz. ASW, 63 mm. **Subject:** National Currency, 15th Anniversary

Date	Mintage	F12	VF20	XF40	MS60	MS63
2008	—	PF63 140	PF65 150			

KM# 195 5000 DRAM
4.30 g., 0.900 Gold 0.1236 oz. AGW, 18 mm. **Subject:** St. Sargis the Commander

Date	Mintage	F12	VF20	XF40	MS60	MS63
2009	—	PF63 350	PF65 400			

KM# 205 5000 DRAM
168.10 g., 0.925 Silver 4.967 oz. ASW, 63 mm. **Subject:** 20th Anniversary of the Republic **Obv:** National arms **Rev:** Two birds in flight, date in color

Date	Mintage	F12	VF20	XF40	MS60	MS63
2011	—	PF63 325	PF65 350			

KM# 107 10000 DRAM
8.60 g., 0.999 Gold 0.2744 oz. AGW, 22 mm. **Obv:** Mesrop Mashtots, creator of the Armenian alphabet **Rev:** Armenian alphabet

Date	Mintage	F12	VF20	XF40	MS60	MS63
2002	1,000	PF63 750	PF65 800			

KM# 108 10000 DRAM
8.60 g., 0.999 Gold 0.2744 oz. AGW, 22 mm. **Obv:** Building above value **Rev:** Aram Khachatryan left birth centennial

Date	Mintage	F12	VF20	XF40	MS60	MS63
2002	500	PF63 750	PF65 800			

KM# 114 10000 DRAM
8.60 g., 0.999 Gold 0.2744 oz. AGW, 22 mm. **Subject:** Arshile Gorky birth April 15, 1904 **Obv:** Bust of Gorky **Rev:** Denomination

Date	Mintage	F12	VF20	XF40	MS60	MS63
2004	1,000	PF63 750	PF65 800			

KM# 116 10000 DRAM
8.60 g., 0.999 Gold 0.2744 oz. AGW, 22 mm. **Subject:** Martiros Saryan 125th Anniversary of Birth **Obv:** Bust of Saryan **Rev:** Landscape, denomination

Date	Mintage	F12	VF20	XF40	MS60	MS63
2005	1,000	PF63 750	PF65 800			

KM# 130 10000 DRAM
8.60 g., 0.999 Gold 0.2744 oz. AGW, 22 mm. **Subject:** Komitas Vardapet **Obv:** Musical notations and score **Rev:** Bust of Vardapet 3/4 right

Date	Mintage	F12	VF20	XF40	MS60	MS63
2006	1,000	PF63 750	PF65 800			

KM# 131 10000 DRAM
8.60 g., 0.900 Gold 0.2472 oz. AGW, 22 mm. **Subject:** 37th Chess Olympiad **Obv:** Chess piece at right **Rev:** National arms within 6 chess pieces in circle

Date	Mintage	F12	VF20	XF40	MS60	MS63
2006	1,000	PF63 750	PF65 800			

KM# 132 10000 DRAM
8.60 g., 0.900 Gold 0.2472 oz. AGW, 22 mm. **Subject:** Hakob Gurjian **Obv:** Seated female sculpture **Rev:** Head 3/4 right

Date	Mintage	F12	VF20	XF40	MS60	MS63
2006	1,000	PF63 750	PF65 800			

KM# 137 10000 DRAM
8.60 g., 0.900 Gold 0.2472 oz. AGW, 22 mm. **Subject:** Jean Carzou **Obv:** National arms with stylized view of shopping bourse **Rev:** Bust of Carzou 3/4 right at laft center

Date	Mintage	F12	VF20	XF40	MS60	MS63
2007	1,000	PF63 750	PF65 800			

KM# 138 10000 DRAM
8.60 g., 0.900 Gold 0.2472 oz. AGW, 22 mm. **Subject:** 15th Anniversary of Armenian Army **Obv:** National arms **Rev:** Military badge

Date	Mintage	F12	VF20	XF40	MS60	MS63
2007	1,000	PF63 750	PF65 800			

KM# 140 10000 DRAM
8.60 g., 0.900 Gold 0.2472 oz. AGW, 22 mm. **Subject:** 15th Anniversary Liberation of Shushi **Obv:** Bird with wings outspread above two shields **Rev:** Swirl in background

Date	Mintage	F12	VF20	XF40	MS60	MS63
2007	1,000	PF63 750	PF65 800			

KM# 175 10000 DRAM
8.60 g., 0.900 Gold 0.2472 oz. AGW, 22 mm. **Subject:** Sagittarius

Date	Mintage	F12	VF20	XF40	MS60	MS63
2008	—	PF63 650	PF65 700			

KM# 166 10000 DRAM
8.60 g., 0.900 Gold 0.2472 oz. AGW, 22 mm. **Subject:** Libra

Date	Mintage	F12	VF20	XF40	MS60	MS63
2008	—	PF63 650	PF65 700			

KM# 168 10000 DRAM
8.60 g., 0.900 Gold 0.2472 oz. AGW, 22 mm. **Subject:** Court, 10th Anniversary

Date	Mintage	F12	VF20	XF40	MS60	MS63
2008	—	PF63 650	PF65 700			

KM# 170 10000 DRAM
8.60 g., 0.900 Gold 0.2472 oz. AGW, 22 mm. **Subject:** William Saroyan, 100th Anniversary of Birth

Date	Mintage	F12	VF20	XF40	MS60	MS63
2008	—	PF63 650	PF65 700			

KM# 173 10000 DRAM
8.60 g., 0.900 Gold 0.2472 oz. AGW, 22 mm. **Subject:** Scorpio

Date	Mintage	F12	VF20	XF40	MS60	MS63
2008	—	PF63 650	PF65 700			

KM# 176 10000 DRAM
8.60 g., 0.900 Gold 0.2472 oz. AGW, 22 mm. **Subject:** Capricorn

Date	Mintage	F12	VF20	XF40	MS60	MS63
2008	—	PF63 650	PF65 700			

KM# 180 10000 DRAM
8.60 g., 0.900 Gold 0.2472 oz. AGW, 22 mm. **Subject:** Aquarius

Date	Mintage	F12	VF20	XF40	MS60	MS63
2008	—	PF63 650	PF65 700			

KM# 181 10000 DRAM
8.60 g., 0.900 Gold 0.2472 oz. AGW, 22 mm. **Subject:** Pisces

Date	Mintage	F12	VF20	XF40	MS60	MS63
2008	—	PF63 650	PF65 700			

KM# 185 10000 DRAM
8.60 g., 0.900 Gold 0.2472 oz. AGW, 22 mm. **Subject:** Aries

Date	Mintage	F12	VF20	XF40	MS60	MS63
2008	—	PF63 650	PF65 700			

KM# 186 10000 DRAM
8.60 g., 0.900 Gold 0.2472 oz. AGW, 22 mm. **Subject:** Taurus

Date	Mintage	F12	VF20	XF40	MS60	MS63
2008	—	PF63 650	PF65 700			

KM# 188 10000 DRAM
8.60 g., 0.900 Gold 0.2472 oz. AGW, 22 mm. **Subject:** Gemini

Date	Mintage	F12	VF20	XF40	MS60	MS63
2008	—	PF63 650	PF65 700			

KM# 189 10000 DRAM
8.60 g., 0.900 Gold 0.2472 oz. AGW, 22 mm. **Subject:** Cancer

Date	Mintage	F12	VF20	XF40	MS60	MS63
2008	—	PF63 650	PF65 700			

KM# 190 10000 DRAM
8.60 g., 0.900 Gold 0.2472 oz. AGW, 22 mm. **Subject:** Leo

Date	Mintage	F12	VF20	XF40	MS60	MS63
2008	—	PF63 650	PF65 700			

KM# 191 10000 DRAM
8.60 g., 0.900 Gold 0.2472 oz. AGW, 22 mm. **Subject:** Virgo

Date	Mintage	F12	VF20	XF40	MS60	MS63
2009	—	PF63 650	PF65 700			

KM# 194 10000 DRAM
8.60 g., 0.900 Gold 0.2472 oz. AGW, 22 mm. **Subject:** Khachatour Aboryan, 200th Anniversary of Birth

Date	Mintage	F12	VF20	XF40	MS60	MS63
2009	—	PF63 750	PF65 800			

KM# 261 10000 DRAM
8.60 g., 0.900 Gold 0.2472 oz. AGW, 22 mm. **Subject:** Vahan Teryan

Date	Mintage	F12	VF20	XF40	MS60	MS63
2010	Est. 1000	PF63 750	PF65 800			

KM# 263 10000 DRAM
8.60 g., 0.900 Gold 0.2472 oz. AGW, 22 mm. **Subject:** Raffi

Date	Mintage	F12	VF20	XF40	MS60	MS63
2010	Est. 1000	PF63 750	PF65 800			

KM# 200 10000 DRAM
8.60 g., 0.900 Gold 0.2472 oz. AGW, 22 mm. **Subject:** Misaq Metsarents, poet, 125th Anniversary of Birth **Edge:** Reeded

Date	Mintage	F12	VF20	XF40	MS60	MS63
2011	1,000	PF63 650	PF65 700			

KM# 211 10000 DRAM
8.60 g., 0.900 Gold 0.2472 oz. AGW, 22 mm. **Subject:** Toros Roslin, 800th Anniversary **Edge:** Reeded

Date	Mintage	F12	VF20	XF40	MS60	MS63
2011	1,000	PF63 650	PF65 700			

KM# 229 10000 DRAM
8.60 g., 0.900 Gold 0.2472 oz. AGW, 20 mm. **Subject:** Army, 20th Anniversary **Rev:** Army emblem and Order of the Motherland **Rev. Designer:** Haroution Samuelian

Date	Mintage	F12	VF20	XF40	MS60	MS63
2012	500	PF65 750				

KM# 247 10000 DRAM
8.60 g., 0.900 Gold 0.2472 oz. AGW, 22 mm. **Subject:** Sayat-Nova

Date	Mintage	F12	VF20	XF40	MS60	MS63
2012	Est. 1000		PF63 650	PF65 700		

KM# 248 10000 DRAM
8.60 g., 0.900 Gold 0.2472 oz. AGW, 22 mm. **Subject:** 20th Anniversary of the Liberation of Shushi

Date	Mintage	F12	VF20	XF40	MS60	MS63
2012	Est. 1000		PF63 650	PF65 700		

KM# 280 10000 DRAM
8.60 g., 0.900 Gold 0.2472 oz. AGW, 22 mm. **Subject:** 20th Anniversary of the Liberation of Sushi

Date	Mintage	F12	VF20	XF40	MS60	MS63
2012	500		PF65 700			

KM# 252 10000 DRAM
8.60 g., 0.900 Gold 0.2472 oz. AGW, 22 mm. **Subject:** Vahram Papazyan

Date	Mintage	F12	VF20	XF40	MS60	MS63
2013	Est. 1000		PF63 650	PF65 700		

KM# 118 50000 DRAM
8.60 g., 0.999 Gold 0.2744 oz. AGW, 22 mm. **Subject:** Armenian Armed Forces **Obv:** Order of the Combat Cross of the Second Degree and the Emblem of the Ministry of Defense of the Republic of Armenia. **Obv. Designer:** H. Samuelian **Rev:** Arms, date and denomination

Date	Mintage	F12	VF20	XF40	MS60	MS63
2005	1,000		PF63 750	PF65 800		

BULLION COINAGE

KM# 198 100 DRAM
7.77 g., 0.999 Silver 0.248 oz. ASW **Obv:** National arms **Rev:** Noah's Ark **Rev. Designer:** Eduard Kurghinyan

Date	Mintage	F12	VF20	XF40	MS60	MS63
2011LEV	—	—	—	—	—	15.00
2012LEV	—	—	—	—	—	15.00
2013	—	—	—	—	—	15.00

KM# 197 200 DRAM
15.55 g., 0.999 Silver 0.4962 oz. ASW **Obv:** National arms **Rev:** Noah's Ark **Rev. Designer:** Eduard Kurghinyan

Date	Mintage	F12	VF20	XF40	MS60	MS63
2011LEV	—	—	—	—	—	25.00
2012LEV	—	—	—	—	—	25.00
2013	—	—	—	—	—	25.00

KM# 196 500 DRAM
31.11 g., 0.999 Silver 0.9926 oz. ASW, 38.6 mm. **Obv:** National arms **Rev:** Dove, Noah's Ark and sun rise over Mt. Ararat **Rev. Designer:** Eduard Kurghinyan

Date	Mintage	F12	VF20	XF40	MS60	MS63
2011LEV	—	—	—	—	—	50.00
2012LEV	—	—	—	—	—	50.00
2013	25.00					

KM# 227 1000 DRAM
155.50 g., 0.999 Silver 4.9623 oz. ASW, 62.2 mm. **Obv:** National arms **Rev:** Noah's Ark **Rev. Designer:** Eduard Kurghinyan

Date	Mintage	F12	VF20	XF40	MS60	MS63
2012LEV	—	—	—	—	—	200

KM# 226 5000 DRAM
311.05 g., 0.999 Silver 9.9262 oz. ASW, 75.5 mm. **Obv:** National arms **Rev:** Noah's Ark **Rev. Designer:** Eduard Kurghinyan **Note:** 7.4mm thick.

Date	Mintage	F12	VF20	XF40	MS60	MS63
2012LEV	—	—	—	—	—	400

KM# 225 10000 DRAM
1000.00 g., 0.999 Silver 31.9118 oz. ASW, 100 mm. **Obv:** National arms **Rev:** Noah's Ark **Rev. Designer:** Eduard Kurghinyan **Note:** 14mm thick.

Date	Mintage	F12	VF20	XF40	MS60	MS63
2012LEV	—	—	—	—	—	1,200

KM# 224 20000 DRAM
5000.00 g., 0.999 Silver 159.5592 oz. ASW, 164.6 mm. **Obv:** National arms **Rev:** Noah's Ark **Rev. Designer:** Eduard Kurghinyan **Note:** 29mm thick

Date	Mintage	F12	VF20	XF40	MS60	MS63
2012LEV	—	—	—	—	—	6,000

ARUBA

The second largest island of the former Netherlands Antilles, Aruba is situated near the Venezuelan coast. The island has an area of 74-1/2 sq. mi. (193 sq. km.) and a population of 105,000. Capital: Oranjestad, named after the Dutch royal family. Aruba was important in the processing and transportation of petroleum products in the first part of the twentieth century, but today the chief industry is tourism.

For earlier issues see Curacao and the Netherlands Antilles.

RULER
Dutch

MINT MARKS
(u) Utrecht - Privy marks only Wine tendril with grapes, 2001-
Wine tendril with grapes plus star, 2002-
Sails of a clipper, 2003-

MONETARY SYSTEM
100 Cents = 1 Florin

DUTCH STATE
Status Aparte
DECIMAL COINAGE

KM# 1 5 CENTS
2.00 g., Nickel Bonded Steel, 16 mm. **Ruler:** Beatrix **Obv:** National arms **Rev:** Geometric design with value **Edge:** Plain

Date	Mintage	F12	VF20	XF40	MS60	MS63
2001(u)	946,900	—	0.10	0.25	0.50	1.00
2002(u)	1,006,000	—	0.10	0.25	0.50	1.00
2003(u)	1,104,100	—	0.10	0.25	0.50	1.00
2004(u)	502,500	—	0.10	0.25	0.50	1.00
2005(u)	602,500	—	0.10	0.25	0.50	1.00
2006(u)	602,000	—	0.10	0.25	0.50	1.00
2007(u)	1,152,000	—	0.10	0.25	0.50	1.00
2008(u)	1,152,000	—	0.10	0.25	0.50	1.00
2009(u)	—	—	0.10	0.25	0.50	1.00
2010(u)	—	—	0.10	0.25	0.50	1.00
2011(u)	—	—	0.10	0.25	0.50	1.00
2012(u)	—	—	0.10	0.25	0.50	1.00
2013(u)	—	—	0.10	0.25	0.60	1.10

KM# 2 10 CENTS
3.00 g., Nickel Bonded Steel, 18 mm. **Ruler:** Beatrix **Obv:** National arms **Rev:** Geometric design with value **Edge:** Reeded

Date	Mintage	F12	VF20	XF40	MS60	MS63
2001(u)	1,006,900	—	0.20	0.35	0.60	1.10
2002(u)	1,006,000	—	0.20	0.35	0.60	1.10
2003(u)	1,004,000	—	0.20	0.35	0.60	1.10
2004(u)	402,500	—	0.20	0.35	0.60	1.10
2005(u)	402,500	—	0.20	0.35	0.60	1.10
2006(u)	452,500	—	0.20	0.35	0.60	1.10
2007(u)	1,102,000	—	0.20	0.35	0.60	1.10
2008(u)	1,442,000	—	0.20	0.35	0.60	1.10
2009(u)	—	—	0.20	0.35	0.60	1.10
2009(u)	—	—	0.20	0.35	0.60	1.10
2010(u)	—	—	0.20	0.35	0.60	1.10
2011	—	—	0.20	0.35	0.60	1.10
2012(u)	—	—	0.20	0.35	0.60	1.10
2013(u)	—	—	0.20	0.35	0.60	1.10

KM# 3 25 CENTS
3.50 g., Nickel Bonded Steel, 20 mm. **Ruler:** Beatrix **Obv:** National arms **Rev:** Geometric design with value **Edge:** Plain

Date	Mintage	F12	VF20	XF40	MS60	MS63
2001(u)	716,900	—	0.20	0.40	0.75	1.50
2002(u)	806,000	—	0.20	0.40	0.75	1.50
2003(u)	804,000	—	0.20	0.40	0.75	1.50
2004(u)	362,500	—	0.20	0.40	0.75	1.50
2005(u)	302,500	—	0.20	0.40	0.75	1.50
2006(u)	302,000	—	0.20	0.40	0.75	1.50
2007(u)	202,000	—	0.20	0.40	0.75	1.50
2008(u)	202,000	—	0.20	0.40	0.75	1.50
2009(u)	—	—	0.20	0.40	0.75	1.50
2010(u)	—	—	0.20	0.40	0.75	1.50
2011(u)	—	—	0.20	0.40	0.75	1.50
2012(u)	—	—	0.20	0.40	0.75	1.50
2013(u)	—	—	0.20	0.40	0.75	1.50

KM# 4 50 CENTS
5.00 g., Nickel Bonded Steel, 20 mm. **Ruler:** Beatrix **Obv:** National arms **Rev:** Geometric design with value **Edge:** Plain **Shape:** 4-sided

Date	Mintage	F12	VF20	XF40	MS60	MS63
2001(u)	506,900	—	0.30	0.50	1.00	1.50
2002(u)	306,000	—	0.30	0.50	1.00	1.50
2003(u)	279,000	—	0.30	0.50	1.00	1.50
2004(u)	402,500	—	0.30	0.50	1.00	1.50
2005(u)	102,500	—	0.30	0.50	1.00	1.50
2006(u)	102,500	—	0.30	0.50	1.00	1.50
2007(u)	32,000	—	0.30	0.60	1.50	2.50
2008(u)	302,000	—	0.30	0.60	1.50	2.50
2009(u)	—	—	0.30	0.60	1.50	2.50
2010(u)	—	—	0.30	0.60	1.50	2.50
2011(u)	—	—	0.30	0.60	1.50	2.50
2012(u)	—	—	0.30	0.60	1.50	2.50
2013(u)	—	—	0.30	0.60	1.50	2.50

KM# 5 FLORIN
8.50 g., Nickel Bonded Steel, 26 mm. **Ruler:** Beatrix **Obv:** Head left **Rev:** National arms and value **Edge:** Lettered **Edge Lettering:** GOD * ZIJ * MET * ONS *

Date	Mintage	F12	VF20	XF40	MS60	MS63
2001(u)	406,900	—	0.60	1.00	2.00	3.00
2002(u)	206,000	—	0.60	1.00	2.00	3.00
2003(u)	179,000	—	0.60	1.00	2.00	3.00
2004(u)	410,000	—	0.60	1.00	2.00	3.00
2005(u)	352,500	—	0.60	1.00	2.00	3.00
2006(u)	402,000	—	0.60	1.00	2.00	3.00
2007(u)	502,000	—	0.60	1.00	2.00	3.00
2008(u)	289,000	—	0.60	1.00	2.00	3.00
2009(u)	—	—	0.60	1.00	2.00	3.00
2010(u)	—	—	0.60	1.00	2.00	3.00
2011(u)	—	—	0.60	1.00	2.00	3.00
2012(u)	—	—	0.60	1.00	2.00	3.00
2013(u)	—	—	0.60	1.00	2.00	3.00

KM# 6 2-1/2 FLORIN
10.30 g., Nickel Bonded Steel, 30 mm. **Ruler:** Beatrix **Obv:** Head left **Rev:** National arms with value **Edge:** Lettered **Edge Lettering:** GOD * ZIJ * MET * ONS *

Date	Mintage	F12	VF20	XF40	MS60	MS63
2001(u) In sets only	6,900	—	—	2.00	3.00	7.00
2002(u) In sets only	6,000	—	—	2.00	3.00	7.00
2003(u) In sets only	4,000	—	—	2.00	3.00	7.00
2004(u) In sets only	2,500	—	—	2.00	3.00	7.00
2005(u) In sets only	2,500	—	—	2.00	3.00	7.00
2006(u) In sets only	2,000	—	—	2.00	3.00	7.00
2007(u) In sets only	2,000	—	—	2.00	3.00	7.00
2008(u) In sets only	2,000	—	—	2.00	3.00	7.00
2009(u) In sets only	2,000	—	—	2.00	3.00	7.00
2010(u) In sets only	—	—	—	2.00	3.00	7.00
2011(u)	—	—	—	2.00	3.00	7.00
2012(u)	—	—	—	2.00	3.00	7.00
2013(u)	—	—	—	2.00	3.00	7.00

KM# 12 5 FLORIN
8.64 g., Nickel Bonded Steel, 26 mm. **Ruler:** Beatrix **Obv:** Head left **Rev:** National arms with value **Edge:** Plain **Shape:** 4-sided

Date	Mintage	F12	VF20	XF40	MS60	MS63
2001(u) In sets only	6,900	—	—	3.00	7.00	9.00
2002(u) In sets only	6,000	—	—	3.00	7.00	9.00
2003(u) In sets only	4,000	—	—	3.00	7.00	9.00
2004(u) In sets only	2,500	—	—	3.00	7.00	9.00
2005(u) In sets only	2,500	—	—	3.00	7.00	9.00

KM# 25 5 FLORIN
11.90 g., 0.925 Silver 0.3516 oz. ASW, 29 mm. **Ruler:** Beatrix **Subject:** 50th Anniversary Charter for the Kingdom of the Netherlands including Netherlands Antilles **Obv:** Head left **Rev:** Royal seal **Rev. Designer:** E. Fingal **Edge Lettering:** GOD * ZIJ * MET * ONS *

Date	Mintage	F12	VF20	XF40	MS60	MS63
2004(u)	4,000		PF63 35.00	PF65 40.00		

KM# 34 5 FLORIN
11.90 g., 0.925 Silver 0.3516 oz. ASW, 29 mm. **Ruler:** Beatrix **Subject:** Queen's Silver Jubilee **Obv:** Head left **Rev:** Flag **Rev. Designer:** F.L. Croes **Edge Lettering:** GOD * ZIJ * MET * ONS

Date	Mintage	F12	VF20	XF40	MS60	MS63
2005(u)	3,100		PF63 28.00	PF65 32.00		

KM# 38 5 FLORIN
8.40 g., Aluminum-Bronze, 22.5 mm. **Ruler:** Beatrix **Obv:** Queen with a half crown on face **Rev:** Value and arms **Edge:** Reeded and lettered **Edge Lettering:** GOD * ZIJ * MET * ONS * **Shape:** Round

Date	Mintage	F12	VF20	XF40	MS60	MS63
2005(u)	827,500	—	—	—	5.00	8.00
2006(u)	102,000	—	—	—	7.00	10.00
2007(u)	52,000	—	—	—	7.00	10.00
2008(u)	22,000	—	—	—	7.00	15.00
2009(u)	—	—	—	—	7.00	15.00
2010(u)	—	—	—	—	7.00	15.00
2011(u)	—	—	—	—	7.00	15.00
2012(u)	—	—	—	—	7.00	15.00
2013	—	—	—	—	7.00	15.00

KM# 41 5 FLORIN
11.90 g., 0.925 Silver 0.3516 oz. ASW, 29 mm. **Ruler:** Beatrix **Subject:** Year of the dolphin **Obv:** Head left **Rev:** Two dolphins bounding out of the water **Edge Lettering:** GOD * ZIJ * MET * ONS *

Date	Mintage	F12	VF20	XF40	MS60	MS63
2007(u)	1,250	PF63 30.00	PF65 35.00			

KM# 42 5 FLORIN
11.90 g., 0.925 Silver 0.3516 oz. ASW, 29 mm. **Ruler:** Beatrix **Subject:** Fiesta de San Juan **Obv:** Head left **Rev:** Harvesting farmer **Edge Lettering:** GOD * ZIJ * MET * ONS

Date	Mintage	F12	VF20	XF40	MS60	MS63
2008(u)	1,250	PF63 35.00	PF65 40.00			

KM# 43 5 FLORIN
11.90 g., 0.925 Silver 0.3516 oz. ASW, 29 mm. **Ruler:** Beatrix **Subject:** Dante at New Year's **Obv:** Head left **Rev:** Dance at New Year's, Hand dropping coins into hat **Edge Lettering:** GOD * ZIJ * MET * ONS

Date	Mintage	F12	VF20	XF40	MS60	MS63
2009(u)	1,250	PF63 35.00	PF65 40.00			

KM# 45 5 FLORIN
11.90 g., 0.925 Silver 0.3516 oz. ASW, 29 mm. **Ruler:** Beatrix **Subject:** Olympic Games 2012 **Obv:** Queen Beatrix **Rev:** Two judoka fight men in action **Edge Lettering:** GOD * ZIJ * MET * ONS *

Date	Mintage	F12	VF20	XF40	MS60	MS63
2010	5,000	PF63 30.00	PF65 35.00			

KM# 46 5 FLORIN
11.90 g., 0.925 Silver 0.3516 oz. ASW, 29 mm. **Ruler:** Beatrix **Obv:** Head left **Rev:** California lighthouse and waves **Edge Lettering:** GOD * ZIJ * MET * ONS *

Date	Mintage	F12	VF20	XF40	MS60	MS63
2010(u)	1,250	PF63 35.00	PF65 40.00			

KM# 47 5 FLORIN
11.90 g., 0.925 Silver 0.3516 oz. ASW, 29 mm. **Ruler:** Beatrix **Obv:** Shield in wreath above mintmarks **Rev:** 25 years Status Aparte with Parliament building **Edge Lettering:** GOD * ZIJ * MET * ONS *

Date	Mintage	G4	VG8	F12	VF20	XF40
2011(u)	1,250	PF63 40.00	PF65 45.00			

KM# 48 5 FLORIN
11.90 g., 0.925 Silver 0.3516 oz. ASW, 29 mm. **Ruler:** Beatrix **Subject:** Royal Vista **Obv:** Shield in wreath above mintmarks **Rev:** Queen Beatrix, Prince Willem-Alexander and Princess Maxima looking left, orange top stripe, blue bottom stripe **Edge Lettering:** GOD * ZIJ * MET * ONS *

Date	Mintage	F12	VF20	XF40	MS60	MS63
2011(u)	1,250	PF63 45.00	PF65 50.00			

KM# 50 5 FLORIN
11.90 g., 0.925 Silver 0.3516 oz. ASW, 29 mm. **Ruler:** Beatrix **Subject:** Alternative reality

Date	Mintage	F12	VF20	XF40	MS60	MS63
2012	—	PF63 30.00	PF65 35.00			

KM# 51 5 FLORIN
11.90 g., 0.925 Silver 0.3516 oz. ASW, 29 mm. **Ruler:** Beatrix **Obv:** National arms **Rev:** Shoco (owl) in color **Edge Lettering:** GOD * ZIJ * MET * ONS * **Designer:** Juan Jose Sanchez Castano

Date	Mintage	F12	VF20	XF40	MS60	MS63
2012(u) Proof	2,500	—	—	—	—	55.00

KM# 52 5 FLORIN
8.40 g., Aluminum-Bronze, 23.5 mm. **Ruler:** Beatrix **Subject:** Abdication of Beatrix **Obv:** National arms **Rev:** Beatrix and Willem Alexander; colored flag **Edge Lettering:** GOD * ZIJ * MET * ONS *

Date	Mintage	F12	VF20	XF40	MS60	MS63
2013(u)	11,000	—	—	—	—	15.00

KM# 53 5 FLORIN
25.00 g., 0.925 Silver 0.7387 oz. ASW, 38 mm. **Ruler:** Willem-Alexander **Subject:** Aruba welcomes Willem Alexander **Obv:** National arms and crown **Rev:** Willem Alexander right **Edge Lettering:** GOD * ZIJ * MET * ONS *

Date	Mintage	F12	VF20	XF40	MS60	MS63
2013(u)	2,000	PF65 75.00				

KM# 54 5 FLORIN
25.00 g., 0.925 Silver 0.7387 oz. ASW, 38 mm. **Ruler:** Willem-Alexander **Subject:** Royal visit **Obv:** National arms within wreath **Rev:** Willem Alexander and Maxima right **Edge Lettering:** GOD * ZIJ * MET * ONS *

Date	Mintage	F12	VF20	XF40	MS60	MS63
2013	1,250	PF65 75.00				

KM# 20 10 FLORIN
25.00 g., 0.925 Silver 0.7387 oz. ASW, 38 mm. **Ruler:** Beatrix

Subject: Green Sea Turtles **Obv:** Head left **Rev:** Seven sea turtles **Edge:** Plain **Designer:** E. Fingal

Date	Mintage	F12	VF20	XF40	MS60	MS63
2001(u) Prooflike	2,000	—	—	—	—	60.00

KM# 24 10 FLORIN
17.80 g., 0.925 Silver 0.526 oz. ASW, 33 mm. **Ruler:** Beatrix **Subject:** Crown Prince's Wedding **Obv:** Head left **Rev:** Conjoined busts of prince and princess Maxima, right **Edge Lettering:** GOD ZIJ MET ONS **Designer:** G. Colley

Date	Mintage	F12	VF20	XF40	MS60	MS63
ND(2002)(u) Prooflike	5,000	—	—	—	—	40.00

KM# 27 10 FLORIN
25.00 g., 0.925 Silver 0.7387 oz. ASW, 38 mm. **Ruler:** Beatrix **Obv:** Head left **Obv. Designer:** E. Fingal **Rev:** Sea shell **Edge:** Plain

Date	Mintage	F12	VF20	XF40	MS60	MS63
2003(u)	2,000	PF63 55.00	PF65 60.00			

KM# 28 10 FLORIN
25.00 g., 0.925 Silver 0.7387 oz. ASW, 38 mm. **Ruler:** Beatrix **Obv:** Head left **Obv. Designer:** E. Fingal **Rev:** Arubia Rattlesnake (Crotalus unicolor). **Edge:** Plain

Date	Mintage	F12	VF20	XF40	MS60	MS63
2003(u)	2,000	PF63 55.00	PF65 60.00			

KM# 29 10 FLORIN
25.00 g., 0.925 Silver 0.7387 oz. ASW, 38 mm. **Ruler:** Beatrix **Obv:** Head left **Obv. Designer:** E. Fingal **Rev:** Burrowing Owl (Athena cunicularia). **Edge:** Plain

Date	Mintage	F12	VF20	XF40	MS60	MS63
2003(u)	1,000	PF63 55.00	PF65 60.00			

KM# 26 10 FLORIN
6.72 g., 0.900 Gold 0.1932 oz. AGW, 22.5 mm. **Ruler:** Beatrix
Subject: 20th Anniversary of Autonomy **Obv:** Head left **Rev:** Royal seal **Edge:** Reeded **Designer:** E. Fingal

Date	Mintage	F12	VF20	XF40	MS60	MS63
2004(u)	1,000	PF63 325	PF65 375			

KM# 30 10 FLORIN
25.00 g., 0.925 Silver 0.7387 oz. ASW, 38 mm. **Ruler:** Beatrix **Obv:** Head left **Obv. Designer:** E. Fingal **Rev:** Cuban Tree Frog (Osteopilus septentrionalis). **Edge:** Plain

Date	Mintage	F12	VF20	XF40	MS60	MS63
2004(u)	1,000	PF63 45.00	PF65 50.00			

KM# 31 10 FLORIN
25.00 g., 0.925 Silver 0.7387 oz. ASW, 38 mm. **Ruler:** Beatrix **Obv:** Head left **Obv. Designer:** E. Fingal **Rev:** Fish right **Edge:** Plain

Date	Mintage	F12	VF20	XF40	MS60	MS63
2004(u)	1,000	PF63 45.00	PF65 50.00			

KM# 33 10 FLORIN
1.24 g., 0.999 Gold 0.0397 oz. AGW, 13.9 mm. **Ruler:** Beatrix **Subject:** Death of Juliana **Obv:** Head left **Obv. Designer:** E. Fingal **Rev:** Juliana in center **Edge:** Reeded

Date	Mintage	F12	VF20	XF40	MS60	MS63
ND (2005)(u)	10,000	PF63 70.00	PF65 75.00			

KM# 35 10 FLORIN
6.72 g., 0.900 Gold 0.1932 oz. AGW, 22.5 mm. **Ruler:** Beatrix **Subject:** Queen's Silver Jubilee **Obv:** Head left **Rev:** Flag **Edge:** Reeded **Designer:** F.L. Croes

Date	Mintage	F12	VF20	XF40	MS60	MS63
2005(u)	750	PF63 325	PF65 375			

KM# 36 10 FLORIN
25.00 g., 0.925 Silver 0.7387 oz. ASW, 38 mm. **Ruler:** Beatrix **Subject:** Status Aparte 20th Anniversary - Flag 30th Anniversary

Obv: Queen's portrait **Rev:** Queen standing next to value and country name **Rev. Designer:** Gustave Nouel **Edge Lettering:** DIOS * TA * CU * NOS *

Date	Mintage	F12	VF20	XF40	MS60	MS63
2006(u)	1,250	PF63 40.00	PF65 45.00			

KM# 44 10 FLORIN
1.24 g., 0.999 Gold 0.0397 oz. AGW, 13.9 mm. **Ruler:** Beatrix **Subject:** Carnival **Obv:** Head left **Rev:** Carnival feathered facemask

Date	Mintage	F12	VF20	XF40	MS60	MS63
2009	5,000	PF63 70.00	PF65 75.00			

KM# 49 10 FLORIN
3.36 g., 0.900 Gold 0.0967 oz. AGW, 18.5 mm. **Ruler:** Beatrix **Subject:** Status Aparte **Obv:** Shield in wreath above mintmarks **Rev:** 25 years Status Aparte with Parliament building **Edge:** Reeded

Date	Mintage	F12	VF20	XF40	MS60	MS63
2011(u)	1,000	PF63 220	PF65 250			

KM# 55 10 FLORIN
1.24 g., 0.999 Gold 0.0396 oz. AGW, 13.92 mm. **Ruler:** Willem-Alexander **Subject:** Aruba welcomes Willem Alexander **Obv:** National arms and crown **Rev:** Willem Alexander right **Edge:** Reeded **Designer:** Elles Kloosterman

Date	Mintage	F12	VF20	XF40	MS60	MS63
2013(u)	750	PF65 130				

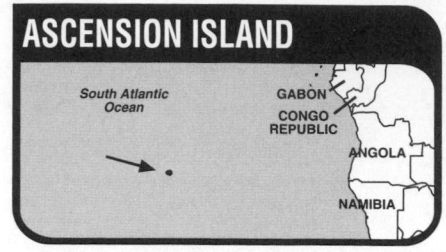

KM# 22 25 FLORIN
25.00 g., 0.925 Silver 0.7387 oz. ASW, 38 mm. **Ruler:** Beatrix **Subject:** 15th Anniversary of Autonomy **Obv:** Head left **Rev:** National arms and inscription **Edge:** Plain

Date	Mintage	F12	VF20	XF40	MS60	MS63
2001(u)	3,000	PF63 45.00	PF65 50.00			

KM# 37 25 FLORIN
6.72 g., 0.900 Gold 0.1932 oz. AGW, 22.5 mm. **Ruler:** Beatrix **Subject:** Status Aparte 20th Anniversary - Flag 30th Anniversary **Obv:** Queen's portrait **Rev:** Queen standing next to value and country name **Rev. Designer:** Gustave Nouel **Edge:** Reeded **Note:** Status Aparte

Date	Mintage	F12	VF20	XF40	MS60	MS63
2006(u)	1,000	PF63 325	PF65 375			

KM# 23 100 FLORIN
6.72 g., Gold AGW, 22.5 mm. **Ruler:** Beatrix **Subject:** Independence **Obv:** Arms, treaty name, dates **Rev:** Head left **Rev. Designer:** Royal Dutch Mint **Edge:** Grained

Date	Mintage	F12	VF20	XF40	MS60	MS63
2001(u)	1,000	PF63 350	PF65 400			

PATTERNS

KM#	Date	Mintage	Identification	Mkt Val
Pn1	2002(u)	—	5 Florin Brass KM#38	700
Pn3	2002(u)	—	5 Florin Nickel Bonded Steel KM#38 with SPECIMEN added	700

MINT SETS

KM#	Date	Mintage	Identification	Issue Price	Mkt Val
MS19	2001 (7)	6,900	KM#1-6, 12	13.25	18.00
MS20	2002 (6)	6,000	KM# 1-6, 12	15.00	20.00
MS21	2003 (7)	4,000	KM# 1-6, 12	15.00	20.00
MS22	2004 (7)	2,500	KM# 1-6, 12	15.00	30.00
MS23	2005 (7)	2,500	KM# 1-6, 12	15.00	30.00
MS24	2006 (7)	2,000	KM# 1-6, 38	15.00	30.00
MS25	2007 (7)	2,500	KM#1-6, 38	20.00	30.00
MS26	2008 (7)	2,000	KM#1-6, 38	26.00	30.00
MS27	2009 (7)	2,000	KM#1-6, 38	26.00	30.00
MS28	2010 (7)	2,000	KM#1-6, 38	26.00	30.00
MS29	2011 (7)	2,000	KM#1-6, 38	26.00	30.00
MS30	2012 (7)	2,000	KM#1-6, 38	28.00	30.00

ASCENSION ISLAND

South Atlantic Ocean — GABON, CONGO REPUBLIC, ANGOLA, NAMIBIA

An island of volcanic origin, Ascension Island lies in the South Atlantic, 700 miles (1,100 km.) northwest of St. Helena. It has an area of 34 sq. mi. (88 sq. km.) on an island 9 miles (14 km.) long and 6 miles (10 km.) wide. Approximate population: 1,146. Although having little vegetation and scant rainfall, the island has a very healthy climate. The island is the nesting place for a large number of sea turtles and sooty terns. Phosphates and guano are the chief natural sources of income. Ascension is a dependency of the British Colony of St. Helena.

RULER
British

MINT MARKS
PM - Pobjoy Mint

BRITISH ADMINISTRATION
STANDARD COINAGE

KM# 13 50 PENCE
28.63 g., Copper-Nickel, 38.6 mm. **Subject:** 75th Birthday of Queen Elizabeth **Obv:** Crowned bust right, denomination below **Obv. Designer:** Raphael Maklouf **Rev:** Crowned monogram above flowers within circle, date below **Edge:** Reeded

Date	Mintage	F12	VF20	XF40	MS60	MS63
2001	—	—	—	—	8.00	9.50

KM# 13a 50 PENCE
28.28 g., 0.925 Silver 0.8356 oz. ASW, 38.6 mm. **Subject:** Queen Elizabeth II's 75th Birthday **Obv:** Crowned bust right, denomination below **Obv. Designer:** Raphael Maklouf **Rev:** Crowned monogram above roses within circle, date below **Edge:** Reeded

Date	Mintage	F12	VF20	XF40	MS60	MS63
2001	10,000	PF63 40.00	PF65 45.00			

KM# 13b 50 PENCE
47.54 g., 0.9166 Gold 1.392 oz. AGW, 38.6 mm. **Subject:** Queen Elizabeth II's 75th Birthday **Obv:** Crowned bust right, denomination below **Obv. Designer:** Raphael Maklouf **Rev:** Crowned monogram above roses within circle, date below **Edge:** Reeded

Date	Mintage	F12	VF20	XF40	MS60	MS63
2001	75	PF65 2,350				

KM# 14 50 PENCE
28.63 g., Copper-Nickel, 38.6 mm. **Subject:** Centennial - Queen Victoria's Death **Obv:** Crowned bust right, denomination below **Obv. Designer:** Raphael Maklouf **Rev:** Crowned bust left, three dates **Edge:** Reeded

Date	Mintage	F12	VF20	XF40	MS60	MS63
2001	—	—	—	—	8.00	9.50

KM# 14a 50 PENCE
28.28 g., 0.925 Silver 0.8356 oz. ASW, 38.6 mm. **Subject:** Centennial of Queen Victoria's Death **Obv:** Crowned bust right, denomination below **Obv. Designer:** Raphael Maklouf **Rev:** Crowned bust left, three dates **Edge:** Reeded

Date	Mintage	F12	VF20	XF40	MS60	MS63
2001	10,000	PF63 40.00	PF65 45.00			

KM# 14b 50 PENCE
47.54 g., 0.9166 Gold 1.392 oz. AGW, 38.6 mm. **Subject:** Centennial of Queen Victoria's Death **Obv:** Crowned bust right, denomination below **Obv. Designer:** Raphael Maklouf **Rev:** Crowned bust left, three dates **Edge:** Reeded

Date	Mintage	F12	VF20	XF40	MS60	MS63
2001	100	PF65 2,500				

KM# 15 50 PENCE
28.35 g., Copper-Nickel, 38.6 mm. **Subject:** Queen's Golden Jubilee **Obv:** Crowned bust right, denomination below **Obv. Designer:** Raphael Maklouf **Rev:** Westminster Abby, monogram at left, circle surrounds, two dates below **Edge:** Reeded

Date	Mintage	F12	VF20	XF40	MS60	MS63
ND(2002)	—	—	—	—	8.00	9.50

KM# 15a 50 PENCE
28.28 g., 0.925 Silver 0.8356 oz. ASW, 38.6 mm. **Subject:** Queen Elizabeth II's Golden Jubilee **Obv:** Gold-plated crowned bust right, denomination below **Obv. Designer:** Raphael Maklouf **Rev:** Monogram and Westminster Abbey within circle, dates below **Edge:** Reeded

Date	Mintage	F12	VF20	XF40	MS60	MS63
ND(2002)	10,000	PF63 40.00	PF65 45.00			

KM# 18 50 PENCE
28.28 g., Copper-Nickel, 38.6 mm. **Subject:** Death of Queen Mother **Obv:** Crowned bust right, denomination below **Obv. Designer:** Raphael Maklouf **Rev:** Queen Mother bust right, between her life dates **Edge:** Reeded

Date	Mintage	F12	VF20	XF40	MS60	MS63
ND(2002)	—	—	—	—	10.00	12.00

KM# 18a 50 PENCE
28.28 g., 0.925 Silver 0.8356 oz. ASW, 38.6 mm. **Subject:** Death of Queen Mother **Obv:** Crowned bust right, denomination below **Rev:** Queen Mother bust right, between her life dates **Edge:** Reeded

Date	Mintage	F12	VF20	XF40	MS60	MS63
ND(2002)	10,000	PF63 40.00	PF65 45.00			

KM# 16 50 PENCE
28.36 g., Copper-Nickel, 38.6 mm. **Subject:** Coronation Jubilee

Obv: Crowned bust right, denomination below **Obv. Designer:** Raphael Maklouf **Rev:** Crown, two scepters and the ampula **Edge:** Reeded

Date	Mintage	F12	VF20	XF40	MS60	MS63
ND (2003) Prooflike	—	—	—	—	10.00	12.00

KM# 16a 50 PENCE
28.28 g., 0.925 Silver 0.8356 oz. ASW, 38.6 mm. **Subject:** Queen Elizabeth II's - 50th Anniversary of Coronation **Obv:** Crowned bust right, denomination below **Obv. Designer:** Raphael Maklouf **Rev:** Crown, two scepters and the ampula **Edge:** Reeded

Date	Mintage	F12	VF20	XF40	MS60	MS63
ND(2003)	5,000	PF63 45.00	PF65 50.00			

KM# 16b 50 PENCE
39.94 g., 0.9166 Gold 1.1694 oz. AGW, 38.6 mm. **Subject:** Queen Elizabeth II's - 50th Anniversary of Coronation **Obv:** Crowned bust right, denomination below **Obv. Designer:** Raphael Maklouf **Rev:** Crown, two scepters and the ampula **Edge:** Reeded

Date	Mintage	F12	VF20	XF40	MS60	MS63
ND(2003)	50	PF65 2,450				

KM# 17 50 PENCE
28.28 g., Copper-Nickel, 38.6 mm. **Subject:** Queen Elizabeth II's- 50th Anniversary of Coronation **Obv:** Crowned head right, denomination below **Obv. Designer:** Raphael Maklouf **Rev:** Crowned monogram **Edge:** Reeded

Date	Mintage	F12	VF20	XF40	MS60	MS63
ND(2003)	—	—	—	—	10.00	12.00

KM# 17a 50 PENCE
28.28 g., 0.925 Silver 0.8356 oz. ASW, 38.6 mm. **Subject:** Queen Elizabeth II's- 50th Anniversary of Coronation **Obv:** Crowned head right, denomination below **Obv. Designer:** Raphael Maklouf **Rev:** Crowned monogram **Edge:** Reeded

Date	Mintage	F12	VF20	XF40	MS60	MS63
ND(2003)	5,000	PF63 45.00	PF65 50.00			

KM# 17b 50 PENCE
39.94 g., 0.9166 Gold 1.1694 oz. AGW, 38.6 mm. **Subject:** Queen Elizabeth II's - 50th Anniversary of Coronation **Obv:** Crowned bust right, denomination below **Obv. Designer:** Raphael Maklouf **Rev:** Crowned monogram **Edge:** Reeded

Date	Mintage	F12	VF20	XF40	MS60	MS63
ND(2003)	50	PF65 2,450				

KM# 19 2 POUNDS
28.28 g., Copper-Nickel, 38.6 mm. **Subject:** Royal Wedding, Prince William and Catherine Middleton **Obv:** Bust in tiara right **Rev:** Two bells and two doves

Date	Mintage	F12	VF20	XF40	MS60	MS63
2011PM	—				10.00	12.50

KM# 19a 2 POUNDS
28.28 g., 0.925 Silver 0.8356 oz. ASW **Subject:** Royal Wedding of Prince William and Catherine Middleton **Obv:** Bust in tiara right **Rev:** Two bells and two doves

Date	Mintage	F12	VF20	XF40	MS60	MS63
2011PM	—	PF63 55.00	PF65 65.00			

KM# 20 2 POUNDS
28.28 g., Copper-Nickel, 38.61 mm. **Subject:** Royal Wedding of Prince William and Catherine Middleton **Obv:** Bust with tiara right **Rev:** Westminster Abbey, profiel portraits conjoined in oval at right

Date	Mintage	F12	VF20	XF40	MS60	MS63
2011PM	—				10.00	12.50

KM# 20a 2 POUNDS
28.28 g., 0.925 Silver 0.8356 oz. ASW, 38.61 mm. **Subject:** Royal Wedding of Prince William and Catherine Middleton **Obv:** Bust in tiara right **Rev:** Westminster Abbey, portraits in oval at right

Date	Mintage	F12	VF20	XF40	MS60	MS63
2011PM	—	PF63 55.00	PF65 65.00			

KM# 21 2 POUNDS
28.28 g., Copper-Nickel, 38.61 mm. **Obv:** Conjoined busts right of 1952 and 2012 portraits **Rev:** 1952 era portrait of Elizabeth II **Rev. Legend:** Life of Queen Elizabeth II

Date	Mintage	F12	VF20	XF40	MS60	MS63
2012PM	—					20.00

KM# 22 2 POUNDS
28.28 g., Copper-Nickel, 38.61 mm. **Subject:** Life of Queen Elizabeth II **Obv:** Conjoined busts right **Rev:** Elizabeth nursing Prince Charles

Date	Mintage	F12	VF20	XF40	MS60	MS63
2012PM	—					15.00

KM# 23 5 POUNDS
62.21 g., 0.999 Silver 1.9852 oz. ASW, 38.61 mm. **Subject:** Elizabeth II 60th Anniversary **Obv:** Conjoined busts of 2012 and 1952 portraits **Rev:** Young postrait wearing state crown in ultra high relief

Date	Mintage	F12	VF20	XF40	MS60	MS63
2012PM	—	PF63 90.00	PF65 100			

KM# 23a 5 POUNDS
31.11 g., 0.999 Gold 0.9926 oz. AGW **Obv:** Conjoined busts right of 2012 and 1952 portraits **Rev:** Youthful Elizabeth II wearing state crown in ultra-high relief

Date	Mintage	F12	VF20	XF40	MS60	MS63
2012PM	—	PF65 2,000				

KM# 25 60 CROWNS
1866.30 g., 0.999 Silver 59.5571 oz. ASW **Obv:** Conjoined busts right of 2012 and 1952 portratis **Rev:** Youthful Elizabeth II wearing gilt state crown inset with 60 diamond chips **Note:** Diamond chip inserts total 1 karat in weight.

Date	Mintage	F12	VF20	XF40	MS60	MS63
2012PM	—	PF65 3,000				

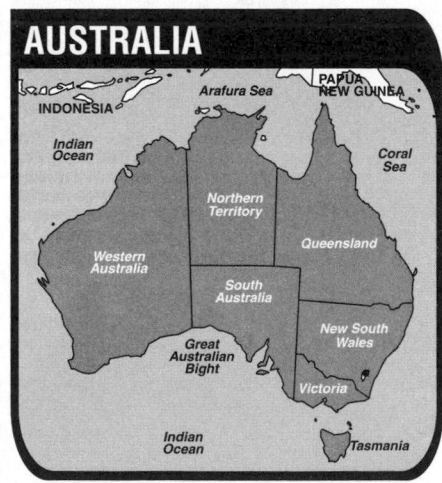

AUSTRALIA

The Commonwealth of Australia, the smallest continent in the world, is located south of Indonesia between the Indian and Pacific oceans. It has an area of 2,967,893 sq. mi. (7,686,850 sq. km.) and an estimated population of 18.84 million. Capital: Canberra. Due to its early and sustained isolation, Australia is the habitat of such curious and unique fauna as the kangaroo, koala, platypus, wombat, echidna and frilled-necked lizard. The continent possesses extensive mineral deposits, the most important of which are iron ore, coal, gold, silver, nickel, uranium, lead and zinc. Raising livestock, mining and manufacturing are the principal industries. Chief exports are wool, meat, wheat, iron ore, coal and nonferrous metals.

Australia is a founding member of the Commonwealth of Nations. Elizabeth II is the Head of State as Queen of Australia; the Prime Minister is Head of Government.

NOTE: Home market grading of Australian coinage is generally stricter than USA practiced standards. The pricing in this catalog reflects strict home market grading standard.

RULER
British until 1942

MONETARY SYSTEM
Decimal Coinage (Commencing 1966)100 Cents = 1 Dollar

COMMONWEALTH OF AUSTRALIA
DECIMAL COINAGE

KM# 62a CENT
2.60 g., 0.999 Silver 0.083 oz. ASW, 17.53 mm. **Ruler:** Elizabeth II **Obv:** Young bust right **Rev:** Feather-tailed glider and value **Rev. Designer:** Stuart Devlin **Edge:** Plain

Date	Mintage	F12	VF20	XF40	MS60	MS63
2006	6,500	PF65 15.00				

KM# 767b CENT
5.61 g., 0.999 Gold 0.179 oz. AGW, 17.53 mm. **Ruler:** Elizabeth II **Obv:** Head with tiara right **Obv. Designer:** Ian Rank-Broadley **Rev:** Feather-tailed glider **Rev. Designer:** Stuart Devlin **Edge:** Plain

Date	Mintage	F12	VF20	XF40	MS60	MS63
2006	300	PF65 650				

KM# 767 CENT
2.60 g., Bronze, 17.65 mm. **Ruler:** Elizabeth II **Obv:** Head with tiara right **Obv. Designer:** Ian Rank-Broadley **Rev:** Feather-tailed glider and value **Rev. Designer:** Stuart Devlin **Edge:** Plain

Date	Mintage	F12	VF20	XF40	MS60	MS63
2006B In sets only	—					15.00
2006B	—	PF65 18.00				

KM# 1249 CENT
2.43 g., 0.999 Silver 0.0775 oz. ASW, 17.6 mm. **Ruler:** Elizabeth II **Subject:** 1966 Decimal Pattern **Obv:** Head right **Obv. Designer:** Ian Rank-Broadley **Rev:** Waratah, flower of New South Wales **Rev. Designer:** Andor Meszaros

Date	Mintage	F12	VF20	XF40	MS60	MS63
2009P	3,344	PF65 15.00				

KM# 767a CENT
2.93 g., 0.999 Silver 0.0935 oz. ASW, 17.53 mm. **Ruler:** Elizabeth II **Obv:** Head with tiara right **Rev:** Feather-tailed glider and value

Date	Mintage	F12	VF20	XF40	MS60	MS63
2011	6,000	PF65 50.00				

KM# 2032 CENT
0.50 g., 0.9999 Gold AGW, 11.15 mm. **Ruler:** Elizabeth II **Subject:** Australian Miniature Money

Date	Mintage	F12	VF20	XF40	MS60	MS63
2012	—	PF65 75.00				

KM# 63a 2 CENTS
5.18 g., 0.999 Silver 0.1653 oz. ASW, 21.6 mm. **Ruler:** Elizabeth II **Obv:** Young bust right **Obv. Designer:** Arnold Machin **Rev:**

Frill-necked lizard and value **Rev. Designer:** Stuart Devlin **Edge:** Plain

Date	Mintage	F12	VF20	XF40	MS60	MS63
2006	6,500	PF65 15.00				

KM# 768b 2 CENTS
11.31 g., 0.999 Gold 0.3609 oz. AGW, 21.6 mm. **Ruler:** Elizabeth II **Obv:** Head with tiara right **Obv. Designer:** Ian Rank-Broadley **Rev:** Frill-necked Lizard and value **Rev. Designer:** Stuart Devlin **Edge:** Plain

Date	Mintage	F12	VF20	XF40	MS60	MS63
2006	300	PF65 700				

KM# 768 2 CENTS
5.20 g., Bronze, 21.59 mm. **Ruler:** Elizabeth II **Obv:** Head with tiara right **Obv. Designer:** Ian Rank-Broadley **Rev:** Frill-necked lizard and value

Date	Mintage	F12	VF20	XF40	MS60	MS63
2006B	—	—	—	—	15.00	
2006B	—	PF65 5.00				

KM# 1250 2 CENTS
5.53 g., 0.999 Silver 0.1765 oz. ASW, 21.6 mm. **Ruler:** Elizabeth II **Subject:** 1966 Decimal Pattern **Obv:** Head right **Obv. Designer:** Ian Rank-Broadley **Rev:** Wattle, national flower **Rev. Designer:** Andor Meszaros

Date	Mintage	F12	VF20	XF40	MS60	MS63
2009P	3,344	PF65 20.00				

KM# 768a 2 CENTS
6.03 g., 0.999 Silver 0.1924 oz. ASW, 21.6 mm. **Ruler:** Elizabeth II **Obv:** Head with tiara right **Rev:** Frill-necked lizard and value

Date	Mintage	F12	VF20	XF40	MS60	MS63
2011	6,000	PF65 100				

KM# 2033 2 CENTS
0.50 g., 0.9999 Gold AGW, 11.15 mm. **Ruler:** Elizabeth II **Subject:** Australian Miniature Money

Date	Mintage	F12	VF20	XF40	MS60	MS63
2012	Est. 2000	PF65 75.00				

KM# 401 5 CENTS
2.83 g., Copper-Nickel, 19.41 mm. **Ruler:** Elizabeth II **Obv:** Head with tiara right **Obv. Designer:** Ian Rank-Broadley **Rev:** Echidna and value **Rev. Designer:** Stuart Devlin **Edge:** Reeded

Date	Mintage	F12	VF20	XF40	MS60	MS63
2001	174,579,000	—	—	—	2.00	3.00
Note: Large obverse head, IRB spaced						
2001	Inc. above			—	2.00	3.00
Note: Smaller obverse head, RB joined						
2001	59,569	PF65 15.00				
2002	148,812,000	—	—	—	2.00	3.00
2002	39,514	PF65 15.00				
2003	115,470,000	—	—	—	2.00	3.00
2003	39,090	PF65 5.00				
2004	147,658,000	—	—	—	2.00	3.00
Note: Normal sized SD						
2004	Inc. above	—	—	—	2.00	3.00
Note: Smaller SD						
2004	50,000	PF65 5.00				
2005	194,300,000	—	—	—	2.00	3.00
Note: Normal sized SD						
2005	Inc. above	—	—	—	2.00	3.00
Note: Smaller SD						
2005	33,520	PF65 5.00				
2006	—	—	—	—	2.00	3.00

Date	Mintage	F12	VF20	XF40	MS60	MS63
2006	—	PF65 5.00				
2007	—	—	—	—	2.00	3.00
2007	—	PF65 5.00				
2008	—	—	—	—	2.00	3.00
2008	—	PF65 5.00				
2009	—	—	—	—	2.00	3.00
2009	—	PF65 5.00				
2010	—	—	—	—	2.00	3.00
2010	—	PF65 5.00				
2011	—	—	—	—	2.00	3.00
2011	—	PF65 5.00				
2012	—	—	—	—	2.00	3.00
2012	—	PF65 5.00				

KM# 401a 5 CENTS
6.03 g., 0.999 Gold 0.1924 oz. AGW, 19.41 mm. **Ruler:** Elizabeth II **Subject:** Federation Centennial **Obv:** Head with tiara right **Obv. Designer:** Ian Rank-Broadley **Rev:** Echidna and value **Rev. Designer:** Stuart Devlin

Date	Mintage	F12	VF20	XF40	MS60	MS63
2001B	650	PF65 650				
2005B	650	PF65 450				
2006B	300	PF65 700				
2013B	500	PF65 450				

KM# 401b 5 CENTS
3.24 g., 0.9999 Silver 0.1035 oz. ASW, 19.41 mm. **Ruler:** Elizabeth II **Obv:** Head with tiara right **Obv. Designer:** Ian Rank-Broadley **Rev:** Echidna and value **Rev. Designer:** Stuart Devlin **Edge:** Reeded

Date	Mintage	F12	VF20	XF40	MS60	MS63
2003B	6,500	PF65 30.00				
2004B	6,500	PF65 20.00				
2005B	6,500	PF65 20.00				
2006B	—	PF65 20.00				
2007B	—	PF65 20.00				
2008B	—	PF65 20.00				
2009B	—	PF65 20.00				
2010B	—	PF65 20.00				
2011B	6,000	PF65 20.00				
2013B	5,000	PF65 25.00				

KM# 64a 5 CENTS
3.24 g., 0.999 Silver 0.1034 oz. ASW, 19.41 mm. **Ruler:** Elizabeth II **Obv:** Young bust right **Obv. Designer:** Arnold Machin **Rev:** Echidna **Rev. Designer:** Stuart Devlin **Edge:** Reeded

Date	Mintage	F12	VF20	XF40	MS60	MS63
2006	6,500	PF65 20.00				

KM# 1251 5 CENTS
2.74 g., 0.999 Silver 0.0874 oz. ASW, 19.6 mm. **Ruler:** Elizabeth II **Subject:** 1966 Decimal Pattern **Obv:** Head right **Obv. Designer:** Ian Rank-Broadley **Rev:** Platypus and yabbie **Rev. Designer:** Andor Meszaros

Date	Mintage	F12	VF20	XF40	MS60	MS63
2009P	3,344	PF65 35.00				

KM# 2034 5 CENTS
0.50 g., 0.9999 Gold AGW, 11.15 mm. **Ruler:** Elizabeth II **Subject:** Australian Miniature Money

Date	Mintage	F12	VF20	XF40	MS60	MS63
2012	Est. 2000	PF65 75.00				

KM# 402 10 CENTS
5.65 g., Copper-Nickel, 23.6 mm. **Ruler:** Elizabeth II **Obv:** Head with tiara right **Obv. Designer:** Ian Rank-Broadley **Rev:**

Lyrebird and value **Rev. Designer:** Stuart Devlin **Edge:** Reeded

Date	Mintage	F12	VF20	XF40	MS60	MS63
2001	109,357,000	—	—	—	3.00	4.00
Note: Large obverse head, IRB spaced						
2001	Inc. above	—	—	—	3.00	4.00
Note: Smaller obverse head, RB joined						
2001	59,569	PF65 15.00				
2002	70,329,000	—	—	—	3.00	4.00
2002	39,514	PF65 5.00				
2003	53,635,000	—	—	—	2.00	3.00
2003	39,090	PF65 5.00				
2004	89,000,000	—	—	—	3.00	4.00
2004	50,000	PF65 5.00				
2005	116,700,000	—	—	—	2.00	3.00
2005	33,520	PF65 5.00				
2006	157,087,000	—	—	—	2.00	3.00
2006	—	PF65 5.00				
2007	61,096,000	—	—	—	3.00	4.00
2007	—	PF65 4.00				
2008	82,860,000	—	—	—	3.00	4.00
2008	—	PF65 5.00				
2009	—	—	—	—	3.00	4.00
2009	—	PF65 5.00				
2010	—	—	—	—	3.00	4.00
2010	—	PF65 5.00				
2011	—	—	—	—	3.00	4.00
2011	—	PF65 5.00				
2012	—	—	—	—	3.00	4.00
2012	—	PF65 5.00				

KM# 402a 10 CENTS
12.14 g., 0.9999 Gold 0.3878 oz. AGW, 23.6 mm. **Ruler:** Elizabeth II **Obv:** Head with tiara right **Obv. Designer:** Ian Rank-Broadley **Rev:** Lyrebird and value **Rev. Designer:** Stuart Devlin **Edge:** Reeded

Date	Mintage	F12	VF20	XF40	MS60	MS63
2001B	650	PF65 750				
2005B	650	PF65 700				
2006B	300	PF65 850				
2013B	500	PF65 700				

KM# 402b 10 CENTS
6.57 g., 0.9999 Silver 0.2098 oz. ASW, 23.6 mm. **Ruler:** Elizabeth II **Obv:** Head with tiara right **Obv. Designer:** Ian Rank-Broadley **Rev:** Lyrebird and value **Rev. Designer:** Stuart Devlin **Edge:** Reeded

Date	Mintage	F12	VF20	XF40	MS60	MS63
2003B	6,500	PF65 20.00				
2004B	6,500	PF65 15.00				
2005B	6,500	PF65 15.00				
2006B	—	PF65 15.00				
2007B	—	PF65 15.00				
2008B	—	PF65 15.00				
2009B	—	PF65 15.00				
2010B	—	PF65 15.00				
2011B	6,000	PF65 15.00				
2013B	5,000	PF65 35.00				

KM# 65a 10 CENTS
6.57 g., 0.999 Silver 0.2097 oz. ASW, 23.6 mm. **Ruler:** Elizabeth II **Obv:** Young bust right **Obv. Designer:** Arnold Machin **Rev:** Superb Lyrebird **Rev. Designer:** Stuart Devlin **Edge:** Reeded

Date	Mintage	F12	VF20	XF40	MS60	MS63
2006	6,500	PF65 15.00				

KM# 1252 10 CENTS
6.07 g., 0.999 Silver 0.1937 oz. ASW, 23.6 mm. **Ruler:** Elizabeth II **Subject:** 1966 Decimal Pattern **Obv:** Head right **Obv. Designer:** Ian Rank-Broadley **Rev:** Kookabura eating snake **Rev. Designer:** Andor Meszaros

Date	Mintage	F12	VF20	XF40	MS60	MS63
2009P	3,344	PF65 45.00				

KM# 1789 10 CENTS
3.12 g., 0.999 Silver 0.0996 oz. ASW, 21 mm. **Ruler:** Elizabeth II **Obv:** Head with tiara right **Rev:** Koala leaning on and hugging branch

Date	Mintage	F12	VF20	XF40	MS60	MS63
2012P	—	—	—	—	—	15.00

KM# 2035 10 CENTS
0.50 g., 0.9999 Gold AGW, 11.15 mm. **Ruler:** Elizabeth II **Subject:** Australian Miniature Money

Date	Mintage	F12	VF20	XF40	MS60	MS63
2012	Est. 2000	PF65 75.00				

KM# 403 20 CENTS
11.30 g., Copper-Nickel, 28.65 mm. **Ruler:** Elizabeth II **Obv:** Head with tiara right **Obv. Designer:** Ian Rank-Broadley **Rev:** Duckbill Platypus **Rev. Designer:** Stuart Devlin **Edge:** Reeded

Date	Mintage	F12	VF20	XF40	MS60	MS63
2001	81,967,000	—	—	—	3.00	4.00
Note: IRB spaced						
2001	Inc. above	—	—	—	3.00	4.00
Note: RB joined						
2001	Inc. above	—	—	—	3.00	4.00
Note: IRB joined						
2001	59,569	PF65 25.00				
2002	27,244,000	—	—	—	3.00	4.00
2002	39,514	PF65 2.00				
2004	74,609,000	—	—	—	3.00	4.00
Note: Small obverse head, flat top A						
2004	Est. 400000	—	—	—	15.00	20.00
Note: Large obverse head, pointed A						
2004	50,000	PF65 10.00				
Note: Large obverse head, pointed top A						
2004	Inc. above	PF65 10.00				
Note: Small obverse head, flat top A						
2005	58,600,000	—	—	—	9.00	10.00
2005	—	PF65 25.00				
2006	102,462,000	—	—	—	3.00	4.00
2006	—	PF65 6.00				
2007	42,712,000	—	—	—	3.00	4.00
2007	—	PF65 25.00				
2008	106,220,000	—	—	—	1.00	2.00
2008	—	PF65 12.00				
2009	—	—	—	—	1.00	2.00
2009	—	PF65 12.00				
2010	—	—	—	—	1.00	2.00
2010	—	PF65 12.00				
2011	—	—	—	—	1.00	2.00
2011	—	PF65 12.00				
2012	—	—	—	—	1.00	2.00
2012	—	PF65 12.00				

KM# 532 20 CENTS
11.30 g., Copper-Nickel, 28.65 mm. **Ruler:** Elizabeth II **Subject:** Centenary of Federation - Norfolk Island **Obv:** Head with tiara right **Obv. Designer:** Ian Rank-Broadley **Rev:** Norfolk Pine over map of island **Rev. Designer:** Megan Cummings **Edge:** Reeded

Date	Mintage	F12	VF20	XF40	MS60	MS63
2001B	2,000,000	—	—	—	3.50	5.00
2001B	—	PF65 10.00				

KM# 550 20 CENTS
11.30 g., Copper-Nickel, 28.65 mm. **Ruler:** Elizabeth II **Series:** Centenary of Federation - New South Wales **Obv:** Head with tiara right **Obv. Designer:** Ian Rank-Broadley **Rev:** Waratah on state map **Rev. Designer:** Joseph Neve **Edge:** Reeded

Date	Mintage	F12	VF20	XF40	MS60	MS63
2001	2,000,000	—	—	—	3.50	5.00
2001	—	PF65 10.00				

KM# 552 20 CENTS
11.30 g., Copper-Nickel, 28.65 mm. **Ruler:** Elizabeth II **Series:** Centenary of Federation - Australian Capital Territory **Obv:** Head with tiara right **Obv. Designer:** Ian Rank-Broadley **Rev:** Parliament House, map, flowers **Rev. Designer:** Stacy Jo-Ann Paine **Edge:** Reeded **Note:** Prev. KM#551.

Date	Mintage	F12	VF20	XF40	MS60	MS63
2001	2,000,000	—	—	—	5.00	6.00
2001	—	PF65 20.00				

KM# 554 20 CENTS
11.30 g., Copper-Nickel, 28.65 mm. **Ruler:** Elizabeth II **Series:** Centenary of Federation - Queensland **Obv:** Head with tiara right **Obv. Designer:** Ian Rank-Broadley **Rev. Designer:** Jennifer Gray **Edge:** Reeded

Date	Mintage	F12	VF20	XF40	MS60	MS63
2001	2,320,000	—	—	—	6.00	8.00
2001	—	PF65 20.00				

KM# 556 20 CENTS
11.30 g., Copper-Nickel, 28.65 mm. **Ruler:** Elizabeth II **Series:** Centenary of Federation - Victoria **Obv:** Head with tiara right **Obv. Designer:** Ian Rank-Broadley **Rev:** Capital building **Rev. Designer:** Ryan Ladd & Mark Kennedy **Edge:** Reeded

Date	Mintage	F12	VF20	XF40	MS60	MS63
2001	2,000,000	—	—	—	6.00	8.00
2001	—	PF65 20.00				

KM# 558 20 CENTS
11.30 g., Copper-Nickel, 28.65 mm. **Ruler:** Elizabeth II **Series:** Centenary of Federation - Northern Territory **Obv:** Head with tiara right **Obv. Designer:** Ian Rank-Broadley **Rev:** Two brolga cranes in ritual dance **Rev. Designer:** Lisa Brett **Edge:** Reeded

Date	Mintage	F12	VF20	XF40	MS60	MS63
2001	2,100,000	—	—	—	6.00	9.00
2001	—	PF65 20.00				

KM# 560 20 CENTS
11.30 g., Copper-Nickel, 28.65 mm. **Ruler:** Elizabeth II **Series:** Centenary of Federation - South Australia **Obv:** Head with tiara right **Obv. Designer:** Ian Rank-Broadley **Rev:** Sturt's Desert Pea, landscape and southern cross **Rev. Designer:** Lisa Murphy **Edge:** Reeded

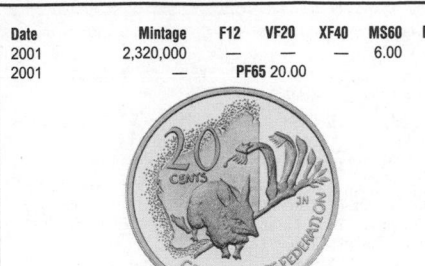

Date	Mintage	F12	VF20	XF40	MS60	MS63
2001	2,320,000	—	—	—	6.00	8.00
2001	—	PF65 20.00				

KM# 562 20 CENTS
11.30 g., Copper-Nickel, 28.65 mm. **Ruler:** Elizabeth II **Series:** Centenary of Federation - Western Australia **Obv:** Head with tiara right **Obv. Designer:** Ian Rank-Broadley **Rev:** Rabbit-eared Bandicoot (bilby), plant and map **Rev. Designer:** Janice Ng **Edge:** Reeded

Date	Mintage	F12	VF20	XF40	MS60	MS63
2001	2,000,000	—	—	—	6.00	10.00
2001	—	PF65 20.00				

KM# 564 20 CENTS
11.30 g., Copper-Nickel, 28.65 mm. **Ruler:** Elizabeth II **Series:** Centenary of Federation - Tasmania **Obv:** Head with tiara right **Obv. Designer:** Ian Rank-Broadley **Rev:** Tasmanian Tiger on map **Rev. Designer:** Abbey MacDonald **Edge:** Reeded

Date	Mintage	F12	VF20	XF40	MS60	MS63
2001	2,000,000	—	—	—	6.00	10.00
2001	—	PF65 20.00				

KM# 589 20 CENTS
11.30 g., Copper-Nickel, 28.65 mm. **Ruler:** Elizabeth II **Subject:** Sir Donald Bradman **Obv:** Head with tiara right **Obv. Designer:** Ian Rank-Broadley **Rev:** Sir Donald Bradman **Rev. Designer:** Vladimir Gottwald **Edge:** Reeded

Date	Mintage	F12	VF20	XF40	MS60	MS63
2001B	10,000,000	—	—	—	35.00	40.00

KM# 819 20 CENTS
24.36 g., 0.999 Gold 0.7774 oz. AGW, 28.52 mm. **Ruler:** Elizabeth II **Obv:** Head with tiara right **Obv. Designer:** Ian Rank-Broadley **Rev:** Platypus with Federation Star **Rev. Designer:** Stuart Devlin **Edge:** Reeded

Date	Mintage	F12	VF20	XF40	MS60	MS63
2001	650	PF65 1,450				

KM# 403a 20 CENTS
13.36 g., 0.9999 Silver 0.4267 oz. ASW, 28.52 mm. **Ruler:** Elizabeth II **Obv:** Head with tiara right **Obv. Designer:** Ian Rank-Broadley **Rev:** Platypus and value **Rev. Designer:** Stuart Devlin **Edge:** Reeded

Date	Mintage	F12	VF20	XF40	MS60	MS63
2003B	6,500	PF65 30.00				
2004B	6,500	PF65 25.00				
2006B	6,500	PF65 25.00				
2007B	—	PF65 25.00				
2008B	—	PF65 25.00				
2009B	—	PF65 25.00				
2010B	—	PF65 25.00				
2011B	6,000	PF65 25.00				
2013B	5,000	PF65 50.00				

KM# 688a 20 CENTS
11.30 g., 0.999 Silver 0.3606 oz. ASW, 28.65 mm. **Ruler:** Elizabeth II **Obv:** Head right **Rev:** Group of Australian Volunteers **Edge:** Reeded

Date	Mintage	F12	VF20	XF40	MS60	MS63
2003B	6,500		PF65 35.00			

KM# 688b 20 CENTS
24.36 g., 0.999 Gold 0.7774 oz. AGW, 28.65 mm. **Ruler:** Elizabeth II **Obv:** Head with tiara right **Obv. Designer:** Ian Rank-Broadley **Rev:** Group of Australian Volunteers **Rev. Designer:** Vladimir Gottwald **Edge:** Reeded

Date	Mintage	F12	VF20	XF40	MS60	MS63
2003B	650		PF65 1,450			

KM# 688 20 CENTS
11.30 g., Copper-Nickel, 28.65 mm. **Ruler:** Elizabeth II **Obv:** Head with tiara right **Obv. Designer:** Ian Rank-Broadley **Rev:** Group of Australian Volunteers **Rev. Designer:** Sir Vladimir Gottwald **Edge:** Reeded

Date	Mintage	F12	VF20	XF40	MS60	MS63
2003B	7,600,000				3.00	4.00
2003B	—		PF65 15.00			

KM# 745a 20 CENTS
13.36 g., 0.999 Silver 0.4263 oz. ASW, 28.65 mm. **Ruler:** Elizabeth II **Obv:** Head right **Rev:** Soldier with wife and child **Edge:** Reeded

Date	Mintage	F12	VF20	XF40	MS60	MS63
2005B	6,500		PF65 35.00			

KM# 745b 20 CENTS
24.36 g., 0.9999 Gold 0.7781 oz. AGW, 28.65 mm. **Ruler:** Elizabeth II **Obv:** Head right **Rev:** Soldier with wife and child **Edge:** Reeded

Date	Mintage	F12	VF20	XF40	MS60	MS63
2005B	650		PF65 1,450			

KM# 745 20 CENTS
11.30 g., Copper-Nickel, 28.65 mm. **Ruler:** Elizabeth II **Subject:** 60th Anniversary - End of WWII **Obv:** Head right. **Designer:** Ian Rank-Broadley **Rev:** Soldier with wife and child **Rev. Designer:** Vladimir Gottwald **Edge:** Reeded

Date	Mintage	F12	VF20	XF40	MS60	MS63
2005B	33,500,000				2.00	3.00
2005B	—		PF65 10.00			

KM# 66a 20 CENTS
13.36 g., 0.999 Silver 0.4263 oz. ASW, 28.52 mm. **Ruler:** Elizabeth II **Obv:** Young bust right **Obv. Designer:** Arnold Machin **Rev:** Platypus **Rev. Designer:** Stuart Devlin **Edge:** Reeded

Date	Mintage	F12	VF20	XF40	MS60	MS63
2006	6,500		PF65 28.00			

KM# 403b 20 CENTS
24.56 g., 0.9999 Gold 0.7845 oz. AGW, 28.52 mm. **Ruler:** Elizabeth II **Subject:** Federation Centennial **Obv:** Head with tiara right **Obv. Designer:** Ian Rank-Broadley **Rev:** Duckbill Platypus and value **Rev. Designer:** Stuart Devlin **Edge:** Reeded

Date	Mintage	F12	VF20	XF40	MS60	MS63
2006B	300		PF65 1,500			
2013B	500		PF65 1,450			

KM# 820a 20 CENTS
13.36 g., 0.999 Silver 0.4263 oz. ASW, 28.52 mm. **Ruler:** Elizabeth II **Subject:** Year of the Surfer Lifesaver **Rev:** Female with rope line

Date	Mintage	F12	VF20	XF40	MS60	MS63
2007B	—		PF65 25.00			

KM# 820 20 CENTS
11.30 g., Copper-Nickel, 28.65 mm. **Ruler:** Elizabeth II **Subject:** Year of the Surf Lifesaver **Obv:** Head with tiara right **Obv. Designer:** Ian Rank-Broadley **Rev:** Female lifesaver working line **Rev. Designer:** Vladimir Gottwald **Edge:** Reeded

Date	Mintage	F12	VF20	XF40	MS60	MS63
2007	—				10.00	7.00
2007	—		PF65 20.00			

KM# 1058 20 CENTS
11.30 g., Copper-Nickel, 28.65 mm. **Ruler:** Elizabeth II **Subject:** Planet earth **Rev:** Map of Australia with water and rocks around **Rev. Designer:** V. Gottwald

Date	Mintage	F12	VF20	XF40	MS60	MS63
2008	—		PF65 12.00			
2008	—				12.00	10.00

KM# 1075 20 CENTS
15.55 g., Copper-Nickel, 28.52 mm. **Ruler:** Elizabeth II **Subject:** Year of Astronomy **Rev:** Star gazers

Date	Mintage	F12	VF20	XF40	MS60	MS63
2009	—		PF65 25.00			
2009	—				10.00	12.00

KM# 1088 20 CENTS
15.55 g., Copper-Nickel, 28.52 mm. **Ruler:** Elizabeth II **Rev:** Poppy

Date	Mintage	F12	VF20	XF40	MS60	MS63
2009	—				10.00	12.00

KM# 1253 20 CENTS
12.86 g., 0.999 Silver 0.4104 oz. ASW, 28.6 mm. **Ruler:** Elizabeth II **Subject:** 1966 Decimal Pattern **Obv:** Head right **Obv. Designer:** Ian Rank-Broadley **Rev:** Black swan in flight **Rev. Designer:** Andor Meszaros

Date	Mintage	F12	VF20	XF40	MS60	MS63
2009P	5,459		PF65 200			

KM# 1433 20 CENTS
11.30 g., Copper-Nickel, 28.65 mm. **Ruler:** Elizabeth II **Subject:** Nurses **Rev:** Nurse looking over serviceman **Rev. Designer:** W. Pietranik

Date	Mintage	F12	VF20	XF40	MS60	MS63
2009C	—				5.00	7.00

KM# 1502 20 CENTS
11.30 g., Copper-Nickel, 28.65 mm. **Ruler:** Elizabeth II **Subject:** Wool Industry **Rev:** Wheel with sheep industry design in spoke wedges

Date	Mintage	F12	VF20	XF40	MS60	MS63
2010C	—		PF65 12.00			
2010C	—				2.00	4.00

KM# 1430 20 CENTS
11.30 g., Copper-Nickel, 28.65 mm. **Ruler:** Elizabeth II **Subject:** Burke & Wills, 150th Anniversary **Rev:** Burke and Wills on camels

Date	Mintage	F12	VF20	XF40	MS60	MS63
2010C	—				5.00	7.00
2010C	—		PF65 10.00			

KM# 1513 20 CENTS
11.30 g., Copper-Nickel, 28.65 mm. **Ruler:** Elizabeth II **Subject:** Taxation office, 100th Anniversary

Date	Mintage	F12	VF20	XF40	MS60	MS63
2010	—				1.50	2.50

KM# 1518 20 CENTS
11.30 g., Copper-Nickel, 28.65 mm. **Ruler:** Elizabeth II **Subject:** Lost Soldiers of Promelles **Rev:** Soldier carrying another on his shoulder

Date	Mintage	F12	VF20	XF40	MS60	MS63
2010	—				1.50	2.50

KM# 1634 20 CENTS
11.30 g., Copper-Nickel, 28.65 mm. **Ruler:** Elizabeth II **Subject:** Year of the Volunteer **Obv:** Head with tiara right **Rev:** Logo within wreath

Date	Mintage	F12	VF20	XF40	MS60	MS63
2011	—				3.00	4.00

KM# 1648 20 CENTS
11.30 g., Copper-Nickel, 28.65 mm. **Ruler:** Elizabeth II **Subject:** War Historians **Obv:** Head with tiara right **Rev:** Man with tripod taking photograph from atop tank

Date	Mintage	F12	VF20	XF40	MS60	MS63
2011	—				3.00	4.00

KM# 1517 20 CENTS
11.30 g., Copper-Nickel, 28.65 mm. **Ruler:** Elizabeth II **Subject:** Ashes Cricket tournament

Date	Mintage	F12	VF20	XF40	MS60	MS63
2011	—			—	1.50	2.50

KM# 1566 20 CENTS
11.30 g., Copper-Nickel, 28.65 mm. **Ruler:** Elizabeth II **Subject:** Royal Wedding **Rev:** Catherine Middleton and Prince William busts left

Date	Mintage	F12	VF20	XF40	MS60	MS63
2011	—			—	4.00	6.00

KM# 1642 20 CENTS
11.30 g., Copper-Nickel, 28.65 mm. **Ruler:** Elizabeth II **Subject:** International Womens Day, 100th Anniversary **Obv:** Head with tiara right **Rev:** Three stylized joyful figures

Date	Mintage	F12	VF20	XF40	MS60	MS63
2011	—			—	3.00	4.00

KM# 1625 20 CENTS
11.30 g., Copper-Nickel, 28.65 mm. **Ruler:** Elizabeth II **Subject:** Australian Wheat **Obv:** Head with tiara right **Rev:** Wheat ear upright

Date	Mintage	F12	VF20	XF40	MS60	MS63
2012	—	PF65 15.00				
2012	—			—	2.00	2.50

KM# 1742 20 CENTS
11.30 g., Copper-Nickel, 28.65 mm. **Ruler:** Elizabeth II **Subject:** World War II, Bombing of Australia **Obv:** Head with tiara right **Rev:** People entering air raid shelter

Date	Mintage	F12	VF20	XF40	MS60	MS63
2012	—			—	3.00	4.00

KM# 1743 20 CENTS
11.30 g., Copper-Nickel, 28.65 mm. **Ruler:** Elizabeth II **Obv:** Head with tiara right **Rev:** Military lookout

Date	Mintage	F12	VF20	XF40	MS60	MS63
2012	—			—	3.00	5.00

KM# 1743a 20 CENTS
13.36 g., 0.999 Silver 0.4263 oz. ASW, 28.65 mm. **Ruler:** Elizabeth II **Subject:** Bombing of Australia - World War II **Obv:** Head with tiara right **Rev:** Military lookout

Date	Mintage	F12	VF20	XF40	MS60	MS63
2012	—	PF65 35.00				

KM# 1857 20 CENTS
11.30 g., Copper-Nickel, 28.65 mm. **Ruler:** Elizabeth II **Subject:** Merchant Navy **Rev:** WWII Freighter sailing left

Date	Mintage	F12	VF20	XF40	MS60	MS63
2012	—			—	4.00	5.00

KM# 2036 20 CENTS
0.50 g., 0.9999 Gold AGW, 11.15 mm. **Ruler:** Elizabeth II **Subject:** Australian Miniature Money

Date	Mintage	F12	VF20	XF40	MS60	MS63
2012	Est. 2000	PF65 75.00				

KM# 403c 20 CENTS
11.30 g., Copper-Nickel, 28.65 mm. **Ruler:** Elizabeth II **Rev:** Platypus in color

Date	Mintage	F12	VF20	XF40	MS60	MS63
2013	—				—	15.00

KM# 403d 20 CENTS
13.36 g., Silver, 28.65 mm. **Ruler:** Elizabeth II **Rev:** Platypus gilt

Date	Mintage	F12	VF20	XF40	MS60	MS63
2013	—	PF65 35.00				

KM# 1961 20 CENTS
11.30 g., Copper-Nickel, 28.52 mm. **Ruler:** Elizabeth II **Subject:** Centenary of Australian Banknotes

Date	Mintage	F12	VF20	XF40	MS60	MS63
2013	—			—	4.00	5.00

KM# 1962 20 CENTS
11.30 g., Copper-Nickel, 28.52 mm. **Ruler:** Elizabeth II **Subject:** Centenary of Australian Banknotes

Date	Mintage	F12	VF20	XF40	MS60	MS63
2013	—			—	4.00	5.00

KM# 1966 20 CENTS
11.30 g., Copper-Nickel, 28.52 mm. **Ruler:** Elizabeth II **Subject:** 25th Anniversary of Australian Parliament House

Date	Mintage	F12	VF20	XF40	MS60	MS63
2013	—			—	4.00	5.00

KM# 1967 20 CENTS
11.30 g., Copper-Nickel, 28.52 mm. **Ruler:** Elizabeth II **Subject:** Royal Australian Army Chaplains **Rev. Designer:** Anna Meszaros

Date	Mintage	F12	VF20	XF40	MS60	MS63
2013	—			—	4.00	5.00

KM# 2010a 20 CENTS
11.30 g., Copper-Nickel, 28.65 mm. **Ruler:** Elizabeth II **Subject:** Mining **Rev:** Mechanisms of mining

Date	Mintage	F12	VF20	XF40	MS60	MS63
2013	Est. 40000				—	8.00

KM# 2010 20 CENTS
11.30 g., Copper-Nickel, 28.65 mm. **Ruler:** Elizabeth II **Subject:** Mining **Rev:** Mechanisms of mining

Date	Mintage	F12	VF20	XF40	MS60	MS63
2013	—			—	4.00	5.00
2013	25,000	PF65 25.00				

KM# 2080 20 CENTS
11.30 g., Silver, 28.65 mm. **Ruler:** Elizabeth II **Subject:** Canberra, 100th Anniversary **Rev:** Map of city

Date	Mintage	F12	VF20	XF40	MS60	MS63
2013	—				—	8.00

KM# 2144 20 CENTS
11.30 g., Copper-Nickel **Ruler:** Elizabeth II **Subject:** Ashes **Obv:** Head with tiara right **Rev:** Cricket player

Date	Mintage	F12	VF20	XF40	MS60	MS63
2013	—				—	4.00

KM# 403a.1 20 CENTS
Silver ASW, 28.65 mm. **Ruler:** Elizabeth II **Obv:** Head with tiara right **Rev:** Duckbill Platypus gilt

Date	Mintage	F12	VF20	XF40	MS60	MS63
2013	—			PF65 25.00		

KM# 599 25 CENTS
7.78 g., 0.999 Silver 0.2481 oz. ASW, 24.8 mm. **Ruler:** Elizabeth II **Obv:** Head with tiara right **Obv. Designer:** Ian Rank-Broadley **Rev:** Parliament House **Edge:** Plain **Shape:** 7-pointed star **Note:** The Dump" portion of the "Holey Dollar" KM#598.

Date	Mintage	F12	VF20	XF40	MS60	MS63
2001 Prooflike	21,668	—				28.00

KM# 1881 25 CENTS
Silver, 18 mm. **Ruler:** Elizabeth II **Subject:** Good Fortune and Prosperity

Date	Mintage	F12	VF20	XF40	MS60	MS63
2007P	5,994			PF65 15.00		

KM# 1917 25 CENTS
5.95 g., 0.999 Silver 0.1898 oz. ASW, 17.6 mm. **Ruler:** Elizabeth II **Subject:** 200th Anniversary of the Australian Holey Dollar & Dump

Date	Mintage	F12	VF20	XF40	MS60	MS63
2013 Proof	Est. 4000	—	—	—	—	10.00

KM# 404 50 CENTS
15.55 g., Copper-Nickel, 31.65 mm. **Ruler:** Elizabeth II **Obv:** Head with tiara right **Obv. Designer:** Ian Rank-Broadley **Rev:** Australian coat of arms with kangaroo and emu supporters **Rev. Designer:** Stuart Devlin **Edge:** Plain **Shape:** 12-sided

Date	Mintage	F12	VF20	XF40	MS60	MS63
2004	17,918,000	—	—	—	9.00	10.00
2004				PF65 25.00		
2005	30,000	—	—	—	25.00	40.00
Note: Issued as part of a PNC only						
2005	—			PF65 10.00		
2006	—	—	—	—	9.00	10.00
2006	—			PF65 25.00		
2007	—	—	—	—	1.00	1.50
2007	—			PF65 10.00		
2008	—	—	—	—	7.00	8.00
2008	—			PF65 10.00		
2009	—	—	—	—	7.00	8.00
2009	—			PF65 10.00		
2010	—	—	—	—	7.00	8.00
2010	—			PF65 10.00		
2011	—	—	—	—	7.00	8.00
2011	—			PF65 10.00		
2012	—	—	—	—	7.00	8.00

KM# 491.1a 50 CENTS
33.88 g., 0.9999 Gold 1.0821 oz. AGW, 31.65 mm. **Ruler:** Elizabeth II **Subject:** Federation Centennial **Obv:** Elizabeth II **Obv. Designer:** Ian Rank-Broadley **Rev:** Commonwealth arms above value

Date	Mintage	F12	VF20	XF40	MS60	MS63
2001B	650			PF65 1,950		

KM# 491.1 50 CENTS
15.55 g., Copper-Nickel, 31.65 mm. **Ruler:** Elizabeth II **Subject:** Centenary of Federation, 1901-2001 **Obv:** Head with tiara right **Obv. Designer:** Ian Rank-Broadley **Rev:** Commonwealth coat of arms **Edge:** Plain **Shape:** 12-sided **Note:** Prev. KM#491.

Date	Mintage	F12	VF20	XF40	MS60	MS63
2001B	43,149,600	—	—	—	5.00	6.00
2001B				PF65 40.00		

KM# 491.2 50 CENTS
15.55 g., Copper-Nickel, 31.65 mm. **Ruler:** Elizabeth II **Subject:** Federation Centennial **Obv:** Elizabeth II right **Obv. Designer:** Ian Rank-Broadley **Rev:** Multicolor arms above value **Edge:** Plain **Shape:** 12-sided

Date	Mintage	F12	VF20	XF40	MS60	MS63
2001B	60,000			PF65 50.00		

KM# 491.2a 50 CENTS
15.55 g., Copper-Nickel, 31.65 mm. **Ruler:** Elizabeth II **Subject:** Centenary of Federation, 1901-2001 **Obv:** Head with tiara right **Obv. Designer:** Ian Rank-Broadley **Rev:** Multicolored Commonwealth coat of arms **Edge:** Plain **Shape:** 12-sided **Note:** Prev. KM#491a.

Date	Mintage	F12	VF20	XF40	MS60	MS63
2001B	—			PF65 50.00		

KM# 533 50 CENTS
15.55 g., Copper-Nickel, 31.65 mm. **Ruler:** Elizabeth II **Subject:** Centennial - Norfolk Island Federation **Obv:** Head with tiara right **Obv. Designer:** Ian Rank-Broadley **Rev:** Norfolk Island coat of arms **Edge:** Plain **Shape:** 12-sided

Date	Mintage	F12	VF20	XF40	MS60	MS63
2001B	2,000,000	—	—	—	6.00	15.00
2001B				PF65 70.00		

KM# 535 50 CENTS
16.89 g., 0.999 Silver 0.5389 oz. ASW, 32.1 mm. **Ruler:** Elizabeth II **Subject:** Year of the Snake **Obv:** Head right **Obv. Designer:** Ian Rank-Broadley **Rev:** Snake with eggs **Edge:** Plain

Date	Mintage	F12	VF20	XF40	MS60	MS63
2001	500,000	—	—	—	—	22.00
2001P	5,000			PF65 65.00		

KM# 551 50 CENTS
15.55 g., Copper-Nickel, 31.65 mm. **Ruler:** Elizabeth II **Series:** Centenary of Federation - New South Wales **Obv:** Head with tiara right **Obv. Designer:** Ian Rank-Broadley **Rev:** New South Wales state arms **Edge:** Plain **Shape:** 12-sided

Date	Mintage	F12	VF20	XF40	MS60	MS63
2001	3,000,000	—	—	—	6.00	7.00
2001				PF65 40.00		

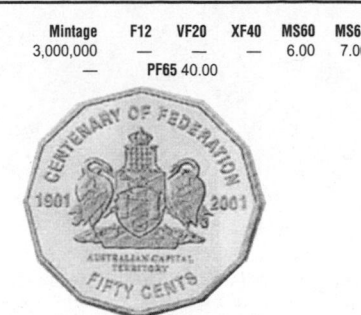

KM# 553 50 CENTS
15.55 g., Copper-Nickel, 31.65 mm. **Ruler:** Elizabeth II **Series:** Centenary of Federation - Australian Capital Territory **Obv:** Head right **Obv. Designer:** Ian Rank-Broadley **Rev:** Australian Capital Territory arms **Edge:** Plain **Shape:** 12-sided

Date	Mintage	F12	VF20	XF40	MS60	MS63
2001	2,000,000	—	—	—	6.00	9.00
2001				PF65 40.00		

KM# 555 50 CENTS
15.55 g., Copper-Nickel, 31.65 mm. **Ruler:** Elizabeth II **Series:** Centenary of Federation - Queensland **Obv:** Head with tiara right **Obv. Designer:** Ian Rank-Broadley **Rev:** Queensland state arms **Edge:** Plain **Shape:** 12-sided

Date	Mintage	F12	VF20	XF40	MS60	MS63
2001	2,300,000	—	—	—	6.00	9.00
2001				PF65 40.00		

KM# 557 50 CENTS
15.55 g., Copper-Nickel, 31.65 mm. **Ruler:** Elizabeth II **Series:** Centenary of Federation - Victoria **Obv:** Head with tiara right **Obv. Designer:** Ian Rank-Broadley **Rev:** Victoria state arms **Edge:** Plain **Shape:** 12-sided

Date	Mintage	F12	VF20	XF40	MS60	MS63
2001	2,800,000	—	—	—	6.00	8.00
2001				PF65 40.00		

KM# 559 50 CENTS
15.55 g., Copper-Nickel, 31.65 mm. **Ruler:** Elizabeth II **Series:** Centenary of Federation - Northern Territory **Obv:** Head with tiara right **Obv. Designer:** Ian Rank-Broadley **Rev:** Northern Territory state arms **Edge:** Plain **Shape:** 12-sided

Date	Mintage	F12	VF20	XF40	MS60	MS63
2001	2,100,000	—	—	—	6.00	10.00
2001				PF65 50.00		

KM# 561 50 CENTS
15.55 g., Copper-Nickel, 31.65 mm. **Ruler:** Elizabeth II **Series:** Centenary of Federation - South Australia **Obv:** Head with tiara right **Obv. Designer:** Ian Rank-Broadley **Rev:** South Australia state arms **Edge:** Plain **Shape:** 12-sided

Date	Mintage	F12	VF20	XF40	MS60	MS63
2001	2,400,000	—	—	—	6.00	20.00
2001			PF65 60.00			

KM# 563 50 CENTS
15.55 g., Copper-Nickel, 31.65 mm. **Ruler:** Elizabeth II **Series:** Centenary of Federation - Western Australia **Obv:** Head with tiara right **Obv. Designer:** Ian Rank-Broadley **Rev:** Western Australia state arms **Edge:** Plain **Shape:** 12-sided

Date	Mintage	F12	VF20	XF40	MS60	MS63
2001	2,400,000	—	—	—	6.00	15.00
2001			PF65 50.00			

KM# 565 50 CENTS
15.55 g., Copper-Nickel, 31.65 mm. **Ruler:** Elizabeth II **Series:** Centenary of Federation - Tasmania **Obv:** Head with tiara right **Obv. Designer:** Ian Rank-Broadley **Rev:** Tasmania state arms **Edge:** Plain **Shape:** 12-sided

Date	Mintage	F12	VF20	XF40	MS60	MS63
2001	2,200,000	—	—	—	6.00	10.00
2001	—		PF65 50.00			

KM# 694 50 CENTS
15.55 g., Copper-Nickel, 31.65 mm. **Ruler:** Elizabeth II **Obv:** Head with tiara right **Obv. Designer:** Ian Rank-Broadley **Rev:** Koala, Lorikeet (bird) and Wombat **Rev. Designer:** John Serranno & Vladimir Gottwald **Edge:** Plain **Shape:** 12-sided

Date	Mintage	F12	VF20	XF40	MS60	MS63
2001	—		PF65 9.00			
2004B	10,577,000	—	—	—	3.00	5.00

KM# 602 50 CENTS
15.55 g., Copper-Nickel, 31.65 mm. **Ruler:** Elizabeth II **Subject:** The Outback Region **Obv:** Head right **Obv. Designer:** Ian Rank-Broadley **Rev:** Windmill **Rev. Designer:** Wojciech Pietranik **Edge:** Plain **Shape:** 12-sided

Date	Mintage	F12	VF20	XF40	MS60	MS63
2002B	11,507,000	—	—	—	6.00	7.00
2002B	39,000		PF65 25.00			

KM# 645 50 CENTS
15.55 g., Copper-Nickel, 31.65 mm. **Ruler:** Elizabeth II **Subject:** Queen's 50th Anniversary of Accession **Obv:** Head right **Rev:** Crown and star **Rev. Designer:** Peter Soobik & Wojciech Pietranik **Shape:** 12-sided

Date	Mintage	F12	VF20	XF40	MS60	MS63
2002B	32,102	—	—	—	30.00	60.00

Note: Issued only in PNC cover

KM# 645a 50 CENTS
18.24 g., 0.999 Silver 0.5821 oz. ASW, 31.65 mm. **Ruler:** Elizabeth II **Subject:** Queen's 50th Anniversary of Accession **Obv:** Head right **Rev:** Crown and star **Rev. Designer:** Peter Soobik & Wojciech Pietranik **Shape:** 12-sided

Date	Mintage	F12	VF20	XF40	MS60	MS63
2002B	13,500		PF65 60.00			

KM# 404a 50 CENTS
18.24 g., 0.9999 Silver 0.5826 oz. ASW, 31.65 mm. **Ruler:** Elizabeth II **Obv:** Head with tiara right **Obv. Designer:** Ian Rank-Broadley **Rev:** Arms and value **Rev. Designer:** Stuart Devlin **Edge:** Plain **Shape:** 12-sided

Date	Mintage	F12	VF20	XF40	MS60	MS63
2003B	6,500		PF65 35.00			
2004B	6,500		PF65 35.00			
2005B	6,500		PF65 35.00			
2006B	—		PF65 35.00			
2007B	—		PF65 35.00			
2008B	—		PF65 35.00			
2009B	—		PF65 35.00			
2010B	—		PF65 35.00			
2011B	6,000		PF65 35.00			
2013B	5,000		PF65 70.00			

KM# 689a 50 CENTS
15.55 g., 0.999 Silver 0.4962 oz. ASW, 31.65 mm. **Ruler:** Elizabeth II **Obv:** Head right **Rev:** Value within circle of volunteer activities

Date	Mintage	F12	VF20	XF40	MS60	MS63
2003B	6,500		PF65 45.00			

KM# 689 50 CENTS
15.55 g., Copper-Nickel, 31.65 mm. **Ruler:** Elizabeth II **Obv:** Head right **Obv. Designer:** Ian Rank-Broadley **Rev:** Value within circle of volunteer activities **Rev. Designer:** Vladimir Gottwald **Edge:** Plain **Shape:** 12-sided

Date	Mintage	F12	VF20	XF40	MS60	MS63
2003B	13,927,000	—	—	—	4.50	5.00
2003B	—		PF65 20.00			

KM# 799 50 CENTS
14.09 g., Aluminum-Bronze, 31.51 mm. **Ruler:** Elizabeth II **Subject:** 50th Anniversary of the Coronation of Elizabeth II **Obv:** Head with tiara right **Obv. Designer:** Ian Rank-Broadley **Rev:** Crown, Federation star, dates **Rev. Designer:** Peter Soobik & Wojciech Pietranik **Edge:** Plain **Shape:** 12-sided

Date	Mintage	F12	VF20	XF40	MS60	MS63
2003	65,003	—	—	—	35.00	40.00

KM# 799a 50 CENTS
18.24 g., 0.999 Silver 0.5821 oz. ASW, 31.51 mm. **Ruler:** Elizabeth II **Subject:** 50th Anniversary of the Coronation of Elizabeth II **Obv:** Head with tiara right **Obv. Designer:** Ian Rank-Broadley **Rev:** Crown, Federation star, dates **Rev. Designer:** Peter Soobik & Wojciech Pietranik **Edge:** Plain **Shape:** 12-sided

Date	Mintage	F12	VF20	XF40	MS60	MS63
2003	6,967		PF65 60.00			

KM# 694a 50 CENTS
18.24 g., 0.999 Silver 0.5821 oz. ASW, 31.65 mm. **Ruler:** Elizabeth II **Obv:** Head with tiara right **Rev:** Wombat, lorikeet and koala **Rev. Designer:** John Serranno & Vladimir Gottwald **Edge:** Plain **Shape:** 12-sided

Date	Mintage	F12	VF20	XF40	MS60	MS63
2004B	8,203		PF65 75.00			

KM# 746 50 CENTS
15.55 g., Copper-Nickel, 31.65 mm. **Ruler:** Elizabeth II **Obv:** Head with tiara right **Obv. Designer:** Ian Rank-Broadley **Rev:** Military cemetery scene **Rev. Designer:** Wojciech Pietranik **Edge:** Plain **Shape:** 12-sided

Date	Mintage	F12	VF20	XF40	MS60	MS63
2005B	11,033,000	—	—	—	3.00	4.00
2005B	—		PF65 20.00			

KM# 746a 50 CENTS
18.24 g., 0.999 Silver 0.5821 oz. ASW, 31.65 mm. **Ruler:** Elizabeth II **Obv:** Head with tiara right **Obv. Designer:** Ian Rank-Broadley **Rev:** Military cemetery scene **Rev. Designer:** Wojciech Pietranik **Edge:** Plain **Shape:** 12-sided

Date	Mintage	F12	VF20	XF40	MS60	MS63
2005B	6,500		PF65 38.00			

KM# 746b 50 CENTS
33.63 g., 0.9999 Gold 1.0742 oz. AGW, 31.65 mm. **Ruler:** Elizabeth II **Obv:** Head with tiara right **Obv. Designer:** Ian Rank-Broadley **Rev:** Military cemetery scene **Rev. Designer:** Wojciech Pietranik **Edge:** Plain **Shape:** 12-sided

Date	Mintage	F12	VF20	XF40	MS60	MS63
2005B	650		PF65 1,950			

KM# 769 50 CENTS
15.55 g., Copper-Nickel, 31.65 mm. **Ruler:** Elizabeth II **Subject:** Commonweath Games, Secondary School Design Competition **Obv:** Head with tiara right **Obv. Designer:** Ian Rank-Broadley **Rev:** Athletes **Rev. Designer:** Kelly Just

Date	Mintage	F12	VF20	XF40	MS60	MS63
2005	20,500,000	—	—	—	2.50	3.50
2005	—		PF65 65.00				

KM# 67a 50 CENTS
18.24 g., 0.999 Silver 0.5821 oz. ASW, 31.51 mm. **Ruler:** Elizabeth II **Obv:** Young bust right **Obv. Designer:** Arnold Machin **Rev:** Australian coat of arms **Rev. Designer:** Stuart Devlin **Edge:** Reeded

Date	Mintage	F12	VF20	XF40	MS60	MS63
2006	6,500		PF65 65.00				

KM# 770 50 CENTS
15.55 g., Copper-Nickel, 31.65 mm. **Ruler:** Elizabeth II **Subject:** Basketball **Obv:** Head with tiara right **Obv. Legend:** ELIZABETH II - AUSTRALIA **Obv. Designer:** Ian Rank-Broadley **Rev:** Basketball player shooting basket, Melbourne 2006 logo at left **Rev. Designer:** Wojciech Pietranik **Rev. Legend:** XVIII COMMONWEALTH GAMES **Shape:** 12-sided

Date	Mintage	F12	VF20	XF40	MS60	MS63
2006	5,002	—	—	—	8.50	10.00

KM# 771 50 CENTS
15.55 g., Copper-Nickel, 31.65 mm. **Ruler:** Elizabeth II **Subject:** Hockey **Obv:** Head with tiara right **Obv. Legend:** ELIZABETH II - AUSTRALIA **Obv. Designer:** Ian Rank-Broadley **Rev:** Hockey player hitting puck, Melboune 2006 logo at upper left **Rev. Designer:** Wojciech Pietranik **Rev. Legend:** XVIII COMMONWEALTH GAMES **Shape:** 12-sided

Date	Mintage	F12	VF20	XF40	MS60	MS63
2006	4,082	—	—	—	8.50	10.00

KM# 772 50 CENTS
15.55 g., Copper-Nickel, 31.65 mm. **Ruler:** Elizabeth II **Subject:** Shooting **Obv:** Head with tiara right **Obv. Legend:** ELIZABETH II - AUSTRALIA **Obv. Designer:** Ian Rank-Broadley **Rev:** Shooter, Melbourne 2006 logo at upper right **Rev. Designer:** Wojciech Pietranik **Rev. Legend:** XVIII COMMONWEALTH GAMES **Shape:** 12-sided

Date	Mintage	F12	VF20	XF40	MS60	MS63
2006	21,070	—	—	—	8.50	10.00

KM# 773 50 CENTS
15.55 g., Copper-Nickel, 31.65 mm. **Ruler:** Elizabeth II **Subject:** Weightlifting **Obv:** Head with tiara right **Obv. Legend:** ELIZABETH II - AUSTRALIA **Obv. Designer:** Ian Rank Broadley **Rev:** Weightlifter holding barbells above head, Melbourne 2006 logo at left **Rev. Designer:** Wojciech Pietranik **Rev. Legend:** XVIII COMMONWEALTH GAMES **Shape:** 12-sided

Date	Mintage	F12	VF20	XF40	MS60	MS63
2006	22,332	—	—	—	8.50	10.00

KM# 774 50 CENTS
15.55 g., Copper-Nickel, 31.65 mm. **Ruler:** Elizabeth II **Subject:** Gymnastics **Obv:** Head with tiara right **Obv. Legend:** ELIZABETH II - AUSTRALIA **Obv. Designer:** Ian Rank-Broadley **Rev:** Gymnast standing with right leg up, Melbourne 2006 logo at left **Rev. Designer:** Wojciech Pietranik **Rev. Legend:** XVIII COMMONWEALTH GAMES **Edge:** Plain **Shape:** 12-sided

Date	Mintage	F12	VF20	XF40	MS60	MS63
2006	3,000	—	—	—	8.50	10.00

KM# 775 50 CENTS
15.55 g., Copper-Nickel, 31.65 mm. **Ruler:** Elizabeth II **Subject:** Rugby 7's **Obv:** Head with tiara right **Obv. Legend:** ELIZABETH II - AUSTRALIA **Obv. Designer:** Ian Rank-Broadley **Rev:** Rugby player running right, Melbourne 2006 logo at upper left **Rev. Designer:** Wojciech Pietranik **Rev. Legend:** XVIII COMMONWEALTH GAMES **Shape:** 12-sided

Date	Mintage	F12	VF20	XF40	MS60	MS63
2006	24,427	—	—	—	8.50	10.00

KM# 776 50 CENTS
15.55 g., Copper-Nickel, 31.65 mm. **Ruler:** Elizabeth II **Subject:** Cycling **Obv:** Head with tiara right **Obv. Legend:** ELIZABETH II - AUSTRALIA **Obv. Designer:** Ian Rank-Broadley **Rev:** Cyclist heading right, Melbourne 2006 logo at upper right **Rev. Designer:** Wojciech Pietranik **Rev. Legend:** XVIII COMMONWEALTH GAMES **Shape:** 12-sided

Date	Mintage	F12	VF20	XF40	MS60	MS63
2006	22,861	—	—	—	8.50	10.00

KM# 777 50 CENTS
15.55 g., Copper-Nickel, 31.65 mm. **Ruler:** Elizabeth II **Subject:** Athletics **Obv:** Head with tiara right **Obv. Legend:** ELIZABETH II - AUSTRALIA **Obv. Designer:** Ian Rank-Broadley **Rev:** Runner right, Melbourne 2006 logo at lower right **Rev. Designer:** Wojciech Pietranik **Rev. Legend:** XVIII COMMONWEALTH GAMES **Shape:** 12-sided

Date	Mintage	F12	VF20	XF40	MS60	MS63
2006	22,475	—	—	—	8.50	10.00

KM# 778 50 CENTS
15.55 g., Copper-Nickel, 31.65 mm. **Ruler:** Elizabeth II **Subject:** Triathlon **Obv:** Head with tiara right **Obv. Legend:** ELIZABETH II - AUSRALIA **Obv. Designer:** Ian Rank-Broadley **Rev:** Bicycle, runner, Melbourne 2006 logo below **Rev. Designer:** Wojciech Pietranik **Rev. Legend:** XVIII COMMONWEALTH GAMES **Shape:** 12-sided

Date	Mintage	F12	VF20	XF40	MS60	MS63
2006	22,302	—	—	—	8.50	10.00

KM# 779 50 CENTS
15.55 g., Copper-Nickel, 31.65 mm. **Ruler:** Elizabeth II **Subject:** Netball **Obv:** Head with tiara right **Obv. Legend:** ELIZABETH II - AUSTRALIA **Obv. Designer:** Ian Rank-Broadley **Rev:** Player shooting basket, Melbourne 2006 logo at upper left **Rev. Designer:** Wojciech Pietranik **Rev. Legend:** XVIII COMMONWEALTH GAMES **Shape:** 12-sided

Date	Mintage	F12	VF20	XF40	MS60	MS63
2006	22,432	—	—	—	8.50	10.00

KM# 780 50 CENTS
15.55 g., Copper-Nickel, 31.65 mm. **Ruler:** Elizabeth II **Subject:** Table tennis **Obv:** Head with tiara right **Obv. Legend:** ELIZABETH II - AUSTRALIA **Obv. Designer:** Ian Rank-Broadley **Rev:** Player hitting ball, Melbourne 2006 logo below **Rev. Designer:** Wojciech Pietranik **Rev. Legend:** XVIII COMMONWEALTH GAMES **Shape:** 12-sided

Date	Mintage	F12	VF20	XF40	MS60	MS63
2006	22,070	—	—	—	8.50	10.00

KM# 781 50 CENTS

15.55 g., Copper-Nickel, 31.65 mm. **Ruler:** Elizabeth II **Subject:** Aquatics **Obv:** Head with tiara right **Obv. Legend:** ELIZABETH II - AUSTRALIA **Obv. Designer:** Ian Rank-Broadley **Rev:** Swimmer, Melbourne 2006 logo **Rev. Designer:** Wojciech Pietranik **Rev. Legend:** XVIII COMMONWEALTH GAMES **Shape:** 12-sided

Date	Mintage	F12	VF20	XF40	MS60	MS63
2006	31,702	—	—	—	8.50	10.00

KM# 801 50 CENTS

15.55 g., Copper-Nickel, 31.65 mm. **Ruler:** Elizabeth II **Subject:** 80th Birthday of Queen Elizabeth II **Obv:** Head with tiara right **Obv. Designer:** Ian Rank-Broadley **Rev:** Royal Cipher **Rev. Designer:** Stuart Devlin **Shape:** 12-sided

Date	Mintage	F12	VF20	XF40	MS60	MS63
2006	28,191	—	—	—	45.00	60.00

KM# 801a 50 CENTS

18.24 g., 0.999 Silver 0.5821 oz. ASW, 31.65 mm. **Ruler:** Elizabeth II **Subject:** 80th Birthday of Queen Elizabeth II **Obv:** Head with tiara right **Obv. Designer:** Ian Rank-Broadley **Rev:** Crowned Royal Cipher on large 80, border of alternating British and Australian flags **Rev. Designer:** Stuart Devlin **Shape:** 12-sided

Date	Mintage	F12	VF20	XF40	MS60	MS63
2006	7,500		PF65 85.00			

KM# 802 50 CENTS

15.55 g., Copper-Nickel, 31.65 mm. **Ruler:** Elizabeth II **Subject:** Visit of Queen Elizabeth II **Obv:** Head with tiara right **Obv. Designer:** Ian Rank-Broadley **Rev:** Australian map and world globe **Rev. Designer:** Stuart Devlin **Shape:** 12-sided

Date	Mintage	F12	VF20	XF40	MS60	MS63
2006	—	—	—	—	30.00	45.00

KM# 802a 50 CENTS

18.24 g., 0.999 Silver 0.5821 oz. ASW, 31.65 mm. **Ruler:** Elizabeth II **Subject:** Visit of Queen Elizabeth II **Obv:** Head with tiara right **Obv. Designer:** Ian Rank-Broadley **Rev:** Australian map and world globe **Rev. Designer:** Stuart Devlin **Shape:** 12-sided

Date	Mintage	F12	VF20	XF40	MS60	MS63
2006	7,500		PF65 90.00			

KM# 821 50 CENTS

13.28 g., 0.800 Silver 0.3394 oz. ASW, 31.51 mm. **Ruler:** Elizabeth II **Obv:** Head with tiara right **Obv. Designer:** Ian Rank-Broadley **Rev:** Australian coat of arms **Rev. Designer:** Stuart Devlin **Edge:** Reeded

Date	Mintage	F12	VF20	XF40	MS60	MS63
2006	—		PF65 70.00			

KM# 821a 50 CENTS

25.30 g., 0.999 Gold 0.8074 oz. AGW, 31.51 mm. **Ruler:** Elizabeth II **Obv:** Head with tiara right **Obv. Designer:** Ian Rank-Broadley **Rev:** Australian coat of arms **Rev. Designer:** Stuart Devlin **Edge:** Reeded

Date	Mintage	F12	VF20	XF40	MS60	MS63
2006	300		PF65 1,500			

KM# 1001 50 CENTS

15.55 g., Copper-Nickel, 31.65 mm. **Ruler:** Elizabeth II **Subject:** XVIII COMMONWEALTH GAMES **Obv:** Head with tiara right **Obv. Legend:** ELIZABETH II - AUSTRALIA **Obv. Designer:** Ian Rank-Broadley **Rev:** Squash player, Melbourne 2006 logo **Rev. Designer:** Wojciech Pietranik **Edge:** Plain **Shape:** 12-sided

Date	Mintage	F12	VF20	XF40	MS60	MS63
2006		—	—	—	12.50	15.00

KM# 1002 50 CENTS

15.55 g., Copper-Nickel, 31.65 mm. **Ruler:** Elizabeth II **Subject:** XVIII COMMONWEALTH GAMES **Obv:** Head with tiara right **Obv. Legend:** ELIZABETH II - AUSTRALIA **Obv. Designer:** Ian Rank-Broadley **Rev:** Lawn bowler, Melbourne 2006 logo **Rev. Designer:** Wojciech Pietranik **Edge:** Plain **Shape:** 12-sided

Date	Mintage	F12	VF20	XF40	MS60	MS63
2006	22,602	—	—	—	12.50	15.00

KM# 1003 50 CENTS

15.55 g., Copper-Nickel, 31.65 mm. **Ruler:** Elizabeth II **Subject:** XVIII COMMONWEALTH GAMES **Obv:** Head with tiara right **Obv. Legend:** ELIZABETH II - AUSTRALIA **Obv. Designer:** Ian Rank-Broadley **Rev:** Boxer, Melbourne 2006 logo **Rev. Designer:** Wojciech Pietranik **Edge:** Plain **Shape:** 12-sided

Date	Mintage	F12	VF20	XF40	MS60	MS63
2006		—	—	—	12.50	15.00

KM# 1004 50 CENTS

Aluminum-Bronze, 30 mm. **Ruler:** Elizabeth II **Obv:** Head with tiara right **Obv. Legend:** ELIZABETH II - AUSTRALIA **Obv. Designer:** Ian Rank-Broadley **Rev:** Everage head facing, multicolor **Rev. Legend:** DAME EDNA EVERAGE - 50TH ANNIVERSARY

Date	Mintage	F12	VF20	XF40	MS60	MS63
ND-2006P	—	—	—	—	20.00	25.00

KM# 1570 50 CENTS

15.55 g., Copper-Nickel, 31.65 mm. **Ruler:** Elizabeth II **Subject:** Commonwealth Games **Rev:** Badminton

Date	Mintage	F12	VF20	XF40	MS60	MS63
2006	—	—	—	—	8.50	10.00

KM# 1041 50 CENTS

15.55 g., Copper-Nickel, 31.65 mm. **Ruler:** Elizabeth II **Subject:** Elizabeth and Philip Wedding Anniversary **Rev:** Profile portraits and diamond at center of circle of trumpets **Rev. Designer:** Stuart Devlin

Date	Mintage	F12	VF20	XF40	MS60	MS63
2007B	60,030	—	—	—	15.00	18.00

KM# 1049 50 CENTS

15.55 g., Copper-Nickel, 31.65 mm. **Ruler:** Elizabeth II **Subject:** Scouting Centennial in Australia **Rev:** Australian Scout Emblem **Rev. Designer:** C. Goodall

Date	Mintage	F12	VF20	XF40	MS60	MS63
2008	49,517	—	—	—	10.00	12.00

KM# 1062 50 CENTS

15.55 g., Copper-Nickel, 31.65 mm. **Ruler:** Elizabeth II **Subject:** 25th Anniversary Australia's Win of the America's Cup **Rev:** Yacht Australia II sailing left **Shape:** 12-sided

Date	Mintage	F12	VF20	XF40	MS60	MS63
2008	32,916	—	—	—	15.00	18.00

KM# 1100 50 CENTS

15.55 g., 0.999 Silver 0.4962 oz. ASW, 36.6 mm. **Ruler:** Elizabeth II **Subject:** Great Barrier Reef **Obv:** Head right **Obv. Designer:** Ian rank-Broadley **Rev:** Lion fish, multicolor **Edge:** reeded

Date	Mintage	F12	VF20	XF40	MS60	MS63
2009P	10,000		PF65 75.00			

KM# 1101 50 CENTS

15.55 g., 0.999 Silver 0.4962 oz. ASW, 36.6 mm. **Ruler:** Elizabeth II **Subject:** Great Barrier Reef **Obv:** Head right **Obv. Designer:** Ian Rank-Broadley **Rev:** Leafy Sea Dragon, multicolor **Edge:** Reeded

Date	Mintage	F12	VF20	XF40	MS60	MS63
2009P	10,000		PF65 75.00			

KM# 1102 50 CENTS
15.55 g., 0.999 Silver 0.4962 oz. ASW, 36.6 mm. **Ruler:**
Elizabeth II **Subject:** Great Barrier Reef **Rev:** Sea turtle,
multicolor

Date	Mintage	F12	VF20	XF40	MS60	MS63
2009P	—	PF65 75.00				

KM# 1432 50 CENTS
15.55 g., Copper-Nickel, 31.65 mm. **Ruler:** Elizabeth II
Subject: Moon Landing 40th Anniversary **Rev:** Earth, moon
and orbiter **Rev. Designer:** C. Goodall

Date	Mintage	F12	VF20	XF40	MS60	MS63
2009C	—	—	—	—	—	10.00

KM# 1571a 50 CENTS
18.24 g., 0.999 Silver 0.5821 oz. ASW, 31.65 mm. **Ruler:**
Elizabeth II **Subject:** Prince William and Catherine Middelton
engagement **Rev:** Bunch of roses, gilt; Royal arms of Prince
William below **Shape:** 12-sided

Date	Mintage	F12	VF20	XF40	MS60	MS63
2010	—	PF65 60.00				

KM# 1328 50 CENTS
15.55 g., 0.999 Silver 0.4962 oz. ASW, 36.6 mm. **Ruler:**
Elizabeth II **Subject:** Great Barrier Reef **Obv:** Head right **Obv.
Designer:** Ian Rank Broadley **Rev:** Clownfish, multicolor

Date	Mintage	F12	VF20	XF40	MS60	MS63
2010P	—	PF65 60.00				

KM# 1329 50 CENTS
15.57 g., 0.999 Silver 0.497 oz. ASW, 36.6 mm. **Ruler:**

Elizabeth II **Subject:** Great Barrier Reef **Rev:** Big belly sea
horse in multicolor

Date	Mintage	F12	VF20	XF40	MS60	MS63
2010P	—	PF65 75.00				

KM# 1389 50 CENTS
15.55 g., 0.999 Silver 0.4962 oz. ASW, 36.6 mm. **Ruler:**
Elizabeth II **Subject:** Great Barrier Reef - Morey Eel **Obv:** Hear
right **Rev:** Tessellate Moray Eel, multicolor

Date	Mintage	F12	VF20	XF40	MS60	MS63
2010P	—	PF65 86.00				

KM# 1450 50 CENTS
15.56 g., 0.999 Silver 0.4965 oz. ASW **Ruler:** Elizabeth II **Rev:**
Australian Sugar Glider, multicolor

Date	Mintage	F12	VF20	XF40	MS60	MS63
2010P	—	PF65 45.00				

KM# 1456 50 CENTS
15.56 g., 0.999 Silver 0.4965 oz. ASW **Ruler:** Elizabeth II **Rev:**
Australian kangaroo, multicolor

Date	Mintage	F12	VF20	XF40	MS60	MS63
2010P	—	PF65 30.00				

KM# 1493 50 CENTS
15.50 g., 0.999 Silver 0.4946 oz. ASW, 36.6 mm. **Ruler:**
Elizabeth II **Rev:** Dingo

Date	Mintage	F12	VF20	XF40	MS60	MS63
2010	—	PF65 50.00				

KM# 1500 50 CENTS
15.55 g., Copper-Nickel, 31.65 mm. **Ruler:** Elizabeth II
Subject: Australia Day **Shape:** 12-sided

Date	Mintage	F12	VF20	XF40	MS60	MS63
2010	—	—	—	—	2.50	4.50

KM# 1501 50 CENTS
15.55 g., Copper-Nickel, 31.65 mm. **Ruler:** Elizabeth II **Subject:**
Melbourne Cup, 150th Anniversary **Rev:** Horses racing right
passing finish pole **Shape:** 12-sided

Date	Mintage	F12	VF20	XF40	MS60	MS63
2010	—	—	—	—	2.50	4.50

KM# 1519 50 CENTS
18.24 g., 0.999 Silver 0.5821 oz. ASW, 31.5 mm. **Ruler:**
Elizabeth II **Subject:** Melbourne Cup, 150th race **Rev:** Trophy,
partially gilt **Shape:** 12-sided

Date	Mintage	F12	VF20	XF40	MS60	MS63
2010	—	PF65 80.00				

KM# 1520 50 CENTS
18.24 g., 0.999 Silver 0.5821 oz. ASW, 31.5 mm. **Ruler:**
Elizabeth II **Subject:** Melbourne Cup **Rev:** Horse and rider,
partially gilt **Shape:** 12-sided

Date	Mintage	F12	VF20	XF40	MS60	MS63
2010	—	PF65 80.00				

KM# 1571 50 CENTS
15.55 g., Copper-Nickel, 31.65 mm. **Ruler:** Elizabeth II
Subject: Prince William and Catherine Middelton engagement
Rev: Bundle of roses, Royal arms of Prince William below
Shape: 12-sided

Date	Mintage	F12	VF20	XF40	MS60	MS63
2010	—	—	—	—	4.00	5.00

KM# 1525a 50 CENTS
18.24 g., Silver, 31.5 mm. **Ruler:** Elizabeth II **Subject:** Australia
day **Rev:** Circle of people clasping hands, partially gilt **Shape:**
12-sided

Date	Mintage	F12	VF20	XF40	MS60	MS63
2011	—	PF65 40.00				

KM# 1567 50 CENTS
15.55 g., Copper-Nickel, 31.65 mm. **Ruler:** Elizabeth II
Subject: Royal Wedding **Rev:** Catherine and William busts left
Shape: 12-sided

Date	Mintage	F12	VF20	XF40	MS60	MS63
2011	—				3.50	5.00

KM# 1567a 50 CENTS
18.24 g., 0.999 Silver 0.5821 oz. ASW, 31.65 mm. **Ruler:**
Elizabeth II **Subject:** Royal Wedding **Rev:** Catherine and
William busts left, gilt flower at bottom **Shape:** 12-sided

Date	Mintage	F12	VF20	XF40	MS60	MS63
2011	—	PF65 60.00				

KM# 1521 50 CENTS
15.55 g., Copper-Nickel, 31.65 mm. **Ruler:** Elizabeth II
Subject: National Service, 60th Anniversary **Shape:** 12-sided

Date	Mintage	F12	VF20	XF40	MS60	MS63
2011	—				4.00	5.00

KM# 1525 50 CENTS
15.55 g., Copper-Nickel, 31.5 mm. **Ruler:** Elizabeth II **Subject:**
Australia Day **Rev:** Circle of people clasping hands

Date	Mintage	F12	VF20	XF40	MS60	MS63
2011	—	—			4.00	5.00

KM# 1532 50 CENTS
15.55 g., 0.999 Silver 0.4962 oz. ASW, 36.6 mm. **Ruler:**
Elizabeth II **Subject:** Bush Baby **Rev:** Koala in color

Date	Mintage	F12	VF20	XF40	MS60	MS63
2011P	—	PF65 65.00				

KM# 1533 50 CENTS
15.55 g., 0.999 Silver 0.4962 oz. ASW **Ruler:** Elizabeth II
Subject: Bush Babies **Rev:** Bilby in color

Date	Mintage	F12	VF20	XF40	MS60	MS63
2011P	—	PF65 65.00				

KM# 1577 50 CENTS
15.59 g., 0.999 Silver 0.4975 oz. ASW, 36.6 mm. **Ruler:**
Elizabeth II **Subject:** Australian Sea Life - Starfish **Rev:**
Starfish in color **Rev. Designer:** Wade Robinson

Date	Mintage	F12	VF20	XF40	MS60	MS63
2011P	10,000	PF65 75.00				

KM# 1579 50 CENTS
15.59 g., 0.999 Silver 0.4975 oz. ASW, 36.6 mm. **Ruler:**
Elizabeth II **Subject:** Australian sea life - Hawksbill Turtle **Rev:**
Color turtle swimming right **Rev. Designer:** Wade Robinson

Date	Mintage	F12	VF20	XF40	MS60	MS63
2011P	10,000	PF65 70.00				

KM# 1624 50 CENTS
15.55 g., Copper-Nickel, 31.65 mm. **Ruler:** Elizabeth II
Subject: Triple Zero Code for Emergency, 50th Anniversary
Obv: Head with tiara right **Rev:** Telephone handset and 000,
in color **Shape:** 12-sided

Date	Mintage	F12	VF20	XF40	MS60	MS63
2011	—	—				20.00

KM# 404b 50 CENTS
15.55 g., Copper-Nickel, 31.65 mm. **Ruler:** Elizabeth II **Obv:**
Head with tiara right **Rev:** Australian coat-of-arms with
Kangaroo and Emu supporters all in color **Shape:** 12-sided

Date	Mintage	F12	VF20	XF40	MS60	MS63
2012	—	—	—	—	—	25.00

KM# 404c 50 CENTS
18.24 g., 0.999 Silver 0.5821 oz. ASW, 31.65 mm. **Ruler:**
Elizabeth II **Obv:** Head with tiara right **Rev:** Australian coat-
of-arms with Kangaroo and Emu supporters all gilt **Shape:**
12-sided

Date	Mintage	F12	VF20	XF40	MS60	MS63
2012	—	PF65 75.00				

KM# 1855 50 CENTS
15.50 g., Copper-Nickel, 31.5 mm. **Ruler:** Elizabeth II **Rev:**
Kokoda Campaign monument **Shape:** 12-sided

Date	Mintage	F12	VF20	XF40	MS60	MS63
2012	—				4.00	5.00

KM# 1578 50 CENTS
15.59 g., 0.999 Silver 0.4975 oz. ASW, 36.6 mm. **Ruler:**
Elizabeth II **Subject:** Australian sea life - Surgeonfish **Rev:**
Surgeonfish in blue, black and yellow colors **Rev. Designer:**
Wade Robinson

Date	Mintage	F12	VF20	XF40	MS60	MS63
2012P	10,000	PF65 75.00				

KM# 1697 50 CENTS
15.59 g., Silver, 36.6 mm. **Ruler:** Elizabeth II **Subject:**
Australian 2012 London Olympic Team **Obv:** Head with tiara
right **Rev:** Male runner, Syndey Harbor Birdge, Tower of
London images **Rev. Designer:** Wade Robinson

Date	Mintage	F12	VF20	XF40	MS60	MS63
2012P	750	PF65 45.00				

KM# 1712 50 CENTS
15.59 g., 0.999 Silver 0.4975 oz. ASW, 36.6 mm. **Ruler:**
Elizabeth II **Obv:** Head with tiara right **Rev:** Reef Octopus in
color **Rev. Designer:** Wade Robinson

Date	Mintage	F12	VF20	XF40	MS60	MS63
2012P	10,000	PF65 50.00				

KM# 1741 50 CENTS
15.55 g., Copper-Nickel, 31.65 mm. **Ruler:** Elizabeth II **Subject:**
Elizabeth II, 60th Anniversary **Obv:** Head with tiara right **Rev:**
State Crown and floral design **Shape:** 12-sided

Date	Mintage	F12	VF20	XF40	MS60	MS63
2012	—	—	—	—	10.00	15.00

KM# 1741a 50 CENTS
18.24 g., 0.999 Silver 0.5821 oz. ASW, 31.65 mm. **Ruler:**
Elizabeth II **Subject:** Elizabeth II, 60th Anniversary **Obv:** Head
with tiara right **Rev:** State Crown and floral **Shape:** 12-sided
Note: Illustration reduced.

Date	Mintage	F12	VF20	XF40	MS60	MS63
2012	—	PF65 75.00				

KM# 1744 50 CENTS
15.55 g., Copper-Nickel, 31.65 mm. **Ruler:** Elizabeth II
Subject: World War II, Bombing of Australia **Obv:** Head with

tiara right **Rev:** Map of Astralia with bombed sites highlighted **Shape:** 12-sided

Date	Mintage	F12	VF20	XF40	MS60	MS63
2012	—	—	—	—	7.50	15.00

KM# 1795 50 CENTS
15.55 g., 0.999 Silver 0.4962 oz. ASW, 36.6 mm. **Ruler:** Elizabeth II **Subject:** Love Koala **Rev:** Two koalas seated in color heart shape

Date	Mintage	F12	VF20	XF40	MS60	MS63
2012P	7,500	PF65 150				

KM# 1801 50 CENTS
15.50 g., 0.999 Silver 0.4946 oz. ASW, 36.6 mm. **Ruler:** Elizabeth II **Subject:** FIFA **Rev:** Soccer player in native costume

Date	Mintage	F12	VF20	XF40	MS60	MS63
2012P	—	PF65 60.00				

KM# 1816 50 CENTS
15.55 g., 0.999 Silver 0.4962 oz. ASW, 36.6 mm. **Ruler:** Elizabeth II **Subject:** Bush Babies - Lemur

Date	Mintage	F12	VF20	XF40	MS60	MS63
2012P	—	PF65 50.00				

KM# 1847 50 CENTS
15.56 g., 0.999 Silver 0.4965 oz. ASW, 36.6 mm. **Ruler:** Elizabeth II **Subject:** Australian Sea Life II, The Reef **Rev:** Manta Ray in color

Date	Mintage	F12	VF20	XF40	MS60	MS63
2012P	—	PF65 45.00				

KM# 1854 50 CENTS
15.55 g., Copper-Nickel, 31.5 mm. **Ruler:** Elizabeth II **Subject:** Australian Ballet, 50th Anniversary **Rev:** Two dancers **Shape:** 12-sided

Date	Mintage	F12	VF20	XF40	MS60	MS63
2012	—	—	—	—	4.00	5.00

KM# 1854a 50 CENTS
18.24 g., 0.999 Silver 0.5821 oz. ASW, 31.5 mm. **Ruler:** Elizabeth II **Subject:** Australian Ballet, 50th Anniversary **Rev:** Two dancers **Shape:** 12-sided

Date	Mintage	F12	VF20	XF40	MS60	MS63
2012	—	PF65 50.00				

KM# 1856 50 CENTS
15.50 g., Copper-Nickel, 31.5 mm. **Ruler:** Elizabeth II **Subject:** Bathurst Endurance Race **Rev:** Racecar and landscape

Date	Mintage	F12	VF20	XF40	MS60	MS63
2012	—	—	—	—	4.00	5.00

KM# 2037 50 CENTS
0.50 g., 0.9999 Gold AGW, 11.15 mm. **Ruler:** Elizabeth II **Subject:** Australian Miniature Money

Date	Mintage	F12	VF20	XF40	MS60	MS63
2012	Est. 2000	PF65 75.00				

KM# 2094a 50 CENTS
15.55 g., 0.999 Silver 0.4962 oz. ASW, 31.5 mm. **Ruler:** Elizabeth II **Subject:** Elizabeth II, 60th Anniversary of reign **Rev:** SIxty stylized crowns in circle **Shape:** 12-sided

Date	Mintage	F12	VF20	XF40	MS60	MS63
2013 Proof	—	—	—	—	—	15.00

KM# 404d 50 CENTS
33.63 g., 0.9999 Gold 1.0742 oz. AGW, 31.51 mm. **Ruler:** Elizabeth II **Obv:** Head with tiara right **Rev:** Arms with supporters, value below

Date	Mintage	F12	VF20	XF40	MS60	MS63
2013	500	PF65 1,950				

KM# 1817 50 CENTS
15.50 g., 0.999 Silver 0.4946 oz. ASW, 36.6 mm. **Ruler:** Elizabeth II **Subject:** Bush Babies - Kookaburra **Rev. Designer:** Elise Martinson

Date	Mintage	F12	VF20	XF40	MS60	MS63
2013P	—	PF65 50.00				

KM# 1818 50 CENTS
15.55 g., Copper-Nickel, 31.65 mm. **Ruler:** Elizabeth II **Subject:** Alesandra Stokic **Rev:** Surfer in wave

Date	Mintage	F12	VF20	XF40	MS60	MS63
2013	—	—	—	—	—	9.00

KM# 1914 50 CENTS
15.50 g., 0.999 Silver 0.4946 oz. ASW, 36.6 mm. **Ruler:** Elizabeth II **Subject:** Australian Bush Babies II - Wombat **Rev. Designer:** Elise Martinson

Date	Mintage	F12	VF20	XF40	MS60	MS63
2013	Est. 10000	PF65 50.00				

KM# 1915 50 CENTS
15.50 g., 0.999 Silver 0.4946 oz. ASW, 36.6 mm. **Ruler:** Elizabeth II **Subject:** Australian Bush Babies II - Platypus **Rev. Designer:** Elise Martinson

Date	Mintage	F12	VF20	XF40	MS60	MS63
2013	Est. 10000	PF65 50.00				

KM# 1923 50 CENTS
15.50 g., 0.999 Silver 0.4946 oz. ASW, 36.6 mm. **Ruler:** Elizabeth II **Subject:** Birds of Australia - Budgerigar **Rev. Designer:** Natasha Muhl

Date	Mintage	F12	VF20	XF40	MS60	MS63
2013 Proof	Est. 10000					

KM# 1924 50 CENTS
15.50 g., 0.999 Silver 0.4946 oz. ASW, 36.6 mm. **Ruler:** Elizabeth II **Subject:** Birds of Australia - Regent Bowerbird **Rev. Designer:** Natasha Muhl

Date	Mintage	F12	VF20	XF40	MS60	MS63
2013P Proof	Est. 10000	—	—	—	—	35.00

KM# 1815 50 CENTS
15.55 g., 0.999 Silver 0.4962 oz. ASW, 36.6 mm. **Ruler:** Elizabeth II **Subject:** Birds - Cockatoo

Date	Mintage	F12	VF20	XF40	MS60	MS63
2013P	—	PF65 50.00				

KM# 1925 50 CENTS
15.50 g., 0.999 Silver 0.4946 oz. ASW, 36.6 mm. **Ruler:** Elizabeth II **Subject:** Birds of Australia - Rainbow Lorikeet **Rev. Designer:** Natasha Muhl

Date	Mintage	F12	VF20	XF40	MS60	MS63
2013	Est. 10000	PF65 50.00				

KM# 1926 50 CENTS
15.50 g., 0.999 Silver 0.4946 oz. ASW, 36.6 mm. **Ruler:** Elizabeth II **Subject:** Newborn Baby **Rev. Designer:** Aleysha Howarth

Date	Mintage	F12	VF20	XF40	MS60	MS63
2013	—	PF65 35.00				

KM# 1960 50 CENTS
15.55 g., Copper-Nickel, 31.51 mm. **Ruler:** Elizabeth II **Subject:** 100 Years of Commonwealth **Rev. Designer:** Aaron Baggio

Date	Mintage	F12	VF20	XF40	MS60	MS63
2013	—	—	—	—	4.00	5.00

KM# 1963 50 CENTS
15.55 g., Copper-Nickel, 31.51 mm. **Ruler:** Elizabeth II **Subject:** Centenary of Australian Banknotes

Date	Mintage	F12	VF20	XF40	MS60	MS63
2013	—	—	—	—	4.00	5.00

KM# 2011 50 CENTS
15.55 g., Copper-Nickel, 31.65 mm. **Ruler:** Elizabeth II **Subject:** Year of the Snake **Edge:** Snake **Shape:** 12 sided

Date	Mintage	F12	VF20	XF40	MS60	MS63
2013	—	—	—	—	4.00	5.00

KM# 2020 50 CENTS
15.37 g., Copper-Nickel, 31.5 mm. **Ruler:** Elizabeth II **Subject:** Year of the Dragon **Rev:** Dragon

Date	Mintage	F12	VF20	XF40	MS60	MS63
2012	—	—	—	—	—	12.50

KM# 2057 50 CENTS
15.59 g., 0.999 Silver 0.4975 oz. ASW, 36.6 mm. **Ruler:** Elizabeth II **Obv:** Head with tiara right **Rev:** Splendid Fairy-Wren in color **Rev. Designer:** Natasha Muhl

Date	Mintage	F12	VF20	XF40	MS60	MS63
2013P	Est. 10000	PF65 50.00				

KM# 2064 50 CENTS
15.59 g., 0.999 Silver 0.4975 oz. ASW, 36.6 mm. **Ruler:** Elizabeth II **Obv:** Head with tiara right **Rev:** Christmas tree in color, stars **Rev. Designer:** Aleysha Howarth

Date	Mintage	F12	VF20	XF40	MS60	MS63
2013P	5,000	PF65 50.00				

KM# 2073 50 CENTS
15.55 g., 0.999 Silver 0.4962 oz. ASW, 36.6 mm. **Ruler:** Elizabeth II **Subject:** Australian-American WWII memorial **Rev:** Eagle monument, flags in background

Date	Mintage	F12	VF20	XF40	MS60	MS63
2013P	—	PF65 35.00				

KM# 2094 50 CENTS
15.55 g., Copper-Nickel, 31.65 mm. **Ruler:** Elizabeth II **Subject:** Elizabeth II, 60th Anniversary of Coronation **Rev:** Sixty stylized crowns in circle **Shape:** 12-sided

Date	Mintage	F12	VF20	XF40	MS60	MS63
2013	—	—	—	—	4.00	5.00

KM# 2094b 50 CENTS
33.63 g., 0.999 Gold 1.0732 oz. AGW, 31.5 mm. **Ruler:** Elizabeth II **Subject:** Elizabeth II, 60th Anniversary of Reign **Rev:** Sixty stylized crowns in circle **Shape:** 12-sided

Date	Mintage	F12	VF20	XF40	MS60	MS63
2013	—	PF65 1,950				

KM# 2140 50 CENTS
15.55 g., 0.999 Silver 0.4962 oz. ASW **Ruler:** Elizabeth II **Obv:** Head with tiara right **Rev:** Regent Bowerbird in color

Date	Mintage	F12	VF20	XF40	MS60	MS63
2013	—	PF65 30.00				

KM# 2141 50 CENTS
Silver ASW **Ruler:** Elizabeth II **Obv:** Head with tiara right **Rev:** Australian red one penny stamp - Kangaroo on map **Shape:** Vertical rectangle

Date	Mintage	F12	VF20	XF40	MS60	MS63
2013	—	PF65 40.00				

KM# 2145 50 CENTS
15.55 g., Copper-Nickel, 31.65 mm. **Ruler:** Elizabeth II **Subject:** Elizabeth II coronation, 60th Anniversary **Obv:** Head with tiara right **Rev:** Sixty crowns **Shape:** 12-sided

Date	Mintage	F12	VF20	XF40	MS60	MS63
2013	—	—	—	—	—	5.00

KM# 2146 50 CENTS
15.55 g., Copper-Nickel **Ruler:** Elizabeth II **Subject:** Birth of Prince George **Obv:** Head with tiara right **Rev:** Crowned W and C in vines **Shape:** 12-sided

Date	Mintage	F12	VF20	XF40	MS60	MS63
2013	—	—	—	—	—	5.00

KM# 2146a 50 CENTS
18.24 g., 0.999 Silver 0.5821 oz. ASW, 31.65 mm. **Ruler:** Elizabeth II **Subject:** Birth of Prince George **Obv:** Head with tiara right **Rev:** Crowned W and C in vines

Date	Mintage	F12	VF20	XF40	MS60	MS63
2013	—	PF65 60.00				

KM# 1254 55 CENTS
15.55 g., 0.999 Silver 0.4962 oz. ASW, 26x38 mm. **Ruler:** Elizabeth II **Subject:** Postal Service, 200th Anniversary **Obv:** Head right **Obv. Designer:** Ian Rank-Broadley **Rev:** Early post box **Edge:** Irregular as with a stamp **Shape:** Vertical rectangle

Date	Mintage	F12	VF20	XF40	MS60	MS63
2009P	8,700	PF65 90.00				

KM# 1255 55 CENTS
15.55 g., 0.999 Silver 0.4962 oz. ASW, 26x38 mm. **Ruler:** Elizabeth II **Subject:** Postal Service, 200th Anniversary **Obv:** Head right **Obv. Designer:** Ian Rank-Broadley **Rev:** Home delivery **Edge:** Irregular as with a stamp **Shape:** Vertical rectangle

Date	Mintage	F12	VF20	XF40	MS60	MS63
2009P	8,700	PF65 90.00				

KM# 1803 60 CENTS
Silver **Ruler:** Elizabeth II **Subject:** London Olympics **Rev:** Scenes of London - Double decker bus; Big Ben; St. Paul's Cathedral, Wheel **Shape:** Vertical rectangle

Date	Mintage	F12	VF20	XF40	MS60	MS63
2012P	—	PF65 100				

KM# 489 DOLLAR
9.00 g., Aluminum-Bronze, 25 mm. **Ruler:** Elizabeth II **Obv:** Head with tiara right **Obv. Designer:** Ian Rank-Broadley **Rev:** Circle of 5 kangaroos **Rev. Designer:** Stuart Devlin **Edge:** Segmented reeding

Date	Mintage	F12	VF20	XF40	MS60	MS63
2001B	1,001,000	PF65 55.00				
2004B	8,800,000	—	—	—	6.00	7.00
2004B	50,000	PF65 75.00				
2005B	5,792,000	—	—	—	6.00	7.00
2005B	33,520	PF65 85.00				
2006B	38,691,000	—	—	—	4.00	5.00
2006B	—	PF65 45.00				
2006B Special Proof	—	PF65 3,500				

Note: Mintage of 25-35 pieces

2007B	—	—	—	—	20.00	25.00
2007B	—	PF65 45.00				
2008B	30,106,000	—	—	—	3.00	5.00
2008B	—	PF65 45.00				
2009B	4,682,000	—	—	—	4.00	6.00
2009C Mintmaster mark	—	—	—	—	—	25.00

Date	Mintage	F12	VF20	XF40	MS60	MS63
2009B	—	PF65 45.00				
2010B	—	—	—	—	—	5.00
2010B	—	PF65 45.00				
2011B	—	—	—	—	—	5.00
2011B	—	PF65 45.00				
2012B	—	—	—	—	—	5.00
2012B	—	PF65 45.00				

KM# 588 DOLLAR
9.00 g., Aluminum-Bronze, 25 mm. **Ruler:** Elizabeth II **Subject:** 90th Anniversary Royal Australian Navy **Obv:** Head with tiara right **Obv. Designer:** Ian Rank-Broadley **Rev:** Navy crest **Rev. Designer:** Vladimir Gottwald **Edge:** Segmented reeding

Date	Mintage	F12	VF20	XF40	MS60	MS63
2001	62,429	—	—	—	60.00	65.00

KM# 530a DOLLAR
11.66 g., 0.999 Silver 0.3721 oz. ASW, 24.9 mm. **Ruler:** Elizabeth II **Subject:** Army Centennial **Obv:** Head with tiara right **Obv. Designer:** Ian Rank-Broadley **Rev:** Army crest **Rev. Designer:** Vladimir Gottwald **Edge:** Segmented reeding

Date	Mintage	F12	VF20	XF40	MS60	MS63
2001	17,839	PF65 50.00				

KM# 530 DOLLAR
9.00 g., Aluminum-Bronze, 25 mm. **Ruler:** Elizabeth II **Subject:** Army Centennial **Obv:** Head with tiara right **Obv. Designer:** Ian Rank-Broadley **Rev:** Army crest **Rev. Designer:** Vladimir Gottwald **Edge:** Segmented reeding

Date	Mintage	F12	VF20	XF40	MS60	MS63
2001C	125,186	—	—	—	18.00	20.00
Note: Large head, IRB spaced						
2001C	Inc. above	—	—	—	18.00	20.00
Note: Small head, IRB joined						
2001S	38,095	—	—	—	25.00	30.00

KM# 531 DOLLAR
9.00 g., Aluminum-Bronze, 25 mm. **Ruler:** Elizabeth II **Subject:** 80th Anniversary Royal Australian Air Force **Obv:** Head with tiara right **Obv. Designer:** Ian Rank-Broadley **Rev:** Air Force crest **Rev. Designer:** Vladimir Gottwald **Edge:** Segmented reeding

Date	Mintage	F12	VF20	XF40	MS60	MS63
2001B	99,281	—	—	—	18.00	20.00
Note: IRB spaced						
2001B	Inc. above	—	—	—	25.00	30.00
Note: IRB joined						

KM# 534.1a DOLLAR
21.70 g., 0.9999 Gold 0.6931 oz. AGW, 25 mm. **Ruler:** Elizabeth II **Subject:** Federation Centennial **Obv:** Elizabeth II **Rev:** Federation logo

Date	Mintage	F12	VF20	XF40	MS60	MS63
2001B	650	PF65 1,300				

KM# 534.1 DOLLAR
9.00 g., Aluminum-Bronze, 25 mm. **Ruler:** Elizabeth II **Subject:** Australian Centenary of Federation - Norfolk Island **Obv:** Head with tiara right **Obv. Designer:** Ian Rank-Broadley **Rev:** Stylized ribbon map of Australia with star. **Rev. Designer:**

Wojciech Pietranik **Edge:** Segmented reeding **Note:** Reverse design raised above field. Prev. KM#534.

Date	Mintage	F12	VF20	XF40	MS60	MS63
2001B	6,781,200	—	—	—	50.00	55.00
Note: IRB joined						
2001B	Inc. above	—	—	—	50.00	55.00
Note: IRB spaced						
2001B			PF65 5.00			

KM# 534.2 DOLLAR
9.00 g., Aluminum-Bronze, 25 mm. **Ruler:** Elizabeth II **Subject:** Australian Centenary of Federation - Norfolk Island **Obv:** Head with tiara right **Obv. Designer:** Ian Rank-Broadley **Rev:** Multicolor ribbon design of Australia with star, printed on the surface. **Rev. Designer:** Wojciech Pietranik **Edge:** Segmented reeding

Date	Mintage	F12	VF20	XF40	MS60	MS63
2001	27,905,000	—	—	—	—	5.00
2001	—	PF65 12.50				

KM# 594 DOLLAR
31.10 g., 0.999 Silver 0.9926 oz. ASW, 40 mm. **Ruler:** Elizabeth II **Subject:** Millennium **Obv:** Head with tiara right **Obv. Designer:** Ian Rank-Broadley **Rev:** Gold inset sun on multicolor earth above Egyptian obelisk **Edge:** Reeded

Date	Mintage	F12	VF20	XF40	MS60	MS63
2001 Prooflike	30,000	—	—	—	37.00	42.00

KM# 598 DOLLAR
31.10 g., 0.999 Silver 0.9925 oz. ASW, 40.4 mm. **Ruler:** Elizabeth II **Subject:** Centenary of Federation "Holey Dollar" **Obv:** Legend around star-shaped center hole **Rev:** Seven coats of arms around star-shaped hole **Edge:** Reeded

Date	Mintage	F12	VF20	XF40	MS60	MS63
ND(2001) Prooflike	21,668	—	—	—	35.00	40.00

KM# 682 DOLLAR
9.00 g., Aluminum-Bronze, 25 mm. **Ruler:** Elizabeth II **Subject:** International Year of Volunteers **Obv:** Head with tiara right **Obv. Designer:** Ian Rank-Broadley **Rev:** Volunteers in wreath **Rev. Designer:** Wojciech Pietranik **Edge:** Segmented reeding

Date	Mintage	F12	VF20	XF40	MS60	MS63
2001B	6,000,000	—	—	—	12.00	15.00

KM# 600.1a DOLLAR
11.66 g., 0.990 Silver 0.3687 oz. ASW, 25 mm. **Ruler:** Elizabeth II **Subject:** Year of the Outback **Obv:** Head with tiara right **Obv. Designer:** Ian Rank-Broadley **Rev:** Stylized map of Australia **Rev. Designer:** Elizabeth Robinson and Wojciech Pietranik **Edge:** Segmented reeding

Date	Mintage	F12	VF20	XF40	MS60	MS63
2002B	12,500	PF65 65.00				

KM# 600.2 DOLLAR
9.00 g., Aluminum-Bronze, 25 mm. **Ruler:** Elizabeth II **Subject:** Year of the Outback **Obv:** Head with tiara right **Obv. Designer:** Ian Rank-Broadley **Rev:** Multicolor stylized map of Australia **Rev. Designer:** Wojciech Pietranik **Edge:** Segmented reeding

Date	Mintage	F12	VF20	XF40	MS60	MS63
2002B	39,514	PF65 15.00				

KM# 600.1 DOLLAR
9.00 g., Aluminum-Bronze, 25 mm. **Ruler:** Elizabeth II **Subject:** Year of the Outback **Obv:** Head with tiara right **Obv. Designer:** Ian Rank-Broadley **Rev:** Stylized map of Australia **Rev. Designer:** Wojciech Pietranik **Edge:** Segmented reeding **Note:** Prev. KM#600.

Date	Mintage	F12	VF20	XF40	MS60	MS63
2002	34,074,000	—	—	—	5.00	7.00
2002	—	PF65 10.00				
2002C	68,447	—	—	—	7.00	9.00
2002B	32,698	—	—	—	7.00	9.00
2002M	31,694	—	—	—	7.00	9.00
2002S	36,931	—	—	—	7.00	9.00

KM# 632 DOLLAR
31.10 g., 0.999 Silver 0.9926 oz. ASW, 40 mm. **Ruler:** Elizabeth II **Subject:** Queen's Golden Jubilee **Obv:** Head right **Rev:** Queen on horse with multicolor flag background **Edge:** Reeded

Date	Mintage	F12	VF20	XF40	MS60	MS63
2002	34,074,000	—	—	—	—	50.00
2002P	26,782	PF65 65.00				

KM# 660 DOLLAR
31.10 g., 0.999 Silver 0.9926 oz. ASW, 40 mm. **Ruler:** Elizabeth II **Subject:** Melbourne Mint **Obv:** Head with tiara right **Obv. Designer:** Ian Rank-Broadley **Rev:** Mint entrance between two gold foil inserts replicating gold sovereign reverse designs **Edge:** Reeded

Date	Mintage	F12	VF20	XF40	MS60	MS63
2002B	13,328	PF65 58.00				

KM# 823 DOLLAR
31.10 g., 0.999 Silver 0.9926 oz. ASW, 40 mm. **Ruler:** Elizabeth II **Subject:** 50th Anniversary - Coronation Elizabeth II **Obv:** Head with tiara right **Obv. Designer:** Ian Rank-Broadley **Rev:** Crown in lettered garland **Note:** Colored design.

Date	Mintage	F12	VF20	XF40	MS60	MS63
2003P	40,400	PF65 45.00				

KM# 489a DOLLAR

11.66 g., 0.999 Silver 0.3721 oz. ASW, 25 mm. **Ruler:** Elizabeth II **Obv:** Head with tiara right **Obv. Designer:** Ian Rank-Broadley **Rev:** Five kangaroos and value **Rev. Designer:** Stuart Devlin **Edge:** Segmented reeding

Date	Mintage	F12	VF20	XF40	MS60	MS63
2003B	6,500	PF65 40.00				
2004B	6,500	PF65 40.00				
2005B	6,500	PF65 40.00				
2006B	—	PF65 40.00				
2007B	—	PF65 40.00				
2008B	—	PF65 40.00				
2009B	—	PF65 40.00				
2010B	—	PF65 40.00				
2011B	6,000	PF65 40.00				
2013B	5,000	PF65 50.00				

KM# 663a DOLLAR

11.66 g., 0.999 Silver 0.3721 oz. ASW, 25 mm. **Ruler:** Elizabeth II **Subject:** Korean War **Obv:** Queens head right **Obv. Designer:** Ian Rank-Broadley **Rev:** Dove of Peace **Rev. Designer:** Vladimir Gottwald **Edge:** Segmented reeding

Date	Mintage	F12	VF20	XF40	MS60	MS63
2003B	15,000	PF65 55.00				

KM# 663 DOLLAR

9.00 g., Aluminum-Bronze, 25 mm. **Ruler:** Elizabeth II **Subject:** 50th Anniversary - End of Korean War **Obv:** Head with tiara right **Obv. Designer:** Ian Rank-Broadley **Rev:** Dove of Peace **Rev. Designer:** Vladimir Gottwald **Edge:** Segmented reeding

Date	Mintage	F12	VF20	XF40	MS60	MS63
2003B	34,949	—	—	—	6.00	8.00
2003C	93,572	—	—	—	6.00	8.00
2003M	36,142	—	—	—	6.00	8.00
2003S	36,091	—	—	—	6.00	8.00

KM# 685 DOLLAR

31.10 g., 0.999 Silver 0.9926 oz. ASW, 40.6 mm. **Ruler:** Elizabeth II **Subject:** 21st Birthday of William **Obv:** Head right **Rev:** Multicolor Prince William **Edge:** Segmented reeding

Date	Mintage	F12	VF20	XF40	MS60	MS63
ND(2003)P	12,500	PF65 45.00				

KM# 690 DOLLAR

9.00 g., Aluminum-Bronze, 25 mm. **Ruler:** Elizabeth II **Obv:** Queens head right **Rev:** Australia Volunteers logo **Edge:** Segmented reeding

Date	Mintage	F12	VF20	XF40	MS60	MS63
2003B	4,149,000	—	—	—	15.00	17.00

KM# 690a DOLLAR

9.00 g., 0.999 Silver 0.2872 oz. ASW, 25 mm. **Ruler:** Elizabeth II **Obv:** Queens head right **Rev:** Australia Volunteers logo

Date	Mintage	F12	VF20	XF40	MS60	MS63
2003B	6,500	PF65 30.00				

KM# 690.1 DOLLAR

9.00 g., Aluminum-Bronze, 25 mm. **Ruler:** Elizabeth II **Subject:** Australia's Volunteers **Obv:** Elizabeth II **Rev:** Multicolor Australia's Volunteers logo **Edge:** Segmented reeding

Date	Mintage	F12	VF20	XF40	MS60	MS63
2003B	39,090	PF65 15.00				

KM# 754 DOLLAR

9.00 g., Aluminum-Bronze, 25 mm. **Ruler:** Elizabeth II **Subject:** Womens Suffrage **Obv:** Queens head right **Obv. Designer:** Ian Rank-Broadley **Rev:** Suffragette talking to Britannia **Rev. Designer:** Vladimir Gottwald **Edge:** Segmented reeding

Date	Mintage	F12	VF20	XF40	MS60	MS63
2003B	10,007,000	—	—	—	5.00	7.00

KM# 763 DOLLAR

13.36 g., 0.999 Silver 0.4263 oz. ASW, 28.5 mm. **Ruler:** Elizabeth II **Series:** Masterpieces in Silver - Port Phillip Patterns **Obv:** 1/4 Ounce design **Rev:** Kangaroo design **Edge:** Reeded

Date	Mintage	F12	VF20	XF40	MS60	MS63
2003B	10,000	PF65 80.00				

KM# 803 DOLLAR

9.00 g., Aluminum-Bronze, 25 mm. **Ruler:** Elizabeth II **Subject:** Vietnam War Veterans 1962-1973 **Obv:** Head with tiara right **Obv. Designer:** Ian Rank-Broadley **Rev:** Australian Vietnam Forces National Memorial **Rev. Designer:** Wojciech Pietranik

Date	Mintage	F12	VF20	XF40	MS60	MS63
2003	57,000	—	—	—	45.00	50.00

KM# 822 DOLLAR

54.30 g., 0.999 Silver 1.7328 oz. ASW, 50 mm. **Ruler:** Elizabeth II **Obv:** Superimposed head above replica of Holey Dollar **Obv. Designer:** Ian Rank-Broadley **Rev:** Replica of Holey Dollar **Edge:** Reeded **Note:** Holey Dollar replica is embedded in silver collar and comes with replica Dump also in 0.999 silver.

Date	Mintage	F12	VF20	XF40	MS60	MS63
2003	11,000	PF65 90.00				

KM# 824 DOLLAR

31.10 g., 0.999 Silver 0.9926 oz. ASW, 40 mm. **Ruler:** Elizabeth II **Subject:** Golden Pipeline **Obv:** Head with tiara right **Obv. Designer:** Ian Rank-Broadley **Rev:** Charles Yelverton O'Connor, innovative engineer, multicolor

Date	Mintage	F12	VF20	XF40	MS60	MS63
2003P	5,000	PF65 130				

KM# 726 DOLLAR

9.00 g., Aluminum-Bronze, 25 mm. **Ruler:** Elizabeth II **Subject:** Eureka Stockade 1854-2004 **Obv:** Head with tiara right **Obv. Designer:** Ian Rank-Broadley **Rev:** Stockade and stylized soldiers **Rev. Designer:** Wojciech Pietranik **Edge:** Segmented reeding

Date	Mintage	F12	VF20	XF40	MS60	MS63
2004B	33,835	—	—	—	5.00	6.00
2004C	70,913	—	—	—	5.00	6.00
2004 E	95,948	—	—	—	5.00	6.00
2004S	45,098	—	—	—	5.00	6.00
2004M	37,526	—	—	—	5.00	6.00
2004 3 known		—	—	—	—	1,000
2004		—	—	—	8.00	10.00

KM# 725 DOLLAR

56.23 g., 0.999 Bi-Metallic 1.7944 oz., 50 mm. **Ruler:** Elizabeth II **Subject:** The Last Penny **Obv:** 1964 dated penny obverse **Rev:** 1964 date penny reverse **Edge:** Reeded

Date	Mintage	F12	VF20	XF40	MS60	MS63
2004B	16,437	PF65 85.00				

KM# 726a DOLLAR

11.66 g., 0.999 Silver 0.3721 oz. ASW, 25 mm. **Ruler:** Elizabeth II **Subject:** Eureka Stockade **Obv:** Head with tiara right **Obv. Designer:** Ian Rank-Broadley **Rev:** Stockade and stylized soldiers **Rev. Designer:** Wojciech Pietranik **Edge:** Segmented reeding

Date	Mintage	F12	VF20	XF40	MS60	MS63
2004B	17,697	PF65 38.00				

KM# 733 DOLLAR

9.00 g., Aluminum-Bronze, 25 mm. **Ruler:** Elizabeth II **Obv:** Head with tiara right **Obv. Designer:** Ian Rank-Broadley **Rev:** Multicolor holographic five kangaroos design **Rev. Designer:** Stuart Devlin **Edge:** Segmented reeding

Date	Mintage	F12	VF20	XF40	MS60	MS63
2004B		PF65 25.00				

KM# 733.1 DOLLAR

9.00 g., Aluminum-Bronze, 25 mm. **Ruler:** Elizabeth II **Rev:** Five kangaroos **Edge:** Segmented reeding

Date	Mintage	F12	VF20	XF40	MS60	MS63
2004B						4.50

KM# 733.1a DOLLAR

11.66 g., 0.9999 Silver 0.3724 oz. ASW, 25 mm. **Ruler:** Elizabeth II **Rev:** Five Kangaroos

Date	Mintage	F12	VF20	XF40	MS60	MS63
2004B	6,500	PF65 35.00				

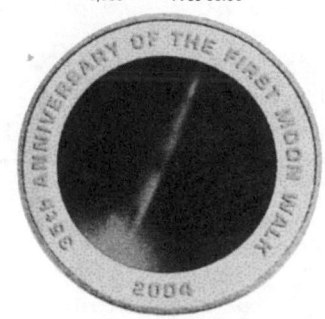

KM# 734 DOLLAR
31.10 g., 0.999 Silver 0.9926 oz. ASW, 40 mm. **Ruler:** Elizabeth II **Subject:** First Moon Walk **Obv:** Head with tiara right **Rev:** Multicolor rocket in flight **Edge:** Reeded

Date	Mintage	F12	VF20	XF40	MS60	MS63
2004P	18,415	PF65 100				

KM# 735 DOLLAR
31.10 g., 0.999 Silver 0.9926 oz. ASW, 40 mm. **Ruler:** Elizabeth II **Subject:** First Moon Walk **Obv:** Head with tiara right **Rev:** Multicolor scene of astronauts planting flag on moon **Edge:** Reeded

Date	Mintage	F12	VF20	XF40	MS60	MS63
2004P	18,415	PF65 110				

KM# 736 DOLLAR
31.10 g., 0.999 Silver 0.9926 oz. ASW, 40 mm. **Ruler:** Elizabeth II **Subject:** First Moon Walk **Obv:** Head with tiara right **Rev:** Multicolor close up of astronaut on moon **Edge:** Reeded

Date	Mintage	F12	VF20	XF40	MS60	MS63
2004P	18,415	PF65 95.00				

KM# 737 DOLLAR
31.10 g., 0.999 Silver 0.9926 oz. ASW, 40 mm. **Ruler:** Elizabeth II **Obv:** Head with tiara right **Rev:** Multicolor Antarctic view of Mawson Station and penguins **Edge:** Reeded

Date	Mintage	F12	VF20	XF40	MS60	MS63
2004P	7,500	PF65 60.00				

KM# 738 DOLLAR
31.10 g., 0.999 Silver 0.9926 oz. ASW, 40 mm. **Ruler:** Elizabeth II **Subject:** 50th Anniversary of Royal Visit **Obv:** Queens head right **Rev:** Gilt lion and kangaroo **Rev. Designer:** Leslie Bowles **Edge:** Reeded

Date	Mintage	F12	VF20	XF40	MS60	MS63
ND (2004)	12,500	PF65 85.00				

KM# 740 DOLLAR
24.38 g., 0.999 Silver 0.7779 oz. ASW, 40.6 mm. **Ruler:** Elizabeth II **Obv:** Crowned head right **Obv. Designer:** Ian Rank-Broadley **Rev:** Eureka Stockade leader, miners and flag **Rev. Designer:** Wojciech Pietranik **Edge:** Reeded

Date	Mintage	F12	VF20	XF40	MS60	MS63
2004	12,500	PF65 145				

KM# 747 DOLLAR
9.00 g., Aluminum-Bronze, 25 mm. **Ruler:** Elizabeth II **Subject:** 60th Anniversary World War II **Obv:** Head with tiara right **Obv. Designer:** Ian Rank-Broadley **Rev:** Rejoicing serviceman **Rev. Designer:** Wojciech Pietranik **Edge:** Segmented reeding

Date	Mintage	F12	VF20	XF40	MS60	MS63
2005B	31,788,000	—	—	—	3.00	4.00
2005B	—	PF65 35.00				

KM# 747a DOLLAR
11.66 g., 0.999 Silver 0.3721 oz. ASW, 25 mm. **Ruler:** Elizabeth II **Obv:** Queen's head right **Rev:** Rejoicing servicemen **Edge:** Segmented reeding

Date	Mintage	F12	VF20	XF40	MS60	MS63
2005B	6,500	PF65 45.00				

KM# 747b DOLLAR
21.52 g., 0.9999 Gold 0.6874 oz. AGW, 25 mm. **Ruler:** Elizabeth II **Obv:** Queen's head right **Rev:** Rejoicing servicemen **Edge:** Segmented reeding

Date	Mintage	F12	VF20	XF40	MS60	MS63
2005B	629	PF65 1,300				

KM# 748a DOLLAR
11.66 g., 0.999 Silver 0.3721 oz. ASW, 25 mm. **Ruler:** Elizabeth II **Subject:** Gallipoli **Obv:** Queen's head right **Rev:** Bugler silhouette **Edge:** Segmented reeding

Date	Mintage	F12	VF20	XF40	MS60	MS63
2005B	17,749	PF65 45.00				
2005B Proof, 2 known	—	PF65 1,500				

KM# 748 DOLLAR
9.00 g., Aluminum-Bronze, 25 mm. **Ruler:** Elizabeth II **Subject:** 90th Anniversary Gallipoli Landing 1915-2005 **Obv:** Head with tiara right **Obv. Designer:** Ian Rank-Broadley **Rev:** Bugler silhouette **Rev. Designer:** Vladimir Gottwald **Edge:** Segmented reeding

Date	Mintage	F12	VF20	XF40	MS60	MS63
2005	15,000	—	—	—	25.00	30.00
2005B	36,108	—	—	—	5.00	6.00
2005C	76,173	—	—	—	5.00	6.00
2005 G	35,452	—	—	—	35.00	40.00
2005M	38,727	—	—	—	5.00	6.00
2005S	39,569	—	—	—	6.00	7.00

KM# 825 DOLLAR
56.45 g., 0.999 Silver 1.8014 oz. ASW, 50 mm. **Ruler:** Elizabeth II **Obv:** Small head with tiara right superimposed above replica of Sydney Mint Sovereign **Obv. Designer:** Ian Rank-Broadley **Rev:** Replica of Sydney Mint Sovereign **Edge:** Reeded

Date	Mintage	F12	VF20	XF40	MS60	MS63
2005	11,845	PF65 90.00				

KM# 830 DOLLAR
31.60 g., 0.999 Silver 1.0084 oz. ASW, 40 mm. **Ruler:** Elizabeth II **Subject:** Centenary Australian Tennis Open 1905-2005 **Obv:** Head with tiara right **Obv. Designer:** Ian Rank-Broadley **Rev:** Tennis players

Date	Mintage	F12	VF20	XF40	MS60	MS63
2005	7,500	PF65 50.00				

KM# 831 DOLLAR
31.60 g., 0.999 Silver 1.0084 oz. ASW, 40 mm. **Ruler:** Elizabeth II **Subject:** Centenary Australian PGA Gold Open 1905-2005 **Obv:** Head with tiara right **Obv. Designer:** Ian Rank-Broadley **Rev:** Golfer

Date	Mintage	F12	VF20	XF40	MS60	MS63
2005	10,000	PF65 85.00				

KM# 832 DOLLAR

31.60 g., 0.999 Silver 1.0084 oz. ASW, 40 mm. **Ruler:** Elizabeth II **Subject:** Rotary International, 100th Anniversary **Obv:** Head with tiara right **Obv. Designer:** Ian Rank-Broadley **Rev:** Rotary International Logo in color

Date	Mintage	F12	VF20	XF40	MS60	MS63
2005	10,870	PF65 90.00				

KM# 833 DOLLAR

31.10 g., 0.999 Silver 0.9926 oz. ASW, 40 mm. **Ruler:** Elizabeth II **Subject:** 90th Anniversary Gallipoli Landings **Obv:** Head with tiara right **Obv. Designer:** Ian Rank-Broadley **Rev:** Multicolor Australian and New Zealand soldiers beneath Australian flag

Date	Mintage	F12	VF20	XF40	MS60	MS63
2005	15,000	PF65 185				

KM# 835 DOLLAR

Aluminum-Bronze, 38.74 mm. **Ruler:** Elizabeth II **Subject:** Living Icons of Australia and New Zealand **Obv:** Head with tiara right **Obv. Designer:** Ian Rank-Broadley **Rev:** Indigenous image of kangaroo **Rev. Designer:** Charmaine Cole

Date	Mintage	F12	VF20	XF40	MS60	MS63
2005	16,547	—	—	—	15.00	20.00

KM# 836 DOLLAR

31.10 g., 0.999 Silver 0.9926 oz. ASW, 40 mm. **Ruler:** Elizabeth II **Subject:** Prince Harry, 21st Birthday **Obv:** Head with tiara right **Obv. Designer:** Ian Rank-Broadley **Rev:** Prince Harry in color

Date	Mintage	F12	VF20	XF40	MS60	MS63
2005	6,088	PF65 80.00				

KM# 1015 DOLLAR

31.60 g., 0.999 Silver 1.0084 oz. ASW, 40.5 mm. **Ruler:** Elizabeth II **Subject:** 50th Anniversary Australian Territory **Obv:** Head with tiara right **Obv. Legend:** ELIZABETH II • AUSTRALIA **Obv. Designer:** Ian Rank-Broadley **Rev:** Red-footed Booby perched on a branch, multicolor **Rev. Legend:** COCOS (KEELING) ISLANDS **Edge:** Reeded

Date	Mintage	F12	VF20	XF40	MS60	MS63
2005P	6,436	PF65 70.00				

KM# 1018 DOLLAR

31.75 g., 0.999 Silver 1.0132 oz. ASW, 40.5 mm. **Ruler:** Elizabeth II **Obv:** Head with tiara right **Obv. Legend:** ELIZABETH II - AUSTRALIA **Obv. Designer:** Ian Rank-Broadley **Rev:** Leopard seal with pup on ice, multicolor **Rev. Legend:** Australian Antarctic Territory **Edge:** Reeded

Date	Mintage	F12	VF20	XF40	MS60	MS63
2005P	7,500	PF65 60.00				

KM# 838 DOLLAR

31.10 g., 0.999 Silver 0.9926 oz. ASW, 40 mm. **Ruler:** Elizabeth II **Subject:** Australain-Japan Year of Exchange **Obv:** Head with tiara right **Obv. Designer:** Ian Rank-Broadley **Rev:** Kangaroo leaping with kangaroo rim decoration

Date	Mintage	F12	VF20	XF40	MS60	MS63
2006	48,279	PF65 50.00				

KM# 77a DOLLAR

11.66 g., 0.999 Silver 0.3721 oz. ASW, 25 mm. **Ruler:** Elizabeth II **Obv:** Young bust right **Obv. Designer:** Arnold Machin **Rev:** Kangaroos **Rev. Designer:** Stuart Devlin **Edge:** Segmented reeding

Date	Mintage	F12	VF20	XF40	MS60	MS63
2006	6,500	PF65 40.00				

KM# 489b DOLLAR

21.52 g., 0.999 Gold 0.6867 oz. AGW, 25 mm. **Ruler:** Elizabeth II **Obv:** Head with tiara right **Obv. Designer:** Ian Rank-Broadley **Rev:** Five kangaroos and value **Rev. Designer:** Stuart Devlin **Edge:** Segmented reeding

Date	Mintage	F12	VF20	XF40	MS60	MS63
2006	300	PF65 1,300				
2013	500	PF65 1,250				

KM# 804 DOLLAR

9.00 g., Aluminum-Bronze, 25 mm. **Ruler:** Elizabeth II **Subject:** XVIII Commonwealth Games **Obv:** Head with tiara right **Rev:** Graphic at left, logo at right

Date	Mintage	F12	VF20	XF40	MS60	MS63
2006	—	—	—	—	3.50	5.00

KM# 805a DOLLAR

11.66 g., 0.999 Silver 0.3721 oz. ASW, 25 mm. **Ruler:** Elizabeth II **Subject:** 50 Years of Television **Obv:** Head with tiara right **Obv. Designer:** Ian Rank-Broadley **Rev:** TV mast and camera **Rev. Designer:** Vladimir Gottwald **Edge:** Segmented reeding

Date	Mintage	F12	VF20	XF40	MS60	MS63
2006	10,790	PF65 45.00				

Date	Mintage	F12	VF20	XF40	MS60	MS63
2006A	3,859	PF65 60.00				

KM# 805 DOLLAR

9.00 g., Aluminum-Bronze, 25 mm. **Ruler:** Elizabeth II **Subject:** 50 Years of Television **Obv:** Head with tiara right **Obv. Designer:** Ian Rank-Broadley **Rev:** TV mast and camera **Rev. Designer:** Vladimir Gottwald **Edge:** Segmented reeding

Date	Mintage	F12	VF20	XF40	MS60	MS63
2006B	47,228	—	—	—	5.00	6.00
2006C	135,221	—	—	—	5.00	6.00
2006M	39,600	—	—	—	5.00	6.00
2006S	48,490	—	—	—	5.00	6.00
2006 TV	46,370	—	—	—	15.00	17.00
2006 Without mint mark, 4 known					—	1,000

KM# 806 DOLLAR

9.00 g., Aluminum-Bronze, 25 mm. **Ruler:** Elizabeth II **Series:** Colored Oceans **Obv:** Head with tiara right **Obv. Designer:** Ian Rank-Broadley **Rev:** Multicolor jumping Bottlenose dolphins **Rev. Designer:** T. Dean **Edge:** Segmented reeding

Date	Mintage	F12	VF20	XF40	MS60	MS63
2006	29,310	—	—	—	—	35.00

KM# 807 DOLLAR

9.00 g., Aluminum-Bronze, 25 mm. **Ruler:** Elizabeth II **Series:** Colored Oceans **Obv:** Head with tiara right **Obv. Designer:** Ian Rank-Broadley **Rev:** Multicolor clown fish **Rev. Designer:** T. Dean **Edge:** Segmented reeding **Note:** Issued in folder.

Date	Mintage	F12	VF20	XF40	MS60	MS63
2006	29,310	—	—	—	25.00	30.00

KM# 826 DOLLAR

60.50 g., 0.999 Silver 1.9307 oz. ASW, 50 mm. **Ruler:** Elizabeth II **Obv:** Replica of 1758 Mexico City Mint 8 Reales **Obv. Legend:** ELIZABETH II (small head right) AUSTRALIA **Rev:** Replica of 1758 Mexico City Mint 8 Reales **Rev. Legend:** PILLAR DOLLAR **Edge:** Reeded

Date	Mintage	F12	VF20	XF40	MS60	MS63
2006	9,846	—	—	—	115	

KM# 841 DOLLAR

31.10 g., 0.999 Silver 0.9926 oz. ASW **Ruler:** Elizabeth II **Subject:** Australia Television, 50th Anniversary **Obv:** Head with tiara right **Obv. Designer:** Ian Rank-Broadley **Rev:** Lenticular display of six historic TV show images **Shape:** Square

Date	Mintage	F12	VF20	XF40	MS60	MS63
2006	9,470	PF65 95.00				

KM# 842 DOLLAR
31.10 g., 0.999 Silver 0.9926 oz. ASW, 40 mm. **Ruler:** Elizabeth II **Subject:** End of Pre-Decimal Coinage, 40th Anniversary **Obv:** Head with tiara right above transparent locket containing small replicas of pre-decimal currency **Obv. Designer:** Ian Rank-Broadley **Rev:** Rim legend about locket

Date	Mintage	F12	VF20	XF40	MS60	MS63
2006P	5,401	PF65 150				

KM# 843 DOLLAR
31.10 g., 0.999 Silver 0.9926 oz. ASW, 40 mm. **Ruler:** Elizabeth II **Subject:** 80th Birthday of Queen Elizabeth II **Obv:** Head with tiara right **Obv. Designer:** Ian Rank-Broadley **Rev:** Queen Elizabeth II

Date	Mintage	F12	VF20	XF40	MS60	MS63
2006P	5,823	PF65 85.00				

KM# 844 DOLLAR
31.10 g., 0.999 Silver 0.9926 oz. ASW, 40 mm. **Ruler:** Elizabeth II **Subject:** Figures of Note **Obv:** Head with tiara right **Obv. Designer:** Ian Rank-Broadley **Rev:** Queen Elizabeth as portrayed on Australia 1 dollar banknote

Date	Mintage	F12	VF20	XF40	MS60	MS63
2006P	2,409	PF65 175				

KM# 845 DOLLAR
31.10 g., 0.999 Silver 0.9926 oz. ASW, 40 mm. **Ruler:** Elizabeth II **Subject:** Figures of Note **Obv:** Head with tiara right **Obv. Designer:** Ian Rank-Broadley **Rev:** MacArthur and Farrer as portrayed on Australia 2 dollar banknote

Date	Mintage	F12	VF20	XF40	MS60	MS63
2006P	2,409	PF65 95.00				

KM# 846 DOLLAR
31.10 g., 0.999 Silver 0.9926 oz. ASW, 40 mm. **Ruler:** Elizabeth II **Subject:** Figures of Note **Obv:** Head with tiara right **Obv. Designer:** Ian Rank-Broadley **Rev:** Banks and Chisholm as portrayed on Australia 5 dollar banknote

Date	Mintage	F12	VF20	XF40	MS60	MS63
2006P	2,271	PF65 95.00				

KM# 847 DOLLAR
31.10 g., 0.999 Silver 0.9926 oz. ASW, 40 mm. **Ruler:** Elizabeth II **Subject:** Figures of Note **Obv:** Head with tiara right **Obv. Designer:** Ian Rank-Broadley **Rev:** Greenway and Lawson as portrayed on Australia 10 dollar banknote

Date	Mintage	F12	VF20	XF40	MS60	MS63
2006P	2,209	PF65 95.00				

KM# 848 DOLLAR
31.10 g., 0.999 Silver 0.9926 oz. ASW, 40 mm. **Ruler:** Elizabeth II **Subject:** Figures of Note **Obv:** Head with tiara right **Obv. Designer:** Ian Rank-Broadley **Rev:** Kingsford-Smith and Hargrave as portrayed on Australia 20 dollar banknote

Date	Mintage	F12	VF20	XF40	MS60	MS63
2006P	2,198	PF65 95.00				

KM# 940 DOLLAR
31.10 g., 0.999 Silver 0.9926 oz. ASW **Ruler:** Elizabeth II **Subject:** Australian Landmarks **Obv:** Head with tiara right **Obv. Designer:** Ian Rank-Broadley **Rev:** Melbourne

Date	Mintage	F12	VF20	XF40	MS60	MS63
2006P	5,923	PF65 50.00				

KM# 941 DOLLAR
31.10 g., 0.999 Silver 0.9926 oz. ASW **Ruler:** Elizabeth II

Subject: Australian Landmarks **Obv:** Head with tiara right **Obv. Designer:** Ian Rank-Broadley **Rev:** Uluru

Date	Mintage	F12	VF20	XF40	MS60	MS63
2006P	5,938	PF65 50.00				

KM# 942 DOLLAR
31.10 g., 0.999 Silver 0.9926 oz. ASW **Ruler:** Elizabeth II **Subject:** Australian Landmarks **Obv:** Head with tiara right **Obv. Designer:** Ian Rank-Broadley **Rev:** Canberra

Date	Mintage	F12	VF20	XF40	MS60	MS63
2006P	4,926	PF65 50.00				

KM# 943 DOLLAR
31.10 g., 0.999 Silver 0.9926 oz. ASW, 40.6 mm. **Ruler:** Elizabeth II **Subject:** Australian Landmarks **Obv:** Head with tiara right **Obv. Designer:** Ian Rank-Broadley **Rev:** Perth

Date	Mintage	F12	VF20	XF40	MS60	MS63
2006P	7,500	PF65 50.00				

KM# 944 DOLLAR
31.10 g., 0.999 Silver 0.9926 oz. ASW **Ruler:** Elizabeth II **Subject:** Australian Landmarks **Obv:** Head with tiara right **Obv. Designer:** Ian Rank-Broadley **Rev:** Great Barrier Reef

Date	Mintage	F12	VF20	XF40	MS60	MS63
2006P	5,751	PF65 50.00				

KM# 849 DOLLAR
31.10 g., 0.999 Silver 0.9926 oz. ASW, 40 mm. **Ruler:** Elizabeth II **Obv:** Head with tiara right **Obv. Legend:** ELIZABETH II - AUSTRALIA **Obv. Designer:** Ian Rank-Broadley **Rev:** Everage head facing, multicolor **Rev. Legend:** DAME EDNA EVERAGE - 50TH ANNIVERSARY

Date	Mintage	F12	VF20	XF40	MS60	MS63
ND-2006P	4,512	PF65 60.00				

KM# 1008 DOLLAR
31.10 g., 0.999 Silver 0.9926 oz. ASW, 40.5 mm. **Ruler:** Elizabeth II **Subject:** 400th Anniversary **Obv:** Head with tiara right **Obv. Legend:** ELIZABETH II - AUSTRALIA **Obv. Designer:** Ian Rank-Broadley **Rev:** Sailing ship at left, early map at right in color **Rev. Legend:** 1606-2006 / Australia on the Map

Date	Mintage	F12	VF20	XF40	MS60	MS63
2006P	9,941	PF65 55.00				

KM# 1019 DOLLAR
31.30 g., 0.999 Silver 0.9988 oz. ASW, 40.5 mm. **Ruler:** Elizabeth II **Subject:** 20th Anniversary of base **Obv:** Head with tiara right **Obv. Legend:** ELIZABETH II - AUSTRALIA **Obv. Designer:** Ian Rank-Broadley **Rev:** Plane above Albatross and chick on ice, multicolor **Rev. Legend:** Australian Antarctic Territory - EDGEWORTH DAVID BASE **Edge:** Reeded

Date	Mintage	F12	VF20	XF40	MS60	MS63
2006P	7,500	PF65 60.00				

KM# 808 DOLLAR
9.00 g., Aluminum-Bronze, 25 mm. **Ruler:** Elizabeth II **Subject:** Ashes Cricket Series 1882-2007 **Obv:** Head with tiara right **Obv. Designer:** Ian Rank-Broadley **Rev:** Urn with supporters **Rev. Designer:** Vladimir Gottwald **Edge:** Segmented reeding

Date	Mintage	F12	VF20	XF40	MS60	MS63
2007	—	—	—	—	3.00	4.00

KM# 809 DOLLAR
9.00 g., Aluminum-Bronze, 25 mm. **Ruler:** Elizabeth II **Subject:** Year of the Pig **Obv:** Head with tiara right **Obv. Designer:** Ian Rank-Broadley **Rev:** Pig **Rev. Designer:** Vladimir Gottwald **Edge:** Segmented reeding

Date	Mintage	F12	VF20	XF40	MS60	MS63
2007	7,500	—	—	—	95.00	—

KM# 809a DOLLAR
11.66 g., 0.999 Silver 0.3721 oz. ASW, 25 mm. **Ruler:** Elizabeth II **Subject:** Year of the Pig **Obv:** Head with tiara right **Obv. Designer:** Ian Rank-Broadley **Rev:** Pig **Rev. Designer:** Vladimir Gottwald **Edge:** Segmented reeding

Date	Mintage	F12	VF20	XF40	MS60	MS63
2007		PF65 28.00				

KM# 828 DOLLAR
9.00 g., Aluminum-Bronze, 25 mm. **Ruler:** Elizabeth II **Subject:** Year of the Surf Lifesaver **Obv:** Head with tiara right **Obv. Designer:** Ian Rank-Broadley **Rev:** Three lifesavers carrying rescued person **Rev. Designer:** Vladimir Gottwald **Edge:** Segmented reeding

Date	Mintage	F12	VF20	XF40	MS60	MS63
2007	34,500	PF65 20.00				

KM# 828a DOLLAR
11.66 g., 0.999 Silver 0.3721 oz. ASW, 25 mm. **Ruler:** Elizabeth II **Subject:** Year of the Surfer Lifesaver **Rev:** Three men saving fourth

Date	Mintage	F12	VF20	XF40	MS60	MS63
2007B	—	PF65 40.00				

KM# 829 DOLLAR
9.00 g., Aluminum-Bronze, 25 mm. **Ruler:** Elizabeth II **Subject:** Norman Lindsay and his Magic Pudding **Obv:** Head with tiara right **Obv. Designer:** Ian Rank-Broadley **Rev:** Lindsay and Pudding characters **Rev. Designer:** Vladimir Gottwald **Edge:** Segmented reeding

Date	Mintage	F12	VF20	XF40	MS60	MS63
2007	33,690	—	—	—	65.00	—

KM# 850 DOLLAR
27.22 g., Copper-Nickel, 38.74 mm. **Ruler:** Elizabeth II **Obv:** Head with tiara right **Obv. Designer:** Ian Rank-Broadley **Rev:** Kangaroo mother and joey **Rev. Designer:** Rolf Harris **Edge:** Reeded

Date	Mintage	F12	VF20	XF40	MS60	MS63
2007	5,000	—	—	—	275	300

KM# 945 DOLLAR
31.10 g., 0.999 Silver 0.9926 oz. ASW **Ruler:** Elizabeth II **Subject:** Australian Landmarks **Obv:** Head with tiara right **Obv. Designer:** Ian Rank-Broadley **Rev:** Gold Coast

Date	Mintage	F12	VF20	XF40	MS60	MS63
2007P	4,558	PF65 60.00				

KM# 946 DOLLAR
31.10 g., 0.999 Silver 0.9926 oz. ASW **Ruler:** Elizabeth II **Subject:** Australian Landmarks **Obv:** Head with tiara right **Obv. Designer:** Ian Rank-Broadley **Rev:** Phillip Island

Date	Mintage	F12	VF20	XF40	MS60	MS63
2007P	4,668	PF65 60.00				

KM# 947 DOLLAR
31.10 g., 0.999 Silver 0.9926 oz. ASW **Ruler:** Elizabeth II **Subject:** Australian Landmarks **Obv:** Head with tiara right **Obv. Designer:** Ian Rank-Broadley **Rev:** Port Arthur

Date	Mintage	F12	VF20	XF40	MS60	MS63
2007P	6,105	PF65 60.00				

KM# 948 DOLLAR
31.10 g., 0.999 Silver 0.9926 oz. ASW **Ruler:** Elizabeth II **Subject:** Australian Landmarks **Obv:** Head with tiara right **Obv. Designer:** Ian Rank-Broadley **Rev:** Adelaide

Date	Mintage	F12	VF20	XF40	MS60	MS63
2007P	6,376	PF65 60.00				

KM# 949 DOLLAR
31.10 g., 0.999 Silver 0.9926 oz. ASW **Ruler:** Elizabeth II **Subject:** Australian Landmarks **Obv:** Head with tiara right **Obv. Designer:** Ian Rank-Broadley **Rev:** Sydney

Date	Mintage	F12	VF20	XF40	MS60	MS63
2007P	5,945	PF65 60.00				

KM# 1009 DOLLAR
31.10 g., 0.999 Silver 0.9926 oz. ASW, 40 mm. **Ruler:** Elizabeth II **Subject:** Phar Lap, 75th Anniversary death **Obv:** Head with tiara right **Obv. Legend:** ELIZABETH II - AUSTRALIA **Rev:** Horse and rider racing right

Date	Mintage	F12	VF20	XF40	MS60	MS63
ND-2007P	5,055	PF65 95.00				

KM# 1011 DOLLAR
31.11 g., 0.999 Silver 0.9926 oz. ASW, 40 mm. **Ruler:** Elizabeth II **Obv:** Crowned bust right at top **Obv. Legend:** ELIZABETH II - AUSTRALIA **Rev:** 12 Lunar figures

Date	Mintage	F12	VF20	XF40	MS60	MS63
2007	5,994	PF65 90.00				

KM# 1012 DOLLAR
31.10 g., 0.999 Silver 0.9926 oz. ASW, 40 mm. **Ruler:** Elizabeth II **Obv:** Bust with tiara right **Obv. Legend:** ELIZABETH II - AUSTRALIA **Obv. Designer:** Ian Rank-Broadley **Rev:** Bridge, multicolor fireworks above **Rev. Designer:** Vladimir Gottwald **Rev. Legend:** 75th ANNIVERSARY - SYDNEY HARBOUR BRIDGE

Date	Mintage	F12	VF20	XF40	MS60	MS63
ND-2007P	8,433	PF65 85.00				

KM# 1016 DOLLAR
11.66 g., 0.999 Silver 0.3721 oz. ASW, 25 mm. **Ruler:** Elizabeth II **Subject:** 75th Anniversary - Sydney Harbor Bridge **Obv:** Head with tiara right **Obv. Legend:** ELIZABETH II _ AUSTRALIA **Obv. Designer:** Ian Rank-Broadley **Rev:** Three men standing at bridge joint **Edge:** Segmented reeding

Date	Mintage	F12	VF20	XF40	MS60	MS63
2007B	12,500	PF65 35.00				

KM# 1016a DOLLAR
9.00 g., Aluminum-Bronze, 25 mm. **Ruler:** Elizabeth II **Subject:** Sydney Harbor Bridge, 75th Anniversary **Obv:** Head with tiara right **Rev:** Three men standing at bridge joint

Date	Mintage	F12	VF20	XF40	MS60	MS63
2007S	—	—	—	—	3.00	4.00

KM# 1020 DOLLAR
31.48 g., 0.999 Silver 1.0046 oz. ASW, 40.5 mm. **Ruler:** Elizabeth II **Subject:** 50th Anniversary of Station **Obv:** Head with tiara right **Obv. Legend:** ELIZABETH II - AUSTRALIA **Obv. Designer:** Ian Rank-Broadley **Rev:** Ship "Kista Dan", multicolor **Rev. Legend:** Australian Antarctic Territory - DAVIS STATION **Edge:** Reeded

Date	Mintage	F12	VF20	XF40	MS60	MS63
2007P	7,500	PF65 60.00				

KM# 1024 DOLLAR
9.00 g., Aluminum-Bronze, 25 mm. **Ruler:** Elizabeth II **Series:** Colored Oceans **Obv:** Head with tiara right **Obv. Designer:** Ian Rank-Broadley **Rev:** Biscuit Star, multicolor **Rev. Designer:** T. Dean **Edge:** Segmented reeding **Note:** Issued in folder.

Date	Mintage	F12	VF20	XF40	MS60	MS63
2007	—	—	—	—	—	22.00

KM# 1025 DOLLAR
9.00 g., Aluminum-Bronze, 25 mm. **Ruler:** Elizabeth II **Series:** Colored Oceans **Obv:** Head with tiara right **Obv. Designer:** Ian Rank-Broadley **Rev:** Longfin Banner fish, multicolor **Rev. Designer:** T. Dean **Edge:** Segmented reeding

Date	Mintage	F12	VF20	XF40	MS60	MS63
2007	25,930	—	—	—	—	22.00

KM# 1026 DOLLAR
9.00 g., Aluminum-Bronze, 25 mm. **Ruler:** Elizabeth II **Series:** Colored Oceans **Obv:** Head with tiara right **Obv. Designer:** Ian Rank-Broadley **Rev:** White Shark, multicolor **Rev. Designer:** T. Dean **Edge:** Segmented reeding **Note:** Issued in folder.

Date	Mintage	F12	VF20	XF40	MS60	MS63
2007	30,416	—	—	—	—	22.00

KM# 1027 DOLLAR
9.00 g., Aluminum-Bronze, 25 mm. **Ruler:** Elizabeth II **Series:** Colored Oceans **Obv:** Head with tiara right **Obv. Designer:** Ian Rank-Broadley **Rev:** Big Belly seahorse **Edge:** Segmented reeding

Date	Mintage	F12	VF20	XF40	MS60	MS63
2007	—	—	—	—	—	22.00

KM# 1040 DOLLAR
9.00 g., Aluminum-Bronze, 25 mm. **Ruler:** Elizabeth II **Subject:** APEC **Rev:** Multiple stars

Date	Mintage	F12	VF20	XF40	MS60	MS63
2007B	20,108,000	—	—	—	3.00	4.00

KM# 1042 DOLLAR
9.00 g., Aluminum-Bronze, 25 mm. **Ruler:** Elizabeth II **Subject:** 60th Anniversary - Peacekeepers **Rev:** Hand holding globe within wreath, dove above

Date	Mintage	F12	VF20	XF40	MS60	MS63
2007B	31,028	—	—	—	—	15.00

KM# 1437 DOLLAR
Silver **Ruler:** Elizabeth II **Subject:** Lunar dollar

Date	Mintage	F12	VF20	XF40	MS60	MS63
2007	—	PF65 50.00				

KM# 1438 DOLLAR
Silver **Ruler:** Elizabeth II **Subject:** One Johanna

Date	Mintage	F12	VF20	XF40	MS60	MS63
2007	—	PF65 50.00				

KM# 1653 DOLLAR
9.00 g., Aluminum-Bronze, 25 mm. **Ruler:** Elizabeth II **Subject:** International Polar Year **Obv:** Head with tiara right **Rev:** Sailing ship in ice

Date	Mintage	F12	VF20	XF40	MS60	MS63
2007	—	—	—	—	6.00	8.00

KM# 1047 DOLLAR
9.00 g., Aluminum-Bronze, 25 mm. **Ruler:** Elizabeth II **Rev:** First coat of arms

Date	Mintage	F12	VF20	XF40	MS60	MS63
2008M	25,202	—	—	—	5.00	6.00
2008B	32,500	—	—	—	5.00	6.00
2008C	104,689	—	—	—	15.00	17.00
2008S	32,500	—	—	—	5.00	6.00

KM# 1063 DOLLAR
9.00 g., Aluminum-Bronze, 25 mm. **Ruler:** Elizabeth II **Subject:** Saint Sister Mary Mackillop **Rev:** Nun and three children, world map in background **Rev. Designer:** V. Gottwald

Date	Mintage	F12	VF20	XF40	MS60	MS63
2008	29,800	—	—	—	15.00	17.00

KM# 1059 DOLLAR
9.00 g., Aluminum-Bronze, 25 mm. **Ruler:** Elizabeth II **Subject:** Planet Earth **Rev:** Four hands and elements **Rev. Designer:** V. Gottwald

Date	Mintage	F12	VF20	XF40	MS60	MS63
2008	—	PF65 25.00				
2008	28,399	—	—	—	20.00	22.00

KM# 1047a DOLLAR
11.60 g., 0.999 Silver 0.3702 oz. ASW, 25 mm. **Ruler:** Elizabeth II **Rev:** First coat of arms

Date	Mintage	F12	VF20	XF40	MS60	MS63
2008C	12,500	PF65 45.00				

KM# 1056a DOLLAR
11.66 g., 0.999 Silver 0.3721 oz. ASW, 25 mm. **Ruler:** Elizabeth II **Subject:** Year of the Rat **Rev:** Mouse at center, flora in arches

Date	Mintage	F12	VF20	XF40	MS60	MS63
2008	10,000	PF65 45.00				

KM# 1076 DOLLAR
9.00 g., Aluminum-Bronze, 25 mm. **Ruler:** Elizabeth II **Subject:** Year of Astronomy **Rev:** Parkes Telescope **Rev. Designer:** Caitlin Goodall

Date	Mintage	F12	VF20	XF40	MS60	MS63
2008	—	PF65 25.00				
2008	—	—	—	—	12.00	14.00

KM# 1039 DOLLAR
9.00 g., Aluminum-Bronze, 25 mm. **Ruler:** Elizabeth II **Subject:** Boy Scouts, 100th Anniversary

Date	Mintage	F12	VF20	XF40	MS60	MS63
2008	—	—	—	—	6.00	7.00

KM# 1052 DOLLAR
9.00 g., Aluminum-Bronze, 25 mm. **Ruler:** Elizabeth II **Subject:** Rugby League Centennial **Rev:** Rugby anniversary logo **Rev. Designer:** V. Gottwald

Date	Mintage	F12	VF20	XF40	MS60	MS63
2008	60,400	—	—	—	15.00	17.00

KM# 1056 DOLLAR
9.00 g., Aluminum-Bronze, 25 mm. **Ruler:** Elizabeth II **Subject:** Year of the Rat **Rev. Designer:** V. Gottwald

Date	Mintage	F12	VF20	XF40	MS60	MS63
2008	—	—	—	—	13.00	15.00

KM# 1064 DOLLAR
9.00 g., Aluminum-Bronze, 25 mm. **Ruler:** Elizabeth II **Subject:** Centennial of Quarantine **Rev:** Beagle and suitcase like map of Australia **Rev. Designer:** W. Pietranik

Date	Mintage	F12	VF20	XF40	MS60	MS63
2008	30,094	—	—	—	15.00	17.00

KM# 1068 DOLLAR
9.00 g., Aluminum-Bronze, 25 mm. **Ruler:** Elizabeth II **Rev:** Multicolor Echidna **Rev. Designer:** S. Foster

Date	Mintage	F12	VF20	XF40	MS60	MS63
2008	20,589	—	—	—	18.00	22.00

KM# 1069 DOLLAR
9.00 g., Aluminum-Bronze, 25 mm. **Ruler:** Elizabeth II **Rev:** Multicolor Rock Wallaby **Rev. Designer:** S. Foster

Date	Mintage	F12	VF20	XF40	MS60	MS63
2008	24,863	—	—	—	18.00	22.00

KM# 1070 DOLLAR
9.00 g., Aluminum-Bronze, 25 mm. **Ruler:** Elizabeth II **Rev:** Multicolor koala **Rev. Designer:** S. Foster

Date	Mintage	F12	VF20	XF40	MS60	MS63
2008	27,045	—	—	—	18.00	22.00

KM# 1071 DOLLAR
9.00 g., Aluminum-Bronze, 25 mm. **Ruler:** Elizabeth II **Rev:** Multicolor wombat **Rev. Designer:** S. Foster

Date	Mintage	F12	VF20	XF40	MS60	MS63
2008	22,295	—	—	—	18.00	22.00

KM# 1090 DOLLAR
13.50 g., Aluminum-Bronze, 29.5 mm. **Ruler:** Elizabeth II **Subject:** Ghost Bat **Obv:** Head right **Rev:** Ghost bat against night sky **Edge:** Reeded

Date	Mintage	F12	VF20	XF40	MS60	MS63
2008	11,914	—	—	—	—	14.00

KM# 1091 DOLLAR
31.11 g., 0.999 Silver 0.9926 oz. ASW, 40.6 mm. **Ruler:** Elizabeth II **Subject:** UNESCO Heritage site - Kakadu National Park **Rev:** Saltwater crocodile and multicolor swamp

Date	Mintage	F12	VF20	XF40	MS60	MS63
2008P	7,500	PF65 75.00				

KM# 1021 DOLLAR
31.11 g., 0.999 Silver 0.9926 oz. ASW, 40 mm. **Ruler:** Elizabeth II **Subject:** Hobart **Rev:** Buildings and harbor **Rev. Legend:** DISCOVER AUSTRALIA

Date	Mintage	F12	VF20	XF40	MS60	MS63
2008P	7,277	PF65 80.00				

KM# 1168 DOLLAR
13.50 g., Aluminum-Bronze, 29.5 mm. **Ruler:** Elizabeth II **Obv:** Head right **Obv. Designer:** Ian Rank-Broadley **Rev:** Common wombat

Date	Mintage	F12	VF20	XF40	MS60	MS63
2008P	11,908	—	—	—	—	14.00

KM# 1169 DOLLAR
13.50 g., Aluminum-Bronze, 29.5 mm. **Ruler:** Elizabeth II **Obv:** Head right **Obv. Designer:** Ian Rank-Broadley **Rev:** Echidna

---

Date	Mintage	F12	VF20	XF40	MS60	MS63
2008P	11,850	—	—	—	—	14.00

KM# 1170 DOLLAR
13.50 g., Aluminum-Bronze, 29.5 mm. **Ruler:** Elizabeth II **Obv:** Head right **Obv. Designer:** Ian Rank-Broadley **Rev:** Frilled-neck lizard

Date	Mintage	F12	VF20	XF40	MS60	MS63
2008P	11,864	—	—	—	—	14.00

KM# 1171 DOLLAR
13.50 g., Aluminum-Bronze, 29.5 mm. **Ruler:** Elizabeth II **Obv:** Head right **Obv. Designer:** Ian Rank-Broadley **Rev:** Grey kangaroo

Date	Mintage	F12	VF20	XF40	MS60	MS63
2008P	14,385	—	—	—	—	14.00

KM# 1172 DOLLAR
13.50 g., Aluminum-Bronze, 29.5 mm. **Ruler:** Elizabeth II **Obv:** Head right **Obv. Designer:** Ian Rank-Broadley **Rev:** Splendid wren

Date	Mintage	F12	VF20	XF40	MS60	MS63
2008P	11,796	—	—	—	—	14.00

KM# 1173 DOLLAR
13.50 g., Aluminum-Bronze, 29.5 mm. **Ruler:** Elizabeth II **Obv:** Head right **Obv. Designer:** Ian Rank-Broadley **Rev:** Palm cockatoo

Date	Mintage	F12	VF20	XF40	MS60	MS63
2008P	11,759	—	—	—	—	14.00

KM# 1174 DOLLAR
13.50 g., Aluminum-Bronze, 29.5 mm. **Ruler:** Elizabeth II **Obv:** Head right **Obv. Designer:** Ian Rank-Broadley **Rev:** Wedge-tailed eagle

Date	Mintage	F12	VF20	XF40	MS60	MS63
2008P	14,034	—	—	—	—	14.00

KM# 1175 DOLLAR
13.50 g., Aluminum-Bronze, 29.5 mm. **Ruler:** Elizabeth II **Obv:** Head right **Obv. Designer:** Ian Rank-Broadley **Rev:** Whale

---

shark

Date	Mintage	F12	VF20	XF40	MS60	MS63
2008P	11,943	—	—	—	—	14.00

KM# 1176 DOLLAR
13.50 g., Aluminum-Bronze, 29.5 mm. **Ruler:** Elizabeth II **Obv:** Head right **Obv. Designer:** Ian Rank-Broadley **Rev:** Green sea turtle

Date	Mintage	F12	VF20	XF40	MS60	MS63
2008P	11,881	—	—	—	—	14.00

KM# 1177 DOLLAR
13.50 g., Aluminum-Bronze, 29.5 mm. **Ruler:** Elizabeth II **Obv:** Head right **Obv. Designer:** Ian Rank-Broadley **Rev:** Platypus

Date	Mintage	F12	VF20	XF40	MS60	MS63
2008P	11,960	—	—	—	—	14.00

KM# 1178 DOLLAR
13.50 g., Aluminum-Bronze, 29.5 mm. **Ruler:** Elizabeth II **Obv:** Head right **Obv. Designer:** Ian Rank-Broadley **Rev:** Australian sea lion

Date	Mintage	F12	VF20	XF40	MS60	MS63
2008P	13,884	—	—	—	—	14.00

KM# 1179 DOLLAR
31.11 g., 0.999 Silver 0.9926 oz. ASW, 40.6 mm. **Ruler:** Elizabeth II **Subject:** 90th Anniversary - End of WWI **Obv:** Head right **Obv. Designer:** Ian Rank-Broadley **Rev:** Silhouette of bugler, multicolor poppies below

Date	Mintage	F12	VF20	XF40	MS60	MS63
2008P	7,554	PF65 90.00				

KM# 1181 DOLLAR
31.11 g., 0.999 Silver 0.9926 oz. ASW, 40 mm. **Ruler:** Elizabeth II **Subject:** Darwin **Obv:** Head right **Obv. Designer:** Ian Rank-Broadley **Rev:** Harbor, multicolor **Rev. Legend:** DISCOVER AUSTRALIA

Date	Mintage	F12	VF20	XF40	MS60	MS63
2008P	7,319	PF65 80.00				

KM# 1182 DOLLAR
31.11 g., 0.999 Silver 0.9926 oz. ASW, 40 mm. **Ruler:** Elizabeth II **Subject:** Kakadu **Obv:** Head right **Obv. Designer:** Ian Rank-Broadley **Rev:** Crocodile, multicolor **Rev. Legend:** DISCOVER AUSTRALIA

Date	Mintage	F12	VF20	XF40	MS60	MS63
2008P	7,252	PF65 80.00				

KM# 1183 DOLLAR
31.11 g., 0.999 Silver 0.9926 oz. ASW **Ruler:** Elizabeth II **Subject:** Brisbane **Obv:** Head right **Obv. Designer:** Ian Rank-Broadley **Rev:** Bridge and view **Rev. Legend:** DISCOVER AUSTRALIA

Date	Mintage	F12	VF20	XF40	MS60	MS63
2008P	7,500	PF65 80.00				

KM# 1184 DOLLAR
31.11 g., 0.999 Silver 0.9926 oz. ASW **Ruler:** Elizabeth II **Subject:** Broome **Obv:** Head right **Obv. Designer:** Ian Rank-Broadley **Rev:** Seascape, pearls, multicolor **Rev. Legend:** DISCOVER AUSTRALIA

Date	Mintage	F12	VF20	XF40	MS60	MS63
2008P	7,252	PF65 80.00				

KM# 1185 DOLLAR
31.11 g., 0.999 Silver 0.9926 oz. ASW **Ruler:** Elizabeth II **Subject:** Sydney **Obv:** Head right **Obv. Designer:** Ian Rank-Broadley **Rev:** Opera House, Harbor Bridge, multicolor **Rev. Legend:** DISCOVER AUSTRALIA

Date	Mintage	F12	VF20	XF40	MS60	MS63
2008P	7,500	PF65 80.00				

KM# 1654 DOLLAR
31.11 g., 0.999 Silver 0.9926 oz. ASW, 40.6 mm. **Ruler:** Elizabeth II **Subject:** HMAS Sydney II

Date	Mintage	F12	VF20	XF40	MS60	MS63
2008	7,430	PF65 90.00				

KM# 1682 DOLLAR
13.80 g., Aluminum-Bronze, 30.6 mm. **Ruler:** Elizabeth II **Subject:** World Youth Day **Rev:** Pope Benedict XVI and WYD logo in color

Date	Mintage	F12	VF20	XF40	MS60	MS63
2008	42,369	—	—	—	—	15.00

KM# 1749 DOLLAR
31.11 g., 0.999 Silver 0.9926 oz. ASW, 40.6 mm. **Ruler:** Elizabeth II **Subject:** Treasurers of Australia, Opals **Obv:** Small head above container of five opals **Rev:** landscape above container

Date	Mintage	F12	VF20	XF40	MS60	MS63
2008P	7,500	PF65 75.00				

KM# 1867 DOLLAR
31.11 g., 0.999 Silver 0.9926 oz. ASW, 40.5 mm. **Ruler:** Elizabeth II **Subject:** World Youth Day

Date	Mintage	F12	VF20	XF40	MS60	MS63
2008P	5,054	PF65 60.00				

KM# 1428 DOLLAR
13.80 g., Aluminum-Bronze, 30.6 mm. **Ruler:** Elizabeth II **Subject:** Citizenship **Obv:** Head in tiara right **Rev:** National arms

Date	Mintage	F12	VF20	XF40	MS60	MS63
2009P	—	—	—	—	—	14.00
2010P	—	—	—	—	—	14.00
2011P	—	—	—	—	—	14.00
2012P	—	—	—	—	—	14.00

KM# 1429 DOLLAR
9.00 g., Aluminum-Bronze, 25 mm. **Ruler:** Elizabeth II **Subject:** Steve Irwin **Rev:** Steve Irwin and animal montage

Date	Mintage	F12	VF20	XF40	MS60	MS63
2009(p)	—	—	—	—	—	12.00

KM# 1078a DOLLAR
11.66 g., 0.999 Silver 0.3721 oz. ASW, 25 mm. **Ruler:** Elizabeth II **Subject:** Year of the Ox **Rev. Designer:** V. Gottwald

Date	Mintage	F12	VF20	XF40	MS60	MS63
2009	10,000	PF65 45.00				

KM# 1087a DOLLAR
11.90 g., 0.999 Silver 0.3798 oz. ASW, 25 mm. **Ruler:** Elizabeth II **Subject:** 60th Anniversary - Citizenship **Rev:** Portraits around globe

Date	Mintage	F12	VF20	XF40	MS60	MS63
2009C	—	PF65 40.00				

KM# 1077 DOLLAR
9.00 g., Aluminum-Bronze, 25 mm. **Ruler:** Elizabeth II **Subject:** Dorothy Wall **Rev:** Portrait and four characters to right **Rev. Designer:** C. Goodall

Date	Mintage	F12	VF20	XF40	MS60	MS63
2009	—	—	—	—	—	12.00

KM# 1078 DOLLAR
9.00 g., Aluminum-Bronze, 25 mm. **Ruler:** Elizabeth II **Subject:** Year of the Ox **Rev:** V. Gottwald

Date	Mintage	F12	VF20	XF40	MS60	MS63
2009	—	—	—	—	12.00	13.00

KM# 1082 DOLLAR
27.22 g., Copper-Nickel, 38.74 mm. **Ruler:** Elizabeth II **Rev:** Kangaroo **Rev. Designer:** K. Done

Date	Mintage	F12	VF20	XF40	MS60	MS63
2009	—	—	—	—	—	25.00

KM# 1087 DOLLAR
9.00 g., Aluminum Bronze, 25 mm. **Ruler:** Elizabeth II **Subject:** 60th Anniversary - Citizenship **Obv:** Head right **Rev:** Portraits around globe

Date	Mintage	F12	VF20	XF40	MS60	MS63
2009C	—	PF65 28.00				

KM# 1089 DOLLAR
Aluminum-Bronze **Ruler:** Elizabeth II **Subject:** Postal Service, 200th Anniversary **Obv:** Head with tiara right **Rev:** Isaac Nichols, first postman

Date	Mintage	F12	VF20	XF40	MS60	MS63
2009	—	—	—	—	—	13.00

KM# 1092 DOLLAR
13.30 g., Aluminum-Bronze, 30.6 mm. **Ruler:** Elizabeth II **Subject:** Celebrate Australia - Western Australia **Rev:** Kangaroo and multicolor Perth city view

Date	Mintage	F12	VF20	XF40	MS60	MS63
2009	13,067	—	—	—	—	13.00

KM# 1093 DOLLAR
13.30 g., Aluminum-Bronze, 30.6 mm. **Ruler:** Elizabeth II **Series:** Celebrate Australia - Victoria **Rev:** Little Penguin and multicolor Melbourne city view

Date	Mintage	F12	VF20	XF40	MS60	MS63
2009	9,499	—	—	—	—	13.00

KM# 1094 DOLLAR
13.30 g., Aluminum-Bronze, 30.6 mm. **Ruler:** Elizabeth II **Subject:** Celebrate Australia - Tasmania **Rev:** Tasmanian Devil and multicolor Cradle Mountain National Park

Date	Mintage	F12	VF20	XF40	MS60	MS63
2009P	9,689	—	—	—	—	13.00

KM# 1095 DOLLAR
13.30 g., Aluminum-Bronze, 30.6 mm. **Ruler:** Elizabeth II **Subject:** Celebrate Australia - South Australia **Rev:** Wombat and multicolor cathedral

Date	Mintage	F12	VF20	XF40	MS60	MS63
2009P	8,591	—	—	—	—	13.00

KM# 1096 DOLLAR
13.30 g., Aluminum-Bronze, 30.6 mm. **Ruler:** Elizabeth II **Subject:** Celebrate Australia - Queensland **Rev:** Sea Turtle with multicolor skyline of Brisbane

Date	Mintage	F12	VF20	XF40	MS60	MS63
2009P	9,666	—	—	—	—	13.00

KM# 1097 DOLLAR
13.30 g., Aluminum-Bronze, 30.6 mm. **Ruler:** Elizabeth II **Subject:** Celebrate Australia - Northern Territoty **Rev:** Saltwater crocodile and multicolor Kakadu National Park

Date	Mintage	F12	VF20	XF40	MS60	MS63
2009P	9,813	—	—	—	—	13.00

KM# 1098 DOLLAR
13.30 g., Aluminum-Bronze, 30.6 mm. **Ruler:** Elizabeth II **Subject:** Celebrate Australia - New South Wales **Rev:** Koala, multicolor Sydney Opera House and Harbor Bridge

Date	Mintage	F12	VF20	XF40	MS60	MS63
2009P	13,657	—	—	—	—	13.00

KM# 1099 DOLLAR
13.30 g., Aluminum-Bronze, 30.6 mm. **Ruler:** Elizabeth II **Subject:** Celebrate Australia - Capital Territory, Canberra **Rev:** Cockatoo and multicolor design

Date	Mintage	F12	VF20	XF40	MS60	MS63
2009P	9,735	—	—	—	—	13.00

KM# 1103 DOLLAR
31.11 g., 0.999 Silver 0.9926 oz. ASW, 27x47 mm. **Ruler:** Elizabeth II **Rev:** Turtle Dreaming **Rev. Designer:** Darryl Bellotti **Shape:** Rectangle

Date	Mintage	F12	VF20	XF40	MS60	MS63
2009	—	PF65 75.00				

KM# 1107 DOLLAR
31.11 g., 0.9999 Silver 0.9935 oz. ASW, 27x47 mm. **Ruler:** Elizabeth II **Rev:** Kangaroo dreaming **Rev. Designer:** Darryl Bellotti **Shape:** Vertical rectangle

Date	Mintage	F12	VF20	XF40	MS60	MS63
2009	—	PF65 75.00				

KM# 1211 DOLLAR
31.11 g., 0.999 Silver 0.9926 oz. ASW, 40.6 mm. **Ruler:** Elizabeth II **Subject:** Antarctic Territory **Obv:** Head right **Designer:** Ian Rank-Broadley **Rev:** Douglas Mawson, one of two men standing on magnetic South Pole

Date	Mintage	F12	VF20	XF40	MS60	MS63
2009P	6,703	PF65 85.00				

KM# 1212 DOLLAR
31.11 g., 0.999 Silver 0.9926 oz. ASW, 40.6 mm. **Ruler:** Elizabeth II **Obv:** Head right **Obv. Designer:** Ian Rank-Broadley **Rev:** Dreaming kangaroo, multicolor **Rev. Designer:** Darryl Bellotti **Rev. Legend:** DISCOVER AUSTRALIA

Date	Mintage	F12	VF20	XF40	MS60	MS63
2009P	10,000	PF63 80.00	PF65 90.00			

KM# 1213 DOLLAR
31.11 g., 0.999 Silver 0.9926 oz. ASW **Ruler:** Elizabeth II **Obv:** Head right **Obv. Designer:** Ian Rank-Broadley **Rev:** Dreaming dolphin, multicolor **Rev. Designer:** Darryl Bellotti **Rev. Legend:** DISCOVER AUSTRALIA **Shape:** 40.6

Date	Mintage	F12	VF20	XF40	MS60	MS63
2009P	10,000	PF63 80.00	PF65 90.00			

KM# 1214 DOLLAR
31.11 g., 0.999 Silver 0.9926 oz. ASW, 40.6 mm. **Ruler:** Elizabeth II **Obv:** Head right **Obv. Designer:** Ian Rank-Broadley **Rev:** Dreaming king brown snake, multicolor **Rev. Designer:** Darryl Bellotti **Rev. Legend:** DISCOVER AUSTRALIA

Date	Mintage	F12	VF20	XF40	MS60	MS63
2009P	10,000	PF63 80.00	PF65 90.00			

KM# 1215 DOLLAR
31.11 g., 0.999 Silver 0.9926 oz. ASW, 40.6 mm. **Ruler:** Elizabeth II **Obv:** Head right **Obv. Designer:** Ian Rank-Broadley **Rev:** Dreaming brolga, multicolor **Rev. Designer:** Darryl Berllotti

Date	Mintage	F12	VF20	XF40	MS60	MS63
2009P	10,000	PF63 80.00	PF65 90.00			

KM# 1216 DOLLAR
31.11 g., 0.999 Silver 0.9926 oz. ASW, 40.6 mm. **Ruler:** Elizabeth II **Obv:** Head right **Obv. Designer:** Ian Rank-Broadley **Rev:** Dreaming echidna, multicolor **Rev. Designer:** Darryl Berllotti

Date	Mintage	F12	VF20	XF40	MS60	MS63
2009P	10,000	PF63 80.00	PF65 90.00			

KM# 1222 DOLLAR
3.11 g., 0.999 Gold 0.0992 oz. AGW, 16 mm. **Ruler:** Elizabeth

II **Obv:** Head right **Obv. Designer:** Ian Rank-Broadley **Rev:** Dreaming kangaroo **Rev. Designer:** Darryl Berttolli

Date	Mintage	F12	VF20	XF40	MS60	MS63
2009P	2,500	PF65 175				

KM# 1242 DOLLAR
31.11 g., 0.999 Silver 0.9926 oz. ASW, 40.6 mm. **Ruler:** Elizabeth II **Subject:** Treasures of Australia **Obv:** Head right **Obv. Designer:** Ian Rank-Broadley **Rev:** Mountains **Note:** Insert container with 1 carat of diamonds.

Date	Mintage	F12	VF20	XF40	MS60	MS63
2009	7,500	PF63 110	PF65 120			

KM# 1245 DOLLAR
31.11 g., 0.999 Silver 0.9926 oz. ASW **Ruler:** Elizabeth II **Subject:** 2010 FIFA World Cup, South Africa **Obv:** Head right **Obv. Designer:** Ian Rank-Broadley **Rev:** Soccer player and kangaroo in background

Date	Mintage	F12	VF20	XF40	MS60	MS63
2009P	15,000	PF63 90.00	PF65 100			

KM# 1248 DOLLAR
31.11 g., 0.999 Silver 0.9926 oz. ASW, 40.6 mm. **Ruler:** Elizabeth II **Subject:** World Masters Games **Obv:** Head right **Obv. Designer:** Ian Rank-Broadley **Rev:** Sydney Harbor Bridge, multicolor logo

Date	Mintage	F12	VF20	XF40	MS60	MS63
2009P	1,742	PF65 100				

KM# 1256 DOLLAR
13.80 g., Aluminum-Bronze, 31 mm. **Ruler:** Elizabeth II **Subject:** Space Topics - Astronomers **Obv:** Head right **Obv. Designer:** Ian Rank-Broadley **Rev:** Galileo Galilei and telescope

Date	Mintage	F12	VF20	XF40	MS60	MS63
2009P	5,316	—	—	—	—	12.00

KM# 1257 DOLLAR
Aluminum-Bronze, 31 mm. **Ruler:** Elizabeth II **Subject:** Space Topics - Craters **Obv:** Head right **Obv. Designer:** Ian Rank-Broadley **Rev:** Moon crater Daedalus

Date	Mintage	F12	VF20	XF40	MS60	MS63
2009P	5,316	—	—	—	—	12.00

KM# 1258 DOLLAR
Aluminum-Bronze, 31 mm. **Ruler:** Elizabeth II **Subject:** Space Topics - Moons **Obv:** Head right **Obv. Designer:** Ian Rank-Broadley **Rev:** Apollo astronaut on moon walk

Date	Mintage	F12	VF20	XF40	MS60	MS63
2009P	5,316	—	—	—	—	12.00

KM# 1259 DOLLAR
Aluminum-Bronze, 31 mm. **Ruler:** Elizabeth II **Subject:** Space Topics - Observatories **Obv:** Head right **Obv. Designer:** Ian

Rank-Broadley **Rev:** Parkes Observatory, New South Wales

Date	Mintage	F12	VF20	XF40	MS60	MS63
2009P	5,316	—	—	—	—	12.00

KM# 1260 DOLLAR
Aluminum-Bronze, 31 mm. **Ruler:** Elizabeth II **Subject:** Space Topics - Rockets **Obv:** Head right **Obv. Designer:** Ian Rank-Broadley **Rev:** Saturn V rocket on launch pad

Date	Mintage	F12	VF20	XF40	MS60	MS63
2009P	5,316	—	—	—	—	12.00

KM# 1261 DOLLAR
Aluminum-Bronze, 31 mm. **Ruler:** Elizabeth II **Subject:** Space Topics - Rovers **Obv:** Head right **Obv. Designer:** Ian Rank-Broadley **Rev:** Mars rover - Spirit and Opportunity

Date	Mintage	F12	VF20	XF40	MS60	MS63
2009P	5,316	—	—	—	—	12.00

KM# 1262 DOLLAR
Aluminum-Bronze, 31 mm. **Ruler:** Elizabeth II **Subject:** Space Topics - Space Shuttles **Obv:** Head right **Obv. Designer:** Ian Rank-Broadley **Rev:** Shuttle Discovery and Space Exploration

Date	Mintage	F12	VF20	XF40	MS60	MS63
2009P	5,316	—	—	—	—	12.00

KM# 1263 DOLLAR
Aluminum-Bronze, 31 mm. **Ruler:** Elizabeth II **Subject:** Space Topics - Probes **Obv:** Head right **Obv. Designer:** Ian Rank-Broadley **Rev:** Deep Space Probes - Pioneer 10 and 11

Date	Mintage	F12	VF20	XF40	MS60	MS63
2009P	5,316	—	—	—	—	12.00

KM# 1264 DOLLAR
Aluminum-Bronze, 31 mm. **Ruler:** Elizabeth II **Subject:** Space Topics - Space Telescope **Obv:** Head right **Obv. Designer:** Ian Rank-Broadley **Rev:** Hubble Space Telescope

Date	Mintage	F12	VF20	XF40	MS60	MS63
2009P	5,316	—	—	—	—	12.00

KM# 1265 DOLLAR
31.11 g., 0.999 Silver 0.9926 oz. ASW, 27x48 mm. **Ruler:** Elizabeth II **Subject:** Chinese Mythological Character - Wealth **Obv:** Head right **Obv. Designer:** Ian Rank-Broadley **Rev:** Man standing, multicolor **Shape:** Vertical rectangle

Date	Mintage	F12	VF20	XF40	MS60	MS63
2009P	—	—	—	—	—	65.00

KM# 1266 DOLLAR
31.11 g., 0.999 Silver 0.9926 oz. ASW, 27x48 mm. **Ruler:** Elizabeth II **Subject:** Chinese Mythological Character - Longevity **Obv:** Head right **Obv. Designer:** Ian Rank-Broadley **Rev:** Man standing with staff, multicolor **Edge Lettering:** Vertical rectangle

Date	Mintage	F12	VF20	XF40	MS60	MS63
2009P	—	—	—	—	—	65.00

KM# 1267 DOLLAR
31.11 g., 0.999 Silver 0.9926 oz. ASW, 27x48 mm. **Ruler:** Elizabeth II **Subject:** Chinese Mythological Character - Success **Obv:** Head right **Obv. Designer:** Ian Rank-Broadley **Rev:** Man standing with deer, multicolor **Shape:** Vertical rectangle

Date	Mintage	F12	VF20	XF40	MS60	MS63
2009P	—	—	—	—	—	65.00

KM# 1268 DOLLAR
31.11 g., 0.999 Silver 0.9926 oz. ASW, 27x48 mm. **Ruler:** Elizabeth II **Subject:** Chinese Mythological Character - Fortune **Obv:** Head right **Obv. Designer:** Ian Rank-Broadley **Rev:** Man standing with scroll, multicolor **Shape:** Vertical rectangle

Date	Mintage	F12	VF20	XF40	MS60	MS63
2009P	—	—	—	—	—	65.00

KM# 1357 DOLLAR
31.14 g., 0.999 Silver 0.9936 oz. ASW, 40.6 mm. **Ruler:** Elizabeth II **Subject:** International Year of Astronomy **Obv:** Head right **Rev:** Youth looking through telescope, pointing at universe

Date	Mintage	F12	VF20	XF40	MS60	MS63
2009P	6,814	PF65 60.00				

KM# 1358 DOLLAR
30.60 g., Aluminum-Bronze, 30.6 mm. **Ruler:** Elizabeth II **Subject:** Swimming **Obv:** Head light **Rev:** Swimmer

Date	Mintage	F12	VF20	XF40	MS60	MS63
2009(p)	8,467	—	—	—	7.50	10.00

KM# 1359 DOLLAR
32.14 g., 0.999 Silver 1.0255 oz. ASW, 40 mm. **Ruler:** Elizabeth

II **Subject:** Swimming **Obv:** Head right **Rev:** Swimmer with hologram effect added

Date	Mintage	F12	VF20	XF40	MS60	MS63
2009(p)	1,993	PF65 70.00				

KM# 1497 DOLLAR
13.80 g., Aluminum-Bronze, 30.6 mm. **Ruler:** Elizabeth II **Subject:** ANZAC **Rev:** Child on lap of grandfather, bugler in background

Date	Mintage	F12	VF20	XF40	MS60	MS63
2009	18,561	—	—	—	7.50	10.00

KM# 1498 DOLLAR
9.00 g., Aluminum-Bronze, 25 mm. **Ruler:** Elizabeth II **Subject:** Age pensions, 100th Anniversary **Rev:** Extended family portrait, elder members seated at front center in detail

Date	Mintage	F12	VF20	XF40	MS60	MS63
2009	—	—	—	—	7.50	10.00

KM# 1499 DOLLAR
9.00 g., Aluminum-Bronze, 25 mm. **Ruler:** Elizabeth II **Subject:** Girl Guides, 100th Anniversary

Date	Mintage	F12	VF20	XF40	MS60	MS63
2009	—	—	—	—	7.50	10.00

KM# 1655 DOLLAR
9.00 g., Aluminum-Bronze, 25 mm. **Ruler:** Elizabeth II **Obv:** Head with tiara right **Rev:** Baby bilby in color right

Date	Mintage	F12	VF20	XF40	MS60	MS63
2009	—	—	—	—	—	10.00

KM# 1656 DOLLAR
9.00 g., Aluminum-Bronze, 25 mm. **Ruler:** Elizabeth II **Obv:** Head with tiara right **Rev:** Frilly lizard in color right

Date	Mintage	F12	VF20	XF40	MS60	MS63
2009	—	—	—	—	—	10.00

KM# 1657 DOLLAR
9.00 g., Aluminum-Bronze, 25 mm. **Ruler:** Elizabeth II **Subject:**

World Masters Games Obv: Head with tiara right **Rev:** Sydney Harbor Bridge, games logo above

Date	Mintage	F12	VF20	XF40	MS60	MS63
2009	—	—	—	—	7.00	10.00

KM# 1403 DOLLAR
31.11 g., 0.999 Silver 0.9926 oz. ASW, 40.6 mm. **Ruler:** Elizabeth II **Obv:** Head right **Rev:** Frill-neck lizard, multicolor

Date	Mintage	F12	VF20	XF40	MS60	MS63
2010(p)	—	PF63 80.00		PF65 90.00		

KM# 1409 DOLLAR
31.11 g., 0.999 Silver 0.9926 oz. ASW, 40.6 mm. **Ruler:** Elizabeth II **Obv:** Head right **Obv. Designer:** Ian Rank Broadley **Rev:** Koala and multicolor

Date	Mintage	F12	VF20	XF40	MS60	MS63
2010(p)	—	PF63 80.00		PF65 90.00		

KM# 1415 DOLLAR
31.11 g., 0.999 Silver 0.9926 oz. ASW, 40.6 mm. **Ruler:** Elizabeth II **Obv:** Head right **Obv. Designer:** Ian Rank Broadley **Rev:** Multicolor platypus

Date	Mintage	F12	VF20	XF40	MS60	MS63
2010(p)	—	PF63 80.00		PF65 90.00		

KM# 1421 DOLLAR
31.11 g., 0.999 Silver 0.9926 oz. ASW, 40.6 mm. **Ruler:** Elizabeth II **Obv:** Head right **Obv. Designer:** Ian Rank-Broadley **Rev:** Multicolor salt water crocodile

Date	Mintage	F12	VF20	XF40	MS60	MS63
2010(p)	—	PF63 80.00		PF65 90.00		

KM# 1427 DOLLAR
31.11 g., 0.999 Silver 0.9926 oz. ASW, 40.6 mm. **Ruler:** Elizabeth II **Obv:** Head right **Obv. Designer:** Ian Rank-Broadley **Rev:** Multicolor wombat

Date	Mintage	F12	VF20	XF40	MS60	MS63
2010(p)	—	PF63 80.00		PF65 90.00		

KM# 1659a DOLLAR
11.66 g., 0.999 Silver 0.3721 oz. ASW, 25 mm. **Ruler:** Elizabeth II **Subject:** Year of the Tiger **Obv:** Head with tiara right **Rev:** Tiger head in circle, floral around

Date	Mintage	F12	VF20	XF40	MS60	MS63
2010	—		PF65 30.00			

KM# 1495 DOLLAR
9.00 g., Aluminum-Bronze, 25 mm. **Ruler:** Elizabeth II **Subject:** Australian coinage, 100th Anniversary **Obv:** Head with tiara right **Rev:** Coinage portraits of Elizabeth II, George VI, George V and Edward VII

Date	Mintage	F12	VF20	XF40	MS60	MS63
2010C	—	—	—	—	4.00	5.00
2010B	—	—	—	—	4.00	5.00
2010M	—	—	—	—	4.00	5.00
2010S	—	—	—	—	4.00	5.00

KM# 1503 DOLLAR
9.00 g., Aluminum-Bronze, 25 mm. **Ruler:** Elizabeth II **Subject:** Wool Industry **Rev:** Sheep sheering and map of Australia

Date	Mintage	F12	VF20	XF40	MS60	MS63
2010	—		PF65 25.00			
2010	—	—	—	—	5.00	6.00

KM# 1324 DOLLAR
31.11 g., 0.999 Silver 0.9926 oz. ASW, 41 mm. **Ruler:** Elizabeth II **Subject:** Lachlan Macquarie, Governor of New South Wales **Obv:** Head right **Obv. Designer:** Ian Rank-Broadley **Rev:** Macquarie, Sydney's "Rum" Hospital, Holey Dollar

Date	Mintage	F12	VF20	XF40	MS60	MS63
2010P	7,500	PF63 80.00		PF65 90.00		

KM# 1325 DOLLAR
31.11 g., 0.999 Silver 0.9926 oz. ASW, 41 mm. **Ruler:** Elizabeth II **Subject:** 2010 Australian Olympic Team **Obv:** Head right **Obv. Designer:** Ian Rank-Broadley **Rev:** Downhill skier, multicolor Australian flag

Date	Mintage	F12	VF20	XF40	MS60	MS63
2010P	5,000	PF63 90.00		PF65 100		

KM# 1326 DOLLAR
31.11 g., 0.999 Silver 0.9926 oz. ASW, 41 mm. **Ruler:** Elizabeth II **Subject:** Century of Flight in Australia **Obv:** Head right **Obv. Designer:** Ian Rank-Broadley **Rev:** Bi-plane, multicolor

Date	Mintage	F12	VF20	XF40	MS60	MS63
2010P	7,500	PF63 80.00		PF65 90.00		

KM# 1380 DOLLAR
13.80 g., Aluminum-Bronze, 30.6 mm. **Ruler:** Elizabeth II **Subject:** Anzac Navy **Obv:** Head right **Rev:** Naval crew member and ship

Date	Mintage	F12	VF20	XF40	MS60	MS63
2010(p)	—	—	—	—	—	12.00

KM# 1381 DOLLAR
31.10 g., 0.999 Silver 0.9926 oz. ASW, 40.5 mm. **Ruler:** Elizabeth II **Subject:** Antarctic - Huskey **Obv:** Head right **Rev:** Huskey in multicolor

Date	Mintage	F12	VF20	XF40	MS60	MS63
2010(p)	7,500		PF65 60.00			

KM# 1382 DOLLAR
13.80 g., Aluminum-Bronze, 30.6 mm. **Ruler:** Elizabeth II **Subject:** Flight Centennial **Obv:** Head right **Rev:** Bi-plane flying right

Date	Mintage	F12	VF20	XF40	MS60	MS63
2010(p)	—	—	—	—	—	13.00

KM# 1383 DOLLAR
31.10 g., 0.999 Silver 0.9926 oz. ASW, 40 mm. **Ruler:** Elizabeth II **Subject:** Edward VII Coinage **Obv:** Head right **Rev:** Coin designs and Edward VII in multicolor

Date	Mintage	F12	VF20	XF40	MS60	MS63
2010(p)	—	—	—	—	—	60.00

KM# 1384 DOLLAR
13.80 g., Aluminum-Bronze, 30.6 mm. **Ruler:** Elizabeth II **Subject:** Celebrate Australia - Barrier Reef **Obv:** Head right

Rev: Sea Turtle and multicolor background

Date	Mintage	F12	VF20	XF40	MS60	MS63
2010P	—	—	—	—	—	15.00

KM# 1385 DOLLAR
13.80 g., Aluminum-Bronze, 30.6 mm. **Ruler:** Elizabeth II **Subject:** Celebrate Australia - Blue Mountain **Obv:** Head right **Rev:** Frog and multicolor background

Date	Mintage	F12	VF20	XF40	MS60	MS63
2010P	—	—	—	—	—	15.00

KM# 1386 DOLLAR
13.80 g., Aluminum-Bronze, 30.6 mm. **Ruler:** Elizabeth II **Subject:** Celebrate Australia - Heard Island **Obv:** Head right **Rev:** Penguins and multicolor background

Date	Mintage	F12	VF20	XF40	MS60	MS63
2010P	—	—	—	—	—	15.00

KM# 1387 DOLLAR
13.80 g., Aluminum-Bronze, 30.6 mm. **Ruler:** Elizabeth II **Subject:** Celebrate Australia - Shark Bay **Obv:** Head right

Date	Mintage	F12	VF20	XF40	MS60	MS63
2010P	—	—	—	—	—	15.00

KM# 1388 DOLLAR
13.80 g., Aluminum-Bronze, 30.6 mm. **Ruler:** Elizabeth II **Subject:** Celebrate Australia - Tasmanian Wilderness **Obv:** Head right **Rev:** Animal before multicolor waterfall background

Date	Mintage	F12	VF20	XF40	MS60	MS63
2010P	—	—	—	—	—	15.00

KM# 1391 DOLLAR
31.11 g., 0.999 Silver 0.9926 oz. ASW **Ruler:** Elizabeth II **Obv:** Head right **Rev:** Panda and koala

Date	Mintage	F12	VF20	XF40	MS60	MS63
2010(p)	—	—	—	—	—	45.00

KM# 1392 DOLLAR
31.11 g., 0.999 Silver 0.9926 oz. ASW **Ruler:** Elizabeth II **Subject:** World Expo **Obv:** Head right **Rev:** Austrlian Panham

Date	Mintage	F12	VF20	XF40	MS60	MS63
2010(p)	—	—	—	—	—	50.00

KM# 1393 DOLLAR
31.11 g., 0.999 Silver 0.9926 oz. ASW **Ruler:** Elizabeth II **Obv:** Head right **Rev:** Kookaburra mascot

Date	Mintage	F12	VF20	XF40	MS60	MS63
2010(p)	—	—	—	—	—	45.00

KM# 1394 DOLLAR
31.11 g., 0.999 Silver 0.9926 oz. ASW **Ruler:** Elizabeth II **Obv:** Head right **Rev:** City scape

Date	Mintage	F12	VF20	XF40	MS60	MS63
2010(p)	—	—	—	—	—	45.00

KM# 1395 DOLLAR
Silver, 40x60 mm. **Ruler:** Elizabeth II **Series:** World Expo **Obv:** Head right **Shape:** Australian outline

Date	Mintage	F12	VF20	XF40	MS60	MS63
2010(p)	—	—	—	—	—	70.00

KM# 1396 DOLLAR
13.80 g., Aluminum-Bronze, 30.6 mm. **Ruler:** Elizabeth II **Subject:** 2010 Shanghai World Expo **Obv:** Head with tiara right **Obv. Designer:** Ian Rank-Broadley **Rev:** Artistic tiger seen from above, advancing forward **Rev. Designer:** Wade Robinson

Date	Mintage	F12	VF20	XF40	MS60	MS63
2010P	—	—	—	—	—	14.00

KM# 1431 DOLLAR
9.00 g., Aluminum-Bronze, 25 mm. **Ruler:** Elizabeth II **Subject:** Burke and Wills 150th Anniversary **Obv:** Head with tiara right **Rev:** King seated under dig tree

Date	Mintage	F12	VF20	XF40	MS60	MS63
2010C	—	—	—	—	—	12.50
2010C	—	PF65 17.50				

KM# 1434 DOLLAR
31.14 g., 0.999 Silver 0.9936 oz. ASW **Ruler:** Elizabeth II **Subject:** Burke & Wills expedition **Rev:** Multicolor scene of explorers

Date	Mintage	F12	VF20	XF40	MS60	MS63
2010P	7,500	PF65 80.00				

KM# 1435 DOLLAR
31.14 g., 0.999 Silver 0.9936 oz. ASW, 40.6 mm. **Ruler:** Elizabeth II **Subject:** Treasures of Australia - Gold **Rev:** Three gold nuggets within insert

Date	Mintage	F12	VF20	XF40	MS60	MS63
2010P	—	PF65 135				

KM# 1440 DOLLAR
13.30 g., Aluminum-Bronze, 30.6 mm. **Ruler:** Elizabeth II **Rev:** Blowfly

Date	Mintage	F12	VF20	XF40	MS60	MS63
2010P	—	—	—	—	—	12.00

KM# 1441 DOLLAR
13.30 g., Aluminum-Bronze, 30.6 mm. **Ruler:** Elizabeth II **Rev:** Bull Ant

Date	Mintage	F12	VF20	XF40	MS60	MS63
2010P	—	—	—	—	—	12.00

KM# 1442 DOLLAR
13.30 g., Aluminum-Bronze, 30.6 mm. **Ruler:** Elizabeth II **Rev:** Burlwing Buttlerfly

Date	Mintage	F12	VF20	XF40	MS60	MS63
2010P	—	—	—	—	—	12.00

KM# 1443 DOLLAR
13.30 g., Aluminum-Bronze, 30.6 mm. **Ruler:** Elizabeth II **Rev:** Cicada

Date	Mintage	F12	VF20	XF40	MS60	MS63
2010P	—	—	—	—	—	12.00

KM# 1444 DOLLAR
13.30 g., Aluminum-Bronze, 30.6 mm. **Ruler:** Elizabeth II **Rev:** Dragonfly

Date	Mintage	F12	VF20	XF40	MS60	MS63
2010P	—	—	—	—	—	12.00

KM# 1445 DOLLAR
13.30 g., Aluminum-Bronze, 30.6 mm. **Ruler:** Elizabeth II **Rev:** Grasshopper

Date	Mintage	F12	VF20	XF40	MS60	MS63
2010P	—	—	—	—	—	12.00

KM# 1446 DOLLAR
13.30 g., Aluminum-Bronze, 30.6 mm. **Ruler:** Elizabeth II **Rev:** Ladybug

Date	Mintage	F12	VF20	XF40	MS60	MS63
2010P	—	—	—	—	—	12.00

KM# 1447 DOLLAR
13.30 g., Aluminum-Bronze, 30.6 mm. **Ruler:** Elizabeth II **Rev:** Praying mantis

Date	Mintage	F12	VF20	XF40	MS60	MS63
2010P	—	—	—	—	—	12.00

KM# 1448 DOLLAR
13.30 g., Aluminum-Bronze, 30.6 mm. **Ruler:** Elizabeth II **Rev:** Red-backed spider

Date	Mintage	F12	VF20	XF40	MS60	MS63
2010P	—	—	—	—	—	12.00

KM# 1451 DOLLAR
31.11 g., 0.999 Silver 0.9926 oz. ASW **Ruler:** Elizabeth II **Subject:** New South Wales - Sidney Coin Show **Rev:** Koala and multicolor opera house and harbor bridge views

Date	Mintage	F12	VF20	XF40	MS60	MS63
2010P	—	PF65 45.00				

KM# 1452 DOLLAR
31.11 g., 0.999 Silver 0.9926 oz. ASW **Ruler:** Elizabeth II **Subject:** Victoria - Melbourne Coin Show **Rev:** Penguin and multicolor tram and building

Date	Mintage	F12	VF20	XF40	MS60	MS63
2010P	—	PF65 45.00				

KM# 1453 DOLLAR
31.11 g., 0.999 Silver 0.9926 oz. ASW, 27x47 mm. **Ruler:** Elizabeth II **Rev:** Dreaming dolphin **Shape:** Vertical rectangle

Date	Mintage	F12	VF20	XF40	MS60	MS63
2010P Proof	—	—	—	—	—	80.00

KM# 1490 DOLLAR
13.30 g., Aluminum-Bronze, 30.6 mm. **Ruler:** Elizabeth II **Rev:** Burke & Willis statue

Date	Mintage	F12	VF20	XF40	MS60	MS63
2010P	—	—	—	—	—	12.00

KM# 1491 DOLLAR
31.11 g., 0.999 Silver 0.9926 oz. ASW, 40.6 mm. **Ruler:** Elizabeth II **Obv:** Head with tiara right **Rev:** Saint Mary Mackillop in color

Date	Mintage	F12	VF20	XF40	MS60	MS63
2010	—	PF65 60.00				

KM# 1494 DOLLAR
31.11 g., 0.999 Silver 0.9926 oz. ASW **Ruler:** Elizabeth II **Subject:** New South Wales

Date	Mintage	F12	VF20	XF40	MS60	MS63
2010		PF65 50.00				

KM# 1495a DOLLAR
11.66 g., 0.999 Silver 0.3721 oz. ASW, 25 mm. **Ruler:** Elizabeth II **Subject:** Centennial of Commonwealth Coins **Obv:** Head in tiara right **Rev:** Four portraits

Date	Mintage	F12	VF20	XF40	MS60	MS63
2010	12,500	PF65 50.00				

KM# 1496 DOLLAR
9.00 g., Aluminum-Bronze, 25 mm. **Ruler:** Elizabeth II **Subject:** Fred Hollows - Inspirational Australians

Date	Mintage	F12	VF20	XF40	MS60	MS63
2010	—	—	—	—	3.50	5.00

KM# 1505 DOLLAR
31.11 g., 0.999 Silver 0.9926 oz. ASW, 40.6 mm. **Ruler:** Elizabeth II **Subject:** Perth-ANDA Bridge **Rev:** City view

Date	Mintage	F12	VF20	XF40	MS60	MS63
2010	—	PF63 60.00	PF65 65.00			

KM# 1568 DOLLAR
31.11 g., 0.999 Silver 0.9926 oz. ASW, 32.6 mm. **Ruler:** Elizabeth II **Subject:** Sidney Cove Medallion, Wedgewood theme **Obv:** Head with tiara right **Rev:** One female standing on rock facing three others, seascape in backgorund **Edge:** Reeded **Note:** High relief

Date	Mintage	F12	VF20	XF40	MS60	MS63
2010P	Est. 5000	PF65 85.00				

KM# 1659 DOLLAR
9.00 g., Aluminum-Bronze, 25 mm. **Ruler:** Elizabeth II **Subject:** Year of the Tiger **Rev:** Tiger head at center in circle, floral around

Date	Mintage	F12	VF20	XF40	MS60	MS63
2010	—	—	—	—	—	10.00

KM# 1504 DOLLAR
9.00 g., Aluminum-Bronze, 25 mm. **Ruler:** Elizabeth II **Subject:** Historical coin designs **Rev:** Sheep head

Date	Mintage	F12	VF20	XF40	MS60	MS63
2011C	—	—	—	—	5.00	6.00

KM# 1523 DOLLAR
31.10 g., 0.999 Silver 0.9926 oz. ASW, 40.6 mm. **Ruler:** Elizabeth II **Subject:** Australia's Bronze Coinagae, 100th Anniversary **Obv:** Head with tiara right **Rev:** George V and coins, in color

Date	Mintage	F12	VF20	XF40	MS60	MS63
2011	—	PF65 75.00				

KM# 1528 DOLLAR
31.11 g., 0.999 Silver 0.9926 oz. ASW, 40.6 mm. **Ruler:** Elizabeth II **Subject:** Famous Battles in Australian History **Rev:** Soldier standing at left, view of Gallipoli, 1915 at right **Rev. Designer:** Wade Robinson

Date	Mintage	F12	VF20	XF40	MS60	MS63
2011P	5,000	PF65 110				

KM# 1529 DOLLAR
13.30 g., Aluminum-Bronze, 30.6 mm. **Ruler:** Elizabeth II **Subject:** ANZAC Day, RAAF **Rev:** Bugler and plane, two airmen at lower right **Rev. Designer:** Wade Robinson

Date	Mintage	F12	VF20	XF40	MS60	MS63
2011P	—	—	—	—	—	13.00

KM# 1530 DOLLAR
31.11 g., 0.999 Silver 0.9926 oz. ASW **Ruler:** Elizabeth II **Subject:** Royal Wedding **Rev:** Catherine Middleton and Prince William in color, Westminster Abbey at left **Rev. Designer:** Aleysha Howarth

Date	Mintage	F12	VF20	XF40	MS60	MS63
2011P	12,500	PF65 110				

KM# 1531 DOLLAR
31.11 g., 0.999 Silver 0.9926 oz. ASW **Ruler:** Elizabeth II **Subject:** Naval Battles **Rev:** Battle of Midway

Date	Mintage	F12	VF20	XF40	MS60	MS63
2011P	5,000	PF65 110				

KM# 1534 DOLLAR
31.11 g., 0.999 Silver 0.9926 oz. ASW **Ruler:** Elizabeth II **Subject:** Dreaming Emu **Rev:** Linear emu in color

Date	Mintage	F12	VF20	XF40	MS60	MS63
2011P	—	PF65 105				

KM# 1540 DOLLAR
31.11 g., 0.999 Silver 0.9926 oz. ASW **Ruler:** Elizabeth II **Subject:** Dreaming Tasmanian Devil **Rev:** Linear tasmanian devil in color

Date	Mintage	F12	VF20	XF40	MS60	MS63
2011P	—	PF65 105				

KM# 1546 DOLLAR
31.11 g., 0.999 Silver 0.9926 oz. ASW **Ruler:** Elizabeth II **Rev:** Linear Kookaburra in color **Rev. Designer:** Dreaming Kookaburra

Date	Mintage	F12	VF20	XF40	MS60	MS63
2011P	—	PF65 115				

KM# 1552 DOLLAR
31.11 g., 0.999 Silver 0.9926 oz. ASW **Ruler:** Elizabeth II **Subject:** Dreaming Shark **Rev:** Linear shark in color

Date	Mintage	F12	VF20	XF40	MS60	MS63
2011P	—	PF65 105				

KM# 1558 DOLLAR
31.11 g., 0.999 Silver 0.9926 oz. ASW **Ruler:** Elizabeth II **Subject:** Dreaming Dingo **Rev:** Linear dingo in color

Date	Mintage	F12	VF20	XF40	MS60	MS63
2011P	—	PF65 105				

KM# 1564 DOLLAR
31.11 g., 0.999 Silver 0.9926 oz. ASW **Ruler:** Elizabeth II **Subject:** Treasures of Australia **Rev:** Keshi pearl engased in mother of pearl locket

Date	Mintage	F12	VF20	XF40	MS60	MS63
2011P	—	PF65 185				

KM# 1565 DOLLAR
31.11 g., 0.999 Silver 0.9926 oz. ASW, 40.6 mm. **Ruler:** Elizabeth II **Subject:** Antarctica **Obv:** Head with tiara right **Rev:** Killer whale in color **Rev. Designer:** Wade Robinson

Date	Mintage	F12	VF20	XF40	MS60	MS63
2011P	7,500	PF65 115				

KM# 1572 DOLLAR

13.00 g., Aluminum-Bronze, 30.6 mm. **Ruler:** Elizabeth II
Subject: Bush Babies - Koala **Rev:** Koala lounging at left **Rev.**
Designer: Elise Martinson

Date	Mintage	F12	VF20	XF40	MS60	MS63
2011(p)	—	—	—	—	—	15.00

KM# 1573 DOLLAR

13.00 g., Aluminum-Bronze, 30.6 mm. **Ruler:** Elizabeth II
Subject: Bush babies - Dingo **Rev:** Dingo seated at left **Rev.**
Designer: Elise Martinson

Date	Mintage	F12	VF20	XF40	MS60	MS63
2011(p)	—	—	—	—	—	15.00

KM# 1574 DOLLAR

13.00 g., Aluminum-Bronze, 30.6 mm. **Ruler:** Elizabeth II
Subject: Bush babies - Bilby **Rev:** Bilby at left **Rev. Designer:**
Elise Martinson

Date	Mintage	F12	VF20	XF40	MS60	MS63
2011(p)	—	—	—	—	—	15.00

KM# 1575 DOLLAR

13.00 g., Aluminum-Bronze, 30.6 mm. **Ruler:** Elizabeth II
Subject: Bush babies - Sugar Glider **Rev:** Sugar Glider at left
Rev. Designer: Elise Martinson

Date	Mintage	F12	VF20	XF40	MS60	MS63
2011(p)	—	—	—	—	—	15.00

KM# 1576 DOLLAR

13.00 g., Aluminum-Bronze, 30.6 mm. **Ruler:** Elizabeth II
Subject: Bush babies - Kangaroo **Rev:** Kangaroo seated at left
Rev. Designer: Elise Martinson

Date	Mintage	F12	VF20	XF40	MS60	MS63
2011(p)	—	—	—	—	—	15.00

KM# 1580 DOLLAR

13.80 g., Aluminum-Bronze, 30.6 mm. **Ruler:** Elizabeth II
Subject: Mythical creatures - Dragon **Rev. Designer:** Tom
Vaughan

Date	Mintage	F12	VF20	XF40	MS60	MS63
2011P	—	—	—	—	—	12.50

KM# 1581 DOLLAR

13.80 g., Aluminum-Bronze, 30.6 mm. **Ruler:** Elizabeth II
Subject: Mythical creatures - Fairy **Rev. Designer:** Tom
Vaughan

Date	Mintage	F12	VF20	XF40	MS60	MS63
2011P	—	—	—	—	—	12.50

KM# 1582 DOLLAR

13.80 g., Aluminum-Bronze, 30.6 mm. **Ruler:** Elizabeth II
Subject: Mythical creatures - Goblin **Rev. Designer:** Tom
Vaughan

Date	Mintage	F12	VF20	XF40	MS60	MS63
2011P	—	—	—	—	—	12.50

KM# 1583 DOLLAR

13.80 g., Aluminum-Bronze, 30.6 mm. **Ruler:** Elizabeth II
Subject: Mythical creatures - Griffin **Rev. Designer:** Tom
Vaughan

Date	Mintage	F12	VF20	XF40	MS60	MS63
2011P	—	—	—	—	—	12.50

KM# 1584 DOLLAR

13.80 g., Aluminum-Bronze, 30.6 mm. **Ruler:** Elizabeth II
Subject: Mythical creatures - Mermaid **Rev. Designer:** Tom
Vaughan

Date	Mintage	F12	VF20	XF40	MS60	MS63
2011P	—	—	—	—	—	12.50

KM# 1585 DOLLAR

13.80 g., Aluminum-Bronze, 30.6 mm. **Ruler:** Elizabeth II
Subject: Mythical creatures - Tree ent **Rev. Designer:** Tom
Vaughan

Date	Mintage	F12	VF20	XF40	MS60	MS63
2011P	—	—	—	—	—	12.50

KM# 1586 DOLLAR

13.80 g., Aluminum-Bronze, 30.6 mm. **Ruler:** Elizabeth II
Subject: Mythical creatures - Ogre **Rev. Designer:** Tom
Vaughan

Date	Mintage	F12	VF20	XF40	MS60	MS63
2011P	—	—	—	—	—	12.50

KM# 1587 DOLLAR

13.80 g., Aluminum-Bronze, 30.6 mm. **Ruler:** Elizabeth II
Subject: Mythical creatures - Phoenix **Rev. Designer:** Tom
Vaughan

Date	Mintage	F12	VF20	XF40	MS60	MS63
2011P	—	—	—	—	—	12.50

KM# 1588 DOLLAR

13.80 g., Aluminum-Bronze, 30.6 mm. **Ruler:** Elizabeth II
Subject: Mythical creatures - Unicorn **Rev. Designer:** Tom
Vaughan

Date	Mintage	F12	VF20	XF40	MS60	MS63
2011P	—	—	—	—	—	12.50

KM# 1589 DOLLAR

13.80 g., Aluminum-Bronze, 30.6 mm. **Ruler:** Elizabeth II **Obv:**
Head in tiara right **Rev:** Christmas tree decorated in color,
presents below, stars around, holly at bottom flanking **Rev.**
Legend: WISHING YOU A MERRY CHRISTMAS / 2011

Date	Mintage	F12	VF20	XF40	MS60	MS63
2011P	—	—	—	—	—	12.50

KM# 1590 DOLLAR
31.10 g., 0.999 Silver 0.9926 oz. ASW, 40 mm. **Ruler:** Elizabeth II **Subject:** Dame Nellie Melba **Obv:** Head with tiara right **Rev:** Colored bust right, musical notes below, flowers at left **Rev. Designer:** Aleysha Howarth

Date	Mintage	F12	VF20	XF40	MS60	MS63
2011P	Est. 5000	PF65 100				

KM# 1591 DOLLAR
13.80 g., Aluminum-Bronze, 30.6 mm. **Ruler:** Elizabeth II **Subject:** Dame Nellie Melba **Obv:** Head with tiara right **Rev:** Bust at left facing right, flowers at right **Rev. Designer:** Aleysha Howarth

Date	Mintage	F12	VF20	XF40	MS60	MS63
2011P	—	—	—	—	—	12.50

KM# 1592 DOLLAR
31.11 g., 0.999 Silver 0.9926 oz. ASW, 40 mm. **Ruler:** Elizabeth II **Subject:** Royal Military College - Duntroon; 100th Anniversary **Obv:** Head with tiara right **Rev:** College emblem gilt above images of soldiers

Date	Mintage	F12	VF20	XF40	MS60	MS63
2011P	Est. 7500	PF65 100				

KM# 1593 DOLLAR
13.80 g., Aluminum-Bronze, 30.6 mm. **Ruler:** Elizabeth II **Subject:** Royal Military College - Duntroon; 100th Anniversary **Obv:** Head with tiara right **Rev:** Military hat badge **Rev. Designer:** Wade Robinson

Date	Mintage	F12	VF20	XF40	MS60	MS63
2011P	—	—	—	—	—	12.50

KM# 1594 DOLLAR
31.11 g., 0.999 Silver 0.9926 oz. ASW, 40 mm. **Ruler:** Elizabeth II **Subject:** Australian Antarctic Territory, Killer Whale **Obv:** Head with tiara right **Rev:** Killer whale, jumping, and in the water with a calf

Date	Mintage	F12	VF20	XF40	MS60	MS63
2011P	Est. 7500	PF65 100				

KM# 1597 DOLLAR
Aluminum-Bronze, 40 mm. **Ruler:** Elizabeth II **Subject:** Wiggles, 20th Anniversary **Obv:** Head with tiara right **Rev:** Wiggles characters in Big Red car **Rev. Designer:** Tom Vaughan **Edge:** Reeded

Date	Mintage	F12	VF20	XF40	MS60	MS63
2011P	—	—	—	—	—	17.50

KM# 1598 DOLLAR
Aluminum-Bronze, 40 mm. **Ruler:** Elizabeth II **Subject:** Wiggles, 20th Anniversary **Obv:** Head in tiara right **Rev:** Wiggles four band members at instruments **Rev. Designer:** Tom Vaughan **Edge:** Reeded

Date	Mintage	F12	VF20	XF40	MS60	MS63
2011P	—	—	—	—	—	17.50

KM# 1599 DOLLAR
Aluminum-Bronze, 40 mm. **Ruler:** Elizabeth II **Subject:** Wiggles, 20th Anniversary **Obv:** Head with tiara right **Rev:** Wiggles Pirate and animal characters **Rev. Designer:** Tom Vaughan

Date	Mintage	F12	VF20	XF40	MS60	MS63
2011P	—	—	—	—	—	17.50

KM# 1600 DOLLAR
Aluminum-Bronze, 40 mm. **Ruler:** Elizabeth II **Subject:** Wiggles, 20th Anniversary **Obv:** Head with tiara right **Rev:** Wiggles charactes in starburst **Rev. Designer:** Tom Vaughan

Date	Mintage	F12	VF20	XF40	MS60	MS63
2011P	—	—	—	—	—	17.50

KM# 1601 DOLLAR
31.11 g., 0.999 Silver 0.9926 oz. ASW, 40 mm. **Ruler:** Elizabeth II **Subject:** Royal Australian Navy, 100th Anniversary **Obv:** Head with tiara right **Rev:** HMAS Yarra, HMAS Anzac and sailors **Edge:** Reeded

Date	Mintage	F12	VF20	XF40	MS60	MS63
2011P		PF65 120				

KM# 1602 DOLLAR
13.80 g., Aluminum-Bronze, 30.6 mm. **Ruler:** Elizabeth II **Subject:** Royal Australian Navy, 100th Anniversary **Obv:** Head with tiara right **Rev:** Navy cap badge **Rev. Designer:** Wade Robinson

Date	Mintage	F12	VF20	XF40	MS60	MS63
2011P	—	—	—	—	—	15.00

KM# 1603 DOLLAR
13.80 g., Aluminum-Bronze, 30.6 mm. **Ruler:** Elizabeth II **Subject:** Elizabeth II's 85th Birthday **Obv:** Head with tiara right **Rev:** Elizabeth II in hat at left, birthday legend and emblem below **Rev. Designer:** Ryan Vanderwiel **Edge:** Reeded

Date	Mintage	F12	VF20	XF40	MS60	MS63
2011P	—	—	—	—	—	15.00

KM# 1604 DOLLAR
31.11 g., 0.999 Silver 0.9926 oz. ASW, 40 mm. **Ruler:** Elizabeth II **Subject:** Wallabies Rugby team **Obv:** Head with tiara right **Rev:** Wallabies logo in color at left, rugby player at right **Rev. Designer:** Ryan Vanderwiel **Edge:** Reeded

Date	Mintage	F12	VF20	XF40	MS60	MS63
2011P	—	PF65 100				

KM# 1606 DOLLAR
31.11 g., 0.999 Silver 0.9926 oz. ASW, 40 mm. **Ruler:** Elizabeth II **Subject:** World War II - Siege of Tobruk **Obv:** Head with tiara right **Rev:** Soldier standing at left, image of solder carried on stretcher at right; Campaign ribbon below **Edge:** Reeded

Date	Mintage	F12	VF20	XF40	MS60	MS63
2011P	Est. 5000	PF65 100				

KM# 1607 DOLLAR
31.11 g., 0.999 Silver 0.9926 oz. ASW, 40 mm. **Ruler:** Elizabeth II **Subject:** Ginger Meggs, 90th Birthday **Obv:** Head with tiara right **Rev:** Cartoon boy riding kangaroo right **Rev. Designer:** Jason Chatfield **Edge:** Reeded

Date	Mintage	F12	VF20	XF40	MS60	MS63
2011P	Est. 3000	PF65 100				

KM# 1609 DOLLAR
31.11 g., 0.999 Silver 0.9926 oz. ASW, 27x47 mm. **Ruler:** Elizabeth II **Obv:** Head with tiara right **Rev:** Dearming Platypus **Rev. Designer:** Darryl Bellotti **Shape:** Vertical rectangle

Date	Mintage	F12	VF20	XF40	MS60	MS63
2011P	—	—	—	—	—	80.00

KM# 1612 DOLLAR
13.80 g., Aluminum-Bronze, 30.6 mm. **Ruler:** Elizabeth II **Subject:** Wet Tropics of Queensland **Obv:** Head with tiara right **Rev:** Bird walking right and color fauna background **Rev. Designer:** Ryan Vanderwiel **Edge:** Reeded

Date	Mintage	F12	VF20	XF40	MS60	MS63
2011P	—	—	—	—	—	15.00

KM# 1613 DOLLAR
13.80 g., Aluminum-Bronze, 30.6 mm. **Ruler:** Elizabeth II **Subject:** Macquarie Island **Obv:** Bust with tiara right **Rev:** Sea lion and color background **Rev. Designer:** Ryan Vanderweil **Edge:** Reeded

Date	Mintage	F12	VF20	XF40	MS60	MS63
2011P	—	—	—	—	—	15.00

KM# 1614 DOLLAR
13.80 g., Aluminum-Bronze, 30.6 mm. **Ruler:** Elizabeth II **Subject:** Goondwana Rainforests **Obv:** Head with tiara right **Rev:** Bird left with color fauna background **Rev. Designer:** Ryan Vanderweil **Edge:** Reeded

Date	Mintage	F12	VF20	XF40	MS60	MS63
2011P	—	—	—	—	—	15.00

KM# 1615 DOLLAR
13.80 g., Aluminum-Bronze, 30.6 mm. **Ruler:** Elizabeth II **Subject:** Australian Fossil Mammal Sites **Obv:** Head with tiara right **Rev:** Dingo left with color landscape in background **Rev. Designer:** Ryan Vanderweil **Edge:** Reeded

Date	Mintage	F12	VF20	XF40	MS60	MS63
2011P	—	—	—	—	—	15.00

KM# 1616 DOLLAR
13.80 g., Aluminum-Bronze, 30.6 mm. **Ruler:** Elizabeth II **Subject:** Purnululu National Park **Obv:** Head with tiara right **Rev:** Kangaroo right with color background **Rev. Designer:** Ryan Vanderweil **Edge:** Reeded

Date	Mintage	F12	VF20	XF40	MS60	MS63
2011P	—	—	—	—	—	15.00

KM# 1617 DOLLAR
9.00 g., Aluminum-Bronze, 25 mm. **Ruler:** Elizabeth II **Obv:** Head with tiara right **Rev:** Crimson Rosella in color

Date	Mintage	F12	VF20	XF40	MS60	MS63
2011	—	—	—	—	—	15.00

KM# 1618 DOLLAR
9.00 g., Aluminum-Bronze, 25 mm. **Ruler:** Elizabeth II **Obv:** Head with tiara right **Rev:** Kookaburra in color

Date	Mintage	F12	VF20	XF40	MS60	MS63
2011	—	—	—	—	—	15.00

KM# 1619 DOLLAR
9.00 g., Aluminum-Bronze, 25 mm. **Ruler:** Elizabeth II **Subject:** CHOGM meeting, Perth **Obv:** Head with tiara right **Rev:** Flags around globe

Date	Mintage	F12	VF20	XF40	MS60	MS63
2011	—	—	—	—	—	10.00

KM# 1620 DOLLAR
9.00 g., Aluminum-Bronze, 25 mm. **Ruler:** Elizabeth II **Subject:** President's Cup **Obv:** Head with tiara right **Rev:** Golfer talking swing

Date	Mintage	F12	VF20	XF40	MS60	MS63
2011	—	—	—	—	—	10.00

KM# 1620a DOLLAR
11.90 g., 0.999 Silver 0.3798 oz. ASW, 25 mm. **Ruler:** Elizabeth II **Subject:** President's Cup **Obv:** Head with tiara right **Rev:** Golfer taking swing

Date	Mintage	F12	VF20	XF40	MS60	MS63
2011	—	PF65 40.00				

KM# 1621 DOLLAR
31.11 g., 0.999 Silver 0.9926 oz. ASW, 40 mm. **Ruler:** Elizabeth II **Subject:** President's Cup **Obv:** Head with tiara right **Rev:** Golf Ball and color trophy and logo, players around edge

Date	Mintage	F12	VF20	XF40	MS60	MS63
2011	—	PF65 100				

KM# 1635 DOLLAR
9.00 g., Aluminum-Bronze, 25 mm. **Ruler:** Elizabeth II **Subject:** Census, 100th Anniversary **Obv:** Head with tiara right **Rev:** Multiple stylized heads at left, geometric Australia outline at right

Date	Mintage	F12	VF20	XF40	MS60	MS63
2011	—	—	—	—	7.00	8.00

KM# 1643 DOLLAR
9.00 g., Aluminum-Bronze, 25 mm. **Ruler:** Elizabeth II **Obv:** Head with tiara right **Rev:** Mitchell Cockatoo in color

Date	Mintage	F12	VF20	XF40	MS60	MS63
2011	—	—	—	—	—	10.00

KM# 1644 DOLLAR
9.00 g., Aluminum-Bronze, 25 mm. **Ruler:** Elizabeth II **Obv:** Head with tiara right **Rev:** Kingfisher in color

Date	Mintage	F12	VF20	XF40	MS60	MS63
2011	—	—	—	—	—	10.00

KM# 1645 DOLLAR
9.00 g., Aluminum-Bronze, 25 mm. **Ruler:** Elizabeth II **Subject:** Dame Joan Sutherland **Obv:** Head with tiara right **Rev:** Sutherland in opera role facing right

Date	Mintage	F12	VF20	XF40	MS60	MS63
2011	—	—	—	—	5.00	7.00

KM# 1646 DOLLAR
9.00 g., Aluminum-Bronze, 25 mm. **Ruler:** Elizabeth II **Obv:** Head with tiara right **Rev:** Birdwing Butterfly in color

Date	Mintage	F12	VF20	XF40	MS60	MS63
2011	—	—	—	—	—	10.00

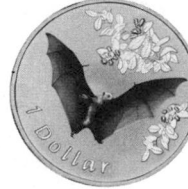

KM# 1647 DOLLAR
9.00 g., Aluminum-Bronze, 25 mm. **Ruler:** Elizabeth II **Obv:** Head with tiara right **Rev:** Flying Fox Bat in color

Date	Mintage	F12	VF20	XF40	MS60	MS63
2011	—	—	—	—	—	10.00

KM# 1661 DOLLAR
9.00 g., Aluminum-Bronze, 25 mm. **Ruler:** Elizabeth II **Subject:** Year of the Rabbit **Obv:** Head with tiara right **Rev:** Rabbit in circle, floral around

Date	Mintage	F12	VF20	XF40	MS60	MS63
2011	—	—	—	—	—	10.00

KM# 1626 DOLLAR
9.00 g., Aluminum-Bronze, 25 mm. **Ruler:** Elizabeth II **Subject:** Australian Wheat **Obv:** Head with tiara right **Rev:** Stylized wheat field and combine harvester

Date	Mintage	F12	VF20	XF40	MS60	MS63
2012	—	PF65 40.00				
2012	—	—	—	—	6.00	10.00

KM# 1680a DOLLAR
11.90 g., 0.999 Silver 0.3798 oz. ASW, 25 mm. **Ruler:** Elizabeth II **Subject:** Year of the Dragon **Rev:** Dragon head within circle, floral around

Date	Mintage	F12	VF20	XF40	MS60	MS63
2012	—	PF65 40.00				

KM# 1699 DOLLAR
31.14 g., 0.999 Silver 0.9936 oz. ASW, 40.6 mm. **Ruler:** Elizabeth II **Subject:** Battle of Kapyong, Korean War **Obv:** Head with tiara right **Rev:** Soldier walking at left, image of soldiers seated at right **Rev. Designer:** Wade Robinson **Edge:** Reeded

Date	Mintage	F12	VF20	XF40	MS60	MS63
2012P	Est. 5000	PF65 100				

KM# 1680 DOLLAR
9.00 g., Aluminum-Bronze, 25 mm. **Ruler:** Elizabeth II **Subject:** Year of the Dragon **Rev:** Dragon head within circle, floral around

Date	Mintage	F12	VF20	XF40	MS60	MS63
2012	—	—	—	—	—	10.00

KM# 1661a DOLLAR
11.66 g., 0.999 Silver 0.3721 oz. ASW, 25 mm. **Ruler:** Elizabeth II **Subject:** Year of the rabbit **Obv:** Head with tiara right **Rev:** Rabbit in circle, floral around

Date	Mintage	F12	VF20	XF40	MS60	MS63
2011	—	PF65 30.00				

KM# 1680b DOLLAR
0.999 Gold AGW, 25 mm. **Ruler:** Elizabeth II **Subject:** Year of the Dragon **Rev:** Dragon at center

Date	Mintage	F12	VF20	XF40	MS60	MS63
2012 Proof	—	—	—	—	—	—

KM# 1808 DOLLAR
13.80 g., Aluminum-Bronze, 30.6 mm. **Ruler:** Elizabeth II **Subject:** Australian 2012 London Olympic Team **Obv:** Head with tiara right **Rev:** Kangaroo with boxing gloves raised **Rev. Designer:** Wade Robinson

Date	Mintage	F12	VF20	XF40	MS60	MS63
2012P	750	—	—	—	—	15.00

KM# 1700 DOLLAR
31.11 g., 0.999 Silver 0.9926 oz. ASW, 40.6 mm. **Ruler:**

Elizabeth II **Subject:** Battle of Kokoda, World War II **Obv:** Head with tiara right **Rev:** Soldier standing at left, image of soldiers walking over bridge at right **Rev. Designer:** Wade Robinson **Edge:** Reeded

Date	Mintage	F12	VF20	XF40	MS60	MS63
2012P	Est. 5000	PF65 100				

KM# 1701 DOLLAR
31.14 g., 0.999 Silver 0.9936 oz. ASW, 40.5 mm. **Ruler:** Elizabeth II **Subject:** Elizabeth II, 60th Anniversary **Obv:** Head with tiara right **Rev:** Dargie's "wattle painting" of Elizabeth II at left, emblem and signature at right **Edge:** Reeded

Date	Mintage	F12	VF20	XF40	MS60	MS63
2012P	7,500	PF65 100				

KM# 1704 DOLLAR
13.80 g., Aluminum-Bronze, 30.6 mm. **Ruler:** Elizabeth II **Subject:** Year of the Dragon

Date	Mintage	F12	VF20	XF40	MS60	MS63
2012P	—	—	—	—	—	15.00

KM# 1705 DOLLAR
31.14 g., 0.999 Silver 0.9936 oz. ASW, 36.6 mm. **Ruler:** Elizabeth II **Obv:** Head with tiara right **Rev:** Koala in a gum tree detailed in an opal at center **Rev. Designer:** Aleysha Howarth

Date	Mintage	F12	VF20	XF40	MS60	MS63
2012P	8,000	PF65 100				

KM# 1706 DOLLAR
31.14 g., Silver, 40.6 mm. **Ruler:** Elizabeth II **Obv:** Head with tiara right **Rev:** Green gold bellfrog, background in color **Edge:** Reeded

Date	Mintage	F12	VF20	XF40	MS60	MS63
2012P	7,500	PF65 100				

KM# 1707 DOLLAR
31.14 g., 0.999 Silver 0.9936 oz. ASW, 40.6 mm. **Ruler:** Elizabeth II **Obv:** Head with tiara right **Rev:** Red kangaroo and color background

Date	Mintage	F12	VF20	XF40	MS60	MS63
2012P	7,500	PF65 100				

KM# 1708 DOLLAR
31.14 g., 0.999 Silver 0.9936 oz. ASW, 40.6 mm. **Ruler:** Elizabeth II **Obv:** Head with tiara right **Rev:** Kookaburra with color background

Date	Mintage	F12	VF20	XF40	MS60	MS63
2012P	7,500	PF65 100				

KM# 1709 DOLLAR
31.14 g., 0.999 Silver 0.9936 oz. ASW, 40.6 mm. **Ruler:** Elizabeth II **Obv:** Head with tiara right **Rev:** Goanna on color background

Date	Mintage	F12	VF20	XF40	MS60	MS63
2012P	7,500	PF65 100				

KM# 1710 DOLLAR
31.14 g., 0.999 Silver 0.9936 oz. ASW, 40.6 mm. **Ruler:** Elizabeth II **Obv:** Head with tiara right **Rev:** Whale shark on color background

Date	Mintage	F12	VF20	XF40	MS60	MS63
2012P	—	PF65 100				

KM# 1711 DOLLAR
9.00 g., Aluminum-Bronze, 25 mm. **Ruler:** Elizabeth II **Subject:** Ethel C. Pedley **Rev:** Bust facing at left, ncharacters Dot and the Kangaroo at right

Date	Mintage	F12	VF20	XF40	MS60	MS63
2012	—	—	—	—	—	12.50

KM# 1714 DOLLAR
13.80 g., Aluminum-Bronze, 30.6 mm. **Ruler:** Elizabeth II **Subject:** ANZAC Day - Nurses **Obv:** Head with tiara right **Rev:** Nurse tending to soldier **Rev. Designer:** Wade Robinson

Date	Mintage	F12	VF40	XF40	MS60	MS63
2012P	—					13.50

KM# 1732 DOLLAR
9.00 g., Aluminum-Bronze, 25 mm. **Ruler:** Elizabeth II **Obv:** Head with tiara right **Rev:** Three wheat ears

Date	Mintage	F12	VF20	XF40	MS60	MS63
2012B	—	—	—	—	—	5.00
2012C	—	—	—	—	3.00	5.00
2012C bluebell	—	—	—	—	—	20.00
2012M	—	—	—	—	—	5.00
2012S	—	—	—	—	—	5.00

KM# 1732a DOLLAR
11.60 g., 0.999 Silver 0.3702 oz. ASW, 25 mm. **Ruler:** Elizabeth II **Obv:** Head with tiara right **Rev:** Three wheat ears

Date	Mintage	F12	VF20	XF40	MS60	MS63
2012	—	PF65 40.00				

KM# 1734 DOLLAR
9.00 g., Aluminum-Bronze, 25 mm. **Ruler:** Elizabeth II **Subject:** Australian Open **Obv:** Head with tiara right **Rev:** Men's Trophy

Date	Mintage	F12	VF20	XF40	MS60	MS63
2012	—	—	—	—	—	15.00

KM# 1735 DOLLAR
9.00 g., Aluminum-Bronze, 25 mm. **Ruler:** Elizabeth II **Subject:** Australian Open **Obv:** Head with tiara right **Rev:** Women's Trophy

Date	Mintage	F12	VF20	XF40	MS60	MS63
2012	—	—	—	—	—	15.00

KM# 1736 DOLLAR
9.00 g., Aluminum-Bronze, 25 mm. **Ruler:** Elizabeth II **Subject:** International Year of Cooperatives **Obv:** Head with tiara right **Rev:** Stick figures moving blocks into position

Date	Mintage	F12	VF20	XF40	MS60	MS63
2012	—	—	—	—	7.00	10.00

KM# 1738 DOLLAR
9.00 g., Aluminum-Bronze, 25 mm. **Ruler:** Elizabeth II **Subject:** Year of the Farmer **Obv:** Head with tiara right **Rev:** Stylized farm layout with produce and animals

Date	Mintage	F12	VF20	XF40	MS60	MS63
2012	—	—	—	—	7.00	10.00

KM# 1745 DOLLAR
9.00 g., Aluminum-Bronze, 25 mm. **Ruler:** Elizabeth II **Obv:** Head with tiara right **Rev:** Asian Elephant at left in color

Date	Mintage	F12	VF20	XF40	MS60	MS63
2012	—	—	—	—	—	15.00

KM# 1746 DOLLAR
9.00 g., Aluminum-Bronze, 25 mm. **Ruler:** Elizabeth II **Obv:** Head with tiara right **Rev:** Western Lowland Gorilla at right in color

Date	Mintage	F12	VF20	XF40	MS60	MS63
2012	—	—	—	—	—	15.00

KM# 1748 DOLLAR
31.14 g., 0.999 Silver 0.9936 oz. ASW, 40.6 mm. **Ruler:** Elizabeth II **Subject:** Australian Olympic Team, 2012 London Games **Obv:** Head with tiara right **Rev:** Runner with Big Ben and Sydney Harbor Bridge in color **Rev. Designer:** Wade Robinson

Date	Mintage	F12	VF20	XF40	MS60	MS63
2012P	7,500	PF65 100				

KM# 1787 DOLLAR
31.14 g., 0.999 Silver 0.9936 oz. ASW, 40.6 mm. **Ruler:** Elizabeth II **Subject:** Elizabeth II's Diamond Jubilee **Obv:** Head with tiara right **Rev:** Elizabeth half-length adjusting shall, gilt royal shield below **Edge:** Reeded

Date	Mintage	F12	VF20	XF40	MS60	MS63
2012P	1,000	PF65 100				

KM# 1788 DOLLAR
31.14 g., 0.999 Silver 0.9936 oz. ASW, 40.6 mm. **Ruler:** Elizabeth II **Subject:** Elizabeth II's Diamond Jubilee **Obv:** Head with tiara right **Rev:** Elizabeth half-length facing at left, royal trumphants at right **Edge:** Reeded

Date	Mintage	F12	VF20	XF40	MS60	MS63
2012P	1,000	PF65 100				

KM# 1791 DOLLAR
31.11 g., 0.999 Silver 0.9926 oz. ASW, 40.6 mm. **Ruler:** Elizabeth II **Rev:** Kookaburra in color **Shape:** Irregular, Map of Australia

Date	Mintage	F12	VF20	XF40	MS60	MS63
2012P	6,000	PF65 150				

KM# 1792 DOLLAR
31.11 g., 0.999 Silver 0.9926 oz. ASW, 40.6 mm. **Ruler:** Elizabeth II **Rev:** Emu in color **Rev. Designer:** Ing Ing Jong **Shape:** Irregular, Map of Australia

Date	Mintage	F12	VF20	XF40	MS60	MS63
2012P	6,000	PF65 120				

KM# 1796 DOLLAR
31.11 g., 0.999 Silver 0.9926 oz. ASW **Ruler:** Elizabeth II **Rev:** Wombat with opal **Rev. Designer:** Aleysha Howarth

Date	Mintage	F12	VF20	XF40	MS60	MS63
2012P	Est. 8000	PF65 100				

KM# 1800 DOLLAR
31.11 g., 0.999 Silver 0.9926 oz. ASW, 40.6 mm. **Ruler:** Elizabeth II **Subject:** Australia-China Friendship, 40th Anniversary **Rev:** kangaroo and Panda under national flags in color

Date	Mintage	F12	VF20	XF40	MS60	MS63
2012P	—	PF65 125				

KM# 1804 DOLLAR
13.50 g., Aluminum-Bronze, 30 mm. **Ruler:** Elizabeth II **Subject:** London Olympics, 2012 **Rev:** Faster - Runner

Date	Mintage	F12	VF20	XF40	MS60	MS63
2012P	—	—	—	—	—	14.00

KM# 1805 DOLLAR
13.50 g., Aluminum-Bronze, 30 mm. **Ruler:** Elizabeth II

Subject: London Olympics, 2012 **Rev:** Higher - Pole Vaulter

Date	Mintage	F12	VF20	XF40	MS60	MS63
2012P	—	—	—	—	—	14.00

KM# 1812 DOLLAR
13.30 g., Aluminum-Bronze, 30.6 mm. **Ruler:** Elizabeth II
Subject: Animal Athletics - Sailfish **Rev. Designer:** Natasha Muhl

Date	Mintage	F12	VF20	XF40	MS60	MS63
2012P	—	—	—	—	—	14.00

KM# 1821 DOLLAR
13.80 g., Aluminum-Bronze, 30.6 mm. **Ruler:** Elizabeth II
Subject: Uluru Kata Tyuta National Park **Rev:** Lizard, color background

Date	Mintage	F12	VF20	XF40	MS60	MS63
2012P	—	—	—	—	—	15.00

KM# 1807 DOLLAR
13.50 g., Aluminum-Bronze, 30 mm. **Ruler:** Elizabeth II
Subject: London Olympics, 2012 **Rev:** Victory - Swimmer, hands raised

Date	Mintage	F12	VF20	XF40	MS60	MS63
2012P	—	—	—	—	—	14.00

KM# 1806 DOLLAR
13.50 g., Aluminum-Bronze, 30 mm. **Ruler:** Elizabeth II
Subject: London Olympics, 2012 **Rev:** Stronger - Weight Lifter

Date	Mintage	F12	VF20	XF40	MS60	MS63
2012P	—	—	—	—	—	14.00

KM# 1813 DOLLAR
13.30 g., Aluminum-Bronze, 30.6 mm. **Ruler:** Elizabeth II **Subject:** Animal Athletics - Rhino Beetle **Rev. Designer:** Natasha Muhl

Date	Mintage	F12	VF20	XF40	MS60	MS63
2012P	—	—	—	—	—	14.00

KM# 1822 DOLLAR
13.80 g., Aluminum-Bronze, 30.6 mm. **Ruler:** Elizabeth II
Subject: Fraser Island **Rev:** Dingo, color background

Date	Mintage	F12	VF20	XF40	MS60	MS63
2012P	—	—	—	—	—	15.00

KM# 1809 DOLLAR
13.30 g., Aluminum-Bronze, 30.6 mm. **Ruler:** Elizabeth II
Subject: Animal Athletics - Cheetah

Date	Mintage	F12	VF20	XF40	MS60	MS63
2012P	—	—	—	—	—	14.00

KM# 1814 DOLLAR
13.30 g., Aluminum-Bronze, 30.6 mm. **Ruler:** Elizabeth II
Subject: Animal Athletics - Rocket Frog **Rev. Designer:** Natasha Muhl

Date	Mintage	F12	VF20	XF40	MS60	MS63
2012P	—	—	—	—	—	14.00

KM# 1823 DOLLAR
13.80 g., Aluminum-Bronze, 30.6 mm. **Ruler:** Elizabeth II **Subject:** Kakadu National Park **Rev:** Two storks, color background

Date	Mintage	F12	VF20	XF40	MS60	MS63
2012P	—	—	—	—	—	15.00

KM# 1810 DOLLAR
13.30 g., Aluminum-Bronze, 30.6 mm. **Ruler:** Elizabeth II
Subject: Animal Athletics - Monarch Butterfly **Rev. Designer:** Natasha Muhl

Date	Mintage	F12	VF20	XF40	MS60	MS63
2012P	—	—	—	—	—	14.00

KM# 1819 DOLLAR
31.11 g., 0.999 Silver 0.9926 oz. ASW, 40.6 mm. **Ruler:** Elizabeth II **Subject:** Famous Battles - Long Tan **Rev. Designer:** Wade Robinson

Date	Mintage	F12	VF20	XF40	MS60	MS63
2012P	—	PF65 100				

KM# 1824 DOLLAR
13.80 g., Aluminum-Bronze, 30.6 mm. **Ruler:** Elizabeth II
Subject: Willandra Lakes Region **Rev:** Eagle, color background

Date	Mintage	F12	VF20	XF40	MS60	MS63
2012P	—	—	—	—	—	15.00

KM# 1811 DOLLAR
13.80 g., Aluminum-Bronze, 30.6 mm. **Ruler:** Elizabeth II **Obv:** Head with tiara right **Rev:** Two boxing kangaroos on color backgorund **Rev. Designer:** Tom Vaughan

Date	Mintage	F12	VF20	XF40	MS60	MS63
2012P	7,500	—	—	—	—	15.00

KM# 1820 DOLLAR
13.80 g., Aluminum-Bronze, 30.6 mm. **Ruler:** Elizabeth II
Subject: Lord Howe Island Group **Rev:** Pair of sparrows in flight, color background

Date	Mintage	F12	VF20	XF40	MS60	MS63
2012P	—	—	—	—	—	15.00

KM# 1826 DOLLAR
31.11 g., 0.999 Silver 0.9926 oz. ASW, 40.6 mm. **Ruler:** Elizabeth II **Subject:** Antarctic Territories **Rev:** Penguins

Date	Mintage	F12	VF20	XF40	MS60	MS63
2012P	—	PF65 100				

KM# 1858 DOLLAR
9.00 g., Aluminum-Bronze, 25 mm. **Ruler:** Elizabeth II **Subject:**
Southern Corrobreee Frog

Date	Mintage	F12	VF20	XF40	MS60	MS63
2012	—	—	—	—	—	10.00

KM# 1859 DOLLAR
9.00 g., Aluminum-Bronze, 25 mm. **Ruler:** Elizabeth II **Subject:**
Sumatran Tiger

Date	Mintage	F12	VF20	XF40	MS60	MS63
2012	—	—	—	—	—	10.00

KM# 1860 DOLLAR
9.00 g., Aluminum-Bronze, 25 mm. **Ruler:** Elizabeth II **Rev:**
Monkey in tree

Date	Mintage	F12	VF20	XF40	MS60	MS63
2012	—	—	—	—	—	10.00

KM# 1861 DOLLAR
9.00 g., Aluminum-Bronze, 25 mm. **Ruler:** Elizabeth II **Subject:**
Sir Douglas Mawson, explorer

Date	Mintage	F12	VF20	XF40	MS60	MS63
2012	—	—	—	—	4.00	5.00

KM# 1865 DOLLAR
31.11 g., 0.999 Silver 0.9926 oz. ASW, 40 mm. **Ruler:** Elizabeth
II **Subject:** Saltwater Crocodile - Bindi

Date	Mintage	F12	VF20	XF40	MS60	MS63
2012	—		PF65 75.00			

KM# 1866 DOLLAR
31.10 g., 0.999 Silver 0.9926 oz. ASW, 40.6 mm. **Ruler:**
Elizabeth II **Obv:** Crystal insert above head with tiara right
Rev: Large snowflakes, crystal insert at top **Rev. Designer:**
Aleysha Howarth

Date	Mintage	F12	VF20	XF40	MS60	MS63
2012P	Est. 5000		PF65 125			

KM# 2009 DOLLAR
Aluminum-Bronze, 30.8 mm. **Ruler:** Elizabeth II **Series:** First
Banknote 100th Anniversary **Rev:** 10 Shilling design

Date	Mintage	F12	VF20	XF40	MS60	MS63
2012P	—	—	—	—	—	15.00

KM# 2008 DOLLAR
13.80 g., Aluminum-Bronze, 30.6 mm. **Ruler:** Elizabeth II
Subject: Christmas **Rev:** Two bells and evergreen in color

Date	Mintage	F12	VF20	XF40	MS60	MS63
2012	—	—	—	—	—	15.00

KM# 2022 DOLLAR
9.00 g., Aluminum-Bronze, 25 mm. **Ruler:** Elizabeth II **Subject:**
AFL Premiers **Rev:** Cup

Date	Mintage	F12	VF20	XF40	MS60	MS63
2012	—	—	—	—	—	20.00

KM# 1824a DOLLAR
31.11 g., 0.999 Silver 0.9926 oz. ASW, 40.6 mm. **Ruler:**
Elizabeth II **Subject:** ANDA Show **Obv:** Head with tiara right
Rev: Wilandra Lakes, Eagle, colored background

Date	Mintage	F12	VF20	XF40	MS60	MS63
2013P	—		PF65 75.00			

KM# 1909 DOLLAR
31.10 g., 0.999 Silver 0.9925 oz. ASW, 33.2 x 33.2 mm. **Ruler:**
Elizabeth II **Subject:** Australian Seasons - Summer

Date	Mintage	F12	VF20	XF40	MS60	MS63
2013	Est. 5000		PF65 75.00			

KM# 1910 DOLLAR
31.14 g., 0.999 Silver 0.9936 oz. ASW, 33.2 x 33.2 mm. **Ruler:**
Elizabeth II **Subject:** Australian Seasons - Autumn **Rev.**
Designer: Ing Ing Jong

Date	Mintage	F12	VF20	XF40	MS60	MS63
2013	Est. 5000		PF65 75.00			

KM# 1911 DOLLAR
31.14 g., 0.999 Silver 0.9936 oz. ASW, 33.2 x 33.2 mm. **Ruler:**
Elizabeth II **Subject:** Australian Seasons - Winter **Obv.**
Designer: Ian Rank-Bradley **Rev:** Green Tree Frog, color
background **Rev. Designer:** Ing Ing Jong **Edge:** Reeded

Date	Mintage	F12	VF20	XF40	MS60	MS63
2013P	Est. 5000		PF65 60.00			

KM# 1912 DOLLAR
31.14 g., 0.999 Silver 0.9936 oz. ASW, 33.2 x 33.2 mm. **Ruler:**
Elizabeth II **Subject:** Australian Seasons - Spring **Obv:** Head

with tiara right **Obv. Designer:** Ian Rank-Broadley **Rev:** Two White Cockatoos, color background **Rev. Designer:** Ing Ing Jong **Edge:** Reeded

Date	Mintage	F12	VF20	XF40	MS60	MS63
2013P	Est. 5000		PF65	75.00		

KM# 1913 DOLLAR
15.50 g., 0.999 Silver 0.4946 oz. ASW, 36.6 mm. **Ruler:** Elizabeth II **Subject:** Australian Bush Babies II - Echidna **Rev. Designer:** Elise Martinson

Date	Mintage	F12	VF20	XF40	MS60	MS63
2013	—		PF65	50.00		

KM# 1916 DOLLAR
25.19 g., 0.999 Silver 0.8038 oz. ASW, 40.6 mm. **Ruler:** Elizabeth II **Subject:** 200th Anniversary of the Australian Holey Dollar & Dump

Date	Mintage	F12	VF20	XF40	MS60	MS63
2013	Est. 4000		PF65	75.00		

KM# 1918 DOLLAR
31.14 g., 0.999 Silver 0.9936 oz. ASW, 40.6 mm. **Ruler:** Elizabeth II **Subject:** 2013 The Land Down Under - Sydney Opera House **Rev. Designer:** Natasha Muhl

Date	Mintage	F12	VF20	XF40	MS60	MS63
2013	Est. 5000		PF65	75.00		

KM# 1920 DOLLAR
31.14 g., 0.999 Silver 0.9936 oz. ASW, 40.6 mm. **Ruler:** Elizabeth II **Subject:** The Land Down Under - Didgeridoo **Rev. Designer:** Tom Vaughan

Date	Mintage	F12	VF20	XF40	MS60	MS63
2013	Est. 5000		PF65	75.00		

KM# 1927 DOLLAR
31.14 g., 0.999 Silver 0.9936 oz. ASW, 40.6 mm. **Ruler:** Elizabeth II **Subject:** HM Queen Elizabeth II - 60th Anniversary of Coronation **Rev. Designer:** Natasha Muhl

Date	Mintage	F12	VF20	XF40	MS60	MS63
2013P	Est. 7500		PF65	75.00		

KM# 1929 DOLLAR
31.14 g., 0.999 Silver 0.9936 oz. ASW, 40.6 mm. **Ruler:** Elizabeth II **Subject:** Australia Map Shaped Coin - Kangaroo **Rev. Designer:** Ing Ing Jong **Shape:** Australia continent

Date	Mintage	F12	VF20	XF40	MS60	MS63
2013P	Est. 6000		PF65	100		

KM# 1930 DOLLAR
31.14 g., 0.999 Silver 0.9936 oz. ASW, 40.6 mm. **Ruler:** Elizabeth II **Subject:** Queen Victoria 175th Anniversary of Coronation **Rev. Designer:** Aleysha Howarth

Date	Mintage	F12	VF20	XF40	MS60	MS63
2013P	Est. 5000		PF65	75.00		

KM# 1932 DOLLAR
31.14 g., 0.999 Silver 0.9936 oz. ASW, 40.6 mm. **Ruler:** Elizabeth II **Subject:** Treasures of the World - Europe - Garnet **Obv:** Head with tiara right **Rev:** Mountainside challet and ferns **Rev. Designer:** Natasha Muhl

Date	Mintage	F12	VF20	XF40	MS60	MS63
2013P	Est. 7500		PF65	100		

KM# 1935 DOLLAR
15.50 g., Silver, 36.6 mm. **Ruler:** Elizabeth II **Subject:** Australian Bush Babies II - Platypus **Rev. Designer:** Elise Martinson

Date	Mintage	F12	VF20	XF40	MS60	MS63
2013	—		PF65	50.00		

KM# 1936 DOLLAR
31.14 g., 0.999 Silver 0.9936 oz. ASW, 40.6 mm. **Ruler:** Elizabeth II **Subject:** Discover Australia - Kangaroo **Rev. Legend:** Ing Ing Jong

Date	Mintage	F12	VF20	XF40	MS60	MS63
2013P	Est. 5000		PF65	75.00		

KM# 1937 DOLLAR
31.14 g., 0.999 Silver 0.9936 oz. ASW, 40.6 mm. **Ruler:** Elizabeth II **Subject:** Discover Australia - Koala **Rev. Legend:** Ing Ing Jong

Date	Mintage	F12	VF20	XF40	MS60	MS63
2013P	Est. 5000		PF65	70.00		

KM# 1938 DOLLAR
31.14 g., 0.999 Silver 0.9936 oz. ASW, 40.6 mm. **Ruler:** Elizabeth II **Subject:** Discover Australia - Emu **Rev. Designer:** Ing Ing Jong

Date	Mintage	F12	VF20	XF40	MS60	MS63
2013P	Est. 5000		PF65	70.00		

KM# 1939 DOLLAR
31.14 g., 0.999 Silver 0.9936 oz. ASW, 40.6 mm. **Ruler:** Elizabeth II **Subject:** Discover Australia - Kookaburra **Rev. Designer:** Ing Ing Jong

Date	Mintage	F12	VF20	XF40	MS60	MS63
2013	Est. 5000		PF65 70.00			

KM# 1940 DOLLAR
31.14 g., 0.999 Silver 0.9936 oz. ASW, 40.6 mm. **Ruler:** Elizabeth II **Subject:** Discover Australia - Platypus **Rev. Designer:** Ing Ing Jong

Date	Mintage	F12	VF20	XF40	MS60	MS63
2013	Est. 5000		PF65 70.00			

KM# 1941 DOLLAR
31.13 g., 0.999 Silver 0.9935 oz. ASW, 40.6 mm. **Ruler:** Elizabeth II **Subject:** The Land Down Under - Captan James Cook **Rev. Designer:** Tom Vaughan

Date	Mintage	F12	VF20	XF40	MS60	MS63
2013P	Est. 5000		PF65 70.00			

KM# 1943 DOLLAR
13.80 g., Aluminum-Bronze, 30.2 mm. **Ruler:** Elizabeth II **Subject:** Experience It Series - Surfing **Obv:** Head in tiara right **Rev:** Surfer, color waves **Rev. Designer:** Natasha Muhl

Date	Mintage	F12	VF20	XF40	MS60	MS63
2013	—	—	—	—	—	15.00

KM# 1944 DOLLAR
13.00 g., Aluminum-Bronze, 30.6 mm. **Ruler:** Elizabeth II **Subject:** Elizabeth II, 60th Anniversary of Coronation **Rev:** Coronation crown

Date	Mintage	F12	VF20	XF40	MS60	MS63
2013	—	—	—	—	—	15.00

KM# 1945 DOLLAR
13.00 g., Aluminum-Bronze, 30.6 mm. **Ruler:** Elizabeth II **Subject:** Victoria, 175th Anniversary of Coronation **Rev:** Coronation crown

Date	Mintage	F12	VF20	XF40	MS60	MS63
2013	—	—	—	—	—	15.00

KM# 1946 DOLLAR
31.10 g., Silver, 40 mm. **Ruler:** Elizabeth II **Subject:** Kangaroos of the World

Date	Mintage	F12	VF20	XF40	MS60	MS63
2013	Est. 10000		PF65 75.00			

KM# 1947 DOLLAR
9.00 g., Aluminum-Bronze, 25 mm. **Ruler:** Elizabeth II **Subject:** Polar Animals - Polar Bear **Rev. Designer:** Aaron Baggio

Date	Mintage	F12	VF20	XF40	MS60	MS63
2013	—	—	—	—	—	15.00

KM# 1948 DOLLAR
Aluminum-Bronze, 25 mm. **Ruler:** Elizabeth II **Subject:** Polar Animals - Walarus **Rev. Designer:** Aaron Baggio

Date	Mintage	F12	VF20	XF40	MS60	MS63
2013	—	—	—	—	—	15.00

KM# 1949 DOLLAR
9.00 g., Aluminum-Bronze, 25 mm. **Ruler:** Elizabeth II **Subject:** Polar Animals - Humpback Whale **Rev. Designer:** Aaron Baggio

Date	Mintage	F12	VF20	XF40	MS60	MS63
2013					—	15.00

KM# 1950 DOLLAR
9.00 g., Aluminum-Bronze, 25 mm. **Ruler:** Elizabeth II **Subject:** Polar Animals - Atlantic Puffin **Rev. Designer:** Aaron Baggio

Date	Mintage	F12	VF20	XF40	MS60	MS63
2013					—	15.00

KM# 1951 DOLLAR
9.00 g., Aluminum-Bronze, 25 mm. **Ruler:** Elizabeth II **Subject:** Polar Animals - Weddell Seal **Rev. Designer:** Aaron Baggio

Date	Mintage	F12	VF20	XF40	MS60	MS63
2013					—	15.00

KM# 1952 DOLLAR
36.31 g., 0.999 Silver 1.1587 oz. ASW, 38.74 mm. **Ruler:** Elizabeth II **Subject:** Centenary of Canberra **Rev. Designer:** Aleksandra Stokic

Date	Mintage	F12	VF20	XF40	MS60	MS63
2013	Est. 5000		PF65 75.00			

KM# 1953 DOLLAR
31.10 g., 0.999 Silver 0.9925 oz. ASW, 40 mm. **Ruler:** Elizabeth II **Subject:** Kangaroo Road Sign **Rev. Designer:** Wojciech Pietranik

Date	Mintage	F12	VF20	XF40	MS60	MS63
2013	Est. 40000		PF65 40.00			

KM# 1968 DOLLAR
9.00 g., Aluminum-Bronze, 25 mm. **Ruler:** Elizabeth II **Subject:** 200 Years of the Benevolent Society

Date	Mintage	F12	VF20	XF40	MS60	MS63
2013	—	—	—	—	—	15.00

KM# 1976 DOLLAR
9.00 g., Aluminum-Nickel-Bronze, 25 mm. **Ruler:** Elizabeth II **Subject:** Polar Animals - Penguin **Rev. Designer:** Aaron Baggio

Date	Mintage	F12	VF20	XF40	MS60	MS63
2013	—	—	—	—	—	15.00

KM# 2004 DOLLAR
13.80 g., Aluminum-Bronze, 30.6 mm. **Ruler:** Elizabeth II **Subject:** Year of the Snake

Date	Mintage	F12	VF20	XF40	MS60	MS63
2013P	—	—	—	—	—	15.00

KM# 2013 DOLLAR
31.11 g., 0.999 Silver 0.9926 oz. ASW **Ruler:** Elizabeth II
Subject: Bindi **Rev:** Crocodile

Date	Mintage	F12	VF20	XF40	MS60	MS63
2013P	—	—	—	—	—	32.00

KM# 2014 DOLLAR
9.00 g., Aluminum-Bronze, 25 mm. **Ruler:** Elizabeth II **Subject:** Slim Dusty

Date	Mintage	F12	VF20	XF40	MS60	MS63
2013	—	—	—	—	—	15.00

KM# 2015 DOLLAR
9.00 g., Aluminum-Bronze, 25 mm. **Ruler:** Elizabeth II **Subject:** Year of the Snake **Rev:** Snake at center

Date	Mintage	F12	VF20	XF40	MS60	MS63
2013	—	—	—	—	—	10.00

KM# 2015a DOLLAR
Silver **Ruler:** Elizabeth II **Subject:** Year of the Snake **Rev:** Snake at center

Date	Mintage	F12	VF20	XF40	MS60	MS63
2013	—	PF65 40.00				

KM# 2015b DOLLAR
Gold AGW **Ruler:** Elizabeth II **Subject:** Year of the Snake **Rev:** Snake at center

Date	Mintage	F12	VF20	XF40	MS60	MS63
2013 Proof	—	—	—	—	—	—

KM# 2016 DOLLAR
9.00 g., Aluminum-Bronze, 25 mm. **Ruler:** Elizabeth II **Subject:** Discovery of Gold **Rev:** Prospector panning in stream bed

Date	Mintage	F12	VF20	XF40	MS60	MS63
2013	Est. 40000	—	—	—	—	15.00
2013	Est. 25000	PF65 30.00				

KM# 2017 DOLLAR
9.00 g., Aluminum-Bronze, 25 mm. **Ruler:** Elizabeth II **Subject:** Black Caviar **Rev:** Horse and jockey right, owners colors

Date	Mintage	F12	VF20	XF40	MS60	MS63
2013	—	—	—	—	—	15.00

KM# 2018 DOLLAR
31.10 g., 0.999 Silver 0.9926 oz. ASW **Ruler:** Elizabeth II **Subject:** Black Caviar **Rev:** Horse and jockey advancing left **Shape:** 40

Date	Mintage	F12	VF20	XF40	MS60	MS63
2013	—	PF63 75.00		PF65 85.00		

KM# 2021 DOLLAR
31.11 g., 0.999 Silver 0.9926 oz. ASW, 40 mm. **Ruler:** Elizabeth II **Subject:** AFL Premiers - Sidney Swans **Rev:** Cup

Date	Mintage	F12	VF20	XF40	MS60	MS63
2013	—	PF65 115				

KM# 2028a DOLLAR
9.00 g., Aluminum-Bronze, 25 mm. **Ruler:** Elizabeth II **Subject:** Holey Dollar **Rev:** NSW coin and Spanish 8 real reverse

Date	Mintage	F12	VF20	XF40	MS60	MS63
2013 B	—	—	—	—	—	6.00

KM# 2028 DOLLAR
9.00 g., Aluminum-Bronze, 25 mm. **Ruler:** Elizabeth II **Subject:** Holey Dollar **Rev:** NSW coin and Spanish 8 real reverse

Date	Mintage	F12	VF20	XF40	MS60	MS63
2013B	—	—	—	—	—	6.00
2013C	—	—	—	—	—	6.00
2013M	—	—	—	—	—	6.00
2013S	—	—	—	—	—	6.00

KM# 2029 DOLLAR
31.11 g., 0.999 Silver 0.9926 oz. ASW, 40.6 mm. **Ruler:** Elizabeth II **Subject:** Bindi - Saltwater Crocodile **Rev:** Crocodile head in color

Date	Mintage	F12	VF20	XF40	MS60	MS63
2013	Est. 5000	PF65 110				

KM# 2038 DOLLAR
0.50 g., 0.9999 Gold AGW, 11.15 mm. **Ruler:** Elizabeth II **Subject:** Australian Miniature Money

Date	Mintage	F12	VF20	XF40	MS60	MS63
2013	Est. 2000	PF65 75.00				

KM# 2043 DOLLAR
31.14 g., 0.999 Silver 0.9936 oz. ASW, 36.6 mm. **Ruler:** Elizabeth II **Rev:** Kangaroo in opal at center **Rev. Designer:** Aleysha Howarth

Date	Mintage	F12	VF20	XF40	MS60	MS63
2013	Est. 8000	PF65 100				

KM# 2045 DOLLAR
13.80 g., Aluminum-Bronze, 30.60 mm. **Ruler:** Elizabeth II **Subject:** Anzac Day - Engineers

Date	Mintage	F12	VF20	XF40	MS60	MS63
2013P	—	—	—	—	—	15.00

KM# 2046 DOLLAR
31.14 g., 0.999 Silver 0.9936 oz. ASW, 40.6 mm. **Ruler:** Elizabeth II **Subject:** Antarctic Territory - Aurora Australis **Obv:** Head with tiara right **Rev:** Researcher and colored Aurora, Antarctic map shape **Rev. Designer:** Wade Robinson

Date	Mintage	F12	VF20	XF40	MS60	MS63
2013P	Est. 7500	PF65 75.00				

KM# 2051 DOLLAR
31.14 g., 0.999 Silver 0.9936 oz. ASW, 40.6 mm. **Ruler:** Elizabeth II **Subject:** Land Down Under - Surfing **Obv:** Head with tiara right **Rev:** Surfer standing holding vertical surfboard, watching waves roll in **Rev. Designer:** Tom Vaughan

Date	Mintage	F12	VF20	XF40	MS60	MS63
2013P	Est. 5000	PF63 75.00		PF65 80.00		

KM# 2058 DOLLAR
13.80 g., Aluminum-Bronze, 30.2 mm. **Ruler:** Elizabeth II **Obv:** Head with tiara right **Rev:** Downhill skier left **Rev. Designer:** Natasha Muhl

Date	Mintage	F12	VF20	XF40	MS60	MS63
2013P	—	—	—	—	—	15.00

KM# 2059 DOLLAR
13.20 g., Aluminum-Bronze, 30.6 mm. **Ruler:** Elizabeth II **Obv:** Head with tiara right **Rev:** Baby Wombat **Rev. Designer:** Elise Martinson

Date	Mintage	F12	VF20	XF40	MS60	MS63
2013P	—	—	—	—	—	15.00

KM# 2060 DOLLAR
31.14 g., 0.999 Silver 0.9936 oz. ASW, 40.6 mm. **Ruler:** Elizabeth II **Subject:** H.R.H. Prince George, Birth **Obv:** Head with tiara right **Rev:** Prince William and Catherine holding infant **Rev. Designer:** Jennifer McKenna

Date	Mintage	F12	VF20	XF40	MS60	MS63
2013P	Est. 10000	PF63 75.00		PF65 85.00		

KM# 2062 DOLLAR
31.14 g., 0.999 Silver 0.9936 oz. ASW, 36.6 mm. **Ruler:** Elizabeth II **Rev:** Pygmy Possum in center opal insert **Rev. Designer:** Aleysha Howarth

Date	Mintage	F12	VF20	XF40	MS60	MS63
2013P	Est. 8000	PF65 100				

KM# 2063 DOLLAR
13.80 g., Aluminum-Bronze, 30.2 mm. **Ruler:** Elizabeth II **Obv:** Head with tiara right **Rev:** Horse and rider **Rev. Designer:** Natasha Muhl

Date	Mintage	F12	VF20	XF40	MS60	MS63
2013P	—	—	—	—	—	15.00

KM# 2065 DOLLAR
31.14 g., 0.999 Silver 0.9936 oz. ASW, 40.6 mm. **Ruler:** Elizabeth II **Subject:** A. B. Banjo Paterson, 150th Anniversary of Birth **Obv:** Head with tiara right **Rev:** Paterson in color **Rev. Designer:** Natasha Muhl

Date	Mintage	F12	VF20	XF40	MS60	MS63
2013P	4,000	PF65 80.00				

KM# 2068 DOLLAR
13.80 g., Aluminum-Bronze, 30.2 mm. **Ruler:** Elizabeth II **Obv:** Head with tiara right **Rev:** Skateboarder **Rev. Designer:** Natasha Muhl

Date	Mintage	F12	VF20	XF40	MS60	MS63
2013P	—	—	—	—	—	15.00

KM# 2069 DOLLAR
13.80 g., Aluminum-Bronze, 30.2 mm. **Ruler:** Elizabeth II **Subject:** Ludwig Leichhardt, explorer **Obv:** Head with tiara right **Rev:** Leichhardt and expedition map

Date	Mintage	F12	VF20	XF40	MS60	MS63
2013P	—	—	—	—	—	15.00

KM# 2070 DOLLAR
31.14 g., 0.999 Silver 0.9936 oz. ASW, 40.6 mm. **Ruler:** Elizabeth II **Obv:** Head with tiara right **Rev:** Platypus along stream in color **Shape:** Irregular

Date	Mintage	F12	VF20	XF40	MS60	MS63
2013P	Est. 6000	PF65 90.00				

KM# 2071 DOLLAR
13.80 g., Aluminum-Bronze, 30.2 mm. **Ruler:** Elizabeth II **Obv:** Head with tiara right **Rev:** Platypus **Rev. Designer:** Elise Martinson

Date	Mintage	F12	VF20	XF40	MS60	MS63
2013P	—	—	—	—	—	15.00

KM# 2075 DOLLAR
13.80 g., Aluminum-Bronze, 30.6 mm. **Ruler:** Elizabeth II **Subject:** Bush babies **Rev:** Possum

Date	Mintage	F12	VF20	XF40	MS60	MS63
2013P	—	—	—	—	—	15.00

KM# 2076 DOLLAR
13.80 g., Aluminum-Bronze, 30.6 mm. **Ruler:** Elizabeth II **Subject:** Bush babies **Rev:** Kookaburra

Date	Mintage	F12	VF20	XF40	MS60	MS63
2013P	—	—	—	—	—	15.00

KM# 2077 DOLLAR
13.80 g., Aluminum-Bronze, 30.6 mm. **Ruler:** Elizabeth II **Subject:** Bush babies **Rev:** Echidna

Date	Mintage	F12	VF20	XF40	MS60	MS63
2013P	—	—	—	—	—	15.00

KM# 2092 DOLLAR
31.11 g., 0.999 Silver 0.9926 oz. ASW **Ruler:** Elizabeth II **Subject:** National Currency, 100th Anniversary **Rev:** 1913 10 Shilling Bank Note in color **Shape:** Rectangle

Date	Mintage	F12	VF20	XF40	MS60	MS63
2013P	—	PF65 100				

KM# 2136 DOLLAR
13.80 g., Aluminum-Bronze, 30.6 mm. **Ruler:** Elizabeth II **Obv:** Head with tiara right **Rev:** BMX riding in color

Date	Mintage	F12	VF20	XF40	MS60	MS63
2013	—	—	—	—	—	15.00

KM# 2137 DOLLAR
13.80 g., Aluminum-Bronze, 30.6 mm. **Ruler:** Elizabeth II **Obv:** Head with tiara right **Rev:** Snorkeling in color

Date	Mintage	F12	VF20	XF40	MS60	MS63
2013	—	—	—	—	—	15.00

KM# 2138 DOLLAR
13.80 g., Aluminum-Bronze, 30.6 mm. **Ruler:** Elizabeth II **Subject:** Christmas **Obv:** Head with tiara right **Rev:** Two candles and greens

Date	Mintage	F12	VF20	XF40	MS60	MS63
2013	—	—	—	—	—	15.00

KM# 2139 DOLLAR
13.80 g., Aluminum-Bronze, 30.6 mm. **Ruler:** Elizabeth II **Subject:** Year of the Snake **Obv:** Head with tiara right **Rev:** Snake coiled on branch

Date	Mintage	F12	VF20	XF40	MS60	MS63
2013	—					15.00

KM# 2142 DOLLAR
31.11 g., 0.999 Silver 0.9926 oz. ASW, 40.6 mm. **Ruler:** Elizabeth II **Subject:** Sister Cities **Obv:** Head with tiara right **Rev:** Lenticular St. Petersburg view of Melbourne view

Date	Mintage	F12	VF20	XF40	MS60	MS63
2013	—	PF65 50.00				

KM# 2143 DOLLAR
31.11 g., 0.999 Silver 0.9926 oz. ASW, 40.6 mm. **Ruler:** Elizabeth II **Obv:** Head with tiara right **Rev:** Kangaroo and joey in color

Date	Mintage	F12	VF20	XF40	MS60	MS63
2013	—	PF65 50.00				

KM# 2147 DOLLAR
9.00 g., Aluminum-Bronze, 25 mm. **Ruler:** Elizabeth II **Subject:** Korean War, 60th Anniversary **Obv:** Head with tiara right **Rev:** Dove in flight

Date	Mintage	F12	VF20	XF40	MS60	MS63
2013	—	—	—	—	—	15.00

KM# 2148 DOLLAR
31.11 g., 0.999 Silver 0.9926 oz. ASW, 40 mm. **Ruler:** Elizabeth II **Subject:** Korean War, 60th Anniversary **Obv:** Head with tiara right **Rev:** Dove in flight

Date	Mintage	F12	VF20	XF40	MS60	MS63
2013	—	PF63 70.00	PF65 75.00			

KM# 2149 DOLLAR
9.00 g., Aluminum-Bronze, 25 mm. **Ruler:** Elizabeth II **Subject:** 40th Anniversary **Obv:** Head with tiara right **Rev:** Sydney Opera House

Date	Mintage	F12	VF20	XF40	MS60	MS63
2013	—					15.00

KM# 2150 DOLLAR
31.11 g., 0.999 Silver 0.9926 oz. ASW, 40 mm. **Ruler:** Elizabeth II **Subject:** 40th Anniversary **Obv:** Head with tiara right **Rev:** Sydney Opera House

Date	Mintage	F12	VF20	XF40	MS60	MS63
2013	5,000	PF63 90.00	PF65 100			

KM# 2151 DOLLAR
9.00 g., Aluminum-Bronze, 25 mm. **Ruler:** Elizabeth II **Subject:** AFL Trophy **Obv:** Head with tiara right **Rev:** Premiers Cup

Date	Mintage	F12	VF20	XF40	MS60	MS63
2013	—					15.00

KM# 2152 DOLLAR
9.00 g., Aluminum-Bronze, 25 mm. **Ruler:** Elizabeth II **Obv:** Head with tiara right **Rev:** Ethel Pedley bust facing

Date	Mintage	F12	VF20	XF40	MS60	MS63
2013	—				—	15.00

KM# 2134 DOLLAR
31.11 g., 0.999 Silver 0.9926 oz. ASW **Ruler:** Elizabeth II **Subject:** New Year **Obv:** Head right **Rev:** Sydney Harbor bridge, holographic fireworks above, eye on bridge

Date	Mintage	F12	VF20	XF40	MS60	MS63
2014	—	PF63 70.00	PF65 75.00			

KM# 406 2 DOLLARS
6.60 g., Aluminum-Bronze, 20.5 mm. **Ruler:** Elizabeth II **Obv:** Head with tiara right **Obv. Designer:** Ian Rank-Broadley **Rev:** Aboriginal elder at left, stars above at right **Rev. Designer:** Horst Hahne **Edge:** Segmented reeding

Date	Mintage	F12	VF20	XF40	MS60	MS63
2001	35,650,000	—	—		5.00	6.00
Note: Large obverse head, IRB spaced						
2001	Inc. above					
Note: Smaller obverse head, IRB joined						
2001	59,569	PF65 8.00				
2002	29,689,000	—	—		4.00	6.00
2002	39,514	PF65 8.00				
2003	13,656,000	—	—		4.00	6.00
2003	39,090	PF65 8.00				
2004	20,084,000	—	—		3.50	5.00
2004	50,000	PF65 7.00				
2005	—	—	—		3.50	5.00
2005	33,520	PF65 7.00				
2006	—	—	—		3.50	5.00
2006	—	PF65 7.00				
2007	—	—	—		3.00	4.50
2007	—	PF65 6.00				
2008	—	—	—		3.00	4.50
2008	—	PF65 6.00				
2009	—	—	—		3.00	4.50

Date	Mintage	F12	VF20	XF40	MS60	MS63
2009	—	PF65 6.00				
2010	—	—	—		3.00	4.50
2010	—	PF65 6.00				
2011	—	—	—		3.00	4.50
2011	—	PF65 6.00				
2012	—	—	—		3.00	4.50
2012	—	PF65 6.00				

KM# 406a 2 DOLLARS
15.88 g., 0.9999 Gold 0.5072 oz. AGW, 20.5 mm. **Ruler:** Elizabeth II **Obv:** Head with tiara right **Obv. Designer:** Ian Rank-Broadley **Rev:** Aboriginal elder and value **Rev. Designer:** Horst Hahne **Edge:** Segmented reeding

Date	Mintage	F12	VF20	XF40	MS60	MS63
2001B	350	PF65 925				
2005B	650	PF65 900				
2006B	300	PF65 950				
2013B	500	PF65 925				

KM# 406b 2 DOLLARS
8.55 g., 0.9999 Silver 0.2731 oz. ASW, 20.5 mm. **Ruler:** Elizabeth II **Obv:** Head with tiara right **Obv. Designer:** Ian Rank-Broadley **Rev:** Aboriginal elder and value **Rev. Designer:** Horst Hahne **Edge:** Segmented reeding

Date	Mintage	F12	VF20	XF40	MS60	MS63
2003B	6,500	PF65 22.00				
2004B	6,500	PF65 22.00				
2005B	6,500	PF65 22.00				
2013B	5,000	PF65 40.00				

KM# 764 2 DOLLARS
18.22 g., 0.999 Silver 0.5814 oz. ASW, 32.5 mm. **Ruler:** Elizabeth II **Series:** Masterpieces in Silver - Port Phillip Patterns **Obv:** 1/2 ounce design **Rev:** Kangaroo design **Edge:** Reeded

Date	Mintage	F12	VF20	XF40	MS60	MS63
2003B	10,000	PF65 35.00				

KM# 755 2 DOLLARS
62.27 g., 0.999 Silver 1.9871 oz. ASW, 50 mm. **Ruler:** Elizabeth II **Series:** Australian Peacekeepers **Obv:** Queen's head right **Rev:** Australian army and color insignia **Edge:** Reeded

Date	Mintage	F12	VF20	XF40	MS60	MS63
2005P	2,500	PF65 90.00				

KM# 756 2 DOLLARS
62.27 g., 0.999 Silver 1.9871 oz. ASW, 50.3 mm. **Ruler:** Elizabeth II **Series:** Australian Peacekeepers **Obv:** Queen's head right **Rev:** Australian navy and color insignia **Edge:** Reeded

Date	Mintage	F12	VF20	XF40	MS60	MS63
2005P	2,500	PF65 90.00				

KM# 757 2 DOLLARS
62.27 g., 0.999 Silver 1.9871 oz. ASW, 50.3 mm. **Ruler:** Elizabeth II **Subject:** Australian Peacekeepers Set **Obv:** Queen's head right **Rev:** Australian airforce and color insignia **Edge:** Reeded

Date	Mintage	F12	VF20	XF40	MS60	MS63
2005P	2,500	PF65 90.00				

KM# 758 2 DOLLARS
62.27 g., 0.999 Silver 1.9871 oz. ASW, 50.3 mm. **Ruler:** Elizabeth II **Series:** Australian Peacekeepers **Obv:** Queen's head right **Rev:** Australian federal police and color insignia **Edge:** Reeded

Date	Mintage	F12	VF20	XF40	MS60	MS63
2005P	2,500	PF65 90.00				

KM# 759 2 DOLLARS
62.27 g., 0.999 Silver 1.9871 oz. ASW, 50.3 mm. **Ruler:** Elizabeth II **Series:** Australian Peacekeepers **Obv:** Queen's head right **Rev:** Australian Agency for International Development and color insignia **Edge:** Reeded

Date	Mintage	F12	VF20	XF40	MS60	MS63
2005P	2,500	PF65 90.00				

KM# 852 2 DOLLARS
8.85 g., 0.999 Silver 0.2824 oz. ASW, 20.5 mm. **Ruler:** Elizabeth II **Obv:** Young bust right **Obv. Designer:** Arnold Machin **Rev:** Aboriginal elder **Rev. Designer:** Horst Hahn **Edge:** Segmented reeding

Date	Mintage	F12	VF20	XF40	MS60	MS63
2006	6,500	PF65 22.00				

KM# 853 2 DOLLARS
1.24 g., 0.999 Gold 0.0397 oz. AGW **Ruler:** Elizabeth II **Obv:** Head with tiara right **Obv. Designer:** Ian Rank-Broadley **Rev:** FIFA World Cup

Date	Mintage	F12	VF20	XF40	MS60	MS63
2006P	50,000	PF65 80.00				

KM# 1246 2 DOLLARS
0.50 g., 0.999 Gold AGW, 12 mm. **Ruler:** Elizabeth II **Subject:** 2010 FIFA World Cup, South Africa **Obv:** Head right **Obv. Designer:** Ian Rank-Broadley **Rev:** Dream kangaroo and soccer ball

Date	Mintage	F12	VF20	XF40	MS60	MS63
2009P	7,500	PF65 85.00				

KM# 1627 2 DOLLARS
31.11 g., 0.999 Silver 0.9926 oz. ASW, 40.6 mm. **Ruler:** Elizabeth II **Subject:** Royal Australian Navy, 100th Anniversary **Obv:** Head with tiara right **Rev:** HMAS AE 2 submarine

Date	Mintage	F12	VF20	XF40	MS60	MS63
2011	—	PF65 100				

KM# 1628 2 DOLLARS
31.11 g., 0.999 Silver 0.9926 oz. ASW, 40.6 mm. **Ruler:** Elizabeth II **Subject:** Royal Australian Navy, 100th Anniversary **Obv:** Head with tiara right **Rev:** HMAS Australia II

Date	Mintage	F12	VF20	XF40	MS60	MS63
2011	—	PF65 100				

KM# 1629 2 DOLLARS
31.11 g., 0.999 Silver 0.9926 oz. ASW, 40.6 mm. **Ruler:** Elizabeth II **Subject:** Royal Australian Navy, 100th Anniversary **Obv:** Head with tiara right **Rev:** HMAS Hobart II

Date	Mintage	F12	VF20	XF40	MS60	MS63
2011	—	PF65 100				

KM# 1630 2 DOLLARS
31.11 g., 0.999 Silver 0.9926 oz. ASW, 40.6 mm. **Ruler:** Elizabeth II **Subject:** Royal Australian Navy, 100th Anniversary **Obv:** Head with tiara right **Rev:** HMAS Yarra III

Date	Mintage	F12	VF20	XF40	MS60	MS63
2011	—	PF65 100				

KM# 1631 2 DOLLARS
31.11 g., 0.999 Silver 0.9926 oz. ASW, 40.6 mm. **Ruler:** Elizabeth II **Subject:** Royal Australian Navy, 100th Anniversary **Obv:** Head with tiara right **Rev:** HMAS Sydney III

Date	Mintage	F12	VF20	XF40	MS60	MS63
2011	—	PF65 100				

KM# 1632 2 DOLLARS
31.11 g., 0.999 Silver 0.9926 oz. ASW, 40.6 mm. **Ruler:** Elizabeth II **Subject:** Royal Australian Navy, 100th Anniversary **Obv:** Head with tiara right **Rev:** HMAS Armidale II

Date	Mintage	F12	VF20	XF40	MS60	MS63
2011	—	PF65 100				

KM# 2007a 2 DOLLARS
6.60 g., Aluminum-Bronze, 20.5 mm. **Ruler:** Elizabeth II **Subject:** Remembrance Day **Rev:** Red and black poppy at center

Date	Mintage	F12	VF20	XF40	MS60	MS63
2012C	—	—	—	—	—	15.00
2012	—	—	—	—	—	15.00

KM# 1740 2 DOLLARS
20.00 g., 0.999 Silver 0.6382 oz. ASW, 34 mm. **Ruler:** Elizabeth II **Subject:** Australian Open **Obv:** Small Queen's portrait above tennis ball **Rev:** Player serving

Date	Mintage	F12	VF20	XF40	MS60	MS63
2012	10,000	PF65 100				

KM# 1802 2 DOLLARS
0.50 g., 0.999 Gold AGW, 11.6 mm. **Ruler:** Elizabeth II **Subject:** FIFA **Rev:** Soccer player and Australia map

Date	Mintage	F12	VF20	XF40	MS60	MS63
2012P	—	PF65 75.00				

KM# 1825 2 DOLLARS
0.50 g., 0.999 Gold AGW, 11.6 mm. **Ruler:** Elizabeth II **Subject:** Mini-Roo **Rev:** Kangaroo

Date	Mintage	F12	VF20	XF40	MS60	MS63
2012P	—	PF65 50.00				

KM# 2007 2 DOLLARS
6.60 g., Aluminum-Bronze, 20.5 mm. **Ruler:** Elizabeth II **Subject:** Remembrance Day **Rev:** Poppy at center

Date	Mintage	F12	VF20	XF40	MS60	MS63
2012	—	—	—	—	—	5.00

KM# 1864 2 DOLLARS
Silver **Ruler:** Elizabeth II **Subject:** Remembrance Day **Rev:** Poppy in color at center

Date	Mintage	F12	VF20	XF40	MS60	MS63
2012	—	PF65 100				

KM# 1922 2 DOLLARS
62.20 g., 0.999 Silver 1.9849 oz. ASW, 55.6 mm. **Ruler:** Elizabeth II **Subject:** Ludwig Leichhardt **Rev. Designer:** Wade Robinson

Date	Mintage	F12	VF20	XF40	MS60	MS63
2013P	Est. 2013	PF65 150				

KM# 1959 2 DOLLARS
0.50 g., 0.9999 Gold AGW, 11 mm. **Ruler:** Elizabeth II **Subject:** Frilled Neck Lizard **Rev. Designer:** Aleksandra Stokic

Date	Mintage	F12	VF20	XF40	MS60	MS63
2013	—	PF65 45.00				

KM# 2039 2 DOLLARS
0.50 g., 0.9999 Gold AGW, 11.15 mm. **Ruler:** Elizabeth II **Subject:** Australian Miniature Money

Date	Mintage	F12	VF20	XF40	MS60	MS63
2013	Est. 2000	PF65 75.00				

KM# 2153 2 DOLLARS
6.60 g., Aluminum-Bronze, 20.5 mm. **Ruler:** Elizabeth II **Subject:** Elizabeth's Coronation, 60th Anniversary **Obv:** Head with tiara right **Rev:** Crown within purple ring

Date	Mintage	F12	VF20	XF40	MS60	MS63
2013	—	—	—	—	—	15.00

KM# 591 5 DOLLARS
36.31 g., 0.999 Silver 1.1587 oz. ASW, 38.74 mm. **Ruler:** Elizabeth II **Subject:** Centennial of Federation Series Finale **Obv:** Queen's head right **Rev:** Multicolor dual hologram: map and rotunda **Edge:** Reeded

Date	Mintage	F12	VF20	XF40	MS60	MS63
2001B	—	PF65 55.00				

KM# 592 5 DOLLARS
36.31 g., 0.999 Silver 1.1587 oz. ASW, 38.74 mm. **Ruler:** Elizabeth II **Subject:** Barton and Reid **Obv:** Queen's head right **Rev:** Portraits of Dame Flora Reid and Lady Jean Barton **Edge:** Reeded

Date	Mintage	F12	VF20	XF40	MS60	MS63
2001B	5,000	PF65 60.00				

KM# 637 5 DOLLARS
36.31 g., 0.999 Silver 1.1587 oz. ASW, 38.74 mm. **Ruler:** Elizabeth II **Subject:** Kingston, Barton and Deakin **Obv:** Queen's head right **Rev:** Three rectangular portraits and value **Edge:** Reeded

Date	Mintage	F12	VF20	XF40	MS60	MS63
2001B	5,000	PF65 60.00				

KM# 638 5 DOLLARS
36.31 g., 0.999 Silver 1.1587 oz. ASW, 38.74 mm. **Ruler:** Elizabeth II **Subject:** Clark, Parkes and Griffith **Obv:** Queen's head right **Rev:** Three rectangular portraits and value **Edge:** Reeded

Date	Mintage	F12	VF20	XF40	MS60	MS63
2001B	5,000	PF65 60.00				

KM# 639 5 DOLLARS
36.31 g., 0.999 Silver 1.1587 oz. ASW, 38.74 mm. **Ruler:** Elizabeth II **Subject:** Spence, Nicholls and Anderson **Obv:** Queen's head right **Rev:** Three circular portraits and value **Edge:** Reeded

Date	Mintage	F12	VF20	XF40	MS60	MS63
2001B	5,000	PF65 60.00				

KM# 640 5 DOLLARS
36.31 g., 0.999 Silver 1.1587 oz. ASW, 38.74 mm. **Ruler:** Elizabeth II **Subject:** Reid, Forrest and Quick **Obv:** Queen's head right **Rev:** Three rectangular portraits and value **Edge:** Reeded

Date	Mintage	F12	VF20	XF40	MS60	MS63
2001B	5,000	PF65 60.00				

KM# 641 5 DOLLARS
36.31 g., 0.999 Silver 1.1587 oz. ASW, 38.74 mm. **Ruler:** Elizabeth II **Subject:** Bathurst Ladies Organizing Committee **Obv:** Queen's head right **Rev:** Circular design with names above value **Edge:** Reeded

Date	Mintage	F12	VF20	XF40	MS60	MS63
2001B	5,000	PF65 60.00				

KM# 662 5 DOLLARS
36.31 g., 0.999 Silver 1.1587 oz. ASW, 38.74 mm. **Ruler:** Elizabeth II **Subject:** Year of the Outback **Obv:** Queen's head right **Rev:** Multicolor holographic landscape **Edge:** Reeded

Date	Mintage	F12	VF20	XF40	MS60	MS63
2002 (2001)B	15,000	PF65 100				

KM# 761 5 DOLLARS
36.31 g., 0.999 Silver 1.1587 oz. ASW **Ruler:** Elizabeth II **Obv:** Queen's head right **Rev:** Sir Donald Bradman

Date	Mintage	F12	VF20	XF40	MS60	MS63
2001	—	PF65 55.00				

KM# 762 5 DOLLARS
20.00 g., Aluminum-Bronze, 38.74 mm. **Ruler:** Elizabeth II **Obv:** Queen's head right **Rev:** Sir Donald Bradman

Date	Mintage	F12	VF20	XF40	MS60	MS63
2001	—	—	—	—	8.50	9.50

KM# 601 5 DOLLARS
10.52 g., Di-Metallic, 27.8 mm. **Ruler:** Elizabeth II **Subject:** Battle of Sunda Strait **Obv:** Head with tiara right **Obv. Designer:** Ian Rank-Broadley **Rev:** Ships bell from the "USS Houston", denomination below **Rev. Designer:** Vladimir Gottwald **Shape:** 24-sided **Note:** Demagnetized.

Date	Mintage	F12	VF20	XF40	MS60	MS63
2002B	—	—	—	—	7.50	9.50

KM# 647 5 DOLLARS
28.00 g., Aluminum-Bronze, 38.74 mm. **Ruler:** Elizabeth II **Subject:** Battle of Sunda Strait **Obv:** Queen's head right **Rev:** Two ships; USS Houston and HMS Perth **Edge:** Reeded

Date	Mintage	F12	VF20	XF40	MS60	MS63
2002B	15,000	PF65 25.00				

KM# 649 5 DOLLARS
20.00 g., Aluminum-Bronze, 38.74 mm. **Ruler:** Elizabeth II **Subject:** Commonwealth Games **Obv:** Head with tiara right, denomination below **Obv. Designer:** Ian Rank-Broadley **Rev:** Eight arms, each represents an event of the games **Edge:** Reeded

Date	Mintage	F12	VF20	XF40	MS60	MS63
2002B	11,145	—	—	—	8.50	9.50

KM# 650 5 DOLLARS
20.00 g., Aluminum-Bronze, 38.74 mm. **Ruler:** Elizabeth II **Subject:** Commonwealth Games **Obv:** Head with tiara right, denomination below **Obv. Designer:** Ian Rank-Broadley **Rev:** Eight arms, each represents an event at the games **Edge:** Reeded

Date	Mintage	F12	VF20	XF40	MS60	MS63
2002B	11,145	—	—	—	8.50	9.50

KM# 651 5 DOLLARS
20.00 g., Aluminum-Bronze, 38.74 mm. **Ruler:** Elizabeth II **Subject:** Commonwealth Games **Obv:** Head with tiara right, denomination below **Rev:** Blue games logo; star above tail of stylized kangaroo and torch **Edge:** Reeded

Date	Mintage	F12	VF20	XF40	MS60	MS63
2002B	11,145	—	—	—	8.50	9.50

KM# 652 5 DOLLARS
36.31 g., 0.999 Silver 1.1587 oz. ASW, 38.74 mm. **Ruler:** Elizabeth II **Subject:** Commonwealth Games **Obv:** Head with tiara right, denomination below **Obv. Designer:** Ian Rank-Broadley **Rev:** Victorious athletes **Edge:** Reeded

Date	Mintage	F12	VF20	XF40	MS60	MS63
2002B	7,581	PF65 50.00				

KM# 653 5 DOLLARS
36.31 g., 0.999 Silver 1.1587 oz. ASW, 38.74 mm. **Ruler:** Elizabeth II **Obv:** Queen's head right **Rev:** Dutch sailing ship, The Duyfken **Edge:** Reeded

Date	Mintage	F12	VF20	XF40	MS60	MS63
2002B	9,096	PF65 47.00				

KM# 654 5 DOLLARS
36.31 g., 0.999 Silver 1.1587 oz. ASW, 38.74 mm. **Ruler:** Elizabeth II **Obv:** Queen's head right **Rev:** HMS Endeavour sailing ship **Edge:** Reeded

Date	Mintage	F12	VF20	XF40	MS60	MS63
2002B	9,096	PF65 47.00				

KM# 655 5 DOLLARS
36.31 g., 0.999 Silver 1.1587 oz. ASW, 38.74 mm. **Ruler:** Elizabeth II **Obv:** Queen's head right **Rev:** HMS Sirius sailing ship **Edge:** Reeded

Date	Mintage	F12	VF20	XF40	MS60	MS63
2002B	9,096	PF65 47.00				

KM# 656 5 DOLLARS
36.31 g., 0.999 Silver 1.1587 oz. ASW, 38.74 mm. **Ruler:** Elizabeth II **Obv:** Queen's head right **Rev:** HMS Investigator sailing ship **Edge:** Reeded

Date	Mintage	F12	VF20	XF40	MS60	MS63
2002B	9,096	PF65 47.00				

KM# 659 5 DOLLARS
31.10 g., 0.999 Silver 0.9926 oz. ASW, 40 mm. **Ruler:** Elizabeth II **Subject:** Queen Mother **Obv:** Queen's head right **Rev:** Queen Mother circa 1927 within wreath of roses **Rev. Designer:** Stuart Devlin **Edge:** Reeded

Date	Mintage	F12	VF20	XF40	MS60	MS63
2002B	30,000	PF65 40.00				

KM# 765 5 DOLLARS
36.31 g., 0.999 Silver 1.1587 oz. ASW, 38.7 mm. **Ruler:** Elizabeth II **Series:** Masterpieces in Silver - Port Phillip Patterns **Obv:** One ounce design **Rev:** Kangaroo design **Edge:** Reeded

Date	Mintage	F12	VF20	XF40	MS60	MS63
2003B	10,000	PF65 45.00				

KM# 810 5 DOLLARS
36.31 g., 0.995 Silver 1.1541 oz. ASW, 40 mm. **Ruler:** Elizabeth II **Subject:** Rugby World Cup **Obv:** Head with tiara right **Obv. Designer:** Ian Rank-Broadley **Rev:** Rugby World Cup and official logos **Edge:** Reeded

Date	Mintage	F12	VF20	XF40	MS60	MS63
2003	20,501	PF65 85.00				

KM# 854 5 DOLLARS
20.00 g., Aluminum-Bronze, 38.74 mm. **Ruler:** Elizabeth II **Subject:** Rugby World Cup **Obv:** Head with tiara right **Obv. Designer:** Ian Rank-Broadley **Rev:** Player kicking ball at posts, official logo **Edge:** Reeded

Date	Mintage	F12	VF20	XF40	MS60	MS63
2003	43,802	—	—	—	15.00	16.50

KM# 1017 5 DOLLARS
36.21 g., 0.999 Silver 1.1555 oz. ASW, 38.7 mm. **Ruler:** Elizabeth II **Obv:** Head with tiara right **Obv. Legend:** ELIZABETH II - AUSTRALIA **Rev:** Faces in oval hologram in ornate frame **Rev. Legend:** AUSTRALIA'S VOLUNTEERS - MAKING A DIFFERENCE **Edge:** Reeded

Date	Mintage	F12	VF20	XF40	MS60	MS63
2003B	15,000	PF65 45.00				

KM# 727 5 DOLLARS
36.31 g., 0.999 Silver 1.1587 oz. ASW, 38.74 mm. **Ruler:** Elizabeth II **Subject:** Olympics **Obv:** Queen's head right **Rev:** Parthenon, Sydney Opera House and shield with multicolor flag and rings **Edge:** Reeded

Date	Mintage	F12	VF20	XF40	MS60	MS63
2004B	17,500	PF65 40.00				

KM# 728 5 DOLLARS
36.31 g., 0.999 Silver 1.1587 oz. ASW, 38.74 mm. **Ruler:** Elizabeth II **Subject:** Tasmania **Obv:** Queen's head right **Rev:** Ship on island map **Edge:** Reeded

Date	Mintage	F12	VF20	XF40	MS60	MS63
2004B	7,500	PF65 47.00				

KM# 728a 5 DOLLARS
20.00 g., Aluminum-Bronze, 38.74 mm. **Ruler:** Elizabeth II **Subject:** Tasmanian Bicentennial **Obv:** Head with tiara right **Obv. Designer:** Ian Rank-Broadley **Rev:** Ship, map, state flower **Rev. Designer:** Vladimir Gottwald **Edge:** Reeded

Date	Mintage	F12	VF20	XF40	MS60	MS63
2004	18,561	—	—	—	12.00	14.00
2004H	2,841	—	—	—	17.50	20.00

KM# 729 5 DOLLARS
31.10 g., 0.999 Silver 0.9926 oz. ASW, 40 mm. **Ruler:** Elizabeth II **Subject:** Adelaide to Darwin Railroad **Obv:** Queen's head right **Rev:** Train, tracks and outline map **Edge:** Reeded

Date	Mintage	F12	VF20	XF40	MS60	MS63
2004B	12,500	PF65 40.00				

KM# 730 5 DOLLARS
31.10 g., 0.999 Silver 0.9926 oz. ASW, 40 mm. **Ruler:** Elizabeth II **Subject:** 150 Years of Australian Steam Railways **Obv:** Queen's head right **Rev:** Old steam train **Edge:** Reeded

Date	Mintage	F12	VF20	XF40	MS60	MS63
2004B	15,000	PF65 37.50				

KM# 812 5 DOLLARS

Aluminum-Bronze, 38.74 mm. **Ruler:** Elizabeth II **Subject:** Olympic Games 2000-2004 **Obv:** Head with tiara right

Date	Mintage	F12	VF20	XF40	MS60	MS63
2004	—				15.00	16.50

KM# 855 5 DOLLARS

27.25 g., Copper-Nickel, 38.74 mm. **Ruler:** Elizabeth II **Subject:** Australia's Own Game **Obv:** Head with tiara right **Obv. Designer:** Ian Rank-Broadley **Rev:** Cup and logos **Edge:** Reeded

Date	Mintage	F12	VF20	XF40	MS60	MS63
2004	16,163	PF65 45.00				

KM# 856 5 DOLLARS

20.00 g., Aluminum-Bronze, 38.74 mm. **Ruler:** Elizabeth II **Subject:** Olympic Games - Sydney To Athens **Obv:** Head with tiara right **Obv. Designer:** Ian Rank-Broadley **Rev:** Silhouettes ancient Greek athlete and Aboriginal **Edge:** Reeded

Date	Mintage	F12	VF20	XF40	MS60	MS63
2004	24,376	—	—	—	15.00	16.50

KM# 750 5 DOLLARS

20.00 g., Aluminum-Bronze, 38.74 mm. **Ruler:** Elizabeth II **Obv:** Queen's head right **Rev:** Tennis player **Edge:** Reeded

Date	Mintage	F12	VF20	XF40	MS60	MS63
2005B	—	—	—	—	7.50	8.50

KM# 859 5 DOLLARS

36.31 g., 0.999 Silver 1.1587 oz. ASW, 38.74 mm. **Ruler:** Elizabeth II **Subject:** 150 Year of State Government **Obv:** Head with tiara right **Obv. Designer:** Ian Rank-Broadley **Rev:** Outline map of State of Victoria **Rev. Designer:** Wojciech Pietranik **Edge:** Reeded

Date	Mintage	F12	VF20	XF40	MS60	MS63
2006	12,500	PF65 85.00				

KM# 782 5 DOLLARS

36.31 g., 0.9999 Silver 1.1598 oz. ASW, 38.74 mm. **Ruler:** Elizabeth II **Subject:** XVIII Commonwealth Games City of Sport **Obv:** Head with tiara right, denomination below **Obv. Designer:** Ian Rank-Broadley **Rev:** City skyline alongside river

Date	Mintage	F12	VF20	XF40	MS60	MS63
2006	10,000	PF63 50.00	PF65 55.00			

KM# 783 5 DOLLARS

20.00 g., Aluminum-Bronze, 38.74 mm. **Ruler:** Elizabeth II **Subject:** XVIII Commonwealth Games in Melbourne **Obv:** Head with tiara right, denomination below **Obv. Designer:** Ian Rank-Broadley **Rev:** Games logo and crown surrounded by stylized athletes **Rev. Designer:** Wojciech Pietranik **Edge:** Reeded

Date	Mintage	F12	VF20	XF40	MS60	MS63
2006	—			—	15.00	16.50

KM# 786 5 DOLLARS

20.00 g., Aluminum-Bronze, 38.74 mm. **Ruler:** Elizabeth II **Subject:** XVIII Commonwealth Games Queen's Baton Relay **Obv:** Head with tiara right **Obv. Designer:** Ian Rank-Broadley **Rev:** Stylized baton runner **Rev. Designer:** Peter Soobik **Edge:** Reeded

Date	Mintage	F12	VF20	XF40	MS60	MS63
2006	20,488	—	—	—	15.00	16.50

KM# 786a 5 DOLLARS

36.31 g., 0.999 Silver 1.1587 oz. ASW, 38.74 mm. **Ruler:** Elizabeth II **Subject:** XVIII Commonwealth Games Queen's Baton Relay **Obv:** Head with tiara right **Obv. Designer:** Ian Rank-Broadley **Rev:** Stylized baton runner **Rev. Designer:** Peter Soobik **Edge:** Reeded

Date	Mintage	F12	VF20	XF40	MS60	MS63
2006	9,100	PF65 75.00				

KM# 787 5 DOLLARS

36.31 g., 0.999 Silver 1.1587 oz. ASW, 38.74 mm. **Ruler:** Elizabeth II **Subject:** Masterpieces in Silver: Australia's Artists **Obv:** Head with tiara right **Obv. Designer:** Ian Rank-Broadley **Rev:** Sidney Nolan: Burke & Wills **Rev. Designer:** Vladimir Gottwald

Date	Mintage	F12	VF20	XF40	MS60	MS63
2006	10,000	PF63 55.00	PF65 60.00			

KM# 788 5 DOLLARS

36.31 g., 0.999 Silver 1.1587 oz. ASW, 38.74 mm. **Ruler:** Elizabeth II **Subject:** Masters in Art - Siding

Date	Mintage	F12	VF20	XF40	MS60	MS63
2006	10,000	PF63 50.00	PF65 55.00			

KM# 789 5 DOLLARS

36.31 g., 0.999 Silver 1.1587 oz. ASW, 38.74 mm. **Ruler:** Elizabeth II **Subject:** Masterpieces in Silver: Australia's Artists **Obv:** Head with tiara right **Obv. Designer:** Ian Rank-Broadley **Rev:** Brett Whitley: Self Portrait in the Studio **Rev. Designer:** Vladimir Gottwald

Date	Mintage	F12	VF20	XF40	MS60	MS63
2006	10,000	PF63 55.00	PF65 60.00			

KM# 790 5 DOLLARS

36.31 g., 0.999 Silver 1.1587 oz. ASW, 38.74 mm. **Ruler:** Elizabeth II **Subject:** Masterpieces in Silver: Australia's Artists **Obv:** Head with tiara right **Obv. Designer:** Ian Rank-Broadley **Rev:** Russell Drysdale: The Drover's Wife **Rev. Designer:** Vladimir Gottwald

Date	Mintage	F12	VF20	XF40	MS60	MS63
2006	10,000	PF63 55.00	PF65 60.00			

KM# 813 5 DOLLARS

20.00 g., Aluminum-Bronze, 38.74 mm. **Ruler:** Elizabeth II **Subject:** Voyage of Discovery 1606 **Obv:** Head with tiara right **Obv. Designer:** Ian Rank-Broadley **Rev:** Dutch yacht Duyfken **Rev. Designer:** Wojciech Pietranik **Edge:** Reeded **Note:** Mint mark: G.

Date	Mintage	F12	VF20	XF40	MS60	MS63
2006	—			—	15.00	16.50

KM# 813a 5 DOLLARS
36.31 g., 0.999 Silver 1.1587 oz. ASW, 38.74 mm. **Ruler:**
Elizabeth II **Subject:** Voyage of Discovery 1606 **Obv:** Head
with tiara right **Obv. Designer:** Ian Rank-Broadley **Rev:** Dutch
yacht Duyfken **Rev. Designer:** Wojciech Pietranik **Edge:**
Reeded **Note:** Mint mark: Tulip.

Date	Mintage	F12	VF20	XF40	MS60	MS63
2006P	8,500	PF65 125				

KM# 857 5 DOLLARS
36.31 g., 0.9999 Silver 1.1598 oz. ASW, 38.74 mm. **Ruler:**
Elizabeth II **Subject:** 150 Year of State Government **Obv:** Head
with tiara right **Obv. Designer:** Ian Rank-Broadley **Rev:** Outline
map of State of New South Wales **Rev. Designer:** Wojciech
Pietranik **Edge:** Reeded

Date	Mintage	F12	VF20	XF40	MS60	MS63
2006	12,500	PF65 85.00				

KM# 858 5 DOLLARS
36.31 g., 0.999 Silver 1.1587 oz. ASW, 38.74 mm. **Ruler:**
Elizabeth II **Subject:** 150 Year of State Government **Obv:** Head
with tiara right **Obv. Designer:** Ian Rank-Broadley **Rev:** Outline
map of State of Tasmania **Rev. Designer:** Wojciech Pietranik
Edge: Reeded

Date	Mintage	F12	VF20	XF40	MS60	MS63
2006	12,500	PF65 85.00				

KM# 860 5 DOLLARS
36.31 g., 0.999 Silver 1.1587 oz. ASW, 38.74 mm. **Ruler:**
Elizabeth II **Subject:** Masterpieces in Silver: Australia's Artists
Obv: Ian Rank-Broadley **Rev:** Jeffrey Smart: Keswick Siding
Rev. Designer: Vladimir Gottwald

Date	Mintage	F12	VF20	XF40	MS60	MS63
2006	10,000	PF63 55.00		PF65 60.00		

KM# 950 5 DOLLARS
1.24 g., 0.999 Gold 0.0397 oz. AGW **Ruler:** Elizabeth II
Subject: Australian Fauna **Obv:** Head with tiara right **Obv.
Designer:** Ian Rank-Broadley **Rev:** Salt water crocodile

Date	Mintage	F12	VF20	XF40	MS60	MS63
2006	4,812	PF65 100				

KM# 953 5 DOLLARS
1.24 g., 0.999 Gold 0.0397 oz. AGW **Ruler:** Elizabeth II
Subject: Australian Fauna **Obv:** Head with tiara right **Obv.
Designer:** Ian Rank-Broadley **Rev:** Grey kangaroo

Date	Mintage	F12	VF20	XF40	MS60	MS63
2006	2,096	PF65 100				

KM# 956 5 DOLLARS
1.24 g., 0.999 Gold 0.0397 oz. AGW **Ruler:** Elizabeth II
Subject: Australian Fauna **Obv:** Head with tiara right **Obv.
Designer:** Ian Rank-Broadley **Rev:** Emu

Date	Mintage	F12	VF20	XF40	MS60	MS63
2006	1,655	PF65 85.00				

KM# 959 5 DOLLARS
1.24 g., 0.999 Gold 0.0397 oz. AGW **Ruler:** Elizabeth II
Subject: Australian Fauna **Obv:** Head with tiara right **Obv.
Designer:** Ian Rank-Broadley **Rev:** Koala

Date	Mintage	F12	VF20	XF40	MS60	MS63
2006	2,519	PF65 100				

KM# 962 5 DOLLARS
1.24 g., 0.999 Gold 0.0397 oz. AGW **Ruler:** Elizabeth II
Subject: Australian Fauna **Obv:** Head with tiara right **Obv.
Designer:** Ian Rank-Broadley **Rev:** Kookaburra

Date	Mintage	F12	VF20	XF40	MS60	MS63
2006	1,697	PF65 100				

KM# 1014 5 DOLLARS
1.24 g., 0.9999 Gold 0.0397 oz. AGW, 19 mm. **Ruler:** Elizabeth
II **Obv:** Bust with tiara right **Obv. Legend:** ELIZABETH II -
AUSTRALIA **Obv. Designer:** Ian Rank-Broadley **Rev:** Sydney
Opera House

Date	Mintage	F12	VF20	XF40	MS60	MS63
2006P	100,000	PF65 75.00				

KM# 861 5 DOLLARS
36.31 g., 0.999 Silver 1.1587 oz. ASW, 38.74 mm. **Ruler:**
Elizabeth II **Subject:** Masterpieces in Silver: Australia's Artists
Obv: Head with tiara right **Obv. Designer:** Ian Rank-Broadley
Rev: Grace Cossington-Smith: Curve of the Bridge **Rev.
Designer:** Vladimir Gottwald

Date	Mintage	F12	VF20	XF40	MS60	MS63
2007	10,000	PF63 50.00		PF65 55.00		

KM# 862 5 DOLLARS
36.31 g., 0.999 Silver 1.1587 oz. ASW, 38.74 mm. **Ruler:**
Elizabeth II **Subject:** Masterpieces in Silver: Australia's Artists
Obv: Head with tiara right **Obv. Designer:** Ian Rank-Broadley
Rev: Clifford Possum Tjpaltjarri: Yuelamu Honey Ant Dreaming
Rev. Designer: Vladimir Gottwald

Date	Mintage	F12	VF20	XF40	MS60	MS63
2007	10,000	PF63 50.00		PF65 55.00		

KM# 863 5 DOLLARS
36.31 g., 0.999 Silver 1.1587 oz. ASW, 38.74 mm. **Ruler:**
Elizabeth II **Subject:** Masterpieces in Silver: Australia's Artists
Obv: Head with tiara right **Obv. Designer:** Ian Rank-Broadley
Rev: William Dobell: Margaret Olley **Rev. Designer:** Vladimir
Gottwald

Date	Mintage	F12	VF20	XF40	MS60	MS63
2007	10,000	PF63 50.00		PF65 55.00		

KM# 864 5 DOLLARS
36.31 g., 0.999 Silver 1.1587 oz. ASW, 38.74 mm. **Ruler:**
Elizabeth II **Subject:** Masterpieces in Silver: Australia's Artists
Obv: Ian Rank-Broadley **Rev:** Margaret Preston: Implement
Blue **Rev. Designer:** Vladimir Gottwald

Date	Mintage	F12	VF20	XF40	MS60	MS63
2007	10,000	PF63 50.00		PF65 55.00		

KM# 865 5 DOLLARS
36.31 g., 0.999 Silver 1.1587 oz. ASW, 38.74 mm. **Ruler:**
Elizabeth II **Subject:** Ashes Cricket Series 1882-2007 **Obv:**
Head with tiara right **Obv. Designer:** Ian Rank-Broadley **Rev:**
Urn with supporters **Rev. Designer:** Vladimir Gottwald **Edge:**
Reeded

Date	Mintage	F12	VF20	XF40	MS60	MS63
2007	12,500	PF63 45.00		PF65 50.00		

KM# 965 5 DOLLARS
1.24 g., 0.999 Gold 0.0397 oz. AGW **Ruler:** Elizabeth II
Subject: Australian Fauna **Obv:** Head with tiara right **Obv.
Designer:** Ian Rank-Broadley **Rev:** Echidna

Date	Mintage	F12	VF20	XF40	MS60	MS63
2007	1,269	PF65 100				

KM# 968 5 DOLLARS
1.24 g., 0.999 Gold 0.0397 oz. AGW **Ruler:** Elizabeth II
Subject: Australian Fauna **Obv:** Head with tiara right **Obv.
Designer:** Ian Rank-Broadley **Rev:** Common wombat

Date	Mintage	F12	VF20	XF40	MS60	MS63
2007	1,242	PF65 100				

KM# 971 5 DOLLARS
1.24 g., 0.999 Gold 0.0397 oz. AGW **Ruler:** Elizabeth II
Subject: Australian Fauna **Obv:** Head with tiara right **Obv.
Designer:** Ian Rank-Broadley **Rev:** Tasmanian devil

Date	Mintage	F12	VF20	XF40	MS60	MS63
2007	1,274	PF65 95.00				

KM# 974 5 DOLLARS
1.24 g., 0.999 Gold 0.0397 oz. AGW **Ruler:** Elizabeth II
Subject: Australian Fauna **Obv:** Head with tiara right **Obv.
Designer:** Ian Rank-Broadley **Rev:** Great white shark

Date	Mintage	F12	VF20	XF40	MS60	MS63
2007	1,656	PF65 100				

KM# 977 5 DOLLARS
1.24 g., 0.999 Gold 0.0397 oz. AGW **Ruler:** Elizabeth II
Subject: Australian Fauna **Obv:** Head with tiara right **Obv.
Designer:** Ian Rank-Broadley **Rev:** Platypus

Date	Mintage	F12	VF20	XF40	MS60	MS63
2007	1,188	PF65 100				

KM# 1013 5 DOLLARS
36.31 g., 0.999 Silver 1.1587 oz. ASW, 38.74 mm. **Ruler:**
Elizabeth II **Subject:** Sydney Harbour Bridge, 75th Anniversary

Obv: Bust with tiara right **Obv. Legend:** ELIZABETH II - AUSTRALIA **Obv. Designer:** Ian Rank-Broadley **Rev:** Bridge **Rev. Inscription:** SYDNEY / HARBOUR / BRIDGE

Date	Mintage	F12	VF20	XF40	MS60	MS63
2007	12,500		PF65 50.00			

KM# 1045 5 DOLLARS
36.31 g., 0.999 Silver 1.1587 oz. ASW, 38.74 mm. **Ruler:** Elizabeth II **Subject:** Year of the surfer lifesaver **Rev:** Rowboat in rough seas

Date	Mintage	F12	VF20	XF40	MS60	MS63
2007B	12,500		PF65 65.00			

KM# 1046 5 DOLLARS
36.31 g., 0.999 Silver 1.1587 oz. ASW, 38.74 mm. **Ruler:** Elizabeth II **Subject:** South Australia State Government **Rev:** Australia map and state enlarged **Rev. Designer:** W. Pietranik

Date	Mintage	F12	VF20	XF40	MS60	MS63
2007B	12,500		PF65 65.00			

KM# 1117 5 DOLLARS
1.24 g., 0.999 Gold 0.0396 oz. AGW, 14 mm. **Ruler:** Elizabeth II **Subject:** Sydney Harbor Bridge **Obv:** Head right **Obv. Designer:** Ian Rank-Broadley **Rev:** Bridge view

Date	Mintage	F12	VF20	XF40	MS60	MS63
2007P	100,000		PF63 100	PF65 110		

KM# 1050 5 DOLLARS
31.11 g., 0.999 Silver 0.9926 oz. ASW, 38.74 mm. **Ruler:** Elizabeth II **Subject:** Scouting Centennial in Australia **Rev:** Scout sign and map **Rev. Designer:** C. Goodall

Date	Mintage	F12	VF20	XF40	MS60	MS63
2008	5,000		PF65 65.00			

KM# 1053 5 DOLLARS
36.31 g., 0.999 Silver 1.1587 oz. ASW, 38.74 mm. **Ruler:** Elizabeth II **Subject:** Rugby League **Rev:** Two players

Date	Mintage	F12	VF20	XF40	MS60	MS63
2008	10,000		PF65 65.00			

KM# 1055 5 DOLLARS
31.11 g., 0.999 Silver 0.9926 oz. ASW, 38.74 mm. **Ruler:** Elizabeth II **Rev:** Antarctic skua in flight over map

Date	Mintage	F12	VF20	XF40	MS60	MS63
2008	12,500		PF65 65.00			

KM# 1065 5 DOLLARS
36.31 g., 0.999 Silver 1.1587 oz. ASW, 38.74 mm. **Ruler:** Elizabeth II **Subject:** 30th Anniversary - Northern Territorial Government **Rev:** Territory map and Australia map **Rev. Designer:** W. Pietranik

Date	Mintage	F12	VF20	XF40	MS60	MS63
2008	12,500		PF65 65.00			

KM# 1066 5 DOLLARS
1.15 g., 0.999 Gold 0.0367 oz. AGW, 14 mm. **Ruler:** Elizabeth II **Rev:** Kisp Koala

Date	Mintage	F12	VF20	XF40	MS60	MS63
2008	10,000		PF63 100	PF65 110		

KM# 1067 5 DOLLARS
1.15 g., 0.999 Gold 0.0367 oz. AGW, 14 mm. **Ruler:** Elizabeth II **Rev:** Binny Bilby

Date	Mintage	F12	VF20	XF40	MS60	MS63
2008	10,000		PF63 100	PF65 110		

KM# 1072 5 DOLLARS
36.31 g., 0.999 Silver 1.1587 oz. ASW, 38.74 mm. **Ruler:** Elizabeth II **Rev:** Avro 504K airplane

Date	Mintage	F12	VF20	XF40	MS60	MS63
2008	10,000		PF63 60.00	PF65 65.00		

KM# 1073 5 DOLLARS
36.31 g., 0.999 Silver 1.1587 oz. ASW, 38.74 mm. **Ruler:** Elizabeth II **Rev:** Airbus A380 airplane

Date	Mintage	F12	VF20	XF40	MS60	MS63
2008	10,000		PF63 60.00	PF65 65.00		

KM# 1084 5 DOLLARS
Aluminum-Bronze, 38.74 mm. **Ruler:** Elizabeth II **Subject:** Sir Donald Bradman 100th Anniversary of Birth **Rev:** Player with cricket bat **Rev. Designer:** V. Gottwald

Date	Mintage	F12	VF20	XF40	MS60	MS63
2008	—	—	—	—	—	10.00

KM# 1080 5 DOLLARS
36.31 g., 0.999 Silver 1.1587 oz. ASW, 38.74 mm. **Ruler:** Elizabeth II **Rev:** Three arctic explorers on map **Rev. Designer:** W. Pietranik

Date	Mintage	F12	VF20	XF40	MS60	MS63
2009	12,500		PF65 65.00			

KM# 1081 5 DOLLARS
36.31 g., 0.999 Silver 1.1587 oz. ASW, 38.74 mm. **Ruler:** Elizabeth II **Subject:** Aurora Australis **Obv:** Head right **Rev:** Sailing ship in Antarctic ice in hologram **Rev. Designer:** W. Pietranik

Date	Mintage	F12	VF20	XF40	MS60	MS63
2009	12,500		PF63 55.00	PF65 60.00		

KM# 1085 5 DOLLARS
1.20 g., 0.999 Gold 0.0383 oz. AGW, 14 mm. **Ruler:** Elizabeth II **Obv:** Head right **Rev:** Lilly Pilly full-neck lizard

Date	Mintage	F12	VF20	XF40	MS60	MS63
2009	10,000		PF63 70.00	PF65 75.00		

KM# 1086 5 DOLLARS
1.20 g., 0.999 Gold 0.0383 oz. AGW, 14 mm. **Ruler:** Elizabeth II **Obv:** Head right **Rev:** Petey Platypus

Date	Mintage	F12	VF20	XF40	MS60	MS63
2009	10,000		PF63 70.00	PF65 75.00		

KM# 1217 5 DOLLARS
1.25 g., 0.999 Gold 0.0399 oz. AGW, 14 mm. **Ruler:** Elizabeth II **Obv:** Head right **Obv. Designer:** Ian Rank-Broadley **Rev:** Dreaming kangaroo **Rev. Designer:** Darryl Berllotti

Date	Mintage	F12	VF20	XF40	MS60	MS63
2009P	25,000		PF63 115	PF65 125		

KM# 1218 5 DOLLARS
1.25 g., 0.999 Gold 0.0399 oz. AGW, 14 mm. **Ruler:** Elizabeth II **Obv:** Head right **Obv. Designer:** Ian Rank-Broadley **Rev:** Dreaming dolphin **Rev. Designer:** Darryl Berttolli

Date	Mintage	F12	VF20	XF40	MS60	MS63
2009P	25,000		PF63 115	PF65 125		

KM# 1219 5 DOLLARS
1.25 g., 0.999 Gold 0.0399 oz. AGW, 14 mm. **Ruler:** Elizabeth II **Obv:** Head right **Obv. Designer:** Ian Rank-Broadley **Rev:** Dreaming king brown snake **Rev. Designer:** Darryl Berttolli

Date	Mintage	F12	VF20	XF40	MS60	MS63
2009P	25,000		PF63 115	PF65 125		

KM# 1220 5 DOLLARS
1.25 g., 0.999 Gold 0.0399 oz. AGW, 14 mm. **Ruler:** Elizabeth II **Obv:** Head right **Obv. Designer:** Ian Rank-Broadley **Rev:** Dreaming brolga **Rev. Designer:** Darryl Berttolli

Date	Mintage	F12	VF20	XF40	MS60	MS63
2009P	25,000		PF63 115	PF65 125		

KM# 1221 5 DOLLARS
1.25 g., 0.999 Gold 0.0399 oz. AGW, 14 mm. **Ruler:** Elizabeth II **Obv:** Head right **Obv. Designer:** Ian Rank-Broadley **Rev:** Dreaming echidna **Rev. Designer:** Darryl Berttolli

Date	Mintage	F12	VF20	XF40	MS60	MS63
2009P	25,000		PF63 115	PF65 125		

KM# 1224 5 DOLLARS
3.11 g., 0.999 Gold 0.0992 oz. AGW, 14 mm. **Ruler:** Elizabeth II **Obv:** Head right **Obv. Designer:** Ian Rank-Broadley **Rev:** Dreaming brown snake **Rev. Designer:** Darryl Berttolli

Date	Mintage	F12	VF20	XF40	MS60	MS63
2009P	2,500		PF65 175			

KM# 1658 5 DOLLARS
36.31 g., 0.999 Silver 1.1587 oz. ASW, 38.74 mm. **Ruler:** Elizabeth II **Subject:** Queensland Government **Rev:** Map of Australian states, Queensland highlighted

Date	Mintage	F12	VF20	XF40	MS60	MS63
2009	—		PF65 85.00			

KM# 1402 5 DOLLARS
1.24 g., 0.999 Gold 0.0396 oz. AGW, 14 mm. **Ruler:** Elizabeth II **Obv:** Head right **Obv. Designer:** Ian Rank Broadley **Rev:** Frill-neck lizard

Date	Mintage	F12	VF20	XF40	MS60	MS63
2010P	25,000	PF63 120	PF65 130			

KM# 1408 5 DOLLARS
1.24 g., 0.999 Gold 0.0396 oz. AGW, 14 mm. **Ruler:** Elizabeth II **Obv:** Head right **Obv. Designer:** Ian Rank-Broadley **Rev:** Koala

Date	Mintage	F12	VF20	XF40	MS60	MS63
2010P	25,000	PF63 120	PF65 130			

KM# 1414 5 DOLLARS
1.24 g., 0.999 Gold 0.0396 oz. AGW, 14 mm. **Ruler:** Elizabeth II **Obv:** Head right **Obv. Designer:** Ian Rank Broadley **Rev:** Platypus

Date	Mintage	F12	VF20	XF40	MS60	MS63
2010P	25,000	PF63 120	PF65 130			

KM# 1420 5 DOLLARS
1.24 g., 0.999 Gold 0.0396 oz. AGW, 14 mm. **Ruler:** Elizabeth II **Obv:** Head right **Obv. Designer:** Ian Rank-Broadley **Rev:** Salt water crocodile

Date	Mintage	F12	VF20	XF40	MS60	MS63
2010P	25,000	PF63 120	PF65 130			

KM# 1426 5 DOLLARS
1.24 g., 0.999 Gold 0.0396 oz. AGW, 14 mm. **Ruler:** Elizabeth II **Obv:** Head right **Obv. Designer:** Ian Rank-Broadley **Rev:** Wombat

Date	Mintage	F12	VF20	XF40	MS60	MS63
2010P	25,000	PF63 120	PF65 130			

KM# 1509 5 DOLLARS
36.31 g., 0.999 Silver 1.1587 oz. ASW, 38.74 mm. **Ruler:** Elizabeth II **Subject:** Aviation - Constellation L749

Date	Mintage	F12	VF20	XF40	MS60	MS63
2010	—		PF63 60.00	PF65 65.00		

KM# 1510 5 DOLLARS
36.31 g., 0.999 Silver 1.1587 oz. ASW, 37.84 mm. **Ruler:** Elizabeth II **Subject:** Aviation - De Havilland DH 86

Date	Mintage	F12	VF20	XF40	MS60	MS63
2010	—		PF63 60.00	PF65 65.00		

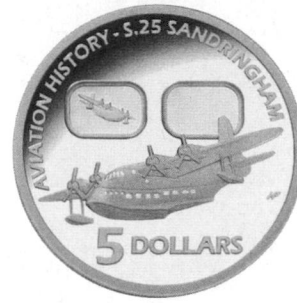

KM# 1511 5 DOLLARS
36.31 g., 0.999 Silver 1.1587 oz. ASW, 38.74 mm. **Ruler:** Elizabeth II **Subject:** Aviation - S.25 Sandringham

Date	Mintage	F12	VF20	XF40	MS60	MS63
2010	—		PF63 60.00	PF65 65.00		

KM# 1512 5 DOLLARS
36.31 g., 0.999 Silver 1.1587 oz. ASW, 38.74 mm. **Ruler:** Elizabeth II **Subject:** Aviation - Boeing 747

Date	Mintage	F12	VF20	XF40	MS60	MS63
2010	—		PF63 60.00	PF65 65.00		

KM# 1535 5 DOLLARS
1.24 g., 0.999 Gold 0.0396 oz. AGW **Ruler:** Elizabeth II **Subject:** Dreaming Emu **Rev:** Linear emu in color

Date	Mintage	F12	VF20	XF40	MS60	MS63
2011P	25,000	PF63 115	PF65 125			

KM# 1541 5 DOLLARS
1.24 g., 0.999 Gold 0.0396 oz. AGW **Ruler:** Elizabeth II **Subject:** Dreaming Tasmanian Devil **Rev:** Linear tasmanian devil in color

Date	Mintage	F12	VF20	XF40	MS60	MS63
2011P	25,000	PF63 115	PF65 125			

KM# 1547 5 DOLLARS
1.24 g., 0.999 Gold 0.0396 oz. AGW **Ruler:** Elizabeth II **Obv:** Dreaming Kookaburra **Edge:** Linear Kookaburra in color

Date	Mintage	F12	VF20	XF40	MS60	MS63
2011P	250,000	PF63 115	PF65 125			

KM# 1553 5 DOLLARS
1.24 g., 0.999 Gold 0.0396 oz. AGW **Ruler:** Elizabeth II **Subject:** Dreaming shark **Rev:** Linear shark in color

Date	Mintage	F12	VF20	XF40	MS60	MS63
2011P	25,000	PF63 115	PF65 125			

KM# 1559 5 DOLLARS
1.24 g., 0.999 Gold 0.0396 oz. AGW **Ruler:** Elizabeth II **Subject:** Dreaming Dingo **Rev:** Linear dingo in color

Date	Mintage	F12	VF20	XF40	MS60	MS63
2011P	25,000	PF63 115	PF65 125			

KM# 1633 5 DOLLARS
20.00 g., Aluminum-Bronze, 38.74 mm. **Ruler:** Elizabeth II **Subject:** Royal Visit **Obv:** Head with tiara right **Rev:** Sixteen crowns **Rev. Designer:** W. Pietranik

Date	Mintage	F12	VF20	XF40	MS60	MS63
2011	—	—	—	—		15.00

KM# 1636 5 DOLLARS
1.24 g., 0.999 Gold 0.0396 oz. AGW, 14 mm. **Ruler:** Elizabeth II **Subject:** Historic Convict Past - Hyde Park Barracks

Date	Mintage	F12	VF20	XF40	MS60	MS63
2011	3,000	PF63 115	PF65 125			

KM# 1637 5 DOLLARS
1.24 g., 0.999 Gold 0.0396 oz. AGW, 14 mm. **Ruler:** Elizabeth II **Subject:** Historic Convict Past - Port Arthur Historic Site

Date	Mintage	F12	VF20	XF40	MS60	MS63
2011	3,000	PF63 115	PF65 125			

KM# 1638 5 DOLLARS
1.24 g., 0.999 Gold 0.0396 oz. AGW, 14 mm. **Ruler:** Elizabeth II **Subject:** Historic Convict Past - Cascades Female Factory

Date	Mintage	F12	VF20	XF40	MS60	MS63
2011	3,000	PF63 115	PF65 125			

KM# 1639 5 DOLLARS
1.24 g., 0.999 Gold 0.0396 oz. AGW, 14 mm. **Ruler:** Elizabeth II **Subject:** Historic Convict Past - Fremantle Prison

Date	Mintage	F12	VF20	XF40	MS60	MS63
2011	3,000	PF63 115	PF65 125			

KM# 1640 5 DOLLARS
1.24 g., 0.999 Gold 0.0396 oz. AGW, 14 mm. **Ruler:** Elizabeth II **Subject:** Historic Convict Past - Coal Mines Historic Site

Date	Mintage	F12	VF20	XF40	MS60	MS63
2011	3,000	PF63 115	PF65 125			

KM# 1641 5 DOLLARS
1.24 g., 0.999 Gold 0.0396 oz. AGW, 14 mm. **Ruler:** Elizabeth II **Subject:** Historic Convict Past - Old Government House and Domain

Date	Mintage	F12	VF20	XF40	MS60	MS63
2011	3,000	PF63 115	PF65 125			

KM# 1652 5 DOLLARS
20.00 g., Aluminum-Bronze, 38.74 mm. **Ruler:** Elizabeth II
Subject: Remembrance Day, 11.11.11 **Obv:** Head with tiara
right **Rev:** Poppy in multicolor

Date	Mintage	F12	VF20	XF40	MS60	MS63
2011	—					17.50

KM# 1739 5 DOLLARS
20.00 g., Aluminum-Bronze, 38.74 mm. **Ruler:** Elizabeth II
Subject: Australian Open **Obv:** Small Queen's head above
tennis ball **Rev:** Player serving

Date	Mintage	F12	VF20	XF40	MS60	MS63
2012	—				—	20.00

KM# 2154 5 DOLLARS
36.31 g., 0.999 Silver 1.1587 oz. ASW, 38.74 mm. **Ruler:**
Elizabeth II **Subject:** Canberra, 100th Anniversary **Obv:** Head
with tiara right **Rev:** Canberra views, old and new

Date	Mintage	F12	VF20	XF40	MS60	MS63
2013	—	PF63 70.00	PF65 75.00			

KM# 1269 8 DOLLARS
5.00 g., 0.999 Gold 0.1596 oz. AGW, 14x23 mm. **Ruler:**
Elizabeth II **Subject:** Chinese Mythological Character **Obv:**
Head right **Obv. Designer:** Ian Rank-Broadley **Rev:** Man
standing, multicolor **Shape:** Vertical rectangle

Date	Mintage	F12	VF20	XF40	MS60	MS63
2008P	1,168	—	—	—	—	435

KM# 1270 8 DOLLARS
5.00 g., 0.999 Gold 0.1596 oz. AGW, 14x23 mm. **Ruler:**
Elizabeth II **Subject:** Chinese Mythological Character -
Longevity **Obv:** Head right **Obv. Designer:** Ian Rank-Broadley
Rev: Nam standing with staff, multicolor **Shape:** Vertical
rectangle

Date	Mintage	F12	VF20	XF40	MS60	MS63
2008P	1,187	—	—	—	—	435

KM# 1716 5 DOLLARS
1.24 g., 0.999 Gold 0.0397 oz. AGW, 14.6 mm. **Ruler:** Elizabeth
II **Rev:** Green and Gold Bell Frog in grease

Date	Mintage	F12	VF20	XF40	MS60	MS63
2012P	2,500	PF63 100	PF65 115			

KM# 1717 5 DOLLARS
1.24 g., 0.999 Gold 0.0397 oz. AGW, 14.6 mm. **Ruler:** Elizabeth
II **Rev:** Kookaburra facing right

Date	Mintage	F12	VF20	XF40	MS60	MS63
2012P	2,500	PF63 100	PF65 115			

KM# 1747 5 DOLLARS
20.00 g., Aluminum-Bronze, 38.74 mm. **Ruler:** Elizabeth II
Obv: Head with tiara right **Rev:** Perth Town Hall

Date	Mintage	F12	VF20	XF40	MS60	MS63
2012 Antique patina	—	—	—	—	20.00	—

KM# 1271 8 DOLLARS
5.00 g., 0.999 Gold 0.1596 oz. AGW, 14x23 mm. **Ruler:**
Elizabeth II **Subject:** Chinese Mythological Character - Success
Obv: Hand right **Obv. Designer:** Ian Rank-Broadley **Rev:** Man
standing with deer, multicolor **Shape:** Vertical rectangle

Date	Mintage	F12	VF20	XF40	MS60	MS63
2008P	1,181	—	—	—	—	435

KM# 1272 8 DOLLARS
5.00 g., 0.999 Gold 0.1596 oz. AGW, 14x23 mm. **Ruler:**
Elizabeth II **Subject:** Mythological Chinese Character - Fortune
Obv: Head right **Obv. Designer:** Ian Rank-Broadley **Rev:** Man
standing with scroll, multicolor **Shape:** Vertical rectangle

Date	Mintage	F12	VF20	XF40	MS60	MS63
2008P	1,181	—	—	—	—	435

KM# 2066 8 DOLLARS
155.67 g., 0.999 Silver 4.9677 oz. ASW, 60.6 mm. **Ruler:**
Elizabeth II **Subject:** A.B. Banjo Paterson, 150th Anniversary
of Birth **Obv:** Head with tiara right **Rev:** Paterson in color **Rev.
Designer:** Natasha Muhl

Date	Mintage	F12	VF20	XF40	MS60	MS63
2013P	250	PF65 600				

KM# 1718 5 DOLLARS
1.24 g., 0.999 Gold 0.0397 oz. AGW, 14.1 mm. **Ruler:** Elizabeth
II **Rev:** Whale shark swimming right

Date	Mintage	F12	VF20	XF40	MS60	MS63
2012P	2,500	PF63 100	PF65 115			

KM# 1719 5 DOLLARS
1.24 g., 0.999 Gold 0.0397 oz. AGW, 14.6 mm. **Ruler:** Elizabeth
II **Rev:** Kangaroo bounding right

Date	Mintage	F12	VF20	XF40	MS60	MS63
2012P	2,500	PF63 100	PF65 115			

KM# 1720 5 DOLLARS
1.24 g., 0.999 Gold 0.0397 oz. AGW, 14.6 mm. **Ruler:** Elizabeth
II **Rev:** Goanna lizard right

Date	Mintage	F12	VF20	XF40	MS60	MS63
2012P	2,500	PF63 100	PF65 115			

KM# 1853 5 DOLLARS
36.31 g., 0.999 Silver 1.1587 oz. ASW, 38.74 mm. **Ruler:**
Elizabeth II **Rev:** Southen Cross in blue sky **Note:** Concave
planchet

Date	Mintage	F12	VF20	XF40	MS60	MS63
2012P	—	PF65 125				

KM# 1965 5 DOLLARS
0.999 Silver **Ruler:** Elizabeth II **Subject:** 25th Anniversary of
Australian Parliament House **Rev. Designer:** Tony Dean

Date	Mintage	F12	VF20	XF40	MS60	MS63
2013	Est. 10000	PF65 125				

KM# 593 10 DOLLARS
33.15 g., Bi-Metallic, 38.74 mm. **Ruler:** Elizabeth II **Subject:**
The Future **Obv:** Queen's portrait **Rev:** Tree, map and
denomination **Rev. Designer:** Peter Soobik and Wojciech
Pietraink **Edge:** Reeded

Date	Mintage	F12	VF20	XF40	MS60	MS63
2001B	—	PF65 55.00				

KM# 1969 5 DOLLARS
31.10 g., 0.999 Silver 0.9925 oz. ASW, 39.62 mm. **Ruler:**
Elizabeth II **Subject:** Southern Sky Pavo **Rev. Designer:**
Aaron Baggio

Date	Mintage	F12	VF20	XF40	MS60	MS63
2013	Est. 10000	PF65 125				

KM# 596 10 DOLLARS
311.04 g., 0.999 Silver 9.9257 oz. ASW, 75.5 mm. **Ruler:**
Elizabeth II **Subject:** Calendar Evolution **Obv:** Head with tiara
right, denomination below **Obv. Designer:** Ian Rank-Broadley
Rev: Multicolor solar system in center, zodiac symbols in outer
circle **Edge:** Segmented reeding **Note:** Illustration reduced.

Date	Mintage	F12	VF20	XF40	MS60	MS63
ND(2001)	1,802	PF65 375				

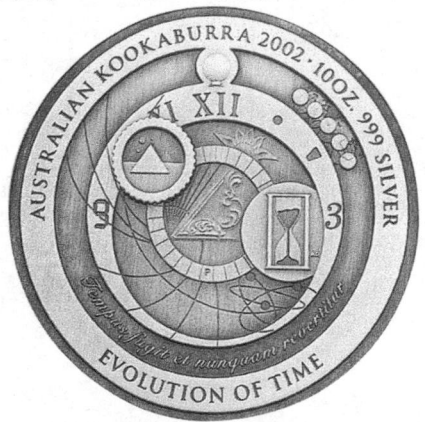

KM# 633 10 DOLLARS
311.04 g., 0.999 Silver 9.9257 oz. ASW, 75.5 mm. **Ruler:**
Elizabeth II **Subject:** Evolution of Time **Obv:** Queen's portrait
right **Rev:** Various time keeping devices **Edge:** Segmented
reeding

Date	Mintage	F12	VF20	XF40	MS60	MS63
2002P	1,533	PF65 425				

KM# 661 10 DOLLARS
60.50 g., 0.999 Silver 1.9307 oz. ASW, 50 mm. **Ruler:** Elizabeth
II **Subject:** The Adelaide Pound **Obv:** Queen's portrait above
gold-plated coin design **Rev:** Legend around gold-plated coin
design **Edge:** Reeded

Date	Mintage	F12	VF20	XF40	MS60	MS63
2002B	10,000	PF65 95.00				

KM# 686 10 DOLLARS
311.00 g., 0.999 Silver 9.9246 oz. ASW, 75.5 mm. **Ruler:**
Elizabeth II **Obv:** Queen's head right **Rev:** Alphabet evolution
design **Edge:** Reeded

Date	Mintage	F12	VF20	XF40	MS60	MS63
2003P	1,041	PF65 425				

KM# 751 10 DOLLARS
60.50 g., 0.999 Silver 1.9307 oz. ASW, 50 mm. **Ruler:** Elizabeth
II **Subject:** 150th Anniversary - Sydney Mint **Obv:** Head with
tiara right above gilt 1853 Sovereign Pattern of Queen Victoria
facing left **Obv. Designer:** Ian Rank-Broadley **Rev:** Gilt reverse
of Sovereign Pattern **Rev. Designer:** Vladimir Gottwald **Edge:**
Reeded

Date	Mintage	F12	VF20	XF40	MS60	MS63
2003B	10,000	PF65 100				
ND(2005)B	10,000	PF65 80.00				

KM# 766 10 DOLLARS
36.31 g., 0.999 Silver 1.1587 oz. ASW, 38.7 mm. **Ruler:**
Elizabeth II **Series:** Masterpieces in Silver - Port Phillip Patterns
Obv: Queen's head right **Rev:** Kangaroo design **Edge:** Reeded

Date	Mintage	F12	VF20	XF40	MS60	MS63
2003B	10,000	PF65 90.00				

KM# 1439 10 DOLLARS
Silver **Ruler:** Elizabeth II **Subject:** Sydney Mint, 100th
Anniversary

Date	Mintage	F12	VF20	XF40	MS60	MS63
2003	10,000	PF63 75.00	PF65 85.00			

KM# 739 10 DOLLARS
311.04 g., 0.999 Silver 9.9257 oz. ASW, 75.5 mm. **Ruler:**
Elizabeth II **Subject:** Evolution of Numbers **Obv:** Queen's head
right **Rev:** Numbers, symbols, abacus and calculator **Edge:**
Reeded

Date	Mintage	F12	VF20	XF40	MS60	MS63
2004	1,051	PF65 425				

KM# 744 10 DOLLARS
311.35 g., 0.999 Silver 9.9356 oz. ASW, 75.5 mm. **Ruler:**
Elizabeth II **Obv:** Queen's head right **Rev:** Multicolor symbolic
design **Edge:** Reeded

Date	Mintage	F12	VF20	XF40	MS60	MS63
2005	1,314	PF65 425				

KM# 866 10 DOLLARS
7.75 g., 0.999 Gold 0.2473 oz. AGW, 17.53 mm. **Ruler:**
Elizabeth II **Subject:** 90th Anniversary Gallipoli Landings **Obv:**
Head with tiara right **Obv. Designer:** Ian Rank-Broadley **Rev:**
Australian slouch hat on inverted rifle before memorial

Date	Mintage	F12	VF20	XF40	MS60	MS63
2005	1,000	PF65 750				

KM# 869 10 DOLLARS
7.78 g., 0.999 Gold 0.2481 oz. AGW, 17.53 mm. **Ruler:**
Elizabeth II **Subject:** FIFA World Cup **Obv:** Head with tiara
right **Obv. Designer:** Ian Rank-Broadley **Rev:** Kangaroo and
players on football

Date	Mintage	F12	VF20	XF40	MS60	MS63
2006P	25,000	PF65 475				

KM# 1118 10 DOLLARS
1.24 g., 0.999 Gold 0.0396 oz. AGW, 14 mm. **Ruler:** Elizabeth II

Obv: Bust right **Obv. Designer:** Ian Rank-Broadley **Rev:** Salt water crocodile **Rev. Legend:** DISCOVER AUSTRALIA

Date	Mintage	F12	VF20	XF40	MS60	MS63
2006P	25,000	PF63 100		PF65 110		

KM# 1119 10 DOLLARS
1.24 g., 0.999 Gold 0.0396 oz. AGW, 14 mm. **Ruler:** Elizabeth II **Obv:** Head right **Obv. Designer:** Ian Rank-Broadley **Rev:** Grey kangaroo **Rev. Legend:** DISCOVER AUSTRALIA

Date	Mintage	F12	VF20	XF40	MS60	MS63
2006P	25,000	PF63 100		PF65 110		

KM# 1120 10 DOLLARS
1.24 g., 0.999 Gold 0.0396 oz. AGW, 14 mm. **Ruler:** Elizabeth II **Obv:** Head right **Obv. Designer:** Ian Rank-Broadley **Rev:** Emu **Rev. Legend:** DISCOVER AUSTRALIA

Date	Mintage	F12	VF20	XF40	MS60	MS63
2006P	25,000	PF63 100		PF65 110		

KM# 1121 10 DOLLARS
1.24 g., 0.999 Gold 0.0396 oz. AGW, 14 mm. **Ruler:** Elizabeth II **Obv:** Head right **Obv. Designer:** Ian Rank-Broadley **Rev:** Koala **Rev. Legend:** DISCOVER AUSTRALIA

Date	Mintage	F12	VF20	XF40	MS60	MS63
2006P	25,000	PF63 100		PF65 110		

KM# 1122 10 DOLLARS
1.24 g., 0.999 Gold 0.0396 oz. AGW, 14 mm. **Ruler:** Elizabeth II **Obv:** Head right **Obv. Designer:** Ian Rank-Broadley **Rev:** Kookaburra **Rev. Legend:** DISCOVER AUSTRALIA

Date	Mintage	F12	VF20	XF40	MS60	MS63
2006P	25,000	PF63 100		PF65 110		

KM# 1133 10 DOLLARS
3.10 g., 0.999 Platinum 0.0989 oz. APW, 16 mm. **Ruler:** Elizabeth II **Obv:** Head right **Obv. Designer:** Ian Rank-Broadley **Rev:** Cooktown orchid, multicolor **Rev. Legend:** DISCOVER AUSTRALIA

Date	Mintage	F12	VF20	XF40	MS60	MS63
2006P	2,500	PF65 300				

KM# 1134 10 DOLLARS
3.10 g., 0.999 Platinum 0.0989 oz. APW, 16 mm. **Ruler:** Elizabeth II **Obv:** Head right **Obv. Designer:** Ian Rank-Broadley **Rev:** Sturt's desert rose, multicolor **Rev. Legend:** DISCOVER AUSTRALIA

Date	Mintage	F12	VF20	XF40	MS60	MS63
2006P	2,500	PF65 300				

KM# 1135 10 DOLLARS
3.10 g., 0.999 Platinum 0.0989 oz. APW, 16 mm. **Ruler:** Elizabeth II **Obv:** Head right **Obv. Designer:** Ian Rank-Broadley **Rev:** Royal Bluebell, multicolor **Rev. Legend:** DISCOVER AUSTRALIA

Date	Mintage	F12	VF20	XF40	MS60	MS63
2006P	2,500	PF65 300				

KM# 1136 10 DOLLARS
3.10 g., 0.999 Platinum 0.0989 oz. APW, 16 mm. **Ruler:** Elizabeth II **Obv:** Head right **Obv. Designer:** Ian Rank-Broadley **Rev:** Red and green kangaroo paw, multicolor **Rev. Legend:** DISCOVER AUSTRALIA

Date	Mintage	F12	VF20	XF40	MS60	MS63
2006P	2,500	PF65 300				

KM# 1137 10 DOLLARS
3.10 g., 0.999 Platinum 0.0989 oz. APW, 16 mm. **Ruler:** Elizabeth II **Obv:** Head right **Obv. Designer:** Ian Rank-Broadley **Rev:** Common pink heath, multicolor **Rev. Legend:** DISCOVER AUSTRALIA

Date	Mintage	F12	VF20	XF40	MS60	MS63
2006P	2,500	PF65 300				

KM# 867 10 DOLLARS
3.11 g., 0.999 Gold 0.0993 oz. AGW **Ruler:** Elizabeth II **Subject:** Ashes Cricket Series 1882-2007 **Obv:** Head with tiara right **Obv. Designer:** Ian Rank-Broadley **Rev:** Urn and supporters **Rev. Designer:** Vladimir Gottwald **Edge:** Reeded

Date	Mintage	F12	VF20	XF40	MS60	MS63
2007	—	PF65 195				

KM# 1000 10 DOLLARS
3.11 g., 0.999 Gold 0.0993 oz. AGW, 17.53 mm. **Ruler:** Elizabeth II **Subject:** Year of the Pig **Obv:** Head with tiara right **Obv. Designer:** Ian Rank-Broadley **Rev:** Mother kangaroo with joey **Rev. Designer:** Rolf Harris **Edge:** Reeded

Date	Mintage	F12	VF20	XF40	MS60	MS63
2007	—	PF65 210				

KM# 1143 10 DOLLARS
1.24 g., 0.999 Gold 0.0396 oz. AGW, 14 mm. **Ruler:** Elizabeth II **Obv:** Head right **Obv. Designer:** Ian Rank-Broadley **Rev:** Echidna **Rev. Legend:** DISCOVER AUSTRALIA

Date	Mintage	F12	VF20	XF40	MS60	MS63
2007P	25,000	PF63 100		PF65 110		

KM# 1144 10 DOLLARS
1.24 g., 0.999 Gold 0.0396 oz. AGW, 14 mm. **Ruler:** Elizabeth

II **Obv:** Head right **Obv. Designer:** Ian rank-Broadley **Rev:** Common wombat **Rev. Legend:** DISCOVER AUSTRALIA

Date	Mintage	F12	VF20	XF40	MS60	MS63
2007P	25,000	PF63 100		PF65 110		

KM# 1145 10 DOLLARS
1.24 g., 0.999 Gold 0.0396 oz. AGW, 14 mm. **Ruler:** Elizabeth II **Obv:** Head right **Obv. Designer:** Ian Rank-Broadley **Rev:** Tasmanian devil **Rev. Legend:** DISCOVER AUSTRALIA

Date	Mintage	F12	VF20	XF40	MS60	MS63
2007P	25,000	PF63 100		PF65 110		

KM# 1146 10 DOLLARS
1.24 g., 0.999 Gold 0.0396 oz. AGW, 14 mm. **Ruler:** Elizabeth II **Obv:** Head right **Obv. Designer:** Ian Rank-Broadley **Rev:** Great white shark **Rev. Legend:** DISCOVER AUSTRALIA

Date	Mintage	F12	VF20	XF40	MS60	MS63
2007P	25,000	PF63 100		PF65 110		

KM# 1147 10 DOLLARS
1.24 g., 0.999 Gold 0.0396 oz. AGW, 14 mm. **Ruler:** Elizabeth II **Obv:** Head right **Obv. Designer:** Ian Rank-Broadley **Rev:** Platypus **Rev. Legend:** DISCOVER AUSTRALIA

Date	Mintage	F12	VF20	XF40	MS60	MS63
2007P	25,000	PF63 100		PF65 110		

KM# 1159 10 DOLLARS
3.10 g., 0.999 Platinum 0.0989 oz. APW, 16 mm. **Ruler:** Elizabeth II **Obv:** Head right **Obv. Designer:** Ian Rank-Broadley **Rev:** Sturt's desert pea, multicolor **Rev. Legend:** DISCOVER AUSTRALIA

Date	Mintage	F12	VF20	XF40	MS60	MS63
2007P	2,500	PF65 300				

KM# 1160 10 DOLLARS
3.10 g., 0.999 Platinum 0.0989 oz. APW, 16 mm. **Ruler:** Elizabeth II **Obv:** Head right **Obv. Designer:** Ian rank-Broadley **Rev:** Tasmanian bluegum, multicolor **Rev. Legend:** DISCOVER AUSTRALIA

Date	Mintage	F12	VF20	XF40	MS60	MS63
2007P	2,500	PF65 300				

KM# 1161 10 DOLLARS
3.10 g., 0.999 Platinum 0.0989 oz. APW, 16 mm. **Ruler:** Elizabeth II **Obv:** Head right **Obv. Designer:** Ian Rank-Broadley **Rev:** Waratah, multicolor **Rev. Legend:** DISCOVER AUSTRALIA

Date	Mintage	F12	VF20	XF40	MS60	MS63
2007P	2,500	PF65 300				

KM# 1162 10 DOLLARS
3.10 g., 0.999 Platinum 0.0989 oz. APW, 16 mm. **Ruler:** Elizabeth II **Obv:** Head right **Obv. Designer:** Ian Rank-Broadley **Rev:** Golden wattle, multicolor **Rev. Legend:** DISCOVER AUSTRALIA

Date	Mintage	F12	VF20	XF40	MS60	MS63
2007P	2,500	PF65 300				

KM# 1051 10 DOLLARS
3.10 g., 0.999 Gold 0.0989 oz. AGW, 17.5 mm. **Ruler:** Elizabeth II **Subject:** Scouting Centennial in Australia **Rev:** Shadow linear portrait of Baden-Powell **Rev. Designer:** C. Goodall

Date	Mintage	F12	VF20	XF40	MS60	MS63
2008	1,500	PF65 335				

KM# 1054 10 DOLLARS
3.11 g., 0.999 Gold 0.0992 oz. AGW, 17.53 mm. **Ruler:** Elizabeth II **Subject:** Rugby League

Date	Mintage	F12	VF20	XF40	MS60	MS63
2008	3,000	PF65 235				

KM# 1622 10 DOLLARS
31.11 g., 0.999 Silver 0.9926 oz. ASW, 40 mm. **Ruler:** Elizabeth II **Subject:** President's Cup **Obv:** Head with tiara right **Rev:** Trophy, gilt

Date	Mintage	F12	VF20	XF40	MS60	MS63
2011	—	PF65 120				

KM# 1662 10 DOLLARS
3.11 g., 0.999 Gold 0.0992 oz. AGW, 17.53 mm. **Ruler:** Elizabeth II **Subject:** Year of the Rabbit **Rev:** Rabbit seated left within circle, floral around

Date	Mintage	F12	VF20	XF40	MS60	MS63
2011		PF65 200				

KM# 1660 10 DOLLARS
3.11 g., 0.999 Gold 0.0992 oz. AGW, 17.53 mm. **Ruler:** Elizabeth II **Subject:** Year of the Tiger **Rev:** Tiger head within circle, floral around

Date	Mintage	F12	VF20	XF40	MS60	MS63
2012	—	PF65 200				

KM# 1681 10 DOLLARS
3.11 g., 0.999 Gold 0.0993 oz. AGW, 17.53 mm. **Ruler:** Elizabeth II **Subject:** Year of the Dragon **Rev:** Dragon head within circle, floral around

Date	Mintage	F12	VF20	XF40	MS60	MS63
2012	—	PF65 200				

KM# 2019 10 DOLLARS
3.11 g., 0.999 Gold 0.0992 oz. AGW, 17.53 mm. **Ruler:** Elizabeth II **Rev:** Three sheafs of wheat

Date	Mintage	F12	VF20	XF40	MS60	MS63
2012 C	Est. 2500	PF65 360				

KM# 1954 10 DOLLARS
155.50 g., 0.999 Silver 4.9623 oz. ASW, 65 mm. **Ruler:**

Elizabeth II **Subject:** Kangaroo Road Sign **Rev. Designer:** Wojciech Pietranik

Date	Mintage	F12	VF20	XF40	MS60	MS63
2013	Est. 5000		PF65 175			

KM# 1964 10 DOLLARS
0.999 Silver **Ruler:** Elizabeth II **Subject:** Bicentenary of the Crossing of the Blue Mountains **Rev. Designer:** Tony Dean

Date	Mintage	F12	VF20	XF40	MS60	MS63
2013	Est. 5000		PF65 200			

KM# 2027 10 DOLLARS
31.11 g., 0.999 Gold 0.9928 oz. AGW, 17.53 mm. **Ruler:** Elizabeth II **Subject:** Holey Dollar **Rev:** NSW coin and 8 real reverse

Date	Mintage	F12	VF20	XF40	MS60	MS63
2013	Est. 2500		PF65 360			

KM# 2031 10 DOLLARS
3.11 g., 0.999 Gold 0.0992 oz. AGW, 17.53 mm. **Ruler:** Elizabeth II **Rev:** Kangaroo standing on rock at left **Rev. Designer:** A. Baggio

Date	Mintage	F12	VF20	XF40	MS60	MS63
2013	Est. 1500		PF65 360			

KM# 2041 10 DOLLARS
311.35 g., 0.999 Silver 9.9357 oz. ASW, 75.6 mm. **Ruler:** Elizabeth II **Subject:** Sydney Opera House **Rev. Designer:** Natasha Muhl

Date	Mintage	F12	VF20	XF40	MS60	MS63
2013	750		PF65 885			

KM# 951 15 DOLLARS
3.11 g., 0.999 Gold 0.0992 oz. AGW **Ruler:** Elizabeth II **Subject:** Australian Fauna **Obv:** Head with tiara right **Obv. Designer:** Ian Rank-Broadley **Rev:** Saltwater crocodile

Date	Mintage	F12	VF20	XF40	MS60	MS63
2006	2,500		PF65 195			

KM# 954 15 DOLLARS
3.11 g., 0.999 Gold 0.0992 oz. AGW **Ruler:** Elizabeth II **Subject:** Australian Fauna **Obv:** Head with tiara right **Obv. Designer:** Ian Rank-Broadley **Rev:** Grey kangaroo

Date	Mintage	F12	VF20	XF40	MS60	MS63
2006	1,999		PF65 195			

KM# 957 15 DOLLARS
3.11 g., 0.999 Gold 0.0992 oz. AGW **Ruler:** Elizabeth II **Subject:** Australian Fauna **Obv:** Head with tiara right **Obv. Designer:** Ian Rank-Broadley **Rev:** Emu

Date	Mintage	F12	VF20	XF40	MS60	MS63
2006	896		PF65 195			

KM# 960 15 DOLLARS
3.11 g., 0.999 Gold 0.0992 oz. AGW **Ruler:** Elizabeth II **Subject:** Australian Fauna **Obv:** Head with tiara right **Obv. Designer:** Ian Rank-Broadley **Rev:** Koala

Date	Mintage	F12	VF20	XF40	MS60	MS63
2006	2,257		PF65 195			

KM# 963 15 DOLLARS
3.11 g., 0.999 Gold 0.0992 oz. AGW **Ruler:** Elizabeth II **Subject:** Australian Fauna **Obv:** Head with tiara right **Obv. Designer:** Ian Rank-Broadley **Rev:** Kookaburra

Date	Mintage	F12	VF20	XF40	MS60	MS63
2006	1,184		PF65 195			

KM# 980 15 DOLLARS
3.11 g., 0.999 Platinum 0.0992 oz. APW **Ruler:** Elizabeth II **Subject:** Australian Flora **Obv:** Head with tiara right **Obv. Designer:** Ian Rank-Broadley **Rev:** Cooktown orchid

Date	Mintage	F12	VF20	XF40	MS60	MS63
2006	1,891		PF65 220			

KM# 982 15 DOLLARS
3.11 g., 0.999 Platinum 0.0992 oz. APW **Ruler:** Elizabeth II **Subject:** Australian Flora **Obv:** Head with tiara right **Obv. Designer:** Ian Rank-Broadley **Rev:** Sturt's desert rose

Date	Mintage	F12	VF20	XF40	MS60	MS63
2006	1,713		PF65 220			

KM# 984 15 DOLLARS
3.11 g., 0.999 Platinum 0.0992 oz. APW **Ruler:** Elizabeth II **Subject:** Australian Flora **Obv:** Head with tiara right **Obv. Designer:** Ian Rank-Broadley **Rev:** Royal bluebell

Date	Mintage	F12	VF20	XF40	MS60	MS63
2006	615		PF65 220			

KM# 986 15 DOLLARS
3.11 g., 0.999 Platinum 0.0992 oz. APW **Ruler:** Elizabeth II **Subject:** Australian Flora **Obv:** Head with tiara right **Obv. Designer:** Ian Rank-Broadley **Rev:** Kangaroo paw

Date	Mintage	F12	VF20	XF40	MS60	MS63
2006	1,606		PF65 220			

KM# 988 15 DOLLARS
3.11 g., 0.999 Platinum 0.0992 oz. APW **Ruler:** Elizabeth II **Subject:** Australian Flora **Obv:** Head with tiara right **Obv. Designer:** Ian Rank-Broadley **Rev:** Common pink heath

Date	Mintage	F12	VF20	XF40	MS60	MS63
2006	500		PF65 220			

KM# 966 15 DOLLARS
3.11 g., 0.999 Gold 0.0992 oz. AGW **Ruler:** Elizabeth II **Subject:** Australian Fauna **Obv:** Head with tiara right **Obv. Designer:** Ian Rank-Broadley **Rev:** Echidna

Date	Mintage	F12	VF20	XF40	MS60	MS63
2007	1,664		PF65 195			

KM# 969 15 DOLLARS
3.11 g., 0.999 Gold 0.0992 oz. AGW **Ruler:** Elizabeth II **Subject:** Australian Fauna **Obv:** Head with tiara right **Obv. Designer:** Ian Rank-Broadley **Rev:** Common wombat

Date	Mintage	F12	VF20	XF40	MS60	MS63
2007	1,678		PF65 195			

KM# 972 15 DOLLARS
3.11 g., 0.999 Gold 0.0992 oz. AGW **Ruler:** Elizabeth II **Subject:** Australian Fauna **Obv:** Head with tiara right **Obv. Designer:** Ian Rank-Broadley **Rev:** Tasmanian devil

Date	Mintage	F12	VF20	XF40	MS60	MS63
2007	1,687		PF65 195			

KM# 975 15 DOLLARS
3.11 g., 0.999 Gold 0.0992 oz. AGW **Ruler:** Elizabeth II **Subject:** Australian Fauna **Obv:** Head with tiara right **Obv. Designer:** Ian Rank-Broadley **Rev:** Great white shark

Date	Mintage	F12	VF20	XF40	MS60	MS63
2007	2,119		PF65 195			

KM# 978 15 DOLLARS
3.11 g., 0.999 Gold 0.0992 oz. AGW **Ruler:** Elizabeth II **Subject:** Australian Fauna **Obv:** Head with tiara right **Obv. Designer:** Ian Rank-Broadley **Rev:** Platypus

Date	Mintage	F12	VF20	XF40	MS60	MS63
2007	1,632		PF65 195			

KM# 990 15 DOLLARS
3.11 g., 0.999 Platinum 0.0992 oz. APW **Ruler:** Elizabeth II **Subject:** Australian Flora **Obv:** Head with tiara right **Obv. Designer:** Ian Rank-Broadley **Rev:** Anemone buttercup

Date	Mintage	F12	VF20	XF40	MS60	MS63
2007	404		PF65 220			

KM# 992 15 DOLLARS
3.11 g., 0.999 Platinum 0.0992 oz. APW **Ruler:** Elizabeth II **Subject:** Australian Flora **Obv:** Head with tiara right **Obv. Designer:** Ian Rank-Broadley **Rev:** Sturt's desert pea

Date	Mintage	F12	VF20	XF40	MS60	MS63
2007	359		PF65 220			

KM# 994 15 DOLLARS
3.11 g., 0.999 Platinum 0.0992 oz. APW **Ruler:** Elizabeth II **Subject:** Australian Flora **Obv:** Head with tiara right **Obv. Designer:** Ian Rank-Broadley **Rev:** Tasmanian bluegum

Date	Mintage	F12	VF20	XF40	MS60	MS63
2007	348		PF65 220			

KM# 996 15 DOLLARS
3.11 g., 0.999 Platinum 0.0992 oz. APW **Ruler:** Elizabeth II **Subject:** Australian Flora **Obv:** Head with tiara right **Obv. Designer:** Ian Rank-Broadley **Rev:** Waratah

Date	Mintage	F12	VF20	XF40	MS60	MS63
2007	364		PF65 220			

KM# 998 15 DOLLARS
3.11 g., 0.999 Platinum 0.0992 oz. APW **Ruler:** Elizabeth II **Subject:** Australian Flora **Obv:** Head with tiara right **Obv. Designer:** Ian Rank-Broadley **Rev:** Golden wattle

Date	Mintage	F12	VF20	XF40	MS60	MS63
2007	414		PF65 220			

KM# 1186 15 DOLLARS
3.11 g., 0.999 Gold 0.0992 oz. AGW, 14 mm. **Ruler:** Elizabeth II **Obv:** Head right **Obv. Designer:** Ian Rank-Broadley **Rev:** Dolphin **Rev. Legend:** DISCOVER AUSTRALIA

Date	Mintage	F12	VF20	XF40	MS60	MS63
2008P	1,857		PF65 110			

KM# 1187 15 DOLLARS
3.11 g., 0.999 Gold 0.0992 oz. AGW, 14 mm. **Ruler:** Elizabeth II **Obv:** Head right **Obv. Designer:** Ian Rank-Broadley **Rev:** King brown snake **Rev. Legend:** DISCOVER AUSTRALIA

Date	Mintage	F12	VF20	XF40	MS60	MS63
2008P	1,308		PF65 110			

KM# 1188 15 DOLLARS
3.11 g., 0.999 Gold 0.0992 oz. AGW, 14 mm. **Ruler:** Elizabeth II **Obv:** Head right **Obv. Designer:** Ian Rank-Broadley **Rev:** Brolga **Rev. Legend:** DISCOVER AUSTRALIA

Date	Mintage	F12	VF20	XF40	MS60	MS63
2008P	1,475		PF65 100			

KM# 1189 15 DOLLARS
3.11 g., 0.999 Gold 0.0992 oz. AGW, 14 mm. **Ruler:** Elizabeth II **Obv:** Head right **Obv. Designer:** Ian Rank-Broadley **Rev:** Dingo **Rev. Legend:** DISCOVER AUSTRALIA

Date	Mintage	F12	VF20	XF40	MS60	MS63
2008P	1,494		PF65 110			

KM# 1190 15 DOLLARS
3.11 g., 0.999 Gold 0.0992 oz. AGW, 14 mm. **Ruler:** Elizabeth II **Obv:** Head right **Obv. Designer:** Ian Rank-Broadley **Rev:** Frill-neck lizard **Rev. Legend:** DISCOVER AUSTRALIA

Date	Mintage	F12	VF20	XF40	MS60	MS63
2008P	1,788		PF65 110			

KM# 1201 15 DOLLARS
3.10 g., 0.999 Platinum 0.0989 oz. APW, 16 mm. **Ruler:** Elizabeth II **Obv:** Head right **Obv. Designer:** Ian Rank-Broadley **Rev:** Black anther fax lilly, multicolor **Rev. Legend:** DISCOVER AUSTRALIA

Date	Mintage	F12	VF20	XF40	MS60	MS63
2008P	352		PF65 300			

KM# 1202 15 DOLLARS
3.10 g., 0.999 Platinum 0.0989 oz. APW, 16 mm. **Ruler:** Elizabeth II **Obv:** Head right **Obv. Designer:** Ian Rank-Broadley **Rev:** Native frangipani, multicolor **Rev. Legend:** DISCOVER AUSTRALIA

Date	Mintage	F12	VF20	XF40	MS60	MS63
2008P	356	PF65 300				

KM# 1203 15 DOLLARS
3.10 g., 0.999 Platinum 0.0989 oz. APW, 16 mm. **Ruler:** Elizabeth II **Obv:** Head right **Rev. Designer:** DISCOVER AUSTRALIA **Rev:** Geraldton wax, multicolor **Rev. Designer:** Ian Rank-Broadley

Date	Mintage	F12	VF20	XF40	MS60	MS63
2008P	373	PF65 300				

KM# 1204 15 DOLLARS
3.10 g., 0.999 Platinum 0.0989 oz. APW, 16 mm. **Ruler:** Elizabeth II **Obv:** Head right **Obv. Designer:** Ian Rank-Broadley **Rev:** Red-flowered kurrajong, multicolor **Rev. Legend:** DISCOVER AUSTRALIA

Date	Mintage	F12	VF20	XF40	MS60	MS63
2008P	338	PF65 300				

KM# 1205 15 DOLLARS
3.10 g., 0.999 Platinum 0.0989 oz. APW, 16 mm. **Ruler:** Elizabeth II **Obv:** Head right **Obv. Designer:** Ian Rank-Broadley **Rev:** Small-leaf lily pilly, multicolor **Rev. Legend:** DISCOVER AUSTRALIA

Date	Mintage	F12	VF20	XF40	MS60	MS63
2008P	380	PF65 300				

KM# 1104 15 DOLLARS
2.50 g., 0.9999 Gold 0.0799 oz. AGW, 13x22 mm. **Ruler:** Elizabeth II **Rev:** Turtle Dreaming **Rev. Designer:** Darryl Bellotti **Shape:** Rectangle

Date	Mintage	F12	VF20	XF40	MS60	MS63
2009	—	PF65 175				

KM# 1108 15 DOLLARS
2.50 g., 0.9999 Gold 0.0799 oz. AGW, 13x22 mm. **Ruler:** Elizabeth II **Rev:** Kangaroo Dreaming **Rev. Designer:** Darryl Bellotti **Shape:** Vertical rectangle

Date	Mintage	G4	VG8	F12	VF20	XF40
2009	—	PF65 175				

KM# 1223 15 DOLLARS
3.11 g., 0.999 Gold 0.0992 oz. AGW, 16 mm. **Ruler:** Elizabeth II **Obv:** Head right **Obv. Designer:** Ian Rank-Broadley **Rev:** Dreaming dolphin **Rev. Designer:** Darryl Berttoli

Date	Mintage	F12	VF20	XF40	MS60	MS63
2009P	2,500	PF65 195				

KM# 1225 15 DOLLARS
3.11 g., 0.999 Gold 0.0992 oz. AGW, 16 mm. **Ruler:** Elizabeth II **Obv:** Head right **Obv. Designer:** Ian Rank-Broadley **Rev:** Dreaming brolga **Rev. Designer:** Darryl Berttolli

Date	Mintage	F12	VF20	XF40	MS60	MS63
2009P	2,500	PF65 195				

KM# 1226 15 DOLLARS
3.11 g., 0.999 Gold 0.0992 oz. AGW, 16 mm. **Ruler:** Elizabeth II **Obv:** Head right **Obv. Designer:** Ian Rank-Broadley **Rev:** Dreaming echidna **Rev. Designer:** Darryl Berttolli

Date	Mintage	F12	VF20	XF40	MS60	MS63
2009P	2,500	PF65 195				

KM# 1228 15 DOLLARS
15.55 g., 0.999 Gold 0.4962 oz. AGW, 25 mm. **Ruler:** Elizabeth II **Obv:** Head right **Obv. Designer:** Ian Rank-Broadley **Rev:** Dreaming dolphin **Rev. Designer:** Darryl Berttolli

Date	Mintage	F12	VF20	XF40	MS60	MS63
2009P	1,000	PF66 1,100				

KM# 1232 15 DOLLARS
3.11 g., 0.999 Platinum 0.0992 oz. APW, 16 mm. **Ruler:** Elizabeth II **Obv:** Head right **Obv. Designer:** Ian Rank-Broadley **Rev:** Dreaming kangaroo, multicolor **Rev. Designer:** Darryl Berttolli

Date	Mintage	F12	VF20	XF40	MS60	MS63
2009P	2,500	PF65 400				

KM# 1233 15 DOLLARS
3.11 g., 0.999 Platinum 0.0992 oz. APW, 16 mm. **Ruler:** Elizabeth II **Obv:** Head right **Obv. Designer:** Ian Rank-Broadley **Rev:** Dreaming dolphin, multicolor **Rev. Designer:** Darryl Berttolli

Date	Mintage	F12	VF20	XF40	MS60	MS63
2009P	2,500	PF65 400				

KM# 1234 15 DOLLARS
3.11 g., 0.999 Platinum 0.0992 oz. APW, 16 mm. **Ruler:** Elizabeth II **Obv:** Head right **Obv. Designer:** Ian Rank-Broadley **Rev:** Dreaming king brown snake, multicolor **Rev. Designer:** Darryl Berttolli

Date	Mintage	F12	VF20	XF40	MS60	MS63
2009P	2,500	PF65 400				

KM# 1235 15 DOLLARS
3.11 g., 0.999 Platinum 0.0992 oz. APW, 16 mm. **Ruler:** Elizabeth II **Obv:** Head right **Obv. Designer:** Ian Rank-Broadley **Rev:** Dreaming brolga **Rev. Designer:** Darryl Berttolli

Date	Mintage	F12	VF20	XF40	MS60	MS63
2009P	2,500	PF65 400				

KM# 1236 15 DOLLARS
3.11 g., 0.999 Platinum 0.0992 oz. APW, 16 mm. **Ruler:** Elizabeth II **Obv:** Head right **Obv. Designer:** Ian Rank-Broadley **Rev:** Dreaming echidna, multicolor **Rev. Designer:** Darryl Berttolli

Date	Mintage	F12	VF20	XF40	MS60	MS63
2009P	2,500	PF65 400				

KM# 1401 15 DOLLARS
3.11 g., 0.999 Gold 0.0992 oz. AGW, 17 mm. **Ruler:** Elizabeth II **Obv:** Head right **Obv. Designer:** Ian Rank-Broadley **Rev:** Frill-neck lizard

Date	Mintage	F12	VF20	XF40	MS60	MS63
2010(p)	2,500	PF65 260				

KM# 1405 15 DOLLARS
3.11 g., 0.999 Platinum 0.0992 oz. APW, 17 mm. **Ruler:** Elizabeth II **Obv:** Head right **Obv. Designer:** Ian Rank-Broadley **Rev:** Multicolor koala

Date	Mintage	F12	VF20	XF40	MS60	MS63
2010(p)	2,500	PF65 335				

KM# 1407 15 DOLLARS
3.11 g., 0.999 Gold 0.0992 oz. AGW, 16 mm. **Ruler:** Elizabeth II **Obv:** Head right **Obv. Designer:** Ian Rank-Broadley **Rev:** Koala

Date	Mintage	F12	VF20	XF40	MS60	MS63
2010(p)	2,500	PF65 260				

KM# 1411 15 DOLLARS
3.11 g., 0.999 Platinum 0.0992 oz. APW, 17 mm. **Ruler:** Elizabeth II **Obv:** Head right **Obv. Designer:** Ian Rank-Broadley **Rev:** Multicolor platypus

Date	Mintage	F12	VF20	XF40	MS60	MS63
2010(p)	2,500	PF65 335				

KM# 1413 15 DOLLARS
0.999 Gold AGW, 16 mm. **Ruler:** Elizabeth II **Obv:** Head right **Obv. Designer:** Ian Rank-Broadley **Rev:** Platypus

Date	Mintage	F12	VF20	XF40	MS60	MS63
2010(p)	2,500	PF65 260				

KM# 1417 15 DOLLARS
0.999 Platinum APW, 17 mm. **Ruler:** Elizabeth II **Obv:** Head right **Obv. Designer:** Ian Rank-Broadley **Rev:** Muticolor saltwater crocodile

Date	Mintage	F12	VF20	XF40	MS60	MS63
2010(p)	2,500	PF65 335				

KM# 1419 15 DOLLARS
3.11 g., 0.999 Gold 0.0992 oz. AGW, 16 mm. **Ruler:** Elizabeth II **Obv:** Head right **Obv. Designer:** Ian Rank-Broadley **Rev:** Saltwater crocodile

Date	Mintage	F12	VF20	XF40	MS60	MS63
2010(p)	2,500	PF65 260				

KM# 1423 15 DOLLARS
3.11 g., 0.999 Platinum 0.0992 oz. APW, 17 mm. **Ruler:** Elizabeth II **Obv:** Head right **Obv. Designer:** Ian Rank-Broadley **Rev:** Multicolor wombat

Date	Mintage	F12	VF20	XF40	MS60	MS63
2010(p)	2,500	PF65 335				

KM# 1425 15 DOLLARS
0.999 Gold AGW, 16 mm. **Ruler:** Elizabeth II **Obv:** Head right **Obv. Designer:** Ian Rank-Broadley **Rev:** Wombat

Date	Mintage	F12	VF20	XF40	MS60	MS63
2010(p)	2,500	PF65 260				

KM# 1454 15 DOLLARS
2.50 g., 0.999 Gold 0.0798 oz. AGW, 13x22 mm. **Ruler:** Elizabeth II **Rev:** Dolphin dreaming **Shape:** Vertical rectangle

Date	Mintage	F12	VF20	XF40	MS60	MS63
2010P	—	PF65 175				

KM# 1492 15 DOLLARS
3.11 g., 0.999 Gold 0.0992 oz. AGW, 17.53 mm. **Ruler:** Elizabeth II **Obv:** Head with tiara right **Rev:** Saint Mary Mackillup in color

Date	Mintage	F12	VF20	XF40	MS60	MS63
2010	2,010	PF65 215				

KM# 1536 15 DOLLARS
3.11 g., 0.999 Gold 0.0992 oz. AGW **Ruler:** Elizabeth II **Subject:** Dreaming Emu **Rev:** Linear emu in color

Date	Mintage	F12	VF20	XF40	MS60	MS63
2011P	2,500	PF65 250				

KM# 1538 15 DOLLARS
3.11 g., 0.999 Platinum 0.0992 oz. APW **Ruler:** Elizabeth II **Subject:** Dreaming Emu **Rev:** Linear emu in color

Date	Mintage	F12	VF20	XF40	MS60	MS63
2011P	2,500	PF65 375				

KM# 1542 15 DOLLARS
3.11 g., 0.999 Gold 0.0992 oz. AGW **Ruler:** Elizabeth II **Subject:** Dreaming Tasmanian Devil **Rev:** Linear tasmanian devil in color

Date	Mintage	F12	VF20	XF40	MS60	MS63
2011P	2,500	PF65 250				

KM# 1544 15 DOLLARS
3.11 g., 0.999 Platinum 0.0992 oz. APW **Ruler:** Elizabeth II **Subject:** Dreaming Tasmanian Devil **Rev:** Linear tasmanian devil in color

Date	Mintage	F12	VF20	XF40	MS60	MS63
2011P	2,500	PF65 375				

KM# 1548 15 DOLLARS
3.11 g., 0.999 Gold 0.0992 oz. AGW **Ruler:** Elizabeth II **Subject:** Dreaming Kookaburra **Rev:** Linear kookaburra in color

Date	Mintage	F12	VF20	XF40	MS60	MS63
2011P	2,500	PF65 250				

KM# 1550 15 DOLLARS
3.11 g., 0.999 Platinum 0.0992 oz. APW **Ruler:** Elizabeth II **Subject:** Dreaming Kookaburra **Rev:** Linear kookaburra in color

Date	Mintage	F12	VF20	XF40	MS60	MS63
2011P	2,500	PF65 375				

KM# 1554 15 DOLLARS
3.11 g., 0.999 Gold 0.0992 oz. AGW **Ruler:** Elizabeth II **Subject:** Dreaming Shark **Rev:** Linear shark in color

Date	Mintage	F12	VF20	XF40	MS60	MS63
2011P	2,500	PF65 250				

KM# 1556 15 DOLLARS
3.11 g., 0.999 Platinum 0.0992 oz. APW **Ruler:** Elizabeth II **Subject:** Dreaming Shark **Rev:** Linear shark in color

Date	Mintage	F12	VF20	XF40	MS60	MS63
2011P	2,500		PF65 375			

KM# 1560 15 DOLLARS
3.11 g., 0.999 Gold 0.0992 oz. AGW **Ruler:** Elizabeth II **Subject:** Dreaming Dingo **Rev:** Linear dingo in color

Date	Mintage	F12	VF20	XF40	MS60	MS63
2011P	2,500		PF65 250			

KM# 1562 15 DOLLARS
3.11 g., 0.999 Platinum 0.0992 oz. APW **Ruler:** Elizabeth II **Subject:** Dreaming Dingo **Rev:** Linear dingo in color

Date	Mintage	F12	VF20	XF40	MS60	MS63
2011P	2,500		PF65 375			

KM# 1610 15 DOLLARS
2.50 g., 0.999 Gold 0.0798 oz. AGW, 13x22 mm. **Ruler:** Elizabeth II **Obv:** Head with tiara right **Rev:** Platypus dreaming **Rev. Designer:** Darryl Bellotti **Shape:** Vertical rectangle

Date	Mintage	F12	VF20	XF40	MS60	MS63
2011P	—		PF65 175			

KM# 1721 15 DOLLARS
3.11 g., 0.999 Gold 0.0993 oz. AGW, 16.6 mm. **Ruler:** Elizabeth II **Rev:** Green and Gold Bell Frog in grass

Date	Mintage	F12	VF20	XF40	MS60	MS63
2012P	1,000		PF65 225			

KM# 1722 15 DOLLARS
3.11 g., 0.999 Gold 0.0993 oz. AGW, 16.6 mm. **Ruler:** Elizabeth II **Rev:** Kookaburra standing right

Date	Mintage	F12	VF20	XF40	MS60	MS63
2012P	1,000		PF65 225			

KM# 1723 15 DOLLARS
3.11 g., 0.999 Gold 0.0993 oz. AGW, 16.6 mm. **Ruler:** Elizabeth II **Rev:** Whale Shark swimming right

Date	Mintage	F12	VF20	XF40	MS60	MS63
2012P	1,000		PF65 225			

KM# 1724 15 DOLLARS
3.11 g., 0.999 Gold 0.0993 oz. AGW, 16.6 mm. **Ruler:** Elizabeth II **Rev:** Kangaroo bounding right

Date	Mintage	F12	VF20	XF40	MS60	MS63
2012P	1,000		PF65 225			

KM# 1725 15 DOLLARS
3.11 g., 0.999 Gold 0.0993 oz. AGW, 16.6 mm. **Ruler:** Elizabeth II **Rev:** Goanna lizard right

Date	Mintage	F12	VF20	XF40	MS60	MS63
2012P	1,000		PF65 225			

KM# 1848 15 DOLLARS
3.11 g., 0.999 Platinum 0.0992 oz. APW, 16.6 mm. **Ruler:** Elizabeth II **Rev:** Bell Frog and color background

Date	Mintage	F12	VF20	XF40	MS60	MS63
2012P	1,000		PF65 325			

KM# 1849 15 DOLLARS
3.11 g., 0.999 Platinum 0.0992 oz. APW, 16.6 mm. **Ruler:** Elizabeth II **Rev:** Kookaburra with color background

Date	Mintage	F12	VF20	XF40	MS60	MS63
2012P	1,000		PF65 325			

KM# 1850 15 DOLLARS
3.11 g., 0.999 Platinum 0.0992 oz. APW, 16.1 mm. **Ruler:** Elizabeth II **Rev:** Whale shark on color background

Date	Mintage	F12	VF20	XF40	MS60	MS63
2012P	1,000		PF65 325			

KM# 1851 15 DOLLARS
3.11 g., 0.999 Platinum 0.0992 oz. APW, 16.1 mm. **Ruler:** Elizabeth II **Rev:** Kangaroo on color background

Date	Mintage	F12	VF20	XF40	MS60	MS63
2012P	1,000		PF65 325			

KM# 1852 15 DOLLARS
3.11 g., 0.999 Platinum 0.0992 oz. APW, 16.1 mm. **Ruler:** Elizabeth II **Rev:** Goanna on color background

Date	Mintage	F12	VF20	XF40	MS60	MS63
2012P	1,000		PF65 325			

KM# 2074 15 DOLLARS
3.11 g., 0.9999 Gold 0.0993 oz. AGW, 17.53 mm. **Ruler:** Elizabeth II **Subject:** Australian - American WWII memorial **Rev:** Eagle monument before US and Australian

Date	Mintage	F12	VF20	XF40	MS60	MS63
2013P	—		PF65 215			

KM# 595 20 DOLLARS
14.03 g., Bi-Metallic, 32.1 mm. **Ruler:** Elizabeth II **Subject:** Gregorian Millennium **Obv:** Head with tiara right **Obv. Designer:** Ian Rank-Broadley **Rev:** Chronograph watch face with observatory in center and three depictions of the earth's rotation **Edge:** Reeded

Date	Mintage	F12	VF20	XF40	MS60	MS63
2001 Prooflike	7,500	—	—	—	—	475

KM# 597 20 DOLLARS
19.63 g., Bi-Metallic, 32.1 mm. **Ruler:** Elizabeth II **Subject:** Centenary of Federation **Obv:** Head with tiara right within star design **Obv. Designer:** Ian Rank-Broadley **Rev:** National arms on a flowery background **Edge:** Reeded

Date	Mintage	F12	VF20	XF40	MS60	MS63
ND(2001) Prooflike	7,635	—	—	—	—	475

KM# 760 20 DOLLARS
Bi-Metallic **Ruler:** Elizabeth II **Rev:** Sir Donald Bradman portrait

Date	Mintage	F12	VF20	XF40	MS60	MS63
2001	8,589		PF65 500			

KM# 634 20 DOLLARS
18.35 g., Bi-Metallic, 32.1 mm. **Ruler:** Elizabeth II **Subject:** Queen's Golden Jubilee **Obv:** Queen's head right **Rev:** Queen before Buckingham Palace **Edge:** Reeded

Date	Mintage	F12	VF20	XF40	MS60	MS63
2002P	7,500		PF65 675			

KM# 687 20 DOLLARS
13.41 g., Bi-Metallic, 32 mm. **Ruler:** Elizabeth II **Subject:** Golden Jubilee of Coronation **Obv:** Head with tiara right **Obv. Designer:** Ian Rank-Broadley **Rev:** Four different coinage portraits of Queen Elizabeth II **Rev. Designer:** Mary Gillick, Arnold Machin, Raphael Maklouf and Ian Rank-Broadley **Edge:** Reeded

Date	Mintage	F12	VF20	XF40	MS60	MS63
2003P	1,338		PF65 625			

KM# 1105 20 DOLLARS
5.00 g., 0.9999 Gold 0.1597 oz. AGW, 14x23.2 mm. **Ruler:** Elizabeth II **Rev:** Turtle Dreaming **Rev. Designer:** Darryl Bellotti **Shape:** Rectangle

Date	Mintage	F12	VF20	XF40	MS60	MS63
2009	—		PF65 325			

KM# 1109 20 DOLLARS
5.00 g., 0.9999 Gold 0.1597 oz. AGW, 14x23.2 mm. **Ruler:** Elizabeth II **Rev:** Kangaroo dreaming **Rev. Designer:** Darryl Bellotti **Shape:** Vertical rectangle

Date	Mintage	F12	VF20	XF40	MS60	MS63
2009	—		PF65 325			

KM# 868 25 DOLLARS
7.99 g., 0.9167 Gold 0.2339 oz. AGW **Ruler:** Elizabeth II **Subject:** 150th Anniversary First Australian Sovereign **Obv:** Head with tiara right **Obv. Designer:** Ian Rank-Broadley

Date	Mintage	F12	VF20	XF40	MS60	MS63
2005	7,500	PF65 475				

KM# 1127 25 DOLLARS
3.10 g., 0.999 Gold 0.0989 oz. AGW, 15.5 mm. **Ruler:** Elizabeth II **Obv:** Head right **Obv. Designer:** Ian Rank-Broadley **Rev:** Kookaburra **Rev. Legend:** DISCOVER AUSTRALIA

Date	Mintage	F12	VF20	XF40	MS60	MS63
2006P	2,500	PF65 195				

KM# 1123 25 DOLLARS
3.10 g., 0.999 Gold 0.0989 oz. AGW, 15.5 mm. **Ruler:** Elizabeth II **Obv:** Head right **Obv. Designer:** Ian Rank-Broadley **Rev:** Saltwater crocodile **Rev. Legend:** DISCOVER AUSTRALIA

Date	Mintage	F12	VF20	XF40	MS60	MS63
2006P	2,500	PF65 195				

KM# 1124 25 DOLLARS
3.10 g., 0.999 Gold 0.0989 oz. AGW, 15.5 mm. **Ruler:** Elizabeth II **Obv:** Head right **Obv. Designer:** Ian Rank-Broadley **Rev:** Grey kangaroo **Rev. Legend:** DISCOVER AUSTRALIA

Date	Mintage	F12	VF20	XF40	MS60	MS63
2006P	2,500	PF65 195				

KM# 1125 25 DOLLARS
3.10 g., 0.999 Gold 0.0989 oz. AGW, 15.5 mm. **Ruler:** Elizabeth II **Obv:** Head right **Obv. Designer:** Ian Rank-Broadley **Rev:** Emu **Rev. Legend:** DISCOVER AUSTRALIA

Date	Mintage	F12	VF20	XF40	MS60	MS63
2006P	2,500	PF65 195				

KM# 1126 25 DOLLARS
3.10 g., 0.999 Gold 0.0989 oz. AGW, 15.5 mm. **Ruler:** Elizabeth II **Obv:** Head right **Obv. Designer:** Ian Rank-Broadley **Rev:** Koala **Rev. Legend:** DISCOVER AUSTRALIA

Date	Mintage	F12	VF20	XF40	MS80	MS63
2006P	2,500	PF65 195				

KM# 1148 25 DOLLARS
3.10 g., 0.999 Gold 0.0989 oz. AGW, 15.5 mm. **Ruler:** Elizabeth II **Obv:** Head right **Obv. Designer:** Ian Rank-Broadley **Rev:** Echinda **Rev. Legend:** DISCOVER AUSTRALIA

Date	Mintage	F12	VF20	XF40	MS60	MS63
2007P	2,500	PF65 195				

KM# 1149 25 DOLLARS
3.10 g., 0.999 Gold 0.0989 oz. AGW, 15.5 mm. **Ruler:** Elizabeth II **Obv:** Head right **Obv. Designer:** Ian Rank-Broadley **Rev:** Common wombat **Rev. Legend:** DISCOVER AUSTRALIA

Date	Mintage	F12	VF20	XF40	MS60	MS63
2007P	2,500	PF65 195				

KM# 1150 25 DOLLARS
3.10 g., 0.999 Gold 0.0989 oz. AGW, 15.5 mm. **Ruler:** Elizabeth II **Obv:** Head right **Obv. Designer:** Ian Rank-Braodley **Rev:** Tasmanian devil **Rev. Legend:** DISCOVER AUSTRALIA

Date	Mintage	F12	VF20	XF40	MS60	MS63
2007P	2,500	PF65 195				

KM# 1151 25 DOLLARS
3.10 g., 0.999 Gold 0.0989 oz. AGW, 15.5 mm. **Ruler:** Elizabeth II **Obv:** Head right **Obv. Designer:** Ian Rank-Broadley **Rev:** Great white shark **Rev. Legend:** DISCOVER AUSTRALIA

Date	Mintage	F12	VF20	XF40	MS60	MS63
2007P	2,500	PF65 195				

KM# 1152 25 DOLLARS
3.10 g., 0.999 Gold 0.0989 oz. AGW, 15.5 mm. **Ruler:** Elizabeth II **Obv:** Head right **Obv. Designer:** Ian Rank-Broadley **Rev:** Platypus **Rev. Legend:** DISCOVER AUSTRALIA

Date	Mintage	F12	VF20	XF40	MS60	MS63
2007P	2,500	PF65 195				

KM# 1158 25 DOLLARS
3.10 g., 0.999 Platinum 0.0989 oz. APW, 16 mm. **Ruler:** Elizabeth II **Obv:** Head right **Obv. Designer:** Ian Rank-Broadley **Rev:** Anemone buttercup, multicolor **Rev. Legend:** DISCOVER AUSTRALIA

Date	Mintage	F12	VF20	XF40	MS60	MS63
2007P	2,500	PF65 325				

KM# 1180 25 DOLLARS
7.77 g., 0.999 Gold 0.248 oz. AGW, 20 mm. **Ruler:** Elizabeth II **Subject:** End of WWI, 90th Anniversary **Obv:** Head right **Rev:** Field cross, multicolor poppies **Rev. Legend:** Ian Rank-

---

Broadley Edge: Reeded

Date	Mintage	F12	VF20	XF40	MS60	MS63
2008P	1,918	PF65 675				

KM# 1191 25 DOLLARS
3.10 g., 0.999 Gold 0.0989 oz. AGW, 15.5 mm. **Ruler:** Elizabeth II **Obv:** Head right **Obv. Designer:** Ian Rank-Broadley **Rev:** Dolphin **Rev. Legend:** DISCOVER AUSTRALIA

Date	Mintage	F12	VF20	XF40	MS60	MS63
2008P	2,500	PF65 195				

KM# 1192 25 DOLLARS
3.10 g., 0.999 Gold 0.0989 oz. AGW, 15.5 mm. **Ruler:** Elizabeth II **Obv:** Head right **Obv. Designer:** Ian Rank-Broadley **Rev:** King brown snake **Rev. Legend:** DISCOVER AUSTRALIA

Date	Mintage	F12	VF20	XF40	MS60	MS63
2008P	2,500	PF65 195				

KM# 1193 25 DOLLARS
3.10 g., 0.999 Gold 0.0989 oz. AGW, 15.5 mm. **Ruler:** Elizabeth II **Obv:** Head right **Obv. Designer:** Ian Rank-Broadley **Rev:** Brolga **Rev. Legend:** DISCOVER AUSTRALIA

Date	Mintage	F12	VF20	XF40	MS60	MS63
2008P	2,500	PF65 195				

KM# 1194 25 DOLLARS
3.10 g., 0.999 Gold 0.0989 oz. AGW, 15.5 mm. **Ruler:** Elizabeth II **Obv:** Head right **Obv. Designer:** Ian Rank-Broadley **Rev:** Dingo **Rev. Legend:** DISCOVER AUSTRALIA

Date	Mintage	F12	VF20	XF40	MS60	MS63
2008P	2,500	PF65 195				

KM# 1195 25 DOLLARS
3.10 g., 0.999 Gold 0.0989 oz. AGW, 15.5 mm. **Ruler:** Elizabeth II **Obv:** Head right **Obv. Designer:** Ian Rank-Broadley **Rev:** Frill-neck lizard **Rev. Legend:** DISCOVER AUSTRALIA

Date	Mintage	F12	VF20	XF40	MS60	MS63
2008P	2,500	PF65 195				

KM# 1273 25 DOLLARS
10.00 g., 0.999 Gold 0.3191 oz. AGW, 15x25 mm. **Ruler:** Elizabeth II **Subject:** Mythological Chinese Character - Wealth **Obv:** Head right **Obv. Designer:** Ian Rank Broadloy **Rev:** Man standing **Shape:** Vertical rectangle

Date	Mintage	F12	VF20	XF40	MS60	MS63
2008P	376	—	—	—	—	800

KM# 1274 25 DOLLARS
10.00 g., 0.999 Gold 0.3191 oz. AGW, 15x25 mm. **Ruler:** Elizabeth II **Subject:** Mythological Chinese Character - Longivity **Obv:** Head right **Obv. Designer:** Ian rank-Broadley **Rev:** Man standing with staff **Shape:** Vertical rectangle

Date	Mintage	F12	VF20	XF40	MS60	MS63
2008P	383	—	—	—	—	825

KM# 1275 25 DOLLARS
10.00 g., 0.999 Gold 0.3191 oz. AGW, 15x25 mm. **Ruler:** Elizabeth II **Subject:** Mythological Chinese Character - Success **Obv:** Head right **Obv. Designer:** Ian Rank-Broadley **Rev:** Man standing with deer **Shape:** Vertical rectangle

Date	Mintage	F12	VF20	XF40	MS60	MS63
2008P	376	—	—	—	—	800

KM# 1276 25 DOLLARS
10.00 g., 0.999 Gold 0.3191 oz. AGW, 15x25 mm. **Ruler:** Elizabeth II **Subject:** Mythological Chinese Character - Fortune **Obv:** Head right **Obv. Designer:** Ian Rank-Broadley **Rev:** Man standing with scroll **Shape:** Vertical rectangle

Date	Mintage	F12	VF20	XF40	MS60	MS63
2008P	374	—	—	—	—	825

KM# 1397 25 DOLLARS
7.99 g., 0.9167 Gold 0.2339 oz. AGW, 22.6 mm. **Ruler:** Elizabeth II **Subject:** Sovereign **Obv:** Head in tiara right **Obv. Designer:** Ian Rank-Broadley **Rev:** National Arms with supporters and flora

Date	Mintage	F12	VF20	XF40	MS60	MS63
2009P	2,500	PF65 825				
2010P	—	PF65 825				
2011P	—	PF65 825				
2012P	—	PF65 825				

KM# 1106 25 DOLLARS
10.00 g., 0.9999 Gold 0.3194 oz. AGW, 15.4x25.4 mm. **Ruler:**

Elizabeth II **Rev:** Turtle dreaming **Rev. Designer:** Darryk Bellotti **Shape:** Verticle rectangle

Date	Mintage	F12	VF20	XF40	MS60	MS63
2009	—	PF65 625				

KM# 1110 25 DOLLARS
10.00 g., 0.9999 Gold 0.3194 oz. AGW, 15.4x25.4 mm. **Ruler:** Elizabeth II **Rev:** Kangaroo dreaming **Rev. Designer:** Darryl Bellotti **Shape:** Vertical rectangle

Date	Mintage	F12	VF20	XF40	MS60	MS63
2009	—	PF65 650				

KM# 1247 25 DOLLARS
7.77 g., 0.000 Gold 0.248 oz. AGW, 21 mm. **Ruler:** Elizabeth II **Subject:** 2010 FIFA World Cup, South Africa **Obv:** Head right **Obv. Designer:** Ian Rank-Broadley **Rev:** Soccer player and kangaroo

Date	Mintage	F12	VF20	XF40	MS60	MS63
2009P	7,500	PF65 775				

KM# 1455 25 DOLLARS
10.00 g., 0.999 Gold 0.3191 oz. AGW, 15.4x25.4 mm. **Ruler:** Elizabeth II **Rev:** Dolphin dreaming **Shape:** Vertical rectangle

Date	Mintage	F12	VF20	XF40	MS60	MS63
2010P	—	PF65 600				

KM# 1611 25 DOLLARS
10.00 g., 0.999 Gold 0.3191 oz. AGW, 15.4x25.4 mm. **Ruler:** Elizabeth II **Obv:** Head with tiara right **Rev:** Platypus dreaming **Rev. Designer:** Darryl Bellotti **Shape:** Vertical rectangle

Date	Mintage	F12	VF20	XF40	MS60	MS63
2011P	—	PF65 625				

KM# 1623 25 DOLLARS
7.77 g., 0.999 Gold 0.248 oz. AGW, 21 mm. **Ruler:** Elizabeth II **Subject:** President's Cup **Obv:** Head with tiara right **Rev:** Golfer taking swing

Date	Mintage	F12	VF20	XF40	MS60	MS63
2011	—	PF65 600				

KM# 1703 25 DOLLARS
7.77 g., 0.9999 Gold 0.2482 oz. AGW, 20.6 mm. **Ruler:** Elizabeth II **Subject:** Elizabeth II, 60th Anniversary **Obv:** Head with tiara right **Rev:** Young bust right **Rev. Designer:** Darryl Bellotti **Edge:** Reeded

Date	Mintage	F12	VF20	XF40	MS60	MS63
2012P	Est. 1000	PF65 550				

KM# 1919 25 DOLLARS
7.77 g., 0.9999 Gold 0.2482 oz. AGW, 20.6 mm. **Ruler:** Elizabeth II **Subject:** The Land Down Under - Sydney Opera House **Rev. Designer:** Natasha Muhl

Date	Mintage	F12	VF20	XF40	MS60	MS63
2013P	Est. 1000	PF65 500				

KM# 1921 25 DOLLARS
7.77 g., 0.9999 Gold 0.2482 oz. AGW, 20.6 mm. **Ruler:** Elizabeth II **Subject:** The Land Down Under - Digeridoo **Rev. Designer:** Tom Vaughan

Date	Mintage	F12	VF20	XF40	MS60	MS63
2013P	Est. 1000	PF65 500				

KM# 1928 25 DOLLARS
7.77 g., 0.9999 Gold 0.2482 oz. AGW, 20.6 mm. **Ruler:** Elizabeth II **Subject:** HM Queen Elizabeth II - 60th Anniversary of Coronation **Rev. Designer:** Natasha Muhl

Date	Mintage	F12	VF20	XF40	MS60	MS63
2013P	Est. 1000	PF65 500				

KM# 1933 25 DOLLARS
7.77 g., 0.9999 Gold 0.2482 oz. AGW, 22.6 mm. **Ruler:** Elizabeth II **Subject:** 2014 FIFA World Cup Brazil **Obv:** Head with tiara right **Obv. Designer:** Ian Rank-Broadley **Rev:** Linear abroiginal figure superimposed on map of Australia **Rev. Designer:** Darryl Bellotti **Edge:** Reeded

Date	Mintage	F12	VF20	XF40	MS60	MS63
2013P	—	PF65 500				

KM# 1934 25 DOLLARS
7.99 g., 0.916 Gold 0.2337 oz. AGW, 22.6 mm. **Ruler:** Elizabeth II **Subject:** Australian Sovereign - Perth Mint **Rev:** Country name within crowned wreath **Rev. Designer:** Ing Ing Jong **Edge:** Reeded

Date	Mintage	F12	VF20	XF40	MS60	MS63
2013P	Est. 1750	PF65 500				

KM# 1942 25 DOLLARS
7.77 g., 0.9999 Gold 0.2482 oz. AGW, 20.6 mm. **Ruler:** Elizabeth II **Subject:** The Land Down Under - Captain James Cook **Obv. Designer:** Tom Vaughan

Date	Mintage	F12	VF20	XF40	MS60	MS63
2013	Est. 1000	PF65 450				

KM# 2052 25 DOLLARS
7.78 g., 0.9999 Gold 0.2484 oz. AGW, 20.6 mm. **Ruler:** Elizabeth II **Subject:** Land Down Under - Surfing **Rev:** Female surfer riding wave **Rev. Designer:** Aleysha Howarth

Date	Mintage	F12	VF20	XF40	MS60	MS63
2013P	1,000	PF65 600				

KM# 2061 25 DOLLARS
7.78 g., 0.9999 Gold 0.2484 oz. AGW, 20.6 mm. **Ruler:** Elizabeth II **Subject:** H.R.H. Prince George, Birth **Obv:** Head with tiara right **Rev:** Prince William and Catherine holding infant **Rev. Designer:** Jennifer McKenna

Date	Mintage	F12	VF20	XF40	MS60	MS63
2013P	Est. 1000	PF65 600				

KM# 2067 25 DOLLARS
7.84 g., 0.9999 Gold 0.2503 oz. AGW, 20.6 mm. **Ruler:** Elizabeth II **Subject:** A.B. Banjo Paterson, 150th Anniversary of Birth **Obv:** Head with tiara right **Rev:** Paterson in color **Rev. Designer:** Natasha Muhl

Date	Mintage	F12	VF20	XF40	MS60	MS63
2013P	5,000	PF65 600				

KM# 784 30 DOLLARS
1000.00 g., 0.999 Silver 31.9118 oz. ASW **Ruler:** Elizabeth II **Subject:** Commonwealth Games **Obv:** Head with tiara right **Rev:** Two figures within circle of all the sports

Date	Mintage	F12	VF20	XF40	MS60	MS63
2006	—	PF65 1,250				

KM# 1955 30 DOLLARS
1000.00 g., 0.999 Silver 31.9118 oz. ASW, 100 mm. **Ruler:** Elizabeth II **Subject:** Kangaroo Road Sign **Rev. Designer:** Wojciech Pietranik

Date	Mintage	F12	VF20	XF40	MS60	MS63
2013	Est. 1500	PF65 900				

KM# 648 50 DOLLARS
36.51 g., Tri-Metallic, 38.74 mm. **Ruler:** Elizabeth II **Subject:** Commonwealth Games **Obv:** Head with tiara right **Obv. Designer:** Ian Rank-Broadley **Rev:** Victorious athletes within inscriptions and runners **Edge:** Reeded

Date	Mintage	F12	VF20	XF40	MS60	MS63
2002B	5,000	PF65 600				

KM# 724 50 DOLLARS
36.51 g., Tri-Metallic, 38.74 mm. **Ruler:** Elizabeth II **Subject:** Olympics - Sydney to Athens **Obv:** Head with tiara right, denomination below **Obv. Designer:** Ian Rank-Broadley **Rev:** Crossed olive and wattle branches about Australian flag and Olympic ring logo **Rev. Designer:** Wojciech Pietranik **Edge:** Reeded

Date	Mintage	F12	VF20	XF40	MS60	MS63
2004B	2,500	PF65 625				

KM# 785 50 DOLLARS
Tri-Metallic, 38.74 mm. **Ruler:** Elizabeth II **Subject:** Melbourne Commonwealth Games **Obv:** Head with tiara right, denomination below **Obv. Designer:** Ian Rank-Broadley **Rev:** Two stylized athletes on central plug surrounded by Games legend and circle of athletes **Rev. Designer:** Wojciech Pietranik

Date	Mintage	F12	VF20	XF40	MS60	MS63
2006	—	PF65 550				

KM# 952 50 DOLLARS
15.50 g., 0.999 Gold 0.4947 oz. AGW, 25 mm. **Ruler:** Elizabeth

II Subject: Australian Fauna **Obv:** Head with tiara right **Obv. Designer:** Ian Rank-Broadley **Rev:** Saltwater crocodile

Date	Mintage	F12	VF20	XF40	MS60	MS63
2006P	588	PF65 900				

KM# 955 50 DOLLARS
15.50 g., 0.999 Gold 0.4947 oz. AGW, 25 mm. **Ruler:** Elizabeth II **Subject:** Australian Fauna **Obv:** Head with tiara right **Obv. Designer:** Ian Rank-Broadley **Rev:** Grey kangaroo

Date	Mintage	F12	VF20	XF40	MS60	MS63
2006P	714	PF65 900				

KM# 958 50 DOLLARS
15.50 g., 0.999 Gold 0.4947 oz. AGW, 25 mm. **Ruler:** Elizabeth II **Subject:** Australian Fauna **Obv:** Head with tiara right **Obv. Designer:** Ian Rank-Broadley **Rev:** Emu

Date	Mintage	F12	VF20	XF40	MS60	MS63
2006P	446	PF65 900				

KM# 961 50 DOLLARS
15.50 g., 0.999 Gold 0.4947 oz. AGW, 25 mm. **Ruler:** Elizabeth II **Subject:** Australian Fauna **Obv:** Head with tiara right **Obv. Designer:** Ian Rank-Broadley **Rev:** Koala

Date	Mintage	F12	VF20	XF40	MS60	MS63
2006P	1,000	PF65 900				

KM# 964 50 DOLLARS
15.50 g., 0.999 Gold 0.4947 oz. AGW, 25 mm. **Ruler:** Elizabeth II **Subject:** Australian Fauna **Obv:** Head with tiara right **Obv. Designer:** Ian Rank-Broadley **Rev:** Kookaburra

Date	Mintage	F12	VF20	XF40	MS60	MS63
2006P	738	PF65 900				

KM# 981 50 DOLLARS
15.50 g., 0.999 Platinum 0.4947 oz. APW **Ruler:** Elizabeth II **Subject:** Australian Flora **Obv:** Head with tiara right **Obv. Designer:** Ian Rank-Broadley **Rev:** Cooktown orchid

Date	Mintage	F12	VF20	XF40	MS60	MS63
2006P	169	PF65 975				

KM# 983 50 DOLLARS
15.50 g., 0.999 Platinum 0.4947 oz. APW **Ruler:** Elizabeth II **Subject:** Australian Flora **Obv:** Head with tiara right **Obv. Designer:** Ian Rank-Broadley **Rev:** Sturt's desert rose

Date	Mintage	F12	VF20	XF40	MS60	MS63
2006P	171	PF65 975				

KM# 985 50 DOLLARS
15.50 g., 0.999 Platinum 0.4947 oz. APW **Ruler:** Elizabeth II **Subject:** Australian Flora **Obv:** Head with tiara right **Obv. Designer:** Ian Rank-Broadley **Rev:** Royal bluebell

Date	Mintage	F12	VF20	XF40	MS60	MS63
2006P	153	PF65 975				

KM# 987 50 DOLLARS
15.50 g., 0.999 Platinum 0.4947 oz. APW **Ruler:** Elizabeth II **Subject:** Australian Flora **Obv:** Head with tiara right **Obv. Designer:** Ian Rank-Broadley **Rev:** Kangaroo paw

Date	Mintage	F12	VF20	XF40	MS60	MS63
2006P	155	PF65 975				

KM# 989 50 DOLLARS
15.50 g., 0.999 Platinum 0.4947 oz. APW **Ruler:** Elizabeth II **Subject:** Australian Flora **Obv:** Head with tiara right **Obv. Designer:** Ian Rank-Broadley **Rev:** Common pink heath

Date	Mintage	F12	VF20	XF40	MS60	MS63
2006P	138	PF65 975				

KM# 967 50 DOLLARS
15.50 g., 0.999 Gold 0.4947 oz. AGW, 25 mm. **Ruler:** Elizabeth II **Subject:** Australian Fauna **Obv:** Head with tiara right **Obv. Designer:** Ian Rank-Broadley **Rev:** Echidna

Date	Mintage	F12	VF20	XF40	MS60	MS63
2007P	269	PF65 900				

KM# 970 50 DOLLARS
15.50 g., 0.999 Gold 0.4947 oz. AGW, 25 mm. **Ruler:** Elizabeth II **Subject:** Australian Fauna **Obv:** Head with tiara right **Obv. Designer:** Ian Rank-Broadley **Rev:** Common wombat

Date	Mintage	F12	VF20	XF40	MS60	MS63
2007P	253	PF65 900				

KM# 973 50 DOLLARS
15.50 g., 0.999 Gold 0.4947 oz. AGW, 25 mm. **Ruler:** Elizabeth II **Subject:** Australian Fauna **Obv:** Head with tiara right **Obv. Designer:** Ian Rank-Broadley **Rev:** Tasmanian devil

Date	Mintage	F12	VF20	XF40	MS60	MS63
2007P	284	PF65 900				

KM# 976 50 DOLLARS
15.50 g., 0.999 Gold 0.4947 oz. AGW, 25 mm. **Ruler:** Elizabeth II **Subject:** Australian Fauna **Obv:** Head with tiara right **Obv. Designer:** Ian Rank-Broadley **Rev:** Great white shark

Date	Mintage	F12	VF20	XF40	MS60	MS63
2007P	706	PF65 900				

KM# 979 50 DOLLARS
15.50 g., 0.999 Gold 0.4947 oz. AGW, 25 mm. **Ruler:** Elizabeth II **Subject:** Australian Fauna **Obv:** Head with tiara right **Obv. Designer:** Ian Rank-Broadley **Rev:** Platypus

Date	Mintage	F12	VF20	XF40	MS60	MS63
2007P	257	PF65 900				

KM# 991 50 DOLLARS
15.50 g., 0.999 Platinum 0.4947 oz. APW, 24 mm. **Ruler:** Elizabeth II **Subject:** Australian Flora **Obv:** Head with tiara right **Obv. Designer:** Ian Rank-Broadley **Rev:** Anemone buttercup

Date	Mintage	F12	VF20	XF40	MS60	MS63
2007P	78	PF65 975				

KM# 993 50 DOLLARS
15.50 g., 0.999 Platinum 0.4947 oz. APW **Ruler:** Elizabeth II **Subject:** Australian Flora **Obv:** Head with tiara right **Obv. Designer:** Ian Rank-Broadley **Rev:** Sturt's desert pea

Date	Mintage	F12	VF20	XF40	MS60	MS63
2007P	78	PF65 975				

KM# 995 50 DOLLARS
15.50 g., 0.999 Platinum 0.4947 oz. APW, 24 mm. **Ruler:** Elizabeth II **Subject:** Australian Flora **Obv:** Head with tiara right **Obv. Designer:** Ian Rank-Broadley **Rev:** Tasmanian Bluegum

Date	Mintage	F12	VF20	XF40	MS60	MS63
2007P	79	PF65 975				

KM# 997 50 DOLLARS
15.50 g., 0.999 Platinum 0.4947 oz. APW **Ruler:** Elizabeth II **Subject:** Australian Flora **Obv:** Head with tiara right **Obv. Designer:** Ian Rank-Broadley **Rev:** Waratah

Date	Mintage	F12	VF20	XF40	MS60	MS63
2007P	83	PF65 975				

KM# 999 50 DOLLARS
15.50 g., 0.999 Platinum 0.4947 oz. APW **Ruler:** Elizabeth II **Subject:** Australian Flora **Obv:** Head with tiara right **Obv. Designer:** Ian Rank-Broadley **Rev:** Golden wattle

Date	Mintage	F12	VF20	XF40	MS60	MS63
2007P	80	PF65 975				

KM# 1167 50 DOLLARS
15.55 g., 0.999 Platinum 0.4962 oz. APW, 25 mm. **Ruler:** Elizabeth II **Subject:** Australian Flora **Rev:** Black-anther flax lily **Rev. Legend:** DISCOVER AUSTRALIA

Date	Mintage	F12	VF20	XF40	MS60	MS63
2008	—	PF65 975				

KM# 1196 50 DOLLARS
15.55 g., 0.999 Gold 0.4962 oz. AGW, 25 mm. **Ruler:** Elizabeth II **Obv:** Head right **Obv. Designer:** Ian Rank-Broadley **Rev:** Dolphin **Rev. Legend:** DISCOVER AUSTRALIA

Date	Mintage	F12	VF20	XF40	MS60	MS63
2008P	673	PF65 900				

KM# 1197 50 DOLLARS
15.55 g., 0.999 Gold 0.4962 oz. AGW, 25 mm. **Ruler:** Elizabeth II **Obv:** Head right **Obv. Designer:** Ian Rank-Broadley **Rev:** King brown snake **Rev. Legend:** DISCOVER AUSTRALIA

Date	Mintage	F12	VF20	XF40	MS60	MS63
2008P	255	PF65 900				

KM# 1198 50 DOLLARS
15.55 g., 0.999 Gold 0.4962 oz. AGW, 25 mm. **Ruler:** Elizabeth II **Obv:** Head right **Obv. Designer:** Ian Rank-Broadley **Rev:** Brolga **Rev. Legend:** DISCOVER AUSTRALIA

Date	Mintage	F12	VF20	XF40	MS60	MS63
2008P	211	PF65 900				

KM# 1199 50 DOLLARS
15.55 g., 0.999 Gold 0.4962 oz. AGW, 25 mm. **Ruler:** Elizabeth II **Obv:** Head right **Obv. Designer:** Ian Rank-Broadley **Rev:** Dingo **Rev. Legend:** DISCOVER AUSTRALIA

Date	Mintage	F12	VF20	XF40	MS60	MS63
2008P	221	PF65 900				

KM# 1200 50 DOLLARS
15.55 g., 0.999 Gold 0.4962 oz. AGW, 25 mm. **Ruler:** Elizabeth II **Obv:** Head right **Obv. Designer:** Ian Rank-Broadley **Rev:** Frill-neck lizard **Rev. Legend:** DISCOVER AUSTRALIA

Date	Mintage	F12	VF20	XF40	MS60	MS63
2008P	219	PF65 900				

KM# 1206 50 DOLLARS
15.55 g., 0.999 Platinum 0.4962 oz. APW, 26 mm. **Ruler:** Elizabeth II **Obv:** Head right **Obv. Designer:** Ian Rank-Broadley **Rev:** Black anther flax lily, multicolor **Rev. Legend:** DISCOVER AUSTRALIA

Date	Mintage	F12	VF20	XF40	MS60	MS63
2008P	104	PF65 1,500				

KM# 1207 50 DOLLARS
15.55 g., 0.999 Platinum 0.4962 oz. APW, 26 mm. **Ruler:** Elizabeth II **Obv:** Head right **Obv. Designer:** Ian Rank-Broadley **Rev:** Native fragipan, multicolor **Rev. Legend:** DISCOVER AUSTRALIA

Date	Mintage	F12	VF20	XF40	MS60	MS63
2008P	105	PF65 1,500				

KM# 1208 50 DOLLARS
15.55 g., 0.999 Platinum 0.4962 oz. APW, 26 mm. **Ruler:** Elizabeth II **Obv:** Head right **Obv. Designer:** Ian Rank-Broadley **Rev:** Geraldton wax, multicolor **Rev. Legend:** DISCOVER AUSTRALIA

Date	Mintage	F12	VF20	XF40	MS60	MS63
2008P	101	PF65 1,500				

KM# 1209 50 DOLLARS
15.55 g., 0.999 Platinum 0.4962 oz. APW, 26 mm. **Ruler:** Elizabeth II **Obv:** Head right **Obv. Designer:** Ian Rank-Broadley **Rev:** Red-flowered kurrajong, multicolor **Rev. Legend:** DISCOVER AUSTRALIA

Date	Mintage	F12	VF20	XF40	MS60	MS63
2008P	101	PF65 1,500				

KM# 1210 50 DOLLARS
15.55 g., 0.999 Platinum 0.4962 oz. APW **Ruler:** Elizabeth II **Obv:** Head right **Obv. Designer:** Ian Rank-Broadley **Rev:** Small-leaf lilly pilly, multicolor **Rev. Legend:** DISCOVER AUSTRALIA

Date	Mintage	F12	VF20	XF40	MS60	MS63
2008P	99	PF65 1,500				

KM# 1229 50 DOLLARS
15.55 g., 0.999 Gold 0.4962 oz. AGW, 25 mm. **Ruler:** Elizabeth II **Obv:** Head right **Obv. Designer:** Ian Rank-Broadley **Rev:** Dreaming king brown snake **Rev. Designer:** Darryl Berttolli

Date	Mintage	F12	VF20	XF40	MS60	MS63
2009P	1,000	PF65 1,100				

KM# 1227 50 DOLLARS
15.55 g., 0.999 Gold 0.4962 oz. AGW, 25 mm. **Ruler:** Elizabeth II **Obv:** Head right **Obv. Designer:** Ian Rank-Broadley **Rev:** Dreaming kangaroo **Rev. Designer:** Darryl Berttolli

Date	Mintage	F12	VF20	XF40	MS60	MS63
2009P	1,000	PF65 1,100				

KM# 1230 50 DOLLARS
15.55 g., 0.999 Gold 0.4962 oz. AGW, 25 mm. **Ruler:** Elizabeth II **Obv:** Head right **Obv. Designer:** Ian Rank-Broadley **Rev:** Dreaming brolga **Rev. Designer:** Darryl Berttolli

Date	Mintage	F12	VF20	XF40	MS60	MS63
2009P	1,000	PF65 1,100				

KM# 1231 50 DOLLARS
15.55 g., 0.999 Gold 0.4962 oz. AGW, 25 mm. **Ruler:** Elizabeth II **Obv:** Head right **Obv. Designer:** Ian Rank-Broadley **Rev:** Dreaming echidna **Rev. Designer:** Darryl Berttolli

Date	Mintage	F12	VF20	XF40	MS60	MS63
2009P	1,000	PF65 1,100				

KM# 1237 50 DOLLARS
15.55 g., 0.999 Platinum 0.4962 oz. APW, 25 mm. **Ruler:** Elizabeth II **Obv:** Head right **Obv. Designer:** Ian Rank-Broadley **Rev:** Dreaming kangaroo, multicolor **Rev. Designer:** Darryl Berttolli

Date	Mintage	F12	VF20	XF40	MS60	MS63
2009P	1,000	PF65 1,500				

KM# 1238 50 DOLLARS
15.55 g., 0.999 Platinum 0.4962 oz. APW, 25 mm. **Ruler:** Elizabeth II **Obv:** Head right **Obv. Designer:** Ian Rank-Broadley **Rev:** Dreaming dolphin, multicolor **Rev. Designer:** Darryl Berttolli

Date	Mintage	F12	VF20	XF40	MS60	MS63
2009P	1,000	PF65 1,500				

KM# 1239 50 DOLLARS
15.55 g., 0.999 Platinum 0.4962 oz. APW, 25 mm. **Ruler:** Elizabeth II **Obv:** Head right **Obv. Designer:** Ian Rank-Broadley **Rev:** Dreaming king brown snake, multicolor **Rev. Designer:** Darryl Berttolli

Date	Mintage	F12	VF20	XF40	MS60	MS63
2009P	1,000	PF65 1,500				

KM# 1240 50 DOLLARS
15.55 g., 0.999 Platinum 0.4962 oz. APW, 25 mm. **Ruler:** Elizabeth II **Obv:** Head right **Obv. Designer:** Ian Rank-Broadley **Rev:** Dreaming brolga, multicolor **Rev. Designer:** Darryl Berttolli

Date	Mintage	F12	VF20	XF40	MS60	MS63
2009P	1,000	PF65 1,500				

KM# 1241 50 DOLLARS
15.55 g., 0.999 Platinum 0.4962 oz. APW, 25 mm. **Ruler:** Elizabeth II **Obv:** Head right **Obv. Designer:** Ian Rank-Broadley **Rev:** Dreaming echidna, multicolor **Rev. Designer:** Darryl Berttolli

Date	Mintage	F12	VF20	XF40	MS60	MS63
2009P	1,000	PF65 1,500				

KM# 1398 50 DOLLARS
15.50 g., 0.999 Platinum 0.4946 oz. APW, 26 mm. **Ruler:** Elizabeth II **Obv:** Head right **Obv. Designer:** Ian Rank-Broadley **Rev:** Multicolor frill-neck lizard **Rev. Designer:** Darryl Bellotti

Date	Mintage	F12	VF20	XF40	MS60	MS63
2010P	1,000	PF65 1,550				

KM# 1400 50 DOLLARS
15.50 g., 0.999 Gold 0.4946 oz. AGW, 26 mm. **Ruler:** Elizabeth II **Obv:** Head right **Obv. Designer:** Ian Rank-Broadley **Rev:** Frill-neck lizard

Date	Mintage	F12	VF20	XF40	MS60	MS63
2010P	1,000	PF65 1,250				

KM# 1404 50 DOLLARS
15.50 g., 0.999 Platinum 0.4946 oz. APW, 26 mm. **Ruler:** Elizabeth II **Obv:** Head right **Rev:** Multicolor koala

Date	Mintage	F12	VF20	XF40	MS60	MS63
2010P	1,000	PF65 1,550				

KM# 1406 50 DOLLARS
15.50 g., 0.999 Gold 0.4946 oz. AGW, 26 mm. **Ruler:** Elizabeth II **Obv:** Head right **Obv. Designer:** Ian Rank-Broadley **Rev:** Koala

Date	Mintage	F12	VF20	XF40	MS60	MS63
2010P	1,000	PF65 1,250				

KM# 1410 50 DOLLARS
15.50 g., 0.999 Platinum 0.4946 oz. APW, 26 mm. **Ruler:** Elizabeth II **Obv:** Head right **Obv. Designer:** Ian Rank-Broadley **Rev:** Multicolor platypus

Date	Mintage	F12	VF20	XF40	MS60	MS63
2010P	1,000	PF65 1,550				

KM# 1412 50 DOLLARS
15.50 g., 0.999 Gold 0.4946 oz. AGW **Ruler:** Elizabeth II **Obv:** Head right **Obv. Designer:** Ian Rank-Broadley **Rev:** Platypus

Date	Mintage	F12	VF20	XF40	MS60	MS63
2010P	1,000	PF65 1,250				

KM# 1416 50 DOLLARS
15.50 g., 0.999 Platinum 0.4946 oz. APW, 26 mm. **Ruler:** Elizabeth II **Obv:** Head right **Obv. Designer:** Ian Rank-Broadley **Rev:** Multicolor saltwater crocodile

Date	Mintage	F12	VF20	XF40	MS60	MS63
2010P	1,000	PF65 1,550				

KM# 1418 50 DOLLARS
15.50 g., 0.999 Gold 0.4946 oz. AGW, 26 mm. **Ruler:** Elizabeth II **Obv:** Head right **Obv. Designer:** Ian Rank-Broadley **Rev:** Saltwater crocodile

Date	Mintage	F12	VF20	XF40	MS60	MS63
2010P	1,000	PF65 1,250				

KM# 1422 50 DOLLARS
15.50 g., 0.999 Platinum 0.4946 oz. APW, 26 mm. **Ruler:** Elizabeth II **Obv:** Head right **Obv. Designer:** Ian Rank-Broadley **Rev:** Multicolor wombat

Date	Mintage	F12	VF20	XF40	MS60	MS63
2010P	1,000	PF65 1,100				

KM# 1424 50 DOLLARS
15.50 g., 0.999 Gold 0.4946 oz. AGW, 26 mm. **Ruler:** Elizabeth II **Obv:** Head right **Obv. Designer:** Ian Rank-Broadley **Rev:** Wombat

Date	Mintage	F12	VF20	XF40	MS60	MS63
2010P	2,500	PF65 1,250				

KM# 1537 50 DOLLARS
15.55 g., 0.999 Gold 0.4962 oz. AGW **Ruler:** Elizabeth II **Subject:** Dreaming Emu **Rev:** Linear emu in color

Date	Mintage	F12	VF20	XF40	MS60	MS63
2011P	—	PF65 1,250				

KM# 1539 50 DOLLARS
15.55 g., 0.999 Platinum 0.4962 oz. APW **Ruler:** Elizabeth II **Subject:** Dreaming Emu **Rev:** Linear emu in color

Date	Mintage	F12	VF20	XF40	MS60	MS63
2011P	1,000	PF65 1,800				

KM# 1543 50 DOLLARS
15.55 g., 0.999 Gold 0.4962 oz. AGW **Ruler:** Elizabeth II **Subject:** Dreaming Tasmanian Devil **Rev:** Linear tasmanian devil in color

Date	Mintage	F12	VF20	XF40	MS60	MS63
2011P	—	PF65 1,250				

KM# 1545 50 DOLLARS
15.55 g., 0.999 Platinum 0.4962 oz. APW **Ruler:** Elizabeth II **Subject:** Dreaming Tasmanian Devil **Rev:** Linear tasmanian devil in color

Date	Mintage	F12	VF20	XF40	MS60	MS63
2011P	—	PF65 1,800				

KM# 1549 50 DOLLARS
15.55 g., 0.999 Gold 0.4962 oz. AGW **Ruler:** Elizabeth II **Series:** Dreaming Kookaburra **Rev:** Linear kookaburra in color

Date	Mintage	F12	VF20	XF40	MS60	MS63
2011P	—	PF65 1,250				

KM# 1551 50 DOLLARS
15.55 g., 0.999 Platinum 0.4962 oz. APW **Ruler:** Elizabeth II **Subject:** Dreaming Kookaburra **Rev:** Linear kookaburra in color

Date	Mintage	F12	VF20	XF40	MS60	MS63
2011P	1,000	PF65 1,800				

KM# 1555 50 DOLLARS
15.55 g., 0.999 Gold 0.4962 oz. AGW **Ruler:** Elizabeth II **Subject:** Dreaming shark **Rev:** Linear shark in color

Date	Mintage	F12	VF20	XF40	MS60	MS63
2011P	—	PF65 1,250				

KM# 1557 50 DOLLARS
15.55 g., 0.999 Platinum 0.4962 oz. APW **Ruler:** Elizabeth II **Subject:** Dreaming shark **Rev:** Linear shark in color

Date	Mintage	F12	VF20	XF40	MS60	MS63
2011P	1,000	PF65 1,800				

KM# 1561 50 DOLLARS
15.55 g., 0.999 Gold 0.4962 oz. AGW **Ruler:** Elizabeth II **Subject:** Dreaming Dingo **Rev:** Linear dingo in color

Date	Mintage	F12	VF20	XF40	MS60	MS63
2011P	—	PF65 1,250				

KM# 1563 50 DOLLARS
15.55 g., 0.999 Platinum 0.4962 oz. APW **Ruler:** Elizabeth II **Subject:** Dreaming Dingo **Rev:** Linear dingo in color

Date	Mintage	F12	VF20	XF40	MS60	MS63
2011P	1,000	PF65 1,800				

KM# 1726 50 DOLLARS
15.55 g., 0.999 Gold 0.4964 oz. AGW, 25.6 mm. **Ruler:** Elizabeth II **Rev:** Green and Gold Bell Frog in grass

Date	Mintage	F12	VF20	XF40	MS60	MS63
2012P	500	PF65 950				

KM# 1727 50 DOLLARS
15.55 g., 0.999 Gold 0.4964 oz. AGW, 25.6 mm. **Ruler:** Elizabeth II **Rev:** Kookaburra standing right

Date	Mintage	F12	VF20	XF40	MS60	MS63
2012P	500	PF65 950				

KM# 1728 50 DOLLARS
15.55 g., 0.999 Gold 0.4964 oz. AGW, 25.6 mm. **Ruler:** Elizabeth II **Rev:** Whale Shark swimming right

Date	Mintage	F12	VF20	XF40	MS60	MS63
2012P	500	PF65 950				

KM# 1729 50 DOLLARS
15.55 g., 0.999 Gold 0.4964 oz. AGW, 25.6 mm. **Ruler:** Elizabeth II **Rev:** Kangaroo bounding right

Date	Mintage	F12	VF20	XF40	MS60	MS63
2012P	500	PF65 950				

KM# 1730 50 DOLLARS
15.55 g., 0.999 Gold 0.4964 oz. AGW, 25.6 mm. **Ruler:** Elizabeth II **Rev:** Goanna lizard right

Date	Mintage	F12	VF20	XF40	MS60	MS63
2012P	500	PF65 950				

KM# 2053 50 DOLLARS
15.55 g., 0.999 Gold 0.4968 oz. AGW, 25.6 mm. **Ruler:** Elizabeth II **Obv:** Head with tiara right **Rev:** Kangaroo, road landscape

Date	Mintage	F12	VF20	XF40	MS60	MS63
2013P	Est. 550	PF65 1,000				

KM# 1696 60 DOLLARS
10.00 g., 0.999 Gold 0.3191 oz. AGW, 22.5 mm. **Ruler:** Elizabeth II **Subject:** Australian 2012 London Olympic Team **Obv:** Head with tiara right **Rev:** Athlete standing on platform with flag **Rev. Designer:** Wade Robinson

Date	Mintage	F12	VF20	XF40	MS60	MS63
2012P	2,012	PF65 675				

KM# 643 100 DOLLARS
10.37 g., 0.9999 Gold 0.3312 oz. AGW, 25 mm. **Ruler:** Elizabeth II **Subject:** Golden Wattle Flower **Obv:** Queen's head right **Rev:** Flower and denomination **Edge:** Reeded

Date	Mintage	F12	VF20	XF40	MS60	MS63
2001B	3,000	—	—	—	600	625
2001B	2,500	PF65 650				

KM# 657 100 DOLLARS
10.37 g., 0.9999 Gold 0.3312 oz. AGW, 25 mm. **Ruler:** Elizabeth II **Obv:** Queen's head right **Rev:** Sturt's Desert Rose **Rev. Designer:** Horst Hahne **Edge:** Reeded

Date	Mintage	F12	VF20	XF40	MS60	MS63
2002B	3,000	—	—	—	600	625
2002B	2,500	PF65 650				

KM# 636 100 DOLLARS
31.10 g., 0.9995 Platinum 0.9931 oz. APW, 32.1 mm. **Ruler:** Elizabeth II **Subject:** Multiculturalism **Obv:** Head with tiara right **Obv. Designer:** Ian Rank-Broadley **Rev:** Six racially diverse portraits against a blue background **Edge:** Reeded

Date	Mintage	F12	VF20	XF40	MS60	MS63
2002	1,000	PF65 1,850				

KM# 646 100 DOLLARS
31.40 g., 0.9999 Gold 1.0029 oz. AGW, 34.1 mm. **Ruler:** Elizabeth II **Subject:** Queen's 50th Anniversary of Accession **Obv:** Queen's head right **Rev:** Silhouette of George VI, queen's portrait and denomination **Rev. Designer:** Peter Soobik **Edge:** Reeded

Date	Mintage	F12	VF20	XF40	MS60	MS63
2002B	2,002	PF65 1,775				

KM# 800 100 DOLLARS
31.10 g., 0.999 Gold 0.9926 oz. AGW, 34 mm. **Ruler:** Elizabeth II **Subject:** 50th Anniversary of the Coronation of Elizabeth II **Obv:** Head with tiara right **Rev:** Young portrait of Queen Elizabeth facing left, royal cipher, crown **Rev. Designer:** Peter Soobik **Edge:** Plain

Date	Mintage	F12	VF20	XF40	MS60	MS63
2003	660	PF65 1,800				

KM# 870 100 DOLLARS
10.37 g., 0.999 Gold 0.3308 oz. AGW, 25 mm. **Ruler:** Elizabeth II **Subject:** State Floral Emblems **Obv:** Head with tiara right **Obv. Designer:** Ian Rank-Broadley **Rev:** Royal Blue Bell flowers **Rev. Designer:** Horst Hahne **Edge:** Reeded

Date	Mintage	F12	VF20	XF40	MS60	MS63
2003	1,383	PF65 650				

KM# 797 100 DOLLARS
31.11 g., 0.999 Gold 0.9927 oz. AGW, 25.1 mm. **Ruler:** Elizabeth II **Subject:** 60th Anniversary of end of World War II **Obv:** Head with tiara right **Obv. Designer:** Ian Rank-Broadley **Rev:** Latent news real photographic images of a dancing man celebrating the end of WWII

Date	Mintage	F12	VF20	XF40	MS60	MS63
2005P	750	PF65 1,800				

KM# 1243 100 DOLLARS
31.11 g., 0.999 Gold 0.9926 oz. AGW, 36 mm. **Ruler:** Elizabeth II **Subject:** Treasures of Australia **Obv:** Head right **Obv. Designer:** Ian Rank-Broadley **Rev:** Mountains **Note:** Insert container with 1 carat of diamonds.

Date	Mintage	F12	VF20	XF40	MS60	MS63
2009P	715	PF65 2,150				

KM# 1436 100 DOLLARS
Gold AGW **Ruler:** Elizabeth II

Date	Mintage	F12	VF20	XF40	MS60	MS63
2010	—	PF65 1,800				

KM# 1595 100 DOLLARS
31.11 g., 0.999 Gold 0.9926 oz. AGW, 36 mm. **Ruler:** Elizabeth II **Subject:** Treasures of Australia **Obv:** Head above pearl container **Rev:** Landscape above pearl container **Edge:** Reeded

Date	Mintage	F12	VF20	XF40	MS60	MS63
2011P	Est. 1000	PF65 2,250				

KM# 1596 100 DOLLARS
31.11 g., 0.999 Gold 0.9926 oz. AGW, 32 mm. **Ruler:** Elizabeth II **Subject:** Gold Coin Program, 25th Anniversary **Obv:** Head with tiara right **Rev:** Nugget **Rev. Designer:** Stuart Devlin

Date	Mintage	F12	VF20	XF40	MS60	MS63
2011P	Est. 1500	PF65 1,850				

KM# 2096 100 DOLLARS
1000.00 g., 0.999 Silver 31.9118 oz. ASW **Ruler:** Elizabeth II **Subject:** Elizabeth II, 60th Anniversary of Reign **Rev:** St. Edward's Crown edged by 60 diamond motifs

Date	Mintage	F12	VF20	XF40	MS60	MS63
2012P	600	PF65 2,000				

KM# 1956 100 DOLLARS
31.10 g., 0.9999 Gold 0.9934 oz. AGW, 38 mm. **Ruler:** Elizabeth II **Subject:** Kangaroo Road Sign **Rev. Designer:** Wojciech Pietranki

Date	Mintage	F12	VF20	XF40	MS60	MS63
2013	Est. 5000	PF65 1,650				

KM# 2079 100 DOLLARS
31.11 g., 0.999 Gold 0.9926 oz. AGW **Ruler:** Elizabeth II **Subject:** Treasures of Europe - Garnet **Rev:** Alpine house and mountain

Date	Mintage	F12	VF20	XF40	MS60	MS63
2013P	—	PF65 1,750				

KM# 2135 100 DOLLARS
13.80 g., Aluminum-Bronze, 30.6 mm. **Ruler:** Elizabeth II **Subject:** Birth of Prince George **Obv:** Head with tiara right **Rev:** Prince William and Katherine with Prince George

Date	Mintage	F12	VF20	XF40	MS60	MS63
2013	—				—	15.00

KM# 644 150 DOLLARS
15.55 g., 0.9999 Gold 0.4967 oz. AGW, 30 mm. **Ruler:** Elizabeth II **Obv:** Queen's head right **Rev:** Golden Wattle flower, value **Edge:** Reeded

Date	Mintage	F12	VF20	XF40	MS60	MS63
2001B	1,500	PF65 900				

KM# 658 150 DOLLARS
15.55 g., 0.9999 Gold 0.4967 oz. AGW, 30 mm. **Ruler:** Elizabeth II **Subject:** State Floral Emblems **Obv:** Queen's head right **Rev:** Sturt's Desert Rose **Rev. Designer:** Horst Hahne **Edge:** Reeded

Date	Mintage	F12	VF20	XF40	MS60	MS63
2002B	1,500	PF65 900				

KM# 872 150 DOLLARS
15.55 g., 0.999 Gold 0.4963 oz. AGW, 30 mm. **Ruler:** Elizabeth II **Subject:** State Floral Emblems **Obv:** Head with tiara right **Obv. Designer:** Ian Rank-Broadley **Rev:** Royal Blue Bell flowers **Rev. Designer:** Horst Hahne **Edge:** Reeded

Date	Mintage	F12	VF20	XF40	MS60	MS63
2003	1,105	PF65 900				

KM# 874 150 DOLLARS
15.55 g., 0.999 Gold 0.4963 oz. AGW, 30 mm. **Ruler:** Elizabeth II **Subject:** Rare Australian Birds **Obv:** Head with tiara right **Obv. Designer:** Ian Rank-Broadley **Rev:** Red-tailed black cockatoo **Rev. Designer:** Wojciech Pietranik **Edge:** Reeded

Date	Mintage	F12	VF20	XF40	MS60	MS63
2003	2,500	PF65 900				

KM# 731 150 DOLLARS
10.37 g., 0.999 Gold 0.3307 oz. AGW, 25 mm. **Ruler:** Elizabeth II **Obv:** Queen's head right **Rev:** Cassowary bird **Edge:** Reeded

Date	Mintage	F12	VF20	XF40	MS60	MS63
2004B	2,500	PF65 625				

KM# 752 150 DOLLARS
10.37 g., 0.9999 Gold 0.3312 oz. AGW, 25 mm. **Ruler:** Elizabeth II **Obv:** Queen's head right **Rev:** Malleefowl bird **Edge:** Reeded

Date	Mintage	F12	VF20	XF40	MS60	MS63
2005B	2,500	PF65 625				

KM# 873 150 DOLLARS
10.37 g., 0.999 Gold 0.3308 oz. AGW, 25 mm. **Ruler:** Elizabeth II **Subject:** Rare Australian Birds **Obv:** Head with tiara right **Obv. Designer:** Ian Rank-Broadley **Rev:** Red-tailed black cockatoo **Rev. Designer:** Wojciech Pietranik **Edge:** Reeded

Date	Mintage	F12	VF20	XF40	MS60	MS63
2006	2,500	PF65 625				

KM# 732 200 DOLLARS
15.55 g., 0.999 Gold 0.4963 oz. AGW, 30 mm. **Ruler:** Elizabeth II **Obv:** Queen's head right **Rev:** Cassowary bird **Edge:** Reeded

Date	Mintage	F12	VF20	XF40	MS60	MS63
2004B	2,500	PF65 900				

KM# 753 200 DOLLARS
15.55 g., 0.9999 Gold 0.4967 oz. AGW, 30 mm. **Ruler:** Elizabeth II **Obv:** Queen's head right **Rev:** Malleefowl bird **Edge:** Reeded

Date	Mintage	F12	VF20	XF40	MS60	MS63
2005B	2,500	PF65 900				

KM# 2006 200 DOLLARS
Gold AGW, 30 mm. **Ruler:** Elizabeth II **Rev:** Bird's head right **Shape:** 12 Sided

Date	Mintage	F12	VF20	XF40	MS60	MS63
2006	—	PF65 900				

KM# 1695 200 DOLLARS
62.21 g., 0.999 Gold 1.9854 oz. AGW **Ruler:** Elizabeth II **Subject:** Australian 2012 London Olympic Team **Rev. Designer:** Wade Robinson

Date	Mintage	F12	VF20	XF40	MS60	MS63
2012	—	PF65 3,750				

KM# 1702 200 DOLLARS
62.22 g., 0.999 Gold 1.9854 oz. AGW, 41.1 mm. **Ruler:** Elizabeth II **Subject:** Elizabeth II, 60th Anniversary **Obv:** Head with tiara right **Rev:** Young head portrait right **Rev. Designer:** Darryl Bellotti

Date	Mintage	F12	VF20	XF40	MS60	MS63
2012P	60	PF65 4,500				

KM# 1931 200 DOLLARS
62.21 g., 0.9999 Gold 1.9871 oz. AGW, 41 mm. Ruler: Elizabeth II Subject: Queen Victoria 175th Anniversary of Coronation Rev. Designer: Aleysha Howarth

Date	Mintage	F12	VF20	XF40	MS60	MS63
2013P	Est. 150	PF65 3,000				

KM# 2042 200 DOLLARS
62.22 g., 0.9999 Gold 1.9872 oz. AGW, 41.1 mm. Ruler: Elizabeth II Subject: Sydney Opera House Rev. Designer: Natasha Muhl

Date	Mintage	F12	VF20	XF40	MS60	MS63
2013	200	PF65 5,120				

KM# 1957 500 DOLLARS
155.50 g., 0.9999 Gold 4.9668 oz. AGW, 60 mm. Ruler: Elizabeth II Subject: Kangaroo Road Sign Rev. Designer: Wojciech Pietranik

Date	Mintage	F12	VF20	XF40	MS60	MS63
2013	—	PF65 7,500				

KM# 2095 1000 DOLLARS
1000.00 g., 0.999 Gold 31.9118 oz. AGW Ruler: Elizabeth II Subject: Elizabeth II, 60th Anniversary of Reign Rev: St. Edward's Crown edged by 60 diamond motifs

Date	Mintage	F12	VF20	XF40	MS60	MS63
2012P	60	PF65 63,000				

KM# 1958 3000 DOLLARS
1000.00 g., 0.9999 Gold 31.9406 oz. AGW, 75 mm. Ruler: Elizabeth II Subject: Kangaroo Road Sign Rev. Designer: Wojciech Pietranik

Date	Mintage	F12	VF20	XF40	MS60	MS63
2013	Est. 100	PF65 47,500				

BULLION - KANGAROO

KM# 1797 50 CENTS
15.50 g., 0.999 Silver 0.4946 oz. ASW, 36.6 mm. Ruler: Elizabeth II Rev: Kangaroo in color

Date	Mintage	F12	VF20	XF40	MS60	MS63
2012P	—	PF65 50.00				

KM# 2087 50 CENTS
15.55 g., 0.9999 Silver 0.4967 oz. ASW, 36.6 mm. Ruler: Elizabeth II Rev: Kangaroo standing right, color background

Date	Mintage	F12	VF20	XF40	MS60	MS63
2013P	—	PF65 50.00				

KM# 590 DOLLAR
31.10 g., 0.999 Silver 0.9926 oz. ASW, 40 mm. Ruler: Elizabeth II Obv: Queen's portrait Rev: Aboriginal-kangaroo design with dots Rev. Designer: Jeanette Timbery Edge: Reeded

Date	Mintage	F12	VF20	XF40	MS60	MS63
2001B Frosted Unc	—					35.00
2001B	—	PF65 40.00				

KM# 642 DOLLAR
31.10 g., 0.999 Silver 0.9926 oz. ASW, 40 mm. Ruler: Elizabeth II Obv: Head with tiara right, denomination below Rev: Aboriginal-style kangaroo with wavy line background Edge: Reeded

Date	Mintage	F12	VF20	XF40	MS60	MS63
2002B	—				35.00	42.00
2002B	—	PF65 50.00				

KM# 798a DOLLAR
31.10 g., 0.999 Silver 0.9926 oz. ASW, 40 mm. Ruler: Elizabeth II Obv: Head with tiara right Obv. Designer: Ian Rank-Broadley Rev: Aboriginal-style kangaroo design Rev. Designer: Wojciech Pietranik Edge: Reeded

Date	Mintage	F12	VF20	XF40	MS60	MS63
2003	7,450	—	—	—	—	125

KM# 798 DOLLAR
31.10 g., 0.999 Silver 0.9926 oz. ASW, 40 mm. Ruler: Elizabeth II Obv: Head with tiara right Obv. Designer: Ian Rank-Broadley Rev: Aboriginal-style kangaroo design Rev. Designer: Wojcieck Pietranik Edge: Reeded

Date	Mintage	F12	VF20	XF40	MS60	MS63
2003	35,230	—	—	—	—	40.00
2003	20,400	PF65 45.00				

KM# 723 DOLLAR
31.10 g., 0.9926 oz. ASW, 40 mm. Ruler: Elizabeth II Obv: Head with tiara right, denomination below Rev: Kangaroo with semi-circle background Edge: Reeded

Date	Mintage	F12	VF20	XF40	MS60	MS63
2004B Frosted Unc					—	37.00
2004B	12,500	PF65 42.00				

KM# 723a DOLLAR
31.10 g., 0.999 Silver 0.9926 oz. ASW, 40 mm. Ruler: Elizabeth II Obv: Head with tiara right, denomination below Rev: Kangaroo with semi-circle background Edge: Reeded

Date	Mintage	F12	VF20	XF40	MS60	MS63
2004B Frosted Unc	—	—	—	—	—	65.00

KM# 749 DOLLAR
31.60 g., 0.999 Silver 1.0084 oz. ASW, 40 mm. Ruler: Elizabeth II Obv: Head with tiara right Obv. Designer: Ian Rank-Broadley Rev: Kangaroo bounding under Southern Cross and above Federation Star Rev. Designer: Wojcieck Pietranik Edge: Reeded

Date	Mintage	F12	VF20	XF40	MS60	MS63
2005	—	—	—	—	35.00	45.00
2005	12,500	PF65 50.00				

KM# 749a DOLLAR
31.10 g., 0.999 Silver 0.9926 oz. ASW, 40 mm. Ruler: Elizabeth II Obv: Head with tiara right Obv. Designer: Ian Rank-Broadley Rev: Kangaroo bounding under Southern Cross and above Federation Star Rev. Designer: Wojcieck Pietranik Edge: Reeded

Date	Mintage	F12	VF20	XF40	MS60	MS63
2005	12,500	PF65 60.00				

KM# 837a DOLLAR
31.60 g., 0.999 Silver 1.0084 oz. ASW, 40 mm. Ruler: Elizabeth II Obv: Head with tiara right Obv. Designer: Ian Rank-Broadley Rev: Kangaroo bounding under Australian sun Rev. Designer: Wojcieck Pietranik Edge: Reeded

Date	Mintage	F12	VF20	XF40	MS60	MS63
2006	7,500	—	—	—	—	55.00

KM# 837 DOLLAR
31.60 g., 0.999 Silver 1.0084 oz. ASW, 40 mm. Ruler: Elizabeth II Obv: Head with tiara right Obv. Designer: Ian Rank-Broadley Rev: Kangaroo bounding under Australian sun Rev. Designer: Wojcieck Pietranik Edge: Reeded

Date	Mintage	F12	VF20	XF40	MS60	MS63
2006	—	—	—	—	—	35.00
2006	12,500	PF65 42.00				

KM# 851 DOLLAR
31.60 g., 0.999 Silver 1.0084 oz. ASW, 40 mm. **Ruler:** Elizabeth II **Obv:** Head with tiara right **Obv. Designer:** Ian Rank-Broadley **Rev:** Kangaroo mother and joey **Rev. Designer:** Rolf Harris **Edge:** Reeded

Date	Mintage	F12	VF20	XF40	MS60	MS63
2007	15,000	—	—	—	—	45.00
2007	12,500	PF65 50.00				

KM# 1061 DOLLAR
27.22 g., Copper-Nickel, 38.74 mm. **Ruler:** Elizabeth II **Rev:** Kangaroo holding football **Rev. Designer:** Reg Mombassa

Date	Mintage	F12	VF20	XF40	MS60	MS63
2008	9,234	—	—	—	—	25.00

KM# 1061a DOLLAR
31.11 g., 0.999 Silver 0.9926 oz. ASW, 40 mm. **Ruler:** Elizabeth II **Rev:** Kangaroo holding football **Rev. Designer:** Reg Mombassa

Date	Mintage	F12	VF20	XF40	MS60	MS63
2008	7,500	—	—	—	—	65.00
2008	10,000	PF65 50.00				

KM# 1061b DOLLAR
31.11 g., 0.999 Silver 0.9926 oz. ASW, 40 mm. **Ruler:** Elizabeth II **Rev:** Kangaroo holding football in color **Rev. Designer:** Reg Mombassa

Date	Mintage	F12	VF20	XF40	MS60	MS63
2008	12,500	PF65 95.00				

KM# 1083 DOLLAR
31.11 g., 0.999 Silver 0.9926 oz. ASW, 40 mm. **Ruler:** Elizabeth II **Rev:** Kangaroo **Rev. Designer:** K. Done

Date	Mintage	F12	VF20	XF40	MS60	MS63
2009	20,000	PF65 65.00				
2009	20,000	—	—	—	—	50.00

KM# 1083a DOLLAR
31.11 g., 0.999 Silver 0.9926 oz. ASW, 40 mm. **Ruler:** Elizabeth II **Rev:** Kangaroo **Rev. Designer:** K. Done

Date	Mintage	F12	VF20	XF40	MS60	MS63
2009	—	—	—	—	—	90.00

KM# 1083b DOLLAR
31.10 g., 0.999 Silver 0.9926 oz. ASW, 40 mm. **Ruler:** Elizabeth II **Rev:** Kangaroo in color

Date	Mintage	F12	VF20	XF40	MS60	MS63
2009	—	PF65 75.00				

KM# 1758 DOLLAR
31.11 g., 0.999 Silver 0.9926 oz. ASW, 40.6 mm. **Ruler:** Elizabeth II **Obv:** Head with tiara right **Rev:** Kangaroo right on rocks

Date	Mintage	F12	VF20	XF40	MS60	MS63
2010P	—	PF65 85.00				
2010P	—	—	—	—	—	75.00

KM# 1762 DOLLAR
31.11 g., 0.999 Silver 0.9926 oz. ASW, 40.6 mm. **Ruler:** Elizabeth II **Obv:** Head with tiara right **Rev:** Kangaroo bounding left at sunset

Date	Mintage	F12	VF20	XF40	MS60	MS63
2010 F15	5,000	PF65 125				
2010 F15	7,000	—	—	—	—	125

KM# 1457 DOLLAR
31.11 g., 0.999 Silver 0.9926 oz. ASW, 40 mm. **Ruler:** Elizabeth II **Rev:** Two kangaroos playing

Date	Mintage	F12	VF20	XF40	MS60	MS63
2010P	—	PF65 42.00				

KM# 1514 DOLLAR
31.11 g., 0.999 Silver 0.9926 oz. ASW, 40. mm. **Ruler:** Elizabeth II **Rev:** Kangaroo in color

Date	Mintage	F12	VF20	XF40	MS60	MS63
2010	—	PF65 60.00				

KM# 1515 DOLLAR
31.11 g., 0.999 Silver 0.9926 oz. ASW, 40 mm. **Ruler:** Elizabeth II **Rev:** Kangaroo in color

Date	Mintage	F12	VF20	XF40	MS60	MS63
2010	—	PF65 60.00				

KM# 1516 DOLLAR
31.11 g., 0.9926 oz. ASW, 40 mm. **Ruler:** Elizabeth II **Rev:** Kangaroo in color

Date	Mintage	F12	VF20	XF40	MS60	MS63
2010	—	PF65 60.00				

KM# 1759 DOLLAR
31.11 g., 0.999 Silver 0.9926 oz. ASW, 40.6 mm. **Ruler:** Elizabeth II **Obv:** Head with tiara right **Rev:** Kangaroo and joey

Date	Mintage	F12	VF20	XF40	MS60	MS63
2011P	—	PF65 85.00				
2011P	—	—	—	—	—	75.00

KM# 1605 DOLLAR
31.11 g., 0.999 Silver 0.9926 oz. ASW, 33 mm. **Ruler:** Elizabeth II **Obv:** Head with tiara right **Rev:** Kangaroo left, sun rays in background **Edge:** Reeded **Note:** Ultra High Relief

Date	Mintage	F12	VF20	XF40	MS60	MS63
2011P	Est. 20000	PF65 110				

KM# 1737 DOLLAR
31.14 g., 0.999 Silver 0.9936 oz. ASW, 40 mm. **Ruler:** Elizabeth II **Obv:** Head with tiara right **Rev:** Mareeba Rock Wallaby **Rev. Designer:** W. Pietranik

Date	Mintage	F12	VF20	XF40	MS60	MS63
2012	20,000	PF65 100				
2012	20,000	—	—	—	—	75.00

KM# 1830 DOLLAR
31.11 g., 0.999 Silver 0.9926 oz. ASW, 33 mm. **Ruler:** Elizabeth II **Rev:** Kangaroo **Rev. Designer:** Wade Robinson **Note:** Ultra High Relief

Date	Mintage	F12	VF20	XF40	MS60	MS63
2012P	—	PF65 110				

KM# 1862 DOLLAR
31.11 g., 0.999 Silver 0.9926 oz. ASW, 40 mm. **Ruler:** Elizabeth II **Obv:** Head in tiara right **Rev:** Kangaroo bounding right

Date	Mintage	F12	VF20	XF40	MS60	MS63
2012	—	PF65 100				

KM# 2030 DOLLAR
31.11 g., 0.999 Silver 0.9926 oz. ASW, 40 mm. **Ruler:** Elizabeth II **Rev:** Kangaroo standing on rock at left **Rev. Designer:** A. Baggio

Date	Mintage	F12	VF20	XF40	MS60	MS63
2013	Est. 20000	PF65 100				
2013	Est. 20000				—	80.00

KM# 1863 DOLLAR
31.11 g., 0.999 Silver 0.9926 oz. ASW, 40 mm. **Ruler:** Elizabeth II **Obv:** Head in tiara right **Rev:** Kangaroo bounding right

Date	Mintage	F12	VF20	XF40	MS60	MS63
2013	Est. 5000	PF65 60.00				

KM# 2005 DOLLAR
6.03 g., 0.999 Silver 0.1924 oz. ASW, 21.69 mm. **Ruler:** Elizabeth II **Subject:** Kangaroo at Sunset

Date	Mintage	F12	VF20	XF40	MS60	MS63
2013	Est. 5000	PF65 15.00				

KM# 2023 DOLLAR
31.10 g., 0.999 Silver 0.9926 oz. ASW, 40 mm. **Ruler:** Elizabeth II **Subject:** Kangaroo Series 20th Anniversary **Rev:** Kangaroo bounding right

Date	Mintage	F12	VF20	XF40	MS60	MS63
2013	Est. 5000	PF65 100				

KM# 2026 DOLLAR
6.03 g., 0.999 Silver 0.1924 oz. ASW, 21.69 mm. **Ruler:** Elizabeth II **Rev:** Kangaroo at sunset

Date	Mintage	F12	VF20	XF40	MS60	MS63
2013	Est. 5000	PF65 65.00				

KM# 2085 DOLLAR
31.11 g., 0.9999 Silver 0.9935 oz. ASW, 40.6 mm. **Ruler:** Elizabeth II **Rev:** Kangaroo standing right **Note:** High relief

Date	Mintage	F12	VF20	XF40	MS60	MS63
2013P	—	PF65 75.00				

KM# 1390 2 DOLLARS
0.50 g., 0.999 Gold AGW **Ruler:** Elizabeth II **Obv:** Head right **Rev:** Kangaroo

Date	Mintage	F12	VF20	XF40	MS60	MS63
2010(p)	—	—	—	—	32.00	35.00

KM# 1527 2 DOLLARS
0.50 g., 0.999 Gold AGW, 11.6 mm. **Ruler:** Elizabeth II **Obv:** Head in tiara right **Rev:** Kangaroo bounding left **Rev. Designer:** Wase Robinson

Date	Mintage	F12	VF20	XF40	MS60	MS63
2010P	—	—	—	—	—	50.00

KM# 1649 2 DOLLARS
0.50 g., 0.999 Gold AGW, 11.6 mm. **Ruler:** Elizabeth II **Obv:** Head with tiara right **Rev:** Kangaroo left

Date	Mintage	F12	VF20	XF40	MS60	MS63
2011	—	PF65 50.00				

KM# 1790 2 DOLLARS
0.50 g., 0.999 Gold AGW, 12 mm. **Ruler:** Elizabeth II **Obv:** Head in tiara right **Rev:** Kangaroo standing right, wind water pump at left **Rev. Designer:** Wade Robinson

Date	Mintage	F12	VF20	XF40	MS60	MS63
2012P	—	—	—	—	—	50.00

KM# 2072 2 DOLLARS
0.50 g., 0.9999 Gold AGW, 14.1 mm. **Ruler:** Elizabeth II **Rev:** Kangaroo standing right

Date	Mintage	F12	VF20	XF40	MS60	MS63
2013P	—	PF65 100				

KM# 893 5 DOLLARS
1.57 g., 0.999 Gold 0.0501 oz. AGW **Ruler:** Elizabeth II **Obv:** Head with tiara right **Obv. Designer:** Ian Rank-Broadley **Rev:** Two kangaroos on map of Australia

Date	Mintage	F12	VF20	XF40	MS60	MS63
2001	10,000	—	—	—	—	115

KM# 1776 10 DOLLARS
3.11 g., 0.999 Gold 0.0992 oz. AGW, 17.53 mm. **Ruler:** Elizabeth II **Rev:** Kangaroo bounding left at sunset

Date	Mintage	F12	VF20	XF40	MS60	MS63
2007P	—	—	—	—	—	225

KM# 1772 10 DOLLARS
3.11 g., 0.999 Gold 0.0992 oz. AGW, 17.53 mm. **Ruler:** Elizabeth II **Rev:** Kangaroo bounding right in grassland

Date	Mintage	F12	VF20	XF40	MS60	MS63
2008P	—	—	—	—	—	225

KM# 1764 10 DOLLARS
3.11 g., 0.999 Gold 0.0992 oz. AGW, 17.53 mm. **Ruler:** Elizabeth II **Obv:** Head with tiara right **Rev:** Kangaroo left, constellation in background

Date	Mintage	F12	VF20	XF40	MS60	MS63
2009P	—	PF65 250				

KM# 1768 10 DOLLARS
3.11 g., 0.999 Gold 0.0992 oz. AGW, 17.53 mm. **Ruler:** Elizabeth II **Rev:** Kangaroo

Date	Mintage	F12	VF20	XF40	MS60	MS63
2010P	—	—	—	—	—	225

KM# 1763 10 DOLLARS
3.11 g., 0.999 Gold 0.0992 oz. AGW, 17.53 mm. **Ruler:** Elizabeth II **Obv:** Head with tiara right **Rev:** Kangaroo right on rocks

Date	Mintage	F12	VF20	XF40	MS60	MS63
2010P	1,500	PF65 250				

KM# 1522 10 DOLLARS
3.11 g., 0.999 Gold 0.0992 oz. AGW, 17.53 mm. **Ruler:** Elizabeth II **Rev:** Two kangaroos

Date	Mintage	F12	VF20	XF40	MS60	MS63
2011	1,500	PF65 265				

KM# 1683 10 DOLLARS
3.11 g., 0.999 Gold 0.0992 oz. AGW, 17.53 mm. **Ruler:** Elizabeth II **Rev:** Kangaroo

Date	Mintage	F12	VF20	XF40	MS60	MS63
2012P	—	PF65 200				

KM# 894 15 DOLLARS
3.11 g., 0.999 Gold 0.0992 oz. AGW **Ruler:** Elizabeth II **Obv:** Head with tiara right **Obv. Designer:** Ian Rank-Broadley **Rev:** Two kangaroos on map of Australia

Date	Mintage	F12	VF20	XF40	MS60	MS63
2001	800	—	—	—	—	195

KM# 897 15 DOLLARS
3.11 g., 0.999 Gold 0.0992 oz. AGW **Ruler:** Elizabeth II **Obv:** Head with tiara right **Obv. Designer:** Ian Rank-Broadley **Rev:** Kangaroo browsing

Date	Mintage	F12	VF20	XF40	MS60	MS63
2002	800	—	—	—	—	195

KM# 902 15 DOLLARS
3.11 g., 0.999 Gold 0.0992 oz. AGW **Ruler:** Elizabeth II **Obv:** Head with tiara right **Obv. Designer:** Ian Rank-Broadley **Rev:** Two kangaroos hopping

Date	Mintage	F12	VF20	XF40	MS60	MS63
2003	500	—	—	—	—	195

KM# 907 15 DOLLARS
3.11 g., 0.999 Gold 0.0992 oz. AGW **Ruler:** Elizabeth II **Obv:** Head with tiara right **Obv. Designer:** Ian Rank-Broadley **Rev:** Crouching kangaroos facing left, Grass tree plant at right

Date	Mintage	F12	VF20	XF40	MS60	MS63
2004	500	—	—	—	—	195

KM# 911 15 DOLLARS
3.11 g., 0.999 Gold 0.0992 oz. AGW **Ruler:** Elizabeth II **Obv:** Head with tiara right **Obv. Designer:** Ian Rank-Broadley **Rev:** Kangaroo in bush

Date	Mintage	F12	VF20	XF40	MS60	MS63
2005	500	—	—	—	—	195

KM# 1362 15 DOLLARS
3.11 g., 0.999 Gold 0.0992 oz. AGW **Ruler:** Elizabeth II **Obv:** Head right **Rev:** Kangaroo

Date	Mintage	F12	VF20	XF40	MS60	MS63
2010(p)	—	—	—	—	—	195

KM# 1989 15 DOLLARS
3.11 g., 0.9999 Gold 0.0994 oz. AGW, 16.6 mm. **Ruler:** Elizabeth II **Subject:** Australian Kangaroo

Date	Mintage	F12	VF20	XF40	MS60	MS63
2013	Est. 200000	PF65 200				

KM# 2081 15 DOLLARS
3.11 g., 0.9999 Gold 0.0993 oz. AGW, 17.53 mm. **Ruler:** Elizabeth II **Rev:** Kangaroo standing right

Date	Mintage	F12	VF20	XF40	MS60	MS63
2013P	—	PF65 195				

KM# 2123 15 DOLLARS
3.11 g., 0.9999 Gold 0.0994 oz. AGW, 16.6 mm. **Ruler:** Elizabeth II **Rev:** Kangaroo set against rural vista

Date	Mintage	F12	VF20	XF40	MS60	MS63
2014P	200,000	—	—	—	—	BV+15%

KM# 895 25 DOLLARS
7.75 g., 0.999 Gold 0.2473 oz. AGW **Ruler:** Elizabeth II **Obv:** Head with tiara right **Obv. Designer:** Ian Rank-Broadley **Rev:** Two kangaroos on map of Australia

Date	Mintage	F12	VF20	XF40	MS60	MS63
2001	500	—	—	—	—	465

KM# 898 25 DOLLARS
7.75 g., 0.999 Gold 0.2473 oz. AGW **Ruler:** Elizabeth II **Obv:** Head with tiara right **Obv. Designer:** Ian Rank-Broadley **Rev:** Kangaroo browsing

Date	Mintage	F12	VF20	XF40	MS60	MS63
2002	500	—	—	—	—	465

KM# 903 25 DOLLARS
7.75 g., 0.999 Gold 0.2473 oz. AGW **Ruler:** Elizabeth II **Obv:** Head with tiara right **Obv. Designer:** Ian Rank-Broadley **Rev:** Two kangaroos hopping

Date	Mintage	F12	VF20	XF40	MS60	MS63
2003	250	—	—	—	—	475

KM# 908 25 DOLLARS
7.75 g., 0.999 Gold 0.2473 oz. AGW **Ruler:** Elizabeth II **Obv:** Head with tiara right **Obv. Designer:** Ian Rank-Broadley **Rev:** Crouching kangaroos facing left, Grass tree plant at right

Date	Mintage	F12	VF20	XF40	MS60	MS63
2004	250	—	—	—	—	475

KM# 912 25 DOLLARS
7.75 g., 0.999 Gold 0.2473 oz. AGW **Ruler:** Elizabeth II **Obv:** Head with tiara right **Obv. Designer:** Ian Rank-Broadley **Rev:** Kangaroo in bush

Date	Mintage	F12	VF20	XF40	MS60	MS63
2005	250	—	—	—	—	475

KM# 1777 25 DOLLARS
7.77 g., 0.999 Gold 0.248 oz. AGW. **Ruler:** Elizabeth II **Rev:** Kangaroo bounding left at sunset

Date	Mintage	F12	VF20	XF40	MS60	MS63
2007P	—	—	—	—	—	475

KM# 1773 25 DOLLARS
7.77 g., 0.999 Gold 0.248 oz. AGW **Ruler:** Elizabeth II **Rev:** Kangaroo bounding right in grassland

Date	Mintage	F12	VF20	XF40	MS60	MS63
2008P	—	—	—	—	—	475

KM# 1765 25 DOLLARS
7.77 g., 0.999 Gold 0.248 oz. AGW, 22 mm. **Ruler:** Elizabeth II **Obv:** Head with tiara right **Rev:** Kangaroo left, constellation in background

Date	Mintage	F12	VF20	XF40	MS60	MS63
2009P	—	PF65 475				

KM# 1769 25 DOLLARS
7.77 g., 0.999 Gold 0.248 oz. AGW **Ruler:** Elizabeth II **Rev:** Kangaroo

Date	Mintage	F12	VF20	XF40	MS60	MS63
2010P	—	—	—	—	—	475

KM# 1363 25 DOLLARS
7.75 g., 0.999 Gold 0.2473 oz. AGW **Ruler:** Elizabeth II **Rev:** Two kangaroos playing

Date	Mintage	F12	VF20	XF40	MS60	MS63
2010P	—	—	—	—	—	465

KM# 1506 25 DOLLARS
6.22 g., 0.999 Gold 0.1985 oz. AGW, 21.69 mm. **Ruler:** Elizabeth II **Obv:** Head with tiara right **Rev:** Kangaroo in outback, windmill at right

Date	Mintage	F12	VF20	XF40	MS60	MS63
2010	1,000	PF65 825				

KM# 1507 25 DOLLARS
6.22 g., 0.999 Gold 0.1985 oz. AGW, 21.69 mm. **Ruler:** Elizabeth II **Obv:** Head in tiara right **Rev:** Kangaroo in outback, windmill at center

Date	Mintage	F12	VF20	XF40	MS60	MS63
2010	1,000	PF65 825				

KM# 1508 25 DOLLARS
6.22 g., 0.999 Gold 0.1985 oz. AGW, 21.69 mm. **Ruler:** Elizabeth II **Obv:** Head in tiara right **Rev:** Kangaroo in outback, windmill at left

Date	Mintage	F12	VF20	XF40	MS60	MS63
2010	1,000	PF65 825				

KM# 1684 25 DOLLARS
7.77 g., 0.999 Gold 0.248 oz. AGW **Ruler:** Elizabeth II **Rev:** Kangaroo

Date	Mintage	F12	VF20	XF40	MS60	MS63
2012P	—	PF65 475				

KM# 1990 25 DOLLARS
7.78 g., 0.9999 Gold 0.2484 oz. AGW, 20.6 mm. **Ruler:** Elizabeth II **Subject:** Australian Kangaroo

Date	Mintage	F12	VF20	XF40	MS60	MS63
2013	Est. 150000	PF65 475				

KM# 2025 25 DOLLARS
6.22 g., 0.999 Gold 0.1985 oz. AGW, 21.7 mm. **Ruler:** Elizabeth II **Rev:** Kangaroo bounding left at sunset

Date	Mintage	F12	VF20	XF40	MS60	MS63
2013	Est. 1000	PF65 650				

KM# 2082 25 DOLLARS
7.77 g., 0.9999 Gold 0.2482 oz. AGW, 21.7 mm. **Ruler:** Elizabeth II **Rev:** Kangaroo standing right

Date	Mintage	F12	VF20	XF40	MS60	MS63
2013P	—	PF65 500				

KM# 2124 25 DOLLARS
7.78 g., 0.9999 Gold 0.2484 oz. AGW, 20.6 mm. **Ruler:** Elizabeth II **Rev:** Kangaroo set against rural vista

Date	Mintage	F12	VF20	XF40	MS60	MS63
2014P	150,000	—	—	—	—	BV+10%

KM# 899 50 DOLLARS
15.50 g., 0.999 Gold 0.4947 oz. AGW **Ruler:** Elizabeth II **Obv:** Head with tiara right **Obv. Designer:** Ian Rank-Broadley **Rev:** Kangaroo browsing

Date	Mintage	F12	VF20	XF40	MS60	MS63
2002	650	—	—	—	900	

KM# 904 50 DOLLARS
15.50 g., 0.999 Gold 0.4947 oz. AGW **Ruler:** Elizabeth II **Obv:** Head with tiara right **Obv. Designer:** Ian Rank-Broadley **Rev:** Two kangaroos hopping

Date	Mintage	F12	VF20	XF40	MS60	MS63
2003	500	—	—	—	900	

KM# 909 50 DOLLARS
15.50 g., 0.999 Gold 0.4947 oz. AGW **Ruler:** Elizabeth II **Obv:** Head with tiara right **Obv. Designer:** Ian Rank-Broadley **Rev:** Crouching kangaroos facing left, Grass tree plant at right

Date	Mintage	F12	VF20	XF40	MS60	MS63
2004	500	—	—	—	900	

Note: In sets only

KM# 913 50 DOLLARS
15.50 g., 0.999 Gold 0.4947 oz. AGW **Ruler:** Elizabeth II **Obv:** Head with tiara right **Obv. Designer:** Ian Rank-Broadley **Rev:** Kangaroo in bush

Date	Mintage	F12	VF20	XF40	MS60	MS63
2005	500	—	—	—	900	

KM# 1778 50 DOLLARS
15.55 g., 0.999 Gold 0.4962 oz. AGW **Ruler:** Elizabeth II **Rev:** Kangaroo bounding left in sunset

Date	Mintage	F12	VF20	XF40	MS60	MS63
2007P	—	—	—	—	—	950

KM# 1774 50 DOLLARS
15.55 g., 0.999 Gold 0.4962 oz. AGW **Ruler:** Elizabeth II **Rev:** Kangaroo bounding right in grassland

Date	Mintage	F12	VF20	XF40	MS60	MS63
2008P	—	—	—	—	—	950

KM# 1766 50 DOLLARS
15.55 g., 0.999 Gold 0.4962 oz. AGW, 25 mm. **Ruler:** Elizabeth II **Obv:** Head with tiara right **Rev:** Kangaroo left, constellation in background

Date	Mintage	F12	VF20	XF40	MS60	MS63
2009P	—	PF65 950				

KM# 1364 50 DOLLARS
15.56 g., 0.999 Gold 0.4965 oz. AGW, 25 mm. **Ruler:** Elizabeth II **Obv:** Head right **Rev:** Two kangaroos playing

Date	Mintage	F12	VF20	XF40	MS60	MS63
2010(p)	—	—	—	—	—	900

KM# 1770 50 DOLLARS
15.55 g., 0.999 Gold 0.4962 oz. AGW, 25 mm. **Ruler:** Elizabeth II **Rev:** Kangaroo

Date	Mintage	F12	VF20	XF40	MS60	MS63
2010P	—	—	—	—	—	950

KM# 1685 50 DOLLARS
15.55 g., 0.999 Gold 0.4962 oz. AGW, 25 mm. **Ruler:** Elizabeth II **Rev:** Kangaroo

Date	Mintage	F12	VF20	XF40	MS60	MS63
2012P	—	PF65 950				

KM# 1991 50 DOLLARS
15.55 g., 0.9999 Gold 0.4968 oz. AGW, 25.6 mm. **Ruler:** Elizabeth II **Subject:** Australian Kangaroo

Date	Mintage	F12	VF20	XF40	MS60	MS63
2013	Est. 100000	PF65 800				

KM# 2083 50 DOLLARS
15.55 g., 0.9999 Gold 0.4967 oz. AGW, 25 mm. **Ruler:** Elizabeth II **Rev:** Kangaroo standing right

Date	Mintage	F12	VF20	XF40	MS60	MS63
2013P	—	PF65 950				

KM# 2125 50 DOLLARS
15.55 g., 0.9999 Gold 0.4967 oz. AGW, 25.6 mm. **Ruler:** Elizabeth II **Rev:** Kangaroo set against rural vista

Date	Mintage	F12	VF20	XF40	MS60	MS63
2014P	100,000	—	—	—	—	BV+7%

KM# 1779 100 DOLLARS
31.11 g., 0.999 Gold 0.9926 oz. AGW, 32 mm. **Ruler:** Elizabeth II **Rev:** Kangaroo bounding left at sunset

Date	Mintage	F12	VF20	XF40	MS60	MS63
2007P	—	—	—	—	—	1,850

KM# 1775 100 DOLLARS
31.11 g., 0.999 Gold 0.9926 oz. AGW, 32 mm. **Ruler:** Elizabeth II **Rev:** Kangaroo bounding right in grassland

Date	Mintage	F12	VF20	XF40	MS60	MS63
2008P	—	—	—	—	—	1,850

KM# 1767 100 DOLLARS
31.11 g., 0.999 Gold 0.9926 oz. AGW, 32 mm. **Ruler:** Elizabeth II **Obv:** Head with tiara right **Rev:** Kangaroo left, constellation in background

Date	Mintage	F12	VF20	XF40	MS60	MS63
2009P	—	PF65 1,850				

KM# 1365 100 DOLLARS
31.10 g., 0.999 Gold 0.9926 oz. AGW, 32 mm. **Ruler:** Elizabeth II **Obv:** Head right **Rev:** Kangaroo

Date	Mintage	F12	VF20	XF40	MS60	MS63
2010(p)	—	—	—	—	—	1,850

KM# 1771 100 DOLLARS
31.11 g., 0.999 Gold 0.9926 oz. AGW, 32 mm. **Ruler:** Elizabeth II **Rev:** Kangaroo

Date	Mintage	F12	VF20	XF40	MS60	MS63
2010P	—	—	—	—	—	1,850

KM# 1686 100 DOLLARS
31.11 g., 0.999 Gold 0.9926 oz. AGW, 32 mm. **Ruler:** Elizabeth
II **Rev:** Kangaroo

Date	Mintage	F12	VF20	XF40	MS60	MS63
2012P	—		PF65 1,850			

KM# 1992 100 DOLLARS
31.11 g., 0.9999 Gold 0.9937 oz. AGW, 32.6 mm. **Ruler:**
Elizabeth II **Subject:** Australian Kangaroo

Date	Mintage	F12	VF20	XF40	MS60	MS63
2013	Est. 350000		PF65 1,650			

KM# 2024 100 DOLLARS
31.10 g., 0.999 Gold 0.9926 oz. AGW, 38.74 mm. **Ruler:**
Elizabeth II **Subject:** Kangaroo Series 20th Anniversary **Rev:**
Kangaroo bounding right

Date	Mintage	F12	VF20	XF40	MS60	MS63
2013	Est. 500		PF65 2,600			

KM# 2084 100 DOLLARS
31.11 g., 0.9999 Gold 0.9935 oz. AGW, 32 mm. **Ruler:** Elizabeth
II **Rev:** Kangaroo standing right

Date	Mintage	F12	VF20	XF40	MS60	MS63
2013P	—		PF65 1,850			

KM# 2126 100 DOLLARS
31.11 g., 0.9999 Gold 0.9937 oz. AGW, 32.6 mm. **Ruler:**
Elizabeth II **Rev:** Kangaroo set against rural vista

Date	Mintage	F12	VF20	XF40	MS60	MS63
2014P	—	—	—	—	BV+3%	

KM# 896 200 DOLLARS
62.21 g., 0.999 Gold 1.9854 oz. AGW, 41 mm. **Ruler:** Elizabeth
II **Obv:** Head with tiara right **Obv. Designer:** Ian Rank-
Broadley **Rev:** Two kangaroos on map of Australia

Date	Mintage	F12	VF20	XF40	MS60	MS63
2001	300	—	—	—	3,500	

KM# 901 200 DOLLARS
62.21 g., 0.999 Gold 1.9854 oz. AGW, 41 mm. **Ruler:** Elizabeth
II **Obv:** Head with tiara right **Obv. Designer:** Ian Rank-
Broadley **Rev:** Kangaroo browsing

Date	Mintage	F12	VF20	XF40	MS60	MS63
2002	300	—	—	—	3,500	

KM# 905 200 DOLLARS
62.21 g., 0.999 Gold 1.9854 oz. AGW, 41 mm. **Ruler:** Elizabeth
II **Obv:** Head with tiara right **Obv. Designer:** Ian Rank-
Broadley **Rev:** Two kangaroos hopping

Date	Mintage	F12	VF20	XF40	MS60	MS63
2003	200		PF65 3,500			

KM# 910 200 DOLLARS
62.21 g., 0.999 Gold 1.9854 oz. AGW, 41 mm. **Ruler:** Elizabeth
II **Obv:** Head with tiara right **Obv. Designer:** Ian Rank-Broadley
Rev: Crouching kangaroos facing left, Grass tree plant at right

Date	Mintage	F12	VF20	XF40	MS60	MS63
2004	200		PF65 3,500			

KM# 1462 300 DOLLARS
1000.00 g., 0.999 Gold 31.9118 oz. AGW **Ruler:** Elizabeth II
Obv: Head with tiara right **Rev:** Two kangaroos playing

Date	Mintage	F12	VF20	XF40	MS60	MS63
2010P	—	—	—	—	55,500	

KM# 1687 3000 DOLLARS
1000.00 g., 0.9999 Gold 31.9406 oz. AGW, 75.6 mm. **Ruler:**
Elizabeth II **Rev:** Red Kangaroo bounding left within circle of
rays

Date	Mintage	F12	VF20	XF40	MS60	MS63
2012P	—					BV+2%
2013P	—					BV+2%
2014P	—					BV+2%

KM# 1993 3000 DOLLARS
1000.00 g., 0.9999 Gold 31.9406 oz. AGW, 75.6 mm. **Ruler:**
Elizabeth II **Subject:** Australian Kangaroo

Date	Mintage	F12	VF20	XF40	MS60	MS63
2013	—		PF65 46,500			

KM# 1569 1000000 DOLLARS
1000000.00 g., 0.9999 Gold 31940.5846 oz. AGW, 800 mm.
Ruler: Elizabeth II **Obv:** Head with tiara right **Rev:** Red
Kangaroo bounding left **Note:** Cast. 120mm thick.

Date	Mintage	F12	VF20	XF40	MS60	MS63
2012P	1	—	—	—	45,000,000	

BULLION - KOOKABURRA

KM# 875 50 CENTS
15.55 g., 0.999 Silver 0.4962 oz. ASW, 38.74 mm. **Ruler:**
Elizabeth II **Obv:** Head with tiara right **Obv. Designer:** Ian
Rank-Broadley **Rev:** Kookaburra on branch, tail above,
two leaves **Edge:** Reeded **Shape:** Square **Note:** Lenticular
technology makes kookaburra appear to move.

Date	Mintage	F12	VF20	XF40	MS60	MS63
2002P	35,788		PF65 35.00			

KM# 684 50 CENTS
15.55 g., 0.999 Silver 0.4962 oz. ASW, 32.1x32.1 mm. **Ruler:**
Elizabeth II **Obv:** Head with tiara right, denomination
below **Obv. Designer:** Ian Rank-Broadley **Rev:** Two kookaburras, one
in flight **Edge:** Reeded **Shape:** Square

Date	Mintage	F12	VF20	XF40	MS60	MS63
2003P	11,585		PF65 32.00			

KM# 876 50 CENTS
15.55 g., 0.999 Silver 0.4962 oz. ASW, 38.74 mm. **Ruler:**
Elizabeth II **Obv:** Head with tiara right **Obv. Designer:** Ian
Rank-Broadley **Rev:** Kookaburra perched on branch, tail below,
four leaves **Edge:** Reeded **Shape:** Square

Date	Mintage	F12	VF20	XF40	MS60	MS63
2004P	9,839		PF65 32.00			

KM# 877 50 CENTS
15.55 g., 0.999 Silver 0.4962 oz. ASW, 25x25 mm. **Ruler:**
Elizabeth II **Obv:** Head with tiara right **Obv. Designer:** Ian
Rank-Broadley **Rev:** Two kookaburras on branch, one laughing
Edge: Reeded **Shape:** Square

Date	Mintage	F12	VF20	XF40	MS60	MS63
2005P	8,433		PF65 32.00			

KM# 1799 50 CENTS
15.50 g., 0.999 Silver 0.4946 oz. ASW, 36.6 mm. **Ruler:**
Elizabeth II **Rev:** Kookaburra in color

Date	Mintage	F12	VF20	XF40	MS60	MS63
2012P	—		PF65 50.00			

KM# 2086 50 CENTS
15.55 g., 0.9999 Silver 0.4967 oz. ASW, 36.6 mm. **Ruler:**
Elizabeth II **Rev:** Two kookaburra on branches, color
background

Date	Mintage	F12	VF20	XF40	MS60	MS63
2013P			PF65 50.00			

KM# 479 DOLLAR
31.97 g., 0.999 Silver 1.0202 oz. ASW **Ruler:** Elizabeth II **Obv:**
Head with tiara right, denomination below **Obv. Designer:** Ian
Rank-Broadley **Rev:** Two kookaburras back-to-back on branch

Date	Mintage	F12	VF20	XF40	MS60	MS63
2001	—	—	—	—	35.00	—
2001	10,000				45.00	—
	Note: Federation star privy mark					
2001	50,000				35.00	—
	Note: Santa Claus privy mark					
2001	1,000				125	—
	Note: Love token personal message					
2001	75,000				42.00	—
	Note: New York State Quarter privy mark					
2001	75,000				42.00	—
	Note: North Carolina State Quarter privy mark					
2001	75,000				42.00	—
	Note: Rhode Island State Quarter privy mark					
2001	75,000				42.00	—
	Note: Vermont State Quarter privy mark					
2001	75,000				42.00	—
	Note: Kentucky State Quarter privy mark					

KM# 691.1 DOLLAR

31.10 g., 0.999 Silver 0.9926 oz. ASW, 40 mm. **Ruler:** Elizabeth II **Obv:** Head with tiara right, denomination below **Obv. Designer:** Ian Rank-Broadley **Rev:** Kookaburra flying over map of Australia **Edge:** Reeded

Date	Mintage	F12	VF20	XF40	MS60	MS63
2001P	4,097	PF65 42.00				
2002P	—	—	—	—	35.00	37.00

KM# 625 DOLLAR

31.10 g., 0.999 Silver 0.9926 oz. ASW, 40.4 mm. **Ruler:** Elizabeth II **Subject:** U.S. State Quarter

Date	Mintage	F12	VF20	XF40	MS60	MS63
2002	75,000	—	—	—	45.00	—
Note: Tennessee State Quarter privy mark						
2002	75,000	—	—	—	45.00	—
Note: Ohio State Quarter privy mark						
2002	75,000	—	—	—	45.00	—
Note: Louisiana State Quarter privy mark						
2002	75,000	—	—	—	45.00	—
Note: Indiana State Quarter privy mark						
2002	75,000	—	—	—	45.00	—
Note: Mississippi State Quarter privy mark						

KM# 666 DOLLAR

31.62 g., 0.999 Silver 1.0091 oz. ASW, 40.3 mm. **Ruler:** Elizabeth II **Obv:** Head with tiara right, denomination below **Obv. Designer:** Ian Rank-Broadley **Rev:** Kookaburra perched on branch **Edge:** Reeded

Date	Mintage	F12	VF20	XF40	MS60	MS63
2002	2,498	PF65 37.00				

KM# 691.2 DOLLAR

31.62 g., 0.999 Silver 1.0091 oz. ASW, 40.5 mm. **Ruler:** Elizabeth II **Obv:** Head with tiara right, denomination below **Obv. Designer:** Ian Rank-Broadley **Rev:** Multicolor US flag above a kookaburra in flight over Australian map **Edge:** Reeded

Date	Mintage	F12	VF20	XF40	MS60	MS63
2002	18,500	—	—	—	35.00	40.00

KM# 683 DOLLAR

31.10 g., 0.999 Silver 0.9926 oz. ASW, 40 mm. **Ruler:** Elizabeth II **Obv:** Head with tiara right, denomination below **Obv. Designer:** Ian Rank-Broadley **Rev:** Two kookaburras, one in flight **Edge:** Reeded **Note:** Gilded.

Date	Mintage	F12	VF20	XF40	MS60	MS63
2003P	2,065	PF65 37.00				
2004	10,000	—	—	—	—	35.00
2004	15,000	PF65 45.00				

KM# 1761 DOLLAR

31.11 g., 0.999 Silver 0.9926 oz. ASW, 40.6 mm. **Ruler:** Elizabeth II **Obv:** Head with tiara right **Rev:** Kookaburra right on branch

Date	Mintage	F12	VF20	XF40	MS60	MS63
2003P	—	—	—	—	—	75.00

KM# 883 DOLLAR

31.11 g., 0.999 Silver 0.9926 oz. ASW, 40.5 mm. **Ruler:** Elizabeth II **Obv:** Head with tiara right **Obv. Designer:** Ian Rank-Broadley **Rev:** Kookaburra perched on branch with four leaves **Edge:** Reeded

Date	Mintage	F12	VF20	XF40	MS60	MS63
2004P	2,156	PF65 35.00				
2005 (2004)	5,000	—	—	—	45.00	—
Note: Gemini privy mark						
2005	5,000	—	—	—	45.00	—
Note: Aquarius privy mark						
2005	5,000	—	—	—	45.00	—
Note: Pisces privy mark						
2005	5,000	—	—	—	45.00	—
Note: Aries privy mark						
2005	5,000	—	—	—	45.00	—
Note: Taurus privy mark						
2005	5,000	—	—	—	45.00	—
Note: Cancer privy mark						
2005	5,000	—	—	—	45.00	—
Note: Leo privy mark						
2005	5,000	—	—	—	45.00	—
Note: Virgo privy mark						
2005	5,000	—	—	—	45.00	—

Date	Mintage	F12	VF20	XF40	MS60	MS63
Note: Libra privy mark						
2005	5,000	—	—	—	45.00	—
Note: Scorpio privy mark						
2005	5,000	—	—	—	45.00	—
Note: Sagittarius privy mark						
2005	5,000	—	—	—	45.00	—
Note: Capricorn privy mark						

KM# 883a DOLLAR

31.10 g., 0.999 Silver 0.9926 oz. ASW, 40 mm. **Ruler:** Elizabeth II **Obv:** Head with tiara right **Obv. Designer:** Ian Rank-Broadley **Rev:** Kookaburra perched on branch with four leaves

Date	Mintage	F12	VF20	XF40	MS60	MS63
2004	10,000	—	—	—	55.00	—

KM# 720 DOLLAR

1.04 g., 0.999 Silver 0.033 oz. ASW, 40 mm. **Ruler:** Elizabeth II **Obv:** Head with tiara right, denomination below **Rev:** Kookaburra, partially gilt **Edge:** Reeded

Date	Mintage	F12	VF20	XF40	MS60	MS63
2005	—	PF65 65.00				

KM# 886 DOLLAR

31.56 g., 0.999 Silver 1.0071 oz. ASW, 40.5 mm. **Ruler:** Elizabeth II **Obv:** Head with tiara right **Obv. Designer:** Ian Rank-Broadley **Rev:** Two kookaburras on branch, one laughing **Edge:** Reeded

Date	Mintage	F12	VF20	XF40	MS60	MS63
2005P	3,457	PF65 40.00				

KM# 886a DOLLAR

31.56 g., 0.999 Silver 1.0071 oz. ASW, 40.5 mm. **Ruler:** Elizabeth II **Obv:** Head with tiara right **Rev:** Two kookaburras on branch, one laughing **Edge:** Reeded

Date	Mintage	F12	VF20	XF40	MS60	MS63
2005P	9,170	PF65 45.00				

KM# 889 DOLLAR

31.56 g., 0.999 Silver 1.0071 oz. ASW, 40.5 mm. **Ruler:** Elizabeth II **Obv:** Head with tiara right **Obv. Designer:** Ian Rank-Broadley **Rev:** Kookaburra on branch, no leaves

Date	Mintage	F12	VF20	XF40	MS60	MS63
2007	300,000	—	—	—	35.00	38.00

KM# 889a DOLLAR

31.56 g., 0.999 Silver 1.0071 oz. ASW, 40.5 mm. **Ruler:** Elizabeth II **Obv:** Head with tiara right **Rev:** Kookaburra on branch, no leaves **Edge:** Reeded

Date	Mintage	F12	VF20	XF40	MS60	MS63
2008P	3,000	PF65 45.00				

KM# 1760 DOLLAR
31.11 g., 0.999 Silver 0.9926 oz. ASW, 40.6 mm. **Ruler:** Elizabeth II **Obv:** Head with tiara right **Rev:** Kookaburra on branch look at spider web at lower left

Date	Mintage	F12	VF20	XF40	MS60	MS63
2008P	—	—	—	—	—	75.00

KM# 1277 DOLLAR
31.11 g., 0.999 Silver 0.9926 oz. ASW, 40 mm. **Ruler:** Elizabeth II **Subject:** Kookaburra 20th Anniversary **Obv:** Head right **Obv. Designer:** Ian Rank-Broadley **Rev:** Kookaburra standing right

Date	Mintage	F12	VF20	XF40	MS60	MS63
2009 P20	10,000	PF63 45.00		PF65 47.00		

KM# 1278 DOLLAR
31.11 g., 0.999 Silver 0.9926 oz. ASW, 40 mm. **Ruler:** Elizabeth II **Subject:** Kookaburra 20th Anniversary **Obv:** Head right **Obv. Designer:** Ian Rank-Broadley **Rev:** Kookaburra on branch, head right

Date	Mintage	F12	VF20	XF40	MS60	MS63
2009 P20	10,000	PF63 45.00		PF65 47.00		

KM# 1279 DOLLAR
31.11 g., 0.999 Silver 0.9926 oz. ASW, 40 mm. **Ruler:** Elizabeth II **Subject:** Kookaburra 20th Anniversary **Obv:** Head right **Obv. Designer:** Ian Rank-Broadley **Rev:** Kookaburra on branch left, head upwards

Date	Mintage	F12	VF20	XF40	MS60	MS63
2009 P20	10,000	PF63 45.00		PF65 47.00		

KM# 1280 DOLLAR
31.11 g., 0.999 Silver 0.9926 oz. ASW, 40 mm. **Ruler:** Elizabeth II **Subject:** Kookaburra 20th Anniversary **Obv:** Head right **Obv. Designer:** Ian Rank-Broadley **Rev:** Kookaburra feeding young in nest at right

Date	Mintage	F12	VF20	XF40	MS60	MS63
2009 P20	10,000	PF63 45.00		PF65 47.00		

KM# 1281 DOLLAR
31.11 g., 0.999 Silver 0.9926 oz. ASW, 40 mm. **Ruler:** Elizabeth II **Subject:** Kookaburra 20th Anniversary **Obv:** Head right **Obv. Designer:** Ian Rank-Broadley **Rev:** Kookaburra pair on branch

Date	Mintage	F12	VF20	XF40	MS60	MS63
2009 P20	10,000	PF63 45.00		PF65 47.00		

KM# 1282 DOLLAR
31.11 g., 0.999 Silver 0.9926 oz. ASW, 40 mm. **Ruler:** Elizabeth II **Obv:** Head right **Obv. Designer:** Ian Rank-Broadley **Rev:** Kookaburra on branch, head left

Date	Mintage	F12	VF20	XF40	MS60	MS63
2009 P20	10,000	PF63 45.00		PF65 47.00		

KM# 1283 DOLLAR
31.11 g., 0.999 Silver 0.9926 oz. ASW, 40 mm. **Ruler:** Elizabeth II **Subject:** Kookaburra 20th Anniversary **Obv:** Head right **Obv. Designer:** Ian rank-Broadley **Rev:** Kookaburra in flight right

Date	Mintage	F12	VF20	XF40	MS60	MS63
2009 P20	10,000	PF63 45.00		PF65 47.00		

KM# 1284 DOLLAR
31.11 g., 0.999 Silver 0.9926 oz. ASW, 40 mm. **Ruler:** Elizabeth II **Subject:** Kookaburra 20th Anniversary **Obv:** Head right **Obv. Designer:** Ian Rank-Broadley **Rev:** Kookaburra by nest at left

Date	Mintage	F12	VF20	XF40	MS60	MS63
2009 P20	10,000	PF63 45.00		PF65 47.00		

KM# 1285 DOLLAR
31.11 g., 0.999 Silver 0.9926 oz. ASW, 40 mm. **Ruler:** Elizabeth II **Subject:** Kookaburra 20th Anniversary **Obv:** Head right **Obv. Designer:** Ian Rank-BroadleyR **Rev:** Kookaburra on fence post

Date	Mintage	F12	VF20	XF40	MS60	MS63
2009 P20	10,000	PF63 45.00		PF65 47.00		

KM# 1286 DOLLAR
31.11 g., 0.999 Silver 0.9926 oz. ASW, 40 mm. **Ruler:** Elizabeth II **Subject:** Kookaburra 20th Anniversary **Obv:** Head right **Obv. Designer:** Ian Rank-Broadleyr **Rev:** Kookaburra pair on branch left

Date	Mintage	F12	VF20	XF40	MS60	MS63
2009 P20	10,000	PF63 45.00		PF65 47.00		

KM# 1287 DOLLAR
31.11 g., 0.999 Silver 0.9926 oz. ASW, 40 mm. **Ruler:** Elizabeth II **Subject:** Kookaburra 20th Anniversary **Obv:** Head right **Obv. Designer:** Ian Rank-Broadley **Rev:** Kookaburra on leafy branch left

Date	Mintage	F12	VF20	XF40	MS60	MS63
2009 P20	10,000	PF63 45.00		PF65 47.00		

KM# 1288 DOLLAR
31.11 g., 0.999 Silver 0.9926 oz. ASW, 40 mm. **Ruler:** Elizabeth II **Subject:** Kookaburra 20th Anniversary **Obv:** Head right **Obv. Designer:** Ian Rank-Broadley **Rev:** Kookaburra pair on branch, beaks upward

Date	Mintage	F12	VF20	XF40	MS60	MS63
2009 P20	10,000	PF63 45.00		PF65 47.00		

KM# 1289 DOLLAR
31.11 g., 0.999 Silver 0.9926 oz. ASW, 40 mm. **Ruler:** Elizabeth II **Subject:** Kookaburra 20th Anniversary **Obv:** Head right **Obv. Designer:** Ian rank-Broadley **Rev:** Kookaburra in flight on map of Australia

Date	Mintage	F12	VF20	XF40	MS60	MS63
2009 P20	10,000	PF63 45.00		PF65 47.00		

KM# 1290 DOLLAR
31.11 g., 0.999 Silver 0.9926 oz. ASW, 40 mm. **Ruler:** Elizabeth II **Subject:** Kookaburra 20th Anniversary **Obv:** Head right **Obv. Designer:** Ian Rank-Broadley **Rev:** Kookaburra on branch right

Date	Mintage	F12	VF20	XF40	MS60	MS63
2009 P20	10,000	PF63 45.00		PF65 47.00		

KM# 1291 DOLLAR
31.11 g., 0.999 Silver 0.9926 oz. ASW, 40 mm. **Ruler:** Elizabeth II **Subject:** Kookaburra 20th Anniversary **Obv:** Head right **Obv. Designer:** Ian Rank-Broadley **Rev:** Two kookaburras, one in flight, one on branch

Date	Mintage	F12	VF20	XF40	MS60	MS63
2009 P20	10,000	PF63 45.00		PF65 47.00		

KM# 1292 DOLLAR
31.11 g., 0.999 Silver 0.9926 oz. ASW, 40 mm. **Ruler:** Elizabeth II **Subject:** Kookaburra 20th Anniversary **Obv:** Head right **Obv. Designer:** Ian Rank-Broadley **Rev:** Kookaburra on branch, head right

Date	Mintage	F12	VF20	XF40	MS60	MS63
2009 P20	10,000	PF63 45.00		PF65 47.00		

KM# 1293 DOLLAR
31.11 g., 0.999 Silver 0.9926 oz. ASW, 40 mm. **Ruler:** Elizabeth II **Subject:** Kookaburra 20th Anniversary **Obv:** Head right **Obv. Designer:** Ian Rank Broadley **Rev:** Kookaburra pair on branch left

Date	Mintage	F12	VF20	XF40	MS60	MS63
2009 P20	10,000	PF63 45.00		PF65 47.00		

KM# 1294 DOLLAR
31.11 g., 0.999 Silver 0.9926 oz. ASW, 40 mm. **Ruler:** Elizabeth II **Subject:** Kookaburra 20th Anniversary **Obv:** Head right **Obv. Designer:** Ian Rank-Broadley **Rev:** Kookaburra on branch left

Date	Mintage	F12	VF20	XF40	MS60	MS63
2009 P20	10,000	PF63 45.00		PF65 47.00		

KM# 1295 DOLLAR
31.11 g., 0.999 Silver 0.9926 oz. ASW, 40 mm. **Ruler:** Elizabeth II **Subject:** Kookaburra 20th Anniversary **Obv:** Head right **Obv. Designer:** Ian Rank-Broadley **Rev:** Kookaburra admiring spider web

Date	Mintage	F12	VF20	XF40	MS60	MS63
2009 P20	10,000	PF63 45.00		PF65 47.00		

KM# 1296 DOLLAR
31.11 g., 0.999 Silver 0.9926 oz. ASW, 40 mm. **Ruler:** Elizabeth II **Subject:** Kookaburra 20th Anniversary **Obv:** Head right **Obv. Designer:** Ian Rank-Broadley **Rev:** Kookaburra on branch, sunburst in background

Date	Mintage	F12	VF20	XF40	MS60	MS63
2009 P20	10,000	PF63 45.00		PF65 47.00		

KM# 1471 DOLLAR
31.11 g., 0.999 Silver 0.9926 oz. ASW, 40 mm. **Ruler:** Elizabeth II **Rev:** Kookabburra on branch

Date	Mintage	F12	VF20	XF40	MS60	MS63
2010P	—	—	—	—	—	45.00

KM# 1692 DOLLAR
31.11 g., 0.999 Silver 0.9926 oz. ASW, 40.5 mm. **Ruler:** Elizabeth II **Rev:** Kookaburra

Date	Mintage	F12	VF20	XF40	MS60	MS63
2012P	—	—	—	—	—	45.00

KM# 1829 DOLLAR
31.11 g., 0.999 Silver 0.9926 oz. ASW, 33 mm. **Ruler:** Elizabeth II **Rev:** Kookaburra **Note:** Ultra High Relief

Date	Mintage	F12	VF20	XF40	MS60	MS63
2012P	—	PF65 110				

KM# 1985 DOLLAR
31.14 g., 0.999 Silver 0.9936 oz. ASW, 40.6 mm. **Ruler:** Elizabeth II **Rev:** Kookaburra

Date	Mintage	F12	VF20	XF40	MS60	MS63
2013P	Est. 1000000	PF63 65.00		PF65 75.00		

KM# 1988 DOLLAR
31.14 g., 0.999 Silver 0.9936 oz. ASW, 32.6 mm. **Ruler:** Elizabeth II **Rev:** Kookaburra **Note:** High Releif.

Date	Mintage	F12	VF20	XF40	MS60	MS63
2013P	Est. 10000	PF63 70.00		PF65 75.00		

KM# 2117 DOLLAR
31.14 g., 0.999 Silver 0.9936 oz. ASW, 40.6 mm. **Ruler:** Elizabeth II **Rev:** Kookaburra sitting on tree branch surrounded by gum leaves

Date	Mintage	F12	VF20	XF40	MS60	MS63
2014P	—	—	—	—	—	45.00

KM# 623.1 2 DOLLARS
62.85 g., 0.999 Silver 2.0057 oz. ASW, 50 mm. **Ruler:** Elizabeth II **Obv:** Head with tiara right, denomination below **Rev:** Two kookaburras back to back **Edge:** Reeded

Date	Mintage	F12	VF20	XF40	MS60	MS63
2001	—	—	—	—	80.00	85.00

KM# 623.2 2 DOLLARS
62.21 g., 0.999 Silver 1.9851 oz. ASW **Ruler:** Elizabeth II **Subject:** USA State Quarters - 2001 **Obv:** Head with tiara right, denomination below **Rev:** Two kookaburras on branch with five

U.S. State Quarter designs added **Edge:** Segmented reeding **Note:** Prev. KM#623

Date	Mintage	F12	VF20	XF40	MS60	MS63
2001	10,000	—	—	—	145	160

KM# 678 2 DOLLARS
62.21 g., 0.999 Silver 1.9851 oz. ASW, 40 mm. **Ruler:** Elizabeth II **Obv:** Head with tiara right, denomination below **Obv. Designer:** Ian Rank-Broadley **Rev:** Kookaburra flying over Australian map **Edge:** Reeded

Date	Mintage	F12	VF20	XF40	MS60	MS63
2001P	1,261	PF65 90.00				
2002	1,500	—	—	—	—	82.00
Note: 1661 Spanish cob privy mark						
2002	1,500	—	—	—	—	82.00
Note: 1771 Spanish pillar dollar privy mark						
2002	1,500	—	—	—	—	82.00
Note: 1881 Gold sovereign privy mark						
2002	1,500	—	—	—	—	82.00
Note: 1991 Gold Australian nugget privy mark						

KM# 879 2 DOLLARS
62.85 g., 0.999 Silver 2.0057 oz. ASW, 40 mm. **Ruler:** Elizabeth II **Obv:** Head with tiara right **Obv. Designer:** Ian Rank-Broadley **Rev:** Kookaburra on branch plus two leaves **Edge:** Reeded

Date	Mintage	F12	VF20	XF40	MS60	MS63
2002P	1,262	PF65 90.00				
2003	1,000	—	—	—	—	115
Note: Boer War privy mark						
2003	1,000	—	—	—	—	115
Note: World War I privy mark						
2003	1,000	—	—	—	—	115
Note: World War II privy mark						
2003	1,000	—	—	—	—	115
Note: Korean War privy mark						
2003	1,000	—	—	—	—	115
Note: Vietnam War privy mark						

KM# 881 2 DOLLARS
62.21 g., 0.999 Silver 1.9851 oz. ASW, 50 mm. **Ruler:** Elizabeth II **Obv:** Head with tiara right **Obv. Designer:** Ian Rank-Broadley **Rev:** Two kookaburras, one in flight **Edge:** Reeded

Date	Mintage	F12	VF20	XF40	MS60	MS63
2003P	821	PF65 90.00				

KM# 884 2 DOLLARS
62.21 g., 0.999 Silver 1.9851 oz. ASW, 50 mm. **Ruler:** Elizabeth II **Obv:** Head with tiara right **Obv. Designer:** Ian Rank-Broadley **Rev:** Kookaburra perched on branch with four leaves **Edge:** Reeded

Date	Mintage	F12	VF20	XF40	MS60	MS63
2004P	800	PF65 90.00				

KM# 887 2 DOLLARS
62.21 g., 0.999 Silver 1.9851 oz. ASW, 50 mm. **Ruler:** Elizabeth II **Obv:** Head with tiara right **Obv. Designer:** Ian Rank-Broadley **Rev:** Two kookaburras on branch, one laughing **Edge:** Reeded

Date	Mintage	F12	VF20	XF40	MS60	MS63
2005P	795	PF65 90.00				

KM# 890 2 DOLLARS
62.21 g., 0.999 Silver 1.9851 oz. ASW, 50 mm. **Ruler:** Elizabeth II **Obv:** Head with tiara right **Obv. Designer:** Ian Rank-Broadley **Rev:** Kookaburra on branch, no leaves

Date	Mintage	F12	VF20	XF40	MS60	MS63
2007	—	—	—	—	85.00	—

KM# 1297 5 DOLLARS
1.55 g., 0.999 Gold 0.0495 oz. AGW, 14 mm. **Ruler:** Elizabeth II **Subject:** Kookaburra 20th Anniversary **Obv:** Head right **Obv. Designer:** Ian Rank-Broadley **Rev:** Kookaburra standing on stump right

Date	Mintage	F12	VF20	XF40	MS60	MS63
2009 P20	2,009	PF63 115	PF65 125			

KM# 1298 5 DOLLARS
1.55 g., 0.999 Gold 0.0495 oz. AGW, 14 mm. **Ruler:** Elizabeth II **Subject:** Kookaburra 20th Anniversary **Obv:** Head right **Obv. Designer:** Ian Rank-Broadley **Rev:** Kookaburra on branch, head right

Date	Mintage	F12	VF20	XF40	MS60	MS63
2009 P20	2,009	PF63 115	PF65 125			

KM# 1299 5 DOLLARS
1.55 g., 0.999 Gold 0.0495 oz. AGW, 14 mm. **Ruler:** Elizabeth II **Subject:** Kookaburra 20th Anniversary **Obv:** Head right **Obv. Designer:** Ian Rank-Broadley **Rev:** Kookaburra on branch left

Date	Mintage	F12	VF20	XF40	MS60	MS63
2009 P20	2,009	PF63 115	PF65 125			

KM# 1300 5 DOLLARS
1.55 g., 0.999 Gold 0.0495 oz. AGW, 14 mm. **Ruler:** Elizabeth II **Subject:** Kookaburra 20th Anniversary **Obv:** Head right **Obv. Designer:** Ian Rank-Broadley **Rev:** Kookaburra on branch feeding young at right

Date	Mintage	F12	VF20	XF40	MS60	MS63
2009 P20	2,009	PF63 115	PF65 125			

KM# 1301 5 DOLLARS
1.55 g., 0.999 Gold 0.0495 oz. AGW, 14 mm. **Ruler:** Elizabeth II **Subject:** Kookaburra 20th Anniversary **Obv:** Head right **Obv. Designer:** Ian Rank-Broadley **Rev:** Kookaburra pair on branch, heads opposite

Date	Mintage	F12	VF20	XF40	MS60	MS63
2009 P20	2,009	PF63 115	PF65 125			

KM# 1302 5 DOLLARS
1.55 g., 0.999 Gold 0.0495 oz. AGW, 14 mm. **Ruler:** Elizabeth II **Subject:** Kookaburra 20th Anniversary **Obv:** Head right **Obv. Designer:** Ian Rank-Broadley **Rev:** Kookaburra on branch, head left

Date	Mintage	F12	VF20	XF40	MS60	MS63
2009 P20	2,009	PF63 115	PF65 125			

KM# 1303 5 DOLLARS
1.55 g., 0.999 Gold 0.0495 oz. AGW, 14 mm. **Ruler:** Elizabeth II **Subject:** Kookaburra 20th Anniversary **Obv:** Head right **Obv. Designer:** Ian Rank-Broadley **Rev:** Kookaburra in flight right

Date	Mintage	F12	VF20	XF40	MS60	MS63
2009 P20	2,009	PF63 115	PF65 125			

KM# 1304 5 DOLLARS
1.55 g., 0.999 Gold 0.0495 oz. AGW, 14 mm. **Ruler:** Elizabeth II **Subject:** Kookaburra 20th Anniversary **Obv:** Head right **Obv. Designer:** Ian Rank-Broadley **Rev:** Kookaburra at nest left, head right

Date	Mintage	F12	VF20	XF40	MS60	MS63
2009 P20	2,009	PF63 115	PF65 125			

KM# 1305 5 DOLLARS
1.55 g., 0.999 Gold 0.0495 oz. AGW, 14 mm. **Ruler:** Elizabeth II **Subject:** Kookaburra 20th Anniversary **Obv:** Head right **Obv. Designer:** Ian Rank-Broadley **Rev:** Kookaburra on fence post

Date	Mintage	F12	VF20	XF40	MS60	MS63
2009 P20	2,009	PF63 115	PF65 125			

KM# 1306 5 DOLLARS
1.55 g., 0.999 Gold 0.0495 oz. AGW, 14 mm. **Ruler:** Elizabeth II **Subject:** Kookaburra 20th Anniversary **Obv:** Head right **Obv. Designer:** Ian Rank-Broadley **Rev:** Kookaburra pair left

Date	Mintage	F12	VF20	XF40	MS60	MS63
2009 P20	2,009	PF63 115	PF65 125			

KM# 1307 5 DOLLARS
1.55 g., 0.999 Gold 0.0495 oz. AGW, 14 mm. **Ruler:** Elizabeth II **Subject:** Kookaburra 20th Anniversary **Obv:** Head right **Obv. Designer:** Ian Rank-Broadley **Rev:** Kookaburra left on leafy branch

Date	Mintage	F12	VF20	XF40	MS60	MS63
2009 P20	2,009	PF63 115	PF65 125			

KM# 1308 5 DOLLARS
1.55 g., 0.999 Gold 0.0495 oz. AGW, 14 mm. **Ruler:** Elizabeth II **Subject:** Kookaburra 20th Anniversary **Obv:** Head right **Obv. Designer:** Ian Rank-Broadley **Rev:** Kookaburra pair facing opposite

Date	Mintage	F12	VF20	XF40	MS60	MS63
2009 P20	2,009	PF63 115	PF65 125			

KM# 1309 5 DOLLARS
1.55 g., 0.999 Gold 0.0495 oz. AGW, 14 mm. **Ruler:** Elizabeth II **Subject:** Kookaburra 20th Anniversary **Obv:** Head right **Obv. Designer:** Ian Rank-Broadley **Rev:** Kookaburra in flight on map of Australia

Date	Mintage	F12	VF20	XF40	MS60	MS63
2009 P20	2,009	PF63 115	PF65 125			

KM# 1310 5 DOLLARS
1.55 g., 0.999 Gold 0.0495 oz. AGW, 14 mm. **Ruler:** Elizabeth II **Subject:** Kookaburra 20th Anniversary **Obv:** Head right **Obv. Designer:** Ian Rank-Broadley **Rev:** Kookaburra on branch right

Date	Mintage	F12	VF20	XF40	MS60	MS63
2009 P20	2,009	PF63 115	PF65 125			

KM# 1311 5 DOLLARS
1.55 g., 0.999 Gold 0.0495 oz. AGW, 14 mm. **Ruler:** Elizabeth II **Subject:** Kookaburra 20th Anniversary **Obv:** Head right **Obv. Designer:** Ian Rank-Broadley **Rev:** Kookaburras, one in flight, one on branch

Date	Mintage	F12	VF20	XF40	MS60	MS63
2009 P20	2,009	PF63 115	PF65 125			

KM# 1312 5 DOLLARS
1.55 g., 0.999 Gold 0.0495 oz. AGW, 14 mm. **Ruler:** Elizabeth II **Subject:** Kookaburra 20th Anniversary **Obv:** Head right **Obv. Designer:** Ian Rank-Broadley **Rev:** Kookaburra on branch, head right

Date	Mintage	F12	VF20	XF40	MS60	MS63
2009 P20	2,009	PF63 115	PF65 125			

KM# 1313 5 DOLLARS
1.55 g., 0.999 Gold 0.0495 oz. AGW, 14 mm. **Ruler:** Elizabeth II **Subject:** Kookaburra 20th Anniversary **Obv:** Head right **Obv. Designer:** Ian Rank-Broadley **Rev:** Kookaburra pair on branch, one with head upward

Date	Mintage	F12	VF20	XF40	MS60	MS63
2009 P20	2,009	PF63 115	PF65 125			

KM# 1314 5 DOLLARS
1.55 g., 0.999 Gold 0.0495 oz. AGW, 14 mm. **Ruler:** Elizabeth II **Subject:** Kookaburra 20th Anniversary **Obv:** Head right **Obv. Designer:** Ian Rank-Broadley **Rev:** Kookaburra on branch left

Date	Mintage	F12	VF20	XF40	MS60	MS63
2009 P20	2,009	PF63 115	PF65 125			

KM# 1315 5 DOLLARS
1.55 g., 0.999 Gold 0.0495 oz. AGW, 14 mm. **Ruler:** Elizabeth II **Subject:** Kookaburra 20th Anniversary **Obv:** Head right **Obv. Designer:** Ian Rank-Broadley **Rev:** Kookaburra on branch admiring spider web

Date	Mintage	F12	VF20	XF40	MS60	MS63
2009 P20	2,009	PF63 115	PF65 125			

KM# 1316 5 DOLLARS
1.55 g., 0.999 Gold 0.0495 oz. AGW, 14 mm. **Ruler:** Elizabeth II **Subject:** Kookaburra 20th Anniversary **Obv:** Head right **Obv. Designer:** Ian Rank-Broadley **Rev:** Kookaburra on branch, sunburst in background

Date	Mintage	F12	VF20	XF40	MS60	MS63
2009 P20	2,009	PF63 115	PF65 125			

KM# 603 10 DOLLARS
311.04 g., 0.999 Silver 9.9257 oz. ASW, 74.9 mm. **Ruler:** Elizabeth II **Subject:** Kookaburra **Obv:** Head with tiara right, denomination below **Obv. Designer:** Ian Rank-Broadley **Rev:** Flying bird over map **Edge:** Reeded

Date	Mintage	F12	VF20	XF40	MS60	MS63
2002	—	PF65 400				

KM# 891 10 DOLLARS
311.04 g., 0.999 Silver 9.9257 oz. ASW, 74.9 mm. **Ruler:** Elizabeth II **Obv:** Head with tiara right **Obv. Designer:** Ian Rank-Broadley **Rev:** Kookaburra on branch, no leaves

Date	Mintage	F12	VF20	XF40	MS60	MS63
2007	—	—	—	—	400	—

KM# 1360 10 DOLLARS
311.04 g., 0.999 Silver 9.9257 oz. ASW, 75.5 mm. **Ruler:** Elizabeth II **Obv:** Head right **Rev:** Kookaburra

Date	Mintage	F12	VF20	XF40	MS60	MS63
2010(p)	—	PF65 425				

KM# 1693 10 DOLLARS
311.04 g., 0.999 Silver 9.9257 oz. ASW **Ruler:** Elizabeth II **Rev:** Kookaburra

Date	Mintage	F12	VF20	XF40	MS60	MS63
2012P	—	PF65 400				

KM# 1986 10 DOLLARS
311.35 g., 0.999 Silver 9.9357 oz. ASW, 75.6 mm. **Ruler:** Elizabeth II **Rev:** Kookaburra

Date	Mintage	F12	VF20	XF40	MS60	MS63
2013P	—	PF65 300				

KM# 2118 10 DOLLARS
311.35 g., 0.999 Silver 9.9357 oz. ASW, 75.6 mm. **Ruler:** Elizabeth II **Rev:** Kookaburra sitting on tree branch surrounded by gum leaves

Date	Mintage	F12	VF20	XF40	MS60	MS63
2014P	—	—	—	—	—	350

KM# 630 20 DOLLARS
62.21 g., 0.999 Silver 1.9851 oz. ASW **Ruler:** Elizabeth II **Subject:** USA State Quarters - 2002 **Obv:** Head with tiara right, denomination below **Rev:** Kookaburra on branch with five state quarter designs added below **Edge:** Reeded and plain sections

Date	Mintage	F12	VF20	XF40	MS60	MS63
2002	10,000	—	—	—	82.00	85.00

KM# 624 30 DOLLARS
1002.50 g., 0.999 Silver 31.9917 oz. ASW, 101 mm. **Ruler:** Elizabeth II **Subject:** USA State Quarters - 2001 **Obv:** Head with tiara right, denomination below **Rev:** Two kookaburras on branch with five state quarter designs added below **Edge:** Reeded and plain sections

Date	Mintage	F12	VF20	XF40	MS60	MS63
2001	1,000	—	—	—	—	1,200

KM# 680 30 DOLLARS
1002.50 g., 0.999 Silver 31.9917 oz. ASW, 101 mm. **Ruler:** Elizabeth II **Obv:** Head with tiara right, denomination below **Obv. Designer:** Ian Rank-Broadley **Rev:** Kookaburra in flight above Australian map **Edge:** Segmented reeding

Date	Mintage	F12	VF20	XF40	MS60	MS63
2001P	212	PF65 1,200				
2002	—	—	—	—	—	1,250

KM# 631 30 DOLLARS
1002.50 g., 0.999 Silver 31.9917 oz. ASW, 101 mm. **Ruler:** Elizabeth II **Subject:** USA State Quarters - 2002 **Obv:** Head with tiara right, denomination below **Rev:** Kookaburra on branch with five state quarter designs added in gold **Edge:** Reeded and plain sections

Date	Mintage	F12	VF20	XF40	MS60	MS63
2002	1,000	—	—	—	—	1,200

KM# 880 30 DOLLARS
1002.50 g., 0.999 Silver 31.9917 oz. ASW, 101 mm. **Ruler:** Elizabeth II **Obv:** Head with tiara right **Rev:** Kookaburra standing on branch **Edge:** Reeded

Date	Mintage	F12	VF20	XF40	MS60	MS63
2002P	190	PF65 1,250				

KM# 882 30 DOLLARS
1002.50 g., 0.999 Silver 31.9917 oz. ASW, 101 mm. **Ruler:** Elizabeth II **Obv:** Head with tiara right **Obv. Designer:** Ian Rank-Broadley **Rev:** Two kookaburras, one in flight **Edge:** Reeded

Date	Mintage	F12	VF20	XF40	MS60	MS63
2003P	135	PF65 1,250				

KM# 885 30 DOLLARS
1002.50 g., 0.999 Silver 31.9917 oz. ASW, 101 mm. **Ruler:** Elizabeth II **Obv:** Head with tiara right **Obv. Designer:** Ian Rank-Broadley **Rev:** Kookaburra perched on branch with four leaves **Edge:** Reeded

Date	Mintage	F12	VF20	XF40	MS60	MS63
2004P	165	PF65 1,250				

KM# 888 30 DOLLARS
1002.50 g., 0.999 Silver 31.9917 oz. ASW, 101 mm. **Ruler:** Elizabeth II **Obv:** Head with tiara right **Obv. Designer:** Ian Rank-Broadley **Rev:** Two kookaburras on branch, one laughing **Edge:** Reeded

Date	Mintage	F12	VF20	XF40	MS60	MS63
2005P	316	PF65 1,250				

KM# 892 30 DOLLARS
1002.50 g., 0.999 Silver 31.9917 oz. ASW, 101 mm. **Ruler:** Elizabeth II **Obv:** Head with tiara right **Obv. Designer:** Ian Rank-Broadley **Rev:** Kookaburras on branch, no leaves

Date	Mintage	F12	VF20	XF40	MS60	MS63
2007	—	—	—	—	1,200	—

KM# 1115 30 DOLLARS
1000.00 g., 0.999 Silver 31.9118 oz. ASW, 101 mm. **Ruler:** Elizabeth II **Rev:** Kookaburra on branch, sunburst background **Rev. Designer:** Darryl Bettolli

Date	Mintage	F12	VF20	XF40	MS60	MS63
2009P	—	PF65 1,300				

KM# 1361 30 DOLLARS
1000.00 g., 0.999 Silver 31.9118 oz. ASW, 100 mm. **Ruler:** Elizabeth II **Obv:** Head right **Rev:** Kookaburra

Date	Mintage	F12	VF20	XF40	MS60	MS63
2010(p)	—	—	—	—	—	1,200

KM# 1694 30 DOLLARS
1000.00 g., 0.999 Silver 31.9118 oz. ASW **Ruler:** Elizabeth II **Rev:** Kookaburra

Date	Mintage	F12	VF20	XF40	MS60	MS63
2012P	—	—	—	—	—	1,200

KM# 1987 30 DOLLARS
1001.00 g., 0.999 Silver 31.9438 oz. ASW, 100.6 mm. **Ruler:** Elizabeth II **Rev:** Kookaburra

Date	Mintage	F12	VF20	XF40	MS60	MS63
2013P	—	PF65 900				

KM# 2119 30 DOLLARS
1001.00 g., 0.999 Silver 31.9437 oz. ASW, 100.6 mm. **Ruler:** Elizabeth II **Rev:** Kookaburra sitting on tree branch surrounded by gum leaves

Date	Mintage	F12	VF20	XF40	MS60	MS63
2014P	—	—	—	—	—	1,000

KM# 2054 50 DOLLARS
15.55 g., 0.9999 Gold 0.4968 oz. AGW, 25.6 mm. **Ruler:** Elizabeth II **Obv:** Head with tiara right **Rev:** Kookaburra seated on branch

Date	Mintage	F12	VF20	XF40	MS60	MS63
2013P	550	PF65 1,000				

KM# 878 200 DOLLARS
31.60 g., 0.999 Silver 1.0084 oz. ASW, 40 mm. **Ruler:** Elizabeth II **Obv:** Head with tiara right with denomination **Obv. Designer:** Ian Rank-Broadley **Rev:** Kookaburra in flight over map of Australia **Note:** Mule.

Date	Mintage	F12	VF20	XF40	MS60	MS63
ND-2001	Est. 20	PF65 2,500				

BULLION - NUGGET

KM# 692 50 DOLLARS
15.50 g., 0.9999 Gold 0.4951 oz. AGW, 25.1 mm. **Ruler:** Elizabeth II **Subject:** Tribute to Liberty **Obv:** Head with tiara right, denomination below **Obv. Designer:** Ian Rank-Broadley **Rev:** Two kangaroos on map above silver Liberty Bell **Edge:** Reeded

Date	Mintage	F12	VF20	XF40	MS60	MS63
2001	419	—	—	—	875	—
2002	1,498	—	—	—	875	—
2002	515	PF65 900				

KM# 693 100 DOLLARS
31.10 g., 0.9999 Gold 0.9935 oz. AGW, 32.1 mm. **Ruler:** Elizabeth II **Subject:** Tribute to Liberty **Obv:** Head with tiara right, denomination below **Obv. Designer:** Ian Rank-Broadley **Rev:** Two kangaroos on map above silver Liberty Bell **Edge:** Reeded

Date	Mintage	F12	VF20	XF40	MS60	MS63
2001	1,498	—	—	—	1,735	—
2002	—	—	—	—	—	1,735

KM# 635 100 DOLLARS
31.10 g., 0.9999 Gold 0.9935 oz. AGW, 32.1 mm. **Ruler:** Elizabeth II **Subject:** Gold Panning **Obv:** Queen's head right **Rev:** Two prospectors dry panning for gold with color highlighted pans and dust **Edge:** Reeded

Date	Mintage	F12	VF20	XF40	MS60	MS63
2002P	1,500	PF65 1,775				

KM# 900 100 DOLLARS
31.10 g., 0.9999 Gold 0.9935 oz. AGW, 32 mm. **Ruler:** Elizabeth II **Obv:** Head with tiara right **Obv. Designer:** Ian Rank-Broadley **Rev:** Prospectors dry-blowing gold dust, colored image

Date	Mintage	F12	VF20	XF40	MS60	MS63
2002	940	—	—	—	1,735	—

KM# 906 100 DOLLARS
31.10 g., 0.999 Gold 0.9926 oz. AGW, 32 mm. **Ruler:** Elizabeth II **Obv:** Head with tiara right **Obv. Designer:** Ian Rank-Broadley **Rev:** Prospectors camp, colored image

Date	Mintage	F12	VF20	XF40	MS60	MS63
2003	658	—	—	—	1,735	—

KM# 741 100 DOLLARS

31.10 g., 0.9999 Gold 0.9935 oz. AGW, 32 mm. **Ruler:** Elizabeth II **Subject:** Eureka Stockade **Obv:** Head with tiara right, denomination below **Obv. Designer:** Ian Rank-Broadley **Rev:** Eureka Stockade leader Peter Lalor and blue flag, colored image **Edge:** Reeded

Date	Mintage	F12	VF20	XF40	MS60	MS63
2004	1,500	—	—	—	1,735	—
2004P	1,500	PF65 1,750				

KM# 915 100 DOLLARS

31.10 g., 0.999 Gold 0.9926 oz. AGW, 32 mm. **Ruler:** Elizabeth II **Subject:** Welcome Stranger Nugget **Obv:** Head with tiara right **Obv. Designer:** Ian Rank-Broadley **Rev:** Welcome Stranger Nugget surrounded by Outback setting, colored image

Date	Mintage	F12	VF20	XF40	MS60	MS63
2005	1,500	—	—	—	1,735	—

KM# 914 200 DOLLARS

62.21 g., 0.999 Gold 1.9854 oz. AGW, 41 mm. **Ruler:** Elizabeth II **Obv:** Head with tiara right **Obv. Designer:** Ian Rank-Broadley **Rev:** Kangaroo in multicolor bush

Date	Mintage	F12	VF20	XF40	MS60	MS63
2005	200	—	—	—	3,500	—

BULLION - KOALA

KM# 1838 10 CENTS

3.11 g., 0.999 Silver 0.0992 oz. ASW, 30 mm. **Ruler:** Elizabeth II **Rev:** Koala sleeping hugging branch **Rev. Designer:** Aleysha Howarth

Date	Mintage	F12	VF20	XF40	MS60	MS63
2012P		PF65 25.00				

KM# 1977 10 CENTS

3.14 g., 0.999 Silver 0.100 oz. ASW, 20.6 mm. **Ruler:** Elizabeth II **Rev:** Koala seated in tree **Rev. Designer:** Tom Vaughan

Date	Mintage	F12	VF20	XF40	MS60	MS63
2013P	—	PF65 20.00				

KM# 1366 50 CENTS

15.55 g., 0.999 Silver 0.4962 oz. ASW **Ruler:** Elizabeth II **Obv:** Head right **Rev:** Koala

Date	Mintage	F12	VF20	XF40	MS60	MS63
2010(p)	—	—	—	—	—	35.00

KM# 1688 50 CENTS

15.50 g., 0.999 Silver 0.4946 oz. ASW, 32 mm. **Ruler:** Elizabeth II **Rev:** Koala

Date	Mintage	F12	VF20	XF40	MS60	MS63
2012P	—	—	—	—	—	20.00

KM# 1798 50 CENTS

15.50 g., 0.999 Silver 0.4946 oz. ASW, 32 mm. **Ruler:** Elizabeth II **Rev:** Koala sleeping hugging branch

Date	Mintage	F12	VF20	XF40	MS60	MS63
2012P	—	—	—	—	—	40.00

KM# 1798a 50 CENTS

15.50 g., 0.999 Silver 0.4946 oz. ASW, 36.6 mm. **Ruler:** Elizabeth II **Rev:** Koala in color

Date	Mintage	F12	VF20	XF40	MS60	MS63
2012P	—	PF65 50.00				

KM# 1978 50 CENTS

15.59 g., 0.999 Silver 0.4975 oz. ASW, 36.6 mm. **Ruler:** Elizabeth II **Rev:** Koala seated in tree

Date	Mintage	F12	VF20	XF40	MS60	MS63
2013P	—	PF65 40.00				

KM# 1978a 50 CENTS

15.55 g., 0.9999 Silver 0.4967 oz. ASW, 36.6 mm. **Ruler:** Elizabeth II **Rev:** Koala seated in tree, color

Date	Mintage	F12	VF20	XF40	MS60	MS63
2013P	—	PF65 30.00				

KM# 1111a DOLLAR

31.11 g., 0.9999 Silver 0.9935 oz. ASW, 40.6 mm. **Ruler:** Elizabeth II **Rev:** Koala seated left on branch, gilt **Rev. Designer:** Darryl Bellotti

Date	Mintage	F12	VF20	XF40	MS60	MS63
2009P	10,000	PF65 60.00				

KM# 1111 DOLLAR

31.11 g., 0.999 Silver 0.9926 oz. ASW, 40.6 mm. **Ruler:** Elizabeth II **Rev:** Koala seated left on branch, shimmer background **Rev. Designer:** Darryl Bellotti

Date	Mintage	F12	VF20	XF40	MS60	MS63
2009P	—	—	—	—	—	45.00

KM# 1464a DOLLAR

31.11 g., 0.9999 Silver 0.9935 oz. ASW **Ruler:** Elizabeth II **Rev:** Koala on branch

Date	Mintage	F12	VF20	XF40	MS60	MS63
2010P	—	PF65 60.00				

KM# 1464 DOLLAR

31.11 g., 0.999 Silver 0.9926 oz. ASW, 40 mm. **Ruler:** Elizabeth II **Rev:** Koala on branch

Date	Mintage	F12	VF20	XF40	MS60	MS63
2010P	—	—	—	—	—	45.00

KM# 1840 DOLLAR

31.11 g., 0.999 Silver 0.9926 oz. ASW, 40.6 mm. **Ruler:** Elizabeth II **Rev:** Koala sleeping hugging branch **Rev. Designer:** Aleysha Howarth

Date	Mintage	F12	VF20	XF40	MS60	MS63
2012P Berlin privy mark	—	—	—	—	—	75.00
2012P	—	—	—	—	—	55.00

KM# 1689 DOLLAR
31.11 g., 0.999 Silver 0.9926 oz. ASW, 40.5 mm. **Ruler:** Elizabeth II **Rev:** Koala

Date	Mintage	F12	VF20	XF40	MS60	MS63
2012P	—	—	—	—	—	45.00

KM# 1828 DOLLAR
31.11 g., 0.999 Silver 0.9926 oz. ASW, 33 mm. **Ruler:** Elizabeth II **Rev:** Koala **Rev. Designer:** Aleysha Howarth **Note:** Ultra High Relief

Date	Mintage	F12	VF20	XF40	MS60	MS63
2012P		PF65 110				

KM# 1840b DOLLAR
31.11 g., 0.999 Silver 0.9926 oz. ASW, 40.6 mm. **Ruler:** Elizabeth II **Rev:** Koala sleeping hugging branch

Date	Mintage	F12	VF20	XF40	MS60	MS63
2012P	—	PF65 70.00				

KM# 1840a DOLLAR
31.11 g., 0.999 Silver 0.9926 oz. ASW, 40.6 mm. **Ruler:** Elizabeth II **Rev:** Gilt Koala sleeping hugging branch

Date	Mintage	F12	VF20	XF40	MS60	MS63
2012P	—	—	—	—	—	75.00

KM# 1979a DOLLAR
31.14 g., 0.999 Silver 0.9936 oz. ASW, 40.6 mm. **Ruler:** Elizabeth II **Rev:** Koala seated in tree, gilt **Rev. Designer:** Tom Vaughan

Date	Mintage	F12	VF20	XF40	MS60	MS63
2013P	Est. 10000	PF65 50.00				

KM# 1979 DOLLAR
31.14 g., 0.999 Silver 0.9936 oz. ASW, 40.6 mm. **Ruler:** Elizabeth II **Rev:** Koala seated in tree

Date	Mintage	F12	VF20	XF40	MS60	MS63
2013P	—	PF65 75.00				

KM# 1979b DOLLAR
31.14 g., 0.999 Silver 0.9936 oz. ASW, 40.6 mm. **Ruler:** Elizabeth II **Rev:** Koala seated in tree, in color **Rev. Designer:** Tom Vaughan

Date	Mintage	F12	VF20	XF40	MS60	MS63
2013 Proof		PF65 65.00				

KM# 2050 DOLLAR
31.14 g., 0.999 Silver 0.9936 oz. ASW, 32.6 mm. **Ruler:** Elizabeth II **Obv:** Head with tiara right **Rev:** Koala seated in tree **Rev. Designer:** Tom Vaughan **Note:** High relief.

Date	Mintage	F12	VF20	XF40	MS60	MS63
2013P	Est. 10000	PF65 90.00				

KM# 2078 2 DOLLARS
0.50 g., 0.9999 Gold AGW **Ruler:** Elizabeth II **Rev:** Seated Koala

Date	Mintage	F12	VF20	XF40	MS60	MS63
2013P Proof	—	—	—	—	—	50.00

KM# 916 5 DOLLARS
1.57 g., 0.999 Platinum 0.0501 oz. APW **Ruler:** Elizabeth II **Obv:** Head with tiara right **Obv. Designer:** Ian Rank-Broadley **Rev:** Two koalas on branch

Date	Mintage	F12	VF20	XF40	MS60	MS63
2001	809	PF65 125				

KM# 1868 5 DOLLARS
1.24 g., 0.999 Platinum 0.0396 oz. APW, 14.1 mm. **Ruler:** Elizabeth II **Rev:** Koala

Date	Mintage	F12	VF20	XF40	MS60	MS63
2002P	714	PF65 150				

KM# 1869 5 DOLLARS
1.24 g., 0.999 Platinum 0.0396 oz. APW, 14.1 mm. **Ruler:** Elizabeth II **Rev:** Koala

Date	Mintage	F12	VF20	XF40	MS60	MS63
2003P	99	PF65 150				

KM# 1870 5 DOLLARS
1.24 g., 0.999 Platinum 0.0396 oz. APW, 14.1 mm. **Ruler:** Elizabeth II **Rev:** Koala

Date	Mintage	F12	VF20	XF40	MS60	MS63
2004P	65	PF65 150				

KM# 1871 5 DOLLARS
1.24 g., 0.999 Platinum 0.0396 oz. APW, 14.1 mm. **Ruler:** Elizabeth II **Rev:** Koala

Date	Mintage	F12	VF20	XF40	MS60	MS63
2005P	200	PF65 150				

KM# 1872 5 DOLLARS
1.24 g., 0.999 Gold 0.0396 oz. AGW, 14.1 mm. **Ruler:** Elizabeth II **Rev:** Koala

Date	Mintage	F12	VF20	XF40	MS60	MS63
2008P	8,957	PF65 125				

KM# 1113 5 DOLLARS
1.24 g., 0.9999 Gold 0.0397 oz. AGW, 14.1 mm. **Ruler:** Elizabeth II **Rev:** Koala seated left on branch **Rev. Designer:** Darryl Bellotti

Date	Mintage	F12	VF20	XF40	MS60	MS63
2009P	15,000	PF65 95.00				

KM# 1467 5 DOLLARS
1.24 g., 0.999 Gold 0.0396 oz. AGW **Ruler:** Elizabeth II **Rev:** Koala on branch

Date	Mintage	F12	VF20	XF40	MS60	MS63
2010P	—	—	—	—	—	90.00

KM# 1843 5 DOLLARS
1.24 g., 0.999 Gold 0.0396 oz. AGW, 14.1 mm. **Ruler:** Elizabeth II **Rev:** Koala sleeping hugging branch

Date	Mintage	F12	VF20	XF40	MS60	MS63
2012P	—	PF65 150				

KM# 1841 8 DOLLARS
155.50 g., 0.999 Silver 4.9623 oz. ASW, 101 mm. **Ruler:** Elizabeth II **Rev:** Koala sleeping hugging branch **Rev. Designer:** Aleysha Howarth

Date	Mintage	F12	VF20	XF40	MS60	MS63
2012P	—	—	—	—	—	350

KM# 2044 8 DOLLARS
155.67 g., 0.999 Silver 4.9678 oz. ASW, 50.6 mm. **Ruler:** Elizabeth II **Rev:** Koala seated in tree **Note:** Ultra High Relief

Date	Mintage	F12	VF20	XF40	MS60	MS63
2013	Est. 5000	PF65 250				

KM# 1368 10 DOLLARS
311.35 g., 0.999 Silver 9.9357 oz. ASW **Ruler:** Elizabeth II **Obv:** Head right **Rev:** Koala

Date	Mintage	F12	VF20	XF40	MS60	MS63
2010P	—	—	—	—	—	400

KM# 1690 10 DOLLARS
311.35 g., 0.999 Silver 9.9357 oz. ASW **Ruler:** Elizabeth II **Rev:** Koala

Date	Mintage	F12	VF20	XF40	MS60	MS63
2012P	—	—	—	—	—	400

KM# 1980 10 DOLLARS
311.35 g., 0.999 Silver 9.9357 oz. ASW, 75.6 mm. **Ruler:** Elizabeth II **Rev:** Koala seated in tree

Date	Mintage	F12	VF20	XF40	MS60	MS63
2013P	—	PF65 300				

KM# 917 15 DOLLARS
3.11 g., 0.999 Platinum 0.0992 oz. APW **Ruler:** Elizabeth II **Obv:** Head with tiara right **Obv. Designer:** Ian Rank-Broadley **Rev:** Two koalas on a branch

Date	Mintage	F12	VF20	XF40	MS60	MS63
2001	407	PF65 210				

KM# 922 15 DOLLARS
3.11 g., 0.999 Platinum 0.0992 oz. APW **Ruler:** Elizabeth II **Obv:** Head with tiara right **Obv. Designer:** Ian Rank-Broadley **Rev:** Koala up a gum tree

Date	Mintage	F12	VF20	XF40	MS60	MS63
2002	665	PF65 210				

KM# 926 15 DOLLARS
3.11 g., 0.999 Platinum 0.0992 oz. APW **Ruler:** Elizabeth II **Obv:** Head with tiara right **Obv. Designer:** Ian Rank-Broadley **Rev:** Mother and baby koala

Date	Mintage	F12	VF20	XF40	MS60	MS63
2003	431	PF65 210				

KM# 931 15 DOLLARS
3.11 g., 0.999 Platinum 0.0992 oz. APW **Ruler:** Elizabeth II **Obv:** Head with tiara right **Obv. Designer:** Ian Rank-Broadley **Rev:** Single koala on branch

Date	Mintage	F12	VF20	XF40	MS60	MS63
2004	302	PF65 210				

KM# 935 15 DOLLARS
3.11 g., 0.999 Platinum 0.0992 oz. APW **Ruler:** Elizabeth II **Obv:** Head with tiara right **Obv. Designer:** Ian Rank-Broadley **Rev:** Single koala with gum leaves

Date	Mintage	F12	VF20	XF40	MS60	MS63
2005	700	PF65 210				

KM# 1873 15 DOLLARS
3.11 g., 0.999 Gold 0.0992 oz. AGW **Ruler:** Elizabeth II **Rev:** Koala

Date	Mintage	F12	VF20	XF40	MS60	MS63
2008P	5,030	PF65 250				

KM# 1114 15 DOLLARS
3.11 g., 0.9999 Gold 0.0993 oz. AGW, 16.1 mm. **Ruler:** Elizabeth II **Rev:** Koala seated left on tree branch **Rev. Designer:** Darryl Bellotti

Date	Mintage	F12	VF20	XF40	MS60	MS63
2009P	5,000	PF65 190				

KM# 1468 15 DOLLARS
3.11 g., 0.999 Gold 0.0992 oz. AGW **Ruler:** Elizabeth II **Rev:** Koala on branch

Date	Mintage	F12	VF20	XF40	MS60	MS63
2010P	—	—	—	—	—	190

KM# 1844 15 DOLLARS
3.11 g., 0.999 Gold 0.0992 oz. AGW **Ruler:** Elizabeth II **Rev:** Koala sleeping hugging branch

Date	Mintage	F12	VF20	XF40	MS60	MS63
2012P	—	PF65 250				

KM# 2049 15 DOLLARS
3.11 g., 0.9999 Gold 0.0993 oz. AGW, 16.1 mm. **Ruler:** Elizabeth II **Obv:** Head with tiara right **Rev:** Koala seated in tree **Rev. Designer:** Tom Vaughan

Date	Mintage	F12	VF20	XF40	MS60	MS63
2013P		PF65 225				

KM# 1982 15 DOLLARS
3.11 g., 0.9999 Gold 0.0994 oz. AGW, 16.1 mm. **Ruler:** Elizabeth II **Subject:** Australian Koala **Rev:** Koala seated in tree

Date	Mintage	F12	VF20	XF40	MS60	MS63
2013P	—	PF65 175				

KM# 2056 15 DOLLARS
3.11 g., 0.9999 Gold 0.0994 oz. AGW, 16.6 mm. **Ruler:** Elizabeth II **Obv:** Head with tiara right **Rev:** Koala seated in tree

Date	Mintage	F12	VF20	XF40	MS60	MS63
2013P	Est. 550	PF65 225				

KM# 918 25 DOLLARS
7.75 g., 0.999 Platinum 0.2473 oz. APW **Ruler:** Elizabeth II **Obv:** Head with tiara right **Obv. Designer:** Ian Rank-Broadley **Rev:** Two koalas on a branch

Date	Mintage	F12	VF20	XF40	MS60	MS63
2001	171	PF65 485				

KM# 923 25 DOLLARS
7.75 g., 0.999 Platinum 0.2473 oz. APW **Ruler:** Elizabeth II **Obv:** Head with tiara right **Obv. Designer:** Ian Rank-Broadley **Rev:** Koala up a gum tree

Date	Mintage	F12	VF20	XF40	MS60	MS63
2002	138	PF65 485				

KM# 927 25 DOLLARS
7.75 g., 0.999 Platinum 0.2473 oz. APW **Ruler:** Elizabeth II **Obv:** Head with tiara right **Obv. Designer:** Ian Rank-Broadley **Rev:** Mother and baby koala

Date	Mintage	F12	VF20	XF40	MS60	MS63
2003	99	PF65 485				

KM# 932 25 DOLLARS
7.75 g., 0.999 Platinum 0.2473 oz. APW **Ruler:** Elizabeth II **Obv:** Head with tiara right **Obv. Designer:** Ian Rank-Broadley **Rev:** Single koala on branch

Date	Mintage	F12	VF20	XF40	MS60	MS63
2004	65	PF65 485				

KM# 936 25 DOLLARS
7.75 g., 0.999 Platinum 0.2473 oz. APW **Ruler:** Elizabeth II **Obv:** Head with tiara right **Obv. Designer:** Ian Rank-Broadley **Rev:** Single koala with gum leaves

Date	Mintage	F12	VF20	XF40	MS60	MS63
2005	200	PF65 485				

KM# 1112 30 DOLLARS
1000.00 g., 0.9999 Silver 31.9406 oz. ASW, 100.6 mm. **Ruler:** Elizabeth II **Rev:** Koala seated left on branch **Rev. Designer:** Darryl Bellotti

Date	Mintage	F12	VF20	XF40	MS60	MS63
2009P Prooflike	—	—	—	—	—	1,150

KM# 1369 30 DOLLARS
1000.00 g., 0.999 Silver 31.9118 oz. ASW, 100.6 mm. **Ruler:** Elizabeth II **Obv:** Head light **Rev:** Koala

Date	Mintage	F12	VF20	XF40	MS60	MS63
2010(p)	—	—	—	—	—	1,150

KM# 1466 30 DOLLARS
1000.00 g., 0.999 Silver 31.9118 oz. ASW, 100.6 mm. **Ruler:** Elizabeth II **Rev:** Koala on branch

Date	Mintage	F12	VF20	XF40	MS60	MS63
2010P	—	—	—	—	—	1,200

KM# 1691 30 DOLLARS
1000.00 g., 0.999 Silver 31.9118 oz. ASW, 100.6 mm. **Ruler:** Elizabeth II **Rev:** Koala **Rev. Designer:** Aleysha Howarth

Date	Mintage	F12	VF20	XF40	MS60	MS63
2012P	—	—	—	—	—	1,200

KM# 1785 30 DOLLARS
1000.00 g., 0.999 Silver 31.9118 oz. ASW, 100.6 mm. **Ruler:** Elizabeth II **Obv:** Head with tiara right **Rev:** Koala hugging and lying on branch **Edge:** Reeded

Date	Mintage	F12	VF20	XF40	MS60	MS63
2012P		PF65 1,250				

KM# 1842 30 DOLLARS
1000.00 g., 0.999 Silver 31.9118 oz. ASW, 101 mm. **Ruler:** Elizabeth II **Rev:** Koala sleeping hugging branch

Date	Mintage	F12	VF20	XF40	MS60	MS63
2012P	—	—	—	—	—	1,400

KM# 1981 30 DOLLARS
1001.00 g., 0.999 Silver 31.9438 oz. ASW, 100.6 mm. **Ruler:** Elizabeth II **Rev:** Koala seated in tree

Date	Mintage	F12	VF20	XF40	MS60	MS63
2013P	—	PF65 1,000				
2013P	—	PF65 1,000				

KM# 919 50 DOLLARS
15.50 g., 0.999 Platinum 0.4947 oz. APW **Ruler:** Elizabeth II **Obv:** Head with tiara right **Obv. Designer:** Ian Rank-Broadley **Rev:** Two koalas on a branch

Date	Mintage	F12	VF20	XF40	MS60	MS63
2001	238	PF65 960				

KM# 924 50 DOLLARS
15.50 g., 0.999 Platinum 0.4947 oz. APW **Ruler:** Elizabeth II **Obv:** Head with tiara right **Obv. Designer:** Ian Rank-Broadley **Rev:** Koala up a gum tree

Date	Mintage	F12	VF20	XF40	MS60	MS63
2002	648	PF65 960				

KM# 928 50 DOLLARS
15.50 g., 0.999 Platinum 0.4947 oz. APW **Ruler:** Elizabeth II **Obv:** Head with tiara right **Obv. Designer:** Ian Rank-Broadley **Rev:** Mother and baby koala

Date	Mintage	F12	VF20	XF40	MS60	MS63
2003	180	PF65 960				

KM# 933 50 DOLLARS
15.50 g., 0.999 Platinum 0.4947 oz. APW **Ruler:** Elizabeth II **Obv:** Head with tiara right **Obv. Designer:** Ian Rank-Broadley **Rev:** Single koala on branch

Date	Mintage	F12	VF20	XF40	MS60	MS63
2004	148	PF65 960				

KM# 937 50 DOLLARS
15.50 g., 0.999 Platinum 0.4947 oz. APW. **Ruler:** Elizabeth II
Obv: Head with tiara right **Obv. Designer:** Ian Rank-Broadley
Rev: Single koala with gum leaves

Date	Mintage	F12	VF20	XF40	MS60	MS63
2005	297	PF65 960				

KM# 2040 50 DOLLARS
15.56 g., 0.9995 Platinum 0.4968 oz. APW, 25.1 mm. **Ruler:** Elizabeth II **Rev:** Koala standing **Rev. Designer:** Michael Tracey

Date	Mintage	F12	VF20	XF40	MS60	MS63
2013	1,200	PF65 1,485				

KM# 2055 50 DOLLARS
15.55 g., 0.9999 Gold 0.4968 oz. AGW, 25.6 mm. **Ruler:** Elizabeth II **Obv:** Head with tiara right **Rev:** Koala seated in tree

Date	Mintage	F12	VF20	XF40	MS60	MS63
2013P	Est. 550	PF65 1,000				

KM# 921 100 DOLLARS
31.10 g., 0.999 Platinum 0.9926 oz. APW **Ruler:** Elizabeth II **Obv:** Head with tiara right **Obv. Designer:** Ian Rank-Broadley **Rev:** Federation: Sir Henry Parkes, flag, parliament house, colored image

Date	Mintage	F12	VF20	XF40	MS60	MS63
2001	228	PF65 1,875				

KM# 1874 100 DOLLARS
31.11 g., 0.999 Platinum 0.9926 oz. APW **Ruler:** Elizabeth II **Rev:** Koala

Date	Mintage	F12	VF20	XF40	MS60	MS63
2002P	1,650	PF65 1,875				

KM# 930 100 DOLLARS
31.10 g., 0.999 Platinum 0.9926 oz. APW **Ruler:** Elizabeth II **Obv:** Head with tiara right **Obv. Designer:** Ian Rank-Broadley **Rev:** The Arts: Dancers, paint brushes, opera house, colored image

Date	Mintage	F12	VF20	XF40	MS60	MS63
2003	1,000	PF65 1,875				

KM# 742 100 DOLLARS
31.10 g., 0.999 Platinum 0.9931 oz. APW, 32.1 mm. **Ruler:** Elizabeth II **Obv:** Head with tiara right, denomination below **Obv. Designer:** Ian Rank-Broadley **Rev:** Sports: Australian sportsmen and women, colored image **Edge:** Reeded

Date	Mintage	F12	VF20	XF40	MS60	MS63
2004P	109	PF65 1,875				

KM# 939 100 DOLLARS
31.10 g., 0.999 Platinum 0.9926 oz. APW **Ruler:** Elizabeth II **Obv:** Head with tiara right **Obv. Designer:** Ian Rank-Broadley **Rev:** Two workers and machine, colored image

Date	Mintage	F12	VF20	XF40	MS60	MS63
2005	247	PF65 1,875				

KM# 1875 100 DOLLARS
31.11 g., 0.999 Gold 0.9926 oz. AGW, 32.1 mm. **Ruler:** Elizabeth II **Rev:** Koala

Date	Mintage	F12	VF20	XF40	MS60	MS63
2008P	1,860	PF65 1,800				

KM# 1469 100 DOLLARS
31.11 g., 0.999 Gold 0.9926 oz. AGW, 32.1 mm. **Ruler:** Elizabeth II **Rev:** Koala on branch

Date	Mintage	F12	VF20	XF40	MS60	MS63
2010P	—	—	—	—	—	1,800

KM# 1608 100 DOLLARS
31.11 g., 0.999 Gold 0.9926 oz. AGW, 28 mm. **Ruler:** Elizabeth II **Obv:** Head with tiara right **Rev:** Two pandas seated in fork of a eucalyptus tree **Edge:** Reeded **Note:** Ultra High Relief

Date	Mintage	F12	VF20	XF40	MS60	MS63
2011P	2,000	PF65 1,950				

KM# 1845 100 DOLLARS
31.11 g., 0.999 Gold 0.9926 oz. AGW, 28 mm. **Ruler:** Elizabeth II **Rev:** Koala sleeping hugging branch **Note:** Ultra High Relief

Date	Mintage	F12	VF20	XF40	MS60	MS63
2012P	—	PF65 1,900				

KM# 1983 100 DOLLARS
31.11 g., 0.9999 Gold 0.9936 oz. AGW, 27.3 mm. **Ruler:** Elizabeth II **Subject:** Australian Koala

Date	Mintage	F12	VF20	XF40	MS60	MS63
2013	Est. 2000	PF65 1,900				

KM# 2048 100 DOLLARS
31.11 g., 0.9999 Gold 0.9936 oz. AGW, 27.3 mm. **Ruler:** Elizabeth II **Obv:** Head with tiara right **Rev:** Koala seated in tree **Rev. Designer:** Tom Vaughan **Note:** High relief.

Date	Mintage	F12	VF20	XF40	MS60	MS63
2013P	—	PF65 2,250				

KM# 920 200 DOLLARS
62.21 g., 0.999 Platinum 1.9854 oz. APW, 41 mm. **Ruler:** Elizabeth II **Obv:** Head with tiara right **Obv. Designer:** Ian Rank-Broadley **Rev:** Two koalas sitting on branch

Date	Mintage	F12	VF20	XF40	MS60	MS63
2001	305	PF65 3,800				

KM# 925 200 DOLLARS
62.21 g., 0.999 Platinum 1.9854 oz. APW, 41 mm. **Ruler:** Elizabeth II **Obv:** Head with tiara right **Obv. Designer:** Ian Rank-Broadley **Rev:** Koala up a gum tree

Date	Mintage	F12	VF20	XF40	MS60	MS63
2002	117	PF65 3,800				

KM# 929 200 DOLLARS
62.21 g., 0.999 Platinum 1.9854 oz. APW, 41 mm. **Ruler:** Elizabeth II **Obv:** Head with tiara right **Obv. Designer:** Ian Rank-Broadley **Rev:** Mother and baby koala

Date	Mintage	F12	VF20	XF40	MS60	MS63
2003	65	PF65 3,800				

KM# 934 200 DOLLARS
62.21 g., 0.999 Platinum 1.9854 oz. APW, 41 mm. **Ruler:** Elizabeth II **Obv:** Head with tiara right **Obv. Designer:** Ian Rank-Broadley **Rev:** Single koala on branch

Date	Mintage	F12	VF20	XF40	MS60	MS63
2004	41	PF65 3,800				

KM# 938 200 DOLLARS
62.21 g., 0.999 Platinum 1.9854 oz. APW, 41 mm. **Ruler:** Elizabeth II **Obv:** Head with tiara right **Obv. Designer:** Ian Rank-Broadley **Rev:** Single koala with gum leaves in color

Date	Mintage	F12	VF20	XF40	MS60	MS63
2005	91	PF65 3,800				

KM# 1876 200 DOLLARS
62.24 g., 0.999 Gold 1.9862 oz. AGW, 40.6 mm. **Ruler:** Elizabeth II **Rev:** Koala

Date	Mintage	F12	VF20	XF40	MS60	MS63
2008P	250	PF65 3,750				

KM# 1470 200 DOLLARS
62.24 g., 0.999 Gold 1.9862 oz. AGW, 41 mm. **Ruler:** Elizabeth II **Rev:** Koala on branch

Date	Mintage	F12	VF20	XF40	MS60	MS63
2010P	—	—	—	—	—	3,750

KM# 1846 200 DOLLARS
62.20 g., 0.999 Gold 1.9849 oz. AGW, 40.6 mm. **Ruler:** Elizabeth II **Rev:** Koala sleeping hugging branch

Date	Mintage	F12	VF20	XF40	MS60	MS63
2012P	—	PF65 3,750				

KM# 1984 200 DOLLARS
62.22 g., 0.9999 Gold 1.9872 oz. AGW, 36.6 mm. **Ruler:** Elizabeth II **Rev:** Koala seated in tree **Note:** High relief.

Date	Mintage	F12	VF20	XF40	MS60	MS63
2013P	Est. 250	PF65 3,250				

KM# 2047 200 DOLLARS
62.22 g., 0.999 Gold 1.9854 oz. AGW, 36.6 mm. **Ruler:**
Elizabeth II **Obv:** Head with tiara right **Rev:** Koala seated in
tree **Rev. Designer:** Tom Vaughan **Note:** High relief.

Date	Mintage	F12	VF20	XF40	MS60	MS63
2013P	250	PF65 4,500				

BULLION - PLATYPUS

KM# 1731 100 DOLLARS
31.12 g., 0.9995 Platinum 0.9936 oz. APW, 32.6 mm. **Ruler:**
Elizabeth II **Obv:** Head with tiara right **Rev:** Platypus swimming
downward **Rev. Designer:** Natasha Muhl **Edge:** Reeded

Date	Mintage	F12	VF20	XF40	MS60	MS63
2012P	30,000	—	—	—	—	1,750
2013P	—	—	—	—	—	1,750
2014P	—	—	—	—	—	1,750

BULLION - LUNAR YEAR

KM# 1010 25 CENTS
0.999 Silver Gilt, 17.8 mm. **Ruler:** Elizabeth II **Obv:** Bust with
tiara right **Obv. Legend:** ELIZABETH II - AUSTRALIA **Obv.
Designer:** Ian Rank-Broadley **Rev:** 4 Chinese characters
Rev. Legend: LUNAR NEW YEAR - GOOD FORTUNE &
PROSPERITY

Date	Mintage	F12	VF20	XF40	MS60	MS63
2007	8,888	PF65 45.00				

KM# 1880 50 CENTS
15.55 g., 0.999 Silver 0.4962 oz. ASW, 32.1 mm. **Ruler:**
Elizabeth II **Subject:** Year of the Snake

Date	Mintage	F12	VF20	XF40	MS60	MS63
2001P	2,023	PF65 35.00				

KM# 579 50 CENTS
15.55 g., 0.999 Silver 0.4963 oz. ASW, 32.1 mm. **Ruler:**
Elizabeth II **Subject:** Year of the Horse **Obv:** Head with tiara
right, denomination below **Obv. Designer:** Ian Rank-Broadley
Rev: Horse running left **Edge:** Reeded

Date	Mintage	F12	VF20	XF40	MS60	MS63
2002P	1,810	PF65 35.00				

KM# 664 50 CENTS
16.40 g., 0.999 Silver 0.5234 oz. ASW, 31.9 mm. **Ruler:**
Elizabeth II **Subject:** Year of the Goat **Obv:** Head with tiara
right, denomination below **Obv. Designer:** Ian Rank-Broadley
Rev: Two goats **Edge:** Reeded

Date	Mintage	F12	VF20	XF40	MS60	MS63
2003	—	—	—	—	20.00	25.00
2003	1,028	PF65 35.00				

KM# 673 50 CENTS
15.55 g., 0.999 Silver 0.4963 oz. ASW, 32.1 mm. **Ruler:**
Elizabeth II **Subject:** Year of the Monkey **Obv:** Head with
tiara right, denomination below **Rev:** Monkey sitting on branch
Edge: Reeded

Date	Mintage	F12	VF20	XF40	MS60	MS63
2004	—	—	—	—	—	20.00
2004	930	PF65 35.00				

KM# 791 50 CENTS
15.57 g., 0.999 Silver 0.4968 oz. ASW, 32.1 mm. **Ruler:**
Elizabeth II **Subject:** Year of the Rooster **Obv:** Elizabeth II
Rev: Standing Rooster looking backwards **Edge:** Reeded

Date	Mintage	F12	VF20	XF40	MS60	MS63
2005P	—	—	—	—	—	20.00
2005P	900	PF65 50.00				

KM# 814 50 CENTS
15.55 g., 0.999 Silver 0.4962 oz. ASW **Ruler:** Elizabeth II
Subject: Bullion Lunar Year - Rooster **Obv:** Head with tiara right

Date	Mintage	F12	VF20	XF40	MS60	MS63
2005	—	—	—	—	—	20.00

KM# 1877 50 CENTS
15.55 g., 0.999 Silver 0.4962 oz. ASW, 32 mm. **Ruler:** Elizabeth
II **Subject:** Year of the Dog

Date	Mintage	F12	VF20	XF40	MS60	MS63
2006P	1,668	—	—	—	—	30.00

KM# 1878 50 CENTS
15.55 g., 0.999 Silver 0.4962 oz. ASW, 32 mm. **Ruler:** Elizabeth
II **Subject:** Year of the Pig

Date	Mintage	F12	VF20	XF40	MS60	MS63
2007P	1,339	—	—	—	—	30.00

KM# 1879 50 CENTS
15.55 g., 0.999 Silver 0.4962 oz. ASW, 32 mm. **Ruler:** Elizabeth
II **Subject:** Year of the Rat

Date	Mintage	F12	VF20	XF40	MS60	MS63
2008P	366	—	—	—	—	30.00

KM# 1750a 50 CENTS
15.55 g., 0.999 Silver 0.4962 oz. ASW, 32 mm. **Ruler:** Elizabeth
II **Subject:** Year of the Ox **Rev:** Two colored oxen standing

Date	Mintage	F12	VF20	XF40	MS60	MS63
2009P	—	—	—	—	—	100

KM# 1750 50 CENTS
15.55 g., 0.999 Silver 0.4962 oz. ASW, 32 mm. **Ruler:** Elizabeth
II **Subject:** Year of the Ox **Obv:** Head with tiara right **Rev:** Two
oxen standing

Date	Mintage	F12	VF20	XF40	MS60	MS63
2009P	—	—	—	—	—	85.00

KM# 1370 50 CENTS
15.55 g., 0.990 Silver 0.4918 oz. ASW, 32 mm. **Ruler:** Elizabeth II
Subject: Year of the Tiger **Obv:** Head right **Rev:** Tiger at rest left

Date	Mintage	F12	VF20	XF40	MS60	MS63
2010P	—	—	—	—	—	20.00

KM# 1474 50 CENTS
15.56 g., 0.999 Silver 0.4965 oz. ASW, 32 mm. **Ruler:** Elizabeth
II **Subject:** Year of the Rabbit **Rev:** Mother and baby rabbit
nose to nose

Date	Mintage	F12	VF20	XF40	MS60	MS63
2011P	—	PF65 30.00				

KM# 1663a 50 CENTS
15.55 g., 0.999 Silver 0.4963 oz. ASW, 32.1 mm. **Ruler:**
Elizabeth II **Subject:** Year of the Dragon **Rev:** Dragon in color

Date	Mintage	F12	VF20	XF40	MS60	MS63
2012P	—	PF65 30.00				

KM# 1663 50 CENTS
15.55 g., 0.999 Silver 0.4963 oz. ASW, 31.9 mm. **Ruler:**
Elizabeth II **Subject:** Year of the Dragon

Date	Mintage	F12	VF20	XF40	MS60	MS63
2012P	—	PF65 25.00				

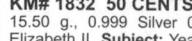

KM# 1832 50 CENTS
15.50 g., 0.999 Silver 0.4946 oz. ASW, 36.6 mm. **Ruler:**
Elizabeth II **Subject:** Year of the Snake **Obv:** Head with tiara
right **Obv. Designer:** Ian Rank Broadley **Rev:** Snake

Date	Mintage	F12	VF20	XF40	MS60	MS63
2013P	—	PF65 40.00				

KM# 1832a 50 CENTS
15.55 g., 0.999 Silver 0.4962 oz. ASW, 36.6 mm. **Ruler:** Elizabeth II **Subject:** Year of the Snake **Rev:** Snake in color

Date	Mintage	F12	VF20	XF40	MS60	MS63
2013P	—	PF65 35.00				

KM# 2110 50 CENTS
15.59 g., 0.9999 Silver 0.498 oz. ASW, 36.6 mm. **Ruler:** Elizabeth II **Subject:** Year of the Horse **Rev:** Two horses standing, one drinking from stream

Date	Mintage	F12	VF20	XF40	MS60	MS63
2014P	—	PF65 25.00				
2014P	—					22.50

KM# 536 DOLLAR
31.10 g., 0.999 Silver 0.9926 oz. ASW, 40.6 mm. **Ruler:** Elizabeth II **Subject:** Year of the Snake **Obv:** Head with tiara right, denomination below **Obv. Designer:** Ian Rank-Broadley **Rev:** Snake with eggs **Edge:** Reeded

Date	Mintage	F12	VF20	XF40	MS60	MS63
2001	300,000	—	—	—	80.00	100
2001P	3,354	PF65 100				

KM# 536a DOLLAR
31.64 g., 0.999 Silver 1.0095 oz. ASW, 40.6 mm. **Ruler:** Elizabeth II **Subject:** Year of the Snake **Obv:** Head with tiara right, denomination below **Rev:** Gold-plated snake **Edge:** Reeded

Date	Mintage	F12	VF20	XF40	MS60	MS63
2001	16,335	—	—	—	45.00	50.00

KM# 580 DOLLAR
31.10 g., 0.999 Silver 0.9926 oz. ASW, 40.6 mm. **Ruler:** Elizabeth II **Subject:** Year of the Horse **Obv:** Head with tiara right, denomination below **Obv. Designer:** Ian Rank-Broadley **Rev:** Horse running left **Edge:** Reeded

Date	Mintage	F12	VF20	XF40	MS60	MS63
2002P	—	—	—	—	75.00	80.00
2002P	2,011	PF65 75.00				

KM# 580a DOLLAR
31.64 g., 0.999 Silver 1.0095 oz. ASW, 40.6 mm. **Ruler:** Elizabeth II **Obv:** Head with tiara right **Rev:** Gold-plated horse **Edge:** Reeded

Date	Mintage	F12	VF20	XF40	MS60	MS63
2002	16,859	—	—	—	40.00	45.00

KM# 665 DOLLAR
31.62 g., 0.999 Silver 1.0091 oz. ASW, 40.3 mm. **Ruler:** Elizabeth II **Subject:** Year of the Goat **Obv:** Head with tiara right, denomination below **Obv. Designer:** Ian Rank-Broadley **Rev:** Two goats **Edge:** Reeded

Date	Mintage	F12	VF20	XF40	MS60	MS63
2003	—	—	—	—	50.00	75.00
2003	1,489	PF65 75.00				

KM# 665a DOLLAR
31.64 g., 0.999 Silver 1.0095 oz. ASW, 40.6 mm. **Ruler:** Elizabeth II **Subject:** Year of the Goat **Obv:** Head with tiara right, denomination below **Rev:** Gold-plated goat **Edge:** Reeded

Date	Mintage	F12	VF20	XF40	MS60	MS63
2003	15,842	—	—	—	50.00	55.00

KM# 674 DOLLAR
31.10 g., 0.999 Silver 0.9926 oz. ASW, 40.6 mm. **Ruler:** Elizabeth II **Subject:** Year of the Monkey **Obv:** Head with tiara right, denomination below **Rev:** Monkey sitting on branch **Edge:** Reeded

Date	Mintage	F12	VF20	XF40	MS60	MS63
2004	—	—	—	—	40.00	45.00
2004	1,187	PF65 55.00				

KM# 674a DOLLAR
31.64 g., 0.999 Silver 1.0095 oz. ASW, 40.6 mm. **Ruler:** Elizabeth II **Subject:** Year of the Monkey **Obv:** Head with tiara right, denomination below **Rev:** Monkey, gilt **Edge:** Reeded

Date	Mintage	F12	VF20	XF40	MS60	MS63
2004	25,599	—	—	—	50.00	55.00

KM# 674b DOLLAR
31.10 g., 0.999 Silver 0.9926 oz. ASW, 40.6 mm. **Ruler:** Elizabeth II **Subject:** Year of the Monkey **Rev:** Monkey in color

Date	Mintage	F12	VF20	XF40	MS60	MS63
2004P	31,406	—	—	—	—	75.00

KM# 695b DOLLAR
31.11 g., 0.999 Silver 0.9926 oz. ASW, 40.5 mm. **Ruler:** Elizabeth II **Subject:** Year of the Rooster **Rev:** Gilt field, colored Rooster

Date	Mintage	F12	VF20	XF40	MS60	MS63
2005P	8,832	—	—	—	—	60.00

KM# 695c DOLLAR
31.11 g., 0.999 Silver 0.9926 oz. ASW, 40.5 mm. **Ruler:** Elizabeth II **Subject:** Year of the Rooster **Rev:** Colored Rooster

Date	Mintage	F12	VF20	XF40	MS60	MS63
2005P	38,000	—	—	—	—	60.00

KM# 695a DOLLAR
31.64 g., 0.999 Silver 1.0095 oz. ASW, 40.5 mm. **Ruler:** Elizabeth II **Subject:** Year of the Rooster **Obv:** Head with tiara right, denomination below **Rev:** Gilt rooster **Edge:** Reeded

Date	Mintage	F12	VF20	XF40	MS60	MS63
2005 Polished fields	28,960	—	—	—	45.00	50.00
2005 Matte fields	—	—	—	—	175	185

KM# 695 DOLLAR
31.11 g., 0.999 Silver 0.9926 oz. ASW, 40.5 mm. **Ruler:** Elizabeth II **Subject:** Year of the Rooster **Obv:** Head with tiara right, denomination below **Rev:** Rooster **Edge:** Reeded

Date	Mintage	F12	VF20	XF40	MS60	MS63
2005	—	—	—	—	75.00	65.00
2005P	1,734	PF65 80.00				

KM# 1882 DOLLAR
31.11 g., 0.999 Silver 0.9926 oz. ASW, 40 mm. **Ruler:** Elizabeth II **Subject:** Year of the Dog

Date	Mintage	F12	VF20	XF40	MS60	MS63
2006P	2,887	PF65 50.00				

KM# 1883 DOLLAR
31.11 g., 0.999 Silver 0.9926 oz. ASW, 40 mm. **Ruler:** Elizabeth II **Subject:** Year of the Pig

Date	Mintage	F12	VF20	XF40	MS60	MS63
2007P	2,833	PF65 50.00				

KM# 1755a DOLLAR
31.11 g., 0.999 Silver 0.9926 oz. ASW, 40 mm. **Ruler:** Elizabeth II **Subject:** Year of the Mouse **Obv:** Head with tiara right **Rev:** Mouse pair in color

Date	Mintage	F12	VF20	XF40	MS60	MS63
2008P	—	—	—	—	—	85.00

KM# 1755 DOLLAR
31.11 g., 0.999 Silver 0.9926 oz. ASW, 40 mm. **Ruler:** Elizabeth II **Subject:** Year of the Mouse **Obv:** Head with tiara right **Rev:** Mouse pair

Date	Mintage	F12	VF20	XF40	MS60	MS63
2008P	4,715	—	—	—	—	75.00

KM# 1755b DOLLAR
31.11 g., 0.999 Silver 0.9926 oz. ASW, 40 mm. **Ruler:** Elizabeth II **Subject:** Year of the Rat **Rev:** Mouse gilt

Date	Mintage	F12	VF20	XF40	MS60	MS63
2008P	—	—	—	—	—	85.00

KM# 1755c DOLLAR
31.11 g., 0.999 Silver 0.9926 oz. ASW, 40.5 mm. **Ruler:** Elizabeth II **Subject:** Year of the Rat **Rev:** Mouse with diamond chip in eye

Date	Mintage	F12	VF20	XF40	MS60	MS63
2008P	—	—	—	—	—	95.00

KM# 1317a DOLLAR
31.11 g., 0.999 Silver 0.9926 oz. ASW, 40.6 mm. **Ruler:** Elizabeth II **Subject:** Year of the Tiger **Obv:** Head right **Obv. Designer:** Ian Rank-Broadley **Rev:** Tiger at rest left, partially gilt

Date	Mintage	F12	VF20	XF40	MS60	MS63
2010P	50,000	PF65 80.00				

KM# 1317 DOLLAR
31.11 g., 0.999 Silver 0.9926 oz. ASW, 40.6 mm. **Ruler:** Elizabeth II **Subject:** Year of the Tiger **Obv:** Head right **Obv. Designer:** Ian Rank-Broadley **Rev:** Tiger at rest left

Date	Mintage	F12	VF20	XF40	MS60	MS63
2010P	—	—	—	—	—	50.00
2010P	1,000	PF65 75.00				

KM# 1317b DOLLAR
31.11 g., 0.999 Silver 0.9926 oz. ASW, 40.6 mm. **Ruler:** Elizabeth II **Subject:** Year of the Tiger **Obv:** Head right **Obv. Designer:** Ian Rank-Broadley **Rev:** Multicolor tiger at rest left

Date	Mintage	F12	VF20	XF40	MS60	MS63
2010P	170,000	PF65 75.00				

KM# 1475a DOLLAR

31.11 g., 0.999 Silver 0.9926 oz. ASW, 40.5 mm. **Ruler:** Elizabeth II **Subject:** Year of the Rabbit **Rev:** Two rabbits, partially gilt

Date	Mintage	F12	VF20	XF40	MS60	MS63
2011P	—			PF65 75.00		

KM# 1475 DOLLAR

31.11 g., 0.999 Silver 0.9926 oz. ASW, 40 mm. **Ruler:** Elizabeth II **Subject:** Year of the Rabbit **Rev:** Mother and baby rabbit nose to nose

Date	Mintage	F12	VF20	XF40	MS60	MS63
2011P	—			PF65 50.00		

KM# 1475b DOLLAR

31.11 g., 0.999 Silver 0.9926 oz. ASW, 40.5 mm. **Ruler:** Elizabeth II **Subject:** Year of the Rabbit **Rev:** Two rabbits in color

Date	Mintage	F12	VF20	XF40	MS60	MS63
2011P	—			PF65 75.00		

KM# 1664.1 DOLLAR

31.11 g., 0.999 Silver 0.9926 oz. ASW, 40.5 mm. **Ruler:** Elizabeth II **Subject:** Year of the Dragon **Rev:** Dragon gilt

Date	Mintage	F12	VF20	XF40	MS60	MS63
2012P	—			PF65 75.00		

KM# 1664.3 DOLLAR

31.11 g., 0.999 Silver 0.9926 oz. ASW, 40 mm. **Ruler:** Elizabeth II **Subject:** Year of the Dragon **Obv:** Head with tiara right **Rev:** Dragon colored red, brown and yellow

Date	Mintage	F12	VF20	XF40	MS60	MS63
2012P	20,000	—	—	—	—	100

KM# 1664.2 DOLLAR

31.11 g., 0.999 Silver 0.9926 oz. ASW, 40.5 mm. **Ruler:** Elizabeth II **Subject:** Year of the Dragon **Rev:** Dragon in black collor

Date	Mintage	F12	VF20	XF40	MS60	MS63
2012P	—				—	70.00
2012P	—			PF65 75.00		

KM# 1664.4 DOLLAR

31.11 g., 0.999 Silver 0.9926 oz. ASW, 40 mm. **Ruler:** Elizabeth II **Subject:** Year of the Dragon **Obv:** Bust with tiara right **Rev:** Dragon colored black and red

Date	Mintage	F12	VF20	XF40	MS60	MS63
2012P	—				—	100

KM# 1664.5 DOLLAR

31.11 g., 0.999 Silver 0.9926 oz. ASW, 40 mm. **Ruler:** Elizabeth II **Subject:** Year of the Dragon **Obv:** Head with tiara right **Rev:** Dragon colored yellow and lavender

Date	Mintage	F12	VF20	XF40	MS60	MS63
2012P	—				—	100

KM# 1664.6 DOLLAR

31.11 g., 0.999 Silver 0.9926 oz. ASW, 40 mm. **Ruler:** Elizabeth II **Subject:** Year of the Dragon **Obv:** Head with tiara right **Rev:** Dragon colored blue and yellow

Date	Mintage	F12	VF20	XF40	MS60	MS63
2012P	—				—	100

KM# 1664.7 DOLLAR

31.11 g., 0.999 Silver 0.9926 oz. ASW, 40 mm. **Ruler:** Elizabeth II **Subject:** Year of the Dragon **Obv:** Head with tiara right **Rev:** Dragon colored purple and yellow

Date	Mintage	F12	VF20	XF40	MS60	MS63
2012P	—				—	100

KM# 1664.8 DOLLAR

31.11 g., 0.999 Silver 0.9926 oz. ASW, 40 mm. **Ruler:** Elizabeth II **Subject:** Year of the Dragon **Obv:** Head with tiara right **Rev:** Dragon colored orange, brown and yellow

Date	Mintage	F12	VF20	XF40	MS60	MS63
2012P	—				—	100

KM# 1664.9 DOLLAR

31.11 g., 0.999 Silver 0.9926 oz. ASW, 40 mm. **Ruler:** Elizabeth II **Subject:** Year of the Dragon **Obv:** Head with tiara right **Rev:** Dragon colored white and blue

Date	Mintage	F12	VF20	XF40	MS60	MS63
2012P	—				—	100

KM# 1664.10 DOLLAR

31.11 g., 0.999 Silver 0.9926 oz. ASW, 40 mm. **Ruler:** Elizabeth II **Subject:** Year of the Dragon **Obv:** Head with tiara right **Rev:** Dragon colored brown and orange

Date	Mintage	F12	VF20	XF40	MS60	MS63
2012P	—				—	100

KM# 1664.11 DOLLAR

31.11 g., 0.999 Silver 0.9926 oz. ASW, 40 mm. **Ruler:** Elizabeth II **Subject:** Year of the Dragon **Obv:** head with tiara right **Rev:** Dragon colored lavender and grey

Date	Mintage	F12	VF20	XF40	MS60	MS63
2012P	—				—	100

KM# 1664 DOLLAR

31.11 g., 0.999 Silver 0.9926 oz. ASW, 40.5 mm. **Ruler:** Elizabeth II **Subject:** Year of the Dragon **Rev:** Dragon

Date	Mintage	F12	VF20	XF40	MS60	MS63
2012P	—				—	40.00
2012P Lion privy mark	—				—	60.00
2012P	—			PF65 45.00		

KM# 1713 DOLLAR

31.14 g., 0.999 Silver 0.9936 oz. ASW, 32.6 mm. **Ruler:** Elizabeth II **Subject:** Year of the Dragon **Obv:** Head with tiara right **Rev:** Dragon **Edge:** Reeded **Note:** High Relief

Date	Mintage	F12	VF20	XF40	MS60	MS63
2012P	7,500			PF65 100		

KM# 1793 DOLLAR

31.11 g., 0.999 Silver 0.9926 oz. ASW **Ruler:** Elizabeth II **Subject:** Year of the Dragon **Note:** High releif

Date	Mintage	F12	VF20	XF40	MS60	MS63
2012P	—			PF65 75.00		

KM# 1831 DOLLAR
31.11 g., 0.999 Silver 0.9926 oz. ASW, 40.6 mm. **Ruler:** Elizabeth II **Subject:** Year of the Snake

Date	Mintage	F12	VF20	XF40	MS60	MS63
2013P	—	PF65 50.00				
2013P	—	—	—	—	—	40.00

KM# 1827 DOLLAR
31.11 g., 0.999 Silver 0.9926 oz. ASW, 32.6 mm. **Ruler:** Elizabeth II **Subject:** Year of the Snake **Note:** Ultra high relief

Date	Mintage	F12	VF20	XF40	MS60	MS63
2013P	7,500	PF65 110				

KM# 1831b DOLLAR
31.11 g., 0.999 Silver 0.9926 oz. ASW, 40.6 mm. **Ruler:** Elizabeth II **Subject:** Year of the Snake **Rev:** Snake in color

Date	Mintage	F12	VF20	XF40	MS60	MS63
2013P	—	—	—	—	—	65.00
2013P	—	PF65 75.00				

KM# 1831a DOLLAR
31.11 g., 0.999 Silver 0.9926 oz. ASW, 40.6 mm. **Ruler:** Elizabeth II **Subject:** Year of the Snake **Rev:** Gilt snake

Date	Mintage	F12	VF20	XF40	MS60	MS63
2013P	—	—	—	—	—	60.00
2013P	—	PF65 75.00				

KM# 1831c DOLLAR
31.14 g., 0.999 Silver 0.9936 oz. ASW, 40.6 mm. **Ruler:** Elizabeth II **Subject:** Year of the Snake **Rev:** Snake in green **Note:** Sold at the Berlin World Money Fair.

Date	Mintage	F12	VF20	XF40	MS60	MS63
2013P	—	PF65 100				

KM# 1970 DOLLAR
31.10 g., 0.999 Silver 0.9925 oz. ASW, 40 mm. **Ruler:** Elizabeth II **Subject:** Year of the Snake **Rev. Designer:** Chrissy Lau

Date	Mintage	F12	VF20	XF40	MS60	MS63
2013 Proof-like Est. 10000	—	—	—	—	—	65.00

KM# 2155 DOLLAR
31.11 g., 0.999 Silver 0.9926 oz. ASW, 40 mm. **Ruler:** Elizabeth II **Subject:** Year of the Snake **Obv:** Head with tiara right **Rev:** Snake coiled upwards

Date	Mintage	F12	VF20	XF40	MS60	MS63
2013	—	PF65 50.00				

KM# 2111 DOLLAR
31.14 g., 0.9999 Silver 0.9945 oz. ASW, 45.6 mm. **Ruler:** Elizabeth II **Subject:** Year of the Horse **Rev:** Two horses standing, one drinking from stream

Date	Mintage	F12	VF20	XF40	MS60	MS63
2014P	—	PF65 50.00				
2014P	300,000	—	—	—	—	45.00

KM# 537 2 DOLLARS
62.21 g., 0.999 Silver 1.9851 oz. ASW, 50.3 mm. **Ruler:** Elizabeth II **Subject:** Year of the Snake **Obv:** Head with tiara right, denomination below **Rev:** Snake with eggs **Edge:** Segmented reeding

Date	Mintage	F12	VF20	XF40	MS60	MS63
2001	—	—	—	—	75.00	85.00
2001P	1,827	PF65 110				

KM# 581 2 DOLLARS
62.21 g., 0.999 Silver 1.9851 oz. ASW, 50 mm. **Ruler:** Elizabeth II **Obv:** Head with tiara right, denomination below **Rev:** Horse running left **Edge:** Reeded

Date	Mintage	F12	VF20	XF40	MS60	MS63
2002	—	—	—	—	75.00	85.00
2002P	1,118	PF65 110				

KM# 679 2 DOLLARS
62.85 g., 0.999 Silver 2.0057 oz. ASW, 50 mm. **Ruler:** Elizabeth II **Subject:** Year of the Goat **Obv:** Head with tiara right, denomination below **Rev:** Two goats **Edge:** Reeded

Date	Mintage	F12	VF20	XF40	MS60	MS63
2003	—	—	—	—	75.00	85.00
2003P	669	PF65 110				

KM# 675 2 DOLLARS
62.21 g., 0.999 Silver 1.9851 oz. ASW, 50 mm. **Ruler:** Elizabeth II **Subject:** Year of the Monkey **Obv:** Head with tiara right, denomination below **Rev:** Monkey sitting on branch **Edge:** Reeded

Date	Mintage	F12	VF20	XF40	MS60	MS63
2004	—	—	—	—	75.00	85.00
2004	520	PF65 110				

KM# 793 2 DOLLARS
62.27 g., 0.999 Silver 1.9871 oz. ASW, 50.3 mm. **Ruler:** Elizabeth II **Subject:** Year of the Rooster **Obv:** Elizabeth II **Rev:** Standing Rooster looking backwards **Edge:** Reeded

Date	Mintage	F12	VF20	XF40	MS60	MS63
2005P	555	PF65 150				

KM# 1884 2 DOLLARS
62.27 g., 0.999 Silver 1.9871 oz. ASW, 50.3 mm. **Ruler:** Elizabeth II **Subject:** Year of the Dog

Date	Mintage	F12	VF20	XF40	MS60	MS63
2006P	1,375	—	—	—	—	125

KM# 1885 2 DOLLARS
62.27 g., 0.999 Silver 1.9871 oz. ASW, 50.3 mm. **Ruler:** Elizabeth II **Subject:** Year of the Pig

Date	Mintage	F12	VF20	XF40	MS60	MS63
2007P	702	—	—	—	—	125

KM# 1886 2 DOLLARS
62.27 g., 0.999 Silver 1.9871 oz. ASW, 50.3 mm. **Ruler:** Elizabeth II **Subject:** Year of the Rat

Date	Mintage	F12	VF20	XF40	MS60	MS63
2008P	366	—	—	—	—	125

KM# 1751a 2 DOLLARS
62.27 g., 0.999 Silver 1.9871 oz. ASW, 50 mm. **Ruler:** Elizabeth II **Subject:** Year of the Ox **Obv:** Head with tiara right **Rev:** Two colored oxen standing

Date	Mintage	F12	VF20	XF40	MS60	MS63
2009P	—	—	—	—	—	125

KM# 1751 2 DOLLARS
62.27 g., 0.999 Silver 1.9871 oz. ASW, 50 mm. **Ruler:** Elizabeth II **Subject:** Year of the Ox **Obv:** Head with tiara right **Rev:** Two oxen standing

Date	Mintage	F12	VF20	XF40	MS60	MS63
2009P	—	—	—	—	—	125

KM# 1320 2 DOLLARS
62.21 g., 0.999 Silver 1.9852 oz. ASW, 50 mm. **Ruler:** Elizabeth II **Subject:** Year of the Tiger **Obv:** Head right **Obv. Designer:** Ian Rank-Broadley **Rev:** Tiger seated left

Date	Mintage	F12	VF20	XF40	MS60	MS63
2010P	1,000	PF65 160				

KM# 1476 2 DOLLARS
62.20 g., 0.999 Silver 1.9849 oz. ASW **Ruler:** Elizabeth II **Subject:** Year of the Rabbit **Rev:** Mother and baby rabbit nose to nose

Date	Mintage	F12	VF20	XF40	MS60	MS63
2011P	—	PF65 110				

KM# 1665 2 DOLLARS
62.27 g., 0.999 Silver 1.9871 oz. ASW, 50.3 mm. **Ruler:** Elizabeth II **Subject:** Year of the Dragon

Date	Mintage	F12	VF20	XF40	MS60	MS63
2012P	—	PF65 150				

KM# 1833 2 DOLLARS
62.20 g., 0.999 Silver 1.9849 oz. ASW, 50.3 mm. **Ruler:** Elizabeth II **Subject:** Year of the Snake

Date	Mintage	F12	VF20	XF40	MS60	MS63
2013P	—	PF65 150				

KM# 1833a 2 DOLLARS
62.27 g., 0.999 Silver 1.9871 oz. ASW, 50.3 mm. **Ruler:** Elizabeth II **Subject:** Year of the Snake **Rev:** Snake in color

Date	Mintage	F12	VF20	XF40	MS60	MS63
2013P	—	—	—	—	—	140
2013P	—	PF65 150				

KM# 2112 2 DOLLARS
62.27 g., 0.9999 Silver 1.9889 oz. ASW, 55.6 mm. **Ruler:** Elizabeth II **Subject:** Year of the Horse **Rev:** Two horses standing, one drinking from stream

Date	Mintage	F12	VF20	XF40	MS60	MS63
2014P	—	PF65 80.00				
2014P	—	—	—	—	—	75.00

KM# 538 5 DOLLARS
1.57 g., 0.999 Gold 0.0501 oz. AGW, 14.1 mm. **Ruler:** Elizabeth II **Subject:** Year of the Snake **Obv:** Head with tiara right, denomination below **Rev:** Snake in tree **Edge:** Reeded

Date	Mintage	F12	VF20	XF40	MS60	MS63
2001	100,000	—	—	—	—	95.00
2001P	100,000	PF65 100				

KM# 582 5 DOLLARS
1.56 g., 0.999 Gold 0.0496 oz. AGW, 14.1 mm. **Ruler:** Elizabeth II **Subject:** Year of the Horse **Obv:** Head with tiara right, denomination below **Rev:** Horse galloping left **Edge:** Reeded

Date	Mintage	F12	VF20	XF40	MS60	MS63
2002P	100,000	—	—	—	—	95.00

KM# 1887 5 DOLLARS
1.57 g., 0.999 Gold 0.0501 oz. AGW, 14.1 mm. **Ruler:** Elizabeth II **Subject:** Year of the Goat

Date	Mintage	F12	VF20	XF40	MS60	MS63
2003P	—	PF65 100				

KM# 668 5 DOLLARS
1.57 g., 0.9999 Gold 0.0502 oz. AGW, 14.1 mm. **Ruler:** Elizabeth II **Subject:** Year of the Monkey **Obv:** Head with tiara right, denomination below **Obv. Designer:** Ian Rank-Broadley **Rev:** Monkey **Edge:** Reeded

Date	Mintage	F12	VF20	XF40	MS60	MS63
2004P	100,000	PF65 100				

KM# 1022 5 DOLLARS
1.57 g., 0.9999 Gold 0.0501 oz. AGW, 13.93 mm. **Ruler:** Elizabeth II **Obv:** Head with tiara right **Rev:** Rooster standing right **Edge:** Reeded **Note:** Polished images with matte fields.

Date	Mintage	F12	VF20	XF40	MS60	MS63
2005	28,000	PF65 110				

KM# 1022a 5 DOLLARS
1.57 g., 0.9999 Gold 0.0501 oz. AGW, 13.93 mm. **Ruler:** Elizabeth II **Subject:** Year of the Rooster **Obv:** Head with tiara right **Rev:** Rooster standing right, multicolor **Edge:** Reeded

Date	Mintage	F12	VF20	XF40	MS60	MS63
2005	22,564	PF65 120				

KM# 1481 5 DOLLARS
1.57 g., 0.9999 Gold 0.0501 oz. AGW, 14.1 mm. **Ruler:** Elizabeth II **Subject:** Year of the Rabbit

Date	Mintage	F12	VF20	XF40	MS60	MS63
2011P	—	PF65 100				

KM# 1666 5 DOLLARS
155.52 g., 0.999 Silver 4.9628 oz. ASW, 65 mm. **Ruler:** Elizabeth II **Subject:** Year of the Dragon

Date	Mintage	F12	VF20	XF40	MS60	MS63
2012P	—	PF65 225				

KM# 1670 5 DOLLARS
1.56 g., 0.999 Gold 0.0496 oz. AGW, 14.1 mm. **Ruler:** Elizabeth II **Subject:** Year of the Dragon **Rev:** Dragon

Date	Mintage	F12	VF20	XF40	MS60	MS63
2012P	—	PF65 110				

KM# 1679 5 DOLLARS
1.55 g., 0.999 Gold 0.0495 oz. AGW, 14.1 mm. **Ruler:** Elizabeth II **Subject:** Year of the Dragon **Rev:** Dragon head facing in color

Date	Mintage	F12	VF20	XF40	MS60	MS63
2012P	—	PF65 125				

KM# 1997 5 DOLLARS
1.55 g., 0.9999 Gold 0.0495 oz. AGW, 14.8 mm. **Ruler:** Elizabeth II **Subject:** Year of the Snake

Date	Mintage	F12	VF20	XF40	MS60	MS63
2013P	—	PF65 100				

KM# 2088 5 DOLLARS
1.55 g., 0.9999 Gold 0.0495 oz. AGW, 14.1 mm. **Ruler:** Elizabeth II **Subject:** Year of the Snake **Rev:** Snake in color

Date	Mintage	F12	VF20	XF40	MS60	MS63
2013P	—	PF65 125				

KM# 2101 5 DOLLARS
1.55 g., 0.9999 Gold 0.0495 oz. AGW, 14.8 mm. **Ruler:** Elizabeth II **Subject:** Year of the Horse **Rev:** Horse galloping left

Date	Mintage	F12	VF20	XF40	MS60	MS63
2014P	—	—	—	—	—	BV+30%

KM# 743 8 DOLLARS
155.52 g., 0.999 Silver 4.9628 oz. ASW, 65 mm. **Ruler:** Elizabeth II **Subject:** Year of the Monkey **Obv:** Head with tiara right, denomination below **Rev:** Gold-plated seated monkey and multicolored ornamentation **Edge:** Reeded **Note:** Illustration reduced.

Date	Mintage	F12	VF20	XF40	MS60	MS63
2004	6,000	—	—	—	—	220

KM# 1023 8 DOLLARS
155.52 g., 0.999 Silver 4.9628 oz. ASW, 65 mm. **Ruler:** Elizabeth II **Subject:** Year of the Rooster **Obv:** Head with tiara right **Rev:** Rooster standing left gilt, floral in color **Edge:** Reeded

Date	Mintage	F12	VF20	XF40	MS60	MS63
2005	10,000	PF65 300				

KM# 1754 8 DOLLARS
155.52 g., 0.999 Silver 4.9628 oz. ASW, 65 mm. **Ruler:** Elizabeth II **Subject:** Year of the Dog **Rev:** German shepard in color seated

Date	Mintage	F12	VF20	XF40	MS60	MS63
2006P	—	—	—	—	—	220

KM# 1756 8 DOLLARS
155.58 g., 0.999 Silver 4.9647 oz. ASW, 65 mm. **Ruler:** Elizabeth II **Subject:** Year of the Pig **Obv:** Head with tiara right **Rev:** Pig in color

Date	Mintage	F12	VF20	XF40	MS60	MS63
2007P	—	—	—	—	—	225

KM# 1757 8 DOLLARS
155.58 g., 0.999 Silver 4.9647 oz. ASW, 65 mm. **Ruler:** Elizabeth II **Subject:** Year of the Mouse **Obv:** Head with tiara right **Rev:** Two mice in color

Date	Mintage	F12	VF20	XF40	MS60	MS63
2008P	—	—	—	—	—	225

KM# 1371 8 DOLLARS
155.52 g., 0.999 Silver 4.9628 oz. ASW, 65 mm. **Ruler:** Elizabeth II **Subject:** Year of the Tiger **Obv:** Head right **Rev:** Tiger at rest left

Date	Mintage	F12	VF20	XF40	MS60	MS63
2010P	—	—	—	—	—	225

KM# 1794 8 DOLLARS
155.50 g., 0.999 Silver 4.9623 oz. ASW, 65 mm. **Ruler:** Elizabeth II **Subject:** Year of the Dragon

Date	Mintage	F12	VF20	XF40	MS60	MS63
2012P	—	PF65 250				

KM# 1994 8 DOLLARS
155.52 g., 0.999 Silver 4.9678 oz. ASW, 65.6 mm. **Ruler:** Elizabeth II **Subject:** Year of the Snake

Date	Mintage	F12	VF20	XF40	MS60	MS63
2013	—	PF65 225				

KM# 2097 8 DOLLARS
155.51 g., 0.9999 Silver 4.9671 oz. ASW, 65 mm. **Ruler:** Elizabeth II **Subject:** Year of the Snake **Rev:** Snake

Date	Mintage	F12	VF20	XF40	MS60	MS63
2013P	—	—	—	—	—	200

KM# 2113 8 DOLLARS
155.67 g., 0.9999 Silver 4.9722 oz. ASW, 65.6 mm. **Ruler:** Elizabeth II **Subject:** Year of the Horse **Rev:** Two horses standing, one drinking from stream

Date	Mintage	F12	VF20	XF40	MS60	MS63
2014P	—	—	—	—	—	175

KM# 539 10 DOLLARS
311.04 g., 0.999 Silver 9.9257 oz. ASW, 75.5 mm. **Ruler:** Elizabeth II **Subject:** Year of the Snake **Obv:** Head with tiara right, denomination below **Rev:** Snake with eggs **Edge:** Segmented reeding

Date	Mintage	F12	VF20	XF40	MS60	MS63
2001	—	—	—	—	375	400
2001P	289	PF65 475				

KM# 583 10 DOLLARS
311.04 g., 0.999 Silver 9.9257 oz. ASW, 75.5 mm. **Ruler:** Elizabeth II **Subject:** Year of the Horse **Obv:** Head with tiara right, denomination below **Rev:** Horse running left **Edge:** Segmented reeding

Date	Mintage	F12	VF20	XF40	MS60	MS63
2002	—	—	—	—	375	400
2002P	68	PF65 450				

KM# 1339 10 DOLLARS
311.04 g., 0.999 Silver 9.9257 oz. ASW, 75.5 mm. **Ruler:** Elizabeth II **Subject:** Year of the Goat **Obv:** Head right

Date	Mintage	F12	VF20	XF40	MS60	MS63
2003P	—	PF65 475				
2003P	—	—	—	—	400	375

KM# 710 10 DOLLARS
311.04 g., 0.999 Silver 9.9257 oz. ASW, 75.5 mm. **Ruler:** Elizabeth II **Subject:** Year of the Goat **Obv:** Head with tiara right, denomination below **Rev:** Goat

Date	Mintage	F12	VF20	XF40	MS60	MS63
2003	—	—	—	—	375	400
2003	78	PF65 450				

KM# 676 10 DOLLARS
311.04 g., 0.999 Silver 9.9257 oz. ASW, 75.5 mm. **Ruler:** Elizabeth II **Subject:** Year of the Monkey **Obv:** Head with tiara right, denomination below **Rev:** Monkey sitting on branch **Edge:** Segmented reeding

Date	Mintage	F12	VF20	XF40	MS60	MS63
2004	—	—	—	—	375	400
2004	84	PF65 475				

KM# 696 10 DOLLARS
311.04 g., 0.999 Silver 9.9257 oz. ASW, 75.5 mm. **Ruler:** Elizabeth II **Subject:** Year of the Rooster **Obv:** Head with tiara right, denomination below **Rev:** Rooster

Date	Mintage	F12	VF20	XF40	MS60	MS63
2005	—	—	—	—	375	400
2005	—	PF65 475				

KM# 1057 10 DOLLARS
3.11 g., 0.999 Gold 0.0992 oz. AGW, 17.53 mm. **Ruler:** Elizabeth II **Subject:** Year of the Rat

Date	Mintage	F12	VF20	XF40	MS60	MS63
2008	2,500	PF65 200				

KM# 1079 10 DOLLARS
3.11 g., 0.999 Gold 0.0992 oz. AGW, 17.53 mm. **Ruler:** Elizabeth II **Subject:** Year of the Ox

Date	Mintage	F12	VF20	XF40	MS60	MS63
2009	2,500	PF65 245				

KM# 1752a 10 DOLLARS
311.04 g., 0.999 Silver 9.9257 oz. ASW, 75.5 mm. **Ruler:** Elizabeth II **Subject:** Year of the Ox **Obv:** Head with tiara right **Rev:** Two colored oxen standing

Date	Mintage	F12	VF20	XF40	MS60	MS63
2009P	—	—	—	—	—	365

KM# 1752 10 DOLLARS
311.04 g., 0.999 Silver 9.9257 oz. ASW, 75.5 mm. **Ruler:** Elizabeth II **Subject:** Year of the Ox **Obv:** Head with tiara right **Rev:** Two oxen standing

Date	Mintage	F12	VF20	XF40	MS60	MS63
2009P	—	—	—	—	—	350

KM# 1321 10 DOLLARS
3.11 g., 0.999 Gold 0.0992 oz. AGW, 19 mm. **Ruler:** Elizabeth II **Subject:** Year of the Tiger **Obv:** Head right **Obv. Designer:** Ian Rank-Broadley **Rev:** Tiger head facing

Date	Mintage	F12	VF20	XF40	MS60	MS63
2010P	8,000			PF65	260	

KM# 1372 10 DOLLARS
311.04 g., 0.999 Silver 9.9257 oz. ASW, 75.5 mm. **Ruler:** Elizabeth II **Subject:** Year of the Tiger **Obv:** Head right **Rev:** Tiger at rest left

Date	Mintage	F12	VF20	XF40	MS60	MS63
2010P	—	—	—	—	—	400

KM# 1478 10 DOLLARS
311.05 g., 0.999 Silver 9.9262 oz. ASW, 75.5 mm. **Ruler:** Elizabeth II **Subject:** Year of the Rabbit **Rev:** Two rabbits nestled under tree

Date	Mintage	F12	VF20	XF40	MS60	MS63
2011P	—			PF65	400	

KM# 1667 10 DOLLARS
311.04 g., 0.999 Silver 9.9257 oz. ASW, 75.5 mm. **Ruler:** Elizabeth II **Subject:** Year of the Dragon **Rev:** Dragon

Date	Mintage	F12	VF20	XF40	MS60	MS63
2012P	—			PF65	400	

KM# 1971 10 DOLLARS
155.50 g., 0.999 Silver 4.9623 oz. ASW, 65 mm. **Ruler:** Elizabeth II **Subject:** Year of the Snake **Rev. Designer:** Chrissy Lau

Date	Mintage	F12	VF20	XF40	MS60	MS63
2013 Proof-like	Est. 5000	—	—	—	—	200

KM# 1995 10 DOLLARS
311.35 g., 0.999 Silver 9.9357 oz. ASW, 85.6 mm. **Ruler:** Elizabeth II **Series:** Year of the Snake

Date	Mintage	F12	VF20	XF40	MS60	MS63
2013	—			PF65	350	

KM# 2098 10 DOLLARS
311.10 g., 0.9999 Silver 9.9367 oz. ASW, 75.5 mm. **Ruler:** Elizabeth II **Subject:** Year of the Snake

Date	Mintage	F12	VF20	XF40	MS60	MS63
2013P	—	—	—	—	—	400

KM# 2156 10 DOLLARS
155.50 g., 0.999 Silver 4.9623 oz. ASW, 65 mm. **Ruler:** Elizabeth II **Subject:** Year of the Snake **Obv:** Head with tiara right **Rev:** Snake coiled upward

Date	Mintage	F12	VF20	XF40	MS60	MS63
2013	—			PF65	225	

KM# 2114 10 DOLLARS
350.00 g., Silver, 85.6 mm. **Ruler:** Elizabeth II **Subject:** Year of the Horse **Rev:** Two horses standing, one drinking from stream

Date	Mintage	F12	VF20	XF40	MS60	MS63
2014P	—	—	—	—	—	350

KM# 540 15 DOLLARS
3.11 g., 0.999 Gold 0.0993 oz. AGW, 16.1 mm. **Ruler:** Elizabeth II **Subject:** Year of the Snake **Obv:** Head with tiara right, denomination below **Rev:** Snake in tree **Edge:** Reeded

Date	Mintage	F12	VF20	XF40	MS60	MS63
2001	80,000	—	—	—	—	175
2001P	3,083			PF65	185	

KM# 584 15 DOLLARS
3.11 g., 0.999 Gold 0.0993 oz. AGW, 16.1 mm. **Ruler:** Elizabeth II **Subject:** Year of the Horse **Obv:** Head with tiara right, denomination below **Rev:** Horse galloping half left **Edge:** Reeded

Date	Mintage	F12	VF20	XF40	MS60	MS63
2002P	—	—	—	—	—	175
2002P	2,812			PF65	185	

KM# 711 15 DOLLARS
3.11 g., 0.9999 Gold 0.0993 oz. AGW, 16.1 mm. **Ruler:** Elizabeth II **Subject:** Year of the Goat **Obv:** Head with tiara right, denomination below **Rev:** Goat

Date	Mintage	F12	VF20	XF40	MS60	MS63
2003	—	—	—	—	—	175
2003P	3,003			PF65	185	

KM# 669 15 DOLLARS
3.11 g., 0.9999 Gold 0.0993 oz. AGW, 16.1 mm. **Ruler:** Elizabeth II **Subject:** Year of the Monkey **Obv:** Head with tiara right, denomination below **Rev:** Monkey **Edge:** Reeded

Date	Mintage	F12	VF20	XF40	MS60	MS63
2004P	—	—	—	—	—	175
2004P	1,966			PF65	185	

KM# 794 15 DOLLARS
3.11 g., 0.9999 Gold 0.0993 oz. AGW, 16.1 mm. **Ruler:** Elizabeth II **Subject:** Year of the Rooster **Obv:** Elizabeth II **Rev:** Standing rooster right **Edge:** Reeded

Date	Mintage	F12	VF20	XF40	MS60	MS63
2005P	1,388			PF65	185	

KM# 794a.1 15 DOLLARS
3.11 g., 0.750 Gold 0.0745 oz. AGW **Ruler:** Elizabeth II **Subject:** Year of the Rooster **Obv:** Head with tiara right **Rev:** Rooster standing right in color **Edge:** Reeded

Date	Mintage	F12	VF20	XF40	MS60	MS63
2005P	16,700			PF65	185	

KM# 794a.2 15 DOLLARS
3.11 g., 0.999 Gold 0.0992 oz. AGW, 16.1 mm. **Ruler:** Elizabeth II **Subject:** Year of the Rooster **Rev:** Rooster in color, pad printed

Date	Mintage	F12	VF20	XF40	MS60	MS63
2005P	7,816			PF65	185	

KM# 794b 15 DOLLARS
3.11 g., 0.999 Gold 0.0992 oz. AGW, 16.1 mm. **Ruler:** Elizabeth II **Subject:** Year of the Rooster **Note:** Rose gold

Date	Mintage	F12	VF20	XF40	MS60	MS63
2005P	7,816			PF65	185	

KM# 1888 15 DOLLARS
3.11 g., 0.999 Gold 0.0992 oz. AGW, 16.1 mm. **Ruler:** Elizabeth II **Subject:** Year of the Dog

Date	Mintage	F12	VF20	XF40	MS60	MS63
2006P	2,894			PF65	185	

KM# 1889 15 DOLLARS
3.11 g., 0.999 Gold 0.0992 oz. AGW, 16.1 mm. **Ruler:** Elizabeth II **Subject:** Year of the Pig

Date	Mintage	F12	VF20	XF40	MS60	MS63
2007P	3,030			PF65	185	

KM# 1890 15 DOLLARS
3.11 g., 0.999 Gold 0.0992 oz. AGW, 16.1 mm. **Ruler:** Elizabeth II **Subject:** Year of the Rat

Date	Mintage	F12	VF20	XF40	MS60	MS63
2008P	2,863			PF65	185	

KM# 1891 15 DOLLARS
3.11 g., 0.999 Gold 0.0992 oz. AGW, 16.1 mm. **Ruler:** Elizabeth II **Subject:** Year of the Ox

Date	Mintage	F12	VF20	XF40	MS60	MS63
2009P	—			PF65	185	

KM# 1373 15 DOLLARS
500.00 g., 0.999 Silver 15.9559 oz. ASW **Ruler:** Elizabeth II **Subject:** Year of the Tiger **Obv:** Head right **Rev:** Tiger at rest left

Date	Mintage	F12	VF20	XF40	MS60	MS63
2010P	—	—	—	—	—	650

KM# 1375 15 DOLLARS
3.11 g., 0.999 Gold 0.0992 oz. AGW, 16.1 mm. **Ruler:** Elizabeth II **Subject:** Year of the Tiger **Obv:** Head right

Date	Mintage	F12	VF20	XF40	MS60	MS63
2010P	—	—	—	—	—	175

KM# 1482 15 DOLLARS
3.10 g., 0.999 Gold 0.0989 oz. AGW, 16.1 mm. **Ruler:** Elizabeth II **Subject:** Year of the Rabbit **Rev:** Rabbit left

Date	Mintage	F12	VF20	XF40	MS60	MS63
2011P	—	PF65 185				

KM# 1671a 15 DOLLARS
3.11 g., 0.999 Gold 0.0992 oz. AGW, 16.1 mm. **Ruler:** Elizabeth II **Subject:** Year of the Dragon **Rev:** Multicolor dragon

Date	Mintage	F12	VF20	XF40	MS60	MS63
2012P	—	PF65 225				

KM# 1671 15 DOLLARS
3.11 g., 0.999 Gold 0.0992 oz. AGW, 16.1 mm. **Ruler:** Elizabeth II **Subject:** Year of the Dragon

Date	Mintage	F12	VF20	XF40	MS60	MS63
2012P	—	PF65 225				

KM# 1835 15 DOLLARS
3.11 g., 0.999 Gold 0.0992 oz. AGW, 16.1 mm. **Ruler:** Elizabeth II **Subject:** Year of the Snake

Date	Mintage	F12	VF20	XF40	MS60	MS63
2013P	—	PF65 250				

KM# 2089 15 DOLLARS
3.11 g., 0.999 Gold 0.0993 oz. AGW, 16.1 mm. **Ruler:** Elizabeth II **Subject:** Year of the Snake **Rev:** Snake in color

Date	Mintage	F12	VF20	XF40	MS60	MS63
2013P	—	PF65 175				

KM# 2102 15 DOLLARS
3.11 g., 0.9999 Gold 0.0993 oz. AGW, 18.6 mm. **Ruler:** Elizabeth II **Subject:** Year of the Horse **Rev:** Horse galloping left

Date	Mintage	F12	VF20	XF40	MS60	MS63
2014P	—	—	—	—	—	BV+15%
2014P	8,000	PF65 BV+17%				

KM# 541 25 DOLLARS
7.75 g., 0.999 Gold 0.2473 oz. AGW, 20.1 mm. **Ruler:** Elizabeth II **Subject:** Year of the Snake **Obv:** Head with tiara right, denomination below **Rev:** Snake in tree **Edge:** Reeded

Date	Mintage	F12	VF20	XF40	MS60	MS63
2001	60,000	—	—	—	—	450
2001P	2,710	PF65 475				

KM# 585 25 DOLLARS
7.78 g., 0.999 Gold 0.2481 oz. AGW, 20.1 mm. **Ruler:** Elizabeth II **Subject:** Year of the Horse **Obv:** Head with tiara right, denomination below **Rev:** Horse galloping half left **Edge:** Reeded

Date	Mintage	F12	VF20	XF40	MS60	MS63
2002P	—	—	—	—	—	450
2002P	2,195	PF65 475				

KM# 712 25 DOLLARS
7.75 g., 0.9999 Gold 0.2475 oz. AGW **Ruler:** Elizabeth II **Subject:** Year of the Goat **Obv:** Head with tiara right, denomination below **Rev:** Goat

Date	Mintage	F12	VF20	XF40	MS60	MS63
2003	—	—	—	—	—	450
2003P	1,969	PF65 475				

KM# 670 25 DOLLARS
7.75 g., 0.9999 Gold 0.2476 oz. AGW, 20.1 mm. **Ruler:** Elizabeth II **Subject:** Year of the Monkey **Obv:** Head with tiara right, denomination below **Rev:** Monkey **Edge:** Reeded

Date	Mintage	F12	VF20	XF40	MS60	MS63
2004P	—	—	—	—	—	450
2004P	1,401	PF65 475				

KM# 795 25 DOLLARS
7.78 g., 0.9999 Gold 0.2484 oz. AGW, 20.1 mm. **Ruler:** Elizabeth II **Subject:** Year of the Rooster **Obv:** Elizabeth II **Rev:** Standing rooster right **Edge:** Reeded

Date	Mintage	F12	VF20	XF40	MS60	MS63
2005P	1,961	PF65 475				

KM# 795a 25 DOLLARS
7.78 g., 0.999 Gold 0.2481 oz. AGW, 20.1 mm. **Ruler:** Elizabeth II **Subject:** Year of the Rooster **Rev:** Rooster in color

Date	Mintage	F12	VF20	XF40	MS60	MS63
2005P	2,889	PF65 475				

KM# 1892 25 DOLLARS
7.78 g., 0.999 Gold 0.2481 oz. AGW, 20.1 mm. **Ruler:** Elizabeth II **Subject:** Year of the Dog

Date	Mintage	F12	VF20	XF40	MS60	MS63
2006P	2,051	PF65 475				

KM# 1893 25 DOLLARS
7.78 g., 0.999 Gold 0.2481 oz. AGW, 20.1 mm. **Ruler:** Elizabeth II **Subject:** Year of the Pig

Date	Mintage	F12	VF20	XF40	MS60	MS63
2007P	2,206	PF65 475				

KM# 1894 25 DOLLARS
7.78 g., 0.999 Gold 0.2481 oz. AGW, 20.1 mm. **Ruler:** Elizabeth II **Subject:** Year of the Rat

Date	Mintage	F12	VF20	XF40	MS60	MS63
2008P	2,088	PF65 475				

KM# 1895 25 DOLLARS
7.78 g., 0.999 Gold 0.2481 oz. AGW, 20.1 mm. **Ruler:** Elizabeth II **Subject:** Year of the Ox

Date	Mintage	F12	VF20	XF40	MS60	MS63
2009P	—	PF65 475				

KM# 1322 25 DOLLARS
7.77 g., 0.999 Gold 0.248 oz. AGW, 22 mm. **Ruler:** Elizabeth II

Subject: Year of the Tiger **Obv:** Head right **Obv. Designer:** Ian Rank-Broadley **Rev:** Tiger head facing

Date	Mintage	F12	VF20	XF40	MS60	MS63
2010P	8,000	PF65 650				

KM# 1483 25 DOLLARS
7.77 g., 0.999 Gold 0.248 oz. AGW **Ruler:** Elizabeth II **Subject:** Year of the Rabbit **Rev:** Rabbit left

Date	Mintage	F12	VF20	XF40	MS60	MS63
2011P	—	PF65 475				

KM# 1672a 25 DOLLARS
7.77 g., 0.999 Gold 0.248 oz. AGW, 22 mm. **Ruler:** Elizabeth II **Subject:** Year of the Dragon **Rev:** Multicolor dragon

Date	Mintage	F12	VF20	XF40	MS60	MS63
2012P	—	PF65 500				

KM# 1672 25 DOLLARS
7.77 g., 0.999 Gold 0.248 oz. AGW, 22 mm. **Ruler:** Elizabeth II **Subject:** Year of the Dragon

Date	Mintage	F12	VF20	XF40	MS60	MS63
2012P	—	PF65 475				

KM# 1836 25 DOLLARS
7.77 g., 0.999 Gold 0.248 oz. AGW, 20 mm. **Ruler:** Elizabeth II **Subject:** Year of the Snake

Date	Mintage	F12	VF20	XF40	MS60	MS63
2013P	—	PF65 550				

KM# 2090 25 DOLLARS
7.77 g., 0.9999 Gold 0.2482 oz. AGW, 22 mm. **Ruler:** Elizabeth II **Subject:** Year of the Snake **Rev:** Snake in color

Date	Mintage	F12	VF20	XF40	MS60	MS63
2013P	—	PF65 650				

KM# 2103 25 DOLLARS
7.78 g., 0.9999 Gold 0.2484 oz. AGW, 22.6 mm. **Ruler:** Elizabeth II **Subject:** Year of the Horse **Rev:** Horse galloping left

Date	Mintage	F12	VF20	XF40	MS60	MS63
2014P	—	—	—	—	—	BV+10%
2014P	8,000	PF66 BV+12%				

KM# 542 30 DOLLARS
1002.50 g., 0.999 Silver 31.9017 oz. ASW, 101 mm. **Ruler:** Elizabeth II **Subject:** Year of the Snake **Obv:** Head with tiara right, denomination below **Rev:** Snake with eggs **Edge:** Segmented reeding

Date	Mintage	F12	VF20	XF40	MS60	MS63
2001	—	—	—	—	—	1,150
2001P	490	PF65 1,350				

KM# 586 30 DOLLARS
1002.50 g., 0.999 Silver 31.9917 oz. ASW, 101 mm. **Ruler:**

Elizabeth II **Subject:** Year of the Horse **Obv:** Head with tiara right, denomination below **Rev:** Horse running left **Edge:** Segmented reeding **Note:** Illustration reduced.

Date	Mintage	F12	VF20	XF40	MS60	MS63
2002	—	—	—	—	—	1,150
2002P	139	PF65 1,350				

KM# 586a 30 DOLLARS
1002.50 g., 0.999 Silver 31.9917 oz. ASW, 101 mm. **Ruler:** Elizabeth II **Subject:** Year of the Horse **Rev:** Horse prancing left, diamond eyes

Date	Mintage	F12	VF20	XF40	MS60	MS63
2002P	883	PF65 1,350				

KM# 681a 30 DOLLARS
1000.00 g., 0.999 Silver 31.9118 oz. ASW, 101 mm. **Ruler:** Elizabeth II **Subject:** Year of the Goat **Rev:** Goat with diamond eyes

Date	Mintage	F12	VF20	XF40	MS60	MS63
2003P	492	PF65 1,350				

KM# 681 30 DOLLARS
1000.00 g., 0.999 Silver 31.9118 oz. ASW, 101 mm. **Ruler:** Elizabeth II **Subject:** Year of the Goat **Obv:** Head with tiara right, denomination below **Rev:** Nanny goat and kid **Edge:** Segmented reeding

Date	Mintage	F12	VF20	XF40	MS60	MS63
2003	—	—	—	—	—	1,150
2003P	105	PF65 1,350				

KM# 677.2 30 DOLLARS
1000.00 g., 0.999 Silver 31.9118 oz. ASW, 101 mm. **Ruler:** Elizabeth II **Subject:** Year of the Monkey **Obv:** Head with tiara right, denomination below **Obv. Designer:** Ian Rank-Broadley **Rev:** Multicolor ornamentation and monkey with diamond chip eyes sitting on branch **Edge:** Segmented reeding **Note:** Illustration reduced.

Date	Mintage	F12	VF20	XF40	MS60	MS63
2004	5,000	PF65 1,300				

KM# 677.1 30 DOLLARS
1000.00 g., 0.999 Silver 31.9118 oz. ASW, 101 mm. **Ruler:** Elizabeth II **Subject:** Year of the Monkey **Obv:** Head with tiara right, denomination below **Rev:** Monkey sitting on branch **Edge:** Segmented reeding

Date	Mintage	F12	VF20	XF40	MS60	MS63
2004	—	—	—	—	—	1,150
2004	5,250	PF65 1,250				

KM# 697 30 DOLLARS
1000.00 g., 0.999 Silver 31.9118 oz. ASW, 101 mm. **Ruler:** Elizabeth II **Subject:** Year of the Rooster **Obv:** Head with tiara right, denomination below **Rev:** Rooster, partially gilt and colored **Note:** Illustration reduced.

Date	Mintage	F12	VF20	XF40	MS60	MS63
2005	2,124	PF65 1,300				

KM# 697a 30 DOLLARS
1000.00 g., 0.999 Silver 31.9118 oz. ASW, 101 mm. **Ruler:** Elizabeth II **Subject:** Year of the Rooster **Rev:** Rooster wiht diamond eye

Date	Mintage	F12	VF20	XF40	MS60	MS63
2005P	588	PF65 1,300				

KM# 1896 30 DOLLARS
1000.00 g., 0.9999 Silver 31.9406 oz. ASW, 101 mm. **Ruler:** Elizabeth II **Subject:** Year of the Dog

Date	Mintage	F12	VF20	XF40	MS60	MS63
2006P	100	PF65 1,300				

KM# 1897 30 DOLLARS
1000.00 g., 0.999 Silver 31.9118 oz. ASW, 101 mm. **Ruler:** Elizabeth II **Subject:** Year of the Pig

Date	Mintage	F12	VF20	XF40	MS60	MS63
2007P	100	PF65 1,300				

KM# 1898 30 DOLLARS
1000.00 g., 0.999 Silver 31.9118 oz. ASW, 101 mm. **Ruler:** Elizabeth II **Subject:** Year of the Rat

Date	Mintage	F12	VF20	XF40	MS60	MS63
2008P	171	PF65 1,300				

KM# 1899 30 DOLLARS
1000.00 g., 0.999 Silver 31.9118 oz. ASW, 101 mm. **Ruler:** Elizabeth II **Subject:** Year of the Ox

Date	Mintage	F12	VF20	XF40	MS60	MS63
2009P	—	PF65 1,300				

KM# 1374 30 DOLLARS
1000.00 g., 0.999 Silver 31.9118 oz. ASW, 101 mm. **Ruler:** Elizabeth II **Subject:** Year of the Tiger **Obv:** Head right

Date	Mintage	F12	VF20	XF40	MS60	MS63
2010P	—	—	—	—	—	1,150

KM# 1319 30 DOLLARS
1000.00 g., 0.999 Silver 31.9118 oz. ASW, 101 mm. **Ruler:** Elizabeth II **Subject:** Year of the Tiger **Obv:** Head right **Obv. Designer:** Ian Rank-Broadley **Rev:** Tiger at rest left **Note:** Illustration reduced.

Date	Mintage	F12	VF20	XF40	MS60	MS63
2010P	5,000	PF65 1,600				

KM# 1479 30 DOLLARS
1000.00 g., 0.999 Silver 31.9118 oz. ASW, 101 mm. **Ruler:** Elizabeth II **Subject:** Year of the Rabbit **Rev:** Mother and baby rabbit nose to nose **Note:** Illustration reduced.

Date	Mintage	F12	VF20	XF40	MS60	MS63
2010P	—	PF65 1,300				

KM# 1668a 30 DOLLARS
1000.00 g., 0.999 Silver 31.9118 oz. ASW, 101 mm. **Ruler:** Elizabeth II **Obv:** Head with tiara right **Rev:** Dragon in color with gemstone

Date	Mintage	F12	VF20	XF40	MS60	MS63
2012P	—	PF65 1,400				

KM# 1668 30 DOLLARS
1000.00 g., 0.999 Silver 31.9118 oz. ASW, 101 mm. **Ruler:** Elizabeth II **Subject:** Year of the Dragon **Rev:** Dragon

Date	Mintage	F12	VF20	XF40	MS60	MS63
2012P	—	PF65 1,250				

KM# 1834 30 DOLLARS
1000.00 g., 0.999 Silver 31.9118 oz. ASW, 101 mm. **Ruler:** Elizabeth II **Subject:** Year of the Snake

Date	Mintage	F12	VF20	XF40	MS60	MS63
2013P	—	PF65 1,500				

KM# 1834a 30 DOLLARS
1000.00 g., 0.999 Silver 31.9118 oz. ASW, 101 mm. **Ruler:** Elizabeth II **Subject:** Year of the Snake **Rev:** Snake in color with diamond chip as eye

Date	Mintage	F12	VF20	XF40	MS60	MS63
2013P	—	PF65 1,750				

KM# 1972 30 DOLLARS
1000.00 g., 0.999 Silver 31.9118 oz. ASW, 100 mm. **Ruler:** Elizabeth II **Subject:** Year of the Snake **Rev. Designer:** Chrissy Lau

Date	Mintage	F12	VF20	XF40	MS60	MS63
2013 Proof-like	Est. 1500	—	—	—	—	800

KM# 2099 30 DOLLARS
1000.00 g., 0.9999 Silver 31.9406 oz. ASW, 101 mm. **Ruler:** Elizabeth II **Subject:** Year of the Snake

Date	Mintage	F12	VF20	XF40	MS60	MS63
2013P						900

KM# 2115 30 DOLLARS
1001.00 g., 0.9999 Silver 31.9725 oz. ASW, 100.6 mm. **Ruler:** Elizabeth II **Subject:** Year of the Horse **Rev:** Two horses standing, one drinking from stream

Date	Mintage	F12	VF20	XF40	MS60	MS63
2014P	—	PF65 1,050				
2014P						1,000

KM# 671 50 DOLLARS
15.59 g., 0.999 Gold 0.4981 oz. AGW, 25.1 mm. **Ruler:** Elizabeth II **Subject:** Year of the Monkey **Obv:** Head with tiara right, denomination below **Rev:** Monkey **Edge:** Reeded

Date	Mintage	F12	VF20	XF40	MS60	MS63
2004P	40,000	PF65 900				

KM# 1900 50 DOLLARS
15.55 g., 0.999 Gold 0.4962 oz. AGW, 25 mm. **Ruler:** Elizabeth II **Subject:** Year of the Rooster

Date	Mintage	F12	VF20	XF40	MS60	MS63
2005P		PF65 900				

KM# 1901 50 DOLLARS
15.55 g., 0.999 Gold 0.4962 oz. AGW, 25 mm. **Ruler:** Elizabeth II **Subject:** Year of the Dog

Date	Mintage	F12	VF20	XF40	MS60	MS63
2006P		PF65 900				

KM# 1902 50 DOLLARS
15.55 g., 0.999 Gold 0.4962 oz. AGW, 25 mm. **Ruler:** Elizabeth II **Subject:** Year of the Pig

Date	Mintage	F12	VF20	XF40	MS60	MS63
2007P		PF65 900				

KM# 1903 50 DOLLARS
15.55 g., 0.999 Gold 0.4962 oz. AGW, 25 mm. **Ruler:** Elizabeth II **Subject:** Year of the Rat

Date	Mintage	F12	VF20	XF40	MS60	MS63
2008P	—	PF65 900				

KM# 1904 50 DOLLARS
15.55 g., 0.999 Gold 0.4962 oz. AGW, 25 mm. **Ruler:** Elizabeth II **Subject:** Year of the Ox

Date	Mintage	F12	VF20	XF40	MS60	MS63
2009P		PF65 900				

KM# 1376 50 DOLLARS
15.59 g., 0.999 Gold 0.4976 oz. AGW, 25 mm. **Ruler:** Elizabeth II **Subject:** Year of the Tiger **Obv:** Head right

Date	Mintage	F12	VF20	XF40	MS60	MS63
2010P	—	PF65 900				

KM# 1484 50 DOLLARS
15.59 g., 0.999 Gold 0.4976 oz. AGW, 25.1 mm. **Ruler:** Elizabeth II **Subject:** Year of the Rabbit

Date	Mintage	F12	VF20	XF40	MS60	MS63
2011P		PF65 950				

KM# 1673 50 DOLLARS
15.55 g., 0.999 Gold 0.4962 oz. AGW, 25 mm. **Ruler:** Elizabeth II **Subject:** Year of the dragon

Date	Mintage	F12	VF20	XF40	MS60	MS63
2012P	—	PF65 950				

KM# 1998 50 DOLLARS
15.55 g., 0.9999 Gold 0.4968 oz. AGW, 30.6 mm. **Ruler:** Elizabeth II **Subject:** Year of the Snake

Date	Mintage	F12	VF20	XF40	MS60	MS63
2013P	—	PF65 775				

KM# 2104 50 DOLLARS
15.55 g., 0.9999 Gold 0.4967 oz. AGW, 30.6 mm. **Ruler:** Elizabeth II **Subject:** Year of the Horse **Rev:** Horse galloping left

Date	Mintage	F12	VF20	XF40	MS60	MS63
2014P	—	—	—	—	—	BV+7%

KM# 543 100 DOLLARS
31.10 g., 0.9999 Gold 0.9926 oz. AGW, 32.1 mm. **Ruler:** Elizabeth II **Subject:** Year of the Snake **Obv:** Head with tiara right, denomination below **Obv. Designer:** Ian Rank-Broadley **Rev:** Snake in tree **Edge:** Reeded

Date	Mintage	F12	VF20	XF40	MS60	MS63
2001	30,000	—	—	—	—	1,750
2001P	1,223	PF65 1,000				

KM# 587 100 DOLLARS
31.10 g., 0.9999 Gold 0.9926 oz. AGW, 32.1 mm. **Ruler:** Elizabeth II **Subject:** Year of the Horse **Obv:** Head with tiara right, denomination below **Rev:** Horse running left **Edge:** Reeded

Date	Mintage	F12	VF20	XF40	MS60	MS63
2002	—	—	—	—	—	1,750
2002P	1,471	PF65 1,800				

KM# 713 100 DOLLARS
31.10 g., 0.9999 Gold 0.9935 oz. AGW, 32.1 mm. **Ruler:** Elizabeth II **Subject:** Year of the Goat **Obv:** Head with tiara right, denomination below **Rev:** Goat

Date	Mintage	F12	VF20	XF40	MS60	MS63
2003P	—	—	—	—	—	1,750
2003P	1,187	PF65 1,800				

KM# 672 100 DOLLARS
31.10 g., 0.9999 Gold 0.9935 oz. AGW, 32.1 mm. **Ruler:** Elizabeth II **Subject:** Year of the Monkey **Obv:** Head with tiara right, denomination below **Rev:** Monkey walking left on branch **Edge:** Reeded

Date	Mintage	F12	VF20	XF40	MS60	MS63
2004	30,000	—	—	—	—	1,750
2004P	999	PF65 1,800				

KM# 796 100 DOLLARS
31.10 g., 0.9999 Gold 0.9935 oz. AGW, 32.1 mm. **Ruler:** Elizabeth II **Subject:** Year of the Rooster **Obv:** Elizabeth II **Rev:** Standing rooster right **Edge:** Reeded

Date	Mintage	F12	VF20	XF40	MS60	MS63
2005P	1,388	PF65 1,800				

KM# 1905 100 DOLLARS
31.10 g., 0.9999 Gold 0.9935 oz. AGW, 32.1 mm. **Ruler:** Elizabeth II **Subject:** Year of the Dog

Date	Mintage	F12	VF20	XF40	MS60	MS63
2006P	1,274	PF65 1,800				

KM# 1906 100 DOLLARS
31.10 g., 0.999 Gold 0.9926 oz. AGW, 32.1 mm. **Ruler:** Elizabeth II **Subject:** Year of the Pig

Date	Mintage	F12	VF20	XF40	MS60	MS63
2007P	1,556	PF65 1,800				

KM# 1907 100 DOLLARS
31.10 g., 0.999 Gold 0.9926 oz. AGW, 32.1 mm. **Ruler:** Elizabeth II **Subject:** Year of the Rat

Date	Mintage	F12	VF20	XF40	MS60	MS63
2008P	1,748	PF65 1,800				

KM# 1908 100 DOLLARS
31.10 g., 0.999 Gold 0.9926 oz. AGW, 32.1 mm. **Ruler:** Elizabeth II **Subject:** Year of the Ox

Date	Mintage	F12	VF20	XF40	MS60	MS63
2009P		PF65 1,800				

KM# 1323 100 DOLLARS
31.11 g., 0.999 Gold 0.9926 oz. AGW, 39.34 mm. **Ruler:** Elizabeth II **Subject:** Year of the Tiger **Obv:** Head right **Obv. Designer:** Ian Rank-Broadley **Rev:** Tiger head facing

Date	Mintage	F12	VF20	XF40	MS60	MS63
2010P	6,000	PF65 2,650				

KM# 1485 100 DOLLARS
31.11 g., 0.999 Gold 0.9926 oz. AGW, 39.34 mm. **Ruler:** Elizabeth II **Subject:** Year of the Rabbit **Rev:** Rabbit seated left

Date	Mintage	F12	VF20	XF40	MS60	MS63
2011P		PF65 1,800				

KM# 1674a 100 DOLLARS
31.11 g., 0.999 Gold 0.9926 oz. AGW, 39.34 mm. **Ruler:** Elizabeth II **Subject:** Year of the Dragon **Rev:** Multicolor dragon

Date	Mintage	F12	VF20	XF40	MS60	MS63
2012P	—	PF65 1,875				

KM# 1674 100 DOLLARS
31.11 g., 0.999 Gold 0.9926 oz. AGW, 27.30 mm. **Ruler:** Elizabeth II **Subject:** Year of the Dragon **Note:** High relief

Date	Mintage	F12	VF20	XF40	MS60	MS63
2012P	38	PF65 2,500				

KM# 1837 100 DOLLARS
31.11 g., 0.999 Gold 0.9926 oz. AGW, 32.1 mm. **Ruler:** Elizabeth II **Subject:** Year of the Snake

Date	Mintage	F12	VF20	XF40	MS60	MS63
2013P	—	PF65 1,900				

KM# 1973 100 DOLLARS
31.10 g., 0.9999 Gold 0.9934 oz. AGW, 38.74 mm. **Ruler:** Elizabeth II **Subject:** Year of the Snake **Rev. Designer:** Chrissy Lau

Date	Mintage	F12	VF20	XF40	MS60	MS63
2013 Proof-like	Est. 1500	—	—	—	—	1,500

KM# 2003 100 DOLLARS
31.11 g., 0.9999 Gold 0.9936 oz. AGW, 27.3 mm. **Ruler:** Elizabeth II **Subject:** Year of the Snake **Note:** High Relief

Date	Mintage	F12	VF20	XF40	MS60	MS63
2013P	Est. 388	PF65 1,550				

KM# 2091 100 DOLLARS
31.11 g., 0.9999 Gold 0.9935 oz. AGW, 32.1 mm. **Ruler:** Elizabeth II **Subject:** Year of the Snake **Rev:** Snake in color

Date	Mintage	F12	VF20	XF40	MS60	MS63
2013P	—	PF65 1,850				

KM# 2157 100 DOLLARS
31.11 g., 0.999 Gold 0.9926 oz. AGW, 32.1 mm. **Ruler:** Elizabeth II **Subject:** Year of the Snake **Obv:** Head with tiara right **Rev:** Snake coiled upward

Date	Mintage	F12	VF20	XF40	MS60	MS63
2013	—	PF65 1,450				

KM# 2105 100 DOLLARS
31.11 g., 0.9999 Gold 0.9937 oz. AGW, 39.34 mm. **Ruler:** Elizabeth II **Subject:** Year of the Horse **Rev:** Horse galloping left

Date	Mintage	F12	VF20	XF40	MS60	MS63
2014P	30,000	—	—	—	—	BV+3%
2014P	6,000	PF65 BV+5%				

KM# 704 200 DOLLARS
62.21 g., 0.9999 Gold 1.9872 oz. AGW, 41.1 mm. **Ruler:** Elizabeth II **Subject:** Year of the Snake **Obv:** Head with tiara right, denomination below **Rev:** Snake

Date	Mintage	F12	VF20	XF40	MS60	MS63
2001	—	PF65 3,500				

KM# 1333 200 DOLLARS
62.21 g., 0.999 Gold 1.9852 oz. AGW, 41.1 mm. **Ruler:** Elizabeth II **Subject:** Year of the Snake **Obv:** Head right

Date	Mintage	F12	VF20	XF40	MS60	MS63
2001P	—	PF65 3,500				

KM# 707 200 DOLLARS
62.21 g., 0.9999 Gold 1.9872 oz. AGW, 41.1 mm. **Ruler:** Elizabeth II **Subject:** Year of the Horse **Rev:** Horse

Date	Mintage	F12	VF20	XF40	MS60	MS63
2002	—	PF65 3,500				

KM# 1336 200 DOLLARS
62.21 g., 0.999 Gold 1.9852 oz. AGW, 41.1 mm. **Ruler:** Elizabeth II **Subject:** Year of the Horse

Date	Mintage	F12	VF20	XF40	MS60	MS63
2002P	—	PF65 3,500				

KM# 714 200 DOLLARS
62.21 g., 0.9999 Gold 1.9872 oz. AGW, 41.1 mm. **Ruler:** Elizabeth II **Subject:** Year of the Goat **Obv:** Head with tiara right **Rev:** Goat

Date	Mintage	F12	VF20	XF40	MS60	MS63
2003	—	PF65 3,500				

KM# 717 200 DOLLARS
62.21 g., 0.9999 Gold 1.987 oz. AGW, 41.1 mm. **Ruler:** Elizabeth II **Subject:** Year of the Monkey **Obv:** Head with tiara right **Rev:** Monkey

Date	Mintage	F12	VF20	XF40	MS60	MS63
2004	—	PF65 3,500				

KM# 698 200 DOLLARS
62.21 g., 0.9999 Gold 1.987 oz. AGW, 41.1 mm. **Ruler:** Elizabeth II **Subject:** Year of the Rooster **Obv:** Head with tiara right **Rev:** Rooster

Date	Mintage	F12	VF20	XF40	MS60	MS63
2005	—	PF65 3,500				

KM# 1377 200 DOLLARS
62.21 g., 0.999 Gold 1.9852 oz. AGW, 41.1 mm. **Ruler:** Elizabeth II **Obv:** Year of the Tiger **Rev:** Tiger head facing

Date	Mintage	F12	VF20	XF40	MS60	MS63
2010P	—	—	—	—	—	3,600

KM# 1486 200 DOLLARS
62.21 g., 0.999 Gold 1.9852 oz. AGW, 41.1 mm. **Ruler:** Elizabeth II **Subject:** Year of the Rabbit

Date	Mintage	F12	VF20	XF40	MS60	MS63
2011P	—	PF65 3,600				

KM# 1675 200 DOLLARS
62.21 g., 0.999 Gold 1.9854 oz. AGW, 41.1 mm. **Ruler:** Elizabeth II **Subject:** Year of the Dragon

Date	Mintage	F12	VF20	XF40	MS60	MS63
2012P	—	PF65 3,550				

KM# 1999 200 DOLLARS
62.22 g., 0.9999 Gold 1.9872 oz. AGW, 41.1 mm. **Ruler:** Elizabeth II **Subject:** Year of the Snake

Date	Mintage	F12	VF20	XF40	MS60	MS63
2013P	—	PF65 3,000				

KM# 2106 200 DOLLARS
62.22 g., 0.9999 Gold 1.9872 oz. AGW, 41.1 mm. **Ruler:** Elizabeth II **Subject:** Year of the Horse **Rev:** Horse galloping left

Date	Mintage	F12	VF20	XF40	MS60	MS63
2014P	—	—	—	—	—	BV+3%

KM# 1006 300 DOLLARS
10000.00 g., 0.999 Silver 319.1184 oz. ASW **Ruler:** Elizabeth II **Series:** Lunar year **Subject:** Year of the Dog **Obv:** Head with tiara right **Obv. Legend:** ELIZABETH II - AUSTRALIA **Obv. Designer:** Ian Rank-Broadley **Rev:** Dog sitting, facing right

Date	Mintage	F12	VF20	XF40	MS60	MS63
2006	—	—	—	—	—	11,500

KM# 1480 300 DOLLARS
10000.00 g., 0.999 Silver 319.1184 oz. ASW **Ruler:** Elizabeth II **Subject:** Year of the Rabbit **Rev:** Two rabbits nestled under tree

Date	Mintage	F12	VF20	XF40	MS60	MS63
2011P	—	PF65 11,750				

KM# 1669 300 DOLLARS
10000.00 g., 0.999 Silver 319.1184 oz. ASW **Ruler:** Elizabeth II **Subject:** Year of the Dragon **Rev:** Dragon

Date	Mintage	F12	VF20	XF40	MS60	MS63
2012P	—	PF65 11,500				

KM# 1996 300 DOLLARS
10010.00 g., 0.999 Silver 319.4375 oz. ASW, 221 mm. **Ruler:** Elizabeth II **Subject:** Year of the Snake

Date	Mintage	F12	VF20	XF40	MS60	MS63
2013	Est. 200	PF65 11,500				

KM# 2116 300 DOLLARS
10010.00 g., 0.9999 Silver 319.7253 oz. ASW, 221 mm. **Ruler:** Elizabeth II **Subject:** Year of the Horse **Rev:** Two horses standing, one drinking from stream

Date	Mintage	F12	VF20	XF40	MS60	MS63
2014P	200	—	—	—	—	9,000

KM# 1974 500 DOLLARS
155.50 g., 0.9999 Gold 4.9668 oz. AGW, 60 mm. **Ruler:** Elizabeth II **Subject:** Year of the Snake **Rev. Designer:** Chrissy Lau

Date	Mintage	F12	VF20	XF40	MS60	MS63
2013 Proof-like	Est. 1000	—	—	—	—	7,000

KM# 705 1000 DOLLARS
311.05 g., 0.9999 Gold 9.9351 oz. AGW, 75.6 mm. **Ruler:**

Elizabeth II **Subject:** Year of the Snake **Obv:** Head with tiara right, denomination below **Rev:** Snake

Date	Mintage	F12	VF20	XF40	MS60	MS63
2001	—	—	—	—	—	18,000

KM# 1334 1000 DOLLARS
311.05 g., 0.999 Gold 9.9261 oz. AGW, 75.6 mm. **Ruler:** Elizabeth II **Subject:** Year of the Snake **Obv:** Head right

Date	Mintage	F12	VF20	XF40	MS60	MS63
2001P	—	—	—	—	—	18,000

KM# 708 1000 DOLLARS
311.05 g., 0.9999 Gold 9.9351 oz. AGW, 75.6 mm. **Ruler:** Elizabeth II **Subject:** Year of the Horse **Obv:** Head with tiara right, denomination below **Rev:** Horse

Date	Mintage	F12	VF20	XF40	MS60	MS63
2002	—	—	—	—	—	18,000

KM# 1337 1000 DOLLARS
311.05 g., 0.999 Gold 9.9261 oz. AGW, 75.6 mm. **Ruler:** Elizabeth II **Subject:** Year of the Horse **Obv:** Head right

Date	Mintage	F12	VF20	XF40	MS60	MS63
2002P	—	—	—	—	—	18,000

KM# 715 1000 DOLLARS
311.05 g., 0.9999 Gold 9.9351 oz. AGW, 75.6 mm. **Ruler:** Elizabeth II **Subject:** Year of the Goat **Obv:** Head with tiara right, denomination below **Rev:** Goat

Date	Mintage	F12	VF20	XF40	MS60	MS63
2003	—	—	—	—	—	18,000

KM# 718 1000 DOLLARS
311.05 g., 0.9999 Gold 9.9351 oz. AGW, 75.6 mm. **Ruler:** Elizabeth II **Subject:** Year of the Monkey **Obv:** Head with tiara right, denomination below **Rev:** Monkey

Date	Mintage	F12	VF20	XF40	MS60	MS63
2004	—	—	—	—	—	18,000

KM# 699 1000 DOLLARS
311.05 g., 0.9999 Gold 9.9351 oz. AGW, 75.6 mm. **Ruler:** Elizabeth II **Subject:** Year of the Rooster **Obv:** Head with tiara right, denomination below **Rev:** Rooster

Date	Mintage	F12	VF20	XF40	MS60	MS63
2005	—	—	—	—	—	18,000

KM# 1378 1000 DOLLARS
311.05 g., 0.999 Gold 9.9261 oz. AGW, 75.6 mm. **Ruler:** Elizabeth II **Subject:** Year of the Tiger **Obv:** Head right

Date	Mintage	F12	VF20	XF40	MS60	MS63
2010(p)	—	—	—	—	—	18,000

KM# 1487 1000 DOLLARS
311.05 g., 0.999 Gold 9.9261 oz. AGW, 75.6 mm. **Ruler:** Elizabeth II **Subject:** Year of the Rabbit

Date	Mintage	F12	VF20	XF40	MS60	MS63
2011P	—	PF65				18,000

KM# 1676 1000 DOLLARS
311.05 g., 0.999 Gold 9.9262 oz. AGW, 75.6 mm. **Ruler:** Elizabeth II **Subject:** Year of the Dragon

Date	Mintage	F12	VF20	XF40	MS60	MS63
2012P	—	PF65				18,000

KM# 2000 1000 DOLLARS
311.07 g., 0.9999 Gold 9.9357 oz. AGW, 75.6 mm. **Ruler:** Elizabeth II **Subject:** Year of the Snake

Date	Mintage	F12	VF20	XF40	MS60	MS63
2013P	—	PF65				15,000

KM# 2107 1000 DOLLARS
321.00 g., 0.9999 Gold 10.2529 oz. AGW, 75.6 mm. **Ruler:** Elizabeth II **Subject:** Year of the Horse **Rev:** Horse galloping left

Date	Mintage	F12	VF20	XF40	MS60	MS63
2014P	—	—	—	—	—	BV+3%

KM# 706 3000 DOLLARS
1000.00 g., 0.9999 Gold 31.9406 oz. AGW, 100.6 mm. **Ruler:** Elizabeth II **Subject:** Year of the Snake **Obv:** Head with tiara right, denomination below **Rev:** Snake

Date	Mintage	F12	VF20	XF40	MS60	MS63
2001	—	—	—	—	—	BV+3%

KM# 1335 3000 DOLLARS
1000.00 g., 0.999 Gold 31.9118 oz. AGW, 100.6 mm. **Ruler:** Elizabeth II **Subject:** Year of the Snake **Obv:** Head right

Date	Mintage	F12	VF20	XF40	MS60	MS63
2001P	—	—	—	—	—	BV+3%

KM# 709 3000 DOLLARS
1000.00 g., 0.9999 Gold 31.9406 oz. AGW, 100.6 mm. **Ruler:** Elizabeth II **Subject:** Year of the Horse **Obv:** Head with tiara right, denomination below **Rev:** Horse

Date	Mintage	F12	VF20	XF40	MS60	MS63
2002	—	—	—	—	—	BV+3%

KM# 1338 3000 DOLLARS
1000.00 g., 0.999 Gold 31.9118 oz. AGW, 100.6 mm. **Ruler:** Elizabeth II **Subject:** Year of the Horse **Obv:** Head right

Date	Mintage	F12	VF20	XF40	MS60	MS63
2002P	—	—	—	—	—	BV+3%

KM# 716 3000 DOLLARS
1000.00 g., 0.9999 Gold 31.9406 oz. AGW, 100.6 mm. **Ruler:** Elizabeth II **Subject:** Year of the Goat **Obv:** Head with tiara right, denomination below **Rev:** Goat

Date	Mintage	F12	VF20	XF40	MS60	MS63
2003	—	—	—	—	—	BV+3%

KM# 719 3000 DOLLARS
1000.00 g., 0.9999 Gold 31.9406 oz. AGW, 100.6 mm. **Ruler:** Elizabeth II **Subject:** Year of the Monkey **Obv:** Head with tiara right, denomination below **Rev:** Monkey

Date	Mintage	F12	VF20	XF40	MS60	MS63
2004	—	—	—	—	—	BV+3%

KM# 700 3000 DOLLARS
1000.00 g., 0.9999 Gold 31.9406 oz. AGW, 100.6 mm. **Ruler:** Elizabeth II **Subject:** Year of the Rooster **Obv:** Head with tiara right, denomination below **Rev:** Rooster

Date	Mintage	F12	VF20	XF40	MS60	MS63
2005	—	—	—	—	—	BV+3%

KM# 1379 3000 DOLLARS
1000.00 g., 0.999 Gold 31.9118 oz. AGW, 100.6 mm. **Ruler:** Elizabeth II **Subject:** Year of the Tiger **Obv:** Head right

Date	Mintage	F12	VF20	XF40	MS60	MS63
2010P	—	—	—	—	—	BV+3%

KM# 1488 3000 DOLLARS
1000.00 g., 0.999 Gold 31.9118 oz. AGW, 100.6 mm. **Ruler:** Elizabeth II **Subject:** Year of the Rabbit

Date	Mintage	F12	VF20	XF40	MS60	MS63
2011P	—	PF65	BV+3%			

KM# 1677 3000 DOLLARS
1000.00 g., 0.999 Gold 31.9118 oz. AGW, 100.6 mm. **Ruler:** Elizabeth II **Subject:** Year of the Dragon

Date	Mintage	F12	VF20	XF40	MS60	MS63
2012P	—	PF65	BV+3%			

KM# 1975 3000 DOLLARS
1000.00 g., 0.9999 Gold 31.9406 oz. AGW, 75 mm. **Ruler:** Elizabeth II **Subject:** Year of the Snake **Rev. Designer:** Chrissy Lau

Date	Mintage	F12	VF20	XF40	MS60	MS63
2013 Proof-like	Est. 100	—	—	—	—	46,500

KM# 2001 3000 DOLLARS
1000.00 g., 0.9999 Gold 31.9406 oz. AGW, 100.6 mm. **Ruler:** Elizabeth II **Subject:** Year of the Snake

Date	Mintage	F12	VF20	XF40	MS60	MS63
2013P	—	PF65				46,500

KM# 2108 3000 DOLLARS
1000.00 g., 0.9999 Gold 31.9406 oz. AGW, 100.1 mm. **Ruler:** Elizabeth II **Subject:** Year of the Horse **Rev:** Horse galloping left

Date	Mintage	F12	VF20	XF40	MS60	MS63
2014P	—	—	—	—	—	BV+3%

KM# 1007 30000 DOLLARS
10000.00 g., 0.9999 Gold 319.4058 oz. AGW, 180.6 mm. **Ruler:** Elizabeth II **Series:** Lunar year **Subject:** Year of the Dog **Obv:** Head with tiara right **Obv. Legend:** ELIZABETH II - AUSTRALIA **Obv. Designer:** Ian Rank-Broadley **Rev:** Dog standing left

Date	Mintage	F12	VF20	XF40	MS60	MS63
2006	100	PF65 BV+2%				

KM# 1489 30000 DOLLARS
10000.00 g., 0.999 Gold 319.1184 oz. AGW, 180.6 mm. **Ruler:** Elizabeth II **Subject:** Year of the Rabbit

Date	Mintage	F12	VF20	XF40	MS60	MS63
2011P	100	PF65 BV+2%				

KM# 1678 30000 DOLLARS
10000.00 g., 0.999 Gold 319.1184 oz. AGW, 180.6 mm. **Ruler:** Elizabeth II **Subject:** Year of the Dragon

Date	Mintage	F12	VF20	XF40	MS60	MS63
2012P	100	PF65 BV+2%				

KM# 2002 30000 DOLLARS
10001.00 g., 0.9999 Gold 319.4378 oz. AGW, 180.6 mm. **Ruler:** Elizabeth II **Subject:** Year of the Snake

Date	Mintage	F12	VF20	XF40	MS60	MS63
2013	Est. 100	PF65 BV+2%				

KM# 2109 30000 DOLLARS
100001.00 g., 0.9999 Gold 3194.0904 oz. AGW, 180 mm. **Ruler:** Elizabeth II **Subject:** Year of the Horse **Rev:** Horse galloping left

Date	Mintage	F12	VF20	XF40	MS60	MS63
2014P	10	—	—	—	—	BV+2%

BABY MINT SETS

KM#	Date	Mintage	Identification	Issue Price	Mkt Val
BMS9	2001 (6)	32,494	KM#401-403, 406, 491.1, 534.1 plus bronze medal	—	110
BMS10	2002 (6)	32,479	KM#401-403, 406, 600.1, 602 plus bronze medal	—	47.50
BMS11	2003 (6)	37,748	KM#401-402, 406, 688-690 plus bronze medal	—	40.00
BMS12	2004 (6)	31,000	KM#401-404, 406, 733.1 plus bronze medal	—	40.00
BMS13	2005 (6)	34,748	KM#401-402, 406, 745-747 plus bronze medal	24.00	27.50
BMS14	2006 (6)	—	KM#401-404, 406, 489 plus bronze medal	24.00	35.00

BABY PROOF SETS

KM#	Date	Mintage	Identification	Issue Price	Mkt Val
BPS7	2001 (6)	15,011	KM#401-403, 406, 491.1, 534.1 plus silver medal	—	165
BPS8	2002 (6)	13,996	KM#401, 403, 406, 600.2, 602 plus silver medal	—	152
BPS9	2003 (6)	14,799	KM#401-402, 406, 688-689, 690.1 plus silver medal	—	125
BPS10	2004 (6)	13,996	KM#401-404, 406, 733 plus silver medal	—	110
BPS11	2005 (6)	—	KM#401-402, 406, 745-747 plus silver medal	—	100
BPS12	2006 (6)	—	KM#401-404, 406, 489 plus silver medal	—	120

MINT SETS

KM#	Date	Mintage	Identification	Issue Price	Mkt Val
MS39	2001 (3)	—	KM532, 533, 534.1	7.80	75.00
MS40	2001 (3)	—	KM534.1, 550, 551	7.80	70.00
MS41	2001 (3)	—	KM534.1, 552, 553	7.80	70.00
MS42	2001 (3)	—	KM534.1, 554, 555	7.80	75.00
MS43	2001 (3)	—	KM534.1, 556, 557	7.80	72.50
MS44	2001 (3)	—	KM534.1, 558, 559	7.80	75.00
MS45	2001 (3)	—	KM534.1, 560, 561	7.80	85.00
MS46	2001 (3)	—	KM534.1, 562, 563	7.80	80.00
MS47	2001 (3)	—	KM534.1, 564, 565	7.80	75.00
MS48	2001 (20)	—	KM532-533, 534.1, 491.1, 550-565	43.68	235
MS49	2001 (6)	—	KM#401-403, 406, 491.1, 534.1	—	80.00
MS50	2002 (6)	—	KM#401-403, 406, 600.1, 602	—	65.00
MS51	2002 (3)	—	KM#691.2, 692, 693	—	2,300
MS52	2003 (5)	—	KM401, 402, 406, 689, 690	—	35.00
MS53	2004 (6)	—	KM#401-404, 406, 733.1	—	32.50
MS54	2005 (6)	—	KM#401, 402, 406, 745-747	—	25.00
MS55	2006 (8)	—	KM#401-404, 406, 489, 767-768	18.50	55.00
MS56	2006 (15)	—	KM#770-781, 1001-1003	80.00	165

PROOF SETS

KM#	Date	Mintage	Identification	Issue Price	Mkt Val
PS107	2001 (3)	—	KM532, 533, 534.2	21.00	95.00
PS108	2001 (3)	—	KM534.2, 550, 551	21.00	65.00
PS109	2001 (3)	—	KM534.2, 552, 553	21.00	75.00
PS110	2001 (3)	—	KM534.2, 554, 555	21.00	75.00
PS111	2001 (3)	—	KM534.2, 556, 557	21.00	75.00
PS112	2001 (3)	—	KM534.2, 558, 559	21.00	85.00
PS113	2001 (3)	—	KM534.2, 560, 561	21.00	95.00
PS114	2001 (3)	—	KM534.2, 562, 563	21.00	85.00
PS115	2001 (3)	—	KM534.2, 564, 565	21.00	85.00
PS116	2001 (20)	—	KM491.2, 532-533, 534.2, 549.2, 550-565	120	665
PS117	2001 (6)	—	KM#401-403, 406, 491.1, 534.1	—	145
PS118	2001 (1)	650	Federation Centennial Set	—	6,000
PS119	2002 (6)	39,513	KM#401-403, 406, 600.2, 602	—	95.00
PS120	2006 (6)	39,090	KM#401-402, 406, 688-689, 690.1	—	70.00
PS121	2003 (6)	6,500	KM#401b, 402b, 406b, 688a, 689a, 690a	—	180
PS122	2003 (4)	10,000	KM763-766	118	250
PS123	2004 (6)	50,000	KM#401-404, 406, 733	—	80.00
PS124	2004 (6)	6,500	KM#401b, 402b, 403b, 404a, 406b, 733.1a	—	150
PS125	2005 (6)	—	KM#401, 402, 406, 745-747	—	85.00
PS126	2005 (6)	6,500	KM#401b, 402b, 406b, 745a, 746a, 747a	—	175
PS127	2005 (6)	650	KM#401a, 402a, 406a, 745b, 746b, 747b	—	5,850
PS128	2006 (8)	—	KM#401-404, 406, 489, 767-768	62.50	120
PS129	2006 (8)	6,500	KM#62a, 63a, 64a, 65a, 66a, 77a, 852	180	220

WEDDING SPECIMEN SETS

KM#	Date	Mintage	Identification	Issue Price	Mkt Val
WSS1	2002 (6)	3,322	KM#401-403, 406, 600.1, 602 Plaque	—	97.50
WSS2	2003 (6)	3,249	KM#401-402, 406, 688-690 Plaque	—	55.00
WSS3	2004 (6)	4,000	KM#401-404, 406, 733.1 Plaque	—	58.50
WSS4	2005 (6)	—	KM#401-402, 406, 745-747 Plaque	60.00	60.00
WSS5	2006 (8)	—	KM#401-404, 406, 489, 767-768 Plaque	60.00	60.00

AUSTRIA

The Republic of Austria, a parliamentary democracy located in mountainous central Europe, has an area of 32,374 sq. mi. (83,850 sq. km.) and a population of 8.08 million. Capital: Wien (Vienna). Austria is primarily an industrial country. Machinery, iron, steel, textiles, yarns and timber are exported.

REPUBLIC

POST WWII DECIMAL COINAGE
100 Groschen - 1 Schilling

KM# 2878 10 GROSCHEN
1.10 g., Aluminum, 20 mm. **Obv:** Small Imperial Eagle with Austrian shield on breast, at top between numbers, scalloped rim, stylized inscription below **Rev:** Large value above date, scalloped rim **Edge:** Plain **Designer:** Hans Köttenstorfer

Date	Mintage	F12	VF20	XF40	MS60	MS63
2001 Special Unc	75,000	—	—	—	—	1.50

KM# 2885 50 GROSCHEN
3.00 g., Aluminum-Bronze, 19.5 mm. **Obv:** Austrian shield **Obv. Designer:** Hans Köttenstorfer **Rev:** Large value above date **Rev. Designer:** Ferdinand Welz **Edge:** Reeded

Date	Mintage	F12	VF20	XF40	MS60	MS63
2001 Special Unc	75,000	—	—	—	—	1.50

KM# 2886 SCHILLING
4.20 g., Aluminum-Bronze, 22.5 mm. **Obv:** Large value above date **Obv. Designer:** Edwin Grienauer **Rev:** Edelweiss flower **Rev. Designer:** Ferdinand Welz **Edge:** Plain

Date	Mintage	F12	VF20	XF40	MS60	MS63
2001 Special Unc	75,000	—	—	—	—	1.00

KM# 2889a 5 SCHILLING
4.80 g., Copper-Nickel, 23.5 mm. **Obv:** Lippizaner stallion with rider, rearing left **Obv. Designer:** Hans Köttenstorfer **Rev:** Austrian shield divides date, value above, sprays below **Rev. Designer:** Josef Köblinger **Edge:** Plain

Date	Mintage	F12	VF20	XF40	MS60	MS63
2001 Special Unc	75,000	—	—	—	—	1.50

KM# 2918 10 SCHILLING
6.20 g., Copper-Nickel Plated Nickel, 26 mm. **Obv:** Imperial Eagle with Austrian shield on breast, holding hammer and sickle **Obv. Designer:** Kurt Bodlak **Rev:** Woman of Wachau left, value and date right of hat **Rev. Designer:** Ferdinand Welz **Edge:** Reeded

Date	Mintage	F12	VF20	XF40	MS60	MS63
2001 Special Unc	75,000	—	—	—	—	1.50

KM# 3075 20 SCHILLING
8.00 g., Copper-Aluminum-Nickel, 27.7 mm. **Subject:** Johann Nepomuk Nestroy **Obv:** Denomination within square **Rev:** Bust half left **Edge:** 19 incuse dots **Designer:** Herbert Wähner

Date	Mintage	F12	VF20	XF40	MS60	MS63
2001	225,000	—	—	—	2.00	—
2001 Special Unc	75,000	—	—	—	—	3.00

KM# 3076 50 SCHILLING
8.15 g., Bi-Metallic, 26.5 mm. **Subject:** The Schilling Era **Obv:** Denomination and shields **Rev:** Four old coin designs **Edge:** Plain

Date	Mintage	F12	VF20	XF40	MS60	MS63
2001	600,000	—	—	—	5.00	—
2001 Special Unc.	100,000	—	—	—	—	5.00

KM# 3073 100 SCHILLING
13.70 g., Bi-Metallic, 34 mm. **Subject:** Transportation **Obv:** Automobile engine **Obv. Designer:** Thomas Pesendorfer **Rev:** Car, train, truck, and plane **Rev. Designer:** Andreas Zanaschka **Edge:** Plain

Date	Mintage	F12	VF20	XF40	MS60	MS63
2001	50,000	PF60 BV+5%				

KM# 3077 100 SCHILLING
20.00 g., 0.900 Silver 0.575 oz. ASW, 34 mm. **Subject:** Charlemagne **Obv:** Holy Roman Emperor's crown above denomination **Obv. Designer:** Thomas Pesendorfer **Rev:** Bust 3/4 facing with scepter, two shields at right **Rev. Designer:** Herbert Wähner **Edge:** Reeded

Date	Mintage	F12	VF20	XF40	MS60	MS63
2001	50,000	PF60 BV+5%				

KM# 3079 100 SCHILLING
20.00 g., 0.900 Silver 0.575 oz. ASW, 34 mm. **Subject:** Duke Rudolf IV **Obv:** University teaching scene **Obv. Designer:** Thomas Pesendorfer **Rev:** Bust on right looking left, St. Stephen's Cathedral at left **Rev. Designer:** Herbert Wähner **Edge:** Reeded

Date	Mintage	F12	VF20	XF40	MS60	MS63
2001	50,000	PF60 BV+5%				

KM# 3074 500 SCHILLING
10.14 g., 0.986 Gold 0.3194 oz. AGW, 22 mm. **Subject:** 2000 Years of Christianity - Bible **Obv:** Bible and symbols of the saints: Matthew, Luke, Mark, and John **Rev:** St. Paul reading from a scroll to two listeners **Designer:** Thomas Pesendorfer

Date	Mintage	F12	VF20	XF40	MS60	MS63
2001	50,000	PF60 600				

KM# 3078 500 SCHILLING
24.00 g., 0.925 Silver 0.7092 oz. ASW, 37 mm. **Subject:** Kufstein Castle **Obv:** Castle view above denomination **Rev:**

Emperor Maximilian being shown one of his new cannons **Edge:** Plain with engraved lettering **Designer:** Thomas Pesendorfer

Date	Mintage	F12	VF20	XF40	MS60	MS63
2001	50,000	—	—	—	45.00	—
2001 Special Unc.	15,000	—	—	—	—	50.00
2001	30,000	PF60 45.00				

KM# 3080 500 SCHILLING
24.00 g., 0.925 Silver 0.7092 oz. ASW, 37 mm. **Subject:** Schattenburg Castle **Obv:** Castle view **Obv. Designer:** Thomas Pesendorfer **Rev:** Two medieval armourers at work **Rev. Designer:** Helmut Andexlinger **Edge:** Plain with engraved lettering

Date	Mintage	F12	VF20	XF40	MS60	MS63
2001	37,000	—	—	—	45.00	—
2001 Special Unc	15,000	—	—	—	—	45.00
2001	43,000	PF60 45.00				

KM# 3081 1000 SCHILLING
16.22 g., 0.986 Gold 0.5109 oz. AGW, 30 mm. **Subject:** Austrian National Library **Obv:** Archduke Maximilian as a student **Obv. Designer:** Thomas Pesendorfer **Rev:** Library interior view **Rev. Designer:** Herbert Wähner **Edge:** Reeded

Date	Mintage	F12	VF20	XF40	MS60	MS63
2001	30,000	PF60 850				

BULLION COINAGE
Philharmonic Issues

KM# 3004 200 SCHILLING
3.12 g., 0.9999 Gold 0.0997 oz. AGW, 16 mm. **Series:** Vienna Philharmonic Orchestra **Obv:** The Golden Hall organ **Rev:** Wind and string instruments **Edge:** Reeded **Designer:** Thomas Pesendorfer

Date	Mintage	F12	VF20	XF40	MS60	MS63
2001	26,400	—	—	—	BV+13%	—

KM# 2989 500 SCHILLING
7.78 g., 0.9999 Gold 0.2484 oz. AGW, 22 mm. **Series:** Vienna Philharmonic Orchestra **Obv:** The Golden Hall organ **Rev:** Wind and string instruments **Edge:** Reeded **Designer:** Thomas Pesendorfer

Date	Mintage	F12	VF20	XF40	MS60	MS63
2001	25,800	—	—	—	BV+10%	—

KM# 3031 1000 SCHILLING
15.55 g., 0.9999 Gold 0.4967 oz. AGW, 28 mm. **Series:** Vienna Philharmonic Orchestra **Obv:** The Golden Hall organ **Rev:** Wind and string instruments **Edge:** Reeded **Designer:** Thomas Pesendorfer

Date	Mintage	F12	VF20	XF40	MS60	MS63
2001	26,800	—	—	—	BV+8%	—

KM# 2990 2000 SCHILLING
31.10 g., 0.9999 Gold 0.9935 oz. AGW, 37 mm. **Series:** Vienna Philharmonic Orchestra **Obv:** The Golden Hall organ **Rev:** Wind and string instruments **Edge:** Reeded **Designer:** Thomas Pesendorfer

Date	Mintage	F12	VF20	XF40	MS60	MS63
2001	54,700	—	—	—	BV+4%	—

EURO COINAGE
European Union Issues

KM# 3082 EURO CENT
2.30 g., Copper Plated Steel, 16.25 mm. **Obv:** Gentian flower **Obv. Legend:** EIN EURO CENT **Obv. Designer:** Josef Kaiser

Rev: Denomination and globe **Rev. Designer:** Luc Luycx **Edge:** Plain

Date	Mintage	F12	VF20	XF40	MS60	MS63
2002	378,400,000	—	—	—	0.35	—
2002 Special Unc	100,000	—	—	—	—	0.50
2002	10,000	PF60 15.00				
2003	10,800,000	—	—	—	0.35	—
2003 Special Unc	125,000	—	—	—	—	0.50
2003	25,000	PF60 3.00				
2004	115,000,000	—	—	—	0.35	—
2004 Special Unc	100,000	—	—	—	—	0.50
2004	20,000	PF60 3.00				
2005	122,900,000	—	—	—	0.35	—
2005 Special Unc	100,000	—	—	—	—	0.50
2005	20,000	PF60 4.00				
2006	48,300,000	—	—	—	0.35	—
2006 Special Unc	100,000	—	—	—	—	0.50
2006	20,000	PF60 4.00				
2007	111,900,000	—	—	—	0.35	—
2007 Special Unc	75,000	—	—	—	—	0.50
2007	20,000	PF60 4.00				
2008	50,900,000	—	—	—	0.35	—
2008 Special Unc	50,000	—	—	—	—	0.50
2008	15,000	PF60 4.00				
2009	158,900,000	—	—	—	0.35	—
2009 Special Unc	75,000	—	—	—	—	0.50
2009	15,000	PF60 4.00				
2010	168,500,000	—	—	—	0.35	—
2010 Special Unc	50,000	—	—	—	—	0.50
2010	15,000	PF60 4.00				
2011	189,600,000	—	—	—	0.35	—
2011 Special Unc	50,000	—	—	—	—	0.50
2011	15,000	PF60 4.00				
2012	169,300,000	—	—	—	0.35	—
2012 Special Unc	50,000	—	—	—	—	0.50
2012	10,000	PF60 4.00				
2013 Special Unc.	50,000	—	—	—	—	0.75
2013	10,000	PF60 4.00				

KM# 3083 2 EURO CENT
3.06 g., Copper Plated Steel, 18.75 mm. **Obv:** Edelweiss flower in inner circle, stars in outer circle **Obv. Legend:** ZWEI EURO CENT **Obv. Designer:** Josef Kaiser **Rev:** Denomination and globe **Rev. Designer:** Luc Luycx **Edge:** Grooved

Date	Mintage	F12	VF20	XF40	MS60	MS63
2002	326,400,000	—	—	—	0.50	—
2002 Special Unc	100,000	—	—	—	—	0.65
2002	10,000	PF60 20.00				
2003	118,500,000	—	—	—	0.50	—
2003 Special Unc	125,000	—	—	—	—	0.65
2003	25,000	PF60 5.00				
2004	156,400,000	—	—	—	0.50	—
2004 Special Unc	100,000	—	—	—	—	0.65
2004	20,000	PF60 5.00				
2005	113,000,000	—	—	—	0.50	—
2005 Special Unc	100,000	—	—	—	—	0.65
2005	20,000	PF60 6.00				
2006	39,800,000	—	—	—	0.35	—
2006 Special Unc	100,000	—	—	—	—	0.65
2006	20,000	PF60 6.00				
2007	72,200,000	—	—	—	0.35	—
2007 Special Unc	75,000	—	—	—	—	0.65
2007	20,000	PF60 6.00				
2008	125,100,000	—	—	—	0.35	—
2008 Special Unc	50,000	—	—	—	—	0.65
2008	15,000	PF60 6.00				
2009	120,400,000	—	—	—	0.35	—
2009 Special Unc	75,000	—	—	—	—	0.65
2009	15,000	PF60 6.00				
2010	104,200,000	—	—	—	0.35	—
2010 Special Unc	50,000	—	—	—	—	0.65
2010	15,000	PF60 6.00				
2011	148,600,000	—	—	—	0.35	—
2011 Special Unc	75,000	—	—	—	—	0.65
2011	15,000	PF60 6.00				
2012	78,100,000	—	—	—	0.35	—
2012 Special Unc	50,000	—	—	—	—	0.65
2012	10,000	PF60 6.00				
2013 Special Unc.	50,000	—	—	—	—	0.75

KM# 3084 5 EURO CENT
3.92 g., Copper Plated Steel, 21.25 mm. **Obv:** Alpine prim rose flower in inner ring, stars in outer ring **Obv. Legend:** FUNF EURO CENT **Obv. Designer:** Josef Kaiser **Rev:** Denomination and globe **Rev. Designer:** Luc Luycx **Edge:** Plain

Date	Mintage	F12	VF20	XF40	MS60	MS63
2002	217,000,000	—	—	—	0.75	—
2002 Special Unc	100,000	—	—	—	—	1.00
2002	10,000	PF60 30.00				
2003	108,500,000	—	—	—	0.75	—
2003 Special Unc	125,000	—	—	—	—	1.00
2003	25,000	PF60 8.50				
2004	89,300,000	—	—	—	0.75	—
2004 Special Unc	100,000	—	—	—	—	1.00
2004	20,000	PF60 9.00				
2005	66,100,000	—	—	—	0.75	—
2005 Special Unc	100,000	—	—	—	—	1.00
2005	20,000	PF60 10.00				
2006	5,600,000	—	—	—	0.75	—
2006 Special Unc	100,000	—	—	—	—	1.00
2006	20,000	PF60 10.00				
2007	52,700,000	—	—	—	0.75	—
2007 Special Unc	75,000	—	—	—	—	1.00
2007	20,000	PF60 10.00				
2008	96,700,000	—	—	—	0.75	—
2008 Special Unc	50,000	—	—	—	—	1.00
2008	15,000	PF60 10.00				
2009	5,800,000	—	—	—	0.75	—
2009 Special Unc	75,000	—	—	—	—	1.00
2009	15,000	PF60 10.00				
2010	63,700,000	—	—	—	0.75	—
2010 Special Unc	50,000	—	—	—	—	1.00
2010	15,000	PF60 10.00				
2011	66,600,000	—	—	—	0.75	—
2011 Special Unc	50,000	—	—	—	—	1.00
2011	15,000	PF60 10.00				
2012	35,300,000	—	—	—	0.75	—
2012 Special Unc	50,000	—	—	—	—	1.00
2012	10,000	PF60 10.00				
2013 Special Unc	50,000	—	—	—	1.00	—
2013	10,000	PF60 10.00				

KM# 3085 10 EURO CENT

4.10 g., Brass, 19.75 mm. **Obv:** St. Stephen's Cathedral spires **Obv. Designer:** Josef Kaiser **Rev:** Relief map of European Union at left, denomination at center right **Rev. Designer:** Luc Luycx **Edge:** Reeded

Date	Mintage	F12	VF20	XF40	MS60	MS63
2002	441,600,000	—	—	—	0.75	—
2002 Special Unc	100,000	—	—	—	—	1.00
2002	10,000	PF60 45.00				
2003 Special Unc	125,000	—	—	—	—	4.00
2003	35,000	PF60 8.50				
2004	5,200,000	—	—	—	0.80	—
2004 Special Unc	100,000	—	—	—	—	1.00
2004	20,000	PF60 9.00				
2005	5,200,000	—	—	—	0.80	—
2005 Special Unc	100,000	—	—	—	—	1.00
2005	20,000	PF60 10.00				
2006	40,000,000	—	—	—	0.75	—
2006 Special Unc	100,000	—	—	—	—	1.00
2006	20,000	PF60 10.00				
2007	81,300,000	—	—	—	0.75	—
2007 Special Unc	75,000	—	—	—	—	1.00
2007	20,000	PF60 10.00				

KM# 3139 10 EURO CENT

4.10 g., Brass, 19.75 mm. **Obv:** St. Stephen's Cathedral spires **Obv. Designer:** Josef Kaiser **Rev:** Relief Map of Western Europe, stars, lines and value **Rev. Designer:** Luc Luycx **Edge:** Reeded

Date	Mintage	F12	VF20	XF40	MS60	MS63
2008	70,200,000	—	—	—	0.75	—
2008 Special Unc	50,000	—	—	—	—	1.00
2008	15,000	PF60 10.00				
2009	15,900,000	—	—	—	0.75	—
2009 Special Unc	75,000	—	—	—	—	1.00
2009	15,000	PF60 10.00				
2010	42,800,000	—	—	—	0.75	—
2010 Special Unc	50,000	—	—	—	—	1.00
2010	15,000	PF60 10.00				
2011	27,600,000	—	—	—	0.75	—
2011 Special Unc	50,000	—	—	—	—	1.00
2011	15,000	PF60 10.00				
2012	25,000,000	—	—	—	0.75	—
2012 Special Unc	50,000	—	—	—	—	1.00
2012	10,000	PF60 10.00				
2013 Special Unc	50,000					
2013	10,000	PF60 1.00				

KM# 3086 20 EURO CENT

5.74 g., Brass, 22.25 mm. **Obv:** Belvedere Palace gate **Obv. Designer:** Josef Kaiser **Rev:** Relief map of European Union at left, denomination at center right **Rev. Designer:** Luc Luycx **Edge:** Notched

Date	Mintage	F12	VF20	XF40	MS60	MS63
2002	203,400,000	—	—	—	1.00	—
2002 Special Unc	100,000	—	—	—	—	1.25
2002	10,000	PF60 60.00				
2003	50,900,000	—	—	—	1.00	—
2003 Special Unc	125,000	—	—	—	—	1.25
2003	25,000	PF60 10.00				
2004	54,800,000	—	—	—	1.00	—
2004 Special Unc	100,000	—	—	—	—	1.25
2004	20,000	PF60 11.50				
2005	4,100,000	—	—	—	1.10	—
2005 Special Unc	100,000	—	—	—	—	1.25
2005	20,000	PF60 12.50				
2006	8,200,000	—	—	—	1.00	—
2006 Special Unc	100,000	—	—	—	—	1.25
2006	20,000	PF60 12.50				
2007	45,000,000	—	—	—	1.00	—
2007 Special Unc	75,000	—	—	—	—	1.25
2007	20,000	PF60 12.50				

KM# 3140 20 EURO CENT

5.74 g., Brass, 22.25 mm. **Obv:** Belvedere Palace gate **Obv. Designer:** Josef Kaiser **Rev:** Expanded relief map of European Union at left, denomination at center right **Rev. Designer:** Luc Luycx **Edge:** Notched

Date	Mintage	F12	VF20	XF40	MS60	MS63
2008	45,300,000	—	—	—	1.00	—
2008 Special Unc.	50,000	—	—	—	—	1.50
2008	15,000	PF60 12.50				
2009	49,800,000	—	—	—	1.00	—
2009 Special Unc.	75,000	—	—	—	—	1.50
2009	15,000	PF60 12.50				
2010	4,200,000	—	—	—	1.00	—
2010 Special Unc.	50,000	—	—	—	—	1.50
2010	15,000	PF60 12.50				
2011	21,300,000	—	—	—	1.00	—
2011 Special Unc.	50,000	—	—	—	—	1.50
2011	15,000	PF60 12.50				
2012	10,800,000	—	—	—	1.00	—
2012 Special Unc.	50,000	—	—	—	—	1.50
2012	10,000	PF60 12.50				
2013 Special Unc	50,000	—	—	—	1.50	—
2013	10,000	PF60 1.50				

KM# 3087 50 EURO CENT

7.80 g., Brass, 24.25 mm. **Obv:** Secession building in Vienna **Obv. Designer:** Josef Kaiser **Rev:** Relief map of European Union at left, denomination at center right **Rev. Designer:** Luc Luycx **Edge:** Reeded

Date	Mintage	F12	VF20	XF40	MS60	MS63
2002	169,100,000	—	—	—	1.25	—
2002 Special Unc	100,000	—	—	—	—	1.50
2002	10,000	PF60 75.00				
2003	9,100,000	—	—	—	1.25	—
2003 Special Unc	125,000	—	—	—	—	1.50
2003	25,000	PF60 12.50				
2004	3,100,000	—	—	—	1.25	—
2004 Special Unc	100,000	—	—	—	—	1.50
2004	20,000	PF60 13.50				
2005	3,100,000	—	—	—	1.25	—
2005 Special Unc	100,000	—	—	—	—	1.50
2005	20,000	PF60 15.00				
2006	3,200,000	—	—	—	1.25	—
2006 Special Unc	100,000	—	—	—	—	1.50
2006	20,000	PF60 15.00				
2007	3,000,000	—	—	—	1.25	—
2007 Special Unc	75,000	—	—	—	—	1.50
2007	20,000	PF60 15.00				

KM# 3141 50 EURO CENT

7.80 g., Brass, 24.25 mm. **Obv:** Secession building in Vienna **Obv. Designer:** Josef Kaiser **Rev:** Expanded relief map of European Union at left, denomination at right **Rev. Designer:** Luc Luycx **Edge:** Reeded

Date	Mintage	F12	VF20	XF40	MS60	MS63
2008	3,000,000	—	—	—	1.25	—
2008 Special Unc	50,000	—	—	—	—	1.50
2008	15,000	PF60 15.00				
2009	14,700,000	—	—	—	1.25	—
2009 Special Unc	75,000	—	—	—	—	1.50
2009	15,000	PF60 15.00				
2010	30,000,000	—	—	—	1.25	—
2010 Special Unc	50,000	—	—	—	—	1.50
2010	15,000	PF60 15.00				
2011	6,000,000	—	—	—	1.25	—
2011 Special Unc	50,000	—	—	—	—	1.50
2011	15,000	PF60 15.00				
2012 Special Unc.	50,000	—	—	—	—	1.50
2012	10,000	PF60 15.00				
2013 Special Unc	50,000	—	—	—	1.50	—
2013	10,000	PF60 15.00				

KM# 3088 EURO

7.50 g., Bi-Metallic, 23.25 mm. **Obv:** Bust of Mozart right within inner circle, stars in outer circle **Obv. Designer:** Josef Kaiser **Rev:** Value at left, relief map of European Union at right **Rev. Designer:** Luc Luycx **Edge:** Segmented reeding

Date	Mintage	F12	VF20	XF40	MS60	MS63
2002	223,500,000	—	—	—	2.50	—
2002 Special Unc	100,000	—	—	—	—	2.75
2002	10,000	PF60 100				
2003 Special Unc	125,000	—	—	—	—	5.00
2003	25,000	PF60 16.50				
2004	2,600,000	—	—	—	2.50	—
2004 Special Unc	100,000	—	—	—	—	2.75
2004	20,000	PF60 17.50				
2005	2,600,000	—	—	—	2.50	—
2005 Special Unc	100,000	—	—	—	—	2.75
2005	20,000	PF60 18.50				
2006	7,700,000	—	—	—	2.50	—
2006 Special Unc	100,000	—	—	—	—	2.75
2006	20,000	PF60 18.50				
2007	41,100,000	—	—	—	2.50	—
2007 Special Unc	75,000	—	—	—	—	2.75
2007	20,000	PF60 18.50				

KM# 3142 EURO

7.50 g., Bi-Metallic, 23.25 mm. **Obv:** Bust of Mozart right within inner circle, stars in outer circle **Obv. Designer:** Josef Kaiser **Rev:** Value at left, expanded relief map of European Union at right **Rev. Designer:** Luc Luycx **Edge:** Segmented reeding

Date	Mintage	F12	VF20	XF40	MS60	MS63
2008	65,500,000	—	—	—	2.00	—
2008 Special Unc	50,000	—	—	—	—	2.75
2008	15,000	PF60 15.00				
2009	40,300,000	—	—	—	2.00	—
2009 Special Unc	75,000	—	—	—	—	2.75
2009	15,000	PF60 15.00				
2010	11,200,000	—	—	—	2.00	—
2010 Special Unc	50,000	—	—	—	—	2.75
2010	15,000	PF60 15.00				
2011	8,000,000	—	—	—	2.00	—
2011 Special Unc	50,000	—	—	—	—	2.75
2011	15,000	PF60 15.00				
2012 Special Unc.	50,000	—	—	—	—	2.75
2012	10,000	PF60 15.00				
2013 Special Unc	50,000	—	—	—	2.75	—
2013	10,000	PF60 15.00				

KM# 3089 2 EURO
8.50 g., Bi-Metallic, 25.75 mm. **Obv:** Bust of Bertha von Suttner, Novelist and winner of 1905 Peace Prize, facing left within inner circle, stars in outer circle **Obv. Designer:** Josef Kaiser **Rev:** Value at left, relief map of European Union at right **Rev. Designer:** Luc Luycx **Edge Lettering:** 2 EURO (star) (star) (star) (star)

Date	Mintage	F12	VF20	XF40	MS60	MS63
2002	196,400,000	—	—	—	3.75	—
2002 Special Unc	100,000	—	—	—	—	4.00
2002	10,000	PF60 125				
2003	4,700,000	—	—	—	3.75	—
2003 Special Unc	125,000	—	—	—	—	4.00
2003	25,000	PF60 25.00				
2004	2,500,000	—	—	—	3.75	—
2004 Special Unc	100,000	—	—	—	—	4.00
2004	20,000	PF60 27.50				
2006	2,300,000	—	—	—	3.75	—
2006 Special Unc	100,000	—	—	—	—	4.00
2006	20,000	PF60 27.50				

KM# 3124 2 EURO
8.50 g., Bi-Metallic, 25.75 mm. **Subject:** 50th Anniversary of the State Treaty **Obv:** Treaty seals and signatures **Rev:** Denomination and map **Edge:** Reeding over lettering **Edge Lettering:** 2 EURO" and 3 stars repeated four times

Date	Mintage	F12	VF20	XF40	MS60	MS63
2005	6,880,000	—	—	—	5.00	—
2005 Special Unc	100,000	—	—	—	—	6.00
2005	20,000	PF60 27.50				

KM# 3150 2 EURO
8.50 g., Bi-Metallic, 25.75 mm. **Subject:** 50th Anniversary - Treaty of Rome **Edge:** Reeded and lettered

Date	Mintage	F12	VF20	XF40	MS60	MS63
2007	8,905,000	—	—	—	4.00	—
2007 Special Unc	75,000	—	—	—	—	5.00
2007	20,000	PF60 27.50				

KM# 3143 2 EURO
8.50 g., Bi-Metallic, 25.75 mm. **Obv:** Bust of Bertha von Suttner, Novelist and winner of 1905 Peace Prize, at right facing left in inner circle, stars in outer circle **Obv. Designer:** Josef Kaiser **Rev:** Value at left, expanded relief map of European Union at right **Rev. Designer:** Luc Luycx **Edge Lettering:** 2 EURO (star) (star) (star)

Date	Mintage	F12	VF20	XF40	MS60	MS63
2008	2,600,000	—	—	—	5.00	—
2008 Special Unc	50,000	—	—	—	—	6.00
2008	15,000	PF60 25.00				
2010	17,000,000	—	—	—	5.00	—
2010 Special Unc	50,000	—	—	—	—	6.00
2010	15,000	PF60 25.00				
2011	27,900,000	—	—	—	5.00	—
2011 Special Unc	50,000	—	—	—	—	6.00
2011	15,000	PF60 25.00				
2012	21,200,000	—	—	—	4.50	—
2013 Special Unc	50,000	—	—	—	—	6.00
2013	10,000	PF60 25.00				

KM# 3175 2 EURO
8.50 g., Bi-Metallic, 25.75 mm. **Subject:** 10th Anniversary - European Monetary Union **Edge:** Reeded and lettered

Date	Mintage	F12	VF20	XF40	MS60	MS63
2009	4,910,000	—	—	—	6.00	—
2009 Special Unc	75,000	—	—	—	—	7.50
2009	15,000	PF60 25.00				

KM# 3205 2 EURO
8.50 g., Bi-Metallic, 25.75 mm. **Subject:** Euro Coinage, 10th Anniversary **Obv:** Euro symbol on globe at center, child-like rendering around

Date	Mintage	F12	VF20	XF40	MS60	MS63
2012	11,000,000	—	—	—	6.00	8.00
2012	10,000	PF60 25.00				
2012 Special Unc.	50,000	—	—	—	—	15.00

KM# 3091 5 EURO
10.00 g., 0.800 Silver 0.2556 oz. ASW, 28.5 mm. **Subject:** Schoenbrunn Zoo **Obv:** Denomination within sun design at center, provincial arms surround **Rev:** Building and animals **Edge:** Plain **Shape:** 9-sided

Date	Mintage	F12	VF20	XF40	MS60	MS63
ND(2002)	500,000	—	—	—	12.50	—
ND(2002) Special Unc	100,000	—	—	—	—	22.50

KM# 3105 5 EURO
10.00 g., 0.800 Silver 0.2556 oz. ASW, 28.5 mm. **Subject:** Water Power **Obv:** Denomination within sun design at center, provincial arms surround **Rev:** Dam with turbine, electric power plant and fish **Edge:** Plain **Shape:** 9-sided

Date	Mintage	F12	VF20	XF40	MS60	MS63
2003	500,000	—	—	—	11.50	—
2003 Special Unc	100,000	—	—	—	—	15.00

KM# 3122 5 EURO
10.00 g., 0.800 Silver 0.2556 oz. ASW, 28.5 mm. **Subject:** Enlargement of the European Union **Obv:** Denomination within sun design at center, provincial arms surround **Rev:** Map of Europe above country names **Edge:** Plain **Shape:** 9-sided

Date	Mintage	F12	VF20	XF40	MS60	MS63
2004	275,000	—	—	—	10.00	—
2004 Special Unc	125,000	—	—	—	—	12.50

KM# 3113 5 EURO
10.00 g., 0.800 Silver 0.2556 oz. ASW, 28.5 mm. **Obv:** Denomination within sun design at center, provincial arms surround **Rev:** Soccer player scoring a goal **Edge:** Plain **Shape:** 9-sided **Note:** Centennial of Austrian Soccer

Date	Mintage	F12	VF20	XF40	MS60	MS63
2004	600,000	—	—	—	10.00	—
2004 Special Unc	100,000	—	—	—	—	12.50

KM# 3117 5 EURO
10.00 g., 0.800 Silver 0.2556 oz. ASW, 28.5 mm. **Subject:** Centennial of Sport Skiing **Obv:** Denomination within sun design at center, provincial arms surround **Rev:** Skier within snowflake design **Edge:** Plain **Shape:** 9-sided

Date	Mintage	F12	VF20	XF40	MS60	MS63
2005	500,000	—	—	—	10.00	—
2005 Special Unc	100,000	—	—	—	—	14.50

KM# 3120 5 EURO
10.00 g., 0.800 Silver 0.2556 oz. ASW, 28.5 mm. **Subject:** 10th Anniversary of Austrian E U Membership **Obv:** Denomination within sun design at center, provincial arms surround **Rev:** Carinthian Gate Theater and Beethoven cameo portrait **Edge:** Plain **Shape:** 9-sided

Date	Mintage	F12	VF20	XF40	MS60	MS63
2005	275,000	—	—	—	12.50	—
2005 Special Unc	125,000	—	—	—	—	14.50

KM# 3131 5 EURO
10.00 g., 0.800 Silver 0.2556 oz. ASW, 28.5 mm. **Subject:** Mozart **Obv:** Denomination within sun design at center, provincial arms surround **Rev:** Mozart and the Salzburg Cathedral **Edge:** Plain **Shape:** Nine sided

Date	Mintage	F12	VF20	XF40	MS60	MS63
2006	375,000	—	—	—	15.00	—
2006 Special Unc	125,000	—	—	—	—	17.50

KM# 3132 5 EURO
10.00 g., 0.800 Silver 0.2556 oz. ASW, 28.5 mm. **Subject:** Austrian Presidency of the EU **Obv:** Value in circle of arms **Rev:** Vienna Hofburg and Josefsplatz view **Edge:** Plain **Shape:** Nine sided

Date	Mintage	F12	VF20	XF40	MS60	MS63
2006	250,000	—	—	—	12.50	—
2006 Special Unc	100,000	—	—	—	—	14.50

KM# 3145 5 EURO

10.00 g., 0.800 Silver 0.2556 oz. ASW, 28.5 mm. **Obv:** Value in circle of shields **Rev:** Mariazell church **Edge:** Plain **Shape:** 9-sided

Date	Mintage	F12	VF20	XF40	MS60	MS63
2007	450,000	—	—	—	15.00	—
2007 Special Unc	100,000	—	—	—	—	20.00

KM# 3144 5 EURO

10.00 g., 0.800 Silver 0.2556 oz. ASW, 28.5 mm. **Subject:** Universal Male Suffrage Centennial **Obv:** Value in circle of shields **Rev:** Cameo portraits of Franz Joseph and von Beck on Reichsrat scene **Edge:** Plain **Shape:** 9-sided

Date	Mintage	F12	VF20	XF40	MS60	MS63
2007	150,000	—	—	—	13.00	—
2007 Special Unc	100,000	—	—	—	—	15.00

KM# 3156 5 EURO

10.00 g., 0.800 Silver 0.2556 oz. ASW, 28.5 mm. **Subject:** Herbert Von Karajan, 100th Birth Anniversary **Obv:** Value and nine provincial shields **Rev:** Bust and notes of Beethoven's Ninth Symphony **Shape:** 9-sided

Date	Mintage	F12	VF20	XF40	MS60	MS63
2008	150,000	—	—	—	17.00	—
2008 Special Unc	100,000	—	—	—	—	20.00

KM# 3163 5 EURO

10.00 g., 0.800 Silver 0.2556 oz. ASW, 28.5 mm. **Obv:** Value within center of nine shields **Rev:** Two soccer players **Shape:** 9-sided

Date	Mintage	F12	VF20	XF40	MS60	MS63
2008	225,000	—	—	—	15.00	—
2008 Special Unc	100,000	—	—	—	—	20.00

KM# 3164 5 EURO

10.00 g., 0.800 Silver 0.2556 oz. ASW, 28.5 mm. **Obv:** Value within center of nine shields **Rev:** One soccer player **Shape:** 9-sided

Date	Mintage	F12	VF20	XF40	MS60	MS63
2008	225,000	—	—	—	15.00	—
2008 Special Unc	100,000	—	—	—	—	20.00

KM# 3177 5 EURO

10.00 g., 0.800 Silver 0.2556 oz. ASW, 28.5 mm. **Subject:** Tyrolean Resistance Fighters, 1809 **Shape:** 9-sided

Date	Mintage	F12	VF20	XF40	MS60	MS63
2009	250,000	—	—	—	20.00	—
2009 Special Unc	100,000	—	—	—	—	30.00

KM# 3170 5 EURO

10.00 g., 0.800 Silver 0.2556 oz. ASW, 28.5 mm. **Subject:** Joseph Haydn, 200th Anniversary of Death **Obv:** Value at center of nine shields **Rev:** Bust facing right at left, pair of violins at right **Shape:** 9-sided

Date	Mintage	F12	VF20	XF40	MS60	MS63
2009	450,000	—	—	—	15.00	—
2009 Special Unc	100,000	—	—	—	—	20.00

KM# 3184 5 EURO

10.00 g., 0.800 Silver 0.2556 oz. ASW, 28.5 mm. **Subject:** Grossglockner - High Alpine Road **Shape:** 9-sided

Date	Mintage	F12	VF20	XF40	MS60	MS63
2010	250,000	—	—	—	15.00	—
2010 Special Unc	50,000	—	—	—	—	20.00

KM# 3192 5 EURO

10.00 g., 0.800 Silver 0.2556 oz. ASW, 28.5 mm. **Subject:** Winter sports **Obv:** Nine provincial shields **Rev:** Snowboarding **Rev. Designer:** Helmut Andexlinger **Shape:** 9-sided

Date	Mintage	F12	VF20	XF40	MS60	MS63
2010	225,000	—	—	—	15.00	—
2010 Special Unc	50,000	—	—	—	—	20.00

KM# 3193 5 EURO

10.00 g., 0.800 Silver 0.2556 oz. ASW, 28.5 mm. **Subject:** Winter Sports **Obv:** Nine provincial shields **Rev:** Ski jumper **Shape:** 9-sided

Date	Mintage	F12	VF20	XF40	MS60	MS63
2010	225,000	—	—	—	15.00	—
2010 Special Unc	50,000	—	—	—	—	20.00

KM# 3195 5 EURO

10.00 g., 0.800 Silver 0.2556 oz. ASW, 28.5 mm. **Subject:** Pummerin, Bell, 1711-2011 **Obv:** Value within circle of shields **Rev:** Large bell **Shape:** 9-sided

Date	Mintage	F12	VF20	XF40	MS60	MS63
2011 Special Unc.	50,000	—	—	—	—	20.00

KM# 3196 5 EURO

10.00 g., 0.800 Silver 0.2556 oz. ASW, 28.5 mm. **Subject:** Land of Forests **Shape:** 9-sided **Designer:** H. Andexlinger

Date	Mintage	F12	VF20	XF40	MS60	MS63
2011 Special Unc.	50,000	—	—	—	—	20.00

KM# 3206 5 EURO

8.90 g., Copper, 28.5 mm. **Subject:** Society of Music Lovers, 200th Anniversary **Obv:** Value at center of circle of nine shields **Obv. Designer:** Thomas Pesendorfer **Rev:** Interior of the "Golden Hall" in Vienna **Rev. Designer:** Helmut Andexlinger **Shape:** 9-sided

Date	Mintage	F12	VF20	XF40	MS60	MS63
2012	300,000	—	—	—	8.00	—

KM# 3206a 5 EURO

10.00 g., 0.800 Silver 0.2556 oz. ASW, 28.5 mm. **Subject:** Society of Music Lovers, 200th Anniversary **Obv:** Value in circle of nine shields **Obv. Designer:** Thomas Pesendorfer **Rev:** Interior of the "Golden Hall" in Vienna **Rev. Designer:** Helmut Andexlinger **Shape:** 9-sided

Date	Mintage	F12	VF20	XF40	MS60	MS63
2012 Special Unc.	50,000	—	—	—	—	28.00

KM# 3215 5 EURO

8.90 g., Copper, 28.5 mm. **Subject:** Schladming **Rev:** Downhill skier **Shape:** 9-sided

Date	Mintage	F12	VF20	XF40	MS60	MS63
2012	300,000	—	—	—	8.00	

KM# 3215a 5 EURO

10.00 g., 0.800 Silver 0.2556 oz. ASW, 28.5 mm. **Subject:** Schladming **Rev:** Downhill skier **Shape:** 9-sided

Date	Mintage	F12	VF20	XF40	MS60	MS63
2012 Special Unc	50,000	—	—	—	—	25.00

KM# 3216 5 EURO

8.90 g., Copper, 28.5 mm. **Subject:** Vienna Waltz **Rev:** Dancers **Shape:** 9-sided

Date	Mintage	F12	VF20	XF40	MS60	MS63
2012	200,000	—	—	—	—	8.00

KM# 3216a 5 EURO

10.00 g., 0.800 Silver 0.2556 oz. ASW, 28.5 mm. **Subject:** Vienna Waltz **Rev:** Two dancers

Date	Mintage	F12	VF20	XF40	MS60	MS63
2012 Special Unc	50,000	—	—	—	—	30.00

KM# 3222 5 EURO

8.90 g., Copper, 28.5 mm. **Subject:** Land of Water, UNESCO Year of Water Cooperation, 2013 **Rev:** Heron in pond, kingfisher and flora **Rev. Designer:** Thomas Pesendorfer **Rev. Legend:** LAND DES WASSERS

Date	Mintage	F12	VF20	XF40	MS60	MS63
2013	200,000	—	—	—	—	8.00

KM# 3222a 5 EURO

10.00 g., 0.800 Silver 0.2556 oz. ASW, 28.5 mm. **Subject:** Land of Water **Obv:** Nine provincial shields **Obv. Designer:** Helmut Andexlinger **Rev:** Heron standing in pond, kingfisher and flora **Rev. Designer:** Thomas Pesendorfer

Date	Mintage	F12	VF20	XF40	MS60	MS63
2013 Special Unc.	50,000	—	—	—	—	30.00

KM# 3096 10 EURO

17.30 g., 0.925 Silver 0.5112 oz. ASW, 32 mm. **Subject:** Ambras Palace **Obv:** Palace, denomination below **Rev:** Three strolling musicians **Edge:** Reeded

Date	Mintage	F12	VF20	XF40	MS60	MS63
2002	130,000	—	—	—	20.00	—
2002 Special Unc	20,000	—	—	—	—	30.00
2002	50,000	PF60 40.00				

KM# 3099 10 EURO

17.30 g., 0.925 Silver 0.5112 oz. ASW, 32 mm. **Subject:** Eggenberg Palace and Johannes Kepler **Obv:** Palace, denomination below **Rev:** Half figure seated with tools **Edge:** Reeded

Date	Mintage	F12	VF20	XF40	MS60	MS63
2002	130,000	—	—	—	20.00	—
2002 Special Unc	20,000	—	—	—	—	30.00
2002	50,000	PF60 32.50				

KM# 3103 10 EURO

17.30 g., 0.925 Silver 0.5112 oz. ASW, 32 mm. **Subject:** Castle of Schlosshof **Obv:** Baroque fountain and palace, denomination below **Rev:** Two gardeners at work

Date	Mintage	F12	VF20	XF40	MS60	MS63
2003	130,000	—	—	—	30.00	—
2003 Special Unc	20,000	—	—	—	—	35.00
2003	50,000	PF60 40.00				

KM# 3106 10 EURO

17.30 g., 0.925 Silver 0.5112 oz. ASW, 32 mm. **Subject:** Schoenbrunn Palace **Obv:** Fountain with palace background, denomination below **Rev:** Palmenhaus greenhouse

Date	Mintage	F12	VF20	XF40	MS60	MS63
2003	100,000	—	—	—	30.00	—
2003 Special Unc	40,000	—	—	—	—	35.00
2003	60,000	PF60 40.00				

KM# 3111 10 EURO

17.30 g., 0.925 Silver 0.5112 oz. ASW, 32 mm. **Obv:** Hellbrunn Castle, denomination below **Rev:** Archbishop Marcus Sitticus and Hellbrunn's "Roman Theatre **Edge:** Reeded

Date	Mintage	F12	VF20	XF40	MS60	MS63
2004	130,000	—	—	—	30.00	—
2004 Special Unc	40,000	—	—	—	—	35.00
2004	60,000	PF60 40.00				

KM# 3115 10 EURO

17.30 g., 0.925 Silver 0.5112 oz. ASW, 32 mm. **Obv:** Artstetten Castle, denomination below **Rev:** Crypt entrance behind portraits of Franz Ferdinand and Sophie

Date	Mintage	F12	VF20	XF40	MS60	MS63
2004	130,000	—	—	—	30.00	—
2004 Special Unc	40,000	—	—	—	—	35.00
2004	60,000	PF60 40.00				

KM# 3121 10 EURO

17.30 g., 0.925 Silver 0.5112 oz. ASW, 32 mm. **Subject:** 60th Anniversary of the Second Republic **Obv:** Statue of Athena, nine provincial shields and denomination at right **Rev:** Parliament building above broken chain, crowd below

Date	Mintage	F12	VF20	XF40	MS60	MS63
2005	130,000	—	—	—	30.00	—
2005 Special Unc	40,000	—	—	—	—	35.00
2005	60,000	PF60 40.00				

KM# 3125 10 EURO

17.30 g., 0.925 Silver 0.5112 oz. ASW, 32 mm. **Subject:** Reopening of the Burg Theater and Opera **Obv:** Two large buildings, denomination at left **Rev:** Comedy and Tragedy Masks

Date	Mintage	F12	VF20	XF40	MS60	MS63
2005	130,000	—	—	—	30.00	—
2005 Special Unc	40,000	—	—	—	—	35.00
2005	60,000	PF60 40.00				

KM# 3129 10 EURO

17.30 g., 0.925 Silver 0.5112 oz. ASW, 32 mm. **Subject:** Nonnenberg Abbey **Obv:** Abbey view, denomination below **Rev:** Statue of St. Erentrudis **Edge:** Reeded

Date	Mintage	F12	VF20	XF40	MS60	MS63
2006	130,000	—	—	—	30.00	—
2006 Special Unc	40,000	—	—	—	—	35.00
2006	60,000	PF60 40.00				

KM# 3137 10 EURO

17.30 g., 0.925 Silver 0.5112 oz. ASW, 32 mm. **Obv:** Gottweig Abby above value **Rev:** Charles VI and staircase

Date	Mintage	F12	VF20	XF40	MS60	MS63
2006	130,000	—	—	—	30.00	—
2006 Special Unc	40,000	—	—	—	—	35.00
2006	60,000	PF60 40.00				

KM# 3146 10 EURO

17.30 g., 0.925 Silver 0.5112 oz. ASW, 32 mm. **Obv:** Melk Abbey view **Rev:** Inner view of the Melk Abbey dome

Date	Mintage	F12	VF20	XF40	MS60	MS63
2007	130,000	—	—	—	30.00	—
2007 Special Unc	40,000	—	—	—	—	35.00
2007	60,000	PF60 40.00				

KM# 3148 10 EURO
17.30 g., 0.925 Silver 0.5112 oz. ASW, 32 mm. **Obv:** St. Paul's Abbey complex **Obv. Legend:** ST. PAUL IM LAVANTTAL **Obv. Inscription:** REPUBLIK / ÖSTERREICH **Rev:** Entrance facade

Date	Mintage	F12	VF20	XF40	MS60	MS63
2007	130,000	—	—	—	30.00	—
2007 Special Unc	60,000	—	—	—	—	35.00
2007	40,000	PF60 40.00				

KM# 3157 10 EURO
17.30 g., 0.925 Silver 0.5112 oz. ASW, 32 mm. **Subject:** Abby of Klosterneuburg **Obv:** Aerial exterior view of church complex **Rev:** Cloister

Date	Mintage	F12	VF20	XF40	MS60	MS63
2008	130,000	—	—	—	30.00	—
2008	60,000	PF60 45.00				
2008 Special Unc	40,000	—	—	—	—	35.00

KM# 3162 10 EURO
17.30 g., 0.925 Silver 0.5112 oz. ASW, 32 mm. **Subject:** Seckau Benedictine Abbey **Obv:** Exterior of abby, value, date and inscriptions "BENEDIKTINERABTEI SECKAU" and "REPUBLIK OESTERREICH" **Rev:** Interior of abbey

Date	Mintage	F12	VF20	XF40	MS60	MS63
2008	130,000	—	—	—	30.00	—
2008 Special Unc	40,000	—	—	—	—	35.00
2008	60,000	PF60 45.00				

KM# 3176 10 EURO
17.30 g., 0.925 Silver 0.5112 oz. ASW, 32 mm. **Series:** Tales and Legends **Subject:** Basilisk of Vienna

Date	Mintage	F12	VF20	XF40	MS60	MS63
2009	130,000	—	—	—	30.00	—
2009	40,000	PF60 45.00				
2009 Special Unc	30,000	—	—	—	—	35.00

KM# 3180 10 EURO
17.30 g., 0.925 Silver 0.5112 oz. ASW, 32 mm. **Series:** Tales and Legends **Subject:** Richard the Lionheart in Dürnstein

Date	Mintage	F12	VF20	XF40	MS60	MS63
2009	130,000	—	—	—	30.00	—
2009	40,000	PF60 45.00				
2009 Special Unc	30,000	—	—	—	—	35.00

KM# 3186 10 EURO
17.30 g., 0.925 Silver 0.5112 oz. ASW, 32 mm. **Subject:** Charlemagne in the Undersberg

Date	Mintage	F12	VF20	XF40	MS60	MS63
2010(h) Special Unc	30,000	—	—	—	—	45.00
2010(h)	130,000	—	—	—	30.00	—
2010(h)	40,000	PF60 45.00				

KM# 3185 10 EURO
17.30 g., 0.925 Silver 0.5112 oz. ASW, 32 mm. **Subject:** Erzberg in Styria **Obv:** Iron Mine **Rev:** Two mermen with cloak

Date	Mintage	F12	VF20	XF40	MS60	MS63
2010	130,000	—	—	—	30.00	—
2010 Special Unc	30,000	—	—	—	—	35.00
2010	40,000	PF60 45.00				

KM# 3197 10 EURO
17.30 g., 0.925 Silver 0.5112 oz. ASW, 32 mm. **Subject:** The Lindworm in Klagenfurt

Date	Mintage	F12	VF20	XF40	MS60	MS63
2011 Special Unc.	30,000	—	—	—	—	45.00
2011	40,000	PF60 55.00				

KM# 3198 10 EURO
17.30 g., 0.925 Silver 0.5112 oz. ASW, 32 mm. **Subject:** My dear old Augustin

Date	Mintage	F12	VF20	XF40	MS60	MS63
2011 Special Unc.	30,000	—	—	—	—	45.00
2011	40,000	PF60 65.00				

KM# 3207 10 EURO
15.00 g., Copper, 32 mm. **Subject:** Steiermark **Obv:** Graz town view **Rev:** Child's drawing of countryside

Date	Mintage	F12	VF20	XF40	MS60	MS63
2012	130,000	—	—	—	17.00	—

KM# 3208 10 EURO
15.00 g., Copper, 32 mm. **Subject:** Carinthia **Obv:** Falconer with bird **Obv. Designer:** Thomas Pesendorfer **Rev:** Child's drawing of countryside **Rev. Designer:** Philip Ogris

Date	Mintage	F12	VF20	XF40	MS60	MS63
2012	130,000	—	—	—	17.00	—

KM# 3208a 10 EURO
17.30 g., 0.925 Silver 0.5112 oz. ASW, 32 mm. **Subject:** Carinthia **Obv:** Falconer and bird **Obv. Designer:** Thomas Pesendorfer **Rev:** Child's drawing of countryside **Rev. Designer:** Philip Ogris

Date	Mintage	F12	VF20	XF40	MS60	MS63
2012	30,000	PF60 55.00				
2012 Special Unc.	40,000	—	—	—	—	50.00

KM# 3211 10 EURO
20.00 g., 0.900 Silver 0.575 oz. ASW, 34 mm. **Series:** Rome on the Danube - Brigantium **Subject:** Brigantium

Date	Mintage	F12	VF20	XF40	MS60	MS63
2012	50,000	PF60 70.00				

KM# 3207a 10 EURO
17.30 g., 0.925 Silver 0.5112 oz. ASW, 32 mm. **Subject:** Steiermark **Obv:** Graz town view **Rev:** Child's design of countryside

Date	Mintage	F12	VF20	XF40	MS60	MS63
2012	30,000	PF60 60.00				
2012 Special Unc	40,000	—	—	—	—	50.00

KM# 3221 10 EURO
15.00 g., Copper **Subject:** Federal Provinces: Lower Austria

Date	Mintage	F12	VF20	XF40	MS60	MS63
2013 Special Unc.	130,000	—	—	—	—	15.00

KM# 3221a 10 EURO
17.30 g., 0.925 Silver 0.5112 oz. ASW, 32 mm. **Subject:** Federal Provinces: Lower Austria

Date	Mintage	F12	VF20	XF40	MS60	MS63
2013	30,000	PF60 55.00				
2013 Special Unc.	40,000	—	—	—	—	50.00

KM# 3224 10 EURO
15.00 g., Copper, 32 mm. **Subject:** Federal Provinces: Vorarlberg

Date	Mintage	F12	VF20	XF40	MS60	MS63
2013	130,000	—	—	—	17.00	—

KM# 3224a 10 EURO
17.30 g., 0.925 Silver 0.5112 oz. ASW, 32 mm. **Subject:**
Federal Provinces: Vorarlberg

Date	Mintage	F12	VF20	XF40	MS60	MS63
2013	30,000	PF60 55.00				
2013 Special Unc.	40,000	—	—	—	—	45.00

KM# 3097 20 EURO
20.00 g., 0.900 Silver 0.575 oz. ASW, 34 mm. **Subject:**
Ferdinand I - Renaissance **Obv:** Hofburg Palace "Swiss Gate"
with two guards, denomination below **Rev:** Bust looking left,
coat of arms at left, dates at right **Edge:** Reeded

Date	Mintage	F12	VF20	XF40	MS60	MS63
2002	—	PF60 37.50				

KM# 3098 20 EURO
20.00 g., 0.900 Silver 0.575 oz. ASW, 34 mm. **Subject:** Prince
Eugen - Baroque Period **Obv:** Baroque staircase with statues,
denomination below **Rev:** Uniformed bust 1/4 left and dates at
right, flags above cannons at left **Edge:** Reeded

Date	Mintage	F12	VF20	XF40	MS60	MS63
2002	—	PF60 50.00				

KM# 3104 20 EURO
20.00 g., 0.900 Silver 0.575 oz. ASW, 34 mm. **Subject:** Prince
Metternich **Obv:** Early steam locomotive, denomination below
Rev: Portrait with map background **Edge:** Reeded

Date	Mintage	F12	VF20	XF40	MS60	MS63
2003	50,000	PF60 50.00				

KM# 3107 20 EURO
20.00 g., 0.900 Silver 0.575 oz. ASW, 34 mm. **Obv:** Republic
of Austria arms, denomination below **Rev:** Four men in a jeep
Edge: Reeded **Note:** Post War Austrian Reconstruction

Date	Mintage	F12	VF20	XF40	MS60	MS63
2003	50,000	PF60 50.00				

KM# 3112 20 EURO
20.00 g., 0.900 Silver 0.575 oz. ASW, 34 mm. **Obv:** S.M.S
Novara under sail in Chinese waters, denomination below **Rev:**
Standing figures behind table with globe and microscope **Edge:**
Reeded **Note:** First Global Circumnavigation by an Austrian ship.

Date	Mintage	F12	VF20	XF40	MS60	MS63
2004	50,000	PF60 50.00				

KM# 3114 20 EURO
20.00 g., 0.900 Silver 0.575 oz. ASW, 34 mm. **Obv:** SMS
Erzherzog Ferdinand Max sailing to the Battle of Lissa,
denomination below **Rev:** Sailors at the wheel with Admiral
Tegetthof in background **Edge:** Reeded

Date	Mintage	F12	VF20	XF40	MS60	MS63
2004	50,000	PF60 52.50				

KM# 3126 20 EURO
20.00 g., 0.900 Silver 0.575 oz. ASW, 34 mm. **Obv:** Ship,
"Admiral Tegetthoff" in arctic waters, denomination below
Rev: Expedition leaders, von Payer and Weyprecht with their
icebound ship behind them **Edge:** Reeded

Date	Mintage	F12	VF20	XF40	MS60	MS63
2005	50,000	PF60 50.00				

KM# 3127 20 EURO
20.00 g., 0.900 Silver 0.575 oz. ASW, 34 mm. **Obv:** SMS St.
George sailing past the Statue of Liberty, denomination below
Rev: Shipyard at Pola, boat on water **Edge:** Reeded

Date	Mintage	F12	VF20	XF40	MS60	MS63
2005	50,000	PF60 50.00				

KM# 3133 20 EURO
20.00 g., 0.900 Silver 0.575 oz. ASW, 34 mm. **Subject:** Austrian
Merchant Marine **Obv:** Two passing steam ships **Rev:** 19th
Century Triest harbor view **Edge:** Reeded

Date	Mintage	F12	VF20	XF40	MS60	MS63
2006	50,000	PF60 50.00				

KM# 3134 20 EURO
20.00 g., 0.900 Silver 0.575 oz. ASW, 34 mm. **Obv:** SMS
Viribus Unitis, flag ship of the Austrian fleet, and other ships
steaming left **Rev:** SMS Viribus Unitis, submarine conning
tower and seaplane **Edge:** Reeded

Date	Mintage	F12	VF20	XF40	MS60	MS63
2006	50,000	PF60 50.00				

KM# 3149 20 EURO
20.00 g., 0.900 Silver 0.575 oz. ASW, 34 mm. **Series:** Austrian
Railways **Obv:** Steam locomotive 1837 with passenger wagons
Obv. Legend: REPUBLIK ÖSTERREICH **Obv. Inscription:**
DAMPFLOKOMOTIVE / AUSTRIA / 1837 **Rev:** People waving
at passenger train crossing a trestle **Rev. Legend:** KAISER -
FERDINANDS - NORDBAHN **Edge:** Reeded

Date	Mintage	F12	VF20	XF40	MS60	MS63
2007	50,000	PF60 70.00				

KM# 3151 20 EURO
20.00 g., 0.900 Silver 0.575 oz. ASW, 34 mm. **Series:** Austrian
Railways **Obv:** Steam locomotive 1848 standing still, viaduct
in background **Obv. Legend:** REPUBLIK ÖSTERREICH **Obv.
Inscription:** DAMPF-/ LOKOMOTIVE / STEINBRØCK / 1848
Rev: Steam train traveling right through city **Rev. Legend:** K.K.
SÜDBAHN WIEN - TRIEST **Edge:** Reeded

Date	Mintage	F12	VF20	XF40	MS60	MS63
2007	50,000	PF60 70.00				

KM# 3154 20 EURO
20.00 g., 0.900 Silver 0.575 oz. ASW, 34 mm. **Subject:**
Southern Railways **Obv:** Steam Locomotive on iron railway
bridge **Obv. Inscription:** KOK kkStB 306 **Rev:** Statue
of Empress Elizabeth and train platform in Vienna's West
Railway station **Rev. Inscription:** KAISERIN-/ ELIZABETH-/
WESTBAHN **Edge:** Reeded

Date	Mintage	F12	VF20	XF40	MS60	MS63
2008	50,000	PF60 70.00				

KM# 3161 20 EURO
20.00 g., 0.900 Silver 0.575 oz. ASW, 34 mm. **Subject:** Imperal
- Royal State Railway **Obv:** Locomotive steaming left **Obv.
Legend:** Nordbahnhof/Wein **Rev:** Female on platform **Edge:**
Reeded

Date	Mintage	F12	VF20	XF40	MS60	MS63
2008	50,000	PF60 70.00				

KM# 3178 20 EURO
20.00 g., 0.900 Silver 0.575 oz. ASW, 34 mm. **Subject:**
The Electric Railway **Obv:** Locomotive model 1189, the
Crocodile **Obv. Designer:** Thomas Pesendorfer **Rev:** Train
on the Trisanna Bridge, Wiesburg Castle in background **Rev.
Designer:** Herbert Wahner **Edge:** Reeded

Date	Mintage	F12	VF20	XF40	MS60	MS63
2009	50,000	PF60 50.00				

KM# 3179 20 EURO
20.00 g., 0.900 Silver 0.575 oz. ASW, 34 mm. **Subject:**
Railways of the Future **Obv:** Railjet highspeed OBB train **Obv.
Designer:** Helmut Andexlinger **Rev:** Electric locomotive of the
1063 class in freight yard **Rev. Designer:** Thomas Pesendorfer
Edge: Reeded

Date	Mintage	F12	VF20	XF40	MS60	MS63
2009	50,000	PF60 70.00				

KM# 3187 20 EURO
20.00 g., 0.900 Silver 0.575 oz. ASW, 34 mm. **Series:** Rome on
the Danube **Subject:** Virunum **Obv:** Emperor Claudium, 2-horse
wagon, gravestone **Obv. Designer:** Helmut Andexlinger **Rev:**
Street scene, wagon and temple facade **Rev. Designer:**
Herbert Waehner **Edge:** Reeded

Date	Mintage	F12	VF20	XF40	MS60	MS63
2010	50,000	PF60 70.00				

KM# 3188 20 EURO
20.00 g., 0.900 Silver 0.575 oz. ASW, 34 mm. **Series:** Rome on
the Danube **Subject:** Vindofona **Edge:** Reeded

Date	Mintage	F12	VF20	XF40	MS60	MS63
2010	50,000	PF60 70.00				

KM# 3199 20 EURO
20.00 g., 0.900 Silver 0.575 oz. ASW, 34 mm. **Series:** Rome on
the Danube **Subject:** Carnuntum **Edge:** Reeded

Date	Mintage	F12	VF20	XF40	MS60	MS63
2011	50,000	PF60 70.00				

KM# 3200 20 EURO
20.00 g., 0.900 Silver 0.575 oz. ASW, 34 mm. **Series:** Rome on
the Danube **Subject:** Aguntum

Date	Mintage	F12	VF20	XF40	MS60	MS63
2011	50,000	PF60 70.00				

KM# 3201 20 EURO
20.00 g., 0.900 Silver 0.575 oz. ASW, 34 mm. **Subject:**
Nikolaus Joseph von Jacquin **Obv:** Bust at left, flower at right
Rev: Karibuk Expedition, Jacquin taking notes of plants in book

Date	Mintage	F12	VF20	XF40	MS60	MS63
2011	50,000	PF60 70.00				

KM# 3209 20 EURO
20.00 g., 0.900 Silver 0.575 oz. ASW, 34 mm. **Series:** European
Artists **Subject:** Egon Schiele **Obv:** Portrait of the artist **Rev:**
Painting of a female

Date	Mintage	F12	VF20	XF40	MS60	MS63
2012	50,000	PF60 70.00				

KM# 3210 20 EURO
20.00 g., 0.900 Silver 0.575 oz. ASW, 34 mm. **Series:** Rome on
the Danube **Subject:** Lauriacum

Date	Mintage	F12	VF20	XF40	MS60	MS63
2012	50,000	PF60 70.00				

KM# 3219 20 EURO
20.00 g., 0.900 Silver 0.575 oz. ASW, 34 mm. **Subject:**
European Writers: Stefan Zweig

Date	Mintage	F12	VF20	XF40	MS60	MS63
2013	50,000	PF60 70.00				

KM# 3220 20 EURO
20.00 g., 0.900 Silver 0.575 oz. ASW, 34 mm. **Series:**
Prehistoric Life **Subject:** Trias - Life in the water

Date	Mintage	F12	VF20	XF40	MS60	MS63
2013	50,000	PF60 70.00				

KM# 3223 20 EURO
20.00 g., 0.900 Silver 0.575 oz. ASW, 34 mm. **Series:** Prehistoric
Life **Subject:** Jura - Life in the Air **Obv:** Rhamphorhynchus and
Jurassic period timeline **Rev:** Two flying Rhamphorhynchus
hunting large dragonfly. Luch tropical vegitation **Designer:**
Thomas Pesendorfer

Date	Mintage	F12	VF20	XF40	MS60	MS63
2013	50,000	PF60 65.00				

KM# 3227 25 EURO
16.50 g., Bi-Metallic, 34 mm. **Subject:** Evolution **Obv:** DNA
and RNA stands **Rev:** Steps in evolution **Designer:** Helmut
Andexlinger **Note:** Two colors of Niobium

Date	Mintage	F12	VF20	XF40	MS60	MS63
2014 Special Unc	65,000	—	—	—	—	80.00

KM# 3101 25 EURO
17.15 g., Bi-Metallic, 34 mm. **Subject:** City of Hall in Tyrol **Obv:**
Satellite mapping the city from outer space **Rev:** Depiction of
the die face used to strike the 1486 guldiner coin **Edge:** Plain

Date	Mintage	F12	VF20	XF40	MS60	MS63
2003 Special Unc	50,000	—	—	—	—	125

KM# 3109 25 EURO
17.15 g., Bi-Metallic, 34 mm. **Subject:** Semmering Alpine Railway **Obv:** Modern and antique locomotives **Rev:** Steam train **Edge:** Plain

Date	Mintage	F12	VF20	XF40	MS60	MS63
2004 Special Unc	50,000	—	—	—	—	100

KM# 3119 25 EURO
17.15 g., Bi-Metallic, 34 mm. **Subject:** 50 Years Austrian Television **Obv:** The original test pattern of the 1950's **Rev:** World globe behind "rabbit ear" antenna; television developmental milestones from 7-1 o'clock **Edge:** Plain

Date	Mintage	F12	VF20	XF40	MS60	MS63
2005 Special Unc	65,000	—	—	—	—	75.00

KM# 3135 25 EURO
17.15 g., Bi-Metallic, 34 mm. **Subject:** European Satellite Navigation **Obv:** Austrian Mint's global location inscribed on a compass face **Rev:** Satellites in orbit around the world globe **Edge:** Plain

Date	Mintage	F12	VF20	XF40	MS60	MS63
2006 Special Unc	65,000	—	—	—	—	75.00

KM# 3147 25 EURO
16.50 g., Bi-Metallic, 34 mm. **Subject:** Austrian Aviation **Obv:** Interior view of modern cockpit **Rev:** Taube airplane flying above glider and pilot **Edge:** Plain

Date	Mintage	F12	VF20	XF40	MS60	MS63
2007 Special Unc	65,000	—	—	—	—	75.00

KM# 3158 25 EURO
16.50 g., Bi-Metallic, 34 mm. **Subject:** Carl Baron Auer von Welsbach, 150th Anniversary of Birth **Obv:** Lighting gas lamp before Vienna City Wall **Obv. Designer:** Herbert Waehner **Rev:** Head of Welsbach, development of light bulbs

Date	Mintage	F12	VF20	XF40	MS60	MS63
2000 Special Unc	65,000	—	—	—	—	80.00

KM# 3174 25 EURO
16.50 g., Bi-Metallic, 34 mm. **Subject:** Year of Astronomy **Obv:** Galileo head and instruments **Rev:** Space exploration satellite

Date	Mintage	F12	VF20	XF40	MS60	MS63
2009 Special Unc	65,000	—	—	—	—	80.00

KM# 3189 25 EURO
16.50 g., Bi-Metallic, 34 mm. **Obv:** Tree and the 4 elements: earth, wind, water, and fire **Rev:** Solar panels, hydroelectric turbine, global thermal energy and wind turbine **Designer:** Helmut Andexlinger

Date	Mintage	F12	VF20	XF40	MS60	MS63
2010 Special Unc	65,000	—	—	—	—	80.00

KM# 3204 25 EURO
16.50 g., Bi-Metallic, 34 mm. **Subject:** Robotics **Rev:** Mars rover

Date	Mintage	F12	VF20	XF40	MS60	MS63
2011 Special Unc	65,000	—	—	—	—	80.00

KM# 3212 25 EURO
16.50 g., Bi-Metallic, 34 mm. **Subject:** Bionics

Date	Mintage	F12	VF20	XF40	MS60	MS63
2012 Special Unc	65,000	—	—	—	—	75.00

KM# 3217 25 EURO
16.50 g., 0.900 Bi-Metallic 0.4744 oz., 34 mm. **Subject:** Tunneling **Obv:** Tunnel boring machine and air vents **Rev:** 19th century tunnel worker and tunnel **Designer:** Herbert Waehner

Date	Mintage	F12	VF20	XF40	MS60	MS63
2013 Special Unc	65,000	PF60 80.00				

KM# 3090 50 EURO
10.14 g., 0.986 Gold 0.3194 oz. AGW, 22 mm. **Subject:** Saints Benedict and Scholastica **Obv:** St. Benedict and his sister St. Scholastica **Rev:** Monk copying a manuscript **Edge:** Reeded

Date	Mintage	F12	VF20	XF40	MS60	MS63
2002	50,000	PF60 600				

KM# 3102 50 EURO
10.14 g., 0.986 Gold 0.3194 oz. AGW, 22 mm. **Subject:** Christian Charity **Obv:** Nursing Sister with hospital patient **Rev:** The Good Samaritan **Edge:** Reeded

Date	Mintage	F12	VF20	XF40	MS60	MS63
2003	50,000	PF60 600				

KM# 3110 50 EURO
10.14 g., 0.986 Gold 0.3194 oz. AGW, 22 mm. **Subject:** Great Composers - Joseph Haydn (1732-1809) **Obv:** Esterhazy Palace **Rev:** Bust 3/4 right

Date	Mintage	F12	VF20	XF40	MS60	MS63
2004	50,000	PF60 600				

KM# 3118 50 EURO
10.14 g., 0.986 Gold 0.3194 oz. AGW, 22 mm. **Subject:** Great Composers - Ludwig Van Beethoven (1770-1827) **Obv:** Lobkowitz Palace above value and document **Rev:** Bust 3/4 facing, dates at left

Date	Mintage	F12	VF20	XF40	MS60	MS63
2005	50,000	PF60 600				

KM# 3130 50 EURO
10.14 g., 0.986 Gold 0.3194 oz. AGW, 22 mm. **Subject:** Great Composers - Mozart **Obv:** Mozart's birthplace, denomination below **Rev:** Leopold and Wolfgang Mozart

Date	Mintage	F12	VF20	XF40	MS60	MS63
2006	50,000	PF60 600				

KM# 3138 50 EURO
10.14 g., 0.986 Gold 0.3194 oz. AGW, 22 mm. **Obv:** Gerard Van Swieten holding book and facing left **Rev:** Akademie der Wissenschaften building

Date	Mintage	F12	VF20	XF40	MS60	MS63
2007	50,000	PF60 600				

KM# 3153 50 EURO
10.14 g., 0.986 Gold 0.3194 oz. AGW, 22 mm. **Subject:** Ignaz Philipp Sammelweis - Personal Hygiene **Obv:** Bust of Sammelweis 3/4 right, staff of Aesculapius at lower right **Obv. Legend:** REPUBLIK ÖSTERREICH **Rev:** Vienna General Hospital, Sammelweis helping patient wash at lower right **Rev. Legend:** ALLGEMEINES KRANKENHAUS WEIN

Date	Mintage	F12	VF20	XF40	MS60	MS63
2008	50,000	PF60 600				

KM# 3171 50 EURO
10.14 g., 0.986 Gold 0.3194 oz. AGW, 22 mm. **Subject:** Theodor Billroth **Obv:** Bust and Aesculapius staff **Rev:** Operation scene

Date	Mintage	F12	VF20	XF40	MS60	MS63
2009	50,000	PF60 600				

KM# 3194 50 EURO
10.14 g., 0.986 Gold 0.3194 oz. AGW, 22 mm. **Subject:** Baron Clemens von Pirquet **Obv:** Portrait of von Pirquet **Designer:** Helmut Andexlinger **Rev:** Facade of Children's Clinic of Vienna

Date	Mintage	F12	VF20	XF40	MS60	MS63
2010	50,000	PF60 600				

KM# 3202 50 EURO
10.14 g., 0.986 Gold 0.3194 oz. AGW, 22 mm. **Subject:** Joanneum Museum **Obv:** Exterior of Art Museum **Rev:** Armor display

Date	Mintage	F12	VF20	XF40	MS60	MS63
2011	50,000	PF60 600				

KM# 3213 50 EURO
10.14 g., 0.986 Gold 0.3194 oz. AGW, 22 mm. **Series:** Klimt and his woman **Subject:** Adele Bloch Bauer **Obv:** Portrait of artist **Rev:** Female subject from painting

Date	Mintage	F12	VF20	XF40	MS60	MS63
2012	30,000	PF60 675				

KM# 3218 50 EURO
10.11 g., 0.986 Gold 0.3184 oz. AGW, 22 mm. **Series:** Klimt and his Women **Subject:** The Expectation **Obv. Designer:** Female subject from painting facing right **Rev. Designer:** Design, country name, date and denomination

Date	Mintage	F12	VF20	XF40	MS60	MS63
2013	30,000	PF60 675				

KM# 3100 100 EURO
16.23 g., 0.986 Gold 0.5111 oz. AGW, 30 mm. **Subject:** Raphael Donner **Obv:** Portrait in front of building **Rev:** Providentia Fountain **Edge:** Reeded

Date	Mintage	F12	VF20	XF40	MS60	MS63
2002	30,000	PF60 900				

KM# 3108 100 EURO
16.23 g., 0.986 Gold 0.5111 oz. AGW, 30 mm. **Obv:** Gustav Klimt standing **Rev:** Klimt's painting "The Kiss **Edge:** Reeded

Date	Mintage	F12	VF20	XF40	MS60	MS63
2003	30,000	PF60 900				

KM# 3116 100 EURO
16.23 g., 0.986 Gold 0.5111 oz. AGW, 30 mm. **Obv:** Secession Exhibit Hall in Vienna **Rev:** Knight in armor, "strength" with two women, "ambition and sympathy

Date	Mintage	F12	VF20	XF40	MS60	MS63
2004	30,000	PF60 900				

KM# 3128 100 EURO
16.23 g., 0.986 Gold 0.5111 oz. AGW, 30 mm. **Subject:** St. Leopold's Church at Steinhof **Obv:** Domed church building, denomination below **Rev:** Two angels flank stained glass portrait

Date	Mintage	F12	VF20	XF40	MS60	MS63
2005	30,000	PF60 900				

KM# 3136 100 EURO
16.23 g., 0.986 Gold 0.5111 oz. AGW, 30 mm. **Subject:** Vienna's River Gate Park **Obv:** Bridge over river scene **Rev:** One of two "sculpted ladies" flanking the park entrance

Date	Mintage	F12	VF20	XF40	MS60	MS63
2006	30,000	PF60 900				

KM# 3155 100 EURO
16.23 g., 0.986 Gold 0.5111 oz. AGW, 30 mm. **Obv:** Building at Linke Wienzeile Nr 38 by architect Otto Koloman Wagner **Rev:** Ornate elevator and stairwell

Date	Mintage	F12	VF20	XF40	MS60	MS63
2007	30,000	PF60 900				

KM# 3160 100 EURO
16.23 g., 0.986 Gold 0.5111 oz. AGW, 30 mm. **Series:** Crowns of the Habsburgs **Obv:** Crown of the Holy Roman Emperor set upon coronation robe **Rev:** Otto I seated facing and old St. Peter's Bastilica, Rome

Date	Mintage	F12	VF20	XF40	MS60	MS63
2008	30,000	PF60 900				

KM# 3181 100 EURO
16.23 g., 0.986 Gold 0.5111 oz. AGW, 30 mm. **Series:** Crowns of the Habsburgs **Subject:** Archducal crown of Austria **Obv:** Crown resting on pillow **Rev:** Procession of the crown, orb and sceptre, Plague memorial column in background

Date	Mintage	F12	VF20	XF40	MS60	MS63
2009	30,000	PF60 800				

KM# 3191 100 EURO
16.23 g., 0.986 Gold 0.5111 oz. AGW, 30 mm. **Series:** Crowns of the Habsburgs **Subject:** St. Stephen's Hungarian Crown **Obv:** Crown of St. Stephen **Rev:** Naria Theresa on horseback

Date	Mintage	F12	VF20	XF40	MS60	MS63
2010	30,000	PF60 900				

KM# 3203 100 EURO
16.23 g., 0.986 Gold 0.5111 oz. AGW, 30 mm. **Series:** Crowns of the Hapsburgs **Subject:** Crown of St. Wenceslas

Date	Mintage	F12	VF20	XF40	MS60	MS63
2011	30,000	PF60 1,000				

KM# 3214 100 EURO
16.23 g., 0.986 Gold 0.5111 oz. AGW, 30 mm. **Series:** Crowns of the hapsburgs **Obv:** Imperial Crown of Austria **Obv. Designer:** Thomas Pesendorfer **Rev:** Emperor Franz Joseph I **Rev. Designer:** Helmut Andexlinger

Date	Mintage	F12	VF20	XF40	MS60	MS63
2012	30,000	PF60	1,000			

KM# 3225 100 EURO
16.23 g., 0.986 Gold 0.5111 oz. AGW, 30 mm. **Series:** Austrian Wildlife **Subject:** Red Deer

Date	Mintage	F12	VF20	XF40	MS60	MS63
2013	30,000	PF60	900			

EURO BULLION COINAGE
Philharmonic Issues

KM# 3159 1-1/2 EURO
31.10 g., 0.999 Silver 0.9926 oz. ASW, 37 mm. **Obv:** Golden Concert Hall **Rev:** Bouquet of Instruments **Edge:** Plain

Date	Mintage	F12	VF20	XF40	MS60	MS63
2008	7,800,000	—	—	—	BV	32.00
2009	9,014,800	—	—	—	BV	32.00
2010	11,358,200	—	—	—	BV	32.00
2011	17,873,700	—	—	—	BV	32.00
2012	8,769,200	—	—	—	BV	32.00
2013	—	—	—	—	BV	32.00

KM# 3226 4 EURO
1.25 g., 0.9999 Gold 0.0399 oz. AGW, 13 mm.

Date	Mintage	F12	VF20	XF40	MS60	MS63
2014	—	—	—	—	BV+25%	50.00

KM# 3092 10 EURO
3.12 g., 0.9999 Gold 0.0997 oz. AGW, 16 mm. **Subject:** Vienna Philharmonic **Obv:** The Golden Hall organ **Rev:** Musical instruments **Edge:** Segmented reeding

Date	Mintage	F12	VF20	XF40	MS60	MS63
2002	75,789	—	—	—	—	BV+13%
2003	59,654	—	—	—	—	BV+13%
2004	67,994	—	—	—	—	BV+13%
2005	62,071	—	—	—	—	BV+13%
2006	39,892	—	—	—	—	BV+13%
2007	76,325	—	—	—	—	BV+13%
2008	176,400	—	—	—	—	BV+13%
2009	437,700	—	—	—	—	BV+13%
2010	226,700	—	—	—	—	BV+13%
2011	268,200	—	—	—	—	BV+13%
2012	176,300	—	—	—	—	BV+13%
2013	—	—	—	—	—	BV+13%

KM# 3093 25 EURO
7.78 g., 0.9999 Gold 0.2484 oz. AGW, 22 mm. **Subject:** Vienna Philharmonic **Obv:** The Golden Hall organ **Rev:** Musical instruments **Edge:** Segmented reeding

Date	Mintage	F12	VF20	XF40	MS60	MS63
2002	40,807	—	—	—	—	BV+10%
2003	34,019	—	—	—	—	BV+10%
2004	32,449	—	—	—	—	BV+10%
2005	32,817	—	—	—	—	BV+10%
2006	29,609	—	—	—	—	BV+10%
2007	34,631	—	—	—	—	BV+10%
2008	97,100	—	—	—	—	BV+10%
2009	172,000	—	—	—	—	BV+10%
2010	84,900	—	—	—	—	BV+10%
2011	102,000	—	—	—	—	BV+10%
2012	64,300	—	—	—	—	BV+10%
2013	—	—	—	—	—	BV+10%
2014 Proof sets only	5,000	PF63	BV+10%			

KM# 3094 50 EURO
15.55 g., 0.9999 Gold 0.4967 oz. AGW, 28 mm. **Subject:** Vienna Philharmonic **Obv:** The Golden Hall organ **Rev:** Musical instruments **Edge:** Segmented reeding

Date	Mintage	F12	VF20	XF40	MS60	MS63
2002	40,922	—	—	—	—	BV+8%
2003	26,848	—	—	—	—	BV+8%
2004	24,269	—	—	—	—	BV+8%
2005	21,049	—	—	—	—	BV+8%
2006	20,085	—	—	—	—	BV+8%
2007	25,091	—	—	—	—	BV+8%
2008	73,800	—	—	—	—	BV+8%
2009	92,300	—	—	—	—	BV+8%
2010	56,600	—	—	—	—	BV+8%
2011	77,500	—	—	—	—	BV+8%
2012	49,500	—	—	—	—	BV+8%
2013	—	—	—	—	—	BV+8%

KM# 3095 100 EURO
31.12 g., 0.9999 Gold 0.994 oz. AGW, 37 mm. **Subject:** Vienna Philharmonic **Obv:** The Golden Hall organ **Rev:** Musical instruments **Edge:** Segmented reeding

Date	Mintage	F12	VF20	XF40	MS60	MS63
2002	164,105	—	—	—	—	BV+4%
2003	179,881	—	—	—	—	BV+4%
2004	176,319	—	—	—	—	BV+4%
2005	158,564	—	—	—	—	BV+4%
2006	82,174	—	—	—	—	BV+4%
2007	108,675	—	—	—	—	BV+4%
2008	715,800	—	—	—	—	BV+4%
2009	835,700	—	—	—	—	BV+4%
2010	501,800	—	—	—	—	BV+4%
2011	586,700	—	—	—	—	BV+4%
2012	341,400	—	—	—	—	BV+4%
2013	—	—	—	—	—	BV+4%
2014 Proof set only	5,000	PF63	BV+10%			

KM# 3182 2000 EURO
622.10 g., 0.9999 Gold 19.8702 oz. AGW, 74 mm. **Subject:** Vienna Philharmonic **Obv:** The Golden Hall Organ **Rev:** Musical instruments **Edge:** Reeded

Date	Mintage	F12	VF20	XF40	MS60	MS63
2009	6,027	—	—	—	—	BV+5%

KM# 3123 100000 EURO
31103.50 g., 0.9999 Gold 993.464 oz. AGW, 370 mm. **Obv:** The Golden Hall organ **Rev:** Musical instruments **Edge:** Reeded

Date	Mintage	F12	VF20	XF40	MS60	MS63
2004	15	PF60	BV+5%			

MINT SETS

KM#	Date	Mintage	Identification	Issue Price	Mkt Val
MS10	2001 (6)	75,000	KM#2878, 2885, 2886, 2889a, 2918, 3075	25.00	40.00
MS11	2002 (8)	100,000	KM#3082-3089, Euro	22.50	25.00
MS12	2003 (8)	125,000	KM#3082-3089, Mozart	22.50	25.00
MS13	2004 (8)	100,000	KM#3082-3089, von Suttner	—	25.00
MS14	2005 (8)	100,000	KM#3082-3088, 3124, State treaty	—	25.00
MS15	2006 (8)	100,000	KM#3082-3089, St. Stephan's Cathedral	—	35.00
MS16	2007 (8)	75,000	KM#3082-3088, 3150, Treaty of Rome	—	25.00
MS17	2008 (8)	50,000	KM#3082-3088, 3139-3143, European Map	—	35.00
MS18	2009 (8)	75,000	KM#3082-3084, 3139-3142, 3175	—	25.00
MS19	2010 (8)	50,000	KM#3082-3084, 3139-3143	—	35.00
MS20	2011 (8)	50,000	KM#3082-3084, 3139-3143	—	35.00
MS21	2012 (8)	50,000	KM#3082-3084, 3139-3142, 3205	—	32.00
MS22	2012 (8)	Inc. Above	KM#3082-3084, 3139-3142, 3205 (Baby Mint Set)	—	35.00

PROOF SETS

KM#	Date	Mintage	Identification	Issue Price	Mkt Val
PS53	2002 (8)	10,000	KM#3082-3089	85.00	485
PS54	2003 (8)	25,000	KM#3082-3089	85.00	95.00
PS55	2004 (8)	20,000	KM#3082-3089	—	105
PS56	2005 (8)	20,000	KM#3082-3088, 3124	—	110
PS57	2006 (8)	20,000	KM#3082-3089	—	110
PS58	2007 (8)	20,000	KM#3082-3088, 3150	—	110
PS59	2008 (8)	15,000	KM#3082-3084, 3139-3143	—	120
PS60	2009 (8)	15,000	KM#3082-3084, 3139-3142, 3175	—	120
PS61	2010 (8)	15,000	KM#3082-3084, 3139-3143	—	110
PS62	2011 (8)	15,000	KM#3082-3084, 3139-3143	—	110
PS63	2012 (8)	10,000	KM#3082-3084, 3139-3142, 3205	—	110

AZERBAIJAN

The Republic of Azerbaijan (formerly Azerbaijan S.S.R.) includes the Nakhichevan Autonomous Republic. Situated in the eastern area of Transcaucasia, it is bordered in the west by Armenia, in the north by Georgia and Dagestan, to the east by the Caspian Sea and to the south by Iran. It has an area of 33,430 sq. mi. (86,600 sq. km.) and a population of 7.8 million. Capital: Baku. The area is rich in mineral deposits of aluminum, copper, iron, lead, salt and zinc, with oil as its leading industry. Agriculture and livestock follow in importance.

MONETARY SYSTEM
100 Qapik = 1 Manat

REPUBLIC
DECIMAL COINAGE

KM# 39 QAPIK
2.80 g., Copper Plated Steel, 16.25 mm. **Obv:** Map above value **Rev:** Value and musical instruments **Edge:** Plain **Designer:** Robert Kalina

Date	Mintage	F12	VF20	XF40	MS60	MS63
ND (2006)	—	—	—	0.60	1.20	2.00

KM# 40 3 QAPIK
3.45 g., Copper Plated Steel, 18 mm. **Obv:** Map above value **Rev:** Value above books **Edge:** Grooved **Designer:** Robert Kalina

Date	Mintage	F12	VF20	XF40	MS60	MS63
ND (2006)	—	—	—	0.75	1.50	2.50

KM# 41 5 QAPIK
4.85 g., Copper Plated Steel, 19.75 mm. **Obv:** Map above value **Rev:** The Maiden Tower, Baku, above value **Edge:** Reeded **Designer:** Robert Kalina

Date	Mintage	F12	VF20	XF40	MS60	MS63
ND (2006)	—	—	—	0.80	1.65	2.75

KM# 42 10 QAPIK
5.25 g., Brass Plated Steel, 22.25 mm. **Obv:** Map above value **Rev:** Value and Military Helmet, Symbolic of desire to regain Nagorno-Karabakh **Edge:** Notched **Designer:** Robert Kalina

Date	Mintage	F12	VF20	XF40	MS60	MS63
ND (2006)	—	—	—	0.85	1.75	3.00
2010						

KM# 43 20 QAPIK
6.60 g., Brass Plated Steel, 24.25 mm. **Obv:** Map above value **Rev:** Value and spiral staircase **Edge:** Segmented reeding **Designer:** Robert Kalina

Date	Mintage	F12	VF20	XF40	MS60	MS63
ND (2006)	—	—	—	1.25	2.50	4.00

KM# 44 50 QAPIK
7.70 g., Bi-Metallic, 25.5 mm. **Obv:** Map above value **Rev:** Two oil wells **Edge:** Reeded and lettered **Designer:** Robert Kalina

Date	Mintage	F12	VF20	XF40	MS60	MS63
ND (2006)	—	—	—	1.50	3.00	5.00

KM# 37 50 MANAT
28.34 g., 0.925 Silver 0.8374 oz. ASW, 38.6 mm. **Subject:** Heydar Aliyev **Obv:** National map **Rev:** Bust 3/4 right **Edge:** Reeded

Date	Mintage	F12	VF20	XF40	MS60	MS63
2004	2,000	PF65 100				

KM# 48 50 MANAT
28.28 g., 0.925 Silver 0.8356 oz. ASW, 38.6 mm. **Subject:** FIFA World Cup, 2006 **Edge:** Plain

Date	Mintage	F12	VF20	XF40	MS60	MS63
2004	200	PF65 175				

KM# 46 100 MANAT
39.94 g., 0.9167 Gold 1.1696 oz. AGW **Subject:** Heydar Aliyev **Obv:** National map **Rev:** Bust 3/4 right **Edge:** Reeded

Date	Mintage	F12	VF20	XF40	MS60	MS63
2004	1,000	PF63 2,000	PF65 2,250			

KM# 47 500 MANAT
50.00 g., 0.999 Platinum 1.5956 oz. APW **Subject:** Heydar Aliyev **Obv:** National map **Rev:** Bust 3/4 right **Edge:** Reeded

Date	Mintage	F12	VF20	XF40	MS60	MS63
2004	100	PF65 3,500				

MINT SETS

KM#	Date	Mintage	Identification	Issue Price	Mkt Val
MS1	2006 (6)	—	KM#39-44.	—	150

BAHAMAS

The Commonwealth of the Bahamas is an archipelago of about 3,000 islands, cays and rocks located in the Atlantic Ocean east of Florida and north of Cuba. The total land area of the 800 mile (1,287 km.) long chain of islands is 5,382 sq. mi. (13,935 sq. km.). They have a population of 302,000. Capital: Nassau. The Bahamas import most of their food and manufactured products and export cement, refined oil, pulpwood and lobsters. Tourism is the principal industry. The Bahamas is a member of the Commonwealth of Nations. Elizabeth II is Head of State as Queen of The Bahamas.

RULER
British

COMMONWEALTH
DECIMAL COINAGE
100 Cents = 1 Dollar

KM# 59a CENT
2.50 g., Copper Plated Zinc, 19 mm. **Ruler:** Elizabeth II **Obv:** National arms above date **Obv. Legend:** COMMONWEALTH OF THE BAHAMAS **Rev:** Starfish, value at top **Edge:** Plain

Date	Mintage	F12	VF20	XF40	MS60	MS63
2001	—	—	—	0.10	0.25	0.75
2004	—	—	—	0.10	0.25	0.75

KM# 218.1 CENT
2.50 g., Copper Plated Zinc, 19 mm. **Ruler:** Elizabeth II **Obv:** National arms, date below **Rev:** Three starfish

Date	Mintage	F12	VF20	XF40	MS60	MS63
2006	—	—	—	—	0.25	0.75
2007	—	—	—	—	0.25	0.75

KM# 218.2 CENT
1.75 g., Copper Plated Zinc, 17 mm. **Ruler:** Elizabeth II **Obv:** National arms, date below **Rev:** Three starfish

Date	Mintage	F12	VF20	XF40	MS60	MS63
2009	—	—	—	—	0.25	0.75

KM# 60 5 CENTS
3.94 g., Copper-Nickel, 21 mm. **Ruler:** Elizabeth II **Obv:** National arms above date **Obv. Legend:** COMMONWEALTH OF THE BAHAMAS **Rev:** Pineapple above garland divides value at top **Rev. Designer:** Arnold Machin **Edge:** Plain

Date	Mintage	F12	VF20	XF40	MS60	MS63
2004	—	—	—	0.10	0.25	0.75
2005	—	—	—	0.10	0.25	0.75
2006	—	—	—	0.10	0.25	0.75

KM# 61 10 CENTS
5.13 g., Copper-Nickel, 23.5 mm. **Ruler:** Elizabeth II **Obv:** National arms, date below, within beaded circle **Rev:** Two bonefish above denomination **Rev. Designer:** Arnold Machin **Edge:** Plain **Shape:** Scalloped

Date	Mintage	F12	VF20	XF40	MS60	MS63
2005	—	—	—	0.25	0.60	0.80

KM# 219 10 CENTS
5.54 g., Copper-Nickel, 23.5 mm. **Ruler:** Elizabeth II **Obv:**

National arms, date below **Rev:** Two fish, value above **Shape:** Scalloped

Date	Mintage	F12	VF20	XF40	MS60	MS63
2007	—			0.25	0.60	0.80

KM# 62 15 CENTS
6.50 g., Copper-Nickel, 25 mm. **Ruler:** Elizabeth II **Obv:** National arms above date **Rev:** Hibiscus, value divided at bottom **Rev. Designer:** Arnold Machin **Edge:** Plain **Shape:** 4-sided

Date	Mintage	F12	VF20	XF40	MS60	MS63
2005	—			0.20	0.50	1.50

KM# 63.2 25 CENTS
5.75 g., Copper-Nickel, 24.26 mm. **Ruler:** Elizabeth II **Obv:** National arms, date below **Rev:** Bahamian Sloop, value above **Edge:** Reeded

Date	Mintage	F12	VF20	XF40	MS60	MS63
2005	—			0.30	0.50	1.50

KM# 217 DOLLAR
Silver **Ruler:** Elizabeth II **Subject:** Queen Mother's 100th Birthday

Date	Mintage	F12	VF20	XF40	MS60	MS63
2002	—	PF65 50.00				

BAHRAIN

The Kingdom of Bahrain, a group of islands in the Persian Gulf off Saudi Arabia, has an area of 268 sq. mi. (622 sq. km.) and a population of 618,000. Capital: Manama. Prior to the depression of the 1930's, the economy was based on pearl fishing. Petroleum and aluminum industries and transit trade are the vital factors in the economy today.

RULERS

Al Khalifa Dynasty
Hamed Bin Isa, 1999-

TITLES

دولة البحرين

State of Bahrain

مملكة البحرين

Kingdom of Bahrain

KINGDOM
STANDARD COINAGE

KM# 30 5 FILS
2.50 g., Brass, 19 mm. **Ruler:** Hamed Bin Isa **Obv:** Palm tree **Obv. Legend:** KINGDOM OF BAHRAIN **Rev:** Denomination in chain link border **Edge:** Plain

Date	Mintage	F12	VF20	XF40	MS60	MS63
AH1426-2005	—				0.50	0.75
AH1428-2007	—				0.50	0.75
AH1430-2009	—				0.50	0.75
AH1431-2010	—				0.50	0.75

KM# 30a 5 FILS
2.50 g., 0.925 Silver 0.0739 oz. ASW, 19 mm. **Ruler:** Hamed Bin Isa **Obv:** Palm tree **Rev:** Denomination in chain link border

Date	Mintage	F12	VF20	XF40	MS60	MS63
AH1431-2010	500	PF60 15.00				

KM# 28 10 FILS
3.35 g., Brass, 21 mm. **Ruler:** Hamed Bin Isa **Obv:** Palm tree **Obv. Legend:** KINGDOM OF BAHRAIN **Rev:** Denomination in chain link border **Edge:** Plain

Date	Mintage	F12	VF20	XF40	MS60	MS63
AH1423-2002	—			0.30	0.75	1.00
AH1424-2004	—			0.30	0.75	1.00
AH1426-2005	—			0.30	0.75	1.00
AH1428-2007	—			0.30	0.75	1.00
AH1429-2008	—			0.30	0.75	1.00
AH1430-2009	—			0.30	0.75	1.00
AH1431-2010	—			0.30	0.75	1.00
AH1432-2011	—			0.30	0.75	1.00

KM# 28a 10 FILS
3.35 g., 0.925 Silver 0.099 oz. ASW, 21 mm. **Ruler:** Hamed Bin Isa **Obv:** Palm tree **Rev:** Denomination in chain link border

Date	Mintage	F12	VF20	XF40	MS60	MS63
AH1431-2010	500	PF60 25.00				

KM# 24 25 FILS
3.50 g., Copper-Nickel, 20 mm. **Ruler:** Hamed Bin Isa **Obv:** Ancient painting **Obv. Legend:** KINGDOM OF BAHRAIN **Rev:** Denomination in chain link border **Edge:** Reeded

Date	Mintage	F12	VF20	XF40	MS60	MS63
AH1423-2002	—			0.45	1.10	1.50
AH1426-2005	—			0.45	1.10	1.50
AH1428-2007	—			0.45	1.10	1.50
AH1429-2008	—			0.45	1.10	1.50
AH1430-2009	—			0.45	1.10	1.50

KM# 24a 25 FILS
3.50 g., 0.925 Silver 0.1034 oz. ASW, 20 mm. **Ruler:** Hamed Bin Isa **Obv:** Ancient painting **Rev:** Denomination in chain link border

Date	Mintage	F12	VF20	XF40	MS60	MS63
AH1431-2010	500	PF60 25.00				

KM# 25 50 FILS
4.50 g., Copper-Nickel, 22 mm. **Ruler:** Hamed Bin Isa **Subject:** Kingdom **Obv:** Stylized sailboats **Obv. Legend:** KINGDOM OF BAHRAIN **Rev:** Denomination in chain link border **Edge:** Reeded

Date	Mintage	F12	VF20	XF40	MS60	MS63
AH1423-2002	—			0.60	1.50	2.00
AH1426-2005	—			0.60	1.50	2.00
AH1428-2007	—			0.60	1.50	2.00
AH1429-2008	—			0.60	1.50	2.00
AH1430-2009	—			0.60	1.50	2.00
AH1431-2010	—			0.60	1.50	2.00

KM# 25a 50 FILS
4.50 g., 0.925 Silver 0.133 oz. ASW, 22 mm. **Ruler:** Hamed Bin Isa **Obv:** Stylized sailboats **Rev:** Denomination in chain link border

Date	Mintage	F12	VF20	XF40	MS60	MS63
AH1431-2010	500	PF60 25.00				

KM# 20 100 FILS
6.00 g., Bi-Metallic, 24 mm. **Obv:** Coat of arms within circle, dates at either side **Obv. Legend:** STATE OF BAHRAIN **Rev:** Numeric denomination back of boxed denomination within circle, chain surrounds **Edge:** Reeded

Date	Mintage	F12	VF20	XF40	MS60	MS63
AH1422-2001	—				3.50	4.00

KM# 26 100 FILS
6.00 g., Bi-Metallic, 24 mm. **Ruler:** Hamed Bin Isa **Subject:** Kingdom **Obv:** National arms **Obv. Legend:** KINGDOM OF BAHRAIN **Rev:** Denomination in chain link border **Edge:** Reeded

Date	Mintage	F12	VF20	XF40	MS60	MS63
AH1423-2002	—			0.90	2.25	3.00
AH1425-2004	—			0.90	2.25	3.00
AH1426-2005	—			0.90	2.25	3.00
AH1427-2006	—			0.90	2.25	3.00
AH1428-2007	—			0.90	2.25	3.00
AH1429-2008	—			0.90	2.25	3.00
AH1430-2009	—			0.90	2.25	3.00
AH1431-2010	—			0.90	2.25	3.00

KM# 29 100 FILS
6.00 g., Bi-Metallic, 24 mm. **Ruler:** Hamed Bin Isa **Subject:** 1st Bahrain Grand Prix **Obv:** Maze design within circle **Rev:** Numeric denomination back of boxed denomination within circle, chain surrounds **Edge:** Reeded

Date	Mintage	F12	VF20	XF40	MS60	MS63
AH1425-2004	30,000			—	30.00	35.00

KM# 26a 100 FILS
6.00 g., 0.925 Silver 0.1773 oz. ASW, 24 mm. **Ruler:** Hamed Bin Isa **Obv:** National arms **Rev:** Denomination in chain link border

Date	Mintage	F12	VF20	XF40	MS60	MS63
AH1431-2010	500	PF60 30.00				

KM# 22 500 FILS
9.00 g., Bi-Metallic, 27 mm. **Ruler:** Hamed Bin Isa **Obv:** Monument and inscription **Obv. Inscription:** STATE OF BAHRAIN **Rev:** Denomination **Edge:** Reeded

Date	Mintage	F12	VF20	XF40	MS60	MS63
2001	—			—	6.00	7.50

KM# 27 500 FILS
9.00 g., Bi-Metallic, 27 mm. **Ruler:** Hamed Bin Isa **Subject:** Kingdom **Obv:** Monument and inscription **Obv. Legend:** KINGDOM OF BAHRAIN **Rev:** Denomination **Edge:** Reeded

Date	Mintage	F12	VF20	XF40	MS60	MS63
2002	—			—	6.50	8.00

KM# 27a 500 FILS
9.00 g., 0.925 Silver 0.2659 oz. ASW, 27 mm. **Ruler:** Hamed Bin Isa **Obv:** Monument and inscription **Rev:** Denomination

Date	Mintage	F12	VF20	XF40	MS60	MS63
AH1431-2010	500	PF60 40.00				

PROOF SETS

KM#	Date	Mintage	Identification	Issue Price	Mkt Val
PS4	2010 (6)	500	KM#30a, 28a, 24a, 25a, 26a, 27a	160	160

BANGLADESH

NEPAL
BHUTAN
PEOPLES REPUBLIC OF CHINA
INDIA
MYANMAR
Bay of Bengal
LAOS

The Peoples Republic of Bangladesh (formerly East Pakistan), a parliamentary democracy located on the Bay of Bengal bordered by India and Burma, has an area of 55,598 sq. mi. (143,998 sq. km.) and a population of 128.1 million. Capital: Dhaka. The economy is predominantly agricultural. Jute products, jute and tea are exported.

Bangladesh is a member of the Commonwealth of Nations. The president is the Head of State and the Government.

MONETARY SYSTEM
100 Poisha = 1 Taka

DATING
Christian era using Bengali numerals.

PEOPLES REPUBLIC

STANDARD COINAGE

KM# 24 50 POISHA
2.60 g., Stainless Steel, 19.3 mm. **Obv:** National emblem, Shapla (water lily) within wreath above water **Rev:** Fish, chicken and produce within inner circle **Edge:** Plain **Shape:** Octagonal

Date	Mintage	F12	VF20	XF40	MS60	MS63
2001	—	—	—	1.50	2.00	3.00

KM# 9b TAKA
4.00 g., Brass, 25 mm. **Obv:** National emblem, Shapla (water lily) **Rev:** Stylized family, value at right **Edge:** Reeded **Note:** Prev. KM # 9.3.

Date	Mintage	F12	VF20	XF40	MS60	MS63
2003	—	—	0.35	1.00	2.25	2.50

KM# 9c TAKA
4.25 g., Stainless Steel, 24.91 mm. **Obv:** National emblem, Shapla (water lily) within wreath above water in octagonal frame **Rev:** Stylized family, value at right within octagonal frame **Edge:** Reeded **Note:** Prev. KM # 9.5.

Date	Mintage	F12	VF20	XF40	MS60	MS63
2001	—	—	—	0.65	1.75	2.25
2002	—	—	—	0.65	1.75	2.25
2003	—	—	—	0.65	1.75	2.25
2007	—	—	—	0.65	1.75	2.25

KM# 32 TAKA
3.25 g., Steel, 21.5 mm. **Obv:** Bank emblem **Rev:** Sheikh Mujibur Rahman facing

Date	Mintage	F12	VF20	XF40	MS60	MS63
2010	500,000	—	—	1.25	2.25	2.75

KM# 25 2 TAKA
7.00 g., Stainless Steel, 26.03 mm. **Obv:** State emblem and "TWO 2 TAKA" within beaded border **Rev:** Two children reading, legend within beaded border **Edge:** Plain

Date	Mintage	F12	VF20	XF40	MS60	MS63
2004	—	—	—	1.25	2.50	3.00
2008	—	—	—	1.25	2.50	3.00

KM# 31 2 TAKA
5.50 g., Stainless Steel, 24 mm. **Obv:** State emblem **Rev:** Bust facing

Date	Mintage	F12	VF20	XF40	MS60	MS63
2010	—	—	—	1.25	2.50	3.50

KM# 26.2 5 TAKA
8.17 g., Steel, 26.8 mm. **Obv:** National emblem, Shapla (water lily) within wreath above water **Rev:** Bridge, date and denomination below, thin characters, extensive clouds above

Date	Mintage	F12	VF20	XF40	MS60	MS63
2008	—	—	—	1.50	3.00	3.25

KM# 26.1 5 TAKA
8.17 g., Steel, 26.8 mm. **Obv:** National emblem, Shapla (water lily) within wreath above water **Rev:** Bridge, date and denomination below, thick characters, limited clouds **Note:** Prev. KM#18.3. The 2006 date is non-magnetic, whereas the 2008 is magnetic. Die varieties exist.

Date	Mintage	F12	VF20	XF40	MS60	MS63
2006	—	—	—	1.50	3.00	3.25

KM# 33 5 TAKA
6.50 g., Steel, 25.5 mm. **Obv:** Urn within wreath **Rev:** Sheikh Mujibur Rahman

Date	Mintage	F12	VF20	XF40	MS60	MS63
2012	600,000	—	—	1.75	3.50	4.00

KM# 27 10 TAKA
0.925 Silver **Subject:** Cricket World Cup **Obv:** Cricket ball logo **Rev:** Trophy

Date	Mintage	F12	VF20	XF40	MS60	MS63
2011	—	PF60 65.00	PF63 75.00			

KM# 28 10 TAKA
22.10 g., 0.925 Silver 0.653 oz. ASW, 38 mm. **Subject:** Rabindranath Tagore, 150th Anniversary of Birth **Obv:** Legend **Rev:** Bust right

Date	Mintage	F12	VF20	XF40	MS60	MS63
2011	—	PF60 75.00	PF63 90.00			

KM# 29 10 TAKA
25.00 g., 0.999 Silver 0.7978 oz. ASW, 38 mm. **Subject:** Nationhood, 40th Anniversary **Obv:** Bangabandhu Sheikh Mujibur Rahman at center **Rev:** Six freedom fighters with hands raised

Date	Mintage	F12	VF20	XF40	MS60	MS63
2011	—	PF60 75.00	PF63 90.00			

KM# 30 10 TAKA
25.00 g., 0.999 Silver 0.7978 oz. ASW, 38 mm. **Subject:** Poem: Bidrohi; 90th Anniversary **Obv:** Legend **Rev:** Kazi Nazrul Islam facing

Date	Mintage	F12	VF20	XF40	MS60	MS63
2011	—	PF60 75.00	PF63 90.00			

KM# 34 100 TAKA
22.00 g., 0.925 Silver 0.6501 oz. ASW, 38 mm. **Subject:** 100th Anniversary of Bangladesh National Museum (1913-2013) **Obv:** 18th century terracotta plaque with image of Horseman **Rev:** Bangladesh Bank monogram

Date	Mintage	F12	VF20	XF40	MS60	MS63
2013	PF60 75.00	PF63 90.00				

BARBADOS

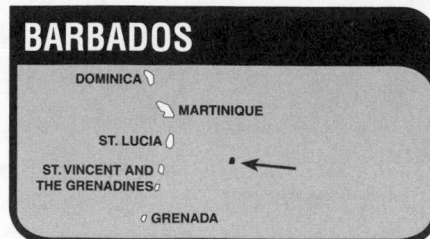

DOMINICA
MARTINIQUE
ST. LUCIA
ST. VINCENT AND THE GRENADINES
GRENADA

Barbados, a Constitutional Monarchy within the Commonwealth of Nations, is located in the Windward Islands of the West Indies east of St. Vincent. The coral island has an area of 166 sq. mi. (430 sq. km.) and a population of 269,000. Capital: Bridgetown. The economy is based on sugar and tourism. Sugar, petroleum products, molasses, and rum are exported.

MONETARY SYSTEM
100 Cents = 1 Dollar

MINT MARKS
(brm) – British Royal Mint
(O) – Ottawa Royal Canadian Mint
(v) - Valcambi

COMMONWEALTH

DECIMAL COINAGE

KM# 10a CENT
2.50 g., Copper Plated Zinc, 19 mm. **Obv:** National arms **Rev:** Trident above value **Rev. Designer:** Philip Nathan **Edge:** Plain

Date	Mintage	F12	VF20	XF40	MS60	MS63
2001	—	—	—	0.10	0.25	0.75
2002	—	—	—	—	0.25	0.75
2003	—	—	—	—	0.25	0.75
2004	—	—	—	—	0.25	0.75
2005	—	—	—	—	0.25	0.75
2006	—	—	—	—	0.25	0.75
2007	—	—	—	—	0.25	0.75

KM# 10b CENT
2.78 g., Copper Plated Steel, 18.86 mm. **Obv:** National arms **Rev:** Trident above value

Date	Mintage	F12	VF20	XF40	MS60	MS63
2008	—	—	—	—	0.25	0.50
2009	—	—	—	—	0.25	0.50
2010	—	—	—	—	0.25	0.50
2011	—	—	—	—	0.25	0.50
2012	—	—	—	—	0.25	0.50

KM# 11 5 CENTS
3.75 g., Brass, 21 mm. **Obv:** National arms **Rev:** South Point Lighthouse, value below **Rev. Designer:** Philip Nathan **Edge:** Plain

Date	Mintage	F12	VF20	XF40	MS60	MS63
2001	—	—	—	—	0.25	0.75
2002	—	—	—	—	0.25	0.75
2004	—	—	—	—	0.25	0.75
2005	—	—	—	—	0.25	0.75
2006	—	—	—	—	0.25	0.75
2007	—	—	—	—	0.25	0.75

KM# 11a 5 CENTS
3.46 g., Brass Plated Steel, 21 mm. **Obv:** National arms **Rev:** South Point Lighthouse, value below

Date	Mintage	F12	VF20	XF40	MS60	MS63
2008	—	—	—	—	0.25	0.75
2009	—	—	—	—	0.25	0.75
2010	—	—	—	—	0.25	0.75
2011	—	—	—	—	0.25	0.75

KM# 12 10 CENTS
2.29 g., Copper-Nickel, 17.77 mm. **Obv:** National arms **Rev:** Tern flying left, value below **Rev. Designer:** Philip Nathan **Edge:** Reeded

Date	Mintage	F12	VF20	XF40	MS60	MS63
2001	—	—	—	0.15	0.50	1.50
2003	—	—	—	0.15	0.50	1.50
2004	—	—	—	0.15	0.50	1.50
2005	—	—	—	0.15	0.50	1.50

KM# 12a 10 CENTS
2.09 g., Nickel Plated Steel, 17.77 mm. **Obv:** National arms **Rev:** Tern flying left, value below **Edge:** Reeded

Date	Mintage	F12	VF20	XF40	MS60	MS63
2007	—	—	—	—	0.50	1.00
2008	—	—	—	—	0.50	1.00
2009	—	—	—	—	0.50	1.00
2012	—	—	—	—	0.50	1.00

KM# 13 25 CENTS
5.65 g., Copper-Nickel, 23.66 mm. **Obv:** National arms **Rev:** Morgan Lewis Windmill, value above **Edge:** Reeded **Designer:** Philip Nathan

Date	Mintage	F12	VF20	XF40	MS60	MS63
2001	—	—	—	0.30	0.60	1.60
2003	—	—	—	0.30	0.60	1.60
2004	—	—	—	0.30	0.60	1.60
2005	—	—	—	0.30	0.60	1.60
2006	—	—	—	0.30	0.60	1.60

KM# 13a 25 CENTS
5.10 g., Nickel Plated Steel, 23.66 mm. **Obv:** National arms **Rev:** Morgan Lewis Windmill, value above **Edge:** Reeded

Date	Mintage	F12	VF20	XF40	MS60	MS63
2007	—	—	—	0.30	0.60	1.00
2008	—	—	—	0.30	0.60	1.00
2009	—	—	—	0.30	0.60	1.00
2011	—	—	—	0.30	0.60	1.00

KM# 14.2 DOLLAR
5.95 g., Copper-Nickel, 25.85 mm. **Obv:** National arms **Rev:** Flying fish left, value below **Shape:** 7-sided **Note:** Thinner planchet.

Date	Mintage	F12	VF20	XF40	MS60	MS63
2004	—	—	—	—	2.25	3.00
2005	—	—	—	—	2.25	3.00

KM# 14.2a DOLLAR
5.95 g., Nickel Plated Steel, 25.85 mm. **Obv:** National arms **Rev:** Flying fish left, value below

Date	Mintage	F12	VF20	XF40	MS60	MS63
2007	—	—	—	—	2.00	2.50
2008	—	—	—	—	2.25	3.00
2009	—	—	—	—	2.00	2.50
2012	—	—	—	—	2.00	2.50

KM# 69 5 DOLLARS
28.28 g., 0.925 Silver 0.8356 oz. ASW, 38.6 mm. **Subject:** UNICEF **Obv:** National arms divide date, denomination below **Rev:** Three boys playing cricket **Edge:** Reeded

Date	Mintage	F12	VF20	XF40	MS60	MS63
2001(v)	100	PF63 60.00	PF65 65.00			

KM# 73 5 DOLLARS
28.28 g., 0.925 Silver 0.8356 oz. ASW, 38.61 mm. **Subject:** 375th Anniversary of the City of Bridgetown **Obv:** Coat of Arms of Barbados **Rev:** Montefiore Fountain (Coleridge Street, Bridgetown)

Date	Mintage	F12	VF20	XF40	MS60	MS63
2003(brm)	200	PF63 55.00	PF65 60.00			

KM# 76 5 DOLLARS
28.28 g., 0.925 Silver 0.8356 oz. ASW, 38.61 mm. **Subject:** 3 W's (Sirs Clyde Walcott, Everton Weekes and Frank Worrell) **Obv:** Coat of Arms of Barbados **Rev:** Sirs Clyde Walcott, Everton Weekes and Frank Worrell relaxing together on the cricket field with a cricket bat and ball beside them, legend, their nickname, circumferential legend, denomination **Rev. Legend:** Barbados - Home of the Masters

Date	Mintage	F12	VF20	XF40	MS60	MS63
2007	250	PF63 90.00	PF65 100			

KM# 78 5 DOLLARS
28.28 g., 0.925 Silver 0.8356 oz. ASW, 38.61 mm. **Subject:** The Right Excellent Sir Garfield Sobers **Obv:** Coat of Arms of Barbados **Rev:** Sir Garfield Sobers in action playing a glorious cover drive, legend, circumferential legend, denomination **Rev. Legend:** The Right Excellent Sir Garfield Sobers; Barbados - Home of the Masters

Date	Mintage	F12	VF20	XF40	MS60	MS63
2007(brm)	250	PF63 90.00	PF65 100			

KM# 74 50 DOLLARS
15.97 g., 0.9167 Gold 0.4676 oz. AGW, 28.4 mm. **Subject:** 375th Anniversary of the City of Bridgetown **Obv:** Coat of Arms of Barbados **Rev:** Montefiore Fountain (Coleridge Street, Bridgetown)

Date	Mintage	F12	VF20	XF40	MS60	MS63
2003	50	PF63 900	PF65 950			

KM# 75 50 DOLLARS
15.97 g., 0.9167 Gold 0.4676 oz. AGW, 28.4 mm. **Subject:** 350th Anniversary of the Bridgetown Synagogue **Obv:** Coat of Arms of Barbados **Rev:** Rum barrel with the initials "mt" on its top (design based on 18th century token used as currency and minted by (and credited with its design) Joseph Tolanto, a Jewish merchant), legend, denomination **Rev. Legend:** 350th ANNIVERSARY OF THE BRIDGETOWN SYNAGOGUE

Date	Mintage	F12	VF20	XF40	MS60	MS63
2004	100	PF63 850	PF65 900			

KM# 77 50 DOLLARS
15.97 g., 0.9167 Gold 0.4676 oz. AGW, 28.4 mm. **Subject:** Sirs Clyde Walcott, Everton Weekes and Frank Worrell **Obv:** Coat of Arms of Barbados **Rev:** Sirs Clyde Walcott, Everton Weekes and Frank Worrell relaxing together on the cricket field with a cricket bat and ball beside them, legend, their nickname, circumferential legend, denomination **Rev. Legend:** Barbados - Home of the Masters

Date	Mintage	F12	VF20	XF40	MS60	MS63
2007(brm)	50	PF63 950	PF65 1,000			

KM# 79 50 DOLLARS
15.97 g., 0.9167 Gold 0.4676 oz. AGW, 28.4 mm. **Subject:** The Right Excellent Sir Garfield Sobers **Obv:** Coat of Arms of Barbados **Rev:** Sir Garfield Sobers in action playing a glorious cover drive, legend, circumferential legend, denomination **Rev. Legend:** The Right Excellent Sir Garfield Sobers; Barbados - Home of the Masters

Date	Mintage	F12	VF20	XF40	MS60	MS63
2007(brm)	50	PF63 950	PF65 1,000			

BELARUS

Belarus (Byelorussia, Belorussia, or White Russia-formerly the Belorussian S.S.R.) is situated along the western Dvina and Dnieper Rivers, bounded in the west by Poland, to the north by Latvia and Lithuania, to the east by Russia and the south by the Ukraine. It has an area of 80,154 sq. mi. (207,600 sq. km.) and a population of 4.8 million. Capital: Minsk. Chief products: peat, salt, and agricultural products including flax, fodder and grasses for cattle breeding and dairy products.

MONETARY SYSTEM
100 Kapeek = 1 Rouble

REPUBLIC
STANDARD COINAGE

KM# 427 ROUBLE
15.50 g., Copper-Nickel, 33 mm. **Subject:** Belarus Bank, 90th Anniversary **Obv:** National arms **Rev:** Bank Building

Date	Mintage	F12	VF20	XF40	MS60	MS63
2012 Prooflike	4,000	—	—	—	—	25.00

KM# 428 ROUBLE
20.00 g., Copper-Nickel, 37.1 mm. **Subject:** Belarus railways, 150th Anniversary **Obv:** National arms and modern trains **Rev:** Old locomotive at station

Date	Mintage	F12	VF20	XF40	MS60	MS63
2012 Prooflike	2,000	—	—	—	—	25.00

KM# 429 ROUBLE
13.16 g., Copper-Nickel, 32 mm. **Subject:** Birds of Belarus **Obv:** National arms and nesting bird **Rev:** Common Swift

Date	Mintage	F12	VF20	XF40	MS60	MS63
2012 Prooflike	2,000	—	—	—	—	25.00

KM# 430 ROUBLE
13.10 g., Copper-Nickel, 32.1 mm. **Subject:** Fatherhood **Obv:** National arms and stylized DNA **Rev:** Stork carrying baby

Date	Mintage	F12	VF20	XF40	MS60	MS63
2012 Prooflike	2,000	—	—	—	—	25.00

KM# 431 ROUBLE
19.50 g., Copper-Nickel, 37 mm. **Subject:** Maxim Tank, 100th Anniversary **Obv:** National arms and landscape **Rev:** Maxim tank and cranes

Date	Mintage	F12	VF20	XF40	MS60	MS63
2012 Prooflike	2,000	—	—	—	—	25.00

KM# 432 ROUBLE
15.50 g., Copper-Nickel, 33 mm. **Subject:** Pottery **Obv:** National arms and wreath **Rev:** Pitcher filled with water

Date	Mintage	F12	VF20	XF40	MS60	MS63
2012 Prooflike	25	—	—	—	—	3,000

KM# 433 ROUBLE

19.60 g., Copper-Nickel, 37.1 mm. **Subject:** War of 1812, 200th Anniversary **Obv:** National arms **Rev:** Memorial stone with inscription

Date	Mintage	F12	VF20	XF40	MS60	MS63
2012 Prooflike	3,000	—	—	—	—	25.00

KM# 434 ROUBLE

27.03 g., Copper-Nickel, 38.61 mm. **Subject:** World Cup Soccer **Obv:** National arms **Rev:** Soccer player

Date	Mintage	F12	VF20	XF40	MS60	MS63
2013 Prooflike	5,000	—	—	—	—	25.00

KM# 435 ROUBLE

19.50 g., Copper-Nickel, 37 mm. **Subject:** Belarus Ballet **Obv:** National arms and National Opera **Rev:** Ballerina

Date	Mintage	F12	VF20	XF40	MS60	MS63
2013	5,000	PF65 20.00				

KM# 436 ROUBLE

13.16 g., Copper-Nickel, 32 mm. **Subject:** BPS-Sberbank, 90th Anniversary **Obv:** National arms and geometric pattern **Rev:** Blossomed tree of life

Date	Mintage	F12	VF20	XF40	MS60	MS63
2013 Prooflike	5,000	—	—	—	—	25.00

KM# 437 ROUBLE

15.50 g., Copper-Nickel, 33 mm. **Subject:** Christianization of the Rus, 1025th Anniversary **Obv:** National arms and stylized cross **Rev:** Dove and angels

Date	Mintage	F12	VF20	XF40	MS60	MS63
2013 Prooflike	5,000	—	—	—	—	25.00

KM# 438 ROUBLE

19.50 g., Copper-Nickel, 37 mm. **Obv:** National arms and Budsalaus' Catholic Church **Rev:** Icon of Virgin Mary

Date	Mintage	F12	VF20	XF40	MS60	MS63
2013	5,000	PF65 20.00				

KM# 47 ROUBLE

13.14 g., Copper-Nickel, 31.9 mm. **Obv:** National arms **Rev:** European Bison **Edge:** Reeded **Designer:** S.P. Zaskevich

Date	Mintage	F12	VF20	XF40	MS60	MS63
2001	5,000	PF65 40.00				

KM# 50 ROUBLE

13.15 g., Copper-Nickel, 28.7 mm. **Subject:** 2002 Winter Olympics **Obv:** National arms **Rev:** Two freestyle skiers **Edge:** Reeded **Designer:** S.P. Zaskevich

Date	Mintage	F12	VF20	XF40	MS60	MS63
2001 Prooflike	2,000	—	—	—	—	35.00

KM# 110 ROUBLE

Copper-Nickel, 32 mm. **Subject:** 900th Anniversary of Euphrasinta **Obv:** National arms **Rev:** Euphrasinta of Polatsk **Designer:** S.P. Zaskevitch

Date	Mintage	F12	VF20	XF40	MS60	MS63
2001	—	—	—	—	50.00	—

KM# 112 ROUBLE

Copper-Nickel, 32 mm. **Subject:** Tower of Kamyantes **Obv:** National arms **Rev:** Kamyanets Tower, seal **Designer:** S.P. Zaskevich

Date	Mintage	F12	VF20	XF40	MS60	MS63
2001	2,000	—	—	—	40.00	—

KM# 44 ROUBLE

13.14 g., Copper-Nickel, 31.9 mm. **Obv:** National arms **Rev:**

Eurasian Beaver and young **Edge:** Reeded **Designer:** S.P. Zaskevich

Date	Mintage	F12	VF20	XF40	MS60	MS63
2002	5,000	PF65 25.00				

KM# 69 ROUBLE

Copper-Nickel, 33 mm. **Subject:** 80th Anniversary of the Savings Bank **Obv:** Folk art design **Obv. Designer:** S.P. Zaskevich **Rev. Designer:** V. Titor

Date	Mintage	F12	VF20	XF40	MS60	MS63
2002 Prooflike	10,000	—	—	—	—	15.00

KM# 106 ROUBLE

Copper-Nickel, 31.9 mm. **Subject:** Jakub Kalas 1881-1956

Date	Mintage	F12	VF20	XF40	MS60	MS63
2002	2,000	PF65 35.00				

KM# 114 ROUBLE

Copper-Nickel, 32 mm. **Subject:** 200th Birthday of Ignatius Dameika **Obv:** National arms **Rev:** Ignatius Dameika, hammer **Rev. Designer:** S.P. Zaskevich

Date	Mintage	F12	VF20	XF40	MS60	MS63
2002 Prooflike	2,000	—	—	—	—	40.00

KM# 116 ROUBLE

Copper-Nickel, 33 mm. **Subject:** 120th Birthday of Yanka Kupala **Obv:** National arms **Rev:** Yanka Kupala, 1882-1942 **Rev. Designer:** S.P. Zaskevich

Date	Mintage	F12	VF20	XF40	MS60	MS63
2002 Prooflike	2,000	—	—	—	—	40.00

KM# 118 ROUBLE

Copper-Nickel, 33 mm. **Subject:** 120th Birthday of Yakub Kolas **Obv:** National arms **Rev:** Yukab Kolas, 1882-1956 **Rev. Designer:** S.P. Zaskevich

Date	Mintage	F12	VF20	XF40	MS60	MS63
2002	2,000	—	—	—	—	40.00

KM# 54 ROUBLE

13.12 g., Copper-Nickel, 31.9 mm. **Obv:** National arms **Rev:** Mute swans on water with reflections **Edge:** Reeded **Designer:** S.P. Zaskevich

Date	Mintage	F12	VF20	XF40	MS60	MS63
2003	5,000	PF65 35.00				

KM# 55 ROUBLE

13.10 g., Copper-Nickel, 31.9 mm. **Obv:** State arms **Rev:** Herring gull in flight **Edge:** Reeded **Designer:** S.P. Zaskevich

Date	Mintage	F12	VF20	XF40	MS60	MS63
2003	5,000	PF65 25.00				

KM# 56 ROUBLE

13.10 g., Copper-Nickel, 32 mm. **Obv:** National arms **Rev:** Church of the Savior and Transfiguration **Edge:** Reeded **Designer:** S.P. Zaskevich

Date	Mintage	F12	VF20	XF40	MS60	MS63
2003	2,000	—	—	—	—	35.00

KM# 61 ROUBLE
13.16 g., Copper-Nickel, 32 mm. **Obv:** National arms **Rev:** Wrestlers **Edge:** Reeded **Designer:** S.P. Zaskevich

Date	Mintage	F12	VF20	XF40	MS60	MS63
2003 Prooflike	5,000	—	—	—	—	10.00

KM# 292 ROUBLE
13.16 g., Copper-Nickel, 32 mm. **Obv:** National arms **Rev:** Church

Date	Mintage	F12	VF20	XF40	MS60	MS63
2003 Prooflike	2,000	—	—	—	—	100

KM# 60 ROUBLE
13.16 g., Copper-Nickel, 32 mm. **Obv:** National arms **Rev:** Two common cranes **Edge:** Reeded **Designer:** S.P. Zaskevich

Date	Mintage	F12	VF20	XF40	MS60	MS63
2004	5,000	PF65 25.00				

KM# 62 ROUBLE
Copper-Nickel, 31.9 mm. **Subject:** Sculling **Obv:** National arms **Obv. Designer:** S.P. Zaskevich **Rev:** Two rowers against a background of stylized oars **Rev. Designer:** S.V. Nekrasova

Date	Mintage	F12	VF20	XF40	MS60	MS63
2004	3,000	—	—	—	15.00	—

KM# 75 ROUBLE
15.92 g., Copper-Nickel, 33 mm. **Subject:** Kupalle **Obv:** Folk art cross design **Rev:** Flower above ferns **Edge:** Reeded **Designer:** S.P. Zaskevich

Date	Mintage	F12	VF20	XF40	MS60	MS63
2004	5,000	—	—	—	40.00	—

KM# 76 ROUBLE
15.92 g., Copper-Nickel, 33 mm. **Subject:** Kalyady **Obv:** Folk art cross design **Rev:** Stylized sunflower **Edge:** Reeded **Designer:** S.P. Zaskevich

Date	Mintage	F12	VF20	XF40	MS60	MS63
2004	5,000	—	—	—	35.00	—

KM# 78 ROUBLE
15.90 g., Copper-Nickel, 33 mm. **Obv:** National arms **Rev:** Radziwill's Castle in Neswizh **Edge:** Reeded **Designer:** S.P. Zaskevich

Date	Mintage	F12	VF20	XF40	MS60	MS63
2004 Prooflike	2,000	—	—	—	—	40.00

KM# 80 ROUBLE
15.90 g., Copper-Nickel, 33 mm. **Subject:** Defenders of Brest

---

Obv: Soviet Patriotic War Order **Rev:** Courage" monument **Edge:** Reeded **Designer:** S.P. Zaskevich

Date	Mintage	F12	VF20	XF40	MS60	MS63
2004	5,000	—	—	—	25.00	—

KM# 83 ROUBLE
Copper-Nickel, 33 mm. **Subject:** Memory of Facist Victims **Obv:** National arms **Obv. Designer:** S.P. Zaskevich **Rev:** Man holding dead **Rev. Designer:** E.N. Vishnyakova

Date	Mintage	F12	VF20	XF40	MS60	MS63
2004	3,000	—	—	—	25.00	—

KM# 85 ROUBLE
Copper-Nickel, 33 mm. **Subject:** Soviet Warriors - Liberators **Obv:** Order of the Patriotic War **Obv. Designer:** S.P. Zaskevich **Rev:** Partisans with blown up railway track **Rev. Designer:** E.N. Vishnyakova

Date	Mintage	F12	VF20	XF40	MS60	MS63
2004	3,000	—	—	—	25.00	—

KM# 293 ROUBLE
14.35 g., Copper-Nickel, 33 mm. **Subject:** Mogilev **Obv:** National arms **Rev:** Shield and town view

Date	Mintage	F12	VF20	XF40	MS60	MS63
2004 Prooflike	2,000	—	—	—	—	40.00

KM# 294 ROUBLE
14.35 g., Copper-Nickel, 33 mm. **Subject:** WWII anniversary **Obv:** Order star **Rev:** Soldier and tank

Date	Mintage	F12	VF20	XF40	MS60	MS63
2004 Prooflike	3,000	—	—	—	—	40.00

KM# 81 ROUBLE
Copper-Nickel, 33 mm. **Subject:** 60th Anniversary of Victory **Obv:** Order of the Victory **Rev:** Star and arrows **Rev. Designer:** S.V. Necrasova

Date	Mintage	F12	VF20	XF40	MS60	MS63
2005	2,000	—	—	—	25.00	—

KM# 97 ROUBLE
14.50 g., Copper-Nickel, 33 mm. **Subject:** Almany Bogs **Obv:** Blooming plant on frosted design **Rev:** Great Grey Owl **Edge:** Lettered **Designer:** S.V. Nekrasova

Date	Mintage	F12	VF20	XF40	MS60	MS63
2005	5,000	PF65 30.00				

KM# 104 ROUBLE
Copper-Nickel, 33 mm. **Subject:** Christmas Egg **Obv:** National arms and folk art cross design **Rev:** Easter egg **Designer:** S.P. Zaskevich

Date	Mintage	F12	VF20	XF40	MS60	MS63
2005	5,000	—	—	—	35.00	—

KM# 107 ROUBLE
Copper-Nickel, 31.9 mm. **Subject:** Bagach - Candle in Basket **Obv:** National arms and solar symbol **Rev:** Basket of grain, candle, ear, table, tablecloth

Date	Mintage	F12	VF20	XF40	MS60	MS63
2005	5,000	—	—	—	35.00	—

KM# 127 ROUBLE
Copper-Nickel, 32 mm. **Subject:** 1000th Anniversary of Vaukavysk **Obv:** National arms **Rev:** National arms of Vaukavysk **Rev. Designer:** S.P. Zaskevitch

Date	Mintage	F12	VF20	XF40	MS60	MS63
2005	2,000	—	—	—	40.00	—

KM# 130 ROUBLE
Copper-Nickel, 32 mm. **Subject:** Jesuit Roman Catholic Church **Obv:** National arms **Rev:** Jesuit Roman Catholic Church in Neswizh **Designer:** S.P. Zaskevich

Date	Mintage	F12	VF20	XF40	MS60	MS63
2005	2,000	—	—	—	40.00	—

KM# 132 ROUBLE
Copper-Nickel, 33 mm. **Subject:** Usyaslau of Polatsk **Obv:** Cathedral of St. Sophia **Rev:** Usyaslav of Polatsk, wolf on a solar disk

Date	Mintage	F12	VF20	XF40	MS60	MS63
2005	5,000	PF65 15.00				

KM# 134 ROUBLE
Copper-Nickel, 33 mm. **Subject:** Tennis **Obv:** National arms **Rev:** Tennis player against racket background **Rev. Designer:** S.V. Nekrasova

Date	Mintage	F12	VF20	XF40	MS60	MS63
2005	5,000	—	—	—	12.00	—

KM# 295 ROUBLE
14.35 g., Copper-Nickel, 33 mm. **Subject:** Grodno **Obv:** National arms **Rev:** Shield and city fortress

Date	Mintage	F12	VF20	XF40	MS60	MS63
2005 Prooflike	2,000	—	—	—	—	40.00

KM# 296 ROUBLE
14.35 g., Copper-Nickel, 33 mm. **Subject:** Brest **Obv:** National arms **Rev:** Shield and city view

Date	Mintage	F12	VF20	XF40	MS60	MS63
2005 Prooflike	2,000	—	—	—	—	40.00

KM# 135 ROUBLE
Copper-Nickel, 32 mm. **Subject:** Vtaselle Wedding **Obv:**

National arms, birds, shamrock **Rev:** Loaf of bread, wedding rings, diadem of flowers, background of honeycomb

Date	Mintage	F12	VF20	XF40	MS60	MS63
2006	5,000	—	—	—	20.00	25.00

KM# 138 ROUBLE

Copper-Nickel, 33 mm. **Subject:** Sophia of Galshany 600th Anniversary **Obv:** Castle of Galshany **Rev:** National arms and Sophia of Galshany **Designer:** S.P. Zaskevich

Date	Mintage	F12	VF20	XF40	MS60	MS63
2006	5,000	—	—	—	20.00	

KM# 140 ROUBLE

Copper-Nickel, 33 mm. **Subject:** Syomukha **Obv:** National arms, solar symbol **Rev:** Chalice, Chaplet of birch, maple, rowan sweet flag leaves **Designer:** S.P. Zaskevich

Date	Mintage	F12	VF20	XF40	MS60	MS63
2006	5,000	—	—	—	25.00	

KM# 146 ROUBLE

Copper-Nickel, 33 mm. **Subject:** Chyrvomy Bar **Obv:** National arms, blooming plant **Rev:** European Mink **Designer:** S.V. Nekrasova

Date	Mintage	F12	VF20	XF40	MS60	MS63
2006	5,000	PF65 17.50				

KM# 273 ROUBLE

13.20 g., Copper-Nickel, 32 mm. **Subject:** Skiing **Edge:** Reeded

Date	Mintage	F12	VF20	XF40	MS60	MS63
2006	5,000	—	—	—	—	20.00

KM# 274 ROUBLE

15.50 g., Copper-Nickel, 33 mm. **Subject:** Rogwald

Date	Mintage	F12	VF20	XF40	MS60	MS63
2006	5,000	—	—	—	—	20.00

KM# 275 ROUBLE

13.16 g., Copper-Nickel, 32 mm. **Subject:** Commonwealth of Independent States, 15th Anniversary **Edge:** Reeded

Date	Mintage	F12	VF20	XF40	MS60	MS63
2006 Prooflike	5,000	—	—	—	—	20.00

KM# 276 ROUBLE

13.20 g., Copper-Nickel, 32 mm. **Subject:** Cycling **Edge:** Plain

Date	Mintage	F12	VF20	XF40	MS60	MS63
2006	5,000	—	—	—	—	20.00

KM# 297 ROUBLE

14.35 g., Copper-Nickel, 33 mm. **Subject:** Gomel **Obv:** National arms **Rev:** Shield and city view

Date	Mintage	F12	VF20	XF40	MS60	MS63
2006 Prooflike	2,000	—	—	—	—	75.00

KM# 298 ROUBLE

15.50 g., Copper-Nickel, 29x29 mm. **Subject:** Struve-Bogen trail **Obv:** National arms and map **Rev:** Eastern Europe map **Shape:** Square

Date	Mintage	F12	VF20	XF40	MS60	MS63
2006 Prooflike	5,000	—	—	—	—	25.00

KM# 417 ROUBLE

15.55 g., Copper-Nickel, 33 mm. **Subject:** Rogvold of Polotsk and Rogneda **Obv:** Ancient fortress of Izyaslavl **Rev:** Rogvold at left with female **Designer:** S. Zaskevich

Date	Mintage	F12	VF20	XF40	MS60	MS63
2006 Prooflike	5,000	—	—	—	—	30.00

KM# 150 ROUBLE

16.00 g., Copper-Nickel, 33 mm. **Subject:** Holidays and Ceremonies **Obv:** Small arms above quilted star design **Rev:** Food, bowl with spoon - Maslenica

Date	Mintage	F12	VF20	XF40	MS60	MS63
2007 Antique	5,000	—	—	—	—	35.00	—

KM# 151 ROUBLE

13.16 g., Copper-Nickel, 32 mm. **Obv:** Thrush Nightingale in hands in oval **Obv. Legend:** РЭСПУБЛІКА БЕЛАРУСЬ **Rev:** Thrush Nightingale perched on branch in oval **Edge:** Reeded

Date	Mintage	F12	VF20	XF40	MS60	MS63
2007 Prooflike	5,000	—	—	—	—	17.50

KM# 217 ROUBLE

14.35 g., Copper-Nickel, 33 mm. **Rev:** Sturgeon

Date	Mintage	F12	VF20	XF40	MS60	MS63
2007	5,000	PF65 15.00				

KM# 299 ROUBLE

13.16 g., Copper-Nickel, 32 mm. **Subject:** Belarus-China relations, 15th anniversary **Obv:** National arms **Rev:** Two archways, with Belerus and China views

Date	Mintage	F12	VF20	XF40	MS60	MS63
2007 Prooflike	3,000	—	—	—	—	25.00

KM# 300 ROUBLE

13.16 g., Copper-Nickel, 32 mm. **Subject:** Naoleon Orda, 200th Anniversary of Birth **Obv:** Three castle views **Rev:** Bust facing, musical notes and sytlized record

Date	Mintage	F12	VF20	XF40	MS60	MS63
2007 Prooflike	7,000	—	—	—	—	25.00

KM# 301 ROUBLE

15.50 g., Copper-Nickel, 33 mm. **Subject:** Gleb Menski **Obv:** Wooden fortress **Rev:** Knight seated left

Date	Mintage	F12	VF20	XF40	MS60	MS63
2007 Prooflike	5,000	—	—	—	—	25.00

KM# 302 ROUBLE

13.16 g., Copper-Nickel, 32 mm. **Subject:** A. Aladawa **Obv:** Building façade **Rev:** Bust and picture frame

Date	Mintage	F12	VF20	XF40	MS60	MS63
2007 Prooflike	4,000	—	—	—	—	25.00

KM# 303 ROUBLE

15.50 g., Copper-Nickel, 33 mm. **Subject:** Legend of the Stork **Obv:** Five stylized storks **Rev:** Large stylized stork

Date	Mintage	F12	VF20	XF40	MS60	MS63
2007 Prooflike	5,000	—	—	—	—	25.00

KM# 215 ROUBLE

13.18 g., Copper-Nickel, 33 mm. **Obv:** Sea chart and compose rose **Rev:** Sailing ship Sedov

Date	Mintage	F12	VF20	XF40	MS60	MS63
2008	7,000	PF65 15.00				

KM# 304 ROUBLE

13.16 g., Copper-Nickel, 32 mm. **Subject:** Zair Azgur **Obv:** Bust sculpture on pedestal **Rev:** Portrait right

Date	Mintage	F12	VF20	XF40	MS60	MS63
2008 Prooflike	3,000	—	—	—	—	25.00

KM# 305 ROUBLE

13.16 g., Copper-Nickel, 32 mm. **Subject:** Vincent Dunin-Martsynkevich **Obv:** Open stage curtian **Rev:** Bust facing, play names at right

Date	Mintage	F12	VF20	XF40	MS60	MS63
2008 Prooflike	3,000	—	—	—	—	25.00

KM# 306 ROUBLE

15.50 g., Copper-Nickel, 33 mm. **Subject:** Legend **Obv:** Five stylized birds **Rev:** Stylized bird

Date	Mintage	F12	VF20	XF40	MS60	MS63
2008 Prooflike	5,000	—	—	—	—	25.00

KM# 307 ROUBLE

13.16 g., Copper-Nickel, 32 mm. **Subject:** House-warming **Obv:** Cat standing left **Rev:** Key in window, house façade **Edge:** Reeded

Date	Mintage	F12	VF20	XF40	MS60	MS63
2008	5,000	—	—	—	—	25.00

KM# 308 ROUBLE

13.16 g., Copper-Nickel, 32 mm. **Subject:** Great White Egret **Obv:** Bird in hand in horizontal oval **Rev:** Great White Egret standing in vertical oval **Edge:** Reeded

Date	Mintage	F12	VF20	XF40	MS60	MS63
2008 Prooflike	5,000	—	—	—	—	30.00

KM# 309 ROUBLE

16.00 g., Copper-Nickel, 33 mm. **Obv:** Folk embroidery star pattern **Rev:** Two angles with candle above log home entrance with festive table set

Date	Mintage	F12	VF20	XF40	MS60	MS63
2008 Antique patina	5,000	—	—	—	—	50.00

KM# 310 ROUBLE
14.35 g., Copper-Nickel, 33 mm. **Subject:** Minsk **Obv:** EurAsEC logo and graphic **Rev:** Old and new city views in two ovals

Date	Mintage	F12	VF20	XF40	MS60	MS63
2008 Prooflike	7,000	—	—	—	—	20.00

KM# 311 ROUBLE
15.50 g., Copper-Nickel, 33 mm. **Subject:** Davyd of Garadzen **Obv:** Fortress **Rev:** Knight standing facing

Date	Mintage	F12	VF20	XF40	MS60	MS63
2008 Prooflike	5,000	—	—	—	—	25.00

KM# 312 ROUBLE
13.16 g., Copper-Nickel, 32 mm. **Series:** Ministry of Finance, 90th Anniversary **Obv:** National arms **Rev:** Ministry of Finance arms

Date	Mintage	F12	VF20	XF40	MS60	MS63
2008 Prooflike	3,000	—	—	—	—	20.00

KM# 313 ROUBLE
14.35 g., Copper-Nickel, 33 mm. **Subject:** Kingfisher **Obv:** Flower **Rev:** Kingfisher on grass near waterway

Date	Mintage	F12	VF20	XF40	MS60	MS63
2008 Prooflike	5,000	—	—	—	—	25.00

KM# 259 ROUBLE
13.16 g., Copper-Nickel, 32 mm. **Obv:** Compass **Rev:** Dar Parmoza at sail

Date	Mintage	F12	VF20	XF40	MS60	MS63
2009	5,000	—	—	—	—	25.00

KM# 218 ROUBLE
13.16 g., Copper-Nickel, 32 mm. **Subject:** Bialowieza Forest, 600th Anniversary **Obv:** Figures joining hands around tree trunk **Rev:** Stylized nature view **Edge:** Reeded

Date	Mintage	F12	VF20	XF40	MS60	MS63
2009 Prooflike	5,000	—	—	—	—	25.00

KM# 219 ROUBLE
13.16 g., Copper-Nickel, 32 mm. **Subject:** Grey Goose **Obv:** Bird in hand **Rev:** Grey goose in oval **Edge:** Reeded

Date	Mintage	F12	VF20	XF40	MS60	MS63
2009 Prooflike	5,000	—	—	—	—	20.00

KM# 220 ROUBLE
15.50 g., Copper-Nickel, 32 mm. **Subject:** Pakatigaroshak **Rev:** Man clubbing dragon

Date	Mintage	F12	VF20	XF40	MS60	MS63
2009	3,500	PF65 17.50				

KM# 221 ROUBLE
15.50 g., Copper-Nickel, 33 mm. **Subject:** Legend of the Skylark **Obv:** five stylized birds in flight **Rev:** Stylized skylark, head left

Date	Mintage	F12	VF20	XF40	MS60	MS63
2009 Prooflike	5,000	—	—	—	—	13.00

KM# 222 ROUBLE
15.50 g., Copper-Nickel, 33 mm. **Subject:** Folk Art - Straw Weaving **Rev:** Horse

Date	Mintage	F12	VF20	XF40	MS60	MS63
2009 Prooflike	5,000	—	—	—	—	13.00

KM# 314 ROUBLE
13.16 g., Copper-Nickel, 32 mm. **Subject:** Academy of Science **Obv:** Earth and spaceship orbits **Rev:** Academy building

Date	Mintage	F12	VF20	XF40	MS60	MS63
2009 Prooflike	4,000	—	—	—	—	20.00

KM# 315 ROUBLE
13.16 g., Copper-Nickel, 32 mm. **Subject:** Zodiac - Pisces **Obv:** Sun and moon **Rev:** Two fish **Edge:** Reeded

Date	Mintage	F12	VF20	XF40	MS60	MS63
2009	10,000	—	—	—	—	20.00

KM# 316 ROUBLE
13.16 g., Copper-Nickel, 32 mm. **Subject:** Zodiac - Aries **Obv:** Sun and moon **Rev:** Ram **Edge:** Reeded

Date	Mintage	F12	VF20	XF40	MS60	MS63
2009	10,000	—	—	—	—	20.00

KM# 317 ROUBLE
13.16 g., Copper-Nickel, 32 mm. **Subject:** Zodiac - Taurus **Obv:** Sun and moon **Rev:** Bull

Date	Mintage	F12	VF20	XF40	MS60	MS63
2009 Prooflike	10,000	—	—	—	—	20.00

KM# 318 ROUBLE
13.16 g., Copper-Nickel, 32 mm. **Subject:** Zodiac - Gemini **Obv:** Sun and moon **Rev:** Twins

Date	Mintage	F12	VF20	XF40	MS60	MS63
2009 Prooflike	10,000	—	—	—	—	20.00

KM# 319 ROUBLE
13.16 g., Copper-Nickel, 32 mm. **Subject:** Zodiac - Cancer **Obv:** Sun and moon **Rev:** Crab

Date	Mintage	F12	VF20	XF40	MS60	MS63
2009 Prooflike	10,000	—	—	—	—	20.00

KM# 320 ROUBLE
13.16 g., Copper-Nickel, 32 mm. **Subject:** Christening **Obv:** Stylized stork **Rev:** Child in a baptism gown **Edge:** Reeded

Date	Mintage	F12	VF20	XF40	MS60	MS63
2009	5,000	—	—	—	—	20.00

KM# 321 ROUBLE
13.16 g., Copper-Nickel, 32 mm. **Subject:** Zodiac - Leo **Obv:** Sun and moon **Rev:** Lion standing left **Edge:** Reeded

Date	Mintage	F12	VF20	XF40	MS60	MS63
2009	10,000	—	—	—	—	20.00

KM# 322 ROUBLE
14.35 g., Copper-Nickel, 33 mm. **Series:** Liberationfrom the Nazis, 65th Anniversary **Rev:** Child looking upwards to birds in flight **Edge:** Reeded

Date	Mintage	F12	VF20	XF40	MS60	MS63
2009 Prooflike	4,000	—	—	—	—	20.00

KM# 323 ROUBLE
13.16 g., Copper-Nickel, 32 mm. **Subject:** Zodiac - Virgo **Obv:** Sun and moon **Rev:** Little girl

Date	Mintage	F12	VF20	XF40	MS60	MS63
2009 Prooflike	10,000	—	—	—	—	20.00

KM# 324 ROUBLE
13.16 g., Copper-Nickel, 32 mm. **Subject:** Zodiac - Libra **Obv:** Sun and moon **Rev:** Scales **Edge:** Reeded

Date	Mintage	F12	VF20	XF40	MS60	MS63
2009	10,000	—	—	—	—	20.00

KM# 325 ROUBLE
16.00 g., Copper-Nickel, 33 mm. **Subject:** Harvesttime **Obv:** Star embroidery pattern **Rev:** Apple, honey and grain harvest

Date	Mintage	F12	VF20	XF40	MS60	MS63
2009 Antique patina	5,000	—	—	—	—	25.00

KM# 326 ROUBLE
13.16 g., Copper-Nickel, 32 mm. **Subject:** Zodiac - Scorpio **Obv:** Sun and moon **Rev:** Scorpion

Date	Mintage	F12	VF20	XF40	MS60	MS63
2009 Proofilke	10,000	—	—	—	—	20.00

KM# 327 ROUBLE
14.35 g., Copper-Nickel, 33 mm. **Subject:** White Stork **Obv:** Stork footprint **Rev:** White Stork and nest

Date	Mintage	F12	VF20	XF40	MS60	MS63
2009 Prooflike	5,000	—	—	—	—	25.00

KM# 329 ROUBLE
13.16 g., Copper-Nickel, 32 mm. **Subject:** Zodiac - Sagittarius **Obv:** Sun and moon **Rev:** Girl with bow and arrow

Date	Mintage	F12	VF20	XF40	MS60	MS63
2009 Prooflike	10,000	—	—	—	—	20.00

KM# 331 ROUBLE
13.16 g., Copper-Nickel, 32 mm. **Subject:** Zodiac - Capricorn **Obv:** Sun and moon **Rev:** Ram

Date	Mintage	F12	VF20	XF40	MS60	MS63
2009 Prooflike	10,000	—	—	—	—	20.00

KM# 332 ROUBLE
13.16 g., Copper-Nickel, 32 mm. **Subject:** Zodiac - Aquarius **Obv:** Sun and moon **Rev:** Child in bathtub **Edge:** Reeded

Date	Mintage	F12	VF20	XF40	MS60	MS63
2009	10,000	—	—	—	—	20.00

KM# 264 ROUBLE
15.50 g., Copper-Nickel, 33 mm. **Subject:** Metalsmith **Rev:** Horseshoe, house within, small horsemen flanking

Date	Mintage	F12	VF20	XF40	MS60	MS63
2010	3,500	PF65 17.50				

KM# 223 ROUBLE
14.35 g., Copper-Nickel, 33 mm. **Subject:** EURASEC, 10th Anniversary **Obv:** Folk embroidery pattern **Rev:** Six flags around globe

Date	Mintage	F12	VF20	XF40	MS60	MS63
2010	3,500	PF65 13.00				

KM# 226 ROUBLE
13.16 g., Copper-Nickel, 33 mm. **Subject:** 1st Belarus Front **Rev:** Gen. Konstantin Rokossovsky

Date	Mintage	F12	VF20	XF40	MS60	MS63
2010	3,000	PF65 13.00				

KM# 227 ROUBLE
13.16 g., Copper-Nickel, 33 mm. **Subject:** 2nd Belarus Front **Rev:** Col. Gen. G.F. Zaharov

Date	Mintage	F12	VF20	XF40	MS60	MS63
2010	3,000	PF65 13.00				

KM# 228 ROUBLE
13.16 g., Copper-Nickel, 33 mm. **Subject:** 3rd Belarus Front **Rev:** Col. Gen. Ivan Chernyakhovsky

Date	Mintage	F12	VF20	XF40	MS60	MS63
2010	3,000	PF65 13.00				

KM# 229 ROUBLE
13.16 g., Copper-Nickel, 33 mm. **Subject:** 1st Baltic Forces **Rev:** Gen. Hovhannes Bagramayn

Date	Mintage	F12	VF20	XF40	MS60	MS63
2010	3,000	PF65 13.00				

KM# 236 ROUBLE
15.50 g., Copper-Nickel, 33 mm. **Subject:** Legend of the Tortoise **Obv:** Five stylized turtles **Rev:** Stylized turtle

Date	Mintage	F12	VF20	XF40	MS60	MS63
2010 Prooflike	3,000	—	—	—	—	20.00

KM# 240 ROUBLE
Copper-Nickel, 32 mm. **Subject:** Age of Majority **Rev:** Flowers and folk patterns

Date	Mintage	F12	VF20	XF40	MS60	MS63
2010	4,000	PF65 13.00				

KM# 262 ROUBLE
14.35 g., Copper-Nickel, 33 mm. **Subject:** End of World War II, 65th Anniversary **Obv:** Broken clock face **Rev:** 5 doves in flight, kiting

Date	Mintage	F12	VF20	XF40	MS60	MS63
2010 Prooflike	3,000	—	—	—	—	25.00

KM# 263 ROUBLE
13.16 g., Copper-Nickel, 32 mm. **Obv:** Compass and chart **Rev:** Amergo Vespucci sailing ship

Date	Mintage	F12	VF20	XF40	MS60	MS63
2010	4,000	PF65 17.50				

KM# 265 ROUBLE
15.55 g., Copper-Nickel, 33 mm. **Subject:** Judaism **Rev:** Valozhyn Yeshiva façade, 1806 date

Date	Mintage	F12	VF20	XF40	MS60	MS63
2010	3,000	PF65 15.00				

KM# 234 ROUBLE
13.16 g., Copper-Nickel, 32 mm. **Rev:** U.S. Frigate Constitution

Date	Mintage	F12	VF20	XF40	MS60	MS63
2010	3,000	PF65 13.00				

KM# 334 ROUBLE
15.50 g., Copper-Nickel, 33 mm. **Subject:** Battle of Grunwald, 600th Anniversary **Obv:** Figure in shape of cross **Rev:** Fingerprint **Edge:** Reeded

Date	Mintage	F12	VF20	XF40	MS60	MS63
2010 Prooflike	3,000	—	—	—	—	25.00

KM# 336 ROUBLE
13.16 g., Copper-Nickel, 32 mm. **Obv:** Bird in hand **Rev:** Kestrel in oval **Edge:** Reeded

Date	Mintage	F12	VF20	XF40	MS60	MS63
2010 Prooflike	4,000	—	—	—	—	25.00

KM# 337 ROUBLE
14.48 g., Copper-Nickel, 32 mm. **Subject:** Winter into Springtime **Obv:** Embroidery pattern **Rev:** Bird emerging from snow, into new fields and sunshine **Edge:** Reeded

Date	Mintage	F12	VF20	XF40	MS60	MS63
2010 Prooflike	3,000	—	—	—	—	20.00

KM# 338 ROUBLE
15.50 g., Copper-Nickel, 33 mm. **Subject:** Leu Sapieha **Obv:** Early document **Rev:** Standing figure in robes

Date	Mintage	F12	VF20	XF40	MS60	MS63
2010 Prooflike	3,000	—	—	—	—	25.00

KM# 270 ROUBLE
13.16 g., Copper-Nickel, 32 mm. **Obv:** Compass rose and chart **Rev:** Cutty Sark sailing right

Date	Mintage	F12	VF20	XF40	MS60	MS63
2011	3,000	PF65 13.00				

KM# 287 ROUBLE
13.16 g., Copper-Nickel, 32 mm. **Subject:** M. Bogdanowicz **Obv:** Embroidery pattern **Rev:** Bust at left center

Date	Mintage	F12	VF20	XF40	MS60	MS63
2011 Prooflike	2,000	—	—	—	—	20.00

KM# 288 ROUBLE
20.00 g., Copper-Nickel, 37 mm. **Subject:** I. Bujnicki **Obv:** Scene of play **Rev:** Bust at left, scene of play

Date	Mintage	F12	VF20	XF40	MS60	MS63
2011 Prooflike	2,000	—	—	—	—	25.00

KM# 291 ROUBLE
13.16 g., Copper-Nickel, 32 mm. **Obv:** National arms **Rev:** Curlew bird standing left, oval background

Date	Mintage	F12	VF20	XF40	MS60	MS63
2011 Prooflike	2,000	—	—	—	—	20.00

KM# 339 ROUBLE
20.00 g., Copper-Nickel, 37 mm. **Subject:** Slavianski Bazaar in Vitebsk **Obv:** Stylized design **Rev:** Historic buildings and stylized designs **Edge:** Reeded

Date	Mintage	F12	VF20	XF40	MS60	MS63
2011 Prooflike	2,500	—	—	—	—	25.00

KM# 340 ROUBLE
13.16 g., Copper-Nickel, 32 mm. **Subject:** Motherhood **Obv:** Embroidery pattern **Rev:** Mother and baby

Date	Mintage	F12	VF20	XF40	MS60	MS63
2011 Prooflike	2,000	—	—	—	—	20.00

KM# 341 ROUBLE
13.16 g., Copper-Nickel, 32 mm. **Subject:** Kruzensztern **Obv:** Compass rose and nautical charts **Rev:** Square-rigged sailing ship

Date	Mintage	F12	VF20	XF40	MS60	MS63
2011 Prooflike	2,000	—	—	—	—	50.00

KM# 419 ROUBLE
13.16 g., Copper-Nickel, 32 mm. **Subject:** Belarus-China Diplomatic Relations, 20th Anniversary **Obv:** National arms **Rev:** Hands clasped at center, national motifs around **Edge:** Reeded

Date	Mintage	F12	VF20	XF40	MS60	MS63
2012	2,000	PF65 20.00				

KM# 448 ROUBLE
27.00 g., Copper-Nickel, 38.61 mm. **Subject:** 2014 FIFA World Cup Brazil

Date	Mintage	F12	VF20	XF40	MS60	MS63
2013	Est. 5,000	PF65 30.00				

KM# 454 ROUBLE
19.50 g., Copper-Nickel, 37 mm. **Subject:** Belarusian Ballet

Date	Mintage	F12	VF20	XF40	MS60	MS63
2013	Est. 5,000	PF65 25.00				

KM# 64 10 ROUBLES
16.82 g., 0.925 Silver 0.497 oz. ASW, 32.9 mm. **Obv:** National arms **Rev:** Jakub Kolas (1882-1956) **Edge:** Reeded **Designer:** S.P. Zaskevich

Date	Mintage	F12	VF20	XF40	MS60	MS63
2002	1,000	PF65 150				

KM# 117 10 ROUBLES
15.55 g., 0.925 Silver 0.4595 oz. ASW, 33 mm. **Subject:** 120th Birthday of Yanka Kupala **Obv:** National arms **Rev:** Yanka Kupala, 1882-1942 **Rev. Designer:** S.P. Zaskevich

Date	Mintage	F12	VF20	XF40	MS60	MS63
2002	1,000	PF65 150				

KM# 129 10 ROUBLES
1.24 g., 0.999 Gold 0.0396 oz. AGW, 13.92 mm. **Subject:** Belarussian Ballet **Obv:** National arms **Obv. Designer:** S.P. Zaskevich **Rev:** Dancing ballerina **Rev. Designer:** Michael Schulze

Date	Mintage	F12	VF20	XF40	MS60	MS63
2005	25,000	—	—	—	100	130

KM# 342 10 ROUBLES
1.24 g., 0.999 Gold 0.0396 oz. AGW, 13.92 mm. **Subject:** Ballet **Obv:** National arms **Rev:** Two ballet performers **Edge:** Reeded

Date	Mintage	F12	VF20	XF40	MS60	MS63
2006	25,000	PF65 150				

KM# 156 10 ROUBLES
16.81 g., 0.925 Silver 0.4967 oz. ASW, 32 mm. **Subject:** Alena Aladana **Rev:** Half-length figure facing, picture in background

Date	Mintage	F12	VF20	XF40	MS60	MS63
2007	4,000	PF65 35.00				

KM# 157 10 ROUBLES
16.81 g., 0.925 Silver 0.4967 oz. ASW, 32 mm. **Subject:** Thrush Nightingale **Rev:** Bird standing right on branch

Date	Mintage	F12	VF20	XF40	MS60	MS63
2007	5,000	PF65 40.00				

KM# 343 10 ROUBLES
1.24 g., 0.999 Gold 0.0396 oz. AGW, 13.92 mm. **Subject:** Ballet **Obv:** National arms **Rev:** Mirror image of ballerina **Edge:** Reeded

Date	Mintage	F12	VF20	XF40	MS60	MS63
2007	10,000	PF65 150				

KM# 172 10 ROUBLES
16.81 g., 0.925 Silver 0.4967 oz. ASW, 32 mm. **Subject:** Zair Azgur **Rev:** Profile right

Date	Mintage	F12	VF20	XF40	MS60	MS63
2008	3,000	PF65 40.00				

KM# 173 10 ROUBLES
16.81 g., 0.925 Silver 0.4967 oz. ASW, 32 mm. **Subject:** Great White Egret **Rev:** Bird standing left

Date	Mintage	F12	VF20	XF40	MS60	MS63
2008	5,000	PF65 45.00				

KM# 174 10 ROUBLES
16.81 g., 0.925 Silver 0.4967 oz. ASW, 32 mm. **Subject:** Vincent Dunin **Rev:** Bust facing

Date	Mintage	F12	VF20	XF40	MS60	MS63
2008	3,000	PF65 35.00				

KM# 175 10 ROUBLES
16.81 g., 0.925 Silver 0.4967 oz. ASW, 32 mm. **Subject:** St. Euphrosyne of Polotsk **Rev:** Half-length figure facing within frame

Date	Mintage	F12	VF20	XF40	MS60	MS63
2008	5,000	PF65 40.00				

KM# 176 10 ROUBLES
16.81 g., 0.925 Silver 0.4967 oz. ASW, 32 mm. **Subject:** St. Steraphin of Sarov **Rev:** Half-length figure standing within frame

Date	Mintage	F12	VF20	XF40	MS60	MS63
2008	5,000	PF65 40.00				

KM# 177 10 ROUBLES
16.81 g., 0.925 Silver 0.4967 oz. ASW, 32 mm. **Subject:** St. Sergii of Radonezh **Rev:** Half-length figure standing within frame

Date	Mintage	F12	VF20	XF40	MS60	MS63
2008	5,000	PF65 40.00				

KM# 178 10 ROUBLES
16.81 g., 0.925 Silver 0.4967 oz. ASW, 32 mm. **Subject:** St. Nicholas **Rev:** Half-length figure standing within frame

Date	Mintage	F12	VF20	XF40	MS60	MS63
2008	5,000	PF65 40.00				

KM# 179 10 ROUBLES
16.81 g., 0.925 Silver 0.4967 oz. ASW, 32 mm. **Subject:** St. Panteleimon **Rev:** Half-length figure standing within frame

Date	Mintage	F12	VF20	XF40	MS60	MS63
2008	5,000	PF65 40.00				

KM# 194 10 ROUBLES
16.81 g., 0.925 Silver 0.4967 oz. ASW, 32 mm. **Subject:** Academy of Science, 80th Anniversary **Rev:** Building

Date	Mintage	F12	VF20	XF40	MS60	MS63
2009	3,000	PF65 40.00				

KM# 195 10 ROUBLES
16.81 g., 0.925 Silver 0.4967 oz. ASW, 32 mm. **Subject:** Greylag goose **Rev:** Goose swimming left

Date	Mintage	F12	VF20	XF40	MS60	MS63
2009	5,000	PF65 40.00				

KM# 344 10 ROUBLES
16.81 g., 0.925 Silver 0.4967 oz. ASW, 33 mm. **Subject:** Establishment of the Federated State, 10th Anniversary **Obv:** National arms **Rev:** Document and ribbon **Edge:** Reeded

Date	Mintage	F12	VF20	XF40	MS60	MS63
2009	3,000	PF65 50.00				

KM# 260 10 ROUBLES
16.81 g., 0.925 Silver 0.4967 oz. ASW, 32 mm. **Obv:** Stylized kestrel in egg **Rev:** Common kestrel

Date	Mintage	F12	VF20	XF40	MS60	MS63
2010	2,500	PF65 75.00				

KM# 230 10 ROUBLES
16.81 g., 0.925 Silver 0.4967 oz. ASW, 33 mm. **Subject:** 1st Belarus Front **Rev:** Gen. Konstantin Rokosovsky

Date	Mintage	F12	VF20	XF40	MS60	MS63
2010	2,500	PF65 35.00				

KM# 231 10 ROUBLES
16.81 g., 0.925 Silver 0.4967 oz. ASW, 33 mm. **Subject:** 2nd Belarus Front **Rev:** Col. Gen. G.F. Zakharov

Date	Mintage	F12	VF20	XF40	MS60	MS63
2010	2,500	PF65 35.00				

KM# 232 10 ROUBLES
16.55 g., 0.925 Silver 0.489 oz. ASW, 33 mm. **Subject:** 3rd Belarus front **Rev:** Col. Gen. Ivan Chernyakovsky

Date	Mintage	F12	VF20	XF40	MS60	MS63
2010	2,500	PF65 35.00				

KM# 233 10 ROUBLES
16.55 g., 0.925 Silver 0.489 oz. ASW, 33 mm. **Subject:** 1st Baltic Front **Rev:** Gen. Hovhannes Bagramgan

Date	Mintage	F12	VF20	XF40	MS60	MS63
2010	2,500	PF65 35.00				

KM# 345 10 ROUBLES
16.81 g., 0.925 Silver 0.4967 oz. ASW, 33 mm. **Subject:** Talmudic School **Obv:** Menorah and writings **Rev:** School façade

Date	Mintage	F12	VF20	XF40	MS60	MS63
2010	300	PF65 75.00				

KM# 346 10 ROUBLES
16.81 g., 0.925 Silver 0.4967 oz. ASW, 37 mm. **Subject:** Slavianski Bazaar **Obv:** Stylized design **Rev:** Historic buildings and stylized design **Edge:** Reeded

Date	Mintage	F12	VF20	XF40	MS60	MS63
2011	2,500	PF65 75.00				

KM# 284 10 ROUBLES
16.81 g., 0.925 Silver 0.4967 oz. ASW, 37 mm. **Subject:** I. Bujnicki **Obv:** Play scene **Rev:** Bust at left, place scene

Date	Mintage	F12	VF20	XF40	MS60	MS63
2011 Prooflike	2,000					75.00

KM# 347 10 ROUBLES
1.00 g., 0.900 Gold 0.0287 oz. AGW, 12 mm. **Subject:** M. Oginski **Obv:** National arms **Rev:** Bust facing

Date	Mintage	F12	VF20	XF40	MS60	MS63
2011	2,000	PF65 150				

KM# 348 10 ROUBLES
16.81 g., 0.925 Silver 0.4967 oz. ASW, 32 mm. **Subject:** Curlew bird **Obv:** Bird in hand **Rev:** Curlew bird in vertical oval

Date	Mintage	F12	VF20	XF40	MS60	MS63
2011 Prooflike	2,000	—	—	—	—	75.00

KM# 349 10 ROUBLES
16.81 g., 0.925 Silver 0.4967 oz. ASW, 32 mm. **Subject:** M. Bogdanowicz **Obv:** Embroidery pattern **Rev:** Bust at left, pattern design

Date	Mintage	F12	VF20	XF40	MS60	MS63
2011 Prooflike	2,000	—	—	—	—	75.00

KM# 424 10 ROUBLES
20.00 g., 0.925 Silver 0.591 oz. ASW, 38.61 mm. **Obv:** National arms **Rev:** Centaurea Cyanus flower

Date	Mintage	F12	VF20	XF40	MS60	MS63
2012	—	PF65 32.50				

KM# 425 10 ROUBLES
0.925 Silver, 38.61 mm. **Subject:** Railways: 150th Anniversary **Obv:** Modern train and station **Rev:** Old time train and station

Date	Mintage	F12	VF20	XF40	MS60	MS63
2012	—	—	—	—	100	120

KM# 446 10 ROUBLES
20.00 g., 0.925 Silver 0.591 oz. ASW, 38.61 mm. **Subject:** 2014 FFIA World Cup Brazil

Date	Mintage	F12	VF20	XF40	MS60	MS63
2013	Est. 10,000	PF65 75.00				

KM# 439 20 ROUBLES
0.925 Silver ASW, 30x45 mm. **Obv:** Stylized cross in ornaments **Rev:** Icon of Barkalabava Madonna

Date	Mintage	F12	VF20	XF40	MS60	MS63
2012	10,000	PF65 100				

KM# 440 20 ROUBLES
33.60 g., 0.925 Silver 0.9928 oz. ASW, 38.61 mm. **Subject:** Belarusbank, 90th Anniversary **Obv:** National arms **Rev:** Bank building

Date	Mintage	F12	VF20	XF40	MS60	MS63
2012	7,000	PF65 65.00				

KM# 441 20 ROUBLES
33.63 g., 0.925 Silver 0.9937 oz. ASW, 38.61 mm. **Subject:** Belarus-China relations, 20th Anniversary **Obv:** National arms **Rev:** Clasped hands

Date	Mintage	F12	VF20	XF40	MS60	MS63
2012	1,500	PF65 65.00				

KM# 442 20 ROUBLES
33.63 g., 0.925 Silver 0.9937 oz. ASW, 38.61 mm. **Obv:** National arms and stylized DNA molecule **Rev:** Stork with baby

Date	Mintage	F12	VF20	XF40	MS60	MS63
2012 Proof	10,000	—	—	—	—	65.00

KM# 443 20 ROUBLES
33.62 g., 0.925 Silver 0.9934 oz. ASW, 38.61 mm. **Subject:** Pottery **Obv:** National arms in stylized wreath **Rev:** Pottery filled with water

Date	Mintage	F12	VF20	XF40	MS60	MS63
2012	3,000	PF65 65.00				

KM# 444 20 ROUBLES
33.63 g., 0.925 Silver 0.9937 oz. ASW, 38.61 mm. **Subject:** Year of the Snake **Obv:** National arms and clockworks **Rev:** Coiled Viper

Date	Mintage	F12	VF20	XF40	MS60	MS63
2012	8,000	PF65 65.00				

KM# 445 20 ROUBLES

33.62 g., 0.925 Silver 0.9934 oz. ASW, 38.61 mm. **Subject:** Christening of the Rus, 1025th Anniversary **Obv:** National arms and stylized cross **Rev:** Dove and angels

Date	Mintage	F12	VF20	XF40	MS60	MS63
2012	3,000	PF65 65.00				

KM# 46 20 ROUBLES

33.73 g., 0.925 Silver 0.9967 oz. ASW, 38.6 mm. **Subject:** Wildlife **Obv:** National arms **Rev:** European Bison **Edge:** Reeded **Designer:** S.P. Zaskevich

Date	Mintage	F12	VF20	XF40	MS60	MS63
2001	2,000	PF65 350				

KM# 49 20 ROUBLES

28.32 g., 0.925 Silver 0.8368 oz. ASW, 38.6 mm. **Subject:** 2002 Winter Olympics **Obv:** National arms **Rev:** Marksman aiming at bullseye **Edge:** Reeded **Designer:** S.P. Zaskevich

Date	Mintage	F12	VF20	XF40	MS60	MS63
2001	15,000	PF65 60.00				

KM# 51 20 ROUBLES

33.65 g., 0.925 Silver 0.9943 oz. ASW, 38.6 mm. **Subject:** 2002 Winter Olympics **Obv:** National arms **Rev:** Two freestyle skiers **Edge:** Reeded **Designer:** S.P. Zaskevich

Date	Mintage	F12	VF20	XF40	MS60	MS63
2001	2,000	PF65 70.00				

KM# 111 20 ROUBLES

31.10 g., 0.925 Silver 0.9189 oz. ASW, 38.61 mm. **Subject:** 900th Anniversary of Euphrasinta **Obv:** National arms **Rev:** Euphrasinta of Polatsk, gold cross **Designer:** S.P. Zaskevitch

Date	Mintage	F12	VF20	XF40	MS60	MS63
2001	Est. 2000	PF65 350				

KM# 113 20 ROUBLES

31.10 g., 0.925 Silver 0.9189 oz. ASW, 38.61 mm. **Subject:** Tower of Kamyantes **Obv:** National arms **Rev:** Kamyanets Tower, seal **Designer:** S.P. Zaskevich

Date	Mintage	F12	VF20	XF40	MS60	MS63
2001	2,000	PF65 110				

KM# 45 20 ROUBLES

33.73 g., 0.925 Silver 0.9967 oz. ASW, 38.8 mm. **Obv:** National arms **Rev:** European beaver and young **Edge:** Reeded **Designer:** S.P. Zaskevich

Date	Mintage	F12	VF20	XF40	MS60	MS63
2002	2,000	PF65 200				

KM# 59 20 ROUBLES

28.63 g., 0.925 Silver 0.846 oz. ASW, 38.6 mm. **Obv:** National arms **Obv. Designer:** S.P. Zaskevich **Rev:** Brown bear with two cubs **Rev. Designer:** Waldemar Vronski **Edge:** Reeded

Date	Mintage	F12	VF20	XF40	MS60	MS63
2002	5,000	PF65 120				

KM# 70 20 ROUBLES

33.85 g., 0.925 Silver 1.0002 oz. ASW, 38.61 mm. **Obv:** National arms **Obv. Designer:** S.P. Zaskevich **Rev:** 80th Anniversary - National Savings Bank **Rev. Designer:** V. Titov **Edge:** Reeded

Date	Mintage	F12	VF20	XF40	MS60	MS63
2002	1,000	PF65 225				

KM# 115 20 ROUBLES

31.10 g., 0.925 Silver 0.9189 oz. ASW, 38.61 mm. **Subject:** 200th Birthday of Ignatius Dameika **Obv:** National arms **Rev:** Ignatius Dameika, hammer and inset with a dameikit stone **Rev. Designer:** S.P. Zaskevich

Date	Mintage	F12	VF20	XF40	MS60	MS63
2002	1,000	PF65 350				

KM# 119 20 ROUBLES

28.28 g., 0.925 Silver 0.8356 oz. ASW, 38.61 mm. **Subject:** 2006 World Cup Football **Obv:** National arms **Rev:** Stylized 2006, football **Designer:** S.P. Zaskevich

Date	Mintage	F12	VF20	XF40	MS60	MS63
2002	25,000	PF65 75.00				

KM# 53 20 ROUBLES

33.84 g., 0.925 Silver 0.9999 oz. ASW, 38.5 mm. **Obv:** State arms **Rev:** Two Mute swans on water with reflections **Edge:** Reeded **Designer:** S.P. Zaskevich

Date	Mintage	F12	VF20	XF40	MS60	MS63
2003	2,000	PF65 250				

KM# 57 20 ROUBLES

31.10 g., 0.925 Silver 0.9189 oz. ASW, 38.6 mm. **Obv:** National arms **Rev:** Church of the Savior and Transfiguration **Edge:** Reeded **Designer:** S.P. Zaskevich

Date	Mintage	F12	VF20	XF40	MS60	MS63
2003	2,000	PF65 100				

KM# 120 20 ROUBLES

31.10 g., 0.925 Silver 0.9189 oz. ASW, 38.61 mm. **Subject:** Freestyle Wrestling **Obv:** National arms **Rev:** Two wrestlers **Designer:** S.P. Zaskevich

Date	Mintage	F12	VF20	XF40	MS60	MS63
2003	3,000	PF65 65.00				

KM# 122 20 ROUBLES

31.10 g., 0.925 Silver 0.9189 oz. ASW, 38.61 mm. **Obv:** National arms **Rev:** Herring gull in flight **Designer:** S.P. Zaskevitch

Date	Mintage	F12	VF20	XF40	MS60	MS63
2003	2,000	PF65 200				

KM# 149 20 ROUBLES

28.28 g., 0.925 Silver 0.8356 oz. ASW, 38.61 mm. **Subject:** 2004 Olympic Games **Obv:** National arms **Rev:** Female shot-putter **Designer:** S.P. Zaskevich

Date	Mintage	F12	VF20	XF40	MS60	MS63
2003	25,000	PF65 65.00				

KM# 71 20 ROUBLES

31.10 g., 0.925 Silver 0.9189 oz. ASW, 38.6 mm. **Subject:** Kupalle **Obv:** Folk art design **Rev:** Fern flower with inset red synthetic crystal **Edge:** Reeded **Designer:** S.P. Zaskevich

Date	Mintage	F12	VF20	XF40	MS60	MS63
2004 Antique finish	3,000	—	—	—	600	—

KM# 72 20 ROUBLES

31.10 g., 0.925 Silver 0.9189 oz. ASW, 38.6 mm. **Subject:** Defense of Brest **Obv:** Multicolor Soviet Order of the Patriotic War **Rev:** Courage" monument **Edge:** Reeded **Designer:** S.P. Zaskevich

Date	Mintage	F12	VF20	XF40	MS60	MS63
2004	3,000	PF65 100				

KM# 73 20 ROUBLES
31.10 g., 0.925 Silver 0.9189 oz. ASW, 38.6 mm. **Obv:** National arms **Rev:** Two common cranes **Edge:** Reeded

Date	Mintage	F12	VF20	XF40	MS60	MS63
2004	2,000	PF65 170				

KM# 77 20 ROUBLES
31.10 g., 0.925 Silver 0.9189 oz. ASW, 38.6 mm. **Subject:** Kalyady **Obv:** Folk art cross design **Rev:** Stylized sunflower with inset blue synthetic crystal **Edge:** Reeded **Designer:** S.P. Zaskevich

Date	Mintage	F12	VF20	XF40	MS60	MS63
2004 Antique finish	5,000	—	—	—	350	—

KM# 79 20 ROUBLES
31.10 g., 0.925 Silver 0.9189 oz. ASW, 38.6 mm. **Obv:** National arms **Rev:** Radziwill's Castle in Neswizh **Edge:** Reeded **Designer:** S.P. Zaskevich

Date	Mintage	F12	VF20	XF40	MS60	MS63
2004	2,000	PF65 100				

KM# 84 20 ROUBLES
31.10 g., 0.925 Silver 0.9189 oz. ASW, 38.61 mm. **Subject:** Memory of Facist Victims **Obv:** Multicolored Order of the Patriotic War **Obv. Designer:** S.P. Zaskevich **Rev:** Man holding dead **Rev. Designer:** E.N. Vishnyakova

Date	Mintage	F12	VF20	XF40	MS60	MS63
2004	2,000	—	—	—	100	—

KM# 86 20 ROUBLES
31.10 g., 0.925 Silver 0.9189 oz. ASW, 38.61 mm. **Subject:** Soviet Warriors - Liberators **Obv:** Multicolored Order of the Patriotic War **Obv. Designer:** S.P. Zaskevich **Rev:** Partisans with blown up railway track **Rev. Designer:** E.N. Vishnyakova

Date	Mintage	F12	VF20	XF40	MS60	MS63
2004	2,000	—	—	—	100	—

KM# 91 20 ROUBLES
31.10 g., 0.925 Silver 0.9189 oz. ASW, 38.61 mm. **Subject:** Trade Union Movement Centennial **Obv:** National arms **Obv. Designer:** S.P. Zaskevich **Rev. Designer:** G.A. Maximor

Date	Mintage	F12	VF20	XF40	MS60	MS63
2004	1,500	PF65 200				

KM# 124 20 ROUBLES
31.10 g., 0.925 Silver 0.9189 oz. ASW, 38.61 mm. **Subject:** Sculling **Obv:** National arms **Obv. Designer:** S.P. Zaskevich **Rev:** Two rowers against a background of stylized oars **Rev. Designer:** S.V. Nekrasova

Date	Mintage	F12	VF20	XF40	MS60	MS63
2004	3,000	—	—	—	50.00	—

KM# 350 20 ROUBLES
33.62 g., 0.925 Silver 0.9934 oz. ASW, 38.61 mm. **Obv:** Russian Order star **Rev:** Soldier with rifle and tank

Date	Mintage	F12	VF20	XF40	MS60	MS63
2004	2,000	PF65 150				

KM# 351 20 ROUBLES
33.62 g., 0.925 Silver 0.9934 oz. ASW, 39 mm. **Subject:** Mogilev **Obv:** National arms **Rev:** Shield and city view

Date	Mintage	F12	VF20	XF40	MS60	MS63
2004	2,000	PF65 200				

KM# 82 20 ROUBLES
28.72 g., 0.925 Silver 0.8486 oz. ASW, 38.6 mm. **Subject:** WW II Victory **Obv:** Multicolor Soviet Order of Victory **Rev:**

Soviet soldiers raising their flag in the Reichstag in Berlin **Rev. Designer:** S.V. Necrasova **Edge:** Reeded

Date	Mintage	F12	VF20	XF40	MS60	MS63
2005	12,000	PF65 60.00				

KM# 92 20 ROUBLES
28.63 g., 0.925 Silver 0.846 oz. ASW, 38.6 mm. **Obv:** Two children sitting on crescent moon **Rev:** Symon the Musician and inset orange color glass crystal **Edge:** Plain **Designer:** S.V. Necrasova

Date	Mintage	F12	VF20	XF40	MS60	MS63
2005 Antique finish	20,000	—	—	—	65.00	—

KM# 93 20 ROUBLES
28.28 g., 0.925 Silver 0.8356 oz. ASW, 38.61 mm. **Subject:** Kalyady's star **Obv:** Two children sitting on a crescent moon **Rev:** Snow Queen, blue glass crystal inset on forehead, flower **Edge:** Plain **Designer:** S.V. Necrasova

Date	Mintage	F12	VF20	XF40	MS60	MS63
2005 Antique finish	20,000	—	—	—	65.00	—

KM# 94 20 ROUBLES
28.63 g., 0.925 Silver 0.846 oz. ASW, 38.6 mm. **Obv:** Two children sitting on a crescent moon **Rev:** White glass crystal inset above landscape with fox, the Little Prince **Edge:** Plain **Designer:** S.V. Necrasova

Date	Mintage	F12	VF20	XF40	MS60	MS63
2005 Antique finish	20,000	—	—	—	65.00	—

KM# 95 20 ROUBLES
28.63 g., 0.925 Silver 0.846 oz. ASW, 38.61 mm. **Obv:** Two children sitting on a crescent moon **Rev:** The Stone Flower, Yellow glass crystal inset in flower design, heads flank **Edge:** Plain **Designer:** S.V. Necrasova

Date	Mintage	F12	VF20	XF40	MS60	MS63
2005 Antique finish	20,000	—	—	—	65.00	—

KM# 96 20 ROUBLES
33.66 g., 0.925 Silver 0.9946 oz. ASW, 38.6 mm. **Subject:** Festivals and Rites - Bogach **Obv:** Small national arms above quilted star design **Rev:** Yellow glass crystal inset in candle flame above basket **Edge:** Reeded **Designer:** S.P. Zaskevich

Date	Mintage	F12	VF20	XF40	MS60	MS63
2005 Antique patina	5,000	—	—	—	170	—

KM# 98 20 ROUBLES
33.63 g., 0.925 Silver 0.9937 oz. ASW, 38.6 mm. **Subject:** Almany Bogs **Obv:** Blooming plant on frosted design **Rev:** Great grey owl in flight **Edge:** Reeded **Designer:** S.V. Nekrasova

Date	Mintage	F12	VF20	XF40	MS60	MS63
2005	5,000	PF65 70.00				

KM# 99 20 ROUBLES
31.10 g., 0.925 Silver 0.9189 oz. ASW, 38.6 mm. **Series:** Easter Egg **Obv:** Quilted cross design **Rev:** Decorated Easter egg with inset pink glass crystal

Date	Mintage	F12	VF20	XF40	MS60	MS63
2005 Antique finish	5,000	—	—	—	250	—

KM# 100 20 ROUBLES
33.62 g., 0.925 Silver 0.9934 oz. ASW, 38.6 mm. **Obv:** Large church **Rev:** Usyaslau of Polatsk

Date	Mintage	F12	VF20	XF40	MS60	MS63
2005		PF65 60.00				

KM# 101 20 ROUBLES
25.00 g., 0.925 Silver 0.7387 oz. ASW, 38.6 mm. **Subject:** 2006 FIFA World Cup Germany **Obv:** National arms **Rev:** Multicolor Europe, Asia and African maps on soccer ball **Rev. Designer:** S.V. Nekrasova **Note:** 2006 World Cup Soccer

Date	Mintage	F12	VF20	XF40	MS60	MS63
2005	50,000	PF65 55.00				

KM# 102 20 ROUBLES
33.94 g., 0.925 Silver 1.0029 oz. ASW, 39 mm. **Obv:** National arms **Rev:** Female tennis player

Date	Mintage	F12	VF20	XF40	MS60	MS63
2005	7,000	PF65 60.00				

KM# 128 20 ROUBLES
31.10 g., 0.925 Silver 0.9189 oz. ASW, 38.61 mm. **Subject:** 1000th Anniversary of Vaukavysk **Obv:** National arms **Rev:** National arms of Vaukavysk **Rev. Designer:** S.P. Zaskevitch

Date	Mintage	F12	VF20	XF40	MS60	MS63
2005	2,000	PF65 100				

KM# 131 20 ROUBLES
31.10 g., 0.925 Silver 0.9189 oz. ASW, 38.61 mm. **Subject:** Jesuit Roman Catholic Church **Obv:** National arms **Rev:** Jesuit Roman Catholic Church in Niasvizh **Designer:** S.P. Zaskevich

Date	Mintage	F12	VF20	XF40	MS60	MS63
2005	2,000	PF65 100				

KM# 133 20 ROUBLES
28.28 g., 0.925 Silver 0.8356 oz. ASW, 38.61 mm. **Subject:** 2006 Olympic Games **Obv:** National arms **Obv. Designer:** S.P. Zaskevich **Rev:** Two hockey players **Rev. Designer:** S.V. Necrasova and Ruth Oswald Koppers

Date	Mintage	F12	VF20	XF40	MS60	MS63
2005	15,000	PF65 60.00				

KM# 352 20 ROUBLES
33.62 g., 0.925 Silver 0.9934 oz. ASW, 39 mm. **Subject:** Grodno **Obv:** National arms **Rev:** Shield and fortress

Date	Mintage	F12	VF20	XF40	MS60	MS63
2005	2,000	PF65 150				

KM# 353 20 ROUBLES
33.62 g., 0.925 Silver 0.9934 oz. ASW, 39 mm. **Subject:** Brest **Obv:** National arms **Rev:** Shield and fortress

Date	Mintage	F12	VF20	XF40	MS60	MS63
2005	2,000	PF65 150				

KM# 136 20 ROUBLES
33.63 g., 0.925 Silver 0.9937 oz. ASW, 38.61 mm. **Subject:** Vtaselle Wedding **Obv:** National arms, birds, shamrock **Rev:** Loaf of bread, golden wedding rings, diadem of flowers, background of honeycomb

Date	Mintage	F12	VF20	XF40	MS60	MS63
2006	25,000	—	—	—	70.00	—

KM# 139 20 ROUBLES
33.62 g., 0.925 Silver 0.9934 oz. ASW, 38.61 mm. **Subject:** Sophia of Galshany 600th Anniversary **Obv:** Castle of Galshany **Rev:** National arms and Sophia of Galshany **Designer:** S.P. Zaskevich

Date	Mintage	F12	VF20	XF40	MS60	MS63
2006	5,000	PF65 70.00				

KM# 147 20 ROUBLES
33.63 g., 0.925 Silver 0.9937 oz. ASW, 38.61 mm. **Subject:** Chyrvomy Bar **Obv:** National arms, blooming plant **Rev:** European mink **Designer:** S.V. Nekrasova

Date	Mintage	F12	VF20	XF40	MS60	MS63
2006	5,000	PF65 100				

KM# 148 20 ROUBLES
28.28 g., 0.925 Silver 0.8356 oz. ASW, 38.5 mm. **Subject:** Twelve Months **Obv:** Two children sitting on a crescent moon **Rev:** Campfire with inset amber in a circle of produce **Edge:** Plain **Note:** Antiqued finish. Prev. duplicate of KM #137.

Date	Mintage	F12	VF20	XF40	MS60	MS63
2006	20,000	—	—	—	65.00	—

KM# 141 20 ROUBLES
33.62 g., 0.925 Silver 0.9934 oz. ASW, 38.61 mm. **Subject:** Festivals and Rites - Syomukha **Obv:** National arms, solar symbol **Rev:** Chalice, Chaplet of birch, maple, rowan, sweet flag leaves inserted in green crystal **Designer:** S.P. Zaskevich

Date	Mintage	F12	VF20	XF40	MS60	MS63
2006 Antique patina	5,000	—	—	—	150	—

KM# 155 20 ROUBLES
33.62 g., 0.925 Silver 0.9934 oz. ASW, 36x36 mm. **Subject:** Struve Geodetic Arc **Rev:** Map of Eastern Europe **Shape:** Square

Date	Mintage	F12	VF20	XF40	MS60	MS63
2006	5,000	PF65 60.00				

KM# 354 20 ROUBLES
33.62 g., 0.925 Silver 0.9934 oz. ASW, 39 mm. **Subject:** Homel **Obv:** National arms **Rev:** Shield and fortress

Date	Mintage	F12	VF20	XF40	MS60	MS63
2006	2,000	PF65 350				

KM# 355 20 ROUBLES
33.62 g., 0.925 Silver 0.9934 oz. ASW, 38.61 mm. **Subject:** CIS, 15th Anniversary **Obv:** Building façade **Rev:** Emblem

Date	Mintage	F12	VF20	XF40	MS60	MS63
2006	5,000	PF65 75.00				

KM# 356 20 ROUBLES
33.62 g., 0.925 Silver 0.9934 oz. ASW, 38.61 mm. **Subject:** Ski Center in Siliczy **Obv:** Skier **Rev:** Town view

Date	Mintage	F12	VF20	XF40	MS60	MS63
2006	5,000	PF65 75.00				

KM# 357 20 ROUBLES
33.62 g., 0.925 Silver 0.9934 oz. ASW, 38.61 mm. **Subject:** Rogwold and Rogneda **Obv:** Fortified circular town **Rev:** Norseman and female, ship

Date	Mintage	F12	VF20	XF40	MS60	MS63
2006	5,000	PF65 85.00				

KM# 358 20 ROUBLES
28.28 g., 0.925 Silver 0.8356 oz. ASW, 38.61 mm. **Subject:** Tale of the Thousand and one nights **Obv:** Boy and girl sitting on crescent moon **Rev:** Arabic window frame and motif

Date	Mintage	F12	VF20	XF40	MS60	MS63
2006 Antique patina	20,000	—	—	—	75.00	—

KM# 359 20 ROUBLES
33.62 g., 0.925 Silver 0.9934 oz. ASW, 38.61 mm. **Subject:** Cycling **Obv:** National arms **Rev:** Two bikes on track

Date	Mintage	F12	VF20	XF40	MS60	MS63
2006	5,000	PF65 80.00				

KM# 360 20 ROUBLES
28.28 g., 0.925 Silver 0.8356 oz. ASW, 38.61 mm. **Subject:** Beijing Olympics, 2008 **Obv:** National arms **Rev:** Runners around center circle

Date	Mintage	F12	VF20	XF40	MS60	MS63
2006	20,000	PF65 80.00				

KM# 166 20 ROUBLES
33.62 g., 0.925 Silver 0.9934 oz. ASW, 38.61 mm. **Subject:** Legend of the Stork **Obv:** Woven basket design **Rev:** Stylized bird

Date	Mintage	F12	VF20	XF40	MS60	MS63
2007	5,000	PF65 65.00				

KM# 158 20 ROUBLES
33.62 g., 0.925 Silver 0.9934 oz. ASW, 38.61 mm. **Subject:**
Belarus - China diplomatic relations **Rev:** Double arches with
country scene

Date	Mintage	F12	VF20	XF40	MS60	MS63
2007	2,000	PF65 100				

KM# 159 20 ROUBLES
33.62 g., 0.925 Silver 0.9934 oz. ASW, 38.61 mm. **Subject:**
Festivals and Rites - Maslenica **Rev:** Pancake and syrup

Date	Mintage	F12	VF20	XF40	MS60	MS63
2007 Antique Patina	5,000	—	—	—	130	—

KM# 160 20 ROUBLES
33.63 g., 0.925 Silver 0.9937 oz. ASW, 38.61 mm. **Subject:**
Napoleon Orda **Rev:** Bust facing, record and musical notes in
background

Date	Mintage	F12	VF20	XF40	MS60	MS63
2007	5,000	PF65 60.00				

KM# 161 20 ROUBLES
28.28 g., 0.925 Silver 0.8356 oz. ASW, 38.61 mm. **Subject:**
Alice in Wonderland **Obv:** Two children sitting on crescent moon
reading book **Rev:** Alice and the March Hare

Date	Mintage	F12	VF20	XF40	MS60	MS63
2007 Matte Proof	20,000	PF65 60.00				

KM# 162 20 ROUBLES
28.28 g., 0.925 Silver 0.8356 oz. ASW, 38.61 mm. **Subject:**
Alice Through the Looking Glass **Obv:** Two children sitting on
crescent moon reading book **Rev:** Alice and chess board

Date	Mintage	F12	VF20	XF40	MS60	MS63
2007 Matte Proof	20,000	PF65 60.00				

KM# 163 20 ROUBLES
31.11 g., 0.999 Silver 0.9926 oz. ASW, 40 mm. **Subject:**
Belarusian Ballet **Rev:** Ballerina and mirror view

Date	Mintage	F12	VF20	XF40	MS60	MS63
2007	10,000	PF65 60.00				

KM# 164 20 ROUBLES
31.10 g., 0.925 Silver 0.9189 oz. ASW, 38.61 mm. **Subject:**
International Polar Year **Obv:** IPY logo **Rev:** Antartic map
behind two penguins

Date	Mintage	F12	VF20	XF40	MS60	MS63
2007	10,000	PF65 60.00				

KM# 165 20 ROUBLES
33.62 g., 0.925 Silver 0.9934 oz. ASW, 38.61 mm. **Subject:**
Prince Gleb of Mensk **Obv:** Wood log building **Rev:** Knight
seated left

Date	Mintage	F12	VF20	XF40	MS60	MS63
2007	5,000	PF65 60.00				

KM# 167 20 ROUBLES
31.11 g., 0.999 Silver 0.9926 oz. ASW, 38.61 mm. **Subject:**
Wolf - Canis Lupus **Rev:** Wolf head facing

Date	Mintage	F12	VF20	XF40	MS60	MS63
2007	7,000	PF65 90.00				

KM# 168 20 ROUBLES
31.11 g., 0.999 Silver 0.9926 oz. ASW, 38.61 mm. **Subject:**
Wolf - Canis Lupis **Rev:** Wolf standing on rock ledge behind
second wolf's head facing

Date	Mintage	F12	VF20	XF40	MS60	MS63
2007	7,000	PF65 90.00				

KM# 169 20 ROUBLES
33.63 g., 0.925 Silver 0.9937 oz. ASW, 38.61 mm. **Subject:**
Dniepra - Sozhsky **Rev:** Sturgeon fish

Date	Mintage	F12	VF20	XF40	MS60	MS63
2007	5,000	PF65 85.00				

KM# 180 20 ROUBLES
33.63 g., 0.925 Silver 0.9937 oz. ASW, 38.61 mm. **Subject:**
Minsk **Rev:** Old and new city views

Date	Mintage	F12	VF20	XF40	MS60	MS63
2008	7,000	PF65 60.00				

KM# 181 20 ROUBLES
33.63 g., 0.925 Silver 0.9937 oz. ASW, 38.61 mm. **Subject:** Financial System, 90th Anniversary **Rev:** Shield

Date	Mintage	F12	VF20	XF40	MS60	MS63
2008	3,000	PF65 60.00				

KM# 182 20 ROUBLES
33.63 g., 0.925 Silver 0.9937 oz. ASW, 38.61 mm. **Subject:** Lipichanskaya Pushcha **Rev:** Kingfisher seated on branch

Date	Mintage	F12	VF20	XF40	MS60	MS63
2008	5,000	PF65 65.00				

KM# 183 20 ROUBLES
33.62 g., 0.925 Silver 0.9934 oz. ASW, 38.61 mm. **Subject:** Festivala and Rites - Dzyady **Rev:** Two angels above table

Date	Mintage	F12	VF20	XF40	MS60	MS63
2008 Antique patina	5,000	—	—	—	90.00	—

KM# 184 20 ROUBLES
33.62 g., 0.925 Silver 0.9934 oz. ASW, 38.61 mm. **Subject:** David of Garadzen **Rev:** Half-length figure of knight

Date	Mintage	F12	VF20	XF40	MS60	MS63
2008	5,000	PF65 60.00				

KM# 185 20 ROUBLES
31.11 g., 0.999 Silver 0.9926 oz. ASW, 40 mm. **Rev:** Figure skater

Date	Mintage	F12	VF20	XF40	MS60	MS63
2008	10,000	PF65 55.00				

KM# 186 20 ROUBLES
31.11 g., 0.999 Silver 0.9926 oz. ASW, 38.61 mm. **Subject:** Lynx **Rev:** Lynx head facing

Date	Mintage	F12	VF20	XF40	MS60	MS63
2008	8,000	PF65 95.00				

KM# 187 20 ROUBLES
31.11 g., 0.999 Silver 0.9926 oz. ASW, 38.61 mm. **Subject:** Lynx **Rev:** Adult lynx with cub

Date	Mintage	F12	VF20	XF40	MS60	MS63
2008	8,000	PF65 95.00				

KM# 188 20 ROUBLES
33.62 g., 0.925 Silver 0.9934 oz. ASW, 38.61 mm. **Subject:** Cuckoo Legend **Rev:** Stylized cuckoo

Date	Mintage	F12	VF20	XF40	MS60	MS63
2008	5,000	PF65 60.00				

KM# 189 20 ROUBLES
28.28 g., 0.925 Silver 0.8356 oz. ASW, 38.61 mm. **Subject:** Turandot **Rev:** Female opera character

Date	Mintage	F12	VF20	XF40	MS60	MS63
2008 Antique	—	—	—	—	65.00	—

KM# 190 20 ROUBLES
33.63 g., 0.925 Silver 0.9937 oz. ASW, 38.61 mm. **Subject:** House Warming **Obv:** Cat **Rev:** Plated key within house facade

Date	Mintage	F12	VF20	XF40	MS60	MS63
2008	25,000	PF65 60.00				

KM# 191 20 ROUBLES
28.28 g., 0.925 Silver 0.8356 oz. ASW, 38.61 mm. **Subject:** Sedov **Obv:** Compass star, multicolor **Rev:** Sailing ship

Date	Mintage	F12	VF20	XF40	MS60	MS63
2008	25,000	PF65 70.00				

KM# 242 20 ROUBLES
28.28 g., 0.925 Silver 0.8356 oz. ASW, 38.61 mm. **Subject:** 3 Musketeers **Rev:** D'Artagnan, with red stone insert

Date	Mintage	F12	VF20	XF40	MS60	MS63
2009	10,000	PF65 85.00				
2009	5,000	—	—	—	—	75.00

KM# 244 20 ROUBLES
28.28 g., 0.925 Silver 0.8356 oz. ASW, 38.61 mm. **Subject:** The Three Musketeers **Rev:** Athos, blue stone insert

Date	Mintage	F12	VF20	XF40	MS60	MS63
2009	5,000	PF65 85.00				
2009	10,000	—	—	—	—	75.00

KM# 245 20 ROUBLES
28.28 g., 0.925 Silver 0.8356 oz. ASW, 38.61 mm. **Subject:** The Three Musketeers **Rev:** Porthos, red stone insert

Date	Mintage	F12	VF20	XF40	MS60	MS63
2009	10,000	PF65 85.00				
2009	5,000	—	—	—	—	75.00

KM# 196 20 ROUBLES
33.63 g., 0.925 Silver 0.9937 oz. ASW, 38.61 mm. **Subject:** 65th Anniversary of Liberation **Rev:** Child looking upward to freeded birds

Date	Mintage	F12	VF20	XF40	MS60	MS63
2009	4,000	PF65 60.00				

KM# 197 20 ROUBLES
28.28 g., 0.925 Silver 0.8356 oz. ASW, 40x28 mm. **Subject:** Llya Repin **Rev:** Bust and house, artist's palet in corner **Shape:** Rectangle

Date	Mintage	F12	VF20	XF40	MS60	MS63
2009	1,500	PF65 60.00				

KM# 198 20 ROUBLES
28.28 g., 0.925 Silver 0.8356 oz. ASW, 38.61 mm. **Subject:** Spasy **Rev:** Bee honey comb, apple tree, grain **Edge:** Reeded

Date	Mintage	F12	VF20	XF40	MS60	MS63
2009 Antique finish	5,000	—	—	—	—	80.00

KM# 199 20 ROUBLES
33.63 g., 0.999 Silver 1.0732 oz. ASW, 38.61 mm. **Subject:** Christening **Rev:** Child in christening gown

Date	Mintage	F12	VF20	XF40	MS60	MS63
2009	5,000	PF65 80.00				

KM# 200 20 ROUBLES
28.28 g., 0.925 Silver 0.8356 oz. ASW, 38.61 mm. **Subject:** Dar Pomorza **Rev:** Sail training vessel

Date	Mintage	F12	VF20	XF40	MS60	MS63
2009	25,000	PF65 60.00				

KM# 201 20 ROUBLES
33.63 g., 0.925 Silver 0.9937 oz. ASW, 38.61 mm. **Subject:** White stork **Rev:** Bird and nest

Date	Mintage	F12	VF20	XF40	MS60	MS63
2009	7,000	PF65 70.00				

KM# 202 20 ROUBLES
33.63 g., 0.925 Silver 0.9937 oz. ASW, 38.61 mm. **Subject:** Belavezhskaya Pushcha **Rev:** Range animals

Date	Mintage	F12	VF20	XF40	MS60	MS63
2009	8,000	PF65 60.00				

KM# 203 20 ROUBLES
28.28 g., 0.925 Silver 0.8356 oz. ASW, 38.61 mm. **Series:** Zodiac - Pisces **Rev:** Two fish

Date	Mintage	F12	VF20	XF40	MS60	MS63
2009 Matte Proof	25,000	PF65 55.00				

KM# 204 20 ROUBLES
28.28 g., 0.925 Silver 0.8356 oz. ASW, 38.61 mm. **Subject:** Zodiac - Aries **Rev:** Ram

Date	Mintage	F12	VF20	XF40	MS60	MS63
2009 Matte Proof	25,000	PF65 55.00				

KM# 205 20 ROUBLES
28.28 g., 0.925 Silver 0.8356 oz. ASW, 38.61 mm. **Subject:** Zodiac - Taurus **Rev:** Bull

Date	Mintage	F12	VF20	XF40	MS60	MS63
2009 Matte Proof	25,000	PF65 55.00				

KM# 206 20 ROUBLES
28.28 g., 0.925 Silver 0.8356 oz. ASW, 38.61 mm. **Subject:** Zodiac - Gemini **Rev:** Twins

Date	Mintage	F12	VF20	XF40	MS60	MS63
2009 Matte Proof	25,000	PF65 55.00				

KM# 207 20 ROUBLES
28.28 g., 0.925 Silver 0.8356 oz. ASW, 38.61 mm. **Subject:** Zodiac - Cancer **Rev:** Crab

Date	Mintage	F12	VF20	XF40	MS60	MS63
2009 Matte Proof	25,000	PF65 55.00				

KM# 208 20 ROUBLES
28.28 g., 0.925 Silver 0.8356 oz. ASW, 38.61 mm. **Subject:** Zodiac - Leo **Rev:** Lion

Date	Mintage	F12	VF20	XF40	MS60	MS63
2009 Matte Proof	25,000		PF65 55.00			

KM# 209 20 ROUBLES
28.28 g., 0.925 Silver 0.8356 oz. ASW, 38.61 mm. **Subject:** Zodiac - Virgo **Rev:** Little girl

Date	Mintage	F12	VF20	XF40	MS60	MS63
2009 Matte Proof	25,000		PF65 55.00			

KM# 210 20 ROUBLES
28.28 g., 0.925 Silver 0.8356 oz. ASW, 38.61 mm. **Subject:** Zodiac - Libra **Rev:** Balance scales

Date	Mintage	F12	VF20	XF40	MS60	MS63
2009 Matte Proof	25,000		PF65 55.00			

KM# 211 20 ROUBLES
28.28 g., 0.925 Silver 0.8356 oz. ASW, 38.61 mm. **Obv. Designer:** Zodiac - Scorpio **Rev:** Scorpion

Date	Mintage	F12	VF20	XF40	MS60	MS63
2009 Matte Proof	25,000		PF65 55.00			

KM# 243 20 ROUBLES
28.28 g., 0.925 Silver 0.8356 oz. ASW, 38.61 mm. **Subject:** The Three Musketeers **Rev:** Aramis, light blue stone insert

Date	Mintage	F12	VF20	XF40	MS60	MS63
2009	5,000	—	—	—	75.00	
2009	10,000		PF65 85.00			

KM# 254 20 ROUBLES
28.28 g., 0.925 Silver 0.8356 oz. ASW, 45.3x35.3 mm. **Subject:** Pushkin's stories **Rev:** Tale of Tsar Saltan **Shape:** Vertical oval

Date	Mintage	F12	VF20	XF40	MS60	MS63
2009	7,000		PF65 85.00			

KM# 361 20 ROUBLES
28.28 g., 0.925 Silver 0.8356 oz. ASW, 38.61 mm. **Subject:** Zodiac - Sagittarius **Obv:** Sun and moon **Rev:** Girl with bow and arrow

Date	Mintage	F12	VF20	XF40	MS60	MS63
2009 Matte Proof	25,000		PF65 55.00			

KM# 362 20 ROUBLES
28.28 g., 0.925 Silver 0.8356 oz. ASW, 38.61 mm. **Subject:** Zodiac - Capricorn **Obv:** Sun and moon **Rev:** Capricorn

Date	Mintage	F12	VF20	XF40	MS60	MS63
2009 Matte Proof	25,000		PF65 55.00			

KM# 363 20 ROUBLES
33.62 g., 0.925 Silver 0.9934 oz. ASW, 38.61 mm. **Subject:** Straw Plaiting **Obv:** National arms within floral wreath **Rev:** Straw horse figure **Edge:** Reeded

Date	Mintage	F12	VF20	XF40	MS60	MS63
2009	5,000		PF65 75.00			

KM# 364 20 ROUBLES
28.28 g., 0.925 Silver 0.8356 oz. ASW, 38.61 mm. **Subject:** Nutcracker **Obv:** Boy and girl on crescent moon **Rev:** scenes from the Nutcracker ballet

Date	Mintage	F12	VF20	XF40	MS60	MS63
2009 Antique patina	25,000	—	—	—	75.00	

KM# 365 20 ROUBLES
28.28 g., 0.925 Silver 0.8356 oz. ASW, 38.61 mm. **Subject:** Zodiac - Aquarius **Obv:** Sun and moon **Rev:** Boy in bathtub

Date	Mintage	F12	VF20	XF40	MS60	MS63
2009 Matte Proof	25,000		PF65 55.00			

KM# 366 20 ROUBLES
33.63 g., 0.925 Silver 0.9937 oz. ASW, 38.61 mm. **Subject:** Legend of the skylark **Obv:** Five stylized birds in flight **Rev:** Stylized bird, head left

Date	Mintage	F12	VF20	XF40	MS60	MS63
2009 Prooflike	5,000		PF65 75.00			

KM# 367 20 ROUBLES
33.63 g., 0.925 Silver 0.9937 oz. ASW, 38.61 mm. **Subject:** Pakatigaroshak - Tale of the Dragon **Obv:** Geometric pattern and EURASAC logo **Rev:** Man clubbing dragon

Date	Mintage	F12	VF20	XF40	MS60	MS63
2009	3,000	PF65 75.00				

KM# 368 20 ROUBLES
31.10 g., 0.999 Silver 0.9925 oz. ASW, 38.61 mm. **Obv:** National arms **Rev:** Squirrel right eating nut **Edge:** Roodod

Date	Mintage	F12	VF20	XF40	MS60	MS63
2009	5,000	PF65 150				

KM# 369 20 ROUBLES
31.10 g., 0.999 Silvor 0.9925 oz. ASW, 38.61 mm. **Obv:** National arms **Rev:** Two squirrels on a branch, crystals in eyes **Edge:** Reeded

Date	Mintage	F12	VF20	XF40	MS60	MS63
2009	5,000	PF65 150				

KM# 370 20 ROUBLES
31.10 g., 0.925 Silver 0.9189 oz. ASW, 40 mm. **Subject:** London Olympics, 2012 **Obv:** Logo and National arms **Rev:** Two stylized players and Tower Bridge

Date	Mintage	F12	VF20	XF40	MS60	MS63
2009	6,000	PF65 75.00				

KM# 258 20 ROUBLES
33.62 g., 0.925 Silver 0.9934 oz. ASW, 38.61 mm. **Subject:** Expo 2010 **Obv:** Folk pattern **Rev:** Exposition buildings of the past

Date	Mintage	F12	VF20	XF40	MS60	MS63
2010	5,000	PF65 100				

KM# 279 20 ROUBLES
31.10 g., 0.999 Silver 0.9925 oz. ASW, 38.61 mm. **Obv:** National arms **Rev:** Two eagle owls, crystals in eyes

Date	Mintage	F12	VF20	XF40	MS60	MS63
2010	5,000	PF65 100				

KM# 224 20 ROUBLES
33.63 g., 0.925 Silver 0.9937 oz. ASW, 38.61 mm. **Subject:** EURASEC, 10th Anniversary **Obv:** Folk embroidery pattern **Rev:** Six flags around multicolor globe

Date	Mintage	F12	VF20	XF40	MS60	MS63
2010	3,000	PF65 60.00				

KM# 225 20 ROUBLES
33.63 g., 0.925 Silver 0.9937 oz. ASW, 38.6 mm. **Subject:** Syaredniaya Pripyat Reserve **Obv:** Eight ferns forming double cross **Rev:** Marsh turtle

Date	Mintage	F12	VF20	XF40	MS60	MS63
2010	3,000	PF65 70.00				

KM# 235 20 ROUBLES
28.28 g., 0.925 Silver 0.8356 oz. ASW, 38.61 mm. **Rev:** U.S. Frigate Constitution

Date	Mintage	F12	VF20	XF40	MS60	MS63
2010	7,000	PF65 75.00				

KM# 237 20 ROUBLES
33.62 g., 0.925 Silver 0.9934 oz. ASW, 38.61 mm. **Subject:** Legend of the tortoise

Date	Mintage	F12	VF20	XF40	MS60	MS63
2010	3,000	PF65 60.00				

KM# 239 20 ROUBLES
28.28 g., 0.925 Silver 0.8356 oz. ASW, 38.6 mm. **Subject:** Battle of Grunwald **Obv:** Figure with outstretched arms **Rev:** Legend within Fingerprint

Date	Mintage	F12	VF20	XF40	MS60	MS63
2010	2,500	PF65 60.00				

KM# 241 20 ROUBLES
33.63 g., 0.925 Silver 0.9937 oz. ASW, 38.61 mm. **Subject:** Age of Majority **Rev:** Multicolor flowers within folk patterns

Date	Mintage	F12	VF20	XF40	MS60	MS63
2010	—	PF65 60.00				

KM# 246 20 ROUBLES
28.28 g., 0.925 Silver 0.8356 oz. ASW, 38.61 mm. **Subject:** Orthodox Churches **Rev:** Cathedral of the Assumption

Date	Mintage	F12	VF20	XF40	MS60	MS63
2010	3,000	PF65 75.00				

KM# 247 20 ROUBLES
28.28 g., 0.925 Silver 0.8356 oz. ASW, 38.61 mm. **Subject:** Orthodox Churches **Rev:** Cathedral of SS Peter and Paul

Date	Mintage	F12	VF20	XF40	MS60	MS63
2010	3,000	PF65 75.00				

KM# 248 20 ROUBLES
28.28 g., 0.925 Silver 0.8356 oz. ASW, 38.61 mm. **Subject:** Orthodox Churches **Rev:** Cathedral of Alexander Nevsky

Date	Mintage	F12	VF20	XF40	MS60	MS63
2010	3,000	PF65 75.00				

KM# 249 20 ROUBLES
28.28 g., 0.925 Silver 0.8356 oz. ASW, 38.61 mm. **Subject:** Orthodox Churches **Rev:** Cathedral of St. Nicholas

Date	Mintage	F12	VF20	XF40	MS60	MS63
2010	3,000	PF65 75.00				

KM# 250 20 ROUBLES
28.28 g., 0.925 Silver 0.8356 oz. ASW, 45.3x35.3 mm. **Subject:** Pushkin's stories **Rev:** Tale of the Golden Cockerel in multicolor **Shape:** Vertical oval

Date	Mintage	F12	VF20	XF40	MS60	MS63
2010	7,000	PF65 85.00				

KM# 251 20 ROUBLES
28.28 g., 0.925 Silver 0.8356 oz. ASW, 45.3x35.3 mm. **Subject:** Pushkin's stories **Rev:** Tale of the fisherman and the fish **Shape:** Vertical oval

Date	Mintage	F12	VF20	XF40	MS60	MS63
2010	7,000	PF65 85.00				

KM# 252 20 ROUBLES
28.28 g., 0.925 Silver 0.8356 oz. ASW, 45.3x35.3 mm. **Subject:** Pushkin's stories **Rev:** Tale of one Dead Princess and Seven Knights **Shape:** Vertical oval

Date	Mintage	F12	VF20	XF40	MS60	MS63
2010	7,000	PF65 85.00				

KM# 253 20 ROUBLES
28.28 g., 0.925 Silver 0.8356 oz. ASW, 45.3x35.3 mm. **Subject:** Pushkin's stories **Rev:** Ruslan and Ludmila **Shape:** Vertical oval

Date	Mintage	F12	VF20	XF40	MS60	MS63
2010	7,000	PF65 85.00				

KM# 256 20 ROUBLES
31.10 g., 0.999 Silver 0.9925 oz. ASW, 38.61 mm. **Subject:** Slavic Woman **Rev:** Madonna and child

Date	Mintage	F12	VF20	XF40	MS60	MS63
2010 Proof	7,000	—				75.00

KM# 257 20 ROUBLES
28.28 g., 0.925 Silver 0.8356 oz. ASW, 28x40 mm. **Subject:** Ivan Khrutsky **Obv:** Color painting of female with fruit basket, arms at lower left **Rev:** Half-length figure of Khrutsky, flowers in vase on table **Shape:** Vertical rectangle

Date	Mintage	F12	VF20	XF40	MS60	MS63
2010	4,000	—				75.00

KM# 261 20 ROUBLES
33.63 g., 0.925 Silver 0.9937 oz. ASW, 38.61 mm. **Subject:** End of World War II, 65th Anniversary **Rev:** Five doves in flight, kiting

Date	Mintage	F12	VF20	XF40	MS60	MS63
2010	2,000	PF65 75.00				

KM# 266 20 ROUBLES
28.28 g., 0.925 Silver 0.8356 oz. ASW, 30x45 mm. **Subject:** Icon of the Most Holy Theotokos of Minsk **Rev:** Madonna icon, partially gilt **Shape:** Vertical rectangle

Date	Mintage	F12	VF20	XF40	MS60	MS63
2010	7,000	PF65 200				

KM# 267 20 ROUBLES
28.28 g., 0.925 Silver 0.8356 oz. ASW, 30x45 mm. **Subject:** Icon of the Mold Holy Theotokos of Smolensk **Rev:** Madonna Icon, partially gilt **Shape:** Vertical rectangle

Date	Mintage	F12	VF20	XF40	MS60	MS63
2010 Prooflike	7,000	—	—	—	—	150

KM# 268 20 ROUBLES
28.28 g., 0.925 Silver 0.8356 oz. ASW, 28x40 mm. **Rev:** Nefertiti bust **Shape:** Vertical rectangle

Date	Mintage	F12	VF20	XF40	MS60	MS63
2010	7,000	PF65 100				

KM# 269 20 ROUBLES
28.28 g., 0.925 Silver 0.8356 oz. ASW, 28x40 mm. **Rev:** Cupid & Psyche **Shape:** Vertical rectangle

Date	Mintage	F12	VF20	XF40	MS60	MS63
2010	7,000	PF65 100				

KM# 271 20 ROUBLES
28.28 g., 0.925 Silver 0.8356 oz. ASW, 38.6 mm. **Obv:** Compass rose and chart **Rev:** Cutty Sark sailing right

Date	Mintage	F12	VF20	XF40	MS60	MS63
2010	—	PF65 55.00				

KM# 374 20 ROUBLES
28.28 g., 0.925 Silver 0.8356 oz. ASW, 28x40 mm. **Subject:** Bernini **Obv:** Portrait facing **Rev:** Ecstasy of St. Theresa

Date	Mintage	F12	VF20	XF40	MS60	MS63
2010	7,000	PF65 125				

KM# 280 20 ROUBLES
28.28 g., 0.925 Silver 0.8356 oz. ASW, 38.61 mm. **Subject:** Krusenstern **Obv:** Compass rose and charts, national arms at top **Rev:** Fully-rigged sailing ship left

Date	Mintage	F12	VF20	XF40	MS60	MS63
2011	7,000	PF65 100				

KM# 281 20 ROUBLES
33.63 g., 0.925 Silver 0.9937 oz. ASW, 38.61 mm. **Subject:** Motherhood **Obv:** Folk embroidery pattern **Rev:** Mother holding baby, bird

Date	Mintage	F12	VF20	XF40	MS60	MS63
2011	10,000	PF65 90.00				

KM# 272 20 ROUBLES
28.28 g., 0.925 Silver 0.8356 oz. ASW, 38.61 mm. **Obv:** Compass rose and chart **Rev:** Amerigo Vespucci sailing left

Date	Mintage	F12	VF20	XF40	MS60	MS63
2010	—	PF65 75.00				

KM# 375 20 ROUBLES
31.10 g., 0.999 Silver 0.9925 oz. ASW, 38.61 mm. **Obv:** National arms **Rev:** Owl head facing, crystal eyes

Date	Mintage	F12	VF20	XF40	MS60	MS63
2010	5,000	PF65 125				

KM# 376 20 ROUBLES
33.63 g., 0.925 Silver 0.9937 oz. ASW, 38.61 mm. **Subject:** Blacksmithing **Obv:** National arms within floral wreath **Rev:** Horseshoe and village church

Date	Mintage	F12	VF20	XF40	MS60	MS63
2010	3,000	PF65 100				

KM# 281a 20 ROUBLES
33.63 g., 0.925 Silver 0.9937 oz. ASW, 38.61 mm. **Obv:** Folk embroidery pattern **Rev:** Mother and child, gilt bird **Rev. Designer:** Mothcrhood

Date	Mintage	F12	VF20	XF40	MS60	MS63
2011	—	PF65 90.00				

KM# 278 20 ROUBLES
7.78 g., 0.999 Gold 0.2483 oz. AGW, 22 mm. **Subject:** Slavic Women **Obv:** Large lis, national arms at top **Rev:** Madonna and Child

Date	Mintage	F12	VF20	XF40	MS60	MS63
2010	Est. 2500	PF65 475				

KM# 371 20 ROUBLES
28.28 g., 0.925 Silver 0.8356 oz. ASW, 38.61 mm. **Obv:** Heart with butterflies within **Rev:** Heart with vine and crystal

Date	Mintage	F12	VF20	XF40	MS60	MS63
2010	10,000	PF65 125				

KM# 282 20 ROUBLES
31.10 g., 0.925 Silver 0.9189 oz. ASW, 30x45 mm. **Subject:** Madonna icon; Theotokos of Kazan **Obv:** Cross at center of design **Rev:** Icon image, ornate frame

Date	Mintage	F12	VF20	XF40	MS60	MS63
2011	10,000	PF65 250				

KM# 372 20 ROUBLES
5.76 g., 0.900 Gold 0.1656 oz. AGW, 19.8 mm. **Subject:** Battle of Grunwald, 600th Anniversary **Obv:** Standard head **Rev:** pellet cross within standard head

Date	Mintage	F12	VF20	XF40	MS60	MS63
2010	500	PF65 400				

KM# 377 20 ROUBLES
33.63 g., 0.925 Silver 0.9937 oz. ASW, 38.61 mm. **Subject:** Candlemas **Obv:** Embroidery pattern **Rev:** Bird rising out of the snow to a flowered field and sunrise **Edge:** Reeded

Date	Mintage	F12	VF20	XF40	MS60	MS63
2010	2,500	PF65 150				

KM# 378 20 ROUBLES
33.63 g., 0.925 Silver 0.9937 oz. ASW, 38.61 mm. **Subject:** Lew Sapieha **Obv:** Ancient document **Rev:** Figure standing

Date	Mintage	F12	VF20	XF40	MS60	MS63
2010	3,000	PF65 125				

KM# 255 20 ROUBLES
28.28 g., 0.925 Silver 0.8356 oz. ASW, 38.61 mm. **Subject:** My Love **Rev:** Two cats, red heart shaped crystal insert at top

Date	Mintage	F12	VF20	XF40	MS60	MS63
2011	15,000	PF65 100				

KM# 283 20 ROUBLES
31.10 g., 0.925 Silver 0.9189 oz. ASW, 30x45 mm. **Subject:** Madonna icon, Theotokos of Zhirovichy **Obv:** Cross within design **Rev:** Madonna icon, angellic corners

Date	Mintage	F12	VF20	XF40	MS60	MS63
2011	10,000	PF65 250				

KM# 373 20 ROUBLES
28.28 g., 0.925 Silver 0.8356 oz. ASW, 28x40 mm. **Subject:** Rodin **Obv:** Portrait facing **Rev:** The Thinker statue

Date	Mintage	F12	VF20	XF40	MS60	MS63
2010	7,000	PF65 125				

KM# 289 20 ROUBLES
28.28 g., 0.925 Silver 0.8356 oz. ASW **Subject:** Paleolithic Venus **Obv:** Cave drawing of steer **Rev:** Carved statue of pregnant female **Shape:** Vertical rectangle

Date	Mintage	F12	VF20	XF40	MS60	MS63
2011	Est. 3500			PF65 90.00		

KM# 290 20 ROUBLES
28.28 g., 0.925 Silver 0.8356 oz. ASW **Subject:** Voltaire **Obv:** Carved portrait bust **Rev:** Statue of seated Voltaire **Shape:** Vertical rectangle

Date	Mintage	F12	VF20	XF40	MS60	MS63
2011	Est. 3500			PF65 90.00		

KM# 379 20 ROUBLES
28.28 g., 0.925 Silver 0.8356 oz. ASW, 38.61 mm. **Subject:** Polotsk **Obv:** Map, ship and national arms **Rev:** Shield and city view

Date	Mintage	F12	VF20	XF40	MS60	MS63
2011	7,000			PF65 110		

KM# 380 20 ROUBLES
28.28 g., 0.925 Silver 0.8356 oz. ASW, 38.61 mm. **Subject:** Arabic Dance

Date	Mintage	F12	VF20	XF40	MS60	MS63
2011	6,000			PF65 110		

KM# 381 20 ROUBLES
31.10 g., 0.999 Silver 0.9925 oz. ASW, 38.61 mm. **Subject:** Hedgehog **Obv:** National arms **Rev:** Hedgehog left, crystal eye

Date	Mintage	F12	VF20	XF40	MS60	MS63
2011	4,000			PF65 125		

KM# 382 20 ROUBLES
31.10 g., 0.999 Silver 0.9925 oz. ASW, 38.61 mm. **Subject:** Hedgehog **Obv:** National arms **Rev:** Hedgehog facing, crystal eyes

Date	Mintage	F12	VF20	XF40	MS60	MS63
2011	4,000			PF65 125		

KM# 383 20 ROUBLES
31.10 g., 0.925 Silver 0.9189 oz. ASW, 45x30 mm. **Subject:** Akhal-Teke Horses **Obv:** Two horses galloping thru low water right **Rev:** Ancient two-horse carriage, horse walking right **Shape:** Rectangle

Date	Mintage	F12	VF20	XF40	MS60	MS63
2011	6,000			PF65 125		

KM# 413 20 ROUBLES
31.11 g., 0.999 Silver 0.9926 oz. ASW, 38.61 mm. **Obv:** National emblem **Rev:** Hedgehog family, Swarovski crystal in eyes

Date	Mintage	F12	VF20	XF40	MS60	MS63
2011	4,000			PF65 100		

KM# 414 20 ROUBLES
31.11 g., 0.999 Silver 0.9926 oz. ASW, 38.61 mm. **Obv:** National emblem **Rev:** Hedgehog facing left, Swarovski crystal in eye

Date	Mintage	F12	VF20	XF40	MS60	MS63
2011	4,000			PF65 100		

KM# 416 20 ROUBLES
0.925 Silver, 30x45 mm. **Obv:** Stylized cross in ornaments **Rev:** Icon of Vladimir Madonna

Date	Mintage	F12	VF20	XF40	MS60	MS63
2012	10,000			PF65 100		

KM# 418 20 ROUBLES
0.925 Silver **Subject:** Reconstruction of Izyaslavl fortress **Rev:** Regvolod of Polotsk **Edge Lettering:** 38.61 **Designer:** S. Zackevich

Date	Mintage	F12	VF20	XF40	MS60	MS63
2012	5,000			PF65 100		

KM# 420 20 ROUBLES
31.11 g., 0.999 Silver 0.9926 oz. ASW, 38.61 mm. **Obv:** National Arms **Rev:** Bison head facing, two crystal eyes

Date	Mintage	F12	VF20	XF40	MS60	MS63
2012	—		PF63 50.00	PF65 55.00		

KM# 422 20 ROUBLES
31.11 g., 0.999 Silver 0.9926 oz. ASW, 38.61 mm. **Obv:** National arms **Rev:** Two bison butting heads

Date	Mintage	F12	VF20	XF40	MS60	MS63
2012	Est. 5000		PF63 50.00	PF65 55.00		

KM# 423 20 ROUBLES
20.00 g., 0.925 Silver 0.591 oz. ASW, 38.61 mm. **Obv:** National arms **Rev:** Nymphaea Alba - flower in color

Date	Mintage	F12	VF20	XF40	MS60	MS63
2012				PF65 32.50		

KM# 426 20 ROUBLES
28.28 g., 0.925 Silver 0.8356 oz. ASW, 38.6 mm. **Subject:** Bear legend **Obv:** National arms and stylized pattern with bears **Rev:** Bear

Date	Mintage	F12	VF20	XF40	MS60	MS63
2012	2,000			PF65 65.00		

KM# 453 20 ROUBLES
20.00 g., 0.999 Silver 0.6382 oz. ASW, 38.61 mm. **Subject:** Belarusian ballet

Date	Mintage	F12	VF20	XF40	MS60	MS63
2013	Est. 10,000			PF65 75.00		

KM# 455 20 ROUBLES
28.28 g., 0.925 Silver 0.8356 oz. ASW, 38.61 mm. **Subject:** Zodiac - Libra

Date	Mintage	F12	VF20	XF40	MS60	MS63
2013	Est. 7,777			PF65 75.00		

KM# 456 20 ROUBLES
28.28 g., 0.925 Silver 0.8356 oz. ASW, 38.61 mm. **Subject:** Zodiac - Scorpio

Date	Mintage	F12	VF20	XF40	MS60	MS63
2013	Est. 7,777			PF65 75.00		

KM# 121 50 ROUBLES
4.45 g., 0.999 Gold 0.142 oz. AGW, 25 mm. **Subject:** Fox **Obv:** National arms **Obv. Designer:** S.P. Zaskevich **Rev:** Red fox with inset diamond eyes **Rev. Designer:** Waldemar Wronski

Date	Mintage	F12	VF20	XF40	MS60	MS63
2002	Est. 2000	—	—	—	1,000	

KM# 126 50 ROUBLES
62.20 g., 0.925 Silver 1.8379 oz. ASW, 50 mm. **Subject:** 60th Anniversary of Victory **Obv:** Order of the Victory, multicolored **Rev:** Stars and arrows **Rev. Designer:** S.V. Necrasova

Date	Mintage	F12	VF20	XF40	MS60	MS63
2005	—			PF65 220		
2005	2,000	—	—	—	—	

KM# 123 50 ROUBLES
8.00 g., 0.900 Gold 0.230 oz. AGW, 21 mm. **Subject:** Herring Gull **Obv:** National arms **Rev:** Herring gull in flight **Designer:** S.P. Zaskevitch

Date	Mintage	F12	VF20	XF40	MS60	MS63
2006	3,000			PF65 800		

KM# 125 50 ROUBLES
8.00 g., 0.900 Gold 0.230 oz. AGW, 21 mm. **Obv:** National arms **Rev:** Pair of common cranes **Designer:** S.P. Zaskevich

Date	Mintage	F12	VF20	XF40	MS60	MS63
2006	3,000			PF65 800		

KM# 142 50 ROUBLES
7.78 g., 0.999 Gold 0.2483 oz. AGW, 25 mm. **Subject:** Peregrine Falcon **Obv:** National arms **Obv. Designer:** S.P. Zaskevich **Rev:** Peregrine falcon with inset diamond eye **Rev. Designer:** S.V. Nekrasova

Date	Mintage	F12	VF20	XF40	MS60	MS63
2006	2,000	—	—	750	1,000	

KM# 143 50 ROUBLES
8.00 g., 0.900 Gold 0.230 oz. AGW, 21 mm. **Subject:** Bison **Obv:** National arms **Rev:** European bison **Designer:** S.P. Zaskevich

Date	Mintage	F12	VF20	XF40	MS60	MS63
2006	3,000			PF65 800		

KM# 144 50 ROUBLES
8.00 g., 0.900 Gold 0.230 oz. AGW, 21 mm. **Subject:** Beaver **Obv:** National arms **Rev:** Family of Eurasian beavers **Designer:** S.P. Zaskovich

Date	Mintage	F12	VF20	XF40	MS60	MS63
2006	3,000			PF65 800		

KM# 145 50 ROUBLES
8.00 g., 0.900 Gold 0.230 oz. AGW, 21 mm. **Subject:** Mute Swan **Obv:** National arms **Rev:** Pair of mute swans **Designer:** S.P. Zaskevich

Date	Mintage	F12	VF20	XF40	MS60	MS63
2006	3,000			PF65 800		

KM# 384 50 ROUBLES
7.78 g., 0.999 Gold 0.2483 oz. AGW, 25 mm. **Obv:** National arms **Rev:** Wolf head facing

Date	Mintage	F12	VF20	XF40	MS60	MS63
2007	2,000			PF65 900		

KM# 385 50 ROUBLES
8.00 g., 0.900 Gold 0.230 oz. AGW, 21 mm. **Obv:** Church within frame **Rev:** Female saint icon

Date	Mintage	F12	VF20	XF40	MS60	MS63
2008	14,000	—	—	—	—	700
2008	1,000			PF65 800		

KM# 386 50 ROUBLES
8.00 g., 0.900 Gold 0.230 oz. AGW, 21 mm. **Obv:** Church within frame **Rev:** Saint Sarowski icon

Date	Mintage	F12	VF20	XF40	MS60	MS63
2008	14,000	—	—	—	—	700
2008	1,000			PF65 800		

KM# 387 50 ROUBLES
8.00 g., 0.900 Gold 0.230 oz. AGW, 21 mm. **Obv:** Church within frame **Rev:** Saint Sergey Radonezski icon

Date	Mintage	F12	VF20	XF40	MS60	MS63
2008	14,000	—	—	—	—	700
2008	1,000			PF65 800		

KM# 388 50 ROUBLES
8.00 g., 0.900 Gold 0.230 oz. AGW, 21 mm. **Obv:** Church within frame **Rev:** Saint Mikplaj the miracle worker icon

Date	Mintage	F12	VF20	XF40	MS60	MS63
2008	14,000	—	—	—	—	700
2008	1,000			PF65 800		

KM# 389 50 ROUBLES
8.00 g., 0.900 Gold 0.230 oz. AGW, 21 mm. **Obv:** Church within frame **Rev:** Saint Pantaleon icon

Date	Mintage	F12	VF20	XF40	MS60	MS63
2008	14,000	—	—	—	—	700
2008	1,000			PF65 800		

KM# 390 50 ROUBLES
7.78 g., 0.999 Silver 0.2483 oz. ASW, 25 mm. **Obv:** National arms **Rev:** Lunx head facing

Date	Mintage	F12	VF20	XF40	MS60	MS63
2008	2,000			PF65 850		

KM# 391 50 ROUBLES
7.78 g., 0.999 Gold 0.2483 oz. AGW, 25 mm. **Obv:** National arms **Rev:** Squirrel right eating nut

Date	Mintage	F12	VF20	XF40	MS60	MS63
2009	2,000	PF65 900				

KM# 277 50 ROUBLES
7.78 g., 0.999 Gold 0.2483 oz. AGW, 25 mm. **Obv:** National arms **Rev:** Owl head facing

Date	Mintage	F12	VF20	XF40	MS60	MS63
2010	—	PF65 900				

KM# 392 50 ROUBLES
8.64 g., 0.900 Gold 0.2484 oz. AGW, 22 mm **Subject:** Battle of Grunwald, 600th Anniversary **Obv:** Stylized figure in shape of cross **Rev:** Stylized fingerprint

Date	Mintage	F12	VF20	XF40	MS60	MS63
2010	500	PF65 800				

KM# 393 50 ROUBLES
7.78 g., 0.999 Gold 0.2483 oz. AGW, 22 mm. **Subject:** Motherhood **Obv:** Lis **Rev:** Mother and child

Date	Mintage	F12	VF20	XF40	MS60	MS63
2010	2,500	PF65 800				

KM# 286 50 ROUBLES
7.78 g., 0.999 Gold 0.2483 oz. AGW, 25 mm. **Obv:** National arms **Rev:** Hedgehog

Date	Mintage	F12	VF20	XF40	MS60	MS63
2011	Est. 1000	PF65 950				

KM# 421 50 ROUBLES
7.78 g., 0.999 Gold 0.2483 oz. AGW, 25 mm. **Obv:** National arms **Rev:** Bison head facing, crystal eyes

Date	Mintage	F12	VF20	XF40	MS60	MS63
2012	Est. 2000	PF65 435				

KM# 450 50 ROUBLES
7.77 g., 0.900 Gold 0.248 oz. AGW, 22 mm. **Subject:** Belarusian Ballet

Date	Mintage	F12	VF20	XF40	MS60	MS63
2013	Ect. 1,000	PF65 350				

KM# 58 100 ROUBLES
155.50 g., 0.925 Silver 4.5947 oz. ASW, 64 mm. **Obv:** Theater building **Rev:** Two ballet dancers **Edge:** Reeded **Designer:** S.P. Zaskevich **Note:** Illustration reduced.

Date	Mintage	F12	VF20	XF40	MS60	MS63
2003	1,000	PF65 750				

KM# 216 100 ROUBLES
17.28 g., 0.900 Gold 0.4968 oz. AGW, 32 mm. **Subject:** China - Belarus relations, 15th Anniversary **Obv:** National arms **Rev:** Two archways, forest in left, Great Wall on right **Edge:** Reeded

Date	Mintage	F12	VF20	XF40	MS60	MS63
2007	1,000	PF65 1,000				

KM# 192 100 ROUBLES
155.50 g., 0.999 Silver 4.9623 oz. ASW, 65 mm. **Subject:** Figure skating **Rev:** Pair of skates and snowflakes **Note:** Illustration reduced.

Date	Mintage	F12	VF20	XF40	MS60	MS63
2008	500	PF65 450				

KM# 193 100 ROUBLES
155.50 g., 0.999 Silver 4.9623 oz. ASW, 65 mm. **Subject:** White Stork Legend **Rev:** Stylized stork

Date	Mintage	F12	VF20	XF40	MS60	MS63
2008	500	PF65 450				

KM# 333 100 ROUBLES
155.50 g., 0.999 Gold 4.9623 oz. AGW, 65 mm. **Subject:** 2012 London Olympics **Obv:** National emblem at center of star design **Rev:** Tower bridge and two stylized handball athletes above

Date	Mintage	F12	VF20	XF40	MS60	MS63
2009	800	PF65 9,500				

KM# 394 100 ROUBLES
155.50 g., 0.999 Silver 4.9623 oz. ASW, 65 mm. **Subject:** London Olympics, 2012 **Obv:** National arms and logo **Rev:** Two stylized players and Tower Bridge

Date	Mintage	F12	VF20	XF40	MS60	MS63
2009 Prooflike	800	—	—	—	—	250

KM# 395 100 ROUBLES
15.50 g., 0.900 Gold 0.4456 oz. AGW, 30 mm. **Subject:** Zodiac - Pisces **Obv:** Sun and moon **Rev:** Two fish

Date	Mintage	F12	VF20	XF40	MS60	MS63
2011	2,000	PF65 1,200				

KM# 396 100 ROUBLES
15.50 g., 0.900 Gold 0.4456 oz. AGW, 30 mm. **Subject:** Zodiac - Ram **Obv:** Sun and moon **Rev:** Ram

Date	Mintage	F12	VF20	XF40	MS60	MS63
2011	2,000	PF65 1,200				

KM# 397 100 ROUBLES
15.50 g., 0.900 Gold 0.4456 oz. AGW, 30 mm. **Subject:** Zodiac - Taurus **Obv:** Sun and moon **Rev:** Bull

Date	Mintage	F12	VF20	XF40	MS60	MS63
2011	2,000	PF65 1,200				

KM# 398 100 ROUBLES
15.50 g., 0.900 Gold 0.4456 oz. AGW, 30 mm. **Subject:** Zodiac - Gemni **Obv:** Sun and moon **Rev:** Twins

Date	Mintage	F12	VF20	XF40	MS60	MS63
2011	2,000	PF65 1,200				

KM# 399 100 ROUBLES
15.50 g., 0.900 Gold 0.4456 oz. AGW, 30 mm. **Subject:** Zodiac - Cancer **Obv:** Sun and moon **Rev:** Crab

Date	Mintage	F12	VF20	XF40	MS60	MS63
2011	2,000	PF65 1,200				

KM# 400 100 ROUBLES
15.50 g., 0.900 Gold 0.4456 oz. AGW, 30 mm. **Subject:** Zodiac - Leo **Obv:** Sun and moon **Rev:** Lion standing left

Date	Mintage	F12	VF20	XF40	MS60	MS63
2011	2,000	PF65 1,200				

KM# 401 100 ROUBLES
15.50 g., 0.900 Gold 0.4456 oz. AGW, 30 mm. **Subject:** Zodiac - Virgo **Obv:** Sun and moon **Rev:** Girl

Date	Mintage	F12	VF20	XF40	MS60	MS63
2011	2,000	PF65 1,200				

KM# 402 100 ROUBLES
15.50 g., 0.900 Gold 0.4456 oz. AGW, 30 mm. **Subject:** Zodiac - Libra **Obv:** Sun and moon **Rev:** Balance scales

Date	Mintage	F12	VF20	XF40	MS60	MS63
2011	2,000	PF65 1,200				

KM# 403 100 ROUBLES
15.50 g., 0.900 Gold 0.4456 oz. AGW, 30 mm. **Subject:** Zodiac - Scorpion **Obv:** Sun and moon **Rev:** Scorpion

Date	Mintage	F12	VF20	XF40	MS60	MS63
2011	2,000	PF65 1,200				

KM# 404 100 ROUBLES
15.50 g., 0.900 Gold 0.4456 oz. AGW, 30 mm. **Subject:** Zodiac - Virgo **Obv:** Sun and moon **Rev:** Girl as angel with bow and arrow

Date	Mintage	F12	VF20	XF40	MS60	MS63
2011	2,000	PF65 1,200				

KM# 405 100 ROUBLES
15.50 g., 0.900 Gold 0.4456 oz. AGW, 30 mm. **Subject:** Zodiac - Capricorn **Obv:** Sun and moon **Rev:** Ram standing left

Date	Mintage	F12	VF20	XF40	MS60	MS63
2011	2,000	PF65 1,200				

KM# 406 100 ROUBLES
15.50 g., 0.900 Gold 0.4456 oz. AGW, 30 mm. **Subject:** Zodiac - Aquarius **Obv:** Sun and moon **Rev:** Child in bathtub

Date	Mintage	F12	VF20	XF40	MS60	MS63
2011	2,000	PF65 1,200				

KM# 447 100 ROUBLES
155.50 g., 0.999 Silver 4.9623 oz. ASW, 65 mm. **Subject:** 2014 FIFA World Cup Brazil

Date	Mintage	F12	VF20	XF40	MS60	MS63
2013	Est. 1,000	PF65 400				

KM# 452 100 ROUBLES
155.50 g., 0.999 Silver 4.9623 oz. ASW, 65 mm. **Subject:** Belarusian Ballet

Date	Mintage	F12	VF20	XF40	MS60	MS63
2013	Est. 750	PF65 400				

KM# 103 200 ROUBLES
31.11 g., 0.999 Gold 0.9926 oz. AGW, 40 mm. **Obv:** National arms **Obv. Designer:** S.P. Zaskevich **Rev:** Belarussian ballerina **Rev. Designer:** Michael Schulze

Date	Mintage	F12	VF20	XF40	MS60	MS63
2005	1,500	PF65 2,000				

KM# 408 200 ROUBLES
34.56 g., 0.900 Gold 0.9936 oz. AGW, 38.61 mm. **Subject:** Ski center in Siliczy **Obv:** Skier **Rev:** Building complex

Date	Mintage	F12	VF20	XF40	MS60	MS63
2006	2,000	PF65 3,000				

KM# 409 200 ROUBLES
31.10 g., 0.999 Gold 0.9925 oz. AGW, 40 mm. **Subject:** Ballet **Obv:** National arms **Rev:** Ballet Pair

Date	Mintage	F12	VF20	XF40	MS60	MS63
2006	1,500	PF65 3,250				

KM# 407 200 ROUBLES
31.10 g., 0.999 Gold 0.9925 oz. AGW, 40 mm. **Subject:** Ballet **Obv:** National arms **Rev:** Ballerina on point right

Date	Mintage	F12	VF20	XF40	MS60	MS63
2007	1,500	PF65 3,000				

KM# 74 1000 ROUBLES
1000.00 g., 0.999 Silver 31.9118 oz. ASW, 100 mm. **Subject:** 2004 Olympics **Obv:** National arms **Rev:** Ancient charioteer **Rev. Designer:** Waldemar Wronski **Note:** Illustration reduced.

Date	Mintage	F12	VF20	XF40	MS60	MS63
2004	650	PF65 1,500				

KM# 410 1000 ROUBLES
155.50 g., 0.999 Gold 4.9623 oz. AGW, 65 mm. **Subject:** Ballet **Obv:** National arms **Rev:** Ballet pair

Date	Mintage	F12	VF20	XF40	MS60	MS63
2006	99	PF65 10,500				

KM# 412 1000 ROUBLES
1000.00 g., 0.999 Silver 31.9118 oz. ASW, 100 mm. **Subject:** Beijing Olympics, 2008 **Obv:** Naitonal arms **Rev:** Classical runners around center circle

Date	Mintage	F12	VF20	XF40	MS60	MS63
2006	2,000	PF65 2,000				

KM# 170 1000 ROUBLES
1000.00 g., 0.999 Silver 31.9118 oz. ASW, 100 mm. **Subject:** Belarussian Ballet **Rev:** Ballerina and mirror image **Note:** Illustration reduced.

Date	Mintage	F12	VF20	XF40	MS60	MS63
2007	300	PF65 2,000				

KM# 171 1000 ROUBLES
1000.00 g., 0.999 Silver 31.9118 oz. ASW, 100 mm. **Subject:** Cross of St. Euphrosyne of Polotsk **Obv:** Church facade **Rev:** Gold-plated pectorial cross **Note:** Illustration reduced.

Date	Mintage	F12	VF20	XF40	MS60	MS63
2007 Proof-like	2,000	PF65 2,000				

KM# 411 1000 ROUBLES
155.50 g., 0.999 Gold 4.9623 oz. AGW, 65 mm. **Subject:** Ballet **Obv:** National arms **Rev:** Mirror image of ballerina

Date	Mintage	F12	VF20	XF40	MS60	MS63
2007	99	PF65 10,500				

KM# 449 1000 ROUBLES
155.50 g., 0.999 Gold 4.9623 oz. AGW, 65 mm. **Subject:** Belarusian Ballet

Date	Mintage	F12	VF20	XF40	MS60	MS63
2013	Est. 49	PF65 9,000				

KM# 451 5 ROUBLE
0.50 g., 0.999 Gold AGW, 11 mm. **Subject:** Belarusian Ballet

Date	Mintage	F12	VF20	XF40	MS60	MS63
2013	Est. 10,000	PF65 50.00				

BELGIUM

The Kingdom of Belgium, a constitutional monarchy in northwest Europe, has an area of 11,780 sq. mi. (30,519 sq. km.) and a population of 10.1 million, chiefly Dutch-speaking Flemish and French-speaking Walloons. Capital: Brussels. Agriculture, dairy farming, and the processing of raw materials for re-export are the principal industries. Beurs voor Diamant in Antwerp is the world's largest diamond trading center. Iron and steel, machinery motor vehicles, chemicals, textile yarns and fabrics comprise the principal exports.

RULER
Albert II, 1993-

MINT MARK
Angel head - Brussels

MINTMASTERS' INITIALS & PRIVY MARKS
Pair of scales – Romain Coenen (1987 -)
Goose feather – Serge Lesens (2010)
NOTE: Beginning in 1987, the letters "qp" (quality proof) appear on non-circulating coins

MONETARY SYSTEM
100 Centimes = 1 Franc
1 Euro = 100 Cents

LEGENDS
Belgian coins are usually inscribed either in Dutch, French or both. However some modern coins are being inscribed in Latin or German. The language used is best told by noting the spelling of the name of the country.

(Fr) French: BELGIQUE or BELGES
(Du) Dutch: BELGIE or BELGEN
(La) Latin: BELGICA
(Ge) German: BELGIEN

KINGDOM
DECIMAL COINAGE

KM# 148.2 50 CENTIMES
2.75 g., Bronze, 19 mm. **Ruler:** Baudouin I **Obv:** Crowned denomination divides date, legend in French **Obv. Legend:** BELGIQUE **Rev:** Helmeted mine worker left, miner's lamp at right, large head, tip of neck 1/2 mm from rim **Edge:** Plain **Designer:** Rau **Note:** Medal alignment.

Date	Mintage	F12	VF20	XF40	MS60	MS63
2001	—	PF65 30.00				

KM# 149.1 50 CENTIMES
2.75 g., Bronze, 19 mm. **Ruler:** Baudouin I **Obv:** Crowned denomination divides date, legend in Dutch **Obv. Legend:** BELGIE **Rev:** Helmeted mine worker left, miner's lamp at right, large head **Edge:** Plain **Designer:** Rau

Date	Mintage	F12	VF20	XF40	MS60	MS63
2001 In sets only	60,000	—	—	—	3.00	—
2001	5,000	PF65 25.00				
Note: Medal alignment						
2007 In sets only	60,000	—	—	—	2.00	—

KM# 149.2 50 CENTIMES
2.75 g., Bronze, 19 mm. **Ruler:** Baudouin I **Obv:** Crowned denomination divides date, legend in French **Obv. Legend:** BELGIQUE **Rev:** Helmeted mine worker left, miner's lamp at right, large head, tip of neck 1/2 mm from rim **Edge:** Plain **Designer:** Rau **Note:** Medal alignment.

Date	Mintage	F12	VF20	XF40	MS60	MS63
2001	—	PF65 30.00				

KM# 148.1 50 CENTIMES
2.70 g., Bronze, 19 mm. **Ruler:** Baudouin I **Obv:** Crowned denomination divides date, legend in French **Obv. Legend:** BELGIQUE **Rev:** Helmeted mine worker left, miner's lamp at right, large head, tip of neck 1/2 mm from rim **Edge:** Plain **Designer:** Rau

Date	Mintage	F12	VF20	XF40	MS60	MS63
2001 In sets only	60,000	—	—	—	2.00	—
2001	5,000	PF65 25.00				
Note: Medal alignment						

KM# 187 FRANC
2.75 g., Nickel Plated Iron, 18 mm. **Ruler:** Albert II **Obv:** Head left, outline around back of head **Rev:** Vertical line divides date and large denomination, legend in French **Rev. Legend:** BELGIQUE **Note:** Mint mark: angel head. Unknown mintmaster's privy mark: scales.

Date	Mintage	F12	VF20	XF40	MS60	MS63
2001 In sets only	60,000	—	—	—	3.00	—
2001	5,000	PF65 25.00				
Note: Medal alignment						

KM# 188 FRANC
2.75 g., Nickel Plated Iron, 18 mm. **Ruler:** Albert II **Obv:** Head left, outline around back of head **Rev:** Vertical line divides date and large denomination, legend in Dutch **Rev. Legend:** BELGIE **Edge:** Plain

Date	Mintage	F12	VF20	XF40	MS60	MS63
2001 In sets only	60,000	—	—	—	3.00	—
2001	5,000	PF65 25.00				
Note: Medal alignment						

KM# 189 5 FRANCS (5 Frank)
5.50 g., Aluminum-Bronze, 24 mm. **Ruler:** Albert II **Obv:** Head left, outline around back of head **Rev:** Vertical line divides date and denomination, legend in French **Rev. Legend:** BELGIQUE **Note:** Mint mark: angel head. Mintmaster R. Coenen's privy mark: scale.

Date	Mintage	F12	VF20	XF40	MS60	MS63
2001 In sets only	60,000	—	—	—	4.00	—
2001	5,000	PF65 25.00				
Note: Medal alignment						

KM# 190 5 FRANCS (5 Frank)
5.50 g., Aluminum-Bronze, 24 mm. **Ruler:** Albert II **Obv:** Head left, outline around back of head **Rev:** Vertical line divides date and large denomination, legend in Dutch **Rev. Legend:** BELGIE **Note:** Mint mark: angel head. Mintmaster R. Coenen's privy mark: scale.

Date	Mintage	F12	VF20	XF40	MS60	MS63
2001 In sets only	60,000	—	—	—	4.00	—
2001	5,000	PF65 25.00				
Note: Medal alignment						

KM# 191 20 FRANCS (20 Frank)
8.50 g., Nickel-Bronze, 25.65 mm. **Ruler:** Albert II **Obv:** Head left, outline around back of head **Rev:** Vertical line divides date and large denomination, legend in French **Rev. Legend:** BELGIQUE **Note:** Mint mark: angel head. Mintmaster R. Coenen's privy mark: scale.

Date	Mintage	F12	VF20	XF40	MS60	MS63
2001 In sets only	60,000	—	—	—	4.00	—
2001	5,000	PF65 25.00				
Note: Medal alignment						

KM# 192 20 FRANCS (20 Frank)
8.50 g., Nickel-Bronze, 25.7 mm. **Ruler:** Albert II **Obv:** Head left, outline around back of head **Rev:** Vertical line divides date and large denomination, legend in Dutch **Rev. Legend:** BELGIE **Note:** Mint mark: angel head. Mintmaster R. Coenen's privy mark: scale.

Date	Mintage	F12	VF20	XF40	MS60	MS63
2001 In sets only	60,000	—	—	—	5.00	—
2001	5,000	PF65 25.00				
Note: Medal alignment						

KM# 193 50 FRANCS (50 Frank)
7.00 g., Nickel, 22.7 mm. **Ruler:** Albert II **Obv:** Head left, outline around back of head **Rev:** Vertical line divides large denomination and date, legend in French **Rev. Legend:** BELGIQUE **Note:** Mint mark: angel head. Mintmaster R. Coenen's privy mark: scale.

Date	Mintage	F12	VF20	XF40	MS60	MS63
2001 In sets only	60,000	—	—	—	8.00	—
2001	5,000	PF65 25.00				
Note: Medal alignment						

KM# 194 50 FRANCS (50 Frank)
7.00 g., Nickel, 22.75 mm. **Ruler:** Albert II **Obv:** Head left, outline around back of head **Rev:** Vertical line divides large denomination and date, legend in Dutch **Rev. Legend:** BELGIE **Note:** Mint mark: angel head. Mintmaster R. Coenen's privy mark: scale.

Date	Mintage	F12	VF20	XF40	MS60	MS63
2001 In sets only	60,000	—	—	—	8.00	—
2001	5,000	PF65 25.00				
Note: Medal alignment						

KM# 222 500 FRANCS (500 Frank)
22.85 g., 0.925 Silver 0.6752 oz. ASW, 37 mm. **Ruler:** Albert II **Subject:** Europe: Europa and the Bull **Obv:** Map and denomination **Rev:** Europa sitting on a bull **Edge:** Plain

Date	Mintage	F12	VF20	XF40	MS60	MS63
2001 (qp)	40,000	PF63 45.00	PF65 50.00			

KM# 223 5000 FRANCS
15.55 g., 0.999 Gold 0.4962 oz. AGW, 29 mm. **Ruler:** Albert II **Subject:** Europe: Europa and the Bull **Obv:** Map and denomination **Rev:** Europa sitting on a bull **Edge:** Plain

Date	Mintage	F12	VF20	XF40	MS60	MS63
2001 (qp)	2,000	PF65 875				

EURO COINAGE
European Union Issues

KM# 224 EURO CENT
2.30 g., Copper Plated Steel, 16.25 mm. **Ruler:** Albert II **Obv:** Head left within inner circle, stars 3/4 surround, date below **Obv. Designer:** Jan Alfons Keustermans **Rev:** Denomination and globe **Rev. Designer:** Luc Luycx **Edge:** Plain

Date	Mintage	F12	VF20	XF40	MS60	MS63
2001	99,840,000	—	—	0.30	0.75	1.00
2001	15,000	PF65 12.00				
2002 In sets only	140,000	—	—	—	18.50	25.00
2002	15,000	PF65 15.00				
2003	10,135,000	—	—	0.25	0.60	0.80
2003	15,000	PF65 12.00				
2004	180,000,000	—	—	0.25	0.60	0.80
2004	—	PF65 12.00				
2005 In sets only	—	—	—	—	—	18.50
2005	3,000	PF65 12.00				
2006	15,000,000	—	—	0.25	0.60	0.80
2006	—	PF65 12.00				
2007	60,000,000	—	—	0.25	0.60	0.80
2007	—	PF65 12.00				

KM# 274 EURO CENT
2.30 g., Copper Plated Steel, 16.25 mm. **Ruler:** Albert II **Obv:** Head of Albert II left, crowned monogram at right, date below

Date	Mintage	F12	VF20	XF40	MS60	MS63
2008	50,000,000	—	—	—	0.35	0.75
2008	—	PF65 12.00				
2009	19,950,000	—	—	—	0.35	0.75
2009	1,500	PF65 12.00				
2010	30,000,000	—	—	—	0.35	0.75
2010	1,850	PF65 12.00				
2011	9,975,000	—	—	—	—	0.75
2011	1,850	PF65 12.00				
2012	19,950,000	—	—	—	—	0.75
2012	1,850	PF65 12.00				

Date	Mintage	F12	VF20	XF40	MS60	MS63
2013	1,850	PF65 12.00				
2013	—	—	—	—	—	0.75

KM# 225 2 EURO CENT
3.06 g., Copper Plated Steel, 18.75 mm. **Ruler:** Albert II **Obv:** Head left within circle, stars 3/4 surround, date below **Obv. Designer:** Jan Alfons Keustermans **Rev:** Denomination and globe **Rev. Designer:** Luc Luycx **Edge:** Grooved

Date	Mintage	F12	VF20	XF40	MS60	MS63
2001 In sets only	40,000	—	—	—	—	9.00

Note: Only available in sets at present, circulation strikes not yet released

Date	Mintage	F12	VF20	XF40	MS60	MS63
2001	15,000	PF65 15.00				
2002 In sets only	140,000	—	—	—	—	6.50
2002	15,000	PF65 12.00				
2003	40,135,000	—	—	0.30	0.75	1.00
2003	15,000	PF65 12.00				
2004	140,000,000	—	—	0.30	0.75	1.00
2004	15,000	PF65 12.00				
2005 In sets only	—	—	—	—	—	1.00
2005	—	PF65 12.00				
2006	30,000,000	—	—	0.30	0.75	1.00
2006	—	PF65 12.00				
2007	70,000,000	—	—	0.30	0.75	1.00
2007	—	PF65 12.00				

KM# 275 2 EURO CENT
3.06 g., Copper Plated Steel, 18.75 mm. **Ruler:** Albert II **Obv:** Head of Albert II left, crowned monogram at right, date below **Edge:** Grooved

Date	Mintage	F12	VF20	XF40	MS60	MS63
2008	40,000,000	—	—	—	0.75	1.00
2008	—	PF65 12.00				
2009	10,000,000	—	—	—	0.75	1.00
2009	1,500	PF65 12.00				
2010	20,000,000	—	—	—	0.75	1.00
2010	1,850	PF65 12.00				
2011	—	—	—	—	—	1.00
2011	1,850	PF65 12.00				
2012	15,000,000	—	—	—	—	1.00
2012	1,850	PF65 12.00				
2013	—	—	—	—	—	1.00
2013	1,850	PF65 12.00				

KM# 226 5 EURO CENT
3.92 g., Copper Plated Steel, 21.25 mm. **Ruler:** Albert II **Obv:** Head left within circle, stars 3/4 surround, date below **Obv. Designer:** Jan Alfons Keustermans **Rev:** Denomination and globe **Rev. Designer:** Luc Luycx **Edge:** Plain

Date	Mintage	F12	VF20	XF40	MS60	MS63
2001 In sets only	40,000	—	—	—	—	12.50
2001	15,000	PF65 15.00				
2002 In sets only	140,000	—	—	—	—	8.00
2002	15,000	PF65 15.00				
2003	30,135,000	—	—	0.30	0.80	1.20
2003	15,000	PF65 12.00				
2004	75,000,000	—	—	0.30	0.80	1.20
2004	—	PF65 12.00				
2005	110,000,000	—	—	0.30	0.80	1.20
2005	—	PF65 12.00				
2006	35,000,000	—	—	0.30	0.80	1.20
2006	—	PF65 12.00				
2007 In sets only	—	—	—	—	—	8.00
2007	—	PF65 12.00				

KM# 276 5 EURO CENT
3.92 g., Copper Plated Steel, 21.25 mm. **Ruler:** Albert II **Obv:** Redesigned head of Albert II left

Date	Mintage	F12	VF20	XF40	MS60	MS63
2008	—	—	—	—	—	2.00
2008	—	PF65 12.00				
2009	—	—	—	—	—	1.20
2009	1,500	PF65 12.00				
2010	25,000,000	—	—	—	0.75	1.20
2010	1,850	PF65 12.00				
2011	25,000,000	—	—	—	—	1.20
2011	1,850	PF65 12.00				

Date	Mintage	F12	VF20	XF40	MS60	MS63
2012	22,500,000	—	—	—	—	1.20
2012	1,850	PF65 12.00				
2013	—	—	—	—	—	1.20
2013	1,850	PF65 12.00				

KM# 227 10 EURO CENT
4.10 g., Brass, 19.75 mm. **Ruler:** Albert II **Obv:** Head left within inner circle, stars 3/4 surround, date below **Obv. Designer:** Jan Alfons Keustermans **Rev:** Denomination and map **Rev. Designer:** Luc Luycx **Edge:** Reeded

Date	Mintage	F12	VF20	XF40	MS60	MS63
2001	145,790,000	—	—	—	0.75	1.25
2001	15,000	PF65 12.00				
2002 In sets only	140,000	—	—	—	6.00	8.00
2002	15,000	PF65 15.00				
2003 In sets only	135,000	—	—	—	6.00	8.00
2003	15,000	PF65 15.00				
2004	20,000,000	—	—	—	1.00	1.50
2004	—	PF65 12.00				
2005	10,000,000	—	—	—	1.00	1.50
2005	—	PF65 12.00				
2006 In sets only	—	—	—	—	1.00	1.50
2006	—	PF65 12.00				

KM# 242 10 EURO CENT
4.10 g., Brass, 19.75 mm. **Ruler:** Albert II **Obv:** King's portrait **Obv. Designer:** Jan Alfons Keustermans **Rev:** Relief map of Western Europe, stars, lines and value **Rev. Designer:** Luc Luycx **Edge:** Reeded

Date	Mintage	F12	VF20	XF40	MS60	MS63
2007	—	—	—	—	1.00	1.50
2007	—	PF65 12.00				

KM# 277 10 EURO CENT
4.10 g., Brass, 19.75 mm. **Ruler:** Albert II **Obv:** Head of Albert II left, crowned monogram right, date below **Edge:** Reeded

Date	Mintage	F12	VF20	XF40	MS60	MS63
2008	—	—	—	—	—	6.00
2008	—	PF65 12.00				
2009	—	—	—	—	—	1.50
2009	1,500	PF65 12.00				
2010	20,000,000	—	—	—	1.00	1.50
2010	1,850	PF65 12.00				
2011	25,000,000	—	—	—	1.00	1.50
2011	1,850	PF65 12.00				
2012	25,000,000	—	—	—	—	1.50
2012	1,850	PF65 12.00				
2013	—	—	—	—	—	1.50
2013	1,850	PF65 12.00				

KM# 228 20 EURO CENT
5.74 g., Brass, 22.25 mm. **Ruler:** Albert II **Obv:** Head left within circle, stars 3/4 surround, date below **Obv. Designer:** Jan Alfons Keustermans **Rev:** Denomination and map **Rev. Designer:** Luc Luycx **Edge:** Notched

Date	Mintage	F12	VF20	XF40	MS60	MS63
2001 In sets only	40,000	—	—	—	10.00	12.50

Note: Only available in sets at present, circulation strikes not yet released

Date	Mintage	F12	VF20	XF40	MS60	MS63
2001	15,000	PF65 15.00				
2002	104,140,000	—	—	—	1.00	1.50
2002	15,000	PF65 12.00				
2003	30,135,000	—	—	—	1.25	1.75
2003	15,000	PF65 12.00				
2004	109,550,000	—	—	—	1.25	1.75
2004	—	PF65 12.00				
2005	10,000,000	—	—	—	1.25	1.75
2005	—	PF65 12.00				
2006	40,000,000	—	—	—	1.25	1.75
2006	—	PF65 12.00				

KM# 243 20 EURO CENT
5.74 g., Brass, 22.25 mm. **Ruler:** Albert II **Obv:** King's portrait **Obv. Designer:** Jan Alfons Keustermans **Rev:** Relief map of Western Europe, stars, lines and value **Rev. Designer:** Luc Luycx **Edge:** Notched

Date	Mintage	F12	VF20	XF40	MS60	MS63
2007	—	—	—	—	1.25	1.75
2007	—	PF65 12.00				

KM# 278 20 EURO CENT
5.74 g., Brass, 22.25 mm. **Ruler:** Albert II **Obv:** Redesigned head of Albert II left **Edge:** Notched

Date	Mintage	F12	VF20	XF40	MS60	MS63
2008	20,000,000	—	—	—	—	2.00
2008	—	PF65 12.00				
2009	30,100,000	—	—	—	1.25	1.75
2009	1,500	PF65 12.00				
2010	15,000,000	—	—	—	1.25	1.75
2010	1,850	PF65 12.00				
2011	—	—	—	—	1.25	1.75
2011	1,850	PF65 12.00				
2012	42,350,000	—	—	—	—	1.75
2012	1,850	PF65 12.00				
2013	—	—	—	—	—	1.75
2013	1,850	PF65 12.00				

KM# 229 50 EURO CENT
7.80 g., Brass, 24.25 mm. **Ruler:** Albert II **Obv:** Head left within circle, stars 3/4 surround, date below **Obv. Designer:** Jan Alfons Keustermans **Rev:** Denomination and map **Rev. Designer:** Luc Luycx **Edge:** Reeded

Date	Mintage	F12	VF20	XF40	MS60	MS63
2001 In sets only	40,000	—	—	—	10.00	12.50
2001	15,000	PF65 15.00				
2002	50,040,000	—	—	—	1.00	1.50
2002	15,000	PF65 12.00				
2003 In sets only	135,000	—	—	—	—	12.50
2003	15,000	PF65 12.00				
2004	8,000,000	—	—	—	1.25	1.75
2004	—	PF65 12.00				
2005 In sets only	—	—	—	—	—	12.50
2005	—	PF65 12.00				
2006 In sets only	—	—	—	—	—	12.50
2006	—	PF65 12.00				

KM# 244 50 EURO CENT
7.80 g., Brass, 24.25 mm. **Ruler:** Albert II **Obv:** King's portrait **Obv. Designer:** Jan Alfons Keustermans **Rev:** Relief map of Western Europe, stars, lines and value **Rev. Designer:** Luc Luycx **Edge:** Reeded

Date	Mintage	F12	VF20	XF40	MS60	MS63
2007	—	—	—	—	1.25	1.75
2007	—	PF65 12.00				

KM# 279 50 EURO CENT
7.80 g., Brass, 24.25 mm. **Ruler:** Albert II **Obv:** Redesigned head of Albert II left **Edge:** Reeded

Date	Mintage	F12	VF20	XF40	MS60	MS63
2008	25,000,000	—	—	—	—	4.00
2008	—	PF65 12.00				
2009	30,000,000	—	—	—	2.00	3.00
2009	1,500	PF65 12.00				
2010	—	—	—	—	—	3.00
2010	1,850	PF65 12.00				
2011	15,000,000	—	—	—	—	3.00
2011	1,850	PF65 12.00				
2012	30,000,000	—	—	—	—	3.00
2012	1,850	PF65 12.00				
2013	1,850	PF65 12.00				
2013	—	—	—	—	—	3.00

KM# 230 EURO

7.50 g., Bi-Metallic, 23.25 mm. **Ruler:** Albert II **Obv:** Head left within circle, stars 3/4 surround, date below **Obv. Designer:** Jan Alfons Keustermans **Rev:** Denomination and map **Rev. Designer:** Luc Luycx **Edge:** Segmented reeding

Date	Mintage	F12	VF20	XF40	MS60	MS63
2001 In sets only	40,000	—	—	—	—	15.00

Note: Only available in sets at present, circulation strikes not yet released

Date	Mintage	F12	VF20	XF40	MS60	MS63
2001	15,000	PF65 18.00				
2002	90,640,000	—	—	—	3.00	5.00

Note: Only a fraction of the mintage released at present

Date	Mintage	F12	VF20	XF40	MS60	MS63
2002	15,000	PF65 15.00				
2003	6,000,000	—	—	—	3.00	5.00
2003	15,000	PF65 15.00				
2004	15,000,000	—	—	—	3.00	5.00
2004	—	PF65 15.00				
2005 In sets only	—	—	—	—	—	15.00
2005	—	PF65 15.00				
2006 In sets only	—	—	—	—	—	15.00
2006	—	PF65 15.00				

KM# 245 EURO

7.50 g., Bi-Metallic, 23.25 mm. **Ruler:** Albert II **Obv:** King's portrait **Obv. Designer:** Jan Alfons Keustermans **Rev:** Relief map of Western Europe, stars, lines and value **Rev. Designer:** Luc Luycx **Edge:** Segmented reeding

Date	Mintage	F12	VF20	XF40	MS60	MS63
2007	—	—	—	—	3.00	5.00
2007	—	PF65 15.00				

KM# 280 EURO

7.50 g., Bi-Metallic, 23.25 mm. **Ruler:** Albert II **Obv:** Redesigned head of Albert II left **Edge:** Segmented reeding

Date	Mintage	F12	VF20	XF40	MS60	MS63
2008	5,000,000	—	—	—	—	6.00
2008	—	PF65 15.00				
2009	10,000,000	—	—	—	3.00	5.00
2009	1,500	PF65 15.00				
2010	—	—	—	—	—	5.00
2010	1,850	PF65 15.00				
2011	15,000,000	—	—	—	—	5.00
2011	1,850	PF65 15.00				
2012	10,000,000	—	—	—	—	5.00
2012	1,850	PF65 15.00				
2013	—	—	—	—	—	5.00
2013	1,850	PF65 15.00				

KM# 231 2 EURO

8.50 g., Bi-Metallic, 25.75 mm. **Ruler:** Albert II **Obv:** Head left within circle, stars 3/4 surround, date below **Obv. Designer:** Jan Alfons Keustermans **Rev:** Denomination and map **Rev. Designer:** Luc Luycx **Edge:** Reeded with 2's and stars

Date	Mintage	F12	VF20	XF40	MS60	MS63
2001 In sets only	40,000	—	—	—	12.50	15.00

Note: Only available in sets at present, circulation strikes not yet released

Date	Mintage	F12	VF20	XF40	MS60	MS63
2001	15,000	PF65 20.00				
2002	50,140,000	—	—	—	3.75	6.00
2002	15,000	PF65 18.00				
2003	30,135,000	—	—	—	3.75	6.00
2003	15,000	PF65 18.00				
2004	65,500,000	—	—	—	3.75	6.00
2004	—	PF65 18.00				
2005	10,500,000	—	—	—	3.75	6.00
2005	—	PF65 18.00				
2006	20,000,000	—	—	—	3.75	6.00
2006	—	PF65 18.00				

KM# 240 2 EURO

8.50 g., Bi-Metallic, 25.75 mm. **Ruler:** Albert II **Subject:** Schengen Agreement **Obv:** Albert II of Belgium and Henri of Luxembourg **Rev:** Value and map **Edge:** Reeded with 2's and stars

Date	Mintage	F12	VF20	XF40	MS60	MS63
2005	5,977,000	—	—	—	5.00	7.50
2005 Prooflike	20,000	—	—	—	—	20.00
2005	—	PF65 25.00				

KM# 241 2 EURO

8.50 g., Bi-Metallic, 25.75 mm. **Ruler:** Albert II **Obv:** Atomic model **Rev:** Value and map **Edge:** Reeded with 2's and stars

Date	Mintage	F12	VF20	XF40	MS60	MS63
2006	4,977,000	—	—	—	4.00	6.00
2006 Prooflike	20,000	—	—	—	—	25.00
2006	3,000	PF63 80.00	PF65 100			

KM# 246 2 EURO

8.50 g., Bi-Metallic, 25.75 mm. **Ruler:** Albert II **Obv:** King's portrait **Obv. Designer:** Jan Alfons Keustermans **Rev:** Relief map of Western Europe, stars, lines and value **Rev. Designer:** Luc Luycx **Edge:** Reeded with 2's and stars

Date	Mintage	F12	VF20	XF40	MS60	MS63
2007	—	—	—	—	3.75	6.00
2007	—	PF65 25.00				

KM# 247 2 EURO

8.50 g., Bi-Metallic, 25.75 mm. **Ruler:** Albert II **Subject:** 50th Anniversary Treaty of Rome **Obv:** Open treaty book **Rev:** Large value at left, modified outline of Europe at right **Edge:** Reeded with stars and 2's

Date	Mintage	F12	VF20	XF40	MS60	MS63
2007	4,960,000	—	—	—	2.00	9.00
2007 Prooflike	35,000	—	—	—	—	25.00
2007	10,000	PF63 65.00	PF65 75.00			

KM# 248 2 EURO

8.50 g., Bi-Metallic, 25.75 mm. **Ruler:** Albert II **Subject:** Universal Declaration of Human Rights **Obv:** Book in bow **Rev:** Large value "2" at left, modified map of Europe at right **Edge:** Reeded with 2's and stars

Date	Mintage	F12	VF20	XF40	MS60	MS63
2008	—	—	—	—	2.00	6.00

KM# 281 2 EURO

8.50 g., Bi-Metallic, 25.75 mm. **Ruler:** Albert II **Obv:** Head of Albert II left, crowned monogram right, date below **Edge:** Reeded with 2's and stars

Date	Mintage	F12	VF20	XF40	MS60	MS63
2008	25,000,000	—	—	—	—	7.50
2008	—	PF65 18.00				
2009	5,000,000	—	—	—	4.00	6.00
2009	—	PF65 18.00				
2010	15,000,000	—	—	—	4.00	6.00
2010	—	PF65 18.00				
2011	32,000,000	—	—	—	4.00	6.00
2011	—	PF65 18.00				
2012	—	—	—	—	4.00	6.00
2013	—	PF65 18.00				
2013	—	—	—	—	4.00	6.00

KM# 282 2 EURO

8.50 g., Bi-Metallic, 25.75 mm. **Ruler:** Albert II **Subject:** 10th Anniversary of EMU **Obv:** Stick figure and E symbol **Edge:** Reeded with 2's and stars

Date	Mintage	F12	VF20	XF40	MS60	MS63
2009	5,000,000	—	—	—	15.00	—
2009 Prooflike	—	—	—	—	—	20.00
2009	—	PF63 60.00	PF65 70.00			

KM# 288 2 EURO

8.50 g., Bi-Metallic, 25.75 mm. **Ruler:** Albert II **Subject:** Louis Braille, 200th Anniversary of Birth **Obv:** Bust right with braile text **Edge:** Reeded with 2's and stars

Date	Mintage	F12	VF20	XF40	MS60	MS63
2009	5,000,000	—	—	—	2.00	5.00

KM# 289 2 EURO

8.50 g., Bi-Metallic, 25.75 mm. **Ruler:** Albert II **Subject:** EU Council Presidency **Rev:** eu in script **Edge:** Reeded with 2's and stars

Date	Mintage	F12	VF20	XF40	MS60	MS63
2010	—	—	—	—	3.00	7.50

KM# 308 2 EURO

8.50 g., Bi-Metallic, 25.75 mm. **Ruler:** Albert II **Subject:** International Women's Day, 100th Anniversary **Obv:** Portraits of I. van Diest and M. Popelin

Date	Mintage	F12	VF20	XF40	MS60	MS63
2011	5,000,000	—	—	—	9.00	12.50
2011 Special Unc.	6,000	—	—	—	—	15.00
2011	7,500	PF65 25.00				

KM# 315 2 EURO
8.50 g., Bi-Metallic, 25.75 mm. **Ruler:** Albert II **Subject:** Euro coinage, 10th Anniversary **Obv:** Euro symbol on globe, child-like rendering around

Date	Mintage	F12	VF20	XF40	MS60	MS63
2012	6,000,000	—	—	—	6.00	8.00
2012 Special Unc.	—	—	—	—	—	15.00
2012	—	PF63 22.00	PF65 25.00			

KM# 317 2 EURO
8.50 g., Bi-Metallic, 25.75 mm. **Ruler:** Albert II **Subject:** Queen Elizabeth Competition **Obv:** Profile of Elizabeth left, crowned monogram at center

Date	Mintage	F12	VF20	XF40	MS60	MS63
2012	5,000,000	—	—	—	—	5.00
2012	—	PF63 25.00	PF65 28.00			

KM# 323 2 EURO
8.50 g., Bi-Metallic, 25.75 mm. **Ruler:** Albert II **Subject:** Meteorological Institute, 100th Anniversary

Date	Mintage	F12	VF20	XF40	MS60	MS63
2013	—	—	—	—	—	5.00
2013	—	PF63 25.00	PF65 28.00			

KM# 270 5 EURO
14.60 g., 0.925 Silver 0.4314 oz. ASW, 30 mm. **Ruler:** Albert II **Subject:** Smurfs - 50th Anniversary **Obv:** Map of Western Europe **Rev:** Smurf

Date	Mintage	F12	VF20	XF40	MS60	MS63
2008	25,000	PF63 45.00	PF65 50.00			

KM# 270a 5 EURO
14.60 g., 0.925 Silver 0.4314 oz. ASW, 30 mm. **Ruler:** Albert II **Subject:** Smurf - 50th Anniversary **Obv:** Map of Western Europe **Rev:** Multicolor 50 and Smurf

Date	Mintage	F12	VF20	XF40	MS60	MS63
2008		PF65 75.00				

KM# 303 5 EURO
14.60 g., 0.925 Silver 0.4314 oz. ASW, 30 mm. **Ruler:** Albert II **Subject:** Belgian Railways, 175th Anniversary

Date	Mintage	F12	VF20	XF40	MS60	MS63
2010		PF63 45.00	PF65 50.00			

KM# 313 5 EURO
14.60 g., 0.925 Silver 0.4314 oz. ASW, 30 mm. **Ruler:** Albert II **Subject:** Helene Dutrieu, Belgium's first female aviator **Obv:** Euro zone map **Rev:** Female portrait at left, biplane at right

Date	Mintage	F12	VF20	XF40	MS60	MS63
2011		PF63 45.00	PF65 50.00			

KM# 327 5 EURO
14.60 g., 0.925 Silver 0.4314 oz. ASW, 30 mm. **Ruler:** Albert II **Subject:** Robert Velter's Spirou, 75th Anniversary **Rev:** Bellboy Spirou from the movies

Date	Mintage	F12	VF20	XF40	MS60	MS63
2013	—	PF63 55.00	PF65 60.00			

KM# 233 10 EURO
18.93 g., 0.925 Silver 0.5593 oz. ASW, 32.9 mm. **Ruler:** Albert II **Subject:** Belgian Railway System **Obv:** Value, head at right transposed on map **Rev:** Train exiting tunnel **Edge:** Reeded

Date	Mintage	F12	VF20	XF40	MS60	MS63
ND (2002)	50,000	PF63 45.00	PF65 50.00			

KM# 235 10 EURO
18.93 g., 0.925 Silver 0.5593 oz. ASW, 32.9 mm. **Ruler:** Albert II **Subject:** Simenon **Edge:** Reeded

Date	Mintage	F12	VF20	XF40	MS60	MS63
2003	50,000	PF63 35.00	PF65 40.00			

KM# 234 10 EURO
18.75 g., 0.925 Silver 0.554 oz. ASW, 33 mm. **Ruler:** Albert II **Obv:** Value **Rev:** Western Europe map and Goddess Europa riding a bull **Edge:** Reeded

Date	Mintage	F12	VF20	XF40	MS60	MS63
2004	50,000	PF63 35.00	PF65 40.00			

KM# 236 10 EURO
18.93 g., 0.925 Silver 0.5593 oz. ASW, 32.9 mm. **Ruler:** Albert II **Subject:** Tintin **Edge:** Reeded

Date	Mintage	F12	VF20	XF40	MS60	MS63
2004	50,000	PF63 75.00	PF65 85.00			

KM# 252 10 EURO
18.75 g., 0.925 Silver 0.554 oz. ASW, 33 mm. **Ruler:** Albert II **Subject:** 60th Anniversary of Liberation **Obv:** Map of Western Europe and stars **Rev:** Phoenix

Date	Mintage	F12	VF20	XF40	MS60	MS63
2005	50,000	PF63 45.00	PF65 50.00			

KM# 251 10 EURO
18.75 g., 0.925 Silver 0.554 oz. ASW, 33 mm. **Ruler:** Albert II **Subject:** Netherland-Belgium Soccer, 75th Anniversary **Obv:** Map of Western Europe and stars **Rev:** Soccer Player

Date	Mintage	F12	VF20	XF40	MS60	MS63
2005	50,000	PF63 40.00	PF65 45.00			

KM# 255 10 EURO
18.75 g., 0.925 Silver 0.554 oz. ASW, 33 mm. **Ruler:** Albert II **Subject:** Justus Lipsius, 400th Anniversary of Death **Obv:** Map of Western Europe and stars **Rev:** Half-length figure of Justus Lipsius

Date	Mintage	F12	VF20	XF40	MS60	MS63
2006	50,000	PF63 40.00	PF65 45.00			

KM# 257 10 EURO
18.75 g., 0.925 Silver 0.554 oz. ASW, 33 mm. **Ruler:** Albert II **Subject:** 50th Anniversary - Mine Accident in Marcinelle **Obv:** Map of Western Europe and stars **Rev:** Male head and industrial mine scene

Date	Mintage	F12	VF20	XF40	MS60	MS63
2006	50,000	PF63 40.00	PF65 45.00			

KM# 257a 10 EURO
18.75 g., 0.925 Silver 0.554 oz. ASW, 33 mm. **Ruler:** Albert II **Subject:** 50th Anniversary, Mine Accident in Marcinelle **Obv:** Map of Western Europe and stars **Rev:** Multicolor male head and industrial mine scene

Date	Mintage	F12	VF20	XF40	MS60	MS63
2006	2,000	PF65 75.00				

KM# 260 10 EURO
18.75 g., 0.925 Silver 0.554 oz. ASW, 33 mm. **Ruler:** Albert II **Subject:** Treaty of Rome, 50th Anniversary **Obv:** Map of Western Europe **Rev:** Document and feather pen

Date	Mintage	F12	VF20	XF40	MS60	MS63
2007	40,000	PF63 40.00	PF65 45.00			

KM# 263 10 EURO
18.75 g., 0.925 Silver 0.554 oz. ASW, 33 mm. **Ruler:** Albert II **Subject:** International Polar Year **Obv:** Map of Western Europe **Rev:** Wind farm and polar station

Date	Mintage	F12	VF20	XF40	MS60	MS63
2007	40,000	PF63 45.00	PF65 50.00			

KM# 266 10 EURO
18.75 g., 0.925 Silver 0.554 oz. ASW, 33 mm. **Ruler:** Albert II **Subject:** 100th Anniversary Maurice Maeterlinck **Obv:** Map of Western Europe **Rev:** Gateway and dome in blue

Date	Mintage	F12	VF20	XF40	MS60	MS63
2008	20,000	PF63 65.00	PF65 75.00			

KM# 268 10 EURO
18.75 g., 0.925 Silver 0.554 oz. ASW, 33 mm. **Ruler:** Albert II **Subject:** Beijing Olympics **Obv:** Map of Western Europe **Rev:** Sport events, logo and torch

Date	Mintage	F12	VF20	XF40	MS60	MS63
2008	20,000	PF63 45.00	PF65 50.00			

KM# 284 10 EURO
18.75 g., 0.925 Silver 0.554 oz. ASW, 33 mm. **Ruler:** Albert II **Subject:** 75th Birthday of the King **Obv:** Head at left, laurel sprigs

Date	Mintage	F12	VF20	XF40	MS60	MS63
2009	—	PF63 45.00	PF65 50.00			

KM# 285 10 EURO
18.75 g., 0.925 Silver 0.554 oz. ASW **Ruler:** Albert II **Subject:** Erasmus

Date	Mintage	F12	VF20	XF40	MS60	MS63
2009	—	—	—	—	—	50.00

KM# 290 10 EURO
18.75 g., 0.925 Silver 0.554 oz. ASW, 33 mm. **Ruler:** Albert II **Subject:** Royal Museum for Central Asia 100th Anniversary

Date	Mintage	F12	VF20	XF40	MS60	MS63
2010	—	—	—	—	—	45.00

KM# 291 10 EURO
18.75 g., 0.925 Silver 0.554 oz. ASW, 33 mm. **Ruler:** Albert II **Subject:** Jean Django' Reinhart Birth Centennial

Date	Mintage	F12	VF20	XF40	MS60	MS63
2010	—	PF63 40.00	PF65 45.00			

KM# 304 10 EURO
18.75 g., 0.925 Silver 0.554 oz. ASW, 33 mm. **Ruler:** Albert II **Subject:** Jean "Django" Reinhardt, 100th Anniversary of Birth

Date	Mintage	F12	VF20	XF40	MS60	MS63
2010	—	PF63 45.00	PF65 50.00			

KM# 309 10 EURO
18.75 g., 0.925 Silver 0.554 oz. ASW, 33 mm. **Ruler:** Albert II **Subject:** Discovery of the South Pole **Obv:** Euro zone map **Rev:** Map, dog sled, Roald Amundsen

Date	Mintage	F12	VF20	XF40	MS60	MS63
2011	—	PF63 45.00	PF65 50.00			

KM# 311 10 EURO
18.75 g., 0.925 Silver 0.554 oz. ASW, 33 mm. **Ruler:** Albert II **Obv:** Euro zone map, partially gilt **Rev:** Belgian deep sea exploration

Date	Mintage	F12	VF20	XF40	MS60	MS63
2011	—	PF63 45.00	PF65 50.00			

KM# 318 10 EURO
18.75 g., 0.925 Silver 0.554 oz. ASW, 33 mm. **Ruler:** Albert II **Subject:** Paul Delvaux, Museum at St. Idesbald, 30th Anniversary **Obv:** Value and map of Euro countries **Rev:** Bust at left, classical scene at right

Date	Mintage	F12	VF20	XF40	MS60	MS63
2012	Est. 15000	PF63 60.00		PF65 70.00		

KM# 319 10 EURO
6.22 g., 0.999 Gold 0.1985 oz. AGW, 22 mm. **Ruler:** Albert II **Subject:** Paul Delvaux, Museum at St. Idesbald, 30th Anniversary **Obv:** Value and map of Euro countries **Rev:** Bust at left, classical scene at right

Date	Mintage	F12	VF20	XF40	MS60	MS63
2012	Est. 1500	PF65 495				

KM# 320 10 EURO
18.75 g., 0.999 Silver 0.5983 oz. ASW, 33 mm. **Ruler:** Albert II **Subject:** 2012 Summer Olympics, London **Obv:** Value and map of Euro countries **Rev:** Half-length figure of Coubertin at right, torch at left

Date	Mintage	F12	VF20	XF40	MS60	MS63
2012	Est. 10000	PF63 60.00		PF65 70.00		

KM# 324 10 EURO
18.75 g., 0.925 Silver 0.554 oz. ASW, 33 mm. **Ruler:** Albert II **Subject:** Hugo Claus **Obv:** Value and map of Euro countries **Rev:** Profile right

Date	Mintage	F12	VF20	XF40	MS60	MS63
2013	Est. 10000	PF63 60.00		PF65 70.00		

KM# 326 10 EURO
18.75 g., 0.925 Silver 0.554 oz. ASW, 33 mm. **Ruler:** Albert II **Subject:** Flanders tour, 100th Anniversary

Date	Mintage	F12	VF20	XF40	MS60	MS63
2013	Est. 10000	PF63 60.00		PF65 70.00		

KM# 259 12 1/2 EURO
1.25 g., 0.999 Gold 0.0399 oz. AGW, 13.92 mm. **Ruler:** Albert II **Subject:** Saxe-Coburg-Gotha, 175th Anniversary **Obv:** Lion and tablet with constitution **Rev:** Head of Leopold I left

Date	Mintage	F12	VF20	XF40	MS60	MS63
2006	15,000	PF63 70.00		PF65 80.00		

KM# 265 12 1/2 EURO
1.25 g., 0.999 Gold 0.0399 oz. AGW, 13.92 mm. **Subject:** 175th Anniversary Saxe-Coburg-Gotha **Obv:** Lion and tablet **Rev:** Leopold II head left

Date	Mintage	F12	VF20	XF40	MS60	MS63
2007	15,000	PF63 70.00		PF65 80.00		

KM# 271 12 1/2 EURO
1.25 g., 0.999 Gold 0.0399 oz. AGW, 13.92 mm. **Ruler:** Albert II **Subject:** 175th Anniversary - Saxe-Coburg-Gotha **Obv:** Lion and tablet **Rev:** Albert I bust right

Date	Mintage	F12	VF20	XF40	MS60	MS63
2008	15,000	PF63 75.00		PF65 85.00		

KM# 292 12 1/2 EURO
1.24 g., 0.999 Gold 0.0397 oz. AGW, 14 mm. **Ruler:** Albert II **Subject:** Leopold III

Date	Mintage	F12	VF20	XF40	MS60	MS63
2009	—	PF63 80.00		PF65 90.00		

KM# 293 12 1/2 EURO
1.24 g., 0.999 Gold 0.0397 oz. AGW, 14 mm. **Ruler:** Albert II

Date	Mintage	F12	VF20	XF40	MS60	MS63
2010	—	PF63 75.00		PF65 85.00		

KM# 316 12 1/2 EURO
1.25 g., 0.999 Gold 0.0399 oz. AGW, 13.92 mm. **Ruler:** Albert II **Obv:** Lion with inscribed tablet **Rev:** Crown and Albert II profile

Date	Mintage	F12	VF20	XF40	MS60	MS63
2011	Est. 6000	PF65 125				

KM# 321 12 1/2 EURO
1.25 g., 0.999 Gold 0.0399 oz. AGW, 13.92 mm. **Ruler:** Albert II **Subject:** Paola Ruffo di Calabria, Queen **Obv:** Lion with inscribed tablet **Rev:** Crown and profile left

Date	Mintage	F12	VF20	XF40	MS60	MS63
2012	Est. 6000	PF65 125				

KM# 328 12 1/2 EURO
1.25 g., 0.999 Gold 0.0399 oz. AGW, 13.92 mm. **Ruler:** Albert II **Subject:** Fabiola de Mora y Aragon

Date	Mintage	F12	VF20	XF40	MS60	MS63
2013	Est. 6000	PF65 225				

KM# 254 20 EURO
22.85 g., 0.999 Silver 0.7292 oz. ASW, 37 mm. **Ruler:** Albert II **Subject:** FIFA World Cup in Germany **Obv:** Albert II head left **Rev:** Soccer player with ball

Date	Mintage	F12	VF20	XF40	MS60	MS63
2005	25,000	PF63 60.00		PF65 65.00		

KM# 262 20 EURO
22.85 g., 0.925 Silver 0.6752 oz. ASW, 37 mm. **Ruler:** Albert II **Subject:** Georges Remi, 100th Anniversary of Birth **Obv:** Map of Western Europe and stars **Rev:** Profile of Georges Renir and his character Tin Tin right

Date	Mintage	F12	VF20	XF40	MS60	MS63
2007	50,000	PF63 65.00		PF65 75.00		

KM# 287 20 EURO
22.85 g., 0.925 Silver 0.6752 oz. ASW, 37 mm. **Ruler:** Albert II **Obv:** Value and map of euro countries **Rev:** Fr. Damien and churches in Tremblo and Molokai, date of canionization below

Date	Mintage	F12	VF20	XF40	MS60	MS63
2009	15,000	PF63 65.00		PF65 75.00		

KM# 305 20 EURO
22.85 g., 0.925 Silver 0.6752 oz. ASW, 37 mm. **Ruler:** Albert II **Subject:** A Dog of Flanders

Date	Mintage	F12	VF20	XF40	MS60	MS63
2010	—	PF63 65.00		PF65 75.00		

KM# 269 25 EURO
3.11 g., 0.999 Gold 0.0992 oz. AGW, 18 mm. **Ruler:** Albert II **Subject:** Beijing Olympics **Obv:** Map of Western Europe **Rev:** Sport events, logo, torch

Date	Mintage	F12	VF20	XF40	MS60	MS63
2008	5,000	PF65 225				

KM# 294 25 EURO
3.11 g., 0.999 Gold 0.0992 oz. AGW, 18 mm. **Ruler:** Albert II **Subject:** Beijing Olympics

Date	Mintage	F12	VF20	XF40	MS60	MS63
2008	4,050	PF65 250				

KM# 250 50 EURO
6.22 g., 0.999 Gold 0.1985 oz. AGW, 21 mm. **Ruler:** Albert II **Subject:** Albert II, 70th Birthday **Obv:** Map of Western Europe and stars **Rev:** Portrait of Albert II

Date	Mintage	F12	VF20	XF40	MS60	MS63
2004	10,000	PF65 350				

KM# 256 50 EURO
6.22 g., 0.999 Gold 0.1985 oz. AGW, 21 mm. **Ruler:** Albert II **Subject:** Justus Lipsius, 400th Anniversary of Death **Obv:** Map of Western Europe and stars **Rev:** Half-length figure of Justus Lipsius right

Date	Mintage	F12	VF20	XF40	MS60	MS63
2006	2,500	PF65 365				

KM# 261 50 EURO
6.22 g., 0.999 Gold 0.1985 oz. AGW, 21 mm. **Ruler:** Albert II **Subject:** Treaty of Rome, 50th Anniversary **Obv:** Map of Western Europe **Rev:** Document and feather pen

Date	Mintage	F12	VF20	XF40	MS60	MS63
2007	2,500	PF65 365				

KM# 267 50 EURO
6.22 g., 0.999 Gold 0.1985 oz. AGW, 21 mm. **Ruler:** Albert II **Subject:** 100th Anniversary Maurice Maeterlinck **Obv:** Map of Western Europe **Rev:** Gate and dove

Date	Mintage	F12	VF20	XF40	MS60	MS63
2008	2,500	PF65 400				

KM# 286 50 EURO
8.45 g., 0.999 Gold 0.2697 oz. AGW **Ruler:** Albert II **Subject:** Erasmus

Date	Mintage	F12	VF20	XF40	MS60	MS63
2009	—	—	—	—	—	475

KM# 306 50 EURO
6.22 g., 0.999 Gold 0.1985 oz. AGW, 22 mm. **Ruler:** Albert II **Subject:** Royal Museum for Central Africa

Date	Mintage	F12	VF20	XF40	MS60	MS63
2010		PF65 400				

KM# 310 50 EURO
8.45 g., 0.999 Gold 0.2697 oz. AGW, 22 mm. **Ruler:** Albert II **Obv:** Euro zone map **Rev:** Four men standing around flag, Roald Amundsen profile at right

Date	Mintage	F12	VF20	XF40	MS60	MS63
2011	—	PF65 550				

KM# 312 50 EURO
6.22 g., 0.999 Gold 0.1985 oz. AGW, 22 mm. **Ruler:** Albert II **Obv:** Euro zone map **Rev:** Belgian deep sea exploration

Date	Mintage	F12	VF20	XF40	MS60	MS63
2011	2,500	PF65 550				

KM# 325 50 EURO
6.22 g., 0.999 Gold 0.1985 oz. AGW, 22 mm. **Ruler:** Albert II **Subject:** Hugo Claus **Obv:** Value and map of Euro countries **Rev:** Profile facing right

Date	Mintage	F12	VF20	XF40	MS60	MS63
2013	Est. 1000	PF65 425				

KM# 237 100 EURO
15.55 g., 0.999 Gold 0.4962 oz. AGW, 29 mm. **Ruler:** Albert II **Subject:** Founding Fathers

Date	Mintage	F12	VF20	XF40	MS60	MS63
2002	5,000	PF65 875				

KM# 238 100 EURO
15.55 g., 0.999 Gold 0.4962 oz. AGW, 29 mm. **Ruler:** Albert II **Subject:** 10th Anniversary of Reign

Date	Mintage	F12	VF20	XF40	MS60	MS63
2003	5,000	PF65 875				

KM# 239 100 EURO
15.55 g., 0.999 Gold 0.4962 oz. AGW, 29 mm. **Ruler:** Albert II **Subject:** Franc Germinal

Date	Mintage	F12	VF20	XF40	MS60	MS63
2004	5,000	PF65 875				

KM# 253 100 EURO
15.55 g., 0.999 Gold 0.4962 oz. AGW, 29 mm. **Ruler:** Albert II **Subject:** 175th Anniversary of Liberty **Obv:** Albert II head left **Rev:** Scene of the 1830 Revolution

Date	Mintage	F12	VF20	XF40	MS60	MS63
2005	5,000	PF65 875				

KM# 258 100 EURO
15.55 g., 0.999 Gold 0.4962 oz. AGW, 29 mm. **Ruler:** Albert II **Subject:** Saxe-Coburg-Gotha, 175th Anniversary **Obv:** Map of Western Europe and stars **Rev:** Church in Laeken, Kings monogram around

Date	Mintage	F12	VF20	XF40	MS60	MS63
2006	5,000	PF65 875				

KM# 264 100 EURO
15.55 g., 0.999 Gold 0.4962 oz. AGW, 29 mm. **Ruler:** Albert II **Subject:** Belgian Coins, 175th Anniversary **Obv:** Map of Western Europe **Rev:** Screw press, coin designs

Date	Mintage	F12	VF20	XF40	MS60	MS63
2007	5,000	PF65 875				

KM# 272 100 EURO
15.55 g., 0.999 Gold 0.4962 oz. AGW, 29 mm. **Ruler:** Albert II **Subject:** 50th Anniversary: Brussels Exposition **Obv:** Map of Western Europe

Date	Mintage	F12	VF20	XF40	MS60	MS63
2008	5,000	PF65 875				

KM# 283 100 EURO
15.55 g., 0.999 Gold 0.4962 oz. AGW **Ruler:** Albert II **Subject:** Royal Wedding Anniversary **Obv:** Conjoined leads at right

Date	Mintage	F12	VF20	XF40	MS60	MS63
2009	—	PF65 875				

KM# 307 100 EURO
15.55 g., 0.999 Gold 0.4962 oz. AGW, 29 mm. **Ruler:** Albert II **Subject:** Prince Philippe, 50th Birthday

Date	Mintage	F12	VF20	XF40	MS60	MS63
2010	2,000	PF65 900				

KM# 314 100 EURO
15.55 g., 0.999 Gold 0.4962 oz. AGW, 29 mm. **Ruler:** Albert II **Subject:** Victor Horta **Obv:** Euro zone map **Rev:** Bust at left, flora

Date	Mintage	F12	VF20	XF40	MS60	MS63
2011	—	PF65 950				

KM# 329 100 EURO
15.55 g., 0.999 Gold 0.4962 oz. AGW, 29 mm. **Ruler:** Albert II
Subject: Baudouin, 20th Anniversary of Death

Date	Mintage	F12	VF20	XF40	MS60	MS63
2013	Est. 1500			PF65 1,000		

KM# 330 20 EURO
22.85 g., 0.925 Silver 0.6752 oz. ASW, 37 mm. **Ruler:** Albert II
Subject: Philippe as king **Rev:** Albert II and Philippe

Date	Mintage	F12	VF20	XF40	MS60	MS63
2013	Est. 15000		PF63 60.00	PF65 70.00		

KM# 322 100 EURO
15.55 g., 0.999 Gold 0.4962 oz. AGW, 29 mm. **Ruler:** Albert II **Subject:** Gerhard Mercator, 500th Anniversary of Birth **Obv:** Value and map of Euro countries **Rev:** Bust at left, globe design background

Date	Mintage	F12	VF20	XF40	MS60	MS63
2012	Est. 2000			PF65 1,000		

MINT SETS

KM#	Date	Mintage	Identification	Issue Price	Mkt Val
MS14	2001 (10)	60,000	KM#148.1, 149.1, 187-194	15.00	45.00
MS15	1999/2000/ 2001 (24)	40,000	Euro Intro	—	250
MS16	2002 (8)	100,000	KM#224-231, 700th Anniversary	—	62.50
MS17	2002 (8)	20,000	KM#224-231, Cycling	—	62.50
MS18	2002 (8)	20,000	KM#224-231, Euros plus waffle francs	—	62.50
MS19	2003 (8)	100,000	KM#224-231, Television 50th	—	37.50
MS20	2003 (8)	15,000	KM#224-231, Ford Production in Belgium Centennial	—	37.50
MS21	2003 (8)	10,000	KM#224-231, Rose	—	37.50
MS22	2003 (8)	10,000	KM#224-231, Baby	—	37.50
MS23.1	2004 (9)	60,000	KM#224-231, Belgian Red Cross, plain medal	—	25.00
MS23.2	2004 (9)	2,000	KM#224-231, Belgian Red Cross, enameled medal	—	175
MS24	2004 (9)	5,000	KM#224-231, Love, medal for engraving	—	37.50
MS25	2004 (9)	5,000	KM#224-231, Baby, medal for engraving	—	37.50
MS26.1	2005 (9)	38,000	KM#224-231, Grand Palace, UNESCO site, plain medal	—	60.00
MS26.2	2005 (9)	2,000	KM#224-231, Grand Palace, UNESCO site, gilt medal	—	85.00
MS27.1	2006 (9)	38,000	KM#224-231, Flemish Houses, UNESCO site, plain medal	—	40.00
MS27.2	2006 (9)	2,000	KM#224-231, Flemish Houses, UNESCO site, colored medal	—	75.00
MS28.1	2007 (9)	38,000	KM#224-226, 242-246, Canal. UNESCO site, plain medal	—	27.50
MS28.2	2007 (9)	2,000	KM#224-226, 242-246, Canal, UNESCO site, colored medal	—	70.00
MS29.1	2008 (9)	25,000	KM#274-281, Bell-tower, UNESCO site, plain medal	—	75.00
MS29.2	2008 (9)	2,000	KM#274-281, Bell-tower, UNESCO site, colored medal	—	85.00
MS30	2009 (8)	25,000	KM#274-281, plus medal	—	45.00
MS31	2010 (8)	30,000	KM#274-281, plus medal	—	45.00
MS32	2011 (8)	30,000	KM#274-281, plus medal	—	45.00

PROOF SETS

KM#	Date	Mintage	Identification	Issue Price	Mkt Val
PS10	2001 (8)	15,000	KM#224-231	80.00	125
PS11	2002 (8)	3,240	KM#224-231	80.00	115
PS12	2003 (8)	3,241	KM#224-231	80.00	110
PS13	2004 (8)	3,006	KM#224-231	80.00	105
PS14	2005 (8)	3,006	KM#224-231	—	110
PS15	2006 (8)	3,006	KM#224-231	—	115
PS17	2007 (8)	3,000	KM#224-226, 242-247	—	175
PS18	2008 (8)	2,500	KM#224-227, 276-278, 280-281	—	100
PS19	2009 (8)	1,500	KM#274-281	—	110
PS20	2010 (8)	1,850	KM#274-281	—	110
PS21	2011 (8)	1,850	KM#274-281	—	110

BELIZE

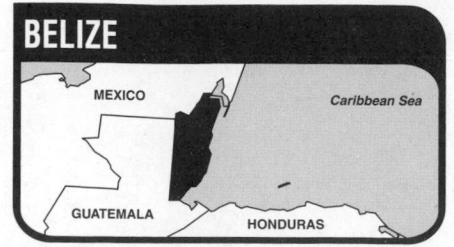

Belize, formerly British Honduras, but now a Constitutional Monarchy within the Commonwealth of Nations, is situated in Central America south of Mexico and east and north of Guatemala, with an area of 8,867 sq. mi. (22,960 sq. km.) and a population of *242,000. Capital: Belmopan. Tourism now augments Belize's economy, in addition to sugar, citrus fruits, chicle and hardwoods, which are exported.

MONETARY SYSTEM
Commencing 1864
100 Cents = 1 Dollar

COMMONWEALTH

DECIMAL COINAGE

KM# 33a CENT
0.80 g., Aluminum, 19.5 mm. **Obv:** Bust of Queen Elizabeth right **Rev:** Denomination within circle **Edge:** Smooth, scalloped

Date	Mintage	F12	VF20	XF40	MS60	MS63
2002	—	—	—	0.10	0.15	0.45
2005	—	—	—	0.10	0.15	0.45
2007	—	—	—	0.10	0.15	0.45
2010	—	—	—	0.10	0.15	0.45

KM# 34a 5 CENTS
1.04 g., Aluminum, 20.2 mm. **Obv:** Bust of Queen Elizabeth II right **Obv. Designer:** Cecil Thomas **Rev:** Denomination within circle **Edge:** Plain

Date	Mintage	F12	VF20	XF40	MS60	MS63
2002	—	—	—	0.10	0.20	0.45
2003	—	—	—	0.10	0.20	0.45
2005	—	—	—	0.10	0.20	0.45
2006	—	—	—	0.10	0.20	0.45
2009	—	—	—	0.10	0.20	0.45

KM# 115 5 CENTS
1.05 g., Aluminum, 20.2 mm.

Date	Mintage	F12	VF20	XF40	MS60	MS63
2002	—	—	—	0.10	0.20	0.40

KM# 36 25 CENTS
5.66 g., Copper-Nickel, 23.6 mm. **Obv:** Crowned bust of Queen Elizabeth II right **Obv. Designer:** Cecil Thomas **Rev:** Denomination within circle, date below **Edge:** Reeded

Date	Mintage	F12	VF20	XF40	MS60	MS63
2003	—	—	0.20	0.35	0.75	1.50
2007	—	—	0.20	0.35	0.75	1.50

KM# 37 50 CENTS
9.07 g., Copper-Nickel, 27.74 mm. **Obv:** Crowned bust of Queen Elizabeth right **Obv. Designer:** Cecil Thomas **Rev:** Denomination within circle, date below **Edge:** Reeded

Date	Mintage	F12	VF20	XF40	MS60	MS63
2010	—	—	—	1.00	2.00	3.00

KM# 99 DOLLAR
8.90 g., Nickel-Brass, 27 mm. **Obv:** Crowned bust of Queen Elizabeth II right **Obv. Designer:** Raphael Maklouf **Rev:** Columbus' three ships, denomination above, date below **Rev. Designer:** Robert Elderton **Edge:** Alternating reeded and plain **Shape:** 10-sided

Date	Mintage	F12	VF20	XF40	MS60	MS63
2003	—	—	—	—	2.25	3.00
2007	—	—	—	—	2.25	3.00

KM# 134 DOLLAR
30.94 g., 0.999 Silver 0.9874 oz. ASW, 39.9 mm. **Subject:** Mayan King **Obv:** National arms **Rev:** Mayan portrait in ornate headdress **Edge:** Reeded

Date	Mintage	F12	VF20	XF40	MS60	MS63
2002	—	—	—	—	40.00	45.00

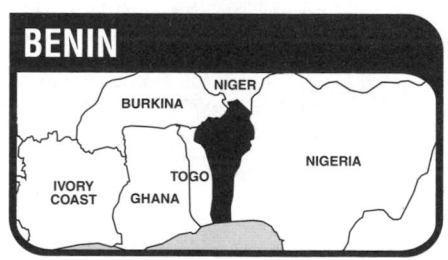

KM# 136 DOLLAR
8.90 g., Nickel-Brass, 27 mm. **Subject:** Central Bank, 30th Anniversary **Obv:** Bird in flight left **Rev:** Central Bank building **Rev. Legend:** Central Bank of Belize 30th Anniversary 1982-2012 **Edge:** alternating plain and reeded **Shape:** 10-sided

Date	Mintage	F12	VF20	XF40	MS60	MS63
2012	—	—	—	—	2.50	3.00

KM# 137 250 DOLLARS
15.98 g., 0.916 Gold 0.4675 oz. AGW, 28.40 mm. **Subject:** Maya Heartland **Obv:** Six glyph carved stones flanked by two Maya Hero Twins **Obv. Legend:** THE MAYA HEARTLAND **Rev:** Large carved jade head of Maya Sun God Kinich Ahau **Rev. Legend:** KINICH AHAU

Date	Mintage	F12	VF20	XF40	MS60	MS63
2012	Est. 500		PF63 800	PF65 1,000		

BENIN

The Republic of Benin (formerly the Republic of Dahomey), located on the south side of the African bulge between Togo and Nigeria, has an area of 43,500 sq. mi. (112,620 sq. km.) and a population of 5.5 million. Capital: Porto-Novo. The principal industry of Benin, one of the poorest countries of West Africa, is the processing of palm oil products. Palm kernel oil, peanuts, cotton, and coffee are exported.

PEOPLES REPUBLIC

STANDARD COINAGE

KM# 53 100 CFA FRANCS
27.00 g., Copper-Nickel, 38.61 mm. **Rev:** Multicolor Cannabis Sativa, Aeromatic

Date	Mintage	F12	VF20	XF40	MS60	MS63
2010	2,500	PF65 65.00				

KM# 53a 100 CFA FRANCS
27.00 g., Copper-Nickel, 38.61 mm. **Rev:** Multicolor Cannabis Sativa, Aeromatic

Date	Mintage	F12	VF20	XF40	MS60	MS63
2010	2,500	PF65 65.00				

KM# 71 100 FRANCS
20.00 g., 0.999 Silver 0.6382 oz. ASW, 36 mm. **Obv:** State arms **Rev:** Steam train in colored forest scene

Date	Mintage	F12	VF20	XF40	MS60	MS63
2010	—	PF65 55.00				

KM# 75 100 FRANCS
Silver Plated Base Metal, 27 mm. **Obv:** National arms **Rev:** Rose in color and fragrant

Date	Mintage	F12	VF20	XF40	MS60	MS63
2011	2,500	PF65 50.00				

KM# 74 100 FRANCS
Silver Plated Base Metal, 38.61 mm. **Subject:** Man in space **Obv:** State arms **Rev:** Gagarin in color

Date	Mintage	F12	VF20	XF40	MS60	MS63
2011 Prooflike	961	—	—	—	—	50.00

KM# 76 100 FRANCS
Silver Plated Base Metal, 27 mm. **Obv:** National arms **Rev:** Convallaria majalis, French lilly in color and fragrant

Date	Mintage	F12	VF20	XF40	MS60	MS63
2011	—	PF65 60.00				

KM# 63 500 FRANCS
Silver, 38.61 mm. **Obv:** National arms **Rev:** Euro coin motifs

Date	Mintage	F12	VF20	XF40	MS60	MS63
2002	—	PF65 45.00				

KM# 72 500 FRANCS
Silver, 38.6 mm. **Subject:** W.A. Mozart

Date	Mintage	F12	VF20	XF40	MS60	MS63
2005	—	PF65 50.00				

KM# 79 1000 FRANCS
25.00 g., 0.925 Silver 0.7387 oz. ASW, 38.61 mm. **Obv:** National arms **Rev:** Lake Baikal in color

Date	Mintage	F12	VF20	XF40	MS60	MS63
2011	PF60 40.00	PF63 50.00				

KM# 64 1000 FRANCS
Silver, 38.61 mm. **Obv:** National arms **Rev:** Zebra

Date	Mintage	F12	VF20	XF40	MS60	MS63
2001	—	PF65 45.00				

KM# 65 1000 FRANCS
Silver, 38.61 mm. **Obv:** National arms **Rev:** Giraffe

Date	Mintage	F12	VF20	XF40	MS60	MS63
2001	—	PF65 45.00				

KM# 66 1000 FRANCS
Silver, 38.61 mm. **Obv:** National arms **Rev:** Whale

Date	Mintage	F12	VF20	XF40	MS60	MS63
2001	—	PF65 65.00				

KM# 62 1000 FRANCS
Silver **Rev:** Klaus Störtebeker and ship

Date	Mintage	F12	VF20	XF40	MS60	MS63
2002	—	PF63 32.50	PF65 37.50			

KM# 54 1000 FRANCS
20.00 g., 0.999 Silver 0.6382 oz. ASW, 36 mm. **Rev:** Multicolor Lockheed Orion

Date	Mintage	F12	VF20	XF40	MS60	MS63
2002	—	PF60 25.00	PF63 35.00			

KM# 55 1000 FRANCS
20.00 g., 0.999 Silver 0.6382 oz. ASW, 36 mm. **Rev:** Multicolor Convair 990 Coronado over mountains

Date	Mintage	F12	VF20	XF40	MS60	MS63
2002	—	PF60 25.00	PF63 35.00			

KM# 60 1000 FRANCS
Silver **Subject:** Sir Francis Drake and the Golden Hind

Date	Mintage	F12	VF20	XF40	MS60	MS63
2003	—	PF63 32.50	PF65 37.50			

KM# 56 1000 FRANCS
20.00 g., 0.999 Silver 0.6382 oz. ASW, 36 mm. **Rev:** Multicolor Douglas DC-8 at airport

Date	Mintage	F12	VF20	XF40	MS60	MS63
2003	—	PF60 25.00	PF63 35.00			

KM# 57 1000 FRANCS
20.00 g., 0.999 Silver 0.6382 oz. ASW, 36 mm. **Rev:** Multicolor Fokker 100 left

Date	Mintage	F12	VF20	XF40	MS60	MS63
2003	—	PF60 25.00	PF63 35.00			

KM# 58 1000 FRANCS
20.00 g., 0.999 Silver 0.6382 oz. ASW, 36 mm. **Rev:** Multicolor Douglas DC-4 right

Date	Mintage	F12	VF20	XF40	MS60	MS63
2004	—	PF60 25.00			PF63 35.00	

KM# 59 1000 FRANCS
20.00 g., 0.999 Silver 0.6382 oz. ASW, 36 mm. **Rev:** Multicolor General Aviation GA-43 against blue sky

Date	Mintage	F12	VF20	XF40	MS60	MS63
2004	—	PF60 35.00			PF63 45.00	

KM# 67 1000 FRANCS
20.00 g., 0.999 Silver 0.6382 oz. ASW, 36 mm. **Obv:** National arms **Rev:** Blue plane at airport in color

Date	Mintage	F12	VF20	XF40	MS60	MS63
2005	—	PF60 35.00			PF63 45.00	

KM# 68 1000 FRANCS
20.00 g., 0.999 Silver 0.6382 oz. ASW, 36 mm. **Obv:** Naitonal arms **Rev:** Red plane in flight with green mountain in background

Date	Mintage	F12	VF20	XF40	MS60	MS63
2005	—	PF60 35.00			PF63 45.00	

KM# 73 1000 FRANCS
Silver, 16 mm. **Subject:** Cannabis **Rev:** Leaf in green **Shape:** Leaf

Date	Mintage	F12	VF20	XF40	MS60	MS63
2011	—	PF65 65.00				

KM# 77 1000 FRANCS
15.55 g., 0.999 Silver 0.4962 oz. ASW, 38.6 mm. **Obv:** National arms **Rev:** Red dragon

Date	Mintage	F12	VF20	XF40	MS60	MS63
2012	—	PF63 22.00			PF65 27.00	

KM# 78 1000 FRANCS
15.55 g., 0.999 Silver 0.4962 oz. ASW, 38.61 mm. **Obv:** National arms **Rev:** Blue dragon

Date	Mintage	F12	VF20	XF40	MS60	MS63
2012	—	PF63 22.00			PF65 27.00	

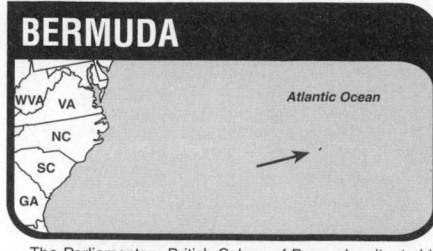

BERMUDA

The Parliamentary British Colony of Bermuda, situated in the western Atlantic Ocean 660 miles (1,062 km.) east of North Carolina, has an area of 20.6 sq. mi. (53 sq. km.) and a population of 61,600. Capital: Hamilton. Concentrated essences, beauty preparations, and cut flowers are exported. Most Bermudians derive their livelihood from tourism. The British monarch is the head of state and is represented by a governor. U.S. Currency circulates in common with the Eastern Caribbean Dollar.

RULER
British

BRITISH COLONY
DECIMAL COINAGE
100 Cents = 1 Dollar

KM# 107 CENT
2.50 g., Copper Plated Zinc, 19 mm. **Ruler:** Elizabeth II **Obv:** Head with tiara right **Obv. Designer:** Ian Rank-Broadley **Rev:** Wild boar left **Rev. Designer:** Michael Rizzello **Edge:** Plain

Date	Mintage	F12	VF20	XF40	MS60	MS63
2001	1,600,000	—	—	—	0.50	0.75
2002	1,120,000	—	—	—	0.50	0.75
2003	800,000	—	—	—	0.50	0.75
2004	1,600,000	—	—	—	0.25	0.50
2005	3,200,000	—	—	—	0.25	0.50
2006	800,000	—	—	—	0.25	0.50
2007	—	—	—	—	0.25	0.50
2008	2,400,000	—	—	—	0.25	0.50

KM# 107a CENT
2.50 g., Copper Plated Steel, 19 mm. **Ruler:** Elizabeth II **Obv:** Head with tiara right **Obv. Designer:** Ian Rank-Broadley **Rev:** Wild boar left **Rev. Designer:** Michael Rizzello

Date	Mintage	F12	VF20	XF40	MS60	MS63
2008	2,400,000	—	—	—	0.25	0.50
2009	4,000,000	—	—	—	0.25	0.50

KM# 108 5 CENTS
5.00 g., Copper-Nickel, 21.2 mm. **Ruler:** Elizabeth II **Obv:** Head with tiara right **Obv. Designer:** Ian Rank-Broadley **Rev:** Queen angel fish left **Rev. Designer:** Michael Rizzello **Edge:** Plain

Date	Mintage	F12	VF20	XF40	MS60	MS63
2001	1,000,000	—	—	—	0.75	1.00
2002	700,000	—	—	—	0.75	1.00
2003	700,000	—	—	—	0.75	1.00
2004	700,000	—	—	—	0.75	1.00
2005	600,000	—	—	—	0.75	1.00
2008	500,000	—	—	—	0.75	1.00
2009	1,500,000	—	—	—	0.50	0.75

KM# 109 10 CENTS
2.50 g., Copper-Nickel, 17.8 mm. **Ruler:** Elizabeth II **Obv:** Head with tiara right **Obv. Designer:** Ian Rank-Broadley **Rev:** Bermuda lily **Rev. Designer:** Michael Rizzello **Edge:** Reeded

Date	Mintage	F12	VF20	XF40	MS60	MS63
2001	1,400,000	—	—	—	0.85	1.00
2002	800,000	—	—	—	0.85	1.00
2003	600,000	—	—	—	0.85	1.00
2004	800,000	—	—	—	0.85	1.00
2005	800,000	—	—	—	0.85	1.00
2008	2,000,000	—	—	—	0.50	0.75
2009	2,000,000	—	—	—	0.50	0.75

KM# 188 25 CENTS
28.28 g., Copper-Nickel, 38.61 mm. **Ruler:** Elizabeth II **Obv:** Head with tiara left **Rev:** Bermuda bluebird and sailboats **Edge:** Reeded

Date	Mintage	F12	VF20	XF40	MS60	MS63
2011	2,000	—	—	—	—	25.00

KM# 189 25 CENTS
28.28 g., Copper-Nickel, 38.61 mm. **Ruler:** Elizabeth II **Obv:** Head with tiara right **Rev:** Bermuda bluebird with sailboats **Edge:** Reeded

Date	Mintage	F12	VF20	XF40	MS60	MS63
2011	2,000	—	—	—	—	25.00

KM# 192 25 CENTS
28.28 g., Copper-Nickel, 38.61 mm. **Ruler:** Elizabeth II **Obv:** Head with tiara right **Rev:** Blue marlin **Edge:** Reeded

Date	Mintage	F12	VF20	XF40	MS60	MS63
2012	2,000	—	—	—	—	25.00

KM# 195 25 CENTS
28.28 g., Copper-Nickel, 36.61 mm. **Ruler:** Elizabeth II **Obv:** Head with tiara right **Rev:** Blue angel fish **Edge:** Reeded

Date	Mintage	F12	VF20	XF40	MS60	MS63
2013	2,000	—	—	—	—	25.00

KM# 110 25 CENTS
Copper-Nickel, 24 mm. **Ruler:** Elizabeth II **Obv:** Head with tiara right **Obv. Designer:** Ian Rank-Broadley **Rev:** Yellow-billed tropical bird right **Rev. Designer:** Michael Rizzello **Edge:** Reeded

Date	Mintage	F12	VF20	XF40	MS60	MS63
2001	800,000	—	—	—	1.50	2.00
2002	800,000	—	—	—	1.50	2.00
2003	800,000	—	—	—	1.50	2.00
2004	800,000	—	—	—	1.50	2.00
2005	1,440,000	—	—	—	1.50	2.00
2006	320,000	—	—	—	1.50	2.00
2007	—	—	—	—	1.50	2.00
2008	1,200,000	—	—	—	1.00	1.50
2009	2,000,000	—	—	—	1.00	1.50

KM# 111 DOLLAR
Nickel-Brass, 26 mm. **Ruler:** Elizabeth II **Obv:** Head with tiara right **Obv. Designer:** Rank-Broadley **Rev:** Sailboat **Rev. Designer:** Eldron Trimingham III

Date	Mintage	F12	VF20	XF40	MS60	MS63
2001	12,000	—	—	—	3.00	3.50
2002	12,000	—	—	—	3.00	3.50
2003	12,000	—	—	—	3.00	3.50
2004	12,000	—	—	—	3.00	3.50
2005	240,000	—	—	—	2.00	3.00
2008	300,000	—	—	—	2.00	3.00
2009	600,000	—	—	—	2.00	3.00

KM# 139 DOLLAR
28.28 g., Copper-Nickel, 38.6 mm. **Ruler:** Elizabeth II **Obv:** Head with tiara right **Obv. Designer:** Ian Rank-Broadley **Rev:** 4 Gombey dancers **Rev. Designer:** Robert Elderton **Edge:** Reeded

Date	Mintage	F12	VF20	XF40	MS60	MS63
2001	—	—	—	—	12.00	14.00

KM# 124 DOLLAR
28.41 g., Copper-Nickel, 38.5 mm. **Ruler:** Elizabeth II **Subject:** Queen's Golden Jubilee **Obv:** Head with tiara right **Obv. Designer:** Ian Rank-Broadley **Rev:** Stylized trumpeters above monogram and date **Edge:** Reeded

Date	Mintage	F12	VF20	XF40	MS60	MS63
2002	—	—	—	—	10.00	12.00

KM# 189 2 DOLLARS
31.60 g., 0.999 Silver 1.0085 oz. ASW, 38.61 mm. **Ruler:** Elizabeth II **Obv:** Head with tiara right **Rev:** Bermuda bluebird and sailboats **Edge:** Reeded

Date	Mintage	F12	VF20	XF40	MS60	MS63
2011	1,000	PF65 110				

KM# 190 2 DOLLARS
31.60 g., 0.999 Silver 1.0085 oz. ASW, 38.61 mm. **Ruler:** Elizabeth II **Obv:** Head with tiara right **Rev:** Color Bermuda bluebird with sailboats **Edge:** Reeded

Date	Mintage	F12	VF20	XF40	MS60	MS63
2011	1,000	PF65 110				

KM# 193 2 DOLLARS
31.60 g., 0.999 Silver 1.0085 oz. ASW, 38.61 mm. **Ruler:** Elizabeth II **Obv:** Head with tiara right **Rev:** Blue marlin in color **Edge:** Reeded

Date	Mintage	F12	VF20	XF40	MS60	MS63
2012	1,000	PF65 110				

KM# 196 2 DOLLARS
31.60 g., 0.999 Silver 1.0085 oz. ASW, 38.61 mm. **Ruler:** Elizabeth II **Obv:** Head with tiara right **Rev:** Blue angel fish in color **Edge:** Reeded

Date	Mintage	F12	VF20	XF40	MS60	MS63
2013	1,000	PF65 110				

KM# 198 2 DOLLARS
31.60 g., 0.999 Silver 1.0085 oz. ASW, 38.61 mm. **Ruler:** Elizabeth II **Subject:** Bermuda Hawksbill Turtle **Obv:** Bust right **Rev:** Turtle **Rev. Legend:** BERMUDA HAWKSBILL TURTLE / TWO DOLLARS

Date	Mintage	F12	VF20	XF40	MS60	MS63
2008	2,500	PF63 45.00			PF65 50.00	

KM# 186 2 DOLLARS
31.60 g., 0.999 Silver 1.0085 oz. ASW, 38.61 mm. **Ruler:** Elizabeth II **Subject:** Cahow **Obv:** Head of Queen Elizabeth II with tiara facing right, legend, country name, date **Obv. Legend:** ELIZABETH II **Rev:** Bird over water surrounding outline of Bermuda, denomination

Date	Mintage	F12	VF20	XF40	MS60	MS63
2010	Est. 1000	PF65 90.00				

KM# 157 3 DOLLARS
33.63 g., 0.925 Silver 0.9937 oz. ASW, 35 mm. **Ruler:** Elizabeth II **Subject:** Shipwrecks Series **Obv:** Elizabeth II **Rev:** Gold-plated image of the Hunter Galley **Edge:** Plain

Date	Mintage	F12	VF20	XF40	MS60	MS63
2006	15,000	PF65 90.00				

KM# 158 3 DOLLARS
33.63 g., 0.925 Silver 0.9937 oz. ASW, 35 mm. **Ruler:** Elizabeth II **Subject:** Shipwrecks Series **Obv:** Elizabeth II **Rev:** Gold-plated image of the North Carolina **Edge:** Plain

Date	Mintage	F12	VF20	XF40	MS60	MS63
2006	15,000	PF65 90.00				

KM# 159 3 DOLLARS
33.63 g., 0.925 Silver 0.9937 oz. ASW, 35 mm. **Ruler:** Elizabeth II **Subject:** Shipwrecks Series **Obv:** Elizabeth II **Rev:** Gold-plated image of the Pollockshields **Edge:** Plain

Date	Mintage	F12	VF20	XF40	MS60	MS63
2006	15,000	PF65 90.00				

KM# 175 3 DOLLARS
31.49 g., 0.999 Gold 1.0049 oz. AGW, 35 mm. **Ruler:** Elizabeth II **Series:** Bermuda Shipwrecks **Subject:** The Constellation **Obv:** Head of Queen Elizabeth II with tiara facing right and legend, country name, date **Obv. Legend:** ELIZABETH II **Rev:** The Constellation, legends, denomination **Rev. Legend:** CONSTELLATION Anno Domini 1943 **Shape:** Triangular

Date	Mintage	F12	VF20	XF40	MS60	MS63
2006	Est. 750	PF63 2,000		PF65 2,200		

KM# 176 3 DOLLARS
31.49 g., 0.999 Gold 1.0049 oz. AGW, 35 mm. **Ruler:** Elizabeth II **Series:** Bermuda Shipwrecks **Subject:** The Hunter Galley **Obv:** Head of Queen Elizabeth II with tiara facing right, legend, country name, date **Obv. Legend:** HUNTER GALLEEY Anno Domini 1752 **Rev:** The Hunter Galley, legend, denomination **Shape:** Triangular

Date	Mintage	F12	VF20	XF40	MS60	MS63
2006	—	PF63 2,000		PF65 2,200		

KM# 177 3 DOLLARS
31.49 g., 0.999 Gold 1.0049 oz. AGW, 35 mm. **Ruler:** Elizabeth II **Series:** Bermuda Shipwrecks **Subject:** The Mary Celestia **Obv:** Head of Queen Elizabeth II wtih tiara facing right, legend, country name, date **Obv. Legend:** ELIZABETH II **Rev:** The Mary Celestia, legends, denomination **Rev. Legend:** MARY CELESTIA Anno Domini 1864 **Shape:** Triangular

Date	Mintage	F12	VF20	XF40	MS60	MS63
2006	Est. 750	PF63 2,000		PF65 2,200		

KM# 178 3 DOLLARS
31.49 g., 0.999 Gold 1.0049 oz. AGW, 35 mm. **Ruler:** Elizabeth II **Series:** Bemuda Shipwrecks **Subject:** The North Carolina **Obv:** Head of Queen Elizabeth II with tiara facing right, legend, country name, date **Obv. Legend:** ELIZABETH II **Rev:** The North Carolina, legends, denomination **Rev. Legend:** NORTH CAROLINA Anno Domini 1880 **Shape:** Triangular

Date	Mintage	F12	VF20	XF40	MS60	MS63
2006	Est. 750	PF63 2,000		PF65 2,200		

KM# 179 3 DOLLARS
31.49 g., 0.999 Gold 1.0049 oz. AGW, 35 mm. **Ruler:** Elizabeth II **Series:** Bermuda Shipwrecks **Subject:** The Pollockshields **Obv:** Head of Queen Elizabeth II with tiara facing right, legend, country name, date **Obv. Legend:** ELIZABETH II **Rev:** The Pollockshields, legends, denomination **Rev. Legend:** POLLOCKSHIELD Anno Domini 1915 **Shape:** Triangular

Date	Mintage	F12	VF20	XF40	MS60	MS63
2006	—	PF63 2,000		PF65 2,200		

KM# 140 3 DOLLARS
33.63 g., 0.925 Silver 0.9937 oz. ASW, 35 mm. **Ruler:** Elizabeth II **Subject:** Shipwrecks Series **Obv:** Elizabeth II **Rev:** The Mary Celestia gold-plated image **Edge:** Plain **Shape:** Triangular

Date	Mintage	F12	VF20	XF40	MS60	MS63
2006	15,000	PF65 90.00				

KM# 141 3 DOLLARS
1.56 g., 0.999 Gold 0.0496 oz. AGW, 15 mm. **Ruler:** Elizabeth II **Subject:** Shipwreck Series **Obv:** Elizabeth II **Rev:** The Mary Celestia **Edge:** Plain **Shape:** Triangular

Date	Mintage	F12	VF20	XF40	MS60	MS63
2006	15,000	PF65 100				

KM# 148 3 DOLLARS
33.63 g., 0.925 Silver 0.9937 oz. ASW, 35 mm. **Ruler:** Elizabeth II **Subject:** Shipwreck Series **Obv:** Elizabeth II **Rev:** The Constellation in gold-plated image **Edge:** Plain **Shape:** Triangular

Date	Mintage	F12	VF20	XF40	MS60	MS63
2006	15,000	PF65 90.00				

KM# 149 3 DOLLARS
1.56 g., 0.999 Gold 0.0496 oz. AGW, 15 mm. **Ruler:** Elizabeth II **Subject:** Shipwreck Series **Obv:** Elizabeth II **Rev:** The Constellation **Edge:** Plain **Shape:** Triangular

Date	Mintage	F12	VF20	XF40	MS60	MS63
2006	15,000	PF65 100				

KM# 156 3 DOLLARS
33.63 g., 0.925 Silver 0.9937 oz. ASW, 35 mm. **Ruler:** Elizabeth II **Subject:** Shipwrecks Series **Obv:** Elizabeth II **Rev:** Gold-plated image of the Sea Venture **Edge:** Plain

Date	Mintage	F12	VF20	XF40	MS60	MS63
2007	15,000	PF65 90.00				

KM# 164 3 DOLLARS
33.63 g., 0.925 Silver 0.9937 oz. ASW, 35 mm. **Ruler:** Elizabeth II **Series:** Bermuda Shipwrecks **Obv:** Head with tiara right, gilt **Obv. Designer:** Ian Rank-Broadley **Rev:** Dutchman sailing ship "Manilla", gilt, 1739 **Edge:** Plain, gilt **Shape:** Triangular

Date	Mintage	F12	VF20	XF40	MS60	MS63
2007	15,000	PF65 85.00				

KM# 180 3 DOLLARS
31.49 g., 0.999 Gold 1.0049 oz. AGW, 35 mm. **Ruler:** Elizabeth II **Series:** Bermuda Shipwrecks **Subject:** The Colonel William G. Ball **Obv:** Head of Queen Elizabeth II with tiara facing right, legend, country name, date **Obv. Legend:** ELIZABETH II **Rev:** The colonel William G. Ball, legends, denomination **Rev. Legend:** WILLIAM G. BALL Anno Domini 1943 **Shape:** Triangular

Date	Mintage	F12	VF20	XF40	MS60	MS63
2007	Est. 750	PF63 2,000		PF65 2,200		

KM# 181 3 DOLLARS
31.49 g., 0.999 Gold 1.0049 oz. AGW, 35 mm. **Ruler:** Elizabeth II **Series:** Bermuda Shipwrecks **Subject:** The Chistobal Colon **Obv:** Head of Queen Elizabeth II with tiara facing right, legend, country name, date **Obv. Legend:** ELIZABETH II **Rev:** The Cristobal Colon, legends, denomination **Rev. Legend:** CRISTOBAL COLON Anno Domini 1936 **Shape:** Triangular

Date	Mintage	F12	VF20	XF40	MS60	MS63
2007	Est. 750	PF63 2,000		PF65 2,200		

KM# 182 3 DOLLARS
31.49 g., 0.999 Gold 1.0049 oz. AGW, 35 mm. **Ruler:** Elizabeth II **Series:** Bermuda Shipwrecks **Subject:** The Kate **Obv:** Head of Queen Elizabeth II with tiara facing right and legend, country name, date **Obv. Legend:** ELIZABETH II **Rev:** The Kate, legends, denomination **Rev. Legend:** KATE Anno Domini 1878 **Shape:** Triangular

Date	Mintage	F12	VF20	XF40	MS60	MS63
2007	Est. 750	PF63 2,000		PF65 2,200		

KM# 183 3 DOLLARS
31.49 g., 0.999 Gold 1.0049 oz. AGW, 35 mm. **Ruler:** Elizabeth II **Series:** Bermuda Shipwrecks **Subject:** The San Pedro **Obv:** Head of Queen Elizabeth II with tiara facing right, legend, country name, date **Obv. Legend:** ELIZABETH II **Rev:** The San Pedro, legends, denomination **Rev. Legend:** SAN PEDRO Anno Domini 1595 **Shape:** Triangular

Date	Mintage	F12	VF20	XF40	MS60	MS63
2007	Est. 750	PF63 2,000		PF65 2,200		

KM# 184 3 DOLLARS
31.49 g., 0.999 Gold 1.0049 oz. AGW, 35 mm. **Ruler:** Elizabeth II **Series:** Bermuda Shipwrecks **Subject:** The Santa Lucia **Obv:** Head of Queen Elizabeth II with tiara facing right, legend, country name, date **Obv. Legend:** ELIZABETH II **Rev:** The Santa Lucia, legends, denomination **Rev. Legend:** SANTA LUCIA Anno Domini 1584 **Shape:** Triangular

Date	Mintage	F12	VF20	XF40	MS60	MS63
2007	Est. 750	PF63 2,000		PF65 2,200		

KM# 185 3 DOLLARS

31.49 g., 0.999 Gold 1.0049 oz. AGW, 35 mm. **Ruler:** Elizabeth II **Series:** Bermuda Shipwrecks **Subject:** The Manilla **Obv:** Head of Queen Elizabeth II with tiara facing right, legend, country name, date **Obv. Legend:** ELIZABETH II **Rev:** The Manilla, legends, denomination **Rev. Legend:** MANILLA Anno Domini 1739 **Shape:** Triangular

Date	Mintage	F12	VF20	XF40	MS60	MS63
2007	—	PF63 2,000	PF65 2,200			

KM# 165 3 DOLLARS

33.63 g., 0.925 Silver 0.9937 oz. ASW, 35 mm. **Ruler:** Elizabeth II **Series:** Bermuda Shipwrecks **Obv:** Head with tiara right, gilt **Obv. Designer:** Ian Rank-Broadley **Rev:** 16th century Spanish sailing ship "Santa Lucia", gilt, 1584 **Edge:** Plain, gilt **Shape:** Triangular

Date	Mintage	F12	VF20	XF40	MS60	MS63
2007	15,000	PF65 85.00				

KM# 166 3 DOLLARS

33.63 g., 0.925 Silver 0.9937 oz. ASW **Ruler:** Elizabeth II **Series:** Bermuda Shipwrecks **Obv:** Head with tiara right, gilt **Obv. Designer:** Ian Rank-Broadley **Rev:** Spanish luxury steamship "Cristobal Colon", gilt, 1936 **Edge:** Plain

Date	Mintage	F12	VF20	XF40	MS60	MS63
2007	15,000	PF65 85.00				

KM# 167 3 DOLLARS

33.63 g., 0.925 Silver 0.9937 oz. ASW, 35 mm. **Ruler:** Elizabeth II **Series:** Bermuda Shipwrecks **Obv:** Head with tiara right, gilt **Obv. Designer:** Ian Rank-Broadley **Rev:** English iron-hulled steamer with sails "Kate", gilt, 1878 **Edge:** Plain **Shape:** Triangular

Date	Mintage	F12	VF20	XF40	MS60	MS63
2007	15,000	PF65 85.00				

KM# 168 3 DOLLARS

33.63 g., 0.925 Silver 0.9937 oz. ASW, 35 mm. **Ruler:** Elizabeth II **Series:** Bermuda Shipwrecks **Obv:** Head with tiara right, gilt **Obv. Designer:** Ian Rank-Broadley **Rev:** 16th century Spanish sailing ship "San Pedro", gilt, 1596 **Edge:** Plain, gilt **Shape:** Triangular

Date	Mintage	F12	VF20	XF40	MS60	MS63
2007	15,000	PF65 85.00				

KM# 169 3 DOLLARS

33.63 g., 0.925 Silver 0.9937 oz. ASW, 35 mm. **Ruler:** Elizabeth II **Series:** Bermuda Shipwrecks **Obv:** Head with tiara right, gilt **Obv. Designer:** Ian Rank-Broadley **Rev:** American luxury yacht "Col. William G. Ball", gilt, 1943 **Edge:** Plain, gilt **Shape:** Triangular

Date	Mintage	F12	VF20	XF40	MS60	MS63
2007	15,000	PF65 85.00				

KM# 199 4 DOLLARS

34.00 g., 0.925 Silver 1.0046 oz. ASW, 40 mm. **Ruler:** Elizabeth II **Obv:** Bust right **Obv. Legend:** Elizabeth II, Value, BERMUDA **Rev:** Sea venture sailing ship **Rev. Legend:** 1609-2009 400th ANNIVERSARY OF THE SETTLEMENT OF BERMUDA **Shape:** Square

Date	Mintage	F12	VF20	XF40	MS60	MS63
ND-2009	2,000	PF65 55.00				

KM# 190 5 DOLLARS

1.55 g., 0.500 Gold 0.0248 oz. AGW, 16 mm. **Ruler:** Elizabeth II **Obv:** Head with tiara right **Rev:** Bermuda bluebird and sailboats **Edge:** Reeded

Date	Mintage	F12	VF20	XF40	MS60	MS63
2011	500	PF65 185				

KM# 191 5 DOLLARS

1.56 g., 0.9999 Gold 0.0497 oz. AGW, 16 mm. **Ruler:** Elizabeth II **Obv:** Head with tiara right **Rev:** Bermuda bluebird with sailboats **Edge:** Reeded

Date	Mintage	F12	VF20	XF40	MS60	MS63
2011	500	PF65 185				

KM# 194 5 DOLLARS

1.56 g., 0.9999 Gold 0.0497 oz. AGW, 16 mm. **Ruler:** Elizabeth II **Obv:** Head with tiara right **Rev:** Blue marlin **Edge:** Reeded

Date	Mintage	F12	VF20	XF40	MS60	MS63
2012	500	PF65 185				

KM# 197 5 DOLLARS

1.56 g., 0.9999 Gold 0.0497 oz. AGW, 16 mm. **Ruler:** Elizabeth II **Obv:** Head with tiara right **Rev:** Blue angle fish **Edge:** Reeded

Date	Mintage	F12	VF20	XF40	MS60	MS63
2013	500	PF65 185				

KM# 120 5 DOLLARS

28.28 g., 0.925 Silver 0.8356 oz. ASW, 38.6 mm. **Ruler:** Elizabeth II **Subject:** Gombey Dancers **Obv:** Head with tiara right **Obv. Designer:** Ian Rank-Broadley **Rev:** Multicolor costumed dancers **Edge:** Reeded

Date	Mintage	F12	VF20	XF40	MS60	MS63
2001	3,500	PF63 55.00	PF65 60.00			

KM# 161 5 DOLLARS

28.28 g., 0.925 Silver 0.8356 oz. ASW, 38.6 mm. **Ruler:** Elizabeth II **Obv:** Bust with tiara right **Rev:** Statehouse facade, St. George's **Edge:** Reeded

Date	Mintage	F12	VF20	XF40	MS60	MS63
2001	3,500	PF63 40.00	PF65 45.00			

KM# 129 5 DOLLARS

28.28 g., 0.925 Silver 0.8356 oz. ASW, 38.6 mm. **Ruler:** Elizabeth II **Subject:** Queen's Jubilee **Obv:** Gold-plated head with tiara right, denomination below **Rev:** Trumpeters, monogram and date below **Edge:** Reeded

Date	Mintage	F12	VF20	XF40	MS60	MS63
2002	20,000	PF63 38.00	PF65 42.00			

KM# 162 5 DOLLARS

28.28 g., 0.925 Silver 0.8356 oz. ASW, 38.6 mm. **Ruler:** Elizabeth II **Subject:** 100th Anniversary Cup Match - Cricket **Obv:** Head with tiara right **Rev:** Two players with caps and teams shields below, multicolor **Edge:** Reeded

Date	Mintage	F12	VF20	XF40	MS60	MS63
2002	3,500	PF63 40.00	PF65 45.00			

KM# 171 5 DOLLARS

28.28 g., 0.925 Silver 0.8356 oz. ASW, 38.6 mm. **Ruler:** Elizabeth II **Subject:** Queen's Golden Jubilee **Obv:** Head with tiara right **Obv. Designer:** Ian Rank-Broadley **Rev:** Stylized trumpeters above monogram and date **Edge:** Reeded

Date	Mintage	F12	VF20	XF40	MS60	MS63
2002	3,500	PF65 50.00				

KM# 130 5 DOLLARS

28.28 g., 0.925 Silver 0.8356 oz. ASW, 38.6 mm. **Ruler:** Elizabeth II **Subject:** Queen's Jubilee **Obv:** Gold-plated head with tiara right **Rev:** Royal visit scene **Edge:** Reeded

Date	Mintage	F12	VF20	XF40	MS60	MS63
2003	20,000	PF63 38.00	PF65 42.00			

KM# 170 5 DOLLARS
28.28 g., 0.925 Silver 0.8356 oz. ASW, 38.6 mm. **Ruler:** Elizabeth II **Subject:** 100th Anniversary Fitted Dinghy Racing **Obv:** Head with tiara right **Rev:** Two dinghies, multicolor sails **Edge:** Reeded

Date	Mintage	F12	VF20	XF40	MS60	MS63
ND-2003	3,500	PF65 50.00				

KM# 131 5 DOLLARS
28.28 g., 0.925 Silver 0.8356 oz. ASW, 38.6 mm. **Ruler:** Elizabeth II **Obv:** Head with tiara right **Rev:** Bermudian stone quarry scene **Edge:** Reeded

Date	Mintage	F12	VF20	XF40	MS60	MS63
2004	3,500	PF63 55.00	PF65 60.00			

KM# 160 5 DOLLARS
14.50 g., 0.925 Silver 0.4284 oz. ASW, 30.9 mm. **Ruler:** Elizabeth II **Subject:** Bermuda Quincentennial **Obv:** Head with tiara right, partially gold-plated **Rev:** Caravel sailing ship partially gold-plated compass face **Edge:** Plain **Shape:** Pentagonal

Date	Mintage	F12	VF20	XF40	MS60	MS63
2005	2,500	PF65 45.00				

KM# 187 5 DOLLARS
1.56 g., 0.999 Gold 0.0496 oz. AGW, 16 mm. **Ruler:** Elizabeth II **Subject:** Cahow **Obv:** Head of Queen Elizabeth II with tiara facing right, legend, country name, date **Obv. Legend:** ELIZABETH II **Rev:** Bird over water surrounding outline of Bermuda, denomination

Date	Mintage	F12	VF20	XF40	MS60	MS63
2010	Est. 500	PF65 150				

KM# 188 5 DOLLARS
28.28 g., 0.925 Silver 0.8356 oz. ASW, 38.6 mm. **Ruler:** Elizabeth II **Rev:** Sword and decorations **Rev. Legend:** THE SYSTEM DOES DISCOVER PEOPLE WHO DO UNSUNG THINGS

Date	Mintage	F12	VF20	XF40	MS60	MS63
2012	—	PF65 75.00				

KM# 142 9 DOLLARS
155.52 g., 0.999 Silver 4.9629 oz. ASW, 65 mm. **Ruler:** Elizabeth II **Subject:** Shipwreck Series **Obv:** Elizabeth II **Rev:** The Mary Celestia **Edge:** Plain **Shape:** Triangular

Date	Mintage	F12	VF20	XF40	MS60	MS63
2007	1,000	PF65 200				

KM# 150 9 DOLLARS
155.52 g., 0.999 Silver 4.9629 oz. ASW, 65 mm. **Ruler:** Elizabeth II **Subject:** Shipwreck Series **Obv:** Elizabeth II **Rev:** The Constellation **Edge:** Plain **Shape:** Triangular

Date	Mintage	F12	VF20	XF40	MS60	MS63
2007	1,000	PF65 200				

KM# 143 30 DOLLARS
31.49 g., 0.999 Gold 1.0049 oz. AGW, 35 mm. **Ruler:** Elizabeth II **Subject:** Shipwreck Series **Obv:** Elizabeth II **Rev:** The Mary Celestia **Edge:** Plain **Shape:** Triangular

Date	Mintage	F12	VF20	XF40	MS60	MS63
2006	750	PF65 1,750				

KM# 151 30 DOLLARS
31.49 g., 0.999 Gold 1.0049 oz. AGW, 35 mm. **Ruler:** Elizabeth II **Subject:** Shipwreck Series **Obv:** Elizabeth II **Rev:** The Constellation **Edge:** Plain **Shape:** Triangular

Date	Mintage	F12	VF20	XF40	MS60	MS63
2006	750	PF65 1,750				

KM# 144 60 DOLLARS
1000.00 g., 0.999 Silver 31.9118 oz. ASW, 100 mm. **Ruler:** Elizabeth II **Subject:** Shipwreck Series **Obv:** Elizabeth II **Rev:** The Mary Celestia **Edge:** Plain

Date	Mintage	F12	VF20	XF40	MS60	MS63
2007	300	PF65 1,200				

KM# 152 60 DOLLARS
1000.00 g., 0.999 Silver 31.9118 oz. ASW, 100 mm. **Ruler:** Elizabeth II **Subject:** Shipwreck Series **Obv:** Elizabeth II **Rev:** The Constellation **Edge:** Plain **Shape:** Triangular

Date	Mintage	F12	VF20	XF40	MS60	MS63
2007	300	PF65 1,200				

KM# 145 90 DOLLARS
155.52 g., 0.999 Gold 4.9629 oz. AGW, 65 mm. **Ruler:** Elizabeth II **Subject:** Shipwreck Series **Obv:** Elizabeth II **Rev:** The Mary Celestia **Edge:** Plain **Shape:** Triangular

Date	Mintage	F12	VF20	XF40	MS60	MS63
2006	90	PF65 8,000				

KM# 153 90 DOLLARS
155.52 g., 0.999 Gold 4.9629 oz. AGW, 65 mm. **Ruler:** Elizabeth II **Subject:** Shipwreck Series **Obv:** Elizabeth II **Rev:** The Constellation **Edge:** Plain **Shape:** Triangular

Date	Mintage	F12	VF20	XF40	MS60	MS63
2006	90	PF65 8,000				

KM# 174 90 DOLLARS
155.52 g., 0.999 Gold 4.9629 oz. AGW, 65 mm. **Ruler:** Elizabeth II **Subject:** Sea Venture, 1609 **Obv:** Head with tiara right **Rev:** Sailing ship left **Shape:** Triangle

Date	Mintage	F12	VF20	XF40	MS60	MS63
2006		PF65 8,000				

KM# 173 100 DOLLARS
1000.00 g., 0.925 Silver 29.548 oz. ASW, 100 mm. **Ruler:** Elizabeth II **Subject:** 500th Anniversary of Discovery **Obv:** Head right **Rev:** Caraval within compass **Shape:** 5-sided

Date	Mintage	F12	VF20	XF40	MS60	MS63
2005	250	PF65 1,150				

KM# 146 300 DOLLARS
155.52 g., 0.9995 Platinum 4.9654 oz. APW, 65 mm. **Ruler:** Elizabeth II **Subject:** Shipwrecks Series **Obv:** Elizabeth II **Rev:** The Mary Celestia **Edge:** Plain **Shape:** Triangular

Date	Mintage	F12	VF20	XF40	MS60	MS63
2006	60	PF65 8,500				

KM# 154 300 DOLLARS
155.52 g., 0.9995 Platinum 4.9654 oz. APW, 65 mm. **Ruler:** Elizabeth II **Subject:** Shipwreck Series **Obv:** Elizabeth II **Rev:** The Constellation **Edge:** Plain **Shape:** Triangular

Date	Mintage	F12	VF20	XF40	MS60	MS63
2006	60	PF65 8,500				

KM# 172 500 DOLLARS
31.11 g., 0.999 Gold 0.9926 oz. AGW, 30.89 mm. **Ruler:** Elizabeth II **Obv:** Queen Elizabeth II **Rev:** Caravel sailing ship in compass face **Edge:** Plain **Shape:** 5-sided **Note:** Bermuda Quincentennial. Prev. KM#160a.

Date	Mintage	F12	VF20	XF40	MS60	MS63
2005	—	PF65 1,800				

KM# 147 600 DOLLARS
1096.00 g., 0.918 Gold 32.1395 oz. AGW, 100 mm. **Ruler:** Elizabeth II **Subject:** Shipwreck Series **Obv:** Elizabeth II **Rev:** The Mary Celestia **Edge:** Plain **Shape:** Triangular

Date	Mintage	F12	VF20	XF40	MS60	MS63
2007	300	PF65 50,000				

KM# 155 600 DOLLARS
1096.00 g., 0.918 Gold 32.1395 oz. AGW, 100 mm. **Ruler:** Elizabeth II **Subject:** Shipwreck Series **Obv:** Elizabeth II **Rev:** The Constellation **Edge:** Plain **Shape:** Triangular

Date	Mintage	F12	VF20	XF40	MS60	MS63
2007	300	PF65 50,000				

PIEDFORT

KM#	Date	Mintage	Identification	Mkt Val
P3	2005	250	5 Dollars 0.925 Silver Gold plated bust and rim Caravel type sailing ship in partially gold plated compass face and rim	—

MINT SETS

KM#	Date	Mintage	Identification	Issue Price	Mkt Val
MS8	2004 (5)	2,300	KM#107-111.	—	10.00

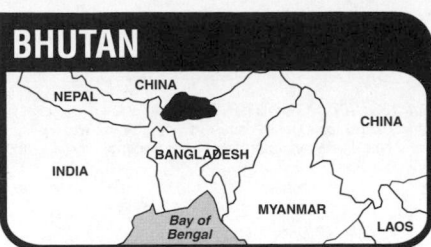

BHUTAN

The Kingdom of Bhutan, a landlocked Himalayan country bordered by Tibet and India, has an area of 18,150 sq. mi. (38,394 sq. km.) and a population of 675,000. Capital: Thimphu. Virtually the entire population is engaged in agricultural and pastoral activities. Rice, wheat, barley, and yak butter are produced in sufficient quantity to make the country self-sufficient in food. The economy of Bhutan is primitive and many transactions are conducted on a barter basis.

RULER
Jigme Singye Wangchuck, 1972-2006
King Jigme Khesar Namgyel Wangchuck, 2006-

KINGDOM
REFORM COINAGE
1974 - 100 Chetrums (Paisa) = 1 Ngultrum (Rupee);
100 Ngultrums = 1 Sertum

X# 105 5 CHETRUMS
3.86 g., Brass, 21.9 mm. **Obv:** Monkey right, date below **Rev:** Effigy of the old "Ma-tam", value below **Edge:** Plain **Note:** This coin is a private issue not authorized by the Royal Monetary Authority of Bhutan

Date	Mintage	F12	VF20	XF40	MS60	MS63
2003		—	—	—	2.00	3.00

KM# 116 NGULTRUM
8.10 g., Nickel Plated Steel **Ruler:** Jigme Khesar Namgyel Wangchuck

Date	Mintage	F12	VF20	XF40	MS60	MS63
2008					5.00	7.00

KM# 115 100 NGULTRUMS
20.20 g., Silver, 38 mm. **Ruler:** Jigme Khesar Namgyel Wangchuck **Subject:** Coronation **Obv:** Portrait left **Rev:** Seal

Date	Mintage	F12	VF20	XF40	MS60	MS63
2008	—	PF63 55.00	PF65 60.00			

KM# 214 100 NGULTRUMS
0.50 g., 0.999 Gold AGW, 11 mm. **Ruler:** Jigme Khesar Namgyel Wangchuck **Subject:** Buddhist Monastery - Taktsang

Date	Mintage	F12	VF20	XF40	MS60	MS63
2010	Est. 5000	PF63 55.00	PF65 60.00			

KM# 224 100 NGULTRUMS
0.50 g., 0.999 Gold AGW, 11 mm. **Ruler:** Jigme Khesar Namgyel Wangchuck **Subject:** Buddhist Monastery - Chorten Kora

Date	Mintage	F12	VF20	XF40	MS60	MS63
2011	Est. 5000	PF63 45.00	PF65 55.00			

KM# 229 100 NGULTRUMS
0.59 g., 0.500 Gold AGW, 11 mm. **Ruler:** Jigme Khesar Namgyel Wangchuck **Subject:** Traditional Archery **Rev:** Archer

Date	Mintage	F12	VF20	XF40	MS60	MS63
2012	7,000	PF63 28.00	PF65 30.00			

KM# 232 100 NGULTRUMS
0.50 g., 0.585 Gold AGW, 11 mm. **Subject:** Mount Everest

Date	Mintage	F12	VF20	XF40	MS60	MS63
2013	Est. 5000	PF63 45.00	PF65 50.00			

KM# 208 200 NGULTRUMS
1.24 g., 0.999 Gold 0.0396 oz. AGW, 13.92 mm. **Ruler:** Jigme Khesar Namgyel Wangchuck **Subject:** Buddha's of the World - Cambodia **Rev:** Head from Angkor Wat

Date	Mintage	F12	VF20	XF40	MS60	MS63
2010	Est. 30000	PF63 80.00	PF65 90.00			

KM# 211 200 NGULTRUMS
1.24 g., 0.999 Gold 0.0396 oz. AGW, 13.92 mm. **Ruler:** Jigme Khesar Namgyel Wangchuck **Subject:** Buddha's of the World - Korea **Rev:** Buddha seated

Date	Mintage	F12	VF20	XF40	MS60	MS63
2010	—	—	—	—	—	90.00

KM# 217 200 NGULTRUMS
1.24 g., 0.999 Gold 0.0396 oz. AGW, 13.92 mm. **Ruler:** Jigme Khesar Namgyel Wangchuck **Subject:** Buddhist World Heritage - Thailand **Rev:** Wat Pho

Date	Mintage	F12	VF20	XF40	MS60	MS63
2011	Est. 30000	—	—	—	—	100

KM# 220 200 NGULTRUMS
1.24 g., 0.999 Gold 0.0396 oz. AGW, 13.92 mm. **Ruler:** Jigme Khesar Namgyel Wangchuck **Subject:** Buddhist World Heritage - China **Rev:** Great Buddha in Leshan

Date	Mintage	F12	VF20	XF40	MS60	MS63
2011	Est. 30000	—	—	—	—	80.00

KM# 181 250 NGULTRUMS
31.11 g., 0.999 Silver 0.9926 oz. ASW, 38.61 mm. **Ruler:** Jigme Singye Wangchuck **Rev:** Sun Yat-Sen bust facing

Date	Mintage	F12	VF20	XF40	MS60	MS63
2003	Est. 4999	PF63 65.00	PF65 70.00			

KM# 185 250 NGULTRUMS
31.11 g., 0.999 Silver 0.9926 oz. ASW, 38.61 mm. **Ruler:** Jigme Singye Wangchuck **Subject:** Wonders of the World - Borobudur Temple in Java

Date	Mintage	F12	VF20	XF40	MS60	MS63
2003	Est. 9999	PF63 60.00	PF65 70.00			

KM# 189 250 NGULTRUMS
31.11 g., 0.999 Silver 0.9926 oz. ASW, 38.61 mm. **Ruler:** Jigme Singye Wangchuck **Subject:** Guanyin, Buddhist godess of mercy

Date	Mintage	F12	VF20	XF40	MS60	MS63
2003	—	PF63 65.00	PF65 70.00			

KM# 191 250 NGULTRUMS
31.11 g., 0.999 Silver 0.9926 oz. ASW, 38.61 mm. **Ruler:** Jigme Singye Wangchuck **Subject:** World Fellowship of Buddhist Youth **Rev:** Lord Buddha, the Enlightenment

Date	Mintage	F12	VF20	XF40	MS60	MS63
2003	Est. 2999	PF63 65.00	PF65 70.00			

KM# 170 250 NGULTRUMS
31.11 g., 0.999 Silver 0.9926 oz. ASW, 38.61 mm. **Ruler:** Jigme Singye Wangchuck **Subject:** Wonders of the World - Pyramids

Date	Mintage	F12	VF20	XF40	MS60	MS63
2004	Est. 4999	PF63 65.00	PF65 70.00			

KM# 172 250 NGULTRUMS
31.11 g., 0.999 Silver 0.9926 oz. ASW, 38.61 mm. **Ruler:** Jigme Singye Wangchuck **Subject:** Wonders of the World - Taj Mahal

Date	Mintage	F12	VF20	XF40	MS60	MS63
2004	Est. 4999	PF63 65.00	PF65 70.00			

KM# 195 250 NGULTRUMS
31.11 g., 0.999 Silver 0.9926 oz. ASW, 38.61 mm. **Ruler:** Jigme Singye Wangchuck **Subject:** Indonesian Games in Palembang **Rev:** Rimau, games mascot

Date	Mintage	F12	VF20	XF40	MS60	MS63
2004	Est. 4999	PF63 65.00	PF65 75.00			

KM# 196 250 NGULTRUMS
31.11 g., 0.999 Silver 0.9926 oz. ASW, 38.61 mm. **Ruler:** Jigme Singye Wangchuck **Subject:** Indonesian Games in Palembang **Rev:** Bridge card hand

Date	Mintage	F12	VF20	XF40	MS60	MS63
2004	4,999	PF63 65.00	PF65 75.00			

KM# 197 250 NGULTRUMS
31.11 g., 0.999 Silver 0.9926 oz. ASW, 38.61 mm. **Ruler:** Jigme Singye Wangchuck **Subject:** Indonesian Games in Palembang **Rev:** Badminton

Date	Mintage	F12	VF20	XF40	MS60	MS63
2004	Est. 4999	PF63 65.00	PF65 75.00			

KM# 198 250 NGULTRUMS
31.11 g., 0.999 Silver 0.9926 oz. ASW, 38.61 mm. **Ruler:** Jigme Singye Wangchuck **Subject:** Indonesian Games in Palembang **Rev:** Sailing

Date	Mintage	F12	VF20	XF40	MS60	MS63
2004	Est. 4999	PF63 65.00	PF65 75.00			

KM# 199 250 NGULTRUMS
31.11 g., 0.999 Silver 0.9926 oz. ASW, 38.61 mm. **Ruler:** Jigme Singye Wangchuck **Subject:** Indonesian Games in Palembang **Rev:** Games logo

Date	Mintage	F12	VF20	XF40	MS60	MS63
2004	Est. 4999	PF63 65.00	PF65 75.00			

KM# 200 250 NGULTRUMS
Bi-Metallic, 38.61 mm. **Ruler:** Jigme Singye Wangchuck **Subject:** Sundial

Date	Mintage	F12	VF20	XF40	MS60	MS63
2004	Est. 9999	—	—	—		125

KM# 201 250 NGULTRUMS
Bi-Metallic, 38.61 mm. **Ruler:** Jigme Singye Wangchuck **Rev:** Compass rose

Date	Mintage	F12	VF20	XF40	MS60	MS63
2004	Est. 9999	—	—	—		125

KM# 207 250 NGULTRUMS
31.11 g., 0.999 Silver 0.9926 oz. ASW, 40.7 mm. **Ruler:** Jigme Khesar Namgyel Wangchuck **Subject:** Buddha's of the World - Cambodia **Rev:** Head from Angkor Wat, in color

Date	Mintage	F12	VF20	XF40	MS60	MS63
2010	Est. 10000	PF63 60.00	PF65 70.00			

KM# 210 250 NGULTRUMS
31.11 g., 0.999 Silver 0.9926 oz. ASW, 40.7 mm. **Ruler:** Jigme Khesar Namgyel Wangchuck **Subject:** Buddha's of the World - Korea **Obv:** Dungkar design in color **Rev:** Buddha seated

Date	Mintage	F12	VF20	XF40	MS60	MS63
2010	Est. 10000	PF63 60.00	PF65 70.00			

KM# 216 250 NGULTRUMS
31.11 g., 0.999 Silver 0.9926 oz. ASW, 40.7 mm. **Ruler:** Jigme Khesar Namgyel Wangchuck **Subject:** Buddhist World heritage - Thailand **Obv:** Dhug in color **Rev:** Wat Pho

Date	Mintage	F12	VF20	XF40	MS60	MS63
2011	Est. 10000	PF63 60.00	PF65 70.00			

KM# 219 250 NGULTRUMS
31.11 g., 0.999 Silver 0.9926 oz. ASW, 40.7 mm. **Ruler:** Jigme Khesar Namgyel Wangchuck **Subject:** Buddhist World Heritage - China **Obv:** Khorto in color **Rev:** Great Buddha in Leshan

Date	Mintage	F12	VF20	XF40	MS60	MS63
2011	Est. 10000	PF63 60.00	PF65 70.00			

KM# 215 300 NGULTRUMS
1.24 g., 0.999 Gold 0.0396 oz. AGW, 13.92 mm. **Ruler:** Jigme Khesar Namgyel Wangchuck **Subject:** Buddhist Monastery - Taktsang

Date	Mintage	F12	VF20	XF40	MS60	MS63
2010	Est. 5000	PF63 85.00	PF65 100			

KM# 226 300 NGULTRUMS
28.28 g., 0.925 Silver 0.8356 oz. ASW, 38.61 mm. **Ruler:** Jigme Khesar Namgyel Wangchuck **Subject:** 2014 Sochi Olympic Games -Cross Country Skiing **Rev:** Two skiers

Date	Mintage	F12	VF20	XF40	MS60	MS63
2012	5,000	PF63 65.00	PF65 70.00			

KM# 227 300 NGULTRUMS
3.11 g., 0.999 Gold 0.0992 oz. AGW, 16.5 mm. **Ruler:** Jigme Khesar Namgyel Wangchuck **Subject:** 2014 FIFA World Cup - Brazil **Rev:** Soccer Player and dragon

Date	Mintage	F12	VF20	XF40	MS60	MS63
2012	1,000	PF65 225				

KM# 228 300 NGULTRUMS
20.00 g., 0.925 Silver 0.591 oz. ASW, 38.61 mm. **Ruler:** Jigme Khesar Namgyel Wangchuck **Subject:** Himalayan Railway **Rev:** Steam Locomotive and outline of mountains

Date	Mintage	F12	VF20	XF40	MS60	MS63
2012	3,000	PF65 60.00				

KM# 230 300 NGULTRUMS
20.00 g., 0.925 Silver 0.591 oz. ASW, 38.61 mm. **Subject:** 2016 Olympics - Table Tennis

Date	Mintage	F12	VF20	XF40	MS60	MS63
2013	Est. 10000	PF63 70.00	PF65 75.00			

KM# 231 300 NGULTRUMS
20.00 g., 0.925 Silver 0.591 oz. ASW, 38.61 mm. **Subject:** 2014 FIFA World Cup Brazil

Date	Mintage	F12	VF20	XF40	MS60	MS63
2013	Est. 10000	PF63 70.00	PF65 75.00			

KM# 233 300 NGULTRUMS
20.00 g., 0.925 Silver 0.591 oz. ASW, 38.61 mm. **Subject:** Kalka Shimla Railway

Date	Mintage	F12	VF20	XF40	MS60	MS63
2013		PF63 70.00	PF65 75.00			

KM# 203 500 NGULTRUM
62.20 g., 0.999 Silver 1.9849 oz. ASW **Ruler:** Jigme Singye Wangchuck **Rev:** Zodiac, partially gilt

Date	Mintage	F12	VF20	XF40	MS60	MS63
2006	—	PF65 110				

KM# 205 500 NGULTRUM
31.11 g., 0.999 Silver 0.9926 oz. ASW, 38.7 mm. **Ruler:** Jigme Khesar Namgyel Wangchuck **Subject:** Coronation

Date	Mintage	F12	VF20	XF40	MS60	MS63
2008	5,000	PF63 75.00	PF65 85.00			

KM# 222 500 NGULTRUM
31.11 g., 0.999 Silver 0.9926 oz. ASW, 40.7 mm. **Ruler:** Jigme Khesar Namgyel Wangchuck **Subject:** Royal Wedding **Rev:** Couple in color

Date	Mintage	F12	VF20	XF40	MS60	MS63
2011	Est. 20000	PF63 135	PF65 150			

KM# 173 1000 NGULTRUM
10.00 g., 0.999 Gold 0.3191 oz. AGW, 26 mm. **Ruler:** Jigme Singye Wangchuck **Subject:** Wonders of the World - Taj Mahal

Date	Mintage	F12	VF20	XF40	MS60	MS63
2002	Est. 3000	PF63 650	PF65 700			

KM# 177 1000 NGULTRUM
10.00 g., 0.999 Gold 0.3191 oz. AGW, 26 mm. **Ruler:** Jigme Singye Wangchuck **Subject:** World Fellowship of Buddhist Youth

Date	Mintage	F12	VF20	XF40	MS60	MS63
2002	Est. 2999	PF63 625	PF65 650			

KM# 182 1000 NGULTRUM
6.22 g., 0.999 Gold 0.1985 oz. AGW, 26 mm. **Ruler:** Jigme Singye Wangchuck **Rev:** Sun Yat-Sen bust facing

Date	Mintage	F12	VF20	XF40	MS60	MS63
2003	Est. 4999	PF63 375	PF65 425			

KM# 183 1000 NGULTRUM
10.00 g., 0.999 Gold 0.3191 oz. AGW, 26 mm. **Ruler:** Jigme Singye Wangchuck **Subject:** Legends of Sports - Rudy Hartono **Rev:** Bust at left, tennis serve at right

Date	Mintage	F12	VF20	XF40	MS60	MS63
2003	Est. 10000	PF63 600	PF65 650			

KM# 186 1000 NGULTRUM
10.00 g., 0.999 Gold 0.3191 oz. AGW, 26 mm. **Ruler:** Jigme Singye Wangchuck **Subject:** Wonders of the World - Borobudur Temple in Java

Date	Mintage	F12	VF20	XF40	MS60	MS63
2003	Est. 9999	PF63 600	PF65 650			

KM# 190 1000 NGULTRUM
10.00 g., 0.999 Gold 0.3191 oz. AGW, 26 mm. **Ruler:** Jigme Singye Wangchuck **Subject:** Guanyin, Buddhist godess of mercy

Date	Mintage	F12	VF20	XF40	MS60	MS63
2003	—	PF63 625	PF65 650			

KM# 192 1000 NGULTRUM
10.00 g., 0.999 Gold 0.3191 oz. AGW, 26 mm. **Ruler:** Jigme Singye Wangchuck **Subject:** World Fellowship of Buddhist Youth **Rev:** Lord Buddha, the Enlightenment

Date	Mintage	F12	VF20	XF40	MS60	MS63
2003	Est. 2999	PF63 625	PF65 650			

KM# 209 1000 NGULTRUM
7.70 g., 0.999 Gold 0.2483 oz. AGW, 22 mm. **Ruler:** Jigme Khesar Namgyel Wangchuck **Subject:** Buddha's of the World - Cambodia **Rev:** Head from Angkor Wat

Date	Mintage	F12	VF20	XF40	MS60	MS63
2010	Est. 6000	PF63 500	PF65 525			

KM# 212 1000 NGULTRUM
7.78 g., 0.999 Gold 0.2483 oz. AGW, 22 mm. **Ruler:** Jigme Khesar Namgyel Wangchuck **Subject:** Buddha's of the World - Korea **Rev:** Buddha seated

Date	Mintage	F12	VF20	XF40	MS60	MS63
2010	Est. 6000	PF63 500	PF65 525			

KM# 213 1000 NGULTRUM
28.28 g., 0.925 Gold 0.8356 oz. AGW, 38.61 mm. **Ruler:** Jigme Khesar Namgyel Wangchuck **Rev:** Charles Lindbergh and Spirit of St. Louis

Date	Mintage	F12	VF20	XF40	MS60	MS63
2010	Est. 5000	PF63 65.00	PF65 70.00			

KM# 218 1000 NGULTRUM
7.78 g., 0.999 Gold 0.2483 oz. AGW, 22 mm. **Ruler:** Jigme Khesar Namgyel Wangchuck **Subject:** Buddhist World Heritage - Thailand **Rev:** Wat Pho

Date	Mintage	F12	VF20	XF40	MS60	MS63
2011	—	PF63 500	PF65 525			

KM# 221 1000 NGULTRUM
7.78 g., 0.999 Gold 0.2483 oz. AGW, 22 mm. **Ruler:** Jigme Khesar Namgyel Wangchuck **Subject:** Buddhist World Heritage - China **Rev:** Great Buddha in Leshan

Date	Mintage	F12	VF20	XF40	MS60	MS63
2011	Est. 6000	PF63 500	PF65 525			

KM# 202 1500 NGULTRUM
155.50 g., 0.999 Silver 4.9623 oz. ASW, 65 mm. **Ruler:** Jigme Singye Wangchuck **Subject:** Wonders of the World - Angkor Wat **Rev:** Angkor Wat temple gilt

Date	Mintage	F12	VF20	XF40	MS60	MS63
2004	—	PF65 250				

KM# 204 1500 NGULTRUM
155.50 g., 0.999 Silver 4.9623 oz. ASW, 65 mm. **Ruler:** Jigme Singye Wangchuck **Subject:** Year of the Dog

Date	Mintage	F12	VF20	XF40	MS60	MS63
2006	Est. 8888	PF63 230	PF65 250			

KM# 167 2000 NGULTRUMS
20.00 g., 0.999 Gold 0.6382 oz. AGW, 33 mm. **Ruler:** Jigme Singye Wangchuck **Subject:** Year of the Horse

Date	Mintage	F12	VF20	XF40	MS60	MS63
2002	—	PF63 1,100	PF65 1,250			

KM# 171 2000 NGULTRUMS
Bi-Metallic **Ruler:** Jigme Singye Wangchuck **Subject:** Wonders of the World - Pyramids

Date	Mintage	F12	VF20	XF40	MS60	MS63
2002	Est. 9999	PF65 550				

KM# 193 2000 NGULTRUMS
20.00 g., 0.999 Gold 0.6382 oz. AGW, 26 mm. **Ruler:** Jigme Singye Wangchuck **Subject:** World Fellowship of Buddhist Youth **Rev:** Lord Buddha, the Enlightenment

Date	Mintage	F12	VF20	XF40	MS60	MS63
2003	—	PF63 1,100	PF65 1,250			

KM# 165 3000 NGULTRUM
31.11 g., 0.999 Gold 0.9926 oz. AGW, 38.61 mm. **Ruler:** Jigme Singye Wangchuck **Subject:** Year of the Snake

Date	Mintage	F12	VF20	XF40	MS60	MS63
2001	Est. 18888	PF63 1,600	PF65 1,750			

KM# 168 3000 NGULTRUM
31.11 g., 0.999 Gold 0.9926 oz. AGW, 38.61 mm. **Ruler:** Jigme Singye Wangchuck **Subject:** Year of the Horse

Date	Mintage	F12	VF20	XF40	MS60	MS63
2002	Est. 18888	PF63 1,600	PF65 1,750			

KM# 174 3000 NGULTRUM
31.11 g., 0.999 Gold 0.9926 oz. AGW, 38.61 mm. **Ruler:** Jigme Singye Wangchuck **Subject:** Wonders of the World - Taj Mahal

Date	Mintage	F12	VF20	XF40	MS60	MS63
2002	Est. 18888	PF63 1,600	PF65 1,750			

KM# 175 3000 NGULTRUM
31.11 g., 0.999 Gold 0.9926 oz. AGW, 38.61 mm. **Ruler:** Jigme Singye Wangchuck **Subject:** Royal Society for the Protection of Nature, 15th Anniversary **Rev:** Elephant head

Date	Mintage	F12	VF20	XF40	MS60	MS63
2002	Est. 10000	PF63 1,650	PF65 1,800			

KM# 176 3000 NGULTRUM
31.11 g., 0.999 Gold 0.9926 oz. AGW, 38.61 mm. **Ruler:** Jigme Singye Wangchuck **Subject:** Royal Society for the Protection of Nature, 15th Anniversary **Rev:** Two tigers

Date	Mintage	F12	VF20	XF40	MS60	MS63
2002	Est. 10000	PF63 1,650	PF65 1,800			

KM# 170 3000 NGULTRUM
31.11 g., 0.999 Gold 0.9926 oz. AGW, 38.61 mm. **Ruler:** Jigme Singye Wangchuck **Subject:** World Fellowship of Buddhist Youth

Date	Mintage	F12	VF20	XF40	MS60	MS63
2002	Est. 10000	PF63 1,650	PF65 1,800			

KM# 179 3000 NGULTRUM
31.11 g., 0.999 Gold 0.9926 oz. AGW, 38.61 mm. **Ruler:** Jigme Singye Wangchuck **Subject:** Year of the Goat **Rev:** Three rams

Date	Mintage	F12	VF20	XF40	MS60	MS63
2003 Proof	Est. 18888	—	—	—	—	1,800

KM# 184 3000 NGULTRUM
31.11 g., 0.999 Gold 0.9926 oz. AGW, 38.61 mm. **Ruler:** Jigme Singye Wangchuck **Subject:** Legends of Sport - Rudy Hartono **Rev:** Bust at left, tennis serve at right

Date	Mintage	F12	VF20	XF40	MS60	MS63
2003	Est. 10000	PF63 1,650	PF65 1,800			

KM# 187 3000 NGULTRUM
31.11 g., 0.999 Gold 0.9926 oz. AGW, 38.61 mm. **Ruler:** Jigme Singye Wangchuck **Subject:** Wonders of the World - Borobudur Temple in Java

Date	Mintage	F12	VF20	XF40	MS60	MS63
2003	Est. 30000	PF63 1,600	PF65 1,750			

KM# 194 3000 NGULTRUM
31.11 g., 0.999 Gold 0.9926 oz. AGW, 38.61 mm. **Ruler:** Jigme Singye Wangchuck **Subject:** World Fellowship of Buddhist Youth **Rev:** Lord Buddha, the Enlightenment

Date	Mintage	F12	VF20	XF40	MS60	MS63
2003	—	PF63 1,600	PF65 1,750			

KM# 166 20000 NGULTRUM
155.52 g., 0.999 Gold 4.9629 oz. AGW, 65 mm. **Ruler:** Jigme Singye Wangchuck **Subject:** Year of the Snake

Date	Mintage	F12	VF20	XF40	MS60	MS63
2001	—	PF65 9,000				

KM# 169 20000 NGULTRUM
155.52 g., 0.999 Gold 4.9629 oz. AGW, 65 mm. **Ruler:** Jigme Singye Wangchuck **Subject:** Year of the Horse

Date	Mintage	F12	VF20	XF40	MS60	MS63
2002	—	PF65 9,000				

KM# 180 20000 NGULTRUM
155.52 g., 0.999 Gold 4.9629 oz. AGW, 65 mm. **Ruler:** Jigme Singye Wangchuck **Subject:** Year of the Goat **Rev:** Three rams

Date	Mintage	F12	VF20	XF40	MS60	MS63
2003	Est. 88	PF65 9,000				

KM# 188 30000 NGULTRUM
155.52 g., 0.999 Gold 4.9629 oz. AGW, 65 mm. **Ruler:** Jigme Singye Wangchuck **Subject:** Wonders of the World - Borobudur Temple in Java

Date	Mintage	F12	VF20	XF40	MS60	MS63
2003	—	PF65 9,000				

KM# 223 100000 NGULTRUM
1000.00 g., 0.999 Silver 31.9118 oz. ASW, 100 mm. **Ruler:** Jigme Khesar Namgyel Wangchuck **Subject:** Royal Wedding **Rev:** Couple

Date	Mintage	F12	VF20	XF40	MS60	MS63
2011	2	PF65 2,000				

KM# 225 5 SERTRUMS
7.78 g., 0.585 Gold 0.1454 oz. AGW, 25 mm. **Ruler:** Jigme Khesar Namgyel Wangchuck **Subject:** 2012 London Olympics - Archery **Rev:** Two archers and target

Date	Mintage	F12	VF20	XF40	MS60	MS63
2012	1,000	PF65 325				

KM# 206 10 SERTUM
31.11 g., 0.999 Gold 0.9926 oz. AGW, 38.7 mm. **Ruler:** Jigme Khesar Namgyel Wangchuck **Subject:** Coronation

Date	Mintage	F12	VF20	XF40	MS60	MS63
2008	1,000	PF65 1,800				

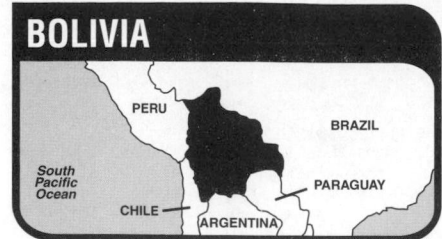

BOLIVIA

The Plurinational State of Bolivia, a landlocked country in west central South America, has an area of 424,165 sq. mi. (1,098,580 sq. km.) and a population of *8.33 million. Its capitals are: La Paz (administrative) and Sucre (constitutional). Principal exports are tin, zinc, antimony, tungsten, petroleum, natural gas, cotton and coffee.

MINT MARK
SA - Paris
(a) - Paris, privy marks only
CHI - Valcambia
H - Heaton
KN - Kings' Norton

REPUBLIC
REFORM COINAGE
1987-; 1,000,000 Peso Bolivianos = 1 Boliviano;
100 Centavos = 1 Boliviano

KM# 202 10 CENTAVOS
1.85 g., Stainless Steel, 19 mm. **Obv:** National arms, star below **Rev:** Denomination within circle, date below

Date	Mintage	F12	VF20	XF40	MS60	MS63
2006	—	—	—	0.20	0.50	0.70

KM# 213 10 CENTAVOS
1.85 g., Copper Clad Steel, 19 mm. **Obv:** National arms **Rev:** Value

Date	Mintage	F12	VF20	XF40	MS60	MS63
2001	—	—	—	—	0.50	1.00
2006	—	—	—	—	0.50	1.00
2008	—	—	—	—	0.50	1.00

Note: Slim and round "0" varieties in 10

KM# 214 10 CENTAVOS
1.85 g., Copper Plated Steel, 19 mm. **Obv:** National arms **Obv. Legend:** ESTADO PLURINACIONAL DE BOLIVIA **Rev:** Value

Date	Mintage	F12	VF20	XF40	MS60	MS63
2010	—	—	—	—	0.10	0.20

KM# 203 20 CENTAVOS
3.25 g., Stainless Steel, 22 mm. **Obv:** National arms, star below **Obv. Legend:** REPUBLICA DE BOLIVIA **Rev:** Denomination within circle, date below **Rev. Legend:** LA UNION ES LA FUERZA **Edge:** Plain

Date	Mintage	F12	VF20	XF40	MS60	MS63
2001	—	—	—	0.25	0.60	0.80
2006	—	—	—	0.25	0.60	0.80
2008	—	—	—	0.25	0.60	0.80

KM# 215 20 CENTAVOS
3.25 g., Stainless Steel, 22 mm. **Obv:** National arms **Obv. Legend:** ESTADO PLURINACIONAL DE BOLIVIA **Rev:** Value

Date	Mintage	F12	VF20	XF40	MS60	MS63
2010	—	—	—	—	0.15	0.25

KM# 204 50 CENTAVOS
3.75 g., Stainless Steel, 24 mm. **Obv:** National arms, star below **Obv. Legend:** REPUBLICA DE BOLIVIA **Rev:** Denomination within circle, date below **Rev. Legend:** LA UNION ES LA FUERZA **Edge:** Plain

Date	Mintage	F12	VF20	XF40	MS60	MS63
2001	—	—	—	0.30	0.75	1.00

Note: Small and large 50 variety

2006	—	—	—	0.30	0.75	1.00
2008	—	—	—	0.30	0.75	1.00

KM# 216 50 CENTAVOS
3.75 g., Stainless Steel, 24 mm. **Obv:** National arms **Obv. Legend:** ESTADO PLURINACIONAL DE BOLIVIA **Rev:** Value

Date	Mintage	F12	VF20	XF40	MS60	MS63
2010	—	—	—	—	0.50	1.00

KM# 205 BOLIVIANO
5.00 g., Stainless Steel, 27 mm. **Obv:** National arms, star below **Obv. Legend:** REPUBLICA DE BOLIVIA **Rev:** Denomination within circle, date below sprays **Rev. Legend:** LA UNION ES LA FUERZA **Edge:** Plain

Date	Mintage	F12	VF20	XF40	MS60	MS63
2001	—	—	—	0.35	0.90	1.20
2004	—	—	—	0.35	0.90	1.20
2008	—	—	—	0.35	0.90	1.20

KM# 217 BOLIVIANO
5.00 g., Stainless Steel, 27 mm. **Obv:** National arms **Obv. Legend:** ESTADO PLURINACIONAL DE BOLIVIA **Rev:** Value

Date	Mintage	F12	VF20	XF40	MS60	MS63
2010	—	—	—	—	1.50	2.00

KM# 206.2 2 BOLIVIANOS
6.25 g., Stainless Steel, 27 mm. **Obv:** National arms, star below **Rev:** Denomination within circle, date below **Note:** Increased size.

Date	Mintage	F12	VF20	XF40	MS60	MS63
2008	—	—	—	—	2.00	3.00

KM# 218 2 BOLIVIANOS
6.25 g., Stainless Steel, 27 mm. **Obv:** National arms **Obv. Legend:** ESTADO PLURINACIONAL DE BOLIVIA **Rev:** Value

Date	Mintage	F12	VF20	XF40	MS60	MS63
2010	—	—	—	—	1.50	2.00
2012	—	—	—	—	1.50	2.00

KM# 212 5 BOLIVIANOS
5.00 g., Bi-Metallic, 23 mm. **Obv:** National arms **Obv. Legend:** REPUBLICA DE BOLIVIA **Rev:** Denomination **Rev. Legend:** LA UNION ES LA FUERZA **Edge:** Reeded

Date	Mintage	F12	VF20	XF40	MS60	MS63
2001	—	—	—	0.90	2.25	3.00
2004	—	—	—	0.90	2.25	3.00

KM# 219 5 BOLIVIANOS
5.00 g., Bi-Metallic, 23 mm. **Obv:** National arms **Obv. Legend:** ESTADO PLURINACIONAL DE BOLIVIA **Rev:** Value **Edge:** Reeded

Date	Mintage	F12	VF20	XF40	MS60	MS63
2010	—	—	—	—	4.00	5.00

BOSNIA - HERZEGOVINA

The Republic of Bosnia and Herzegovina borders Croatia to the north and west, Serbia to the east and Montenegro in the southeast with only 12.4 mi. of coastline. The total land area is 19,735 sq. mi. (51,129 sq. km.). They have a population of *4.34 million. Capital: Sarajevo. Electricity, mining and agriculture are leading industries.

MONETARY SYSTEM
1 Convertible Marka = 100 Convertible Feniga =
1 Deutschemark 1998-
NOTE: Euros circulate freely.

REPUBLIC
REFORM COINAGE
1998-

KM# 121 5 FENINGA
2.66 g., Nickel Plated Steel, 18 mm. **Obv:** Denomination on map **Rev:** Triangle and stars **Edge:** Reeded

Date	Mintage	F12	VF20	XF40	MS60	MS63
2005	—	—	—	—	1.00	1.25
2008	—	—	—	—	1.00	1.25
2011	—	—	—	—	1.00	1.25

KM# 115 10 FENINGA
3.90 g., Copper Plated Steel, 20 mm. **Obv:** Denomination on map within circle **Rev:** Triangle and stars, date at left within circle **Edge:** Plain

Date	Mintage	F12	VF20	XF40	MS60	MS63
2004	—	—	—	—	0.50	0.75
2007	—	—	—	—	0.50	0.75
2008	—	—	—	—	0.50	0.75
2011	—	—	—	—	0.50	0.75

KM# 116 20 FENINGA
4.50 g., Copper Plated Steel, 22 mm. **Obv:** Denomination on map within circle **Rev:** Triangle and stars, date at left within circle **Edge:** Reeded

Date	Mintage	F12	VF20	XF40	MS60	MS63
2004	—	—	—	—	1.00	1.25
2007	—	—	—	—	1.00	1.25
2008	—	—	—	—	1.00	1.25
2009	—	—	—	—	1.00	1.25

KM# 117 50 FENINGA
5.15 g., Copper Plated Steel, 24 mm. **Obv:** Denomination on map within circle **Rev:** Triangle and stars, date at left within circle

Date	Mintage	F12	VF20	XF40	MS60	MS63
2007	—	—	—	—	—	3.00

KM# 118 KONVERTIBLE MARKA
4.95 g., Nickel Plated Steel, 23.23 mm. **Obv:** Denomination **Rev:** Coat of arms above date **Edge:** Segmented reeding

Date	Mintage	F12	VF20	XF40	MS60	MS63
2002	—	—	—	—	5.50	6.00
2003	—	—	—	—	5.50	6.00
2004	—	—	—	—	5.50	6.00
2006	—	—	—	—	4.00	5.00
2007	—	—	—	—	4.00	5.00
2008	—	—	—	—	4.00	5.00
2009	—	—	—	—	4.00	5.00

KM# 119 2 KONVERTIBLE MARKA
6.90 g., Bi-Metallic, 25.75 mm. **Obv:** Denomination within circle **Rev:** Dove of Peace, date at right within circle **Edge:** Segmented reeding

Date	Mintage	F12	VF20	XF40	MS60	MS63
2002	—	—	—	—	13.50	15.00
2003	—	—	—	—	13.50	15.00
2008	—	—	—	—	13.50	15.00

KM# 120 5 KONVERTIBLE MARKA
10.35 g., Bi-Metallic, 30 mm. **Obv:** Denomination within circle **Rev:** Dove of Peace in flight **Edge:** Reeded

Date	Mintage	F12	VF20	XF40	MS60	MS63
2005	—	—	—	—	17.50	20.00
2009	—	—	—	—	17.50	20.00

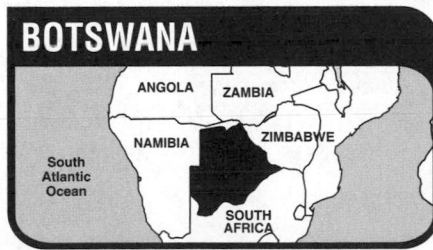

BOTSWANA

The Republic of Botswana (formerly Bechuanaland), located in south central Africa between Namibia and Zimbabwe, has an area of 224,607 sq. mi. (600,370 sq. km.) and a population of *1.62 million. Capital: Gaborone. Botswana is a member of a Customs Union with South Africa, Lesotho, and Swaziland. The economy is primarily pastoral with a rapidly developing mining industry, of which diamonds, copper and nickel are the chief elements. Meat products and diamonds comprise 85 percent of the exports.

Botswana is a member of the Commonwealth of Nations. The president is Chief of State and Head of government.

MINT MARK
B - Berne

MONETARY SYSTEM
100 Cents = 1 Thebe

REPUBLIC
REFORM COINAGE
100 Thebe = 1 Pula

KM# 26 5 THEBE
2.41 g., Copper Plated Steel, 16.9 mm. **Obv:** National arms, date below **Rev:** Toko bird left, value above **Rev. Designer:** Mike Hibbit **Edge:** Plain **Shape:** 7-sided

Date	Mintage	F12	VF20	XF40	MS60	MS63
2002	—	—	—	0.25	0.50	1.00
2007	—	—	—	0.25	0.50	1.00
2009	—	—	—	0.25	0.50	1.00

KM# 27 10 THEBE
2.80 g., Nickel Plated Steel, 18 mm. **Obv:** National arms above date **Rev:** South African Oryx right, value above **Rev. Designer:** Mike Hibbit

Date	Mintage	F12	VF20	XF40	MS60	MS63
2002	—	—	—	0.30	0.75	1.25
2008	—	—	—	0.30	0.75	1.25

KM# 28 25 THEBE
3.50 g., Nickel Plated Steel, 21 mm. **Obv:** National arms, date below **Rev:** Zebu left, value above **Rev. Designer:** Mike Hibbit **Shape:** 7-sided

Date	Mintage	F12	VF20	XF40	MS60	MS63
2007	—	—	0.30	0.60	1.50	2.00
2009	—	—	0.30	0.60	1.50	2.00

KM# 29 50 THEBE
4.82 g., Nickel Plated Steel, 21.5 mm. **Obv:** National arms, date below **Rev:** African Fish Eagle left, value above **Rev. Designer:** Mike Hibbit

Date	Mintage	F12	VF20	XF40	MS60	MS63
2001	—	—	0.50	1.00	2.00	2.50

KM# 24 PULA
8.70 g., Nickel-Brass, 23.5 mm. **Obv:** National arms, date below **Rev:** Zebra left, denomination above **Rev. Designer:** Mike Hibbit **Shape:** 7-sided

Date	Mintage	F12	VF20	XF40	MS60	MS63
2007	—	—	1.00	1.75	3.50	6.00

KM# 25a 2 PULA
6.00 g., Brass Plated Steel, 24.5 mm. **Subject:** Wildlife **Obv:** National arms, date below **Rev:** Rhinoceros left, denomination above **Shape:** 7-sided

Date	Mintage	F12	VF20	XF40	MS60	MS63
2004	—	—	—	—	2.75	3.50

KM# 30 5 PULA
6.20 g., Bi-Metallic, 23.4 mm. **Obv:** National arms, date below **Rev:** Mophane worm on a mophane leaf, denomination below within circle **Edge:** Reeded

Date	Mintage	F12	VF20	XF40	MS60	MS63
2007	—	—	—	—	6.50	10.00

BRAZIL

The Federative Republic of Brazil, which comprises half the continent of South America and is the only Latin American country deriving its culture and language from Portugal, has an area of 3,286,488 sq. mi. (8,511,965 sq. km.) and a population of *169.2 million. Capital: Brasilia. The economy of Brazil is as varied and complex as any in the developing world. Agriculture is a mainstay of the economy, while only 4 percent of the area is under cultivation. Known mineral resources are almost unlimited in variety and size of reserves. A large, relatively sophisticated industry ranges from basic steel and chemical production to finished consumer goods. Coffee, cotton, iron ore and cocoa are the chief exports.

MINT MARKS
(a) - Paris, privy marks only
B - Bahia

REPUBLIC
REFORM COINAGE
2750 Cruzeiros Reais = 1 Real;
100 Centavos = 1 Real
1994-present

KM# 647 CENTAVO
2.43 g., Copper Plated Steel, 17 mm. **Obv:** Cabral bust at right **Rev:** Denomination on linear design at left, 3/4 globe with sash on right, date below **Edge:** Plain

Date	Mintage	F12	VF20	XF40	MS60	MS63
2001	242,924,000	—	—	—	0.10	0.20
2002	161,824,000	—	—	—	0.10	0.20
2003	250,000,000	—	—	—	0.10	0.20
2004	167,232,000	—	—	—	0.10	0.20

KM# 648 5 CENTAVOS
4.10 g., Copper Plated Steel, 22 mm. **Obv:** Tiradente bust at right, dove at left **Rev:** Denomination on linear design at left, 3/4 globe with sash on right, date below **Edge:** Plain

Date	Mintage	F12	VF20	XF40	MS60	MS63
2001	175,940,000	—	—	—	0.45	0.65
2002	153,088,000	—	—	—	0.45	0.65
2003	260,000,000	—	—	—	0.45	0.65
2004	262,656,000	—	—	—	0.45	0.65
2005	230,144,000	—	—	—	0.45	0.65
2006	255,488,000	—	—	—	0.45	0.65
2007	403,968,000	—	—	—	0.45	0.65
2008	28,672,000	—	—	—	0.45	0.65
2009	400,128,000	—	—	—	0.30	0.50
2010	550,144,000	—	—	—	0.30	0.50
2011	437,504,000	—	—	—	0.30	0.50
2012	400,128,000	—	—	—	0.30	0.50
2013	—	—	—	—	0.30	0.50

KM# 649.2 10 CENTAVOS
4.80 g., Bronze Plated Steel, 20 mm. **Obv:** Bust of Pedro at right, horseman with sword in right hand at left **Rev:** Denomination on linear design at left, 3/4 globe with sash on right, date below **Edge:** Reeded

Date	Mintage	F12	VF20	XF40	MS60	MS63
2001	134,701,000	—	—	—	0.60	0.80
2002	172,032,000	—	—	—	0.60	0.80
2003	252,666,000	—	—	—	0.60	0.80
2004	348,480,000	—	—	—	0.60	0.80
2005	362,112,000	—	—	—	0.60	0.80
2006	265,728,000	—	—	—	0.60	0.80
2007	316,800,000	—	—	—	0.60	0.80
2008	534,412,000	—	—	—	0.50	0.75
2009	205,748,000	—	—	—	0.50	0.75
2010	520,128,000	—	—	—	0.50	0.75
2011	415,104,000	—	—	—	0.50	0.75
2012	454,464,000	—	—	—	0.50	0.75
2013	380,352,000	—	—	—	0.50	0.75

KM# 650 25 CENTAVOS
7.55 g., Bronze Plated Steel, 25 mm. **Obv:** Deodoro bust at right, national arms at left **Rev:** Denomination on linear design at left, 3/4 globe with sash on right, date below **Edge:** Reeded

Date	Mintage	F12	VF20	XF40	MS60	MS63
2001	92,642,000	—	—	—	0.75	1.00
2002	100,096,000	—	—	—	0.75	1.00
2003	147,200,000	—	—	—	0.75	1.00
2004	160,000,000	—	—	—	0.75	1.00
2005	100,096,000	—	—	—	0.75	1.00
2006	110,720,000	—	—	—	0.75	1.00
2007	118,784,000	—	—	—	0.75	1.00
2008	269,031,000	—	—	—	0.60	0.75
2009	200,985,000	—	—	—	0.60	0.75
2010	240,000,000	—	—	—	0.60	0.75
2011	142,592,000	—	—	—	0.60	0.75
2012	100,096,000	—	—	—	0.60	0.75
2013	190,976,000	—	—	—	0.60	0.75

KM# 651 50 CENTAVOS
9.25 g., Copper-Nickel, 23 mm. **Obv:** Rio Branco bust at right, map at left **Rev:** Denomination on linear design at left, 3/4 globe with sash on right, date below **Edge Lettering:** BRASIL ORDEM E PROGRESSO

Date	Mintage	F12	VF20	XF40	MS60	MS63
2001	14,735,000	—	—	—	1.50	1.75

KM# 651a 50 CENTAVOS
6.80 g., Stainless Steel, 23 mm. **Obv:** Rio Branco bust at right, map at left **Rev:** Denomination on linear design at left, 3/4 globe with sash on right, date below **Edge Lettering:** BRASIL ORDEM E PROGRESSO

Date	Mintage	F12	VF20	XF40	MS60	MS63
2002	189,952,000	—	—	—	1.25	1.50
2003	143,696,000	—	—	—	1.25	1.50
2005	122,416,000	—	—	—	1.25	1.50
2006	39,984,000	—	—	—	1.25	1.50
2007	130,032,000	—	—	—	1.25	1.50
2008	290,080,000	—	—	—	1.25	1.50
2009	300,048,000	—	—	—	1.25	1.50
2010	170,016,000	—	—	—	1.25	1.50
2011	116,928,000	—	—	—	1.25	1.50
2012	100,016,000	—	—	—	1.25	1.50
2013	259,728,000	—	—	—	1.25	1.50

KM# 683 50 CENTAVOS
6.80 g., Stainless Steel, 23 mm. **Obv:** Rio Branco bust at right, map at left **Rev:** Denomination on linear design at left, 3/4 globe with sash on right, date below **Edge Lettering:** BRASIL ORDEM E PROGRESSO **Note:** Mule with the reverse for the 5 centavos coin on the 50 centavos planchet.

Date	Mintage	F12	VF20	XF40	MS60	MS63
2012	—	—	—	—	—	250

KM# 652a REAL
7.00 g., Bi-Metallic, 27 mm. **Obv:** Allegorical portrait **Rev:** Denomination on linear design at left, 3/4 globe with sash on right, date below **Edge:** Segmented reeding

Date	Mintage	F12	VF20	XF40	MS60	MS63
2002	54,192,000	—	—	—	3.00	4.00
2003	100,000,000	—	—	—	3.00	4.00
2004	150,016,000	—	—	—	3.00	4.00

Date	Mintage	F12	VF20	XF40	MS60	MS63
2005	43,776,000	—	—	—	3.00	4.00
2006	179,968,000	—	—	—	2.00	2.50
2007	275,712,000	—	—	—	2.00	2.50
2008	664,833,000	—	—	—	2.00	2.50
2009	245,247,000	—	—	—	1.50	2.00
2010	220,032,000	—	—	—	1.50	2.00
2011	140,032,000	—	—	—	1.50	2.00
2012	150,016,000	—	—	—	1.50	2.00
2013	263,936,000	—	—	—	1.50	2.00
2014	150,016,000	—	—	—	1.50	2.00

KM# 656 REAL
7.00 g., Bi-Metallic, 27 mm. **Subject:** Centennial of Juscelino Kubitschek, president **Obv:** Head left **Obv. Designer:** Alzira Duim **Rev:** Denomination on linear design at left, 3/4 globe with sash on right, date below **Edge:** Segmented reeding

Date	Mintage	F12	VF20	XF40	MS60	MS63
2002	50,000,000	—	—	—	3.50	4.50

KM# 668 REAL
7.00 g., Bi-Metallic, 27 mm. **Subject:** 40th Anniversary of Central Bank **Obv:** Monument **Rev:** Value on flag **Edge:** Segmented reeding

Date	Mintage	F12	VF20	XF40	MS60	MS63
2005	40,000,000	—	—	—	5.00	6.50

KM# 679 REAL
7.00 g., Bi-Metallic, 27 mm. **Subject:** Olympic Flag Delivery London 2012 - Rio 2016 **Obv:** Monument **Obv. Legend:** ENTREGA DA BANDEIRA OLIMPICA, LONDRES 2012 - RIO 2016 **Rev:** Value on flag **Edge:** Segmented Reeding

Date	Mintage	F12	VF20	XF40	MS60	MS63
2012	1,952,000	—	—	—	5.00	6.50

KM# 657 2 REAIS
28.00 g., 0.999 Silver 0.8935 oz. ASW, 40 mm. **Subject:** Centennial - Carlos Drummond de Andrade **Obv:** Denomination and writer **Rev:** Stylized portrait **Edge:** Reeded

Date	Mintage	F12	VF20	XF40	MS60	MS63
ND(2002)	4,693	PF63 65.00	PF65 75.00			

KM# 658 2 REAIS
28.00 g., 0.999 Silver 0.8935 oz. ASW, 40 mm. **Subject:** Centennial - Juscelino Kubitschek **Obv:** Bust facing in upper right, initials at left **Rev:** Denomination **Edge:** Reeded

Date	Mintage	F12	VF20	XF40	MS60	MS63
2002	8,476	PF63 55.00	PF65 65.00			

KM# 663 2 REAIS
27.00 g., 0.925 Silver 0.7978 oz. ASW, 40 mm. **Obv:** Value and piano player **Rev:** Ary Barroso singing **Edge:** Reeded

Date	Mintage	F12	VF20	XF40	MS60	MS63
2003	3,663	PF63 55.00	PF65 65.00			

KM# 665 2 REAIS
27.00 g., 0.925 Silver 0.7978 oz. ASW, 40 mm. **Subject:** Centennial - Cándido Con Portinari **Obv:** Starving family scene, value and country name **Rev:** Portinari's portrait, stars in squares design **Edge:** Reeded

Date	Mintage	F12	VF20	XF40	MS60	MS63
ND(2003)	2,000	PF63 325	PF65 350			

KM# 666 2 REAIS
27.00 g., 0.925 Silver 0.7978 oz. ASW, 40 mm. **Subject:** FIFA Centennial **Obv:** Soccer ball and value **Rev:** Center part of a Brazilian flag and stars **Edge:** Reeded

Date	Mintage	F12	VF20	XF40	MS60	MS63
2004	12,166	PF63 150	PF65 175			

KM# 671 2 REAIS
27.00 g., 0.925 Silver 0.7978 oz. ASW, 40 mm. **Subject:** Centennial of Flight 14 bis **Obv:** Image of 14 Bis **Obv. Legend:** Centenario Do Voo Do 14 Bis Brasil 1906-2006 **Rev:** Image and signature of Santos Dumont and value **Edge:** Reeded

Date	Mintage	F12	VF20	XF40	MS60	MS63
2006	4,000	PF63 95.00	PF65 110			

KM# 672 2 REAIS
10.17 g., Copper-Nickel, 30 mm. **Subject:** Pan-American Games XV **Obv:** Official logo of Pan-American Games XV **Rev:** Image of running athlete, XV Jogos Pan-Americanos, value, Brasil and date. **Edge:** Reeded

Date	Mintage	F12	VF20	XF40	MS60	MS63
2007	10,000	—	—	—	—	12.00

KM# 675 2 REAIS
10.17 g., Copper-Nickel, 30 mm. **Subject:** Japanese immigration to Brazil, 100th Anniversary **Obv:** Farmer and persimmon crop **Rev:** Ship "Kasato Maru **Edge:** Reeded

Date	Mintage	F12	VF20	XF40	MS60	MS63
2008	10,000	—	—	—	—	16.00

KM# 684 5 REAIS
27.00 g., 0.925 Silver 0.7978 oz. ASW, 40 mm. **Subject:** UNESCO World Heritage Site - Diamantina **Obv:** Musicians on balcony of historic house **Rev:** House of Glory footbridge

Date	Mintage	F12	VF20	XF40	MS60	MS63
2013	3,000	PF63 85.00	PF65 100			

KM# 661 5 REAIS
28.00 g., 0.999 Silver 0.8935 oz. ASW, 40 mm. **Subject:** Brazil's 5th World Cup Championship **Obv:** Soccer ball and value **Rev:** Soccer ball and value **Edge:** Reeded

Date	Mintage	F12	VF20	XF40	MS60	MS63
2002	10,149	PF63 60.00	PF65 65.00			

KM# 673 5 REAIS
27.00 g., 0.925 Silver 0.7978 oz. ASW, 40 mm. **Subject:** Pan-American Games XV **Obv:** Official logo of Pan-American Games XV **Rev:** Sugar Loaf, lines of Copacabana sidewalk, "XV Jogos Pan-Americanos", value, Brasil and date. **Edge:** Reeded

Date	Mintage	F12	VF20	XF40	MS60	MS63
2007	4,000	PF63 60.00	PF65 70.00			

KM# 674 5 REAIS
27.00 g., 0.925 Silver 0.7978 oz. ASW, 40 mm. **Subject:** Royal Family's arrival in Brazil, 200th Anniversary **Obv:** Ship "Martim de Freitas **Rev:** Names and dates of institutions created by Dom John **Edge:** Reeded

Date	Mintage	F12	VF20	XF40	MS60	MS63
2008	2,000	PF63 275	PF65 300			

KM# 676 5 REAIS
27.00 g., 0.925 Silver 0.7978 oz. ASW, 40 mm. **Subject:** World Heritage Sites, Brasilia, 50th Anniversary **Obv:** Schematic city plan **Rev:** Brasilia's architecture montage: Congress, Cathedral, Presidential palace and Warriors sculpture **Edge:** Reeded

Date	Mintage	F12	VF20	XF40	MS60	MS63
2010	6,000	PF63 95.00	PF65 110			

KM# 677 5 REAIS
27.00 g., 0.925 Silver 0.7978 oz. ASW, 40 mm. **Subject:** 2010 World Cup, South Africa **Obv:** Two players with soccer ball, Brazil flag in background **Rev:** Map of Africa, South african savannah, soccer player at left **Edge:** Reeded

Date	Mintage	F12	VF20	XF40	MS60	MS63
2010	9,000	PF63 85.00	PF65 110			

KM# 678 5 REAIS
27.00 g., 0.925 Silver 0.7978 oz. ASW, 40 mm. **Subject:** UNESCO World Heritage site. 300th Anniversary of the Foundling of the Pilar Vila Rica of Ouro Preto **Obv:** Houses and churches representing the city's architecture **Rev:** Three angels and baroque scrolls **Rev. Legend:** PATRIMONIO DA HUMANIDADE • UNESCO OURO PRETO and BRAZIL **Edge:** Reeded

Date	Mintage	F12	VF20	XF40	MS60	MS63
2011	2,000	PF65 150				

KM# 680 5 REAIS
27.00 g., 0.925 Silver 0.7978 oz. ASW, 40 mm. **Subject:** Delivery of Olympic Flag London 2012 - Rio 2016 **Obv:** Olympic flag, logo of 2016 Rio de Janeiro Olympic games, legend, date **Obv. Legend:** ENTREGA DA BANDEIRA OLIMPICA **Rev:** Illustration illuding to London's Tower Bridge, Rio de Janeiro's Christ the Redeemer statue, legend, denomination, country name **Rev. Legend:** LONDRES 2012 - RIO 2016 **Edge:** Reeded

Date	Mintage	F12	VF20	XF40	MS60	MS63
2012	6,000	PF63 95.00	PF65 110			

KM# 681 5 REAIS
27.00 g., 0.925 Silver 0.7978 oz. ASW, 40 mm. **Subject:** International Year of Cooperatives **Obv:** Official logo of International Year of Cooperatives, legend, date **Obv. Legend:** ANO INTERNACTIONAL DAS COOPERATIVAS **Rev:** Globe supported by three pairs of hands, legend, denomination, country name **Rev. Legend:** COOPERATIVAS CONSTROEM UM MUNDO MELHOR **Edge:** Reeded

Date	Mintage	F12	VF20	XF40	MS60	MS63
2012	5,000	PF63 85.00	PF65 100			

KM# 682 5 REAIS
27.00 g., 0.925 Silver 0.7978 oz. ASW, 40 mm. **Subject:** UNESCO World Heritage site. City of Goiás **Obv:** House representing the architecture of Goiá City with Cora Coralina's house, an important poetess born in this city, on first view. **Obv. Legend:** GOIÁS 2012 **Rev:** Houses representing the architecture of Goiás City and face value on the left and part of a poem by Cora Coralina ("Eu sou estas casas encostadas cochichando umas com as outras") **Rev. Legend:** PATRIMONIO DA HUMANIDADE • UNESCO **Edge:** Reeded

Date	Mintage	F12	VF20	XF40	MS60	MS63
2012	3,000	PF63 85.00	PF65 100			

KM# 659 20 REAIS
8.00 g., 0.900 Gold 0.230 oz. AGW, 22 mm. **Obv:** Juscelino Kubitschek de Oliveira's portrait **Rev:** Value **Edge:** Reeded

Date	Mintage	F12	VF20	XF40	MS60	MS63
2002	2,499	PF63 425	PF65 475			

KM# 660 20 REAIS
8.00 g., 0.900 Gold 0.230 oz. AGW, 22 mm. **Obv:** Carlos Drummond de Andrade portrait and value **Rev:** Andrade caricature, name and dates **Edge:** Reeded

Date	Mintage	F12	VF20	XF40	MS60	MS63
ND(2002)	2,499	PF63 375	PF65 400			

KM# 662 20 REAIS
8.00 g., 0.900 Gold 0.230 oz. AGW, 22 mm. **Subject:** World Cup 2002 **Obv:** Soccer player **Rev:** Value, inscription and shooting stars **Edge:** Reeded

Date	Mintage	F12	VF20	XF40	MS60	MS63
2002	2,499	PF63 375	PF65 400			

KM# 664 20 REAIS
8.00 g., 0.900 Gold 0.230 oz. AGW, 22 mm. **Subject:** Centennial - Ary Barroso **Obv:** Piano keyboard and musical notes above value **Rev:** Caricature of Ary Barroso **Edge:** Reeded

Date	Mintage	F12	VF20	XF40	MS60	MS63
2003	2,500	PF63 375	PF65 400			

KM# 670 20 REAIS
8.00 g., 0.900 Gold 0.230 oz. AGW, 22 mm. **Subject:** FIFA Centennial **Obv:** Soccer ball, value, date **Obv. Legend:** BRASIL **Rev:** Christ the Redeemer, Sugar Loaf **Rev. Legend:** FUTEBUL MUNDIAL CENTENARIO DA FIFA **Edge:** Reeded

Date	Mintage	F12	VF20	XF40	MS60	MS63
2004	4,060	PF63 600	PF65 700			

BRITISH ANTARCTIC TERRITORY

BRITISH TERRITORY
DECIMAL COINAGE

KM# 1 2 POUNDS
28.28 g., Copper-Nickel, 38.6 mm. **Ruler:** Elizabeth II **Subject:** 200th Anniversary of the Granting of Letters Patent **Obv:** Elizabeth II bust facing right **Rev:** Arms with denomination below **Rev. Legend:** 1908 . CENTENARY OF GRANTING OF LETTERS PATENT . 2008

Date	Mintage	F12	VF20	XF40	MS60	MS63
2008	Est. 50000	—	—	—	17.50	20.00

KM# 1a 2 POUNDS
28.28 g., 0.925 Silver 0.8356 oz. ASW, 38.6 mm. **Ruler:** Elizabeth II **Obv:** Bust right **Rev:** Supported arms

Date	Mintage	F12	VF20	XF40	MS60	MS63
2008	Est. 10000	PF63 55.00	PF65 60.00			

KM# 5a 2 POUNDS
28.28 g., 0.925 Silver 0.8356 oz. ASW, 38.6 mm. **Ruler:** Elizabeth II **Obv:** Bust right **Rev:** Whale and other Antarctic wildlife

Date	Mintage	F12	VF20	XF40	MS60	MS63
2009	10,000	PF63 40.00	PF65 45.00			

KM# 5 2 POUNDS
28.28 g., Copper-Nickel, 38.6 mm. **Ruler:** Elizabeth II **Subject:** Antarctic treaty **Obv:** Bust right **Rev:** Whale and other Antarctic wildlife

Date	Mintage	F12	VF20	XF40	MS60	MS63
2009	50,000	—	—	—	15.00	18.00

KM# 6 2 POUNDS
28.28 g., Copper-Nickel, 38.61 mm. **Ruler:** Elizabeth II
Subject: Scott's Terra Nova Expedition **Obv:** Bust in tiara right
Rev: Captain scott, ship and men on ice flow

Date	Mintage	F12	VF20	XF40	MS60	MS63
2012	—	—	—	—	17.50	20.00

KM# 8 2 POUNDS
28.28 g., Copper-Nickel, 38.61 mm. **Ruler:** Elizabeth II **Subject:**
Queen Elizabeth Land **Rev:** Antarctic map with boundries

Date	Mintage	F12	VF20	XF40	MS60	MS63
2013	—	—	—	—	—	15.00

KM# 9 2 POUNDS
28.28 g., Copper-Nickel, 38.61 mm. **Ruler:** Elizabeth II
Subject: Emperor Penguin **Rev:** Three penguin chicks

Date	Mintage	F12	VF20	XF40	MS60	MS63
2013	—	—	—	—	—	15.00

KM# 2 4 POUNDS
1.24 g., 0.9999 Gold 0.0396 oz. AGW, 13.92 mm. **Ruler:**
Elizabeth II **Obv:** Bust right **Rev:** Supported arms

Date	Mintage	F12	VF20	XF40	MS60	MS63
2008	Est. 10000	PF63 80.00		PF65 100		

KM# 3 20 POUNDS
6.22 g., 0.9999 Gold 0.1987 oz. AGW **Ruler:** Elizabeth II **Obv:**
Bust right **Rev:** Supported arms

Date	Mintage	F12	VF20	XF40	MS60	MS63
2008	Est. 2000	PF63 350		PF65 375		

BRITISH INDIAN OCEAN TERRITORY

TERRITORY
DECIMAL COINAGE

KM# 1 2 POUNDS
28.28 g., Copper-Nickel, 38.61 mm. **Ruler:** Elizabeth II **Obv:**
Bust with tiara right **Rev:** Arms with supporters

Date	Mintage	F12	VF20	XF40	MS60	MS63
2009PM	—	—	—	—	—	25.00

KM# 1a 2 POUNDS
28.28 g., 0.925 Silver 0.8356 oz. ASW, 38.61 mm. **Ruler:**
Elizabeth II **Subject:** First commemorative coin

Date	Mintage	F12	VF20	XF40	MS60	MS63
2009PM	Est. 10000	PF63 50.00		PF65 55.00		

KM# 2 2 POUNDS
22.00 g., 0.925 Silver 0.6501 oz. ASW, 38.61 mm. **Ruler:**
Elizabeth II **Obv:** Small head at top, sea turtle insert **Rev:**
Circle of life of the sea turtle

Date	Mintage	F12	VF20	XF40	MS60	MS63
2009PM	Est. 5000	PF63 80.00		PF65 90.00		

KM# 3 2 POUNDS
28.28 g., Copper-Nickel, 38.61 mm. **Ruler:** Elizabeth II **Subject:**
Engagement **Rev:** Prince William and Catherine Middleton

Date	Mintage	F12	VF20	XF40	MS60	MS63
2010PM	—	—	—	—	14.00	17.50

KM# 3a 2 POUNDS
28.28 g., 0.925 Silver 0.8356 oz. ASW, 38.61 mm. **Ruler:**
Elizabeth II **Subject:** Engagement

Date	Mintage	F12	VF20	XF40	MS60	MS63
2011PM	Est. 10000	PF63 50.00		PF65 55.00		

KM# 4 2 POUNDS
28.28 g., Copper-Nickel, 38.61 mm. **Ruler:** Elizabeth II **Subject:**
Royal Wedding **Obv:** Bust with tiara right **Rev:** Conjoined busts
left of Catherine Middleton and Prince William

Date	Mintage	F12	VF20	XF40	MS60	MS63
2011PM	—	—	—	—	10.00	12.50

KM# 5 2 POUNDS
28.28 g., Copper-Nickel, 38.61 mm. **Ruler:** Elizabeth II
Subject: Prince Philip, 90th Birthday **Obv:** Bust in tiara right
Rev: Crowned EP cipher within circle of crosses and anchors

Date	Mintage	F12	VF20	XF40	MS60	MS63
2011PM	—	—	—	—	17.50	20.00

KM# 4a 2 POUNDS
28.28 g., 0.925 Silver 0.8356 oz. ASW, 38.61 mm. **Ruler:**
Elizabeth II **Subject:** Royal Wedding

Date	Mintage	F12	VF20	XF40	MS60	MS63
2011PM	Est. 10000	PF63 50.00		PF65 55.00		

KM# 5a 2 POUNDS
28.28 g., 0.925 Silver 0.8356 oz. ASW **Ruler:** Elizabeth II
Subject: Prince Philip, 90th Birthday

Date	Mintage	F12	VF20	XF40	MS60	MS63
2011PM	Est. 10000	PF63 50.00		PF65 55.00		

KM# 6 2 POUNDS
28.28 g., Copper-Nickel, 38.6 mm. **Ruler:** Elizabeth II **Subject:**
Life of Queen Elizabeth II **Obv:** Conjoined busts left **Rev:**
Elizabeth and Margaret as children riding a rocking horse

Date	Mintage	F12	VF20	XF40	MS60	MS63
2012PM	—	—	—	—	—	15.00

KM# 7 2 POUNDS
28.28 g., Copper-Nickel, 38.61 mm. **Ruler:** Elizabeth II
Subject: Life of Queen Elizabeth II **Obv:** Conjoined busts right,
young and current portraits **Rev:** Queen Mother waving at left,
Queen Elizabeth at right

Date	Mintage	F12	VF20	XF40	MS60	MS63
2012PM	—	—	—	—	—	20.00

KM# 6a 2 POUNDS
28.28 g., 0.925 Silver 0.8356 oz. ASW, 38.61 mm. **Ruler:**
Elizabeth II **Subject:** Elizabeth II, 60th Anniversary as Queen
Rev: Princess Elizabeth and Margaret

Date	Mintage	F12	VF20	XF40	MS60	MS63
2012PM	Est. 10000	PF63 50.00		PF65 55.00		

KM# 8 2 POUNDS
28.28 g., Copper-Nickel, 38.61 mm. **Ruler:** Elizabeth II
Subject: The Drive, first anniversary **Rev:** Prince William and
Kate in Aston Martin DB-6 on wedding day

Date	Mintage	F12	VF20	XF40	MS60	MS63
2012PM	—	—	—	—	14.00	17.50

KM# 7a 2 POUNDS
28.28 g., 0.925 Silver 0.8356 oz. ASW, 38.61 mm. **Ruler:**
Elizabeth II **Subject:** Elizabeth II, 60th Anniversary of reign
Rev: Queen Mother and Elizabeth

Date	Mintage	F12	VF20	XF40	MS60	MS63
2012PM	Est. 10000	PF63 50.00		PF65 55.00		

KM# 8a 2 POUNDS
28.28 g., 0.925 Silver 0.8356 oz. ASW, 38.61 mm. **Ruler:**
Elizabeth II **Subject:** Wedding, 1st Anniversary **Rev:** Duke and
Duchess of Cambridge in Aston Martin DB-6 drive about

Date	Mintage	F12	VF20	XF40	MS60	MS63
2012PM	Est. 10000	PF63 50.00		PF65 55.00		

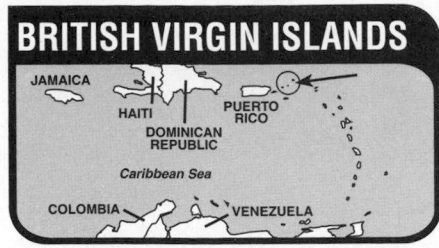

BRITISH VIRGIN ISLANDS

JAMAICA

HAITI

PUERTO RICO

DOMINICAN REPUBLIC

Caribbean Sea

COLOMBIA — VENEZUELA

The Colony of the Virgin Islands, a British colony situated in the Caribbean Sea northeast of Puerto Rico and west of the Leeward Islands, has an area of 59 sq. mi. (155 sq. km.) and a population of 13,000. Capital: Road Town. The principal islands of the 36-island group are Tortola, Virgin Gorda, Anegada, and Jost Van Dyke. The chief industries are fishing and stock raising. Fish, livestock and bananas are exported.

BRITISH COLONY

STANDARD COINAGE

KM# 429 $1.50 DOLLAR
47.00 g., Copper, 48 mm. **Ruler:** Elizabeth II **Subject:** Father of the Modern Olympics

Date	Mintage	F12	VF20	XF40	MS60	MS63
2012	Est. 3000	—	—	—	—	—

KM# 196 DOLLAR
28.28 g., Copper-Nickel, 38.6 mm. **Subject:** Queen's Golden Jubilee **Obv:** Queen's bust right **Obv. Designer:** Ian Rank-Broadley **Rev:** Carnival dancers **Edge:** Reeded

Date	Mintage	F12	VF20	XF40	MS60	MS63
2002	—	—	—	—	7.50	9.50

KM# 180 DOLLAR
28.28 g., Copper-Nickel, 38.6 mm. **Subject:** Sir Francis Drake **Obv:** Queen's bust right **Obv. Designer:** Ian Rank-Broadley **Rev:** Ship, portrait and map **Edge:** Reeded

Date	Mintage	F12	VF20	XF40	MS60	MS63
2002	—	—	—	—	7.50	9.50

KM# 183 DOLLAR
28.28 g., Copper-Nickel, 38.6 mm. **Subject:** Sir Walter Raleigh **Obv:** Queen's bust right **Obv. Designer:** Ian Rank-Broadley **Rev:** Ship, portrait and map **Edge:** Reeded

Date	Mintage	F12	VF20	XF40	MS60	MS63
2002	—	—	—	—	7.50	9.50

KM# 187 DOLLAR
28.28 g., Copper Nickel, 38.6 mm. **Subject:** Queen's Golden Jubilee **Obv:** Queen's bust right **Obv. Designer:** Ian Rank-Broadley **Rev:** Queen on horse **Edge:** Reeded

Date	Mintage	F12	VF20	XF40	MS60	MS63
2002	—	—	—	—	7.50	9.50

KM# 190 DOLLAR
28.28 g., Copper-Nickel, 38.6 mm. **Subject:** Queen's Golden Jubilee **Obv:** Queen's bust right **Obv. Designer:** Ian Rank-Broadley **Rev:** Queen on throne **Edge:** Reeded

Date	Mintage	F12	VF20	XF40	MS60	MS63
2002	—	—	—	—	7.50	9.50

KM# 193 DOLLAR
28.28 g., Copper-Nickel, 38.6 mm. **Subject:** Queen's Golden Jubilee **Obv:** Queen's bust right **Obv. Designer:** Ian Rank-Broadley **Rev:** Queen with President Ronald Reagan and First Lady Nancy Reagan **Edge:** Reeded

Date	Mintage	F12	VF20	XF40	MS60	MS63
2002	—	—	—	—	7.50	9.50

KM# 199 DOLLAR
28.28 g., Copper-Nickel, 38.6 mm. **Subject:** Teddy Bear Centennial **Obv:** Queen's bust right **Obv. Designer:** Ian Rank-Broadley **Rev:** Teddy bear **Edge:** Reeded

Date	Mintage	F12	VF20	XF40	MS60	MS63
2002	—	—	—	—	8.50	15.00

KM# 204 DOLLAR
28.28 g., Copper-Nickel, 38.6 mm. **Subject:** Princess Diana **Obv:** Queen's bust right **Obv. Designer:** Ian Rank-Broadley **Rev:** Diana's portrait **Edge:** Reeded

Date	Mintage	F12	VF20	XF40	MS60	MS63
2002	—	—	—	—	7.50	9.50

KM# 207 DOLLAR
28.28 g., Copper-Nickel, 38.6 mm. **Subject:** September 11, 2001 **Obv:** Queen's bust right **Obv. Designer:** Ian Rank-Broadley **Rev:** World Trade Center twin towers **Edge:** Reeded

Date	Mintage	F12	VF20	XF40	MS60	MS63
2002	—	—	—	—	12.00	13.50

KM# 210 DOLLAR
28.28 g., Copper-Nickel, 38.6 mm. **Subject:** September 11, 2001 **Obv:** Queen's bust right **Obv. Designer:** Ian Rank-Broadley **Rev:** Statue of Liberty **Edge:** Reeded

Date	Mintage	F12	VF20	XF40	MS60	MS63
2002	—	—	—	—	12.00	13.50

KM# 213 DOLLAR
28.28 g., Copper-Nickel, 38.6 mm. **Subject:** Queen Mother **Obv:** Queen's bust right **Obv. Designer:** Ian Rank-Broadley **Rev:** Queen Mother and a young Prince Charles **Edge:** Reeded

Date	Mintage	F12	VF20	XF40	MS60	MS63
2002PM	—	—	—	—	10.00	12.00

KM# 216 DOLLAR
28.28 g., Copper-Nickel, 38.6 mm. **Subject:** Queen Mother **Obv:** Queen's bust right **Obv. Designer:** Ian Rank-Broadley **Rev:** Queen Mother with four grandchildren **Edge:** Reeded

Date	Mintage	F12	VF20	XF40	MS60	MS63
2002PM	—	—	—	—	10.00	12.00

KM# 219 DOLLAR
28.28 g., Copper-Nickel, 38.6 mm. **Subject:** Queen Mother Series **Obv:** Queen's bust right **Obv. Designer:** Ian Rank-Broadley **Rev:** Queen Mother with uniformed Prince Charles **Edge:** Reeded

Date	Mintage	F12	VF20	XF40	MS60	MS63
2002PM	—	—	—	—	10.00	12.00

KM# 222 DOLLAR
28.28 g., Copper-Nickel, 38.6 mm. **Subject:** Queen Mother Series **Obv:** Queen's bust right **Obv. Designer:** Ian Rank-Broadley **Rev:** Queen Mother's coffin **Edge:** Reeded

Date	Mintage	F12	VF20	XF40	MS60	MS63
2002PM	—	—	—	—	10.00	12.00

KM# 225 DOLLAR
28.44 g., Copper-Nickel, 38.6 mm. **Subject:** Kennedy Assassination **Obv:** Queen's bust right **Obv. Designer:** Ian Rank-Broadley **Rev:** President Kennedy's portrait left **Edge:** Reeded

Date	Mintage	F12	VF20	XF40	MS60	MS63
2003	—	—	—	—	10.00	12.00

KM# 229 DOLLAR
28.28 g., Copper-Nickel, 38.6 mm. **Subject:** Powered Flight Centennial **Obv:** Queen's bust right **Obv. Designer:** Ian Rank-Broadley **Rev:** Three historic airplanes and rocket **Edge:** Reeded

Date	Mintage	F12	VF20	XF40	MS60	MS63
2003	—	—	—	—	10.00	12.00

KM# 232 DOLLAR
28.28 g., Copper-Nickel, 38.6 mm. **Obv:** Queen's bust right **Obv. Designer:** Ian Rank-Broadley **Rev:** Henry VIII and Elizabeth I **Edge:** Reeded

Date	Mintage	F12	VF20	XF40	MS60	MS63
2003	—	—	—	—	10.00	12.00

KM# 235 DOLLAR
28.28 g., Copper-Nickel, 38.6 mm. **Obv:** Queen's bust right **Obv. Designer:** Ian Rank-Broadley **Rev:** Matthew Parker, Archbishop of Canterbury **Edge:** Reeded

Date	Mintage	F12	VF20	XF40	MS60	MS63
2003	—	—	—	—	10.00	12.00

KM# 238 DOLLAR
28.28 g., Copper Nickel, 38.6 mm. **Obv:** Queen's bust right **Obv. Designer:** Ian Rank-Broadley **Rev:** Sir Francis Drake and ships **Edge:** Reeded

Date	Mintage	F12	VF20	XF40	MS60	MS63
2003	—	—	—	—	10.00	12.00

KM# 241 DOLLAR
28.28 g., Copper-Nickel, 38.6 mm. **Obv:** Queen's bust right **Obv. Designer:** Ian Rank-Broadley **Rev:** Sir Walter Raleigh **Edge:** Reeded

Date	Mintage	F12	VF20	XF40	MS60	MS63
2003	—	—	—	—	10.00	12.00

KM# 244 DOLLAR
28.28 g., Copper-Nickel, 38.6 mm. **Obv:** Queen's bust right **Obv. Designer:** Ian Rank-Broadley **Rev:** Sir William Shakespeare **Edge:** Reeded

Date	Mintage	F12	VF20	XF40	MS60	MS63
2003	—	—	—	—	10.00	12.00

KM# 247 DOLLAR
28.28 g., Copper-Nickel, 38.6 mm. **Obv:** Queen's bust right **Obv. Designer:** Ian Rank-Broadley **Rev:** Elizabeth I above her funeral procession **Edge:** Reeded

Date	Mintage	F12	VF20	XF40	MS60	MS63
2003	—	—	—	—	10.00	12.00

KM# 250 DOLLAR
28.28 g., Copper-Nickel, 38.6 mm. **Subject:** Olympics **Obv:** Queen's bust right **Obv. Designer:** Ian Rank-Broadley **Rev:** Ancient bust, runners and coin **Edge:** Reeded

Date	Mintage	F12	VF20	XF40	MS60	MS63
2003	—	—	—	—	10.00	12.00

KM# 253 DOLLAR
28.28 g., Copper-Nickel, 38.6 mm. **Subject:** Olympics **Obv:** Queen's bust right **Obv. Designer:** Ian Rank-Broadley **Rev:** Ancient bust, charioteer and coin **Edge:** Reeded

Date	Mintage	F12	VF20	XF40	MS60	MS63
2003	—	—	—	—	10.00	12.00

KM# 303 DOLLAR
28.28 g., Copper-Nickel, 38.6 mm. **Subject:** 2004 Athens Olympics **Obv:** Queen's bust right **Obv. Designer:** Ian Rank-Broadley **Rev:** Ancient athlete's bust right, runners at lower right, ancient coin with owl at upper right **Edge:** Reeded

Date	Mintage	F12	VF20	XF40	MS60	MS63
2003	—	—	—	—	10.00	12.00

KM# 306 DOLLAR
28.28 g., Copper-Nickel, 38.6 mm. **Subject:** 2004 Athens Olympics **Obv:** Queen's bust right **Obv. Designer:** Ian Rank-Broadley **Rev:** Ancient athlete bust left, chariot race at lower left, ancient coin at upper left **Edge:** Reeded

Date	Mintage	F12	VF20	XF40	MS60	MS63
2003	—	—	—	—	10.00	12.00

KM# 310 DOLLAR
28.28 g., Copper-Nickel, 38.6 mm. **Subject:** Queen Elizabeth's Golden Coronation Jubilee **Obv:** Elizabeth II **Rev:** Cameo portraits above the ship "Gothic **Edge:** Reeded

Date	Mintage	F12	VF20	XF40	MS60	MS63
2003	—	—	—	—	7.50	9.50

KM# 319 DOLLAR
28.28 g., Copper-Nickel **Subject:** 50th Anniversary of Coronation **Rev:** Queen riding in automobile

Date	Mintage	F12	VF20	XF40	MS60	MS63
2003	—	—	—	—	12.00	15.00

KM# 320 DOLLAR
28.28 g., Copper-Nickel **Subject:** Golden Jubilee of Coronation **Rev:** Sir. Edmond Hillary on Mt. Everest, Queen II above mountain climbers

Date	Mintage	F12	VF20	XF40	MS60	MS63
2003	—	—	—	—	12.00	15.00

KM# 321 DOLLAR
28.28 g., Copper-Nickel **Rev:** Queen presenting Ascot Horse Racing prize

Date	Mintage	F12	VF20	XF40	MS60	MS63
2003	—	—	—	—	10.00	12.00

KM# 265 DOLLAR
28.28 g., Copper-Nickel, 38.6 mm. **Obv:** Queen's bust right **Obv. Designer:** Ian Rank-Broadley **Rev:** Sir Francis Drake, ship and map **Edge:** Reeded

Date	Mintage	F12	VF20	XF40	MS60	MS63
2004	—	—	—	—	10.00	12.00

KM# 267.1 DOLLAR
28.28 g., Copper-Nickel, 38.6 mm. **Obv:** Queen's bust right **Obv. Designer:** Ian Rank-Broadley **Rev:** Peter Rabbit **Edge:** Reeded

Date	Mintage	F12	VF20	XF40	MS60	MS63
2004	—	—	—	—	15.00	17.00

KM# 267.2 DOLLAR
28.28 g., Copper-Nickel, 38.6 mm. **Obv:** Queen's bust right **Obv. Designer:** Ian Rank-Broadley **Rev:** Multicolor Peter Rabbit **Edge:** Reeded

Date	Mintage	F12	VF20	XF40	MS60	MS63
2004	—	—	—	—	20.00	22.00

KM# 268 DOLLAR
3.11 g., 0.999 Silver 0.0992 oz. ASW, 18 mm. **Obv:** Queen's bust right **Obv. Designer:** Ian Rank-Broadley **Rev:** Peter Rabbit **Edge:** Reeded

Date	Mintage	F12	VF20	XF40	MS60	MS63
2004	10,000		PF65 25.00			

KM# 281 DOLLAR
28.28 g., Copper-Nickel, 38.6 mm. **Obv:** Queen's bust right **Obv. Designer:** Ian Rank-Broadley **Rev:** Sailor above two D-Day landing craft **Edge:** Reeded

Date	Mintage	F12	VF20	XF40	MS60	MS63
2004	—	—	—	—	10.00	12.00

KM# 286 DOLLAR
28.28 g., Copper-Nickel, 38.6 mm. **Obv:** Queen's bust right **Obv. Designer:** Ian Rank-Broadley **Rev:** Dolphin **Edge:** Reeded

Date	Mintage	F12	VF20	XF40	MS60	MS63
2004	—	—	—	—	12.00	14.00

KM# 297 DOLLAR
28.28 g., Copper-Nickel, 38.6 mm. **Obv:** Queen's bust right **Obv. Designer:** Ian Rank-Broadley **Rev:** Soldier above tank and jeeps **Edge:** Reeded

Date	Mintage	F12	VF20	XF40	MS60	MS63
2004	—	—	—	—	10.00	12.00

KM# 300 DOLLAR
28.28 g., Copper-Nickel, 38.6 mm. **Obv:** Queen's bust right **Obv. Designer:** Ian Rank-Broadley **Rev:** Pilot and planes above D-Day landing **Edge:** Reeded

Date	Mintage	F12	VF20	XF40	MS60	MS63
2004	—	—	—	—	10.00	12.00

KM# 330 DOLLAR
Copper-Nickel **Ruler:** Elizabeth II **Rev:** Battle of Britain

Date	Mintage	F12	VF20	XF40	MS60	MS63
2005	—	—	—	—	15.00	17.00

KM# 331 DOLLAR
Copper-Nickel **Ruler:** Elizabeth II **Rev:** Battle of Berlin

Date	Mintage	F12	VF20	XF40	MS60	MS63
2005	—	—	—	—	15.00	17.00

KM# 312 DOLLAR
28.28 g., Copper-Nickel, 38.6 mm. **Obv:** Bust of Queen Elizabeth II right **Rev:** Mother and baby dolphins **Edge:** Reeded

Date	Mintage	F12	VF20	XF40	MS60	MS63
2005	—	—	—	—	12.00	14.00

KM# 322 DOLLAR
28.28 g., Copper-Nickel **Rev:** VJ Day, McArthur and U.S.S. Missiouri Battleship

Date	Mintage	F12	VF20	XF40	MS60	MS63
2005	—	—	—	—	10.00	12.00

KM# 323 DOLLAR
28.28 g., Copper-Nickel **Rev:** Warships near Atlantic coast, West Indies islands

Date	Mintage	F12	VF20	XF40	MS60	MS63
2005	—	—	—	—	10.00	12.00

KM# 324 DOLLAR
28.28 g., Copper-Nickel **Rev:** Death of Nelson

Date	Mintage	F12	VF20	XF40	MS60	MS63
2005	—	—	—	—	10.00	12.00

KM# 325 DOLLAR
28.28 g., Copper-Nickel **Rev:** Nelson and Order Star above ships

Date	Mintage	F12	VF20	XF40	MS60	MS63
2005	—	—	—	—	10.00	12.00

KM# 326 DOLLAR
28.28 g., Copper-Nickel **Rev:** Nelson and Napoleon

Date	Mintage	F12	VF20	XF40	MS60	MS63
2005	—	—	—	—	10.00	12.00

KM# 327 DOLLAR
28.28 g., Copper-Nickel **Rev:** Nelson's Column, statue and ships

Date	Mintage	F12	VF20	XF40	MS60	MS63
2005	—	—	—	—	10.00	12.00

KM# 328 DOLLAR
28.28 g., Copper-Nickel **Rev:** V.E. Day, Montgomery and Eisenhower

Date	Mintage	F12	VF20	XF40	MS60	MS63
2005	—	—	—	—	10.00	12.00

KM# 403 DOLLAR
28.28 g., Copper-Nickel, 38.61 mm. **Ruler:** Elizabeth II **Obv:** Bust in tiara right **Rev:** Inverted Swan postage stamp

Date	Mintage	F12	VF20	XF40	MS60	MS63
2005PM	—	—	—	—	17.50	20.00

KM# 329 DOLLAR
Copper-Nickel **Rev:** Two dolphins

Date	Mintage	F12	VF20	XF40	MS60	MS63
2006	—	—	—	—	10.00	12.00

KM# 349 DOLLAR
28.28 g., Copper-Nickel, 38.6 mm. **Ruler:** Elizabeth II **Subject:** 5th Anniversary Attack on Twin Towers, New York City **Obv:** Crowned bust right **Obv. Legend:** BRITISH VIRGIN ISLANDS - QUEEN ELIZABETH II **Rev:** Twin Towers in sprays, remembrance ribbon privy mark at upper right **Rev. Legend:** LEST WE FORGET **Edge:** Reeded

Date	Mintage	F12	VF20	XF40	MS60	MS63
2006	—	—	—	—	15.00	17.00

KM# 332 DOLLAR
28.28 g., Copper-Nickel, 38.60 mm. **Ruler:** Elizabeth II **Subject:** 400th Anniversary Founding of Jamestown **Obv:** Bust with tiara right **Obv. Legend:** BRITISH VIRGIN ISLANDS - QUEEN ELIZABETH II **Rev:** British lion laying, American eagle perched on sprays **Rev. Legend:** UNITED IN FRIENDSHIP **Edge:** Reeded

Date	Mintage	F12	VF20	XF40	MS60	MS63
2007	—	—	—	—	16.50	18.50

KM# 404 DOLLAR
28.28 g., Copper-Nickel, 38.61 mm. **Ruler:** Elizabeth II **Obv:** Bust in tiara right **Rev:** George Washington 5 cent postage stamp

Date	Mintage	F12	VF20	XF40	MS60	MS63
2007PM	—	—	—	—	17.50	20.00

KM# 370 DOLLAR
28.28 g., Copper-Nickel, 38.6 mm. **Ruler:** Elizabeth II **Obv:** Bust right **Rev:** Two soccer players and leopard

Date	Mintage	F12	VF20	XF40	MS60	MS63
2009	—	—	—	—	12.00	15.00

KM# 373 DOLLAR
28.28 g., Copper-Nickel, 38.6 mm. **Ruler:** Elizabeth II **Obv:** Bust right **Rev:** Queen Elizabeth I aboard ship

Date	Mintage	F12	VF20	XF40	MS60	MS63
2000	—	—	—	—	12.00	15.00

KM# 375 DOLLAR
28.28 g., Copper-Nickel, 38.6 mm. **Ruler:** Elizabeth II **Obv:** Bust right **Rev:** Elizabeth I between two columns

Date	Mintage	F12	VF20	XF40	MS60	MS63
2009	—	—	—	—	12.00	15.00

KM# 393 DOLLAR
28.28 g., Copper-Nickel, 38.6 mm. **Ruler:** Elizabeth II **Subject:** Peanuts 60th Anniversary **Rev:** Snoopy sleeping atop doghouse

Date	Mintage	F12	VF20	XF40	MS60	MS63
2010PM	—	—	—	—	—	25.00

KM# 396 DOLLAR
28.28 g., Bronze, 38.6 mm. **Ruler:** Elizabeth II **Subject:** Elgin Marbles **Rev:** Two horsemen

Date	Mintage	F12	VF20	XF40	MS60	MS63
2010PM	—	—	—	—	25.00	—

KM# 402 DOLLAR
28.28 g., Copper-Nickel, 38.61 mm. **Ruler:** Elizabeth II **Subject:** Birth of Venus

Date	Mintage	F12	VF20	XF40	MS60	MS63
2010PM	—	—	—	—	—	15.00

KM# 436 DOLLAR
28.28 g., Copper-Nickel, 38.61 mm. **Ruler:** Elizabeth II **Subject:** Orient Express

Date	Mintage	F12	VF20	XF40	MS60	MS63
2011PM	—	—	—	—	—	15.00

KM# 436a DOLLAR
28.28 g., Copper-Nickel, 38.61 mm. **Ruler:** Elizabeth II **Subject:** Royal Husdon Steam Locomotive **Rev:** Locomotive in color

Date	Mintage	F12	VF20	XF40	MS60	MS63
2011	—	—	—	—	—	20.00

KM# 431 DOLLAR
28.28 g., Copper-Nickel, 38.6 mm. **Ruler:** Elizabeth II **Subject:** Father of the Modern Olympics

Date	Mintage	F12	VF20	XF40	MS60	MS63
2012	—	—	—	—	—	15.00

KM# 439 DOLLAR
28.28 g., Copper-Nickel, 38.61 mm. **Ruler:** Elizabeth II **Subject:** Birth of Prince George **Rev:** Prince William and blue footprints added at right

Date	Mintage	F12	VF20	XF40	MS60	MS63
2013PM	—	—	—	—	—	15.00

KM# 441 DOLLAR
28.28 g., Copper-Nickel, 38.61 mm. **Ruler:** Elizabeth II **Subject:** Birth of Prince George **Rev:** Catherine and blue footprints added at right

Date	Mintage	F12	VF20	XF40	MS60	MS63
2013PM	—	—	—	—	—	15.00

KM# 443 DOLLAR
28.28 g., Copper-Nickel, 38.61 mm. **Ruler:** Elizabeth II **Subject:** Last Concord Flight, 10th Anniversary **Rev:** Concord, NY and London Skyline

Date	Mintage	F12	VF20	XF40	MS60	MS63
2013PM	—	—	—	—	—	15.00

KM# 443a DOLLAR
28.28 g., Copper-Nickel, 38.61 mm. **Ruler:** Elizabeth II **Subject:** Last flight of Concorde, 10th Anniversary **Rev:** Concord with tailfin in color, NY and London skyline

Date	Mintage	F12	VF20	XF40	MS60	MS63
2013PM	—	—	—	—	—	20.00

KM# 446 DOLLAR
28.28 g., Copper-Nickel, 38.8 mm. **Ruler:** Elizabeth II **Obv:** Bust right **Rev:** Sea horse

Date	Mintage	F12	VF20	XF40	MS60	MS63
2014	—	—	—	—	—	15.00

KM# 278 2 DOLLARS
58.00 g., Bronze, 50 mm. **Obv:** Queen's bust right **Obv. Designer:** Ian Rank-Broadley **Rev:** 1896 Olympic medal design **Edge:** Reeded

Date	Mintage	F12	VF20	XF40	MS60	MS63
2004	3,500	PF65 20.00				

KM# 380 2 DOLLARS
Bronze, 50 mm. **Ruler:** Elizabeth II **Rev:** Turtle

Date	Mintage	F12	VF20	XF40	MS60	MS63
2008PM	—	—	—	—	—	20.00

KM# 269.1 2.50 DOLLARS
7.78 g., 0.999 Silver 0.2481 oz. ASW, 26 mm. **Obv:** Queen's bust right **Obv. Designer:** Ian Rank-Broadley **Rev:** Peter Rabbit **Edge:** Reeded

Date	Mintage	F12	VF20	XF40	MS60	MS63
2004	—	PF65 18.00				

KM# 269.2 2.50 DOLLARS
7.78 g., 0.999 Silver 0.2481 oz. ASW, 26 mm. **Obv:** Queen's bust right **Obv. Designer:** Ian Rank-Broadley **Rev:** Multicolor Peter Rabbit **Edge:** Reeded

Date	Mintage	F12	VF20	XF40	MS60	MS63
2004	7,500	PF65 25.00				

KM# 381 4 DOLLARS
Silver **Ruler:** Elizabeth II **Subject:** 400th Anniversary of Settlement

Date	Mintage	F12	VF20	XF40	MS60	MS63
2009PM	—	—	—	—	—	35.00

KM# 284 5 DOLLARS
10.00 g., 0.3162 oz. Titanium, 36.1 mm. **Obv:** Queen's bust right **Obv. Designer:** Ian Rank-Broadley **Rev:** British Guiana stamp design **Edge:** Reeded

Date	Mintage	F12	VF20	XF40	MS60	MS63
2004	7,500	PF65 95.00				

KM# 340 5 DOLLARS
0.9999 Bi-Metallic **Ruler:** Elizabeth II **Obv:** Conjoined busts with Philip right, within gold ring **Obv. Legend:** BRITISH VIRGIN ISLANDS — QUEEN ELIZABETH II **Rev:** Conjoined busts of Princess Elizabeth and Prince Philip right within gold ring **Rev. Legend:** WITH THIS RING, I THEE WED **Edge:** Reeded

Date	Mintage	F12	VF20	XF40	MS60	MS63
2007	—	PF65 500				

KM# 405 5 DOLLARS
28.28 g., Copper-Nickel, 38.61 mm. **Ruler:** Elizabeth II **Obv:** Bust in tiara right **Rev:** Benjamin Franklin postage stamp

Date	Mintage	F12	VF20	XF40	MS60	MS63
2007PM	—	—	—	—	17.50	20.00

KM# 414 5 DOLLARS
28.28 g., Copper-Nickel, 38.61 mm. **Ruler:** Elizabeth II **Subject:** Bejing Olympics **Obv:** Bust in tiara right **Rev:** Tennis plays against Great Wall background

Date	Mintage	F12	VF20	XF40	MS60	MS63
2008PM	—	PF65 25.00				

KM# 426 5 DOLLARS
28.28 g., Silver, 38.61 mm. **Ruler:** Elizabeth II **Subject:** Bejing Olympics **Obv:** Bust in tiara right **Rev:** Tennis plays against Great Wall background

Date	Mintage	F12	VF20	XF40	MS60	MS63
2008PM	—	PF65 50.00				

KM# 383 5 DOLLARS
Titanium **Ruler:** Elizabeth II **Subject:** Bejing Olympics - Tennis

Date	Mintage	F12	VF20	XF40	MS60	MS63
2009PM	—	PF65 55.00				

KM# 384 5 DOLLARS
Titanium **Ruler:** Elizabeth II **Subject:** Bejing Olympics - Swimming

Date	Mintage	F12	VF20	XF40	MS60	MS63
2009PM	—	PF65 55.00				

KM# 385 5 DOLLARS
Titanium **Ruler:** Elizabeth II **Subject:** Bejing Olympics

Date	Mintage	F12	VF20	XF40	MS60	MS63
2009PM	—	PF65 55.00				

KM# 386 5 DOLLARS
Titanium **Ruler:** Elizabeth II **Subject:** Bejing Olympics

Date	Mintage	F12	VF20	XF40	MS60	MS63
2009PM	—	PF65 55.00				

KM# 387 5 DOLLARS
Titanium **Ruler:** Elizabeth II **Subject:** Bejing Olympics

Date	Mintage	F12	VF20	XF40	MS60	MS63
2009PM	—	PF65 55.00				

KM# 399 5 DOLLARS
7.00 g., Bi-Metallic, 38.6 mm. **Ruler:** Elizabeth II **Subject:** 175th Anniversary of Publication of Hans Christian Anderson's first book **Rev:** Scene from the Little Mermaid

Date	Mintage	F12	VF20	XF40	MS60	MS63
2010PM	Est. 5000	PF65 120				

KM# 400 5 DOLLARS
10.00 g., Tri-Metallic, 38.6 mm. **Ruler:** Elizabeth II **Subject:** 175th Anniversary of Publication of Hans Christian Andersen's first book **Rev:** Scene from the Little Mermaid

Date	Mintage	F12	VF20	XF40	MS60	MS63
2010PM	Est. 7500	PF65 120				

KM# 433 5 DOLLARS
35.50 g., Bronze, 50 mm. **Ruler:** Elizabeth II **Subject:** RMS Titanic Remembered

Date	Mintage	F12	VF20	XF40	MS60	MS63
2012	Est. 7500	—	—	—	—	—
Uncirculated						

KM# 208.1 10 DOLLARS
28.28 g., 0.925 Silver 0.8356 oz. ASW, 38.6 mm. **Subject:** September 11, 2001 **Obv:** Queen's bust right **Obv. Designer:** Ian Rank-Broadley **Rev:** World Trade Center twin towers **Edge:** Reeded

Date	Mintage	F12	VF20	XF40	MS60	MS63
2002	10,000	PF65 50.00				

KM# 181 10 DOLLARS
28.28 g., 0.925 Silver 0.8356 oz. ASW, 38.6 mm. **Subject:** Sir Francis Drake **Obv:** Queen's bust right **Obv. Designer:** Ian Rank-Broadley **Rev:** Ship, portrait and map **Edge:** Reeded

Date	Mintage	F12	VF20	XF40	MS60	MS63
2002	—	PF65 45.00				

KM# 184 10 DOLLARS
28.28 g., 0.925 Silver 0.8356 oz. ASW, 38.6 mm. **Subject:** Sir Walter Raleigh **Obv:** Queen's bust right **Obv. Designer:** Ian Rank-Broadley **Rev:** Ship, portrait and map **Edge:** Reeded

Date	Mintage	F12	VF20	XF40	MS60	MS63
2002	—	PF65 45.00				

KM# 188 10 DOLLARS
28.28 g., 0.925 Gold Clad Silver 0.8356 oz., 38.6 mm. **Subject:** Queen's Golden Jubilee **Obv:** Queen's bust right **Obv. Designer:** Ian Rank-Broadley **Rev:** Queen on horse trotting left **Edge:** Reeded

Date	Mintage	F12	VF20	XF40	MS60	MS63
2002	10,000	PF65 42.50				

KM# 191 10 DOLLARS
28.28 g., 0.925 Gold Clad Silver 0.8356 oz., 38.6 mm. **Subject:** Queen's Golden Jubilee **Obv:** Queen's bust right **Obv. Designer:** Ian Rank-Broadley **Rev:** 3/4-length Queen seated on throne **Edge:** Reeded

Date	Mintage	F12	VF20	XF40	MS60	MS63
2002	10,000	PF65 45.00				

KM# 194 10 DOLLARS
28.28 g., 0.925 Gold Clad Silver 0.8356 oz., 38.6 mm. **Subject:** Queen's Golden Jubilee **Obv:** Queen's bust right **Obv. Designer:** Ian Rank-Broadley **Rev:** Queen with President Ronald Reagan and First Lady Nancy Reagan **Edge:** Reeded

Date	Mintage	F12	VF20	XF40	MS60	MS63
2002		PF65 45.00				

KM# 197 10 DOLLARS
28.28 g., 0.925 Gold Clad Silver 0.8356 oz., 38.6 mm. **Subject:** Queen's Golden Jubilee **Obv:** Queen's bust right **Obv. Designer:** Ian Rank-Broadley **Rev:** Carnival dancers **Edge:** Reeded

Date	Mintage	F12	VF20	XF40	MS60	MS63
2002	10,000	PF65 45.00				

KM# 200 10 DOLLARS
28.28 g., 0.925 Silver 0.8356 oz. ASW, 38.6 mm. **Subject:** Teddy Bear Centennial **Obv:** Queen's bust right **Obv. Designer:** Ian Rank-Broadley **Rev:** Teddy bear **Edge:** Reeded

Date	Mintage	F12	VF20	XF40	MS60	MS63
2002	10,000	PF65 40.00				

KM# 205 10 DOLLARS
28.28 g., 0.925 Silver 0.8356 oz. ASW, 38.6 mm. **Subject:** Princess Diana **Obv:** Queen's bust right **Obv. Designer:** Ian Rank-Broadley **Rev:** Diana's portrait **Edge:** Reeded

Date	Mintage	F12	VF20	XF40	MS60	MS63
2002	10,000	PF65 40.00				

KM# 208.2 10 DOLLARS
28.28 g., 0.925 Silver 0.8356 oz. ASW, 38.6 mm. **Subject:** September 11, 2001 **Obv:** Queen's bust right **Obv. Designer:** Ian Rank-Broadley **Rev:** Holographic multicolor World Trade Center twin towers **Edge:** Reeded

Date	Mintage	F12	VF20	XF40	MS60	MS63
2002	10,000	PF65 45.00				

KM# 211 10 DOLLARS
28.28 g., 0.925 Silver 0.8356 oz. ASW, 38.6 mm. **Subject:** September 11, 2001 **Obv:** Queen's bust right **Obv. Designer:** Ian Rank-Broadley **Rev:** Statue of Liberty **Edge:** Reeded

Date	Mintage	F12	VF20	XF40	MS60	MS63
2002	10,000	PF65 40.00				

KM# 214 10 DOLLARS
28.28 g., 0.925 Silver 0.8356 oz. ASW, 38.6 mm. **Subject:** Queen Mother **Obv:** Queen's bust right **Obv. Designer:** Ian Rank-Broadley **Rev:** Queen Mother with young Prince Charles **Edge:** Reeded

Date	Mintage	F12	VF20	XF40	MS60	MS63
2002PM	10,000	PF65 40.00				

KM# 217 10 DOLLARS
28.28 g., 0.925 Silver 0.8356 oz. ASW, 38.6 mm. **Subject:** Queen Mother Series **Obv:** Queen's bust right **Obv. Designer:** Ian Rank-Broadley **Rev:** Queen Mother with four grandchildren **Edge:** Reeded

Date	Mintage	F12	VF20	XF40	MS60	MS63
2002PM	10,000	PF65 40.00				

KM# 220 10 DOLLARS
28.28 g., 0.925 Silver 0.8356 oz. ASW, 38.6 mm. **Subject:** Queen Mother Series **Obv:** Queen's bust right **Obv. Designer:** Ian Rank-Broadley **Rev:** Queen Mother with uniformed Prince Charles **Edge:** Reeded

Date	Mintage	F12	VF20	XF40	MS60	MS63
2002PM	10,000	PF65 40.00				

KM# 223   10 DOLLARS
28.28 g., 0.925 Silver 0.8356 oz. ASW, 38.6 mm. **Subject:** Queen Mother Series **Obv:** Queen's bust right **Obv. Designer:** Ian Rank-Broadley **Rev:** Queen Mother's coffin **Edge:** Reeded

Date	Mintage	F12	VF20	XF40	MS60	MS63
2002PM	10,000	PF65 40.00				

KM# 226   10 DOLLARS
28.28 g., 0.925 Silver 0.8356 oz. ASW, 38.6 mm. **Subject:** Kennedy Assassination **Obv:** Queen's bust right **Obv. Designer:** Ian Rank-Broadley **Rev:** President Kennedy's head left **Edge:** Reeded

Date	Mintage	F12	VF20	XF40	MS60	MS63
2003	10,000	PF65 50.00				

KM# 230   10 DOLLARS
28.28 g., 0.925 Silver 0.8356 oz. ASW, 38.6 mm. **Subject:** Powered Flight Centennial **Obv:** Queen's bust right **Obv. Designer:** Ian Rank-Broadley **Rev:** Three historic airplanes and rocket **Edge:** Reeded

Date	Mintage	F12	VF20	XF40	MS60	MS63
2003	10,000	PF65 45.00				

KM# 233   10 DOLLARS
28.28 g., 0.925 Silver 0.8356 oz. ASW, 38.6 mm. **Obv:** Queen's bust right **Obv. Designer:** Ian Rank-Broadley **Rev:** Henry VIII and Elizabeth I **Edge:** Reeded

Date	Mintage	F12	VF20	XF40	MS60	MS63
2003	10,000	PF65 42.00				

KM# 236   10 DOLLARS
28.28 g., 0.925 Silver 0.8356 oz. ASW, 38.6 mm. **Obv:** Queen's bust right **Obv. Designer:** Ian Rank-Broadley **Rev:** Matthew Parker, Archbishop of Canterbury **Edge:** Reeded

Date	Mintage	F12	VF20	XF40	MS60	MS63
2003	10,000	PF65 42.00				

KM# 239   10 DOLLARS
28.28 g., 0.925 Silver 0.8356 oz. ASW, 38.6 mm. **Obv:** Queen's bust right **Obv. Designer:** Ian Rank-Broadley **Rev:** Sir Francis Drake and ships **Edge:** Reeded

Date	Mintage	F12	VF20	XF40	MS60	MS63
2003	10,000	PF65 42.00				

KM# 242   10 DOLLARS
28.28 g., 0.925 Silver 0.8356 oz. ASW, 38.6 mm. **Obv:** Queen's bust right **Obv. Designer:** Ian Rank-Broadley **Rev:** Sir Walter Raleigh **Edge:** Reeded

Date	Mintage	F12	VF20	XF40	MS60	MS63
2003	10,000	PF65 42.00				

KM# 245   10 DOLLARS
28.28 g., 0.925 Silver 0.8356 oz. ASW, 38.6 mm. **Obv:** Queen's bust right **Obv. Designer:** Ian Rank-Broadley **Rev:** Sir William Shakespeare **Edge:** Reeded

Date	Mintage	F12	VF20	XF40	MS60	MS63
2003	10,000	PF65 42.00				

KM# 248   10 DOLLARS
28.28 g., 0.925 Silver 0.8356 oz. ASW, 38.6 mm. **Obv:** Queen's bust right **Obv. Designer:** Ian Rank-Broadley **Rev:** Elizabeth I above her funeral procession **Edge:** Reeded

Date	Mintage	F12	VF20	XF40	MS60	MS63
2003	10,000	PF65 42.00				

KM# 251   10 DOLLARS
28.28 g., 0.925 Silver 0.8356 oz. ASW, 38.6 mm. **Subject:** Olympics **Obv:** Queen's bust right **Obv. Designer:** Ian Rank-Broadley **Rev:** Ancient bust, runners and coin **Edge:** Reeded

Date	Mintage	F12	VF20	XF40	MS60	MS63
2003	10,000	PF65 42.00				

KM# 254   10 DOLLARS
28.28 g., 0.925 Silver 0.8356 oz. ASW, 38.6 mm. **Subject:** Olympics **Obv:** Queen's bust right **Obv. Designer:** Ian Rank-Broadley **Rev:** Ancient bust, charioteer and coin **Edge:** Reeded

Date	Mintage	F12	VF20	XF40	MS60	MS63
2003	10,000	PF65 42.00				

KM# 311   10 DOLLARS
28.30 g., 0.925 Gold Clad Silver 0.8362 oz., 38.6 mm. **Subject:** Queen Elizabeth's Golden Coronation Jubilee **Obv:** Elizabeth II **Rev:** Cameo portrait above ship "Gothic **Edge:** Reeded

Date	Mintage	F12	VF20	XF40	MS60	MS63
2003	—	PF65 50.00				

KM# 266   10 DOLLARS
28.28 g., 0.925 Silver 0.8356 oz. ASW, 38.6 mm. **Obv:** Queen's bust right **Obv. Designer:** Ian Rank-Broadley **Rev:** Sir Francis Drake, ship and map **Edge:** Reeded

Date	Mintage	F12	VF20	XF40	MS60	MS63
2004	10,000	PF65 45.00				

KM# 270.1   10 DOLLARS
28.28 g., 0.925 Silver 0.8356 oz. ASW, 38.6 mm. **Obv:** Queen's bust right **Obv. Designer:** Ian Rank-Broadley **Rev:** Peter Rabbit **Edge:** Reeded

Date	Mintage	F12	VF20	XF40	MS60	MS63
2004	5,000	PF65 47.50				

KM# 270.2   10 DOLLARS
28.28 g., 0.925 Silver 0.8356 oz. ASW, 38.6 mm. **Obv:** Queen's bust right **Obv. Designer:** Ian Rank-Broadley **Rev:** Multicolor Peter Rabbit **Edge:** Reeded

Date	Mintage	F12	VF20	XF40	MS60	MS63
2004	—	PF65 65.00				

KM# 274   10 DOLLARS
1.24 g., 0.9999 Gold 0.0397 oz. AGW, 14 mm. **Obv:** Queen's bust right **Obv. Designer:** Ian Rank-Broadley **Rev:** Hernando Pizarro **Edge:** Reeded

Date	Mintage	F12	VF20	XF40	MS60	MS63
2004	350	PF65 85.00				

KM# 282   10 DOLLARS
28.28 g., 0.925 Silver 0.8356 oz. ASW, 38.6 mm. **Obv:** Queen's bust right **Obv. Designer:** Ian Rank-Broadley **Rev:** Sailor above two D-Day landing craft **Edge:** Reeded

Date	Mintage	F12	VF20	XF40	MS60	MS63
2004	10,000	PF65 50.00				

KM# 287 10 DOLLARS
31.10 g., 0.999 Silver 0.9926 oz. ASW, 38.6 mm. Obv: Queen's bust right Obv. Designer: Ian Rank-Broadley Rev: Dolphin Edge: Reeded

Date	Mintage	F12	VF20	XF40	MS60	MS63
2004	10,000	PF65 55.00				

KM# 288 10 DOLLARS
1.24 g., 0.9999 Gold 0.0397 oz. AGW, 14 mm. Obv: Queen's bust right Obv. Designer: Ian Rank-Broadley Rev: Dolphin Edge: Reeded

Date	Mintage	F12	VF20	XF40	MS60	MS63
2004	10,000	PF63 70.00	PF65 75.00			

KM# 298 10 DOLLARS
28.28 g., 0.925 Silver 0.8356 oz. ASW, 38.6 mm. Obv: Queen's bust right Obv. Designer: Ian Rank-Broadley Rev: Soldier above tank and jeeps Edge: Reeded

Date	Mintage	F12	VF20	XF40	MS60	MS63
2004	10,000	PF65 50.00				

KM# 301 10 DOLLARS
28.28 g., 0.925 Silver 0.8356 oz. ASW, 38.6 mm. Obv: Queen's bust right Obv. Designer: Ian Rank-Broadley Rev: Pilot and planes above D-Day landing Edge: Reeded

Date	Mintage	F12	VF20	XF40	MS60	MS63
2004	10,000	PF65 50.00				

KM# 304 10 DOLLARS
28.28 g., 0.925 Silver 0.8356 oz. ASW, 38.6 mm. Obv: Queen's bust right Obv. Designer: Ian Rank-Broadley Rev: Ancient Olympic bust, runners and owl coin Edge: Reeded

Date	Mintage	F12	VF20	XF40	MS60	MS63
2004	10,000	PF65 50.00				

KM# 307 10 DOLLARS
28.28 g., 0.925 Silver 0.8356 oz. ASW, 38.6 mm. Obv: Queen's bust right Obv. Designer: Ian Rank-Broadley Rev: Ancient Olympic bust, charioteer and Zeus coin Edge: Reeded

Date	Mintage	F12	VF20	XF40	MS60	MS63
2004	10,000	PF65 50.00				

KM# 313 10 DOLLARS
31.10 g., 0.999 Silver 0.9926 oz. ASW, 38.6 mm. Obv: Bust of Queen Elizabeth II right Rev: Mother and baby dolphin Edge: Reeded

Date	Mintage	F12	VF20	XF40	MS60	MS63
2005	10,000	PF65 55.00				

KM# 314 10 DOLLARS
1.24 g., 0.9999 Gold 0.0397 oz. AGW, 13.92 mm. Obv: Bust of Queen Elizabeth II right Rev: Mother and baby dolphin Edge: Reeded

Date	Mintage	F12	VF20	XF40	MS60	MS63
2005	10,000	PF63 70.00	PF65 75.00			

KM# 350 10 DOLLARS
28.28 g., 0.925 Silver 0.8356 oz. ASW, 38.60 mm. Ruler: Elizabeth II Subject: 5th Anniversary - Attack on Twin Towers, New York City Obv: Crowned bust right Obv. Legend: BRITISH VIRGIN ISLANDS — QUEEN ELIZABETH II Rev: Twin Towers in sprays, remembrance ribbon privy mark at upper right Rev. Inscription: LEST WE FORGET Edge: Reeded

Date	Mintage	F12	VF20	XF40	MS60	MS63
2006	10,000	PF65 77.50				

KM# 333 10 DOLLARS
28.28 g., 0.9167 Silver 0.8281 oz. ASW, 38.60 mm. Ruler: Elizabeth II Subject: 400th Anniversary Founding of Jamestown Obv: Bust with tiara right Obv. Legend: BRITISH VIRGIN ISLANDS — QUEEN ELIZABETH II Rev: British lion laying, American eagle perched on sprays Rev. Legend: UNITED IN FRIENDSHIP Edge: Reeded

Date	Mintage	F12	VF20	XF40	MS60	MS63
2007	25,000	PF63 65.00	PF65 75.00			

KM# 334 10 DOLLARS
1.24 g., 0.9999 Gold 0.0397 oz. AGW, 13.92 mm. Ruler: Elizabeth II Subject: 400th Anniversary Founding of Jamestown Obv: Bust with tiara right Obv. Legend: BRITISH VIRGIN ISLANDS — QUEEN ELIZABETH II Rev: British lion laying, American eagle perched on sprays Rev. Legend: UNITED IN FRIENDSHIP Edge: Reeded

Date	Mintage	F12	VF20	XF40	MS60	MS63
2007	20,000	PF63 65.00	PF65 75.00			

KM# 339 10 DOLLARS
28.28 g., Copper-Nickel Ruler: Elizabeth II Subject: 10th Anniversary Death of Princess Diana Obv: Bust with tiara right Obv. Legend: BRITISH VIRGIN ISLANDS — QUEEN ELIZABETH II Rev: Mother Teresa at left, Princess Diana at right Rev. Legend: MOTHER TERESA • IN LOVING MEMORY • PRINCESS DIANA Edge: Reeded

Date	Mintage	F12	VF20	XF40	MS60	MS63
2007					18.50	—

KM# 341 10 DOLLARS
28.28 g., Copper-Nickel Ruler: Elizabeth II Subject: Diamond Wedding Anniversary Obv: Conjoined busts with Philip right Obv. Legend: BRITISH VIRGIN ISLANDS — QUEEN ELIZABETH II Rev: Bride to be and King George VI standing facing Rev. Legend: Diamond Wedding of H.M. Queen Elizabeth II & H.R.H. Prince Philip Rev. Inscription: THE GIVING AWAY Edge: Reeded

Date	Mintage	F12	VF20	XF40	MS60	MS63
2007		—	—	—	16.50	18.50

KM# 342 10 DOLLARS
28.28 g., Copper-Nickel Ruler: Elizabeth II Subject: Diamond Wedding Anniversary Obv: Conjoined busts with Philip right Obv. Legend: BRITISH VIRGIN ISLANDS — QUEEN ELIZABETH II Rev. Legend: Diamond Wedding of H.M. Queen Elizabeth II & H.R.H. Prince Philip Rev. Inscription: THE GLASS COACH Edge: Reeded

Date	Mintage	F12	VF20	XF40	MS60	MS63
2007		—	—	—	16.50	18.50

KM# 343 10 DOLLARS
28.28 g., Copper-Nickel Ruler: Elizabeth II Subject: Diamond Wedding Anniversary Obv: Conjoined busts with Philip right Obv. Legend: BRITISH VIRGIN ISLANDS — QUEEN ELIZABETH II Rev. Legend: Diamond Wedding of H.M. Queen Elizabeth II & H.R.H. Prince Philip Rev. Inscription: THE HONEYMOON Edge: Reeded

Date	Mintage	F12	VF20	XF40	MS60	MS63
2007		—	—	—	16.50	18.50

KM# 344 10 DOLLARS
28.28 g., Copper-Nickel Ruler: Elizabeth II Subject: Diamond Wedding Anniversary Obv: Conjoined busts with Philip right Obv. Legend: BRITISH VIRGIN ISLANDS — QUEEN ELIZABETH II Rev. Legend: Diamond Wedding of H.M. Queen Elizabeth II & H.R.H. Prince Philip Rev. Inscription: THE WEDDING PROGRAM Edge: Reeded

Date	Mintage	F12	VF20	XF40	MS60	MS63
2007		—	—	—	16.50	18.50

KM# 411 10 DOLLARS
28.28 g., 0.925 Silver 0.8356 oz. ASW, 38.61 mm. Ruler: Elizabeth II Subject: Act of Union, 300th Anniversary Obv: Bust in tiara right Rev: Flags above Queen Anne's portrait, lion and unicorn supporters flanking

Date	Mintage	F12	VF20	XF40	MS60	MS63
2007PM	—	PF65 42.00				

KM# 339a 10 DOLLARS
0.9167 Silver Ruler: Elizabeth II Subject: 10th Anniversary - Death of Princess Diana Obv: Bust with tiara right Obv. Legend: BRITISH VIRGIN ISLANDS — QUEEN ELIZABETH II Rev: Mother Teresa at left, Princess Diana at right Rev. Legend: MOTHER TERESA • IN LOVING MEMORY • PRINCESS DIANA Edge: Reeded

Date	Mintage	F12	VF20	XF40	MS60	MS63
2007		PF65 75.00				

KM# 341a 10 DOLLARS
28.28 g., 0.925 Silver 0.8356 oz. ASW Ruler: Elizabeth II Subject: Diamond Wedding Anniversary Obv: Conjoined busts with Philip right Obv. Legend: BRITISH VIRGIN ISLANDS — QUEEN ELIZABETH II Rev: Bride to be and King George VI standing facing Rev. Legend: Diamond Wedding of H.M. Queen Elizabeth II & H.R.H. Prince Philip Rev. Inscription: THE GIVING AWAY Edge: Reeded

Date	Mintage	F12	VF20	XF40	MS60	MS63
2007		PF65 75.00				

KM# 342a 10 DOLLARS
28.28 g., 0.925 Silver 0.8356 oz. ASW Ruler: Elizabeth II Subject: Diamond Wedding Anniversary Obv: Conjoined busts with Philip right Obv. Legend: BRITISH VIRGIN ISLANDS — QUEEN ELIZABETH II Rev. Legend: Diamond Wedding of H.M. Queen Elizabeth II & H.R.H. Prince Philip Rev. Inscription: THE GLASS COACH Edge: Reeded

Date	Mintage	F12	VF20	XF40	MS60	MS63
2007		PF65 75.00				

KM# 343a 10 DOLLARS
28.28 g., 0.925 Silver 0.8356 oz. ASW Ruler: Elizabeth II Subject: Diamond Wedding Anniversary Obv: Conjoined busts with Philip right Obv. Legend: BRITISH VIRGIN ISLANDS — QUEEN ELIZABETH II Rev. Legend: Diamond Wedding of H.M. Queen Elizabeth II & H.R.H. Prince Philip Rev. Inscription: THE HONEYMOON Edge: Reeded

Date	Mintage	F12	VF20	XF40	MS60	MS63
2007		PF65 75.00				

KM# 344a 10 DOLLARS
28.28 g., 0.925 Silver 0.8356 oz. ASW Ruler: Elizabeth II Subject: Diamond Wedding Anniversary Obv: Conjoined busts with Philip right Obv. Legend: BRITISH VIRGIN ISLANDS — QUEEN ELIZABETH II Rev. Legend: Diamond Wedding of H.M. Queen Elizabeth II & H.R.H. Prince Philip Rev. Inscription: THE WEDDING PROGRAM Edge: Reeded

Date	Mintage	F12	VF20	XF40	MS60	MS63
2007		PF65 75.00				

KM# 371 10 DOLLARS
28.28 g., 0.925 Silver 0.8356 oz. ASW, 38.6 mm. Ruler: Elizabeth II Obv: Bust right Rev: Two soccer players and leopard

Date	Mintage	F12	VF20	XF40	MS60	MS63
2009	10,000	PF65 40.00				
2010	—	PF65 40.00				

KM# 372 10 DOLLARS
1.24 g., 0.999 Gold 0.0396 oz. AGW, 13.92 mm. Ruler: Elizabeth II Obv: Bust right Rev: Henry VIII facing

Date	Mintage	F12	VF20	XF40	MS60	MS63
2009PM	5,000	PF63 75.00	PF65 80.00			

KM# 374 10 DOLLARS
28.28 g., 0.925 Silver 0.8356 oz. ASW, 38.6 mm. Ruler: Elizabeth II Obv: Bust right Rev: Elizabeth I aboard ship

Date	Mintage	F12	VF20	XF40	MS60	MS63
2009	10,000	PF65 42.00				

KM# 376 10 DOLLARS
28.28 g., 0.925 Silver 0.8356 oz. ASW, 38.6 mm. Ruler: Elizabeth II Obv: Bust right Rev: Elizabeth I between two columns

Date	Mintage	F12	VF20	XF40	MS60	MS63
2009	10,000	PF65 42.00				

KM# 382 10 DOLLARS
28.28 g., Copper-Nickel, 38.6 mm. Ruler: Elizabeth II Subject: Centennial of Naval Aviation Rev: 1936 Fairey Swordfish returning to carrier HMS Fencer

Date	Mintage	F12	VF20	XF40	MS60	MS63
2009	—	—	—	—	—	7.50

KM# 382a 10 DOLLARS
28.28 g., Silver, 38.6 mm. Ruler: Elizabeth II Subject: Centennial of Naval Aviation Rev: 1936 Fairey Swordfish returing to carrier HMS Fencer

Date	Mintage	F12	VF20	XF40	MS60	MS63
2009	10,000	PF65 40.00				

KM# 394 10 DOLLARS
28.28 g., 0.925 Silver 0.8356 oz. ASW, 38.6 mm. **Ruler:** Elizabeth II **Subject:** Peanuts 60th Anniversary **Rev:** Multicolor Snoopy asleep atop doghouse

Date	Mintage	F12	VF20	XF40	MS60	MS63
2010PM	10,000	PF65 40.00				

KM# 395 10 DOLLARS
1.24 g., 0.999 Gold 0.0396 oz. AGW, 13.92 mm. **Ruler:** Elizabeth II **Series:** Peanuts 60th Anniversary **Rev:** Snoopy asleep atop doghouse

Date	Mintage	F12	VF20	XF40	MS60	MS63
2010PM	10,000	PF63 85.00	PF65 95.00			

KM# 397 10 DOLLARS
31.11 g., 0.999 Silver 0.9926 oz. ASW, 38.6 mm. **Ruler:** Elizabeth II **Subject:** Elgin Marbles **Rev:** Two horsemen

Date	Mintage	F12	VF20	XF40	MS60	MS63
2010PM	10,000	PF65 50.00				

KM# 398 10 DOLLARS
1.22 g., 0.999 Gold 0.0389 oz. AGW, 13.92 mm. **Ruler:** Elizabeth II **Subject:** Birth of Venus

Date	Mintage	F12	VF20	XF40	MS60	MS63
2010PM	Est. 10000	PF63 85.00	PF65 95.00			

KM# 401 10 DOLLARS
28.28 g., 0.925 Silver 0.8356 oz. ASW, 38.6 mm. **Ruler:** Elizabeth II **Subject:** Birth of Venus

Date	Mintage	F12	VF20	XF40	MS60	MS63
2010	Est. 10000	PF65 50.00				

KM# 406 10 DOLLARS
28.28 g., 0.925 Silver 0.8356 oz. ASW, 38.61 mm. **Ruler:** Elizabeth II **Obv:** Bust in tiara right **Rev:** World Trade Center complex

Date	Mintage	F12	VF20	XF40	MS60	MS63
2011PM		PF65 45.00				

KM# 407 10 DOLLARS
28.28 g., 0.925 Silver 0.8356 oz. ASW, 38.61 mm. **Ruler:** Elizabeth II **Subject:** Queen Elizabeth II's 85th Birthday **Obv:** Older and young busts conjoined right **Rev:** Queen on horseback left

Date	Mintage	F12	VF20	XF40	MS60	MS63
2011PM	—	PF65 42.00				

KM# 408 10 DOLLARS
28.28 g., 0.925 Silver 0.8356 oz. ASW, 38.61 mm. **Ruler:** Elizabeth II **Subject:** Royal Wedding - Prince William and Catherine Middleton **Obv:** Bust in tiara right **Rev:** Busts of Catherine and William

Date	Mintage	F12	VF20	XF40	MS60	MS63
2011PM	—	PF65 42.00				

KM# 409 10 DOLLARS
1.22 g., 0.999 Gold 0.0389 oz. AGW, 13.92 mm. **Ruler:** Elizabeth II **Obv:** Bust in tiara right **Rev:** Anne Boylen bust 1/4 left

Date	Mintage	F12	VF20	XF40	MS60	MS63
2011PM	—	PF63 90.00	PF65 100			

KM# 410 10 DOLLARS
28.28 g., Silver, 38.61 mm. **Ruler:** Elizabeth II **Subject:** Life cycle of a tree frog **Obv:** Frog at center **Rev:** Life cycle of a tree frog

Date	Mintage	F12	VF20	XF40	MS60	MS63
2011PM	—	PF65 120				

KM# 417 10 DOLLARS
28.28 g., 0.925 Silver 0.8356 oz. ASW, 38.61 mm. **Ruler:** Elizabeth II **Subject:** Life of Queen Elizabeth II **Obv:** Current

and young busts conjoined right **Rev:** Half length bust facing wearing Order sash and tiara

Date	Mintage	F12	VF20	XF40	MS60	MS63
2012PM	—	PF65 50.00				

KM# 418 10 DOLLARS
28.28 g., Silver, 38.6 mm. **Ruler:** Elizabeth II **Subject:** Life of Queen Elizabeth II **Obv:** Conjoined busts right **Rev:** Elizabeth II on horseback as if reviewing troops

Date	Mintage	F12	VF20	XF40	MS60	MS63
2012PM Proof	—	—	—	—	—	50.00

KM# 419 10 DOLLARS
28.28 g., Copper-Nickel, 38.6 mm. **Ruler:** Elizabeth II **Subject:** Valentine's day **Obv:** Conjoined busts right **Rev:** Crescent moon and pixi

Date	Mintage	F12	VF20	XF40	MS60	MS63
2012PM	—	—	—	—		15.00

KM# 420 10 DOLLARS
28.28 g., 0.925 Silver 0.8356 oz. ASW, 38.6 mm. **Ruler:** Elizabeth II **Subject:** Summer Olympics, London **Obv:** Conjoined busts right **Rev:** Gymnast on pommel horse, Union Jack in color below

Date	Mintage	F12	VF20	XF40	MS60	MS63
2012PM	—	PF65 50.00				

KM# 421 10 DOLLARS
28.28 g., 0.925 Silver 0.8356 oz. ASW, 38.6 mm. **Ruler:** Elizabeth II **Subject:** Summer Olympics, London **Obv:** Conjoined busts right **Rev:** Dressage, Union Jack in color below

Date	Mintage	F12	VF20	XF40	MS60	MS63
2012PM	—	PF65 50.00				

KM# 422 10 DOLLARS

28.28 g., 0.925 Silver 0.8356 oz. ASW, 38.6 mm. **Ruler:** Elizabeth II **Subject:** Summer Olympics, London **Obv:** Conjoined busts right **Rev:** Fencing, Union Jack in color below

Date	Mintage	F12	VF20	XF40	MS60	MS63
2012PM	—		PF65 50.00			

KM# 423 10 DOLLARS

28.28 g., 0.925 Silver 0.8356 oz. ASW, 38.6 mm. **Ruler:** Elizabeth II **Subject:** Summer Olympics, London **Obv:** Conjoined busts right **Rev:** Soccer players, Union Jack in color below

Date	Mintage	F12	VF20	XF40	MS60	MS63
2012PM	—		PF65 50.00			

KM# 424 10 DOLLARS

28.28 g., Copper-Nickel, 38.61 mm. **Ruler:** Elizabeth II **Rev:** Prince William

Date	Mintage	F12	VF20	XF40	MS60	MS63
2012PM	—					15.00

KM# 425 10 DOLLARS

28.28 g., Copper-Nickel, 38.61 mm. **Ruler:** Elizabeth II **Rev:** Duchess of Cambridge

Date	Mintage	F12	VF20	XF40	MS60	MS63
2012PM	—					15.00

KM# 427 10 DOLLARS

23.40 g., Silver, 38.6 mm. **Ruler:** Elizabeth II **Subject:** Year of the Dragon **Obv:** Dragon at center **Rev:** Dragon at center, Zodiac around

Date	Mintage	F12	VF20	XF40	MS60	MS63
2012 Proof	Est. 5000					

KM# 428 10 DOLLARS

21.11 g., Silver, 62x61 mm. **Ruler:** Elizabeth II **Obv:** Bust with crown right **Rev:** Nefertiti Bust **Shape:** Head

Date	Mintage	F12	VF20	XF40	MS60	MS63
2012	—		PF65 65.00			

KM# 432 10 DOLLARS

28.28 g., Silver, 38.6 mm. **Ruler:** Elizabeth II **Subject:** Father of the Modern Olympics

Date	Mintage	F12	VF20	XF40	MS60	MS63
2012 Proof	Est. 10000	—	—	—	—	—

KM# 437 10 DOLLARS

31.10 g., 0.999 Silver 0.9926 oz. ASW, 30 mm. **Ruler:** Elizabeth II **Rev:** Layout of pyramids in Giza, sand encased **Note:** High relief, 4.5mm

Date	Mintage	F12	VF20	XF40	MS60	MS63
2013PM	1,999	—	—	—	—	35.00

KM# 438 10 DOLLARS

28.28 g., Copper-Nickel, 38.61 mm. **Ruler:** Elizabeth II **Subject:** Orient Express

Date	Mintage	F12	VF20	XF40	MS60	MS63
2013PM	—					15.00

KM# 438a 10 DOLLARS

28.28 g., 0.925 Silver 0.8356 oz. ASW, 38.61 mm. **Ruler:** Elizabeth II **Subject:** Orient Express

Date	Mintage	F12	VF20	XF40	MS60	MS63
2013PM	10,000		PF65 60.00			

KM# 440 10 DOLLARS

28.28 g., 0.925 Silver 0.8356 oz. ASW, 38.61 mm. **Ruler:** Elizabeth II **Subject:** Birth of Prince George **Rev:** Prince William with blue footprints added at right

Date	Mintage	F12	VF20	XF40	MS60	MS63
2013PM	10,000		PF65 60.00			

KM# 442 10 DOLLARS

28.28 g., 0.925 Silver 0.8356 oz. ASW, 38.61 mm. **Ruler:** Elizabeth II **Subject:** Birth of Prince George **Rev:** Katherine and blue footprints added at right

Date	Mintage	F12	VF20	XF40	MS60	MS63
2013PM	10,000		PF65 60.00			

KM# 444 10 DOLLARS

28.28 g., 0.925 Silver 0.8356 oz. ASW, 38.61 mm. **Ruler:** Elizabeth II **Subject:** Last flight of Concorde, 10th Anniversary **Rev:** Concorde, NY and London skyline

Date	Mintage	F12	VF20	XF40	MS60	MS63
2013PM	10,000		PF65 60.00			

KM# 444a 10 DOLLARS

28.28 g., 0.925 Silver 0.8356 oz. ASW, 38.61 mm. **Ruler:** Elizabeth II **Subject:** Last flight of Concorde, 10th Anniversary **Rev:** Concorde with tailfin in color, NY and London skyline

Date	Mintage	F12	VF20	XF40	MS60	MS63
2013PM	10,000		PF65 60.00			

KM# 201 20 DOLLARS

1.24 g., 0.9999 Gold 0.0397 oz. AGW, 13.92 mm. **Subject:** Teddy Bear Centennial **Obv:** Queen's bust right **Obv. Designer:** Ian Rank-Broadley **Rev:** Teddy bear **Edge:** Reeded

Date	Mintage	F12	VF20	XF40	MS60	MS63
2002	10,000		PF63 70.00	PF65 75.00		

KM# 227 20 DOLLARS

1.24 g., 0.9999 Gold 0.0396 oz. AGW, 13.92 mm. **Subject:** Kennedy Assassination **Obv:** Queen's bust right **Obv. Designer:** Ian Rank-Broadley **Rev:** President Kennedy's portrait **Edge:** Reeded

Date	Mintage	F12	VF20	XF40	MS60	MS63
2003	10,000		PF63 70.00	PF65 75.00		

KM# 271 20 DOLLARS

1.24 g., 0.9999 Gold 0.0397 oz. AGW, 14 mm. **Obv:** Queen's bust right **Obv. Designer:** Ian Rank-Broadley **Rev:** Peter Rabbit **Edge:** Reeded

Date	Mintage	F12	VF20	XF40	MS60	MS63
2004	5,000		PF63 75.00	PF65 80.00		

KM# 279 20 DOLLARS

58.00 g., 0.999 Silver 1.8509 oz. ASW, 50 mm. **Subject:** XXVIII Olympic Games **Obv:** Bust with tiara right **Obv. Designer:** Ian Rank Broadley **Rev:** 1896 Olympic medal design **Edge:** Reeded

Date	Mintage	F12	VF20	XF40	MS60	MS63
2004PM	2,004		PF63 75.00	PF65 90.00		

KM# 279a 20 DOLLARS

63.59 g., 0.999 Silver Gilt 2.0293 oz., 49.93 mm. **Ruler:** Elizabeth II **Subject:** XXVII Olympic Games **Obv:** Bust with tiara right **Rev:** 1896 Olympic medal design **Edge:** Reeded

Date	Mintage	F12	VF20	XF40	MS60	MS63
2004PM	—		PF65 100			

KM# 345 20 DOLLARS

3.96 g., 0.750 Gold 0.0949 oz. AGW, 21.78 mm. **Ruler:** Elizabeth II **Subject:** 500th Anniversary - Death of Columbus **Obv:** Crowned bust right **Obv. Legend:** BRITISH VIRGIN ISLANDS - QUEEN ELIZABETH II **Rev:** Bust of Columbus facing 3/4 left at right, outlined map of the Americas at left **Rev. Legend:** 1451 - CHRISTOPHER COLUMBUS - 1506 **Edge:** Reeded **Note:** Struck in white gold.

Date	Mintage	F12	VF20	XF40	MS60	MS63
2006	1,506		PF65 185			

KM# 346 20 DOLLARS
4.02 g., 0.750 Gold 0.0963 oz. AGW, 21.78 mm. **Ruler:** Elizabeth II **Subject:** 500th Anniversary - Death of Columbus **Obv:** Crowned bust right **Obv. Legend:** BRITISH VIRGIN ISLANDS - QUEEN ELIZABETH II **Rev:** Sailing ship "Santa Maria **Rev. Legend:** 1451 - CHRISTOPHER COLUMBUS - 1506 **Edge:** Reeded **Note:** Struck in rose gold.

Date	Mintage	F12	VF20	XF40	MS60	MS63
2006	1,506	PF65 185				

KM# 347 20 DOLLARS
3.99 g., 0.750 Gold 0.0956 oz. AGW, 21.78 mm. **Ruler:** Elizabeth II **Subject:** 500th Anniversary - Death of Columbus **Obv:** Crowned bust right **Obv. Legend:** BRITISH VIRGIN ISLANDS - QUEEN ELIZABETH II **Rev:** Sailing ships "Niña" and "Pinta **Rev. Legend:** 1451 - CHRISTOPHER COLUMBUS - 1506 **Edge:** Reeded **Note:** Struck in yellow gold.

Date	Mintage	F12	VF20	XF40	MS60	MS63
2006	1,506	PF65 200				

KM# 379 30 DOLLARS
155.50 g., 0.999 Silver 4.9623 oz. ASW **Ruler:** Elizabeth II **Subject:** Nelson's Victory at Trafalgar **Rev:** Two ships

Date	Mintage	F12	VF20	XF40	MS60	MS63
2008	—	PF63 200	PF65 225			

KM# 275 25 DOLLARS
3.11 g., 0.9999 Gold 0.0993 oz. AGW, 18 mm. **Obv:** Queen's bust right **Obv. Designer:** Ian Rank-Broadley **Rev:** Hernando Pizarro portrait and life events pictorial **Edge:** Reeded

Date	Mintage	F12	VF20	XF40	MS60	MS63
2004	350	PF65 185				

KM# 289 25 DOLLARS
3.11 g., 0.9999 Gold 0.0993 oz. AGW, 18 mm. **Obv:** Queen's bust right **Obv. Designer:** Ian Rank-Broadley **Rev:** Dolphin **Edge:** Reeded

Date	Mintage	F12	VF20	XF40	MS60	MS63
2004	6,000	PF65 180				

KM# 315 25 DOLLARS
3.11 g., 0.9999 Gold 0.0993 oz. AGW, 18 mm. **Obv:** Bust of Queen Elizabeth II right **Rev:** Mother and baby dolphins **Edge:** Reeded

Date	Mintage	F12	VF20	XF40	MS60	MS63
2005	6,000	PF65 180				

KM# 335 25 DOLLARS
3.11 g., 0.9999 Gold 0.0994 oz. AGW, 17.95 mm. **Ruler:** Elizabeth II **Subject:** 400th Anniversary Founding of Jamestown **Obv:** Bust with tiara right **Obv. Legend:** BRITISH VIRGIN ISLANDS - QUEEN ELIZABETH II **Rev:** British lion laying, American eagle perched on sprays **Rev. Legend:** UNITED IN FRIENDSHIP **Edge:** Reeded

Date	Mintage	VG8	F12	VF20	XF40	MS60	MS63
2007	7,500	PF65 180					

KM# 412 25 DOLLARS
6.22 g., 0.999 Gold 0.1985 oz. AGW, 22 mm. **Ruler:** Elizabeth II **Subject:** Nelson's victory at Trafalgar **Obv:** Bust in tiara right **Rev:** Victory crowned Britannia standing on prow

Date	Mintage	F12	VF20	XF40	MS60	MS63
2008PM	—	PF65 450				

KM# 202 50 DOLLARS
3.11 g., 0.9999 Gold 0.0993 oz. AGW, 17.95 mm. **Subject:** Teddy Bear Centennial **Obv:** Queen's bust right **Obv. Designer:** Ian Rank-Broadley **Rev:** Teddy bear **Edge:** Reeded

Date	Mintage	F12	VF20	XF40	MS60	MS63
2002	—	PF65 185				

KM# 272 50 DOLLARS
3.11 g., 0.9999 Gold 0.0993 oz. AGW, 18 mm. **Obv:** Queen's bust right **Obv. Designer:** Ian Rank-Broadley **Rev:** Peter Rabbit **Edge:** Reeded

Date	Mintage	F12	VF20	XF40	MS60	MS63
2004	3,000	PF65 190				

KM# 276 50 DOLLARS
6.22 g., 0.9999 Gold 0.1987 oz. AGW, 22 mm. **Obv:** Queen's bust right **Obv. Designer:** Ian Rank-Broadley **Rev:** Treasure ship with blue color sail **Edge:** Reeded

Date	Mintage	F12	VF20	XF40	MS60	MS63
2004	350	PF65 400				

KM# 290 50 DOLLARS
6.22 g., 0.9999 Gold 0.1987 oz. AGW, 22 mm. **Obv:** Queen's bust right **Obv. Designer:** Ian Rank-Broadley **Rev:** Dolphin **Edge:** Reeded

Date	Mintage	F12	VF20	XF40	MS60	MS63
2004	3,500	PF65 350				

KM# 316 50 DOLLARS
6.22 g., 0.9999 Gold 0.1987 oz. AGW, 22 mm. **Obv:** Bust of Queen Elizabeth II right **Rev:** Large and small dolphins **Edge:** Reeded

Date	Mintage	F12	VF20	XF40	MS60	MS63
2005	3,500	PF65 350				

KM# 351 50 DOLLARS
6.22 g., 0.9999 Gold 0.1987 oz. AGW, 22 mm. **Ruler:** Elizabeth II **Subject:** 5th Anniversary - Attack on Twin Towers, New York City **Obv:** Crowned bust right **Obv. Legend:** BRITISH VIRGIN ISLANDS - QUEEN ELIZABETH II **Rev:** Twin Towers in sprays, remembrance ribbon privy mark at upper right **Rev. Inscription:** LEST WE FORGET **Edge:** Reeded

Date	Mintage	F12	VF20	XF40	MS60	MS63
2006	2,000	PF65 365				

KM# 336 50 DOLLARS
6.22 g., 0.9999 Gold 0.1988 oz. AGW, 22 mm. **Ruler:** Elizabeth II **Subject:** 400th Anniversary Founding of Jamestown **Obv:** Bust with tiara right **Obv. Legend:** BRITISH VIRGIN ISLANDS - QUEEN ELIZABETH II **Rev:** British lion laying, American eagle perched on sprays **Rev. Legend:** UNITED IN FRIENDSHIP **Edge:** Reeded

Date	Mintage	F12	VF20	XF40	MS60	MS63
2007	5,000	PF65 360				

KM# 413 50 DOLLARS
6.22 g., 0.999 Gold 0.1985 oz. AGW, 22 mm. **Ruler:** Elizabeth II **Subject:** Color photography, 100th Anniversary **Obv:** Bust in tiara right **Rev:** Conjoined portraits right in photo frame

Date	Mintage	F12	VF20	XF40	MS60	MS63
2007PM	—	PF65 450				

KM# 377 50 DOLLARS
6.22 g., 0.999 Gold 0.1985 oz. AGW, 22 mm. **Ruler:** Elizabeth II **Obv:** Bust right **Rev:** Elizabeth II aboard ship with 1mm pearl

Date	Mintage	F12	VF20	XF40	MS60	MS63
2009	750	PF65 375				

KM# 378 50 DOLLARS
6.22 g., 0.999 Gold 0.1985 oz. AGW, 22 mm. **Ruler:** Elizabeth II **Obv:** Bust right **Rev:** Elizabeth II between two columns, .01ct ruby insert

Date	Mintage	F12	VF20	XF40	MS60	MS63
2009	750	PF65 375				

KM# 285 75 DOLLARS
11.00 g., Bi-Metallic, 36.5 mm. **Obv:** Queen's bust right **Obv. Designer:** Ian Rank-Broadley **Rev:** British Guiana stamp design **Edge:** Reeded

Date	Mintage	F12	VF20	XF40	MS60	MS63
2004	2,500	PF65 450				

KM# 389 75 DOLLARS
Bi-Metallic **Ruler:** Elizabeth II **Subject:** Mozart

Date	Mintage	F12	VF20	XF40	MS60	MS63
2006PM	—	PF65 450				

KM# 388 75 DOLLARS
Bi-Metallic, 36.5 mm. **Ruler:** Elizabeth II **Subject:** Beijing Olympics **Obv:** Bust in tiara right **Rev:** Tennis plays against Great Wall background

Date	Mintage	F12	VF20	XF40	MS60	MS63
2009PM	—	PF65 450				

KM# 209.1 100 DOLLARS
6.22 g., 0.9999 Gold 0.1987 oz. AGW, 22 mm. **Subject:** September 11, 2001 **Obv:** Queen's bust right **Obv. Designer:** Ian Rank-Broadley **Rev:** World Trade Center twin towers **Edge:** Reeded

Date	Mintage	F12	VF20	XF40	MS60	MS63
2002		PF65 350				

KM# 182 100 DOLLARS
6.22 g., 0.999 Gold 0.1985 oz. AGW, 22 mm. **Subject:** Sir Francis Drake **Obv:** Queen's bust right **Obv. Designer:** Ian Rank-Broadley **Rev:** Ship, portrait and map **Edge:** Reeded

Date	Mintage	F12	VF20	XF40	MS60	MS63
2002	5,000	PF65 350				

KM# 185 100 DOLLARS
6.22 g., 0.999 Gold 0.1985 oz. AGW, 22 mm. **Subject:** Sir Walter Raleigh **Obv:** Queen's bust right **Obv. Designer:** Ian Rank-Broadley **Rev:** Ship, portrait and map **Edge:** Reeded

Date	Mintage	F12	VF20	XF40	MS60	MS63
2002	5,000	PF65 350				

KM# 189 100 DOLLARS
6.22 g., 0.9999 Gold 0.1987 oz. AGW, 22 mm. **Subject:** Queen's Golden Jubilee **Obv:** Queen's bust right **Obv. Designer:** Ian Rank-Broadley **Rev:** Queen on horse **Edge:** Reeded

Date	Mintage	F12	VF20	XF40	MS60	MS63
2002	—	PF65 365				

KM# 192 100 DOLLARS
6.22 g., 0.9999 Gold 0.1987 oz. AGW, 22 mm. **Subject:** Queen's Golden Jubilee **Obv:** Queen's bust right **Obv. Designer:** Ian Rank-Broadley **Rev:** Queen on throne **Edge:** Reeded

Date	Mintage	F12	VF20	XF40	MS60	MS63
2002	—	PF65 365				

KM# 195 100 DOLLARS
6.22 g., 0.9999 Gold 0.1987 oz. AGW, 22 mm. **Subject:** Queen's Golden Jubilee **Obv:** Queen's bust right **Obv. Designer:** Ian Rank-Broadley **Rev:** Queen with President Ronald Reagan and Mrs. Nancy Reagan **Edge:** Reeded

Date	Mintage	F12	VF20	XF40	MS60	MS63
2002	—	PF65 365				

KM# 198 100 DOLLARS
6.22 g., 0.9999 Gold 0.1987 oz. AGW, 22 mm. **Subject:** Queen's Golden Jubilee **Obv:** Queen's bust right **Obv. Designer:** Ian Rank-Broadley **Rev:** Carnival dancers **Edge:** Reeded

Date	Mintage	F12	VF20	XF40	MS60	MS63
2002		PF65 365				

KM# 203 100 DOLLARS
6.22 g., 0.9999 Gold 0.1987 oz. AGW, 22 mm. **Subject:** Teddy Bear Centennial **Obv:** Queen's bust right **Obv. Designer:** Ian Rank-Broadley **Rev:** Teddy bear **Edge:** Reeded

Date	Mintage	F12	VF20	XF40	MS60	MS63
2002	—	PF65 350				

KM# 206 100 DOLLARS
6.22 g., 0.9999 Gold 0.1987 oz. AGW, 22 mm. **Subject:** Princess Diana **Obv:** Queen's bust right **Obv. Designer:** Ian Rank-Broadley **Rev:** Diana's portrait **Edge:** Reeded

Date	Mintage	F12	VF20	XF40	MS60	MS63
2002	—	PF65 350				

KM# 209.2 100 DOLLARS
6.22 g., 0.9999 Gold 0.1987 oz. AGW, 22 mm. **Subject:** September 11, 2001 **Obv:** Queen's bust right **Obv. Designer:** Ian Rank-Broadley **Rev:** Holographic multicolor World Trade Center twin towers **Edge:** Reeded

Date	Mintage	F12	VF20	XF40	MS60	MS63
2002	—	PF65 350				

KM# 212 100 DOLLARS
6.22 g., 0.9999 Gold 0.1987 oz. AGW, 22 mm. **Subject:** September 11, 2001 **Obv:** Queen's bust right **Obv. Designer:** Ian Rank-Broadley **Rev:** Statue of Liberty **Edge:** Reeded

Date	Mintage	F12	VF20	XF40	MS60	MS63
2002	—	PF65 350				

KM# 215 100 DOLLARS
6.22 g., 0.9999 Gold 0.1987 oz. AGW, 22 mm. **Subject:** Queen Mother Series **Obv:** Queen's bust right **Obv. Designer:** Ian Rank-Broadley **Rev:** Queen Mother with young Prince Charles **Edge:** Reeded

Date	Mintage	F12	VF20	XF40	MS60	MS63
2002PM	5,000	PF65 350				

KM# 218 100 DOLLARS
6.22 g., 0.9999 Gold 0.1987 oz. AGW, 22 mm. **Subject:** Queen Mother Series **Obv:** Queen's bust right **Obv. Designer:** Ian Rank-Broadley **Rev:** Queen Mother with four grandchildren **Edge:** Reeded

Date	Mintage	F12	VF20	XF40	MS60	MS63
2002PM	5,000	PF65 350				

KM# 221 100 DOLLARS
6.22 g., 0.9999 Gold 0.1987 oz. AGW, 22 mm. **Subject:** Queen Mother Series **Obv:** Queen's bust right **Obv. Designer:** Ian Rank-Broadley **Rev:** Queen Mother with uniformed Prince Charles **Edge:** Reeded

Date	Mintage	F12	VF20	XF40	MS60	MS63
2002PM	5,000	PF65 350				

KM# 224 100 DOLLARS
6.22 g., 0.9999 Gold 0.1987 oz. AGW, 22 mm. **Subject:** Queen Mother Series **Obv:** Queen's bust right **Obv. Designer:** Ian Rank-Broadley **Rev:** Queen Mother's coffin **Edge:** Reeded

Date	Mintage	F12	VF20	XF40	MS60	MS63
2002PM	5,000	PF65 350				

KM# 228 100 DOLLARS
6.22 g., 0.9999 Gold 0.1987 oz. AGW, 22 mm. **Subject:** Kennedy Assassination **Obv:** Queen's bust right **Obv. Designer:** Ian Rank-Broadley **Rev:** President Kennedy's portrait **Edge:** Reeded

Date	Mintage	F12	VF20	XF40	MS60	MS63
2003	5,000	PF65 350				

KM# 231 100 DOLLARS
15.55 g., 0.9999 Gold 0.4967 oz. AGW, 30 mm. **Subject:** Powered Flight Centennial **Obv:** Queen's bust right **Obv. Designer:** Ian Rank-Broadley **Rev:** Three historic airplanes and rocket **Edge:** Reeded

Date	Mintage	F12	VF20	XF40	MS60	MS63
2003	—	PF65 875				

KM# 234 100 DOLLARS
6.22 g., 0.9999 Gold 0.1987 oz. AGW, 22 mm. **Obv:** Queen's bust right **Obv. Designer:** Ian Rank-Broadley **Rev:** Henry VIII and Elizabeth I **Edge:** Reeded

Date	Mintage	F12	VF20	XF40	MS60	MS63
2003	5,000	PF65 350				

KM# 237 100 DOLLARS
6.22 g., 0.9999 Gold 0.1987 oz. AGW, 22 mm. **Obv:** Queen's bust right **Obv. Designer:** Ian Rank-Broadley **Rev:** Matthew Parker, Archbishop of Canterbury **Edge:** Reeded

Date	Mintage	F12	VF20	XF40	MS60	MS63
2003	5,000	PF65 350				

KM# 240 100 DOLLARS
6.22 g., 0.9999 Gold 0.1987 oz. AGW, 22 mm. **Obv:** Queen's bust right **Obv. Designer:** Ian Rank-Broadley **Rev:** Sir Francis Drake and ships **Edge:** Reeded

Date	Mintage	F12	VF20	XF40	MS60	MS63
2003	5,000	PF65 350				

KM# 243 100 DOLLARS
6.22 g., 0.9999 Gold 0.1987 oz. AGW, 22 mm. **Obv:** Queen's bust right **Obv. Designer:** Ian Rank-Broadley **Rev:** Sir Walter Raleigh **Edge:** Reeded

Date	Mintage	F12	VF20	XF40	MS60	MS63
2003	5,000	PF65 350				

KM# 246 100 DOLLARS
6.22 g., 0.9999 Gold 0.1987 oz. AGW, 22 mm. **Obv:** Queen's bust right **Obv. Designer:** Ian Rank-Broadley **Rev:** Sir William Shakespeare **Edge:** Reeded

Date	Mintage	F12	VF20	XF40	MS60	MS63
2003	5,000	PF65 350				

KM# 249 100 DOLLARS
6.22 g., 0.9999 Gold 0.1987 oz. AGW, 22 mm. **Obv:** Queen's bust right **Obv. Designer:** Ian Rank-Broadley **Rev:** Elizabeth I above her funeral procession **Edge:** Reeded

Date	Mintage	F12	VF20	XF40	MS60	MS63
2003	5,000	PF65 350				

KM# 252 100 DOLLARS
6.22 g., 0.9999 Gold 0.1987 oz. AGW, 22 mm. **Subject:** Olympics **Obv:** Queen's bust right **Obv. Designer:** Ian Rank-Broadley **Rev:** Ancient Olympic bust, runners in background and coin upper right **Edge:** Reeded

Date	Mintage	F12	VF20	XF40	MS60	MS63
2003	5,000	PF65 350				

KM# 255 100 DOLLARS
6.22 g., 0.9999 Gold 0.1987 oz. AGW, 22 mm. **Subject:** Olympics **Obv:** Queen's bust right **Obv. Designer:** Ian Rank-Broadley **Rev:** Ancient bust, charioteer and coin **Edge:** Reeded

Date	Mintage	F12	VF20	XF40	MS60	MS63
2003	5,000	PF65 350				

KM# 273.1 100 DOLLARS
6.22 g., 0.9999 Gold 0.1987 oz. AGW, 22 mm. **Obv:** Queen's bust right **Obv. Designer:** Ian Rank-Broadley **Rev:** Peter Rabbit **Edge:** Reeded

Date	Mintage	F12	VF20	XF40	MS60	MS63
2004	2,000	PF65 365				

KM# 273.2 100 DOLLARS
6.22 g., 0.9999 Gold 0.1987 oz. AGW, 22 mm. **Obv:** Queen's bust right **Obv. Designer:** Ian Rank-Broadley **Rev:** Multicolor Peter Rabbit **Edge:** Reeded

Date	Mintage	F12	VF20	XF40	MS60	MS63
2004		PF65 365				

KM# 283 100 DOLLARS
6.22 g., 0.9999 Gold 0.1987 oz. AGW, 22 mm. **Obv:** Queen's bust right **Obv. Designer:** Ian Rank-Broadley **Rev:** Sailor above two D-Day landing craft **Edge:** Reeded

Date	Mintage	F12	VF20	XF40	MS60	MS63
2004	5,000	PF65 350				

KM# 299 100 DOLLARS
6.22 g., 0.9999 Gold 0.1987 oz. AGW, 22 mm. **Obv:** Queen's bust right **Obv. Designer:** Ian Rank-Broadley **Rev:** Soldier above tank and jeeps **Edge:** Reeded

Date	Mintage	F12	VF20	XF40	MS60	MS63
2004	5,000	PF65 350				

KM# 302 100 DOLLARS
6.22 g., 0.9999 Gold 0.1987 oz. AGW, 22 mm. **Obv:** Queen's bust right **Obv. Designer:** Ian Rank-Broadley **Rev:** Pilot and planes above D-Day landing **Edge:** Reeded

Date	Mintage	F12	VF20	XF40	MS60	MS63
2004	5,000	PF65 350				

KM# 305 100 DOLLARS
6.22 g., 0.9999 Gold 0.1987 oz. AGW, 22 mm. **Obv:** Queen's bust right **Obv. Designer:** Ian Rank-Broadley **Rev:** Ancient Olympic bust, runners and owl coin **Edge:** Reeded

Date	Mintage	F12	VF20	XF40	MS60	MS63
2004	5,000	PF65 350				

KM# 308 100 DOLLARS
6.22 g., 0.9999 Gold 0.1987 oz. AGW, 22 mm. **Obv:** Queen's bust right **Obv. Designer:** Ian Rank-Broadley **Rev:** Ancient Olympic bust, charioteer and Zeus coin **Edge:** Reeded

Date	Mintage	F12	VF20	XF40	MS60	MS63
2004	5,000	PF65 350				

KM# 434 100 DOLLARS
1000.00 g., Silver, 120 mm. **Ruler:** Elizabeth II **Subject:** RMS

Titanic Remembered

Date	Mintage	F12	VF20	XF40	MS60	MS63
2012 Proof	—	—	—	—	—	—

KM# 317 125 DOLLARS
15.55 g., 0.9999 Gold 0.4967 oz. AGW, 30 mm. **Obv:** Bust of Queen Elizabeth II right **Rev:** Mother and baby dolphin **Edge:** Reeded

Date	Mintage	F12	VF20	XF40	MS60	MS63
2005	1,500	PF65 900				

KM# 337 125 DOLLARS
15.56 g., 0.9999 Gold 0.497 oz. AGW, 30 mm. **Ruler:** Elizabeth II **Subject:** 400th Anniversary Founding of Jamestown **Obv:** Bust with tiara right **Obv. Legend:** BRITISH VIRGIN ISLANDS - QUEEN ELIZABETH II **Rev:** British lion laying, American eagle perched on sprays **Rev. Legend:** UNITED IN FRIENDSHIP **Edge:** Reeded

Date	Mintage	F12	VF20	XF40	MS60	MS63
2007	3,000	PF65 875				

KM# 309 250 DOLLARS
15.55 g., 0.999 Gold 0.4963 oz. AGW, 30 mm. **Obv:** Queen's bust right **Obv. Designer:** Ian Rank-Broadley **Rev:** Statue of Liberty and the date "11 Sept. 2001 **Edge:** Reeded

Date	Mintage	F12	VF20	XF40	MS60	MS63
2002	250	PF65 950				

KM# 280 250 DOLLARS
58.00 g., 0.500 Gold 0.9264 oz. AGW, 50 mm. **Obv:** Queen's bust right **Obv. Designer:** Ian Rank-Broadley **Rev:** 1896 Olympic medal design **Edge:** Reeded

Date	Mintage	F12	VF20	XF40	MS60	MS63
2004	1,000	PF65 1,650				

KM# 318 250 DOLLARS
31.10 g., 0.9999 Gold 0.9934 oz. AGW, 32.7 mm. **Obv:** Bust of Queen Elizabeth II right **Rev:** Mother and baby dolphin **Edge:** Reeded

Date	Mintage	F12	VF20	XF40	MS60	MS63
2005	750	PF65 1,750				

KM# 390 250 DOLLARS
Gold AGW **Ruler:** Elizabeth II **Subject:** Mozart

Date	Mintage	F12	VF20	XF40	MS60	MS63
2006PM	—	PF65 1,750				

KM# 338 250 DOLLARS
31.10 g., 0.9999 Gold 0.9934 oz. AGW, 32.7 mm. **Ruler:** Elizabeth II **Subject:** 400th Anniversary Founding of Jamestown **Obv:** Bust with tiara right **Obv. Legend:** BRITISH VIRGIN ISLANDS - QUEEN ELIZABETH II **Rev:** British lion laying, American eagle perched on sprays **Rev. Legend:** UNITED IN FRIENDSHIP **Edge:** Reeded

Date	Mintage	F12	VF20	XF40	MS60	MS63
2007	1,000	PF65 1,750				

KM# 277 500 DOLLARS
160.76 g., 0.999 Gold 5.130 oz. AGW, 150 mm. **Obv:** Queen's bust right **Obv. Designer:** Ian Rank-Broadley **Rev:** Gold-plated portrait of Hernando Pizarro, small inset emerald above Pizarro's life events pictoral **Edge:** Reeded **Note:** Photo reduced.

Date	Mintage	F12	VF20	XF40	MS60	MS63
2004	500	PF65 9,000				

KM# 348 500 DOLLARS
160.76 g., 0.999 Gold 5.130 oz. AGW, 150 mm. **Ruler:** Elizabeth II **Subject:** 500th Anniversary - Death of Columbus **Obv:** Crowned bust right **Obv. Legend:** BRITISH VIRGIN ISLANDS - QUEEN ELIZABETH II **Rev:** Ship in background at left, Columbus standing at right with right arm outstreched looking right, compass below. **Rev. Legend:** 1451 - DISCOVERER OF AMERICA - CHRISTOPHER COLUMBUS - 1506 **Edge:** Reeded

Date	Mintage	F12	VF20	XF40	MS60	MS63
2006	1,506	PF63 8,700	PF65 8,900			

KM# 392 500 DOLLARS
160.76 g., 0.999 Silver 5.130 oz. ASW, 150 mm. **Ruler:** Elizabeth II **Subject:** Battle of Trafalgar **Rev:** Two naval ships in battle

Date	Mintage	F12	VF20	XF40	MS60	MS63
2008PM	—	PF63 225	PF65 250			

KM# 435 500 DOLLARS
155.51 g., Gold AGW, 65 mm. **Ruler:** Elizabeth II **Subject:** RMS Titanic Remembered

Date	Mintage	F12	VF20	XF40	MS60	MS63
2012 Proof	Est. 99	—	—	—	—	—

KM# 430
47.00 g., Silver, 48 mm. **Ruler:** Elizabeth II **Subject:** Father of the Modern Olympics

Date	Mintage	F12	VF20	XF40	MS60	MS63
2012 Proof	Est. 2000	—	—	—	—	—

MINT SETS

KM#	Date	Mintage	Identification	Issue Price	Mkt Val
MS12	2007 (4)	—	KM# 341 - 344	65.00	80.00

PROOF SETS

KM#	Date	Mintage	Identification	Issue Price	Mkt Val
PS20	2007 (4)	—	KM# 341a - 344a	300	300

BRUNEI

Negara Brunei Darussalam (Brunei, Adobe of Peace), an independent sultanate on the northwest coast of the island of Borneo, has an area of 2,226 sq. mi. (5,765 sq. km.) and a population of *326,000. Capital: Bandar Seri Begawan. Crude oil and rubber are exported.

TITLES

نكري بروني

RULERS
Sultan Hassanal Bolkiah, 1967-

SULTANATE
DECIMAL COINAGE
100 Sen = 1 Dollar (Ringgit)

KM# 34 SEN
1.75 g., Copper Clad Steel, 17.7 mm. **Ruler:** Sultan Hassanal Bolkiah **Obv:** Uniformed bust facing **Rev:** Native design, denomination below, date at right **Edge:** Plain

Date	Mintage	F12	VF20	XF40	MS60	MS63
2001	576,000	—	—	—	0.75	1.00
2002	804,900	—	—	—	0.75	1.00
2004	—	—	—	—	0.75	1.00
2005	—	—	—	—	0.75	1.00
2006	—	—	—	—	0.75	1.00

KM# 34b SEN
1.70 g., Brass, 17.7 mm. **Ruler:** Sultan Hassanal Bolkiah **Obv:** Uniformed bust facing **Rev:** Native design, denomination below, date at right

Date	Mintage	F12	VF20	XF40	MS60	MS63
2008	—	—	—	—	0.75	1.00
2009	—	—	—	—	0.75	1.00
2010	—	—	—	—	0.75	1.00

KM# 35 5 SEN
1.41 g., Copper-Nickel, 16.26 mm. **Ruler:** Sultan Hassanal Bolkiah **Obv:** Uniformed bust facing **Rev:** Native design, denomination below, date at right **Edge:** Reeded

Date	Mintage	F12	VF20	XF40	MS60	MS63
2001	808,000	—	—	—	1.00	1.50
2002	1,418,178	—	—	—	1.00	1.50
2004	—	—	—	—	1.00	1.50
2005	—	—	—	—	1.00	1.50
2006	—	—	—	—	1.00	1.50
2007	—	—	—	—	1.00	1.50
2008	—	—	—	—	1.00	1.50
2009	—	—	—	—	1.00	1.50
2010	—	—	—	—	1.00	1.50

KM# 36 10 SEN
2.82 g., Copper-Nickel, 19.4 mm. **Ruler:** Sultan Hassanal Bolkiah **Obv:** Uniformed bust facing **Rev:** Native design, denomination below, date at right **Edge:** Reeded

Date	Mintage	F12	VF20	XF40	MS60	MS63
2001	164,000	—	—	—	1.00	1.50
2002	476,452	—	—	—	1.00	1.50
2004	—	—	—	—	1.00	1.50
2005	—	—	—	—	1.00	1.50
2006	—	—	—	—	1.00	1.50
2007	—	—	—	—	1.00	1.50
2008	—	—	—	—	1.00	1.50
2009	—	—	—	—	1.00	1.50

KM# 37 20 SEN
5.65 g., Copper-Nickel, 23.5 mm. **Ruler:** Sultan Hassanal Bolkiah **Obv:** Uniformed bust facing **Rev:** Native design, denomination below, date at right **Edge:** Reeded

Date	Mintage	F12	VF20	XF40	MS60	MS63
2001	270,647	—	—	0.45	1.10	1.50
2002	597,272	—	—	0.45	1.10	1.50
2004	—	—	—	0.45	1.10	1.50
2005	—	—	—	0.45	1.10	1.50
2008	—	—	—	0.45	1.10	1.50
2009	—	—	—	0.45	1.10	1.50
2010	—	—	—	0.45	1.10	1.50

KM# 38 50 SEN
9.33 g., Copper-Nickel, 27.7 mm. **Ruler:** Sultan Hassanal Bolkiah **Obv:** Uniformed bust facing **Rev:** National arms within circle, denomination below, date at right **Edge:** Security

Date	Mintage	F12	VF20	XF40	MS60	MS63
2001	50,000	—	—	1.00	2.50	3.00
2002	1,325	—	—	1.75	3.50	5.00
2004	—	—	—	0.75	2.00	3.00
2005	—	—	—	0.75	2.00	3.00
2006	—	—	—	0.75	2.00	3.00
2007	—	—	—	0.75	2.00	3.00
2008	—	—	—	0.75	2.00	3.00
2009	—	—	—	0.75	2.00	3.00
2010	—	—	—	0.75	2.00	3.00

KM# 80 2 DOLLARS
31.10 g., Copper-Nickel, 40.7 mm. **Ruler:** Sultan Hassanal Bolkiah **Subject:** 20th Anniversary of Independence **Obv:** Bust 3/4 left, facing **Obv. Legend:** SULTAN HAJI HASSANAL BOLKIAH **Rev:** National arms **Rev. Legend:** NEGARI BRUNEI DARUSSALAM

Date	Mintage	F12	VF20	XF40	MS60	MS63
2004	4,000	PF63 55.00	PF65 65.00			

KM# 86 2 DOLLARS
31.10 g., Copper-Nickel, 40.7 mm. **Ruler:** Sultan Hassanal Bolkiah **Subject:** 60th Birthday **Obv:** Bust 3/4 left, facing **Obv. Legend:** SULTAN HAJI HASSANAL BOLKIAH **Rev:** Multicolor 1/2-length figure in civilian clothes, facing

Date	Mintage	F12	VF20	XF40	MS60	MS63
2006	200	PF65 120				

KM# 77 3 DOLLARS
24.00 g., Copper-Nickel, 40 mm. **Ruler:** Sultan Hassanal Bolkiah **Obv:** Uniformed bust facing **Obv. Legend:** SULTAN

HAJI HASSANAL BOLKIAH **Rev:** Logo at center **Rev. Legend:** COMMONWEALTH FINANCE MINISTERS MEETING **Edge:** Reeded

Date	Mintage	F12	VF20	XF40	MS60	MS63
2003	4,000	PF63 40.00		PF65 45.00		

KM# 83 3 DOLLARS
31.10 g., Copper-Nickel, 40.7 mm. **Ruler:** Sultan Hassanal Bolkiah **Subject:** Royal Wedding **Obv:** Multicolor portraits of Royal couple

Date	Mintage	F12	VF20	XF40	MS60	MS63
2004	5,000	PF63 45.00		PF65 50.00		

KM# 81 20 DOLLARS
31.10 g., 0.999 Silver 0.9925 oz. ASW, 40.7 mm. **Ruler:** Sultan Hassanal Bolkiah **Subject:** 20th Anniversary of Independence **Obv:** Bust 3/4 left, facing **Obv. Legend:** SULTAN HAJI HASSANAL BOLKIAH **Rev:** National arms **Rev. Legend:** NEGARI BRUNEI DARUSSALAM

Date	Mintage	F12	VF20	XF40	MS60	MS63
2004	1,000	PF65 120				

KM# 87 20 DOLLARS
31.10 g., 0.999 Silver 0.9925 oz. ASW, 40.7 mm. **Ruler:** Sultan Hassanal Bolkiah **Subject:** 60th Birthday **Obv:** Bust 3/4 left, facing **Obv. Legend:** SULTAN HAJI HASSANAL BOLKIAH **Rev:** Multicolor 1/2-length figure in civilian clothes, facing

Date	Mintage	F12	VF20	XF40	MS60	MS63
2006	200	PF65 275				

KM# 78 30 DOLLARS
62.20 g., 0.999 Silver 1.9849 oz. ASW **Ruler:** Sultan Hassanal Bolkiah **Subject:** Commonwealth Finance Ministers' Meeting **Obv:** Logo at upper left, multicolor bust of Sultan 3/4 left, facing at right **Obv. Legend:** SULTAN HAJI HASSANAL BOLIAH **Rev:** World map at left - center, national arms at upper right **Shape:** Rectangular, 65 x 31 mm

Date	Mintage	F12	VF20	XF40	MS60	MS63
2003	1,000	PF65 210				

KM# 84 30 DOLLARS
31.10 g., 0.999 Silver 0.9925 oz. ASW, 40.7 mm. **Ruler:** Sultan Hassanal Bolkiah **Subject:** Royal Wedding **Obv:** Multicolor portraits of Royal couple

Date	Mintage	F12	VF20	XF40	MS60	MS63
2004	1,000	PF65 180				

KM# 90 50 DOLLARS
31.10 g., 0.999 Silver 0.9925 oz. ASW, 40.7 mm. **Subject:** ASEAN 2013 Presidency **Obv:** Sultan in color **Rev:** ASEAN logo at center in color **Shape:** 8-sided

Date	Mintage	F12	VF20	XF40	MS60	MS63
2013	400	PF65 125				

KM# 89 100 DOLLARS
Gold AGW **Subject:** ASEAN 2013 Presidency **Rev:** ASEAN logo at center in color **Shape:** 8-sided

Date	Mintage	F12	VF20	XF40	MS60	MS63
2013 Proof	—	—	—	—	—	—

KM# 82 200 DOLLARS
31.10 g., 0.9999 Gold 0.9934 oz. AGW, 32.1 mm. **Ruler:** Sultan Hassanal Bolkiah **Subject:** 20th Anniversary of Independence **Obv:** Bust 3/4 left, facing **Obv. Legend:** SULTAN HAJI HASSANAL BOLKIAH **Rev:** National arms **Rev. Legend:** NEGARI BRUNEI DARUSSALAM

Date	Mintage	F12	VF20	XF40	MS60	MS63
2004	200	PF65 2,400				

KM# 85 200 DOLLARS
31.10 g., 0.9999 Gold 0.9934 oz. AGW, 32 mm. **Ruler:** Sultan Hassanal Bolkiah **Subject:** Royal Wedding **Obv:** Multicolor portraits of Royal couple

Date	Mintage	F12	VF20	XF40	MS60	MS63
2004	200	PF65 2,400				

KM# 88 200 DOLLARS
31.10 g., 0.9999 Gold 0.9934 oz. AGW, 32.1 mm. **Ruler:** Sultan Hassanal Bolkiah **Subject:** 60th Birthday **Obv:** Bust 3/4 left, facing **Obv. Legend:** SULTAN HAJI HASSANAL BOLKIAH **Rev:** Multicolor 1/2-length figure in civilian clothes, facing

Date	Mintage	F12	VF20	XF40	MS60	MS63
2006	200	PF65 2,500				

PROOF SETS

KM#	Date	Mintage	Identification	Issue Price	Mkt Val
PS20	2003 (2)	500	KM#77-78	—	250
PS21	2004 (3)	200	KM80-82	—	2,600
PS22	2004 (3)	200	KM83-85	—	2,650
PS23	2006 (3)	200	KM86-88	—	2,900

BULGARIA

The Republic of Bulgaria, formerly the Peoples Republic of Bulgaria, a Balkan country on the Black Sea in southeastern Europe, has an area of 42,855 sq. mi. (110,910 sq. km.) and a population of *8.31 million. Capital: Sofia. Agriculture remains a key component of the economy but industrialization, particularly heavy industry, has been emphasized since the late 1940s. Machinery, tobacco and cigarettes, wines and spirits, clothing and metals are the chief exports. Bulgaria joined the European Union in January 2007.

MONETARY SYSTEM
100 Stotinki = 1 Lev

REPUBLIC
REFORM COINAGE

KM# 237 STOTINKA
1.80 g., Aluminum-Bronze, 16 mm. **Obv:** Madara horseman right, animal below **Rev:** Denomination above date **Edge:** Plain

Date	Mintage	F12	VF20	XF40	MS60	MS63
2002	10,000	PF60 1.00				

KM# 237a STOTINKA
1.80 g., Brass Plated Steel, 16 mm. **Obv:** Madara horseman right **Rev:** Denomination above date

Date	Mintage	F12	VF20	XF40	MS60	MS63
2002	10,000	PF60 1.00				

KM# 238 2 STOTINKI
2.50 g., Aluminum-Bronze, 18 mm. **Obv:** Madara horseman right, animal below **Rev:** Denomination above date **Edge:** Plain

Date	Mintage	F12	VF20	XF40	MS60	MS63
2002	10,000	PF60 1.50				

KM# 238a 2 STOTINKI
2.50 g., Brass Plated Steel, 18 mm. **Obv:** Madara horseman right **Rev:** Denomination above date

Date	Mintage	F12	VF20	XF40	MS60	MS63
2002	10,000	PF60 1.50				

KM# 239 5 STOTINKI
3.50 g., Aluminum-Bronze, 20 mm. **Obv:** Madara horseman right, animal below **Rev:** Denomination above date **Edge:** Plain **Note:** Prev. KM#A239.

Date	Mintage	F12	VF20	XF40	MS60	MS63
2002	10,000	PF60 2.00				

KM# 239a 5 STOTINKI
3.50 g., Brass Plated Steel, 20 mm. **Obv:** Madara horseman right **Rev:** Denomination above date

Date	Mintage	F12	VF20	XF40	MS60	MS63
2002	10,000	PF60 2.00				

KM# 240 10 STOTINKI
3.00 g., Copper-Nickel-Zinc, 18.5 mm. **Obv:** Madara horseman right, animal below **Rev:** Denomination above date **Edge:** Reeded

Date	Mintage	F12	VF20	XF40	MS60	MS63
2002	10,000	PF60 2.50				

KM# 241 20 STOTINKI
4.00 g., Copper-Nickel-Zinc, 20.5 mm. **Obv:** Madara horseman right, animal below **Rev:** Denomination above date **Edge:** Reeded

Date	Mintage	F12	VF20	XF40	MS60	MS63
2002	10,000	PF60 3.00				

KM# 242 50 STOTINKI
5.00 g., Copper-Nickel-Zinc, 22.5 mm. **Obv:** Madara horseman right, animal below **Rev:** Denomination above date **Edge:** Reeded

Date	Mintage	F12	VF20	XF40	MS60	MS63
2002	10,000	PF60 5.00				

KM# 272 50 STOTINKI
5.00 g., Copper-Nickel-Zinc, 22.5 mm. **Obv:** Stylized Bulgarian arms, lion left, NATO - 2004 under lion **Rev:** Denomination above date **Edge:** Reeded

Date	Mintage	F12	VF20	XF40	MS60	MS63
2004	—	—	—	—	2.00	3.00

KM# 282 50 STOTINKI
5.00 g., Copper-Nickel-Zinc, 22.5 mm. **Obv:** European Union seated woman allegory **Rev:** Value above date **Edge:** Reeded **Note:** Prev. KM#274.

Date	Mintage	F12	VF20	XF40	MS60	MS63
2005	—	—	—	—	1.25	1.75

KM# 291 50 STOTINKI
5.00 g., Copper-Nickel-Zinc, 22.5 mm. **Obv:** Value **Rev:** Pillar behind open book **Edge:** Reeded **Note:** Prev. KM#276.

Date	Mintage	F12	VF20	XF40	MS60	MS63
2007	500,000	—	—	—	—	1.50

KM# 257 LEV
15.55 g., 0.999 Gold 0.4962 oz. AGW **Obv:** St. Ivan of Rila **Rev:** Large number one **Edge:** Plain

Date	Mintage	F12	VF20	XF40	MS60	MS63
2002	2,000	PF65 875				

KM# 254 LEV
7.00 g., Bi-Metallic, 24.5 mm. **Obv:** St. Ivan of Rila **Rev:** Denomination **Edge:** Segmented reeding

Date	Mintage	F12	VF20	XF40	MS60	MS63
2002	24,842,000				3.00	4.00
2002	10,000	PF63 10.00		PF65 12.00		

KM# 281 1.95583 LEVA
20.00 g., 0.999 Silver 0.6382 oz. ASW, 40 mm. **Subject:** Bulgaria - EU **Obv:** National Arms, value below **Rev:** Female seated within stars **Rev. Designer:** Bogomil Nikolov

Date	Mintage	F12	VF20	XF40	MS60	MS63
2005	14,000	PF65 50.00				

KM# 290 1.95583 LEVA
20.00 g., 0.999 Silver 0.6382 oz. ASW, 40 mm. **Subject:** Bulgaria in the EU **Obv:** National Arms **Rev:** Column and open window design **Rev. Designer:** Bogomil Nikolov and Elena Dimitrova

Date	Mintage	F12	VF20	XF40	MS60	MS63
2007	14,000	PF65 45.00				

KM# 304 2 LEVA
16.40 g., 0.999 Copper 0.5234 oz., 34.2 mm. **Subject:** Dechko, Uzunov 110th Anniversary of Birth **Obv:** National arms **Rev:** Petar Stoikov

Date	Mintage	F12	VF20	XF40	MS60	MS63
2009	8,000	PF63 12.00	PF65 15.00			

KM# 310 2 LEVA
16.40 g., Copper-Nickel, 34.2 mm. **Obv:** National arms, value below **Rev:** Zahariy Zograf's self-portrait

Date	Mintage	F12	VF20	XF40	MS60	MS63
2010	—	PF63 20.00	PF65 25.00			

KM# 317 2 LEVA
16.40 g., Copper, 34.2 mm. **Subject:** Dimcho Debelyanov, 125th Anniversary of Birth **Obv:** National arms **Rev:** Portrait facing **Edge:** Plain

Date	Mintage	F12	VF20	XF40	MS60	MS63
2012	5,000	PF65 20.00				

KM# 258 5 LEVA
1.24 g., 0.999 Gold 0.0396 oz. AGW **Obv:** Denomination **Rev:** Olympic archer **Edge:** Plain

Date	Mintage	F12	VF20	XF40	MS60	MS63
2002	12,000	PF65 75.00				

KM# 259 5 LEVA
1.24 g., 0.999 Gold 0.0396 oz. AGW **Obv:** Denomination **Rev:** Olympic cyclist **Edge:** Plain

Date	Mintage	F12	VF20	XF40	MS60	MS63
2002	12,000	PF65 75.00				

KM# 260 5 LEVA
1.24 g., 0.999 Gold 0.0396 oz. AGW **Obv:** Denomination **Rev:** Olympic fencing **Edge:** Plain

Date	Mintage	F12	VF20	XF40	MS60	MS63
2002	12,000	PF65 75.00				

KM# 261 5 LEVA
1.24 g., 0.999 Gold 0.0396 oz. AGW **Obv:** Denomination **Rev:** Olympic wrestling **Edge:** Plain

Date	Mintage	F12	VF20	XF40	MS60	MS63
2002	12,000	PF65 75.00				

KM# 262 5 LEVA
1.24 g., 0.999 Gold 0.0396 oz. AGW, 14 mm. **Obv:** Denomination **Rev:** Olympic gymnastics **Edge:** Plain

Date	Mintage	F12	VF20	XF40	MS60	MS63
2002	12,000	PF65 75.00				

KM# 263 5 LEVA
1.24 g., 0.999 Gold 0.0396 oz. AGW, 14 mm. **Obv:** Denomination **Rev:** Olympics founder Pierre du Coubertin **Edge:** Plain

Date	Mintage	F12	VF20	XF40	MS60	MS63
2002	17,000	PF65 75.00				

KM# 264 5 LEVA
1.24 g., 0.999 Gold 0.0396 oz. AGW, 14 mm. **Obv:** Denomination **Rev:** Olympic running **Edge:** Plain

Date	Mintage	F12	VF20	XF40	MS60	MS63
2002	12,000	PF65 75.00				

KM# 265 5 LEVA
1.24 g., 0.999 Gold 0.0396 oz. AGW, 14 mm. **Obv:** Denomination **Rev:** Olympic swimming **Edge:** Plain

Date	Mintage	F12	VF20	XF40	MS60	MS63
2002	12,000	PF65 75.00				

KM# 266 5 LEVA
1.24 g., 0.999 Gold 0.0396 oz. AGW, 14 mm. **Obv:** Denomination **Rev:** Olympic tennis **Edge:** Plain

Date	Mintage	F12	VF20	XF40	MS60	MS63
2002	12,000	PF65 75.00				

KM# 267 5 LEVA
1.24 g., 0.999 Gold 0.0396 oz. AGW, 14 mm. **Obv:** Denomination **Rev:** Olympic weight lifting **Edge:** Plain

Date	Mintage	F12	VF20	XF40	MS60	MS63
2002	12,000	PF65 75.00				

KM# 274 5 LEVA
15.00 g., Copper-Nickel, 34.2 mm. **Subject:** Sourvakari **Obv:** National arms **Rev:** Multicolor children in winter clothes **Rev. Designer:** Stephan Nenov

Date	Mintage	F12	VF20	XF40	MS60	MS63
2002	5,000	PF63 15.00	PF65 17.00			

KM# 268 5 LEVA
28.28 g., 0.925 Silver 0.8356 oz. ASW, 38.5 mm. **Obv:** Denomination **Rev:** FIFA Soccer trophy cup **Edge:** reeded

Date	Mintage	F12	VF20	XF40	MS60	MS63
2003	50,000	PF63 37.00	PF65 42.00			

KM# 276 5 LEVA
15.00 g., Copper-Nickel, 34.2 mm. **Obv:** National arms, date and denomination below **Rev:** Multicolor child on rocking horse **Edge:** Plain **Note:** Prev. KM#275.

Date	Mintage	F12	VF20	XF40	MS60	MS63
2003	10,000	PF63 32.00	PF65 35.00			

KM# 277 5 LEVA
15.00 g., Copper-Nickel, 34.2 mm. **Subject:** Palm Sunday **Obv:** National Arms **Rev:** Bogomil Nikolov and Elena Dimitrova

Date	Mintage	F12	VF20	XF40	MS60	MS63
2004	10,000	PF63 15.00	PF65 17.00			

KM# 279 5 LEVA
15.00 g., Copper-Nickel, 34.2 mm. **Subject:** Baba Marta **Obv:** National Arms **Rev:** Multicolor flora and butterfly **Rev. Designer:** Vanya Dimitrova

Date	Mintage	F12	VF20	XF40	MS60	MS63
2005	10,000	PF63 15.00	PF65 17.00			

KM# 284 5 LEVA
23.30 g., 0.500 Silver 0.3721 oz. ASW, 38.6 mm. **Subject:** Bulgaria Crafts - winemaking **Obv:** National Arms **Rev:** Multicolor grapes - wine caraffe **Rev. Designer:** Ivan Todorov and Plamen Dzhermanov

Date	Mintage	F12	VF20	XF40	MS60	MS63
2006	10,000	PF63 25.00	PF65 30.00			

KM# 296 5 LEVA
23.30 g., 0.500 Silver 0.3721 oz. ASW, 38.6 mm. **Subject:** Bulgarian Crafts - Carpet Weaving **Obv:** National Arms **Rev:** Ivan Todorov and Plamen Dzhermanov

Date	Mintage	F12	VF20	XF40	MS60	MS63
2007	7,000	PF63 25.00	PF65 30.00			

KM# 305 5 LEVA
23.30 g., 0.999 Silver 0.7435 oz. ASW, 38.6 mm. **Subject:** Bulgarian National Bank, 130th Anniversary **Obv:** Bank emblem **Obv. Designer:** Razvigor Kolev and Borislav Kyossev **Rev:** Multicolor lion mozaic, fragment of stained glass

Date	Mintage	F12	VF20	XF40	MS60	MS63
2009	4,000	PF65 45.00				

KM# 306 5 LEVA
0.500 Silver **Subject:** Traditional Bulgarian Crafts - Pottery **Rev:** Color pot and design

Date	Mintage	F12	VF20	XF40	MS60	MS63
2009	—	—	—	—	—	35.00

KM# 322 5 LEVA
23.300 Silver ASW, 38.6 mm. **Subject:** Kose Bose Tale **Obv:** National arms **Rev:** Boy and Fox in color

Date	Mintage	F12	VF20	XF40	MS60	MS63
2011	6,000	—	—	—	—	45.00

KM# 321 5 LEVA
23.30 g., 0.500 Silver 0.3721 oz. ASW, 38.6 mm. **Obv:** National arms **Rev:** Boy and the wind in color

Date	Mintage	F12	VF20	XF40	MS60	MS63
2012	—	PF65 50.00				

KM# 246 10 LEVA
23.60 g., 0.925 Silver 0.6973 oz. ASW, 38.5 mm. **Subject:** Higher Education **Obv:** National arms, date and denomination below **Rev:** Graduate before building **Edge:** Plain

Date	Mintage	F12	VF20	XF40	MS60	MS63
2001	10,000	PF63 40.00	PF65 45.00			

KM# 247 10 LEVA
23.33 g., 0.925 Silver 0.6894 oz. ASW, 38.5 mm. **Subject:** Olympics **Obv:** National arms, date and denomination below **Rev:** Ski jumper **Edge:** Plain with serial number

Date	Mintage	F12	VF20	XF40	MS60	MS63
2001	25,000	PF63 40.00	PF65 45.00			

KM# 275 10 LEVA
23.30 g., 0.925 Silver 0.6885 oz. ASW, 38.6 mm. **Obv:** National arms **Rev:** Head and Star of David **Rev. Designer:** Peter Stoikov

Date	Mintage	F12	VF20	XF40	MS60	MS63
2003	2,000	PF65 50.00				

KM# 270 10 LEVA
23.33 g., 0.999 Silver 0.7445 oz. ASW, 38.6 mm. **Subject:** National Theater Centennial **Edge:** Plain

Date	Mintage	F12	VF20	XF40	MS60	MS63
2004	5,000	PF65 50.00				

KM# 273 10 LEVA
23.20 g., 0.925 Silver 0.6855 oz. ASW, 38.5 mm. **Obv:** National arms, date and denomination below **Rev:** St. Nikolay Mirlikiisky Chudofvorez with gold-plated crosses and halo **Edge:** Plain

Date	Mintage	F12	VF20	XF40	MS60	MS63
2004	10,000	PF63 42.00	PF65 45.00			

KM# 280 10 LEVA
23.30 g., 0.925 Silver 0.6885 oz. ASW, 38.6 mm. **Subject:** XX Olympic Games - Turino, Italy **Obv:** National arms **Rev:** Short track speed skater **Rev. Designer:** Plamen Chernev

Date	Mintage	F12	VF20	XF40	MS60	MS63
2005	4,000	PF65 40.00				

KM# 283 10 LEVA
20.00 g., 0.999 Silver 0.6382 oz. ASW, 40 mm. **Obv:** National arms **Rev:** Ancient sculpture

Date	Mintage	F12	VF20	XF40	MS60	MS63
2005	10,000	PF65 45.00				

KM# 285 10 LEVA
23.30 g., 0.925 Silver 0.6885 oz. ASW, 38.6 mm. **Subject:** National Parks - Black Sea Coast **Obv:** National arms **Rev:** Map and three circular motifs **Rev. Designer:** Eugenia Isankoa and Plamen Chernev

Date	Mintage	F12	VF20	XF40	MS60	MS63
2006	7,000	PF65 40.00				

KM# 286 10 LEVA
20.00 g., 0.999 Silver 0.6382 oz. ASW, 40 mm. **Subject:** Treasures of Bulgaria - Letnitsa **Obv:** National arms **Rev:** Horseman statue **Rev. Designer:** Eugenio Evtimov

Date	Mintage	F12	VF20	XF40	MS60	MS63
2006	10,000	PF65 45.00				

KM# 292 10 LEVA
31.10 g., 0.999 Silver 0.9925 oz. ASW, 40 mm. **Subject:** Boris Christov **Obv:** National arms **Obv. Legend:** БЪЛГАРСКА НАРОДНА БАНКА **Rev:** Early regal 1/2-length male figure facing holding orb **Rev. Legend:** ИМЕНИТИ БЪЛГАРСКИ ГЛАСОВЕ **Note:** Prev. KM#277.

Date	Mintage	F12	VF20	XF40	MS60	MS63
2007	10,000	PF63 45.00	PF65 50.00			

KM# 295 10 LEVA
23.30 g., 0.925 Silver 0.6885 oz. ASW, 38.6 mm. **Subject:** National Parks - Pirin Mountain **Obv:** National arms **Rev:** Vanya Dimitrova

Date	Mintage	F12	VF20	XF40	MS60	MS63
2007	6,000	PF63 35.00	PF65 40.00			

KM# 297 10 LEVA
20.00 g., 0.999 Silver 0.6382 oz. ASW, 40 mm. **Subject:** Treasures of Bulgaria - Pegasus from Vayovo **Obv:** National arms **Rev:** Pegasus forepart **Rev. Designer:** Razvigor Klov, Borislav Kyossev and Krassimis Angelov

Date	Mintage	F12	VF20	XF40	MS60	MS63
2007	10,000	PF65 45.00				

KM# 298 10 LEVA
23.30 g., 0.925 Silver 0.6885 oz. ASW, 38.6 mm. **Subject:** 130th Anniversary Bulgarian Liberation **Obv:** National arms **Rev:** Two figures in 19th century coats

Date	Mintage	F12	VF20	XF40	MS60	MS63
2008	10,000	PF63 35.00	PF65 40.00			

KM# 299 10 LEVA
23.30 g., 0.925 Silver 0.6885 oz. ASW, 38.6 mm. **Subject:** Shooting sports **Obv:** National Arms **Rev:** Target, bowhunter, rifleman **Rev. Designer:** Todor Todorov and Yana Vassileva

Date	Mintage	F12	VF20	XF40	MS60	MS63
2008	5,000	PF63 35.00	PF65 40.00			

KM# 300 10 LEVA
20.00 g., 0.999 Silver 0.6382 oz. ASW, 40 mm. **Subject:** Treasures of Bulgaria - Sevt III **Obv:** Statue head of King Sevt III **Rev:** Elena Todorova and Todor Todorav

Date	Mintage	F12	VF20	XF40	MS60	MS63
2008	8,000	PF65 45.00				

KM# 301 10 LEVA
23.30 g., 0.925 Silver 0.6885 oz. ASW, 38.6 mm. **Subject:** Bulgarian Independence - 100th Anniversary **Rev:** Crowned shield **Rev. Designer:** Ivan Todorov

Date	Mintage	F12	VF20	XF40	MS60	MS63
2008	5,000	PF63 35.00	PF65 40.00			

KM# 302 10 LEVA
31.10 g., 0.999 Silver 0.9925 oz. ASW, 40 mm. **Subject:** Great Bulgarian Voices: Nikolay Gyaurov **Obv:** National arms **Rev:** Elena Todorov and Todor Todorov

Date	Mintage	F12	VF20	XF40	MS60	MS63
2008	6,000	PF65 50.00				

KM# 308 10 LEVA
31.11 g., 0.999 Silver 0.9926 oz. ASW, 40 mm. **Obv:** National arms **Rev:** Belogradchick rock formations

Date	Mintage	F12	VF20	XF40	MS60	MS63
2010	—	PF65 50.00				

KM# 309 10 LEVA
23.33 g., 0.925 Silver 0.6894 oz. ASW, 38.61 mm. **Subject:** Unification, 125th Anniversary **Obv:** National arms **Rev:** Document seal gilt

Date	Mintage	F12	VF20	XF40	MS60	MS63
2010	5,000	PF65 50.00				

KM# 312 10 LEVA
23.33 g., 0.925 Silver 0.6894 oz. ASW, 38.61 mm. **Obv:** St. George Zograf at right, National arms and value at left **Rev:** St. George Zograf Monastery

Date	Mintage	F12	VF20	XF40	MS60	MS63
2011	6,000	PF65 75.00				

KM# 313 10 LEVA
31.10 g., 0.999 Silver 0.9925 oz. ASW, 40 mm. **Obv:** National arms **Rev:** Gena Dimitrova as Princess Turandot

Date	Mintage	F12	VF20	XF40	MS60	MS63
2011	4,000	PF65 75.00				

KM# 314 10 LEVA
23.33 g., 0.925 Silver 0.6894 oz. ASW, 38.61 mm. **Subject:** Khan Krum **Obv:** Fragment miniture from Constantine Manasses' Chronicle, Khan Krum drinks a toast **Rev:** Khan Krum pursuing the Byzantines

Date	Mintage	F12	VF20	XF40	MS60	MS63
2011	5,000	PF65 75.00				

KM# 318 10 LEVA
23.33 g., 0.925 Silver 0.6894 oz. ASW, 38.6 mm. **Subject:** Slavo-Bulgraian History, 250th Anniversary **Obv:** National arms with gilt design above **Rev:** Gilt seal on documnet

Date	Mintage	F12	VF20	XF40	MS60	MS63
2012	4,000	PF65 75.00				

KM# 319 10 LEVA
23.33 g., 0.925 Silver 0.6894 oz. ASW, 38.61 mm. **Subject:** Chudnite Mostove **Obv:** National arms, value below **Rev:** Natural Bridge

Date	Mintage	F12	VF20	XF40	MS60	MS63
2012	4,000	PF65 75.00				

KM# 320 10 LEVA
Silver, 38.61 mm. **Subject:** Death of Tsar Samuel **Obv:** Knights mourning Samuel **Rev:** Knights on horseback

Date	Mintage	F12	VF20	XF40	MS60	MS63
2013	—	PF65 100				

KM# 269 20 LEVA
1.55 g., 0.999 Gold 0.0495 oz. AGW, 16 mm. **Obv:** Denomination **Rev:** Mother of God **Edge:** Plain

Date	Mintage	F12	VF20	XF40	MS60	MS63
2003	20,000	PF63 75.00	PF65 95.00			

KM# 287 20 LEVA
1.55 g., 0.999 Gold 0.0495 oz. AGW, 13.9 mm. **Subject:** Iconography St John the Baptist **Obv:** National arms **Rev:** Saint facing **Rev. Designer:** Rada Dimitroua

Date	Mintage	F12	VF20	XF40	MS60	MS63
2006	12,000		PF63 75.00		PF65 95.00	

KM# 294 20 LEVA
1.55 g., 0.999 Gold 0.0495 oz. AGW, 13.9 mm. **Subject:** Iconography - St. George the Victorious **Rev:** St. George slaying dragon **Rev. Designer:** Plamen Chernev

Date	Mintage	F12	VF20	XF40	MS60	MS63
2007	8,000		PF65 100			

KM# 303 20 LEVA
1.55 g., 0.999 Gold 0.0495 oz. AGW, 13.9 mm. **Subject:** Tsar Boris I, the Baptist **Obv:** Half-length figure facing **Rev:** Krassimir Angelov, Borislav Kyossev, Razvigov Kolev

Date	Mintage	F12	VF20	XF40	MS60	MS63
2008	8,000		PF65 100			

KM# 316 20 LEVA
1.55 g., 0.999 Gold 0.0495 oz. AGW, 13.9 mm. **Obv:** National arms **Rev:** Virgin Mary and Child

Date	Mintage	F12	VF20	XF40	MS60	MS63
2011	—		PF65 100			

KM# 293 100 LEVA
8.64 g., 0.999 Gold 0.2757 oz. AGW **Subject:** Iconography - St. George the Victorious **Obv:** National arms **Rev:** Plamen Chernev

Date	Mintage	F12	VF20	XF40	MS60	MS63
2007	1,500		PF65 500			

KM# 307 100 LEVA
7.77 g., 0.999 Gold 0.248 oz. AGW, 22 mm. **Subject:** Bulgarian Iconography - St. Dimitar the Wonder Worker

Date	Mintage	F12	VF20	XF40	MS60	MS63
2009	—		PF65 475			

KM# 311 100 LEVA
8.64 g., 0.999 Gold 0.2757 oz. AGW, 24 mm. **Obv:** National arms, value below **Rev:** St. Naum and Monastery of St. Naum in Ohrid

Date	Mintage	F12	VF20	XF40	MS60	MS63
2010	3,000		PF65 500			

KM# 271 125 LEVA
7.78 g., 0.999 Gold 0.2483 oz. AGW, 21 mm. **Subject:** Bulgarian National Bank 125th Anniversary

Date	Mintage	F12	VF20	XF40	MS60	MS63
2004	3,000		PF65 475			

PIEDFORT

KM#	Date	Mintage	Identification	Mkt Val
P4	2004	5,000	10 Leva 0.999 Silver 100 Years - National Theatre, 38.61mm.	75.00

PROOF SETS

KM#	Date	Mintage	Identification	Issue Price	Mkt Val
PS8	2002 (7)	10,000	KM#237-242, 254	—	25.00

BURUNDI

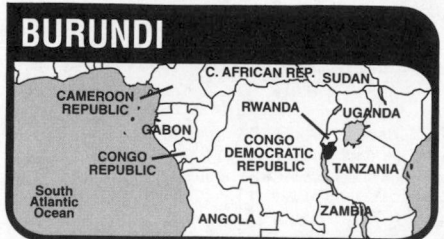

The Republic of Burundi, a landlocked country in central Africa, was a kingdom with a feudalistic society, caste system and Mwami (king) for more than 400 years before independence. It has an area of 10,740 sq. mi. (27,830 sq. km.) and a population of 6.3 million. Capital: Bujumbura. Plagued by poor soil, irregular rainfall and a single-crop economy, coffee, Burundi is barely able to feed itself. Coffee and tea are exported.

Burundi gained independence as a kingdom under Mwami Mwambutsa IV on July 1, 1962. The republic was established by military coup in 1966.

MINT MARKS
PM - Pobjoy Mint
(b) - Privy Marks, Brussels

MONETARY SYSTEM
100 Centimes = 1 Franc

REPUBLIC
1966-

STANDARD COINAGE

KM# 19 FRANC
0.87 g., Aluminum, 18.91 mm. **Obv:** Denomination **Rev:** Arms above date **Edge:** Reeded

Date	Mintage	F12	VF20	XF40	MS60	MS63
2003PM	—			0.50	1.50	2.00

KM# 21 10 FRANCS
6.25 g., Nickel Plated Steel, 27 mm. **Obv:** Country name in three languages **Rev:** Value at center of wreath of bananas and wheat

Date	Mintage	F12	VF20	XF40	MS60	MS63
2011	—				1.00	2.00

KM# 22 50 FRANCS
7.25 g., Nickel Plated Steel, 29 mm. **Obv:** Country name in three languages **Rev:** Drum and drummer

Date	Mintage	F12	VF20	XF40	MS60	MS63
2011	—				2.50	3.00

CAMBODIA

The Kingdom of Cambodia, formerly Democratic Kampuchea and the Khmer Republic, a land of paddy fields and forest-clad hills located on the Indo-Chinese peninsula, fronting on the Gulf of Thailand, has an area of 70,238 sq. mi. (181,040 sq. km.) and a population of *11.21 million. Capital: Phnom Penh. Agriculture is the basis of the economy, with rice the chief crop. Native industries include cattle breeding, weaving and rice milling. Rubber, cattle, corn, and timber are exported.

RULERS
Norodom Sihanouk, 1991-1993
Chairman, Supreme National Council King, 1993-2012

KINGDOM
1993 -

DECIMAL COINAGE

KM# 98 500 RIELS
19.92 g., Brass, 38.7 mm. **Subject:** Angkor Wat **Obv:** Armless statue of Jayavarman VII **Rev:** View of Angkor Wat in center **Edge:** Reeded

Date	Mintage	F12	VF20	XF40	MS60	MS63
2001	28,000				7.50	10.00

KM# 99 3000 RIELS
1.24 g., 0.9999 Gold 0.0397 oz. AGW, 13.92 mm. **Subject:** Angkor Wat **Obv:** Armless statue of Jayavarman VII **Rev:** View of Angkor Wat in center **Edge:** Reeded

Date	Mintage	F12	VF20	XF40	MS60	MS63
2001	28,000	—		—	75.00	85.00

KM# 100 3000 RIELS
20.00 g., 0.925 Silver 0.591 oz. ASW, 38.7 mm. **Subject:** Buddha **Obv:** Armless statue of Jayavarman VII **Rev:** Radiant Buddha next to a carved Buddha face **Edge:** Reeded

Date	Mintage	F12	VF20	XF40	MS60	MS63
2001	10,000	PF63 45.00	PF65 55.00			

KM# 101 3000 RIELS
20.00 g., 0.925 Silver 0.591 oz. ASW, 38.7 mm. **Subject:** Apsara Dance **Obv:** Armless statue of Jayavarman VII **Rev:** Dancer next to multicolor carpet pattern **Edge:** Reeded

Date	Mintage	F12	VF20	XF40	MS60	MS63
2001	10,000	PF65 60.00				

KM# 103 3000 RIELS
20.00 g., 0.999 Silver 0.6382 oz. ASW, 38.7 mm. **Obv:** King Jayavarman VII (1162-1201) **Rev:** Multicolor Tutankhamen's mask **Edge:** Reeded

Date	Mintage	F12	VF20	XF40	MS60	MS63
2004	9,100	PF65 65.00				

KM# 104 3000 RIELS
1.24 g., 0.999 Gold 0.0397 oz. AGW, 13.92 mm. **Obv:** King Jayavarman VII (1162-1201) **Rev:** Sphinx and pyramid **Edge:** Reeded

Date	Mintage	F12	VF20	XF40	MS60	MS63
2004	27,900	PF63 85.00	PF65 95.00			

KM# 124 3000 RIELS
1.24 g., 0.999 Gold 0.0396 oz. AGW, 13.92 mm. **Rev:** Pyramids

Date	Mintage	F12	VF20	XF40	MS60	MS63
2004	—				75.00	85.00

KM# 139 3000 RIELS
31.11 g., 0.999 Silver 0.9926 oz. ASW **Subject:** 2006 FIFA World Cup - Germany **Obv:** King Jayayarman VII **Rev:** Temple above half of a soccer ball

Date	Mintage	F12	VF20	XF40	MS60	MS63
2004		PF63 65.00	PF65 75.00			

KM# 126 3000 RIELS
1.22 g., 0.999 Gold 0.0389 oz. AGW, 13.92 mm.   **Rev:** Taj Mahal

Date	Mintage	F12	VF20	XF40	MS60	MS63
2005	—	—	—	—	75.00	85.00

KM# 127 3000 RIELS
31.11 g., Silver, 38.7 mm. **Rev:** Indian Dancer, multicolor

Date	Mintage	F12	VF20	XF40	MS60	MS63
2005	—	PF65 65.00				

KM# 129 3000 RIELS
1.22 g., 0.999 Gold 0.0389 oz. AGW, 13.92 mm.   **Rev:** Colosseum in Rome

Date	Mintage	F12	VF20	XF40	MS60	MS63
2006	—	—	—	—	75.00	85.00

KM# 130 3000 RIELS
Silver, 38.7 mm. **Rev:** Multicolor Roman soldier

Date	Mintage	F12	VF20	XF40	MS60	MS63
2006	—	PF65 80.00				

KM# 110 3000 RIELS
31.11 g., 0.999 Silver 0.9926 oz. ASW, 40.7 mm. **Subject:** Year of the Dog **Rev:** Multicolor St. Bernard

Date	Mintage	F12	VF20	XF40	MS60	MS63
2006 Prooflike	4,000	—	—	—	—	80.00

KM# 111 3000 RIELS
31.11 g., 0.999 Silver 0.9926 oz. ASW, 40.7 mm. **Subject:** Year of the Dog **Rev:** Multicolor Bloodhound

Date	Mintage	F12	VF20	XF40	MS60	MS63
2006 Prooflike	4,000	—	—	—	—	80.00

KM# 112 3000 RIELS
31.11 g., 0.999 Silver 0.9926 oz. ASW, 40.7 mm. **Subject:** Year of the Dog **Rev:** Multicolor Siberian Husky

Date	Mintage	F12	VF20	XF40	MS60	MS63
2006 Prooflike	4,000	—	—	—	—	80.00

KM# 113 3000 RIELS
31.11 g., 0.999 Silver 0.9926 oz. ASW, 40.7 mm. **Subject:** Year of the Dog **Rev:** Multicolor Shar Pei

Date	Mintage	F12	VF20	XF40	MS60	MS63
2006 Prooflike	4,000	—	—	—	—	80.00

KM# 114 3000 RIELS
31.11 g., 0.999 Silver 0.9926 oz. ASW, 40.7 mm. **Subject:** Year of the Dog **Rev:** Multicolor Borzaya

Date	Mintage	F12	VF20	XF40	MS60	MS63
2006 Prooflike	51,000	—	—	—	—	80.00

KM# 115 3000 RIELS
31.11 g., 0.999 Silver 0.9926 oz. ASW, 40.7 mm. **Subject:** Year of the Dog **Rev:** Multicolor Labrador

Date	Mintage	F12	VF20	XF40	MS60	MS63
2006 Prooflike	51,000	—	—	—	—	80.00

KM# 116 3000 RIELS
31.11 g., 0.999 Silver 0.9926 oz. ASW, 40.7 mm. **Subject:** Year of the Dog **Rev:** Multicolor Russian Spaniel

Date	Mintage	F12	VF20	XF40	MS60	MS63
2006 Prooflike	51,000	—	—	—	—	80.00

KM# 117 3000 RIELS
31.11 g., 0.999 Silver 0.9926 oz. ASW, 40.7 mm. **Subject:** Year of the Dog **Rev:** Multicolor Newfoundland

Date	Mintage	F12	VF20	XF40	MS60	MS63
2006 Prooflike	51,000	—	—	—	—	80.00

KM# 132 3000 RIELS
1.22 g., 0.999 Gold 0.0389 oz. AGW, 13.92 mm.   **Rev:** Borobudur Temple, Indonesia

Date	Mintage	F12	VF20	XF40	MS60	MS63
2007	28,000	—	—	—	75.00	85.00

KM# 133 3000 RIELS
31.11 g., 0.999 Silver 0.9926 oz. ASW, 38.7 mm. **Rev:** Legomo dancer, multicolor

Date	Mintage	F12	VF20	XF40	MS60	MS63
2007	10,000	PF65 80.00				

KM# 118 3000 RIELS
31.11 g., 0.999 Silver 0.9926 oz. ASW, 40.7 mm. **Subject:** Year of the Pig **Rev:** Multicolor pig

Date	Mintage	F12	VF20	XF40	MS60	MS63
2007 Prooflike	—	—	—	—	—	80.00

KM# 135 3000 RIELS
31.11 g., 0.999 Silver 0.9926 oz. ASW, 40.7 mm. **Subject:** Year of the Pig **Rev:** Multicolor pig

Date	Mintage	F12	VF20	XF40	MS60	MS63
2007 Prooflike	30,000	—	—	—	—	90.00

KM# 136 3000 RIELS
31.11 g., 0.999 Silver 0.9926 oz. ASW, 40.7 mm. **Subject:** Year of the Pig **Rev:** Multicolor pig

Date	Mintage	F12	VF20	XF40	MS60	MS63
2007 Prooflike	30,000	—	—	—	—	90.00

KM# 137 3000 RIELS
31.11 g., 0.999 Silver 0.9926 oz. ASW, 40.7 mm. **Subject:** Year of the Pig **Rev:** Multicolor pig

Date	Mintage	F12	VF20	XF40	MS60	MS63
2007 Prooflike	30,000	—	—	—	—	90.00

KM# 138 3000 RIELS
31.11 g., 0.999 Silver 0.9926 oz. ASW, 40.7 mm. **Subject:** Year of the Pig **Rev:** Multicolor pig

Date	Mintage	F12	VF20	XF40	MS60	MS63
2007 Prooflike	30,000	—	—	—	—	90.00

KM# 121 3000 RIELS
1.24 g., 0.999 Gold 0.0396 oz. AGW, 13.9 mm. **Subject:** Statue torso **Rev:** Shwe Dragon Pagoda, Mynamar

Date	Mintage	F12	VF20	XF40	MS60	MS63
2008	—	PF63 85.00	PF65 95.00			

KM# 123 3000 RIELS
31.10 g., 0.999 Silver 0.9926 oz. ASW, 40.7 mm. **Obv:** Statue torso **Rev:** Multicolor Padaung

Date	Mintage	F12	VF20	XF40	MS60	MS63
2009	—	PF65 75.00				

KM# 102 10000 RIELS
31.10 g., 0.999 Bi-Metallic 0.9926 oz., 40.7 mm. **Subject:**
Angkor Wat **Obv:** Armless statue of Jayavarman **Rev:** Multicolor
holographic view of Angkor Wat in center **Edge:** Reeded

Date	Mintage	F12	VF20	XF40	MS60	MS63
2001	—	PF65 350				

KM# 125 10000 RIELS
31.11 g., 0.999 Silver 0.9926 oz. ASW, 40.7 mm. **Rev:** Great
Wall of China, holographic insert

Date	Mintage	F12	VF20	XF40	MS60	MS63
2003	—	PF65 300				

KM# 105 10000 RIELS
31.10 g., 0.999 Silver 0.9926 oz. ASW, 40.7 mm. **Obv:** King
Jayavarman VII (1162-1201) **Rev:** Sphinx and pyramid on
holographic gold insert **Edge:** Reeded

Date	Mintage	F12	VF20	XF40	MS60	MS63
2004	2,100	PF65 300				

KM# 119 10000 RIELS
31.11 g., 0.999 Silver 0.9926 oz. ASW, 38.7 mm. **Subject:**
Zheng He 600th Anniversary **Rev:** Sailing ship with latent image

Date	Mintage	F12	VF20	XF40	MS60	MS63
2005	200	PF65 165				

KM# 120 10000 RIELS
31.11 g., 0.999 Silver 0.9926 oz. ASW, 38.7 mm. **Subject:**
Zheng He 600th Anniversary **Rev:** Multicolor figure standing

Date	Mintage	F12	VF20	XF40	MS60	MS63
2005	200	PF65 150				

KM# 128 10000 RIELS
31.11 g., 0.999 Silver 0.9926 oz. ASW, 40.7 mm. **Rev:** Taj
Mahal in multicolor hologram at center

Date	Mintage	F12	VF20	XF40	MS60	MS63
2005	—	PF65 300				

KM# 131 10000 RIELS
31.11 g., 0.999 Silver 0.9926 oz. ASW, 40.7 mm. **Rev:**
Colosseum in multicolor hologram

Date	Mintage	F12	VF20	XF40	MS60	MS63
2006	—	PF65 300				

KM# 134 10000 RIELS
31.11 g., 0.999 Silver 0.9926 oz. ASW, 40.7 mm. **Rev:**
Boraburdur temple, Indonesia

Date	Mintage	F12	VF20	XF40	MS60	MS63
2007	300	PF65 300				

KM# 122 10000 RIELS
31.10 g., 0.999 Silver 0.9926 oz. ASW, 40.7 mm. **Obv:** Statue
torso **Rev:** Hologram of Shwe Dragon Pagoda, Mynamar

Date	Mintage	F12	VF20	XF40	MS60	MS63
2009	—	PF65 150				

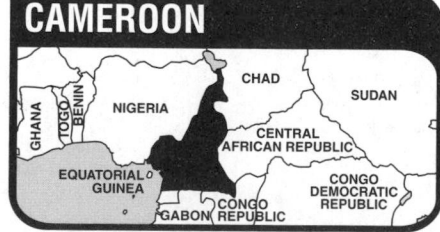

CAMEROON

The Republic of Cameroon, located in west-central Africa
on the Gulf of Guinea, has an area of 183,569 sq. mi. (475,445
sq. km.) and a population of *15.13 million. Capital: Yaounde.
About 90 percent of the labor force is employed on the land;
cash crops account for 80 percent of the country's export
revenue. Cocoa, coffee, aluminum, cotton, rubber, and timber
are exported. Cameroon is a member of the Commonwealth of
Nations. The President is the Head of State; the Prime Minister
is the Head of Government.

MINT MARKS
(a) - Paris, privy marks only
SA - Pretoria, 1943

MONETARY SYSTEM
100 Centimes = 1 Franc

REPUBLIC
STANDARD COINAGE

KM# 56 100 FRANCS
27.00 g., Silver Plated Copper, 40 mm. **Subject:** Soccer
Championships **Obv:** National arms **Rev:** Soccer player,
Brandenburg gate, map of Germany

Date	Mintage	F12	VF20	XF40	MS60	MS63
2012	10,000	PF63 20.00	PF65 30.00			

KM# 57 100 FRANCS
27.00 g., Silver Plated Copper, 40 mm. **Subject:** Soccer
Championship **Obv:** National arms **Rev:** Brazilian player
kneeling

Date	Mintage	F12	VF20	XF40	MS60	MS63
2012	10,000	PF63 20.00	PF65 30.00			

KM# 28 500 FRANCS
15.55 g., 0.925 Silver 0.4595 oz. ASW, 33 mm. **Subject:** Zodiac
- Cancer **Obv:** National arms

Date	Mintage	F12	VF20	XF40	MS60	MS63
2010	3,000	—	—	—	—	50.00

KM# 29 500 FRANCS
15.55 g., 0.925 Silver 0.4595 oz. ASW **Subject:** Zodiac - Leo
Obv: National arms

Date	Mintage	F12	VF20	XF40	MS60	MS63
2010	3,000	—	—	—	—	50.00

KM# 30 500 FRANCS
15.55 g., 0.925 Silver 0.4595 oz. ASW, 33 mm. **Subject:** Zodiac
- Virgo **Obv:** National arms

Date	Mintage	F12	VF20	XF40	MS60	MS63
2010	3,000	—	—	—	—	50.00

KM# 31 500 FRANCS
15.55 g., 0.925 Silver 0.4595 oz. ASW, 33 mm. **Subject:** Zodiac
- Libra **Obv:** National arms

Date	Mintage	F12	VF20	XF40	MS60	MS63
2010	3,000	—	—	—	—	50.00

KM# 32 500 FRANCS
15.55 g., 0.999 Silver 0.4962 oz. ASW, 33 mm. **Subject:** Zodiac
- Scorpius **Obv:** National arms

Date	Mintage	F12	VF20	XF40	MS60	MS63
2010	3,000	—	—	—	—	50.00

KM# 33 500 FRANCS
15.55 g., 0.925 Silver 0.4595 oz. ASW, 33 mm. **Subject:** Zodiac
- Sagittarius **Obv:** National arms

Date	Mintage	F12	VF20	XF40	MS60	MS63
2010	3,000	—	—	—	—	50.00

KM# 34 500 FRANCS
15.55 g., 0.925 Silver 0.4595 oz. ASW, 33 mm. **Subject:** Zodiac
- Capricorn **Obv:** National Arms

Date	Mintage	F12	VF20	XF40	MS60	MS63
2010	3,000	—	—	—	—	50.00

KM# 25 500 FRANCS
15.55 g., 0.925 Silver 0.4595 oz. ASW, 33 mm. **Subject:** Zodiac
- Aries **Obv:** National arms

Date	Mintage	F12	VF20	XF40	MS60	MS63
2010	3,000	—	—	—	—	50.00

KM# 35 500 FRANCS
15.55 g., 0.925 Silver 0.4595 oz. ASW, 33 mm. **Subject:** Zodiac
- Aquarius **Obv:** National arms

Date	Mintage	F12	VF20	XF40	MS60	MS63
2010	3,000	—	—	—	—	50.00

KM# 26 500 FRANCS
15.55 g., 0.925 Silver 0.4595 oz. ASW, 33 mm. **Subject:** Zodiac
- Taurus **Obv:** National arms

Date	Mintage	F12	VF20	XF40	MS60	MS63
2010	3,000	—	—	—	—	50.00

KM# 36 500 FRANCS
15.55 g., 0.925 Silver 0.4595 oz. ASW, 33 mm. **Subject:** Zodiac
- Pisces **Obv:** National arms

Date	Mintage	F12	VF20	XF40	MS60	MS63
2010	3,000	—	—	—	—	50.00

KM# 27 500 FRANCS
15.55 g., 0.925 Silver 0.4595 oz. ASW, 33 mm. **Subject:** Zodiac
- Gemini **Obv:** National arms

Date	Mintage	F12	VF20	XF40	MS60	MS63
2010	3,000	—	—	—	—	50.00

KM# 24 1000 FRANCS
25.00 g., 0.925 Copper-Nickel 0.7387 oz., 38.61 mm. **Obv:**
Arms **Rev:** Papillons D'Amour butterfly **Edge:** Reeded

Date	Mintage	F12	VF20	XF40	MS60	MS63
2010	2,500	PF63 55.00	PF65 65.00			

KM# 37 1000 FRANCS
25.00 g., 0.999 Silver 0.7978 oz. ASW, 38.61 mm. **Subject:** Ange de l'amour **Obv:** National arms **Rev:** Cupuid

Date	Mintage	F12	VF20	XF40	MS60	MS63
2010	2,500	PF65 80.00				

KM# 38 1000 FRANCS
20.00 g., 0.925 Silver 0.591 oz. ASW, 38.61 mm. **Obv:** National arms **Rev:** Heat sensetive image of the Shroud of Turin

Date	Mintage	F12	VF20	XF40	MS60	MS63
2010	2,010	PF65 75.00				

KM# 49 1000 FRANCS
25.00 g., Copper-Nickel, 39 mm. **Obv:** National arms **Rev:** Two swans, hologram between them

Date	Mintage	F12	VF20	XF40	MS60	MS63
2011 Antique Finish	—	—	—	—	—	75.00
2011		PF65 55.00				

KM# 50 1000 FRANCS
25.00 g., Copper-Nickel, 39 mm. **Obv:** National arms **Rev:** Monarch Butterfly in 3-D and color

Date	Mintage	F12	VF20	XF40	MS60	MS63
2011	—	PF65 55.00				

KM# 51 1000 FRANCS
31.11 g., 0.999 Silver 0.9926 oz. ASW, 38.61 mm. **Subject:** Year of the Dragon **Obv:** National arms **Rev:** Dragon in color

Date	Mintage	F12	VF20	XF40	MS60	MS63
2012		PF65 75.00				

KM# 52 1000 FRANCS
20.00 g., 0.999 Silver 0.6382 oz. ASW, 38.61 mm. **Subject:** Year of the Dragon **Obv:** National arms **Rev:** Gilt dragon and Great Wall of China

Date	Mintage	F12	VF20	XF40	MS60	MS63
2012	888	PF65 60.00				

KM# 53 1000 FRANCS
20.00 g., 0.999 Silver 0.6382 oz. ASW, 38.61 mm. **Obv:** National arms **Rev:** Unicorn and opal

Date	Mintage	F12	VF20	XF40	MS60	MS63
2012	888	PF65 75.00				

KM# 58 1000 FRANCS
20.00 g., 0.999 Silver 0.6382 oz. ASW, 38.61 mm. **Obv:** National arms **Rev:** Two Cross River Gorillas

Date	Mintage	F12	VF20	XF40	MS60	MS63
2012	—	—	—	—	—	50.00

KM# 54 1000 FRANCS
31.11 g., 0.999 Silver 0.9926 oz. ASW, 40 mm. **Rev:** Cross River Gorilla

Date	Mintage	F12	VF20	XF40	MS60	MS63
2013 Antique patina	1,000	PF65 100				

KM# 40 1500 FRANCS
62.20 g., 0.999 Silver 1.9849 oz. ASW, 40x40 mm. **Obv:** National arms **Rev:** Black Rhinoceros head profile facing right

Date	Mintage	F12	VF20	XF40	MS60	MS63
2010	—	PF63 85.00	PF65 95.00			

KM# 55 1500 FRANCS
62.20 g., 0.999 Silver 1.9849 oz. ASW, 42 x 42 mm. **Subject:** Rare Wildlife - Black Rhino

Date	Mintage	F12	VF20	XF40	MS60	MS63
2010	Est. 999	PF65 250				

CANADA

Canada is located to the north of the United States, and spans the full breadth of the northern portion of North America from Atlantic to Pacific oceans, except for the State of Alaska. It has a total area of 3,850,000 sq. mi. (9,971,550 sq. km.) and a population of 30.29 million. Capital: Ottawa. Canada is a member of the Commonwealth of Nations. Elizabeth II is Head of State as Queen of Canada.

RULER
British 1763-

MONETARY SYSTEM
1 Dollar = 100 Cents

CONFEDERATION
CIRCULATION COINAGE

KM# 289 CENT
2.25 g., Copper Plated Steel, 19.05 mm. **Ruler:** Elizabeth II **Obv:** Crowned head right **Rev:** Maple twig design **Edge:** Round and plain

Date	Mintage	VF20	XF40	MS60	MS63
2001	919,358,000	—	—	—	0.30
2001P	—	PF63 3.50	PF65 5.00		
2003	92,219,775	—	—	—	0.30
2003P	—	PF63 3.50	PF65 5.00		
2003P	235,936,799	—	—	—	1.50

KM# 445 CENT
2.25 g., Copper Plated Steel, 19.1 mm. **Ruler:** Elizabeth II **Subject:** Elizabeth II Golden Jubilee **Obv:** Crowned head right, Jubilee commemorative dates 1952-2002 **Rev:** Denomination above maple leaves **Edge:** Plain

Date	Mintage	VF20	XF40	MS60	MS63
1952 2002	716,366,000			—	0.76
1952-2002P	114,212,000	—	—	—	1.00
1952-2002P	32,642	PF63 4.00	PF65 5.00		

KM# 445a CENT
0.925 Silver **Ruler:** Elizabeth II **Subject:** Elizabeth II Golden Jubilee **Obv:** Crowned head right, Jubilee commemorative dates 1952-2002 **Rev:** Denomination above maple leaves

Date	Mintage	VF20	XF40	MS60	MS63
1952-2002	21,537	PF63 2.50	PF65 3.00		

KM# 490a CENT
2.25 g., Copper Plated Steel, 19.05 mm. **Ruler:** Elizabeth II **Obv:** Bust right **Rev:** Two maple leaves

Date	Mintage	VF20	XF40	MS60	MS63
2003P	591,257,000	—	—	—	0.25
2003 WP	Inc. above	—	—	—	0.25
2004P	134,906,000	—	—	—	0.25
2005P	30,525,000	—	—	—	0.25
2006P	137,733,000	—	—	—	0.25
2006(ml)	Inc. above	—	—	—	0.25
2007(ml)	938,270,000	—	—	—	0.25
2007(ml)		PF63 2.00	PF65 2.50		
2008(ml)	787,625,000	—	—	—	0.25

Date	Mintage	VF20	XF40	MS60	MS63
2008(ml)	—	PF63 2.00	PF65 2.50	—	—
2009(ml)	455,680,000	—	—	—	0.25
2009(ml)	—	PF63 2.00	PF65 2.50	—	—
2010(ml)	—	—	—	—	0.25
2010(ml)	—	PF63 2.00	PF65 2.50	—	—
2011(ml)	—	—	—	—	0.25
2011(ml)	—	PF63 2.00	PF65 2.50	—	—
2012(ml)	—	—	—	—	0.25
2012(ml)	—	PF63 2.00	PF65 2.50	—	—

KM# 468 CENT
2.50 g., Copper **Ruler:** Elizabeth II **Subject:** 50th Anniversary of the Coronation of Elizabeth II **Obv:** 1953 Effigy of the Queen, Jubilee commemorative dates 1953-2003

Date	Mintage	VF20	XF40	MS60	MS63
1953-2003	—	PF63 1.50	PF65 2.50	—	—

KM# 490 CENT
2.25 g., Copper Plated Zinc, 19.05 mm. **Ruler:** Elizabeth II **Obv:** New effigy of Queen Elizabeth II right **Rev:** Two maple leaves **Edge:** Plain

Date	Mintage	VF20	XF40	MS60	MS63
2003	56,877,144	—	—	—	0.25
2004	653,317,000	—	—	—	0.25
2004	—	PF63 1.50	PF65 2.50	—	—
2005	759,658,000	—	—	—	0.25
2005	—	PF63 1.50	PF65 2.50	—	—
2006	886,275,000	—	—	—	0.25
2006	—	PF63 1.50	PF65 2.50	—	—

KM# 490b CENT
2.25 g., Copper Plated Zinc **Ruler:** Elizabeth II **Obv:** Head right **Rev:** Maple leaf, selectively gold plated **Note:** Bound into Annual Report.

Date	Mintage	VF20	XF40	MS60	MS63
2003	7,746	PF63 25.00	PF65 35.00	—	—

KM# 1023 CENT
Copper, 19.1 mm. **Ruler:** Elizabeth II **Obv:** George V bust left **Rev:** Value within wreath, dual dates below

Date	Mintage	VF20	XF40	MS60	MS63
1935-2010	—	PF63 8.00	PF65 10.00	—	—

KM# 1153 CENT
5.67 g., Copper, 19.1 mm. **Ruler:** Elizabeth II **Obv:** George V bust **Rev:** Value within wreath

Date	Mintage	VF20	XF40	MS60	MS63
1911-2011	6,000	PF63 8.00	PF65 10.00	—	—

KM# 1520 CENT
1.27 g., 0.9999 Gold 0.0406 oz. AGW, 13.92 mm. **Ruler:** Elizabeth II **Subject:** End of the Cent **Edge:** Reeded

Date	Mintage	VF20	XF40	MS60	MS63
2012 Proof	Est. 12000	—	—	—	—

KM# 1342 CENT
Silver, 25.5 mm. **Ruler:** Elizabeth II **Obv:** Edward VI bust left **Rev:** Small leaves in wreath around value

Date	Mintage	VF20	XF40	MS60	MS63
2012	—	PF65 20.00			

KM# 1343 CENT
Silver, 25.5 mm. **Ruler:** Elizabeth II **Obv:** George V bust right **Rev:** Small leaves in wreath around value

Date	Mintage	VF20	XF40	MS60	MS63
2012	—	PF65 20.00			

KM# 1344 CENT
0.925 Silver, 19.1 mm. **Ruler:** Elizabeth II **Obv:** Elizabeth II bust right **Rev:** Two maple leaves

Date	Mintage	VF20	XF40	MS60	MS63
2012	—	PF65 20.00			

KM# 1345 CENT
0.925 Silver, 19.1 mm. **Ruler:** Elizabeth II **Obv:** Elizabeth II Malouf bust right **Rev:** Dove in flight

Date	Mintage	VF20	XF40	MS60	MS63
2012	—	PF65 20.00			

KM# 1427 CENT
157.60 g., 0.999 Silver 5.0293 oz. ASW, 65 mm. **Ruler:** Elizabeth II **Subject:** Farewell to the cent **Rev:** Two maple leaves

Date	Mintage	VF20	XF40	MS60	MS63
2012	Est. 1500	PF65 500			

KM# 1428 CENT
15.87 g., 0.999 Silver 0.5064 oz. ASW, 34 mm. **Ruler:** Elizabeth II **Rev:** Two maple leaves selectively gilt

Date	Mintage	F12	VF20	XF40	MS60	MS63
2013	Est. 3000	PF63 45.00		PF65 55.00		

KM# 410 3 CENTS
3.11 g., 0.925 Silver 0.0919 oz. ASW, 21.3 mm. **Ruler:** Elizabeth II **Subject:** 1st Canadian Postage Stamp **Obv:** Crowned head right **Rev:** Partial stamp design **Edge:** Plain

Date	Mintage	VF20	XF40	MS60	MS63
2001	59,573	PF63 11.00	PF65 12.50	—	—

KM# 182 5 CENTS
4.60 g., Copper-Nickel, 19.55 mm. **Ruler:** Elizabeth II **Obv:** Crowned head right **Rev:** Beaver on rock divides dates and denomination **Edge:** Plain

Date	Mintage	VF20	XF40	MS60	MS63
2001	30,035,000	—	—	6.50	12.50
2001P	—	PF63 8.00	PF65 10.00	—	—
2003	—	—	—	0.15	0.30

KM# 182a 5 CENTS
5.35 g., 0.925 Silver 0.1581 oz. ASW, 21.2 mm. **Ruler:** Elizabeth II **Obv:** Crowned head right **Rev:** Beaver on rock divides date and denomination

Date	Mintage	VF20	XF40	MS60	MS63
2001	—	PF63 7.00	PF65 8.00	—	—
2003	—	PF63 7.00	PF65 8.00	—	—

KM# 182b 5 CENTS
3.90 g., Nickel Plated Steel, 21.2 mm. **Ruler:** Elizabeth II **Obv:** Crowned head right **Rev:** Beaver on rock divides date and denomination **Edge:** Plain

Date	Mintage	VF20	XF40	MS60	MS63
2001 P	136,650,000	—	—	0.20	0.35
2003 P	32,986,921	—	—	—	0.35

KM# 413 5 CENTS
5.35 g., 0.925 Silver 0.1581 oz. ASW, 21.2 mm. **Ruler:** Elizabeth II **Subject:** Royal Military College **Obv:** Crowned head right
Rev: Marching cadets and arch **Edge:** Plain

Date	Mintage	VF20	XF40	MS60	MS63
2001	—	PF63 7.00	PF65 8.00	—	—

KM# 446a 5 CENTS
5.35 g., 0.925 Silver 0.1581 oz. ASW, 21.2 mm. **Ruler:** Elizabeth II **Subject:** Elizabeth II Golden Jubilee **Obv:** Queen, Jubilee commemorative dates 1952-2002

Date	Mintage	VF20	XF40	MS60	MS63
1952-2002	21,573	PF63 10.00	PF65 11.50	—	—

KM# 446 5 CENTS
3.95 g., Nickel Plated Steel, 21.2 mm. **Ruler:** Elizabeth II **Subject:** Elizabeth II Golden Jubilee **Obv:** Crowned head right, Jubilee commemorative dates 1952-2002 **Note:** Magnetic.

Date	Mintage	VF20	XF40	MS60	MS63
1952-2002P	135,960,000	—	—	—	0.45
1952-2002P	32,642	PF63 8.00	PF65 10.00	—	—

KM# 453 5 CENTS
5.35 g., 0.925 Silver 0.1581 oz. ASW, 21.2 mm. **Ruler:** Elizabeth II **Subject:** Vimy Ridge - WWI **Obv:** Crowned head right **Rev:** Vimy Ridge Memorial, allegorical figure and dates 1917-2002

Date	Mintage	VF20	XF40	MS60	MS63
2002	—	PF63 10.00	PF65 11.50	—	—

KM# 491 5 CENTS
3.95 g., Nickel Plated Steel, 21.2 mm. **Ruler:** Elizabeth II **Obv:** Bare head right **Rev:** Beaver divides date and denomination **Note:** Magnetic.

Date	Mintage	VF20	XF40	MS60	MS63
2003P	61,392,180	—	—	—	0.45
2004P	132,097,000	—	—	—	0.45
2004P	—	PF63 1.50	PF65 2.50	—	—
2005P	89,664,000	—	—	—	0.45
2005P	—	PF63 1.50	PF65 2.50	—	—
2006P	139,308,000	—	—	—	0.50
2006P	—	PF63 1.50	PF65 2.50	—	—
2006(ml)	184,874,000	—	—	—	0.45
2006(ml)	—	PF63 1.50	PF65 2.50	—	—
2007(ml)	221,472,000	—	—	—	0.45
2007(ml)	—	PF63 1.50	PF65 2.50	—	—
2008(ml)	278,530,000	—	—	—	0.45
2008(ml)	—	PF63 1.50	PF65 2.50	—	—
2009(ml)	266,488,000	—	—	—	0.45
2009(ml)	—	PF63 1.50	PF65 2.50	—	—
2010(ml)	—	—	—	—	0.45
2010(ml)	—	PF63 1.50	PF65 2.50	—	—
2011(ml)	—	—	—	—	0.45
2011(ml)	—	PF63 1.50	PF65 2.50	—	—
2012(ml)	—	—	—	—	0.45
2012(ml)	—	PF63 1.50	PF65 2.50	—	—
2013(ml)	—	—	—	—	0.45
2013(ml)	—	PF63 1.50	PF65 2.50	—	—

KM# 469 5 CENTS
5.35 g., 0.925 Silver 0.1581 oz. ASW, 21.2 mm. **Ruler:** Elizabeth II **Subject:** 50th Anniversary of the Coronation of Elizabeth II **Obv:** Crowned head right, Jubilee commemorative dates 1953-2003

Date	Mintage	VF20	XF40	MS60	MS63
1953-2003	21,573	PF63 10.00	PF65 11.50	—	—

KM# 491a 5 CENTS
5.35 g., 0.925 Silver 0.1581 oz. ASW, 21.1 mm. **Ruler:** Elizabeth II **Obv:** Crowned head right **Rev:** Beaver divides date and denomination **Edge:** Plain

Date	Mintage	VF20	XF40	MS60	MS63
2004	—	PF63 5.00	PF65 6.50	—	—

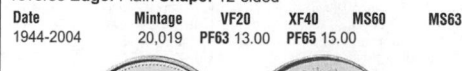

KM# 506 5 CENTS
5.35 g., 0.925 Silver 0.1581 oz. ASW, 21.3 mm. **Ruler:** Elizabeth II **Obv:** Bare head right **Rev:** Victory " design of the KM-40 reverse **Edge:** Plain **Shape:** 12-sided

Date	Mintage	VF20	XF40	MS60	MS63
1944-2004	20,019	PF63 13.00	PF65 15.00	—	—

KM# 627 5 CENTS
3.95 g., Nickel Plated Steel, 21.2 mm. **Ruler:** Elizabeth II **Subject:** 60th Anniversary, Victory in Europe 1945-2005 **Obv:** Head right **Rev:** Large V **Edge:** Plain

Date	Mintage	VF20	XF40	MS60	MS63
2005P	59,269,192	—	—	—	4.50

KM# 758 5 CENTS
5.30 g., 0.925 Silver 0.1566 oz. ASW **Ruler:** Elizabeth II **Obv:** George VI head left **Rev:** Torch and large V

Date	Mintage	VF20	XF40	MS60	MS63
2005	42,792	PF63 30.00	PF65 35.00		

KM# 758a 5 CENTS
5.30 g., 0.925 Silver 0.1566 oz. ASW **Ruler:** Elizabeth II **Obv:** George VI head left **Rev:** Torch and large V **Note:** Bound into Annual Report.

Date	Mintage	VF20	XF40	MS60	MS63
2005	6,065	PF63 35.00	PF65 40.00		

KM# 491b 5 CENTS
4.60 g., Copper-Nickel **Ruler:** Elizabeth II **Obv:** Bust right **Rev:** Beaver

Date	Mintage	VF20	XF40	MS60	MS63
2006	43,008,000	—	—	—	5.00

KM# 1024 5 CENTS
Nickel, 21.2 mm. **Ruler:** Elizabeth II **Obv:** George V bust left **Rev:** Denomination and 1935-2010 anniversary dates, two maple leaves below

Date	Mintage	VF20	XF40	MS60	MS63
1935-2010			PF63 12.00	PF65 15.00	

KM# 1154 5 CENTS
1.56 g., 0.925 Silver 0.0461 oz. ASW, 15.5 mm. **Ruler:** Elizabeth II **Obv:** George V bust **Rev:** Value within wreath

Date	Mintage	VF20	XF40	MS60	MS63
1911-2011	6,000		PF63 12.00	PF65 15.00	

KM# 183a 10 CENTS
2.40 g., 0.925 Silver 0.0709 oz. ASW, 18.03 mm. **Ruler:** Elizabeth II **Obv:** Crowned head right **Rev:** Bluenose sailing left, date at right, denomination below

Date	Mintage	VF20	XF40	MS60	MS63
2001	—	PF63 4.00	PF65 5.00		
2002	—	PF63 6.50	PF65 7.50		
2003	—	PF63 6.50	PF65 7.50		

KM# 183b 10 CENTS
1.77 g., Nickel Plated Steel, 18.03 mm. **Ruler:** Elizabeth II **Obv:** Crowned head right **Rev:** Bluenose sailing left, date at right, denomination below **Edge:** Reeded

Date	Mintage	VF20	XF40	MS60	MS63
2001 P	266,000,000	—	—	0.20	0.45
2003 P	162,398,000	—	—	—	0.20

KM# 412a 10 CENTS
2.40 g., 0.925 Silver 0.0709 oz. ASW, 18 mm. **Ruler:** Elizabeth II **Subject:** Year of the Volunteer **Obv:** Crowned head right **Rev:** Three portraits left above banner, radiant sun below **Edge:** Reeded

Date	Mintage	VF20	XF40	MS60	MS63
2001P	40,634	PF63 8.00	PF65 9.00		

KM# 412 10 CENTS
1.77 g., Nickel Plated Steel, 18 mm. **Ruler:** Elizabeth II **Subject:** Year of the Volunteer **Obv:** Crowned head right **Rev:** Three portraits left and radiant sun **Edge:** Reeded

Date	Mintage	VF20	XF40	MS60	MS63
2001P	224,714,000	—	—	—	4.50

KM# 447 10 CENTS
1.77 g., Nickel Plated Steel, 18 mm. **Ruler:** Elizabeth II **Subject:** Elizabeth II Golden Jubilee **Obv:** Crowned head right, Jubilee commemorative dates 1952-2002

Date	Mintage	VF20	XF40	MS60	MS63
1952-2002P	252,563,000				1.00
1952-2002	32,642	PF63 1.50	PF65 2.50		

KM# 447a 10 CENTS
2.32 g., 0.925 Silver 0.0686 oz. ASW, 18 mm. **Ruler:** Elizabeth II **Subject:** Elizabeth II Golden Jubilee **Obv:** Crowned head right, Jubilee commemorative dates 1952-2002

Date	Mintage	VF20	XF40	MS60	MS63
2002	21,537	PF63 11.00	PF65 12.50		

KM# 470 10 CENTS
2.32 g., 0.925 Silver 0.0686 oz. ASW **Ruler:** Elizabeth II **Subject:** 50th Anniversary of the Coronation of Elizabeth II **Obv:** Head right **Rev:** Bluenose sailing left

Date	Mintage	VF20	XF40	MS60	MS63
1953-2003	21,537	PF63 11.00	PF65 12.00		

KM# 492 10 CENTS
1.77 g., Nickel Plated Steel, 18 mm. **Ruler:** Elizabeth II **Obv:** Head right **Rev:** Bluenose sailing left

Date	Mintage	VF20	XF40	MS60	MS63
2003P	—	—	—	—	1.25
2004P	211,924,000	—	—	—	0.60
2004P		PF63 1.50	PF65 2.50		
2005P	212,175,000	—	—	—	0.60
2005P		PF63 1.50	PF65 2.50		
2006P	312,122,000	—	—	—	0.60
2006P		PF63 1.50	PF65 2.50		
2007(ml) Straight 7	304,110,000	—	—	—	0.60
2007(ml) Curved 7	Inc. above	—	—	—	0.60
2008(ml)		PF63 1.50	PF65 2.50		
2008(ml)	467,495,000	—	—	—	0.60
2009(ml)		PF63 1.50	PF65 2.50		
2009(ml)	370,700,000	—	—	—	0.60
2010(ml)		PF63 1.50	PF65 2.50		
2010(ml)		—	—	—	0.60
2011(ml)		PF63 1.50	PF65 2.50		
2011(ml)		—	—	—	0.60
2012(ml)		PF63 1.50	PF65 2.50		
2012(ml)		—	—	—	0.60
2013(ml)		PF63 1.50	PF65 2.50		
2013(ml)		—	—	—	0.60

KM# 492a 10 CENTS
2.40 g., 0.925 Silver 0.0709 oz. ASW, 18 mm. **Ruler:** Elizabeth II **Obv:** Bare head right **Rev:** Sailboat **Edge:** Reeded

Date	Mintage	VF20	XF40	MS60	MS63
2004	—	PF65 6.00			

KM# 524 10 CENTS
2.40 g., 0.925 Silver 0.0709 oz. ASW, 18 mm. **Ruler:** Elizabeth II **Subject:** Golf, Championship of Canada, Centennial. **Obv:** Head right

Date	Mintage	VF20	XF40	MS60	MS63
2004	39,486	—	—	—	12.50

KM# 1025 10 CENTS
Silver, 18.03 mm. **Ruler:** Elizabeth II **Obv:** George V bust left **Rev:** Value within wreath, dual dates below

Date	Mintage	VF20	XF40	MS60	MS63
1935-2010			PF63 17.00	PF65 20.00	

KM# 1155 10 CENTS
2.40 g., 0.925 Silver 0.0709 oz. ASW, 18.03 mm. **Ruler:** Elizabeth II **Obv:** George V bust **Rev:** Value within wreath

Date	Mintage	VF20	XF40	MS60	MS63
1911-2011	6,000		PF63 17.00	PF65 20.00	

KM# 184 25 CENTS
5.07 g., Nickel, 23.88 mm. **Ruler:** Elizabeth II **Obv:** Crowned head right **Rev:** Caribou left, denomination above, date at right

Date	Mintage	VF20	XF40	MS60	MS63
2001	8,415,000	—	—	3.00	5.00
2001	—	PF63 6.50	PF65 7.50		

KM# 184a 25 CENTS
5.90 g., 0.925 Silver 0.1743 oz. ASW, 23.88 mm. **Ruler:** Elizabeth II **Obv:** Crowned head right **Rev:** Caribou left, denomination above, date at right

Date	Mintage	VF20	XF40	MS60	MS63
2001	—	PF63 835	PF65 9.50		
2003	—	PF63 8.50	PF65 9.50		

KM# 184b 25 CENTS
4.40 g., Nickel Plated Steel, 23.88 mm. **Ruler:** Elizabeth II **Obv:** Crowned head right **Rev:** Caribou left, denomination above, date at right

Date	Mintage	VF20	XF40	MS60	MS63
2001 P	55,773,000	—	—	1.25	0.95
2001 P	—	PF65 5.00			
2002 P	156,105,000	—	—	—	2.50
2002 P	—	PF65 5.00			
2003 P	87,647,000	—	—	—	2.50
2003 P	—	PF65 5.00			

KM# 419 25 CENTS
4.40 g., Nickel Plated Steel, 23.9 mm. **Ruler:** Elizabeth II **Subject:** Canada Day **Obv:** Crowned head right **Rev:** Maple leaf at center, children holding hands below **Edge:** Reeded

Date	Mintage	VF20	XF40	MS60	MS63
2001	96,352	—	—	—	7.00

KM# 448 25 CENTS
4.40 g., Nickel Plated Steel, 23.9 mm. **Ruler:** Elizabeth II **Subject:** Elizabeth II Golden Jubilee **Obv:** Crowned head right **Rev:** Caribou left

Date	Mintage	VF20	XF40	MS60	MS63
1952-2002P	152,485,000	—	—	—	2.00
1952-2002P	32,642	PF63 5.00	PF65 6.00		

KM# 448a 25 CENTS
5.90 g., 0.925 Silver 0.1743 oz. ASW, 23.9 mm. **Ruler:** Elizabeth II **Subject:** Elizabeth II Golden Jubilee **Obv:** Crowned head right, Jubilee commemorative dates 1952-2002

Date	Mintage	VF20	XF40	MS60	MS63
1952-2002	100,000	PF63 11.00	PF65 12.50		

KM# 451 25 CENTS
4.40 g., Nickel Plated Steel, 23.9 mm. **Ruler:** Elizabeth II **Rev:** Small human figures supporting large maple leaf

Date	Mintage	VF20	XF40	MS60	MS63
2002P	30,627,000	—	—	—	5.00

KM# 451a 25 CENTS
4.40 g., Nickel Plated Steel, 23.9 mm. **Ruler:** Elizabeth II **Subject:** Canada Day **Obv:** Crowned head right **Rev:** Human figures supporting large red maple leaf **Edge:** Reeded

Date	Mintage	VF20	XF40	MS60	MS63
2002P	49,901	—	—	—	6.00

KM# 471 25 CENTS
5.90 g., 0.925 Silver 0.1743 oz. ASW, 23.9 mm. **Ruler:** Elizabeth II **Subject:** 50th Anniversary of the Coronation of Elizabeth II **Obv:** 1953 Effigy of the Queen, Coronation Jubilee dates 1953-2003

Date	Mintage	VF20	XF40	MS60	MS63
1953-2003	21,537	PF63 11.00	PF65 12.50		

KM# 474 25 CENTS
4.40 g., 0.925 Silver 0.130 oz. ASW, 23.9 mm. **Ruler:** Elizabeth II **Subject:** Canada Day **Obv:** Queen's head right **Rev:** Polar bear and red colored maple leaves

Date	Mintage	VF20	XF40	MS60	MS63
2003	63,511	PF63 11.00	PF65 12.00		

KM# 493 25 CENTS
4.40 g., Nickel Plated Steel, 23.9 mm. **Ruler:** Elizabeth II **Obv:**

Bare head right **Rev:** Caribou left, denomination above, date at right

Date	Mintage	VF20	XF40	MS60	MS63
2003P	66,861,633	—	—	—	2.00
2003P W	—	—	—	—	—
2004P	177,466,000	—	—	—	2.50
2004P		PF63 4.00	PF65 5.00		
2005P	206,346,000	—	—	—	2.50
2005P		PF63 4.00	PF65 5.00		
2006P	423,189,000	—	—	—	2.50
2006P		PF63 4.00	PF65 5.00		
2006(ml)		—	—	—	2.50
2007(ml)	386,763,000	—	—	—	2.50
2007(ml)		PF63 4.00	PF65 5.00		
2008(ml)	387,222,000	—	—	—	2.50
2008(ml)		PF63 4.00	PF65 5.00		
2009(ml)	266,766,000	—	—	—	2.50
2009(ml)		PF63 4.00	PF65 5.00		
2010(ml)		—	—	—	2.50
2010(ml)		PF63 4.00	PF65 5.00		
2011(ml)		—	—	—	2.50
2011(ml)		PF63 4.00	PF65 5.00		
2012(ml)		—	—	—	2.50
2012(ml)		PF63 4.00	PF65 5.00		
2013(ml)		—	—	—	2.50
2013(ml)		PF63 4.00	PF65 5.00		

KM# 493a 25 CENTS

5.90 g., 0.925 Silver 0.1743 oz. ASW, 23.9 mm. **Ruler:** Elizabeth II **Obv:** Bare head right **Rev:** Caribou **Edge:** Reeded

Date	Mintage	VF20	XF40	MS60	MS63
2004	—	PF63 5.00	PF65 6.50		

KM# 510 25 CENTS

4.40 g., Nickel Plated Steel, 23.9 mm. **Ruler:** Elizabeth II **Obv:** Bare head right **Rev:** Red poppy in center of maple leaf **Edge:** Reeded

Date	Mintage	VF20	XF40	MS60	MS63
2004	28,500,000	—	—	—	5.00

KM# 510a 25 CENTS

5.90 g., 0.925 Silver 0.1743 oz. ASW, 23.9 mm. **Ruler:** Elizabeth II **Obv:** Bare head right **Rev:** Poppy at center of maple leaf, selectively gold plated **Edge:** Reeded **Note:** Housed in Annual Report.

Date	Mintage	VF20	XF40	MS60	MS63
2004	12,677	PF63 18.00	PF65 20.00		

KM# 525 25 CENTS

4.40 g., Nickel Plated Steel, 23.9 mm. **Ruler:** Elizabeth II **Obv:** Bare head right **Rev:** Maple leaf, colorized

Date	Mintage	VF20	XF40	MS60	MS63
2004	16,028	—	—	—	8.00

KM# 628 25 CENTS

4.40 g., Nickel Plated Steel, 23.9 mm. **Ruler:** Elizabeth II **Subject:** First Settlement, Ile Ste Croix 1604-2004 **Obv:** Bare head right **Rev:** Sailing ship Bonne-Renommee

Date	Mintage	VF20	XF40	MS60	MS63
2004P	15,400,000	—	—	—	5.00

KM# 698 25 CENTS

4.40 g., Nickel Plated Steel, 23.88 mm. **Ruler:** Elizabeth II **Rev:** Santa, colorized

Date	Mintage	VF20	XF40	MS60	MS63
2004	62,777	—	—	—	5.00

KM# 699 25 CENTS

4.40 g., Nickel Plated Steel, 23.9 mm. **Ruler:** Elizabeth II **Series:** Canada Day **Rev:** Moose head, humorous

Date	Mintage	VF20	XF40	MS60	MS63
2004	44,752	—	—	—	5.00

KM# 529 25 CENTS

4.40 g., Nickel Plated Steel, 23.9 mm. **Ruler:** Elizabeth II **Subject:** WWII, 60th Anniversary **Obv:** Head right **Rev:** Three soldiers and flag

Date	Mintage	VF20	XF40	MS60	MS63
1945-2005	3,500	—	—	—	20.00

KM# 530 25 CENTS

4.40 g., Nickel Plated Steel, 23.9 mm. **Ruler:** Elizabeth II **Subject:** Alberta **Obv:** Head right **Rev:** Oil rig and sunset

Date	Mintage	VF20	XF40	MS60	MS63
2005P	20,640,000	—	—	—	7.00

KM# 531 25 CENTS

4.40 g., Nickel Plated Steel, 23.9 mm. **Ruler:** Elizabeth II **Subject:** Canada Day **Obv:** Head right **Rev:** Beaver, colorized

Date	Mintage	VF20	XF40	MS60	MS63
2005P	58,370	—	—	—	8.50

KM# 532 25 CENTS

4.40 g., Nickel Plated Steel, 23.9 mm. **Ruler:** Elizabeth II **Subject:** Saskatchewan **Obv:** Head right **Rev:** Bird on fencepost

Date	Mintage	VF20	XF40	MS60	MS63
2005P	19,290,000	—	—	—	7.00

KM# 533 25 CENTS

4.40 g., Nickel Plated Steel, 23.9 mm. **Ruler:** Elizabeth II **Obv:** Head right **Rev:** Stuffed bear in Christmas stocking, colorized

Date	Mintage	VF20	XF40	MS60	MS63
2005P	72,831	—	—	—	10.00

KM# 535 25 CENTS

4.40 g., Nickel Plated Steel, 23.9 mm. **Ruler:** Elizabeth II **Subject:** Year of the Veteran **Obv:** Head right **Rev:** Conjoined busts of young and veteran left **Edge:** Reeded

Date	Mintage	VF20	XF40	MS60	MS63
2005P	29,390,000	—	—	—	7.00

KM# 576 25 CENTS

4.40 g., Nickel Plated Steel, 23.9 mm. **Ruler:** Elizabeth II **Subject:** Quebec Winter Carnival **Obv:** Head right **Rev:** Snowman, colorized

Date	Mintage	VF20	XF40	MS60	MS63
2006	8,200	—	—	—	10.00

KM# 534 25 CENTS

4.40 g., Nickel Plated Steel, 23.9 mm. **Ruler:** Elizabeth II **Subject:** Toronto Maple Leafs **Obv:** Head right **Rev:** Colorized team logo

Date	Mintage	VF20	XF40	MS60	MS63
2006P	11,765	—	—	—	12.50

KM# 575 25 CENTS

4.40 g., Nickel Plated Steel, 23.9 mm. **Ruler:** Elizabeth II **Subject:** Montreal Canadiens **Obv:** Head right **Rev:** Colorized logo

Date	Mintage	VF20	XF40	MS60	MS63
2006P	11,765	—	—	—	12.50

KM# 629 25 CENTS

4.40 g., Nickel Plated Steel, 23.9 mm. **Ruler:** Elizabeth II **Obv:** Head right **Rev:** Medal of Bravery (maple leaf within wreath) **Edge:** Reeded

Date	Mintage	VF20	XF40	MS60	MS63
2006(ml)	20,045,111	—	—	—	2.50

KM# 632 25 CENTS

12.61 g., Nickel Plated Steel, 35 mm. **Ruler:** Elizabeth II **Subject:** Queen Elizabeth II 80th Birthday **Rev:** Crown, colorized

Date	Mintage	VF20	XF40	MS60	MS63
1926-2006 Specimen	24,977	—	—	—	25.00

KM# 633 25 CENTS

4.43 g., Nickel Plated Steel, 23.9 mm. **Ruler:** Elizabeth II **Subject:** Canada Day **Obv:** Crowned head right **Rev:** Boy marching with flag, colorized

Date	Mintage	VF20	XF40	MS60	MS63
2006P	30,328	—	—	—	6.00

KM# 634 25 CENTS

4.43 g., Nickel Plated Steel, 23.88 mm. **Ruler:** Elizabeth II **Subject:** Breast Cancer **Rev:** Four ribbons, all colorized **Note:** Sold housed in a bookmark.

Date	Mintage	VF20	XF40	MS60	MS63
2006P	40,911	—	—	—	10.00

KM# 635 25 CENTS

4.43 g., Nickel Plated Steel, 23.88 mm. **Ruler:** Elizabeth II **Subject:** Breast Cancer **Rev:** Colorized pink ribbon applique in center.

Date	Mintage	VF20	XF40	MS60	MS63
2006P	29,798,000	—	—	—	1.50

KM# 637 25 CENTS
4.43 g., Nickel Plated Steel, 23.88 mm. **Ruler:** Elizabeth II **Subject:** Wedding **Rev:** Colorized bouquet of flowers

Date	Mintage	VF20	XF40	MS60	MS63
2006(ml)	10,318	—	—	—	5.00

KM# 642 25 CENTS
4.43 g., Nickel Plated Steel, 23.88 mm. **Ruler:** Elizabeth II **Subject:** Ottawa Senators **Obv:** Head right **Rev:** Logo

Date	Mintage	VF20	XF40	MS60	MS63
2006P	11,765	—	—	—	12.50

KM# 644 25 CENTS
4.43 g., Nickel Plated Steel, 23.88 mm. **Ruler:** Elizabeth II **Subject:** Calgary Flames **Obv:** Head right **Rev:** Logo

Date	Mintage	VF20	XF40	MS60	MS63
2006(ml)	1,082	—	—	—	12.50

KM# 645 25 CENTS
4.43 g., Nickel Plated Steel, 23.88 mm. **Ruler:** Elizabeth II **Subject:** Edmonton Oilers **Obv:** Head right **Rev:** Logo

Date	Mintage	VF20	XF40	MS60	MS63
2006(ml)	2,214	—	—	—	12.50

KM# 647 25 CENTS
4.43 g., Nickel Plated Steel **Ruler:** Elizabeth II **Subject:** Santa and Rudolph **Rev:** Colorized Santa in sled lead by Rudolph

Date	Mintage	VF20	XF40	MS60	MS63
2006P	99,258	—	—	—	5.00

KM# 638 25 CENTS
4.43 g., Nickel Plated Steel, 23.88 mm. **Ruler:** Elizabeth II **Subject:** Birthday **Rev:** Colorized balloons

Date	Mintage	VF20	XF40	MS60	MS63
2007(ml)	24,531	—	—	—	5.00

KM# 639 25 CENTS
4.43 g., Nickel Plated Steel, 23.88 mm. **Ruler:** Elizabeth II **Subject:** Baby birth **Rev:** Colorized baby rattle **Edge:** Reeded

Date	Mintage	VF20	XF40	MS60	MS63
2007(ml)	30,090	—	—	—	5.00

KM# 640 25 CENTS
4.43 g., Nickel Plated Steel, 23.88 mm. **Ruler:** Elizabeth II **Subject:** Oh Canada **Obv:** Head right **Rev:** Maple leaf, colorized

Date	Mintage	VF20	XF40	MS60	MS63
2006 (2007)(ml)	23,582	—	—	—	8.50

KM# 641 25 CENTS
4.43 g., Nickel Plated Steel, 23.88 mm. **Ruler:** Elizabeth II **Subject:** Congratulations **Obv:** Head right **Rev:** Fireworks, colorized

Date	Mintage	VF20	XF40	MS60	MS63
2006 (2007)(ml)	9,671	—	—	—	8.00

KM# 643 25 CENTS
4.43 g., Nickel Plated Steel, 23.88 mm. **Ruler:** Elizabeth II **Subject:** Vancouver Canucks **Obv:** Head right **Rev:** Logo

Date	Mintage	VF20	XF40	MS60	MS63
2007(ml)	1,526	—	—	—	12.50

KM# 682 25 CENTS
4.43 g., Nickel Plated Steel **Ruler:** Elizabeth II **Subject:** Curling **Obv:** Head right

Date	Mintage	VF20	XF40	MS60	MS63
2007	22,400,000	—	—	—	7.50
2008 Mule					

KM# 683 25 CENTS
4.43 g., Nickel Plated Steel **Ruler:** Elizabeth II **Subject:** Ice Hockey **Obv:** Head right

Date	Mintage	VF20	XF40	MS60	MS63
2007	22,400,000	—	—	—	7.50
2008 Mule					

KM# 684 25 CENTS
4.43 g., Nickel Plated Steel, 23.8 mm. **Ruler:** Elizabeth II **Subject:** Paralympic Winter Games **Obv:** Head right **Rev:** Wheelchair curling

Date	Mintage	VF20	XF40	MS60	MS63
2007	22,400,000	—	—	—	7.50
2008 Mule					

KM# 685 25 CENTS
4.43 g., Nickel Plated Steel **Ruler:** Elizabeth II **Subject:** Biathlon **Obv:** Head right

Date	Mintage	VF20	XF40	MS60	MS63
2007	22,400,000	—	—	—	7.50
2008 Mule					

KM# 686 25 CENTS
4.43 g., Nickel Plated Steel, 23.8 mm. **Ruler:** Elizabeth II **Subject:** Alpine Skiing **Obv:** Head right

Date	Mintage	VF20	XF40	MS60	MS63
2007	22,400,000	—	—	—	7.50
2008 Mule					

KM# 701 25 CENTS
4.43 g., Nickel Plated Steel, 23.88 mm. **Ruler:** Elizabeth II **Subject:** Birthday **Rev:** Party hat, multicolor

Date	Mintage	VF20	XF40	MS60	MS63
2007	11,376	—	—	—	8.00

KM# 702 25 CENTS
4.43 g., Nickel Plated Steel, 23.88 mm. **Ruler:** Elizabeth II **Subject:** Congratulations **Rev:** Trophy, multicolor

Date	Mintage	VF20	XF40	MS60	MS63
2007		—	—	—	8.00

KM# 703 25 CENTS
4.43 g., Nickel Plated Steel, 23.88 mm. **Ruler:** Elizabeth II **Subject:** Wedding **Rev:** Cake, multicolor

Date	Mintage	VF20	XF40	MS60	MS63
2007		—	—	—	8.00

KM# 704 25 CENTS
4.43 g., Nickel Plated Steel, 23.88 mm. **Ruler:** Elizabeth II **Subject:** Canada Day **Rev:** Mountie, colorized

Date	Mintage	VF20	XF40	MS60	MS63
2007(ml)	27,743	—	—	—	8.00

KM# 705 25 CENTS
4.43 g., Nickel Plated Steel, 23.88 mm. **Ruler:** Elizabeth II **Subject:** Christmas **Rev:** Multicolor tree

Date	Mintage	VF20	XF40	MS60	MS63
2007	66,267	—	—	—	8.00

KM# 706 25 CENTS
12.61 g., Nickel Plated Steel, 35.0 mm. **Ruler:** Elizabeth II **Subject:** Red-breasted Nuthatch **Obv:** Head right **Obv. Legend:** ELIZABETH II - D · G · REGINA **Rev:** Nuthatch perched on pine branch multicolor **Rev. Legend:** CANADA **Edge:** Plain

Date	Mintage	VF20	XF40	MS60	MS63
2007(ml) Specimen	11,909	—	—	—	295

KM# 707 25 CENTS
12.61 g., Nickel Plated Steel, 35 mm. **Ruler:** Elizabeth II **Obv:** Elizabeth II **Rev:** Multicolor ruby-throated hummingbird and flower **Edge:** Plain

Date	Mintage	VF20	XF40	MS60	MS63
2007 Specimen	17,174	—	—	—	135

KM# 708 25 CENTS
12.61 g., Nickel Plated Steel, 35 mm. **Ruler:** Elizabeth II **Subject:** Queen's 60th Wedding Anniversary **Rev:** Royal carriage in color

Date	Mintage	VF20	XF40	MS60	MS63
1947-2007 Specimen	15,235	—	—	—	25.00

KM# 713 25 CENTS
4.40 g., Nickel Plated Steel **Ruler:** Elizabeth II **Rev:** Toronto Maple Leaf logo, colorized

Date	Mintage	VF20	XF40	MS60	MS63
2007(ml)	5,365	—	—	—	5.00

KM# 714 25 CENTS
4.40 g., Nickel Plated Steel **Ruler:** Elizabeth II **Rev:** Ottawa Senators logo, colorized

Date	Mintage	VF20	XF40	MS60	MS63
2007(ml)	2,474	—	—	—	5.00

KM# 723 25 CENTS
4.40 g., Nickel Plated Steel **Ruler:** Elizabeth II **Rev:** Montreal Canadiens logo, colorized

Date	Mintage	VF20	XF40	MS60	MS63
2007(ml)	4,091	—	—	—	5.00

KM# 1039 25 CENTS
4.43 g., Nickel Plated Steel, 23.9 mm. **Ruler:** Elizabeth II
Subject: Canada Day **Rev:** Colorized moose head

Date	Mintage	VF20	XF40	MS60	MS63
2008	11,538	—	—	—	12.50

KM# 760 25 CENTS
4.43 g., Nickel Plated Steel, 23.88 mm. **Ruler:** Elizabeth II
Subject: Baby **Rev:** Multicolor blue teddy bear

Date	Mintage	VF20	XF40	MS60	MS63
2008	29,639	—	—	—	8.00

KM# 761 25 CENTS
4.43 g., Nickel Plated Steel, 23.88 mm. **Ruler:** Elizabeth II
Subject: Birthday **Rev:** Multicolor party hat

Date	Mintage	VF20	XF40	MS60	MS63
2008	11,376	—	—	—	8.00

KM# 762 25 CENTS
4.43 g., Nickel Plated Steel, 23.88 mm. **Ruler:** Elizabeth II
Subject: Congratulations **Rev:** Multicolor trophy

Date	Mintage	VF20	XF40	MS60	MS63
2008	6,821	—	—	—	8.00

KM# 763 25 CENTS
4.43 g., Nickel Plated Steel, 23.88 mm. **Ruler:** Elizabeth II
Subject: Wedding **Rev:** Multicolor wedding cake

Date	Mintage	VF20	XF40	MS60	MS63
2008	7,407	—	—	—	8.00

KM# 764 25 CENTS
4.43 g., Nickel Plated Steel, 23.88 mm. **Ruler:** Elizabeth II
Subject: Santa Claus **Rev:** Multicolor Santa

Date	Mintage	VF20	XF40	MS60	MS63
2008	42,344	—	—	—	8.00

KM# 765 25 CENTS
4.43 g., Nickel Plated Steel, 23.9 mm. **Ruler:** Elizabeth II
Subject: Vancouver Olympics **Rev:** Freestyle skiing

Date	Mintage	VF20	XF40	MS60	MS63
2008	—	—	—	—	2.00

KM# 766 25 CENTS
4.43 g., Nickel Plated Steel, 23.8 mm. **Ruler:** Elizabeth II
Subject: Vancouver Olympics **Rev:** Figure skating

Date	Mintage	VF20	XF40	MS60	MS63
2008	—	—	—	—	2.00

KM# 768 25 CENTS
4.43 g., Nickel Plated Steel, 23.88 mm. **Ruler:** Elizabeth II
Subject: Vancouver Olympics **Rev:** Snowboarding

Date	Mintage	VF20	XF40	MS60	MS63
2008	—	—	—	—	2.00

KM# 769 25 CENTS
4.43 g., Nickel Plated Steel, 23.88 mm. **Ruler:** Elizabeth II
Subject: Vancouver Olympics **Rev:** Olympic mascot - Miga

Date	Mintage	VF20	XF40	MS60	MS63
2008	—	—	—	—	3.00

KM# 770 25 CENTS
4.43 g., Nickel Plated Steel, 23.88 mm. **Ruler:** Elizabeth II
Subject: Vancouver Olympics **Rev:** Olympic mascot - Quatchi

Date	Mintage	VF20	XF40	MS60	MS63
2008	—	—	—	—	3.00

KM# 771 25 CENTS
4.43 g., Nickel Plated Steel, 23.88 mm. **Ruler:** Elizabeth II
Subject: Vancouver Olympics **Rev:** Olympic mascot - Sumi

Date	Mintage	VF20	XF40	MS60	MS63
2008	—	—	—	—	3.00

KM# 772 25 CENTS
4.43 g., Nickel Plated Steel, 23.88 mm. **Ruler:** Elizabeth II
Subject: Oh Canada **Rev:** Multicolor red flag

Date	Mintage	VF20	XF40	MS60	MS63
2008	—	—	—	—	8.00

KM# 773 25 CENTS
12.61 g., Nickel Plated Steel, 35 mm. **Ruler:** Elizabeth II **Obv:** Bust right **Rev:** Downy woodpecker in tree, multicolor **Edge:** Plain **Note:** Prev. KM#717.

Date	Mintage	VF20	XF40	MS60	MS63
2008(ml) Specimen	14,282	—	—	—	275

KM# 774 25 CENTS
12.61 g., Nickel Plated Steel, 35 mm. **Ruler:** Elizabeth II **Obv:** Bust right **Rev:** Northern cardinal perched on branch - multicolor **Edge:** Plain **Note:** Prev. KM#718.

Date	Mintage	VF20	XF40	MS60	MS63
2008(ml) Specimen	11,604	—	—	—	275

KM# 775 25 CENTS
4.43 g., Nickel Plated Steel, 23.8 mm. **Ruler:** Elizabeth II
Subject: End of WWI, 90th Anniversary **Rev:** Multicolor poppy

Date	Mintage	VF20	XF40	MS60	MS63
1918-2008	10,167	—	—	—	8.00

KM# 776 25 CENTS
12.61 g., Nickel Plated Steel, 35 mm. **Ruler:** Elizabeth II
Subject: Anne of Green Gables **Rev:** Image of young girl, multicolor

Date	Mintage	VF20	XF40	MS60	MS63
1908-2008 Specimen	32,795	—	—	—	20.00

KM# 841 25 CENTS
4.43 g., Nickel Plated Steel, 23.8 mm. **Ruler:** Elizabeth II
Subject: Vancouver Olympics **Rev:** Bobsleigh

Date	Mintage	VF20	XF40	MS60	MS63
2008	—	—	—	—	3.00

KM# 1041 25 CENTS
4.43 g., Nickel Plated Steel **Ruler:** Elizabeth II **Subject:** WWI
Rev: Three military men standing over tomb

Date	Mintage	VF20	XF40	MS60	MS63
2008(ml)	10,167	—	—	—	12.50

KM# 1063a 25 CENTS
Nickel Plated Steel **Ruler:** Elizabeth II **Subject:** Men's Hockey
Rev: Hockey player and maple leaf outline in red

Date	Mintage	VF20	XF40	MS60	MS63
2009	—	—	—	—	7.50

KM# 1064a 25 CENTS
Nickel Plated Steel **Ruler:** Elizabeth II **Subject:** Women's Hockey **Rev:** Hockey player and male leaf outline in red

Date	Mintage	VF20	XF40	MS60	MS63
2009	—	—	—	—	7.50

KM# 1065a 25 CENTS

Nickel Plated Steel **Ruler:** Elizabeth II **Subject:** Klassen - female skater **Rev:** Skater and maple leaf outline in red

Date	Mintage	VF20	XF40	MS60	MS63
2009	—	—	—	—	7.50

KM# 840 25 CENTS

4.43 g., Nickel Plated Steel, 23.8 mm. **Ruler:** Elizabeth II **Subject:** Valcouver 2010 Olympics **Rev:** Cross-country skiing

Date	Mintage	VF20	XF40	MS60	MS63
2009	—	—	—	—	3.00

KM# 842 25 CENTS

4.43 g., Nickel Plated Steel, 23.9 mm. **Ruler:** Elizabeth II **Subject:** Edmonton Olympics **Rev:** Speed skating

Date	Mintage	VF20	XF40	MS60	MS63
2009	—	—	—	—	3.00

KM# 885 25 CENTS

4.40 g., Nickel Plated Steel, 23.88 mm. **Ruler:** Elizabeth II **Subject:** Canada Day **Rev:** Animals in boat with flag **Rev. Legend:** Canada 25 cents

Date	Mintage	VF20	XF40	MS60	MS63
2009	11,091	—	—	—	5.00

KM# 886 25 CENTS

12.61 g., Nickel Plated Steel, 35 mm. **Ruler:** Elizabeth II **Subject:** Notre-Dame-Du-Saguenay **Obv:** Bust right **Obv. Legend:** Elizabeth II DG Regina **Rev:** Color photo of fjord and statue **Rev. Legend:** Canada 25 cents

Date	Mintage	VF20	XF40	MS60	MS63
2009 Specimen	16,653	—	—	—	25.00

KM# 915 25 CENTS

4.43 g., Nickel Plated Steel, 23.9 mm. **Ruler:** Elizabeth II **Subject:** Surprise Birthday **Obv:** Bust right **Rev:** Colorized

Date	Mintage	VF20	XF40	MS60	MS63
2009	9,663	—	—	—	12.50

KM# 916 25 CENTS

4.43 g., Nickel Plated Steel, 23.9 mm. **Ruler:** Elizabeth II **Subject:** Share the Excitement **Obv:** Bust right **Rev:** Colorized

Date	Mintage	VF20	XF40	MS60	MS63
2009	4,126	—	—	—	12.50

KM# 917 25 CENTS

4.43 g., Nickel Plated Steel, 23.9 mm. **Ruler:** Elizabeth II **Subject:** Share the Love **Obv:** Bust right **Rev:** Two doves, coolored

Date	Mintage	VF20	XF40	MS60	MS63
2009	7,571	—	—	—	12.50

KM# 918 25 CENTS

4.43 g., Nickel Plated Steel, 23.9 mm. **Ruler:** Elizabeth II **Subject:** Thank You **Obv:** Bust right **Rev:** Colorized

Date	Mintage	VF20	XF40	MS60	MS63
2009	4,415	—	—	—	12.50

KM# 933 25 CENTS

4.40 g., Nickel Plated Steel, 23.9 mm. **Ruler:** Elizabeth II **Rev:** Santa Claus, multicolor

Date	Mintage	VF20	XF40	MS60	MS63
2009	—	—	—	—	16.50

KM# 934 25 CENTS

4.40 g., Nickel Plated Steel, 23.9 mm. **Ruler:** Elizabeth II **Rev:** Multicolor teddy bear, crescent moon

Date	Mintage	VF20	XF40	MS60	MS63
2009	25,182	—	—	—	16.50

KM# 935 25 CENTS

4.40 g., Nickel Plated Steel, 23.9 mm. **Ruler:** Elizabeth II **Subject:** Oh Canada **Rev:** Maple leaves, yellow color

Date	Mintage	VF20	XF40	MS60	MS63
2009	14,451	—	—	—	16.50

KM# 952 25 CENTS

4.40 g., Nickel Plated Steel, 23.9 mm. **Ruler:** Elizabeth II **Rev:** Sledge hockey

Date	Mintage	VF20	XF40	MS60	MS63
2009	—	—	—	—	3.00

KM# 1063 25 CENTS

Nickel Plated Steel **Ruler:** Elizabeth II **Subject:** Men's Hockey **Rev:** Hockey player and maple leaf outline

Date	Mintage	VF20	XF40	MS60	MS63
2009	—	—	—	—	2.50

KM# 1064 25 CENTS

Nickel Plated Steel, 23.9 mm. **Ruler:** Elizabeth II **Subject:** Women's Hockey **Rev:** Hockey player and maple leaf outline

Date	Mintage	VF20	XF40	MS60	MS63
2009	—	—	—	—	2.50

KM# 1065 25 CENTS

Nickel Plated Steel, 23.9 mm. **Ruler:** Elizabeth II **Subject:** Klassen - Female speed skater **Rev:** Skater and maple leaf outline

Date	Mintage	VF20	XF40	MS60	MS63
2009	—	—	—	—	2.50

KM# 880 25 CENTS

4.40 g., Nickel Plated Steel, 23.88 mm. **Ruler:** Elizabeth II **Subject:** Miga Mascot Vancouver Olympics **Rev:** Mica Mascot - color **Rev. Legend:** Vancouver 2010 25 cents

Date	Mintage	VF20	XF40	MS60	MS63
2010	14,654	—	—	—	3.00

KM# 881 25 CENTS

4.40 g., Nickel Plated Steel, 23.88 mm. **Ruler:** Elizabeth II **Subject:** Quatchi Mascot - Vancouver Olympics **Obv:** Bust right **Rev:** Quatchi Mascot color **Rev. Legend:** Vancouver 2010 25 cents

Date	Mintage	VF20	XF40	MS60	MS63
2010	15,310	—	—	—	3.00

KM# 882 25 CENTS

4.40 g., Nickel Plated Steel, 23.88 mm. **Ruler:** Elizabeth II **Subject:** Sumi Mascot **Rev:** Sumi Mascot color **Rev. Legend:** Vancouver 2010 25 cents

Date	Mintage	VF20	XF40	MS60	MS63
2010	15,333	—	—	—	3.00

KM# 953 25 CENTS

4.40 g., Nickel Plated Steel, 23.9 mm. **Ruler:** Elizabeth II **Rev:** Ice hockey

Date	Mintage	VF20	XF40	MS60	MS63
2010	—	—	—	—	3.00

KM# 953a 25 CENTS

4.40 g., Nickel Plated Steel, 23.9 mm. **Ruler:** Elizabeth II **Rev:** Ice Hockey - red enamel

Date	Mintage	VF20	XF40	MS60	MS63
2010	—	—	—	—	8.00

KM# 954 25 CENTS

4.40 g., Nickel Plated Steel, 23.9 mm. **Ruler:** Elizabeth II **Rev:** Curling

Date	Mintage	VF20	XF40	MS60	MS63
2010	—	—	—	—	3.00

KM# 954a 25 CENTS
4.40 g., Nickel Plated Steel, 23.9 mm. **Ruler:** Elizabeth II **Rev:** Curling red enamel

Date	Mintage	VF20	XF40	MS60	MS63
2010	—	—	—	—	8.00

KM# 955 25 CENTS
4.40 g., Nickel Plated Steel, 23.9 mm. **Ruler:** Elizabeth II **Rev:** Wheelchair curling

Date	Mintage	VF20	XF40	MS60	MS63
2010	—	—	—	—	3.00

KM# 955a 25 CENTS
4.40 g., Nickel Plated Steel, 23.9 mm. **Ruler:** Elizabeth II **Rev:** Wheelchair curling - red enamel

Date	Mintage	VF20	XF40	MS60	MS63
2010	—	—	—	—	8.00

KM# 956 25 CENTS
4.40 g., Nickel Plated Steel, 23.9 mm. **Ruler:** Elizabeth II **Rev:** Biathlon

Date	Mintage	VF20	XF40	MS60	MS63
2010	—	—	—	—	3.00

KM# 956a 25 CENTS
4.40 g., Nickel Plated Steel, 23.9 mm. **Ruler:** Elizabeth II **Rev:** Biathlon - red enamel

Date	Mintage	VF20	XF40	MS60	MS63
2010	—	—	—	—	8.00

KM# 957 25 CENTS
4.40 g., Nickel Plated Steel, 23.9 mm. **Ruler:** Elizabeth II **Rev:** Alpine skiing

Date	Mintage	VF20	XF40	MS60	MS63
2010	—	—	—	—	3.00

KM# 957a 25 CENTS
4.40 g., Nickel Plated Steel, 23.9 mm. **Ruler:** Elizabeth II **Rev:** Alpine skiing - red enamel

Date	Mintage	VF20	XF40	MS60	MS63
2010	—	—	—	—	8.00

KM# 958 25 CENTS
4.40 g., Nickel Plated Steel, 23.9 mm. **Ruler:** Elizabeth II **Rev:** Snowboarding

Date	Mintage	VF20	XF40	MS60	MS63
2010	—	—	—	—	3.00

KM# 958a 25 CENTS
4.40 g., Nickel Plated Steel, 23.9 mm. **Ruler:** Elizabeth II **Rev:** Snowboarding - red enamel

Date	Mintage	VF20	XF40	MS60	MS63
2010	—	—	—	—	8.00

KM# 959 25 CENTS
23.90 g., Nickel Plated Steel, 23.9 mm. **Ruler:** Elizabeth II **Rev:** Free-style skiing

Date	Mintage	VF20	XF40	MS60	MS63
2010	—	—	—	—	3.00

KM# 959a 25 CENTS
4.40 g., Nickel Plated Steel, 23.9 mm. **Ruler:** Elizabeth II **Rev:** Free-style skiing - red enamel

Date	Mintage	VF20	XF40	MS60	MS63
2010	—	—	—	—	8.00

KM# 960 25 CENTS
4.40 g., Nickel Plated Steel, 23.9 mm. **Ruler:** Elizabeth II **Rev:** Alpine skiing

Date	Mintage	VF20	XF40	MS60	MS63
2010	—	—	—	—	3.00

KM# 960a 25 CENTS
4.40 g., Nickel Plated Steel, 23.9 mm. **Ruler:** Elizabeth II **Rev:** Alpine skiing - red enamel

Date	Mintage	VF20	XF40	MS60	MS63
2010	—	—	—	—	8.00

KM# 988 25 CENTS
4.40 g., Nickel Plated Steel, 23.88 mm. **Ruler:** Elizabeth II **Rev:** Blue baby carriage

Date	Mintage	VF20	XF40	MS60	MS63
2010	—	—	—	—	10.00

KM# 989 25 CENTS
4.40 g., Nickel Plated Steel, 23.9 mm. **Ruler:** Elizabeth II **Rev:** Purple gift box

Date	Mintage	VF20	XF40	MS60	MS63
2010	—	—	—	—	10.00

KM# 990 25 CENTS
4.40 g., Nickel Plated Steel, 23.9 mm. **Ruler:** Elizabeth II **Rev:** Four stars

Date	Mintage	VF20	XF40	MS60	MS63
2010	—	—	—	—	10.00

KM# 991 25 CENTS
4.40 g., Nickel Plated Steel, 23.9 mm. **Ruler:** Elizabeth II **Rev:** Three maple leaves

Date	Mintage	VF20	XF40	MS60	MS63
2010	—	—	—	—	12.50

KM# 992 25 CENTS
4.40 g., Nickel Plated Steel, 23.9 mm. **Ruler:** Elizabeth II **Rev:** Three zinnias

Date	Mintage	VF20	XF40	MS60	MS63
2010	—	—	—	—	12.50

KM# 993 25 CENTS
4.43 g., Nickel Plated Steel, 23.9 mm. **Ruler:** Elizabeth II **Rev:** Pink hearts and roses

Date	Mintage	VF20	XF40	MS60	MS63
2010	—	—	—	—	10.00

KM# 994 25 CENTS
12.61 g., Nickel Plated Steel, 35 mm. **Ruler:** Elizabeth II **Rev:** Goldfinch, multicolor

Date	Mintage	VF20	XF40	MS60	MS63
2010 Specimen	Est. 14000	—	—	—	90.00

KM# 1001 25 CENTS
12.61 g., Nickel Plated Steel, 35 mm. **Ruler:** Elizabeth II **Subject:** Blue Jay **Rev:** Multicolor blue jay on yellow maple leaves

Date	Mintage	VF20	XF40	MS60	MS63
2010 Specimen	Est. 14000	—	—	—	90.00

KM# 1006 25 CENTS
0.50 g., 0.999 Gold AGW, 11 mm. **Ruler:** Elizabeth II **Rev:** Caribou head left

Date	Mintage	VF20	XF40	MS60	MS63
2010	15,000	PF63 70.00	PF65 80.00		

KM# 1021 25 CENTS
Nickel Plated Steel, 23.9 mm. **Ruler:** Elizabeth II **Rev:** Santa Claus in color

Date	Mintage	VF20	XF40	MS60	MS63
2010	—	—	—	—	15.00

KM# 1026 25 CENTS
Silver, 23.8 mm. **Ruler:** Elizabeth II **Obv:** George V bust left **Rev:** Value within wreath, dual dates below

Date	Mintage	VF20	XF40	MS60	MS63
1935-2010	—	PF63 22.00	PF65 25.00		

KM# 1028 25 CENTS
4.40 g., Nickel Plated Steel, 23.9 mm. **Ruler:** Elizabeth II **Rev:** Soldier standing, two red poppies, large maple leaf behind

Date	Mintage	VF20	XF40	MS60	MS63
2010	—	—	—	—	15.00

KM# 1110 25 CENTS
12.61 g., Nickel Plated Steel, 35 mm. **Ruler:** Elizabeth II **Subject:** Royal Wedding **Rev:** Colored portraits left of William and Katherine

Date	Mintage	VF20	XF40	MS60	MS63
2011 Specimen	—	—	—	—	25.00

KM# 1156 25 CENTS
5.90 g., 0.925 Silver 0.1743 oz. ASW, 23.8 mm. **Ruler:** Elizabeth II **Obv:** George V bust **Rev:** Value within wreath

Date	Mintage	VF20	XF40	MS60	MS63
1911-2011	6,000	PF63 22.00	PF65 25.00		

KM# 1168a 25 CENTS
4.40 g., Nickel Plated Steel, 23.9 mm. **Ruler:** Elizabeth II **Obv:** Bust right **Rev:** Stylized bison, green circle in background

Date	Mintage	VF20	XF40	MS60	MS63
2011	—	—	—	—	9.50

KM# 1169a 25 CENTS
4.40 g., Nickel Plated Steel, 23.9 mm. **Ruler:** Elizabeth II **Obv:** Bust right **Rev:** Stylized falcon with yellow circle in background

Date	Mintage	VF20	XF40	MS60	MS63
2011	—	—	—	—	9.50

KM# 1170a 25 CENTS
4.40 g., Nickel Plated Steel, 23.9 mm. **Ruler:** Elizabeth II **Obv:** Bust right **Rev:** Stylized orca whale with blue circle in background

Date	Mintage	VF20	XF40	MS60	MS63
2011	—	—	—	—	9.50

KM# 1079 25 CENTS
12.61 g., Nickel Plated Steel, 35 mm. **Ruler:** Elizabeth II **Rev:** Barn Swallow in color

Date	Mintage	VF20	XF40	MS60	MS63
2011 Specimen	Est. 14000	—	—	—	55.00

KM# 1080 25 CENTS
4.43 g., Nickel Plated Steel, 23.88 mm. **Ruler:** Elizabeth II **Subject:** Oh Canada! **Rev:** Maple leaf and circular legend

Date	Mintage	VF20	XF40	MS60	MS63
2011	—	—	—	—	2.50

KM# 1081 25 CENTS
4.43 g., Nickel Plated Steel, 23.88 mm. **Ruler:** Elizabeth II **Subject:** Wedding **Rev:** Two rings

Date	Mintage	VF20	XF40	MS60	MS63
2011	—	—	—	—	2.50

KM# 1082 25 CENTS
4.43 g., Nickel Plated Steel, 23.88 mm. **Ruler:** Elizabeth II **Subject:** Birthday **Rev:** Year in four baloons

Date	Mintage	VF20	XF40	MS60	MS63
2011	—	—	—	—	2.50

KM# 1083 25 CENTS
4.43 g., Nickel Plated Steel, 23.88 mm. **Ruler:** Elizabeth II **Subject:** New Baby! **Rev:** Baby's feet

Date	Mintage	VF20	XF40	MS60	MS63
2011	—	—	—	—	2.50

KM# 1084 25 CENTS
4.43 g., Nickel Plated Steel, 23.88 mm. **Ruler:** Elizabeth II **Rev:** Tooth Fairy

Date	Mintage	VF20	XF40	MS60	MS63
2011	—	—	—	—	2.50

KM# 1113 25 CENTS
12.61 g., Nickel Plated Steel, 35 mm. **Ruler:** Elizabeth II **Rev:** Fantasy Furry Woods creature in color

Date	Mintage	VF20	XF40	MS60	MS63
2011	—	—	—	—	20.00

KM# 1114 25 CENTS
12.61 g., Nickel Plated Steel, 35 mm. **Ruler:** Elizabeth II **Rev:** Fantasy sea serpent in color

Date	Mintage	VF20	XF40	MS60	MS63
2011	—	—	—	—	20.00

KM# 1115 25 CENTS
12.61 g., Nickel Plated Steel, 35 mm. **Ruler:** Elizabeth II **Rev:** Tulip and ladybug in color

Date	Mintage	VF20	XF40	MS60	MS63
2011	—	—	—	—	35.00

KM# 1116 25 CENTS
12.61 g., Nickel Plated Steel, 35 mm. **Ruler:** Elizabeth II **Rev:** Black capped chickadee in color

Date	Mintage	VF20	XF40	MS60	MS63
2011 Specimen	—	—	—	—	55.00

KM# 1148 25 CENTS
4.43 g., Nickel Plated Steel, 23.9 mm. **Ruler:** Elizabeth II **Obv:** Bust right **Rev:** Snowflake

Date	Mintage	VF20	XF40	MS60	MS63
2011	—	—	—	—	7.50

KM# 1168 25 CENTS
4.40 g., Nickel Plated Steel, 23.9 mm. **Ruler:** Elizabeth II **Obv:** Bust right **Rev:** Stylized bison

Date	Mintage	VF20	XF40	MS60	MS63
2011	—	—	—	—	2.50

KM# 1169 25 CENTS
4.40 g., Nickel Plated Steel, 23.9 mm. **Ruler:** Elizabeth II **Obv:** Bust right **Rev:** Stylized falcon

Date	Mintage	VF20	XF40	MS60	MS63
2011	—	—	—	—	2.50

KM# 1170 25 CENTS
4.40 g., Nickel Plated Steel, 23.9 mm. **Ruler:** Elizabeth II **Obv:**

Bust right **Rev:** Stylized orca whale

Date	Mintage	VF20	XF40	MS60	MS63
2011	—	—	—	—	2.50

KM# 1171 25 CENTS
0.50 g., 0.999 Gold AGW, 11 mm. **Ruler:** Elizabeth II **Obv:** Bust right **Rev:** Cougar head left

Date	Mintage	VF20	XF40	MS60	MS63
2011	—	PF63 70.00	PF65 80.00		

KM# 1172 25 CENTS
12.61 g., Copper Plated Silver, 35 mm. **Ruler:** Elizabeth II **Obv:** Bust right **Rev:** Wayne Greskey in hockey helmet left

Date	Mintage	VF20	XF40	MS60	MS63
2011 Specimen	—	—	—	—	35.00

KM# 1192 25 CENTS
4.43 g., Nickel Plated Steel, 23.9 mm. **Ruler:** Elizabeth II **Subject:** Canadian Broadcasting Company, 75th Anniversary **Obv:** Bust right **Rev:** Old-time radio microphone

Date	Mintage	VF20	XF40	MS60	MS63
2011	—	—	—	—	2.50

KM# 1193 25 CENTS
12.61 g., Nickel Plated Steel, 35 mm. **Ruler:** Elizabeth II **Subject:** Mythical Creature - Mishepishu **Obv:** Bust right **Rev:** Horned lizard in color

Date	Mintage	VF20	XF40	MS60	MS63
2011	—	—	—	—	15.00

KM# 1322a 25 CENTS
4.43 g., Nickel Plated Steel, 23.9 mm. **Ruler:** Elizabeth II **Subject:** War of 1812 - Brock **Rev:** Portrait at right, red maple leaf

Date	Mintage	VF20	XF40	MS60	MS63
2012	—	—	—	—	10.00

KM# 1227 25 CENTS
4.43 g., Nickel Plated Steel, 23.9 mm. **Ruler:** Elizabeth II **Obv:**

Bust right **Rev:** Tooth Fairy in flight

Date	Mintage	VF20	XF40	MS60	MS63
2012	—	—	—	—	2.50

KM# 1228 25 CENTS
4.43 g., Nickel Plated Steel, 23.9 mm. **Ruler:** Elizabeth II **Subject:** Baby **Rev:** Baby's mobile

Date	Mintage	VF20	XF40	MS60	MS63
2012	—	—	—	—	2.50

KM# 1229 25 CENTS
4.43 g., Nickel Plated Steel, 23.9 mm. **Ruler:** Elizabeth II **Subject:** Wedding **Rev:** Two wedding rings with small feet

Date	Mintage	VF20	XF40	MS60	MS63
2012	—	—	—	—	2.50

KM# 1230 25 CENTS
4.43 g., Nickel Plated Steel, 23.9 mm. **Ruler:** Elizabeth II **Subject:** Birthday **Rev:** Cone with character face

Date	Mintage	VF20	XF40	MS60	MS63
2012	—	—	—	—	2.50

KM# 1231 25 CENTS
4.43 g., Nickel Plated Steel, 23.9 mm. **Ruler:** Elizabeth II **Subject:** Oh, Canada ! **Rev:** Maple leaves with character faces

Date	Mintage	VF20	XF40	MS60	MS63
2012	—	—	—	—	2.50

KM# 1232 25 CENTS
4.43 g., Nickel Plated Steel, 23.88 mm. **Ruler:** Elizabeth II **Subject:** Winnipeg Jets **Rev:** Jet superimposed on Maple leaf

Date	Mintage	VF20	XF40	MS60	MS63
2012	—	—	—	—	2.50

KM# 1233 25 CENTS
12.61 g., Nickel Plated Steel, 35 mm. **Ruler:** Elizabeth II **Subject:** Titanic, 100th Anniversary **Obv:** Bust right **Rev:** Two views of Titanic, one at dockside, one nighttime at sea

Date	Mintage	VF20	XF40	MS60	MS63
2012	—	—	—	—	20.00

KM# 1247 25 CENTS
12.61 g., Nickel Plated Steel, 35 mm. **Ruler:** Elizabeth II **Subject:** Coast Guard, 100th anniversary **Rev:** Rescue craft in rough seas

Date	Mintage	VF20	XF40	MS60	MS63
2012	—	—	—	—	30.00

KM# 1252 25 CENTS
12.61 g., Nickel Plated Steel, 35 mm. **Ruler:** Elizabeth II **Subject:** Pachyrhinosaurus Lakusta **Note:** Skelton glows in the dark.

Date	Mintage	VF20	XF40	MS60	MS63
2012	—	—	—	—	25.00

KM# 1253 25 CENTS
12.61 g., Nickel Plated Steel, 35 mm. **Ruler:** Elizabeth II **Subject:** Rose Breasted Grosbeak

Date	Mintage	VF20	XF40	MS60	MS63
2012	—	—	—	—	35.00

KM# 1265 25 CENTS
12.61 g., Nickel Plated Steel, 35 mm. **Ruler:** Elizabeth II **Subject:** Aster and Bee

Date	Mintage	VF20	XF40	MS60	MS63
2012	—	—	—	—	35.00

KM# 1313 25 CENTS
0.50 g., Silver, 35 mm. **Ruler:** Elizabeth II **Subject:** Grey Cup, 100th Anniversary **Obv:** Bust right **Rev:** B.C. Lions logo in color

Date	Mintage	VF20	XF40	MS60	MS63
2012	—	PF65 25.00			

KM# 1314 25 CENTS
0.50 g., Copper-Nickel, 35 mm. **Ruler:** Elizabeth II **Subject:** Grey Cup, 100th Anniversary **Obv:** Bust right **Rev:** Calgary Stampeeders logo in color

Date	Mintage	VF20	XF40	MS60	MS63
2012	—	PF65 25.00			

KM# 1315 25 CENTS
0.50 g., Copper-Nickel, 35 mm. **Ruler:** Elizabeth II **Subject:** Grey Cup, 100th Anniversary **Obv:** Bust right **Rev:** Edmonton Eskimos logo in color

Date	Mintage	VF20	XF40	MS60	MS63
2012	—	PF65 25.00			

KM# 1316 25 CENTS
0.50 g., Copper-Nickel, 35 mm. **Ruler:** Elizabeth II **Subject:** Grey Cup, 100th Anniversary **Obv:** Bust right **Rev:** Hamilton Tiger-Cats logo in color

Date	Mintage	F12	VF20	XF40	MS60	MS63
2012	—	PF65 25.00				

KM# 1317 25 CENTS
0.50 g., Copper-Nickel, 35 mm. **Ruler:** Elizabeth II **Subject:** Grey Cup, 100th Anniversary **Obv:** Bust right **Rev:** Montreal Alouettes logo in color

Date	Mintage	VF20	XF40	MS60	MS63
2012	—	PF65 25.00			

KM# 1318 25 CENTS
0.50 g., Copper-Nickel, 35 mm. **Ruler:** Elizabeth II **Subject:** Grey Cup, 100th Anniversary **Obv:** Bust right **Rev:** Saskatchewan Roughriders logo in color

Date	Mintage	VF20	XF40	MS60	MS63
2012	—	PF65 25.00			

KM# 1319 25 CENTS
0.50 g., Copper-Nickel, 35 mm. **Ruler:** Elizabeth II **Subject:** Grey Cup, 100th Anniversary **Obv:** Bust right **Rev:** Toronto Argonauts logo in color

Date	Mintage	VF20	XF40	MS60	MS63
2012	—	PF65 25.00			

KM# 1320 25 CENTS
0.50 g., Copper-Nickel, 35 mm. **Ruler:** Elizabeth II **Subject:** Grey Cup, 100th Anniversary **Obv:** Bust right **Rev:** Winnipeg Blue Bombers logo in color

Date	Mintage	VF20	XF40	MS60	MS63
2012	—	PF65 25.00			

KM# 1321 25 CENTS
12.61 g., Nickel Plated Steel, 35 mm. **Ruler:** Elizabeth II **Subject:** Calgary Stampeed **Rev:** Cowboy on bucking horse in color

Date	Mintage	VF20	XF40	MS60	MS63
2012 Specimen	—	—	—	—	45.00

KM# 1322 25 CENTS
4.43 g., Nickel Plated Steel, 23.9 mm. **Ruler:** Elizabeth II **Subject:** War of 1812 - Brock **Rev:** Porrait at right

Date	Mintage	VF20	XF40	MS60	MS63
2012	—	—	—	—	2.50

KM# 1324 25 CENTS
4.43 g., Nickel Plated Steel, 23.9 mm. **Ruler:** Elizabeth II **Subject:** War of 1812 - Tecumseh **Rev:** Portrait at right

Date	Mintage	VF20	XF40	MS60	MS63
2012	—	—	—	—	2.50

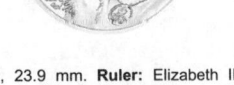

KM# 1324a 25 CENTS
4.42 g., Nickel Plated Steel, 23.9 mm. **Ruler:** Elizabeth II **Subject:** War of 1812 - Tecumseh **Rev:** Portrait at right, red maple leaf

Date	Mintage	VF20	XF40	MS60	MS63
2012	—	—	—	—	10.00

KM# 1326 25 CENTS
12.61 g., Nickel Plated Steel, 35 mm. **Ruler:** Elizabeth II **Rev:** Evening Grosbeak in color

Date	Mintage	VF20	XF40	MS60	MS63
2012 Specimen	—	—	—	—	35.00

KM# 1341 25 CENTS
12.16 g., Copper-Nickel, 35 mm. **Ruler:** Elizabeth II **Subject:** Christmas Lenticular **Rev:** Santa Claus with bag of presents

Date	Mintage	VF20	XF40	MS60	MS63
2012 Specimen	25,000	—	—	—	30.00

KM# 1351 25 CENTS
Nickel Plated Steel, 35 mm. **Ruler:** Elizabeth II **Subject:** Quetzalcoatlus **Rev:** Dinosaur in color and as glow-in-the-dark skelton

Date	Mintage	VF20	XF40	MS60	MS63
2013	—	—	—	—	40.00

KM# 1353 25 CENTS
12.61 g., Copper-Nickel, 35 mm. **Ruler:** Elizabeth II **Rev:** Purple cone flower and butterfly in color

Date	Mintage	VF20	XF40	MS60	MS63
2013 Specimen	17,500	—	—	—	30.00

KM# 1354 25 CENTS
12.61 g., Copper-Nickel, 35 mm. **Ruler:** Elizabeth II **Rev:** Male and female mallards in color

Date	Mintage	VF20	XF40	MS60	MS63
2013 Specimen	17,500	—	—	—	30.00

KM# 1368 25 CENTS
4.43 g., Nickel Plated Steel, 23.9 mm. **Ruler:** Elizabeth II **Subject:** Oh Canada **Rev:** Maple Leaf

Date	Mintage	VF20	XF40	MS60	MS63
2013	—	PF63 8.00	PF65 10.00		

KM# 1373 25 CENTS
12.61 g., Nickel Plated Steel, 35 mm. **Ruler:** Elizabeth II **Rev:** American Robin in color

Date	Mintage	VF20	XF40	MS60	MS63
2013 Specimen	—	—	—	—	35.00

KM# 1380 25 CENTS
0.50 g., 0.9999 Gold AGW, 11 mm. **Ruler:** Elizabeth II **Rev:** Hummingbird in flight right

Date	Mintage	VF20	XF40	MS60	MS63
2013	Est. 10000	PF63 70.00	PF65 80.00		

KM# 1419 25 CENTS
4.43 g., Nickel Plated Steel, 23.9 mm. **Ruler:** Elizabeth II **Subject:** Birthday **Rev:** Birthday cake and candle

Date	Mintage	VF20	XF40	MS60	MS63
2013	—	PF63 17.00	PF65 20.00		

KM# 1420 25 CENTS
4.43 g., Nickel Plated Steel, 23.9 mm. **Ruler:** Elizabeth II **Rev:** Two Rings

Date	Mintage	VF20	XF40	MS60	MS63
2013	—	PF63 17.00	PF65 20.00		

KM# 1432 25 CENTS
15.50 g., Copper-Nickel, 35 mm. **Ruler:** Elizabeth II **Subject:** Coronation Anniversary **Rev:** Elizabeth standing, Victoria painting in background in color.

Date	Mintage	VF20	XF40	MS60	MS63
2013 Specimen	Est. 15000	—	—	—	25.00

KM# 1443 25 CENTS
Copper-Nickel, 35 mm. **Ruler:** Elizabeth II **Obv:** Bust right **Rev:** Barn owl in flight left, in color

Date	Mintage	VF20	XF40	MS60	MS63
2013	17,500	PF63 30.00	PF65 35.00		

KM# 1460 25 CENTS
0.50 g., Nickel Plated Steel, 35 mm. **Ruler:** Elizabeth II **Rev:** Baby carriage - William and Catherine names around

Date	Mintage	VF20	XF40	MS60	MS63
2013 Specimen	—	—	—	—	25.00

KM# 1465 25 CENTS
12.61 g., Nickel Plated Steel, 35 mm. **Ruler:** Elizabeth II **Rev:** Christmas wreath in color

Date	Mintage	VF20	XF40	MS60	MS63
2013	—	—	—	—	25.00

KM# 1491 25 CENTS
15.50 g., Copper-Nickel, 35 mm. **Ruler:** Elizabeth II **Subject:** Eastern Prickly Pear Cactus **Rev:** Partial flower in color

Date	Mintage	VF20	XF40	MS60	MS63
2013	17,500	PF63 20.00	PF65 25.00		

KM# 1494 25 CENTS
0.50 g., 0.999 Gold AGW, 11 mm. **Ruler:** Elizabeth II **Subject:** Rocky Mountain Bighorn Sheep **Rev:** Head right

Date	Mintage	VF20	XF40	MS60	MS63
2013	10,000	PF63 70.00	PF65 80.00		

KM# 1521 25 CENTS
Copper-Nickel, 28 mm. **Ruler:** Elizabeth II **Rev:** Tylosaurus Pembinensis glow in the dark

Date	Mintage	VF20	XF40	MS60	MS63
2013	30,000	PF63 25.00	PF65 30.00		

KM# 1524 25 CENTS
Copper-Nickel, 35 mm. **Ruler:** Elizabeth II **Rev:** Wood duck pair

Date	Mintage	VF20	XF40	MS60	MS63
2013	—	—	—	30.00	

KM# 1539 25 CENTS
Nickel Plated Steel, 23.9 mm. **Ruler:** Elizabeth II **Obv:** Birthday cake

Date	Mintage	VF20	XF40	MS60	MS63
2013	—	—	—	2.50	

KM# 1547 25 CENTS
Copper-Nickel, 23.9 mm. **Ruler:** Elizabeth II **Rev:** Artic Explorers, compass rose

Date	Mintage	VF20	XF40	MS60	MS63
2013 Frosted compass arc	—	—	—	2.50	
2013 Frosted explorers	—	—	—	2.50	

KM# 1572 25 CENTS
12.61 g., Nickel Plated Steel, 35 mm. **Ruler:** Elizabeth II **Obv:** Bust right **Rev:** Montreal Canadians logo in color

Date	Mintage	VF20	XF40	MS60	MS63
2014	—	—	—	10.00	

KM# 1573 25 CENTS
12.61 g., Nickel Plated Steel, 35 mm. **Ruler:** Elizabeth II **Obv:** Bust right **Rev:** Canucks logo in color

Date	Mintage	VF20	XF40	MS60	MS63
2014	—	—	—	10.00	

KM# 1574 25 CENTS
12.61 g., Nickel Plated Steel, 35 mm. **Ruler:** Elizabeth II **Obv:** Bust right **Rev:** Calgary Flames logo in color

Date	Mintage	VF20	XF40	MS60	MS63
2014	—	—	—	10.00	

KM# 1575 25 CENTS
12.61 g., Nickel Plated Steel, 35 mm. **Ruler:** Elizabeth II **Obv:** Bust right **Rev:** Winnipeg Jets logo in color

Date	Mintage	VF20	XF40	MS60	MS63
2014	—	—	—	10.00	

KM# 1576 25 CENTS
12.61 g., Nickel Plated Steel, 35 mm. **Ruler:** Elizabeth II **Obv:** Bust right **Rev:** Toronto Maple Leafs logo in color

Date	Mintage	VF20	XF40	MS60	MS63
2014	—	—	—	10.00	

KM# 1577 25 CENTS
12.61 g., Nickel Plated Steel, 35 mm. **Ruler:** Elizabeth II **Obv:** Bust right **Rev:** Edmonton Oilers logo in color

Date	Mintage	VF20	XF40	MS60	MS63
2014	—	—	—	10.00	

KM# 1578 25 CENTS
12.610 Nickel Plated Steel, 35 mm. **Ruler:** Elizabeth II **Obv:** Bust right **Rev:** Senators logo in color

Date	Mintage	VF20	XF40	MS60	MS63
2014	—	—	—	10.00	

KM# 1602 25 CENTS
0.50 g., 0.999 Gold AGW, 11 mm. **Ruler:** Elizabeth II **Obv:** Bust right **Rev:** Chipmonk

Date	Mintage	VF20	XF40	MS60	MS63
2014	—	PF63 70.00	PF65 80.00		

KM# 1618 25 CENTS
12.61 g., Nickel Plated Steel, 35 mm. **Ruler:** Elizabeth II **Obv:** Bust right **Rev:** Eastern Meadowlark in color

Date	Mintage	VF20	XF40	MS60	MS63
2014	—	—	—	—	35.00

KM# 1619 25 CENTS
12.61 g., Nickel Plated Steel, 35 mm. **Ruler:** Elizabeth II **Obv:** Bust right **Rev:** Tikaalik creature in glow in the dark format

Date	Mintage	VF20	XF40	MS60	MS63
2014	—	—	—	—	25.00

KM# 1630 25 CENTS
12.61 g., Nickel Plated Steel, 35 mm. **Ruler:** Elizabeth II **Obv:** Bust right **Rev:** Pintail ducks in color

Date	Mintage	VF20	XF40	MS60	MS63
2014	—	—	—	—	25.00

KM# 290 50 CENTS
8.10 g., Nickel, 27.1 mm. **Ruler:** Elizabeth II **Obv:** Crowned head right **Rev:** Redesigned arms **Edge:** Reeded

Date	Mintage	VF20	XF40	MS60	MS63
2001P	—	—	—	—	1.50
2001P	—	PF63 3.50	PF65 5.00		
2003P	—	—	—	—	1.50
2003P	—	PF63 3.50	PF65 5.00		

KM# 290a 50 CENTS
11.66 g., 0.925 Silver 0.3446 oz. ASW, 27.13 mm. **Ruler:** Elizabeth II **Obv:** Crowned head right **Rev:** Redesigned arms **Edge:** Reeded

Date	Mintage	VF20	XF40	MS60	MS63
2001	—	PF65 13.00			
2003	—	PF65 13.00			

KM# 290b 50 CENTS
6.90 g., Nickel Plated Steel, 27.13 mm. **Ruler:** Elizabeth II **Obv:** Crowned head right **Rev:** Redesigned arms **Edge:** Reeded

Date	Mintage	VF20	XF40	MS60	MS63
2001 P	389,000	—	—	1.00	1.50
2003 P	—	—	—	—	5.00

KM# 420 50 CENTS
9.30 g., 0.925 Silver 0.2748 oz. ASW, 27.13 mm. **Ruler:** Elizabeth II **Series:** Festivals - Quebec **Obv:** Crowned head right **Rev:** Snowman and Chateau Frontenac **Edge:** Reeded

Date	Mintage	VF20	XF40	MS60	MS63
2001	58,123	PF63 7.50	PF65 8.50		

KM# 421 50 CENTS
9.30 g., 0.925 Silver 0.2748 oz. ASW, 27.13 mm. **Ruler:** Elizabeth II **Series:** Festivals - Nunavut **Obv:** Crowned head right **Rev:** Dancer, dog sled and snowmobiles **Edge:** Reeded

Date	Mintage	VF20	XF40	MS60	MS63
2001	—	PF63 7.50	PF65 8.50		

KM# 422 50 CENTS
9.30 g., 0.925 Silver 0.2748 oz. ASW, 27.13 mm. **Ruler:** Elizabeth II **Series:** Festivals - Newfoundland **Obv:** Crowned head right **Rev:** Sailor and musical people **Edge:** Reeded

Date	Mintage	VF20	XF40	MS60	MS63
2001	58,123	PF63 7.50	PF65 8.50		

KM# 423 50 CENTS
9.30 g., 0.925 Silver 0.2748 oz. ASW, 27.13 mm. **Ruler:** Elizabeth II **Series:** Festivals - Prince Edward Island **Obv:** Crowned head right **Rev:** Family, juggler and building **Edge:** Reeded

Date	Mintage	VF20	XF40	MS60	MS63
2001	58,123	PF63 7.50	PF65 8.50		

KM# 424 50 CENTS
9.30 g., 0.925 Silver 0.2748 oz. ASW, 27.13 mm. **Ruler:** Elizabeth II **Series:** Folklore - The Sled **Obv:** Crowned head right **Rev:** Family scene **Edge:** Reeded

Date	Mintage	VF20	XF40	MS60	MS63
2001	28,979	PF63 8.00	PF65 9.00		

KM# 425 50 CENTS
9.30 g., 0.925 Silver 0.2748 oz. ASW, 27.13 mm. **Ruler:** Elizabeth II **Series:** Folklore - The Maiden's Cave **Obv:** Crowned head right **Rev:** Woman shouting **Edge:** Reeded

Date	Mintage	VF20	XF40	MS60	MS63
2001	28,979	PF63 8.00	PF65 9.00		

KM# 426 50 CENTS
9.30 g., 0.925 Silver 0.2748 oz. ASW, 27.13 mm. **Ruler:** Elizabeth II **Series:** Folklore - The Small Jumpers **Obv:** Crowned head right **Rev:** Jumping children on seashore **Edge:** Reeded

Date	Mintage	VF20	XF40	MS60	MS63
2001	28,979	PF63 8.00	PF65 9.00		

KM# 509 50 CENTS
6.90 g., Nickel Plated Steel, 27.13 mm. **Ruler:** Elizabeth II **Obv:** Crowned head right **Rev:** National arms **Edge:** Reeded

Date	Mintage	VF20	XF40	MS60	MS63
2001 P	—	—	—	—	1.50

KM# 444 50 CENTS
6.90 g., Nickel Plated Steel, 27.13 mm. **Ruler:** Elizabeth II **Subject:** Queen's Golden Jubilee **Obv:** Coronation crowned head right and monogram **Rev:** Canadian arms **Edge:** Reeded

Date	Mintage	VF20	XF40	MS60	MS63
1952-2002P	14,440,000	—	—	—	2.50

KM# 444a 50 CENTS
9.30 g., 0.925 Silver 0.2748 oz. ASW, 27.13 mm. **Ruler:** Elizabeth II **Subject:** Elizabeth II Golden Jubilee **Obv:** Crowned head right, Jubilee commemorative dates 1952-2002

Date	Mintage	VF20	XF40	MS60	MS63
1952-2002	100,000	PF63 15.00	PF65 17.50		

KM# 444b 50 CENTS
9.30 g., 0.925 Silver Gilt 0.2748 oz., 27.13 mm. **Ruler:** Elizabeth II **Subject:** Queen's Golden Jubilee **Obv:** Crowned head right and monogram **Rev:** Canadian arms **Edge:** Reeded **Note:** Special 24 karat gold-plated issue of KM#444.

Date	Mintage	VF20	XF40	MS60	MS63
1952-2002	32,642	PF63 30.00	PF65 35.00		

KM# 454 50 CENTS
9.30 g., 0.925 Silver 0.2748 oz. ASW, 27.13 mm. **Ruler:** Elizabeth II **Subject:** Nova Scotia Annapolis Valley Apple Blossom Festival **Obv:** Crowned head right

Date	Mintage	VF20	XF40	MS60	MS63
2002	59,998	PF63 7.50	PF65 9.50		

KM# 455 50 CENTS
9.30 g., 0.925 Silver 0.2748 oz. ASW, 27.13 mm. **Ruler:** Elizabeth II **Subject:** Stratford Festival **Obv:** Crowned head right **Rev:** Couple with building in background

Date	Mintage	VF20	XF40	MS60	MS63
2002	59,998	PF63 7.50	PF65 9.50		

KM# 456 50 CENTS
9.30 g., 0.925 Silver 0.2748 oz. ASW, 27.13 mm. **Ruler:**
Elizabeth II **Subject:** Folklorama **Obv:** Crowned head right

Date	Mintage	VF20	XF40	MS60	MS63
2002	59,998	PF63 7.50	PF65 9.50		

KM# 457 50 CENTS
9.30 g., 0.925 Silver 0.2748 oz. ASW, 27.13 mm. **Ruler:**
Elizabeth II **Subject:** Calgary Stampede **Obv:** Crowned head
right

Date	Mintage	VF20	XF40	MS60	MS63
2002	59,998	PF63 7.50	PF65 9.50		

KM# 458 50 CENTS
9.30 g., 0.925 Silver 0.2748 oz. ASW, 27.13 mm. **Ruler:**
Elizabeth II **Subject:** Squamish Days Logger Sports **Obv:**
Crowned head right

Date	Mintage	VF20	XF40	MS60	MS63
2002	59,998	PF63 7.50	PF65 9.50		

KM# 459 50 CENTS
9.30 g., 0.925 Silver 0.2748 oz. ASW, 27.13 mm. **Ruler:**
Elizabeth II **Series:** Folklore and Legends **Obv:** Crowned head
right **Rev:** The Shoemaker in Heaven

Date	Mintage	VF20	XF40	MS60	MS63
2002	19,267	PF63 10.00	PF65 11.00		

KM# 460 50 CENTS
9.30 g., 0.925 Silver 0.2748 oz. ASW, 27.13 mm. **Ruler:**
Elizabeth II **Series:** Folklore and Legends **Subject:** The Ghost
Ship **Obv:** Crowned head right

Date	Mintage	VF20	XF40	MS60	MS63
2002	19,267	PF63 10.00	PF65 11.00		

KM# 461 50 CENTS
9.30 g., 0.925 Silver 0.2748 oz. ASW, 27.13 mm. **Ruler:**
Elizabeth II **Series:** Folklore and Legends **Subject:** The Pig
That Wouldn't Get Over the Stile **Obv:** Crowned head right

Date	Mintage	VF20	XF40	MS60	MS63
2002	19,267	PF63 10.00	PF65 11.00		

KM# 472 50 CENTS
11.62 g., 0.925 Silver 0.3433 oz. ASW, 27.13 mm. **Ruler:**
Elizabeth II **Subject:** 50th Anniversary of the Coronation of
Elizabeth II **Obv:** Crowned head right, Jubilee commemorative
dates 1952-2002

Date	Mintage	VF20	XF40	MS60	MS63
2003	30,000	PF63 12.00	PF65 15.00		

KM# 475 50 CENTS
9.30 g., 0.925 Silver 0.2748 oz. ASW, 27.13 mm. **Ruler:**
Elizabeth II **Obv:** Crowned head right **Rev:** Golden daffodil

Date	Mintage	VF20	XF40	MS60	MS63
2003	36,293	PF63 20.00	PF65 25.00		

KM# 476 50 CENTS
9.30 g., 0.925 Silver 0.2748 oz. ASW, 27.13 mm. **Ruler:**
Elizabeth II **Subject:** Yukon International Storytelling Festival
Obv: Crowned head right

Date	Mintage	VF20	XF40	MS60	MS63
2003	—	PF63 10.00	PF65 11.00		

KM# 477 50 CENTS
9.30 g., 0.925 Silver 0.2748 oz. ASW, 27.13 mm. **Ruler:**
Elizabeth II **Subject:** Festival Acadien de Caraquet **Obv:**
Crowned head right **Rev:** Sailboat and couple

Date	Mintage	VF20	XF40	MS60	MS63
2003	—	PF63 10.00	PF65 11.00		

KM# 478 50 CENTS
9.30 g., 0.925 Silver 0.2748 oz. ASW, 27.13 mm. **Ruler:**
Elizabeth II **Subject:** Back to Batoche **Obv:** Crowned head right

Date	Mintage	VF20	XF40	MS60	MS63
2003	—	PF63 10.00	PF65 11.00		

KM# 479 50 CENTS
9.30 g., 0.925 Silver 0.2748 oz. ASW, 27.13 mm. **Ruler:**
Elizabeth II **Subject:** Great Northern Arts Festival **Obv:**
Crowned head right

Date	Mintage	VF20	XF40	MS60	MS63
2003	—	PF63 10.00	PF65 11.00		

KM# 494 50 CENTS
6.90 g., Nickel Plated Steel, 27.13 mm. **Ruler:** Elizabeth II **Obv:**
Crowned head right **Rev:** National arms **Edge:** Reeded

Date	Mintage	VF20	XF40	MS60	MS63
2003P W	—	—	—	—	5.00
2003P W	—	PF63 6.50	PF65 7.50		
2004P	—	—	—	—	5.00
2004P	—	PF63 6.50	PF65 7.50		
2005P	200,000	—	—	—	1.50
2005P	—	PF63 4.00	PF65 5.00		
2006P	98,000	—	—	—	1.50
2006P	—	PF63 4.00	PF65 5.00		
2007(ml)	250,000	—	—	—	1.50
2007(ml)	—	PF63 4.00	PF65 5.00		
2008(ml)	211,000	—	—	—	1.50
2008(ml)	—	PF63 4.00	PF65 5.00		
2009(ml)	150,000	—	—	—	1.50
2009(ml)	—	PF63 4.00	PF65 5.00		
2010(ml)	—	—	—	—	1.50
2010(ml)	—	PF63 4.00	PF65 5.00		
2011(ml)	—	—	—	—	1.50
2011(ml)	—	PF63 4.00	PF65 5.00		
2012(ml)	—	—	—	—	1.50
2012(ml)	—	PF63 4.00	PF65 5.00		
2013(ml)	—	—	—	—	1.50
2013(ml)	—	PF63 4.00	PF65 5.00		

KM# 494a 50 CENTS
9.30 g., 0.925 Silver 0.2748 oz. ASW, 27.13 mm. **Ruler:**
Elizabeth II **Obv:** Crowned head right **Rev:** Canadian coat of
arms **Edge:** Reeded

Date	Mintage	VF20	XF40	MS60	MS63
2004	—	PF63 6.00	PF65 7.50		

KM# 526 50 CENTS
1.27 g., 0.9999 Gold 0.0406 oz. AGW, 14 mm. **Ruler:** Elizabeth
II **Subject:** Moose **Obv:** Head right **Rev:** Moose head facing
right

Date	Mintage	VF20	XF40	MS60	MS63
2004	—	PF65 85.00			

KM# 606 50 CENTS
9.30 g., 0.925 Silver 0.2748 oz. ASW, 27.13 mm. **Ruler:**
Elizabeth II **Obv:** Head right **Rev:** Clouded Sulphur Butterfly,
hologram

Date	Mintage	VF20	XF40	MS60	MS63
2004	15,281	PF63 40.00	PF65 45.00		

KM# 712 50 CENTS
9.30 g., 0.925 Silver 0.2748 oz. ASW, 27.13 mm. **Ruler:**
Elizabeth II **Rev:** Hologram of Tiger Swallowtail butterfly

Date	Mintage	VF20	XF40	MS60	MS63
2004	20,462	PF63 42.00	PF65 45.00		

KM# 536 50 CENTS
9.30 g., 0.925 Silver 0.2748 oz. ASW, 27.13 mm. **Ruler:**

Elizabeth II Subject: Golden rose **Obv:** Head right

Date	Mintage	VF20	XF40	MS60	MS63
2005	17,418	PF63 35.00	PF65 40.00		

KM# 537 50 CENTS
9.30 g., 0.925 Silver 0.2748 oz. ASW, 27.13 mm. **Ruler:**
Elizabeth II **Obv:** Head right **Rev:** Great Spangled Fritillary
butterfly, hologram

Date	Mintage	VF20	XF40	MS60	MS63
2005	20,000	PF63 45.00	PF65 50.00		

KM# 538 50 CENTS
9.30 g., 0.925 Silver 0.2748 oz. ASW, 27.13 mm. **Ruler:**
Elizabeth II **Subject:** Toronto Maple Leafs **Obv:** Head right
Rev: Darryl Sittler

Date	Mintage	VF20	XF40	MS60	MS63
2005 Specimen	25,000	PF65 16.00			

KM# 539 50 CENTS
9.30 g., 0.925 Silver 0.2748 oz. ASW, 27.13 mm. **Ruler:**
Elizabeth II **Subject:** Toronto Maple Leafs **Obv:** Head right
Rev: Dave Keon

Date	Mintage	VF20	XF40	MS60	MS63
2005 Specimen	25,000	PF65 16.00			

KM# 540 50 CENTS
9.30 g., 0.925 Silver 0.2748 oz. ASW, 27.13 mm. **Ruler:**
Elizabeth II **Subject:** Toronto Maple Leafs **Obv:** Head right
Rev: Jonny Bover, goalie

Date	Mintage	VF20	XF40	MS60	MS63
2005 Specimen	25,000	PF65 16.00			

KM# 541 50 CENTS
9.30 g., 0.925 Silver 0.2748 oz. ASW, 27.13 mm. **Ruler:**
Elizabeth II **Subject:** Toronto Maple Leafs **Obv:** Head right
Rev: Tim Horton

Date	Mintage	VF20	XF40	MS60	MS63
2005 Specimen	25,000	PF65 16.00			

KM# 543 50 CENTS
9.30 g., 0.925 Silver 0.2748 oz. ASW **Ruler:** Elizabeth II
Subject: WWII - Battle of Britain **Obv:** Head right **Rev:** Fighter
plane in sky

Date	Mintage	VF20	XF40	MS60	MS63
2005 Specimen	20,000	PF63 20.00	PF65 22.50		

KM# 544 50 CENTS
9.30 g., 0.925 Silver 0.2748 oz. ASW, 27.13 mm. **Ruler:**
Elizabeth II **Subject:** WWII - Battle of Scheldt **Obv:** Head right
Rev: Four soldiers walking down road

Date	Mintage	VF20	XF40	MS60	MS63
2005 Specimen	20,000	PF65 19.00			

KM# 545 50 CENTS
9.30 g., 0.925 Silver 0.2748 oz. ASW, 27.13 mm. **Ruler:**
Elizabeth II **Subject:** WWII - Battle of the Atlantic **Obv:** Head
right **Rev:** Merchant ship sinking

Date	Mintage	VF20	XF40	MS60	MS63
2005 Specimen	20,000	PF65 19.00			

KM# 546 50 CENTS
9.30 g., 0.925 Silver 0.2748 oz. ASW, 27.13 mm. **Ruler:**
Elizabeth II **Subject:** WWII - Conquest of Sicily **Obv:** Head right
Rev: Tank among town ruins

Date	Mintage	VF20	XF40	MS60	MS63
2005 Specimen	20,000	PF65 19.00			

KM# 547 50 CENTS
9.30 g., 0.925 Silver 0.2748 oz. ASW, 27.13 mm. **Ruler:**
Elizabeth II **Subject:** WWII - Liberation of the Netherlands **Obv:**
Head right **Rev:** Soldiers in parade, one holding flag

Date	Mintage	VF20	XF40	MS60	MS63
2005 Specimen	20,000	PF65 19.00			

KM# 548 50 CENTS
9.30 g., 0.925 Silver 0.2748 oz. ASW, 27.13 mm. **Ruler:**
Elizabeth II **Subject:** WWII - Raid of Dieppe **Obv:** Head right
Rev: Three soldiers exiting landing craft

Date	Mintage	VF20	XF40	MS60	MS63
2005 Specimen	20,000	PF65 19.00			

KM# 577 50 CENTS
9.30 g., 0.925 Silver 0.2748 oz. ASW, 27.13 mm. **Ruler:** Elizabeth II **Subject:** Montreal Canadiens **Obv:** Head right **Rev:** Guy LaFleur

Date	Mintage	VF20	XF40	MS60	MS63
2005 Specimen	25,000			PF65 17.50	

KM# 578 50 CENTS
9.30 g., 0.925 Silver 0.2748 oz. ASW, 27.13 mm. **Ruler:** Elizabeth II **Subject:** Montreal Canadiens **Obv:** Head right **Rev:** Jaque Plante

Date	Mintage	VF20	XF40	MS60	MS63
2005 Specimen	25,000			PF65 17.50	

KM# 579 50 CENTS
9.30 g., 0.925 Silver 0.2748 oz. ASW, 27.13 mm. **Ruler:** Elizabeth II **Subject:** Montreal Canadiens **Obv:** Head right **Rev:** Jean Beliveau

Date	Mintage	VF20	XF40	MS60	MS63
2005 Specimen	25,000			PF65 17.50	

KM# 580 50 CENTS
9.30 g., 0.925 Silver 0.2748 oz. ASW, 27.13 mm. **Ruler:** Elizabeth II **Subject:** Montreal Canadiens **Obv:** Head right **Rev:** Maurice Richard

Date	Mintage	VF20	XF40	MS60	MS63
2005 Specimen	25,000			PF65 17.50	

KM# 599 50 CENTS
9.30 g., 0.925 Silver 0.2748 oz. ASW, 27.13 mm. **Ruler:** Elizabeth II **Obv:** Head right **Rev:** Monarch butterfly, colorized

Date	Mintage	VF20	XF40	MS60	MS63
2005	20,000	PF63 45.00	PF65 50.00		

KM# 648 50 CENTS
9.30 g., 0.925 Silver 0.2748 oz. ASW, 27.13 mm. **Ruler:** Elizabeth II **Subject:** Golden Daisy **Obv:** Head right

Date	Mintage	VF20	XF40	MS60	MS63
2006	18,190	PF63 27.00	PF65 30.00		

KM# 649 50 CENTS
9.30 g., 0.925 Silver 0.2748 oz. ASW, 27.13 mm. **Ruler:** Elizabeth II **Subject:** Short-tailed swallowtail **Obv:** Head right **Rev:** Colorized butterfly

Date	Mintage	VF20	XF40	MS60	MS63
2006	24,568	PF63 42.00	PF65 45.00		

KM# 650 50 CENTS
9.30 g., 0.925 Silver 0.2748 oz. ASW, 27.13 mm. **Ruler:** Elizabeth II **Obv:** Head right **Rev:** Butterfly, silvery blue hologram

Date	Mintage	VF20	XF40	MS60	MS63
2000	10,000	PF63 42.00	PF65 45.00		

KM# 651 50 CENTS
9.30 g., 0.925 Silver 0.2748 oz. ASW **Ruler:** Elizabeth II **Subject:** Cowboy **Obv:** Head right

Date	Mintage	VF20	XF40	MS60	MS63
2006	—	—	—	—	17.50

KM# 494b 50 CENTS
6.90 g., Nickel Plated Steel, 27.13 mm. **Ruler:** Elizabeth II **Rev:** State Arms, gilt **Note:** Housed in Mint Annual Report

Date	Mintage	VF20	XF40	MS60	MS63
2006	—				15.00

KM# 716 50 CENTS
9.30 g., 0.925 Silver 0.2748 oz. ASW **Ruler:** Elizabeth II **Rev:** Multicolor holiday ornaments

Date	Mintage	VF20	XF40	MS60	MS63
2006	16,989	—	—	—	17.50

KM# 715 50 CENTS
9.30 g., 0.925 Silver 0.2748 oz. ASW, 27.12 mm. **Ruler:** Elizabeth II **Rev:** Forget-me-not flower

Date	Mintage	VF20	XF40	MS60	MS63
2007	22,882	PF63 35.00	PF65 40.00		

KM# 778 50 CENTS
20.00 g., 0.925 Silver 0.591 oz. ASW, 34.06 mm. **Ruler:** Elizabeth II **Subject:** Milk delivery **Obv:** Bust right **Rev:** Cow head and milk can **Shape:** Triangle

Date	Mintage	VF20	XF40	MS60	MS63
2008	24,448	PF63 25.00	PF65 35.00		

KM# 779 50 CENTS
9.30 g., 0.925 Silver 0.2748 oz. ASW, 35 mm. **Ruler:** Elizabeth II **Rev:** Multicolor snowman

Date	Mintage	VF20	XF40	MS60	MS63
2008	21,679	—	—	—	17.50

KM# 780 50 CENTS
9.30 g., 0.925 Silver 0.2748 oz. ASW, 29.72 mm. **Ruler:** Elizabeth II **Subject:** Ottawa Mint Centennial 1908-2008 **Obv:** Edward bust right **Rev:** Crowned value and dates within wreath

Date	Mintage	VF20	XF40	MS60	MS63
2008	3,248	PF65 20.00			

KM# 845 50 CENTS
9.30 g., 0.925 Silver 0.2748 oz. ASW, 27.13 mm. **Ruler:**

Elizabeth II **Rev:** Calgary Flames lenticular design, old and new logos

Date	Mintage	VF20	XF40	MS60	MS63
2009	—	—	—	—	12.00

KM# 846 50 CENTS
9.30 g., 0.925 Silver 0.2748 oz. ASW, 27.13 mm. **Ruler:** Elizabeth II **Rev:** Edmonton Oiler's lenticular design, old and new logos

Date	Mintage	VF20	XF40	MS60	MS63
2009	—	—	—	—	12.00

KM# 847 50 CENTS
9.30 g., 0.925 Silver 0.2748 oz. ASW, 27.13 mm. **Ruler:** Elizabeth II **Rev:** Montreal Canadiens lenticular design, old and new logos

Date	Mintage	VF20	XF40	MS60	MS63
2009	—	—	—	—	12.00

KM# 848 50 CENTS
9.30 g., 0.925 Silver 0.2748 oz. ASW, 27.13 mm. **Ruler:** Elizabeth II **Rev:** Ottawa Senators lenticular design, old and new logos

Date	Mintage	VF20	XF40	MS60	MS63
2009	—	—	—	—	12.00

KM# 849 50 CENTS
9.30 g., 0.925 Silver 0.2748 oz. ASW, 27.13 mm. **Ruler:** Elizabeth II **Rev:** Toronto Maple Leafs lenticular design, old and new logos

Date	Mintage	VF20	XF40	MS60	MS63
2009	—	—	—	—	12.00

KM# 850 50 CENTS
9.30 g., 0.925 Silver 0.2748 oz. ASW, 27.13 mm. **Ruler:** Elizabeth II **Rev:** Vancouver Canucks lenticular design, old and new logos

Date	Mintage	VF20	XF40	MS60	MS63
2009	—	—	—	—	12.00

KM# 857 50 CENTS
6.90 g., Nickel Plated Steel, 35 mm. **Ruler:** Elizabeth II **Rev:** Calgary Flames lenticular old and new logos

Date	Mintage	VF20	XF40	MS60	MS63
2009					25.00

KM# 858 50 CENTS
6.90 g., Nickel Plated Steel, 35 mm. **Ruler:** Elizabeth II **Rev:** Edmonton Oilers lenticular old and new logos

Date	Mintage	VF20	XF40	MS60	MS63
2009					25.00

KM# 859 50 CENTS
35.00 g., Nickel Plated Steel, 35 mm. **Ruler:** Elizabeth II **Rev:** Montreal Canadians lenticular old and new logo

Date	Mintage	VF20	XF40	MS60	MS63
2009					25.00

KM# 860 50 CENTS
6.90 g., Nickel Plated Steel, 35 mm. **Ruler:** Elizabeth II **Rev:** Ottawa Senators lenticular old and new logos

Date	Mintage	VF20	XF40	MS60	MS63
2009	—	—	—	—	25.00

KM# 861 50 CENTS
6.90 g., Nickel Plated Steel, 35 mm. **Ruler:** Elizabeth II **Rev:** Toronto Maple Leafs lenticular old and new logos

Date	Mintage	VF20	XF40	MS60	MS63
2009	—	—	—	—	25.00

KM# 862 50 CENTS
6.90 g., Nickel Plated Steel, 35 mm. **Ruler:** Elizabeth II **Rev:** Vancouver Canucks lenticular old and new logos

Date	Mintage	VF20	XF40	MS60	MS63
2009	—	—	—	—	25.00

KM# 887 50 CENTS
19.10 g., Copper-Nickel, 34.06 mm. **Ruler:** Elizabeth II **Subject:** Six-string national guitar **Obv:** Bust right **Obv. Legend:** Elizabeth II DG Regina **Rev:** Hologram with 6 "strings **Rev. Legend:** 50 CENTS Canada **Shape:** Triangle

Date	Mintage	VF20	XF40	MS60	MS63
2009	13,602	PF63 45.00	PF65 50.00		

KM# 936 50 CENTS
9.30 g., Nickel **Ruler:** Elizabeth II **Rev:** Vancouver Canucks goalie jersey

Date	Mintage	VF20	XF40	MS60	MS63
2009	3,563	—	—	—	15.00

KM# 937 50 CENTS
6.90 g., Nickel Plated Steel, 35 mm. **Ruler:** Elizabeth II **Rev:** Calgary Flames player - colorized

Date	Mintage	VF20	XF40	MS60	MS63
2009	3,518	—	—	—	15.00

KM# 938 50 CENTS
6.90 g., Nickel Plated Steel, 35 mm. **Ruler:** Elizabeth II **Rev:** Edmonton Oilers player

Date	Mintage	VF20	XF40	MS60	MS63
2009	3,562	—	—	—	15.00

KM# 939 50 CENTS
6.90 g., Nickel Plated Steel, 35 mm. **Ruler:** Elizabeth II **Rev:** Toronto Maple Leafs player

Date	Mintage	VF20	XF40	MS60	MS63
2009	5,918	—	—	—	15.00

KM# 940 50 CENTS
6.90 g., Nickel Plated Steel, 35 mm. **Ruler:** Elizabeth II **Rev:** Montreal Canadiens player

Date	Mintage	VF20	XF40	MS60	MS63
2009	9,865	—	—	—	15.00

KM# 941 50 CENTS
6.90 g., Nickel Plated Steel, 35 mm. **Ruler:** Elizabeth II **Rev:** Ottawa Senators player

Date	Mintage	VF20	XF40	MS60	MS63
2009	3,293	—	—	—	15.00

KM# 1035 50 CENTS
12.61 g., Brass Plated Steel, 35 mm. **Ruler:** Elizabeth II **Subject:** Christmas toy train **Rev:** movement from far to close

Date	Mintage	VF20	XF40	MS60	MS63
2009	19,103	—	—	—	17.50

KM# 961 50 CENTS
6.90 g., Nickel Plated Steel, 35 mm. **Ruler:** Elizabeth II **Rev:** Bob sleigh

Date	Mintage	VF20	XF40	MS60	MS63
2010	—	—	—	—	12.00

KM# 961a 50 CENTS
6.90 g., Nickel Plated Steel, 35 mm. **Ruler:** Elizabeth II **Rev:** Bob sleigh - red enamel

Date	Mintage	VF20	XF40	MS60	MS63
2010	—	—	—	—	12.00

KM# 962 50 CENTS
6.90 g., Nickel Plated Steel, 35 mm. **Ruler:** Elizabeth II **Rev:** Speed skating

Date	Mintage	VF20	XF40	MS60	MS63
2010	—	—	—	—	12.00

KM# 962a 50 CENTS
6.90 g., Nickel Plated Steel, 35 mm. **Ruler:** Elizabeth II **Rev:** Speed skating - red enamel

Date	Mintage	VF20	XF40	MS60	MS63
2010	—	—	—	—	12.00

KM# 963 50 CENTS
6.90 g., Nickel Plated Steel, 35 mm. **Ruler:** Elizabeth II **Rev:** Migaand Quatchi in bob sleigh

Date	Mintage	VF20	XF40	MS60	MS63
2010	2,119	—	—	—	12.00

KM# 964 50 CENTS
6.90 g., Nickel Plated Steel, 35 mm. **Ruler:** Elizabeth II **Rev:** Miga in hockey

Date	Mintage	VF20	XF40	MS60	MS63
2010	5,275	—	—	—	12.00

KM# 965 50 CENTS
6.90 g., Nickel Plated Steel, 35 mm. **Ruler:** Elizabeth II **Rev:** Quatchi in ice hockey

Date	Mintage	VF20	XF40	MS60	MS63
2010	5,614	—	—	—	12.00

KM# 966 50 CENTS
6.90 g., Nickel Plated Steel, 35 mm. **Ruler:** Elizabeth II **Rev:** Sumi Para Sledge

Date	Mintage	VF20	XF40	MS60	MS63
2010	3,707	—	—	—	12.00

KM# 967 50 CENTS
6.90 g., Nickel Plated Steel, 35 mm. **Ruler:** Elizabeth II **Rev:** Miga and Quatchi Figure-skating **Edge:** Reeded

Date	Mintage	VF20	XF40	MS60	MS63
2010	2,981	—	—	—	12.00

KM# 968 50 CENTS
6.90 g., Nickel Plated Steel, 35 mm. **Ruler:** Elizabeth II **Rev:** Free-style mascot

Date	Mintage	VF20	XF40	MS60	MS63
2010	2,114	—	—	—	12.00

KM# 969 50 CENTS
6.90 g., Nickel Plated Steel, 35 mm. **Ruler:** Elizabeth II **Rev:** Skeleton mascot

Date	Mintage	VF20	XF40	MS60	MS63
2010	1,672	—	—	—	12.00

KM# 970 50 CENTS
6.90 g., Nickel Plated Steel, 35 mm. **Ruler:** Elizabeth II **Rev:** Parallel giant slalom mascot

Date	Mintage	VF20	XF40	MS60	MS63
2010	1,730	—	—	—	12.00

KM# 971 50 CENTS
6.90 g., Nickel Plated Steel, 35 mm. **Ruler:** Elizabeth II **Rev:** Alpine skiing mascot

Date	Mintage	VF20	XF40	MS60	MS63
2010	2,309	—	—	—	12.00

KM# 972 50 CENTS
6.90 g., Nickel Plated Steel, 35 mm. **Ruler:** Elizabeth II **Rev:** Para Olympic alpine skiing mascott

Date	Mintage	VF20	XF40	MS60	MS63
2010	1,902	—	—	—	12.00

KM# 973 50 CENTS
6.90 g., Nickel Plated Steel, 35 mm. **Ruler:** Elizabeth II **Rev:** Snowboard mascot

Date	Mintage	VF20	XF40	MS60	MS63
2010	2,090	—	—	—	12.00

KM# 974 50 CENTS
6.90 g., Nickel Plated Steel, 35 mm. **Ruler:** Elizabeth II **Rev:** Speed-skating mascott

Date	Mintage	VF20	XF40	MS60	MS63
2010	1,825	—	—	—	12.00

KM# 986 50 CENTS
12.61 g., Brass Plated Steel, 35 mm. **Ruler:** Elizabeth II **Rev:** Dasplerosaurus Torosus - 3-D lenticular movement

Date	Mintage	VF20	XF40	MS60	MS63
2010	—	—	—	—	20.00

KM# 1015 50 CENTS
12.61 g., Brass Plated Steel, 35 mm. **Ruler:** Elizabeth II **Rev:** Sinosauropteryx

Date	Mintage	VF20	XF40	MS60	MS63
2010	—	—	—	—	20.00

KM# 1016 50 CENTS
12.61 g., Brass Plated Steel, 35 mm. **Ruler:** Elizabeth II **Rev:** Albertosaurus

Date	Mintage	VF20	XF40	MS60	MS63
2010	—			—	20.00

KM# 1043 50 CENTS
Nickel Plated Steel, 34 mm. **Ruler:** Elizabeth II **Rev:** Santa Claus transforms into Rudolf the red-nosed reindeer

Date	Mintage	VF20	XF40	MS60	MS63
2010	—	—	—	—	17.50

KM# 1157 50 CENTS
11.62 g., 0.925 Silver 0.3433 oz. ASW, 29.72 mm. **Ruler:** Elizabeth II **Obv:** George V bust **Rev:** Value within wreath

Date	Mintage	VF20	XF40	MS60	MS63
1911-2011	6,000	PF63 40.00	PF65 45.00		

KM# 1180 50 CENTS
6.90 g., Nickel Plated Steel, 27.13 mm. **Ruler:** Elizabeth II **Obv:** Bust right **Rev:** Winnipeg Jets Logo, jet over maple leaf **Edge:** Reeded

Date	Mintage	VF20	XF40	MS60	MS63
2011	—	—	—	—	15.00

KM# 1191 50 CENTS
12.61 g., Copper Plated Steel, 35 mm. **Ruler:** Elizabeth II **Obv:** Bust right **Rev:** Santa Claus checking list, and in sled over house

Date	Mintage	VF20	XF40	MS60	MS63
2011	—	—	—	—	27.50

KM# 1202 50 CENTS
1.27 g., 0.9999 Gold 0.0406 oz. AGW, 13.92 mm. **Ruler:** Elizabeth II **Rev:** Wood Bison **Edge:** Reeded

Date	Mintage	VF20	XF40	MS60	MS63
2011	Est. 2500	PF63 95.00	PF65 100		

KM# 1204 50 CENTS
1.27 g., 0.9999 Gold 0.0406 oz. AGW, 13.92 mm. **Ruler:** Elizabeth II **Subject:** Boreal Forest **Rev:** Bird and tree **Edge:** Reeded

Date	Mintage	VF20	XF40	MS60	MS63
2011	Est. 2500	PF63 95.00	PF65 100		

KM# 1206 50 CENTS
1.27 g., 0.9999 Gold 0.0406 oz. AGW, 13.92 mm. **Ruler:** Elizabeth II **Rev:** Peregrine Falcon perched on branch

Date	Mintage	VF20	XF40	MS60	MS63
2011	Est. 2500	PF63 95.00	PF65 100		

KM# 1208 50 CENTS
1.27 g., 0.9999 Gold 0.0406 oz. AGW, 13.92 mm. **Ruler:** Elizabeth II **Rev:** Orca Whale **Edge:** Reeded

Date	Mintage	VF20	XF40	MS60	MS63
2011	Est. 2500	PF63 95.00	PF65 100		

KM# 1234 50 CENTS
12.61 g., Nickel Plated Steel, 35 mm. **Ruler:** Elizabeth II **Subject:** Titanic, 100th Anniversary **Obv:** Bust right **Rev:** Titanic sailing forward towards iceberg, colored sea

Date	Mintage	VF20	XF40	MS60	MS63
2012	—	PF65 65.00			

KM# 1264 50 CENTS
1.27 g., 0.999 Gold 0.0405 oz. AGW, 13.92 mm. **Ruler:** Elizabeth II **Subject:** Gold Rush

Date	Mintage	F12	VF20	XF40	MS60	MS63
2012	—	PF63 90.00	PF65 100			

KM# 1293 50 CENTS
9.30 g., 0.925 Silver 0.2748 oz. ASW, 27.13 mm. **Ruler:** Elizabeth II **Subject:** Elizabeth II Diamond Jubilee **Rev:** Crowned monogram within wreath in color

Date	Mintage	VF20	XF40	MS60	MS63
2012	—	—	—	—	

KM# 1435 50 CENTS
Silver Plated Copper-Nickel, 35 mm. **Ruler:** Elizabeth II **Rev:** Canadian Tiger Swallowtail Butterfly in color

Date	Mintage	VF20	XF40	MS60	MS63
2013	Est. 20000	PF63 30.00	PF65 35.00		

KM# 1444 50 CENTS
12.51 g., Copper-Nickel, 35 mm. **Ruler:** Elizabeth II **Subject:** 75th Anniversary of Superman **Rev:** Superman lenticular background - then and now

Date	Mintage	VF20	XF40	MS60	MS63
2013	—	PF63 25.00	PF65 30.00		

KM# 1493 50 CENTS
1.27 g., 0.9999 Gold 0.0406 oz. AGW, 13.92 mm. **Ruler:** Elizabeth II **Rev:** Starfish

Date	Mintage	VF20	XF40	MS60	MS63
2013	10,000	PF63 120	PF65 130		

KM# 1496 50 CENTS
1.27 g., 0.9999 Gold 0.0406 oz. AGW, 13.92 mm. **Ruler:** Elizabeth II **Subject:** Louisbourg, 300th Anniversary **Rev:** Ship, fort gate and fish

Date	Mintage	VF20	XF40	MS60	MS63
2013	1,000	PF63 120	PF65 130		

KM# 1523 50 CENTS
Copper-Nickel, 35 mm. **Ruler:** Elizabeth II **Rev:** Snowman, lenticular

Date	Mintage	VF20	XF40	MS60	MS63
2013	20,000	—	—	—	30.00

KM# 1545 50 CENTS
Silver 31.9118 oz. ASW **Ruler:** Elizabeth II **Rev:** Superman in color

Date	Mintage	VF20	XF40	MS60	MS63
2013 Proof	—	—	—	—	—

KM# 1584 50 CENTS
1.27 g., 0.999 Gold 0.0405 oz. AGW, 13.92 mm. **Ruler:** Elizabeth II **Obv:** Bust right **Rev:** Beaver left from 5 Cent coin

Date	Mintage	VF20	XF40	MS60	MS63
2014	PF63 80.00	PF65 90.00			

KM# 1585 50 CENTS
Silver Plated, 35 mm. **Ruler:** Elizabeth II **Subject:** 100 Blessings of Good Fortune **Obv:** Bust right

Date	Mintage	VF20	XF40	MS60	MS63
2014	PF63 45.00	PF65 50.00			

KM# 186 DOLLAR
7.00 g., Aureate-Bronze Plated Nickel, 26.5 mm. **Ruler:** Elizabeth II **Obv:** Crowned head right **Rev:** Loon right, date and denomination **Shape:** 11-sided

Date	Mintage	VF20	XF40	MS60	MS63
2001					6.00
2001	74,194	PF63 7.00	PF65 8.00		
2002					4.50
2002	65,315	PF63 6.50	PF65 7.50		
2003					5.50

Note: Mintage of 5,101,000 includes both KM186 and KM495 examples.

| 2003 | — | PF63 10.00 | PF65 12.00 | | |

KM# 414 DOLLAR
25.18 g., 0.925 Silver 0.7439 oz. ASW, 36 mm. **Ruler:** Elizabeth II **Subject:** National Ballet **Obv:** Crowned head right **Rev:** Ballet dancers **Edge:** Reeded

Date	Mintage	VF20	XF40	MS60	MS63
2001	65,000				27.50
2001		PF63 25.00	PF65 35.00		

KM# 434 DOLLAR
25.18 g., 0.925 Silver 0.7439 oz. ASW, 36 mm. **Ruler:** Elizabeth II **Obv:** Crowned head right **Rev:** Recycled 1911 pattern dollar design: denomination, country name and dates in crowned wreath **Edge:** Reeded

Date	Mintage	VF20	XF40	MS60	MS63
1911-2001	24,996	PF63 45.00	PF65 55.00		

KM# 186a DOLLAR
Gilt, 26.5 mm. **Ruler:** Elizabeth II **Subject:** Olympic Win

Date	Mintage	VF20	XF40	MS60	MS63
2002	—	PF63 35.00	PF65 40.00		

KM# 443 DOLLAR
25.18 g., 0.925 Silver 0.7439 oz. ASW, 36 mm. **Ruler:** Elizabeth II **Subject:** Queen's Golden Jubilee **Obv:** Crowned head right, with anniversary date at left **Rev:** Queen in her coach and a view of the coach, denomination below **Edge:** Reeded

Date	Mintage	VF20	XF40	MS60	MS63
1952-2002	65,140	—	—	—	28.50
1952-2002	29,688	PF63 30.00	PF65 40.00		

KM# 443a DOLLAR
25.18 g., 0.925 Silver Gilt 0.744 oz., 36 mm. **Ruler:** Elizabeth II **Subject:** Queen's Golden Jubilee **Obv:** Crowned head right with anniversary date **Rev:** Queen in her coach and a view of the coach **Edge:** Reeded **Note:** Special 24 karat gold plated issue of KM#443.

Date	Mintage	VF20	XF40	MS60	MS63
2002	32,642	PF63 40.00	PF65 45.00		

KM# 462 DOLLAR
7.00 g., Aureate-Bronze Plated Nickel **Ruler:** Elizabeth II **Obv:** Commemorative dates 1952-2002 **Rev:** Family of Loons

Date	Mintage	VF20	XF40	MS60	MS63
2002 Specimen	67,672	—	—	—	25.00

KM# 467a DOLLAR
Gold AGW **Ruler:** Elizabeth II **Subject:** 50th Anniversary, Accession to the Throne **Obv:** Crowned head right **Note:** Sold on the internet.

Date	Mintage	VF20	XF40	MS60	MS63
2002	1	PF65 55,500			

KM# 467 DOLLAR
7.00 g., Aureate-Bronze Plated Nickel **Ruler:** Elizabeth II **Subject:** Elizabeth II Golden Jubilee **Obv:** Crowned head right, Jubilee commemorative dates 1952-2002

Date	Mintage	VF20	XF40	MS60	MS63
2002	2,302,000	—	—	—	2.50
2002	—	PF63 7.00	PF65 8.00		

KM# 503 DOLLAR
25.18 g., 0.925 Silver 0.7439 oz. ASW, 36 mm. **Ruler:** Elizabeth II **Subject:** Queen Mother **Obv:** Crowned head right **Rev:** Queen Mother facing

Date	Mintage	VF20	XF40	MS60	MS63
2002	9,994	PF65 250			

KM# 450 DOLLAR
25.18 g., 0.9999 Silver 0.8041 oz. ASW, 36 mm. **Ruler:** Elizabeth II **Subject:** Cobalt Mining Centennial **Obv:** Queens portrait right **Rev:** Mine tower and fox **Edge:** Reeded

Date	Mintage	VF20	XF40	MS60	MS63
2003	51,130	—	—		30.00
2003	88,536	PF63 35.00	PF65 45.00		

KM# 495 DOLLAR
7.00 g., Aureate-Bronze Plated Nickel, 26.5 mm. **Ruler:** Elizabeth II **Obv:** Bare head right **Rev:** Loon right **Shape:** 11-sided

Date	Mintage	VF20	XF40	MS60	MS63
2003	5,102,000	—	—		5.50
Note: Mintage of 5,101,000 includes both KM 186 and 495 examples.					
2003W Proof-like	—	—	—		7.50
2003	62,507	PF63 6.50	PF65 7.50		
2004	10,894,000	—	—	—	1.75
2004	—	PF63 10.00	PF65 12.00		
2005	44,375,000	—	—		3.00
2005	—	PF63 6.50	PF65 7.50		
2006	49,111,000	—	—		3.00
2006	—	PF63 6.50	PF65 7.50		
2006(ml)	49,111,000	—	—		3.00
2006(ml)	—	PF63 6.50	PF65 7.50		
2007(ml)	38,045,000	—	—		3.00
2007(ml)	—	PF63 6.50	PF65 7.50		
2008(ml)	29,561,000	—	—		3.00
2008(ml)	—	PF63 6.50	PF65 7.50		
2009(ml)	39,601,000	—	—		3.00
2009(ml)	—	PF63 6.50	PF65 7.50		
2010(ml)	—	—	—		3.00
2010(ml)	—	PF63 6.50	PF65 7.50		
2011(ml)	—	—	—		3.00
2011(ml)	—	PF63 6.50	PF65 7.50		
2012(ml)	—	—	—		3.00
2012(ml)	—	PF63 6.50	PF65 7.50		

KM# 473 DOLLAR
25.18 g., 0.9999 Silver 0.8041 oz. ASW **Ruler:** Elizabeth II **Subject:** 50th Anniversary of the Coronation of Elizabeth II **Obv:** 1953 effigy of the Queen, Jubilee dates 1953-2003 **Rev:** Voyageur, date and denomination below

Date	Mintage	VF20	XF40	MS60	MS63
1953-2003	21,537	PF63 35.00	PF65 45.00		

KM# 480 DOLLAR
25.18 g., 0.9999 Silver 0.8041 oz. ASW **Ruler:** Elizabeth II **Subject:** Coronation of Queen Elizabeth II **Obv:** Head right **Rev:** Voyaguers

Date	Mintage	VF20	XF40	MS60	MS63
1953-2003	29,586	PF63 40.00	PF65 50.00		

KM# 480a DOLLAR
Gold AGW **Ruler:** Elizabeth II **Subject:** 50th Anniversary of Coronation **Rev:** Voyageur **Note:** Sold on the internet.

Date	Mintage	VF20	XF40	MS60	MS63
1953-2003	1	PF65 62,750			

KM# 507 DOLLAR
7.00 g., Aureate-Bronze Plated Nickel, 26.5 mm. **Ruler:**

Elizabeth II **Obv:** Bare head right, date below **Rev:** Loon **Edge:** Plain **Shape:** 11-sided

Date	Mintage	VF20	XF40	MS60	MS63
2004	25,105	**PF65** 75.00			

KM# 511 DOLLAR
25.18 g., 0.9999 Silver 0.8041 oz. ASW, 36 mm. **Ruler:** Elizabeth II **Obv:** Elizabeth II **Rev:** Poppy on maple leaf **Edge:** Reeded

Date	Mintage	VF20	XF40	MS60	MS63
2004	24,527	**PF63** 45.00	**PF65** 50.00		

KM# 513 DOLLAR
7.00 g., Aureate-Bronze Plated Nickel, 26.5 mm. **Ruler:** Elizabeth II **Subject:** Olympics **Obv:** Bare head right **Rev:** Maple leaf, Olympic flame and rings above loon **Edge:** Plain **Shape:** 11-sided

Date	Mintage	VF20	XF40	MS60	MS63
2004	6,526,000	—	—	—	8.00

KM# 513a DOLLAR
9.31 g., 0.925 Silver 0.2751 oz. ASW, 26.5 mm. **Ruler:** Elizabeth II **Subject:** Olympics **Obv:** Bare head right **Rev:** Multicolor maple leaf, Olympic flame and rings above loon **Edge:** Plain **Shape:** 11-sided

Date	Mintage	VF20	XF40	MS60	MS63
2004	19,994	**PF63** 45.00	**PF65** 50.00		

KM# 512 DOLLAR
25.18 g., 0.9999 Silver 0.8041 oz. ASW, 36 mm. **Ruler:** Elizabeth II **Subject:** First French Settlement in America **Obv:** Crowned head right **Rev:** Sailing ship **Edge:** Reeded

Date	Mintage	VF20	XF40	MS60	MS63
2004	42,582	—	—	—	30.00
2004 Fleur-dis-lis privy mark	8,315	—	—	—	60.00
2004	106,974	**PF63** 45.00	**PF65** 50.00		

KM# 549 DOLLAR
25.18 g., 0.925 Silver 0.7439 oz. ASW, 36.07 mm. **Ruler:** Elizabeth II **Subject:** 40th Anniversary of National Flag **Obv:** Head right

Date	Mintage	VF20	XF40	MS60	MS63
2005	50,948	—	—	—	27.50
2005	95,431	**PF63** 35.00	**PF65** 40.00		

KM# 549a DOLLAR
25.18 g., 0.925 Silver 0.7439 oz. ASW, 36.07 mm. **Ruler:** Elizabeth II **Subject:** 40th Anniversary of National Flag **Obv:** Head right

Date	Mintage	VF20	XF40	MS60	MS63
2005	62,562	—	—	—	75.00

KM# 549b DOLLAR
25.18 g., 0.925 Silver 0.744 oz. ASW, 36.07 mm. **Ruler:** Elizabeth II **Subject:** 40th Anniversary National Flag **Rev:** National flag, colorized

Date	Mintage	VF20	XF40	MS60	MS63
2005	4,898	**PF65** 350			

KM# 552 DOLLAR
7.00 g., Aureate-Bronze Plated Nickel, 26.5 mm. **Ruler:** Elizabeth II **Obv:** Head right **Rev:** Terry Fox walking left

Date	Mintage	VF20	XF40	MS60	MS63
2005	1,290,900	—	—	—	3.50

KM# 553 DOLLAR
7.00 g., Aureate-Bronze Plated Nickel **Ruler:** Elizabeth II **Subject:** Tuffed Puffin **Obv:** Head right

Date	Mintage	VF20	XF40	MS60	MS63
2005	39,818	**PF63** 25.00	**PF65** 30.00		

KM# 581 DOLLAR
9.31 g., 0.925 Silver 0.2751 oz. ASW **Ruler:** Elizabeth II **Subject:** Lullabies Loonie **Obv:** Head right **Rev:** Loon and moon, teddy bear in stars

Date	Mintage	VF20	XF40	MS60	MS63
2006	18,103	—	—	—	4.50

KM# 582 DOLLAR
7.00 g., Aureate-Bronze Plated Nickel, 26.5 mm. **Ruler:** Elizabeth II **Subject:** Snowy owl **Obv:** Head right **Rev:** Snowy owl with year above

Date	Mintage	VF20	XF40	MS60	MS63
2006 Specimen	39,935	**PF65** 30.00			

KM# 583 DOLLAR
25.18 g., 0.925 Silver 0.7439 oz. ASW, 36 mm. **Ruler:** Elizabeth II **Obv:** Head right **Rev:** Victoria Cross

Date	Mintage	VF20	XF40	MS60	MS63
2006	27,254	—	—	—	25.00
2006	53,822	**PF63** 40.00	**PF65** 45.00		

KM# 583a DOLLAR
25.18 g., 0.925 Silver 0.7439 oz. ASW, 36 mm. **Ruler:** Elizabeth II **Obv:** Head right **Rev:** Victoria Cross gilt

Date	Mintage	VF20	XF40	MS60	MS63
2006	53,822	**PF63** 65.00	**PF65** 75.00		

KM# 630 DOLLAR
7.00 g., Aureate Bronze, 26.5 mm. **Ruler:** Elizabeth II **Obv:** Bust right **Rev:** Loon splashing in water

Date	Mintage	VF20	XF40	MS60	MS63
2006		—	—	—	3.00

KM# 630a DOLLAR
9.31 g., 0.925 Silver 0.2751 oz. ASW, 26.5 mm. **Ruler:** Elizabeth II **Subject:** Olympic Games **Obv:** Crowned head right **Rev:** Loon in flight, colored olympic logo above

Date	Mintage	VF20	XF40	MS60	MS63
2006	19,956	—	—	—	30.00

KM# 654 DOLLAR
7.00 g., 0.925 Silver 0.2068 oz. ASW **Ruler:** Elizabeth II **Obv:** Head right **Rev:** Snowflake, colorized **Note:** Sold in a CD package.

Date	Mintage	VF20	XF40	MS60	MS63
2006(ml)	34,014	—	—	—	35.00

KM# 655 DOLLAR
7.00 g., 0.925 Silver 0.2068 oz. ASW **Ruler:** Elizabeth II **Subject:** Baby Rattle **Obv:** Head right **Rev:** Baby rattle

Date	Mintage	VF20	XF40	MS60	MS63
2006	3,207	—	—	—	20.00

KM# 655a DOLLAR
7.00 g., 0.925 Silver 0.2068 oz. ASW **Ruler:** Elizabeth II **Obv:** Bust right **Rev:** Baby Rattle, partially gilt

Date	Mintage	VF20	XF40	MS60	MS63
2006	1,911	—	—	—	15.00

KM# 656 DOLLAR
28.18 g., 0.925 Silver 0.8325 oz. ASW **Ruler:** Elizabeth II **Subject:** Medal of Bravery **Obv:** Head right

Date	Mintage	VF20	XF40	MS60	MS63
2006	8,343	**PF63** 45.00	**PF65** 50.00		

KM# 656a DOLLAR
28.18 g., 0.925 Silver 0.8325 oz. ASW **Ruler:** Elizabeth II **Subject:** Medal of Bravery **Obv:** Head right **Rev:** Maple leaf within wreath. Colorized.

Date	Mintage	VF20	XF40	MS60	MS63
2006	4,999	**PF65** 150			

KM# 1287 DOLLAR
7.00 g., Aureate Bronze, 26.5 mm. **Ruler:** Elizabeth II **Rev:** Goose in flight

Date	Mintage	VF20	XF40	MS60	MS63
2006	—	**PF65** 20.00			

KM# 688 DOLLAR
7.00 g., Aureate-Bronze Plated Nickel, 26.5 mm. **Ruler:** Elizabeth II **Obv:** Head right **Rev:** Trumpeter Swan

Date	Mintage	VF20	XF40	MS60	MS63
2007(ml)	40,000	—	—	—	20.00

KM# 653 DOLLAR
25.18 g., 0.925 Silver 0.7439 oz. ASW, 36.07 mm. **Ruler:** Elizabeth II **Subject:** Thayendanegea **Obv:** Head right **Rev:** Bust 3/4 facing right

Date	Mintage	VF20	XF40	MS60	MS63
2007	16,378	—	—	—	30.00
2007	—	PF63 37.00	PF65 40.00		

KM# 653a DOLLAR
25.18 g., 0.925 Silver 0.7439 oz. ASW, 36.07 mm. **Ruler:** Elizabeth II **Subject:** Thayendanega **Rev:** Bust 3/4 right, partially gold plated

Date	Mintage	VF20	XF40	MS60	MS63
2007	60,000	PF65 125			

KM# 720 DOLLAR
25.18 g., 0.925 Silver 0.744 oz. ASW, 36.07 mm. **Ruler:** Elizabeth II **Obv:** Bust right **Rev:** Thayendanega multicolor

Date	Mintage	VF20	XF40	MS60	MS63
2007	4,760	PF63 110	PF65 120		

KM# 700 DOLLAR
7.00 g., 0.925 Silver 0.2068 oz. ASW, 23.88 mm. **Ruler:** Elizabeth II **Rev:** Alphabet Letter Blocks

Date	Mintage	VF20	XF40	MS60	MS63
2007	3,207	PF63 22.00	PF65 25.00		

KM# 719 DOLLAR
25.18 g., 0.925 Silver 0.744 oz. ASW, 36.07 mm. **Ruler:** Elizabeth II **Subject:** Celebration of the Arts **Rev:** Book, TV set, musical instruments, film montage **Edge:** Reeded

Date	Mintage	VF20	XF40	MS60	MS63
2007	6,466	PF63 50.00	PF65 55.00		

KM# A727 DOLLAR
7.00 g., Aureate-Bronze Plated Nickel, 26.5 mm. **Ruler:** Elizabeth II **Subject:** Vancouver Olympic Games **Rev:** Loon splashing in water, Olympics logo at right

Date	Mintage	VF20	XF40	MS60	MS63
2007(ml)	19,973	—	—	—	3.00

KM# 721 DOLLAR
7.00 g., Aureate-Bronze Plated Nickel, 26.5 mm. **Ruler:** Elizabeth II **Obv:** Bust right **Rev:** Calgary flames, multicolor in circle

Date	Mintage	VF20	XF40	MS60	MS63
2008	—	—	—	—	25.00

KM# 722 DOLLAR
7.00 g., Aureate-Bronze Plated Nickel, 26.5 mm. **Ruler:** Elizabeth II **Obv:** Bust **Rev:** Edmonton Oilers logo, multicolor in logo

Date	Mintage	VF20	XF40	MS60	MS63
2008	1,584	—	—	—	25.00

KM# 723A DOLLAR
7.00 g., Aureate-Bronze Plated Nickel, 26.5 mm. **Ruler:** Elizabeth II **Obv:** Bust right **Rev:** Montreal Canadians, multicolor logo in circle

Date	Mintage	VF20	XF40	MS60	MS63
2008	2,659	—	—	—	25.00

KM# 724 DOLLAR
7.00 g., Nickel, 26.5 mm. **Ruler:** Elizabeth II **Rev:** Ottawa Senators, multicolor logo in circle

Date	Mintage	VF20	XF40	MS60	MS63
2008	1,633	—	—	—	25.00

KM# 725 DOLLAR
7.00 g., Aureate-Bronze Plated Nickel, 26.5 mm. **Ruler:** Elizabeth II **Obv:** Bust right **Rev:** Toronto Maple Leafs, multicolor logo in circle

Date	Mintage	VF20	XF40	MS60	MS63
2008	—	—	—	—	25.00

KM# 726 DOLLAR
7.00 g., Aureate-Bronze Plated Nickel, 26.5 mm. **Ruler:** Elizabeth II **Obv:** Bust left **Rev:** Vancouver Canucks, logo in center

Date	Mintage	VF20	XF40	MS60	MS63
2008	1,302	—	—	—	25.00

KM# 767 DOLLAR
25.18 g., 0.925 Silver 0.744 oz. ASW, 36.07 mm. **Ruler:** Elizabeth II **Rev:** Poppy at center of large maple leaf

Date	Mintage	VF20	XF40	MS60	MS63
2008	—	PF63 40.00	PF65 50.00		

KM# 781 DOLLAR
25.18 g., 0.925 Silver 0.744 oz. ASW, 36.07 mm. **Ruler:** Elizabeth II **Subject:** Ottawa Mint Centennial 1908-2008 **Rev:** Maple leaf transforming into a common loon, gilt rim and 100

Date	Mintage	VF20	XF40	MS60	MS63
2008	15,000	PF63 55.00	PF65 65.00		

KM# 784 DOLLAR
7.00 g., Aureate-Bronze Plated Nickel, 26.5 mm. **Ruler:** Elizabeth II **Rev:** Common elder

Date	Mintage	VF20	XF40	MS60	MS63
2008 Specimen	21,227	PF65 50.00			

KM# 785 DOLLAR
25.18 g., 0.925 Silver 0.744 oz. ASW, 36.07 mm. **Ruler:** Elizabeth II **Subject:** Founding of Quebec 400th Anniversary **Rev:** Samuel de Champlain, ship and town view

Date	Mintage	VF20	XF40	MS60	MS63
2008	35,000	—	—	—	25.00
2008	65,000	PF63 35.00	PF65 40.00		

KM# 785a DOLLAR
25.18 g., 0.925 Silver 0.744 oz. ASW, 36.07 mm. **Ruler:** Elizabeth II **Subject:** Founding of Quebec 400th Anniversary **Rev:** Samuel de Champlain selectively gold plated, ship, town view

Date	Mintage	VF20	XF40	MS60	MS63
2008	38,630	PF63 65.00	PF65 75.00		

KM# 787 DOLLAR
7.00 g., Aureate-Bronze Plated Nickel, 26.5 mm. **Ruler:** Elizabeth II **Subject:** Lucky Loonie **Rev:** Loon splashing and Olympic logo at right

Date	Mintage	VF20	XF40	MS60	MS63
2008	—	—	—	—	20.00

KM# 787a DOLLAR
9.31 g., 0.925 Silver 0.2751 oz. ASW, 26.5 mm. **Ruler:** Elizabeth II **Rev:** Loon splashing with Olympic logo and maple leaf in color above

Date	Mintage	VF20	XF40	MS60	MS63
2008	52,987	PF63 22.00	PF65 25.00		

KM# 790 DOLLAR
6.50 g., Nickel, 26.5 mm. **Ruler:** Elizabeth II **Rev:** Calgary Flames

Date	Mintage	VF20	XF40	MS60	MS63
2008	—	—	—	—	25.00

KM# 791 DOLLAR
6.50 g., Nickel, 26.5 mm. **Ruler:** Elizabeth II **Rev:** Edmonton Oilers

Date	Mintage	VF20	XF40	MS60	MS63
2008	—	—	—	—	25.00

KM# 792 DOLLAR
6.50 g., Nickel, 26.5 mm. **Ruler:** Elizabeth II **Rev:** Montreal Canadiens

Date	Mintage	VF20	XF40	MS60	MS63
2008	—	—	—	—	25.00

KM# 793 DOLLAR
6.50 g., Nickel, 26.5 mm. **Ruler:** Elizabeth II **Rev:** Ottawa Senators

Date	Mintage	VF20	XF40	MS60	MS63
2008	—				25.00

KM# 794 DOLLAR
6.50 g., Nickel, 26.5 mm. **Ruler:** Elizabeth II **Rev:** Toronto Maple Leafs

Date	Mintage	VF20	XF40	MS60	MS63
2008	—				25.00

KM# 795 DOLLAR
6.50 g., Nickel, 26.5 mm. **Ruler:** Elizabeth II **Rev:** Vancouver Canucks

Date	Mintage	VF20	XF40	MS60	MS63
2008	—	—	—	—	25.00

KM# 851 DOLLAR
33.65 g., Nickel, 26.5 mm. **Ruler:** Elizabeth II **Rev:** Calgary Flames Road Jersey

Date	Mintage	VF20	XF40	MS60	MS63
2009	382	—	—	—	25.00

KM# 852 DOLLAR
33.65 g., Nickel, 26.5 mm. **Ruler:** Elizabeth II **Rev:** Edmonton Oilers Road Jersey

Date	Mintage	VF20	XF40	MS60	MS63
2009	472	—	—	—	25.00

KM# 853 DOLLAR
33.65 g., Nickel, 26.5 mm. **Ruler:** Elizabeth II **Rev:** Montreal Canadians Road Jersey

Date	Mintage	VF20	XF40	MS60	MS63
2009	4,857	—	—	—	25.00

KM# 854 DOLLAR
33.65 g., Nickel, 26.5 mm. **Ruler:** Elizabeth II **Rev:** Ottawa Senators Road Jersey

Date	Mintage	VF20	XF40	MS60	MS63
2009	387				25.00

KM# 855 DOLLAR
33.65 g., Nickel, 26.5 mm. **Ruler:** Elizabeth II **Rev:** Toronto Maple Leafs Road Jersey

Date	Mintage	VF20	XF40	MS60	MS63
2009	1,328	—	—	—	25.00

KM# 856 DOLLAR
33.65 g., Nickel, 26.5 mm. **Ruler:** Elizabeth II **Rev:** Vancouver Canucks Road Jersey

Date	Mintage	VF20	XF40	MS60	MS63
2009	794	—	—	—	25.00

KM# 864 DOLLAR
7.00 g., Aureate-Bronze Plated Nickel, 26.5 mm. **Ruler:** Elizabeth II **Subject:** Montreal Canadiens, 100th Anniversary **Obv:** Bust right **Rev:** Montreal Canadiens logo and large 100 **Shape:** 11-sided

Date	Mintage	VF20	XF40	MS60	MS63
2009	—	—	—	—	25.00

KM# 865 DOLLAR
25.17 g., 0.925 Silver 0.7437 oz. ASW, 36.07 mm. **Ruler:** Elizabeth II **Subject:** Montreal Canadiens 100th Anniversary **Obv:** Bust right **Rev:** Montreal Canadiens logo partially gilt

Date	Mintage	VF20	XF40	MS60	MS63
2009 Proof in black case	15,000	PF65 75.00			
2009 Proof in acrilic stand	5,000	PF65 150			

KM# 889 DOLLAR
25.18 g., 0.925 Silver 0.744 oz. ASW, 36.07 mm. **Ruler:** Elizabeth II **Subject:** 100th Anniversary of flight in Canada **Obv:** Bust right **Obv. Legend:** Elizabeth II DG Regina **Rev:** Silhouette with arms spread, 3 planes, plane cutout **Rev. Legend:** Canada Dollar 1909-2009

Date	Mintage	VF20	XF40	MS60	MS63
2009	13,074	—			40.00
2009	52,549	PF63 40.00	PF65 50.00		

KM# 889a DOLLAR
25.18 g., 0.925 Silver 0.744 oz. ASW, 36.07 mm. **Ruler:** Elizabeth II **Rev:** Bust right **Rev:** Boy silouette with arms spread, 3 planes, plane shadow partially gilt

Date	Mintage	VF20	XF40	MS60	MS63
2009(ml)	27,549	PF63 55.00	PF65 65.00		

KM# 914 DOLLAR
7.00 g., Aureate-Bronze Plated Nickel, 26.5 mm. **Ruler:** Elizabeth II **Obv:** Bust right **Rev:** Blue heron in flight

Date	Mintage	VF20	XF40	MS60	MS63
2009 Specimen	21,677	—	—	—	50.00

KM# 883 DOLLAR
7.00 g., Aureate-Bronze Plated Nickel, 26.5 mm. **Ruler:** Elizabeth II **Subject:** Lucky Loonie **Obv:** Bust right **Obv. Legend:** Elizabeth II DG Regina **Rev:** Canadian Olympic logo **Rev. Legend:** Canada Dollar

Date	Mintage	VF20	XF40	MS60	MS63
2010	12,000	—	—	—	20.00

KM# 883a DOLLAR
9.31 g., 0.925 Silver 0.2751 oz. ASW, 26.5 mm. **Ruler:** Elizabeth II **Subject:** Lucky Loonie **Obv:** Bust right **Obv. Legend:** Elizabeth II DG Regina **Rev:** Canadian Olympic logo in color **Rev. Legend:** Vancouver 2010 Canada Dollar **Shape:** 11-sided

Date	Mintage	VF20	XF40	MS60	MS63
2010	40,000	PF63 45.00	PF65 55.00		

KM# 1046 DOLLAR
Aureate-Bronze Plated Nickel, 26.5 mm. **Ruler:** Elizabeth II **Subject:** Roughriders **Rev:** S logo **Shape:** 11-sided

Date	Mintage	VF20	XF40	MS60	MS63
2010(ml)	—	—	—	—	7.50

KM# 975 DOLLAR
0.925 Silver, 36 mm. **Ruler:** Elizabeth II **Rev:** Sun mask

Date	Mintage	VF20	XF40	MS60	MS63
2010	1,278	PF65 200			

KM# 995 DOLLAR

25.17 g., 0.925 Silver 0.7437 oz. ASW, 36.07 mm. **Ruler:** Elizabeth II **Rev:** HMCS Sackville

Date	Mintage	VF20	XF40	MS60	MS63
2010	—	PF63 45.00	PF65 55.00		

KM# 995a DOLLAR

25.17 g., 0.925 Silver 0.7437 oz. ASW, 36.07 mm. **Ruler:** Elizabeth II **Subject:** Navy Centennial **Rev:** HMCS Sackville, sea waves in gilt

Date	Mintage	VF20	XF40	MS60	MS63
2010	—	PF63 100	PF65 110		

KM# 996 DOLLAR

7.00 g., Aureate-Bronze Plated Nickel, 26.5 mm. **Ruler:** Elizabeth II **Rev:** Northern Harrier Hawk

Date	Mintage	VF20	XF40	MS60	MS63
2010	35,000	—	—		30.00
2010(ml)	—	PF63 40.00	PF65 50.00		

KM# 1017 DOLLAR

7.00 g., Aureate-Bronze Plated Nickel, 26.5 mm. **Ruler:** Elizabeth II **Rev:** Male and female sailors saluting, HMCS Halifax and anchor above

Date	Mintage	VF20	XF40	MS60	MS63
2010	—	—	—	—	5.00

KM# 1017a DOLLAR

7.00 g., Aureate Bronze, 26.5 mm. **Ruler:** Elizabeth II **Rev:** Male and female sailors saluting, HMCS Halifax in background and anchor above

Date	Mintage	VF20	XF40	MS60	MS63
2010	—	PF63 45.00	PF65 50.00		

KM# 1027 DOLLAR

25.18 g., 0.925 Silver 0.744 oz. ASW, 36.07 mm. **Ruler:** Elizabeth II **Obv:** George V bust left **Rev:** Voyaguers, dual dates below

Date	Mintage	VF20	XF40	MS60	MS63
2010	7,500	PF63 60.00	PF65 70.00		

KM# 1050 DOLLAR

25.18 g., 0.925 Silver 0.744 oz. ASW, 36.07 mm. **Ruler:** Elizabeth II **Rev:** Red poppy in large field of poppies **Edge:** Reeded

Date	Mintage	VF20	XF40	MS60	MS63
2010	5,000	PF63 140	PF65 150		

KM# 1087 DOLLAR

25.18 g., 0.925 Silver 0.744 oz. ASW, 36.07 mm. **Ruler:** Elizabeth II **Subject:** Parks Canada, 100th Anniversary **Rev:** Female head looking downward into hands holding nature scene

Date	Mintage	VF20	XF40	MS60	MS63
2011	—	PF63 50.00	PF65 60.00		
2011	25,000				50.00

KM# 1087a DOLLAR

25.18 g., 0.925 Silver 0.744 oz. ASW, 36.07 mm. **Ruler:** Elizabeth II **Subject:** Parks Canada, 100th Anniversary **Rev:** Female head looking downward to hands holding nature scene, partially gilt

Date	Mintage	VF20	XF40	MS60	MS63
2011	45,000	PF63 65.00	PF65 75.00		

KM# 1086 DOLLAR

7.00 g., Aureate-Bronze Plated Nickel, 26.5 mm. **Ruler:** Elizabeth II **Rev:** Great Grey Owl

Date	Mintage	VF20	XF40	MS60	MS63
2011	35,000	—	—	—	13.50

KM# 1112 DOLLAR

25.17 g., 0.925 Silver 0.7437 oz. ASW, 36.07 mm. **Ruler:** Elizabeth II **Obv:** Crowned bust left of George V **Rev:** Value and date within maple wreath

Date	Mintage	VF20	XF40	MS60	MS63
2011	Est. 15000	PF63 110	PF65 115		

KM# 1166 DOLLAR

7.00 g., Aureate-Bronze Plated Nickel, 26.5 mm. **Ruler:** Elizabeth II **Subject:** Canada Parks **Obv:** Bust right **Rev:** Stylized animals

Date	Mintage	VF20	XF40	MS60	MS63
2011	—	—	—	—	5.00

KM# 1225 DOLLAR

25.18 g., 0.925 Silver 0.744 oz. ASW, 36.07 mm. **Ruler:** Elizabeth II **Subject:** War of 1812, 200th Anniversary **Obv:** Bust right **Rev:** Two soldiers and guide on patrol

Date	Mintage	VF20	XF40	MS60	MS63
2012	—	PF63 50.00	PF65 60.00		
2012	—				50.00

KM# 1225a DOLLAR

25.18 g., 0.925 Silver 0.744 oz. ASW, 36.07 mm. **Ruler:** Elizabeth II **Subject:** War of 1812, 200th Anniversary **Obv:** Bust right, gilt rim **Rev:** Two solders and guide, partially gilt

Date	Mintage	VF20	XF40	MS60	MS63
2012	—	PF63 55.00	PF65 65.00		

KM# 1256 DOLLAR

6.27 g., Brass Plated Steel, 26.5 mm. **Ruler:** Elizabeth II **Subject:** Lucky Loonie **Rev:** Loon and Olympic logo **Shape:** 11-sided

Date	Mintage	VF20	XF40	MS60	MS63
2012	—	—	—	—	10.00

KM# 1336a DOLLAR

7.89 g., 0.999 Silver 0.2518 oz. ASW, 26.5 mm. **Ruler:** Elizabeth II **Subject:** Lucky Loonie **Rev:** Loon with wings spread on water, maple leaf and olympic logo

Date	Mintage	VF20	XF40	MS60	MS63
2012	20,000	PF63 35.00	PF65 40.00		

KM# 1216 DOLLAR

9.31 g., 0.925 Silver 0.2751 oz. ASW, 26.5 mm. **Ruler:** Elizabeth II **Obv:** Bust right, SP/PA below **Rev:** Loon, 1987-2012 below

Date	Mintage	VF20	XF40	MS60	MS63
2012 Specimen	—	PF65 55.00			

KM# 1222 DOLLAR

7.00 g., Aureate-Bronze Plated Nickel, 26.5 mm. **Ruler:**

Elizabeth II **Obv:** Bust right **Rev:** Loon and two young, 1987-2012 dates

Date	Mintage	VF20	XF40	MS60	MS63
2012 Specimen	—	PF65 40.00			

KM# 1244 DOLLAR
25.18 g., 0.925 Silver 0.744 oz. ASW, 36.07 mm. **Ruler:** Elizabeth II **Subject:** Calgary Stampede

Date	Mintage	VF20	XF40	MS60	MS63
2012	—	PF63 45.00	PF65 55.00		

KM# 1254 DOLLAR
7.89 g., 0.999 Silver 0.2518 oz. ASW, 26.5 mm. **Ruler:** Elizabeth II **Subject:** Loonie, 25th Anniversary **Rev:** Two loons and large 25

Date	Mintage	VF20	XF40	MS60	MS63
1987-2012	15,000	PF63 32.00	PF65 35.00		

KM# 1255 DOLLAR
6.27 g., Brass Plated Steel, 26.5 mm. **Ruler:** Elizabeth II **Rev:** Loon with security feature above **Shape:** 11-sided

Date	Mintage	VF20	XF40	MS60	MS63
2012	—	—	—	—	5.00
2012	—	PF65 7.50			
2013	—	—	—	—	5.00
2013	—	PF65 7.50			

KM# 1256a DOLLAR
12.16 g., 0.925 Silver 0.3593 oz. ASW, 26.5 mm. **Ruler:** Elizabeth II **Subject:** Lucky loonie **Rev:** Loon and olympic logo in color

Date	Mintage	VF20	XF40	MS60	MS63
2012	—	PF63 30.00	PF65 35.00		

KM# 1274 DOLLAR
25.18 g., 0.925 Silver 0.744 oz. ASW, 36.07 mm. **Ruler:** Elizabeth II **Subject:** Artistic Loonie **Rev:** Four Loons in color

Date	Mintage	VF20	XF40	MS60	MS63
2012	—	PF65 125			

KM# 1294 DOLLAR
6.27 g., Brass Plated Steel, 26.5 mm. **Ruler:** Elizabeth II **Subject:** Grey Cup, 100th Anniversary **Obv:** Bust right **Shape:** 11-sided

Date	Mintage	VF20	XF40	MS60	MS63
2012	—	—	—	—	5.00

KM# 1295 DOLLAR
25.18 g., 0.925 Silver 0.744 oz. ASW, 36.07 mm. **Ruler:** Elizabeth II **Subject:** Grey Cup, 100th Anniversary

Date	Mintage	VF20	XF40	MS60	MS63
2012	—	PF63 75.00	PF65 85.00		

KM# 1360 DOLLAR
7.00 g., Bronze Plated Nickel, 26.5 mm. **Ruler:** Elizabeth II **Rev:** Blue wing teal standing on log

Date	Mintage	VF20	XF40	MS60	MS63
2013	50,000	PF63 35.00	PF65 40.00		

KM# 1387 DOLLAR
23.17 g., 0.999 Silver 0.7394 oz. ASW, 36.07 mm. **Ruler:** Elizabeth II **Subject:** Arctic Exploration - 100th Anniversary **Rev:** Three explorers and dog sled team, Company Rose in background

Date	Mintage	VF20	XF40	MS60	MS63
2013	Est. 40000	PF63 50.00	PF65 60.00		
2013	20,000	—	—	—	55.00

KM# 1387a DOLLAR
23.17 g., 0.999 Silver 0.7394 oz. ASW, 36.07 mm. **Ruler:** Elizabeth II **Subject:** Arctic Exploration - 100th Anniversary **Rev:** Map of North Pole, Arctic Explorers, Selectively Gilt

Date	Mintage	VF20	XF40	MS60	MS63
2013	—	PF65 225			

KM# 1388 DOLLAR
23.17 g., 0.999 Silver 0.7394 oz. ASW, 36.07 mm. **Ruler:** Elizabeth II **Subject:** End of 7 Years War - 250th Anniversary **Rev:** Soldiers and Settlers

Date	Mintage	VF20	XF40	MS60	MS63
2013	Est. 10000	PF63 60.00	PF65 70.00		

KM# 1394 DOLLAR
25.11 g., 0.925 Silver 0.7419 oz. ASW, 36.07 mm. **Ruler:** Elizabeth II **Obv:** Elizabeth II, Mary Glick portrait

Date	Mintage	VF20	XF40	MS60	MS63
2013	—	PF63 55.00	PF65 65.00		

KM# 1464 DOLLAR
23.17 g., 0.925 Silver 0.6846 oz. ASW, 36 mm. **Ruler:** Elizabeth II **Subject:** Korean War Armistice, 60th Anniversary **Rev:** Hercules slaying Hydra **Note:** Based on the design of the Korean Service Medal

Date	Mintage	VF20	XF40	MS60	MS63
2013	10,000	PF63 65.00	PF65 75.00		

KM# 1586 DOLLAR
25.18 g., 0.925 Silver 0.744 oz. ASW, 36.07 mm. **Ruler:** Elizabeth II **Subject:** WWI **Obv:** Bust right **Rev:** Soldier and woman kissing, soldiers boarding train

Date	Mintage	VF20	XF40	MS60	MS63
2014	—	—	—	—	50.00
2014	PF63 55.00	PF65 65.00			

KM# 1587 DOLLAR
7.00 g., Aluminum-Bronze, 26.5 mm. **Ruler:** Elizabeth II **Subject:** Lucky Loon **Obv:** Bust right **Rev:** Loon, Olympic logo at left

Date	Mintage	VF20	XF40	MS60	MS63
2014	—	—	—	5.00	

KM# 1588 DOLLAR
7.00 g., Aluminum-Bronze, 26.5 mm. **Ruler:** Elizabeth II **Subject:** Baby loon **Obv:** Bust right **Rev:** Stork in flight left with baby bundle

Date	Mintage	VF20	XF40	MS60	MS63
2014	—	—	—	—	5.00

KM# 1589 DOLLAR
7.00 g., Aluminum-Bronze, 26.5 mm. **Ruler:** Elizabeth II **Subject:** Birthday Loon **Obv:** Bust right **Rev:** Party hats, decorations, presents

Date	Mintage	VF20	XF40	MS60	MS63
2014	—	—	—	—	—

KM# 1591 DOLLAR
7.00 g., Aluminum-Bronze **Ruler:** Elizabeth II **Subject:** Oh Canada Loonie **Obv:** Bust right **Rev:** Maple leaf

Date	Mintage	VF20	XF40	MS60	MS63
2014	—	—	—	—	5.00

KM# 1627 DOLLAR
6.27 g., Brass Plated Nickel, 26.5 mm. **Ruler:** Elizabeth II **Subject:** Wedding **Rev:** Two birds

Date	Mintage	VF20	XF40	MS60	MS63
2014	—	—	—	—	20.00

KM# 1628 DOLLAR
6.27 g., Bronze Plated Nickel, 26.5 mm. **Ruler:** Elizabeth II **Rev:** Ferruginous Hawk in flight right

Date	Mintage	VF20	XF40	MS60	MS63
2014 Specimen	50,000	—	—	—	50.00

KM# 652 DOLLAR (Louis)
1.50 g., 0.999 Gold 0.0479 oz. AGW, 14.1 mm. **Ruler:** Elizabeth II **Subject:** Gold Louis **Obv:** Bust right **Rev:** Crowned double L monogram within wreath

Date	Mintage	VF20	XF40	MS60	MS63
2006	5,648	PF63 100	PF65 110		

KM# 756 DOLLAR (Louis)
1.56 g., 0.999 Gold 0.0496 oz. AGW, 14.1 mm. **Ruler:** Elizabeth II **Obv:** Bust right **Rev:** Crown above two oval shields

Date	Mintage	VF20	XF40	MS60	MS63
2007	4,023	PF65 110			

KM# 834 DOLLAR (Louis)
1.56 g., 0.999 Gold 0.0496 oz. AGW, 14.1 mm. **Ruler:** Elizabeth II **Obv:** Bust right **Rev:** Crowned double L monogram, three lis around

Date	Mintage	VF20	XF40	MS60	MS63
2008	3,793	PF65 110			

KM# 270c 2 DOLLARS
8.83 g., 0.925 Silver 0.2609 oz. ASW, 28 mm. **Ruler:** Elizabeth II **Obv:** Crowned head right within circle, date below **Rev:** Polar bear right within circle, denomination below **Note:** 1.9mm thick.

Date	Mintage	VF20	XF40	MS60	MS63
2001	—	PF65 12.00			

KM# 270 2 DOLLARS
7.30 g., Bi-Metallic, 28 mm. **Ruler:** Elizabeth II **Obv:** Crowned head right within circle, date below **Rev:** Polar bear right within circle, denomination below **Edge:** Segmented reeding

Date	Mintage	VF20	XF40	MS60	MS63
2001	27,008,000	—	—	—	5.00
2001	74,944	PF63 11.00	PF65 12.50		
2002	11,910,000	—	—	—	5.00
2002	65,315	PF63 11.00	PF65 12.50		
2003	7,123,697	—	—	—	5.00
2003	62,007	PF63 11.00	PF65 12.50		

KM# 449 2 DOLLARS
7.30 g., Bi-Metallic, 28 mm. **Ruler:** Elizabeth II **Subject:** Elizabeth II Golden Jubilee **Obv:** Crowned head right, jubilee commemorative dates below **Edge:** Segmented reeding

Date	Mintage	VF20	XF40	MS60	MS63
1952-2002	27,020,000	—	—	—	4.00

KM# 449a 2 DOLLARS
8.83 g., 0.925 Silver 0.2609 oz. ASW, 28 mm. **Ruler:** Elizabeth II **Subject:** Elizabeth II Golden Jubilee **Obv:** Crowned head right, jubilee commemorative dates below

Date	Mintage	VF20	XF40	MS60	MS63
1952-2002	100,000	PF63 12.00	PF65 14.00		

KM# 270d 2 DOLLARS
8.83 g., 0.925 Silver 0.2609 oz. ASW **Ruler:** Elizabeth II **Subject:** 100th Anniversary of the Cobalt Silver Strike **Obv:** Crowned head right, within circle, date below **Rev:** Polar bear right, within circle, denomination below

Date	Mintage	VF20	XF40	MS60	MS63
2003	100,000	PF65 25.00			

KM# 496 2 DOLLARS
7.30 g., Bi-Metallic, 28 mm. **Ruler:** Elizabeth II **Obv:** Head right **Rev:** Polar bear advancing right **Edge:** Segmented reeding

Date	Mintage	VF20	XF40	MS60	MS63
2003	11,244,000	—	—	—	5.00
2003W	71,142	—	—	—	25.00
2004	12,908,000	—	—	—	5.00
2004	—	PF63 11.00	PF65 12.50		
2005	38,317,000	—	—	—	5.00
2005	—	PF63 11.00	PF65 12.50		
2006(ml)	35,319,000	—	—	—	5.00
2006(ml)	—	PF63 11.00	PF65 12.50		
2007(ml)	38,957,000	—	—	—	5.00
2007(ml)	—	PF63 11.00	PF65 12.50		
2008(ml)	18,400,000	—	—	—	5.00
2008(ml)	—	PF63 11.00	PF65 12.50		
2009(ml)	38,430,000	—	—	—	5.00
2009(ml)	—	PF63 11.00	PF65 12.50		
2010(ml)	—	—	—	—	5.00
2010(ml)	—	PF63 11.00	PF65 12.50		
2011(ml)	—	—	—	—	5.00
2011(ml)	—	PF63 11.00	PF65 12.50		
2012(ml)	—	—	—	—	5.00
2012(ml)	—	PF63 11.00	PF65 12.50		

KM# 835 2 DOLLARS
8.80 g., 0.925 Silver 0.260 oz. ASW, 27.95 mm. **Ruler:** Elizabeth II **Rev:** Proud Polar Bear advancing right

Date	Mintage	VF20	XF40	MS60	MS63
2004	12,607	PF63 30.00	PF65 40.00		

KM# 496a 2 DOLLARS
10.84 g., 0.925 Bi-Metallic 0.3203 oz., 28 mm. **Ruler:** Elizabeth II **Obv:** Head right **Rev:** Polar Bear **Edge:** Segmented reeding

Date	Mintage	VF20	XF40	MS60	MS63
2004	—	PF63 22.00	PF65 25.00		

KM# 631 2 DOLLARS
7.30 g., Bi-Metallic, 28 mm. **Ruler:** Elizabeth II **Subject:** 10th Anniversary of $2 coin **Obv:** Crowned head right **Edge:** Segmented reeding

Date	Mintage	VF20	XF40	MS60	MS63
2006(ml)	5,005,000	—	—	—	25.00
2006(ml)	—	PF63 37.00	PF65 40.00		

KM# 631a 2 DOLLARS
Bi-Metallic **Ruler:** Elizabeth II **Subject:** 10th Anniversary of $2 coin **Obv:** Crowned head right **Rev:** Polar bear

Date	Mintage	VF20	XF40	MS60	MS63
2006	2,068	PF65 400			

KM# 836 2 DOLLARS
7.30 g., Bi-Metallic, 28 mm. **Ruler:** Elizabeth II **Subject:** $2 coin, 10th Anniversary **Rev:** Churchill" Polar Bear, northern lights **Edge:** Segmented reeding

Date	Mintage	VF20	XF40	MS60	MS63
2006(ml)	31,636	—	—	—	7.50

KM# 837 2 DOLLARS
7.30 g., Bi-Metallic **Ruler:** Elizabeth II **Obv:** Bust left, date at top **Rev:** Polar Bear advancing right

Date	Mintage	VF20	XF40	MS60	MS63
2006(ml)	—	—	—	—	7.50
2007(ml)	38,957,000	—	—	—	7.50

KM# 796 2 DOLLARS
8.83 g., 0.925 Silver 0.2609 oz. ASW, 28.07 mm. **Ruler:** Elizabeth II **Rev:** Bear, gold plated center

Date	Mintage	VF20	XF40	MS60	MS63
2008	—	—	—	—	25.00

KM# 1040 2 DOLLARS
7.30 g., Bi-Metallic, 28 mm. **Ruler:** Elizabeth II **Subject:** Quebec 400th Anniversary **Rev:** Lis and small sailing ship **Edge:** Segmented reeding

Date	Mintage	VF20	XF40	MS60	MS63
2008	—	—	—	—	7.50

KM# 1020 2 DOLLARS
7.30 g., Bi-Metallic, 28 mm. **Ruler:** Elizabeth II **Rev:** Two lynx cubs **Edge:** Segmented reeding

Date	Mintage	VF20	XF40	MS60	MS63
2010 Specimen	15,000	PF63 40.00			

KM# 1088 2 DOLLARS
7.30 g., Bi-Metallic, 28 mm. **Ruler:** Elizabeth II **Rev:** Elk Calf **Edge:** Segmented reeding

Date	Mintage	VF20	XF40	MS60	MS63
2011	—	—	—	—	7.50

KM# 1167 2 DOLLARS
7.30 g., Bi-Metallic, 28 mm. **Ruler:** Elizabeth II **Subject:** Canada Parks **Obv:** Bust right **Rev:** Stylized trees

Date	Mintage	VF20	XF40	MS60	MS63
2011	—	—	—	—	7.50

KM# 1257 2 DOLLARS
6.92 g., Bi-Metallic, 28 mm. **Ruler:** Elizabeth II **Rev:** Polar bear with security device above **Edge:** Lettered and segmented reeding

Date	Mintage	VF20	XF40	MS60	MS63
2012	—	—	—	—	7.50
2012	—	PF65 10.00			
2013	—	—	—	—	7.50
2013	—	PF65 10.00			

KM# 1258 2 DOLLARS
6.92 g., Bi-Metallic, 28 mm. **Ruler:** Elizabeth II **Subject:** H.M.S. Shannon **Edge:** Lettered and segmented reeding

Date	Mintage	VF20	XF40	MS60	MS63
2012	—	—	—	—	10.00

KM# 1263 2 DOLLARS
7.30 g., Bi-Metallic, 28 mm. **Ruler:** Elizabeth II **Rev:** Wolf cubs

Date	Mintage	VF20	XF40	MS60	MS63
2012	—	—	—	—	10.00

KM# 1463 2 DOLLARS
(No Composition), 28 mm. **Ruler:** Elizabeth II **Rev:** Two black bear cubs playing

Date	Mintage	VF20	XF40	MS60	MS63
2013	17,500	PF63 45.00	PF65 50.00		

KM# 657 3 DOLLARS
11.72 g., 0.925 Silver 0.3463 oz. ASW, 27x27 mm. **Ruler:** Elizabeth II **Rev:** Beaver within wreath **Shape:** Square

Date	Mintage	VF20	XF40	MS60	MS63
2006	19,963	PF65 225			

KM# 1051 3 DOLLARS
11.60 g., 0.925 Silver 0.3428 oz. ASW, 27x27 mm. **Ruler:** Elizabeth II **Subject:** Wildlife conservation **Rev:** Stylized polar bear and northern lights **Shape:** square

Date	Mintage	VF20	XF40	MS60	MS63
2010 Specimen	15,000	—	—	—	55.00

KM# 978 3 DOLLARS
7.96 g., Silver, 27 mm. **Ruler:** Elizabeth II **Rev:** Return of the Tyee (giant salmon)

Date	Mintage	VF20	XF40	MS60	MS63
2010	15,000	PF63 40.00	PF65 50.00		

KM# 1011 3 DOLLARS
11.60 g., 0.925 Silver 0.3428 oz. ASW, 27x27 mm. **Ruler:** Elizabeth II **Rev:** Barn Owl **Shape:** Square

Date	Mintage	VF20	XF40	MS60	MS63
2010	15,000	PF63 55.00	PF65 65.00		

KM# 1089 3 DOLLARS
11.60 g., 0.925 Silver 0.3428 oz. ASW, 27x27 mm. **Ruler:** Elizabeth II **Rev:** Orca Whale **Shape:** Square

Date	Mintage	VF20	XF40	MS60	MS63
2011	15,000	PF63 55.00	PF65 65.00		

KM# 1090 3 DOLLARS
7.96 g., 0.999 Silver 0.254 oz. ASW, 27 mm. **Ruler:** Elizabeth II **Obv:** Bust right **Rev:** Eskimo mother kneeling, child on back, partially gilt

Date	Mintage	VF20	XF40	MS60	MS63
2011	10,000	PF63 55.00	PF65 65.00		

KM# 1117 3 DOLLARS
7.96 g., 0.9999 Silver 0.2542 oz. ASW, 27 mm. **Ruler:** Elizabeth II **Subject:** January birthstone, Garnet **Obv:** Bust left **Rev:** Birthstone at cener of artistic sunburst **Edge:** Reeded

Date	Mintage	VF20	XF40	MS60	MS63
2011	—	PF63 40.00	PF65 45.00		

KM# 1118 3 DOLLARS
7.96 g., 0.9999 Silver 0.2542 oz. ASW, 27 mm. **Ruler:** Elizabeth II **Subject:** February birthstone, Amythest **Obv:** Bust right **Rev:** Birthstone at cener of artistic sunburst **Edge:** Reeded

Date	Mintage	VF20	XF40	MS60	MS63
2011	—	PF63 40.00	PF65 45.00		

KM# 1119 3 DOLLARS
7.96 g., 0.9999 Silver 0.2542 oz. ASW, 27 mm. **Ruler:** Elizabeth II **Subject:** March birthstone, Aquamarine **Obv:** Bust right **Rev:** Birthstone at cener of artistic sunburst **Edge:** Reeded

Date	Mintage	VF20	XF40	MS60	MS63
2011	—	PF63 40.00	PF65 45.00		

KM# 1120 3 DOLLARS
7.96 g., 0.9999 Silver 0.2542 oz. ASW, 27 mm. **Ruler:** Elizabeth II **Subject:** April birthstone, diamond **Obv:** Bust right **Rev:** Birthstone at cener of artistic sunburst **Edge:** Reeded

Date	Mintage	VF20	XF40	MS60	MS63
2011	—	PF63 40.00	PF65 45.00		

KM# 1121 3 DOLLARS
7.96 g., 0.9999 Silver 0.2542 oz. ASW, 27 mm. **Ruler:** Elizabeth II **Subject:** May birthstone **Obv:** Bust right **Rev:** Birthstone at cener of artistic sunburst **Edge:** Reeded

Date	Mintage	VF20	XF40	MS60	MS63
2011	—	PF63 40.00	PF65 45.00		

KM# 1122 3 DOLLARS
7.96 g., 0.9999 Silver 0.2542 oz. ASW, 27 mm. **Ruler:** Elizabeth II **Subject:** June birthstone, Alexandrite **Obv:** Bust right **Rev:** Birthstone at cener of artistic sunburst

Date	Mintage	VF20	XF40	MS60	MS63
2011	—	PF63 40.00	PF65 45.00		

KM# 1123 3 DOLLARS
7.96 g., 0.9999 Silver 0.2542 oz. ASW, 27 mm. **Ruler:** Elizabeth II **Subject:** July birthstone, Ruby **Obv:** Bust right **Rev:** Birthstone at cener of artistic sunburst

KM# 1124 3 DOLLARS
7.96 g., 0.9999 Silver 0.2542 oz. ASW, 27 mm. **Ruler:** Elizabeth II **Subject:** August birthstone, Priedot **Obv:** Bust right **Rev:** Birthstone at cener of artistic sunburst

Date	Mintage	VF20	XF40	MS60	MS63
2011	—	PF63 40.00	PF65 45.00		

KM# 1125 3 DOLLARS
7.96 g., 0.9999 Silver 0.2542 oz. ASW, 27 mm. **Ruler:** Elizabeth II **Subject:** September birhtstone **Obv:** Bust right **Rev:** Birthstone at cener of artistic sunburst **Edge:** Reeded

Date	Mintage	VF20	XF40	MS60	MS63
2011	—	PF63 40.00	PF65 45.00		

KM# 1126 3 DOLLARS
7.96 g., 0.9999 Silver 0.2542 oz. ASW, 27 mm. **Ruler:** Elizabeth II **Subject:** October birthstone **Obv:** Bust right **Rev:** Birthstone at cener of artistic sunburst

Date	Mintage	VF20	XF40	MS60	MS63
2011	—	PF63 40.00	PF65 45.00		

KM# 1127 3 DOLLARS
7.96 g., 0.9999 Silver 0.2542 oz. ASW, 27 mm. **Ruler:** Elizabeth II **Subject:** November birthstone **Obv:** Bust right **Rev:** Birthstone at cener of artistic sunburst

Date	Mintage	VF20	XF40	MS60	MS63
2011	—	PF63 40.00	PF65 45.00		

KM# 1128 3 DOLLARS
7.96 g., 0.9999 Silver 0.2542 oz. ASW, 27 mm. **Ruler:** Elizabeth II **Subject:** December birhtstone **Obv:** Bust right **Rev:** Birthstone at cener of artistic sunburst

Date	Mintage	VF20	XF40	MS60	MS63
2011	—	PF63 40.00	PF65 45.00		

KM# 1151 3 DOLLARS
11.80 g., 0.925 Silver 0.3487 oz. ASW, 27x27 mm. **Ruler:** Elizabeth II **Obv:** Bust right **Rev:** Black footed ferret

Date	Mintage	VF20	XF40	MS60	MS63
2011	Est. 15000	PF63 55.00	PF65 65.00		

KM# 1300 3 DOLLARS
7.96 g., 0.9999 Silver 0.2542 oz. ASW, 27 mm. **Ruler:** Elizabeth II **Subject:** January birthstone, Garnet **Obv:** Bust right **Rev:** Birthstone at center of wreath

Date	Mintage	VF20	XF40	MS60	MS63
2013	—	PF65 50.00			

M# 1301 3 DOLLARS
7.96 g., 0.999 Silver 0.254 oz. ASW, 27 mm. **Ruler:** Elizabeth II **Subject:** February birthstone, Amythest **Obv:** Bust right **Rev:** Birthstone at center of wreath

Date	Mintage	VF20	XF40	MS60	MS63
2013	—	PF65 65.00			

KM# 1302 3 DOLLARS
7.96 g., 0.999 Silver 0.254 oz. ASW, 27 mm. **Ruler:** Elizabeth II **Subject:** March birthstone, Aquamarine **Obv:** Bust right **Rev:** Birthstone at center of wreath

Date	Mintage	VF20	XF40	MS60	MS63
2013	—	PF65 50.00			

M# 1303 3 DOLLARS
7.96 g., 0.999 Silver 0.254 oz. ASW, 27 mm. **Ruler:** Elizabeth II **Subject:** April birthstone, Diamond **Obv:** Bust right **Rev:** Birthstone at center of wreath

Date	Mintage	VF20	XF40	MS60	MS63
2013	—	PF65 50.00			

KM# 1304 3 DOLLARS
7.96 g., 0.999 Silver 0.254 oz. ASW, 27 mm. **Ruler:** Elizabeth II **Subject:** May birthstone **Obv:** Bust right **Rev:** Birthstone at center of wreath

Date	Mintage	VF20	XF40	MS60	MS63
2013	—	PF65 50.00			

KM# 1305 3 DOLLARS
7.96 g., 0.999 Silver 0.254 oz. ASW, 27 mm. **Ruler:** Elizabeth II **Subject:** June birthstone, Alexandrite **Obv:** Bust right **Rev:** Birthstone at center of wreath

Date	Mintage	VF20	XF40	MS60	MS63
2013	—	PF65 50.00			

KM# 1306 3 DOLLARS
7.96 g., 0.999 Silver 0.254 oz. ASW, 27 mm. **Ruler:** Elizabeth II **Subject:** July birthstone - Ruby **Obv:** Bust right **Rev:** Birthstone at center of wreath

Date	Mintage	VF20	XF40	MS60	MS63
2013	—	PF65 50.00			

KM# 1307 3 DOLLARS
7.96 g., 0.999 Silver 0.254 oz. ASW, 27 mm. **Ruler:** Elizabeth II **Subject:** August birthstone - Priedot **Obv:** Bust right **Rev:** Birthstone at center of wreath

Date	Mintage	VF20	XF40	MS60	MS63
2013	—	PF65 50.00			

KM# 1308 3 DOLLARS
7.96 g., 0.999 Silver 0.254 oz. ASW, 27 mm. **Ruler:** Elizabeth II **Subject:** September birthstone **Obv:** Bust right **Rev:** Birthstone at center of wreath

Date	Mintage	VF20	XF40	MS60	MS63
2013	—	PF65 50.00			

KM# 1309 3 DOLLARS
7.96 g., 0.999 Silver 0.254 oz. ASW, 27 mm. **Ruler:** Elizabeth II **Subject:** October birthstone **Obv:** Bust right **Rev:** Birthstone at center of wreath

Date	Mintage	VF20	XF40	MS60	MS63
2013	—	PF65 50.00			

KM# 1310 3 DOLLARS
7.96 g., 0.999 Silver 0.254 oz. ASW, 27 mm. **Ruler:** Elizabeth II **Subject:** November birthstone **Obv:** Bust right **Rev:** Birthstone at center of wreath

Date	Mintage	VF20	XF40	MS60	MS63
2013	—	PF65 50.00			

KM# 1311 3 DOLLARS
7.96 g., 0.999 Silver 0.254 oz. ASW, 27 mm. **Ruler:** Elizabeth II **Subject:** December birthstone **Obv:** Bust right **Rev:** Birthstone at center of wreath

Date	Mintage	VF20	XF40	MS60	MS63
2013	—	PF65 50.00			

KM# 1352 3 DOLLARS
7.96 g., 0.9999 Silver 0.2542 oz. ASW, 27 mm. **Ruler:** Elizabeth II **Rev:** Hummingbirds around crystal

Date	Mintage	VF20	XF40	MS60	MS63
2013	20,000	PF63 65.00	PF65 70.00		

KM# 1367 3 DOLLARS
7.96 g., 0.9999 Silver 0.2542 oz. ASW, 27 mm. **Ruler:** Elizabeth II **Subject:** Animal Architects: Bee **Rev:** Bee and Hive in color

Date	Mintage	VF20	XF40	MS60	MS63
2013	Est. 10000	PF63 60.00	PF65 70.00		

KM# 1451 3 DOLLARS
7.96 g., 0.9999 Silver 0.2542 oz. ASW, 27 mm. **Ruler:** Elizabeth II **Rev:** Large maple leaf and many small maple leaves

Date	Mintage	VF20	XF40	MS60	MS63
2013	10,000	PF63 50.00	PF65 60.00		

KM# 1481 3 DOLLARS
19.20 g., 0.950 Copper 0.5827 oz., 35.75 mm. **Ruler:** Elizabeth II **Subject:** Banknote Allegory **Rev:** Female seated

Date	Mintage	VF20	XF40	MS60	MS63
2013	15,000	PF63 35.00	PF65 40.00		

KM# 1485 3 DOLLARS
31.11 g., 0.999 Silver 0.9926 oz. ASW, 38 mm. **Ruler:** Elizabeth II **Rev:** Gradfather and grandson fishing from lake dock, dog at their side

Date	Mintage	VF20	XF40	MS60	MS63
2013	—	PF63 45.00	PF65 50.00		

KM# 1492 3 DOLLARS
7.96 g., 0.9999 Silver 0.2542 oz. ASW, 27 mm. **Ruler:** Elizabeth II **Rev:** Hummingbird and morning glory - crystal insert

Date	Mintage	VF20	XF40	MS60	MS63
2013	20,000	PF63 50.00	PF65 60.00		

KM# 1528 3 DOLLARS
7.96 g., 0.999 Silver 0.254 oz. ASW, 27 mm. **Ruler:** Elizabeth II **Rev:** Spider on web

Date	Mintage	VF20	XF40	MS60	MS63
2013	10,000	PF63 60.00	PF65 70.00		

KM# 1537 3 DOLLARS
7.96 g., 0.999 Silver 0.254 oz. ASW, 27 mm. **Ruler:** Elizabeth II **Rev:** Whale, realistic and Inuit designs

Date	Mintage	VF20	XF40	MS60	MS63
2013	10,000	PF63 30.00	PF65 35.00		
2013 Reverse Proof	PF65 35.00				

KM# 1617 3 DOLLARS
7.96 g., 0.999 Silver 0.254 oz. ASW, 27 mm. **Ruler:** Elizabeth II **Subject:** Jewel of Life **Obv:** Bust right **Rev:** Tree and crystals

Date	Mintage	VF20	XF40	MS60	MS63
2014	15,000	PF63 50.00	PF65 60.00		

KM# 728 4 DOLLARS
15.87 g., 0.925 Silver 0.4689 oz. ASW, 34 mm. **Ruler:** Elizabeth II **Subject:** Dinosaur fossil **Obv:** Bust right **Rev:** Parasaurolophus, selective enameling

Date	Mintage	VF20	XF40	MS60	MS63
2007	14,946	PF63 115	PF65 125		

KM# 797 4 DOLLARS
15.87 g., 0.999 Silver 0.5064 oz. ASW, 34 mm. **Ruler:** Elizabeth II **Subject:** Dinosaur fossil **Obv:** Bust right **Rev:** Triceratops, enameled

Date	Mintage	VF20	XF40	MS60	MS63
2008	13,046	PF63 65.00	PF65 75.00		

KM# 890 4 DOLLARS
15.87 g., 0.999 Silver 0.5064 oz. ASW, 34 mm. **Ruler:** Elizabeth II **Subject:** Tyrannosaurus Rex **Obv:** Bust right **Obv. Legend:** Elizabeth II DG Regina **Rev:** T-Rex skeleton in selective aging **Rev. Legend:** Canada 4 Dollars

Date	Mintage	VF20	XF40	MS60	MS63
2009	13,572	PF63 50.00	PF65 60.00		

KM# 942 4 DOLLARS
15.87 g., Silver, 34 mm. **Ruler:** Elizabeth II **Rev:** Kids hanging stocking on fireplace, Christmas tree on right

Date	Mintage	VF20	XF40	MS60	MS63
2009	6,011	PF63 40.00	PF65 45.00		

KM# 1014 4 DOLLARS
15.87 g., 0.999 Silver 0.5064 oz. ASW, 34 mm. **Ruler:** Elizabeth II **Rev:** Euoplocephalus

Date	Mintage	VF20	XF40	MS60	MS63
2010	Est. 13000	PF63 50.00	PF65 60.00		

KM# 1022 4 DOLLARS
Silver **Ruler:** Elizabeth II **Rev:** Dromaeosaurus

Date	Mintage	VF20	XF40	MS60	MS63
2010	8,982	PF63 75.00	PF65 85.00		

KM# 1129 4 DOLLARS
15.87 g., 0.9999 Silver 0.5069 oz. ASW, 34 mm. **Ruler:** Elizabeth II **Obv:** Bust right **Rev:** Baby's footprint **Edge:** Reeded

Date	Mintage	VF20	XF40	MS60	MS63
2011	Est. 10000	PF63 50.00	PF65 60.00		

KM# 1325 4 DOLLARS
7.96 g., 0.999 Silver 0.254 oz. ASW, 27 mm. **Ruler:** Elizabeth II **Subject:** War of 1812 - Tecumseh **Rev:** Portrait at right, red maple leaf

Date	Mintage	VF20	XF40	MS60	MS63
2012	10,000	PF63 45.00	PF65 50.00		

KM# 1323 4 DOLLARS
7.96 g., 0.999 Silver 0.254 oz. ASW, 27 mm. **Ruler:** Elizabeth II **Subject:** War of 1812 - Brock **Rev:** Portrait at right, red maple leaf

Date	Mintage	VF20	XF40	MS60	MS63
2012	10,000	PF63 45.00	PF65 50.00		

KM# 1356 4 DOLLARS
7.96 g., 0.9999 Silver 0.2542 oz. ASW, 27 mm. **Ruler:** Elizabeth II **Subject:** War of 1812 - Salaberry **Rev:** Bust at right, red maple leaf

Date	Mintage	VF20	XF40	MS60	MS63
2013	10,000	PF63 45.00	PF65 50.00		

KM# 1452 4 DOLLARS
7.96 g., 0.999 Silver 0.254 oz. ASW, 27 mm. **Ruler:** Elizabeth II **Subject:** Heroes of 1812 **Rev:** Bust at right, maple leaf in color

Date	Mintage	VF20	XF40	MS60	MS63
2013	Est. 10000	PF63 40.00	PF65 50.00		

KM# 435 5 DOLLARS
16.86 g., 0.925 Silver 0.4982 oz. ASW, 28.4 mm. **Ruler:** Elizabeth II **Subject:** Guglielmo Marconi **Obv:** Crowned head right **Rev:** Gold-plated cameo portrait of Marconi **Edge:** Reeded **Note:** Only issued in two coin set with British 2 pounds KM#1014a.

Date	Mintage	VF20	XF40	MS60	MS63
2001	15,011	PF63 22.00	PF65 30.00		

KM# 519 5 DOLLARS
8.36 g., 0.900 Gold 0.2403 oz. AGW, 21.6 mm. **Ruler:** Elizabeth II **Obv:** Crowned head right **Rev:** National arms **Edge:** Reeded

Date	Mintage	VF20	XF40	MS60	MS63
1912-2002	2,002	PF65 450			

KM# 603 5 DOLLARS
31.11 g., 0.9999 Silver 0.9935 oz. ASW **Ruler:** Elizabeth II **Obv:** Head right **Rev:** Loon splashing in the water, hologram

Date	Mintage	VF20	XF40	MS60	MS63
2002 Satin Proof	30,000	PF65 50.00			

KM# 518 5 DOLLARS
31.12 g., 0.9999 Silver 0.994 oz. ASW, 38 mm. **Ruler:** Elizabeth II **Subject:** F.I.F.A. World Cup Soccer , Germany 2006 **Obv:** Crowned head right, denomination **Rev:** Goalie on knees **Edge:** Reeded

Date	Mintage	VF20	XF40	MS60	MS63
2003	21,542	PF63 35.00	PF65 40.00		

KM# 514 5 DOLLARS
31.12 g., 0.9999 Silver 0.994 oz. ASW, 38 mm. **Ruler:** Elizabeth II **Obv:** Crowned head right **Rev:** Moose **Edge:** Reeded

Date	Mintage	VF20	XF40	MS60	MS63
2004	12,822	PF65 175			

KM# 527 5 DOLLARS
31.12 g., 0.9999 Silver 0.994 oz. ASW **Ruler:** Elizabeth II **Subject:** Golf, Championship of Canada, Centennial **Obv:** Head right

Date	Mintage	VF20	XF40	MS60	MS63
2004	18,750	PF63 25.00	PF65 30.00		

KM# 554 5 DOLLARS
31.12 g., 0.9999 Silver 0.994 oz. ASW **Ruler:** Elizabeth II **Subject:** Alberta

Date	Mintage	VF20	XF40	MS60	MS63
2005	20,000	PF63 30.00	PF65 35.00		

KM# 555 5 DOLLARS
31.12 g., 0.9999 Silver 0.994 oz. ASW **Ruler:** Elizabeth II **Subject:** Saskatchewan **Obv:** Head right

Date	Mintage	VF20	XF40	MS60	MS63
2005	20,000	PF63 30.00	PF65 35.00		

KM# 556.1 5 DOLLARS
31.12 g., 0.999 Silver 0.9931 oz. ASW, 38.02 mm. **Ruler:** Elizabeth II **Subject:** 60th Annivesay Victory WWII - Veterans **Obv:** Bust right **Rev:** Large V and heads of sailor, soldier and aviator on large maple leaf **Edge:** Reeded

Date	Mintage	VF20	XF40	MS60	MS63
2005	25,000	—	—	—	32.00

KM# 556.2 5 DOLLARS
31.12 g., 0.9999 Silver 0.994 oz. ASW, 38.02 mm. **Ruler:** Elizabeth II **Subject:** 60th Anniversary Victory WW II - Veterans **Obv:** Bust right **Rev:** Large V and heads of sailor, soldier and aviator on maple leaf with small maple leaf added at left and right **Edge:** Reeded

Date	Mintage	VF20	XF40	MS60	MS63
2005	10,000	—	—	—	125

KM# 557 5 DOLLARS
31.12 g., 0.9999 Silver 0.994 oz. ASW, 36 mm. **Ruler:** Elizabeth II **Subject:** Walrus and calf **Obv:** Head right **Rev:** Two walrusus and calf

Date	Mintage	VF20	XF40	MS60	MS63
2005	5,519	PF63 40.00	PF65 45.00		

KM# 558 5 DOLLARS
31.12 g., 0.9999 Silver 0.994 oz. ASW, 36 mm. **Ruler:** Elizabeth II **Subject:** White tailed deer **Obv:** Head right **Rev:** Two deer standing

Date	Mintage	VF20	XF40	MS60	MS63
2005	6,439	PF63 40.00	PF65 45.00		

KM# 585 5 DOLLARS
31.12 g., 0.9999 Silver 0.994 oz. ASW, 36 mm. **Ruler:** Elizabeth II **Obv:** Head right **Rev:** Peregrine Falcon feeding young ones

Date	Mintage	VF20	XF40	MS60	MS63
2006	7,226	PF63 45.00	PF65 50.00		

KM# 586 5 DOLLARS
31.12 g., 0.9999 Silver 0.994 oz. ASW, 36 mm. **Ruler:** Elizabeth II **Subject:** Sable Island horses **Obv:** Head right **Rev:** Horse and foal standing

Date	Mintage	VF20	XF40	MS60	MS63
2006	10,108	PF63 45.00	PF65 50.00		

KM# 658 5 DOLLARS
31.12 g., 0.9999 Silver 0.994 oz. ASW, 36.07 mm. **Ruler:** Elizabeth II **Subject:** Breast Cancer Awareness **Rev:** Colorized pink ribbon

Date	Mintage	VF20	XF40	MS60	MS63
2006	11,048	PF63 45.00	PF65 50.00		

KM# 659 5 DOLLARS
31.12 g., 0.9999 Silver 0.994 oz. ASW **Ruler:** Elizabeth II **Subject:** C.A.F. Snowbirds Acrobatic Jet Flying Team **Rev:** Image of fighter jets and piolt

Date	Mintage	VF20	XF40	MS60	MS63
2006	10,034	PF63 45.00	PF65 50.00		

KM# 1036 5 DOLLARS
31.12 g., 0.999 Silver 0.9931 oz. ASW **Ruler:** Elizabeth II **Subject:** 80th Anniversary **Rev:** Two deer standing, one eating branch

Date	Mintage	VF20	XF40	MS60	MS63
2009	27,872	PF63 60.00	PF65 70.00		

KM# 1130 5 DOLLARS
8.50 g., Bi-Metallic, 28 mm. **Ruler:** Elizabeth II **Subject:** Summer - Buck Moon **Obv:** Bust right **Rev:** Buck against summer moon

Date	Mintage	VF20	XF40	MS60	MS63
2011	7,500	PF63 115	PF65 125		

KM# 1131 5 DOLLARS
8.50 g., Bi-Metallic, 28 mm. **Ruler:** Elizabeth II **Subject:** Fall Moon **Obv:** Bust right **Rev:** Native American hunter seated tracking prey before Harvest Moon

Date	Mintage	VF20	XF40	MS60	MS63
2011	7,500	PF63 115	PF65 125		

KM# 1149 5 DOLLARS
3.13 g., 0.9999 Gold 0.100 oz. AGW, 16 mm. **Ruler:** Elizabeth II **Subject:** Norman Bethune **Obv:** Bust right **Rev:** Half-length figure at right, looking left

Date	Mintage	VF20	XF40	MS60	MS63
2011	Est. 5000	PF65 300			

KM# 1236 5 DOLLARS
8.36 g., 0.900 Gold 0.2403 oz. AGW, 21.6 mm. **Ruler:** Elizabeth II **Obv:** Bust right **Rev:** Crowned monogram in wreath

Date	Mintage	VF20	XF40	MS60	MS63
1952-2012	—	PF65 500			

KM# 1132 5 DOLLARS
8.50 g., Bi-Metallic, 28 mm. **Ruler:** Elizabeth II **Subject:** Winter Moon **Obv:** Bust right **Rev:** Wolf howling before Winter Moon

Date	Mintage	VF20	XF40	MS60	MS63
2012	7,500	PF63 115	PF65 125		

KM# 1133 5 DOLLARS
8.50 g., Bi-Metallic, 28 mm. **Ruler:** Elizabeth II **Subject:** Spring Moon **Rev:** Phlox blossoming against a Spring Moon, field in color

Date	Mintage	VF20	XF40	MS60	MS63
2012	—	PF63 115	PF65 125		

KM# 1194 5 DOLLARS
3.13 g., 0.999 Gold 0.0999 oz. AGW, 16 mm. **Ruler:** Elizabeth II **Obv:** Bust right **Rev:** Royal Cypher, wreath below

Date	Mintage	VF20	XF40	MS60	MS63
2012	—	PF65 200			

KM# 1220 5 DOLLARS
3.13 g., 0.9999 Gold 0.100 oz. AGW, 16 mm. **Ruler:** Elizabeth II **Subject:** Year of the Dragon **Obv:** Bust right **Rev:** Dragon forpart right

Date	Mintage	VF20	XF40	MS60	MS63
2012 Specimen	—	PF65 225			

KM# 1248 5 DOLLARS
31.12 g., 0.999 Silver 0.9931 oz. ASW, 36 mm. **Ruler:** Elizabeth II **Subject:** Rick Hansen **Rev:** Wheelchair bound athlete

Date	Mintage	VF20	XF40	MS60	MS63
2012	—	PF63 65.00	PF65 75.00		

KM# 1281 5 DOLLARS
3.13 g., 0.999 Gold 0.0999 oz. AGW, 16 mm. **Ruler:** Elizabeth II
Subject: Year of the Dragon

Date	Mintage	VF20	XF40	MS60	MS63
2012	—	PF65 200			

KM# 1332 5 DOLLARS
31.11 g., 0.999 Silver 0.9926 oz. ASW, 36 mm. **Ruler:** Elizabeth II **Subject:** Georgia Pope **Rev:** Four female soldiers

Date	Mintage	VF20	XF40	MS60	MS63
2012	—	PF63 70.00	PF65 75.00		

KM# 1298 5 DOLLARS
3.13 g., 0.999 Gold 0.0999 oz. AGW **Ruler:** Elizabeth II
Subject: Year of the Snake

Date	Mintage	VF20	XF40	MS60	MS63
2013	—	PF65 225			

KM# 1395 5 DOLLARS
3.13 g., 0.9999 Gold 0.100 oz. AGW, 16 mm. **Ruler:** Elizabeth II
Rev: Beaver swimming with branch in mouth

Date	Mintage	VF20	XF40	MS60	MS63
2013	Est. 4000	PF65 280			

KM# 1401 5 DOLLARS
3.13 g., 0.9999 Gold 0.100 oz. AGW, 16 mm. **Ruler:** Elizabeth II **Rev:** Polar Bear head

Date	Mintage	VF20	XF40	MS60	MS63
2013	Est. 4000	PF65 275			

KM# 1426 5 DOLLARS
23.17 g., 0.9999 Silver 0.7401 oz. ASW, 36 mm. **Ruler:** Elizabeth II **Subject:** Traditions: Hunting **Rev:** Deer and hunter teaching child

Date	Mintage	VF20	XF40	MS60	MS63
2013	Est. 10000	PF63 60.00	PF65 70.00		

KM# 1453 5 DOLLARS
3.13 g., 0.999 Gold 0.0999 oz. AGW, 16 mm. **Ruler:** Elizabeth II **Rev:** Caribou head

Date	Mintage	VF20	XF40	MS60	MS63
2013	4,000	PF65 275			

KM# 1454 5 DOLLARS
3.13 g., 0.999 Gold 0.0999 oz. AGW, 16 mm. **Ruler:** Elizabeth II **Rev:** Wolf head

Date	Mintage	VF20	XF40	MS60	MS63
2013	4,000	PF65 275			

KM# 1461a 5 DOLLARS
23.17 g., 0.9999 Gilt 0.7401 oz., 36 mm. **Ruler:** Elizabeth II **Subject:** Birth of Prince George **Rev:** W and C crowned in gilt center, infant toys around

Date	Mintage	VF20	XF40	MS60	MS63
2013	Est. 15000	PF63 65.00	PF65 75.00		

KM# 1461 5 DOLLARS
23.17 g., 0.9999 Silver 0.7401 oz. ASW, 36 mm. **Ruler:** Elizabeth II **Subject:** Birth of Prince George **Rev:** W and C crowned in gilt center, Infant toys around

Date	Mintage	VF20	XF40	MS60	MS63
2013	Est. 15000	PF63 65.00	PF65 75.00		

KM# 1475 5 DOLLARS
8.50 g., 0.9999 Silver 0.2715 oz. ASW, 28 mm. **Ruler:** Elizabeth II **Subject:** Father Ice

Date	Mintage	VF20	XF40	MS60	MS63
2013	6,500	PF63 130	PF65 140		

KM# 1476 5 DOLLARS
8.50 g., 0.9999 Silver 0.2715 oz. ASW, 28 mm. **Ruler:** Elizabeth II **Subject:** Mother Ice

Date	Mintage	VF20	XF40	MS60	MS63
2013	6,500	PF63 130	PF65 140		

KM# 1497 5 DOLLARS
7.80 g., 0.999 Gold 0.2489 oz. AGW, 20 mm. **Ruler:** Elizabeth II **Subject:** US / Canada Devil's Brigade **Rev:** Special Forces Emblem

Date	Mintage	VF20	XF40	MS60	MS63
2013	2,000	PF65 650			

KM# 1498 5 DOLLARS
23.17 g., 0.9999 Silver 0.7401 oz. ASW, 36 mm. **Ruler:** Elizabeth II **Subject:** US / Canada Devil's Brigade **Rev:** Special Forces Emblem

Date	Mintage	VF20	XF40	MS60	MS63
2013	20,000	PF63 70.00	PF66 80.00		

KM# 1534 5 DOLLARS
23.00 g., 0.999 Silver 0.734 oz. ASW, 36 mm. **Ruler:** Elizabeth II **Subject:** Traditional Hunting - Bison **Rev:** Natives advancing upon Bison herd in distance

Date	Mintage	VF20	XF40	MS60	MS63
2013	10,000	PF63 65.00	PF65 70.00		

KM# 1543 5 DOLLARS
3.13 g., 0.999 Gold 0.0999 oz. AGW, 16 mm. **Ruler:** Elizabeth II **Subject:** Oh Canada **Rev:** Orca surfacing

Date	Mintage	VF20	XF40	MS60	MS63
2013	4,000	PF65 275			

KM# 1551 5 DOLLARS
Silver ASW **Ruler:** Elizabeth II **Subject:** Banknote design

Date	Mintage	VF20	XF40	MS60	MS63
2013 Proof	—	—	—	—	

KM# 1559 5 DOLLARS
23.00 g., 0.9999 Silver 0.7346 oz. ASW, 36 mm. **Ruler:** Elizabeth II **Rev:** St. George slaying dragon

Date	Mintage	VF20	XF40	MS60	MS63
2014	8,500	PF63 65.00	PF65 75.00		

KM# 1611 5 DOLLARS
3.13 g., 0.999 Gold 0.0999 oz. AGW, 16 mm. **Ruler:** Elizabeth II **Obv:** Bust right **Rev:** Grizzly bear

Date	Mintage	VF20	XF40	MS60	MS63
2014	4,000	PF65 280			

KM# 1615 5 DOLLARS
23.17 g., 0.999 Silver 0.7394 oz. ASW, 36.07 mm. **Ruler:** Elizabeth II **Subject:** Traditions of the Hunt - Seal Spearing **Obv:** Bust right **Rev:** Two men ready to spear seal

Date	Mintage	VF20	XF40	MS60	MS63
2014	10,000	PF63 60.00	PF65 70.00		

KM# 515 8 DOLLARS
28.80 g., 0.925 Silver 0.851 oz. ASW, 39 mm. **Ruler:** Elizabeth II **Obv:** Head right **Rev:** Grizzly bear walking left **Edge:** Reeded

Date	Mintage	VF20	XF40	MS60	MS63
2004	12,942	PF65 85.00			

KM# 597 8 DOLLARS
32.15 g., 0.999 Silver 1.0269 oz. ASW **Ruler:** Elizabeth II **Subject:** Canadian Pacific Railway, 120th Anniversary **Obv:** Head right **Rev:** Railway bridge, center is gilt

Date	Mintage	VF20	XF40	MS60	MS63
2005	9,892	PF63 60.00	PF65 65.00		

KM# 598 8 DOLLARS
32.15 g., 0.9999 Silver 1.0269 oz. ASW **Ruler:** Elizabeth II **Subject:** Canadian Pacific Railway, 120th Anniversary **Obv:** Head right **Rev:** Railway memorial to the Chinese workers, center gilt

Date	Mintage	VF20	XF40	MS60	MS63
2005	9,892	PF63 60.00	PF65 65.00		

KM# 730 8 DOLLARS
25.18 g., 0.9999 Silver 0.8043 oz. ASW, 36.07 mm. **Ruler:** Elizabeth II **Obv:** Queens's head at top in circle, three Chinese characters **Rev:** Dragon and other creatures

Date	Mintage	VF20	XF40	MS60	MS63
2007	19,996	PF63 45.00	PF65 50.00		

KM# 731 8 DOLLARS
25.18 g., 0.999 Silver 0.8035 oz. ASW, 36.1 mm. **Ruler:** Elizabeth II **Rev:** Maple leaf, long life hologram

Date	Mintage	VF20	XF40	MS60	MS63
2007	15,000	PF65 55.00			

KM# 943 8 DOLLARS
25.18 g., 0.925 Silver 0.744 oz. ASW, 36.1 mm. **Ruler:** Elizabeth II **Rev:** Hologram maple of wisdom at top left, crystal in center, dragons around

Date	Mintage	VF20	XF40	MS60	MS63
2009	7,273	PF63 85.00	PF65 90.00		

KM# 1012 8 DOLLARS
25.30 g., 0.925 Silver 0.7476 oz. ASW, 36.07 mm. **Ruler:** Elizabeth II **Rev:** Horses around central maple leaf hologram

Date	Mintage	VF20	XF40	MS60	MS63
2010	8,888	PF63 90.00	PF65 100		

KM# 1535 8 DOLLARS
46.65 g., 0.999 Silver 1.4887 oz. ASW, 38 mm. **Ruler:** Elizabeth II **Rev:** Polar bear advancing left

Date	Mintage	VF20	XF40	MS60	MS63
2013	PF65 125				

KM# 520 10 DOLLARS
16.72 g., 0.900 Gold 0.4807 oz. AGW, 26.92 mm. **Ruler:** Elizabeth II **Obv:** Crowned head right **Rev:** National arms **Edge:** Reeded

Date	Mintage	VF20	XF40	MS60	MS63
1912-2002	2,002	PF65 850			

KM# 559 10 DOLLARS
25.18 g., 0.9999 Silver 0.8041 oz. ASW, 36 mm. **Ruler:** Elizabeth II **Subject:** Pope John Paul II **Obv:** Head right

Date	Mintage	VF20	XF40	MS60	MS63
2005	24,716	PF63 40.00	PF65 45.00		

KM# 757 10 DOLLARS
25.18 g., 0.9999 Silver 0.8041 oz. ASW **Ruler:** Elizabeth II **Subject:** Year of the Veteran **Rev:** Profile left of young and old veteran

Date	Mintage	VF20	XF40	MS60	MS63
2005	6,549	PF65 225			

KM# 661 10 DOLLARS
25.18 g., 0.9999 Silver 0.8041 oz. ASW **Ruler:** Elizabeth II **Subject:** National Historic Sites **Obv:** Head right **Rev:** Fortress of Louisbourg

Date	Mintage	VF20	XF40	MS60	MS63
2006	5,544	PF63 35.00	PF65 40.00		

KM# 1010 10 DOLLARS
15.87 g., 0.999 Silver 0.5064 oz. ASW **Ruler:** Elizabeth II **Subject:** 75th Anniversary Canadian Bank Notes **Rev:** Female seated

Date	Mintage	VF20	XF40	MS60	MS63
2010	7,500	PF63 45.00	PF65 50.00		

KM# 1096 10 DOLLARS
27.78 g., 0.925 Silver 0.8208 oz. ASW, 40 mm. **Ruler:** Elizabeth II **Obv:** Bust right **Rev:** Blue whale diving in sea

Date	Mintage	VF20	XF40	MS60	MS63
2010	10,000	PF63 75.00	PF65 85.00		

KM# 1199 10 DOLLARS
15.87 g., 0.9999 Silver 0.5069 oz. ASW, 34 mm. **Ruler:** Elizabeth II **Subject:** Winter Scene - Skating **Rev:** Three kids skating on pond, colored holly at left

Date	Mintage	VF20	XF40	MS60	MS63
2011	Est. 8000	PF63 35.00	PF65 40.00		

KM# 1198 10 DOLLARS
15.87 g., 0.999 Silver 0.5064 oz. ASW, 34 mm. **Ruler:** Elizabeth II **Subject:** Highway of Heroes **Obv:** Bust right **Rev:** Citizens on Highway 401 overpass with signs and flags, large maple leaf in background, Memorial Cross medal at top left. **Edge:** Reeded

Date	Mintage	VF20	XF40	MS60	MS63
2011	25,000	PF63 60.00	PF65 70.00		

KM# 1200 10 DOLLARS
15.87 g., 0.9999 Silver 0.5069 oz. ASW, 34 mm. **Ruler:** Elizabeth II **Subject:** Winter scene - Two houses **Rev:** Two houses in snowy lane, colored holly flanking

Date	Mintage	VF20	XF40	MS60	MS63
2011	—	PF63 35.00	PF65 40.00		

KM# 1201 10 DOLLARS
15.87 g., 0.9999 Silver 0.5069 oz. ASW, 34 mm. **Ruler:** Elizabeth II **Obv:** Bust right **Rev:** Wood Bison

Date	Mintage	VF20	XF40	MS60	MS63
2011	Est. 10000	PF63 40.00	PF65 50.00		

KM# 1203 10 DOLLARS
15.87 g., 0.9999 Silver 0.5069 oz. ASW, 34 mm. **Ruler:** Elizabeth II **Subject:** Boreal Forest **Rev:** Bird and tree

Date	Mintage	VF20	XF40	MS60	MS63
2011	Est. 10000	PF63 40.00	PF65 50.00		

KM# 1205 10 DOLLARS
15.87 g., 0.9999 Silver 0.5069 oz. ASW, 34 mm. **Ruler:** Elizabeth II **Obv:** Bust right **Rev:** Peregrine Falcon perched on branch

Date	Mintage	VF20	XF40	MS60	MS63
2011	Est. 10000	PF63 40.00	PF65 50.00		

KM# 1207 10 DOLLARS
15.87 g., 0.9999 Silver 0.5069 oz. ASW, 34 mm. **Ruler:** Elizabeth II **Obv:** Bust right **Rev:** Orca Whale

Date	Mintage	VF20	XF40	MS60	MS63
2011	Est. 10000	PF63 40.00	PF65 50.00		

KM# 1221 10 DOLLARS
15.87 g., 0.999 Silver 0.5064 oz. ASW, 34 mm. **Ruler:** Elizabeth II **Subject:** Year of the Dragon **Obv:** Bust right **Rev:** Dragon forepart right

Date	Mintage	VF20	XF40	MS60	MS63
2012 Specimen	58,888	—	—	—	40.00

KM# 1235 10 DOLLARS
25.18 g., 0.999 Silver 0.8034 oz. ASW, 36 mm. **Ruler:** Elizabeth II **Obv:** Bust right **Rev:** Titanic sailing at right, map of Eastern Canada at left

Date	Mintage	VF20	XF40	MS60	MS63
2012	—	PF63 90.00	PF65 100		

KM# 1249 10 DOLLARS
15.87 g., 0.999 Silver 0.5064 oz. ASW, 34 mm. **Ruler:** Elizabeth II **Subject:** H.M.S. Shannon

Date	Mintage	VF20	XF40	MS60	MS63
2012	—	PF63 55.00	PF65 65.00		

KM# 1259 10 DOLLARS
15.87 g., 0.999 Silver 0.5064 oz. ASW, 34 mm. **Ruler:** Elizabeth II **Subject:** Praying Mantis

Date	Mintage	VF20	XF40	MS60	MS63
2012	—	PF63 40.00	PF65 45.00		

KM# 1282 10 DOLLARS
7.77 g., 0.999 Gold 0.248 oz. AGW, 20 mm. **Ruler:** Elizabeth II **Subject:** Year of the Dragon

Date	Mintage	VF20	XF40	MS60	MS63
2012	—	PF65 450			

KM# 1346 10 DOLLARS
15.55 g., 0.999 Silver 0.4962 oz. ASW, 34 mm. **Ruler:** Elizabeth II **Rev:** Baby's feet

Date	Mintage	VF20	XF40	MS60	MS63
2012 Specimen	—	—	—	—	27.50
2013	—	—	—	—	27.50

KM# 1299 10 DOLLARS
31.11 g., 0.999 Silver 0.9926 oz. ASW, 34 mm. **Ruler:** Elizabeth II **Subject:** Year of the Snake

Date	Mintage	VF20	XF40	MS60	MS63
2013	—	PF65 50.00			

KM# 1355 10 DOLLARS
30.00 g., 0.999 Silver 0.9574 oz. ASW, 36.5 mm. **Ruler:** Elizabeth II **Rev:** Male and female mallards in color

Date	Mintage	VF20	XF40	MS60	MS63
2013	—	PF63 75.00	PF65 85.00		

KM# 1357 10 DOLLARS
15.87 g., 0.999 Silver 0.5064 oz. ASW, 34 mm. **Ruler:** Elizabeth II **Subject:** Year of the Snake **Rev:** Circular coiled snake

Date	Mintage	VF20	XF40	MS60	MS63
2013	18,888	PF63 40.00	PF65 45.00		

KM# 1383 10 DOLLARS
15.87 g., 0.999 Silver 0.5064 oz. ASW, 34 mm. **Ruler:** Elizabeth II **Subject:** Ice Skating on Frozen Lake **Rev:** Winter Scene in Color

Date	Mintage	VF20	XF40	MS60	MS63
2013	Est. 8000	PF63 55.00	PF65 65.00		

KM# 1392 10 DOLLARS
15.87 g., 0.999 Silver 0.5064 oz. ASW, 35 mm. **Ruler:** Elizabeth II **Subject:** Oh Canada - R.C.M.P. **Rev:** Mountie on horseback

Date	Mintage	VF20	XF40	MS60	MS63
2013	—	PF63 32.00	PF65 40.00		

KM# 1392a 10 DOLLARS
15.87 g., 0.999 Silver 0.5064 oz. ASW, 35 mm. **Ruler:** Elizabeth II **Subject:** Oh Canada - R.C.M.P. **Rev:** Mountie on horseback

Date	Mintage	VF20	XF40	MS60	MS63
2013	PF63 65.00	PF65 75.00			

KM# 1393 10 DOLLARS
15.87 g., 0.999 Silver 0.5064 oz. ASW, 34 mm. **Ruler:** Elizabeth II **Rev:** Twelve Spotted Skimmer Dragonfly in color

Date	Mintage	VF20	XF40	MS60	MS63
2013	Est. 10000	PF63 70.00	PF65 80.00		

KM# 1396 10 DOLLARS
15.87 g., 0.9999 Silver 0.5069 oz. ASW, 34 mm. **Ruler:**
Elizabeth II **Rev:** Bever Felling Tree

Date	Mintage	VF20	XF40	MS60	MS63
2013	Est. 40000	PF63 35.00	PF65 40.00		

KM# 1396a 10 DOLLARS
15.87 g., 0.999 Silver 0.5064 oz. ASW, 34 mm. **Ruler:** Elizabeth
II **Subject:** Oh Canada - Beaver **Rev:** Beaver knawing on tree

Date	Mintage	VF20	XF40	MS60	MS63
2013	PF63 65.00	PF65 75.00			

KM# 1400 10 DOLLARS
15.87 g., 0.999 Silver 0.5064 oz. ASW, 34 mm. **Ruler:** Elizabeth
II **Rev:** Stone formation at sea side

Date	Mintage	VF20	XF40	MS60	MS63
2013	40,000	PF63 35.00	PF65 40.00		

KM# 1400a 10 DOLLARS
15.87 g., 0.999 Silver 0.5064 oz. ASW, 34 mm. **Ruler:** Elizabeth
II **Subject:** Oh Canada **Rev:** Stone formation at sea side

Date	Mintage	VF20	XF40	MS60	MS63
2013	PF63 65.00	PF65 75.00			

KM# 1402 10 DOLLARS
15.57 g., 0.999 Silver 0.4969 oz. ASW, 34 mm. **Ruler:** Elizabeth
II **Rev:** Polar Bear walking right

Date	Mintage	VF20	XF40	MS60	MS63
2013	—	PF63 35.00	PF65 40.00		

KM# 1402a 10 DOLLARS
15.57 g., 0.999 Silver 0.4969 oz. ASW **Ruler:** Elizabeth II
Subject: Oh Canada **Rev:** Polar bear advancing right

Date	Mintage	VF20	XF40	MS60	MS63
2013	PF63 65.00	PF65 75.00			

KM# 1421 10 DOLLARS
15.87 g., 0.9999 Silver 0.5069 oz. ASW, 34 mm. **Ruler:**
Elizabeth II **Rev:** Caribou

Date	Mintage	VF20	XF40	MS60	MS63
2013	Est. 40000	PF63 25.00	PF65 30.00		

KM# 1421a 10 DOLLARS
15.87 g., 0.9999 Silver 0.5069 oz. ASW, 34 mm. **Ruler:**
Elizabeth II **Subject:** Oh Canada **Rev:** Caribou

Date	Mintage	VF20	XF40	MS60	MS63
2013	PF63 65.00	PF65 75.00			

KM# 1422 10 DOLLARS
15.87 g., 0.9999 Silver 0.5069 oz. ASW, 34 mm. **Ruler:**
Elizabeth II **Rev:** Niagra Falls

Date	Mintage	VF20	XF40	MS60	MS63
2013	Est. 40000	PF63 32.00	PF65 40.00		

KM# 1422a 10 DOLLARS
15.87 g., 0.9999 Silver 0.5069 oz. ASW, 34 mm. **Ruler:**
Elizabeth II **Subject:** Oh Canada **Rev:** Niagra Falls

Date	Mintage	VF20	XF40	MS60	MS63
2013	PF63 65.00	PF65 75.00			

KM# 1423 10 DOLLARS
15.57 g., 0.9999 Silver 0.4973 oz. ASW, 34 mm. **Ruler:**
Elizabeth II **Rev:** Summer lake swimming

Date	Mintage	VF20	XF40	MS60	MS63
2013	Est. 40000	PF63 32.00	PF65 40.00		

KM# 1423a 10 DOLLARS
15.87 g., 0.9999 Silver 0.5069 oz. ASW, 34 mm. **Ruler:**
Elizabeth II **Subject:** Oh Canada **Rev:** Summertime lake
swimming

Date	Mintage	VF20	XF40	MS60	MS63
2013	PF63 65.00	PF65 75.00			

KM# 1424 10 DOLLARS
15.87 g., 0.9999 Silver 0.5069 oz. ASW, 34 mm. **Ruler:**
Elizabeth II **Rev:** Hand holding three Fall colored maple leaves

Date	Mintage	VF20	XF40	MS60	MS63
2013	Est. 40000	PF63 32.00	PF65 40.00		

KM# 1424a 10 DOLLARS
15.87 g., 0.9999 Silver 0.5069 oz. ASW, 34 mm. **Ruler:**
Elizabeth II **Subject:** Oh Canada **Rev:** Hand holding three
color maple leaves

Date	Mintage	VF20	XF40	MS60	MS63
2013	PF63 65.00	PF65 75.00			

KM# 1425 10 DOLLARS
15.87 g., 0.9999 Silver 0.5069 oz. ASW, 34 mm. **Ruler:**
Elizabeth II **Rev:** Outdoor ice hockey rink

Date	Mintage	VF20	XF40	MS60	MS63
2013	Est. 40000	PF63 32.00	PF65 40.00		

KM# 1425a 10 DOLLARS
15.87 g., 0.9999 Silver 0.5069 oz. ASW, 34 mm. **Ruler:**
Elizabeth II **Subject:** Oh Canada **Rev:** Winter ice rink

Date	Mintage	VF20	XF40	MS60	MS63
2013	PF63 65.00	PF65 75.00			

KM# 1442 10 DOLLARS
15.87 g., 0.999 Silver 0.5064 oz. ASW, 34 mm. **Ruler:** Elizabeth II **Obv:** Bust right **Rev:** Dreamcatcher in color **Edge:** Reeded

Date	Mintage	F12	VF20	XF40	MS60	MS63
2013	10,000	PF63 70.00		PF65 80.00		

KM# 1445 10 DOLLARS
7.06 g., 0.999 Silver 0.2253 oz. ASW, 27 mm. **Ruler:** Elizabeth II **Subject:** 75th Anniversary of Superman **Rev:** Superman breaking chains **Rev. Legend:** Joe Shuster, DC Comics

Date	Mintage	VF20	XF40	MS60	MS63
2013	Est. 15000	PF63 40.00		PF65 45.00	

KM# 1455 10 DOLLARS
15.57 g., 0.999 Silver 0.4969 oz. ASW, 34 mm. **Ruler:** Elizabeth II **Rev:** Wolf standing right

Date	Mintage	VF20	XF40	MS60	MS63
2013	Est. 40000	PF63 35.00		PF65 40.00	

KM# 1455a 10 DOLLARS
15.57 g., 0.999 Silver 0.4969 oz. ASW **Ruler:** Elizabeth II **Rev:** Wolf standing right

Date	Mintage	VF20	XF40	MS60	MS63
2013		PF63 65.00		PF65 75.00	

KM# 1529 10 DOLLARS
15.87 g., 0.999 Silver 0.5064 oz. ASW, 34 mm. **Ruler:** Elizabeth II **Rev:** Three red candles

Date	Mintage	VF20	XF40	MS60	MS63
2013	10,000	PF63 55.00		PF65 65.00	

KM# 1530 10 DOLLARS
15.87 g., 0.999 Silver 0.5064 oz. ASW, 34 mm. **Ruler:** Elizabeth II **Rev:** Partridge in a pear tree, colored greens below

Date	Mintage	VF20	XF40	MS60	MS63
2013	10,000	PF63 55.00		PF65 65.00	

KM# 1533 10 DOLLARS
15.87 g., 0.999 Silver 0.5064 oz. ASW, 34 mm. **Ruler:** Elizabeth II **Subject:** World Cup, 2014 **Rev:** Soccer player, maple leaf, fans

Date	Mintage	VF20	XF40	MS60	MS63
2013	10,000	PF63 50.00		PF65 55.00	

KM# 1536 10 DOLLARS
15.87 g., 0.999 Silver 0.5064 oz. ASW, 34 mm. **Ruler:** Elizabeth II **Subject:** Oh Canada - Holiday season **Rev:** Sleigh and Christmas Tree

Date	Mintage	VF20	XF40	MS60	MS63
2013	40,000	PF63 35.00		PF65 40.00	

KM# 1536a 10 DOLLARS
15.87 g., 0.999 Silver 0.5064 oz. ASW, 34 mm. **Ruler:** Elizabeth II **Subject:** Oh Canada - Holiday Season **Rev:** Sleigh and tree

Date	Mintage	VF20	XF40	MS60	MS63
2013		PF63 65.00		PF65 75.00	

KM# 1540 10 DOLLARS
15.870 Silver ASW, 34 mm. **Ruler:** Elizabeth II **Subject:** Oh Canada **Rev:** Orca surfacing

Date	Mintage	VF20	XF40	MS60	MS63
2013	40,000	PF63 35.00		PF65 40.00	

KM# 1540a 10 DOLLARS
15.87 g., 0.999 Silver 0.5064 oz. ASW, 34 mm. **Ruler:** Elizabeth II **Subject:** Oh Canada **Rev:** Orca surfacing

Date	Mintage	VF20	XF40	MS60	MS63
2013		PF63 65.00		PF65 75.00	

KM# 1546 10 DOLLARS
30.00 g., 0.999 Silver 0.9574 oz. ASW, 36.5 mm. **Ruler:** Elizabeth II **Rev:** Wood Ducks

Date	Mintage	VF20	XF40	MS60	MS63
2013		PF63 75.00		PF65 85.00	

KM# 1517 10 DOLLARS
15.87 g., 0.9999 Silver 0.5069 oz. ASW, 34 mm. **Ruler:** Elizabeth II **Subject:** Year of the Horse **Rev:** Horse head left

Date	Mintage	VF20	XF40	MS60	MS63
2014	58,888	PF63 35.00		PF65 40.00	

KM# 1580 10 DOLLARS
15.87 g., 0.999 Silver 0.5064 oz. ASW, 34 mm. **Ruler:** Elizabeth II **Obv:** Bust right **Rev:** Igloo

Date	Mintage	VF20	XF40	MS60	MS63
2014		PF63 55.00		PF65 65.00	

KM# 1590 10 DOLLARS
15.87 g., 0.999 Silver 0.5064 oz. ASW, 34 mm. **Ruler:** Elizabeth II **Obv:** Bust right **Rev:** Adult teaching child how to ice skate, in color

Date	Mintage	VF20	XF40	MS60	MS63
2014		PF63 50.00		PF65 60.00	

KM# 1607 10 DOLLARS
15.87 g., 0.999 Silver 0.5064 oz. ASW, 34 mm. **Ruler:** Elizabeth II **Rev:** Pintail ducks in color

Date	Mintage	VF20	XF40	MS60	MS63
2014	10,000	—	—	—	35.00

KM# 1612 10 DOLLARS
15.87 g., 0.999 Silver 0.5064 oz. ASW, 34 mm. **Ruler:** Elizabeth II **Obv:** Bust right **Rev:** Grizzly bear left

Date	Mintage	VF20	XF40	MS60	MS63
2014	40,000	PF63 35.00	PF65 40.00		

KM# 1613 10 DOLLARS
0.999 Silver ASW, 34 mm. **Ruler:** Elizabeth II **Subject:** World War I - Mobilization of a nation **Obv:** Bust right **Rev:** Soldier with gear walking up ship's gangway

Date	Mintage	VF20	XF40	MS60	MS63
2014	40,000	PF63 40.00	PF65 45.00		

KM# 1625 10 DOLLARS
15.87 g., 0.999 Silver 0.5064 oz. ASW, 34 mm. **Ruler:** Elizabeth II **Obv:** Bust right **Rev:** Downhill skiing

Date	Mintage	VF20	XF40	MS60	MS63
2014	40,000	PF63 35.00	PF65 40.00		

KM# 1629 10 DOLLARS
0.999 Silver ASW, 34 mm. **Ruler:** Elizabeth II **Obv:** Bust right **Rev:** Two baby's feet

Date	Mintage	VF20	XF40	MS60	MS63
2014	—	PF63 45.00	PF65 50.00		

KM# 415 15 DOLLARS
33.63 g., 0.925 Silver 0.9937 oz. ASW, 40 mm. **Ruler:** Elizabeth II **Subject:** Year of the Snake **Obv:** Crowned head right **Rev:** Snake within circle of lunar calendar signs **Edge:** Reeded

Date	Mintage	VF20	XF40	MS60	MS63
2001	—	PF63 75.00	PF65 85.00		

KM# 463 15 DOLLARS
33.63 g., 0.925 Silver 0.9937 oz. ASW **Ruler:** Elizabeth II **Subject:** Year of the Horse **Obv:** Crowned head right **Rev:** Horse in center with Chinese Lunar calendar around

Date	Mintage	VF20	XF40	MS60	MS63
2002	59,395	PF63 75.00	PF65 85.00		

KM# 481 15 DOLLARS
33.63 g., 0.925 Silver 0.9937 oz. ASW, 40 mm. **Ruler:** Elizabeth II **Subject:** Year of the Sheep **Obv:** Crowned head right **Rev:** Sheep in center with Chinese Lunar calendar around

Date	Mintage	VF20	XF40	MS60	MS63
2003	53,714	PF63 75.00	PF65 85.00		

KM# 610 15 DOLLARS
33.63 g., 0.925 Silver 0.9937 oz. ASW **Ruler:** Elizabeth II **Subject:** Year of the Monkey **Obv:** Crowned head right **Rev:** Monkey in center with Chinese Lunar calendar around

Date	Mintage	VF20	XF40	MS60	MS63
2004	46,175	PF65 150			

KM# 560 15 DOLLARS
33.63 g., 0.925 Silver 0.9937 oz. ASW **Ruler:** Elizabeth II **Subject:** Year of the Rooster **Obv:** Crowned head right **Rev:** Rooster in center with Chinese Lunar calendar around

Date	Mintage	VF20	XF40	MS60	MS63
2005	44,690	PF65 125			

KM# 587 15 DOLLARS
33.63 g., 0.925 Silver 0.9937 oz. ASW **Ruler:** Elizabeth II **Subject:** Year of the Dog **Obv:** Crowned head left **Rev:** Dog in center with Chinese Lunar calendar around

Date	Mintage	VF20	XF40	MS60	MS63
2006	41,617	PF63 85.00	PF65 100		

KM# 732 15 DOLLARS
33.63 g., 0.925 Silver 0.9937 oz. ASW, 40 mm. **Ruler:** Elizabeth II **Subject:** Year of the Pig **Rev:** Pig at center of lunar characters

Date	Mintage	VF20	XF40	MS60	MS63
2007	48,888	PF63 90.00	PF65 100		

KM# 801 15 DOLLARS
33.63 g., 0.925 Silver 0.9937 oz. ASW, 40 mm. **Ruler:** Elizabeth II **Subject:** Year of the Rat **Rev:** Rat, gold octagonal insert at center

Date	Mintage	VF20	XF40	MS60	MS63
2008	48,888	PF63 80.00	PF65 90.00		

KM# 803 15 DOLLARS
30.00 g., 0.925 Silver 0.8864 oz. ASW, 36.15 mm. **Ruler:** Elizabeth II **Rev:** Queen Victoria's coinage portrait

Date	Mintage	VF20	XF40	MS60	MS63
2008	3,442	—	—		100

KM# 804 15 DOLLARS
30.00 g., 0.925 Silver 0.8864 oz. ASW, 36.15 mm. **Ruler:** Elizabeth II **Rev:** Edward VII coinage portrait

Date	Mintage	VF20	XF40	MS60	MS63
2008	6,261	—	—		100

KM# 805 15 DOLLARS
20.00 g., 0.925 Silver 0.591 oz. ASW, 36.15 mm. **Ruler:** Elizabeth II **Rev:** George V coinage portrait

Date	Mintage	VF20	XF40	MS60	MS63
2008	—	—	—		100

KM# 806 15 DOLLARS
31.56 g., 0.925 Silver 0.9325 oz. ASW, 49.8 x 28.6 mm. **Ruler:** Elizabeth II **Rev:** Queen of Spades, multicolor playing card

Date	Mintage	VF20	XF40	MS60	MS63
2008	8,714	PF63 80.00	PF65 90.00		

KM# 807 15 DOLLARS
31.56 g., 0.925 Silver 0.9325 oz. ASW, 28.6x49.8 mm. **Ruler:** Elizabeth II **Rev:** Jack of Hearts, multicolor playing card

Date	Mintage	VF20	XF40	MS60	MS63
2008	11,362	PF63 75.00	PF65 85.00		

KM# 919 15 DOLLARS
31.56 g., 0.925 Silver 0.9325 oz. ASW, 49.8 x 28.6 mm. **Ruler:** Elizabeth II **Obv:** Bust right **Rev:** Ten of spades, multicolor **Shape:** rectangle

Date	Mintage	VF20	XF40	MS60	MS63
2009	5,921	PF63 140	PF65 150		

KM# 920 15 DOLLARS
31.56 g., 0.925 Silver 0.9325 oz. ASW, 49.8 x 28.6 mm. **Ruler:**

Elizabeth II **Obv:** Bust right **Rev:** King of hearts, multicolor **Shape:** Rectangle

Date	Mintage	VF20	XF40	MS60	MS63
2009	5,798	PF63 110	PF65 120		

KM# 866 15 DOLLARS
33.63 g., 0.925 Silver 0.9937 oz. ASW, 40 mm. **Ruler:** Elizabeth II **Subject:** Year of the Ox **Rev:** Ox, octagon gold insert

Date	Mintage	VF20	XF40	MS60	MS63
2009	48,888	PF63 80.00	PF65 90.00		

KM# 922 15 DOLLARS
30.00 g., 0.925 Silver 0.8864 oz. ASW, 36.15 mm. **Ruler:** Elizabeth II **Obv:** Bust right **Rev:** Paget portrait of George VI

Date	Mintage	VF20	XF40	MS60	MS63
2009(ml) Prooflike	—	—	—	—	100

KM# 923 15 DOLLARS
30.00 g., 0.925 Silver 0.8864 oz. ASW, 36.15 mm. **Ruler:** Elizabeth II **Obv:** Bust right **Rev:** Gillick portrait of Queen Elizabeth II

Date	Mintage	VF20	XF40	MS60	MS63
2009(ml) Prooflike	2,643	—	—	—	100

KM# 1038 15 DOLLARS
Silver, 38 mm. **Ruler:** Elizabeth II **Subject:** Year of the tiger **Rev:** Tiger in forest **Shape:** scalloped

Date	Mintage	VF20	XF40	MS60	MS63
2009	10,268	PF63 75.00	PF65 85.00		

KM# 980 15 DOLLARS
34.00 g., 0.925 Silver 1.0046 oz. ASW, 40 mm. **Ruler:** Elizabeth II **Rev:** Tiger in gold insert

Date	Mintage	VF20	XF40	MS60	MS63
2010	48,888	PF63 90.00	PF65 100		

KM# 1032 15 DOLLARS
0.999 Silver **Ruler:** Elizabeth II **Subject:** Year of the tiger **Rev:** Tiger walking tiger

Date	Mintage	VF20	XF40	MS60	MS63
2010	9,999	PF63 75.00	PF65 85.00		

KM# 1055 15 DOLLARS
31.11 g., 0.999 Silver 0.9926 oz. ASW, 38 mm. **Ruler:** Elizabeth II **Rev:** Rabbit sitting, head turned left **Shape:** scalloped

Date	Mintage	VF20	XF40	MS60	MS63
2011	19,888	PF63 75.00	PF65 85.00		

KM# 1091 15 DOLLARS
25.11 g., 0.925 Silver 0.742 oz. ASW, 36.15 mm. **Ruler:** Elizabeth II **Rev:** Prince Charles bust

Date	Mintage	VF20	XF40	MS60	MS63
2011 Prooflike	10,000				110

KM# 1092 15 DOLLARS
25.11 g., 0.925 Silver 0.742 oz. ASW, 36.15 mm. **Ruler:** Elizabeth II **Rev:** Prince William

Date	Mintage	VF20	XF40	MS60	MS63
2011 Prooflike	10,000				110

KM# 1093 15 DOLLARS
25.18 g., 0.925 Silver 0.744 oz. ASW, 36.15 mm. **Ruler:** Elizabeth II **Rev:** Prince Harry bust 1/4 right

Date	Mintage	VF20	XF40	MS60	MS63
2011 Prooflike	10,000	—	—	—	110

KM# 1094 15 DOLLARS
31.39 g., 0.999 Silver 1.0017 oz. ASW, 38 mm. **Ruler:** Elizabeth II **Rev:** Rabbit bounding left

Date	Mintage	VF20	XF40	MS60	MS63
2011	9,999	PF63 90.00	PF65 100		

KM# 1152 15 DOLLARS
31.39 g., 0.9999 Silver 1.0026 oz. ASW, 38 mm. **Ruler:** Elizabeth II **Obv:** Bust right **Rev:** Magpie, bird of happyness in flight at top, lotus flowers at bottom, maple leaf hologram at center

Date	Mintage	VF20	XF40	MS60	MS63
2011	—	PF63 90.00	PF65 100		

KM# 1183 15 DOLLARS
31.11 g., 0.999 Silver 0.9926 oz. ASW, 36.5 mm. **Ruler:** Elizabeth II **Subject:** Year of the Dragon **Obv:** Bust right **Rev:** Dragon right

Date	Mintage	VF20	XF40	MS60	MS63
2012	—	PF63 65.00	PF65 75.00		

KM# 1186 15 DOLLARS
31.11 g., 0.999 Silver 0.9926 oz. ASW, 36.5 mm. **Ruler:** Elizabeth II **Subject:** Year of the Dragon **Obv:** Bust right **Rev:** Dragon left **Shape:** Scalloped

Date	Mintage	VF20	XF40	MS60	MS63
2012	—	PF63 65.00	PF65 75.00		

KM# 1260 15 DOLLARS
31.39 g., 0.999 Silver 1.0017 oz. ASW, 36.5 mm. **Ruler:** Elizabeth II **Subject:** Good Fortune **Rev:** Deer and doe froclicking around central hologram

Date	Mintage	VF20	XF40	MS60	MS63
2012	—	PF63 65.00	PF65 75.00		

KM# 1358 15 DOLLARS
31.39 g., 0.999 Silver 1.0017 oz. ASW, 36.5 mm. **Ruler:** Elizabeth II **Subject:** Year of the Snake **Rev:** Snake vertically between two Chinese characters

Date	Mintage	VF20	XF40	MS60	MS63
2013	28,888	PF65 100			

KM# 1359 15 DOLLARS
26.70 g., 0.999 Silver 0.852 oz. ASW, 38 mm. **Ruler:** Elizabeth II **Subject:** Year of the Snake **Rev:** Snake under maple leaves **Shape:** Scalloped

Date	Mintage	VF20	XF40	MS60	MS63
2013	28,888	PF63 65.00	PF65 75.00		

KM# 1439 15 DOLLARS
31.39 g., 0.9999 Silver 1.0026 oz. ASW, 38 mm. **Ruler:** Elizabeth II **Subject:** Maple of Peace **Obv:** Elephant right - Maple leaf and hologram at center

Date	Mintage	VF20	XF40	MS60	MS63
2013	Est. 8888	PF63 90.00	PF65 100		

KM# 1446 15 DOLLARS
15.87 g., 0.999 Silver 0.5064 oz. ASW, 34 mm. **Ruler:** Elizabeth II **Subject:** 75th Anniversary of Superman **Obv:** Superman in color flying forward

Date	Mintage	VF20	XF40	MS60	MS63
2013	15,000	PF63 60.00	PF65 70.00		

KM# 1514 15 DOLLARS
31.11 g., 0.9999 Silver 0.9935 oz. ASW, 38 mm. **Ruler:** Elizabeth II **Subject:** Year of the Horse **Rev:** Horse prancing left

Date	Mintage	VF20	XF40	MS60	MS63
2014	28,888	PF63 90.00	PF65 100		

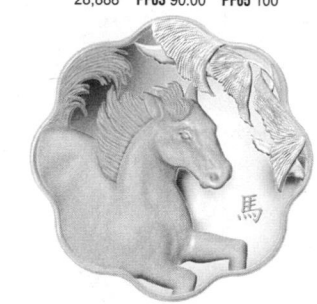

KM# 1516 15 DOLLARS
26.70 g., 0.999 (No Composition) 0.852 oz., 38 mm. **Ruler:** Elizabeth II **Subject:** Year of the Horse **Rev:** Horse forepart right **Shape:** Scalloped

Date	Mintage	VF20	XF40	MS60	MS63
2014	2,888	PF63 90.00	PF65 100		

KM# 411 20 DOLLARS
31.10 g., 0.925 Silver 0.919 oz. ASW, 38 mm. **Ruler:** Elizabeth II **Subject:** Transportation - Steam Locomotive **Obv:** Crowned head right **Rev:** First Canadian Steel Steam Locomotive and cameo hologram **Edge:** Segmented reeding

Date	Mintage	VF20	XF40	MS60	MS63
2001	15,000	PF63 35.00	PF65 45.00		

KM# 427 20 DOLLARS
31.10 g., 0.925 Silver 0.919 oz. ASW, 38 mm. **Ruler:** Elizabeth II **Series:** Transportation - The Marco Polo **Obv:** Crowned head right **Rev:** Sailship with hologram cameo **Edge:** Segmented reeding

Date	Mintage	VF20	XF40	MS60	MS63
2001	15,000	PF63 35.00	PF65 45.00		

KM# 428 20 DOLLARS
31.10 g., 0.925 Silver 0.919 oz. ASW, 38 mm. **Ruler:** Elizabeth II **Series:** Transportation - Russell Touring Car **Obv:** Crowned head right **Rev:** Russell touring car with hologram cameo **Edge:** Segmented reeding

Date	Mintage	VF20	XF40	MS60	MS63
2001	15,000	PF63 35.00	PF65 45.00		

KM# 464 20 DOLLARS
31.10 g., 0.925 Silver 0.919 oz. ASW **Ruler:** Elizabeth II **Obv:** Crowned head right **Rev:** Gray-Dort Model 25-SM with cameo hologram

Date	Mintage	VF20	XF40	MS60	MS63
2002	15,000	PF63 35.00	PF65 45.00		

KM# 465 20 DOLLARS
31.10 g., 0.925 Silver 0.919 oz. ASW **Ruler:** Elizabeth II **Obv:** Crowned head right **Rev:** Sailing ship William D. Lawrence

Date	Mintage	VF20	XF40	MS60	MS63
2002	15,000	PF63 35.00	PF65 45.00		

KM# 482 20 DOLLARS
31.39 g., 0.9999 Silver 1.0026 oz. ASW, 38 mm. **Ruler:** Elizabeth II **Obv:** Crowned head right **Rev:** Niagara Falls hologram

Date	Mintage	VF20	XF40	MS60	MS63
2003	29,967	PF63 65.00	PF65 75.00		

KM# 483 20 DOLLARS
31.10 g., 0.925 Silver 0.919 oz. ASW **Ruler:** Elizabeth II **Subject:** The HMCS Bras d'or (FHE-400) **Obv:** Crowned head right **Rev:** Ship in water

Date	Mintage	VF20	XF40	MS60	MS63
2003	15,000	PF63 35.00	PF65 45.00		

KM# 523 20 DOLLARS
31.39 g., 0.999 Silver 1.0017 oz. ASW, 38 mm. **Ruler:** Elizabeth II **Obv:** Crowned head right **Rev:** Canadian Rockies, multicolor

Date	Mintage	VF20	XF40	MS60	MS63
2003	29,967	PF63 45.00	PF65 50.00		

KM# 484 20 DOLLARS
31.10 g., 0.925 Silver 0.919 oz. ASW **Ruler:** Elizabeth II **Subject:** Canadian National FA-1 diesel-electric locomotive **Obv:** Crowned head right

Date	Mintage	VF20	XF40	MS60	MS63
2003	15,000	PF63 35.00	PF65 45.00		

KM# 485 20 DOLLARS
31.10 g., 0.925 Silver 0.919 oz. ASW **Ruler:** Elizabeth II **Obv:** Crowned head right **Rev:** The Bricklin SV-1

Date	Mintage	VF20	XF40	MS60	MS63
2003	15,000	PF63 35.00	PF65 45.00		

KM# 611 20 DOLLARS
31.39 g., 0.9999 Silver 1.0026 oz. ASW, 38 mm. **Ruler:** Elizabeth II **Obv:** Head right **Rev:** Iceberg, hologram

Date	Mintage	VF20	XF40	MS60	MS63
2004	24,879	PF63 40.00	PF65 45.00		

KM# 838 20 DOLLARS
31.39 g., 0.9999 Silver 1.0026 oz. ASW, 38 mm. **Ruler:** Elizabeth II **Rev:** Hopewell Rocks, gilt

Date	Mintage	VF20	XF40	MS60	MS63
2004	16.918	PF63 35.00	PF65 45.00		

KM# 561 20 DOLLARS
31.39 g., 0.9999 Silver 1.0026 oz. ASW, 38 mm. **Ruler:** Elizabeth II **Obv:** Head right **Rev:** Three-masted sailing ship, hologram of the sea

Date	Mintage	VF20	XF40	MS60	MS63
2005	18,276	PF63 50.00	PF65 55.00		

KM# 562 20 DOLLARS
31.39 g., 0.9999 Silver 1.0026 oz. ASW, 38 mm. **Ruler:** Elizabeth II **Subject:** Northwest Territories Diamonds **Obv:** Head right **Rev:** Multicolor diamond hologram on landscape **Edge:** Reeded

Date	Mintage	VF20	XF40	MS60	MS63
2005	35,000	PF63 45.00	PF65 50.00		

KM# 563 20 DOLLARS
31.39 g., 0.9999 Silver 1.0026 oz. ASW **Ruler:** Elizabeth II **Subject:** Mingan Archepelago **Obv:** Head right **Rev:** Cliffs with whale tail out of water

Date	Mintage	VF20	XF40	MS60	MS63
2005	—	PF63 470	PF65 45.00		

KM# 564 20 DOLLARS
31.39 g., 0.9999 Silver 1.0026 oz. ASW **Ruler:** Elizabeth II **Subject:** Rainforests of the Pacific Northwest **Obv:** Head right **Rev:** Open winged bird

Date	Mintage	VF20	XF40	MS60	MS63
2005	—	PF63 40.00	PF65 45.00		

KM# 565 20 DOLLARS
31.39 g., 0.9999 Silver 1.0026 oz. ASW, 38 mm. **Ruler:** Elizabeth II **Subject:** Toronto Island National Park **Obv:** Head right **Rev:** Toronto Island Lighthouse, Toronto skyline in background

Date	Mintage	VF20	XF40	MS60	MS63
2005	—	PF63 50.00	PF65 55.00		

KM# 588 20 DOLLARS
31.39 g., 0.9999 Silver 1.0026 oz. ASW **Ruler:** Elizabeth II **Subject:** Georgian Bay National Park **Obv:** Head right **Rev:** Canoe and small trees on island

Date	Mintage	VF20	XF40	MS60	MS63
2006	—	PF63 50.00	PF65 60.00		

KM# 589 20 DOLLARS
31.10 g., 0.9999 Silver 0.9934 oz. ASW, 38 mm. **Ruler:** Elizabeth II **Obv:** Head right **Rev:** Notre Dame Basilica, Montreal, as a hologram

Date	Mintage	VF20	XF40	MS60	MS63
2006	15,000	PF63 45.00	PF65 50.00		

KM# 663 20 DOLLARS
31.39 g., 0.9999 Silver 1.0026 oz. ASW, 38 mm. **Ruler:** Elizabeth II **Subject:** Nahanni National Park **Obv:** Head right **Rev:** Bear walking along sream, cliff in background

Date	Mintage	VF20	XF40	MS60	MS63
2006	—	PF63 55.00	PF65 60.00		

KM# 664 20 DOLLARS
31.39 g., 0.9999 Silver 1.0026 oz. ASW, 38 mm. **Ruler:** Elizabeth II **Subject:** Jasper National Park **Obv:** Head right **Rev:** Cowboy on horseback in majestic scene

Date	Mintage	VF20	XF40	MS60	MS63
2006	—	PF63 55.00	PF65 60.00		

KM# 665 20 DOLLARS
31.10 g., 0.9999 Silver 0.9934 oz. ASW, 38 mm. **Ruler:** Elizabeth II **Obv:** Head right **Rev:** Holographic rendering of CN Tower

Date	Mintage	VF20	XF40	MS60	MS63
2006	15,000	PF63 55.00	PF65 60.00		

KM# 666 20 DOLLARS
31.10 g., 0.9999 Silver 0.9934 oz. ASW **Ruler:** Elizabeth II **Obv:** Head right **Rev:** Holographic view of Pengrowth Saddledome in Calgary

Date	Mintage	VF20	XF40	MS60	MS63
2006	15,000	PF63 50.00	PF65 55.00		

KM# 667 20 DOLLARS
31.39 g., 0.9999 Silver 1.0026 oz. ASW **Ruler:** Elizabeth II **Subject:** Tall Ship **Obv:** Head right **Rev:** Ketch and holographic image of thunderstorm in sky

Date	Mintage	VF20	XF40	MS60	MS63
2006	10,299	PF63 55.00	PF65 60.00		

KM# 734 20 DOLLARS
31.10 g., 0.999 Silver 0.9925 oz. ASW, 38 mm. **Ruler:** Elizabeth II **Rev:** Holiday sleigh ride

Date	Mintage	VF20	XF40	MS60	MS63
2007	6,804	PF63 65.00	PF65 70.00		

KM# 735 20 DOLLARS
31.10 g., 0.999 Silver 0.9925 oz. ASW, 38 mm. **Ruler:** Elizabeth II **Rev:** Snowflake, aquamarine crystal

Date	Mintage	VF20	XF40	MS60	MS63
2007	4,989	PF65 175			

KM# 737 20 DOLLARS
31.10 g., 0.999 Silver 0.9925 oz. ASW, 38 mm. **Ruler:** Elizabeth II **Subject:** International Polar Year

Date	Mintage	VF20	XF40	MS60	MS63
2007	9,164	PF63 60.00	PF65 65.00		

KM# 737a 20 DOLLARS
27.78 g., 0.925 Silver 0.8208 oz. ASW, 40 mm. **Ruler:** Elizabeth II **Subject:** International Polar Year **Rev:** Blue plasma coating

Date	Mintage	VF20	XF40	MS60	MS63
2007	3,005	PF65 250			

KM# 738 20 DOLLARS
31.39 g., 0.9999 Silver 1.0026 oz. ASW, 38 mm. **Ruler:** Elizabeth II **Subject:** Tall ships **Rev:** Brigantine in harbor, hologram

Date	Mintage	VF20	XF40	MS60	MS63
2007	16,000	PF63 55.00	PF65 60.00		

KM# 839 20 DOLLARS
31.39 g., 0.9999 Silver 1.0026 oz. ASW **Ruler:** Elizabeth II **Rev:** Northern lights in hologram

Date	Mintage	VF20	XF40	MS60	MS63
2007	—	—	—	—	35.00

KM# 808 20 DOLLARS
31.50 g., 0.925 Silver 0.9308 oz. ASW, 38 mm. **Ruler:** Elizabeth II **Subject:** Agriculture trade **Rev:** Team of horses plowing

Date	Mintage	VF20	XF40	MS60	MS63
2008	5,802	PF63 65.00	PF65 70.00		

KM# 809 20 DOLLARS
31.11 g., 0.999 Silver 0.9926 oz. ASW, 38 mm. **Ruler:** Elizabeth II **Rev:** Royal Hudson Steam locomotive

Date	Mintage	VF20	XF40	MS60	MS63
2008	8,345	PF63 65.00	PF65 70.00		

KM# 810 20 DOLLARS
31.39 g., 0.999 Silver 1.0017 oz. ASW, 38 mm. **Ruler:** Elizabeth II **Rev:** Green leaf and crystal raindrop

Date	Mintage	VF20	XF40	MS60	MS63
2008	15,000	PF63 165	PF65 175		

KM# 811 20 DOLLARS
31.11 g., 0.999 Silver 0.9926 oz. ASW **Ruler:** Elizabeth II **Rev:** Snowflake, amethyst crystal

Date	Mintage	VF20	XF40	MS60	MS63
2008	7,172	PF63 90.00	PF65 95.00		

KM# 813 20 DOLLARS
31.11 g., 0.999 Silver 0.9926 oz. ASW, 38 mm. **Ruler:** Elizabeth II **Rev:** Carolers around tree

Date	Mintage	VF20	XF40	MS60	MS63
2008	10,000	PF63 60.00	PF65 70.00		

KM# 872 20 DOLLARS
31.11 g., 0.999 Silver 0.9926 oz. ASW, 38 mm. **Ruler:** Elizabeth II **Rev:** Snowflake, sapphire crystal

Date	Mintage	VF20	XF40	MS60	MS63
2008	7,765	PF63 90.00	PF65 95.00		

KM# 891 20 DOLLARS
31.39 g., 0.999 Silver 1.0017 oz. ASW, 38 mm. **Ruler:** Elizabeth II **Subject:** Great Canadian Locomotives - Jubilee **Obv:** Bust right **Obv. Legend:** Elizabeth II DG Regina **Rev:** Jubilee locomotive side view **Rev. Legend:** Canada 20 Dollars **Edge Lettering:** Jubilee

Date	Mintage	VF20	XF40	MS60	MS63
2009	6,036	PF63 65.00	PF65 70.00		

KM# 893 20 DOLLARS
31.39 g., 0.999 Silver 1.0017 oz. ASW, 38 mm. **Ruler:** Elizabeth II **Subject:** Coal mining trade **Obv:** Bust right **Obv. Legend:** Elizabeth II DG Regina **Rev:** Miner pushing cart with coal **Rev. Legend:** Canada 20 Dollars

Date	Mintage	VF20	XF40	MS60	MS63
2009	10,000	PF63 65.00	PF65 75.00		

KM# 870 20 DOLLARS
27.78 g., 0.925 Silver 0.8208 oz. ASW, 40 mm. **Ruler:** Elizabeth II **Rev:** Calgary Flames goalie mask multicolor on goal net

Date	Mintage	VF20	XF40	MS60	MS63
2009	10,000	PF63 60.00	PF65 70.00		

KM# 871 20 DOLLARS
27.78 g., 0.925 Silver 0.8208 oz. ASW, 40 mm. **Ruler:** Elizabeth II **Rev:** Edmonton Oilers goalie mask, multicolor on goal net

Date	Mintage	VF20	XF40	MS60	MS63
2009	10,000	PF63 60.00	PF65 70.00		

KM# 872A 20 DOLLARS
27.78 g., 0.925 Silver 0.8208 oz. ASW, 40 mm. **Ruler:** Elizabeth II **Rev:** Montreal Canadians goalie mask multicolor

Date	Mintage	VF20	XF40	MS60	MS63
2009	10,000	PF63 60.00	PF65 70.00		

KM# 873 20 DOLLARS
27.78 g., 0.925 Silver 0.8208 oz. ASW, 40 mm. **Ruler:** Elizabeth II **Rev:** Ottawa Senators goalie mask on goal net

Date	Mintage	VF20	XF40	MS60	MS63
2009	10,000	PF63 60.00	PF65 70.00		

KM# 874 20 DOLLARS
27.78 g., 0.925 Silver 0.8208 oz. ASW, 40 mm. **Ruler:** Elizabeth II **Rev:** Toronto Maple Leafs goalie mask, multicolor on goal net

Date	Mintage	VF20	XF40	MS60	MS63
2009	10,000	PF63 60.00	PF65 70.00		

KM# 875 20 DOLLARS
27.78 g., 0.925 Silver 0.8208 oz. ASW, 40 mm. **Ruler:** Elizabeth II **Rev:** Vancouver Canucks goalie mask, multicolor on goal net

Date	Mintage	VF20	XF40	MS60	MS63
2009	10,000	PF63 60.00	PF65 70.00		

KM# 876 20 DOLLARS
31.50 g., 0.925 Silver 0.9308 oz. ASW, 40 mm. **Ruler:** Elizabeth II **Rev:** Summer moon mask

Date	Mintage	VF20	XF40	MS60	MS63
2009	2,834	PF65 225			

KM# 944 20 DOLLARS
31.11 g., 0.999 Silver 0.9926 oz. ASW, 38 mm. **Ruler:** Elizabeth II **Rev:** Snowflake - light blue crystal

Date	Mintage	VF20	XF40	MS60	MS63
2009	7,477	PF63 95.00	PF65 100		

KM# 945 20 DOLLARS
31.11 g., 0.999 Silver 0.9926 oz. ASW, 38 mm. **Ruler:** Elizabeth II **Rev:** Snowflake - light red crystal

Date	Mintage	VF20	XF40	MS60	MS63
2009	7,004	PF63 95.00	PF65 100		

KM# 892 20 DOLLARS
31.39 g., 0.999 Silver 1.0017 oz. ASW, 38 mm. **Ruler:** Elizabeth II **Subject:** Crystal raindrop **Obv:** Bust right **Rev:** Maple leaf and rain drop - fall colors

Date	Mintage	VF20	XF40	MS60	MS63
2009	9,998	PF63 75.00	PF65 85.00		

KM# 987 20 DOLLARS
31.39 g., 0.9999 Silver 1.0026 oz. ASW, 38 mm. **Ruler:** Elizabeth II **Rev:** Lotus Water Lilly in multicolor and crystal

Date	Mintage	VF20	XF40	MS60	MS63
2010	10,000	PF63 110	PF65 120		

KM# 1009 20 DOLLARS
31.39 g., 0.999 Silver 1.0017 oz. ASW **Ruler:** Elizabeth II **Subject:** 75th Anniversary of Canadian Bank Notes **Rev:** Female and farmer seated

Date	Mintage	VF20	XF40	MS60	MS63
2010	7,500	PF63 65.00	PF65 70.00		

KM# 1013 20 DOLLARS
31.39 g., 0.999 Silver 1.0017 oz. ASW, 38 mm. **Ruler:** Elizabeth II **Rev:** Maple leaf and crystal

Date	Mintage	VF20	XF40	MS60	MS63
2010	10,000	PF63 90.00	PF65 100		

KM# 1018 20 DOLLARS
31.39 g., 0.999 Silver 1.0017 oz. ASW, 38 mm. **Ruler:** Elizabeth II **Rev:** Steam Locomotive Selkirk

Date	Mintage	VF20	XF40	MS60	MS63
2010	10,000	PF65 80.00			

KM# 1048 20 DOLLARS
31.11 g., 0.9999 Silver 0.9935 oz. ASW, 38 mm. **Ruler:** Elizabeth II **Rev:** Snowflake, blue crystals

Date	Mintage	VF20	XF40	MS60	MS63
2010	7,500	PF63 85.00	PF65 95.00		

KM# 1049 20 DOLLARS
31.11 g., 0.9999 Silver 0.9935 oz. ASW, 38 mm. **Ruler:** Elizabeth II **Rev:** Snowflake, tanzanite crystals

Date	Mintage	VF20	XF40	MS60	MS63
2010	7,500	PF63 85.00	PF65 95.00		

KM# 1066 20 DOLLARS
31.99 g., 0.999 Silver 1.0209 oz. ASW, 38 mm. **Ruler:** Elizabeth II **Rev:** Pinecone with ruby crystals

Date	Mintage	VF20	XF40	MS60	MS63
2010	5,000	PF63 110	PF65 120		

KM# 1067 20 DOLLARS
31.99 g., 0.999 Silver 1.0209 oz. ASW, 38 mm. **Ruler:** Elizabeth II **Rev:** Pinecone with moonlight blue crystals

Date	Mintage	VF20	XF40	MS60	MS63
2010	5,000	PF63 110	PF65 120		

KM# 1075 20 DOLLARS
27.78 g., 0.925 Silver 0.8208 oz. ASW, 40 mm. **Ruler:** Elizabeth II **Subject:** Winter Scene **Rev:** Horse pulling cut Christmas Tree

Date	Mintage	VF20	XF40	MS60	MS63
2011	8,000	PF63 60.00	PF65 70.00		

KM# 1111 20 DOLLARS
31.39 g., 0.999 Silver 1.0017 oz. ASW, 40 mm. **Ruler:** Elizabeth II **Subject:** Royal Wedding **Rev:** Portraits of Katherine and William facing each other, crystal insert

Date	Mintage	VF20	XF40	MS60	MS63
2011	—	PF63 70.00	PF65 80.00		

KM# 1134 20 DOLLARS
31.39 g., 0.9999 Silver 1.0026 oz. ASW, 38 mm. **Ruler:** Elizabeth II **Subject:** Canadian Pacific's D-10 Steam Locomotive **Obv:** Bust right **Rev:** Steam locomotive right **Edge:** Lettered

Date	Mintage	VF20	XF40	MS60	MS63
2011	10,000	PF63 70.00	PF65 80.00		

KM# 1135 20 DOLLARS
31.39 g., 0.9999 Silver 1.0026 oz. ASW, 38 mm. **Ruler:** Elizabeth II **Obv:** Bust right **Rev:** Tulip in color and Vienitian glass lady bug

Date	Mintage	VF20	XF40	MS60	MS63
2011	5,000	PF65 1,000			

KM# 1145 20 DOLLARS
31.39 g., 0.9999 Silver 1.0026 oz. ASW, 38 mm. **Ruler:** Elizabeth II **Obv:** Bust right **Rev:** Wild rose in color, swarovski crystrals

Date	Mintage	VF20	XF40	MS60	MS63
2011	Est. 10000	PF63 125	PF65 135		

KM# 1147 20 DOLLARS
31.39 g., 0.9999 Silver 1.0026 oz. ASW, 38 mm. **Ruler:** Elizabeth II **Obv:** Bust right **Rev:** Maple leaves, seeds in color, swarovski crystal drop

Date	Mintage	VF20	XF40	MS60	MS63
2011	—	PF63 100	PF65 110		

KM# 1181 20 DOLLARS
31.39 g., 0.9999 Silver 1.0017 oz. ASW, 38 mm. **Ruler:** Elizabeth II **Obv:** Bust right **Rev:** Winnipeg Jets Logo, jet over maple leaf

Date	Mintage	VF20	XF40	MS60	MS63
2011	15,000	PF63 85.00	PF65 95.00		

KM# 1182 20 DOLLARS
31.99 g., 0.9999 Silver 1.0218 oz. ASW, 38 mm. **Ruler:** Elizabeth II **Obv:** Bust right **Rev:** Christmas tree with six crystals

Date	Mintage	VF20	XF40	MS60	MS63
2011	—	PF63 65.00	PF65 75.00		

KM# 1187 20 DOLLARS
31.39 g., 0.9999 Silver 1.0017 oz. ASW, 38 mm. **Ruler:** Elizabeth II **Obv:** Bust right **Rev:** Snowflake with emerald crystals

Date	Mintage	VF20	XF40	MS60	MS63
2011	15,000	PF63 75.00	PF65 85.00		

KM# 1188 20 DOLLARS
31.89 g., 0.999 Silver 1.0177 oz. ASW, 38 mm. **Ruler:** Elizabeth II **Obv:** Bust right **Rev:** Snowflake with topaz crystals

Date	Mintage	VF20	XF40	MS60	MS63
2011	15,000	PF63 75.00	PF65 85.00		

KM# 1189 20 DOLLARS
31.89 g., 0.999 Silver 1.0177 oz. ASW, 38 mm. **Ruler:** Elizabeth II **Obv:** Bust right **Rev:** Three snowflakes with three Hyacinth red crystals

Date	Mintage	VF20	XF40	MS60	MS63
2011	15,000	PF63 75.00	PF65 85.00		

KM# 1190 20 DOLLARS
31.89 g., 0.999 Silver 1.0177 oz. ASW, 38 mm. **Ruler:** Elizabeth II **Obv:** Bust right **Rev:** Three snowflakes with three Montana blue crystals

Date	Mintage	VF20	XF40	MS60	MS63
2011	15,000	PF63 75.00	PF65 85.00		

KM# 1137 20 DOLLARS
31.39 g., 0.999 Silver 1.0017 oz. ASW, 38 mm. **Ruler:** Elizabeth II **Subject:** Elizabeth II, 60th Anniversary of reign **Obv:** Bust right **Rev:** Crowned bust right with swarovski crystal insert **Edge:** Reeded

Date	Mintage	VF20	XF40	MS60	MS63
1952-2012	15,000	PF63 70.00	PF65 80.00		

KM# 1177 20 DOLLARS
27.78 g., 0.925 Silver 0.8208 oz. ASW, 38 mm. **Ruler:** Elizabeth II **Obv:** Bust right **Rev:** Youthful busts right of Elizabeth II and Prince Philip

Date	Mintage	VF20	XF40	MS60	MS63
1952-2012	—	PF63 75.00	PF65 85.00		

KM# 1178 20 DOLLARS
27.78 g., 0.925 Silver 0.8208 oz. ASW, 38 mm. **Ruler:** Elizabeth II **Obv:** Bust right **Rev:** Royal cypher, wreath below

Date	Mintage	VF20	XF40	MS60	MS63
1952-2012	—	PF63 75.00	PF65 85.00		

KM# 1238 20 DOLLARS
30.75 g., 0.9999 Silver 0.9822 oz. ASW, 36 mm. **Ruler:** Elizabeth II **Subject:** Elizabeth II, Diamond Jubilee **Obv:** Bust right **Rev:** Elizabeth II profile left, high releif

Date	Mintage	VF20	XF40	MS60	MS63
2012	7,500	PF63 65.00	PF65 75.00		

KM# 1239 20 DOLLARS
7.96 g., 0.999 Silver 0.254 oz. ASW, 27 mm. **Ruler:** Elizabeth II **Subject:** Royal visit to Canada **Obv:** Young portrait right **Rev:** Elizabeth II with Mountie and horse

Date	Mintage	VF20	XF40	MS60	MS63
1952-2012	25,000	PF63 25.00	PF65 30.00		

KM# 1246 20 DOLLARS
27.78 g., 0.925 Silver 0.8208 oz. ASW, 38 mm. **Ruler:** Elizabeth II **Subject:** Coast Guard, 50th Anniversary

Date	Mintage	VF20	XF40	MS60	MS63
2012	—	PF63 90.00	PF65 100		

KM# 1250 20 DOLLARS
27.78 g., 0.925 Silver 0.8208 oz. ASW, 38 mm. **Ruler:** Elizabeth II **Subject:** F.H. Varley

Date	Mintage	VF20	XF40	MS60	MS63
2012	—	PF63 65.00	PF65 75.00		

KM# 1251 20 DOLLARS
27.78 g., 0.925 Silver 0.8208 oz. ASW, 38 mm. **Ruler:** Elizabeth II **Subject:** Arthur Lismer

Date	Mintage	VF20	XF40	MS60	MS63
2012	—	PF63 65.00	PF65 75.00		

KM# 1266 20 DOLLARS
31.10 g., 0.999 Silver 0.9925 oz. ASW, 38 mm. **Ruler:** Elizabeth II **Subject:** Aster and bee

Date	Mintage	VF20	XF40	MS60	MS63
2012	—	PF63 90.00	PF65 100		

KM# 1269 20 DOLLARS
31.39 g., 0.999 Silver 1.0017 oz. ASW, 38 mm. **Ruler:** Elizabeth II **Subject:** Sugar Maple Leaf **Rev:** Leaves in color, crystal

Date	Mintage	VF20	XF40	MS60	MS63
2012	—	PF65 130			

KM# 1270 20 DOLLARS
31.39 g., 0.999 Silver 1.0017 oz. ASW, 38 mm. **Ruler:** Elizabeth II **Rev:** Rhododendron

Date	Mintage	VF20	XF40	MS60	MS63
2012	—	PF65 125			

KM# 1280 20 DOLLARS
31.11 g., 0.999 Silver 0.9926 oz. ASW, 38 mm. **Ruler:** Elizabeth II **Subject:** Bateman Moose

Date	Mintage	VF20	XF40	MS60	MS63
2012	—	PF65 135			

KM# 1283 20 DOLLARS
15.55 g., 0.999 Gold 0.4962 oz. AGW, 25 mm. **Ruler:** Elizabeth II **Subject:** Year of the Dragon

Date	Mintage	VF20	XF40	MS60	MS63
2012	—	PF65 900			

KM# 1333 20 DOLLARS
31.11 g., 0.999 Silver 0.9926 oz. ASW, 38 mm. **Ruler:** Elizabeth
II **Rev:** Snowstorm

Date	Mintage	VF20	XF40	MS60	MS63
2012	—	PF63 45.00	PF65 50.00		

KM# 1334 20 DOLLARS
28.02 g., 0.999 Silver 0.8942 oz. ASW **Ruler:** Elizabeth II
Subject: Christmas Play **Rev:** Three childred as the Magi,
crystal

Date	Mintage	VF20	XF40	MS60	MS63
2012	10,000	PF63 110	PF65 115		

KM# 1335 20 DOLLARS
27.78 g., 0.925 Silver 0.8208 oz. ASW, 38 mm. **Ruler:** Elizabeth
II **Subject:** Franklin Carmichael **Rev:** Snowy Landscape

Date	Mintage	VF20	XF40	MS60	MS63
2012	—	PF63 70.00	PF65 75.00		

KM# 1347 20 DOLLARS
31.39 g., 0.999 Silver 1.0017 oz. ASW, 38 mm. **Ruler:** Elizabeth
II **Rev:** Blue flag iris in color with three crystals

Date	Mintage	VF20	XF40	MS60	MS63
2013	10,000	PF63 110	PF65 120		

KM# 1361 20 DOLLARS
31.39 g., 0.999 Silver 1.0017 oz. ASW, 35 mm. **Ruler:** Elizabeth
II **Rev:** Purple cone flower, butterfly in color and high relief

Date	Mintage	VF20	XF40	MS60	MS63
2013	—	PF63 50.00	PF65 60.00		

KM# 1363 20 DOLLARS
31.39 g., 0.9999 Silver 1.0026 oz. ASW, 38 mm. **Ruler:**
Elizabeth II **Subject:** Canadian Maple Canopy - Spring **Rev:**
Forest Canopy in Spring, Colorized

Date	Mintage	VF20	XF40	MS60	MS63
2013	Est. 7500	PF63 90.00	PF65 100		

KM# 1374 20 DOLLARS
31.40 g., 0.999 Silver 1.0019 oz. ASW, 38 mm. **Ruler:** Elizabeth
II **Subject:** Baseball **Rev:** Baseball Batter

Date	Mintage	VF20	XF40	MS60	MS63
2013	Est. 7500	PF63 110	PF65 115		

KM# 1375 20 DOLLARS
31.39 g., 0.999 Silver 1.0017 oz. ASW, 38 mm. **Ruler:** Elizabeth
II **Subject:** Baseball **Rev:** Baseball Fielder

Date	Mintage	VF20	XF40	MS60	MS63
2013	Est. 7500	PF63 110	PF65 115		

KM# 1376 20 DOLLARS
31.39 g., 0.999 Silver 1.0017 oz. ASW, 38 mm. **Ruler:** Elizabeth
II **Subject:** Baseball **Rev:** Baseball Pitcher

Date	Mintage	VF20	XF40	MS60	MS63
2013	—	PF63 110	PF65 115		

KM# 1377 20 DOLLARS
31.39 g., 0.999 Silver 1.0017 oz. ASW, 38 mm. **Ruler:** Elizabeth
II **Subject:** Baseball **Rev:** Baseball Runner

Date	Mintage	VF20	XF40	MS60	MS63
2013	Est. 7500	PF63 110	PF65 115		

KM# 1381 20 DOLLARS
31.11 g., 0.999 Silver 0.9926 oz. ASW, 38 mm. **Ruler:** Elizabeth
II **Subject:** Snow Flake With Crystal

Date	Mintage	VF20	XF40	MS60	MS63
2013	—	PF63 110	PF65 120		

KM# 1384 20 DOLLARS
31.39 g., 0.999 Silver 1.0017 oz. ASW, 38 mm. **Ruler:** Elizabeth
II **Subject:** Frank Johnston - Painter **Rev:** Painting: Guardian
of the Gorge

Date	Mintage	VF20	XF40	MS60	MS63
2013	Est. 7000	PF63 80.00	PF65 90.00		

KM# 1385 20 DOLLARS
31.39 g., 0.999 Silver 1.0017 oz. ASW, 38 mm. **Ruler:** Elizabeth
II **Subject:** Lauren S. Harris - Painter **Rev:** Painting: Toronto
Street, Winter Morning

Date	Mintage	VF20	XF40	MS60	MS63
2013	Est. 7000	PF63 80.00	PF65 90.00		

KM# 1397 20 DOLLARS
31.39 g., 0.9999 Silver 1.0026 oz. ASW, 38 mm. **Ruler:**
Elizabeth II **Rev:** Beaver gnawing on tree

Date	Mintage	VF20	XF40	MS60	MS63
2013	8,500	PF63 90.00	PF65 100		

KM# 1404 20 DOLLARS
28.20 g., 0.9999 Silver 0.9007 oz. ASW, 40 mm. **Ruler:** Elizabeth II **Rev:** Arctic Fox and Northern lights in background

Date	Mintage	VF20	XF40	MS60	MS63
2013	—	PF63 75.00	PF65 85.00		

KM# 1436 20 DOLLARS
28.02 g., 0.999 Silver 0.8942 oz. ASW, 40 mm. **Ruler:** Elizabeth II **Rev:** Canadian Tiger Swallowtail Butterfly in color

Date	Mintage	VF20	XF40	MS60	MS63
2013	Est. 10000	PF63 90.00	PF65 100		

KM# 1440 20 DOLLARS
31.39 g., 0.9999 Silver 1.0026 oz. ASW, 38 mm. **Ruler:** Elizabeth II **Obv:** Eagle head left

Date	Mintage	VF20	XF40	MS60	MS63
2013	Est. 7500	PF63 90.00	PF65 100		

KM# 1447 20 DOLLARS
31.39 g., 0.999 Silver 1.0017 oz. ASW, 38 mm. **Ruler:** Elizabeth II **Rev:** Superman standing right, cape blowing

Date	Mintage	VF20	XF40	MS60	MS63
2013	Est. 10000	PF63 100	PF65 110		

KM# 1448 20 DOLLARS
31.39 g., 0.999 Silver 1.0017 oz. ASW, 38 mm. **Ruler:** Elizabeth II **Subject:** 75th Anniversary of Superman **Rev:** Superman flying forward, multi-color background hologram

Date	Mintage	VF20	XF40	MS60	MS63
2013	Est. 10000	PF63 120	PF65 130		

KM# 1449 20 DOLLARS
31.39 g., 0.999 Silver 1.0017 oz. ASW, 38 mm. **Ruler:** Elizabeth II **Subject:** 75th Anniversary of Superman **Rev:** 'S' shield logo in color

Date	Mintage	VF20	XF40	MS60	MS63
2013	Est. 10000	PF63 110	PF65 120		

KM# 1451a 20 DOLLARS
7.96 g., 0.999 Silver 0.2542 oz. ASW, 38 mm. **Ruler:** Elizabeth II **Rev:** Red maple leaf in center of many small maple leaves

Date	Mintage	F12	VF20	XF40	MS60	MS63
2013	Est. 10000		PF63 100	PF65 115		

KM# 1459 20 DOLLARS
31.39 g., 0.999 Silver 1.0017 oz. ASW, 38 mm. **Ruler:** Elizabeth II **Rev:** Pronghorn Antelope with northern lights in the background

Date	Mintage	VF20	XF40	MS60	MS63
2013	Est. 8500	PF63 80.00	PF65 90.00		

KM# 1466 20 DOLLARS
31.39 g., 0.9999 Silver 1.0026 oz. ASW, 38 mm. **Ruler:** Elizabeth II **Subject:** Birth of Prince George **Rev:** Baby sleeping in crib

Date	Mintage	VF20	XF40	MS60	MS63
2013	7,500	PF63 70.00	PF65 80.00		

KM# 1467 20 DOLLARS
31.39 g., 0.9999 Silver 1.0026 oz. ASW, 38 mm. **Ruler:** Elizabeth II **Subject:** Birth of Prince George **Rev:** Parents hands holding baby's head

Date	Mintage	VF20	XF40	MS60	MS63
2013	7,500	PF63 70.00	PF65 80.00		

KM# 1468 20 DOLLARS
31.39 g., 0.9999 Silver 1.0026 oz. ASW, 38 mm. **Ruler:** Elizabeth II **Subject:** Birth of Prince George **Rev:** Mint Mascot Moose and Beaver Mountie plush dolls in crib with sleeping baby

Date	Mintage	VF20	XF40	MS60	MS63
2013	7,500	PF63 70.00	PF65 80.00		

KM# 1469 20 DOLLARS
31.39 g., 0.9999 Silver 1.0026 oz. ASW, 38 mm. **Ruler:** Elizabeth II **Subject:** Autumn Bliss **Rev:** Color view of canoe, lake and trees

Date	Mintage	VF20	XF40	MS60	MS63
2013	7,500	PF63 90.00	PF65 100		

KM# 1470 20 DOLLARS
31.39 g., 0.9999 Silver 1.0026 oz. ASW, 38 mm. **Ruler:** Elizabeth II **Subject:** A.Y. Jackson, painter **Rev:** Detail of painting, Sant Tile de Caps

Date	Mintage	VF20	XF40	MS60	MS63
2013	7,000	PF63 90.00	PF65 100		

KM# 1471 20 DOLLARS
31.39 g., 0.9999 Silver 1.0026 oz. ASW, 38 mm. **Ruler:** Elizabeth II **Subject:** J.E.H. MacDonald, painter **Rev:** Detail of painting, Sumacs

Date	Mintage	VF20	XF40	MS60	MS63
2013	7,000	PF63 90.00	PF65 100		

KM# 1474 20 DOLLARS
31.39 g., 0.999 Silver 1.0017 oz. ASW, 38 mm. **Ruler:** Elizabeth II **Subject:** Dinosaurs of Canada **Rev:** Bathygnathus advancing left

Date	Mintage	VF20	XF40	MS60	MS63
2013	8,500	PF63 80.00	PF65 90.00		

KM# 1479 20 DOLLARS
31.39 g., 0.999 Silver 1.0017 oz. ASW, 38 mm. **Ruler:** Elizabeth II **Rev:** Eagle in flight left

Date	Mintage	VF20	XF40	MS60	MS63
2013	—	PF63 80.00	PF65 90.00		

KM# 1484 20 DOLLARS
31.11 g., 0.999 Silver 0.9926 oz. ASW, 38 mm. **Ruler:** Elizabeth II **Subject:** Louisburg Settlement **Rev:** Colonial sea-side scene

Date	Mintage	VF20	XF40	MS60	MS63
2013	8,500	PF63 80.00	PF65 90.00		

KM# 1507 20 DOLLARS
0.999 Silver, 38 mm. **Ruler:** Elizabeth II **Subject:** Carlito Dalceggio, artist

Date	Mintage	VF20	XF40	MS60	MS63
2013	7,500	PF63 80.00	PF65 90.00		

KM# 1510 20 DOLLARS
31.39 g., 0.9999 Silver 1.0026 oz. ASW, 38 mm. **Ruler:** Elizabeth II **Rev:** Two eagles standing on rock

Date	Mintage	VF20	XF40	MS60	MS63
2013	7,500	PF63 75.00	PF65 80.00		

KM# 1513 20 DOLLARS
31.39 g., 0.9999 Silver 1.0026 oz. ASW, 38 mm. **Ruler:** Elizabeth II **Subject:** Northern Lights, the great Hare **Rev:** Hare seated watching hologram of Northern Lights

Date	Mintage	VF20	XF40	MS60	MS63
2013	8,500	PF63 100	PF65 110		

KM# 1522 20 DOLLARS
31.39 g., 0.999 Silver 1.0017 oz. ASW, 38 mm. **Ruler:** Elizabeth II **Rev:** Maple forest canopy, two fall leaves in color

Date	Mintage	VF20	XF40	MS60	MS63
2013	7,500	PF63 90.00	PF65 100		

KM# 1526 20 DOLLARS
31.39 g., 0.999 Silver 1.0017 oz. ASW, 38 mm. **Ruler:** Elizabeth II **Rev:** Pointsettia, ornament, star and candy cane in color **Note:** Venitian glass used for coloring

Date	Mintage	VF20	XF40	MS60	MS63
2013	10,000	PF63 140	PF65 150		

KM# 1527 20 DOLLARS
31.39 g., 0.999 Silver 1.0017 oz. ASW, 38 mm. **Ruler:** Elizabeth II **Rev:** Snowflake, crystal at center

Date	Mintage	VF20	XF40	MS60	MS63
2013	10,000	PF63 110	PF65 115		

KM# 1531 20 DOLLARS
31.39 g., 0.999 Silver 1.0017 oz. ASW, 38 mm. **Ruler:** Elizabeth II **Rev:** Holiday Wreath with five colored crystals

Date	Mintage	VF20	XF40	MS60	MS63
2013	10,000	PF65 175			

KM# 1532 20 DOLLARS
31.39 g., 0.999 Silver 1.0017 oz. ASW, 38 mm. **Ruler:** Elizabeth II **Rev:** Scutellosaurus advancing left

Date	Mintage	VF20	XF40	MS60	MS63
2013	850	PF63 80.00	PF65 90.00		

KM# 1548 20 DOLLARS
Silver ASW **Ruler:** Elizabeth II **Rev:** Stained glass window pattern in color

Date	Mintage	VF20	XF40	MS60	MS63
2013		PF63 65.00	PF65 75.00		

KM# 1553 20 DOLLARS
Silver ASW, 38 mm. **Ruler:** Elizabeth II **Subject:** Pond Hockey in color

Date	Mintage	VF20	XF40	MS60	MS63
2014	8,500	PF63 90.00	PF65 100		

KM# 1556 20 DOLLARS
31.39 g., 0.9999 Silver 1.0026 oz. ASW, 38 mm. **Ruler:** Elizabeth II **Rev:** Polar bear walking on rocks in color

Date	Mintage	VF20	XF40	MS60	MS63
2014	8,500	PF63 90.00	PF65 100		

KM# 1558 20 DOLLARS
31.39 g., 0.999 Silver 1.0017 oz. ASW, 38 mm. **Ruler:** Elizabeth II **Rev:** Canadian UN Peacekeeper with binoculars, blue beret

Date	Mintage	VF20	XF40	MS60	MS63
2014	8,500	PF65 115			

KM# 1565 20 DOLLARS
31.39 g., 0.9999 Silver 1.0026 oz. ASW, 38 mm. **Ruler:** Elizabeth II **Rev:** Lake Superior in blue color

Date	Mintage	VF20	XF40	MS60	MS63
2014	10,000	PF63 110	PF65 115		

KM# 1566 20 DOLLARS
31.39 g., 0.999 Silver 1.0017 oz. ASW, 38 mm. **Rev:** Lake Huron in color

Date	Mintage	VF20	XF40	MS60	MS63
2014	10,000	PF63 110	PF65 115		

KM# 1567 20 DOLLARS
31.39 g., 0.999 Silver 1.0017 oz. ASW, 38 mm. **Ruler:** Elizabeth II **Rev:** Lake Michigan in color

Date	Mintage	VF20	XF40	MS60	MS63
2014	10,000	PF63 110	PF65 115		

KM# 1568 20 DOLLARS
31.39 g., 0.999 Silver 1.0017 oz. ASW, 38 mm. **Ruler:** Elizabeth II **Rev:** Lake Erie in color

Date	Mintage	VF20	XF40	MS60	MS63
2014	10,000	PF63 110	PF65 115		

KM# 1569 20 DOLLARS
31.39 g., 0.999 Silver 1.0017 oz. ASW, 38 mm. **Ruler:** Elizabeth II **Rev:** Lake Ontario in color

Date	Mintage	VF20	XF40	MS60	MS63
2014	10,000	PF63 110	PF65 115		

KM# 1570 20 DOLLARS
31.39 g., 0.9999 Silver 1.0026 oz. ASW, 38 mm. **Ruler:** Elizabeth II **Rev:** Caribou in color

Date	Mintage	VF20	XF40	MS60	MS63
2014	8,500	PF63 90.00	PF65 100		

KM# 1609 20 DOLLARS
31.39 g., 0.999 Silver 1.0017 oz. ASW, 38 mm. **Ruler:** Elizabeth II **Obv:** Bust right **Rev:** Bison head facing

Date	Mintage	VF20	XF40	MS60	MS63
2014	7,500	PF63 90.00	PF65 100		

KM# 1610 20 DOLLARS
31.39 g., .999 Silver ASW, 38 mm. **Ruler:** Elizabeth II **Obv:** Bust right **Rev:** Bison pair advancing left

Date	Mintage	VF20	XF40	MS60	MS63
2014	7,500	PF63 90.00	PF65 100		

KM# 1614 20 DOLLARS

31.11 g., 0.999 Silver 0.9926 oz. ASW, 40 mm. **Ruler:** Elizabeth II **Obv:** Bust right **Rev:** Wolverine with northern lights in background

Date	Mintage	VF20	XF40	MS60	MS63
2014	8,500	PF63 80.00	PF65 90.00		

KM# 742 25 DOLLARS

27.78 g., 0.925 Silver 0.8208 oz. ASW, 40 mm. **Ruler:** Elizabeth II **Subject:** Vancouver Olympics **Rev:** Alpine skiing, hologram

Date	Mintage	VF20	XF40	MS60	MS63
2007	45,000	PF63 45.00	PF65 50.00		

KM# 743 25 DOLLARS

27.78 g., 0.925 Silver 0.8208 oz. ASW, 40 mm. **Ruler:** Elizabeth II **Subject:** Vancouver Olympics **Rev:** Athletics pride hologram

Date	Mintage	VF20	XF40	MS60	MS63
2007	45,000	PF63 60.00	PF65 65.00		

KM# 744 25 DOLLARS

27.75 g., 0.925 Silver 0.820 oz. ASW, 40 mm. **Ruler:** Elizabeth II **Subject:** Vancouver Olympics **Rev:** Biathleon hologram

Date	Mintage	VF20	XF40	MS60	MS63
2007	54,000	PF63 45.00	PF65 50.00		

KM# 745 25 DOLLARS

27.78 g., 0.925 Silver 0.8208 oz. ASW, 40 mm. **Ruler:** Elizabeth II **Subject:** Vancouver Olympics **Rev:** Curling hologram

Date	Mintage	VF20	XF40	MS60	MS63
2007	—	PF63 45.00	PF65 50.00		

KM# 746 25 DOLLARS

27.78 g., 0.925 Silver 0.8208 oz. ASW, 40 mm. **Ruler:** Elizabeth II **Subject:** Vancouver Olympics **Rev:** Hockey, hologram

Date	Mintage	VF20	XF40	MS60	MS63
2007	45,000	PF63 45.00	PF65 50.00		

KM# 814 25 DOLLARS

27.78 g., 0.925 Silver 0.8208 oz. ASW, 40 mm. **Ruler:** Elizabeth II **Subject:** Vancouver Olympics **Rev:** Bobsleigh, hologram

Date	Mintage	VF20	XF40	MS60	MS63
2008	45,000	PF63 40.00	PF65 50.00		

KM# 815 25 DOLLARS

27.78 g., 0.925 Silver 0.8208 oz. ASW, 40 mm. **Ruler:** Elizabeth II **Subject:** Vancouver Olympics **Rev:** Figure skating, hologram

Date	Mintage	VF20	XF40	MS60	MS63
2008	45,000	PF63 40.00	PF65 50.00		

KM# 816 25 DOLLARS

27.78 g., 0.925 Silver 0.8208 oz. ASW, 40 mm. **Ruler:** Elizabeth II **Subject:** Vancouver Olympics **Rev:** Freestyle skating, hologram

Date	Mintage	VF20	XF40	MS60	MS63
2008	45,000	PF63 40.00	PF65 50.00		

KM# 817 25 DOLLARS

27.78 g., 0.925 Silver 0.8208 oz. ASW, 40 mm. **Ruler:** Elizabeth II **Subject:** Vancouver Olympics **Rev:** Snowboarding, hologram

Date	Mintage	VF20	XF40	MS60	MS63
2008	45,000	PF63 40.00	PF65 50.00		

KM# 818 25 DOLLARS

27.78 g., 0.925 Silver 0.8208 oz. ASW, 40 mm. **Ruler:** Elizabeth II **Subject:** Vancouver Olympics **Rev:** Home of the 2010 Olympics

Date	Mintage	VF20	XF40	MS60	MS63
2008	45,000	PF63 40.00	PF65 50.00		

KM# 903 25 DOLLARS

27.78 g., 0.925 Silver 0.8208 oz. ASW, 40 mm. **Ruler:** Elizabeth II **Subject:** 2010 Vancouver Olympics **Obv:** Bust right **Rev:** Cross Country Skiing and hologram at left

Date	Mintage	VF20	XF40	MS60	MS63
2009	45,000	PF63 45.00	PF65 50.00		

KM# 904 25 DOLLARS
27.78 g., 0.925 Silver 0.8208 oz. ASW, 40 mm. **Ruler:** Elizabeth II **Subject:** 2010 Vancouver Olympics **Obv:** Bust right **Rev:** Olympians holding torch, hologram at left

Date	Mintage	VF20	XF40	MS60	MS63
2009	45,000	PF63 45.00	PF65 50.00		

KM# 905 25 DOLLARS
27.78 g., 0.925 Silver 0.8208 oz. ASW, 40 mm. **Ruler:** Elizabeth II **Subject:** 2010 Vancouver Olympics **Obv:** Bust right **Rev:** Sled, hologram at left

Date	Mintage	VF20	XF40	MS60	MS63
2009	45,000	PF63 45.00	PF65 50.00		

KM# 906 25 DOLLARS
27.78 g., 0.925 Silver 0.8208 oz. ASW, 40 mm. **Ruler:** Elizabeth II **Subject:** 2010 Vancouver Olympics **Obv:** Bust right **Rev:** Ski Jumper, hologram at left

Date	Mintage	VF20	XF40	MS60	MS63
2009	45,000	PF63 45.00	PF65 50.00		

KM# 907 25 DOLLARS
27.78 g., 0.925 Silver 0.8208 oz. ASW, 40 mm. **Ruler:** Elizabeth II **Subject:** 2010 Vancouver Olympics **Obv:** Bust right **Rev:** Speed Skaters, hologram at left

Date	Mintage	VF20	XF40	MS60	MS63
2009	45,000	PF63 45.00	PF65 50.00		

KM# 1146 25 DOLLARS
62.41 g., 0.9999 Silver 1.9934 oz. ASW, 60 mm. **Ruler:** Elizabeth II **Obv:** Bust right **Rev:** Toronto map and skyline, partilly gilt **Edge:** Reeded

Date	Mintage	VF20	XF40	MS60	MS63
2011	Est. 7500	PF63 170	PF65 180		

KM# 1173 25 DOLLARS
31.39 g., 0.9999 Silver 1.0026 oz. ASW, 38 mm. **Ruler:** Elizabeth II **Obv:** Bust right **Rev:** Wayne Greskey skating right, father's portrait in circle at right, 99 in hologram at lower right

Date	Mintage	VF20	XF40	MS60	MS63
2011	—	PF63 75.00	PF65 85.00		

KM# 1330 25 DOLLARS
31.11 g., 0.999 Silver 0.9926 oz. ASW, 38 mm. **Ruler:** Elizabeth II **Rev:** Grandmother Moon Mask

Date	Mintage	VF20	XF40	MS60	MS63
2012	—	PF63 70.00	PF65 75.00		

KM# 1398 25 DOLLARS
31.39 g., 0.9999 Silver 1.0026 oz. ASW, 38 mm. **Ruler:** Elizabeth II **Rev:** Beaver with two kits

Date	Mintage	VF20	XF40	MS60	MS63
2013	Est. 8500	PF63 80.00	PF65 90.00		

KM# 1403 25 DOLLARS
31.39 g., 0.999 Silver 1.0017 oz. ASW, 38 mm. **Ruler:** Elizabeth II **Rev:** Polar Bear and two cubs

Date	Mintage	VF20	XF40	MS60	MS63
2013	Est. 8500	PF63 80.00	PF65 90.00		

KM# 1405 25 DOLLARS
7.77 g., 0.999 Gold 0.248 oz. AGW, 20 mm. **Ruler:** Elizabeth II **Rev:** Arctic Fox with Northern lights in the background

Date	Mintage	VF20	XF40	MS60	MS63
2013	Est. 1500	PF65 650			

KM# 1456 25 DOLLARS
31.39 g., 0.999 Silver 1.0017 oz. ASW, 38 mm. **Ruler:** Elizabeth II **Rev:** Caribou mother and calf

Date	Mintage	VF20	XF40	MS60	MS63
2013	Est. 8500	PF63 80.00	PF65 90.00		

KM# 1457 25 DOLLARS
31.39 g., 0.999 Silver 1.0017 oz. ASW, 38 mm. **Ruler:** Elizabeth II **Rev:** Wolf mother and two pups

Date	Mintage	VF20	XF40	MS60	MS63
2013	Est. 8500	PF63 80.00	PF65 90.00		

KM# 1458 25 DOLLARS
7.77 g., 0.999 Gold 0.248 oz. AGW, 20 mm. **Ruler:** Elizabeth II **Rev:** Pronghorn Antelope with northern lights in background

Date	Mintage	VF20	XF40	MS60	MS63
2013	Est. 1500	PF65 650			

KM# 1482 25 DOLLARS
31.11 g., 0.999 Silver 0.9926 oz. ASW, 38 mm. **Ruler:** Elizabeth II **Subject:** Banknote Allegory **Rev:** Female seated

Date	Mintage	F12	VF20	XF40	MS60	MS63
2013 Proof	8,500	—	—	—	—	90.00

KM# 1483 25 DOLLARS
7.80 g., 0.9999 Gold 0.2491 oz. AGW, 20 mm. **Ruler:** Elizabeth II **Subject:** Banknote Allegory **Rev:** Seated female

Date	Mintage	VF20	XF40	MS60	MS63
2013	2,000	PF65 650			

KM# 1508 25 DOLLARS
30.76 g., 0.9999 Silver 0.9825 oz. ASW, 36.15 mm. **Ruler:** Elizabeth II **Subject:** Grandmother Moon Mask **Rev:** Mask carving

Date	Mintage	VF20	XF40	MS60	MS63
2013	6,000	PF63 140	PF65 150		

KM# 1541 25 DOLLARS
31.39 g., 0.999 Silver 1.0017 oz. ASW, 38 mm. **Ruler:** Elizabeth II **Subject:** Oh Canada **Rev:** Orca surfacing

Date	Mintage	VF20	XF40	MS60	MS63
2013	8,500	PF63 80.00	PF65 90.00		

KM# 1581 25 DOLLARS
31.39 g., 0.999 Silver 1.0017 oz. ASW, 38 mm. **Ruler:** Elizabeth II **Obv:** Bust right **Rev:** Igloo

Date	Mintage	VF20	XF40	MS60	MS63
2014		PF63 65.00	PF65 75.00		

KM# 1608 25 DOLLARS
7.
7.97 g., 0.999 Gold AGW, 20 mm. **Ruler:** Elizabeth II **Obv:** Bust right **Rev:** Wolverine with northern lights in background

Date	Mintage	VF20	XF40	MS60	MS63
2014	1,500	PF65 650			

KM# 1626 25 DOLLARS
31.39 g., 0.999 Silver 1.0017 oz. ASW, 38 mm. **Ruler:** Elizabeth II **Obv:** Bust right **Rev:** Downhill skiing

Date	Mintage	VF20	XF40	MS60	MS63
2014	—	PF63 80.00	PF65 90.00		

KM# 590 30 DOLLARS
31.50 g., 0.925 Silver 0.9308 oz. ASW **Ruler:** Elizabeth II **Subject:** Pacific Northwest Wood Carvings **Obv:** Head right **Rev:** Welcome figure totem pole

Date	Mintage	VF20	XF40	MS60	MS63
2006	9,904			PF63 65.00	PF65 75.00

KM# 668 30 DOLLARS
31.50 g., 0.925 Silver 0.9308 oz. ASW **Ruler:** Elizabeth II **Subject:** Canadarm and Col. C. Hadfield **Obv:** Head right **Rev:** Hologram of Canadarm

Date	Mintage	VF20	XF40	MS60	MS63
2006	9,357			PF63 85.00	PF65 90.00

KM# 669 30 DOLLARS
31.50 g., 0.925 Silver 0.9308 oz. ASW **Ruler:** Elizabeth II **Subject:** National War Memorial **Obv:** Head right **Rev:** Statue of three soldiers

Date	Mintage	VF20	XF40	MS60	MS63
2006	8,876			PF63 80.00	PF65 85.00

KM# 670 30 DOLLARS
31.50 g., 0.925 Silver 0.9308 oz. ASW **Ruler:** Elizabeth II **Subject:** Beaumont Hamel Newfoundland **Obv:** Head right **Rev:** Caribou statue on rock outcrop

Date	Mintage	VF20	XF40	MS60	MS63
2006	15,325			PF63 90.00	PF65 95.00

KM# 671 30 DOLLARS
31.50 g., 0.925 Silver 0.9308 oz. ASW **Ruler:** Elizabeth II **Obv:** Head right **Rev:** Dog Sled Team in color

Date	Mintage	VF20	XF40	MS60	MS63
2006	7,384			PF63 80.00	PF65 85.00

KM# 739 30 DOLLARS
31.50 g., 0.925 Silver 0.9308 oz. ASW, 40 mm. **Ruler:** Elizabeth II **Rev:** Niagra Falls panoramic hologram

Date	Mintage	VF20	XF40	MS60	MS63
2007	7,384			PF63 75.00	PF65 85.00

KM# 741 30 DOLLARS
31.50 g., 0.925 Silver 0.9308 oz. ASW, 40 mm. **Ruler:** Elizabeth II **Rev:** War Memorial, Vimy Ridge

Date	Mintage	VF20	XF40	MS60	MS63
2007	5,335			PF65 85.00	

KM# 819 30 DOLLARS
31.50 g., 0.925 Silver 0.9308 oz. ASW, 40 mm. **Ruler:** Elizabeth II **Subject:** IMAX **Rev:** Youth reaching out to shark on large screen

Date	Mintage	VF20	XF40	MS60	MS63
2008	3,861			PF63 65.00	PF65 75.00

KM# 895 30 DOLLARS
33.75 g., 0.925 Silver 0.9972 oz. ASW, 40 mm. **Ruler:** Elizabeth II **Subject:** International year of astronomy **Obv:** Bust right **Obv. Legend:** Elizabeth II 30 Dollars DG Regina **Rev:** Observatory with planets and colored sky **Rev. Legend:** Canada

Date	Mintage	VF20	XF40	MS60	MS63
2009	7,174			PF63 80.00	PF65 90.00

KM# 1623 30 DOLLARS
62.70 g., 0.999 Silver 2.0009 oz. ASW, 54 mm. **Ruler:** Elizabeth II **Subject:** Canada thru the eyes of Tim Barnard **Obv:** Bust

---

right Rev: Multitude of designs

Date	Mintage	VF20	XF40	MS60	MS63
2014	5,000			PF65 250	

KM# 566 50 DOLLARS
12.00 g., 0.5833 Gold 0.2236 oz. AGW, 27 mm. **Ruler:** Elizabeth II **Subject:** End of World War II, 60th Anniversary **Obv:** Head right **Rev:** Large V and three portraits

Date	Mintage	VF20	XF40	MS60	MS63
2005 Specimen	4,000			PF65 375	

KM# 672 50 DOLLARS
31.16 g., 0.9995 Palladium 0.9949 oz. APW **Ruler:** Elizabeth II **Subject:** Constellation in Spring sky position **Rev:** Large Bear at top

Date	Mintage	VF20	XF40	MS60	MS63
2006	297			PF65 1,250	

KM# 673 50 DOLLARS
31.16 g., 0.9995 Palladium 0.9949 oz. APW **Ruler:** Elizabeth II **Subject:** Constellation in Summer sky position **Rev:** Large Bear at left

Date	Mintage	VF20	XF40	MS60	MS63
2006	296			PF65 1,250	

KM# 674 50 DOLLARS
31.16 g., 0.9995 Palladium 0.9949 oz. APW **Ruler:** Elizabeth II **Subject:** Constellation in Autumn sky position **Rev:** Large Bear towards bottom

Date	Mintage	VF20	XF40	MS60	MS63
2006	296			PF65 1,250	

KM# 675 50 DOLLARS
31.16 g., 0.9995 Palladium 0.9949 oz. APW **Ruler:** Elizabeth II **Subject:** Constellation in Winter sky position **Rev:** Large Bear towards right

Date	Mintage	VF20	XF40	MS60	MS63
2006	293			PF65 1,250	

KM# 709 50 DOLLARS

155.50 g., 0.9999 Silver 4.9668 oz. ASW **Ruler:** Elizabeth II **Subject:** Queen's 60th Wedding Anniversary **Rev:** Coat of Arms and Mascots of Elizabeth and Philip

Date	Mintage	VF20	XF40	MS60	MS63
2007	1,957	PF65 350			

KM# 783 50 DOLLARS

156.77 g., 0.999 Silver 5.0028 oz. ASW, 65 mm. **Ruler:** Elizabeth II **Subject:** Ottawa Mint Centennial 1908-2008 **Rev:** Mint building facade **Note:** Photo reduced.

Date	Mintage	VF20	XF40	MS60	MS63
2008	2,078	PF65 400			

KM# 896 50 DOLLARS

156.77 g., 0.999 Silver 5.0028 oz. ASW, 65.25 mm. **Ruler:** Elizabeth II **Subject:** 150 Anniversary of the start of construction of the parliament buildings **Obv:** Bust right **Obv. Legend:** Elizabeth II Canada DG Regina **Rev:** Incomplete west block, original architecture **Rev. Legend:** 50 Dollars 1859-2009

Date	Mintage	VF20	XF40	MS60	MS63
2009	910	PF65 450			

KM# 1008 50 DOLLARS

157.60 g., 0.999 Silver 5.0293 oz. ASW, 65.25 mm. **Ruler:** Elizabeth II **Subject:** 75th Anniverary of Canadian Bank Notes **Rev:** Female seated speaking into microphone **Note:** Photo reduced.

Date	Mintage	VF20	XF40	MS60	MS63
2010	2,000	PF65 400			

KM# 1243 50 DOLLARS

156.77 g., 0.925 Silver 4.6322 oz. ASW, 65.25 mm. **Ruler:** Elizabeth II **Subject:** Calgary Stampede

Date	Mintage	VF20	XF40	MS60	MS63
2012	—	PF65 400			

KM# 1284 50 DOLLARS

31.11 g., 0.999 Gold 0.9926 oz. AGW, 30 mm. **Ruler:** Elizabeth II **Subject:** Year of the Dragon

Date	Mintage	VF20	XF40	MS60	MS63
2012	—	PF65 1,750			

KM# 1296 50 DOLLARS

Gold AGW **Ruler:** Elizabeth II **Obv:** Bust right **Rev:** High relief bust **Note:** Ultra high relief

Date	Mintage	VF20	XF40	MS60	MS63
2012	500	—	—		

KM# 1399 50 DOLLARS

155.55 g., 0.999 Silver 4.9639 oz. ASW, 65 mm. **Ruler:** Elizabeth II **Rev:** Beaver gnawing standing tree, two others with felled tree

Date	Mintage	VF20	XF40	MS60	MS63
2013	—	PF65 450			

KM# 1417 50 DOLLARS

155.55 g., 0.9999 Silver 4.9684 oz. ASW, 65.25 mm. **Ruler:** Elizabeth II **Obv:** Four Seasons: Spring/Fall Scene **Rev:** Winter/Summer/Large Tree

Date	Mintage	VF20	XF40	MS60	MS63
2013	—	PF65 250			

KM# 1429 50 DOLLARS

157.60 g., 0.999 Silver 5.0293 oz. ASW, 65 mm. **Ruler:** Elizabeth II **Subject:** War of 1812 - Naval Battle **Rev:** HMS Shannon and Chesapeak

Date	Mintage	VF20	XF40	MS60	MS63
2013	Est. 1500	PF65 500			

KM# 1433 50 DOLLARS

157.60 g., 0.999 Silver 5.0293 oz. ASW, 62.25 mm. **Ruler:** Elizabeth II **Subject:** Coronation Anniversary **Rev:** Elizabeth II in Coronation robes - Loman image in the Victoria & Albert Museum

Date	Mintage	VF20	XF40	MS60	MS63
2013	Est. 1500	PF65 525			

KM# 1557 50 DOLLARS
157.60 g., 0.999 Silver 5.0293 oz. ASW, 65 mm. **Ruler:** Elizabeth II **Rev:** Beaver swimming with birch branch in mouth

Date	Mintage	VF20	XF40	MS60	MS63
2014	1,500	PF65 520			

KM# 567 75 DOLLARS
31.44 g., 0.4166 Gold 0.4184 oz. AGW, 36.07 mm. **Ruler:** Elizabeth II **Subject:** Pope John Paul II **Obv:** Head right **Rev:** Pope giving blessing

Date	Mintage	VF20	XF40	MS60	MS63
2005	1,870	PF65 825			

KM# 747 75 DOLLARS
12.00 g., 0.583 Gold 0.2235 oz. AGW, 27 mm. **Ruler:** Elizabeth II **Subject:** Vancouver Olympics - Athletics Pride **Rev:** Athletics celebrating, holding flag aloft

Date	Mintage	VF20	XF40	MS60	MS63
2007	4,524	PF65 440			

KM# 748 75 DOLLARS
12.00 g., 0.583 Gold 0.2235 oz. AGW, 27 mm. **Ruler:** Elizabeth II **Obv:** Bust right **Rev:** Canada geese in flight left, multicolor

Date	Mintage	VF20	XF40	MS60	MS63
2007	4,418	PF65 440			

KM# 749 75 DOLLARS
12.00 g., 0.583 Gold 0.2235 oz. AGW, 27 mm. **Ruler:** Elizabeth II **Rev:** Mountie, multicolor

Date	Mintage	VF20	XF40	MS60	MS63
2007	6,687	PF65 440			

KM# 820 75 DOLLARS
12.00 g., 0.583 Gold 0.2235 oz. AGW, 27 mm. **Ruler:** Elizabeth II **Rev:** 2010 Olympic Inukshuk Stone man, partially silver plated

Date	Mintage	VF20	XF40	MS60	MS63
2008	—	PF65 420			

KM# 821 75 DOLLARS
12.00 g., 0.583 Gold 0.2235 oz. AGW, 27 mm. **Ruler:** Elizabeth II **Rev:** Four Host Nations mask emblems, colored

Date	Mintage	VF20	XF40	MS60	MS63
2008	8,000	PF65 440			

KM# 947 75 DOLLARS
12.00 g., 0.583 Gold 0.2235 oz. AGW, 27 mm. **Ruler:** Elizabeth II **Subject:** Vancouver Olympics **Rev:** Tent building at Olympic site, color

Date	Mintage	VF20	XF40	MS60	MS63
2008	8,000	PF63 430	PF65 440		

KM# 908 75 DOLLARS
12.00 g., 0.583 Gold 0.2235 oz. AGW, 27 mm. **Ruler:** Elizabeth II **Subject:** 2010 Vancouver Olympics **Obv:** Bust right **Rev:** Multicolor moose

Date	Mintage	VF20	XF40	MS60	MS63
2009	4,075	PF65 440			

KM# 909 75 DOLLARS
12.00 g., 0.583 Gold 0.2235 oz. AGW, 27 mm. **Ruler:** Elizabeth II **Subject:** 2010 Vancouver Olympics **Obv:** Bust right **Rev:** Multicolor athletics and torch

Date	Mintage	VF20	XF40	MS60	MS63
2009	4,479	PF65 440			

KM# 910 75 DOLLARS
12.00 g., 0.583 Gold 0.2235 oz. AGW, 27 mm. **Ruler:** Elizabeth

II **Subject:** 2010 Vancouver Olympics **Obv:** Bust right **Rev:** Wolf, multicolor

Date	Mintage	VF20	XF40	MS60	MS63
2009	4,161	PF65 440			

KM# 1002 75 DOLLARS
12.00 g., 0.583 Gold 0.2235 oz. AGW, 27 mm. **Ruler:** Elizabeth II **Rev:** Spring color maple leaves

Date	Mintage	VF20	XF40	MS60	MS63
2010	1,000	PF65 500			

KM# 1003 75 DOLLARS
12.00 g., 0.583 Gold 0.2235 oz. AGW, 27 mm. **Ruler:** Elizabeth II **Rev:** Summer color maple leaves

Date	Mintage	VF20	XF40	MS60	MS63
2010	1,000	PF65 500			

KM# 1004 75 DOLLARS
12.00 g., 0.583 Gold 0.2235 oz. AGW, 27 mm. **Ruler:** Elizabeth II **Rev:** Fall color maple leaves

Date	Mintage	VF20	XF40	MS60	MS63
2010	1,000	PF65 500			

KM# 1005 75 DOLLARS
12.00 g., 0.583 Gold 0.2235 oz. AGW, 27 mm. **Ruler:** Elizabeth II **Rev:** Winter color maple leaves

Date	Mintage	VF20	XF40	MS60	MS63
2010	1,000	PF65 500			

KM# 1378 75 DOLLARS
7.77 g., 0.999 Gold 0.248 oz. AGW, 20 mm. **Ruler:** Elizabeth II **Subject:** Baseball **Rev:** Baseball Diamond and Crossed Bats

Date	Mintage	VF20	XF40	MS60	MS63
2013	—	PF65 900			

KM# 1379 75 DOLLARS
7.77 g., 0.999 Gold 0.248 oz. AGW, 20 mm. **Ruler:** Elizabeth II **Subject:** Baseball **Rev:** Baseball

Date	Mintage	VF20	XF40	MS60	MS63
2013	Est. 3500	PF65 900			

KM# 1450 75 DOLLARS
12.00 g., 0.583 Gold 0.2235 oz. AGW, 27 mm. **Ruler:** Elizabeth II **Subject:** 75th Anniversary of Superman **Rev:** Superman in color, jumping on rooftop, logo name above

Date	Mintage	VF20	XF40	MS60	MS63
2013	Est. 2000	PF65 750			

KM# 416 100 DOLLARS
13.34 g., 0.583 Gold 0.2484 oz. AGW, 27 mm. **Ruler:** Elizabeth II **Subject:** Library of Parliament **Obv:** Crowned head right **Rev:** Statue in domed building **Edge:** Reeded

Date	Mintage	VF20	XF40	MS60	MS63
2001	—	PF65 475			

KM# 452 100 DOLLARS
13.34 g., 0.583 Gold 0.2484 oz. AGW, 27 mm. **Ruler:** Elizabeth II **Subject:** Discovery of Oil in Alberta **Obv:** Crowned head right **Rev:** Oil well with black oil spill on ground **Edge:** Reeded

Date	Mintage	VF20	XF40	MS60	MS63
2002	9,994	PF65 475			

KM# 486 100 DOLLARS
13.34 g., 0.583 Gold 0.2484 oz. AGW **Ruler:** Elizabeth II **Subject:** 100th Anniversary of the Discovery of Marquis Wheat **Obv:** Head right

Date	Mintage	VF20	XF40	MS60	MS63
2003	9,993	PF65 475			

KM# 528 100 DOLLARS
12.00 g., 0.583 Gold 0.2235 oz. AGW **Ruler:** Elizabeth II **Subject:** St. Lawrence Seaway, 50th Anniversary **Obv:** Head right

Date	Mintage	VF20	XF40	MS60	MS63
2004	7,454	PF65 425			

KM# 593 100 DOLLARS
12.00 g., 0.5833 Gold 0.2236 oz. AGW **Ruler:** Elizabeth II **Subject:** 130th Anniversary, Supreme Court **Obv:** Head right

Date	Mintage	VF20	XF40	MS60	MS63
2005	5,092	PF65 425			

KM# 591 100 DOLLARS
12.00 g., 0.5833 Gold 0.2236 oz. AGW **Ruler:** Elizabeth II **Subject:** 75th Anniversary, Hockey Classic between Royal Military College and U.S. Military Academy **Obv:** Head right

Date	Mintage	VF20	XF40	MS60	MS63
2006	5,439	PF65 425			

KM# 689 100 DOLLARS
12.00 g., 0.5833 Gold 0.2236 oz. AGW, 27 mm. **Ruler:** Elizabeth II **Subject:** 140th Anniversary Dominion **Obv:** Head right

Date	Mintage	VF20	XF40	MS60	MS63
2007	4,453	PF65 425			

KM# 823 100 DOLLARS
12.00 g., 0.583 Gold 0.2235 oz. AGW, 27 mm. **Ruler:** Elizabeth II **Rev:** Fraser River

Date	Mintage	VF20	XF40	MS60	MS63
2008	3,089	PF65 425			

KM# 898 100 DOLLARS
12.00 g., 0.583 Gold 0.2235 oz. AGW, 27 mm. **Ruler:** Elizabeth II **Subject:** 10th Anniversary of Nunavut **Obv:** Bust right **Obv. Legend:** Elizabeth II DG Regina **Rev:** Inuit dancer with 3 faces behind **Rev. Legend:** Canada 100 Dollars 1999-2009

Date	Mintage	VF20	XF40	MS60	MS63
2009	2,309	PF65 425			

KM# 997 100 DOLLARS
12.00 g., 0.583 Gold 0.2235 oz. AGW, 27 mm. **Ruler:** Elizabeth II **Rev:** Henry Hudson, Map of Hudson's Bay

Date	Mintage	VF20	XF40	MS60	MS63
2010	Est. 5000	PF65 425			

KM# 1073 100 DOLLARS
12.00 g., 0.583 Gold 0.2235 oz. AGW, 27 mm. **Ruler:** Elizabeth II **Subject:** Canadian Railroads, 175th Anniversary **Rev:** Early steam locomotive

Date	Mintage	VF20	XF40	MS60	MS63
2011	3,000	PF65 425			

KM# 1389 100 DOLLARS
12.00 g., 0.5833 Gold 0.2236 oz. AGW, 27 mm. **Ruler:** Elizabeth II **Subject:** Arctic Exploration - 100th Anniversary **Rev:** Map of the North Pole, Explorers

Date	Mintage	VF20	XF40	MS60	MS63
2013	—	PF65 600			

KM# 1441 100 DOLLARS
31.60 g., 0.999 Silver 1.0084 oz. ASW, 40 mm. **Ruler:** Elizabeth II **Rev:** Three bison advancing left

Date	Mintage	VF20	XF40	MS60	MS63
2013 Matte Proof	Est. 50000	PF63 100			

KM# 1582 100 DOLLARS
13.34 g., 0.999 Gold 0.4256 oz. AGW, 27 mm. **Ruler:** Elizabeth II **Subject:** Charlottetown Quebec, 1864 **Obv:** Bust right **Rev:** Building views

Date	Mintage	VF20	XF40	MS60	MS63
2014		PF65 475			

KM# 417 150 DOLLARS
13.61 g., 0.750 Gold 0.3261 oz. AGW, 28 mm. **Ruler:** Elizabeth II **Subject:** Year of the Snake **Obv:** Crowned head right **Rev:** Multicolor snake hologram **Edge:** Reeded

Date	Mintage	VF20	XF40	MS60	MS63
2001	—	PF65 625			

KM# 604 150 DOLLARS
13.61 g., 0.750 Gold 0.3261 oz. AGW **Ruler:** Elizabeth II **Obv:** Head right **Rev:** Stylized horse left

Date	Mintage	VF20	XF40	MS60	MS63
2002	6,843	PF65 625			

KM# 487 150 DOLLARS
13.61 g., 0.750 Gold 0.3261 oz. AGW, 28 mm. **Ruler:** Elizabeth II **Subject:** Year of the Ram **Obv:** Crowned head right **Rev:** Stylized ram left, hologram

Date	Mintage	VF20	XF40	MS60	MS63
2003	3,927	PF65 625			

KM# 614 150 DOLLARS
13.61 g., 0.750 Gold 0.3261 oz. AGW **Ruler:** Elizabeth II **Obv:** Head right **Rev:** Year of the Monkey, hologram

Date	Mintage	VF20	XF40	MS60	MS63
2004	3,392	PF65 625			

KM# 568 150 DOLLARS
13.61 g., 0.750 Gold 0.3261 oz. AGW **Ruler:** Elizabeth II **Subject:** Year of the Rooster **Obv:** Head right **Rev:** Rooster left, hologram

Date	Mintage	VF20	XF40	MS60	MS63
2005	3,731	PF65 625			

KM# 592 150 DOLLARS
13.61 g., 0.750 Gold 0.3261 oz. AGW, 28 mm. **Ruler:** Elizabeth II **Subject:** Year of the Dog, hologram **Obv:** Head right **Rev:** Stylized dog left

Date	Mintage	VF20	XF40	MS60	MS63
2006	2,604	PF65 625			

KM# 733 150 DOLLARS
11.84 g., 0.750 Gold 0.2837 oz. AGW, 28 mm. **Ruler:** Elizabeth II **Subject:** Year of the Pig **Obv:** Head right **Rev:** Pig in center with Chinese lunar calendar around, hologram

Date	Mintage	VF20	XF40	MS60	MS63
2007	826	PF65 675			

KM# 802 150 DOLLARS
11.84 g., 0.750 Gold 0.2837 oz. AGW, 28 mm. **Ruler:** Elizabeth II **Subject:** Year of the Rat **Rev:** Rat, hologram

Date	Mintage	VF20	XF40	MS60	MS63
2008	582	PF65 675			

KM# 899 150 DOLLARS
10.40 g., 0.999 Gold 0.3319 oz. AGW, 22.5 mm. **Ruler:** Elizabeth II **Subject:** Blessings of wealth **Obv:** Bust right **Obv. Legend:** Elizabeth II, DG Regina, Fine Gold 99999 or PUR **Rev:** Three goldfish surround peony, clouds **Rev. Legend:** Canada 150 Dollars (Chinese symbols of good fortune) **Edge:** Scalloped

Date	Mintage	VF20	XF40	MS60	MS63
2009	1,273	PF65 650			

KM# 867 150 DOLLARS
11.84 g., 0.750 Gold 0.2837 oz. AGW, 28 mm. **Ruler:** Elizabeth II **Subject:** Year of the Ox **Rev:** Ox, hologram

Date	Mintage	VF20	XF40	MS60	MS63
2009	486	PF65 550			

KM# 979 150 DOLLARS
11.84 g., 0.750 Gold 0.2837 oz. AGW, 28 mm. **Ruler:** Elizabeth II **Subject:** Year of the Tiger **Rev:** Tiger in hologram

Date	Mintage	VF20	XF40	MS60	MS63
2010	1,507	PF65 550			

KM# 1030 150 DOLLARS
10.40 g., 0.9999 Gold 0.3322 oz. AGW **Ruler:** Elizabeth II **Subject:** Blessing of Wealth **Shape:** Scalloped

Date	Mintage	VF20	XF40	MS60	MS63
2010	1,388	PF65 650			

KM# 1031 150 DOLLARS
Gold AGW **Ruler:** Elizabeth II **Subject:** Year of the Tiger **Rev:** Tiger walking

Date	Mintage	VF20	XF40	MS60	MS63
2010	2,500	PF65 600			

KM# 1054 150 DOLLARS
Gold AGW **Ruler:** Elizabeth II **Subject:** Year of the rabbit **Rev:** Rabit hopping left, character at left

Date	Mintage	VF20	XF40	MS60	MS63
2011	2,500	PF65 600			

KM# 1053 150 DOLLARS
13.61 g., 0.750 Gold 0.3261 oz. AGW, 28 mm. **Ruler:** Elizabeth II **Subject:** Year of the rabbit **Rev:** Rabbit hologram

Date	Mintage	VF20	XF40	MS60	MS63
2011	—	PF65 600			

KM# 1184 150 DOLLARS
13.61 g., 0.750 Gold 0.3261 oz. AGW, 28 mm. **Ruler:** Elizabeth II **Subject:** Year of the Dragon **Obv:** Bust right **Rev:** Dragon left

Date	Mintage	VF20	XF40	MS60	MS63
2012	—	PF65 650			

KM# 1262 150 DOLLARS
10.40 g., 0.999 Gold 0.3319 oz. AGW, 22.5 mm. **Ruler:** Elizabeth II **Subject:** Good Fortune Panda

Date	Mintage	VF20	XF40	MS60	MS63
2012	—	PF65 650			

KM# 1362 150 DOLLARS
11.84 g., 0.750 Gold 0.2837 oz. AGW, 28 mm. **Ruler:** Elizabeth II **Subject:** Year of the Snake **Rev:** Snake vertical between two Chinese characters

Date	Mintage	VF20	XF40	MS60	MS63
2013	2,500	PF65 700			

KM# 1418 150 DOLLARS
15.59 g., Gold AGW, 25 mm. **Ruler:** Elizabeth II **Subject:** Baseball **Rev:** Runner with hands raised

Date	Mintage	VF20	XF40	MS60	MS63
2013	Est. 3500	PF65 1,550			

KM# 1437 150 DOLLARS
10.40 g., 0.999 Gold 0.3319 oz. AGW, 22.5 mm. **Ruler:** Elizabeth II **Subject:** Blessings of Peace **Rev:** Clouds, phoenix and feathers **Shape:** Scalloped

Date	Mintage	VF20	XF40	MS60	MS63
2013	Est. 888	PF65 700			

KM# 1515 150 DOLLARS
11.84 g., 0.750 Gold 0.2837 oz. AGW, 28 mm. **Ruler:** Elizabeth II **Subject:** Year of the Horse **Rev:** Horse prancing left

Date	Mintage	VF20	XF40	MS60	MS63
2014	2,500	PF65 700			

KM# 418 200 DOLLARS
17.14 g., 0.9166 Gold 0.5017 oz. AGW, 29 mm. **Ruler:** Elizabeth II **Subject:** Cornelius D. Krieghoff's "The Habitant farm **Obv:** Queens head right **Edge:** Reeded

Date	Mintage	VF20	XF40	MS60	MS63
2001		PF65 975			

KM# 466 200 DOLLARS
17.14 g., 0.9166 Gold 0.5017 oz. AGW, 29 mm. **Ruler:** Elizabeth II **Subject:** Thomas Thompson "The Jack Pine" (1916-17) **Obv:** Crowned head right

Date	Mintage	VF20	XF40	MS60	MS63
2002	5,264	PF65 975			

KM# 488 200 DOLLARS
17.14 g., 0.9166 Gold 0.5017 oz. AGW **Ruler:** Elizabeth II

Subject: Fitzgerald's "Houses" (1929) **Obv:** Crowned head right **Rev:** House with trees

Date	Mintage	VF20	XF40	MS60	MS63
2003	4,118	PF65 975			

KM# 516 200 DOLLARS
16.00 g., 0.9166 Gold 0.4685 oz. AGW, 29 mm. **Ruler:** Elizabeth II **Subject:** Fragments **Obv:** Crowned head right **Rev:** Fragmented face **Edge:** Reeded

Date	Mintage	VF20	XF40	MS60	MS63
2004	3,917	PF65 900			

KM# 569 200 DOLLARS
16.00 g., 0.9166 Gold 0.4685 oz. AGW **Ruler:** Elizabeth II **Subject:** Fur traders **Obv:** Head right **Rev:** Men in canoe riding wave

Date	Mintage	VF20	XF40	MS60	MS63
2005	3,669	PF65 900			

KM# 594 200 DOLLARS
16.00 g., 0.9166 Gold 0.4685 oz. AGW **Ruler:** Elizabeth II **Subject:** Timber trade **Obv:** Head right **Rev:** Lumberjacks felling tree

Date	Mintage	VF20	XF40	MS60	MS63
2006	3,218	PF65 900			

KM# 691 200 DOLLARS
16.00 g., 0.9166 Gold 0.4685 oz. AGW, 29 mm. **Ruler:** Elizabeth II **Subject:** Fishing Trade **Obv:** Head right **Rev:** Two fishermen hauling net

Date	Mintage	VF20	XF40	MS60	MS63
2007	2,137	PF65 900			

KM# 824 200 DOLLARS
16.00 g., 0.917 Gold 0.4687 oz. AGW, 29 mm. **Ruler:** Elizabeth II **Subject:** Commerce **Rev:** Horse drawn plow

Date	Mintage	VF20	XF40	MS60	MS63
2008	1,951	PF65 900			

KM# 894 200 DOLLARS
16.00 g., 0.916 Gold 0.4682 oz. AGW, 29 mm. **Ruler:** Elizabeth II **Subject:** Coal mining trade **Obv:** Bust right **Obv. Legend:** Elizabeth II DG Regina **Rev:** Miner pushing cart with black coal **Rev. Legend:** Canada 200 Dollars

Date	Mintage	VF20	XF40	MS60	MS63
2009	2,241	PF65 900			

KM# 1000 200 DOLLARS
16.00 g., 0.916 Gold 0.4682 oz. AGW, 29 mm. **Ruler:** Elizabeth II **Subject:** Petroleum and Oil Trade **Rev:** Oil railcar and well head

Date	Mintage	VF20	XF40	MS60	MS63
2010	Est. 4000	PF65 900			

KM# 1060 200 DOLLARS
16.00 g., 0.9167 Gold 0.4685 oz. AGW, 29 mm. **Ruler:** Elizabeth II **Rev:** Olympic athletics with medal, flag and flowers

Date	Mintage	VF20	XF40	MS60	MS63
2010	—	PF65 900			

KM# 1074 200 DOLLARS
16.00 g., 0.9167 Gold 0.4685 oz. AGW, 29 mm. **Ruler:** Elizabeth II **Rev:** SS Beaver - Seam Sail ship

Date	Mintage	VF20	XF40	MS60	MS63
2011	2,800	PF65 900			

KM# 1143 200 DOLLARS
16.00 g., 0.9167 Gold 0.4685 oz. AGW, 27 mm. **Ruler:** Elizabeth II **Subject:** Wedding, Prince William and Katherine Middleton **Obv:** Bust right **Rev:** Half-length figures facing, swarovski crystal **Edge:** Reeded

Date	Mintage	VF20	XF40	MS60	MS63
2011	2,000	PF65 900			

KM# 1174 200 DOLLARS
16.00 g., 0.916 Gold 0.4682 oz. AGW, 29 mm. **Ruler:** Elizabeth II **Obv:** Bust right **Rev:** Wayne Greskey skating right, father's portrait in circle at right, 99 in color at lower right

Date	Mintage	VF20	XF40	MS60	MS63
2011	999	PF65 900			

KM# 1219 200 DOLLARS
16.00 g., 0.9167 Gold 0.4685 oz. AGW, 29 mm. **Ruler:** Elizabeth II **Obv:** Bust right **Rev:** Prospector panning for gold in stream

Date	Mintage	VF20	XF40	MS60	MS63
2012	—	PF65 900			

KM# 1223 200 DOLLARS
16.00 g., 0.9167 Gold 0.4685 oz. AGW, 29 mm. **Ruler:** Elizabeth II **Obv:** Bust right **Rev:** Vikings and ship

Date	Mintage	VF20	XF40	MS60	MS63
2012	—	PF65 900			

KM# 1279 200 DOLLARS
31.11 g., 0.999 Gold 0.9926 oz. AGW, 30 mm. **Ruler:** Elizabeth II **Subject:** Bateman Moose

Date	Mintage	VF20	XF40	MS60	MS63
2012	—	PF65 1,850			

KM# 1331 200 DOLLARS
33.33 g., 0.999 Gold 1.0636 oz. AGW, 30 mm. **Ruler:** Elizabeth II **Rev:** Grandmother Moon Mask

Date	Mintage	VF20	XF40	MS60	MS63
2012	500	PF65 3,000			

KM# 1390 200 DOLLARS
15.43 g., 0.999 Gold 0.4924 oz. AGW, 29 mm. **Ruler:** Elizabeth II **Subject:** Explorer Jacques Cartier

Date	Mintage	VF20	XF40	MS60	MS63
2013	Est. 2000	PF65 1,200			

KM# 1480 200 DOLLARS
31.11 g., 0.999 Gold 0.9926 oz. AGW, 30 mm. **Ruler:** Elizabeth II **Rev:** Eagle in nest with two chicks

Date	Mintage	F12	VF20	XF40	MS60	MS63
2013 Proof	350	—	—	—	—	2,750

KM# 1500 200 DOLLARS
33.33 g., 0.9999 Gold 1.0646 oz. AGW, 30 mm. **Ruler:** Elizabeth II **Subject:** Grandmother Moon Mask **Rev:** Mask carving

Date	Mintage	VF20	XF40	MS60	MS63
2013	500	PF65 3,000			

KM# 1583 200 DOLLARS
16.00 g., 0.9167 Gold 0.4685 oz. AGW, 29 mm. **Ruler:** Elizabeth II **Obv:** Bust right **Rev:** Indian and explorer standing next to canoes

Date	Mintage	VF20	XF40	MS60	MS63
2014		PF65 900			

KM# 1G1G 200 DOLLARS
31.11 g., 0.999 Gold 0.9926 oz. AGW, 30 mm. **Ruler:** Elizabeth
II **Obv:** Bust right **Rev:** Howling wolf

Date	Mintage	VF20	XF40	MS60	MS63
2014	2,000	PF65 2,800			

KM# 677 250 DOLLARS
45.00 g., 0.5833 Gold 0.8385 oz. AGW, 40 mm. **Ruler:** Elizabeth
II **Rev:** Dog Sled Team

Date	Mintage	VF20	XF40	MS60	MS63
2006	953	PF65 1,625			

KM# 751 250 DOLLARS
1000.00 g., 0.9999 Silver 31.9406 oz. ASW, 101.6 mm. **Ruler:**
Elizabeth II **Subject:** Vancouver Olympics, 2010 **Rev:** Early
Canada motif **Note:** Illustration reduced.

Date	Mintage	VF20	XF40	MS60	MS63
2007	2,500	PF66 1,250			

KM# 833 250 DOLLARS
1000.00 g., 0.999 Silver 31.9118 oz. ASW, 101.6 mm. **Ruler:**
Elizabeth II **Subject:** Vancouver Olympics 2010 **Rev:** Towards
confederation **Note:** Illustration reduced.

Date	Mintage	VF20	XF40	MS60	MS63
2008	2,500	PF65 1,350			

KM# 913 250 DOLLARS
1000.00 g., 0.9999 Silver 31.9406 oz. ASW, 101.5 mm. **Ruler:**
Elizabeth II **Obv:** Bust right **Rev:** Mask with fish - Surviving the
flood **Note:** Illustration reduced.

Date	Mintage	VF20	XF40	MS60	MS63
2009	815	PF65 1,350			

KM# 949 250 DOLLARS
1000.00 g., 0.999 Silver 31.9118 oz. ASW, 101.6 mm. **Ruler:**
Elizabeth II **Rev:** Modern Canada

Date	Mintage	VF20	XF40	MS60	MS63
2009	905	PF65 1,350			

KM# 981 250 DOLLARS
1000.00 g., 0.999 Silver 31.9118 oz. ASW, 101.6 mm. **Ruler:**
Elizabeth II **Rev:** Eagle head

Date	Mintage	VF20	XF40	MS60	MS63
2010 Antique Patina	500	—	—		1,350
2010	500	PF65 1,400			

KM# 981a 250 DOLLARS
1000.00 g., 0.999 Silver 31.9118 oz. ASW, 101.6 mm. **Ruler:**
Elizabeth II **Rev:** Eagle head, blue enamel

Date	Mintage	VF20	XF40	MS60	MS63
2010	500	PF65 1,400			

KM# 1044 250 DOLLARS
1000.00 g., 0.999 Silver 31.9118 oz. ASW, 101.6 mm. **Ruler:**
Elizabeth II **Subject:** Baniff, 125th Anniversary of resort
founding **Rev:** Features of Baniff

Date	Mintage	VF20	XF40	MS60	MS63
2010	750	PF65 1,650			

KM# 1285 250 DOLLARS
1000.00 g., 0.999 Silver 31.9118 oz. ASW, 101 mm. **Ruler:**
Elizabeth II **Subject:** Olympic views

Date	Mintage	VF20	XF40	MS60	MS63
2010	—	PF65 1,350			

KM# 1150 250 DOLLARS
1000.00 g., 0.9999 Silver 31.9406 oz. ASW, 100 mm. **Ruler:**
Elizabeth II **Rev:** Lacrosse

Date	Mintage	VF20	XF40	MS60	MS63
2011	—	PF65 1,350			

KM# 1185 250 DOLLARS
1000.00 g., 0.999 Silver 31.9118 oz. ASW, 101.6 mm. **Ruler:**
Elizabeth II **Subject:** Year of the Dragon **Obv:** Bust left **Rev:**
Dragon left

Date	Mintage	VF20	XF40	MS60	MS63
2012	—	PF65 1,550			

KM# 1277 250 DOLLARS
1000.00 g., 0.999 Silver 31.9118 oz. ASW, 101 mm. **Ruler:**
Elizabeth II **Subject:** Bateman Moose

Date	Mintage	VF20	XF40	MS60	MS63
2012	—	PF65 1,650			

KM# 1340 250 DOLLARS
1000.00 g., 0.9999 Silver 31.9406 oz. ASW, 102 mm. **Ruler:**
Elizabeth II **Subject:** War of 1812, Battle of Queenstown
Heights **Rev:** Battle scene

Date	Mintage	VF20	XF40	MS60	MS63
2012	7,000	PF65 2,250			

KM# 1366 250 DOLLARS
1000.00 g., 0.9999 Silver 31.9406 oz. ASW **Ruler:** Elizabeth II
Subject: Year of the Snake **Rev:** Snake under maple leaves

Date	Mintage	VF20	XF40	MS60	MS63
2013	Est. 888	PF65 2,250			

KM# 1369 250 DOLLARS
1000.00 g., 0.999 Silver 31.9118 oz. ASW **Ruler:** Elizabeth II
Subject: End of 7 Years War **Rev:** Map of North America with
Arms of France and Great Britain

Date	Mintage	VF20	XF40	MS60	MS63
2013	Est. 500	PF65 2,250			

KM# 1371 250 DOLLARS
1000.00 g., 0.999 Silver 31.9118 oz. ASW, 101 mm. **Ruler:**
Elizabeth II **Subject:** Arctic Coastline

Date	Mintage	VF20	XF40	MS60	MS63
2013	Est. 750	PF65 2,250			

KM# 1438 250 DOLLARS
1000.00 g., 0.9999 Silver 31.9406 oz. ASW, 102.1 mm. **Ruler:**
Elizabeth II **Rev:** Two maple leaves - gilt

Date	Mintage	VF20	XF40	MS60	MS63
2013	Est. 600	PF65 2,300			

KM# 1477 250 DOLLARS
1000.00 g., 0.9999 Silver 31.9406 oz. ASW, 102.1 mm. **Ruler:**
Elizabeth II **Subject:** Battle of Chateauguay **Rev:** Henri
Julien's painting of the battle

Date	Mintage	VF20	XF40	MS60	MS63
2013	500	PF65 2,250			

KM# 1502 250 DOLLARS
1000.00 g., 0.9999 Silver 31.9406 oz. ASW, 102.1 mm. **Ruler:**
Elizabeth II **Rev:** Two caribou advancing left

Date	Mintage	VF20	XF40	MS60	MS63
2013	500	PF65 2,500			

KM# 1518 250 DOLLARS
1000.00 g., 0.9999 Silver 31.9406 oz. ASW, 102.1 mm. **Ruler:**
Elizabeth II **Subject:** Year of the Horse **Rev:** Horse rearing
up left

Date	Mintage	VF20	XF40	MS60	MS63
2014	388	PF65 2,250			

KM# 1579 250 DOLLARS
1000.00 g., 0.9999 Silver 31.9406 oz. ASW, 101 mm. **Ruler:**
Elizabeth II **Subject:** Year of the Horse

Date	Mintage	VF20	XF40	MS60	MS63
2014	PF65 1,350				

KM# 1605 250 DOLLARS
1000.00 g., 0.9999 Silver 31.9406 oz. ASW, 101 mm. **Ruler:**
Elizabeth II **Obv:** Bust right **Rev:** Snowy owl, yellow eyes

Date	Mintage	VF20	XF40	MS60	MS63
2014	—	PF65 1,650			

KM# 1622 250 DOLLARS
62.34 g., 0.999 Gold 1.9894 oz. AGW, 42 mm. **Ruler:** Elizabeth
II **Subject:** Canada thru the eyes of Tim Barnard **Obv:** Bust
right **Rev:** Multitude of designs

Date	Mintage	VF20	XF40	MS60	MS63
2014	300	PF65 5,200			

KM# 501 300 DOLLARS
60.00 g., 0.5833 Gold 1.118 oz. AGW, 50 mm. **Ruler:** Elizabeth
II **Obv:** Triple cameo portraits of Queen Elizabeth II by Gillick,
Machin and de Pedery-Hunt, each in 14K gold, rose in center
Rev: Dates "1952-2002" and denomination in legend, rose in
center **Note:** Housed in anodized gold-colored aluminum box
with cherrywood stained siding

Date	Mintage	VF20	XF40	MS60	MS63
1952-2002	999	PF65 2,150			

KM# 517 300 DOLLARS
60.00 g., 0.5833 Gold 1.118 oz. AGW, 50 mm. **Ruler:** Elizabeth
II **Obv:** Four coinage portraits of Elizabeth II **Rev:** Canadian
arms above value **Edge:** Plain

Date	Mintage	VF20	XF40	MS60	MS63
2004	998	PF65 2,150			

KM# 600 300 DOLLARS
60.00 g., 0.5833 Gold 1.118 oz. AGW, 40 mm. **Ruler:** Elizabeth
II **Subject:** Welcome Figure Totem Pole **Obv:** Head right **Rev:**
Men with totem pole

Date	Mintage	VF20	XF40	MS60	MS63
2005	948	PF65 2,150			

KM# 570.1 300 DOLLARS
45.00 g., 0.5833 Gold 0.8385 oz. AGW, 40 mm. **Ruler:** Elizabeth
II **Subject:** Standard Time - 4 AM Pacific **Obv:** Head right **Rev:**
Roman numeral clock with world inside

Date	Mintage	VF20	XF40	MS60	MS63
2005	200	PF65 1,650			

KM# 570.2 300 DOLLARS
45.00 g., 0.583 Gold 0.838 oz. AGW, 40 mm. **Ruler:** Elizabeth II
Subject: Standard Time - Mountian 5 AM **Obv:** Head right **Rev:**
Roman numeral clock with world inside.

Date	Mintage	VF20	XF40	MS60	MS63
2005	200	PF65 1,650			

KM# 570.3 300 DOLLARS
45.00 g., 0.583 Gold 0.838 oz. AGW, 40 mm. **Ruler:** Elizabeth II
Subject: Standard Time - Central 6 PM **Obv:** Head right **Rev:**
Roman numeral clock with world inside

Date	Mintage	VF20	XF40	MS60	MS63
2005	200	PF65 1,650			

KM# 570.4 300 DOLLARS
45.00 g., 0.583 Gold 0.838 oz. AGW, 40 mm. **Ruler:** Elizabeth II
Subject: Standard Time - Eastern 7 AM **Obv:** Head right **Rev:**
Roman numeral clock with world inside

Date	Mintage	VF20	XF40	MS60	MS63
2005	200	PF65 1,650			

KM# 570.5 300 DOLLARS
45.00 g., 0.583 Gold 0.838 oz. AGW, 40 mm. **Ruler:** Elizabeth II
Subject: Standard Time - Atlantic 8 AM **Obv:** Head right **Rev:**
Roman numeral clock with world inside

Date	Mintage	VF20	XF40	MS60	MS63
2005	200	PF65 1,650			

KM# 570.6 300 DOLLARS
45.00 g., 0.583 Gold 0.838 oz. AGW, 40 mm. **Ruler:** Elizabeth II
Subject: Standard Time - Newfoundland 8:30 **Obv:** Head right
Rev: Roman numeral clock with world inside

Date	Mintage	VF20	XF40	MS60	MS63
2005	200	PF65 1,650			

KM# 596 300 DOLLARS
60.00 g., 0.5833 Gold 1.118 oz. AGW, 50 mm. **Ruler:** Elizabeth
II **Subject:** Shinplaster **Obv:** Head right **Rev:** Britannia bust,
spear over shoulder

Date	Mintage	VF20	XF40	MS60	MS63
2005	994	PF65 2,150			

KM# 678 300 DOLLARS
45.00 g., 0.5833 Gold 0.8385 oz. AGW, 40 mm. **Ruler:** Elizabeth
II **Rev:** Hologram of Canadarm, Col. C. Hadfield in spacewalk

Date	Mintage	VF20	XF40	MS60	MS63
2006	581	PF65 1,650			

KM# 679 300 DOLLARS
60.00 g., 0.5833 Gold 1.118 oz. AGW, 50 mm. **Ruler:** Elizabeth
II **Subject:** Queen Elizabeth's 80th Birthday **Rev:** State Crown,
colorized

Date	Mintage	VF20	XF40	MS60	MS63
2006	996	PF65 2,150			

KM# 680 300 DOLLARS
60.00 g., 0.5833 Gold 1.118 oz. AGW, 50 mm. **Ruler:** Elizabeth
II **Subject:** Crystal Snowflake

Date	Mintage	VF20	XF40	MS60	MS63
2006	998	PF65 2,150			

KM# 595 300 DOLLARS
60.00 g., 0.5833 Gold 1.118 oz. AGW, 50 mm. **Ruler:** Elizabeth
II **Subject:** Shinplaster **Obv:** Head right **Rev:** Seated Britannia
with shield

Date	Mintage	VF20	XF40	MS60	MS63
2006	940	PF65 2,150			

KM# 692 300 DOLLARS
60.00 g., 0.5833 Gold 1.118 oz. AGW, 50 mm. **Ruler:** Elizabeth
II **Subject:** Shinplaster **Rev:** 1923 25 cent bank note

Date	Mintage	VF20	XF40	MS60	MS63
2007	778	PF65 2,150			

KM# 740 300 DOLLARS
45.00 g., 0.583 Gold 0.838 oz. AGW, 40 mm. **Ruler:** Elizabeth II
Rev: Canadian Rockies panoramic hologram

Date	Mintage	VF20	XF40	MS60	MS63
2007	511	PF65 1,750			

KM# 752 300 DOLLARS
60.00 g., 0.583 Gold 1.1174 oz. AGW, 50 mm. **Ruler:** Elizabeth
II **Subject:** Vancouver Olympics **Rev:** Olympic ideals, classic
figures and torch

Date	Mintage	VF20	XF40	MS60	MS63
2007	953	PF65 2,150			

KM# 825 300 DOLLARS
45.00 g., 0.583 Gold 0.838 oz. AGW, 50 mm. **Ruler:** Elizabeth II
Rev: Alberta Coat of Arms

Date	Mintage	VF20	XF40	MS60	MS63
2000	344	PF65 1,750			

KM# 826 300 DOLLARS
60.00 g., 0.583 Gold 1.1174 oz. AGW, 50 mm. **Ruler:** Elizabeth
II **Rev:** Newfoundland and Labrador Coat of Arms

Date	Mintage	VF20	XF40	MS60	MS63
2008	472	PF65 2,150			

KM# 827 300 DOLLARS
45.00 g., 0.583 Gold 0.838 oz. AGW, 40 mm. **Ruler:** Elizabeth II
Subject: Canadian achievements IMAX **Rev:** Kid in audience reaching out to shark on big screen

Date	Mintage	VF20	XF40	MS60	MS63
2008	—	PF65 1,650			

KM# 828 300 DOLLARS
60.00 g., 0.583 Gold 1.1174 oz. AGW, 50 mm. **Ruler:** Elizabeth II **Rev:** Four seasons moon mask in color, blue design in border

Date	Mintage	VF20	XF40	MS60	MS63
2008	544	PF65 3,800			

KM# 830 300 DOLLARS
60.00 g., 0.583 Gold 1.1174 oz. AGW, 50 mm. **Ruler:** Elizabeth II **Subject:** Vancouver Olympics **Rev:** Olympic competition, athletics and torch

Date	Mintage	VF20	XF40	MS60	MS63
2008	334	PF65 2,250			

KM# 900 300 DOLLARS
60.00 g., 0.583 Gold 1.1174 oz. AGW, 50 mm. **Ruler:** Elizabeth II **Subject:** Yukon Coat of Arms **Obv:** Bust right **Obv. Legend:** Elizabeth II DG Regina **Rev:** Yukon Coat of Arms **Rev. Legend:** Canada 300 Dollars

Date	Mintage	VF20	XF40	MS60	MS63
2009	325	PF65 2,150			

KM# 877 300 DOLLARS
60.00 g., 0.583 Gold 1.1174 oz. AGW, 50 mm. **Ruler:** Elizabeth II **Rev:** Summer moon mask, enameled

Date	Mintage	VF20	XF40	MS60	MS63
2009	—	PF65 2,250			

KM# 911 300 DOLLARS
60.00 g., 0.583 Gold 1.1174 oz. AGW, 50 mm. **Ruler:** Elizabeth II **Subject:** 2010 Vancouver Olympics **Obv:** Bust right **Rev:** Athletics with torch - Olympic firendship

Date	Mintage	VF20	XF40	MS60	MS63
2009	880	PF65 2,150			

KM# 999 300 DOLLARS
54.00 g., 0.583 Gold 1.0057 oz. AGW, 50 mm. **Ruler:** Elizabeth II **Rev:** British Columbia Arms

Date	Mintage	VF20	XF40	MS60	MS63
2010	500	PF65 1,900			

KM# 1047 300 DOLLARS
60.00 g., 0.583 Gold 1.1174 oz. AGW, 50 mm. **Ruler:** Elizabeth

II **Rev:** Snowflake, white crystals

Date	Mintage	VF20	XF40	MS60	MS63
2010	750	PF65 2,150			

KM# 1078 300 DOLLARS
60.00 g., 0.583 Gold 1.1174 oz. AGW, 50 mm. **Ruler:** Elizabeth II **Rev:** New Brunswick Coat of arms

Date	Mintage	VF20	XF40	MS60	MS63
2010	500	PF65 2,150			

KM# 1095 300 DOLLARS
60.00 g., 0.9167 Gold 1.757 oz. AGW, 50 mm. **Ruler:** Elizabeth II **Rev:** Manitoba Coat of arms

Date	Mintage	VF20	XF40	MS60	MS63
2011	500	PF65 3,300			

KM# 1215 300 DOLLARS
60.00 g., 0.917 Gold 1.7575 oz. AGW, 50 mm. **Ruler:** Elizabeth II **Obv:** Bust right **Rev:** Arms of Nova Scotia

Date	Mintage	VF20	XF40	MS60	MS63
2011	—	PF65 3,300			

KM# 1195 300 DOLLARS
45.00 g., 0.583 Gold 0.838 oz. AGW, 40 mm. **Ruler:** Elizabeth II **Subject:** Elizabeth II, Diamond Jubilee **Obv:** Bust right **Rev:**

Youthful bust with crown right, insert crystal at right

Date	Mintage	VF20	XF40	MS60	MS63
1952-2012	—	PF65 1,600			

KM# 1224 300 DOLLARS
60.00 g., 0.9167 Gold 1.757 oz. AGW, 50 mm. **Ruler:** Elizabeth II **Obv:** Bust right **Rev:** Shield of Quebec

Date	Mintage	VF20	XF40	MS60	MS63
2012	—	PF65 3,300			

KM# 1242 300 DOLLARS
16.00 g., 0.016 Gold 0.4682 oz. AGW, 29 mm. **Ruler:** Elizabeth II **Subject:** Calgary Stampede

Date	Mintage	VF20	XF40	MS60	MS63
2012	—	PF65 900			

KM# 1278 300 DOLLARS
31.11 g., 0.999 Platinum 0.9927 oz. APW, 30 mm. **Ruler:** Elizabeth II **Subject:** Bateman Moose

Date	Mintage	VF20	XF40	MS60	MS63
2012	—	PF65 1,750			

KM# 1338 300 DOLLARS
60.00 g., 0.917 Gold 1.7575 oz. AGW, 50 mm. **Ruler:** Elizabeth II **Subject:** Nunavut Province **Rev:** Provincial Arms

Date	Mintage	VF20	XF40	MS60	MS63
2012	—	PF65 4,000			

KM# 1430 300 DOLLARS
31.16 g., 0.9995 Platinum 0.9949 oz. APW, 30 mm. **Ruler:** Elizabeth II **Subject:** War of 1812 - Naval Battle **Rev:** HMS Shannon and Chesapeake

Date	Mintage	VF20	XF40	MS60	MS63
2013	Est. 250	PF65 3,000			

KM# 1549 300 DOLLARS
60.00 g., 0.9176 Gold 1.7587 oz. AGW, 50 mm. **Ruler:** Elizabeth II **Subject:** Northwest Territories **Rev:** Provincial Arms

Date	Mintage	VF20	XF40	MS60	MS63
2013	PF65 4,000				

KM# 1571 300 DOLLARS
60.00 g., 0.917 Gold 1.7575 oz. AGW, 50 mm. **Ruler:** Elizabeth II **Obv:** Bust right **Rev:** Arms of Ontario

Date	Mintage	VF20	XF40	MS60	MS63
2013 Proof	3,300	—	—	—	—

KM# 1592 300 DOLLARS
60.00 g., 0.999 Gold 1.9147 oz. AGW **Ruler:** Elizabeth II **Obv:** Bust right **Rev:** Saskashawan coat of arms

Date	Mintage	VF20	XF40	MS60	MS63
2014	PF65 3,300				

KM# 433 350 DOLLARS
38.05 g., 0.9999 Gold 1.2153 oz. AGW, 34 mm. **Ruler:** Elizabeth II **Subject:** The Mayflower Flower **Obv:** Crowned head right **Rev:** Two flowers **Edge:** Reeded

Date	Mintage	VF20	XF40	MS60	MS63
2001	1,988	PF65 2,350			

KM# 502 350 DOLLARS
38.05 g., 0.9999 Gold 1.2153 oz. AGW, 34 mm. **Ruler:** Elizabeth II **Subject:** The Wild Rose **Obv:** Crowned head right **Rev:** Wild rose plant

Date	Mintage	VF20	XF40	MS60	MS63
2002	2,001	PF65 2,350			

KM# 504 350 DOLLARS
38.05 g., 0.9999 Gold 1.2153 oz. AGW, 34 mm. **Ruler:** Elizabeth II **Subject:** The White Trillium **Obv:** Crowned head right **Rev:** White Trillium

Date	Mintage	VF20	XF40	MS60	MS63
2003	1,865	PF65 2,350			

KM# 601 350 DOLLARS
38.05 g., 0.9999 Gold 1.2153 oz. AGW **Ruler:** Elizabeth II **Subject:** Western Red Lilly **Obv:** Head right **Rev:** Western Red Lilies

Date	Mintage	VF20	XF40	MS60	MS63
2005	1,634	PF65 2,350			

KM# 626 350 DOLLARS
38.05 g., 0.9999 Gold 1.2153 oz. AGW, 34 mm. **Ruler:** Elizabeth II **Subject:** Iris Vericolor **Obv:** Crowned head right **Rev:** Iris

Date	Mintage	VF20	XF40	MS60	MS63
2006	1,995	PF65 2,350			

KM# 754 350 DOLLARS
35.00 g., 0.9999 Gold 1.1179 oz. AGW, 34 mm. **Ruler:** Elizabeth II **Rev:** Purple violet

Date	Mintage	VF20	XF40	MS60	MS63
2007	1,392	PF65 2,200			

KM# 832 350 DOLLARS
35.00 g., 0.9999 Gold 1.1179 oz. AGW, 34 mm. **Ruler:** Elizabeth II **Rev:** Purple saxifrage

Date	Mintage	VF20	XF40	MS60	MS63
2008	1,313	PF65 2,200			

KM# 901 350 DOLLARS
35.00 g., 1.000 Gold 1.118 oz. AGW, 34 mm. **Ruler:** Elizabeth II **Obv:** Bust right **Obv. Legend:** Elizabeth II Canada DG Regina Fine Gold 350 Dollars or PUR 99999 **Rev:** Cluster of pitcher flowers **Rev. Legend:** Julie Wilson

Date	Mintage	VF20	XF40	MS60	MS63
2009	1,003	PF65 2,200			

KM# 1019 350 DOLLARS
35.00 g., 0.999 Gold 1.1169 oz. AGW, 34 mm. **Ruler:** Elizabeth II **Rev:** Praire Crocus

Date	Mintage	VF20	XF40	MS60	MS63
2010	Est. 1400	PF65 2,200			

KM# 1136 350 DOLLARS
35.00 g., 0.9999 Gold 1.1179 oz. AGW, 34 mm. **Ruler:** Elizabeth II **Obv:** Bust right **Rev:** Mountain Avens in bloom **Edge:** Reeded

Date	Mintage	VF20	XF40	MS60	MS63
2011	1,300	PF65 2,200			

KM# 1327 350 DOLLARS
35.00 g., 0.999 Gold 1.1169 oz. AGW, 34 mm. **Ruler:** Elizabeth II **Subject:** War of 1812 - Sir Issac Brock **Rev:** Putti crowning funeral urn, design of 1816 Half-penny token

Date	Mintage	VF20	XF40	MS60	MS63
2012	1,000	PF65 2,800			

KM# 1499 350 DOLLARS
35.00 g., 0.9999 Gold 1.1179 oz. AGW, 34 mm. **Ruler:** Elizabeth II **Rev:** Polar Bear

Date	Mintage	VF20	XF40	MS60	MS63
2013	600	PF65 2,800			

KM# 710 500 DOLLARS
156.50 g., 0.9999 Gold 4.9987 oz. AGW, 60 mm. **Ruler:** Elizabeth II **Subject:** Queen's 60th Wedding **Rev:** Coat of Arms and Mascots of Elizabeth and Philip

Date	Mintage	VF20	XF40	MS60	MS63
2007	198	—	—	—	9,150

KM# 782 500 DOLLARS
155.76 g., 0.999 Gold 4.9706 oz. AGW, 60 mm. **Ruler:** Elizabeth II **Subject:** Ottawa Mint Centennial 1908-2008 **Rev:** Mint building facade **Note:** Illustration reduced.

Date	Mintage	VF20	XF40	MS60	MS63
2008	248	—	—	—	9,150

KM# 897 500 DOLLARS
156.05 g., 0.999 Gold 4.9798 oz. AGW, 60 mm. **Ruler:** Elizabeth II **Subject:** 150th Anniversary of the start of construction of the Parliament Buildings **Obv:** Bust right **Rev:** Incomplete west block, original architecture **Rev. Legend:** 500 Dollars 1859-2009

Date	Mintage	VF20	XF40	MS60	MS63
2009	77	PF65 9,150			

KM# 1007 500 DOLLARS
156.50 g., 0.999 Gold 4.9942 oz. AGW, 60 mm. **Ruler:** Elizabeth II **Subject:** 75th Anniversary of Canadian Bank Notes **Rev:** Abundance seated under tree

Date	Mintage	VF20	XF40	MS60	MS63
2010	200	PF65 9,150			

KM# 1179 500 DOLLARS
156.50 g., 0.9999 Gold 4.9987 oz. AGW, 60 mm. **Ruler:** Elizabeth II **Obv:** Crowned bust of George V **Rev:** Arms of Canada, dual dates and denomination below **Edge:** Serially numbered

Date	Mintage	VF20	XF40	MS60	MS63
1912-2012	200	PF65 9,150			

KM# 1431 500 DOLLARS
156.05 g., Gold AGW, 60 mm. **Ruler:** Elizabeth II **Subject:** War of 1812 - Naval Battle **Rev:** HMS Shannon and Chesapeake

Date	Mintage	VF20	XF40	MS60	MS63
2013	Est. 200	PF65 12,000			

KM# 1495 500 DOLLARS
156.00 g., 0.9999 Gold 4.9827 oz. AGW, 60.15 mm. **Ruler:** Elizabeth II **Subject:** Aboriginal art **Rev:** Artic animals, aboriginal in canoe

Date	Mintage	VF20	XF40	MS60	MS63
2013	1,000	PF65 12,000			

KM# 1538 500 DOLLARS
5000.00 g., 0.999 Silver 159.5592 oz. ASW, 180 mm. **Ruler:** Elizabeth II **Rev:** Tsatsisnukomi

Date	Mintage	VF20	XF40	MS60	MS63
2013	100	PF65 10,500			

KM# 681 2500 DOLLARS
1000.00 g., 0.9999 Gold 31.9406 oz. AGW, 101.6 mm. **Ruler:** Elizabeth II **Subject:** Kilo **Rev:** Common Characters, Early Canada

Date	Mintage	VF20	XF40	MS60	MS63
2007 (2006)	20	—	—	—	57,000

KM# 1288 2500 DOLLARS
1000.00 g., 0.999 Gold 31.9118 oz. AGW, 101 mm. **Ruler:** Elizabeth II **Subject:** Old town view

Date	Mintage	VF20	XF40	MS60	MS63
2008	—	PF65 57,000			

KM# 902 2500 DOLLARS
1000.00 g., 0.999 Silver 31.9118 oz. ASW, 101.6 mm. **Ruler:** Elizabeth II **Series:** History and Culture Collection **Subject:** Modern Canada **Obv:** Bust right **Obv. Legend:** Vancouver 2010, 2500 Dollars, Elizabeth II **Rev:** Canadian landscape with modern elements

Date	Mintage	VF20	XF40	MS60	MS63
2009	2,500	PF65 1,250			

KM# 902a 2500 DOLLARS
1000.00 g., 0.999 Gold 31.9118 oz. AGW, 101.6 mm. **Ruler:** Elizabeth II **Series:** History and Culture Collection **Subject:** Modern Canada **Obv:** Bust right **Obv. Legend:** Vancouver 2010, 2500 Dollars, Elizabeth II **Rev:** Canadian landscape with modern elements

Date	Mintage	VF20	XF40	MS60	MS63
2009	50	PF65 57,000			

KM# 912 2500 DOLLARS
1000.00 g., 0.9999 Gold 31.9406 oz. AGW, 101 mm. **Ruler:** Elizabeth II **Obv:** Bust right **Rev:** Mask with fish - Surviving the flood

Date	Mintage	VF20	XF40	MS60	MS63
2009	40	PF65 58,000			

KM# 984 2500 DOLLARS
1000.00 g., 0.999 Gold 31.9118 oz. AGW, 101 mm. **Ruler:** Elizabeth II

Date	Mintage	VF20	XF40	MS60	MS63
2010	20	PF65 60,000			

KM# 1045 2500 DOLLARS
1000.00 g., 0.9999 Gold 31.9406 oz. AGW, 101 mm. **Ruler:** Elizabeth II **Subject:** Baniff, 125th Anniversary **Rev:** Highlights of Baniff

Date	Mintage	VF20	XF40	MS60	MS63
2010	—	PF65 60,000			

KM# 1286 2500 DOLLARS
1000.00 g., 0.999 Gold 31.9118 oz. AGW, 101 mm. **Ruler:** Elizabeth II **Subject:** Olympic views

Date	Mintage	VF20	XF40	MS60	MS63
2010	—	PF65 60,000			

KM# 1197 2500 DOLLARS
1000.00 g., 0.9999 Gold 31.9406 oz. AGW, 101 mm. **Ruler:** Elizabeth II **Obv:** Bust right **Rev:** Early lacrosse game

Date	Mintage	VF20	XF40	MS60	MS63
2011	35	PF65 60,000			

KM# 1276 2500 DOLLARS
1000.00 g., 0.999 Gold 31.9118 oz. AGW, 101 mm. **Ruler:** Elizabeth II **Subject:** Bateman Moose

Date	Mintage	VF20	XF40	MS60	MS63
2012	—	PF65 58,000			

KM# 1339 2500 DOLLARS
1000.00 g., 0.9999 Gold 31.9406 oz. AGW, 101 mm. **Ruler:** Elizabeth II **Subject:** War of 1812, Battle of Queenston Heights **Rev:** Battle scene

Date	Mintage	VF20	XF40	MS60	MS63
2012	20	PF65 60,000			

KM# 1364 2500 DOLLARS
1000.00 g., 0.9999 Gold 31.9406 oz. AGW, 101.6 mm. **Ruler:**
Elizabeth II **Subject:** Year of the Snake **Rev:** Snake under
maple leaves

Date	Mintage	VF20	XF40	MS60	MS63
2013	Est. 25	**PF65** 69,000			

KM# 1370 2500 DOLLARS
1000.00 g., 0.999 Gold 31.9118 oz. AGW, 102 mm. **Ruler:**
Elizabeth II **Series:** End of 7 Years War - 250th Anniversary
Rev: Map of North America and Arms of France and Great
Britain.

Date	Mintage	VF20	XF40	MS60	MS63
2013	Est. 20	**PF65** 69,000			

KM# 1372 2500 DOLLARS
1000.00 g., 0.999 Gold 31.9118 oz. AGW, 101.6 mm. **Ruler:**
Elizabeth II **Subject:** Arctic Coastline

Date	Mintage	VF20	XF40	MS60	MS63
2013	Est. 20	**PF65** 69,000			

KM# 1478 2500 DOLLARS
1000.00 g., 0.9999 Gold 31.9406 oz. AGW, 101 mm. **Ruler:**
Elizabeth II **Subject:** Battle of Chateauguay and Crysler's Farm

Date	Mintage	VF20	XF40	MS60	MS63
2013	20	**PF65** 69,000			

KM# 1501 2500 DOLLARS
1000.00 g., 0.9999 Gold 31.9406 oz. AGW, 101.6 mm. **Ruler:**
Elizabeth II **Rev:** Two caribou advancing left

Date	Mintage	VF20	XF40	MS60	MS63
2013	20	**PF65** 69,000			

KM# 1519 2500 DOLLARS
1000.00 g., 0.9999 Gold 31.9406 oz. AGW, 101.6 mm. **Ruler:**
Elizabeth II **Subject:** Year of the Horse **Rev:** Horse rearing
up left

Date	Mintage	VF20	XF40	MS60	MS63
2014	18	**PF65** 69,000			

KM# 1606 2500 DOLLARS
1000.00 g., 0.9999 Gold 31.9406 oz. AGW, 101 mm. **Ruler:**
Elizabeth II **Obv:** Bust right **Rev:** Snowy owl, colored eyes

Date	Mintage	VF20	XF40	MS60	MS63
2014	—	**PF65** 60,000			

SILVER BULLION COINAGE

KM# 617 DOLLAR
1.56 g., 0.9999 Silver 0.0497 oz. ASW, 16 mm. **Ruler:** Elizabeth
II **Obv:** Crowned head right **Rev:** Holographic Maple leaf
Edge: Reeded

Date	Mintage	VF20	XF40	MS60	MS63
2003	—	**PF65** 4.50			

KM# 621 DOLLAR
1.56 g., 0.9999 Silver 0.0497 oz. ASW, 17 mm. **Ruler:** Elizabeth
II **Obv:** Crowned head right **Rev:** Maple leaf **Edge:** Reeded

Date	Mintage	VF20	XF40	MS60	MS63
2004 Mint logo privy mark	13,859	**PF63** 3.50	**PF65** 4.50		

KM# 718 DOLLAR
15.55 g., 0.999 Silver 0.4962 oz. ASW, 32 mm. **Ruler:** Elizabeth
II **Obv:** Bust right **Rev:** Grey Wolf standing with moon in
background **Edge:** Reeded

Date	Mintage	VF20	XF40	MS60	MS63
2005	106,800	—	—	—	40.00
2006	—	—	—	—	40.00
2007	—	—	—	—	40.00

KM# 1489 DOLLAR
1.000 Silver **Ruler:** Elizabeth II **Rev:** Maple leaf tilted left **Note:**
Thick planchet.

Date	Mintage	VF20	XF40	MS60	MS63
2010	—	**PF63** 65.00	**PF65** 75.00		

KM# 1406 DOLLAR
1.55 g., 0.9999 Silver 0.0495 oz. ASW, 17 mm. **Ruler:** Elizabeth
II **Rev:** Three Maple Leaves

Date	Mintage	VF20	XF40	MS60	MS63
2013	—	**PF63** 18.00	**PF65** 20.00		

KM# 1593 DOLLAR
1.56 g., 0.9999 Silver 0.0497 oz. ASW, 16 mm. **Ruler:** Elizabeth II **Obv:** Bust right **Rev:** Two maple leaves, one gilt

Date	Mintage	VF20	XF40	MS60	MS63
2014	—	—	—		5.00

KM# 618 2 DOLLARS
3.11 g., 0.9999 Silver 0.0993 oz. ASW, 20.1 mm. **Ruler:** Elizabeth II **Obv:** Crowned head right **Rev:** Holographic Maple leaf **Edge:** Reeded

Date	Mintage	VF20	XF40	MS60	MS63
2003	—			PF65 7.50	

KM# 622 2 DOLLARS
3.11 g., 0.9999 Silver 0.0993 oz. ASW, 21 mm. **Ruler:** Elizabeth II **Obv:** Crowned head right **Rev:** Maple leaf **Edge:** Reeded

Date	Mintage	VF20	XF40	MS60	MS63
2004 Mint logo privy mark	13,859	PF63 6.50		PF65 7.50	

KM# 571 2 DOLLARS
3.11 g., 0.9999 Silver 0.0993 oz. ASW, 21 mm. **Ruler:** Elizabeth II **Obv:** Head right **Rev:** Lynx

Date	Mintage	VF20	XF40	MS60	MS63
2005	—	PF63 6.50		PF65 7.50	

KM# 1407 2 DOLLARS
3.11 g., 0.999 Silver 0.0992 oz. ASW **Ruler:** Elizabeth II **Rev:** Three Maple Leaves

Date	Mintage	VF20	XF40	MS60	MS63
2013	—	PF63 25.00		PF65 30.00	

KM# 1594 2 DOLLARS
3.11 g., 0.9999 Silver 0.0993 oz. ASW, 20.1 mm. **Ruler:** Elizabeth II **Obv:** Bust right **Rev:** Two maple leaves, one gilt

Date	Mintage	VF20	XF40	MS60	MS63
2014	—	—	—	10.00	

KM# 619 3 DOLLARS
7.78 g., 0.9999 Silver 0.2484 oz. ASW, 26.9 mm. **Ruler:** Elizabeth II **Obv:** Crowned head right **Rev:** Holographic Maple leaf **Edge:** Reeded

Date	Mintage	VF20	XF40	MS60	MS63
2003	—			PF65 15.00	

KM# 623 3 DOLLARS
7.78 g., 0.9999 Silver 0.2484 oz. ASW, 27 mm. **Ruler:** Elizabeth II **Obv:** Crowned head right **Rev:** Maple leaf **Edge:** Reeded

Date	Mintage	VF20	XF40	MS60	MS63
2004 Mint logo privy mark	13,859	PF63 11.00		PF65 12.50	

KM# 1415 3 DOLLARS
7.77 g., 0.999 Silver 0.248 oz. ASW, 27 mm. **Ruler:** Elizabeth II **Rev:** Fox

Date	Mintage	VF20	XF40	MS60	MS63
2004	—	PF63 30.00		PF65 35.00	

KM# 572 3 DOLLARS
7.78 g., 0.9999 Silver 0.2484 oz. ASW, 27 mm. **Ruler:** Elizabeth II **Obv:** Head right **Rev:** Lynx

Date	Mintage	VF20	XF40	MS60	MS63
2005	—	PF63 11.00		PF65 12.50	

KM# 1408 3 DOLLARS
7.78 g., 0.9999 Silver 0.2484 oz. ASW, 27 mm. **Ruler:** Elizabeth II **Rev:** Three Maple Leaves

Date	Mintage	VF20	XF40	MS60	MS63
2012	—	PF63 35.00		PF65 40.00	

KM# 1595 3 DOLLARS
7.77 g., 0.9999 Silver 0.2482 oz. ASW, 27 mm. **Ruler:** Elizabeth II **Obv:** Bust right **Rev:** Two maple leaves, one gilt

Date	Mintage	VF20	XF40	MS60	MS63
2014	—	—	—	15.00	

KM# 620 4 DOLLARS
15.55 g., 0.9999 Silver 0.4967 oz. ASW, 33.9 mm. **Ruler:** Elizabeth II **Obv:** Crowned head right **Rev:** Holographic Maple leaf **Edge:** Reeded

Date	Mintage	VF20	XF40	MS60	MS63
2003	—	PF63 22.00		PF65 25.00	

KM# 624 4 DOLLARS
15.55 g., 0.9999 Silver 0.4967 oz. ASW, 34 mm. **Ruler:** Elizabeth II **Obv:** Crowned head right **Rev:** Maple leaf **Edge:** Reeded

Date	Mintage	VF20	XF40	MS60	MS63
2004 Mint logo privy mark Reverse Proof	13,859	PF65 22.50			

KM# 573 4 DOLLARS
15.55 g., 0.9999 Silver 0.4967 oz. ASW, 34 mm. **Ruler:** Elizabeth II **Obv:** Head right **Rev:** Lynx

Date	Mintage	VF20	XF40	MS60	MS63
2005	—	PF63 20.00		PF65 22.50	

KM# 1409 4 DOLLARS
15.55 g., 0.9999 Silver 0.4967 oz. ASW, 33.9 mm. **Ruler:** Elizabeth II **Rev:** Three maple leaves

Date	Mintage	VF20	XF40	MS60	MS63
2013	—	PF63 35.00		PF65 40.00	

KM# 1596 4 DOLLARS
15.55 g., 0.9999 Silver 0.4967 oz. ASW, 34 mm. **Ruler:** Elizabeth II **Obv:** Bust right **Rev:** Two maple leaves, one gilt

Date	Mintage	VF20	XF40	MS60	MS63
2014	—	—	—	22.50	

KM# 187 5 DOLLARS
31.10 g., 0.9999 Silver 0.9934 oz. ASW **Ruler:** Elizabeth II **Obv:** Crowned head right, date and denomination below **Rev:** Maple leaf flanked by 9999

Date	Mintage	VF20	XF40	MS60	MS63
2001	398,563				35.00
2001 Reverse proof, Snake privy mark	25,000	PF63 35.00		PF65 45.00	
2002	576,196	—		—	35.00

Date	Mintage	VF20	XF40	MS60	MS63
2002 Reverse proof, Horse privy mark	25,000	PF63 35.00	PF65 45.00		
2003	—			—	35.00
2003 Reverse proof, sheep privy mark	25,000	PF63 35.00	PF65 45.00		

KM# 437 5 DOLLARS
31.10 g., 0.9999 Silver 0.9935 oz. ASW, 38 mm. **Ruler:** Elizabeth II **Obv:** Crowned head right, date and denomination below **Rev:** Radiant maple leaf hologram **Edge:** Reeded

Date	Mintage	VF20	XF40	MS60	MS63
2001 Good fortune privy mark	29,906	—	—	—	75.00

KM# 436 5 DOLLARS
31.10 g., 0.9999 Silver 0.9935 oz. ASW, 38 mm. **Ruler:** Elizabeth II **Obv:** Crowned head right, date and denomination below **Rev:** Three maple leaves in autumn colors, 9999 flanks **Edge:** Reeded

Date	Mintage	VF20	XF40	MS60	MS63
2001	49,709	PF63 30.00	PF65 40.00		

KM# 505 5 DOLLARS
31.10 g., 0.9999 Silver 0.9935 oz. ASW, 38 mm. **Ruler:** Elizabeth II **Obv:** Crowned head right, date and denomination below **Rev:** Two maple leaves in spring color (green) **Edge:** Reeded

Date	Mintage	VF20	XF40	MS60	MS63
2002	29,509	—	—	—	37.50

KM# 521 5 DOLLARS
31.10 g., 0.9999 Silver 0.9935 oz. ASW **Ruler:** Elizabeth II **Obv:** Head right **Rev:** Maple leaf, summer colors

Date	Mintage	VF20	XF40	MS60	MS63
2003	29,416	—	—	—	37.50

KM# 508 5 DOLLARS
31.10 g., 0.9999 Silver 0.9935 oz. ASW, 38 mm. **Ruler:** Elizabeth II **Obv:** Crowned head right, date and denomination below **Rev:** Holographic Maple leaf flanked by 9999 **Edge:** Reeded

Date	Mintage	VF20	XF40	MS60	MS63
2003 (2004)	—	PF63 35.00	PF65 37.50		

KM# 607 5 DOLLARS
31.12 g., 0.9999 Silver 0.994 oz. ASW **Ruler:** Elizabeth II **Obv:** Head right **Rev:** Maple leaf, winter colors

Date	Mintage	VF20	XF40	MS60	MS63
2004	—	—	—	—	37.50

KM# 625 5 DOLLARS
31.10 g., 0.9999 Silver 0.9935 oz. ASW, 38 mm. **Ruler:** Elizabeth II **Obv:** Bust right **Rev:** Maple leaf **Edge:** Reeded

Date	Mintage	VF20	XF40	MS60	MS63
2004 Mint logo privy mark Specimen	13,859	PF65 37.50			
2004 Monkey privy mark Specimen	25,000	PF65 37.50			
2004 D-Day privy mark Specimen	11,698	PF65 37.50			
2004 Desjardins privy mark	15,000	—	—	—	37.50
2004 Capricorn privy Mark Reverse proof	5,000	PF65 37.50			
2004 Aquarius privy mark Reverse proof	5,000	PF65 37.50			
2004 Pisces privy mark Reverse proof	5,000	PF65 37.50			
2004 Aries privy mark Reverse proof	5,000	PF65 37.50			
2004 Taurus privy mark Reverse proof	5,000	PF65 37.50			
2004 Gemini privy mark Reverse proof	5,000	PF65 37.50			
2004 Cancer privy mark Reverse proof	5,000	PF65 37.50			
2004 Leo privy mark Reverse proof	5,000	PF65 37.50			
2004 Virgo privy mark Reverse proof	5,000	PF65 37.50			
2004 Libra privy mark Reverse proof	5,000	PF65 37.50			
2004 Scorpio privy mark Reverse proof	5,000	PF65 37.50			
2004 Sagittarius privy mark Reverse proof	5,000	PF65 50.00			
2005	—	—	—	—	35.00
2005 Tulip privy mark Reverse proof	3,500	PF65 50.00			
2005 Tank privy mark Reverse proof	7,000	PF65 60.00			
2005 USS Missouri privy mark Reverse proof	7,000	PF65 60.00			
2005 Rooster privy mark Reverse proof	15,000	PF65 50.00			

Date	Mintage	VF20	XF40	MS60	MS63
2006	—	—		—	35.00
2006 Dog privy mark Reverse proof	—	PF65 50.00			
2007	—	—		—	35.00
2007 F12 privy mark Reverse proof	—	PF65 130			
2007 Pig privy mark Reverse proof	—	PF65 50.00			
2008	—	—		—	35.00
2008 F12 privy mark Reverse proof	—	PF65 130			
2008 Rat privy mark Reverse proof	—	PF65 50.00			
2009	—	—		—	35.00
2009 Brandenberg Gate privy mark Reverse proof	—	PF65 50.00			
2009 Tower Bridge privy mark Reverse proof	—	PF65 50.00			
2009 Ox Privy mark Reverse proof	—	PF65 50.00			
2010	—	—		—	35.00
2010 Fabulous 15 privy mark Reverse proof	—	PF65 50.00			
2011	—	—		—	35.00
2012	—	—		—	35.00
2012 Dragon privy mark Reverse proof	—	PF65 50.00			
2012 Titanic privy mark Reverse proof	—	PF65 50.00			
2012 Pisa privy mark	—	—		—	35.00
2012 Fabulous 15 privy mark Reverse proof	—	PF65 75.00			
2013	—	—		—	35.00
2014	—	—		—	35.00

KM# 522 5 DOLLARS
31.11 g., 0.9999 Silver 0.9935 oz. ASW **Ruler:** Elizabeth II **Obv:** Head right **Rev:** Maple leaf, winter color

Date	Mintage	VF20	XF40	MS60	MS63
2004	26,763	—	—	—	35.00

KM# 574 5 DOLLARS
31.10 g., 0.9999 Silver 0.9935 oz. ASW, 38 mm. **Ruler:** Elizabeth II **Obv:** Head right **Rev:** Lynx

Date	Mintage	VF20	XF40	MS60	MS63
2005	—	PF63 35.00	PF65 37.50		

KM# 924 5 DOLLARS
31.11 g., 0.9999 Silver 0.9935 oz. ASW **Ruler:** Elizabeth II **Rev:** Maple Leaf, laser engraved

Date	Mintage	VF20	XF40	MS60	MS63
2005	25,000	PF63 50.00	PF65 60.00		

KM# 550 5 DOLLARS
31.10 g., 0.9999 Silver 0.9935 oz. ASW, 38 mm. **Ruler:** Elizabeth II **Obv:** Head right **Rev:** Big Leaf Maple and seed pod, color

Date	Mintage	VF20	XF40	MS60	MS63
2005	21,233	—	—	—	35.00

KM# 660 5 DOLLARS
31.10 g., 0.999 Silver 0.9926 oz. ASW **Ruler:** Elizabeth II **Obv:** Bust right **Rev:** Silver maple, colorized

Date	Mintage	VF20	XF40	MS60	MS63
2006	14,157	—	—	—	37.50

KM# 625a 5 DOLLARS
31.11 g., 0.9999 Silver 0.9935 oz. ASW, 38 mm. **Ruler:** Elizabeth II **Rev:** Maple leaf, gilt

Date	Mintage	VF20	XF40	MS60	MS63
2007	—	—	—	—	75.00
2008	—	—	—	—	75.00
2009	—	—	—	—	75.00
2009 Tower Bridge Privy Mark	—	—	—	—	76.00
2010	—	—	—	—	75.00

KM# 729 5 DOLLARS
31.11 g., 0.999 Silver 0.9926 oz. ASW, 38 mm. **Ruler:** Elizabeth II **Obv:** Bust right **Rev:** Maple leaf orange multicolor

Date	Mintage	VF20	XF40	MS60	MS63
2007	—	PF63 40.00	PF65 45.00		

KM# 925 5 DOLLARS
31.11 g., 0.999 Silver 0.9926 oz. ASW **Ruler:** Elizabeth II **Obv:** Bust right **Rev:** Sugar maple, colorized

Date	Mintage	VF20	XF40	MS60	MS63
2007	11,495	—	—	—	37.50

KM# 928 5 DOLLARS
31.39 g., 0.999 Silver 1.0017 oz. ASW, 38 mm. **Ruler:** Elizabeth II **Rev:** Orange sugar maple leaf

Date	Mintage	VF20	XF40	MS60	MS63
2007 Specimen	20,000	—	—	—	100

KM# 798 5 DOLLARS
31.11 g., 0.999 Silver 0.9926 oz. ASW, 38 mm. **Ruler:** Elizabeth

II **Subject:** Maple Leaf 20th Anniversary **Rev:** Maple Leaf, selective gold plating

Date	Mintage	VF20	XF40	MS60	MS63
2008	10,000	PF63 65.00	PF65 75.00		

KM# 799 5 DOLLARS
31.11 g., 0.999 Silver 0.9926 oz. ASW, 38 mm. **Ruler:** Elizabeth II **Subject:** Breast Cancer Awareness **Rev:** Multicolor, green maple leaf and pink ribbon

Date	Mintage	VF20	XF40	MS60	MS63
2008	11,048	—	—	—	85.00

KM# 800 5 DOLLARS
31.11 g., 0.999 Silver 0.9926 oz. ASW, 38 mm. **Ruler:** Elizabeth II **Subject:** Vancouver Olympics **Obv:** Bust right **Rev:** Maple leaf, Olympic logo at left, turtle

Date	Mintage	VF20	XF40	MS60	MS63
2008	—	—	—	—	37.50
2009	—	—	—	—	37.50
2010	—	—	—	—	37.50

KM# 800a 5 DOLLARS
31.11 g., 0.9999 Silver 0.9935 oz. ASW, 38 mm. **Ruler:** Elizabeth II **Rev:** Maple leaf gilt, olympic logo at left

Date	Mintage	VF20	XF40	MS60	MS63
2008	—	—	—	—	50.00

KM# 1056 5 DOLLARS
31.11 g., 0.9999 Silver 0.9935 oz. ASW, 38 mm. **Ruler:** Elizabeth II **Rev:** Maple leaf in brown color, card diamond

Date	Mintage	VF20	XF40	MS60	MS63
2008	—	—	—	—	50.00

KM# 1057 5 DOLLARS
31.11 g., 0.9999 Silver 0.9935 oz. ASW, 38 mm. **Ruler:** Elizabeth II **Rev:** Maple Leaf in green color, card heart

Date	Mintage	VF20	XF40	MS60	MS63
2008	—	—	—	—	50.00

KM# 1058 5 DOLLARS
31.11 g., 0.9999 Silver 0.9935 oz. ASW, 38 mm. **Ruler:** Elizabeth II **Rev:** Maple leaf in green color, card club

Date	Mintage	VF20	XF40	MS60	MS63
2008	—	—	—	—	50.00

KM# 1059 5 DOLLARS
31.11 g., 0.9999 Silver 0.9935 oz. ASW, 38 mm. **Ruler:** Elizabeth II **Rev:** Maple Leaf in red color, card spade

Date	Mintage	VF20	XF40	MS60	MS63
2008	—	—	—	—	50.00

KM# 863 5 DOLLARS
31.11 g., 0.9999 Silver 0.9935 oz. ASW, 38 mm. **Ruler:** Elizabeth II **Subject:** Vancouver Olympics **Rev:** Thunderbird Totem

Date	Mintage	VF20	XF40	MS60	MS63
2009	—	—	—	—	50.00

KM# 863a 5 DOLLARS
31.11 g., 0.9999 Silver 0.9935 oz. ASW, 38 mm. **Ruler:** Elizabeth II **Rev:** Thunderbird, gilt

Date	Mintage	VF20	XF40	MS60	MS63
2009	—	—	—	—	60.00

KM# 1061 5 DOLLARS
31.11 g., 0.9999 Silver 0.9935 oz. ASW, 38 mm. **Ruler:** Elizabeth II **Rev:** Maple leaf in red color, support our troops yellow ribbon

Date	Mintage	VF20	XF40	MS60	MS63
2009	—	—	—	—	70.00

KM# 998 5 DOLLARS
31.12 g., 0.999 Silver 0.9931 oz. ASW, 38 mm. **Ruler:** Elizabeth II **Rev:** Olympic Hockey

Date	Mintage	VF20	XF40	MS60	MS63
2010	—	PF63 38.00	PF65 42.00		

KM# 998a 5 DOLLARS
31.11 g., 0.9999 Silver 0.9935 oz. ASW, 38 mm. **Ruler:** Elizabeth II **Rev:** Hockey player, gilt maple leaves flanking

Date	Mintage	VF20	XF40	MS60	MS63
2010	—	—	—	—	50.00

KM# 1077 5 DOLLARS
31.39 g., 0.999 Silver 1.0017 oz. ASW, 34 mm. **Ruler:** Elizabeth II **Rev:** Maple leaf on 45 degree angle left **Note:** Piedfort.

Date	Mintage	VF20	XF40	MS60	MS63
2010 Reverse Proof	9,000	PF65 80.00			

KM# 1289 5 DOLLARS
31.11 g., 0.9999 Silver 0.9935 oz. ASW, 38 mm. **Ruler:** Elizabeth II **Rev:** Maple leaf in green with crystal

Date	Mintage	VF20	XF40	MS60	MS63
2010	—	—	—	—	65.00

KM# 1290 5 DOLLARS
31.11 g., 0.999 Silver 0.9926 oz. ASW, 38 mm. **Ruler:** Elizabeth II **Rev:** Maple leaf in red with crystal

Date	Mintage	VF20	XF40	MS60	MS63
2010	—	—	—	—	65.00

KM# 1291 5 DOLLARS
31.11 g., 0.9999 Silver 0.9935 oz. ASW, 38 mm. **Ruler:** Elizabeth II **Rev:** Maple leaf in dark green with crystal

Date	Mintage	VF20	XF40	MS60	MS63
2010	—	—	—	—	65.00

KM# 1292 5 DOLLARS
31.11 g., 0.9999 Silver 0.9935 oz. ASW, 38 mm. **Ruler:** Elizabeth II **Rev:** Maple leaf in color with crystal

Date	Mintage	F12	VF20	XF40	MS60	MS63
2010	—	—	—	—	—	65.00

KM# 1052 5 DOLLARS
31.11 g., 0.9999 Silver 0.9935 oz. ASW, 38 mm. **Ruler:** Elizabeth II **Rev:** Wolf standing with moonlight in background

Date	Mintage	VF20	XF40	MS60	MS63
2011	1,000,000	—	—	—	42.00

KM# 1109 5 DOLLARS
31.11 g., 0.999 Silver 0.9926 oz. ASW, 38 mm. **Ruler:** Elizabeth II **Rev:** Grizzly Bear walking right

Date	Mintage	VF20	XF40	MS60	MS63
2011	1,000,000	—	—	—	40.00

KM# 1164 5 DOLLARS
31.11 g., 0.999 Silver 0.9926 oz. ASW, 38 mm. **Ruler:** Elizabeth II **Rev:** Cougar

Date	Mintage	VF20	XF40	MS60	MS63
2012	1,000,000	—	—	—	40.00

KM# 1241 5 DOLLARS
31.14 g., 0.9999 Silver 0.9945 oz. ASW, 38 mm. **Ruler:** Elizabeth II **Obv:** Bust right **Rev:** Moose left **Edge:** Reeded

Date	Mintage	VF20	XF40	MS60	MS63
2012	1,000,000	—	—	—	42.00

KM# 1297 5 DOLLARS
31.11 g., 0.999 Silver 0.9926 oz. ASW, 38 mm. **Ruler:** Elizabeth II **Obv:** Bust right **Rev:** Antelope

Date	Mintage	VF20	XF40	MS60	MS63
2013	—	—	—	—	42.00

KM# 1350 5 DOLLARS
31.11 g., 0.999 Silver 0.9926 oz. ASW, 38 mm. **Ruler:** Elizabeth II **Rev:** Antelope

Date	Mintage	VF20	XF40	MS60	MS63
2013	—	—	—	—	35.00

KM# 1382 5 DOLLARS
31.11 g., 0.999 Silver 0.9926 oz. ASW, 38 mm. **Ruler:** Elizabeth
II **Subject:** Silver Maple Leaf - 25th Anniversary **Rev:** Maple
leaf and gilt shadow of maple leaf

Date	Mintage	VF20	XF40	MS60	MS63
2013	Est. 10000	PF63 100	PF65 110		

KM# 1410 5 DOLLARS
31.11 g., 0.9999 Silver 0.9935 oz. ASW, 38 mm. **Ruler:**
Elizabeth II **Rev:** Three maple leaves

Date	Mintage	VF20	XF40	MS60	MS63
2013	—	—	—	—	45.00

KM# 1434 5 DOLLARS
31.11 g., 0.9999 Silver 0.9935 oz. ASW, 38 mm. **Ruler:**
Elizabeth II **Rev:** Wood bison advancing left

Date	Mintage	VF20	XF40	MS60	MS63
2013	—	—	—	—	40.00

KM# 1525 5 DOLLARS
31.39 g., 0.999 Silver 1.0017 oz. ASW, 34 mm. **Ruler:** Elizabeth
II **Rev:** Maple leaves **Note:** High relief piefort

Date	Mintage	VF20	XF40	MS60	MS63
2013	10,000	PF63 45.00	PF65 50.00		

KM# 1542 5 DOLLARS
31.39 g., 0.9999 Silver 1.0026 oz. ASW, 38 mm. **Ruler:**
Elizabeth II **Rev:** Large 25 on maple leaf

Date	Mintage	VF20	XF40	MS60	MS63
2013	—	—	—	75.00	

KM# 1597 5 DOLLARS
31.10 g., 0.9999 Silver 0.9935 oz. ASW, 38 mm. **Ruler:**
Elizabeth II **Obv:** Bust right **Rev:** Two maple leaves, one gilt

Date	Mintage	VF20	XF40	MS60	MS63
2014	—	—	—	40.00	

KM# 1601 5 DOLLARS
31.11 g., 0.9999 Silver 0.9935 oz. ASW, 38 mm. **Ruler:** Elizabeth
II **Obv:** Bust right, rays in field **Rev:** Maple leaf, rays in field

Date	Mintage	VF20	XF40	MS60	MS63
2014	—	—	—	50.00	

KM# 1158 10 DOLLARS
31.11 g., 0.9999 Silver 0.9935 oz. ASW, 38 mm. **Ruler:** Elizabeth
II **Obv:** Bust right **Rev:** Branch with three maple leaves

Date	Mintage	VF20	XF40	MS60	MS63
2011	—	PF63 45.00	PF65 50.00		

KM# 1268 10 DOLLARS
31.11 g., 0.999 Silver 0.9926 oz. ASW, 38 mm. **Ruler:** Elizabeth
II **Subject:** Maple Leaf Forever

Date	Mintage	VF20	XF40	MS60	MS63
2012	—	PF63 40.00	PF65 50.00		

KM# 1473 10 DOLLARS
15.87 g., 0.9999 Silver 0.5069 oz. ASW, 34 mm. **Ruler:**
Elizabeth II **Rev:** Two maple leaves

Date	Mintage	VF20	XF40	MS60	MS63
2013	5,000	PF63 35.00	PF65 40.00		

KM# 1062 20 DOLLARS
7.96 g., 0.9999 Silver 0.2542 oz. ASW, 27 mm. **Ruler:** Elizabeth
II **Rev:** Five Maple leaves at left **Note:** Thick planchet

Date	Mintage	VF20	XF40	MS60	MS63
2011	200,000	—	—	—	25.00

KM# 1176 20 DOLLARS
7.96 g., 0.9999 Silver 0.2542 oz. ASW, 27 mm. **Ruler:** Elizabeth
II **Obv:** Bust right **Rev:** Canoe and reflection **Edge:** Reeded
Note: Thick planchet.

Date	Mintage	VF20	XF40	MS60	MS63
2011	200,000	—	—	—	30.00

KM# 1226 20 DOLLARS
7.96 g., 0.9999 Silver 0.2542 oz. ASW, 27 mm. **Ruler:** Elizabeth
II **Obv:** Bust right **Rev:** Waterline view of polar bear swimming
Edge: Reeded

Date	Mintage	VF20	XF40	MS60	MS63
2012	250,000	—	—	—	25.00

KM# 1237 20 DOLLARS
7.96 g., 0.9999 Silver 0.2542 oz. ASW, 27 mm. **Ruler:** Elizabeth
II **Subject:** Commemorating the end of the Canadian Cent
Obv: Bust right **Rev:** Maple leaves floating on water

Date	Mintage	VF20	XF40	MS60	MS63
2012	—	—	—	—	20.00

KM# 1337 20 DOLLARS
15.55 g., 0.999 Silver 0.4962 oz. ASW, 27 mm. **Ruler:** Elizabeth
II **Rev:** Reindeer

Date	Mintage	VF20	XF40	MS60	MS63
2012	—	—	—	—	27.50

KM# 1554 20 DOLLARS
7.96 g., 0.999 Silver 0.254 oz. ASW, 27 mm. **Ruler:** Elizabeth
II **Rev:** Santa

Date	Mintage	VF20	XF40	MS60	MS63
2013	225,000	—	—	—	20.00

KM# 1365 20 DOLLARS
15.55 g., 0.999 Silver 0.4962 oz. ASW, 27 mm. **Ruler:** Elizabeth
II **Subject:** Year of the Snake **Rev:** Snake in Tree

Date	Mintage	VF20	XF40	MS60	MS63
2013	Est. 128888	PF63 25.00	PF65 30.00		

KM# 1511 20 DOLLARS
7.96 g., 0.999 Silver 0.254 oz. ASW, 27 mm. **Ruler:** Elizabeth II **Rev:** Wolf

Date	Mintage	VF20	XF40	MS60	MS63
2013	250,000	—	—	—	25.00

KM# 1512 20 DOLLARS
7.70 g., 0.9999 Silver 0.2459 oz. ASW, 27 mm. **Ruler:** Elizabeth II **Rev:** Iceberg and whale

Date	Mintage	VF20	XF40	MS60	MS63
2013	225,000	—	—	—	25.00

KM# 1561 20 DOLLARS
7.96 g., 0.999 Silver 0.254 oz. ASW **Ruler:** Elizabeth II **Rev:** Goose in flight right

Date	Mintage	VF20	XF40	MS60	MS63
2014	225,000	—	—	—	20.00

KM# 1562 20 DOLLARS
7.96 g., 0.999 Silver 0.254 oz. ASW, 27 mm. **Ruler:** Elizabeth II **Rev:** Bobcat

Date	Mintage	VF20	XF40	MS60	MS63
2014	225,000	—	—	—	20.00

KM# 1563 20 DOLLARS
7.96 g., 0.999 Silver 0.254 oz. ASW, 27 mm. **Ruler:** Elizabeth II **Rev:** Summertime

Date	Mintage	VF20	XF40	MS60	MS63
2014	225,000	—	—	—	20.00

KM# 1564 20 DOLLARS
7.96 g., 0.999 Silver 0.254 oz. ASW, 27 mm. **Ruler:** Elizabeth II **Rev:** Holiday Candles

Date	Mintage	VF20	XF40	MS60	MS63
2014	225,000	—	—	—	20.00

KM# 1509 50 DOLLARS
157.60 g., 0.9999 Silver 5.0338 oz. ASW, 65 mm. **Ruler:** Elizabeth II **Subject:** Maple Leaf Bullion, 25th Anniversary **Rev:** Three maple leaves

Date	Mintage	VF20	XF40	MS60	MS63
2013	2,500	PF65 500			

KM# 1550 50 DOLLARS
Silver ASW **Ruler:** Elizabeth II **Subject:** Silver Maple Leaf, 25th Anniversary

Date	Mintage	VF20	XF40	MS60	MS63
2013					

KM# 1624 50 DOLLARS
157.60 g., 0.999 Silver 5.0293 oz. ASW, 65.25 mm. **Ruler:** Elizabeth II **Obv:** Bust right **Rev:** Three maple leaves

Date	Mintage	VF20	XF40	MS60	MS63
2014	2,500	PF65 520			

KM# 1555 100 DOLLARS
31.60 g., 0.9999 Silver 1.0093 oz. ASW, 40 mm. **Ruler:** Elizabeth II **Rev:** Bear eating salmon in river

Date	Mintage	VF20	XF40	MS60	MS63
2014	50,000	—	—	—	100

KM# 1620 100 DOLLARS
31.60 g., 0.999 Silver 1.0084 oz. ASW, 40 mm. **Ruler:** Elizabeth II **Obv:** Bust right **Rev:** Eagle in flight

Date	Mintage	VF20	XF40	MS60	MS63
2014 Matte Proof	50,000	PF63 115			

KM# 1621 100 DOLLARS
31.60 g., 0.999 Silver 1.0084 oz. ASW, 40 mm. **Ruler:** Elizabeth II **Obv:** Bust right **Rev:** Two big horn sheep butting heads

Date	Mintage	VF20	XF40	MS60	MS63
2014 Matte Proof	50,000	PF63 115			

KM# 676 250 DOLLARS
1000.00 g., 0.9999 Silver 31.9406 oz. ASW **Ruler:** Elizabeth II **Subject:** Kilo

Date	Mintage	VF20	XF40	MS60	MS63
2006					1,350

KM# 1160 250 DOLLARS
1000.00 g., 0.9999 Silver 31.9406 oz. ASW, 101 mm. **Ruler:** Elizabeth II **Obv:** Bust right **Rev:** Three maple leaves on branch

Date	Mintage	VF20	XF40	MS60	MS63
2011	999	PF65 2,000			

KM# 1272 250 DOLLARS
1000.00 g., 0.999 Silver 31.9118 oz. ASW, 101 mm. **Ruler:** Elizabeth II **Subject:** Maple Leaf Forever

Date	Mintage	VF20	XF40	MS60	MS63
2012	—	PF65 1,450			

KM# 1472 250 DOLLARS
1000.00 g., 0.999 Silver 31.9118 oz. ASW, 102.1 mm. **Ruler:** Elizabeth II **Rev:** Two maple leaves, gilt

Date	Mintage	VF20	XF40	MS60	MS63
2013	600	PF65 2,300			

KM# 1245 500 DOLLARS
5000.00 g., 0.9999 Silver 159.7029 oz. ASW, 101 mm. **Ruler:** Elizabeth II **Subject:** Haida sculpture

Date	Mintage	VF20	XF40	MS60	MS63
2012	100	PF65 7,500			

GOLD BULLION COINAGE

KM# 542 50 CENTS
1.27 g., 0.999 Gold 0.0405 oz. AGW, 13.92 mm. **Ruler:** Elizabeth II **Rev:** Voyagers with northern lights above

Date	Mintage	VF20	XF40	MS60	MS63
2005	—	PF65 100			

KM# 717 50 CENTS
1.24 g., 0.999 Gold 0.0396 oz. AGW, 13.9 mm. **Ruler:** Elizabeth II **Rev:** Wolf

Date	Mintage	VF20	XF40	MS60	MS63
2006	—	PF63 90.00	PF65 100		

KM# 926 50 CENTS
1.24 g., 0.999 Gold 0.0396 oz. AGW, 13.9 mm. **Ruler:** Elizabeth II **Rev:** Cowboy and bronco rider

Date	Mintage	VF20	XF40	MS60	MS63
2006	—	PF63 90.00	PF65 100		

KM# 927 50 CENTS
1.24 g., 0.999 Gold 0.0396 oz. AGW, 13.9 mm. **Ruler:** Elizabeth II **Subject:** Gold Louis

Date	Mintage	VF20	XF40	MS60	MS63
2007	—	PF63 90.00	PF65 100		

KM# 777 50 CENTS
1.24 g., 0.999 Gold 0.0396 oz. AGW, 13.9 mm. **Ruler:** Elizabeth II **Subject:** DeHavilland beaver

Date	Mintage	VF20	XF40	MS60	MS63
2008	20,000	PF63 90.00	PF65 100		

KM# 888 50 CENTS
1.27 g., 0.999 Gold 0.0405 oz. AGW, 13.92 mm. **Ruler:** Elizabeth II **Subject:** Red maple **Obv:** Bust right **Obv. Legend:** Elizabeth II 50 cents **Rev:** Two maple leaves **Rev. Legend:** Canada, Fine gold 1/25 oz or PUR 9999

Date	Mintage	VF20	XF40	MS60	MS63
2009	150,000	PF63 75.00	PF65 90.00		

KM# 985 50 CENTS
1.24 g., 0.999 Gold 0.0396 oz. AGW, 13.92 mm. **Ruler:** Elizabeth II **Subject:** RCMP **Obv:** Bust right **Rev:** Mountie on horseback

Date	Mintage	VF20	XF40	MS60	MS63
2010	Est. 14000	PF63 90.00	PF65 100		

KM# 1085 50 CENTS
1.27 g., 0.999 Gold 0.0405 oz. AGW, 13.92 mm. **Ruler:** Elizabeth II **Rev:** Geese in flight left

Date	Mintage	VF20	XF40	MS60	MS63
2011	10,000	PF63 80.00	PF65 90.00		

KM# 1214 50 CENTS
1.27 g., 1.000 Gold 0.0406 oz. AGW, 13.92 mm. **Ruler:** Elizabeth II **Obv:** Bust right **Rev:** Three maple leaves, 2007-2012 above

Date	Mintage	VF20	XF40	MS60	MS63
2012	—	PF63 80.00	PF65 90.00		

KM# 1218 50 CENTS
1.27 g., 0.9999 Gold 0.0406 oz. AGW, 13.92 mm. **Ruler:** Elizabeth II **Obv:** Bust right **Rev:** Schooner sailing left

Date	Mintage	VF20	XF40	MS60	MS63
2012	—	PF65 90.00			

KM# 1348 50 CENTS
1.27 g., 0.9999 Gold 0.0406 oz. AGW, 13.92 mm. **Ruler:** Elizabeth II **Rev:** Bald eagle head left

Date	Mintage	VF20	XF40	MS60	MS63
2013	10,000	PF63 120	PF65 130		

KM# 1349 50 CENTS
1.27 g., 0.9999 Gold 0.0406 oz. AGW, 13.92 mm. **Ruler:** Elizabeth II **Subject:** Inuit Art by Joanassie Nowkawalk

Date	Mintage	VF20	XF40	MS60	MS63
2013	10,000	PF63 120	PF65 130		

KM# 238 DOLLAR
1.56 g., 0.9999 Gold 0.0497 oz. AGW **Ruler:** Elizabeth II **Obv:** Crowned head right, denomination and date below **Rev:** Maple leaf flanked by 9999

Date	Mintage	VF20	XF40	MS60	MS63
2001	—	—	—	—	BV+30%

KM# 438 DOLLAR
1.58 g., 0.999 Gold 0.0505 oz. AGW, 14.1 mm. **Ruler:** Elizabeth II **Subject:** Holographic Maple Leaves **Obv:** Crowned head right **Rev:** Three maple leaves multicolor hologram **Edge:** Reeded

Date	Mintage	VF20	XF40	MS60	MS63
2001	600	—	—	—	85.00

KM# 1416 DOLLAR
1.55 g., 0.9999 Gold 0.0495 oz. AGW, 14 mm. **Ruler:** Elizabeth II **Obv:** Bust right **Rev:** Maple Leaf

Date	Mintage	VF20	XF40	MS60	MS63
2009	—	PF63 115	PF65 125		

KM# 1490 DOLLAR
1.000 Gold AGW **Ruler:** Elizabeth II **Rev:** Maple leaf tilted left **Note:** Thick planchet.

Date	Mintage	VF20	XF40	MS60	MS63
2010 Proof	—	—	—	—	—

KM# 1138 DOLLAR
1.56 g., 0.9999 Gold 0.0498 oz. AGW, 14 mm. **Ruler:** Elizabeth II **Obv:** Bust right **Rev:** Maple leaf

Date	Mintage	VF20	XF40	MS60	MS63
1911-2011	—	—	—	—	100

KM# 1213 DOLLAR
1.58 g., 1.000 Gold 0.0505 oz. AGW, 14.1 mm. **Ruler:** Elizabeth II **Obv:** Bust right **Rev:** Three maple leaves, 2007-2012 above

Date	Mintage	VF20	XF40	MS60	MS63
2012	—	PF63 100	PF65 110		

KM# 1411 DOLLAR
1.55 g., 0.9999 Gold 0.0495 oz. AGW **Ruler:** Elizabeth II **Rev:** Two maple leaves

Date	Mintage	F12	VF20	XF40	MS60	MS63
2013	—	PF63 115	PF65 125			

KM# 1506 DOLLAR
1.58 g., 0.9999 Gold 0.0505 oz. AGW, 14.1 mm. **Ruler:** Elizabeth II **Rev:** Two maple leaves

Date	Mintage	VF20	XF40	MS60	MS63
2013 Reverse proof	—	PF65 150			

KM# 188 5 DOLLARS
3.12 g., 0.9999 Gold 0.0997 oz. AGW **Ruler:** Elizabeth II **Obv:** Elizabeth II effigy **Rev:** Maple leaf

Date	Mintage	VF20	XF40	MS60	MS63
2001	—	—	—	—	BV+14%

KM# 439 5 DOLLARS
3.13 g., 0.9999 Gold 0.100 oz. AGW, 16 mm. **Ruler:** Elizabeth II **Subject:** Holographic Maple Leaves **Obv:** Crowned head right **Rev:** Three maple leaves multicolor hologram **Edge:** Reeded

Date	Mintage	VF20	XF40	MS60	MS63
2001	600	—	—	—	200

KM# 929 5 DOLLARS
3.13 g., 0.999 Gold 0.0999 oz. AGW, 16 mm. **Ruler:** Elizabeth II **Rev:** Maple leaf

Date	Mintage	VF20	XF40	MS60	MS63
2007	—	PF65 200			
2008	—	PF65 200			
2009	—	PF65 200			
2010	—	PF65 200			
2011	—	PF65 200			

KM# 1139 5 DOLLARS
3.13 g., 0.999 Gold 0.0999 oz. AGW, 16 mm. **Ruler:** Elizabeth II **Obv:** Bust right **Rev:** Maple leaf

Date	Mintage	VF20	XF40	MS60	MS63
1911-2011	—	—	—	—	225

KM# 1212 5 DOLLARS
3.13 g., 1.000 Gold 0.100 oz. AGW, 16 mm. **Ruler:** Elizabeth II **Obv:** Bust right **Rev:** Three maple leaves, 2007-2012 above

Date	Mintage	VF20	XF40	MS60	MS63
2012	—	PF65 200			

KM# 1267 5 DOLLARS
3.13 g., 0.999 Gold 0.0999 oz. AGW, 16 mm. **Ruler:** Elizabeth II **Subject:** Maple Leaf Forever

Date	Mintage	VF20	XF40	MS60	MS63
2012	—	PF65 200			

KM# 1412 5 DOLLARS
3.11 g., 0.9999 Gold 0.0993 oz. AGW **Ruler:** Elizabeth II **Rev:** Two maple leaves

Date	Mintage	VF20	XF40	MS60	MS63
2013	—	PF65 250			

KM# 1505 5 DOLLARS
3.13 g., 0.9999 Gold 0.100 oz. AGW, 16 mm. **Ruler:** Elizabeth II **Rev:** Two maple leaves

Date	Mintage	VF20	XF40	MS60	MS63
2013 Reverse Proof	—	PF65 225			

KM# 1598 5 DOLLARS
3.11 g., 0.9999 Gold 0.0993 oz. AGW, 16 mm. **Ruler:** Elizabeth II **Obv:** Bust right **Rev:** Three maple leaves

Date	Mintage	VF20	XF40	MS60	MS63
2014	—	PF65 200			

KM# 189 10 DOLLARS
7.79 g., 0.9999 Gold 0.2487 oz. AGW **Ruler:** Elizabeth II **Obv:** Crowned head right, date and denomination below **Rev:** Maple leaf flanked by 9999

Date	Mintage	VF20	XF40	MS60	MS63
2001	—	—	—	—	BV+15%

KM# 440 10 DOLLARS
7.80 g., 0.9999 Gold 0.249 oz. AGW, 20 mm. **Ruler:** Elizabeth II **Subject:** Holographic Maples Leaves **Obv:** Crowned head right **Rev:** Three maple leaves multicolor hologram **Edge:** Reeded

Date	Mintage	VF20	XF40	MS60	MS63
2001	15,000	—	—	—	475

KM# 1140 10 DOLLARS
7.80 g., 0.9999 Gold 0.249 oz. AGW, 20 mm. **Ruler:** Elizabeth II **Obv:** Bust right **Rev:** Maple leaf

Date	Mintage	VF20	XF40	MS60	MS63
1911-2011	—	—	—	—	485

KM# 1312 10 DOLLARS
6.22 g., 0.999 Gold 0.1985 oz. AGW **Ruler:** Elizabeth II **Obv:** Bust right **Rev:** Maple leaf **Note:** Piedfort

Date	Mintage	VF20	XF40	MS60	MS63
2011	—	—	—	—	400

KM# 1211 10 DOLLARS
7.80 g., 1.000 Gold 0.2491 oz. AGW, 20 mm. **Ruler:** Elizabeth II **Obv:** Bust right **Rev:** Three maple leaves, 2007-2012 above

Date	Mintage	VF20	XF40	MS60	MS63
2012	—	PF65 475			

KM# 1275 10 DOLLARS
7.77 g., 0.9999 Gold 0.2482 oz. AGW, 20 mm. **Ruler:** Elizabeth II **Subject:** War of 1812

Date	Mintage	VF20	XF40	MS60	MS63
2012	—	PF65 500			

KM# 1413 10 DOLLARS
7.77 g., 0.9999 Gold 0.2482 oz. AGW **Ruler:** Elizabeth II **Rev:** Two maple leaves

Date	Mintage	VF20	XF40	MS60	MS63
2013	—	PF65 500			

KM# 1504 10 DOLLARS
7.77 g., 0.999 Gold 0.248 oz. AGW, 20 mm. **Ruler:** Elizabeth II
Rev: Two maple leaves

Date	Mintage	VF20	XF40	MS60	MS63
2013 Reverse proof	600	PF65 400			

KM# 1599 10 DOLLARS
7.77 g., 0.9999 Gold 0.2482 oz. AGW, 20 mm. **Ruler:** Elizabeth II **Obv:** Bust right **Rev:** Three maple leaves

Date	Mintage	VF20	XF40	MS60	MS63
2014	PF65 475				

KM# 190 20 DOLLARS
15.55 g., 0.9999 Gold 0.4967 oz. AGW **Ruler:** Elizabeth II **Obv:** Crowned head right, date and denomination below **Rev:** Maple leaf flanked by 9999

Date	Mintage	VF20	XF40	MS60	MS63
2001	—	—	—	—	BV+12%

KM# 441 20 DOLLARS
15.58 g., 0.9999 Gold 0.4978 oz. AGW, 25 mm. **Ruler:** Elizabeth II **Subject:** Holographic Maples Leaves **Obv:** Crowned head right **Rev:** Three maple leaves multicolor hologram **Edge:** Reeded

Date	Mintage	VF20	XF40	MS60	MS63
2001	600	—	—	—	925

KM# 191 50 DOLLARS
31.10 g., 0.9999 Gold 0.9934 oz. AGW **Ruler:** Elizabeth II **Obv:** Crowned head right, date and denomination below **Rev:** Maple leaf flanked by .9999

Date	Mintage	VF20	XF40	MS60	MS63
2001	—	—	—	—	BV+7%

KM# 442 50 DOLLARS
31.15 g., 0.9999 Gold 0.9949 oz. AGW, 30 mm. **Ruler:** Elizabeth II **Subject:** Holographic Maples Leaves **Obv:** Crowned head right **Rev:** Three maple leaves multicolor hologram **Edge:** Reeded

Date	Mintage	VF20	XF40	MS60	MS63
2001	600	—	—	—	1,850

KM# 1042 50 DOLLARS
31.11 g., 0.999 Gold 0.9926 oz. AGW, 30 mm. **Ruler:** Elizabeth II **Rev:** Vancouver logo and maple leaf **Edge:** Reeded

Date	Mintage	VF20	XF40	MS60	MS63
2008P	—	—	—	—	1,850

KM# 1042a 50 DOLLARS
31.11 g., 0.9999 Gold 0.9935 oz. AGW, 30 mm. **Ruler:** Elizabeth II **Rev:** Maple leaf in red enamel, olympic logo at left

Date	Mintage	VF20	XF40	MS60	MS63
2008	—	—	—	—	1,850

KM# 1037 50 DOLLARS
31.11 g., 0.9999 Gold 0.9935 oz. AGW, 30 mm. **Ruler:** Elizabeth II **Rev:** Thunderbird **Edge:** Reeded

Date	Mintage	VF20	XF40	MS60	MS63
2009	—	—	—	—	1,850

KM# 1037a 50 DOLLARS
31.11 g., 0.9999 Gold 0.9935 oz. AGW, 30 mm. **Ruler:** Elizabeth II **Rev:** Thunderbird, stars in red enamel highlights

Date	Mintage	VF20	XF40	MS60	MS63
2009	—	—	—	—	1,850

KM# 1029 50 DOLLARS
31.11 g., 0.9999 Gold 0.9935 oz. AGW, 30 mm. **Ruler:** Elizabeth II **Rev:** Hockey player flanked by maple leaves

Date	Mintage	VF20	XF40	MS60	MS63
2010	—	—	—	—	1,850

KM# 1029a 50 DOLLARS
31.11 g., 0.9999 Gold 0.9935 oz. AGW, 30 mm. **Ruler:** Elizabeth II **Rev:** Hockey player, red enameled maple leaves flanking

Date	Mintage	VF20	XF40	MS60	MS63
2010	—	—	—	—	1,850

KM# 1141 50 DOLLARS
31.11 g., 0.9999 Gold 0.9935 oz. AGW, 30 mm. **Ruler:** Elizabeth II **Obv:** Bust right **Rev:** Maple leaf

Date	Mintage	VF20	XF40	MS60	MS63
1911-2011	—	—	—	—	1,850

KM# 1210 50 DOLLARS
31.11 g., 1.000 Gold 0.9936 oz. AGW, 30 mm. **Ruler:** Elizabeth II **Obv:** Bust right **Rev:** Three maple leaves, 2007-2012 above

Date	Mintage	VF20	XF40	MS60	MS63
2012	—	PF65 1,850			

KM# 1414 50 DOLLARS
31.10 g., 0.9999 Gold 0.9934 oz. AGW, 30 mm. **Ruler:** Elizabeth II **Rev:** Two Maple Leaves

Date	Mintage	VF20	XF40	MS60	MS63
2013	—	—	—	—	1,800

KM# 1488 50 DOLLARS
31.11 g., 0.9999 Gold 0.9935 oz. AGW, 30 mm. **Ruler:** Elizabeth II **Rev:** Maple Leaf, security feature added

Date	Mintage	VF20	XF40	MS60	MS63
2013	—	—	—	—	BV+3%
2014	—	—	—	BV+3%	

KM# 1503 50 DOLLARS
31.11 g., 0.9999 Gold 0.9935 oz. AGW, 30 mm. **Ruler:** Elizabeth II **Rev:** Two maple leaves

Date	Mintage	VF20	XF40	MS60	MS63
2013 Reverse Proof	600	PF65 1,800			

KM# 1600 50 DOLLARS
31.11 g., 0.9999 Gold 0.9935 oz. AGW, 30 mm. **Ruler:** Elizabeth II **Obv:** Bust right **Rev:** Three maple leaves

Date	Mintage	VF20	XF40	MS60	MS63
2014	PF65 1,500				

KM# 750 200 DOLLARS
31.11 g., 1.000 Gold 0.9936 oz. AGW, 30 mm. **Ruler:** Elizabeth II **Rev:** Three maple leaves

Date	Mintage	VF20	XF40	MS60	MS63
2007 Proof, T/E privy mark	500	PF65 1,850			

KM# 786 200 DOLLARS
31.11 g., 1.000 Gold 0.9936 oz. AGW, 30 mm. **Ruler:** Elizabeth II **Obv:** Bust right on lathe-work background **Rev:** Two maple leaves on lathe-work background

Date	Mintage	VF20	XF40	MS60	MS63
2008	—	PF65 1,850			

KM# 1162 200 DOLLARS
31.11 g., 1.000 Gold 0.9936 oz. AGW **Ruler:** Elizabeth II **Rev:** Maple leaf with lathe backgound

Date	Mintage	VF20	XF40	MS60	MS63
2009	—	PF65 1,850			

KM# 1163 200 DOLLARS
31.11 g., 0.999 Gold 0.9926 oz. AGW **Ruler:** Elizabeth II **Subject:** Celebrating win **Rev:** Three athletics with hands raised

Date	Mintage	VF20	XF40	MS60	MS63
2010	—	PF65 1,850			

KM# 1165 200 DOLLARS
31.11 g., 1.000 Gold 0.9936 oz. AGW, 30 mm. **Ruler:** Elizabeth II **Rev:** Mountie on horseback, lathe backgound

Date	Mintage	VF20	XF40	MS60	MS63
2011	—	—	—	—	1,850

KM# 1487 200 DOLLARS
31.11 g., 0.9999 Gold 0.9935 oz. AGW, 30 mm. **Ruler:** Elizabeth II **Rev:** Three maple leaves, engine turned background

Date	Mintage	VF20	XF40	MS60	MS63
2012	—	PF65 1,800			

KM# 1328 500 DOLLARS
155.55 g., 0.9999 Gold 4.9684 oz. AGW, 55 mm. **Ruler:** Elizabeth II **Rev:** Three Maple Leaves

Date	Mintage	VF20	XF40	MS60	MS63
2012	—	PF65 10,000			

KM# 1161 2500 DOLLARS
1000.00 g., 0.9999 Gold 31.9406 oz. AGW, 101 mm. **Ruler:** Elizabeth II **Rev:** Three maple leaves on branch

Date	Mintage	VF20	XF40	MS60	MS63
2011	—	PF65 56,000			

KM# 1271 2500 DOLLARS
1000.00 g., 0.999 Gold 31.9118 oz. AGW, 101 mm. **Ruler:** Elizabeth II **Subject:** Maple Leaf Forever

Date	Mintage	VF20	XF40	MS60	MS63
2012	—	PF65 56,000			

KM# 1486 2500 DOLLARS
1000.00 g., 0.9999 Gold 31.9406 oz. AGW, 101 mm. **Ruler:** Elizabeth II **Rev:** Three maple leaves

Date	Mintage	VF20	XF40	MS60	MS63
2012	—	PF65 69,000			

KM# 1209 100000 DOLLARS
10000.00 g., 1.000 Gold 319.4346 oz. AGW **Ruler:** Elizabeth II **Obv:** Bust right **Rev:** Bill Reid's sculpture: Spirit of Haida Gwaii **Note:** The sculpture is at the Canadian Embassy in Washington, D.C.

Date	Mintage	VF20	XF40	MS60	MS63
2011	—	PF65 565,000			

KM# 755 1000000 DOLLARS
100000.00 g., 0.9999 Gold 3194.0585 oz. AGW **Ruler:** Elizabeth II **Obv:** Bust right **Rev:** Three maple leaves **Note:** Cast

Date	Mintage	VF20	XF40	MS60	MS63
2007	10	—	—	—	5,630,000

PLATINUM BULLION COINAGE

KM# 429 30 DOLLARS
3.11 g., 0.9995 Platinum 0.0993 oz. APW, 16 mm. **Ruler:** Elizabeth II **Obv:** Crowned head right **Rev:** Harlequin duck's head **Edge:** Reeded

Date	Mintage	VF20	XF40	MS60	MS63
2001	448	PF65 200			

KM# 1097 30 DOLLARS
3.11 g., 0.9995 Platinum 0.0993 oz. APW, 16 mm. **Ruler:** Elizabeth II **Rev:** Great Blue Heron

Date	Mintage	VF20	XF40	MS60	MS63
2002	344	PF65 200			

KM# 1101 30 DOLLARS
3.11 g., 0.9995 Platinum 0.0993 oz. APW, 16 mm. **Ruler:** Elizabeth II **Rev:** Atlantic Walrus

Date	Mintage	VF20	XF40	MS60	MS63
2003	365	PF65 250			

KM# 1105 30 DOLLARS
3.11 g., 0.9995 Platinum 0.0993 oz. APW, 16 mm. **Ruler:** Elizabeth II **Rev:** Grizzly Bear

Date	Mintage	VF20	XF40	MS60	MS63
2004	380	PF65 250			

KM# 430 75 DOLLARS
7.78 g., 0.9995 Platinum 0.2483 oz. APW, 20 mm. **Ruler:** Elizabeth II **Obv:** Crowned head right **Rev:** Harlequin duck in flight **Edge:** Reeded

Date	Mintage	VF20	XF40	MS60	MS63
2001	448	PF65 500			

KM# 1098 75 DOLLARS
7.77 g., 0.9995 Platinum 0.2481 oz. APW, 20 mm. **Ruler:** Elizabeth II **Rev:** Great Blue Heron

Date	Mintage	VF20	XF40	MS60	MS63
2002	344	PF65 525			

KM# 1102 75 DOLLARS
7.77 g., 0.9995 Platinum 0.2481 oz. APW, 20 mm. **Ruler:** Elizabeth II **Rev:** Atlantic Walrus

Date	Mintage	VF20	XF40	MS60	MS63
2003	365	PF65 550			

KM# 1106 75 DOLLARS
7.77 g., 0.9995 Platinum 0.2481 oz. APW, 20 mm. **Ruler:** Elizabeth II **Rev:** Grizzly Bear

Date	Mintage	VF20	XF40	MS60	MS63
2004	380	PF65 550			

KM# 431 150 DOLLARS
15.55 g., 0.9995 Platinum 0.4965 oz. APW, 25 mm. **Ruler:** Elizabeth II **Obv:** Crowned head right **Rev:** Two harlequin ducks **Edge:** Reeded

Date	Mintage	VF20	XF40	MS60	MS63
2001	448	PF65 1,000			

KM# 1099 150 DOLLARS
15.55 g., 0.9995 Platinum 0.4965 oz. APW, 25 mm. **Ruler:** Elizabeth II **Rev:** Great Blue Heron

Date	Mintage	VF20	XF40	MS60	MS63
2002	344	PF65 1,000			

KM# 1103 150 DOLLARS
15.55 g., 0.9995 Platinum 0.4965 oz. APW, 25 mm. **Ruler:** Elizabeth II **Rev:** Atlantic Walrus

Date	Mintage	VF20	XF40	MS60	MS63
2003	365	PF65 1,000			

KM# 1107 150 DOLLARS
15.55 g., 0.9995 Platinum 0.4965 oz. APW, 25 mm. **Ruler:** Elizabeth II **Rev:** Grizzly Bear

Date	Mintage	VF20	XF40	MS60	MS63
2004	380	PF65 1,000			

KM# 432 300 DOLLARS
31.10 g., 0.9995 Platinum 0.9931 oz. APW, 30 mm. **Ruler:** Elizabeth II **Obv:** Crowned head right **Rev:** Two standing harlequin ducks **Edge:** Reeded

Date	Mintage	VF20	XF40	MS60	MS63
2001	448	PF65 1,900			

KM# 1100 300 DOLLARS
31.11 g., 0.9995 Platinum 0.9931 oz. APW, 30 mm. **Ruler:** Elizabeth II **Rev:** Great Blue Heron

Date	Mintage	VF20	XF40	MS60	MS63
2002	344	PF65 1,950			

KM# 1104 300 DOLLARS
31.11 g., 0.9995 Platinum 0.9931 oz. APW, 30 mm. **Ruler:** Elizabeth II **Rev:** Atlantic Walrus

Date	Mintage	VF20	XF40	MS60	MS63
2003	365	PF65 1,950			

KM# 1108 300 DOLLARS
31.11 g., 0.9995 Platinum 0.9931 oz. APW, 30 mm. **Ruler:** Elizabeth II **Rev:** Grizzly Bear

Date	Mintage	VF20	XF40	MS60	MS63
2004	380	PF65 1,950			

KM# 753 300 DOLLARS
31.11 g., 0.9999 Platinum 0.9935 oz. APW **Ruler:** Elizabeth II **Rev:** Wooly mammoth

Date	Mintage	VF20	XF40	MS60	MS63
2007	400	PF65 3,200			

KM# 831 300 DOLLARS
31.11 g., 0.999 Platinum 0.9926 oz. APW **Ruler:** Elizabeth II **Rev:** Saber Tooth Scimitar cat

Date	Mintage	VF20	XF40	MS60	MS63
2008	200	PF65 3,500			

KM# 951 300 DOLLARS
31.16 g., 0.999 Platinum 0.9944 oz. APW, 30 mm. **Ruler:** Elizabeth II **Rev:** Steppe Bison

Date	Mintage	VF20	XF40	MS60	MS63
2009	200	PF65 3,500			

KM# 1159 300 DOLLARS
31.11 g., 0.999 Platinum 0.9926 oz. APW, 30 mm. **Ruler:** Elizabeth II **Rev:** Ground Sloth

Date	Mintage	VF20	XF40	MS60	MS63
2010	200	PF65 1,900			

KM# 1175 300 DOLLARS
31.11 g., 0.9995 Platinum 0.9931 oz. APW, 30 mm. **Ruler:** Elizabeth II **Obv:** Bust right **Rev:** Cougar head left

Date	Mintage	VF20	XF40	MS60	MS63
2011	200	PF65 1,950			

KM# 1273 300 DOLLARS
31.11 g., 0.999 Platinum 0.9926 oz. APW, 30 mm. **Ruler:** Elizabeth II **Subject:** Maple Leaf Forever

Date	Mintage	VF20	XF40	MS60	MS63
2012	—	PF65 1,950			

KM# 1386 300 DOLLARS
31.11 g., 0.999 Platinum 0.9926 oz. APW, 30 mm. **Ruler:** Elizabeth II **Subject:** Maple Leaf - 25th Anniversary **Rev:** Maple Leaf - Gilt Shadow

Date	Mintage	VF20	XF40	MS60	MS63
2013	Est. 250	PF65 3,000			

KM# 1391 300 DOLLARS
31.11 g., 0.999 Platinum 0.9927 oz. APW, 30 mm. **Ruler:** Elizabeth II **Rev:** The Bald Eagles at Nest

Date	Mintage	VF20	XF40	MS60	MS63
2013	—	PF65 2,250			

KM# 1544 300 DOLLARS
31.11 g., 0.999 Platinum 0.9927 oz. APW, 30 mm. **Ruler:** Elizabeth II **Rev:** Two bison

Date	Mintage	VF20	XF40	MS60	MS63
2013	PF65 2,250				

KM# 1552 300 DOLLARS
31.16 g., 0.9995 Platinum 0.9949 oz. APW, 30 mm. **Ruler:** Elizabeth II **Rev:** Two bison with heads butting

Date	Mintage	VF20	XF40	MS60	MS63
2014	200	PF65 3,000			

KM# 1560 300 DOLLARS
31.16 g., 0.9995 Platinum 0.9949 oz. APW, 30 mm. **Ruler:** Elizabeth II **Rev:** Bighorn Sheep

Date	Mintage	VF20	XF40	MS60	MS63
2014	250	PF65 3,000			

MINT SETS

KM#	Date	Mintage	Identification	Issue Price	Mkt Val
MS8	2001 (5)	600	KM438-442	1,996	2,950
MS9	2002 (7)	135,000	Double-dated 1952-2002, KM#444-449, 467	11.75	16.00
MS10	2002 (7)	—	KM#444-449, 467, Oh! Canada! 135th Birthday Gift set.	17.00	16.00
MS11	2002 (7)	—	KM#444-449, 467, Tiny Treasures Uncirculated Gift Set	17.00	16.00
MS12	2003 (7)	135,000	KM#289, 182b, 183b, 184b, 290, 186, 270	12.00	16.00
MS13	2003 (7)	75,000	KM490-496	13.25	20.00
MS14	2003 (7)	—	KM289, 182-184, 290, 186, 270, Oh! Canada!	17.75	16.00
MS15	2003 (7)	—	KM289, 182-184, 290, 186, 270, Tiny Treasures Uncirculated Gift Set	17.75	16.00

PROOF SETS

KM#	Date	Mintage	Identification	Issue Price	Mkt Val
PS51	2001 (4)	—	KM429, 430, 431, 432	—	3,600
PS52	2002 (8)	100,000	KM#443, 444a, 445, 446a-449a, 467	60.00	125
PS53	2002 (3)	—	KM#459-461	57.50	35.00
PS54	2002 (2)	—	KM#519, 520	750	1,125
PS55	2003 (8)	100,000	KM#182a,183a,184a, 186, 270d, 289, 290a, 450	62.50	125
PS56	2003 (6)	30,000	KM#468-473	75.00	100
PS57	2004 (8)	—	KM#490, 491a-494a, 495, 496a, 512	—	115
PS58	2004 (5)	25,000	KM#621-625	—	100

SPECIMEN SETS (SS)

KM#	Date	Mintage	Identification	Issue Price	Mkt Val
SS90	2002 (7)	75,000	KM#444-449,462	30.00	65.00
SS91	2003 (3)	75,000	KM#(uncertain), 270, 289, 290	30.00	50.00

CAPE VERDE

The Republic of Cape Verde, Africa's smallest republic, is located in the Atlantic Ocean, about 370 miles (595 km.) west of Dakar, Senegal, off the coast of Africa. The 14-island republic has an area of 1,557 sq. mi. (4,033 sq. km.) and a population of 435,983. Capital: Praia. The refueling of ships and aircraft is the chief economic function of the country. Fishing is important and agriculture is widely practiced, but the Cape Verdes are not self-sufficient in food. Fish products, salt, bananas, and shellfish are exported.

After 500 years of Portuguese rule, the Cape Verdes became independent on July 5, 1975. At the first general election, all seats of the new national assembly were won by the Party for the Independence of Guinea-Bissau and Cape Verde (PAIGC). The PAIGC linked the two former colonies into one state. Antonio Mascarenhas Monteiro won the first free presidential election in 1991.

MONETARY SYSTEM
100 Centavos = 1 Escudo

REPUBLIC
DECIMAL COINAGE

KM# 46 25 ESCUDOS
15.55 g., 0.999 Silver 0.4963 oz. ASW, 30.4 mm. **Obv:** Value above national arms **Rev:** Jesus **Edge:** Plain

Date	Mintage	F12	VF20	XF40	MS60	MS63
2006	—	PF63 35.00	PF65 40.00			

KM# 47 50 ESCUDOS
1.56 g., 0.999 Gold 0.0496 oz. AGW, 16 mm. **Obv:** Value above national arms **Rev:** Jesus **Edge:** Plain

Date	Mintage	F12	VF20	XF40	MS60	MS63
2006	—	PF63 90.00	PF65 100			

KM# 48 50 ESCUDOS
25.00 g., 0.925 Silver 0.7387 oz. ASW, 38.8 mm. **Subject:** 500th Anniversary Death of Christopher Columbus **Obv:** National arms **Obv. Legend:** CABO VERDE **Rev:** Sailing ship "Santa Maria **Rev. Legend:** A SANTA MARIA DE CHRIST?V?O COLOMBO **Edge:** Reeded

Date	Mintage	F12	VF20	XF40	MS60	MS63
2006	—	PF63 50.00	PF65 55.00			

KM# 49 50 ESCUDOS
25.00 g., 0.925 Silver 0.7387 oz. ASW, 38.6 mm. **Subject:** Appearance in Grotto **Obv:** National arms **Obv. Legend:** CABO VERDE **Rev:** Maria standing facing 3/4 left at right **Rev. Legend:** AVE MARIA - LOURDES **Edge:** Reeded

Date	Mintage	F12	VF20	XF40	MS60	MS63
2006	—	PF63 60.00	PF65 65.00			

KM# 50 50 ESCUDOS
25.00 g., 0.925 Silver 0.7387 oz. ASW **Obv:** National arms **Rev:** Red Kite bird

Date	Mintage	F12	VF20	XF40	MS60	MS63
2006	—	PF63 60.00	PF65 65.00			

KM# 52 50 ESCUDOS
25.00 g., 0.925 Silver 0.7387 oz. ASW, 38.6 mm. **Rev:** East India Company's Princess Louisa and 1/2 real from shipwreck

Date	Mintage	F12	VF20	XF40	MS60	MS63
2006	Est. 1500	PF63 75.00	PF65 80.00			

KM# 53 50 ESCUDOS
25.00 g., 0.925 Silver 0.7387 oz. ASW, 38.6 mm. **Rev:** Princess Louisa hitting the reef, 1/2 real from shipwreck

Date	Mintage	F12	VF20	XF40	MS60	MS63
2006	Est. 1500	PF63 75.00	PF65 80.00			

KM# 45 200 ESCUDOS
7.80 g., Copper-Nickel, 29.5 mm. **Subject:** 30th Anniversary of Independence **Obv:** National arms in number 2 of 200 **Rev:** Symbolic education design **Edge:** Reeded **Shape:** Round

Date	Mintage	F12	VF20	XF40	MS60	MS63
2005	—	—	—	—	8.50	10.00

KM# 45a 200 ESCUDOS
18.28 g., 0.925 Silver 0.5401 oz. ASW **Subject:** 30th Anniversary of Independence **Obv:** National arms in number 2 of 200 **Rev:** Symbolic education design **Edge:** Reeded **Shape:** Round

Date	Mintage	F12	VF20	XF40	MS60	MS63
2005	—	PF63 60.00	PF65 70.00			

KM# 51 250 ESCUDOS
Copper-Nickel **Subject:** Independence, 35th Anniversary **Obv:** Ship sailing forward **Rev:** Arms

Date	Mintage	F12	VF20	XF40	MS60	MS63
2010	—	—	—	—	12.00	15.00

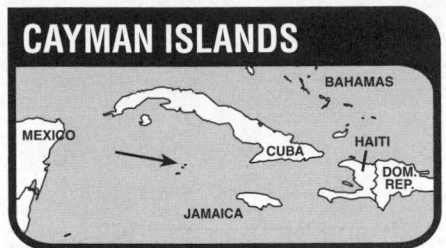

CAYMAN ISLANDS

The Cayman Islands are a British Crown Colony situated about 180 miles (280 km) northwest of Jamaica. It consists of three islands: Grand Cayman, Little Cayman, and Cayman Brac. The islands have an area of 102 sq. mi. (259 sq. km.) and a population of 33,200. Capital: George Town. Seafaring, commerce, banking, and tourism are the principal industries. Rope, turtle shells, and sharkskins are exported.

RULER
British

MINT
MARKSCHI - Valcambi

MONETARY SYSTEM
100 Cents = 1 Dollar

BRITISH COLONY
DECIMAL COINAGE

KM# 131 CENT
2.55 g., Copper Plated Steel, 17 mm. **Ruler:** Elizabeth II **Obv:** Crowned head right **Rev:** Grand Caiman thrush **Edge:** Plain

Date	Mintage	F12	VF20	XF40	MS60	MS63
2002	10,000,000	—	—	0.15	0.35	0.75
2005	16,220,000	—	—	0.15	0.35	0.75
2008	12,000,000	—	—	0.15	0.35	0.75

KM# 132 5 CENTS
2.00 g., Nickel Plated Steel, 18 mm. **Ruler:** Elizabeth II **Obv:** Crowned head right **Rev:** Pink-spotted shrimp **Edge:** Plain

Date	Mintage	F12	VF20	XF40	MS60	MS63
2002	2,500,000	—	—	0.15	0.35	1.00
2005	2,500,000	—	—	0.15	0.35	1.00
2008	3,000,000	—	—	0.15	0.35	1.00

KM# 133 10 CENTS
3.45 g., Nickel Plated Steel, 21 mm. **Ruler:** Elizabeth II **Obv:** Head with tiara right **Rev:** Green turtle surfacing **Edge:** Reeded

Date	Mintage	F12	VF20	XF40	MS60	MS63
2002	3,000,000	—	0.25	0.40	1.00	1.25
2005	3,000,000	—	0.25	0.40	1.00	1.25
2008	3,500,000	—	0.25	0.40	1.00	1.25

KM# 134 25 CENTS
5.10 g., Nickel Plated Steel, 24.26 mm. **Ruler:** Elizabeth II **Obv:** Head with tiara right **Rev:** Schooner sailing right **Edge:** Reeded

Date	Mintage	F12	VF20	XF40	MS60	MS63
2002	2,500,000	—	—	0.75	1.25	1.50
2005	2,500,000	—	—	0.75	1.25	1.50
2008	3,000,000	—	—	0.75	1.25	1.50

KM# 136 2 DOLLARS
28.34 g., 0.925 Silver 0.8374 oz. ASW, 38.6 mm. **Ruler:** Elizabeth II **Obv:** Gold plated Queen Elizabeth II **Rev:** British crown and value **Edge:** Reeded

Date	Mintage	F12	VF20	XF40	MS60	MS63
2002		PF60 55.00		PF63 50.00		

KM# 135 2 DOLLARS
28.28 g., 0.925 Silver 0.8356 oz. ASW, 38.6 mm. **Ruler:** Elizabeth II **Subject:** 500th Anniversary - Christopher Columbus First Recorded Sighting of the Cayman Islands **Obv:** Crowned head right **Rev:** Quincentennial Celebrations Logo in color

Date	Mintage	F12	VF20	XF40	MS60	MS63
2003	1,500	PF60 55.00		PF63 50.00		

KM# 138 2 DOLLARS
28.28 g., 0.925 Silver 0.8356 oz. ASW, 38.61 mm. **Ruler:** Elizabeth II **Subject:** Royal Horticulture Society **Obv:** Head right, gilt portrait **Rev:** RHS Tent and flowers

Date	Mintage	F12	VF20	XF40	MS60	MS63
2003	—	PF60 55.00		PF63 50.00		

KM# 137 5 DOLLARS
28.28 g., 0.925 Silver 0.8356 oz. ASW, 38.6 mm. **Ruler:** Elizabeth II **Subject:** Elizabeth II's 80th Birthday **Obv:** Crowned head right - gilt **Obv. Legend:** CAYMAN ISLANDS - ELIZABETH II **Rev:** Queen crowning Charles as Prince of Wales

Date	Mintage	F12	VF20	XF40	MS60	MS63
2006	25,000	PF60 50.00		PF63 45.00		

KM# 145 5 DOLLARS
28.28 g., 0.925 Silver 0.8356 oz. ASW, 38.61 mm. **Ruler:** Elizabeth II **Subject:** Queen Elizabeth, 80th Birthday **Rev:** Elizabeth and Philip in the state coach

Date	Mintage	F12	VF20	XF40	MS60	MS63
2006	Est. 25000	PF60 50.00		PF63 45.00		

KM# 149 5 DOLLARS
28.28 g., 0.925 Silver 0.8356 oz. ASW, 38.6 mm. **Ruler:** Elizabeth II **Obv:** Head in tiara right, gilt face and rim **Rev:** Queen and Prince Philip in carriage, gilt 80 above

Date	Mintage	F12	VF20	XF40	MS60	MS63
2006		PF60 55.00		PF63 50.00		

KM# 139 5 DOLLARS
28.28 g., 0.925 Silver 0.8356 oz. ASW, 38.61 mm. **Ruler:** Elizabeth II **Subject:** Cayman Islands Monetary Authority, 10th Anniversary **Obv:** Bust right **Rev:** Island's coat of arms

Date	Mintage	F12	VF20	XF40	MS60	MS63
2007	200	PF60 110		PF63 100		

KM# 146 5 DOLLARS
28.28 g., 0.925 Silver 0.8356 oz. ASW, 38.61 mm. **Ruler:** Elizabeth II **Subject:** End of World War I, 90th Anniversary

Date	Mintage	F12	VF20	XF40	MS60	MS63
2008	—	PF60 55.00		PF63 50.00		

KM# 147 5 DOLLARS
28.28 g., 0.925 Silver 0.8356 oz. ASW, 38.61 mm. **Ruler:** Elizabeth II **Subject:** End of World War I, 90th Anniversary

Date	Mintage	F12	VF20	XF40	MS60	MS63
2008	—	PF60 55.00		PF63 50.00		

KM# 141 5 DOLLARS
28.28 g., 0.925 Silver 0.8356 oz. ASW, 38.6 mm. **Ruler:** Elizabeth II **Subject:** Constitutional Government, 50th Anniversary **Obv:** Bust right **Rev:** Coat of arms

Date	Mintage	F12	VF20	XF40	MS60	MS63
2009	300	PF60 85.00		PF63 75.00		

KM# 150 5 DOLLARS
28.28 g., 0.925 Silver 0.8356 oz. ASW, 38.61 mm. **Ruler:** Elizabeth II **Subject:** Royal Yacht Britannia, 60th Anniversary **Rev:** HMY Britannia, flags **Rev. Legend:** I NAME THIS SHIP BRITANNIA

Date	Mintage	F12	VF20	XF40	MS60	MS63
2012	—	PF60 110				

KM# 151 5 DOLLARS
28.28 g., 0.925 Silver 0.8356 oz. ASW, 38.61 mm. **Ruler:** Elizabeth II **Subject:** Heroes Day, 10th Anniversary **Obv:** Coat of arms, gilt **Rev:** Statues of father and son sitting on ship's deck, woman holding the earth in her hands, three small catboats in the water

Date	Mintage	F12	VF20	XF40	MS60	MS63
2013	200	PF60 115				

KM# 140 10 DOLLARS
7.99 g., 0.9167 Gold 0.2339 oz. AGW, 22.1 mm. **Ruler:** Elizabeth II **Subject:** Cayman Islands Monetary Authority, 10th Anniversary **Obv:** Bust right **Rev:** Island's coat of arms

Date	Mintage	F12	VF20	XF40	MS60	MS63
2007	75	PF60 500		PF63 450		

KM# 152 10 DOLLARS
28.28 g., 0.925 Silver 0.8356 oz. ASW, 38.61 mm. **Ruler:** Elizabeth II **Subject:** Royal Family **Shape:** 7-Sided

Date	Mintage	F12	VF20	XF40	MS60	MS63
2007	Est. 30000	PF60 40.00	PF63 35.00			

KM# 153 10 DOLLARS
28.28 g., 0.925 Silver 0.8356 oz. ASW, 38.61 mm. **Ruler:** Elizabeth II **Subject:** Royal Yacht Britannia **Shape:** 7-Sided

Date	Mintage	F12	VF20	XF40	MS60	MS63
2007	Est. 30000	PF60 40.00	PF63 35.00			

KM# 154 10 DOLLARS
28.28 g., 0.925 Silver 0.8356 oz. ASW, 38.61 mm. **Ruler:** Elizabeth II **Shape:** 7-Sided

Date	Mintage	F12	VF20	XF40	MS60	MS63
2007	Est. 30000	PF60 40.00	PF63 35.00			

KM# 142 10 DOLLARS
7.99 g., 0.9167 Gold 0.2339 oz. AGW, 22.1 mm. **Ruler:** Elizabeth II **Subject:** Constitutional Government, 50th Anniversary **Obv:** Bust right **Rev:** Coat of Arms

Date	Mintage	F12	VF20	XF40	MS60	MS63
2009	125	PF60 475	PF63 425			

KM# 148 50 DOLLARS
155.50 g., 0.925 Silver 4.5947 oz. ASW, 65 mm. **Ruler:** Elizabeth II **Subject:** End of World War I, 90th Anniversary **Rev:** Soldier in the field with barbed wire

Date	Mintage	F12	VF20	XF40	MS60	MS63
2008	Est. 150	PF60 300	PF63 250			

CENTRAL AFRICAN STATES

The Central African States, a monetary union comprised of Equatorial Guinea (a former Spanish possession), the former French possessions and now independent states of the Republic of Congo (Brazzaville), Gabon, Central African Republic, Chad and Cameroon, issues a common currency for the member states from a common central bank. The monetary unit, the African Financial Community franc, is tied to and supported by the French franc.

In 1960, an attempt was made to form a union of the newly independent republics of Chad, Congo, Central Africa and Gabon. The proposal was discarded when Chad refused to become a constituent member. The four countries then linked into an Equatorial Customs Unit, to which Cameroon became an associate member in 1961. A more extensive cooperation of the five republics, identified as the Central African Customs and Economic Union, was entered into force at the beginning of 1966.

In 1974 the Central Bank of the Equatorial African States, which had issued coins and paper currency in its own name and with the names of the constituent member nations, changed its name to the Bank of the Central African States. Equatorial Guinea converted to the CFA currency system issuing its first 100 Franc in 1985.

MONETARY UNION
STANDARD COINAGE

KM# 8 FRANC
1.30 g., Aluminum, 23 mm. **Obv:** Three giant eland left, date below **Obv. Designer:** G.B.L. Bazor **Rev:** Denomination within wreath

Date	Mintage	F12	VF20	XF40	MS60	MS63
2003	—	0.20	0.40	0.80	2.00	—

KM# 16 FRANC
1.61 g., Stainless Steel, 14.9 mm. **Obv:** Value **Rev:** Value above produce **Edge:** Plain

Date	Mintage	F12	VF20	XF40	MS60	MS63
2006(a)	—	—	—	—	0.15	0.25

KM# 17 2 FRANCS
2.43 g., Stainless Steel, 17.9 mm. **Obv:** Value **Rev:** Value above produce **Edge:** Plain

Date	Mintage	F12	VF20	XF40	MS60	MS63
2006(a)	—	—	—	—	0.25	0.35

KM# 7 5 FRANCS
3.00 g., Aluminum-Bronze, 20 mm. **Obv:** Three giant eland left, date below **Obv. Designer:** G.B.L. Bazor **Rev:** Denomination within wreath

Date	Mintage	F12	VF20	XF40	MS60	MS63
2003	—	0.15	0.30	0.60	1.25	—

KM# 18 5 FRANCS
2.41 g., Brass, 15.9 mm. **Obv:** Value **Rev:** Value above produce **Edge:** Reeded

Date	Mintage	F12	VF20	XF40	MS60	MS63
2006(a)	—	—	—	—	0.50	0.65

KM# 9 10 FRANCS
4.00 g., Aluminum-Bronze, 23 mm. **Obv:** Three giant eland left, date below **Obv. Designer:** G.B.L. Bazor **Rev:** Denomination within wreath

Date	Mintage	F12	VF20	XF40	MS60	MS63
2003(a)	—	0.20	0.35	0.75	1.50	—

KM# 19 10 FRANCS
3.00 g., Brass, 17.9 mm. **Obv:** Value **Rev:** Value above produce **Edge:** Reeded

Date	Mintage	F12	VF20	XF40	MS60	MS63
2006(a)	—	—	—	—	0.75	1.00

KM# 10 25 FRANCS
8.00 g., Aluminum-Bronze, 27.2 mm. **Obv:** Three giant eland left, date below **Obv. Designer:** G.B.L. Bazor **Rev:** Denomination within wreath

Date	Mintage	F12	VF20	XF40	MS60	MS63
2003(a)	—	0.25	0.50	1.00	2.00	—

KM# 20 25 FRANCS
4.20 g., Brass, 22.7 mm. **Obv:** Value **Rev:** Value above produce **Edge:** Reeded

Date	Mintage	F12	VF20	XF40	MS60	MS63
2006(a)	—	—	—	—	1.00	1.25

KM# 11 50 FRANCS
4.70 g., Nickel, 21.5 mm. **Obv:** Three giant eland left, date below **Obv. Designer:** G.B.L. Bazor **Rev:** Denomination within flower design **Edge:** Reeded **Note:** Starting in 1996 an extra flora item was added where the mintmark was formerly located.

Date	Mintage	F12	VF20	XF40	MS60	MS63
2003(a)	—	0.75	1.50	3.50	6.00	—

KM# 21 50 FRANCS
4.90 g., Stainless Steel, 22 mm. **Obv:** Value **Rev:** Value above produce **Edge:** Reeded

Date	Mintage	F12	VF20	XF40	MS60	MS63
2006(a)	—	—	—	—	1.25	1.50

KM# 13 100 FRANCS
7.05 g., Nickel, 25.5 mm. **Obv:** Three giant eland **Rev:** Denomination

Date	Mintage	F12	VF20	XF40	MS60	MS63
2003	—	—	—	—	4.50	6.00

KM# 15 100 FRANCS
6.00 g., Bi-Metallic, 23.9 mm. **Obv:** Denomination above initials within beaded circle **Rev:** Value above produce **Edge:** Reeded

Date	Mintage	F12	VF20	XF40	MS60	MS63
2006(a)	—	—	—	—	5.00	6.50

KM# 22 500 FRANCS

8.10 g., Copper Nickel, 26 mm. **Obv:** Value above produce
Rev: Value **Edge:** Segmented reeding and lettering

Date	Mintage	F12	VF20	XF40	MS60	MS63
2006(a)	—				8.00	10.00

KM# 23 1000 FRANCS

22.20 g., 0.900 Silver 0.6382 oz. ASW, 37 mm. **Subject:** FIFA
World Cup, England, 2004 **Edge:** Plain

Date	Mintage	F12	VF20	XF40	MS60	MS63
2004(a)	—					35.00
2004(a)	—	PF63 40.00		PF65 45.00		

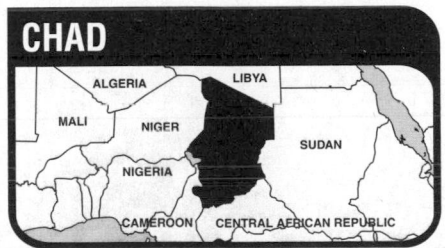

CHAD

The Republic of Chad, a landlocked country of central
Africa, is the largest country of former French Equatorial Africa.
It has an area of 495,755 sq. mi. (1,284,000 sq. km.) and a
population of *7.27 million. Capital: N'Djamena. An expanding
livestock industry produces camels, cattle and sheep. Cotton
(the chief product), ivory and palm oil are important exports.

NOTE: For earlier and related coinage see French
Equatorial Africa and the Equatorial African States. For later
coinage see Central African States.

MINT MARKS
(a) - Paris, privy marks only
(b) = Brussels
NI - Numismatica Italiana, Arezzo, Italy

REPUBLIC
DECIMAL COINAGE

KM# 30 500 FRANCS

Silver, 31 mm. **Obv:** Native portrait within circle **Rev:** Rhino
mom and baby

Date	Mintage	F12	VF20	XF40	MS60	MS63
2001	—	PF65 30.00				

KM# 20 1000 FRANCS

15.00 g., 0.999 Silver 0.4787 oz. ASW, 35 mm. **Obv:** Native
portrait within circle, denomination below **Rev:** Ancient Arabic
war ship **Edge:** Plain

Date	Mintage	F12	VF20	XF40	MS60	MS63
2001	—	PF65 40.00				

KM# 21 1000 FRANCS

25.10 g., 0.999 Silver 0.801 oz. ASW, 40 mm. **Obv:** Native
portrait within circle, denomination below **Rev:** Soccer player
and stadium **Edge:** Reeded

Date	Mintage	F12	VF20	XF40	MS60	MS63
2001	—	PF63 45.00		PF65 50.00		

KM# 35 1000 FRANCS

20.00 g., Silver, 40 mm. **Subject:** African Fauna **Obv:** Native
portrait within circle **Rev:** Balearica Pavonina (two birds)

Date	Mintage	F12	VF20	XF40	MS60	MS63
2001	—	PF63 40.00		PF65 45.00		

KM# 29 1000 FRANCS

15.00 g., 0.999 Silver 0.4787 oz. ASW, 36 mm. **Obv:** Native
portrait within circle **Rev:** Multicolor orang-outan

Date	Mintage	F12	VF20	XF40	MS60	MS63
2001	—	PF65 35.00				

KM# 22 1000 FRANCS

20.00 g., 0.999 Silver 0.6382 oz. ASW, 40 mm. **Obv:** Native
portrait within circle, denomination below **Rev:** Horizontal
soccer player above stadium **Edge:** Reeded

Date	Mintage	F12	VF20	XF40	MS60	MS63
2002	5,000	PF63 40.00		PF65 45.00		

KM# 23 1000 FRANCS

20.15 g., 0.999 Silver 0.643 oz. ASW, 40 mm. **Obv:** Native
portrait within circle, denomination below **Rev:** Soccer player
and Arch of Triumph **Edge:** Reeded

Date	Mintage	F12	VF20	XF40	MS60	MS63
2002	—	PF63 37.00		PF65 42.00		

KM# 31 1000 FRANCS

15.00 g., 0.985 Silver 0.472 oz. ASW, 34 mm. **Rev:** Multicolor
McDonnell-Douglass DC-10 landing left

Date	Mintage	F12	VF20	XF40	MS60	MS63
2002	—	PF65 35.00				

KM# 32 1000 FRANCS

15.00 g., 0.985 Silver 0.472 oz. ASW, 34 mm. **Rev:** Multicolor
Boeing 747 taking-off right

Date	Mintage	F12	VF20	XF40	MS60	MS63
2002	—	PF65 35.00				

KM# 36 1000 FRANCS
20.00 g., Silver, 40 mm. **Subject:** Animals in Peril **Obv:** Native portrait within circle **Rev:** Leopard

Date	Mintage	F12	VF20	XF40	MS60	MS63
2003	—	PF63 35.00		PF65 40.00		

KM# 33 1000 FRANCS
15.00 g., 0.985 Silver 0.472 oz. ASW, 34 mm. **Rev:** Multicolor McDonnell-Douglass DC-9 over mountains

Date	Mintage	F12	VF20	XF40	MS60	MS63
2003	—	PF65 35.00				

KM# 34 1000 FRANCS
15.00 g., 0.985 Silver 0.472 oz. ASW, 34 mm. **Rev:** Multicolor Fokker F-7a top wing

Date	Mintage	F12	VF20	XF40	MS60	MS63
2003	—	PF65 35.00				

CHILE

The Republic of Chile, a ribbon-like country on the Pacific coast of southern South America, has an area of 292,135 sq. mi. (756,950 sq. km.) and a population of *15.21 million. Capital: Santiago. Historically, the economic base of Chile has been the rich mineral deposits of its northern provinces. Copper has accounted for more than 75 percent of Chile's export earnings in recent years. Other important mineral exports are iron ore, iodine and nitrate of soda. Fresh fruits and vegetables, as well as wine are increasingly significant in inter-hemispheric trade.

MINT MARK
So – Santiago
(ml) – Maple leaf – Royal Canadian Mint (RCM)

REPUBLIC
REFORM COINAGE
100 Centavos = 1 Peso; 1000 Old Escudos = 1 Peso

KM# 231 PESO
0.70 g., Aluminum, 15.5 mm. **Obv:** Gen. Bernardo O'Higgins bust right **Obv. Legend:** REPUBLICA - DE CHILE **Rev:** Denomination above date within wreath **Edge:** Plain **Shape:** 8-sided **Note:** Varieties exist.

Date	Mintage	F12	VF20	XF40	MS60	MS63
2001So Narrow date	—	—	—	—	0.10	0.20
2002So Narrow date	—	—	—	—	0.10	0.20
2003So Narrow date	—	—	—	—	0.10	0.20
2004So Wide date	—	—	—	—	0.10	0.20
2005So Wide date	—	—	—	—	0.10	0.20
2006So Wide date	—	—	—	—	0.10	0.20
2008So Wide date	—	—	—	—	0.10	0.20
2009So Wide date	—	—	—	—	0.10	0.20
2011So Wide date	—	—	—	—	0.10	0.20
2012So Wide date	—	—	—	—	0.10	0.20

KM# 232 5 PESOS
2.20 g., Aluminum-Bronze, 15.5 mm. **Obv:** Gen. Bernardo O'Higgins bust right **Obv. Legend:** REPUBLICA - DE CHILE **Rev:** Denomination above date within wreath **Edge:** Plain **Shape:** 8-sided **Note:** Varieties exist.

Date	Mintage	F12	VF20	XF40	MS60	MS63
2001So Narrow date	—	—	—	—	0.10	0.35	0.60
2001 (sa) Wide date	—	—	—	0.15	0.50	0.75
Note: Without name of sculptor						
2002So Narrow date	—	—	—	0.15	0.50	0.75
2002 (a) Wide date	—	—	—	0.10	0.35	0.60
2003So	—	—	—	0.10	0.35	0.60
2004So	—	—	—	0.10	0.35	0.60
2005So	—	—	—	0.10	0.35	0.60
2006So	—	—	—	0.10	0.35	0.60
2007So	—	—	—	0.10	0.35	0.60
2008So	—	—	—	0.10	0.35	0.60
2009So	—	—	—	0.10	0.35	0.60
2010So	—	—	—	0.10	0.35	0.60
2011So	—	—	—	0.10	0.35	0.60
2012So (Minted in Madrid)	—	—	—	0.10	0.35	0.60

KM# 228.2 10 PESOS
3.50 g., Aluminum-Bronze, 21 mm. **Obv:** Bust of Gen. Bernardo O'Higgins right **Obv. Legend:** REPUBLICA - DE CHILE **Rev:** Denomination above date within sprays **Edge:** Reeded **Note:** All 9's are curl tail 9's except for the 1999 date, these are straight tail 9's. Normal rim.

Date	Mintage	F12	VF20	XF40	MS60	MS63
2001So	—	—	—	0.20	0.50	0.65
2002So	—	—	—	0.20	0.50	0.65
2003So	—	—	—	0.20	0.50	0.65
2004So	—	—	—	0.20	0.50	0.65
2005So	—	—	—	0.20	0.50	0.65
2006So	—	—	—	0.20	0.50	0.65
2007	—	—	—	0.20	0.50	0.65
Note: Struck in Canada						
2008So	—	—	—	0.20	0.50	0.65
2009So	—	—	—	0.20	0.50	0.65
2010So	—	—	—	0.20	0.50	0.65
2011So	—	—	—	0.20	0.50	0.65
2012So	—	—	—	0.20	0.50	0.65
2013So	—	—	—	0.20	0.50	0.65

KM# 219.2 50 PESOS
7.00 g., Aluminum-Bronze, 25 mm. **Obv:** Bust of Gen. Bernardo O'Higgins right **Obv. Legend:** REPUBLICA - DE CHILE **Rev:** Denomination above date within sprays **Edge:** Ornamented **Shape:** 10-sided **Note:** Narrow date.

Date	Mintage	F12	VF20	XF40	MS60	MS63
2001So	—	—	—	0.50	1.25	1.50
2002So	—	—	—	0.50	1.25	1.50
2005So	—	—	—	0.50	1.00	1.25
2006So	—	—	—	0.50	1.00	1.25
2007	—	—	—	0.50	1.00	1.25
Note: Struck in Canada						
2009So	—	—	—	0.50	1.00	1.25
2010So	—	—	—	0.50	1.00	1.25
2011So	—	—	—	0.50	1.00	1.25
2012So	—	—	—	0.50	1.00	1.25
2013So	—	—	—	0.50	1.00	1.25

KM# 219.3 50 PESOS
7.00 g., Aluminum-Bronze, 25 mm. **Obv:** Bust of Gen. Bernardo O'Higgins right **Obv. Legend:** REPUBLICA DE CHIIE **Rev:** Denomination above date within sprays **Note:** Error spelling in legend of CHILE.

Date	Mintage	F12	VF20	XF40	MS60	MS63
2008	—	—	—	—	1.50	2.50
2009	—	—	—	—	1.50	2.50

KM# 236 100 PESOS
7.58 g., Bi-Metallic, 23.5 mm. **Subject:** Native people **Obv:** Bust of native Mapuche girl facing **Obv. Legend:** REPUBLICA DE CHILE - PUEBLOS ORIGINARIOS **Rev:** National arms above denomination **Edge:** Segmented reeding

Date	Mintage	F12	VF20	XF40	MS60	MS63
2001So	—	—	0.35	0.90	2.25	3.00
2003So	—	—	0.35	0.90	2.25	3.00
2004So	—	—	0.35	0.90	2.25	3.00
2005So	—	—	0.35	0.90	2.25	3.00
2006So	—	—	0.35	0.90	2.25	3.00
2008So	—	—	0.35	0.90	2.25	3.00
2009So	—	—	0.35	0.90	2.25	3.00
2010So	—	—	0.35	0.90	2.25	3.00
2011So	—	—	0.35	0.90	2.25	3.00
2012So	—	—	0.35	0.90	2.25	3.00

KM# 235 500 PESOS
6.50 g., Bi-Metallic, 26 mm. **Subject:** Cardinal Raul Silva Henriquez **Obv:** Bust of cardinal within inner ring facing left **Rev:** Denomination above date within wreath **Edge:** Reeded

Date	Mintage	F12	VF20	XF40	MS60	MS63
2001So	—	—	—	—	6.00	6.50
2002So 4.1mm date	—	—	—	—	6.00	6.50
2002So 5.2mm date	—	—	—	—	6.00	6.50
2003So	—	—	—	—	6.00	6.50
2008So	—	—	—	—	6.00	6.50
2009So	—	—	—	—	6.00	6.50
2010So	—	—	—	—	6.00	6.50
2011So	—	—	—	—	6.00	6.50
2012So	—	—	—	—	6.00	6.50

CHINA / Peoples Republic

The Peoples Republic of China, located in eastern Asia, has an area of 3,696,100 sq. mi. (9,596,960 sq. km.) (including Manchuria and Tibet) and a population of *1.20 billion. Capital: Peking (Beijing). The economy is based on agriculture, mining, and manufacturing. Textiles, clothing, metal ores, tea and rice are exported.

MONETARY SYSTEM
10 Fen (Cents) = 1 Jiao
10 Jiao = 1 Renminbi Yuan

MINT MARKS
(b) - Beijing (Peking)
(s) - Shanghai
(y) - Shenyang (Mukden)

OBVERSE LEGENDS

中华人民共和国

ZHONGHUA RENMIN GONGHEGUO
(Peoples Republic of China)

中国人民银行

ZHONGGUO RENMIN YINHANG
(Peoples Bank of China)

PEOPLES REPUBLIC
STANDARD COINAGE

KM# 1 FEN
0.70 g., Aluminum, 18 mm. **Obv:** National emblem **Rev:** Value in wreath, date below **Edge:** Reeded **Note:** Prev. Y#1.

Date	Mintage	F12	VF20	XF40	MS60	MS63
2005	—	—	—	—	0.15	0.25
2006	—	—	—	—	0.15	0.25
2007	—	—	—	—	0.15	0.25
2008	—	—	—	—	0.15	0.25
2009	—	—	—	—	0.15	0.25
2010	—	—	—	—	0.15	0.25
2011	—	—	—	—	0.15	0.25

KM# 1210 JIAO
1.12 g., Aluminum, 19 mm. **Obv:** Denomination, date below **Rev:** Orchid **Rev. Legend:** ZHONGGUA RENMIN YINHANG **Edge:** Plain **Note:** Prev. Y#1068.

Date	Mintage	F12	VF20	XF40	MS60	MS63
2001	—	—	—	—	0.50	0.75
2002	—	—	—	—	0.50	0.75
2003	—	—	—	—	0.50	0.75

KM# 1210a JIAO
Copper-Nickel, 19 mm. **Obv:** Denomination, date below **Note:** Prev. Y#1068a.

Date	Mintage	F12	VF20	XF40	MS60	MS63
2005	—	—	—	—	0.50	0.75

KM# 1210b JIAO
3.20 g., Stainless Steel, 19 mm. **Obv:** Value, date below **Rev:** Orchid **Rev. Legend:** ZHONGGUA RENMIN YINHANG **Edge:** Plain **Note:** Prev. Y#1068b.

Date	Mintage	F12	VF20	XF40	MS60	MS63
2005	—	—	—	—	—	2.00
2006	—	—	—	—	—	0.25
2007	—	—	—	—	—	0.25
2008	—	—	—	—	—	0.25
2009	—	—	—	—	—	0.25
2010	—	—	—	—	—	0.25
2011	—	—	—	—	—	0.25
2012	—	—	—	—	—	0.25

KM# 336 5 JIAO
3.80 g., Brass, 20.5 mm. **Obv:** National emblem, date below **Rev:** Denomination above flowers **Edge:** Segmented reeding **Note:** Prev. Y#329.

Date	Mintage	F12	VF20	XF40	MS60	MS63
2001	—	—	—	—	1.00	1.25

KM# 1411 5 JIAO
3.80 g., Brass, 20.5 mm. **Obv:** Denomination **Rev:** Flower **Rev. Legend:** ZHONGGUA RENMIN YINHANG **Edge:** Segmented reeding **Note:** Prev. Y#1106.

Date	Mintage	F12	VF20	XF40	MS60	MS63
2002	—	—	—	—	1.50	1.75
2003	—	—	—	—	1.50	1.75
2004	—	—	—	—	1.50	1.75
2005	—	—	—	—	1.50	1.75
2006	—	—	—	—	1.50	1.75
2007	—	—	—	—	1.50	1.75
2008	—	—	—	—	1.50	1.75
2009	—	—	—	—	1.50	1.75
2010	—	—	—	—	1.50	1.75
2011	—	—	—	—	1.50	1.75
2012	—	—	—	—	1.50	1.75
2013	—	—	—	—	1.50	1.75

KM# 1212 YUAN
6.10 g., Nickel Plated Steel, 24.9 mm. **Obv:** Denomination, date below **Rev:** Chrysanthemum **Rev. Legend:** ZHONGGUA RENMIN YINHANG **Edge:** RMB" three times **Note:** Prev. Y#1069.

Date	Mintage	F12	VF20	XF40	MS60	MS63
2001	—	—	—	—	2.00	2.50
2002	—	—	—	—	2.00	2.50
2003	—	—	—	—	2.00	2.50
2004	—	—	—	—	2.00	2.50
2005	—	—	—	—	2.00	2.50
2006	—	—	—	—	2.00	2.50
2007	—	—	—	—	2.00	2.50
2008	—	—	—	—	2.00	2.50
2009	—	—	—	—	2.00	2.50
2010	—	—	—	—	2.00	2.50
2011	—	—	—	—	2.00	2.50
2012	—	—	—	—	2.00	2.50
2013	—	—	—	—	2.00	2.50

KM# 1465 YUAN
6.85 g., Brass, 25 mm. **Obv:** Value **Rev:** Celebrating child and ram **Edge:** Lettered **Edge Lettering:** RMB" three times **Note:** Prev. Y#1125.

Date	Mintage	F12	VF20	XF40	MS60	MS63
2003	—	—	—	—	5.00	6.00

KM# 1521 YUAN
Brass **Obv:** Denomination **Rev:** Celebrating Child **Note:** Prev. Y#1247.

Date	Mintage	F12	VF20	XF40	MS60	MS63
2004	—	—	—	—	2.50	3.00

KM# 1522 YUAN
6.00 g., Nickel Clad Steel, 25 mm. **Obv:** Palace **Rev:** Deng Xiao Ping 1904-2004 **Note:** Prev. Y#1248.

Date	Mintage	F12	VF20	XF40	MS60	MS63
2004	—	—	—	—	3.50	4.00

KM# 1523 YUAN
Nickel Clad Steel **Subject:** 50th Year of Peoples Congress **Obv:** Congress building **Note:** Prev. Y#1249.

Date	Mintage	F12	VF20	XF40	MS60	MS63
2004	—	—	—	—	3.50	4.00

KM# 1574 YUAN
5.96 g., Nickel Clad Steel, 25 mm. **Obv:** Building **Rev:** Bust of Chenyun **Edge:** Lettered **Note:** Prev. Y#1208.

Date	Mintage	F12	VF20	XF40	MS60	MS63
2005	—	—	—	—	3.50	4.00

KM# 1575 YUAN
Brass **Subject:** Year of the Rooster **Obv:** Denomination **Rev:** Celebrating Child **Note:** Prev. Y#1250.

Date	Mintage	F12	VF20	XF40	MS60	MS63
2005	—	—	—	—	3.00	3.50

KM# 1650 YUAN
Brass **Subject:** Year of the Dog **Obv:** Denomination **Rev:** Celebrating Child **Note:** Prev. Y#1251.

Date	Mintage	F12	VF20	XF40	MS60	MS63
2006	—	—	—	—	7.00	8.00

KM# 1775 YUAN
6.75 g., Brass, 25 mm. **Subject:** 29th Olympics **Obv:** Stylized Olympics logo **Rev:** Cartoon swimmer **Edge:** Reeded **Note:** Prev. Y#1256.

Date	Mintage	F12	VF20	XF40	MS60	MS63
2008 (2006)(y)	—	—	—	—	5.00	6.00

KM# 1776 YUAN
6.75 g., Brass, 25 mm. **Subject:** 29th Olympics **Obv:** Stylized Olympics logo **Rev:** Cartoon Weight Lifter **Edge:** Reeded **Note:** Prev. Y#1257.

Date	Mintage	F12	VF20	XF40	MS60	MS63
2008 (2006)	—	—	—	—	5.00	6.00

KM# 1652 YUAN
6.75 g., Brass, 25 mm. **Subject:** Year of the Pig

Date	Mintage	F12	VF20	XF40	MS60	MS63
2007	10,000,000	—	—	—	—	8.00

KM# 1671 YUAN
6.75 g., Brass, 25 mm. **Subject:** 29th Summer Olympics, Bejing **Obv:** Olympic Logo **Rev:** Yingying mascot on pomel horse, latent image

Date	Mintage	F12	VF20	XF40	MS60	MS63
2008	—	—	—	—	—	5.00

KM# 1672 YUAN
6.75 g., Brass, 25 mm. **Subject:** 29th Summer Olympics, Bejing **Obv:** Olympic games logo **Rev:** Jingjing mascot with bow and arrow, latent images

Date	Mintage	F12	VF20	XF40	MS60	MS63
2008	—	—	—	—	—	5.00

KM# 1673 YUAN
6.75 g., Brass, 25 mm. **Subject:** 29th Summer Olympics, Bejing **Obv:** Olympics logo **Rev:** Huanhuan mascot playing soccer, latent image

Date	Mintage	F12	VF20	XF40	MS60	MS63
2008	—	—	—	—	—	5.00

KM# 1810 YUAN
Brass, 25 mm. **Obv:** Beijing Olympic logo **Rev:** Character playing ping-pong

Date	Mintage	F12	VF20	XF40	MS60	MS63
2008	—	—	—	—	2.50	3.00

KM# 1811 YUAN
Brass, 25 mm. **Obv:** Beijing Olympic logo **Rev:** Character fencing with bow and arrow

Date	Mintage	F12	VF20	XF40	MS60	MS63
2008	—				2.50	3.00

KM# 1812 YUAN
Brass, 25 mm. **Obv:** Beijing Olympic logo **Rev:** Character on horseback

Date	Mintage	F12	VF20	XF40	MS60	MS63
2008	—				2.50	3.00

KM# 1813 YUAN
Brass, 25 mm. **Obv:** Large value **Rev:** Boy with rat pattern chinese knot & cluster of fireworks

Date	Mintage	F12	VF20	XF40	MS60	MS63
2008	10,000,000				2.50	3.00

KM# 1790 YUAN
6.75 g., Brass, 25 mm. **Subject:** Year of the Bull

Date	Mintage	F12	VF20	XF40	MS60	MS63
2009	30,000,000				—	5.00

KM# 1791 YUAN
6.75 g., Brass, 25 mm. **Subject:** Conservation **Rev:** Eye and leaf on globe

Date	Mintage	F12	VF20	XF40	MS60	MS63
2009	10,000,000				—	5.00

KM# 1792 YUAN
6.75 g., Brass, 25 mm. **Subject:** Harmony **Rev:** Haromony in seal script

Date	Mintage	F12	VF20	XF40	MS60	MS63
2009	10,000,000				—	5.00

KM# 1988 YUAN
Nickel Plated Brass, 25 mm. **Subject:** Shanghai Expo **Obv:** Expo logo **Rev:** Skyline and expo mascot

Date	Mintage	F12	VF20	XF40	MS60	MS63
2010	60,000,000				6.00	8.00

KM# 1989 YUAN
Brass, 25 mm. **Subject:** Year of the Tiger **Obv:** Large value **Rev:** Child dancing

Date	Mintage	F12	VF20	XF40	MS60	MS63
2010	60,000,000				5.00	7.50

KM# 1990 YUAN
Brass, 25 mm. **Subject:** Enviornmental protection **Obv:** State emblem **Rev:** Caligraphy - Peace-Harmony

Date	Mintage	F12	VF20	XF40	MS60	MS63
2010	10,000,000				6.00	8.00

KM# 1991 YUAN
Brass, 25 mm. **Subject:** Environmental protection **Obv:** National emblem **Rev:** Family dancing, globe

Date	Mintage	F12	VF20	XF40	MS60	MS63
2010	10,000,000				6.00	8.00

KM# 1993 YUAN
Brass, 25 mm. **Subject:** Year of the Rabbit **Obv:** Large value **Rev:** Child playing

Date	Mintage	F12	VF20	XF40	MS60	MS63
2011	60,000,000				6.00	8.00

KM# 2041 YUAN
6.75 g., Brass, 25 mm. **Subject:** Year of the Dragon **Obv:** Large numeral value **Rev:** Child dancing with lantern, dragon in background

Date	Mintage	F12	VF20	XF40	MS60	MS63
2012	80,000,000					3.00

KM# 2058 3 YUAN
7.78 g., 0.999 Silver 0.2483 oz. ASW, 25 mm. **Subject:** Panda, 30th Anniversary **Obv:** Temple of Heaven **Rev:** Panda

Date	Mintage	F12	VF20	XF40	MS60	MS63
2012	300,000	PF63 25.00		PF65 30.00		

KM# 1068 5 YUAN
22.00 g., 0.900 Silver 0.6325 oz. ASW, 36 mm. **Obv:** Great Wall **Rev:** Gymnast, denomination at right **Edge:** Reeded **Note:** Prev. Y#1189.

Date	Mintage	F12	VF20	XF40	MS60	MS63
2005(y)	—				75.00	85.00

KM# 1363 5 YUAN
12.80 g., Brass, 30 mm. **Subject:** 50th Anniversary - Chinese Occupation of Tibet **Obv:** National emblem **Rev:** Potala Palace, value and two dancers **Edge:** Reeded **Note:** Prev. Y#1126.

Date	Mintage	F12	VF20	XF40	MS60	MS63
2001(y)	10,000,000					8.00

KM# 1364 5 YUAN
12.80 g., Brass, 30 mm. **Subject:** Revolution: 90th Anniversary **Obv:** National emblem **Rev:** Battle scene **Edge:** Reeded **Note:** Prev. Y#1109.

Date	Mintage	F12	VF20	XF40	MS60	MS63
2001	—				7.50	8.50

KM# 1412 5 YUAN
12.80 g., Brass, 30 mm. **Subject:** The Great Wall **Obv:** State arms, icroscopic inscription repeated four times on the inner raised rim **Obv. Inscription:** SHI JIE WEN HUA YI CHAN **Rev:** Two views of the Great Wall **Edge:** Reeded **Note:** Prev. Y#1107.

Date	Mintage	F12	VF20	XF40	MS60	MS63
2002	—				7.00	8.00

KM# 1413 5 YUAN
12.80 g., Brass, 30 mm. **Subject:** Terra Cotta Army **Obv:** State arms and the microscopic inscription repeated four times on the raised inner rim. **Obv. Inscription:** SHI JIE WEN HUA YI CHAN **Rev:** Terra Cotta Soldier close-up with many more in background **Edge:** Reeded **Note:** Prev. Y#1108.

Date	Mintage	F12	VF20	XF40	MS60	MS63
2002	—				7.00	8.00

KM# 1461 5 YUAN
12.80 g., Brass, 30 mm. **Obv:** National emblem **Rev:** Chaotian Temple in Beigang Taiwan **Edge:** Reeded **Note:** Prev. Y#1127.

Date	Mintage	F12	VF20	XF40	MS60	MS63
2003	10,000,000				7.00	8.00

KM# 1462 5 YUAN
12.80 g., Brass, 30 mm. **Obv:** National emblem **Rev:** Chikan Tower on Treasure Island Taiwan **Edge:** Reeded **Note:** Prev. Y#1128.

Date	Mintage	F12	VF20	XF40	MS60	MS63
2003(y)	10,000,000				7.00	8.00

KM# 1463 5 YUAN
12.80 g., Brass, 30 mm. **Subject:** Chaotian Temple in Beijing **Obv:** State emblem **Rev:** Buildings **Edge:** Reeded **Note:** Prev. Y#1230.

Date	Mintage	F12	VF20	XF40	MS60	MS63
2003	10,000,000				7.00	8.00

KM# 1464 5 YUAN
Brass, 30 mm. **Obv:** National emblem **Rev:** Imperial Palace **Note:** Prev. Y#1252.

Date	Mintage	F12	VF20	XF40	MS60	MS63
2003	—				7.00	8.00

KM# 1524 5 YUAN
Brass, 30 mm. **Obv:** National emblem **Rev:** Island scene **Note:** Prev. Y#1253.

Date	Mintage	F12	VF20	XF40	MS60	MS63
2004	—				6.00	7.00

KM# 1525 5 YUAN
Brass, 30 mm. **Obv:** National emblem **Rev:** Lighthouse **Note:** Prev. Y#1254.

Date	Mintage	F12	VF20	XF40	MS60	MS63
2004	—				6.00	7.00

KM# 1526 5 YUAN
12.70 g., Brass, 30 mm. **Obv:** National emblem **Rev:** Peking Man bust and discovery site view **Edge:** Reeded **Note:** Prev. Y#1201.

Date	Mintage	F12	VF20	XF40	MS60	MS63
2004	6,000,000				6.00	7.00

KM# 1527 5 YUAN
12.70 g., Brass, 30 mm. **Obv:** National emblem **Rev:** Pavillion and bridge **Edge:** Reeded **Note:** Prev. Y#1202.

Date	Mintage	F12	VF20	XF40	MS60	MS63
2004	6,000,000				6.00	7.00

KM# 1576 5 YUAN
12.92 g., Brass, 30 mm. **Obv:** National emblem **Rev:** Lijiang building **Edge:** Reeded **Note:** Prev. Y#1209.

Date	Mintage	F12	VF20	XF40	MS60	MS63
2005	—				6.00	7.00

KM# 1577 5 YUAN
12.80 g., Brass, 30 mm. **Subject:** Taiwan **Obv:** State emblem **Rev:** Tower and terrace **Edge:** Reeded **Note:** Prev. Y#1231.

Date	Mintage	F12	VF20	XF40	MS60	MS63
2005	—	—	—	—	6.00	7.00

KM# 1578 5 YUAN
12.92 g., Brass, 30 mm. **Obv:** National emblem **Rev:** Green City Hall **Edge:** Reeded **Note:** Prev. Y#1210.

Date	Mintage	F12	VF20	XF40	MS60	MS63
2005	—	—	—	—	6.00	7.00

KM# 1651 5 YUAN
12.80 g., Brass, 30 mm. **Subject:** UNESCO World Heritage site - Summer Palace Pagoda

Date	Mintage	F12	VF20	XF40	MS60	MS63
2006	—	—	—	—	6.00	7.00

KM# 1731 5 YUAN
Brass, 30 mm. **Obv:** State emblem **Rev:** Large statue head

Date	Mintage	F12	VF20	XF40	MS60	MS63
2006	10,000,000	PF65 3.00				

KM# 1826 5 YUAN
15.57 g., 0.999 Silver 0.4969 oz. ASW, 33 mm. **Subject:** 12th Special Olympics in Shanghai **Obv:** Logo in color

Date	Mintage	F12	VF20	XF40	MS60	MS63
2007	40,000	PF65 60.00				

KM# 1992 5 YUAN
Brass, 30 mm. **Subject:** Chinese Communist Party, 90th Anniversary **Obv:** National emblem **Rev:** Banner, hammer and sythe, stars, birds in flight

Date	Mintage	F12	VF20	XF40	MS60	MS63
2011	60,000,000	—	—	—	7.50	9.00

KM# 1395 10 YUAN
31.10 g., 0.999 Silver 0.9926 oz. ASW, 40 mm. **Subject:** 2008 Olympics Beijing bid **Obv:** Gold-plated "V" design **Rev:** Radiant Temple of Heaven **Edge:** Reeded **Note:** Prev. Y#1103.

Date	Mintage	F12	VF20	XF40	MS60	MS63
2001	60,000	PF63 45.00	PF65 50.00			

KM# 1384 10 YUAN
31.10 g., 0.999 Silver 0.9926 oz. ASW **Series:** Folk Fairy Tales **Rev:** Heroic figure putting ax to mountains

Date	Mintage	F12	VF20	XF40	MS60	MS63
2001	30,000	PF65 120				

KM# 1385 10 YUAN
31.10 g., 0.999 Silver 0.9926 oz. ASW, 40 mm. **Series:** Folk Fairy Tales **Rev:** Multicolor angelic figure

Date	Mintage	F12	VF20	XF40	MS60	MS63
2001	30,000	PF65 120				

KM# 1396 10 YUAN
31.10 g., 0.999 Silver 0.9926 oz. ASW, 40 mm. **Series:** Folk customs - Mid Autumn Festival **Rev:** Flora and sun

Date	Mintage	F12	VF20	XF40	MS60	MS63
2001	40,000	PF65 180				

KM# 1397 10 YUAN
31.10 g., 0.999 Silver 0.9926 oz. ASW, 32 mm. **Subject:** Bejing International Coin Expo **Obv:** Globe hemisphere view **Rev:** Bejing city view

Date	Mintage	F12	VF20	XF40	MS60	MS63
2001	40,000	PF65 125				

KM# 1398 10 YUAN
31.10 g., 0.999 Silver 0.9926 oz. ASW, 40 mm. **Subject:** Bejing opera **Rev:** Two multicolor actors, one with hankie

Date	Mintage	F12	VF20	XF40	MS60	MS63
2001	38,000	PF65 100				

KM# 1399 10 YUAN
31.10 g., 0.9926 Silver 0.9926 oz. ASW, 40 mm. **Subject:** Bejing opera **Rev:** Two actors, one with blue ribbon

Date	Mintage	F12	VF20	XF40	MS60	MS63
2001	38,000	PF65 120				

KM# 1400 10 YUAN
31.10 g., 0.9926 Silver 0.9926 oz. ASW, 40 mm. **Subject:** Bejing opera **Rev:** Two multicolor actors, one with tassles

Date	Mintage	F12	VF20	XF40	MS60	MS63
2001	38,000	PF65 60.00				

KM# 1401 10 YUAN
31.10 g., 0.999 Silver 0.9926 oz. ASW, 40 mm. **Subject:** Bejing opera **Rev:** Two multicolor actors, white or black beard

Date	Mintage	F12	VF20	XF40	MS60	MS63
2001	38,000	PF65 120				

KM# 1428 10 YUAN
31.10 g., 0.999 Silver 0.9926 oz. ASW, 40 mm. **Series:** Folk Fairy Tales **Rev:** Multicolor male figure seated

Date	Mintage	F12	VF20	XF40	MS60	MS63
2002	30,000	PF65 120				

KM# 1429 10 YUAN
31.10 g., 0.999 Silver 0.9926 oz. ASW, 40 mm. **Series:** Folk fairy tails **Rev:** Male figure brandishing sword

Date	Mintage	F12	VF20	XF40	MS60	MS63
2002	30,000	PF65 120				

KM# 1438 10 YUAN
31.10 g., 0.999 Silver 0.9926 oz. ASW, 40 mm. **Series:** Folk customs **Rev:** Dragon boat

Date	Mintage	F12	VF20	XF40	MS60	MS63
2002	40,000	PF65 120				

KM# 1441 10 YUAN
31.10 g., 0.999 Silver 0.9926 oz. ASW, 40 mm. **Series:** Classic literature **Rev:** Black and red dressed women seated **Shape:** Octagon

Date	Mintage	F12	VF20	XF40	MS60	MS63
2002	38,000	PF65 100				

KM# 1442 10 YUAN
31.10 g., 0.999 Silver 0.9926 oz. ASW, 40 mm. **Series:** Classic literature **Rev:** Multicolor white dressed woman standing **Shape:** Octagon

Date	Mintage	F12	VF20	XF40	MS60	MS63
2002	38,000	PF65 100				

KM# 1443 10 YUAN
31.10 g., 0.999 Silver 0.9926 oz. ASW, 40 mm. **Series:** Classic literature **Rev:** Multicolor yellow dressed woman walking left **Shape:** Octagon

Date	Mintage	F12	VF20	XF40	MS60	MS63
2002	38,000	PF65 100				

KM# 1444 10 YUAN
31.10 g., 0.999 Silver 0.9926 oz. ASW, 40 mm. **Series:** Classic literature **Obv:** Multicolor purple dressed woman **Shape:** Octagon

Date	Mintage	F12	VF20	XF40	MS60	MS63
2002	38,000	PF65 100				

KM# 1447 10 YUAN
31.10 g., 0.999 Silver 0.9926 oz. ASW, 40 mm. **Subject:** Bejing Coin and Stamp Fair **Obv:** Hemisphere map **Rev:** Highway design

Date	Mintage	F12	VF20	XF40	MS60	MS63
2002	40,000	PF65 95.00				

KM# 1448 10 YUAN
31.10 g., 0.999 Silver 0.9926 oz. ASW, 40 mm. **Subject:** Table tennis, 50th anniversary **Rev:** Trophies, flag

Date	Mintage	F12	VF20	XF40	MS60	MS63
2002	50,000	PF65 100				

KM# 1449 10 YUAN
31.10 g., 0.999 Silver 0.9926 oz. ASW, 40 mm. **Series:** Bejing opera **Rev:** Two multicolor characters, one seated

Date	Mintage	F12	VF20	XF40	MS60	MS63
2002	38,000	PF65 65.00				

KM# 1450 10 YUAN
31.10 g., 0.999 Silver 0.9926 oz. ASW, 40 mm. **Series:** Bejing opera **Rev:** Two multicolor characters, white and green

Date	Mintage	F12	VF20	XF40	MS60	MS63
2002	38,000	PF65 125				

KM# 1451 10 YUAN
31.10 g., 0.999 Silver 0.9926 oz. ASW, 40 mm. **Series:** Bejing opera **Rev:** Bearded character, black

Date	Mintage	F12	VF20	XF40	MS60	MS63
2002	38,000	PF65 125				

KM# 1452 10 YUAN
31.10 g., 0.999 Silver 0.9926 oz. ASW, 40 mm. **Series:** Bejing opera **Rev:** Multicolor bearded character, red

Date	Mintage	F12	VF20	XF40	MS60	MS63
2002	38,000	PF65 125				

KM# 1455 10 YUAN
31.10 g., 0.999 Silver 0.9926 oz. ASW, 40 mm. **Subject:** Shanghai World Expo of 2010 **Obv:** Flower design with inset pearl **Rev:** 2010 Logo incorporating a tower **Edge:** Reeded **Note:** Prev. Y#1233.

Date	Mintage	F12	VF20	XF40	MS60	MS63
2002	50,000	PF63 115	PF65 125			

KM# A1455 10 YUAN
31.10 g., 0.999 Silver 0.9926 oz. ASW, 40 mm. **Subject:** World Expo 2010 **Rev:** Tower

Date	Mintage	F12	VF20	XF40	MS60	MS63
2002	50,000	PF63 90.00	PF65 100			

KM# 1507 10 YUAN
31.10 g., 0.999 Silver 0.9926 oz. ASW, 40 mm. **Obv:** Stylized forest **Rev:** Cyclists in forest **Edge:** Reeded **Note:** Prev. Y#1132.

Date	Mintage	F12	VF20	XF40	MS60	MS63
2003	30,000	PF63 115	PF65 125			

KM# 1508 10 YUAN
31.10 g., 0.999 Silver 0.9926 oz. ASW, 40 mm. **Obv:** Stylized forest **Rev:** Birds flying over forest **Edge:** Reeded **Note:** Prev. Y#1133.

Date	Mintage	F12	VF20	XF40	MS60	MS63
2003(y)	30,000	PF63 115	PF65 125			

KM# 1510 10 YUAN
31.10 g., 0.999 Silver 0.9926 oz. ASW, 40 mm. **Obv:** Solar system design **Rev:** Multicolor Chinese Astronaut **Edge:** Reeded **Note:** Prev. Y#1134.

Date	Mintage	F12	VF20	XF40	MS60	MS63
2003(y)	60,000	PF65 90.00				

KM# 1487 10 YUAN
31.10 g., 0.999 Silver 0.9926 oz. ASW, 40 mm. **Rev:** Two Koi

Date	Mintage	F12	VF20	XF40	MS60	MS63
2003	100,000	PF63 75.00	PF65 90.00			

KM# 1489 10 YUAN
31.10 g., 0.999 Silver 0.9926 oz. ASW, 40 mm. **Subject:** Arbor Day **Rev:** Trees with bike riders

Date	Mintage	F12	VF20	XF40	MS60	MS63
2003	30,000	PF63 80.00	PF65 90.00			

KM# 1490 10 YUAN
31.10 g., 0.999 Silver 0.9926 oz. ASW, 40 mm. **Subject:** Arbor Day **Rev:** Close-up of leaves, birds in flight

Date	Mintage	F12	VF20	XF40	MS60	MS63
2003	30,000	PF63 110	PF65 120			

KM# 1491 10 YUAN
31.10 g., 0.999 Silver 0.9926 oz. ASW, 40 mm. **Series:** Fairy tails **Rev:** Multicolor blue female

Date	Mintage	F12	VF20	XF40	MS60	MS63
2003	30,000	PF65 120				

KM# 1492 10 YUAN
31.10 g., 0.999 Silver 0.9926 oz. ASW, 40 mm. **Subject:** Fairy tails **Rev:** Multicolor red bloused girl

Date	Mintage	F12	VF20	XF40	MS60	MS63
2003	30,000	PF65 120				

KM# 1496 10 YUAN
31.10 g., 0.999 Silver 0.9926 oz. ASW, 40 mm. **Series:** Class literature **Rev:** Multicolor purple cloaked man and monkey

Date	Mintage	F12	VF20	XF40	MS60	MS63
2003	38,000	PF65 120				

KM# 1497 10 YUAN
31.10 g., 0.999 Silver 0.9926 oz. ASW, 40 mm. **Series:** Classic literature **Rev:** Two multicolor men fighting in clouds

Date	Mintage	F12	VF20	XF40	MS60	MS63
2003	38,000	PF65 120				

KM# 1498 10 YUAN
31.10 g., 0.999 Silver 0.9926 oz. ASW, 40 mm. **Rev:** Multicolor female standing, black dress **Shape:** Octagon

Date	Mintage	F12	VF20	XF40	MS60	MS63
2003	38,000	PF65 120				

KM# 1499 10 YUAN
31.10 g., 0.999 Silver 0.9926 oz. ASW, 40 mm. **Series:** Classic Literature **Rev:** Multicolor female kneeling **Shape:** Octagon

Date	Mintage	F12	VF20	XF40	MS60	MS63
2003	38,000	PF65 120				

KM# 1500 10 YUAN
31.10 g., 0.999 Silver 0.9926 oz. ASW, 40 mm. **Series:** Classic literature **Rev:** Multicolor female walking, rose dress **Shape:** Octagon

Date	Mintage	F12	VF20	XF40	MS60	MS63
2003	—	PF65 120				

KM# 1501 10 YUAN
31.10 g., 0.999 Silver 0.9926 oz. ASW, 40 mm. **Series:** Classic literature **Rev:** Multicolor female kneeling, red dress **Shape:** Octagon

Date	Mintage	F12	VF20	XF40	MS60	MS63
2003	—	PF65 120				

KM# 1558 10 YUAN
31.10 g., 0.999 Silver 0.9926 oz. ASW, 40 mm. **Obv:** Monkey King leading the Master over bridge **Rev:** Multicolor Pig carrying Monkey King piggy-back style **Edge:** Reeded **Note:** Prev. Y#1215.

Date	Mintage	F12	VF20	XF40	MS60	MS63
2004	38,000	PF65 110				

KM# 1559 10 YUAN
31.10 g., 0.999 Silver 0.9926 oz. ASW, 40 mm. **Obv:** Monkey King leading the Master over bridge **Rev:** Multicolor Monkey King fighting the "Ox Fiend **Edge:** Reeded **Note:** Prev. Y#1214.

Date	Mintage	F12	VF20	XF40	MS60	MS63
2004	38,000	PF65 110				

KM# 1566 10 YUAN
31.10 g., 0.999 Silver 0.9926 oz. ASW, 40 mm. **Obv:** Guangan Exposition Hall **Rev:** Deng Xiaoping and value **Edge:** Reeded **Note:** Prev. Y#1240. Photo reduced.

Date	Mintage	F12	VF20	XF40	MS60	MS63
2004	80,000	PF63 75.00	PF65 90.00			

KM# 1570 10 YUAN
31.10 g., 0.999 Silver 0.9926 oz. ASW, 40 mm. **Obv:** National arms above People's Congress Hall and ornamental column **Rev:** Multicolor hologram depicting the hall's overhead lighting **Edge:** Reeded **Note:** Prev. KM#1212.

Date	Mintage	F12	VF20	XF40	MS60	MS63
2004	50,000	PF65 100				

KM# 1539 10 YUAN
31.10 g., 0.999 Silver 0.9926 oz. ASW, 40 mm. **Subject:** 20th Anniversary / Bank of China Industrial and Commercial **Rev:** Panda walking with cub

Date	Mintage	F12	VF20	XF40	MS60	MS63
2004	120,000	PF63 75.00	PF65 90.00			

KM# 1541 10 YUAN
31.10 g., 0.999 Silver 0.9926 oz. ASW, 40 mm. **Subject:** 50th Anniversary China Construction Bank **Rev:** Panda walking with cub

Date	Mintage	F12	VF20	XF40	MS60	MS63
2004	170,000	PF63 75.00	PF65 90.00			

KM# 1543 10 YUAN
31.10 g., 0.999 Silver 0.9926 oz. ASW, 40 mm. **Subject:** Bejing International Coin Expo **Rev:** Panda walking with cub, gold plated center

Date	Mintage	F12	VF20	XF40	MS60	MS63
2004	30,000	PF63 110	PF65 120			

KM# 1555 10 YUAN
31.10 g., 0.999 Silver 0.9926 oz. ASW, 40 mm. **Subject:** 100th Anniversary Red Cross **Obv:** Red Cross within wreath **Rev:** Dove **Note:** Colorized

Date	Mintage	F12	VF20	XF40	MS60	MS63
2004	60,000	PF65 85.00				

KM# 1557 10 YUAN
31.10 g., 0.999 Silver 0.9926 oz. ASW, 40 mm. **Series:** Folk customs **Subject:** Lantern Festival **Rev:** Boy holding lantern **Note:** Colorized

Date	Mintage	F12	VF20	XF40	MS60	MS63
2004	60,000	PF65 100				

KM# 1580 10 YUAN
31.10 g., 0.999 Silver 0.9926 oz. ASW, 40 mm. **Subject:** 600th Anniversary of Zheng He's voyage **Obv:** Multicolor stylized sailboat on water **Rev:** Ancient Chinese navigational instruments **Edge:** Reeded **Note:** Prev. Y#1239.

Date	Mintage	F12	VF20	XF40	MS60	MS63
2005(y)	—	PF65 100				

KM# 1592 10 YUAN
31.11 g., 0.999 Silver 0.9926 oz. ASW, 40 mm. **Obv:** Temple of Heaven **Rev:** Panda cub and mom seated in bamboo **Note:** Gilt rim

Date	Mintage	F12	VF20	XF40	MS60	MS63
2005	30,000	PF63 75.00	PF65 85.00			

KM# 1601 10 YUAN
31.11 g., 0.999 Silver 0.9926 oz. ASW, 40 mm. **Subject:** Foundation of Industrial & Commercial Bank **Obv:** Temple of Heaven, gilt rim **Rev:** Panda cub and mom seated in bamboo

Date	Mintage	F12	VF20	XF40	MS60	MS63
2005	100,000	PF63 65.00	PF65 75.00			

KM# 1603 10 YUAN
31.11 g., 0.999 Silver 0.9926 oz. ASW, 40 mm. **Subject:** 100th Anniversary of Bank of Shanghai **Obv:** Temple of Heaven **Rev:** Panda cub and mom seated in bamboo

Date	Mintage	F12	VF20	XF40	MS60	MS63
2005	50,000	PF63 70.00	PF65 80.00			

KM# 1618 10 YUAN
31.11 g., 0.999 Silver 0.9926 oz. ASW, 40 mm. **Subject:** 2006 World Cup - Germany **Obv:** Multicolor logo **Rev:** Classical soccer player and goal net **Note:** Prev - Y1255, KM1670

Date	Mintage	F12	VF20	XF40	MS60	MS63
2005	50,000	PF63 75.00	PF65 85.00			

KM# 1626 10 YUAN
31.11 g., 0.999 Silver 0.9926 oz. ASW, 40 mm. **Subject:** 600th Anniversary - Zheng He's Voyages **Obv:** Multicolor logo **Rev:** Nautical invention

Date	Mintage	F12	VF20	XF40	MS60	MS63
2005	60,000	PF63 65.00	PF65 75.00			

KM# 1628 10 YUAN
31.11 g., 0.999 Silver 0.9926 oz. ASW, 40 mm. **Subject:** Chen Yun Birth Centennial **Obv:** House **Rev:** Half-length figure facing

Date	Mintage	F12	VF20	XF40	MS60	MS63
2005	15,000	PF65 150				

KM# 1629 10 YUAN
31.11 g., 0.999 Silver 0.9926 oz. ASW, 40 mm. **Subject:** Chen Yun Birth Centennial **Obv:** House **Rev:** Figure seated in chair, arm outstretched

Date	Mintage	F12	VF20	XF40	MS60	MS63
2005	15,000	PF65 150				

KM# 1631 10 YUAN
31.11 g., 0.999 Silver 0.9926 oz. ASW, 40 mm. **Subject:** 60th Anniversary of Victory - War of Resistance **Obv:** Monument **Rev:** People celebrating

Date	Mintage	F12	VF20	XF40	MS60	MS63
2005	30,000	PF63 130	PF65 140			

KM# 1636 10 YUAN
31.11 g., 0.999 Silver 0.9926 oz. ASW, 40 mm. **Series:** Classical Literature **Obv:** Horseman on arch bridge **Rev:** Multicolor monkey and female

Date	Mintage	F12	VF20	XF40	MS60	MS63
2005	38,000	PF65 130				

KM# 1637 10 YUAN

31.11 g., 0.999 Silver 0.9926 oz. ASW, 40 mm. **Series:** Classical Literature **Obv:** Horseman on arch bridge **Rev:** Multicolor man slaying spider on web

Date	Mintage	F12	VF20	XF40	MS60	MS63
2005	38,000	PF65 130				

KM# 1639 10 YUAN

31.11 g., 0.999 Silver 0.9926 oz. ASW, 40 mm. **Subject:** Chinese Movie Centennial **Obv:** Winged column **Rev:** Old time movie camera

Date	Mintage	F12	VF20	XF40	MS60	MS63
2005	60,000	PF63 75.00		PF65 85.00		

KM# 1670 10 YUAN

31.10 g., 0.999 Silver 0.9926 oz. ASW **Subject:** World Cup Soccer **Obv:** Colorized logo **Rev:** Classically dressed athlete scoring goal **Note:** Prev. Y#1255.

Date	Mintage	F12	VF20	XF40	MS60	MS63
2006	—	PF65 100				

KM# A1670 10 YUAN

31.11 g., 0.999 Silver 0.9926 oz. ASW, 40 mm. **Subject:** Shengang Horticultural Expo **Obv:** Temple of Heaven **Rev:** Two pandas seated with bamboo

Date	Mintage	F12	VF20	XF40	MS60	MS63
2006	30,000	PF63 75.00		PF65 85.00		

KM# 1666 10 YUAN

31.11 g., 0.999 Silver 0.9926 oz. ASW, 40 mm. **Obv:** Temple of Heaven **Rev:** Two pandas seated with bamboo

Date	Mintage	F12	VF20	XF40	MS60	MS63
2006	50,000	PF63 65.00		PF65 75.00		

KM# 1668 10 YUAN

31.11 g., 0.999 Silver 0.9926 oz. ASW, 40 mm. **Subject:** 10th Anniversary of China Minsheng Banking Corp **Obv:** Temple of Heaven **Rev:** Two pandas seated with bamboo

Date	Mintage	F12	VF20	XF40	MS60	MS63
2006	70,000	PF63 75.00		PF65 85.00		

KM# 1675 10 YUAN

31.11 g., 0.999 Silver 0.9926 oz. ASW, 40 mm. **Subject:** 10th Anniversary Jinan City Commercial Bank **Obv:** Temple of Heaven **Rev:** Two pandas seated with bamboo

Date	Mintage	F12	VF20	XF40	MS60	MS63
2006	20,000	PF63 75.00		PF65 85.00		

KM# 1676 10 YUAN

31.11 g., 0.999 Silver 0.9926 oz. ASW, 40 mm. **Subject:** Beijing International Stamp and Coin Expo **Obv:** Temple of Heaven **Rev:** Two pandas seated with bamboo

Date	Mintage	F12	VF20	XF40	MS60	MS63
2006	20,000	PF63 90.00		PF65 100		

KM# 1690 10 YUAN

31.11 g., 0.999 Silver 0.9926 oz. ASW, 40 mm. **Subject:** Yvelv Academy **Obv:** Front door of Academy **Rev:** Exterior view

Date	Mintage	F12	VF20	XF40	MS60	MS63
2006	40,000	PF63 75.00		PF65 85.00		

KM# 1691 10 YUAN

31.11 g., 0.999 Silver 0.9926 oz. ASW, 40 mm. **Subject:** Qinghai - Tibet Railway Opening **Obv:** Lhasa Railway Station with mountains in background **Rev:** Yvante Bridge over the Yangtze River and tibetan antelope and yak

Date	Mintage	F12	VF20	XF40	MS60	MS63
2006	36,000	PF65 150				

KM# 1693 10 YUAN

31.11 g., 0.999 Silver 0.9926 oz. ASW, 40 mm. **Obv:** Map of marches and hammer and sickle **Rev:** Group of marchers in snow

Date	Mintage	F12	VF20	XF40	MS60	MS63
2006	25,000	PF65 110				

KM# 1653 10 YUAN

31.10 g., 0.999 Silver 0.9926 oz. ASW, 40 mm. **Subject:** Chengdu multi-purpose warplanes, 10th Anniversary

Date	Mintage	F12	VF20	XF40	MS60	MS63
2007	20,000	PF63 65.00		PF65 75.00		

KM# 1729 10 YUAN

31.11 g., 0.999 Silver 0.9926 oz. ASW, 40 mm. **Subject:** 60th Anniversary - Foundry of Mongolia Autonomous Region **Obv:** Wheel of Mongolian Lele Cart **Rev:** Grassland view of Mongolia, huts and horsemen

Date	Mintage	F12	VF20	XF40	MS60	MS63
2007	20,000	PF65 110				

KM# 1828 10 YUAN

31.10 g., 0.999 Silver 0.9926 oz. ASW, 40 mm. **Subject:** Chinese aerospace **Obv:** Solar System **Rev:** Chang'e 1 in lunar orbit

Date	Mintage	F12	VF20	XF40	MS60	MS63
2007	40,000	PF63 65.00		PF65 75.00		

KM# 1863 10 YUAN

31.10 g., 0.999 Silver 0.9926 oz. ASW, 40 mm. **Subject:** Xi'an City Commercial Bank **Obv:** Temple of Heaven **Rev:** Panda

Date	Mintage	F12	VF20	XF40	MS60	MS63
2007	20,000	—	—	—		300

KM# 1864 10 YUAN

31.10 g., 0.999 Silver 0.9926 oz. ASW, 40 mm. **Subject:** China International Trust and Investment Co., 20th Anniversary **Obv:** Temple of Heaven **Rev:** Panda

Date	Mintage	F12	VF20	XF40	MS60	MS63
2007	20,000	—	—	—		300

KM# 1674 10 YUAN

31.11 g., 0.999 Silver 0.9926 oz. ASW, 40 mm. **Subject:** 29th Summer Olympics, Bejing **Rev:** Great Wall, ornament at left in color

Date	Mintage	F12	VF20	XF40	MS60	MS63
2008 S	160,000	PF65 75.00				
2008 Y	Inc. above	PF65 75.00				
2008 Z	Inc. above	PF65 75.00				

KM# 1688 10 YUAN

31.11 g., 0.999 Silver 0.9926 oz. ASW, 40 mm. **Subject:** 29th Summer Olympics, Bejing **Rev:** Summer Palace, Bejing; flower at left in color

Date	Mintage	F12	VF20	XF40	MS60	MS63
2008 S	160,000	PF65 75.00				
2008 Y	Inc. above	PF65 75.00				
2008 Z	Inc. above	PF65 75.00				

KM# 1702 10 YUAN
31.11 g., 0.999 Silver 0.9926 oz. ASW, 40 mm. **Subject:** 2007 Summer Olympics **Obv:** Beijing Olympic logo **Rev:** Child with kite, multicolor design **Note:** Issued in 2006

Date	Mintage	F12	VF20	XF40	MS60	MS63
2008 S	160,000	PF65 75.00				
2008 Y	Inc. above	PF65 75.00				
2008 Z	Inc. above	PF65 75.00				

KM# 1703 10 YUAN
31.11 g., 0.999 Silver 0.9926 oz. ASW, 40 mm. **Subject:** 2007 Summer Olympics **Obv:** Beijing Olympics logo **Rev:** Two children playing leapfrog, multicolor **Note:** Issued in 2006

Date	Mintage	F12	VF20	XF40	MS60	MS63
2008 S	160,000	PF65 75.00				
2008 Y	Inc. above	PF65 75.00				
2008 Z	Inc. above	PF65 75.00				

KM# 1704 10 YUAN
31.11 g., 0.999 Silver 0.9926 oz. ASW, 40 mm. **Subject:** 2007 Summer Olympics **Obv:** Beijing Olympics logo **Rev:** Child rolling ring with stick, multicolor **Note:** Issued in 2006

Date	Mintage	F12	VF20	XF40	MS60	MS63
2008 S	160,000	PF65 75.00				
2008 Y	Inc. above	PF65 75.00				
2008 Z	Inc. above	PF65 75.00				

KM# 1705 10 YUAN
31.11 g., 0.999 Silver 0.9926 oz. ASW, 40 mm. **Subject:** 2007 Summer Olympics **Obv:** Beijing Olympic's logo **Rev:** Young girl dancing, multicolor **Note:** Issued in 2006

Date	Mintage	F12	VF20	XF40	MS60	MS63
2008 S	160,000	PF65 75.00				
2008 Y	Inc. above	PF65 75.00				
2008 Z	Inc. above	PF65 75.00				

KM# 1732 10 YUAN
31.11 g., 0.999 Silver 0.9926 oz. ASW, 40 mm. **Subject:** 29th Summer Games, Beijing **Rev:** White Pagoda, North Sea Park

Date	Mintage	F12	VF20	XF40	MS60	MS63
2008	160,000	PF65 75.00				
2008	Inc. above	PF65 75.00				
2008	Inc. above	PF65 75.00				

KM# 1733 10 YUAN
31.11 g., 0.999 Silver 0.9926 oz. ASW, 40 mm. **Subject:** 29th Summer Olympics, Beijing **Obv:** Olympics logo **Rev:** Traditonal residence, flower at left in color

Date	Mintage	F12	VF20	XF40	MS60	MS63
2008 S	160,000	PF65 75.00				
2008 Y	Inc. above	PF65 75.00				
2008 Z	Inc. above	PF65 75.00				

KM# 1734 10 YUAN
31.10 g., 0.999 Silver 0.9926 oz. ASW, 40 mm. **Obv:** Solar system **Rev:** Man walkking in space in color

Date	Mintage	F12	VF20	XF40	MS60	MS63
2008	60,000	PF65 75.00				

KM# 1736 10 YUAN
31.11 g., 0.999 Silver 0.9926 oz. ASW, 40 mm. **Subject:** Economic Reform in China, 30th Anniversary **Rev:** Economic Growth

Date	Mintage	F12	VF20	XF40	MS60	MS63
2008	80,000	PF63 55.00	PF65 65.00			

KM# 1739 10 YUAN
31.10 g., 0.999 Silver 0.9926 oz. ASW, 40 mm. **Subject:** Banknote Printing Works, Beijing, 100th Anniversary **Obv:** Temple of Heaven **Rev:** Two pandas

Date	Mintage	F12	VF20	XF40	MS60	MS63
2008	20,000	—	—	—	—	275

KM# 1825 10 YUAN
31.11 g., 0.999 Silver 0.9926 oz. ASW, 40 mm. **Subject:** Bank of Communications, Centennial

Date	Mintage	F12	VF20	XF40	MS60	MS63
2008	—	PF63 75.00	PF65 85.00			

KM# 1843 10 YUAN
31.11 g., 0.999 Silver 0.9926 oz. ASW, 40 mm. **Subject:** Beijing Olympics **Rev:** Multicolor mask, stall tea scene

Date	Mintage	F12	VF20	XF40	MS60	MS63
2008	160,000	PF65 55.00				

KM# 1844 10 YUAN
31.11 g., 0.999 Silver 0.9926 oz. ASW, 40 mm. **Subject:** Beijing Olympics **Rev:** Multicolor mask, lion dancer

Date	Mintage	F12	VF20	XF40	MS60	MS63
2008	160,000	PF65 55.00				

KM# 1845 10 YUAN
31.11 g., 0.999 Silver 0.9926 oz. ASW, 40 mm. **Subject:** Beijing Olympics **Rev:** Multicolor mask, Yangtze dancer

Date	Mintage	F12	VF20	XF40	MS60	MS63
2008	160,000	PF65 55.00				

KM# 1846 10 YUAN
31.11 g., 0.999 Silver 0.9926 oz. ASW, 40 mm. **Subject:** Beijing Olympics **Rev:** Multicolor mask, Beijing Opera

Date	Mintage	F12	VF20	XF40	MS60	MS63
2008	160,000	PF65 55.00				

KM# 1852 10 YUAN
31.11 g., 0.999 Silver 0.9926 oz. ASW, 40 mm. **Subject:** Hainan Special Economic Zone

Date	Mintage	F12	VF20	XF40	MS60	MS63
2008	20,000	PF63 80.00	PF65 90.00			

KM# 1854 10 YUAN
31.11 g., 0.999 Silver 0.9926 oz. ASW, 40 mm. **Subject:** Para Olympics

Date	Mintage	F12	VF20	XF40	MS60	MS63
2008	30,000	PF63 90.00	PF65 100			

KM# 1856 10 YUAN
31.11 g., 0.999 Silver 0.9926 oz. ASW, 40 mm. **Subject:** Ningxia Hui Autonomous Region

Date	Mintage	F12	VF20	XF40	MS60	MS63
2008	20,000	PF63 110	PF65 120			

KM# 1858 10 YUAN
31.11 g., 0.999 Silver 0.9926 oz. ASW, 40 mm. **Subject:** Beijing Coin and Stamp Expo

Date	Mintage	F12	VF20	XF40	MS60	MS63
2008	30,000	PF63 65.00	PF65 75.00			

KM# 1859 10 YUAN
31.11 g., 0.999 Silver 0.9926 oz. ASW, 40 mm. **Subject:** Guangxi Zhuang Autonomous Region

Date	Mintage	F12	VF20	XF40	MS60	MS63
2008	20,000	PF63 100	PF65 110			

KM# 1907 10 YUAN
31.11 g., 0.999 Silver 0.9926 oz. ASW, 40 mm. **Subject:** Shanghai Expo

Date	Mintage	F12	VF20	XF40	MS60	MS63
2009	—	PF65 60.00				

KM# 1891 10 YUAN
31.11 g., 0.999 Silver 0.9926 oz. ASW, 40 mm. **Subject:** Precious Metal Commemoratives, 30th Anniversary

Date	Mintage	F12	VF20	XF40	MS60	MS63
2009	300,000	—	—	—	—	40.00

KM# 1892 10 YUAN
31.11 g., 0.999 Silver 0.9926 oz. ASW, 40 mm. **Subject:** Beijing International Coin & Stamp Show

Date	Mintage	F12	VF20	XF40	MS60	MS63
2009	30,000	—	—	—	—	60.00

KM# 1896 10 YUAN
31.10 g., 0.999 Silver 0.9926 oz. ASW, 40 mm. **Subject:** Stock Exchange trading in Shenzhen **Obv:** Temple of Heaven **Rev:** Two pandas

Date	Mintage	F12	VF20	XF40	MS60	MS63
2009	30,000	PF65 150				

KM# 1898 10 YUAN
31.11 g., 0.999 Silver 0.9926 oz. ASW, 40 mm. **Subject:** P.R.C. 60th Anniversary **Rev:** Multicolor

Date	Mintage	F12	VF20	XF40	MS60	MS63
2009	100,000	PF65 65.00				

KM# 1902 10 YUAN
31.11 g., 0.999 Silver 0.9926 oz. ASW, 40 mm. **Subject:** Outlaws of the Marsh, series 1 **Rev:** Multicolor

Date	Mintage	F12	VF20	XF40	MS60	MS63
2009	60,000	PF65 95.00				

KM# 1903 10 YUAN
31.11 g., 0.999 Silver 0.9926 oz. ASW, 40 mm. **Subject:** Outlaws of the Marsh, series 1 **Rev:** Multicolor

Date	Mintage	F12	VF20	XF40	MS60	MS63
2009	60,000	PF65 95.00				

KM# 1905 10 YUAN
31.11 g., 0.999 Silver 0.9926 oz. ASW, 40 mm. **Subject:** 16th Asian Games

Date	Mintage	F12	VF20	XF40	MS60	MS63
2009	60,000	PF63 45.00	PF65 50.00			

KM# 1908 10 YUAN
31.11 g., 0.999 Silver 0.9926 oz. ASW, 40 mm. **Subject:** Shanghai Expo

Date	Mintage	F12	VF20	XF40	MS60	MS63
2009	—	PF63 45.00	PF65 50.00			

KM# 1910 10 YUAN
31.11 g., 0.999 Silver 0.9926 oz. ASW, 40 mm. **Subject:** China Agricultural Bank

Date	Mintage	F12	VF20	XF40	MS60	MS63
2009	100,000	—	—	—	—	45.00

KM# 1793 10 YUAN
31.11 g., 0.999 Silver 0.9926 oz. ASW **Subject:** Agricultural Bank, IPO **Obv:** Temple of Heaven **Rev:** Panda

Date	Mintage	F12	VF20	XF40	MS60	MS63
2010	70,000					275

KM# 1795 10 YUAN
31.10 g., 0.999 Silver 0.9926 oz. ASW, 40 mm. **Subject:** Capital Market in the Peoples Republic of China, 20th Anniversary **Obv:** Temple of Heaven **Rev:** Panda

Date	Mintage	F12	VF20	XF40	MS60	MS63
2010 Proof	40,000	—	—	—	—	120

KM# 1796 10 YUAN
31.10 g., 0.999 Silver 0.9926 oz. ASW, 40 mm. **Subject:** Shanghai Mint, 90th Anniversary **Obv:** Temple of Heaven **Rev:** Panda

Date	Mintage	F12	VF20	XF40	MS60	MS63
2010	20,000	—	—	—	—	275

KM# 1939 10 YUAN
31.11 g., 0.999 Silver 0.9926 oz. ASW, 40 mm. **Series:** Outlaws of the Marsh, series 2 **Rev:** Multicolor

Date	Mintage	F12	VF20	XF40	MS60	MS63
2010	70,000	PF65 90.00				

KM# 1940 10 YUAN
31.11 g., 0.999 Silver 0.9926 oz. ASW, 40 mm. **Series:** Outlaws of the Marsh, series 2 **Rev:** Multicolor

Date	Mintage	F12	VF20	XF40	MS60	MS63
2010	70,000	PF65 90.00				

KM# 1942 10 YUAN
10.36 g., 0.999 Gold 0.3306 oz. AGW **Subject:** Shanghai World Expo, 2010

Date	Mintage	F12	VF20	XF40	MS60	MS63
2010	60,000	PF65 600				

KM# 1943 10 YUAN
31.11 g., 0.999 Silver 0.9926 oz. ASW, 40 mm. **Subject:** Shanghai World Expo, 2010

Date	Mintage	F12	VF20	XF40	MS60	MS63
2010	80,000	PF63 60.00	PF65 70.00			

KM# 1944 10 YUAN
31.11 g., 0.999 Silver 0.9926 oz. ASW, 40 mm. **Subject:** Shanghai World Expo, 2010

Date	Mintage	F12	VF20	XF40	MS60	MS63
2010	80,000	PF63 60.00	PF65 70.00			

KM# 1946 10 YUAN
31.11 g., 0.999 Silver 0.9926 oz. ASW, 40 mm. **Subject:** Wudang Mountain

Date	Mintage	F12	VF20	XF40	MS60	MS63
2010	60,000	PF63 65.00	PF65 75.00			

KM# 1953 10 YUAN
31.11 g., 0.999 Silver 0.9926 oz. ASW **Subject:** Shenzhen Economic Zone

Date	Mintage	F12	VF20	XF40	MS60	MS63
2010	30,000	PF63 60.00	PF65 70.00			

KM# 1955 10 YUAN
31.11 g., 0.999 Silver 0.9926 oz. ASW, 40 mm. **Subject:** 16th Asian Games

Date	Mintage	F12	VF20	XF40	MS60	MS63
2010	60,000	PF63 55.00	PF65 65.00			

KM# 1957 10 YUAN
31.11 g., 0.999 Silver 0.9926 oz. ASW, 40 mm. **Subject:** Bejing Opera, series 1 **Rev:** Multicolor face mask

Date	Mintage	F12	VF20	XF40	MS60	MS63
2010	50,000	PF65 65.00				

KM# 1958 10 YUAN
31.11 g., 0.999 Silver 0.9926 oz. ASW, 40 mm. **Subject:** Bejing Opera, series 1 **Rev:** Multicolor face mask

Date	Mintage	F12	VF20	XF40	MS60	MS63
2010	50,000	PF65 65.00				

KM# 1959 10 YUAN
31.11 g., 0.999 Silver 0.9926 oz. ASW, 40 mm. **Subject:** Bejing Stamp & Coin Expo

Date	Mintage	F12	VF20	XF40	MS60	MS63
2010	30,000	PF63 50.00	PF65 60.00			

KM# 1985 10 YUAN
31.11 g., 0.999 Silver 0.9926 oz. ASW, 40 mm. **Subject:** Peking Opera art **Rev:** Lu Zhishen, the "Flowery Monk" character from Water Margin

Date	Mintage	F12	VF20	XF40	MS60	MS63
2011	50,000	PF63 75.00	PF65 85.00			

KM# 1986 10 YUAN
31.11 g., 0.999 Silver 0.9926 oz. ASW, 40 mm. **Subject:** Peking Opera art **Rev:** Shan Ziongxin

Date	Mintage	F12	VF20	XF40	MS60	MS63
2011	50,000	PF63 75.00	PF65 85.00			

KM# 1798 10 YUAN
31.10 g., 0.999 Silver 0.9926 oz. ASW, 40 mm. **Subject:** World Wildlife Fund, 50th Anniversary **Rev:** Tibetian antelope

Date	Mintage	F12	VF20	XF40	MS60	MS63
2011	30,000	PF63 60.00	PF65 70.00			

KM# 1800 10 YUAN
31.10 g., 0.999 Silver 0.9926 oz. ASW, 40 mm. **Subject:** Tsinghua University, 100th Anniversary **Rev:** Old University entrance

Date	Mintage	F12	VF20	XF40	MS60	MS63
2011	Est. 50000	PF63 65.00	PF65 75.00			

KM# 1804 10 YUAN
31.11 g., 0.999 Silver 0.9926 oz. ASW, 40 mm. **Subject:** 23rd Beijing International Stamp and Coin Exposition **Rev:** Byzantine coin and Song Dynasty coin

Date	Mintage	F12	VF20	XF40	MS60	MS63
2011	Est. 30000	PF65 125				

KM# 1805 10 YUAN
31.10 g., 0.999 Silver 0.9926 oz. ASW, 40 mm. **Subject:** Chinese Literature **Rev:** Archer and geese in color

Date	Mintage	F12	VF20	XF40	MS60	MS63
2011	70,000	PF65 75.00				

KM# 1806 10 YUAN
31.11 g., 0.999 Silver 0.9926 oz. ASW, 40 mm. **Subject:** Chinese Literature **Rev:** Li Kui as black wind in color

Date	Mintage	F12	VF20	XF40	MS60	MS63
2011	70,000	PF65 75.00				

KM# 1994 10 YUAN
31.11 g., 0.999 Silver 0.9926 oz. ASW, 40 mm. **Subject:** Bejing-Shanghai High Speed Rail **Obv:** Temple of Heaven **Rev:** Two pandas

Date	Mintage	F12	VF20	XF40	MS60	MS63
2011	30,000	PF65 200				

KM# 1996 10 YUAN
31.11 g., 0.999 Silver 0.9926 oz. ASW, 40 mm. **Subject:** Xi-an Hortaculture Exposition **Obv:** Temple of Heaven **Rev:** Two pandas

Date	Mintage	F12	VF20	XF40	MS60	MS63
2011	20,000	PF65 235				

KM# 1998 10 YUAN
31.11 g., 0.999 Silver 0.9926 oz. ASW, 40 mm. **Subject:** 26th Summer Universade, Shezhuan **Obv:** Colored wreath logo **Rev:** Cubic building

Date	Mintage	F12	VF20	XF40	MS60	MS63
2011	30,000	PF65 200				

KM# 2000 10 YUAN
31.11 g., 0.999 Silver 0.9926 oz. ASW, 40 mm. **Subject:** Peaceful liberation, 60th Anniversary **Obv:** National emblem **Rev:** Ornate design

Date	Mintage	F12	VF20	XF40	MS60	MS63
2011 Proof	30,000	—	—	—	—	200

KM# 2002 10 YUAN
31.11 g., 0.999 Silver 0.9926 oz. ASW, 40 mm. **Subject:** 100th Anniversary of the Revolution **Obv:** National emblem **Rev:** Revolutionary army advancing right - Wuchang Uprising

Date	Mintage	F12	VF20	XF40	MS60	MS63
2011	160,000	PF65 100				

KM# 2004 10 YUAN
31.11 g., 0.999 Silver 0.9926 oz. ASW, 40 mm. **Subject:** Avation Industry in the P.R.C., 60th Anniversary **Obv:** Temple of Heaven **Rev:** Two pandas

Date	Mintage	F12	VF20	XF40	MS60	MS63
2011	20,000	PF65 200				

KM# 2007 10 YUAN
31.11 g., 0.999 Silver 0.9926 oz. ASW, 40 mm. **Subject:** World Heritage Site **Obv:** National emblem **Rev:** Songyue Temple Pagoda

Date	Mintage	F12	VF20	XF40	MS60	MS63
2011	60,000	PF65 150				

KM# 2034 10 YUAN
31.10 g., 0.999 Silver 0.9926 oz. ASW **Subject:** National Committee of the Chinese Financial Workers Union, 60th Anniversary **Rev:** Mother and cub panda

Date	Mintage	F12	VF20	XF40	MS60	MS63
2011	30,000	—	—	—	—	200

KM# 2035 10 YUAN
31.10 g., 0.999 Silver 0.9926 oz. ASW, 40 mm. **Subject:** Shanghai Gold Exchange, 10th Anniversary **Rev:** Mother and cub panda

Date	Mintage	F12	VF20	XF40	MS60	MS63
2011	30,000	—	—	—	—	140

KM# 2037 10 YUAN
31.10 g., 0.999 Silver 0.9926 oz. ASW, 40 mm. **Subject:** Xiamen Special Economic Zone, 30th Anniversary **Rev:** Mother and cub panda

Date	Mintage	F12	VF20	XF40	MS60	MS63
2011	20,000	—	—	—	—	200

KM# 2039 10 YUAN
31.10 g., 0.999 Silver 0.9926 oz. ASW, 40 mm. **Subject:** Rual Credit Cooperatives, 60th Anniversary **Rev:** Mother and cub panda

Date	Mintage	F12	VF20	XF40	MS60	MS63
2011	60,000	—	—	—	—	100

KM# 2047 10 YUAN
31.10 g., 0.999 Silver 0.9926 oz. ASW, 40 mm. **Subject:** Bejing Opera Masks **Rev:** Zhang Fei mask in color

Date	Mintage	F12	VF20	XF40	MS60	MS63
2012	50,000	PF65 85.00				

KM# 2048 10 YUAN
31.10 g., 0.999 Silver 0.9926 oz. ASW, 40 mm. **Subject:** Bejing Opera Mask **Rev:** Tao Hong mask in color

Date	Mintage	F12	VF20	XF40	MS60	MS63
2012	50,000	PF65 80.00				

KM# 2052 10 YUAN
31.10 g., 0.999 Silver 0.9926 oz. ASW, 40 mm. **Subject:** Bronze Age vessels **Rev:** Three water vessels from the Shang Dynasty, Zianwen find

Date	Mintage	F12	VF20	XF40	MS60	MS63
2012	80,000	PF63 70.00	PF65 80.00			

KM# 2057 10 YUAN
31.10 g., Silver, 40 mm. **Subject:** Beijing International Stamp and Coin Exposition

Date	Mintage	F12	VF20	XF40	MS60	MS63
2012	30,000	PF63 115	PF65 125			

KM# 2063 10 YUAN
31.10 g., 0.999 Silver 0.9926 oz. ASW, 40 mm. **Subject:** Bank of China, 100th Anniversary **Obv:** Temple of Heaven **Rev:** Mother and cub panda seated

Date	Mintage	F12	VF20	XF40	MS60	MS63
2012	260,000	—	—	—	—	85.00

KM# 1388 20 YUAN
62.21 g., 0.999 Silver 1.9851 oz. ASW, 40 mm. **Subject:** Mogao Grottos **Obv:** 8-story building **Rev:** Buddha-like statue **Edge:** Reeded **Note:** Prev. Y#1082.

Date	Mintage	F12	VF20	XF40	MS60	MS63
2001	—	PF65 150				

KM# 1432 20 YUAN
62.21 g., 0.999 Silver 1.9851 oz. ASW, 40 mm. **Rev:** Buddha-like statue

Date	Mintage	F12	VF20	XF40	MS60	MS63
2002	30,000	PF65 150				

KM# 1563 20 YUAN
31.10 g., 0.999 Silver 0.9926 oz. ASW, 40 mm. **Series:** Maijishan grotto art **Rev:** Two figures standing

Date	Mintage	F12	VF20	XF40	MS60	MS63
2004	20,000	PF65 90.00				

KM# 2042 20 YUAN
62.27 g., 0.999 Silver 1.9871 oz. ASW, 40 mm. **Subject:** UNESCO **Rev:** Budda statue in Riwo Tsenga

Date	Mintage	F12	VF20	XF40	MS60	MS63
2012	Est. 100000	PF63 135	PF65 150			

KM# 1389 50 YUAN
3.11 g., 0.999 Gold 0.0993 oz. AGW **Subject:** Mogao Grottoes **Obv:** Eight story building **Rev:** Buddha-like statue **Edge:** Reeded. **Note:** Prev. Y#1084.

Date	Mintage	F12	VF20	XF40	MS60	MS63
2001	—	PF65 250				

KM# 1390 50 YUAN
155.52 g., 0.999 Silver 4.9628 oz. ASW, 70 mm. **Subject:** Mogao Grottoes **Obv:** Eight story building **Rev:** Four musicians **Edge:** Reeded. **Note:** Prev. Y#1083.

Date	Mintage	F12	VF20	XF40	MS60	MS63
2001	—	PF65 300				

KM# 1394 50 YUAN
155.52 g., 0.999 Silver 4.9628 oz. ASW, 90 x 40 mm. **Subject:** Han Xizai's Dinner Party **Obv:** Tang Dynasty buildings **Rev:** Multicolor "Five Dynasties" painting **Edge:** Plain **Shape:** Rectangular **Note:** Prev. Y#1104.

Date	Mintage	F12	VF20	XF40	MS60	MS63
2001	18,800	PF65 275				

KM# 1386 50 YUAN
155.52 g., 0.999 Silver 4.9628 oz. ASW, 90 x 40 mm. **Series:** Folk fairy tails **Rev:** Seven multicolor figures on beach **Shape:** Rectangle

Date	Mintage	F12	VF20	XF40	MS60	MS63
2001	10,000	PF65 300				

KM# 1402 50 YUAN
155.52 g., 0.999 Silver 4.9629 oz. ASW, 90 x 50 mm. **Subject:** Bejing opera **Rev:** Four multicolor actors **Shape:** Rectangle

Date	Mintage	F12	VF20	XF40	MS60	MS63
2001	11,800	PF65 300				

KM# 1433 50 YUAN
155.52 g., 0.999 Silver 4.9629 oz. ASW, 70 mm. **Series:** Long men grottoes **Rev:** Two figures

Date	Mintage	F12	VF20	XF40	MS60	MS63
2002	8,000	PF65 300				

KM# 1445 50 YUAN
155.52 g., 0.999 Silver 4.9629 oz. ASW, 65 x 26 mm. **Series:** Classic literature **Rev:** Multicolor crowd of women **Shape:** Fan-like

Date	Mintage	F12	VF20	XF40	MS60	MS63
2002	11,800	PF65 250				

KM# 1430 50 YUAN
155.79 g., 0.999 Silver 4.9715 oz. ASW, 90 x 40 mm. **Series:** Folk fairy tails **Rev:** Multicolor female with red ribbon **Shape:** Rectangle

Date	Mintage	F12	VF20	XF40	MS60	MS63
2002	—	PF65 375				

KM# 1437 50 YUAN
3.11 g., 0.999 Gold 0.0992 oz. AGW, 18 mm. **Subject:** Kuan yin **Rev. Designer:** Female holding child, hologram

Date	Mintage	F12	VF20	XF40	MS60	MS63
2002	33,000	PF65 225				

KM# 1453 50 YUAN
155.52 g., 0.999 Silver 4.9629 oz. ASW, 90 x 40 mm. **Series:** Bejing opera **Rev:** Three multicolor characters one with spikes in costume **Shape:** Rectangle

Date	Mintage	F12	VF20	XF40	MS60	MS63
2002	11,800	PF65 300				

KM# 1493 50 YUAN
155.35 g., 0.999 Silver 4.9575 oz. ASW, 90 x 40 mm. **Series:** Fairy tails **Rev:** Multicolor man with two boys in buckets, jenole in flight at left **Shape:** Rectangle

Date	Mintage	F12	VF20	XF40	MS60	MS63
2003	10,000	PF65 350				

KM# 1512 50 YUAN
3.11 g., 0.999 Gold 0.0993 oz. AGW, 18 mm. **Obv:** Putuo Mountain Pilgrimage Gate **Rev:** Seated Kuanyin with holographic background **Edge:** Reeded **Note:** Prev. Y#1234.

Date	Mintage	F12	VF20	XF40	MS60	MS63
2003	33,000	PF65 225				

KM# 1502 50 YUAN
155.50 g., 0.999 Silver 4.9623 oz. ASW, 80 x 50 mm. **Series:** Class literature **Rev:** Multicolor man lying on couch **Shape:** Rectangle **Note:** Illustration reduced.

Date	Mintage	F12	VF20	XF40	MS60	MS63
2003	10,000	PF65 350				

KM# 1503 50 YUAN
155.15 g., 0.999 Silver 4.9511 oz. ASW, 65 x 125 mm. **Series:** Class literature **Rev:** Six people **Shape:** Arc **Note:** Colorized

Date	Mintage	F12	VF20	XF40	MS60	MS63
2003	11,800	PF65 350				

KM# 1560 50 YUAN
155.52 g., 0.999 Silver 4.9628 oz. ASW, 80x50 mm. **Obv:** Monkey King leading the Master over bridge **Rev:** Multicolor Monkey King fighting the Pig Demon of Bones **Edge:** Plain **Shape:** Rectangle **Note:** Prev. Y#1216.

Date	Mintage	F12	VF20	XF40	MS60	MS63
2004	10,000	PF65 375				

KM# 1572 50 YUAN
3.11 g., 0.999 Gold 0.0992 oz. AGW, 18 mm. **Obv:** Putuo Mountain Pilgrimage Gate **Rev:** Kuanyin and value **Edge:** Reeded **Note:** Prev. Y#1237.

Date	Mintage	F12	VF20	XF40	MS60	MS63
2004	33,000	PF65 225				

KM# 1635 50 YUAN
155.00 g., 0.999 Silver 4.9463 oz. ASW, 80 x 50 mm. **Series:** Classical Literature **Obv:** Horseman on arch bridge **Rev:** Multicolor female and lion **Shape:** Rectangle **Note:** Illustration reduced.

Date	Mintage	F12	VF20	XF40	MS60	MS63
2005	10,000	PF65 350				

KM# 1901 50 YUAN
155.50 g., 0.999 Silver 4.9623 oz. ASW, 80x50 mm. **Subject:** Outlaws of the Marsh, series 1 **Rev:** Multicolor **Shape:** Rectangle **Note:** Illustration reduced.

Date	Mintage	F12	VF20	XF40	MS60	MS63
2003	10,000	PF65 350				
2009	10,000	PF65 250				

KM# 1938 50 YUAN
155.50 g., 0.999 Silver 4.9623 oz. ASW, 80x50 mm. **Subject:** Outlaws of the Marsh, series 2 **Rev:** Multicolor **Shape:** Regtangle **Note:** Illustration reduced.

Date	Mintage	F12	VF20	XF40	MS60	MS63
2003	10,000	PF65 350				
2010	12,000	PF65 225				

KM# 1951 50 YUAN
62.10 g., 0.999 Silver 1.9817 oz. ASW **Subject:** Yungang Grotto Art

Date	Mintage	F12	VF20	XF40	MS60	MS63
2010	20,000	PF65 120				

KM# 1807 50 YUAN
155.67 g., 0.999 Silver 4.9677 oz. ASW, 80x50 mm. **Subject:** Chinese Literature **Rev:** Yan Qing and Ren Yuan in color

Date	Mintage	F12	VF20	XF40	MS60	MS63
2011	12,000	PF65 325				

KM# 2049 50 YUAN
155.67 g., 0.999 Silver 4.9677 oz. ASW, 70 mm. **Subject:** Beijing Opera Masks **Rev:** Zhong Kui mask in color

Date	Mintage	F12	VF20	XF40	MS60	MS63
2012	10,000	PF65 350				

KM# 2053 50 YUAN
155.67 g., 0.999 Silver 4.9677 oz. ASW, 70 mm. **Subject:** Vessels of the Bronze Age **Rev:** Shang Dynasty kettle

Date	Mintage	F12	VF20	XF40	MS60	MS63
2012	10,000	PF65 350				

KM# 2059 50 YUAN
155.67 g., 0.999 Silver 4.9677 oz. ASW, 70 mm. **Subject:** Panda, 30th Anniversary **Obv:** Temple of Heaven **Rev:** Panda

Date	Mintage	F12	VF20	XF40	MS60	MS63
2012	30,000	PF65 350				

KM# 2060 50 YUAN
3.11 g., 0.999 Gold 0.0992 oz. AGW, 18 mm. **Subject:** Panda, 30th Anniversary **Obv:** Temple of Heaven **Rev:** Panda

Date	Mintage	F12	VF20	XF40	MS60	MS63
2012	100,000	PF65 300				

KM# 1514 100 YUAN
3.10 g., 0.999 Platinum 0.099 oz. APW, 18 mm. **Series:** Guan Yi

Date	Mintage	F12	VF20	XF40	MS60	MS63
2003	33,000	PF65 225				

KM# 1534 100 YUAN
15.55 g., 0.999 Palladium 0.4962 oz. APW, 27 mm. **Obv:** Temple of Heaven **Rev:** Panda mother and cub, "kissing pandas **Edge:** Reeded **Note:** Prev. Y#1211.

Date	Mintage	F12	VF20	XF40	MS60	MS63
2004	8,000	PF65 550				

KM# 1573 100 YUAN
3.11 g., 0.9995 Platinum 0.0993 oz. APW, 18 mm. **Obv:** Putuo Mountain Pilgrimage Gate **Rev:** Kuanyin and value **Edge:** Reeded **Note:** Prev. Y#1238.

Date	Mintage	F12	VF20	XF40	MS60	MS63
2004	33,000	PF65 225				

KM# 1540 100 YUAN
7.85 g., 0.999 Gold 0.2505 oz. AGW, 22 mm. **Subject:** 20th Anniversary / Bank of China Industrial and Commercial **Rev:** Panda walking with cub

Date	Mintage	F12	VF20	XF40	MS60	MS63
2004	50,000	PF65 500				

KM# 1542 100 YUAN
7.84 g., 0.999 Gold 0.2502 oz. AGW, 22 mm. **Subject:** 50th Anniversary China Construction Bank **Rev:** Panda walking with cub

Date	Mintage	F12	VF20	XF40	MS60	MS63
2004	60,000	PF65 500				

KM# 1600 100 YUAN
7.77 g., 0.999 Gold 0.248 oz. AGW, 22 mm. **Subject:** Foundation of Industrial & Commercial Bank **Obv:** Temple of Heaven **Rev:** Panda cub and mom seated in bamboo

Date	Mintage	F12	VF20	XF40	MS60	MS63
2005	40,000	PF65 500				

KM# 1602 100 YUAN
7.77 g., 0.999 Gold 0.248 oz. AGW, 22 mm. **Subject:** 100th Anniversary of Bank of Shanghai **Obv:** Temple of Heaven **Rev:** Panda cub and mom seated in bamboo

Date	Mintage	F12	VF20	XF40	MS60	MS63
2005	40,000	PF65 500				

KM# 1616 100 YUAN
7.70 g., 0.999 Gold 0.2457 oz. AGW, 22 mm. **Subject:** 2006 World Cup - Germany **Obv:** Multicolor logo **Rev:** Temple of Heaven and soccer ball

Date	Mintage	F12	VF20	XF40	MS60	MS63
2005	10,000	PF65 550				

KM# A979 100 YUAN
8.50 g., 0.999 Gold 0.2713 oz. AGW, 22 mm. **Subject:** 10th Anniversary Bank of Beijing **Obv:** Temple of Heaven **Rev:** Two pandas

Date	Mintage	F12	VF20	XF40	MS60	MS63
2006	100	—	—	—	—	800

KM# A980 100 YUAN
8.50 g., 0.999 Gold 0.2713 oz. AGW, 22 mm. **Subject:** 10th Anniversary China Minsheng Banking Corp. **Obv:** Temple of Heaven **Rev:** Two Pandas munching on bamboo

Date	Mintage	F12	VF20	XF40	MS60	MS63
2006	100	—	—	—	—	800

KM# 1694 100 YUAN
7.77 g., 0.999 Gold 0.248 oz. AGW, 22 mm. **Subject:** Qinghai - Tibet Railway Opening **Obv:** Map of railway route and track layer **Rev:** Kun Lun Tunnel Portal

Date	Mintage	F12	VF20	XF40	MS60	MS63
2006	16,000	PF65 550				

KM# 1665 100 YUAN
7.77 g., 0.999 Gold 0.248 oz. AGW, 22 mm. **Subject:** 10th Anniversary Bank of Beijing **Obv:** Temple of Heaven **Rev:** Two pandas seated with bamboo

Date	Mintage	F12	VF20	XF40	MS60	MS63
2006	150,000	PF65 500				

KM# 1667 100 YUAN
7.77 g., 0.999 Silver 0.248 oz. ASW, 22 mm. **Subject:** 10th Anniversary - China Minsheng Banking Corp **Obv:** Temple of Heaven **Rev:** Two pandas seated with bamboo

Date	Mintage	F12	VF20	XF40	MS60	MS63
2006	20,000	PF65 550				

KM# 1669 100 YUAN
7.77 g., 0.999 Gold 0.248 oz. AGW, 22 mm. **Subject:** Shenyang Horticultural Expo **Obv:** Temple of Heaven **Rev:** Two pandas seated with bamboo

Date	Mintage	F12	VF20	XF40	MS60	MS63
2006	10,000	PF65 550				

KM# 1730 100 YUAN
7.77 g., 0.999 Gold 0.248 oz. AGW, 22 mm. **Subject:** 60th Anniversary - Foundry of Mongolia Autonomous Region **Obv:** Wheel of Mongolian Lele Cart **Rev:** Female Mongolian in posture of welcome

Date	Mintage	F12	VF20	XF40	MS60	MS63
2007	10,000	PF65 550				

KM# 1827 100 YUAN
7.78 g., 0.999 Gold 0.2483 oz. AGW, 22 mm. **Subject:** 12th Special Olympics in Shanghai **Obv:** Logo in color **Rev:** Runner

Date	Mintage	F12	VF20	XF40	MS60	MS63
2007	20,000	PF65 650				

KM# 1737 100 YUAN
7.78 g., 0.999 Gold 0.2483 oz. AGW, 22 mm. **Subject:** Economic Reform in China, 30th Anniversary **Rev:** Flowers and fireworks

Date	Mintage	F12	VF20	XF40	MS60	MS63
2008	30,000	PF65 600				

KM# 1824 100 YUAN
7.77 g., 0.999 Gold 0.248 oz. AGW, 23 mm. **Subject:** Bank of Communications, Centennial **Rev:** Panda

Date	Mintage	F12	VF20	XF40	MS60	MS63
2008	10,000	PF65 550				

KM# 1853 100 YUAN
7.77 g., 0.999 Gold 0.248 oz. AGW **Subject:** Hainan Special Economic Zone

Date	Mintage	F12	VF20	XF40	MS60	MS63
2008	10,000	PF65 550				

KM# 1857 100 YUAN
7.77 g., 0.999 Gold 0.248 oz. AGW **Subject:** Ningxia Hui Autonomous Region

Date	Mintage	F12	VF20	XF40	MS60	MS63
2008	10,000	PF65 550				

KM# 1860 100 YUAN
7.77 g., 0.999 Gold 0.248 oz. AGW **Subject:** Guangzi Zhuang Autonomous Region

Date	Mintage	F12	VF20	XF40	MS60	MS63
2008	10,000	PF65 550				

KM# 1890 100 YUAN
7.77 g., 0.999 Gold 0.248 oz. AGW, 23 mm. **Subject:** Precious Metal Commemoratives, 30th Anniversary **Obv:** Temple of Heaven **Rev:** Two pandas seated

Date	Mintage	F12	VF20	XF40	MS60	MS63
2009	10,000	—	—	—	—	550

KM# 1895 100 YUAN
7.77 g., 0.999 Gold 0.248 oz. AGW, 22 mm. **Subject:** P.R.C. 60th Anniversary

Date	Mintage	F12	VF20	XF40	MS60	MS63
2009	100,000	PF65 500				

KM# 1904 100 YUAN
7.77 g., 0.999 Gold 0.248 oz. AGW, 22 mm. **Subject:** 16th Asian Games

Date	Mintage	F12	VF20	XF40	MS60	MS63
2009	30,000	PF65 525				

KM# 1909 100 YUAN
7.77 g., 0.999 Gold 0.248 oz. AGW, 22 mm. **Subject:** China Agricultural Bank

Date	Mintage	F12	VF20	XF40	MS60	MS63
2009	100,000	—	—	—	—	500

KM# 1794 100 YUAN
7.78 g., 0.999 Gold 0.2483 oz. AGW, 22 mm. **Subject:** Agricultural Bank, IPO **Obv:** Temple of Heaven **Rev:** Panda

Date	Mintage	F12	VF20	XF40	MS60	MS63
2010	60,000	—	—	—	—	500

KM# 1797 100 YUAN
7.78 g., 0.999 Gold 0.2483 oz. AGW, 22 mm. **Subject:** Shanghai Mint, 90th Anniversary **Obv:** Temple of Heaven **Rev:** Panda

Date	Mintage	F12	VF20	XF40	MS60	MS63
2010	5,000	—	—	—	—	500

KM# 1945 100 YUAN
7.77 g., 0.999 Gold 0.248 oz. AGW **Subject:** Wudang Mountain

Date	Mintage	F12	VF20	XF40	MS60	MS63
2010	30,000	PF65 525				

KM# 1952 100 YUAN
7.77 g., 0.999 Gold 0.248 oz. ACW **Subject:** Shenzhen Economic Zone

Date	Mintage	F12	VF20	XF40	MS60	MS63
2010	20,000	PF65 525				

KM# 1954 100 YUAN
7.77 g., 0.999 Gold 0.248 oz. AGW **Subject:** 16th Asian Games

Date	Mintage	F12	VF20	XF40	MS60	MS63
2010	30,000	PF65 525				

KM# 1956 100 YUAN
7.77 g., 0.999 Gold 0.248 oz. AGW **Subject:** Bejing Opera, series 1 **Rev:** Multicolor

Date	Mintage	F12	VF20	XF40	MS60	MS63
2010	30,000	PF65 525				

KM# 1987 100 YUAN
7.77 g., 0.999 Gold 0.248 oz. AGW, 22 mm. **Subject:** Peking Opera art **Rev:** Mask of Guan Yu

Date	Mintage	F12	VF20	XF40	MS60	MS63
2011	30,000	PF65 525				

KM# 1799 100 YUAN
7.78 g., 0.999 Gold 0.2483 oz. AGW, 22 mm. **Subject:** World Wildlife Fund, 50th Anniversary **Rev:** Large 50 and WWF logo

Date	Mintage	F12	VF20	XF40	MS60	MS63
2011	10,000	PF65 600				

KM# 1801 100 YUAN
7.78 g., 0.999 Gold 0.2483 oz. AGW, 22 mm. **Subject:** Tsinghua University **Rev:** Original main building

Date	Mintage	F12	VF20	XF40	MS60	MS63
2011	Est. 20000	PF65 550				

KM# 1995 100 YUAN
7.77 g., 0.999 Gold 0.248 oz. AGW, 22 mm. **Subject:** Bejing-Shanghai High Speed Rail **Obv:** Temple of Heaven **Rev:** Two pandas

Date	Mintage	F12	VF20	XF40	MS60	MS63
2011	10,000	PF65 600				

KM# 1997 100 YUAN
7.77 g., 0.999 Gold 0.248 oz. AGW, 22 mm. **Subject:** Xi-an Horticulture Exposition **Obv:** Temple of Heaven **Rev:** Two pandas

Date	Mintage	F12	VF20	XF40	MS60	MS63
2011	3,000	PF65 750				

KM# 1999 100 YUAN
7.77 g., 0.999 Gold 0.248 oz. AGW, 22 mm. **Subject:** 26th Summer Universade, Shezhuan **Obv:** Colored wreath logo

Rev: Rays and smile face design

Date	Mintage	F12	VF20	XF40	MS60	MS63
2011	20,000	PF65 750				

KM# 2001 100 YUAN
7.77 g., 0.999 Gold 0.248 oz. AGW, 22 mm. **Subject:** Peaceful Liberation, 60th Anniversary **Obv:** National emblem **Rev:** Ornate design

Date	Mintage	F12	VF20	XF40	MS60	MS63
2011	20,000	PF65 750				

KM# 2003 100 YUAN
7.77 g., 0.999 Gold 0.248 oz. AGW, 22 mm. **Subject:** 100th Anniversary of the Revolution **Obv:** National emblem **Rev:** Sun Yat-sen bust facing

Date	Mintage	F12	VF20	XF40	MS60	MS63
2011	100,000	PF65 650				

KM# 2005 100 YUAN
7.77 g., 0.999 Gold 0.248 oz. AGW, 22 mm. **Subject:** Avation Industry in the P.R.C., 60th Anniversary **Obv:** Temple of Heaven **Rev:** Two pandas

Date	Mintage	F12	VF20	XF40	MS60	MS63
2011	5,000	PF65 750				

KM# 2008 100 YUAN
7.77 g., 0.999 Gold 0.248 oz. AGW, 22 mm. **Subject:** World Heritage Site **Obv:** National emblem **Rev:** Gate of the Shaolin Temple

Date	Mintage	F12	VF20	XF40	MS60	MS63
2011	30,000	PF65 650				

KM# 2036 100 YUAN
7.78 g., 0.999 Gold 0.2483 oz. AGW, 22 mm. **Subject:** Shanghai Gold Exchange **Rev:** Mother and cub panda

Date	Mintage	F12	VF20	XF40	MS60	MS63
2011	6,000	—	—	—	—	550

KM# 2038 100 YUAN
7.78 g., 0.999 Gold 0.2483 oz. AGW, 22 mm. **Subject:** Xiamen Special Economic Zone, 30th Anniversary **Rev:** Mother and cub panda

Date	Mintage	F12	VF20	XF40	MS60	MS63
2011	5,000	—	—	—	—	550

KM# 2040 100 YUAN
7.78 g., 0.999 Gold 0.2483 oz. AGW, 22 mm. **Subject:** Rural Credit Cooperatives, 60th Anniversary **Rev:** Mother and cub panda

Date	Mintage	F12	VF20	XF40	MS60	MS63
2011	25,000	—	—	—	—	550

KM# 2044 100 YUAN
7.78 g., 0.999 Gold 0.2483 oz. AGW, 22 mm. **Subject:** UNESCO **Rev:** Pusading Temple

Date	Mintage	F12	VF20	XF40	MS60	MS63
2012	60,000	PF65 550				

KM# 2050 100 YUAN
7.78 g., 0.999 Gold 0.2483 oz. AGW, 22 mm. **Subject:** Beijing Opera Mask **Rev:** Monkey King in color

Date	Mintage	F12	VF20	XF40	MS60	MS63
2012	30,000	PF65 550				

KM# 2055 100 YUAN
7.78 g., 0.999 Gold 0.2483 oz. AGW, 22 mm. **Subject:** Bronze Age vessels **Rev:** Tripod drinking glass, Xia Dynasty, Yanshi find

Date	Mintage	F12	VF20	XF40	MS60	MS63
2012	50,000	PF65 550				

KM# 2064 100 YUAN
7.78 g., 0.999 Gold 0.2483 oz. AGW, 22 mm. **Subject:** Bank of China, 100th Anniversary **Obv:** Temple of Heaven **Rev:** Mother and cub panda

Date	Mintage	F12	VF20	XF40	MS60	MS63
2012	55,000	—	—	—	—	550

KM# 1488 150 YUAN
10.05 g., 0.999 Gold 0.3207 oz. AGW, 23 mm. **Subject:** Spring festival **Obv:** Tree with berries **Rev:** Two Koi in ribbon sea

Date	Mintage	F12	VF20	XF40	MS60	MS63
2003	50,000	PF65 600				

KM# 1511 150 YUAN
10.13 g., 0.999 Gold 0.3233 oz. AGW, 23 mm. **Subject:** Space flight **Rev:** Multicolor astronaut and ship

Date	Mintage	F12	VF20	XF40	MS60	MS63
2003	30,000	PF65 625				

KM# 1556 150 YUAN
10.50 g., 0.999 Gold 0.3351 oz. AGW, 23 mm. **Series:** Folk customs **Subject:** Lantern Festival **Rev:** Boy holding lantern **Note:** Colorized

Date	Mintage	F12	VF20	XF40	MS60	MS63
2004	20,000	PF65 650				

KM# 1638 150 YUAN
10.05 g., 0.999 Gold 0.3207 oz. AGW, 23 mm. **Subject:** Chinese Movie Centennial **Obv:** Winged column **Rev:** Movie clipboard

Date	Mintage	F12	VF20	XF40	MS60	MS63
2005	20,000	PF65 650				

KM# 1654 150 YUAN
10.36 g., 0.999 Gold 0.3306 oz. AGW, 23 mm. **Subject:** Chengdu multi-purpose war planes, 10th Anniversary

Date	Mintage	F12	VF20	XF40	MS60	MS63
2007	10,000	PF65 850				

KM# 1829 150 YUAN
10.36 g., 0.999 Gold 0.3306 oz. AGW, 23 mm. **Subject:** Chinese aerospace **Obv:** Solar system **Rev:** Chang'e 1 in lunar orbit

Date	Mintage	F12	VF20	XF40	MS60	MS63
2007	20,000	PF65 850				

KM# 1847 150 YUAN
10.10 g., 0.999 Gold 0.3223 oz. AGW, 23 mm. **Subject:** Beijing Olympics **Rev:** Classical wrestlers

Date	Mintage	F12	VF20	XF40	MS60	MS63
2008	60,000	PF65 600				

KM# 1848 150 YUAN
10.10 g., 0.999 Gold 0.3223 oz. AGW, 23 mm. **Subject:** Beijing Olympics **Obv:** Beijing Olympics **Rev:** Classical soccer player

Date	Mintage	F12	VF20	XF40	MS60	MS63
2008	60,000	PF65 600				

KM# 1696 150 YUAN
10.36 g., 0.999 Gold 0.3306 oz. AGW, 23 mm. **Subject:** 29th Summer Olympics, Beijing **Rev:** Swimmer entering water at race start

Date	Mintage	F12	VF20	XF40	MS60	MS63
2008 S	60,000	PF65 600				
2008 Y	Inc. above	PF65 600				
2008 Z	Inc. above	PF65 600				

KM# 1697 150 YUAN
10.36 g., 0.999 Gold 0.3306 oz. AGW, 23 mm. **Subject:** 29th Summer Olympics, Beijing **Obv:** Olympics Logo **Rev:** Ancient Chinese weightlifter

Date	Mintage	F12	VF20	XF40	MS60	MS63
2008 S	60,000	PF65 600				
2008 Y	Inc. above	PF65 600				
2008 Z	Inc. above	PF65 600				

KM# 1700 150 YUAN
10.05 g., 0.999 Gold 0.3207 oz. AGW, 23 mm. **Subject:** 29th Summer Olympics **Obv:** Beijing Olympic logo **Rev:** Ancient horsemaid and new logo **Note:** Issued in 2006

Date	Mintage	F12	VF20	XF40	MS60	MS63
2008 S	60,000	PF65 600				
2008 Y	Inc. above	PF65 600				
2008 Z	Inc. above	PF65 600				

KM# 1701 150 YUAN
10.05 g., 0.999 Gold 0.3207 oz. AGW, 23 mm. **Subject:** 29th Summer Olympics **Obv:** Beijing Olympic logo **Rev:** Ancient archer and new logo **Note:** Issued in 2006

Date	Mintage	F12	VF20	XF40	MS60	MS63
2008 S	60,000	PF65 600				
2008 Y	Inc. above	PF65 600				
2008 Z	Inc. above	PF65 600				

KM# 1735 150 YUAN
10.36 g., 0.999 Gold 0.3306 oz. AGW, 23 mm. **Obv:** Solar system **Rev:** Man walking in space

Date	Mintage	F12	VF20	XF40	MS60	MS63
2008	30,000	PF65 900				

KM# 1855 150 YUAN
10.10 g., 0.999 Gold 0.3223 oz. AGW **Subject:** Para Olympics

Date	Mintage	F12	VF20	XF40	MS60	MS63
2008	15,000	PF65 700				

KM# 1900 150 YUAN
10.36 g., 0.999 Gold 0.3306 oz. AGW, 23 mm. **Subject:** Outlaws of the Marsh, series 1 **Rev:** Multicolor

Date	Mintage	F12	VF20	XF40	MS60	MS63
2009	30,000	PF65 650				

KM# 1906 150 YUAN
10.35 g., 0.999 Gold 0.3303 oz. AGW **Subject:** Shanghai Expo

Date	Mintage	F12	VF20	XF40	MS60	MS63
2009	—	PF65 650				

KM# 1937 150 YUAN
10.35 g., 0.999 Gold 0.3303 oz. AGW **Subject:** Outlaws of the Marsh, series 2 **Rev:** Multicolor

Date	Mintage	F12	VF20	XF40	MS60	MS63
2010	35,000	PF65 650				

KM# 1941 150 YUAN
155.55 g., 0.999 Gold 4.9639 oz. AGW **Subject:** Shanghai World Expo, 2010

Date	Mintage	F12	VF20	XF40	MS60	MS63
2010	1,000	PF65 9,500				

KM# 1809 150 YUAN
1036.00 g., 0.999 Gold 33.0607 oz. AGW, 23 mm. **Subject:** Chinese Literature **Rev:** Wu Yong reviewing the plan in color

Date	Mintage	F12	VF20	XF40	MS60	MS63
2011	35,000	PF65 60,000				

KM# 1387 200 YUAN
15.55 g., 0.999 Gold 0.4963 oz. AGW, 27 mm. **Series:** Folk fairy tails **Rev:** Multicolor heroic figure putting ax to clouds

Date	Mintage	F12	VF20	XF40	MS60	MS63
2001	8,800	PF65 1,050				

KM# 1391 200 YUAN
15.55 g., 0.999 Gold 0.4963 oz. AGW, 27 mm. **Subject:** Mogao Grottoes **Obv:** Eight story building **Rev:** Dancing drummer **Edge:** Reeded. **Note:** Prev. Y#1085.

Date	Mintage	F12	VF20	XF40	MS60	MS63
2001	—	PF65 1,050				

KM# 1393 200 YUAN
15.55 g., 0.999 Gold 0.4963 oz. AGW, 27 mm. **Subject:** 50th Anniversary Chinese Occupation of Tibet **Obv:** Five stars **Rev:** Denomination in flower **Edge:** Reeded **Note:** Prev. Y#1087.

Date	Mintage	F12	VF20	XF40	MS60	MS63
2001	15,000	PF65 950				

KM# 1403 200 YUAN
15.55 g., 0.999 Gold 0.4963 oz. AGW, 27 mm. **Subject:** Bejing opera **Rev:** Multicolor ribbon dancer

Date	Mintage	F12	VF20	XF40	MS60	MS63
2001	8,000	PF65 1,100				

KM# 1431 200 YUAN
15.50 g., 0.999 Gold 0.4946 oz. AGW **Subject:** Art **Rev:** Multicolor male with snake and staff **Note:** Prev. Y#1148.

Date	Mintage	F12	VF20	XF40	MS60	MS63
2002	8,800	PF65 1,050				

KM# 1434 200 YUAN
15.55 g., 0.999 Gold 0.4962 oz. AGW, 27 mm. **Subject:** Buddha **Note:** Prev. Y#1145.

Date	Mintage	F12	VF20	XF40	MS60	MS63
2002	8,800	PF65 1,050				

KM# 1439 200 YUAN
15.52 g., 0.999 Gold 0.4952 oz. AGW, 27 mm. **Subject:** Sichuan Sanxingdui relics **Obv:** Museum building **Rev:** Face mask

Date	Mintage	F12	VF20	XF40	MS60	MS63
2002	8,800	PF65 1,050				

KM# 1440 200 YUAN
15.50 g., 0.999 Gold 0.4946 oz. AGW **Subject:** Ceremonial Mask **Note:** Prev. Y#1149.

Date	Mintage	F12	VF20	XF40	MS60	MS63
2002	5,000	PF65 1,100				

KM# 1446 200 YUAN
15.50 g., 0.999 Gold 0.4946 oz. AGW **Subject:** Dream of the Red Mansion **Shape:** Octagon **Note:** Prev. Y#1147.

Date	Mintage	F12	VF20	XF40	MS60	MS63
2002	8,000	PF65 1,100				

KM# 1454 200 YUAN
15.50 g., 0.999 Gold 0.4946 oz. AGW **Subject:** Peking Opera **Note:** Prev. Y#1146.

Date	Mintage	F12	VF20	XF40	MS60	MS63
2002	8,000	PF65 1,050				

KM# 1456 200 YUAN
15.52 g., 0.999 Gold 0.4952 oz. AGW, 27 mm. **Subject:** World Expo 2010 **Rev:** Skyline

Date	Mintage	F12	VF20	XF40	MS60	MS63
2002	5,000	PF65 1,100				

KM# 1494 200 YUAN
15.55 g., 0.9999 Gold 0.4967 oz. AGW **Subject:** Chinese Mythical Folk Tales **Note:** Prev. Y#1160.

Date	Mintage	F12	VF20	XF40	MS60	MS63
2003	8,800	PF65 1,050				

KM# 1495 200 YUAN
15.52 g., 0.999 Gold 0.4951 oz. AGW, 27 mm. **Subject:** Finger Sarira of Sakyanmunt **Obv:** Tall tower **Rev:** Flora design

Date	Mintage	F12	VF20	XF40	MS60	MS63
2003	12,000	PF65 950				

KM# 1504 200 YUAN
15.55 g., 0.9999 Gold 0.4967 oz. AGW **Subject:** Pilgrimage to the West **Note:** Prev. Y#1159.

Date	Mintage	F12	VF20	XF40	MS60	MS63
2003	11,800	PF65 950				

KM# 1506 200 YUAN
15.51 g., 0.999 Gold 0.495 oz. AGW, 40 mm. **Series:** Classical literature **Rev:** Multicolor blue seated female **Shape:** Hexagon

Date	Mintage	F12	VF20	XF40	MS60	MS63
2003	8,000	PF65 1,050				

KM# 1509 200 YUAN
15.52 g., 0.999 Gold 0.4951 oz. AGW, 27 mm. **Series:** Wulingyan Scenic Resort

Date	Mintage	F12	VF20	XF40	MS60	MS63
2003	8,000	PF65 950				

KM# 1561 200 YUAN
15.55 g., 0.999 Gold 0.4962 oz. AGW, 27 mm. **Obv:** Monkey King leading the Master over bridge **Rev:** Multicolor Monkey King on one knee meeting the Master **Edge:** Reeded **Note:** Prev. Y#1217.

Date	Mintage	F12	VF20	XF40	MS60	MS63
2004	11,800	PF65 950				

KM# 1564 200 YUAN
15.56 g., 0.999 Gold 0.4965 oz. AGW, 27 mm. **Series:** Maijishan grotto art **Rev:** Buddha statue

Date	Mintage	F12	VF20	XF40	MS60	MS63
2004	8,800	PF65 1,050				

KM# 1567 200 YUAN
15.55 g., 0.999 Gold 0.4963 oz. AGW, 27 mm. **Obv:** Guangan Exposition Hall **Rev:** Deng Xiaoping and value **Edge:** Reeded **Note:** Prev. Y#1241.

Date	Mintage	F12	VF20	XF40	MS60	MS63
2004	10,000	PF65 950				

KM# 1571 200 YUAN
15.55 g., 0.999 Gold 0.4962 oz. AGW, 27 mm. **Obv:** National arms above People's Congress Hall and ornamental column **Rev:** Multicolor hologram depicting the hall's overhead lighting **Edge:** Reeded **Note:** Prev. Y#1213.

Date	Mintage	F12	VF20	XF40	MS60	MS63
2004	5,000	PF65 1,050				

KM# 1625 200 YUAN
15.55 g., 0.999 Gold 0.4962 oz. AGW, 27 mm. **Subject:** 600th Anniversary of Zheng He's Voyages **Obv:** Multicolor logo **Rev:** Zheng He portrait in linear form

Date	Mintage	F12	VF20	XF40	MS60	MS63
2005	6,000	PF65 950				

KM# 1627 200 YUAN
15.55 g., 0.999 Gold 0.4962 oz. AGW, 27 mm. **Subject:** Chen Yun Birth Centennial **Obv:** House **Rev:** Head 3/4 right

Date	Mintage	F12	VF20	XF40	MS60	MS63
2005	5,000	PF65 1,100				

KM# 1630 200 YUAN
15.55 g., 0.999 Gold 0.4962 oz. AGW, 27 mm. **Subject:** 60th Anniversary of Victory - War of Resistance **Obv:** Monument **Rev:** Mob of Peoples Army

Date	Mintage	F12	VF20	XF40	MS60	MS63
2005	5,000	PF65 1,100				

KM# 1633 200 YUAN
15.55 g., 0.999 Gold 0.4962 oz. AGW, 27 mm. **Series:** Classical Literature **Obv:** Horseman on arch bridge **Rev:** Two multicolor women, one with monkey, other with rabbit

Date	Mintage	F12	VF20	XF40	MS60	MS63
2005	11,800	PF65 950				

KM# 1689 200 YUAN
15.55 g., 0.999 Gold 0.4962 oz. AGW, 27 mm. **Subject:** Yvelv Academy **Obv:** Front door of Academy **Rev:** Interior room

Date	Mintage	F12	VF20	XF40	MS60	MS63
2006	7,000	PF65 950				

KM# 1692 200 YUAN
15.55 g., 0.999 Gold 0.4962 oz. AGW, 27 mm. **Subject:** 70th Anniversary of Long March **Obv:** Route of the marches, hammer and sickle symbol **Rev:** Group of marchers advancing with rifles

Date	Mintage	F12	VF20	XF40	MS60	MS63
2006	10,000	PF65 950				

KM# 1862 200 YUAN
15.57 g., 0.999 Gold 0.4969 oz. AGW, 27 mm. **Subject:** Chinese Peoples Liberation Army, 80th Anniversary **Obv:** Three military men saluting, flag in background **Rev:** Ship, tank, plane

Date	Mintage	F12	VF20	XF40	MS60	MS63
2007	10,000	PF65 1,100				

KM# 1949 200 YUAN
15.55 g., 0.999 Gold 0.4962 oz. AGW **Subject:** Yungang Grotto Art

Date	Mintage	F12	VF20	XF40	MS60	MS63
2010	10,000	PF65 975				

KM# 1435 300 YUAN
1000.00 g., 0.999 Silver 31.9118 oz. ASW, 100 mm. **Series:** Long men grottoes **Rev:** Large female statue

Date	Mintage	F12	VF20	XF40	MS60	MS63
2002	8,000	PF65 1,750				

KM# 1513 300 YUAN
1000.00 g., 0.999 Silver 31.9118 oz. ASW, 100 mm. **Series:** Guan Yi

Date	Mintage	F12	VF20	XF40	MS60	MS63
2003	3,800	PF65 3,500				

KM# 1568 300 YUAN
1000.00 g., 0.999 Silver 31.9118 oz. ASW, 100 mm. **Obv:** Guangan Exposition Hall **Rev:** Deng Xiaoping and value **Edge:** Reeded **Note:** Prev. Y#1242.

Date	Mintage	F12	VF20	XF40	MS60	MS63
2004	5,000	PF65 1,850				

KM# 1579 300 YUAN
1000.00 g., 0.999 Silver 31.9118 oz. ASW, 100 mm. **Series:** Kuan Yin **Rev:** Female seated holding flower

Date	Mintage	F12	VF20	XF40	MS60	MS63
2004	3,800	PF65 2,000				

KM# 1617 300 YUAN
1000.00 g., 0.999 Silver 31.9118 oz. ASW, 100 mm. **Subject:** 2006 World Cup - Germany **Obv:** Multicolor logo **Rev:** World Cup Trophy

Date	Mintage	F12	VF20	XF40	MS60	MS63
2005	3,000	PF65 2,250				

KM# 1634 300 YUAN
1000.00 g., 0.999 Silver 31.9118 oz. ASW, 100 mm. **Series:** Classical Literature **Obv:** Horseman on arch bridge **Rev:** Multicolor heavenly buddha

Date	Mintage	F12	VF20	XF40	MS60	MS63
2005	5,000	PF65 2,250				

KM# 1695 300 YUAN
1000.00 g., 0.999 Silver 31.9118 oz. ASW, 100 mm. **Subject:** 29th Summer Olympics, Beijing **Obv:** Olympics Logo **Rev:** Riding and rowing

Date	Mintage	F12	VF20	XF40	MS60	MS63
2008	20,008	PF65 2,000				

KM# 1849 300 YUAN
1000.00 g., 0.999 Silver 31.9118 oz. ASW, 100 mm. **Subject:** Beijing Olympics **Obv:** Multicolor logo **Rev:** Classical tug of war **Note:** Photo reduced.

Date	Mintage	F12	VF20	XF40	MS60	MS63
2008	20,008	PF65 2,250				

KM# 1897 300 YUAN
1000.00 g., 0.999 Silver 31.9118 oz. ASW, 100 mm. **Subject:** P.R.C. 60th Anniversary

Date	Mintage	F12	VF20	XF40	MS60	MS63
2009	6,000	PF65 2,100				

KM# 1950 300 YUAN
1000.00 g., 0.999 Silver 31.9118 oz. ASW **Subject:** Yungang Grotto Art

Date	Mintage	F12	VF20	XF40	MS60	MS63
2010	3,800	PF65 2,100				

KM# 1808 300 YUAN
1000.00 g., 0.999 Silver 31.9118 oz. ASW, 100 mm. **Subject:** Chinese Literature **Rev:** Meeting of the Heroes in the great hall in color

Date	Mintage	F12	VF20	XF40	MS60	MS63
2011	10,000	PF65 1,650				

KM# 2006 300 YUAN
1000.00 g., 0.999 Silver 31.9118 oz. ASW, 100 mm. **Subject:** World Heritage Site **Obv:** National emblem **Rev:** Tianzhong Pavillon at the Zhongyue Temple

Date	Mintage	F12	VF20	XF40	MS60	MS63
2011	5,000	PF65 1,750				

KM# 2043 300 YUAN
1000.00 g., 0.999 Silver 31.9118 oz. ASW, 100 mm. **Subject:**
UNESCO **Rev:** Tayuan Temple

Date	Mintage	F12	VF20	XF40	MS60	MS63
2012	—	PF65 1,600				

KM# 2061 500 YUAN
31.10 g., 0.999 Gold 0.9926 oz. AGW, 32 mm. **Subject:** Panda,
30th Anniversary **Obv:** Temple of Heaven **Rev:** Panda

Date	Mintage	F12	VF20	XF40	MS60	MS63
2012	30,000	PF65 2,250				

KM# 1392 2000 YUAN
155.52 g., 0.999 Gold 4.9628 oz. AGW, 60 mm. **Subject:**
Mogao Grottoes **Obv:** Eight story building **Rev:** Two dancers
Edge: Reeded **Note:** Prev. #Y1086.

Date	Mintage	F12	VF20	XF40	MS60	MS63
2001	—	PF65 25,000				

KM# 1436 2000 YUAN
155.52 g., 0.999 Gold 4.9628 oz. AGW, 60 mm. **Subject:**
Chinese grottos art - Longmen **Note:** Prev. #Y1151.

Date	Mintage	F12	VF20	XF40	MS60	MS63
2002	288	PF65 13,500				

KM# 1505 2000 YUAN
155.50 g., 0.999 Gold 4.9623 oz. AGW, 64 x 40 mm. **Series:**
Class literature **Rev:** Two multicolor monkey kings **Shape:**
Rectangle **Note:** Illustration reduced.

Date	Mintage	F12	VF20	XF40	MS60	MS63
2003	500	PF65 11,500				

KM# 1562 2000 YUAN
155.52 g., 0.999 Gold 4.9628 oz. AGW, 64x40 mm. **Obv:**
Monkey King leading Master over bridge **Rev:** Multicolor
Monkey King fighting the Pig "Demon of Bones **Edge:** Plain
Shape: Ingot **Note:** Prev. #Y1218. Illustration reduced.

Date	Mintage	F12	VF20	XF40	MS60	MS63
2004	500	PF65 11,500				

KM# 1565 2000 YUAN
155.52 g., 0.999 Gold 4.9628 oz. AGW, 60 mm. **Subject:**
Maijishan Grottos **Obv:** Grotto view **Rev:** Buddha portrait within
halo of flying devatas **Edge:** Reeded **Note:** Prev. #Y1206.

Date	Mintage	F12	VF20	XF40	MS60	MS63
2004(y)	288	PF65 14,500				

KM# 1569 2000 YUAN
155.52 g., 0.999 Gold 4.9628 oz. AGW, 60 mm. **Obv:** Guangan
Exposition Hall **Rev:** Deng Xiaoping and value **Edge:** Reeded
Note: Prev. #Y1243.

Date	Mintage	F12	VF20	XF40	MS60	MS63
2004	600	PF65 13,500				

KM# 1632 2000 YUAN
155.00 g., 0.999 Gold 4.9463 oz. AGW, 64 x 40 mm. **Series:**
Classic Literature Pilgrimage To The West **Obv:** Horseback rider
on arch bridge **Rev:** Multicolor court scene **Shape:** Rectangle

Date	Mintage	F12	VF20	XF40	MS60	MS63
2005	500	PF65 13,500				

KM# 1698 2000 YUAN
155.52 g., 0.999 Gold 4.9629 oz. AGW, 60 mm. **Subject:** 29th
Summer Olympics, Beijing **Obv:** Olympics Logo **Rev:** Athletics
and team sports

Date	Mintage	F12	VF20	XF40	MS60	MS63
2008	2,008	PF65 9,000				

KM# 1738 2000 YUAN
155.67 g., 0.999 Gold 4.9677 oz. AGW, 60 mm. **Subject:**
Economic Reform in China, 30th Anniversary **Rev:** Flowers and
Fireworks

Date	Mintage	F12	VF20	XF40	MS60	MS63
2008	800	PF65 9,500				

KM# 1850 2000 YUAN
155.55 g., 0.999 Gold 4.9639 oz. AGW, 60 mm. **Subject:**
Beijing Olympics **Obv:** Multicolor logo **Rev:** Four sports

Date	Mintage	F12	VF20	XF40	MS60	MS63
2008	—	PF65 16,500				

KM# 1894 2000 YUAN
155.50 g., 0.999 Gold 4.9623 oz. AGW, 60 mm. **Subject:**
P.R.C. 60th Anniversary

Date	Mintage	F12	VF20	XF40	MS60	MS63
2009	600	PF65 12,000				

KM# 1899 2000 YUAN
155.50 g., 0.999 Gold 4.9623 oz. AGW, 64c40 mm. **Subject:**
Outlaws of the Marsh, series 1 **Rev:** Multicolor **Shape:**
Rectangle

Date	Mintage	F12	VF20	XF40	MS60	MS63
2009	800	PF65 12,000				

KM# 1936 2000 YUAN
155.55 g., 0.999 Gold 4.9639 oz. AGW, 64x40 mm. **Series:** Outlaws of the Marsh, series 2 **Rev:** Multicolor **Shape:** Rectangle

Date	Mintage	F12	VF20	XF40	MS60	MS63
2010	900	PF65 12,000				

KM# 1948 2000 YUAN
155.50 g., 0.999 Gold 4.9623 oz. AGW **Subject:** Yungang Grotto Art

Date	Mintage	F12	VF20	XF40	MS60	MS63
2010	800	PF65 12,000				

KM# 1802 2000 YUAN
155.67 g., 0.999 Gold 4.9677 oz. AGW, 90 mm. **Subject:** UNESCO **Rev:** Taishi Que

Date	Mintage	F12	VF20	XF40	MS60	MS63
2011	Est. 1000	PF65 10,000				

KM# 1819 2000 YUAN
155.67 g., 0.999 Gold 4.9677 oz. AGW, 64x40 mm. **Subject:** Chinese Literature **Rev:** Huyan Zhuo and Guan Sheng in color

Date	Mintage	F12	VF20	XF40	MS60	MS63
2011	900	PF65 11,000				

KM# 2045 2000 YUAN
155.67 g., 0.999 Gold 4.9677 oz. AGW, 60 mm. **Subject:** UNESCO **Rev:** Xiantong Temple

Date	Mintage	F12	VF20	XF40	MS60	MS63
2012	3,000	PF65 11,000				

KM# 2051 2000 YUAN
155.67 g., 0.999 Gold 4.9677 oz. AGW, 60 mm. **Subject:** Beijing Opera Masks **Rev:** Guan Yu mask in color

Date	Mintage	F12	VF20	XF40	MS60	MS63
2012	2,000	PF65 11,000				

KM# 2056 2000 YUAN
155.67 g., 0.999 Gold 4.9677 oz. AGW, 40 mm. **Subject:** Bronze Age Containers **Rev:** Storrage vessel from the Shang Dynastie, Zhengzhou find

Date	Mintage	F12	VF20	XF40	MS60	MS63
2012	30,000	PF65 8,500				

KM# 2062 2000 YUAN
155.67 g., 0.999 Gold 4.9677 oz. AGW, 60 mm. **Subject:** Panda, 30th Anniversary **Obv:** Temple of Heaven **Rev:** Panda

Date	Mintage	F12	VF20	XF40	MS60	MS63
2012	3,000	PF65 11,500				

KM# 2054 3000 YUAN
1000.00 g., 0.999 Silver 31.9118 oz. ASW, 100 mm. **Subject:** Bronze Age Vessels **Rev:** Shang Dynasty wine container

Date	Mintage	F12	VF20	XF40	MS60	MS63
2012	6,000	PF65 1,750				

KM# 1893 10000 YUAN
1000.00 g., 0.999 Gold 31.9118 oz. AGW, 90 mm. **Subject:** P.R.C. 60th Anniversary

Date	Mintage	F12	VF20	XF40	MS60	MS63
2009	100	PF65 60,000				

KM# 1947 10000 YUAN
1000.00 g., 0.999 Gold 31.9118 oz. AGW **Subject:** Yungang Grotto Art

Date	Mintage	F12	VF20	XF40	MS60	MS63
2010	100	PF65 60,000				

KM# 1803 10000 YUAN
1000.00 g., 0.999 Gold 31.9118 oz. AGW, 90 mm. **Subject:** UNESCO **Rev:** Observatory

Date	Mintage	F12	VF20	XF40	MS60	MS63
2011	200	PF65 60,000				

KM# 1869 10000 YUAN
1000.00 g., 0.999 Gold 31.9118 oz. AGW, 90 mm. **Subject:** Chinese Literature **Rev:** Meeting in the great hall in color

Date	Mintage	F12	VF20	XF40	MS60	MS63
2011	200	PF65 60,000				

KM# 2046 10000 YUAN
1000.00 g., 0.999 Gold 31.9118 oz. AGW, 90 mm. **Subject:** UNESCO **Rev:** Foguang Temple

Date	Mintage	F12	VF20	XF40	MS60	MS63
2012	300	PF65 60,000				

KM# 1851 100000 YUAN
10000.00 g., 0.999 Gold 319.1184 oz. AGW, 180 mm. **Subject:** Beijing Olympics **Obv:** Multicolor logo **Rev:** Sports montage, Temple of Heaven

Date	Mintage	F12	VF20	XF40	MS60	MS63
2008	29	PF65 650,000				

SILVER BULLION COINAGE
Lunar Series

KM# 1379 10 YUAN
30.84 g., 0.999 Silver 0.9842 oz. ASW, 39.9 mm. **Subject:** Year of the Snake **Obv:** Traditional style building **Rev:** Snake **Shape:** Scalloped **Note:** Prev. Y#1041.

Date	Mintage	F12	VF20	XF40	MS60	MS63
2001	6,800	PF65 165				

KM# 1382 10 YUAN
31.10 g., 0.999 Silver 0.9926 oz. ASW **Subject:** Year of the Snake **Shape:** Fan-like **Note:** Prev. Y#1042.

Date	Mintage	F12	VF20	XF40	MS60	MS63
2001	66,000	—	—	—	100	115

KM# 1375 10 YUAN
31.10 g., 0.999 Silver 0.9926 oz. ASW, 40 mm. **Subject:** Year of the Snake **Rev:** Multicolor

Date	Mintage	F12	VF20	XF40	MS60	MS63
2001	6,800	PF65 150				

KM# 1418 10 YUAN
31.10 g., 0.999 Silver 0.9926 oz. ASW, 40 mm. **Subject:** Year of the Horse **Obv:** Da Zheng Hall **Rev:** Stylized horse head **Edge:** Reeded **Note:** Prev. Y#1232.

Date	Mintage	F12	VF20	XF40	MS60	MS63
2002	50,000	—	—	—	—	140

KM# 1414 10 YUAN
31.10 g., 0.999 Silver 0.9926 oz. ASW, 40 mm. **Subject:** Year of the Horse **Rev:** Multicolor horse prancing right

Date	Mintage	F12	VF20	XF40	MS60	MS63
2002	10,000	PF65 150				

KM# 1423 10 YUAN
31.10 g., 0.999 Silver 0.9926 oz. ASW, 40 mm. **Subject:** Year of the Horse **Shape:** Fan-like

Date	Mintage	F12	VF20	XF40	MS60	MS63
2002	50,000	PF65 175				

KM# 1425 10 YUAN
31.10 g., 0.999 Silver 0.9926 oz. ASW, 40 mm. **Subject:** Year of the Horse **Shape:** Scalloped

Date	Mintage	F12	VF20	XF40	MS60	MS63
2002	6,800	PF65 400				

KM# A1477 10 YUAN
31.10 g., 0.999 Silver 0.9926 oz. ASW, 40 mm. **Subject:** Year of the Sheep

Date	Mintage	F12	VF20	XF40	MS60	MS63
2003	66,000	PF65 150				

KM# 1477 10 YUAN
31.10 g., 0.999 Silver 0.9926 oz. ASW, 40 mm. **Subject:** Year of the Sheep **Rev:** Multicolor

Date	Mintage	F12	VF20	XF40	MS60	MS63
2003	6,800	PF65 150				

KM# 1480 10 YUAN
31.10 g., 0.999 Silver 0.9926 oz. ASW, 40 mm. **Subject:** Year of the sheep **Shape:** Scalloped

Date	Mintage	F12	VF20	XF40	MS60	MS63
2003	50,000	PF65 70.00				

KM# 1485 10 YUAN
31.10 g., 0.999 Silver 0.9926 oz. ASW, 30 x 85 mm. **Subject:** Year of the Sheep **Shape:** Fan-like

Date	Mintage	F12	VF20	XF40	MS60	MS63
2003	66,000	PF65 175				

KM# 1545 10 YUAN
31.10 g., 0.999 Silver 0.9926 oz. ASW, 40 mm. **Series:** Lunar New Year **Subject:** Year of the Monkey

Date	Mintage	F12	VF20	XF40	MS60	MS63
2004	80,000	PF65 150				

KM# A1545 10 YUAN
31.10 g., 0.999 Silver 0.9926 oz. ASW, 40 mm. **Series:** Lunar New Year **Subject:** Year of the Monkey **Rev:** Multicolor monkey

Date	Mintage	F12	VF20	XF40	MS60	MS63
2004	—	PF65 150				

KM# 1548 10 YUAN
31.10 g., 0.999 Silver 0.9926 oz. ASW, 40 mm. **Subject:** Lunar New Year **Rev:** Monkey **Shape:** Scalloped

Date	Mintage	F12	VF20	XF40	MS60	MS63
2004	6,800	PF65 190				

KM# 1553 10 YUAN
31.10 g., 0.999 Silver 0.9926 oz. ASW, 30 x 85 mm. **Series:** Lunar New Year **Subject:** Year of the Monkey **Rev:** Monkey **Shape:** Fan-like

Date	Mintage	F12	VF20	XF40	MS60	MS63
2004	66,000	PF65 175				

KM# 1612 10 YUAN
31.11 g., 0.999 Silver 0.9926 oz. ASW, 40 mm. **Subject:** Year of the rooster **Obv:** Classical rooster **Rev:** Multicolor rooster

Date	Mintage	F12	VF20	XF40	MS60	MS63
2005	100,000	PF65 190				

KM# 1613 10 YUAN
31.11 g., 0.999 Silver 0.9926 oz. ASW, 40 mm. **Subject:** Year of the rooster **Obv:** Classical rooster **Rev:** Rooster, hen and chicks **Shape:** Scallop

Date	Mintage	F12	VF20	XF40	MS60	MS63
2005	60,000	PF65 125				

KM# 1614 10 YUAN
31.11 g., 0.999 Silver 0.9926 oz. ASW, 40 mm. **Subject:** Year of the rooster **Obv:** Classical rooster **Rev:** Rooster, hen and chicks

Date	Mintage	F12	VF20	XF40	MS60	MS63
2005	8,000	PF65 150				

KM# 1615 10 YUAN
31.11 g., 0.999 Silver 0.9926 oz. ASW, 30 x 85 mm. **Subject:** Year of the rooster **Obv:** Temple **Rev:** Rooster, hen and chicks **Shape:** Fan-like **Note:** Photo reduced.

Date	Mintage	F12	VF20	XF40	MS60	MS63
2005	66,000	PF65 190				

KM# 1684 10 YUAN
31.10 g., 0.999 Silver 0.9926 oz. ASW, 40 mm. **Obv:** Dog-shaped belt-hook from ancient Chinese bronze ware, decorative design of dog tail-shaped plant leaves **Rev:** 2 smart dogs **Note:** Prev. Y#1225; 1657.

Date	Mintage	F12	VF20	XF40	MS60	MS63
2006	80,000	—	—	—	—	125

KM# 1685 10 YUAN
31.10 g., 0.999 Silver 0.9926 oz. ASW, 40 mm. **Obv:** Dog-shaped belt-hook depicted from ancient Chinese bronze ware and a decorative design of dog tail-shaped plant leaves **Rev:** 2 smart dogs **Shape:** Scalloped **Note:** Prev. Y#1223; KM#1655.

Date	Mintage	F12	VF20	XF40	MS60	MS63
2006	60,000	PF65 140				

KM# 1686 10 YUAN
31.10 g., 0.999 Silver 0.9926 oz. ASW **Obv:** Qing Yuan Gate of the China Great Wall **Rev:** 2 dogs at play **Shape:** Fan-like **Note:** Prev. Y#1219; KM#1651. Photo reduced.

Date	Mintage	F12	VF20	XF40	MS60	MS63
2006	66,000	PF65 165				

KM# 1687 10 YUAN
31.10 g., 0.999 Silver 0.9926 oz. ASW, 40 mm. **Obv:** Belt-hook in dog shape from Chinese ancient bronze ware and a decorative design of dog tail-shaped plant leaves **Rev:** 2 dogs at play **Note:** Prev. Y#1221; KM#1653.

Date	Mintage	F12	VF20	XF40	MS60	MS63
2006	100,000	PF65 125				

KM# 1716 10 YUAN
31.11 g., 0.999 Silver 0.9926 oz. ASW, 40 mm. **Subject:** Year of the Pig **Obv:** Classical pig **Rev:** Pig walking right

Date	Mintage	F12	VF20	XF40	MS60	MS63
2007	80,000	PF65 140				

KM# 1717 10 YUAN
31.11 g., 0.999 Silver 0.9926 oz. ASW, 40 mm. **Subject:** Year of the Pig **Obv:** Classical pig **Rev:** Multicolor sow and four piglets sucking

Date	Mintage	F12	VF20	XF40	MS60	MS63
2007	100,000	PF65 125				

KM# 1718 10 YUAN
31.11 g., 0.999 Silver 0.9926 oz. ASW, 85 x 60 mm. **Subject:** Year of the Pig **Obv:** Temple **Rev:** Sow and four piglets **Shape:** Fan-like

Date	Mintage	F12	VF20	XF40	MS60	MS63
2007	66,000	PF65 190				

KM# 1719 10 YUAN
31.11 g., 0.999 Silver 0.9926 oz. ASW, 40 mm. **Subject:** Year of the Pig **Obv:** Classical pig **Rev:** Pig walking right **Shape:** Scalloped

Date	Mintage	F12	VF20	XF40	MS60	MS63
2007	60,000	PF65 140				

KM# 1830 10 YUAN
31.11 g., 0.999 Silver 0.9926 oz. ASW, 40 mm. **Rev:** Multicolor

Date	Mintage	F12	VF20	XF40	MS60	MS63
2008	—	PF65 60.00				

KM# 1831 10 YUAN
31.11 g., 0.999 Silver 0.9926 oz. ASW, 40 mm. **Subject:** Year of the Rat

Date	Mintage	F12	VF20	XF40	MS60	MS63
2008	—	PF65 140				

KM# 1832 10 YUAN
31.11 g., 0.999 Silver 0.9926 oz. ASW, 40 mm. **Subject:** Year of the Rat **Shape:** Scallop

Date	Mintage	F12	VF20	XF40	MS60	MS63
2008	—	PF65 140				

KM# 1833 10 YUAN
31.11 g., 0.999 Silver 0.9926 oz. ASW, 85 x 60 mm. **Subject:** Year of the Rat **Shape:** Fan-like

Date	Mintage	F12	VF20	XF40	MS60	MS63
2008	—	PF65 190				

KM# 1875 10 YUAN
31.11 g., 0.999 Silver 0.9926 oz. ASW, 40 mm. **Rev:** Multicolor

Date	Mintage	F12	VF20	XF40	MS60	MS63
2009	—	PF65 125				

KM# 1876 10 YUAN
31.11 g., 0.999 Silver 0.9926 oz. ASW, 40 mm. **Subject:** Year of the Ox

Date	Mintage	F12	VF20	XF40	MS60	MS63
2009	100,000	PF63 115	PF65 125			

KM# 1877 10 YUAN
31.11 g., 0.999 Silver 0.9926 oz. ASW **Subject:** Year of the Ox

Date	Mintage	F12	VF20	XF40	MS60	MS63
2009	66,000	PF63 135	PF65 145			

KM# 1878 10 YUAN
31.11 g., 0.999 Silver 0.9926 oz. ASW **Shape:** Fan-like

Date	Mintage	F12	VF20	XF40	MS60	MS63
2009	66,000	PF65 190				

KM# 1922 10 YUAN
31.11 g., 0.999 Silver 0.9926 oz. ASW **Subject:** Year of the Tiger **Shape:** Arc

Date	Mintage	F12	VF20	XF40	MS60	MS63
2010	66,000	—	—	—	—	100

KM# 1923 10 YUAN
31.11 g., 0.999 Silver 0.9926 oz. ASW **Subject:** Year of the Tiger **Shape:** Scalloped

Date	Mintage	F12	VF20	XF40	MS60	MS63
2010	60,000	PF65 145				

KM# 1924 10 YUAN
31.11 g., 0.999 Silver 0.9926 oz. ASW **Subject:** Year of the Tiger

Date	Mintage	F12	VF20	XF40	MS60	MS63
2010	100,000	PF65 115				

KM# 1925 10 YUAN
31.11 g., 0.999 Silver 0.9926 oz. ASW **Subject:** Year of the Tiger **Rev:** Multicolor

Date	Mintage	F12	VF20	XF40	MS60	MS63
2010	100,000	PF65 135				

KM# 1971 10 YUAN
31.11 g., 0.999 Silver 0.9926 oz. ASW **Subject:** Year of the Rabbit **Shape:** Arc

Date	Mintage	F12	VF20	XF40	MS60	MS63
2011	66,000	—	—	—	—	100

KM# 1972 10 YUAN
31.11 g., 0.999 Silver 0.9926 oz. ASW **Subject:** Year of the Rabbit **Shape:** Scalloped

Date	Mintage	F12	VF20	XF40	MS60	MS63
2011	60,000	PF65 120				

KM# 1973 10 YUAN
31.11 g., 0.999 Silver 0.9926 oz. ASW, 40 mm. **Subject:** Year of the Rabbit

Date	Mintage	F12	VF20	XF40	MS60	MS63
2011	100,000	PF65 100				

KM# 1974 10 YUAN
31.11 g., 0.999 Silver 0.9926 oz. ASW **Subject:** Year of the Rabbit **Rev:** Multicolor

Date	Mintage	F12	VF20	XF40	MS60	MS63
2011	100,000	PF65 100				

KM# 2020 10 YUAN
31.11 g., 0.999 Silver 0.9926 oz. ASW **Subject:** Year of the Dragon **Shape:** Fan

Date	Mintage	F12	VF20	XF40	MS60	MS63
2012	—	PF65 145				

KM# 2021 10 YUAN
31.11 g., 0.999 Silver 0.9926 oz. ASW, 40 mm. **Subject:** Year of the Dragon **Shape:** Scalloped

Date	Mintage	F12	VF20	XF40	MS60	MS63
2012 proof	—	PF65 125				

KM# 2022 10 YUAN
31.11 g., 0.999 Silver 0.9926 oz. ASW, 40 mm. **Subject:** Year of the Dragon

Date	Mintage	F12	VF20	XF40	MS60	MS63
2012	—	PF65 75.00				

KM# 2023 10 YUAN
31.11 g., 0.999 Silver 0.9926 oz. ASW **Subject:** Year of the Dragon **Rev:** Colored dragon

Date	Mintage	F12	VF20	XF40	MS60	MS63
2012	—	PF65 110				

KM# 1377 50 YUAN
155.44 g., 0.999 Silver 4.9604 oz. ASW, 80.6 x 50.5 mm. **Subject:** Year of the Snake **Obv:** Traditional style building **Rev:** Snake **Edge:** Plain **Shape:** Rectangle **Note:** Illustration reduced. Prev. Y#1040.

Date	Mintage	F12	VF20	XF40	MS60	MS63
2001	1,888	PF65 1,250				

KM# 1421 50 YUAN
155.52 g., 0.999 Silver 4.9629 oz. ASW, 80 x 50 mm. **Subject:** Year of the Horse **Rev:** Three horses running left **Shape:** Rectangle

Date	Mintage	F12	VF20	XF40	MS60	MS63
2002	1,888	PF65 2,000				

KM# 1484 50 YUAN
155.50 g., 0.999 Silver 4.9623 oz. ASW, 80 x 50 mm. **Subject:** Year of the Sheep **Shape:** Rectangle

Date	Mintage	F12	VF20	XF40	MS60	MS63
2003	1,888	PF65 1,250				

KM# 1551 50 YUAN
155.50 g., 0.999 Silver 4.9623 oz. ASW, 80 x 50 mm. **Series:** Lunar New Year **Subject:** Year of the Monkey **Rev:** Monkey **Shape:** Rectangle **Note:** Photo reduced.

Date	Mintage	F12	VF20	XF40	MS60	MS63
2004	1,888	PF65 1,250				

KM# 1611 50 YUAN
155.00 g., 0.999 Silver 4.9463 oz. ASW, 80 x 50 mm. **Subject:** Year of the Rooster **Obv:** Classical rooster **Rev:** Rooster, hen and chicks **Shape:** Rectangle **Note:** Photo reduced.

Date	Mintage	F12	VF20	XF40	MS60	MS63
2005	1,888	PF65 1,250				

KM# 1683 50 YUAN
155.44 g., 0.999 Silver 4.9604 oz. ASW, 60 x 50 mm. **Subject:** Year of the Dog **Obv:** Classical dog **Rev:** Two dogs **Shape:** Rectangle **Note:** Photo reduced.

Date	Mintage	F12	VF20	XF40	MS60	MS63
2006	1,888	PF65 1,250				

KM# 1720 50 YUAN
155.55 g., 0.999 Silver 4.9639 oz. ASW, 80 x 50 mm. **Subject:** Year of the Pig **Obv:** Classical pig **Rev:** Sow and four pigletts **Shape:** Rectangle

Date	Mintage	F12	VF20	XF40	MS60	MS63
2007	1,888	PF65 1,250				

KM# 1834 50 YUAN
155.50 g., 0.999 Silver 4.9623 oz. ASW, 80 x 50 mm. **Subject:** Year of the Rat **Shape:** Rectangle

Date	Mintage	F12	VF20	XF40	MS60	MS63
2008	—	PF65 1,250				

KM# 1879 50 YUAN
Silver **Subject:** Year of the Ox

Date	Mintage	F12	VF20	XF40	MS60	MS63
2009	1,888	PF65 1,250				

KM# 1920 50 YUAN
155.50 g., 0.999 Silver 4.9623 oz. ASW **Subject:** Year of the Tiger **Shape:** Rectangle

Date	Mintage	F12	VF20	XF40	MS60	MS63
2010	1,888	PF65 1,250				

KM# 1921 50 YUAN
155.50 g., 0.999 Silver 4.9623 oz. ASW **Subject:** Year of the Tiger

Date	Mintage	F12	VF20	XF40	MS60	MS63
2010	8,800	PF65 850				

KM# 1969 50 YUAN
155.50 g., 0.999 Silver 4.9623 oz. ASW, 80x50 mm. **Subject:** Year of the Rabbit **Shape:** Rectangle **Note:** Photo reduced.

Date	Mintage	F12	VF20	XF40	MS60	MS63
2011	1,888	PF65 1,250				

KM# 1970 50 YUAN
155.50 g., 0.999 Silver 4.9623 oz. ASW **Subject:** Year of the Rabbit **Rev:** Multicolor

Date	Mintage	F12	VF20	XF40	MS60	MS63
2011	8,800	PF65 750				

KM# 2018 50 YUAN
155.55 g., 0.999 Silver 4.9639 oz. ASW, 80x50 mm. **Subject:** Year of the Dragon **Shape:** Rectangle

Date	Mintage	F12	VF20	XF40	MS60	MS63
2012	—	PF65 850				

KM# 2019 50 YUAN
155.55 g., 0.999 Silver 4.9639 oz. ASW **Subject:** Year of the Dragon **Rev:** Colored dragon

Date	Mintage	F12	VF20	XF40	MS60	MS63
2012 proof	—	PF65 750				

KM# 1420 300 YUAN
1000.00 g., 0.999 Silver 31.9118 oz. ASW, 100 mm. **Series:** Lunar **Subject:** Year of the Horse

Date	Mintage	F12	VF20	XF40	MS60	MS63
2002	3,800	PF65 6,500				

KM# 1479 300 YUAN
1000.00 g., 0.999 Silver 31.9118 oz. ASW, 100 mm. **Subject:** Year of the Sheep

Date	Mintage	F12	VF20	XF40	MS60	MS63
2003	3,800	PF65 7,500				

KM# 1547 300 YUAN
1000.00 g., 0.999 Silver 31.9118 oz. ASW, 100 mm. **Series:** Lunar New Year **Subject:** Year of the Monkey **Rev:** Monkey

Date	Mintage	F12	VF20	XF40	MS60	MS63
2004	3,800	PF65 9,000				

KM# 1610 300 YUAN
1000.00 g., 0.999 Silver 31.9118 oz. ASW, 100 mm. **Subject:** Year of the Rooster **Obv:** Classical rooster **Rev:** Rooster strutting **Note:** Photo reduced.

Date	Mintage	F12	VF20	XF40	MS60	MS63
2005	3,800	PF65 5,000				

KM# 1682 300 YUAN
1000.00 g., 0.999 Silver 31.9118 oz. ASW, 100 mm. **Obv:** Dog-shaped belt-hook from ancient Chinese bronze ware, decorative design of dog tail-shaped plant leaves **Rev:** 2 dogs **Note:** Prev. Y#1227; KM#1659. Photo reduced.

Date	Mintage	F12	VF20	XF40	MS60	MS63
2006	3,800	PF65 4,500				

KM# 1725 300 YUAN
1000.00 g., 0.999 Silver 31.9118 oz. ASW, 100 mm. **Subject:** Year of the Pig **Obv:** Classical pig **Rev:** Three pigs

Date	Mintage	F12	VF20	XF40	MS60	MS63
2007	3,800	PF65 5,000				

KM# 1839 300 YUAN
1000.00 g., 0.999 Silver 31.9118 oz. ASW, 100 mm. **Subject:** Year of the Rat

Date	Mintage	F12	VF20	XF40	MS60	MS63
2008	—	PF65 5,000				

KM# 1884 300 YUAN
1000.00 g., 0.999 Silver 31.9118 oz. ASW **Subject:** Year of the Ox

Date	Mintage	F12	VF20	XF40	MS60	MS63
2009	3,800	PF65 5,000				

KM# 1919 300 YUAN
1000.00 g., 0.999 Silver 31.9118 oz. ASW **Subject:** Year of the Tiger

Date	Mintage	F12	VF20	XF40	MS60	MS63
2010	3,800	PF65 4,500				

KM# 1968 300 YUAN
1000.00 g., 0.999 Silver 31.9118 oz. ASW, 100 mm. **Subject:** Year of the Rabbit **Note:** Photo reduced.

Date	Mintage	F12	VF20	XF40	MS60	MS63
2011	1,888	PF65 4,500				

KM# 2017 300 YUAN
1000.00 g., 0.999 Silver 31.9118 oz. ASW, 100 mm. **Subject:** Year of the Dragon

Date	Mintage	F12	VF20	XF40	MS60	MS63
2012	—	PF65 1,250				

SILVER BULLION COINAGE
Panda Series

KM# 1772 3 YUAN
7.77 g., 0.999 Silver 0.248 oz. ASW, 25 mm. **Obv:** Temple of Heaven **Rev:** Panda seated on rock

Date	Mintage	F12	VF20	XF40	MS60	MS63
2007	30,000	PF63 25.00		PF65 30.00		

KM# 1780 3 YUAN
7.77 g., 0.999 Silver 0.248 oz. ASW, 25 mm. **Obv:** Temple of Heaven **Rev:** Panda looking forward

Date	Mintage	F12	VF20	XF40	MS60	MS63
2007	30,000	PF63 25.00		PF65 30.00		

KM# 1740 3 YUAN
7.77 g., 0.999 Silver 0.248 oz. ASW, 25 mm. **Obv:** Temple of Heaven **Rev:** Panda seated with branch

Date	Mintage	F12	VF20	XF40	MS60	MS63
2007	30,000	PF63 25.00		PF65 30.00		

KM# 1742 3 YUAN
7.77 g., 0.999 Silver 0.248 oz. ASW, 25 mm. **Obv:** Temple of Heaven **Rev:** Panda walking right

Date	Mintage	F12	VF20	XF40	MS60	MS63
2007	30,000	PF63 25.00		PF65 30.00		

KM# 1744 3 YUAN
7.77 g., 0.999 Silver 0.248 oz. ASW, 25 mm. **Obv:** Temple of Heaven **Rev:** Panda seated with bamboo branch

Date	Mintage	F12	VF20	XF40	MS60	MS63
2007	30,000	PF63 25.00		PF65 30.00		

KM# 1746 3 YUAN
7.77 g., 0.999 Silver 0.248 oz. ASW **Obv:** Temple of Heaven **Rev:** Panda hanging from branch

Date	Mintage	F12	VF20	XF40	MS60	MS63
2007	30,000	PF63 25.00		PF65 30.00		

KM# 1748 3 YUAN
7.77 g., 0.999 Silver 0.248 oz. ASW, 25 mm. **Obv:** Temple of Heaven **Rev:** Panda walking forward

Date	Mintage	F12	VF20	XF40	MS60	MS63
2007	30,000	PF63 25.00	PF65 30.00			

KM# 1750 3 YUAN
7.77 g., 0.999 Silver 0.248 oz. ASW, 25 mm. **Obv:** Temple of Heaven **Rev:** Panda drinking water

Date	Mintage	F12	VF20	XF40	MS60	MS63
2007	30,000	PF63 25.00	PF65 30.00			

KM# 1752 3 YUAN
7.77 g., 0.999 Silver 0.248 oz. ASW, 25 mm. **Obv:** Temple of Heaven **Rev:** Panda seated in oval with branch

Date	Mintage	F12	VF20	XF40	MS60	MS63
2007	30,000	PF63 25.00	PF65 30.00			

KM# 1754 3 YUAN
7.77 g., 0.999 Silver 0.248 oz. ASW, 25 mm. **Obv:** Temple of Heaven **Rev:** Panda seated on geometric background

Date	Mintage	F12	VF20	XF40	MS60	MS63
2007	30,000	PF63 25.00	PF65 30.00			

KM# 1756 3 YUAN
7.77 g., 0.999 Silver 0.248 oz. ASW, 10 mm. **Obv:** Temple of Heaven **Rev:** Panda on rock

Date	Mintage	F12	VF20	XF40	MS60	MS63
2007	30,000	PF63 25.00	PF65 30.00			

KM# 1758 3 YUAN
7.77 g., 0.999 Silver 0.248 oz. ASW, 25 mm. **Obv:** Temple of Heaven **Rev:** Panda seated on river bank

Date	Mintage	F12	VF20	XF40	MS60	MS63
2007	30,000	PF63 25.00	PF65 30.00			

KM# 1760 3 YUAN
7.77 g., 0.999 Silver 0.248 oz. ASW, 25 mm. **Obv:** Temple of Heaven **Rev:** Panda on tree branch

Date	Mintage	F12	VF20	XF40	MS60	MS63
2007	30,000	PF63 25.00	PF65 30.00			

KM# 1762 3 YUAN
7.77 g., 0.999 Silver 0.248 oz. ASW, 25 mm. **Obv:** Temple of Heaven **Rev:** Panda on rock ledge

Date	Mintage	F12	VF20	XF40	MS60	MS63
2007	30,000	PF63 25.00	PF65 30.00			

KM# 1764 3 YUAN
7.77 g., 0.999 Silver 0.248 oz. ASW, 25 mm. **Obv:** Temple of Heaven **Rev:** Panda seated munching bamboo

Date	Mintage	F12	VF20	XF40	MS60	MS63
2007	30,000	PF63 25.00	PF65 30.00			

KM# 1766 3 YUAN
7.77 g., 0.999 Silver 0.248 oz. ASW, 25 mm. **Obv:** Temple of Heaven **Rev:** Panda pulling bamboo

Date	Mintage	F12	VF20	XF40	MS60	MS63
2007	30,000	PF63 25.00	PF65 30.00			

KM# 1768 3 YUAN
7.77 g., 0.999 Silver 0.248 oz. ASW, 25 mm. **Obv:** Temple of Heaven **Rev:** Panda in tree

Date	Mintage	F12	VF20	XF40	MS60	MS63
2007	30,000	PF63 25.00	PF65 30.00			

KM# 1770 3 YUAN
7.77 g., 0.999 Silver 0.248 oz. ASW, 25 mm. **Obv:** Temple of Heaven **Rev:** Panda looking over branch

Date	Mintage	F12	VF20	XF40	MS60	MS63
2007	30,000	PF63 25.00	PF65 30.00			

KM# 1774 3 YUAN
7.77 g., 0.999 Silver 0.248 oz. ASW, 25 mm. **Obv:** Temple of Heaven **Rev:** Panda looking out over rock

Date	Mintage	F12	VF20	XF40	MS60	MS63
2007	30,000	PF63 25.00	PF65 30.00			

KM# A1776 3 YUAN
7.77 g., 0.999 Silver 0.248 oz. ASW, 25 mm. **Obv:** Temple of Heaven **Rev:** Panda seated on frosted background

Date	Mintage	F12	VF20	XF40	MS60	MS63
2007	30,000	PF63 25.00	PF65 30.00			

KM# 1778 3 YUAN
7.77 g., 0.999 Silver 0.248 oz. ASW, 25 mm. **Obv:** Temple of Heaven **Rev:** Panda walking amongst bamboo

Date	Mintage	F12	VF20	XF40	MS60	MS63
2007	30,000	PF63 25.00	PF65 30.00			

KM# 1782 3 YUAN
7.77 g., 0.999 Silver 0.248 oz. ASW, 25 mm. **Obv:** Temple of Heaven **Rev:** Panda and cub walking right

Date	Mintage	F12	VF20	XF40	MS60	MS63
2007	30,000	PF63 25.00	PF65 30.00			

KM# 1784 3 YUAN
7.77 g., 0.999 Silver 0.248 oz. ASW, 25 mm. **Obv:** Temple of Heaven **Rev:** Panda seated with cub on left

Date	Mintage	F12	VF20	XF40	MS60	MS63
2007	30,000	PF63 25.00	PF65 30.00			

KM# 1786 3 YUAN
7.77 g., 0.999 Silver 0.248 oz. ASW, 25 mm. **Obv:** Temple of Heaven **Rev:** Panda seated with cub on right

Date	Mintage	F12	VF20	XF40	MS60	MS63
2007	30,000	PF63 25.00	PF65 30.00			

KM# 1788 3 YUAN
7.77 g., 0.999 Silver 0.248 oz. ASW, 25 mm. **Obv:** Temple of Heaven **Rev:** Panda seated with cub, both munching bamboo

Date	Mintage	F12	VF20	XF40	MS60	MS63
2007	30,000	PF63 25.00	PF65 30.00			

KM# 1365 10 YUAN
31.10 g., 0.999 Silver 0.9926 oz. ASW, 40.1 mm. **Obv:** Temple of Heaven with incuse legend **Rev:** Panda walking left through bamboo **Edge:** Oblique reeding **Note:** Large and small date varieties exist. Prev. Y#1111.

Date	Mintage	F12	VF20	XF40	MS60	MS63
2001	250,000	—	—		50.00	45.00
2001 D		PF63 65.00	PF65 75.00			
2002		PF63 65.00	PF65 75.00			

KM# A1365 10 YUAN
31.23 g., 0.999 Silver 0.9966 oz. ASW, 40 mm. **Obv:** Temple of Heaven, incuse legend **Rev:** Multicolor panda walking in bamboo **Edge:** Slanted reeding **Note:** Large and small date varieties exist.

Date	Mintage	F12	VF20	XF40	MS60	MS63
2002	—	PF63 80.00	PF65 90.00			

Note: Privately colored

KM# 1466 10 YUAN
31.10 g., 0.999 Silver 0.9926 oz. ASW, 40 mm. **Obv:** Temple of Heaven **Rev:** Panda eating bamboo in a frosted circle **Edge:** Slant reeded **Note:** Prev. Y#1244.

Date	Mintage	F12	VF20	XF40	MS60	MS63
2003	—	PF63 80.00	PF65 90.00			

KM# 1528 10 YUAN
31.10 g., 0.999 Silver 0.9926 oz. ASW, 40 mm. **Obv:** Temple of Heaven **Rev:** Panda nuzzling her cub **Edge:** Slant reeded **Note:** Prev. Y#1245.

Date	Mintage	F12	VF20	XF40	MS60	MS63
2004	—	PF63 80.00	PF65 90.00			

KM# 1589 10 YUAN
31.11 g., 0.999 Silver 0.9926 oz. ASW, 40 mm. **Obv:** Temple of Heaven **Rev:** Panda cub and mom seated in bamboo

Date	Mintage	F12	VF20	XF40	MS60	MS63
2005	60,000	PF63 80.00	PF65 90.00			

KM# 1664 10 YUAN
31.11 g., 0.999 Silver 0.9926 oz. ASW, 40 mm. **Obv:** Temple of Heaven **Rev:** Two pandas seated with bamboo

Date	Mintage	F12	VF20	XF40	MS60	MS63
2006	600,000	PF63 65.00	PF65 75.00			

KM# 1706 10 YUAN
31.11 g., 0.999 Silver 0.9926 oz. ASW, 40 mm. **Obv:** Temple of Heaven **Rev:** Two pandas, one walking, one seated

Date	Mintage	F12	VF20	XF40	MS60	MS63
2007	600,000	PF63 65.00	PF65 75.00			

KM# 1865 10 YUAN
31.11 g., 0.999 Silver 0.9926 oz. ASW, 40 mm. **Obv:** Temple of Heaven **Rev:** Adult panda at left, facing left, cub on right facing left, cub seated

Date	Mintage	F12	VF20	XF40	MS60	MS63
2008	—	PF63 60.00	PF65 70.00			

KM# 1814 10 YUAN
31.11 g., 0.999 Silver 0.9926 oz. ASW, 40 mm. **Rev:** Panda cub pawing mom

Date	Mintage	F12	VF20	XF40	MS60	MS63
2008	—	PF63 60.00	PF65 70.00			

KM# 1931 10 YUAN
31.11 g., 0.999 Silver 0.9926 oz. ASW, 40 mm. **Obv:** Temple of Heaven **Rev:** Two pandas, one lying on back

Date	Mintage	F12	VF20	XF40	MS80	MS83
2010	800,000	—	—		—	60.00

KM# 1980 10 YUAN
31.11 g., 0.999 Silver 0.9926 oz. ASW, 40 mm.

Date	Mintage	F12	VF20	XF40	MS60	MS63
2011	—	—	—		—	45.00

KM# 2029 10 YUAN
31.11 g., 0.999 Silver 0.9926 oz. ASW, 40 mm.

Date	Mintage	F12	VF20	XF40	MS60	MS63
2012	—	—	—		—	50.00

KM# 1468 50 YUAN
151.50 g., 0.999 Silver 4.8346 oz. ASW, 80 x 50 mm. **Rev: Designer:** Panda and bamboo **Shape:** Rectangle

Date	Mintage	F12	VF20	XF40	MS60	MS63
2003	1,888	PF65 1,150				

KM# 1530 50 YUAN
155.50 g., 0.999 Silver 4.9623 oz. ASW, 70 mm. **Rev:** Panda walking with cub **Note:** Illustration reduced.

Date	Mintage	F12	VF20	XF40	MS60	MS63
2004	10,000	PF65 600				

KM# 1588 50 YUAN
155.00 g., 0.999 Silver 4.9463 oz. ASW, 70 mm. **Obv:** Temple of Heaven **Rev:** Panda cub and mom seated in bamboo

Date	Mintage	F12	VF20	XF40	MS60	MS63
2005	10,000	PF65 550				

KM# 1663 50 YUAN
155.55 g., 0.999 Silver 4.9639 oz. ASW, 70 mm. **Obv:** Temple of Heaven **Rev:** Two pandas seated with bamboo

Date	Mintage	F12	VF20	XF40	MS60	MS63
2006	10,000	PF65 550				

KM# 1708 50 YUAN
155.55 g., 0.999 Silver 4.9639 oz. ASW, 70 mm. **Obv:** Temple of Heaven **Rev:** Two pandas, one walking, one seated

Date	Mintage	F12	VF20	XF40	MS60	MS63
2007	10,000	PF65 550				

KM# 1867 50 YUAN
155.50 g., 0.999 Silver 4.9623 oz. ASW

Date	Mintage	F12	VF20	XF40	MS60	MS63
2008		PF65 550				

KM# 1816 50 YUAN
155.50 g., Silver, 70 mm. **Rev:** Panda cub pawing mom

Date	Mintage	F12	VF20	XF40	MS60	MS63
2008		PF65 550				

KM# 1935 50 YUAN
155.55 g., 0.999 Silver 4.9639 oz. ASW **Obv:** Temple of Heaven **Rev:** Two pandas, one lying on back

Date	Mintage	F12	VF20	XF40	MS60	MS63
2010	10,000	PF65 650				

KM# 1984 50 YUAN
155.55 g., 0.999 Silver 4.9639 oz. ASW

Date	Mintage	F12	VF20	XF40	MS60	MS63
2011	—	PF65 500				

KM# 2033 50 YUAN
155.55 g., 0.999 Silver 4.9639 oz. ASW, 70 mm.

Date	Mintage	F12	VF20	XF40	MS60	MS63
2012	—	PF65 650				

KM# 1370 300 YUAN
1000.00 g., 0.999 Silver 31.9118 oz. ASW, 100 mm. **Rev:** Panda walking thru bamboo

Date	Mintage	F12	VF20	XF40	MS60	MS63
2001 D	2,000	PF65 2,500				

KM# 1416 300 YUAN
1000.00 g., 0.999 Silver 31.9118 oz. ASW, 100 mm. **Subject:** Panda Coinage 20th Anniversary **Obv:** Temple of Heaven **Rev:** Two gold inserts with the 1982 and 2002 panda designs on bamboo leaves **Edge:** Plain **Note:** Large and small date varieties exist. Prev. Y#1116.

Date	Mintage	F12	VF20	XF40	MS60	MS63
2002	6,000	PF65 3,000				

KM# 1473 300 YUAN
1000.00 g., 0.999 Silver 31.9118 oz. ASW **Rev:** Panda and bamboo **Shape:** 100

Date	Mintage	F12	VF20	XF40	MS60	MS63
2003	7,500	PF65 2,000				

KM# 1536 300 YUAN
1000.00 g., 0.999 Silver 31.9118 oz. ASW, 100 mm. **Rev:** Panda walking with cub

Date	Mintage	F12	VF20	XF40	MS60	MS63
2004	4,000	PF65 2,000				

KM# 1587 300 YUAN
1000.00 g., 0.999 Silver 31.9118 oz. ASW, 100 mm. **Obv:** Temple of Heaven **Rev:** Panda cub and mom seated in bamboo **Note:** Photo reduced.

Date	Mintage	F12	VF20	XF40	MS60	MS63
2005	4,000	PF65 2,250				

KM# 1662 300 YUAN
1000.00 g., 0.999 Silver 31.9118 oz. ASW, 100 mm. **Obv:** Temple of Heaven **Rev:** Two pandas seated with bamboo **Note:** Photo reduced.

Date	Mintage	F12	VF20	XF40	MS60	MS63
2006	4,000	PF65 2,250				

KM# 1712 300 YUAN
1000.00 g., 0.999 Silver 31.9118 oz. ASW, 100 mm. **Obv:** Temple of Heaven **Rev:** Two pandas, one walking, one seated

Date	Mintage	F12	VF20	XF40	MS60	MS63
2007	4,000	PF65 2,250				

KM# 1820 300 YUAN
1000.00 g., 0.999 Silver 31.9118 oz. ASW, 100 mm. **Rev:** Panda cub pawing mom

Date	Mintage	F12	VF20	XF40	MS60	MS63
2008	—	PF65 2,000				

KM# 1871 300 YUAN
1000.00 g., 0.999 Silver 31.9118 oz. ASW

Date	Mintage	F12	VF20	XF40	MS60	MS63
2008	—	PF65 2,000				

KM# 1934 300 YUAN
1000.00 g., 0.999 Silver 31.9118 oz. ASW **Obv:** Temple of Heaven **Rev:** Two pandas, one lying on back

Date	Mintage	F12	VF20	XF40	MS60	MS63
2010	4,000	PF65 1,500				

KM# 1983 300 YUAN
1000.00 g., 0.999 Silver 31.9118 oz. ASW, 100 mm.

Date	Mintage	F12	VF20	XF40	MS60	MS63
2011	—	PF65 1,250				

KM# 2032 300 YUAN
1000.00 g., 0.999 Silver 31.9118 oz. ASW, 100 mm.

Date	Mintage	F12	VF20	XF40	MS60	MS63
2012	—	PF65 1,500				

GOLD BULLION COINAGE
Panda Series

KM# 1779 15 YUAN
1.24 g., 0.999 Gold 0.0396 oz. AGW, 12 mm. **Obv:** Temple of Heaven **Rev:** Panda walking amongst bamboo

Date	Mintage	F12	VF20	XF40	MS60	MS63
2007	18,000	PF65 95.00				

KM# 1741 15 YUAN
1.24 g., 0.999 Gold 0.0396 oz. AGW, 12 mm. **Obv:** Temple of Heaven **Rev:** Panda seated with branch

Date	Mintage	F12	VF20	XF40	MS60	MS63
2007	18,000	PF65 95.00				

KM# 1743 15 YUAN
1.24 g., 0.999 Gold 0.0396 oz. AGW, 12 mm. **Obv:** Temple of heaven **Rev:** Panda walking right

Date	Mintage	F12	VF20	XF40	MS60	MS63
2007	18,000	PF65 95.00				

KM# 1745 15 YUAN
1.24 g., 0.999 Gold 0.0396 oz. AGW, 12 mm. **Obv:** Temple of heaven **Rev:** Panda seated with bamboo branch

Date	Mintage	F12	VF20	XF40	MS60	MS63
2007	18,000	PF65 95.00				

KM# 1747 15 YUAN
1.24 g., 0.999 Gold 0.0396 oz. AGW, 12 mm. **Obv:** Temple of Heaven **Rev:** Panda hanging from branch

Date	Mintage	F12	VF20	XF40	MS60	MS63
2007	18,000	PF65 95.00				

KM# 1749 15 YUAN
1.24 g., 0.999 Gold 0.0396 oz. AGW, 12 mm. **Obv:** Temple of Heaven **Rev:** Panda walking forward

Date	Mintage	F12	VF20	XF40	MS60	MS63
2007	18,000	PF65 95.00				

KM# 1751 15 YUAN
1.24 g., 0.999 Gold 0.0396 oz. AGW, 12 mm. **Obv:** Temple of Heaven **Rev:** Panda drinking water

Date	Mintage	F12	VF20	XF40	MS60	MS63
2007	18,000	PF65 95.00				

KM# 1753 15 YUAN
1.24 g., 0.999 Gold 0.0396 oz. AGW, 12 mm. **Obv:** Temple of Heaven **Rev:** Panda seated in oval with branch

Date	Mintage	F12	VF20	XF40	MS60	MS63
2007	18,000	PF65 95.00				

KM# 1755 15 YUAN
1.24 g., 0.999 Gold 0.0396 oz. AGW, 12 mm. **Rev:** Panda seated on geometric background

Date	Mintage	F12	VF20	XF40	MS60	MS63
2007	18,000	PF65 95.00				

KM# 1757 15 YUAN
1.24 g., 0.999 Gold 0.0396 oz. AGW, 12 mm. **Obv:** Temple of Heaven **Rev:** Panda on rock

Date	Mintage	F12	VF20	XF40	MS60	MS63
2007	18,000	PF65 95.00				

KM# 1759 15 YUAN
1.24 g., 0.999 Gold 0.0396 oz. AGW, 12 mm. **Obv:** Temple of Heaven **Rev:** Panda seated on river bank

Date	Mintage	F12	VF20	XF40	MS60	MS63
2007	18,000	PF65 95.00				

KM# 1761 15 YUAN
1.24 g., 0.999 Gold 0.0396 oz. AGW, 12 mm. **Obv:** Temple of Heaven **Rev:** Panda on tree branch

Date	Mintage	F12	VF20	XF40	MS60	MS63
2007	18,000	PF65 95.00				

KM# 1763 15 YUAN
1.24 g., 0.999 Gold 0.0396 oz. AGW, 12 mm. **Obv:** Temple of Heaven **Rev:** Panda on rock ledge

Date	Mintage	F12	VF20	XF40	MS60	MS63
2007	18,000	PF65 95.00				

KM# 1765 15 YUAN
1.24 g., 0.999 Gold 0.0396 oz. AGW, 12 mm. **Obv:** Temple of Heaven **Rev:** Panda seated munching bamboo

Date	Mintage	F12	VF20	XF40	MS60	MS63
2007	18,000	PF65 95.00				

KM# 1767 15 YUAN
1.24 g., 0.999 Gold 0.0396 oz. AGW **Obv:** Temple of Heaven **Rev:** Panda pulling bamboo **Shape:** 12

Date	Mintage	F12	VF20	XF40	MS60	MS63
2007	1,800	PF65 95.00				

KM# 1769 15 YUAN
1.24 g., 0.999 Gold 0.0396 oz. AGW, 12 mm. **Obv:** Temple of Heaven **Rev:** Panda in tree

Date	Mintage	F12	VF20	XF40	MS60	MS63
2007	18,000	PF65 95.00				

KM# 1771 15 YUAN
1.24 g., 0.999 Gold 0.0396 oz. AGW **Obv:** Temple of Heaven **Rev:** Panda looking over branch

Date	Mintage	F12	VF20	XF40	MS60	MS63
2007	18,000	PF65 95.00				

KM# 1773 15 YUAN
1.24 g., 0.999 Gold 0.0396 oz. AGW, 12 mm. **Obv:** Temple of Heaven **Rev:** Panda seated on rock

Date	Mintage	F12	VF20	XF40	MS60	MS63
2007	18,000	PF65 95.00				

KM# A1775 15 YUAN
1.24 g., 0.999 Gold 0.0396 oz. AGW, 12 mm. **Obv:** Temple of Heaven **Rev:** Panda looking out from rock

Date	Mintage	F12	VF20	XF40	MS60	MS63
2007	18,000	PF65 95.00				

KM# 1777 15 YUAN
1.24 g., 0.999 Gold 0.0396 oz. AGW, 12 mm. **Obv:** Temple of Heaven **Rev:** Panda seated on frosted background

Date	Mintage	F12	VF20	XF40	MS60	MS63
2007	18,000	PF65 95.00				

KM# 1781 15 YUAN
1.24 g., 0.999 Gold 0.0396 oz. AGW, 12 mm. **Obv:** Temple of Heaven **Rev:** Panda looking forward

Date	Mintage	F12	VF20	XF40	MS60	MS63
2007	18,000	PF65 95.00				

KM# 1783 15 YUAN
1.24 g., 0.999 Gold 0.0396 oz. AGW, 12 mm. **Obv:** Temple of Heaven **Rev:** Panda and cub walking right

Date	Mintage	F12	VF20	XF40	MS60	MS63
2007	18,000	PF65 95.00				

KM# 1785 15 YUAN
1.24 g., 0.999 Gold 0.0396 oz. AGW, 12 mm. **Obv:** Temple of Heaven **Rev:** Panda seated with cub on left

Date	Mintage	F12	VF20	XF40	MS60	MS63
2007	18,000	PF65 95.00				

KM# 1787 15 YUAN
1.24 g., 0.999 Gold 0.0396 oz. AGW, 12 mm. **Obv:** Temple of Heaven **Rev:** Panda seated with cub on right

Date	Mintage	F12	VF20	XF40	MS60	MS63
2007	18,000	PF65 95.00				

KM# 1789 15 YUAN
1.24 g., 0.999 Gold 0.0396 oz. AGW, 12 mm. **Obv:** Temple of Heaven **Rev:** Panda seated with cub, both munching bamboo

Date	Mintage	F12	VF20	XF40	MS60	MS63
2007	18,000	PF65 95.00				

KM# 1366 20 YUAN
1.56 g., 0.999 Gold 0.0498 oz. AGW, 14 mm. **Obv:** Temple of Heaven **Rev:** Panda walking left through bamboo **Edge:** Reeded **Note:** Large and small date varieties exist. Prev. Y#1112.

Date	Mintage	F12	VF20	XF40	MS60	MS63
2001	200,000	—	—	—	100	115
2001 D	Inc. above	—	—	—	100	115
2002	74,601	—	—	—	100	115

KM# 1467 20 YUAN
1.56 g., 0.9999 Gold 0.0497 oz. AGW, 14.5 mm. **Subject:** Panda **Obv:** Temple of Heaven **Rev:** Panda facing, walking through bamboo **Edge:** Reeded **Note:** Large and small date varieties exist. Prev. Y#1154.

Date	Mintage	F12	VF20	XF40	MS60	MS63
2003	117,000	—	—	—	—	110

KM# 1529 20 YUAN
1.56 g., 0.9999 Gold 0.0497 oz. AGW, 14 mm. **Rev:** Panda walking with cub **Note:** Large and small date varieties exist. Prev. Y#1172.

Date	Mintage	F12	VF20	XF40	MS60	MS63
2004	101,000	—	—	—	—	120

KM# 1586 20 YUAN
1.55 g., 0.999 Gold 0.0495 oz. AGW, 14 mm. **Obv:** Temple of Heaven **Rev:** Panda cub and mom seated in bamboo

Date	Mintage	F12	VF20	XF40	MS60	MS63
2005	89,500	PF65 125				

KM# 1661 20 YUAN
1.56 g., 0.999 Gold 0.0496 oz. AGW, 14 mm. **Obv:** Temple of Heaven **Rev:** Two pandas seated with bamboo

Date	Mintage	F12	VF20	XF40	MS60	MS63
2006	62,000	PF65 145				

KM# 1707 20 YUAN
1.56 g., 0.999 Gold 0.0496 oz. AGW, 14 mm. **Obv:** Temple of Heaven **Rev:** Two pandas, one walking, one seated

Date	Mintage	F12	VF20	XF40	MS60	MS63
2007	200,000	PF65 100				

KM# 1815 20 YUAN
1.56 g., 0.999 Gold 0.0496 oz. AGW, 14 mm. **Rev:** Panda cut pawing mom

Date	Mintage	F12	VF20	XF40	MS60	MS63
2008	—	PF65 100				

KM# 1866 20 YUAN
1.56 g., 0.999 Gold 0.0496 oz. AGW

Date	Mintage	F12	VF20	XF40	MS60	MS63
2008	—	PF65 100				

KM# 1930 20 YUAN
1.55 g., 0.999 Gold 0.0495 oz. AGW **Obv:** Temple of Heaven **Rev:** Two pandas, one lying on back

Date	Mintage	F12	VF20	XF40	MS60	MS63
2010	120,000	—	—	—	—	110

KM# 1979 20 YUAN
1.55 g., 0.999 Gold 0.0495 oz. AGW, 14 mm.

Date	Mintage	F12	VF20	XF40	MS60	MS63
2011	—	—	—	—	—	110

KM# 2028 20 YUAN
1.55 g., 0.999 Gold 0.0495 oz. AGW, 14 mm.

Date	Mintage	F12	VF20	XF40	MS60	MS63
2012	—	—	—	—	—	110

KM# 1817 30 YUAN
3.11 g., 0.999 Gold 0.0992 oz. AGW, 18 mm. **Rev:** Panda cub pawing mom

Date	Mintage	F12	VF20	XF40	MS60	MS63
2008	—	PF65 215				

KM# 1367 50 YUAN
3.11 g., 0.999 Gold 0.0993 oz. AGW, 18 mm. **Obv:** Temple of Heaven **Rev:** Panda walking left through bamboo **Edge:** Reeded **Note:** Large and small date varieties exist. Prev. Y#1113.

Date	Mintage	F12	VF20	XF40	MS60	MS63
2001 D	150,000	—	—	—	—	250
2001	50,000	—	—	—	—	200

KM# 1457 50 YUAN
3.11 g., 0.9999 Gold 0.0993 oz. AGW **Subject:** Temple of Heaven **Rev:** Panda walking

Date	Mintage	F12	VF20	XF40	MS60	MS63
2002	36,092	—	—	—	—	225

KM# 1469 50 YUAN
3.11 g., 0.9999 Gold 0.0993 oz. AGW **Subject:** Panda **Note:** Large and small date varieties exist. Prev. Y#1157.

Date	Mintage	F12	VF20	XF40	MS60	MS63
2003	47,500	—	—	—	—	215

KM# 1531 50 YUAN
3.11 g., 0.9999 Gold 0.0993 oz. AGW **Subject:** Panda **Note:** Large and small date varieties exist. Prev. Y#1173.

Date	Mintage	F12	VF20	XF40	MS60	MS63
2004	—	—	—	—	—	200

KM# 1585 50 YUAN
3.11 g., 0.999 Gold 0.0992 oz. AGW, 18 mm. **Obv:** Temple of Heaven **Rev:** Panda cub and mom seated in bamboo

Date	Mintage	F12	VF20	XF40	MS60	MS63
2005	150,000	—	—	—	—	200

KM# 1660 50 YUAN
3.11 g., 0.999 Gold 0.0992 oz. AGW, 18 mm. **Obv:** Temple of Heaven **Rev:** Two pandas seated with bamboo

Date	Mintage	F12	VF20	XF40	MS60	MS63
2006	150,000	—	—	—	—	200

KM# 1709 50 YUAN
3.11 g., 0.999 Gold 0.0992 oz. AGW, 18 mm. **Obv:** Temple of Heaven **Rev:** Two pandas, one walking, one seated

Date	Mintage	F12	VF20	XF40	MS60	MS63
2007	150,000	—	—	—	—	200

KM# 1868 50 YUAN
3.10 g., 0.999 Gold 0.0989 oz. AGW, 18 mm. **Rev:** Panda cub pawing mom

Date	Mintage	F12	VF20	XF40	MS60	MS63
2008	—	—	—	—	—	200

KM# 1929 50 YUAN
3.11 g., 0.999 Gold 0.0992 oz. AGW **Obv:** Temple of Heaven **Rev:** Two pandas, one lying on back

Date	Mintage	F12	VF20	XF40	MS60	MS63
2010	120,000	—	—	—	—	200

KM# 1978 50 YUAN
3.11 g., 0.999 Gold 0.0992 oz. AGW, 18 mm.

Date	Mintage	F12	VF20	XF40	MS60	MS63
2011	—	—	—	—	—	200

KM# 2027 50 YUAN
3.11 g., 0.999 Gold 0.0992 oz. AGW, 18 mm.

Date	Mintage	F12	VF20	XF40	MS60	MS63
2012	—	—	—	—	—	200

KM# 1368 100 YUAN
7.78 g., 0.999 Gold 0.2481 oz. AGW, 22 mm. **Obv:** Temple of Heaven **Rev:** Panda walking left through bamboo **Edge:** Reeded **Note:** Large and small date varieties exist. Prev. Y#1114.

Date	Mintage	F12	VF20	XF40	MS60	MS63
2001	85,010	—	—	—	—	475
2001 D	Inc. above	—	—	—	—	525

KM# 1458 100 YUAN
7.78 g., 0.9999 Gold 0.2484 oz. AGW **Obv:** Temple of Heaven **Rev:** Panda walking

Date	Mintage	F12	VF20	XF40	MS60	MS63
2002	19,205	—	—	—	—	500

KM# 1471 100 YUAN
7.78 g., 0.9999 Gold 0.2484 oz. AGW **Subject:** Panda **Note:** Large and small date varieties exist. Prev. Y#1158.

Date	Mintage	F12	VF20	XF40	MS60	MS63
2003	28,000	—	—	—	—	475

KM# 1533 100 YUAN
7.78 g., 0.9999 Gold 0.2484 oz. AGW **Subject:** Panda **Note:** Large and small date varieties exist. Prev. Y#1174. Photo reduced.

Date	Mintage	F12	VF20	XF40	MS60	MS63
2004	41,000	—	—	—	—	475

KM# 1584 100 YUAN
7.77 g., 0.999 Gold 0.248 oz. AGW, 22 mm. **Obv:** Temple of Heaven **Rev:** Panda cub and mom seated in bamboo

Date	Mintage	F12	VF20	XF40	MS60	MS63
2005	40,000	—	—	—	—	475

KM# 1659 100 YUAN
7.77 g., 0.999 Gold 0.248 oz. AGW, 22 mm. **Obv:** Temple of Heaven **Rev:** Two pandas seated with bamboo

Date	Mintage	F12	VF20	XF40	MS60	MS63
2006	28,500	—	—	—	—	500

KM# 1710 100 YUAN
7.77 g., 0.999 Gold 0.248 oz. AGW, 22 mm. **Obv:** Temple of Heaven **Rev:** Two pandas, one walking, one seated

Date	Mintage	F12	VF20	XF40	MS60	MS63
2007	60,000	—	—	—	—	475

KM# 1818 100 YUAN
7.77 g., 0.999 Gold 0.248 oz. AGW, 22 mm. **Rev:** Panda cub pawing mom

Date	Mintage	F12	VF20	XF40	MS60	MS63
2008	—	—	—	—	—	475

KM# 1928 100 YUAN
7.77 g., 0.999 Gold 0.248 oz. AGW **Obv:** Temple of Heaven **Rev:** Two panda, one lying on back

Date	Mintage	F12	VF20	XF40	MS60	MS63
2010	120,000	—	—	—	—	500

KM# 1977 100 YUAN
7.77 g., 0.999 Gold 0.248 oz. AGW, 22 mm.

Date	Mintage	F12	VF20	XF40	MS60	MS63
2011	—	—	—	—	—	500

KM# 2026 100 YUAN
7.77 g., 0.999 Gold 0.248 oz. AGW, 22 mm.

Date	Mintage	F12	VF20	XF40	MS60	MS63
2012	—	—	—	—	—	450

KM# 1369 200 YUAN
15.55 g., 0.999 Gold 0.4963 oz. AGW, 27 mm. **Obv:** Temple of Heaven **Rev:** Panda in bamboo forest **Edge:** Slanted reeding **Note:** Illustration reduced. Large and small date varieties exist. Prev. Y#1105.

Date	Mintage	F12	VF20	XF40	MS60	MS63
2001 D	100,000	—	—	—	—	875
2001	33,215	—	—	—	—	900

KM# 1459 200 YUAN
15.55 g., 0.9999 Gold 0.4967 oz. AGW **Rev:** Panda

Date	Mintage	F12	VF20	XF40	MS60	MS63
2002	28,514	—	—	—	—	900

KM# 1472 200 YUAN
15.55 g., 0.9999 Gold 0.4967 oz. AGW **Subject:** Panda **Note:** Large and small date varieties exist. Prev. Y#1162.

Date	Mintage	F12	VF20	XF40	MS60	MS63
2003	25,000	—	—	—	—	900

KM# 1535 200 YUAN
15.55 g., 0.999 Gold 0.4963 oz. AGW **Subject:** Panda **Note:** Large and small date varieties exist. Prev. Y#1175.

Date	Mintage	F12	VF20	XF40	MS60	MS63
2004	42,000	—	—	—	—	875

KM# 1583 200 YUAN
15.55 g., 0.999 Gold 0.4963 oz. AGW, 27 mm. **Obv:** Temple of Heaven **Rev:** Panda cub and mom seated in bamboo

Date	Mintage	F12	VF20	XF40	MS60	MS63
2005	36,410	—	—	—	—	875

KM# 1658 200 YUAN
15.55 g., 0.999 Gold 0.4962 oz. AGW, 27 mm. **Obv:** Temple of Heaven **Rev:** Two pandas seated with bamboo

Date	Mintage	F12	VF20	XF40	MS60	MS63
2006	25,600	—	—	—	—	900

KM# 1711 200 YUAN
15.55 g., 0.999 Gold 0.4962 oz. AGW **Obv:** Temple of Heaven **Rev:** Two pandas, one walking, one seated

Date	Mintage	F12	VF20	XF40	MS60	MS63
2007	60,000	—	—	—	—	875

KM# 1870 200 YUAN
15.50 g., 0.999 Gold 0.4946 oz. AGW

Date	Mintage	F12	VF20	XF40	MS60	MS63
2009	—	—	—	—	—	875

KM# 1927 200 YUAN
15.55 g., 0.999 Gold 0.4962 oz. AGW **Obv:** Temple of Heaven **Rev:** Two pandas, one lying on back

Date	Mintage	F12	VF20	XF40	MS60	MS63
2010	120,000	—	—	—	—	900

KM# 1976 200 YUAN
15.55 g., 0.999 Gold 0.4962 oz. AGW

Date	Mintage	F12	VF20	XF40	MS60	MS63
2011	—	—	—	—	—	900

KM# 2025 200 YUAN
15.55 g., 0.999 Gold 0.4962 oz. AGW, 27 mm.

Date	Mintage	F12	VF20	XF40	MS60	MS63
2012	—	—	—	—	—	900

KM# 1371 500 YUAN
31.10 g., 0.999 Gold 0.9926 oz. AGW, 32 mm. **Obv:** Temple of Heaven **Rev:** Panda walking through bamboo **Edge:** Reeded **Note:** Prev. Y#1088.

Date	Mintage	F12	VF20	XF40	MS60	MS63
2001 D	150,000	—	—	—	—	BV+10%
2001		—	—	—	—	BV+10%

KM# 1405 500 YUAN
31.11 g., 0.9999 Gold 0.9935 oz. AGW **Rev:** Panda

Date	Mintage	F12	VF20	XF40	MS60	MS63
2001	41,411	—	—	—	—	BV+10%

KM# 1460 500 YUAN
31.11 g., 0.9999 Gold 0.9935 oz. AGW **Rev:** Panda

Date	Mintage	F12	VF20	XF40	MS60	MS63
2002	28,345	—	—	—	—	BV+15%

KM# 1474 500 YUAN
31.13 g., 0.9999 Gold 0.9944 oz. AGW **Subject:** Panda **Note:** Large and small date varieties exist. Prev. Y#1164.

Date	Mintage	F12	VF20	XF40	MS60	MS63
2003	36,300	—	—	—	—	BV+12%

KM# 1537 500 YUAN
31.10 g., 0.9999 Gold 0.9935 oz. AGW **Subject:** Panda **Note:** Large and small date varieties exist. Prev. Y#1176.

Date	Mintage	F12	VF20	XF40	MS60	MS63
2004	55,000	—	—	—	—	BV+10%

KM# 1582 500 YUAN
31.11 g., 0.999 Gold 0.9926 oz. AGW, 32 mm. **Obv:** Temple of
Heaven **Rev:** Panda cub and mom seated in bamboo

Date	Mintage	F12	VF20	XF40	MS60	MS63
2005	50,300	PF65 BV+10%				

KM# 1657 500 YUAN
31.11 g., 0.999 Gold 0.9926 oz. AGW, 32 mm. **Obv:** Temple of
Heaven **Rev:** Two panda's seated with bamboo

Date	Mintage	F12	VF20	XF40	MS60	MS63
2006	115,600	PF65 BV+10%				

KM# 1713 500 YUAN
31.11 g., 0.999 Gold 0.9926 oz. AGW, 32 mm. **Obv:** Temple of
Heaven **Rev:** Two pandas, one walking, one seated

Date	Mintage	F12	VF20	XF40	MS60	MS63
2007	150,000	PF65 BV+10%				

KM# 1821 500 YUAN
31.11 g., 0.999 Gold 0.9926 oz. AGW, 32 mm. **Rev:** Panda
cub pawing mom

Date	Mintage	F12	VF20	XF40	MS60	MS63
2008	—	PF65 BV+10%				

KM# 1872 500 YUAN
31.11 g., 0.999 Gold 0.9926 oz. AGW

Date	Mintage	F12	VF20	XF40	MS60	MS63
2009	—	PF65 BV+10%				

KM# 1926 500 YUAN
31.11 g., 0.999 Gold 0.9926 oz. AGW **Obv:** Temple of Heaven
Rev: Two pandas, one lying on back

Date	Mintage	F12	VF20	XF40	MS60	MS63
2010	300,000	—	—	—	—	BV+10%

KM# 1975 500 YUAN
31.11 g., 0.999 Gold 0.9926 oz. AGW

Date	Mintage	F12	VF20	XF40	MS60	MS63
2011	—	—	—	—	—	BV+10%

KM# 2024 500 YUAN
31.11 g., 0.999 Gold 0.9926 oz. AGW, 32 mm.

Date	Mintage	F12	VF20	XF40	MS60	MS63
2012	—	—	—	—	—	BV+10%

KM# 1581 2000 YUAN
155.00 g., 0.999 Gold 4.9463 oz. AGW, 60 mm. **Obv:** Temple
of Heaven **Rev:** Panda cub and mom seated in bamboo **Note:**
Photo reduced.

Date	Mintage	F12	VF20	XF40	MS60	MS63
2005	1,000	PF65 BV+15%				

KM# 1656 2000 YUAN
155.55 g., 0.999 Gold 4.9639 oz. AGW, 60 mm. **Obv:** Temple
of Heaven **Rev:** Two pandas seated with bamboo **Note:** Photo
reduced.

Date	Mintage	F12	VF20	XF40	MS60	MS63
2006	1,000	PF65 BV+15%				

KM# 1714 2000 YUAN
155.55 g., 0.999 Gold 4.9639 oz. AGW, 60 mm. **Obv:** Temple of
Heaven **Rev:** Two pandas, one walking, one seated

Date	Mintage	F12	VF20	XF40	MS60	MS63
2007	1,000	PF65 BV+15%				

KM# 1822 2000 YUAN
155.55 g., 0.999 Gold 4.9623 oz. AGW, 60 mm. **Rev:** Panda
cub pawing mom

Date	Mintage	F12	VF20	XF40	MS60	MS63
2008	1,000	PF65 BV+15%				

KM# 1873 2000 YUAN
155.50 g., 0.999 Gold 4.9623 oz. AGW

Date	Mintage	F12	VF20	XF40	MS60	MS63
2009	1,000	PF65 BV+15%				

KM# 1914 2000 YUAN
155.50 g., 0.999 Gold 4.9623 oz. AGW **Subject:** Year of the
Tiger **Rev:** Multicolor

Date	Mintage	F12	VF20	XF40	MS60	MS63
2010	1,800	PF65 BV+10%				

KM# 1933 2000 YUAN
155.50 g., 0.999 Gold 4.9623 oz. AGW **Obv:** Temple of Heaven
Rev: Two pandas, one lying on back

Date	Mintage	F12	VF20	XF40	MS60	MS63
2010	1,000	PF65 BV+15%				

KM# 1982 2000 YUAN
155.55 g., 0.999 Gold 4.9639 oz. AGW, 60 mm.

Date	Mintage	F12	VF20	XF40	MS60	MS63
2011	—	PF65 BV+10%				

KM# 1372 10000 YUAN
1000.00 g., 0.999 Gold 31.9118 oz. AGW **Subject:** Panda
Note: Large and small date varieties exist. Prev. #Y1138.

Date	Mintage	F12	VF20	XF40	MS60	MS63
2001	68	—	—	—	—	BV+25%

KM# A1475 10000 YUAN
1000.00 g., 0.9999 Gold 31.9406 oz. AGW **Subject:** Panda
Note: Large and small date varieties exist. Prev. #Y1165.

Date	Mintage	F12	VF20	XF40	MS60	MS63
2002	68	—	—	—	—	BV+25%

KM# 1475 10000 YUAN
1000.00 g., 0.999 Gold 31.9118 oz. AGW, 100 mm. **Rev:**
Panda and bamboo

Date	Mintage	F12	VF20	XF40	MS60	MS63
2003	68	PF65 BV+25%				

KM# 1538 10000 YUAN
1000.00 g., 0.9999 Gold 31.9406 oz. AGW **Subject:** Panda
Note: Large and small date varieties exist. Prev. #Y1177.

Date	Mintage	F12	VF20	XF40	MS60	MS63
2004	68	—	—	—	—	BV+25%

KM# A1580 10000 YUAN
1000.00 g., 0.999 Gold 31.9118 oz. AGW, 90 mm. **Obv:** Temple
of Heaven **Rev:** Panda cub and mom seated in bamboo **Note:**
Photo reduced.

Date	Mintage	F12	VF20	XF40	MS60	MS63
2005	100	PF65 BV+25%				

KM# 1655 10000 YUAN
1000.00 g., 0.999 Gold 31.9118 oz. AGW, 90 mm. **Obv:** Temple
of Heaven **Rev:** Two pandas seated with bamboo **Note:** Photo
reduced.

Date	Mintage	F12	VF20	XF40	MS60	MS63
2006	200	PF65 BV+20%				

KM# 1715 10000 YUAN
1000.00 g., 0.999 Gold 31.9118 oz. AGW **Obv:** Temple of
Heaven **Rev:** Two pandas, one walking, one seated

Date	Mintage	F12	VF20	XF40	MS60	MS63
2007	200	PF65 BV+20%				

KM# 1823 10000 YUAN
1000.00 g., 0.999 Gold 31.9118 oz. AGW, 90 mm. **Rev:** Panda
cub pawing mom

Date	Mintage	F12	VF20	XF40	MS60	MS63
2008	200	PF65 BV+20%				

KM# 1874 10000 YUAN
1000.00 g., 0.999 Gold 31.9118 oz. AGW

Date	Mintage	F12	VF20	XF40	MS60	MS63
2009	200	PF65 BV+20%				

KM# 1932 10000 YUAN
1000.00 g., 0.999 Gold 31.9118 oz. AGW **Obv:** Temple of
Heaven **Rev:** Two pandas, one lying on back

Date	Mintage	F12	VF20	XF40	MS60	MS63
2010	200	PF65 BV+20%				

KM# 1981 10000 YUAN
1000.00 g., 0.999 Gold 31.9118 oz. AGW, 90 mm.

Date	Mintage	F12	VF20	XF40	MS60	MS63
2011	—	PF05 BV+20%				

KM# 2030 10000 YUAN
1000.00 g., 0.999 Gold 31.9118 oz. AGW, 90 mm.

Date	Mintage	F12	VF20	XF40	MS60	MS63
2012	—	PF65 BV+20%				

GOLD BULLION COINAGE
Lunar Series

KM# 1967 20 YUAN
3.11 g., 0.999 Gold 0.0992 oz. AGW, 18 mm. **Subject:** Year of the Rabbit **Rev:** Multicolor

Date	Mintage	F12	VF20	XF40	MS60	MS63
2011	80,000	PF65 225				

KM# 1374 50 YUAN
3.11 g., 0.999 Gold 0.0993 oz. AGW, 18 mm. **Subject:** Year of the Snake **Note:** Prev. Y#1141.1; 1043.

Date	Mintage	F12	VF20	XF40	MS60	MS63
2001	48,000	—	—	—	—	265

KM# 1376 50 YUAN
3.11 g., 0.9999 Gold 0.0994 oz. AGW **Subject:** Year of the Snake **Rev:** Multicolor. **Note:** Prev. Y#1141.2.

Date	Mintage	F12	VF20	XF40	MS60	MS63
2001	30,000	—	—	—	—	350

KM# 1417 50 YUAN
3.11 g., 0.9999 Gold 0.0992 oz. AGW **Subject:** Year of the Horse **Rev:** Multicolor horse prancing forward **Note:** Prev. Y#1143.2.

Date	Mintage	F12	VF20	XF40	MS60	MS63
2002	30,000	—	—	—	—	425

KM# 1419 50 YUAN
3.11 g., 0.9999 Gold 0.0992 oz. AGW **Subject:** Year of the Horse **Rev:** Dramatic horse profile right **Note:** Prev. Y#1143.1.

Date	Mintage	F12	VF20	XF40	MS60	MS63
2002	48,000	—	—	—	—	240

KM# 1478 50 YUAN
3.11 g., 0.9999 Gold 0.0993 oz. AGW **Subject:** Year of the Goat **Note:** Prev. Y#1155.1.

Date	Mintage	F12	VF20	XF40	MS60	MS63
2003	48,000	—	—	—	—	275

KM# A1478 50 YUAN
3.11 g., 0.9999 Gold 0.0994 oz. AGW **Subject:** Year of the Goat **Rev:** Multicolor. **Note:** Prev. Y#1155.2

Date	Mintage	F12	VF20	XF40	MS60	MS63
2003	30,000	—	—	—	—	400

KM# 1544 50 YUAN
3.11 g., 0.9999 Gold 0.0993 oz. AGW, 18 mm. **Subject:** Year of the Monkey **Note:** Prev. Y#1167.1.

Date	Mintage	F12	VF20	XF40	MS60	MS63
2004	48,000	—	—	—	—	275

KM# 1546 50 YUAN
3.11 g., 0.9999 Gold 0.0993 oz. AGW **Subject:** Year of the Monkey **Rev:** Multicolor monkey and baby **Note:** Prev. Y#1167.2

Date	Mintage	F12	VF20	XF40	MS60	MS63
2004	30,000	—	—	—	—	425

KM# 1608 50 YUAN
3.11 g., 0.999 Gold 0.0992 oz. AGW, 18 mm. **Subject:** Year of the Rooster **Obv:** Classical rooster **Rev:** Multicolor rooster

Date	Mintage	F12	VF20	XF40	MS60	MS63
2005	30,000	PF65 375				

KM# 1609 50 YUAN
3.11 g., 0.999 Gold 0.0992 oz. AGW, 18 mm. **Subject:** Year of the Rooster **Obv:** Classical rooster **Rev:** Rooster, hen and chicks

Date	Mintage	F12	VF20	XF40	MS60	MS63
2005	60,000	PF65 300				

KM# 1680 50 YUAN
3.11 g., 0.999 Gold 0.0993 oz. AGW, 18 mm. **Obv:** Dog-shaped belt-hook from ancient Chinese bronze ware, decorative design of dog tail-shaped plant leaves **Rev:** 2 smart dogs **Note:** Prev. Y#1226; KM#1658.

Date	Mintage	F12	VF20	XF40	MS60	MS63
2006	60,000	—	—	—	—	225

KM# 1681 50 YUAN
3.11 g., 0.999 Gold 0.0993 oz. AGW, 18 mm. **Obv:** Dog-shaped belt-hook , an ancient Chinese bronze ware, decorative disign of dog tail-shaped plant leaves **Rev:** 2 dogs at play **Note:** Prev. Y#1222; KM#1654.

Date	Mintage	F12	VF20	XF40	MS60	MS63
2006	30,000	PF65 220				

KM# 1721 50 YUAN
3.10 g., 0.999 Gold 0.0989 oz. AGW, 18 mm. **Subject:** Year of the Pig **Obv:** Classical pig **Rev:** Pig walking right

Date	Mintage	F12	VF20	XF40	MS60	MS63
2007	—	PF65 225				

KM# 1722 50 YUAN
3.10 g., 0.999 Gold 0.0989 oz. AGW, 18 mm. **Subject:** Year of the Pig **Obv:** Classical pig **Rev:** Multicolor sow and piglets sucking

Date	Mintage	F12	VF20	XF40	MS60	MS63
2007	30,000	PF65 550				

KM# 1835 50 YUAN
3.11 g., 0.999 Gold 0.0992 oz. AGW **Subject:** Year of the Rat **Rev:** Multicolor **Shape:** 18

Date	Mintage	F12	VF20	XF40	MS60	MS63
2008	30,000	PF65 350				

KM# 1836 50 YUAN
3.11 g., 0.999 Gold 0.0992 oz. AGW, 18 mm. **Subject:** Year of the Rat

Date	Mintage	F12	VF20	XF40	MS60	MS63
2008	60,000	PF65 225				

KM# 1880 50 YUAN
3.11 g., 0.999 Gold 0.0992 oz. AGW, 18 mm. **Subject:** Year of the Ox colorized

Date	Mintage	F12	VF20	XF40	MS60	MS63
2009	30,000	PF65 400				

KM# 1881 50 YUAN
3.11 g., 0.999 Gold 0.0992 oz. AGW, 18 mm. **Subject:** Year of the Ox

Date	Mintage	F12	VF20	XF40	MS60	MS63
2009	80,000	PF65 200				

KM# 1917 50 YUAN
3.11 g., 0.999 Gold 0.0992 oz. AGW **Subject:** Year of the Tiger

Date	Mintage	F12	VF20	XF40	MS60	MS63
2010	80,000	PF65 225				

KM# 1918 50 YUAN
3.11 g., 0.999 Gold 0.0992 oz. AGW **Subject:** Year of the Tiger **Rev:** Multicolor

Date	Mintage	F12	VF20	XF40	MS60	MS63
2010	80,000	PF65 225				

KM# 1966 50 YUAN
3.11 g., 0.999 Gold 0.0992 oz. AGW, 18 mm. **Subject:** Year of the Rabbit

Date	Mintage	F12	VF20	XF40	MS60	MS63
2011	80,000	PF65 225				

KM# 2015 50 YUAN
3.11 g., 0.999 Gold 0.0991 oz. AGW, 18 mm. **Subject:** Year of the Dragon

Date	Mintage	F12	VF20	XF40	MS60	MS63
2012	—	PF65 225				

KM# 2016 50 YUAN
3.11 g., 0.999 Gold 0.0991 oz. AGW, 18 mm. **Subject:** Year of the Dragon **Rev:** Colored

Date	Mintage	F12	VF20	XF40	MS60	MS63
2012	—	PF65 225				

KM# 1380 200 YUAN
15.55 g., 0.999 Gold 0.4963 oz. AGW **Subject:** Year of the Snake **Shape:** Flower **Note:** Prev. Y#1045.

Date	Mintage	F12	VF20	XF40	MS60	MS63
2001	2,300	PF65 1,250				

KM# 1383 200 YUAN
15.55 g., 0.999 Gold 0.4963 oz. AGW **Subject:** Year of the Snake **Rev:** Fan **Note:** Prev. Y#1044.

Date	Mintage	F12	VF20	XF40	MS60	MS63
2001	6,600	—	—	—	—	950

KM# 1424 200 YUAN
15.55 g., 0.999 Gold 0.4962 oz. AGW **Subject:** Year of the Horse **Shape:** Fan

Date	Mintage	F12	VF20	XF40	MS60	MS63
2002	6,600	—	—	—	—	1,000

KM# 1426 200 YUAN
15.50 g., 0.999 Gold 0.4946 oz. AGW **Subject:** Year of the Horse **Shape:** Flower **Note:** Prev. Y#1150.

Date	Mintage	F12	VF20	XF40	MS60	MS63
2002	2,300	—	—	—	—	1,350

KM# 1475.1 200 YUAN
15.55 g., 0.9999 Gold 0.4967 oz. AGW **Subject:** Year of the Goat **Shape:** Fan

Date	Mintage	F12	VF20	XF40	MS60	MS63
2003	6,600	—	—	—	—	950

KM# 1481 200 YUAN
15.55 g., 0.9999 Gold 0.4967 oz. AGW **Subject:** Year of the Goat **Shape:** Flower **Note:** Prev. Y#1161.

Date	Mintage	F12	VF20	XF40	MS60	MS63
2003	2,300	—	—	—	—	1,350

KM# 1486 200 YUAN
15.51 g., 0.999 Gold 0.495 oz. AGW, 58 x 30 mm. **Subject:** Year of the Sheep **Shape:** Fan

Date	Mintage	F12	VF20	XF40	MS60	MS63
2003	6,600	PF65 1,100				

KM# 1549 200 YUAN
15.55 g., 0.9999 Gold 0.4967 oz. AGW **Subject:** Year of the Monkey **Shape:** Flower **Note:** Prev. Y#1169.

Date	Mintage	F12	VF20	XF40	MS60	MS63
2004	2,300	—	—	—	—	1,350

KM# 1554 200 YUAN
15.55 g., 0.9999 Gold 0.4967 oz. AGW **Subject:** Year of the Monkey **Shape:** Fan **Note:** Illustration reduced. Prev. Y#1168.

Date	Mintage	F12	VF20	XF40	MS60	MS63
2004	6,600	—	—	—	—	1,100

KM# 1606 200 YUAN
15.55 g., 0.999 Gold 0.4962 oz. AGW, 27 mm. **Series:** Classical rooster **Subject:** Year of the Rooster **Obv:** Rooster, hen and chicks **Shape:** Scallops

Date	Mintage	F12	VF20	XF40	MS60	MS63
2005	8,000	PF65 925				

KM# 1607 200 YUAN
15.55 g., 0.999 Gold 0.4962 oz. AGW, 58 x 30 mm. **Subject:** Year of the Rooster **Obv:** Temple **Rev:** Rooster, hen and chicks **Shape:** Fan **Note:** Illustration reduced.

Date	Mintage	F12	VF20	XF40	MS60	MS63
2005	6,600	PF65 950				

KM# 1677 200 YUAN
15.63 g., 0.999 Gold 0.4988 oz. AGW, 27 mm. **Subject:** Year of the Dog **Obv:** Dog-shaped belt-hook from ancient Chinese bronze ware, decorative design of dog tail-shaped plant leaves **Rev:** 2 smart dogs **Shape:** Scalloped **Note:** Prev. Y#1224; KM#1656.

Date	Mintage	F12	VF20	XF40	MS60	MS63
2006	8,000	PF65 1,350				

KM# 1679 200 YUAN
15.63 g., 0.999 Gold 0.4988 oz. AGW **Subject:** Year of the Dog **Obv:** Qing Yuan Gate of the China Great Wall **Rev:** 2 dogs at play **Shape:** 30× Fan **Note:** Prev. Y#1220; KM#1652. Illustration reduced.

Date	Mintage	F12	VF20	XF40	MS60	MS63
2006	6,600	PF65 1,100				

KM# 1723 200 YUAN
15.50 g., 0.999 Gold 0.4946 oz. AGW, 58 x 39 mm. **Subject:** Year of the Pig **Obv:** Temple **Rev:** Sow and four piglets **Shape:** Fan

Date	Mintage	F12	VF20	XF40	MS60	MS63
2007	6,600	PF65 1,150				

KM# 1724 200 YUAN
15.55 g., 0.999 Gold 0.4962 oz. AGW, 27 mm. **Subject:** Year of the Pig **Obv:** Classical pig **Rev:** Pig walking right **Shape:** Flower

Date	Mintage	F12	VF20	XF40	MS60	MS63
2007	8,000	PF65 950				

KM# 1837 200 YUAN
15.50 g., 0.999 Gold 0.4946 oz. AGW, 27 mm. **Subject:** Year of the Rat **Shape:** Flower

Date	Mintage	F12	VF20	XF40	MS60	MS63
2008	8,000	PF65 950				

KM# 1838 200 YUAN
15.50 g., 0.999 Gold 0.4946 oz. AGW, 58 x 39 mm. **Subject:** Year of the Rat **Shape:** Fan

Date	Mintage	F12	VF20	XF40	MS60	MS63
2008	6,600	PF65 1,000				

KM# 1883 200 YUAN
15.50 g., 0.999 Gold 0.4946 oz. AGW **Subject:** Year of the Ox **Shape:** Fan

Date	Mintage	F12	VF20	XF40	MS60	MS63
2009	6,600	PF65 1,000				

KM# 1882 200 YUAN
15.50 g., 0.999 Gold 0.4946 oz. AGW **Subject:** Year of the Ox **Shape:** Flower

Date	Mintage	F12	VF20	XF40	MS60	MS63
2009	8,000	PF65 950				

KM# 1915 200 YUAN
15.55 g., 0.999 Gold 0.4962 oz. AGW **Subject:** Year of the Tiger **Shape:** Arc

Date	Mintage	F12	VF20	XF40	MS60	MS63
2010	6,600	—	—	—	—	975

KM# 1916 200 YUAN
15.55 g., 0.999 Gold 0.4962 oz. AGW **Subject:** Year of the Tiger **Shape:** Scalloped

Date	Mintage	F12	VF20	XF40	MS60	MS63
2010	8,000	PF65 925				

KM# 1964 200 YUAN
15.50 g., 0.999 Gold 0.4946 oz. AGW **Subject:** Year of the Rabbit **Shape:** Arc **Note:** Photo reduced.

Date	Mintage	F12	VF20	XF40	MS60	MS63
2011	6,600	—	—	—	—	975

KM# 1965 200 YUAN
15.55 g., 0.999 Gold 0.4962 oz. AGW **Subject:** Year of the Rabbit **Shape:** Scallop

Date	Mintage	F12	VF20	XF40	MS60	MS63
2011	8,000	PF65 925				

KM# 2013 200 YUAN
15.55 g., 0.999 Gold 0.4962 oz. AGW **Subject:** Year of the Dragon **Shape:** Fan

Date	Mintage	F12	VF20	XF40	MS60	MS63
2012	—	PF65 1,000				

KM# 2014 200 YUAN
15.55 g., 0.999 Gold 0.4962 oz. AGW **Subject:** Year of the Dragon **Shape:** Scalloped

Date	Mintage	F12	VF20	XF40	MS60	MS63
2012	—	PF65 950				

KM# 1378 2000 YUAN
155.52 g., 0.999 Gold 4.9628 oz. AGW, 80 x 50 mm. **Subject:** Year of the Snake **Shape:** Rectangle **Note:** Prev. #Y1046.

Date	Mintage	F12	VF20	XF40	MS60	MS63
2001	118	PF65 22,500				

KM# 1422 2000 YUAN
155.52 g., 0.9999 Gold 4.9673 oz. AGW **Subject:** Year of the Horse **Shape:** Rectangle **Note:** Prev. #Y1152.

Date	Mintage	F12	VF20	XF40	MS60	MS63
2002	118	PF65 22,500				

KM# 1483 2000 YUAN
155.52 g., 0.9999 Gold 4.9674 oz. AGW **Subject:** Year of the Goat **Note:** Prev. #Y1163.

Date	Mintage	F12	VF20	XF40	MS60	MS63
2003	118	PF65 22,500				

KM# 1552 2000 YUAN
155.18 g., 0.9999 Gold 4.9564 oz. AGW **Subject:** Year of the Monkey **Note:** Prev. #Y1170. Illustration reduced.

Date	Mintage	F12	VF20	XF40	MS60	MS63
2004	118	PF65 22,500				

KM# 1605 2000 YUAN
155.55 g., 0.999 Gold 4.9639 oz. AGW, 64 x 40 mm. **Subject:** Year of the Rooster **Obv:** Classical rooster **Rev:** Rooster, hen and chicks **Shape:** Rectangle **Note:** Photo reduced.

Date	Mintage	F12	VF20	XF40	MS60	MS63
2005	118	PF65 22,500				

KM# 1678 2000 YUAN
155.55 g., 0.999 Gold 4.9639 oz. AGW, 64 x 40 mm. **Subject:** Year of the Dog **Obv:** Classical dog **Rev:** Two dogs **Note:** Photo reduced.

Date	Mintage	F12	VF20	XF40	MS60	MS63
2006	118	PF65 22,500				

KM# 1726 2000 YUAN
155.55 g., 0.999 Gold 4.9639 oz. AGW, 64 x 40 mm. **Subject:** Year of the Pig **Obv:** Classical pig **Rev:** Sow and four piglets **Shape:** Rectangle

Date	Mintage	F12	VF20	XF40	MS60	MS63
2007	118	PF65 22,500				

KM# 1840 2000 YUAN
155.00 g., 0.999 Gold 4.9463 oz. AGW, 64 x 40 mm. **Subject:** Year of the Rat **Shape:** Rectangle

Date	Mintage	F12	VF20	XF40	MS60	MS63
2008	118	PF65 22,500				

KM# 1885 2000 YUAN
155.50 g., 0.999 Gold 4.9623 oz. AGW, 64x40 mm. **Subject:** Year of the Ox **Shape:** Rectangle

Date	Mintage	F12	VF20	XF40	MS60	MS63
2009	118	PF65 22,500				

KM# 1913 2000 YUAN
155.20 g., 0.999 Gold 4.9527 oz. AGW, 64x40 mm. **Subject:** Year of the Tiger **Shape:** Rectangle

Date	Mintage	F12	VF20	XF40	MS60	MS63
2010	118	PF65 20,000				

KM# 1962 2000 YUAN
155.50 g., 0.999 Gold 4.9623 oz. AGW, 64x40 mm. **Subject:** Year of the Rabbit **Shape:** Rectangle **Note:** Photo reduced.

Date	Mintage	F12	VF20	XF40	MS60	MS63
2011	118	PF65 20,000				

KM# 1963 2000 YUAN
155.50 g., 0.999 Gold 4.9623 oz. AGW **Subject:** Year of the Rabbit **Rev:** Multicolor **Note:** Photo reduced.

Date	Mintage	F12	VF20	XF40	MS60	MS63
2011	1,800	PF65 9,500				

KM# 2011 2000 YUAN
155.55 g., 0.999 Gold 4.9639 oz. AGW, 64x40 mm. **Subject:** Year of the Dragon **Shape:** Rectangle

Date	Mintage	F12	VF20	XF40	MS60	MS63
2012	—	PF65 20,000				

KM# 2012 2000 YUAN
155.55 g., 0.999 Gold 4.9639 oz. AGW **Subject:** Year of the Dragon **Rev:** Colored Dragon

Date	Mintage	F12	VF20	XF40	MS60	MS63
2012	—	PF65 9,500				

KM# 2031 2000 YUAN
155.55 g., 0.999 Gold 4.9639 oz. AGW, 60 mm.

Date	Mintage	F12	VF20	XF40	MS60	MS63
2012	—	PF65 11,000				

KM# 1381 10000 YUAN
1000.00 g., 0.999 Gold 31.9118 oz. AGW **Subject:** Year of the Snake **Shape:** Scalloped **Note:** Prev. #Y1047.

Date	Mintage	F12	VF20	XF40	MS60	MS63
2001	15	PF65 125,000				

KM# 1427 10000 YUAN
1000.00 g., 0.9999 Gold 31.9406 oz. AGW **Subject:** Year of the Horse **Shape:** Scalloped **Note:** Prev. #Y1153.

Date	Mintage	F12	VF20	XF40	MS60	MS63
2002	15	PF65 90,000				

KM# 1482 10000 YUAN
1000.00 g., 0.9999 Gold 31.9406 oz. AGW, 100 mm. **Subject:** Year of the Goat **Shape:** Scalloped **Note:** Prev. #Y1166.

Date	Mintage	F12	VF20	XF40	MS60	MS63
2003	15	PF65 75,000				

KM# 1550 10000 YUAN
1000.00 g., 0.9999 Gold 31.9406 oz. AGW, 100 mm. **Subject:** Year of the Monkey **Shape:** Scalloped **Note:** Prev. #Y1171.

Date	Mintage	F12	VF20	XF40	MS60	MS63
2004	15	PF65 90,000				

KM# 1604 10000 YUAN
1000.00 g., 0.999 Gold 31.9118 oz. AGW, 100 mm. **Obv:** Classical rooster **Rev:** Rooster strutting **Edge:** Scalloped **Note:** Photo reduced.

Date	Mintage	F12	VF20	XF40	MS60	MS63
2005	15	PF65 75,000				

KM# 1727 10000 YUAN
1000.00 g., 0.999 Gold 31.9118 oz. AGW, 100 mm. **Subject:** Year of the Pig **Obv:** Classical pig **Rev:** Three pigs **Shape:** Scalloped

Date	Mintage	F12	VF20	XF40	MS60	MS63
2007	118	PF65 70,000				

KM# 1841 10000 YUAN
1000.00 g., 0.999 Gold 31.9118 oz. AGW, 100 mm. **Subject:** Year of the Rat **Shape:** Scalloped

Date	Mintage	F12	VF20	XF40	MS60	MS63
2008	118	PF65 70,000				

KM# 1912 10000 YUAN
1000.00 g., 0.999 Gold 31.9118 oz. AGW, 100 mm. **Subject:** Year of the Tiger **Shape:** Scalloped

Date	Mintage	F12	VF20	XF40	MS60	MS63
2010	118	PF65 68,000				

KM# 1961 10000 YUAN
1000.00 g., 0.999 Gold 31.9118 oz. AGW, 100 mm. **Subject:** Year of the Rabbit **Shape:** Scalloped **Note:** Photo reduced.

Date	Mintage	F12	VF20	XF40	MS60	MS63
2011	118	PF65 68,000				

KM# 2010 10000 YUAN
1000.00 g., 0.999 Gold 31.9118 oz. AGW, 100 mm. **Subject:** Year of the Dragon

Date	Mintage	F12	VF20	XF40	MS60	MS63
2012	—	PF65 75,000				

KM# 1728 100000 YUAN
10000.00 g., 0.999 Gold 319.1184 oz. AGW, 180 mm. **Subject:** Year of the Pig **Obv:** Classical pig **Rev:** Sow with four pigletts sucking

Date	Mintage	F12	VF20	XF40	MS60	MS63
2007	18	PF65 600,000				

KM# 1842 100000 YUAN
10000.00 g., 0.999 Gold 319.1184 oz. AGW, 180 mm.

Date	Mintage	F12	VF20	XF40	MS60	MS63
2008	18	PF65 600,000				

KM# 1886 100000 YUAN
1000.00 g., 0.999 Gold 31.9118 oz. AGW, 180 mm. **Subject:** Year of the Ox

Date	Mintage	F12	VF20	XF40	MS60	MS63
2009	118	PF65 70,000				

KM# 1887 100000 YUAN
10000.00 g., 0.999 Gold 319.1184 oz. AGW, 180 mm. **Subject:** Year of the Ox

Date	Mintage	F12	VF20	XF40	MS60	MS63
2009	—	PF65 700,000				

KM# 1911 100000 YUAN
10000.00 g., 0.999 Gold 319.1184 oz. AGW, 180 mm. **Subject:** Year of the Tiger

Date	Mintage	F12	VF20	XF40	MS60	MS63
2010	18	PF65 700,000				

KM# 1960 100000 YUAN
10000.00 g., 0.999 Gold 319.1184 oz. AGW, 180 mm. **Subject:** Year of the Rabbit **Note:** Photo reduced.

Date	Mintage	F12	VF20	XF40	MS60	MS63
2011	18	PF65 700,000				

KM# 2009 100000 YUAN
10000.00 g., 0.999 Gold 319.1184 oz. AGW, 180 mm. **Subject:** Year of the Dragon

Date	Mintage	F12	VF20	XF40	MS60	MS63
2012	—	PF65 700,000				

PALLADIUM BULLION COINAGE
Panda Series

KM# A1531 100 YUAN
15.56 g., 0.999 Palladium 0.4965 oz. APW, 14 mm. **Rev:** Panda walking with cub

Date	Mintage	F12	VF20	XF40	MS60	MS63
2004	8,000	PF65 500				

KM# 1590 100 YUAN
15.55 g., 0.999 Palladium 0.4962 oz. APW, 30 mm. **Obv:** Temple of Heaven **Rev:** Panda cub and mom seated in bamboo

Date	Mintage	F12	VF20	XF40	MS60	MS63
2005	8,000	PF65 530				

PLATINUM BULLION COINAGE
Panda Series

KM# 1470 50 YUAN
1.55 g., 0.9995 Platinum 0.0495 oz. APW, 14.03 mm. **Obv:** Temple of Heaven, incuse legend **Rev:** Panda standing facing eating bamboo **Edge:** Reeded

Date	Mintage	F12	VF20	XF40	MS60	MS63
2003	50,000	PF65 135				

KM# 1532 50 YUAN
1.45 g., 0.9995 Platinum 0.0463 oz. APW, 14 mm. **Obv:** Temple of Heaven, incuse legend **Rev:** Panda standing facing with cub **Edge:** Reeded

Date	Mintage	F12	VF20	XF40	MS60	MS63
2004	50,000	PF65 135				

KM# 1415 100 YUAN
3.11 g., 0.9995 Platinum 0.0993 oz. APW, 18 mm. **Subject:** Panda Coinage 20th Anniversary **Obv:** Seated panda design of 1982 **Rev:** Walking panda design of 2002 **Edge:** Reeded **Note:** Prev. Y#1115.

Date	Mintage	F12	VF20	XF40	MS60	MS63
2002	20,000	PF65 250				

KM# 1591 100 YUAN
3.11 g., 0.999 Platinum 0.0992 oz. APW, 18 mm. **Obv:** Temple of Heaven **Rev:** Panda cub and mom seated in bamboo

Date	Mintage	F12	VF20	XF40	MS60	MS63
2005	30,000	PF65 200				

CHINA, REPUBLIC OF

TAIWAN

The Republic of China, comprising Taiwan (an island located 90 miles (145 km.) off the southeastern coast of mainland China), the offshore islands of Quemoy and Matsu and nearby islets of the Pescadores chain, has an area of 14,000 sq. mi. (35,980 sq. km.) and a population of 20.2 million. Capital: Taipei. During the past decade, manufacturing has replaced agriculture in importance. Fruits, vegetables, plywood, textile yarns and fabrics and clothing are exported.

The coins of Nationalist China do not carry A.D. dating, but are dated according to the year of the republic, which was established in 1911. However, republican years are added to 1911 to find the western year. Thus republican year 90 plus 1911 equals Gregorian calendar year 2001AD.

REPUBLIC
STANDARD COINAGE

Y# 550 1/2 YUAN
3.00 g., Bronze, 18 mm. **Obv:** Orchid **Rev:** Value and Chinese symbols **Edge:** Plain

Date	Mintage	F12	VF20	XF40	MS60	MS63
90(2001)	—	PF60 10.00				
92(2003)	—	PF60 10.00				
92(2003)	—	—	—	0.30	1.00	1.25
93(2004)	—	—	—	0.30	1.00	1.25

Y# 551 YUAN
3.80 g., Aluminum-Bronze, 20 mm. **Obv:** Bust of Chiang Kai-shek left **Rev:** Chinese value in center, 1 below **Edge:** Reeded

Date	Mintage	F12	VF20	XF40	MS60	MS63
90(2001)	—	PF60 12.50				
92(2003)	—	—	—	0.15	0.30	0.45
92(2003)	—	PF60 12.50				
94 (2005)	—	—	—	0.15	0.30	0.45
95(2006)	—	—	—	0.15	0.30	0.45
96(2007)	—	—	—	0.15	0.30	0.45
97(2008)	—	—	—	0.15	0.30	0.45
98(2009)	—	—	—	0.15	0.30	0.45
99(2010)	—	—	—	0.15	0.30	0.45
100(2011)	—	—	—	0.15	0.30	0.45
101(2012)	—	—	—	0.15	0.30	0.45

Y# 552 5 YUAN
4.40 g., Copper-Nickel, 22 mm. **Obv:** Bust of Chiang Kai-shek left **Rev:** Chinese value in center, 5 below **Edge:** Reeded

Date	Mintage	F12	VF20	XF40	MS60	MS63
90(2001)	—	PF60 12.50				
92(2003)	—	—	—	0.25	0.50	0.75
92(2003)	—	PF60 12.50				
97(2008)	—	—	—	0.25	0.50	0.75
100(2011)	—	—	—	0.25	0.50	0.75
101 (2012)	—	—	—	0.25	0.50	0.75

Y# 553 10 YUAN
7.50 g., Copper-Nickel, 26 mm. **Obv:** Bust of Chiang Kai-shek left **Rev:** Chinese value in center, 10 below **Edge:** Reeded

Date	Mintage	F12	VF20	XF40	MS60	MS63
90(2001)	—	PF60 15.00				
92(2003)	—	—	0.25	0.45	0.75	1.00
92(2003)	—	PF60 15.00				
93(2004)	—	—	—	0.45	0.75	1.00
94(2005)	—	—	—	0.45	0.75	1.00
95(2006)	—	—	—	0.45	0.75	1.00
96(2007)	—	—	—	0.45	0.75	1.00
96(2007)	—	PF60 15.00				
97(2008)	—	—	—	0.45	0.75	1.00
98(2009)	—	—	—	0.45	0.75	1.00
99(2010)	—	—	—	0.45	0.75	1.00

Y# 567 10 YUAN
7.43 g., Copper-Nickel, 26 mm. **Subject:** 90th Anniversary of the Republic **Obv:** Bust of Sun Yat-sen facing **Rev:** Holographic design and denomination **Edge:** Reeded

Date	Mintage	F12	VF20	XF40	MS60	MS63
90 (2001)	30,000,000	—	—	—	2.50	3.00

Y# 572 10 YUAN
7.50 g., Copper-Nickel, 26 mm. **Subject:** Chiang Ching-kuo, president **Obv:** Portrait facing **Rev:** Two legends in latent format, large value below

Date	Mintage	F12	VF20	XF40	MS60	MS63
100 (2010)	—	—	—	—	2.00	3.00

Y# 573 10 YUAN
7.50 g., Copper-Nickel, 26 mm. **Subject:** Chiang Wei-shui **Obv:** Portrait facing **Rev:** Two legends as latent images, large value below

Date	Mintage	F12	VF20	XF40	MS60	MS63
100 (2010)	—	—	—	—	2.00	3.00

Y# 574 10 YUAN
7.50 g., Copper-Nickel, 26 mm. **Subject:** Dr. Sun Yat-sen **Obv:** Bust facing **Rev:** Two legends as latent images, large value below

Date	Mintage	F12	VF20	XF40	MS60	MS63
100 (2011)	—	—	—	—	2.00	3.00
101 (2012)	—	—	—	—	2.00	3.00

Y# 565 20 YUAN
8.50 g., Bi-Metallic, 26.85 mm. **Subject:** Mona Rudao, Sediq chieftain **Obv:** Male portrait **Rev:** Three boats **Edge:** Reeded

Date	Mintage	F12	VF20	XF40	MS60	MS63
90(2001)	—	—	—	—	3.50	4.50
90(2001)	—	PF60 18.00				
92(2003)	—	—	—	—	3.50	4.50
92(2003)	—	PF60 18.00				
101(2012)	—	—	—	—	3.50	4.50

Y# 568 50 YUAN
10.00 g., Aluminum-Bronze, 28 mm. **Obv:** Bust **Rev:** Denomination above latent image denomination **Edge:** Reeding and denomination

Date	Mintage	F12	VF20	XF40	MS60	MS63
90-2001	—	PF60 20.00				
91-2002	—	—	—	—	7.50	10.00
92-2003	—	—	—	—	7.50	10.00
92-2003	—	PF60 20.00				
93-2004	—	—	—	—	7.50	10.00
94-2005	—	—	—	—	7.50	10.00
95-2006	—	—	—	—	7.50	10.00
95-2006	—	PF60 20.00				
96-2007	—	—	—	—	7.50	10.00
97-2008	—	—	—	—	7.50	10.00
101-2012	—	—	—	—	7.50	10.00

Y# 570 50 YUAN
15.57 g., 0.999 Silver 0.4968 oz. ASW, 33 mm. **Subject:** World Cup Baseball **Obv:** Player at bat with ball background **Rev:** Mount Jade above denomination **Edge:** Reeded

Date	Mintage	F12	VF20	XF40	MS60	MS63
90(2001)	130,000	—	—	—	25.00	27.50

Y# 569 50 YUAN
15.57 g., 0.999 Silver 0.4968 oz. ASW, 33 mm. **Subject:** 90th Anniversary of the Republic **Obv:** Portrait of Sun Yat-sen **Rev:** Latent image above denomination **Edge:** Reeded

Date	Mintage	F12	VF20	XF40	MS60	MS63
90(2001) (2002)	230,000	—	—	—	25.00	27.50

Y# 571 50 YUAN
31.10 g., 0.999 Silver 0.9926 oz. ASW, 38 mm. **Subject:** Third National Expressway **Obv:** Multicolor island map **Rev:** Kao Ping Hsi bridge **Edge:** Reeded

Date	Mintage	F12	VF20	XF40	MS60	MS63
93-2004	20,000	—	—	—	45.00	50.00

Y# 578 100 YUAN
31.14 g., 0.999 Silver 0.9936 oz. ASW, 38 mm. **Subject:** Year of the Rooster

Date	Mintage	F12	VF20	XF40	MS60	MS63
2005	150,000	PF63 130		PF65 150		

Y# 579 100 YUAN
31.14 g., 0.999 Silver 0.9936 oz. ASW, 38 mm. **Subject:** Asian International Stamp Exhibition 2005, Taipei

Date	Mintage	F12	VF20	XF40	MS60	MS63
2005	25,000	PF63 100		PF65 115		

Y# 580 100 YUAN
31.14 g., 0.999 Silver 0.9936 oz. ASW **Subject:** Lunar Year of the Dog

Date	Mintage	F12	VF20	XF40	MS60	MS63
2006	150,000	PF63 125		PF65 140		

Y# 581 100 YUAN
31.14 g., 0.999 Silver 0.9936 oz. ASW, 38 mm. **Subject:** Taiwan High Speed Rail

Date	Mintage	F12	VF20	XF40	MS60	MS63
2006	30,000	PF63 100		PF65 115		

Y# 582 100 YUAN
31.14 g., 0.999 Silver 0.9936 oz. ASW **Subject:** Lunar Year of the Pig

Date	Mintage	F12	VF20	XF40	MS60	MS63
2007	150,000	PF63 125		PF65 140		

Y# 583 100 YUAN
31.14 g., 0.999 Silver 0.9936 oz. ASW **Subject:** Lunar Year of the Rat

Date	Mintage	F12	VF20	XF40	MS60	MS63
2008	150,000	PF63 125		PF65 140		

Y# 584 100 YUAN
31.14 g., 0.999 Silver 0.9936 oz. ASW, 38 mm. **Subject:** 2008 Asian International Stamp Exposition, Taipai

Date	Mintage	F12	VF20	XF40	MS60	MS63
2008	20,000	PF63 100		PF65 115		

Y# 587 100 YUAN
31.14 g., 0.999 Silver 0.9936 oz. ASW, 38 mm. **Subject:** Lunar Year of the Buffalo

Date	Mintage	F12	VF20	XF40	MS60	MS63
2009	150,000	PF63 125		PF65 140		

Y# 588 100 YUAN
31.14 g., 0.999 Silver 0.9936 oz. ASW, 38 mm. **Subject:** Lunar Year of the Tiger

Date	Mintage	F12	VF20	XF40	MS60	MS63
2010	150,000	PF63 130		PF65 150		

Y# 589 100 YUAN
31.14 g., 0.999 Silver 0.9936 oz. ASW, 38 mm. **Subject:** Lunar Year of the Rabbit

Date	Mintage	F12	VF20	XF40	MS60	MS63
2011	150,000	PF63 125		PF65 140		

Y# 590 100 YUAN
31.14 g., 0.999 Silver 0.9936 oz. ASW, 38 mm. **Subject:** 100th Anniversary of the Republic of China

Date	Mintage	F12	VF20	XF40	MS60	MS63
2011	120,000	PF63 90.00		PF65 110		

Y# 591 100 YUAN
31.14 g., 0.999 Silver 0.9936 oz. ASW, 38 mm. **Subject:** Lunar Year of the Water Dragon

Date	Mintage	F12	VF20	XF40	MS60	MS63
2012	150,000	PF63 125		PF65 140		

Y# 576 200 YUAN
31.14 g., 0.999 Silver 0.9936 oz. ASW, 38 mm. **Subject:** Inauguration of the President of the People's Republic of China

Date	Mintage	F12	VF20	XF40	MS60	MS63
2004	65,000	PF63 100		PF65 115		

Y# 585 200 YUAN
31.14 g., 0.999 Silver 0.9936 oz. ASW, 38 mm. **Subject:** Inauguration of the President and Vice President of the People's Republic of China

Date	Mintage	F12	VF20	XF40	MS60	MS63
2008	120,000	PF63 100		PF65 115		

Y# 592 200 YUAN
31.14 g., 0.925 Silver 0.920 oz. ASW, 38 mm. **Subject:** Election of the President of the People's Republic of China

Date	Mintage	F12	VF20	XF40	MS60	MS63
2012	—	PF63 100		PF65 115		

Y# 577 2000 YUAN
31.11 g., 0.9999 Gold 0.9936 oz. AGW, 33 mm. **Subject:** Inauguration of the President of the People's Republic of China

Date	Mintage	F12	VF20	XF40	MS60	MS63
2004	—	PF63 1,500		PF65 1,900		

Y# 586 2000 YUAN
31.11 g., 0.9999 Gold 0.9936 oz. AGW, 33 mm. **Subject:** Inauguration of the President and Vice President of The People's Republic of China

Date	Mintage	F12	VF20	XF40	MS60	MS63
2008	60,000	PF63 1,750		PF65 2,000		

Y# 593 2000 YUAN
31.11 g., 0.9999 Gold 0.9936 oz. AGW, 33 mm. **Subject:** Election of the President of the People's Republic of China

Date	Mintage	F12	VF20	XF40	MS60	MS63
2012	—	PF63 1,750		PF65 2,000		

MINT SETS

KM#	Date	Mintage	Identification	Issue Price	Mkt Val
MS9	92(2003) (6)	—	Y#550-553, 565, 568 plus C-N Year of the Goat medal	—	20.00

PROOF SETS

KM#	Date	Mintage	Identification	Issue Price	Mkt Val
PS10	90(2001) (6)	210,000	Y#550-553, 565, 568 plus medal	29.40	90.00
PS12	92(2003) (6)	—	Y550-553, 565, 568 plus silver Year of the Goat Medal	—	100

COLOMBIA

The Republic of Colombia, in the northwestern corner of South America, has an area of 440,831 sq. mi. (1,138,910 sq. km.) and a population of 42.3 million. Capital: Bogota. The economy is primarily agricultural with a mild, rich coffee being the chief crop. Colombia has the world's largest platinum deposits and important reserves of coal, iron ore, petroleum and limestone; other precious metals and emeralds are also mined. Coffee, crude oil, bananas, sugar and emeralds are exported.

REPUBLIC

DECIMAL COINAGE
100 Centavos = 1 Peso

KM# 282.2 20 PESOS
3.60 g., Aluminum-Bronze, 20.25 mm. **Obv:** Flagged arms, 68 beads circle around the rim **Rev:** Denomination within wreath

Date	Mintage	F12	VF20	XF40	MS60	MS63
2003	15,900,000	—	—	—	0.50	0.75

KM# 294 20 PESOS
2.00 g., Brass, 17.2 mm. **Obv:** Head of Simon Bolivar left **Rev:** Value **Edge:** Reeded

Date	Mintage	F12	VF20	XF40	MS60	MS63
2004	22,700,000	—	—	—	0.15	0.25
2005	56,100,000	—	—	—	0.15	0.25
2006	63,012,500	—	—	—	0.15	0.25
2007	87,300,000	—	—	—	0.15	0.25
2008	5,850,000	—	—	—	0.20	0.30

KM# 283.2 50 PESOS
4.60 g., Copper-Nickel-Zinc, 21.8 mm. **Obv:** National arms, date below **Rev:** Denomination within wreath, 72 beads circle around rim **Edge:** Reeded

Date	Mintage	F12	VF20	XF40	MS60	MS63
2003	59,842,620	—	—	0.30	0.80	1.20
2004	51,700,000	—	—	0.30	0.80	1.20
2005	47,200,000	—	—	0.30	0.80	1.20
2006	22,000,000	—	—	0.30	0.80	1.20
2007	14,500,000	—	—	0.30	0.80	1.20
2008	67,500,000	—	—	0.30	0.80	1.20

KM# 283.2a 50 PESOS
Stainless Steel, 21.8 mm. **Obv:** National Arms, date below **Rev:** Denomination within wreath, 72 beads circle around rim **Edge:** Reeded

Date	Mintage	F12	VF20	XF40	MS60	MS63
2007	14,824,000	—	—	—	0.75	1.00
2008	67,500,000	—	—	—	0.75	1.00
2009	3,000,000	—	—	—	0.75	1.20
2010	55,100,000	—	—	—	0.75	1.00
2011	19,100,000	—	—	—	0.75	1.00
2012	22,300,000	—	—	—	0.75	1.00

KM# 295 50 PESOS
2.00 g., Nickel Plated Steel, 17 mm. **Obv:** Value at center **Rev:** Spectacled bear (Tremarctos ornatus)

Date	Mintage	F12	VF20	XF40	MS60	MS63
2012	30,816,000	—	—	—	0.75	1.00

KM# 285.2 100 PESOS
5.31 g., Aluminum-Bronze, 23 mm. **Obv:** Flagged arms above date **Rev:** Denomination within wreath, numerals 6mm tall **Edge:** Segmented reeding and lettered **Edge Lettering:** CIEN PESOS (twice) **Note:** Edge varieties exist.

Date	Mintage	F12	VF20	XF40	MS60	MS63
2006	59,000,000	—	—	0.60	1.50	2.00
2007	55,000,000	—	—	0.60	1.50	2.00
2008	120,200,000	—	—	0.60	1.50	2.00
2009	41,800,000	—	—	0.60	1.50	2.00
2010	85,400,000	—	—	0.50	1.25	1.50
2011	108,500,000	—	—	0.50	1.25	1.50
2012	20,000,000	—	—	0.50	1.25	1.50

KM# 296 100 PESOS
3.24 g., Brass Plated Steel, 20.3 mm. **Obv:** Value at center **Rev:** Colombian fruit frailejon

Date	Mintage	F12	VF20	XF40	MS60	MS63
2012	—	—	—	—	1.00	1.50
2013	—	—	—	—	1.00	1.25

KM# 287 200 PESOS
7.08 g., Copper-Nickel-Zinc, 24.4 mm. **Obv:** Denomination within lined circle, date below **Rev:** Quimbaya artwork **Edge Lettering:** MOTIVO QUIMBAYA - 200 PESOS

Date	Mintage	F12	VF20	XF40	MS60	MS63
2003	26,600,000	—	—	0.60	1.50	2.00
2004	31,200,000	—	—	0.60	1.50	2.00
2005	49,700,000	—	—	0.60	1.50	2.00
2006	75,462,500	—	—	0.60	1.50	2.00
2007	85,000,000	—	—	0.60	1.50	2.00
2008	110,400,000	—	—	0.60	1.50	2.00
2009	42,200,000	—	—	0.60	1.50	2.00
2010	85,600,000	—	—	0.60	1.50	2.00
2011	104,000,000	—	—	0.60	1.50	2.00
2012	45,000,000	—	—	0.60	1.50	2.50

KM# 297 200 PESOS
4.61 g., Copper-Nickel-Zinc, 22.4 mm. **Obv:** Value at center **Rev:** Scarlet macaw (Ara macao)

Date	Mintage	F12	VF20	XF40	MS60	MS63
2012	55,000,000	—	—	—	1.25	1.50
2013		—	—	—	1.25	1.50

KM# 286 500 PESOS
7.14 g., Bi-Metallic, 23.7 mm. **Obv:** Guacari tree within circle **Rev:** Denomination within circle, date below **Edge:** Segmented reeding

Date	Mintage	F12	VF20	XF40	MS60	MS63
2002	38,800,000	—	—	1.20	3.00	4.00
2003	26,410,000	—	—	1.20	3.00	4.00
2004	90,454,000	—	—	1.20	3.00	4.00
2005	97,664,000	—	—	1.20	3.00	4.00
2006	70,700,000	—	—	1.20	3.00	4.00
2007	109,624,000	—	—	1.20	3.00	4.00
2008	132,400,000	—	—	1.20	3.00	4.00
2009	39,700,000	—	—	1.20	3.00	4.00
2010	35,800,000	—	—	1.00	2.00	3.00
2011	76,200,000	—	—	1.00	2.00	3.00
2012	40,000,000	—	—	1.00	2.00	3.00

KM# 298 500 PESOS
7.14 g., Bi-Metallic, 23.7 mm. **Obv:** Value at center **Rev:** Glass frog (Hyalinobatrachium pellucidum) **Edge:** Segmented reeding

Date	Mintage	F12	VF20	XF40	MS60	MS63
2012	22,738,000	—	—	—	1.50	2.00

KM# 299 1000 PESOS
9.95 g., Bi-Metallic, 26.7 mm. **Obv:** Value at center with waves below **Rev:** Loggerhead sea turtle (Caretta caretta) and sea waves design **Edge:** Reeded & Security

Date	Mintage	F12	VF20	XF40	MS60	MS63
2012	—	—	—	—	5.00	7.50
2013	—	—	—	—	2.00	2.50

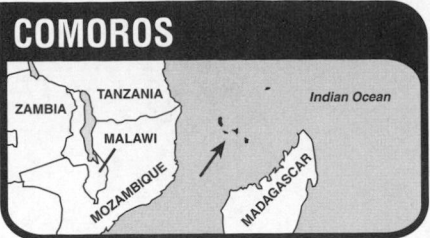

COMOROS

The Federal Islamic Republic of the Comoros, a volcanic archipelago located in the Mozambique Channel of the Indian Ocean 300 miles (483 km.) northwest of Madagascar, has an area of 719 sq. mi. (2,171 sq. km.) and a population of *714,000. Capital: Moroni. The economy of the islands is based on agriculture. There are practically no mineral resources. Vanilla, essence for perfumes, copra, and sisal are exported.

Ancient Phoenician traders were probably the first visitors to the Comoro Islands, but the first detailed knowledge of the area was gathered by Arab sailors. Arab dominion and culture were firmly established when the Portuguese, Dutch, and French arrived in the 16th century. In 1843 a Malagasy ruler ceded the island of Mayotte to France; the other three principal islands of the archipelago-Anjouan, Moheli, and Grand Comore came under French protection in 1886. The islands were joined administratively with Madagascar in 1912. The Comoros became partially autonomous, with the status of a French overseas territory, in 1946, and achieved complete internal autonomy in 1961. On Dec. 31, 1975, after 133 years of French association, the Comoro Islands became the independent Republic of the Comoros.

Mayotte retained the option of determining its future ties and in 1976 voted to remain French. Its present status is that of a French Territorial Collectivity. French currency now circulates there.

MINT MARKS
(a) - Paris, privy marks only
A - Paris

MONETARY SYSTEM
100 Centimes = 1 Franc

FEDERAL ISLAMIC REPUBLIC

BANQUE CENTRAL COINAGE

KM# 19 10 FRANCS
2.40 g., Steel, 17 mm. **Obv:** Crescent and four stars **Rev:** Value

Date	Mintage	F12	VF20	XF40	MS60	MS63
2001(a)	—	—	—	—	7.50	15.00

KM# 14a 25 FRANCS
3.97 g., Steel, 20 mm. **Series:** F.A.O. **Obv:** Chickens **Rev:** Denomination above date

Date	Mintage	F12	VF20	XF40	MS60	MS63
2001(a) Horseshoe	—	0.20	0.40	0.80	2.00	—

KM# 16 50 FRANCS
5.60 g., Nickel, 23.93 mm. **Obv:** Crescent and stars above denomination, date below **Rev:** Building with tall tower **Edge:** Reeded

Date	Mintage	F12	VF20	XF40	MS60	MS63
2001(a) horseshoe	—	—	—	—	2.50	3.50

KM# 16a 50 FRANCS
Nickel Plated Steel, 23.9 mm. **Obv:** Crescent and stars above denomination, date below **Rev:** Building with tall tower **Edge:** Reeded

Date	Mintage	F12	VF20	XF40	MS60	MS63
2001(a)	—	0.25	0.50	1.00	2.50	3.50

KM# 18a 100 FRANCS
10.20 g., Copper-Nickel, 28 mm. **Obv:** Crescent and stars above denomination, date below **Rev:** Boat and fish

Date	Mintage	F12	VF20	XF40	MS60	MS63
2003(a)	—	—	—	—	3.50	5.00

KM# 20 1000 FRANCS
22.20 g., 0.900 Silver 0.6382 oz. ASW, 37 mm. **Obv:** Crescent and four stars **Rev:** Mosque of the Sultans

Date	Mintage	F12	VF20	XF40	MS60	MS63
2002	500	PF63 100	PF65 120			

KM# 21 250 FRANCS
Bi-Metallic **Subject:** Central Bank, 30th Anniversary **Obv:** Large value at center **Rev:** Crescent and vertical stars

Date	Mintage	F12	VF20	XF40	MS60	MS63
2013	—	—	—	—	10.00	15.00

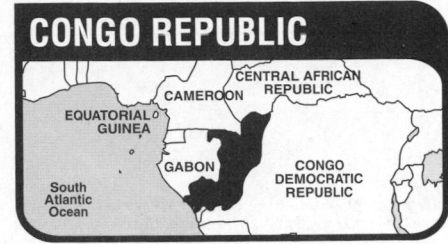

CONGO REPUBLIC

The Republic of the Congo (formerly the Peoples Republic of the Congo), located on the equator in west-central Africa, has an area of 132,047 sq. mi. (342,000 sq. km.) and a population of *2.98 million. Capital: Brazzaville. Agriculture forestry, mining, and food processing are the principal industries. Timber, industrial diamonds, potash, peanuts, and cocoa beans are exported.

NOTE: For earlier and related coinage see French Equatorial Africa and the Equatorial African States. For later coinage see Central African States.

MINT MARK
(a) - Paris, privy marks only

MONETARY SYSTEM
100 Centimes = 1 Franc

REPUBLIC
Republique du Congo

DECIMAL COINAGE

KM# 110 500 FRANCS
Silver **Subject:** History of aviation **Rev:** Swiss Air jet over mountains, 1931-2001, in color

Date	Mintage	F12	VF20	XF40	MS60	MS63
2002	—	PF65 50.00				

KM# 47 1000 FRANCS
15.00 g., 0.999 Silver 0.4787 oz. ASW, 35 mm. **Obv:** Seated woman with tablet **Rev:** Two soccer players and colosseum **Edge:** Plain

Date	Mintage	F12	VF20	XF40	MS60	MS63
2001	—	PF65 42.00				

KM# 48 1000 FRANCS
20.00 g., 0.999 Silver 0.6382 oz. ASW, 38 mm. **Obv:** Seated woman with tablet **Rev:** Two soccer players and Mexican pyramid **Edge:** Reeded

Date	Mintage	F12	VF20	XF40	MS60	MS63
2001	—	PF65 45.00				

KM# 112 1000 FRANCS
Silver, 38 mm. **Subject:** Thomas W. Lawson **Obv:** Female holding tablets **Rev:** Seven-masted Great Lakes Sconner sailing right

Date	Mintage	F12	VF20	XF40	MS60	MS63
2001	—	PF63 35.00	PF65 40.00			

KM# 109 1000 FRANCS
20.00 g., 0.999 Silver 0.6382 oz. ASW, 38.6 mm. **Obv:** Seated woman with tablets **Rev:** Portuguese merchant ship

Date	Mintage	F12	VF20	XF40	MS60	MS63
2002	—	PF63 40.00	PF65 45.00			

KM# 113 1000 FRANCS
Silver, 38 mm. **Obv:** Female with tablets **Rev:** Hohenzollern castle

Date	Mintage	F12	VF20	XF40	MS60	MS63
2002	—	PF63 35.00	PF65 40.00			

KM# 114 1000 FRANCS
Silver, 38 mm. **Obv:** Female seated with tablets **Rev:** Nymphenburg palace

Date	Mintage	F12	VF20	XF40	MS60	MS63
2002	—	PF63 35.00	PF65 40.00			

KM# 67 1000 FRANCS
31.11 g., 0.999 Silver 0.9926 oz. ASW, 40 mm. **Rev:** Eifle tower and franc coin in color

Date	Mintage	F12	VF20	XF40	MS60	MS63
2002	Est. 2001	PF65 90.00				

KM# 68 1000 FRANCS
Silver **Subject:** African Wildlife **Shape:** Rectangle

Date	Mintage	F12	VF20	XF40	MS60	MS63
2002 Proof	—	—	—	—	—	—

KM# 115 1000 FRANCS
20.00 g., 0.999 Silver 0.6382 oz. ASW, 38.6 mm. **Obv:** Seated female with two tablets **Rev:** DC-3 aircraft in clouds

Date	Mintage	F12	VF20	XF40	MS60	MS63
2002	—	PF65 50.00				

KM# 116 1000 FRANCS
20.00 g., 0.999 Silver 0.6382 oz. ASW, 38.6 mm. **Obv:** Seated female with two tablets **Rev:** Swiss A-3000 flying over mountains

Date	Mintage	F12	VF20	XF40	MS60	MS63
2002	—	PF65 50.00				

KM# 50 1000 FRANCS
20.20 g., Silver, 40 mm. **Series:** Endangered Wildlife **Obv:** Seated woman with tablet **Obv. Legend:** REPUBLIQUE DU CONGO **Rev:** Gorilla seated with infant **Rev. Legend:** - LE MONDE ANIMAL EN PERIL **Edge:** Reeded

Date	Mintage	F12	VF20	XF40	MS60	MS63
2003	—	PF65 50.00				

KM# 108 1000 FRANCS
20.00 g., 0.999 Silver 0.6382 oz. ASW, 38.6 mm. **Obv:** Seated woman with two tablets **Rev:** James Cook and the Endeavour

Date	Mintage	F12	VF20	XF40	MS60	MS63
2003	—	PF63 40.00	PF65 45.00			

KM# 117 1000 FRANCS
20.00 g., 0.999 Silver 0.6382 oz. ASW, 38.6 mm. **Obv:** Seated female with two tablets **Rev:** MD-11 aircraft on runway

Date	Mintage	F12	VF20	XF40	MS60	MS63
2003	—	PF65 50.00				

KM# 111 1000 FRANCS
Silver, 38 mm. **Subject:** Konrad Duden **Obv:** Female holding tablets **Rev:** Bust facing, writing

Date	Mintage	F12	VF20	XF40	MS60	MS63
2004	—	PF63 35.00	PF65 40.00			

KM# 118 1000 FRANCS
20.00 g., 0.999 Silver 0.6382 oz. ASW, 38.6 mm. **Obv:** Seated female with two tablets **Rev:** BAC-111 on grasy runway

Date	Mintage	F12	VF20	XF40	MS60	MS63
2004	—	PF65 50.00				

KM# 119 1000 FRANCS
20.00 g., 0.999 Silver 0.6382 oz. ASW, 38.6 mm. **Obv:** Seated female with two tablets **Rev:** DC-2 in clouds

Date	Mintage	F12	VF20	XF40	MS60	MS63
2004	—	PF65 50.00				

KM# 120 1000 FRANCS
20.00 g., 0.999 Silver 0.6382 oz. ASW, 38.6 mm. **Obv:** Seated female with two tablets **Rev:** DC-7 at airport

Date	Mintage	F12	VF20	XF40	MS60	MS63
2004	—	PF65 50.00				

KM# 51 1000 FRANCS
15.50 g., Silver, 35.02 mm. **Obv:** Seated woman with tablet **Obv. Legend:** REPUBLIQUE DU CONGO **Rev:** Head of Michelangelo 3/4 right **Edge:** Plain

Date	Mintage	F12	VF20	XF40	MS60	MS63
2005	—	PF63 35.00 PF65 40.00				

KM# 72 1000 FRANCS
0.999 Silver **Obv:** National Arms **Rev:** Steamlocomotive Limmat and Spanish Bon trasport (1847) from Baden to Zurich

Date	Mintage	F12	VF20	XF40	MS60	MS63
2007	—	PF65 75.00				

KM# 69 1500 FRANCS
1.24 g., 0.999 Gold 0.0396 oz. AGW, 13.92 mm. **Rev:** Ferdinand Graf von Zeppelin

Date	Mintage	F12	VF20	XF40	MS60	MS63
2005	—	PF63 90.00 PF65 100				

KM# 70 1500 FRANCS
1.24 g., 0.999 Gold 0.0396 oz. AGW, 13.92 mm. **Rev:** Spinx and Pyramids

Date	Mintage	F12	VF20	XF40	MS60	MS63
2005	—	PF63 90.00 PF65 100				

KM# 71 1500 FRANCS
1.24 g., 0.999 Gold 0.0396 oz. AGW, 13.94 mm. **Rev:** Neuschwanstein castle

Date	Mintage	F12	VF20	XF40	MS60	MS63
2005	—	PF63 90.00 PF65 100				

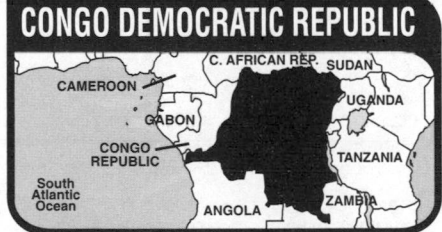

CONGO DEMOCRATIC REPUBLIC

The Democratic Republic of the Congo (formerly the Republic of Zaire, and earlier the Belgian Congo), located in the south-central part of Africa, has an area of 905,568 sq. mi. (2,345,410 sq. km.) and a population of *47.4 million. Capital: Kinshasa. The mineral-rich country produces copper, tin, diamonds, gold, zinc, cobalt and uranium.

DEMOCRATIC REPUBLIC
1998 -

REFORM COINAGE
Congo Francs; July 1998

KM# 76 25 CENTIMES
0.88 g., Aluminum, 19.90 mm. **Obv:** Lion left **Rev:** Mongoose **Edge:** Plain

Date	Mintage	F12	VF20	XF40	MS60	MS63
2002	—				0.75	1.00

KM# 77 25 CENTIMES
0.85 g., Aluminum, 20 mm. **Obv:** Lion left **Rev:** Ram right, looking left **Edge:** Plain

Date	Mintage	F12	VF20	XF40	MS60	MS63
2002	—				0.75	1.00

KM# 83 25 CENTIMES
1.30 g., Aluminum, 20 mm. **Obv:** Lion left **Rev:** Wild leaping dog right **Edge:** Plain

Date	Mintage	F12	VF20	XF40	MS60	MS63
2002	—				0.75	1.00

KM# 75 50 CENTIMES
2.20 g., Aluminum, 20.97 mm. **Obv:** Lion left **Rev:** Soccer player right, bumping ball with head **Edge:** Plain

Date	Mintage	F12	VF20	XF40	MS60	MS63
2002	—				1.25	1.50

KM# 78 50 CENTIMES
2.16 g., Aluminum, 27 mm. **Obv:** Lion left **Rev:** Giraffe right, looking left **Edge:** Plain

Date	Mintage	F12	VF20	XF40	MS60	MS63
2002	—				1.25	1.50

KM# 79 50 CENTIMES
2.20 g., Aluminum, 26.92 mm. **Obv:** Lion left **Rev:** Gorilla facing, looking left **Edge:** Plain

Date	Mintage	F12	VF20	XF40	MS60	MS63
2002	—				1.00	1.25

KM# 80 50 CENTIMES
2.16 g., Aluminum, 27 mm. **Obv:** Lion left **Rev:** Butterfly **Edge:** Plain

Date	Mintage	F12	VF20	XF40	MS60	MS63
2002	—				1.50	1.75

KM# 123 50 CENTIMES
3.92 g., Stainless Steel, 22.3 mm. **Obv:** Lion left above denomination **Rev:** Verney L. Camereon **Edge:** Plain

Date	Mintage	F12	VF20	XF40	MS60	MS63
2002	—				1.00	1.25

KM# 81 FRANC
4.57 g., Brass, 20.31 mm. **Obv:** Lion left **Rev:** Turtle **Edge:** Plain

Date	Mintage	F12	VF20	XF40	MS60	MS63
2002	—				1.25	1.50

KM# 82 FRANC
4.52 g., Brass, 20.32 mm. **Obv:** Lion left **Rev:** Chicken **Edge:** Plain

Date	Mintage	F12	VF20	XF40	MS60	MS63
2002	—				1.50	1.75

KM# 156 FRANC
5.00 g., Nickel Clad Steel, 24.8 mm. **Subject:** 25th Anniversary - Pope John Paul II's Visit **Obv:** Lion left **Rev:** Pope John Paul II as a priest in 1946 **Edge:** Plain

Date	Mintage	F12	VF20	XF40	MS60	MS63
2004	—				2.00	2.50

KM# 157 FRANC
5.00 g., Nickel Clad Steel, 24.8 mm. **Subject:** 25th Anniversary - Pope John Paul II's Visit **Obv:** Lion left **Rev:** Pope John Paul II as a Cardinal in 1967 **Edge:** Plain

Date	Mintage	F12	VF20	XF40	MS60	MS63
2004	—				2.00	2.50

KM# 158 FRANC
5.00 g., Nickel Clad Steel, 24.8 mm. **Subject:** 25th Anniversary - Pope John Paul II's Visit **Obv:** Lion left **Rev:** Pope John Paul II as newly elected pope in 1978 **Edge:** Plain

Date	Mintage	F12	VF20	XF40	MS60	MS63
2004	—				2.00	2.50

KM# 159 FRANC

5.00 g., Nickel Clad Steel, 24.8 mm. **Subject:** 25th Anniversary - Pope John Paul II's Visit **Obv:** Lion left **Rev:** Pope John Paul II wearing a mitre **Edge:** Plain

Date	Mintage	F12	VF20	XF40	MS60	MS63
2004	—	—	—	—	2.00	2.50

KM# 174 FRANC

6.00 g., Copper-Nickel, 21 mm. **Obv:** Lion left **Rev:** African Golden Cat right **Edge:** Plain

Date	Mintage	F12	VF20	XF40	MS60	MS63
2004	5,000	—	—	—	7.25	9.00

KM# 174a FRANC

8.00 g., 0.999 Silver 0.2553 oz. ASW, 21 mm. **Obv:** Lion left **Rev:** African Golden Cat right **Edge:** Plain

Date	Mintage	F12	VF20	XF40	MS60	MS63
2004	25	—	—	—	270	300

KM# 56 5 FRANCS

22.40 g., Copper-Nickel, 39.8 mm. **Series:** Wild Life Protection **Obv:** Lion left **Rev:** Multicolor swallowtail butterfly hologram **Edge:** Reeded **Note:** Prev. KM#79.

Date	Mintage	F12	VF20	XF40	MS60	MS63
2002(2001)	20,000	—	—	—	35.00	40.00

KM# 57 5 FRANCS

22.40 g., Copper-Nickel, 39.8 mm. **Series:** Wild Life Protection **Obv:** Lion left **Rev:** Multicolor dark greenish butterfly hologram **Edge:** Reeded **Note:** Prev. KM#80.

Date	Mintage	F12	VF20	XF40	MS60	MS63
2002(2001)	20,000	—	—	—	35.00	40.00

KM# 58 5 FRANCS

22.40 g., Copper-Nickel, 39.8 mm. **Series:** Wild Life Protection **Obv:** Lion left **Rev:** Multicolor red and black butterfly hologram **Edge:** Reeded **Note:** Prev. KM#81.

Date	Mintage	F12	VF20	XF40	MS60	MS63
2002(2001)	20,000	—	—	—	35.00	40.00

KM# 170 5 FRANCS

24.30 g., Copper-Nickel, 38.5 mm. **Obv:** Lion left **Rev:** Multicolor German 1 mark coin dated 2001 **Edge:** Reeded

Date	Mintage	F12	VF20	XF40	MS60	MS63
2002	—	—	—	—	15.00	20.00

KM# 198 5 FRANCS

Copper-Nickel, 38.6 mm. **Obv:** Lion left **Rev:** Cameleon on branch in color

Date	Mintage	F12	VF20	XF40	MS60	MS63
2003	—	—	—	—	—	25.00

KM# 214 5 FRANCS

22.40 g., Copper-Nickel, 38.6 mm. **Subject:** Wild Life protection **Obv:** Lion left **Rev:** Loggerhead sea turtle

Date	Mintage	F12	VF20	XF40	MS60	MS63
2003	—	—	—	—	—	45.00

KM# 215 5 FRANCS

22.40 g., Copper-Nickel, 38.6 mm. **Subject:** Wild Life Protection **Obv:** Lion left **Rev:** Dolphin as prism

Date	Mintage	F12	VF20	XF40	MS60	MS63
2003	—	—	—	—	—	40.00

KM# 216 5 FRANCS

22.40 g., Copper-Nickel, 38.6 mm. **Subject:** Wild Life Protection **Obv:** Lion left **Rev:** Orca whale as prism

Date	Mintage	F12	VF20	XF40	MS60	MS63
2003	—	—	—	—	—	40.00

KM# 128 5 FRANCS

8.00 g., Iron, 27.26x14.13 mm. **Obv:** Country name, lion and date in the bowl part of the spoon; value on the handle part **Edge:** Reeded **Note:** This is the Spoon part of the Compass and Spoon set. See also KM#127 (The spoon is the compass needle.)

Date	Mintage	F12	VF20	XF40	MS60	MS63
2004	5,000	—	—	—	—	15.00

KM# 164 5 FRANCS

25.40 g., Copper-Nickel, 38.8 mm. **Subject:** Papal Visit **Obv:** Lion left **Rev:** Pope John Paul II with staff and mitre **Edge:** Reeded

Date	Mintage	F12	VF20	XF40	MS60	MS63
ND (2004)	—	PF65 25.00				

KM# 165 5 FRANCS

49.50 g., Copper-Nickel, 45.1 mm. **Obv:** Lion left **Rev:** Rotating 50 year calender **Edge:** Reeded

Date	Mintage	F12	VF20	XF40	MS60	MS63
ND-2004 Matte	—	—	—	—	75.00	—

KM# 146 5 FRANCS

27.00 g., Copper-Nickel, 38.6 mm. **Obv:** Lion left **Rev:**

Multicolor Quetzal bird **Edge:** Reeded

Date	Mintage	F12	VF20	XF40	MS60	MS63
2004	5,000	PF65 35.00				

KM# 147 5 FRANCS
27.00 g., Copper-Nickel, 38.6 mm. **Obv:** Lion left **Rev:** Multicolor Bird of Paradise **Edge:** Reeded

Date	Mintage	F12	VF20	XF40	MS60	MS63
2004	5,000	PF65 35.00				

KM# 148 5 FRANCS
27.00 g., Copper-Nickel, 38.6 mm. **Obv:** Lion left **Rev:** Multicolor Kingfisher bird **Edge:** Reeded

Date	Mintage	F12	VF20	XF40	MS60	MS63
2004	5,000	PF65 35.00				

KM# 166 5 FRANCS
2.16 g., Wood, 39.4 mm. **Obv:** Lion, brown ink **Rev:** Gorilla, brown ink **Edge:** Plain

Date	Mintage	F12	VF20	XF40	MS60	MS63
2005	2,000				21.00	—

KM# 179 5 FRANCS
25.92 g., Copper-Nickel, 38.6 mm. **Series:** Wildlife Protection **Obv:** Lion standing left **Obv. Legend:** REPUBLIQUE DEMOCRATIQUE DU CONGO **Rev:** Butterfly Fish, multicolor **Edge:** Reeded

Date	Mintage	F12	VF20	XF40	MS60	MS63
2005	5,000	—	—	—	—	26.00

KM# 180 5 FRANCS
25.92 g., Copper-Nickel, 38.6 mm. **Series:** Wildlife Protection **Obv:** Lion standing left **Obv. Legend:** REPUBLIQUE DEMOCRATIQYE DU CONGO **Rev:** African Moony Fish, multicolor **Edge:** Reeded

Date	Mintage	F12	VF20	XF40	MS60	MS63
2005	5,000	—	—	—	—	26.00

KM# 181 5 FRANCS
25.92 g., Copper-Nickel, 38.6 mm. **Series:** Wildlife Protection **Obv:** Lion standing laft **Obv. Legend:** REPUBLIQUE DENOCRATIQYE DU CONGO **Rev:** Red Perch, multicolor **Edge:** Reeded

Date	Mintage	F12	VF20	XF40	MS60	MS63
2005	5,000	—	—	—	—	20.00

KM# 182 5 FRANCS
Copper-Nickel, 38.6 mm. **Obv:** Lion standing left **Rev:** Two cupids embracing, roses - multicolor **Rev. Legend:** Endless Love **Edge:** Reeded **Shape:** Heart

Date	Mintage	F12	VF20	XF40	MS60	MS63
2005	5,000	PF65 35.00				

KM# 220 5 FRANCS
Silver, 38.6 mm. **Obv:** Lion standing left **Rev:** Swiss Guard standing at right in hallway

Date	Mintage	F12	VF20	XF40	MS60	MS63
2006	—	PF65 50.00				

KM# 178 5 FRANCS
26.30 g., Silver Plated Bronze, 38.6 mm. **Obv:** Lion **Rev:** Multicolor Pope John Paul II wearing a mitre **Edge:** Reeded

Date	Mintage	F12	VF20	XF40	MS60	MS63
2007	—	PF65 40.00				

KM# 38 10 FRANCS
31.30 g., 0.925 Silver 0.9249 oz. ASW, 27 x 47.1 mm. **Subject:** Illusion **Obv:** Lion left **Rev:** Multicolor couple in flower picture **Edge:** Plain **Shape:** Rectangular **Note:** Prev. KM#61.

Date	Mintage	F12	VF20	XF40	MS60	MS63
2001	—	PF65 50.00				

KM# 59 10 FRANCS
25.95 g., 0.925 Silver 0.7668 oz. ASW, 39.9 mm. **Series:** Wild Life Protection **Obv:** Lion left **Rev:** Multicolor swallowtail butterfly hologram **Edge:** Reeded **Note:** Prev. KM#82.

Date	Mintage	F12	VF20	XF40	MS60	MS63
2002 (2001)	15,000	PF65 65.00				

KM# 60 10 FRANCS
25.95 g., 0.925 Silver 0.7668 oz. ASW, 39.9 mm. **Series:** Wild Life Protection **Obv:** Lion left **Rev:** Multicolor dark greenish butterfly hologram **Edge:** Reeded **Note:** Prev. KM#83.

Date	Mintage	F12	VF20	XF40	MS60	MS63
2002 (2001)	15,000	PF65 65.00				

KM# 61 10 FRANCS
25.95 g., 0.925 Silver 0.7668 oz. ASW, 39.9 mm. **Series:** Wild Life Protection **Obv:** Lion left **Rev:** Multicolor red and black butterfly hologram **Edge:** Reeded **Note:** Prev. KM#84.

Date	Mintage	F12	VF20	XF40	MS60	MS63
2002 (2001)	15,000	PF65 65.00				

KM# 65 10 FRANCS
20.00 g., 0.925 Silver 0.591 oz. ASW, 40.1 mm. **Series:** Airplanes **Obv:** Lion left **Rev:** Vickers Vimy twin engine biplane flying left **Edge:** Reeded **Note:** Prev. KM#88.

Date	Mintage	F12	VF20	XF40	MS60	MS63
2001	—	PF63 42.00	PF65 45.00			

KM# 66 10 FRANCS
20.00 g., 0.925 Silver 0.591 oz. ASW, 40.1 mm. **Series:** Airplanes **Obv:** Lion left **Rev:** Fokker DR1 triplane flying left **Edge:** Reeded **Note:** Prev. KM#89.

Date	Mintage	F12	VF20	XF40	MS60	MS63
2001	—	PF63 42.00	PF65 45.00			

KM# 67 10 FRANCS
20.00 g., 0.925 Silver 0.591 oz. ASW, 40.1 mm. **Series:** Airplanes **Obv:** Lion left **Rev:** Lockheed Vega flying left **Edge:** Reeded **Note:** Prev. KM#90.

Date	Mintage	F12	VF20	XF40	MS60	MS63
2001	—	PF63 42.00	PF65 45.00			

KM# 68 10 FRANCS
20.00 g., 0.925 Silver 0.591 oz. ASW, 40.1 mm. **Series:** Airplanes **Obv:** Lion left **Rev:** Boeing 314 Clipper flying left **Edge:** Reeded **Note:** Prev. KM#91.

Date	Mintage	F12	VF20	XF40	MS60	MS63
2001	—	PF63 42.00	PF65 45.00			

KM# 69 10 FRANCS
20.00 g., 0.925 Silver 0.591 oz. ASW, 40.1 mm. **Series:** Airplanes **Obv:** Lion left **Rev:** Junkers JU-87 Stuka in a dive **Edge:** Reeded **Note:** Prev. KM#92.

Date	Mintage	F12	VF20	XF40	MS60	MS63
2001	—	PF63 42.00	PF65 45.00			

KM# 70 10 FRANCS
20.00 g., 0.925 Silver 0.591 oz. ASW, 40.1 mm. **Series:** Airplanes **Obv:** Lion left **Rev:** B-29 Enola Gay flying left **Edge:** Reeded **Note:** Prev. KM#93.

Date	Mintage	F12	VF20	XF40	MS60	MS63
2001	—	PF63 42.00	PF65 45.00			

KM# 71 10 FRANCS
20.00 g., 0.925 Silver 0.591 oz. ASW, 40.1 mm. **Series:** Airplanes **Obv:** Lion left **Rev:** Bell X-1 rocket plane flying left **Edge:** Reeded **Note:** Prev. KM#94.

Date	Mintage	F12	VF20	XF40	MS60	MS63
2001	—	PF63 42.00	PF65 45.00			

KM# 72 10 FRANCS
20.00 g., 0.925 Silver 0.591 oz. ASW, 40.1 mm. **Series:** Airplanes **Obv:** Lion left **Rev:** Mikoyan-Gurevich Mig 21 fighter flying left **Edge:** Reeded

Date	Mintage	F12	VF20	XF40	MS60	MS63
2001	—	PF63 42.00	PF65 45.00			

KM# 74 10 FRANCS
31.10 g., 0.999 Silver 0.9926 oz. ASW, 40 mm. **Subject:** 2004 Olympics **Obv:** Lion left **Rev:** Convex chariot **Edge:** Reeded

Date	Mintage	F12	VF20	XF40	MS60	MS63
2001 Antique Finish	15,000	—	—	—	45.00	—

KM# 167 10 FRANCS
20.00 g., 0.925 Silver 0.591 oz. ASW, 40.1 mm. **Obv:** Lion left **Rev:** SS Bremen ship at sea **Edge:** Reeded

Date	Mintage	F12	VF20	XF40	MS60	MS63
2001	—	PF65 35.00				

KM# 168 10 FRANCS
20.00 g., 0.925 Silver 0.591 oz. ASW, 40.1 mm. **Obv:** Lion left **Rev:** RMS Queen Elizabeth 2 at sea **Edge:** Reeded

Date	Mintage	F12	VF20	XF40	MS60	MS63
2001	—	PF65 35.00				

KM# 169 10 FRANCS
20.00 g., 0.925 Silver 0.591 oz. ASW, 30 mm. **Obv:** Lion left
Rev: Sail Ship America **Edge:** Reeded

Date	Mintage	F12	VF20	XF40	MS60	MS63
2001	—	PF65 35.00				

KM# 175 10 FRANCS
25.83 g., Silver, 40 mm. **Obv:** Lion left **Rev:** 3 players **Edge:**
Reeded

Date	Mintage	F12	VF20	XF40	MS60	MS63
2001	—	—	—	—	—	50.00

KM# 197 10 FRANCS
20.00 g., 0.5948 Silver 0.380 oz. ASW, 40.1 mm. **Obv:** Lion left
Rev: SS Andrea Doria sailing left

Date	Mintage	F12	VF20	XF40	MS60	MS63
2001	—	PF65 45.00				

KM# 199 10 FRANCS
Silver, 40.1 mm. **Obv:** Lion left **Rev:** M.S. Voyager of the Seas
sailing left

Date	Mintage	F12	VF20	XF40	MS60	MS63
2001	—	PF65 45.00				

KM# 91 10 FRANCS
31.10 g., 0.999 Silver 0.9925 oz. ASW, 40 mm. **Subject:**
Olympics **Obv:** Lion left **Rev:** Ancient athlete incuse design
Edge: Plain **Note:** Design hubs with the design of the 500 sika
coin KM-42 of Ghana

Date	Mintage	F12	VF20	XF40	MS60	MS63
2002 Antiqued finish	—	—	—	40.00	—	—

KM# 93 10 FRANCS
31.23 g., 0.999 Silver 0.9966 oz. ASW, 38.7 mm. **Obv:** Lion left
Rev: Bearded portrait of Verney L. Camereon **Edge:** Reeded

Date	Mintage	F12	VF20	XF40	MS60	MS63
2002	—	—	—	—	40.00	45.00

KM# 94 10 FRANCS
26.15 g., Copper-Nickel, 40.3 mm. **Subject:** Historic
Automobiles **Obv:** Lion left **Rev:** 1908 Berliet car **Edge:** Reeded

Date	Mintage	F12	VF20	XF40	MS60	MS63
2002	—	PF63 13.50		PF65 15.00		

KM# 95 10 FRANCS
26.15 g., Copper-Nickel, 40.3 mm. **Subject:** Historic
Automobiles **Obv:** Lion left **Rev:** 1919 Hispano Suiza H6 car
right **Edge:** Reeded

Date	Mintage	F12	VF20	XF40	MS60	MS63
2002	—	PF63 13.50		PF65 15.00		

KM# 96 10 FRANCS
32.00 g., Silver Plated Copper, 40 mm. **Subject:** World Cup
Soccer **Obv:** Lion left **Rev:** Soccer player and multicolor
American flag **Edge:** Reeded

Date	Mintage	F12	VF20	XF40	MS60	MS63
2002	20,000	PF65 50.00				

KM# 97 10 FRANCS
32.00 g., Silver Plated Copper, 40 mm. **Subject:** World Cup
Soccer **Obv:** Lion left **Rev:** Two soccer players and multicolor
flag of Ecuador **Edge:** Reeded

Date	Mintage	F12	VF20	XF40	MS60	MS63
2002	20,000	PF65 50.00				

KM# 103 10 FRANCS
19.00 g., 0.999 Silver 0.6063 oz. ASW, 40 mm. **Series:**
Airplanes **Obv:** Lion left **Rev:** WWI German Gotha Ursinus G
bomber flying left at 8 o'clock **Edge:** Reeded

Date	Mintage	F12	VF20	XF40	MS60	MS63
2002	—	PF63 42.00		PF65 45.00		

KM# 104 10 FRANCS
19.00 g., 0.999 Silver 0.6063 oz. ASW, 40 mm. **Series:**
Airplanes **Obv:** Lion left **Rev:** WWII ME 109 German fighter
plane flying left **Edge:** Reeded

Date	Mintage	F12	VF20	XF40	MS60	MS63
2002	—	PF63 42.00		PF65 45.00		

KM# 105 10 FRANCS
19.00 g., 0.999 Silver 0.6063 oz. ASW, 40 mm. **Series:** Airplanes **Obv:** Lion left **Rev:** Savoia-Marchetti S 55 seaplane flying left **Edge:** Reeded

Date	Mintage	F12	VF20	XF40	MS60	MS63
2002	—	PF63 42.00	PF65 45.00			

KM# 106 10 FRANCS
19.00 g., 0.999 Silver 0.6063 oz. ASW, 40 mm. **Series:** Airplanes **Obv:** Lion left **Rev:** B-58 Hustler Delta wing bomber flying left at 8 o'clock **Edge:** Reeded

Date	Mintage	F12	VF20	XF40	MS60	MS63
2002	—	PF63 42.00	PF65 45.00			

KM# 107 10 FRANCS
19.00 g., 0.999 Silver 0.6063 oz. ASW, 40 mm. **Series:** Airplanes **Obv:** Lion left **Rev:** CF-105 Arrow jet fighter plane flying right, nose up **Edge:** Reeded

Date	Mintage	F12	VF20	XF40	MS60	MS63
2002	—	PF63 42.00	PF65 45.00			

KM# 108 10 FRANCS
19.00 g., 0.999 Silver 0.6063 oz. ASW, 40 mm. **Series:** Airplanes **Obv:** Lion left **Rev:** XB-70 Valkyrie experimental jet bomber flying right **Edge:** Reeded

Date	Mintage	F12	VF20	XF40	MS60	MS63
2002	—	PF63 42.00	PF65 45.00			

KM# 124 10 FRANCS
26.00 g., 0.925 Silver 0.7682 oz. ASW, 40 mm. **Subject:** Field Marshal Erwin Rommel **Obv:** Lion left above value **Rev:** Rommel, tank and map **Edge:** Reeded

Date	Mintage	F12	VF20	XF40	MS60	MS63
2002	15,000	PF65 42.50				

KM# 125 10 FRANCS
26.00 g., 0.925 Silver 0.7682 oz. ASW, 40 mm. **Subject:** George S. Patton **Obv:** Lion left above value **Rev:** Patton, tank and map **Edge:** Reeded

Date	Mintage	F12	VF20	XF40	MS60	MS63
2002	15,000	PF65 42.50				

KM# 162 10 FRANCS
20.20 g., 0.999 Silver 0.6446 oz. ASW, 40 mm. **Obv:** Lion left **Rev:** Space shuttle and five astronauts **Edge:** Reeded

Date	Mintage	F12	VF20	XF40	MS60	MS63
2002	—	PF65 40.00				

KM# 189 10 FRANCS
26.15 g., Copper-Nickel, 40.3 mm. **Series:** Automobiles **Obv:** Lion standing left **Rev:** Rolls Royce **Edge:** Reeded

Date	Mintage	F12	VF20	XF40	MS60	MS63
2002	—	PF63 13.50	PF65 15.00			

KM# 190 10 FRANCS
26.15 g., Copper-Nickel, 40.3 mm. **Series:** Automobiles **Obv:** Lion standing left **Rev:** Peugeot

Date	Mintage	F12	VF20	XF40	MS60	MS63
2002	—	PF63 13.50	PF65 15.00			

KM# 191 10 FRANCS
26.15 g., Copper-Nickel, 40.3 mm. **Series:** Automobiles **Obv:** Lion standing left **Rev:** Opel **Edge:** Reeded

Date	Mintage	F12	VF20	XF40	MS60	MS63
2002	—	PF63 13.50	PF65 15.00			

KM# 192 10 FRANCS
26.15 g., Copper-Nickel, 40.3 mm. **Series:** Automobiles **Obv:** Lion standing left **Rev:** Cadillac

Date	Mintage	F12	VF20	XF40	MS60	MS63
2002	—	PF63 13.50	PF65 15.00			

KM# 187 10 FRANCS
26.15 g., Copper-Nickel, 40.3 mm. **Series:** Automobiles **Obv:** Lion standing left **Rev:** Buick **Edge:** Reeded

Date	Mintage	F12	VF20	XF40	MS60	MS63
2002	—	PF63 13.50	PF65 15.00			

KM# 188 10 FRANCS
26.15 g., Copper-Nickel, 40.3 mm. **Series:** Automobiles **Obv:** Lion standing left **Rev:** Land Rover **Edge:** Reeded

Date	Mintage	F12	VF20	XF40	MS60	MS63
2002	—	PF63 13.50	PF65 15.00			

KM# 193 10 FRANCS
26.15 g., Copper-Nickel, 40.3 mm. **Series:** Automobiles **Obv:** Lion standing left **Rev:** Benz **Shape:** Reeded

Date	Mintage	F12	VF20	XF40	MS60	MS63
2002	—	PF63 13.50	PF65 15.00			

KM# 194 10 FRANCS
26.15 g., Copper-Nickel, 40.3 mm. **Series:** Automobiles **Obv:** Lion standing left **Rev:** Audi **Edge:** Reeded

Date	Mintage	F12	VF20	XF40	MS60	MS63
2002	—	PF63 13.50	PF65 15.00			

KM# 195 10 FRANCS
26.15 g., Copper-Nickel, 40.3 mm. **Series:** Automobiles **Obv:** Lion standing left **Rev:** Alfa Romero

Date	Mintage	F12	VF20	XF40	MS60	MS63
2002	—	PF63 13.50	PF65 15.00			

KM# 196 10 FRANCS
26.15 g., Copper-Nickel, 40.3 mm. **Series:** Automobiles **Obv:** Lion standing left **Rev:** Ford Model 'T' **Edge:** Reeded

Date	Mintage	F12	VF20	XF40	MS60	MS63
2002	—	PF63 13.50	PF65 15.00			

KM# 99.1 10 FRANCS
24.91 g., 0.925 Silver 0.736 oz. ASW, 38.6 mm. **Obv:** Lion left **Rev:** Chameleon **Edge:** Reeded

Date	Mintage	F12	VF20	XF40	MS60	MS63
2003	—	PF65 45.00				

KM# 99.2 10 FRANCS
24.91 g., 0.925 Silver 0.736 oz. ASW, 38.6 mm. **Obv:** Lion left **Rev:** Multicolor chameleon **Edge:** Reeded

Date	Mintage	F12	VF20	XF40	MS60	MS63
2003	—	PF65 50.00				

KM# 100 10 FRANCS
24.91 g., 0.925 Silver 0.736 oz. ASW, 38.6 mm. **Obv:** Lion left **Rev:** Striped skunk **Edge:** Reeded

Date	Mintage	F12	VF20	XF40	MS60	MS63
2003	—	PF65 475				

KM# 101 10 FRANCS
24.91 g., 0.925 Silver 0.736 oz. ASW, 38.6 mm. **Obv:** Lion left **Rev:** Porcupine on rock, right **Edge:** Reeded

Date	Mintage	F12	VF20	XF40	MS60	MS63
2003	—	PF65 50.00				

KM# 102 10 FRANCS
24.91 g., 0.925 Silver 0.736 oz. ASW, 38.6 mm. **Obv:** Lion left
Rev: Giant Pangolin on rock right **Edge:** Reeded

Date	Mintage	F12	VF20	XF40	MS60	MS63
2003	—	PF65 50.00				

KM# 109 10 FRANCS
19.00 g., 0.999 Silver 0.6063 oz. ASW, 40 mm. **Obv:** Lion left
Rev: 14 BIS early aircraft in flight **Edge:** Reeded

Date	Mintage	F12	VF20	XF40	MS60	MS63
2003	—	PF63 42.00	PF65 45.00			

KM# 110 10 FRANCS
19.00 g., 0.999 Silver 0.6063 oz. ASW, 40 mm. **Obv:** Lion left **Rev:** WWI Sopwith Camel fighter plane flying right **Edge:** Reeded

Date	Mintage	F12	VF20	XF40	MS60	MS63
2003	—	PF63 42.00	PF65 45.00			

KM# 111 10 FRANCS
19.00 g., 0.999 Silver 0.6063 oz. ASW, 40 mm. **Obv:** Lion left
Rev: Curtiss NC-4 early seaplane flying left **Edge:** Reeded

Date	Mintage	F12	VF20	XF40	MS60	MS63
2003	—	PF63 42.00	PF65 45.00			

KM# 112 10 FRANCS
19.00 g., 0.999 Silver 0.6063 oz. ASW, 40 mm. **Obv:** Lion left
Rev: Macchi-Castoldi MC-72 seaplane flying left at 8 o'clock
Edge: Reeded

Date	Mintage	F12	VF20	XF40	MS60	MS63
2003	—	PF63 42.00	PF65 45.00			

KM# 113 10 FRANCS
19.00 g., 0.999 Silver 0.6063 oz. ASW, 40 mm. **Obv:** Lion left
Rev: WWII CA-12 Boomerang fighter plane flying above map at 10 o'clock **Edge:** Reeded

Date	Mintage	F12	VF20	XF40	MS60	MS63
2003	—	PF63 42.00	PF65 45.00			

KM# 114 10 FRANCS
19.00 g., 0.999 Silver 0.6063 oz. ASW, 40 mm. **Obv:** Lion left
Rev: B-50A Superfortress bomber flying left **Edge:** Reeded

Date	Mintage	F12	VF20	XF40	MS60	MS63
2003	—	PF63 42.00	PF65 45.00			

KM# 115 10 FRANCS
19.00 g., 0.999 Silver 0.6063 oz. ASW, 40 mm. **Obv:** Lion left **Rev:** WWII Heinkel-178 German jet plane flying left **Edge:** Reeded

Date	Mintage	F12	VF20	XF40	MS60	MS63
2003	—	PF63 42.00	PF65 45.00			

KM# 116 10 FRANCS
19.00 g., 0.999 Silver 0.6063 oz. ASW, 40 mm. **Obv:** Lion left
Rev: Early De Havilland Comet jet liner flying left **Edge:** Reeded

Date	Mintage	F12	VF20	XF40	MS60	MS63
2003	—	PF63 42.00	PF65 45.00			

KM# 117 10 FRANCS
19.00 g., 0.999 Silver 0.6063 oz. ASW, 40 mm. **Obv:** Lion
left **Rev:** Panavia Tornado jet fighter-bomber flying left **Edge:** Reeded

Date	Mintage	F12	VF20	XF40	MS60	MS63
2003	—	PF63 42.00	PF65 45.00			

KM# 118 10 FRANCS
19.00 g., 0.999 Silver 0.6063 oz. ASW, 40 mm. **Obv:** Lion left
Rev: Hindustan HF24 jet fighter flying left **Edge:** Reeded

Date	Mintage	F12	VF20	XF40	MS60	MS63
2003	—	PF63 42.00	PF65 45.00			

KM# 119 10 FRANCS
19.00 g., 0.999 Silver 0.6063 oz. ASW, 40 mm. **Obv:** Lion left
Rev: Lockheed F-117 Stealth fighter flying left **Edge:** Reeded

Date	Mintage	F12	VF20	XF40	MS60	MS63
2003	—	PF63 42.00	PF65 45.00			

KM# 120 10 FRANCS
19.00 g., 0.999 Silver 0.6063 oz. ASW, 40 mm. **Obv:** Lion left
Rev: North American X-15 experimental rocket plane flying right at 1 o'clock **Edge:** Reeded

Date	Mintage	F12	VF20	XF40	MS60	MS63
2003	—	PF63 42.00	PF65 45.00			

KM# 122 10 FRANCS
25.00 g., 0.925 Silver 0.7387 oz. ASW, 38.6 mm. **Obv:** Lion
left **Rev:** Multicolor 3D hologram view of Victoria Falls **Edge:**
Reeded

Date	Mintage	F12	VF20	XF40	MS60	MS63
2003	5,000	PF63 50.00	PF65 70.00			

KM# 132 10 FRANCS
25.00 g., 0.900 Silver 0.7187 oz. ASW, 40 mm. **Obv:** Lion left
Rev: Multicolor dolphin leaping left **Edge:** Reeded

Date	Mintage	F12	VF20	XF40	MS60	MS63
2003	5,000	PF65 30.00				

KM# 133 10 FRANCS
25.00 g., 0.900 Silver 0.7187 oz. ASW, 40 mm. **Obv:** Lion left
Rev: Multicolor sea turtle left **Edge:** Reeded

Date	Mintage	F12	VF20	XF40	MS60	MS63
2003	5,000	PF65 30.00				

KM# 134 10 FRANCS
25.00 g., 0.900 Silver 0.7187 oz. ASW, 40 mm. **Obv:** Lion left
Rev: Multicolor killer whale jumping right **Edge:** Reeded

Date	Mintage	F12	VF20	XF40	MS60	MS63
2003	5,000	PF65 30.00				

KM# 135 10 FRANCS
26.00 g., 0.999 Silver 0.8297 oz. ASW, 40 mm. **Obv:** Lion
left **Rev:** Pope John Paul II with staff and mitre, waving **Edge:**
Reeded

Date	Mintage	F12	VF20	XF40	MS60	MS63
2003	—	PF65 55.00				

KM# 163 10 FRANCS
39.10 g., Acrylic, 49.9 mm. **Obv:** Old World Swallowtail butterfly
above lion and value **Rev:** Rear view of the obverse **Edge:**
Plain

Date	Mintage	F12	VF20	XF40	MS60	MS63
2003	—	—	—	—	75.00	—

KM# 171 10 FRANCS
39.10 g., Acrylic, 49.9 mm. **Obv:** Gorch Fock sail ship above
lion and value **Rev:** Rear view of the obverse design **Edge:**
Plain

Date	Mintage	F12	VF20	XF40	MS60	MS63
2003	1,000	—	—	—	75.00	—

KM# 126 10 FRANCS
25.00 g., 0.925 Silver 0.7387 oz. ASW, 38.6 mm. **Obv:** Lion left
above value **Rev:** Sundial face with collapsible gnomon **Edge:**
Reeded

Date	Mintage	F12	VF20	XF40	MS60	MS63
2004	5,000	PF65 50.00				

KM# 127 10 FRANCS
25.00 g., 0.925 Silver 0.7387 oz. ASW, 38.6 mm. **Obv:** Lion
left above value **Rev:** Compass face **Edge:** Reeded **Note:**

Compass part of the compass and spoon set (KM#128)

Date	Mintage	F12	VF20	XF40	MS60	MS63
2004	5,000	PF65 50.00				

KM# 141 10 FRANCS
25.00 g., 0.925 Silver 0.7387 oz. ASW, 38.6 mm. **Obv:** Lion
left **Rev:** Multicolor Emperor fish swimming left **Edge:** Reeded

Date	Mintage	F12	VF20	XF40	MS60	MS63
2004	5,000	PF65 55.00				

KM# 142 10 FRANCS
25.00 g., 0.925 Silver 0.7387 oz. ASW, 38.6 mm. **Obv:** Lion left
Rev: Multicolor octopus facing **Edge:** Reeded

Date	Mintage	F12	VF20	XF40	MS60	MS63
2004	5,000	PF65 75.00				

KM# 143 10 FRANCS
25.00 g., 0.925 Silver 0.7387 oz. ASW, 38.6 mm. **Obv:** Lion left
Rev: Formula 1 and GT race cars **Edge:** Reeded

Date	Mintage	F12	VF20	XF40	MS60	MS63
2004	5,000	PF65 45.00				

KM# 145 10 FRANCS
25.00 g., 0.925 Silver 0.7387 oz. ASW, 27x47 mm. **Obv:** Lion
left **Rev:** Pope with crucifix **Edge:** Plain **Shape:** Rectangular

Date	Mintage	F12	VF20	XF40	MS60	MS63
2004	5,000	PF65 50.00				

KM# 149 10 FRANCS
25.00 g., 0.925 Silver 0.7387 oz. ASW, 38.6 mm. **Obv:** Lion left
Rev: Multicolor Quetzal bird **Edge:** Reeded

Date	Mintage	F12	VF20	XF40	MS60	MS63
2004	5,000	**PF65** 35.00				

KM# 150 10 FRANCS
25.00 g., 0.925 Silver 0.7387 oz. ASW, 38.6 mm. **Obv:** Lion left
Rev: Multicolor Bird of Paradise on branch left **Edge:** Reeded

Date	Mintage	F12	VF20	XF40	MS60	MS63
2004	5,000	**PF65** 35.00				

KM# 151 10 FRANCS
25.00 g., 0.925 Silver 0.7387 oz. ASW, 38.6 mm. **Obv:** Lion left
Rev: Multicolor Kingfisher bird left **Edge:** Reeded

Date	Mintage	F12	VF20	XF40	MS60	MS63
2004	5,000	**PF65** 35.00				

KM# 155 10 FRANCS
Acrylic, 50 mm. **Obv:** Etched nine-masted sailing junk above
lion, value and country name **Edge:** Plain

Date	Mintage	F12	VF20	XF40	MS60	MS63
2004	2,000	—	—	—	—	55.00

KM# 179a 10 FRANCS
25.00 g., 0.925 Silver 0.7387 oz. ASW, 38.58 mm. **Series:**
Wildlife Protection **Obv:** Lion standing left **Obv. Legend:**
REPUBLIQUE DEMOCRATIQUE DU CONGO **Rev:** Butterfly
Fish, multicolor **Edge:** Reeded

Date	Mintage	F12	VF20	XF40	MS60	MS63
2005	5,000	**PF65** 45.00				

KM# 180a 10 FRANCS
25.00 g., 0.925 Silver 0.7387 oz. ASW, 38.50 mm. **Series:**
Wildlife Protection **Obv:** Lion standing left **Obv. Legend:**
REPUBLIQUE DEMOCRATIQUE DU CONGO **Rev:** African
Moony Fish, multicolor **Edge:** Reeded

Date	Mintage	F12	VF20	XF40	MS60	MS63
2005	5,000	**PF65** 45.00				

KM# 181a 10 FRANCS
25.00 g., 0.925 Silver 0.7387 oz. ASW, 38.58 mm. **Series:**
Wildlife Protection **Obv:** Lion standing left **Obv. Legend:**
REPUBLIQUE DEMOCRATIQUE DU CONGO **Rev:** Red
Perch, multicolor **Edge:** Reeded

Date	Mintage	F12	VF20	XF40	MS60	MS63
2005	5,000	**PF65** 45.00				

KM# 172 10 FRANCS
25.00 g., Silver, 38.6 mm. **Obv:** Lion left **Rev:** Pope waving half
facing at left, cross at upper right, Vatican at lower right

Date	Mintage	F12	VF20	XF40	MS60	MS63
2005	3,000	**PF65** 50.00				

KM# 217 10 FRANCS
39.00 g., Acrylic, 50 mm. **Obv:** John Paul II, lion and cross

Date	Mintage	F12	VF20	XF40	MS60	MS63
2005	—	—	—	—	—	50.00

KM# 218 10 FRANCS
39.10 g., Acrylic, 50 mm. **Obv:** Sailing training vessel Amergo
Vespucci

Date	Mintage	F12	VF20	XF40	MS60	MS63
2005	—	—	—	—	—	50.00

KM# 176 10 FRANCS
32.00 g., 0.999 Silver 1.0212 oz. ASW, 40 mm. **Obv:** Lion
standing left **Obv. Legend:** REPUBLIQUE DEMOCRATIQUE
DU CONGO **Rev:** World Trade Center Twin Towers as they
were before 9-11 **Edge:** Reeded

Date	Mintage	F12	VF20	XF40	MS60	MS63
2006	—	**PF65** 50.00				

KM# 219 10 FRANCS
39.00 g., Acrylic, 50 mm. **Obv:** Sailing ship Shtandart

Date	Mintage	F12	VF20	XF40	MS60	MS63
2006	—	—	—	—	—	50.00

KM# 221 10 FRANCS
Silver, 38.6 mm. **Obv:** Lion standing left **Rev:** Swiss Guard
standing taking oath on flag

Date	Mintage	F12	VF20	XF40	MS60	MS63
2006	—	**PF65** 70.00				

KM# 222 10 FRANCS
39.10 g., Acrylic, 50 mm. **Obv:** Admiral Michiel de Ruyter and sailing ship

Date	Mintage	F12	VF20	XF40	MS60	MS63
2007	—					50.00

KM# 200 10 FRANCS
Silver Plated Copper, 40 mm. **Subject:** Aviation Centennial 1903-2003 **Obv:** National arms **Rev:** Early aircraft and bust

Date	Mintage	F12	VF20	XF40	MS60	MS63
2008	—	PF65 15.00				

KM# 201 10 FRANCS
Silver Plated Copper, 40 mm. **Subject:** Warriors of the World
Obv: National arms **Rev:** Spartan standing

Date	Mintage	F12	VF20	XF40	MS60	MS63
2010	—	PF63 25.00	PF65 30.00			

KM# 202 10 FRANCS
Silver Plated Copper, 40 mm. **Subject:** Warriors of the World
Obv: National arms **Rev:** Centurian

Date	Mintage	F12	VF20	XF40	MS60	MS63
2010	—	PF63 25.00	PF65 30.00			

KM# 203 10 FRANCS
Silver Plated Copper, 40 mm. **Subject:** Warriors of the World
Obv: National arms **Rev:** Gladiator standing

Date	Mintage	F12	VF20	XF40	MS60	MS63
2010	—	PF63 25.00	PF65 30.00			

KM# 204 10 FRANCS
Silver Plated Copper, 40 mm. **Subject:** Warriors of the World
Obv: Naitonal arms **Rev:** Chinese warrior

Date	Mintage	F12	VF20	XF40	MS60	MS63
2010	—	PF63 25.00	PF65 30.00			

KM# 205 10 FRANCS
Silver Plated Copper, 40 mm. **Subject:** Warriors of the World
Obv: Naitonal Arms **Rev:** Celtic Warrior

Date	Mintage	F12	VF20	XF40	MS60	MS63
2010	—	PF63 25.00	PF65 30.00			

KM# 206 10 FRANCS
Silver Plated Copper, 40 mm. **Subject:** Warriors of the World
Obv: National arms **Rev:** Mongolian warrior on horseback

Date	Mintage	F12	VF20	XF40	MS60	MS63
2010	—	PF63 25.00	PF65 30.00			

KM# 207 10 FRANCS
Silver Plated Copper, 40 mm. **Subject:** Warriors of the World
Obv: National arms **Rev:** Viking standing

Date	Mintage	F12	VF20	XF40	MS60	MS63
2010	—	PF63 25.00	PF65 30.00			

KM# 208 10 FRANCS
Silver Plated Copper, 40 mm. **Subject:** Warriors of the World
Obv: National arms **Rev:** English Archer

Date	Mintage	F12	VF20	XF40	MS60	MS63
2010	—	PF63 25.00	PF65 30.00			

KM# 209 10 FRANCS
Silver Plated Copper, 40 mm. **Subject:** Warriors of the World
Obv: National arms **Rev:** Templar Knight on horseback

Date	Mintage	F12	VF20	XF40	MS60	MS63
2010	—	PF63 25.00	PF65 30.00			

KM# 210 10 FRANCS
Silver Plated Copper, 40 mm. **Subject:** Warriors of the World
Obv: National arms **Rev:** Ninja standing

Date	Mintage	F12	VF20	XF40	MS60	MS63
2010	—	PF63 25.00	PF65 30.00			

KM# 211 10 FRANCS
Silver Plated Copper, 40 mm. **Subject:** Warriors of the World
Obv: National arms **Rev:** Samurai warrior standing

Date	Mintage	F12	VF20	XF40	MS60	MS63
2010	—	PF63 25.00	PF65 30.00			

KM# 212 10 FRANCS
Silver Plated Copper, 40 mm. **Subject:** Warriors of the World
Obv: National arms **Rev:** Zulu warrior standing

Date	Mintage	F12	VF20	XF40	MS60	MS63
2010	—	PF63 25.00	PF65 30.00			

KM# 136 20 FRANCS
1.24 g., 0.9999 Gold 0.0397 oz. AGW, 13.92 mm. **Obv:** Lion left
Rev: Pope John Paul II with staff and mitre, waving **Edge:** Plain

Date	Mintage	F12	VF20	XF40	MS60	MS63
2003	—	PF65 75.00				

KM# 137 20 FRANCS
1.24 g., 0.9999 Gold 0.0397 oz. AGW, 13.92 mm. **Obv:** Lion left
Rev: Skunk **Edge:** Plain

Date	Mintage	F12	VF20	XF40	MS60	MS63
2003	25,000	PF65 75.00				

KM# 138 20 FRANCS
1.24 g., 0.9999 Gold 0.0397 oz. AGW, 13.92 mm. **Obv:** Lion left
Rev: Giant anteater right **Edge:** Plain

Date	Mintage	F12	VF20	XF40	MS60	MS63
2003	25,000	PF65 75.00				

KM# 139 20 FRANCS
1.24 g., 0.9999 Gold 0.0397 oz. AGW, 13.92 mm. **Obv:** Lion left
Rev: Porcupine right **Edge:** Plain

Date	Mintage	F12	VF20	XF40	MS60	MS63
2003	25,000	PF65 75.00				

KM# 140 20 FRANCS
1.24 g., 0.9999 Gold 0.0397 oz. AGW, 13.92 mm. **Obv:** Lion left
Rev: Chameleon **Edge:** Plain

Date	Mintage	F12	VF20	XF40	MS60	MS63
2003	25,000	PF65 75.00				

KM# 184 20 FRANCS
1.22 g., 0.9999 Gold 0.039 oz. AGW, 13.74 mm. **Subject:**
XXVIII Summer Olympics - Athens **Obv:** Lion standing right
Rev: Athenian tetradrachm featuring owl perched **Edge:**
Reeded

Date	Mintage	F12	VF20	XF40	MS60	MS63
2003	25,000	PF65 75.00				

KM# 144 20 FRANCS
1.24 g., 0.9999 Gold 0.0397 oz. AGW, 13.92 mm. **Obv:** Lion left
Rev: Ferrari coat of arms **Edge:** Plain

Date	Mintage	F12	VF20	XF40	MS60	MS63
2004	5,000	PF65 75.00				

KM# 186 20 FRANCS
1.24 g., 0.9999 Gold 0.0397 oz. AGW, 13.92 mm. **Subject:**
Christmas **Obv:** Lion standing left **Rev:** Jesus lying in manger

Date	Mintage	F12	VF20	XF40	MS60	MS63
ND-2004	25,000	PF65 75.00				

KM# 173 20 FRANCS
1.53 g., 0.999 Gold 0.0488 oz. AGW, 13.9 mm. **Obv:** Lion left
Rev: Pope waving at left, cross at upper right, Vatican at lower
right

Date	Mintage	F12	VF20	XF40	MS60	MS63
2005	25,000	PF65 95.00				

KM# 213 25 FRANCS
Acrylic, 50mm mm. **Rev:** H.M. Bark Endeavour at center;
Captian James Cook bust at top left, National arms at bottom
center

Date	Mintage	F12	VF20	XF40	MS60	MS63
2009	—	—	—	—	—	55.00

KM# 223 30 FRANCS
20.00 g., 0.999 Silver 0.6382 oz. ASW, 38.61 mm. **Subject:**
Big Cats - Lion

Date	Mintage	F12	VF20	XF40	MS60	MS63
2011	3,000	PF65 50.00				

KM# 224 30 FRANCS
20.00 g., 0.999 Silver 0.6382 oz. ASW, 38.61 mm. **Subject:**
Big cats - Leopard

Date	Mintage	F12	VF20	XF40	MS60	MS63
2011	3,000	PF65 50.00				

KM# 225 30 FRANCS
20.00 g., 0.999 Silver 0.6382 oz. ASW, 38.61 mm. **Subject:**
Big cats - Chetah

Date	Mintage	F12	VF20	XF40	MS60	MS63
2011	3,000	PF65 50.00				

KM# 226 30 FRANCS
20.00 g., 0.999 Silver 0.6382 oz. ASW, 38.61 mm. **Subject:**
Big cats - Tiger

Date	Mintage	F12	VF20	XF40	MS60	MS63
2011	3,000	PF65 50.00				

KM# 185 75 FRANCS
15.55 g., 0.9999 Gold 0.4967 oz. AGW **Subject:** XXVIII
Summer Olympics - Athens **Obv:** Lion standing right **Rev:**
Athenian tetradrachm featuring owl perched **Edge:** Reeded

Date	Mintage	F12	VF20	XF40	MS60	MS63
2003	500	PF65 900				

KM# 129 100 FRANCS
31.10 g., 0.9999 Gold 0.9934 oz. AGW, 40 mm. **Series:**
Wild Life Protection **Obv:** Lion left **Rev:** Reflective multicolor
swallowtail butterfly **Edge:** Reeded

Date	Mintage	F12	VF20	XF40	MS60	MS63
2002	50	PF65 1,800				

KM# 130 100 FRANCS
31.10 g., 0.9999 Gold 0.9934 oz. AGW, 40 mm. **Series:** Wild
Life Protection **Obv:** Lion left **Rev:** Reflective multicolor dark
greenish butterfly **Edge:** Reeded

Date	Mintage	F12	VF20	XF40	MS60	MS63
2002	50	PF65 1,800				

KM# 131 100 FRANCS
31.10 g., 0.9999 Gold 0.9934 oz. AGW, 40 mm. **Series:** Wild
Life Protection **Obv:** Lion left **Rev:** Reflective multicolor red and
black butterfly **Edge:** Reeded

Date	Mintage	F12	VF20	XF40	MS60	MS63
2002	50	PF65 1,800				

KM# 152 100 FRANCS
31.10 g., 0.9999 Gold 0.9935 oz. AGW, 38.6 mm. **Obv:** Lion left
Rev: Multicolor Quetzal bird **Edge:** Reeded

Date	Mintage	F12	VF20	XF40	MS60	MS63
2004	25	PF65 1,800				

KM# 153 100 FRANCS
31.10 g., 0.9999 Gold 0.9935 oz. AGW, 38.6 mm. **Obv:** Lion left
Rev: Multicolor Bird of Paradise left **Edge:** Reeded

Date	Mintage	F12	VF20	XF40	MS60	MS63
2004	25	PF65 1,800				

KM# 154 100 FRANCS
31.10 g., 0.9999 Gold 0.9935 oz. AGW, 38.6 mm. **Obv:** Lion left
Rev: Multicolor Kingfisher bird **Edge:** Reeded

Date	Mintage	F12	VF20	XF40	MS60	MS63
2004	25	PF65 1,800				

KM# 179b 100 FRANCS
31.10 g., 0.999 Gold 0.9925 oz. AGW, 38.58 mm. **Series:**
Wildlife Protection **Obv:** Lion standing left **Obv. Legend:**
REPUBLIQUE DEMOCRATIQUE DU CONGO **Rev:** Butterfly
Fish, multicolor **Edge:** Reeded

Date	Mintage	F12	VF20	XF40	MS60	MS63
2005	25	PF65 1,800				

KM# 180b 100 FRANCS
31.10 g., 0.999 Gold 0.9925 oz. AGW, 38.58 mm. **Series:**
Wildlife Protection **Obv:** Lion standing left **Obv. Legend:**
REPUBLIQUE DEMOCRATIQUE DU CONGO **Rev:** African
Mooney Fish, muticolor **Edge:** Reeded

Date	Mintage	F12	VF20	XF40	MS60	MS63
2005	25	PF65 1,800				

KM# 181b 100 FRANCS
31.10 g., 0.999 Gold 0.9925 oz. AGW, 38.58 mm. **Series:** Wildlife Protection **Obv:** Lion standing left **Obv. Legend:** REPUBLIQUE DEMOCRATIQUE DU CONGO **Rev:** Red Perch, multicolor **Edge:** Reeded

Date	Mintage	F12	VF20	XF40	MS60	MS63
2005	25	PF65 1,800				

MINT SETS

KM#	Date	Mintage	Identification	Issue Price	Mkt Val
MS2	2004 (4)	—	KM#156-159		12.50

COOK ISLANDS

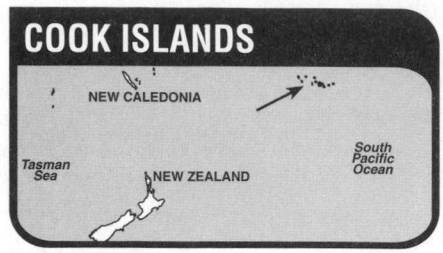

Cook Islands, a self-governing dependency of New Zealand consisting of 15 islands, is located in the South Pacific Ocean about 2,000 miles (3,218 km.) northeast of New Zealand. It has an area of 93 sq. mi. (234 sq. km.) and a population of 17,185. Capital: Avarua. The United States claims the islands of Danger, Manahiki, Penrhyn, and Rakahanga atolls. Citrus and canned fruits and juices, copra, clothing, jewelry, and mother-of-pearl shell are exported.

RULER
British

MINT MARK
PM - Pobjoy Mint

MONETARY SYSTEM
100 Cents = 1 Dollar

DEPENDENCY OF NEW ZEALAND
DECIMAL COINAGE

KM# 419 CENT
1.44 g., Aluminum, 21.9 mm. **Ruler:** Elizabeth II **Obv:** Crowned head right, date below **Rev:** Bust of Capt. James Cook right, denomination below **Edge:** Plain

Date	Mintage	F12	VF20	XF40	MS60	MS63
2003	—	—	—	—	1.25	1.50

KM# 420 CENT
1.44 g., Aluminum, 21.9 mm. **Ruler:** Elizabeth II **Obv:** Crowned head right, date below **Rev:** Collie dog right, denomination below **Edge:** Plain

Date	Mintage	F12	VF20	XF40	MS60	MS63
2003	—	—	—	—	0.75	1.00

KM# 421 CENT
1.44 g., Aluminum, 21.9 mm. **Ruler:** Elizabeth II **Obv:** Crowned head right, date below **Rev:** Pointer dog right, denomination above **Edge:** Plain

Date	Mintage	F12	VF20	XF40	MS60	MS63
2003	—	—	—	—	0.75	1.00

KM# 422 CENT
1.44 g., Aluminum, 21.9 mm. **Ruler:** Elizabeth II **Obv:** Crowned head right, date below **Rev:** Rooster right, denomination above **Edge:** Plain

Date	Mintage	F12	VF20	XF40	MS60	MS63
2003	—	—	—	—	0.75	1.00

KM# 423 CENT
1.44 g., Aluminum, 22 mm. **Ruler:** Elizabeth II **Obv:** Crowned head right, date below **Rev:** Monkey on branch, denomination at left **Edge:** Plain

Date	Mintage	F12	VF20	XF40	MS60	MS63
2003	—	—	—	—	0.75	1.00

KM# 756 CENT
3.64 g., Brass Plated Steel, 11.8 mm. **Ruler:** Elizabeth II **Obv:** Bust right **Rev:** Female Hula dancer

Date	Mintage	F12	VF20	XF40	MS60	MS63
2010	—	—	—	—	0.75	1.00

KM# 757 2 CENTS
5.10 g., Brass Plated Steel, 19.8 mm. **Ruler:** Elizabeth II **Obv:** Bust right **Rev:** The Endeavor

Date	Mintage	F12	VF20	XF40	MS60	MS63
2010	—	—	—	—	0.75	1.00

KM# 758 5 CENTS
6.15 g., Brass Plated Steel, 21.7 mm. **Ruler:** Elizabeth II **Obv:** Bust right **Rev:** Tiare Maori flower

Date	Mintage	F12	VF20	XF40	MS60	MS63
2010	—	—	—	—	1.00	1.50

KM# 759 10 CENTS
11.50 g., Nickel Plated Steel, 20.5 mm. **Ruler:** Elizabeth II **Obv:** Bust right **Rev:** Yellowfin tuna

Date	Mintage	F12	VF20	XF40	MS60	MS63
2010	—	—	—	—	1.00	1.50

KM# 760 20 CENTS
14.13 g., Nickel Plated Steel, 21.75 mm. **Ruler:** Elizabeth II **Obv:** Bust right **Rev:** Bird

Date	Mintage	F12	VF20	XF40	MS60	MS63
2010	—	—	—	—	1.50	2.00

KM# 1116 50 CENTS
28.28 g., Copper-Nickel, 38.61 mm. **Ruler:** Elizabeth II **Subject:** Elizabeth II Corronation, 50th Anniversary

Date	Mintage	F12	VF20	XF40	MS60	MS63
2002	—	—	—	—	—	20.00

KM# 1144 50 CENTS
Copper-Nickel **Ruler:** Elizabeth II **Rev:** Edward "Ned" Kelley in color

Date	Mintage	F12	VF20	XF40	MS60	MS63
2004	Est. 10000	PF65 15.00				

KM# 761 50 CENTS
Nickel Plated Steel, 34 mm. **Ruler:** Elizabeth II **Obv:** Bust right **Rev:** The Endeavor **Edge Lettering:** Reeded

Date	Mintage	F12	VF20	XF40	MS60	MS63
2010	—	—	—	—	2.00	2.50

KM# 1114 DOLLAR
32.00 g., Copper-Nickel, 40 mm. **Ruler:** Elizabeth II **Subject:** 2002 Winter Olympics, Salt Lake City

Date	Mintage	F12	VF20	XF40	MS60	MS63
2001	—	—	—	—	—	15.00

KM# 1115 DOLLAR
9.50 g., 0.999 Silver 0.3032 oz. ASW, 22.5 mm. **Ruler:** Elizabeth II **Series:** 2002 Commonwealth Games, Manchester **Rev:** Track field and medals on ribbons

Date	Mintage	F12	VF20	XF40	MS60	MS63
2001	Est. 5000	PF65 20.00				

KM# 396 DOLLAR
24.88 g., 0.999 Silver 0.7941 oz. ASW, 40.6 mm. **Ruler:** Elizabeth II **Subject:** Crown Jewels **Obv:** Crowned head right, legend **Rev:** Crowns and royal regalia **Edge:** Reeded

Date	Mintage	F12	VF20	XF40	MS60	MS63
2002	50,000	PF65 32.50				

KM# 1117 DOLLAR
0.999 Silver **Ruler:** Elizabeth II **Subject:** 2002 Winter Olumpics, Salt Lake City **Rev:** Figure skating

Date	Mintage	F12	VF20	XF40	MS60	MS63
2002	—	PF65 37.50				

KM# 1118 DOLLAR
Copper-Nickel **Ruler:** Elizabeth II **Subject:** XVII World Cup, Korea and Japan **Rev:** Soccer player and ball

Date	Mintage	F12	VF20	XF40	MS60	MS63
2002	—	PF65 15.00				

KM# 416 DOLLAR
10.75 g., Copper-Nickel, 28.5 mm. **Ruler:** Elizabeth II **Obv:** Queen's new portrait **Rev:** Tangaroa statue and value **Shape:** Scalloped

Date	Mintage	F12	VF20	XF40	MS60	MS63
2003	—	—	—	—	2.50	3.00
2010	—	—	—	—	2.50	3.00

KM# 455 DOLLAR
23.90 g., Copper-Nickel, 38.5 mm. **Ruler:** Elizabeth II **Obv:**

Queen Elizabeth II **Rev:** 50th Anniversary - Playboy magazine logo **Edge:** Reeded

Date	Mintage	F12	VF20	XF40	MS60	MS63
2003	—	—	—	—	7.00	9.00

KM# 462 DOLLAR
Copper-Nickel, 41 mm. **Ruler:** Elizabeth II **Rev:** Face of 5 Euro Banknote

Date	Mintage	F12	VF20	XF40	MS60	MS63
2003	—	—	—	—	7.00	9.00

KM# 463 DOLLAR
Copper-Nickel, 41 mm. **Ruler:** Elizabeth II **Rev:** Face of 10 Euro Banknote

Date	Mintage	F12	VF20	XF40	MS60	MS63
2003	—	—	—	—	7.00	9.00

KM# 464 DOLLAR
Copper-Nickel, 41 mm. **Ruler:** Elizabeth II **Rev:** Face of 20 Euro Banknote

Date	Mintage	F12	VF20	XF40	MS60	MS63
2003	—	—	—	—	7.00	9.00

KM# 465 DOLLAR
Copper-Nickel, 41 mm. **Ruler:** Elizabeth II **Rev:** Face of 50 Euro Banknote

Date	Mintage	F12	VF20	XF40	MS60	MS63
2003	—	—	—	—	7.00	9.00

KM# 466 DOLLAR
Copper-Nickel, 41 mm. **Ruler:** Elizabeth II **Rev:** Face of 100 Euro Banknote

Date	Mintage	F12	VF20	XF40	MS60	MS63
2003	—	—	—	—	7.00	9.00

KM# 467 DOLLAR
Copper-Nickel, 41 mm. **Ruler:** Elizabeth II **Rev:** Face of 500 Euro Banknote

Date	Mintage	F12	VF20	XF40	MS60	MS63
2003	—	—	—	—	7.00	9.00

KM# 455a DOLLAR
25.27 g., Copper-Nickel, 38.3 mm. **Ruler:** Elizabeth II **Obv:** Elizabeth II **Rev:** Playboy magazine's 50th Anniversary logo **Edge:** Reeded

Date	Mintage	F12	VF20	XF40	MS60	MS63
2003	50,000	PF63 18.00	PF65 20.00			

KM# 455b DOLLAR
25.27 g., 0.999 Silver 0.8064 oz. ASW, 38.3 mm. **Ruler:** Elizabeth II **Obv:** Elizabeth II **Rev:** Playboy magazine's 50th Anniversary logo **Edge:** Reeded

Date	Mintage	F12	VF20	XF40	MS60	MS63
2003	—	PF63 37.00	PF65 40.00			

KM# 455c DOLLAR
25.27 g., 0.999 Silver Gilt 0.8064 oz., 38.3 mm. **Ruler:** Elizabeth II **Obv:** Elizabeth II **Rev:** Playboy magazine's 50th Anniversary logo **Edge:** Reeded

Date	Mintage	F12	VF20	XF40	MS60	MS63
2003	—	PF63 45.00	PF65 50.00			

KM# 424 DOLLAR
8.50 g., 0.999 Silver 0.2713 oz. ASW, 25.1 mm. **Ruler:** Elizabeth II **Subject:** Zodiac Gemstones - Cancer **Obv:** Crowned head above ornamental center **Rev:** Encapsulated emeralds above Crab (Cancer) **Edge:** Reeded

Date	Mintage	F12	VF20	XF40	MS60	MS63
ND(2003)	10,000	PF65 25.00				

KM# 424a DOLLAR
8.50 g., 0.999 Silver Gilt 0.2713 oz., 25.1 mm. **Ruler:** Elizabeth II **Obv:** Crowned head above ornamental center **Rev:** Encapsulated emeralds above Crab (cancer)

Date	Mintage	F12	VF20	XF40	MS60	MS63
ND(2003)	10,000	PF65 60.00				

KM# 425 DOLLAR
8.50 g., 0.999 Silver 0.2713 oz. ASW, 25.1 mm. **Ruler:** Elizabeth II **Subject:** Zodiac Gemstones - Aquarius **Obv:** Crowned head above ornamental center **Rev:** Encapsulated garnets with Aquarius in background **Edge:** Reeded

Date	Mintage	F12	VF20	XF40	MS60	MS63
ND(2004) (2003)	10,000	PF65 25.00				

KM# 425a DOLLAR
8.50 g., 0.999 Silver Gilt 0.2713 oz., 25.1 mm. **Ruler:** Elizabeth II **Obv:** Crowned head above ornamental center **Rev:** Encapsulated garnets with Aquarius in background

Date	Mintage	F12	VF20	XF40	MS60	MS63
ND(2003)	10,000	PF65 60.00				

KM# 426 DOLLAR
8.50 g., 0.999 Silver 0.2713 oz. ASW, 25.1 mm. **Ruler:** Elizabeth II **Subject:** Zodiac Gemstones - Aries **Obv:** Crowned head above ornamental center **Rev:** Encapsulated Bloodstones in center with ram at left **Edge:** Reeded

Date	Mintage	F12	VF20	XF40	MS60	MS63
ND(2003)	10,000	PF65 25.00				

KM# 426a DOLLAR
8.50 g., 0.999 Silver Gilt 0.2713 oz., 25.1 mm. **Ruler:** Elizabeth II **Obv:** Crowned head above ornamental center **Rev:** Encapsulated Bloodstones in center with ram at left

Date	Mintage	F12	VF20	XF40	MS60	MS63
ND(2003)	10,000	PF65 60.00				

KM# 427 DOLLAR
8.50 g., 0.999 Silver 0.2713 oz. ASW, 25.1 mm. **Ruler:** Elizabeth II **Subject:** Zodiac Gemstones - Taurus **Obv:** Crowned head above ornamental center **Rev:** Encapsulated Sapphires with bull in background **Edge:** Reeded

Date	Mintage	F12	VF20	XF40	MS60	MS63
ND(2003)	10,000	PF65 25.00				

KM# 427a DOLLAR
8.50 g., 0.999 Silver Gilt 0.2713 oz., 25.1 mm. **Ruler:** Elizabeth II **Subject:** Zodiac Gemstones - Taurus **Obv:** Crowned head above ornamental center **Rev:** Encapsulated Sapphires with bull in background **Edge:** Reeded

Date	Mintage	F12	VF20	XF40	MS60	MS63
ND(2003)	10,000	PF65 60.00				

KM# 428 DOLLAR
8.50 g., 0.999 Silver 0.2713 oz. ASW, 25.1 mm. **Ruler:** Elizabeth II **Obv:** Crowned head above ornamental center **Rev:** Encapsulated Agates between twins **Edge:** Reeded

Date	Mintage	F12	VF20	XF40	MS60	MS63
ND(2003)	10,000	PF65 25.00				

KM# 428a DOLLAR
8.50 g., 0.999 Silver Gilt 0.2713 oz., 25.1 mm. **Ruler:** Elizabeth II **Obv:** Crowned head above ornamental center **Rev:** Encapsulated Agates between twins **Edge:** Reeded

Date	Mintage	F12	VF20	XF40	MS60	MS63
ND(2003)	10,000	PF65 60.00				

KM# 429 DOLLAR
8.50 g., 0.999 Silver 0.2713 oz. ASW, 25.1 mm. **Ruler:** Elizabeth II **Obv:** Crowned head above ornamental center **Rev:** Encapsulated Onyx stones with lion at right **Edge:** Reeded

Date	Mintage	F12	VF20	XF40	MS60	MS63
ND(2003)	10,000	PF65 25.00				

KM# 429a DOLLAR
8.50 g., 0.999 Silver Gilt 0.2713 oz., 25.1 mm. **Ruler:** Elizabeth II **Obv:** Crowned head above ornamental center **Rev:** Encapsulated Onyx stones with lion at right **Edge:** Reeded

Date	Mintage	F12	VF20	XF40	MS60	MS63
ND(2003)	10,000	PF65 60.00				

KM# 430 DOLLAR
8.50 g., 0.999 Silver 0.2713 oz. ASW, 25.1 mm. **Ruler:** Elizabeth II **Subject:** Zodiac Gemstones - Virgo **Obv:** Crowned head above ornamented center **Rev:** Encapsulated Carnelian stones with woman at right **Edge:** Reeded

Date	Mintage	F12	VF20	XF40	MS60	MS63
ND(2003)	10,000	PF65 25.00				

KM# 430a DOLLAR
8.50 g., 0.999 Silver Gilt 0.2713 oz., 25.1 mm. **Ruler:** Elizabeth II **Subject:** Zodiac Gemstones - Virgo **Obv:** Crowned head above ornamented center **Rev:** Encapsulated Carnelian stones with Virgo at right **Edge:** Reeded

Date	Mintage	F12	VF20	XF40	MS60	MS63
ND(2003)	10,000	PF65 60.00				

KM# 431 DOLLAR
8.50 g., 0.999 Silver 0.2713 oz. ASW, 25.1 mm. **Ruler:** Elizabeth II **Subject:** Zodiac Gemstones - Libra **Obv:** Crowned head above ornamented center **Rev:** Encapsulated Peridot stones with balance scale **Edge:** Reeded

Date	Mintage	F12	VF20	XF40	MS60	MS63
ND(2003)	10,000	PF65 25.00				

KM# 431a DOLLAR
8.50 g., 0.999 Silver Gilt 0.2713 oz., 25.1 mm. **Ruler:** Elizabeth II **Subject:** Zodiac Gemstones - Libra **Obv:** Crowned head above ornamented center **Rev:** Encapsulated Peridot stones with balance scale **Edge:** Reeded

Date	Mintage	F12	VF20	XF40	MS60	MS63
ND(2003)	10,000	PF65 60.00				

KM# 432 DOLLAR
8.50 g., 0.999 Silver 0.2713 oz. ASW, 25.1 mm. **Ruler:** Elizabeth II **Subject:** Zodiac Gemstones - Scorpio **Obv:** Crowned head above ornamented center **Rev:** Encapsulated Aquamarine stones with scorpion at lower right **Edge:** Reeded

Date	Mintage	F12	VF20	XF40	MS60	MS63
ND(2003)	10,000	PF65 25.00				

KM# 432a DOLLAR
8.50 g., 0.999 Silver Gilt 0.2713 oz., 25.1 mm. **Ruler:** Elizabeth II **Subject:** Zodiac Gemstones - Scorpio **Obv:** Crowned head above ornamented center **Rev:** Encapsulated Aquamarine stones with scorpion at lower right **Edge:** Reeded

Date	Mintage	F12	VF20	XF40	MS60	MS63
ND(2003)	10,000	PF65 60.00				

KM# 433 DOLLAR
8.50 g., 0.999 Silver 0.2713 oz. ASW, 25.1 mm. **Ruler:** Elizabeth II **Subject:** Zodiac Gemstones - Sagittarius **Obv:** Crowned head above ornamented center **Rev:** Encapsulated Topaz stones with centaur at right **Edge:** Reeded

Date	Mintage	F12	VF20	XF40	MS60	MS63
ND(2003)	10,000	PF65 25.00				

KM# 433a DOLLAR
8.50 g., 0.999 Silver Gilt 0.2713 oz., 25.1 mm. **Ruler:** Elizabeth II **Subject:** Zodiac Gemstones - Sagittarius **Obv:** Crowned head above ornamented center **Rev:** Encapsulated Topaz stones with centaur at right **Edge:** Reeded

Date	Mintage	F12	VF20	XF40	MS60	MS63
ND(2003)	10,000	PF65 60.00				

KM# 434 DOLLAR
8.50 g., 0.999 Silver 0.2713 oz. ASW, 25.1 mm. **Ruler:** Elizabeth II **Subject:** Zodiac Gemstones - Capricorn **Obv:** Crowned head above ornamental center **Rev:** Encapsulated rubies with goat at right **Edge:** Reeded

Date	Mintage	F12	VF20	XF40	MS60	MS63
ND(2003)	10,000	PF65 25.00				

KM# 434a DOLLAR
8.50 g., 0.999 Silver Gilt 0.2713 oz., 25.1 mm. **Ruler:** Elizabeth II **Subject:** Zodiac Gemstones - Capricorn **Obv:** Crowned head above ornamented center **Rev:** Encapsulated Rubies with goat at right **Edge:** Reeded

Date	Mintage	F12	VF20	XF40	MS60	MS63
ND(2003)	10,000	PF65 60.00				

KM# 435 DOLLAR
8.50 g., 0.999 Silver 0.2713 oz. ASW, 25.1 mm. **Ruler:** Elizabeth II **Subject:** Zodiac Gemstones - Pices **Obv:** Crowned head above ornamented center **Rev:** Encapsulated Amethyst stones and two fish **Edge:** Reeded

Date	Mintage	F12	VF20	XF40	MS60	MS63
ND(2003)	10,000	PF65 25.00				

KM# 435a DOLLAR
8.50 g., 0.999 Silver Gilt 0.2713 oz., 25.1 mm. **Ruler:** Elizabeth II **Subject:** Zodiac Gemstones - Pices **Obv:** Crowned head above ornamented center **Rev:** Encapsulated Amethyst stones and 2 fish **Edge:** Reeded

Date	Mintage	F12	VF20	XF40	MS60	MS63
ND(2003)	10,000	PF65 60.00				

KM# 746 DOLLAR
24.90 g., Copper-Nickel, 38 mm. **Ruler:** Elizabeth II **Subject:** Historic ships - Espusi

Date	Mintage	F12	VF20	XF40	MS60	MS63
2003	—	—	—	—	15.00	20.00

KM# 747 DOLLAR
24.90 g., Copper-Nickel, 38 mm. **Ruler:** Elizabeth II **Subject:** Historic ships - Gorch Foch

Date	Mintage	F12	VF20	XF40	MS60	MS63
2003	—	—	—	—	15.00	20.00

KM# 748 DOLLAR
24.90 g., Copper-Nickel, 38 mm. **Ruler:** Elizabeth II **Subject:** Historic ships - Constitution

Date	Mintage	F12	VF20	XF40	MS60	MS63
2003	—	—	—	—	15.00	20.00

KM# 749 DOLLAR
24.90 g., Copper-Nickel, 38 mm. **Ruler:** Elizabeth II **Subject:** Historic ships - Beagle

Date	Mintage	F12	VF20	XF40	MS60	MS63
2003	—	—	—	—	15.00	20.00

KM# 750 DOLLAR
24.90 g., Copper-Nickel, 38 mm. **Ruler:** Elizabeth II **Subject:** Historic ship - Endeavour

Date	Mintage	F12	VF20	XF40	MS60	MS63
2003	—	—	—	—	15.00	20.00

KM# 751 DOLLAR
24.90 g., Copper-Nickel, 38 mm. **Ruler:** Elizabeth II **Subject:** Historic Ship - Vasa

Date	Mintage	F12	VF20	XF40	MS60	MS63
2003	—			—	15.00	20.00

KM# 1127 DOLLAR
31.64 g., 0.999 Silver 1.0095 oz. ASW, 40.5 mm. **Ruler:** Elizabeth II **Rev:** James Cook and sailing ship

Date	Mintage	F12	VF20	XF40	MS60	MS63
2003	Est. 4999	PF65 50.00				

KM# 1130 DOLLAR
31.11 g., 0.999 Silver 0.9926 oz. ASW, 38.6 mm. **Ruler:** Elizabeth II **Subject:** Full Gospel Business Men's Fellowship, 50th Anniversary

Date	Mintage	F12	VF20	XF40	MS60	MS63
2003	Est. 4999	PF65 55.00				

KM# 1143 DOLLAR
28.28 g., 0.925 Silver 0.8356 oz. ASW, 38.61 mm. **Ruler:** Elizabeth II **Series:** Elizabeth II, 50th Anniversary of Corronation

Date	Mintage	F12	VF20	XF40	MS60	MS63
2003 Proof	Est. 20000	—	—	—	—	45.00

KM# 438 DOLLAR
31.10 g., 0.999 Silver 0.9926 oz. ASW, 40.5 mm. **Ruler:** Elizabeth II **Obv:** Crowned head right **Rev:** Multicolor Deng Xiaoping on Chinese map **Edge:** Plain **Shape:** As a map

Date	Mintage	F12	VF20	XF40	MS60	MS63
2004	20,000	—	—	—	70.00	75.00

KM# 454 DOLLAR
27.53 g., 0.999 Silver Clad Copper-Nickel 0.8785 oz., 38.6 mm. **Ruler:** Elizabeth II **Subject:** 60th Anniversary - D-Day Invasion **Obv:** Crowned bust right, new portrait **Rev:** Invasion scene of soldiers storming the beaches (Sword, Gold, Juno, Omaha, and Utah) of Normandy

Date	Mintage	F12	VF20	XF40	MS60	MS63
2004	—	—	—	—	18.00	20.00

KM# 1146 DOLLAR
31.64 g., 0.999 Silver 1.0095 oz. ASW **Ruler:** Elizabeth II **Subject:** Cobb & Co. 150th Anniversary **Rev:** Hackney Cab in color

Date	Mintage	F12	VF20	XF40	MS60	MS63
2004	—	PF65 60.00				

KM# 1147 DOLLAR
31.64 g., 0.999 Silver 1.0095 oz. ASW **Ruler:** Elizabeth II **Subject:** 90th Anniversary, Battle of the Emden and Sydney I

Date	Mintage	F12	VF20	XF40	MS60	MS63
2004	Est. 5000	PF65 60.00				

KM# 1148 DOLLAR
10.75 g., Copper-Nickel, 28.28 mm. **Ruler:** Elizabeth II **Rev:** Elvis Presley

Date	Mintage	F12	VF20	XF40	MS60	MS63
2004						15.00

KM# 1150 DOLLAR
31.11 g., 0.999 Silver 0.9926 oz. ASW, 45 mm. **Ruler:** Elizabeth II **Subject:** XXVIII Summer Olympics, Athens **Rev:** Cyclist in color

Date	Mintage	F12	VF20	XF40	MS60	MS63
2004	Est. 5000	—				45.00

KM# 1151 DOLLAR
31.11 g., 0.999 Silver 0.9926 oz. ASW, 45 mm. **Ruler:** Elizabeth II **Rev:** Gymnast

Date	Mintage	F12	VF20	XF40	MS60	MS63
2004	Est. 5000	—				45.00

KM# 1152 DOLLAR
31.11 g., 0.999 Silver 0.9926 oz. ASW, 45 mm. **Ruler:** Elizabeth II **Subject:** XXVIII Summer Olympics, Athens **Rev:** Two basketball players in color

Date	Mintage	F12	VF20	XF40	MS60	MS63
2004	Est. 5000	—				45.00

KM# 1153 DOLLAR
31.11 g., 0.999 Silver 0.9926 oz. ASW, 45 mm. **Ruler:** Elizabeth II **Subject:** XVIII Summer Olympics, Athens **Rev:** Sprinter in color

Date	Mintage	F12	VF20	XF40	MS60	MS63
2004	Est. 5000	—				45.00

KM# 1154 DOLLAR
31.11 g., 0.999 Silver 0.9926 oz. ASW, 45 mm. **Ruler:** Elizabeth II **Subject:** XXVIII Summer Olympics, Athens **Rev:** Archer in color

Date	Mintage	F12	VF20	XF40	MS60	MS63
2004	Est. 5000	—				45.00

KM# 1155 DOLLAR
31.11 g., 0.999 Silver 0.9926 oz. ASW, 45 mm. **Ruler:** Elizabeth II **Subject:** XXVIII Summer Olympics, Athens **Rev:** Weightlifter in color

Date	Mintage	F12	VF20	XF40	MS60	MS63
2004 Proof	Est. 5000	—				45.00

KM# 1156 DOLLAR
24.00 g., Copper-Nickel, 38 mm. **Ruler:** Elizabeth II **Rev:** Mohandas Ghandhi

Date	Mintage	F12	VF20	XF40	MS60	MS63
2004	—				15.00	18.00

KM# 443 DOLLAR
23.90 g., Copper-Nickel, 38.5 mm. **Ruler:** Elizabeth II **Subject:** Battle of Trafalgar **Obv:** Crowned bust right, new portrait **Rev:** HMS Victory and color portrait of Nelson **Edge:** Reeded

Date	Mintage	F12	VF20	XF40	MS60	MS63
2005	—	—	—	—	15.00	18.00

KM# 470 DOLLAR
31.16 g., 0.999 Silver 0.9944 oz. ASW, 39.02 mm. **Ruler:** Elizabeth II **Obv:** Twin Towers and Statue of Liberty, Queens Head below **Obv. Legend:** COOK ISLANDS / WE WILL NEVER FORGET **Rev:** Freedoom Tower and Statue of Liberty **Rev. Inscription:** LET / FREEDOM / RING - FREEDOM TOWER **Edge:** Reeded and plain with lettering **Edge Lettering:** 1 TROY OZ. .999 FINE SILVER

Date	Mintage	F12	VF20	XF40	MS60	MS63
2005	—	PF65 35.00				
2006	—	PF65 30.00				
2007	—	PF65 30.00				
2008	—	PF65 30.00				

KM# 1107 DOLLAR
31.11 g., 0.999 Silver 0.9926 oz. ASW, 40 mm. **Ruler:** Elizabeth II **Rev:** Pope Benedict XVI partially gilt

Date	Mintage	F12	VF20	XF40	MS60	MS63
2005	—	PF65 45.00				

KM# 1133 DOLLAR
Copper-Nickel, 38.6 mm. **Ruler:** Elizabeth II **Subject:** Star Wars, 30th Anniversary

Date	Mintage	F12	VF20	XF40	MS60	MS63
2005	Est. 9999	PF65 20.00				

KM# 1157 DOLLAR
31.64 g., 0.999 Silver 1.0095 oz. ASW **Ruler:** Elizabeth II **Subject:** Australian Automobiles

Date	Mintage	F12	VF20	XF40	MS60	MS63
2005	Est. 1500	PF65 60.00				

KM# 1158 DOLLAR
31.64 g., 0.999 Silver 1.0095 oz. ASW **Ruler:** Elizabeth II **Subject:** Australian Automobiles

Date	Mintage	F12	VF20	XF40	MS60	MS63
2005	Est. 1500	PF65 60.00				

KM# 1159 DOLLAR
31.64 g., 0.999 Silver 1.0095 oz. ASW **Ruler:** Elizabeth II **Subject:** Australian Automobiles

Date	Mintage	F12	VF20	XF40	MS60	MS63
2005	Est. 1500	PF65 60.00				

KM# 1160 DOLLAR
31.64 g., 0.999 Silver 1.0095 oz. ASW **Ruler:** Elizabeth II **Subject:** Australian Automobiles

Date	Mintage	F12	VF20	XF40	MS60	MS63
2005	Est. 1500	PF65 60.00				

KM# 1161 DOLLAR
31.64 g., 0.999 Silver 1.0095 oz. ASW **Ruler:** Elizabeth II **Subject:** Australian Automobiles

Date	Mintage	F12	VF20	XF40	MS60	MS63
2005	Est. 1500	PF65 60.00				

KM# 1162 DOLLAR
31.64 g., 0.999 Silver 1.0095 oz. ASW **Ruler:** Elizabeth II **Subject:** Australian Automobiles

Date	Mintage	F12	VF20	XF40	MS60	MS63
2005	Est. 1500	PF65 60.00				

KM# 1163 DOLLAR
31.64 g., 0.999 Silver 1.0095 oz. ASW **Ruler:** Elizabeth II **Subject:** Australian Automobiles

Date	Mintage	F12	VF20	XF40	MS60	MS63
2005	Est. 1500	PF65 60.00				

KM# 1164 DOLLAR
31.64 g., 0.999 Silver 1.0095 oz. ASW **Ruler:** Elizabeth II **Subject:** Australian Automobiles

Date	Mintage	F12	VF20	XF40	MS60	MS63
2005	Est. 1500	PF65 60.00				

KM# 1165 DOLLAR
31.64 g., 0.999 Silver 1.0095 oz. ASW **Ruler:** Elizabeth II **Subject:** Australian Automobiles

Date	Mintage	F12	VF20	XF40	MS60	MS63
2005	Est. 1500	PF65 60.00				

KM# 1166 DOLLAR
31.64 g., 0.999 Silver 1.0095 oz. ASW **Ruler:** Elizabeth II **Subject:** Australian Automobiles

Date	Mintage	F12	VF20	XF40	MS60	MS63
2005	1,500	PF65 60.00				

KM# 1167 DOLLAR
31.64 g., 0.999 Silver 1.0095 oz. ASW **Ruler:** Elizabeth II **Subject:** Australian Automobiles

Date	Mintage	F12	VF20	XF40	MS60	MS63
2005	Est. 1500	PF65 60.00				

KM# 1168 DOLLAR
31.64 g., 0.999 Silver 1.0095 oz. ASW **Ruler:** Elizabeth II **Subject:** Australian Automobiles

Date	Mintage	F12	VF20	XF40	MS60	MS63
2005	Est. 1500	PF65 60.00				

KM# 1173 DOLLAR
32.00 g., Copper-Nickel, 40 mm. **Ruler:** Elizabeth II **Rev:** Snowflake, building tower hockey play and figure skater

Date	Mintage	F12	VF20	XF40	MS60	MS63
2005	20,000	—	—	—	10.00	12.00

KM# 1174 DOLLAR
Copper-Nickel **Ruler:** Elizabeth II **Subject:** Marriage of Prince Charles and Camilla Parker-Bowles

Date	Mintage	F12	VF20	XF40	MS60	MS63
2005	Est. 5000	—				15.00

KM# 1177 DOLLAR
31.64 g., 0.999 Silver 1.0095 oz. ASW **Ruler:** Elizabeth II **Rev:** Pope John Paul II in color

Date	Mintage	F12	VF20	XF40	MS60	MS63
2005	5,000	PF65 125				

KM# 479 DOLLAR
Copper-Nickel, 38.6 mm. **Ruler:** Elizabeth II **Subject:** Gun ships of the world **Rev:** HMS Redoutable

Date	Mintage	F12	VF20	XF40	MS60	MS63
2006	—	—	—	—	—	25.00

KM# 480 DOLLAR
24.90 g., Copper-Nickel, 38 mm. **Ruler:** Elizabeth II **Subject:** Gunships of the world **Obv:** Crowned bust right **Rev:** Ark Royal in color **Edge:** Reeded

Date	Mintage	F12	VF20	XF40	MS60	MS63
2006	—	—	—	—	—	25.00

KM# 752 DOLLAR
24.90 g., Copper-Nickel, 38 mm. **Ruler:** Elizabeth II **Subject:** Gun ships - Chesapeak **Rev:** Multicolor naval ship

Date	Mintage	F12	VF20	XF40	MS60	MS63
2006	—	—	—	—	15.00	20.00

KM# 753 DOLLAR
24.90 g., Copper-Nickel, 38 mm. **Ruler:** Elizabeth II **Subject:** Gun ships - Syvende **Rev:** Multicolor naval ship

Date	Mintage	F12	VF20	XF40	MS60	MS63
2006	—	—	—	—	15.00	20.00

KM# 754 DOLLAR
24.90 g., Copper-Nickel, 38 mm. **Ruler:** Elizabeth II **Rev:** Multicolor Naval ship

Date	Mintage	F12	VF20	XF40	MS60	MS63
2006	—	—	—	—	15.00	20.00

KM# 755 DOLLAR
24.90 g., Copper-Nickel, 38 mm. **Ruler:** Elizabeth II **Subject:** Gun Ships - Mary Rose **Rev:** Multicolor Naval ship

Date	Mintage	F12	VF20	XF40	MS60	MS63
2006	—	—	—	—	15.00	20.00

KM# 1137 DOLLAR
31.64 g., 0.999 Silver 1.0095 oz. ASW **Ruler:** Elizabeth II **Subject:** 1923 New South Wales Garford Fire

Date	Mintage	F12	VF20	XF40	MS60	MS63
2006	Est. 5000	PF65 55.00				

KM# 1169 DOLLAR
0.50 g., 0.999 Gold AGW **Ruler:** Elizabeth II **Rev:** Pope Benedict XVI

Date	Mintage	F12	VF20	XF40	MS60	MS63
2006	—	PF65 45.00				

KM# 1179 DOLLAR
Silver **Ruler:** Elizabeth II **Subject:** David Livingstone

Date	Mintage	F12	VF20	XF40	MS60	MS63
2006	—	PF65 45.00				

KM# 1180 DOLLAR
Silver **Ruler:** Elizabeth II **Subject:** Ferdinanad Magellan

Date	Mintage	F12	VF20	XF40	MS60	MS63
2006	—	PF65 45.00				

KM# 1181 DOLLAR
Silver **Ruler:** Elizabeth II **Subject:** Roald Amundsen

Date	Mintage	F12	VF20	XF40	MS60	MS63
2006	—	PF65 45.00				

KM# 1182 DOLLAR
Silver **Ruler:** Elizabeth II **Subject:** Christopher Columbus

Date	Mintage	F12	VF20	XF40	MS60	MS63
2006	—	PF65 45.00				

KM# 1183 DOLLAR
Silver **Ruler:** Elizabeth II **Subject:** Juan Sebastian de Elcano

Date	Mintage	F12	VF20	XF40	MS60	MS63
2006	—	PF65 45.00				

KM# 1428 DOLLAR
Copper-Nickel, 38.61 mm. **Ruler:** Elizabeth II **Subject:** Television, 80th anniversary

Date	Mintage	F12	VF20	XF40	MS60	MS63
2006	—	—	—	—	10.00	12.00

KM# 471 DOLLAR
35.80 g., 0.999 Silver 1.1424 oz. ASW **Ruler:** Elizabeth II **Subject:** Sputnik 50th Anniversary - 1957-2007 **Obv:** Small bust divides legend above, center globe with color applique **Rev:** Satellite orbiting Earth with color applique **Rev. Legend:** SPUTNIK 50th ANNIVERSARY 1957 - 2007 **Edge:** Plain **Note:** Center piece rotates freely

Date	Mintage	F12	VF20	XF40	MS60	MS63
2007	—	PF65 95.00				

KM# 733 DOLLAR
25.09 g., Copper-Nickel, 38.8 mm. **Ruler:** Elizabeth II **Rev:** HMS Victory **Rev. Legend:** England expects that every man will do his duty

Date	Mintage	F12	VF20	XF40	MS60	MS63
2007	—	—	—	—	—	15.00

KM# 734 DOLLAR
25.09 g., Copper-Nickel, 38.8 mm. **Ruler:** Elizabeth II **Rev:** Admiral Nelson and two naval vessels **Rev. Legend:** England expects that every man will do his duty

Date	Mintage	F12	VF20	XF40	MS60	MS63
2007	—	—	—	—	—	15.00

KM# 735 DOLLAR
0.50 g., 0.999 Gold AGW, 11 mm. **Ruler:** Elizabeth II **Rev:** Treaty of Rome - Slovenia

Date	Mintage	F12	VF20	XF40	MS60	MS63
2007	—	PF65 40.00				

KM# 736 DOLLAR
0.50 g., 0.999 Gold AGW **Ruler:** Elizabeth II **Rev:** Benedict XVI's 2 Euro Coin

Date	Mintage	F12	VF20	XF40	MS60	MS63
2007	—	PF65 40.00				

KM# 490 DOLLAR
31.10 g., 0.999 Silver 0.9926 oz. ASW, 40.6 mm. **Ruler:** Elizabeth II **Subject:** Historical Australian Coins **Obv:** Head with tiara right **Rev:** 1757 New South Wales Holey Dollar **Edge:** Reeded

Date	Mintage	F12	VF20	XF40	MS60	MS63
2007	1,500	PF65 125				

KM# 491 DOLLAR
31.10 g., 0.999 Silver 0.9926 oz. ASW, 40.6 mm. **Ruler:** Elizabeth II **Subject:** Historical Australian Coins **Obv:** Head with tiara right **Rev:** Gilt 1857 Sydney Mint Sovereign **Edge:** Reeded

Date	Mintage	F12	VF20	XF40	MS60	MS63
2007	1,500	PF65 125				

KM# 492 DOLLAR
31.10 g., 0.999 Silver 0.9926 oz. ASW, 40.6 mm. **Ruler:** Elizabeth II **Subject:** Historical Australian Coins **Obv:** Head with tiarra right **Rev:** Copper 1937 pattern penny **Edge:** Reeded

Date	Mintage	F12	VF20	XF40	MS60	MS63
2007	1,500	PF65 125				

KM# 1138 DOLLAR
0.50 g., 0.999 Gold AGW, 11 mm. **Ruler:** Elizabeth II **Subject:** Treaty of Rome, 50th Anniversary **Rev:** San Marino

Date	Mintage	F12	VF20	XF40	MS60	MS63
2007	—	PF65 50.00				

KM# 1196 DOLLAR
25.00 g., Copper-Nickel, 38.6 mm. **Ruler:** Elizabeth II **Rev:**

Photo of Elizabeth II and Prince Philip in State Crown and uniform

Date	Mintage	F12	VF20	XF40	MS60	MS63
2007	Est. 50000	PF65 17.50				

KM# 1197 DOLLAR
25.00 g., Copper-Nickel, 38.6 mm. **Ruler:** Elizabeth II **Rev:** Photo of Elizabeth II and Prince Philip riding in state coach

Date	Mintage	F12	VF20	XF40	MS60	MS63
2007	—	PF65 17.50				

KM# 1198 DOLLAR
25.00 g., Copper-Nickel, 38.6 mm. **Ruler:** Elizabeth II **Rev:** Photo Elizabeth II in wedding dress and Prince Philip in uniform

Date	Mintage	F12	VF20	XF40	MS60	MS63
2007	—	PF65 17.50				

KM# 1199 DOLLAR
25.00 g., Copper-Nickel, 38.6 mm. **Ruler:** Elizabeth II **Rev:** Photo of Elizabeth II in wedding dress and Prince Philip in uniform, both waving

Date	Mintage	F12	VF20	XF40	MS60	MS63
2007	Est. 50000	PF65 17.50				

KM# 1200 DOLLAR
25.00 g., Copper-Nickel, 38.6 mm. **Ruler:** Elizabeth II **Rev:** Recent photo of Elizabeth in blue hat and Prince Philip in uniform

Date	Mintage	F12	VF20	XF40	MS60	MS63
2007	Est. 50000	PF65 17.50				

KM# 1466 DOLLAR
28.28 g., 0.925 Silver 0.8356 oz. ASW, 38.61 mm. **Ruler:** Elizabeth II **Rev:** Horatio Nelson and the Battle of Trafalgar

Date	Mintage	F12	VF20	XF40	MS60	MS63
2007	Est. 5000	PF65 55.00				

KM# 1468 DOLLAR
0.50 g., 0.999 Gold AGW, 11 mm. **Ruler:** Elizabeth II **Rev:** Sugar Maple leaf

Date	Mintage	F12	VF20	XF40	MS60	MS63
2007	Est. 5000	PF65 50.00				

KM# 1520 DOLLAR
0.50 g., 1.000 Gold AGW **Ruler:** Elizabeth II **Subject:** 2007 Walking Liberty

Date	Mintage	F12	VF20	XF40	MS60	MS63
2007	Est. 15000	PF65 70.00				

KM# 1521 DOLLAR
0.50 g., 1.000 Gold AGW, 11 mm. **Ruler:** Elizabeth II **Subject:** 2007 Eagle

Date	Mintage	F12	VF20	XF40	MS60	MS63
2007	Est. 15000	PF65 50.00				

KM# 1209a DOLLAR
0.50 g., 0.999 Platinum APW, 11 mm. **Ruler:** Elizabeth II **Subject:** British Monarchs - Henry VIII

Date	Mintage	F12	VF20	XF40	MS60	MS63
2008	Est. 50000	PF65 50.00				

KM# 493 DOLLAR
31.10 g., 0.999 Silver 0.9926 oz. ASW, 40.6 mm. **Ruler:** Elizabeth II **Subject:** Historical Australian Coins **Obv:** Head with tiara right **Rev:** 1823 MacIntosh and Degraves Shilling **Edge:** Reeded

Date	Mintage	F12	VF20	XF40	MS60	MS63
2008	1,500	PF65 125				

KM# 494 DOLLAR
31.10 g., 0.999 Silver 0.9926 oz. ASW, 40.6 mm. **Ruler:** Elizabeth II **Subject:** Historic Australian Coins **Obv:** Head with tiara right **Rev:** Gilt 1788 George III Spade Guinea **Edge:** Reeded

Date	Mintage	F12	VF20	XF40	MS60	MS63
2008	1,500	PF65 125				

KM# 495 DOLLAR
31.10 g., 0.999 Silver 0.9926 oz. ASW, 40.6 mm. **Ruler:**

Elizabeth II **Subject:** Historic Australian Coins **Obv:** Head with tiara right **Rev:** Australian 1910 Florin **Edge:** Reeded

Date	Mintage	F12	VF20	XF40	MS60	MS63
2008	1,500	PF65 125				

KM# 496 DOLLAR
31.10 g., 0.999 Silver 0.9926 oz. ASW, 40.6 mm. **Ruler:** Elizabeth II **Subject:** Historic Australian Coins **Obv:** Head with tiara right **Rev:** Gilt 1808-1815 Gold Pagoda **Edge:** Reeded

Date	Mintage	F12	VF20	XF40	MS60	MS63
2008	1,500	PF65 125				

KM# 497 DOLLAR
31.10 g., 0.999 Silver 0.9926 oz. ASW, 40.6 mm. **Ruler:** Elizabeth II **Subject:** Historic Australian Coins **Obv:** Head with tiara right **Rev:** 1850's Taylor's sixpence pattern **Edge:** Reeded

Date	Mintage	F12	VF20	XF40	MS60	MS63
2008	1,500	PF65 125				

KM# 498 DOLLAR
31.11 g., 0.999 Silver 0.9926 oz. ASW, 40.6 mm. **Ruler:** Elizabeth II **Subject:** Historic Australian Coins **Obv:** Head with tiara right **Rev:** Copper Australian WWII Interment Camp Token **Edge:** Reeded

Date	Mintage	F12	VF20	XF40	MS60	MS63
2008	1,500	PF65 125				

KM# 499 DOLLAR
31.10 g., 0.999 Silver 0.9926 oz. ASW, 40.6 mm. **Ruler:** Elizabeth II **Subject:** Historic Australian Coins **Obv:** Head with tiara right **Rev:** Australian 1946 Perth Mint Shilling **Edge:** Reeded

Date	Mintage	F12	VF20	XF40	MS60	MS63
2008	1,500	PF65 125				

KM# 500 DOLLAR
31.10 g., 0.999 Silver 0.9926 oz. ASW, 40.6 mm. **Ruler:** Elizabeth II **Subject:** Historic Australian Coins **Obv:** Head with tiara right **Rev:** Australian 1938 Crown **Edge:** Reeded

Date	Mintage	F12	VF20	XF40	MS60	MS63
2008	1,500	PF65 125				

KM# 501 DOLLAR
31.10 g., 0.999 Silver 0.9926 oz. ASW, 40.6 mm. **Ruler:** Elizabeth II **Subject:** Historic Australian Coins **Obv:** Head with tiara right **Rev:** Copper Australian 1930 Penny **Edge:** Reeded

Date	Mintage	F12	VF20	XF40	MS60	MS63
2008	1,500	PF65 125				

KM# 502 DOLLAR
31.10 g., 0.999 Silver 0.9926 oz. ASW, 40.6 mm. **Ruler:** Elizabeth II **Subject:** World War I **Obv:** Head with tiara right **Rev:** Multicolor image of Australian WWI soldier in Europe **Edge:** Reeded

Date	Mintage	F12	VF20	XF40	MS60	MS63
2008	1,918	PF65 85.00				

KM# 504 DOLLAR
31.10 g., 0.999 Silver 0.9926 oz. ASW, 40.6 mm. **Ruler:** Elizabeth II **Subject:** World War I **Obv:** Head with tiara right **Rev:** Multicolor image of Australian WWI soldier in Mid-East scene **Edge:** Reeded

Date	Mintage	F12	VF20	XF40	MS60	MS63
2008	1,918	PF65 85.00				

KM# 506 DOLLAR
31.10 g., 0.999 Silver 0.9926 oz. ASW, 40.6 mm. **Ruler:** Elizabeth II **Subject:** Captain Cook **Obv:** Head with tiara right **Rev:** Multicolor image of James Cook within letter C **Edge:** Reeded

Date	Mintage	F12	VF20	XF40	MS60	MS63
2008	1,779	PF65 100				

KM# 507 DOLLAR
31.10 g., 0.999 Silver 0.9926 oz. ASW, 40.6 mm. **Ruler:** Elizabeth II **Subject:** Captain Cook **Obv:** Head with tiara right **Rev:** Multicolor image of James Cook, Bottany Bay all within letter O **Edge:** Reeded

Date	Mintage	F12	VF20	XF40	MS60	MS63
2008	1,779	PF65 100				

KM# 508 DOLLAR
31.10 g., 0.999 Silver 0.9926 oz. ASW, 40.6 mm. **Ruler:** Elizabeth II **Subject:** Captain Cook **Obv:** Head with tiara right **Rev:** Multicolor image of James Cook, a new world all within letter O **Edge:** Reeded

Date	Mintage	F12	VF20	XF40	MS60	MS63
2008	1,779	PF65 100				

KM# 509 DOLLAR
31.10 g., 0.999 Silver 0.9926 oz. ASW, 40.6 mm. **Ruler:** Elizabeth II **Subject:** Captain Cook **Obv:** Head with tiara right **Rev:** Multicolor image of James Cook, striking the reef, large letter K in background **Edge:** Reeded

Date	Mintage	F12	VF20	XF40	MS60	MS63
2008	1,779	PF65 100				

KM# 765 DOLLAR
35.80 g., 0.999 Silver 1.1424 oz. ASW, 40 mm. **Ruler:** Elizabeth II **Subject:** 1961 First man in Space

Date	Mintage	F12	VF20	XF40	MS60	MS63
2008	—	PF65 115				

KM# 801 DOLLAR
31.11 g., 0.999 Silver 0.9926 oz. ASW, 40 mm. **Ruler:** Elizabeth II **Rev:** An-2, partially gilt

Date	Mintage	F12	VF20	XF40	MS60	MS63
2008	—	PF65 50.00				

KM# 802 DOLLAR
31.11 g., 0.999 Silver 0.9926 oz. ASW, 40 mm. **Ruler:** Elizabeth II **Rev:** An-74, partially gilt

Date	Mintage	F12	VF20	XF40	MS60	MS63
2008	—	PF65 50.00				

KM# 803 DOLLAR
31.11 g., 0.999 Silver 0.9926 oz. ASW, 40 mm. **Ruler:** Elizabeth II **Rev:** An-124, partially gilt

Date	Mintage	F12	VF20	XF40	MS60	MS63
2008	—	PF65 50.00				

KM# 804 DOLLAR
31.11 g., 0.999 Silver 0.9926 oz. ASW, 40 mm. **Ruler:** Elizabeth II **Rev:** An-148, partially gilt

Date	Mintage	F12	VF20	XF40	MS60	MS63
2008	—	PF65 50.00				

KM# 805 DOLLAR
31.11 g., 0.999 Silver 0.9926 oz. ASW, 40 mm. **Ruler:** Elizabeth II **Rev:** An-225, partially gilt

Date	Mintage	F12	VF20	XF40	MS60	MS63
2008	—	PF65 50.00				

KM# 1208 DOLLAR
0.50 g., 0.999 Gold AGW, 11 mm. **Ruler:** Elizabeth II **Subject:** British Monarchs - Henry V

Date	Mintage	F12	VF20	XF40	MS60	MS63
2008	Est. 14500	PF65 45.00				

KM# 1209 DOLLAR
0.50 g., 0.999 Gold AGW, 11 mm. **Ruler:** Elizabeth II **Subject:** British Monarchs - Henry VIII

Date	Mintage	F12	VF20	XF40	MS60	MS63
2008	Est. 50000	PF65 45.00				

KM# 1210 DOLLAR
0.50 g., 0.999 Gold AGW, 11 mm. **Ruler:** Elizabeth II **Subject:** British Monarchs - Elizabeth II

Date	Mintage	F12	VF20	XF40	MS60	MS63
2008	Est. 50000	PF65 45.00				

KM# 1522 DOLLAR
0.50 g., 1.000 Gold AGW, 11 mm. **Ruler:** Elizabeth II **Subject:** 2008 Indian Head

Date	Mintage	F12	VF20	XF40	MS60	MS63
2008	Est. 15000	PF65 70.00				

KM# 1571 DOLLAR
34.00 g., Gold Plated Copper, 38.6 mm. **Ruler:** Elizabeth II **Subject:** World MOnuments - Memorial Church in Berlin

Date	Mintage	F12	VF20	XF40	MS60	MS63
2009	Est. 7500					80.00

KM# 701 DOLLAR
31.11 g., 0.999 Silver 0.9926 oz. ASW, 39 mm. **Ruler:** Elizabeth II **Subject:** First Man on the Moon, 40th Anniversary **Obv:** Head right at top, multicolor moon in center **Rev:** Rocket, orbiter, moon walk. moon in multicolor at center

Date	Mintage	F12	VF20	XF40	MS60	MS63
2009	25,000	PF65 110				

KM# 702 DOLLAR
31.11 g., 0.999 Silver 0.9926 oz. ASW, 33x33 mm. **Ruler:** Elizabeth II **Subject:** Cook's Cottage, 75th Anniversary of relocation **Obv:** Head right **Rev:** Cottage and multicolor Captain Cook image **Shape:** Square

Date	Mintage	F12	VF20	XF40	MS60	MS63
2009	5,000	PF65 95.00				

KM# 706 DOLLAR
0.50 g., 0.999 Gold AGW, 11 mm. **Ruler:** Elizabeth II **Subject:** Pope Benedict XVI visits the Holy Land **Rev:** Dome of the Rock

Date	Mintage	F12	VF20	XF40	MS60	MS63
2009	25,000	PF65 35.00				

KM# 772 DOLLAR
27.00 g., Copper, 40 mm. **Ruler:** Elizabeth II **Subject:** Year of Astronomy **Rev:** Sun, multicolor

Date	Mintage	F12	VF20	XF40	MS60	MS63
2009	—	—	—	—	—	20.00

KM# 773 DOLLAR
27.00 g., Copper, 40 mm. **Ruler:** Elizabeth II **Subject:** Year of Astronomy **Rev:** Mercury, multicolor

Date	Mintage	F12	VF20	XF40	MS60	MS63
2009						20.00

KM# 774 DOLLAR
27.00 g., Copper, 40 mm. **Ruler:** Elizabeth II **Subject:** Year of Astronomy **Rev:** Venus, multicolor

Date	Mintage	F12	VF20	XF40	MS60	MS63
2009	—	—	—	—	—	25.00

KM# 775 DOLLAR
27.00 g., Copper, 40 mm. **Ruler:** Elizabeth II **Subject:** Year of Astronomy **Rev:** Earth, multicolor

Date	Mintage	F12	VF20	XF40	MS60	MS63
2009	—	—	—	—	—	22.00

KM# 776 DOLLAR
27.00 g., Copper, 40 mm. **Ruler:** Elizabeth II **Subject:** Year of Astronomy **Rev:** Mars, multicolor

Date	Mintage	F12	VF20	XF40	MS60	MS63
2009	—	—	—	—	—	22.00

KM# 777 DOLLAR
27.00 g., Copper, 40 mm. **Ruler:** Elizabeth II **Subject:** Year of Astronomy **Rev:** Jupiter, multicolor

Date	Mintage	F12	VF20	XF40	MS60	MS63
2009	—	—	—	—	—	22.00

KM# 778 DOLLAR
27.00 g., Copper, 40 mm. **Ruler:** Elizabeth II **Subject:** Year of Astronomy **Rev:** Saturn, multicolor

Date	Mintage	F12	VF20	XF40	MS60	MS63
2009	—	—	—	—	—	22.00

KM# 779 DOLLAR
27.00 g., Copper, 40 mm. **Ruler:** Elizabeth II **Subject:** Year of Astronomy **Rev:** Uranus, multicolor

Date	Mintage	F12	VF20	XF40	MS60	MS63
2009	—	—	—	—	—	22.00

KM# 780 DOLLAR
27.00 g., Copper, 40 mm. **Ruler:** Elizabeth II **Subject:** Year of Astronomy **Rev:** Neptune, multicolor

Date	Mintage	F12	VF20	XF40	MS60	MS63
2009	—	—	—	—	—	22.00

KM# 781 DOLLAR
27.00 g., Copper, 40 mm. **Ruler:** Elizabeth II **Subject:** Year of Astronomy **Rev:** Solar System, multicolor

Date	Mintage	F12	VF20	XF40	MS60	MS63
2009	—	—	—	—	—	22.00

KM# 794 DOLLAR
Copper-Nickel, 40 mm. **Ruler:** Elizabeth II **Rev:** Nessie, multicolor

Date	Mintage	F12	VF20	XF40	MS60	MS63
2009	—	—	—	—	—	22.00

KM# 795 DOLLAR
Copper-Nickel, 40 mm. **Ruler:** Elizabeth II **Rev:** Bigfoot, multicolor

Date	Mintage	F12	VF20	XF40	MS60	MS63
2009	—	—	—	—	—	22.00

KM# 796 DOLLAR
Copper-Nickel, 40 mm. **Ruler:** Elizabeth II **Rev:** Medussa, multicolor

Date	Mintage	F12	VF20	XF40	MS60	MS63
2009	—	—	—	—	—	22.00

KM# 797 DOLLAR
Copper-Nickel, 40 mm. **Ruler:** Elizabeth II **Rev:** Pegasus, multicolor

Date	Mintage	F12	VF20	XF40	MS60	MS63
2009	—	—	—	—	—	22.00

KM# 798 DOLLAR
Silver, 40 mm. **Ruler:** Elizabeth II **Rev:** Baba Yaga, multicolor

Date	Mintage	F12	VF20	XF40	MS60	MS63
2009	—	—	—	—	—	22.00

KM# 799 DOLLAR
Copper-Nickel, 40 mm. **Ruler:** Elizabeth II **Rev:** Phoenix, multicolor

Date	Mintage	F12	VF20	XF40	MS60	MS63
2009	—	—	—	—	—	22.00

KM# 1172 DOLLAR
27.00 g., Copper-Nickel, 38.6 mm. **Ruler:** Elizabeth II **Subject:** Moon Landing, 40th Anniversary **Rev:** Landing module Eagle and moon in color

Date	Mintage	F12	VF20	XF40	MS60	MS63
2009	—	—	—	—	—	17.50

KM# 1231 DOLLAR
25.00 g., Copper-Nickel, 38.6 mm. **Ruler:** Elizabeth II **Subject:** British Monarchs - Henry VIII

Date	Mintage	F12	VF20	XF40	MS60	MS63
2009	Est. 50000	—	—	—	—	17.50

KM# 1241 DOLLAR
31.14 g., 0.999 Silver 0.9936 oz. ASW, 38.61 mm. **Ruler:** Elizabeth II **Subject:** Battle of Gettysburg and General Meade **Rev:** Battle scene at left, Meade in color at right

Date	Mintage	F12	VF20	XF40	MS60	MS63
2009	—	PF65 65.00				

KM# 1327 DOLLAR
Silver **Ruler:** Elizabeth II **Subject:** Mystical creatures - Drago **Rev:** Dragon in color

Date	Mintage	F12	VF20	XF40	MS60	MS63
2009	—	PF65 75.00				

KM# 1328 DOLLAR
Copper-Nickel **Ruler:** Elizabeth II **Subject:** Wonders of the World **Rev:** Ayers Rock in color

Date	Mintage	F12	VF20	XF40	MS60	MS63
2009	—	—	—	—	—	20.00

KM# 1478 DOLLAR
27.00 g., Silver Plated Copper, 40 mm. **Ruler:** Elizabeth II **Rev:** Mount Everest in color

Date	Mintage	F12	VF20	XF40	MS60	MS63
2009	Est. 5000	—	—	—	—	25.00

KM# 1479 DOLLAR
27.00 g., Silver Plated Copper, 40 mm. **Ruler:** Elizabeth II **Rev:** Niagara Falls in color

Date	Mintage	F12	VF20	XF40	MS60	MS63
2009	Est. 5000	—	—	—	—	25.00

KM# 1480 DOLLAR
27.00 g., Silver Plated Copper, 40 mm. **Ruler:** Elizabeth II **Rev:** Grand Canyon in color

Date	Mintage	F12	VF20	XF40	MS60	MS63
2009	Est. 5000	—	—	—	—	25.00

KM# 1481 DOLLAR
27.00 g., Silver Plated Copper, 40 mm. **Ruler:** Elizabeth II **Rev:** Mt. Aetna volcano in color

Date	Mintage	F12	VF20	XF40	MS60	MS63
2009	Est. 5000	—	—	—	—	25.00

KM# 1482 DOLLAR
27.00 g., Silver Plated Copper, 40 mm. **Ruler:** Elizabeth II **Rev:** Northern lights in color

Date	Mintage	F12	VF20	XF40	MS60	MS63
2009	Est. 5000	—	—	—	—	25.00

KM# 1483 DOLLAR
27.00 g., Silver Plated Copper, 40 mm. **Ruler:** Elizabeth II **Rev:** Strokkur geyser in Iceland

Date	Mintage	F12	VF20	XF40	MS60	MS63
2009	Est. 5000	—	—	—	—	25.00

KM# 1493 DOLLAR
0.50 g., 0.999 Gold AGW, 11 mm. **Ruler:** Elizabeth II **Subject:** James Cook, 200th Anniversary of Death **Rev:** H.M.S. Endeavour

Date	Mintage	F12	VF20	XF40	MS60	MS63
2009	Est. 10000	PF65 35.00				

KM# 1517 DOLLAR
26.03 g., Silver Plated Copper, 38.61 mm. **Ruler:** Elizabeth II **Subject:** 2012 London Olympic Games - Sailing

Date	Mintage	F12	VF20	XF40	MS60	MS63
2009	Est. 30000	PF65 12.00				

KM# 1534 DOLLAR
5.67 g., 0.999 Silver 0.1809 oz. ASW, 35 mm. **Ruler:** Elizabeth II **Subject:** Ships and Explorers - Amundsen and Fram

Date	Mintage	F12	VF20	XF40	MS60	MS63
2009	Est. 5000	PF65 15.00				

KM# 1535 DOLLAR
5.67 g., 0.999 Silver 0.1809 oz. ASW, 35 mm. **Ruler:** Elizabeth II **Series:** Sips and Explorers - Gorch Fock

Date	Mintage	F12	VF20	XF40	MS60	MS63
2009	—	PF65 15.00				

KM# 1536 DOLLAR
5.67 g., 0.999 Silver 0.1809 oz. ASW, 35 mm. **Ruler:** Elizabeth II
Subject: Ships and Explorers - Henry the Seafarer

Date	Mintage	F12	VF20	XF40	MS60	MS63
2009	Est. 5000	PF65 15.00				

KM# 1568 DOLLAR
34.00 g., Gold Plated Copper, 38.6 mm. **Ruler:** Elizabeth II
Subject: World Monuments - Brandenburg Gate Berlin

Date	Mintage	F12	VF20	XF40	MS60	MS63
2009	Est. 20000	—	—	—	—	65.00

KM# 1569 DOLLAR
34.00 g., Gold Plated Copper, 38.6 mm. **Ruler:** Elizabeth II
Subject: World Monuments - Holsten Gate in Lubeck

Date	Mintage	F12	VF20	XF40	MS60	MS63
2009	Est. 7500	—	—	—	—	80.00

KM# 1570 DOLLAR
34.00 g., Gold Plated Copper, 38.6 mm. **Ruler:** Elizabeth II
Subject: World Monuments - Semper Opera in Dresden

Date	Mintage	F12	VF20	XF40	MS60	MS63
2009	—	—	—	—	—	80.00

KM# 1572 DOLLAR
34.00 g., Gold Plated Copper, 38.6 mm. **Ruler:** Elizabeth II
Subject: World Monuments - CHurch of Our Lady in Dresden

Date	Mintage	F12	VF20	XF40	MS60	MS63
2009	—	—	—	—	—	80.00

KM# 1576 DOLLAR
34.00 g., Gold Plated Copper, 38.6 mm. **Ruler:** Elizabeth II
Subject: World Monuments - Porta Nigra in Trier

Date	Mintage	F12	VF20	XF40	MS60	MS63
2009	Est. 7500	—	—	—	—	80.00

KM# 762 DOLLAR
10.93 g., Bi-Metallic **Ruler:** Elizabeth II **Obv:** Bust right **Rev:** Carved Maori figure (Tangaroa)

Date	Mintage	F12	VF20	XF40	MS60	MS63
2010	—	—	—	—	5.00	6.00

KM# 720 DOLLAR
0.12 g., 0.999 Silver, 4 mm. **Ruler:** Elizabeth II **Rev:** Fisherman's God statue **Note:** Illustration enlarged.

Date	Mintage	F12	VF20	XF40	MS60	MS63
2010 Prooflike	5,000	—	—	—	—	10.00

KM# 739 DOLLAR
31.11 g., 0.999 Silver 0.9926 oz. ASW, 37.65 mm. **Ruler:** Elizabeth II **Subject:** Niko & the way to the stars **Obv:** Head crowned left **Rev:** Multicolor deer **Shape:** 7-sided

Date	Mintage	F12	VF20	XF40	MS60	MS63
2010	3,500	PF65 60.00				

KM# 740 DOLLAR
31.11 g., 0.999 Silver 0.9926 oz. ASW, 37.65 mm. **Ruler:** Elizabeth II **Subject:** Niko & the way to the stars **Obv:** Head crowned left **Rev:** Multicolor wolf **Shape:** 7-sided

Date	Mintage	F12	VF20	XF40	MS60	MS63
2010	3,500	PF65 60.00				

KM# 741 DOLLAR
31.11 g., 0.999 Silver 0.9926 oz. ASW, 37.65 mm. **Ruler:** Elizabeth II **Subject:** Niko & the way to the stars **Obv:** Head crowned left **Rev:** Multicolor flying squirrel **Shape:** 7-sided

Date	Mintage	F12	VF20	XF40	MS60	MS63
2010	3,500	PF65 60.00				

KM# 742 DOLLAR
31.11 g., 0.999 Silver 0.9926 oz. ASW, 37.65 mm. **Ruler:** Elizabeth II **Subject:** Niko and the way to the stars **Obv:** Head crowned right **Rev:** Multicolor Ermine **Shape:** 7-sided

Date	Mintage	F12	VF20	XF40	MS60	MS63
2010	3,500	PF65 60.00				

KM# 743 DOLLAR
31.11 g., 0.999 Silver 0.9926 oz. ASW, 37.65 mm. **Ruler:** Elizabeth II **Subject:** Niko and the way to the stars **Obv:** Head crowned right **Rev:** Multicolor deer, flying squirrel and ermine **Shape:** 7-sided

Date	Mintage	F12	VF20	XF40	MS60	MS63
2010	3,500	PF65 60.00				

KM# 744 DOLLAR
31.14 g., 0.999 Silver 0.9936 oz. ASW, 40.6 mm. **Ruler:** Elizabeth II **Subject:** Battle of Trafalgar, 1805 **Rev:** Multicolor battle scene, HMS Victory

Date	Mintage	F12	VF20	XF40	MS60	MS63
2010	5,000	PF65 80.00				

KM# 770 DOLLAR
31.11 g., 0.999 Silver 0.9926 oz. ASW, 40 mm. **Ruler:** Elizabeth II **Subject:** Battle of Hampton Roads, Va. **Rev:** Monitor, multicolor background

Date	Mintage	F12	VF20	XF40	MS60	MS63
2010	5,000	PF65 80.00				

KM# 771 DOLLAR
31.11 g., 0.999 Silver 0.9926 oz. ASW, 40 mm. **Ruler:** Elizabeth II **Subject:** Battle of Salams **Rev:** Trireame, multicolor insert

Date	Mintage	F12	VF20	XF40	MS60	MS63
2010	5,000	PF65 100				

KM# 1243 DOLLAR
31.14 g., 0.999 Silver 0.9936 oz. ASW, 40.6 mm. **Ruler:** Elizabeth II **Subject:** Battle of Midway **Rev:** Aircraft carrier

Date	Mintage	F12	VF20	XF40	MS60	MS63
2010	5,000	PF65 100				

KM# 1256 DOLLAR
31.14 g., 0.999 Silver 0.9936 oz. ASW, 40.6 mm. **Ruler:** Elizabeth II **Subject:** Battle of Grunwald

Date	Mintage	F12	VF20	XF40	MS60	MS63
2010	—	PF65 50.00				

KM# 1257 DOLLAR
31.11 g., 0.999 Silver 0.9926 oz. ASW, 40.6 mm. **Ruler:** Elizabeth II **Subject:** Trafalgar **Rev:** H.M.S. Victory and Battle scene in color

Date	Mintage	F12	VF20	XF40	MS60	MS63
2010	5,000	PF65 80.00				

KM# 1295 DOLLAR
0.50 g., 0.999 Gold AGW, 11 mm. **Ruler:** Elizabeth II **Rev:** Martin Luther King

Date	Mintage	F12	VF20	XF40	MS60	MS63
2010	—	PF65 50.00				

KM# 1458 DOLLAR
25.00 g., Copper-Nickel, 38.61 mm. **Ruler:** Elizabeth II **Rev:** Photo of William and Kate

Date	Mintage	F12	VF20	XF40	MS60	MS63
2010	—	PF65 20.00				

KM# 1573 DOLLAR
34.00 g., Gold Plated Copper, 38.6 mm. **Ruler:** Elizabeth II **Subject:** World Monuments - Cathedral of Cologne

Date	Mintage	F12	VF20	XF40	MS60	MS63
2010	Est. 7500	—	—	—	—	80.00

KM# 1574 DOLLAR
34.00 g., Gold Plated Copper, 38.6 mm. **Ruler:** Elizabeth II **Subject:** World Monuments - Memorial of the Battle of the Peoples

Date	Mintage	F12	VF20	XF40	MS60	MS63
2010	Est. 7500	—	—	—	—	80.00

KM# 1575 DOLLAR
34.00 g., Gold Plated Copper, 38.6 mm. **Ruler:** Elizabeth II **Subject:** World Monuments - Castle Neuschwanstein

Date	Mintage	F12	VF20	XF40	MS60	MS63
2010	Est. 7500	—	—	—	—	80.00

KM# 1577 DOLLAR
34.00 g., Gold Plated Copper, 38.6 mm. **Ruler:** Elizabeth II **Subject:** World Monuments - German Reichstag in Berlin

Date	Mintage	F12	VF20	XF40	MS60	MS63
2010	—	—	—	—	—	80.00

KM# 1578 DOLLAR
34.00 g., Gold Plated Copper, 38.6 mm. **Ruler:** Elizabeth II **Subject:** World Monuments - Wartburg

Date	Mintage	F12	VF20	XF40	MS60	MS63
2010	—	—	—	—	—	80.00

KM# 1579 DOLLAR
34.00 g., Gold Plated Copper, 38.6 mm. **Ruler:** Elizabeth II **Series:** World Monuments - Castle Sanssouci

Date	Mintage	F12	VF20	XF40	MS60	MS63
2010	Est. 7500	—	—	—	—	80.00

KM# 1580 DOLLAR
34.00 g., Gold Plated Copper, 38.6 mm. **Ruler:** Elizabeth II **Subject:** World Monuments - Elbphilharmonie in Hamburg

Date	Mintage	F12	VF20	XF40	MS60	MS63
2010	—	—	—	—	—	80.00

KM# 1581 DOLLAR
34.00 g., Gold Plated Copper, 38.6 mm. **Ruler:** Elizabeth II **Subject:** World Monuments - Bellevue Palace in Berlin

Date	Mintage	F12	VF20	XF40	MS60	MS63
2010	Est. 7500	—	—	—	—	80.00

KM# 1582 DOLLAR
34.00 g., Gold Plated Copper, 38.6 mm. **Ruler:** Elizabeth II **Subject:** World Monuments - Ulmer Munster

Date	Mintage	F12	VF20	XF40	MS60	MS63
2010	—	—	—	—	—	80.00

KM# 1283 DOLLAR
31.10 g., 0.999 Silver 0.9925 oz. ASW, 40.6 mm. **Ruler:**
Elizabeth II **Subject:** Florin - 1927 design

Date	Mintage	F12	VF20	XF40	MS60	MS63
2011	1,500	PF65 75.00				

KM# 1313 DOLLAR
27.00 g., Silver Plated Copper, 38.61 mm. **Ruler:** Elizabeth II
Subject: Marilyn Monroe, 85th Birthday

Date	Mintage	F12	VF20	XF40	MS60	MS63
2011	2,500	PF65 25.00				

KM# 1235 DOLLAR
31.14 g., 0.999 Silver 0.9936 oz. ASW, 40.6 mm. **Ruler:**
Elizabeth II **Subject:** Battle of Jutland, 1916 **Rev:** Multicolor
battleship

Date	Mintage	F12	VF20	XF40	MS60	MS63
2011	5,000	PF65 85.00				

KM# 1269 DOLLAR
31.14 g., 0.999 Silver 0.9936 oz. ASW, 47.6x27.6 mm. **Ruler:**
Elizabeth II **Subject:** Year of the Rabbit **Rev:** Two brown
rabbits **Shape:** Rectangle

Date	Mintage	F12	VF20	XF40	MS60	MS63
2011	3,000	PF65 100				

KM# 1270 DOLLAR
31.14 g., 0.999 Silver 0.9936 oz. ASW, 47.6x27.6 mm. **Ruler:**
Elizabeth II **Subject:** Year of the Rabbit **Rev:** Two white rabbits
Shape: Rectangle

Date	Mintage	F12	VF20	XF40	MS60	MS63
2011	3,000	PF65 100				

KM# 1271 DOLLAR
31.14 g., 0.999 Silver 0.9936 oz. ASW, 47.6x27.6 mm. **Ruler:**
Elizabeth II **Subject:** Year of the Rabbit **Rev:** One black rabbit
Shape: Rectangle

Date	Mintage	F12	VF20	XF40	MS60	MS63
2011	3,000	PF65 100				

KM# 1272 DOLLAR
31.14 g., 0.999 Silver 0.9936 oz. ASW, 47.6x27.6 mm. **Ruler:**
Elizabeth II **Subject:** Year of the Rabbit **Rev:** One black rabbit
Shape: Rectangle

Date	Mintage	F12	VF20	XF40	MS60	MS63
2011	3,000	PF65 100				

KM# 1284 DOLLAR
31.10 g., 0.999 Silver 0.9925 oz. ASW, 40.6 mm. **Ruler:**
Elizabeth II **Subject:** Florin - 1934-35 Centenary

Date	Mintage	F12	VF20	XF40	MS60	MS63
2011	1,500	PF65 75.00				

KM# 1285 DOLLAR
31.10 g., 0.999 Silver 0.9925 oz. ASW, 40.6 mm. **Ruler:**
Elizabeth II **Subject:** Florin - 1901-51 Jubilee

Date	Mintage	F12	VF20	XF40	MS60	MS63
2011	1,500	PF65 75.00				

KM# 1286 DOLLAR
31.10 g., 0.999 Silver 0.9925 oz. ASW, 40.6 mm. **Ruler:**
Elizabeth II **Subject:** Florin - 1954 Royal Visit

Date	Mintage	F12	VF20	XF40	MS60	MS63
2011	1,500	PF65 75.00				

KM# 1342 DOLLAR
31.11 g., 0.999 Silver 0.9926 oz. ASW, 38.61 mm. **Ruler:**
Elizabeth II **Subject:** Planets - Mercury **Rev:** with color

Date	Mintage	F12	VF20	XF40	MS60	MS63
2011	—	PF65 75.00				

KM# 1343 DOLLAR
31.11 g., 0.999 Silver 0.9926 oz. ASW, 38.61 mm. **Ruler:**
Elizabeth II **Subject:** Plants - Venus **Rev:** with color

Date	Mintage	F12	VF20	XF40	MS60	MS63
2011	—	PF65 75.00				

KM# 1344 DOLLAR
31.11 g., 0.999 Silver 0.9926 oz. ASW, 30.61 mm. **Ruler:**
Elizabeth II **Subject:** Planets - Earth **Rev:** with color

Date	Mintage	F12	VF20	XF40	MS60	MS63
2011	—	PF65 75.00				

KM# 1345 DOLLAR
31.11 g., 0.999 Silver 0.9926 oz. ASW, 38.61 mm. **Ruler:**
Elizabeth II **Subject:** Plants - Mars **Rev:** with color

Date	Mintage	F12	VF20	XF40	MS60	MS63
2011	—	PF65 75.00				

KM# 1346 DOLLAR
31.11 g., 0.999 Silver 0.9926 oz. ASW, 38.61 mm. **Ruler:**
Elizabeth II **Subject:** Planets - Jupiter **Rev:** Jupiter and
Sagittarius with color

Date	Mintage	F12	VF20	XF40	MS60	MS63
2011	—	PF65 75.00				

KM# 1347 DOLLAR
31.11 g., 0.999 Silver 0.9926 oz. ASW, 38.61 mm. **Ruler:**
Elizabeth II **Subject:** Planets - Saturn **Rev:** Saturn and
Capricorn with color

Date	Mintage	F12	VF20	XF40	MS60	MS63
2011	—	PF65 75.00				

KM# 1348 DOLLAR
31.11 g., 0.999 Silver 0.9926 oz. ASW, 38.61 mm. **Ruler:** Elizabeth II **Subject:** Planets - Uranis **Rev:** Uranis and Aquarius with color

Date	Mintage	F12	VF20	XF40	MS60	MS63
2011	—	PF65 75.00				

KM# 1385 DOLLAR
31.11 g., 0.999 Silver 0.9926 oz. ASW, 38.61 mm. **Ruler:** Elizabeth II **Subject:** Marylin Monroe, 80th Birthday **Rev:** Marylin Monroe in color pose

Date	Mintage	F12	VF20	XF40	MS60	MS63
2011	—	PF65 125				

KM# 1396 DOLLAR
31.11 g., 0.999 Silver 0.9926 oz. ASW, 38.61 mm. **Ruler:** Elizabeth II **Subject:** Hollywood Legends - Elizabeth Taylor **Rev:** Elizabeth Taylor facing photo

Date	Mintage	F12	VF20	XF40	MS60	MS63
2011	—	PF65 125				

KM# 1459 DOLLAR
25.00 g., Copper-Nickel, 38.61 mm. **Ruler:** Elizabeth II **Rev:** Photo of William and Kate

Date	Mintage	F12	VF20	XF40	MS60	MS63
2011	—	PF65 25.00				

KM# 1375 DOLLAR
0.50 g., 0.999 Gold AGW, 11 mm. **Ruler:** Elizabeth II **Obv:** Head with tiara right **Rev:** Titanic sailing left

Date	Mintage	F12	VF20	XF40	MS60	MS63
2012	—	PF65 50.00				

KM# 1391 DOLLAR
31.11 g., 0.999 Silver 0.9926 oz. ASW, 47.6x27.6 mm. **Ruler:** Elizabeth II **Obv:** Head with crown right **Rev:** Orange dragon at right

Date	Mintage	F12	VF20	XF40	MS60	MS63
2012	3,000	PF65 125				

KM# 1392 DOLLAR
31.11 g., 0.999 Silver 0.9926 oz. ASW, 47.6x27.6 mm. **Ruler:** Elizabeth II **Obv:** Head with crown right **Rev:** Blue dragon at left center

Date	Mintage	F12	VF20	XF40	MS60	MS63
2012	3,000	PF65 125				

KM# 1393 DOLLAR
31.11 g., 0.999 Silver 0.9926 oz. ASW, 47.6x27.6 mm. **Ruler:** Elizabeth II **Obv:** Head with crown right **Rev:** Brown dragon at center

Date	Mintage	F12	VF20	XF40	MS60	MS63
2012	3,000	PF65 125				

KM# 1394 DOLLAR
31.11 g., 0.999 Silver 0.9926 oz. ASW, 47.6x27.6 mm. **Ruler:** Elizabeth II **Obv:** Head with crown right **Rev:** Orange dragon at left

Date	Mintage	F12	VF20	XF40	MS60	MS63
2012	3,000	PF65 125				

KM# 1424 DOLLAR
Silver Plated Copper-Nickel, 38.61 mm. **Ruler:** Elizabeth II **Subject:** Ctyrlistek Cartoons **Rev:** Characters in color

Date	Mintage	F12	VF20	XF40	MS60	MS63
2012	100	PF65 35.00				

KM# 1441 DOLLAR
15.50 g., 0.999 Silver 0.4946 oz. ASW **Ruler:** Elizabeth II **Subject:** Year of the Dragon **Rev:** Blue dragon **Shape:** Arc **Note:** One of four which form circle.

Date	Mintage	F12	VF20	XF40	MS60	MS63
2012	—	PF65 50.00				

KM# 1442 DOLLAR
15.50 g., 0.999 Silver 0.4946 oz. ASW **Ruler:** Elizabeth II **Subject:** Year of the Dragon **Rev:** Orange dragon **Shape:** Arc **Note:** One of four which form circle.

Date	Mintage	F12	VF20	XF40	MS60	MS63
2012	—	PF65 50.00				

KM# 1443 DOLLAR
15.50 g., 0.999 Silver 0.4946 oz. ASW **Ruler:** Elizabeth II **Subject:** Year of the Dragon **Rev:** Red dragon **Shape:** Arc **Note:** One of four which form circle.

Date	Mintage	F12	VF20	XF40	MS60	MS63
2012	—	PF65 50.00				

KM# 1444 DOLLAR
15.50 g., 0.999 Silver 0.4946 oz. ASW **Ruler:** Elizabeth II **Subject:** Year of the Dragon **Rev:** Green dragon **Shape:** Arc **Note:** One of four which form circle.

Date	Mintage	F12	VF20	XF40	MS60	MS63
2012	—	PF65 50.00				

KM# 1449 DOLLAR
Silver Plated Copper, 38.61 mm. **Ruler:** Elizabeth II **Subject:** Abu Simbel **Rev:** Statues in color

Date	Mintage	F12	VF20	XF40	MS60	MS63
2012	—	PF65 40.00				

KM# 1456 DOLLAR
25.00 g., Copper-Nickel, 38.61 mm. **Ruler:** Elizabeth II **Subject:** Space Walk **Rev:** Photo of Space Walk

Date	Mintage	F12	VF20	XF40	MS60	MS63
2012	—	PF65 60.00				

KM# 1457 DOLLAR
Silver **Ruler:** Elizabeth II **Subject:** Everlasting love **Rev:** Flowers in color **Shape:** Heart

Date	Mintage	F12	VF20	XF40	MS60	MS63
2012	—	PF65 100				

KM# 1599 DOLLAR
20.12 g., 0.925 Silver 0.5945 oz. ASW, 38.6 mm. **Ruler:** Elizabeth II **Subject:** Gold Cup, Royal Ascot **Rev:** Gold Cup trophy, horse forepart at right

Date	Mintage	F12	VF20	XF40	MS60	MS63
2012	—	PF65 75.00				

KM# 1460 DOLLAR
31.11 g., 0.999 Silver 0.9926 oz. ASW, 27x47 mm. **Ruler:** Elizabeth II **Subject:** Year of the Snake **Rev:** Blue lipped sea snake **Shape:** Rectangle

Date	Mintage	F12	VF20	XF40	MS60	MS63
2013	3,000	PF65 100				

KM# 1461 DOLLAR
31.11 g., 0.999 Silver 0.9926 oz. ASW, 27x47 mm. **Ruler:** Elizabeth II **Subject:** Year of the Snake **Rev:** Yellow banded wolf snake **Shape:** Rectangle

Date	Mintage	F12	VF20	XF40	MS60	MS63
2013	3,000	PF65 100				

KM# 1462 DOLLAR
31.11 g., 0.999 Silver 0.9926 oz. ASW, 38.61 mm. **Ruler:** Elizabeth II **Subject:** Year of the Snake **Rev:** Red bamboo rat snake

Date	Mintage	F12	VF20	XF40	MS60	MS63
2013	3,000	PF65 100				

KM# 1463 DOLLAR
31.11 g., 0.999 Silver 0.9926 oz. ASW, 38.61 mm. **Ruler:** Elizabeth II **Subject:** Year of the Snake **Rev:** Chinese green tree viper

Date	Mintage	F12	VF20	XF40	MS60	MS63
2013	3,000	PF65 100				

KM# 1464 DOLLAR
15.50 g., 0.999 Silver 0.4946 oz. ASW, 49x24 mm. **Ruler:** Elizabeth II **Subject:** Year of the Snake **Shape:** Fan

Date	Mintage	F12	VF20	XF40	MS60	MS63
2013	7,500	PF65 75.00				

KM# 1595 DOLLAR
27.00 g., Copper-Nickel, 38.61 mm. **Ruler:** Elizabeth II **Subject:** Cyrlistek Cartoons - Pinda

Date	Mintage	F12	VF20	XF40	MS60	MS63
2013	Est. 1000	PF65 80.00				

KM# 1597 DOLLAR
27.00 g., Copper-Nickel, 38.61 mm. **Ruler:** Elizabeth II **Subject:** Ctyrlistek Cartoons - Fifinka

Date	Mintage	F12	VF20	XF40	MS60	MS63
2013	Est. 1000	PF65 80.00				

KM# 1598 DOLLAR
27.00 g., Copper-Nickel, 38.61 mm. **Ruler:** Elizabeth II **Subject:** Ctyrlistek Cartoons - Bobik

Date	Mintage	F12	VF20	XF40	MS60	MS63
2013	Est. 1000	PF65 80.00				

KM# 1603 DOLLAR
0.925 Silver ASW **Ruler:** Elizabeth II **Subject:** 2016 Olympics Transfer from London to Rio

Date	Mintage	F12	VF20	XF40	MS60	MS63
2013	Est. 10000	PF65 50.00				

KM# 1604 DOLLAR
0.50 g., 0.999 Gold AGW, 11 mm. **Ruler:** Elizabeth II **Subject:** 2016 Olympics - Transfer from London to Rio

Date	Mintage	F12	VF20	XF40	MS60	MS63
2013	Est. 1000	PF65 50.00				

KM# 1607 DOLLAR
0.50 g., 0.585 Gold AGW, 11 mm. **Ruler:** Elizabeth II **Subject:** Vincent van Gogh

Date	Mintage	F12	VF20	XF40	MS60	MS63
2013	Est. 5000	PF65 50.00				

KM# 1612 DOLLAR
7.30 g., 0.333 Silver 0.0777 oz. ASW, 30 mm. **Ruler:** Elizabeth II **Subject:** 2014 FIFA World Cup - Brazil Trophy

Date	Mintage	F12	VF20	XF40	MS60	MS63
2013	Est. 25000	PF65 40.00				

KM# 1613 DOLLAR
7.30 g., 0.333 Silver 0.0777 oz. ASW, 30 mm. **Ruler:** Elizabeth II **Subject:** 2014 FIFA World Cup Brazil - Mascot

Date	Mintage	F12	VF20	XF40	MS60	MS63
2013	Est. 25000	PF65 50.00				

KM# 554 2 DOLLARS
31.11 g., 0.999 Silver 0.9926 oz. ASW, 40.5 mm. **Ruler:** Elizabeth II **Subject:** Asian wildlife **Rev:** Multicolored pheasant-tailed Jacana

Date	Mintage	F12	VF20	XF40	MS60	MS63
2001	3,000	PF65 85.00				

KM# 551 2 DOLLARS
31.11 g., 0.999 Silver 0.9926 oz. ASW, 40.5 mm. **Ruler:** Elizabeth II **Subject:** Asian wildlife **Rev:** Multicolor Mikado Pheasant

Date	Mintage	F12	VF20	XF40	MS60	MS63
2001	5,000	PF65 85.00				

KM# 552 2 DOLLARS
31.11 g., 0.999 Silver 0.9926 oz. ASW, 40.5 mm. **Ruler:** Elizabeth II **Subject:** Asian wildlife **Rev:** Multicolor black-faced spoonbill

Date	Mintage	F12	VF20	XF40	MS60	MS63
2001	5,000	PF65 85.00				

KM# 553 2 DOLLARS
31.11 g., 0.999 Silver 0.9926 oz. ASW, 40.5 mm. **Ruler:** Elizabeth II **Subject:** Asian wildlife **Rev:** Multicolor Indian Pitta

Date	Mintage	F12	VF20	XF40	MS60	MS63
2001	3,000	PF65 85.00				

KM# 468 2 DOLLARS
Copper-Nickel **Ruler:** Elizabeth II **Rev:** Football championship

Date	Mintage	F12	VF20	XF40	MS60	MS63
2002	—	—	—	—	5.00	7.00

KM# 1119 2 DOLLARS
Copper-Nickel, 30 mm. **Ruler:** Elizabeth II **Subject:** XXVIII Summer Olympics, Athens **Rev:** Discus thrower

Date	Mintage	F12	VF20	XF40	MS60	MS63
2002	PF65 15.00					

KM# 1120 2 DOLLARS
Silver **Ruler:** Elizabeth II **Subject:** Endangered Wildlife **Rev:** Lion family

Date	Mintage	F12	VF20	XF40	MS60	MS63
2002	PF65 25.00					

KM# 1282 2 DOLLARS
31.14 g., 0.999 Silver 0.9936 oz. ASW, 40.6 mm. **Ruler:** Elizabeth II **Subject:** Taiwan New Koala Family **Obv:** Head crowned right **Rev:** Multicolor Koala seated with leaves

Date	Mintage	F12	VF20	XF40	MS60	MS63
2002	—	PF65 135				

KM# 417 2 DOLLARS
7.55 g., Copper-Nickel, 26 mm. **Ruler:** Elizabeth II **Obv:** Crowned bust right, new portrait **Rev:** Mortar and pestle from Atiu Island **Shape:** Triangle

Date	Mintage	F12	VF20	XF40	MS60	MS63
2003	—	—	—	—	3.00	3.50
2010	—	—	—	—	3.00	3.50

KM# 1123 2 DOLLARS
62.77 g., 0.999 Silver 2.0031 oz. ASW, 50 mm. **Ruler:** Elizabeth II **Rev:** Edward "Ned" Kelly in color

Date	Mintage	F12	VF20	XF40	MS60	MS63
2003	Est. 2500	PF65 125				

KM# 1124 2 DOLLARS
62.77 g., 0.999 Silver 2.0031 oz. ASW, 50 mm. **Ruler:** Elizabeth II **Rev:** Daniel Morgan in color

Date	Mintage	F12	VF20	XF40	MS60	MS63
2003	—	PF65 125				

KM# 1125 2 DOLLARS
62.77 g., 0.999 Silver 2.0031 oz. ASW **Ruler:** Elizabeth II **Rev:** Ben Hall in color

Date	Mintage	F12	VF20	XF40	MS60	MS63
2003	Est. 2500	PF65 125				

KM# 1126 2 DOLLARS
62.77 g., 0.999 Silver 2.0031 oz. ASW, 50 mm. **Ruler:** Elizabeth II **Rev:** Fred Ward "Captain Thunderbolt" in color

Date	Mintage	F12	VF20	XF40	MS60	MS63
2003	Est. 2500	PF65 125				

KM# 1139 2 DOLLARS
0.999 Silver, 30 mm. **Ruler:** Elizabeth II **Subject:** John F. Kennedy, 40th Anniversary of Death

Date	Mintage	F12	VF20	XF40	MS60	MS63
2003	—	PF65 45.00				

KM# 1141 2 DOLLARS
Gold AGW **Ruler:** Elizabeth II **Rev:** Red cardinal in color

Date	Mintage	F12	VF20	XF40	MS60	MS63
2003	Est. 5000	PF65 85.00				

KM# 1142 2 DOLLARS
Gold AGW **Ruler:** Elizabeth II **Subject:** Love swing **Rev:** Bird in color

Date	Mintage	F12	VF20	XF40	MS60	MS63
2003	Est. 5000	PF65 85.00				

KM# 536 2 DOLLARS
31.11 g., 0.999 Silver 0.9926 oz. ASW, 40.7 mm. **Ruler:** Elizabeth II **Subject:** Birds of New Zealand **Rev:** Multicolor tui

Date	Mintage	F12	VF20	XF40	MS60	MS63
2005 Prooflike	8,000	—	—	—	—	85.00

KM# 537 2 DOLLARS
31.11 g., 0.999 Silver 0.9926 oz. ASW, 40.7 mm. **Ruler:** Elizabeth II **Subject:** Birds of New Zealand **Rev:** Multicolor bell bird

Date	Mintage	F12	VF20	XF40	MS60	MS63
2005 Prooflike	8,000	—	—	—	—	85.00

KM# 538 2 DOLLARS
31.11 g., 0.999 Silver 0.9926 oz. ASW, 40.7 mm. **Ruler:** Elizabeth II **Subject:** Birds of New Zealand **Rev:** Multicolor New Zealand Pigeon

Date	Mintage	F12	VF20	XF40	MS60	MS63
2005 Prooflike	8,000	—	—	—	—	85.00

KM# 539 2 DOLLARS
31.11 g., 0.999 Silver 0.9926 oz. ASW, 40.7 mm. **Ruler:** Elizabeth II **Subject:** Birds of New Zealand **Rev:** Multicolor yellow crowned parakeet

Date	Mintage	F12	VF20	XF40	MS60	MS63
2005 Prooflike	8,000	—	—	—	—	85.00

KM# 524 2 DOLLARS
31.11 g., 0.999 Silver 0.9926 oz. ASW, 40.7 mm. **Ruler:** Elizabeth II **Subject:** Classic Speedsters from the 1930's **Rev:** Multicolor 1935 Auburn 851 Speedster

Date	Mintage	F12	VF20	XF40	MS60	MS63
2006 Prooflike	6,000	—	—	—	—	75.00

KM# 525 2 DOLLARS
31.11 g., 0.999 Silver 0.9926 oz. ASW, 40.7 mm. **Ruler:** Elizabeth II **Subject:** Classic Speedsters from the 1930's **Rev:** Multicolor 1935 Bugatti Type 57SC Atlantic Speedster

Date	Mintage	F12	VF20	XF40	MS60	MS63
2006 Prooflike	6,000	—	—	—	—	75.00

KM# 526 2 DOLLARS
31.11 g., 0.999 Silver 0.9926 oz. ASW, 40.7 mm. **Ruler:** Elizabeth II **Subject:** Speedsters from the 1930's **Rev:** Multicolor 1936 Duesenberg SSJ Speedster

Date	Mintage	F12	VF20	XF40	MS60	MS63
2006 Prooflike	—	—	—	—	—	75.00

KM# 527 2 DOLLARS
31.11 g., 0.999 Silver 0.9926 oz. ASW, 40.7 mm. **Ruler:** Elizabeth II **Subject:** Speedsters from the 1930's **Rev:** Multicolor 1930 Packard 734 Boattail Speedster

Date	Mintage	F12	VF20	XF40	MS60	MS63
2006 Prooflike	6,000	—	—	—	—	75.00

KM# 1170 2 DOLLARS
10.00 g., 0.925 Silver 0.2955 oz. ASW, 30 mm. **Ruler:** Elizabeth II **Rev:** Motion Pictures, 100th Anniversary

Date	Mintage	F12	VF20	XF40	MS60	MS63
2006	Est. 2500	—	—	—	—	35.00

KM# 1288 2 DOLLARS
31.11 g., 0.999 Silver 0.9926 oz. ASW, 40.7 mm. **Ruler:** Elizabeth II **Rev:** Supermarine S-6B race plane in color

Date	Mintage	F12	VF20	XF40	MS60	MS63
2006 Prooflike	6,000	—	—	—	—	65.00

KM# 1289 2 DOLLARS
31.11 g., 0.999 Silver 0.9926 oz. ASW, 40.7 mm. **Ruler:** Elizabeth II **Rev:** GeeBee race plane in color

Date	Mintage	F12	VF20	XF40	MS60	MS63
2006 Prooflike	6,000	—	—	—	—	65.00

KM# 1290 2 DOLLARS
31.11 g., 0.999 Silver 0.9926 oz. ASW, 40.7 mm. **Ruler:** Elizabeth II **Rev:** Hughes H-1 race plane in color

Date	Mintage	F12	VF20	XF40	MS60	MS63
2006 Prooflike	6,000	—	—	—	—	65.00

KM# 1291 2 DOLLARS
31.11 g., 0.999 Silver 0.9926 oz. ASW, 40.7 mm. **Ruler:** Elizabeth II **Rev:** Polikarpov I-16 race plane in color

Date	Mintage	F12	VF20	XF40	MS60	MS63
2006 Prooflike	6,000	—	—	—	—	65.00

KM# 1316 2 DOLLARS
Silver **Ruler:** Elizabeth II **Rev:** Motorcycle - Brough in color

Date	Mintage	F12	VF20	XF40	MS60	MS63
2007	—	PF65 45.00				

KM# 1317 2 DOLLARS
Silver **Ruler:** Elizabeth II **Rev:** Motorcycle - BSA Sloper in color

Date	Mintage	F12	VF20	XF40	MS60	MS63
2007	—	PF65 45.00				

KM# 1318 2 DOLLARS
Silver **Ruler:** Elizabeth II **Rev:** Motorcycle - IZH 8

Date	Mintage	F12	VF20	XF40	MS60	MS63
2007	—	PF65 45.00				

KM# 514 2 DOLLARS
31.11 g., 0.999 Silver 0.9926 oz. ASW, 40.7 mm. **Ruler:** Elizabeth II **Subject:** Great Motorcycles from the 1930's **Rev:** Multicolor 1930 BSA Sloper

Date	Mintage	F12	VF20	XF40	MS60	MS63
2007 Prooflike	6,000	—	—	—	—	70.00

KM# 515 2 DOLLARS
31.11 g., 0.999 Silver 0.9926 oz. ASW, 40.7 mm. **Ruler:** Elizabeth II **Subject:** Great motorcycles from the 1930's **Rev:** Multicolor 1937 Ariel 1000 Squarefour

Date	Mintage	F12	VF20	XF40	MS60	MS63
2007 Prooflike	6,000	—	—	—	—	70.00

KM# 516 2 DOLLARS
31.11 g., 0.999 Silver 0.9926 oz. ASW, 40.7 mm. **Ruler:** Elizabeth II **Subject:** Great motorcycles from the 1930's **Rev:** Multicolor 1938 12H 8

Date	Mintage	F12	VF20	XF40	MS60	MS63
2007 Prooflike	6,000	—	—	—	—	70.00

KM# 517 2 DOLLARS
31.11 g., 0.999 Silver 0.9926 oz. ASW, 40.7 mm. **Ruler:** Elizabeth II **Subject:** Great motorcycles from the 1930's **Rev:** Multicolor 1931 Matchless Silver Hawk

Date	Mintage	F12	VF20	XF40	MS60	MS63
2007 Prooflike	6,000	—	—	—	—	70.00

KM# 518 2 DOLLARS
31.11 g., 0.999 Silver 0.9926 oz. ASW, 40.7 mm. **Ruler:** Elizabeth II **Subject:** Great motocycles from the 1930's **Rev:** Multicolor 1932 Brough Superior SS100

Date	Mintage	F12	VF20	XF40	MS60	MS63
2007 Prooflike	6,000	—	—	—	—	70.00

KM# 529 2 DOLLARS
31.11 g., 0.999 Silver 0.9926 oz. ASW, 40.7 mm. **Ruler:** Elizabeth II **Subject:** International Women's Day **Rev:** Multicolor tulips, large 8

Date	Mintage	F12	VF20	XF40	MS60	MS63
2007 Prooflike	4,000	—	—	—	—	65.00

KM# 532 2 DOLLARS
31.11 g., 0.999 Silver 0.9926 oz. ASW, 40.7 mm. **Ruler:** Elizabeth II **Subject:** Sherlock Holmes **Rev:** Multicolor portrait

Date	Mintage	F12	VF20	XF40	MS60	MS63
2007 Prooflike	8,000	—	—	—	—	100

KM# 1184 2 DOLLARS
31.11 g., 0.999 Silver 0.9926 oz. ASW, 40.7 mm. **Ruler:** Elizabeth II **Subject:** Birds of Fiji **Rev:** Island Thrush in color

Date	Mintage	F12	VF20	XF40	MS60	MS63
2007	—	—	—	—	—	45.00

KM# 1185 2 DOLLARS
31.11 g., 0.999 Silver 0.9926 oz. ASW, 40.7 mm. **Ruler:** Elizabeth II **Subject:** Birds of Fiji **Rev:** Vampire Bat in color

Date	Mintage	F12	VF20	XF40	MS60	MS63
2007	Est. 4000	—	—	—	—	45.00

KM# 1186 2 DOLLARS
31.11 g., 0.999 Silver 0.9926 oz. ASW, 40.7 mm. **Ruler:** Elizabeth II **Subject:** Birds of Fiji **Rev:** Kingfisher in color

Date	Mintage	F12	VF20	XF40	MS60	MS63
2007	4,000	—	—	—	—	45.00

KM# 1187 2 DOLLARS
31.11 g., 0.999 Silver 0.9926 oz. ASW, 40.7 mm. **Ruler:** Elizabeth II **Subject:** Birds of Fiji **Rev:** Lori in color

Date	Mintage	F12	VF20	XF40	MS60	MS63
2007	4,000	—	—	—	—	45.00

KM# 510 2 DOLLARS
31.11 g., 0.999 Silver 0.9926 oz. ASW, 40.7 mm. **Ruler:** Elizabeth II **Subject:** Year of the Rat **Rev:** Multicolor scene of little girl from Russian animated cartoon

Date	Mintage	F12	VF20	XF40	MS60	MS63
2008 Prooflike	10,000	—	—	—	—	80.00

KM# 511 2 DOLLARS
31.11 g., 0.999 Silver 0.9926 oz. ASW, 40.7 mm. **Ruler:** Elizabeth II **Subject:** Year of the Rat **Rev:** Multicolor scene of nutcracker from Russian animated cartoon

Date	Mintage	F12	VF20	XF40	MS60	MS63
2008 Prooflike	10,000	—	—	—	—	80.00

KM# 512 2 DOLLARS
39.11 g., 0.999 Silver 1.2479 oz. ASW, 40.7 mm. **Ruler:** Elizabeth II **Rev:** Multicolor scene of Adventure of Cat Leopold Russian animated cartoon

Date	Mintage	F12	VF20	XF40	MS60	MS63
2008 Prooflike	10,000	—	—	—	—	100

KM# 513 2 DOLLARS
31.11 g., 0.999 Silver 0.9926 oz. ASW, 40.7 mm. **Ruler:** Elizabeth II **Subject:** Year of the Rat **Rev:** Multicolor scene of tough toy soldier from Russian animated cartoon

Date	Mintage	F12	VF20	XF40	MS60	MS63
2008 Prooflike	10,000	—	—	—	—	80.00

KM# 519 2 DOLLARS
31.11 g., 0.999 Silver 0.9926 oz. ASW, 40.7 mm. **Ruler:** Elizabeth II **Subject:** Racers from the 1930's **Rev:** Multicolor Gee Bee

Date	Mintage	F12	VF20	XF40	MS60	MS63
2008 Prooflike	6,000	—	—	—	—	70.00

KM# 520 2 DOLLARS
31.11 g., 0.999 Silver 0.9926 oz. ASW, 40.7 mm. **Ruler:** Elizabeth II **Subject:** Racers from the 1930's **Rev:** Multicolor, Hughes H-1 Racer

Date	Mintage	F12	VF20	XF40	MS60	MS63
2008 Prooflike	6,000	—	—	—	—	70.00

KM# 521 2 DOLLARS
31.11 g., 0.999 Silver 0.9926 oz. ASW, 40.7 mm. **Ruler:** Elizabeth II **Subject:** Racers from the 1930's **Rev:** Multicolor Laird Turner LTR-14 Meteor

Date	Mintage	F12	VF20	XF40	MS60	MS63
2008 Prooflike	6,000	—	—	—	—	70.00

KM# 522 2 DOLLARS
31.11 g., 0.999 Silver 0.9926 oz. ASW, 40.7 mm. **Ruler:** Elizabeth II **Subject:** Racers from the 1930's **Rev:** Multicolor Spuermarine S.6B Floatplane

Date	Mintage	F12	VF20	XF40	MS60	MS63
2008 Prooflike	6,000	—	—	—	—	70.00

KM# 523 2 DOLLARS
31.11 g., 0.999 Silver 0.9926 oz. ASW, 40.7 mm. **Ruler:** Elizabeth II **Subject:** Racers from the 1930's **Rev:** Multicolor Polikarpov I-16

Date	Mintage	F12	VF20	XF40	MS60	MS63
2008 Prooflike	6,000	—	—	—	—	70.00

KM# 528 2 DOLLARS
31.11 g., 0.999 Silver 0.9926 oz. ASW, 40.7 mm. **Ruler:** Elizabeth II **Subject:** Valentines (Love) **Rev:** Multicolor pair of swans **Rev. Legend:** Love is precious

Date	Mintage	F12	VF20	XF40	MS60	MS63
2008 Prooflike	16,000	—	—	—	—	90.00

KM# 530 2 DOLLARS
31.11 g., 0.999 Silver 0.9926 oz. ASW, 40.7 mm. **Ruler:** Elizabeth II **Subject:** Mikhail Kalasknikov **Rev:** Multicolor portrait in uniform with siver gun

Date	Mintage	F12	VF20	XF40	MS60	MS63
2008 Prooflike	20,000	—	—	—	—	100

KM# 531 2 DOLLARS
31.11 g., 0.999 Silver 0.9926 oz. ASW, 40.7 mm. **Ruler:** Elizabeth II **Subject:** Mikhail Kalashnikov **Rev:** Multicolor red star, soldier and gun

Date	Mintage	F12	VF20	XF40	MS60	MS63
2008 Prooflike	20,000	—	—	—	—	100

KM# 533 2 DOLLARS
31.11 g., 0.999 Silver 0.9926 oz. ASW, 40.7 mm. **Ruler:** Elizabeth II **Subject:** Sherlock Holmes **Rev:** Multicolor scene from Hound of the Baskervilles

Date	Mintage	F12	VF20	XF40	MS60	MS63
2008 Prooflike	8,000	—	—	—	—	100

KM# 534 2 DOLLARS
31.11 g., 0.999 Silver 0.9926 oz. ASW, 40.7 mm. **Ruler:** Elizabeth II **Subject:** Sherlock Holmes **Rev:** Multicolor scehe from the Final Problem

Date	Mintage	F12	VF20	XF40	MS60	MS63
2008 Prooflike	8,000	—	—	—	—	100

KM# 535 2 DOLLARS
31.11 g., 0.999 Silver 0.9926 oz. ASW, 40.7 mm. **Ruler:** Elizabeth II **Subject:** Sherlock Holmes **Rev:** Multicolor scene from the Sign of the Four

Date	Mintage	F12	VF20	XF40	MS60	MS63
2008 Prooflike	8,000	—	—	—	—	100

KM# 540 2 DOLLARS
31.11 g., 0.999 Silver 0.9926 oz. ASW, 40.7 mm. **Ruler:** Elizabeth II **Subject:** Ballet dancers **Rev:** Multicolor Vasley Nijinnsky

Date	Mintage	F12	VF20	XF40	MS60	MS63
2008 Prooflike	8,000	—	—	—	—	85.00

KM# 541 2 DOLLARS
31.11 g., 0.999 Silver 0.9926 oz. ASW, 40.7 mm. **Ruler:** Elizabeth II **Subject:** Ballet Dancers **Rev:** Multicolor Matuilda Kshesinskaya

Date	Mintage	F12	VF20	XF40	MS60	MS63
2008 Prooflike	8,000	—	—	—	—	85.00

KM# 542 2 DOLLARS
31.11 g., 0.999 Silver 0.9926 oz. ASW, 40.7 mm. **Ruler:** Elizabeth II **Subject:** Ballet dancers **Rev:** Multicolor Sergey Lifar

Date	Mintage	F12	VF20	XF40	MS60	MS63
2008 Prooflike	8,000	—	—	—	—	85.00

KM# 543 2 DOLLARS
31.11 g., 0.999 Silver 0.9926 oz. ASW, 40.7 mm. **Ruler:** Elizabeth II **Subject:** Ballet dancers **Rev:** Multicolor Anna Pavlova

Date	Mintage	F12	VF20	XF40	MS60	MS63
2008 Prooflike	—	—	—	—	—	85.00

KM# 544 2 DOLLARS
31.11 g., 0.999 Silver 0.9926 oz. ASW, 40.7 mm. **Ruler:** Elizabeth II **Subject:** White Army **Rev:** Multicolor Anton Denkin

Date	Mintage	F12	VF20	XF40	MS60	MS63
2008 Prooflike	6,000	—	—	—	—	85.00

KM# 545 2 DOLLARS
31.11 g., 0.999 Silver 0.9926 oz. ASW, 40.7 mm. **Ruler:** Elizabeth II **Subject:** White Army **Rev:** Multicolor Pytor Vrangel

Date	Mintage	F12	VF20	XF40	MS60	MS63
2008 Prooflike	6,000	—	—	—	—	85.00

KM# 546 2 DOLLARS
31.11 g., 0.999 Silver 0.9926 oz. ASW, 40.7 mm. **Ruler:** Elizabeth II **Subject:** White Army **Rev:** Multicolor Alexander Kutepov

Date	Mintage	F12	VF20	XF40	MS60	MS63
2008 Prooflike	6,000	—	—	—	—	85.00

KM# 547 2 DOLLARS
31.11 g., 0.999 Silver 0.9926 oz. ASW, 40.7 mm. **Ruler:** Elizabeth II **Subject:** White Army **Rev:** Multicolor Alexander Kolchak

Date	Mintage	F12	VF20	XF40	MS60	MS63
2008 Prooflike	6,000	—	—	—	—	85.00

KM# 721 2 DOLLARS
0.12 g., 0.999 Gold AGW, 4 mm. **Ruler:** Elizabeth II **Rev:** Lady Penrhyn sailing ship **Note:** Illustration enlarged.

Date	Mintage	F12	VF20	XF40	MS60	MS63
2010 Prooflike	5,000	—	—	—	—	12.00

KM# 722 2 DOLLARS
0.12 g., 0.995 Platinum APW, 4 mm. **Ruler:** Elizabeth II **Rev:** Humpback whale **Note:** Illustration enlarged.

Date	Mintage	F12	VF20	XF40	MS60	MS63
2010 Prooflike	5,000	—	—	—	—	15.00

KM# 1294 2 DOLLARS
31.11 g., 0.999 Silver 0.9926 oz. ASW, 33 mm. **Ruler:** Elizabeth II **Rev:** Fish with crown partially gilt

Date	Mintage	F12	VF20	XF40	MS60	MS63
2010		—	PF65 55.00			

KM# 1312 2 DOLLARS
15.55 g., 0.925 Silver 0.4595 oz. ASW, 33 mm. **Ruler:** Elizabeth II **Subject:** Good Luck

Date	Mintage	F12	VF20	XF40	MS60	MS63
2010	1,000	—	—	—	—	45.00

KM# 1384 2 DOLLARS
31.11 g., 0.999 Silver 0.9926 oz. ASW, 40.7 mm. **Ruler:** Elizabeth II **Subject:** Polish President's death, 1st Anniversary **Rev:** Portrait at right, plane crash site in color at left

Date	Mintage	F12	VF20	XF40	MS60	MS63
2011	—	—	—	—	—	75.00

KM# 1405 2 DOLLARS
15.50 g., 0.925 Silver 0.458 oz. ASW, 15.5x35 mm. **Ruler:** Elizabeth II **Subject:** Hieronymus Bosch, pater **Rev:** Paradise in color **Shape:** Vertical rectangle

Date	Mintage	F12	VF20	XF40	MS60	MS63
2011	500	PF65 150				

KM# 1407 2 DOLLARS
15.50 g., 0.925 Silver 0.458 oz. ASW, 15.5x35 mm. **Ruler:** Elizabeth II **Subject:** Hieronymus Bosch, pater **Rev:** Hell in color **Shape:** Vertical rectangle

Date	Mintage	F12	VF20	XF40	MS60	MS63
2011	500	PF65 150				

KM# 1411 2 DOLLARS
31.11 g., 0.999 Silver 0.9926 oz. ASW, 38.61 mm. **Ruler:** Elizabeth II **Subject:** Soyuzmultfilm - Old dog and wolf **Rev:** Wolf in color

Date	Mintage	F12	VF20	XF40	MS60	MS63
2011	2,000	PF65 100				

KM# 1412 2 DOLLARS
31.11 g., 0.999 Silver 0.9927 oz. ASW, 38.61 mm. **Ruler:** Elizabeth II **Subject:** Kipling's Jungle Book **Rev:** Mowgli and Aklea in color

Date	Mintage	F12	VF20	XF40	MS60	MS63
2011	2,000	PF65 100				

KM# 1413 2 DOLLARS
31.11 g., 0.999 Silver 0.9926 oz. ASW, 38.61 mm. **Ruler:** Elizabeth II **Subject:** Kipling's Jungle Book characters **Rev:** Kaa, snake

Date	Mintage	F12	VF20	XF40	MS60	MS63
2011	2,000	PF65 100				

KM# 1414 2 DOLLARS
31.11 g., 0.999 Silver 0.9926 oz. ASW, 38.61 mm. **Ruler:** Elizabeth II **Subject:** Kipling's Jungle Book characters **Rev:** Baloo (bear) in color

Date	Mintage	F12	VF20	XF40	MS60	MS63
2011	2,000	PF65 100				

KM# 1415 2 DOLLARS
31.11 g., 0.999 Silver 0.9926 oz. ASW, 38.61 mm. **Ruler:** Elizabeth II **Subject:** Kipling's Jungle Book characters **Rev:** Bagheera and Kaa, panther and crow

Date	Mintage	F12	VF20	XF40	MS60	MS63
2011	2,000	PF65 100				

KM# 1416 2 DOLLARS
31.11 g., 0.999 Silver 0.9926 oz. ASW, 38.61 mm. **Ruler:** Elizabeth II **Subject:** Kipling's Jungle Book characters **Rev:** Shere Khan (tiger) in color

Date	Mintage	F12	VF20	XF40	MS60	MS63
2011	2,000	PF65 100				

KM# 1593 2 DOLLARS
15.55 g., 0.925 Silver 0.4595 oz. ASW, 35 mm. **Ruler:** Elizabeth II **Subject:** Venomous Spiders - Brazilian Wandering Spider

Date	Mintage	F12	VF20	XF40	MS60	MS63
2013	Est. 1000	PF65 60.00				

KM# 1121 5 DOLLARS
Silver **Ruler:** Elizabeth II **Rev:** Sir Francis Drake

Date	Mintage	F12	VF20	XF40	MS60	MS63
2002	—	PF65 35.00				

KM# 1122 5 DOLLARS
Silver **Ruler:** Elizabeth II **Rev:** Kon Tiki and Thor Heyerdahl

Date	Mintage	F12	VF20	XF40	MS60	MS63
2002	—	PF65 45.00				

KM# 418 5 DOLLARS
14.00 g., Aluminum-Bronze, 31.5 mm. **Ruler:** Elizabeth II **Obv:** Crowned bust right, new portrait **Rev:** Conch shell and value **Shape:** 12-sided

Date	Mintage	F12	VF20	XF40	MS60	MS63
2003	—	—	—	—	6.00	8.00

KM# 1140 5 DOLLARS
20.00 g., 0.999 Silver 0.6382 oz. ASW **Ruler:** Elizabeth II **Subject:** Vincent van Gogh, 150th Anniversary of Birth

Date	Mintage	F12	VF20	XF40	MS60	MS63
2003	—	PF65 35.00				

KM# 469 5 DOLLARS
Copper-Nickel, 40 mm. **Ruler:** Elizabeth II **Obv:** USPS logo, Queens head above **Rev:** 5 cent 1847 Benjamin Franklin stamp

Date	Mintage	F12	VF20	XF40	MS60	MS63
2004	—	—	—	—	10.00	12.00

KM# 469a 5 DOLLARS
Silver, 40 mm. **Ruler:** Elizabeth II **Obv:** USPS logo, Queens head above **Rev:** 5 cent 1847 Benjamin Franklin stamp **Edge:** Reeded

Date	Mintage	F12	VF20	XF40	MS60	MS63
2004	—	PF65 30.00				

KM# 1149 5 DOLLARS
31.64 g., 0.999 Silver 1.0095 oz. ASW **Ruler:** Elizabeth II **Subject:** Apollo Moon Landing, 35th Anniversary **Rev:** Astronaut in Solar System

Date	Mintage	F12	VF20	XF40	MS60	MS63
2004	Est. 10000	PF65 55.00				

KM# 1108 5 DOLLARS
25.00 g., 0.925 Silver 0.7387 oz. ASW **Ruler:** Elizabeth II **Subject:** Ferrari F2

Date	Mintage	F12	VF20	XF40	MS60	MS63
2005	Est. 8000	PF63 25.00	PF65 30.00			

KM# 1109 5 DOLLARS
25.00 g., 0.925 Silver 0.7387 oz. ASW **Ruler:** Elizabeth II **Rev:** Ferrari F 2004 in color

Date	Mintage	F12	VF20	XF40	MS60	MS63
2005	Est. 8000	PF63 25.00	PF65 30.00			

KM# 1134 5 DOLLARS
31.11 g., 0.999 Silver 0.9926 oz. ASW, 38.6 mm. **Ruler:** Elizabeth II **Subject:** Star Wars, 30th Anniversary

Date	Mintage	F12	VF20	XF40	MS60	MS63
2005	—	PF65 50.00				

KM# 1135 5 DOLLARS
31.11 g., 0.999 Silver 0.9926 oz. ASW, 38.6 mm. **Ruler:** Elizabeth II **Subject:** Star Wars, 30th Anniversary

Date	Mintage	F12	VF20	XF40	MS60	MS63
2005	Est. 9999	PF65 50.00				

KM# 1175 5 DOLLARS
25.00 g., 0.925 Silver 0.7387 oz. ASW **Ruler:** Elizabeth II **Subject:** Marriage of Prince Charles and Camilla Parker-Bowles

Date	Mintage	F12	VF20	XF40	MS60	MS63
2005	—	PF65 45.00				

KM# 478 5 DOLLARS
Silver Gilt **Ruler:** Elizabeth II **Subject:** Pope Benedict XVI's visit to Valencia, Spain **Obv:** Bust right **Rev:** Valencia Cathedral **Shape:** Cathedral outline **Note:** Jeweled cathedral.

Date	Mintage	F12	VF20	XF40	MS60	MS63
2006	2,500	PF65 100				

KM# 560 5 DOLLARS
25.00 g., 0.925 Silver 0.7387 oz. ASW, 35x31 mm. **Ruler:** Elizabeth II **Subject:** Benedict XVI Annus Secundus **Rev:** Cross in crystals and gilt Papal Arms **Shape:** 6-sided

Date	Mintage	F12	VF20	XF40	MS60	MS63
2006	5,000	PF63 65.00	PF65 75.00			

KM# 561 5 DOLLARS
25.00 g., 0.999 Silver 0.7978 oz. ASW, 42x49 mm. **Ruler:** Elizabeth II **Subject:** Benedict XVI visits Germany **Rev:** Cathedral gilt, crystal inserts **Shape:** oval

Date	Mintage	F12	VF20	XF40	MS60	MS63
2006	5,000	PF63 65.00	PF65 75.00			

KM# 562 5 DOLLARS
25.00 g., 0.999 Silver 0.7978 oz. ASW, 35x35 mm. **Ruler:** Elizabeth II **Subject:** Benedict XVI **Rev:** Profile at left, cross in crystal inserts **Shape:** Square

Date	Mintage	F12	VF20	XF40	MS60	MS63
2006	5,000	PF63 65.00	PF65 75.00			

KM# 563 5 DOLLARS
25.00 g., 0.999 Silver 0.7978 oz. ASW, 35x38 mm. **Ruler:** Elizabeth II **Subject:** Christmas in St. Peter's Square **Rev:** St. Peter's partially gilt, star crystal insert **Shape:** Triange

Date	Mintage	F12	VF20	XF40	MS60	MS63
2006	5,000	PF63 65.00	PF65 75.00			

KM# 564 5 DOLLARS
25.00 g., 0.999 Silver 0.7978 oz. ASW, 20x44 mm. **Ruler:** Elizabeth II **Subject:** benedict XVI visits Poland **Rev:** Polish icon, partially gilt, crystal insert **Shape:** Candle

Date	Mintage	F12	VF20	XF40	MS60	MS63
2006	564	PF63 65.00	PF65 75.00			

KM# 565 5 DOLLARS
25.00 g., 0.999 Silver 0.7978 oz. ASW, 38.6 mm. **Ruler:** Elizabeth II **Rev:** St. Peter's Basilica, partially gilt, crystals as stars

Date	Mintage	F12	VF20	XF40	MS60	MS63
2006	5,000	PF63 65.00	PF65 75.00			

KM# 566 5 DOLLARS
25.00 g., 0.999 Silver 0.7978 oz. ASW, 35x35 mm. **Ruler:** Elizabeth II **Subject:** Swiss Guards, 500th Anniversary **Rev:** Four Swiss guards, partially gilt, crystal insert **Shape:** Diamond

Date	Mintage	F12	VF20	XF40	MS60	MS63
2006	5,000	PF63 65.00	PF65 75.00			

KM# 567 5 DOLLARS
25.00 g., 0.999 Silver 0.7978 oz. ASW, 40x25 mm. **Ruler:** Elizabeth II **Subject:** Benedict XVI visits Turkey **Rev:** Pope and Patrarch, partially gilt, crystal insert **Shape:** Rectangle

Date	Mintage	F12	VF20	XF40	MS60	MS63
2006	5,000	PF63 65.00	PF65 75.00			

KM# 568 5 DOLLARS
25.00 g., 0.999 Silver 0.7978 oz. ASW, 40x25 mm. **Ruler:** Elizabeth II **Subject:** Urbi et Orbi message **Rev:** Benedict XVI giving blessing, partially gilt, crystal insert **Shape:** Rectangle

Date	Mintage	F12	VF20	XF40	MS60	MS63
2006	5,000	PF63 65.00	PF65 75.00			

KM# 569 5 DOLLARS
0.25 g., 0.999 Silver, 29x42 mm. **Ruler:** Elizabeth II **Subject:** Benedict XVI visits Vallencia **Rev:** Valencia cathedral façade, partially gilt, crystal inserts **Shape:** Irregular

Date	Mintage	F12	VF20	XF40	MS60	MS63
2006	5,000	PF65 75.00				

KM# 570 5 DOLLARS
31.10 g., 0.999 Silver 0.9925 oz. ASW, 38.6 mm. **Ruler:** Elizabeth II **Rev:** Statue of Liberty gilt pop-up

Date	Mintage	F12	VF20	XF40	MS60	MS63
2006	5,000	PF65 90.00				

KM# 571 5 DOLLARS
31.10 g., 0.999 Silver 0.9925 oz. ASW, 38.6 mm. **Ruler:** Elizabeth II **Rev:** Ludwig's castle gilt pop-up

Date	Mintage	F12	VF20	XF40	MS60	MS63
2006	5,000	PF65 90.00				

KM# 572 5 DOLLARS
25.00 g., 0.999 Silver 0.7978 oz. ASW, 35x35 mm. **Ruler:** Elizabeth II **Subject:** Benedict XVI visits Marianzell **Rev:** Our Lady or Marianzell, partially gilt, crystal inserts **Shape:** Tablet

Date	Mintage	F12	VF20	XF40	MS60	MS63
2007	5,000	PF63 75.00	PF65 85.00			

KM# 573 5 DOLLARS
25.00 g., 0.999 Silver 0.7978 oz. ASW, 35x35 mm. **Ruler:** Elizabeth II **Rev:** St. Francis, tau cross, partially gilt, crystal insert **Shape:** Dove

Date	Mintage	F12	VF20	XF40	MS60	MS63
2007	5,000	PF63 65.00	PF65 75.00			

KM# 574 5 DOLLARS
25.00 g., 0.999 Silver 0.7978 oz. ASW, 31x40 mm. **Ruler:** Elizabeth II **Rev:** Benedict XVI bust left, partially gilt, crystal insert **Shape:** Irregular

Date	Mintage	F12	VF20	XF40	MS60	MS63
2007	5,000	PF63 65.00	PF65 75.00			

KM# 575 5 DOLLARS
25.00 g., 0.999 Silver 0.7978 oz. ASW, 35x45 mm. **Ruler:** Elizabeth II **Subject:** Benedict XVI visits Brazil **Rev:** Christ statue in Rio, partially gilt, crystal insert **Shape:** Diamond

Date	Mintage	F12	VF20	XF40	MS60	MS63
2007	5,000	PF63 65.00	PF65 75.00			

KM# 576 5 DOLLARS
25.00 g., 0.999 Silver 0.7978 oz. ASW, 37 mm. **Ruler:** Elizabeth II **Subject:** Princess Diana, 10th Anniversary of death **Rev:** Bust at left, multicolored rose **Shape:** Heart

Date	Mintage	F12	VF20	XF40	MS60	MS63
2007	1,997	PF65 75.00				

KM# 577 5 DOLLARS
25.00 g., 0.999 Silver 0.7978 oz. ASW, 39x24 mm. **Ruler:** Elizabeth II **Subject:** Docrine of the Immaculate Conception **Rev:** Virgin Mary and cathedral, partially gilt, crystal insert **Shape:** Rectangle

Date	Mintage	F12	VF20	XF40	MS60	MS63
2007	5,000	PF63 65.00	PF65 75.00			

KM# 578 5 DOLLARS
25.00 g., 0.999 Silver 0.7978 oz. ASW, 31x35 mm. **Ruler:** Elizabeth II **Subject:** Benedict XVI visits Loredo **Rev:** Pope blessing crowd, cathedral, partially gilt, crystal insert **Shape:** 6-sided

Date	Mintage	F12	VF20	XF40	MS60	MS63
2007	5,000	PF63 65.00	PF65 75.00			

KM# 579 5 DOLLARS
25.00 g., 0.999 Silver 0.7978 oz. ASW, 35x35 mm. **Ruler:** Elizabeth II **Subject:** Santo Subito **Rev:** Pope John Paul II, partially gilt, crystal insert **Shape:** Cross

Date	Mintage	F12	VF20	XF40	MS60	MS63
2007	5,000	PF65 100				

KM# 580 5 DOLLARS
25.00 g., 0.999 Silver 0.7978 oz. ASW, 30x45 mm. **Ruler:** Elizabeth II **Subject:** Way of the Cross **Rev:** Benedict XVI holdign cross, collesum in background, partially gilt, crystal insert **Shape:** Vertical oval

Date	Mintage	F12	VF20	XF40	MS60	MS63
2007	5,000	PF63 65.00	PF65 75.00			

KM# 581 5 DOLLARS
31.10 g., 0.999 Silver 0.9925 oz. ASW, 38.6 mm. **Ruler:** Elizabeth II **Rev:** Parthenon gilt pop-up

Date	Mintage	F12	VF20	XF40	MS60	MS63
2007	5,000	PF65 90.00				

KM# 583 5 DOLLARS
31.10 g., 0.999 Silver 0.9925 oz. ASW, 38.6 mm. **Ruler:** Elizabeth II **Rev:** Rio's Christ statue gilt pop-up

Date	Mintage	F12	VF20	XF40	MS60	MS63
2007	5,000	PF65 100				

KM# 584 5 DOLLARS
31.10 g., 0.999 Silver 0.9925 oz. ASW, 38.6 mm. **Ruler:** Elizabeth II **Rev:** Collesum gilt pop-up

Date	Mintage	F12	VF20	XF40	MS60	MS63
2007	5,000	PF65 90.00				

KM# 586 5 DOLLARS
31.10 g., 0.999 Silver 0.9925 oz. ASW, 38.6 mm. **Ruler:** Elizabeth II **Rev:** Eifle Tower gilt pop-up

Date	Mintage	F12	VF20	XF40	MS60	MS63
2007	5,000	PF65 90.00				

KM# 763 5 DOLLARS
20.00 g., Silver, 38.61 mm. **Ruler:** Elizabeth II **Subject:** Drenham Meteor **Obv:** Bust right **Rev:** Meteorite and fragment inset

Date	Mintage	F12	VF20	XF40	MS60	MS63
2007	2,500	PF65 100				

KM# 1188 5 DOLLARS
20.00 g., 0.925 Silver 0.591 oz. ASW, 38.61 mm. **Ruler:** Elizabeth II **Subject:** Elvis Presley, 30th Anniversary of death

Date	Mintage	F12	VF20	XF40	MS60	MS63
2007	Est. 50000	PF65 70.00				

KM# 1189 5 DOLLARS
20.00 g., 0.925 Silver 0.591 oz. ASW, 38.61 mm. **Ruler:** Elizabeth II **Subject:** Elvis Presely, 30th Anniversary of Death **Rev:** Love me Tender, 1956

Date	Mintage	F12	VF20	XF40	MS60	MS63
2007	Est. 50000	PF65 70.00				

KM# 1201 5 DOLLARS
25.00 g., Copper-Nickel, 38.6 mm. **Ruler:** Elizabeth II **Subject:** Lady Diana, 10th Anniversary of Death **Rev:** Diana partially gilt

Date	Mintage	F12	VF20	XF40	MS60	MS63
2007	Est. 50000	PF65 22.50				

KM# 1202 5 DOLLARS
25.00 g., Copper-Nickel, 38.6 mm. **Ruler:** Elizabeth II **Subject:** Princess Diana, 10th Anniversary of Death **Rev:** Diana in wedding dress, partially gilt

Date	Mintage	F12	VF20	XF40	MS60	MS63
2007	Est. 14500	PF65 22.50				

KM# 1203 5 DOLLARS
155.50 g., Copper-Nickel, 65 mm. **Ruler:** Elizabeth II **Subject:** Princess Diana, 10th Anniversary of Death **Rev:** Lady Diana, partially gilt

Date	Mintage	F12	VF20	XF40	MS60	MS63
2007	Est. 1961	PF65 85.00				

KM# 1320 5 DOLLARS
Silver **Ruler:** Elizabeth II **Rev:** Copernicus with solar system, partially gilt

Date	Mintage	F12	VF20	XF40	MS60	MS63
2008	—	PF65 50.00				

KM# 594 5 DOLLARS
25.00 g., 0.999 Silver 0.7978 oz. ASW, 35x35 mm. **Ruler:** Elizabeth II **Subject:** Pope John Paul II Election 30th Anniversary **Rev:** John Paul II coat-of-arms, aprtially gilt, crystal insert **Shape:** Diamond

Date	Mintage	F12	VF20	XF40	MS60	MS63
2008	5,000	PF65 120				

KM# 595 5 DOLLARS
25.00 g., 0.999 Silver 0.7978 oz. ASW, 30x45 mm. **Ruler:** Elizabeth II **Subject:** Lourdes, 150th Anniversary **Rev:** Statue of Our Lady of Lourdes, partially gilt, crystal insert **Shape:** Vertical oval

Date	Mintage	F12	VF20	XF40	MS60	MS63
2008	5,000	PF65 110				

KM# 596 5 DOLLARS
25.00 g., 0.999 Silver 0.7978 oz. ASW, 30x45 mm. **Ruler:** Elizabeth II **Subject:** Lourdes, 150th Anniversary **Rev:** Our Lady of Lourdes, holigram, partially gilt, crystal insert **Shape:** Vertical oval

Date	Mintage	F12	VF20	XF40	MS60	MS63
2008	5,000	PF65 120				

KM# 597 5 DOLLARS
25.00 g., 0.999 Silver 0.7978 oz. ASW, 40x25 mm. **Ruler:** Elizabeth II **Subject:** Benedict XVI Annus Novas **Rev:** Benedict XVI and dove **Shape:** Oval

Date	Mintage	F12	VF20	XF40	MS60	MS63
2008	5,000	PF65 100				

KM# 598 5 DOLLARS
25.00 g., 0.999 Silver 0.7978 oz. ASW, 32x41 mm. **Ruler:** Elizabeth II **Rev:** St. Peter's Square, cresch and christmas tree, partially gilt, crystal insert **Shape:** Triangle

Date	Mintage	F12	VF20	XF40	MS60	MS63
2008	5,000	PF65 100				

KM# 599 5 DOLLARS
25.00 g., 0.999 Silver 0.7978 oz. ASW, 35x35 mm. **Ruler:** Elizabeth II **Subject:** Crufifixio Domini **Rev:** Benedict XVI before cross, partially gilt, crystal inserts **Shape:** Cross

Date	Mintage	F12	VF20	XF40	MS60	MS63
2008	5,000	PF65 100				

KM# 600 5 DOLLARS
25.00 g., 0.999 Silver 0.7978 oz. ASW, 29x42 mm. **Ruler:** Elizabeth II **Subject:** Paulus year **Rev:** Benedict XVI in Basicilica, partially gilt, crystal insert **Shape:** Vertical rectangle

Date	Mintage	F12	VF20	XF40	MS60	MS63
2008	5,000	PF65 100				

KM# 601 5 DOLLARS
25.00 g., 0.999 Silver 0.7978 oz. ASW, 40x25 mm. **Ruler:** Elizabeth II **Subject:** Sistine Chapel, 500th Anniversary **Rev:** Adam and god, Sistine Chapel ceiling, partially gilt, crystal insert **Shape:** Rectangle

Date	Mintage	F12	VF20	XF40	MS60	MS63
2008	5,000	PF65 120				

KM# 602 5 DOLLARS
25.00 g., 0.999 Silver 0.7978 oz. ASW, 40x42 mm. **Ruler:** Elizabeth II **Rev:** St Martin on horseback, partially gilt, crystal insert **Shape:** 8-sided

Date	Mintage	F12	VF20	XF40	MS60	MS63
2008	5,000	PF65 100				

KM# 603 5 DOLLARS
25.00 g., 0.999 Silver 0.7978 oz. ASW, 45x34 mm. **Ruler:** Elizabeth II **Subject:** Benedict XVI visits Sydney **Rev:** Sydney Harbor Bridge and Sydney Opera House, partially gilt, crystal insert **Shape:** Irregular oval

Date	Mintage	F12	VF20	XF40	MS60	MS63
2008	5,000	PF65 100				

KM# 604 5 DOLLARS
25.00 g., 0.999 Silver 0.7978 oz. ASW, 35x35 mm. **Ruler:** Elizabeth II **Subject:** Tu Es Peterus **Rev:** Cross Keys, Christ handing keys to kneeling St. Peter. Partially gilt, crystal insert. **Shape:** Square

Date	Mintage	F12	VF20	XF40	MS60	MS63
2008	5,000	PF65 120				

KM# 605 5 DOLLARS
25.00 g., 0.999 Silver 0.7978 oz. ASW, 38.6 mm. **Ruler:** Elizabeth II **Rev:** Pope blessing crowd, partially gilt, crystal inserts

Date	Mintage	F12	VF20	XF40	MS60	MS63
2008	5,000	PF65 110				

KM# 606 5 DOLLARS
25.00 g., 0.999 Silver 0.7978 oz. ASW, 42x29 mm. **Ruler:** Elizabeth II **Subject:** Benedict XVI visits the United States **Rev:** Benedict XVI, the White House, Statue of Liberty, UN Building, partially gilt, crystal inserts **Shape:** Irregular US Map shape

Date	Mintage	F12	VF20	XF40	MS60	MS63
2008	5,000	PF65 110				

KM# 607 5 DOLLARS
25.00 g., 0.999 Silver 0.7978 oz. ASW, 40x42 mm. **Ruler:** Elizabeth II **Rev:** St. George slaying dragon, partially gilt, crystal insert **Shape:** 8-sided

Date	Mintage	F12	VF20	XF40	MS60	MS63
2008	5,000	PF65 100				

KM# 608 5 DOLLARS
31.11 g., 0.999 Silver 0.9926 oz. ASW, 38.6 mm. **Ruler:** Elizabeth II **Subject:** Conversion of Russia, 1000th Anniversary **Rev:** Baptism scene **Note:** Exclusive to the Russian Market.

Date	Mintage	F12	VF20	XF40	MS60	MS63
2008	500	PF65 120				

KM# 609 5 DOLLARS
31.11 g., 0.999 Silver 0.9926 oz. ASW, 47x27 mm. **Ruler:** Elizabeth II **Subject:** Orthodox Communication **Rev:** Patriarch's meeting **Shape:** Rectangle **Note:** Exclusive to the Russian Market.

Date	Mintage	F12	VF20	XF40	MS60	MS63
2008	500	PF65 120				

KM# 610 5 DOLLARS
25.00 g., 0.999 Silver 0.7978 oz. ASW, 30x38 mm. **Ruler:** Elizabeth II **Rev:** Icon - Theotokos of Vladimir, wood insert **Shape:** Rectangle **Note:** Exclusive to the Russian Market.

Date	Mintage	F12	VF20	XF40	MS60	MS63
2008	2,500	PF65 120				

KM# 611 5 DOLLARS
31.11 g., 0.999 Silver 0.9926 oz. ASW, 38.6 mm. **Ruler:** Elizabeth II **Subject:** Kiev Churches **Rev:** Church of All Saints **Note:** Exclusive to the Russian Market.

Date	Mintage	F12	VF20	XF40	MS60	MS63
2008	500	PF65 120				

KM# 612 5 DOLLARS
31.11 g., 0.999 Silver 0.9926 oz. ASW, 38.6 mm. **Ruler:** Elizabeth II **Subject:** Kiev Churches **Rev:** Dormotion of Theotokos **Note:** Exclusive to the Russian Market.

Date	Mintage	F12	VF20	XF40	MS60	MS63
2008	500	PF65 120				

KM# 613 5 DOLLARS
31.11 g., 0.999 Silver 0.9926 oz. ASW **Ruler:** Elizabeth II **Subject:** Kiev Churches **Rev:** Refractory of Pechersky **Shape:** 38.6 **Note:** Exclusive to the Russian Market.

Date	Mintage	F12	VF20	XF40	MS60	MS63
2008	500	PF65 120				

KM# 614 5 DOLLARS
31.11 g., 0.999 Silver 0.9926 oz. ASW, 38.6 mm. **Ruler:** Elizabeth II **Subject:** Kiev Churches **Rev:** Troitskaya Barbican **Note:** Exclusive to the Russian Market.

Date	Mintage	F12	VF20	XF40	MS60	MS63
2008	500	PF65 120				

KM# 615 5 DOLLARS
25.00 g., 0.925 Silver 0.7387 oz. ASW, 37 mm. **Ruler:** Elizabeth II **Rev:** Cupid and roses **Rev. Legend:** My Everlasting Love **Shape:** Heart

Date	Mintage	F12	VF20	XF40	MS60	MS63
2008	2,500	PF65 70.00				

KM# 616 5 DOLLARS
25.00 g., 0.925 Silver 0.7387 oz. ASW, 38.6 mm. **Ruler:** Elizabeth II **Subject:** Endangered Wildlife - Arctic **Rev:** Polar bear and cubs, crystal inserts

Date	Mintage	F12	VF20	XF40	MS60	MS63
2008	2,500	PF65 70.00				

KM# 617 5 DOLLARS
25.00 g., 0.925 Silver 0.7387 oz. ASW, 38.6 mm. **Ruler:**
Elizabeth II **Subject:** Engangered wildlife - Antarctic **Rev:**
Penguin, crystal insert

Date	Mintage	F12	VF20	XF40	MS60	MS63
2008	2,500	**PF65** 70.00				

KM# 618 5 DOLLARS
25.00 g., 0.925 Silver 0.7387 oz. ASW, 38.6 mm. **Ruler:**
Elizabeth II **Subject:** Pultusk Meteorite **Rev:** Earth and
Meteorite fragment insert

Date	Mintage	F12	VF20	XF40	MS60	MS63
2008	2,500	**PF65** 85.00				

KM# 666 5 DOLLARS
141.40 g., 0.999 Silver 4.5123 oz. ASW, 65 mm. **Ruler:**
Elizabeth II **Subject:** Tall ships **Obv:** Bust right **Rev:** Germany's
Preussen, 5-masted square rigger

Date	Mintage	F12	VF20	XF40	MS60	MS63
2008	—	**PF65** 285				

KM# 667 5 DOLLARS
141.40 g., 0.999 Silver 4.5123 oz. ASW, 65 mm. **Ruler:**
Elizabeth II **Subject:** Tall ships **Rev:** France's France II

Date	Mintage	F12	VF20	XF40	MS60	MS63
2008	—	**PF65** 285				

KM# 668 5 DOLLARS
141.40 g., 0.999 Silver 4.5123 oz. ASW, 65 mm. **Ruler:**
Elizabeth II **Subject:** Tall Ships **Rev:** America's Thomas W.
Lawson, 7-masted schooner

Date	Mintage	F12	VF20	XF40	MS60	MS63
2008	—	**PF65** 285				

KM# 669 5 DOLLARS
141.40 g., 0.999 Silver 4.5123 oz. ASW, 65 mm. **Ruler:**
Elizabeth II **Subject:** Tall Ships **Rev:** Russia's Sedov, 4-masted
barque

Date	Mintage	F12	VF20	XF40	MS60	MS63
2008	—	**PF65** 285				

KM# 670 5 DOLLARS
141.40 g., 0.999 Silver 4.5123 oz. ASW, 65 mm. **Ruler:** Elizabeth
II **Subject:** Tall Ships **Rev:** Norway's Christian Radich

Date	Mintage	F12	VF20	XF40	MS60	MS63
2008	—	**PF65** 285				

KM# 671 5 DOLLARS
141.40 g., 0.999 Silver 4.5123 oz. ASW, 65 mm. **Ruler:**
Elizabeth II **Subject:** Tall Ships **Rev:** Russian 4-masted barque
Kruzenshtern

Date	Mintage	F12	VF20	XF40	MS60	MS63
2008	—	**PF65** 285				

KM# 766 5 DOLLARS
31.11 g., 0.999 Silver 0.9926 oz. ASW, 40 mm. **Ruler:** Elizabeth
II **Subject:** First man on the Moon **Rev:** Moon and rock
fragment

Date	Mintage	F12	VF20	XF40	MS60	MS63
2008	—	**PF65** 120				

KM# 1207 5 DOLLARS
0.50 g., 0.999 Gold AGW, 11 mm. **Ruler:** Elizabeth II **Rev:**
American Bison

Date	Mintage	F12	VF20	XF40	MS60	MS63
2008	Est. 10000	**PF65** 70.00				

KM# 1211 5 DOLLARS
155.50 g., Copper-Nickel, 65 mm. **Ruler:** Elizabeth II **Subject:**
British Monarchs - Elizabeth I

Date	Mintage	F12	VF20	XF40	MS60	MS63
2008	Est. 450	**PF65** 85.00				

KM# 1526 5 DOLLARS
0.50 g., 1.000 Gold AGW, 11 mm. **Ruler:** Elizabeth II **Subject:** Aristotle

Date	Mintage	F12	VF20	XF40	MS60	MS63
2008	Est. 10000	PF65 50.00				

KM# 1330 5 DOLLARS
Silver **Ruler:** Elizabeth II **Rev:** European Bison, partially gilt

Date	Mintage	F12	VF20	XF40	MS60	MS63
2009	—	PF65 50.00				

KM# 640 5 DOLLARS
25.00 g., 0.999 Silver 0.7978 oz. ASW, 38.6 mm. **Ruler:** Elizabeth II **Rev:** Papal Tiara above crossed keys, partially gilt, crystal inserts

Date	Mintage	F12	VF20	XF40	MS60	MS63
2009	5,000	PF65 120				

KM# 641 5 DOLLARS
25.00 g., 0.999 Silver 0.7978 oz. ASW **Ruler:** Elizabeth II **Subject:** Benedict XVI visits Israel **Rev:** Benedict XVI and "Dome of the Rock", partially gilt, crystal inserts **Shape:** Diamond

Date	Mintage	F12	VF20	XF40	MS60	MS63
2009	5,000	PF65 115				

KM# 642 5 DOLLARS
25.00 g., 0.999 Silver 0.7978 oz. ASW **Ruler:** Elizabeth II **Subject:** Benedict XVI visits Africa **Rev:** Bust at left, partially gilt, crystal inserts **Shape:** Irregular, Africa shape

Date	Mintage	F12	VF20	XF40	MS60	MS63
2009	5,000	PF65 115				

KM# 643 5 DOLLARS
25.00 g., 0.999 Silver 0.7978 oz. ASW **Ruler:** Elizabeth II **Subject:** Easter 2009 **Rev:** Statue of the risen Christ, partially gilt, crystal inserts **Shape:** Fish

Date	Mintage	F12	VF20	XF40	MS60	MS63
2009	5,000	PF65 115				

KM# 644 5 DOLLARS
25.00 g., 0.999 Silver 0.7978 oz. ASW, 35 mm. **Ruler:** Elizabeth II **Rev:** Star of the Magi, partially gilt, crystal inserts **Shape:** Star

Date	Mintage	F12	VF20	XF40	MS60	MS63
2009	5,000	PF65 115				

KM# 645 5 DOLLARS
25.00 g., 0.999 Silver 0.7978 oz. ASW, 35x35 mm. **Ruler:** Elizabeth II **Rev:** Cathedral of Santiago de Composetla, partially gilt, crystal inserts

Date	Mintage	F12	VF20	XF40	MS60	MS63
2009	5,000	PF65 120				

KM# 646 5 DOLLARS
25.00 g., 0.999 Silver 0.7978 oz. ASW, 25x35 mm. **Ruler:** Elizabeth II **Rev:** Michangelo's Pieta, partially gilt, crystal inserts **Shape:** Rectangle

Date	Mintage	F12	VF20	XF40	MS60	MS63
2009	5,000	PF65 115				

KM# 647 5 DOLLARS
25.00 g., 0.999 Silver 0.7978 oz. ASW, 30x34 mm. **Ruler:** Elizabeth II **Rev:** St. Christopher, partially gilt, crystal inserts **Shape:** Oval

Date	Mintage	F12	VF20	XF40	MS60	MS63
2009	5,000	PF65 115				

KM# 648 5 DOLLARS
25.00 g., 0.999 Silver 0.7978 oz. ASW, 40x25 mm. **Ruler:** Elizabeth II **Subject:** Benedict XVI visits the Czech Republic **Rev:** Benedict XVI in Wenceleses square, partially gilt, crystal inserts **Shape:** Rectangle

Date	Mintage	F12	VF20	XF40	MS60	MS63
2009	5,000	PF65 115				

KM# 649 5 DOLLARS
25.00 g., 0.999 Silver 0.7978 oz. ASW **Ruler:** Elizabeth II **Rev:** Christmas, village scene, partially gilt, crystal inserts **Shape:** Diamond

Date	Mintage	F12	VF20	XF40	MS60	MS63
2009	5,000	PF65 115				

KM# 650 5 DOLLARS
31.11 g., 0.999 Silver 0.9926 oz. ASW, 38.6 mm. **Ruler:** Elizabeth II **Subject:** Kiev Churches **Rev:** Andreevskaya Church **Note:** Exclusive to the Russian Market.

Date	Mintage	F12	VF20	XF40	MS60	MS63
2009	500	PF65 125				

KM# 651 5 DOLLARS
31.11 g., 0.999 Silver 0.9926 oz. ASW, 38.6 mm. **Ruler:** Elizabeth II **Subject:** Kiev Churches **Rev:** Kirillovskaya Church **Note:** Exclusive to the Russian Market.

Date	Mintage	F12	VF20	XF40	MS60	MS63
2009	500	PF65 125				

KM# 652 5 DOLLARS
31.11 g., 0.999 Silver 0.9926 oz. ASW, 38.6 mm. **Ruler:** Elizabeth II **Subject:** Kiev Chruches **Rev:** Mikailovsky Monastery **Note:** Exclusive to the Russian Market.

Date	Mintage	F12	VF20	XF40	MS60	MS63
2009	500	PF65 125				

KM# 653 5 DOLLARS
31.11 g., 0.999 Silver 0.9926 oz. ASW, 38.6 mm. **Ruler:**

Elizabeth II **Subject:** Kiev Churches **Rev:** Cathedral of St. Sophia **Note:** Exclusive to the Russian Market.

Date	Mintage	F12	VF20	XF40	MS60	MS63
2009	500	PF65 125				

KM# 654 5 DOLLARS
31.11 g., 0.999 Silver 0.9926 oz. ASW, 38.61 mm. **Ruler:** Elizabeth II **Subject:** Ukraine Landmarks - Bendrological park, Sofiyivka **Rev:** Statue and gardens **Note:** Exclusive to the Russian Market.

Date	Mintage	F12	VF20	XF40	MS60	MS63
2009	500	PF65 120				

KM# 655 5 DOLLARS
31.11 g., 0.999 Silver 0.9926 oz. ASW, 38.61 mm. **Ruler:** Elizabeth II **Subject:** Ukraine Landmarks - Holy Dormition Kiev Pechersk Lavra **Rev:** Churches **Note:** Exclusive to the Russian Market.

Date	Mintage	F12	VF20	XF40	MS60	MS63
2009	500	PF65 120				

KM# 656 5 DOLLARS
31.11 g., 0.999 Silver 0.9926 oz. ASW, 38.61 mm. **Ruler:** Elizabeth II **Subject:** Ukraine Landmarks - Holy Dormition Pochayiv Lavra **Rev:** Buildings **Note:** Exclusive to the Russian Market.

Date	Mintage	F12	VF20	XF40	MS60	MS63
2009	500	PF65 120				

KM# 657 5 DOLLARS
31.11 g., 0.999 Silver 0.9926 oz. ASW, 38.61 mm. **Ruler:** Elizabeth II **Subject:** Ukraine Landmarks - Holy Dormition Sviatohirsk Lavra **Rev:** Virgin Mary and Church **Note:** Exclusive to the Russian Market.

Date	Mintage	F12	VF20	XF40	MS60	MS63
2009	500	PF65 120				

KM# 658 5 DOLLARS
31.11 g., 0.999 Silver 0.9926 oz. ASW, 38.61 mm. **Ruler:** Elizabeth II **Subject:** Ukraine Landmarks - Kamyanets National Reserve **Rev:** Fortress **Note:** Exclusive to the Russian Market.

Date	Mintage	F12	VF20	XF40	MS60	MS63
2009	500	PF65 120				

KM# 659 5 DOLLARS
31.11 g., 0.999 Silver 0.9926 oz. ASW, 38.6 mm. **Ruler:** Elizabeth II **Subject:** Ukraine Landmarks - Khersones Tavrijsky National Reserve **Rev:** Roman ruins **Note:** Exclusive to the Russian Market.

Date	Mintage	F12	VF20	XF40	MS60	MS63
2009	500	PF65 120				

KM# 660 5 DOLLARS
31.11 g., 0.999 Silver 0.9926 oz. ASW, 38.6 mm. **Ruler:** Elizabeth II **Subject:** Ukraine Landmarks - Khortytsia National Reserve **Rev:** Stone carvings and bridge **Note:** Exclusive to the Russian Market.

Date	Mintage	F12	VF20	XF40	MS60	MS63
2009	500	PF65 120				

KM# 661 5 DOLLARS
31.11 g., 0.999 Silver 0.9926 oz. ASW, 38.6 mm. **Ruler:** Elizabeth II **Subject:** Ukraine Landmarks - National Theatre of Odessa **Rev:** Opera House **Note:** Exclusive to the Russian Market.

Date	Mintage	F12	VF20	XF40	MS60	MS63
2009	500	PF65 120				

KM# 662 5 DOLLARS
31.11 g., 0.999 Silver 0.9926 oz. ASW, 38.6 mm. **Ruler:** Elizabeth II **Subject:** Ukraine Landmarks - Olesko Castle **Rev:** Hillside dwelling **Note:** Exclusive to the Russian Market.

Date	Mintage	F12	VF20	XF40	MS60	MS63
2009	500	PF65 120				

KM# 663 5 DOLLARS
31.11 g., 0.999 Silver 0.9926 oz. ASW, 38.6 mm. **Ruler:** Elizabeth II **Subject:** Ukraine Landmarks - Palanok Castle in Mukachevo **Rev:** Hilltop fortress **Note:** Exclusive to the Russian Market.

Date	Mintage	F12	VF20	XF40	MS60	MS63
2009	500	PF65 120				

KM# 664 5 DOLLARS
31.11 g., 0.999 Silver 0.9926 oz. ASW, 38.6 mm. **Ruler:** Elizabeth II **Subject:** Ukraine Landmarks - Khotyn Fortress Reserve **Rev:** Road to castle **Note:** Exclusive to the Russian Market.

Date	Mintage	F12	VF20	XF40	MS60	MS63
2009	500	PF65 120				

KM# 665 5 DOLLARS
31.11 g., 0.999 Silver 0.9926 oz. ASW, 38.6 mm. **Ruler:** Elizabeth II **Subject:** Ukraine Landmarks - Upper Castle of Lutsk **Rev:** Tower **Note:** Exclusive to the Russian Market.

Date	Mintage	F12	VF20	XF40	MS60	MS63
2009	500	PF65 120				

KM# 672 5 DOLLARS
25.00 g., 0.925 Silver 0.7387 oz. ASW, 38.6 mm. **Ruler:** Elizabeth II **Rev:** HMS Endeavour and James Cook portrait

Date	Mintage	F12	VF20	XF40	MS60	MS63
2009	2,500	PF65 45.00				

KM# 673 5 DOLLARS
25.00 g., 0.500 Silver 0.3993 oz. ASW, 38.6 mm. **Ruler:** Elizabeth II **Rev:** Ferrari F-2008 Carbon

Date	Mintage	F12	VF20	XF40	MS60	MS63
ND2009	2,008	PF65 50.00				

KM# 674 5 DOLLARS
20.00 g., 0.925 Silver 0.591 oz. ASW, 38.61 mm. **Ruler:** Elizabeth II **Subject:** Endangered Wildlife **Rev:** Giant Anteater

Date	Mintage	F12	VF20	XF40	MS60	MS63
2009	5,000	PF65 50.00				

KM# 675 5 DOLLARS
31.11 g., 0.925 Silver 0.9191 oz. ASW, 38.6 mm. **Ruler:** Elizabeth II **Series:** International Womens Day **Rev:** Roses and butterfly **Note:** Exclusive to the Russian Market

Date	Mintage	F12	VF20	XF40	MS60	MS63
2009	500	PF65 120				

KM# 676 5 DOLLARS
25.00 g., 0.925 Silver 0.7387 oz. ASW, 38.6 mm. **Ruler:** Elizabeth II **Rev:** Sir Lancelot, multicolor

Date	Mintage	F12	VF20	XF40	MS60	MS63
2009	2,500	PF65 75.00				

KM# 677 5 DOLLARS
0.925 Silver **Ruler:** Elizabeth II **Subject:** Masters of Europe - Vermeer **Rev:** Girl with a pearl earing, multicolor **Shape:** Vertical rectangle

Date	Mintage	F12	VF20	XF40	MS60	MS63
2009	—	PF65 65.00				

KM# 678 5 DOLLARS
0.925 Silver **Ruler:** Elizabeth II **Subject:** Masters of Europe - DaVinci **Rev:** Lady with an ermine, multicolor **Shape:** Vertical rectangle

Date	Mintage	F12	VF20	XF40	MS60	MS63
2009	—	PF65 75.00				

KM# 679 5 DOLLARS
0.925 Silver **Ruler:** Elizabeth II **Subject:** Masters of Europe - Jan Matejko **Rev:** Wernyhora, multicolor **Shape:** Vertical rectangle

Date	Mintage	F12	VF20	XF40	MS60	MS63
2009	—	PF65 65.00				

KM# 680 5 DOLLARS
Silver **Ruler:** Elizabeth II **Subject:** 50th Anniversary of Space exploration, 40th Anniversary of Apollo 11 **Obv:** Moon **Rev:** Moonscape and moon rock implant

Date	Mintage	F12	VF20	XF40	MS60	MS63
2009 Matte	1,969	—	—	—	—	300

KM# 681 5 DOLLARS
25.00 g., 0.925 Silver 0.7387 oz. ASW **Ruler:** Elizabeth II **Subject:** 400th Anniversary of Mars observations **Obv:** Bust with tiara right **Rev:** Mars landscape

Date	Mintage	F12	VF20	XF40	MS60	MS63
2009 Matte	2,500	—	—	—	—	250

KM# 682 5 DOLLARS
25.00 g., 0.925 Silver 0.7387 oz. ASW, 38.61 mm. **Ruler:** Elizabeth II **Subject:** Year of the Ox **Rev:** Child riding oxen, partially gilt **Note:** Exclusive to the Russian market

Date	Mintage	F12	VF20	XF40	MS60	MS63
2009	1,000	PF65 200				

KM# 683 5 DOLLARS
25.00 g., 0.999 Silver 0.7978 oz. ASW **Ruler:** Elizabeth II **Subject:** World of Flowers - Pansey **Rev:** Pansey, multicolor cloisonne

Date	Mintage	F12	VF20	XF40	MS60	MS63
2009	2,500	PF65 75.00				

KM# 684 5 DOLLARS
25.00 g., 0.999 Silver 0.7978 oz. ASW, 38.6 mm. **Ruler:** Elizabeth II **Subject:** World of flowers - Poppy **Rev:** Poppy, multicolor closinne

Date	Mintage	F12	VF20	XF40	MS60	MS63
2009	2,500	PF65 75.00				

KM# 685 5 DOLLARS
25.00 g., 0.925 Silver 0.7387 oz. ASW, 30x43 mm. **Ruler:** Elizabeth II **Obv:** Bust right **Rev:** Easter chick, thermal image changing **Shape:** Egg

Date	Mintage	F12	VF20	XF40	MS60	MS63
2009	2,500	PF65 70.00				

KM# 686 5 DOLLARS
25.00 g., 0.925 Silver 0.7387 oz. ASW, 35x35 mm. **Ruler:** Elizabeth II **Rev:** Season's greetings, rocking horse **Shape:** Square

Date	Mintage	F12	VF20	XF40	MS60	MS63
2009	2,500	PF65 60.00				

KM# 687 5 DOLLARS
25.00 g., 0.999 Silver 0.7978 oz. ASW, 30x38 mm. **Ruler:** Elizabeth II **Rev:** Kazan Virgin icon **Shape:** Vertical rectangle
Note: Exclusive to the Russian market

Date	Mintage	F12	VF20	XF40	MS60	MS63
2009	2,500	PF65 125				

KM# 764 5 DOLLARS
Silver, 25x40 mm. **Ruler:** Elizabeth II **Subject:** Ferrari, the Legend **Rev:** Car and enameled shield **Shape:** Vertical rectangle

Date	Mintage	F12	VF20	XF40	MS60	MS63
2009	—	PF65 125				

KM# 782 5 DOLLARS
20.00 g., 0.999 Silver 0.6382 oz. ASW, 40 mm. **Ruler:** Elizabeth II **Subject:** Year of Astronomy **Rev:** Sun, multicolor

Date	Mintage	F12	VF20	XF40	MS60	MS63
2009	—	—	—	—	—	50.00

KM# 783 5 DOLLARS
20.00 g., 0.999 Silver 0.6382 oz. ASW, 40 mm. **Ruler:** Elizabeth II **Subject:** Year of Astronomy **Rev:** Mercury, multicolor

Date	Mintage	F12	VF20	XF40	MS60	MS63
2009	—	—	—	—	—	50.00

KM# 784 5 DOLLARS
20.00 g., 0.999 Silver 0.6382 oz. ASW, 40 mm. **Ruler:** Elizabeth II **Subject:** Year of Astronomy **Rev:** Venus, multicolor

Date	Mintage	F12	VF20	XF40	MS60	MS63
2009	—	—	—	—	—	55.00

KM# 785 5 DOLLARS
20.00 g., 0.999 Silver 0.6382 oz. ASW, 40 mm. **Ruler:** Elizabeth II **Subject:** Year of Astronomy **Rev:** Earth, multicolor

Date	Mintage	F12	VF20	XF40	MS60	MS63
2009	—	—	—	—	—	50.00

KM# 786 5 DOLLARS
20.00 g., 0.999 Silver 0.6382 oz. ASW, 40 mm. **Ruler:** Elizabeth II **Subject:** Year of Astronomy **Rev:** Mars, multicolor

Date	Mintage	F12	VF20	XF40	MS60	MS63
2009	—	—	—	—	—	50.00

KM# 787 5 DOLLARS
20.00 g., 0.999 Silver 0.6382 oz. ASW, 40 mm. **Ruler:** Elizabeth II **Subject:** Year of Astronomy **Rev:** Jupiter, multicolor

Date	Mintage	F12	VF20	XF40	MS60	MS63
2009	—	—	—	—	—	50.00

KM# 788 5 DOLLARS
20.00 g., 0.999 Silver 0.6382 oz. ASW, 40 mm. **Ruler:** Elizabeth II **Subject:** Year of Astronomy **Rev:** Saturn, multicolor

Date	Mintage	F12	VF20	XF40	MS60	MS63
2009	—	—	—	—	—	50.00

KM# 789 5 DOLLARS
20.00 g., 0.999 Silver 0.6382 oz. ASW, 40 mm. **Ruler:** Elizabeth II **Subject:** Year of Astronomy **Rev:** Uranus, multicolor

Date	Mintage	F12	VF20	XF40	MS60	MS63
2009	—	—	—	—	—	50.00

KM# 790 5 DOLLARS
20.00 g., 0.999 Silver 0.6382 oz. ASW, 40 mm. **Ruler:** Elizabeth II **Subject:** Year of Astronomy **Rev:** Neptune, multicolor

Date	Mintage	F12	VF20	XF40	MS60	MS63
2009	—	—	—	—	—	50.00

KM# 791 5 DOLLARS
20.00 g., 0.999 Silver 0.6382 oz. ASW, 40 mm. **Ruler:** Elizabeth II **Subject:** Year of Astronomy **Rev:** Solar System, multicolor

Date	Mintage	F12	VF20	XF40	MS60	MS63
2009	—	—	—	—	—	50.00

KM# 1225 5 DOLLARS
28.28 g., 0.925 Silver 0.8356 oz. ASW, 38.6 mm. **Ruler:** Elizabeth II **Subject:** Ikuko Shimizu's Hello Kitty **Rev:** Kitty and London Buss in multicolor

Date	Mintage	F12	VF20	XF40	MS60	MS63
2009	Est. 3000	PF65 110				

KM# 1226 5 DOLLARS
28.28 g., 0.925 Silver 0.8356 oz. ASW, 38.6 mm. **Ruler:** Elizabeth II **Subject:** Ikuko Shimizu's Hello Kitty **Rev:** Kitty playing polo in multicolor

Date	Mintage	F12	VF20	XF40	MS60	MS63
2009	Est. 3000	PF65 110				

KM# 1227 5 DOLLARS
28.28 g., 0.925 Silver 0.8356 oz. ASW, 38.6 mm. **Ruler:** Elizabeth II **Subject:** Ikuko Shimizu's Hello Kitty **Rev:** Kitty and Daniel with Tower Bridge in multicolor

Date	Mintage	F12	VF20	XF40	MS60	MS63
2009		PF65 110				

KM# 1236 5 DOLLARS
25.00 g., 0.925 Silver 0.7387 oz. ASW, 38.61 mm. **Ruler:** Elizabeth II **Subject:** Lady of the Lake

Date	Mintage	F12	VF20	XF40	MS60	MS63
2009	2,500	PF65 75.00				

KM# 1237 5 DOLLARS
25.00 g., 0.925 Silver 0.7387 oz. ASW, 38.61 mm. **Ruler:** Elizabeth II **Rev:** Excalibur set into rock in color

Date	Mintage	F12	VF20	XF40	MS60	MS63
2009	2,500	PF65 75.00				

KM# 1238 5 DOLLARS
25.00 g., 0.925 Silver 0.7387 oz. ASW, 38.61 mm. **Ruler:** Elizabeth II **Subject:** King Arthur

Date	Mintage	F12	VF20	XF40	MS60	MS63
2009	2,500	PF65 75.00				

KM# 1239 5 DOLLARS
25.00 g., 0.925 Silver 0.7387 oz. ASW, 38.61 mm. **Ruler:** Elizabeth II **Subject:** Sir Galahad

Date	Mintage	F12	VF20	XF40	MS60	MS63
2009	2,500	PF65 75.00				

KM# 1240 5 DOLLARS
25.00 g., 0.925 Silver 0.7387 oz. ASW, 38.61 mm. **Ruler:** Elizabeth II **Subject:** The Holy Grail

Date	Mintage	F12	VF20	XF40	MS60	MS63
2009	2,500	PF65 75.00				

KM# 1329 5 DOLLARS
Silver **Ruler:** Elizabeth II **Subject:** Banker's Day **Rev:** Map of Ukraine, locations pinpointed

Date	Mintage	F12	VF20	XF40	MS60	MS63
2009 Antique patina	—	—	—	—	—	85.00

KM# 1331 5 DOLLARS
Silver **Ruler:** Elizabeth II **Rev:** Napoleon on horseback in battle in color

Date	Mintage	F12	VF20	XF40	MS60	MS63
2009	—	PF65 65.00				

KM# 1430 5 DOLLARS
Copper-Nickel, 38.61 mm. **Ruler:** Elizabeth II **Subject:** First Crusade

Date	Mintage	F12	VF20	XF40	MS60	MS63
2009	—	—	—	—	—	25.00

KM# 1490 5 DOLLARS
0.50 g., 0.999 Gold AGW, 11 mm. **Ruler:** Elizabeth II **Rev:** Man with golden helmet by Rembrant

Date	Mintage	F12	VF20	XF40	MS60	MS63
2009	Est. 10000	PF65 60.00				

KM# 1523 5 DOLLARS
0.50 g., 1.000 Gold AGW, 11 mm. **Ruler:** Elizabeth II **Subject:** Greek Mythology Artemis

Date	Mintage	F12	VF20	XF40	MS60	MS63
2009	Est. 10000	PF65 50.00				

KM# 1524 5 DOLLARS
0.50 g., 1.000 Gold AGW, 11 mm. **Ruler:** Elizabeth II **Subject:** Greek Mythology Ares

Date	Mintage	F12	VF20	XF40	MS60	MS63
2009	Est. 10000	PF65 50.00				

KM# 1525 5 DOLLARS
0.50 g., 1.000 Gold AGW, 11 mm. **Ruler:** Elizabeth II **Subject:** Greek Mythology Helios

Date	Mintage	F12	VF20	XF40	MS60	MS63
2009	Est. 10000	PF65 50.00				

KM# 1527 5 DOLLARS
0.50 g., 1.000 Gold AGW, 11 mm. **Ruler:** Elizabeth II **Subject:** 10 Years of Euro Introduction

Date	Mintage	F12	VF20	XF40	MS60	MS63
2009	Est. 10000	PF65 50.00				

KM# 1528 5 DOLLARS
0.50 g., 0.999 Gold AGW, 11 mm. **Ruler:** Elizabeth II **Subject:** Orpheus

Date	Mintage	F12	VF20	XF40	MS60	MS63
2009	Est. 10000	PF65 50.00				

KM# 1529 5 DOLLARS
0.50 g., 0.999 Gold AGW, 11 mm. **Ruler:** Elizabeth II **Subject:** Eurydice

Date	Mintage	F12	VF20	XF40	MS60	MS63
2009	Est. 10000	PF65 60.00				

KM# 1337 5 DOLLARS
Silver **Ruler:** Elizabeth II **Subject:** Clothed and nude Maya **Shape:** Rectangle **Note:** Detachable clothing over image.

Date	Mintage	F12	VF20	XF40	MS60	MS63
2010	—	PF65 80.00				

KM# 1340 5 DOLLARS
Silver **Ruler:** Elizabeth II **Subject:** Trafalgar **Rev:** HMS Victory in color

Date	Mintage	F12	VF20	XF40	MS60	MS63
2010	—	PF65 80.00				

KM# 723 5 DOLLARS
31.11 g., 0.999 Silver 0.9926 oz. ASW, 24x47 mm. **Ruler:** Elizabeth II **Subject:** War of 1812 **Rev:** Peter Bagraton

Date	Mintage	F12	VF20	XF40	MS60	MS63
2010 Antique patina	2,000	—	—	—	—	55.00

KM# 724 5 DOLLARS
31.11 g., 0.999 Silver 0.9926 oz. ASW **Ruler:** Elizabeth II **Subject:** War of 1812 **Rev:** Mikhail Kutuzov **Shape:** 24x47

Date	Mintage	F12	VF20	XF40	MS60	MS63
2010 Antique patina	2,000	—	—	—	—	55.00

KM# 725 5 DOLLARS
31.11 g., 0.999 Silver 0.9926 oz. ASW, 27x47 mm. **Ruler:** Elizabeth II **Subject:** War of 1812 **Rev:** Bikoly Raevsky

Date	Mintage	F12	VF20	XF40	MS60	MS63
2010 Antique finish	2,000	—	—	—	—	55.00

KM# 726 5 DOLLARS
20.00 g., 0.999 Silver 0.6382 oz. ASW, 30x43 mm. **Ruler:** Elizabeth II **Subject:** Imperial Eggs **Rev:** Blue egg

Date	Mintage	F12	VF20	XF40	MS60	MS63
2010	2,500	PF65 65.00				

KM# 727 5 DOLLARS
20.00 g., 0.999 Silver 0.6382 oz. ASW, 30x43 mm. **Ruler:** Elizabeth II **Subject:** Imperial Egg **Rev:** Green cloisonne

Date	Mintage	F12	VF20	XF40	MS60	MS63
2010	2,500	PF65 65.00				

KM# 728 5 DOLLARS
20.00 g., 0.999 Silver 0.6382 oz. ASW, 30x43 mm. **Ruler:** Elizabeth II **Subject:** Imperial Egg **Rev:** Yellow cloisonne and Bohemian crystals

Date	Mintage	F12	VF20	XF40	MS60	MS63
2010	2,500	PF65 65.00				

KM# 729 5 DOLLARS
25.00 g., 0.999 Silver 0.7978 oz. ASW, 38.6 mm. **Ruler:** Elizabeth II **Rev:** Martin Luther King, pointing **Note:** Fits together with KM#730.

Date	Mintage	F12	VF20	XF40	MS60	MS63
2010 Antique finish	2,500	—	—	—	—	45.00

KM# 730 5 DOLLARS
25.00 g., 0.999 Silver 0.7978 oz. ASW, 38.6 mm. **Ruler:** Elizabeth II **Rev:** Barack Obama, pointing **Note:** Fits together with KM#729.

Date	Mintage	F12	VF20	XF40	MS60	MS63
2010 Antique finish	2,500	—	—	—	—	45.00

KM# 731 5 DOLLARS
25.00 g., 0.925 Silver 0.7387 oz. ASW, 38.6 mm. **Ruler:** Elizabeth II **Subject:** Tender Love **Rev:** Rose in relief hologram

Date	Mintage	F12	VF20	XF40	MS60	MS63
2010	2,500	PF65 50.00				

KM# 732 5 DOLLARS
25.00 g., 0.925 Silver 0.7387 oz. ASW, 30x38 mm. **Ruler:** Elizabeth II **Rev:** Holy Trinity icon

Date	Mintage	F12	VF20	XF40	MS60	MS63
2010	2,500	PF65 65.00				

KM# 1244 5 DOLLARS
25.00 g., 0.925 Silver 0.7387 oz. ASW, 30x38 mm. **Ruler:** Elizabeth II **Subject:** Vasily Tropinin, 1776-1857 **Rev:** The Lacemaker, multicolor **Shape:** Vertical rectangle

Date	Mintage	F12	VF20	XF40	MS60	MS63
2010	2,500	PF65 65.00				

KM# 1245 5 DOLLARS
25.00 g., 0.925 Silver 0.7387 oz. ASW, 40.6 mm. **Ruler:** Elizabeth II **Subject:** Don Juan, Battle of Lepanto

Date	Mintage	F12	VF20	XF40	MS60	MS63
2010	1,000	PF65 75.00				

KM# 1250 5 DOLLARS
26.00 g., 0.925 Silver 0.7682 oz. ASW, 30x38 mm. **Ruler:** Elizabeth II **Subject:** Peter Brandl **Shape:** Vertical rectangle

Date	Mintage	F12	VF20	XF40	MS60	MS63
2010	2,500	PF65 60.00				

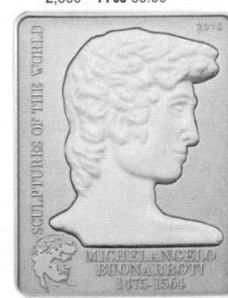

KM# 1251 5 DOLLARS
25.00 g., 0.925 Silver 0.7387 oz. ASW, 30x38 mm. **Ruler:** Elizabeth II **Subject:** Michangelo's David **Shape:** Vertical rectangle

Date	Mintage	F12	VF20	XF40	MS60	MS63
2010	2,500	PF65 45.00				

KM# 1252 5 DOLLARS
25.00 g., 0.925 Silver 0.7387 oz. ASW, 38.61 mm. **Ruler:** Elizabeth II **Subject:** Hollywood Stars - Ginger Rogers

Date	Mintage	F12	VF20	XF40	MS60	MS63
2010	2,500	PF65 55.00				

KM# 1254 5 DOLLARS
25.00 g., 0.925 Silver 0.7387 oz. ASW, 38.61 mm. **Ruler:** Elizabeth II **Subject:** Hollywood Stars - Clark Gable

Date	Mintage	F12	VF20	XF40	MS60	MS63
2010	2,500	PF65 55.00				

KM# 1255 5 DOLLARS
25.00 g., 0.925 Silver 0.7387 oz. ASW, 38.61 mm. **Ruler:** Elizabeth II **Subject:** Gdansk **Rev:** Town view, statue in copper **Note:** Antique patina.

Date	Mintage	F12	VF20	XF40	MS60	MS63
2010	1,000	PF65 60.00				

KM# 1281 5 DOLLARS
Silver, 27x47 mm. **Ruler:** Elizabeth II **Subject:** Ferrari 250 GTO and 599 GTO **Rev:** Car at top and bottom, yellow logo at center **Shape:** Vertical rectangle

Date	Mintage	F12	VF20	XF40	MS60	MS63
2010	1,010	PF65 135				

KM# 1253 5 DOLLARS
25.00 g., 0.925 Silver 0.7387 oz. ASW, 38.61 mm. **Ruler:** Elizabeth II **Subject:** Hollywood Stars - John Wayne

Date	Mintage	F12	VF20	XF40	MS60	MS63
2010	2,500	PF65 55.00				

KM# 1292 5 DOLLARS
25.00 g., 0.999 Silver 0.7978 oz. ASW, 30x38 mm. **Ruler:** Elizabeth II **Subject:** Russian Icons **Rev:** Icon of St. Nicolas **Shape:** Vertical rectangle

Date	Mintage	F12	VF20	XF40	MS60	MS63
2010	—	PF65 120				

KM# 1299 5 DOLLARS
25.00 g., 0.925 Silver 0.7387 oz. ASW, 38.61 mm. **Ruler:** Elizabeth II **Rev:** HAH 280 Meteorite in color

Date	Mintage	F12	VF20	XF40	MS60	MS63
2010 Antique Patina	2,500	—	—	—	—	250

KM# 1300 5 DOLLARS
31.11 g., 0.925 Silver 0.9191 oz. ASW, 38.61 mm. **Ruler:** Elizabeth II **Subject:** Yugra district **Rev:** Bear

Date	Mintage	F12	VF20	XF40	MS60	MS63
2010	2,000	PF65 75.00				

KM# 1301 5 DOLLARS
31.11 g., 0.925 Silver 0.9191 oz. ASW, 38.61 mm. **Ruler:** Elizabeth II **Subject:** Yugra District **Rev:** Crude Oil

Date	Mintage	F12	VF20	XF40	MS60	MS63
2010	2,000	PF65 75.00				

KM# 1302 5 DOLLARS
31.11 g., 0.925 Silver 0.9191 oz. ASW, 38.61 mm. **Ruler:** Elizabeth II **Subject:** Yugra District **Rev:** Sledge Jump

Date	Mintage	F12	VF20	XF40	MS60	MS63
2010	2,000	PF65 75.00				

KM# 1303 5 DOLLARS
31.11 g., 0.999 Silver 0.9926 oz. ASW, 38.61 mm. **Ruler:** Elizabeth II **Subject:** Day of Prudence

Date	Mintage	F12	VF20	XF40	MS60	MS63
2010 Antique patina	500	—	—	—	—	75.00

KM# 1304 5 DOLLARS
25.00 g., 0.999 Silver 0.7978 oz. ASW, 30x38 mm. **Ruler:** Elizabeth II **Subject:** Russian Icons **Rev:** The Holy Face of Christ **Shape:** Vertical rectangle

Date	Mintage	F12	VF20	XF40	MS60	MS63
2010	2,500	PF65 75.00				

KM# 1305 5 DOLLARS
25.00 g., 0.999 Silver 0.7978 oz. ASW, 30x38 mm. **Ruler:** Elizabeth II **Subject:** Russian Icons **Rev:** St. Sergius of Radonezh **Shape:** Vertical rectangle

Date	Mintage	F12	VF20	XF40	MS60	MS63
2010	2,500	PF65 75.00				

KM# 1307 5 DOLLARS
25.00 g., 0.925 Silver 0.7387 oz. ASW, 38.61 mm. **Ruler:** Elizabeth II **Rev:** Wedding day, color and partially gilt

Date	Mintage	F12	VF20	XF40	MS60	MS63
2010	2,000	PF65 75.00				

KM# 1308 5 DOLLARS
31.11 g., 0.999 Silver 0.9926 oz. ASW, 38.61 mm. **Ruler:** Elizabeth II **Subject:** Dear Grandmother

Date	Mintage	F12	VF20	XF40	MS60	MS63
2010	500	PF65 75.00				

KM# 1309 5 DOLLARS
25.00 g., 0.925 Silver 0.7387 oz. ASW, 38.61 mm. **Ruler:** Elizabeth II **Rev:** Cats at night

Date	Mintage	F12	VF20	XF40	MS60	MS63
2010	2,000	PF65 75.00				

KM# 1310 5 DOLLARS
25.00 g., 0.999 Silver 0.7978 oz. ASW, 30x38 mm. **Ruler:** Elizabeth II **Subject:** Patron saints **Rev:** St. Helena **Shape:** Vertical rectangle

Date	Mintage	F12	VF20	XF40	MS60	MS63
2010	2,500	PF65 75.00				

KM# 1311 5 DOLLARS
25.00 g., 0.999 Silver 0.7978 oz. ASW, 30x38 mm. **Ruler:** Elizabeth II **Subject:** Patron Saints **Rev:** St. Constantine **Shape:** Vertical rectangle

Date	Mintage	F12	VF20	XF40	MS60	MS63
2010	2,500	PF65 75.00				

KM# 1334 5 DOLLARS
Silver, 40 mm. **Ruler:** Elizabeth II **Subject:** 2nd Crusade

Date	Mintage	F12	VF20	XF40	MS60	MS63
2010 Antique patina	—	—	—	—	—	100

KM# 1335 5 DOLLARS
Silver, 40 mm. **Ruler:** Elizabeth II **Subject:** 3rd Crusade

Date	Mintage	F12	VF20	XF40	MS60	MS63
2010 Antique patina	—					100

KM# 1336 5 DOLLARS
Silver **Ruler:** Elizabeth II **Subject:** 4th Crusade

Date	Mintage	F12	VF20	XF40	MS60	MS63
2010 Antique patina	—					100

KM# 1338 5 DOLLARS
Silver **Ruler:** Elizabeth II **Subject:** Lubek

Date	Mintage	F12	VF20	XF40	MS60	MS63
2010 Antique patina	—				—	100

KM# 1339 5 DOLLARS
Silver **Ruler:** Elizabeth II **Subject:** Zutphen

Date	Mintage	F12	VF20	XF40	MS60	MS63
2010 Antque patina	—				—	100

KM# 1429 5 DOLLARS
Silver, 38.61 mm. **Ruler:** Elizabeth II **Rev:** Boticelli's Natalis Domini, partially gilt, crystal inserts above **Shape:** Half-circle

Date	Mintage	F12	VF20	XF40	MS60	MS63
2010	—	PF65 75.00				

KM# 1530 5 DOLLARS
0.50 g., 1.000 Gold AGW, 11 mm. **Ruler:** Elizabeth II **Subject:** Rose of Dubai

Date	Mintage	F12	VF20	XF40	MS60	MS63
2010	—	PF65 70.00				

KM# 1531 5 DOLLARS
0.50 g., 0.9999 Gold AGW, 11 mm. **Ruler:** Elizabeth II **Subject:** Mexican Gold

Date	Mintage	F12	VF20	XF40	MS60	MS63
2010	Est. 5000	PF65 50.00				

KM# 1532 5 DOLLARS
0.50 g., 0.999 Gold AGW, 11 mm. **Ruler:** Elizabeth II **Subject:** St. George and the Dragon

Date	Mintage	F12	VF20	XF40	MS60	MS63
2010	Est. 10000	PF65 50.00				

KM# 1617 5 DOLLARS
25.00 g., 0.925 Silver 0.7387 oz. ASW, 40 mm. **Ruler:** Elizabeth II **Subject:** Kaliningrad (Koingsberg) **Rev:** Copper-plated knight standing at left, town view at right

Date	Mintage	F12	VF20	XF40	MS60	MS63
2010 Antique patina	—				—	60.00

KM# 1314 5 DOLLARS
25.00 g., 0.925 Silver 0.7387 oz. ASW, 38.61 mm. **Ruler:** Elizabeth II **Subject:** Marilyn Monroe, 85th Birthday

Date	Mintage	F12	VF20	XF40	MS60	MS63
2011	1,926	PF65 95.00				

KM# 1380 5 DOLLARS
Silver, 30x28.5 mm. **Ruler:** Elizabeth II **Subject:** Seeds of Love **Rev:** Vine and half of a heart shaped red crystal

Date	Mintage	F12	VF20	XF40	MS60	MS63
2011 Antique patina	—	PF65 75.00				

KM# 1261 5 DOLLARS
25.00 g., 0.925 Silver 0.7387 oz. ASW, 38.61 mm. **Ruler:** Elizabeth II **Subject:** Flowers - Daisy

Date	Mintage	F12	VF20	XF40	MS60	MS63
2011	2,500	PF65 75.00				

KM# 1262 5 DOLLARS
25.00 g., 0.925 Silver 0.7387 oz. ASW, 38.61 mm. **Ruler:** Elizabeth II **Subject:** Hollywood Stars - Sophia Loren

Date	Mintage	F12	VF20	XF40	MS60	MS63
2011	2,500	PF65 55.00				

KM# 1263 5 DOLLARS
25.00 g., 0.925 Silver 0.7387 oz. ASW, 38.61 mm. **Ruler:** Elizabeth II **Subject:** Hollywood Stars - Elizabeth Taylor

Date	Mintage	F12	VF20	XF40	MS60	MS63
2011	2,500	PF65 55.00				

KM# 1264 5 DOLLARS
25.00 g., 0.925 Silver 0.7387 oz. ASW, 38.61 mm. **Ruler:** Elizabeth II **Subject:** Hollywood Stars - Marylin Monroe

Date	Mintage	F12	VF20	XF40	MS60	MS63
2011	2,500	PF65 85.00				

KM# 1265 5 DOLLARS
25.00 g., 0.925 Silver 0.7387 oz. ASW, 38.61 mm. **Ruler:** Elizabeth II **Subject:** Terminator-2, 20th Anniversary **Rev:** Walking through flames

Date	Mintage	F12	VF20	XF40	MS60	MS63
2011	—	PF65 60.00				

KM# 1266 5 DOLLARS
25.00 g., 0.925 Silver 0.7387 oz. ASW, 38.61 mm. **Ruler:** Elizabeth II **Subject:** Terminator-2, 20th Anniversary **Rev:** Riding motorcycle

Date	Mintage	F12	VF20	XF40	MS60	MS63
2011	—	PF65 60.00				

KM# 1267 5 DOLLARS
25.00 g., 0.925 Silver 0.7387 oz. ASW **Ruler:** Elizabeth II
Subject: Terminator-2, 20th Anniversary **Rev:** Head shot
Shape: 38.61

Date	Mintage	F12	VF20	XF40	MS60	MS63
2011	—	PF65 60.00				

KM# 1287 5 DOLLARS
31.10 g., 0.925 Silver 0.9189 oz. ASW, 38.6 mm. **Ruler:**
Elizabeth II **Subject:** Scent of Austalia - Eucalyptus **Rev:**
Koala, eucalyptus leaves and gum berries

Date	Mintage	F12	VF20	XF40	MS60	MS63
2011	2,500	—	—	—	—	100

KM# 1353 5 DOLLARS
25.00 g., 0.925 Silver 0.7387 oz. ASW, 30x38 mm. **Ruler:**
Elizabeth II **Subject:** Patron Saints **Rev:** St. Mary Magalene
Shape: Vertical rectangle

Date	Mintage	F12	VF20	XF40	MS60	MS63
2011	—	PF65 75.00				

KM# 1355 5 DOLLARS
25.00 g., 0.925 Silver 0.7387 oz. ASW, 30x38 mm. **Ruler:**

Elizabeth II **Subject:** Patron Saints **Rev:** St. Catherine Icon
Shape: Vertical rectangle

Date	Mintage	F12	VF20	XF40	MS60	MS63
2011	—	PF65 75.00				

KM# 1357 5 DOLLARS
25.00 g., Silver, 30x38 mm. **Ruler:** Elizabeth II **Subject:** Patrol
Saints **Rev:** St. Oleg Icon **Shape:** Vertical rectangle

Date	Mintage	F12	VF20	XF40	MS60	MS63
2011	—	PF65 75.00				

KM# 1358 5 DOLLARS
25.00 g., 0.925 Silver 0.7387 oz. ASW, 30x38 mm. **Ruler:**
Elizabeth II **Subject:** Patron Saints **Rev:** St. Vladimir Icon
Shape: Vertical rectangle

Date	Mintage	F12	VF20	XF40	MS60	MS63
2011	—	PF65 75.00				

KM# 1361 5 DOLLARS
31.11 g., 0.999 Silver 0.9926 oz. ASW, 38.61 mm. **Ruler:**
Elizabeth II **Subject:** Soyuzmultfilm 75th Anniversary - Winnie
the Pooh **Rev:** Winnie the Pooh in color **Edge:** Reeded

Date	Mintage	F12	VF20	XF40	MS60	MS63
2011	2,000	PF65 90.00				

KM# 1362 5 DOLLARS
31.11 g., 0.999 Silver 0.9926 oz. ASW, 38.61 mm. **Ruler:**
Elizabeth II **Subject:** Soyuzmultfilm 75th Anniversary - Winnie
the Pooh **Rev:** Piglet in color

Date	Mintage	F12	VF20	XF40	MS60	MS63
2011	2,000	PF65 85.00				

KM# 1363 5 DOLLARS
31.11 g., 0.999 Silver 0.9926 oz. ASW, 38.61 mm. **Ruler:**
Elizabeth II **Subject:** Soyuzmultfilm 75th Anniversary - Winnie
the Pooh **Rev:** Owl in color **Edge:** Reeded

Date	Mintage	F12	VF20	XF40	MS60	MS63
2011	2,000	PF65 85.00				

KM# 1364 5 DOLLARS
31.11 g., 0.999 Silver 0.9926 oz. ASW, 38.61 mm. **Ruler:**
Elizabeth II **Subject:** Soyuzmultfilm 75th Anniversary - Winnie
the Pooh **Rev:** Eyore in color **Edge:** Reeded

Date	Mintage	F12	VF20	XF40	MS60	MS63
2011	2,000	PF65 85.00				

KM# 1365 5 DOLLARS
31.11 g., 0.999 Silver 0.9926 oz. ASW, 38.61 mm. **Ruler:**
Elizabeth II **Subject:** Soyuzmultfilm 75th Anniversary - Winnie
the Pooh **Rev:** Rabbit in color **Edge:** Reeded

Date	Mintage	F12	VF20	XF40	MS60	MS63
2011	2,000	PF65 85.00				

KM# 1367 5 DOLLARS
31.11 g., 0.999 Silver 0.9926 oz. ASW, 38.61 mm. **Ruler:**
Elizabeth II **Subject:** Soyuzmultfilm 75th Anniversary - Little
Boy and Karlsson-on-the-Roof **Rev:** Little Boy and dog in color
Edge: Reeded

Date	Mintage	F12	VF20	XF40	MS60	MS63
2011	2,000	PF65 85.00				

KM# 1368 5 DOLLARS
31.11 g., 0.999 Silver 0.9926 oz. ASW, 38.61 mm. **Ruler:** Elizabeth II **Subject:** Soyuzmultfilm 75th Anniversary - Little Boy and Karlsson-on-the-Roof **Rev:** Karlsson in color **Edge:** Reeded

Date	Mintage	F12	VF20	XF40	MS60	MS63
2011	2,000	PF65 90.00				

KM# 1369 5 DOLLARS
31.11 g., 0.999 Silver 0.9926 oz. ASW, 38.61 mm. **Ruler:** Elizabeth II **Subject:** Soyuzmultfilm 75th Anniversary - Little Boy and Karlsson-on-the-Roof **Rev:** Freken Bok in color **Edge:** Reeded

Date	Mintage	F12	VF20	XF40	MS60	MS63
2011	2,000	PF65 90.00				

KM# 1371 5 DOLLARS
31.11 g., 0.999 Silver 0.9926 oz. ASW, 38.61 mm. **Ruler:** Elizabeth II **Subject:** Soyuzmultfilm 75th Anniversary - Cheburashka and Crocodile Gena **Rev:** Cheburashka with orange in color **Edge:** Reeded

Date	Mintage	F12	VF20	XF40	MS60	MS63
2011	2,000	PF65 85.00				

KM# 1372 5 DOLLARS
31.11 g., 0.999 Silver 0.9926 oz. ASW, 38.61 mm. **Ruler:** Elizabeth II **Subject:** Soyuzmultfilm 75th Anniversary - Cheburashka and Crocodile Gena **Rev:** Madame Shapoklyak and dog in color **Edge:** Reeded

Date	Mintage	F12	VF20	XF40	MS60	MS63
2011	2,000	PF65 90.00				

KM# 1373 5 DOLLARS
31.11 g., 0.999 Silver 0.9926 oz. ASW, 38.61 mm. **Ruler:** Elizabeth II **Subject:** Soyuzmultfilm 75th Anniversary - Cheburashka and Crocodile Gena **Rev:** Crocodile Gena in color **Edge:** Reeded

Date	Mintage	F12	VF20	XF40	MS60	MS63
2011	2,000	PF65 85.00				

KM# 1374 5 DOLLARS
31.11 g., 0.999 Silver 0.9926 oz. ASW, 38.61 mm. **Ruler:** Elizabeth II **Subject:** Soyuzmultfilm 75th Anniversary - Hedgehog in a fog **Rev:** Hedgehog in a fog in color **Edge:** Reeded

Date	Mintage	F12	VF20	XF40	MS60	MS63
2011	2,000	PF65 90.00				

KM# 1381 5 DOLLARS
20.00 g., 0.925 Silver 0.591 oz. ASW, 40 mm. **Ruler:** Elizabeth II **Subject:** Muonionalusta Meteor **Obv:** Head with tiara right **Rev:** View of meteor falling and fragment insert

Date	Mintage	F12	VF20	XF40	MS60	MS63
2011	2,500	PF65 125				

KM# 1398 5 DOLLARS
31.14 g., 0.999 Silver 0.9936 oz. ASW, 38.61 mm. **Ruler:** Elizabeth II **Subject:** Soyuzmultfilm animation - Cat named Woof **Obv:** Head with crown right **Rev:** Dog and kitten in color **Edge:** Reeded

Date	Mintage	F12	VF20	XF40	MS60	MS63
2011	2,000	PF65 90.00				

KM# 1399 5 DOLLARS
31.14 g., 0.999 Silver 0.9936 oz. ASW, 38.61 mm. **Ruler:** Elizabeth II **Subject:** Soyuzmultfilm animation - Umka **Obv:** Head with crown right **Rev:** Polar bear and cub in color **Edge:** Reeded

Date	Mintage	F12	VF20	XF40	MS60	MS63
2011	2,000	PF65 90.00				

KM# 1400 5 DOLLARS
31.14 g., 0.999 Silver 0.9936 oz. ASW, 38.61 mm. **Ruler:** Elizabeth II **Subject:** Soyuzmultfilm animation - Cat named Woof **Obv:** Head with crown right **Rev:** Cat and dog in color **Edge:** Reeded

Date	Mintage	F12	VF20	XF40	MS60	MS63
2011	2,000	PF65 90.00				

KM# 1401 5 DOLLARS
31.14 g., 0.999 Silver 0.9936 oz. ASW, 38.61 mm. **Ruler:** Elizabeth II **Subject:** Soyuzmultfilm animation - Lion and turtle **Obv:** Head with crown right **Rev:** Turtle and lion **Edge:** Reeded

Date	Mintage	F12	VF20	XF40	MS60	MS63
2011	2,000	PF65 90.00				

KM# 1406 5 DOLLARS
31.10 g., 0.925 Silver 0.9189 oz. ASW, 35x35 mm. **Ruler:** Elizabeth II **Subject:** Hieronymus Bosch, pater **Rev:** The Garden (of Eden), in color **Shape:** Square

Date	Mintage	F12	VF20	XF40	MS60	MS63
2011	500	PF65 300				

KM# 1409 5 DOLLARS
31.11 g., 0.999 Silver 0.9926 oz. ASW, 38.61 mm. **Ruler:** Elizabeth II **Subject:** Holidays of Bonifaciya **Rev:** Lion in color

Date	Mintage	F12	VF20	XF40	MS60	MS63
2011	2,000	PF65 100				

KM# 1410 5 DOLLARS
31.11 g., 0.999 Silver 0.9926 oz. ASW, 38.61 mm. **Ruler:** Elizabeth II **Subject:** Soyuzmultfilm Anniversary - Old dog and wolf **Rev:** Wolf dog in color

Date	Mintage	F12	VF20	XF40	MS60	MS63
2011	2,000	PF65 100				

KM# 1417 5 DOLLARS
155.50 g., 0.999 Silver 4.9623 oz. ASW, 65 mm. **Ruler:** Elizabeth II **Subject:** Brothers Grimm - Bremen Town Musicians **Rev:** Troubador and animals on cart

Date	Mintage	F12	VF20	XF40	MS60	MS63
2011	500	PF65 250				

KM# 1418 5 DOLLARS
31.11 g., 0.999 Silver 0.9926 oz. ASW, 38.61 mm. **Ruler:** Elizabeth II **Subject:** Brothers Grimm - Bremen Town Musicians **Rev:** Troubador in color

Date	Mintage	F12	VF20	XF40	MS60	MS63
2011	2,000	PF65 100				

KM# 1419 5 DOLLARS
31.11 g., 0.999 Silver 0.9926 oz. ASW, 38.61 mm. **Ruler:** Elizabeth II **Subject:** Brothers Grimm - Bremen Town Musicians **Rev:** Musical coach in color

Date	Mintage	F12	VF20	XF40	MS60	MS63
2011	2,000	PF65 100				

KM# 1420 5 DOLLARS
31.11 g., 0.999 Silver 0.9926 oz. ASW, 38.61 mm. **Ruler:** Elizabeth II **Subject:** Brothers Grimm - Bremen Town Musicians **Rev:** Queen and cannoner in color

Date	Mintage	F12	VF20	XF40	MS60	MS63
2011	2,000	PF65 100				

KM# 1421 5 DOLLARS
31.11 g., 0.999 Silver 0.9926 oz. ASW, 38.61 mm. **Ruler:** Elizabeth II **Subject:** Brothers Grimm - Bremen Town Musicians **Rev:** Polynesian dancers in color

Date	Mintage	F12	VF20	XF40	MS60	MS63
2011	2,000	PF65 100				

KM# 1422 5 DOLLARS
31.11 g., 0.999 Silver 0.9926 oz. ASW, 38.61 mm. **Ruler:** Elizabeth II **Subject:** Brothers Grimm - Bremen Town Musicians **Rev:** Rock and Roll group in color

Date	Mintage	F12	VF20	XF40	MS60	MS63
2011	2,000	PF65 100				

KM# 1427 5 DOLLARS
25.00 g., 0.925 Silver 0.7387 oz. ASW, 38.61 mm. **Ruler:** Elizabeth II **Subject:** 5th Crusade **Rev:** John of Brienne

Date	Mintage	F12	VF20	XF40	MS60	MS63
2011 Antique patina	1,000	PF65 75.00				

KM# 1431 5 DOLLARS
Silver, 38.61 mm. **Ruler:** Elizabeth II **Subject:** Muonionalusta meteorite **Rev:** Meteorite fragment flying over forest lake

Date	Mintage	F12	VF20	XF40	MS60	MS63
2011	—		PF65 125			

KM# 1503 5 DOLLARS
145.00 g., Copper Plated Tombac, 65 mm. **Ruler:** Elizabeth II **Subject:** Elizabeth II, 60th anniversary of reign **Rev:** Elizabeth II photo in color by Julian Calder

Date	Mintage	F12	VF20	XF40	MS60	MS63
2011	Est. 2012		PF65 45.00			

KM# 1504 5 DOLLARS
0.50 g., 0.999 Gold AGW, 11 mm. **Ruler:** Elizabeth II **Rev:** Tiki Art Tangaroa

Date	Mintage	F12	VF20	XF40	MS60	MS63
2011	Est. 10000		PF65 55.00			

KM# 1533 5 DOLLARS
0.50 g., 1.000 Gold AGW, 11 mm. **Ruler:** Elizabeth II **Subject:** 20 Years of Ballerina

Date	Mintage	F12	VF20	XF40	MS60	MS63
2011	Est. 5000		PF65 50.00			

KM# 1376 5 DOLLARS
25.00 g., 0.925 Silver 0.7387 oz. ASW, 45x30 mm. **Ruler:** Elizabeth II **Obv:** Head with tiara right **Rev:** Titanic sailing left in color, coal fragment insert **Shape:** Horizontal oval

Date	Mintage	F12	VF20	XF40	MS60	MS63
2012	2,012		PF65 70.00			

KM# 1377 5 DOLLARS
20.00 g., 0.999 Silver 0.6382 oz. ASW, 30x43 mm. **Ruler:** Elizabeth II **Subject:** Imperial Egg - Swan **Obv:** Head with tiara right **Rev:** Pink coloring

Date	Mintage	F12	VF20	XF40	MS60	MS63
2012	—		PF65 65.00			

KM# 1378 5 DOLLARS
20.00 g., 0.999 Silver 0.6382 oz. ASW, 30x43 mm. **Ruler:** Elizabeth II **Subject:** Imperial egg - Elephant **Obv:** Head with tiara right **Rev:** Blue coloring

Date	Mintage	F12	VF20	XF40	MS60	MS63
2012	—		PF65 65.00			

KM# 1379 5 DOLLARS
20.00 g., 0.999 Silver 0.6382 oz. ASW, 30x43 mm. **Ruler:** Elizabeth II **Subject:** Imperial egg **Obv:** Head in tiara right **Rev:** Multicolor closonne

Date	Mintage	F12	VF20	XF40	MS60	MS63
2012	—		PF65 65.00			

KM# 1382 5 DOLLARS
31.11 g., 0.999 Silver 0.9926 oz. ASW, 38.61 mm. **Ruler:** Elizabeth II **Subject:** History of Egypt **Rev:** Tutankhamun's gold mask in color

Date	Mintage	F12	VF20	XF40	MS60	MS63
2012	—		PF65 85.00			

KM# 1390 5 DOLLARS
31.11 g., 0.999 Silver 0.9926 oz. ASW, 38.61 mm. **Ruler:** Elizabeth II **Subject:** Titanic, 100th Anniversary **Rev:** Titanic side view sailing left, recovered coal fragment insert

Date	Mintage	F12	VF20	XF40	MS60	MS63
2012	—		PF65 125			

KM# 1395 5 DOLLARS
31.11 g., 0.999 Silver 0.9926 oz. ASW, 38.61 mm. **Ruler:**

Elizabeth II Obv: Head with tiara right **Rev:** Cherry Blossom in color

Date	Mintage	F12	VF20	XF40	MS60	MS63
2012	—		PF65 60.00			

KM# 1425 5 DOLLARS
20.00 g., 0.925 Silver 0.591 oz. ASW, 30x35 mm. **Ruler:** Elizabeth II **Subject:** Love conquers all **Rev:** Roman Cupids by Caravaggio **Shape:** Vertical oval

Date	Mintage	F12	VF20	XF40	MS60	MS63
2012	1,000		PF65 80.00			

KM# 1437 5 DOLLARS
25.00 g., 0.925 Silver 0.7387 oz. ASW, 38.61 mm. **Ruler:** Elizabeth II **Subject:** Hollywood Stars - Marlene Dietrich

Date	Mintage	F12	VF20	XF40	MS60	MS63
2012	2,500		PF65 65.00			

KM# 1438 5 DOLLARS
25.00 g., 0.925 Silver 0.7387 oz. ASW, 38.61 mm. **Ruler:** Elizabeth II **Subject:** Hollywood Stars - Anita Ekberg

Date	Mintage	F12	VF20	XF40	MS60	MS63
2012	2,500		PF65 65.00			

KM# 1439 5 DOLLARS
25.00 g., 0.925 Silver 0.7387 oz. ASW, 38.61 mm. **Ruler:** Elizabeth II **Subject:** Hollywood Stars - Robert Mitchum

Date	Mintage	F12	VF20	XF40	MS60	MS63
2012	2,500		PF65 65.00			

KM# 1440 5 DOLLARS
20.00 g., 0.925 Silver 0.591 oz. ASW, 38.6 mm. **Ruler:** Elizabeth II **Subject:** Seymchan Meteorite **Rev:** Meteorite fragment in color scene

Date	Mintage	F12	VF20	XF40	MS60	MS63
2012	2,500		PF65 125			

KM# 1446 5 DOLLARS
31.11 g., 0.999 Silver 0.9926 oz. ASW, 38.61 mm. **Ruler:** Elizabeth II **Subject:** Yes of the Dragon **Rev:** Golden dragon

Date	Mintage	F12	VF20	XF40	MS60	MS63
2012	—	PF65 165				

KM# 1447 5 DOLLARS
31.11 g., 0.999 Silver 0.9926 oz. ASW, 38.61 mm. **Ruler:** Elizabeth II **Subject:** Year of the Dragon **Rev:** Blue dragon

Date	Mintage	F12	VF20	XF40	MS60	MS63
2012	—	PF65 165				

KM# 1450 5 DOLLARS
20.00 g., 0.925 Silver 0.591 oz. ASW, 38.61 mm. **Ruler:** Elizabeth II **Subject:** PGA Tour - Golf ball insert

Date	Mintage	F12	VF20	XF40	MS60	MS63
2012	2,500	PF65 55.00				

KM# 1451 5 DOLLARS
20.00 g., 0.925 Silver 0.591 oz. ASW, 38.61 mm. **Ruler:** Elizabeth II **Subject:** Amerigo Vespucci, 500th Anniversary of voyage of discovery **Rev:** Sailing ship

Date	Mintage	F12	VF20	XF40	MS60	MS63
2012	2,500	PF65 75.00				

KM# 1452 5 DOLLARS
25.00 g., 0.925 Silver 0.7387 oz. ASW, 30x38 mm. **Ruler:** Elizabeth II **Rev:** Nativity of the Blessed Virgin Mary **Shape:** Vertical rectangle

Date	Mintage	F12	VF20	XF40	MS60	MS63
2012	2,500	PF65 100				

KM# 1453 5 DOLLARS
31.11 g., 0.999 Silver 0.9926 oz. ASW, 38.61 mm. **Ruler:** Elizabeth II **Subject:** Year of the Dragon **Rev:** Color dragon

Date	Mintage	F12	VF20	XF40	MS60	MS63
2012	—	PF65 100				

KM# 1587 5 DOLLARS
0.50 g., 0.585 Gold AGW, 11 mm. **Ruler:** Elizabeth II **Subject:** Smallest Gold Coins - James Cook

Date	Mintage	F12	VF20	XF40	MS60	MS63
2012	Est. 10000	PF65 32.00				

KM# 1594 5 DOLLARS
20.00 g., 0.925 Silver 0.591 oz. ASW, 38.61 mm. **Ruler:** Elizabeth II **Subject:** Black Squirrel

Date	Mintage	F12	VF20	XF40	MS60	MS63
2013	Est. 999	PF65 75.00				

KM# 1605 5 DOLLARS
0.50 g., 0.585 Gold AGW, 11 mm. **Ruler:** Elizabeth II **Subject:** Zeppelin

Date	Mintage	F12	VF20	XF40	MS60	MS63
2013	Est. 5000	PF65 50.00				

KM# 1606 5 DOLLARS
0.50 g., 0.585 Gold AGW, 11 mm. **Ruler:** Elizabeth II **Subject:** Ned Kelly

Date	Mintage	F12	VF20	XF40	MS60	MS63
2013	Est. 5000	PF65 50.00				

KM# 1608 5 DOLLARS
0.50 g., 0.999 Gold AGW, 11 mm. **Ruler:** Elizabeth II **Subject:** Vincent van Gogh

Date	Mintage	F12	VF20	XF40	MS60	MS63
2013	Est. 5000	PF65 50.00				

KM# 1609 5 DOLLARS
0.50 g., 0.999 Gold AGW, 11 mm. **Ruler:** Elizabeth II **Subject:** Buffalo, 100th Anniversary

Date	Mintage	F12	VF20	XF40	MS60	MS63
2013	Est. 5000	PF65 50.00				

KM# 1610 5 DOLLARS
0.50 g., 0.999 Gold AGW, 11 mm. **Ruler:** Elizabeth II **Subject:** Troy

Date	Mintage	F12	VF20	XF40	MS60	MS63
2013	Est. 7500	PF65 50.00				

KM# 473 10 DOLLARS
20.12 g., Silver, 38.62 mm. **Ruler:** Elizabeth II **Subject:** 2004 Summer Olympics - Athens **Obv:** Crowned bust right **Rev:** Male discus thrower **Edge:** Reeded

Date	Mintage	F12	VF20	XF40	MS60	MS63
2001	—	PF65 37.50				

KM# 549 10 DOLLARS
10.00 g., 0.9999 Gold 0.3194 oz. AGW, 25 mm. **Ruler:** Elizabeth II **Rev:** Multicolored Mikado Pheasant

Date	Mintage	F12	VF20	XF40	MS60	MS63
2001	1,000	PF65 600				

KM# 550 10 DOLLARS
10.00 g., 0.9999 Gold 0.3194 oz. AGW, 25 mm. **Ruler:** Elizabeth II **Rev:** Multicolor black-faced spoonbill

Date	Mintage	F12	VF20	XF40	MS60	MS63
2001	1,000	PF65 600				

KM# 453 10 DOLLARS
186.83 g., 0.999 Silver Gilt 5.9621 oz., 89 mm. **Ruler:** Elizabeth II **Obv:** Crowned bust right, unique portrait for Cook Is. **Rev:** Queen Victoria standing with lion **Edge:** Reeded

Date	Mintage	F12	VF20	XF40	MS60	MS63
2003	198	PF65 375				

KM# 1110 10 DOLLARS
1.24 g., 0.999 Gold 0.0396 oz. AGW **Ruler:** Elizabeth II **Rev:** Emblem

Date	Mintage	F12	VF20	XF40	MS60	MS63
2005	Est. 8000	PF65 85.00				

KM# 1136 10 DOLLARS
1.24 g., 0.999 Gold 0.0396 oz. AGW, 13.92 mm. **Ruler:** Elizabeth II **Subject:** Star Wars, 30th Anniversary

Date	Mintage	F12	VF20	XF40	MS60	MS63
2005	9,999	PF63 85.00	PF65 95.00			

KM# 1176 10 DOLLARS
1.24 g., 0.999 Gold 0.0396 oz. AGW **Ruler:** Elizabeth II **Subject:** Marriage of Prince Charles and Camilla Parker-Bowles

Date	Mintage	F12	VF20	XF40	MS60	MS63
2005	—	PF63 85.00	PF65 95.00			

KM# 1178 10 DOLLARS
1.24 g., 0.999 Gold 0.0396 oz. AGW, 13.92 mm. **Ruler:** Elizabeth II **Rev:** Pope John Paul II

Date	Mintage	F12	VF20	XF40	MS60	MS63
2005	—	PF63 85.00	PF65 95.00			

KM# 582 10 DOLLARS
31.10 g., 0.999 Silver 0.9925 oz. ASW, 38.6 mm. **Ruler:** Elizabeth II **Rev:** Chichen Itza gilt pop-up

Date	Mintage	F12	VF20	XF40	MS60	MS63
2007	5,000	PF65 65.00				

KM# 585 10 DOLLARS
31.10 g., 0.999 Silver 0.9925 oz. ASW, 38.6 mm. **Ruler:**
Elizabeth II **Rev:** Easter Island status gilt pop-up

Date	Mintage	F12	VF20	XF40	MS60	MS63
2007	5,000	PF65 100				

KM# 587 10 DOLLARS
31.10 g., 0.999 Silver 0.9925 oz. ASW, 38.6 mm. **Ruler:**
Elizabeth II **Rev:** Pyrmids gilt pop-up

Date	Mintage	F12	VF20	XF40	MS60	MS63
2007	5,000	PF65 65.00				

KM# 588 10 DOLLARS
31.10 g., 0.999 Silver 0.9925 oz. ASW, 38.6 mm. **Ruler:**
Elizabeth II **Rev:** Golden Gate Bridge gilt pop-up

Date	Mintage	F12	VF20	XF40	MS60	MS63
2007	5,000	PF65 65.00				

KM# 589 10 DOLLARS
31.10 g., 0.999 Silver 0.9925 oz. ASW, 38.6 mm. **Ruler:**
Elizabeth II **Rev:** Great Wall of China gilt pop-up

Date	Mintage	F12	VF20	XF40	MS60	MS63
2007	5,000	PF65 65.00				

KM# 590 10 DOLLARS
31.10 g., 0.999 Silver 0.9925 oz. ASW, 38.6 mm. **Ruler:**
Elizabeth II **Rev:** Sydney Harbor Bridge gilt pop-up

Date	Mintage	F12	VF20	XF40	MS60	MS63
2007	5,000	PF65 65.00				

KM# 591 10 DOLLARS
31.10 g., 0.999 Silver 0.9925 oz. ASW, 38.6 mm. **Ruler:**
Elizabeth II **Rev:** Machu Pichu gilt pop-up

Date	Mintage	F12	VF20	XF40	MS60	MS63
2007	5,000	PF65 65.00				

KM# 592 10 DOLLARS
31.10 g., 0.999 Silver 0.9925 oz. ASW, 38.6 mm. **Ruler:**
Elizabeth II **Rev:** Petra Treasury gilt pop-up

Date	Mintage	F12	VF20	XF40	MS60	MS63
2007	5,000	PF65 65.00				

KM# 593 10 DOLLARS
31.10 g., 0.999 Silver 0.9925 oz. ASW, 38.6 mm. **Ruler:**
Elizabeth II **Rev:** Taj mahal gilt pop-up

Date	Mintage	F12	VF20	XF40	MS60	MS63
2007	5,000	PF65 65.00				

KM# 1113 10 DOLLARS
0.50 g., 0.999 Gold AGW, 11 mm. **Ruler:** Elizabeth II **Subject:**
Treaty of rome, 50th Anniversary **Rev:** Monaco

Date	Mintage	F12	VF20	XF40	MS60	MS63
2007	Est. 5000	PF65 50.00				

KM# 1171 10 DOLLARS
0.50 g., 0.999 Gold AGW, 11 mm. **Ruler:** Elizabeth II **Subject:**
Treaty of Rome, 50th Anniversary **Rev:** Vatican City

Date	Mintage	F12	VF20	XF40	MS60	MS63
2007	Est. 5000	PF65 50.00				

KM# 1192 10 DOLLARS
1.24 g., 0.999 Gold 0.0396 oz. AGW, 13.92 mm. **Ruler:**
Elizabeth II **Subject:** European Monarchs **Rev:** Elizabeth II

Date	Mintage	F12	VF20	XF40	MS60	MS63
2007	Est. 10000	PF65 85.00				

KM# 1193 10 DOLLARS
1.24 g., 0.999 Gold 0.0396 oz. AGW **Ruler:** Elizabeth II
Subject: European Monarchs **Rev:** Juan Carlos I

Date	Mintage	F12	VF20	XF40	MS60	MS63
2007	Est. 10000	PF65 85.00				

KM# 1195 10 DOLLARS
1.24 g., Gold AGW, 13.92 mm. **Ruler:** Elizabeth II **Subject:**
European Monarchs **Rev:** Beatrix

Date	Mintage	F12	VF20	XF40	MS60	MS63
2007	Est. 10000	PF65 85.00				

KM# 1204 10 DOLLARS
1.24 g., 0.999 Gold 0.0396 oz. AGW, 13.92 mm. **Ruler:**
Elizabeth II **Subject:** Christmas **Rev:** Cherib seated on rock

Date	Mintage	F12	VF20	XF40	MS60	MS63
2007 proof	Est. 15000	PF65 85.00				

KM# 1194 10 DOLLARS
1.24 g., 0.999 Gold 0.0396 oz. AGW **Ruler:** Elizabeth II
Subject: European Monarchs **Rev:** Carl XVI Gustaf

Date	Mintage	F12	VF20	XF40	MS60	MS63
2007	Est. 10000	PF65 85.00				

KM# 619 10 DOLLARS
31.10 g., 0.999 Silver 0.9925 oz. ASW, 38.6 mm. **Ruler:**
Elizabeth II **Rev:** Angor Wat temple gilt pop-up

Date	Mintage	F12	VF20	XF40	MS60	MS63
2008	5,000	PF65 65.00				

KM# 620 10 DOLLARS
31.10 g., 0.999 Silver 0.9925 oz. ASW, 38.6 mm. **Ruler:**
Elizabeth II **Rev:** Ayer's Rock gilt pop-up

Date	Mintage	F12	VF20	XF40	MS60	MS63
2008	5,000	PF65 65.00				

KM# 621 10 DOLLARS
31.10 g., 0.999 Silver 0.9925 oz. ASW, 38.6 mm. **Ruler:**
Elizabeth II **Rev:** Parliament Buildings and Big Ben pop-up

Date	Mintage	F12	VF20	XF40	MS60	MS63
2008	5,000	PF65 65.00				

KM# 622 10 DOLLARS
31.10 g., 0.999 Silver 0.9925 oz. ASW, 38.6 mm. **Ruler:**
Elizabeth II **Rev:** Mt. Rushmore figures gilt pop-up

Date	Mintage	F12	VF20	XF40	MS60	MS63
2008	5,000	PF65 65.00				

KM# 623 10 DOLLARS
31.10 g., 0.999 Silver 0.9925 oz. ASW, 38.6 mm. **Ruler:**
Elizabeth II **Rev:** Sydney Opera House gilt pop-up

Date	Mintage	F12	VF20	XF40	MS60	MS63
2008	5,000	PF65 65.00				

KM# 624 10 DOLLARS
31.10 g., 0.999 Silver 0.9925 oz. ASW, 38.6 mm. **Ruler:**
Elizabeth II **Rev:** Malaysian Twin Towers gilt pop-up

Date	Mintage	F12	VF20	XF40	MS60	MS63
2008	5,000	PF65 65.00				

KM# 625 10 DOLLARS
31.10 g., 0.999 Silver 0.9925 oz. ASW, 38.6 mm. **Ruler:**
Elizabeth II **Rev:** Sphinx gilt pop-up

Date	Mintage	F12	VF20	XF40	MS60	MS63
2008	5,000	PF65 65.00				

KM# 626 10 DOLLARS
31.10 g., 0.999 Silver 0.9925 oz. ASW, 38.6 mm. **Ruler:**
Elizabeth II **Rev:** Stonehedge gilt pop-up

Date	Mintage	F12	VF20	XF40	MS60	MS63
2008	5,000	PF65 65.00				

KM# 627 10 DOLLARS
62.21 g., 0.999 Silver 1.9851 oz. ASW, 50 mm. **Ruler:** Elizabeth II **Rev:** Tsar Alexander II, multicolor **Note:** Exclusive to the Russian Market.

Date	Mintage	F12	VF20	XF40	MS60	MS63
2008	500	PF65 350				

KM# 628 10 DOLLARS
62.21 g., 0.999 Silver 1.9851 oz. ASW **Ruler:** Elizabeth II **Rev:** Tsar Alexi, multicolor **Note:** Exclusive to the Russian Market.

Date	Mintage	F12	VF20	XF40	MS60	MS63
2008	500	PF65 350				

KM# 629 10 DOLLARS
62.21 g., 0.999 Silver 1.9851 oz. ASW, 50 mm. **Ruler:** Elizabeth II **Rev:** Tsarina Anna, multicolor

Date	Mintage	F12	VF20	XF40	MS60	MS63
2008	500	PF65 350				

KM# 630 10 DOLLARS
62.21 g., 0.999 Silver 1.9851 oz. ASW, 50 mm. **Ruler:** Elizabeth II **Rev:** Tsarina Elizabeth, multicolor

Date	Mintage	F12	VF20	XF40	MS60	MS63
2008	500	PF65 350				

KM# 631 10 DOLLARS
62.21 g., 0.999 Silver 1.9851 oz. ASW, 50 mm. **Ruler:** Elizabeth II **Rev:** Tsar Mikhail, multicolor

Date	Mintage	F12	VF20	XF40	MS60	MS63
2008	500	PF65 350				

KM# 632 10 DOLLARS
62.21 g., 0.999 Silver 1.9851 oz. ASW, 50 mm. **Ruler:** Elizabeth II **Rev:** Tsar Paul I, multicolor

Date	Mintage	F12	VF20	XF40	MS60	MS63
2008	500	PF65 350				

KM# 633 10 DOLLARS
31.10 g., 0.999 Silver 0.9925 oz. ASW, 40 mm. **Ruler:** Elizabeth II **Rev:** Nathan Rothschild bust at right, partially gilt

Date	Mintage	F12	VF20	XF40	MS60	MS63
2008	10,000	PF65 55.00				

KM# 634 10 DOLLARS
31.11 g., 0.999 Silver 0.9926 oz. ASW, 40 mm. **Ruler:** Elizabeth II **Rev:** Henry Ford at left and Model-A car at right, partially gilt

Date	Mintage	F12	VF20	XF40	MS60	MS63
2008	10,000	PF65 55.00				

KM# 635 10 DOLLARS
31.10 g., 0.999 Silver 0.9925 oz. ASW, 40 mm. **Ruler:** Elizabeth II **Rev:** John D. Rockefeller Sr., bust right, oil derrick partially gilt.

Date	Mintage	F12	VF20	XF40	MS60	MS63
2008	10,000	PF65 60.00				

KM# 704 10 DOLLARS
1.00 g., 0.999 Gold 0.0319 oz. AGW, 13.9 mm. **Ruler:** Elizabeth II **Subject:** Gorch Fock **Rev:** Sailing vessel right

Date	Mintage	F12	VF20	XF40	MS60	MS63
2008	15,000	PF65 70.00				

KM# 705 10 DOLLARS
62.21 g., 0.999 Silver 1.9852 oz. ASW, 50 mm. **Ruler:** Elizabeth II **Subject:** Kiev Churches **Rev:** Lavra bell tower

Date	Mintage	F12	VF20	XF40	MS60	MS63
2008 Proof	500	—	—	—	—	200

KM# 1205 10 DOLLARS
1.00 g., 0.999 Gold 0.0319 oz. AGW, 13.92 mm. **Ruler:** Elizabeth II **Rev:** Gorch Fock I, 1933

Date	Mintage	F12	VF20	XF40	MS60	MS63
2008	—	PF65 70.00				

KM# 1206 10 DOLLARS
1.00 g., 0.999 Gold 0.0319 oz. AGW, 13.92 mm. **Ruler:** Elizabeth II **Subject:** Endangered Wildlife **Rev:** Polar Bear

Date	Mintage	F12	VF20	XF40	MS60	MS63
2008	Est. 25000	PF65 60.00				

KM# 1469 10 DOLLARS
31.11 g., 0.999 Silver 0.9926 oz. ASW, 38.61 mm. **Ruler:** Elizabeth II **Rev:** Koln Cathedral 4 gr. gold pop-up

Date	Mintage	F12	VF20	XF40	MS60	MS63
2008	Est. 5000	—	—	—	—	80.00

KM# 1515 10 DOLLARS
7.78 g., 0.585 Gold 0.1454 oz. AGW, 25 mm. **Ruler:** Elizabeth II **Subject:** 2008 Vancouver Olympic Games - Transfer Coin

Date	Mintage	F12	VF20	XF40	MS60	MS63
2008	Est. 1000	PF65 320				

KM# 1543 10 DOLLARS
28.28 g., 0.925 Silver 0.8356 oz. ASW, 38.61 mm. **Ruler:**
Elizabeth II **Subject:** Railways - Big Boy

Date	Mintage	F12	VF20	XF40	MS60	MS63
2008	Est. 5000	PF65 45.00				

KM# 688 10 DOLLARS
31.11 g., 0.999 Silver 0.9926 oz. ASW, 38.6 mm. **Ruler:**
Elizabeth II **Subject:** World Monuments - Egypt, Abu Simbel
Rev: Statues of Ramesses II at Abu Simbel gilt pop-up

Date	Mintage	F12	VF20	XF40	MS60	MS63
2009	Est. 3000	PF65 75.00				

KM# 689 10 DOLLARS
31.11 g., 0.999 Silver 0.9926 oz. ASW, 38.6 mm. **Ruler:**
Elizabeth II **Subject:** World Monuments- France, Arc de
Triomphe **Rev:** Arc de Triumph gilt pop-up

Date	Mintage	F12	VF20	XF40	MS60	MS63
2009	Est. 3000	PF65 75.00				

KM# 690 10 DOLLARS
31.11 g., 0.999 Silver 0.9926 oz. ASW, 38.6 mm. **Ruler:**
Elizabeth II **Subject:** Wold Monuments - Turkey, Hagia Sophia
Rev: Hagia Sofia gilt pop-up

Date	Mintage	F12	VF20	XF40	MS60	MS63
2009	Est. 3000	PF65 75.00				

KM# 691 10 DOLLARS
31.11 g., 0.999 Silver 0.9926 oz. ASW, 38.6 mm. **Ruler:**
Elizabeth II **Subject:** World Monuments - China, Temple of
Heaven **Rev:** Temple of Heaven gilt pop-up

Date	Mintage	F12	VF20	XF40	MS60	MS63
2009	—	PF65 75.00				

KM# 692 10 DOLLARS
31.11 g., 0.999 Silver 0.9926 oz. ASW, 38.6 mm. **Ruler:**
Elizabeth II **Subject:** World Monuments - Germany Holsten
Gate Lubeck **Rev:** Holstein Gate gilt pop-up

Date	Mintage	F12	VF20	XF40	MS60	MS63
2009	Est. 3000	PF65 75.00				

KM# 693 10 DOLLARS
31.11 g., 0.999 Silver 0.9926 oz. ASW, 38.6 mm. **Ruler:**
Elizabeth II **Subject:** World Monuments - Germany, Kaiser
Wilhelm Memorial Church **Rev:** Ruins of Kaiser Church in
Berlin, gilt pop-up

Date	Mintage	F12	VF20	XF40	MS60	MS63
2009	Est. 3000	PF65 75.00				

KM# 694 10 DOLLARS
31.11 g., 0.999 Silver 0.9926 oz. ASW, 38.6 mm. **Ruler:**
Elizabeth II **Rev:** Statue of Peter I gilt pop-up

Date	Mintage	F12	VF20	XF40	MS60	MS63
2009	5,000	PF65 65.00				

KM# 695 10 DOLLARS
31.11 g., 0.999 Silver 0.9926 oz. ASW, 38.6 mm. **Ruler:**
Elizabeth II **Subject:** World Monuments - Italy, Venice Rialto
Bridge **Rev:** Bridge in Venice, gilt pop-up

Date	Mintage	F12	VF20	XF40	MS60	MS63
2009	Est. 3000	PF65 75.00				

KM# 696 10 DOLLARS
31.11 g., 0.999 Silver 0.9926 oz. ASW, 38.6 mm. **Ruler:**
Elizabeth II **Subject:** World Monuments - Germany Semper
Opera **Rev:** Opera house, gilt pop-up

Date	Mintage	F12	VF20	XF40	MS60	MS63
2009	Est. 3000	PF65 75.00				

KM# 703 10 DOLLARS
25.00 g., 0.999 Silver 0.7978 oz. ASW, 38.6 mm. **Ruler:**
Elizabeth II **Subject:** Nicolaus Copernicus **Rev:** Bust facing
and orbit of the planets, crystal insert, partially gold plated

Date	Mintage	F12	VF20	XF40	MS60	MS63
2009	7,500	PF65 75.00				

KM# 708 10 DOLLARS
1.00 g., 0.999 Gold 0.0319 oz. AGW, 13.9 mm. **Ruler:** Elizabeth
II **Rev:** Bridge

Date	Mintage	F12	VF20	XF40	MS60	MS63
2009	250	PF65 70.00				

KM# 709 10 DOLLARS
1.00 g., 0.999 Gold 0.0319 oz. AGW, 13.9 mm. **Ruler:** Elizabeth
II **Rev:** Statue and gardens

Date	Mintage	F12	VF20	XF40	MS60	MS63
2009	250	PF65 70.00				

KM# 710 10 DOLLARS
1.00 g., 0.999 Gold 0.0319 oz. AGW, 13.9 mm. **Ruler:** Elizabeth II **Rev:** City Gate tower

Date	Mintage	F12	VF20	XF40	MS60	MS63
2009	250	PF65 70.00				

KM# 711 10 DOLLARS
1.00 g., 0.999 Gold 0.0319 oz. AGW, 13.9 mm. **Ruler:** Elizabeth II **Rev:** Virgin Mary statue and church in background

Date	Mintage	F12	VF20	XF40	MS60	MS63
2009	250	PF65 70.00				

KM# 712 10 DOLLARS
1.00 g., 0.999 Gold 0.0319 oz. AGW, 13.9 mm. **Ruler:** Elizabeth II **Rev:** Multiple church spires

Date	Mintage	F12	VF20	XF40	MS60	MS63
2009	250	PF65 70.00				

KM# 713 10 DOLLARS
1.00 g., 0.999 Gold 0.0319 oz. AGW, 13.9 mm. **Ruler:** Elizabeth II **Rev:** National Theater

Date	Mintage	F12	VF20	XF40	MS60	MS63
2009	250	PF65 70.00				

KM# 714 10 DOLLARS
1.00 g., 0.999 Gold 0.0319 oz. AGW, 13.9 mm. **Ruler:** Elizabeth II **Rev:** Castle

Date	Mintage	F12	VF20	XF40	MS60	MS63
2009	250	PF65 70.00				

KM# 715 10 DOLLARS
1.00 g., 0.999 Gold 0.0319 oz. AGW, 13.9 mm. **Ruler:** Elizabeth II **Rev:** Castle on a hill

Date	Mintage	F12	VF20	XF40	MS60	MS63
2009	250	PF65 70.00				

KM# 716 10 DOLLARS
1.00 g., 0.999 Gold 0.0319 oz. AGW, 13.9 mm. **Ruler:** Elizabeth II **Rev:** Castle

Date	Mintage	F12	VF20	XF40	MS60	MS63
2009	250	PF65 70.00				

KM# 717 10 DOLLARS
1.00 g., 0.999 Gold 0.0319 oz. AGW, 13.9 mm. **Ruler:** Elizabeth II **Rev:** Castle

Date	Mintage	F12	VF20	XF40	MS60	MS63
2009	250	PF65 70.00				

KM# 718 10 DOLLARS
1.00 g., 0.999 Gold 0.0319 oz. AGW, 13.9 mm. **Ruler:** Elizabeth II **Rev:** Church

Date	Mintage	F12	VF20	XF40	MS60	MS63
2009	250	PF65 70.00				

KM# 719 10 DOLLARS
1.00 g., 0.999 Gold 0.0319 oz. AGW, 13.9 mm. **Ruler:** Elizabeth II **Rev:** Ancient ruins

Date	Mintage	F12	VF20	XF40	MS60	MS63
2009	250	PF65 70.00				

KM# 792 10 DOLLARS
31.11 g., 0.999 Silver 0.9926 oz. ASW, 40 mm. **Ruler:** Elizabeth II **Subject:** Tycoons - Alfred Nobel **Rev:** Nobel bust at right, Prize Medal partially gilt at right

Date	Mintage	F12	VF20	XF40	MS60	MS63
2009	10,000	PF65 55.00				

KM# 793 10 DOLLARS
31.11 g., 0.999 Silver 0.9926 oz. ASW, 40 mm. **Ruler:** Elizabeth II **Subject:** Tycoons **Rev:** Cecil Rhodes, partially gilt

Date	Mintage	F12	VF20	XF40	MS60	MS63
2009	10,000	PF65 55.00				

KM# 1228 10 DOLLARS
155.50 g., 0.925 Silver 4.5947 oz. ASW, 65 mm. **Ruler:** Elizabeth II **Subject:** Ikuko Shimizu's Hello Kitty **Rev:** Kitty and Buckingham Palace in multicolor

Date	Mintage	F12	VF20	XF40	MS60	MS63
2009	Est. 1500	PF65 350				

KM# 1232 10 DOLLARS
1.24 g., 0.999 Gold 0.0396 oz. AGW, 13.92 mm. **Ruler:** Elizabeth II **Subject:** Knut Hamsun, 150th Anniversary of Birth

Date	Mintage	F12	VF20	XF40	MS60	MS63
2009	Est. 1000	PF65 85.00				

KM# 1233 10 DOLLARS
1.24 g., 0.999 Gold 0.0396 oz. AGW, 13.92 mm. **Ruler:** Elizabeth II **Subject:** Sweedish King Oscar II

Date	Mintage	F12	VF20	XF40	MS60	MS63
2009	Est. 10000	PF65 85.00				

KM# 1332 10 DOLLARS
1.24 g., 0.999 Gold 0.0396 oz. AGW, 13.92 mm. **Ruler:** Elizabeth II **Subject:** 40th Anniversary of Moon landing

Date	Mintage	F12	VF20	XF40	MS60	MS63
2009	—	PF65 100				

KM# 1333 10 DOLLARS
1.24 g., 0.999 Gold 0.0396 oz. AGW, 13.92 mm. **Ruler:** Elizabeth II **Subject:** James Cook and the H.M.S Endeavor

Date	Mintage	F12	VF20	XF40	MS60	MS63
2009	—	PF65 100				

KM# 1484 10 DOLLARS
31.11 g., 0.999 Silver 0.9926 oz. ASW, 38.61 mm. **Ruler:** Elizabeth II **Subject:** World Monuments - Germany, Porta Nigra **Rev:** Porta Nigra in Trier

Date	Mintage	F12	VF20	XF40	MS60	MS63
2009	Est. 3000	—	—	—	—	80.00

KM# 1485 10 DOLLARS
31.11 g., 0.999 Silver 0.9926 oz. ASW, 38.61 mm. **Ruler:** Elizabeth II **Rev:** Semper Opera House in Dresden

Date	Mintage	F12	VF20	XF40	MS60	MS63
2009	Est. 3000	—	—	—	—	80.00

KM# 1486 10 DOLLARS
31.11 g., 0.999 Silver 0.9926 oz. ASW, 38.61 mm. **Ruler:** Elizabeth II **Subject:** World Monuments - Germany, Memorial for the Battle of the Peoples in Leipzig **Rev:** Battle monument in Leipzig

Date	Mintage	F12	VF20	XF40	MS60	MS63
2009	—	—	—	—	—	80.00

KM# 1487 10 DOLLARS
31.11 g., 0.999 Silver 0.9926 oz. ASW, 38.61 mm. **Ruler:** Elizabeth II **Subject:** World Monuments - Spain, Sagrada Familia **Rev:** Holy Family Cathedral in Barcelona

Date	Mintage	F12	VF20	XF40	MS60	MS63
2009	Est. 3000	—	—	—	—	80.00

KM# 1488 10 DOLLARS
31.11 g., 0.999 Silver 0.9926 oz. ASW, 38.61 mm. **Ruler:** Elizabeth II **Subject:** World Monuments - United Arab Emirates, Burj Al Arab **Rev:** Burj al Arab ni Dubai

Date	Mintage	F12	VF20	XF40	MS60	MS63
2009 Proof	Est. 3000	—	—	—	—	80.00

KM# 1489 10 DOLLARS
28.28 g., 0.925 Silver 0.8356 oz. ASW, 38.61 mm. **Ruler:** Elizabeth II **Subject:** Railways - Steam Locomotive GS4 The Daylight **Rev:** Southern Pacific's GS-4 Daylight Limited

Date	Mintage	F12	VF20	XF40	MS60	MS63
2009	Est. 5000	PF65 55.00				

KM# 1491 10 DOLLARS
Silver **Ruler:** Elizabeth II **Subject:** Wold Cup Soccer, South Africa

Date	Mintage	F12	VF20	XF40	MS60	MS63
2009	Est. 10000	PF65 55.00				

KM# 1492 10 DOLLARS
1.00 g., 0.999 Gold 0.0319 oz. AGW, 13.92 mm. **Ruler:** Elizabeth II **Subject:** World Cup Soccer in South Africa

Date	Mintage	F12	VF20	XF40	MS60	MS63
2009	Est. 5000	PF65 70.00				

KM# 1516 10 DOLLARS
28.28 g., 0.925 Silver 0.8356 oz. ASW, 38.61 mm. **Ruler:** Elizabeth II **Subject:** 2012 London Olympic Games - Sailing

Date	Mintage	F12	VF20	XF40	MS60	MS63
2009	Est. 10000	PF65 55.00				

KM# 1249 10 DOLLARS
31.14 g., 0.999 Silver 0.9936 oz. ASW, 45 mm. **Ruler:** Elizabeth II **Subject:** Albert Durer **Rev:** Rabbit illustration with crystals

Date	Mintage	F12	VF20	XF40	MS60	MS63
2010	3,000	PF65 75.00				

KM# 1258 10 DOLLARS
50.00 g., 0.925 Silver 1.4774 oz. ASW, 50 mm. **Ruler:** Elizabeth II **Subject:** Windows of Heaven **Rev:** Cologne Cathedral, stained glass windows, facade and ceiling arch plan

Date	Mintage	F12	VF20	XF40	MS60	MS63
2010	2,000	PF65 500				

KM# 1293 10 DOLLARS
31.11 g., 0.999 Silver 0.9926 oz. ASW, 45 mm. **Ruler:** Elizabeth II **Subject:** Oberg **Rev:** Rural Russian folk scene

Date	Mintage	F12	VF20	XF40	MS60	MS63
2010	—	PF65 75.00				

KM# 1296 10 DOLLARS
0.50 g., 0.999 Gold AGW, 11 mm. **Ruler:** Elizabeth II **Rev:** Barack Obama

Date	Mintage	F12	VF20	XF40	MS60	MS63
2010	—	PF65 50.00				

KM# 1297 10 DOLLARS
1.00 g., 0.999 Gold 0.0319 oz. AGW, 13.92 mm. **Ruler:** Elizabeth II **Rev:** Martin Luther King

Date	Mintage	F12	VF20	XF40	MS60	MS63
2010	—	PF65 75.00				

KM# 1298 10 DOLLARS
1.00 g., 0.999 Gold 0.0319 oz. AGW, 13.92 mm. **Ruler:** Elizabeth II **Rev:** Barack Obama

Date	Mintage	F12	VF20	XF40	MS60	MS63
2010	—	PF65 75.00				

KM# 1495 10 DOLLARS
31.11 g., 0.999 Silver 0.9926 oz. ASW, 38.61 mm. **Ruler:** Elizabeth II **Rev:** Sanssouci Palace in Potsdam

Date	Mintage	F12	VF20	XF40	MS60	MS63
2010	Est. 3000	—	—	—	—	80.00

KM# 1496 10 DOLLARS
31.11 g., 0.999 Silver 0.9926 oz. ASW, 38.61 mm. **Ruler:** Elizabeth II **Subject:** World Monuments - Bellevue Palace Berlin **Rev:** Castle in Eisenach

Date	Mintage	F12	VF20	XF40	MS60	MS63
2010	Est. 3000	—	—	—	—	80.00

KM# 1497 10 DOLLARS
31.11 g., 0.999 Silver 0.9926 oz. ASW, 38.61 mm. **Ruler:**

Elizabeth II **Subject:** World Monuments - Belgium Atomium **Rev:** The Atomium in Brussels

Date	Mintage	F12	VF20	XF40	MS60	MS63
2010 Proof	—	—	—	—	—	80.00

KM# 1498 10 DOLLARS
31.11 g., 0.999 Silver 0.9926 oz. ASW, 38.61 mm. **Ruler:** Elizabeth II **Subject:** World Monuments - Denmark, Little Mermaid **Rev:** Little Mermaid statue in Copenhagen

Date	Mintage	F12	VF20	XF40	MS60	MS63
2010	Est. 3000	—	—	—	—	80.00

KM# 1499 10 DOLLARS
31.11 g., 0.999 Silver 0.9926 oz. ASW, 38.61 mm. **Ruler:** Elizabeth II **Subject:** World Monuments - France, Fort Carcassonne **Rev:** Comtal castle in Carcassonne

Date	Mintage	F12	VF20	XF40	MS60	MS63
2010	Est. 3000	—	—	—	—	80.00

KM# 1500 10 DOLLARS
31.11 g., 0.999 Silver 0.9926 oz. ASW, 38.61 mm. **Ruler:** Elizabeth II **Rev:** Belem tower in Lisbon

Date	Mintage	F12	VF20	XF40	MS60	MS63
2010	Est. 3000	—	—	—	—	80.00

KM# 1501 10 DOLLARS
31.11 g., 0.999 Silver 0.9926 oz. ASW, 38.61 mm. **Ruler:** Elizabeth II **Subject:** World Monuments - Laos, That Luang **Rev:** That Luang in Viet Nam

Date	Mintage	F12	VF20	XF40	MS60	MS63
2010 Proof	Est. 3000	—	—	—	—	80.00

KM# 1502 10 DOLLARS
31.11 g., 0.999 Silver 0.9926 oz. ASW, 38.61 mm. **Ruler:** Elizabeth II **Subject:** World Monuments - Tibet, Portala Palace **Rev:** Dala Lama's palace in Tibet

Date	Mintage	F12	VF20	XF40	MS60	MS63
2010	Est. 3000	—	—	—	—	80.00

KM# 1518 10 DOLLARS
28.28 g., 0.925 Silver 0.8356 oz. ASW, 38.61 mm. **Ruler:** Elizabeth II **Subject:** 2014 Sochi Olympic Games - Transfer Coin "From Vancouver to Sochi", Colorized

Date	Mintage	F12	VF20	XF40	MS60	MS63
2010	Est. 5000		PF65	55.00		
2011	Est. 5000		PF65	55.00		

KM# 1519 10 DOLLARS
7.78 g., 0.585 Gold 0.1454 oz. AGW, 25 mm. **Ruler:** Elizabeth II **Subject:** 2014 Sotchi Olympic Games - Transfer Coin "From Vancouver to Sotchi", Colorized

Date	Mintage	F12	VF20	XF40	MS60	MS63
2010	Est. 500		PF65	350		
2011	—		PF65	350		

KM# 1544 10 DOLLARS
28.28 g., 0.925 Silver 0.8356 oz. ASW, 38.61 mm. **Ruler:** Elizabeth II **Subject:** Railways - California Zephyr

Date	Mintage	F12	VF20	XF40	MS60	MS63
2010	Est. 5000		PF65	45.00		

KM# 1545 10 DOLLARS
31.11 g., 0.999 Silver 0.9926 oz. ASW, 38.61 mm. **Ruler:** Elizabeth II **Subject:** World Monuments - Germany, Wartburg

Date	Mintage	F12	VF20	XF40	MS60	MS63
2010	Est. 3000	—	—	—	—	80.00

KM# 1546 10 DOLLARS
31.11 g., 0.999 Silver 0.9926 oz. ASW, 38.61 mm. **Ruler:** Elizabeth II **Subject:** World Monuments - Ukraine - St. Sophia Cathedral

Date	Mintage	F12	VF20	XF40	MS60	MS63
2010	Est. 3000	—	—	—	—	80.00

KM# 1547 10 DOLLARS
31.11 g., 0.999 Silver 0.9926 oz. ASW, 38.61 mm. **Ruler:** Elizabeth II **Subject:** World Monuments - United Arab Emirates, Burj Dubai

Date	Mintage	F12	VF20	XF40	MS60	MS63
2010	Est. 3000	—	—	—	—	80.00

KM# 1548 10 DOLLARS
31.11 g., 0.999 Silver 0.9926 oz. ASW, 38.61 mm. **Ruler:** Elizabeth II **Subject:** World Monuments - USA, Empire State Building

Date	Mintage	F12	VF20	XF40	MS60	MS63
2010	Est. 3000		PF65	80.00		

KM# 1549 10 DOLLARS
31.11 g., 0.999 Silver 0.9926 oz. ASW, 38.61 mm. **Ruler:** Elizabeth II **Subject:** World Monuments - England, Buckingham Palace

Date	Mintage	F12	VF20	XF40	MS60	MS63
2010	—	—	—	—	—	80.00

KM# 1550 10 DOLLARS
31.11 g., 0.999 Silver 0.9926 oz. ASW, 38.61 mm. **Ruler:** Elizabeth II **Subject:** World Monuments - Liechtenstein, Vaduz Castle

Date	Mintage	F12	VF20	XF40	MS60	MS63
2010	Est. 3000	—	—	—	—	80.00

KM# 1551 10 DOLLARS
31.11 g., 0.999 Silver 0.9926 oz. ASW, 38.61 mm. **Ruler:** Elizabeth II **Subject:** World Monuments - German Reunification

Date	Mintage	F12	VF20	XF40	MS60	MS63
2010	—	—	—	—	—	80.00

KM# 1552 10 DOLLARS
31.11 g., 0.999 Silver 0.9926 oz. ASW, 38.61 mm. **Ruler:** Elizabeth II **Subject:** World Monuments - Portugal, Sintra

Date	Mintage	F12	VF20	XF40	MS60	MS63
2010	—	—	—	—	—	80.00

KM# 1553 10 DOLLARS
31.11 g., 0.999 Silver 0.9926 oz. ASW, 38.61 mm. **Ruler:** Elizabeth II **Subject:** World Monuments - German Reunification

Date	Mintage	F12	VF20	XF40	MS60	MS63
2010	3000	—	—	—	—	80.00

KM# 1555 10 DOLLARS
31.11 g., 0.999 Silver 0.9926 oz. ASW, 38.61 mm. **Ruler:** Elizabeth II **Subject:** World Monuments - USA Space Needle

Date	Mintage	F12	VF20	XF40	MS60	MS63
2011	Est. 3000		PF65	80.00		

KM# 1259 10 DOLLARS
50.00 g., 0.999 Silver 1.5956 oz. ASW, 50 mm. **Ruler:** Elizabeth II **Subject:** Windows of Heaven **Rev:** Westminister Abbey, stained glass windows, floor plan and facade

Date	Mintage	F12	VF20	XF40	MS60	MS63
2011	2,000	PF65 350				

KM# 1388 10 DOLLARS
50.00 g., 0.999 Silver 1.5956 oz. ASW, 50 mm. **Ruler:** Elizabeth II **Subject:** St. Issac's Cathedral, St. Petersburg **Rev:** Stained glass window and floor plan

Date	Mintage	F12	VF20	XF40	MS60	MS63
2011	2,000	PF65 300				

KM# 1389 10 DOLLARS
50.00 g., 0.999 Silver 1.5956 oz. ASW, 50 mm. **Ruler:** Elizabeth II **Subject:** Seville Cathedral **Rev:** Stained glass window, floor plan and façade

Date	Mintage	F12	VF20	XF40	MS60	MS63
2011	2,000	PF65 250				

KM# 1505 10 DOLLARS
31.11 g., 0.999 Silver 0.9926 oz. ASW, 65 mm. **Ruler:** Elizabeth II **Series:** Biggest Silver Ounces of the World **Subject:** The Five Continents: Europe **Rev:** Moose before Bandenburg Gate and European Tuscany

Date	Mintage	F12	VF20	XF40	MS60	MS63
2011	Est. 3000	PF65 85.00				

KM# 1506 10 DOLLARS
31.11 g., 0.999 Silver 0.9926 oz. ASW, 65 mm. **Ruler:** Elizabeth II **Series:** Biggest Silver Ounces of the World **Subject:** The Five Continents: America **Rev:** Grizley bear before Statue of Liberty and cattle ranchers in America

Date	Mintage	F12	VF20	XF40	MS60	MS63
2011	Est. 3000	PF65 85.00				

KM# 1507 10 DOLLARS
31.11 g., 0.999 Silver 0.9926 oz. ASW, 65 mm. **Ruler:** Elizabeth II **Series:** Biggest Silver Ounces of the World **Subject:** The Five Continents: Asia **Rev:** Panda before Taj Mahal and Great Wall of China

Date	Mintage	F12	VF20	XF40	MS60	MS63
2011	—	PF65 85.00				

KM# 1508 10 DOLLARS
31.11 g., 0.999 Silver 0.9926 oz. ASW, 65 mm. **Ruler:** Elizabeth II **Series:** Biggest Silver Ounces of the World **Subject:** The Five Continents: Australia **Rev:** Kangaroo before Harbor Bridge and Ayers Rock in Australia

Date	Mintage	F12	VF20	XF40	MS60	MS63
2011	Est. 3000	PF65 85.00				

KM# 1509 10 DOLLARS
31.11 g., 0.999 Silver 0.9926 oz. ASW, 65 mm. **Ruler:** Elizabeth II **Series:** Biggest Silver Ounces of the World **Subject:** The Five Continents: Africa **Rev:** Elephant before Great Sphinx and Mt. Kilimanjaro in Africa

Date	Mintage	F12	VF20	XF40	MS60	MS63
2011	Est. 3000	PF65 85.00				

KM# 1537 10 DOLLARS
15.55 g., 0.999 Silver 0.4962 oz. ASW, 33 mm. **Ruler:** Elizabeth II **Series:** History of Silver - Black Swan Treasure

Date	Mintage	F12	VF20	XF40	MS60	MS63
2011	Est. 8000	PF65 30.00				

KM# 1538 10 DOLLARS
15.55 g., 0.999 Silver 0.4962 oz. ASW, 33 mm. **Ruler:** Elizabeth II **Subject:** History of Silver - ANcient Coins of Lydia

Date	Mintage	F12	VF20	XF40	MS60	MS63
2011	Est. 8000	PF65 30.00				

KM# 1539 10 DOLLARS
15.55 g., 0.999 Silver 0.4962 oz. ASW, 33 mm. **Ruler:** Elizabeth II **Subject:** History of Silver - Chinese Acupuntcture

Date	Mintage	F12	VF20	XF40	MS60	MS63
2011	Est. 8000	PF65 30.00				

KM# 1540 10 DOLLARS
15.55 g., 0.999 Silver 0.4962 oz. ASW, 33 mm. **Ruler:** Elizabeth II **Subject:** History of Silver - Rio de la Plata

Date	Mintage	F12	VF20	XF40	MS60	MS63
2011	Est. 8000	PF65 30.00				

KM# 1541 10 DOLLARS
15.55 g., 0.999 Silver 0.4962 oz. ASW, 33 mm. **Ruler:** Elizabeth II **Subject:** History of Silver - Navajo

Date	Mintage	F12	VF20	XF40	MS60	MS63
2011	Est. 8000	PF65 30.00				

KM# 1542 10 DOLLARS
15.55 g., 0.999 Silver 0.4962 oz. ASW, 33 mm. **Ruler:** Elizabeth II **Subject:** History of Silver - Cerro Rico - Potosi

Date	Mintage	F12	VF20	XF40	MS60	MS63
2011	Est. 8000	PF65 30.00				

KM# 1554 10 DOLLARS
31.11 g., 0.999 Silver 0.9926 oz. ASW, 38.61 mm. **Ruler:** Elizabeth II **Subject:** World Monuments - Japan, Giant Kamakura Buddha

Date	Mintage	F12	VF20	XF40	MS60	MS63
2011	Est. 3000	—	—	—	—	80.00

KM# 1556 10 DOLLARS
31.11 g., 0.999 Silver 0.9926 oz. ASW, 38.61 mm. **Ruler:** Elizabeth II **Subject:** World Monuments - France, Notre Dame

Date	Mintage	F12	VF20	XF40	MS60	MS63
2011	Est. 3000	—	—	—	—	80.00

KM# 1557 10 DOLLARS
31.11 g., 0.999 Silver 0.9926 oz. ASW, 38.61 mm. **Ruler:** Elizabeth II **Subject:** World Monuments - Germany, Eltz Castle

Date	Mintage	F12	VF20	XF40	MS60	MS63
2011	Est. 3000	—	—	—	80.00	—

KM# 1559 10 DOLLARS
31.11 g., 0.999 Silver 0.9926 oz. ASW, 38.61 mm. **Ruler:** Elizabeth II **Subject:** World Monuments - USA, White House

Date	Mintage	F12	VF20	XF40	MS60	MS63
2011	Est. 3000	—	—	—	—	80.00

KM# 1560 10 DOLLARS
31.11 g., 0.999 Silver 0.9926 oz. ASW, 38.61 mm. **Ruler:** Elizabeth II **Subject:** World Monuments - Holland Kinderdijk Windmills

Date	Mintage	F12	VF20	XF40	MS60	MS63
2011	Est. 3000					80.00

KM# 1561 10 DOLLARS
31.11 g., 0.999 Silver 0.9926 oz. ASW **Ruler:** Elizabeth II **Subject:** World Monuments - Italy. Famous Landmarks **Edge:** 38.61

Date	Mintage	F12	VF20	XF40	MS60	MS63
2011	Est. 3000	—	—	—	—	80.00

KM# 1562 10 DOLLARS
31.11 g., 0.999 Silver 0.9926 oz. ASW, 38.61 mm. **Ruler:** Elizabeth II **Subject:** World Monuments - Temple Mount

Date	Mintage	F12	VF20	XF40	MS60	MS63
2011	Est. 3000	—	—	—	—	80.00

KM# 1563 10 DOLLARS
31.11 g., 0.999 Silver 0.9926 oz. ASW, 38.61 mm. **Ruler:** Elizabeth II **Subject:** World Monuments - Germany, Speyer Cathedral

Date	Mintage	F12	VF20	XF40	MS60	MS63
2011	Est. 3000	—	—	—	—	80.00

KM# 1564 10 DOLLARS
31.11 g., 0.999 Silver 0.9926 oz. ASW, 38.61 mm. **Ruler:** Elizabeth II **Subject:** World Monuments - UK, Windsor Castle

Date	Mintage	F12	VF20	XF40	MS60	MS63
2011	Est. 3000	—	—	—	—	80.00

KM# 1565 10 DOLLARS
31.11 g., 0.999 Silver 0.9926 oz. ASW, 38.61 mm. **Ruler:** Elizabeth II **Subject:** World Monuments - Castle Schwerin

Date	Mintage	F12	VF20	XF40	MS60	MS63
2011	Est. 3000	—	—	—	—	80.00

KM# 1566 10 DOLLARS
31.11 g., 0.999 Silver 0.9926 oz. ASW, 38.61 mm. **Ruler:** Elizabeth II **Subject:** World Monuments - England, Westminister Abby

Date	Mintage	F12	VF20	XF40	MS60	MS63
2011	Est. 3000	—	—	—	—	85.00

KM# 1567 10 DOLLARS
31.11 g., 0.999 Silver 0.9926 oz. ASW **Ruler:** Elizabeth II **Subject:** World Monuments - Austria, Famous Landmarks **Shape:** 38.61

Date	Mintage	F12	VF20	XF40	MS60	MS63
2011	Est. 3000	—	—	—	—	85.00

KM# 1583 10 DOLLARS
31.10 g., 0.999 Silver 0.9925 oz. ASW, 40.6 mm. **Ruler:** Elizabeth II **Subject:** Diamond Jubilee of Queen Elizabeth II - Trooping the Color, Colorized

Date	Mintage	F12	VF20	XF40	MS60	MS63
2011	Est. 10000	PF65 60.00				

KM# 1434 10 DOLLARS
50.00 g., 0.925 Silver 1.4774 oz. ASW, 50 mm. **Ruler:** Elizabeth II **Subject:** Window's of Heaven - St. Isaac's Cathedral, St. Petersburg, Russia **Rev:** Stained glass window

Date	Mintage	F12	VF20	XF40	MS60	MS63
2012	2,000	PF65 285				

KM# 1433 10 DOLLARS
50.00 g., 0.925 Silver 1.4774 oz. ASW, 50 mm. **Ruler:** Elizabeth II **Subject:** Window's of Heaven, Church of St. Francis, Krakow, Poland **Rev:** Stained glass window

Date	Mintage	F12	VF20	XF40	MS60	MS63
2012	2,000	PF65 250				

KM# 1510 10 DOLLARS
31.11 g., 0.999 Silver 0.9926 oz. ASW, 65 mm. **Ruler:** Elizabeth II **Subject:** Ancient Cultures - Babylon

Date	Mintage	F12	VF20	XF40	MS60	MS63
2012	—	PF65 75.00				

KM# 1511 10 DOLLARS
31.11 g., 0.999 Silver 0.9926 oz. ASW, 65 mm. **Ruler:** Elizabeth II **Subject:** Ancient Cultures - Chinese

Date	Mintage	F12	VF20	XF40	MS60	MS63
2012	—	PF65 75.00				

KM# 1512 10 DOLLARS
31.11 g., 0.999 Silver 0.9926 oz. ASW, 65 mm. **Ruler:** Elizabeth II **Subject:** Ancient Cultures - Egyptian

Date	Mintage	F12	VF20	XF40	MS60	MS63
2012	—	PF65 75.00				

KM# 1513 10 DOLLARS
31.11 g., 0.999 Silver 0.9926 oz. ASW, 65 mm. **Ruler:** Elizabeth II **Subject:** Ancient Cultures - Greek

Date	Mintage	F12	VF20	XF40	MS60	MS63
2012	—	PF65 75.00				

KM# 1514 10 DOLLARS
31.11 g., 0.999 Silver 0.9926 oz. ASW, 65 mm. **Ruler:** Elizabeth II **Subject:** Ancient Cultures - Aztec

Date	Mintage	F12	VF20	XF40	MS60	MS63
2012	—	PF65 75.00				

KM# 1585 10 DOLLARS
20.00 g., 0.925 Gold 0.591 oz. AGW, 38.61 mm. **Ruler:** Elizabeth II **Subject:** 2016 Rio Olympic Games - Transfer Coin "From London to Rio

Date	Mintage	F12	VF20	XF40	MS60	MS63
2012	Est. 10000	PF65 1,380				

KM# 1586 10 DOLLARS
28.28 g., 0.925 Silver 0.8356 oz. ASW, 38.61 mm. **Ruler:** Elizabeth II **Subject:** 2014 Sochi Olympic Games - Halfpipe Skiing

Date	Mintage	F12	VF20	XF40	MS60	MS63
2012	Est. 5000	PF65 40.00				

KM# 1588 10 DOLLARS
20.00 g., 0.925 Silver 0.591 oz. ASW, 38.61 mm. **Ruler:** Elizabeth II **Subject:** 2014 FIFA World Cup Brazil - Indian and Soccer Player

Date	Mintage	F12	VF20	XF40	MS60	MS63
2012	Est. 10000	PF65 35.00				

KM# 1589 10 DOLLARS
20.00 g., 0.925 Silver 0.591 oz. ASW, 38.61 mm. **Ruler:** Elizabeth II **Subject:** Raliways - Empire State Express No. 999

Date	Mintage	F12	VF20	XF40	MS60	MS63
2012	—	PF65 35.00				

KM# 1590 10 DOLLARS
31.10 g., 0.999 Silver 0.9925 oz. ASW, 38.61 mm. **Ruler:** Elizabeth II **Subject:** Tiki Silver Ounce

Date	Mintage	F12	VF20	XF40	MS60	MS63
2012	Est. 5000	PF65 40.00				

KM# 1600 10 DOLLARS
Silver **Ruler:** Elizabeth II **Subject:** Sistine Chapel

Date	Mintage	F12	VF20	XF40	MS60	MS63
2012	—	PF65 75.00				

KM# 1616 10 DOLLARS
1.00 g., 0.999 Gold 0.0319 oz. AGW, 11 mm. **Ruler:** Elizabeth II **Rev:** Trans-Atlantic Liner "Deutschland"

Date	Mintage	F12	VF20	XF40	MS60	MS63
2012	—	PF65 75.00				

KM# 1611 10 DOLLARS
20.00 g., 0.925 Silver 0.591 oz. ASW, 38.61 mm. **Ruler:** Elizabeth II **Subject:** 2014 FIFA World Cup - Brazil Mascot

Date	Mintage	F12	VF20	XF40	MS60	MS63
2013	Est. 10000	PF65 75.00				

KM# 1615 10 DOLLARS
31.11 g., 0.999 Silver 0.9926 oz. ASW, 65 mm. **Ruler:** Elizabeth II **Subject:** Christopher Columbus

Date	Mintage	F12	VF20	XF40	MS60	MS63
2013	Est. 3000	PF65 50.00				

KM# 1558 10 DOLLARS
31.11 g., 0.999 Silver 0.9926 oz. ASW, 38.61 mm. **Ruler:** Elizabeth II **Subject:** World Monuments - USA, World Trade Center

Date	Mintage	F12	VF20	XF40	MS60	MS63
3000	Est. 3000	PF65 80.00				

KM# 1131 12 DOLLARS
10.00 g., 0.9999 Gold 0.3194 oz. AGW, 26 mm. **Ruler:** Elizabeth II **Subject:** Full Gospel Business Men's Fellowship, 50th Anniversary **Rev:** Jesus Christ

Date	Mintage	F12	VF20	XF40	MS60	MS63
2003	Est. 4999	PF65 600				

KM# 894 20 DOLLARS
31.11 g., 0.925 Silver 0.9191 oz. ASW **Ruler:** Elizabeth II **Rev:** Marco Polo visits the Khubla Khan in China

Date	Mintage	F12	VF20	XF40	MS60	MS63
2007	—	PF65 60.00				

KM# 636 20 DOLLARS
93.30 g., 0.999 Silver 2.9774 oz. ASW, 55 mm. **Ruler:** Elizabeth II **Rev:** Michangelo, Creation of Adam, multicolor with crystal inserts

Date	Mintage	F12	VF20	XF40	MS60	MS63
2008	1,000	PF65 650				

KM# 637 20 DOLLARS
93.30 g., 0.999 Silver 2.9774 oz. ASW, 55 mm. **Ruler:** Elizabeth II **Rev:** DaVinci, Last Supper, multicolor with crystal inserts

Date	Mintage	F12	VF20	XF40	MS60	MS63
2008	1,000	PF65 750				

KM# 638 20 DOLLARS
93.30 g., 0.999 Silver 2.9774 oz. ASW, 55 mm. **Ruler:** Elizabeth II **Rev:** Raffaello, School of Athens, multicolor with crystal inserts

Date	Mintage	F12	VF20	XF40	MS60	MS63
2008	1,000	PF65 600				

KM# 639 20 DOLLARS
93.30 g., 0.999 Silver 2.9774 oz. ASW, 55 mm. **Ruler:** Elizabeth II **Rev:** Botticelli, Birth of Venus, multicolor with crystal inserts

Date	Mintage	F12	VF20	XF40	MS60	MS63
2008	1,458	PF65 425				

KM# 1477 20 DOLLARS
93.30 g., 0.999 Silver 2.9774 oz. ASW, 55 mm. **Ruler:** Elizabeth II **Rev:** Vatican City 100 Euro design

Date	Mintage	F12	VF20	XF40	MS60	MS63
2008	Est. 960	PF65 225				

KM# 697 20 DOLLARS
93.32 g., 0.999 Silver 2.9779 oz. ASW, 55 mm. **Ruler:** Elizabeth II **Subject:** European Masters - DaVinci **Rev:** Mona Lisa, 12 crystals imbedded

Date	Mintage	F12	VF20	XF40	MS60	MS63
2009	999	PF65 1,450				

KM# 698 20 DOLLARS
93.32 g., 0.999 Silver 2.9779 oz. ASW, 55 mm. **Ruler:** Elizabeth II **Subject:** European Masters - Rembrandt **Rev:** The Night watch, crystals embedded

Date	Mintage	F12	VF20	XF40	MS60	MS63
2009	1,642	PF65 475				

KM# 699 20 DOLLARS
93.32 g., 0.999 Silver 2.9779 oz. ASW, 55 mm. **Ruler:** Elizabeth II **Subject:** European Masters - Raffaelo **Rev:** Sistine Chapel Madonna, crystals embedded

Date	Mintage	F12	VF20	XF40	MS60	MS63
2009	1,512	PF65 475				

KM# 700 20 DOLLARS
93.32 g., 0.999 Silver 2.9779 oz. ASW, 55 mm. **Ruler:** Elizabeth II **Subject:** European Masters - Spltzwlg **Rev:** The Poor Poet, crystals embedded

Date	Mintage	F12	VF20	XF40	MS60	MS63
2009	—	PF65 425				

KM# 769 20 DOLLARS
93.32 g., 0.999 Silver 2.9779 oz. ASW, 55 mm. **Ruler:** Elizabeth II **Rev:** Vetruvian man

Date	Mintage	F12	VF20	XF40	MS60	MS63
2010	—	PF65 550				

KM# 1246 20 DOLLARS
93.30 g., 0.999 Silver 2.9774 oz. ASW, 55 mm. **Ruler:** Elizabeth II **Subject:** Carlo Maratta **Rev:** Holy Night, color image of Mary and child, crystals

Date	Mintage	F12	VF20	XF40	MS60	MS63
2010	1,655	—	—	—	—	450

KM# 1248 20 DOLLARS
93.30 g., 0.999 Silver 2.9774 oz. ASW, 55 mm. **Ruler:** Elizabeth II **Subject:** Rembrandt **Rev:** Man in a Golden Helmet, plus crystals

Date	Mintage	F12	VF20	XF40	MS60	MS63
2010	1,655	PF65 450				

KM# 1341 20 DOLLARS
93.14 g., 0.999 Silver 2.9721 oz. ASW, 55 mm. **Ruler:** Elizabeth II **Subject:** Van Gogh, Sunflowers

Date	Mintage	F12	VF20	XF40	MS60	MS63
2010	—	PF65 435				

KM# 1494 20 DOLLARS
93.30 g., 0.999 Silver 2.9774 oz. ASW, 55 mm. **Ruler:** Elizabeth II **Rev:** Man drawing by DaVinci

Date	Mintage	F12	VF20	XF40	MS60	MS63
2010	Est. 999	PF65 525				

KM# 1387 20 DOLLARS
93.14 g., 0.999 Silver 2.9721 oz. ASW, 55 mm. **Ruler:** Elizabeth II **Subject:** Charles LeBrun, painter **Obv:** Head with tiara right **Rev:** Adoration of the Shepards painting **Edge:** Reeded

Date	Mintage	F12	VF20	XF40	MS60	MS63
2011	1,689	PF65 450				

KM# 1402 20 DOLLARS
93.30 g., 0.999 Silver 2.9774 oz. ASW, 55 mm. **Ruler:** Elizabeth II **Subject:** Vincent van Gogh **Rev:** Sunflowers

Date	Mintage	F12	VF20	XF40	MS60	MS63
2011	1,655	PF65 400				

KM# 1403 20 DOLLARS
93.30 g., 0.999 Silver 2.9774 oz. ASW, 55 mm. **Ruler:** Elizabeth II **Subject:** Franz Marc, painter **Rev:** Blue Horse

Date	Mintage	F12	VF20	XF40	MS60	MS63
2011 proof	1,911	PF65 415				

KM# 1404 20 DOLLARS
93.30 g., 0.999 Silver 2.9774 oz. ASW, 55 mm. **Ruler:** Elizabeth II **Subject:** Giovanni Canalello Bucentoro **Rev:** St. Mark's and Doge's Palace, Venice

Date	Mintage	F12	VF20	XF40	MS60	MS63
2011	1,732	PF65 450				

KM# 1448 20 DOLLARS
93.30 g., 0.999 Silver 2.9774 oz. ASW, 65 mm. **Ruler:** Elizabeth II **Subject:** Vatican Art **Rev:** Giovanni Canaletto's St. Mark's Square and the Doge's palace

Date	Mintage	F12	VF20	XF40	MS60	MS63
2011	—	PF65 450				

KM# 1454 20 DOLLARS
100.00 g., 0.999 Silver 3.1912 oz. ASW, 25x36 mm. **Ruler:** Elizabeth II **Subject:** The Luxury lifestyle **Rev:** Large blue crystal insert **Shape:** Vertical rectangle

Date	Mintage	F12	VF20	XF40	MS60	MS63
2011	2,000	PF65 550				

KM# 1397 20 DOLLARS
93.30 g., 0.999 Silver 2.9774 oz. ASW, 55 mm. **Ruler:** Elizabeth II **Obv:** Bust with tiara right **Rev:** Nefertiti head in color at center, crystal frame around

Date	Mintage	F12	VF20	XF40	MS60	MS63
2012		PF65 350				

KM# 1432 20 DOLLARS
93.30 g., 0.999 Silver 2.9774 oz. ASW, 55 mm. **Ruler:** Elizabeth II **Subject:** Portrait of Adele **Rev:** Painting image

Date	Mintage	F12	VF20	XF40	MS60	MS63
2012	1,897	PF65 250				

KM# 1435 20 DOLLARS
93.30 g., 0.999 Silver 2.9774 oz. ASW, 55 mm. **Ruler:** Elizabeth II **Subject:** Vatican Art **Rev:** Renoir's Sleeping Bather

Date	Mintage	F12	VF20	XF40	MS60	MS63
2012	—	PF65 325				

KM# 1436 20 DOLLARS
93.30 g., 0.999 Silver 2.9774 oz. ASW, 55 mm. **Ruler:** Elizabeth II **Subject:** Vatican Art **Rev:** Neferititi

Date	Mintage	F12	VF20	XF40	MS60	MS63
2012		PF65 450				

KM# 1455 20 DOLLARS
93.30 g., 0.999 Silver 2.9774 oz. ASW, 65 mm. **Ruler:** Elizabeth II **Subject:** Art - Gustav Klemt **Rev:** Adele 3 in color

Date	Mintage	F12	VF20	XF40	MS60	MS63
2012		PF65 400				

KM# 1145 25 DOLLARS
7.87 g., 0.9999 Gold 0.2514 oz. AGW **Ruler:** Elizabeth II **Rev:** Edward "Ned"Kelley in color

Date	Mintage	F12	VF20	XF40	MS60	MS63
2004 proof	Est. 1000	PF63 350	PF65 425			

KM# 1190 25 DOLLARS
155.50 g., 0.925 Silver 4.5947 oz. ASW, 65 mm. **Ruler:** Elizabeth II **Subject:** Elvis Presely, 30th Anniversary of death **Rev:** That's All right, Mama

Date	Mintage	F12	VF20	XF40	MS60	MS63
2007	Est. 1977	PF65 350				

KM# 1321 25 DOLLARS
Silver **Ruler:** Elizabeth II **Rev:** Christian Radish

Date	Mintage	F12	VF20	XF40	MS60	MS63
2008	—	PF65 85.00				

KM# 1322 25 DOLLARS
Silver **Ruler:** Elizabeth II **Rev:** France II

Date	Mintage	F12	VF20	XF40	MS60	MS63
2008	—	PF65 85.00				

KM# 1325 25 DOLLARS
Silver **Ruler:** Elizabeth II **Rev:** Sedov

Date	Mintage	F12	VF20	XF40	MS60	MS63
2008	—	PF65 85.00				

KM# 1326 25 DOLLARS
Silver **Ruler:** Elizabeth II **Rev:** Thomas Lawson

Date	Mintage	F12	VF20	XF40	MS60	MS63
2008	—	PF65 85.00				

KM# 1423 25 DOLLARS
7.77 g., 0.999 Gold 0.248 oz. AGW **Ruler:** Elizabeth II **Subject:** Pultusk Meteorite

Date	Mintage	F12	VF20	XF40	MS60	MS63
2008	—	PF65 500				

KM# 767 25 DOLLARS
155.50 g., 0.999 Silver 4.9623 oz. ASW, 65 mm. **Ruler:** Elizabeth II **Subject:** Year of the Ox **Rev:** Child riding back of ox, partially gilt **Note:** Photo reduced.

Date	Mintage	F12	VF20	XF40	MS60	MS63
2009	—	PF65 675				

KM# 1229 25 DOLLARS
7.98 g., 0.916 Gold 0.2335 oz. AGW, 22.05 mm. **Ruler:** Elizabeth II **Subject:** Ikuko Shimizu's Hello Kitty **Rev:** Kitty and Union Jack flag in multicolor

Date	Mintage	F12	VF20	XF40	MS60	MS63
2009	Est. 1000	PF65 650				

KM# 1584 25 DOLLARS
92.05 g., 0.999 Silver 2.9375 oz. ASW, 55 mm. **Ruler:** Elizabeth II **Subject:** World Monuments - Sculpture Coin, Fall of the Berlin Wall

Date	Mintage	F12	VF20	XF40	MS60	MS63
2009	1,989	—	—	—	—	130

KM# 1242 25 DOLLARS
4.00 g., 0.999 Gold 0.1276 oz. AGW, 14x23.3 mm. **Ruler:** Elizabeth II **Subject:** Shroud of Turin **Rev:** Image of the face of Jesus, 3 red crystals

Date	Mintage	F12	VF20	XF40	MS60	MS63
2010	2,000	PF65 500				

KM# 1323 25 DOLLARS
Silver **Ruler:** Elizabeth II **Rev:** Krulzernen

Date	Mintage	F12	VF20	XF40	MS60	MS63
2011	—	PF65 85.00				

KM# 1324 25 DOLLARS
Silver **Ruler:** Elizabeth II **Rev:** Preussen

Date	Mintage	F12	VF20	XF40	MS60	MS63
2011	—	PF65 85.00				

KM# 1360 25 DOLLARS
155.50 g., 0.999 Silver 4.9623 oz. ASW, 65 mm. **Ruler:** Elizabeth II **Subject:** Soyuzmultfilm 75th Anniversary - Winnie the Pooh **Rev:** Winnie the Pooh characters in color **Edge:** Reeded **Note:** Photo reduced.

Date	Mintage	F12	VF20	XF40	MS60	MS63
2011	500	PF65 420				

KM# 1366 25 DOLLARS
155.50 g., 0.999 Silver 4.9623 oz. ASW, 65 mm. **Ruler:** Elizabeth II **Subject:** Soyuzmultfilm 75th Anniversary - Little Boy and Karlsson-on-the-Roof **Rev:** Little Boy, Karlsson and Freken Bok in color **Edge:** Reeded **Note:** Photo reduced.

Date	Mintage	F12	VF20	XF40	MS60	MS63
2011	500	PF65 425				

KM# 1370 25 DOLLARS
155.50 g., 0.999 Silver 4.9623 oz. ASW, 65 mm. **Ruler:** Elizabeth II **Subject:** Soyuzmultfilm 75th Anniversary - Cheburashka and Crocodile Gena **Rev:** Cheburashka, Crocodile Gena and Madame Shapoklyak in color **Edge:** Reeded **Note:** Photo reduced.

Date	Mintage	F12	VF20	XF40	MS60	MS63
2011	500	PF65 420				

KM# 1408 25 DOLLARS
155.50 g., 0.999 Silver 4.9623 oz. ASW, 65 mm. **Ruler:** Elizabeth II **Subject:** Kipling's Mowgli story characters **Rev:** Characters in color

Date	Mintage	F12	VF20	XF40	MS60	MS63
2011	Est. 500	PF65 250				

KM# 1426 25 DOLLARS
25.00 g., 0.925 Silver 0.7387 oz. ASW, 38.61 mm. **Ruler:** Elizabeth II **Rev:** King Cobra (Ophiophagus hannah)

Date	Mintage	F12	VF20	XF40	MS60	MS63
2011	1,000	PF65 75.00				

KM# 439 30 DOLLARS
10.00 g., 0.9999 Gold 0.3194 oz. AGW, 16.1 mm. **Ruler:** Elizabeth II **Obv:** Crowned head right, date below **Rev:** Multicolor Peony flower and denomination **Edge:** Reeded

Date	Mintage	F12	VF20	XF40	MS60	MS63
2004	10,000	—	—	—	—	600

KM# 1128 35 DOLLARS
10.02 g., 0.999 Gold 0.3198 oz. AGW, 25 mm. **Ruler:** Elizabeth II **Rev:** James Cook and sailing ship

Date	Mintage	F12	VF20	XF40	MS60	MS63
2003	Est. 4999	PF65 625				

KM# 440 35 DOLLARS
10.00 g., 0.9999 Gold 0.3194 oz. AGW, 16.1 mm. **Ruler:** Elizabeth II **Obv:** Crowned head right, date below **Rev:** Multicolor Chinese man beating a tiger and denomination **Edge:** Reeded

Date	Mintage	F12	VF20	XF40	MS60	MS63
2004	6,000	—	—	—	—	600

KM# 441 35 DOLLARS
10.00 g., 0.9999 Gold 0.3194 oz. AGW, 16.1 mm. **Ruler:** Elizabeth II **Obv:** Crowned head right, date below **Rev:** Multicolor Chinese man riding a horse and denomination **Edge:** Reeded

Date	Mintage	F12	VF20	XF40	MS60	MS63
2004	10,000	—	—	—	—	600

KM# 442 35 DOLLARS
10.00 g., 0.9999 Gold 0.3194 oz. AGW, 25 x 15 mm. **Ruler:** Elizabeth II **Obv:** Crowned head right, date below **Rev:** Multicolor "Eight immortals crossing the sea" and denomination **Edge:** Plain **Shape:** Ingot

Date	Mintage	F12	VF20	XF40	MS60	MS63
2004	3,000					650

KM# 1132 50 DOLLARS
31.11 g., 0.9999 Gold 0.9935 oz. AGW, 38.6 mm. **Ruler:** Elizabeth II **Subject:** Full Gospel Business Men's Fellowship, 50th Anniversary **Rev:** Jesus Christ

Date	Mintage	F12	VF20	XF40	MS60	MS63
2003	Est. 2999	PF65 1,800				

KM# 1319 50 DOLLARS
Silver **Ruler:** Elizabeth II **Subject:** Worlf Wildlife Fund **Rev:** Two deer

Date	Mintage	F12	VF20	XF40	MS60	MS63
2007	—	PF65 100				

KM# 1191 50 DOLLARS
7.78 g., 0.750 Gold 0.1864 oz. AGW, 26 mm. **Ruler:** Elizabeth II **Subject:** Elvis Presley, 30th Anniversary of death

Date	Mintage	F12	VF20	XF40	MS60	MS63
2007	500	PF65 420				

KM# 800 50 DOLLARS
155.50 g., 0.999 Silver 4.9623 oz. ASW, 65 mm. **Ruler:** Elizabeth II **Subject:** Tales of the Carribean **Rev:** Sea monster atacking Pirate ship

Date	Mintage	F12	VF20	XF40	MS60	MS63
2008	500	—	—	—	—	1,000

KM# 1230 50 DOLLARS
15.61 g., 0.999 Gold 0.4981 oz. AGW, 26.5 mm. **Ruler:** Elizabeth II **Subject:** Ikuko Shimizu's Hello Kitty **Rev:** Kitty and Daniel in automobile near Westminster and Big Ben in multicolor

Date	Mintage	F12	VF20	XF40	MS60	MS63
2009	Est. 1000	PF65 1,000				

KM# 738 50 DOLLARS
31.11 g., 0.9999 Palladium 0.9935 oz. APW **Ruler:** Elizabeth II **Rev:** Ship model left

Date	Mintage	F12	VF20	XF40	MS60	MS63
2010					—	900

KM# 1465 50 DOLLARS
155.50 g., 0.999 Silver 4.9623 oz. ASW, 65 mm. **Ruler:** Elizabeth II **Rev:** Airship Hindenburg in flight over New York skyline engraved on mother-of-pearl insert **Note:** Photo reduced.

Date	Mintage	F12	VF20	XF40	MS60	MS63
2013	750	PF65 350				

KM# 1591 50 DOLLARS
155.50 g., Silver, 65 mm. **Ruler:** Elizabeth II **Subject:** Year of the Snake **Obv:** Head and Tiara right **Rev:** Snake on hand in green mother of pearl

Date	Mintage	F12	VF20	XF40	MS60	MS63
2013		PF65 350				

KM# 1592 50 DOLLARS
155.55 g., 0.999 Silver 4.9639 oz. ASW, 65 mm. **Ruler:** Elizabeth II **Subject:** Jules Verne's 20,000 Leagues Under the Sea **Obv:** Nautalus and sea creature in mother of pearl

Date	Mintage	F12	VF20	XF40	MS60	MS63
2014	750	PF65 350				

KM# 1601 50 DOLLARS
155.50 g., 0.999 Silver 4.9623 oz. ASW, 65 mm. **Ruler:** Elizabeth II **Subject:** Year of the Horse **Rev:** Horse engraved in mother of pearl

Date	Mintage	F12	VF20	XF40	MS60	MS63
2014	888	PF65 500				

KM# 397 100 DOLLARS
23.33 g., 0.9999 Gold 0.7451 oz. AGW, 32.1 mm. **Ruler:** Elizabeth II **Subject:** Crown Jewels **Obv:** Crowned bust right, legend **Rev:** Crowns and royal regalia **Edge:** Reeded

Date	Mintage	F12	VF20	XF40	MS60	MS63
2002	5,000	PF65 1,350				

KM# 1129 100 DOLLARS
31.16 g., 0.999 Gold 0.9944 oz. AGW, 32 mm. **Ruler:** Elizabeth II **Rev:** James Cook and sailing ship

Date	Mintage	F12	VF20	XF40	MS60	MS63
2003	Est. 2999	PF65 1,700				

KM# 503 100 DOLLARS
31.10 g., 0.9999 Gold 0.9934 oz. AGW, 40.6 mm. **Ruler:** Elizabeth II **Subject:** WWI **Obv:** Head with tiara right **Rev:** Multicolor image of Australian WWI soldier in Europe **Edge:** Reeded

Date	Mintage	F12	VF20	XF40	MS60	MS63
2008	90	PF65 2,000				

KM# 505 100 DOLLARS
31.10 g., 0.9999 Gold 0.9934 oz. AGW, 40.6 mm. **Ruler:** Elizabeth II **Subject:** WWI **Obv:** Head with tiara right **Rev:** Multicolor image of Australian WWI soldier in Mid-East scene **Edge:** Reeded

Date	Mintage	F12	VF20	XF40	MS60	MS63
2008	90	PF65 2,000				

KM# 737 100 DOLLARS
31.11 g., 0.9999 Platinum 0.9935 oz. APW **Ruler:** Elizabeth II **Rev:** Ship model left

Date	Mintage	F12	VF20	XF40	MS60	MS63
2010	—	—	—	—	—	2,250

KM# 1614 100 DOLLARS
3.11 g., 0.999 Gold 0.0992 oz. AGW, 16.5 mm. **Ruler:** Elizabeth II **Subject:** 2014 FIFA World Cup - Brazil Mascot

Date	Mintage	F12	VF20	XF40	MS60	MS63
2013	Est. 1000	PF65 175				

KM# 1212 200 DOLLARS
31.16 g., 0.9999 Gold 0.9953 oz. AGW, 32 mm. **Ruler:** Elizabeth II **Subject:** John Marshall's Cow Parade **Rev:** Cow in multicolor

Date	Mintage	F12	VF20	XF40	MS60	MS63
2008	Est. 100	—	—	—	—	1,850

KM# 1213 200 DOLLARS
31.16 g., 0.999 Gold 0.9944 oz. AGW, 32 mm. **Ruler:** Elizabeth II **Subject:** John Marshall's Cow Parade **Rev:** African Moonlight Cow in multicolor

Date	Mintage	F12	VF20	XF40	MS60	MS63
2008	Est. 100	—	—	—	—	1,850

KM# 1214 200 DOLLARS
31.17 g., 0.999 Gold 0.9945 oz. AGW, 32 mm. **Ruler:** Elizabeth II **Subject:** John Marshall's Cow Parade **Rev:** Discount Motivated in multicolor

Date	Mintage	F12	VF20	XF40	MS60	MS63
2008	Est. 100	—	—	—	—	1,850

KM# 1215 200 DOLLARS
31.17 g., 0.9999 Gold 0.9954 oz. AGW. **Ruler:** Elizabeth II **Subject:** John Marshall's Cow Parade **Rev:** Moodonna in multicolor

Date	Mintage	F12	VF20	XF40	MS60	MS63
2008	Est. 100	—	—	—	—	1,850

KM# 1216 200 DOLLARS
31.17 g., 0.999 Gold 0.9945 oz. AGW, 32 mm. **Ruler:** Elizabeth II **Subject:** John Marshall's Cow Parade **Rev:** Moodiba in multicolor

Date	Mintage	F12	VF20	XF40	MS60	MS63
2008	Est. 100	—	—	—	—	1,850

KM# 1217 200 DOLLARS
31.17 g., 0.9999 Gold 0.9954 oz. AGW, 32 mm. **Ruler:** Elizabeth II **Subject:** John Marshall's Cow Parade **Rev:** Railbow Cowwow in multicolor

Date	Mintage	F12	VF20	XF40	MS60	MS63
2008	Est. 100	—	—	—	—	1,850

KM# 1218 200 DOLLARS
31.17 g., 0.9999 Gold 0.9954 oz. AGW, 32 mm. **Ruler:** Elizabeth II **Subject:** John Marshall's Cow Parade **Rev:** Picowso in multicolor

Date	Mintage	F12	VF20	XF40	MS60	MS63
2008	Est. 100	—	—	—	—	1,850

KM# 1219 200 DOLLARS
31.17 g., 0.999 Gold 0.9945 oz. AGW, 32 mm. **Ruler:** Elizabeth II **Subject:** John Marshall's Cow Parade **Rev:** Location Cow in multicolor

Date	Mintage	F12	VF20	XF40	MS60	MS63
2008	Est. 100	—	—	—	—	1,850

KM# 1220 200 DOLLARS
31.17 g., 0.9999 Gold 0.9954 oz. AGW, 32 mm. **Ruler:** Elizabeth II **Subject:** John Marshall's Cow Parade **Rev:** Milking in the Farmhouse in multicolor

Date	Mintage	F12	VF20	XF40	MS60	MS63
2008	Est. 100	—	—	—	—	1,850

KM# 1221 200 DOLLARS
31.17 g., 0.9999 Gold 0.9954 oz. AGW, 32 mm. **Ruler:** Elizabeth II **Subject:** John Marshall's Cow Parade **Rev:** Evening Cows in multicolor

Date	Mintage	F12	VF20	XF40	MS60	MS63
2008	Est. 100	—	—	—	—	1,850

KM# 1222 200 DOLLARS
31.17 g., 0.9999 Gold 0.9954 oz. AGW, 32 mm. **Ruler:** Elizabeth II **Subject:** John Marshall's Cow Parade **Rev:** Cultural Moosic Cow in multicolor

Date	Mintage	F12	VF20	XF40	MS60	MS63
2008	Est. 100	—	—	—	—	1,850

KM# 1223 200 DOLLARS
31.17 g., 0.9999 Gold 0.9954 oz. AGW, 32 mm. **Ruler:** Elizabeth II **Subject:** John Marshall's Cow Parade **Rev:** Freedomoo Cow in multicolor

Date	Mintage	F12	VF20	XF40	MS60	MS63
2008	Est. 100	—	—	—	—	1,850

KM# 1224 200 DOLLARS
31.17 g., 0.9999 Gold 0.9954 oz. AGW, 32 mm. **Ruler:** Elizabeth II **Subject:** John Marshall's Cow Parade **Rev:** Bovingham Palace Cow in multicolor

Date	Mintage	F12	VF20	XF40	MS60	MS63
2008	Est. 100	—	—	—	—	1,850

KM# 768 200 DOLLARS
31.11 g., 0.9999 Gold 0.9926 oz. AGW, 40.6 mm. **Ruler:** Elizabeth II **Subject:** Year of the Ox **Rev:** Child riding back of ox

Date	Mintage	F12	VF20	XF40	MS60	MS63
2009	—	PF65 1,850				

KM# 389 500 DOLLARS
2000.00 g., 0.999 Silver 63.8237 oz. ASW, 105 mm. **Ruler:** Elizabeth II **Subject:** Moby Dick **Obv:** Crowned head right **Rev:** Whale jumping over a six-man rowboat **Edge:** Plain **Note:** Illustration reduced.

Date	Mintage	F12	VF20	XF40	MS60	MS63
2001	—	PF65 2,300				

KM# 548 500 DOLLARS
113.00 g., 1.000 Gold 3.6096 oz. AGW, 50 mm. **Ruler:** Elizabeth II **Subject:** Jack Nicklaus **Rev:** Portrait facing - two golf poses flanking

Date	Mintage	F12	VF20	XF40	MS60	MS63
2006	113	PF65 6,250				

KM# 1602
155.50 g., 0.999 Gold 4.9623 oz. AGW **Ruler:** Elizabeth II **Subject:** Year of the Horse **Rev:** Horse in mother of pearl

Date	Mintage	F12	VF20	XF40	MS60	MS63
2014 Proof	25	—	—	—	—	—

BULLION COINAGE

KM# 1473 DOLLAR
31.11 g., 0.999 Silver 0.9926 oz. ASW, 39 mm. **Ruler:** Elizabeth II **Rev:** H.M.A.V. Bounty

Date	Mintage	F12	VF20	XF40	MS60	MS63
2009	—	—	—	—	—	40.00

KM# 1596 DOLLAR
27.00 g., Silver, 38.61 mm. **Ruler:** Elizabeth II **Subject:** Ctyrlistek Cartoon - Myspulin

Date	Mintage	F12	VF20	XF40	MS60	MS63
2013	Est. 1000	PF65 80.00				

KM# 1470 5 DOLLARS
100.00 g., 0.999 Silver 3.1912 oz. ASW **Ruler:** Elizabeth II **Rev:** H.M.A.V. Bounty

Date	Mintage	F12	VF20	XF40	MS60	MS63
2009	—	—	—	—	—	135

KM# 1474 10 DOLLARS
3.11 g., 0.999 Gold 0.0992 oz. AGW **Ruler:** Elizabeth II **Rev:** H.M.A.V. Bounty

Date	Mintage	F12	VF20	XF40	MS60	MS63
2009	—	—	—	—	—	185

KM# 1475 25 DOLLARS
7.78 g., 0.999 Gold 0.2483 oz. AGW **Ruler:** Elizabeth II **Rev:** H.M.A.V. Bounty

Date	Mintage	F12	VF20	XF40	MS60	MS63
2009	—	—	—	—	—	475

KM# 1467 30 DOLLARS
1000.00 g., 0.999 Silver 31.9118 oz. ASW, 50x105 mm. **Ruler:** Elizabeth II **Shape:** Rectangle

Date	Mintage	F12	VF20	XF40	MS60	MS63
2007	—	—	—	—	—	1,200

KM# 1234 50 DOLLARS
31.11 g., 0.999 Palladium 0.9926 oz. APW, 38.6 mm. **Ruler:** Elizabeth II **Rev:** H.M.A.V. Bounty, as full hull model

Date	Mintage	F12	VF20	XF40	MS60	MS63
2009	—	—	—	—	—	1,000

KM# 1471 100 DOLLARS
3110.00 g., 0.999 Silver 99.2458 oz. ASW, 89x182 mm. **Ruler:** Elizabeth II **Rev:** H.M.A.V. Bounty

Date	Mintage	F12	VF20	XF40	MS60	MS63
2008	—	—	—	—	—	3,500

KM# 1476 100 DOLLARS
31.11 g., 0.999 Gold 0.9926 oz. AGW **Ruler:** Elizabeth II **Rev:** H.M.A.V. Bounty

Date	Mintage	F12	VF20	XF40	MS60	MS63
2009	—	—	—	—	—	1,900

KM# 1472 150 DOLLARS
5000.00 g., 0.999 Silver 159.5592 oz. ASW, 89x182 mm. **Ruler:** Elizabeth II **Rev:** H.M.A.V. Bounty

Date	Mintage	F12	VF20	XF40	MS60	MS63
2008	—	—	—	—	—	5,500

MAUNDY MONEY
Ceremonial Sterling Pence

KM# 449 PENNY
0.48 g., 0.999 Silver, 11.1 mm. **Ruler:** Elizabeth II **Subject:** Maundy **Obv:** Crowned bust right **Rev:** Crowned denomination divides date within wreath **Edge:** Plain

Date	Mintage	F12	VF20	XF40	MS60	MS63
2002	5,000	PF65 8.00				

KM# 450 2 PENCE
0.94 g., 0.999 Silver, 13.4 mm. **Ruler:** Elizabeth II **Subject:** Maundy **Obv:** Crowned bust right **Rev:** Crowned denomination divides date within wreath **Edge:** Plain

Date	Mintage	F12	VF20	XF40	MS60	MS63
2002	5,000	PF65 10.00				

KM# 451 3 PENCE
1.44 g., 0.999 Silver 0.046 oz. ASW, 16.1 mm. **Ruler:** Elizabeth II **Subject:** Maundy **Obv:** Crowned bust right **Rev:** Crowned denomination divides date within wreath **Edge:** Plain

Date	Mintage	F12	VF20	XF40	MS60	MS63
2002	5,000	PF65 12.00				

KM# 452 4 PENCE
1.93 g., 0.999 Silver 0.0616 oz. ASW, 17.5 mm. **Ruler:** Elizabeth II **Subject:** Maundy **Obv:** Crowned bust right **Rev:** Crowned denomination divides date within wreath **Edge:** Plain

Date	Mintage	F12	VF20	XF40	MS60	MS63
2002	5,000	PF65 15.00				

PROOF SETS

KM#	Date	Mintage	Identification	Issue Price	Mkt Val
PS25	2002 (4)	5,000	KM#449-452	—	45.00

COSTA RICA

The Republic of Costa Rica, located in southern Central America between Nicaragua and Panama, has an area of 19,730 sq. mi. (51,100 sq. km.) and a population of 3.4 million. Capital: San Jose. Agriculture predominates; tourism and coffee, bananas, beef and sugar contribute heavily to the country's export earnings.

KEY TO MINT IDENTIFICATION

Key Letter	Mint
(a)	Armant Metalurgica, Santiago, Chile
(c)	Casa de Moneda, Mexico City Mint
(cc)	Casa de Moneda, Brazil
(co)	Colombia Republican Banko
(g)	Guatemala Mint
(i)	Italcambio Mint
(p) or (P)	Philadelphia Mint, USA
(r)	RCM – Royal Canadian Mint
(rm)	Royal Mint, London
(s)	San Francisco
(sj)	San Jose
(sm)	Sherrit Mint, Toronto
(v)	Vereingte Deutsche Metallwerke, Karlsruhe
(w)	Westain, Toronto

REPUBLIC

REFORM COINAGE

1920, 100 Centimos = 1 Colon

KM# 227a.2 5 COLONES

4.00 g., Brass, 21.6 mm. **Obv:** National arms, date below, large letters in legend, large date, shield is not outlined **Rev:** Denomination above spray, B.C.C.R. below, thin '5' **Edge:** Segmented reeding

Date	Mintage	F12	VF20	XF40	MS60	MS63
2001(a)	35,000,000	—	—	—	0.65	1.00

KM# 227b 5 COLONES

0.90 g., Aluminum, 21.4 mm. **Obv:** National arms **Obv. Legend:** REPUBLICA DE COSTA RICA **Rev:** Denomination above sprays, B.C.C.R. **Edge:** Plain

Date	Mintage	F12	VF20	XF40	MS60	MS63
2005	55,000,000	—	—	—	0.35	0.50
2008	300,000,000	—	—	—	0.35	0.50

KM# 228.2 10 COLONES

5.00 g., Copper-Aluminum-Nickel, 23.5 mm. **Obv:** National arms, date below, large legend and date, shield not outlined **Rev:** Denomination above spray, B.C.C.R. below, thick '1' **Edge:** Segmented reeding

Date	Mintage	F12	VF20	XF40	MS60	MS63
2002(a)	15,000,000	—	—	—	0.75	1.00

KM# 228b 10 COLONES

1.13 g., Aluminum, 22.97 mm. **Obv:** National arms **Obv. Legend:** REPUBLICA DE COSTA RICA **Rev:** Denomination above sprays, B.C.C.R. **Edge:** Reeded

Date	Mintage	F12	VF20	XF40	MS60	MS63
2005	50,000,000	—	—	—	0.50	0.75
Note: Fine letters						
2008	200,000,000	—	—	—	0.50	0.75
Note: Bold letters						
2012	230,000,000	—	—	—	0.50	0.75

KM# 229a 25 COLONES

7.00 g., Copper-Aluminum-Nickel, 25.5 mm. **Obv:** National arms **Obv. Legend:** REPUBLICA DE COSTA RICA **Rev:** Value above sprays, B.C.C.R. below **Edge:** Segmented reeding

Date	Mintage	F12	VF20	XF40	MS60	MS63
2001(a)	10,000,000	—	—	—	1.00	1.50
2003	15,000,000	—	—	—	1.00	1.50

KM# 229b 25 COLONES

7.00 g., Brass, 25.5 mm. **Obv:** National arms, date below **Rev:** Value above sprays, B.C.C.R. below **Edge:** Plain **Note:** Prev.#229a.1

Date	Mintage	F12	VF20	XF40	MS60	MS63
2005	30,000,000	—	—	—	1.00	1.50

KM# 229c 25 COLONES

Brass Plated Steel, 25.5 mm. **Obv:** National arms, country name and date **Rev:** Sprays, legend B.C.C.R. and denomination

Date	Mintage	F12	VF20	XF40	MS60	MS63
2007	90,000,000	—	—	—	1.00	1.50

KM# 231.1a 50 COLONES

7.92 g., Copper-Aluminum-Nickel, 27.5 mm. **Obv:** National arms, date below **Rev:** Value with spray below **Rev. Legend:** B. C. C. R. **Edge:** Segmented reeding

Date	Mintage	F12	VF20	XF40	MS60	MS63
2002	15,000,000	—	—	—	1.00	1.50

KM# 231.1b 50 COLONES

7.84 g., Brass Plated Steel, 27.5 mm. **Obv:** National arms above date **Rev:** Value above sprays, B.C.C.R. below **Edge:** Segmented reeding

Date	Mintage	F12	VF20	XF40	MS60	MS63
2006	5,000,000	—	—	—	1.00	1.50
2007	36,000,000	—	—	—	1.00	1.50

KM# 240a 100 COLONES

9.00 g., Brass Plated Steel, 29.5 mm. **Obv:** National arms above date **Rev:** Value above sprays **Edge:** Reeded

Date	Mintage	F12	VF20	XF40	MS60	MS63
2006	14,000,000	—	—	—	1.00	1.50
2007	108,000,000	—	—	—	1.00	1.50

KM# 239.1 500 COLONES

11.00 g., Copper-Aluminum-Nickel, 33 mm. **Obv:** National arms **Obv. Legend:** REPUBLICA DE COSTA RICA **Rev:** Value above sprays, B.C.C.R. below, thick numerals **Edge:** Segmented reeding

Date	Mintage	F12	VF20	XF40	MS60	MS63
2003(a)	15,000,000	—	—	0.85	1.25	1.75
2005	10,000,000	—	—	0.85	1.25	1.75

KM# 239.2 500 COLONES

Brass, 32.9 mm. **Obv:** National arms, date below **Obv. Legend:** REPUBLICA DE COSTA RICA **Rev:** Denomination above sprays, B.C.C.R. below, thin numerals **Edge:** Segmented reeding

Date	Mintage	F12	VF20	XF40	MS60	MS63
2003	100	—	—	—	—	250

KM# 239.1a 500 COLONES

11.00 g., Brass Plated Steel, 33 mm. **Obv:** National arms, date below **Rev:** Value above sprays, B.C.C.R. below **Edge:** Segmented reeding

Date	Mintage	F12	VF20	XF40	MS60	MS63
2006	6,000,000	—	—	0.85	1.25	1.75
2007	38,200,000	—	—	0.85	1.25	1.75

CREEK NATION

POARCH CREEK INDIANS

SOVEREIGN NATION

MILLED COINAGE

KM# 1 DOLLAR

31.13 g., 0.999 Silver 0.9935 oz. ASW, 39 mm. **Subject:** Peace **Obv:** Tribal seal **Obv. Legend:** CREEK NATION OF INDIANS **Rev:** Indian on horseback left **Rev. Legend:** PEACE **Edge:** Reeded

Date	Mintage	F12	VF20	XF40	MS60	MS63
2004	10,000	PF63 45.00	PF65 50.00			
2004	20,000	—	—	—	—	35.00

KM# 2 DOLLAR
31.11 g., 0.999 Silver 0.9926 oz. ASW, 39 mm. **Subject:** 20th
Anniversary of Recognition **Obv:** Young sky dancer right, symbol
Obv. Legend: CREEK NATION OF INDIANS **Rev:** Busts of 5
tribal chiefs, symbol below **Rev. Legend:** SOVEREIGN NATION
Edge: Reeded

Date	Mintage	F12	VF20	XF40	MS60	MS63
2004	10,000	PF63 45.00	PF65 50.00			
2004	20,000	—	—	—	—	35.00

KM# 7 DOLLAR
31.11 g., 0.999 Silver 0.9926 oz. ASW, 40.52 mm. **Obv:** Tribal
seal **Obv. Legend:** CREEK NATION OF INDIANS **Rev:** Bust
of Chief Menawa 3/4 left **Rev. Legend:** CHIEF MENAWA "THE
GREAT WARRIOR **Edge:** Reeded

Date	Mintage	F12	VF20	XF40	MS60	MS63
2005	20,000	—	—	—	—	35.00
2005	10,000	PF63 45.00	PF65 50.00			

KM# 8 DOLLAR
31.11 g., 0.999 Silver 0.9926 oz. ASW, 40.55 mm. **Obv:** Tribal
seal **Obv. Legend:** CREEK NATION OF INDIANS **Rev:** Tchow-
ee-put-o-kaw 3/4 right **Rev. Legend:** TCOW-EE-PUT-O-KAW
Edge: Reeded

Date	Mintage	F12	VF20	XF40	MS60	MS63
2005	10,000	PF63 45.00	PF65 50.00			
2005	20,000	—	—	—	—	35.00

KM# 10 DOLLAR
31.12 g., 0.999 Silver 0.9931 oz. ASW, 41.61 mm. **Obv:** Dancer
left at center right, a tribal seal at lower left **Obv. Legend:**
CREEK NATION - OF INDIANS **Rev:** Warrior horseback 3/4
right **Rev. Legend:** SOVEREIGN NATION **Edge:** Reeded

Date	Mintage	F12	VF20	XF40	MS60	MS63
2006	20,000	—	—	—	—	35.00
2006	10,000	PF63 45.00	PF65 50.00			

KM# 11 DOLLAR
31.17 g., 0.999 Silver 0.9947 oz. ASW, 40.58 mm. **Obv:** Tribal
seal **Obv. Legend:** CREEK NATION OF INDIANS **Rev:** Facing
busts of Chief Tomochichi and his son with eagle **Rev. Legend:**
CHIEF TOMOCHICHI **Edge:** Reeded

Date	Mintage	F12	VF20	XF40	MS60	MS63
2006	20,000	—	—	—	—	35.00
2006	10,000	PF63 45.00	PF65 50.00			

KM# 13 DOLLAR
31.11 g., 0.999 Silver 0.9926 oz. ASW, 40.58 mm. **Obv:** Sky
Dancer **Obv. Legend:** CREEK NATION OF INDIANS **Rev:**
Warrior on horseback **Rev. Legend:** CHIEF OPOTHLE
YOHOLO **Edge:** Reeded

Date	Mintage	F12	VF20	XF40	MS60	MS63
2007	10,000	PF63 45.00	PF65 50.00			
2007		—	—	—	—	35.00

KM# 4 5 DOLLARS
6.17 g., 0.999 Gold 0.1969 oz. AGW, 22 mm. **Subject:** Peace
Obv: Symbol **Obv. Legend:** CREEK NATION OF INDIANS
Rev: Indian horseback left **Edge:** Reeded

Date	Mintage	F12	VF20	XF40	MS60	MS63
2004	—	PF63 350	PF65 375			

KM# 9 5 DOLLARS
6.17 g., 0.999 Gold 0.1969 oz. AGW, 22.18 mm. **Obv:** Tribal
seal **Obv. Legend:** CREEK NATION OF INDIANS **Rev:** Busts
of Chief Hopothle Mico and George Washington 3/4 left **Rev.
Legend:** CHIEF HOPOTHLE MICO • GEORGE WASHINGTON
Edge: Reeded

Date	Mintage	F12	VF20	XF40	MS60	MS63
2005	2,500	PF63 350	PF65 375			

KM# 12 5 DOLLARS
6.17 g., 0.999 Gold 0.1969 oz. AGW, 22.2 mm. **Obv:** Tribal
seal **Obv. Legend:** CREEK NATION OF INDIANS **Rev:** Bust
of Chief Stee•Chaco•Me•Co **Rev. Legend:** CHIEF STEE •
CHACO • ME • CO **Edge:** Reeded

Date	Mintage	F12	VF20	XF40	MS60	MS63
2006	2,500	PF63 350	PF65 375			

KM# 14 5 DOLLARS
6.17 g., 0.999 Gold 0.1969 oz. AGW, 22.2 mm. **Obv:** Tribal seal
Obv. Legend: CREEK NATION OF INDIANS **Rev. Legend:**
CHIEF CALVIN MCGHEE **Edge:** Reeded

Date	Mintage	F12	VF20	XF40	MS60	MS63
2007	2,500	PF63 350	PF65 375			

KM# 5 10 DOLLARS
15.55 g., 0.9995 Palladium 0.4965 oz. APW, 30 mm. **Subject:**
20th Anniversary of Recognition **Obv:** Young sky dancer
right, symbol **Obv. Legend:** CREEK NATION OF INDIANS
Rev: Busts of 5 tribal chiefs, symbol below **Rev. Legend:**
SOVEREIGN NATION **Edge:** Reeded

Date	Mintage	F12	VF20	XF40	MS60	MS63
2004	250	PF65 650				

KM# 6 100 DOLLARS
31.11 g., 0.999 Gold 0.9926 oz. AGW, 31.94 mm. **Subject:**
Treaty for Autonomy, 20th Anniversary **Obv:** Native dancer right
at left center, tribal seal at right **Obv. Legend:** CREEK NATION
- OF INDIANS **Rev:** Five portraits left to right, tribal seal below
Rev. Legend: • SOVEREIGN NATION • **Edge:** Reeded

Date	Mintage	F12	VF20	XF40	MS60	MS63
2004	250	PF65 1,850				

CROATIA

AUSTRIA HUNGARY
SLOVENIA ROMANIA
BOSNIA & HERZEGOVINA
ITALY Adriatic SERBIA BULGARIA
MONTENEGRO

The Republic of Croatia, (Hrvatska) bordered on the west by the Adriatic Sea and the northeast by Hungary, has an area of 21,829 sq. mi. (56,538 sq. km.) and a population of 4.7 million. Capital: Zagreb.

NOTE: Coin dates starting with 1994 are followed with a period. Example: 1994.

REPUBLIC

REFORM COINAGE

For the circulating minor coins, the reverse legend (name of item) is in Croatian for odd dated years and Latin for even dated years.May 30, 1994 - 1000 Dinara = 1 Kuna; 100 Lipa = 1 Kuna

KM# 3 LIPA
0.70 g., Aluminum, 17 mm. **Obv:** Denomination above crowned arms **Obv. Legend:** REPUBLIKA HRVATSKA **Rev:** Ears of corn, date below **Rev. Legend:** KUKURUZ **Edge:** Plain

Date	Mintage	F12	VF20	XF40	MS60	MS63
2001	2,000,000	—	—	0.20	0.50	—
2001	1,000	PF60 2.50				
2003	1,500,000	—	—	0.20	0.50	—
2003	1,000	PF60 2.50				
2005	—	—	—	0.20	0.50	—
2005	2,000	PF60 2.00				
2007	—	—	—	0.20	0.50	—
2007	1,000	PF60 2.00				
2009 In sets only	—	—	—	—	1.00	—
2009	—	PF60 2.00				
2011	—	PF60 2.00				

KM# 12 LIPA
0.70 g., Aluminum, 17 mm. **Obv:** Denomination above crowned arms **Obv. Legend:** REPUBLIKA HRVATSKA **Rev:** Ears of corn, date below **Rev. Legend:** ZEA MAYS **Edge:** Plain

Date	Mintage	F12	VF20	XF40	MS60	MS63
2002	3,000,000	—	—	0.40	1.00	—
2002	1,000	PF60 2.50				
2004	2,000,000	—	—	0.40	1.00	—
2004	2,000	PF60 1.50				
2006	—	—	—	0.40	1.00	—
2006	1,000	PF60 1.50				
2008	—	—	—	0.40	1.00	—
2008	1,000	PF60 1.50				
2010	—	PF60 1.50				
2012	—	—	—	0.40	1.00	—
2012	—	PF60 1.50				

KM# 4 2 LIPE
0.92 g., Aluminum, 19 mm. **Obv:** Denomination above crowned arms on half braid **Obv. Legend:** REPUBLIKA HRVATSKA **Rev:** Grapevine, date below **Rev. Legend:** VINOVA LOZA **Edge:** Plain

Date	Mintage	F12	VF20	XF40	MS60	MS63
2001	2,986,000	—	—	0.40	1.00	—
2001	1,000	PF60 3.00				
2003	2,000,000	—	—	0.40	1.00	—
2003	1,000	PF60 3.00				
2005	—	—	—	0.40	1.00	—
2005	2,000	PF60 3.00				
2007	—	—	—	0.40	1.00	—
2007	1,000	PF60 3.00				
2009 In sets only	—	—	—	—	2.00	—
2009	—	PF60 3.00				

Date	Mintage	F12	VF20	XF40	MS60	MS63
2011	—	PF60 3.00				

KM# 14 2 LIPE
0.92 g., Aluminum, 19 mm. **Obv:** Denomination above crowned arms on half braid **Obv. Legend:** REPUBLIKA HRVATSKA **Rev:** Grapevine, date below **Rev. Legend:** VITIS VINIFERA **Edge:** Plain

Date	Mintage	F12	VF20	XF40	MS60	MS63
2002	2,000,000	—	—	0.80	2.00	—
2002	1,000	PF60 3.00				
2004	2,000,000	—	—	0.80	2.00	—
2004	2,000	PF60 2.50				
2006	—	—	—	0.80	2.00	—
2006	1,000	PF60 2.50				
2008	—	—	—	0.80	2.00	—
2008	1,000	PF60 2.50				
2010	—	PF60 2.50				
2012	—	—	—	0.80	2.00	—
2012	—	PF60 2.50				

KM# 5 5 LIPA
2.50 g., Brass Plated Steel, 18 mm. **Obv:** Denomination above crowned arms **Obv. Legend:** REPUBLIKA HRVATSKA **Rev:** Oak leaves, date below **Rev. Legend:** HRAST LUZNJAK **Edge:** Plain

Date	Mintage	F12	VF20	XF40	MS60	MS63
2001	6,598,000	—	—	0.40	1.00	—
2001	1,000	PF60 4.00				
2003	13,000,000	—	—	0.40	1.00	—
2003	2,000	PF60 3.50				
2005	—	—	—	0.40	1.00	—
2005	2,000	PF60 3.50				
2007	—	—	—	0.40	1.00	—
2007	1,000	PF60 3.50				
2009	—	—	—	0.40	1.00	—
2009	—	PF60 3.50				
2011	—	—	—	0.40	1.00	—
2011	—	PF60 3.50				

KM# 15 5 LIPA
2.50 g., Brass Plated Steel, 18 mm. **Obv:** Denomination above crowned arms **Obv. Legend:** REPUBLIKA HRVATSKA **Rev:** Oak leaves, date below **Rev. Legend:** QUERCUS ROBUR **Edge:** Plain

Date	Mintage	F12	VF20	XF40	MS60	MS63
2002	3,500,000	—	—	0.80	2.00	—
2002	1,000	PF60 4.00				
2004	2,000,000	—	—	0.80	2.00	—
2004	2,000	PF60 3.00				
2006	—	—	—	0.80	2.00	—
2006	1,000	PF60 3.00				
2008	—	—	—	0.80	2.00	—
2008	1,000	PF60 3.00				
2010	—	—	—	0.80	2.00	—
2010	—	PF60 3.00				
2012	—	—	—	0.80	2.00	—
2012	—	PF60 3.00				

KM# 6 10 LIPA
3.25 g., Brass Plated Steel, 20 mm. **Obv:** Denomination above crowned arms **Obv. Legend:** REPUBLIKA HRVATSKA **Rev:** Tobacco plant, date below **Rev. Legend:** DUHAN **Edge:** Plain

Date	Mintage	F12	VF20	XF40	MS60	MS63
2001	31,500,000	—	—	0.40	1.50	—
2001	1,000	PF60 5.00				
2003	12,000,000	—	—	0.40	1.50	—
2003	1,000	PF60 5.00				
2005	—	—	—	0.40	1.50	—
2005	2,000	PF60 5.00				

Date	Mintage	F12	VF20	XF40	MS60	MS63
2011	—	PF60 3.00				

Date	Mintage	F12	VF20	XF40	MS60	MS63
2007	—	—	—	0.40	1.50	—
2007	1,000	PF60 5.00				
2009	—	—	—	0.40	1.50	—
2009	1,000	PF60 5.00				
2011	—	—	—	0.40	1.50	—
2011	—	PF60 5.00				

KM# 16 10 LIPA
3.25 g., Brass Plated Steel, 20 mm. **Obv:** Denomination above crowned arms on half braid **Obv. Legend:** REPUBLIKA HRVATSKA **Rev:** Tobacco plant, date below **Rev. Legend:** NICOTIANA TABACUM **Edge:** Plain

Date	Mintage	F12	VF20	XF40	MS60	MS63
2002	2,000,000	—	—	0.80	2.50	—
2002	1,000	PF60 5.00				
2004	2,000,000	—	—	0.80	2.50	—
2004	2,000	PF60 4.50				
2006	—	—	—	0.80	2.50	—
2006	1,000	PF60 4.50				
2008	—	—	—	0.80	2.50	—
2008	1,000	PF60 4.50				
2010	—	—	—	0.80	2.50	—
2010	1,000	PF60 4.50				
2012	—	—	—	0.80	2.50	—
2012	—	PF60 4.50				

KM# 7 20 LIPA
2.90 g., Nickel Plated Steel, 18.5 mm. **Obv:** Denomination above crowned arms on half braid **Obv. Legend:** REPUBLIKA HRVATSKA **Rev:** Olive branch, date below **Rev. Legend:** MASLINA **Edge:** Plain

Date	Mintage	F12	VF20	XF40	MS60	MS63
2001	23,000,000	—	—	0.45	1.50	—
2001	1,000	PF60 5.00				
2003	12,500,000	—	—	0.45	1.50	—
2003	1,000	PF60 5.00				
2005	—	—	—	0.45	1.50	—
2005	2,000	PF60 5.00				
2007	—	—	—	0.45	1.50	—
2007	1,000	PF60 5.00				
2009	—	—	—	0.45	1.50	—
2009	—	PF60 5.00				
2011	—	—	—	0.45	1.50	—
2011	—	PF60 5.00				

KM# 17 20 LIPA
2.90 g., Nickel Plated Steel, 18.5 mm. **Obv:** Denomination above crowned arms on half braid **Obv. Legend:** REPUBLIKA HRVATSKA **Rev:** Olive branch, date below **Rev. Legend:** OLEA EUROPAEA **Edge:** Plain

Date	Mintage	F12	VF20	XF40	MS60	MS63
2002	2,000,000	—	—	0.80	2.50	—
2002	1,000	PF60 5.00				
2004	2,000,000	—	—	0.80	2.50	—
2004	2,000	PF60 4.50				
2006	—	—	—	0.80	2.50	—
2006	1,000	PF60 4.50				
2008	—	—	—	0.80	2.50	—
2008	1,000	PF60 4.50				
2010	—	—	—	0.80	2.50	—
2010	1,000	PF60 4.50				
2012	—	—	—	0.80	2.50	—
2012	—	PF60 4.50				

KM# 8 50 LIPA
3.65 g., Nickel Plated Steel, 20.5 mm. **Obv:** Denomination above crowned arms on half braid **Obv. Legend:** REPUBLIKA HRVATSKA **Rev:** Flowers, date below **Rev. Legend:** VELEBITSKA DEGENIJA **Edge:** Plain

Date	Mintage	F12	VF20	XF40	MS60	MS63
2001	5,500,000	—	—	0.60	1.50	—
2001	1,000	PF60 5.50				
2003	8,000,000	—	—	0.60	1.50	—
2003	1,000	PF60 5.50				
2005	—	—	—	0.60	1.50	—
2005	2,000	PF60 5.00				
2007	—	—	—	0.60	1.50	—
2007	1,000	PF60 5.00				
2009	—	—	—	0.60	1.50	—
2009	—	PF60 5.00				
2011	—	—	—	0.60	1.50	—
2011	—	PF60 5.00				

KM# 19 50 LIPA
3.65 g., Nickel Plated Steel, 20.5 mm. **Obv:** Denomination above crowned arms on half braid **Obv. Legend:** REPUBLIKA HRVATSKA **Rev:** Flowers, date below **Rev. Legend:** DEGENIA VELEBITICA **Edge:** Plain

Date	Mintage	F12	VF20	XF40	MS60	MS63
2002	2,000,000	—	—	0.80	2.50	—
2002	1,000	PF60 5.00				
2004	2,000,000	—	—	0.80	2.50	—
2004	2,000	PF60 4.50				
2006	—	—	—	0.80	2.50	—
2006	1,000	PF60 4.50				
2008	—	—	—	0.80	2.50	—
2008	1,000	PF60 4.50				
2010	—	—	—	0.80	2.50	—
2010	1,000	PF60 4.50				
2012	—	—	—	0.80	2.50	—
2012	—	PF60 4.50				

KM# 9.1 KUNA
5.00 g., Copper-Nickel-Zinc, 22.5 mm. **Obv:** Marten back of numeral, arms divide branches below **Obv. Legend:** REPUBLIKA HRVATSKA **Rev:** Nightingale left, two dates **Rev. Legend:** SLAVUJ **Edge:** Reeded

Date	Mintage	F12	VF20	XF40	MS60	MS63
2001	1,000,000	—	—	0.75	1.65	2.00
2001	1,000	PF60 4.50				
2003	2,000,000	—	—	0.75	1.65	2.00
2003	1,000	PF60 4.50				
2005	—	—	—	0.75	1.65	2.00
2005	2,000	PF60 4.50				
2007	—	—	—	0.75	1.65	2.00
2007	1,000	PF60 4.50				
2009	—	—	—	0.75	1.65	2.00
2009	—	PF60 4.50				
2011	—	—	—	0.75	1.65	2.00
2011	—	PF60 4.50				

KM# 9.2 KUNA
5.00 g., Copper-Nickel-Zinc, 22.5 mm. **Obv:** Crowned arms flanked by sprays, denomination above on marten **Rev:** Nightingale, left, '1994' above, date below **Edge:** Reeded

Date	Mintage	F12	VF20	XF40	MS60	MS63
2001	—	PF60 4.00				

KM# 20.1 KUNA
5.00 g., Copper-Nickel-Zinc, 22.5 mm. **Obv:** Marten back of numeral, arms divide branches below **Rev:** Nightingale left, date below **Rev. Legend:** Error spelling "LUSCINNIA" MEGARHYNCHOS **Edge:** Reeded **Note:** Formerly KM-20

Date	Mintage	F12	VF20	XF40	MS60	MS63
2002	—	—	—	—	—	2.00

KM# 20.2 KUNA
5.00 g., Copper-Nickel-Zinc, 22.5 mm. **Obv:** Marten back of numeral, arms divide branches below **Obv. Legend:** REPUBLIKA HRVATSKA **Rev:** Nightingale left, date below **Rev. Legend:** Correct spelling "LUSCINIA" MEGARHYNCHOS **Edge:** Reeded

Date	Mintage	F12	VF20	XF40	MS60	MS63
2002	1,000,000	—	—	1.00	3.00	—

Date	Mintage	F12	VF20	XF40	MS60	MS63
2002	1,000	PF60 5.00				
2006	—	—	—	1.00	3.00	—
2006	1,000	PF60 5.00				
2008	—	—	—	1.00	3.00	—
2008	1,000	PF60 5.00				
2010	—	—	—	1.00	3.00	—
2010	—	PF60 5.00				
2012	—	—	—	1.00	3.00	—
2012	—	PF60 5.00				

KM# 79 KUNA
5.00 g., Copper-Nickel-Zinc, 22.5 mm. **Subject:** 10th Anniversary of National Currency **Obv:** Crowned arms flanked by sprays, denomination above on marten **Obv. Legend:** REPUBLIKA HRVATSKA **Rev:** Nightingale left, date below **Rev. Legend:** MEGARHYNCHOS **Edge:** Reeded

Date	Mintage	F12	VF20	XF40	MS60	MS63
ND(2004)	30,000	—	—	1.00	3.00	—
ND(2004)	2,000	PF60 5.00				

KM# 10 2 KUNE
6.20 g., Copper Nickel Zinc, 24.6 mm. **Obv:** Marten back of numeral, arms divide branches below **Obv. Legend:** REPUBLIKA HRVATSKA **Rev:** Bluefin tuna right, date below **Rev. Legend:** TUNJ **Edge:** Reeded

Date	Mintage	F12	VF20	XF40	MS60	MS63
2001	1,250,000	—	—	1.00	2.00	—
2001	1,000	PF60 6.50				
2003	7,250,000	—	—	1.00	2.00	—
2003	1,000	PF60 6.50				
2005	—	—	—	1.00	2.00	—
2005	2,000	PF60 6.50				
2007	—	—	—	1.00	2.00	—
2007	1,000	PF60 6.50				
2009	—	—	—	1.00	2.00	—
2009	—	PF60 6.50				
2011	—	—	—	1.00	2.00	—
2011	—	PF60 6.50				

KM# 21 2 KUNE
6.20 g., Copper-Nickel-Zinc, 24.5 mm. **Obv:** Marten back of numeral, arms divide branches below **Obv. Legend:** REPUBLIKA HRVATSKA **Rev:** Bluefin tuna right, date below **Rev. Legend:** THUNNUS - THYNNUS **Edge:** Reeded

Date	Mintage	F12	VF20	XF40	MS60	MS63
2002	1,000,000	—	—	1.50	3.00	—
2002	1,000	PF60 6.00				
2004	2,000,000	—	—	1.50	3.00	—
2004	2,000	PF60 5.50				
2006	—	—	—	1.50	3.00	—
2006 (2007)	1,000	PF60 5.50				
2008	—	—	—	1.50	3.00	—
2008	1,000	PF60 5.50				
2010	—	—	—	1.50	3.00	—
2010	—	PF60 5.50				
2012	—	—	—	1.50	3.00	—
2012	—	PF60 5.50				

KM# 11 5 KUNA
7.45 g., Copper-Nickel-Zinc, 26.7 mm. **Obv:** Marten back of numeral, arms divide branches below **Obv. Legend:**

REPUBLIKA HRVATSKA **Rev:** Brown bear left, date below **Rev. Legend:** MRKI MEDVJED **Edge:** Reeded

Date	Mintage	F12	VF20	XF40	MS60	MS63
2001	17,300,000	—	—	1.50	5.00	10.00
2001	1,000	PF60 9.00				
2003	1,000,000	—	—	1.50	5.00	10.00
2003	1,000	PF60 9.00				
2005	—	—	—	1.50	5.00	10.00
2005	2,000	PF60 9.00				
2007	—	—	—	1.50	5.00	10.00
2007	1,000	PF60 9.00				
2009	—	—	—	1.50	5.00	10.00
2009	—	PF60 9.00				
2011	—	—	—	1.50	5.00	10.00
2011	—	PF60 9.00				

KM# 23 5 KUNA
7.45 g., Copper-Nickel-Zinc, 26.5 mm. **Obv:** Marten back of numeral, arms divide branches below **Obv. Legend:** REPUBLIKA HRVATSKA **Rev:** Brown bear left, date below **Rev. Legend:** URSUS ARCTOS **Edge:** Reeded

Date	Mintage	F12	VF20	XF40	MS60	MS63
2002	2,000,000	—	—	2.00	5.00	9.00
2002	1,000	PF60 9.00				
2004	2,000,000	—	—	2.00	5.00	9.00
2004	2,000	PF60 8.00				
2006	—	—	—	2.00	5.00	9.00
2006	1,000	PF60 8.00				
2008	—	—	—	2.00	5.00	9.00
2008	1,000	PF60 8.00				
2010	—	—	—	2.00	5.00	9.00
2010	—	PF60 8.00				
2012	—	—	—	2.00	5.00	9.00
2012	—	PF60 8.00				

KM# 66 25 KUNA
12.75 g., Bi-Metallic, 32 mm. **Subject:** 10th Anniversary of International Recognition **Obv:** Denomination in 3-D on outlined marten within circle, arms divide sprays below **Rev:** National map **Edge:** Plain **Shape:** 12-sided

Date	Mintage	F12	VF20	XF40	MS60	MS63
ND-2002	200,000	—	—	—	—	8.50

KM# 78 25 KUNA
12.75 g., Bi-Metallic, 32 mm. **Subject:** Croatian European Union Candidacy **Obv:** Denomination in 3-D on outlined marten within circle, arms divide sprays below **Rev:** Joined squares within circle of stars **Edge:** Plain **Shape:** 12-sided

Date	Mintage	F12	VF20	XF40	MS60	MS63
ND (2004)	30,000	—	—	—	—	10.00
ND (2004)	—	PF63 22.00	PF65 25.00			

KM# 93   25 KUNA
12.75 g., Bi-Metallic, 32 mm.   **Subject:** EBRD Annual Meeting, Zagreb **Obv:** Large value at center **Rev:** Stylized old and new skyline

Date	Mintage	F12	VF20	XF40	MS60	MS63
2010	—	—	—	—	—	10.00

KM# 94   25 KUNA
12.75 g., Bi-Metallic, 32 mm.   **Subject:** Croatian entry into European Union **Obv:** Shield and country names **Rev:** Group of 28 stars **Shape:** 12-sided

Date	Mintage	F12	VF20	XF40	MS60	MS63
2013	—	PF63 25.00		PF65 30.00		

KM# 83   150 KUNA
24.00 g., 0.925 Silver 0.7092 oz. ASW, 37 mm.   **Subject:** 2006 Winter Olympics - Italy **Obv:** National arms below denomination **Rev:** Slalom skiing

Date	Mintage	F12	VF20	XF40	MS60	MS63
ND-2006	15,000	PF63 35.00		PF65 40.00		

KM# 84   150 KUNA
24.00 g., 0.925 Silver 0.7092 oz. ASW, 37 mm.   **Subject:** 2006 World Soccer Championship - Germany **Obv:** National arms below denomination **Rev:** Soccer player

Date	Mintage	F12	VF20	XF40	MS60	MS63
ND-2006	50,000	PF63 30.00		PF65 35.00		

KM# 85   150 KUNA
24.00 g., 0.925 Silver 0.7092 oz. ASW, 37 mm.   **Subject:** 2006 World Soccer Championship - Germany **Obv:** National arms above denomination **Rev:** Vignette

Date	Mintage	F12	VF20	XF40	MS60	MS63
ND-2006	10,000	PF63 40.00		PF65 45.00		

KM# 86   150 KUNA
24.00 g., 0.925 Silver 0.7092 oz. ASW, 37 mm.   **Subject:** 150th Anniversary - Birth of Nikola Tesla **Obv:** National arms above induction motor and denomination **Rev:** Bust of Tesla

Date	Mintage	F12	VF20	XF40	MS60	MS63
ND-2006	5,000	PF63 47.00		PF65 50.00		

KM# 87   150 KUNA
24.00 g., 0.925 Silver 0.7092 oz. ASW, 37 mm.   **Subject:** 2008 Olympic Games - Peoples Republic of China **Obv:** National arms, value in laurel wreath **Rev:** T'ai-ho Tien gate in Beijing, athlete **Edge:** Plain **Edge Lettering:** Ag 925/1000 24 g 37 mm PP HNZ

Date	Mintage	F12	VF20	XF40	MS60	MS63
ND-2006	20,000	PF63 35.00		PF65 40.00		

KM# 88   150 KUNA
24.00 g., 0.925 Silver 0.7092 oz. ASW, 37 mm.   **Subject:** Ican Mestrovic **Obv:** Squares and shamrocks **Rev:** Female kneeling with Irish harp

Date	Mintage	F12	VF20	XF40	MS60	MS63
2007	4,000	—	—	—	—	45.00

KM# 89   150 KUNA
24.00 g., 0.925 Silver 0.7092 oz. ASW, 37 mm.   **Subject:** Benedikt Kotruljevic **Obv:** Pile of coins **Rev:** Bust right

Date	Mintage	F12	VF20	XF40	MS60	MS63
2007	10,000	—	—	—	—	40.00

KM# 90   150 KUNA
24.00 g., 0.925 Silver 0.7092 oz. ASW, 37 mm.   **Subject:** Historic Ships - Dubrovnik Karaka **Obv:** Sail within compass **Rev:** Ship

Date	Mintage	F12	VF20	XF40	MS60	MS63
2007	10,000	—	—	—	—	40.00

KM# 91   1000 KUNA
7.00 g., 0.986 Gold 0.2205 oz. AGW, 22 mm.   **Subject:** Andrija Monorovicic, 150th Anniversary of Birth **Obv:** Globe bisected showing layers **Rev:** Bust facing

Date	Mintage	F12	VF20	XF40	MS60	MS63
2007	2,000	—	—	—	—	425

KM# 92   1000 KUNA
7.00 g., 0.986 Gold 0.2205 oz. AGW, 22 mm.   **Subject:** Marin Drzic **Obv:** Shield flanked by comedy and tragedy masks **Rev:** Half-length figure right

Date	Mintage	F12	VF20	XF40	MS60	MS63
2008	2,000	—	—	—	—	425

KM# 95   1000 KUNA
7.00 g., 0.986 Gold 0.2205 oz. AGW, 22 mm.   **Subject:** Croatian entry into European Union **Obv:** Three stars and shield **Rev:** Group of 28 stars

Date	Mintage	F12	VF20	XF40	MS60	MS63
2013	—	PF63 425		PF65 450		

MINT SETS

KM#	Date	Mintage	Identification	Issue Price	Mkt Val
MS2	2002 (9)	—	KM#12, 14-17, 19, 20.1, 21, 23	—	25.00
MSX1	2003 (8)	30,000	X#Pn1-Pn8	—	30.00
MSX2	2004 (8)	10,000	X#Pn9-Pn16	—	30.00
MSX3	ND(2006) (8)	20,000	X#Pn17-Pn24.	—	30.00
MSX4	2006 (8)	10,000	X#Pn25-Pn32.	—	30.00
MSX5	2007 (8)	30,000	X#Pn1-Pn8.	—	30.00

PROOF SETS

KM#	Date	Mintage	Identification	Issue Price	Mkt Val
PS36	2001 (9)	—	KM#3-8, 9.2, 10, 11	—	45.00
PS37	2002 (9)	—	KM#12, 14-17, 19, 20.1, 21, 23	—	45.00
PS38	2003 (9)	—	KM#3-8, 9.1, 10, 11	—	45.00
PS39	2004 (9)	—	KM#12, 14-17, 19, 21, 23, 79	—	40.00
PS40	2005 (9)	—	KM#3-8, 9.1, 10-11	—	45.00
PS41	2006 (9)	—	KM#12, 14-17, 19, 20.2, 21, 23	—	40.00
PS42	2007 (9)	—	KM#3-8, 9.1, 10-11	—	45.00
PS43	2008 (9)	—	KM#12, 14-17, 19, 20.2, 21, 23	—	40.00
PS44	2009 (9)	—	KM#3-8, 9.1, 10-11.	—	45.00
PS45	2010 (9)	—	KM#12, 14-17, 19, 20.2, 21, 23	—	45.00
PS46	2011 (9)	—	KM#3-8, 9.1, 10-11.	—	45.00
PS47	2012 (9)	—	KM#12, 14-17, 19, 20.2, 21, 23.	—	45.00

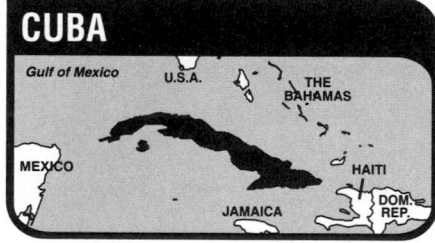

CUBA

The Republic of Cuba, situated at the northern edge of the Caribbean Sea about 90 miles (145 km.) south of Florida, has an area of 42,804 sq. mi. (110,860 sq. km.) and a population of *11.2 million. Capital: Havana. The Cuban economy is based on the cultivation and refining of sugar, which provides 80 percent of export earnings.

MINT MARK
Key - Havana, 1977-

MONETARY SYSTEM
100 Centavos = 1 Peso

SECOND REPUBLIC
1962 - Present
DECIMAL COINAGE

KM# 33.3   CENTAVO
0.75 g., Aluminum, 16.76 mm.   **Obv:** Cuban arms within wreath, denomination below **Rev:** Roman denomination within circle of star, date below **Edge:** Plain **Note:** Shield varieties exist.

Date	Mintage	F12	VF20	XF40	MS60	MS63
2001	—	—	—	0.40	0.80	1.75
2002	—	—	—	0.40	0.80	1.75
2003	—	—	—	0.40	0.80	1.75
2004	—	—	—	0.40	0.80	1.75
2005	—	—	—	0.40	0.80	1.75
2006	—	—	—	0.40	0.80	1.75
2007	—	—	—	0.40	0.80	1.75
2008	—	—	—	—	0.80	1.75
2010	—	—	—	—	0.80	1.75
2012	—	—	—	—	0.80	1.75

KM# 34   5 CENTAVOS
1.50 g., Aluminum, 21.21 mm.   **Obv:** National arms within wreath, denomination below **Rev:** Roman denomination within circle of star, date below **Note:** Shield varieties exist.

Date	Mintage	F12	VF20	XF40	MS60	MS63
2001	6,703,331	—	0.10	0.25	0.75	1.50
2002	14,830,000	—	—	0.25	0.75	1.50
	Note: High or low dates exist.					
2003	62,520,000	—	—	0.25	0.75	1.50
2004	62,520,000	—	—	0.25	0.75	1.50
2006	62,520,000	—	—	0.25	0.75	1.50
2007	62,520,000	—	—	0.25	0.75	1.50
2008	—	—	—	0.25	0.75	1.50
2009	—	—	—	0.25	0.75	1.50
2010	—	—	—	0.25	0.75	1.50

KM# 35.1   20 CENTAVOS
2.00 g., Aluminum, 24 mm.   **Obv:** Cuban arms within wreath, denomination below **Rev:** Roman denomination within circle of star, date below **Note:** Shield varieties exist.

Date	Mintage	F12	VF20	XF40	MS60	MS63
2002	25,000,000	—	0.50	1.00	2.00	4.00
2003	11,911,000	—	0.50	1.00	2.00	4.00
2005	—	—	0.50	1.00	2.00	4.00
2006	—	—	0.50	1.00	2.00	4.00
2007	—	—	0.50	1.00	2.00	4.00

KM# 35.2   20 CENTAVOS
2.00 g., Aluminum, 24 mm.   **Obv:** National arms, revised shield **Rev:** Roman denomination within circle of star

Date	Mintage	F12	VF20	XF40	MS60	MS63
2002	—	4.00	7.00	10.00	15.00	—
	Note: Large and small dates exist.					
2003	—	4.00	7.00	10.00	15.00	—
2005	—	4.00	7.00	10.00	15.00	—
2006	—	4.00	7.00	10.00	15.00	—

KM# 347   PESO
5.52 g., Brass Plated Steel, 24.5 mm.   **Subject:** Jose Marti **Obv:** National arms within wreath, denomination below **Rev:** Smaller Bust facing, denomination at left **Rev. Legend:** PATRIA O MUERTE **Note:** Rim varieties exist.

Date	Mintage	F12	VF20	XF40	MS60	MS63
2001	—	—	—	1.00	2.00	4.00
2002	—	—	—	1.00	2.00	4.00
2012	—	—	—	1.00	2.00	4.00

KM# 829   PESO
12.70 g., Nickel Plated Steel, 32.5 mm.   **Obv:** National arms **Rev:** Carpenter bird perched - multicolor **Rev. Legend:** FAUNA CUBANA - PAJERO CARPINTERO **Edge:** Plain

Date	Mintage	F12	VF20	XF40	MS60	MS63
2001	—	—	—	—	15.00	—

KM# 844   PESO
26.00 g., Copper-Nickel, 38 mm.   **Subject:** Bolivar, 175th Anniversary of Liberation **Rev:** Bust

Date	Mintage	F12	VF20	XF40	MS60	MS63
2001	—	—	—	—	15.00	

KM# 845 PESO
26.00 g., Copper-Nickel, 38 mm. **Subject:** Bolivar - 175th Anniversary of Liberation **Rev:** Birthplace

Date	Mintage	F12	VF20	XF40	MS60	MS63
2001	—	—	—	—	—	15.00

KM# 846 PESO
Copper-Nickel, 38 mm. **Subject:** Boliver, 175th Anniversary of Liberation **Rev:** Battle scene

Date	Mintage	F12	VF20	XF40	MS60	MS63
2001	—	—	—	—	—	15.00

KM# 847 PESO
12.70 g., Nickel Plated Steel, 32.5 mm. **Subject:** Cuban Fauna - Avellaneda Butterfly **Rev:** Butterfly

Date	Mintage	F12	VF20	XF40	MS60	MS63
2001	—	—	—	—	—	15.00

KM# 848 PESO
26.00 g., Copper-Nickel, 38 mm. **Subject:** Global Conference Three

Date	Mintage	F12	VF20	XF40	MS60	MS63
2001	200	—	—	—	—	50.00

KM# 849 PESO
26.00 g., Copper-Nickel, 38 mm. **Subject:** Monuments of Cuba **Rev:** Havana Cathedral

Date	Mintage	F12	VF20	XF40	MS60	MS63
2001	—	—	—	—	—	15.00

KM# 850 PESO
26.00 g., Copper-Nickel, 38 mm. **Subject:** Monuments of Cuba **Rev:** Trinidad Cathedral

Date	Mintage	F12	VF20	XF40	MS60	MS63
2001	—	—	—	—	—	15.00

KM# 851 PESO
Copper-Nickel, 38 mm. **Subject:** Monuments of Cuba **Rev:** Templete

Date	Mintage	F12	VF20	XF40	MS60	MS63
2001	—	—	—	—	—	15.00

KM# 852 PESO
26.00 g., Copper-Nickel, 38 mm. **Subject:** Playa Giron

Date	Mintage	F12	VF20	XF40	MS60	MS63
2001	—	—	—	—	—	15.00

KM# 830 PESO
12.70 g., Nickel Plated Steel, 32.5 mm. **Obv:** National arms **Rev:** Parrot perched - multicolor **Rev. Legend:** FAUNA CUBANA - COTORRA **Edge:** Plain

Date	Mintage	F12	VF20	XF40	MS60	MS63
2001	—	—	—	—	15.00	—

KM# 831 PESO
12.70 g., Nickel Plated Steel, 32.5 mm. **Obv:** National arms **Rev:** Pink orchid - multicolor **Rev. Legend:** FLORA CUBANA - ORQUIDEAS **Edge:** Plain

Date	Mintage	F12	VF20	XF40	MS60	MS63
2001	—	—	—	—	20.00	—

KM# 832 PESO
12.70 g., Nickel Plated Steel, 32.5 mm. **Obv:** National arms **Rev:** Yellow orchid - multicolor **Rev. Legend:** FLORA CUBANA - ORQUIDEAS **Edge:** Plain

Date	Mintage	F12	VF20	XF40	MS60	MS63
2001	—	—	—	—	20.00	—

KM# 833 PESO
12.70 g., Nickel Plated Steel, 32.5 mm. **Obv:** National arms **Rev:** White orchid - multicolor **Rev. Legend:** FLORA CUBANA - ORQUIDEAS **Edge:** Plain

Date	Mintage	F12	VF20	XF40	MS60	MS63
2001	—	—	—	—	20.00	—

KM# 853 PESO
26.00 g., Copper-Nickel, 38 mm. **Subject:** Federico Engels

Date	Mintage	F12	VF20	XF40	MS60	MS63
2002	—	—	—	—	—	15.00

KM# 854 PESO
26.00 g., Copper-Nickel, 38 mm. **Subject:** Lenin

Date	Mintage	F12	VF20	XF40	MS60	MS63
2002	—	—	—	—	—	15.00

KM# 855 PESO
26.00 g., Copper-Nickel, 38 mm. **Subject:** Mao Tse Tung

Date	Mintage	F12	VF20	XF40	MS60	MS63
2002	—	—	—	—	—	15.00

KM# 856 PESO
26.00 g., Copper-Nickel, 38 mm. **Subject:** Karl Marx

Date	Mintage	F12	VF20	XF40	MS60	MS63
2002	—	—	—	—	—	15.00

KM# 951 PESO
Copper-Nickel **Rev:** Birds in color

Date	Mintage	F12	VF20	XF40	MS60	MS63
2002	—	PF65 60.00				

KM# 857 PESO
26.00 g., Copper-Nickel, 38 mm. **Subject:** Che Guevara, 75th Anniversary of Birth

Date	Mintage	F12	VF20	XF40	MS60	MS63
2003	—	—	—	—	—	15.00

KM# 858 PESO
26.00 g., Copper-Nickel, 38 mm. **Subject:** Che Guevara, 75th Anniversary of Birth

Date	Mintage	F12	VF20	XF40	MS60	MS63
2003	—	—	—	—	—	15.00

KM# 953 PESO
20.00 g., Copper, 38 mm. **Subject:** Ernesto "Che" Guevara, 75th Birthday **Rev:** Bust

Date	Mintage	F12	VF20	XF40	MS60	MS63
2003	—	—	—	—	—	50.00

KM# 728 PESO
Silver **Subject:** Endangered Wildlife **Rev:** Crocodile

Date	Mintage	F12	VF20	XF40	MS60	MS63
2003	—	PF65 45.00				

KM# 859 PESO
26.00 g., Copper-Nickel, 38 mm. **Subject:** Fauna - Hawk Pilgrin

Date	Mintage	F12	VF20	XF40	MS60	MS63
2004	—	—	—	—	—	17.00

KM# 860 PESO
26.00 g., Copper-Nickel, 38 mm. **Subject:** Fauna Iberian Lynx

Date	Mintage	F12	VF20	XF40	MS60	MS63
2004	—	—	—	—	—	17.00

KM# 861 PESO
26.00 g., Copper-Nickel, 38 mm. **Subject:** Fauna - Imperial Eagle

Date	Mintage	F12	VF20	XF40	MS60	MS63
2004	—	—	—	—	—	17.00

KM# 862 PESO
26.00 g., Copper-Nickel, 38 mm. **Subject:** Fauna Lobo Gris

Date	Mintage	F12	VF20	XF40	MS60	MS63
2004	—	—	—	—	—	17.00

KM# 863 PESO
26.00 g., Copper-Nickel, 38 mm. **Subject:** Fauna - Oso Pards

Date	Mintage	F12	VF20	XF40	MS60	MS63
2004	—	—	—	—	—	17.00

KM# 864 PESO
26.00 g., Copper-Nickel, 38 mm. **Subject:** Fauna - Osprey

Date	Mintage	F12	VF20	XF40	MS60	MS63
2004	—	—	—	—	—	17.00

KM# 865 PESO
Copper-Nickel, 38 mm. **Subject:** Cuban Tobacco

Date	Mintage	F12	VF20	XF40	MS60	MS63
2005	—	—	—	—	—	17.00

KM# 866 PESO
26.00 g., Nickel Plated Steel, 32.8 mm. **Subject:** Tropical Fish - Pygoplites **Obv:** National arms within wreath **Rev:** Pyglopites dicanthus

Date	Mintage	F12	VF20	XF40	MS60	MS63
2005	—	—	—	—	—	15.00

KM# 867 PESO
26.00 g., Nickel Plated Steel, 32.8 mm. **Subject:** Tropical Fish - Zanclus **Obv:** National arms within wreath **Rev:** Zanclus canescens

Date	Mintage	F12	VF20	XF40	MS60	MS63
2005	—	—	—	—	—	15.00

KM# 868 PESO
26.00 g., Nickel Plated Steel, 32.8 mm. **Subject:** Tropical Fish - Rhinecanthus **Obv:** National arms

Date	Mintage	F12	VF20	XF40	MS60	MS63
2005	—	—	—	—	—	15.00

KM# 924 PESO
Nickel Plated Steel **Subject:** Cuban Tobacco, 500th Anniversary **Rev:** Tobacco traders before caraval sailing ship

Date	Mintage	F12	VF20	XF40	MS60	MS63
2005 Proof	—	—	—	—	—	10.00

KM# 869 PESO
26.00 g., Nickel Plated Steel, 38 mm. **Obv:** National arms within wreath **Rev:** Toucan

Date	Mintage	F12	VF20	XF40	MS60	MS63
2006	—	—	—	—	—	15.00

KM# 870 PESO
26.00 g., Copper-Nickel, 38 mm. **Subject:** 29th Summer Olympics

Date	Mintage	F12	VF20	XF40	MS60	MS63
2006	—	—	—	—	—	15.00

KM# 871 PESO
26.00 g., Copper-Nickel, 38 mm. **Subject:** Che Guevara, 40th Anniversary of his Death **Obv:** National arms within wreath **Rev:** Bust facing

Date	Mintage	F12	VF20	XF40	MS60	MS63
2007	—	—	—	—	—	15.00

KM# 873 PESO
26.00 g., Copper-Nickel **Subject:** Fauna - Buitre (Condor)

Date	Mintage	F12	VF20	XF40	MS60	MS63
2007	—	—	—	—	—	17.00

KM# 874 PESO
26.00 g., Copper-Nickel, 38 mm. **Subject:** Fauna - Burro

Date	Mintage	F12	VF20	XF40	MS60	MS63
2007	—	—	—	—	—	17.00

KM# 875 PESO
26.00 g., Copper-Nickel, 38 mm. **Subject:** Fauna - Cobra Montesa

Date	Mintage	F12	VF20	XF40	MS60	MS63
2007	—	—	—	—	—	17.00

KM# 876 PESO
26.00 g., Copper-Nickel **Subject:** Fauna - Gato Montes

Date	Mintage	F12	VF20	XF40	MS60	MS63
2007	—	—	—	—	—	17.00

KM# 877 PESO
26.00 g., Copper-Nickel, 38 mm. **Subject:** Fauma - Mastin Espanol

Date	Mintage	F12	VF20	XF40	MS60	MS63
2007	—	—	—	—	—	17.00

KM# 878 PESO
26.00 g., Copper-Nickel, 26 mm. **Subject:** Fauna - Urogallo

Date	Mintage	F12	VF20	XF40	MS60	MS63
2007	—	—	—	—	—	17.00

KM# 879 PESO
26.00 g., Copper-Nickel, 38 mm. **Subject:** Fortress - El Morro

Date	Mintage	F12	VF20	XF40	MS60	MS63
2007	—	—	—	—	—	17.00

KM# 880 PESO
26.00 g., Copper-Nickel, 38 mm. **Subject:** Fortress - La Fuerza

Date	Mintage	F12	VF20	XF40	MS60	MS63
2007	—	—	—	—	—	15.00

KM# 881 PESO
26.00 g., Copper-Nickel, 38 mm. **Subject:** Fortress - La Punta

Date	Mintage	F12	VF20	XF40	MS60	MS63
2007	—	—	—	—	—	15.00

KM# 882 PESO
26.00 g., Copper-Nickel, 38 mm. **Subject:** Garibaldi

Date	Mintage	F12	VF20	XF40	MS60	MS63
2007	—	—	—	—	—	15.00

KM# 883 PESO
26.00 g., Copper-Nickel, 38 mm. **Subject:** Santa Ana Ship

Date	Mintage	F12	VF20	XF40	MS60	MS63
2007	—	—	—	—	—	15.00

KM# 884 PESO
26.00 g., Copper-Nickel, 38 mm. **Subject:** Sputnik

Date	Mintage	F12	VF20	XF40	MS60	MS63
2007	—	—	—	—	—	15.00

KM# 871a PESO
26.00 g., Copper, 38 mm. **Obv:** Che Guevara, 40th Anniversary of his Death

Date	Mintage	F12	VF20	XF40	MS60	MS63
2007	—	—	—	—	—	15.00

KM# 901 PESO
38.00 g., Copper-Nickel, 38 mm. **Subject:** Ship - Principe Asturias

Date	Mintage	F12	VF20	XF40	MS60	MS63
2008	—	—	—	—	15.00	—

KM# 902 PESO
26.00 g., Copper-Nickel, 38 mm. **Subject:** Ship San Carlos

Date	Mintage	F12	VF20	XF40	MS60	MS63
2008	—	—	—	—	15.00	—

KM# 903 PESO
38.00 g., Copper-Nickel, 38 mm. **Subject:** Ship- San Hermene

Date	Mintage	F12	VF20	XF40	MS60	MS63
2008	—	—	—	—	—	15.00

KM# 907 PESO
41.00 g., Copper, 45 mm. **Subject:** Revolution, 50th Anniversary **Obv:** National arms within wreath **Rev:** Five scenes in medallions

Date	Mintage	F12	VF20	XF40	MS60	MS63
2009 Antique patina	2,009	—	—	—	—	15.00

KM# 908 PESO
26.00 g., Copper-Nickel, 38 mm. **Subject:** Fidel & Raul Castro **Obv:** National arms within wreath

Date	Mintage	F12	VF20	XF40	MS60	MS63
2009	5,000	—	—	—	—	15.00

KM# 910 PESO
26.00 g., Copper-Nickel, 38 mm. **Subject:** Manatee

Date	Mintage	F12	VF20	XF40	MS60	MS63
2009	—	—	—	—	—	15.00

KM# 956 PESO
Gold AGW, 45 mm. **Subject:** Revolution, 50th Anniversary

Date	Mintage	F12	VF20	XF40	MS60	MS63
2009	50	PF65 2,000				

KM# 908a PESO
26.00 g., Copper, 38 mm. **Subject:** Fidel and Raul Castro

Date	Mintage	F12	VF20	XF40	MS60	MS63
2009	5,000	—	—	—	—	15.00

KM# 954 PESO
26.00 g., Copper-Nickel, 38 mm. **Obv:** National arms within wreath **Rev:** Castro and Hemingway

Date	Mintage	F12	VF20	XF40	MS60	MS63
2010	5,000	—	—	—	—	15.00

KM# 954a PESO
26.00 g., Copper, 38 mm. **Obv:** National arms within wreath **Rev:** Castro and Hemingway

Date	Mintage	F12	VF20	XF40	MS60	MS63
2010	5,000	—	—	—	—	15.00

KM# 954b PESO
20.00 g., 0.999 Silver 0.6382 oz. ASW, 38 mm. **Obv:** National arms within wreath **Rev:** Castro and Hemingway

Date	Mintage	F12	VF20	XF40	MS60	MS63
2010	5,000	PF65 45.00				

KM# 955 PESO
26.00 g., Copper-Nickel, 38 mm. **Subject:** Independence of the Americas, 200th Anniversary **Obv:** National arms at left and legend at right **Rev:** Sunburst and map of the Americas

Date	Mintage	F12	VF20	XF40	MS60	MS63
2011	—	—	—	—	—	15.00

KM# 955a PESO
26.00 g., Copper, 38 mm. **Subject:** Independence of the Americas, 200th Anniversary **Obv:** National arms within wreath at left, legend at right **Rev:** Sunburst and map of the Americas

Date	Mintage	F12	VF20	XF40	MS60	MS63
2011	—	—	—	—	—	15.00

KM# 955b PESO
20.00 g., 0.999 Silver 0.6382 oz. ASW, 38 mm. **Subject:** Independence of the Americas, 200th Anniversary **Obv:** National arms at left, legend at right **Rev:** Sunburst and map of the Americas

Date	Mintage	F12	VF20	XF40	MS60	MS63
2011	1,810	PF65 45.00				

KM# 346a 3 PESOS
8.00 g., Nickel Plated Steel, 26.5 mm. **Obv:** National arms within wreath, denomination below **Rev:** Head facing, date below **Note:** Shield varieties exist.

Date	Mintage	F12	VF20	XF40	MS60	MS63
2002	—	—	—	2.50	5.00	7.00

KM# 739 5 PESOS
1.24 g., Gold AGW, 14 mm. **Subject:** Wonders of the Ancient World **Obv:** Cuban arms **Rev:** Ancient lighthouse of Alexandria

Date	Mintage	F12	VF20	XF40	MS60	MS63
2005	5,000	PF65 85.00				

KM# 740 5 PESOS
1.24 g., Gold AGW, 14 mm. **Subject:** Wonders of the Ancient World **Obv:** Cuban arms **Rev:** Colossus of Rhodes

Date	Mintage	F12	VF20	XF40	MS60	MS63
2005	5,000	PF65 75.00				

KM# 741 5 PESOS
1.24 g., Gold AGW, 14 mm. **Subject:** Wonders of the Ancient World **Obv:** Cuban arms **Rev:** Hanging Gardens of Babylon

Date	Mintage	F12	VF20	XF40	MS60	MS63
2005	5,000	PF65 75.00				

KM# 742 5 PESOS
1.24 g., Gold AGW, 14 mm. **Subject:** Wonders of the Ancient World **Obv:** Cuban arms **Rev:** Egyptian Pyramids

Date	Mintage	F12	VF20	XF40	MS60	MS63
2005	5,000	PF65 75.00				

KM# 743 5 PESOS
1.24 g., Gold AGW, 14 mm. **Subject:** Wonders of the Ancient World **Obv:** Cuban arms **Rev:** Temple of Artemis

Date	Mintage	F12	VF20	XF40	MS60	MS63
2005	5,000	PF65 75.00				

KM# 744 5 PESOS
1.24 g., Gold AGW, 14 mm. **Subject:** Wonders of the Ancient World **Obv:** Cuban arms **Rev:** Statue of Jupiter

Date	Mintage	F12	VF20	XF40	MS60	MS63
2005	5,000	PF65 75.00				

KM# 745 5 PESOS
1.24 g., Gold AGW, 14 mm. **Subject:** Wonders of the Ancient World **Obv:** Cuban arms **Rev:** Mausoleum of Halicarnas

Date	Mintage	F12	VF20	XF40	MS60	MS63
2005	5,000	PF65 75.00				

KM# 746 5 PESOS
1.24 g., Gold AGW, 14 mm. **Obv:** Cuban arms **Rev:** Cortes, Montezuma and Aztec Pyramid

Date	Mintage	F12	VF20	XF40	MS60	MS63
2005	15,000	PF65 75.00				

KM# 885 5 PESOS
12.00 g., Silver, 30 mm. **Subject:** Che Guevara, 40th Anniversary of his Death

Date	Mintage	F12	VF20	XF40	MS60	MS63
2007	—	PF63 40.00	PF65 45.00			

KM# 762 10 PESOS
31.10 g., 0.999 Silver 0.9926 oz. ASW, 38 mm. **Obv:** Cuban arms **Rev:** Two Bee hummingbirds

Date	Mintage	F12	VF20	XF40	MS60	MS63
2001	20,000	PF63 35.00	PF65 40.00			

KM# 763 10 PESOS
20.00 g., 0.999 Silver 0.6382 oz. ASW, 38 mm. **Subject:** Third Globalization Conference **Obv:** Cuban arms **Rev:** World map

Date	Mintage	F12	VF20	XF40	MS60	MS63
2001	100	PF65 200				

KM# 765 10 PESOS
31.10 g., 0.999 Silver 0.9926 oz. ASW, 38 mm. **Subject:** 106th Anniversary - Jose Marti's **Obv:** Cuban arms **Rev:** Monument

Date	Mintage	F12	VF20	XF40	MS60	MS63
2001	—	PF63 40.00	PF65 45.00			

KM# 766 10 PESOS
15.00 g., 0.999 Silver 0.4787 oz. ASW, 35 mm. **Subject:** Cuban Fauna **Obv:** Cuban arms **Rev:** Red-splashed Sulphur butterfly

Date	Mintage	F12	VF20	XF40	MS60	MS63
2001	—	PF65 35.00				

KM# 767 10 PESOS
15.00 g., 0.999 Silver 0.4787 oz. ASW, 35 mm. **Subject:** Cuban Fauna **Obv:** Cuban arms **Rev:** Cuban Parrot

Date	Mintage	F12	VF20	XF40	MS60	MS63
2001	—	PF65 35.00				

KM# 768 10 PESOS
15.00 g., 0.999 Silver 0.4787 oz. ASW, 35 mm. **Obv:** National arms **Rev:** Cuban (Green) woodpecker

Date	Mintage	F12	VF20	XF40	MS60	MS63
2001	—	PF65 35.00				

KM# 769 10 PESOS
15.00 g., 0.999 Silver 0.4787 oz. ASW, 35 mm. **Obv:** Cuban arms **Rev:** Multicolor white orchid

Date	Mintage	F12	VF20	XF40	MS60	MS63
2001	—	PF65 30.00				

KM# 770 10 PESOS
15.00 g., 0.999 Silver 0.4787 oz. ASW, 35 mm. **Subject:** Cuban Flora **Obv:** Cuban arms **Rev:** Multicolor yellow orchid

Date	Mintage	F12	VF20	XF40	MS60	MS63
2001	—	PF65 30.00				

KM# 771 10 PESOS
15.00 g., 0.999 Silver 0.4787 oz. ASW, 35 mm. **Subject:** Cuban Flora **Obv:** Cuban arms **Rev:** Multicolor pink orchid

Date	Mintage	F12	VF20	XF40	MS60	MS63
2001	—	PF65 30.00				

KM# 772 10 PESOS
31.10 g., 0.999 Silver 0.9926 oz. ASW, 42 mm. **Obv:** Cuban arms **Rev:** Multicolor Santa Maria

Date	Mintage	F12	VF20	XF40	MS60	MS63
2001	—	PF65 50.00				

KM# 773 10 PESOS
15.00 g., 0.999 Silver 0.4787 oz. ASW, 35 mm. **Subject:** World Cup Soccer Champions **Obv:** Cuban arms **Rev:** Soccer player and stadium

Date	Mintage	F12	VF20	XF40	MS60	MS63
2001	—	PF63 25.00 PF65 30.00				

KM# 774 10 PESOS
20.00 g., 0.999 Silver 0.6382 oz. ASW, 38 mm. **Subject:** Cuban Monuments **Obv:** Cuban arms **Rev:** Trinidad street view

Date	Mintage	F12	VF20	XF40	MS60	MS63
2001	—	PF63 35.00 PF65 40.00				

KM# 775 10 PESOS
20.00 g., 0.999 Silver 0.6382 oz. ASW, 38 mm. **Subject:** Cuban Monuments **Obv:** Cuban arms **Rev:** Havana Cathedral

Date	Mintage	F12	VF20	XF40	MS60	MS63
2001	—	PF63 35.00 PF65 40.00				

KM# 776 10 PESOS
20.00 g., 0.999 Silver 0.6382 oz. ASW, 38 mm. **Subject:** Cuban Monuments **Obv:** Cuban arms **Rev:** Template building

Date	Mintage	F12	VF20	XF40	MS60	MS63
2001	—	PF63 35.00 PF65 40.00				

KM# 777 10 PESOS
31.10 g., 0.999 Silver 0.9926 oz. ASW, 38 mm. **Obv:** Cuban arms **Rev:** Bolivar standing at his birthplace

Date	Mintage	F12	VF20	XF40	MS60	MS63
2001	—	PF63 45.00 PF65 50.00				

KM# 778 10 PESOS
31.10 g., 0.999 Silver 0.9926 oz. ASW, 38 mm. **Obv:** Cuban arms **Rev:** Bolivar and map of South America

Date	Mintage	F12	VF20	XF40	MS60	MS63
2001	—	PF63 45.00 PF65 50.00				

KM# 779 10 PESOS
31.10 g., 0.999 Silver 0.9926 oz. ASW, 38 mm. **Subject:** 180th Anniversary of the Battle of Carabobo **Obv:** Cuban arms **Rev:** Bolivar leading troops

Date	Mintage	F12	VF20	XF40	MS60	MS63
2001	—	PF63 45.00 PF65 50.00				

KM# 828 10 PESOS
20.00 g., 0.999 Silver 0.6382 oz. ASW **Subject:** XVII World Soccer Championship - Korea and Japan 2002 **Obv:** National arms

Date	Mintage	F12	VF20	XF40	MS60	MS63
2001 proof	—	PF65 45.00				

KM# 764 10 PESOS
20.00 g., 0.999 Silver 0.6382 oz. ASW, 38 mm. **Subject:** 40th Anniversary - Battle of Giron **Obv:** Cuban arms **Rev:** Soldiers

on tank

Date	Mintage	F12	VF20	XF40	MS60	MS63
2001	—					30.00
2001	3,000	PF63 40.00	PF65 45.00			

KM# 734 10 PESOS
20.00 g., 0.999 Silver 0.6382 oz. ASW, 37.9 mm. **Subject:** Olympics **Obv:** Cuban arms **Rev:** Runner and ancient ruins **Edge:** Reeded

Date	Mintage	F12	VF20	XF40	MS60	MS63
2002	—	PF65 38.00				

KM# 780 10 PESOS
20.00 g., 0.999 Silver 0.6382 oz. ASW, 38 mm. **Subject:** World Cup Soccer Champions **Obv:** Cuban arms **Rev:** Soccer player and map above "CHILE 1962

Date	Mintage	F12	VF20	XF40	MS60	MS63
2002	—	PF63 32.00	PF65 38.00			

KM# 781 10 PESOS
20.00 g., 0.999 Silver 0.6382 oz. ASW, 38 mm. **Subject:** World Cup Soccer Champions **Obv:** Cuban arms **Rev:** Soccer player and Cuauhtemoc head below MEXICO 1970

Date	Mintage	F12	VF20	XF40	MS60	MS63
2002	—	PF63 32.00	PF65 38.00			

KM# 782 10 PESOS
20.00 g., 0.999 Silver 0.6382 oz. ASW, 38 mm. **Obv:** Cuban arms **Rev:** Vasco De Gama and ship

Date	Mintage	F12	VF20	XF40	MS60	MS63
2002	—	PF63 35.00	PF65 40.00			

KM# 783 10 PESOS
20.00 g., 0.999 Silver 0.6382 oz. ASW, 38 mm. **Obv:** Cuban arms **Rev:** Americo Vespucio and ship

Date	Mintage	F12	VF20	XF40	MS60	MS63
2002	—	PF63 35.00	PF65 40.00			

KM# 784 10 PESOS
31.10 g., 0.999 Silver 0.9926 oz. ASW, 38 mm. **Subject:** Leaders of Communism **Obv:** Cuban arms **Rev:** Head of Mao Tse Tung left

Date	Mintage	F12	VF20	XF40	MS60	MS63
2002	—	PF65 50.00				

KM# 785 10 PESOS
31.10 g., 0.999 Silver 0.9926 oz. ASW, 38 mm. **Subject:** Leaders of Communism **Obv:** Cuban arms **Rev:** Head of Karl Marx 3/4 left

Date	Mintage	F12	VF20	XF40	MS60	MS63
2002	—	PF65 50.00				

KM# 786 10 PESOS
31.10 g., 0.999 Silver 0.9926 oz. ASW, 38 mm. **Subject:** Leaders of Communism **Obv:** Cuban arms **Rev:** Head of Vladimir Lenin right

Date	Mintage	F12	VF20	XF40	MS60	MS63
2002	—	PF65 60.00				

KM# 787 10 PESOS
31.10 g., 0.999 Silver 0.9926 oz. ASW, 38 mm. **Subject:** Leaders of Communism **Obv:** Cuban arms **Rev:** Head of Federico Engels 3/4 right

Date	Mintage	F12	VF20	XF40	MS60	MS63
2002	—	PF65 50.00				

KM# 788 10 PESOS
27.00 g., 0.999 Silver 0.8616 oz. ASW, 40 mm. **Subject:** IBERO-AMERICA Series **Obv:** Circle of arms around Cuban arms **Rev:** Santisima Trinidad ship

Date	Mintage	F12	VF20	XF40	MS60	MS63
2002	14,000	PF63 40.00	PF65 45.00			

KM# 952 10 PESOS
27.00 g., 0.925 Silver 0.7978 oz. ASW **Obv:** National Arms surrounded by 10 older arms **Rev:** Santisima Trinidad, sailing ship

Date	Mintage	F12	VF20	XF40	MS60	MS63
2002	—	PF63 50.00	PF65 55.00			

KM# 789 10 PESOS
31.10 g., 0.999 Silver 0.9926 oz. ASW, 38 mm. **Subject:** Jose Marti's 150th Birthday **Obv:** Cuban arms **Rev:** Numbered infield behind head right

Date	Mintage	F12	VF20	XF40	MS60	MS63
2003	150	PF65 150				

KM# 790 10 PESOS
20.00 g., 0.999 Silver 0.6382 oz. ASW, 38 mm. **Obv:** Cuban arms **Rev:** Ferdinand Magellan, ship, and astrolab

Date	Mintage	F12	VF20	XF40	MS60	MS63
2003	5,000	PF63 35.00	PF65 40.00			

KM# 791 10 PESOS
20.00 g., 0.999 Silver 0.6382 oz. ASW, 38 mm. **Obv:** Cuban arms **Rev:** Sailing ship, Sovereign of the Seas

Date	Mintage	F12	VF20	XF40	MS60	MS63
2003	5,000	PF63 35.00	PF65 40.00			

KM# 792 10 PESOS
20.00 g., 0.999 Silver 0.6382 oz. ASW, 38 mm. **Obv:** Cuban arms **Rev:** Che Guevara, 75th Anniversary of Birth

Date	Mintage	F12	VF20	XF40	MS60	MS63
2003	5,000	PF63 35.00	PF65 40.00			

KM# 793 10 PESOS
31.10 g., 0.999 Silver 0.9925 oz. ASW, 38 mm. **Subject:** World Cup Soccer - Germany 2006 **Obv:** Cuban arms **Rev:** 5 soccer players

Date	Mintage	F12	VF20	XF40	MS60	MS63
2003	50,000	PF63 40.00	PF65 45.00			

KM# 794 10 PESOS
20.00 g., 0.999 Silver 0.6382 oz. ASW, 38 mm. **Subject:** Endangered Wildlife **Obv:** Cuban arms **Rev:** Cuban Crocodile

Date	Mintage	F12	VF20	XF40	MS60	MS63
2003	5,000	PF65 45.00				

KM# 795 10 PESOS
20.00 g., 0.999 Silver 0.6382 oz. ASW, 38 mm. **Subject:** Endangered Wildlife **Obv:** Cuban arms **Rev:** Ocelot

Date	Mintage	F12	VF20	XF40	MS60	MS63
2003	5,000	PF65 45.00				

KM# 727 10 PESOS
Silver **Subject:** Endangered wildlife **Rev:** Iguana

Date	Mintage	F12	VF20	XF40	MS60	MS63
2003	—	PF65 40.00				

KM# 921 10 PESOS
Silver **Subject:** World Cup, Germany **Rev:** Five soccer players

Date	Mintage	F12	VF20	XF40	MS60	MS63
2003	50,000	PF65 55.00				

KM# 796 10 PESOS
20.00 g., 0.999 Silver 0.6382 oz. ASW, 38 mm. **Obv:** Cuban arms **Rev:** John Cabot's portrait in cameo above ship

Date	Mintage	F12	VF20	XF40	MS60	MS63
2004	5,000	PF63 35.00	PF65 40.00			

KM# 797 10 PESOS
15.00 g., 0.999 Silver 0.4787 oz. ASW, 35 mm. **Subject:** Hippocampus Kuda **Obv:** Cuban arms **Rev:** Spotted seahorse

Date	Mintage	F12	VF20	XF40	MS60	MS63
2004	5,000	PF65 45.00				

KM# 798 10 PESOS
20.00 g., 0.999 Silver 0.6382 oz. ASW, 38 mm. **Obv:** Cuban arms **Rev:** Murphy's Petrel bird on rock

Date	Mintage	F12	VF20	XF40	MS60	MS63
2004	5,000	PF65 45.00				

KM# 799 10 PESOS
20.00 g., 0.999 Silver 0.6382 oz. ASW, 38 mm. **Obv:** Cuban arms **Rev:** Cuban Rock Iguana on branch

Date	Mintage	F12	VF20	XF40	MS60	MS63
2004	5,000	PF65 45.00				

KM# 800 10 PESOS
31.10 g., 0.999 Silver 0.9925 oz. ASW, 38 mm. **Obv:** Cuban

arms **Rev:** Imperial eagle perched on branch

Date	Mintage	F12	VF20	XF40	MS60	MS63
2004	1,000	PF65 58.00				

KM# 801 10 PESOS
31.10 g., 0.999 Silver 0.9925 oz. ASW, 38 mm. **Obv:** Cuban arms **Rev:** Bearded vulture in flight

Date	Mintage	F12	VF20	XF40	MS60	MS63
2004	1,000	PF65 58.00				

KM# 802 10 PESOS
31.10 g., 0.999 Silver 0.9925 oz. ASW, 38 mm. **Obv:** Cuban arms **Rev:** Iberian Lynx

Date	Mintage	F12	VF20	XF40	MS60	MS63
2004	1,000	PF65 58.00				

KM# 803 10 PESOS
31.10 g., 0.999 Silver 0.9925 oz. ASW, 38 mm. **Obv:** Cuban arms **Rev:** 2 grey wolves

Date	Mintage	F12	VF20	XF40	MS60	MS63
2004	1,000	PF65 60.00				

KM# 804 10 PESOS
31.10 g., 0.999 Silver 0.9925 oz. ASW, 38 mm. **Obv:** Cuban arms **Rev:** Brown bear

Date	Mintage	F12	VF20	XF40	MS60	MS63
2004	—	—	—	—	—	40.00
2004	1,000	PF65 60.00				

KM# 805 10 PESOS
31.10 g., 0.999 Silver 0.9925 oz. ASW, 38 mm. **Obv:** Cuban arms **Rev:** Peregrine Falcon perches on branch

Date	Mintage	F12	VF20	XF40	MS60	MS63
2004	1,000	PF65 60.00				

KM# 806 10 PESOS
20.00 g., 0.999 Silver 0.6382 oz. ASW, 38 mm. **Subject:** Monuments of Cuba **Obv:** Cuban arms **Rev:** University of Havana building

Date	Mintage	F12	VF20	XF40	MS60	MS63
2004	1,500	PF63 47.00	PF65 50.00			

KM# 807 10 PESOS
20.00 g., 0.999 Silver 0.6382 oz. ASW, 38 mm. **Subject:** Monuments of Cuba **Obv:** Cuban arms **Rev:** Fountain of India

Date	Mintage	F12	VF20	XF40	MS60	MS63
2004	1,500	PF63 47.00	PF65 50.00			

KM# 808 10 PESOS
20.00 g., 0.999 Silver 0.6382 oz. ASW, 38 mm. **Subject:** Monuments of Cuba **Obv:** Cuban arms **Rev:** Plaza building

Date	Mintage	F12	VF20	XF40	MS60	MS63
2004	1,500	PF63 47.00	PF65 50.00			

KM# 923 10 PESOS
15.00 g., 0.999 Silver 0.4787 oz. ASW **Rev:** Sea Horse and coral reef in color

Date	Mintage	F12	VF20	XF40	MS60	MS63
2004	—	PF65 35.00				

KM# 809 10 PESOS
27.00 g., 0.925 Silver 0.7978 oz. ASW, 40 mm. **Obv:** Cuban arms within circle of arms **Rev:** Portions of the old Havana Wall

Date	Mintage	F12	VF20	XF40	MS60	MS63
2005	12,000	PF63 60.00	PF65 70.00			

KM# 810 10 PESOS
20.00 g., 0.999 Silver 0.6382 oz. ASW, 38 mm. **Subject:** Tobacco **Obv:** Cuban arms **Rev:** Indian showing tobacco to Columbus, ship in background

Date	Mintage	F12	VF20	XF40	MS60	MS63
2005	2,000	PF65 50.00				

KM# 811 10 PESOS
20.00 g., 0.925 Silver 0.591 oz. ASW, 38 mm. **Subject:** Columbus' Ships **Obv:** Cuban arms **Rev:** The Santa Maria under sail

Date	Mintage	F12	VF20	XF40	MS60	MS63
2005	5,000	PF63 40.00	PF65 42.00			

KM# 812 10 PESOS
20.00 g., 0.925 Silver 0.591 oz. ASW, 38 mm. **Subject:** Columbus' Ships **Obv:** Cuban arms **Rev:** The Nina under sail

Date	Mintage	F12	VF20	XF40	MS60	MS63
2005	5,000	PF63 40.00	PF65 42.00			

KM# 813 10 PESOS
20.00 g., 0.925 Silver 0.591 oz. ASW, 38 mm. **Subject:** Columbus' Ships **Obv:** Cuban arms **Rev:** The Pinta under sail

Date	Mintage	F12	VF20	XF40	MS60	MS63
2005	5,000	PF63 40.00	PF65 42.00			

KM# 814 10 PESOS
20.00 g., 0.925 Silver 0.591 oz. ASW, 38 mm. **Obv:** Cuban arms **Rev:** Cuban Solenodon on branch

Date	Mintage	F12	VF20	XF40	MS60	MS63
2005	5,000	PF65 42.00				

KM# 815 10 PESOS
15.00 g., 0.999 Silver 0.4787 oz. ASW, 35 mm. **Obv:** Cuban arms **Rev:** Multicolor Solenodon on branch

Date	Mintage	F12	VF20	XF40	MS60	MS63
2005	5,000	PF65 40.00				

KM# 816 10 PESOS
15.00 g., 0.925 Silver 0.4432 oz. ASW, 35 mm. **Subject:** Tropical Fish **Obv:** Cuban arms **Rev:** Picassofish (triggerfish)

Date	Mintage	F12	VF20	XF40	MS60	MS63
2005	2,000	PF65 40.00				

KM# 817 10 PESOS
15.00 g., 0.925 Silver 0.4432 oz. ASW, 35 mm. **Subject:** Tropical Fish **Obv:** Cuban arms **Rev:** Moorish Idol fish

Date	Mintage	F12	VF20	XF40	MS60	MS63
2005	2,000	PF65 40.00				

KM# 818 10 PESOS
15.00 g., 0.925 Silver 0.4432 oz. ASW, 35 mm. **Subject:**
Tropical Fish **Obv:** Cuban arms **Rev:** Regal Angel fish

Date	Mintage	F12	VF20	XF40	MS60	MS63
2005	2,000	PF65 40.00				

KM# 819 10 PESOS
20.00 g., 0.999 Silver 0.6382 oz. ASW, 38 mm. **Subject:** Don
Quijote, 400th Anniversary **Obv:** Cuban arms **Rev:** Don Quijote
and Sancho looking at two windmills

Date	Mintage	F12	VF20	XF40	MS60	MS63
2005	5,000	PF63 45.00	PF65 50.00			

KM# 820 10 PESOS
31.10 g., 0.999 Silver 0.9925 oz. ASW, 38 mm. **Subject:**
Maximo Gomez Centennial of Death **Obv:** Cuban arms **Rev:**
Bust 3/4 left, numbered behind neck

Date	Mintage	F12	VF20	XF40	MS60	MS63
2005	100	PF65 220				

KM# 925 10 PESOS
27.00 g., 0.925 Silver 0.7978 oz. ASW, 40 mm. **Subject:** Ibero
American sites **Rev:** Old City Wall

Date	Mintage	F12	VF20	XF40	MS60	MS63
2005	—	PF63 50.00	PF65 55.00			

KM# 821 10 PESOS
20.00 g., 0.925 Silver 0.591 oz. ASW, 38 mm. **Subject:** XXIX
Olympics **Obv:** Cuban arms **Rev:** Baseball player with bat,
baseball background

Date	Mintage	F12	VF20	XF40	MS60	MS63
2006	15,000	PF63 35.00	PF65 40.00			

KM# 886 10 PESOS
20.00 g., Silver, 38 mm. **Subject:** Che Guevara, 40th
Anniversary of his Death

Date	Mintage	F12	VF20	XF40	MS60	MS63
2007	—	PF65 40.00				

KM# 887 10 PESOS
20.00 g., Silver, 38 mm. **Subject:** Fauna - Buitre (Condor)

Date	Mintage	F12	VF20	XF40	MS60	MS63
2007	—	PF65 40.00				

KM# 888 10 PESOS
20.00 g., Silver **Subject:** Fauna Burro

Date	Mintage	F12	VF20	XF40	MS60	MS63
2007	—	PF65 40.00				

KM# 889 10 PESOS
20.00 g., Silver, 38 mm. **Subject:** Fauna - Cobra Montesa

Date	Mintage	F12	VF20	XF40	MS60	MS63
2007	—	PF65 45.00				

KM# 890 10 PESOS
20.00 g., Silver, 38 mm. **Subject:** Fauna - Gato Montes

Date	Mintage	F12	VF20	XF40	MS60	MS63
2007	—					

KM# 891 10 PESOS
20.00 g., Silver, 38 mm. **Subject:** Fauna - Mastin Espanol

Date	Mintage	F12	VF20	XF40	MS60	MS63
2007	—	PF65 40.00				

KM# 892 10 PESOS
20.00 g., Silver, 38 mm. **Subject:** Fauna - Urogallo

Date	Mintage	F12	VF20	XF40	MS60	MS63
2007	—	PF65 40.00				

KM# 893 10 PESOS
20.00 g., Silver, 38 mm. **Subject:** Fortress - El Morro

Date	Mintage	F12	VF20	XF40	MS60	MS63
2007	—	PF65 40.00				

KM# 894 10 PESOS
20.00 g., Silver, 38 mm. **Subject:** Fortress - La Fuerza

Date	Mintage	F12	VF20	XF40	MS60	MS63
2007	—	PF65 40.00				

KM# 895 10 PESOS
20.00 g., Silver, 38 mm. **Subject:** La Punta

Date	Mintage	F12	VF20	XF40	MS60	MS63
2007	—	PF65 40.00				

KM# 896 10 PESOS
20.00 g., Silver, 38 mm. **Subject:** Garabaldi

Date	Mintage	F12	VF20	XF40	MS60	MS63
2007	—	PF65 40.00				

KM# 897 10 PESOS
27.00 g., 0.925 Silver 0.7978 oz. ASW, 40 mm. **Subject:** Ibero
- American Series - Javelin

Date	Mintage	F12	VF20	XF40	MS60	MS63
2007	—	PF63 40.00	PF65 45.00			

KM# 898 10 PESOS
20.00 g., Silver, 38 mm. **Subject:** Sputnik

Date	Mintage	F12	VF20	XF40	MS60	MS63
2007	—	PF63 35.00	PF65 40.00			

KM# 899 10 PESOS
20.00 g., Silver, 38 mm. **Subject:** World Championship Soccer
England

Date	Mintage	F12	VF20	XF40	MS60	MS63
2007	—	PF63 35.00	PF65 40.00			

KM# 904 10 PESOS
20.00 g., 0.999 Silver 0.6382 oz. ASW, 38 mm. **Subject:** Ship
Principe Asturias

Date	Mintage	F12	VF20	XF40	MS60	MS63
2008	—	PF65 40.00				

KM# 905 10 PESOS
20.00 g., 0.999 Silver 0.6382 oz. ASW, 40 mm. **Subject:** Ship -
San Carlos **Obv:** National arms within wreath

Date	Mintage	F12	VF20	XF40	MS60	MS63
2008	—	PF65 40.00				

KM# 906 10 PESOS
20.00 g., 0.999 Silver 0.6382 oz. ASW, 40 mm. **Subject:** Ship
- San Hermene

Date	Mintage	F12	VF20	XF40	MS60	MS63
2008	—	PF65 40.00				

KM# 911 10 PESOS
20.00 g., 0.999 Silver 0.6382 oz. ASW, 38 mm. **Subject:** Fidel
and Raul Castro

Date	Mintage	F12	VF20	XF40	MS60	MS63
2009	5,000	PF65 40.00				

KM# 912 10 PESOS
20.00 g., 0.999 Silver 0.6382 oz. ASW, 38 mm. **Subject:**
Manatee **Obv:** National arms in wreath

Date	Mintage	F12	VF20	XF40	MS60	MS63
2009	—	PF65 40.00				

KM# 926 10 PESOS
27.00 g., 0.925 Silver 0.7978 oz. ASW, 40 mm. **Subject:** Ibero-
American series - Historic coins **Obv:** Cuban arms at center of
circle of other national arms **Rev:** Historic coin

Date	Mintage	F12	VF20	XF40	MS60	MS63
2010	12,000	PF63 50.00	PF65 55.00			

KM# 900 20 PESOS
62.20 g., 0.999 Silver 1.9849 oz. ASW, 45 mm. **Subject:** Che Guevara - 40th Anniversary of Death

Date	Mintage	F12	VF20	XF40	MS60	MS63
2007	—	PF63 85.00		PF65 95.00		

KM# 913 20 PESOS
62.21 g., 0.999 Silver 1.9852 oz. ASW, 45 mm. **Subject:** Revolution 50th Anniversary

Date	Mintage	F12	VF20	XF40	MS60	MS63
2009	1,959	PF63 130		PF65 150		

KM# 922 25 PESOS
7.78 g., 0.999 Gold 0.2483 oz. AGW **Subject:** Wold Cup, Germany **Rev:** Socer player and globe

Date	Mintage	F12	VF20	XF40	MS60	MS63
2004	25,000	PF63 425		PF65 475		

KM# 822 100 PESOS
31.10 g., 0.999 Gold 0.9925 oz. AGW, 38 mm. **Subject:** 100th Anniversary - Death of Marti **Obv:** Cuban arms **Rev:** Monument

Date	Mintage	F12	VF20	XF40	MS60	MS63
2001	100	PF65 1,850				

PESO CONVERTIBLE SERIES

KM# 729 CENTAVO
1.70 g., Copper Plated Steel, 15 mm. **Obv:** National arms within wreath, denomination below **Rev:** Tower and denomination **Edge:** Reeded

Date	Mintage	F12	VF20	XF40	MS60	MS63
2002	—	—	—	—	3.00	—
2006	—	—	—	—	3.00	—
2007	—	—	—	—	3.00	—
2013	—	—	—	—	3.00	—

KM# 733 CENTAVO
0.75 g., Aluminum, 16.75 mm. **Obv:** Cuban arms **Rev:** Tower and denomination **Edge:** Plain

Date	Mintage	F12	VF20	XF40	MS60	MS63
2001	—	—	—	—	2.00	—
2002	—	—	—	—	2.00	—
2003	—	—	—	—	2.00	—
2005	—	—	—	—	2.00	—
2007	—	—	—	—	2.00	—

KM# 575.2 5 CENTAVOS
2.65 g., Nickel Plated Steel, 18 mm. **Obv:** National arms **Rev:** Casa Colonial **Note:** Coin alignment, recut designs.

Date	Mintage	F12	VF20	XF40	MS60	MS63
2001	—	—	—	—	1.00	—
2002	—	—	—	—	1.00	—
2003	—	—	—	—	1.00	—
2004	—	—	—	—	1.00	—
2006	—	—	—	—	1.00	—
2007	—	—	—	—	1.00	—
2008	—	—	—	—	1.00	—
2009	—	—	—	—	1.00	—

KM# 576.2 10 CENTAVOS
4.00 g., Nickel Plated Steel, 20 mm. **Obv:** National arms **Rev:** Castillo de la Fuerza **Note:** Coin alignment, recut designs.

Date	Mintage	F12	VF20	XF40	MS60	MS63
2002	—	—	—	—	2.00	—
2003	—	—	—	—	2.00	—
2008	—	—	—	—	2.00	—
2009	—	—	—	—	2.00	—

KM# 577.2 25 CENTAVOS
5.65 g., Nickel Plated Steel, 23 mm. **Obv:** National arms **Rev:** Trinidad **Note:** Coin alignment.

Date	Mintage	F12	VF20	XF40	MS60	MS63
2001	—	—	—	—	3.00	—
2002	—	—	—	—	3.00	—
2003	—	—	—	—	3.00	—
2006	—	—	—	—	3.00	—
2007	—	—	—	—	3.00	—
2008	—	—	—	—	3.00	—

KM# 578.2 50 CENTAVOS
7.53 g., Nickel Plated Steel, 25 mm. **Obv:** Cuban arms **Rev:** Havana Cathedral **Note:** Coin alignment.

Date	Mintage	F12	VF20	XF40	MS60	MS63
2002	—	—	—	—	5.00	—
2007	—	—	—	—	5.00	—

KM# 579.2 PESO
8.50 g., Nickel Plated Steel, 27 mm. **Obv:** National arms **Rev:** Guama **Edge:** Reeded **Note:** Coin alignment.

Date	Mintage	F12	VF20	XF40	MS60	MS63
2001	—	—	—	—	—	5.00
2007	—	—	—	—	—	5.00
2012	—	—	—	—	—	5.00

MINT SETS

KM#	Date	Mintage	Identification	Issue Price	Mkt Val
MS3	2001 (3)	—	KM#831-833	—	62.50

CYPRUS

The island of Cyprus lies in the eastern Mediterranean Sea 44 miles (71 km.) south of Turkey and 60 miles (97 km.) off the Syrian coast. It is the third largest island in the Mediterranean Sea, having an area of 3,572 sq. mi. (9,251 sq. km.) and a population of 736,636. Capital: Nicosia. Agriculture, light manufacturing and tourism are the chief industries. Citrus fruit, potatoes, footwear and clothing are exported

Cyprus is a member of the Commonwealth of Nations. The president is Chief of State and Head of Government. Cyprus is also a member of the European Union since May 2004.

MINT MARKS
no mint mark - Royal Mint, London, England
H - Birmingham, England

REPUBLIC
REFORM COINAGE
100 Cents = 1 Pound

KM# 53.3 CENT
2.00 g., Nickel-Brass, 16.5 mm. **Obv:** Shielded arms within altered wreath, date below **Rev:** Stylized bird on a branch, denomination at left **Edge:** Plain

Date	Mintage	F12	VF20	XF40	MS60	MS63
2003	5,000,000	—	—	0.10	0.20	0.30
2004 Narrow figures	12,000,000	—	—	0.10	0.20	0.30

KM# 54.3 2 CENTS
2.50 g., Nickel-Brass, 19 mm. **Obv:** Shielded arms within altered wreath, date below **Rev:** Stylized goats, denomination upper right **Edge:** Plain

Date	Mintage	F12	VF20	XF40	MS60	MS63
2003	5,000,000	—	—	0.15	0.25	0.35
2004	7,000,000	—	—	0.15	0.25	0.35

KM# 55.3 5 CENTS
3.75 g., Nickel-Brass, 22 mm. **Obv:** Altered wreath around arms **Rev:** Stylized bull's head above denomination **Edge:** Plain

Date	Mintage	F12	VF20	XF40	MS60	MS63
2001	15,000,000	—	—	0.20	0.50	0.75
2004	15,000,000	—	—	0.20	0.50	0.75

KM# 56.3 10 CENTS
5.50 g., Nickel-Brass, 24.5 mm. **Obv:** Altered wreath around arms **Rev:** Decorative vase, denomination above **Edge:** Reeded

Date	Mintage	F12	VF20	XF40	MS60	MS63
2002	10,000,000	—	—	0.35	0.75	1.00
2004 Narrow figures	7,000,000	—	—	0.35	0.75	1.00

KM# 62.2 20 CENTS
7.75 g., Nickel-Brass, 27.25 mm. **Obv:** Altered wreath around arms **Rev:** Head left, denomination at right **Edge:** Reeded

Date	Mintage	F12	VF20	XF40	MS60	MS63
2001	15,000,000	—	—	—	1.00	1.50
2004	4,000,000	—	—	—	1.00	1.50

KM# 66 50 CENTS
7.00 g., Copper-Nickel, 26 mm. **Subject:** Abduction of Europa **Obv:** National arms, date below **Rev:** Female figure riding bull right within square, denomination below **Edge:** Plain **Shape:** 7-sided

Date	Mintage	F12	VF20	XF40	MS60	MS63
2002	7,000,000	—	—	—	2.50	3.25
2004	5,000,000	—	—	—	2.50	3.25

KM# 96 POUND
28.28 g., Copper-Nickel, 38.6 mm. **Obv:** National arms **Rev:** Butterfly on branch

Date	Mintage	F12	VF20	XF40	MS60	MS63
2002		PF63 45.00	PF65 50.00			

KM# 75 POUND
28.28 g., Copper-Nickel, 38.6 mm. **Subject:** Cyprus Joins the European Union **Obv:** National arms **Rev:** Map in center with Triton trumpeting through a seashell **Edge:** Plain

Date	Mintage	F12	VF20	XF40	MS60	MS63
2004	3,000	—	—	—	25.00	50.00

KM# 75a POUND
28.28 g., 0.925 Silver 0.8356 oz. ASW, 38.6 mm. **Subject:** Cyprus Joins the European Union **Obv:** National arms **Rev:** Map and Triton trumpeting through a sea shell **Edge:** Plain

Date	Mintage	F12	VF20	XF40	MS60	MS63
2004	3,000	PF63 75.00	PF65 80.00			

KM# 76 POUND
28.27 g., Copper-Nickel, 38.5 mm. **Obv:** National arms **Rev:** Mediterranean Monk Seal **Edge:** Plain

Date	Mintage	F12	VF20	XF40	MS60	MS63
2005	4,000	PF63 45.00	PF65 50.00			

KM# 76a POUND
28.28 g., 0.925 Silver 0.8356 oz. ASW, 38.61 mm. **Obv:** National arms **Rev:** Mediterranean Monk Seal **Edge:** Plain

Date	Mintage	F12	VF20	XF40	MS60	MS63
2005	4,000	PF63 60.00	PF65 65.00			

KM# 77a POUND
28.28 g., 0.925 Silver 0.8356 oz. ASW, 38.61 mm. **Obv:** National arms **Rev:** Akamas Centaurea flowers **Edge:** Plain

Date	Mintage	F12	VF20	XF40	MS60	MS63
2006	3,000	PF63 70.00	PF65 75.00			

KM# 77 POUND
28.28 g., Copper-Nickel, 38.6 mm. **Obv:** National arms **Rev:** Akamas Centaurea flowers **Edge:** Plain

Date	Mintage	F12	VF20	XF40	MS60	MS63
2006	6,000	PF63 25.00	PF65 30.00			

KM# 86 POUND
28.28 g., Copper-Nickel, 38.6 mm. **Subject:** 50th Anniversary Treaty of Rome **Obv:** National arms **Rev:** Open Treaty Book **Edge:** Plain

Date	Mintage	F12	VF20	XF40	MS60	MS63
2007 Prooflike	10,000	PF63 28.00	PF65 32.00			

KM# 87 20 POUNDS
7.99 g., Gold AGW, 22.05 mm. **Obv:** National arms **Rev:** Greek god Triton, trumpeter (messenger) of the deep sea below outlined map of Cyprus

Date	Mintage	F12	VF20	XF40	MS60	MS63
2004	1,500	PF65 1,000				

EURO COINAGE
European Union Issues

KM# 78 EURO CENT
2.30 g., Copper Plated Steel, 16.25 mm. **Obv:** Two Mouflons **Rev:** Large value at left, globe at lower right **Edge:** Plain

Date	Mintage	F12	VF20	XF40	MS60	MS63
2008	40,000,000	—	—	—	0.35	0.50
2009	20,000,000	—	—	—	0.35	0.50
2010	200,000	—	—	—	0.35	0.50
2011	15,200,000	—	—	—	0.35	0.50
2012	988,000	—	—	—	0.35	0.50

KM# 79 2 EURO CENT
3.06 g., Copper Plated Steel, 18.75 mm. **Obv:** Two Mouflons **Rev:** Large value at left, globe at lower right **Edge:** Grooved

Date	Mintage	F12	VF20	XF40	MS60	MS63
2008	100,000,000	—	—	—	0.50	0.75
2009	1,000,000	—	—	—	0.50	0.75
2010	200,000	—	—	—	0.50	0.75
2011	200,000	—	—	—	0.50	0.75
2012	988,000	—	—	—	0.50	0.75

KM# 80 5 EURO CENT
3.92 g., Copper Plated Steel, 21.25 mm. **Obv:** Two Mouflons **Rev:** Large value at left, globe at lower right **Edge:** Plain

Date	Mintage	F12	VF20	XF40	MS60	MS63
2008	60,000,000	—	—	—	1.00	1.25
2009	6,000,000	—	—	—	1.00	1.25
2010	200,000	—	—	—	1.00	1.25
2011	30,200,000	—	—	—	1.00	1.25
2012	988,000	—	—	—	1.00	1.25

KM# 81 10 EURO CENT
4.10 g., Brass, 19.75 mm. **Obv:** Early sailing boat **Rev:** Modified outline of Europe at left, large value at right **Edge:** Reeded

Date	Mintage	F12	VF20	XF40	MS60	MS63
2008	70,000,000	—	—	—	1.25	1.50
2009	1,000,000	—	—	—	1.25	1.50
2010	200,000	—	—	—	1.25	1.50
2011	200,000	—	—	—	1.25	1.50
2012	988,000	—	—	—	1.25	1.50

KM# 82 20 EURO CENT
5.74 g., Brass, 22.25 mm. **Obv:** Early sailing boat **Rev:** Modified outline of Europe at left, large value at right **Edge:** Notched

Date	Mintage	F12	VF20	XF40	MS60	MS63
2008	65,000,000	—	—	—	1.50	2.00
2009	1,000,000	—	—	—	1.50	2.00
2010	200,000	—	—	—	1.50	2.00
2011	200,000	—	—	—	1.50	2.00
2012	988,000	—	—	—	1.50	2.00

KM# 83 50 EURO CENT
7.80 g., Brass, 24.25 mm. **Obv:** Early sailing boat **Rev:** Modified outline of Europe at left, large value at right **Edge:** Reeded

Date	Mintage	F12	VF20	XF40	MS60	MS63
2008	30,000,000	—	—	—	2.00	2.50
2009	1,000,000	—	—	—	2.00	2.50
2010	200,000	—	—	—	2.00	2.50
2011	200,000	—	—	—	2.00	2.50
2012	988,000	—	—	—	2.00	2.50

KM# 84 EURO
7.50 g., Bi-Metallic, 23.25 mm. **Obv:** Ancient cross shaped idol discovered in the village of Pomos in the distrct of Paphos. **Rev:** Large value at left, modified outline of Europe at right **Edge:**

Segmented reeding

Date	Mintage	F12	VF20	XF40	MS60	MS63
2008	28,000,000	—	—	—	3.50	5.00
2009	4,000,000	—	—	—	3.50	5.00
2010	200,000	—	—	—	3.50	5.00
2011	200,000	—	—	—	3.50	5.00
2012	988,000	—	—	—	3.50	5.00

KM# 85 2 EURO
8.50 g., Bi-Metallic, 25.75 mm. **Obv:** Ancient cross shaped idol discovered in the village of Pomos in the distrct of Paphos. **Rev:** Large value at left, modified outline of Europe at right

Date	Mintage	F12	VF20	XF40	MS60	MS63
2008	25,000,000	—	—	—	5.00	7.00
2009	5,000,000	—	—	—	5.00	7.00
2010	200,000	—	—	—	5.00	7.00
2011	200,000	—	—	—	5.00	7.00
2012	988,000	—	—	—	5.00	7.00

KM# 89 2 EURO
8.50 g., Bi-Metallic, 25.75 mm. **Subject:** 10th Anniversary of Euro **Obv:** Ancient statue wearing a cross found in Solol **Rev:** Childs drawing of a stick figure and 2E

Date	Mintage	F12	VF20	XF40	MS60	MS63
2009	980,000	—	—	—	5.00	7.00
2009 Special Unc.	20,000	—	—	—	—	15.00
2009		PF65 25.00				

KM# 98 2 EURO
8.50 g., Bi-Metallic, 25.75 mm. **Subject:** Cyprian presidency of European Council

Date	Mintage	F12	VF20	XF40	MS60	MS63
2012		PF65 7.00				

KM# 97 2 EURO
8.50 g., Bi-Metallic, 25.75 mm. **Subject:** Euro Coinage, 10th Anniversary **Obv:** Euro symbol on globe, child-like rendering around

Date	Mintage	F12	VF20	XF40	MS60	MS63
2012 Special Unc.	5,000	—	—	—	—	15.00
2012	1,000,000	—	—	—	6.00	8.00
2012	8,000	PF65 25.00				

KM# 88 5 EURO
28.28 g., 0.925 Silver 0.8356 oz. ASW, 38.61 mm. **Subject:** Entry into Euro Zone **Obv:** National arms **Rev:** Euro band around outlined Europe and Cyprus **Edge:** Reeded

Date	Mintage	F12	VF20	XF40	MS60	MS63
2008	15,000	PF63 70.00	PF65 75.00			

KM# 94 5 EURO
28.28 g., 0.925 Silver 0.8356 oz. ASW, 38.61 mm. **Subject:** Republic of Cyprus, 50th Anniversary **Obv:** National arms **Rev:** Bird in stylized tree

Date	Mintage	F12	VF20	XF40	MS60	MS63
2010	5,000	PF63 60.00	PF65 65.00			

KM# 95 20 EURO
7.99 g., 0.900 Gold 0.2297 oz. AGW, 22 mm. **Subject:** Republic of Cyprus, 50th Anniversary **Obv:** National arms **Rev:** Bird in stylized tree **Edge:** Reeded

Date	Mintage	F12	VF20	XF40	MS60	MS63
2010	750	PF65 450				

MINT SETS

KM#	Date	Mintage	Identification	Issue Price	Mkt Val
MS20	2008 (8)	70,000	KM#78-85	—	50.00
MS21	2009 (9)	15,000	KM#78-85, 89	—	60.00
MS22	2011 (8)	10,000	KM#78-85	—	50.00
MS23	2012 (8)	—	KM#78-85	—	50.00
XMS1	2004 (8)	18,000	X#Pn1-Pn8	—	30.00

PROOF SETS

KM#	Date	Mintage	Identification	Issue Price	Mkt Val
XPS1	2004 (9)	12,500	X#Pn1-Pn9	—	55.00
XPS2	2004 (9)	400	X#Pn1a-Pn9a	—	165

CZECH REPUBLIC

The Czech Republic was formerly united with Slovakia as Czechoslovakia. It is bordered in the west by Germany, to the north by Poland, to the east by Slovakia and to the south by Austria. It consists of 3 major regions: Bohemia, Moravia and Silesia and has an area of 30,450 sq. mi. (78,864 sq. km.) and a population of 10.4 million. Capital: Prague (Praha). Agriculture and livestock are chief occupations while coal deposits are the main mineral resources.

MINT MARKS
(c) - castle = Hamburg
(cr) - cross = British Royal Mint
(l) - leaf = Royal Canadian
(m) - crowned *b* or *CM* = Jablonec nad Nisou
(mk) - *MK* in circle = Kremnica
(o) - broken circle = Vienna (Wien)

MONETARY SYSTEM
1 Czechoslovak Koruna (Kcs) = 1 Czech Koruna (Kc)
1 Koruna = 100 Haleru

REPUBLIC

STANDARD COINAGE

KM# 6 10 HALERU
0.60 g., Aluminum, 15.5 mm. **Obv:** Crowned Czech lion left, date below **Rev:** Denomination and stylized river **Edge:** Plain **Note:** Two varieties of mint marks exist for 1994.

Date	Mintage	F12	VF20	XF40	MS60	MS63
2001(m)	40,525,000	—	—	—	0.20	—
2001(m)	—	PF65 10.00				
2002(m)	81,496,000	—	—	—	0.20	—
2002(m)	—	PF65 10.00				
2003(m)	3,022,350	—	—	—	0.20	—
2003(m)	—	PF65 7.00				
2004(m)	—	—	—	—	0.20	—
2004(m)	—	PF65 7.00				
2005(m)	—	—	—	—	0.20	—

KM# 2.3 20 HALERU
0.74 g., Aluminum, 17 mm. **Obv:** Crowned Czech lion left, date above **Rev:** Open 2 in denomination, "h" above angle line **Edge:** Reeded **Note:** Medal alignment.

Date	Mintage	F12	VF20	XF40	MS60	MS63
2001(m)	44,425,000	—	—	—	0.30	—
2001(m)	—	PF65 12.50				
2002(m)	20,000	—	—	—	0.30	—
2002(m)	—	PF65 12.50				
2003(m)	22,200	—	—	—	0.30	—
2003(m)	3,000	PF65 7.50				
2004(m)	—	—	—	—	0.30	—
2004(m)	—	PF65 7.50				

KM# 3.1 50 HALERU
0.90 g., Aluminum, 19 mm. **Obv:** Crowned Czech lion left, date below **Rev:** Large denomination **Edge:** Segmented reeding **Note:** Prev. KM#3.

Date	Mintage	F12	VF20	XF40	MS60	MS63
2001(m)	21,425,000	—	—	—	0.50	—
2001(m)	2,500	PF65 12.50				

KM# 3.2 50 HALERU
0.90 g., Aluminum, 19 mm. **Obv:** Crowned Czech lion left, date below **Rev:** Large denomination **Edge:** Segmented reeding **Note:** Outlined lettering and larger mint mark

Date	Mintage	F12	VF20	XF40	MS60	MS63
2001(m)	21,425,000	—	—	—	0.50	—
2001(m)	—	PF65 12.50				
2002(m)	26,246,298	—	—	—	0.50	—
2002(m)	3,490	PF65 12.50				
2003(m)	41,548,000	—	—	—	0.50	—
2003(m)	3,000	PF65 7.50				
2004(m)	931,145	—	—	—	0.50	—
2004(m)	4,000	PF65 7.50				
2005(m)	36,814,000	—	—	—	0.50	—
2005(m)	3,000	PF65 7.50				
2006(m)	40,030,500	—	—	—	0.50	—
2006(m)	2,500	PF65 7.50				
2007(m)	35,020,500	—	—	—	0.50	—
2007(m)	2,500	PF65 7.50				
2008(m)	17,000	—	—	—	0.50	—
2008(m)	2,500	PF65 3.00				
2009(m)	—	—	—	—	0.50	—
2009(m)	2,500	PF65 3.00				

KM# 7 KORUNA
3.60 g., Nickel Plated Steel, 20 mm. **Obv:** Crowned Czech lion left, date below. **Rev:** Denomination above crown **Edge:** Reeded **Note:** Two varieties of mint marks exist for 1996. 2000-03 have two varieties in the artist monogram.

Date	Mintage	F12	VF20	XF40	MS60	MS63
2001(m)	15,938,353	—	—	—	0.60	—
2001(m)	—	PF65 20.00				
2002(m)	26,244,666	—	—	—	0.60	—
2002(m)	—	PF65 20.00				
2003(m)	36,877,440	—	—	—	0.60	—
2003(m)	3,000	PF65 10.00				
2004(m)	30,500	—	—	—	0.60	—
2004(m)	—	PF65 10.00				
2005(m)	14,000	—	—	—	0.60	—
2005(m)	3,000	PF65 10.00				
2006(m)	27,097,500	—	—	—	0.60	—
2006(m)	2,500	PF65 10.00				
2007(m)	14,170,500	—	—	—	0.60	—
2007(m)	2,500	PF65 10.00				

Date	Mintage	F12	VF20	XF40	MS60	MS63
2008(m)	29,617,000	—	—	—	0.60	—
2008(m)	2,500	PF65 6.00				
2009(m)	38,367,400	—	—	—	0.60	—
2009(m)	3,200	PF65 6.00				
2010(m)	15,004,602	—	—	—	0.60	—
2010(m)	3,200	PF65 6.00				
2011(m)	4,000,600	—	—	—	0.60	—
2011(m)	2,500	PF65 6.00				
2012(m)	19,000,000	—	—	—	0.60	—
2012(m)	—	PF63 6.00				
2013(m)		—	—	—	0.60	—

KM# 9 2 KORUNY
3.70 g., Nickel Plated Steel, 21.5 mm. **Obv:** Crowned Czech lion left, date below **Rev:** Large denomination, pendant design at left **Edge:** Plain **Shape:** 11-sided **Note:** Two varieties of designer monograms exist for 2001-04.

Date	Mintage	F12	VF20	XF40	MS60	MS63
2001(m)	26,117,000	—	—	—	0.65	—
2001(m)	—	PF65 20.00				
2002(m)	20,941,084	—	—	—	0.65	—
2002(m)	—	PF65 20.00				
2003(m)	20,955,000	—	—	—	0.65	—
2003(m)	—	PF65 12.50				
2004(m)	15,658,556	—	—	—	0.65	—
2004(m)	—	PF65 10.00				
2005(m)	14,000	—	—	—	0.65	—
2005(m)	3,000	PF65 7.50				
2006(m)	30,500	—	—	—	0.65	—
2006(m)	2,500	PF65 7.50				
2007(m)	30,020,500	—	—	—	0.65	—
2007(m)	2,500	PF65 7.50				
2008(m)	26,267,000	—	—	—	0.65	—
2008(m)	2,500	PF65 5.00				
2009(m)	25,418,000	—	—	—	0.65	—
2009(m)	3,200	PF65 5.00				
2010(m)	26,054,000	—	—	—	0.65	—
2010(m)	3,200	PF65 5.00				
2011(m)	12,000,000	—	—	—	0.65	—
2011(m)	2,500	PF65 5.00				
2012(m)	13,000,000	—	—	—	0.65	—
2012(m)	—	PF65 5.00				
2013(m)		—	—	—	0.65	—
2013	—	PF65 5.00				

KM# 8 5 KORUN
4.80 g., Nickel Plated Steel, 23 mm. **Obv:** Crowned Czech lion left, date below **Rev:** Large denomination, Charles bridge and linden leaf **Edge:** Plain

Date	Mintage	F12	VF20	XF40	MS60	MS63
2001(m)	25,000	—	—	—	1.00	—
2001(m)	—	PF65 27.50				
2002(m)	21,344,995	—	—	—	1.00	—
2002(m)	—	PF65 27.50				
2003(m)	22,000	—	—	—	1.00	—
2003(m)	—	PF65 15.00				
2004(m)	34,940	—	—	—	1.00	—
2004(m)	—	PF65 12.00				
2005(m)	14,000	—	—	—	1.00	—
2005(m)	3,000	PF65 10.00				
2006(m)	25,030,500	—	—	—	1.00	—
2006(m)	2,500	PF65 10.00				
2007(m)	20,500	—	—	—	1.00	—
2007(m)	2,500	PF65 10.00				
2008(m)	11,617,000	—	—	—	1.00	—
2008(m)	2,500	PF65 6.00				
2009(m)	19,911,000	—	—	—	1.00	—
2009(m)	3,200	PF65 6.00				
2010(m)	14,711,000	—	—	—	1.00	—
2010(m)	3,200	PF65 6.00				
2011(m)	—	—	—	—	1.00	—
2011(m)	5,500	PF65 6.00				
2012(m)	—	—	—	—	1.00	—
2012(m)	—	PF65 6.00				
2013(m)		—	—	—	1.00	—

KM# 4 10 KORUN
7.62 g., Copper Plated Steel, 24.5 mm. **Obv:** Crowned Czech lion left, date below **Rev:** Brno Cathedral, denomination below **Edge:** Reeded **Note:** Position of designer's initials on reverse change during the 1995 strike.

Date	Mintage	F12	VF20	XF40	MS60	MS63
2001(m)	25,000	—	—	—	1.50	—
2001(m)	2,500	PF65 28.00				
2002(m)	20,156	—	—	—	1.50	—
2002(m)	—	PF65 28.00				
2003(m)	18,747,000	—	—	—	1.50	—
2003(m)	—	PF65 17.50				
2004(m)	2,255,740	—	—	—	1.50	—
2004(m)	—	PF65 14.00				
2005(m)	14,000	—	—	—	1.50	—
2005(m)	3,000	PF65 10.00				
2006(m)	30,500	—	—	—	1.50	—
2006(m)	2,500	PF65 10.00				
2007(m)	20,500	—	—	—	1.50	—
2007(m)	2,500	PF65 10.00				
2008(m)	10,092,000	—	—	—	1.50	—
2008(m)	2,500	PF65 7.00				
2009(m)	10,511,000	—	—	—	1.50	—
2009(m)	3,200	PF65 7.00				
2010(m)	16,811,000	—	—	—	1.50	—
2010(m)	3,200	PF65 7.00				
2011(m)	—	—	—	—	1.50	—
2011(m)	5,500	PF65 7.00				
2012(m)	—	—	—	—	1.50	—
2012(m)	—	PF65 7.00				
2013(m)		—	—	—	1.50	—

KM# 5 20 KORUN
8.43 g., Brass Plated Steel, 26 mm. **Obv:** Crowned Czech lion left, date below **Rev:** St. Wenceslas (Duke Vaclav) on horse **Edge:** Plain **Shape:** 13-sided **Note:** Two varieties of mint marks and style of 9's exist for 1997.

Date	Mintage	F12	VF20	XF40	MS60	MS63
2001(m)	25,000	—	—	—	2.50	—
2001(m)	—	PF65 40.00				
2002(m)	20,996,500	—	—	—	2.50	—
2002(m)	—	PF65 40.00				
2003(m)	22,000	—	—	—	2.50	—
2003(m)	—	PF65 25.00				
2004(m)	8,249,507	—	—	—	2.50	—
2004(m)	—	PF65 22.50				
2005(m)	9,866,778	—	—	—	2.50	—
2005(m)	3,000	PF65 22.50				
2006(m)	2,096,500	—	—	—	2.50	—
2006(m)	2,500	PF65 22.50				
2007(m)	20,500	—	—	—	2.50	—
2007(m)	2,500	PF65 22.50				
2008(m)	17,000	—	—	—	2.50	—
2008(m)	2,500	PF65 10.00				
2009(m)	11,000	—	—	—	2.50	—
2009(m)	3,200	PF65 10.00				
2010(m)	11,000	—	—	—	2.50	—
2010(m)	3,200	PF65 10.00				
2011(m)	8,000,000	—	—	—	2.50	—
2011(m)	5,500	PF65 10.00				
2012(m)	8,000,000	—	—	—	2.50	—
2012(m)	—	PF65 10.00				
2013		—	—	—	2.50	—

KM# 1 50 KORUN
9.70 g., Bi-Metallic, 27.5 mm. **Obv:** Crowned Czech lion left **Rev:** Prague city view **Edge:** Plain

Date	Mintage	F12	VF20	XF40	MS60	MS63
2001(m)	16,000	—	—	—	9.00	—

Date	Mintage	F12	VF20	XF40	MS60	MS63
2001(m)	—	PF65 80.00				
2002(m)	16,771	—	—	—	9.00	—
2002(m)	—	PF65 80.00				
2003(m)	22,000	—	—	—	9.00	—
2003(m)	—	PF65 50.00				
2004(m)	34,555	—	—	—	9.00	—
2004(m)	—	PF65 40.00				
2005(m)	14,000	—	—	—	9.00	—
2005(m)	3,000	PF65 25.00				
2006(m)	30,500	—	—	—	9.00	—
2006(m)	2,500	PF65 25.00				
2007(m)	20,500	—	—	—	9.00	—
2007(m)	2,500	PF65 25.00				
2008(m)	9,528,300	—	—	—	9.00	—
2008(m)	2,500	PF65 20.00				
2009(m)	36,719,050	—	—	—	9.00	—
2009(m)	3,200	PF65 20.00				
2010(m)	17,210,000	—	—	—	9.00	—
2010(m)	32,000	PF65 20.00				
2011(m)	10,000,000	—	—	—	9.00	—
2011(m)	5,500	PF65 20.00				
2012(m)	10,000,000	—	—	—	9.00	—
2012(m)	—	PF65 20.00				
2013(m)		—	—	—	9.00	—

KM# 51 200 KORUN
13.00 g., 0.900 Silver 0.3737 oz. ASW, 31 mm. **Subject:** Jaroslav Seifert **Obv:** Quartered arms above denomination **Rev:** Head right, dates at left **Note:** 1,680 pieces uncirculated and 2 proof remelted.

Date	Mintage	F12	VF20	XF40	MS60	MS63
ND-2001	11,746	—	—	—	18.00	20.00
Note: Milled edge						
ND-2001	3,186	PF65 165				

Note: Plain edge with CESKA NARODNI BANKA *0.900* 13g

KM# 52 200 KORUN
13.00 g., 0.900 Silver 0.3737 oz. ASW, 31 mm. **Subject:** Soccer **Obv:** Quartered arms on square, denomination below **Rev:** Rampant lion on soccer ball **Note:** 2,350 pieces uncirculated and 1 proof remelted.

Date	Mintage	F12	VF20	XF40	MS60	MS63
ND-2001	12,050	—	—	—	18.00	20.00
Note: Milled edge						
ND-2001	3,896	PF65 165				

Note: Plain edge with CESKA NARODNI BANKA *0.900* 13g

KM# 53 200 KORUN
13.00 g., 0.900 Silver 0.3737 oz. ASW, 31 mm. **Subject:** 250th Anniversary - Death of Kilian Ignac Dientzenhofer **Obv:** Quartered arms, denomination at right **Rev:** Doorway and caliper **Note:** 1,840 pieces uncirculated and 104 proof remelted.

Date	Mintage	F12	VF20	XF40	MS60	MS63
ND(2001)	11,565	—	—	—	18.00	20.00
Note: Milled edge						
ND(2001)	3,282	PF65 150				

Note: Plain edge with CESKA NARODNI BANKA *0.900* 13g

KM# 54 200 KORUN
13.00 g., 0.900 Silver 0.3737 oz. ASW, 31 mm. **Subject:** Euro Currency System **Obv:** National arms **Rev:** Prague gros coin design **Note:** 134 pieces uncirculated and 1 proof remelted.

Date	Mintage	F12	VF20	XF40	MS60	MS63
ND-2001	3,995	PF65 200				
Note: Plain edge with CESKA NARODNI BANKA *0.900* 13g						
ND-2001	13,730	—	—	—	18.00	20.00
Note: Milled edge						

KM# 58 200 KORUN
13.00 g., 0.900 Silver 0.3737 oz. ASW, 31 mm. **Subject:** Frantisek Skroup **Obv:** Quartered, elongated arms above date **Rev:** Portrait and name **Note:** 1,480 pieces uncirculated and 13 proof remelted.

Date	Mintage	F12	VF20	XF40	MS60	MS63
ND-2001	11,944	—	—	—	18.00	20.00
Note: Milled edge						
ND-2001	3,179	PF65 175				
Note: Plain edge with CESKA NARODNI BANKA *0.900* 13g						

KM# 55 200 KORUN
13.00 g., 0.900 Silver 0.3737 oz. ASW, 31 mm. **Subject:** St. Zdislava **Obv:** Old and new arms form diamond above denomination **Rev:** Saint feeding sick person **Note:** 865 pieces uncirculated remelted.

Date	Mintage	F12	VF20	XF40	MS60	MS63
ND-2002	12,083	—	—	—	18.00	20.00
Note: Milled edge						
ND-2002	3,596	PF65 300				
Note: Plain edge with CESKA NARODNI BANKA *0.900* 13g						

KM# 56 200 KORUN
13.00 g., 0.900 Silver 0.3737 oz. ASW, 30.9 mm. **Subject:** Emil Holub **Obv:** National arms, eagles and lions, denomination below **Rev:** Traveler and African dancers **Note:** 1,350 pieces uncirculated and 7 proof remelted.

Date	Mintage	F12	VF20	XF40	MS60	MS63
ND-2002	3,588	PF65 165				
Note: Plain edge with CESKA NARODNI BANKA *0.900* 13g						
ND-2002	11,602	—	—	—	18.00	20.00
Note: Milled edge						

KM# 57 200 KORUN
13.00 g., 0.900 Silver 0.3737 oz. ASW, 30.9 mm. **Subject:** Jiri of Podebrady **Obv:** Overlapped arms **Rev:** Head right **Note:** 1,200 pieces uncirculated and 5 proof remelted.

Date	Mintage	F12	VF20	XF40	MS60	MS63
ND-2002	11,729	—	—	—	18.00	20.00
Note: Milled edge						
ND-2002	3,591	PF65 200				
Note: Plain edge with CESKA NARODNI BANKA *0.900* 13g						

KM# 59 200 KORUN
13.00 g., 0.900 Silver 0.3737 oz. ASW, 31 mm. **Subject:** Mikolas Ales **Obv:** Four coats of arms above denomination **Rev:** Horse and rider **Note:** 573 pieces uncirculated and 130 proof remelted.

Date	Mintage	F12	VF20	XF40	MS60	MS63
ND(2002)	11,879	—	—	—	18.00	20.00
Note: Milled edge						
ND-2002(m)	4,258	PF65 165				
Note: Plain edge with CESKA NARODNI BANKA *0.900* 13g						

KM# 60 200 KORUN
13.00 g., 0.900 Silver 0.3737 oz. ASW, 31 mm. **Subject:** Jaroslav Vrchlicky **Obv:** Denomination and quill **Rev:** Bust with hat facing **Note:** 889 pieces uncirculated and 5 proof remelted.

Date	Mintage	F12	VF20	XF40	MS60	MS63
ND-2003	10,583	—	—	—	18.00	20.00
Note: Milled edge						
ND-2003	3,692	PF65 135				
Note: Plain edge with CESKA NARODNI BANKA *0.900* 13g						

KM# 62 200 KORUN
13.00 g., 0.900 Silver 0.3737 oz. ASW, 30.9 mm. **Subject:** Josef Thomayer **Obv:** National arms **Rev:** Portrait **Note:** 783 uncirculated and 12 proof were remelted.

Date	Mintage	F12	VF20	XF40	MS60	MS63
ND(2003)	10,525	—	—	—	18.00	20.00
Note: Milled edge						
ND-2003	3,981	PF65 135				
Note: Plain edge with CESKA NARODNI BANKA *0.900* 13g						

KM# 63 200 KORUN
13.00 g., 0.900 Silver 0.3737 oz. ASW, 31 mm. **Subject:** Tabor-Bechyne Electric Railway **Rev:** Railroad station scene **Note:** 808 Uncirculated were remelted.

Date	Mintage	F12	VF20	XF40	MS60	MS63
ND(2003)	10,986	—	—	—	18.00	20.00
Note: Milled edge						
ND-2003	4,097	PF65 125				
Note: Plain edge with CESKA NARODNI BANKA *0.900* 13g						

KM# 64 200 KORUN
13.00 g., 0.900 Silver 0.3737 oz. ASW, 31 mm. **Subject:** Bohemian Skiers' Union **Obv:** Head 3/4 left **Rev:** Skier **Note:** 680 Uncirculated and 13 proof were remelted.

Date	Mintage	F12	VF20	XF40	MS60	MS63
ND(2003)	10,801	—	—	—	18.00	20.00
Note: Milled edge						
ND-2003	4,284	PF65 120				
Note: Plain edge with CESKA NARODNI BANKA *0.900* 13g						

KM# 77 200 KORUN
13.00 g., 0.900 Silver 0.3737 oz. ASW, 31 mm. **Obv:** Prokop Divis **Rev:** Lightning conductor

Date	Mintage	F12	VF20	XF40	MS60	MS63
2004	4,600	PF65 85.00				
Note: Plain edge with CESKA NARODNI BANKA * Ag 0.900 * 13g *						
2004	14,000	—	—	—	18.00	20.00
Note: Reeded						

KM# 70 200 KORUN
13.00 g., 0.900 Silver 0.3737 oz. ASW, 31 mm. **Subject:** 300th Anniversary - Death of pond builder Jakub Krcin **Obv:** Coat of arms above value with reflected design below **Rev:** Two fishermen in boat with reflection on water below **Note:** 656 uncirculated remelted.

Date	Mintage	F12	VF20	XF40	MS60	MS63
ND(2004)(m)	10,685	—	—	—	18.00	20.00
Note: Milled edge						
ND-2004	3,995	PF65 120				
Note: Plain edge with CESKA NARODNI BANKA *0.900* 13g						

KM# 71 200 KORUN
13.00 g., 0.900 Silver 0.3737 oz. ASW **Subject:** Entry into the European Union **Rev:** State emblems of 15 members of the European Union

Date	Mintage	F12	VF20	XF40	MS60	MS63
2004	13,918	—	—	—	18.00	20.00

Note: Plain edge with codes for EU countries

2004	9,994	PF65 65.00				

Note: Plain edge with CESKA NARODNI BANKA *0.900* 13g

KM# 72 200 KORUN
13.00 g., 0.900 Silver 0.3737 oz. ASW, 31 mm. **Subject:** Prokop Diviš **Obv:** Lighting conductor modulator **Rev:** Head of Diviš

Date	Mintage	F12	VF20	XF40	MS60	MS63
2004	10,145	—	—	—	18.00	20.00

Note: Milled edge

2004	3,897	PF65 85.00				

Note: Plain edge with CESKA NARODNI BANKA *0.900* 13g

KM# 73 200 KORUN
13.00 g., 0.900 Silver 0.3737 oz. ASW **Subject:** Leos Janacek **Rev:** Head of Janacek

Date	Mintage	F12	VF20	XF40	MS60	MS63
2004	10,143	—	—	—	18.00	20.00

Note: Milled edge

2004		—	PF65 75.00			

Note: Plain edge with CESKA NARODNI BANKA *0.900* 13g

KM# 74 200 KORUN
13.00 g., 0.900 Silver 0.3737 oz. ASW **Subject:** Kralice Bible **Obv:** Enlargement of bible page **Rev:** Bible page

Date	Mintage	F12	VF20	XF40	MS60	MS63
2004	10,975	—	—	—	18.00	20.00

Note: Reeded

2004		—	PF65 95.00			

KM# 78 200 KORUN
13.00 g., 0.900 Silver 0.3737 oz. ASW, 31 mm. **Subject:** 100th Anniversary of Jan Werich and Jiri Voskovec

Date	Mintage	F12	VF20	XF40	MS60	MS63
2005	4,997	PF65 135				

Note: Plain edge with CESKA NARODNI BANKA *0.900* 13g

2005	10,884	—	—	—	18.00	20.00

Note: Milled edge

KM# 80 200 KORUN
13.00 g., 0.900 Silver 0.3737 oz. ASW, 31 mm. **Subject:** 450th Anniversary - Birth of Mikulas Dacicky **Obv:** Arms of Dacicky **Rev:** Head of Mikulas Dacicky z Heslova

Date	Mintage	F12	VF20	XF40	MS60	MS63
2005	5,597	PF65 70.00				

Note: Plain edge with CESKA NARODNI BANKA *0.900* 13g

2005	10,076	—	—	—	18.00	20.00

Note: Milled edge

KM# 79 200 KORUN
13.00 g., 0.900 Silver 0.3737 oz. ASW, 31 mm. **Subject:** 100th Anniversary of Production of 1st Car in Mlada Boleslav **Rev:** 1st car of LK factory

Date	Mintage	F12	VF20	XF40	MS60	MS63
2005	10,797	PF65 65.00				

Note: Plain edge with CESKA NARODNI BANKA *0.900* 13g

2005	13,225	—	—	—	18.00	20.00

KM# 84 200 KORUN
13.00 g., 0.900 Silver 0.3737 oz. ASW, 31 mm. **Subject:** 700th Anniversary - Death of Vaclav III **Obv:** Sword between two shields positioned top-to-top **Rev:** King Vaclav III between shields of Bohemia and Moravia

Date	Mintage	F12	VF20	XF40	MS60	MS63
2006	10,471	—	—	—	18.00	20.00

Note: Milled edge

2006	7,497	PF65 50.00				

Note: Plain edge with CESKA NARODNI BANKA *0.900* 13g

KM# 85 200 KORUN
13.00 g., 0.900 Silver 0.3737 oz. ASW, 31 mm. **Subject:** 100th Anniversary - Birth of Jaroslav Jezek **Obv:** Musical score **Rev:** Caricature looking at score

Date	Mintage	F12	VF20	XF40	MS60	MS63
2006(m)	15,442	PF65 30.00				

Note: Plain edge with CESKA NARODNI BANKA *0.900* 13g

2006(m)	10,192	—	—	—	18.00	20.00

Note: Milled edge

KM# 81 200 KORUN
13.00 g., 0.900 Silver 0.3737 oz. ASW, 31 mm. **Subject:** 250th Anniversary - Birth of F.J. Gerstner

Date	Mintage	F12	VF20	XF40	MS60	MS63
2006	6,194	PF65 50.00				

Note: Plain edge with CESKA NARODNI BANKA *0.900* 13g

2006	11,101	—	—	—	18.00	20.00

Note: Milled edge

KM# 82 200 KORUN
13.00 g., 0.900 Silver 0.3737 oz. ASW, 31 mm. **Subject:** 150th Anniversary - School of Glass Making in Kamenicky Senov **Obv:** Image of National Arms within glass cube **Rev:** Artistic image within glass cube

Date	Mintage	F12	VF20	XF40	MS60	MS63
2006	6,494	PF65 50.00				

Note: Plain edge with CESKA NARODNI BANKA *0.900* 13g

2006	9,546	—	—	—	20.00	22.00

Note: Milled edge

KM# 83 200 KORUN
13.00 g., 0.900 Silver 0.3737 oz. ASW, 31 mm. **Subject:** 500th Anniversary - Death of Matej Rejsek **Obv:** Pulpit in the church of St. Laurer in Kank **Rev:** Portrait of Rejsek on the Prasna gate in Prague

Date	Mintage	F12	VF20	XF40	MS60	MS63
2006	6,494	PF65 50.00				

Note: Plain edge with CESKA NARODNI BANKA *0.900* 13g

2006	9,594	—	—	—	20.00	22.00

Note: Milled edge

KM# 91 200 KORUN
13.00 g., 0.900 Silver 0.3737 oz. ASW, 31 mm. **Subject:** Founding of Jednota Bratrska, 550th Anniversary **Obv:** Emblem of Jednota Bratrska, tree, ram with flag. **Rev:** Chalice with ram with flag

Date	Mintage	F12	VF20	XF40	MS60	MS63
2007	8,297	PF65 65.00				

Note: Plain edge with CESKA NARODNI BANKA *0.900* 13g

2007	10,471	—	—	—	20.00	22.00

Note: Milled edge

KM# 92 200 KORUN
13.00 g., 0.900 Silver 0.3737 oz. ASW, 31 mm. **Subject:**
Charles Bridge cornerstone, 650th anniversary

Date	Mintage	F12	VF20	XF40	MS60	MS63
2007	18,746	PF65 32.00				

Note: Plain edge with CESKA NARODNI BANKA *0.900*
13g

2007	10,772	—	—	—	20.00	22.00

Note: Milled edge

KM# 93 200 KORUN
13.00 g., 0.900 Silver 0.3737 oz. ASW, 31 mm. **Subject:**
Jarmila Novotná, 100th Anniversary of Birth **Obv:** Names of the
operas in which Novotna sang **Rev:** Head of Novotna

Date	Mintage	F12	VF20	XF40	MS60	MS63
2007 Proof	12,788	PF65 32.00				

Note: Plain edge with CESKA NARODNI BANKA *0.900*
13g

2007	9,584	—	—	—	20.00	22.00

Note: Milled edge

KM# 94 200 KORUN
13.00 g., 0.900 Silver 0.3737 oz. ASW, 31 mm. **Subject:** Earth
Satelite Launch, 50th Anniversary **Obv:** Satelite and sound
signal of satelite **Rev:** Plentary system with satelite

Date	Mintage	F12	VF20	XF40	MS60	MS63
2007	10,148	—	—	—	30.00	50.00

Note: Milled edge

2007	14,797	PF65 42.50				

Note: Plain edge with CESKA NARODNI BANKA *0.900*
13g

KM# 101 200 KORUN
13.00 g., 0.900 Silver 0.3737 oz. ASW, 31 mm. **Subject:**
National Technical Museum **Obv:** Steam Locomotive and
driving wheel **Rev:** Museum façade and clock face

Date	Mintage	F12	VF20	XF40	MS60	MS63
2008	14,997	PF65 35.00				

Note: Plain edge with CESKA NARODNI BANKA *0.900*
13g

2008	9,972	—	—	—	22.00	25.00

Note: Milled edge

KM# 99 200 KORUN
13.00 g., 0.900 Silver 0.3737 oz. ASW, 31 mm. **Subject:**
Schengen Convention **Obv:** Arms **Rev:** Opening of the frontiers

Date	Mintage	F12	VF20	XF40	MS60	MS63
2008	15,743	PF65 32.00				

Note: Plain edge with CESKA NARODNI BANKA *0.900*
13g

2008	9,739	—	—	—	20.00	22.00

Note: Milled edge

KM# 97 200 KORUN
13.00 g., 0.900 Silver 0.3737 oz. ASW, 31 mm. **Subject:**
Charles IV Vineyard Planting decree

Date	Mintage	F12	VF20	XF40	MS60	MS63
2008	9,768	—	—	—	20.00	22.00

Note: Milled edge

2008	16,997	PF65 32.00				

Note: Plain edge with CESKA NARODNI BANKA *0.900*
13g

KM# 98 200 KORUN
13.00 g., 0.900 Silver 0.3737 oz. ASW **Subject:** Josef Hlavka,
100th Anniversary of Death **Obv:** Wing over architectural
element **Rev:** Facing portrait of Hlavka

Date	Mintage	F12	VF20	XF40	MS60	MS63
2008	9,559	—	—	—	20.00	22.00

Note: Milled edge

2008	15,976	PF65 32.00				

Note: Plain edge with CESKA NARODNI BANKA *0.900*
13g

KM# 102 200 KORUN
13.00 g., 0.900 Silver 0.3737 oz. ASW, 31 mm. **Subject:** Czech
Ice Hockey Association - 100th Anniversary **Obv:** Hockey
Player **Rev:** Logo

Date	Mintage	F12	VF20	XF40	MS60	MS63
2008	10,272	—	—	—	20.00	22.00

Note: Milled edge

2008	15,097	PF65 55.00				

Note: Plain edge with CESKA NARODNI BANKA *0.900*
13g

KM# 106 200 KORUN
13.00 g., 0.900 Silver 0.3737 oz. ASW, 31 mm. **Subject:** Nordic
World Ski Championships in Liberec **Obv:** Logo with skis **Rev:**
Cross country skiers and ski jumpers

Date	Mintage	F12	VF20	XF40	MS60	MS63
2009	15,197	PF65 32.00				

Note: Plain edge with CESKA NARODNI BANKA *0.900*
13g

2009	10,772	—	—	—	20.00	22.00

Note: Milled edge

KM# 108 200 KORUN
13.00 g., 0.900 Silver 0.3737 oz. ASW, 31 mm. **Subject:** Rabbi
Jehuda Löw **Obv:** Star of David and dates **Rev:** Symbols of
Rabbi Low

Date	Mintage	F12	VF20	XF40	MS60	MS63
2009	18,100	PF65 32.00				

Note: Plain edge with CESKA NARODNI BANKA *0.900*
13g

2009	11,275	—	—	—	20.00	22.00

Note: Milled edge

KM# 105 200 KORUN
13.00 g., 0.900 Silver 0.3737 oz. ASW, 31 mm. **Subject:** Czech
Presidency to Council of the European Union **Obv:** Arms in
circle **Rev:** Czech flag and circle of stars

Date	Mintage	F12	VF20	XF40	MS60	MS63
2009	13,172	—	—	—	20.00	22.00

Note: Milled edge

2009	19,697	PF65 32.00				

Note: Plain edge with CESKA NARODNI BANKA *0.900*
13g

KM# 100 200 KORUN
13.00 g., 0.900 Silver 0.3737 oz. ASW, 31 mm. **Subject:**
Viktor Ponrepo,150th Anniversary **Obv:** Tripod camera **Rev:**
Mustache and top hat

Date	Mintage	F12	VF20	XF40	MS60	MS63
2008	14,997	PF65 32.00				

Note: Plain edge with CESKA NARODNI BANKA *0.900*
13g

2008	9,572	—	—	—	20.00	22.00

Note: Milled edge

KM# 107 200 KORUN

13.00 g., 0.900 Silver 0.3737 oz. ASW, 31 mm. **Subject:** North Pole Exploration **Obv:** Facing Explorer **Rev:** Sled and Northern Lights

Date	Mintage	F12	VF20	XF40	MS60	MS63
2009	10,172	—	—	—	20.00	22.00
Note: Milled edge						
2009	16,767	**PF65** 37.50				
Note: Plain edge with CESKA NARODNI BANKA *0.900* 13g						

KM# 109 200 KORUN

13.00 g., 0.900 Silver 0.3737 oz. ASW, 31 mm. **Subject:** Kepler's Planetary Motion Laws **Obv:** Kepler's plan of Mars **Rev:** Portrait of Kepler

Date	Mintage	F12	VF20	XF40	MS60	MS63
2009	10,472	—	—	—	20.00	22.00
Note: Milled edge						
2009	19,687	**PF65** 95.00				
Note: Plain edge with CESKA NARODNI BANKA *0.900* 13g						

KM# 112 200 KORUN

13.00 g., 0.900 Silver 0.3737 oz. ASW, 31 mm. **Subject:** Astronomical Clock, Prague **Obv:** Figures of four apostles and rooster **Rev:** Clock works

Date	Mintage	F12	VF20	XF40	MS60	MS63
2010	10,372	—	—	—	18.00	20.00
Note: Milled edge						
2010	16,097	**PF65** 32.50				
Note: Plain edge with CESKA NARODNI BANKA *0.900* 13g						

KM# 113 200 KORUN

13.00 g., 0.900 Silver 0.3737 oz. ASW, 31 mm. **Subject:** Gustav Mahler **Obv:** Part of Mahler's 5th symphony **Rev:** Portrait of Mahler

Date	Mintage	F12	VF20	XF40	MS60	MS63
2010	9,672	—	—	—	18.00	20.00
Note: Milled edge						
2010	15,047	**PF65** 32.50				
Note: Plain edge with CESKA NARODNI BANKA *0.900* 13g						

KM# 114 200 KORUN

13.00 g., 0.900 Silver 0.3737 oz. ASW, 31 mm. **Subject:** Alfons Mucha **Obv:** Print of Music by Mucha **Rev:** Facing portrait of Mucha

Date	Mintage	F12	VF20	XF40	MS60	MS63
2010	10,072	—	—	—	18.00	20.00
Note: Milled edge						
2010	15,897	**PF65** 75.00				
Note: Plain edge with CESKA NARODNI BANKA *0.900* 13g						

KM# 115 200 KORUN

13.00 g., 0.900 Silver 0.3737 oz. ASW, 31 mm. **Subject:** John of Luxembourg, 700th Wedding Anniversary **Obv:** Czech lion on tapestry background **Rev:** John and wife standing

Date	Mintage	F12	VF20	XF40	MS60	MS63
2010	9,572	—	—	—	18.00	20.00
Note: Milled edge						
2010	13,897	**PF65** 32.00				
Note: Plain edge with CESKA NARODNI BANKA *0.900* 13g						

KM# 116 200 KORUN

13.00 g., 0.900 Silver 0.3737 oz. ASW, 31 mm. **Subject:** Karel Zeman, 100th Anniversary of Birth **Obv:** Marionettes of Zeman's cinemas **Rev:** Submarine, airship, octopus of Zeman's cinemas

Date	Mintage	F12	VF20	XF40	MS60	MS63
2010	9,275	—	—	—	18.00	20.00
Note: Milled edge						
2010	13,000	**PF65** 32.00				
Note: Plain edge with CESKA NARODNI BANKA *0.900* 13g						

KM# 119 200 KORUN

13.00 g., 0.925 Silver 0.3841 oz. ASW, 31 mm. **Subject:** Prague Conservatory, 200th Anniversary

Date	Mintage	F12	VF20	XF40	MS60	MS63
2011	11,500	**PF65** 32.00				
Note: Plain edge with CESKA NARODNI BANKA *0.925* 13g						
2011	7,777	—	—	—	18.00	20.00
Note: Milled edge						

KM# 120 200 KORUN

13.00 g., 0.925 Silver 0.3841 oz. ASW, 31 mm. **Subject:** Jan Kaspar, 100th Anniversary of First Flight

Date	Mintage	F12	VF20	XF40	MS60	MS63
2011	7,777	—	—	—	18.00	20.00
Note: Milled edge						
2011	11,600	**PF65** 32.00				
Note: Plain edge with CESKA NARODNI BANKA *0.925* 13g						

KM# 121 200 KORUN

13.00 g., 0.925 Silver 0.3841 oz. ASW, 31 mm. **Subject:** Jiri Melantrich, 500th Anniversary of Birth

Date	Mintage	F12	VF20	XF40	MS60	MS63
2011	7,877	—	—	—	18.00	20.00
Note: Milled edge						
2011	11,600	**PF65** 32.00				
Note: Plain edge with CESKA NARODNI BANKA *0.925* 13g						

KM# 122 200 KORUN

13.00 g., 0.925 Silver 0.3841 oz. ASW, 31 mm. **Subject:** Petr Vok, 400th Anniversary of Death

Date	Mintage	F12	VF20	XF40	MS60	MS63
2011	8,200	—	—	—	18.00	20.00
Note: Milled edge						
2011	12,200	**PF65** 32.00				
Note: Plain edge with CESKA NARODNI BANKA *0.925* 13g						

KM# 129 200 KORUN

13.00 g., 0.925 Silver 0.3841 oz. ASW, 31 mm. **Subject:** Kamil Lhoták, 100th Anniversary of Birth

Date	Mintage	F12	VF20	XF40	MS60	MS63
2012	13,200	**PF65** 32.00				
2012	7,700	—	—	—	—	25.00

KM# 126 200 KORUN

13.00 g., 0.925 Silver 0.3841 oz. ASW, 31 mm. **Subject:** Emperor Rudolf II, 400th Anniversary of Death **Obv:** Emperor on horseback, Prague city view in backgorund **Rev:** Portrait, signature and arms

Date	Mintage	F12	VF20	XF40	MS60	MS63
2012	12,600	PF65 32.00				
2012	8,100	—	—	—	—	25.00

Note: Milled edge

KM# 127 200 KORUN

13.00 g., 0.925 Silver 0.3841 oz. ASW, 31 mm. **Subject:** Sokol, 150th Anniversary **Obv:** SOKOL logo and stylized gymnasts in background **Rev:** Falcon, stylized gymnasts in background

Date	Mintage	F12	VF20	XF40	MS60	MS63
2012	12,200	PF65 32.00				
2012	8,000	—	—	—	—	25.00

Note: Milled edge

KM# 128 200 KORUN

13.00 g., 0.925 Silver 0.3841 oz. ASW, 31 mm. **Subject:** Czech Scouts - Junak, 100th Anniversary **Obv:** Scouting emblems **Rev:** A. B. Svojsik, founder of Czeck scouting

Date	Mintage	F12	VF20	XF40	MS60	MS63
2012	12,200	PF65 32.00				
2012	8,000	—	—	—	—	50.00

Note: Milled edge

KM# 130 200 KORUN

13.00 g., 0.925 Silver 0.3841 oz. ASW, 31 mm. **Subject:** Prague Municipal House, 100th Anniversary

Date	Mintage	F12	VF20	XF40	MS60	MS63
2012	7,700	—	—	—	—	25.00
2012	13,600	PF65 32.00				

KM# 123 500 KORUN

25.00 g., 0.925 Silver 0.7387 oz. ASW, 40 mm. **Subject:** Karel Jaromir Erben, 200th Anniversary of Birth **Obv:** Floral bouquet **Rev:** Portrait 1/4 left

Date	Mintage	F12	VF20	XF40	MS60	MS63
2011	7,300	—	—	—	—	35.00

Note: Milled edge

2011	10,800	PF65 45.00				

Note: Plain edge with CESKA NARODNI BANKA *0.925* 13g

KM# 131 500 KORUN

25.00 g., 0.925 Silver 0.7387 oz. ASW, 40 mm. **Subject:** Jiri Trnka, 100th Anniversary of Birth **Rev:** Profile left

Date	Mintage	F12	VF20	XF40	MS60	MS63
2012	12,100	PF65 40.00				
2012	6,800	—	—	—	—	35.00

Note: Milled edge.

GOLD BULLION COINAGE

KM# 65 2000 KORUN

6.22 g., 0.9999 Gold 0.1987 oz. AGW, 20 mm. **Subject:** Romanesque - Znojmo Rotunda **Obv:** Three heraldic animals **Rev:** Farmer and round building

Date	Mintage	F12	VF20	XF40	MS60	MS63
ND-2001	2,197	—	—	—	—	375

Note: Milled edge

ND-2001		—	PF65 400			

Note: Plain edge

KM# 66 2000 KORUN

6.22 g., 0.9999 Gold 0.1987 oz. AGW, 20 mm. **Subject:** Gothic - Cloister of the Vyssi Brod Monastery **Obv:** Three heraldic animals above Gothic design **Rev:** Man holding church building model

Date	Mintage	F12	VF20	XF40	MS60	MS63
2001	2,195	—	—	—	—	375

Note: Milled edge

2001		—	PF65 400			

Note: Plain edge

KM# 61 2000 KORUN

6.22 g., 0.9999 Gold 0.1987 oz. AGW, 20 mm. **Subject:** Renaissance - Litomysl Castle **Obv:** Three heraldic animals above mermaid **Rev:** Aerial castle view and mythical creature

Date	Mintage	F12	VF20	XF40	MS60	MS63
2002	2,094	—	—	—	—	375

Note: Milled edge

2002		—	PF65 400			

Note: Plain edge

KM# 67 2000 KORUN

6.22 g., 0.9999 Gold 0.1987 oz. AGW, 20 mm. **Subject:** Gothic - Fountain in Kutna Hora **Obv:** Three heraldic animals **Rev:** Fountain enclosure

Date	Mintage	F12	VF20	XF40	MS60	MS63
2002	2,195	—	—	—	—	375

Note: Milled edge

2002		—	PF65 400			

Note: Plain edge

KM# 68 2000 KORUN

6.22 g., 0.9999 Gold 0.1987 oz. AGW, 20 mm. **Subject:** Renaissance - Slavonice House Gables **Obv:** Three heraldic animals above city view **Rev:** City arms

Date	Mintage	F12	VF20	XF40	MS60	MS63
2003	1,994	—	—	—	—	375

Note: Milled edge

2003	2,996	PF65 400				

Note: Plain edge

KM# 69 2000 KORUN

6.22 g., 0.9999 Gold 0.1987 oz. AGW, 20 mm. **Subject:** Baroque - Buchlovice Palace **Obv:** Three heraldic animals above palace **Rev:** Palace view

Date	Mintage	F12	VF20	XF40	MS60	MS63
2003	1,994	—	—	—	—	375

Note: Milled edge

2003		—	PF65 400			

Note: Plain edge

KM# 75 2000 KORUN

6.22 g., 0.9999 Gold 0.1987 oz. AGW, 20 mm. **Obv:** Ornamental porch below three heraldic animals **Rev:** Hluboka Castle with coat of arms in foreground

Date	Mintage	F12	VF20	XF40	MS60	MS63
2004	1,994	—	—	—	—	375

Note: Milled edge

2004	2,997	PF65 400				

Note: Plain edge

KM# 86 2000 KORUN

6.22 g., 0.999 Gold 0.1985 oz. AGW, 20 mm. **Subject:** Kacina Castle

Date	Mintage	F12	VF20	XF40	MS60	MS63
2004	2,996	PF65 400				

Note: Plain edge

2004	1,994	—	—	—	—	375

Note: Milled edge

KM# 87 2000 KORUN

6.22 g., 0.999 Gold 0.1985 oz. AGW, 20 mm. **Subject:** Lazne Bohdanec Spa **Obv:** Gocar Spa Pavillion, full facade **Rev:** Gocar Spa Pavillion central area

Date	Mintage	F12	VF20	XF40	MS60	MS63
2005	2,996	PF65 400				

Note: Plain edge

2005	1,997	—	—	—	—	375

Note: Milled edge

KM# 88 2000 KORUN
6.22 g., 0.999 Gold 0.1985 oz. AGW, 20 mm. **Subject:** Dancing House in Prague **Rev:** Exterior view of Dancing House

Date	Mintage	F12	VF20	XF40	MS60	MS63
2005	3,297	PF65 400				
Note: Plain edge						
2005	1,996	—	—	—	—	375
Note: Milled edge						

KM# 76 2500 KORUN
31.10 g., Bi-Metallic, 40 mm. **Subject:** Czech entry into the European Union **Obv:** Value within circle of shields **Rev:** 1.5.2004" within circle of dates and text **Edge:** Lettered **Edge Lettering:** CNB * Ag 0.999 * 23,328 g CNB Au 999.9 * 7,776g *

Date	Mintage	F12	VF20	XF40	MS60	MS63
ND (2004)	8,117	PF65 500				

KM# 90 2500 KORUN
7.79 g., 0.999 Gold 0.2484 oz. AGW, 22 mm. **Subject:** Observatory at Prague Klementinum **Obv:** Sun's rays thru clouds **Rev:** Building tower, rays and moon **Note:** Prev. KM #86.

Date	Mintage	F12	VF20	XF40	MS60	MS63
2006	3,797	PF65 1,000				
Note: Plain edge						
2006	1,897	—	—	—	—	700
Note: Milled edge						

KM# 89 2500 KORUN
7.78 g., 0.999 Gold 0.2482 oz. AGW, 22 mm. **Subject:** Hand Paper Mill at Velke Losiny

Date	Mintage	F12	VF20	XF40	MS60	MS63
2006	3,000	PF65 3,000				
Note: Plain edge						
2006	1,800	—	—	—	1,500	—
Note: Milled edge						

KM# 95 2500 KORUN
7.78 g., 0.999 Gold 0.2482 oz. AGW, 22 mm. **Subject:** Sevcinsky Mine at Pribram-Brezove Hory **Rev:** Head-gear tower at mine

Date	Mintage	F12	VF20	XF40	MS60	MS63
2007	5,097	PF65 500				
Note: Plain edge						
2007	2,097	—	—	—	—	475
Note: Milled edge						

KM# 96 2500 KORUN
7.78 g., 0.999 Gold 0.2482 oz. AGW, 22 mm. **Subject:** Water mill at Slup **Obv:** Water Mill **Rev:** Water Mill

Date	Mintage	F12	VF20	XF40	MS60	MS63
2007	6,297	PF65 500				
2007	2,297	—	—	—	—	475

KM# 103 2500 KORUN
7.78 g., 0.999 Gold 0.2483 oz. AGW, 22 mm. **Subject:** Stadlec Suspension Bridge **Obv:** Side view of bridge **Rev:** View of bridge thru arch

Date	Mintage	F12	VF20	XF40	MS60	MS63
2008	10,897	PF65 500				
Note: Plain edge						
2008	3,097	—	—	—	—	475
Note: Milled edge						

KM# 104 2500 KORUN
7.78 g., 0.999 Gold 0.2483 oz. AGW, 22 mm. **Subject:** Plzen Brewery **Obv:** Copper vats **Rev:** Plzen Brewery façade and wooden barrels

Date	Mintage	F12	VF20	XF40	MS60	MS63
2008	10,797	PF65 500				
Note: Plain edge						
2008	3,197	—	—	—	—	475
Note: Milled edge						

KM# 110 2500 KORUN
7.78 g., 0.999 Gold 0.2482 oz. AGW, 22 mm. **Subject:** Elbe Sluice under Strekov Castle **Obv:** Turbine in sluice in the Labe (Elbe) river **Rev:** Sluice under Strekov castle

Date	Mintage	F12	VF20	XF40	MS60	MS63
2009	10,497	PF65 500				
Note: Plain edge						
2009	3,497	—	—	—	—	475
Note: Milled edge						

KM# 111 2500 KORUN
7.78 g., 0.999 Gold 0.2482 oz. AGW, 22 mm. **Subject:** Windmill at Ruprechtov

Date	Mintage	F12	VF20	XF40	MS60	MS63
2009	10,497	PF65 500				
2009	3,497	—	—	—	—	475

KM# 117 2500 KORUN
7.77 g., 0.999 Gold 0.248 oz. AGW, 22 mm. **Subject:** Hammer Mill in Dobriv

Date	Mintage	F12	VF20	XF40	MS60	MS63
2010	3,797	—	—	—	—	475
Note: Milled edge						
2010	9,997	PF65 500				
Note: Plain edge						

KM# 118 2500 KORUN
7.77 g., 0.999 Gold 0.248 oz. AGW, 22 mm. **Subject:** Michael Mine in Ostrana **Obv:** Turbine **Rev:** Mine shaft

Date	Mintage	F12	VF20	XF40	MS60	MS63
2010	3,697	—	—	—	—	475
Note: Milled edge						
2010	9,097	PF65 500				
Note: Plain edge						

KM# 124 5000 KORUN
15.55 g., 0.9999 Gold 0.4968 oz. AGW, 28 mm. **Subject:** Gothic Bridge in Pisek

Date	Mintage	F12	VF20	XF40	MS60	MS63
2011	2,600	—	—	—	—	900
2011	6,900	PF65 950				

KM# 125 5000 KORUN
15.55 g., 0.9999 Gold 0.4968 oz. AGW, 28 mm. **Subject:** Renaissance Bridge in Stribro

Date	Mintage	F12	VF20	XF40	MS60	MS63
2011	2,700	—	—	—	—	900
Note: Milled edge						
2011	7,300	PF65 950				
Note: Plain edge						

KM# 132 5000 KORUN
15.55 g., 0.9999 Gold 0.4968 oz. AGW, 28 mm. **Subject:** Banocco Bridge in Namest nad Oslavou

Date	Mintage	F12	VF20	XF40	MS60	MS63
2012	3,200	—	—	—	—	950
2012	9,000	PF65 950				

KM# 133 5000 KORUN
15.55 g., 0.9999 Gold 0.4968 oz. AGW, 28 mm. **Subject:** Negrelli viaduct in Prague

Date	Mintage	F12	VF20	XF40	MS60	MS63
2012	3,900	—	—	—	—	900
2012	12,200	PF65 950				

KM# 134 10000 KORUN
31.11 g., 0.9999 Gold 0.9936 oz. AGW, 34 mm. **Subject:** Gold Bulla of Sicily, 800th Anniversary

Date	Mintage	F12	VF20	XF40	MS60	MS63
2012	3,100	—	—	—	—	1,900
2012	10,900	PF65 2,000				

MINT SETS

KM#	Date	Mintage	Identification	Issue Price	Mkt Val
MS14	2001 (9)	11,500	KM#1, 2.3, 3.2, 4-9, Tyn Church folder	—	17.50
MS15	2002 (9)	11,885	KM#1, 2.3, 3.2, 4-9, Castles	—	60.00
MS16	2002 (9)	5,115	KM#1, 2.3, 3.2, 4-9, NATO Summit folder	—	17.50
MS17	2003 (9)	22,000	KM#1, 2.3, 3.2, 4-9, CNB 10th Anniversary	—	30.00
MS18	2004 (7)	7,500	KM#1, 3.2, 4-5, 7-9, Football	—	30.00
MS19	2004 (7)	13,000	KM#1, 3.2, 4-5, 7-9, EU Entry	—	40.00
MS20	2004 (7)	10,000	KM#1, 3.2, 4-5, 7-9	—	16.00
MS21	2005 (8)	13,015	KM#1, 3.2, 4-5, 7-9, plus Smetna/Dvorak Medal and CD	—	17.50
MS22	2006 (7)	9,000	KM#1, 3.2, 4-5, 7-9, UNESCO Folder	—	16.00
MS23	2006 (7)	5,139	KM#1, 3.2, 4-5, 7-9, Football Championship	—	40.00
MS24	2006 (7)	9,784	KM#1, 3.2, 4-5, 7-9, plus Euro Medal	—	45.00
MS25	2007 (7)	8,500	KM#1, 3.2, 4-5, 7-9, UNESCO Kunta Hora folder	—	25.00
MS26	2007 (14)	10,000	KM#1, 3.2, 4-5, 7-9. Natural beauties with Slovakia coins	—	35.00
MS27	2008 (7)	9,000	KM#1, 3.2, 4-5, 7-9, plus UNESCO Medal	—	30.00
MS28	2008 (8)	6,000	KM#1, 3.2, 4-5, 7-9, Soccer medal and package	—	17.50
MS29	2009 (8)	10,000	KM#1, 3.2, 4-5, 7-9 plus brass Southern Bohemia Medal	—	17.50
MS30	2010 (6)	10,000	KM#1, 3.2, 4-5, 7-9, Zlin Region folder	—	17.50
MS31	2011 (6)	10,000	KM#1, 4-5, 7-9, Plzen Region folder	—	17.50
MS32	2011 (6)	5,000	KM#1, 4-5, 7-9. Baby set.	—	17.50
MS33	2011 (6)	450	KM# 1, 4-5, 7-9. ENA and CNB official distribution	12.00	15.00

PROOF SETS

KM#	Date	Mintage	Identification	Issue Price	Mkt Val
PS6	2001 (9)	2,500	KM#1, 2.3, 3.1, 4-9	35.00	250
PS7	2002 (9)	3,490	KM#1, 2.3, 3.2, 4-9	35.00	250
PS8	2003 (9)	3,000	KM#1, 2.3, 3.2, 4-9	35.00	150
PS9	2004 (7)	4,000	KM#1, 3.2, 4-5, 7-9	35.00	100
PS10	2005 (8)	3,000	KM#1, 3.2, 4-5, 7-9, and silver strike of Czechoslovakia KM#4	—	100
PS11	2006 (8)	2,500	KM#1, 3.2, 4-5, 7-9, and silver strike of Czechoslovakia KM#2	—	120
PS12	2007 (8)	2,500	KM#1, 3.2, 4-5, 7-9, and silver Unesco medal	—	120
PS13	2008 (8)	2,500	KM#1, 3.2, 4-5, 7-9, and silver medal for 15th Anniversary of Republic	—	150
PS14	2009 (8)	3,200	KM#1, 3.2, 4-5, 7-9, and silver medal for the Czech Presidency of the EU	—	85.00
PS15	2010 (7)	3,200	KM#1, 4-5, 7-9, plus silver T. G. Masaryk medal	—	85.00
PS16	2011 (7)	3,500	KM#1, 4-5, 7-9, plus silver Ema Destinnova medal in a velvet case	—	85.00
PS17	2011 (7)	2,000	KM#1, 4-5, 7-9, plus silver Ema Destinnova medal in a leather case	—	120

DENMARK

The Kingdom of Denmark (Danmark), a constitutional monarchy located at the mouth of the Baltic Sea, has an area of 16,639 sq. mi. (43,070 sq. km.) and a population of 5.2 million. Capital: Copenhagen. Most of the country is arable. Agriculture is conducted by large farms served by cooperatives. The largest industries are food processing, iron and metal, and shipping. Machinery, meats (chiefly bacon), dairy products and chemicals are exported.

As a result of a referendum held September 28, 2000, the currency of the European Monetary Union, the Euro, will not be introduced in Denmark in the foreseeable future.

RULER
Margrethe II, 1972—

MINT MARKS
(h) - Copenhagen, heart

MINT OFFICIALS' INITIALS

Copenhagen Mint

Letter	Date	Name
LG	1989-2001	Laust Grove

MONEYERS' INITIALS

Copenhagen Mint

Letter	Date	Name
A	1986-	Johan Alkjaer (designer)
HV	1986-	Hanne Varming (sculptor)
JP	1989-	Jan Petersen

MONETARY SYSTEM
100 Øre = 1 Krone

KINGDOM

DECIMAL COINAGE

100 ÿre = 1 Krone; 1874-present

KM# 868.1 25 ØRE
2.80 g., Bronze, 17.5 mm. **Ruler:** Margrethe II **Obv:** Large crown divides date above, initial to right of country **Rev:** Denomination, small heart above, mint mark and initials LG-JP below **Note:** Beginning in 1996 and ending with 1998, the words "DANMARK" and "ØRE" have raised edges. Heart mint mark under "ØRE"; Prev. KM#868.

Date	Mintage	VF20	XF40	MS60	MS63	MS65
2001 LG; JP; A	10,530,000	—	—	—	—	0.15

KM# 868.2 25 ØRE
2.80 g., Bronze, 17.5 mm. **Ruler:** Margrethe II **Obv:** Large crown divides date above **Rev:** Denomination, small heart above **Edge:** Plain **Note:** Without initials

Date	Mintage	XF40	MS60	MS63	MS65
2002	12,000,000	—	—	—	0.15
2003	17,590,000	—	—	—	0.15
2004	7,040,304	—	—	—	0.15
2004	3,000	PF63 15.00	PF65 18.00		
2005	19,039,000	—	—	—	0.15
2005	2,650	PF63 15.00	PF65 18.00		
2006	16,796,000	—	—	—	0.15
2006	1,800	PF63 15.00	PF65 18.00		
2007	20,592,000	—	—	—	0.15
2007	1,400	PF63 15.00	PF65 18.00		
2008	2,049,000	—	—	—	0.15
2008	1,000	PF63 15.00	PF65 18.00		

KM# 866.2 50 ØRE
4.30 g., Bronze, 21.5 mm. **Ruler:** Margrethe II **Obv:** Large crown divides date above, initial to right of country name **Rev:** Large heart above value, mint mark and initials LG-JP below **Note:** Beginning in 1996 and ending in 1998, the words "DANMARK" and "ØRE" have raised edges. Heart mint mark under the word "ØRE".

Date	Mintage	VF20	XF40	MS60	MS63	MS65
2001 LG; JP; A	12,270,000	—	—	—	—	0.30

KM# 866.3 50 ØRE
4.30 g., Bronze, 21.5 mm. **Ruler:** Margrethe II **Obv:** Large crown divides date above **Rev:** Small heart above denomination **Edge:** Plain **Note:** No initials

Date	Mintage	XF40	MS60	MS63	MS65
2002	3,900,000	—	—	—	0.50
2003	8,817,000	—	—	—	0.30
2004	10,040,706	—	—	—	0.25
2004	3,000	PF63 15.00	PF65 18.00		
2005	12,037,000	—	—	—	0.25
2005	2,650	PF63 15.00	PF65 18.00		
2006	14,843,000	—	—	—	0.25
2006	1,800	PF63 15.00	PF65 18.00		
2007	10,198,000	—	—	—	0.25
2007	1,400	PF63 15.00	PF65 18.00		
2008	2,573,000	—	—	—	0.25
2008	1,000	PF63 15.00	PF65 18.00		
2009	1,050	PF63 15.00	PF65 18.00		
2010	1,010	PF63 15.00	PF65 18.00		
2011	1,000	PF63 15.00	PF65 18.00		
2012	1,090	PF63 15.00	PF65 18.00		
2013	—	PF63 15.00	PF65 18.00		
2013		—	—	—	1.00

KM# 873.1 KRONE
3.60 g., Copper-Nickel, 20.25 mm. **Ruler:** Margrethe II **Obv:** 3 crowned MII monograms around center hole, date, mint mark, and initials LG-JP-A below **Rev:** Wave design surrounds center hole, value above, hearts flank **Edge:** Reeded **Note:** Prev. KM#873.

Date	Mintage	VF20	XF40	MS60	MS63	MS65
2001 LG; JP; A	14,640,000	—	—	—	—	0.40

KM# 873.2 KRONE
3.60 g., Copper-Nickel, 20.25 mm. **Ruler:** Margrethe II **Obv:** 3 crowned MII monograms around center hole, date below **Rev:** Design surounds center hole, value above, hearts flank **Edge:** Reeded **Note:** Without initials

Date	Mintage	XF40	MS60	MS63	MS65
2002	9,000,000	—	—	—	0.40
2003	5,231,000	—	—	—	0.40
2004	16,139,596	—	—	—	0.40
2004	3,000	PF63 18.00	PF65 22.00		
2005	16,757,000	—	—	—	0.40
2005	2,650	PF63 18.00	PF65 22.00		
2006	21,026,000	—	—	—	0.40
2006	1,800	PF63 18.00	PF65 22.00		
2007	11,729,000	—	—	—	0.40
2007	1,400	PF63 18.00	PF65 22.00		
2008	13,339,000	—	—	—	0.40
2008	1,000	PF63 18.00	PF65 22.00		
2009	624,000	—	—	—	2.00
2009	1,050	PF63 18.00	PF65 22.00		
2010 In sets only	26,000	—	—	—	2.00
2010	1,010	PF63 18.00	PF65 22.00		
2011 In sets only	21,000	—	—	—	2.00
2011	1,000	PF63 18.00	PF65 22.00		
2012	17,170	—	—	—	2.00
2012	1,090	PF63 18.00	PF65 22.00		
2013	—	PF63 18.00	PF65 22.00		
2013		—	—	—	0.40

KM# 874.1 2 KRONER
5.90 g., Copper-Nickel, 24.5 mm. **Ruler:** Margrethe II **Obv:** 3 crowned MII monograms around center hole, date and initials LG-JP-A below **Rev:** Design surrounds center hole, denomination above, hearts flank **Edge:** Segmented reeding **Note:** Prev. KM#874.

Date	Mintage	VF20	XF40	MS60	MS63	MS65
2001 LG; JP; A	11,180,000	—	—	—	—	0.80

KM# 874.2 2 KRONER
5.90 g., Copper-Nickel, 24.5 mm. **Ruler:** Margrethe II **Obv:** 3 crowned MII monograms around center hole, date and initials

LGpJP-A below **Rev:** Wave design surrounds center hole, denomination above, hearts flank **Edge:** Segmented reeding **Note:** Without initials

Date	Mintage	XF40	MS60	MS63	MS65
2002	6,159,000	—	—	—	0.80
2004	7,381,531	—	—	—	0.80
2004	3,000	PF63 22.00		PF65 25.00	
2005	16,684,000	—	—	—	0.80
2005	2,650	PF63 22.00		PF65 25.00	
2006	7,331,000	—	—	—	0.80
2006	1,800	PF63 22.00		PF65 25.00	
2007	22,060,000	—	—	—	0.80
2007	1,400	PF63 22.00		PF65 25.00	
2008	2,623,000	—	—	—	0.80
2008	1,000	PF63 22.00		PF65 25.00	
2009 In sets only	27,000	—	—	—	2.50
2009	1,050	PF63 22.00		PF65 25.00	
2010 In sets only	25,000	—	—	—	2.50
2010	1,010	PF63 22.00		PF65 25.00	
2011	920,000	—	—	—	1.00
2011	1,000	PF63 22.00		PF65 25.00	
2012 In sets only	18,000	—	—	—	1.00
2012	1,090	PF63 22.00		PF65 25.00	
2013	—	PF63 22.00		PF65 25.00	
2013		—	—	—	0.80

KM# 869.1 5 KRONER
9.20 g., Copper-Nickel, 28.5 mm. **Ruler:** Margrethe II **Obv:** 3 crowned MII monograms around center hole, date and initials LG-JP-A below **Rev:** Wave design surrounds center hole, denomination above, hearts flank **Edge:** Reeded **Note:** Large and small date varieties exist.

Date	Mintage	VF20	XF40	MS60	MS63	MS65
2001 LG; JP; A	5,700,000	—	—	—	—	1.75

KM# 869.2 5 KRONER
9.20 g., Copper-Nickel, 28.5 mm. **Ruler:** Margrethe II **Obv:** 3 crowned MII monograms around center hole, date below **Rev:** Wave design surrounds center hole, denomination above, hearts flank **Edge:** Reeded **Note:** Without initials

Date	Mintage	XF40	MS60	MS63	MS65
2002	5,980,000	—	—	—	1.75
2004	1,415,925	—	—	—	1.50
2004	3,000	PF63 30.00		PF65 35.00	
2005	7,073,000	—	—	—	1.50
2005	2,650	PF63 30.00		PF65 35.00	
2006	3,431,000	—	—	—	1.50
2006	1,800	PF63 30.00		PF65 35.00	
2007	4,983,000	—	—	—	1.50
2007	1,400	PF63 30.00		PF65 35.00	
2008	7,506,000	—	—	—	1.50
2008	1,000	PF63 30.00		PF65 35.00	
2009 In sets only	25,700	—	—	—	3.00
2009	1,050	PF63 30.00		PF65 35.00	
2010 In sets only	24,300	—	—	—	3.00
2010	1,010	PF63 30.00		PF65 35.00	
2011 In sets only	19,900	—	—	—	3.00
2011	1,000	PF63 30.00		PF65 35.00	
2012 In sets only	17,170	—	—	—	3.00
2012	1,090	PF63 30.00		PF65 35.00	
2013		PF63 30.00		PF65 35.00	
2013		—	—	—	1.50

KM# 887.1 10 KRONER
7.00 g., Aluminum-Bronze, 23.35 mm. **Ruler:** Margrethe II **Obv:** Crowned head right within inner circle, date, initials LG-JP-A below, mint mark after II in title **Obv. Legend:** MARGRETHE II - DANMARKS DRONNING **Rev:** Crowned arms within inner circle above denomination **Edge:** Plain

Date	Mintage	XF40	MS60	MS63	MS65
2001(h) LG; JP; A	4,800,000	—	—	—	4.00

KM# 887.2 10 KRONER
7.00 g., Aluminum-Bronze, 23.35 mm. **Ruler:** Margrethe II **Obv:** Crowned bust right, mint mark after II in title **Obv. Legend:** MARGRETHE II - DANMARKS DRONNING **Rev:** Crowned arms and denomination **Edge:** Plain **Note:** Without initials

Date	Mintage	XF40	MS60	MS63	MS65
2002(h)	7,299,900	—	—	—	3.00

KM# 896 10 KRONER
7.00 g., Aluminum-Bronze, 23.35 mm. **Ruler:** Margrethe II **Obv:** Crowned bust right within circle, date below **Obv. Legend:** MARGRETHE II - DANMARKS DRONNING **Rev:** Crowned arms above denomination **Edge:** Plain

Date	Mintage	XF40	MS60	MS63	MS65
2004(h)	5,835,426	—	—	—	3.00
2004(h)	3,000	PF63 35.00		PF65 40.00	
2005(h)	2,614,000	—	—	—	3.00
2005(h)	2,650	PF63 35.00		PF65 40.00	
2006(h)	3,530,000	—	—	—	3.00
2006(h)	1,800	PF63 35.00		PF65 40.00	
2007(h)	3,294,000	—	—	—	3.00
2007(h)	1,400	PF63 35.00		PF65 40.00	
2008(h)	2,258,000	—	—	—	3.00
2008(h)	1,000	PF63 35.00		PF65 40.00	
2009(h)	1,701,000	—	—	—	4.00
2009(h)	1,050	PF63 35.00		PF65 40.00	
2010(h) In sets only	24,300	—	—	—	7.00
2010(h)	1,010	PF63 35.00		PF65 40.00	

KM# 898 10 KRONER
7.00 g., Aluminum-Bronze, 23.35 mm. **Ruler:** Margrethe II **Series:** Fairy Tales **Subject:** Hans Christian Andersen's Ugly duckling story **Obv:** Crowned bust right within circle, date below **Obv. Legend:** MARGRETHE II - DANMARKS DRONNING **Rev:** Swan and reflection on water within circle, value below **Edge:** Plain

Date	Mintage	XF40	MS60	MS63	MS65
2005(h)	1,206,675	—	—	2.75	4.00

KM# 900 10 KRONER
7.00 g., Aluminum-Bronze, 23.35 mm. **Ruler:** Margrethe II **Series:** Fairy Tales **Subject:** Hans Christian Andersen's Little Mermaid **Obv:** Crowned bust right within circle, date below **Obv. Legend:** MARGRETHE II - DANMARKS DRONNING **Rev:** Little Mermaid **Edge:** Plain

Date	Mintage	XF40	MS60	MS63	MS65
2005(h)	1,206,675	—	—	2.75	4.00

KM# 906 10 KRONER
31.10 g., 0.999 Silver 0.9925 oz. ASW, 38 mm. **Ruler:** Margrethe II **Series:** Fairy Tales **Subject:** Hans Christian Andersen's The Ugly Duckling **Obv:** Crowned bust right **Obv. Legend:** MARGRETHE II - DANMARKS DRONNING **Rev:** Swan and reflection on water

Date	Mintage	XF40	MS60	MS63	MS65
2005(h)	75,000	—	—	—	35.00

KM# 907 10 KRONER
8.65 g., 0.900 Gold 0.2487 oz. AGW, 22 mm. **Ruler:** Margrethe II **Series:** Fairy Tales **Subject:** Hans Christian Andersen's The Ugly Duckling **Obv:** Crowned bust right **Obv. Legend:** MARGRETHE II - DANMARKS DRONNING **Rev:** Swan and reflection on water

Date	Mintage	XF40	MS60	MS63	MS65
2005(h)	7,000	—	—	425	—

KM# 908 10 KRONER
31.10 g., 0.999 Silver 0.9925 oz. ASW, 38 mm. **Ruler:** Margrethe II **Series:** Fairy Tales **Subject:** Hans Christian Andersen's Little Mermaid **Obv:** Crowned bust right, date below **Obv. Legend:** MARGRETHE II - DANMARKS DRONNING **Rev:** Little Mermaid

Date	Mintage	XF40	MS60	MS63	MS65
2005(h)	40,220	PF63 35.00		PF65 40.00	

KM# 911 10 KRONER
8.65 g., 0.900 Gold 0.2487 oz. AGW, 22 mm. **Ruler:** Margrethe II **Series:** Fairy Tales **Subject:** Hans Christian Andersen's Little Mermaid **Obv:** Crowned bust right **Obv. Legend:** MARGRETHE II - DANMARKS DRONNING **Rev:** Little Mermaid

Date	Mintage	XF40	MS60	MS63	MS65
2005(h)	4,220	—	—	425	—

KM# 903 10 KRONER
7.00 g., Aluminum-Bronze, 23.35 mm. **Ruler:** Margrethe II **Series:** Fairy Tales **Subject:** H.C. Andersen's "The Shadow" **Obv:** Crowned bust right within circle, date below **Obv. Legend:** MARGRETHE II - DANMARKS DRONNING **Rev:** Stylized figures **Edge:** Plain

Date	Mintage	XF40	MS60	MS63	MS65
2006(h)	1,206,675	—	—	2.75	4.00

KM# 909 10 KRONER
31.10 g., 0.999 Silver 0.9925 oz. ASW, 38 mm. **Ruler:** Margrethe II **Series:** Fairy Tales **Subject:** H.C. Andersen's "Skyggen" (The Shadow) **Obv:** Crowned bust right **Obv. Legend:** MARGRETHE II - DANMARKS DRONNING **Rev:** Stylized figures

Date	Mintage	XF40	MS60	MS63	MS65
2006(h)	22,317	PF63 45.00		PF65 50.00	

KM# 910 10 KRONER
8.65 g., 0.900 Gold 0.2487 oz. AGW, 22 mm. **Ruler:** Margrethe II **Series:** Fairy Tales **Subject:** H.C. Andersen's "Skyggen" (The Shadow) **Obv:** Crowned bust right **Obv. Legend:** MARGRETHE II - DANMARKS DRONNING **Rev:** Stylized figures

Date	Mintage	XF40	MS60	MS63	MS65
2006(h)	3,070	—	—	425	—

KM# 951 10 KRONER
31.10 g., 0.999 Silver 0.9925 oz. ASW, 38 mm. **Ruler:** Margrethe II **Series:** Fairy Tales **Subject:** Hans Christian Andersen's Snow Queen **Obv:** Crowned bust right **Obv. Legend:** MARGRETHE II - DANMARKS DRONNING **Rev:** Ice pieces

Date	Mintage	XF40	MS60	MS63	MS65
2006(h)	25,758	—	—	40.00	—

KM# 952 10 KRONER
8.65 g., 0.900 Gold 0.2487 oz. AGW, 22 mm. **Ruler:** Margrethe II **Series:** Fairy Tales **Subject:** The Snow Queen **Obv:** Crowned bust right **Obv. Legend:** MARGRETHE II - DANMARKS DRONNING **Rev:** Ice pieces

Date	Mintage	XF40	MS60	MS63	MS65
2006(h)	3,075	—	—	475	—

KM# 914 10 KRONER
7.00 g., Aluminum-Bronze, 23.35 mm. **Ruler:** Margrethe II **Series:** Fairy Tales **Subject:** Hans Christian Andersen's Snow Queen **Obv:** Crowned bust right **Obv. Legend:** MARGRETHE II - DANMARKS DRONNING **Rev:** Ice pieces

Date	Mintage	XF40	MS60	MS63	MS65
2006(h)	1,206,675	—	—	2.75	4.00

KM# 916 10 KRONER
7.00 g., Aluminum-Bronze, 23.35 mm. **Ruler:** Margrethe II **Subject:** International Polar Year 2007-2009 **Obv:** Head with tiara right **Obv. Legend:** MARGRETHE II - DANMARKS DRONNING **Rev:** Polar bear facing, walking on ice flow **Rev. Legend:** POLARÅR 2007-2009 **Edge:** Plain

Date	Mintage	XF40	MS60	MS63	MS65
2007(h)	1,200,000	—	—	2.75	4.00

KM# 949 10 KRONER
31.10 g., 0.999 Silver 0.9925 oz. ASW, 38 mm. **Ruler:** Margrethe II **Series:** Fairy Tales **Subject:** H.C. Anderson's 'The Nightengale' **Rev:** Bird

Date	Mintage	XF40	MS60	MS63	MS65
2007	18,117		PF63 40.00	PF65 45.00	

KM# 923 10 KRONER
7.00 g., Aluminum-Bronze, 23.35 mm. **Ruler:** Margrethe II **Series:** Fairy Tales **Subject:** H.C. Anderson's 'The Nightengale' **Rev:** Bird

Date	Mintage	XF40	MS60	MS63	MS65
2007	1,206,675	—	—	2.75	4.00

KM# 950 10 KRONER
8.65 g., 0.900 Gold 0.2487 oz. AGW, 22 mm. **Ruler:** Margrethe II **Series:** Fairy Tales **Subject:** H.C. Anderson's 'The Nightengale' **Rev:** Bird

Date	Mintage	XF40	MS60	MS63	MS65
2007	2,964	—	—	475	—

KM# 925 10 KRONER
7.00 g., Aluminum Bronze, 23.36 mm. **Ruler:** Margretho II **Series:** International Polar Year 2007-2009 **Obv:** Head with tiara right **Rev:** Outlined globe **Rev. Legend:** POLARÁR 2007-2009 **Edge:** Plain

Date	Mintage	XF40	MS60	MS63	MS65
2008(h)	1,200,000	—	—	2.75	4.00

KM# 932 10 KRONER
7.00 g., Aluminum-Bronze, 23.35 mm. **Ruler:** Margrethe II **Rev:** Ice scape, Northern Lights

Date	Mintage	XF40	MS60	MS63	MS65
2009	1,200,000	—	—	2.75	4.00

KM# 943 10 KRONER
7.00 g., Aluminum-Bronze, 23.35 mm. **Ruler:** Margrethe II **Obv:** Head right **Obv. Legend:** MARGRETHE II DANMARKS DRONNING **Rev:** Crowned shield and value **Edge:** Plain

Date	Mintage	XF40	MS60	MS63	MS65
2011(h)	2,339,000	—	—	2.75	4.00
2011 Special Unc	3,010	—	—	25.00	—
2011(h)	1,000	PF63 25.00	PF65 28.00		
2012 In sets only	24,000	—	—		6.00
2012	1,090	PF63 25.00	PF65 28.00		

KM# 954 10 KRONER
7.00 g., Aluminum-Bronze, 23.35 mm. **Ruler:** Margrethe II **Obv:** Bust right **Rev:** Crown, three lions and denomination **Edge:** Plain

Date	Mintage	XF40	MS60	MS63	MS65
2013	—	—	—	5.00	—
2013		PF63 28.00	PF65 32.00		

KM# 888.1 20 KRONER
9.30 g., Aluminum-Bronze, 27 mm. **Ruler:** Margrethe II **Obv:** Crowned bust right within circle, date and initials LG-JP-A below, mint mark after II in legend **Obv. Legend:** MARGRETHE II - DANMARKS DRONNING **Rev:** Crowned arms within ornaments and value **Edge:** Alternating reeded and plain sections

Date	Mintage	XF40	MS60	MS63	MS65
2001(h) LG; JP; A	2,900,000				5.00

KM# 888.2 20 KRONER
9.30 g., Aluminum-Bronze, 27 mm. **Ruler:** Margrethe II **Obv:** Crowned bust right within circle, mint mark after II in legend **Obv. Legend:** MARGRETHE II - DANMARKS DRONNING **Rev:** Crowned arms within ornaments and value **Edge:** Alternate reeded and plain sections **Note:** Without initials.

Date	Mintage	XF40	MS60	MS63	MS65
2002(h)	5,500,000	—			5.00

KM# 889 20 KRONER
9.30 g., Aluminum-Bronze, 27 mm. **Ruler:** Margrethe II **Series:** Danish Towers **Obv:** Crowned bust right within circle date below, mint mark after II in legend **Obv. Legend:** MARGRETHE II - DANMARKS DRONNING **Rev:** Aarhus City Hall **Edge:** Reeded and plain sections

Date	Mintage	XF40	MS60	MS63	MS65
2002(h)	1,208,600	—			5.00

KM# 890 20 KRONER
9.30 g., Aluminum-Bronze, 27 mm. **Ruler:** Margrethe II **Series:** Danish Towers **Obv:** Crowned bust right within circle, mint mark and date **Obv. Legend:** MARGRETHE II - DANMARKS DRONNING **Rev:** Copenhagen Old Stock Exchange spire with four intertwined dragon tails **Edge:** Alternate reeded and plain sections

Date	Mintage	XF40	MS60	MS63	MS65
2003(h)	1,208,600	—			5.00

KM# 891 20 KRONER
9.30 g., Aluminum-Bronze, 27 mm. **Ruler:** Margrethe II **Obv:** Crowned bust right within circle, mint mark and date **Obv. Legend:** MARGRETHE II - DANMARKS DRONNING **Rev:** Crowned arms above denomination **Edge:** Alternate reeded and plain sections

Date	Mintage	XF40	MS60	MS63	MS65
2003(h)	5,720,000	—	—	—	5.00
2004(h)	6,922,182	—			5.00
2004(h)	3,000	PF63 50.00	PF65 55.00		
2005(h)	4,194,000	—			5.00
2005(h)	2,650	PF63 50.00	PF65 55.00		
2006(h)	3,051,000	—			5.00
2006(h)	1,800	PF63 50.00	PF65 55.00		
2007(h)	2,409,000	—			5.00
2007(h)	1,400	PF63 50.00	PF65 55.00		
2008(h)	1,982,000	—			5.00
2008(h)	1,000	PF63 50.00	PF65 55.00		
2009(h)	2,021,000	—			5.00
2009(h)	1,050	PF63 50.00	PF65 55.00		
2010(h) In sets only	24,300	—			7.00
2010(h)	1,010	PF63 50.00	PF65 55.00		

KM# 892 20 KRONER
9.30 g., Aluminum-Bronze, 27 mm. **Ruler:** Margrethe II **Series:** Danish towers **Obv:** Crowned bust right within circle, mint mark and date **Obv. Legend:** MARGRETHE II - DANMARKS DRONNING **Rev:** Christiansborg Castle (parliament) tower and Danish flag **Edge:** Alternate reeded and plain sections

Date	Mintage	XF40	MS60	MS63	MS65
2003(h)	1,208,600	—			5.00

KM# 893 20 KRONER
9.30 g., Aluminum-Bronze, 27 mm. **Ruler:** Margrethe II **Series:** Danish Towers **Obv:** Crowned bust right within circle, date below **Obv. Legend:** MARGRETHE II - DANMARKS DRONNING **Rev:** Gåsetårnet tower **Edge:** Alternate reeded and plain sections

Date	Mintage	XF40	MS60	MS63	MS65
2004(h)	1,208,600	—			5.00

KM# 894 20 KRONER
9.30 g., Aluminum-Bronze, 27 mm. **Ruler:** Margrethe II **Subject:** Crown Prince's Wedding **Obv:** Crowned bust right within circle, date below **Obv. Legend:** MARGRETHE II - DANMARKS DRONNING **Rev:** Crown Prince Frederik and Crown Princess Mary **Edge:** Alternate reeded and plain sections

Date	Mintage	XF40	MS60	MS63	MS65
2004(h)	1,200,000	—			5.00

KM# 897 20 KRONER
9.30 g., Aluminum-Bronze, 27 mm. **Ruler:** Margrethe II **Series:** Danish Towers **Obv:** Crowned bust right within circle, date below **Obv. Legend:** MARGRETHE II - DANMARKS DRONNING **Rev:** Svaneke water tower, Bornholm **Edge:** Alternate reeded and plain sections

Date	Mintage	XF40	MS60	MS63	MS65
2004(h)	1,208,600	—	—	—	5.00

KM# 899 20 KRONER
9.30 g., Aluminum-Bronze, 27 mm. **Ruler:** Margrethe II **Series:** Danish Towers **Obv:** Crowned bust right within circle, date below **Obv. Legend:** MARGRETHE II - DANMARKS DRONNING **Rev:** Landet Kirke, with elements from the story of Elvira Madigan and Sixten Sparre, including a revolver among leaves of chestnut-trees **Edge:** Segmented reeding

Date	Mintage	XF40	MS60	MS63	MS65
2005(h)	1,208,600	—	—	—	5.00

KM# 901 20 KRONER
9.30 g., Aluminum-Bronze, 27 mm. **Ruler:** Margrethe II **Series:** Danish Towers **Obv:** Crowned bust right within circle, date below **Obv. Legend:** MARGRETHE II - DANMARKS DRONNING **Rev:** Lighthouse of Nolsoy (Faeroe Islands) **Edge:** Alternate plain and reeded segments

Date	Mintage	XF40	MS60	MS63	MS65
2005(h)	1,208,600	—	—	—	5.00

KM# 902 20 KRONER
9.30 g., Aluminum-Bronze, 27 mm. **Ruler:** Margrethe II **Series:** Danish Towers **Obv:** Crowned bust right within circle, date below **Obv. Legend:** MARGRETHE II - DANMARKS DRONNING **Rev:** Gråsten Castle Bell Tower **Edge:** Segmented reeding

Date	Mintage	XF40	MS60	MS63	MS65
2006(h)	1,208,600	—	—	—	5.00

KM# 913 20 KRONER
9.30 g., Aluminum-Bronze, 27 mm. **Ruler:** Margrethe II **Series:** Danish Towers **Obv:** Crowned bust right within circle, date below **Obv. Legend:** MARGRETHE II - DANMARKS DRONNING **Rev:** The Greenland Cairns: Nukaritt/Three Brothers **Rev. Legend:** TRE BRØDRE **Edge:** Alternate plain and reeded segments

Date	Mintage	XF40	MS60	MS63	MS65
2006(h)	1,208,600	—	—	—	5.00

KM# 919 20 KRONER
9.30 g., Aluminum-Bronze, 27 mm. **Ruler:** Margrethe II **Series:** Danish Towers **Obv:** Bust with tiarra right **Obv. Legend:** MARGRETHE II - DANMARKS DRONNING **Rev:** City Hall in Copenhagen **Rev. Legend:** KØBENHAVNS RÅDHUS **Edge:** Alternate plain and reeded segments

Date	Mintage	XF40	MS60	MS63	MS65
2007(h)	1,208,600	—	—	—	5.00

KM# 920 20 KRONER
9.30 g., Aluminum-Bronze, 27 mm. **Ruler:** Margrethe II **Series:** Danish Ships **Obv:** Crowned bust right **Obv. Legend:** MARGRETHE II - DANMARKS DRONNING **Rev:** Sailing ship Jylland **Rev. Legend:** FREGATTEN - JYLLAND **Edge:** Segmented reeding

Date	Mintage	XF40	MS60	MS63	MS65
2007(h)	1,200,000	—	—	—	5.00

KM# 921 20 KRONER
9.30 g., Aluminum-Bronze, 27 mm. **Ruler:** Margrethe II **Series:** Danish ships **Subject:** The Galathea 3 expedition **Obv:** Crowned bust right **Obv. Legend:** MARGRETHE II - DANMARKS DRONNING **Rev:** Ship Vaedderen, route map in background **Rev. Legend:** VAEDDEREN **Edge:** Segmented reeding

Date	Mintage	XF40	MS60	MS63	MS65
2007(h)	1,200,000	—	—	—	5.00

KM# 926 20 KRONER
9.30 g., Aluminum-Bronze, 27 mm. **Ruler:** Margrethe II **Series:** Danish Ships **Obv:** Head with tiara right **Rev:** World's first ocean-going diesel-engine merchant ship, built 1912 **Rev. Legend:** SELANDIA **Edge:** Segmented reeding

Date	Mintage	XF40	MS60	MS63	MS65
2008(h)	1,200,000	—	—	—	5.00
2008(h)	1,500	PF63 60.00	PF65 65.00		

KM# 927 20 KRONER
9.30 g., Aluminum-Bronze, 27 mm. **Ruler:** Margrethe II **Series:** Danish Ships **Subject:** Voyage to Dublin, Ireland, with full size replica Viking ship, HAVHINGSTEN **Obv:** Crowned bust right **Obv. Legend:** MARGRETHE II - DANMARKS DRONNING **Rev:** Sailing vessel at sea **Rev. Legend:** HAVHINGSTEN / 20 KRONER **Edge:** Segmented reeding

Date	Mintage	XF40	MS60	MS63	MS65
2008	1,200,000	—	—	—	5.00
2008	1,500	PF63 60.00	PF65 65.00		

KM# 928 20 KRONER
9.30 g., Aluminum-Bronze, 27 mm. **Ruler:** Margrethe II **Series:** Danish Ships **Rev:** Royal Yacht Dannebrog **Edge:** Segmented reeding

Date	Mintage	XF40	MS60	MS63	MS65
2008	1,200,000	—	—	5.00	—
2008	1,500	PF63 60.00	PF65 65.00		

KM# 935 20 KRONER
9.30 g., Aluminum-Bronze, 27 mm. **Ruler:** Margrethe II **Series:** Danish Ships **Obv:** Crowned bust right **Obv. Legend:** MARGRETHE II - DANMARKS DRONNING **Rev:** Lightship XVII (built 1895) on duty **Edge:** Segmented reeding

Date	Mintage	XF40	MS60	MS63	MS65
2009	1,100,000	—	—	9.00	—
2009	1,500	PF63 60.00	PF65 65.00		

KM# 936 20 KRONER
9.30 g., Aluminum-Bronze, 27 mm. **Ruler:** Margrethe II **Series:** Danish Ships **Obv:** Crowned bust facing right **Rev:** FAERØBÅD (Boat of Faeroe Islands) **Edge:** Segmented reeding

Date	Mintage	XF40	MS60	MS63	MS65
2009	900,000	—	—	—	5.00
2009	2,825	PF63 60.00	PF65 65.00		

KM# 942 20 KRONER
9.30 g., Aluminum-Bronze, 27 mm. **Ruler:** Margrethe II **Subject:** The Emma Maersk, a container ship **Obv:** Head right **Obv. Legend:** MARGRETHE II DANMARKS DRONNING **Rev:** Emma Maersk, container ship, right **Edge:** Segmented reeding

Date	Mintage	XF40	MS60	MS63	MS65
2011	800,000	—	—	—	5.00
2011	3,810	PF63 60.00	PF65 65.00		
2012	—	PF63 30.00	PF65 35.00		

KM# 937 20 KRONER
9.30 g., Aluminum-Bronze, 27 mm. **Ruler:** Margrethe II **Subject:** Queen's 70th Birthday **Obv:** Head right **Rev:** Crowned shield against background of daisies

Date	Mintage	XF40	MS60	MS63	MS65
2010	1,440,000	—	—	—	5.00
2010	4,100	PF63 60.00	PF65 65.00		

KM# 940 20 KRONER
9.30 g., Aluminum-Bronze, 27 mm. **Ruler:** Margrethe II **Series:** Danish Ships **Subject:** Greenland kayak - women's ship **Obv:** Bust facing right **Rev:** Kayak-Umak **Rev. Legend:** KAJAK • KONEBÅD **Edge:** Segmented reeding

Date	Mintage	XF40	MS60	MS63	MS65
2010	972,000	—	—	—	5.00
2010	1,877	PF63 60.00	PF65 65.00		

KM# 941 20 KRONER
9.30 g., Aluminum-Bronze, 27 mm. **Ruler:** Margrethe II **Series:** Danish Ships **Subject:** The Hjejlen, a paddle steamer **Obv:** Head right **Obv. Legend:** MARGRETHE II DANMARKS DRONNING **Rev:** The Hjejlen and value **Edge:** Segmented reeding

Date	Mintage	XF40	MS60	MS63	MS65
2011	700,000	—	—	—	5.00
2011	2,662	PF63 60.00	PF65 65.00		

KM# 944 20 KRONER
9.30 g., Aluminum-Bronze, 27 mm. **Ruler:** Margrethe II **Obv:** Head right **Obv. Legend:** MARGRETHE II DANMARKS DRONNING **Rev:** Crowned shield and value **Edge:** Segmented reeding

Date	Mintage	XF40	MS60	MS63	MS65
2011(h)	1,035,000	—	6.25	—	—
2011 Special Unc	3,019	—		6.00	—
2011(h)	1,000	PF63 50.00	PF65 55.00		
2012 In sets only	276,000	—	6.25	—	—
2011 (2012)	1,090	PF63 50.00	PF65 55.00		

KM# 945 20 KRONER
9.30 g., Aluminum-Bronze, 27 mm. **Ruler:** Margrethe II **Subject:** 40th Jubilee of Queen Margrethe II **Obv:** Bust of Queen Margrethe II facing right **Obv. Legend:** MARGRETHE II DANMARKS DRONNING **Rev:** Design, legend 1972 14 JANUAR 2012 and denomination **Edge:** Segmented reeding

Date	Mintage	XF40	MS60	MS63	MS65
2012	750,000	—	—	—	5.00
2012	3,180	PF63 60.00	PF65 65.00		

KM# 948 20 KRONER
9.30 g., Aluminum-Bronze, 27 mm. **Ruler:** Margrethe II **Series:** Danish Ships **Subject:** The Kong Frederik IX, a ferry **Obv:** Bust of Queen Margrethe II facing right **Obv. Legend:** MARGRETHE II DANMARKS DRONNING **Rev:** The Kong Frederik IX, legend KONG FREDERIK IX and denomination **Edge:** Segmented reeding

Date	Mintage	XF40	MS60	MS63	MS65
2012	349,000	—	—	—	5.00
2012	2,331	PF63 60.00	PF65 65.00		

KM# 953 20 KRONER
9.30 g., Aluminum-Bronze, 27 mm. **Ruler:** Margrethe II **Obv:** Bust right **Rev:** Fishing vessel and denomination **Rev. Inscription:** FISKEKUTTER **Edge:** Segmented reeding

Date	Mintage	XF40	MS60	MS63	MS65
2012	257,000	—	—	5.00	—
2012	1,732	PF63 28.00	PF65 32.00		

KM# 955 20 KRONER
9.30 g., Aluminum-Bronze, 27 mm. **Ruler:** Margrethe II **Obv:** Bust right **Rev:** Crown, three lions and denomination **Edge:** Segmented reeding

Date	Mintage	XF40	MS60	MS63	MS65
2013	—	—	—	5.00	—
2013	—	PF63 35.00	PF65 38.00		

KM# 956 20 KRONER
9.30 g., Aluminum-Bronze, 27 mm. **Ruler:** Margrethe II **Subject:** Niels Bohr **Obv:** Bust right **Rev:** Atom design **Edge:** Segmented reeding

Date	Mintage	XF40	MS60	MS63	MS65
2013	250,000	—	—	5.50	—
2013	—	PF63 35.00	PF65 38.00		

KM# 958 20 KRONER
9.30 g., Aluminum-Bronze, 27 mm. **Ruler:** Margrethe II **Subject:** H.C. Ørsted **Obv:** Bust right **Rev:** Electromagnet with poles connected **Edge:** Segmented reeding

Date	Mintage	XF40	MS60	MS63	MS65
2013	250,000	—	—	5.50	—
2013	—	PF63 35.00	PF65 38.00		

KM# 960 20 KRONER
9.30 g., Aluminum-Bronze, 27 mm. **Ruler:** Margrethe II **Subject:** Ole Rømer **Obv:** Bust right **Rev:** Sun and orbiting planets and moons

Date	Mintage	XF40	MS60	MS63	MS65
2013	250,000	—	—	5.50	—
2013	—	PF63 35.00	PF65 38.00		

KM# 962 20 KRONER
9.30 g., Aluminum-Bronze, 27 mm. **Ruler:** Margrethe II **Subject:** Tycho Brahe **Obv:** Bust right **Rev:** Sun and constellations **Edge:** Segmented reeding

Date	Mintage	XF40	MS60	MS63	MS65
2013	250,000	—	—	5.50	—
2013	—	PF63 35.00	PF65 38.00		

KM# 917 100 KRONER
31.00 g., 0.999 Silver 0.9893 oz. ASW, 38 mm. **Ruler:** Margrethe II **Subject:** International Polar Year 2007-2009 **Obv:** Crowned bust right **Obv. Legend:** MARGRETHE II - DANMARKS DRONNING **Rev:** Polar bear facing, walking on ice flow **Rev. Legend:** POLARÅR 2007-2009

Date	Mintage	XF40	MS60	MS63	MS65
2007(h)	43,048	—	—	—	45.00

KM# 930 100 KRONER
31.10 g., 0.999 Silver 0.9925 oz. ASW, 38 mm. **Ruler:** Margrethe II **Subject:** International Polar Year 2007-2009 **Rev:** Globe and dog sled

Date	Mintage	XF40	MS60	MS63	MS65
2008	15,631	—	—	—	50.00

KM# 933 100 KRONER
31.10 g., 0.999 Silver 0.9925 oz. ASW, 38 mm. **Ruler:** Margrethe II **Subject:** International Polar Year 2007-2009 **Rev:** Ice scape, Northern Lights

Date	Mintage	XF40	MS60	MS63	MS65
2009	10,600	—	—	—	55.00

KM# 895 200 KRONER
31.10 g., 0.999 Silver 0.9925 oz. ASW, 38.3 mm. **Ruler:** Margrethe II **Subject:** Wedding of Crown Prince **Obv:** Crowned bust right within circle, date below **Obv. Legend:** MARGRETHE II - DANMARKS DRONNING **Rev:** Crown Prince Frederik and Crown Princess Mary **Edge:** Plain **Note:** No initials.

Date	Mintage	XF40	MS60	MS63	MS65
2004(h)	125,000	—	—	45.00	—

KM# 929 500 KRONER
31.10 g., 0.999 Silver 0.9925 oz. ASW, 38 mm. **Ruler:** Margrethe II **Rev:** Royal Yacht Dannebrog

Date	Mintage	XF40	MS60	MS63	MS65
2008	31,700	—	—	—	100

KM# 938 500 KRONER
31.10 g., 0.999 Silver 0.9925 oz. ASW, 38 mm. **Ruler:** Margrethe II **Subject:** Queen's 70th Birthday **Obv:** Head right **Rev:** Crowned shield against a background of daisies

Date	Mintage	XF40	MS60	MS63	MS65
2010	28,236	—	—	—	100

KM# 946 500 KRONER
31.10 g., 0.999 Silver 0.9925 oz. ASW, 38 mm. **Ruler:** Margrethe II **Subject:** 40th Jubilee of Queen Margrethe II **Obv:** Bust of the Queen Margrethe II facing right **Obv. Legend:** MARGRETHE II DANMARKS DRONNING **Rev:** Design, legend 1972, 14 JANUAR 2012 and denomination

Date	Mintage	XF40	MS60	MS63	MS65
2012	16,881	—	—	—	100

KM# 957 500 KRONER
31.11 g., 0.999 Silver 0.9926 oz. ASW, 38 mm. **Ruler:** Margrethe II **Subject:** Niels Bohr **Obv:** Bust right **Rev:** Design of atom

Date	Mintage	XF40	MS60	MS63	MS65
2013	—	—	—	95.00	—

KM# 959 500 KRONER
31.11 g., 0.999 Silver 0.9926 oz. ASW, 38 mm. **Ruler:** Margrethe II **Subject:** H.C. Ørsted **Obv:** Bust right **Rev:** Electromagnet with wire connecting poles

Date	Mintage	XF40	MS60	MS63	MS65
2013	—	—	—	95.00	—

KM# 961 500 KRONER
31.11 g., 0.999 Silver 0.9926 oz. ASW, 38 mm. **Ruler:** Margrethe II **Subject:** Ole Rømer **Obv:** Bust right **Rev:** Sun and orbiting planets and moon

Date	Mintage	XF40	MS60	MS63	MS65
2013	—	—	—	95.00	—

KM# 963 500 KRONER
31.11 g., 0.999 Silver 0.9926 oz. ASW, 38 mm. **Ruler:** Margrethe II **Subject:** Tycho Brahe **Obv:** Bust right **Rev:** Sun and constellation of stars

Date	Mintage	XF40	MS60	MS63	MS65
2013	—	—	—	95.00	—

KM# 918 1000 KRONER
8.65 g., 0.900 Gold 0.2487 oz. AGW, 22 mm. **Ruler:** Margrethe II **Subject:** International Polar Year 2007-2009 **Obv:** Crowned bust right **Obv. Legend:** MARGRETHE II - DANMARKS DRONNING **Rev:** Polar bear facing, walking on ice flow **Rev. Legend:** POLARÅR 2007-2009 **Note:** Struck from gold from Greenland having a small polar bear to right of denomination.

Date	Mintage	XF40	MS60	MS63	MS65
2007(h)	6,000	PF63 425	PF65 450		

KM# 931 1000 KRONER
8.65 g., 0.900 Gold 0.2487 oz. AGW, 22 mm. **Ruler:** Margrethe II **Subject:** International Polar Year 2007-2009 **Rev:** Globe and dog sled

Date	Mintage	XF40	MS60	MS63	MS65
2008	3,604	PF63 425		PF65 450	

KM# 934 1000 KRONER
8.65 g., 0.900 Gold 0.2487 oz. AGW, 22 mm. **Ruler:** Margrethe II **Subject:** International Polar Year 2007-2009 **Rev:** Ice scape, Northern Lights

Date	Mintage	XF40	MS60	MS63	MS65
2009	2,400	PF63 425		PF65 450	

KM# 939 1000 KRONER
8.65 g., 0.900 Gold 0.2487 oz. AGW, 22 mm. **Ruler:** Margrethe II **Subject:** Queen's 70th Birthday **Obv:** Bust right **Rev:** Crowned shield against background of daisies

Date	Mintage	XF40	MS60	MS63	MS65
2010	2,639	PF63 475		PF65 500	

KM# 947 3000 KRONER
8.65 g., 0.900 Gold 0.2487 oz. AGW, 22 mm. **Ruler:** Margrethe II **Subject:** 40th Jubilee of Queen Margrethe II **Obv:** Bust of Queen Margrethe II facing right **Obv. Legend:** MARGRETHE II DANMARKS DRONNING **Rev:** Design, legend 1972 14 JANUAR 2012 and denomination **Edge:** Segmented reeding

Date	Mintage	XF40	MS60	MS63	MS65
2012	2,325	—	—	—	600

MINT SETS

KM# Date	Mintage Identification	Issue Price	Mkt Val
MS46 2001 (5)	28,000 KM866.2, 868, 869, 873, 874, 887, 888	15.00	37.50
MS47 2002 (7)	28,000 KM866.3, 868.2, 869.2, 873.2, 874.2, 887.2, 888.2	17.50	35.00
MS48 2003 (6)	30,000 KM866.3, 868.2, 873.2, 889, 890, 891	17.50	35.00
MS49 2004 (8)	33,000 KM#866.3, 868.2, 869.2, 873.2, 874.2, 891, 894, 896, plus Battle of Köge Bay medal in Nordic gold	34.50	75.00
MS50 2005 (8)	26,700 KM#866.3, 868.2, 869.2, 873.2, 874.2, 891, 896, 898, plus Battle of Copenhagen medal in Nordic gold	34.50	50.00
MS51 2006 (8)	25,000 KM#866.3, 868.2, 869.2, 873.2, 874.2, 891, 896, plus Floating Dock medal in Copenhagen sound medal in Nordic gold	40.00	42.00
MS52 2006 (8)	5,000 KM#866.3, 868.2, 869.2, 873.2, 874.2, 891, 896 plus children's medal in Nordic gold. (Children's coin set)	—	48.00
MS53 2002-07 (9)	8,600 KM#889, 890, 892, 893, 897, 899, 901, 902, 913, 919. (Tower coin set)	—	100
MS54 2005-07 (6)	6,675 KM#898, 900, 903, 914, 923 plus Hans Christian Anderson medal in Nordic gold (Fairy tale coin set).	—	55.00

KM# Date	Mintage Identification	Issue Price	Mkt Val
MS55 2007 (8)	23,000 KM#866.3, 868.2, 869.2, 873.2, 874.2, 891, 896 plus Galathea medal in Nordic gold.	—	42.00
MS56 2007 (7)	2,700 KM#866.3, 868.2, 869.2, 873.2, 874.2, 891, 896 plus Children's medal in Nordic gold (Children's coin set)	46.00	50.00
MS57 2008 (7)	1,000 KM#866.3, 868.2, 869.2, 873.2, 874.2, 891, 896 plus Children's medal in Nordic gold (Children's coin set).	—	50.00
MS58 2008 (8)	20,350 KM#866.3, 868.2, 869.2, 873.2, 874.2, 891, 896 plus Battle of Kronberg Castle Coast (Elsinore) medal in Nordic gold.	—	45.00
MS59 2009 (6)	1,450 KM#866.3, 869.2, 873.2, 874.2, 891, 896 plus Children's medal in Nordic gold (Children's coin set)	—	65.00
MS60 2009 (7)	24,250 KM#866.3, 869.2, 873.2, 874.2, 891, 896 plus Neptune admiring Naval fleet medal in Nordic gold.	—	60.00
MS61 2010 (7)	1,300 KM#866.3, 869.2, 873.2, 874.2, 891, 896 plus children's medal in Nordic gold (Children's coin set).	—	45.00
MS62 2010 (7)	23,000 KM#866.3, 869.2, 873.2, 874.2, 891, 896 plus Danish Navy's first dry dock medal in Nordic gold	—	45.00
MS63 2011 (6)	1,750 KM#866.3, 869.2, 873.2, 874.2, 943-944 plus children's medal in Nordic gold.	—	45.00
MS64 2011 (6)	17,150 KM#866.3, 869.2, 873.2, 874.2, 943-944	—	40.00
MS65 2012 (6)	— KM#866.3, 869.2, 873.2, 874.2, 943, 944	—	40.00
MS66 2012 (6)	— KM#866.3, 869.2, 873.2, 874.2, 943, 944, plus Children's medal in Nordic gold (Children's coin set)	—	45.00

PROOF SETS

KM# Date	Mintage Identification	Issue Price	Mkt Val
PS1 2004 (8)	3,000 KM#866.3, 868.2, 869.2, 873.2, 874.2, 891, 896, plus Royal Wedding medal in .925 Silver	150	250
PS2 2005 (8)	2,650 KM866.3, 868.2, 869.2, 873.2, 874.2, 896, 891 plus 1801 Battle of Copenhagen medal in .925 Silver	150	185
PS3 2006 (8)	1,800 KM#866.3, 868.2, 869.2, 873.2, 874.2, 896, 891 plus 1691 Floating Dock medal in .925 Silver	160	185
PS4 2007 (8)	1,400 KM#866.3, 868.2, 869.2, 873.2, 874.2, 896, 891, plus Galathea medal in .925 silver	160	185
PS5 2008 (8)	1,000 KM#866.3, 868.2, 869.2, 873.2, 874.2, 896, 891, plus medal in .925 Silver	—	200
PS6 2009 (7)	1,050 KM#866.3, 869.2, 873.2, 874.2, 891, 896 plus Neptune admiring Naval fleet medal in .925 Silver.	—	250
PS7 2010 (7)	1,010 KM#866.3, 869.2, 873.2, 874.2, 891, 896 plus Danish Navy's first dry dock medal in .925 Silver	—	185
PS8 2011 (2)	3,010 KM#943-944	—	75.00
PS9 2011 (6)	1,000 KM#866.3, 869.2, 873.2, 874.2, 943-944	—	185

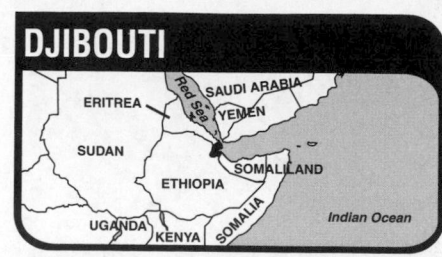

DJIBOUTI

The Republic of Djibouti (formerly French Somaliland and the French Overseas Territory of Afars and Issas), located in northeast Africa at the Bab el Mandeb Strait connecting the Suez Canal and the Red Sea with the Gulf of Aden and the Indian Ocean, has an area of 8,950 sq. mi. (22,000 sq. km.) and a population of 421,320. Capital: Djibouti. The tiny nation has less than one sq. mi. of arable land, and no natural resources except salt, sand, and camels. The commercial activities of the transshipment port of Djibouti and the Addis Abada-Djibouti railroad are the basis of the economy. Salt, fish and hides are exported.

REPUBLIC
STANDARD COINAGE

KM# 23 10 FRANCS
3.00 g., Aluminum-Bronze, 20 mm. **Obv:** National arms within wreath, date below **Rev:** Boats on water, denomination above **Note:** Varieties exist.

Date	Mintage	F12	VF20	XF40	MS60	MS63
2004(a)	—	—	—	—	2.50	4.50
2007(a)	—	—	—	—	2.50	4.50
2010(a)	—	—	—	—	2.50	4.50

KM# 34 10 FRANCS
3.40 g., Copper-Nickel, 20.9 mm. **Obv:** National arms **Rev:** Chimpanzee **Edge:** Plain

Date	Mintage	F12	VF20	XF40	MS60	MS63
2003	—	—	—	—	2.00	4.00

KM# 24 20 FRANCS
4.00 g., Aluminum-Bronze, 23.5 mm. **Obv:** National arms within wreath, date below **Rev:** Boats on water, denomination above **Note:** Varieties exist.

Date	Mintage	F12	VF20	XF40	MS60	MS63
2007(a)	—	—	—	—	2.50	4.50
2010(a)	—	—	—	—	2.50	4.50

KM# 25 50 FRANCS
7.05 g., Copper-Nickel, 25.7 mm. **Obv:** National arms within wreath, date below **Rev:** Pair of dromedary camels right, denomination above

Date	Mintage	F12	VF20	XF40	MS60	MS63
2007(a)	—	—	—	—	6.00	9.00
2010(a)	—	—	—	—	6.00	9.00

KM# 26 100 FRANCS
12.00 g., Copper-Nickel, 30 mm. **Obv:** National arms within wreath, date below **Rev:** Pair of dromedary camels right, denomination above

Date	Mintage	F12	VF20	XF40	MS60	MS63
2004(a)	—	—	—	2.50	7.00	9.00
2007(a)	—	—	—	2.50	7.00	9.00
2010(a)	—	—	—	2.50	7.00	9.00

KM# 38 100 FRANCS
Nickel, 35 mm. **Subject:** 25th Anniversary of Independence **Obv:** Small national arms on state flag **Obv. Legend:** REPUBLIQUE DE DJIBOUTI **Rev:** UNITÉ in color **Rev. Legend:** UNITÉ ... ÉGALITÉ ... PAIX

Date	Mintage	F12	VF20	XF40	MS60	MS63
ND(2002)	—	—	—	—	—	160

KM# 39 100 FRANCS
Nickel, 35 mm. **Subject:** 25th Anniversary of Independence **Obv:** Small national arms on state flag **Obv. Legend:** REPUBLIQUE DE DJIBOUTI **Rev:** É/GAL/ITÉ in color **Rev. Legend:** UNITÉ ... ÉGALITÉ ... PAIX

Date	Mintage	F12	VF20	XF40	MS60	MS63
AH(2002)	—	—	—	—	—	160

KM# 40 100 FRANCS
Nickel, 35 mm. **Subject:** 25th Anniversary of Independence **Obv:** Small national arms on state flag **Obv. Legend:** REPUBLIQUE DE DJIBOUTI **Rev:** PAI/X in color **Rev. Legend:** UNITÉ ... ÉGALITÉ ... PAIX

Date	Mintage	F12	VF20	XF40	MS60	MS63
ND(2002)	—	—	—	—	—	160

KM# 41 250 FRANCS
22.20 g., 0.900 Silver 0.6382 oz. ASW **Obv:** National arms **Obv. Legend:** REPUBLIQUE DE DJIBOUTI **Rev:** Two dromedary camels right **Rev. Legend:** UNITÉ - ÉGALITÉ - PAIX

Date	Mintage	F12	VF20	XF40	MS60	MS63
2002(a) Proof						

Note: Confirmation requested

KM# 42 250 FRANCS
10.00 g., Bi-Metallic **Obv:** National arms **Rev:** Djibouti Francolin

Date	Mintage	F12	VF20	XF40	MS60	MS63
(2012)	—	—	—	5.00	9.00	12.00

KM# 27 500 FRANCS
Aluminum-Bronze **Obv:** National arms within wreath, date below **Rev:** Denomination within sprays

Date	Mintage	F12	VF20	XF40	MS60	MS63
2010(a)	—	—	—	6.00	12.00	15.00

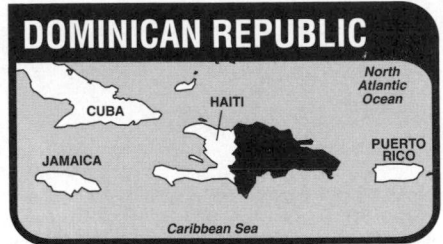

DOMINICAN REPUBLIC

The Dominican Republic, which occupies the eastern two-thirds of the island of Hispaniola, has an area of 18,704 sq. mi. (48,734 sq. km.) and a population of 7.9 million. Capital: Santo Domingo. The largely agricultural economy produces sugar, coffee, tobacco and cocoa. Tourism and casino gaming are also a rising source of revenue.

REPUBLIC
REFORM COINAGE
1937: 100 Centavos = 1 Peso Oro

KM# 80.2 PESO
6.49 g., Brass, 25 mm. **Subject:** Juan Pablo Duarte **Obv:** National arms and denomination **Rev:** DUARTE below bust, date below **Note:** Coin die alignment.

Date	Mintage	F12	VF20	XF40	MS60	MS63
2002	—	—	—	—	2.00	2.50
2005	—	—	—	—	2.00	2.50
2008	—	—	—	—	2.00	2.50

KM# 90 PESO
12.50 g., Copper-Nickel, 30.6 mm. **Obv:** Pan American Games logo **Rev:** National arms and denomination **Edge:** Reeded

Date	Mintage	F12	VF20	XF40	MS60	MS63
2003	—	PF63 12.00	PF65 15.00			

KM# 89 5 PESOS
6.06 g., Bi-Metallic, 23 mm. **Subject:** Sanchez **Obv:** National arms and denomination **Rev:** Portrait facing within circle, date below **Edge:** Segmented reeding

Date	Mintage	F12	VF20	XF40	MS60	MS63
2002	—	—	—	—	2.50	3.00
2005	—	—	—	—	2.50	3.00
2007	—	—	—	—	2.50	3.00
2008	—	—	—	—	2.50	3.00

KM# 106 10 PESOS
8.20 g., Bi-Metallic, 27 mm. **Obv:** Value at left of national arms **Obv. Legend:** • REPUBLICA DOMINICANA • **Rev:** Bust of General Mella facing **Rev. Legend:** BANCO CENTRAL DE LA REPUBLICA DOMINICANA **Edge:** Segmented reeding

Date	Mintage	F12	VF20	XF40	MS60	MS63
2005	—	—	—	—	6.00	8.00
2007	—	—	—	—	6.00	8.00
2008	—	—	—	—	6.00	8.00
2010	—	—	—	—	6.00	8.00

KM# 107 25 PESOS
8.56 g., Copper-Nickel, 28.82 mm. **Obv:** Value at left of national arms **Obv. Legend:** REPUBLICA DOMINICANA **Rev:** Bust of General Luperon facing **Rev. Legend:** BANCO CENTRAL DE LA REPUBLICA DOMINICANA **Rev. Inscription:** HEROE DE LA RESTAURACION **Edge:** Reeded

Date	Mintage	F12	VF20	XF40	MS60	MS63
2005	—	—	—	—	5.00	7.00
2008	—	—	—	—	5.00	7.00
2010	—	—	—	—	5.00	7.00

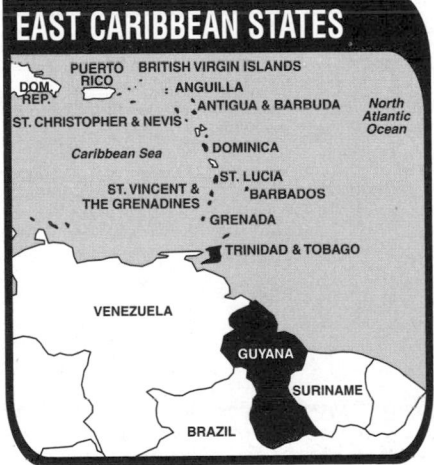

EAST CARIBBEAN STATES

The East Caribbean States, formerly the British Caribbean Territories (Eastern Group), formed a currency board in 1950 to provide the constituent territories of Trinidad & Tobago, Barbados, British Guiana (now Guyana), British Virgin Islands, Anguilla, St. Kitts, Nevis, Antigua, Dominica, St. Lucia, St. Vincent and Grenada with a common currency, thereby permitting withdrawal of the regular British Pound currency. This was dissolved in 1965 and after the breakup, the East Caribbean Territories, a grouping including Barbados, the Leeward and Windward Islands, came into being. Coinage of the dissolved 'Eastern Group' continues to circulate. Paper currency of the East Caribbean Authority was first issued in 1965 and although Barbados withdrew from the group they continued using them prior to 1973 when Barbados issued a decimal coinage.

A series of 4-dollar coins tied to the FAO coinage program were released in 1970 under the name of the Caribbean Development Bank by eight loosely federated island groupings in the eastern Caribbean. These issues are listed individually in this volume under Antigua, Barbados, Dominica, Grenada, Montserrat, St. Kitts, St. Lucia and St. Vincent.

STANDARD COINAGE
100 Cents = 1 Dollar

KM# 10 CENT
0.90 g., Aluminum, 18.4 mm. **Ruler:** Elizabeth II **Obv:** Young bust right **Rev:** Wreath divides denomination, date upper right **Shape:** Scalloped **Note:** Prev. KM#1.

Date	Mintage	F12	VF20	XF40	MS60	MS63
2001	—	—	—	—	0.20	0.30

KM# 34 CENT
1.03 g., Aluminum, 18.42 mm. **Ruler:** Elizabeth II **Obv:** Crowned head right **Rev:** Denomination **Edge:** Plain

Date	Mintage	F12	VF20	XF40	MS60	MS63
2002	—	—	—	—	0.20	0.30
2004	—	—	—	—	0.20	0.30
2008	—	—	—	—	0.20	0.30
2011	—	—	—	—	0.20	0.30

KM# 35 2 CENTS
1.42 g., Aluminum, 21.46 mm. **Ruler:** Elizabeth II **Obv:** Crowned head right **Rev:** Denomination **Edge:** Plain

Date	Mintage	F12	VF20	XF40	MS60	MS63
2002	—	—	—	—	0.25	0.35
2004	—	—	—	—	0.25	0.35
2008	—	—	—	—	0.25	0.35

KM# 36 5 CENTS
1.74 g., Aluminum, 23.11 mm. **Ruler:** Elizabeth II **Obv:** Crowned head right **Rev:** Denomination **Edge:** Plain

Date	Mintage	F12	VF20	XF40	MS60	MS63
2002	—	—	—	—	0.30	0.45
2004	—	—	—	—	0.30	0.45
2008	—	—	—	—	0.30	0.45
2010	—	—	—	—	0.30	0.45

KM# 37 10 CENTS
2.59 g., Copper-Nickel, 18.06 mm. **Ruler:** Elizabeth II **Obv:** Crowned head right **Rev:** Sir Francis Drake's Golden Hind and denomination **Edge:** Reeded

Date	Mintage	F12	VF20	XF40	MS60	MS63
2002	—	—	—	—	0.40	0.60
2004	—	—	—	—	0.40	0.60
2007	—	—	—	—	0.40	0.60

KM# 37a 10 CENTS
Nickel Plated Steel, 18 mm. **Ruler:** Elizabeth II **Obv:** Crowned head right **Rev:** Sir Francis Drake's Golden Hind and denomination **Edge:** Reeded

Date	Mintage	F12	VF20	XF40	MS60	MS63
2009	—	—	—	—	0.40	0.60

KM# 38 25 CENTS
6.48 g., Copper-Nickel, 23.98 mm. **Ruler:** Elizabeth II **Obv:** Crowned head right **Rev:** Sir Francis Drake's Golden Hind and denomination **Edge:** Reeded

Date	Mintage	F12	VF20	XF40	MS60	MS63
2002	—	—	—	—	0.50	0.75
2004	—	—	—	—	0.50	0.75
2007	—	—	—	—	0.50	0.75

KM# 38a 25 CENTS
Nickel Plated Steel, 24 mm. **Ruler:** Elizabeth II **Obv:** Crowned head right **Rev:** Sir Francis Drake's Golden Hind and denomination **Edge:** Reeded

Date	Mintage	F12	VF20	XF40	MS60	MS63
2010	—	—	—	—	0.50	0.75

KM# 39 DOLLAR
7.98 g., Copper-Nickel, 26.5 mm. **Ruler:** Elizabeth II **Obv:** Crowned head right **Rev:** Sir Francis Drake's Golden Hind and denomination **Edge:** Segmented reeding

Date	Mintage	F12	VF20	XF40	MS60	MS63
2002	—	—	—	—	2.00	3.00
2004	—	—	—	—	2.00	3.00
2007	—	—	—	—	2.00	3.00

KM# 40 DOLLAR
28.28 g., Copper-Nickel Gilt, 38.6 mm. **Ruler:** Elizabeth II **Subject:** Golden Jubilee Monarchs **Obv:** Crowned head right **Rev:** Henry III (1216-1277) **Edge:** Reeded

Date	Mintage	F12	VF20	XF40	MS60	MS63
2002	5,000	—	—	—	22.50	25.00

KM# 42 DOLLAR
28.28 g., Copper-Nickel Gilt, 38.6 mm. **Ruler:** Elizabeth II **Subject:** Golden Jubilee Monarchs **Obv:** Crowned head right **Rev:** Edward III (1327-1377) **Edge:** Reeded

Date	Mintage	F12	VF20	XF40	MS60	MS63
2002	5,000	—	—	—	22.50	25.00

KM# 44 DOLLAR
28.28 g., Copper-Nickel Gilt, 38.6 mm. **Ruler:** Elizabeth II **Subject:** Golden Jubilee Monarchs **Obv:** Crowned head right **Rev:** George III (1760-1820) **Edge:** Reeded

Date	Mintage	F12	VF20	XF40	MS60	MS63
2002	5,000	—	—	—	22.50	25.00

KM# 46 DOLLAR
28.28 g., Copper-Nickel Gilt, 38.6 mm. **Ruler:** Elizabeth II **Subject:** Golden Jubilee Monarchs **Obv:** Crowned head right **Rev:** Queen Victoria (1837-1901) **Edge:** Reeded

Date	Mintage	F12	VF20	XF40	MS60	MS63
2002	5,000	—	—	—	22.50	25.00

KM# 48 DOLLAR
28.28 g., Copper-Nickel Gilt, 38.6 mm. **Ruler:** Elizabeth II **Subject:** Golden Jubilee Monarchs **Obv:** Crowned head right **Rev:** Queen Elizabeth II (1952-) **Edge:** Reeded

Date	Mintage	F12	VF20	XF40	MS60	MS63
2002	5,000	—	—	—	22.50	25.00

KM# 86 DOLLAR
27.73 g., Copper-Nickel, 38.5 mm. **Ruler:** Elizabeth II **Subject:** Coronation Jubilee **Obv:** Crowned head right **Rev:** Fireworks display above building **Edge:** Reeded

Date	Mintage	F12	VF20	XF40	MS60	MS63
2002	—	—	—	—	10.00	12.00

KM# 58 DOLLAR
7.98 g., Copper-Nickel, 26.5 mm. **Ruler:** Elizabeth II **Subject:** 25th Anniversary **Obv:** Head right **Rev:** Motto within wreath

Date	Mintage	F12	VF20	XF40	MS60	MS63
2008	500,000	—	—	—	—	5.00

KM# 51 2 DOLLARS
56.56 g., Copper-Nickel Gilt, 38.6 mm. **Ruler:** Elizabeth II **Subject:** British Military Leaders **Obv:** Crowned head right **Rev:** Wellington's portrait and battle scene **Edge:** Reeded

Date	Mintage	F12	VF20	XF40	MS60	MS63
2002	10,000	PF63 35.00		PF65 45.00		

KM# 54 2 DOLLARS
56.56 g., Copper-Nickel Gilt, 38.6 mm. **Ruler:** Elizabeth II **Subject:** British Military Leaders **Obv:** Crowned head right **Rev:** Admiral Nelson's portrait and naval battle scene **Edge:** Reeded

Date	Mintage	F12	VF20	XF40	MS60	MS63
2003	10,000	PF63 35.00		PF65 45.00		

KM# 57 2 DOLLARS
56.56 g., Copper-Nickel Gilt, 38.6 mm. **Ruler:** Elizabeth II **Subject:** British Military Leaders **Obv:** Crowned head right **Rev:** Churchill's portrait and air battle scene **Edge:** Reeded

Date	Mintage	F12	VF20	XF40	MS60	MS63
2003	10,000	PF63 35.00		PF65 45.00		

KM# 87 2 DOLLARS
11.35 g., Copper-Nickel, 30 mm. **Ruler:** Elizabeth II **Subject:** Financial Information Month, 10th Anniversary **Rev:** Hands holding tree **Edge:** Reeded

Date	Mintage	F12	VF20	XF40	MS60	MS63
2011	—	—	—	—	4.00	5.00

KM# 60 2 DOLLARS
Copper-Nickel, 38.6 mm. **Ruler:** Elizabeth II **Subject:** Financial Information Month **Obv:** Head in tiara right **Rev:** Tree seedling growing in palm of hand

Date	Mintage	F12	VF20	XF40	MS60	MS63
2011	—	PF63 35.00		PF65 45.00		

KM# 61 8 DOLLARS
Copper-Nickel, 38.61 mm. **Ruler:** Elizabeth II **Subject:** OECS Economic Union **Obv:** Head in tiara right **Rev:** Flags in color

Date	Mintage	F12	VF20	XF40	MS60	MS63
2011	—	PF65 100				

KM# 41 10 DOLLARS
28.28 g., 0.925 Silver 0.8356 oz. ASW, 38.6 mm. **Ruler:** Elizabeth II **Subject:** Golden Jubilee Monarchs **Obv:** Crowned head right **Rev:** Henry III (1216-1272) **Edge:** Reeded

Date	Mintage	F12	VF20	XF40	MS60	MS63
2002	10,000	PF65 65.00				

KM# 41a 10 DOLLARS
39.94 g., 0.9166 Gold 1.1694 oz. AGW, 38.6 mm. **Ruler:** Elizabeth II **Subject:** Golden Jubilee Monarchs **Obv:** Crowned head right **Rev:** Henry III (1216-1272) **Edge:** Reeded

Date	Mintage	F12	VF20	XF40	MS60	MS63
2002	100	PF65 2,150				

KM# 43 10 DOLLARS
28.28 g., 0.925 Silver 0.8356 oz. ASW, 38.6 mm. **Ruler:** Elizabeth II **Subject:** Golden Jubile Monarchs **Obv:** Crowned head right **Rev:** Edward III (1327-1377) **Edge:** Reeded

Date	Mintage	F12	VF20	XF40	MS60	MS63
2002	10,000	PF65 65.00				

KM# 43a 10 DOLLARS
39.94 g., 0.9166 Gold 1.1694 oz. AGW, 38.6 mm. **Ruler:** Elizabeth II **Subject:** Golden Jubilee Monarchs **Obv:** Crowned head right **Rev:** Edward III (1327-1377) **Edge:** Reeded

Date	Mintage	F12	VF20	XF40	MS60	MS63
2002	100	PF65 2,150				

KM# 45 10 DOLLARS
28.28 g., 0.925 Silver 0.8356 oz. ASW, 38.6 mm. **Subject:** Golden Jubilee Monarchs **Obv:** Crowned head right **Rev:** George III (1760-1820) **Edge:** Reeded

Date	Mintage	F12	VF20	XF40	MS60	MS63
2002	10,000	PF65 65.00				

KM# 45a 10 DOLLARS
39.94 g., 0.9166 Gold 1.1694 oz. AGW, 38.6 mm. **Ruler:** Elizabeth II **Subject:** Golden Jubilee Monarchs **Obv:** Crowned head right **Rev:** George III (1760-1820) **Edge:** Reeded

Date	Mintage	F12	VF20	XF40	MS60	MS63
2002	100	PF65 2,150				

KM# 47 10 DOLLARS
28.28 g., 0.925 Silver 0.8356 oz. ASW, 38.6 mm. **Ruler:** Elizabeth II **Subject:** Golden Jubilee Monarchs **Obv:** Crowned

head right **Rev:** Queen Victoria (1837-1901) **Edge:** Reeded

Date	Mintage	F12	VF20	XF40	MS60	MS63
2002	10,000	PF65 65.00				

KM# 47a 10 DOLLARS
39.94 g., 0.9166 Gold 1.1694 oz. AGW, 38.6 mm. **Ruler:** Elizabeth II **Subject:** Golden Jubilee Monarchs **Obv:** Crowned head right **Rev:** Queen Victoria (1837-1901) **Edge:** Reeded

Date	Mintage	F12	VF20	XF40	MS60	MS63
2002	100	PF65 2,150				

KM# 49 10 DOLLARS
28.28 g., 0.925 Silver 0.8356 oz. ASW, 38.6 mm. **Ruler:** Elizabeth II **Subject:** Golden Jubilee Monarchs **Obv:** Crowned head right **Rev:** Queen Elizabeth II (1952-) **Edge:** Reeded

Date	Mintage	F12	VF20	XF40	MS60	MS63
2002	10,000	PF65 65.00				

KM# 49a 10 DOLLARS
39.94 g., 0.9166 Gold 1.1694 oz. AGW, 38.6 mm. **Ruler:** Elizabeth II **Subject:** Golden Jubilee Monarchs **Obv:** Crowned head right **Rev:** Queen Elizabeth II (1952-) **Edge:** Reeded

Date	Mintage	F12	VF20	XF40	MS60	MS63
2002	100	PF65 2,150				

KM# 59 10 DOLLARS
Silver, 39 mm. **Ruler:** Elizabeth II **Obv:** Head right, partially gilt **Rev:** Fireworks display above Buckingham Palace

Date	Mintage	F12	VF20	XF40	MS60	MS63
2002	—	PF63 45.00		PF65 50.00		

KM# 88 10 DOLLARS
28.28 g., 0.925 Silver 0.8356 oz. ASW, 38.61 mm. **Ruler:** Elizabeth II **Subject:** Queen Elizabeth II Celebration **Shape:** 7-Sided

Date	Mintage	F12	VF20	XF40	MS60	MS63
2007	Est. 30000	PF63 32.00		PF65 40.00		

KM# 89 10 DOLLARS
28.28 g., 0.925 Silver 0.8356 oz. ASW, 38.61 mm. **Ruler:** Elizabeth II **Subject:** Queen Elizabeth II - Country Life **Shape:** 7-Sided

Date	Mintage	F12	VF20	XF40	MS60	MS63
2007	Est. 30000	PF63 32.00	PF65 40.00			

KM# 90 10 DOLLARS
28.28 g., 0.925 Silver 0.8356 oz. ASW, 38.61 mm. **Ruler:** Elizabeth II **Subject:** Queen Elizabeth II 60th Wedding Anniversary **Shape:** 7-Sided

Date	Mintage	F12	VF20	XF40	MS60	MS63
2007	Est. 30000	PF63 32.00	PF65 40.00			

KM# 91 10 DOLLARS
28.28 g., 0.925 Silver 0.8356 oz. ASW, 38.6 mm. **Ruler:** Elizabeth II **Rev:** Military colors and trumpants **Rev. Legend:** THE COLOURS THAT I AM PRESENTING TO YOU

Date	Mintage	F12	VF20	XF40	MS60	MS63
2012	—	PF65 75.00				

EAST TIMOR

East Timor, population: 522,433, area: 7332 sq. miles, capital: Dili, is primarily located on the eastern half of the island of Timor, just northwest of Australia at the eastern end of the Indonesian archipelago. Formerly a Portuguese colony, Timor declared its independence from Portugal on November 28, 1975. After nine short days of fledgling autonomy, a guerilla faction sympathetic to the Indonesian territorial claim to East Timor seized the government. On July 17, 1976 the Provisional government enacted a law, which dissolved the free republic and made East Timor the 24th province of Indonesia. Violent rule and civil unrest plagued the province, with great loss of life and extreme damage to property and natural resources until independence was again achieved with United Nations assistance during a period from 1999 to 2002. Emerging as the Democratic Republic of Timor-Leste and commonly known as East Timor the country has worked, with international assistance to rebuild its decimated infrastructure. Natural resources waiting to be tapped include rich oil reserves, though current exports are most dependent on coffee, sandalwood and marble. The first coins of the new republic were issued in 2003.

DEMOCRATIC REPUBLIC OF TIMOR-LESTE
DECIMAL COINAGE

KM# 1 CENTAVO
3.10 g., Nickel Clad Steel, 17 mm. **Obv:** Nautilus above date **Rev:** Denomination within circle **Edge:** Plain

Date	Mintage	F12	VF20	XF40	MS60	MS63
2003	1,500,000	—			1.50	2.50
2003	12,500	PF63 8.00				
2004	1,500,000	—			1.50	2.50
2005	—				1.50	2.50
2005	12,500	PF63 8.00				
2012	—				1.50	2.50
2012	2,000	PF63 8.00				

KM# 2 5 CENTAVOS
4.10 g., Nickel Clad Steel, 18.75 mm. **Obv:** Rice plant above date **Rev:** Denomination within circle **Edge:** Plain

Date	Mintage	F12	VF20	XF40	MS60	MS63
2003	1,500,000	—			2.00	3.00
2003	12,500	PF63 10.00				
2004	1,500,000	—			2.00	3.00
2005	—				2.00	3.00
2005	12,500	PF63 10.00				
2006	—				2.00	3.00
2010	—				2.00	3.00
2012	—	—			2.00	3.00
2012	2,000	PF63 10.00				

KM# 3 10 CENTAVOS
5.20 g., Nickel Clad Steel, 20.75 mm. **Obv:** Rooster left above date **Rev:** Denomination within circle **Edge:** Plain

Date	Mintage	F12	VF20	XF40	MS60	MS63
2003	2,500,000	—			2.50	4.00
2003	12,500	PF63 12.00				
2004	2,500,000	—			2.50	4.00
2005	—				2.50	4.00
2005	12,500	PF63 12.00				
2006	—				2.50	4.00
2010	—				2.50	4.00
2011	—				2.50	4.00
2012	—				2.50	2.50
2012	—	PF63 12.00				

KM# 4 25 CENTAVOS
5.85 g., Nickel-Brass, 21.25 mm. **Obv:** Sail boat above date **Rev:** Denomination within circle **Edge:** Reeded

Date	Mintage	F12	VF20	XF40	MS60	MS63
2003	1,500,000	—			3.50	5.00
2003	12,500	PF63 16.00				
2004	1,500,000	—			3.50	5.00
2005	—				3.50	5.00
2005	12,500	PF63 16.00				
2006	—				3.50	5.00
2011	—				3.50	5.00
2012	—				3.50	5.00
2012	2,000	PF63 16.00				

KM# 5 50 CENTAVOS
6.50 g., Nickel-Brass, 25 mm. **Obv:** Coffee plant with beans above date **Rev:** Denomination within circle **Edge:** Reeded

Date	Mintage	F12	VF20	XF40	MS60	MS63
2003	1,000,000	—			5.00	7.00
2003	12,500	PF63 22.00				
2004	1,000,000	—			5.00	7.00
2005	—				5.00	7.00
2005	12,500	PF63 22.00				
2006	—				5.00	7.00
2011	—				5.00	7.00
2012	—				5.00	7.00
2012	2,000	PF63 22.00				

KM# 6 50 CENTAVOS
Nickel-Brass

Date	Mintage	F12	VF20	XF40	MS60	MS63
2012	—				10.00	15.00
2012	2,000	PF63 25.00				

ECUADOR

North Pacific Ocean · COLOMBIA · BRAZIL · PERU

The Republic of Ecuador, located astride the equator on the Pacific Coast of South America, has an area of 105,037 sq. mi. (283,560 sq. km.) and a population of 10.9 million. Capital: Quito. Agriculture is the mainstay of the economy but there are appreciable deposits of minerals and petroleum. It is one of the world's largest exporters of bananas and balsa wood. Coffee, cacao, sugar and petroleum are also valuable exports.

REPUBLIC
REFORM COINAGE
100 Centavos = 1 Dollar

KM# 104 CENTAVO (Un)
2.52 g., Brass, 19 mm. **Obv:** Map of the Americas within circle **Rev:** Denomination **Edge:** Plain

Date	Mintage	F12	VF20	XF40	MS60	MS63
2003	—				0.20	0.40
2004	—				0.20	0.40

KM# 104a CENTAVO (Un)
2.42 g., Copper Plated Steel, 19 mm. **Obv:** Map of the Americas **Rev:** Denomination **Edge:** Plain

Date	Mintage	F12	VF20	XF40	MS60	MS63
2003	—				0.30	0.50

KM# 105 5 CENTAVOS (Cinco)
5.00 g., Steel, 21.2 mm. **Subject:** Juan Montalvo **Obv:** Bust 3/4 facing and arms **Rev:** Denomination **Edge:** Plain

Date	Mintage	F12	VF20	XF40	MS60	MS63
2003	—	—	—	—	0.50	0.75

KM# 115 SUCRE (Un)
8.36 g., 0.900 Gold 0.2403 oz. AGW, 22 mm. **Subject:** Homage to Jefferson Pérez Quezada **Obv:** National arms **Obv. Legend:** BANCO CENTRAL DEL ECUADOR **Rev:** 3/4 length figure of Perez running **Rev. Legend:** BICAMPEON MUNDIAL - CAMPEON OLIMPICO ATLANTA 1996

Date	Mintage	F12	VF20	XF40	MS60	MS63
2006	—	PF60 450				

KM# 116 SUCRE (Un)
31.10 g., 0.999 Silver 0.9925 oz. ASW, 39 mm. **Subject:** Independence 200th Anniversary

Date	Mintage	F12	VF20	XF40	MS60	MS63
2009	200	PF60 75.00				

KM# 117 SUCRE (Un)
(No Composition) **Subject:** Masacre

Date	Mintage	F12	VF20	XF40	MS60	MS63
2010	—	**PF60** 100				

KM# 118 SUCRE (Un)
8.36 g., 0.900 Gold 0.2403 oz. AGW, 13.9 mm. **Subject:** World Cup Soccer **Obv:** National arms **Rev:** Ecuadorian Soccer plaer torso holding a soccer ball

Date	Mintage	F12	VF20	XF40	MS60	MS63
2006	—	**PF60** 150				

KM# 119 SUCRE (Un)
27.10 g., 0.925 Silver 0.8008 oz. ASW, 40 mm. **Obv:** National arms within circle of other state arms **Rev:** Runner on track

Date	Mintage	F12	VF20	XF40	MS60	MS63
2007	—	**PF60** 60.00				

KM# 112 25000 SUCRES
27.10 g., 0.925 Silver 0.8008 oz. ASW, 40 mm. **Subject:** IBERO-AMERICA Series **Obv:** Coats of arms **Rev:** Balsawood sailing raft **Edge:** Reeded

Date	Mintage	F12	VF20	XF40	MS60	MS63
2002	—	**PF60** 30.00	**PF63** 45.00	**PF65** 60.00		

KM# 113 25000 SUCRES
27.00 g., 0.925 Silver 0.7978 oz. ASW, 40 mm. **Obv:** National arms **Rev:** Capital building in Quito **Edge:** Reeded

Date	Mintage	F12	VF20	XF40	MS60	MS63
2004	1,000	**PF60** 45.00	**PF63** 60.00	**PF65** 75.00		

KM# 114 25000 SUCRES
27.20 g., 0.925 Silver 0.8037 oz. ASW, 40 mm. **Subject:** 2006 World Cup Soccer **Obv:** National arms **Rev:** Ecuadorian Soccer player torso holding a soccer ball **Edge:** Reeded

Date	Mintage	F12	VF20	XF40	MS60	MS63
ND(2006)	—	**PF60** 35.00	**PF63** 45.00	**PF65** 55.00		

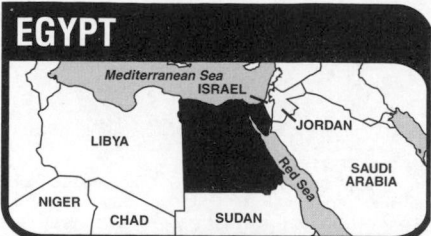

EGYPT

The Arab Republic of Egypt, located on the northeastern corner of Africa, has an area of 385,229 sq. mi. (1,1001,450 sq. km.) and a population of 62.4 million. Capital: Cairo. Although Egypt is an almost rainless expanse of desert, its economy is predominantly agricultural. Cotton, rice and petroleum are exported. Other main sources of income are revenues from the Suez Canal, remittances of Egyptian workers abroad and tourism.

ARAB REPUBLIC
AH1391- / 1971- AD
DECIMAL COINAGE

KM# 941 5 PIASTRES
1.95 g., Brass, 18 mm. **Obv:** Denomination divides dates below, legend above **Rev:** Antique pottery vase **Edge:** Plain

Date	Mintage	XF40	MS60	MS63	MS65
AH1425-2004	—	—	1.50	2.00	—

KM# 941a 5 PIASTRES
1.50 g., Copper Plated Steel, 18 mm. **Obv:** Denomination divides dates below, legend above **Rev:** Antique pottery vase

Date	Mintage	XF40	MS60	MS63	MS65
AH1429/2008	—	—	1.50	2.00	—

KM# 922 10 PIASTRES
4.52 g., Copper-Nickel, 24.8 mm. **Subject:** National Women's Council **Obv:** Value **Rev:** Woman standing next to Sphinx **Edge:** Reeded

Date	Mintage	XF40	MS60	MS63	MS65
AH1425-2004	—	—	1.50	2.00	—

KM# 990 10 PIASTRES
3.41 g., Nickel Plated Steel, 19.03 mm. **Obv:** Text, date and value **Rev:** Mosque

Date	Mintage	XF40	MS60	MS63	MS65
AH1429 (2008)	—	—	1.00	1.50	—

KM# 923 20 PIASTRES
6.00 g., Copper-Nickel, 26.8 mm. **Subject:** National Women's Council **Obv:** Value **Rev:** Woman standing next to Sphinx **Edge:** Reeded

Date	Mintage	XF40	MS60	MS63	MS65
AH1425-2004	—	—	2.50	3.50	—

KM# 991 25 PIASTRES
4.50 g., Nickel Plated Steel, 21 mm. **Obv:** Value at center, Arabic legend at top, dates below **Rev:** Value at center, Arabic at top, English value below **Edge:** Reeded

Date	Mintage	XF40	MS60	MS63	MS65
AH1429-2008	—	—	2.50	3.50	—
AH1430-2009	—	—	2.50	3.50	—
AH1431-2010	—	—	2.50	3.50	—

KM# 942.1 50 PIASTRES
6.50 g., Brass, 25 mm. **Obv:** Value **Rev:** Bust of Cleopatra left **Edge:** Reeded **Note:** Non-magnetic.

Date	Mintage	XF40	MS60	MS63	MS65
AH1426-2005	—	1.20	3.00	4.00	—
AH1427-2006	—	1.20	3.00	4.00	—

KM# 942.2 50 PIASTRES
6.50 g., Brass Plated Steel, 23 mm. **Obv:** Value **Rev:** Bust of Cleopatra left **Edge:** Reeded **Note:** Magnetic

Date	Mintage	XF40	MS60	MS63	MS65
AH1428-2007	—	—	1.00	1.50	—
AH1429-2008	—	—	1.00	1.50	—
AH1430-2009	—	—	1.00	1.50	—
AH1431-2010	—	—	1.00	1.50	—
AH1433-2012	—	—	1.00	1.50	—

KM# 903 1/2 POUND
4.00 g., 0.875 Gold 0.1118 oz. AGW, 18 mm. **Subject:** Egyptian Museum Centennial **Obv:** Value **Rev:** Building **Edge:** Reeded

Date	Mintage	XF40	MS60	MS63	MS65
AH1423-2002	—	—	250	275	300

KM# 930 POUND
15.00 g., 0.720 Silver 0.345 oz. ASW, 35 mm. **Subject:** National Women's Council **Obv:** Value **Rev:** Woman standing next to Sphinx **Edge:** Reeded

Date	Mintage	XF40	MS60	MS63	MS65
AH1421-2001	600	—	45.00	50.00	60.00

KM# 904 POUND
15.00 g., 0.720 Silver 0.345 oz. ASW, 35 mm. **Subject:** Egyptian Museum Centennial **Obv:** Value **Rev:** Building, centennial numerals in background **Edge:** Reeded

Date	Mintage	XF40	MS60	MS63	MS65
AH1423-2002	1,500	—	35.00	40.00	45.00

KM# 905 POUND
8.00 g., 0.875 Gold 0.2236 oz. AGW, 24 mm. **Subject:** Egyptian Museum Centennial **Obv:** Value **Rev:** Building, centennial numerals in background **Edge:** Reeded

Date	Mintage	XF40	MS60	MS63	MS65
AH1423-2002	300	—	400	425	450

KM# 909 POUND
15.00 g., 0.720 Silver 0.345 oz. ASW, 35 mm. **Subject:** International Ear, Nose and Throat Conference **Obv:** King Tut's Gold Mask **Rev:** IFOS" on world map **Edge:** Reeded

Date	Mintage	XF40	MS60	MS63	MS65
AH1423-2002	2,500	—	30.00	35.00	40.00

KM# 910 POUND
15.00 g., 0.720 Silver 0.345 oz. ASW, 35 mm. **Subject:** 50th Anniversary of Egyptian Revolution **Obv:** Value **Rev:** Soldier with flag **Edge:** Reeded

Date	Mintage	XF40	MS60	MS63	MS65
AH1423-2002	1,500	—	35.00	40.00	45.00

KM# 912 POUND
15.00 g., 0.720 Silver 0.345 oz. ASW, 35 mm. **Subject:** Alexandria Library **Obv:** Legend and inscription **Rev:** Inscribed arches above library roof **Edge:** Reeded

Date	Mintage	XF40	MS60	MS63	MS65
AH1423-2002	8,000	—	30.00	35.00	40.00

KM# 913 POUND
15.00 g., 0.720 Silver 0.345 oz. ASW, 35 mm. **Subject:** Body Building Championships **Obv:** Arabic and English legends **Rev:** Mr. Universe cartoon **Edge:** Reeded

Date	Mintage	XF40	MS60	MS63	MS65
AH1423-2002	1,000	—	30.00	35.00	40.00

KM# 936 POUND
8.00 g., 0.875 Gold 0.2236 oz. AGW, 24 mm. **Subject:** 50th Anniversary of Egyptian Revolution **Obv:** Value **Rev:** Soldier with flag, pyramids and radiant sun **Edge:** Reeded

Date	Mintage	XF40	MS60	MS63	MS65
AH1423-2002	400	—	400	425	450

KM# 938 POUND
8.00 g., 0.875 Gold 0.2236 oz. AGW, 24 mm. **Subject:**

Alexandria Library **Obv:** Cufic text in center **Rev:** Arched inscription above slanted library roof **Edge:** Reeded

Date	Mintage	XF40	MS60	MS63	MS65
AH1423-2002	750	—	400	425	450

KM# 955 POUND
8.00 g., 0.875 Gold 0.2236 oz. AGW, 24 mm. **Subject:** Golden Jubilee Ein Shams University **Obv:** Value **Rev:** Obelisk with bird standing at left and right **Edge:** Reeded

Date	Mintage	XF40	MS60	MS63	MS65
AH1422-2002	400	—	400	425	450

KM# 956 POUND
8.00 g., 0.875 Gold 0.2236 oz. AGW, 24 mm. **Subject:** Police Day **Obv:** Police eagle with wings spread, value **Rev:** Police badge **Edge:** Reeded

Date	Mintage	XF40	MS60	MS63	MS65
AH1422-2002	400	—	400	425	450

KM# 915 POUND
15.00 g., 0.720 Silver 0.345 oz. ASW, 35 mm. **Subject:** 30th Anniversary of the October War **Obv:** Value, dates and legend **Rev:** Soldier with flag above pyramids **Edge:** Reeded

Date	Mintage	XF40	MS60	MS63	MS65
AH1424-2003	1,000	—	30.00	35.00	40.00

KM# 917 POUND
15.00 g., 0.720 Silver 0.345 oz. ASW, 35 mm. **Subject:** 25th Anniversary of the Commerce Society **Obv:** Value, dates and legend **Rev:** Radiant sun above lattice work **Edge:** Reeded

Date	Mintage	XF40	MS60	MS63	MS65
AH1424-2003	1,200	—	30.00	35.00	40.00

KM# 957 POUND
8.00 g., 0.875 Gold 0.2236 oz. AGW, 24 mm. **Subject:** 30th Anniversary October War Victory **Obv:** Value **Rev:** Soldier holding flag on top of pyramid **Edge:** Reeded

Date	Mintage	XF40	MS60	MS63	MS65
AH1424-2003	200	—	425	445	475

KM# 958 POUND
8.00 g., 0.875 Gold 0.2236 oz. AGW, 24 mm. **Series:** Value **Subject:** Radio and Television Festival **Obv:** Modern abstract design **Edge:** Reeded

Date	Mintage	XF40	MS60	MS63	MS65
AH1424-2003	1,000	—	375	400	425

KM# 959 POUND
8.00 g., 0.875 Gold 0.2236 oz. AGW, 24 mm. **Subject:** 50th Anniversary El Gomhoreya Newspaper - Hosni Mubarak **Obv:** Value **Rev:** Bust facing at left, building in background **Edge:** Reeded

Date	Mintage	XF40	MS60	MS63	MS65
AH1424-2003	400	—	400	425	450

KM# 924 POUND
15.00 g., 0.720 Silver 0.345 oz. ASW, 35 mm. **Subject:** 90th Anniversary Scouts **Obv:** Value **Rev:** Combined scouting badge **Edge:** Reeded

Date	Mintage	XF40	MS60	MS63	MS65
AH1425-2004	2,000	—	30.00	35.00	40.00

KM# 934 POUND
15.00 g., 0.725 Silver 0.3474 oz. ASW, 35 mm. **Subject:** Golden Jubilee - Military Production **Obv:** Value **Rev:** Ancient chariot, horse and rider **Edge:** Reeded

Date	Mintage	XF40	MS60	MS63	MS65
AH1425-2004	1,000	—	30.00	35.00	40.00

KM# 960 POUND
8.00 g., 0.875 Gold 0.2236 oz. AGW, 24 mm. **Subject:** Golden Jubilee Military Production **Obv:** Value **Rev:** Ancient chariot, horse and rider left **Edge:** Reeded

Date	Mintage	XF40	MS60	MS63	MS65
AH1425-2004	750	—	375	400	425

KM# 940 POUND
8.50 g., Bi-Metallic, 25.1 mm. **Obv:** Value **Rev:** King Tutankhaman's gold mask **Edge:** Reeded

Date	Mintage	XF40	MS60	MS63	MS65
AH1426-2005	—	—	3.00	5.00	—
AH1427-2006	—	—	3.00	5.00	—

KM# 961 POUND
8.00 g., 0.875 Gold 0.2236 oz. AGW, 24 mm. **Subject:** World Environment Day **Obv:** Value **Rev:** Stylized tree, emblem at left, bird standing at right **Edge:** Reeded

Date	Mintage	XF40	MS60	MS63	MS65
AH1427-2006	200	—	425	445	475

KM# 962 POUND
8.00 g., 0.875 Gold 0.2236 oz. AGW, 24 mm. **Subject:** Golden Jubilee Suez Canal Nationalization **Obv:** Value **Rev:** Large "50" above government buildings **Edge:** Reeded

Date	Mintage	XF40	MS60	MS63	MS65
AH1427-2006	1,000	—	375	400	425

KM# 965 POUND
15.00 g., 0.720 Silver 0.345 oz. ASW, 35 mm. **Subject:** Golden Jubilee Suez Canal Nationalization **Obv:** Value **Rev:** Large "50" above government buildings **Edge:** Reeded

Date	Mintage	XF40	MS60	MS63	MS65
AH1427-2006	1,750	—	35.00	40.00	45.00

KM# 966 POUND
15.00 g., 0.720 Silver 0.345 oz. ASW, 35 mm. **Subject:** 60th Anniversary UNESCO **Obv:** Value **Rev:** Logo **Edge:** Reeded

Date	Mintage	XF40	MS60	MS63	MS65
AH1427-2006	800	—	100	125	145

KM# 967 POUND
15.00 g., 0.720 Silver 0.345 oz. ASW, 35 mm. **Subject:** 13th General Population Census **Obv:** Value **Rev:** Stylized couple leaning left at left **Edge:** Reeded

Date	Mintage	XF40	MS60	MS63	MS65
AH1427-2006	2,000	—	45.00	50.00	55.00

KM# 944 POUND
15.00 g., 0.720 Silver 0.345 oz. ASW, 35.00 mm. **Subject:** Air Force Diamond Jubilee **Obv:** Value **Rev:** Air Force insignia **Edge:** Reeded

Date	Mintage	XF40	MS60	MS63	MS65
AH1428-2007	—	—	45.00	50.00	55.00

KM# 963 POUND
8.00 g., 0.875 Gold 0.2236 oz. AGW, 24 mm. **Subject:** Silver Jubilee Egyptian Enviromental Protection **Obv:** Value **Rev:** World globe **Edge:** Reeded

Date	Mintage	XF40	MS60	MS63	MS65
AH1428-2007	300	—	420	440	465

KM# 964 POUND
8.00 g., 0.875 Gold 0.2236 oz. AGW, 24 mm. **Subject:** Diamond Jubilee Air Force **Obv:** Value **Rev:** Air Force emblem **Edge:** Reeded

Date	Mintage	XF40	MS60	MS63	MS65
AH1428-2007	130	—	500	550	600

KM# 968 POUND
15.00 g., 0.720 Silver 0.345 oz. ASW, 35 mm. **Subject:** 100th Anniversary Ahly Club **Obv:** Value **Rev:** Large "100" with linked zeroes **Edge:** Reeded

Date	Mintage	XF40	MS60	MS63	MS65
AH1428-2007	5,000	—	45.00	50.00	55.00

KM# 940a POUND
8.50 g., Bi-Metallic, 25.1 mm. **Obv:** Value at center **Rev:** King Tutankhaman's gold mask **Edge:** Reeded **Note:** Magnetic

Date	Mintage	XF40	MS60	MS63	MS65
AH1428-2007	—	—	3.00	5.00	—
AH1429-2008	—	—	3.00	4.00	—
AH1430-2009	—	—	3.00	4.00	—
AH1431-2010	—	—	3.00	4.00	—

KM# 996 POUND
15.00 g., 0.720 Silver 0.345 oz. ASW, 35 mm. **Subject:** Susan Mubarak

Date	Mintage	XF40	MS60	MS63	MS65
AH1431-2010	—	—	45.00	50.00	55.00

KM# 998 POUND
15.00 g., 0.720 Silver 0.345 oz. ASW, 35 mm. **Subject:** 50th Anniversary

Date	Mintage	XF40	MS60	MS63	MS65
AH1431-2010	—	—	45.00	50.00	55.00

KM# 931 5 POUNDS
17.50 g., 0.720 Silver 0.4025 oz. ASW, 37 mm. **Subject:** National Women's Council **Obv:** Value **Rev:** Woman standing next to Sphinx **Edge:** Reeded

Date	Mintage	XF40	MS60	MS63	MS65
AH1421-2001	600	—	55.00	60.00	70.00

KM# 906 5 POUNDS
17.50 g., 0.720 Silver 0.4025 oz. ASW, 37 mm. **Subject:** Egyptian Museum Centennial **Obv:** Value **Rev:** Building, centennial numerals in background **Edge:** Reeded

Date	Mintage	XF40	MS60	MS63	MS65
AH1423-2002	1,500	—	45.00	48.00	52.00

KM# 907 5 POUNDS
26.00 g., 0.875 Gold 0.7267 oz. AGW, 33 mm. **Subject:** Egyptian Museum Centennial **Obv:** Value **Rev:** Building, centennial numerals in background **Edge:** Reeded

Date	Mintage	XF40	MS60	MS63	MS65
AH1423-2002	250	—	1,250	1,350	1,500

KM# 911 5 POUNDS
17.55 g., 0.925 Silver 0.5186 oz. ASW, 37 mm. **Subject:** 50th Anniversary of the Egyptian Revolution **Obv:** Value **Rev:** Soldier with flag **Edge:** Reeded

Date	Mintage	XF40	MS60	MS63	MS65
AH1423-2002	1,500	—	45.00	48.00	52.00

KM# 914 5 POUNDS
17.50 g., 0.720 Silver 0.4025 oz. ASW, 37 mm. **Subject:** Body Building Championships **Obv:** Arabic and English legends **Rev:** Mr. Universe cartoon **Edge:** Reeded

Date	Mintage	XF40	MS60	MS63	MS65
AH1423-2002	800	—	40.00	45.00	55.00

KM# 932 5 POUNDS
17.50 g., 0.720 Silver 0.4025 oz. ASW, 37 mm. **Subject:** 50th Anniversary of the National Police **Obv:** Value and police logo **Rev:** Ceremonial design **Edge:** Reeded

Date	Mintage	XF40	MS60	MS63	MS65
AH1422-2002	750	—	45.00	50.00	60.00

KM# 916 5 POUNDS
17.50 g., 0.720 Silver 0.4025 oz. ASW, 37 mm. **Subject:** 30th Anniversary of the October War **Obv:** Value and legend **Rev:** Soldier with flag above pyramids **Edge:** Reeded

Date	Mintage	XF40	MS60	MS63	MS65
AH1424-2003	800	—	40.00	45.00	55.00

KM# 918 5 POUNDS
17.50 g., 0.720 Silver 0.4025 oz. ASW, 37 mm. **Obv:** Value and legend **Rev:** Geo-Physical Institute **Edge:** Reeded

Date	Mintage	XF40	MS60	MS63	MS65
AH1424-2003	800	—	40.00	45.00	55.00

KM# 919 5 POUNDS
17.50 g., 0.720 Silver 0.4025 oz. ASW, 37 mm. **Subject:** 50th Anniversary of the Republic **Obv:** Value and legend **Rev:** Portrait and building **Edge:** Reeded

Date	Mintage	XF40	MS60	MS63	MS65
AH1424-2003	3,000	—	37.00	42.00	48.00

KM# 920 5 POUNDS
17.50 g., 0.720 Silver 0.4025 oz. ASW, 37 mm. **Subject:** 25th Anniversary of the Delta Bank **Obv:** Value and legend **Rev:** Delta on world globe **Edge:** Reeded

Date	Mintage	XF40	MS60	MS63	MS65
AH1424-2004	1,500	—	37.00	42.00	48.00

KM# 925 5 POUNDS
17.50 g., 0.720 Silver 0.4025 oz. ASW, 37 mm. **Obv:** Value **Rev:** Balance scale **Edge:** Reeded

Date	Mintage	XF40	MS60	MS63	MS65
AH1425-2004	3,300	—	37.00	42.00	48.00

KM# 933 5 POUNDS
17.50 g., 0.720 Silver 0.4025 oz. ASW, 37 mm. **Subject:** 90th Anniversary - Egyptian Scouts Organization - 1914-2004 **Obv:** Value **Rev:** Combined scouting emblem **Edge:** Reeded

Date	Mintage	XF40	MS60	MS63	MS65
AH1425-2004	—	—	37.00	42.00	48.00

KM# 935 5 POUNDS
17.50 g., 0.720 Silver 0.4025 oz. ASW, 37 mm. **Subject:** Golden Jubilee - Military Production **Obv:** Value **Rev:** Ancient chariot, horse and rider left **Edge:** Reeded

Date	Mintage	XF40	MS60	MS63	MS65
AH1425-2004	800	—	40.00	45.00	55.00

KM# 974 5 POUNDS
17.50 g., 0.720 Silver 0.4025 oz. ASW, 37 mm. **Subject:** Golden Jubilee Cairo Mint **Obv:** Value **Rev:** National arms above mint building **Edge:** Reeded

Date	Mintage	XF40	MS60	MS63	MS65
AH1425-2004	1,750	—	45.00	50.00	55.00

KM# 975 5 POUNDS
17.50 g., 0.720 Silver 0.4025 oz. ASW, 37 mm. **Subject:** 60th Anniversary Arab League **Obv:** Value **Rev:** Logo in center of ornate background **Edge:** Reeded

Date	Mintage	XF40	MS60	MS63	MS65
AH1426-2005	2,000	—	55.00	60.00	65.00

KM# 976 5 POUNDS
17.50 g., 0.720 Silver 0.4025 oz. ASW, 37 mm. **Subject:** World Environment Day **Obv:** Value **Rev:** Stylized tree with logo at left, bird at right **Edge:** Reeded

Date	Mintage	XF40	MS60	MS63	MS65
AH1427-2006	1,000	—	70.00	80.00	90.00

KM# 977 5 POUNDS
17.50 g., 0.720 Silver 0.4025 oz. ASW, 35 mm. **Subject:** Golden jubilee Suez Canal Nationalization **Obv:** Value **Rev:** Large "50" above government buildings **Edge:** Reeded

Date	Mintage	XF40	MS60	MS63	MS65
AH1427-2006	1,750	—	45.00	50.00	55.00

KM# 978 5 POUNDS
17.50 g., 0.720 Silver 0.4025 oz. ASW, 37 mm. **Subject:** 60th Anniversary UNESCO **Obv:** Value **Rev:** Logo **Edge:** Reeded

Date	Mintage	XF40	MS60	MS63	MS65
AH1427-2006	800	—	100	125	145

KM# 979 5 POUNDS
17.50 g., 0.720 Silver 0.4025 oz. ASW, 37 mm. **Subject:** Diamond Jubilee Academy of Arab Language **Obv:** Value **Rev:** Globe on open book **Edge:** Reeded

Date	Mintage	XF40	MS60	MS63	MS65
AH1427-2006	1,000	—	70.00	80.00	90.00

KM# 980 5 POUNDS
17.50 g., 0.720 Silver 0.4025 oz. ASW, 37 mm. **Subject:** 13th General Population Census **Obv:** Circle with inscription in center **Rev:** Stylized couple leaning left at left **Edge:** Reeded

Date	Mintage	XF40	MS60	MS63	MS65
AH1427-2006	1,500	—	65.00	75.00	85.00

KM# 943 5 POUNDS
17.50 g., 0.720 Silver 0.4025 oz. ASW, 37 mm. **Subject:** 11th Pan-Arab Games **Obv:** Value **Rev:** Logo with outlined map of Arab nations in background **Edge:** Reeded

Date	Mintage	XF40	MS60	MS63	MS65
AH1428-2007	6,300	—	30.00	35.00	40.00

KM# 945 5 POUNDS
17.50 g., 0.720 Silver 0.4025 oz. ASW, 37 mm. **Subject:** Air Force Diamond Jubilee **Obv:** Value **Rev:** Air Force insignia **Edge:** Reeded

Date	Mintage	XF40	MS60	MS63	MS65
AH1428-2007	600	—	55.00	60.00	70.00

KM# 981 5 POUNDS
17.50 g., 0.720 Silver 0.4025 oz. ASW, 37 mm. **Subject:** 100th Anniversary Ahly Club **Obv:** Value **Rev:** Large "100" With linked zeroes **Edge:** Reeded

Date	Mintage	XF40	MS60	MS63	MS65
AH1428-2007	3,000	—	45.00	50.00	55.00

KM# 982 5 POUNDS
17.50 g., 0.720 Silver 0.4025 oz. ASW, 37 mm. **Subject:** Diamond Jubilee Court of Cassation **Obv:** Balance scale above inscriptions **Rev:** Court building **Edge:** Reeded

Date	Mintage	XF40	MS60	MS63	MS65
AH1428-2007	450	—	125	150	175

KM# 983 5 POUNDS
17.50 g., 0.720 Silver 0.4025 oz. ASW, 37 mm. **Subject:** Silver Jubilee Enviromental Protection Agency **Obv:** Value **Rev:** World globe **Edge:** Reeded

Date	Mintage	XF40	MS60	MS63	MS65
AH1428-2007	1,300	—	55.00	60.00	70.00

KM# 984 5 POUNDS
17.50 g., 0.720 Silver 0.4025 oz. ASW, 37 mm. **Subject:** 11th Arab Sports Championship - Egypt **Obv:** Value **Rev:** Stylized player on map of Arab countries **Edge:** Reeded

Date	Mintage	XF40	MS60	MS63	MS65
AH1428-2007	6,300	—	45.00	50.00	55.00

KM# 994 5 POUNDS
17.50 g., 0.720 Silver 0.4025 oz. ASW, 37 mm. **Subject:** Ras Muhammad Reserve protection

Date	Mintage	XF40	MS60	MS63	MS65
AH1431-2010	—	—	37.00	42.00	48.00

KM# 995 5 POUNDS
17.50 g., 0.720 Silver 0.4025 oz. ASW, 37 mm. **Subject:** Egypt Olympic Committee

Date	Mintage	XF40	MS60	MS63	MS65
AH1431-2010	—	—	37.00	42.00	48.00

KM# 997 5 POUNDS
17.50 g., 0.720 Silver 0.4025 oz. ASW, 37 mm. **Subject:** Susan Mubarak

Date	Mintage	XF40	MS60	MS63	MS65
AH1431-2010	—	—	45.00	50.00	55.00

KM# 999 5 POUNDS
17.50 g., 0.720 Silver 0.4025 oz. ASW, 37 mm. **Subject:** 50th Anniversary

Date	Mintage	XF40	MS60	MS63	MS65
AH1431-2010	—	—	45.00	50.00	55.00

KM# 908 10 POUNDS
40.00 g., 0.875 Gold 1.118 oz. AGW, 37 mm. **Subject:** Egyptian Museum Centennial **Obv:** Denomination **Rev:** Building, centennial numerals in background **Edge:** Reeded

Date	Mintage	XF40	MS60	MS63	MS65
AH1423-2002	150	—	1,900	2,000	2,200

KM# 989 10 POUNDS
40.00 g., 0.875 Gold 1.118 oz. AGW, 37 mm. **Subject:** Golden Jubilee Police Day **Obv:** Eagle left with wings spread **Rev:** Police emblem **Edge:** Reeded

Date	Mintage	XF40	MS60	MS63	MS65
AH1422-2002	150	—	1,900	2,000	2,200

KM# 985 10 POUNDS
40.00 g., 0.875 Gold 1.118 oz. AGW, 37 mm. **Subject:** 50th Anniversary El Gomhoreya News **Obv:** Value **Rev:** Bust of Hosni Mubarak facing at left, building in background **Edge:** Reeded

Date	Mintage	XF40	MS60	MS63	MS65
AH1424-2003	50	—	2,000	2,150	2,350

KM# 986 10 POUNDS
40.00 g., 0.875 Gold 1.118 oz. AGW, 37 mm. **Subject:** Golden Jubilee Military Production **Obv:** Value **Rev:** Ancient chariot, horse and rider left **Edge:** Reeded

Date	Mintage	XF40	MS60	MS63	MS65
AH1425-2004	85	—	1,950	2,100	2,300

KM# 987 10 POUNDS
40.00 g., 0.875 Gold 1.118 oz. AGW, 37 mm. **Subject:** 60th Anniversary Arab League **Obv:** Value **Rev:** Emblem at center, ornate background **Edge:** Reeded

Date	Mintage	XF40	MS60	MS63	MS65
AH1426-2005	50	—	2,000	2,150	2,350

KM# 988 10 POUNDS
40.00 g., 0.875 Gold 1.118 oz. AGW, 37 mm. **Subject:** Diamond Jubilee Air Force **Obv:** Value **Rev:** Air Force emblem **Edge:** Reeded

Date	Mintage	XF40	MS60	MS63	MS65
AH1428-2007	25	—	2,100	2,250	2,500

ESTONIA

The Republic of Estonia (formerly the Estonian Soviet Socialist Republic of the U.S.S.R.) is the northernmost of the three Baltic States in Eastern Europe. It has an area of 17,462 sq. mi. (45,100 sq. km.) and a population of 1.6 million. Capital: Tallinn. Agriculture and dairy farming are the principal industries. Butter, eggs, bacon, timber and petroleum are exported.

MODERN REPUBLIC
1991 - present

STANDARD COINAGE

KM# 22 10 SENTI
1.85 g., Aluminum-Bronze, 17.1 mm. **Obv:** Three lions left divide date **Rev:** Denomination **Rev. Legend:** EESTI VABARIIK **Edge:** Plain

Date	Mintage	F12	VF20	XF40	MS60	MS63
2002	30,000,000	—	—	0.20	0.50	0.80
2006	31,000,000	—	—	0.20	0.50	0.80
2008	15,000,000	—	—	0.20	0.50	0.80

KM# 23a 20 SENTI
2.00 g., Nickel Plated Steel, 18.9 mm. **Obv:** National arms divide date **Rev:** Denomination **Rev. Legend:** EESTI VABARIIK **Edge:** Plain

Date	Mintage	F12	VF20	XF40	MS60	MS63
2003	11,100,000	—	—	—	0.60	1.00
2004	20,000,000	—	—	—	0.60	1.00
2006	2,000,000	—	—	—	0.60	1.00
2008	12,000,000	—	—	—	0.60	1.00

KM# 24 50 SENTI
2.90 g., Aluminum-Bronze, 19.5 mm. **Obv:** National arms divide date **Rev:** Denomination **Rev. Legend:** EESTI VABARIIK **Edge:** Plain

Date	Mintage	F12	VF20	XF40	MS60	MS63
2004	10,000,000	—	—	—	1.00	1.50
2006	7,000,000	—	—	—	1.00	1.50
2007	17,000,000	—	—	—	1.00	1.50

KM# 35 KROON
5.00 g., Aluminum-Bronze, 23.5 mm. **Obv:** National arms **Rev:** Large, thick denomination **Rev. Legend:** EESTI VABARIIK **Edge:** Segmented reeding

Date	Mintage	F12	VF20	XF40	MS60	MS63
2001	15,000,000	—	—	0.50	1.50	2.00
2003	15,000,000	—	—	0.50	1.50	2.00
2006	15,170,000	—	—	0.50	1.50	2.00

KM# 44 KROON
4.80 g., Brass, 23.21 mm. **Obv:** National arms **Rev:** Stylized plant in circle **Rev. Legend:** EESTI VABARIIK **Edge:** Segmented reeding

Date	Mintage	F12	VF20	XF40	MS60	MS63
2008	20,000,000	—	—	1.00	2.00	3.00

KM# 38 10 KROONI
28.28 g., 0.999 Silver 0.9025 oz. ASW, 38.6 mm. **Subject:** Tartu University **Obv:** National arms **Rev:** Building in oval, value at left **Edge:** Reeded

Date	Mintage	F12	VF20	XF40	MS60	MS63
2002	10,000	PF63 70.00		PF65 80.00		

KM# 40 10 KROONI
28.28 g., 0.999 Silver 0.9025 oz. ASW, 38.6 mm. **Subject:** Estonian Flag **Obv:** National arms **Rev:** Round multicolor flag design **Edge:** Reeded

Date	Mintage	F12	VF20	XF40	MS60	MS63
2004	10,000	PF63 65.00		PF65 75.00		

KM# 42 10 KROONI
28.28 g., 0.999 Silver 0.9025 oz. ASW, 38.6 mm. **Subject:** Torino Winter Olympics **Obv:** National arms **Rev:** Gold inset cross country skier in semi-circle above Olympic flame **Edge:** Reeded

Date	Mintage	PF65	VF20	XF40	MS60	MS63
2006	10,000	PF65 150				

KM# 46 10 KROONI
28.28 g., 0.999 Silver 0.9025 oz. ASW, 38.61 mm. **Subject:** 90th Anniversary of Independence **Obv:** National arms **Obv. Legend:** EESTI VARBARIIK **Rev:** Wiiralt oak tree **Edge:** Plain

Date	Mintage	F12	VF20	XF40	MS60	MS63
2008	10,000	PF65 85.00				

KM# 48 10 KROONI
28.28 g., 0.999 Silver 0.9025 oz. ASW, 38.61 mm. **Subject:** Olympics **Obv:** Arms **Rev:** Torch and geometric patterns

Date	Mintage	F12	VF20	XF40	MS60	MS63
2008	—	PF65 50.00				

KM# 49 10 KROONI
24.10 g., 0.999 Silver 0.7691 oz. ASW, 38.61 mm. **Subject:** National Museum **Obv:** National arms within starburst **Rev:** Design in star

Date	Mintage	F12	VF20	XF40	MS60	MS63
2008	—	PF65 85.00				

KM# 51 10 KROONI
31.11 g., 0.999 Silver 0.9926 oz. ASW, 40.6 mm. **Subject:** Song and Dance Festival **Obv:** National Arms **Rev:** Circle of dancers

Date	Mintage	F12	VF20	XF40	MS60	MS63
2009	—	PF65 75.00				

KM# 53 10 KROONI
28.28 g., 0.999 Silver 0.9025 oz. ASW, 38.61 mm. **Subject:** Vancouver Winter Olympics **Obv:** National arms within wreath, date below **Rev:** Two stylized cross county skiers right

Date	Mintage	F12	VF20	XF40	MS60	MS63
2010	—	PF65 60.00				

KM# 55 25 KROONI
24.10 g., 0.9999 Silver 0.7698 oz. ASW, 38.61 mm.

Date	Mintage	F12	VF20	XF40	MS60	MS63
2010	—	PF65 75.00				

KM# 50 50 KROONI
8.64 g., 0.999 Gold 0.2757 oz. AGW, 22 mm. **Obv:** National Arms and laurel branch **Rev:** Windmill

Date	Mintage	F12	VF20	XF40	MS60	MS63
2008	—	PF65 650				

KM# 54 50 KROONI
24.50 g., 0.999 Silver 0.7818 oz. ASW, 38.61 mm. **Subject:** Estonian Nature **Obv:** Arms and legned

Date	Mintage	F12	VF20	XF40	MS60	MS63
2010	—	PF65 60.00				

KM# 39 100 KROONI
7.78 g., 0.9999 Gold 0.2484 oz. AGW **Subject:** Monetary Reform **Obv:** National arms **Rev:** Cross design **Edge:** Reeded

Date	Mintage	F12	VF20	XF40	MS60	MS63
2002	2,000	—	—	—	—	625

KM# 41 100 KROONI
7.78 g., 0.9999 Gold 0.2484 oz. AGW, 22 mm. **Subject:** Olympic Games **Obv:** National arms within wreath **Rev:** Olympic flame above rings in center **Edge:** Reeded

Date	Mintage	F12	VF20	XF40	MS60	MS63
2004 Prooflike	5,000	—	—	—	—	550

KM# 43 100 KROONI
28.28 g., 0.999 Silver 0.9025 oz. ASW, 38.6 mm. **Subject:** National Opera **Obv:** National arms **Rev:** Building front **Edge:** Plain

Date	Mintage	F12	VF20	XF40	MS60	MS63
2006	10,000	PF63 75.00	PF65 85.00			

KM# 45 100 KROONI
7.78 g., 0.9999 Gold 0.2485 oz. AGW **Subject:** 15th Anniversary Reintroduction of the Estonian Kroon **Obv:** National arms **Obv. Legend:** EESTI VARBARIIK **Rev:** Cornflower **Rev. Legend:** KROONI TAAS- / KEHTESTAMISE / 15. AASTAPAEV **Edge:** Plain **Shape:** Triangular

Date	Mintage	F12	VF20	XF40	MS60	MS63
2007 Prooflike	6,000	—	—	—	—	525

KM# 47 100 KROONI
7.78 g., 0.999 Platinum 0.2481 oz. APW, 18 mm. **Subject:** 90th Anniversary of Republic **Rev:** Three birds on wire

Date	Mintage	F12	VF20	XF40	MS60	MS63
2008	3,000	PF65 675				

KM# 52 100 KROONI
7.78 g., 0.999 Gold 0.2483 oz. AGW, 22 mm. **Subject:** Song and dance festival **Obv:** Arms **Rev:** Stylized chorus on stage

Date	Mintage	F12	VF20	XF40	MS60	MS63
2009	—	PF65 600				

KM# 56 100 KROONI
7.78 g., 0.999 Gold 0.2483 oz. AGW, 22 mm.

Date	Mintage	F12	VF20	XF40	MS60	MS63
2010	—	PF65 650				

EURO COINAGE

KM# 61 EURO CENT
2.30 g., Copper Plated Steel, 16.25 mm. **Obv:** Map of Estonia **Rev:** Denomination and globe

Date	Mintage	F12	VF20	XF40	MS60	MS63
2011	32,000,000	—	—	—	0.35	0.50
2011	3,500	PF63 6.00				
2012	25,000,000	—	—	—	0.35	0.50

KM# 62 2 EURO CENT
3.06 g., Copper Plated Steel, 18.75 mm. **Obv:** Map of Estonia **Rev:** Denomination and globe **Edge:** Grooved

Date	Mintage	F12	VF20	XF40	MS60	MS63
2011	30,000,000	—	—	—	0.50	0.75
2011	3,500	PF63 7.00				
2012	25,000,000	—	—	—	0.50	0.75

KM# 63 5 EURO CENT
3.92 g., Copper Plated Steel, 21.25 mm. **Obv:** Map of Estonia **Rev:** Denomination and globe

Date	Mintage	F12	VF20	XF40	MS60	MS63
2011	30,000,000	—	—	—	0.75	1.50
2011	3,500	PF63 7.00				

KM# 64 10 EURO CENT
4.10 g., Brass, 19.75 mm. **Obv:** Map of Estonia **Rev:** Relief map of Western Europe, stars, line and value **Edge:** Reeded

Date	Mintage	F12	VF20	XF40	MS60	MS63
2011	30,000,000	—	—	—	1.50	2.00
2011	3,500	PF63 7.00				

KM# 65 20 EURO CENT
5.74 g., Brass, 22.25 mm. **Obv:** Map of Estonia **Rev:** Relief map of Western Europe, stars, line and value **Edge:** Notched

Date	Mintage	F12	VF20	XF40	MS60	MS63
2011	25,000,000	—	—	—	1.00	1.50
2011	3,500	PF63 9.00				

KM# 66 50 EURO CENT
7.80 g., Brass, 24.25 mm. **Obv:** Map of Estonia **Rev:** Relief map of Western Europe, stars, line and value **Edge:** Reeded

Date	Mintage	F12	VF20	XF40	MS60	MS63
2011	20,000,000	—	—	—	1.50	2.00
2011	3,500	PF63 15.00				

KM# 67 EURO
7.50 g., Bi-Metallic, 23.35 mm. **Obv:** Map of Estonia **Rev:** Relief map of Western Europe, stars, lines and value **Edge:** Segmented reeding

Date	Mintage	F12	VF20	XF40	MS60	MS63
2011	16,000,000	—	—	—	2.50	4.00
2011	3,500	PF63 15.00				

KM# 68 2 EURO
8.50 g., Bi-Metallic, 25.75 mm. **Obv:** Map of Estonia **Rev:** Relief map of Western Europe, stars, lines and value **Edge:** Reeded and lettered

Date	Mintage	F12	VF20	XF40	MS60	MS63
2011	11,000,000	—	—	—	4.00	6.00
2011	3,500	PF63 30.00				

KM# 70 2 EURO
8.50 g., Bi-Metallic, 25.75 mm. **Subject:** Euro Coinage, 10th Anniversary **Obv:** Euro symbol on globe at center, child-like rendering around

Date	Mintage	F12	VF20	XF40	MS60	MS63
2012	2,000,000	—	—	—	4.00	6.00

KM# 73 7 EURO
28.28 g., 0.925 Silver 0.8356 oz. ASW, 38.61 mm. **Subject:** Raymond Valgre **Obv:** National arms **Rev:** Musical notes and Valgre signature

Date	Mintage	F12	VF20	XF40	MS60	MS63
2013	7,500	PF65 70.00				

KM# 71 10 EURO
28.80 g., 0.9999 Silver 0.9199 oz. ASW, 38.61 mm. **Subject:** Estonia's Future **Obv:** National arms **Rev:** Two dancing figures, value at top **Edge Lettering:** Ag 999.9

Date	Mintage	F12	VF20	XF40	MS60	MS63
2011	30,000	PF63 65.00	PF65 75.00			

KM# 72 12 EURO
28.28 g., 0.999 Silver 0.9025 oz. ASW, 38.61 mm. **Subject:** London Olympics **Obv:** National arms **Rev:** Ribbons, Olympic rings and flame

Date	Mintage	F12	VF20	XF40	MS60	MS63
2012	7,500	PF65 100				

KM# 69 20 EURO
14.60 g., Bi-Metallic, 27.25 mm. **Subject:** Estonia's entry into Eurozone **Obv:** National arms **Rev:** Lace

Date	Mintage	F12	VF20	XF40	MS60	MS63
2011	10,000	PF65 650				

MINT SETS

KM#	Date	Mintage	Identification	Issue Price	Mkt Val
MS2	2011 (8)	50,000	KM#61-68	—	25.00

PROOF SETS

KM#	Date	Mintage	Identification	Issue Price	Mkt Val
PS1	2011 (8)	3,500	KM#61-68	—	95.00

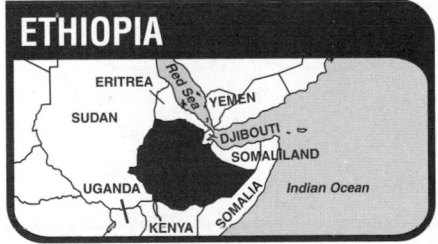

ETHIOPIA

The People's Federal Republic of Ethiopia (formerly the Peoples Democratic Republic and the Empire of Ethiopia), Africa's oldest independent nation, faces the Red Sea in East-Central Africa. The country has an area of 424,214 sq. mi. (1,004,390 sq. km.) and a population of 56 million people who are divided among 40 tribes that speak some 270 languages and dialects. Capital: Addis Ababa. The economy is predominantly agricultural and pastoral. Gold and platinum are mined and petroleum fields are being developed. Coffee, oilseeds, hides and cereals are exported.

DATING
Ethiopian coinage is dated by the Ethiopian Era calendar (E.E.), which commenced 7 years and 8 months after the advent of A.D. dating.

EXAMPLE
1900 (10 and 9 = 19 x 100)
　36 (Add 30 and 6)
1936 E.E.
　8 (Add)
1943/4 AD

PEOPLES DEMOCRATIC REPUBLIC

DECIMAL COINAGE
100 Santeems (Cents) = 1 Birr (Dollar)
100 Matonas = 100 Santeems

KM# 44.3 5 CENTS
3.00 g., Brass Plated Steel, 20 mm. **Obv:** Large lion head, right **Rev:** Denomination left of figure

Date	Mintage	F12	VF20	XF40	MS60	MS63
EE1996 (2004)	—	—	—	—	—	1.00
EE1998 (2006)	—	—	—	—	—	1.00
EE1999 (2007)	—	—	—	—	—	1.00
EE2000 (2008)	—	—	—	—	—	1.00
EE2004 (2012)	—	—	—	—	—	1.00

KM# 45.3 10 CENTS
4.50 g., Brass Plated Steel, 23 mm. **Obv:** Large lion head right **Rev:** Mountain Nyala, denomination at right

Date	Mintage	F12	VF20	XF40	MS60	MS63
EE1996 (2004)	—	—	—	—	—	1.25
EE1997 (2005)	—	—	—	—	—	1.25
EE1998 (2006) (2005)	—	—	—	—	—	1.25
EE2000 (2008)	—	—	—	—	—	1.25
EE2004 (2012)	—	—	—	—	—	1.25

KM# 46.3 25 CENTS
3.70 g., Copper-Nickel Plated Steel, 21.45 mm. **Obv:** Large lion head right **Rev:** Man and woman with arms raised divide denomination

Date	Mintage	F12	VF20	XF40	MS60	MS63
EE1996 (2004)	—	—	—	—	—	1.25
EE1997 (2005)	—	—	—	—	—	1.25
EE2000 (2008)	—	—	—	—	—	1.25
EE2004 (2012)	—	—	—	—	—	1.25

KM# 47.2 50 CENTS
6.00 g., Copper-Nickel Plated Steel, 25 mm. **Obv:** Small lion head, two long chin whiskers at left nearly touch date **Rev:** People of the republic, denomination above

Date	Mintage	F12	VF20	XF40	MS60	MS63
EE1996 (2004)	—	—	—	—	1.75	3.00
EE1997 (2005)	—	—	—	—	1.75	3.00
EE2000 (2008)	—	—	—	—	1.75	3.00
EE2004 (2012)	—	—	—	—	1.75	3.00

KM# 78 BIRR
6.82 g., Bi-Metallic, 27 mm. **Obv:** Large lion right in center **Rev:** Balance scale

Date	Mintage	F12	VF20	XF40	MS60	MS63
EE2002 (2010)	416,000,000	—	—	—	2.25	4.50

KM# 76 20 BIRR
30.00 g., 0.900 Silver 0.8625 oz. ASW, 40 mm. **Obv:** Vertical symbol with ribbon **Rev:** Reconstructed skeleton

Date	Mintage	F12	VF20	XF40	MS60	MS63
EE2000 (2007)	Est. 50000	PF60 75.00	PF63 65.00			

KM# 77 600 BIRR
20.00 g., Gold AGW, 34 mm. **Rev:** Selam Skull

Date	Mintage	F12	VF20	XF40	MS60	MS63
EE2000 (2007)	Est. 1000	PF60 1,250	PF63 1,100			

FALKLAND ISLANDS

The Colony of the Falkland Islands and Dependencies, a British colony located in the South Atlantic about 500 miles northeast of Cape Horn, has an area of 4,700 sq. mi. (12,170 sq. km.) and a population of 2,121. East Falkland, West Falkland, South Georgia, and South Sandwich are the largest of the 200 islands. Capital: Stanley. Sheep grazing is the main industry. Wool, whale oil, and seal oil are exported.

RULER
British

MONETARY SYSTEM
100 Pence = 1 Pound

BRITISH COLONY

DECIMAL COINAGE

KM# 130 PENNY
3.56 g., Copper Plated Steel, 20.3 mm. **Ruler:** Elizabeth II **Obv:** Head with tiara right **Obv. Legend:** QUEEN ELIZABETH THE SECOND **Rev:** Two Gentoo penguins flank value **Rev. Legend:** FALKLAND ISLANDS **Edge:** Plain

Date	Mintage	F12	VF20	XF40	MS60	MS63
2004	—	—	—	—	0.50	0.75

KM# 131 2 PENCE
7.12 g., Copper Plated Steel, 25.9 mm. **Ruler:** Elizabeth II **Obv:** Head with tiara right **Obv. Legend:** QUEEN ELIZABETH THE SECOND **Rev:** Upland goose alighting, value above **Rev. Legend:** FALKLAND ISLANDS **Edge:** Plain

Date	Mintage	F12	VF20	XF40	MS60	MS63
2004	—	—	—	—	0.50	1.00

KM# 132 5 PENCE
3.25 g., Copper-Nickel, 18 mm. **Ruler:** Elizabeth II **Obv:** Head with tiara right **Obv. Legend:** QUEEN ELIZABETH THE SECOND **Rev:** Black-browed Albatross in flight, value below **Rev. Legend:** FALKLAND - ISLANDS **Edge:** Reeded

Date	Mintage	F12	VF20	XF40	MS60	MS63
2004	—	—	—	—	0.75	1.00

KM# 133 10 PENCE
6.50 g., Copper-Nickel, 24.5 mm. **Ruler:** Elizabeth II **Obv:** Head with tiara right **Obv. Legend:** QUEEN ELIZABETH THE SECOND **Rev:** Ursine seal with cub, value below **Rev. Legend:** FALKLAND ISLANDS **Edge:** Reeded

Date	Mintage	F12	VF20	XF40	MS60	MS63
2004	—	—	—	—	1.50	3.00

KM# 134 20 PENCE
5.00 g., Copper-Nickel, 21.4 mm. **Ruler:** Elizabeth II **Obv:** Head with tiara right **Legend:** QUEEN ELIZABETH THE SECOND **Rev:** Romney marsh sheep standing left, value above **Rev. Legend:** FALKLAND ISLANDS **Edge:** Plain **Shape:** 7-sided

Date	Mintage	F12	VF20	XF40	MS60	MS63
2004	—	—	—	—	2.00	4.00

KM# 70 50 PENCE
29.10 g., Copper-Nickel, 38.6 mm. **Ruler:** Elizabeth II **Subject:** Centennial of Queen Victoria's Death **Obv:** Crowned bust right, denomination below **Rev:** Crowned head left, three dates **Edge:** Reeded

Date	Mintage	F12	VF20	XF40	MS60	MS63
2001	—	—	—	—	6.00	7.00

KM# 70a 50 PENCE
28.28 g., 0.925 Silver 0.8356 oz. ASW, 38.6 mm. **Ruler:** Elizabeth II **Obv:** Crowned bust right, denomination below **Rev:** Crowned head left, three dates **Edge:** Reeded

Date	Mintage	F12	VF20	XF40	MS60	MS63
2001	10,000	PF65 50.00				

KM# 70b 50 PENCE
47.54 g., 0.917 Gold 1.3926 oz. AGW, 38.61 mm. **Ruler:** Elizabeth II **Subject:** Centennial of Queen Victoria's Death **Obv:** Crowned bust right, denomination below **Rev:** Victoria's crowned bust left, three dates **Edge:** Reeded

Date	Mintage	F12	VF20	XF40	MS60	MS63
2001	100	PF65 2,500				

KM# 71 50 PENCE
29.10 g., Copper-Nickel, 38.6 mm. **Ruler:** Elizabeth II **Subject:**

Queen Elizabeth's 75th Birthday **Obv:** Crowned bust right, denomination below **Rev:** Bust of Queen Elizabeth II left **Edge:** Reeded

Date	Mintage	F12	VF20	XF40	MS60	MS63
2001	—	—	—	—	6.00	7.00

KM# 71b 50 PENCE
47.54 g., 0.917 Gold 1.3926 oz. AGW, 38.61 mm. **Ruler:** Elizabeth II **Subject:** Queen Elizabeth's 75th Birthday **Obv:** Crowned bust right, denomination below **Rev:** Bust of Queen Elizabeth II left

Date	Mintage	F12	VF20	XF40	MS60	MS63
2001	Est. 100	PF65 2,500				

KM# 86 50 PENCE
28.28 g., Copper-Nickel, 38.6 mm. **Ruler:** Elizabeth II **Obv:** Crowned bust right, denomination below **Rev:** Edward IV (1461-83) with Rose Ryal gold coin design **Edge:** Reeded

Date	Mintage	F12	VF20	XF40	MS60	MS63
2001	—	—	—	—	9.00	10.00

KM# 86a 50 PENCE
28.28 g., 0.925 Silver 0.8356 oz. ASW, 38.6 mm. **Ruler:** Elizabeth II **Obv:** Crowned bust right, denomination below **Rev:** Edward IV (1461-83) with gold-plated Rose Ryal gold coin design **Edge:** Reeded

Date	Mintage	F12	VF20	XF40	MS60	MS63
2001	5,000	PF65 50.00				

KM# 87 50 PENCE
28.28 g., Copper-Nickel, 38.6 mm. **Ruler:** Elizabeth II **Obv:** Crowned bust right, denomination below **Rev:** Henry VII (1485-1509) with 1489 Gold Sovereign coin design **Edge:** Reeded

Date	Mintage	F12	VF20	XF40	MS60	MS63
2001	—	—	—	—	9.00	10.00

KM# 87a 50 PENCE
28.28 g., 0.925 Silver 0.8356 oz. ASW, 38.6 mm. **Ruler:** Elizabeth II **Obv:** Crowned bust right, denomination below **Rev:** Henry VII (1485-1509) with gold-plated 1489 gold Sovereign coin design **Edge:** Reeded

Date	Mintage	F12	VF20	XF40	MS60	MS63
2001	5,000	PF65 50.00				

KM# 88 50 PENCE
28.28 g., Copper-Nickel, 38.6 mm. **Ruler:** Elizabeth II **Obv:** Crowned bust right, denomination below **Rev:** Charles II (1660-85) with 1663 gold Guinea coin design **Edge:** Reeded

Date	Mintage	F12	VF20	XF40	MS60	MS63
2001	—	—	—	—	9.00	10.00

KM# 88a 50 PENCE
28.28 g., 0.925 Silver 0.8356 oz. ASW, 38.6 mm. **Ruler:** Elizabeth II **Obv:** Crowned bust right, denomination below **Rev:** Charles II (1660-85) with gold-plated Gold Guinea coin design **Edge:** Reeded

Date	Mintage	F12	VF20	XF40	MS60	MS63
2001	5,000	PF65 50.00				

KM# 89 50 PENCE
28.28 g., Copper-Nickel, 38.6 mm. **Ruler:** Elizabeth II **Obv:** Crowned bust right, denomination below **Rev:** Queen Victoria with Gold Sovereign coin design **Edge:** Reeded

Date	Mintage	F12	VF20	XF40	MS60	MS63
2001	—	—	—	—	9.00	10.00

KM# 89a 50 PENCE
28.28 g., 0.925 Silver 0.8356 oz. ASW, 38.6 mm. **Ruler:** Elizabeth II **Obv:** Crowned bust right, denomination below **Rev:** Queen Victoria with gold-plated Gold Sovereign coin design **Edge:** Reeded

Date	Mintage	F12	VF20	XF40	MS60	MS63
2001	5,000	PF65 50.00				

KM# 73.1 50 PENCE
28.13 g., Copper-Nickel, 38.6 mm. **Ruler:** Elizabeth II **Subject:** Queen's Golden Jubilee **Obv:** Crowned head right, denomination below **Rev:** Queen Elizabeth II on throne in inner circle below multicolor bunting **Edge:** Reeded

Date	Mintage	F12	VF20	XF40	MS60	MS63
2002(2001) (2002)	—	PF65 8.00				

KM# 73.2 50 PENCE
Copper-Nickel **Ruler:** Elizabeth II **Subject:** Queen's Golden Jubilee **Obv:** Crowned bust right, denomination below **Rev:** With plain bunting

Date	Mintage	F12	VF20	XF40	MS60	MS63
2002	—	—	—	—	6.00	7.00

KM# 73a.1 50 PENCE
28.28 g., 0.925 Silver 0.8356 oz. ASW, 38.6 mm. **Ruler:** Elizabeth II **Subject:** Queen's Golden Jubilee **Obv:** Crowned bust right, denomination below **Rev:** Queen on throne below multicolor bunting **Edge:** Reeded

Date	Mintage	F12	VF20	XF40	MS60	MS63
2002	25,000	PF65 45.00				

KM# 73a.2 50 PENCE
28.28 g., 0.925 Silver 0.8356 oz. ASW, 38.61 mm. **Ruler:** Elizabeth II **Obv:** Crowned bust right, denomination below **Rev:** With plain bunting

Date	Mintage	F12	VF20	XF40	MS60	MS63
2002	—	PF65 45.00				

KM# 73b.1 50 PENCE
39.94 g., 0.917 Gold 1.1699 oz. AGW, 38.61 mm. **Ruler:**

Obv: Crowned bust right, denomination below **Rev:** Crowned queen with scepter and orb below multicolor bunting **Edge:** Reeded

Date	Mintage	F12	VF20	XF40	MS60	MS63
2002	150	PF65 2,100				

KM# 74.1 50 PENCE
28.13 g., Copper-Nickel, 38.6 mm. **Ruler:** Elizabeth II **Subject:** Queen's Golden Jubilee **Obv:** Crowned bust right, denomination below **Rev:** Queen on horse half left in inner circle below multicolor bunting **Edge:** Reeded

Date	Mintage	F12	VF20	XF40	MS60	MS63
2002(2001)	PF65 8.00					

KM# 74.2 50 PENCE
Copper-Nickel **Ruler:** Elizabeth II **Subject:** Queen's Golden Jubilee **Obv:** Crowned bust right, denomination below **Rev:** With plain bunting

Date	Mintage	F12	VF20	XF40	MS60	MS63
2002	—	—	—	—	7.00	8.00

KM# 74a.1 50 PENCE
28.28 g., 0.925 Silver 0.8356 oz. ASW, 38.6 mm. **Ruler:** Elizabeth II **Subject:** Queen's Golden Jubilee **Obv:** Crowned bust right, denomination below **Edge:** Reeded

Date	Mintage	F12	VF20	XF40	MS60	MS63
2002	25,000	PF65 45.00				

KM# 74a.2 50 PENCE
28.28 g., 0.925 Silver 0.8356 oz. ASW, 38.61 mm. **Ruler:** Elizabeth II **Subject:** Queen's Golden Jubilee **Obv:** Crowned bust right, denomination below **Rev:** With plain bunting

Date	Mintage	F12	VF20	XF40	MS60	MS63
2002	—	PF65 45.00				

KM# 74b.1 50 PENCE
39.94 g., 0.917 Gold 1.1699 oz. AGW, 38.61 mm. **Ruler:** Elizabeth II **Subject:** Queen's Golden Jubilee **Obv:** Crowned bust right, denomination below **Rev:** Queen on horseback below multicolored bunting **Edge:** Reeded

Date	Mintage	F12	VF20	XF40	MS60	MS63
2002	150	PF65 2,050				

KM# 74b.2 50 PENCE
39.94 g., 0.917 Gold 1.1699 oz. AGW, 38.61 mm. **Ruler:** Elizabeth II **Subject:** Queen's Golden Jubilee **Obv:** Crowned bust right, denomination below **Rev:** With plain bunting

Date	Mintage	F12	VF20	XF40	MS60	MS63
2002	—	PF65 2,100				

KM# 75.1 50 PENCE
28.13 g., Copper-Nickel, 38.6 mm. **Ruler:** Elizabeth II **Subject:** Queen's Golden Jubilee **Obv:** Crowned bust right, denomination below **Rev:** Queen Elizabeth II talking into microphone below multicolor bunting **Edge:** Reeded

Date	Mintage	F12	VF20	XF40	MS60	MS63
2002(2001) (2002)	—	PF65 8.00				

KM# 75.2 50 PENCE
Copper-Nickel **Ruler:** Elizabeth II **Subject:** Queen's Golden Jubilee **Obv:** Crowned bust right, denomination below **Rev:** With plain bunting

Date	Mintage	F12	VF20	XF40	MS60	MS63
2002	—	—	—	—	6.00	7.00

KM# 75a.1 50 PENCE
28.28 g., 0.925 Silver 0.8356 oz. ASW, 38.6 mm. **Ruler:** Elizabeth II **Subject:** Queen's Golden Jubilee **Obv:** Crowned bust right, denomination below **Rev:** Queen speaking into a radio microphone below multicolored bunting **Edge:** Reeded

Date	Mintage	F12	VF20	XF40	MS60	MS63
2002	25,000	PF65 45.00				

KM# 75a.2 50 PENCE
28.28 g., 0.925 Silver 0.8356 oz. ASW, 38.61 mm. **Ruler:** Elizabeth II **Subject:** Queen's Golden Jubilee **Obv:** Crowned bust right, denomination below **Rev:** With plain bunting

Date	Mintage	F12	VF20	XF40	MS60	MS63
2002	—	PF65 45.00				

KM# 75b.1 50 PENCE
39.94 g., 0.917 Gold 1.1699 oz. AGW, 38.61 mm. **Ruler:** Elizabeth II **Subject:** Queen's Golden Jubilee **Obv:** Crowned bust right, denomination below **Rev:** Elizabeth speaking into a radio microphone below multicolored bunting **Edge:** Reeded

Date	Mintage	F12	VF20	XF40	MS60	MS63
2002	50	PF65 2,150				

KM# 75b.2 50 PENCE
39.94 g., 0.917 Gold 1.1699 oz. AGW, 38.61 mm. **Ruler:** Elizabeth II **Subject:** Queen's Golden Jubilee **Obv:** Crowned bust right, denomination below **Rev:** With plain bunting

Date	Mintage	F12	VF20	XF40	MS60	MS63
2002	—	PF65 2,100				

KM# 76.1 50 PENCE
28.13 g., Copper-Nickel, 38.6 mm. **Ruler:** Elizabeth II **Subject:** Queen's Golden Jubilee **Obv:** Crowned bust right, denomination below **Rev:** Queen walking to left in front of a crowd below multicolored bunting **Edge:** Reeded

Date	Mintage	F12	VF20	XF40	MS60	MS63
2002(2001) (2002)	—	PF65 8.00				

KM# 76.2 50 PENCE
Copper-Nickel **Ruler:** Elizabeth II **Subject:** Queen's Golden Jubilee **Obv:** Crowned bust right, denomination below **Rev:** With plain bunting

Date	Mintage	F12	VF20	XF40	MS60	MS63
2002	—	—	—	—	6.00	7.00

KM# 76a.1 50 PENCE
28.28 g., 0.925 Silver 0.8356 oz. ASW, 38.6 mm. **Ruler:** Elizabeth II **Subject:** Queen's Golden Jubilee **Obv:** Crowned bust right, denomination below **Rev:** Queen standing before crowd below multicolored bunting **Edge:** Reeded

Date	Mintage	F12	VF20	XF40	MS60	MS63
2002	15,000	PF65 45.00				

KM# 76a.2 50 PENCE
28.28 g., 0.925 Silver 0.8356 oz. ASW, 38.61 mm. **Ruler:** Elizabeth II **Subject:** Queen's Golden Jubilee **Obv:** Crowned bust right, denomination below **Rev:** With plain bunting

Date	Mintage	F12	VF20	XF40	MS60	MS63
2002	—	PF65 45.00				

KM# 76b.1 50 PENCE
39.94 g., 0.917 Gold 1.1699 oz. AGW, 38.61 mm. **Ruler:** Elizabeth II **Subject:** Queen's Golden Jubilee **Obv:** Crowned bust right, denomination below **Rev:** Queen standing before a crowd below multicolored bunting **Edge:** Reeded

Date	Mintage	F12	VF20	XF40	MS60	MS63
2002	50	PF65 2,150				

KM# 76b.2 50 PENCE
39.94 g., 0.917 Gold 1.1699 oz. AGW, 38.61 mm. **Ruler:** Elizabeth II **Subject:** Queen's Golden Jubilee **Obv:** Crowned bust right, denomination below **Rev:** With plain bunting

Date	Mintage	F12	VF20	XF40	MS60	MS63
2002	—	PF65 2,100				

KM# 77.1 50 PENCE
28.13 g., Copper-Nickel, 38.6 mm. **Ruler:** Elizabeth II **Subject:** Queen's Golden Jubilee **Obv:** Crowned bust right, denomination below **Rev:** Conjoined busts of Queen Elizabeth, Prince Charles, Prince William facing left in inner circle below multicolor bunting **Edge:** Reeded

Date	Mintage	F12	VF20	XF40	MS60	MS63
2002(2001) (2002)		PF65 8.00				

KM# 77.2 50 PENCE
Copper-Nickel **Ruler:** Elizabeth II **Subject:** Queen's Golden Jubilee **Obv:** Crowned bust right, denomination below **Rev:** With plain bunting

Date	Mintage	F12	VF20	XF40	MS60	MS63
2002	—	—	—	—	6.00	7.00

KM# 77a.1 50 PENCE
28.28 g., 0.925 Silver 0.8356 oz. ASW, 38.6 mm. **Ruler:** Elizabeth II **Subject:** Queen's Golden Jubilee **Obv:** Crowned bust right, denomination below **Rev:** Queen, Prince Charles and Prince William below multicolor bunting **Edge:** Reeded

Date	Mintage	F12	VF20	XF40	MS60	MS63
2002	15,000	PF65 45.00				

KM# 77a.2 50 PENCE
28.28 g., 0.925 Silver 0.8356 oz. ASW, 38.61 mm. **Ruler:** Elizabeth II **Subject:** Queen's Golden Jubilee **Obv:** Crowned bust right, denomination below **Rev:** With plain bunting

Date	Mintage	F12	VF20	XF40	MS60	MS63
2002	—	PF65 45.00				

KM# 77b.1 50 PENCE
39.94 g., 0.917 Gold 1.1699 oz. AGW, 38.61 mm. **Ruler:** Elizabeth II **Subject:** Queen's Golden Jubilee **Obv:** Crowned bust right, denomination below **Rev:** Elizabeth II, Prince Charles and his son William below multicolored bunting **Edge:** Reeded

Date	Mintage	F12	VF20	XF40	MS60	MS63
2002	50	PF65 2,150				

KM# 77b.2 50 PENCE
39.94 g., 0.917 Gold 1.1699 oz. AGW, 38.61 mm. **Ruler:** Elizabeth II **Subject:** Queen's Golden Jubilee **Obv:** Crowned bust right, denomination below **Rev:** With plain bunting

Date	Mintage	F12	VF20	XF40	MS60	MS63
2002	—	PF65 2,100				

KM# 78.1 50 PENCE
28.13 g., Copper-Nickel, 38.6 mm. **Ruler:** Elizabeth II **Subject:** Queen's Golden Jubilee **Obv:** Crowned bust right, denomination below **Rev:** Royal coach below multicolor bunting **Edge:** Reeded

Date	Mintage	F12	VF20	XF40	MS60	MS63
2002		PF65 8.00				

KM# 78.2 50 PENCE
Copper-Nickel **Ruler:** Elizabeth II **Subject:** Queen's Golden Jubilee **Obv:** Crowned bust right, denomination below **Rev:** With plain bunting

Date	Mintage	F12	VF20	XF40	MS60	MS63
2002	—	—	—	—	6.00	7.00

KM# 78a.1 50 PENCE
28.28 g., 0.925 Silver 0.8356 oz. ASW, 38.6 mm. **Ruler:** Elizabeth II **Subject:** Queen's Golden Jubilee **Obv:** Crowned bust right, denomination below **Rev:** Coronation coach below multicolor bunting **Edge:** Reeded

Date	Mintage	F12	VF20	XF40	MS60	MS63
2002	15,000	PF65 45.00				

KM# 78b.1 50 PENCE
39.94 g., 0.917 Gold 1.1699 oz. AGW, 38.61 mm. **Ruler:** Elizabeth II **Subject:** Queen's Golden Jubilee **Obv:** Crowned bust right, denomination below **Rev:** Coronation coach below multicolor bunting **Edge:** Reeded

Date	Mintage	F12	VF20	XF40	MS60	MS63
2002	150	PF65 2,150				

KM# 78b.2 50 PENCE
39.94 g., 0.917 Gold 1.1699 oz. AGW, 38.61 mm. **Ruler:** Elizabeth II **Subject:** Queen's Golden Jubilee **Obv:** Crowned bust right, denomination below **Rev:** With plain bunting

Date	Mintage	F12	VF20	XF40	MS60	MS63
2002	—	PF65 2,100				

KM# 79.1 50 PENCE
28.13 g., Copper-Nickel, 38.6 mm. **Ruler:** Elizabeth II **Subject:** Queen's Golden Jubilee **Obv:** Crowned bust right, denomination below **Rev:** Scepter and orb below multicolor bunting **Edge:** Reeded

Date	Mintage	F12	VF20	XF40	MS60	MS63
2002	—	PF65 8.00				

KM# 79.2 50 PENCE
Copper-Nickel **Ruler:** Elizabeth II **Subject:** Queen's Golden Jubilee **Obv:** Crowned bust right, denomination below **Rev:** With plain bunting

Date	Mintage	F12	VF20	XF40	MS60	MS63
2002	—	—	—	—	6.00	7.00

KM# 79a.1 50 PENCE
28.28 g., 0.925 Silver 0.8356 oz. ASW, 38.6 mm. **Ruler:** Elizabeth II **Subject:** Queen's Golden Jubilee **Obv:** Crowned bust right, denomination below **Rev:** Orb and scepter below multicolor bunting **Edge:** Reeded

Date	Mintage	F12	VF20	XF40	MS60	MS63
2002	15,000	PF65 45.00				

KM# 79a.2 50 PENCE
28.28 g., 0.925 Silver 0.8356 oz. ASW, 38.61 mm. **Ruler:** Elizabeth II **Subject:** Queen's Golden Jubilee **Obv:** Crowned bust right, denomination below **Rev:** With plain bunting

Date	Mintage	F12	VF20	XF40	MS60	MS63
2002	—	PF65 45.00				

KM# 79b.1 50 PENCE
39.94 g., 0.917 Gold 1.1699 oz. AGW, 38.61 mm. **Ruler:** Elizabeth II **Subject:** Queen's Golden Jubilee **Obv:** Crowned bust right, denomination below **Rev:** Orb and scepter below multicolor bunting **Edge:** Reeded

Date	Mintage	F12	VF20	XF40	MS60	MS63
2002	150	PF65 2,150				

KM# 79b.2 50 PENCE
39.94 g., 0.917 Gold 1.1699 oz. AGW, 38.61 mm. **Ruler:** Elizabeth II **Subject:** Queen's Golden Jubilee **Obv:** Crowned bust right, denomination below **Rev:** With plain bunting

Date	Mintage	F12	VF20	XF40	MS60	MS63
2002	—	PF65 2,100				

KM# 80.1 50 PENCE
28.13 g., Copper-Nickel, 38.6 mm. **Ruler:** Elizabeth II **Subject:** Queen's Golden Jubilee **Obv:** Crowned bust right, denomination below **Rev:** Crown below multicolor bunting **Edge:** Reeded

Date	Mintage	F12	VF20	XF40	MS60	MS63
2002	—	PF65 8.00				

KM# 80.2 50 PENCE
Copper-Nickel **Ruler:** Elizabeth II **Subject:** Queen's Golden Jubilee **Obv:** Crowned bust right, denomination below **Rev:** With plain bunting

Date	Mintage	F12	VF20	XF40	MS60	MS63
2002	—	—	—	—	6.00	7.00

KM# 80a.1 50 PENCE
28.28 g., 0.925 Silver 0.8356 oz. ASW, 38.6 mm. **Ruler:** Elizabeth II **Subject:** Queen's Golden Jubilee **Obv:** Crowned bust right, denomination below **Rev:** Crown below multicolor bunting **Edge:** Reeded

Date	Mintage	F12	VF20	XF40	MS60	MS63
2002	15,000	PF65 45.00				

KM# 80a.2 50 PENCE
28.28 g., 0.925 Silver 0.8356 oz. ASW, 38.61 mm. **Ruler:** Elizabeth II **Subject:** Queen's Golden Jubilee **Obv:** Crowned bust right, denomination below **Rev:** With plain bunting

Date	Mintage	F12	VF20	XF40	MS60	MS63
2002	—	PF65 45.00				

KM# 80b.1 50 PENCE
39.94 g., 0.917 Gold 1.1699 oz. AGW, 38.61 mm. **Ruler:** Elizabeth II **Subject:** Queen's Golden Jubilee **Obv:** Crowned bust right, denomination below **Rev:** Crown below multicolor bunting **Edge:** Reeded

Date	Mintage	F12	VF20	XF40	MS60	MS63
2002	150	PF65 2,150				

KM# 80b.2 50 PENCE
39.94 g., 0.917 Gold 1.1699 oz. AGW, 38.61 mm. **Ruler:** Elizabeth II **Subject:** Queen's Golden Jubilee **Obv:** Crowned bust right, denomination below **Rev:** With plain bunting

Date	Mintage	F12	VF20	XF40	MS60	MS63
2002	—	PF65 2,100				

KM# 81.1 50 PENCE
28.13 g., Copper-Nickel, 38.6 mm. **Ruler:** Elizabeth II **Subject:** Queen's Golden Jubilee **Obv:** Crowned bust right, denomination below **Rev:** Throne below multicolor bunting **Edge:** Reeded

Date	Mintage	F12	VF20	XF40	MS60	MS63
2002	—	PF65 8.00				

KM# 81.2 50 PENCE
Copper-Nickel **Ruler:** Elizabeth II **Subject:** Queen's Golden Jubilee **Obv:** Crowned bust right, denomination below **Rev:** With plain bunting

Date	Mintage	F12	VF20	XF40	MS60	MS63
2002	—	—	—	—	6.00	7.00

KM# 81a.1 50 PENCE
28.28 g., 0.925 Silver 0.8356 oz. ASW, 38.6 mm. **Ruler:** Elizabeth II **Subject:** Queen's Golden Jubilee **Obv:** Crowned bust right, denomination below **Rev:** Coronation throne below multicolor bunting **Edge:** Reeded

Date	Mintage	F12	VF20	XF40	MS60	MS63
2002	15,000	PF65 45.00				

KM# 81a.2 50 PENCE
28.28 g., 0.925 Silver 0.8356 oz. ASW, 38.61 mm. **Ruler:** Elizabeth II **Subject:** Queen's Golden Jubilee **Obv:** Crowned bust right, denomination below **Rev:** With plain bunting

Date	Mintage	F12	VF20	XF40	MS60	MS63
2002	—	PF65 45.00				

KM# 81b.1 50 PENCE
39.94 g., 0.917 Gold 1.1699 oz. AGW, 38.61 mm. **Ruler:** Elizabeth II **Subject:** Queen's Golden Jubilee **Obv:** Crowned bust right, denomination below **Rev:** Coronation Throne below multicolored bunting **Edge:** Reeded

Date	Mintage	F12	VF20	XF40	MS60	MS63
2002	150	PF65 2,150				

KM# 81b.2 50 PENCE
39.94 g., 0.917 Gold 1.1699 oz. AGW, 38.61 mm. **Ruler:** Elizabeth II **Subject:** Queen's Golden Jubilee **Obv:** Crowned bust right, denomination below **Rev:** With plain bunting

Date	Mintage	F12	VF20	XF40	MS60	MS63
2002	—	PF65 2,100				

KM# 82.1 50 PENCE
28.13 g., Copper-Nickel, 38.6 mm. **Ruler:** Elizabeth II **Subject:** Queen's Golden Jubilee **Obv:** Crowned bust right, denomination below **Rev:** Queen on throne below multicolor bunting **Edge:** Reeded

Date	Mintage	F12	VF20	XF40	MS60	MS63
2002 Proof	—	—	—	—	6.00	7.00

KM# 82.2 50 PENCE
Copper-Nickel **Ruler:** Elizabeth II **Subject:** Queen's Golden Jubilee **Obv:** Crowned bust right, denomination below **Rev:** With plain bunting

Date	Mintage	F12	VF20	XF40	MS60	MS63
2002	—	—	—	—	6.00	7.00

KM# 82a.1 50 PENCE
28.28 g., 0.925 Silver 0.8356 oz. ASW, 38.6 mm. **Ruler:** Elizabeth II **Subject:** Queen's Golden Jubilee **Obv:** Crowned bust right, denomination below **Rev:** Queen on throne below multicolor bunting **Edge:** Reeded

Date	Mintage	F12	VF20	XF40	MS60	MS63
2002	15,000	PF65 45.00				

KM# 82a.2 50 PENCE
28.28 g., 0.925 Silver 0.8356 oz. ASW, 38.61 mm. **Ruler:** Elizabeth II **Subject:** Queen's Golden Jubilee **Obv:** Crowned bust right, denomination below **Rev:** With plain bunting

Date	Mintage	F12	VF20	XF40	MS60	MS63
2002	—	PF65 45.00				

KM# 82b.1 50 PENCE
39.94 g., 0.917 Gold 1.1699 oz. AGW, 38.61 mm. **Ruler:** Elizabeth II **Subject:** Queen's Golden Jubilee **Obv:** Crowned bust right, denomination below **Rev:** Queen seated on throne below multicolor bunting **Edge:** Reeded

Date	Mintage	F12	VF20	XF40	MS60	MS63
2002	50	PF65 2,150				

KM# 82b.2 50 PENCE
39.94 g., 0.917 Gold 1.1699 oz. AGW, 38.61 mm. **Ruler:** Elizabeth II **Subject:** Queen's Golden Jubilee **Obv:** Crowned bust right, denomination below **Rev:** With plain bunting

Date	Mintage	F12	VF20	XF40	MS60	MS63
2002	—	PF65 2,100				

KM# 83.1 50 PENCE
28.13 g., Copper-Nickel, 38.6 mm. **Ruler:** Elizabeth II **Subject:** Queen's Golden Jubilee **Obv:** Crowned bust right, denomination below **Rev:** Queen and young family below multicolor bunting **Edge:** Reeded

Date	Mintage	F12	VF20	XF40	MS60	MS63
2002 Proof	—	—	—	—	6.00	7.00

KM# 83a.1 50 PENCE
28.28 g., 0.925 Silver 0.8356 oz. ASW, 38.6 mm. **Ruler:** Elizabeth II **Subject:** Queen's Golden Jubilee **Obv:** Crowned bust right, denomination below **Rev:** Royal family below multicolor bunting **Edge:** Reeded

Date	Mintage	F12	VF20	XF40	MS60	MS63
2002	15,000	PF65 45.00				

KM# 83a.2 50 PENCE
28.28 g., 0.925 Silver 0.8356 oz. ASW, 38.61 mm. **Ruler:** Elizabeth II **Subject:** Queen's Golden Jubilee **Obv:** Crowned bust right, denomination below **Rev:** With plain bunting

Date	Mintage	F12	VF20	XF40	MS60	MS63
2002	—	PF65 45.00				

KM# 83b.1 50 PENCE
39.94 g., 0.917 Gold 1.1699 oz. AGW, 38.61 mm. **Ruler:** Elizabeth II **Subject:** Queen's Golden Jubilee **Obv:** Crowned bust right, denomination below **Rev:** Royal Family below multicolor bunting **Edge:** Reeded

Date	Mintage	F12	VF20	XF40	MS60	MS63
2002	50	PF65 2,150				

KM# 83b.2 50 PENCE
39.94 g., 0.917 Gold 1.1699 oz. AGW, 38.61 mm. **Ruler:** Elizabeth II **Subject:** Queen's Golden Jubilee **Obv:** Crowned bust right, denomination below **Rev:** With plain bunting

Date	Mintage	F12	VF20	XF40	MS60	MS63
2002	—	PF65 2,100				

KM# 84.1 50 PENCE
28.13 g., Copper-Nickel, 38.6 mm. **Ruler:** Elizabeth II **Subject:** Queen's Golden Jubilee **Obv:** Crowned bust right, denomination below **Rev:** Queens head and tree house below multicolor bunting **Edge:** Reeded

Date	Mintage	F12	VF20	XF40	MS60	MS63
2002	—	PF65 8.00				

KM# 84.2 50 PENCE
Copper-Nickel **Ruler:** Elizabeth II **Subject:** Queen's Golden Jubilee **Obv:** Crowned bust right, denomination below **Rev:** With plain bunting

Date	Mintage	F12	VF20	XF40	MS60	MS63
2002	—	—	—	—	6.00	7.00

KM# 84a.1 50 PENCE
28.28 g., 0.925 Silver 0.8356 oz. ASW, 38.6 mm. **Ruler:** Elizabeth II **Subject:** Queen's Golden Jubilee **Obv:** Crowned bust right, denomination below **Rev:** Queen and tree house below multicolor bunting **Edge:** Reeded

Date	Mintage	F12	VF20	XF40	MS60	MS63
2002	25,000	PF65 45.00				

KM# 84a.2 50 PENCE
28.28 g., 0.925 Silver 0.8356 oz. ASW, 38.61 mm. **Ruler:** Elizabeth II **Subject:** Queen's Golden Jubilee **Obv:** Crowned bust right, denomination below **Rev:** With plain bunting

Date	Mintage	F12	VF20	XF40	MS60	MS63
2002		PF65 45.00				

KM# 84b.1 50 PENCE
39.94 g., 0.917 Gold 1.1699 oz. AGW, 38.61 mm. **Ruler:** Elizabeth II **Subject:** Queen's Golden Jubilee **Obv:** Crowned bust right, denomination below **Rev:** Queen and tree house below multicolor bunting **Edge:** Reeded

Date	Mintage	F12	VF20	XF40	MS60	MS63
2002	50	PF65 2,150				

KM# 84b.2 50 PENCE
39.94 g., 0.917 Gold 1.1699 oz. AGW, 38.61 mm. **Ruler:** Elizabeth II **Subject:** Queen's Golden Jubilee **Obv:** Crowned bust right, denomination below **Rev:** With plain bunting

Date	Mintage	F12	VF20	XF40	MS60	MS63
2002	—	PF65 2,100				

KM# 90 50 PENCE
28.28 g., Copper-Nickel, 38.6 mm. **Ruler:** Elizabeth II **Obv:** Crowned bust right, denomination below **Rev:** Conjoined busts of Elizabeth and Philip below multicolor bunting **Edge:** Reeded

Date	Mintage	F12	VF20	XF40	MS60	MS63
2002	—	—	—	—	6.00	7.00

KM# 90a.1 50 PENCE
28.28 g., 0.925 Silver 0.8356 oz. ASW, 38.6 mm. **Ruler:** Elizabeth II **Obv:** Crowned bust right, denomination below **Rev:** Elizabeth and Philip below multicolor bunting **Edge:** Reeded

Date	Mintage	F12	VF20	XF40	MS60	MS63
2002	15,000	PF65 45.00				

KM# 90a.2 50 PENCE
28.28 g., 0.925 Silver 0.8356 oz. ASW, 38.6 mm. **Ruler:** Elizabeth II **Obv:** Crowned bust right, denomination below **Rev:** With plain bunting

Date	Mintage	F12	VF20	XF40	MS60	MS63
2002	—	PF65 45.00				

KM# 90b.1 50 PENCE
39.94 g., 0.917 Gold 1.1699 oz. AGW, 38.61 mm. **Ruler:** Elizabeth II **Obv:** Crowned bust right, denomination below **Rev:** Elizabeth and Philip below multicolor bunting **Edge:** Reeded

Date	Mintage	F12	VF20	XF40	MS60	MS63
2002	50	PF65 2,150				

KM# 90b.2 50 PENCE
39.94 g., 0.917 Gold 1.1699 oz. AGW, 38.61 mm. **Ruler:** Elizabeth II **Obv:** Crowned bust right, denomination below **Rev:** With plain bunting **Edge:** Reeded

Date	Mintage	F12	VF20	XF40	MS60	MS63
2002	—	PF65 2,100				

KM# 91 50 PENCE
28.28 g., Copper-Nickel, 38.6 mm. **Ruler:** Elizabeth II **Obv:** Crowned bust right, denomination below **Rev:** Queen and Aborigine dancers below multicolor bunting **Edge:** Reeded

Date	Mintage	F12	VF20	XF40	MS60	MS63
2002	—	—	—	—	6.00	7.00

KM# 91a.1 50 PENCE
28.28 g., 0.925 Silver 0.8356 oz. ASW, 38.6 mm. **Ruler:** Elizabeth II **Obv:** Crowned bust right, denomination below **Rev:** Queen and Aborigine dancers below multicolor bunting **Edge:** Reeded

Date	Mintage	F12	VF20	XF40	MS60	MS63
2002	15,000	PF65 45.00				

KM# 91a.2 50 PENCE
28.28 g., 0.925 Silver 0.8356 oz. ASW, 38.6 mm. **Ruler:** Elizabeth II **Obv:** Crowned bust right, denomination below **Rev:** With plain bunting **Edge:** Reeded

Date	Mintage	F12	VF20	XF40	MS60	MS63
2002		PF65 45.00				

KM# 91b.1 50 PENCE
39.94 g., 0.917 Gold 1.1699 oz. AGW, 38.61 mm. **Ruler:** Elizabeth II **Obv:** Crowned bust right, denomination below **Rev:** Queen and Aborigine dancers below multicolor bunting **Edge:** Reeded

Date	Mintage	F12	VF20	XF40	MS60	MS63
2002	50	PF65 2,150				

KM# 91b.2 50 PENCE
39.94 g., 0.917 Gold 1.1699 oz. AGW, 38.61 mm. **Ruler:** Elizabeth II **Obv:** Crowned bust right, denomination below **Rev:** With plain bunting **Edge:** Reeded

Date	Mintage	F12	VF20	XF40	MS60	MS63
2002	—	PF65 2,100				

KM# 92 50 PENCE
28.28 g., Copper-Nickel, 38.6 mm. **Ruler:** Elizabeth II **Obv:** Crowned bust right, denomination below **Rev:** Queen and St. Paul's Cathedral dome below multicolor bunting **Edge:** Reeded

Date	Mintage	F12	VF20	XF40	MS60	MS63
2002	—	—	—	—	6.00	7.00

KM# 92a.1 50 PENCE
28.28 g., 0.925 Silver 0.8356 oz. ASW, 38.6 mm. **Ruler:** Elizabeth II **Obv:** Crowned bust right, denomination below **Rev:** Queen and St. Paul's Cathedral dome below multicolor bunting

Date	Mintage	F12	VF20	XF40	MS60	MS63
2002	15,000	PF65 45.00				

KM# 92a.2 50 PENCE
28.28 g., 0.925 Silver 0.8356 oz. ASW, 38.6 mm. **Ruler:** Elizabeth II **Obv:** Crowned bust right, denomination below **Rev:** With plain bunting **Edge:** Reeded

Date	Mintage	F12	VF20	XF40	MS60	MS63
2002	—	PF65 45.00				

KM# 92b.1 50 PENCE
39.94 g., 0.917 Gold 1.1699 oz. AGW, 38.61 mm. **Ruler:** Elizabeth II **Obv:** Crowned bust right, denomination below **Rev:** Queen and St. Paul's Cathedral dome below multicolor bunting **Edge:** Reeded

Date	Mintage	F12	VF20	XF40	MS60	MS63
2002	50	PF65 2,150				

KM# 92b.2 50 PENCE
39.94 g., 0.917 Gold 1.1699 oz. AGW, 38.61 mm. **Ruler:** Elizabeth II **Obv:** Crowned bust right, denomination below **Rev:** With plain bunting **Edge:** Reeded

Date	Mintage	F12	VF20	XF40	MS60	MS63
2002	—	PF65 2,100				

KM# 93 50 PENCE
28.28 g., Copper-Nickel, 38.6 mm. **Ruler:** Elizabeth II **Obv:** Crowned bust right, denomination below **Rev:** Elizabeth and Philip in coronation coach below multicolor bunting **Edge:** Reeded

Date	Mintage	F12	VF20	XF40	MS60	MS63
2002	—	—	—	—	6.00	7.00

KM# 93a.1 50 PENCE
28.28 g., 0.925 Silver 0.8356 oz. ASW, 38.6 mm. **Ruler:** Elizabeth II **Obv:** Crowned bust right, denomination below **Rev:** Elizabeth and Philip in coronation coach below multicolor bunting

Date	Mintage	F12	VF20	XF40	MS60	MS63
2002	15,000	PF65 45.00				

KM# 93a.2 50 PENCE
28.28 g., 0.925 Silver 0.8356 oz. ASW, 38.6 mm. **Ruler:** Elizabeth II **Obv:** Crowned bust right, denomination below **Rev:** With plain bunting **Edge:** Reeded

Date	Mintage	F12	VF20	XF40	MS60	MS63
2002		PF65 45.00				

KM# 93b.1 50 PENCE
39.94 g., 0.917 Gold 1.1699 oz. AGW, 38.61 mm. **Ruler:** Elizabeth II **Obv:** Crowned bust right, denomination below **Rev:** Elizabeth and Philip in coronation coach below multicolor bunting **Edge:** Reeded

Date	Mintage	F12	VF20	XF40	MS60	MS63
2002	50	PF65 2,150				

KM# 93b.2 50 PENCE
39.94 g., 0.917 Gold 1.1699 oz. AGW, 38.61 mm. **Ruler:** Elizabeth II **Obv:** Crowned bust right, denomination below **Rev:** With plain bunting **Edge:** Reeded

Date	Mintage	F12	VF20	XF40	MS60	MS63
2002	—	PF65 2,100				

KM# 94 50 PENCE
28.28 g., Copper-Nickel, 38.6 mm. **Ruler:** Elizabeth II **Obv:** Crowned bust right, denomination below **Rev:** Elizabeth and Prince Charles at flower show below multicolor bunting **Edge:** Reeded

Date	Mintage	F12	VF20	XF40	MS60	MS63
2002	—	—	—	—	6.00	7.00

KM# 94a.1 50 PENCE
28.28 g., 0.925 Silver 0.8356 oz. ASW, 38.6 mm. **Ruler:** Elizabeth II **Obv:** Crowned bust right, denomination below **Rev:** Queen and Prince Charles at flower show below multicolor bunting **Edge:** Reeded

Date	Mintage	F12	VF20	XF40	MS60	MS63
2002	15,000	PF65 45.00				

KM# 94a.2 50 PENCE
28.28 g., 0.925 Silver 0.8356 oz. ASW, 38.6 mm. **Ruler:** Elizabeth II **Obv:** Crowned bust right, denomination below **Rev:** With plain bunting **Edge:** Reeded

Date	Mintage	F12	VF20	XF40	MS60	MS63
2002		PF65 45.00				

KM# 94b.1 50 PENCE
39.94 g., 0.917 Gold 1.1699 oz. AGW, 38.61 mm. **Ruler:** Elizabeth II **Obv:** Crowned bust right, denomination below **Rev:** Queen and Prince Charles at flower show below multicolor bunting **Edge:** Reeded

Date	Mintage	F12	VF20	XF40	MS60	MS63
2002	50	PF65 2,150				

KM# 94b.2 50 PENCE
39.94 g., 0.917 Gold 1.1699 oz. AGW, 38.61 mm. **Ruler:** Elizabeth II **Obv:** Crowned bust right, denomination below **Rev:** With plain bunting **Edge:** Reeded

Date	Mintage	F12	VF20	XF40	MS60	MS63
2002	—	PF65 2,100				

KM# 95 50 PENCE
28.28 g., Copper-Nickel, 38.6 mm. **Ruler:** Elizabeth II **Obv:** Crowned bust right, denomination below **Rev:** Elizabeth and Philip on balcony below multicolor bunting **Edge:** Reeded

Date	Mintage	F12	VF20	XF40	MS60	MS63
2002	—	—	—	—	6.00	7.00

KM# 95a.1 50 PENCE
28.28 g., 0.925 Silver 0.8356 oz. ASW, 38.61 mm. **Ruler:** Elizabeth II **Obv:** Crowned bust right, denomination below **Rev:** Elizabeth and Philip on balcony below colored bunting **Edge:** Reeded

Date	Mintage	F12	VF20	XF40	MS60	MS63
2002	15,000	PF65 45.00				

KM# 95a.2 50 PENCE
28.28 g., 0.925 Silver 0.8356 oz. ASW, 38.6 mm. **Ruler:** Elizabeth II **Obv:** Crowned bust right, denomination below **Rev:** With plain bunting **Edge:** Reeded

Date	Mintage	F12	VF20	XF40	MS60	MS63
2002	—	PF65 45.00				

KM# 95b.1 50 PENCE
39.94 g., 0.917 Gold 1.1699 oz. AGW, 38.61 mm. **Ruler:** Elizabeth II **Obv:** Crowned bust right, denomination below **Rev:** Elizabeth and Philip on balcony below multicolor bunting **Edge:** Reeded

Date	Mintage	F12	VF20	XF40	MS60	MS63
2002	50	PF65 2,150				

KM# 95b.2 50 PENCE
39.94 g., 0.917 Gold 1.1699 oz. AGW, 38.61 mm. **Ruler:** Elizabeth II **Obv:** Crowned bust right, denomination below **Rev:** With plain bunting **Edge:** Reeded

Date	Mintage	F12	VF20	XF40	MS60	MS63
2002	—	PF65 2,100				

KM# 96 50 PENCE
28.28 g., Copper-Nickel, 38.6 mm. **Ruler:** Elizabeth II **Obv:** Crowned bust right, denomination below **Rev:** Multicolor jets below multicolor bunting **Edge:** Reeded

Date	Mintage	F12	VF20	XF40	MS60	MS63
2002	—	—	—	—	6.00	7.00

KM# 96a.1 50 PENCE
28.28 g., 0.925 Silver 0.8356 oz. ASW, 38.6 mm. **Ruler:** Elizabeth II **Obv:** Crowned bust right, denomination below **Rev:** Multicolor jets below multicolor bunting **Edge:** Reeded

Date	Mintage	F12	VF20	XF40	MS60	MS63
2002	15,000	PF65 45.00				

KM# 96a.2 50 PENCE
28.28 g., 0.925 Silver 0.8356 oz. ASW, 38.6 mm. **Ruler:** Elizabeth II **Obv:** Crowned bust right, denomination below **Rev:** With plain bunting **Edge:** Reeded

Date	Mintage	F12	VF20	XF40	MS60	MS63
2002	—	PF65 45.00				

KM# 96b.1 50 PENCE
39.94 g., 0.917 Gold 1.1699 oz. AGW, 38.61 mm. **Ruler:** Elizabeth II **Obv:** Crowned bust right, denomination below **Rev:** Multicolor jets below multicolor bunting **Edge:** Reeded

Date	Mintage	F12	VF20	XF40	MS60	MS63
2002	50	PF65 2,150				

KM# 96b.2 50 PENCE
39.94 g., 0.917 Gold 1.1699 oz. AGW, 38.61 mm. **Ruler:** Elizabeth II **Obv:** Crowned bust right, denomination below **Rev:** With plain bunting **Edge:** Reeded

Date	Mintage	F12	VF20	XF40	MS60	MS63
2002	—	PF65 2,100				

KM# 97 50 PENCE
28.28 g., Copper-Nickel, 38.6 mm. **Ruler:** Elizabeth II **Obv:** Crowned bust right, denomination below **Rev:** Queen and fireworks below multicolor bunting **Edge:** Reeded

Date	Mintage	F12	VF20	XF40	MS60	MS63
2002	—	—	—	—	6.00	7.00

KM# 97a.1 50 PENCE
28.28 g., 0.925 Silver 0.8356 oz. ASW, 38.61 mm. **Ruler:** Elizabeth II **Obv:** Crowned bust right, denomination below **Rev:** Queen and fireworks below multicolor bunting **Edge:** Reeded

Date	Mintage	F12	VF20	XF40	MS60	MS63
2002	15,000	PF65 45.00				

KM# 97a.2 50 PENCE
28.28 g., 0.925 Silver 0.8356 oz. ASW, 38.6 mm. **Ruler:** Elizabeth II **Obv:** Crowned bust right, denomination below **Rev:** With plain bunting **Edge:** Reeded

Date	Mintage	F12	VF20	XF40	MS60	MS63
2002	—	PF65 45.00				

KM# 97b.1 50 PENCE
39.94 g., 0.917 Gold 1.1699 oz. AGW, 38.61 mm. **Ruler:** Elizabeth II **Obv:** Crowned bust right, denomination below **Rev:** Queen and fireworks below multicolor bunting **Edge:** Reeded

Date	Mintage	F12	VF20	XF40	MS60	MS63
2002	50	PF65 2,150				

KM# 97b.2 50 PENCE
39.94 g., 0.917 Gold 1.1699 oz. AGW, 38.61 mm. **Ruler:** Elizabeth II **Obv:** Crowned bust right, denomination below **Rev:** With plain bunting **Edge:** Reeded

Date	Mintage	F12	VF20	XF40	MS60	MS63
2002	—	PF65 2,100				

KM# 98 50 PENCE
28.28 g., Copper-Nickel, 38.6 mm. **Ruler:** Elizabeth II **Obv:** Crowned bust right, denomination below **Rev:** UK map and flags below multicolor bunting **Edge:** Reeded

Date	Mintage	F12	VF20	XF40	MS60	MS63
2002	—	—	—	—	6.00	7.00

KM# 98a.1 50 PENCE
28.28 g., 0.925 Silver 0.8356 oz. ASW, 38.6 mm. **Ruler:** Elizabeth II **Obv:** Crowned bust right, denomination below **Rev:** UK and four flags below multicolor bunting **Edge:** Reeded

Date	Mintage	F12	VF20	XF40	MS60	MS63
2002	15,000	PF65 45.00				

KM# 98a.2 50 PENCE
28.28 g., 0.925 Silver 0.8356 oz. ASW, 38.6 mm. **Ruler:** Elizabeth II **Obv:** Crowned bust right, denomination below **Rev:** With plain bunting **Edge:** Reeded

Date	Mintage	F12	VF20	XF40	MS60	MS63
2002		PF65 45.00				

KM# 98b.1 50 PENCE
39.94 g., 0.917 Gold 1.1699 oz. AGW, 38.61 mm. **Ruler:** Elizabeth II **Obv:** Crowned bust right, denomination below **Rev:** UK map and four flags below multicolor bunting **Edge:** Reeded

Date	Mintage	F12	VF20	XF40	MS60	MS63
2002	50	PF65 2,150				

KM# 98b.2 50 PENCE
39.94 g., 0.917 Gold 1.1699 oz. AGW, 38.61 mm. **Ruler:** Elizabeth II **Obv:** Crowned bust right, denomination below **Rev:** With plain bunting **Edge:** Reeded

Date	Mintage	F12	VF20	XF40	MS60	MS63
2002	—	PF65 2,100				

KM# 99 50 PENCE
28.28 g., Copper-Nickel, 38.6 mm. **Ruler:** Elizabeth II **Obv:** Crowned bust right, denomination below **Rev:** Queen and two Commonwealth Games athletes below multicolor bunting **Edge:** Reeded

Date	Mintage	F12	VF20	XF40	MS60	MS63
2002	—	—	—	—	6.00	7.00

KM# 99a.1 50 PENCE
28.28 g., 0.925 Silver 0.8356 oz. ASW, 38.6 mm. **Ruler:** Elizabeth II **Obv:** Crowned bust right, denomination below **Rev:** Queen and two Commonwealth Games athletes below multicolor bunting **Edge:** Reeded

Date	Mintage	F12	VF20	XF40	MS60	MS63
2002	15,000	PF65 45.00				

KM# 99a.2 50 PENCE
28.28 g., 0.925 Silver 0.8356 oz. ASW, 38.6 mm. **Ruler:** Elizabeth II **Obv:** Crowned bust right, denomination below **Rev:** With plain bunting **Edge:** Reeded

Date	Mintage	F12	VF20	XF40	MS60	MS63
2002	—	PF65 45.00				

KM# 99b.1 50 PENCE
39.94 g., 0.917 Gold 1.1699 oz. AGW, 38.61 mm. **Ruler:** Elizabeth II **Obv:** Crowned bust right, denomination below **Rev:** Queen and two Commonwealth Games athletes below multicolor bunting **Edge:** Reeded

Date	Mintage	F12	VF20	XF40	MS60	MS63
2002	50	PF65 2,150				

KM# 99b.2 50 PENCE
39.94 g., 0.917 Gold 1.1699 oz. AGW, 38.61 mm. **Ruler:** Elizabeth II **Obv:** Crowned bust right, denomination below **Rev:** With plain bunting **Edge:** Reeded

Date	Mintage	F12	VF20	XF40	MS60	MS63
2002	—	PF65 2,100				

KM# 100 50 PENCE
28.28 g., Copper-Nickel, 38.6 mm. **Ruler:** Elizabeth II **Obv:** Crowned bust right, denomination below **Rev:** Royal Ascot Carriage scene below multicolor bunting **Edge:** Reeded

Date	Mintage	F12	VF20	XF40	MS60	MS63
2002	—	—	—	—	6.00	7.00

KM# 100a.1 50 PENCE
28.28 g., 0.925 Silver 0.8356 oz. ASW, 38.6 mm. **Ruler:** Elizabeth II **Obv:** Crowned bust right, denomination below **Rev:** Royal Ascot Carriage scene below multicolor bunting **Edge:** Reeded

Date	Mintage	F12	VF20	XF40	MS60	MS63
2002	15,000				PF65 45.00	

KM# 100a.2 50 PENCE
28.28 g., 0.925 Silver 0.8356 oz. ASW, 38.6 mm. **Ruler:** Elizabeth II **Obv:** Crowned bust right, denomination below **Rev:** With plain bunting **Edge:** Reeded

Date	Mintage	F12	VF20	XF40	MS60	MS63
2002					PF65 45.00	

KM# 100b.1 50 PENCE
39.94 g., 0.917 Gold 1.1699 oz. AGW, 38.61 mm. **Ruler:** Elizabeth II **Obv:** Crowned bust right, denomination below **Rev:** Royal Ascot Carriage scene below multicolor bunting **Edge:** Reeded

Date	Mintage	F12	VF20	XF40	MS60	MS63
2002	50				PF65 2,150	

KM# 100b.2 50 PENCE
39.94 g., 0.917 Gold 1.1699 oz. AGW, 38.61 mm. **Ruler:** Elizabeth II **Obv:** Crowned bust right, denomination below **Rev:** With plain bunting **Edge:** Reeded

Date	Mintage	F12	VF20	XF40	MS60	MS63
2002					PF65 2,100	

KM# 101 50 PENCE
28.28 g., Copper-Nickel, 38.6 mm. **Ruler:** Elizabeth II **Obv:** Crowned bust right, denomination below **Rev:** Queen and two hockey players below multicolor bunting **Edge:** Reeded

Date	Mintage	F12	VF20	XF40	MS60	MS63
2002	—	—	—	—	6.00	7.00

KM# 101a.1 50 PENCE
28.28 g., 0.925 Silver 0.8356 oz. ASW, 38.6 mm. **Ruler:** Elizabeth II **Obv:** Crowned bust right, denomination below **Rev:** Queen and two hockey players below multicolor bunting **Edge:** Reeded

Date	Mintage	F12	VF20	XF40	MS60	MS63
2002	15,000	PF65 45.00				

KM# 101a.2 50 PENCE
28.28 g., 0.925 Silver 0.8356 oz. ASW, 38.6 mm. **Ruler:** Elizabeth II **Obv:** Crowned bust right, denomination below **Rev:** With plain bunting **Edge:** Reeded

Date	Mintage	F12	VF20	XF40	MS60	MS63
2002	—	PF65 45.00				

KM# 101b.1 50 PENCE
39.94 g., 0.917 Gold 1.1699 oz. AGW, 38.61 mm. **Ruler:** Elizabeth II **Obv:** Crowned bust right, denomination below **Rev:** Queen and two hockey players below multicolor bunting **Edge:** Reeded

Date	Mintage	F12	VF20	XF40	MS60	MS63
2002	50	PF65 2,150				

KM# 101b.2 50 PENCE
39.94 g., 0.917 Gold 1.1699 oz. AGW, 38.61 mm. **Ruler:** Elizabeth II **Obv:** Crowned bust right, denomination below **Rev:** With plain bunting **Edge:** Reeded

Date	Mintage	F12	VF20	XF40	MS60	MS63
2002	—	PF65 2,100				

KM# 102 50 PENCE
28.28 g., Copper-Nickel, 38.6 mm. **Ruler:** Elizabeth II **Obv:** Crowned bust right, denomination below **Rev:** Queen Mother as a young lady and as an elderly lady **Edge:** Reeded

Date	Mintage	F12	VF20	XF40	MS60	MS63
ND(2002)	—	—	—	—	9.00	10.00

KM# 102a 50 PENCE
28.28 g., 0.925 Silver 0.8356 oz. ASW, 38.6 mm. **Ruler:** Elizabeth II **Obv:** Crowned bust right, denomination below **Rev:** Queen Mother as a young lady and as an elderly lady **Edge:** Reeded

Date	Mintage	F12	VF20	XF40	MS60	MS63
ND(2002)	10,000	PF65 45.00				

KM# 135 50 PENCE
8.00 g., Copper-Nickel, 27.3 mm. **Ruler:** Elizabeth II **Obv:** Crowned bust right **Rev:** Fox standing right **Shape:** 7-sided

Date	Mintage	F12	VF20	XF40	MS60	MS63
2003	—	—	—	—	5.00	7.50
2004	—	—	—	—	5.00	7.50

KM# 149 50 PENCE
28.28 g., 0.925 Silver 0.8356 oz. ASW, 38.6 mm. **Ruler:** Elizabeth II **Subject:** Queen's 80th Birthday **Obv:** Head with tiara right - gilt **Obv. Legend:** QUEEN ELIZABETH II - FALKLAND ISLANDS **Rev:** Elizabeth seated at left, Queen Mother at right holding baby

Date	Mintage	F12	VF20	XF40	MS60	MS63
2006	—	PF65 45.00				

KM# 163 50 PENCE
8.00 g., Copper-Nickel, 27.3 mm. **Ruler:** Elizabeth II **Subject:** 25th Annivery of Liberation **Obv:** Head in tiara right **Rev:** Soldier in full gear standing before map of Falklands **Shape:** 7-sided

Date	Mintage	F12	VF20	XF40	MS60	MS63
2007PM	—	—	—	—	5.00	7.50

KM# 136 POUND
9.50 g., Nickel-Brass, 22.5 mm. **Ruler:** Elizabeth II **Obv:** Crowned bust right **Rev:** Shield

Date	Mintage	F12	VF20	XF40	MS60	MS63
2004	—	—	—	—	3.50	5.00

KM# 137 2 POUNDS
12.00 g., Bi-Metallic, 28.4 mm. **Ruler:** Elizabeth II **Obv:** Head with tiara right **Obv. Legend:** QUEEN ELIZABETH THE SECOND **Rev:** Sun and map surrounded by wildlife **Edge:** Reeded and lettered **Edge Lettering:** 30 YEARS OF FALKLAND ISLANDS COINAGE

Date	Mintage	F12	VF20	XF40	MS60	MS63
2004	—	—	—	5.00	10.00	12.00

KM# 103 25 POUNDS
7.81 g., 0.9999 Gold 0.2495 oz. AGW, 22 mm. **Ruler:** Elizabeth II **Obv:** Crowned bust right, denomination below **Rev:** Queen Mother as a young lady and as an elderly lady **Edge:** Reeded

Date	Mintage	F12	VF20	XF40	MS60	MS63
ND(2002)	1,000	PF65 475				

KM# 170 CROWN
28.28 g., Copper-Nickel, 38.6 mm. **Subject:** Margaret Thatcher bust facing

Date	Mintage	F12	VF20	XF40	MS60	MS63
2013	—	—	—	—	—	15.00

CROWN COINAGE

KM# 161 1/25 CROWN
0.50 g., 0.999 Gold AGW, 11 mm. **Ruler:** Elizabeth II **Subject:** Henry Dunant, Founder, International Red Cross and 1901 Nobel Peace Prize winner **Obv:** Bust with tiara right **Rev:** Dunant bust facing

Date	Mintage	F12	VF20	XF40	MS60	MS63
2010PM	—	PF65 80.00				

KM# 141 1/5 CROWN
6.22 g., 0.9999 Gold 0.1987 oz. AGW **Ruler:** Elizabeth II **Subject:** Diamond Wedding Anniversary **Obv:** Conjoined busts with Prince Philip right **Obv. Legend:** QUEEN ELIZABETH II - FALKLAND ISLANDS **Rev:** Bride and groom standing facing at wedding cake; .01 carat x 1.3mm diamond embedded at top **Rev. Legend:** Diamond Wedding of H.M. Queen Elizabeth II & H.R.H. Prince Philip **Edge:** Reeded

Date	Mintage	F12	VF20	XF40	MS60	MS63
2007PM	—	PF65 450				

KM# 129 CROWN
Copper-Nickel **Ruler:** Elizabeth II **Rev:** Nelson and the H.M.S. Victory

Date	Mintage	F12	VF20	XF40	MS60	MS63
2005	—	—	—	—	10.00	12.00

KM# 151 CROWN
Copper-Nickel, 38.61 mm. **Ruler:** Elizabeth II **Subject:** I. K. Burnel **Rev:** S. S. Great Britain sailing right

Date	Mintage	F12	VF20	XF40	MS60	MS63
2006PM	—					15.00

KM# 152 CROWN
Copper-Nickel, 38.61 mm. **Ruler:** Elizabeth II **Subject:** Artic and Antarctic - John Ross and James Clark Ross **Rev:** Ships Victory and Erebus

Date	Mintage	F12	VF20	XF40	MS60	MS63
2006PM	—					15.00

KM# 138 CROWN
Copper-Nickel **Ruler:** Elizabeth II **Rev:** Winston Churchill

Date	Mintage	F12	VF20	XF40	MS60	MS63
2007	—				15.00	17.50

KM# 139 CROWN
Copper-Nickel **Ruler:** Elizabeth II **Rev:** Queen Elizabeth I

Date	Mintage	F12	VF20	XF40	MS60	MS63
2007	—				15.00	17.50

KM# 140 CROWN
Copper-Nickel **Ruler:** Elizabeth II **Rev:** Charles Darwin

Date	Mintage	F12	VF20	XF40	MS60	MS63
2007	—				15.00	17.50

KM# 142 CROWN
Copper-Nickel **Ruler:** Elizabeth II **Subject:** Diamond Wedding Anniversary **Obv:** Conjoined busts with Prince Philip right **Obv. Legend:** QUEEN ELIZABETH II - FALKLAND ISLANDS **Rev:** King George VI standing at left giving Philip standing at right his consent to a contract of matrimony **Rev. Legend:** Diamond Wedding of H.M. Queen Elizabeth II & H.R.H. Prince Philip **Edge:** Reeded

Date	Mintage	F12	VF20	XF40	MS60	MS63
2007PM	—				17.00	20.00

KM# 143 CROWN
Copper-Nickel **Ruler:** Elizabeth II **Subject:** Diamond Wedding Anniversary **Obv:** Conjoined busts with Prince Philip right **Obv. Legend:** QUEEN ELIZABETH II - FALKLAND ISLANDS **Rev:** Bride and groom standing facing at wedding cake **Rev. Legend:** Diamond Wedding of H.M. Queen Elizabeth II & H.R.H. Prince Philip **Edge:** Reeded

Date	Mintage	F12	VF20	XF40	MS60	MS63
2007PM	—				17.00	20.00

KM# 144 CROWN
Copper-Nickel **Ruler:** Elizabeth II **Subject:** Diamond Wedding Anniversary **Obv:** Conjoined busts with Prince Philip right **Obv. Legend:** QUEEN ELIZABETH II - FALKLAND ISLANDS **Rev:** Bridesmaids and Page Boys **Rev. Legend:** Diamond Wedding of H.M. Queen Elizabeth II & H.R.H. Prince Philip **Edge:** Reeded

Date	Mintage	F12	VF20	XF40	MS60	MS63
2007PM	—				17.00	20.00

KM# 145 CROWN
Copper-Nickel **Ruler:** Elizabeth II **Subject:** Diamond Wedding Anniversary **Obv:** Conjoined busts with Prince Philip right **Obv. Legend:** QUEEN ELIZABETH II - FALKLAND ISLANDS **Rev:** Buckingham Palace facade **Rev. Legend:** Diamond Wedding of H.M. Queen Elizabeth II & H.R.H. Prince Philip **Edge:** Reeded

Date	Mintage	F12	VF20	XF40	MS60	MS63
2007PM	—				17.00	20.00

KM# 146 CROWN
Copper-Nickel **Ruler:** Elizabeth II **Subject:** 10th Anniversary - Death of Princess Diana **Obv:** Bust with tiara right **Obv. Legend:** QUEEN ELIZABETH II - FALKLAND ISLANDS **Rev:** Bust of Princess Diana facing 3/4 right **Rev. Legend:** 1961 - 1997 • DIANA — PRINCESS OF WALES **Edge:** Reeded

Date	Mintage	F12	VF20	XF40	MS60	MS63
2007PM	—				17.00	20.00

KM# 147 CROWN
Copper-Nickel, 38 mm. **Ruler:** Elizabeth II **Subject:** 20th Anniversary - Falkland Islands Fishery **Obv:** Bust right of Queen Elizabeth II **Rev:** Shortfin Squid (Illex Argentinca) **Edge:** Reeded

Date	Mintage	F12	VF20	XF40	MS60	MS63
2007PM	—				17.00	20.00

KM# 148 CROWN
Copper-Nickel, 39 mm. **Ruler:** Elizabeth II **Subject:** Scouting Centennial **Obv:** Crowned bust right **Obv. Legend:** QUEEN ELIZABETH II FALKLAND ISLANDS 2007 **Rev:** Baden-Powell bust 3/4 left, scout saluting, tent flanking within circle on animal tracks **Rev. Legend:** 1857 ROBERT BADEN-POWELL 1941 ONE CROWN **Edge:** Reeded

Date	Mintage	F12	VF20	XF40	MS60	MS63
2007PM	—				12.50	15.00

KM# 142a CROWN
0.9167 Silver **Ruler:** Elizabeth II **Subject:** Diamond Wedding Anniversary **Obv:** Conjoined busts with Prince Philip right **Obv. Legend:** QUEEN ELIZABETH II - FALKLAND ISLANDS **Rev:** King George VI, standing at left, giving Philip, standing at right, his consent to a contract of matrimony **Rev. Legend:** Diamond Wedding of H.M. Queen Elizabeth II & H.R.H. Prince Philip **Edge:** Reeded

Date	Mintage	F12	VF20	XF40	MS60	MS63
2007PM	—	PF65 40.00				

KM# 143a CROWN
0.9167 Silver **Ruler:** Elizabeth II **Subject:** Diamond Wedding Anniversary **Obv:** Conjoined busts with Prince Philip right **Obv. Legend:** QUEEN ELIZABETH II - FALKLAND ISLANDS **Rev:** Bride and groom standing facing at wedding cake **Rev. Legend:** Diamond Wedding of H.M. Queen Elizabeth II & H.R.H. Prince Philip **Edge:** Reeded

Date	Mintage	VG8	F12	VF20	XF40	MS60
2007PM	—	PF65 40.00				

KM# 144a CROWN
0.9167 Silver **Ruler:** Elizabeth II **Subject:** Diamond Wedding Anniversary **Obv:** Conjoined busts with Prince Philip right **Obv. Legend:** QUEEN ELIZABETH II - FALKLAND ISLANDS **Rev:** Bridesmaids and Page Boys **Rev. Legend:** Diamond Wedding of H.M. Queen Elizabeth II & H.R.H. Prince Philip **Edge:** Reeded

Date	Mintage	F12	VF20	XF40	MS60	MS63
2007PM	—	PF65 40.00				

KM# 145a CROWN
0.9167 Silver **Ruler:** Elizabeth II **Subject:** Diamond Wedding Anniversary **Obv:** Conjoined busts with Prince Philip right **Obv. Legend:** QUEEN ELIZABETH II - FALKLAND ISLANDS **Rev:** Buckingham Palace facade **Rev. Legend:** Diamond Wedding of H.M. Queen Elizabeth II & H.R.H. Prince Philip **Edge:** Reeded

Date	Mintage	F12	VF20	XF40	MS60	MS63
2007PM	—	PF65 40.00				

KM# 146a CROWN
0.9167 Silver **Ruler:** Elizabeth II **Subject:** 10th Anniversary Death of Princess Diana **Obv:** Bust with tiara right **Obv. Legend:** QUEEN ELIZABETH II - FALKLAND ISLANDS **Rev:** Bust of Princess Diana facing 3/4 right **Rev. Legend:** 1961 - 1997 ? DIANA ? PRINCESS OF WALES **Edge:** Reeded

Date	Mintage	F12	VF20	XF40	MS60	MS63
2007PM	—	PF65 75.00				

KM# 148a CROWN
28.28 g., 0.925 Silver 0.8356 oz. ASW, 38.5 mm. **Ruler:** Elizabeth II **Subject:** Scouting Centennial **Obv:** Crowned bust right **Obv. Legend:** QUEEN ELIZABETH II FALKLAND ISLANDS 2007 **Rev:** Baden-Powell bust 3/4 facing left, scout saluting and tent flanking, within circle of animal tracks and rope **Rev. Legend:** 1857 ROBERT BADEN-POWELL 1941 ONE CROWN **Edge:** Reeded

Date	Mintage	F12	VF20	XF40	MS60	MS63
2007PM	10,000	PF65 65.00				

KM# 156 CROWN
28.28 g., Copper-Nickel, 38.61 mm. **Ruler:** Elizabeth II **Subject:** International Polar Year - Discovery **Obv:** Bust in tiara right **Rev:** Icebound ship

Date	Mintage	F12	VF20	XF40	MS60	MS63
2007PM	—				17.50	20.00

KM# 157 CROWN
Copper-Nickel, 38.61 mm. **Ruler:** Elizabeth II **Subject:** 25th Anniversary of Liberation **Obv:** Bust in tiara right **Rev:** Britannia standing before map of the Falkland Islands

Date	Mintage	F12	VF20	XF40	MS60	MS63
2007PM	—				17.50	20.00

KM# 158 CROWN
28.28 g., Copper-Nickel, 38.61 mm. **Ruler:** Elizabeth II **Subject:** Race for the South Pole **Obv:** Bust in tiara right **Rev:** Portraits of Scott and Amundsen, dog-sleds, and man-pulled sleds.

Date	Mintage	F12	VF20	XF40	MS60	MS63
2007PM	—				17.50	20.00

KM# 150 CROWN
28.28 g., Copper-Nickel, 38.6 mm. **Ruler:** Elizabeth II **Subject:** Royal Air Force, 90th anniversary

Date	Mintage	F12	VF20	XF40	MS60	MS63
2008	—					12.00

KM# 153 CROWN
Copper-Nickel, 38.61 mm. **Ruler:** Elizabeth II **Subject:** Spitfire **Obv:** Bust in tiara right **Rev:** Two planes in flight

Date	Mintage	F12	VF20	XF40	MS60	MS63
2008	—	—	—	—	12.50	15.00

KM# 154 CROWN
Copper-Nickel, 38.61 mm. **Ruler:** Elizabeth II **Subject:** Port Louis **Obv:** Bust in tiara right **Rev:** Flag raising over fort

Date	Mintage	F12	VF20	XF40	MS60	MS63
2008	—	—	—	—	12.50	15.00

KM# 162 CROWN
28.28 g., Copper-Nickel, 38.61 mm. **Ruler:** Elizabeth II **Obv:** Bust in tiara right **Rev:** Charles Darwin bust left

Date	Mintage	F12	VF20	XF40	MS60	MS63
2009PM	—	—	—	—	18.50	22.00

KM# 159 CROWN
Copper-Nickel, 38.61 mm. **Ruler:** Elizabeth II **Subject:** RAF Search and Rescue 70th anniversary **Obv:** Bust in tiara right **Rev:** RAF Search and Rescue Helicopter

Date	Mintage	F12	VF20	XF40	MS60	MS63
2011PM	—	—	—	—	17.50	20.00

KM# 160 CROWN
Copper-Nickel, 38.61 mm. **Ruler:** Elizabeth II **Subject:** Royal Wedding - Prince William and Catherine Middleton **Obv:** Bust in tiara right **Rev:** Busts left

Date	Mintage	F12	VF20	XF40	MS60	MS63
2011PM	—	—	—	—	17.50	20.00

KM# 164 CROWN
Copper-Nickel, 38.61 mm. **Ruler:** Elizabeth II **Subject:** Elizabeth and Philip 60th Wedding anniversary **Obv:** Bust in tiara right **Rev:** Lion on crown and Plumes

Date	Mintage	F12	VF20	XF40	MS60	MS63
2011PM	—	—	—	—	17.50	20.00

KM# 165 CROWN
28.28 g., Copper-Nickel, 38.6 mm. **Ruler:** Elizabeth II **Subject:** Life of Queen Elizabeth II **Obv:** Conjoined busts right **Rev:** Elizabeth, the Queen mother in robes of the Order of the Garter

Date	Mintage	F12	VF20	XF40	MS60	MS63
2012PM	—	—	—	—	—	15.00

KM# 166 CROWN
28.28 g., Copper-Nickel, 38.6 mm. **Ruler:** Elizabeth II **Subject:** Life of Queen Elizabeth II **Obv:** Conjoined busts right **Rev:** Elizabeth as WWII nurse

Date	Mintage	F12	VF20	XF40	MS60	MS63
2012PM	—	—	—	—	—	15.00

KM# 167 CROWN
Silver, 38.6 mm. **Ruler:** Elizabeth II **Obv:** Head at top, butterfly in glass **Rev:** Life of the butterfly around central image

Date	Mintage	F12	VF20	XF40	MS60	MS63
2012PM	—	PF65 85.00				

KM# 168 CROWN
Copper-Nickel **Ruler:** Elizabeth II **Subject:** Stanley Sports Association, 100th Anniversary **Obv:** Double busts right **Rev:** Horse facing left

Date	Mintage	F12	VF20	XF40	MS60	MS63
2012 Proof	—	—	—	—	—	—

KM# 169 CROWN
28.28 g., Copper-Nickel, 38.6 mm. **Ruler:** Elizabeth II **Subject:** Falkland Islands Referendum

Date	Mintage	F12	VF20	XF40	MS60	MS63
2013	—	—	—	—	—	15.00

KM# 169a CROWN
28.28 g., 0.925 Silver 0.8356 oz. ASW, 38.6 mm. **Ruler:** Elizabeth II **Subject:** Falkland Islands Referendum

Date	Mintage	F12	VF20	XF40	MS60	MS63
2013 Proof	Est. 10000	—	—	—	—	—

PIEDFORT

KM#	Date	Mintage	Identification	Mkt Val
P4	2001	500	50 Pence 0.925 Silver Proof KM#86a.	95.00
P5	2001	500	50 Pence 0.925 Silver Proof KM#70a.	110
P6	2001	—	50 Pence 0.925 Silver Queen's portrait Edward's portrait with two gold plated coin designs	—
P7	2001	—	50 Pence 0.925 Silver Queen's portrait Henry's portrait with two gold plated coin designs	—
P8	2001	—	50 Pence 0.925 Silver Queen's portrait Charles' portrait with two gold plated coin designs	—
P9	2001	—	50 Pence 0.925 Silver Queen's portrait Victoria's portrait with two gold plated coin designs	—
P10	2001	500	50 Pence 0.925 Silver	90.00
P11	2001	500	50 Pence 0.925 Silver	95.00
P12	2001	500	50 Pence 0.925 Silver	95.00
P13	2001	500	50 Pence 0.925 Silver	110
P14	2002	500	50 Pence 0.925 Silver Proof KM#73a.	95.00
P15	2002	500	50 Pence 0.925 Silver Proof KM#74a.	110
P16	2002	500	50 Pence 0.925 Silver Proof KM#75a.	95.00
P17	2002	500	50 Pence 0.925 Silver Proof KM#76a.	95.00
P18	2002	500	50 Pence 0.925 Silver Proof KM#77a.	95.00
P19	2002	500	50 Pence 0.925 Silver Proof KM#78a.	95.00
P20	2002	500	50 Pence 0.925 Silver Proof KM#79a.	95.00
P21	2002	500	50 Pence 0.925 Silver Proof KM#80a.	95.00
P22	2002	500	50 Pence 0.925 Silver Proof KM#81a.	95.00
P23	2002	500	50 Pence 0.925 Silver Proof KM#82a.	95.00
P24	2002	500	50 Pence 0.925 Silver Proof KM#83a.	95.00
P25	2002	500	50 Pence 0.925 Silver Proof KM#84a.	95.00
P26	ND(2002)	500	50 Pence 0.925 Silver Proof KM#102a.	95.00

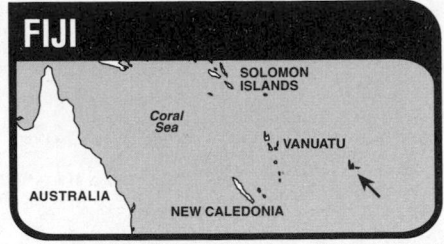

FIJI

The Republic of Fiji consists of about 320 islands located in the southwestern Pacific 1,100 miles (1,770 km.) north of New Zealand. The islands have a combined area of 7,056 sq. mi. (18,274 sq. km.) and a population of 772,891. Capital: Suva. Fiji's economy is based on agriculture and mining. Sugar, coconut products, manganese, and gold are exported. Fiji is a member of the Commonwealth of Nations, but has been subject to periodic short suspensions.

MINT MARK
(o) - Royal Canadian Mint, Ottawa

REPUBLIC
British Administration until 1970

DECIMAL COINAGE
100 Cents = 1 Dollar

KM# 49a CENT
1.58 g., Copper Plated Zinc, 17.53 mm. **Ruler:** Elizabeth II **Obv:** Crowned head right, date at right **Rev:** Tanoa kava bowl divides denomination

Date	Mintage	F12	VF20	XF40	MS60	MS63
2001(o)	—	—	—	—	0.20	0.65
2002(o)	5,880,000	—	—	—	0.20	0.65
2003(o)	8,030,000	—	—	—	0.20	0.65
2004(o)	8,840,000	—	—	—	0.20	0.65
2005(o)	9,720,000	—	—	—	0.20	0.65

KM# 49b CENT
1.76 g., Copper Plated Steel, 17.5 mm. **Ruler:** Elizabeth II **Obv:** Crowned head right, date at right **Rev:** Tanoa kava bowl

Date	Mintage	F12	VF20	XF40	MS60	MS63
2006(o)	—	—	—	—	0.25	0.50

KM# 50a 2 CENTS
3.16 g., Copper Plated Zinc, 21.08 mm. **Ruler:** Elizabeth II **Obv:** Crowned head right, date at right **Rev:** Palm fan and denomination

Date	Mintage	F12	VF20	XF40	MS60	MS63
2001(o)	2,830,000	—	—	—	0.30	0.85
2002(o)	5,000,000	—	—	—	0.30	0.85
2003(o)	6,410,000	—	—	—	0.30	0.85
2004(o)	7,050,000	—	—	—	0.30	0.85
2005(o)	7,760,000	—	—	—	0.30	0.85

KM# 51a 5 CENTS
2.34 g., Nickel Plated Steel, 19.41 mm. **Ruler:** Elizabeth II **Obv:** Crowned head right **Rev:** Fijian drum - lali divides denomination **Edge:** Reeded

Date	Mintage	F12	VF20	XF40	MS60	MS63
2006(l)	—	—	—	—	0.75	1.00

KM# 119 5 CENTS
2.34 g., Nickel Plated Steel, 19.5 mm. **Ruler:** Elizabeth II **Obv:** Crowned head right **Rev:** Fijian drum - Lali divides denomination **Edge:** Plain

Date	Mintage	F12	VF20	XF40	MS60	MS63
2009	—	—	—	—	0.75	1.00
2010	—	—	—	—	0.75	1.00

KM# 332 5 CENTS
2.34 g., Nickel Plated Steel, 19.5 mm. **Ruler:** Elizabeth II **Obv:** Luga roro (Foxfaced Rabbit Fish) **Rev:** Lalt (Wooden drum)

Date	Mintage	F12	VF20	XF40	MS60	MS63
2012	—	—	—	—	—	0.50

KM# 52a 10 CENTS
4.75 g., Nickel Plated Steel, 23.6 mm. **Ruler:** Elizabeth II **Obv:** Crowned head right **Rev:** Throwing club - ula tava tava divides value **Edge:** Reeded

Date	Mintage	F12	VF20	XF40	MS60	MS63
2006	—	—	—	—	1.00	1.25

KM# 120 10 CENTS
3.55 g., Nickel Plated Steel, 21.5 mm. **Ruler:** Elizabeth II **Obv:** Crowned head right **Rev:** Throwing club - ula tava tava divides value **Edge:** Reeded

Date	Mintage	F12	VF20	XF40	MS60	MS63
2009	—	—	—	—	1.00	1.25

KM# 333 10 CENTS
3.55 g., Nickel Plated Steel, 21.5 mm. **Ruler:** Elizabeth II **Obv:** Beka Mirimiri (Fiji Flying Fox) handing upside down **Rev:** Lula Tavatava (War club)

Date	Mintage	F12	VF20	XF40	MS60	MS63
2012	—	—	—	—	—	0.50
2013	—	—	—	—	—	0.50

KM# 53a 20 CENTS
10.50 g., Nickel Plated Steel, 28.5 mm. **Ruler:** Elizabeth II **Obv:** Crowned head right **Rev:** Tabua on braided connit cord divides denomination **Edge:** Reeded

Date	Mintage	F12	VF20	XF40	MS60	MS63
2006(l)	—	—	0.20	0.35	1.25	1.50

KM# 95 20 CENTS
11.24 g., Copper-Nickel, 28.5 mm. **Ruler:** Elizabeth II **Obv:** Crowned head right, date at right **Rev:** South Pacific Games flame logo **Edge:** Reeded **Note:** Prooflike examples issued in special cards.

Date	Mintage	F12	VF20	XF40	MS60	MS63
2003	1,540,000	—	—	—	1.50	2.50
2003 Prooflike	—	—	—	—	—	6.00

KM# 121 20 CENTS
4.68 g., Nickel Plated Steel, 24 mm. **Ruler:** Elizabeth II **Obv:** Crowned head right **Rev:** Tabua, a ceremonial whale's tooth divides denomination **Edge:** Segmented reeding

Date	Mintage	F12	VF20	XF40	MS60	MS63
2009	—	—	—	0.35	1.25	1.50
2010	—	—	—	0.35	1.25	1.50

KM# 334 20 CENTS
4.68 g., Nickel Plated Steel, 24 mm. **Ruler:** Elizabeth II **Obv:** Kaka (Kadavu Shining Parrot) **Rev:** Tabua (Whale's tooth)

Date	Mintage	F12	VF20	XF40	MS60	MS63
2012	—	—	—	—	—	1.50
2013	—	—	—	—	—	1.50

KM# 259 50 CENTS
Copper-Nickel **Ruler:** Elizabeth II **Subject:** Taiwan Wildlife, a Blackfaced Loffler

Date	Mintage	F12	VF20	XF40	MS60	MS63
2003	—	—	—	—	—	15.00

KM# 260 50 CENTS
Copper-Nickel **Ruler:** Elizabeth II **Subject:** Taiwan Wildlife - Neon pitta

Date	Mintage	F12	VF20	XF40	MS60	MS63
2003	—	—	—	—	—	15.00

KM# 122 50 CENTS
6.50 g., Nickel Plated Steel, 26.5 mm. **Ruler:** Elizabeth II **Obv:** Crowned head right **Rev:** Sailing canoe - Takia, denomination below **Edge:** Reeded

Date	Mintage	F12	VF20	XF40	MS60	MS63
2009	—	—	—	—	1.00	2.00

KM# 164 50 CENTS
27.22 g., Copper-Nickel, 38.74 mm. **Ruler:** Elizabeth II **Subject:** Year of the Tiger **Obv:** Female goddess facing **Rev:** Multicolor Formosan Tiger

Date	Mintage	F12	VF20	XF40	MS60	MS63
2010(c)	6,000	—	—	—	—	50.00

KM# 335 50 CENTS
6.50 g., Nickel Plated Steel, 26.5 mm. **Ruler:** Elizabeth II **Obv:** Varivoce (Humphead Urasse Fish) **Rev:** Camakau (Sail Catamaran)

Date	Mintage	F12	VF20	XF40	MS60	MS63
2012	—	—	—	—	—	1.50
2013	—	—	—	—	—	1.50

KM# 254 DOLLAR
28.28 g., Copper-Nickel, 38.61 mm. **Ruler:** Elizabeth II **Subject:** Elizabeth II, 50th Anniversary of Reign **Rev:** Draped sword

Date	Mintage	F12	VF20	XF40	MS60	MS63
2002	—	—	—	—	—	20.00

KM# 255 DOLLAR
28.28 g., Copper-Nickel, 38.61 mm. **Ruler:** Elizabeth II **Subject:** Elizabeth II, 50th Anniversary of Reign **Rev:** Boys Choir in Westminster Abbey

Date	Mintage	F12	VF20	XF40	MS60	MS63
2002	—	—	—	—	—	20.00

KM# 261 DOLLAR
31.11 g., 0.999 Silver 0.9926 oz. ASW, 38.7 mm. **Ruler:** Elizabeth II **Subject:** Song Meiling, 1st Anniversary of Death **Obv:** National arms **Rev:** Song Meiling and Jiang Jieshi

Date	Mintage	F12	VF20	XF40	MS60	MS63
2004	—	PF65 55.00				

KM# 262 DOLLAR
31.11 g., 0.999 Silver 0.9926 oz. ASW, 38.7 mm. **Ruler:** Elizabeth II **Subject:** Song Meiling, 1st Anniversary of Death **Rev:** Song Meiling and Chrysanthemen

Date	Mintage	F12	VF20	XF40	MS60	MS63
2004	—	PF65 55.00				

KM# 114 DOLLAR
31.11 g., 0.999 Silver 0.9926 oz. ASW, 40.7 mm. **Ruler:** Elizabeth II **Subject:** Sputnik I, 50th Anniversary **Rev:** Multicolor earth, satellite rocket

Date	Mintage	F12	VF20	XF40	MS60	MS63
2007 Prooflike	6,000	—	—	—	—	110

KM# 233 DOLLAR
0.50 g., 0.9999 Gold AGW, 11 mm. **Ruler:** Elizabeth II **Obv:** Head in tiara right **Rev:** Britannia seated left

Date	Mintage	F12	VF20	XF40	MS60	MS63
2007	15,000	PF65 50.00				

KM# 234 DOLLAR

0.50 g., 0.9999 Gold AGW, 11 mm. **Ruler:** Elizabeth II **Obv:** Head in tiara right **Rev:** Victory from Mexico's Libertad bullion coinage

Date	Mintage	F12	VF20	XF40	MS60	MS63
2007	15,000	PF65 50.00				

KM# 115 DOLLAR

31.11 g., 0.999 Silver 0.9926 oz. ASW **Ruler:** Elizabeth II **Subject:** Birds of Fiji **Rev:** Multicolor - blue crested broadbill

Date	Mintage	F12	VF20	XF40	MS60	MS63
2008 Prooflike	4,000	—	—	—	—	95.00

KM# 116 DOLLAR

31.11 g., 0.999 Silver 0.9926 oz. ASW **Ruler:** Elizabeth II **Subject:** Birds of Fiji **Rev:** Multicolor collared lory

Date	Mintage	F12	VF20	XF40	MS60	MS63
2008 Prooflike	4,000	—	—	—	—	95.00

KM# 117 DOLLAR

31.11 g., 0.999 Silver 0.9926 oz. ASW **Ruler:** Elizabeth II **Subject:** Birds of Fiji **Rev:** Multicolor - Island Thrush

Date	Mintage	F12	VF20	XF40	MS60	MS63
2008 Prooflike	4,000	—	—	—	—	95.00

KM# 118 DOLLAR

31.11 g., 0.999 Silver 0.9926 oz. ASW **Ruler:** Elizabeth II **Subject:** Birds of Fiji **Rev:** Multicolor white collared kingfisher

Date	Mintage	F12	VF20	XF40	MS60	MS63
2008 Prooflike	4,000	—	—	—	—	95.00

KM# 237 DOLLAR

28.28 g., 0.925 Silver 0.8356 oz. ASW, 38.61 mm. **Ruler:** Elizabeth II **Subject:** History fo Seafaring **Obv:** Head with tiara right **Rev:** Pamir sailing right

Date	Mintage	F12	VF20	XF40	MS60	MS63
2008	1,500	PF63 32.00	PF65 35.00			

KM# 124 DOLLAR

Copper-Nickel **Ruler:** Elizabeth II **Subject:** Barack Obama elected U.S. President

Date	Mintage	F12	VF20	XF40	MS60	MS63
2009	—	—	—	—	—	15.00

KM# 139a DOLLAR

Copper-Nickel, 38.61 mm. **Ruler:** Elizabeth II **Subject:** Great animals of the World - Zebra

Date	Mintage	F12	VF20	XF40	MS60	MS63
2009	—	—	—	—	—	15.00

KM# 137a DOLLAR

Copper-Nickel **Ruler:** Elizabeth II **Subject:** Great animals of the World - Panda

Date	Mintage	F12	VF20	XF40	MS60	MS63
2009	—	—	—	—	—	15.00

KM# 138a DOLLAR

Copper-Nickel **Ruler:** Elizabeth II **Subject:** Great animals of the World - Koi

Date	Mintage	F12	VF20	XF40	MS60	MS63
2009	—	—	—	—	—	15.00

KM# 140a DOLLAR

Copper-Nickel **Ruler:** Elizabeth II **Subject:** Great animals of the World - Elephant

Date	Mintage	F12	VF20	XF40	MS60	MS63
2009	—	—	—	—	—	15.00

KM# 141a DOLLAR

Copper-Nickel **Ruler:** Elizabeth II **Subject:** Great animals of the World - Cheeta

Date	Mintage	F12	VF20	XF40	MS60	MS63
2009	—	—	—	—	—	15.00

KM# 142a DOLLAR

Copper-Nickel **Ruler:** Elizabeth II **Subject:** Great animals of the World - Leopard

Date	Mintage	F12	VF20	XF40	MS60	MS63
2009	—	—	—	—	—	15.00

KM# 143a DOLLAR

Copper-Nickel **Ruler:** Elizabeth II **Subject:** Great animals of the World - Giraffe

Date	Mintage	F12	VF20	XF40	MS60	MS63
2009	—	—	—	—	—	15.00

KM# 144a DOLLAR

Copper-Nickel **Ruler:** Elizabeth II **Subject:** Great animals of the World - Tiger

Date	Mintage	F12	VF20	XF40	MS60	MS63
2009	—	—	—	—	—	15.00

KM# 130 DOLLAR

Copper-Nickel, 40 mm. **Ruler:** Elizabeth II **Subject:** Pacific Explorers - Sir Francis Drake **Rev:** Ship, portrait in oval

Date	Mintage	F12	VF20	XF40	MS60	MS63
2009	—	PF65 15.00				

KM# 131 DOLLAR

Copper-Nickel, 40 mm. **Ruler:** Elizabeth II **Subject:** Pacific Explorers - Ferdinand Magellan **Rev:** Ship, portrait in oval

Date	Mintage	F12	VF20	XF40	MS60	MS63
2009	—	PF65 15.00				

KM# 132 DOLLAR

Copper-Nickel, 40 mm. **Ruler:** Elizabeth II **Subject:** Pacific Explorers - James Cook **Rev:** Ship, portrait in oval

Date	Mintage	F12	VF20	XF40	MS60	MS63
2009	—	PF65 15.00				

KM# 133 DOLLAR

Copper-Nickel, 40 mm. **Ruler:** Elizabeth II **Subject:** Pacific Explorers - Abel Tasman **Rev:** Ship, portrait in oval

Date	Mintage	F12	VF20	XF40	MS60	MS63
2009	—	PF65 15.00				

KM# 134 DOLLAR

Copper-Nickel **Ruler:** Elizabeth II **Subject:** Pacific Explorers - Jacob DeMare & William Schouten **Rev:** Ship, portraits in oval

Date	Mintage	F12	VF20	XF40	MS60	MS63
2009	—	PF65 15.00				

KM# 135 DOLLAR

Copper-Nickel **Ruler:** Elizabeth II **Subject:** Pacific Explorers - William Bligh **Rev:** Ship, portrait in oval

Date	Mintage	F12	VF20	XF40	MS60	MS63
2009	—	—	—	—	—	15.00

KM# 137 DOLLAR

Copper-Nickel, 38.61 mm. **Ruler:** Elizabeth II **Subject:** Great animals of the World - Panda **Rev:** Panda seated, fur pattern as background

Date	Mintage	F12	VF20	XF40	MS60	MS63
2009	—	—	—	—	—	15.00

KM# 138 DOLLAR

Copper-Nickel, 38.61 mm. **Ruler:** Elizabeth II **Subject:** Great animals of the World - Koi **Rev:** Koi fish swimming right, scale pattern as background

Date	Mintage	F12	VF20	XF40	MS60	MS63
2009	—	—	—	—	—	15.00

KM# 139 DOLLAR

Copper-Nickel **Ruler:** Elizabeth II **Subject:** Great animals of the World - Zebra

Date	Mintage	F12	VF20	XF40	MS60	MS63
2009	—	—	—	—	—	15.00

KM# 140 DOLLAR

Copper-Nickel **Ruler:** Elizabeth II **Subject:** Great animals of the World - Elephant

Date	Mintage	F12	VF20	XF40	MS60	MS63
2009	—	—	—	—	—	15.00

KM# 141 DOLLAR
Copper-Nickel, 38.61 mm. **Ruler:** Elizabeth II **Subject:** Great animals of the world - Cheeta **Rev:** Cheets standing left, fur pattern background

Date	Mintage	F12	VF20	XF40	MS60	MS63
2009	—	—	—	—	—	15.00

KM# 142 DOLLAR
Copper-Nickel, 38.61 mm. **Ruler:** Elizabeth II **Subject:** Great animals of teh World - Leopard **Rev:** Leopard walking left, leopard skin background

Date	Mintage	F12	VF20	XF40	MS60	MS63
2009	—	—	—	—	—	15.00

KM# 143 DOLLAR
Copper-Nickel **Ruler:** Elizabeth II **Subject:** Great animals of the World - Giraffe

Date	Mintage	F12	VF20	XF40	MS60	MS63
2009	—	—	—	—	—	15.00

KM# 144 DOLLAR
Copper-Nickel, 38.61 mm. **Ruler:** Elizabeth II **Subject:** Great animals of the World - Tiger **Rev:** Tiger advancing right, fur pattern as background

Date	Mintage	F12	VF20	XF40	MS60	MS63
2009	—	—	—	—	—	15.00

KM# 145 DOLLAR
Copper-Nickel **Ruler:** Elizabeth II **Subject:** Tropical fish - Yellow pointed nose

Date	Mintage	F12	VF20	XF40	MS60	MS63
2009	—	—	—	—	—	15.00

KM# 146 DOLLAR
Copper-Nickel **Ruler:** Elizabeth II **Subject:** Tropical fish - Albino yellow fish

Date	Mintage	F12	VF20	XF40	MS60	MS63
2009	—	—	—	—	—	15.00

KM# 147 DOLLAR
Copper-Nickel **Ruler:** Elizabeth II **Subject:** Tropical fish - Striped Butterfly fish

Date	Mintage	F12	VF20	XF40	MS60	MS63
2009	—	—	—	—	—	15.00

KM# 148 DOLLAR
Copper-Nickel **Ruler:** Elizabeth II **Subject:** Tropical fish - Damsel fish

Date	Mintage	F12	VF20	XF40	MS60	MS63
2009	—	—	—	—	—	15.00

KM# 149 DOLLAR
Copper-Nickel, 38.6 mm. **Ruler:** Elizabeth II **Subject:** Tropical fish - Surgern fish **Rev:** Colored fish below ship

Date	Mintage	F12	VF20	XF40	MS60	MS63
2009	—	—	—	—	—	15.00

KM# 150 DOLLAR
Copper-Nickel **Ruler:** Elizabeth II **Subject:** Tropical fish - Clown fish

Date	Mintage	F12	VF20	XF40	MS60	MS63
2009	—	—	—	—	—	15.00

KM# 293 DOLLAR
25.00 g., Aluminum-Bronze, 38.61 mm. **Ruler:** Elizabeth II **Rev:** Mary and Christ child

Date	Mintage	F12	VF20	XF40	MS60	MS63
2009	—	—	—	—	—	10.00

KM# 126 DOLLAR
Silver **Ruler:** Elizabeth II **Subject:** H.C. Andersen - Steadfast Tin Soldier **Rev:** Multicolor toy soldier in flames

Date	Mintage	F12	VF20	XF40	MS60	MS63
2010	—	PF65 50.00				

KM# 127 DOLLAR
Silver **Ruler:** Elizabeth II **Subject:** H.C. Andersen - The Nightengale **Rev:** Multicolor bird

Date	Mintage	F12	VF20	XF40	MS60	MS63
2010	—	PF65 65.00				

KM# 128 DOLLAR
Silver **Ruler:** Elizabeth II **Subject:** H.C. Andersen - Thumbelina **Rev:** Multicolor Pixi

Date	Mintage	F12	VF20	XF40	MS60	MS63
2010	—	PF65 50.00				

KM# 129 DOLLAR
Silver **Ruler:** Elizabeth II **Subject:** H.C. Andersen - The little match girl **Rev:** Multicolor girl with match

Date	Mintage	F12	VF20	XF40	MS60	MS63
2010	—	PF65 50.00				

KM# 152 DOLLAR
31.11 g., 0.999 Silver 0.9926 oz. ASW, 46x29 mm. **Ruler:** Elizabeth II **Subject:** Siberian Tiger **Shape:** Irregular

Date	Mintage	F12	VF20	XF40	MS60	MS63
2010	10,000	PF65 60.00				

KM# 153 DOLLAR
31.11 g., 0.999 Silver 0.9926 oz. ASW, 46x29 mm. **Ruler:** Elizabeth II **Subject:** Bengal Tiger **Shape:** Irregular

Date	Mintage	F12	VF20	XF40	MS60	MS63
2010	10,000	PF65 60.00				

KM# 154 DOLLAR
Tri-Metallic, 40 mm. **Ruler:** Elizabeth II **Subject:** FIAA World Cup - South Africa **Rev:** Pretoria stadium and antelopes

Date	Mintage	F12	VF20	XF40	MS60	MS63
2010	—	—	—	—	—	20.00

KM# 155 DOLLAR
Tri-Metallic, 40 mm. **Ruler:** Elizabeth II **Subject:** FIAA World Cup - South Africa **Rev:** Kapstadt stadium and Zebra

Date	Mintage	F12	VF20	XF40	MS60	MS63
2010	—	—	—	—	—	20.00

KM# 156 DOLLAR
Tri-Metallic, 40 mm. **Ruler:** Elizabeth II **Subject:** FIAA World Cup - South Africa **Rev:** Johannesburg Stadium and Rhinos

Date	Mintage	F12	VF20	XF40	MS60	MS63
2010	—	—	—	—	—	20.00

KM# 157 DOLLAR
Tri-Metallic, 40 mm. **Ruler:** Elizabeth II **Subject:** FIAA World Cup - South Africa **Rev:** Johannesburg Stadium and Leopard

Date	Mintage	F12	VF20	XF40	MS60	MS63
2010	—	—	—	—	—	20.00

KM# 158 DOLLAR
Tri-Metallic, 40 mm. **Ruler:** Elizabeth II **Subject:** FIAA World Cup - South Africa **Rev:** Rustenburg Stadium and Lion

Date	Mintage	F12	VF20	XF40	MS60	MS63
2010	—	—	—	—	—	20.00

KM# 159 DOLLAR
Tri-Metallic, 40 mm. **Ruler:** Elizabeth II **Subject:** FIAA World Cup - South Africa **Rev:** Durban Stadium and Giraffes

Date	Mintage	F12	VF20	XF40	MS60	MS63
2010	—	—	—	—	—	20.00

KM# 160 DOLLAR
Tri-Metallic, 40 mm. **Ruler:** Elizabeth II **Subject:** FIAA World Cup - South Africa **Rev:** Polokwane Stadium and Elephant

Date	Mintage	F12	VF20	XF40	MS60	MS63
2010	—	—	—	—	—	20.00

KM# 161 DOLLAR
Tri-Metallic, 40 mm. **Ruler:** Elizabeth II **Subject:** FIAA World Cup - South Africa **Rev:** Nelspruit stadium and Water buffalo

Date	Mintage	F12	VF20	XF40	MS60	MS63
2010	—	—	—	—	—	20.00

KM# 162 DOLLAR
Tri-Metallic, 40 mm. **Ruler:** Elizabeth II **Subject:** FIAA World Cup - South Africa **Rev:** Bloemfontein stadium and Lemurs

Date	Mintage	F12	VF20	XF40	MS60	MS63
2010	—	—	—	—	—	20.00

KM# 163 DOLLAR
Tri-Metallic, 40 mm. **Ruler:** Elizabeth II **Subject:** FIAA World Cup - South Africa **Rev:** Port Elizabeth stadium and Animal

Date	Mintage	F12	VF20	XF40	MS60	MS63
2010	—	—	—	—	—	20.00

KM# 181 DOLLAR
31.11 g., 0.999 Silver 0.9926 oz. ASW, 38.61 mm. **Ruler:** Elizabeth II **Subject:** Year of the Tiger **Obv:** Head with crown right **Rev:** Bengal Tiger in color **Shape:** Yin-Yang

Date	Mintage	F12	VF20	XF40	MS60	MS63
2010	—	PF65 50.00				

KM# 182 DOLLAR
31.11 g., 0.999 Silver 0.9926 oz. ASW, 38.61 mm. **Ruler:**
Elizabeth II **Obv:** Head with crown right **Rev:** Siberian tiger in
color **Shape:** Yin-Yang

Date	Mintage	F12	VF20	XF40	MS60	MS63
2010	—	PF65 50.00				

KM# 238 DOLLAR
0.50 g., 0.999 Gold AGW, 11 mm. **Ruler:** Elizabeth II **Subject:**
Johann Philipp Reis **Obv:** Head in tiara right **Rev:** Reis portrait

Date	Mintage	F12	VF20	XF40	MS60	MS63
2010	5,000	PF65 50.00				

KM# 240 DOLLAR
26.03 g., Copper Plated Silver, 38.61 mm. **Ruler:** Elizabeth II
Subject: London Olympics, 2012 **Obv:** Head with tiara right
Rev: Triathlon sports

Date	Mintage	F12	VF20	XF40	MS60	MS63
2010	10,000	PF63 20.00	PF65 22.00			

KM# 242 DOLLAR
6.22 g., 0.999 Silver 0.1985 oz. ASW, 35 mm. **Ruler:** Elizabeth
II **Subject:** Vitus Bering **Obv:** Head with tiara right **Rev:** Vitus
J. Bering and ship Saint Peter

Date	Mintage	F12	VF20	XF40	MS60	MS63
2010	5,000	PF63 32.00	PF65 35.00			

KM# 170 DOLLAR
31.11 g., 0.999 Silver 0.9926 oz. ASW, 38.6 mm. **Ruler:**
Elizabeth II **Subject:** Year of the Dragon **Obv:** Characters,
Filigree center **Rev:** Characters, Filigree center

Date	Mintage	F12	VF20	XF40	MS60	MS63
2011	10,000	PF65 120				

KM# 176 DOLLAR
31.11 g., 0.999 Silver 0.9926 oz. ASW, 38.61 mm. **Ruler:**
Elizabeth II **Subject:** Year of the Rabbit **Obv:** Head with crown
right **Rev:** Rabbit eating carrot, carrots in color

Date	Mintage	F12	VF20	XF40	MS60	MS63
2011	—	PF65 60.00				

KM# 177 DOLLAR
31.11 g., 0.999 Silver 0.9926 oz. ASW, 38.61 mm. **Ruler:**
Elizabeth II **Subject:** Year of the Rabbit **Obv:** Head at left,
rabbit in center cut-out **Rev:** Rabbit in center, leatuce leaves
around

Date	Mintage	F12	VF20	XF40	MS60	MS63
2011	—	PF65 145				

KM# 179 DOLLAR
31.11 g., 0.999 Silver 0.9926 oz. ASW, 38.61 mm. **Ruler:**
Elizabeth II **Subject:** Year of the Rabbit **Obv:** Head in crown
right **Rev:** Snow rabbit in color **Shape:** Yin-Yang

Date	Mintage	F12	VF20	XF40	MS60	MS63
2011	—	PF65 90.00				

KM# 180 DOLLAR
31.11 g., 0.999 Silver 0.9926 oz. ASW, 38.61 mm. **Ruler:**
Elizabeth II **Subject:** Year of the Rabbit **Obv:** Head with crown
right **Rev:** Summer rabbit **Shape:** Yin-Yang

Date	Mintage	F12	VF20	XF40	MS60	MS63
2011	—	PF65 90.00				

KM# 183 DOLLAR
Copper-Nickel, 38.61 mm. **Ruler:** Elizabeth II **Obv:** Bust right
Rev: Sun, gilt figure

Date	Mintage	F12	VF20	XF40	MS60	MS63
2011	—	—	—	—	—	30.00

KM# 184 DOLLAR
Copper-Nickel, 38.61 mm. **Ruler:** Elizabeth II **Obv:** Bust right
Rev: Mercury, gilt figure

Date	Mintage	F12	VF20	XF40	MS60	MS63
2011	—	—	—	—	—	30.00

KM# 185 DOLLAR
Copper-Nickel, 38.6 mm. **Ruler:** Elizabeth II **Obv:** Bust right
Rev: Venus, gilt statue

Date	Mintage	F12	VF20	XF40	MS60	MS63
2011	—	—	—	—	—	30.00

KM# 186 DOLLAR
Copper-Nickel, 38.61 mm. **Ruler:** Elizabeth II **Obv:** Bust right
Rev: Earth, gilt statue

Date	Mintage	F12	VF20	XF40	MS60	MS63
2011	—	—	—	—	—	30.00

KM# 187 DOLLAR
Copper-Nickel, 38.61 mm. **Ruler:** Elizabeth II **Obv:** Bust right
Rev: Mars, gilt statue

Date	Mintage	F12	VF20	XF40	MS60	MS63
2011	—	—	—	—	—	30.00

KM# 188 DOLLAR
Copper-Nickel, 38.61 mm. **Ruler:** Elizabeth II **Obv:** Bust right
Rev: Jupiter, gilt statue

Date	Mintage	F12	VF20	XF40	MS60	MS63
2011	—	—	—	—	—	30.00

KM# 189 DOLLAR
Copper-Nickel, 38.61 mm. **Ruler:** Elizabeth II **Obv:** Bust right
Rev: Saturn, gilt statue

Date	Mintage	F12	VF20	XF40	MS60	MS63
2011	—	—	—	—	—	30.00

KM# 190 DOLLAR
Copper-Nickel, 38.6 mm. **Ruler:** Elizabeth II **Obv:** Bust right
Rev: Uranus, gilt statue

Date	Mintage	F12	VF20	XF40	MS60	MS63
2011	—	—	—	—	—	30.00

KM# 191 DOLLAR
Copper-Nickel, 38.61 mm. **Ruler:** Elizabeth II **Obv:** Bust right
Rev: Neptune, gilt statue

Date	Mintage	F12	VF20	XF40	MS60	MS63
2011	—	—	—	—	—	30.00

KM# 192 DOLLAR
Copper-Nickel, 38.61 mm. **Ruler:** Elizabeth II **Obv:** Bust right
Rev: Pluto, gilt statue

Date	Mintage	F12	VF20	XF40	MS60	MS63
2011	—	—	—	—	—	30.00

KM# 246 DOLLAR
0.50 g., 0.999 Gold AGW, 11 mm. **Ruler:** Elizabeth II **Obv:**
Head with tiara right **Rev:** Nero head right

Date	Mintage	F12	VF20	XF40	MS60	MS63
2011	5,000	PF65 50.00				

KM# 171 DOLLAR
15.55 g., 0.999 Silver 0.4962 oz. ASW, 38.6 mm. **Ruler:**
Elizabeth II **Subject:** Year of the Dragon **Rev:** Red dragon
Shape: Yin

Date	Mintage	F12	VF20	XF40	MS60	MS63
2012	10,000	PF65 85.00				

KM# 172 DOLLAR
15.55 g., 0.999 Silver 0.4962 oz. ASW, 38.6 mm. **Ruler:**
Elizabeth II **Subject:** Year of the Dragon **Rev:** Blue dragon
Shape: Yang

Date	Mintage	F12	VF20	XF40	MS60	MS63
2012	—	PF65 85.00				

KM# 200 DOLLAR
20.00 g., Copper-Nickel, 38.61 mm. **Ruler:** Elizabeth II
Subject: Carnival - Rio

Date	Mintage	F12	VF20	XF40	MS60	MS63
2012	2,500	—	—	—	—	40.00

KM# 201 DOLLAR
20.00 g., Copper-Nickel, 38.6 mm. **Ruler:** Elizabeth II **Subject:**
Carnival - Venice **Obv:** Head with tiara right

Date	Mintage	F12	VF20	XF40	MS60	MS63
2012	2,500	—	—	—	—	50.00

KM# 202 DOLLAR
20.00 g., Copper-Nickel, 38.6 mm. **Ruler:** Elizabeth II **Subject:**
Carnival - Nice **Obv:** Head with tiara right

Date	Mintage	F12	VF20	XF40	MS60	MS63
2012	2,500	—	—	—	—	50.00

KM# 203 DOLLAR
20.00 g., Copper-Nickel, 38.6 mm. **Ruler:** Elizabeth II **Subject:**
Carnival - New Orleans **Obv:** Head with tiara right

Date	Mintage	F12	VF20	XF40	MS60	MS63
2012	2,500	—	—	—	—	50.00

KM# 204 DOLLAR
20.00 g., Copper-Nickel, 38.6 mm. **Ruler:** Elizabeth II **Subject:**
Carnival - Cologne **Obv:** Head with tiara right

Date	Mintage	F12	VF20	XF40	MS60	MS63
2012	2,500	—	—	—	—	50.00

KM# 205 DOLLAR
20.00 g., Copper-Nickel, 38.6 mm. **Ruler:** Elizabeth II **Subject:**
Carnival - Basel **Obv:** Head with tiara right

Date	Mintage	F12	VF20	XF40	MS60	MS63
2012	2,500	—	—	—	—	50.00

KM# 212 DOLLAR
20.00 g., Copper-Nickel, 38.6 mm. **Ruler:** Elizabeth II **Subject:**
Music - Chanson

Date	Mintage	F12	VF20	XF40	MS60	MS63
2012	2,500	PF65 30.00				

KM# 213 DOLLAR
20.00 g., Copper-Nickel, 38.6 mm. **Ruler:** Elizabeth II **Subject:**
Music - Bob Marley

Date	Mintage	F12	VF20	XF40	MS60	MS63
2012	2,500	PF65 30.00				

KM# 214 DOLLAR
20.00 g., Copper-Nickel, 38.6 mm. **Ruler:** Elizabeth II **Subject:** Music - Elvis Presley

Date	Mintage	F12	VF20	XF40	MS60	MS63
2012	2,500	PF65 30.00				

KM# 319 DOLLAR
0.50 g., 0.585 Gold AGW, 11 mm. **Ruler:** Elizabeth II **Subject:** Smallest Gold Coins Pirogue of the Fiji Islands

Date	Mintage	F12	VF20	XF40	MS60	MS63
2012	—	PF65 35.00				

KM# 320 DOLLAR
0.50 g., 0.9999 Gold AGW, 11 mm. **Ruler:** Elizabeth II **Subject:** Smallest Gold Coins - Diamond Jubilee

Date	Mintage	F12	VF20	XF40	MS60	MS63
2012	Est. 5000	PF65 50.00				

KM# 336 DOLLAR
5.05 g., Brass Plated Steel, 23 mm. **Ruler:** Elizabeth II **Obv:** Vokai (Banded Iguana) **Rev:** Saqamoli (Drinking vessel)

Date	Mintage	F12	VF20	XF40	MS60	MS63
2012	—	—	—	—	—	2.00
2013	—	—	—	—	—	2.00

KM# 349 DOLLAR
0.50 g., 0.585 Gold AGW, 11 mm. **Ruler:** Elizabeth II **Subject:** H.M.S. Bounty

Date	Mintage	F12	VF20	XF40	MS60	MS63
2013	Est. 5000	PF65 40.00				

KM# 351 DOLLAR
0.50 g., 0.585 Gold AGW, 11 mm. **Ruler:** Elizabeth II **Subject:** Gutenberg

Date	Mintage	F12	VF20	XF40	MS60	MS63
2013	Est. 5000	PF65 40.00				

KM# 108 2 DOLLARS
10.00 g., 0.925 Silver 0.2955 oz. ASW, 30 mm. **Ruler:** Elizabeth II **Subject:** XVIII FIFA World Football Championship - Germany 2006 **Obv:** Crowned head right **Obv. Legend:** ELIZABETH II - FIJI **Rev:** World cup

Date	Mintage	F12	VF20	XF40	MS60	MS63
2004	50,000	PF60 17.00	PF63 20.00	PF65 22.00		

KM# 193 2 DOLLARS
Silver, 38.61 mm. **Ruler:** Elizabeth II **Obv:** Head crowned right **Rev:** Orthodox church in color

Date	Mintage	F12	VF20	XF40	MS60	MS63
2009	—	PF65 50.00				

KM# 194 2 DOLLARS
Silver, 38.61 mm. **Ruler:** Elizabeth II **Obv:** Head crowned right **Rev:** Nicholas II Romanoff wedding portrait in color

Date	Mintage	F12	VF20	XF40	MS60	MS63
2009	—	PF65 50.00				

KM# 273 2 DOLLARS
0.999 Silver, 45x31 mm. **Ruler:** Elizabeth II **Rev:** British airship R34 in color **Shape:** Oval

Date	Mintage	F12	VF20	XF40	MS60	MS63
2009	20,000	PF63 90.00	PF65 100			

KM# 274 2 DOLLARS
0.999 Silver, 45x31 mm. **Ruler:** Elizabeth II **Rev:** Soviet airship B6 in color **Shape:** Oval

Date	Mintage	F12	VF20	XF40	MS60	MS63
2009	20,000	PF63 90.00	PF65 100			

KM# 276 2 DOLLARS
0.999 Silver, 45x31 mm. **Ruler:** Elizabeth II **Rev:** U.S. Airship Akron in color **Shape:** Oval

Date	Mintage	F12	VF20	XF40	MS60	MS63
2009	20,000	PF63 90.00	PF65 100			

KM# 276 2 DOLLARS
0.999 Silver, 45x31 mm. **Ruler:** Elizabeth II **Rev:** German airship Hindenburg in color **Shape:** Oval

Date	Mintage	F12	VF20	XF40	MS60	MS63
2009	20,000	PF63 90.00	PF65 100			

KM# 195 2 DOLLARS
Silver, 38.61 mm. **Ruler:** Elizabeth II **Obv:** Head crowned right **Rev:** Romanoff family portrait in color

Date	Mintage	F12	VF20	XF40	MS60	MS63
2009	—	PF65 50.00				

KM# 166 2 DOLLARS
31.11 g., 0.999 Silver 0.9926 oz. ASW, 45x31 mm. **Ruler:** Elizabeth II **Rev:** Submarine Ohio in color **Shape:** Oval

Date	Mintage	F12	VF20	XF40	MS60	MS63
2010 Prooflike	15,000	—	—	—	—	90.00

KM# 167 2 DOLLARS
31.11 g., 0.999 Silver 0.9926 oz. ASW, 45x31 mm. **Ruler:** Elizabeth II **Rev:** Submarine Triomphant in color **Shape:** Oval

Date	Mintage	F12	VF20	XF40	MS60	MS63
2010 Prooflike	15,000	—	—	—	—	90.00

KM# 168 2 DOLLARS
31.11 g., 0.999 Silver 0.9926 oz. ASW, 45x31 mm. **Ruler:** Elizabeth II **Rev:** Submarine Typhoon in color **Shape:** Oval

Date	Mintage	F12	VF20	XF40	MS60	MS63
2010 Prooflike	15,000	—	—	—	—	90.00

KM# 169 2 DOLLARS
31.11 g., 0.999 Silver 0.9926 oz. ASW, 45x31 mm. **Ruler:** Elizabeth II **Rev:** Submarine Vanguard in color **Shape:** Oval

Date	Mintage	F12	VF20	XF40	MS60	MS63
2010 Prooflike	15,000	—	—	—	—	90.00

KM# 252 2 DOLLARS
31.11 g., 0.999 Silver 0.9926 oz. ASW **Ruler:** Elizabeth II **Rev:** Muhammad Ali, color portrait

Date	Mintage	F12	VF20	XF40	MS60	MS63
2012	7,500	PF65 100				

KM# 337 2 DOLLARS
(No Composition), 27.5 mm. **Ruler:** Elizabeth II **Obv:** Gani Yatu (Peregrine Falcon) **Rev:** Tanoa (Drinking vessel)

Date	Mintage	F12	VF20	XF40	MS60	MS63
2012	—	—	—	—	—	4.00
2013	—	—	—	—	—	4.00

KM# 338 2 DOLLARS
31.11 g., 0.999 Silver 0.9926 oz. ASW **Ruler:** Elizabeth II **Obv:**
National Arms **Rev:** Yorkshire Terrier (My Little Puppy)

Date	Mintage	F12	VF20	XF40	MS60	MS63
2013	Est. 5000	PF65 50.00				

KM# 339 2 DOLLARS
31.11 g., 0.999 Silver 0.9926 oz. ASW, 40 mm. **Ruler:** Elizabeth
II **Obv:** National arms **Rev:** Basset Hound (My Best Friend)

Date	Mintage	F12	VF20	XF40	MS60	MS63
2013	Est. 5000	PF65 50.00				

KM# 340 2 DOLLARS
31.11 g., 0.999 Silver 0.9926 oz. ASW, 40 mm. **Ruler:** Elizabeth
II **Obv:** National arms **Rev:** Boxer (My Great Protector)

Date	Mintage	F12	VF20	XF40	MS60	MS63
2013	Est. 5000	PF65 50.00				

KM# 341 2 DOLLARS
31.11 g., 0.999 Silver 0.9926 oz. ASW, 40 mm. **Ruler:** Elizabeth
II **Obv:** National arms **Rev:** American Curl (Fluffy Cat)

Date	Mintage	F12	VF20	XF40	MS60	MS63
2013	Est. 5000	PF65 50.00				

KM# 342 2 DOLLARS
31.11 g., 0.999 Silver 0.9926 oz. ASW, 40 mm. **Ruler:** Elizabeth
II **Obv:** National arms **Rev:** Sphynx (Super Cat)

Date	Mintage	F12	VF20	XF40	MS60	MS63
2013 Proof	Est. 5000	—	—	—	—	—

KM# 343 2 DOLLARS
31.10 g., 0.999 Silver 0.9926 oz. ASW, 40 mm. **Ruler:** Elizabeth
II **Obv:** National arms **Rev:** Felis Margarita (Wild Cat)

Date	Mintage	F12	VF20	XF40	MS60	MS63
2013 Proof	Est. 5000	—	—	—	—	—

KM# 93 5 DOLLARS
1.56 g., 0.9999 Gold 0.0497 oz. AGW **Ruler:** Elizabeth II **Obv:**
Crowned head right, date at right **Rev:** Arms

Date	Mintage	F12	VF20	XF40	MS60	MS63
2002	3,000	PF63 90.00	PF65 100			

KM# 115A 5 DOLLARS
1.56 g., 0.9999 Gold 0.0498 oz. AGW, 13.9 mm. **Ruler:**
Elizabeth II **Rev:** Coat of Arms

Date	Mintage	F12	VF20	XF40	MS60	MS63
2002	3,000	PF63 200	PF65 220			

KM# 173 5 DOLLARS
Silver, 39 mm. **Ruler:** Elizabeth II **Subject:** Queen Elizabeth
II, 80th Birthday

Date	Mintage	F12	VF20	XF40	MS60	MS63
2006	—	PF65 50.00				

KM# 265 5 DOLLARS
Silver **Ruler:** Elizabeth II **Subject:** Christopher Columbus,
500th Anniversary of Death **Rev:** Santa Maria and Columbus
portrait

Date	Mintage	F12	VF20	XF40	MS60	MS63
2006	3,000	PF65 35.00				

KM# 266 5 DOLLARS
1.24 g., 0.585 Gold 0.0232 oz. AGW, 13.92 mm. **Ruler:**
Elizabeth II **Rev:** Stonehedge

Date	Mintage	F12	VF20	XF40	MS60	MS63
2006	7,500	PF63 45.00	PF65 50.00			

KM# 267 5 DOLLARS
1.24 g., 0.585 Gold 0.0232 oz. AGW, 13.92 mm. **Ruler:**
Elizabeth II **Rev:** Easter Island rock sculptures

Date	Mintage	F12	VF20	XF40	MS60	MS63
2006	7,500	PF63 45.00	PF65 50.00			

KM# 268 5 DOLLARS
1.24 g., 0.585 Gold 0.0232 oz. AGW, 13.92 mm. **Ruler:**
Elizabeth II **Rev:** Bird glyph on Nazca Plateau

Date	Mintage	F12	VF20	XF40	MS60	MS63
2006	7,500	PF63 45.00	PF65 50.00			

KM# 269 5 DOLLARS
1.24 g., 0.585 Gold 0.0232 oz. AGW, 13.92 mm. **Ruler:**
Elizabeth II **Rev:** Seven castles

Date	Mintage	F12	VF20	XF40	MS60	MS63
2006	7,500	PF63 45.00	PF65 50.00			

KM# 270 5 DOLLARS
1.24 g., 0.585 Gold 0.0232 oz. AGW, 13.92 mm. **Ruler:**
Elizabeth II **Rev:** Atlantis

Date	Mintage	F12	VF20	XF40	MS60	MS63
2006	7,500	PF63 45.00	PF65 50.00			

KM# 271 5 DOLLARS
1.24 g., 0.585 Gold 0.0232 oz. AGW, 13.92 mm. **Ruler:**
Elizabeth II **Rev:** Ayers Rock

Date	Mintage	F12	VF20	XF40	MS60	MS63
2006	7,500	PF63 45.00	PF65 50.00			

KM# 272 5 DOLLARS
1.24 g., 0.585 Gold 0.0232 oz. AGW, 13.92 mm. **Ruler:**
Elizabeth II **Rev:** Sailing ship in Bermuda triangle

Date	Mintage	F12	VF20	XF40	MS60	MS63
2006	7,500	PF63 45.00	PF65 50.00			

KM# 206 5 DOLLARS
62.20 g., 0.999 Silver 1.9849 oz. ASW, 60 mm. **Ruler:** Elizabeth
II **Subject:** Map - New York City, Manhattan Island

Date	Mintage	F12	VF20	XF40	MS60	MS63
2011	5,000	PF65 125				

KM# 207 5 DOLLARS
62.20 g., 0.999 Silver 1.9849 oz. ASW, 60 mm. **Ruler:** Elizabeth
II **Subject:** Map - Paris

Date	Mintage	F12	VF20	XF40	MS60	MS63
2011	5,000	PF65 125				

KM# 208 5 DOLLARS
62.20 g., 0.999 Silver 1.9849 oz. ASW, 60 mm. **Ruler:** Elizabeth
II **Subject:** Map - Tokyo

Date	Mintage	F12	VF20	XF40	MS60	MS63
2011	5,000	PF65 125				

KM# 209 5 DOLLARS
62.20 g., 0.999 Silver 1.9849 oz. ASW, 60 mm. **Ruler:** Elizabeth
II **Subject:** Map - Sidney

Date	Mintage	F12	VF20	XF40	MS60	MS63
2011	5,000	PF65 125				

KM# 210 5 DOLLARS
62.20 g., 0.999 Silver 1.9849 oz. ASW, 60 mm. **Ruler:** Elizabeth
II **Subject:** Map - Berlin

Date	Mintage	F12	VF20	XF40	MS60	MS63
2011	5,000	PF65 125				

KM# 318 5 DOLLARS
28.28 g., 0.925 Silver 0.8356 oz. ASW, 38.61 mm. **Ruler:**

Elizabeth II **Subject:** Diamond Jubilee of Queen Elizabeth II
- Imperial State Crown

Date	Mintage	F12	VF20	XF40	MS60	MS63
2012	Est. 10000	PF65 50.00				

KM# 82 10 DOLLARS
31.62 g., 0.925 Silver 0.9343 oz. ASW, 38.6 mm. **Ruler:**
Elizabeth II **Obv:** Crowned head right, date at right **Rev:**
William Bligh's - HMS Providence **Edge:** Reeded

Date	Mintage	F12	VF20	XF40	MS60	MS63
2001	—	PF63 35.00	PF65 40.00			

KM# 83 10 DOLLARS
28.28 g., 0.925 Silver 0.8356 oz. ASW, 38.6 mm. **Ruler:**
Elizabeth II **Subject:** Queen Elizabeth II - 50 Years of Reign
Obv: Queen's head right, gilded **Rev:** Cloth draped sword hilt,
legend and denomination **Rev. Legend:** Defender of the Faith...
Edge: Reeded

Date	Mintage	F12	VF20	XF40	MS60	MS63
2002	15,000	PF63 37.00	PF65 42.00			

KM# 84 10 DOLLARS
28.28 g., 0.925 Silver 0.8356 oz. ASW, 38.6 mm. **Ruler:**
Elizabeth II **Subject:** Queen Elizabeth II - 50th Year of Reign
Obv: Head right, gilded **Rev:** Four man chorus, legend, and
denomination **Rev. Legend:** Westminster Abbey June 1953.
Edge: Reeded

Date	Mintage	F12	VF20	XF40	MS60	MS63
2002	15,000	PF63 37.00	PF65 42.00			

KM# 94 10 DOLLARS
3.11 g., 0.9999 Gold 0.0993 oz. AGW **Ruler:** Elizabeth II **Obv:**
Crowned head right, date at right **Rev:** Arms **Edge:** Reeded

Date	Mintage	F12	VF20	XF40	MS60	MS63
2002	2,000	PF63 175	PF65 200			

KM# 101 10 DOLLARS
31.10 g., 0.999 Silver 0.9925 oz. ASW, 40 mm. **Ruler:** Elizabeth
II **Series:** Save the Whales **Obv:** Crowned head right, date at

right **Obv. Legend:** ELIZABETH II - FIJI **Rev:** Sperm Whale on
mother-of-pearl inset **Edge:** Plain

Date	Mintage	F12	VF20	XF40	MS60	MS63
2002	2,000	PF65 85.00				

KM# 114A 10 DOLLARS
3.11 g., 0.9999 Gold 0.0993 oz. AGW, 16 mm. **Ruler:** Elizabeth
II **Rev:** Coat of Arms

Date	Mintage	F12	VF20	XF40	MS60	MS63
2002	2,000	PF63 325	PF65 350			

KM# 104 10 DOLLARS
28.28 g., 0.925 Silver 0.8356 oz. ASW, 38.6 mm. **Ruler:**
Elizabeth II **Series:** Endangered Wildlife **Obv:** Crowned
head right **Obv. Legend:** ELIZABETH II - FIJI **Rev:** Head of
Peregrine Falcon right

Date	Mintage	F12	VF20	XF40	MS60	MS63
2002	—	PF63 42.00	PF65 45.00			

KM# 105 10 DOLLARS
28.28 g., 0.925 Silver 0.8356 oz. ASW, 38.6 mm. **Ruler:**
Elizabeth II **Obv:** Crowned head right **Obv. Legend:**
ELIZABETH II - FIJI **Rev:** Sailing ship "Vostok

Date	Mintage	F12	VF20	XF40	MS60	MS63
2002	—	PF63 35.00	PF65 40.00			

KM# 106 10 DOLLARS
1.24 g., 0.9999 Gold 0.0396 oz. AGW, 13.88 mm. **Ruler:**
Elizabeth II **Obv:** Crowned head right **Obv. Legend:**
ELIZABETH II - FIJI **Rev:** Sailing ship at left, naval bust 3/4
left at right **Rev. Legend:** HMS INVESTIGATOR * MATTHEW
FLINDERS **Edge:** Reeded

Date	Mintage	F12	VF20	XF40	MS60	MS63
2002	—	PF63 75.00	PF65 85.00			

KM# 258 10 DOLLARS
31.11 g., 0.999 Silver 0.9926 oz. ASW, 40 mm. **Ruler:** Elizabeth
II **Subject:** Fairwell to the Irish Pfund **Rev:** Coin motif in color

Date	Mintage	F12	VF20	XF40	MS60	MS63
2002	Est. 2001	PF65 80.00				

KM# 107 10 DOLLARS
28.26 g., 0.925 Silver 0.835 oz. ASW, 38.61 mm. **Ruler:**
Elizabeth II **Obv:** Crowned head right **Obv. Legend:**
ELIZABETH II - FIJI **Rev:** Sailing ship at left, naval bust 3/4
left at right **Rev. Legend:** HMS INVESTIGATOR * MATTHEW
FLINDERS **Edge:** Reeded

Date	Mintage	F12	VF20	XF40	MS60	MS63
2003	—	PF63 42.00	PF65 45.00			

KM# 113 10 DOLLARS
1.24 g., Gold AGW, 13.91 mm. **Ruler:** Elizabeth II **Subject:**
Lost Treasure of King Richard **Obv:** Crowned head right **Rev:**
Bust of King Richard facing **Edge:** Reeded

Date	Mintage	F12	VF20	XF40	MS60	MS63
2003	—	PF63 70.00	PF65 80.00			

KM# 109 10 DOLLARS
28.28 g., 0.925 Silver 0.8356 oz. ASW, 38.61 mm. **Ruler:**
Elizabeth II **Subject:** XXVIII Summer Olympics - Athens 2004
Obv: Crowned head right **Obv. Legend:** ELIZABETH II - FIJI
Rev: Regatta **Edge:** Reeded

Date	Mintage	F12	VF20	XF40	MS60	MS63
2004	—	PF63 38.00	PF65 42.00			

KM# 110 10 DOLLARS
Copper-Nickel-Zinc, 38.6 mm. **Ruler:** Elizabeth II **Subject:**
XVIII FIFA World Football Championship - Germany 2006 **Obv:**
Crowned head right **Obv. Legend:** ELIZABETH II - FIJI **Rev:**
Digital countdown clock

Date	Mintage	F12	VF20	XF40	MS60	MS63
2005	50,000	—	—	—	—	45.00

KM# 263 10 DOLLARS
31.11 g., 0.999 Silver 0.9926 oz. ASW, 38.61 mm. **Ruler:** Elizabeth II **Subject:** FIFA World Cup **Rev:** Trophy

Date	Mintage	F12	VF20	XF40	MS60	MS63
2005	—				—	80.00

KM# 111 10 DOLLARS
1.24 g., 0.9999 Gold 0.0396 oz. AGW **Ruler:** Elizabeth II **Subject:** 500th Anniversary Death of Christopher Columbus **Obv:** Crowned head right **Obv. Legend:** ELIZABETH II - FIJI **Rev:** Sailing ship "Santa Maria

Date	Mintage	F12	VF20	XF40	MS60	MS63
2006	15,000	PF63 70.00		PF65 80.00		

KM# 330 10 DOLLARS
28.28 g., 0.925 Silver 0.8356 oz. ASW, 38.61 mm. **Ruler:** Elizabeth II **Subject:** Queen Elizabeth II 60th Wedding Anniversary **Shape:** 7-Sided

Date	Mintage	F12	VF20	XF40	MS60	MS63
2007	—	PF65 40.00				

KM# 331 10 DOLLARS
28.28 g., 0.925 Silver 0.8356 oz. ASW, 38.61 mm. **Ruler:** Elizabeth II **Subject:** Balmoral Castle **Shape:** 7-Sided

Date	Mintage	F12	VF20	XF40	MS60	MS63
2007	Est. 30000	PF65 40.00				

KM# 235 10 DOLLARS
28.28 g., 0.925 Silver 0.8356 oz. ASW, 38.61 mm. **Ruler:** Elizabeth II **Subject:** James Watt **Obv:** Head in tiara right **Rev:** James Watt and steam engine

Date	Mintage	F12	VF20	XF40	MS60	MS63
2008	5,000	PF65 35.00				

KM# 236 10 DOLLARS
1.00 g., 0.9999 Gold 0.0319 oz. AGW, 13.92 mm. **Ruler:** Elizabeth II **Subject:** Lapita art **Obv:** Head with Tiara right **Rev:** Artistic design

Date	Mintage	F12	VF20	XF40	MS60	MS63
2008	15,000	PF65 75.00				

KM# 125 10 DOLLARS
31.11 g., 0.999 Silver 0.9926 oz. ASW **Ruler:** Elizabeth II **Obv:** Crowned head right **Rev:** Yes we can!

Date	Mintage	F12	VF20	XF40	MS60	MS63
2009	—	PF65 50.00				

KM# 178 10 DOLLARS
28.28 g., 0.925 Silver 0.8356 oz. ASW, 38.61 mm. **Ruler:** Elizabeth II **Obv:** Head with tiara right **Rev:** Barak Obama at left

Date	Mintage	F12	VF20	XF40	MS60	MS63
2009	—	PF65 50.00				

KM# 277 10 DOLLARS
28.28 g., 0.925 Silver 0.8356 oz. ASW, 38.61 mm. **Ruler:** Elizabeth II **Rev:** Butterfly fish in color

Date	Mintage	F12	VF20	XF40	MS60	MS63
2009	—	PF65 45.00				

KM# 277a 10 DOLLARS
39.00 g., 0.916 Gold 1.1412 oz. AGW, 38.61 mm. **Ruler:** Elizabeth II **Rev:** Butterfly fish

Date	Mintage	F12	VF20	XF40	MS60	MS63
2009	—	PF63 1,950		PF65 2,100		

KM# 278 10 DOLLARS
28.28 g., 0.925 Silver 0.8356 oz. ASW, 38.61 mm. **Ruler:** Elizabeth II **Rev:** Imperial Angler fish in color

Date	Mintage	F12	VF20	XF40	MS60	MS63
2009	—	PF65 45.00				

KM# 278a 10 DOLLARS
39.00 g., 0.916 Gold 1.1412 oz. AGW, 38.61 mm. **Ruler:** Elizabeth II **Rev:** Imperial Angler

Date	Mintage	F12	VF20	XF40	MS60	MS63
2009	—	PF63 1,950		PF65 2,100		

KM# 279 10 DOLLARS
28.28 g., 0.925 Silver 0.8356 oz. ASW, 38.61 mm. **Ruler:** Elizabeth II **Rev:** Clown fish in color

Date	Mintage	F12	VF20	XF40	MS60	MS63
2009	—	PF65 45.00				

KM# 279a 10 DOLLARS
39.00 g., 0.916 Gold 1.1412 oz. AGW, 38.61 mm. **Ruler:** Elizabeth II **Rev:** Clown fish

Date	Mintage	F12	VF20	XF40	MS60	MS63
2009	—	PF63 1,950		PF65 2,100		

KM# 280 10 DOLLARS
28.28 g., 0.925 Silver 0.8356 oz. ASW, 38.61 mm. **Ruler:** Elizabeth II **Rev:** Flame dwarf angel fish in color

Date	Mintage	F12	VF20	XF40	MS60	MS63
2009	—	PF65 45.00				

KM# 280a 10 DOLLARS
39.00 g., 0.916 Gold 1.1412 oz. AGW, 38.61 mm. **Ruler:** Elizabeth II **Rev:** Flame dwarf angel fish

Date	Mintage	F12	VF20	XF40	MS60	MS63
2009	—	PF63 1,950		PF65 2,100		

KM# 281 10 DOLLARS
28.28 g., 0.925 Silver 0.8356 oz. ASW, 38.61 mm. **Ruler:** Elizabeth II **Rev:** Pallet surgeon fish in color

Date	Mintage	F12	VF20	XF40	MS60	MS63
2009	—	PF65 45.00				

KM# 281a 10 DOLLARS
39.00 g., 0.916 Gold 1.1412 oz. AGW, 38.61 mm. **Ruler:** Elizabeth II **Rev:** Pallet surgeon fish

Date	Mintage	F12	VF20	XF40	MS60	MS63
2009	—	PF63 1,950		PF65 2,100		

KM# 282 10 DOLLARS
28.28 g., 0.925 Silver 0.8356 oz. ASW, 38.61 mm. **Ruler:** Elizabeth II **Rev:** Yellow nose surgeon fish in color

Date	Mintage	F12	VF20	XF40	MS60	MS63
2009 Proof	—				—	45.00

KM# 282a 10 DOLLARS
39.00 g., 0.916 Gold 1.1412 oz. AGW, 38.61 mm. **Ruler:** Elizabeth II **Rev:** Yellow nose surgeon fish

Date	Mintage	F12	VF20	XF40	MS60	MS63
2009	—	PF63 1,950		PF65 2,100		

KM# 283 10 DOLLARS
28.28 g., 0.925 Silver 0.8356 oz. ASW, 38.61 mm. **Ruler:** Elizabeth II **Rev:** Cheetah

Date	Mintage	F12	VF20	XF40	MS60	MS63
2009	—	PF65 45.00				

KM# 283a 10 DOLLARS
39.00 g., 0.916 Gold 1.1412 oz. AGW, 38.61 mm. **Ruler:** Elizabeth II **Rev:** Cheetah

Date	Mintage	F12	VF20	XF40	MS60	MS63
2009	—	PF63 1,950		PF65 2,100		

KM# 284 10 DOLLARS
28.28 g., 0.925 Silver 0.8356 oz. ASW, 38.61 mm. **Ruler:** Elizabeth II **Rev:** Elephant

Date	Mintage	F12	VF20	XF40	MS60	MS63
2009	—	PF65 45.00				

KM# 284a 10 DOLLARS
39.00 g., 0.916 Gold 1.1412 oz. AGW, 38.61 mm. **Ruler:** Elizabeth II **Rev:** Elephant

Date	Mintage	F12	VF20	XF40	MS60	MS63
2009	—	PF63 1,950		PF65 2,100		

KM# 285a 10 DOLLARS
39.00 g., 0.916 Gold 1.1412 oz. AGW, 38.61 mm. **Ruler:** Elizabeth II **Rev:** Giraffe

Date	Mintage	F12	VF20	XF40	MS60	MS63
2009	—	PF63 1,950		PF65 2,100		

KM# 285 10 DOLLARS
28.28 g., 0.925 Silver 0.8356 oz. ASW, 38.61 mm. **Ruler:** Elizabeth II **Rev:** Giraffe

Date	Mintage	F12	VF20	XF40	MS60	MS63
2009	—	PF65 45.00				

KM# 286 10 DOLLARS
28.28 g., 0.925 Silver 0.8356 oz. ASW, 38.61 mm. **Ruler:** Elizabeth II **Rev:** Koi

Date	Mintage	F12	VF20	XF40	MS60	MS63
2009	—	PF65 45.00				

KM# 286a 10 DOLLARS
39.00 g., 0.916 Gold 1.1412 oz. AGW, 38.61 mm. **Ruler:** Elizabeth II **Rev:** Koi

Date	Mintage	F12	VF20	XF40	MS60	MS63
2009	—	PF63 1,950		PF65 2,100		

KM# 287 10 DOLLARS
28.28 g., 0.925 Silver 0.8356 oz. ASW, 38.61 mm. **Ruler:** Elizabeth II **Rev:** Leopard

Date	Mintage	F12	VF20	XF40	MS60	MS63
2009	—	PF65 45.00				

KM# 287a 10 DOLLARS
39.00 g., 0.916 Gold 1.1412 oz. AGW, 38.61 mm. **Ruler:** Elizabeth II **Rev:** Leopard

Date	Mintage	F12	VF20	XF40	MS60	MS63
2009	—	PF63 1,950		PF65 2,100		

KM# 288 10 DOLLARS
28.28 g., 0.925 Silver 0.8356 oz. ASW, 38.61 mm. **Ruler:** Elizabeth II **Rev:** Panda

Date	Mintage	F12	VF20	XF40	MS60	MS63
2009	—	PF65 45.00				

KM# 288a 10 DOLLARS
39.00 g., 0.916 Gold 1.1412 oz. AGW, 38.61 mm. **Ruler:** Elizabeth II **Rev:** Panda

Date	Mintage	F12	VF20	XF40	MS60	MS63
2009	—	PF63 1,950		PF65 2,100		

KM# 289 10 DOLLARS
28.28 g., 0.925 Silver 0.8356 oz. ASW, 38.61 mm. **Ruler:** Elizabeth II **Rev:** Tiger

Date	Mintage	F12	VF20	XF40	MS60	MS63
2009	—	PF65 45.00				

KM# 289a 10 DOLLARS
39.00 g., 0.916 Gold 1.1412 oz. AGW, 38.61 mm. **Ruler:** Elizabeth II **Rev:** Tiger

Date	Mintage	F12	VF20	XF40	MS60	MS63
2009	—	PF63 1,950		PF65 2,100		

KM# 290 10 DOLLARS
28.28 g., 0.925 Silver 0.8356 oz. ASW, 38.61 mm. **Ruler:** Elizabeth II **Rev:** Zebra

Date	Mintage	F12	VF20	XF40	MS60	MS63
2009	—	PF65 45.00				

KM# 290a 10 DOLLARS
39.00 g., 0.916 Gold 1.1412 oz. AGW, 38.61 mm. **Ruler:** Elizabeth II **Rev:** Zebra

Date	Mintage	F12	VF20	XF40	MS60	MS63
2009	—	PF63 1,950		PF65 2,100		

KM# 291 10 DOLLARS
Silver **Ruler:** Elizabeth II **Subject:** Wold Cup Soccer, South Africa

Date	Mintage	F12	VF20	XF40	MS60	MS63
2009	Est. 10000	PF65 55.00				

KM# 292 10 DOLLARS
1.00 g., 0.999 Gold 0.0319 oz. AGW, 13.92 mm. **Ruler:** Elizabeth II **Subject:** World Cup Soccer, South Africa

Date	Mintage	F12	VF20	XF40	MS60	MS63
2009	Est. 5000	PF65 70.00				

KM# 294 10 DOLLARS
28.28 g., 0.925 Silver 0.8356 oz. ASW, 38.61 mm. **Ruler:** Elizabeth II **Rev:** Mary and Christ child

Date	Mintage	F12	VF20	XF40	MS60	MS63
2009	—	PF65 45.00				

KM# 294a 10 DOLLARS
39.00 g., 0.916 Gold 1.1412 oz. AGW, 38.61 mm. **Ruler:** Elizabeth II **Rev:** Mary and Christ child

Date	Mintage	F12	VF20	XF40	MS60	MS63
2009	—	PF63 1,950		PF65 2,100		

KM# 216 10 DOLLARS
0.50 g., 0.999 Gold AGW, 11 mm. **Ruler:** Elizabeth II **Obv:** Head in tiara right **Rev:** Sun, statue and symbol

Date	Mintage	F12	VF20	XF40	MS60	MS63
2010	2,000	PF65 40.00				

KM# 217 10 DOLLARS
0.50 g., 0.999 Gold AGW, 11 mm. **Ruler:** Elizabeth II **Obv:** Head with tiara right **Rev:** Mercury, statue and symbol

Date	Mintage	F12	VF20	XF40	MS60	MS63
2010	2,000	PF65 40.00				

KM# 218 10 DOLLARS
0.50 g., 0.999 Gold AGW, 11 mm. **Ruler:** Elizabeth II **Obv:** Head with tiara right **Rev:** Venus, statue and symbol

Date	Mintage	F12	VF20	XF40	MS60	MS63
2010	2,000	PF65 40.00				

KM# 219 10 DOLLARS
0.50 g., 0.999 Gold AGW, 11 mm. **Ruler:** Elizabeth II **Obv:** Head with tiara right **Rev:** Earth, statue and symbol

Date	Mintage	F12	VF20	XF40	MS60	MS63
2010	2,000	PF65 40.00				

KM# 220 10 DOLLARS
0.50 g., 0.999 Gold AGW, 11 mm. **Ruler:** Elizabeth II **Obv:** Head with tiara right **Rev:** Mars, statue and symbol

Date	Mintage	F12	VF20	XF40	MS60	MS63
2010	2,000	PF65 40.00				

KM# 221 10 DOLLARS
0.50 g., 0.999 Gold AGW, 11 mm. **Ruler:** Elizabeth II **Obv:** Head with tiara right **Rev:** Jupiter, statue and symbol

Date	Mintage	F12	VF20	XF40	MS60	MS63
2010	2,000	PF65 40.00				

KM# 222 10 DOLLARS
0.50 g., 0.999 Gold AGW, 11 mm. **Ruler:** Elizabeth II **Obv:** Head with tiara right **Rev:** Saturn, statue and symbol

Date	Mintage	F12	VF20	XF40	MS60	MS63
2010	2,000	PF65 40.00				

KM# 223 10 DOLLARS
0.50 g., 0.999 Gold AGW, 11 mm. **Ruler:** Elizabeth II **Obv:** Head with tiara right **Rev:** Uranus, statue and symbol

Date	Mintage	F12	VF20	XF40	MS60	MS63
2010	2,000	PF65 40.00				

KM# 224 10 DOLLARS
0.50 g., 0.999 Gold AGW, 11 mm. **Ruler:** Elizabeth II **Obv:** Head with tiara right **Rev:** Neptune, statue and symbol

Date	Mintage	F12	VF20	XF40	MS60	MS63
2010	2,000	PF65 40.00				

KM# 225 10 DOLLARS
0.50 g., 0.999 Gold AGW, 11 mm. **Ruler:** Elizabeth II **Obv:** Head with tiara right **Rev:** Pluto, statue and symbol

Date	Mintage	F12	VF20	XF40	MS60	MS63
2010	2,000	PF65 40.00				

KM# 239 10 DOLLARS
28.28 g., 0.925 Silver 0.8356 oz. ASW, 38.61 mm. **Ruler:** Elizabeth II **Subject:** John Bull, steam locomotive **Obv:** Head with tiara right **Rev:** Steam locomotive left

Date	Mintage	F12	VF20	XF40	MS60	MS63
2010	5,000	PF65 35.00				

KM# 241 10 DOLLARS
28.28 g., 0.925 Silver 0.8356 oz. ASW, 38.61 mm. **Ruler:** Elizabeth II **Subject:** London Olympics, 2012 **Obv:** Head with tiara right **Rev:** Triathlon sports

Date	Mintage	F12	VF20	XF40	MS60	MS63
2010	5,000	PF65 35.00				

KM# 295 10 DOLLARS
0.50 g., 0.999 Gold AGW, 11 mm. **Ruler:** Elizabeth II **Rev:** Eye of Horus

Date	Mintage	F12	VF20	XF40	MS60	MS63
2010	—	PF63 3.00	PF65 35.00			

KM# 296 10 DOLLARS
0.50 g., 0.999 Gold AGW, 11 mm. **Ruler:** Elizabeth II **Rev:** Gold mask of Tutanchamun

Date	Mintage	F12	VF20	XF40	MS60	MS63
2010	—	PF63 32.00	PF65 35.00			

KM# 297 10 DOLLARS
0.50 g., 0.999 Gold AGW, 11 mm. **Ruler:** Elizabeth II **Rev:** Egyptian dog-headed god

Date	Mintage	F12	VF20	XF40	MS60	MS63
2010	—	PF63 32.00	PF65 35.00			

KM# 243 10 DOLLARS
28.28 g., 0.925 Silver 0.8356 oz. ASW, 38.61 mm. **Ruler:** Elizabeth II **Subject:** Etrich II Taube **Obv:** Head with tiara right **Rev:** Early experimental aircraft

Date	Mintage	F12	VF20	XF40	MS60	MS63
2011	5,000	PF63 32.00	PF65 35.00			

KM# 245 10 DOLLARS
28.28 g., 0.925 Silver 0.8356 oz. ASW, 38.6 mm. **Ruler:** Elizabeth II **Subject:** Lady Diana Spencer **Obv:** Head with tiara right **Rev:** Bust at right, gilt rose at left

Date	Mintage	F12	VF20	XF40	MS60	MS63
2011	7,500	PF65 35.00				

KM# 247 10 DOLLARS
28.28 g., 0.925 Silver 0.8356 oz. ASW, 38.61 mm. **Ruler:** Elizabeth II **Subject:** London Olympics, 2012 **Obv:** Head with tiara right **Rev:** Rowing

Date	Mintage	F12	VF20	XF40	MS60	MS63
2011	5,000	PF63 32.00	PF65 35.00			

KM# 249 10 DOLLARS
28.28 g., 0.925 Silver 0.8356 oz. ASW, 38.6 mm. **Ruler:** Elizabeth II **Subject:** Lady Diana **Obv:** Head with tiara right **Rev:** Diana with Prince William and Prince Harry

Date	Mintage	F12	VF20	XF40	MS60	MS63
2011	7,500	PF65 35.00				

KM# 250 10 DOLLARS
28.28 g., 0.925 Silver 0.8356 oz. ASW, 38.6 mm. **Ruler:** Elizabeth II **Subject:** Princess Diana **Obv:** Head with tiara right **Rev:** Diana and AIDS baby, gilt rose at left

Date	Mintage	F12	VF20	XF40	MS60	MS63
2011	7,500	PF65 35.00				

KM# 251 10 DOLLARS
28.28 g., 0.925 Silver 0.8356 oz. ASW, 38.6 mm. **Ruler:** Elizabeth II **Subject:** Lady Diana **Obv:** Head with tiara right **Rev:** Bust left, gilt rose to left

Date	Mintage	F12	VF20	XF40	MS60	MS63
2011	7,500	PF65 35.00				

KM# 298 10 DOLLARS
0.50 g., 0.999 Gold AGW, 11 mm. **Ruler:** Elizabeth II **Rev:** Matterhorn

Date	Mintage	F12	VF20	XF40	MS60	MS63
2011	Est. 5000	PF63 32.00	PF65 35.00			

KM# 299 10 DOLLARS
0.50 g., 0.999 Gold AGW, 11 mm. **Ruler:** Elizabeth II **Rev:** Bay of Halong, Viet Nam

Date	Mintage	F12	VF20	XF40	MS60	MS63
2011	Est. 5000	PF63 32.00	PF65 35.00			

KM# 300 10 DOLLARS
0.50 g., 0.999 Gold AGW, 11 mm. **Ruler:** Elizabeth II **Rev:** Amazon in Brazil

Date	Mintage	F12	VF20	XF40	MS60	MS63
2011	—	PF63 32.00	PF65 35.00			

KM# 301 10 DOLLARS
0.50 g., 0.999 Gold AGW, 11 mm. **Ruler:** Elizabeth II **Rev:** Monument Valley in the USA

Date	Mintage	F12	VF20	XF40	MS60	MS63
2011	Est. 5000	PF63 32.00	PF65 35.00			

KM# 302 10 DOLLARS
0.50 g., 0.999 Gold AGW, 11 mm. **Ruler:** Elizabeth II **Rev:** Pamukkale in Turkey

Date	Mintage	F12	VF20	XF40	MS60	MS63
2011	—	PF63 32.00	PF65 35.00			

KM# 303 10 DOLLARS
0.50 g., 0.999 Gold AGW, 11 mm. **Ruler:** Elizabeth II **Rev:** Mesa in South Africa

Date	Mintage	F12	VF20	XF40	MS60	MS63
2011	Est. 5000	PF63 32.00	PF65 35.00			

KM# 304 10 DOLLARS
0.50 g., 0.999 Gold AGW, 11 mm. **Ruler:** Elizabeth II **Rev:** Namibia feature

Date	Mintage	F12	VF20	XF40	MS60	MS63
2011	—	PF63 32.00	PF65 35.00			

KM# 305 10 DOLLARS
0.50 g., 0.999 Gold AGW, 11 mm. **Ruler:** Elizabeth II **Subject:** Euro motif **Rev:** Map of Estonia

Date	Mintage	F12	VF20	XF40	MS60	MS63
2011	—	PF63 32.00	PF65 35.00			

KM# 198 10 DOLLARS
Silver, 38.61 mm. **Ruler:** Elizabeth II **Obv:** Jewels at center **Rev:** Sunset

Date	Mintage	F12	VF20	XF40	MS60	MS63
2012	—	PF65 60.00				

KM# 199 10 DOLLARS
Silver, 38.6 mm. **Ruler:** Elizabeth II **Obv:** Foral with blue jewel insert as cut out **Rev:** Flowers around blue jewel insert

Date	Mintage	F12	VF20	XF40	MS60	MS63
2012	—	PF65 60.00				

KM# 226 10 DOLLARS
20.00 g., 0.925 Silver 0.591 oz. ASW, 54x32 mm. **Ruler:** Elizabeth II **Subject:** Aztec Calender **Obv:** Head with tiara right, insert at left **Rev:** Aztec design, insert at left **Shape:** Horizontal oval

Date	Mintage	F12	VF20	XF40	MS60	MS63
2012	1,000	—	—	—	—	125

KM# 227 10 DOLLARS
20.00 g., 0.925 Silver 0.591 oz. ASW, 32x54 mm. **Ruler:** Elizabeth II **Obv:** Head in tiara right, insert **Rev:** Atlas holding up world on shoulders, insert **Shape:** Vertical oval

Date	Mintage	F12	VF20	XF40	MS60	MS63
2012	1,000	—	—	—	—	75.00

KM# 230 10 DOLLARS
31.11 g., 0.999 Silver 0.9926 oz. ASW, 40 mm. **Ruler:** Elizabeth II **Subject:** Year of the Dragon **Obv:** Head with tiara right **Rev:** Gilt dragon and pearl

Date	Mintage	F12	VF20	XF40	MS60	MS63
2012	8,888	PF65 100				

KM# 253 10 DOLLARS
20.00 g., 0.999 Silver 0.6382 oz. ASW **Ruler:** Elizabeth II **Subject:** End of World War I **Rev:** Fireworks in color over Kremlin skyline

Date	Mintage	F12	VF20	XF40	MS60	MS63
2012	—	PF65 100				

KM# 308 10 DOLLARS
28.28 g., 0.925 Silver 0.8356 oz. ASW, 38.61 mm. **Ruler:** Elizabeth II **Subject:** 2014 Sochi Olympic Games - Men's Giant Slalom

Date	Mintage	F12	VF20	XF40	MS60	MS63
2012	Est. 5000	PF65 32.00				

KM# 309 10 DOLLARS
20.00 g., 0.925 Silver 0.591 oz. ASW, 38.61 mm. **Ruler:** Elizabeth II **Subject:** 2014 FIFA World Cup Brazil - Colorized Soccer Players

Date	Mintage	F12	VF20	XF40	MS60	MS63
2012	Est. 10000	PF65 28.00				

KM# 310 10 DOLLARS
2.84 g., 0.999 Gold 0.0905 oz. AGW, 16.5 mm. **Ruler:** Elizabeth II **Subject:** 2014 FIFA World Cup Brazil

Date	Mintage	F12	VF20	XF40	MS60	MS63
2012	Est. 1000	PF65 180				

KM# 317 10 DOLLARS
20.00 g., 0.925 Silver 0.591 oz. ASW, 38.61 mm. **Ruler:** Elizabeth II **Subject:** Ruler Series - Constantine the Great

Date	Mintage	F12	VF20	XF40	MS60	MS63
2012	Est. 30000	PF65 28.00				

KM# 321 10 DOLLARS
20.00 g., 0.925 Silver 0.591 oz. ASW, 38.61 mm. **Ruler:** Elizabeth II **Subject:** Intercity Railways in Europe

Date	Mintage	F12	VF20	XF40	MS60	MS63
2012	Est. 5000	PF65 40.00				

KM# 322 10 DOLLARS
28.35 g., 0.999 Silver 0.9047 oz. ASW, 53x36 mm. **Ruler:** Elizabeth II **Subject:** Cities at Night - New York

Date	Mintage	F12	VF20	XF40	MS60	MS63
2012	Est. 3500	PF65 80.00				

KM# 323 10 DOLLARS
28.35 g., 0.999 Silver 0.9047 oz. ASW, 53x36 mm. **Ruler:** Elizabeth II **Subject:** Cities at Night - London

Date	Mintage	F12	VF20	XF40	MS60	MS63
2012	Est. 3500	PF65 80.00				

KM# 324 10 DOLLARS
28.35 g., 0.999 Silver 0.9047 oz. ASW, 53x36 mm. **Ruler:** Elizabeth II **Subject:** Cities at Night - Paris

Date	Mintage	F12	VF20	XF40	MS60	MS63
2012	Est. 3500	PF65 80.00				

KM# 325 10 DOLLARS
20.00 g., 0.999 Silver 0.6382 oz. ASW, 40 mm. **Ruler:** Elizabeth II **Subject:** Kainsaz Russia 1937 Meteorite **Obv:** Bust right above fragments **Rev:** Color application of Kainsaz Meteorite

Date	Mintage	F12	VF20	XF40	MS60	MS63
2012	Est. 999	PF65 65.00				

KM# 326 10 DOLLARS
31.11 g., 0.999 Silver 0.9926 oz. ASW, 38.61 mm. **Ruler:** Elizabeth II **Obv:** Michaelangelo's head gilt

Date	Mintage	F12	VF20	XF40	MS60	MS63
2012	—	PF65 50.00				

KM# 327 10 DOLLARS
31.11 g., 0.999 Silver 0.9926 oz. ASW, 38.61 mm. **Ruler:** Elizabeth II **Subject:** Raphael - gilt bust

Date	Mintage	F12	VF20	XF40	MS60	MS63
2012	—	PF65 50.00				

KM# 329 10 DOLLARS
20.00 g., 0.999 Silver 0.6382 oz. ASW, 40 mm. **Ruler:** Elizabeth II **Subject:** Abee 1952 Meteorite **Rev:** Color application of meteorite

Date	Mintage	F12	VF20	XF40	MS60	MS63
2012	Est. 999	PF65 65.00				

KM# 346 10 DOLLARS
20.00 g., 0.925 Silver 0.591 oz. ASW, 38.61 mm. **Ruler:** Elizabeth II **Subject:** 2016 Olympics - Rugby

Date	Mintage	F12	VF20	XF40	MS60	MS63
2013	Est. 5000	PF63 65.00	PF65 75.00			

KM# 344 10 DOLLARS
31.11 g., 0.999 Silver 0.9926 oz. ASW, 40 mm. **Ruler:** Elizabeth II **Subject:** Year of the Horse **Rev:** Horse head left in color

Date	Mintage	F12	VF20	XF40	MS60	MS63
2014	3,888	PF63 75.00	PF65 85.00			

KM# 345 10 DOLLARS
31.11 g., 0.999 Silver 0.9926 oz. ASW, 40 mm. **Ruler:** Elizabeth II **Subject:** Year of the Horse **Obv:** National arms in center **Rev:** Three gilt horses around center red stone

Date	Mintage	F12	VF20	XF40	MS60	MS63
2014	8,800	PF63 90.00	PF65 100			

KM# 256 20 DOLLARS
Platinum APW **Ruler:** Elizabeth II **Subject:** Elizabeth II, 50th Anniversary of Reign **Rev:** Draped sword

Date	Mintage	F12	VF20	XF40	MS60	MS63
2002 Proof	—	—	—	—	—	—

KM# 257 20 DOLLARS
Platinum APW **Ruler:** Elizabeth II **Subject:** Elizabeth II, 50th Anniversary of Reign **Rev:** Boys Choir in Westminister Abbey

Date	Mintage	F12	VF20	XF40	MS60	MS63
2002 Proof	—	—	—	—	—	—

KM# 231 20 DOLLARS
62.20 g., 0.999 Silver 1.9849 oz. ASW, 50.2 mm. **Ruler:** Elizabeth II **Subject:** Year of the Dragon **Obv:** Head with tiara right **Rev:** Fire Red Dragon with ruby insert

Date	Mintage	F12	VF20	XF40	MS60	MS63
2012	888	PF63 225	PF65 250			

KM# 313 20 DOLLARS
56.70 g., 0.999 Silver 1.8094 oz. ASW, 32x66 mm. **Ruler:** Elizabeth II **Subject:** Painter Series - Colorized Sixtine Madonna (Complete Painting)

Date	Mintage	F12	VF20	XF40	MS60	MS63
2012	—	PF65 100				

KM# 314 20 DOLLARS
56.70 g., 0.999 Silver 1.8094 oz. ASW, 66x32 mm. **Ruler:** Elizabeth II **Subject:** Painter Series - Colorized, Sixtine Madonna (Angels)

Date	Mintage	F12	VF20	XF40	MS60	MS63
2012	Est. 500	PF65 100				

KM# 315 20 DOLLARS
56.70 g., 0.999 Silver 1.8094 oz. ASW, 66x32 mm. **Ruler:** Elizabeth II **Subject:** Painter Series - Colorized, The Creation of Adam

Date	Mintage	F12	VF20	XF40	MS60	MS63
2012	Est. 500	PF65 100				

KM# 316 20 DOLLARS
56.70 g., 0.999 Silver 1.8094 oz. ASW, 66 x 32 mm. **Ruler:** Elizabeth II **Subject:** Painter Series - The Creation of Adam (Hands)

Date	Mintage	F12	VF20	XF40	MS60	MS63
2012	Est. 500	PF65 100				

KM# 348 20 DOLLARS
62.20 g., 0.999 Silver 1.9849 oz. ASW, 50 mm. **Ruler:** Elizabeth II **Subject:** Year of the Snake

Date	Mintage	F12	VF20	XF40	MS60	MS63
2013	Est. 888	PF63 200	PF65 200			

KM# 112 25 DOLLARS
155.50 g., 0.999 Silver 4.9623 oz. ASW **Ruler:** Elizabeth II **Obv:** Crowned head right **Obv. Legend:** ELIZABETH II - FIJI **Rev:** Sailing ship "Vostok

Date	Mintage	F12	VF20	XF40	MS60	MS63
2002	—	PF63 105	PF65 220			

KM# 350 25 DOLLARS
93.30 g., 0.999 Silver 2.9774 oz. ASW, 55 mm. **Ruler:** Elizabeth II **Subject:** 2014 FIFA World Cup - Brazil

Date	Mintage	F12	VF20	XF40	MS60	MS63
2013	Est. 500	PF65 400				

KM# 264 50 DOLLARS
155.00 g., 0.999 Silver 4.9463 oz. ASW, 65 mm. **Ruler:** Elizabeth II **Rev:** Marine life - coral reef

Date	Mintage	F12	VF20	XF40	MS60	MS63
2005	500	PF65 275				

KM# 244 50 DOLLARS
7.78 g., 0.9999 Gold 0.2485 oz. AGW, 22 mm. **Ruler:** Elizabeth II **Subject:** Diana Princess of Wales **Obv:** Head with tiara right **Rev:** Bust right, while colored rose at right

Date	Mintage	F12	VF20	XF40	MS60	MS63
2011	Est. 3000	PF63 450	PF65 475			

KM# 248 50 DOLLARS
7.77 g., 0.5833 Gold 0.1448 oz. AGW, 25 mm. **Ruler:** Elizabeth II **Subject:** London Olympics, 2012 **Obv:** Head with tiara right **Rev:** Rowing

Date	Mintage	F12	VF20	XF40	MS60	MS63
2011	1,000	PF65 325				

KM# 196 50 DOLLARS
155.50 g., 0.999 Silver 4.9623 oz. ASW, 65 mm. **Ruler:** Elizabeth II **Subject:** Year of the Dragon **Obv:** Head crowned right **Rev:** Dragon etched in mother of pearl

Date	Mintage	F12	VF20	XF40	MS60	MS63
2012	750	PF65 400				

KM# 197 50 DOLLARS
155.50 g., 0.999 Silver 4.9623 oz. ASW, 65 mm. **Ruler:** Elizabeth II **Obv:** Head crowned right **Rev:** Titanic etched mother of pearl

Date	Mintage	F12	VF20	XF40	MS60	MS63
2012	750	PF65 450				

KM# 228 50 DOLLARS
62.20 g., 0.999 Silver 1.9849 oz. ASW, 65 mm. **Ruler:** Elizabeth II **Obv:** Head in tiara right **Rev:** Tutankhamun in color

Date	Mintage	F12	VF20	XF40	MS60	MS63
2012	999	PF63 175	PF65 200			

KM# 229 50 DOLLARS
62.20 g., 0.999 Silver 1.9849 oz. ASW, 65 mm. **Ruler:** Elizabeth II **Obv:** Head in tiara right **Rev:** Neferititi head in color

Date	Mintage	F12	VF20	XF40	MS60	MS63
2012	999	PF63 175	PF65 200			

KM# 306 50 DOLLARS
155.50 g., 0.999 Silver 4.9623 oz. ASW, 65 mm. **Ruler:** Elizabeth II **Rev:** Dragon with the pearl of wisdom in gold

Date	Mintage	F12	VF20	XF40	MS60	MS63
2012	888	PF63 225	PF65 250			

KM# 312 50 DOLLARS
155.50 g., 0.999 Silver 4.9623 oz. ASW, 65 mm. **Ruler:** Elizabeth II **Subject:** Lunar Year of the Dragon with Mother of Pearl Inlay

Date	Mintage	F12	VF20	XF40	MS60	MS63
2012	—	PF65 250				

KM# 99 100 DOLLARS
7.78 g., 0.585 Gold 0.1454 oz. AGW **Ruler:** Elizabeth II **Subject:** 2006 FIFA World Cup - Germany **Obv:** Crowned head right, date at right **Rev:** World Cup **Edge:** Reeded

Date	Mintage	F12	VF20	XF40	MS60	MS63
2003	25,000	PF63 250	PF65 275			

KM# 347 200 DOLLARS
31.11 g., 0.999 Gold 0.9926 oz. AGW, 38.61 mm. **Ruler:** Elizabeth II **Subject:** 2014 FIFA World Cup - Brazil

Date	Mintage	F12	VF20	XF40	MS60	MS63
2013	Est. 150	PF63 1,500	PF65 1,500			

KM# 311 1000 DOLLARS
141.75 g., 0.999 Gold 4.5235 oz. AGW, 65 mm. **Ruler:** Elizabeth II **Subject:** R.M.S. Titanic with Blue Mother of Pearl

Date	Mintage	F12	VF20	XF40	MS60	MS63
2012	Est. 25	PF65 9,600				

SILVER BULLION COINAGE

KM# 211 DOLLAR
15.50 g., 0.999 Silver 0.4946 oz. ASW, 32.5 mm. **Ruler:** Elizabeth II **Obv:** Head with crown right **Rev:** Hawksbill turtle

Date	Mintage	F12	VF20	XF40	MS60	MS63
2012 Prooflike	—					22.50

KM# 151a 2 DOLLARS
31.11 g., 0.999 Silver 0.9926 oz. ASW, 40 mm. **Ruler:** Elizabeth II **Rev:** Hawksbill Taku Turtle, gilt

Date	Mintage	F12	VF20	XF40	MS60	MS63
2010	Est. 5000	PF65 65.00				
2012		PF65 65.00				

KM# 151 2 DOLLARS
31.11 g., 0.999 Silver 0.9926 oz. ASW, 40.5 mm. **Ruler:** Elizabeth II **Rev:** Hawksbill Taku Turtle

Date	Mintage	F12	VF20	XF40	MS60	MS63
2010 Prooflike	—	—	—	—	—	50.00
2011 Prooflike	—	—	—	—	—	50.00
2012 Prooflike	—	—	—	—	—	50.00

KM# 165 2 DOLLARS
31.11 g., 0.999 Silver 0.9926 oz. ASW, 40.7 mm. **Ruler:** Elizabeth II **Rev:** Pacific Swordfish gilt

Date	Mintage	F12	VF20	XF40	MS60	MS63
2011 Prooflike	5,000	—	—	—	—	80.00

KM# 232 10 DOLLARS
155.50 g., 0.999 Silver 4.9623 oz. ASW **Ruler:** Elizabeth II **Obv:** Head with tiara right **Rev:** Hawksbill turtle

Date	Mintage	F12	VF20	XF40	MS60	MS63
2012 Prooflike	—	—	—	—	—	185

GOLD BULLION COINAGE

KM# 136 PACIFIC SOVEREIGN
31.11 g., 0.999 Gold 0.9926 oz. AGW, 32 mm. **Ruler:** Elizabeth II **Rev:** Beach scene, two palm trees at right

Date	Mintage	F12	VF20	XF40	MS60	MS63
2009 Proof-like	—	—	—	—	—	1,650

KM# 215 PACIFIC SOVEREIGN
31.14 g., 0.999 Gold 0.9936 oz. AGW, 32.1 mm. **Ruler:** Elizabeth II **Obv:** Head crowned right **Rev:** Beach scene, one palm tree at left

Date	Mintage	F12	VF20	XF40	MS60	MS63
2011	—	PF63 1,700	PF65 1,800			

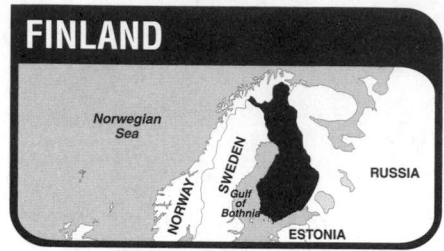

FINLAND

The Republic of Finland, the third most northerly state of the European continent, has an area of 130,559 sq. mi. (338,127 sq. km.) and a population of 5.1 million. Capital: Helsinki. Lumbering, shipbuilding, metal and woodworking are the leading industries. Paper, timber, wood pulp, plywood and metal products are exported.

MONETARY SYSTEM
100 Pennia = 1 Markka until 2001
100 Euro Cent = 1 Euro 2001 -
MINT MARKS
H - Birmingham 1921Heart
(h) - Copenhagen 1922No mm – Helsinki
M – 1987-2006
FI – FINLAND – 2007-
Rampant lion in a circle – 2010-

MINT OFFICIALS' INITIALS

Letter Date		Name
J-M	2002	Toivo Jaatinen & Raimo Makkonen
L-M	2000-03	Maija Lavonen & Raimo Makkonen
K-M	2004	Heli Kauhanen & Raimo Makkonen
K-M	2005-2006	Tapio Kettunen & Raimo Makkonen
M-M	2002-2006	Pertti Mäkinen & Raimo Makkone
N-M	2001	Antti Neuvonen & Raimo Makkonen
P-M	2003	Matti Peltokangas & Raimo Makkonen
P-M	2001, 2005-2007	Reijo Paavilainen & Raimo Makkonen
S-M	2003	Anneli Sigriläinen & Raimo Makkonen
V-M	2002	Erikki Vainio & Hannu Veijalainen & Raimo Makkonen

REPUBLIC

REFORM COINAGE
100 Old Markkaa = 1 New Markkaa 1963

KM# 65 10 PENNI'A'
1.80 g., Copper-Nickel, 16.3 mm. **Obv:** Flower pods and stems, date at right **Rev:** Denomination to right of honeycombs

Date	Mintage	F12	VF20	XF40	MS60	MS63
2001 M	25,000,000	—	—	—	1.00	1.50
2001 M		PF60 7.00				

KM# 66 50 PENNI'A'
3.30 g., Copper-Nickel, 19.7 mm. **Obv:** Polar bear, date below **Rev:** Denomination above flower heads **Edge:** Reeded

Date	Mintage	F12	VF20	XF40	MS60	MS63
2001 M	200,000	—	—	0.20	1.00	1.50
2001 M		PF60 8.00				

KM# 76 MARKKA
5.00 g., Aluminum-Bronze, 22.2 mm. **Obv:** Rampant lion left within circle, date below **Rev:** Ornaments flank denomination within circle

Date	Mintage	F12	VF20	XF40	MS60	MS63
2001 M	200,000	—	—	0.50	1.00	1.50
2001 M		PF60 10.00				

KM# 95 MARKKA
8.64 g., 0.750 Gold 0.207 oz. AGW, 22 mm. **Subject:** Last

Markka Coin Obv: Rampant lion with sword left **Rev:** Stylized tree with roots **Edge:** Reeded

Date	Mintage	F12	VF20	XF40	MS60	MS63
2001 P-M	55,000	PF63 350	PF65 375			

KM# 106 MARKKA
6.10 g., Copper-Nickel, 24 mm. **Subject:** Remembrance Markka **Obv:** Rampant lion with sword left **Rev:** Denomination and pine tree **Edge:** Plain **Note:** This coin is encased in acrylic resin and sealed in a display card.

Date	Mintage	F12	VF20	XF40	MS60	MS63
2001M N-M	500,000	—			5.00	6.50

KM# 73 5 MARKKAA
5.50 g., Copper-Aluminum-Nickel, 24.5 mm. **Obv:** Lake Saimaa ringed seal, date below **Rev:** Denomination, dragonfly and lily pad leaves

Date	Mintage	F12	VF20	XF40	MS60	MS63
2001 M	200,000	—	—	—	2.00	3.00
2001 M		PF60 12.00				

KM# 77 10 MARKKAA
8.80 g., Bi-Metallic, 27.25 mm. **Obv:** Capercaillie bird within circle, date above **Rev:** Denomination and branches

Date	Mintage	F12	VF20	XF40	MS60	MS63
2001 M	200,000	—	—	2.00	3.00	4.00
2001 M		PF60 18.00				

KM# 96 25 MARKKAA
20.20 g., Bi-Metallic, 35 mm. **Subject:** First Nordic Ski Championship, "Lahti 2001 **Obv:** Stylized woman's face **Rev:** Female torso, landscape **Edge:** Plain

Date	Mintage	F12	VF20	XF40	MS60	MS63
2001M Prooflike	100,000	—	—	25.00	30.00	35.00

KM# 97 100 MARKKAA
31.00 g., 0.925 Silver 0.916 oz. ASW, 35 mm. **Subject:** Aino Ackte **Obv:** Partial portrait **Rev:** High heel boot and trouser bottom **Edge:** Plain

Date	Mintage	F12	VF20	XF40	MS60	MS63
2001M	33,000	—	—	—	32.00	45.00
2001M	12,000	PF63 60.00	PF65 70.00			

EURO COINAGE
European Union Issues

KM# 98 EURO CENT
2.30 g., Copper Plated Steel, 16.25 mm. **Obv:** Rampant lion left surrounded by stars, date at left **Rev:** Denomination and globe **Edge:** Plain

Date	Mintage	F12	VF20	XF40	MS60	MS63
2001M	500,000	—	—	—	10.00	
2001M Proof	15,000	—	—	—		
2002M	659,000	—	—	—	5.00	
2002M	13,000	PF63 15.00				
2003M	6,790,000	—	—	—	1.00	

Column 1 (top table - continuation):

Date	Mintage	F12	VF20	XF40	MS60	MS63
2003M	14,500	PF63 15.00				
2004M	9,690,000	—	—	—	1.00	—
2004M	5,000	PF63 15.00				
2005M	5,800,000	—	—	—	1.00	—
2005M	3,000	PF63 15.00				
2006M	4,000,000	—	—	—	1.00	—
2006M	3,300	PF63 15.00				
2007FI	3,000,000	—	—	—	1.00	—
2007FI	—	PF63 15.00				
2008FI	1,500,000	—	—	—	1.00	—
2008FI	2,500	PF63 15.00				
2009FI	936,500	—	—	—	1.00	—
2009FI	2,500	PF63 15.00				
2010FI	738,000	—	—	—	1.00	—
2010FI	2,000	PF63 15.00				
2011FI	755,000	—	—	—	1.00	—
2011FI	755,000	PF63 15.00				
2012FI	724,000	—	—	—	1.00	—
2012FI	724,000	PF63 15.00				
2013FI	—	—	—	—	1.00	—
2013FI	—	PF63 15.00				

KM# 99 2 EURO CENT
3.06 g., Copper Plated Steel, 18.75 mm. **Obv:** Rampant lion surrounded by stars, date at left **Rev:** Denomination and globe **Edge:** Grooved

Date	Mintage	F12	VF20	XF40	MS60	MS63
2001M	500,000	—	—	—	10.00	—
2001M	15,000	PF63 15.00				
2002M	659,000	—	—	—	5.00	—
2002M	13,000	PF63 15.00				
2003M	6,790,000	—	—	—	2.00	—
2003M	14,500	PF63 15.00				
2004M	8,024,000	—	—	—	2.00	—
2004M	5,000	PF63 15.00				
2005M	5,800,000	—	—	—	2.50	—
2005M	3,000	PF63 15.00				
2006M	4,000,000	—	—	—	2.00	—
2006M	3,300	PF63 15.00				
2007FI	3,000,000	—	—	—	2.00	—
2007FI	—	PF63 15.00				
2008FI	1,500,000	—	—	—	2.00	—
2008FI	2,500	PF63 15.00				
2009FI	936,500	—	—	—	2.00	—
2009FI	2,500	PF63 15.00				
2010FI	738,000	—	—	—	2.00	—
2010FI	2,000	PF63 15.00				
2011FI	755,000	—	—	—	3.00	—
2011FI	—	PF63 15.00				
2012FI	—	—	—	—	3.00	—
2012FI	724,000	PF63 15.00				
2013FI	—	—	—	—	3.00	—
2013FI	—	PF63 15.00				

KM# 100 5 EURO CENT
3.92 g., Copper Plated Steel, 21.25 mm. **Obv:** Rampant lion left surrounded by stars, date at left **Rev:** Denomination and globe **Edge:** Plain

Date	Mintage	F12	VF20	XF40	MS60	MS63
2001M	213,756,000	—	—	—	0.50	—
2001M	15,000	PF63 15.00				
2002M	101,824,000	—	—	—	0.50	—
2002M	13,000	PF63 15.00				
2003M	790,000	—	—	—	2.00	—
2003M	14,500	PF63 15.00				
2004M	629,000	—	—	—	2.00	—
2004M	5,000	PF63 15.00				
2005M	800,000	—	—	—	2.00	—
2005M	3,000	PF63 15.00				
2006M	1,000,000	—	—	—	1.00	—
2006M	3,000	PF63 15.00				
2007FI	1,000,000	—	—	—	1.00	—
2007FI	—	PF63 15.00				
2008FI	1,000,000	—	—	—	1.00	—
2008FI	2,500	PF63 15.00				
2009FI	936,500	—	—	—	1.00	—
2009FI	2,500	PF63 15.00				
2010FI	738,000	—	—	—	1.00	—
2010FI	2,000	PF63 15.00				
2011FI	755,000	—	—	—	1.00	—
2011FI	—	PF63 15.00				
2012FI	—	—	—	—	1.00	—
2012FI	724,000	PF63 15.00				

Date	Mintage	F12	VF20	XF40	MS60	MS63
2013FI	—	—	—	—	1.00	—
2013FI	—	PF63 15.00				

KM# 101 10 EURO CENT
4.10 g., Brass, 19.75 mm. **Obv:** Rampant lion left surrounded by stars, date at left **Rev:** Denomination and map **Edge:** Reeded

Date	Mintage	F12	VF20	XF40	MS60	MS63
2001M	14,730,000	—	—	—	10.00	—
2001M	15,000	PF63 18.00				
2002M	1,499,000	—	—	—	10.00	—
2002M	13,000	PF63 18.00				
2003M	790,000	—	—	—	5.00	—
2003M	14,500	PF63 18.00				
2004M	629,000	—	—	—	5.00	—
2004M	5,000	PF63 18.00				
2005M	800,000	—	—	—	3.00	—
2005M	3,000	PF63 18.00				
2006M	1,000,000	—	—	—	3.00	—
2006M	3,300	PF63 18.00				

KM# 126 10 EURO CENT
4.10 g., Brass, 19.75 mm. **Obv:** Rampant lion surrounded by stars **Rev:** Relief map of Western Europe, stars, lines and value **Edge:** Reeded **Note:** In different years, varieties exist in the position of the mint mark and mintmaster symbols.

Date	Mintage	F12	VF20	XF40	MS60	MS63
2007FI	1,000,000	—	—	—	2.50	—
2007FI	—	PF63 18.00				
2008FI	1,000,000	—	—	—	2.50	—
2008FI	2,500	PF63 18.00				
2009FI	936,500	—	—	—	2.50	—
2009FI	2,500	PF63 18.00				
2010FI	730,000	—	—	—	2.50	—
2010FI	2,000	PF63 18.00				
2011FI	—	—	—	—	2.50	—
2011FI	755,000	PF63 18.00				
2012FI	10,724,000	—	—	—	2.50	—
2012FI	—	PF63 18.00				
2013FI	—	—	—	—	2.50	—
2013FI	—	PF63 18.00				

KM# 102 20 EURO CENT
5.74 g., Brass, 22.25 mm. **Obv:** Rampant lion left surrounded by stars, date at left **Rev:** Denomination and map **Edge:** Notched

Date	Mintage	F12	VF20	XF40	MS60	MS63
2001M	121,763,000	—	—	—	2.00	—
2001M	15,000	PF63 20.00				
2002M	100,759,000	—	—	—	2.00	—
2002M	13,000	PF63 20.00				
2003M	790,000	—	—	—	3.00	—
2003M	14,500	PF63 20.00				
2004M	629,000	—	—	—	3.00	—
2004M	5,000	PF63 20.00				
2005M	800,000	—	—	—	3.00	—
2005M	3,000	PF63 20.00				
2006M	1,000,000	—	—	—	2.00	—
2006M	3,300	PF63 20.00				

KM# 127 20 EURO CENT
5.74 g., Brass, 22.25 mm. **Obv:** Rampant lion surrounded by stars **Rev:** Relief map of Western Europe, stars, lines and value **Edge:** Notched

Date	Mintage	F12	VF20	XF40	MS60	MS63
2007FI	1,000,000	—	—	—	2.00	—
2007FI	—	PF63 20.00				
2008FI	1,000,000	—	—	—	2.00	—
2008FI	2,500	PF63 20.00				
2009FI	936,500	—	—	—	2.00	—
2009FI	2,500	PF63 20.00				
2010FI	738,000	—	—	—	1.75	—
2010FI	2,000	PF63 20.00				
2011FI	8,755,000	—	—	—	1.75	—
2011FI	—	PF63 20.00				
2012FI	10,724,000	—	—	—	1.75	—
2012FI	—	PF63 20.00				
2013FI	—	—	—	—	1.75	—
2013FI	—	PF63 20.00				

KM# 103 50 EURO CENT
7.80 g., Brass, 24.25 mm. **Obv:** Rampant lion left surrounded by stars, date at left **Rev:** Denomination and map **Edge:** Reeded

Date	Mintage	F12	VF20	XF40	MS60	MS63
2001M	4,432,000	—	—	—	5.00	—

Date	Mintage	F12	VF20	XF40	MS60	MS63
2001M	15,000	PF63 22.00				
2002M	1,147,000	—	—	—	10.00	—
2002M	13,000	PF63 22.00				
2003M	790,000	—	—	—	5.00	—
2003M	14,500	PF63 22.00				
2004M	629,000	—	—	—	5.00	—
2004M	5,000	PF63 22.00				
2005M	4,800,000	—	—	—	5.00	—
2005M	3,000	PF63 22.00				
2006M	6,850,000	—	—	—	3.00	—
2006M	3,300	PF63 22.00				

KM# 128 50 EURO CENT
7.80 g., Brass, 24.25 mm. **Obv:** Rampant lion surrounded by stars **Rev:** Relief map of Western Europe, stars, lines and value **Edge:** Reeded

Date	Mintage	F12	VF20	XF40	MS60	MS63
2007FI	1,000,000	—	—	—	3.00	—
2007FI	—	PF63 22.00				
2008FI	8,000,000	—	—	—	3.00	—
2008FI	2,500	PF63 22.00				
2009FI	6,936,500	—	—	—	3.00	—
2009FI	2,500	PF63 22.00				
2010FI	738,000	—	—	—	3.00	—
2010FI	2,000	PF63 22.00				
2011FI	—	—	—	—	5.00	—
2011FI	3,755,000	PF63 22.00				
2012FI	4,724,000	—	—	—	3.00	—
2012FI	—	PF63 22.00				
2013FI	—	—	—	—	5.00	—
2013FI	—	PF63 22.00				

KM# 104 EURO
7.50 g., Bi-Metallic, 23.25 mm. **Obv:** 2 flying swans, date below, surrounded by stars on outer ring **Rev:** Denomination and map **Edge:** Segmented reeding

Date	Mintage	F12	VF20	XF40	MS60	MS63
2001M	13,862,000	—	—	—	5.00	—
2001M	15,000	PF63 25.00				
2002M	14,114,000	—	—	—	5.00	—
2002M	13,000	PF63 25.00				
2003M	790,000	—	—	—	10.00	—
2003M	14,500	PF63 25.00				
2004M	5,529,000	—	—	—	6.50	—
2004M	5,000	PF63 25.00				
2005M	7,935,000	—	—	—	6.50	—
2005M	3,000	PF63 25.00				
2006M	1,705,000	—	—	—	5.00	—
2006M	3,300	PF63 25.00				

KM# 129 EURO
7.50 g., Bi-Metallic, 23.25 mm. **Obv:** 2 flying swans surrounded by stars on outer ring **Rev:** Relief map of western Europe, stars, lines and value **Edge:** Segmented reeding **Note:** In different years, varieties exist in the position of the mint mark and mintmaster symbols.

Date	Mintage	F12	VF20	XF40	MS60	MS63
2007FI	1,000,000	—	—	—	5.00	—
2007FI	—	PF63 25.00				
2008FI	1,000,000	—	—	—	5.00	—
2008FI	2,500	PF63 25.00				
2009FI	936,500	—	—	—	5.00	—
2009FI	2,500	PF63 25.00				
2010FI	738,000	—	—	—	5.00	—
2010FI	2,000	PF63 25.00				
2011FI	755,000	—	—	—	6.50	—
2011FI	—	PF63 25.00				
2012FI	724,000	—	—	—	6.50	—
2012FI	—	PF63 25.00				
2013FI	—	—	—	—	6.50	—
2013FI	—	PF63 25.00				

KM# 105 2 EURO
8.50 g., Bi-Metallic, 25.75 mm. **Obv:** 2 cloudberry flowers surrounded by stars on outer ring **Rev:** Denomination and map **Edge:** Reeded and lettered **Edge Lettering:** SUOMI FINLAND

Date	Mintage	F12	VF20	XF40	MS60	MS63
2001M	29,132,000	—	—	—	5.00	—
2001M	15,000	PF63 30.00				
2002M	1,386,000	—	—	—	15.00	—

Date	Mintage	F12	VF20	XF40	MS60	MS63
2002M	13,000	PF63 30.00				
2003M	9,080,000	—	—	—	7.50	—
2003M	14,500	PF63 30.00				
2004M	10,029,000	—	—	—	7.00	—
2004M	5,000	PF63 30.00				
2005M	10,800,000	—	—	—	7.00	—
2005M	3,000	PF63 30.00				
2006M	11,000,000	—	—	—	5.00	—
2006M	3,300	PF63 30.00				

KM# 114 2 EURO
8.50 g., Bi-Metallic, 25.75 mm. **Subject:** EU Expansion **Obv:** Stylized flower **Rev:** Denomination and map **Edge:** Reeded and lettered

Date	Mintage	F12	VF20	XF40	MS60	MS63
2004M M	1,000,000	—	—	—	30.00	11.50
2004M M Proof	—	—	—	—	—	—

KM# 119 2 EURO
8.50 g., Bi-Metallic, 25.75 mm. **Subject:** 60th Anniversary - Finland - UN **Obv:** Dove on a puzzle **Rev:** Denomination over map **Edge Lettering:** YK 1945-2005 FN

Date	Mintage	F12	VF20	XF40	MS60	MS63
2005M K	2,000,000	—	—	—	6.00	7.50

KM# 125 2 EURO
8.50 g., Bi-Metallic, 25.75 mm. **Subject:** Centennial of Universal Suffrage **Obv:** Two faces **Rev:** Value and map **Edge Lettering:** SUOMI FINLAND

Date	Mintage	F12	VF20	XF40	MS60	MS63
2006M M	2,500,000	—	—	—	6.00	7.50

KM# 130 2 EURO
8.50 g., Bi-Metallic, 25.75 mm. **Obv:** 2 cloudberry flowers surrounded by stars on outer ring **Rev:** Relief map of Western Europe, stars, lines and value **Edge:** Reeded and lettered **Edge Lettering:** SUOMI FINLAND

Date	Mintage	F12	VF20	XF40	MS60	MS63
2006M Error die pairing	—	—	—	50.00	75.00	100
2007FI	8,600,000	—	—	—	6.00	7.50
2007FI	—	PF63 30.00				
2008FI	9,800,000	—	—	—	6.00	7.50
2008FI	2,500	PF63 30.00				
2009FI	6,256,500	—	—	—	6.00	7.50
2009FI	2,500	PF63 30.00				
2010FI	3,938,000	—	—	—	6.00	7.50
2010FI	2,000	PF63 30.00				
2011FI	5,155,000	—	—	—	6.00	7.50
2011FI	—	PF63 30.00				
2012FI	—	—	—	—	6.00	7.50
2012FI	3,234,000	PF63 30.00				
2013FI	—	—	—	—	6.00	7.50
2013FI	—	PF63 30.00				

KM# 139 2 EURO
8.50 g., Bi-Metallic, 25.75 mm. **Subject:** 90th Anniversary of Independence **Obv:** Longboat rowing together **Edge:** Reeded and lettered

Date	Mintage	F12	VF20	XF40	MS60	MS63
2007M	2,000,000	—	—	—	—	6.00
2007M	20,000	PF65 20.00				

KM# 138 2 EURO
8.50 g., Bi-Metallic, 25.75 mm. **Subject:** 50th Anniversary Treaty of Rome **Obv:** Open treaty book **Rev:** Large value at left, modified outline of Europe at right **Edge:** Reeded and lettered

Date	Mintage	F12	VF20	XF40	MS60	MS63
2007	—	—	—	—	7.00	9.00
2007	—	PF65 75.00				

KM# 143 2 EURO
8.50 g., Bi-Metallic, 25.75 mm. **Subject:** Universal Declaration of Human Rights **Obv:** Human figure within heart in landscape **Rev:** Segmented reeding

Date	Mintage	F12	VF20	XF40	MS60	MS63
2008	2,500,000	—	—	—	6.00	7.50
2008	2,500	PF63 22.00	PF65 25.00			

KM# 149 2 EURO
8.50 g., Bi-Metallic, 25.75 mm. **Subject:** Finnish Autonomy, 200th Anniversary **Obv:** Classical Pyramid **Edge:** Lettered

Date	Mintage	F12	VF20	XF40	MS60	MS63
2009	2,500	PF63 25.00	PF65 30.00			
2009	1,600,000	—	—	—	6.00	7.50

KM# 144 2 EURO
8.50 g., Bi-Metallic, 25.75 mm. **Subject:** EMU 10th Anniversary **Obv:** Stick figure and E symbol **Edge:** Reeded and lettered

Date	Mintage	F12	VF20	XF40	MS60	MS63
2009	25,000	PF63 28.00	PF65 30.00			
2009	1,400,000	—	—	—	6.00	7.50

KM# 154 2 EURO
8.50 g., Bi-Metallic, 25.75 mm. **Subject:** Finnish Currency, 150th Anniversary

Date	Mintage	F12	VF20	XF40	MS60	MS63
2010	25,000	PF63 25.00	PF65 30.00			
2010	1,600,000	—	—	—	6.00	7.50

KM# 163 2 EURO
8.50 g., Bi-Metallic, 25.75 mm. **Subject:** Bank of Finland, 200th Anniversary **Obv:** Swan in Flight

Date	Mintage	F12	VF20	XF40	MS60	MS63
2011	25,000	PF63 25.00	PF65 30.00			
2011	—	—	—	—	6.00	7.50

KM# 178 2 EURO
8.50 g., Bi-Metallic, 25.75 mm. **Subject:** Euro coinage, 10th Anniversary **Obv:** Euro symbol on globe at center, child-like rendering around

Date	Mintage	F12	VF20	XF40	MS60	MS63
2012M Special Unc.	—	—	—	—	—	15.00
2012M	1,500,000	—	—	—	6.00	8.00
2012	25,000	PF63 20.00	PF65 25.00			

KM# 182 2 EURO
8.50 g., Bi-Metallic, 25.75 mm. **Subject:** Helene Schjerfbeck, 150th Anniversary of Birth **Obv:** Helene Schjerfbeck

Date	Mintage	F12	VF20	XF40	MS60	MS63
2012	13,000	PF63 25.00	PF65 30.00			
2012	1,987,000	—	—	—	6.00	7.50

KM# 190 2 EURO
8.50 g., Bi-Metallic, 25.75 mm. **Subject:** Finnish Parliament

Date	Mintage	F12	VF20	XF40	MS60	MS63
2013	—	—	—	—	7.00	8.00

KM# 193 2 EURO
8.50 g., Bi-Metallic, 25.75 mm. **Subject:** Frans Eemil Sillanpaa, 125th Anniversary of Birth

Date	Mintage	F12	VF20	XF40	MS60	MS63
2013	1,000,000	—	—	—	6.00	8.00
2013	11,000	PF63 30.00	PF65 35.00			

KM# 194 2 EURO
8.50 g., Bi-Metallic, 25.75 mm. **Subject:** Parliament, 150th Anniversary **Obv:** Stylized 1863 date

Date	Mintage	F12	VF20	XF40	MS60	MS63
2013	989,000	—	—	—	6.00	8.00
2013	11,000	PF63 30.00	PF65 35.00			

KM# 111 5 EURO
20.10 g., Bi-Metallic, 34.9 mm. **Subject:** Ice Hockey World Championships **Obv:** Summer landscape and denomination **Rev:** Three hockey sticks and a puck **Edge:** Plain

Date	Mintage	F12	VF20	XF40	MS60	MS63
2003M M-M	150,000	—	—	—	25.00	30.00

KM# 118 5 EURO
19.80 g., Bi-Metallic, 35 mm. **Subject:** 10th Anniversary - IAAF World Championships in Athletics **Obv:** Female javelin thrower, denomination **Rev:** Running feet **Edge:** Plain

Date	Mintage	F12	VF20	XF40	MS60	MS63
2005M K-M	170,000	—	—	—	15.00	20.00
2005M K-M	5,000	PF63 25.00		PF65 30.00		

KM# 123 5 EURO
18.70 g., Brass, 35 mm. **Subject:** 150th Anniversary - Demilitarization of Aland **Obv:** Boat, Dove of Peace on the helm **Rev:** Tree **Edge Lettering:** AHVENANMAAN DEMILITARISOINTI 150 VUOTTA*

Date	Mintage	F12	VF20	XF40	MS60	MS63
2006 M-M	55,000	—	—	—	20.00	25.00

KM# 131 5 EURO
9.81 g., Bi-Metallic, 27.25 mm. **Subject:** Finland Presidency of European Union **Obv:** Letter decorations with 2006 and SUOMI-FINLAND **Rev:** 5 EURO below letter decoration

Date	Mintage	F12	VF20	XF40	MS60	MS63
2006M P-M	100,000	—	—	—	15.00	20.00

KM# 146 5 EURO
19.81 g., Bi-Metallic, 35 mm. **Subject:** Independence, 90th Anniversary **Obv:** Potroglif of a longboat

Date	Mintage	F12	VF20	XF40	MS60	MS63
2007P	20,000	PF63 30.00		PF65 35.00		
2007P	130,000	—	—	—	—	15.00

KM# 135 5 EURO
19.81 g., Bi-Metallic, 35 mm. **Subject:** 90th Anniversary of Finland's Independence

Date	Mintage	F12	VF20	XF40	MS60	MS63
2007 P	130,000	—	—	—	15.00	20.00
2007 P	20,000	PF63 25.00		PF65 30.00		

KM# 141 5 EURO
19.81 g., Bi-Metallic, 35 mm. **Subject:** Science and Research

Date	Mintage	F12	VF20	XF40	MS60	MS63
2008K	20,000	PF63 25.00		PF65 30.00		
2008K	25,000	—	—	—	15.00	20.00

KM# 158 5 EURO
9.80 g., Bi-Metallic, 27.5 mm. **Subject:** Provinces - Varsinais - Suomi

Date	Mintage	F12	VF20	XF40	MS60	MS63
2010T	90,000	—	—	—	—	12.00
2010T	30,000	PF63 25.00		PF65 30.00		

KM# 156 5 EURO
9.80 g., Bi-Metallic, 27.25 mm. **Subject:** Provinces - Satakunta

Date	Mintage	F12	VF20	XF40	MS60	MS63
2010T	—	—	—	—	—	12.00
2010T	—	PF63 25.00		PF65 30.00		

KM# 159 5 EURO
9.80 g., Bi-Metallic, 27.25 mm. **Subject:** Provinces - Karjala **Rev:** Shield

Date	Mintage	F12	VF20	XF40	MS60	MS63
2011T	20,000	PF63 25.00		PF65 30.00		
2011T	100,000	—	—	—	13.00	15.00

KM# 176 5 EURO
9.80 g., Bi-Metallic, 27.25 mm. **Subject:** Provinces-Karjala **Rev:** Shield

Date	Mintage	F12	VF20	XF40	MS60	MS63
2011T	20,000	PF63 30.00		PF65 35.00		
2011T	100,000	—	—	—	—	25.00

KM# 177 5 EURO
9.80 g., Bi-Metallic, 27.25 mm. **Series:** Provinces - Ahvenamnas **Obv:** Needle sewing fishing net **Rev:** Shield

Date	Mintage	F12	VF20	XF40	MS60	MS63
2011T	20,000	PF63 25.00		PF65 30.00		
2011T	100,000	—	—	—	—	18.00

KM# 160 5 EURO
9.80 g., Bi-Metallic, 27.5 mm. **Subject:** Provinces - Uusimaa

Date	Mintage	F12	VF20	XF40	MS60	MS63
2011T	100,000	—	—	—	15.00	20.00
2011T	20,000	PF63 25.00		PF65 30.00		

KM# 161 5 EURO
9.80 g., Bi-Metallic, 27.5 mm. **Subject:** Provinces - Häme

Date	Mintage	F12	VF20	XF40	MS60	MS63
2011T	100,000	—	—	—	—	12.00
2011T	20,000	PF63 20.00		PF65 25.00		

KM# 162 5 EURO
9.80 g., Bi-Metallic, 27.5 mm. **Subject:** Provinces - Savo

Date	Mintage	F12	VF20	XF40	MS60	MS63
2011T	100,000	—	—	—	15.00	20.00
2011T	20,000	PF63 25.00		PF65 30.00		

KM# 170 5 EURO
9.80 g., Bi-Metallic, 27.25 mm. **Subject:** Provinces - Lappi **Obv:** Shield **Rev:** Antler

Date	Mintage	F12	VF20	XF40	MS60	MS63
2011T	100,000	—	—	—	13.00	15.00
2011T	20,000	PF63 25.00		PF65 30.00		

KM# 171 5 EURO
9.80 g., Bi-Metallic, 27.25 mm. **Subject:** Provinces - Pohjanmea **Obv:** Shield **Rev:** Wood

Date	Mintage	F12	VF20	XF40	MS60	MS63
2011T	—	—	—	—	—	12.00
2011T	—	PF63 25.00		PF65 30.00		

KM# 175 5 EURO
9.80 g., Bi-Metallic, 27.25 mm. **Subject:** Provinces - Häme **Rev:** Shield

Date	Mintage	F12	VF20	XF40	MS60	MS63
2011T	100,000	—	—	—	—	25.00
2011T	20,000	PF63 30.00		PF65 35.00		

KM# 181 5 EURO
9.00 g., Aluminum-Bronze, 27.25 mm. **Subject:** World Design Capital Helsinki 2012 **Obv:** Angular **Rev:** Angular

Date	Mintage	F12	VF20	XF40	MS60	MS63
2012	100,000	—	—	—	—	105

KM# 183 5 EURO
9.80 g., Bi-Metallic, 27.25 mm. **Subject:** IIHF Ice Hockey World Championship **Obv:** Puck flying into the goal **Rev:** Hockey player

Date	Mintage	F12	VF20	XF40	MS60	MS63
2012N	180,000	—	—	—	—	5.00
2012N	20,000	PF65 18.00				

KM# 184 5 EURO
9.80 g., Bi-Metallic, 27.25 mm. **Subject:** Northern Nature - Flora **Obv:** Crowfoot framed by moss and lichen

Date	Mintage	F12	VF20	XF40	MS60	MS63
2012P	7,000	PF65 45.00				
2012P	50,000	—	—	—	7.00	8.00

KM# 185 5 EURO
9.80 g., Bi-Metallic, 27.25 mm. **Subject:** Northern Nature - Fauna **Obv:** Paw trail of the arctic fox **Rev:** 5 EURO SUOMI FINLAND

Date	Mintage	F12	VF20	XF40	MS60	MS63
2012P	50,000	—	—	—	7.00	8.00
2012P	7,000	PF65 45.00				

KM# 186 5 EURO
9.80 g., Bi-Metallic, 27.25 mm. **Subject:** Northern Nature - Winter **Obv:** Northern lights **Rev:** Animal tracks in the snow

Date	Mintage	F12	VF20	XF40	MS60	MS63
2012P	50,000	—	—	—	7.00	8.00
2012P	7,000	PF65 45.00				

KM# 191 5 EURO
9.80 g., Bi-Metallic, 27.25 mm. **Subject:** Buildings of the Provinces **Obv:** Helsinki and Uspenski Cathedral **Rev:** Shield and Denomination

Date	Mintage	F12	VF20	XF40	MS60	MS63
2012T	Est. 55000	—	—	—	7.00	8.00
2012T	Est. 10000	PF65 40.00				

KM# 192 5 EURO
9.80 g., Bi-Metallic, 27.25 mm. **Subject:** Buildings of the Provinces-Lappi **Obv:** Jätkänkynttilä Bridge in Rovaniemi **Rev:** Shield and denomination

Date	Mintage	F12	VF20	XF40	MS60	MS63
2012T	10,000	PF65 40.00				
2012T	55,000	—	—	—	7.00	8.00

KM# 195 5 EURO
9.00 g., Bi-Metallic, 27.25 mm. **Obv:** Imatra Dam **Rev:** Shield and denomination

Date	Mintage	F12	VF20	XF40	MS60	MS63
2013	55,000	—	—	—	17.00	20.00
2013	10,000	PF63 30.00	PF65 35.00			

KM# 196 5 EURO
9.80 g., Bi-Metallic, 27.25 mm. **Subject:** Northern Nature - Summer **Obv:** Water lilies **Rev:** Lakeside landscape

Date	Mintage	F12	VF20	XF40	MS60	MS63
2013	50,000	—	—	—	17.00	20.00
2013	7,000	PF63 32.00	PF65 40.00			

KM# 197 5 EURO
9.80 g., Bi-Metallic, 27.25 mm. **Obv:** Turku Cathedral **Rev:** Shield and denomination

Date	Mintage	F12	VF20	XF40	MS60	MS63
2013	55,000	—	—	—	17.00	20.00
2013	10,000	PF63 30.00	PF65 35.00			

KM# 198 5 EURO
9.80 g., Bi-Metallic, 27.25 mm. **Obv:** Sammallahdenmaki Satakunta **Rev:** Shield and denomination

Date	Mintage	F12	VF20	XF40	MS60	MS63
2013	55,000	—	—	—	17.00	20.00
2013	10,000	PF63 30.00	PF65 35.00			

KM# 199 5 EURO
9.80 g., Bi-Metallic, 27.25 mm. **Obv:** St. Olaf's Castle **Rev:** Shield and denomination

Date	Mintage	F12	VF20	XF40	MS60	MS63
2013	55,000	—	—	—	17.00	20.00
2013	10,000	PF63 30.00	PF65 35.00			

KM# 200 5 EURO
9.80 g., Bi-Metallic, 27.25 mm. **Obv:** Salskar Lighthouse, Aland **Rev:** Shield and denomination

Date	Mintage	F12	VF20	XF40	MS60	MS63
2013	55,000	—	—	—	17.00	20.00
2013	10,000	PF63 30.00	PF65 35.00			

KM# 107 10 EURO
27.40 g., 0.925 Silver 0.8096 oz. ASW, 38.6 mm. **Subject:** 50th Anniversary - Helsinki Olympics **Obv:** Flames and denomination above globe with map of Finland **Rev:** Tower and partial coin design **Edge:** Plain

Date	Mintage	F12	VF20	XF40	MS60	MS63
2002M VV-M	10,000	—	—	—	25.00	30.00
2002M VV-M	34,800	PF63 35.00	PF65 40.00			

KM# 108 10 EURO
27.40 g., 0.925 Silver 0.8096 oz. ASW, 38.6 mm. **Subject:** Elias Lönnrot **Obv:** Ribbon with stars **Rev:** Quill and signature **Edge:** Plain

Date	Mintage	F12	VF20	XF40	MS60	MS63
2002M M-M	40,000	—	—	—	25.00	30.00
2002M M-M	40,000	PF63 35.00	PF65 40.00			

KM# 110 10 EURO
27.40 g., 0.925 Silver 0.8096 oz. ASW, 38.6 mm. **Subject:** Anders Chydenius **Obv:** Stylized design **Rev:** Name and book **Edge:** Plain

Date	Mintage	F12	VF20	XF40	MS60	MS63
2003M	30,000	PF63 40.00	PF65 45.00			
2003M L-M	30,000	—	—	—	25.00	30.00

KM# 112 10 EURO
27.40 g., 0.925 Silver 0.8096 oz. ASW, 38.6 mm. **Subject:** Mannerheim and St. Petersburg **Obv:** Head 3/4 facing **Rev:** Fortress, denomination at right

Date	Mintage	F12	VF20	XF40	MS60	MS63
2003 S-M	29,000	PF63 35.00		PF65 40.00		
2003 S-M	6,000	—	—	—	30.00	35.00

KM# 116 10 EURO
27.40 g., 0.925 Silver 0.8096 oz. ASW, 38.6 mm. **Subject:** Tove Jansson **Obv:** Three "muumi" figures **Rev:** Head of Tove Jansson

Date	Mintage	F12	VF20	XF40	MS60	MS63
2004 M-M	20,000	PF65 50.00				
2004 M-M	50,000	—	—	—	30.00	40.00

KM# 115 10 EURO
27.40 g., 0.925 Silver 0.8096 oz. ASW, 38.6 mm. **Subject:** 200th Birthday of Johan Ludwig Runeberg **Obv:** Head of Runeberg **Rev:** Text of 1831 Helsingfors Tidningar newspaper

Date	Mintage	F12	VF20	XF40	MS60	MS63
2004 K-M	5,600	—	—	—	30.00	35.00
2004 K-M	22,750	PF65 40.00				

KM# 122 10 EURO
25.50 g., 0.925 Silver 0.7535 oz. ASW, 38.6 mm. **Subject:** Unknown Soldier and Finnish Film Art **Obv:** Trench **Rev:** Soldier with helmet on top of a film

Date	Mintage	F12	VF20	XF40	MS60	MS63
2005 P-M	25,000	—	—	—	30.00	32.00
2005 P-M	15,000	PF63 37.00		PF65 40.00		

KM# 120 10 EURO
25.50 g., 0.925 Silver 0.7535 oz. ASW, 38.6 mm. **Subject:** 60 years of Peace **Obv:** Dove of peace **Rev:** Flowering plant

Date	Mintage	F12	VF20	XF40	MS60	MS63
2005 M-M	55,000	—	—	—	28.00	35.00
2005	5,000	PF63 40.00		PF65 45.00		

KM# 124 10 EURO
25.50 g., 0.925 Silver 0.7535 oz. ASW, 38.6 mm. **Subject:** 200th Birthday - Johan Vilhelm Snellman **Obv:** Sun rising over the lake **Rev:** Snellman

Date	Mintage	F12	VF20	XF40	MS60	MS63
2006 K-M		—	—	—	30.00	35.00
2006 K-M		—	PF63 30.00		PF65 35.00	

KM# 132 10 EURO
25.50 g., 0.925 Silver 0.7535 oz. ASW, 38.6 mm. **Subject:** 100th Anniversary of Parliamentary Reform **Obv:** Two stylist heads female and male with text SUOMI FINLAND 10 EURO **Rev:** Male and female fingers inserting ballot paper into ballot box with text 100V EDUSKUNTAUUDISTUS 2006 **Edge Lettering:** LANTDAGSREFORMEN 1906

Date	Mintage	F12	VF20	XF40	MS60	MS63
2006M M-M	40,000	—	—	—	30.00	40.00
2006M M-M	20,000	PF63 40.00		PF65 45.00		

KM# 134 10 EURO
25.50 g., 0.925 Silver 0.7535 oz. ASW, 38.6 mm. **Subject:** A.E. Nordenskiöld and the Northeast Passage **Rev:** Sailor at ship's wheel during foul weather

Date	Mintage	F12	VF20	XF40	MS60	MS63
2007M P	7,000	—	—	—	30.00	35.00
2007M P	33,000	PF63 37.00		PF65 40.00		

KM# 136 10 EURO
25.50 g., 0.925 Silver 0.7535 oz. ASW, 38.6 mm. **Subject:** Mikael Agricola - Finnish Language **Obv:** Quill pen and lettering **Rev:** Alphabet Letters

Date	Mintage	F12	VF20	XF40	MS60	MS63
2007 P	6,000	—	—	—	30.00	35.00
2007 P	24,000	PF63 40.00		PF65 50.00		

KM# 140 10 EURO
25.50 g., 0.925 Silver 0.7535 oz. ASW, 38.6 mm. **Subject:** Finnish Flag **Obv:** SUOMI FINLAND 2008 and flag **Rev:** SUOMEN LIPPU 1918-2008-FINLANDS FLAGGA and value

Date	Mintage	F12	VF20	XF40	MS60	MS63
2008K	26,000	PF63 35.00		PF65 40.00		
2008K	9,000	—	—	—	30.00	32.00

KM# 142 10 EURO
25.50 g., 0.925 Silver 0.7535 oz. ASW, 38.6 mm. **Subject:** Mika Waltari **Obv:** Signature and 1908-1879 **Rev:** Egyptian pharaoh hound and value

Date	Mintage	F12	VF20	XF40	MS60	MS63
2008P	15,000	PF63 35.00		PF65 40.00		
2008P	5,000	—	—	—	30.00	32.00

KM# 173 10 EURO
25.50 g., 0.925 Silver 0.7535 oz. ASW **Subject:** Council of State, 200th Anniversary

Date	Mintage	F12	VF20	XF40	MS60	MS63
2009P	15,000	PF63 70.00		PF65 80.00		
2009P	5,000	—	—	—	—	50.00

KM# 148 10 EURO
25.50 g., 0.925 Silver 0.7535 oz. ASW, 38.6 mm. **Subject:** Fredrik Pacius **Obv:** Opening notes to Kung Karls Jakt, first opera of Pacius **Rev:** Stage curtian opening

Date	Mintage	F12	VF20	XF40	MS60	MS63
2009M	7,000	—	—	—	35.00	58.00
2009M	28,000	PF63 75.00		PF65 80.00		

KM# 151 10 EURO
25.50 g., 0.925 Silver 0.7535 oz. ASW, 38.6 mm. **Subject:** Eero Saarinen, 100th Anniversary of Birth **Obv:** Tulip chair **Rev:** St. Louis Arch

Date	Mintage	F12	VF20	XF40	MS60	MS63
2010K	20,000	PF63 75.00		PF65 80.00		
2010K	6,000	—	—	—	—	50.00

KM# 152 10 EURO
25.50 g., 0.925 Silver 0.7535 oz. ASW, 38.6 mm. **Subject:** Minna Cauth, author

Date	Mintage	F12	VF20	XF40	MS60	MS63
2010P	16,000	PF63 75.00		PF65 80.00		
2010P	4,000	—	—	—	—	50.00

KM# 157 10 EURO
25.50 g., 0.925 Silver 0.7535 oz. ASW, 38.6 mm. **Subject:** Konsta Jylhä, 100th Anniversary of Birth

Date	Mintage	F12	VF20	XF40	MS60	MS63
2010P	—	PF63 75.00		PF65 80.00		
2010P	—	—	—	—	32.00	50.00

KM# 165 10 EURO
25.50 g., 0.925 Silver 0.7535 oz. ASW, 38.6 mm. **Subject:** Hella Wuolijoki and Equality

Date	Mintage	F12	VF20	XF40	MS60	MS63
2011P	7,000	PF63 75.00		PF65 80.00		
2011P	5,000	—	—	—	30.00	70.00

KM# 166 10 EURO
25.50 g., 0.925 Silver 0.7535 oz. ASW, 38.6 mm. **Subject:** Kaj Franck and industrial art **Obv:** Franck's signature

Date	Mintage	F12	VF20	XF40	MS60	MS63
2011P	10,000	PF63 75.00	PF65 80.00			
2011P	5,000	—	—	—	30.00	70.00

KM# 167 10 EURO
25.50 g., 0.925 Silver 0.7535 oz. ASW, 38.6 mm. **Subject:** Pehr Kalm and European Explorers **Obv:** Mountain laurel - kalmia latifolia **Rev:** Surveyor before Niagara Falls

Date	Mintage	F12	VF20	XF40	MS60	MS63
2011V	14,000	PF63 65.00	PF65 70.00			
2011V	6,000	—	—	—	30.00	35.00

KM# 168 10 EURO
25.50 g., 0.500 Silver 0.4073 oz. ASW, 38.6 mm. **Subject:** Juhani Aho and Finnish Literature **Rev:** Pen point and manuscript

Date	Mintage	F12	VF20	XF40	MS60	MS63
2011P	8,000	—	—	—	—	50.00

KM# 168a 10 EURO
25.50 g., 0.925 Silver 0.7535 oz. ASW, 38.6 mm. **Subject:** Juhani Aho and Finnish Literature

Date	Mintage	F12	VF20	XF40	MS60	MS63
2011P	7,000	PF60 80.00				

KM# 179 10 EURO
25.50 g., 0.925 Silver 0.7535 oz. ASW, 38.6 mm. **Subject:** Henrik Wigström, 150th Anniversary of Birth **Obv:** Swan swimming left, Lilly pads nearby **Rev:** Floral Easter egg ball

Date	Mintage	F12	VF20	XF40	MS60	MS63
2012M	15,000	PF65 75.00				
2012M	15,000	—	—	—	30.00	70.00

KM# 187 10 EURO
25.50 g., 0.925 Silver 0.7535 oz. ASW, 38.6 mm. **Subject:** Arvo Ylppö and Medicin **Obv:** Colored alphabet letters **Rev:** Baby nestled in stethoscope

Date	Mintage	F12	VF20	XF40	MS60	MS63
2012M	20,000	—	—	—	—	70.00
2012M	20,000	PF65 80.00				

KM# 188 10 EURO
25.50 g., 0.925 Silver 0.7535 oz. ASW, 38.6 mm. **Subject:** Armi Ratia and Industrial Art **Obv:** Armi Ratia 1912-1973 **Rev:** Unikko flower

Date	Mintage	F12	VF20	XF40	MS60	MS63
2012	20,000	—	—	—	—	70.00
2012	20,000	PF65 80.00				

KM# 201 10 EURO
25.50 g., 0.925 Silver 0.7535 oz. ASW, 38.6 mm. **Obv:** Frans Eemil Sillanpaa **Rev:** Art of Sillanpaa

Date	Mintage	F12	VF20	XF40	MS60	MS63
2013	20,000	—	—	—	—	70.00
2013	20,000	PF65 80.00				

KM# 202 10 EURO
25.50 g., 0.925 Silver 0.7535 oz. ASW, 38.6 mm. **Subject:** Sophie Mannerheim, 150th Anniversary **Obv:** Sophie Mannerheim **Rev:** Woman and children

Date	Mintage	F12	VF20	XF40	MS60	MS63
2013	20,000	—	—	—	—	70.00
2013	20,000	PF65 80.00				

KM# 204 10 EURO
25.50 g., 0.925 Silver 0.7535 oz. ASW, 38.6 mm. **Subject:** Multicultural

Date	Mintage	F12	VF20	XF40	MS60	MS63
2013	—	PF65 75.00				

KM# 121 20 EURO
1.73 g., 0.900 Gold 0.0497 oz. AGW, 13.9 mm. **Subject:** 10th Anniversary - IAAF World Championships in Athletics **Obv:** Helsinki Stadium **Rev:** Two faces

Date	Mintage	F12	VF20	XF40	MS60	MS63
2005 M-M	30,000	PF63 90.00	PF65 100			

KM# 172 20 EURO
25.50 g., 0.925 Silver 0.7535 oz. ASW, 38.6 mm. **Subject:** Peace and security **Obv:** Two peace doves with a twig

Date	Mintage	F12	VF20	XF40	MS60	MS63
2009K	11,500	PF65 120				
2009K	3,500	—	—	—	32.00	40.00

KM# 153 20 EURO
33.62 g., 0.925 Silver 0.9934 oz. ASW, 38.61 mm. **Subject:** Children's creativity

Date	Mintage	F12	VF20	XF40	MS60	MS63
2010M	10,000	PF65 120				
2010M	3,500	—	—	—	—	100

KM# 169a 20 EURO
33.62 g., 0.925 Silver 0.9934 oz. ASW, 38.6 mm. **Subject:** Protecting the Baltic **Obv:** Fishing boat and map of the Baltic Sea **Rev:** Seal and fish

Date	Mintage	F12	VF20	XF40	MS60	MS63
2011K	8,000	PF60 110				

KM# 169 20 EURO

33.62 g., 0.500 Silver 0.537 oz. ASW, 38.6 mm. **Subject:** Protecting Baltic Sea **Obv:** Fishing boat and map of the Baltic Sea **Rev:** Seal and fish

Date	Mintage	F12	VF20	XF40	MS60	MS63
2011K	7,000	—	—	—	—	80.00

KM# 189 20 EURO

33.62 g., 0.925 Silver 0.9934 oz. ASW, 38.6 mm. **Subject:** Equity and Tolerance **Obv:** World map **Rev:** Human faces and value

Date	Mintage	F12	VF20	XF40	MS60	MS63
2012P	20,000	—	—	—	—	110
2012P	20,000	PF65 120				

KM# 113 50 EURO

13.20 g., Bi-Metallic, 27.25 mm. **Subject:** Finnish art and design **Obv:** Snowflake design within box, beaded circle surrounds **Rev:** Snowflake design within beaded circle

Date	Mintage	F12	VF20	XF40	MS60	MS63
2003 P-M	10,600	PF65 375				

KM# 133 50 EURO

12.80 g., Bi-Metallic, 27.25 mm. **Subject:** Finland Presidency of European Union **Obv:** Letter decorations with 2006 and SUOMI-FINLAND **Rev:** 50 EURO below letter decoration

Date	Mintage	F12	VF20	XF40	MS60	MS63
2006M P-M	8,000	PF65 400				

KM# 180 50 EURO

10.80 g., Bi-Metallic, 27.25 mm. **Subject:** World Design Capital Helsinki 2012 **Obv:** WORLD DESIGN CAPITAL HELSINKI around angular patterns **Rev:** 50 above angular patterns

Date	Mintage	F12	VF20	XF40	MS60	MS63
2012L	5,000	PF65 600				

KM# 109 100 EURO

8.64 g., 0.900 Gold 0.2484 oz. AGW, 22 mm. **Subject:** Lapland **Obv:** Small tree and mountain stream **Rev:** Lake landscape beneath the midnight sun **Edge:** Plain with serial number

Date	Mintage	F12	VF20	XF40	MS60	MS63
2002M J-M	25,000	PF65 450				

KM# 117 100 EURO

8.64 g., 0.900 Gold 0.2484 oz. AGW, 22 mm. **Subject:** 150th Birthday of Albert Edelfelt **Obv:** Flower **Rev:** Head of Edelfelt

Date	Mintage	F12	VF20	XF40	MS60	MS63
2004 M-M	8,500	PF65 475				

KM# 137 100 EURO

8.48 g., 0.917 Gold 0.2484 oz. AGW **Subject:** 90th Anniversary of Finland's Independence **Obv:** Finland and the years of independence **Rev:** Abstract composition

Date	Mintage	F12	VF20	XF40	MS60	MS63
2007 P	—	—	—	—	450	465
2007 P		PF65 475				

KM# 174 100 EURO

8.48 g., 0.917 Gold 0.2484 oz. AGW, 22 mm. **Subject:** Finnish War and the Birth of Autonomy **Obv:** Half of an Eagle at left **Rev:** Half of a Crown at right

Date	Mintage	F12	VF20	XF40	MS60	MS63
2008P	9,000	PF65 625				

KM# 145 100 EURO

6.78 g., 0.917 Gold 0.1986 oz. AGW, 22 mm. **Subject:** Diet of Porvoo **Rev:** Porvoo

Date	Mintage	F12	VF20	XF40	MS60	MS63
2009P	7,500	PF65 375				

KM# 150 100 EURO

5.65 g., 0.917 Gold 0.1655 oz. AGW, 22 mm. **Subject:** Finnish Currency, 150th Anniversary **Obv:** Finnish Lion **Rev:** Composition of figures

Date	Mintage	F12	VF20	XF40	MS60	MS63
2010P	—	PF65 550				

KM# 164 100 EURO

5.65 g., 0.917 Gold 0.1655 oz. AGW, 22 mm. **Subject:** Bank of Finland, 200th Anniversary **Obv:** Swan in flight **Rev:** Left wing of swan SUOMI FINLAND value and date

Date	Mintage	F12	VF20	XF40	MS60	MS63
2011V	8,000	PF65 525				

KM# 203 100 EURO

5.65 g., 0.917 Gold 0.1655 oz. AGW, 22 mm. **Subject:** Parliament, 150th Anniversary

Date	Mintage	F12	VF20	XF40	MS60	MS63
2013	—	PF65 525				

MINT SETS

KM#	Date	Mintage	Identification	Issue Price	Mkt Val
MS58	2001 (5)	20,000	KM#65, 66, 73, 76, 77	18.00	22.50
MS59	2001 (5)	—	KM#65, 66, 73, 76, 77, medal	—	22.50
MS60	2002 (8)	130,000	KM#98-105, Church medal	—	40.00
MS61	2003 (8)	170,000	KM#98-105, Golden medal, goldpanning in Lappland	—	37.50
MS62	2002 (8)	2,000	KM#98-105, Baby	—	100
MS63	2003 (9)	8,000	KM#98-105, Silver medal, goldpanning in Lappland	—	125
MS64	2003 (8)	15,000	KM#98-105, Ice Hockey	—	60.00
MS65	2003 (9)	3,000	KM#98-105, medal and teddy bear	—	—
MS66	2003 (9)	5,000	KM#98-105, Baby, medal	—	37.50
MS67	2003 (9)	4,000	KM#98-105, Rose, medal	—	60.00
MS68	2003 (9)	30,000	KM#98-105, Christmas, golden medal	—	37.50
MS69	2004 (8)	55,000	KM#98-105, Euro zone, medal	—	40.00
MS70	2004 (8)	5,000	KM#98-105, 114, baby, medal	—	35.00
MS71	2004 (8)	18,000	KM#98-105, Tove Jansson, 90th Birthday	—	42.50
MS72	2004 (9)	4,000	KM#98-105, Music, medal	—	60.00
MS73	2005 (8)	40,000	KM#98-105, Wildlife, medal	—	42.50
MS74	2005 (9)	30,000	KM#98-105, 118, Paraolympics	—	55.00
MS75	2005 (9)	4,000	KM#98-105, Baby, medal	—	45.00
MS76	2005 (9)	3,000	KM#98-105, Music, medal	—	55.00
MS77	2006 (9)	40,000	KM#98-105, 119, Lighthouse	—	45.00
MS78	2006 (9)	20,000	KM#98-105, 125, Centennial of Parliament reform, suffrage	—	55.00
MS79	2006 (9)	3,200	KM#98-105, Music, medal	—	55.00
MS380	2006 (9)	4,000	KM#98-105, Wedding, medal	—	55.00
MS81	2006 (9)	4,600	KM#98-105, Baby, medal	—	55.00
MS82	2006 (9)	4,000	KM#98-105, Aland	—	45.00
MS83	2007 (9)	30,000	KM#98-100, 126-130, Lighthouse, medal	—	30.00
MS84	2007 (9)	3,000	KM#98-100, 126-130, Rose, medal	—	70.00
MS85	2007 (9)	3,000	KM#98-100, 126-130, Marriage, medal	—	55.00
MS86	2007 (9)	4,000	KM#98-100, 126-130, Baby, medal	—	65.00
MS87	2007 (10)	20,000	KM#98-100, 126-130, 138, European Song Festival, medal	—	45.00
MS88	2007 (8)	4,000	KM#98-100, 126-130, Aland	—	40.00
MS89	2007 (9)	20,000	KM#98-100, 126-130, 139, Swans	—	50.00
MS90	2007 (3)	—	KM98-100	—	10.00
MS91	2008 (9)	30,000	KM#98-100, 126-130, Lighthouse, medal	—	35.00
MS92	2008 (9)	3,000	KM#98-100, 126-130, Rose, medal	—	55.00
MS93	2008 (9)	3,000	KM#98-100, 126-130, Wedding, medal	—	45.00
MS94	2008 (9)	4,000	KM#98-100, 126-130, Baby, medal	—	50.00
MS95	2008 (9)	4,000	KM#98-100, 126-130, Aland medal	—	25.00
MS96	2008 (9)	30,000	KM#98-100, 126-130, 143	—	25.00
MS97	2009 (10)	20,000	KM#98-100, 126-130, 149 plus medal	—	40.00
MS98	2009 (10)	30,000	KM#98-100, 126-130, 149 plus lighthouse medal	—	45.00
MS99	2009 (10)	2,200	KM#98-100, 126-130, 149 Aland	—	40.00
MS100	2009 (10)	1,500	KM#98-100, 126-130, 149, Wedding, plus medal	—	45.00
MS101	2009 (10)	3,000	KM#98-100, 126-130, 149, Music plus medal	—	45.00
MS102	2009 (10)	4,000	KM#98-100, 126-130, 149, Baby, plus medal	—	45.00
MS103	2010 (10)	30,000	KM#98-100, 126-130, 154 and Lighthouse medal	—	45.00
MS104	2010 (10)	15,000	KM#98-100, 126-130, 154 plus Biology medal	—	45.00
MS105	2010 (10)	2,500	KM#98-100, 126-130, 154 plus Music medal	—	45.00

MS106 2010 (10)	2	KM#98-100, 126-130, 154 plus Wedding medal	—	45.00
MS107 2010 (10)	3,000	KM#98-105, 126-130, 154 plus Kids medal	—	45.00
MS108 2010 (3)	7,000	KM#98-100	—	12.50
MS109 2011 (10)	20,000	KM#98-100, 126-130, 163 plus Lighthouse medal	—	45.00
MS110 2011 (10)	15,000	KM#98-100, 126-130, 163 plus Nature medal	—	45.00
MS111 2011 (10)	3,000	KM#98-100, 126-130, 163 plus Kids medal	—	45.00
MS112 2011 (10)	2,500	KM#98-100, 126-130, 163 plus Music medal	—	45.00
MS113 2011 (10)	2,500	KM#98-100, 126-130, 163 plus Wedding medal	—	45.00
MS114 2011 (3)	10,000	KM#98-100	—	15.00

PROOF SETS

KM#	Date	Mintage	Identification	Issue Price	Mkt Val
PS9	2001 (6)	—	KM#65-66, 73, 76-77, medal	—	60.00
PS10	2002 (9)	5,000	KM#98-105, European Union gold medal	—	550
PS11	2002 (9)	8,000	KM#98-105, National Theater silver medal	—	185
PS12	2003 (9)	500	KM#98-105, Gold medal	—	350
PS13	2003 (9)	5,000	KM#98-105, Gold medal with diamond chip	—	500
PS14	2003 (9)	1,000	KM#98-105, Silver medal	—	400
PS15	2003 (9)	8,000	KM#98-105, Silver medal with diamond chip	—	150
PS16	2004 (10)	5,000	KM#98-105, 114, Silver medal	—	225
PS17	2005 (10)	3,000	KM#98-105, 118, Silver medal	—	200
PS18	2005 (4)	2,005	KM#118, 121 plus 2 older coins.	—	225
PS19	2006 (10)	3,300	KM#98-105, 125, Salmon medal	—	200
PS20	2007 (10)	2,500	KM#98-100, 126-130, 138, Silver medal.	—	150
PS21	2008 (10)	2,500	KM#98-100, 126-130, 143 plus medal	—	185
PS22	2009 (11)	2,500	KM#98-100, 126-130, 144, 149, plus medal	—	225
PS23	2010 (10)	2,000	KM#98-100, 126-130, 154 plus medal	—	200
PS24	2011 (10)	—	KM#98-100, 126-130, 163 plus medal	—	200
PS25	2010 (3)	7,000	KM#150 plus Russian 1863 Kopek and Finnish 1864 Pennia	—	475

FRANCE

The French Republic, largest of the West European nations, has an area of 210,026 sq. mi. (547,030 sq. km.) and a population of 58.1 million. Capital: Paris. Agriculture, manufacturing, tourist industry and financial services are the most important elements of France's diversified economy. Textiles and clothing, steel products, machinery and transportation equipment, chemicals, pharmaceuticals, nuclear electricity, agricultural products and wine are exported.

ENGRAVER GENERALS' PRIVY MARKS

Mark	Desc.	Date	Name
⌒	Horseshoe	2000-2002	Gérard Buquoi

	SL Heart-shaped monogram	2002-2003	Serge Levet
	French horn w/fish in water	2003-2010	Hubert Larivière

MINT DIRECTORS' PRIVY MARKS

Some modern coins struck from dies produced at the Paris Mint have the 'A' mint mark. In the absence of a mint mark, the cornucopia privy mark serves to attribute a coin to Paris design.

A - Paris, Central Mint

MODERN REPUBLICS
1870-present

REFORM COINAGE
1 Old Franc = 1 New Centime;
100 New Centimes = 1 New FrancCommencing 1960

KM# 928 CENTIME
1.65 g., Stainless Steel, 15 mm. **Obv:** Cursive legend surrounds grain sprig **Rev:** Cursive denomination, date at top **Edge:** Plain **Note:** 1991-1993 dated coins, non-Proof, exist in both coin and medal alignment. Values given here are for medal alignment examples. Pieces struck in coin alignment have been traded for as much as $50.00.

Date	Mintage	F12	VF20	XF40	MS60	MS63
2001 In sets only	—	—	—	—	—	1.50
2001	—	PF60 2.00				

KM# 928a CENTIME
2.50 g., 0.750 Gold 0.0599 oz. AGW **Obv:** Cursive legend surrounds grain sprig, medallic alignment **Rev:** Cursive denomination, date above, medallic alignment **Edge:** Plain **Note:** Last Centime.

Date	Mintage	F12	VF20	XF40	MS60	MS63
2001	—	—	—	—	—	250

KM# 933 5 CENTIMES
2.00 g., Aluminum-Bronze, 17 mm. **Obv:** Liberty bust left **Rev:** Denomination above date, grain sprig below, laurel branch at left **Edge:** Plain **Note:** 1991-1993 dated coins, non-Proof exist in both coin and medal alignment.

Date	Mintage	F12	VF20	XF40	MS60	MS63
2001 In sets only	—	—	—	—	1.50	2.50
2001	—	PF60 1.00				

KM# 929 10 CENTIMES
3.00 g., Aluminum-Bronze, 20 mm. **Obv:** Liberty bust left **Rev:** Denomination above date, grain sprig below, laurel branch at left **Edge:** Plain **Note:** Without mint mark. 1991-1993 dated coins, non-Proof, exist in both coin and medal alignment.

Date	Mintage	F12	VF20	XF40	MS60	MS63
2001 In sets only	—	—	—	—	—	3.00
2001	—	PF60 1.00				

KM# 930 20 CENTIMES
4.00 g., Aluminum-Bronze, 23.5 mm. **Obv:** Liberty bust left **Rev:** Denomination above date, grain sprig below, laurel branch at left **Edge:** Plain **Note:** Without mint mark. 1991-1993 dated coins, non-Proof, exist in both coin and medal alignment.

Date	Mintage	F12	VF20	XF40	MS60	MS63
2001 In sets only	—	—	—	—	—	3.00
2001	—	PF60 1.00				

KM# 931.1 1/2 FRANC
4.50 g., Nickel, 19.5 mm. **Obv:** The Seed Sower **Rev:** Laurel divides denomination and date **Edge:** Reeded **Note:** Without mint mark.

Date	Mintage	F12	VF20	XF40	MS60	MS63
2001 In sets only	—	—	—	—	2.00	3.00

KM# 931.2 1/2 FRANC
4.50 g., Nickel, 19.5 mm. **Obv:** Modified sower, engraver's signature: "O. ROTY" preceded by "D'AP" **Rev:** Laurel divides date and denomination **Edge:** Plain

Date	Mintage	F12	VF20	XF40	MS60	MS63
2001	—	—	—	—	0.40	0.60
2001	—	PF60 1.50				

KM# 925.1 FRANC
6.00 g., Nickel, 24 mm. **Obv:** The Seed Sower **Rev:** Laurel branch divides denomination and date **Edge:** Reeded **Note:** Without mint mark.

Date	Mintage	F12	VF20	XF40	MS60	MS63
2001	20,000,000	—	—	—	0.40	0.60

KM# 925.2 FRANC
6.00 g., Nickel, 24 mm. **Obv:** Modified sower, engraver's signature: O. ROTY, preceded by D'AP **Rev:** Laurel divides date and denomination **Edge:** Plain

Date	Mintage	F12	VF20	XF40	MS60	MS63
2001	—	—	—	—	0.40	0.60
2001	—	PF60 2.50				

KM# 925.1a FRANC
8.00 g., 0.750 Gold 0.1917 oz. AGW, 24 mm. **Obv:** The Seed Sower **Rev:** Laurel divides date and denomination **Edge:** Reeded **Note:** Medallic alignment.

Date	Mintage	F12	VF20	XF40	MS60	MS63
2001	Est. 9941	—	—	—	BV	365

KM# 1290 FRANC
17.77 g., 0.980 Silver 0.5563 oz. ASW **Subject:** The Last Franc **Obv:** Legend on polished field **Obv. Legend:** UN ULTIME FRANC **Rev:** Number "1" on polished field **Edge Lettering:** REPUBLIQUE FRANCAISE STARCK LIBERTE EGALITE FRATERNITE (2001). **Note:** The coin is intentionally warped and the edge inscription is very faint. Struck at Paris Mint.

Date	Mintage	F12	VF20	XF40	MS60	MS63
2001 Matte	49,838	PF63 150				

KM# 1290a FRANC
26.10 g., 0.750 Gold 0.6253 oz. AGW **Subject:** The Last Franc **Obv:** Legend on polished field **Obv. Legend:** UN ULTIME FRANC **Rev:** Number "1" on polished field **Edge Lettering:** REPUBLIQUE FRANCAISE. STARCK. LIBERTE. EGALITE. FRATERNITE (cornucopia) 2001 **Note:** This coin has an intentionally warped surface and the edge inscription is very weak.

Date	Mintage	F12	VF20	XF40	MS60	MS63
2001 Matte	4,963	—	—	—	1,250	1,700

KM# 942.1 2 FRANCS
7.50 g., Nickel, 26.5 mm. **Obv:** The Seed Sower **Rev:** Denomination on branches, date below **Edge:** Wide reeded

Date	Mintage	F12	VF20	XF40	MS60	MS63
2001 Bee	—	—	—	—	0.75	1.25

KM# 942.2 2 FRANCS
7.50 g., Nickel, 26.5 mm. **Obv:** The Seed Sower **Rev:** Denomination on branches, date below **Edge:** Plain

Date	Mintage	F12	VF20	XF40	MS60	MS63
2001	—	—	—	—	0.75	1.25
2001	—	PF60 3.50				

KM# 926a.1 5 FRANCS
10.00 g., Nickel Clad Copper-Nickel, 29 mm. **Obv:** The Seed Sower **Rev:** Branches divide denomination and date **Edge:** Reeded

Date	Mintage	F12	VF20	XF40	MS60	MS63
2001 In sets only	—	—	—	—	5.00	7.50

KM# 926a.2 5 FRANCS
10.00 g., Nickel Clad Copper-Nickel, 29 mm. **Obv:** Modified sower, engraver's signature: "O. ROTY" preceded by "D'AP" **Rev:** Branches divide date and denomination **Edge:** Plain

Date	Mintage	F12	VF20	XF40	MS60	MS63
2001	—	PF63 6.50				
2001	—	—	—	—	1.65	2.50

KM# 1309 5 FRANCS
12.00 g., 0.900 Silver 0.345 oz. ASW, 29 mm. **Subject:** Last Year of the Franc **Obv:** The Seed Sower **Rev:** Denomination and date **Edge:** Lettered **Edge Lettering:** * LIBERTY * EGALITE * FRATERNITE *

Date	Mintage	F12	VF20	XF40	MS60	MS63
2001	25,000	—	—	—	22.50	25.00

KM# 1265.1 6.55957 FRANCS
13.00 g., 0.900 Silver 0.3737 oz. ASW **Subject:** Last Year of the French Franc **Obv:** French and other European euro currency equivalents **Rev:** Europa allegorical portrait, date below, "last year of the franc" logo after the date **Edge:** Reeded

Date	Mintage	F12	VF20	XF40	MS60	MS63
2001	—	—	—	—	25.00	50.00

KM# 1265.2 6.55957 FRANCS
22.20 g., 0.900 Silver 0.6382 oz. ASW **Obv:** French and other European euro currency equivalents **Rev:** Europa allegorical portrait, date below, "last year of the franc" logo after the date **Edge:** Plain

Date	Mintage	F12	VF20	XF40	MS60	MS63
2001	Est. 10000	PF63 60.00	PF65 65.00			

KM# 1276 6.55957 FRANCS
22.20 g., 0.900 Silver 0.6382 oz. ASW **Subject:** Mottos **Obv:** Denomination **Rev:** FRATERNITE in red letters **Edge:** Reeded

Date	Mintage	F12	VF20	XF40	MS60	MS63
2001	2,171	PF63 50.00	PF65 55.00			

KM# 1277 6.55957 FRANCS
22.20 g., 0.900 Silver 0.6382 oz. ASW **Subject:** Mottos **Obv:** Denomination **Rev:** EGALITE in white letters

Date	Mintage	F12	VF20	XF40	MS60	MS63
2001	2,190	PF63 50.00	PF65 55.00			

KM# 1278 6.55957 FRANCS
22.20 g., 0.900 Silver 0.6382 oz. ASW **Subject:** Mottos **Obv:** Denomination **Rev:** LIBERTE in red letters

Date	Mintage	F12	VF20	XF40	MS60	MS63
2001	2,259	PF63 50.00	PF65 55.00			

KM# 964.2 10 FRANCS
Aluminum-Bronze, 23 mm. **Obv:** Winged figure divides RF **Rev:** Patterned denomination above date **Edge:** Plain

Date	Mintage	F12	VF20	XF40	MS60	MS63
2001	—	PF63 15.00				
2001	—	—	—	—	6.00	7.50

KM# 1268 10 FRANCS
22.20 g., 0.900 Silver 0.6382 oz. ASW **Subject:** Monuments of France - Palace of Versailles **Obv:** Stylized French map **Rev:** 1/2 bust of Louis XIV at right, Internal and external palace views at left **Edge:** Plain

Date	Mintage	F12	VF20	XF40	MS60	MS63
2001	Est. 2561	PF63 50.00	PF65 55.00			

KM# 1270 10 FRANCS
22.20 g., 0.900 Silver 0.6382 oz. ASW **Subject:** Monuments of France - Arch of Triumph **Obv:** Stylized French map **Rev:** Arch of Triumph on the Champs Elysees partial close up and aerial views

Date	Mintage	F12	VF20	XF40	MS60	MS63
2001	Est. 2882	PF63 50.00	PF65 55.00			

KM# 1272 10 FRANCS
22.20 g., 0.900 Silver 0.6382 oz. ASW **Subject:** Monuments of France - Notre Dame Cathedral **Obv:** Stylized French map **Rev:** Gargoyle at left, cathedral views at right

Date	Mintage	F12	VF20	XF40	MS60	MS63
2001	Est. 2877	PF63 50.00	PF65 55.00			

KM# 1274 10 FRANCS
22.20 g., 0.900 Silver 0.6382 oz. ASW **Subject:** Monuments of France - Eiffel Tower **Obv:** Stylized French map **Rev:** Two tower views

Date	Mintage	F12	VF20	XF40	MS60	MS63
2001	Est. 3888	PF63 45.00	PF65 50.00			

KM# 1008.2 20 FRANCS
9.00 g., Tri-Metallic, 27 mm. **Obv:** Mont St. Michel **Rev:** Patterned denomination above date **Edge:** 5 milled bands, reeded or plain

Date	Mintage	F12	VF20	XF40	MS60	MS63
2001	—	PF63 25.00				
2001	—	—	—	—	8.00	10.00

KM# 1266 65.5997 FRANCS
8.45 g., 0.920 Gold 0.2483 oz. AGW **Subject:** Last Year of the French Franc **Obv:** French and other European euro currency equivalents **Rev:** Europa allegorical portrait, date below, "last year of the franc" logo after the date **Edge:** Reeded

Date	Mintage	F12	VF20	XF40	MS60	MS63
2001	3,000	PF65 600				

KM# 1269 100 FRANCS
17.00 g., 0.920 Gold 0.4996 oz. AGW **Subject:** Palace of Versailles **Obv:** Stylized French map **Rev:** Louis XIV with internal and external palace views **Edge:** Plain

Date	Mintage	F12	VF20	XF40	MS60	MS63
2001	105	PF63 875	PF65 900			

KM# 1271 100 FRANCS
17.00 g., 0.920 Gold 0.4996 oz. AGW **Obv:** Champs-Elysees **Rev:** Arch of Triumph partial close up and aerial views

Date	Mintage	F12	VF20	XF40	MS60	MS63
2001	115	PF63 875	PF65 900			

KM# 1273 100 FRANCS
17.00 g., 0.920 Gold 0.4996 oz. AGW **Obv:** Notre-Dame Cathedral **Rev:** Gargoyle and cathedral views

Date	Mintage	F12	VF20	XF40	MS60	MS63
2001	116	PF63 875	PF65 900			

KM# 1275 100 FRANCS
17.00 g., 0.920 Gold 0.4996 oz. AGW **Obv:** Eiffel Tower **Rev:** Two tower views

Date	Mintage	F12	VF20	XF40	MS60	MS63
2001	170	PF63 875	PF65 900			

KM# 1994 100 FRANCS
155.55 g., 0.999 Gold 4.9639 oz. AGW **Obv:** Cruved cross with coins **Rev:** Europa facing at right, flags at left

Date	Mintage	F12	VF20	XF40	MS60	MS63
2003	99	PF65 9,500				

KM# 2001 100 FRANCS
155.55 g., 0.999 Gold 4.9639 oz. AGW **Subject:** Athletic World Championships **Obv:** Winner Podium before buildings **Rev:** Runner

Date	Mintage	F12	VF20	XF40	MS60	MS63
2003	369	PF65 10,000				

KM# 2002 100 FRANCS
155.55 g., 0.999 Gold 4.9639 oz. AGW **Subject:** Louisana Purchase, 200th Anniversary **Obv:** Thomas Jefferson and Napoleon Bonaparte with map of purchase **Rev:** Celebration of Lousiana: plantation mansion, jazz, riverboat

Date	Mintage	F12	VF20	XF40	MS60	MS63
2003	99	PF65 10,000				

KM# 1267 655.957 FRANCS
31.10 g., 0.999 Gold 0.9926 oz. AGW **Subject:** Last Year of the French Franc **Obv:** French and other European euro currency equivalents **Rev:** Europa allegorical portrait, date below, "last year of the franc" logo after the date **Edge:** Plain

Date	Mintage	F12	VF20	XF40	MS60	MS63
2001	2,000	PF65 2,100				

KM# 1267.1 655.957 FRANCS
155.52 g., 0.999 Gold 4.9628 oz. AGW **Obv:** French and other European euro currency equivalents **Rev:** Europa allegorical portrait, date below, "last year of the franc" after the date **Edge:** Plain

Date	Mintage	F12	VF20	XF40	MS60	MS63
2001	99	PF65 9,500				

KM# 1279 655.957 FRANCS
17.00 g., 0.920 Gold 0.4996 oz. AGW **Subject:** Motto Series **Obv:** Denomination **Rev:** FRATERNITE **Edge:** Reeded

Date	Mintage	F12	VF20	XF40	MS60	MS63
2001	62	PF63 1,000	PF65 1,100			

KM# 1280 655.957 FRANCS
17.00 g., 0.920 Gold 0.4996 oz. AGW **Subject:** Motto Series **Obv:** Denomination **Rev:** EGALITE

Date	Mintage	F12	VF20	XF40	MS60	MS63
2001	64	PF63 1,000	PF65 1,100			

KM# 1281 655.957 FRANCS
17.00 g., 0.920 Gold 0.4996 oz. AGW **Subject:** Motto Series **Obv:** Denomination **Rev:** LIBERTE

Date	Mintage	F12	VF20	XF40	MS60	MS63
2001	63	PF63 1,000	PF65 1,100			

EURO COINAGE
European Union Issues

KM# 1282 EURO CENT
2.27 g., Copper Plated Steel, 16.3 mm. **Obv:** Human face **Rev:** Denomination and globe **Edge:** Plain

Date	Mintage	F12	VF20	XF40	MS60	MS63
2001	300,681,580	—	—	—	0.35	0.50
2001	15,000	PF63 10.00				
2002	200,000	—	—	—	—	10.00
2002	21,453	PF63 8.00				
2003	160,017,000	—	—	—	1.00	1.50
2003	40,000	PF63 8.00				
2004	400,032,000	—	—	—	0.35	0.50
2004	20,000	PF63 10.00				
2005	240,320,000	—	—	—	0.35	0.50
2005	10,000	PF63 12.00				
2006	343,078,000	—	—	—	0.35	0.50
2006	10,000	PF63 12.00				
2007	300,058,000	—	—	—	0.35	0.50
2007	7,500	PF63 14.00				
2008	462,757,000	—	—	—	0.35	0.50
2008	7,500	PF63 14.00				
2009	404,050,500	—	—	—	0.35	0.50
2009	7,500	PF63 14.00				
2010	336,000,000	—	—	—	0.35	0.50
2010	—	PF63 15.00				
2011	320,118,000	—	—	—	0.35	0.50
2011	—	PF63 15.00				
2012	358,566,000	—	—	—	0.35	0.50
2012	—	PF63 15.00				
2013	—	—	—	—	0.35	0.50
2013	—	PF63 15.00				

KM# 1283 2 EURO CENT
3.03 g., Copper Plated Steel, 18.7 mm. **Obv:** Human face **Rev:** Denomination and globe **Edge:** Grooved

Date	Mintage	F12	VF20	XF40	MS60	MS63
2001	249,101,580	—	—	—	0.50	0.75
2001	15,000	PF63 10.00				
2002 In sets only	100,000	—	—	—	—	12.50
2002	21,453	PF63 8.00				
2003	160,175,000	—	—	—	1.25	2.00
2003	40,000	PF63 8.00				
2004	300,024,000	—	—	—	—	1.00
2004	20,000	PF63 10.00				
2005	2,603,202,000	—	—	—	—	1.00
2005	10,000	PF63 12.00				
2006	283,278,000	—	—	—	—	1.00
2006	10,000	PF63 12.00				
2007	213,258,000	—	—	—	—	1.00
2007	7,500	PF63 14.00				
2008	386,557,000	—	—	—	—	1.00
2008	7,500	PF63 14.00				
2009	317,050,500	—	—	—	—	1.00
2009	7,500	PF63 14.00				
2010	277,000,000	—	—	—	—	1.00
2010	—	PF63 14.00				
2011	250,128,000	—	—	—	—	1.00
2011	—	PF63 14.00				
2012	277,668,000	—	—	—	—	1.00
2012	—	PF63 14.00				
2013	—	—	—	—	—	1.00
2013	—	PF63 14.00				

KM# 1284 5 EURO CENT
3.86 g., Copper Plated Steel, 21.2 mm. **Obv:** Human face **Rev:** Denomination and globe **Edge:** Plain

Date	Mintage	F12	VF20	XF40	MS60	MS63
2001	217,324,477	—	—	—	0.75	1.25
2001	15,000	PF63 12.00				
2002	186,400,000	—	—	—	0.75	1.25
2002	21,453	PF63 10.00				
2003	101,175,000	—	—	—	1.00	1.50
2003	40,000	PF63 10.00				
2004	60,162,000	—	—	—	—	1.25

Date	Mintage	F12	VF20	XF40	MS60	MS63
2004	20,000	PF63 12.00				
2005	20,320,000	—	—	—	—	1.25
2005	10,000	PF63 14.00				
2006	132,078,000	—	—	—	—	1.25
2006	10,000	PF63 14.00				
2007	130,058,000	—	—	—	—	1.25
2007	7,500	PF63 16.00				
2008	218,257,000	—	—	—	—	1.25
2008	7,500	PF63 16.00				
2009	184,550,500	—	—	—	—	1.25
2009	7,500	PF63 16.00				
2010	184,000,000	—	—	—	—	1.25
2010	—	PF63 16.00				
2011	144,900,000	—	—	—	—	1.25
2011	—	PF63 16.00				
2012	139,104,000	—	—	—	—	1.25
2012	—	PF63 16.00				
2013	—	—	—	—	—	1.25
2013	—	PF63 16.00				

KM# 1285 10 EURO CENT
4.07 g., Brass, 19.7 mm. **Obv:** The seed sower divides date and RF **Rev:** Denomination and map **Edge:** Reeded

Date	Mintage	F12	VF20	XF40	MS60	MS63
2001	144,513,261	—	—	—	1.25	2.00
2001	15,000	PF63 12.00				
2002	206,700,000	—	—	—	0.75	1.25
2002	21,453	PF63 10.00				
2003	180,875,000	—	—	—	1.25	2.00
2003	40,000	PF63 10.00				
2004	5,000,000	—	—	—	—	1.50
2004 In sets only	140,000					
2004	20,000	PF63 12.00				
2005	45,120,000	—	—	—	—	1.50
2005	10,000	PF63 14.00				
2006	60,278,000	—	—	—	—	1.50
2006	10,000	PF63 14.00				

KM# 1410 10 EURO CENT
4.07 g., Brass, 19.7 mm. **Obv:** Sower **Rev:** Relief map of Western Europe, stars, lines and value **Edge:** Reeded

Date	Mintage	F12	VF20	XF40	MS60	MS63
2007	90,158,000	—	—	—	—	1.50
2007	7,500	PF63 14.00				
2008	178,757,000	—	—	—	—	1.50
2008	7,500	PF63 14.00				
2009	142,550,500	—	—	—	—	1.50
2009	7,500	PF63 14.00				
2010	—	—	—	—	—	1.50
2010	—	PF63 14.00				
2011	—	—	—	—	—	1.50
2011	—	PF63 14.00				
2012	—	—	—	—	—	1.50
2012	—	PF63 14.00				
2013	—	—	—	—	—	1.50
2013	—	PF63 14.00				

KM# 1286 20 EURO CENT
5.73 g., Brass, 22.2 mm. **Obv:** The seed sower divides date and RF **Rev:** Denomination and map **Edge:** Notched

Date	Mintage	F12	VF20	XF40	MS60	MS63
2001	256,342,108	—	—	—	1.00	1.50
2001	15,000	PF63 14.00				
2002	192,100,000	—	—	—	1.00	1.50
2002	21,453	PF63 12.00				
2003 In sets only	180,000	—	—	—	—	9.50
2003	40,000	PF63 12.00				
2004 In sets only	160,000	—	—	—	—	9.50
2004	20,000	PF63 14.00				
2005 In sets only	120,000	—	—	—	—	9.50
2005	10,000	PF63 16.00				
2006 In sets only	67,600	—	—	—	—	9.50
2006	10,000	PF63 16.00				

KM# 1411 20 EURO CENT
5.73 g., Brass, 22.2 mm. **Obv:** Sower **Rev:** Relief map of Western Europe, stars, lines and value **Edge:** Notched

Date	Mintage	F12	VF20	XF40	MS60	MS63
2007	40,258,000	—	—	—	—	1.50
2007	7,500	PF63 14.00				
2008	25,557,000	—	—	—	—	1.50
2008	7,500	PF63 14.00				
2009	82,550,500	—	—	—	—	1.50
2009	7,500	PF63 14.00				
2010	—	—	—	—	—	1.50
2010	—	PF63 14.00				
2011	—	—	—	—	—	1.50
2011	—	PF63 14.00				
2012	—	—	—	—	—	1.50
2012	—	PF63 14.00				
2013	—	—	—	—	—	1.50
2013	—	PF63 14.00				

KM# 1293 1/4 EURO
12.50 g., Aluminum-Bronze, 30 mm. **Subject:** Childrens Design **Obv:** Euro globe with children **Rev:** Denomination and stars **Edge:** Plain

Date	Mintage	F12	VF20	XF40	MS60	MS63
2002	61,431	—	—	—	6.50	8.50

KM# 1300 1/4 EURO
13.00 g., 0.900 Silver 0.3737 oz. ASW, 30 mm. **Subject:** Europa **Obv:** Eight French euro coin designs **Rev:** Portrait and flags design of 6.55957 francs coin KM-1265 **Edge:** Reeded

Date	Mintage	F12	VF20	XF40	MS60	MS63
2002	20,000	—	—	—	20.00	22.00

KM# 1331 1/4 EURO
3.11 g., 0.999 Gold 0.0992 oz. AGW, 15 mm. **Subject:** Children's Design **Obv:** Euro globe with children **Rev:** Denomination **Edge:** Plain

Date	Mintage	F12	VF20	XF40	MS60	MS63
2002	5,000	PF63 185	PF65 200			

KM# 1293a 1/4 EURO
13.00 g., 0.900 Silver 0.3737 oz. ASW, 30 mm. **Subject:** Childrens Design **Obv:** Euro globe with children **Rev:** Denomination **Edge:** Plain

Date	Mintage	F12	VF20	XF40	MS60	MS63
2002	10,000	PF63 45.00	PF65 50.00			

KM# 1983 1/4 EURO
13.00 g., 0.900 Silver 0.3737 oz. ASW **Obv:** Soccer ball and syylized map of France **Rev:** Two soccer players and stadium plan

Date	Mintage	F12	VF20	XF40	MS60	MS63
2002	9,033	—	—	—	—	35.00

KM# 1350 1/4 EURO
3.11 g., 0.9999 Gold 0.0993 oz. AGW, 15 mm. **Obv:** Obverse design of first one franc coin **Rev:** Reverse design of first one franc coin **Edge:** Plain

Date	Mintage	F12	VF20	XF40	MS60	MS63
2003	1,143	PF63 185		PF65 200		

KM# 1991 1/4 EURO
13.00 g., 0.900 Silver 0.3737 oz. ASW **Obv:** Curved cross pattern with coins **Rev:** Europa head at right, flags at left

Date	Mintage	F12	VF20	XF40	MS60	MS63
2003	16,035	—	—	—	—	25.00

KM# 1995 1/4 EURO
13.00 g., 0.900 Silver 0.3737 oz. ASW **Subject:** Tour de France, 100th Anniversary

Date	Mintage	F12	VF20	XF40	MS60	MS63
2003	71,257	—	—	—	—	20.00

KM# 1372 1/4 EURO
22.20 g., 0.900 Silver 0.6382 oz. ASW, 37 mm. **Obv:** Samuel de Champlain **Rev:** Sail ship **Edge:** Plain

Date	Mintage	F12	VF20	XF40	MS60	MS63
2004	15,105	—	—	—	27.50	32.50

KM# 1390 1/4 EURO
13.00 g., 0.900 Silver 0.3737 oz. ASW, 30 mm. **Subject:** European Union Expansion **Obv:** Partial face and flags **Rev:** Puzzle map **Edge:** Plain

Date	Mintage	F12	VF20	XF40	MS60	MS63
2004	10,066	—	—	—	22.00	25.00

KM# 2017 1/4 EURO
22.20 g., 0.900 Silver 0.6382 oz. ASW **Subject:** Chinese - French culture **Obv:** Rooster and dragon **Rev:** Temple of Heaven and Eiffel tower

Date	Mintage	F12	VF20	XF40	MS60	MS63
2004	10,000	—	—	—	—	100

KM# 1402 1/4 EURO
11.00 g., Aluminum-Bronze, 30 mm. **Subject:** Jules Verne **Obv:** Various scenes from Jules Verne's novels **Rev:** Jules Verne's portrait left of value and date

Date	Mintage	F12	VF20	XF40	MS60	MS63
2005	22,256	—	—	—	—	10.00

KM# 1415 1/4 EURO
22.20 g., 0.900 Silver 0.6382 oz. ASW, 37 mm. **Obv:** Jean de la Fontaine, value, Chinese astrological animals, date, Paris mint privy marks but without national identification **Rev:** Dog in wreath **Edge:** Reeded **Note:** Anonymous coinage

Date	Mintage	F12	VF20	XF40	MS60	MS63
2006	10,000	—	—	—	32.00	35.00

KM# 1442 1/4 EURO
22.20 g., 0.900 Silver 0.6382 oz. ASW, 37 mm. **Obv:** Bust of Franklin facing slightly right at left, his diplomatic and technical successes at right **Obv. Legend:** BENJAMIN FRANKLIN 1706-2006 **Obv. Inscription:** AMI DE LA FRANCE **Rev:** French flag at left, American flag at right **Rev. Inscription:** PHILOSOPHE / DIPLOMATE / ÉCRIVAIN / SAVANT

Date	Mintage	F12	VF20	XF40	MS60	MS63
2006	15,000	—	—	—	32.00	35.00

KM# 1445 1/4 EURO
22.20 g., 0.900 Silver 0.6382 oz. ASW, 37 mm. **Subject:** Marshall Bernadotte under Napoleon **Rev:** Military bust facing 3/4 right at left, building in backgound at right **Rev. Legend:** LIBERTÉ / ÉGALITÉ / FRATERNITÉ - KARL XIV JOHAN ROI DE SUÈDE

Date	Mintage	F12	VF20	XF40	MS60	MS63
2006 Proof	10,000	—	—	—	32.00	35.00

KM# 1457 1/4 EURO
22.20 g., 0.900 Silver 0.6382 oz. ASW, 37 mm. **Subject:** Hôpitaux de France Foundation **Obv:** Foundation logo **Rev:** TGV train, money box on outlined map of France

Date	Mintage	F12	VF20	XF40	MS60	MS63
2006	50,000	—	—	—	28.00	30.00

KM# 2061 1/4 EURO
22.20 g., 0.900 Silver 0.6382 oz. ASW **Subject:** Wolfgang Amadeus Mozart, 250th Anniversary of Birth **Obv:** Youthful bust **Rev:** Hand on piano keys, music above

Date	Mintage	F12	VF20	XF40	MS60	MS63
2006	5,000	—	—	—	—	55.00

KM# 1417 1/4 EURO
22.20 g., 0.900 Silver 0.6382 oz. ASW, 37 mm. **Obv:** Jean de la Fontaine, value, Chinese astrological animals, date, Paris mint privy marks but without national identification **Rev:** Pig in wreath **Edge:** Reeded **Note:** Anonymous issue.

Date	Mintage	F12	VF20	XF40	MS60	MS63
2007	10,000	—	—	—	32.00	35.00

KM# 1419 1/4 EURO
13.00 g., 0.900 Silver 0.3737 oz. ASW, 30 mm. **Obv:** Military bust of Lafayette facing 3/4 left **Obv. Legend:** LA FAYETTE. HÉROS DE LA RÉVOLUTION AMÉRICAINE **Obv. Inscription:** 1757/1854 at left, RF monogram at right **Rev:** Sailing ship L' Hermione **Rev. Legend:** LA FAYETTE, HERO OF THE AMERICAN REVOLUTION **Edge:** Plain

Date	Mintage	F12	VF20	XF40	MS60	MS63
2007 (a) Proof-like	4,740	—	—	—	32.00	35.00

KM# 1421 1/4 EURO
15.00 g., 0.900 Silver 0.4312 oz. ASW **Subject:** 90th Anniversary Death of Degas **Obv:** Ballerina "The Star" at left **Obv. Inscription:** Degas **Rev:** Paint brushes and oils multicolor at left, self portrait at right **Rev. Inscription:** LIBERTÉ / ÉGALITÉ / FRATERNITÉ **Shape:** rectangular, 30 x 21 mm

Date	Mintage	F12	VF20	XF40	MS60	MS63
2007	5,000	—	—	—	42.00	45.00

KM# 1461 1/4 EURO
13.00 g., 0.900 Silver 0.3737 oz. ASW, 30 mm. **Subject:** Sebastien Le Prestre de Vauban, 300th Anniversary of Death **Obv:** Arms above funeral coach, book at left **Rev:** Vauban standing; plans of fortress

Date	Mintage	F12	VF20	XF40	MS60	MS63
2007	4,051	PF63 22.00		PF65 25.00		

KM# 1483 1/4 EURO
13.00 g., 0.900 Silver 0.3737 oz. ASW, 37 mm. **Subject:** 2007 Rugby World Cup **Obv:** Two Rugby players **Rev:** Logo and goal

Date	Mintage	F12	VF20	XF40	MS60	MS63
2007	Est. 4944	—	—	—	32.00	35.00

KM# 1570 1/4 EURO
15.00 g., 0.900 Silver 0.4312 oz. ASW, 30 x 21 mm. **Subject:** Edward Manet **Obv:** Manet's "Olympia" painting **Rev:** Multicolor paint brushes and Manet's portrait **Shape:** Rectangle

Date	Mintage	F12	VF20	XF40	MS60	MS63
2008	7,695	—	—	—	—	65.00

KM# 1572 1/4 EURO
22.20 g., 0.900 Silver 0.6382 oz. ASW, 37 mm. **Subject:** Lunar New Year - Year of the Rat **Obv:** Bust of Jean de la Fontaine and twelve awards **Rev:** Rat within border

Date	Mintage	F12	VF20	XF40	MS60	MS63
2008	5,267	—	—	—	32.00	35.00

KM# 1287 50 EURO CENT
7.81 g., Brass, 24.2 mm. **Obv:** The Seed Sower divides date and RF **Rev:** Denomination and map **Edge:** Reeded

Date	Mintage	F12	VF20	XF40	MS60	MS63
2001	276,287,274	—	—	—	1.25	2.00
2001	15,000	PF63 15.00				
2002	226,500,000	—	—	—	1.25	2.00
2002	21,453	PF63 14.00				
2003 In sets only	180,000	—	—	—	—	11.50
2003	40,000	PF63 14.00				
2004 In sets only	160,000	—	—	—	—	11.50
2004	20,000	PF63 15.00				
2005 In sets only	120,000	—	—	—	—	11.50
2005	10,000	PF63 17.00				
2006 In sets only	67,600	—	—	—	—	11.50
2006	10,000	PF63 17.00				

KM# 1412 50 EURO CENT
7.81 g., Brass, 24.2 mm. **Obv:** Sower **Rev:** Relief map of Western Europe, stars, lines and value **Edge:** Reeded

Date	Mintage	F12	VF20	XF40	MS60	MS63
2007 In sets only	58,000	—	—	—	—	11.50
2007	7,500	PF63 16.00				
2008 In sets only	57,000	—	—	—	—	2.00
2008	7,500	PF63 16.00				
2009 In sets only	50,500	—	—	—	—	2.00
2009	7,500	PF63 16.00				
2010	—	—	—	—	—	2.00
2010	—	PF63 16.00				
2011	—	—	—	—	—	2.00
2011	—	PF63 16.00				
2012	—	—	—	—	—	2.00
2012	—	PF63 16.00				
2013	—	—	—	—	—	2.00
2013	—	PF63 16.00				

KM# 1288 EURO
7.50 g., Bi-Metallic, 23.25 mm. **Obv:** Stylized tree divides RF within circle, date below **Rev:** Denomination and map **Edge:** Segmented reeding

Date	Mintage	F12	VF20	XF40	MS60	MS63
2001	150,251,624	—	—	—	2.75	4.00
2001	15,000	PF63 18.00				
2002	129,400,000	—	—	—	2.50	3.75
2002	21,453	PF63 16.00				
2003 In sets only	100,000	—	—	—	8.00	12.50
2003	20,000	PF63 18.00				
2004 In sets only	160,000	—	—	—	—	2.50
2004	20,000	PF63 18.00				
2005 In sets only	120,000	—	—	—	—	2.50
2005	10,000	PF63 20.00				
2006 In sets only	78,000	—	—	—	—	2.50
2006	10,000	PF63 20.00				

KM# 1413 EURO
7.50 g., Bi-Metallic, 23.25 mm. **Obv:** Stylized tree **Rev:** Relief map of Western Europe, stars, lines and value **Edge:** Segmented reeding

Date	Mintage	F12	VF20	XF40	MS60	MS63
2007 In sets only	58,000	—	—	—	—	11.50
2007	7,500	PF63 20.00				
2008 In sets only	57,000	—	—	—	—	2.50
2008	7,500	PF63 20.00				
2009 In sets only	50,500	—	—	—	—	2.50

Date	Mintage	F12	VF20	XF40	MS60	MS63
2009	7,500	PF63 20.00				
2010	—	—	—	—	—	2.50
2010	—	PF63 20.00				
2011	—	—	—	—	—	2.50
2011	—	PF63 20.00				
2012	—	—	—	—	—	2.50
2012	—	PF63 20.00				
2013	—	—	—	—	—	2.50
2013	—	PF63 20.00				

KM# 1464 EURO
155.55 g., 0.950 Silver 4.7204 oz. ASW, 50 mm. **Subject:** Sebastien Le Prestre de Vauban, 300th Anniversary of Death

Date	Mintage	F12	VF20	XF40	MS60	MS63
2007	500	PF63 350	PF65 375			

KM# 1470 EURO
17.00 g., 0.920 Gold 0.4996 oz. AGW, 31 mm. **Subject:** Le Petit Prince, 60th Anniversary **Obv:** Prince standing with rabbit

Date	Mintage	F12	VF20	XF40	MS60	MS63
2007	2,000	PF63 875	PF65 900			

KM# 1486 EURO
17.00 g., 0.920 Gold 0.4996 oz. AGW, 31 mm. **Subject:** 2007 Rugby World Cup **Obv:** Two players and goal **Rev:** Logo and goal

Date	Mintage	F12	VF20	XF40	MS60	MS63
2007	500	PF63 875	PF65 900			

KM# 1490 EURO
22.00 g., 0.900 Silver 0.6325 oz. ASW **Subject:** Unesco **Obv:** Great Wall of China

Date	Mintage	F12	VF20	XF40	MS60	MS63
2007	5,000	PF63 60.00	PF65 70.00			

KM# 1491 EURO
8.45 g., 0.920 Gold 0.2483 oz. AGW, 22 mm. **Subject:** Unesco **Obv:** Great Wall of China **Rev:** Unesco Building and emblem

Date	Mintage	F12	VF20	XF40	MS60	MS63
2007	500	PF63 450	PF65 475			

KM# 1492 EURO
22.20 g., 0.900 Silver 0.6382 oz. ASW, 37 mm. **Subject:** Point Neuf 400th Anniversary **Obv:** Monuments of France logo **Rev:** Point Neuf Bridge, Paris Mint Museum

Date	Mintage	F12	VF20	XF40	MS60	MS63
2007	3,000	PF63 80.00	PF65 90.00			

KM# 1493 EURO
8.45 g., 0.920 Gold 0.2483 oz. AGW, 22 mm. **Subject:** Point Neuf, 400th Anniversary **Obv:** Monuments of France logo **Rev:** Point Neuf Brudge, Paris Mint Building

Date	Mintage	F12	VF20	XF40	MS60	MS63
2007	500	PF63 450	PF65 475			

KM# 1495 EURO
8.45 g., 0.920 Gold 0.2483 oz. AGW, 22 mm. **Subject:** Cannes Film Festival **Obv:** Cinema screen and stage, Golden Palm Award

Date	Mintage	F12	VF20	XF40	MS60	MS63
2007	500	PF63 450	PF65 475			

KM# 1514 EURO
17.00 g., 0.920 Gold 0.4996 oz. AGW, 31 mm. **Subject:** Stanislas Lesczynski **Obv:** Bust, shield **Rev:** Palac Stanislas - Nancy

Date	Mintage	F12	VF20	XF40	MS60	MS63
2007	500	PF63 875	PF65 900			

KM# 1587 EURO
8.45 g., 0.920 Gold 0.2483 oz. AGW, 22 mm. **Subject:** Court of Human Rights, 50th Anniversary **Obv:** Sower left **Rev:** Text

Date	Mintage	F12	VF20	XF40	MS60	MS63
2009P	500	PF63 450	PF65 475			

KM# 1301 1-1/2 EURO
22.20 g., 0.900 Silver 0.6382 oz. ASW, 37 mm. **Subject:** Europa **Obv:** Eight French euro coins design **Rev:** Portrait and flags design of 6.55957 francs KM-1265 **Edge:** Plain

Date	Mintage	F12	VF20	XF40	MS60	MS63
2002	50,000	PF63 45.00	PF65 50.00			

KM# 1305 1-1/2 EURO
22.20 g., 0.900 Silver 0.6382 oz. ASW, 37 mm. **Subject:** French Landmarks **Obv:** French map **Rev:** Le Mont St. Michel **Edge:** Plain

Date	Mintage	F12	VF20	XF40	MS60	MS63
2002	9,520	PF63 50.00	PF65 55.00			

KM# 1307 1-1/2 EURO
22.20 g., 0.900 Silver 0.6382 oz. ASW, 37 mm. **Subject:** French Landmarks **Obv:** French map **Rev:** La Butte Montmartre **Edge:** Plain

Date	Mintage	F12	VF20	XF40	MS60	MS63
2002	6,095	PF63 47.50	PF65 50.00			

KM# 1310 1-1/2 EURO
22.20 g., 0.900 Silver 0.6382 oz. ASW, 37 mm. **Subject:** First West to East Transatlantic Flight **Obv:** Denomination, map and Lindbergh portrait **Rev:** Spirit of St. Louis (airplane) and map **Edge:** Plain

Date	Mintage	F12	VF20	XF40	MS60	MS63
2002	10,000	PF63 50.00	PF65 55.00			

KM# 1332 1-1/2 EURO
22.20 g., 0.900 Silver 0.6382 oz. ASW, 37 mm. **Obv:** Victor Hugo, denomination and map **Rev:** Multicolor "Gavroche **Edge:** Plain

Date	Mintage	F12	VF20	XF40	MS60	MS63
2002	10,000	PF63 55.00	PF65 60.00			

KM# 1840 1-1/2 EURO
22.20 g., 0.900 Silver 0.6382 oz. ASW, 37 mm. **Subject:** Snow White **Rev:** Scenes from the book, color

Date	Mintage	F12	VF20	XF40	MS60	MS63
2002	9,751	PF63 55.00	PF65 60.00			

KM# 1841 1-1/2 EURO
22.20 g., 0.900 Silver 0.6382 oz. ASW, 37 mm. **Subject:** Cinderella **Rev:** Scenes from the book, color

Date	Mintage	F12	VF20	XF40	MS60	MS63
2002	9,907	PF63 55.00	PF65 60.00			

KM# 1842 1-1/2 EURO
22.20 g., 0.900 Silver 0.6382 oz. ASW, 37 mm. **Subject:** Pinocchio **Rev:** Scenes form the book, color

Date	Mintage	F12	VF20	XF40	MS60	MS63
2002	—	PF63 55.00	PF65 60.00			

KM# 1321 1-1/2 EURO
22.20 g., 0.900 Silver 0.6382 oz. ASW, 37 mm. **Obv:** Tour de France logo **Rev:** Cyclist going left **Edge:** Plain

Date	Mintage	F12	VF20	XF40	MS60	MS63
2003	22,905	PF63 50.00	PF65 55.00			

KM# 1322 1-1/2 EURO
22.20 g., 0.900 Silver 0.6382 oz. ASW, 37 mm. **Obv:** Tour de France logo **Rev:** Group of cyclists and Arch de Triumph **Edge:** Plain

Date	Mintage	F12	VF20	XF40	MS60	MS63
2003 (Ht)	16,532	PF63 50.00	PF65 55.00			

KM# 1323 1-1/2 EURO
22.20 g., 0.900 Silver 0.6382 oz. ASW, 37 mm. **Obv:** Tour de France logo **Rev:** Two cyclists and spectators **Edge:** Plain

Date	Mintage	F12	VF20	XF40	MS60	MS63
2003 (Ht)	15,934	PF63 50.00	PF65 55.00			

KM# 1324 1-1/2 EURO
22.20 g., 0.900 Silver 0.6382 oz. ASW, 37 mm. **Obv:** Tour de France logo **Rev:** Two groups of cyclists **Edge:** Plain

Date	Mintage	F12	VF20	XF40	MS60	MS63
2003 (Ht)	16,317	PF63 50.00	PF65 55.00			

KM# 1325 1-1/2 EURO
22.20 g., 0.900 Silver 0.6382 oz. ASW, 37 mm. **Obv:** Tour de France logo **Rev:** Cyclists, stopwatch and gears **Edge:** Plain

Date	Mintage	F12	VF20	XF40	MS60	MS63
2003 (Ht)	5,589	PF63 50.00	PF65 55.00			

KM# 1336 1-1/2 EURO
22.20 g., 0.900 Silver 0.6382 oz. ASW, 37 mm. **Obv:** Jefferson and Napoleon with Louisiana Purchase map **Rev:** Jazz musician, mansion and river boat **Edge:** Plain

Date	Mintage	F12	VF20	XF40	MS60	MS63
2003	10,000	PF63 55.00	PF65 60.00			

KM# 1338 1-1/2 EURO
22.20 g., 0.900 Silver 0.6382 oz. ASW, 37 mm. **Obv:** Curved cross design with multiple values **Rev:** Goddess Europa and flags **Edge:** Plain

Date	Mintage	F12	VF20	XF40	MS60	MS63
2003	24,501	PF63 50.00	PF65 55.00			

KM# 1341 1-1/2 EURO
22.20 g., 0.900 Silver 0.6382 oz. ASW, 37 mm. **Obv:** Denomination and compass face **Rev:** SS Normandie and New York City **Edge:** Plain

Date	Mintage	F12	VF20	XF40	MS60	MS63
2003	2,422	PF63 55.00	PF65 60.00			

KM# 1343 1-1/2 EURO
22.20 g., 0.900 Silver 0.6382 oz. ASW, 37 mm. **Obv:** Denomination and compass face **Rev:** Airplane and Tokyo Geisha **Edge:** Plain

Date	Mintage	F12	VF20	XF40	MS60	MS63
2003	2,285	PF63 55.00	PF65 60.00			

KM# 1345 1-1/2 EURO
22.20 g., 0.900 Silver 0.6382 oz. ASW, 37 mm. **Obv:** Paul Gauguin **Rev:** Native woman **Edge:** Plain

Date	Mintage	F12	VF20	XF40	MS60	MS63
2003	3,198	PF63 70.00	PF65 80.00			

KM# 1351 1-1/2 EURO
22.20 g., 0.900 Silver 0.6382 oz. ASW, 37 mm. **Obv:** Obverse design of first one franc coin **Rev:** Reverse design of first one franc coin **Edge:** Plain

Date	Mintage	F12	VF20	XF40	MS60	MS63
2003	15,000	PF63 55.00	PF65 60.00			

KM# 1353 1-1/2 EURO
22.20 g., 0.900 Silver 0.6382 oz. ASW, 37 mm. **Obv:** Mona Lisa **Rev:** Leonardo da Vinci **Edge:** Plain

Date	Mintage	F12	VF20	XF40	MS60	MS63
2003	8,139	PF63 55.00	PF65 60.00			

KM# 1355 1-1/2 EURO
22.20 g., 0.900 Silver 0.6382 oz. ASW, 37 mm. **Obv:** Map and denomination **Rev:** Chateau Chambord **Edge:** Plain

Date	Mintage	F12	VF20	XF40	MS60	MS63
2003	3,094	PF63 50.00	PF65 55.00			

KM# 1357 1-1/2 EURO
22.20 g., 0.900 Silver 0.6382 oz. ASW, 37 mm. **Obv:** Denomination in swirling design **Rev:** Multicolor Hansel and Gretel, witch and house **Edge:** Plain

Date	Mintage	F12	VF20	XF40	MS60	MS63
2003	3,124	PF63 55.00	PF65 60.00			

KM# 1359 1-1/2 EURO
22.20 g., 0.900 Silver 0.6382 oz. ASW, 37 mm. **Obv:** Denomination in swirling design **Rev:** Multicolor Alice in Wonderland **Edge:** Plain

Date	Mintage	F12	VF20	XF40	MS60	MS63
2003	3,096	PF63 55.00	PF65 60.00			

KM# 1361 1-1/2 EURO
22.20 g., 0.900 Silver 0.6382 oz. ASW, 37 mm. **Obv:** Pierre de Coubertin **Rev:** Olympic runners **Edge:** Plain

Date	Mintage	F12	VF20	XF40	MS60	MS63
2003	50,000	PF63 50.00	PF65 55.00			

KM# 1843 1-1/2 EURO
22.20 g., 0.900 Silver 0.6382 oz. ASW, 37 mm. **Subject:** Athletic Games **Rev:** Shot Put athlete and stadium

Date	Mintage	F12	VF20	XF40	MS60	MS63
2003	4,195	PF63 55.00	PF65 60.00			

KM# 1996 1-1/2 EURO
22.20 g., 0.900 Silver 0.6382 oz. ASW **Subject:** Athletic World Championships **Obv:** Winner podium before buildigns **Rev:** Runners by Pont des Arts

Date	Mintage	F12	VF20	XF40	MS60	MS63
2003	4,425	PF63 45.00	PF65 50.00			

KM# 1997 1-1/2 EURO
22.20 g., 0.900 Silver 0.6382 oz. ASW **Subject:** Athletic Wordl Championships **Obv:** Winner podium before buildings **Rev:** High jumper before Pont au Double

Date	Mintage	F12	VF20	XF40	MS60	MS63
2003	4,169	PF63 45.00	PF65 50.00			

KM# 2003 1-1/2 EURO
22.20 g., 0.900 Silver 0.6382 oz. ASW **Obv:** Sower advancing left **Rev:** Stars and map of European Union

Date	Mintage	F12	VF20	XF40	MS60	MS63
2003	6,100	PF63 55.00	PF65 65.00			

KM# 2006 1-1/2 EURO
22.20 g., 0.900 Silver 0.6382 oz. ASW **Subject:** Orient Express, Hagia Sophia in Istanbul

Date	Mintage	F12	VF20	XF40	MS60	MS63
2003	Est. 3821	PF63 45.00	PF65 50.00			

KM# 2008 1-1/2 EURO
22.20 g., 0.900 Silver 0.6382 oz. ASW **Subject:** Childhood Fairy Tales **Rev:** Sleeping Beauty

Date	Mintage	F12	VF20	XF40	MS60	MS63
2003	3,246	PF63 55.00	PF65 65.00			

KM# 1364 1-1/2 EURO
22.20 g., 0.900 Silver 0.6382 oz. ASW, 37 mm. **Obv:** Map with denomination **Rev:** Avignon Popes Palace **Edge:** Plain

Date	Mintage	F12	VF20	XF40	MS60	MS63
2004	3,504	PF63 50.00	PF65 55.00			

KM# 1366 1-1/2 EURO
22.20 g., 0.900 Silver 0.6382 oz. ASW, 37 mm. **Obv:** Book, eagle and denomination **Rev:** Napoleon and coronation scene in background **Edge:** Plain

Date	Mintage	F12	VF20	XF40	MS60	MS63
2004	9,705	PF63 45.00	PF65 50.00			

KM# 1369 1-1/2 EURO
22.20 g., 0.900 Silver 0.6382 oz. ASW, 37 mm. **Obv:** Soldiers and Normandy invasion scene **Rev:** D-DAY™ above denomination **Edge:** Plain

Date	Mintage	F12	VF20	XF40	MS60	MS63
2004	3,343	PF63 50.00	PF65 55.00			

KM# 1373 1-1/2 EURO
22.20 g., 0.900 Silver 0.6382 oz. ASW, 37 mm. **Obv:** Emile Loubet and King Edward VII **Rev:** Marianne and Britannia **Edge:** Plain

Date	Mintage	F12	VF20	XF40	MS60	MS63
2004	4,022	PF63 50.00	PF65 55.00			

KM# 1374 1-1/2 EURO
22.20 g., 0.900 Silver 0.6382 oz. ASW, 37 mm. **Obv:** Soccer ball and denomination **Rev:** Rooster and quill **Edge:** Plain

Date	Mintage	F12	VF20	XF40	MS60	MS63
2004	25,000	PF63 55.00	PF65 60.00			

KM# 1378 1-1/2 EURO
22.20 g., 0.900 Silver 0.6382 oz. ASW, 37 mm. **Obv:** Compass rose **Rev:** Ocean liner **Edge:** Plain

Date	Mintage	F12	VF20	XF40	MS60	MS63
2004	1,708	PF63 50.00	PF65 55.00			

KM# 1380 1-1/2 EURO
22.20 g., 0.900 Silver 0.6382 oz. ASW, 37 mm. **Obv:** Compass rose **Rev:** Trans-Siberian Railroad **Edge:** Plain

Date	Mintage	F12	VF20	XF40	MS60	MS63
2004	2,958	PF63 50.00	PF65 55.00			

KM# 1382 1-1/2 EURO
22.20 g., 0.900 Silver 0.6382 oz. ASW, 37 mm. **Obv:** Compass rose **Rev:** Half-track vehicle **Edge:** Plain

Date	Mintage	F12	VF20	XF40	MS60	MS63
2004	1,743	PF63 47.50	PF65 50.00			

KM# 1384 1-1/2 EURO
22.20 g., 0.900 Silver 0.6382 oz. ASW, 37 mm. **Obv:** Compass rose **Rev:** Biplane airliner **Edge:** Plain

Date	Mintage	F12	VF20	XF40	MS60	MS63
2004	1,548	PF63 47.50	PF65 50.00			

KM# 1386 1-1/2 EURO
22.20 g., 0.900 Silver 0.6382 oz. ASW, 37 mm. **Obv:** F.A. Bartholdi **Rev:** Statue of Liberty **Edge:** Plain

Date	Mintage	F12	VF20	XF40	MS60	MS63
2004	3,303	PF63 47.50	PF65 50.00			

KM# 1391 1-1/2 EURO
22.20 g., 0.900 Silver 0.6382 oz. ASW, 37 mm. **Subject:** European Union Expansion **Obv:** Puzzle map of Europe **Rev:** Partial face and flags **Edge:** Plain

Date	Mintage	F12	VF20	XF40	MS60	MS63
2004	40,000	PF63 42.50	PF65 50.00			

KM# 1844 1-1/2 EURO
22.20 g., 0.900 Silver 0.6382 oz. ASW, 37 mm. **Obv:** Sower advancing left within stars **Rev:** Head at left, stars at right

Date	Mintage	F12	VF20	XF40	MS60	MS63
2004	Est. 5000	PF63 55.00	PF65 60.00			

KM# 2013 1-1/2 EURO
22.20 g., 0.900 Silver 0.6382 oz. ASW **Subject:** Childhood stories **Rev:** Aladdin and lamp in color

Date	Mintage	F12	VF20	XF40	MS60	MS63
2004	2,222	PF63 70.00	PF65 80.00			

KM# 2014 1-1/2 EURO
22.20 g., 0.900 Silver 0.6382 oz. ASW **Subject:** Childhood stories **Rev:** Peter Pan in color

Date	Mintage	F12	VF20	XF40	MS60	MS63
2004	2,469	PF63 70.00	PF65 80.00			

KM# 1423 1-1/2 EURO
22.20 g., 0.900 Silver 0.6382 oz. ASW, 37 mm. **Subject:** Biathlon **Rev:** Skier at right facing 3/4 left, mountain peaks in background **Rev. Inscription:** JEUX D'HIVER

Date	Mintage	F12	VF20	XF40	MS60	MS63
2005	4,903	PF63 45.00	PF65 50.00			

KM# 1425 1-1/2 EURO
22.20 g., 0.900 Silver 0.6382 oz. ASW, 37 mm. **Series:** Jules Verne **Subject:** From the Earth to the Moon **Rev:** Crowd observing at lower left, volcano erupting above, moon at upper right, Verne in spaceship at lower right, factory chimneys belching smoke in background **Rev. Legend:** DE LA TERRE... LA LUNE

Date	Mintage	F12	VF20	XF40	MS60	MS63
2005	1,336	PF63 65.00	PF65 75.00			

KM# 1427 1-1/2 EURO
22.20 g., 0.900 Silver 0.6382 oz. ASW, 37 mm. **Rev:** Kitty and poodle at table at cafe, multicolor **Rev. Legend:** Hello Kitty

Date	Mintage	F12	VF20	XF40	MS60	MS63
2005	4,000	PF63 65.00	PF65 75.00			

KM# 1428 1-1/2 EURO
22.20 g., 0.900 Silver 0.6382 oz. ASW, 37 mm. **Rev:** Kitty on the Champs-Elysees, multicolor **Rev. Legend:** Hello Kitty

Date	Mintage	F12	VF20	XF40	MS60	MS63
2005	4,000	PF63 65.00	PF65 75.00			

KM# 1431 1-1/2 EURO
22.20 g., 0.900 Silver 0.6382 oz. ASW, 37 mm. **Subject:** Bicentennial Victory at Austerlitz **Rev:** Battle scene **Rev. Legend:** LIBERTÉ ÉGALITÉ FRATERNITÉ

Date	Mintage	F12	VF20	XF40	MS60	MS63
2005	7,203	PF63 50.00	PF65 55.00			

KM# 1434 1-1/2 EURO
22.20 g., 0.900 Silver 0.6382 oz. ASW, 37 mm. **Subject:** 50th Anniversary of the Europe flag **Rev:** Stars at left, partial flag at center right

Date	Mintage	F12	VF20	XF40	MS60	MS63
2005	7,861	PF63 50.00	PF65 55.00			

KM# 1436 1-1/2 EURO
22.20 g., 0.900 Silver 0.6382 oz. ASW, 37 mm. **Subject:** Centenary Law of Dec. 9, 1905 **Obv:** Sower" left in ring of stars

Date	Mintage	F12	VF20	XF40	MS60	MS63
2005	3,110	PF63 50.00	PF65 55.00			
2006	10,000	PF63 50.00	PF65 55.00			

KM# 1438 1-1/2 EURO
22.20 g., 0.900 Silver 0.6382 oz. ASW, 37 mm. **Series:** Jules Verne **Subject:** 20,000 Leagues Under the Sea **Rev:** Submarine above plants and divers **Rev. Legend:** VINGT MILLE LIEUES SOUS LES MERS

Date	Mintage	F12	VF20	XF40	MS60	MS63
2005	4,463	PF63 65.00	PF65 75.00			

KM# 1440 1-1/2 EURO
22.20 g., 0.900 Silver 0.6382 oz. ASW, 37 mm. **Subject:** 150th Anniversary of Classification of Bordeax Wines **Rev:** Stylized female with grapes between various names of wines at her feet

Date	Mintage	F12	VF20	XF40	MS60	MS63
2005	2,832	PF63 65.00	PF65 75.00			

KM# 1441 1-1/2 EURO
22.20 g., 0.900 Silver 0.6382 oz. ASW, 37 mm. **Subject:** 60th Anniversary - End of World War II **Rev:** Doves in flight **Rev. Inscription:** L'EUROPE FAIT LA PAIX

Date	Mintage	F12	VF20	XF40	MS60	MS63
2005	44,532	PF63 45.00	PF65 50.00			

KM# 2020 1-1/2 EURO
22.20 g., 0.900 Silver 0.6382 oz. ASW **Subject:** World Cup Soccer **Obv:** Trophy and soccer ball motif **Rev:** Value within map of France

Date	Mintage	F12	VF20	XF40	MS60	MS63
2005	1,883	PF63 45.00	PF65 50.00			

KM# 2027 1-1/2 EURO
22.20 g., 0.900 Silver 0.6382 oz. ASW **Subject:** Frederic Chopin, 195th Anniversary of Birth **Obv:** Profile at left, piano keys at right vertically **Rev:** Monument in Wausau park at left, piano keys at right vertically

Date	Mintage	F12	VF20	XF40	MS60	MS63
2005	3,000	PF63 300	PF65 325			

KM# 2029 1-1/2 EURO
22.20 g., 0.900 Silver 0.6382 oz. ASW, 37 mm. **Subject:** Jules Verne, 100th Anniversary of Death **Obv:** Around the World in 80 days

Date	Mintage	F12	VF20	XF40	MS60	MS63
2005	4,998	PF63 100	PF65 120			

KM# 2036 1-1/2 EURO
22.20 g., 0.900 Silver 0.6382 oz. ASW **Subject:** Hello Kitty **Rev:** Kitty with umbrella in color flying above Paris skyline

Date	Mintage	F12	VF20	XF40	MS60	MS63
2005	Est. 4000	PF63 55.00	PF65 65.00			

KM# 1444 1-1/2 EURO
22.20 g., 0.900 Silver 0.6382 oz. ASW, 37 mm. **Subject:** 100th Anniversary - French Grand Prix **Obv:** Steering wheel with early race car in upper segment, two gauges at lower left, R / F at lower right **Obv. Legend:** LE MANS 1906 - CENTENAIRE du 1er GRAND PRIX de l'AUTOMOBILE CLUB de FRANCE **Rev:** Modern racing car's steering wheel **Rev. Legend:** MAGNY-COURS

Date	Mintage	F12	VF20	XF40	MS60	MS63
2006	4,235	PF63 65.00	PF65 75.00			

KM# 1447 1-1/2 EURO
22.20 g., 0.900 Silver 0.6382 oz. ASW, 37 mm. **Obv:** Strogoff on horseback wielding sword, city at left, soldiers at lower left, cavalry at right **Obv. Legend:** MICHEL STROGOFF **Rev:** Head of Verne facing 3/4 right at left center, instruments and anchor in curved band **Rev. Legend:** 1828 JULES VERNE 1905 - LIBERTÉ . ÉGALITÉ . FRATERNITÉ

Date	Mintage	F12	VF20	XF40	MS60	MS63
2006	2,468	PF63 100	PF65 125			

KM# 1450 1-1/2 EURO
22.20 g., 0.900 Silver 0.6382 oz. ASW, 37 mm. **Subject:** Jules Verne **Obv:** Hot air balloon, parrots at left, native masks at lower left, foliage at right, native huts below, map of Africa in background **Obv. Legend:** CINQ SEMAINES EN BAILON **Rev:** Head of Verne facing 3/4 right at left center, instruments and anchor in curved band **Rev. Legend:** 1828 JULES VERNE 1905

Date	Mintage	F12	VF20	XF40	MS60	MS63
2006	2,287	PF63 65.00	PF65 75.00			

KM# 1452 1-1/2 EURO
22.20 g., 0.900 Silver 0.6382 oz. ASW, 37 mm. **Subject:** Formula 1 World Championship **Obv:** Race car outline on checker board background **Obv. Legend:** LIBERTÉ ÉGALITÉ FRATERNITÉ **Rev:** Race car outline in victory sprays with star **Rev. Legend:** RENAULT - CHAMPION DU MONDE FIA 2005 DES CONSTRUCTEURS DE FORMULE 1

Date	Mintage	F12	VF20	XF40	MS60	MS63
2006	10,000	PF63 50.00	PF65 55.00			

KM# 1453 1-1/2 EURO
22.20 g., 0.900 Silver 0.6382 oz. ASW, 37 mm. **Subject:** 100th Anniversary - Death of Paul Cézanne **Obv:** Self portrait **Obv. Inscription:** PAUL / CÉZANNE **Rev:** The Card Players **Rev. Legend:** LIBERTÉ ÉGALITÉ FRATERNITÉ

Date	Mintage	F12	VF20	XF40	MS60	MS63
2006	5,000	PF63 65.00	PF65 75.00			

KM# 1455 1-1/2 EURO
22.20 g., 0.900 Silver 0.6382 oz. ASW, 37 mm. **Obv:** Map of the Basilica **Rev:** Bust of Pope Benedict XVI with arms outstretched facing 3/4 right at lower left, Basilica in background **Rev. Legend:** 500 ANS de la BASILIQUE SAINT-PIERRE

Date	Mintage	F12	VF20	XF40	MS60	MS63
2006	5,000	PF63 65.00	PF65 75.00			

KM# 1456 1-1/2 EURO
22.20 g., 0.900 Silver 0.6382 oz. ASW, 37 mm. **Rev:** Half of Arc

at left, eternal flame above WW I plaque at right **Rev. Legend:** ARC DE TRIOMPHE

Date	Mintage	F12	VF20	XF40	MS60	MS63
2006	3,620	PF63 50.00	PF65 55.00			

KM# 1458 1-1/2 EURO
22.20 g., 0.900 Silver 0.6382 oz. ASW, 37 mm. **Subject:** 300th Anniversary - Completion of the Dome of Les Invalides **Obv:** Dome between Jules-Hardouin Mansart at left, Louis XIV at right **Rev. Legend:** SAINT-LOUIS - DES INVALIDES **Rev. Inscription:** 28/AOÛT - 1706

Date	Mintage	F12	VF20	XF40	MS60	MS63
2006	2,891	PF63 50.00	PF65 55.00			

KM# 2037 1-1/2 EURO
22.20 g., 0.900 Silver 0.6382 oz. ASW **Subject:** Robert Schuman, 120th Anniversary of Birth

Date	Mintage	F12	VF20	XF40	MS60	MS63
2006	21,517	PF63 35.00	PF65 40.00			

KM# 2041 1-1/2 EURO
22.20 g., 0.900 Silver 0.6382 oz. ASW **Subject:** Bejing Olympics **Obv:** Three fencing foils on globe map pointing at Bejing **Rev:** Two fencers

Date	Mintage	F12	VF20	XF40	MS60	MS63
2006	10,000	PF63 45.00	PF65 50.00			

KM# 2048 1-1/2 EURO
22.20 g., 0.900 Silver 0.6382 oz. ASW **Subject:** Marie Amélie of Orleans and Carlos I of Portugal, 120th Anniversary of Marriage **Obv:** Bust in tiara left **Rev:** Two shields crowned

Date	Mintage	F12	VF20	XF40	MS60	MS63
2006	3,000	PF63 150	PF65 175			

KM# 2055 1-1/2 EURO
22.20 g., 0.900 Silver 0.6382 oz. ASW **Subject:** Abolition of the Death Penalty, 25th Anniversary **Obv:** Sower advancing left **Rev:** Guillotine

Date	Mintage	F12	VF20	XF40	MS60	MS63
2006	3,110	PF63 45.00	PF65 50.00			

KM# 2064 1-1/2 EURO
22.20 g., 0.900 Silver 0.6382 oz. ASW **Subject:** Jules Verne, 100th Anniversary of Death **Obv:** Voyage to the center of the Earth

Date	Mintage	F12	VF20	XF40	MS60	MS63
2006	2,411	PF63 100	PF65 120			

KM# 1484 1-1/2 EURO
22.20 g., 0.900 Silver 0.6382 oz. ASW, 37 mm. **Subject:** 2007 Rugby World Cup **Obv:** Two players and goal **Rev:** Logo and goal

Date	Mintage	F12	VF20	XF40	MS60	MS63
2007	4,915	PF63 50.00	PF65 55.00			

KM# 1501 1-1/2 EURO
22.20 g., 0.900 Silver 0.6382 oz. ASW, 37 mm. **Subject:** Georges Pompendev Center, 30th Anniversary

Date	Mintage	F12	VF20	XF40	MS60	MS63
2007	—	PF63 50.00	PF65 55.00			

KM# 1462 1-1/2 EURO
22.00 g., 0.900 Silver 0.6325 oz. ASW, 37 mm. **Subject:** Sebastien Le Prestre de Vauban, 300th Anniversary of Death

Date	Mintage	F12	VF20	XF40	MS60	MS63
2007	14,364	PF63 40.00	PF65 45.00			

KM# 1465 1-1/2 EURO
22.20 g., 0.900 Silver 0.6382 oz. ASW, 37 mm. **Subject:** Le Petit Prince, 60th Anniversary **Obv:** Prince standing, multicolor

Date	Mintage	F12	VF20	XF40	MS60	MS63
2007	3,000	PF63 55.00	PF65 60.00			

KM# 1467 1-1/2 EURO
22.20 g., 0.900 Silver 0.6382 oz. ASW, 37 mm. **Subject:** Le Petit Prince, 60th Anniversary **Obv:** Prince lying in field, multicolor

Date	Mintage	F12	VF20	XF40	MS60	MS63
2007	3,000	PF63 55.00	PF65 60.00			

KM# 1469 1-1/2 EURO
22.20 g., 0.900 Silver 0.6382 oz. ASW, 37 mm. **Subject:** Le Petite Prince, 60th Anniversary **Obv:** Prince standing with fox, multicolor

Date	Mintage	F12	VF20	XF40	MS60	MS63
2007	3,000	PF63 55.00	PF65 60.00			

KM# 1473 1-1/2 EURO
22.20 g., 0.900 Silver 0.6382 oz. ASW, 37 mm. **Subject:** Paul E. Victor, 100th Birthday **Obv:** International Polar Year Logo **Rev:** Bust at left, Islands

Date	Mintage	F12	VF20	XF40	MS60	MS63
2007	5,000	PF63 55.00	PF65 60.00			

KM# 1475 1-1/2 EURO
22.20 g., 0.900 Silver 0.6382 oz. ASW, 37 mm. **Obv:** Formula 1 race car on checkered background **Rev:** Legend in wreath on checkered background

Date	Mintage	F12	VF20	XF40	MS60	MS63
2007//2006 (2007)	4,554	PF63 55.00	PF65 60.00			

KM# 1477 1-1/2 EURO
22.20 g., 0.900 Silver 0.6382 oz. ASW, 37 mm. **Subject:** 29th Summer Olympic Games Beijing **Obv:** Rider on horseback, globe map of China **Rev:** Equestrian jump over orienteal fence

Date	Mintage	F12	VF20	XF40	MS60	MS63
2007	10,000	PF63 50.00	PF65 55.00			

KM# 1479 1-1/2 EURO
22.20 g., 0.900 Silver 0.6382 oz. ASW, 37 mm. **Subject:** Airbus A380 **Obv:** Airplane **Rev:** Europa head and flags

Date	Mintage	F12	VF20	XF40	MS60	MS63
2007	5,000	PF63 50.00	PF65 55.00			

KM# 1488 1-1/2 EURO
22.20 g., 0.900 Silver 0.6382 oz. ASW, 37 mm. **Obv:** Christian Dior bust **Rev:** Dior Museum building

Date	Mintage	F12	VF20	XF40	MS60	MS63
2007	4,799	PF63 75.00	PF65 85.00			

KM# 1505 1-1/2 EURO
22.20 g., 0.900 Silver 0.6382 oz. ASW, 37 mm. **Subject:** George Remir Centennial **Obv:** Wand and sparkles **Rev:** Tin Tin and the Professor calculus in multicolor

Date	Mintage	F12	VF20	XF40	MS60	MS63
2007	10,000	PF63 60.00	PF65 70.00			

KM# 1506 1-1/2 EURO
22.20 g., 0.900 Silver 0.6382 oz. ASW, 37 mm. **Subject:** Georges Remi Centennial **Obv:** Wand and sparkles **Rev:** Tin Tin and Captain Haddock in multicolor

Date	Mintage	F12	VF20	XF40	MS60	MS63
2007	5,043	PF63 65.00	PF65 75.00			

KM# 1507 1-1/2 EURO
22.20 g., 0.900 Silver 0.6382 oz. ASW, 37 mm. **Subject:** Georges Remi Centennial **Obv:** Wand and sparkles **Rev:** Tin Tin and Chang in multicolor

Date	Mintage	F12	VF20	XF40	MS60	MS63
2007	4,648	PF63 65.00	PF65 75.00			

KM# 1511 1-1/2 EURO
22.20 g., 0.900 Silver 0.6382 oz. ASW, 37 mm. **Subject:** Aristides de Sousa Mendes, Portuguese diplomat **Obv:** Bust right **Rev:** Plaque

Date	Mintage	F12	VF20	XF40	MS60	MS63
2007	3,000	PF63 55.00	PF65 60.00			

KM# 1516 1-1/2 EURO
22.20 g., 0.900 Silver 0.6382 oz. ASW, 37 mm. **Subject:** Asterix **Rev:** The Banquet

Date	Mintage	F12	VF20	XF40	MS60	MS63
2007	2,994	PF63 60.00	PF65 70.00			

KM# 1517 1-1/2 EURO
22.20 g., 0.900 Silver 0.6382 oz. ASW, 37 mm. **Subject:** Asterix **Rev:** The posion

Date	Mintage	F12	VF20	XF40	MS60	MS63
2007	2,996	PF63 60.00	PF65 70.00			

KM# 1518 1-1/2 EURO
22.20 g., 0.900 Silver 0.6382 oz. ASW, 37 mm. **Subject:** Asterix **Rev:** The Chase

Date	Mintage	F12	VF20	XF40	MS60	MS63
2007	2,996	PF63 60.00	PF65 70.00			

KM# 1527 1-1/2 EURO
22.20 g., 0.900 Silver 0.6382 oz. ASW, 37 mm. **Subject:** French Presidency of European Union **Obv:** Text written stars **Rev:** Europa head and flags

Date	Mintage	F12	VF20	XF40	MS60	MS63
2008	4,412	PF63 50.00	PF65 55.00			

KM# 1532 1-1/2 EURO
22.20 g., 0.900 Silver 0.6382 oz. ASW **Subject:** Eurpean Parliament, 50th Anniversary **Obv:** Map of EU within stars **Rev:** European Parliament Building in Strasboury **Shape:** 37

Date	Mintage	F12	VF20	XF40	MS60	MS63
2008	13,802	PF63 50.00	PF65 55.00			

KM# 1537 1-1/2 EURO
22.20 g., 0.900 Silver 0.6382 oz. ASW, 37 mm. **Subject:** 5th Republic, 50th Anniversasry **Obv:** Sower **Rev:** deGaulle head right

Date	Mintage	F12	VF20	XF40	MS60	MS63
2008	6,631	PF63 50.00	PF65 55.00			

KM# 1543 1-1/2 EURO
22.20 g., 0.900 Silver 0.6382 oz. ASW, 37 mm. **Subject:** 29th Summer Olympic Games - Beijing **Obv:** Swimmer and globe **Rev:** Diver and oriental screen

Date	Mintage	F12	VF20	XF40	MS60	MS63
2008	3,824	PF63 65.00	PF65 75.00			

KM# 1546 1-1/2 EURO
22.20 g., 0.900 Silver 0.6382 oz. ASW, 37 mm. **Subject:** UEFA **Obv:** French soccer team **Rev:** UEFA logo

Date	Mintage	F12	VF20	XF40	MS60	MS63
2008	5,000	PF63 55.00	PF65 60.00			

KM# 1548 1-1/2 EURO
22.20 g., 0.900 Silver 0.6382 oz. ASW, 37 mm. **Subject:** Franco - Japanese Relators, 150th Anniversary **Obv:** Eiffel Tower and Kimono forming logo **Rev:** Delacroix "La Liberte

Date	Mintage	F12	VF20	XF40	MS60	MS63
2008	4,866	PF63 65.00	PF65 75.00			

KM# 1549 1-1/2 EURO
22.20 g., 0.900 Silver 0.6382 oz. ASW, 37 mm. **Subject:** Franco - Japanese Relators - 150th Anniversary **Obv:** Eillfel Tower and Kimono forming logo **Rev:** Ichikawa Ebizo IV portrait painting

Date	Mintage	F12	VF20	XF40	MS60	MS63
2008	4,735	PF63 65.00	PF65 75.00			

KM# 1550 1-1/2 EURO
22.20 g., 0.900 Silver 0.6382 oz. ASW, 37 mm. **Subject:** Franco - Japanese Relators - 150th Anniversary **Obv:** Eillfel Tower and Kimono forming logo **Rev:** Scenes of Paris and Tokyo - Eillfel Tower and Pagoda Sensoji

Date	Mintage	F12	VF20	XF40	MS60	MS63
2008	48,914	PF63 65.00	PF65 75.00			

KM# 1551 1-1/2 EURO
22.20 g., 0.900 Silver 0.6382 oz. ASW, 37 mm. **Subject:** Franco - Japanese Relators - 150th Anniversary **Obv:** Eiflfel Tower and Kimono forming logo **Rev:** Japanese cash coin of "Kanei Tsuho

Date	Mintage	F12	VF20	XF40	MS60	MS63
2008	4,873	PF63 65.00	PF65 75.00			

KM# 1555 1-1/2 EURO
22.20 g., 0.900 Silver 0.6382 oz. ASW, 37 mm. **Subject:** André Citronën **Obv:** First front wheel drive auto **Rev:** Bust 1/4 left

Date	Mintage	F12	VF20	XF40	MS60	MS63
2008	3,814	PF63 65.00	PF65 75.00			

KM# 1558 1-1/2 EURO
22.20 g., 0.900 Silver 0.6382 oz. ASW, 37 mm. **Subject:** Rouen Armada **Obv:** Cape Horn, sextant, hour glass **Rev:** Sailing ship

Date	Mintage	F12	VF20	XF40	MS60	MS63
2008	2,790	PF63 65.00	PF65 75.00			

KM# 1561 1-1/2 EURO
22.20 g., 0.900 Silver 0.6382 oz. ASW, 37 mm. **Subject:** Lourdes, 150th Anniversary **Obv:** Church of Notre Dame at Lourdes **Rev:** Cross with Pope John Paul II, Pope Benedict XVI and Bernadette Soubirous in quadrants

Date	Mintage	F12	VF20	XF40	MS60	MS63
2008	8,001	PF63 60.00	PF65 70.00			

KM# 1566 1-1/2 EURO
22.20 g., 0.900 Silver 0.6382 oz. ASW, 37 mm. **Subject:** Gabrielle Chanel **Obv:** Bust right in hat **Rev:** Value on "Matelassé" pattern

Date	Mintage	F12	VF20	XF40	MS60	MS63
2008	9,987	PF63 65.00	PF65 75.00			

KM# 1574 1-1/2 EURO
22.20 g., 0.900 Silver 0.6382 oz. ASW, 37 mm. **Subject:** UNESCO - Grand Canyon **Obv:** Grand Canyon **Rev:** UNESCO logos

Date	Mintage	F12	VF20	XF40	MS60	MS63
2008	3,647	PF63 65.00	PF65 75.00			

KM# 1576 1-1/2 EURO
22.20 g., 0.900 Silver 0.6382 oz. ASW, 37 mm. **Subject:** International Polar Year **Obv:** IPY logo **Rev:** Emperor Penguin and map of Antartica

Date	Mintage	F12	VF20	XF40	MS60	MS63
2008	3,553	PF63 65.00	PF65 75.00			

KM# 1578 1-1/2 EURO
22.20 g., 0.900 Silver 0.6382 oz. ASW, 37 mm. **Subject:** Spirou, 70th Anniversary **Obv:** Character Spirou in thought **Rev:** 70th Anniversary logo

Date	Mintage	F12	VF20	XF40	MS60	MS63
2008	3,672	PF63 60.00	PF65 70.00			

KM# 1633 1-1/2 EURO
11.00 g., Aluminum-Bronze, 30 mm. **Obv:** Stadium view, soccer player **Rev:** Shield of Olympique Lyonnais

Date	Mintage	F12	VF20	XF40	MS60	MS63
2009	8,455	—	—		15.00	20.00

KM# 1723 1-1/2 EURO
11.00 g., Aluminum-Bronze, 30 mm. **Obv:** Soccer player **Rev:** Girondins de Bordeaux logo

Date	Mintage	F12	VF20	XF40	MS60	MS63
2010	25,000	—	—		15.00	20.00

KM# 1754 1-1/2 EURO
11.00 g., Aluminum-Bronze, 30 mm. **Subject:** Olympique de Marseille **Obv:** Soccer player **Rev:** OM logo

Date	Mintage	F12	VF20	XF40	MS60	MS63
2011	25,000	—	—			15.00

KM# 1918 1-1/2 EURO
11.00 g., Aluminum-Bronze, 30 mm. **Subject:** Paris Saint Germain **Obv:** Stadium and player **Rev:** Team logo

Date	Mintage	F12	VF20	XF40	MS60	MS63
2012(a)	25,000	—	—			15.00

KM# 1289 2 EURO
8.50 g., Bi-Metallic, 25.75 mm. **Obv:** Stylized tree divides RF within circle, date below **Rev:** Denomination and map **Edge:** Reeded with 2's and stars

Date	Mintage	F12	VF20	XF40	MS60	MS63
2001	237,950,793	—	—		3.75	6.00
2001	15,000	PF63 20.00				
2002	153,700,000	—	—		3.75	6.00
2002	21,453	PF63 18.00				
2003 In sets only	180,000	—	—			13.50
2003	40,000	PF63 20.00				
2004 In sets only	160,000	—	—			13.50
2004	20,000	PF63 20.00				
2005 In sets only	120,000	—	—			13.50
2005	10,000	PF63 20.00				
2006 In sets only	67,600	—	—			13.50
2006	10,000	PF63 20.00				

KM# 1414 2 EURO
8.50 g., Bi-Metallic, 25.75 mm. **Obv:** Stylized tree divides RF within circle, date below **Rev:** Relief map of Western Europe, stars, lines and value **Edge:** Reeded with 2's and stars

Date	Mintage	F12	VF20	XF40	MS60	MS63
2007 In sets only	58,000	—	—			15.00
2007	7,500	PF63 25.00				
2008 In sets only	57,000	—	—			6.00
2008	7,500	PF63 25.00				
2009 In sets only	50,500	—	—			6.00
2009	7,500	PF63 25.00				
2010	—	—	—			6.00
2010	—	PF63 25.00				
2011	—	—	—			6.00
2011	—	PF63 25.00				
2012	—	—	—			6.00
2012	—	PF63 25.00				
2013	—	—	—			6.00
2013	—	PF63 25.00				

KM# 1460 2 EURO
8.50 g., Bi-Metallic, 25.75 mm. **Subject:** Treaty of Rome 50th Anniversary **Edge:** Reeded with 2's and stars

Date	Mintage	F12	VF20	XF40	MS60	MS63
2007	9,600,000	—	—		5.50	6.50

KM# 1459 2 EURO
8.50 g., Bi-Metallic, 25.75 mm. **Subject:** European Union Presidency **Obv:** Inscription **Obv. Inscription:** PRÉSIDENCE / FRANÇAISE / UNION / EUROPÉENNE / RF **Rev:** Large value "2" at left, modified map of Europe at right **Edge:** Reeded with 2's and stars

Date	Mintage	F12	VF20	XF40	MS60	MS63
2008(a)	20,100,000	—	—		5.50	6.50

KM# 1542 2 EURO
8.50 g., Bi-Metallic, 25.75 mm. **Subject:** 5th Republic, 50th Anniversary **Obv:** Text within stars **Rev:** Value at left, relief map of the EU at right **Edge:** Reeded with 2's and stars

Date	Mintage	F12	VF20	XF40	MS60	MS63
2008(a) Sets only	20,000	—	—			20.00
2008(a)	10,000,000	—	—		6.50	7.50
2008(a)	10,000	PF63 40.00	PF65 45.00			

KM# 1590 2 EURO
8.50 g., Bi-Metallic, 25.75 mm. **Subject:** EMU 10th Anniversary **Obv:** Stick figure and E design **Edge:** Reeded with 2's and stars

Date	Mintage	F12	VF20	XF40	MS60	MS63
2009	6,801	PF63 15.00	PF65 18.00			
2009	7,284	—	—		8.00	10.00

KM# 1676 2 EURO
8.50 g., Bi-Metallic, 25.75 mm. **Subject:** 70th Anniversary, June 18th Appeal **Obv:** General Charles DeGaulle giving BBC speech **Rev:** Value and map **Edge:** Reeded with 2's and stars

Date	Mintage	F12	VF20	XF40	MS60	MS63
2010	20,000	—	—		8.00	10.00
2010	10,000	PF63 15.00	PF65 18.00			

KM# 1789 2 EURO
8.50 g., Bi-Metallic, 25.75 mm. **Subject:** International Music Day, 30th Anniversary **Obv:** Youth jamming **Rev:** Value and map of Western Europe **Edge:** Reeded with 2's and stars

Date	Mintage	F12	VF20	XF40	MS60	MS63
2011	10,000,000	—	—		5.00	—
2011 Special Unc.	20,000	—	—			8.00
2011	10,000	PF63 15.00	PF65 18.00			

KM# 1846 2 EURO
8.50 g., Bi-Metallic, 25.75 mm. **Subject:** Euro coinage, 10th Anniversary **Obv:** Euro symbol on globe, child-like drawing around

Date	Mintage	F12	VF20	XF40	MS60	MS63
2012(a) Special Unc.	—	—	—			10.00
2012(a)	10,000,000	—	—		6.50	7.50
2012(a)	—	PF63 15.00	PF65 18.00			

KM# 1894 2 EURO
8.50 g., Bi-Metallic, 25.75 mm. **Subject:** abbé Pierre, 100th anniversary of Birth **Obv:** Portrait facing of abbé Pierre, wearing beret

Date	Mintage	F12	VF20	XF40	MS60	MS63
2012(a) Special Unc.	10,000	—	—			10.00
2012(a)	1,000,000	—	—		6.00	7.00
2012(a)	10,000	PF63 25.00	PF65 30.00			

KM# 1847 2 EURO
22.20 g., 0.900 Silver 0.6382 oz. ASW, 37 mm. **Obv:** Sailing ship L'Hermione **Rev:** Ship figurehead at right, ship's wheel at bottom

Date	Mintage	F12	VF20	XF40	MS60	MS63
2012(a)	10,000	PF63 35.00	PF65 40.00			

KM# 2102 2 EURO
8.50 g., Bi-Metallic, 25.75 mm. **Subject:** Pierre de Coubertin 150th Anniversary of Birth **Rev:** Rings at left, facing bust at right

Date	Mintage	F12	VF20	XF40	MS60	MS63
2013	—	—	—			8.00
2013 Special Unc	—	—	—			8.00
2013	—	PF63 15.00	PF65 18.00			

KM# 2094 2 EURO
8.50 g., Bi-Metallic, 25.75 mm. **Subject:** French-German
Friendship, 50th Anniversary

Date	Mintage	F12	VF20	XF40	MS60	MS63
2013	—				7.00	10.00
2013	—	PF63 15.00	PF65 18.00			

KM# 1347 5 EURO
24.90 g., 0.900 Bi-Metallic 0.7159 oz., 37 mm. **Obv:** The Seed
Sower on gold insert **Rev:** Denomination and map **Edge:** Plain

Date	Mintage	F12	VF20	XF40	MS60	MS63
2002	8,408	PF63 550	PF65 575			

KM# 1371 5 EURO
24.90 g., Bi-Metallic, 37 mm. **Obv:** The Seed Sower on gold
insert **Rev:** French face map and denomination **Edge:** Plain

Date	Mintage	F12	VF20	XF40	MS60	MS63
2004	3,000	PF63 550	PF65 575			

KM# 2010 5 EURO
12.00 g., 0.900 Silver 0.345 oz. ASW, 29 mm. **Obv:** Tree within
hexagon **Rev:** Pantheon and large value

Date	Mintage	F12	VF20	XF40	MS60	MS63
2004	—	PF63 25.00	PF65 30.00			
2005	—	PF63 25.00	PF65 30.00			
2006	—	PF63 25.00	PF65 30.00			

KM# 1523 5 EURO
22.20 g., 0.900 Silver 0.6382 oz. ASW, 37 mm. **Subject:** Euro
- 5th Anniversary **Obv:** The Seed Sower

Date	Mintage	F12	VF20	XF40	MS60	MS63
2007	5,000	PF63 55.00	PF65 60.00			

KM# 1524 5 EURO
163.80 g., 0.950 Silver 4.9708 oz. ASW, 50 mm. **Subject:** Euro
5th Anniversary **Obv:** Sower

Date	Mintage	F12	VF20	XF40	MS60	MS63
2007	493	PF63 325	PF65 350			

KM# 1525 5 EURO
1.24 g., 0.999 Gold 0.0396 oz. AGW, 13.9 mm. **Subject:** Euro
5th Anniversary **Obv:** The Seed Sower

Date	Mintage	F12	VF20	XF40	MS60	MS63
2007	9,951	PF63 75.00	PF65 85.00			

KM# 1526 5 EURO
31.11 g., 0.920 Gold 0.9141 oz. AGW, 31 mm. **Subject:** Euro
5th Anniversary **Obv:** The Seed Sower

Date	Mintage	F12	VF20	XF40	MS60	MS63
2007	472	PF65 1,600				

KM# 1534 5 EURO
10.00 g., 0.500 Silver 0.1597 oz. ASW, 27 mm. **Obv:** Sower, full
length **Rev:** Value within hexagon design

Date	Mintage	F12	VF20	XF40	MS60	MS63
2008	2,000,000	PF63 15.00	PF65 18.00			

KM# 1538 5 EURO
1.24 g., 0.999 Gold 0.0396 oz. AGW, 13.9 mm. **Subject:** 5th
Republic, 50th Anniversary **Obv:** Sower **Rev:** de Gaulle head
right

Date	Mintage	F12	VF20	XF40	MS60	MS63
2008	9,757	PF63 75.00	PF65 85.00			

KM# 1586 5 EURO
1.24 g., 0.999 Gold 0.0396 oz. AGW, 13.9 mm. **Subject:** Court
of Human Rights, 50th Anniversary **Obv:** The Seed Sower left
Rev: Text

Date	Mintage	F12	VF20	XF40	MS60	MS63
2009P	8,118	PF63 75.00	PF65 85.00			

KM# 1625 5 EURO
15.00 g., 0.900 Silver 0.4312 oz. ASW, 30 x 21 mm. **Subject:**
Monet **Obv:** Le Bassin Aux Nympheas, 1900 painting **Rev:**

Multicolor pallet and brushes, portrait **Shape:** Rectangle

Date	Mintage	F12	VF20	XF40	MS60	MS63
2009P	3,865	—	—	—	—	45.00

KM# 1627 5 EURO
22.20 g., 0.900 Silver 0.6382 oz. ASW, 37 mm. **Subject:** Year
of the Ox **Obv:** Oxen within Asia screen garden **Rev:** Portrait
of La Fontaine

Date	Mintage	F12	VF20	XF40	MS60	MS63
2009P	4,738	PF63 35.00	PF65 40.00			

KM# 1643 5 EURO
15.00 g., 0.900 Silver 0.4312 oz. ASW **Subject:** Pierre Auguste
Renoir **Obv:** Boaters Lunch in color **Rev:** Portrait and paint
brushes **Shape:** Rectangle

Date	Mintage	F12	VF20	XF40	MS60	MS63
2009	2,799	—	—	—	—	45.00

KM# 1674 5 EURO
1.24 g., 0.999 Gold 0.0396 oz. AGW, 13.9 mm. **Obv:** The Seed
Sower left **Rev:** Wheat and olive branch

Date	Mintage	F12	VF20	XF40	MS60	MS63
2010	10,000	PF63 75.00	PF65 85.00			

KM# 1680 5 EURO
0.50 g., 0.999 Gold AGW, 11 mm. **Subject:** Cluny Abbey, 1100th
Anniversary **Obv:** Europa head facing **Rev:** Cluny Abbey

Date	Mintage	F12	VF20	XF40	MS60	MS63
2010	20,000	PF63 45.00	PF65 50.00			

KM# 1715 5 EURO
22.20 g., 0.900 Silver 0.6382 oz. ASW, 37 mm. **Obv:** Tiger
within border **Rev:** La Fontaine bust at left, animals at right

Date	Mintage	F12	VF20	XF40	MS60	MS63
2010	10,000	PF63 65.00	PF65 75.00			

KM# 1785 5 EURO
1.24 g., 0.999 Gold 0.0397 oz. AGW, 13.9 mm. **Subject:** Euro
Starter Kit, 10th Anniversary **Obv:** Sower **Rev:** Euro starter kit

Date	Mintage	F12	VF20	XF40	MS60	MS63
2011	10,000	PF63 100	PF65 120			

KM# 1791 5 EURO
0.50 g., 0.999 Gold AGW, 11 mm. **Subject:** International Music
Day, 30th Anniversary **Obv:** Europa **Rev:** Youth jamming

Date	Mintage	F12	VF20	XF40	MS60	MS63
2011	20,000	PF63 100	PF65 120			

KM# 1810 5 EURO
0.50 g., 0.999 Gold AGW, 11 mm. **Subject:** UNESCO World
Heritage Site - Palace of Versailles

Date	Mintage	F12	VF20	XF40	MS60	MS63
2011	20,000	PF63 100	PF65 120			

KM# 1833 5 EURO
22.20 g., 0.900 Silver 0.6382 oz. ASW, 37 mm. **Subject:** Year
of the Rabbit **Obv:** Rabbit seated facing right **Rev:** Fontaine
and animals

Date	Mintage	F12	VF20	XF40	MS60	MS63
2011	10,000	PF63 50.00	PF65 55.00			

KM# 1851 5 EURO
0.50 g., 0.999 Gold AGW, 11 mm. **Subject:** Eurocorps, 20th
Anniversary **Obv:** Mitterrand and Kohl standing clasping hands
Rev: Europa facing

Date	Mintage	F12	VF20	XF40	MS60	MS63
2012(a)	10,000	PF63 65.00	PF65 75.00			

KM# 1890 5 EURO
0.50 g., 0.999 Gold AGW, 11 mm. **Subject:** Euro, 10th
Anniversary **Obv:** The Sower advancing left **Rev:** Value on
globe with child-like renderings around

Date	Mintage	F12	VF20	XF40	MS60	MS63
2012(a)	10,000	PF63 75.00	PF65 85.00			

KM# 1896 5 EURO
1.24 g., 0.999 Gold 0.0397 oz. AGW, 13.9 mm. **Subject:** abbé
Pierre, 100th anniversary of Birth **Obv:** Pierre's bust at left,
shaddow figure at right **Rev:** Emmaus International logo and
quote

Date	Mintage	F12	VF20	XF40	MS60	MS63
2012(a)	10,000	PF63 100	PF65 120			

KM# 1907 5 EURO
0.50 g., 0.999 Gold AGW, 11 mm. **Subject:** UNESCO - World
Heritage Site **Obv:** Abu Simbel temple **Rev:** Sphinx and
Pyramids

Date	Mintage	F12	VF20	XF40	MS60	MS63
2012(a)	10,000	PF63 75.00	PF65 85.00			

KM# 2092 5 EURO
0.50 g., 0.999 Gold AGW, 11 mm. **Subject:** French - German
Friendship **Rev:** Europa head facing at right, banners at left

Date	Mintage	F12	VF20	XF40	MS60	MS63
2013	—	PF63 75.00	PF65 85.00			

KM# 2099 5 EURO
0.50 g., 0.999 Gold AGW, 11 mm. **Subject:** Notre Dame, 850th
Anniversary **Obv:** Seal at right, cathedral details **Rev:** Seal at
left, cathedral details

Date	Mintage	F12	VF20	XF40	MS60	MS63
2013	15,000	PF63 100	PF65 120			

KM# 1302 10 EURO
8.45 g., 0.999 Gold 0.2697 oz. AGW, 22 mm. **Subject:** Europa **Obv:** Eight French euro coin designs **Rev:** Portrait and flags design of 6.55957 francs KM-1265 **Edge:** Reeded

Date	Mintage	F12	VF20	XF40	MS60	MS63
2002	3,000				PF65 525	

KM# 1326 10 EURO
8.45 g., 0.920 Gold 0.2483 oz. AGW, 22 mm. **Obv:** Tour de France logo **Rev:** Cyclist going left **Edge:** Reeded

Date	Mintage	F12	VF20	XF40	MS60	MS63
2003 (Ht)	5,000	PF63 500		PF65 525		

KM# 1348 10 EURO
8.45 g., 0.920 Gold 0.2483 oz. AGW, 22 mm. **Obv:** The seed sower **Rev:** Denomination and map **Edge:** Plain

Date	Mintage	F12	VF20	XF40	MS60	MS63
2003	5,779	PF63 475		PF65 500		

KM# 1352 10 EURO
8.45 g., 0.920 Gold 0.2483 oz. AGW, 22 mm. **Obv:** Obverse design of first one franc coin **Rev:** Reverse design of first one franc coin **Edge:** Plain

Date	Mintage	F12	VF20	XF40	MS60	MS63
2003	1,761	PF63 475		PF65 500		

KM# 1362 10 EURO
8.45 g., 0.920 Gold 0.2483 oz. AGW, 22 mm. **Obv:** Pierre de Coubertin **Rev:** Olympic runners **Edge:** Plain

Date	Mintage	F12	VF20	XF40	MS60	MS63
2003	1,635	PF63 475		PF65 500		

KM# 1992 10 EURO
8.45 g., 0.920 Gold 0.2483 oz. AGW **Obv:** Curved cross with coins **Rev:** Europa head at right, flags at left

Date	Mintage	F12	VF20	XF40	MS60	MS63
2003	Est. 7000	PF63 550		PF65 575		

KM# 1367 10 EURO
6.41 g., 0.900 Gold 0.1843 oz. AGW, 22 mm. **Obv:** Book, denomination and eagle **Rev:** Napoleon and coronation scene **Edge:** Plain

Date	Mintage	F12	VF20	XF40	MS60	MS63
2004	5,000	PF63 400		PF65 425		

KM# 1375 10 EURO
8.45 g., 0.920 Gold 0.2483 oz. AGW, 22 mm. **Obv:** Half soccer ball and denomination **Rev:** Eiffel tower and soccer balls **Edge:** Plain

Date	Mintage	F12	VF20	XF40	MS60	MS63
2004	10,000	PF63 475		PF65 500		

KM# 1392 10 EURO
8.45 g., 0.920 Gold 0.2483 oz. AGW, 22 mm. **Subject:** European Union Expansion **Obv:** Partial face and flags **Rev:** Puzzle map **Edge:** Reeded

Date	Mintage	F12	VF20	XF40	MS60	MS63
2004	5,000	PF63 500		PF65 525		

KM# 1403 10 EURO
8.45 g., 0.920 Gold 0.2483 oz. AGW, 22 mm. **Subject:** Jules Verne **Obv:** Various scenes from Verne's novel "Around The World in 80 Days **Rev:** Jules Verne's portrait left of value and date

Date	Mintage	F12	VF20	XF40	MS60	MS63
2005	811	PF63 575		PF65 600		

KM# 1424 10 EURO
8.45 g., 0.920 Gold 0.2483 oz. AGW, 22 mm. **Subject:** Biathlon **Rev:** Skier at right facing 3/4 left, mountain peaks in background **Rev. Inscription:** JEUX D'HIVER

Date	Mintage	F12	VF20	XF40	MS60	MS63
2005	700	PF63 475		PF65 500		

KM# 1426 10 EURO
8.45 g., 0.920 Gold 0.2483 oz. AGW, 22 mm. **Series:** Jules Verne **Subject:** From the earth to the moon **Rev:** Crowd observing at lower left, volcano erupting above, moon at upper right, Verne in spaceship at lower right, chimneys belching smoke in backgroud **Rev. Legend:** DE LA TERRE À LA LUNE

Date	Mintage	F12	VF20	XF40	MS60	MS63
2005	414	PF63 500		PF65 525		

KM# 1429 10 EURO
8.45 g., 0.920 Gold 0.2483 oz. AGW, 22 mm. **Rev:** Kitty at the Spectacle, multicolor **Rev. Legend:** Hello Kitty

Date	Mintage	F12	VF20	XF40	MS60	MS63
2005	1,000	PF63 550		PF65 575		

KM# 1432 10 EURO
6.41 g., 0.900 Gold 0.1843 oz. AGW, 21 mm. **Subject:** Bicentennial - Victory at Austerlitz **Rev:** Battle scene **Rev. Legend:** LIBERTÉ ÉGALITÉ FRATERNITÉ

Date	Mintage	F12	VF20	XF40	MS60	MS63
2005	451	PF63 400		PF65 425		

KM# 1435 10 EURO
8.45 g., 0.920 Gold 0.2483 oz. AGW, 22 mm. **Subject:** 50th Anniversary - Flag of Europe **Rev:** Stars at left, partial flag at center right

Date	Mintage	F12	VF20	XF40	MS60	MS63
2005	1,798	PF63 475		PF65 500		

KM# 1439 10 EURO
8.45 g., 0.920 Gold 0.2483 oz. AGW, 22 mm. **Series:** Jules Verne **Subject:** 20,000 Leagues Under the Sea **Rev:** Submarine above plants and divers **Rev. Legend:** VINGT MILLE LIEUES SOUS LES MERS

Date	Mintage	F12	VF20	XF40	MS60	MS63
2005	490	PF63 500		PF65 525		

KM# 2021 10 EURO
8.45 g., 0.920 Gold 0.2483 oz. AGW **Subject:** World Cup Soccer **Obv:** World Cup Trophy and soccer ball **Rev:** Large value and map of France

Date	Mintage	F12	VF20	XF40	MS60	MS63
2005	1,518	PF63 550		PF65 575		

KM# 2023 10 EURO
8.45 g., 0.920 Gold 0.2483 oz. AGW **Obv:** Globe and map of Europe **Rev:** Doves in flight above globe

Date	Mintage	F12	VF20	XF40	MS60	MS63
2005	3,000	PF63 550		PF65 575		

KM# 2026 10 EURO
8.45 g., 0.920 Gold 0.2483 oz. AGW **Subject:** Bordeaux, 150th Anniversary **Obv:** Female holding bounty **Rev:** Stylized fingers and a grape

Date	Mintage	F12	VF20	XF40	MS60	MS63
2005	500	PF63 550		PF65 575		

KM# 1416 10 EURO
8.45 g., 0.920 Gold 0.2483 oz. AGW, 22 mm. **Obv:** Jean de la Fontaine, value, Chinese astrological animals, date, Paris mint privy marks but without national identification **Rev:** Dog in wreath **Edge:** Reeded

Date	Mintage	F12	VF20	XF40	MS60	MS63
2006	500	PF63 525		PF65 550		

KM# 1446 10 EURO
8.45 g., 0.920 Gold 0.2483 oz. AGW, 22 mm. **Subject:** Marshal Bernadotte under Napoleon **Rev:** Military bust facing 3/4 right at left, building in backgound at right **Rev. Legend:** LIBERTÉ GALITÉ FRATERNITÉ - KARL XIV JOHAN ROI DE SUÉDE

Date	Mintage	F12	VF20	XF40	MS60	MS63
2006	1,000	PF63 500		PF65 525		

KM# 1448 10 EURO
8.45 g., 0.920 Gold 0.2483 oz. AGW, 22 mm. **Subject:** 20,000 Leagues Under the Sea **Obv:** Strogoff horseback wielding a sword, city at left, soldiers at lower left, calvary at right - the Tartars, Siberia and the Tsar's Army **Obv. Legend:** MICHEL STROGOFF **Rev:** Head of Verne facing 3/4 right at left center, instruments and anchor in curved band **Rev. Legend:** 1828 JULES VERNE 1905

Date	Mintage	F12	VF20	XF40	MS60	MS63
2006	500	PF63 525		PF65 550		

KM# 1449 10 EURO
8.45 g., 0.920 Gold 0.2483 oz. AGW, 22 mm. **Subject:** 20,000 Leagues Under the Sea **Obv:** Hot air balloon, parrots at left, native masks below left, foliage at right, huts below, map of Africa in background. **Obv. Legend:** CINQ SEMAINES EN BALLON **Rev:** Head of Verne facing 3/4 right at left center, instruments and anchor in curved band **Rev. Legend:** 1828 JULES VERNE 1905 - LIBERTÉ . ÉGALITÉ . FRATERNITÉ

Date	Mintage	F12	VF20	XF40	MS60	MS63
2006	500	PF63 525		PF65 550		

KM# 1451 10 EURO
8.45 g., 0.920 Gold 0.2483 oz. AGW, 22 mm. **Subject:** 100th Anniversary - French Grand Prix **Obv:** Steering wheel with early race car in upper segment, two gauges at lower left, R / F at lower right **Obv. Legend:** LE MANS 1906 - CENTENAIRE du 1er GRAND PRIX de l'AUTOMOBILE CLUB de France **Rev. Legend:** MAGNY-COURS

Date	Mintage	F12	VF20	XF40	MS60	MS63
2006	500	PF63 525		PF65 550		

KM# 2038 10 EURO
8.45 g., 0.920 Gold 0.2483 oz. AGW **Subject:** Robert Schuman, 120th Anniversary of Birth

Date	Mintage	F12	VF20	XF40	MS60	MS63
2006	—	PF63 550		PF65 575		

KM# 2042 10 EURO
8.45 g., 0.920 Gold 0.2483 oz. AGW **Subject:** Bejing Olympics **Obv:** Three fencing foils on globe map pointing toward Bejing **Rev:** Two fencers

Date	Mintage	F12	VF20	XF40	MS60	MS63
2006	1,000	PF63 550		PF65 575		

KM# 2043 10 EURO
8.45 g., 0.920 Gold 0.2483 oz. AGW **Subject:** Benjamin Franklin, 300th anniversary of Birth **Obv:** Bust at left, kite in thunderclouds at right **Rev:** French and American flags

Date	Mintage	F12	VF20	XF40	MS60	MS63
2006	1,000	PF63 525		PF65 550		

KM# 2045 10 EURO
8.45 g., 0.920 Gold 0.2483 oz. AGW **Subject:** St. Peter's Basilica, 500th Anniversary **Obv:** Floorplan of St. Peter's **Rev:** Façade and Pope Benedict XVI

Date	Mintage	F12	VF20	XF40	MS60	MS63
2006	1,000	PF63 525		PF65 550		

KM# 2049 10 EURO
8.45 g., 0.920 Gold 0.2483 oz. AGW **Subject:** Marie Amélie of Orleans and Carlos I of Portugal, 120th Anniversary of Marriage **Obv:** Bust with tiara left **Rev:** Two shields crowned

Date	Mintage	F12	VF20	XF40	MS60	MS63
2006	500	PF63 600		PF65 625		

KM# 2053 10 EURO
8.45 g., 0.920 Gold 0.2483 oz. AGW **Obv:** Partial monuments forming map of France **Rev:** Arc de Triomphe and Tomb of Unknown Soldier

Date	Mintage	F12	VF20	XF40	MS60	MS63
2006	500	PF63 525		PF65 550		

KM# 2054 10 EURO
8.45 g., 0.920 Gold 0.2483 oz. AGW **Subject:** Church of St. Louis des Invalides **Obv:** Monument fragments forming map of France **Rev:** Church Façade flanked by two men

Date	Mintage	F12	VF20	XF40	MS60	MS63
2006	500	PF63 525		PF65 550		

KM# 2063 10 EURO
8.45 g., 0.920 Gold 0.2483 oz. AGW **Subject:** Wolfgang Amadeus Mozart, 250th Anniversary of Birth **Obv:** Youthful bust **Rev:** Hands at piano keys, music above

Date	Mintage	F12	VF20	XF40	MS60	MS63
2006	1,000	PF63 525		PF65 550		

KM# 2068 10 EURO
8.45 g., 0.920 Gold 0.2483 oz. AGW **Subject:** Jules Verne, 100th Anniversary of Death **Obv:** Voyage to the center of the Earth

Date	Mintage	F12	VF20	XF40	MS60	MS63
2006	500	PF63 525		PF65 550		

KM# 1418 10 EURO
8.45 g., 0.920 Gold 0.2483 oz. AGW, 22 mm. **Obv:** Jean de la Fontaine, value, Chinese astrological animals, date, Paris mint privy marks but without national identification **Rev:** Pig in wreath **Edge:** Reeded **Note:** anonymous issue

Date	Mintage	F12	VF20	XF40	MS60	MS63
2007	500	PF63 525		PF65 550		

KM# 1420 10 EURO
8.45 g., 0.920 Gold 0.2483 oz. AGW, 22 mm. **Obv:** Military bust of Lafayette facing 3/4 left **Obv. Legend:** LA FAYETTE. HÉROS DELA RÉVOLUTION AMÉRICAINE **Obv. Inscription:** 1757/1854 at left, RF monogram at right **Rev:** Sailing ship L' Hermione **Rev. Legend:** LA FAYETTE, HERO OF THE AMERICAN REVOLUTION **Edge:** Plain

Date	Mintage	F12	VF20	XF40	MS60	MS63
2007 (a)	499	PF63 525		PF65 550		

KM# 1502 10 EURO
8.45 g., 0.920 Gold 0.2483 oz. AGW, 22 mm. **Subject:** Georges Pompidou Center, 30th Anniversary

Date	Mintage	F12	VF20	XF40	MS60	MS63
2007	—	PF63 525	PF65 550			

KM# 1463 10 EURO
8.45 g., 0.920 Gold 0.2483 oz. AGW, 22 mm. **Subject:** Sebastien Le Prestre de Vauban, 300th Anniversary of Death

Date	Mintage	F12	VF20	XF40	MS60	MS63
2007	1,838	PF63 475	PF65 500			

KM# 1474 10 EURO
8.45 g., 0.920 Gold 0.2483 oz. AGW, 22 mm. **Subject:** Paul E. Victor, 100th birthday **Obv:** International polar year logo **Rev:** Bust at left, Islands

Date	Mintage	F12	VF20	XF40	MS60	MS63
2007	500	—	—	—	—	500

KM# 1476 10 EURO
8.45 g., 0.920 Gold 0.2483 oz. AGW, 22 mm. **Obv:** Formula 1 race car on checkered background **Rev:** Legend in wreath on checkered background

Date	Mintage	F12	VF20	XF40	MS60	MS63
2007//2006 (2007)	500	PF63 525	PF65 550			

KM# 1478 10 EURO
8.45 g., 0.920 Gold 0.2483 oz. AGW, 22 mm. **Subject:** 29th Summer Olympic Games Beijing **Obv:** Rider on horseback, globe map of China **Rev:** Equestrian jump over oriental fence

Date	Mintage	F12	VF20	XF40	MS60	MS63
2007	1,000	PF63 525	PF65 550			

KM# 1480 10 EURO
8.45 g., 0.920 Gold 0.2483 oz. AGW, 22 mm. **Subject:** Airbus A380 **Obv:** Airplane **Rev:** Europa head and flags

Date	Mintage	F12	VF20	XF40	MS60	MS63
2007	1,000	PF63 500	PF65 525			

KM# 1485 10 EURO
8.45 g., 0.920 Gold 0.2483 oz. AGW, 22 mm. **Subject:** 2007 Rugby World Cup **Obv:** Two players and goal **Rev:** Logo and goal

Date	Mintage	F12	VF20	XF40	MS60	MS63
2007	500	PF63 525	PF65 550			

KM# 1489 10 EURO
8.45 g., 0.920 Gold 0.2483 oz. AGW, 22 mm. **Obv:** Christian Dior **Rev:** Dior Museum building

Date	Mintage	F12	VF20	XF40	MS60	MS63
2007	500	PF63 525	PF65 550			

KM# 1508 10 EURO
8.45 g., 0.920 Gold 0.2483 oz. AGW, 22 mm. **Subject:** Georges Remi Centennial **Obv:** Wand and sparkles **Rev:** Tin Tin raising cap

Date	Mintage	F12	VF20	XF40	MS60	MS63
2007	1,000	PF63 500	PF65 525			

KM# 1512 10 EURO
8.45 g., 0.920 Gold 0.2483 oz. AGW, 22 mm. **Subject:** Aristides de Sousa Mendes, Portuguese diplomat **Obv:** Bust right **Rev:** Plaque

Date	Mintage	F12	VF20	XF40	MS60	MS63
2007	500	PF63 525	PF65 550			

KM# 1519 10 EURO
8.45 g., 0.920 Gold 0.2483 oz. AGW, 22 mm. **Subject:** Asterix **Rev:** Character with torch

Date	Mintage	F12	VF20	XF40	MS60	MS63
2007	480	PF63 525	PF65 550			

KM# 1544 10 EURO
8.45 g., 0.920 Gold 0.2483 oz. AGW, 22 mm. **Subject:** 29th Summer Olympic Games - Beijing **Obv:** Swimmer and globe **Rev:** Diver and oriental screen

Date	Mintage	F12	VF20	XF40	MS60	MS63
2008	988	PF63 500	PF65 525			

KM# 1528 10 EURO
8.45 g., 0.920 Gold 0.2483 oz. AGW, 22 mm. **Subject:** French Presidency of European Union **Obv:** Text within stars **Rev:** Europa head and flags

Date	Mintage	F12	VF20	XF40	MS60	MS63
2008	999	PF63 500	PF65 525			

KM# 1533 10 EURO
8.45 g., 0.920 Gold 0.2483 oz. AGW, 22 mm. **Subject:** European Parliament, 50th Anniversary **Obv:** Map of EU within stars **Rev:** European Parliament Building in Strasbourg

Date	Mintage	F12	VF20	XF40	MS60	MS63
2008	1,845	PF63 475	PF65 500			

KM# 1539 10 EURO
8.45 g., 0.999 Gold 0.2697 oz. AGW, 22 mm. **Subject:** 5th Republic, 50th Anniversary **Obv:** The Seed Sower **Rev:** de Gaulle head right

Date	Mintage	F12	VF20	XF40	MS60	MS63
2008	620	PF63 500	PF65 525			

KM# 1547 10 EURO
8.45 g., 0.920 Gold 0.2483 oz. AGW, 22 mm. **Subject:** UEFA **Obv:** French soccer team **Rev:** UEFA logo

Date	Mintage	F12	VF20	XF40	MS60	MS63
2008	500	PF63 525	PF65 550			

KM# 1552 10 EURO
8.45 g., 0.920 Gold 0.2483 oz. AGW, 22 mm. **Subject:** Franco - Japanese Relators - 150th Anniversary **Obv:** Eiffel Tower and Kimono forming logo **Rev:** Delacroix's "La Liberte"

Date	Mintage	F12	VF20	XF40	MS60	MS63
2008	1,726	PF63 475	PF65 500			

KM# 1553 10 EURO
8.45 g., 0.920 Gold 0.2483 oz. AGW, 22 mm. **Subject:** Franco - Japanese Relators - 150th Anniversary **Obv:** Eiffel Tower and Kimono forming logo **Rev:** Ichikawa Ebizo IV" portrait painting

Date	Mintage	F12	VF20	XF40	MS60	MS63
2008	1,657	PF63 475	PF65 500			

KM# 1554 10 EURO
8.45 g., 0.920 Gold 0.2483 oz. AGW, 22 mm. **Subject:** Franco - Japanese Relators - 150th Anniversary **Obv:** Eiffel Tower and Kimono forming logo **Rev:** Japanese cash coin from "Kanci Tsuho"

Date	Mintage	F12	VF20	XF40	MS60	MS63
2008	1,848	PF63 475	PF65 500			

KM# 1556 10 EURO
0.45 g., 0.920 Gold AGW, 22 mm. **Subject:** André Citronë **Obv:** First front wheel drive auto **Rev:** Bust 1/4 left

Date	Mintage	F12	VF20	XF40	MS60	MS63
2008	500	PF63 525	PF65 550			

KM# 1559 10 EURO
8.45 g., 0.920 Gold 0.2483 oz. AGW, 22 mm. **Subject:** Rouen Armada **Obv:** Cape Hown, sextant, hour glass **Edge:** Sailing ship

Date	Mintage	F12	VF20	XF40	MS60	MS63
2008	500	PF63 525	PF65 550			

KM# 1562 10 EURO
8.45 g., 0.920 Gold 0.2483 oz. AGW, 22 mm. **Subject:** Lourdes, 150th Anniversary **Obv:** Church of Notre Dame at Lourdes **Rev:** Cross with Pope John Paul II, Pope Benedict XVI and Bernadette Soubirous in quadrants

Date	Mintage	F12	VF20	XF40	MS60	MS63
2008	999	PF63 500	PF65 525			

KM# 1567 10 EURO
8.45 g., 0.920 Gold 0.2483 oz. AGW, 22 mm. **Subject:** Gabrielle Chanel **Obv:** Portrait in hat, right **Rev:** Value on "Matelassé" pattern

Date	Mintage	F12	VF20	XF40	MS60	MS63
2008	500	PF63 475	PF65 500			

KM# 1573 10 EURO
8.45 g., 0.920 Gold 0.2483 oz. AGW, 22 mm. **Subject:** Lunar New Year - Year of the Rat **Obv:** Bust of Jean de la Fontaine and twelve awards **Rev:** Rat within border

Date	Mintage	F12	VF20	XF40	MS60	MS63
2008	500	PF63 525	PF65 550			

KM# 1575 10 EURO
8.45 g., 0.920 Gold 0.2483 oz. AGW, 22 mm. **Subject:** UNESCO - Grand Canyon **Obv:** Grand Canyon **Rev:** UNESCO logos

Date	Mintage	F12	VF20	XF40	MS60	MS63
2008	500	PF63 525	PF65 550			

KM# 1577 10 EURO
8.45 g., 0.920 Gold 0.2483 oz. AGW, 22 mm. **Subject:** International Polar Year **Obv:** IPY logo **Rev:** Emperor Penguin and map of Antartica

Date	Mintage	F12	VF20	XF40	MS60	MS63
2008	500	PF63 525	PF65 550			

KM# 1579 10 EURO
8.45 g., 0.920 Gold 0.2483 oz. AGW, 22 mm. **Subject:** Spirou, 70th Anniversary **Obv:** Character Spirou in thought **Rev:** 70th Aniversary logo

Date	Mintage	F12	VF20	XF40	MS60	MS63
2008	387	PF63 525	PF65 550			

KM# 1591 10 EURO
27.20 g., 0.900 Silver 0.782 oz. ASW, 37 mm. **Subject:** Europa - Fall of Berlin Wall **Obv:** Brandenburg gate and doves in flight **Rev:** Head facing and flags

Date	Mintage	F12	VF20	XF40	MS60	MS63
2009P	10,000	PF63 37.50	PF65 40.00			

KM# 1580 10 EURO
12.00 g., 0.900 Silver 0.345 oz. ASW, 29 mm. **Obv:** Modernistic sower advancing right **Rev:** Wreath and value

Date	Mintage	F12	VF20	XF40	MS60	MS63
2009P	2,000,000	—	—	—	—	17.50

KM# 1584 10 EURO
22.20 g., 0.900 Silver 0.6382 oz. ASW, 37 mm. **Subject:** Court of Human Rights, 50th Anniversary **Obv:** Sower left **Rev:** Text

Date	Mintage	F12	VF20	XF40	MS60	MS63
2009P	8,284	PF63 35.00	PF65 40.00			

KM# 1596 10 EURO
22.20 g., 0.900 Silver 0.6382 oz. ASW, 37 mm. **Subject:** Concorde 40th Anniversary **Obv:** Concorde in flight **Rev:** Tail emblems

Date	Mintage	F12	VF20	XF40	MS60	MS63
2009P	15,077	PF63 40.00	PF65 45.00			

KM# 1601 10 EURO
20.89 g., 0.900 Silver 0.6006 oz. ASW, 37 mm. **Obv:** Eiffel Tower Structure **Rev:** Gustave Eiffel at left

Date	Mintage	F12	VF20	XF40	MS60	MS63
2009P	7,989	PF63 35.00	PF65 40.00			

KM# 1606 10 EURO
27.20 g., 0.900 Silver 0.782 oz. ASW, 37 mm. **Subject:** Bugatti 100th Anniversary **Obv:** Ettore Bugatti at left **Rev:** Race car and quilt motif

Date	Mintage	F12	VF20	XF40	MS60	MS63
2009P	3,547	PF63 40.00	PF65 45.00			

KM# 1611 10 EURO
22.20 g., 0.900 Silver 0.6382 oz. ASW, 37 mm. **Subject:** Curie Institute, 100th Anniversary

Date	Mintage	F12	VF20	XF40	MS60	MS63
2009P	10,000	PF63 35.00	PF65 40.00			

KM# 1616 10 EURO
27.20 g., 0.900 Silver 0.782 oz. ASW, 37 mm. **Subject:** Unesco site - The Kremlin in Moscow **Obv:** Wall Tower and cathedral

Date	Mintage	F12	VF20	XF40	MS60	MS63
2009P	5,205	PF63 37.00	PF65 42.00			

KM# 1621 10 EURO
22.20 g., 0.900 Silver 0.6382 oz. ASW, 37 mm. **Subject:** First Moon Landing, 40th Anniversary **Obv:** Footprint on the moon

Date	Mintage	F12	VF20	XF40	MS60	MS63
2009P	9,996	PF63 35.00	PF65 40.00			

KM# 1629 10 EURO
22.20 g., 0.900 Silver 0.6382 oz. ASW, 37 mm. **Subject:** Comic strip heroes **Obv:** Wanted posted **Rev:** Lucky Luke on horseback

Date	Mintage	F12	VF20	XF40	MS60	MS63
2009P	5,000	PF63 45.00	PF65 50.00			

KM# 1631 10 EURO
22.20 g., 0.900 Silver 0.6382 oz. ASW, 37 mm. **Obv:** Soccer player **Rev:** Shield of Stade Francais in color

Date	Mintage	F12	VF20	XF40	MS60	MS63
2009P	2,206	PF63 40.00	PF65 45.00			

KM# 1634 10 EURO
27.20 g., 0.900 Silver 0.782 oz. ASW, 37 mm. **Subject:** Alpine skiing **Obv:** Globe and downhill skier **Rev:** Downhill skier on mountainside

Date	Mintage	F12	VF20	XF40	MS60	MS63
2009P	10,000	PF63 37.00	PF65 42.00			

KM# 1636 10 EURO
22.20 g., 0.900 Silver 0.6382 oz. ASW, 37 mm. **Subject:** FIFA World Cup, South Africa **Obv:** Soccer player on field **Rev:** Soccerball, map of Africa, Prorea flower

Date	Mintage	F12	VF20	XF40	MS60	MS63
2009P	6,404	PF63 35.00	PF65 40.00			

KM# 1675 10 EURO
22.20 g., 0.900 Silver 0.6382 oz. ASW, 37 mm. **Obv:** Sower left **Rev:** Wheat and olive branch

Date	Mintage	F12	VF20	XF40	MS60	MS63
2009					30.00	
2010	10,000	PF63 35.00	PF65 40.00			

KM# 1645 10 EURO
12.00 g., 0.900 Silver 0.345 oz. ASW, 29 mm. **Subject:** Aquitaine **Rev:** Value at center, wreath horizontal

Date	Mintage	F12	VF20	XF40	MS60	MS63
2010	7,690	—	—	—	—	22.50

KM# 1646 10 EURO
12.00 g., 0.900 Silver 0.345 oz. ASW, 29 mm. **Subject:** Auvergne **Rev:** Value at center, wreath horizontal

Date	Mintage	F12	VF20	XF40	MS60	MS63
2010	7,690	—	—	—	—	22.50

KM# 1647 10 EURO
12.00 g., 0.900 Silver 0.345 oz. ASW, 29 mm. **Subject:** Basse - Normandie **Rev:** Value at center, wreath horizontal

Date	Mintage	F12	VF20	XF40	MS60	MS63
2010	7,690	—	—	—	—	22.50

KM# 1648 10 EURO
12.00 g., 0.900 Silver 0.345 oz. ASW, 29 mm. **Subject:** Bretagne **Rev:** Value at center, wreath horizontal

Date	Mintage	F12	VF20	XF40	MS60	MS63
2010	7,690	—	—	—	—	22.50

KM# 1649 10 EURO
12.00 g., 0.900 Silver 0.345 oz. ASW, 29 mm. **Subject:** Burgundy **Rev:** Value at center, wreath horizontal

Date	Mintage	F12	VF20	XF40	MS60	MS63
2010	7,690	—	—	—	—	22.50

KM# 1650 10 EURO
12.00 g., 0.900 Silver 0.345 oz. ASW, 29 mm. **Subject:** Centre **Rev:** Value at center, wreath horizontal

Date	Mintage	F12	VF20	XF40	MS60	MS63
2010	7,690	—	—	—	—	22.50

KM# 1651 10 EURO
12.00 g., 0.900 Silver 0.345 oz. ASW, 29 mm. **Subject:** Champagne - Ardenne **Rev:** Value at center, wreath horizontal

Date	Mintage	F12	VF20	XF40	MS60	MS63
2010	7,690	—	—	—	—	22.50

KM# 1652 10 EURO
12.00 g., 0.900 Silver 0.345 oz. ASW, 29 mm. **Subject:** Alsace **Rev:** Value at center, wreath horizontal

Date	Mintage	F12	VF20	XF40	MS60	MS63
2010	7,690	—	—	—	—	22.50

KM# 1653 10 EURO
12.00 g., 0.900 Silver 0.345 oz. ASW, 29 mm. **Subject:** French - Comte **Rev:** Value at center, wreath horizontal

Date	Mintage	F12	VF20	XF40	MS60	MS63
2010	7,690	—	—	—	—	22.50

KM# 1654 10 EURO
12.00 g., 0.900 Silver 0.345 oz. ASW, 29 mm. **Subject:** French Guiana **Rev:** Value at center, wreath horizontal

Date	Mintage	F12	VF20	XF40	MS60	MS63
2010	7,690	—	—	—	—	25.00

KM# 1655 10 EURO
12.00 g., 0.900 Silver 0.345 oz. ASW, 29 mm. **Subject:** Guadeloupe **Rev:** Value at center, wreath horizontal

Date	Mintage	F12	VF20	XF40	MS60	MS63
2010	7,690	—	—	—	—	25.00

KM# 1656 10 EURO
12.00 g., 0.900 Silver 0.345 oz. ASW, 29 mm. **Subject:** Haute - Normandie **Rev:** Value at center, wreath horizontal

Date	Mintage	F12	VF20	XF40	MS60	MS63
2010	7,690	—	—	—	—	22.50

KM# 1657 10 EURO
12.00 g., 0.900 Silver 0.345 oz. ASW, 29 mm. **Subject:** Ile-de-France **Rev:** Value at center, wreath horizontal

Date	Mintage	F12	VF20	XF40	MS60	MS63
2010	7,690	—	—	—	—	22.50

KM# 1658 10 EURO
12.00 g., 0.900 Silver 0.345 oz. ASW, 29 mm. **Subject:** Corsica **Rev:** Value at center, wreath horizontal

Date	Mintage	F12	VF20	XF40	MS60	MS63
2010	7,690	—	—	—	—	25.00

KM# 1659 10 EURO
12.00 g., 0.900 Silver 0.345 oz. ASW, 29 mm. **Subject:** Languedoc - Roussillon **Rev:** Value at center, wreath horizontal

Date	Mintage	F12	VF20	XF40	MS60	MS63
2010	7,690	—	—	—	—	22.50

KM# 1660 10 EURO
12.00 g., 0.900 Silver 0.345 oz. ASW, 29 mm. **Subject:** Limousin **Rev:** Value at center, wreath horizontal

Date	Mintage	F12	VF20	XF40	MS60	MS63
2010	7,690	—	—	—	—	22.50

KM# 1661 10 EURO
12.00 g., 0.900 Silver 0.345 oz. ASW, 29 mm. **Subject:** Lorroaine **Rev:** Value at center, wreath horizontal

Date	Mintage	F12	VF20	XF40	MS60	MS63
2010	7,690	—	—	—	—	22.50

KM# 1662 10 EURO
12.00 g., 0.900 Silver 0.345 oz. ASW, 29 mm. **Subject:** Martinique **Rev:** Value at center, wreath horizontal

Date	Mintage	F12	VF20	XF40	MS60	MS63
2010	7,690	—	—	—	—	25.00

KM# 1663 10 EURO
12.00 g., 0.900 Silver 0.345 oz. ASW, 29 mm. **Subject:** Midi - Pyrenees **Rev:** Value at center, wreath horizontal

Date	Mintage	F12	VF20	XF40	MS60	MS63
2010	7,690	—	—	—	—	22.50

KM# 1664 10 EURO
12.00 g., 0.900 Silver 0.345 oz. ASW, 29 mm. **Subject:** Nord - Pas de - Calais **Rev:** Value at center, wreath horizontal

Date	Mintage	F12	VF20	XF40	MS60	MS63
2010	7,690	—	—	—	—	22.50

KM# 1665 10 EURO
12.00 g., 0.900 Silver 0.345 oz. ASW, 29 mm. **Subject:** Pays de la Loire **Rev:** Value at center, wreath horizontal

Date	Mintage	F12	VF20	XF40	MS60	MS63
2010	7,690	—	—	—	—	22.50

KM# 1666 10 EURO
12.00 g., 0.900 Silver 0.345 oz. ASW, 29 mm. **Subject:** Picardie **Rev:** Value at center, wreath horizontal

Date	Mintage	F12	VF20	XF40	MS60	MS63
2010	7,690	—	—	—	—	22.50

KM# 1667 10 EURO
12.00 g., 0.900 Silver 0.345 oz. ASW, 29 mm. **Subject:** Poitou - Charentes **Rev:** Value at center, wreath horizontal

Date	Mintage	F12	VF20	XF40	MS60	MS63
2010	7,690	—	—	—	—	22.50

KM# 1668 10 EURO
12.00 g., 0.900 Silver 0.345 oz. ASW, 29 mm. **Subject:** Provence - Alpes - Cote d'Azur **Rev:** Value at center, wreath horizontal

Date	Mintage	F12	VF20	XF40	MS60	MS63
2010	7,690	—	—	—	—	22.50

KM# 1669 10 EURO
12.00 g., 0.900 Silver 0.345 oz. ASW, 29 mm. **Subject:** Reunion **Rev:** Value at center, wreath horizontal

Date	Mintage	F12	VF20	XF40	MS60	MS63
2010	7,690	—	—	—	—	25.00

KM# 1670 10 EURO
12.00 g., 0.900 Silver 0.345 oz. ASW, 29 mm. **Subject:** Rhone - Alpes **Rev:** Value at center, wreath horizontal

Date	Mintage	F12	VF20	XF40	MS60	MS63
2010	7,690	—	—	—	—	22.50

KM# 1681 10 EURO
22.20 g., 0.999 Silver 0.7084 oz. ASW, 37 mm. **Subject:** Cluny Abbey, 1100th Anniversary **Obv:** Europa head facing **Rev:** Cluny Abbey

Date	Mintage	F12	VF20	XF40	MS60	MS63
2010	10,000	PF63 50.00	PF65 55.00			

KM# 1686 10 EURO
22.20 g., 0.900 Silver 0.6382 oz. ASW, 37 mm. **Obv:** Georges Pompidou Center design **Rev:** Design detail

Date	Mintage	F12	VF20	XF40	MS60	MS63
2010	30,000	PF63 40.00	PF65 45.00			

KM# 1691 10 EURO
22.20 g., Nickel-Copper, 37 mm. **Obv:** Marcel Dassault **Rev:** Mirage III plane

Date	Mintage	F12	VF20	XF40	MS60	MS63
2010	20,000	PF63 45.00	PF65 50.00			

KM# 1695 10 EURO
22.20 g., 0.900 Silver 0.6382 oz. ASW, 37 mm. **Obv:** Mother Teresa and child **Rev:** Mother Teresa and Pope John Paul II

Date	Mintage	F12	VF20	XF40	MS60	MS63
2010	20,000	PF63 40.00	PF65 45.00			

KM# 1700 10 EURO
22.20 g., 0.900 Silver 0.6382 oz. ASW, 37 mm. **Obv:** Taj Mahal **Rev:** UNESCO offices

Date	Mintage	F12	VF20	XF40	MS60	MS63
2010	10,000	PF63 55.00	PF65 65.00			

KM# 1705 10 EURO
22.20 g., 0.900 Silver 0.6382 oz. ASW, 37 mm. **Obv:** Lille station and route map **Rev:** Three TGV trains

Date	Mintage	F12	VF20	XF40	MS60	MS63
2010	30,000	PF63 35.00	PF65 40.00			

KM# 1708 10 EURO
15.00 g., 0.900 Silver 0.4312 oz. ASW, 30x21 mm. **Rev:** Georges Braque **Shape:** Rectangle

Date	Mintage	F12	VF20	XF40	MS60	MS63
2010	20,000	PF63 60.00	PF65 70.00			

KM# 1713 10 EURO
15.00 g., 0.900 Silver 0.4312 oz. ASW, 30x21 mm. **Rev:** Picasso **Shape:** Rectangle

Date	Mintage	F12	VF20	XF40	MS60	MS63
2010	20,000	PF63 70.00	PF65 80.00			

KM# 1717 10 EURO
22.20 g., 0.900 Silver 0.6382 oz. ASW, 37 mm. **Obv:** Blake and Mortimer **Rev:** Secret of the Swordfish" scene, arrest of Col. Olrik.

Date	Mintage	F12	VF20	XF40	MS60	MS63
2010	10,000	PF63 50.00	PF65 60.00			

KM# 1720 10 EURO
22.20 g., 0.900 Silver 0.6382 oz. ASW, 37 mm. **Obv:** Handball player and globe **Rev:** Handball player, net and Big Ben

Date	Mintage	F12	VF20	XF40	MS60	MS63
2010	10,000	PF63 40.00	PF65 45.00			

KM# 1722 10 EURO
22.20 g., 0.900 Silver 0.6382 oz. ASW, 37 mm. **Obv:** Soccer player **Rev:** Stade Toulousain logo, multicolor

Date	Mintage	F12	VF20	XF40	MS60	MS63
2010	5,000	PF63 50.00	PF65 55.00			

KM# 1726 10 EURO
10.00 g., 0.500 Silver 0.1597 oz. ASW, 29 mm. **Subject:** Mayotte **Obv:** Value at center, wreath horizontal

Date	Mintage	F12	VF20	XF40	MS60	MS63
2011	50,000	—	—	—	—	20.00

KM# 1727 10 EURO
10.00 g., 0.500 Silver 0.1597 oz. ASW, 29 mm. **Subject:** Aquitaine

Date	Mintage	F12	VF20	XF40	MS60	MS63
2011	150,000	—	—	—	—	20.00

KM# 1728 10 EURO
10.00 g., 0.500 Silver 0.1597 oz. ASW, 29 mm. **Subject:** Auvergne

Date	Mintage	F12	VF20	XF40	MS60	MS63
2011	80,000	—	—	—	—	20.00

KM# 1729 10 EURO
10.00 g., 0.500 Silver 0.1597 oz. ASW, 29 mm. **Subject:** Basse - Normindie

Date	Mintage	F12	VF20	XF40	MS60	MS63
2011	100,000	—	—	—	—	20.00

KM# 1730 10 EURO
10.00 g., 0.500 Silver 0.1597 oz. ASW, 29 mm. **Subject:** Bretagne

Date	Mintage	F12	VF20	XF40	MS60	MS63
2011	150,000	—	—	—	—	20.00

KM# 1731 10 EURO
10.00 g., 0.500 Silver 0.1597 oz. ASW, 29 mm. **Subject:** Burgundy

Date	Mintage	F12	VF20	XF40	MS60	MS63
2011	—	—	—	—	—	20.00

KM# 1732 10 EURO
10.00 g., 0.500 Silver 0.1597 oz. ASW, 29 mm. **Subject:** Centre

Date	Mintage	F12	VF20	XF40	MS60	MS63
2011	80,000	—	—	—	—	20.00

KM# 1733 10 EURO
10.00 g., 0.500 Silver 0.1597 oz. ASW, 29 mm. **Subject:** Campagne - Ardenne

Date	Mintage	F12	VF20	XF40	MS60	MS63
2011	50,000	—	—	—	—	20.00

KM# 1734 10 EURO
10.00 g., 0.500 Silver 0.1597 oz. ASW, 29 mm. **Subject:** Alsace

Date	Mintage	F12	VF20	XF40	MS60	MS63
2011	100,000	—	—	—	—	20.00

KM# 1735 10 EURO
10.00 g., 0.500 Silver 0.1597 oz. ASW, 29 mm. **Subject:** France - Comte

Date	Mintage	F12	VF20	XF40	MS60	MS63
2011	80,000	—	—	—	—	20.00

KM# 1736 10 EURO
10.00 g., 0.500 Silver 0.1597 oz. ASW, 29 mm. **Subject:** Guyane

Date	Mintage	F12	VF20	XF40	MS60	MS63
2011	50,000	—	—	—	—	25.00

KM# 1737 10 EURO
10.00 g., 0.500 Silver 0.1597 oz. ASW, 29 mm. **Subject:** Guadeloupe

Date	Mintage	F12	VF20	XF40	MS60	MS63
2011	50,000	—	—	—	—	25.00

KM# 1738 10 EURO
10.00 g., 0.500 Silver 0.1597 oz. ASW, 29 mm. **Subject:** Haute - Normandie

Date	Mintage	F12	VF20	XF40	MS60	MS63
2011	80,000	—	—	—	—	20.00

KM# 1739 10 EURO
10.00 g., 0.500 Silver 0.1597 oz. ASW, 29 mm. **Subject:** Ile de France

Date	Mintage	F12	VF20	XF40	MS60	MS63
2011	310,000	—	—	—	—	20.00

KM# 1740 10 EURO
10.00 g., 0.500 Silver 0.1597 oz. ASW, 29 mm. **Subject:** Corsica

Date	Mintage	F12	VF20	XF40	MS60	MS63
2011	80,000	—	—	—	—	25.00

KM# 1741 10 EURO
10.00 g., 0.500 Silver 0.1597 oz. ASW, 29 mm. **Subject:** Languedoc - Rossillon

Date	Mintage	F12	VF20	XF40	MS60	MS63
2011	120,000	—	—	—	—	20.00

KM# 1742 10 EURO
10.00 g., 0.500 Silver 0.1597 oz. ASW, 29 mm. **Subject:** Limousin

Date	Mintage	F12	VF20	XF40	MS60	MS63
2011	80,000	—	—	—	—	20.00

KM# 1743 10 EURO
10.00 g., 0.500 Silver 0.1597 oz. ASW, 29 mm. **Subject:** Lorraine

Date	Mintage	F12	VF20	XF40	MS60	MS63
2011	100,000	—	—	—	—	20.00

KM# 1744 10 EURO
10.00 g., 0.500 Silver 0.1597 oz. ASW, 29 mm. **Subject:** Martinique

Date	Mintage	F12	VF20	XF40	MS60	MS63
2011	50,000	—	—	—	—	25.00

KM# 1745 10 EURO
10.00 g., 0.500 Silver 0.1597 oz. ASW, 29 mm. **Subject:** Nord Pas de Calais

Date	Mintage	F12	VF20	XF40	MS60	MS63
2011	180,000	—	—	—	—	20.00

KM# 1746 10 EURO
10.00 g., 0.500 Silver 0.1597 oz. ASW, 29 mm. **Subject:** Pays de la Loire

Date	Mintage	F12	VF20	XF40	MS60	MS63
2011	—	—	—	—	—	20.00

KM# 1747 10 EURO
10.00 g., 0.500 Silver 0.1597 oz. ASW, 29 mm. **Subject:** Picardie

Date	Mintage	F12	VF20	XF40	MS60	MS63
2011	100,000	—	—	—	—	20.00

KM# 1748 10 EURO
10.00 g., 0.500 Silver 0.1597 oz. ASW, 29 mm. **Subject:** Poitou - Charentes

Date	Mintage	F12	VF20	XF40	MS60	MS63
2011	100,000	—	—	—	—	20.00

KM# 1749 10 EURO
10.00 g., 0.500 Silver 0.1597 oz. ASW, 29 mm. **Subject:** Province - Alpes - Cote d'Azur

Date	Mintage	F12	VF20	XF40	MS60	MS63
2011	220,000	—	—	—	—	20.00

KM# 1750 10 EURO
10.00 g., 0.500 Silver 0.1597 oz. ASW, 29 mm. **Subject:** Reunion

Date	Mintage	F12	VF20	XF40	MS60	MS63
2011	70,000	—	—	—	—	25.00

KM# 1751 10 EURO
10.00 g., 0.500 Silver 0.1597 oz. ASW, 29 mm. **Subject:** Rhone - Alpes

Date	Mintage	F12	VF20	XF40	MS60	MS63
2011	220,000	—	—	—	—	20.00

KM# 1752 10 EURO
10.00 g., 0.500 Silver 0.1597 oz. ASW, 29 mm. **Subject:** Midi - Pyreneis

Date	Mintage	F12	VF20	XF40	MS60	MS63
2011	120,000	—	—	—	—	20.00

KM# 1784 10 EURO
22.20 g., 0.900 Silver 0.6382 oz. ASW, 37 mm. **Subject:** Euro Starter Kit, 10th Anniversary **Obv:** Sower left **Rev:** Euro starter kit

Date	Mintage	F12	VF20	XF40	MS60	MS63
2011	10,000	PF63 40.00		PF65 45.00		

KM# 1790 10 EURO
22.20 g., 0.900 Silver 0.6382 oz. ASW, 37 mm. **Subject:** International Music Day, 30th Anniversary **Obv:** Europa **Rev:** Youth jamming

Date	Mintage	F12	VF20	XF40	MS60	MS63
2011	10,000	PF63 40.00		PF65 45.00		

KM# 1795 10 EURO
22.20 g., 0.900 Silver 0.6382 oz. ASW, 37 mm. **Subject:** Great Explorers - Jacques Cartier **Obv:** The Grand Hermine sailing away **Rev:** Cartier, globe and compass rose

Date	Mintage	F12	VF20	XF40	MS60	MS63
2011	30,000	PF63 50.00		PF65 55.00		

KM# 1800 10 EURO
22.20 g., 0.900 Silver 0.6382 oz. ASW, 37 mm. **Subject:** Colvis, 481-511 **Obv:** Hands over chalice, reign dates at left, value at right **Rev:** Crowned head left

Date	Mintage	F12	VF20	XF40	MS60	MS63
2011	20,000	PF63 50.00		PF65 55.00		

KM# 1802 10 EURO
22.20 g., 0.900 Silver 0.6382 oz. ASW, 37 mm. **Subject:** Charlemagne, 768-814 **Obv:** Cross on orb, reight dates at left, value at right **Rev:** Crowned head left

Date	Mintage	F12	VF20	XF40	MS60	MS63
2011	20,000	PF63 50.00		PF65 55.00		

KM# 1804 10 EURO
22.20 g., 0.900 Silver 0.6382 oz. ASW, 37 mm. **Subject:** Charles II, 840-877 **Obv:** KARLOS monogram **Rev:** Crowned head left

Date	Mintage	F12	VF20	XF40	MS60	MS63
2011	20,000	PF63 50.00		PF65 55.00		

KM# 1806 10 EURO
22.20 g., 0.900 Silver 0.6382 oz. ASW, 37 mm. **Subject:** WWF - Audouin's Gull **Obv:** Gull in flight right **Rev:** Gull standing right, WWF panda logo

Date	Mintage	F12	VF20	XF40	MS60	MS63
2011	20,000	PF63 55.00		PF65 60.00		

KM# 1809 10 EURO
22.20 g., 0.900 Silver 0.6382 oz. ASW, 37 mm. **Subject:** UNESCO World Heritage Site - Palace of Versailles **Obv:** Building and garden plan **Rev:** Top view of UNESCO's Paris headquarters

Date	Mintage	F12	VF20	XF40	MS60	MS63
2011	20,000	PF63 50.00		PF65 55.00		

KM# 1814 10 EURO
22.20 g., 0.900 Silver 0.6382 oz. ASW, 37 mm. **Obv:** Metz railroad station **Rev:** TGV and ICE trains

Date	Mintage	F12	VF20	XF40	MS60	MS63
2011	10,000	PF63 50.00		PF65 55.00		

KM# 1819 10 EURO
15.00 g., 0.900 Silver 0.4312 oz. ASW, 30x21 mm. **Subject:** Vassily Kandinsky **Shape:** Rectangle

Date	Mintage	F12	VF20	XF40	MS60	MS63
2011	10,000	PF63 70.00		PF65 80.00		

KM# 1823 10 EURO
15.00 g., 0.900 Silver 0.4312 oz. ASW, 31 mm. **Subject:** Andy Warhol **Obv:** Portrait facing **Rev:** Dollar sign in color

Date	Mintage	F12	VF20	XF40	MS60	MS63
2011	10,000	PF63 65.00		PF65 75.00		

KM# 1827 10 EURO
22.20 g., 0.900 Silver 0.6382 oz. ASW, 37 mm. **Obv:** Cosette - Les Miserables **Rev:** Victor Hugo

Date	Mintage	F12	VF20	XF40	MS60	MS63
2011	10,000	PF63 50.00		PF65 55.00		

KM# 1829 10 EURO
22.20 g., 0.900 Silver 0.6382 oz. ASW, 37 mm. **Obv:** Nana **Rev:** Emile Zola

Date	Mintage	F12	VF20	XF40	MS60	MS63
2011	5,000	PF63 50.00		PF65 55.00		

KM# 1831 10 EURO
22.20 g., 0.900 Silver 0.6382 oz. ASW, 37 mm. **Obv:** The
Stranger **Rev:** Albert Camus

Date	Mintage	F12	VF20	XF40	MS60	MS63
2011	—	PF63 50.00	PF65 55.00			

KM# 1835 10 EURO
22.20 g., 0.900 Silver 0.6382 oz. ASW, 37 mm. **Subject:** Comic
Strip XIII **Obv:** Montage of characters **Rev:** Profile left and large
XIII

Date	Mintage	F12	VF20	XF40	MS60	MS63
2011	10,000	PF63 50.00	PF65 55.00			

KM# 1755 10 EURO
22.20 g., 0.900 Silver 0.6382 oz. ASW, 37 mm. **Obv:** Bicycle
racer **Rev:** Metro 92 logo

Date	Mintage	F12	VF20	XF40	MS60	MS63
2011	5,000	PF63 50.00	PF65 55.00			

KM# 1838 10 EURO
22.20 g., 0.900 Silver 0.6382 oz. ASW, 37 mm. **Obv:** Female
figure skater and globe **Rev:** Figure skating pair

Date	Mintage	F12	VF20	XF40	MS60	MS63
2011	10,000	PF63 50.00	PF65 55.00			

KM# 1850 10 EURO
22.20 g., 0.900 Silver 0.6382 oz. ASW, 27 mm. **Subject:**
Eurocorps, 20th Anniversary **Obv:** Mitterrand and Kohl standing
clasping hands **Rev:** Europa facing

Date	Mintage	F12	VF20	XF40	MS60	MS63
2012(a)	10,000	PF63 35.00	PF65 40.00			

KM# 1856 10 EURO
22.20 g., 0.900 Silver 0.6382 oz. ASW, 37 mm. **Subject:**
Hugues Capet **Obv:** Crowned head faicing **Rev:** Right hand
raised in benidiction

Date	Mintage	F12	VF20	XF40	MS60	MS63
2012(a)	20,000	PF63 35.00	PF65 40.00			

KM# 1857 10 EURO
22.20 g., 0.900 Silver 0.6382 oz. ASW, 37 mm. **Subject:** Saint
Louis **Obv:** Crowned head faicing **Rev:** Oak tree

Date	Mintage	F12	VF20	XF40	MS60	MS63
2012(a)	20,000	PF63 35.00	PF65 40.00			

KM# 1859 10 EURO
22.20 g., 0.900 Silver 0.6382 oz. ASW, 37 mm. **Subject:** The
Three Musketeers **Obv:** D'Artagnan, cross emblem and three
musketeers standing with swords raised **Rev:** Musketeers
motto: "Un pour tours…" at left, Alexandre Dumas portrait at
right

Date	Mintage	F12	VF20	XF40	MS60	MS63
2012(a)	5,000	PF63 35.00	PF65 40.00			

KM# 1862 10 EURO
10.00 g., 0.500 Silver 0.1597 oz. ASW, 29 mm. **Subject:**
Mayotte **Obv:** Value at center, wreath horizontal

Date	Mintage	F12	VF20	XF40	MS60	MS63
2012(a)	—	—	—	—	—	20.00

KM# 1863 10 EURO
10.00 g., 0.500 Silver 0.1597 oz. ASW, 29 mm. **Subject:**
Aquitaine **Obv:** Value at center, wreath horizontal

Date	Mintage	F12	VF20	XF40	MS60	MS63
2012(a)	—	—	—	—	—	20.00

KM# 1864 10 EURO
10.00 g., 0.500 Silver 0.1597 oz. ASW, 29 mm. **Subject:**
Auvergne **Obv:** Value at center, wreath horizontal

Date	Mintage	F12	VF20	XF40	MS60	MS63
2012(a)	—	—	—	—	—	20.00

KM# 1865 10 EURO
10.00 g., 0.500 Silver 0.1597 oz. ASW, 29 mm. **Subject:** Basse
- Normandie **Obv:** Value at center, wreath horizontal

Date	Mintage	F12	VF20	XF40	MS60	MS63
2012(a)	—	—	—	—	—	20.00

KM# 1866 10 EURO
10.00 g., 0.500 Silver 0.1597 oz. ASW, 29 mm. **Subject:**
Bretagne **Obv:** Value at center, wreath horizontal

Date	Mintage	F12	VF20	XF40	MS60	MS63
2012(a)	—	—	—	—	—	20.00

KM# 1867 10 EURO
10.00 g., 0.500 Silver 0.1597 oz. ASW, 29 mm. **Subject:**
Burgundy **Obv:** Value at center, wreath horizontal

Date	Mintage	F12	VF20	XF40	MS60	MS63
2012(a)	—	—	—	—	—	20.00

KM# 1868 10 EURO
10.00 g., 0.500 Silver 0.1597 oz. ASW, 29 mm. **Subject:** Centre
Obv: Value at center, wreath horizontal

Date	Mintage	F12	VF20	XF40	MS60	MS63
2012(a)	—	—	—	—	—	20.00

KM# 1869 10 EURO
10.00 g., 0.500 Silver 0.1597 oz. ASW, 29 mm. **Subject:**
Champagne - Ardenne **Obv:** Value at center, wreath horizontal

Date	Mintage	F12	VF20	XF40	MS60	MS63
2012(a)	—	—	—	—	—	20.00

KM# 1870 10 EURO
10.00 g., 0.500 Silver 0.1597 oz. ASW, 29 mm. **Subject:** Alsace
Obv: Value at center, wreath horizontal

Date	Mintage	F12	VF20	XF40	MS60	MS63
2012(a)	—	—	—	—	—	20.00

KM# 1871 10 EURO
10.00 g., 0.500 Silver 0.1597 oz. ASW, 29 mm. **Subject:**
France - Comte

Date	Mintage	F12	VF20	XF40	MS60	MS63
2012(a)	—	—	—	—	—	20.00

KM# 1872 10 EURO
10.00 g., 0.500 Silver 0.1597 oz. ASW, 29 mm. **Subject:**
French Guiana **Obv:** Value at center, wreath horizontal

Date	Mintage	F12	VF20	XF40	MS60	MS63
2012(a)	—	—	—	—	—	25.00

KM# 1873 10 EURO
10.00 g., 0.500 Silver 0.1597 oz. ASW, 29 mm. **Subject:**
Guadeloupe **Obv:** Value at center, wreath horizontal

Date	Mintage	F12	VF20	XF40	MS60	MS63
2012(a)	—	—	—	—	—	25.00

KM# 1874 10 EURO
10.00 g., 0.500 Silver 0.1597 oz. ASW, 29 mm. **Subject:** Haute
- Normandie **Obv:** Value at center, wreath horizontal

Date	Mintage	F12	VF20	XF40	MS60	MS63
2012(a)	—	—	—	—	—	20.00

KM# 1875 10 EURO
10.00 g., 0.500 Silver 0.1597 oz. ASW, 29 mm. **Subject:** Ile de
France **Obv:** Value at center, wreath horizontal

Date	Mintage	F12	VF20	XF40	MS60	MS63
2012(a)	—	—	—	—	—	20.00

KM# 1876 10 EURO
10.00 g., 0.500 Silver 0.1597 oz. ASW, 29 mm. **Subject:**
Corsica **Obv:** Value at center, wreath horizontal

Date	Mintage	F12	VF20	XF40	MS60	MS63
2012(a)	—	—	—	—	—	25.00

KM# 1877 10 EURO
10.00 g., 0.500 Silver 0.1597 oz. ASW, 29 mm. **Subject:**
Languedoc - Rossillon **Obv:** Value at center, wreath horizontal

Date	Mintage	F12	VF20	XF40	MS60	MS63
2012(a)	—	—	—	—	—	20.00

KM# 1878 10 EURO
10.00 g., 0.500 Silver 0.1597 oz. ASW, 29 mm. **Subject:**
Limousin **Obv:** Value at center, wreath horizontal

Date	Mintage	F12	VF20	XF40	MS60	MS63
2012(a)	—	—	—	—	—	20.00

KM# 1879 10 EURO
10.00 g., 0.500 Silver 0.1597 oz. ASW, 29 mm. **Subject:**
Martinique **Obv:** Value at center, wreath horizontal

Date	Mintage	F12	VF20	XF40	MS60	MS63
2012(a)	—	—	—	—	—	25.00

KM# 1880 10 EURO
10.00 g., 0.500 Silver 0.1597 oz. ASW, 29 mm. **Subject:** Nord
Pas de Calais **Obv:** Value at center, wreath horizontal

Date	Mintage	F12	VF20	XF40	MS60	MS63
2012(a)	—	—	—	—	—	20.00

KM# 1881 10 EURO
10.00 g., 0.500 Silver 0.1597 oz. ASW, 29 mm. **Subject:** Pays
de la Loire **Obv:** Value at center, wreath horizontal

Date	Mintage	F12	VF20	XF40	MS60	MS63
2012(a)	—	—	—	—	—	20.00

KM# 1882 10 EURO
10.00 g., 0.500 Silver 0.1597 oz. ASW, 29 mm. **Subject:**
Picardie **Obv:** Value at center, wreath horizontal

Date	Mintage	F12	VF20	XF40	MS60	MS63
2012(a)	—	—	—	—	—	20.00

KM# 1883 10 EURO
10.00 g., 0.500 Silver 0.1597 oz. ASW, 29 mm. **Subject:** Poitou
- Charentes **Obv:** Value at center, wreath horizontal

Date	Mintage	F12	VF20	XF40	MS60	MS63
2012(a)	—	—	—	—	—	20.00

KM# 1884 10 EURO
10.00 g., 0.500 Silver 0.1597 oz. ASW, 29 mm. **Subject:**
Province - Alpes - Cote d'Azur **Obv:** Value at center, wreath
horizontal

Date	Mintage	F12	VF20	XF40	MS60	MS63
2012(a)	—	—	—	—	—	20.00

KM# 1885 10 EURO
10.00 g., 0.500 Silver 0.1597 oz. ASW, 29 mm. **Subject:** Reunion **Obv:** Value at center, wreath horizontal

Date	Mintage	F12	VF20	XF40	MS60	MS63
2012(a)	—	—	—	—	—	25.00

KM# 1886 10 EURO
10.00 g., 0.500 Silver 0.1597 oz. ASW, 29 mm. **Subject:** Rhone - Alpes **Obv:** Value at center, wreath horizontal

Date	Mintage	F12	VF20	XF40	MS60	MS63
2012(a)	—	—	—	—	—	20.00

KM# 1887 10 EURO
10.00 g., 0.500 Silver 0.1597 oz. ASW, 29 mm. **Subject:** Midi - Pyrenees **Obv:** Value at center, wreath horizontal

Date	Mintage	F12	VF20	XF40	MS60	MS63
2012(a)	—	—	—	—	—	20.00

KM# 1888 10 EURO
10.00 g., 0.500 Silver 0.1597 oz. ASW, 29 mm. **Subject:** Lorraine **Obv:** Value at center, wreath horizontal

Date	Mintage	F12	VF20	XF40	MS60	MS63
2012(a)	—	—	—	—	—	20.00

KM# 1889 10 EURO
22.20 g., 0.900 Silver 0.6382 oz. ASW, 37 mm. **Subject:** Euro, 10th Anniversary **Obv:** The Sower advancing left **Rev:** Value at center on globe, child-like drawings around

Date	Mintage	F12	VF20	XF40	MS60	MS63
2012(a)	15,000	PF63 35.00		PF65 40.00		

KM# 1895 10 EURO
22.20 g., 0.900 Silver 0.6382 oz. ASW, 37 mm. **Subject:** abbé Pierre, 100th anniversary of Birth **Obv:** Pierre at left, shadow at right **Rev:** Emmaus International logo and quote

Date	Mintage	F12	VF20	XF40	MS60	MS63
2012(a)	10,000	PF63 35.00		PF65 40.00		

KM# 1905 10 EURO
22.20 g., 0.900 Silver 0.6382 oz. ASW, 37 mm. **Subject:** UNESCO - World Heritage Site **Obv:** Abu Simbel temple

Date	Mintage	F12	VF20	XF40	MS60	MS63
2012(a)	10,000	PF63 35.00		PF65 40.00		

KM# 1911 10 EURO
22.20 g., 0.900 Silver 0.6382 oz. ASW, 37 mm. **Subject:** TGV South-East **Obv:** Lyon Saint-Exupery station **Rev:** Two modern locomotives

Date	Mintage	F12	VF20	XF40	MS60	MS63
2012(a)	5,000	PF63 35.00		PF65 40.00		

KM# 1916 10 EURO
22.20 g., 0.900 Silver 0.6382 oz. ASW, 37 mm. **Subject:** Comic strip hero **Obv:** Largo Winch and building **Rev:** Winch riding motorcycle being chased by two cars

Date	Mintage	F12	VF20	XF40	MS60	MS63
2012(a)	5,000	PF63 35.00		PF65 40.00		

KM# 1919 10 EURO
22.20 g., 0.900 Silver 0.6382 oz. ASW, 37 mm. **Subject:** Toulonnais Rugby Club **Obv:** Value and Stadium field view **Rev:** Colored shield and portrait Felix Mayol

Date	Mintage	F12	VF20	XF40	MS60	MS63
2012(a)	5,000	PF63 45.00		PF65 50.00		

KM# 1921 10 EURO
22.20 g., 0.900 Silver 0.6382 oz. ASW, 37 mm. **Subject:** 2012 Summer Olympics, London **Obv:** Two judo athletes and map of Europe **Rev:** Two judo athletes

Date	Mintage	F12	VF20	XF40	MS60	MS63
2012(a)	10,000	PF63 35.00		PF65 40.00		

KM# 1924 10 EURO
22.20 g., 0.900 Silver 0.6382 oz. ASW, 37 mm. **Subject:** Year of the Dragon **Obv:** Dragon **Rev:** La Fontaine and zodiac animals

Date	Mintage	F12	VF20	XF40	MS60	MS63
2012(a)	10,000	PF63 55.00		PF65 65.00		

KM# 2073 10 EURO
10.00 g., 0.500 Silver 0.1597 oz. ASW, 29 mm. **Obv:** Horizontal wreath, value within **Rev:** Hercules group standing

Date	Mintage	F12	VF20	XF40	MS60	MS63
2012	491,000	—	—	—	—	15.00
2012	19,000	PF63 35.00		PF65 40.00		
2013	—	—	—	—	—	15.00
2013	—	PF63 35.00		PF65 40.00		

KM# 2075 10 EURO
22.20 g., 0.900 Silver 0.6382 oz. ASW, 37 mm. **Obv:** Palice de Louvre **Rev:** Philipp II August, head facing

Date	Mintage	F12	VF20	XF40	MS60	MS63
2012	Est. 20000	—	—	—	—	65.00

KM# 2078 10 EURO
22.20 g., 0.900 Silver 0.6382 oz. ASW, 37 mm. **Obv:** Aircraft Carrier Jean de Arc **Rev:** Anchor chain below convoy of ships

Date	Mintage	F12	VF20	XF40	MS60	MS63
2012	Est. 10000	PF63 45.00		PF65 50.00		

KM# 2079 10 EURO
22.20 g., 0.900 Silver 0.6382 oz. ASW, 37 mm. **Obv:** Trans-atlantic liner France **Rev:** Two winged smoke-stacks, partial porthole

Date	Mintage	F12	VF20	XF40	MS60	MS63
2012	Est. 10000	PF63 45.00		PF65 50.00		

KM# 2084 10 EURO
22.20 g., 0.900 Silver 0.6382 oz. ASW, 37 mm. **Obv:** Roxane on the Balcony **Rev:** Edmond Rostand and quote

Date	Mintage	F12	VF20	XF40	MS60	MS63
2012	Est. 5000	PF63 35.00	PF65 40.00			

KM# 2085 10 EURO
22.20 g., 0.900 Silver 0.6382 oz. ASW, 37 mm. **Obv:** Puss in boots **Rev:** Charles Perrault and quote

Date	Mintage	F12	VF20	XF40	MS60	MS63
2012	Est. 5000	PF63 35.00	PF65 40.00			

KM# 2087 10 EURO
22.20 g., 0.900 Silver 0.6382 oz. ASW, 37 mm. **Obv:** Yves Klein, blue hand **Rev:** Klein artwork

Date	Mintage	F12	VF20	XF40	MS60	MS63
2012	—	PF63 40.00	PF65 45.00			

KM# 2091 10 EURO
22.20 g., 0.900 Silver 0.6382 oz. ASW, 37 mm. **Subject:** French-German Friendship, 50th Anniversary **Rev:** Europa head facing at right, banners at left

Date	Mintage	F12	VF20	XF40	MS60	MS63
2013	—	PF63 35.00	PF65 40.00			

KM# 2095 10 EURO
22.20 g., 0.900 Silver 0.6382 oz. ASW, 37 mm. **Subject:** Rudolf Noureev **Obv:** Portrait at right **Rev:** Dancer and National Theater

Date	Mintage	F12	VF20	XF40	MS60	MS63
2013	—	PF63 35.00	PF65 40.00			

KM# 2097 10 EURO
22.20 g., 0.900 Silver 0.6382 oz. ASW, 37 mm. **Subject:** Notre Dame, 850th Anniversary **Obv:** Seal at right, cathedral details, blue highlights **Rev:** Seal at left, cathedral details, blue highlights

Date	Mintage	F12	VF20	XF40	MS60	MS63
2013	—	PF63 50.00	PF65 55.00			

KM# A1450 15 EURO
31.00 g., 0.900 Silver 0.8912 oz. ASW, 31 mm. **Rev:** Pantheon

Date	Mintage	F12	VF20	XF40	MS60	MS63
2007	7,500	PF63 75.00	PF65 85.00			

KM# 1535 15 EURO
15.00 g., 0.900 Silver 0.4312 oz. ASW, 31 mm. **Obv:** Sower, half length advancing right **Rev:** Value within hexagon

Date	Mintage	F12	VF20	XF40	MS60	MS63
2008	7,500	PF63 55.00	PF65 60.00			
2008	500,000	—	—	—		45.00
2009	7,500	PF63 55.00	PF65 60.00			
2010	9,000	PF63 55.00	PF65 60.00			

KM# 1306 20 EURO
17.00 g., 0.920 Gold 0.4996 oz. AGW, 31 mm. **Subject:** French Landmarks **Obv:** French map **Rev:** Le Mont St. Michel **Edge:** Plain

Date	Mintage	F12	VF20	XF40	MS60	MS63
2002	1,000	PF63 950	PF65 1,000			

KM# 1308 20 EURO
17.00 g., 0.920 Gold 0.4996 oz. AGW, 31 mm. **Subject:** French Landmarks **Obv:** French map **Rev:** La Butte Montmartre **Edge:** Plain

Date	Mintage	F12	VF20	XF40	MS60	MS63
2002	1,000	PF63 875	PF65 900			

KM# 1333 20 EURO
17.00 g., 0.920 Gold 0.4996 oz. AGW, 31 mm. **Obv:** Victor Hugo, denomination and map **Rev:** Gavroche **Edge:** Plain

Date	Mintage	F12	VF20	XF40	MS60	MS63
2002	2,000	PF63 900	PF65 925			

KM# 1982 20 EURO
17.00 g., 0.920 Gold 0.4996 oz. AGW **Obv:** French euro coin designs **Rev:** Europa head facing, flags at left

Date	Mintage	F12	VF20	XF40	MS60	MS63
2002	3,000	PF63 1,000	PF65 1,100			

KM# 1984 20 EURO
17.00 g., 0.920 Gold 0.4996 oz. AGW **Subject:** Charles Lindburg's Flight, 75th Anniversary **Obv:** Map of Northern France, portrait of Lindburg **Rev:** Spirit of St. Louis plane and U.S. Coastline

Date	Mintage	F12	VF20	XF40	MS60	MS63
2002	1,000	PF63 1,000	PF65 1,100			

KM# 1986 20 EURO
163.80 g., 0.950 Silver 4.9708 oz. ASW, 50 mm. **Obv:** Victor Hugo bust facing at left **Rev:** Street scene from Les Miserables **Rev. Legend:** GAVROCHE

Date	Mintage	F12	VF20	XF40	MS60	MS63
2002	500	PF63 1,400	PF65 1,500			

KM# 1987 20 EURO
17.00 g., 0.920 Gold 0.4996 oz. AGW **Subject:** Children's stories **Rev:** Cinderilla

Date	Mintage	F12	VF20	XF40	MS60	MS63
2002	926	PF63 1,000	PF65 1,100			

KM# 1988 20 EURO
17.00 g., 0.920 Gold 0.4996 oz. AGW **Subject:** Children's Stories **Rev:** Snow White

Date	Mintage	F12	VF20	XF40	MS60	MS63
2002	950	PF63 1,000	PF65 1,100			

KM# 1989 20 EURO
17.00 g., 0.920 Gold 0.4996 oz. AGW **Subject:** Children's Stories **Rev:** Pinocchio

Date	Mintage	F12	VF20	XF40	MS60	MS63
2002	1,000	PF63 1,000	PF65 1,100			

KM# 1990 20 EURO
17.00 g., 0.920 Gold 0.4996 oz. AGW **Obv:** Sower advancing left **Rev:** Large value and map of Europe

Date	Mintage	F12	VF20	XF40	MS60	MS63
2002	4,182	PF63 1,000	PF65 1,100			

KM# 1327 20 EURO
8.45 g., 0.920 Gold 0.2483 oz. AGW, 31 mm. **Obv:** Tour de France logo **Rev:** Group of cyclists and Arch de Triumph **Edge:** Reeded

Date	Mintage	F12	VF20	XF40	MS60	MS63
2003A	2,127	PF63 475	PF65 500			

KM# 1328 20 EURO
8.45 g., 0.920 Gold 0.2483 oz. AGW, 31 mm. **Obv:** Tour de France logo **Rev:** Two cyclists and spectators **Edge:** Reeded

Date	Mintage	F12	VF20	XF40	MS60	MS63
2003A	2,100	PF63 475	PF65 500			

KM# 1329 20 EURO
8.45 g., 0.920 Gold 0.2483 oz. AGW, 31 mm. **Obv:** Tour de France logo **Rev:** Two groups of cyclists **Edge:** Reeded

Date	Mintage	F12	VF20	XF40	MS60	MS63
2003A	2,103	PF63 475	PF65 500			

KM# 1330 20 EURO
8.45 g., 0.920 Gold 0.2483 oz. AGW, 31 mm. **Obv:** Tour de France logo **Rev:** Cyclist, stop watch and gears **Edge:** Reeded

Date	Mintage	F12	VF20	XF40	MS60	MS63
2003A	2,107	PF63 475	PF65 500			

KM# 1334 20 EURO
17.00 g., 0.920 Gold 0.4996 oz. AGW, 31 mm. **Obv:** Tour de France logo **Rev:** Cyclist going left **Edge:** Plain

Date	Mintage	F12	VF20	XF40	MS60	MS63
2003	5,000	PF63 875	PF65 900			

KM# 1337 20 EURO
17.00 g., 0.920 Gold 0.4996 oz. AGW, 31 mm. **Obv:** Jefferson and Napoleon with Louisiana Purchase map **Rev:** Jazz musician, mansion and river boat **Edge:** Plain

Date	Mintage	F12	VF20	XF40	MS60	MS63
2003	761	PF63 900	PF65 925			

KM# 1339 20 EURO
17.00 g., 0.920 Gold 0.4996 oz. AGW, 31 mm. **Obv:** Curved cross design with multiple values **Rev:** Goddess Europa and flags **Edge:** Plain

Date	Mintage	F12	VF20	XF40	MS60	MS63
2003	2,322	PF63 875	PF65 900			

KM# 1342 20 EURO
17.00 g., 0.920 Gold 0.4996 oz. AGW, 31 mm. **Obv:** Denomination and compass face **Rev:** SS Normandie and New York City skyline **Edge:** Plain

Date	Mintage	F12	VF20	XF40	MS60	MS63
2003	389	PF63 900	PF65 925			

KM# 1344 20 EURO
17.00 g., 0.920 Gold 0.4996 oz. AGW, 31 mm. **Obv:** Denomination and compass face **Rev:** Airplane and Tokyo Geisha **Edge:** Plain

Date	Mintage	F12	VF20	XF40	MS60	MS63
2003	580	PF63 900	PF65 925			

KM# 1346 20 EURO
17.00 g., 0.920 Gold 0.4996 oz. AGW, 31 mm. **Obv:** Paul Gauguin **Rev:** Native woman **Edge:** Plain

Date	Mintage	F12	VF20	XF40	MS60	MS63
2003	628	PF63 875				

KM# 1349 20 EURO
17.00 g., 0.920 Gold 0.4996 oz. AGW, 31 mm. **Obv:** The Seed Sower **Rev:** Denomination and map **Edge:** Plain

Date	Mintage	F12	VF20	XF40	MS60	MS63
2003	1,166	PF63 875	PF65 900			

KM# 1354 20 EURO
17.00 g., 0.920 Gold 0.4996 oz. AGW, 31 mm. **Obv:** Mona Lisa **Rev:** Leonardo da Vinci and denomination **Edge:** Plain

Date	Mintage	F12	VF20	XF40	MS60	MS63
2003	808	PF63 900	PF65 925			

KM# 1356 20 EURO
17.00 g., 0.920 Gold 0.4996 oz. AGW, 31 mm. **Obv:** Map and denomination **Rev:** Chateau Chambord **Edge:** Plain

Date	Mintage	F12	VF20	XF40	MS60	MS63
2003	561	PF63 900	PF65 925			

KM# 1358 20 EURO
17.00 g., 0.920 Gold 0.4996 oz. AGW, 31 mm. **Obv:** Denomination in swirling design **Rev:** Hansel and Gretel, witch and house **Edge:** Plain

Date	Mintage	F12	VF20	XF40	MS60	MS63
2003	310	PF63 900		PF65 925		

KM# 1360 20 EURO
17.00 g., 0.920 Gold 0.4996 oz. AGW, 31 mm. **Obv:** Denomination in swirling design **Rev:** Alice in Wonderland **Edge:** Plain

Date	Mintage	F12	VF20	XF40	MS60	MS63
2003	314	PF63 900		PF65 925		

KM# 1363 20 EURO
17.00 g., 0.920 Gold 0.4996 oz. AGW, 31 mm. **Obv:** Pierre de Coubertin **Rev:** Olympic runners **Edge:** Plain

Date	Mintage	F12	VF20	XF40	MS60	MS63
2003	334	PF63 875		PF65 900		

KM# 1998 20 EURO
17.00 g., 0.920 Gold 0.4996 oz. AGW **Subject:** Athletic World Championships **Obv:** Winner podium before buildings **Rev:** Runner

Date	Mintage	F12	VF20	XF40	MS60	MS63
2003	1,165	PF63 1,000		PF65 1,100		

KM# 1999 20 EURO
17.00 g., 0.920 Gold 0.4996 oz. AGW **Subject:** Athletic World Championships **Obv:** Winner podium before buildings **Rev:** High jumper

Date	Mintage	F12	VF20	XF40	MS60	MS63
2003	863	PF63 1,000		PF65 1,100		

KM# 2000 20 EURO
17.00 g., 0.920 Gold 0.4996 oz. AGW **Subject:** Athletic World Championships **Obv:** Winner podium before buildings

Date	Mintage	F12	VF20	XF40	MS60	MS63
2003	867	PF63 1,000		PF65 1,100		

KM# 2004 20 EURO
163.80 g., 0.950 Silver 4.9708 oz. ASW, 50 mm. **Obv:** Mona Lisa **Rev:** Leonardo DaVinci bust at left, large value at right

Date	Mintage	F12	VF20	XF40	MS60	MS63
2003	999	PF63 400		PF65 425		

KM# 2007 20 EURO
17.00 g., 0.920 Gold 0.4996 oz. AGW **Subject:** Orient Express, Hagia Sophia in Istanbul **Obv:** Compass Rose **Rev:** Steam locomotive

Date	Mintage	F12	VF20	XF40	MS60	MS63
2003	402	PF63 1,000		PF65 1,100		

KM# 2009 20 EURO
17.00 g., 0.920 Gold 0.4996 oz. AGW **Subject:** Childhood Fairy Tales **Rev:** Sleeping Beauty

Date	Mintage	F12	VF20	XF40	MS60	MS63
2003	309	PF63 1,250		PF65 1,350		

KM# 1365 20 EURO
17.00 g., 0.920 Gold 0.4996 oz. AGW, 31 mm. **Obv:** Map with denomination **Rev:** Avignon Popes Palace **Edge:** Plain

Date	Mintage	F12	VF20	XF40	MS60	MS63
2004	595	PF63 900		PF65 925		

KM# 1370 20 EURO
17.00 g., 0.920 Gold 0.4996 oz. AGW, 31 mm. **Obv:** Soldiers and Normandy invasion scene **Rev:** D-DAY" above denomination **Edge:** Plain

Date	Mintage	F12	VF20	XF40	MS60	MS63
2004	531	PF63 875		PF65 900		

KM# 1376 20 EURO
17.00 g., 0.920 Gold 0.4996 oz. AGW, 31 mm. **Subject:** Centenary Law of Dec. 9, 1905 **Obv:** Sower" left in ring of stars **Rev:** Denomination and French map face design **Edge:** Plain

Date	Mintage	F12	VF20	XF40	MS60	MS63
2004	874	PF63 875		PF65 900		
2006	1,000	PF63 900		PF65 925		

KM# 1379 20 EURO
17.00 g., 0.920 Gold 0.4996 oz. AGW, 31 mm. **Obv:** Compass rose **Rev:** Ocean liner **Edge:** Plain

Date	Mintage	F12	VF20	XF40	MS60	MS63
2004	281	PF63 900		PF65 925		

KM# 1381 20 EURO
17.00 g., 0.920 Gold 0.4996 oz. AGW, 31 mm. **Obv:** Compass rose **Rev:** Trans-Siberian Railroad **Edge:** Plain

Date	Mintage	F12	VF20	XF40	MS60	MS63
2004	299	PF63 900		PF65 925		

KM# 1383 20 EURO
17.00 g., 0.920 Gold 0.4996 oz. AGW, 31 mm. **Obv:** Compass rose **Rev:** Half-track vehicle **Edge:** Plain

Date	Mintage	F12	VF20	XF40	MS60	MS63
2004	273	PF63 900		PF65 925		

KM# 1385 20 EURO
17.00 g., 0.920 Gold 0.4996 oz. AGW, 31 mm. **Obv:** Compass rose **Rev:** Biplane airliner **Edge:** Plain

Date	Mintage	F12	VF20	XF40	MS60	MS63
2004	273	PF63 900		PF65 925		

KM# 1388 20 EURO
17.00 g., 0.920 Gold 0.4996 oz. AGW, 31 mm. **Obv:** Statue of Liberty **Rev:** F. A. Bartholdi **Edge:** Plain

Date	Mintage	F12	VF20	XF40	MS60	MS63
2004	320	PF63 875		PF65 900		

KM# 1393 20 EURO
17.00 g., 0.920 Gold 0.4996 oz. AGW, 31 mm. **Subject:** European Union Expansion **Obv:** Partial face and flags **Rev:** Puzzle map **Edge:** Plain

Date	Mintage	F12	VF20	XF40	MS60	MS63
2004	1,280	PF63 875		PF65 900		

KM# 2016 20 EURO
17.00 g., 0.920 Gold 0.4996 oz. AGW **Subject:** Childhood stories **Rev:** Peter Pan

Date	Mintage	F12	VF20	XF40	MS60	MS63
2004	362	PF63 1,000		PF65 1,100		

KM# 2011 20 EURO
17.00 g., 0.920 Gold 0.4996 oz. AGW **Subject:** French-English Treaty, 100th Anniversary **Obv:** Two busts and treaty document **Rev:** Marianne and Britannia

Date	Mintage	F12	VF20	XF40	MS60	MS63
2004	339	PF63 1,500		PF65 1,600		

KM# 2015 20 EURO
17.00 g., 0.920 Gold 0.4996 oz. AGW **Subject:** Childhood stories **Rev:** Aladdin

Date	Mintage	F12	VF20	XF40	MS60	MS63
2004	316	PF63 1,200		PF65 1,300		

KM# 1433 20 EURO
17.00 g., 0.920 Gold 0.4996 oz. AGW, 31 mm. **Subject:** Bicentennial Victory at Austerlitz **Rev:** Battle scene **Rev. Legend:** LIBERTÉ ÉGALITÉ FRATERNITÉ

Date	Mintage	F12	VF20	XF40	MS60	MS63
2005	1,431	PF63 875		PF65 900		

KM# 1437 20 EURO
17.00 g., 0.920 Gold 0.4996 oz. AGW, 31 mm. **Subject:** Centenary - Law of Dec. 9, 1905 **Obv:** Sower" at left in ring of stars

Date	Mintage	F12	VF20	XF40	MS60	MS63
2005	436	PF63 875		PF65 900		

KM# 2022 20 EURO
17.00 g., 0.920 Gold 0.4996 oz. AGW **Subject:** World Cup Soccer **Obv:** World Cup trophy and soccer ball **Rev:** Large value and map of France

Date	Mintage	F12	VF20	XF40	MS60	MS63
2005	Est. 102	PF63 1,000		PF65 1,100		

KM# 2028 20 EURO
17.00 g., 0.920 Gold 0.4996 oz. AGW **Subject:** Frederic Chopin, 195th Anniversary of Birth **Obv:** Profile at left, piano keys at right vertically **Rev:** Statue in Wausau park at left, piano keys at right vertically

Date	Mintage	F12	VF20	XF40	MS60	MS63
2005	500			PF65 3,000		

KM# 2030 20 EURO
163.80 g., 0.950 Silver 4.9708 oz. ASW, 50 mm. **Subject:** Jules Verne, 100th Anniversary of Death **Obv:** Around the World in 80 days

Date	Mintage	F12	VF20	XF40	MS60	MS63
2005	500	PF63 350		PF65 375		

KM# 2031 20 EURO
163.50 g., 0.950 Silver 4.9617 oz. ASW, 50 mm. **Subject:** Jules Verne, 100th Anniversary of Death **Obv:** 20,000 leagues under the sea

Date	Mintage	F12	VF20	XF40	MS60	MS63
2005	500	PF63 350		PF65 375		

KM# 2032 20 EURO
163.50 g., 0.950 Silver 4.9617 oz. ASW, 50 mm. **Subject:** Jules Verne, 100th Anniversary of Death **Rev:** From the earth to the moon

Date	Mintage	F12	VF20	XF40	MS60	MS63
2005	500	PF63 350		PF65 375		

KM# 1443 20 EURO
155.52 g., 0.950 Silver 4.7195 oz. ASW, 50 mm. **Obv:** Bust of Franklin facing slightly right at left, his diplomatic and technical successes at right **Legend:** BENJAMIN FRANKLIN 1706-2006 **Obv. Inscription:** AMI DE LA FRANCE

Date	Mintage	F12	VF20	XF40	MS60	MS63
2006	500	PF63 300		PF65 325		

KM# 1454 20 EURO
155.50 g., 0.950 Silver 4.7189 oz. ASW, 50 mm. **Subject:** 100th Anniversary - Paul Cézanne's death **Obv:** Self portrait **Rev:** The Card Players **Rev. Legend:** LIBERTÉ ÉGALITÉ FRATERNITÉ

Date	Mintage	F12	VF20	XF40	MS60	MS63
2006	500	PF63 300		PF65 325		

KM# 2050 20 EURO
163.80 g., 0.950 Silver 4.9708 oz. ASW, 50 mm. **Subject:** Marie Curie, 100th Anniversary of Sorbonne Professorship **Obv:** Bust and atom **Rev:** Building tower and students

Date	Mintage	F12	VF20	XF40	MS60	MS63
2006	500	PF63 500		PF65 525		

KM# 2051 20 EURO
17.00 g., 0.920 Gold 0.4996 oz. AGW **Subject:** Marie Curie, 100th Anniversary of Sorbonne Professorship **Obv:** Bust and atom **Rev:** Building tower and students

Date	Mintage	F12	VF20	XF40	MS60	MS63
2006	500	PF63 1,400		PF65 1,500		

KM# 2052 20 EURO
163.80 g., 0.950 Silver 4.9708 oz. ASW, 50 mm. **Obv:** Monument parts as map of France **Rev:** Arc de Triomphe and tomb of Unknown soldier

Date	Mintage	F12	VF20	XF40	MS60	MS63
2006	500	PF63 300		PF65 325		

Note: Individually numbered

KM# 2056 20 EURO
17.00 g., 0.920 Gold 0.4996 oz. AGW **Subject:** Abolition of the Death Penalty, 25th Anniversary **Obv:** Sower advancing left **Rev:** Guillotine

Date	Mintage	F12	VF20	XF40	MS60	MS63
2006	652	PF63 1,000		PF65 1,100		

KM# 2059 20 EURO
17.00 g., 0.920 Gold 0.4996 oz. AGW **Subject:** Paul Cézanne, 100th Anniversary of Death **Obv:** Bust **Rev:** Two men seated at table, wine bottle between them

Date	Mintage	F12	VF20	XF40	MS60	MS63
2006	500	PF63 1,100		PF65 1,200		

KM# 2062 20 EURO
163.80 g., 0.950 Silver 4.9708 oz. ASW, 50 mm. **Subject:** Wolfgang Amadeus Mozart, 250th Anniversary of Birth **Obv:** Youthful bust **Rev:** Hands at piano keys, music above

Date	Mintage	F12	VF20	XF40	MS60	MS63
2006	500	PF63 400		PF65 425		

Note: Individually numbered

KM# 2065 20 EURO
163.80 g., 0.950 Silver 4.9708 oz. ASW, 50 mm. **Subject:** Jules Verne, 100th Anniversary of Death **Obv:** Voyage to the center of the earth

Date	Mintage	F12	VF20	XF40	MS60	MS63
2006	500	PF63 400		PF65 425		

KM# 2066 20 EURO
165.30 g., 0.999 Silver 5.275 oz. ASW, 50 mm. **Subject:** Jules Verne, 100th Anniversary of Death **Obv:** Michel Strogoff, the curier of the Tsar

Date	Mintage	F12	VF20	XF40	MS60	MS63
2006	500	PF63 400		PF65 425		

KM# 2067 20 EURO
163.80 g., 0.999 Silver 5.2272 oz. ASW, 50 mm. **Subject:** Jules Verne, 100th Anniversary of Death **Obv:** Five weeks in a balloon

Date	Mintage	F12	VF20	XF40	MS60	MS63
2006	500	PF63 400		PF65 425		

KM# 1520 20 EURO
155.50 g., 0.950 Silver 4.7189 oz. ASW, 50 mm. **Subject:** Asterix **Rev:** Character running downhill

Date	Mintage	F12	VF20	XF40	MS60	MS63
2007	500	PF63 425		PF65 450		

KM# 1422 20 EURO
17.00 g., 0.920 Gold 0.4996 oz. AGW, 30 x 21 mm. **Subject:**

Edgar Degas, 90th Anniversary of Seuth **Obv:** Degas painting of dancer **Rev:** Brushes and Degas portrait **Shape:** Rectangle

Date	Mintage	F12	VF20	XF40	MS60	MS63
2007	500	PF63 1,000	PF65 1,100			

KM# 1468 20 EURO
17.00 g., 0.920 Gold 0.4996 oz. AGW, 31 mm. **Subject:** Le Petit Prince, 60th Anniversary **Obv:** Prince lying in field

Date	Mintage	F12	VF20	XF40	MS60	MS63
2007	1,475	PF63 875	PF65 900			

KM# 1471 20 EURO
155.55 g., 0.950 Silver 4.7204 oz. ASW, 50 mm. **Obv:** Two dragons in flight **Rev:** Merlin and Excalibur

Date	Mintage	F12	VF20	XF40	MS60	MS63
2007	498	PF63 400	PF65 425			

KM# 1472 20 EURO
17.00 g., 0.920 Gold 0.4996 oz. AGW, 31 mm. **Obv:** Two dragons in flight **Rev:** Merlin & Excalibur

Date	Mintage	F12	VF20	XF40	MS60	MS63
2007	500	PF63 900	PF65 925			

KM# 1494 20 EURO
155.55 g., 0.950 Silver 4.7204 oz. ASW, 50 mm. **Subject:** Point Neuf - 400th Anniversary **Obv:** Moments of France logo **Rev:** Point Neuf Bridge and Paris Mint Building

Date	Mintage	F12	VF20	XF40	MS60	MS63
2007	434	PF63 300	PF65 325			

KM# 1496 20 EURO
155.55 g., 0.950 Silver 4.7204 oz. ASW, 50 mm. **Subject:** Cannes Film Festival, 60th Anniversary **Obv:** Cinema screen and stage, Golden Palm Award

Date	Mintage	F12	VF20	XF40	MS60	MS63
2007	369	PF63 300	PF65 325			

KM# 1509 20 EURO
100.00 g., 0.950 Silver 3.0347 oz. ASW, 49 mm. **Subject:** Georges Remi Centennial **Rev:** Tin Tin and Snowy

Date	Mintage	F12	VF20	XF40	MS60	MS63
2007	488	PF63 325	PF65 350			

KM# 1513 20 EURO
155.50 g., 0.950 Silver 4.7189 oz. ASW, 50 mm. **Subject:** Stanislas Leszczynski **Obv:** Bust and shield **Rev:** Palace Stanislas - Nancy

Date	Mintage	F12	VF20	XF40	MS60	MS63
2007	500	PF63 325	PF65 350			

KM# 1521 20 EURO
17.00 g., 0.920 Gold 0.4996 oz. AGW, 31 mm. **Subject:** Asterix **Rev:** Asterix and Cleopatria

Date	Mintage	F12	VF20	XF40	MS60	MS63
2007	490	PF63 900	PF65 925			

KM# 1529 20 EURO
163.80 g., 0.950 Silver 4.9708 oz. ASW, 50 mm. **Subject:** French Presidency of European Union **Obv:** Text within stars **Rev:** Europa head and flags

Date	Mintage	F12	VF20	XF40	MS60	MS63
2008	500	PF63 300	PF65 325			

KM# 1540 20 EURO
163.80 g., 0.950 Silver 4.9708 oz. ASW, 50 mm. **Subject:** 5th Republic, 50th Anniversary **Obv:** Sower **Rev:** de Gaulle head right

Date	Mintage	F12	VF20	XF40	MS60	MS63
2008	500	PF63 300	PF65 325			

KM# 1541 20 EURO
17.00 g., 0.9205 Gold 0.4999 oz. AGW, 31 mm. **Subject:** 5th Republic, 50th Anniversary **Obv:** Sower **Rev:** de Gaulle head right

Date	Mintage	F12	VF20	XF40	MS60	MS63
2008	500	PF63 900	PF65 925			

KM# 1557 20 EURO
163.80 g., 0.950 Silver 4.9708 oz. ASW, 50 mm. **Subject:** André Citronë **Obv:** First front wheel drive auto **Rev:** Bust 1/4 left

Date	Mintage	F12	VF20	XF40	MS60	MS63
2008	500	PF63 425	PF65 450			

KM# 1560 20 EURO
163.80 g., 0.950 Silver 4.9708 oz. ASW, 50 mm. **Subject:** Rouen Armada **Obv:** Cape Horn, sextant, hour glass **Rev:** Sailing ship

Date	Mintage	F12	VF20	XF40	MS60	MS63
2008	—	PF63 450	PF65 475			

KM# 1563 20 EURO
163.80 g., 0.950 Silver 4.9708 oz. ASW, 50 mm. **Subject:** Lourdes, 150th Anniversary **Obv:** Church of Notre Dame at Lourdes **Rev:** Cross with Pope John Paul II, Pope Benedict XVI and Bernadette Soubirous in quadrants

Date	Mintage	F12	VF20	XF40	MS60	MS63
2008	500	PF63 400	PF65 425			

KM# 1568 20 EURO
163.80 g., 0.950 Silver 4.9708 oz. ASW, 50 mm. **Subject:** Gabrielle Chanel **Obv:** Portrait in hat, right **Rev:** Value on "Matelassé" pattern

Date	Mintage	F12	VF20	XF40	MS60	MS63
2008	499	PF63 400	PF65 425			

KM# 1571 20 EURO
17.00 g., 0.920 Gold 0.4996 oz. AGW, 30 x 21 mm. **Subject:** Edward Manet **Obv:** Manet's "Olympia" painting **Rev:** Paint brushes and Manet's portrait **Shape:** Rectangle

Date	Mintage	F12	VF20	XF40	MS60	MS63
2008	500	PF63 950	PF65 975			

KM# 1602 20 EURO
44.40 g., 0.900 Silver 1.2765 oz. ASW, 37 mm. **Obv:** Eiffel Tower Structure **Rev:** Gustave Eiffel at left

Date	Mintage	F12	VF20	XF40	MS60	MS63
2009P	2,522	PF63 100	PF65 120			

KM# 1607 20 EURO
44.40 g., 0.900 Silver 1.2765 oz. ASW, 37 mm. **Subject:** Bugatti 100th Anniversary **Obv:** Ettore Bugatti at left **Rev:** Race car and grill motif

Date	Mintage	F12	VF20	XF40	MS60	MS63
2009P	789	PF63 100	PF65 120			

KM# 1612 20 EURO
44.40 g., 0.900 Silver 1.2765 oz. ASW, 37 mm. **Subject:** Curie Institute, 100th Anniversary

Date	Mintage	F12	VF20	XF40	MS60	MS63
2009P	5,000	PF63 70.00	PF65 80.00			

KM# 1617 20 EURO
163.80 g., 0.950 Silver 4.9708 oz. ASW, 50 mm. **Subject:** Unesco site - The Kremlin in Moscow **Obv:** Wall Tower and cathedral

Date	Mintage	F12	VF20	XF40	MS60	MS63
2009P	500	PF63 300	PF65 325			

KM# 1690 20 EURO
44.40 g., 0.900 Silver 1.2765 oz. ASW, 37 mm. **Obv:** Marcel Dassault **Rev:** Mirage III plane

Date	Mintage	F12	VF20	XF40	MS60	MS63
2010	2,000	PF63 75.00	PF65 85.00			

KM# 1704 20 EURO
44.40 g., 0.900 Silver 1.2765 oz. ASW, 37 mm. **Obv:** Lille station and route map **Rev:** Three TGV trains

Date	Mintage	F12	VF20	XF40	MS60	MS63
2010	2,000	PF63 75.00	PF65 85.00			

KM# 1815 20 EURO
44.40 g., 0.900 Silver 1.2765 oz. ASW, 37 mm. **Obv:** Metz railroad station **Rev:** TGV and ICE trains

Date	Mintage	F12	VF20	XF40	MS60	MS63
2011	1,000	PF63 100	PF65 120			

KM# 2070 20 EURO
15.00 g., 0.900 Silver 0.4312 oz. ASW, 31 mm. **Subject:** G-20 Meeting in Cannes **Obv:** Sower advancing right **Rev:** Laurel tree and oak tree in the shape of a Euro symbol with value specification in the hexagon as stylization national borders

Date	Mintage	F12	VF20	XF40	MS60	MS63
2011	2,000	—	—	—	—	100

KM# 1912 20 EURO
44.40 g., 0.900 Silver 1.2765 oz. ASW, 37 mm. **Subject:** TGV South East **Obv:** Lyon Saint-Exupery station **Rev:** Two modern locomotives

Date	Mintage	F12	VF20	XF40	MS60	MS63
2012(a)	1,000	PF63 75.00	PF65 85.00			

KM# 1581 25 EURO
18.00 g., 0.900 Silver 0.5175 oz. ASW, 33 mm. **Obv:** Modernistic sower advancing right **Rev:** Value and wreath

Date	Mintage	F12	VF20	XF40	MS60	MS63
2009P	250,000	—	—	—	—	35.00

KM# 1303 50 EURO
31.00 g., 0.999 Gold 0.9893 oz. AGW, 37 mm. **Subject:** Europa **Obv:** Eight French euro coin designs **Rev:** Portrait and flags design of 6.55957 francs KM-1265 **Edge:** Plain

Date	Mintage	F12	VF20	XF40	MS60	MS63
2002	2,000	PF65 1,800				

KM# 1335 50 EURO
31.10 g., 0.999 Gold 0.9925 oz. AGW, 37 mm. **Obv:** Tour de France logo **Rev:** Cyclist going left **Edge:** Plain

Date	Mintage	F12	VF20	XF40	MS60	MS63
2002 (2003)	5,000	PF65 1,750				

KM# 1340 50 EURO
1000.00 g., 0.950 Silver 30.3466 oz. ASW, 100 mm. **Obv:** Curved cross design with multiple values **Rev:** Goddess Europa and flags **Edge:** Plain with three line inscription at six o'clock

Date	Mintage	F12	VF20	XF40	MS60	MS63
2003	5,528	PF63 1,150	PF65 1,200			

KM# 1993 50 EURO
31.11 g., 0.999 Gold 0.9926 oz. AGW **Obv:** Curved cross with coins **Rev:** Europa head at right, flags at left

Date	Mintage	F12	VF20	XF40	MS60	MS63
2003	2,000	PF65 1,850				

KM# 1368 50 EURO
31.10 g., 0.999 Gold 0.9925 oz. AGW, 37 mm. **Obv:** Book, denomination and eagle **Rev:** Napoleon and coronation scene **Edge:** Plain

Date	Mintage	F12	VF20	XF40	MS60	MS63
2004	2,000	PF65 1,800				

KM# 1394 50 EURO
31.10 g., 0.999 Gold 0.9926 oz. AGW, 37 mm. **Subject:** European Union Expansion **Obv:** Partial face and flags **Rev:** Puzzle map **Edge:** Plain

Date	Mintage	F12	VF20	XF40	MS60	MS63
2004	618	PF65 1,800				

KM# 1430 50 EURO
31.10 g., 0.999 Gold 0.9926 oz. AGW, 37 mm. **Rev:** Kitty and Daniel in Versailles **Rev. Legend:** Hello Kitty

Date	Mintage	F12	VF20	XF40	MS60	MS63
2005	1,260	PF65 1,850				

KM# 2018 50 EURO
31.10 g., 0.999 Gold 0.9925 oz. AGW **Subject:** European Union, 50th Anniversary **Obv:** Flag of the European Union **Rev:** Europa head facing at right, banners at left

Date	Mintage	F12	VF20	XF40	MS60	MS63
2005	500	PF65 1,800				

KM# 2039 50 EURO
31.10 g., 0.999 Gold 0.9925 oz. AGW **Subject:** Robert Schuman, 120th Anniversary of Birth **Rev:** Europa head facing at right, with color highlights

Date	Mintage	F12	VF20	XF40	MS60	MS63
2006	500	PF65 1,900				

KM# 2046 50 EURO
31.11 g., 0.999 Gold 0.9926 oz. AGW **Subject:** St. Peter's Bascilica, 500th Anniversary **Obv:** St. Peter's floor plan **Rev:** Façade of St. Peter's, Pope Benedict XVI

Date	Mintage	F12	VF20	XF40	MS60	MS63
2006	500	PF65 1,900				

KM# 2057 50 EURO
31.11 g., 0.999 Gold 0.9926 oz. AGW **Subject:** Abolishment of the Death Penalty, 25th Anniversary **Obv:** Sower advancing left **Rev:** Guillotine

Date	Mintage	F12	VF20	XF40	MS60	MS63
2006	Est. 500	PF65 1,800				

KM# 1466 50 EURO
31.11 g., 0.999 Gold 0.9926 oz. AGW, 37 mm. **Subject:** Le Petit Prince, 60th Anniversary **Obv:** Prince standing

Date	Mintage	F12	VF20	XF40	MS60	MS63
2007	1,491	PF65 1,800				

KM# 1481 50 EURO
31.10 g., 0.999 Gold 0.9925 oz. AGW, 37 mm. **Subject:** Airbus A380 **Obv:** Airplane **Rev:** Europa and flags

Date	Mintage	F12	VF20	XF40	MS60	MS63
2007	500	PF65 1,900				

KM# 1487 50 EURO
1000.00 g., 0.950 Silver 30.3466 oz. ASW **Subject:** 2007 Rugby World Cup **Obv:** Two players and goal **Rev:** Logo and goal **Shape:** Oval

Date	Mintage	F12	VF20	XF40	MS60	MS63
2007	298	PF65 1,500				

KM# 1510 50 EURO
31.11 g., 0.999 Gold 0.9926 oz. AGW, 37 mm. **Subject:** Georges Remi Centennial **Obv:** Wand and sparkles **Rev:** Tin Tin and dog Snowy

Date	Mintage	F12	VF20	XF40	MS60	MS63
2007	500	PF65 1,900				

KM# 1522 50 EURO
31.05 g., 0.999 Gold 0.9909 oz. AGW, 37 mm. **Subject:** Asterix **Rev:** Asterix and the Butcher of Arverne

Date	Mintage	F12	VF20	XF40	MS60	MS63
2007	500	PF65 1,900				

KM# 1530 50 EURO
31.10 g., 0.999 Gold 0.9926 oz. AGW, 37 mm. **Subject:** French Presidency of the Euopean Union **Obv:** Text within stars **Rev:** Europa head within flags

Date	Mintage	F12	VF20	XF40	MS60	MS63
2008	497	PF65 1,900				

KM# 1564 50 EURO
31.10 g., 0.999 Gold 0.9926 oz. AGW, 37 mm. **Subject:** Lourdes, 150th Anniversary **Obv:** Church of Notre Dame at Lourdes **Rev:** Cross with Pope John Paul II, Pope Benedict XVI and Bernadette Soubirous in quadrants

Date	Mintage	F12	VF20	XF40	MS60	MS63
2008	500	PF65 1,900				

KM# 1597 50 EURO
163.80 g., 0.950 Silver 4.9708 oz. ASW, 50 mm. **Subject:** Concorde 40th Anniversary **Obv:** Concorde in flight **Rev:** Tail emblems

Date	Mintage	F12	VF20	XF40	MS60	MS63
2009P	1,000	PF63 300	PF65 325			

KM# 1603 50 EURO
163.80 g., 0.950 Silver 4.9708 oz. ASW, 50 mm. **Obv:** Eiffel Tower Structure **Rev:** Gustave Eiffel at left

Date	Mintage	F12	VF20	XF40	MS60	MS63
2009P	554	PF63 400	PF65 425			

KM# 1585 50 EURO
163.80 g., 0.950 Silver 4.9708 oz. ASW, 50 mm. **Subject:** Court of Human Rights, 50th Anniversary **Obv:** Sower left **Rev:** Text

Date	Mintage	F12	VF20	XF40	MS60	MS63
2009P	251	PF63 325	PF65 350			

KM# 1592 50 EURO
8.45 g., 0.920 Gold 0.2483 oz. AGW, 22 mm. **Subject:** Europa - Fall of Berlin Wall **Obv:** Brandenburg gate and doves in flight **Rev:** Head facing and flags

Date	Mintage	F12	VF20	XF40	MS60	MS63
2009P	1,000	PF63 500	PF65 525			

KM# 1598 50 EURO
8.45 g., 0.920 Gold 0.2483 oz. AGW, 22 mm. **Subject:** Concorde 40th Anniversary **Obv:** Concorde in flight **Rev:** Tail emblems

Date	Mintage	F12	VF20	XF40	MS60	MS63
2009P	2,135	PF63 475	PF65 500			

KM# 1604 50 EURO
8.45 g., 0.920 Gold 0.2483 oz. AGW, 22 mm. **Obv:** Eiffel Tower Structure **Rev:** Gustave Eiffel at left

Date	Mintage	F12	VF20	XF40	MS60	MS63
2009P	793	PF63 500	PF65 525			

KM# 1608 50 EURO
163.80 g., 0.950 Silver 4.9708 oz. ASW, 50 mm. **Subject:** Bugatti 100th Anniverary **Obv:** Ettore Bugatti at left **Rev:** Race car and grill motif

Date	Mintage	F12	VF20	XF40	MS60	MS63
2009P	269	PF63 475	PF65 500			

KM# 1609 50 EURO
8.45 g., 0.920 Gold 0.2483 oz. AGW, 22 mm. **Subject:** Bugatti 100th Anniversary **Obv:** Ettore Bugatti at left **Rev:** Race car and grill motif

Date	Mintage	F12	VF20	XF40	MS60	MS63
2009P	854	PF63 500	PF65 525			

KM# 1613 50 EURO
163.80 g., 0.950 Silver 4.9708 oz. ASW, 50 mm. **Subject:** Curie Institute, 100th Anniversary

Date	Mintage	F12	VF20	XF40	MS60	MS63
2009P	500	PF63 350	PF65 375			

KM# 1614 50 EURO
8.45 g., 0.920 Gold 0.2483 oz. AGW, 22 mm. **Subject:** Curie Institute, 100th Anniversary

Date	Mintage	F12	VF20	XF40	MS60	MS63
2009P	1,000	PF63 500	PF65 525			

KM# 1618 50 EURO
163.80 g., 0.950 Silver 4.9708 oz. ASW, 50 mm. **Subject:** UNESCO Site - The Kremlin in Moscow

Date	Mintage	F12	VF20	XF40	MS60	MS63
2009	497	PF63 300	PF65 325			

KM# 1622 50 EURO
163.80 g., 0.950 Silver 4.9708 oz. ASW, 50 mm. **Subject:** First Moon Landing, 40th Anniversary **Obv:** Footprint on the moon

Date	Mintage	F12	VF20	XF40	MS60	MS63
2009P	371	PF63 350	PF65 375			

KM# 1623 50 EURO
8.45 g., 0.920 Gold 0.2483 oz. AGW, 22 mm. **Subject:** First Moon Landing, 40th Anniversary **Obv:** Footprint on the moon

Date	Mintage	F12	VF20	XF40	MS60	MS63
2009P	986	PF63 475	PF65 500			

KM# 1628 50 EURO
8.45 g., 0.920 Gold 0.2483 oz. AGW, 22 mm. **Subject:** Year of the Ox **Obv:** Oxen within Asian screen **Rev:** Portrait of LaFontaine

Date	Mintage	F12	VF20	XF40	MS60	MS63
2009P	497	PF63 525	PF65 550			

KM# 1630 50 EURO
8.45 g., 0.920 Gold 0.2483 oz. AGW, 22 mm. **Subject:** Comic strip heroes **Obv:** Wanted Poster **Rev:** Lucky Luke on horseback

Date	Mintage	F12	VF20	XF40	MS60	MS63
2009P	967	PF63 500	PF65 525			

KM# 1632 50 EURO
8.45 g., 0.920 Gold 0.2483 oz. AGW, 22 mm. **Obv:** Rugby player **Rev:** State Francais

Date	Mintage	F12	VF20	XF40	MS60	MS63
2009P	325	PF63 525	PF65 550			

KM# 1635 50 EURO
8.45 g., 0.920 Gold 0.2483 oz. AGW, 22 mm. **Subject:** Alpine skiing **Obv:** Globe and downhill skier **Rev:** Downhill skier on mountainside

Date	Mintage	F12	VF20	XF40	MS60	MS63
2009P	974	PF63 500	PF65 525			

KM# 1637 50 EURO
163.80 g., 0.950 Silver 4.9708 oz. ASW, 50 mm. **Subject:** FIFA World Cup, South Africa 2010 **Obv:** Soccer player on field **Rev:** Soccerball, Map of Africa, Protrea flower

Date	Mintage	F12	VF20	XF40	MS60	MS63
2009P	500	PF63 400	PF65 425			

KM# 1638 50 EURO
8.45 g., 0.920 Gold 0.2483 oz. AGW, 22 mm. **Subject:** FIFA World Cup, South Africa 2010 **Obv:** Soccer Player on field **Rev:** Soccerball, Map of Africa, Protea flower

Date	Mintage	F12	VF20	XF40	MS60	MS63
2009P	6,287	PF63 475	PF65 500			

KM# 1644 50 EURO
36.00 g., 0.900 Silver 1.035 oz. ASW, 36 mm. **Obv:** The Seed Sower advancing right, sun rays from above **Rev:** Value at center, wreath horizontal

Date	Mintage	F12	VF20	XF40	MS60	MS63
2010	100,000	—	—	—	—	45.00

KM# 1673 50 EURO
8.45 g., 0.920 Gold 0.2483 oz. AGW, 22 mm. **Obv:** The Seed Sower left **Rev:** Wheat and olive branch

Date	Mintage	F12	VF20	XF40	MS60	MS63
2010	500	PF63 525	PF65 550			

KM# 1679 50 EURO
8.45 g., 0.925 Gold 0.2497 oz. AGW, 22 mm. **Subject:** Cluny Abbey, 1100th Anniversary **Obv:** Europa head facing **Rev:** Cluney Abbey

Date	Mintage	F12	VF20	XF40	MS60	MS63
2010	1,000	PF63 500	PF65 525			

KM# 1684 50 EURO
8.45 g., 0.920 Gold 0.2483 oz. AGW, 22 mm. **Obv:** Georges Pompidou Center design **Rev:** Design detail

Date	Mintage	F12	VF20	XF40	MS60	MS63
2010	3,000	PF63 475	PF65 500			

KM# 1685 50 EURO
163.80 g., 0.950 Silver 4.9708 oz. ASW, 50 mm. **Obv:** Georges Pompidou Center design **Rev:** Design detail

Date	Mintage	F12	VF20	XF40	MS60	MS63
2010	1,000	PF63 300	PF65 325			

KM# 1688 50 EURO
8.45 g., 0.920 Gold 0.2483 oz. AGW, 22 mm. **Obv:** Marcel Dassault **Rev:** Mirage III plane

Date	Mintage	F12	VF20	XF40	MS60	MS63
2010	1,000	PF63 500	PF65 525			

KM# 1694 50 EURO
8.45 g., 0.920 Gold 0.2483 oz. AGW, 22 mm. **Obv:** Mother Teresa and child **Rev:** Mother Teresa and Pope John Paul II

Date	Mintage	F12	VF20	XF40	MS60	MS63
2010	1,000	PF63 500	PF65 525			

KM# 1699 50 EURO
8.45 g., 0.920 Gold 0.2483 oz. AGW, 22 mm. **Obv:** Taj Mahal **Rev:** UNESCO offices

Date	Mintage	F12	VF20	XF40	MS60	MS63
2010	1,000	PF63 500	PF65 525			

KM# 1702 50 EURO
0.45 g., 0.920 Gold 0.2483 oz. AGW, 22 mm. **Obv:** Lille station and route map **Rev:** Three TGV trains

Date	Mintage	F12	VF20	XF40	MS60	MS63
2010	1,000	PF63 500	PF65 525			

KM# 1703 50 EURO
163.80 g., 0.950 Silver 4.9708 oz. ASW, 50 mm. **Obv:** Lille station and route map **Rev:** Three TGV trains

Date	Mintage	F12	VF20	XF40	MS60	MS63
2010	500	PF63 350	PF65 375			

KM# 1714 50 EURO
8.45 g., 0.920 Gold 0.2483 oz. AGW, 22 mm. **Obv:** Tiger within border **Rev:** La Fontaine bust at left, animals at right

Date	Mintage	F12	VF20	XF40	MS60	MS63
2010	500	PF63 525	PF65 550			

KM# 1716 50 EURO
8.45 g., 0.920 Gold 0.2483 oz. AGW, 22 mm. **Obv:** Blake and Mortimer **Rev:** Secret of the Swordfish" scene, the arrest of Col. Olrik

Date	Mintage	F12	VF20	XF40	MS60	MS63
2010	500	PF63 525	PF65 550			

KM# 1719 50 EURO
8.45 g., 0.920 Gold 0.2483 oz. AGW, 22 mm. **Obv:** Handball player on globe **Rev:** Handball player, net, Big Ben

Date	Mintage	F12	VF20	XF40	MS60	MS63
2010	1,000	PF63 500	PF65 525			

KM# 1721 50 EURO
8.45 g., 0.920 Gold 0.2483 oz. AGW, 22 mm. **Obv:** Soccer player **Rev:** Stade Toulousain logo, multicolor

Date	Mintage	F12	VF20	XF40	MS60	MS63
2010	500	PF63 525	PF65 550			

KM# 1786 50 EURO
8.45 g., 0.920 Gold 0.2483 oz. AGW, 22 mm. **Subject:** Euro Starter Kit, 10th Anniversary **Obv:** Sower **Rev:** Euro starter kit

Date	Mintage	F12	VF20	XF40	MS60	MS63
2011	3,000	PF63 475	PF65 500			

KM# 1792 50 EURO
8.45 g., 0.920 Gold 0.2483 oz. AGW, 22 mm. **Subject:** International Music Day, 30th Anniversary **Obv:** Europa **Rev:** Youth jamming

Date	Mintage	F12	VF20	XF40	MS60	MS63
2011	3,000	PF63 475	PF65 500			

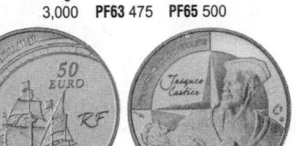

KM# 1796 50 EURO
8.45 g., 0.920 Gold 0.2483 oz. AGW, 22 mm. **Subject:** Great Explorers - Jacques Cartier **Obv:** The Grande Hermine sailing away **Rev:** Carter, globe and compass rose

Date	Mintage	F12	VF20	XF40	MS60	MS63
2011	3,000	PF63 475	PF65 500			

KM# 1801 50 EURO
8.45 g., 0.920 Gold 0.2483 oz. AGW, 22 mm. **Subject:** Clovis, 481-511 **Obv:** Hands over chalice, reign dates at left, value at right **Rev:** Crowned head left

Date	Mintage	F12	VF20	XF40	MS60	MS63
2011	1,500	PF63 485	PF65 500			

KM# 1803 50 EURO
8.45 g., 0.920 Gold 0.2483 oz. AGW, 22 mm. **Subject:** Charlemagne, 768-814 **Obv:** Cross on orb, reight dates at left, value at right **Rev:** Crowned head left

Date	Mintage	F12	VF20	XF40	MS60	MS63
2011	1,500	PF63 485	PF65 500			

KM# 1805 50 EURO
8.45 g., 0.920 Gold 0.2483 oz. AGW, 22 mm. **Subject:** Charles II, 840-877 **Obv:** KARLOS monogram **Rev:** Crowned head left

Date	Mintage	F12	VF20	XF40	MS60	MS63
2011	1,500	PF63 485	PF65 500			

KM# 1807 50 EURO
8.45 g., 0.920 Gold 0.2483 oz. AGW, 22 mm. **Subject:** WWF - Audouin's Gull **Obv:** Gull in flight right **Rev:** Gull standing right, WWF logo at right

Date	Mintage	F12	VF20	XF40	MS60	MS63
2011	1,000	PF63 500	PF65 525			

KM# 1811 50 EURO
8.45 g., 0.920 Gold 0.2483 oz. AGW, 22 mm. **Subject:** UNESCO World Heritage Site - Palace of Versailles

Date	Mintage	F12	VF20	XF40	MS60	MS63
2011	1,000	PF63 500	PF65 525			

KM# 1816 50 EURO
163.80 g., 0.950 Silver 4.9708 oz. ASW, 50 mm. **Obv:** Metz railroad station **Rev:** TGV and ICE trains

Date	Mintage	F12	VF20	XF40	MS60	MS63
2011	500	PF63 300	PF65 325			

KM# 1817 50 EURO
8.45 g., 0.920 Gold 0.2483 oz. AGW, 22 mm. **Obv:** Metz railroad station **Rev:** TGV and ICE trains

Date	Mintage	F12	VF20	XF40	MS60	MS63
2011	1,000	PF63 500	PF65 525			

KM# 1828 50 EURO
8.45 g., 0.920 Gold 0.2483 oz. AGW, 22 mm. **Obv:** Cosette - Les Miserables **Rev:** Victor Hugo

Date	Mintage	F12	VF20	XF40	MS60	MS63
2011	3,000	PF63 475	PF65 500			

KM# 1830 50 EURO
8.45 g., 0.920 Gold 0.2483 oz. AGW, 22 mm. **Obv:** Nana **Rev:** Emile Zola

Date	Mintage	F12	VF20	XF40	MS60	MS63
2011	1,000	PF63 500	PF65 525			

KM# 1832 50 EURO
8.45 g., 0.920 Gold 0.2483 oz. AGW, 22 mm. **Obv:** The Stranger **Rev:** Albert Camus

Date	Mintage	F12	VF20	XF40	MS60	MS63
2011	—	PF63 500	PF65 525			

KM# 1834 50 EURO
8.45 g., 0.920 Gold 0.2483 oz. AGW, 22 mm. **Subject:** Year of the Rabbit **Obv:** Rabbit seated facing right **Rev:** Fontaine and animals

Date	Mintage	F12	VF20	XF40	MS60	MS63
2011	500	PF63 525	PF65 550			

KM# 1837 50 EURO
8.45 g., 0.920 Gold 0.2483 oz. AGW, 22 mm. **Obv:** Comic Characters **Rev:** Profile left and large XIII

Date	Mintage	F12	VF20	XF40	MS60	MS63
2011	1,000	PF63 500	PF65 525			

KM# 1839 50 EURO
8.45 g., 0.920 Gold 0.2483 oz. AGW, 22 mm. **Obv:** Female figure skater on globe **Rev:** Figure skating pair

Date	Mintage	F12	VF20	XF40	MS60	MS63
2011	1,000	PF63 500	PF65 525			

KM# 1756 50 EURO
8.45 g., 0.920 Gold 0.2483 oz. AGW, 22 mm. **Obv:** Bicycle racer **Rev:** Metro 92 logo

Date	Mintage	F12	VF20	XF40	MS60	MS63
2011	500	PF63 500	PF65 525			

KM# 2071 50 EURO
36.00 g., 0.900 Silver 1.035 oz. ASW, 41 mm. **Subject:** G-20 Meeting in Cannes **Obv:** Sower advancing right **Rev:** Laurel tree and oak tree in the shape of a Euro symbol with value specification in the hexagon as stylization national borders

Date	Mintage	F12	VF20	XF40	MS60	MS63
2011	200	—	—	—	—	200

KM# 1848 50 EURO
163.80 g., 0.925 Silver 4.840 oz. ASW, 50 mm. **Obv:** Battleship Jeanne de Arc **Rev:** WWII convoy image, anchor chain below

Date	Mintage	F12	VF20	XF40	MS60	MS63
2012(a)	500	PF63 350	PF65 375			

KM# 1849 50 EURO
8.45 g., 0.920 Gold 0.2483 oz. AGW, 22 mm. **Obv:** SS France waterline view **Rev:** Winged funnels, porthole detail below

Date	Mintage	F12	VF20	XF40	MS60	MS63
2012(a)	1,500	PF63 485	PF65 500			

KM# 1852 50 EURO
8.45 g., 0.920 Gold 0.2483 oz. AGW, 22 mm. **Subject:** Eurocorps, 20th Anniversary **Obv:** Mitterrand and Kohl standing clasping hands **Rev:** Europa facing

Date	Mintage	F12	VF20	XF40	MS60	MS63
2012(a)	1,500	PF63 475	PF65 500			

KM# 1858 50 EURO
8.45 g., 0.920 Gold 0.2483 oz. AGW, 22 mm. **Subject:** Philippe II Auguste **Obv:** Crowned head facing **Rev:** The Louvre's original design

Date	Mintage	F12	VF20	XF40	MS60	MS63
2012(a)	1,500	PF63 485	PF65 500			

KM# 1860 50 EURO
8.45 g., 0.920 Gold 0.2483 oz. AGW, 22 mm. **Subject:** Savinien Cyrano de Bergerac **Obv:** Half-length figure of Cyrano at left, Roxane on balcony at top right **Rev:** Quote at left, Edmond Rostand portrait at right

Date	Mintage	F12	VF20	XF40	MS60	MS63
2012(a)	1,000	PF63 500	PF65 525			

KM# 1861 50 EURO
8.45 g., 0.920 Gold 0.2483 oz. AGW, 22 mm. **Subject:** Puss in boots **Obv:** Puss in boots standing, castle in background **Rev:** Quote at left, Charles Perrault portrait at right

Date	Mintage	F12	VF20	XF40	MS60	MS63
2012(a)	1,000	PF63 500	PF65 525			

KM# 1891 50 EURO
8.45 g., 0.920 Gold 0.2483 oz. AGW, 22 mm. **Subject:** Euro, 10th Anniversary **Obv:** The Sower advancing left **Rev:** Value on globe, child-like renderings around

Date	Mintage	F12	VF20	XF40	MS60	MS63
2012(a)	1,000	PF63 500	PF65 525			

KM# 1897 50 EURO
8.45 g., 0.920 Gold 0.2483 oz. AGW, 22 mm. **Subject:** abbé Pierre, 100th anniversary of Birth **Obv:** Pierre's bust at left, shaddow figure at right **Rev:** Emmaus International logo and quote

Date	Mintage	F12	VF20	XF40	MS60	MS63
2012(a)	1,000	PF63 500	PF65 525			

KM# 1906 50 EURO
163.80 g., 0.950 Silver 4.9708 oz. ASW, 50 mm. **Subject:** UNESCO - World Heritage Site **Obv:** Abu Simbel temple

Date	Mintage	F12	VF20	XF40	MS60	MS63
2012(a)	500	PF63 375	PF65 400			

KM# 1908 50 EURO
8.45 g., 0.920 Gold 0.2483 oz. AGW, 22 mm. **Subject:** UNESCO - World Heritage Site **Obv:** Abu Simbel temple

Date	Mintage	F12	VF20	XF40	MS60	MS63
2012(a)	1,500	PF63 485	PF65 500			

KM# 1913 50 EURO
163.80 g., 0.950 Silver 4.9708 oz. ASW, 50 mm. **Subject:** TGV South-East **Obv:** Lyon Saint-Exupery station **Rev:** Two modern locomotives

Date	Mintage	F12	VF20	XF40	MS60	MS63
2012(a)	500	PF63 300		PF65 325		

KM# 1914 50 EURO
8.45 g., 0.920 Gold 0.2483 oz. AGW, 22 mm. **Subject:** TGV Sud-Est **Obv:** Lyon Saint-Exupery station **Rev:** Two modern locomotives

Date	Mintage	F12	VF20	XF40	MS60	MS63
2012(a)	1,000	PF63 500		PF65 525		

KM# 1917 50 EURO
8.45 g., 0.920 Gold 0.2483 oz. AGW, 22 mm. **Subject:** Comic strip hero **Obv:** Largo Winch and building **Rev:** Winch riding motocycle being chased by two cars

Date	Mintage	F12	VF20	XF40	MS60	MS63
2012(a)	500	PF63 525		PF65 550		

KM# 1920 50 EURO
8.45 g., 0.920 Gold 0.2483 oz. AGW, 22 mm. **Subject:** Toulonnais Rugby Club **Obv:** Value and stadium field view **Rev:** Shield and portrait of Felix Mayol

Date	Mintage	F12	VF20	XF40	MS60	MS63
2012(a)	500	PF63 525		PF65 550		

KM# 1922 50 EURO
8.45 g., 0.920 Gold 0.2483 oz. AGW, 22 mm. **Subject:** 2012 Summer Olympics, London **Obv:** Two judo athletes and map of Europe **Rev:** Two judo athletes

Date	Mintage	F12	VF20	XF40	MS60	MS63
2012(a)	1,000	PF63 500		PF65 525		

KM# 1925 50 EURO
8.45 g., 0.920 Gold 0.2483 oz. AGW, 22 mm. **Subject:** Year of the Dragon **Obv:** Dragon **Rev:** La Fontaine and zodiac animals

Date	Mintage	F12	VF20	XF40	MS60	MS63
2012(a)	1,000	PF63 500		PF65 525		

KM# 2076 50 EURO
8.45 g., 0.920 Gold 0.2483 oz. AGW, 22 mm. **Obv:** Hand raised in benidiction **Rev:** Hugues Capet head facing

Date	Mintage	F12	VF20	XF40	MS60	MS63
2012	Est. 1500	—		—		500

KM# 2077 50 EURO
8.45 g., 0.920 Gold 0.2483 oz. AGW **Obv:** Oak tree **Rev:** Saint Louis head facing

Date	Mintage	F12	VF20	XF40	MS60	MS63
2012	Est. 1500	—	—	—	—	500

KM# 2080 50 EURO
163.80 g., 0.950 Silver 4.9708 oz. ASW, 50 mm. **Obv:** Sailing ship Hermione **Rev:** Ship wheel, sails, figurehead

Date	Mintage	F12	VF20	XF40	MS60	MS63
2012	Est. 500	PF63 300		PF65 325		

KM# 2081 50 EURO
163.80 g., 0.950 Silver 4.9708 oz. ASW, 50 mm. **Obv:** Trans-atlantic liner France **Rev:** Winged smoke stacks, partial porthole

Date	Mintage	F12	VF20	XF40	MS60	MS63
2012	Est. 500	PF63 300		PF65 325		

KM# 2082 50 EURO
8.45 g., 0.920 Gold 0.2483 oz. AGW, 22 mm. **Obv:** Sailing ship Hermione **Rev:** Ship wheel, sails, figurehead

Date	Mintage	F12	VF20	XF40	MS60	MS63
2012	Est. 1500	PF63 500		PF65 525		

KM# 2083 50 EURO
8.45 g., 0.920 Gold 0.2483 oz. AGW, 22 mm. **Obv:** Cruiser Jean d'Arc **Rev:** Anchor chain below convoy of ships

Date	Mintage	F12	VF20	XF40	MS60	MS63
2012	Est. 1500	PF63 500		PF65 525		

KM# 2086 50 EURO
8.45 g., 0.920 Gold 0.2483 oz. AGW **Obv:** d'Artagnan **Rev:** Alexander Dumas and quote

Date	Mintage	F12	VF20	XF40	MS60	MS63
2012	Est. 1000	PF63 500		PF65 525		

KM# 2088 50 EURO
163.80 g., 0.950 Silver 4.9708 oz. ASW, 50 mm. **Obv:** Yves Klein, blue hand **Rev:** Klein artwork

Date	Mintage	F12	VF20	XF40	MS60	MS63
2012	—	PF63 300	PF65 325			

KM# 2090 50 EURO
8.45 g., 0.920 Gold 0.2483 oz. AGW, 22 mm. **Obv:** Yves Klein and hand **Rev:** Klein artwork

Date	Mintage	F12	VF20	XF40	MS60	MS63
2012	—	PF63 525	PF65 550			

KM# 2093 50 EURO
8.45 g., 0.920 Gold 0.2483 oz. AGW, 22 mm. **Subject:** French-German Friendship, 50th Anniversary **Rev:** Europa head facing at right, banners at left

Date	Mintage	F12	VF20	XF40	MS60	MS63
2013	—	PF63 525	PF65 550			

KM# 2096 50 EURO
8.45 g., 0.920 Gold 0.2483 oz. AGW, 22 mm. **Subject:** Rudolf Noureev **Obv:** Portrait at right **Rev:** Dancer and National Theater

Date	Mintage	F12	VF20	XF40	MS60	MS63
2013	—	PF63 525	PF65 550			

KM# 2098 50 EURO
163.80 g., 0.950 Silver 4.9708 oz. ASW, 50 mm. **Subject:** Notre Dame, 850th Anniversary **Obv:** Seal at right, cathedral details, blue highlights **Rev:** Seal at left, cathedral details, blue highlights

Date	Mintage	F12	VF20	XF40	MS60	MS63
2013	850	PF63 300	PF65 325			

KM# 2100 50 EURO
8.45 g., 0.920 Gold 0.2483 oz. AGW, 22 mm. **Subject:** Notre Dame, 850th Anniversary **Obv:** Seal at right, cathedral details **Rev:** Seal at left, cathedral details

Date	Mintage	F12	VF20	XF40	MS60	MS63
2013	1,000	PF63 600	PF65 625			

KM# 1304 100 EURO
155.52 g., 0.999 Gold 4.9628 oz. AGW, 50 mm. **Subject:** Europa **Obv:** Eight French euro coin designs **Rev:** Portrait and flags design of 6.55957 francs KM-1265 **Edge:** Plain

Date	Mintage	F12	VF20	XF40	MS60	MS63
2002	99	PF65 10,000				

KM# 1985 100 EURO
155.55 g., 0.999 Gold 4.9639 oz. AGW **Subject:** Charles Lindburg, 75th Anniverversary of Flight **Obv:** Map of Northern France **Rev:** Spirit of St. Louis, U.S. Coastline

Date	Mintage	F12	VF20	XF40	MS60	MS63
2002	99	PF65 12,500				

KM# 2005 100 EURO
155.55 g., 0.999 Gold 4.9639 oz. AGW **Obv:** Mona Lisa **Rev:** Leonardo DaVinci head left, large value right

Date	Mintage	F12	VF20	XF40	MS60	MS63
2003	99	PF65 10,000				

KM# 1377 100 EURO
155.52 g., 0.999 Gold 4.9628 oz. AGW, 50 mm. **Subject:** D-Day 60th Anniversary **Obv:** Soldiers and Normandy invasion scene **Rev:** D-Day" inscription above denomination **Edge:** Plain

Date	Mintage	F12	VF20	XF40	MS60	MS63
2004	68	PF65 9,500				

KM# 1387 100 EURO
155.50 g., 0.950 Gold 4.7189 oz. AGW, 50 mm. **Obv:** Statue of Liberty **Rev:** F. A. Bartholdi **Edge:** Plain

Date	Mintage	F12	VF20	XF40	MS60	MS63
2004	99	PF65 10,000				

KM# 1389 100 EURO
155.50 g., 0.999 Gold 4.9623 oz. AGW, 50 mm. **Obv:** Statue of Liberty **Rev:** F. A. Bartholdi **Edge:** Plain

Date	Mintage	F12	VF20	XF40	MS60	MS63
2004	99	PF65 10,000				

KM# 1395 100 EURO
155.55 g., 0.999 Gold 4.9639 oz. AGW, 50 mm. **Subject:** European Union Expansion **Obv:** Partial face and flags **Rev:** Puzzle map **Edge:** Plain

Date	Mintage	F12	VF20	XF40	MS60	MS63
2004	99	PF65 10,000				

KM# 2012 100 EURO
155.55 g., 0.999 Gold 4.9639 oz. AGW **Subject:** Napoleon's coronation, 200th Anniversary **Obv:** Napoleon, laureate **Rev:** Notre Dame cathedral façade

Date	Mintage	F12	VF20	XF40	MS60	MS63
2004	99	PF65 10,000				

KM# 2019 100 EURO
155.55 g., 0.999 Gold 4.9639 oz. AGW **Subject:** European Union, 50th Anniversary **Obv:** European Union Flag **Rev:** Europa head facing at right, banners at left

Date	Mintage	F12	VF20	XF40	MS60	MS63
2005	99	PF65 10,000				

KM# 2024 100 EURO
155.55 g., 0.999 Gold 4.9639 oz. AGW **Obv:** Stars and map of Europe **Rev:** Doves in flight above globe

Date	Mintage	F12	VF20	XF40	MS60	MS63
2005	Est. 99	PF65 10,000				

KM# 2025 100 EURO
155.55 g., 0.999 Gold 4.9639 oz. AGW **Obv:** Napoleon looking out over land towards Sunrise **Rev:** Napoleon and troops in the field

Date	Mintage	F12	VF20	XF40	MS60	MS63
2005	Est. 99	PF65 10,000				

KM# 2033 100 EURO
155.55 g., 0.999 Gold 4.9639 oz. AGW **Subject:** Jules Verne, 100th Anniversary of Death **Obv:** Around the world in 80 days

Date	Mintage	F12	VF20	XF40	MS60	MS63
2005	80	PF65 11,000				

KM# 2034 100 EURO
155.55 g., 0.999 Gold 4.9639 oz. AGW **Subject:** Jules Verne, 100th Anniversary of Death **Obv:** 20,000 leagues under the sea

Date	Mintage	F12	VF20	XF40	MS60	MS63
2005	71	PF65 11,000				

KM# 2035 100 EURO
155.55 g., 0.999 Gold 4.9639 oz. AGW **Subject:** Jules Verne, 100th Anniversary of Death **Obv:** From the earth to the moon

Date	Mintage	F12	VF20	XF40	MS60	MS63
2005	71	PF65 11,000				

KM# 2040 100 EURO
155.55 g., 0.999 Gold 4.9639 oz. AGW **Subject:** Robert Schuman, 120th Anniversary of Birth **Rev:** Europa head facing at right, color highlights

Date	Mintage	F12	VF20	XF40	MS60	MS63
2006	99	PF65 10,000				

Note: Individually numbered

KM# 2044 100 EURO
155.55 g., 0.999 Gold 4.9639 oz. AGW **Subject:** Benjamin Franklin, 300th Anniversary of Birth **Obv:** Bust at left, kite in thunderclouds at right **Rev:** French and American flags

Date	Mintage	F12	VF20	XF40	MS60	MS63
2006	99	PF65 10,000				

Note: Individually numbered

KM# 2047 100 EURO
155.55 g., 0.999 Gold 4.9639 oz. AGW **Subject:** St. Peter's Basilica, 500th Anniversary **Obv:** St. Peter's floor plan **Rev:** Façade of St. Peter's, Pope Benedict XVI

Date	Mintage	F12	VF20	XF40	MS60	MS63
2006	99	PF65 10,000				

Note: Individually numbered

KM# 2058 100 EURO
155.55 g., 0.999 Gold 4.9639 oz. AGW **Subject:** Abolishment of the Death Penalty, 25th Anniversary **Obv:** Sower advancing left **Rev:** Guillotine

Date	Mintage	F12	VF20	XF40	MS60	MS63
2006	—	PF65 10,000				

Note: Individually numbered

KM# 2060 100 EURO
155.55 g., 0.999 Gold 4.9639 oz. AGW **Subject:** Paul Cézanne, 100th Anniversary of Death **Obv:** Bust **Rev:** Two men seated at table, wine bottle between them

Date	Mintage	F12	VF20	XF40	MS60	MS63
2006	—	PF65 10,000				

Note: Individually numbered

KM# 2069 100 EURO
155.55 g., 0.999 Gold 4.9623 oz. AGW **Subject:** Jules Verne, 100th Anniversary of Death **Obv:** Voyage to the center of the Earth

Date	Mintage	F12	VF20	XF40	MS60	MS63
2006	92	PF65 10,000				

KM# 1482 100 EURO
155.55 g., 0.999 Gold 4.9639 oz. AGW, 50 mm. **Subject:** Airbus A380 **Rev:** Europa head and flags

Date	Mintage	F12	VF20	XF40	MS60	MS63
2007	99	PF65 10,000				

KM# 1497 100 EURO
155.50 g., 0.999 Gold 4.9623 oz. AGW, 50 mm. **Subject:** Cannes Film Festival, 60th Anniversary **Obv:** Cinema screen and stage, Golden Palm Award

Date	Mintage	F12	VF20	XF40	MS60	MS63
2007	99	PF65 10,000				

KM# 1531 100 EURO
155.50 g., 0.999 Gold 4.9623 oz. AGW, 50 mm. **Subject:** French Presidency of the European Union **Obv:** Text within stars **Rev:** Europa head and flags

Date	Mintage	F12	VF20	XF40	MS60	MS63
2008	99	PF65 10,000				

KM# 1536 100 EURO
3.10 g., 0.999 Gold 0.0989 oz. AGW, 15 mm. **Obv:** Modernistic sower advancing right **Rev:** Value and wreath

Date	Mintage	F12	VF20	XF40	MS60	MS63
2008	50,000	—	—	—	—	180
2009	50,000	—	—	—	—	180
2010	50,000	—	—	—	—	180

KM# 1545 100 EURO
155.50 g., 0.999 Gold 4.9623 oz. AGW, 50 mm. **Subject:** 29th
Summer Olympic Games - Beijing **Obv:** Swimmer and globe
Rev: Diver and oriental screen

Date	Mintage	F12	VF20	XF40	MS60	MS63
2008	98					
	PF65 10,000					

KM# 1565 100 EURO
155.50 g., 0.999 Gold 4.9623 oz. AGW, 50 mm. **Subject:**
Lourdes, 150th Anniversary **Obv:** Church of Notre Dame at
Lourdes **Rev:** Cross with Pope John Paul II, Pope Benedict XVI
and Bernadette Soubirous in quadrants

Date	Mintage	F12	VF20	XF40	MS60	MS63
2008	99					
	PF65 10,000					

KM# 1582 100 EURO
155.50 g., 0.999 Gold 4.9623 oz. AGW **Subject:** CoCo Chanel,
125th Anniversary of Birth **Obv:** Profile at left **Rev:** Diamond
handbag pattern

Date	Mintage	F12	VF20	XF40	MS60	MS63
2008	Est. 99					
	PF65 9,500					

KM# 1588 100 EURO
31.11 g., 0.920 Gold 0.9141 oz. AGW, 47 mm. **Subject:** Court
of Human Rights, 50th Anniversary **Obv:** The Seed Sower left
Rev: Text

Date	Mintage	F12	VF20	XF40	MS60	MS63
2009P	500					
	PF65 1,750					

KM# 1626 100 EURO
17.00 g., 0.920 Gold 0.4996 oz. AGW, 30 x 21 mm. **Subject:**
Renoir **Obv:** Le dejuner des canotiers, 1881 painting **Rev:**
Brushes and portrait **Shape:** Rectangle

Date	Mintage	F12	VF20	XF40	MS60	MS63
2009P	317					
	PF65 1,000					

KM# 1641 100 EURO
17.00 g., 0.920 Gold 0.4996 oz. AGW **Subject:** Claude Monet
Obv: Bassin of the Nymphs in color **Rev:** Portrait and paint
brushes **Shape:** Rectangle

Date	Mintage	F12	VF20	XF40	MS60	MS63
2009	361					
	PF63 950 PF65 975					

KM# 1672 100 EURO
17.00 g., 0.920 Gold 0.4996 oz. AGW, 18 mm. **Obv:** The Seed
Sower left **Rev:** Wheat and olive branch

Date	Mintage	F12	VF20	XF40	MS60	MS63
2010	500					
	PF63 925 PF65 950					

KM# 1689 100 EURO
327.60 g., 0.950 Silver 9.9415 oz. ASW, 65 mm. **Obv:** Marcel
Dassault **Rev:** Mirage III plane

Date	Mintage	F12	VF20	XF40	MS60	MS63
2010	500					
	PF63 400 PF65 425					

KM# 1707 100 EURO
17.00 g., 0.920 Gold 0.4996 oz. AGW, 30x21 mm. **Rev:**
Georges Braque **Shape:** Rectangle

Date	Mintage	F12	VF20	XF40	MS60	MS63
2010	500					
	PF63 975 PF65 1,000					

KM# 1711 100 EURO
17.00 g., 0.920 Gold 0.4996 oz. AGW, 30x21 mm. **Rev:**
Picasso **Shape:** Rectangle

Date	Mintage	F12	VF20	XF40	MS60	MS63
2010	500					
	PF63 1,000 PF65 1,100					

KM# 1724 100 EURO
50.00 g., 0.900 Silver 1.4375 oz. ASW, 47 mm. **Obv:** Value at
center, wreath horizontal **Rev:** Hercules goup

Date	Mintage	F12	VF20	XF40	MS60	MS63
2011	50,000	—	—	—	—	150
2012	50,000	—	—	—	—	150

KM# 1787 100 EURO
17.00 g., 0.920 Gold 0.4996 oz. AGW, 31 mm. **Subject:** Euro
Starter Kit, 10th Anniversary **Obv:** Sower **Rev:** Euro starter kit

Date	Mintage	F12	VF20	XF40	MS60	MS63
2011	500	PF63 925	PF65 950			

KM# 1820 100 EURO
17.00 g., 0.920 Gold 0.4996 oz. AGW, 30x21 mm. **Subject:**
Vasslly Kandlnsky **Shape:** Rectangle

Date	Mintage	F12	VF20	XF40	MS60	MS63
2011	500	PF63 975	PF65 1,000			

KM# 1824 100 EURO
17.00 g., 0.920 Gold 0.4996 oz. AGW, 31 mm. **Subject:** Andy
Warhol **Obv:** Portrait facing **Rev:** Dollar sign

Date	Mintage	F12	VF20	XF40	MS60	MS63
2011	500	PF63 975	PF65 1,000			

KM# 1836 100 EURO
327.60 g., 0.950 Silver 9.9415 oz. ASW, 75 mm. **Obv:** Commic
characters **Rev:** Profile left and large XIII

Date	Mintage	F12	VF20	XF40	MS60	MS63
2011	500	PF63 400	PF65 425			

KM# 1892 100 EURO
17.00 g., 0.920 Gold 0.4996 oz. AGW, 31 mm. **Subject:** Euro,
10th Anniversary **Obv:** The Sower advancing left **Rev:** Value on
globe at center, child-like renderings around

Date	Mintage	F12	VF20	XF40	MS60	MS63
2012(a)	500	PF63 950	PF65 975			

KM# 2089 100 EURO
327.60 g., 0.950 Silver 9.9415 oz. ASW, 75 mm. **Obv:** Yves
Klein and blue hand **Rev:** Klein artwork

Date	Mintage	F12	VF20	XF40	MS60	MS63
2012	500	PF63 1,250	PF65 1,350			

KM# 1589 200 EURO
31.10 g., 0.999 Gold 0.9926 oz. AGW, 37 mm. **Subject:** Court
of Human Rights - 50th Anniversary **Obv:** The Seed Sower left
Rev: Text

Date	Mintage	F12	VF20	XF40	MS60	MS63
2009P	500	PF65 1,850				

KM# 1593 200 EURO
31.10 g., 0.999 Gold 0.9926 oz. AGW, 37 mm. **Subject:** Europa
- Fall of Berlin Wall **Obv:** Brandenburg gate and doves in flight
Rev: Head facing and flags

Date	Mintage	F12	VF20	XF40	MS60	MS63
2009P	500	PF65 1,850				

KM# 1624 200 EURO
31.10 g., 0.999 Gold 0.9926 oz. AGW, 37 mm. **Subject:** First
Moon Landing, 40th Anniversary **Obv:** Footprint on the moon

Date	Mintage	F12	VF20	XF40	MS60	MS63
2009P	1,000	PF65 1,850				

KM# 1639 200 EURO
31.10 g., 0.999 Gold 0.9926 oz. AGW, 37 mm. **Subject:** FIFA
World Cup, South Africa 2010 **Obv:** Soccer player on field **Rev:**
Soccerball, Map of Africa, Protea flower

Date	Mintage	F12	VF20	XF40	MS60	MS63
2009P	125	PF65 1,850				

KM# 1678 200 EURO
31.10 g., 0.999 Gold 0.9926 oz. AGW, 37 mm. **Subject:** Cluny
Abbey, 1100th Anniversary **Obv:** Europa head facing **Rev:**
Cluny Abbey

Date	Mintage	F12	VF20	XF40	MS60	MS63
2010	500	PF65 1,850				

KM# 1683 200 EURO
31.10 g., 0.999 Gold 0.9926 oz. AGW, 37 mm. **Obv:** Georges
Pompidou Center design **Rev:** Design detail

Date	Mintage	F12	VF20	XF40	MS60	MS63
2010	500	PF65 1,850				

KM# 1693 200 EURO
31.10 g., 0.999 Gold 0.9926 oz. AGW, 37 mm. **Obv:** Mother
Teresa and child **Rev:** Mother Teresa and Pope John Paul II

Date	Mintage	F12	VF20	XF40	MS60	MS63
2010	500	PF65 1,850				

KM# 1698 200 EURO
31.10 g., 0.999 Gold 0.9926 oz. AGW, 37 mm. **Obv:** Taj Mahal
Rev: UNESCO offices

Date	Mintage	F12	VF20	XF40	MS60	MS63
2010	1,000	PF65 1,800				

KM# 1701 200 EURO
31.10 g., 0.999 Gold 0.9926 oz. AGW, 37 mm. **Obv:** Lille station
and route map **Rev:** Three TGV trains

Date	Mintage	F12	VF20	XF40	MS60	MS63
2010	500	PF65 1,850				

KM# 1818 200 EURO
31.10 g., 0.999 Gold 0.9926 oz. AGW, 37 mm. **Obv:** Metz

railroad station **Rev:** TGV and ICE trains

Date	Mintage	F12	VF20	XF40	MS60	MS63
2011	—	PF65 1,850				

KM# 1757 200 EURO
4.00 g., 0.999 Gold 0.1276 oz. AGW, 21 mm. **Obv:** French region names around RF within stylized map of France **Rev:** Value within wreath

Date	Mintage	F12	VF20	XF40	MS60	MS63
2011(a) Proof	50,000	—	—	—	—	265

KM# 1793 200 EURO
31.10 g., 0.999 Gold 0.9926 oz. AGW, 37 mm. **Subject:** International Music Day, 30th Anniversary **Obv:** Europa **Rev:** Youth jamming

Date	Mintage	F12	VF20	XF40	MS60	MS63
2011	500	PF65 1,900				

KM# 1797 200 EURO
31.10 g., 0.999 Gold 0.9926 oz. AGW, 37 mm. **Subject:** Great Explorers - Jacques Cartier **Obv:** The Grande Hermine sailing away **Rev:** Cartier, globe and compass rose

Date	Mintage	F12	VF20	XF40	MS60	MS63
2011	500	PF65 1,850				

KM# 1808 200 EURO
31.10 g., 0.999 Gold 0.9926 oz. AGW, 37 mm. **Subject:** WWF - Audouin's Gull **Obv:** Gull in flight right **Rev:** Gull standing right, WWF logo right

Date	Mintage	F12	VF20	XF40	MS60	MS63
2011	500	PF65 1,850				

KM# 2072 200 EURO
4.00 g., 0.999 Gold 0.1276 oz. AGW, 21 mm. **Subject:** G-20 Meeting in Cannes **Obv:** Sower advancing right **Rev:** Laurel tree and oak tree in the shape of a Euro symbol with value specification in the hexagon as stylization national borders

Date	Mintage	F12	VF20	XF40	MS60	MS63
2011	100	—	—	—	—	400

KM# 1853 200 EURO
31.10 g., 0.999 Gold 0.9926 oz. AGW, 37 mm. **Subject:** Eurocorps, 20th Anniversary **Obv:** Mitterrand and Kohl standing clasping hands **Rev:** Europa facing

Date	Mintage	F12	VF20	XF40	MS60	MS63
2012(a)	500	PF65 1,850				

KM# 1898 200 EURO
31.10 g., 0.999 Gold 0.9926 oz. AGW, 37 mm. **Subject:** abbé Pierre, 100th anniversary of Birth **Obv:** Pierre's bust at left, shaddow figure at right **Rev:** Emmaus International logo, quote below

Date	Mintage	F12	VF20	XF40	MS60	MS63
2012(a)	500	PF65 1,850				

KM# 1915 200 EURO
31.10 g., 0.999 Gold 0.9926 oz. AGW, 37 mm. **Subject:** TGV South-East **Obv:** Lyon Saint-Exupery station **Rev:** Two modern locomotives

Date	Mintage	F12	VF20	XF40	MS60	MS63
2012(a)	500	PF65 1,850				

KM# 1923 200 EURO
31.10 g., 0.999 Gold 0.9926 oz. AGW, 37 mm. **Subject:** 2012 Summer Olympics, London **Obv:** Two judo athletes and map of Europe **Rev:** Two judo athletes

Date	Mintage	F12	VF20	XF40	MS60	MS63
2012(a)	500	PF65 1,850				

KM# 1926 200 EURO
31.10 g., 0.999 Gold 0.9926 oz. AGW, 37 mm. **Subject:** Year of the Dragon **Obv:** Dragon **Rev:** La Fontaine and zodiac animals

Date	Mintage	F12	VF20	XF40	MS60	MS63
2012(a)	500	PF65 1,850				

KM# 2074 200 EURO
4.00 g., 0.999 Gold 0.1276 oz. AGW, 21 mm. **Obv:** French province names in horizontal lines, RF in center in stylized map of France **Rev:** Laural and oak wreath, value within

Date	Mintage	F12	VF20	XF40	MS60	MS63
2012	50,000	—	—	—	—	325

KM# 2101 200 EURO
31.11 g., 0.999 Gold 0.9926 oz. AGW, 37 mm. **Subject:** Notre Dame, 850th Anniversary **Obv:** Seal at right, cathedral details **Rev:** Seal at left, cathedral details

Date	Mintage	F12	VF20	XF40	MS60	MS63
2013	500	PF65 2,750				

KM# 1583 250 EURO
8.45 g., 0.920 Gold 0.2483 oz. AGW, 22 mm. **Obv:** Modernistic sower advancing right **Rev:** Value and wreath

Date	Mintage	F12	VF20	XF40	MS60	MS63
2009P	25,000	—	—	—	—	500

KM# 1671 250 EURO
62.21 g., 0.999 Gold 1.9852 oz. AGW, 37 mm. **Obv:** The Seed Sower left **Rev:** Wheat and olive branch

Date	Mintage	F12	VF20	XF40	MS60	MS63
2010	500	PF65 3,550				

KM# 1788 250 EURO
62.21 g., 0.999 Gold 1.9852 oz. AGW, 37 mm. **Subject:** Euro Starter Kit, 10th Anniversary **Obv:** Sower **Rev:** Euro starter kit **Note:** Thick planchet.

Date	Mintage	F12	VF20	XF40	MS60	MS63
2011	500	PF65 3,550				

KM# 1893 250 EURO
62.21 g., 0.999 Gold 1.9852 oz. AGW, 37 mm. **Subject:** Euro, 10th Anniversary **Obv:** The Sower advancing left **Rev:** Value on globe at center, child-like renderings around

Date	Mintage	F12	VF20	XF40	MS60	MS63
2012(a)	500	PF65 3,600				

KM# 1396 500 EURO
1000.00 g., 0.999 Gold 31.9118 oz. AGW, 85 mm. **Subject:** European Union Expansion **Obv:** Partial face and flags **Rev:** Puzzle map **Edge:** Plain **Note:** Illustration reduced.

Date	Mintage	F12	VF20	XF40	MS60	MS63
2004	20	PF65 60,000				

KM# 1594 500 EURO
155.50 g., 0.999 Gold 4.9623 oz. AGW, 50 mm. **Subject:** Europa - Fall of Berlin Wall **Obv:** Brandenburg gate and doves in flight **Rev:** Head facing and flags

Date	Mintage	F12	VF20	XF40	MS60	MS63
2009P	99	PF65 9,250				

KM# 1599 500 EURO
155.50 g., 0.999 Gold 4.9623 oz. AGW, 50 mm. **Subject:** Concorde 40th Anniversary **Obv:** Concorde in flight **Rev:** Tail emblems

Date	Mintage	F12	VF20	XF40	MS60	MS63
2009P	90	PF65 9,250				

KM# 1605 500 EURO
155.50 g., 0.999 Gold 4.9623 oz. AGW, 50 mm. **Obv:** Eiffel Tower Structure **Rev:** Gustave Eiffel at left

Date	Mintage	F12	VF20	XF40	MS60	MS63
2009P	65	PF65 9,250				

KM# 1610 500 EURO
155.50 g., 0.999 Gold 4.9623 oz. AGW, 50 mm. **Subject:** Bugatti 100th Anniversary **Obv:** Ettore Bugatti at left **Rev:** Race car and grill motif

Date	Mintage	F12	VF20	XF40	MS60	MS63
2009P	85	PF65 9,975				

KM# 1615 500 EURO
155.50 g., 0.999 Gold 4.9623 oz. AGW, 50 mm. **Subject:** Curie Institute, 100th Anniversary

Date	Mintage	F12	VF20	XF40	MS60	MS63
2009P	99	PF65 9,250				

KM# 1619 500 EURO
155.50 g., 0.999 Gold 4.9623 oz. AGW, 50 mm. **Subject:** Unesco site - The Kremlin in Moscow **Obv:** Wall Tower and cathedral

Date	Mintage	F12	VF20	XF40	MS60	MS63
2009P	99	PF65 925				

KM# 1640 500 EURO
155.50 g., 0.999 Gold 4.9623 oz. AGW, 50 mm. **Subject:** FIFA World Cup, South Africa 2010 **Obv:** Soccer player on field **Rev:** Soccerball, Map of Africa, Protea flower

Date	Mintage	F12	VF20	XF40	MS60	MS63
2009P	22	PF65 9,250				

KM# 1642 500 EURO
12.00 g., 0.999 Gold 0.3829 oz. AGW, 31 mm. **Obv:** The Seed Sower advancing right, sun rays from below **Rev:** Value in center, wreath horizontal

Date	Mintage	F12	VF20	XF40	MS60	MS63
2010	25,000	—	—	—	—	700

KM# 1687 500 EURO
155.50 g., 0.999 Gold 4.9623 oz. AGW, 50 mm. **Obv:** Marcel Dassault **Rev:** Mirage III plane

Date	Mintage	F12	VF20	XF40	MS60	MS63
2010	99	PF65 9,250				

KM# 1692 500 EURO
155.50 g., 0.999 Gold 4.9623 oz. AGW, 50 mm. **Obv:** Mother Teresa and child **Rev:** Mother Teresa and Pope John Paul II

Date	Mintage	F12	VF20	XF40	MS60	MS63
2010	99	PF65 9,250				

KM# 1697 500 EURO
155.50 g., 0.999 Gold 4.9623 oz. AGW, 50 mm. **Obv:** Taj Mahal **Rev:** UNESCO offices

Date	Mintage	F12	VF20	XF40	MS60	MS63
2010	99	PF65 9,250				

KM# 1706 500 EURO
155.50 g., 0.999 Gold 4.9623 oz. AGW **Obv:** Doves **Rev:** Georges Baraque **Shape:** 50

Date	Mintage	F12	VF20	XF40	MS60	MS63
2010	99	PF65 9,250				

KM# 1710 500 EURO
155.50 g., 0.999 Gold 4.9623 oz. AGW, 50 mm. **Rev:** Picasso

Date	Mintage	F12	VF20	XF40	MS60	MS63
2010	99	PF65 9,250				

KM# 1712 500 EURO
1000.00 g., 0.950 Silver 30.3466 oz. ASW, 100 mm. **Rev:** Picasso

Date	Mintage	F12	VF20	XF40	MS60	MS63
2010	500	PF63 1,200	PF65 1,300			

KM# 1718 500 EURO
155.50 g., 0.999 Gold 4.9623 oz. AGW, 50 mm. **Obv:** Handball player on globe **Rev:** Handball player, net, Big Ben

Date	Mintage	F12	VF20	XF40	MS60	MS63
2010	99	PF65 9,250				

KM# 1798 500 EURO
155.50 g., 0.999 Gold 4.9623 oz. AGW, 50 mm. **Subject:** Great Explorers - Jacques Cartier **Obv:** The Grande Hermine sailing away **Rev:** Cartier, globe and compass rose

Date	Mintage	F12	VF20	XF40	MS60	MS63
2011	99	PF65 9,500				

KM# 1812 500 EURO
155.50 g., 0.999 Gold 4.9623 oz. AGW, 50 mm. **Subject:** UNESCO World Heritage Site - Palace of Versailles

Date	Mintage	F12	VF20	XF40	MS60	MS63
2011	99	PF65 9,250				

KM# 1821 500 EURO
155.50 g., 0.999 Gold 4.9623 oz. AGW, 53x37 mm. **Subject:** Vassily Kandinsky **Shape:** Rectangle

Date	Mintage	F12	VF20	XF40	MS60	MS63
2011	99	PF65 9,975				

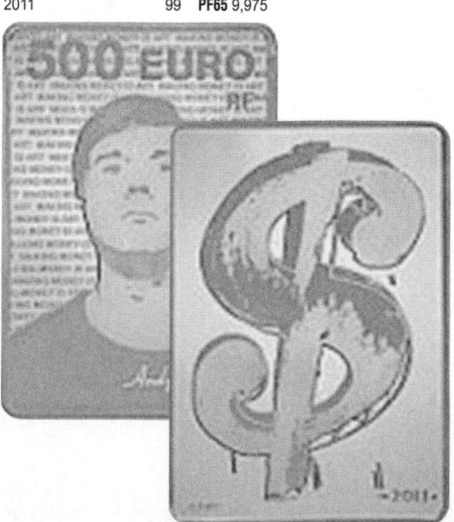

KM# 1825 500 EURO
155.50 g., 0.999 Gold 4.9623 oz. AGW, 53x37 mm. **Subject:** Andy Warhol **Shape:** Rectangle

Date	Mintage	F12	VF20	XF40	MS60	MS63
2011	99	PF65 9,500				

KM# 1854 500 EURO
155.59 g., 0.999 Gold 4.9652 oz. AGW, 50 mm. **Subject:**
Eurocorps, 20th Anniversary **Obv:** Mitterrand and Kohl standing
clasping hands **Rev:** Europa facing

Date	Mintage	F12	VF20	XF40	MS60	MS63
2012(a)	99	PF65 9,250				

KM# 1899 500 EURO
155.50 g., 0.999 Gold 4.9623 oz. AGW, 50 mm. **Subject:** abbé
Pierre, 100th anniversary of Birth **Obv:** Pierre's bust at left,
shadow at right **Rev:** Emmaus International logo, quote below

Date	Mintage	F12	VF20	XF40	MS60	MS63
2012(a)	99	PF65 9,250				

KM# 1909 500 EURO
155.50 g., 0.999 Gold 4.9623 oz. AGW, 50 mm. **Subject:**
UNESCO - World Heritage Site **Obv:** Abu Simbel temple **Rev:**
Sphinx and Pyramids

Date	Mintage	F12	VF20	XF40	MS60	MS63
2012(a)	99	PF65 9,250				

KM# 1927 500 EURO
155.50 g., 0.999 Gold 4.9623 oz. AGW, 50 mm. **Subject:** Year
of the Dragon **Obv:** Dragon **Rev:** La Fontaine and zodiac
animals

Date	Mintage	F12	VF20	XF40	MS60	MS63
2012(a)	99	PF65 9,250				

KM# 1595 1000 EURO
311.00 g., 0.999 Gold 9.9246 oz. AGW, 65 mm. **Subject:**
Europa - Fall of Berlin Wall **Obv:** Brandenburg gate and doves
in flight **Rev:** Head facing and flags

Date	Mintage	F12	VF20	XF40	MS60	MS63
2009P	20	PF65 18,500				

KM# 1600 1000 EURO
311.00 g., 0.999 Gold 9.9246 oz. AGW, 65 mm. **Subject:**
Concorde 40 Anniversary **Obv:** Concorde in flight **Rev:** Tail
emblems

Date	Mintage	F12	VF20	XF40	MS60	MS63
2009P	20	PF65 1,850				

KM# 1677 1000 EURO
31.10 g., 0.999 Gold 0.9925 oz. AGW, 65 mm. **Subject:** Cluny
Abbey, 1100th Anniversary **Obv:** Europa head facing **Rev:**
Cluny Abby view

Date	Mintage	F12	VF20	XF40	MS60	MS63
2010	39	PF65 18,500				

KM# 1682 1000 EURO
311.00 g., 0.999 Gold 9.9246 oz. AGW, 65 mm. **Obv:** Georges
Pompidou Center design **Rev:** Design detail

Date	Mintage	F12	VF20	XF40	MS60	MS63
2010	39	PF65 18,500				

KM# 1725 1000 EURO
20.00 g., 0.999 Gold 0.6382 oz. AGW, 39 mm. **Obv:** Value at
center, wreath horizontal **Rev:** Hercules goup

Date	Mintage	F12	VF20	XF40	MS60	MS63
2011	10,000	—	—	—	—	1,250
2012	10,000	—	—	—	—	1,250

KM# 1794 1000 EURO
311.00 g., 0.999 Gold 9.9246 oz. AGW, 65 mm. **Subject:**
International Music Day, 30th Anniversary **Obv:** Europa **Rev:**
Youth jamming

Date	Mintage	F12	VF20	XF40	MS60	MS63
2011	39	PF65 18,500				

KM# 1799 1000 EURO
311.00 g., 0.999 Gold 9.9246 oz. AGW, 65 mm. **Subject:** Great
Explorers - Jacques Cartier **Obv:** The Grande Hermine sailing
away **Rev:** Cartier, globe and compass rose

Date	Mintage	F12	VF20	XF40	MS60	MS63
2011	39	PF65 18,500				

KM# 1855 1000 EURO
311.00 g., 0.999 Gold 9.9246 oz. AGW, 65 mm. **Subject:**
Eurocorps, 20th Anniversary **Obv:** Mitterrand and Kohl standing
clasping hands **Rev:** Europa facing

Date	Mintage	F12	VF20	XF40	MS60	MS63
2012(a)	39	PF65 18,500				

KM# 1620 5000 EURO
1000.00 g., 0.999 Gold 31.9118 oz. AGW, 85 mm. **Subject:**
Unesco site - The Kremlin in Moscow **Obv:** Wall Tower and
cathedral

Date	Mintage	F12	VF20	XF40	MS60	MS63
2009P	23	PF65 60,000				

KM# 1696 5000 EURO
1000.00 g., 0.999 Gold 31.9118 oz. AGW, 85 mm. **Obv:** Taj
Mahal and diamond inserts **Rev:** UNESCO offices

Date	Mintage	F12	VF20	XF40	MS60	MS63
2010	29	PF65 60,000				

KM# 1709 5000 EURO
1000.00 g., 0.999 Gold 31.9118 oz. AGW, 85 mm. **Rev:**
Picasso

Date	Mintage	F12	VF20	XF40	MS60	MS63
2010	29	PF65 60,000				

KM# 1813 5000 EURO
1000.00 g., 0.999 Gold 31.9118 oz. AGW, 85 mm. **Subject:**
UNESCO World Heritage Site - Palace of Versailles

Date	Mintage	F12	VF20	XF40	MS60	MS63
2011	29	PF65 60,000				

KM# 1822 5000 EURO
1000.00 g., 0.999 Gold 31.9118 oz. AGW, 90x63 mm. **Subject:** Vassily Kandinsky **Shape:** Rectangle

Date	Mintage	F12	VF20	XF40	MS60	MS63
2011	29	PF65 60,000				

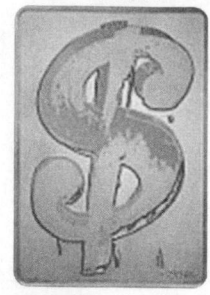

KM# 1826 5000 EURO
1000.00 g., 0.999 Gold 31.9118 oz. AGW, 90x63 mm. **Subject:** Andy Warhol **Shape:** Rectangle

Date	Mintage	F12	VF20	XF40	MS60	MS63
2011	29	PF65 60,000				

KM# 1910 5000 EURO
1000.00 g., 0.999 Gold 31.9118 oz. AGW, 85 mm. **Subject:** UNESCO - World Heritage Site **Obv:** Abu Simbel temple **Rev:** Sphinx and Pyramids

Date	Mintage	F12	VF20	XF40	MS60	MS63
2012(a)	29	PF65 60,000				

KM# 1928 5000 EURO
75.00 g., 0.999 Gold 2.3934 oz. AGW, 45 mm. **Obv:** Value at center, wreath horizontal **Rev:** Hercules group

Date	Mintage	F12	VF20	XF40	MS60	MS63
2012(a)	2,000	—	—	—	—	4,500

MINT SETS

KM#	Date	Mintage	Identification	Issue Price	Mkt Val
MS20	2001 (2)	10,000	KM#925.1a, 928a		590
MS21	2001 (8)	35,000	KM#1282-1289	20.25	20.00
MS22	2002 (8)	35,000	KM#1282-1289	20.25	40.00
MS23	2003 (8)	—	KM#1282-89		55.00
MS24	2004 (8)	—	KM#1282-1289		45.00
MS25	2005 (8)	—	KM#1282-1289		45.00
MS26	2005 (8)	40,000	KM#1282-1289 Moebius set plus token	45.00	55.00
MS27	2005 (8)	10,000	KM1282-1289, French Memories - Bordeaux	45.00	45.00
MS28	2006 (8)	70,000	KM#1282-1289	36.50	42.50
MS29	2006 (8)	500	KM#1282-1289, Denver, Colorado special ANA Coin Convention Set	45.00	70.00
MS30	2006 (8)	500	KM#1282-1289, Berlin Coin Fair set	45.00	55.00
MS31	2006 (8)	500	KM1282-1289, Pierre Curie set	45.00	50.00
MS32	2006 (8)	500	KM#1282-1289, Musee de la Monnaie set	45.00	50.00
MS33	2006 (8)	500	KM#1282-1289, Journ-ees du Patrimoine set	45.00	50.00
MS34	2006 (8)	500	KM#1282-1289, Bour-gogne set	45.00	50.00
MS35	2006 (8)	500	KM#1282-1289, "Coree set" (Korea)	45.00	50.00
MS36	2006 (8)	500	KM#1282-1289, Nord Pas-de-Calais set	45.00	50.00
MS37	2006 (8)	500	KM#1282-1289, Jacques Chirac set	45.00	50.00
MS38	2006 (8)	500	KM#1282-1289, Mit-terand & Khol	45.00	50.00
MS39	2006 (8)	500	KM#1282-1289, Birthday 1 set	45.00	45.00
MS40	2006 (8)	500	KM#1282-1289, Birthday 2 set	45.00	45.00
MS41	2006 (8)	500	KM#1282-1289, Tokyo set	45.00	50.00
MS42	2006 (8)	500	KM#1282-1289, Viaduc de Millau set	45.00	50.00
MS43	2006 (8)	500	KM#1282-1289, Ile-de-France set	45.00	50.00

PROOF SETS

KM#	Date	Mintage	Identification	Issue Price	Mkt Val
PS21	2001 (8)	15,000	KM#1282-1289	59.00	125
PS22	2002 (8)	40,000	KM#1282-1289	59.00	110
PS23	2003 (5)	150,000	KM1321, 1322, 1323, 1324, 1325	—	260
PS24	2003 (5)	5,000	KM#1326, 1327, 1328, 1329, 1330	—	1,900
PS25	2003 (8)	—	KM#1282-1289	—	110
PS26	2004 (9)	20,000	KM#1282-1289 plus Pantheon 5 Euro	—	150
PS27	2005 (9)	10,000	KM#1282-1289 plus Pantheon 5 Euro	—	150
PS28	2006 (9)	10,000	KM#1282-1289 plus Pantheon 5 Euro	—	150
PS29	2007 (9)	7,500	KM#1282-84, 1410-1414 plus 15 Euro	—	150
PS30	2008 (10)	7,500	KM#1282-84, 1410-1414, 1535	—	200
PS31	2009 (10)	7,500	KM#1282-84, 1410-1414, 1535	—	200
PS32	2010 (9)	9,000	KM#1282-84, 1410-1414 plus 15 Euro	—	150
PS33	2011 (9)	9,000	KM#1282-84, 1410-1414, 1795	—	200
PS34	2012 (9)	10,000	KM#1282-84, 1410-1414 plus Hercules 10 Euro	—	150

FRENCH POLYNESIA

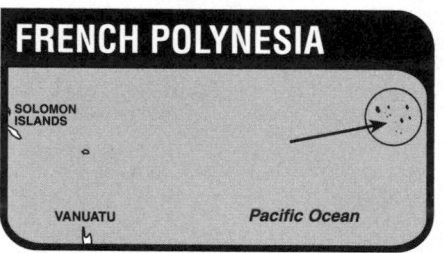

SOLOMON ISLANDS

VANUATU — Pacific Ocean

The Territory of French Polynesia (formerly French Oceania) has an area of 1,544 sq. mi. (3,941 sq. km.) and a population of 220,000. It is comprised of the same five archipelagoes that were grouped administratively to form French Oceania.

The colony of French Oceania became the Territory of French Polynesia by act of the French National Assembly in March, 1957. In Sept. of 1958 it voted in favor of the new constitution of the Fifth Republic, thereby electing to remain within the new French Community.

Picturesque, mountainous Tahiti, the setting of many tales of adventure and romance, is one of the most inspiringly beautiful islands in the world. Robert Louis Stevenson called it 'God's sweetest works'. It was there that Paul Gaugin, one of the pioneers of the Impressionist movement, painted the brilliant, exotic pictures that later made him famous. The arid coral atolls of Tuamotu comprise the most economically valuable area of French Polynesia. Pearl oysters thrive in the warm, limpid lagoons, and extensive portions of the atolls are valuable phosphate rock.

RULER
French

MINT MARKS
(a) - Paris, privy marks only

MONETARY SYSTEM
100 Centimes = 1 Franc

FRENCH OVERSEAS TERRITORY

DECIMAL COINAGE

KM# 11 FRANC
1.30 g., Aluminum, 23 mm. **Obv:** Seated Liberty with torch and cornucopia right, date below, legend added flanking figure's feet **Obv. Legend:** I. E. O. M. **Rev:** Legend and island scene divide denomination

Date	Mintage	F12	VF20	XF40	MS60	MS63
2001(a)	2,900,000	—	—	—	0.50	1.00
2002(a)	1,600,000	—	—	—	0.50	1.00
2003(a)	4,200,000	—	—	—	0.50	1.00
2004(a)	2,400,000	—	—	—	0.50	1.00
2005(a)		—	—	—	0.50	1.00
2006(a)	2,100,000	—	—	—	0.50	1.00
2007(a) Coin rotation	3,400,000	—	—	—	0.50	1.00
2007(a) Medal rotation	Inc. above	—	—	—	—	30.00
2008(a)	4,800,000	—	—	—	0.50	1.00
2009(a)	3,200,000	—	—	—	0.50	1.00
2010(a)	2,100,000	—	—	—	0.50	1.00
2011(a)		—	—	—	0.50	1.00

KM# 10 2 FRANCS
2.30 g., Aluminum, 27 mm. **Obv:** Seated Liberty with torch and cornucopia right, date below, legend added flanking figure's feet **Obv. Legend:** I. E. O. M. **Rev:** Legend and island scene divide denomination

Date	Mintage	F12	VF20	XF40	MS60	MS63
2001(a)	2,400,000	—	—	—	0.75	1.50
2002(a)	2,500,000	—	—	—	0.75	1.50
2003(a)	3,200,000	—	—	—	0.75	1.50
2004(a)	3,000,000	—	—	—	0.75	1.50
2005(a)	900,000	—	—	—	0.75	1.50
2006(a)	1,600,000	—	—	—	0.75	1.50
2007(a)	640,000	—	—	—	0.75	1.50
2008(a)	1,900,000	—	—	—	0.75	1.50
2009(a)	1,600,000	—	—	—	0.75	1.50
2010(a)	2,400,000	—	—	—	0.75	1.50
2011(a)	1,600,000	—	—	—	0.75	1.50

KM# 12 5 FRANCS
3.75 g., Aluminum, 31 mm. **Obv:** Seated Liberty with torch and cornucopia right, date below, legend added flanking figure's feet **Obv. Legend:** I. E. O. M. **Rev:** Legend and island divide denomination

Date	Mintage	F12	VF20	XF40	MS60	MS63
2001(a)	1,600,000	—	—	—	1.00	2.00
2002(a)	400,000	—	—	—	1.00	2.00
2003(a)	1,000,000	—	—	—	1.00	2.00
2004(a)	600,000	—	—	—	1.00	2.00
2005(a)	600,000	—	—	—	1.00	2.00
2006(a)	720,000	—	—	—	1.00	2.00
2007(a)	1,000,000	—	—	—	1.00	2.00
2008(a)	1,060,000	—	—	—	1.00	2.00
2009(a)	900,000	—	—	—	1.00	2.00
2010(a)	700,000	—	—	—	1.00	2.00
2011(a)	900,000	—	—	—	1.00	2.00

KM# 8 10 FRANCS
6.00 g., Nickel, 24 mm. **Obv:** Capped head left, date and legend below **Obv. Legend:** I. E. O. M. **Rev:** Native art, denomination below **Edge:** Reeded

Date	Mintage	F12	VF20	XF40	MS60	MS63
2001(a)	500,000	—	—	—	1.25	2.75
2002(a)	600,000	—	—	—	1.25	2.75
2003(a)	1,000,000	—	—	—	1.25	2.75
2004(a)	600,000	—	—	—	1.25	2.75
2005(a)	200,000	—	—	—	1.25	2.75

KM# 8a 10 FRANCS
6.00 g., Copper-Nickel, 24 mm. **Obv:** Capped head left, date and legend below **Obv. Legend:** I. E. O. M. **Rev:** Native art, denomination below **Edge:** Reeded

Date	Mintage	F12	VF20	XF40	MS60	MS63
2006(a)	620,000	—	—	—	1.25	2.75
2007(a)	800,000	—	—	—	1.25	2.75
2008(a)	820,000	—	—	—	1.25	2.75
2009(a)	1,000,000	—	—	—	1.25	2.75
2010(a)	500,000	—	—	—	1.25	2.75
2011(a)	200,000	—	—	—	1.25	2.75

KM# 9 20 FRANCS
10.00 g., Nickel, 28.3 mm. **Obv:** Capped head left, date and legend below **Obv. Legend:** I. E. O. M. **Rev:** Flowers, vanilla shoots, bread fruit **Edge:** Reeded

Date	Mintage	F12	VF20	XF40	MS60	MS63
2001(a)	500,000	—	—	—	1.75	3.25
2002(a)	300,000	—	—	—	1.75	3.25
2003(a)	700,000	—	—	—	1.75	3.00
2004(a)	600,000	—	—	—	1.75	3.00
2005(a)	30,000	—	—	—	20.00	35.00

KM# 9a 20 FRANCS
10.00 g., Copper-Nickel, 28.3 mm. **Obv:** Capped head left, date and legend below **Obv. Legend:** I. E. O. M. **Rev:** Flowers, vanilla shoots, bread fruit **Edge:** Reeded

Date	Mintage	F12	VF20	XF40	MS60	MS63
2006(a)	300,000	—	—	—	1.75	3.00
2007(a)	450,000	—	—	—	1.75	3.00
2008(a)	610,000	—	—	—	1.75	3.00
2009(a)	750,000	—	—	—	1.75	3.00
2010(a)	200,000	—	—	—	1.75	3.00
2011(a)	400,000	—	—	—	1.75	3.00

KM# 13 50 FRANCS
15.00 g., Nickel, 33 mm. **Obv:** Capped head left, date and legend below **Obv. Legend:** I. E. O. M. **Rev:** Denomination above Moorea Harbor **Edge:** Reeded

Date	Mintage	F12	VF20	XF40	MS60	MS63
2001(a)	300,000	—	—	—	2.00	4.00
2002(a)		—	—	—	2.00	4.00
2003(a)	240,000	—	—	—	2.00	4.00
2004(a)	100,000	—	—	—	2.00	4.00
2005(a)	100,000	—	—	—	2.00	4.00

KM# 13a 50 FRANCS

15.00 g., Copper-Nickel, 33 mm. **Obv:** Capped head left, date and legend below **Obv. Legend:** I. E. O. M. **Rev:** Denomination above Moorea Harbor **Edge:** Reeded

Date	Mintage	F12	VF20	XF40	MS60	MS63
2006(a)	15,000	—	—	—	3.00	5.00
2007(a)	310,000	—	—	—	2.00	4.00
2008(a)	200,000	—	—	—	2.00	4.00
2009(a)	300,000	—	—	—	2.00	4.00
2010(a)	120,000	—	—	—	2.00	4.00
2011(a)	130,000	—	—	—	2.00	4.00

KM# 14 100 FRANCS

10.00 g., Nickel-Bronze, 30 mm. **Obv:** Capped head left, date below **Rev:** Denomination above Moorea Harbor **Edge:** Reeded

Date	Mintage	F12	VF20	XF40	MS60	MS63
2001(a)	200,000	—	—	—	3.00	5.00
2002(a)	—	—	—	—	3.00	5.00
2003(a)	600,000	—	—	—	2.75	5.00
2004(a)	450,000	—	—	—	2.75	5.00
2005(a)	300,000	—	—	—	2.75	5.00

KM# 14a 100 FRANCS

10.00 g., Aluminum-Bronze, 30 mm. **Obv:** Capped head left, date below **Obv. Legend:** I. E. O. M. **Rev:** Denomination above Moorea Harbor **Edge:** Reeded

Date	Mintage	F12	VF20	XF40	MS60	MS63
2006(a)	200,000	—	—	—	2.75	5.00
2007(a)	650,000	—	—	—	2.75	5.00
2008(a)	690,000	—	—	—	2.75	5.00
2009(a)	—	—	—	—	2.75	5.00
2010(a)	—	—	—	—	2.75	5.00
2011(a)	—	—	—	—	2.75	5.00

MINT SETS

KM#	Date	Mintage	Identification	Issue Price	Mkt Val
MS1	2001 (7)	3,000	KM#8-14	—	22.50
MS2	2002 (7)	5,000	KM#8-14	—	22.50
MS3	2003 (7)	3,000	KM#8-14	—	22.50

GABON

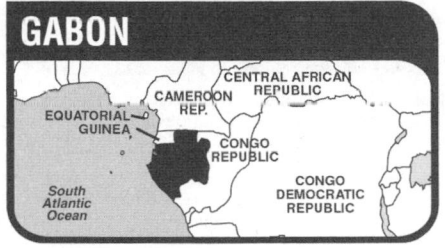

The Gabonese Republic, a member of the French Community, straddles the equator on the west coast of Africa. The hot and humid rain forest country has an area of 103,347 sq. mi. (267,670 sq. km.) and a population of 1.2 million, almost all of Bantu origin. Capital: Libreville. Extravagantly rich in resources, Gabon exports crude oil, manganese ore, gold and timbers.

MINT MARKS
(a) - Paris, privy marks only
(t) - Poissy, privy marks only, thunderbolt

REPUBLIC

DECIMAL COINAGE

KM# 19 1000 FRANCS

31.14 g., 0.999 Silver 0.9936 oz. ASW, 40 mm. **Obv:** National arms **Rev:** Elephant

Date	Mintage	F12	VF20	XF40	MS60	MS63
2012	2,000	PF63 55.00		PF65 60.00		

KM# 20 1000 FRANCS

31.14 g., 0.999 Silver 0.9936 oz. ASW, 40 mm. **Obv:** National arms **Rev:** Gazelle

Date	Mintage	F12	VF20	XF40	MS60	MS63
2012	2,000	PF63 55.00		PF65 60.00		

KM# 21 1000 FRANCS

31.14 g., 0.999 Silver 0.9936 oz. ASW, 40 mm. **Obv:** National arms **Rev:** Baby elephants

Date	Mintage	F12	VF20	XF40	MS60	MS63
2012	2,000	PF63 55.00		PF65 60.00		

KM# 18 1000 FRANCS

31.14 g., 0.999 Silver 0.9936 oz. ASW, 40 mm. **Obv:** National arms **Rev:** Male lion

Date	Mintage	F12	VF20	XF40	MS60	MS63
2012	2,000	PF63 55.00		PF65 60.00		

KM# 22 1000 FRANCS

31.11 g., 0.999 Silver 0.9926 oz. ASW, 38.61 mm. **Rev:** Elephant facing

Date	Mintage	F12	VF20	XF40	MS60	MS63
2012	—	PF63 70.00		PF65 75.00		

GAMBIA

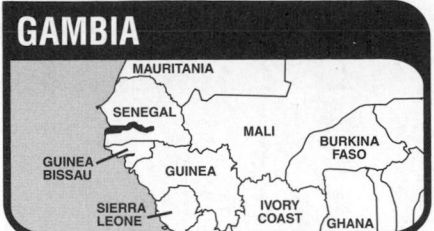

The Republic of The Gambia, occupies a strip of land 7 miles (11km.) to 20 miles (32 km.) wide and 200 miles (322 km.) long encompassing both sides of West Africa's Gambia River, and completely surrounded by Senegal. The republic, one of Africa's smallest countries, has an area of 4,127 sq. mi. (11,300 sq. km.) and a population of 989,273. Capital: Banjul. Agriculture and tourism are the principal industries. Peanuts constitute 95 per cent of export earnings.

The Gambia was once part of the great empires of Ghana and Songhay. When Portuguese gold seekers and slave traders visited The Gambia in the 15th century, it was part of the Kingdom of Mali. In 1588 the territory became, through purchase, the first British colony in Africa. English slavers established Fort James, the first settlement, on a small island a dozen miles up the Gambia River in 1664. After alternate periods of union with Sierra Leone and existence as a separate colony The Gambia became a British colony in 1888. On Feb. 18, 1965, The Gambia achieved independence as a constitutional monarchy within the Commonwealth of Nations, with Elizabeth II as Head of State as Queen of The Gambia. It became a republic on April 24, 1970, remaining a member of the Commonwealth, but with the president as Chief of State and Head of Government.

Together with Senegal, The Gambia formed a confederation on February 1, 1982. This confederation was officially dissolved on September 21, 1989. In July, 1994 a military junta took control of The Gambia and disbanded its elected government.

RULER
British until 1970

REPUBLIC

DECIMAL COINAGE

100 Bututs = 1 Dalasi

KM# 58 50 BUTUTS

Nickel Plated Steel, 28.8 mm. **Obv:** National arms, date below **Rev:** African domestic ox divides denomination

Date	Mintage	F12	VF20	XF40	MS60	MS63
2008	—	—	—	—	1.50	2.00
2011	—	—	—	—	1.50	2.00

KM# 72 DALASI

Gold AGW **Subject:** 7th Conference of the African Union in Banjul

Date	Mintage	F12	VF20	XF40	MS60	MS63
2006 Proof						

KM# 59a DALASI

8.67 g., Nickel Plated Steel **Obv:** National arms, date below **Rev:** Slender-snouted crocodile, denomination at right **Shape:** 7-sided

Date	Mintage	F12	VF20	XF40	MS60	MS63
2008	—	—	—	2.75	6.00	7.50
2011	—	—	—	2.75	6.00	7.50

GEORGIA

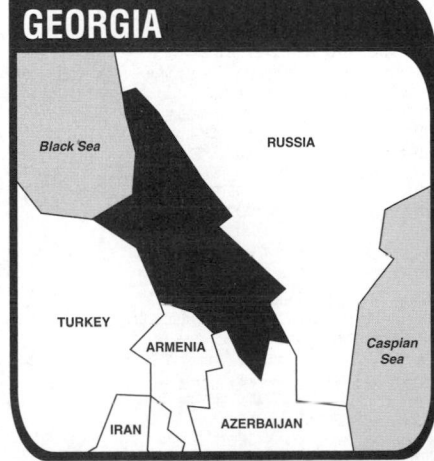

Georgia (formerly the Georgian Social Democratic Republic under the U.S.S.R.), is bounded by the Black Sea to the west and by Turkey, Armenia and Azerbaijan. It occupies the western part of Transcaucasia covering an area of 26,900 sq. mi. (69,700 sq. km.) and a population of 5.7 million. Capitol: Tbilisi. Hydro-electricity, minerals, forestry and agriculture are the chief industries.

Germano-- Georgian treaty was signed on May 28, 1918, followed by a Turko-Georgian peace treaty on June 4. The end of WW I and the collapse of the central powers allowed free The collapse of the U.S.S.R. allowed full transition to independence and on April 9, 1991 a unanimous vote declared the republic an independent state based on its original treaty of independence of May 1918.

INDEPENDENT STATE (C.I.S.)

STANDARD COINAGE

100 Thetri = 1 Lari

KM# 89 50 THETRI

6.50 g., Copper-Nickel, 24 mm. **Obv:** National arms **Rev:** Value **Edge:** Reeded and lettered

Date	Mintage	F12	VF20	XF40	MS60	MS63
2006	—	—	—	—	3.00	4.00

KM# 95 LARI

28.28 g., 0.999 Silver 0.9025 oz. ASW, 38.61 mm. **Subject:** World Cup Soccer, 2006 Germany **Obv:** Map of Georgia, flag **Rev:** World Cup trophy, two soccer players

Date	Mintage	F12	VF20	XF40	MS60	MS63
2004	50,000	PF63 40.00		PF65 45.00		

KM# 90 LARI

7.80 g., Copper-Nickel, 26.2 mm. **Obv:** National arms **Rev:** Value **Edge:** Reeded and lettered

Date	Mintage	F12	VF20	XF40	MS60	MS63
2006	—	—	—	—	5.00	6.50

KM# 92 2 LARI

12.92 g., Copper-Nickel, 31 mm. **Obv:** Trophy cup, value and date **Rev:** UEFA Winners Cup and soccer player **Edge:** Plain

Date	Mintage	F12	VF20	XF40	MS60	MS63
2006	10,000	—	—	—	—	18.00

KM# 94 2 LARI
8.00 g., Bi-Metallic, 27 mm. **Obv:** National arms **Rev:** Large value **Edge:** Reeded and lettered

Date	Mintage	F12	VF20	XF40	MS60	MS63
2006					7.50	9.00

KM# 103 2 LARI
28.28 g., 0.925 Silver 0.8356 oz. ASW, 38.61 mm. **Obv:** Trophy cup, value and date **Rev:** UEFA Winners Cup and soccer player

Date	Mintage	F12	VF20	XF40	MS60	MS63
2006	6,000	PF63 60.00	PF65 65.00			

KM# 93 3 LARI
12.80 g., Copper-Nickel, 31 mm. **Obv:** Three oil wells **Rev:** Map with "Baku-Tbilisi-Ceyhan" route **Edge:** Lettered

Date	Mintage	F12	VF20	XF40	MS60	MS63
2006	3,000	—	—	—	—	25.00

KM# 102 3 LARI
28.28 g., Silver, 38.61 mm. **Obv:** Three oil wells **Rev:** Map with "Baku-Tbilisi-Ceyhan" route

Date	Mintage	F12	VF20	XF40	MS60	MS63
2006	5,000	PF63 60.00	PF65 65.00			

KM# 106 10 LARI
28.28 g., 0.925 Silver 0.8356 oz. ASW, 38.61 mm. **Subject:** St. George's Day **Obv:** Drawing of church by Don Christoforo de Castelli **Rev:** Church of St. george in Ilora

Date	Mintage	F12	VF20	XF40	MS60	MS63
2009	1,500	PF63 75.00	PF65 85.00			

KM# 104 20 LARI
28.28 g., 0.925 Silver 0.8356 oz. ASW, 38.61 mm. **Obv:** Two classical runners **Rev:** Exterior of Bird's Nest Stadium, torch

Date	Mintage	F12	VF20	XF40	MS60	MS63
2008	1,500	PF63 75.00	PF65 85.00			

KM# 105 20 LARI
8.50 g., 0.900 Gold 0.2444 oz. AGW, 25 mm. **Obv:** Two classical runners **Rev:** Exterior of Bird's Nest Stadium, torch

Date	Mintage	F12	VF20	XF40	MS60	MS63
2008	—	PF63 450	PF65 500			

BULLION COINAGE

KM# 96 10 LARI
3.11 g., 0.999 Gold 0.0992 oz. AGW, 16 mm. **Obv:** Ancient sailing vessel, trade route **Rev:** Golden Fleece

Date	Mintage	F12	VF20	XF40	MS60	MS63
2006	4,000	—	—	—	—	175

KM# 97 25 LARI
7.78 g., 0.999 Gold 0.2483 oz. AGW, 22 mm. **Obv:** Ancient sailing ship trade route map **Rev:** Golden Feece

Date	Mintage	F12	VF20	XF40	MS60	MS63
2006	—	—	—	—	—	450

KM# 98 50 LARI
28.00 g., 0.999 Gold 0.8935 oz. AGW, 28 mm. **Obv:** Ancient sailing ship, trade route map **Rev:** Golden Fleece

Date	Mintage	F12	VF20	XF40	MS60	MS63
2006	—	—	—	—	—	1,600

KM# 99 100 LARI
31.11 g., 0.999 Gold 0.9926 oz. AGW, 37 mm. **Obv:** Ancient sailing ship, trade route map **Rev:** Golden Fleece

Date	Mintage	F12	VF20	XF40	MS60	MS63
2006	—	—	—	—	—	1,750

KM# 100 300 LARI
155.50 g., 0.999 Gold 4.9623 oz. AGW, 50 mm. **Obv:** Ancient sailing ship, trade route map **Rev:** Golden Fleece

Date	Mintage	F12	VF20	XF40	MS60	MS63
2006	—	—	—	—	—	9,000

KM# 101 1000 LARI
311.00 g., 0.999 Gold 9.9246 oz. AGW, 60 mm. **Obv:** Ancient sailing ship, trade route map **Rev:** Golden Fleece

Date	Mintage	F12	VF20	XF40	MS60	MS63
2006	—	—	—	—	—	17,500

GERMANY-FEDERAL REPUBLIC

The Federal Republic of Germany, located in north-central Europe, has an area of 137,744 sq. mi. (356,910sq. km.) and a population of 81.1 million. Capital: Berlin. The economy centers about one of the world's foremost industrial establishments. Machinery, motor vehicles, iron, steel, yarns and fabrics are exported.

MINT MARKS
A - Berlin
D - Munich
F - Stuttgart
G - Karlsruhe
J - Hamburg

MONETARY SYSTEM
100 Pfennig = 1 Deutsche Mark (DM)

FEDERAL REPUBLIC
STANDARD COINAGE

KM# 105 PFENNIG
2.00 g., Copper Plated Steel, 16.5 mm. **Obv:** Five oak leaves, date below **Obv. Legend:** BUNDESREPUBLIK DEUTSCHLAND **Rev:** Denomination

Date	Mintage	F12	VF20	XF40	MS60	MS63
2001A In sets only	130,000	—	—	—	5.00	—
2001A	78,000	PF60 5.00				
2001D In sets only	130,000	—	—	—	5.00	—
2001D	78,000	PF60 5.00				
2001F In sets only	130,000	—	—	—	5.00	—
2001F	78,000	PF60 5.00				
2001G In sets only	130,000	—	—	—	5.00	—
2001G	78,000	PF60 5.00				
2001J In sets only	130,000	—	—	—	5.00	—
2001J	78,000	PF60 5.00				

KM# 106a 2 PFENNIG
2.90 g., Copper Plated Steel, 19.25 mm. **Obv:** Five oak leaves, date below **Rev:** Denomination

Date	Mintage	F12	VF20	XF40	MS60	MS63
2001A In sets only	130,000	—	—	—	5.00	—
2001A	78,000	PF65 5.00				
2001D In sets only	130,000	—	—	—	5.00	—
2001D	78,000	PF65 5.00				
2001F In sets only	130,000	—	—	—	5.00	—
2001F	78,000	PF65 5.00				
2001G In sets only	130,000	—	—	—	5.00	—
2001G	78,000	PF65 5.00				
2001J In sets only	130,000	—	—	—	5.00	—
2001J	78,000	PF65 5.00				

KM# 107 5 PFENNIG
3.00 g., Brass Clad Steel, 18.5 mm. **Obv:** Five oak leaves, date below **Obv. Legend:** BUNDESREPUBLIK DEUTSCHLAND **Rev:** Denomination

Date	Mintage	F12	VF20	XF40	MS60	MS63
2001A In sets only	130,000	—	—	—	5.00	—
2001A	78,000	PF60 5.00				
2001D In sets only	130,000	—	—	—	5.00	—
2001D	78,000	PF60 5.00				
2001F In sets only	130,000	—	—	—	5.00	—
2001F	78,000	PF60 5.00				
2001G In sets only	130,000	—	—	—	5.00	—
2001G	78,000	PF60 5.00				
2001J In sets only	130,000	—	—	—	5.00	—
2001J	78,000	PF60 5.00				

KM# 108 10 PFENNIG
4.00 g., Brass Clad Steel, 21.5 mm. **Obv:** Five oak leaves, date below **Obv. Legend:** BUNDESREPUBLIK DEUTSCHLAND **Rev:** Denomination **Edge:** Plain

Date	Mintage	F12	VF20	XF40	MS60	MS63
2001A In sets only	135,808	—	—	—	5.00	—
2001A	78,000	PF60 5.00				
2001D In sets only	135,808	—	—	—	5.00	—
2001D	78,000	PF60 5.00				
2001F In sets only	135,808	—	—	—	5.00	—
2001F	78,000	PF60 5.00				
2001G In sets only	153,018	—	—	—	5.00	—
2001G	78,000	PF60 5.00				
2001J In sets only	135,808	—	—	—	5.00	—
2001J	78,000	PF60 5.00				

KM# 109.2 50 PFENNIG
3.50 g., Copper-Nickel, 20 mm. **Obv:** Denomination **Obv. Legend:** BUNDESREPUBLIK DEUTSCHLAND **Rev:** Woman planting an oak seedling **Edge:** Plain

Date	Mintage	F12	VF20	XF40	MS60	MS63
2001A In sets only	130,000	—	—	—	10.00	—
2001A	78,000	PF60 10.00				
2001D In sets only	130,000	—	—	—	10.00	—
2001D	78,000	PF60 10.00				
2001F In sets only	130,000	—	—	—	10.00	—
2001F	78,000	PF60 10.00				
2001G In sets only	130,000	—	—	—	10.00	—
2001G	78,000	PF60 10.00				
2001J In sets only	130,000	—	—	—	10.00	—
2001J	78,000	PF60 10.00				

KM# 110 MARK
5.50 g., Copper-Nickel, 23.5 mm. **Obv:** Eagle **Rev:** Denomination flanked by oak leaves, date below

Date	Mintage	F12	VF20	XF40	MS60	MS63
2001A In sets only	130,000	—	—	—	15.00	—
2001A	78,000	PF60 15.00				

Date	Mintage	F12	VF20	XF40	MS60	MS63
2001D In sets only	130,000	—	—	—	15.00	—
2001D	78,000	PF60 15.00				
2001F In sets only	130,000	—	—	—	15.00	—
2001F	78,000	PF60 15.00				
2001G In sets only	130,000	—	—	—	15.00	—
2001G	78,000	PF60 15.00				
2001J In sets only	130,000	—	—	—	15.00	—
2001J	78,000	PF60 15.00				

KM# 203 MARK

12.00 g., 0.9999 Gold 0.3833 oz. AGW, 23.5 mm. **Subject:** Retirement of the Mark Currency **Obv:** Eagle **Rev:** Denomination flanked by oak leaves, date below **Edge:** Arabeskes

Date	Mintage	F12	VF20	XF40	MS60	MS63
2001A	200,000	PF60 750				
2001D	200,000	PF60 750				
2001G	200,000	PF60 750				
2001J	200,000	PF60 750				
2001F	200,000	PF60 750				

KM# 170 2 MARK

7.00 g., Copper-Nickel Clad Nickel, 26.75 mm. **Subject:** Ludwig Erhard **Obv:** Eagle above denomination **Rev:** Head facing dates **Edge Lettering:** EINIGKEIT UND RECHT UND FREIHEIT

Date	Mintage	F12	VF20	XF40	MS60	MS63
2001A In sets only	130,000	—	—	—	10.00	—
2001A	78,000	PF60 10.00				
2001D In sets only	130,000	—	—	—	10.00	—
2001D	78,000	PF60 10.00				
2001F In sets only	130,000	—	—	—	10.00	—
2001F	78,000	PF60 10.00				
2001G In sets only	130,000	—	—	—	10.00	—
2001G	78,000	PF60 10.00				
2001J In sets only	130,000	—	—	—	10.00	—
2001J	78,000	PF60 10.00				

KM# 175 2 MARK

7.04 g., Copper-Nickel Clad Nickel, 26.8 mm. **Subject:** Franz Joseph Strauss **Obv:** Eagle above denomination **Rev:** Head left divides dates **Edge Lettering:** EINIGKEIT UND RECHT UND FREIHEIT

Date	Mintage	F12	VF20	XF40	MS60	MS63
2001A In sets only	130,000	—	—	—	10.00	—
2001A	78,000	PF60 10.00				
2001D In sets only	130,000	—	—	—	10.00	—
2001D	78,000	PF60 10.00				
2001F In sets only	130,000	—	—	—	10.00	—
2001F	78,000	PF60 10.00				
2001G In sets only	130,000	—	—	—	10.00	—
2001G	78,000	PF60 10.00				
2001J In sets only	130,000	—	—	—	10.00	—
2001J	78,000	PF60 10.00				

KM# 183 2 MARK

7.00 g., Copper-Nickel Clad Nickel, 26.75 mm. **Subject:** Willy Brandt **Obv:** Eagle above denomination **Rev:** Head facing divides dates **Edge Lettering:** EINIGKEIT UND RECHT UND FREIHEIT

Date	Mintage	F12	VF20	XF40	MS60	MS63
2001A In sets only	130,000	—	—	—	10.00	—
2001A	78,000	PF60 10.00				
2001D In sets only	130,000	—	—	—	10.00	—
2001D	78,000	PF60 10.00				
2001F In sets only	130,000	—	—	—	10.00	—
2001F	78,000	PF60 10.00				
2001G In sets only	130,000	—	—	—	10.00	—
2001G	78,000	PF60 10.00				
2001J In sets only	130,000	—	—	—	10.00	—
2001J	78,000	PF60 10.00				

KM# 140.1 5 MARK

10.00 g., Copper-Nickel Clad Nickel, 29 mm. **Obv:** Denomination within rounded square therefore nicknamed "TV-Fives" **Rev:** Eagle above date **Edge Lettering:** EINIGKEIT UND RECHT UND FREIHEIT

Date	Mintage	F12	VF20	XF40	MS60	MS63
2001A In sets only	130,000	—	—	—	30.00	—
2001A	78,000	PF60 30.00				
2001D In sets only	130,000	—	—	—	30.00	—
2001D	78,000	PF60 30.00				
2001F In sets only	130,000	—	—	—	30.00	—
2001F	78,000	PF60 30.00				
2001G In sets only	130,000	—	—	—	30.00	—
2001G	78,000	PF60 30.00				
2001J In sets only	130,000	—	—	—	30.00	—
2001J	78,000	PF60 30.00				

COMMEMORATIVE COINAGE

KM# 205 10 MARK

15.50 g., 0.925 Silver 0.458 oz. ASW, 32.5 mm. **Subject:** 200th Anniversary - Birth of Albert Gustav Lortzing **Obv:** Stylized eagle above denomination **Rev:** Portrait and music **Edge Lettering:** * WILDSCHUETZ * UNDINE * ZAR UND ZIMMERMANN *

Date	Mintage	F12	VF20	XF40	MS60	MS63
2001J	2,500,000	—	—	17.50	18.50	
2001J	163,000	PF60 22.00				
2001	163,000	PF60 22.00				
2001	163,000	PF60 22.00				
2001	163,000	PF60 22.00				
2001	163,000	PF60 22.00				

KM# 206 10 MARK

15.50 g., 0.925 Silver 0.458 oz. ASW, 32.5 mm. **Subject:** Federal Court of Constitution: 50th Anniversary **Obv:** Stylized eagle above denomination **Rev:** Justice holding books and scale **Edge:** Lettered **Edge Lettering:** FÜR DAS GESAMTE DEUTSCHE VOLK

Date	Mintage	F12	VF20	XF40	MS60	MS63
2001G	2,000,000	—	—	17.50	18.50	
2001G	151,000	PF60 22.00				
2001A	151,000	PF60 22.00				
2001D	151,000	PF60 22.00				
2001F	151,000	PF60 22.00				
2001J	151,000	PF60 22.00				

KM# 204 10 MARK

15.50 g., 0.925 Silver 0.458 oz. ASW, 32.5 mm. **Obv:** Imperial eagle above denomination **Rev:** Naval Museum, Stralsund **Edge Lettering:** OHNE WASSER KEIN LEBEN

Date	Mintage	F12	VF20	XF40	MS60	MS63
2001A	2,500,000	—	—	17.50	18.50	
2001A	163,000	PF60 22.00				
2001D	163,000	PF60 22.00				
2001F	163,000	PF60 22.00				
2001G	163,000	PF60 22.00				
2001J	163,000	PF60 22.00				

EURO COINAGE
European Union Issues

KM# 207 EURO CENT

2.30 g., Copper Plated Steel, 16.25 mm. **Obv:** Oak leaves **Rev:** Denomination and globe **Edge:** Plain

Date	Mintage	F12	VF20	XF40	MS60	MS63
2002A	800,090,000	—	—	—	0.35	—
2002A	75,000	PF65 1.00				
2002D	840,090,000	—	—	—	0.35	—
2002D	75,000	PF65 1.00				
2002F	960,090,000	—	—	—	0.35	—
2002F	75,000	PF65 1.00				
2002G	560,090,000	—	—	—	0.35	—
2002G	75,000	PF65 1.00				
2002J	840,090,000	—	—	—	0.35	—
2002J	75,000	PF65 1.00				
2003A In sets only	90,000	—	—	—	4.50	—
2003A	75,000	PF65 1.00				
2003D In sets only	90,000	—	—	—	4.50	—
2003D	75,000	PF65 1.00				
2003F In sets only	90,000	—	—	—	4.50	—
2003F	75,000	PF65 1.00				
2003G In sets only	90,000	—	—	—	4.50	—
2003G	75,000	PF65 1.00				
2003J In sets only	90,000	—	—	—	4.50	—
2003J	75,000	PF65 1.00				
2004A	280,090,000	—	—	—	0.35	—
2004A	75,000	PF65 1.00				
2004D	294,090,000	—	—	—	0.35	—
2004D	75,000	PF65 1.00				
2004F	336,090,000	—	—	—	0.35	—
2004F	75,000	PF65 1.00				
2004G	196,090,000	—	—	—	0.35	—
2004G	75,000	PF65 1.00				
2004J	294,090,000	—	—	—	0.35	—
2004J	75,000	PF65 1.00				
2005A	120,090,000	—	—	—	0.35	—
2005A	75,000	PF65 1.00				
2005D	126,090,000	—	—	—	0.35	—
2005D	75,000	PF65 1.00				
2005F	144,090,000	—	—	—	0.35	—
2005F	75,000	PF65 1.00				
2005G	84,090,000	—	—	—	0.35	—
2005G	75,000	PF65 1.00				
2005J	126,090,000	—	—	—	0.35	—
2005J	75,000	PF65 1.00				
2006A In sets only	90,000	—	—	—	4.50	—
2006A	75,000	PF65 1.00				
2006D In sets only	90,000	—	—	—	4.50	—
2006D	75,000	PF65 1.00				
2006F In sets only	90,000	—	—	—	4.50	—
2006F	75,000	PF05 1.00				
2006G In sets only	90,000	—	—	—	4.50	—
2006G	75,000	PF65 1.00				
2006J In sets only	90,000	—	—	—	4.50	—
2006J	75,000	PF65 1.00				
2007A	119,490,000	—	—	—	0.35	—
2007A	75,000	PF65 1.00				
2007D	125,460,000	—	—	—	0.35	—
2007D	75,000	PF65 1.00				
2007F	143,370,000	—	—	—	0.35	—
2007F	75,000	PF65 1.00				
2007G	83,670,000	—	—	—	0.35	—
2007G	75,000	PF65 1.00				
2007J	125,460,000	—	—	—	0.35	—
2007J	75,000	PF65 1.00				
2008A	101,280,000	—	—	—	0.35	—
2008A	70,000	PF65 1.00				
2008D	106,340,000	—	—	—	0.35	—
2008D	70,000	PF65 1.00				
2008F	121,520,000	—	—	—	0.35	—
2008F	70,000	PF65 1.00				
2008G	70,920,000	—	—	—	0.35	—
2008G	70,000	PF65 1.00				
2008J	106,340,000	—	—	—	0.35	—
2008J	70,000	PF65 1.00				
2009A	100,060,000	—	—	—	0.35	—
2009A	50,000	PF65 1.00				
2009D	105,060,000	—	—	—	0.35	—
2009D	50,000	PF65 1.00				
2009F	120,060,000	—	—	—	0.35	—
2009F	50,000	PF65 1.00				
2009G	70,060,000	—	—	—	0.35	—
2009G	50,000	PF65 1.00				
2009J	105,060,000	—	—	—	0.35	—
2009J	50,000	PF65 1.00				
2010A	94,454,000	—	—	—	0.35	—
2010A	45,150	PF65 1.00				
2010D	99,167,000	—	—	—	0.35	—
2010D	40,120	PF65 1.00				
2010F	113,327,000	—	—	—	0.35	—
2010F	40,120	PF65 1.00				
2010G	66,127,000	—	—	—	0.35	—
2010G	40,120	PF65 1.00				
2010J	99,167,000	—	—	—	0.35	—
2010J	40,120	PF65 1.00				
2011A	118,448,000	—	—	—	0.35	—
2011A	43,000	PF65 1.25				
2011D	124,364,000	—	—	—	0.35	—
2011D	37,000	PF65 1.25				
2011F	142,124,000	—	—	—	0.35	—
2011F	37,000	PF65 1.25				
2011G	82,924,000	—	—	—	0.35	—
2011G	37,000	PF65 1.25				
2011J	124,364,000	—	—	—	0.35	—
2011J	37,000	PF65 1.25				
2012A	104,245,000	—	—	—	0.35	—
2012A	40,000	PF65 1.25				
2012D	109,450,000	—	—	—	0.35	—
2012D	Est. 40000	PF65 1.25				

Date	Mintage	F12	VF20	XF40	MS60	MS63
2012F	125,080,000	—	—	—	0.35	—
2012F	Est. 40000	PF65 1.25				
2012G	Est. 72990	—	—	—	0.35	—
2012G	Est. 40000	PF65 1.25				
2012J	109,450,000	—	—	—	0.35	—
2012J	32,000	PF65 1.25				
2013A	Est. 60045000	—	—	—	0.20	—
2013A	35,000	PF65 1.25				
2013D	—	—	—	—	0.20	—
2013D	Est. 40000	PF65 1.25				
2013F	Est. 72040000	—	—	—	0.20	—
2013F	Est. 40000	PF65 1.25				
2013G	—	—	—	—	0.20	—
2013G	Est. 40000	PF65 1.25				
2013J	Est. 63040000	—	—	—	0.20	—
2013J	Est. 40000	PF65 1.25				

KM# 208 2 EURO CENT
3.06 g., Copper Plated Steel, 18.75 mm. **Obv:** Oak leaves **Rev:** Denomination and globe **Edge:** Grooved

Date	Mintage	F12	VF20	XF40	MS60	MS63
2002A	360,090,000	—	—	—	0.50	—
2002A	75,000	PF65 1.50				
2002D	483,090,000	—	—	—	0.50	—
2002D	75,000	PF65 1.50				
2002F	507,890,000	—	—	—	0.50	—
2002F	75,000	PF65 1.50				
2002G	311,890,000	—	—	—	0.50	—
2002G	75,000	PF65 1.50				
2002J	419,490,000	—	—	—	0.50	—
2002J	75,000	PF65 1.50				
2003A	200,090,000	—	—	—	0.50	—
2003A	75,000	PF65 1.50				
2003D	105,090,000	—	—	—	0.50	—
2003D	75,000	PF65 1.50				
2003F	164,290,000	—	—	—	0.50	—
2003F	75,000	PF65 1.50				
2003G	80,290,000	—	—	—	0.50	—
2003G	75,000	PF65 1.50				
2003J	168,690,000	—	—	—	0.50	—
2003J	75,000	PF65 1.50				
2004A	127,090,000	—	—	—	0.50	—
2004A	75,000	PF65 1.50				
2004D	133,440,000	—	—	—	0.50	—
2004D	75,000	PF65 1.50				
2004F	152,490,000	—	—	—	0.50	—
2004F	75,000	PF65 1.50				
2004G	88,990,000	—	—	—	0.50	—
2004G	75,000	PF65 1.50				
2004J	133,440,000	—	—	—	0.50	—
2004J	75,000	PF65 1.50				
2005A	73,090,000	—	—	—	0.50	—
2005A	75,000	PF65 1.50				
2005D	76,740,000	—	—	—	0.50	—
2005D	75,000	PF65 1.50				
2005F	87,690,000	—	—	—	0.50	—
2005F	75,000	PF65 1.50				
2005G	51,590,000	—	—	—	0.50	—
2005G	75,000	PF65 1.50				
2005J	76,740,000	—	—	—	0.50	—
2005J	75,000	PF65 1.50				
2006A	108,090,000	—	—	—	0.50	—
2006A	75,000	PF65 1.50				
2006D	113,490,000	—	—	—	0.50	—
2006D	75,000	PF65 1.50				
2006F	129,690,000	—	—	—	0.50	—
2006F	75,000	PF65 1.50				
2006G	75,690,000	—	—	—	0.50	—
2006G	75,000	PF65 1.50				
2006J	148,490,000	—	—	—	0.50	—
2006J	75,000	PF65 1.50				
2007A	100,090,000	—	—	—	0.50	—
2007A	75,000	PF65 1.50				
2007D	105,090,000	—	—	—	0.50	—
2007D	75,000	PF65 1.50				
2007F	120,090,000	—	—	—	0.50	—
2007F	75,000	PF65 1.50				
2007G	70,090,000	—	—	—	0.50	—
2007G	75,000	PF65 1.50				
2007J	105,090,000	—	—	—	0.50	—
2007J	75,000	PF65 1.50				
2008A	80,080,000	—	—	—	0.50	—
2008A	70,000	PF65 1.50				
2008D	84,080,000	—	—	—	0.50	—
2008D	70,000	PF65 1.50				
2008F	96,080,000	—	—	—	0.50	—
2008F	70,000	PF65 1.50				
2008G	56,080,000	—	—	—	0.50	—
2008G	70,000	PF65 1.50				
2008J	84,080,000	—	—	—	0.50	—
2008J	70,000	PF65 1.50				

Date	Mintage	F12	VF20	XF40	MS60	MS63
2009A	59,060,000	—	—	—	0.50	—
2009A	50,000	PF65 1.50				
2009D	62,010,000	—	—	—	0.50	—
2009D	50,000	PF65 1.50				
2009F	70,860,000	—	—	—	0.50	—
2009F	50,000	PF65 1.50				
2009G	41,360,000	—	—	—	0.50	—
2009G	50,000	PF65 1.50				
2009J	62,010,000	—	—	—	0.50	—
2009J	50,000	PF65 1.50				
2010A	72,854,000	—	—	—	0.50	—
2010A	45,150	PF65 1.50				
2010D	76,487,000	—	—	—	0.50	—
2010D	40,120	PF65 1.50				
2010F	87,407,000	—	—	—	0.50	—
2010F	40,120	PF65 1.50				
2010G	51,007,000	—	—	—	0.50	—
2010G	40,120	PF65 1.50				
2010J	76,487,000	—	—	—	0.50	—
2010J	40,120	PF65 1.50				
2011A	100,448,000	—	—	—	0.50	—
2011A	Est. 43000	PF65 1.50				
2011D	105,464,000	—	—	—	0.50	—
2011D	37,000	PF65 1.50				
2011F	120,524,000	—	—	—	0.50	—
2011F	Est. 37000	PF65 1.50				
2011G	70,324,000	—	—	—	0.50	—
2011G	37,000	PF65 1.50				
2011G	105,464,000	—	—	—	0.50	—
2011J	Est. 37000	PF65 1.50				
2012A	Est. 77490000	—	—	—	0.50	—
2012A	Est. 40000	PF65 1.75				
2012D	Est. 81320000	—	—	—	0.50	—
2012D	Est. 40000	PF65 1.75				
2012F	Est. 92930000	—	—	—	0.50	—
2012F	32,000	PF65 1.75				
2012G	Est. 54230000	—	—	—	0.50	—
2012G	Est. 40000	PF65 1.75				
2012J	Est. 81320000	—	—	—	0.50	—
2012J	Est. 40000	PF65 1.75				
2013A	Est. 60045000	—	—	—	0.50	—
2013A	Est. 35000	PF65 1.75				
2013D	Est. 63040000	—	—	—	0.50	—
2013D	Est. 30000	PF65 1.75				
2013F	Est. 72040000	—	—	—	0.50	—
2013F	Est. 30000	PF65 1.75				
2013G	Est. 42040000	—	—	—	0.50	—
2013G	Est. 30000	PF65 1.75				
2013J	Est. 63040000	—	—	—	0.50	—
2013J	Est. 30000	PF65 1.75				

KM# 209 5 EURO CENT
3.92 g., Copper Plated Steel, 21.25 mm. **Obv:** Oak leaves **Rev:** Denomination and globe **Edge:** Plain

Date	Mintage	F12	VF20	XF40	MS60	MS63
2002A	480,090,000	—	—	—	0.75	—
2002A	75,000	PF65 2.00				
2002D	504,090,000	—	—	—	0.75	—
2002D	75,000	PF65 2.00				
2002F	576,090,000	—	—	—	0.75	—
2002F	75,000	PF65 2.00				
2002G	336,090,000	—	—	—	0.75	—
2002G	75,000	PF65 2.00				
2002J	504,090,000	—	—	—	0.75	—
2002J	90,000	PF65 2.00				
2003A In sets only	75,000	—	—	—	4.50	—
2003A	90,000	PF65 2.00				
2003D In sets only	75,000	—	—	—	4.50	—
2003D	90,000	PF65 2.00				
2003F In sets only	75,000	—	—	—	4.50	—
2003F	90,000	PF65 2.00				
2003G In sets only	75,000	—	—	—	4.50	—
2003G	90,000	PF65 2.00				
2003J In sets only	90,000	—	—	—	4.50	—
2003J	75,000	PF65 2.00				
2004A	112,090,000	—	—	—	0.75	—
2004A	75,000	PF65 2.00				
2004D	117,690,000	—	—	—	0.75	—
2004D	75,000	PF65 2.00				
2004F	134,490,000	—	—	—	0.75	—
2004F	75,000	PF65 2.00				
2004G	78,490,000	—	—	—	0.75	—
2004G	75,000	PF65 2.00				
2004J	117,690,000	—	—	—	0.75	—
2004J	75,000	PF65 2.00				
2005A	44,090,000	—	—	—	0.75	—
2005A	75,000	PF65 2.00				
2005D	46,290,000	—	—	—	0.75	—
2005D	75,000	PF65 2.00				
2005F	52,890,000	—	—	—	0.75	—

Date	Mintage	F12	VF20	XF40	MS60	MS63
2005F	75,000	PF65 2.00				
2005G	30,890,000	—	—	—	0.75	—
2005G	75,000	PF65 2.00				
2005J	46,290,000	—	—	—	0.75	—
2005J	75,000	PF65 2.00				
2006A	27,090,000	—	—	—	0.75	—
2006A	75,000	PF65 2.00				
2006D	28,440,000	—	—	—	0.75	—
2006D	75,000	PF65 2.00				
2006F	32,490,000	—	—	—	0.75	—
2006F	75,000	PF65 2.00				
2006G	18,990,000	—	—	—	0.75	—
2006G	75,000	PF65 2.00				
2006J	28,440,000	—	—	—	0.75	—
2006J	75,000	PF65 2.00				
2007A	52,490,000	—	—	—	0.75	—
2007A	75,000	PF65 2.00				
2007D	55,110,000	—	—	—	0.75	—
2007D	75,000	PF65 2.00				
2007F	62,970,000	—	—	—	0.75	—
2007F	75,000	PF65 2.00				
2007G	36,770,000	—	—	—	0.75	—
2007G	75,000	PF65 2.00				
2007J	55,110,000	—	—	—	0.75	—
2007J	75,000	PF65 2.00				
2008A	29,280,000	—	—	—	0.75	—
2008A	70,000	PF65 2.00				
2008D	30,740,000	—	—	—	0.75	—
2008D	70,000	PF65 2.00				
2008F	35,120,000	—	—	—	0.75	—
2008F	70,000	PF65 2.00				
2008G	24,520,000	—	—	—	0.75	—
2008G	70,000	PF65 2.00				
2008J	30,740,000	—	—	—	0.75	—
2008J	70,000	PF65 2.00				
2009A	39,660,000	—	—	—	0.75	—
2009A	50,000	PF65 2.00				
2009D	41,640,000	—	—	—	0.75	—
2009D	50,000	PF65 2.00				
2009F	47,580,000	—	—	—	0.75	—
2009F	50,000	PF65 2.00				
2009G	27,780,000	—	—	—	0.75	—
2009G	50,000	PF65 2.00				
2009J	41,640,000	—	—	—	0.75	—
2009J	50,000	PF65 2.00				
2010A	39,854,000	—	—	—	0.75	—
2010A	45,150	PF65 2.00				
2010D	41,837,000	—	—	—	0.75	—
2010D	40,120	PF65 2.00				
2010F	47,807,000	—	—	—	0.75	—
2010F	40,120	PF65 2.00				
2010G	20,903,000	—	—	—	0.75	—
2010G	40,120	PF65 2.00				
2010J	41,837,000	—	—	—	0.75	—
2010J	40,120	PF65 2.00				
2011A	59,248,000	—	—	—	0.75	—
2011A	Est. 43000	PF65 2.25				
2011D	62,204,000	—	—	—	0.75	—
2011D	Est. 37000	PF65 2.25				
2011F	71,084,000	—	—	—	0.75	—
2011F	Est. 37000	PF65 2.25				
2011G	41,484,000	—	—	—	0.75	—
2011G	37,000	PF65 2.25				
2011J	62,204,000	—	—	—	0.75	—
2011J	Est. 37000	PF65 2.25				
2012A	41,845,000	—	—	—	0.75	—
2012A	40,000	PF65 2.25				
2012D	43,930,000	—	—	—	0.75	—
2012D	Est. 40000	PF65 2.25				
2012F	50,200,000	—	—	—	0.75	—
2012F	Est. 40000	PF65 2.25				
2012G	29,300,000	—	—	—	0.75	—
2012G	Est. 40000	PF65 2.25				
2012J	43,930,000	—	—	—	0.75	—
2012J	Est. 40000	PF65 2.25				
2013A	Est. 32040000	—	—	—	0.40	—
2013A	Est. 40000	PF65 2.25				
2013D	Est. 33640000	—	—	—	0.40	—
2013D	Est. 40000	PF65 2.25				
2013F	Est. 38440000	—	—	—	0.40	—
2013F	Est. 40000	PF65 2.25				
2013G	Est. 22040000	—	—	—	0.40	—
2013G	Est. 40000	PF65 2.25				
2013J	Est. 33640000	—	—	—	0.40	—
2013J	Est. 40000	PF65 2.50				

KM# 210 10 EURO CENT
4.10 g., Brass, 19.75 mm. **Obv:** Brandenburg Gate **Rev:** Denomination and map **Edge:** Reeded

Date	Mintage	F12	VF20	XF40	MS60	MS63
2002A	696,240,000	—	—	—	0.75	—

Date	Mintage	F12	VF20	XF40	MS60	MS63
2002A	75,000	PF65 2.00				
2002D	722,040,000	—	—	—	0.75	—
2002D	75,000	PF65 2.00				
2002F	838,890,000	—	—	—	0.75	—
2002F	75,000	PF65 2.00				
2002G	494,390,000	—	—	—	0.75	—
2002G	75,000	PF65 2.00				
2002J	758,730,000	—	—	—	0.75	—
2002J	75,000	PF65 2.00				
2003A	50,750,000	—	—	—	1.25	—
2003A	75,000	PF65 2.00				
2003D	50,940,000				1.25	
2003D	75,000	PF65 2.00				
2003F	6,090,000	—	—	—	2.00	—
2003F	75,000	PF65 2.00				
2003G	13,090,000	—	—	—	1.25	—
2003G	75,000	PF65 2.00				
2003J	25,590,000	—	—	—	1.25	—
2003J	75,000	PF65 2.00				
2004A In sets only	99,000	—	—	—	4.50	—
2004A	75,000	PF65 2.00				
2004D	11,290,000	—	—	—	1.25	—
2004D	75,000	PF65 2.00				
2004F	51,450,000	—	—	—	1.25	—
2004F	75,000	PF65 2.00				
2004G	15,550,000	—	—	—	1.25	—
2004G	75,000	PF65 2.00				
2004J In sets only	90,000	—	—	—	4.50	—
2004J	75,000	PF65 2.00				
2005A In sets only	90,000	—	—	—	4.50	—
2005A	75,000	PF65 2.00				
2005D In sets only	90,000	—	—	—	4.50	—
2005D	75,000	PF65 2.00				
2005F In sets only	90,000	—	—	—	4.50	—
2005F	75,000	PF65 2.00				
2005G In sets only	90,000	—	—	—	4.50	—
2005G	75,000	PF65 2.00				
2005J In sets only	90,000	—	—	—	4.50	—
2005J	75,000	PF65 2.00				
2006A In sets only	90,000	—	—	—	4.50	—
2006A	75,000	PF65 2.00				
2006D In sets only	90,000	—	—	—	4.50	—
2006D	75,000	PF65 2.00				
2006F In sets only	90,000	—	—	—	4.50	—
2006F	75,000	PF65 2.00				
2006G In sets only	90,000	—	—	—	4.50	—
2006G	75,000	PF65 2.00				
2006J In sets only	90,000	—	—	—	4.50	—
2006J	75,000	PF65 2.00				

KM# 254 10 EURO CENT
4.10 g., Brass, 19.75 mm. **Obv:** Brandenburg Gate **Rev:** Relief map of Western Europe, stars, lines and value **Edge:** Reeded

Date	Mintage	F12	VF20	XF40	MS60	MS63
2007A In sets only	90,000	—	—	—	4.50	—
2007A	75,000	PF65 2.00				
2007D In sets only	90,000	—	—	—	4.50	—
2007D	75,000	PF65 2.00				
2007F In sets only	90,000	—	—	—	4.50	—
2007F	75,000	PF65 2.00				
2007G In sets only	90,000	—	—	—	4.50	—
2007G	75,000	PF65 2.00				
2007J In sets only	90,000	—	—	—	4.50	—
2007J	75,000	PF65 2.00				
2008A In sets only	80,000	—	—	—	4.50	—
2008A	70,000	PF65 2.00				
2008D In sets only	80,000	—	—	—	4.50	—
2008D	70,000	PF65 2.00				
2008F In sets only	80,000	—	—	—	4.50	—
2008F	70,000	PF65 2.00				
2008G In sets only	80,000	—	—	—	4.50	—
2008G	70,000	PF65 2.00				
2008J In sets only	80,000	—	—	—	4.50	—
2008J	70,000	PF65 2.00				
2009A In sets only	60,000	—	—	—	4.50	—
2009A	50,000	PF65 2.00				
2009D In sets only	60,000	—	—	—	4.50	—
2009D	50,000	PF65 2.00				
2009F In sets only	60,000	—	—	—	4.50	—
2009F	50,000	PF65 2.00				
2009G In sets only	60,000	—	—	—	4.50	—
2009G	50,000	PF65 2.00				
2009J In sets only	60,000	—	—	—	4.50	—
2009J	50,000	PF65 2.00				
2010A In sets only	53,800	—	—	—	4.00	—
2010A	45,150	PF65 2.00				
2010D In sets only	46,800	—	—	—	4.00	—
2010D	40,120	PF65 2.00				
2010F In sets only	46,800	—	—	—	4.00	—
2010F	40,120	PF65 2.00				
2010G In sets only	46,800	—	—	—	4.00	—
2010G	40,120	PF65 2.00				
2010J In sets only	46,800	—	—	—	4.00	—
2010J	40,120	PF65 2.00				
2011A In sets only	Est. 55000	—	—	—	4.00	—
2011A	48,000	PF65 2.75				
2011D In sets only	44,000	—	—	—	4.00	—
2011D	37,000	PF65 2.75				
2011F In sets only	44,000	—	—	—	4.00	—

Date	Mintage	F12	VF20	XF40	MS60	MS63
2011F	37,000	PF65 2.75				
2011G In sets only	44,000	—	—	—	4.00	—
2011G	37,000	PF65 2.75				
2011J In sets only	44,000	—	—	—	4.00	—
2011J	37,000	PF65 2.75				
2012A In sets only	40,000	—	—	—	3.00	—
2012A	—	PF65 2.75				
2012D In sets only	Est. 50000	—	—	—	3.00	—
2012D	Est. 40000	PF65 2.75				
2012F In sets only	Est. 50000	—	—	—	3.00	—
2012F	Est. 40000	PF65 2.75				
2012G In sets only	Est. 50000	—	—	—	3.00	—
2012G	Est. 40000	PF65 2.75				
2012J In sets only	Est. 50000	—	—	—	3.00	—
2012J	Est. 40000	PF65 2.75				
2013A In sets only	Est. 40000	—	—	—	—	—
2013A	35,000	PF65 2.75				
2013D In sets only	Est. 35000	—	—	—	—	—
2013D	30,000	PF65 2.75				
2013F In sets only	Est. 35000	—	—	—	—	—
2013F	Est. 40000	PF65 2.75				
2013F In sets only	Est. 30000	—	—	—	—	—
2013G	—	PF65 2.75				
2013J In sets only	Est. 35000	—	—	—	—	—
2013J	Est. 40000	PF65 2.75				

KM# 211 20 EURO CENT
5.74 g., Brass, 22.25 mm. **Obv:** Brandenburg Gate **Rev:** Denomination and map **Edge:** Notched

Date	Mintage	F12	VF20	XF40	MS60	MS63
2002A	378,240,000	—	—	—	1.00	—
2002A	75,000	PF65 3.00				
2002D	367,090,000	—	—	—	1.00	—
2002D	75,000	PF65 3.00				
2002F	421,690,000	—	—	—	1.00	—
2002F	75,000	PF65 3.00				
2002G	251,990,000	—	—	—	1.00	—
2002G	75,000	PF65 3.00				
2002J	441,090,000	—	—	—	1.00	—
2002J	75,000	PF65 3.00				
2003A	41,950,000	—	—	—	1.00	—
2003A	75,000	PF65 3.00				
2003D	24,190,000	—	—	—	1.00	—
2003D	75,000	PF65 3.00				
2003F	82,490,000	—	—	—	1.00	—
2003F	75,000	PF65 3.00				
2003G	42,190,000	—	—	—	1.00	—
2003G	75,000	PF65 3.00				
2003J In sets only	90,000	—	—	—	4.50	—
2003J	75,000	PF65 3.00				
2004A In sets only	90,000	—	—	—	4.50	—
2004A	75,000	PF65 3.00				
2004D	49,850,000	—	—	—	2.50	—
2004D	75,000	PF65 3.00				
2004F In sets only	90,000	—	—	—	4.50	—
2004F	75,000	PF65 3.00				
2004G In sets only	90,000	—	—	—	4.50	—
2004G	75,000	PF65 3.00				
2004J In sets only	90,000	—	—	—	4.50	—
2004J	75,000	PF65 3.00				
2005A	8,090,000	—	—	—	1.00	—
2005A	75,000	PF65 3.00				
2005D	8,490,000	—	—	—	1.00	—
2005D	75,000	PF65 3.00				
2005F	9,690,000	—	—	—	1.00	—
2005F	75,000	PF65 3.00				
2005G	5,690,000	—	—	—	1.00	—
2005G	75,000	PF65 3.00				
2005J	8,490,000	—	—	—	1.00	—
2005J	75,000	PF65 3.00				
2006A	39,090,000	—	—	—	1.00	—
2006A	75,000	PF65 3.00				
2006D	41,040,000	—	—	—	1.00	—
2006D	75,000	PF65 3.00				
2006F	46,890,000	—	—	—	1.00	—
2006F	75,000	PF65 3.00				
2006G	27,390,000	—	—	—	1.00	—
2006G	75,000	PF65 3.00				
2006J	41,040,000	—	—	—	1.00	—
2006J	75,000	PF65 3.00				
2007F Error die paring	—	—	—	—	60.00	75.00

KM# 255 20 EURO CENT
5.74 g., Brass, 22.25 mm. **Obv:** Brandenburg Gate **Rev:** Relief map of Western Europe, stars, lines and value **Edge:** Notched

Date	Mintage	F12	VF20	XF40	MS60	MS63
2007A	21,690,000	—	—	—	1.00	—
2007A	75,000	PF65 3.00				
2007D	22,770,000	—	—	—	1.00	—
2007D	75,000	PF65 3.00				
2007F	26,010,000	—	—	—	1.00	—
2007F	75,000	PF65 3.00				
2007G	15,210,000	—	—	—	1.00	—
2007G	75,000	PF65 3.00				
2007J	23,020,000	—	—	—	1.00	—
2007J	75,000	PF65 3.00				
2008A	15,880,000	—	—	—	1.00	—
2008A	70,000	PF65 3.00				
2008D	16,670,000	—	—	—	1.00	—
2008D	70,000	PF65 3.00				
2008F	19,040,000	—	—	—	1.00	—
2008F	70,000	PF65 3.00				
2008G	11,140,000	—	—	—	1.00	—
2008G	70,000	PF65 3.00				
2008J	16,420,000	—	—	—	1.00	—
2008J	70,000	PF65 3.00				
2009A	21,660,000	—	—	—	1.00	—
2009A	50,000	PF65 3.00				
2009D	22,740,000	—	—	—	1.00	—
2009D	50,000	PF65 3.00				
2009F	25,980,000	—	—	—	1.00	—
2009F	50,000	PF65 3.00				
2009G	15,180,000	—	—	—	1.00	—
2009G	50,000	PF65 3.00				
2009J	22,740,000	—	—	—	1.00	—
2009J	50,000	PF65 3.00				
2010A	24,454,000	—	—	—	1.00	—
2010A	45,150	PF65 3.00				
2010D	25,667,000	—	—	—	1.00	—
2010D	40,120	PF65 3.00				
2010F	29,327,000	—	—	—	1.00	—
2010F	40,120	PF65 3.00				
2010G	17,127,000	—	—	—	1.00	—
2010G	40,120	PF65 3.00				
2010J	25,667,000	—	—	—	1.00	—
2010J	40,120	PF65 3.00				
2011A	33,048,000	—	—	—	1.00	—
2011A	43,000	PF65 3.00				
2011D	34,694,000	—	—	—	1.00	—
2011D	37,000	PF65 3.00				
2011F	39,644,000	—	—	—	1.00	—
2011F	37,000	PF65 3.00				
2011G	23,144,000	—	—	—	1.00	—
2011G	37,000	PF65 3.00				
2011J	34,694,000	—	—	—	1.00	—
2011J	37,000	PF65 3.00				
2012A	21,245,000	—	—	—	1.00	—
2012A	Est. 40000	PF65 3.00				
2012D	Est. 23810000	—	—	—	1.00	—
2012D	32,000	PF65 3.00				
2012F	Est. 25490000	—	—	—	1.00	—
2012F	Est. 40000	PF65 3.00				
2012G	Est. 11240000	—	—	—	1.00	—
2012G	Est. 40000	PF65 3.00				
2012J	Est. 22310000	—	—	—	1.00	—
2012J	Est. 40000	PF65 3.00				
2013A	Est. 16045000	—	—	—	0.70	—
2013A	35,000	PF65 3.00				
2013D	Est. 16840000	—	—	—	0.70	—
2013D	Est. 40000	PF65 3.00				
2013F	Est. 19240000	—	—	—	0.70	—
2013F	30,000	PF65 3.00				
2013G	—	—	—	—	0.70	—
2013G	Est. 40000	PF65 3.00				
2013J	Est. 16840000	—	—	—	0.70	—
2013J	Est. 40000	PF65 3.00				

KM# 212 50 EURO CENT
7.80 g., Brass, 24.25 mm. **Obv:** Brandenburg Gate **Rev:** Denomination and map **Edge:** Reeded

Date	Mintage	F12	VF20	XF40	MS60	MS63
2002A	337,840,000	—	—	—	1.75	—
2002A	75,000	PF65 4.00				
2002D	370,330,000	—	—	—	1.75	—
2002D	75,000	PF65 4.00				
2002F	430,570,000	—	—	—	1.75	—
2002F	75,000	PF65 4.00				
2002G	256,650,000	—	—	—	1.75	—
2002G	75,000	PF65 4.00				
2002J	401,490,000	—	—	—	1.75	—
2002J	75,000	PF65 4.00				
2003A In sets only	90,000	—	—	—	4.50	—

Date	Mintage	F12	VF20	XF40	MS60	MS63
2003A	75,000	PF65 4.00				
2003D	70,710,000	—	—	—	2.00	—
2003D	75,000	PF65 4.00				
2003F In sets only	90,000	—	—	—	4.50	—
2003F	75,000	PF65 4.00				
2003G In sets only	90,000	—	—	—	4.50	—
2003G	75,000	PF65 4.00				
2003J	39,690,000	—	—	—	1.75	—
2003J	75,000	PF65 4.00				
2004A	82,350,000	—	—	—	1.75	—
2004A	75,000	PF65 4.00				
2004D In sets only	90,000	—	—	—	4.50	—
2004D	75,000	PF65 4.00				
2004F	73,610,000	—	—	—	1.75	—
2004F	75,000	PF65 4.00				
2004G	37,530,000	—	—	—	1.75	—
2004G	75,000	PF65 4.00				
2004J In sets only	90,000	—	—	—	4.50	—
2004J	75,000	PF65 4.00				
2005A In sets only	90,000	—	—	—	4.50	—
2005A	75,000	PF65 4.00				
2005D In sets only	90,000	—	—	—	4.50	—
2005D	75,000	PF65 4.00				
2005F In sets only	90,000	—	—	—	4.50	—
2005F	75,000	PF65 4.00				
2005G In sets only	90,000	—	—	—	4.50	—
2005G	75,000	PF65 4.00				
2005J In sets only	90,000	—	—	—	4.50	—
2005J	75,000	PF65 4.00				
2006A In sets only	90,000	—	—	—	4.50	—
2006A	75,000	PF65 4.00				
2006D In sets only	90,000	—	—	—	4.50	—
2006D	75,000	PF65 4.00				
2006F In sets only	90,000	—	—	—	4.50	—
2006F	75,000	PF65 4.00				
2006G In sets only	90,000	—	—	—	4.50	—
2006G	75,000	PF65 4.00				
2006J In sets only	90,000	—	—	—	4.50	—
2006J	75,000	PF65 4.00				

KM# 256 50 EURO CENT

7.80 g., Brass, 24.25 mm. **Obv:** Brandenburg Gate **Rev:** Relief map of Western Europe, stars, lines and value **Edge:** Reeded

Date	Mintage	F12	VF20	XF40	MS60	MS63
2007A In sets only	90,000	—	—	—	4.50	—
2007A	75,000	PF65 4.00				
2007D In sets only	90,000	—	—	—	4.50	—
2007D	75,000	PF65 4.00				
2007F In sets only	90,000	—	—	—	4.50	—
2007F	75,000	PF65 4.00				
2007G In sets only	90,000	—	—	—	4.50	—
2007G	75,000	PF65 4.00				
2007J In sets only	90,000	—	—	—	4.50	—
2007J	75,000	PF65 4.00				
2008A In sets only	80,000	—	—	—	4.50	—
2008A	70,000	PF65 4.00				
2008D In sets only	80,000	—	—	—	4.50	—
2008D	70,000	PF65 4.00				
2008F In sets only	80,000	—	—	—	4.50	—
2008F	70,000	PF65 4.00				
2008G In sets only	80,000	—	—	—	4.50	—
2008G	70,000	PF65 4.00				
2008J In sets only	80,000	—	—	—	4.50	—
2008J	70,000	PF65 4.00				
2009A In sets only	60,000	—	—	—	4.50	—
2009A	50,000	PF65 4.00				
2009D In sets only	60,000	—	—	—	4.50	—
2009D	50,000	PF65 4.00				
2009F In sets only	60,000	—	—	—	4.50	—
2009F	50,000	PF65 4.00				
2009G In sets only	60,000	—	—	—	4.50	—
2009G	50,000	PF65 4.00				
2009J In sets only	60,000	—	—	—	4.50	—
2009J	50,000	PF65 4.00				
2010A In sets only	53,800	—	—	—	4.00	—
2010A	45,150	PF65 4.00				
2010D In sets only	46,800	—	—	—	4.00	—
2010D	40,120	PF65 4.00				
2010F In sets only	46,800	—	—	—	4.00	—
2010F	40,120	PF65 4.00				
2010G In sets only	46,800	—	—	—	4.00	—
2010G	40,120	PF65 4.00				
2010J In sets only	46,800	—	—	—	4.00	—
2010J	40,120	PF65 4.00				
2011A In sets only	48,000	—	—	—	4.00	—
2011A	Est. 43000	PF65 4.00				
2011D In sets only	Est. 44000	—	—	—	4.00	—
2011D	37,000	PF65 4.00				
2011F In sets only	Est. 44000	—	—	—	4.00	—
2011F	37,000	PF65 4.00				
2011G In sets only	Est. 44000	—	—	—	4.00	—
2011G	Est. 37000	PF65 4.00				
2011J In sets only	Est. 44000	—	—	—	4.00	—
2011J	Est. 37000	PF65 4.00				
2012A In sets only	40,000	—	—	—	4.00	—
2012A	Est. 40000	PF65 4.00				
2012D In sets only	40,000	—	—	—	4.00	—
2012D	Est. 40000	PF65 4.00				
2012F In sets only	Est. 50000	—	—	—	4.00	—

Date	Mintage	F12	VF20	XF40	MS60	MS63
2012F	Est. 40000	PF65 4.00				
2012G In sets only	Est. 50000	—	—	—	4.00	—
2012G	Est. 40000	PF65 4.00				
2012J In sets only	Est. 50000	—	—	—	4.00	—
2012J	Est. 40000	PF65 4.00				
2013A In sets only	Est. 40000	—	—	—	—	—
2013A	Est. 40000	PF65 4.00				
2013D In sets only	Est. 35000	—	—	—	4.00	—
2013D	Est. 40000	PF65 4.00				
2013F In sets only	Est. 35000	—	—	—	4.00	—
2013F	Est. 40000	PF65 4.00				
2013G In sets only	Est. 35000	—	—	—	4.00	—
2013G	Est. 40000	PF65 4.00				
2013J In sets only	Est. 35000	—	—	—	4.00	—
2013J	Est. 40000	PF65 4.00				

KM# 213 EURO

7.50 g., Bi-Metallic, 23.25 mm. **Obv:** Stylized eagle **Rev:** Denomination over map **Edge:** Segmented reeding

Date	Mintage	F12	VF20	XF40	MS60	MS63
2002A	367,990,000	—	—	—	2.50	—
2002A	75,000	PF65 6.50				
2002D	372,690,000	—	—	—	2.50	—
2002D	75,000	PF65 6.50				
2002F	439,890,000	—	—	—	2.50	—
2002F	75,000	PF65 6.50				
2002G	266,440,000	—	—	—	2.50	—
2002G	75,000	PF65 6.50				
2002J	372,400,000	—	—	—	2.50	—
2002J	75,000	PF65 6.50				
2003A	50,340,000	—	—	—	2.50	—
2003A	75,000	PF65 6.50				
2003D In sets only	90,000	—	—	—	5.50	—
2003D	75,000	PF65 6.50				
2003F In sets only	90,000	—	—	—	5.50	—
2003F	75,000	PF65 6.50				
2003G In sets only	90,000	—	—	—	5.50	—
2003G	75,000	PF65 6.50				
2003J	29,940,000	—	—	—	2.50	—
2003J	75,000	PF65 6.50				
2004A	21,950,000	—	—	—	2.50	—
2004A	75,000	PF65 6.50				
2004D	89,350,000	—	—	—	2.50	—
2004D	75,000	PF65 6.50				
2004F	88,290,000	—	—	—	2.50	—
2004F	75,000	PF65 6.50				
2004G	41,740,000	—	—	—	2.50	—
2004G	75,000	PF65 6.50				
2004J In sets only	90,000	—	—	—	5.50	—
2004J	75,000	PF65 6.50				
2005A In sets only	90,000	—	—	—	5.50	—
2005A	75,000	PF65 5.00				
2005D In sets only	90,000	—	—	—	5.50	—
2005D	75,000	PF65 5.00				
2005F In sets only	90,000	—	—	—	5.50	—
2005F	75,000	PF65 5.00				
2005G In sets only	90,000	—	—	—	5.50	—
2005G	75,000	PF65 5.00				
2005J	59,930,000	—	—	—	2.50	—
2005J	75,000	PF65 5.00				
2006A In sets only	90,000	—	—	—	5.50	—
2006A	75,000	PF65 5.00				
2006D In sets only	90,000	—	—	—	5.50	—
2006D	75,000	PF65 5.00				
2006F In sets only	90,000	—	—	—	5.50	—
2006F	75,000	PF65 5.00				
2006G In sets only	90,000	—	—	—	5.50	—
2006G	75,000	PF65 5.00				
2006J In sets only	90,000	—	—	—	5.50	—
2006J	75,000	PF65 5.00				

KM# 257 EURO

7.50 g., Bi-Metallic, 23.25 mm. **Obv:** Stylized eagle **Rev:** Relief map of Western Europe, stars, lines and value **Edge:** Segmented reeding

Date	Mintage	F12	VF20	XF40	MS60	MS63
2007A In sets only	90,000	—	—	—	5.50	—
2007A	75,000	PF65 5.00				
2007D In sets only	90,000	—	—	—	5.50	—
2007D	75,000	PF65 5.00				
2007F In sets only	90,000	—	—	—	5.50	—
2007F	75,000	PF65 5.00				
2007G In sets only	90,000	—	—	—	5.50	—
2007G	75,000	PF65 5.00				
2007J In sets only	90,000	—	—	—	5.50	—
2007J	75,000	PF65 5.00				
2008A In sets only	80,000	—	—	—	5.50	—
2008A	70,000	PF65 5.00				
2008D In sets only	80,000	—	—	—	5.50	—
2008D	70,000	PF65 5.00				

Date	Mintage	F12	VF20	XF40	MS60	MS63
2008F In sets only	80,000	—	—	—	5.50	—
2008F	70,000	PF65 5.00				
2008G In sets only	80,000	—	—	—	5.50	—
2008G	70,000	PF65 5.00				
2008J In sets only	80,000	—	—	—	5.50	—
2008J	70,000	PF65 5.00				
2009A In sets only	60,000	—	—	—	5.50	—
2009A	50,000	PF65 5.00				
2009D In sets only	60,000	—	—	—	5.50	—
2009D	50,000	PF65 5.00				
2009F In sets only	60,000	—	—	—	5.50	—
2009F	50,000	PF65 5.00				
2009G In sets only	60,000	—	—	—	5.50	—
2009G	50,000	PF65 5.00				
2009J In sets only	60,000	—	—	—	5.50	—
2009J	50,000	PF65 5.00				
2010A In sets only	53,800	—	—	—	4.00	—
2010A	45,150	PF65 5.00				
2010D In sets only	46,800	—	—	—	4.00	—
2010D	40,120	PF65 5.00				
2010F In sets only	46,800	—	—	—	4.00	—
2010F	40,120	PF65 5.00				
2010G In sets only	46,800	—	—	—	4.00	—
2010G	40,120	PF65 5.00				
2010J In sets only	46,800	—	—	—	4.00	—
2010J	40,120	PF65 5.00				
2011A In sets only	48,000	—	—	—	4.00	—
2011A	43,000	PF65 5.00				
2011D In sets only	44,000	—	—	—	4.00	—
2011D	37,000	PF65 5.00				
2011F In sets only	44,000	—	—	—	4.00	—
2011F	37,000	PF65 5.00				
2011G In sets only	44,000	—	—	—	4.00	—
2011G	37,000	PF65 5.00				
2011J In sets only	44,000	—	—	—	4.00	—
2011J	37,000	PF65 5.00				
2012A In sets only	45,000	—	—	—	4.00	—
2012A	40,000	PF65 5.00				
2012D In sets only	Est. 50000	—	—	—	4.00	—
2012D	Est. 40000	PF65 5.00				
2012F In sets only	Est. 50000	—	—	—	4.00	—
2012F	32,000	PF65 5.00				
2012G In sets only	Est. 50000	—	—	—	4.00	—
2012G	Est. 40000	PF65 5.00				
2012J In sets only	Est. 50000	—	—	—	4.00	—
2012J	30,000	PF65 5.00				
2013A In sets only	Est. 50000	—	—	—	4.00	—
2013A	Est. 40000	PF65 5.00				
2013D In sets only	Est. 50000	—	—	—	4.00	—
2013D	Est. 40000	PF65 5.00				
2013F In sets only	Est. 50000	—	—	—	4.00	—
2013F	Est. 40000	PF65 5.00				
2013G In sets only	Est. 50000	—	—	—	4.00	—
2013G	Est. 40000	PF65 5.00				
2013J In sets only	Est. 50000	—	—	—	4.00	—
2013J	Est. 40000	PF65 5.00				

KM# 214 2 EURO

8.50 g., Bi-Metallic, 25.75 mm. **Obv:** Stylized eagle **Rev:** Denomination and map **Edge:** Reeded and "EINIGKEIT UND RECHT UND FREIHEIT"

Date	Mintage	F12	VF20	XF40	MS60	MS63
2002A	239,010,000	—	—	—	4.50	—
2002A	75,000	PF65 12.50				
2002D	231,390,000	—	—	—	4.50	—
2002D	75,000	PF65 12.50				
2002F	281,180,000	—	—	—	4.50	—
2002F	75,000	PF65 12.50				
2002G	181,040,000	—	—	—	4.50	—
2002G	75,000	PF65 12.50				
2002J	257,910,000	—	—	—	4.50	—
2002J	75,000	PF65 12.50				
2003A	20,560,000	—	—	—	4.50	—
2003A	75,000	PF65 12.50				
2003D	22,260,000	—	—	—	4.50	—
2003D	75,000	PF65 12.50				
2003F	24,550,000	—	—	—	4.50	—
2003F	75,000	PF65 12.50				
2003G	29,230,000	—	—	—	4.50	—
2003G	75,000	PF65 12.50				
2003J	19,590,000	—	—	—	4.50	—
2003J	75,000	PF65 12.50				
2004A	31,660,000	—	—	—	4.50	—
2004A	75,000	PF65 12.50				
2004D	19,930,000	—	—	—	4.50	—
2004D	75,000	PF65 12.50				
2004F In sets only	90,000	—	—	—	5.50	—
2004F	75,000	PF65 12.50				

Date	Mintage	F12	VF20	XF40	MS60	MS63
2004G In sets only	90,000	—	—	—	5.50	—
2004G	75,000	PF65 12.50				
2004J	22,600,000	—	—	—	4.50	—
2004J	75,000	PF65 12.50				
2005A In sets only	90,000	—	—	—	5.50	—
2005A	75,000	PF65 10.00				
2005D In sets only	90,000	—	—	—	5.50	—
2005D	75,000	PF65 10.00				
2005F In sets only	90,000	—	—	—	5.50	—
2005F	75,000	PF65 10.00				
2005G In sets only	90,000	—	—	—	5.50	—
2005G	75,000	PF65 10.00				
2005J In sets only	90,000	—	—	—	5.50	—
2005J	75,000	PF65 10.00				
2006A In sets only	90,000	—	—	—	5.50	—
2006A	75,000	PF65 10.00				
2006D In sets only	90,000	—	—	—	5.50	—
2006D	75,000	PF65 10.00				
2006F In sets only	90,000	—	—	—	5.50	—
2006F	75,000	PF65 10.00				
2006G In sets only	90,000	—	—	—	5.50	—
2006G	75,000	PF65 10.00				
2006J In sets only	90,000	—	—	—	5.50	—
2006J	75,000	PF65 10.00				

KM# 253 2 EURO
8.50 g., Bi-Metallic, 25.75 mm. **Obv:** Schleswig Holstein castle **Obv. Legend:** BUNDESREPULIK DEUTSCHLAND **Obv. Inscription:** SCHLESWIG- / HOLSTEIN **Rev:** Denomination over map

Date	Mintage	F12	VF20	XF40	MS60	MS63
2006A	6,170,000	—	—	—	5.00	6.00
2006A	145,000	PF63 8.00	PF65 10.00			
2006D	6,470,000	—	—	—	5.00	6.00
2006D	145,000	PF63 8.00	PF65 10.00			
2006F	7,370,000	—	—	—	5.00	6.00
2006F	145,000	PF63 8.00	PF65 10.00			
2006G	4,370,000	—	—	—	5.00	6.00
2006G	145,000	PF63 8.00	PF65 10.00			
2006J	6,470,000	—	—	—	5.00	6.00
2006J	145,000	PF63 8.00	PF65 10.00			

KM# 259 2 EURO
8.50 g., Bi-Metallic, 25.75 mm. **Subject:** 50th Anniversary Treaty of Rome **Obv:** Open treaty book **Obv. Legend:** BUNDESREPUBLIK DEUTSCHLAND **Rev:** Large value at left, modified outline of Europe at right **Edge Lettering:** EINIGKEIT UND RECHT UND FREIHEIT

Date	Mintage	F12	VF20	XF40	MS60	MS63
2007A	1,090,000	—	—	—	4.00	5.00
2007A	125,000	PF63 8.00	PF65 10.00			
2007D	14,590,000	—	—	—	4.00	5.50
2007D	125,000	PF63 8.00	PF65 10.00			
2007F	8,090,000	—	—	—	4.00	5.50
2007F	125,000	PF63 8.00	PF65 10.00			
2007G	5,090,000	—	—	—	4.00	5.50
2007G	125,000	PF63 8.00	PF65 10.00			
2007J	1,590,000	—	—	—	4.00	5.50
2007J	125,000	PF63 8.00	PF65 10.00			

KM# 260 2 EURO
8.50 g., Bi-Metallic, 25.75 mm. **Obv:** City buildings, Mecklenburg's Schwerin Castle **Obv. Legend:** BUNDESREPUBLIK DEUTSCHLAND **Obv. Inscription:** MECKLENBURG- / VORPOMMERN **Rev:** Large value at left, modified map of Europe at right **Edge Lettering:** EINIGKEIT UND RECHT UND FREIHEIT

Date	Mintage	F12	VF20	XF40	MS60	MS63
2007A	1,210,000	—	—	—	4.00	5.50
2007A	145,000	PF63 8.00	PF65 10.00			
2007D	12,010,000	—	—	—	4.00	5.50
2007D	145,000	PF63 8.00	PF65 10.00			
2007F	12,110,000	—	—	—	4.00	5.50
2007F	145,000	PF63 8.00	PF65 10.00			
2007G	4,370,000	—	—	—	4.00	5.50
2007G	145,000	PF63 8.00	PF65 10.00			
2007J	1,240,000	—	—	—	4.00	5.50
2007J	145,000	PF63 8.00	PF65 10.00			

KM# 258 2 EURO
8.50 g., Bi-Metallic, 25.75 mm. **Obv:** Stylized eagle **Rev:** Relief map of Western Europe, stars, lines and value **Edge Lettering:** EINIGKEIT UND RECHT UND FREIHEIT

Date	Mintage	F12	VF20	XF40	MS60	MS63
2008A	11,480,000	—	—	—	4.50	—
2008A	70,000	PF63 8.00	PF65 10.00			
2008D	12,050,000	—	—	—	4.50	—
2008D	70,000	PF63 8.00	PF65 10.00			
2008F	13,760,000	—	—	—	4.50	—
2008F	70,000	PF63 8.00	PF65 10.00			
2008G	8,060,000	—	—	—	4.50	—
2008G	70,000	PF63 8.00	PF65 10.00			
2008J	12,050,000	—	—	—	4.50	—
2008J	70,000	PF63 8.00	PF65 10.00			
2010A	19,654,000	—	—	—	4.50	—
2010A	45,150	PF63 8.00	PF65 10.00			
2010D	20,627,000	—	—	—	4.50	—
2010D	40,120	PF63 8.00	PF65 10.00			
2010F	23,567,000	—	—	—	4.50	—
2010F	40,120	PF63 8.00	PF65 10.00			
2010G	13,767,000	—	—	—	4.50	—
2010G	40,120	PF63 8.00	PF65 10.00			
2010J	20,627,000	—	—	—	4.50	—
2010J	40,120	PF63 8.00	PF65 10.00			
2011A	23,848,000	—	—	—	4.50	—
2011A	43,000	PF63 8.00	PF65 10.00			
2011D	25,034,000	—	—	—	4.50	—
2011D	37,000	PF63 8.00	PF65 10.00			
2011F	28,604,000	—	—	—	4.50	—
2011F	37,000	PF63 8.00	PF65 10.00			
2011G	16,704,000	—	—	—	4.50	—
2011G	37,000	PF63 8.00	PF65 10.00			
2011J	25,034,000	—	—	—	4.50	—
2011J	37,000	PF63 8.00	PF65 10.00			

KM# 261A 2 EURO
8.50 g., Bi-Metallic, 25.75 mm. **Obv:** Hamburg Cathedral **Rev:** Denomination over map **Edge Lettering:** EINIGKEIT UND RECHT UND FREIHEIT **Note:** Mule with old reverse Euro Zone map.

Date	Mintage	F12	VF20	XF40	MS60	MS63
2008F	Inc. above	—	—	—	—	30.00

KM# 277 2 EURO
8.50 g., Bi-Metallic, 25.75 mm. **Subject:** EMU, 10th Anniversary **Obv:** Stick figure and E symbol

Date	Mintage	F12	VF20	XF40	MS60	MS63
2009A	6,060,000	—	—	—	4.50	5.00
2009A	80,000	PF63 8.00	PF65 10.00			
2009D	6,360,000	—	—	—	4.50	5.00
2009D	80,000	PF63 8.00	PF65 10.00			
2009F	7,260,000	—	—	—	4.50	5.00
2009F	80,000	PF63 8.00	PF65 10.00			
2009G	4,260,000	—	—	—	4.50	5.00
2009G	80,000	PF63 8.00	PF65 10.00			
2009J	6,360,000	—	—	—	4.50	5.00
2009J	80,000	PF63 8.00	PF65 10.00			

KM# 276 2 EURO
8.50 g., Bi-Metallic, 25.75 mm. **Obv:** Building in Saarland **Rev:** Value and map

Date	Mintage	F12	VF20	XF40	MS60	MS63
2009A	6,110,000	—	—	—	4.50	5.00
2009A	100,000	PF63 8.00	PF65 10.00			
2009D	6,410,000	—	—	—	4.50	5.00
2009D	100,000	PF63 8.00	PF65 10.00			
2009F	7,310,000	—	—	—	4.50	5.00
2009F	100,000	PF63 8.00	PF65 10.00			
2009G	4,310,000	—	—	—	4.50	5.00
2009G	100,000	PF63 8.00	PF65 10.00			
2009J	6,410,000	—	—	—	4.50	5.00
2009J	100,000	PF63 8.00	PF65 10.00			

KM# 285 2 EURO
8.50 g., Bi-Metallic, 25.75 mm. **Obv:** Bremen town hall and statue and knight statue **Rev:** Value and map

Date	Mintage	F12	VF20	XF40	MS60	MS63
2010A	6,104,000	—	—	—	4.50	5.00
2010A	100,000	PF63 8.00	PF65 10.00			
2010D	6,397,000	—	—	—	4.50	5.00
2010D	100,000	PF63 8.00	PF65 10.00			
2010F	7,297,000	—	—	—	4.50	5.00
2010F	100,000	PF63 8.00	PF65 10.00			
2010G	4,297,000	—	—	—	4.50	5.00
2010G	100,000	PF63 8.00	PF65 10.00			
2010J	6,397,000	—	—	—	4.50	5.00
2010J	100,000	PF63 8.00	PF65 10.00			

KM# 261 2 EURO
8.50 g., Bi-Metallic, 25.75 mm. **Obv:** Hamburg Cathedral **Obv. Legend:** BUNDESREPUBLIK DEUTSCHLAND **Obv. Inscription:** HAMBURG **Rev:** Large value at left, modified outline of Europe at right **Edge Lettering:** EINIGKEIT UND RECHT UND FREIHEIT

Date	Mintage	F12	VF20	XF40	MS60	MS63
2008A	1,160,000	—	—	—	4.00	5.50
2008A	140,000	PF63 8.00	PF65 10.00			
2008D	9,060,000	—	—	—	4.00	5.50
2008D	140,000	PF63 8.00	PF65 10.00			
2008F	9,760,000	—	—	—	4.00	5.50
2008F	140,000	PF63 8.00	PF65 10.00			
2008G	4,360,000	—	—	—	4.00	5.50
2008G	140,000	PF63 8.00	PF65 10.00			
2008J	6,460,000	—	—	—	4.00	5.50
2008J	140,000	PF63 8.00	PF65 10.00			

KM# 293 2 EURO
8.50 g., Bi-Metallic, 25.75 mm. **Obv:** Cologne Cathedral **Obv. Legend:** NORDRHEIN - WESTFALEN

Date	Mintage	F12	VF20	XF40	MS60	MS63
2011A	6,102,000	—	—	—	5.00	7.50
2011A	102,000	PF63 8.00	PF65 10.00			
2011D	6,402,000	—	—	—	5.00	7.50
2011D	102,000	PF63 8.00	PF65 10.00			
2011F	7,302,000	—	—	—	5.00	7.50
2011F	102,000	PF63 8.00	PF65 10.00			
2011G	4,302,000	—	—	—	5.00	7.50
2011G	102,000	PF63 8.00	PF65 10.00			
2011J	6,402,000	—	—	—	5.00	7.50
2011J	102,000	PF63 8.00	PF65 10.00			

KM# 305 2 EURO

8.50 g., Bi-Metallic, 25.75 mm. **Series:** German States **Subject:** Bavaria, Neuschwanstein Castle **Rev:** Relief map of Europe, stars, lines and value **Edge Lettering:** EINIGKEIT UND RECHT UND FREIHEIT

Date	Mintage	F12	VF20	XF40	MS60	MS63
2012A	Est. 6100000	—	—	—	4.00	5.00
2012A	95,000	PF63 8.00	PF65 10.00			
2012D	Est. 6400000	—	—	—	4.00	5.00
2012D	87,000	PF63 8.00	PF65 10.00			
2012F	Est. 7300000	—	—	—	4.00	5.00
2012F	87,000	PF63 8.00	PF65 10.00			
2012G	Est. 4300000	—	—	—	4.00	5.00
2012G	87,000	PF63 8.00	PF65 10.00			
2012J	Est. 6400000	—	—	—	4.00	5.00
2012J	87,000	PF63 8.00	PF65 10.00			

KM# 306 2 EURO

8.50 g., Bi-Metallic, 25.75 mm. **Subject:** Euro coinage, 10th Anniversary **Obv:** Euro symbol on globe at center, child-like rendering around **Rev:** Reliev map of Europe, stars, lines and value **Edge Lettering:** EINIGKEIT UND RECHT UND FREIHEIT

Date	Mintage	F12	VF20	XF40	MS60	MS63
2012A	Est. 6100000	—	—	—	4.00	5.00
2012A	95,000	PF63 8.00	PF65 10.00			
2012D	Est. 6400000	—	—	—	4.00	5.00
2012D	87,000	PF63 8.00	PF65 10.00			
2012F	Est. 7300000	—	—	—	4.00	5.00
2012F	87,000	PF63 8.00	PF65 10.00			
2012G	4,240,000	—	—	—	4.00	5.00
2012G	87,000	PF63 8.00	PF65 10.00			
2012J	Est. 6400000	—	—	—	4.00	5.00
2012J	87,000	PF63 8.00	PF65 10.00			

KM# 315 2 EURO

8.50 g., Bi-Metallic, 25.75 mm. **Subject:** Fiftieth Anniversary of the Elysée (Paris) Treaty **Obv:** Heads of Konrad Adenauer and Charles de Gaulle **Rev:** Relief map of Europe, stars, lines and value **Rev. Legend:** TRAITÉ DE L' ÉLYSÉE, ÉLYSÉE-VERTAG and 50 ANS JAHRE **Edge Lettering:** EINIGKEIT UND RECHT UND FREIHEIT

Date	Mintage	F12	VF20	XF40	MS60	MS63
2013F	Est. 77000	PF63 7.00	PF65 9.00			
2013D	Est. 77000	PF63 7.00	PF65 9.00			
2013F	Est. 2740000	—	—	—	4.00	5.00
2013J	Est. 2410000	—	—	—	4.00	5.00
2013A	Est. 84000	PF63 7.00	PF65 9.00			
2013G	Est. 77000	PF63 7.00	PF65 9.00			
2013J	Est. 77000	PF63 7.00	PF65 9.00			
2013A	Est. 2300000	—	—	—	4.00	5.00
2013G	Est. 1575000	—	—	—	4.00	5.00
2013D	Est. 2410000	—	—	—	4.00	5.00

KM# 314 2 EURO

8.50 g., Bi-Metallic, 25.75 mm. **Series:** German States **Subject:** Baden-Wurttemberg, Maulbrunn Cloister **Obv:** Maulbrunn Cloiser **Obv. Legend:** BADEN-WURTTEMBERG **Rev:** Relief map of Europe, stars, lines and value **Edge Lettering:** EINIGKEIT UND RECHT UND FREIHEIT

Date	Mintage	F12	VF20	XF40	MS60	MS63
2013A	Est. 6087000	—	—	—	4.00	5.00
2013A	Est. 89000	PF63 7.00	PF65 9.00			
2013D	Est. 6400000	—	—	—	4.00	5.00
2013D	Est. 82000	PF63 7.00	PF65 9.00			
2013F	Est. 7282000	—	—	—	4.00	5.00
2013F	Est. 82000	PF63 7.00	PF65 9.00			
2013G	Est. 4300000	—	—	—	4.00	5.00
2013G	Est. 82000	PF63 7.00	PF65 9.00			

Date	Mintage	F12	VF20	XF40	MS60	MS63
2013J	Est. 6400000	—	—	—	4.00	5.00
2013J	Est. 82000	PF63 7.00	PF65 9.00			

KM# 215 10 EURO

18.00 g., 0.925 Silver 0.5319 oz. ASW, 32.5 mm. **Subject:** Introduction of the Euro Currency **Obv:** Stylized round eagle **Rev:** Euro symbol and map **Edge Lettering:** IM ZEICHEN DER EINIGUNG EUROPAS

Date	Mintage	F12	VF20	XF40	MS60	MS63
2002F	2,000,000	—	—	—	22.00	25.00
2002F	400,000	PF63 28.00	PF65 30.00			

KM# 216 10 EURO

18.00 g., 0.925 Silver 0.5319 oz. ASW, 32.5 mm. **Subject:** Berlin Subway Centennial **Obv:** Stylized squarish eagle **Rev:** Elevated and subterranean train views **Edge Lettering:** HISTORISCH UND ZUKUNFTS WEISEND

Date	Mintage	F12	VF20	XF40	MS60	MS63
2002D	2,000,000	—	—	—	22.00	25.00
2002D	400,000	PF63 28.00	PF65 30.00			

KM# 217 10 EURO

18.00 g., 0.925 Silver 0.5319 oz. ASW, 32.5 mm. **Subject:** Documenta Kassel Art Exposition **Obv:** Stylized eagle above inscription **Rev:** Exposition logo **Edge Lettering:** ART (in nine languages)

Date	Mintage	F12	VF20	XF40	MS60	MS63
2002J	2,000,000	—	—	—	22.00	25.00
2002J	300,000	PF63 28.00	PF65 30.00			

KM# 218 10 EURO

18.00 g., 0.925 Silver 0.5319 oz. ASW, 32.5 mm. **Subject:** Museum Island, Berlin **Obv:** Stylized eagle **Rev:** Aerial view of museum complex **Edge Lettering:** FREISTÄTTE FÜR KUNST UND WISSENSCHAFT

Date	Mintage	F12	VF20	XF40	MS60	MS63
2002A	2,000,000	—	—	—	22.00	25.00
2002A	280,000	PF63 28.00	PF65 30.00			

KM# 219 10 EURO

18.00 g., 0.925 Silver 0.5319 oz. ASW, 32.5 mm. **Subject:** 50 Years - German Television **Obv:** Stylized eagle silhouette **Rev:** Television screen silhouette **Edge Lettering:** BILDUNG UNTERHALTUNG INFORMATION

Date	Mintage	F12	VF20	XF40	MS60	MS63
2002G	2,000,000	—	—	—	22.00	25.00
2002G	290,000	PF63 30.00	PF65 32.00			

KM# 227 10 EURO

18.00 g., 0.925 Silver 0.5319 oz. ASW, 32.5 mm. **Obv:** Stylized eagle above denomination **Rev:** Gottfried Semper and floor plan **Edge Lettering:** ARCHITEKT • FORSCHER • KOSMOPOLIT • DEMOKRAT•

Date	Mintage	F12	VF20	XF40	MS60	MS63
2003G	350,000	PF63 28.00	PF65 30.00			
2003G	2,050,000	—	—	—	22.00	25.00

KM# 222 10 EURO

18.00 g., 0.925 Silver 0.5319 oz. ASW, 32.5 mm. **Subject:** Justus von Liebig **Obv:** Eagle above denomination **Rev:** Liebig's portrait **Edge Lettering:** FORSCHEN • LEHREN • ANWENDEN •

Date	Mintage	F12	VF20	XF40	MS60	MS63
2003J	2,050,000	—	—	—	22.00	25.00
2003J	350,000	PF63 28.00	PF65 30.00			

KM# 225 10 EURO

18.00 g., 0.925 Silver 0.5319 oz. ASW, 32.5 mm. **Subject:** German Museum München Centennial **Obv:** Stylized eagle, denomination at left **Rev:** Abstract design **Edge Lettering:** SAMMELN • AUSSTELLEN • FORSCHEN • BILDEN •

Date	Mintage	F12	VF20	XF40	MS60	MS63
2003D	350,000	PF63 28.00	PF65 30.00			
2003D	2,050,000	—	—	—	22.00	25.00

KM# 223 10 EURO

18.00 g., 0.925 Silver 0.5319 oz. ASW, 32.5 mm. **Subject:** World Cup Soccer **Obv:** Stylized round eagle above denomination **Rev:** German map on soccer ball **Edge Lettering:** DIE WELT ZU GAST BEI FREUNDEN A • D • F • G • J • **Note:** Mint is determined by which letter "E" in the edge inscription has a short center bar. If the first letter "E" has the short center bar the coin is from the Berlin mint. Second "E"= Munich, third "E"=Stuttgart, fourth "E"=Karlsruhe, fifth "E"=Hamburg

Date	Mintage	F12	VF20	XF40	MS60	MS63
2003A	710,000	—	—	—	22.00	25.00
2003A	80,000	PF63 30.00		PF65 32.00		
2003D	710,000	—	—	—	22.00	25.00
2003D	80,000	PF63 30.00		PF65 32.00		
2003F	710,000	—	—	—	22.00	25.00
2003F	80,000	PF63 30.00		PF65 32.00		
2003G	710,000	—	—	—	22.00	25.00
2003G	80,000	PF63 30.00		PF65 32.00		
2003J	710,000	—	—	—	22.00	25.00
2003J	80,000	PF63 30.00		PF65 32.00		

KM# 224 10 EURO
18.00 g., 0.925 Silver 0.5319 oz. ASW, 32.5 mm. **Subject:** Ruhr Industrial District **Obv:** Stylized eagle, denomination below **Rev:** Various city views **Edge Lettering:** RUHRPOTT KULTURLANDSCHAFT

Date	Mintage	F12	VF20	XF40	MS60	MS63
2003F	2,050,000	—	—	—	22.00	25.00
2003F	350,000	PF63 28.00		PF65 30.00		

KM# 226 10 EURO
18.00 g., 0.925 Silver 0.5319 oz. ASW, 32.5 mm. **Subject:** 50th Anniversary of the Ill-fated East German Revolution **Obv:** Stylized eagle, denomination at left **Rev:** Tank tracks over slogans **Edge Lettering:** ERINNERUNG AN DEN VOLKSAUFSTAND IN DER DDR

Date	Mintage	F12	VF20	XF40	MS60	MS63
2003A	2,050,000	—	—	—	22.00	25.00
2003A	350,000	PF63 28.00		PF65 30.00		

KM# 230 10 EURO
18.00 g., 0.925 Silver 0.5319 oz. ASW, 32.5 mm. **Obv:** Stylized eagle, stars and denomination **Rev:** Bauhaus Dessau geometric shapes design **Edge Lettering:** KUNST TECHNIK LEHRE

Date	Mintage	F12	VF20	XF40	MS60	MS63
2004A	1,800,000	—	—	—	22.00	25.00
2004A	300,000	PF63 28.00		PF65 30.00		

KM# 232 10 EURO
18.00 g., 0.925 Silver 0.5319 oz. ASW, 32.5 mm. **Obv:** Stylized eagle and denomination **Rev:** Geese flying over Wattenmeer National Park **Edge Lettering:** MEERESGRUND TRIFFT HORIZONT

Date	Mintage	F12	VF20	XF40	MS60	MS63
2004J	300,000	PF63 28.00		PF65 30.00		
2004J	1,800,000	—	—	—	22.00	25.00

KM# 233 10 EURO
18.00 g., 0.925 Silver 0.5319 oz. ASW, 32.5 mm. **Obv:** Stylized eagle **Rev:** Eduard Moerike **Edge Lettering:** OHNE DAS SCHÖNE WAS SOLL DER GEWINN

Date	Mintage	F12	VF20	XF40	MS60	MS63
2004F	300,000	PF63 28.00		PF65 30.00		
2004F	1,800,000	—	—	—	22.00	25.00

KM# 234 10 EURO
18.00 g., 0.925 Silver 0.5319 oz. ASW, 32.5 mm. **Obv:** Stylized eagle, denomination below **Rev:** Space station above the earth **Edge Lettering:** RAUMFAHRT VERBINDET DIE WELT

Date	Mintage	F12	VF20	XF40	MS60	MS63
2004D	300,000	PF63 28.00		PF65 30.00		
2004D	1,800,000	—	—	—	22.00	25.00

KM# 231 10 EURO
18.00 g., 0.925 Silver 0.5319 oz. ASW, 32.5 mm. **Obv:** Stylized eagle above denomination **Rev:** European Union country names and dates **Edge Lettering:** FREUDE SCHÖNER GÖTTERFUNKEN

Date	Mintage	F12	VF20	XF40	MS60	MS63
2004G	1,800,000	—	—	—	22.00	25.00
2004G	300,000	PF63 28.00		PF65 30.00		

KM# 229 10 EURO
18.00 g., 0.925 Silver 0.5319 oz. ASW, 32.5 mm. **Obv:** Stylized eagle, denomination below **Rev:** Soccer ball orbiting the earth **Edge Lettering:** DIE WELT ZU GAST BEI FREUNDEN A D F G J **Note:** Soccer Series: Mint determination same as KM-223

Date	Mintage	F12	VF20	XF40	MS60	MS63
2004A	800,000	—	—	—	22.00	25.00
2004A	80,000	PF63 28.00		PF65 30.00		
2004D	800,000	—	—	—	22.00	25.00
2004D	80,000	PF63 28.00		PF65 30.00		
2004F	800,000	—	—	—	22.00	25.00
2004F	80,000	PF63 28.00		PF65 30.00		
2004G	800,000	—	—	—	22.00	25.00
2004G	80,000	PF63 28.00		PF65 30.00		
2004J	800,000	—	—	—	22.00	25.00
2004J	80,000	PF63 28.00		PF65 30.00		

KM# 238 10 EURO
18.00 g., 0.925 Silver 0.5319 oz. ASW, 32.5 mm. **Subject:** Albert Einstein **Obv:** Stylized eagle within circle, denomination below **Rev:** E=mc2 on a sphere resting on a net **Edge Lettering:** NICHT AUFHOREN ZU FRAGEN

Date	Mintage	F12	VF20	XF40	MS60	MS63
2005J	1,800,000	—	—	—	22.00	25.00
2005J	300,000	PF63 28.00		PF65 30.00		

KM# 239 10 EURO
18.00 g., 0.925 Silver 0.5319 oz. ASW, 32.5 mm. **Subject:** Friedrich von Schiller **Obv:** Stylized eagle **Rev:** Schiller portrait **Edge Lettering:** ERNST IST DAS LEBEN. HEITER IST DIE KUNST

Date	Mintage	F12	VF20	XF40	MS60	MS63
2005G	1,800,000	—	—	—	22.00	25.00
2005G	300,000	PF63 28.00		PF65 30.00		

KM# 240 10 EURO
18.00 g., 0.925 Silver 0.5319 oz. ASW, 32.5 mm. **Subject:** Magdeburg **Obv:** Stylized eagle, denomination below **Rev:** Church flanked by landmarks and objects **Edge Lettering:** MAGADOBURG 805 • MAGDEBURG 2005 •

Date	Mintage	F12	VF20	XF40	MS60	MS63
2005A	300,000	PF63 28.00		PF65 30.00		
2005A	1,800,000	—	—	—	22.00	25.00

KM# 241 10 EURO
18.00 g., 0.925 Silver 0.5319 oz. ASW, 32.5 mm. **Subject:** Bavarian Forest National Park **Obv:** Stylized eagle **Rev:** Various park scenes **Edge:** Lettered

Date	Mintage	F12	VF20	XF40	MS60	MS63
2005D	1,800,000	—	—	—	22.00	25.00
2005D	300,000	PF63 28.00		PF65 30.00		

KM# 242 10 EURO

18.00 g., 0.925 Silver 0.5319 oz. ASW, 32.5 mm. **Subject:** Bertha von Suttner **Obv:** Stylized eagle above stars **Rev:** Suttner's portrait **Edge Lettering:** EIPHNH PAX FRIEDEN twice

Date	Mintage	F12	VF20	XF40	MS60	MS63
2005F	300,000	PF63 28.00	PF65 30.00			
2005F	1,800,000	—	—	—	22.00	25.00

KM# 243 10 EURO

18.00 g., 0.925 Silver 0.5319 oz. ASW, 32.5 mm. **Subject:** World Cup Soccer **Obv:** Round stylized eagle **Rev:** Ball and legs seen through a net **Edge Lettering:** DIE WELT ZU GAST BEI FREUNDEN

Date	Mintage	F12	VF20	XF40	MS60	MS63
2005A	800,000	—	—	—	22.00	25.00
2005A	80,000	PF63 30.00	PF65 32.00			
2005D	800,000	—	—	—	22.00	25.00
2005D	80,000	PF63 30.00	PF65 32.00			
2005F	800,000	—	—	—	22.00	25.00
2005F	80,000	PF63 30.00	PF65 32.00			
2005G	800,000	—	—	—	22.00	25.00
2005G	80,000	PF63 30.00	PF65 32.00			
2005J	800,000	—	—	—	22.00	25.00
2005J	80,000	PF63 30.00	PF65 32.00			

KM# 245 10 EURO

18.00 g., 0.925 Silver 0.5319 oz. ASW, 32.5 mm. **Subject:** Karl Friedrich Schinkel **Obv:** Stylized eagle **Rev:** Kneeling brick layer **Edge Lettering:** DER MENSCH BILDE SICH IN ALLEM SCHÖN

Date	Mintage	F12	VF20	XF40	MS60	MS63
2006F	300,000	PF63 28.00	PF65 30.00			
2006F	1,600,000	—	—	—	22.00	25.00

KM# 247 10 EURO

18.00 g., 0.925 Silver 0.5319 oz. ASW, 32.5 mm. **Subject:** Hanseatic League **Obv:** Stylized eagle **Rev:** Old sail boat **Edge Lettering:** Wandel durch Handel - von der Hanse nach Europa

Date	Mintage	F12	VF20	XF40	MS60	MS63
2006J	300,000	PF63 28.00	PF65 30.00			
2006J	1,600,000	—	—	—	22.00	25.00

KM# 248 10 EURO

18.00 g., 0.925 Silver 0.5319 oz. ASW, 32.5 mm. **Subject:** Mozart **Obv:** Stylized eagle, music and denomination above **Rev:** Bust left, dates above **Edge Lettering:** -- MOZART -- DIE WELT HAT EINEN SINN

Date	Mintage	F12	VF20	XF40	MS60	MS63
2006D	1,600,000	—	—	—	22.00	25.00
2006D	300,000	PF63 28.00	PF65 30.00			

KM# 249 10 EURO

18.00 g., 0.925 Silver 0.5319 oz. ASW, 32.5 mm. **Subject:** World Cup Soccer **Obv:** Stylized eagle **Rev:** Brandenburg Gate on ball on globe **Edge Lettering:** DIE WELT ZU GAST BEI FREUNDEN - ADFGJ **Note:** Mint is determined by which letter "E" in the edge inscription has a short center bar. If the first letter "E" has the short center bar the coin is from the Berlin mint. Second "E"= Munich, third "E"=Stuttgart, fourth "E"=Karlsruhe, fifth "E"=Hamburg

Date	Mintage	F12	VF20	XF40	MS60	MS63
2006A	800,000	—	—	—	20.00	22.00
2006A	80,000	PF63 23.00	PF65 25.00			
2006D	800,000	—	—	—	20.00	22.00
2006D	80,000	PF63 23.00	PF65 25.00			
2006F	800,000	—	—	—	20.00	22.00
2006F	80,000	PF63 23.00	PF65 25.00			
2006G	800,000	—	—	—	20.00	22.00
2006G	80,000	PF63 23.00	PF65 25.00			
2006J	800,000	—	—	—	20.00	22.00
2006J	80,000	PF63 23.00	PF65 25.00			

KM# 263 10 EURO

18.00 g., 0.925 Silver 0.5319 oz. ASW, 32.5 mm. **Subject:** Saarland, 50th Anniversary of German control **Obv:** Eagle **Rev:** Modern town view, four stylized heads

Date	Mintage	F12	VF20	XF40	MS60	MS63
2007G	1,600,000	—	—	—	22.00	25.00
2007G	300,000	PF63 28.00	PF65 30.00			

KM# 264 10 EURO

18.00 g., 0.925 Silver 0.5319 oz. ASW, 32.5 mm. **Subject:** Treaty of Rome, 50th Anniversary **Obv:** Eagle **Rev:** Map of Central Europe and stars

Date	Mintage	F12	VF20	XF40	MS60	MS63
2007F	1,600,000	—	—	—	22.00	25.00
2007F	300,000	PF63 28.00	PF65 30.00			

KM# 265 10 EURO

18.00 g., 0.925 Silver 0.5319 oz. ASW, 32.5 mm. **Subject:** Wilhelm Busch, 175th Anniversary of Birth **Obv:** Eagle within square **Rev:** Portrait of Busch, characters Helene, Max and Moritz flanking

Date	Mintage	F12	VF20	XF40	MS60	MS63
2007D	1,600,000	—	—	—	22.00	25.00
2007D	300,000	PF63 28.00	PF65 30.00			

KM# 266 10 EURO

18.00 g., 0.925 Silver 0.5319 oz. ASW, 32.5 mm. **Subject:** Deutsche Bundesbank, 50th Aniversary **Obv:** Eagle on rectangle design **Rev:** Buildings on graph

Date	Mintage	F12	VF20	XF40	MS60	MS63
2007J	1,600,000	—	—	—	22.00	25.00
2007J	300,000	PF63 28.00	PF65 30.00			

KM# 268 10 EURO

18.00 g., 0.925 Silver 0.5319 oz. ASW, 32.5 mm. **Subject:** Eagle **Rev:** St. Elisabeth von Thuringen

Date	Mintage	F12	VF20	XF40	MS60	MS63
2007A	1,600,000	—	—	—	22.00	25.00
2007A	300,000	PF63 28.00	PF65 30.00			

KM# 271 10 EURO

18.00 g., 0.925 Silver 0.5319 oz. ASW, 32.5 mm. **Subject:** Franz Kafka, 125th Anniversary of Birth **Obv:** Eagle **Rev:**

Prague Cathedral, writings & portrait **Edge Lettering:** EIN KÄFIG GING EINEN VOGEL SUCHEN

Date	Mintage	F12	VF20	XF40	MS60	MS63
2008G	1,500,000	—	—	—	22.00	25.00
2008G	260,000	PF63 28.00	PF65 30.00			

KM# 272 10 EURO
18.00 g., 0.925 Silver 0.5319 oz. ASW, 32.5 mm. **Subject:** Max Planck, 150th Anniversary of Birth **Obv:** Eagle **Rev:** Graph and portrait **Edge Lettering:** DEM ANWENDEN MUSS DAS + ERKENNEN VORAUSGEHEN

Date	Mintage	F12	VF20	XF40	MS60	MS63
2008F	1,500,000	—	—	—	22.00	25.00
2008F	260,000	PF63 28.00	PF65 30.00			

KM# 273 10 EURO
18.00 g., 0.925 Silver 0.6310 oz. ASW **Subject:** Carl Spitzweg - 200th Anniversary of Birth **Obv:** Eagle **Rev:** Spitzweg reclining in bed with books, umbrella above **Edge Lettering:** ACH, DIE VERGANGENHEIT IST SCHÖN **Shape:** 32.5

Date	Mintage	F12	VF20	XF40	MS60	MS63
2008D	1,500,000	—	—	—	22.00	25.00
2008D	260,000	PF63 28.00	PF65 30.00			

KM# 274 10 EURO
18.00 g., 0.925 Silver 0.5319 oz. ASW, 32.5 mm. **Subject:** Gorch Fock II, 50th Anniversary **Obv:** Eagle **Rev:** Naval training sailing ship Gorch Fock II **Edge Lettering:** SEEFAHRT IST NOT

Date	Mintage	F12	VF20	XF40	MS60	MS63
2008J	1,500,000	—	—	—	22.00	25.00
2008J	260,000	PF63 28.00	PF65 30.00			

KM# 294 10 EURO
18.00 g., 0.925 Silver 0.5319 oz. ASW, 32.5 mm. **Subject:** Archaology in Germany **Obv:** Eagle, stars flanking **Rev:** Sun, moon and star shield

Date	Mintage	F12	VF20	XF40	MS60	MS63
2008A	1,500,000	—	—	—	22.00	25.00
2008A	260,000	PF63 28.00	PF65 30.00			

KM# 280 10 EURO
18.00 g., 0.925 Silver 0.5319 oz. ASW, 32.5 mm. **Subject:** Kepler's Laws - 400th Anniversary **Obv:** Eagle above value **Rev:** Portrait and geometric diagram demonstrating planetary orbits

Date	Mintage	F12	VF20	XF40	MS60	MS63
2009F	1,643,000	—	—	—	22.00	25.00
2009F	200,000	PF63 28.00	PF65 30.00			

KM# 281 10 EURO
18.00 g., 0.925 Silver 0.5319 oz. ASW, 32.5 mm. **Subject:** International Aerospace Expo, 100th Anniversary **Obv:** Eagle above value **Rev:** Plane landing, montage of plane development

Date	Mintage	F12	VF20	XF40	MS60	MS63
2009D	1,650,000	—	—	—	22.00	25.00
2009D	200,000	PF63 28.00	PF65 30.00			

KM# 282 10 EURO
18.00 g., 0.925 Silver 0.5319 oz. ASW, 32.5 mm. **Subject:** Leipzig University - 600th Anniversary **Obv:** Eagle above value **Rev:** University seal, portrait of Gottfried Wilhelm Leibniz

Date	Mintage	F12	VF20	XF40	MS60	MS63
2009A	1,613,000	—	—	—	22.00	25.00
2009G	200,000	PF63 28.00	PF65 30.00			

KM# 284 10 EURO
18.00 g., 0.925 Silver 0.5319 oz. ASW, 32.5 mm. **Subject:** Marion Countess Donhoff - 100th Anniversary of Birth **Obv:** Eagle and value **Rev:** Profile right

Date	Mintage	F12	VF20	XF40	MS60	MS63
2009J	1,600,000	—	—	—	22.00	25.00
2009J	200,000	PF63 28.00	PF65 30.00			

KM# 279 10 EURO
18.00 g., 0.925 Silver 0.5319 oz. ASW, 32.5 mm. **Subject:** IAAF World Championships - Berlin **Obv:** Eagle and value **Rev:**

Female javelin thrower in stadium **Note:** Mint Marks letters are in Morse Code.

Date	Mintage	F12	VF20	XF40	MS60	MS63
2009A	362,000	—	—	—	22.00	25.00
2009A	40,000	PF63 28.00	PF65 30.00			
2009D	362,000	—	—	—	22.00	25.00
2009D	40,000	PF63 28.00	PF65 30.00			
2009F	362,000	PF63 5.00				
2009F	40,000	PF63 28.00	PF65 30.00			
2009G	362,000	—	—	—	22.00	25.00
2009G	40,000	PF63 28.00	PF65 30.00			
2009J	362,000	—	—	—	22.00	25.00
2009J	40,000	PF63 28.00	PF66 30.00			

KM# 281a 10 EURO
18.00 g., 0.925 Silver 0.5319 oz. ASW, 32.5 mm. **Subject:** International Air Travel, 100th Anniversary **Obv:** Stylized eagle **Rev:** Airplanes, partially gilt

Date	Mintage	F12	VF20	XF40	MS60	MS63
2009D	1,650,000	—	—	—	22.00	25.00
2009D	200,000	PF63 28.00	PF65 30.00			

KM# 283 10 EURO
18.00 g., 0.925 Silver 0.5319 oz. ASW, 32.5 mm. **Subject:** Youth hostels - 100th Anniversary **Obv:** Eagle and value **Rev:** Stylized mountain, Alternal hostel in Westphalia

Date	Mintage	F12	VF20	XF40	MS60	MS63
2009G	1,610,000	—	—	—	22.00	25.00
2009G	200,000	PF63 28.00	PF65 30.00			

KM# 291 10 EURO
18.00 g., 0.925 Silver 0.5319 oz. ASW **Subject:** 175th Anniversary of German Railroads **Edge Lettering:** AUF VEREINTEN GLEISEN 1835-2010

Date	Mintage	F12	VF20	XF40	MS60	MS63
2010D	2,041,000	—	—	—	21.00	23.00
2010D	186,000	PF63 28.00	PF65 30.00			

KM# 290 10 EURO
18.00 g., 0.925 Silver 0.5319 oz. ASW, 32.5 mm. **Subject:** German Unification, 20th Anniversary **Edge Lettering:** EINIGKEIT UND RECHT UND FREIHEIT

Date	Mintage	F12	VF20	XF40	MS60	MS63
2010A	2,100,000	—	—	—	20.00	22.00
2010A	184,200	PF63 23.00	PF65 25.00			

KM# 287 10 EURO
18.00 g., 0.925 Silver 0.5319 oz. ASW, 32.5 mm. **Subject:** Porcelain Production in Germany, 300th Anniversary

Date	Mintage	F12	VF20	XF40	MS60	MS63
2010F	1,749,000	—	—	—	20.00	22.00
2010F	182,900	PF63 23.00	PF65 25.00			

KM# 288 10 EURO
18.00 g., 0.925 Silver 0.5319 oz. ASW, 32.5 mm. **Subject:** Robert Schumann - 200th Birth Anniversary

Date	Mintage	F12	VF20	XF40	MS60	MS63
2010J	1,700,000	—	—	—	20.00	22.00
2010J	182,900	PF63 23.00	PF65 25.00			

KM# 289 10 EURO
14.00 g., 0.925 Silver 0.4137 oz. ASW, 32.5 mm. **Subject:** Konrad Zuse, 100th Birth Anniversary

Date	Mintage	F12	VF20	XF40	MS60	MS63
2010G	1,706,000	—	—	—	20.00	22.00
2010G	182,900	PF63 23.00		PF65 25.00		

KM# 299a 10 EURO
16.00 g., 0.625 Silver 0.3194 oz. ASW, 32.5 mm. **Subject:** Soccer (Football) Women's World Cup in Germany **Edge Lettering:** DIE ZUKUNFT DES FUSSBALLS IST WEIBLICH

Date	Mintage	F12	VF20	XF40	MS60	MS63
2011A	47,000	PF63 28.00		PF65 30.00		
2011D	47,000	PF63 28.00		PF65 30.00		
2011F	47,000	PF63 28.00		PF65 30.00		
2011G	47,000	PF63 28.00		PF65 30.00		
2011J	47,000	PF63 28.00		PF65 30.00		

KM# 299 10 EURO
14.00 g., Copper-Nickel, 32.5 mm. **Subject:** Soccer (Football) Women's World Cup in Germany **Edge Lettering:** DIE ZUKUNFT DES FUSSBALLS IST WEIBLICH

Date	Mintage	F12	VF20	XF40	MS60	MS63
2011A	444,800	—	—	—	15.00	16.00
2011D	444,800	—	—	—	15.00	16.00
2011F	444,800	—	—	—	15.00	16.00
2011G	444,800	—	—	—	15.00	16.00
2011J	444,800	—	—	—	15.00	16.00

KM# 298 10 EURO
18.00 g., 0.925 Silver 0.5319 oz. ASW, 32.5 mm. **Subject:** FIS World Alpine Ski Championships **Edge Lettering:** FESTSPIELE IM SHNEE (Issued in 2010)

Date	Mintage	F12	VF20	XF40	MS60	MS63
2011A	400,000	—	—	—	21.00	23.00
2011A	41,400	PF63 28.00		PF65 30.00		
2011D	400,000	—	—	—	21.00	23.00
2011D	41,400	PF63 28.00		PF65 30.00		
2011F	400,000	—	—	—	21.00	23.00
2011F	41,400	PF63 28.00		PF65 30.00		
2011G	400,000	—	—	—	21.00	23.00
2011G	41,400	PF63 28.00		PF65 30.00		
2011J	400,000	—	—	—	21.00	23.00
2011J	41,400	PF63 28.00		PF65 30.00		

KM# 295 10 EURO
16.00 g., 0.625 Silver 0.3194 oz. ASW, 32.5 mm. **Subject:** Franz Liszt, 200th Anniversary of Birth **Edge Lettering:** CGME OBLICE - GENIE VEPPUCHIT

Date	Mintage	F12	VF20	XF40	MS60	MS63
2011G	2,187,000	—	—	—	15.00	16.00
2011G	178,000	PF63 28.00		PF65 30.00		

KM# 296a 10 EURO
14.00 g., 0.625 Silver 0.2795 oz. ASW, 32.5 mm. **Subject:** 125th Anniversary of the Automobile **Obv:** Stylized eagle, stars, country name, denomination and date **Obv. Legend:** 125 JAHRE AUTOMOBIL **Rev:** Hand on steering wheel, zig-sag roadway **Edge Lettering:** WAS UNS BEWEGT

Date	Mintage	F12	VF20	XF40	MS60	MS63
2011F	223,000	PF63 28.00		PF65 30.00		

KM# 300 10 EURO
14.00 g., Copper-Nickel, 32.5 mm. **Subject:** Till Eulenspiegel, 500th Anniversary **Edge Lettering:** SO BIN ICH DOCH HIE GEWESEN

Date	Mintage	F12	VF20	XF40	MS60	MS63
2011D	Est. 1800000	—	—	—	15.00	16.00

KM# 300a 10 EURO
16.00 g., 0.625 Silver 0.3194 oz. ASW, 32.5 mm. **Subject:** Til Eulenspiegel, 500th Anniversary **Edge Lettering:** SO BIN ICH DOCH HIE GEWESEN

Date	Mintage	F12	VF20	XF40	MS60	MS63
2011D	223,000	PF63 28.00		PF65 30.00		

KM# 301 10 EURO
14.00 g., Copper-Nickel, 32.5 mm. **Subject:** Discovery of the Archaeopteryx, 150th Anniversary **Edge Lettering:** ARCHAEOPTERYX - ZEUGE DER EVOLUTION

Date	Mintage	F12	VF20	XF40	MS60	MS63
2011A	Est. 2093000	—	—	—	15.00	16.00

KM# 301a 10 EURO
16.00 g., 0.625 Silver 0.3194 oz. ASW, 32.5 mm. **Subject:** Discovery of the Archaeopteryx, 150th Anniversary **Edge Lettering:** ARCHAEOPTERYX - ZEUGE DER EVOLUTION

Date	Mintage	F12	VF20	XF40	MS60	MS63
2011A	223,000	PF63 28.00		PF65 30.00		

KM# 302 10 EURO
14.00 g., Copper-Nickel, 32.5 mm. **Subject:** Elbe Tunnel, Hamburg, 100th Anniversary **Edge Lettering:** VERBINDUNG VON STADT UND HAFEN

Date	Mintage	F12	VF20	XF40	MS60	MS63
2011J	Est. 1900000	—	—	—	15.00	16.00

KM# 302a 10 EURO
16.00 g., 0.625 Silver 0.3194 oz. ASW, 32.5 mm. **Subject:** Elbe Tunnel, Hamburg, 100th Anniversary **Edge Lettering:** VERBINDUNG VON STADT UND HAFEN

Date	Mintage	F12	VF20	XF40	MS60	MS63
2011J	223,000	PF63 28.00		PF65 30.00		

KM# 308 10 EURO
16.00 g., 0.925 Silver 0.3194 oz. ASW, 32.5 mm. **Subject:** Friedrich der Grosse, 300th Anniversary of Birth **Obv:** Head of Friedrich the Great facing left **Obv. Legend:** 300 GEBURTSTAG FRIEDRICH II 1712-1786 **Rev:** Stylized eagle, stars, country name, denomination and date **Edge Lettering:** MICH MEINEN MITBÜRGERN NÜTZLICH ERWEISEN

Date	Mintage	F12	VF20	XF40	MS60	MS63
2012A	230,000	PF63 18.00		PF65 20.00		

KM# 309 10 EURO
14.00 g., Copper-Nickel, 32.5 mm. **Subject:** German Argo Action, 50th Anniversary of **Obv:** Sprouting seedling **Obv. Legend:** 50 JAHRE DEUTSCHE WELTHUNGERHILFE **Rev:** Stylized eagle, stars, country name, denomination and date **Edge Lettering:** HILFE ZUR SELBSTHILFE

Date	Mintage	F12	VF20	XF40	MS60	MS63
2012G	Est. 1579000	—	—	—	14.50	15.00

KM# 310 10 EURO
16.00 g., 0.625 Silver 0.3194 oz. ASW, 32.5 mm. **Subject:** Brothers Grimm, 200th Anniversary **Obv:** Conjoined heads of Grimm Brothers facing left **Obv. Legend:** 200 JAHRE GRIMMS MARCHEN **Rev:** Stylized eagle, stars, country name, denomination and date **Edge Lettering:** UND WENN SIE NICHT GESTORBEN SIND...

Date	Mintage	F12	VF20	XF40	MS60	MS63
2012F	Est. 210000	PF63 18.00		PF65 20.00		

KM# 311 10 EURO
14.00 g., 0.925 Silver 0.4137 oz. ASW, 32.5 mm. **Subject:** German National Library, 100th Anniversary **Obv:** Head facing left, design **Obv. Legend:** DEUTSCHE NATIONAL BIBLIOTECK 100 JAHRE **Rev:** Stylized eagle, country name, denomination and date **Edge Lettering:** BÜCHER SIND DER EINGANG ZUR WELT

Date	Mintage	F12	VF20	XF40	MS60	MS63
2012D	1,490,000	PF63 18.00		PF65 20.00		

KM# 312 10 EURO
14.00 g., Copper-Nickel, 32.5 mm. **Subject:** Gerhart Hauptmann, 150th Anniversary of Birth **Obv:** Head of Gerhart Hauptmann **Obv. Legend:** 150 GEBURTSTAG GERHART HAUPTMANN **Rev:** Stylized eagle, stars country name, denomination and date **Edge Lettering:** A JEDER MENSCH HAT HALT 'NE SEHNSUCHT

Date	Mintage	F12	VF20	XF40	MS60	MS63
2012J	1,432,000	—	—	—	14.50	15.00

KM# 318 10 EURO
16.00 g., 0.925 Silver 0.4728 oz. ASW, 32.5 mm. **Subject:** Georg Buchner, 200th Anniversary of Birth

Date	Mintage	F12	VF20	XF40	MS60	MS63
2012	—	—	—	—		25.00
2012	—	PF63 28.00		PF65 30.00		

KM# 316 10 EURO
18.00 g., 0.925 Silver 0.5319 oz. ASW **Subject:** Richard Wagner, 200th Anniversary of Birth

Date	Mintage	F12	VF20	XF40	MS60	MS63
2013	—	—	—	—		25.00
2013	—	PF63 28.00		PF65 30.00		

KM# 317 10 EURO
18.00 g., 0.925 Silver 0.5319 oz. ASW, 32.5 mm. **Subject:** Friedrich III

Date	Mintage	F12	VF20	XF40	MS60	MS63
2013	—	—	—	—		25.00
2013	—	PF63 28.00		PF65 30.00		

KM# 319 10 EURO
16.00 g., 0.925 Silver 0.4728 oz. ASW, 32.5 mm. **Subject:** Heinrich Herz, Electric Rays, 125th Anniversary

Date	Mintage	F12	VF20	XF40	MS60	MS63
2013	—	—	—	—		25.00
2013	—	PF63 28.00		PF65 30.00		

KM# 320 10 EURO
16.00 g., 0.925 Silver 0.4728 oz. ASW, 32.5 mm. **Subject:** Red Cross, 150th Anniversary

Date	Mintage	F12	VF20	XF40	MS60	MS63
2013	—	—	—	—		25.00
2013	—	PF63 28.00		PF65 30.00		

KM# 321 10 EURO
16.00 g., 0.925 Silver 0.4728 oz. ASW **Subject:** German Fairy Tales - Snow White

Date	Mintage	F12	VF20	XF40	MS60	MS63
2013	—	—	—	—		25.00
2013	—	PF63 28.00		PF65 30.00		

KM# 329 10 EURO
14.00 g., Copper-Nickel, 32.5 mm. **Subject:** Johann Gottfried Schadow, 250th Anniversary of Birth **Obv:** Eagle **Rev:** Portrait facing, two ladies at left

Date	Mintage	F12	VF20	XF40	MS60	MS63
2014A	—	—	—	—		20.00

KM# 330 10 EURO
14.00 g., Copper-Nickel, 32.5 mm. **Subject:** Richard Strauss, 150th Anniversary of Birth **Obv:** Eagle **Rev:** Head right

Date	Mintage	F12	VF20	XF40	MS60	MS63
2014	—	—	—	—		20.00

KM# 331 10 EURO

14.00 g., Copper-Nickel, 32.5 mm. **Subject:** Chronicles of Ulrich Richental - King Sigismund, the Pope and Jan Hus, 600th Anniversary **Obv:** Eagle **Rev:** Council of Bishops

Date	Mintage	F12	VF20	XF40	MS60	MS63
2014F	—	—	—	—	—	20.00

KM# 332 10 EURO

14.00 g., Copper-Nickel, 32.5 mm. **Subject:** Daniel Gabriel Fahrenheit's invention of the mercury thermometer **Obv:** Eagle

Date	Mintage	F12	VF20	XF40	MS60	MS63
2014J	—	—	—	—	—	20.00

KM# 322a 10 EURO

16.00 g., 0.625 Silver 0.3194 oz. ASW, 32.5 mm. **Subject:** Daniel Gabriel Fahrenheit's invention of the mercury thermometer, 300th Anniversary **Obv:** Eagle

Date	Mintage	F12	VF20	XF40	MS60	MS63
2014J	—	PF63 38.00	PF65 40.00			

KM# 328a 10 EURO

16.00 g., 0.625 Silver 0.3194 oz. ASW, 32.5 mm. **Obv:** Eagle **Rev:** Old lady with Hansel and Gretel

Date	Mintage	F12	VF20	XF40	MS60	MS63
2014G	—	PF63 38.00	PF65 40.00			

KM# 329a 10 EURO

16.00 g., 0.625 Silver 0.3194 oz. ASW, 32.5 mm. **Subject:** Johann Gottfried Schadow, 250th Anniversary of Birth **Obv:** Eagle **Rev:** Bust facing, two women at left

Date	Mintage	F12	VF20	XF40	MS60	MS63
2014A	—	PF63 38.00	PF65 40.00			

KM# 330a 10 EURO

16.00 g., 0.625 Silver 0.3194 oz. ASW, 32.5 mm. **Obv:** Eagle **Rev:** Richard Strauss, 150th Anniversary of Birth

Date	Mintage	F12	VF20	XF40	MS60	MS63
2014D	—	PF63 38.00	PF65 40.00			

KM# 331a 10 EURO

16.00 g., 0.625 Silver 0.3194 oz. ASW, 32.5 mm. **Subject:** Chronicles of Ulrich Richental on King Sigismund, the Pope and Jan Hus, 600th Anniversary **Obv:** Eagle **Rev:** Council of Bishops

Date	Mintage	F12	VF20	XF40	MS60	MS63
2014F	—	PF63 38.00	PF65 40.00			

KM# 297 20 EURO

3.89 g., 0.9999 Gold 0.1242 oz. AGW, 17.5 mm. **Series:** German Forest **Subject:** Oak Tree **Obv:** Stylized eagle, stars, legend "BUNDESREPUBLIK DEUTSCHLAND", date and value **Rev:** Oak leaf and legends "DEUTSCHER WALD" and "EICHE **Edge:** Reeded

Date	Mintage	F12	VF20	XF40	MS60	MS63
2010D	40,000	—	—	—	—	250
2010F	40,000	—	—	—	—	250
2010A	40,000	—	—	—	—	250
2010G	40,000	—	—	—	—	250
2010J	40,000	—	—	—	—	250

KM# 303 20 EURO

3.89 g., 0.9999 Gold 0.1242 oz. AGW, 17.5 mm. **Series:** German Forest **Subject:** Beech Tree **Obv:** Stylized eagle, stars, legend, date and value **Obv. Legend:** BUNDERSREPUBLIK DEUTSCHLAND **Rev:** Beech leaf and legends **Rev. Legend:** DEUTSCHER WALD / BUCHE **Edge:** Reeded

Date	Mintage	F12	VF20	XF40	MS60	MS63
2011A	40,000	—	—	—	—	250
2011D	40,000	—	—	—	—	250
2011F	40,000	—	—	—	—	250
2011G	40,000	—	—	—	—	250
2011J	40,000	—	—	—	—	250

KM# 307 20 EURO

3.89 g., 0.9999 Gold 0.1242 oz. AGW, 17.5 mm. **Series:** German Forest **Subject:** Spruce Tree **Obv:** Stylized eagle, stars, date and value **Obv. Legend:** BUNDESREPUBLIK DEUTSCHLAND **Rev:** Spruce branch end and legends **Rev. Legend:** DEUTSCHER WALD / FICHTE **Edge:** Reeded

Date	Mintage	F12	VF20	XF40	MS60	MS63
2012A	40,000	—	—	—	—	250
2012D	40,000	—	—	—	—	250
2012F	40,000	—	—	—	—	250
2012G	40,000	—	—	—	—	250
2012J	40,000	—	—	—	—	250

KM# 324 20 EURO

3.89 g., 0.9999 Gold 0.1242 oz. AGW, 17.5 mm. **Series:** German Forest **Subject:** Pine Tree **Obv:** Stylized eagle, stars, country name, date and denomination **Rev:** Pine needles **Rev. Legend:** DEUTSCHER WALD and KIEFER **Edge:** Reeded

Date	Mintage	F12	VF20	XF40	MS60	MS63
2013	—	—	—	—	—	275
2013	Est. 40000	—	—	—	—	275
2013	—	—	—	—	—	275
2013	Est. 40000	—	—	—	—	275
2013	Est. 40000	—	—	—	—	275

KM# 220 100 EURO

15.55 g., 0.9999 Gold 0.4967 oz. AGW, 28 mm. **Subject:** Introduction of the Euro Currency **Obv:** Stylized round eagle **Rev:** Euro symbol and arches **Edge:** Reeded

Date	Mintage	F12	VF20	XF40	MS60	MS63
2002A	100,000	PF63 825	PF65 850			
2002D	100,000	PF63 825	PF65 850			
2002F	100,000	PF63 825	PF65 850			
2002G	100,000	PF63 825	PF65 850			
2002J	100,000	PF63 825	PF65 850			

KM# 228 100 EURO

15.55 g., 0.9999 Gold 0.4967 oz. AGW, 28 mm. **Obv:** Stylized eagle, denomination below **Rev:** Quedlinburg Abbey in monogram **Edge:** Reeded

Date	Mintage	F12	VF20	XF40	MS60	MS63
2003D (2003)	80,000	PF63 825	PF65 850			
2003F (2003)	00,000	PF63 825	PF65 850			
2003J (2003)	80,000	PF63 825	PF65 850			
2003A	80,000	PF63 825	PF65 850			
2003G (2003)	80,000	PF63 825	PF65 850			

KM# 235 100 EURO

15.55 g., 0.9999 Gold 0.4967 oz. AGW, 28 mm. **Obv:** Stylized eagle, denomination below **Rev:** Bamberg city view **Edge:** Reeded

Date	Mintage	F12	VF20	XF40	MS60	MS63
2004A	80,000	PF63 825	PF65 850			
2004F	80,000	PF63 825	PF65 850			
2004D	80,000	PF63 825	PF65 850			
2004J	80,000	PF63 825	PF65 850			
2004G	80,000	PF63 825	PF65 850			

KM# 236 100 EURO

15.55 g., 0.9999 Gold 0.4967 oz. AGW **Subject:** UNESCO - Weimar **Obv:** Stylized eagle **Rev:** Historical City of Weimar buildings **Edge:** Reeded

Date	Mintage	F12	VF20	XF40	MS60	MS63
2006 (2005)A	70,000	PF63 825	PF65 850			
2006 (2005)D	70,000	PF63 825	PF65 850			
2006 (2005)F	70,000	PF63 825	PF65 850			
2006 (2005)G	70,000	PF63 825	PF65 850			
2006 (2005)J	70,000	PF63 825	PF65 850			

KM# 237 100 EURO

15.55 g., 0.9999 Gold 0.4967 oz. AGW, 28 mm. **Subject:** Soccer - Germany 2006 **Obv:** Round stylized eagle **Rev:** Aerial view of stadium

Date	Mintage	F12	VF20	XF40	MS60	MS63
2005A	70,000	PF63 825	PF65 850			
2005D	70,000	PF63 825	PF65 850			
2005F	70,000	PF63 825	PF65 850			
2005G	70,000	PF63 825	PF65 850			
2005J	70,000	PF63 825	PF65 850			

KM# 267 100 EURO

15.55 g., 0.9999 Gold 0.4967 oz. AGW, 28 mm. **Subject:** Lubeck - UNESCO Heritage site **Obv:** Eagle **Rev:** City view

Date	Mintage	F12	VF20	XF40	MS60	MS63
2007A	66,000	PF63 825	PF65 850			
2007D	66,000	PF63 825	PF65 850			
2007F	66,000	PF63 825	PF65 850			
2007G	66,000	PF63 825	PF65 850			
2007J	66,000	PF63 825	PF65 850			

KM# 270 100 EURO

15.55 g., 0.9999 Gold 0.4967 oz. AGW, 28 mm. **Subject:** Goslar - UNESCO Heritage site **Obv:** Eagle **Edge:** Reeded

Date	Mintage	F12	VF20	XF40	MS60	MS63
2008A	64,000	PF63 825	PF65 850			
2008D	64,000	PF63 825	PF65 850			
2008F	64,000	PF63 825	PF65 850			
2008G	64,000	PF63 825	PF65 850			
2008J	64,000	PF63 825	PF65 850			

KM# 278 100 EURO

15.55 g., 0.9999 Gold 0.4967 oz. AGW, 28 mm. **Subject:** Trier - UNESCO Heritage site **Obv:** Eagle and denomination **Rev:** Riverside montage of buildings **Edge:** Reeded

Date	Mintage	F12	VF20	XF40	MS60	MS63
2009A	64,000	PF63 825	PF65 850			
2009D	64,000	PF63 825	PF65 850			
2009F	64,000	PF63 825	PF65 850			
2009G	64,000	PF63 825	PF65 850			
2009J	64,000	PF63 825	PF65 850			

KM# 286 100 EURO

15.55 g., 0.9999 Gold 0.4967 oz. AGW, 28 mm. **Subject:** Würzburg - UNESCO Heritage site **Rev:** Würzburg residence and court garden

Date	Mintage	F12	VF20	XF40	MS60	MS63
2010A	64,000	PF63 825	PF65 850			
2010D	64,000	PF63 825	PF65 850			
2010F	64,000	PF63 825	PF65 850			
2010G	64,000	PF63 825	PF65 850			
2010J	64,000	PF63 825	PF65 850			

KM# 304 100 EURO

15.55 g., 0.9999 Gold 0.4967 oz. AGW **Subject:** UNESCO World Heritage Site - Wartburg Castle **Obv:** Stylized eagle, stars, legend date and value **Obv. Legend:** BUNDESREPUBLIK DEUTSCHLAND **Rev:** Wartburg Castle and legends **Rev. Legend:** UNESCO WELTERE WARTBURG / GEGR 1067 LUDWIG DER SPRINGER HERMANN I... **Edge:** Reeded

Date	Mintage	F12	VF20	XF40	MS60	MS63
2011A	60,000	PF63 825	PF65 850			
2011D	60,000	PF63 825	PF65 850			
2011F	60,000	PF63 825	PF65 850			
2011G	60,000	PF63 825	PF65 850			
2011J	60,000	PF63 825	PF65 850			

KM# 313 100 EURO
15.55 g., 0.9999 Gold 0.4967 oz. AGW, 28 mm. **Subject:** UNESCO - Aachen Cathedral **Obv:** Eagle **Rev:** Side view of Cathedral

Date	Mintage	F12	VF20	XF40	MS60	MS63
2012A	54,000	PF63 825	PF65 850			
2012D	54,000	PF63 825	PF65 850			
2012F	54,000	PF63 825	PF65 850			
2012G	54,000	PF63 825	PF65 850			
2012J	54,000	PF63 825	PF65 850			

KM# 322 100 EURO
15.55 g., 0.999 Gold 0.4962 oz. AGW, 28 mm. **Subject:** Aachen Cathedral, European Heritage Site.

Date	Mintage	F12	VF20	XF40	MS60	MS63
2012A	44,000	PF63 825	PF65 850			
2012D	44,000	PF63 825	PF65 850			
2012F	44,000	PF63 825	PF65 850			
2012G	44,000	PF63 825	PF65 850			
2012J	44,000	PF63 825	PF65 850			

KM# 333 100 EURO
15.55 g., 0.999 Gold 0.4962 oz. AGW, 28 mm. **Subject:** Lorsch Cloister **Obv:** Eagle

Date	Mintage	F12	VF20	XF40	MS60	MS63
2014D	—	PF63 950	PF65 975			
2014F	—	PF63 950	PF65 975			
2014G	—	PF63 950	PF65 975			
2014J	—	PF63 950	PF65 975			
2014A	—	PF63 950	PF65 975			

KM# 221 200 EURO
31.10 g., 0.9999 Gold 0.9934 oz. AGW, 32.5 mm. **Subject:** Introduction of the Euro Currency **Obv:** Stylized round eagle **Rev:** Euro symbol and arches **Edge Lettering:** IM ... ZEICHEN ... DER ... EINIGUNG ... EUROPAS

Date	Mintage	F12	VF20	XF40	MS60	MS63
2002A	1,700	PF63 1,850	PF65 1,950			
2002D	1,700	PF63 1,850	PF65 1,950			
2002F	1,700	PF63 1,850	PF65 1,950			
2002G	1,700	PF63 1,850	PF65 1,950			
2002J	1,700	PF63 1,850	PF65 1,950			

KM# 328 10 EURO
14.00 g., Copper-Nickel, 32.5 mm. **Obv:** Eagle **Rev:** Old lady with Hansel and Gretel

Date	Mintage	F12	VF20	XF40	MS60	MS63
2014G	—	—	—	—	20.00	—

MINT SETS

KM#	Date	Mintage	Identification	Issue Price	Mkt Val
MS119	2001A (10)	130,000	KM105,100, 107, 108, 109.2, 110, 140.1, 170, 175,183	—	40.00
MS120	2001D (10)	130,000	KM105, 106a, 107-108, 109.2, 110, 140.1, 170, 175, 183	—	40.00
MS121	2001F (10)	130,000	KM105, 106a, 107-108, 109.2, 110, 140.1, 170, 175, 183	—	40.00
MS122	2001G (10)	130,000	KM105, 106a, 107-108, 109.2, 110, 140.1, 170, 175, 183	—	40.00
MS123	2001J (10)	130,000	KM105, 106a, 107-108, 109.2, 110, 140.1, 170, 175, 183	—	40.00
MS124	2002A (8)	90,000	KM#207-214	—	20.00
MS125	2002D (8)	90,000	KM#207-214	—	20.00
MS126	2002F (8)	90,000	KM#207-214	—	20.00
MS127	2002G (8)	90,000	KM#207-214	—	20.00
MS128	2002J (8)	90,000	KM#207-214	—	20.00
MS129	2003A (8)	90,000	KM#207-214	—	25.00
MS130	2003D (8)	90,000	KM#207-214	—	27.50
MS131	2003F (8)	90,000	KM#207-214	—	27.50
MS132	2003G (8)	90,000	KM#207-214	—	27.50
MS133	2003J (8)	90,000	KM#207-214	—	25.00
MS134	2004A (8)	90,000	KM#207-214	—	24.00
MS135	2004D (8)	90,000	KM#207-214	—	22.00
MS136	2004F (8)	90,000	KM#207-214	—	24.00
MS137	2004G (8)	90,000	KM#207-214	—	24.00
MS138	2004J (8)	90,000	KM#207-214	—	28.00
MS139	2005A (8)	90,000	KM#207-214	—	28.00
MS140	2005D (8)	90,000	KM#207-214	—	28.00
MS141	2005F (8)	90,000	KM#207-214	—	28.00
MS142	2005G (8)	90,000	KM#207-214	—	28.00
MS143	2005J (8)	90,000	KM#207-214	—	26.00
MS144	2006A (9)	90,000	KM#207-214, 253	—	35.00
MS145	2006D (9)	90,000	KM#207-214, 253	—	35.00
MS146	2006F (9)	90,000	KM#207-214, 253	—	35.00
MS147	2006G (9)	90,000	KM#207-214, 253	—	35.00
MS148	2006J (9)	90,000	KM#207-214, 253	—	35.00
MS149	2006 (5)	80,000	KM#253 (A, D, F, G and J)	—	23.00
MS150	2007A (9)	90,000	KM#207-209, 254-257, 259, 260	—	27.00
MS151	2007D (9)	90,000	KM#207-209, 254-257, 259, 260	—	27.00
MS152	2007F (9)	90,000	KM#207-209, 254-257, 259, 260	—	27.00
MS153	2007G (9)	90,000	KM#207-209, 254-257, 259, 260	—	27.00
MS154	2007J (9)	90,000	KM#207-209, 254-257, 259, 260	—	27.00
MS155	2007 (5)	80,000	KM#260 (A, D, F, G and J)	—	23.00
MS156	2008A (9)	80,000	KM#207-209, 254-258, 261	—	27.00
MS157	2008D (9)	80,000	KM#207-209, 254-258, 261	—	27.00
MS158	2008F (9)	80,000	KM#207-209, 254-258, 261	—	27.00
MS159	2008G (9)	80,000	KM#207-209, 254-258, 261	—	27.00
MS160	2008J (9)	80,000	KM#207-209, 254-258, 261	—	27.00
MS161	2008 (5)	80,000	KM#261 (A, D, F, G, J)	—	23.00
MS162	2009A (9)	60,000	KM#207-209, 254-257, 276, 277	—	27.00
MS163	2009D (9)	60,000	KM#207-209, 254-257, 276, 277	—	27.00
MS164	2009F (9)	60,000	KM#207-209, 254-257, 276, 277	—	27.00
MS165	2009G (9)	60,000	KM#207-209, 254-257, 276, 277	—	27.00
MS166	2009J (9)	60,000	KM#207-209, 254-257, 276, 277	—	27.00
MS167	2009 (5)	50,000	KM#276 (A, D, F, G, J)	—	23.00
MS168	2010A (9)	53,800	KM#207-209, 254-258, 285	—	20.00
MS169	2010D (9)	46,800	KM#207-209, 254-258, 285	—	20.00
MS170	2010F (9)	46,800	KM#207-209, 254-258, 285	—	20.00
MS171	2010G (9)	46,800	KM#207-209, 254-258, 285	—	20.00
MS172	2010J (9)	46,800	KM#207-209, 254-258, 285	—	20.00
MS173	2010 (5)	45,000	KM#285 (A, D, F, G, J)	—	23.00
MS174	2011A (9)	48,000	KM#207-209, 254-258, 293	—	20.00
MS175	2011D (9)	44,000	KM#207-209, 254-258, 293	—	20.00
MS176	2011F (9)	44,000	KM#207-209, 254-258, 293	—	20.00
MS177	2011G (9)	44,000	KM#207-209, 254-258, 293	—	20.00
MS178	2011J (9)	44,000	KM#207-209, 254-258, 293	—	20.00
MS179	2011 (5)	147,000	KM#293 (A, D, F, G, J)	—	23.00
MS180	2012A (9)	50,000	KM#207-209, 254-257, 305, 306	—	20.00
MS181	2012D (9)	50,000	KM#207-209, 254-257, 305, 306	—	20.00
MS182	2012G (9)	50,000	KM#207-209, 254-257, 305, 306	—	20.00
MS183	2012G (9)	50,000	KM#207-209, 254-257, 305, 306	—	20.00
MS184	2012J (9)	50,000	KM#207-209, 254-257, 305, 306	—	20.00
MS185	2012 (5)	45,000	KM#305 (A, D, F, G and J)	—	24.00
MS186	2012 (6)	45,000	KM#306 (A, D, F, G and J)	—	38.00

PROOF SETS

KM#	Date	Mintage	Identification	Issue Price	Mkt Val
PS150	2001A (10)	78,000	KM105,106a, 107-108, 109.2, 110, 140.1, 170, 175, 183	—	45.00
PS151	2001D (10)	78,000	KM105,106a, 107-108, 109.2, 110, 140.1, 170, 175, 183	—	45.00
PS152	2001F (10)	78,000	KM105, 106a, 107-108, 110, 140.1, 170, 175, 183	—	45.00
PS153	2001G (10)	78,000	KM105, 106a, 107-108, 109.2, 110, 140.1, 170, 175, 183	—	45.00
PS154	2001J (10)	78,000	KM105, 106a, 107-108, 109.2, 110, 140.1, 170, 175, 183	—	45.00
PS155	2002A (8)	75,000	KM#207-214	—	20.00
PS156	2002D (8)	75,000	KM#207-214	—	20.00
PS157	2002F (8)	75,000	KM#207-214	—	20.00
PS158	2002G (8)	75,000	KM#207-214	—	20.00
PS159	2002J (8)	75,000	KM#207-214	—	20.00
PS160	2003A (8)	75,000	KM#207-214	—	20.00
PS161	2003D (8)	75,000	KM#207-214	—	20.00
PS162	2003F (8)	75,000	KM#207-214	—	20.00
PS163	2003G (8)	75,000	KM#207-214	—	20.00
PS164	2003J (8)	75,000	KM#207-214	—	20.00
PS165	2004A (8)	75,000	KM#207-214	—	20.00
PS166	2004D (8)	75,000	KM#207-214	—	20.00
PS167	2004F (8)	75,000	KM#207-214	—	20.00
PS168	2004G (8)	75,000	KM#207-214	—	20.00
PS169	2004J (8)	75,000	KM#207-214	—	20.00
PS170	2005A (8)	75,000	KM#207-214	—	30.00
PS171	2005D (8)	75,000	KM#207-214	—	30.00
PS172	2005F (8)	75,000	KM#207-214	—	30.00
PS173	2005G (8)	75,000	KM#207-214	—	30.00
PS174	2005J (8)	75,000	KM#207-214	—	30.00
PS175	2006A (9)	75,000	KM#207-214, 253	—	35.00
PS176	2006D (9)	75,000	KM#207-214, 253	—	35.00
PS177	2006F (9)	75,000	KM#207-214, 253	—	35.00
PS178	2006G (9)	75,000	KM#207-214, 253	—	35.00
PS179	2006J (9)	75,000	KM#207-214, 253	—	35.00
PS180	2006 (5)	70,000	KM#253 (A, D, F, G, J)	—	30.00
PS181	2007A (9)	70,000	KM#207-209, 254-257, 259, 260	—	35.00
PS182	2007D (9)	70,000	KM#207-209, 254-257, 259, 260	—	35.00
PS183	2007F (9)	70,000	KM#207-209, 254-257, 259, 260	—	35.00
PS184	2007G (9)	75,000	KM#207-209, 254-257, 259, 260	—	35.00
PS185	2007J (9)	75,000	KM#207-209, 254-257, 259, 260	—	35.00
PS186	2007 (5)	70,000	KM#260 (A, D, F, G, J)	—	40.00
PS187	2008A (9)	70,000	KM#207-209, 254-258, 261	—	35.00
PS188	2008D (9)	70,000	KM#207-209, 254-258, 261	—	35.00
PS189	2008F (9)	70,000	KM#207-209, 254-258, 261	—	35.00
PS190	2008G (9)	70,000	KM#207-209, 254-258, 261	—	35.00
PS191	2008J (9)	70,000	KM#207-209, 254-258, 261	—	35.00
PS192	2008 (5)	70,000	KM#261 (A, D, F, G, J)	—	40.00

PS193	2009A (9)	50,000	KM#207-209, 254-258, 276	—	35.00
PS194	2009D (9)	50,000	KM#207-209, 254-258, 276	—	35.00
PS195	2009F (9)	50,000	KM#207-209, 254-258, 276	—	35.00
PS196	2009G (9)	50,000	KM#207-209, 254-258, 276	—	35.00
PS197	2009J (9)	50,000	KM#207-209, 254-258, 276	—	35.00
PS198	2009 (5)	50,000	KM#276 (A, D, F, G, J)	—	40.00
PS199	2010A (9)	45,150	KM#207-209, 254-258, 285	—	40.00
PS200	2010D (9)	40,120	KM#207-209, 254-258, 285	—	40.00
PS201	2010F (9)	40,120	KM#207-209, 254-258, 285	—	40.00
PS202	2010G (9)	40,120	KM#207-209, 254-258, 285	—	40.00
PS203	2010J (9)	40,120	KM#207-209, 254-258, 285	—	40.00
PS204	2010 (5)	45,000	KM#285 (A, D, F, G, J)	—	40.00
PS215	2011A (9)	43,000	KM#207-209, 254-258, 293	—	40.00
PS216	2011D (9)	37,000	KM#207-209, 254-258, 293	—	40.00
PS217	2011F (9)	37,000	KM#207-209, 254-258, 293	—	40.00
PS218	2011G (9)	37,000	KM#207-209, 254-258, 293	—	40.00
PS219	2011J (9)	37,000	KM#207-209, 254-258, 293	—	40.00
PS220	2011 (5)	55,000	KM#293 (A, D, F, G, J)	—	40.00
PS221	2002 (5)	80,000	KM#215-219	—	150
PS222	2003 (6)	80,000	KM#222-227	—	180
PS223	2004 (6)	80,000	KM#229-234	—	180
PS224	2005 (6)	80,000	KM#238-243	—	200
PS225	2006 (6)	80,000	KM#245-249	—	150
PS226	2007 (5)	50,000	KM#259 (A, D, F, G and J)	—	42.00
PS227	2007 (5)	80,000	KM#263-266, 268	—	150
PS228	2008 (5)	80,000	KM#271-274, 294	—	150
PS229	2008 (5)	20,000	KM#277 (A, D, F, G and J)	—	42.00
PS230	2009 (6)	60,000	KM#279, 281, 281a, 282-284	—	180
PS231	2010 (5)	57,900	KM#287-291, 298a	—	180
PS232	2011 (6)	63,000	KM#295, 296a, 299a-302a	—	180
PS233	2012A (9)	40,000	KM#207-209, 254-258, 305, 306	—	30.00
PS234	2012D (9)	32,000	KM#207-209, 254-257, 305, 306	—	30.00
PS235	2012F (9)	32,000	KM#207-209, 254-257, 305, 306	—	30.00
PS236	2012G (9)	40,000	KM#207-209, 254-257, 305, 306	—	30.00
PS237	2012J (10)	32,000	KM#207-209, 254-258, 305, 306	—	30.00
PS238	2012 (5)	55,000	KM#306 (A, D, F, G and J)	—	42.00
PS239	2012 (0)	60,000	KM#308a-312a	—	150

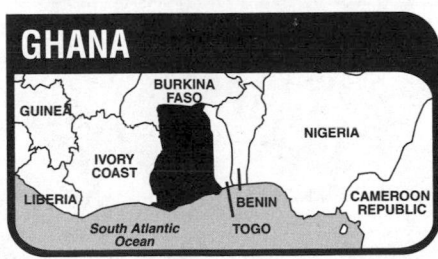

GHANA

The Republic of Ghana, a member of the Commonwealth of Nations situated on the West Coast of Africa between Ivory Coast and Togo, has an area of 92,100 sq. mi. (238,540 sq. km.) and a population of 14 million, almost entirely African. Capital: Accra. Cocoa (the major crop), coconuts, palm kernels and coffee are exported. Mining, second in importance to agriculture, is concentrated on gold, manganese and industrial diamonds.

MONETARY SYSTEM
1 Cedi = 100 Pesewas, 1965-2007
1 (new) Cedi = 10,000 (old) Cedis, 2007-

REPUBLIC
DECIMAL COINAGE

KM# 36 10 CEDIS
4.41 g., Copper-Nickel, 22.9 mm. **Obv:** National arms divides date and denomination **Rev:** Gorilla family **Edge:** Plain

Date	Mintage	F12	VF20	XF40	MS60	MS63
2003	—	—	—	—	1.50	2.00

REFORM COINAGE
2007-

KM# 37 PESEWA
1.82 g., Copper Plated Steel, 17 mm. **Obv:** National arms **Obv. Legend:** GHANA **Rev:** Adomi Bridge **Edge:** Plain

Date	Mintage	F12	VF20	XF40	MS60	MS63
2007	—	—	—	—	—	0.75

KM# 38 5 PESEWAS
2.50 g., Nickel Clad Steel, 18 mm. **Obv:** National arms **Obv. Legend:** GHANA **Rev:** Native male blowing horn **Edge:** Plain

Date	Mintage	F12	VF20	XF40	MS60	MS63
2007	—	—	—	—	—	1.25

KM# 39 10 PESEWAS
3.23 g., Nickel Clad Steel, 20.4 mm. **Obv:** National arms **Obv. Legend:** GHANA **Rev:** Open book, pen **Edge:** Reeded

Date	Mintage	F12	VF20	XF40	MS60	MS63
2007	—	—	—	—	—	2.50

KM# 40 20 PESEWAS
4.40 g., Nickel Plated Steel, 23.5 mm. **Obv:** National arms **Obv. Legend:** GHANA **Rev:** Split open cocoa pod **Edge:** Plain

Date	Mintage	F12	VF20	XF40	MS60	MS63
2007	—	—	—	—	—	3.50

KM# 41 50 PESEWAS
6.08 g., Nickel Plated Steel, 26.4 mm. **Obv:** National arms **Obv. Legend:** GHANA **Rev:** 1/2 length figure of market woman facing **Edge:** Reeded

Date	Mintage	F12	VF20	XF40	MS60	MS63
2007	—	—	—	—	—	6.00

KM# 42 CEDI
7.40 g., Bi-Metallic, 28 mm. **Obv:** National arms **Obv. Legend:** GHANA **Rev:** Scale of Justice in sprays **Edge:** Segmented reeding

Date	Mintage	F12	VF20	XF40	MS60	MS63
2007	—	—	—	—	—	10.00

KM# 43 5 CEDIS
31.14 g., 0.999 Silver 0.9936 oz. ASW, 40 mm. **Obv:** Elizabeth II **Rev:** Elephants

Date	Mintage	F12	VF20	XF40	MS60	MS63
2013	2,000	PF63 65.00		PF65 70.00		

GIBRALTAR

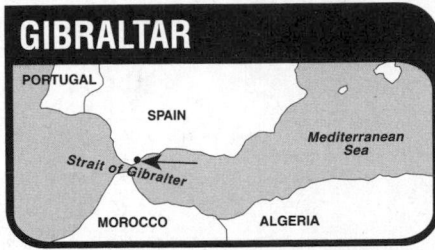

The British Colony of Gibraltar, located at the southernmost point of the Iberian Peninsula, has an area of 2.25 sq. mi. (6.5 sq. km.) and a population of 29,651. Capital (and only town): Gibraltar. Aside from its strategic importance as guardian of the western entrance to the Mediterranean Sea, Gibraltar is also a free port and a British naval base.

RULERS
British

MINT MARKS
PM - Pobjoy Mint

MINT PRIVY MARKS
U - Unc finish

BRITISH COLONY
DECIMAL COINAGE
100 Pence = 1 Pound

KM# 773 PENNY
3.56 g., Copper Plated Steel, 20.32 mm. **Ruler:** Elizabeth II **Obv:** Head with tiara right **Rev:** Barbary partridge left divides denomination

Date	Mintage	F12	VF20	XF40	MS60	MS63
2001 AA	—	—	—	—	0.35	0.50
2002 AA	—	—	—	—	0.35	0.50
2003 AA	—	—	—	—	0.35	0.50

KM# 1046 PENNY
3.56 g., Copper Plated Steel, 20.32 mm. **Ruler:** Elizabeth II **Subject:** 300th Anniversary **Obv:** Crowned bust right **Rev:** Monkey **Edge:** Plain

Date	Mintage	F12	VF20	XF40	MS60	MS63
2004	—	—	—	—	0.30	0.50

KM# 1079 PENNY
3.56 g., Copper Plated Steel, 20.32 mm. **Ruler:** Elizabeth II **Obv:** Bust right **Rev:** Sceptre

Date	Mintage	F12	VF20	XF40	MS60	MS63
2005	—	—	—	—	0.35	0.50
2006	—	—	—	—	0.35	0.50
2007	—	—	—	—	0.35	0.50
2008	—	—	—	—	0.35	0.50
2009	—	—	—	—	0.35	0.50
2010	—	—	—	—	0.35	0.50
2011 (2012)	—	—	—	—	0.35	0.50

KM# 1098 PENNY
3.54 g., Bronze Plated Steel, 20.5 mm. **Ruler:** Elizabeth II **Rev:** Bird left

Date	Mintage	F12	VF20	XF40	MS60	MS63
2010	—	—	—	—	0.35	0.50

KM# 1099 PENNY
3.56 g., Copper Plated Steel, 20.32 mm. **Ruler:** Elizabeth II **Obv:** Bust right **Obv. Legend:** ELIZABETH II QUEEN OF GIBRALTAR **Rev:** Bird left

Date	Mintage	F12	VF20	XF40	MS60	MS63
2012	—	—	—	—	0.35	0.50

KM# 774 2 PENCE
7.12 g., Copper Plated Steel, 25.91 mm. **Ruler:** Elizabeth II **Obv:** Head with tiara right

Date	Mintage	F12	VF20	XF40	MS60	MS63
2001 AA	—	—	—	—	0.50	0.85
2001PM AB	—	—	—	—	0.50	0.85
2002	—	—	—	—	0.50	0.85
2003 AA	—	—	—	—	0.50	0.85

KM# 1044 2 PENCE
7.12 g., Copper Plated Steel, 25.91 mm. **Ruler:** Elizabeth II **Subject:** 300th Anniversary **Obv:** Crowned bust right **Rev:** Four old keys **Edge:** Plain

Date	Mintage	F12	VF20	XF40	MS60	MS63
2004	—	—	—	—	0.50	0.65

KM# 1065 2 PENCE
7.12 g., Copper Plated Steel, 25.91 mm. **Ruler:** Elizabeth II **Subject:** Operation Torch, 1942 **Rev:** Three soldiers

Date	Mintage	F12	VF20	XF40	MS60	MS63
2005	—	—	—	—	0.50	0.65
2006	—	—	—	—	0.50	0.65
2007	—	—	—	—	0.50	0.65
2008	—	—	—	—	0.50	0.65
2009	—	—	—	—	0.50	0.65
2010	—	—	—	—	0.50	0.65
2011	—	—	—	—	0.50	0.65

KM# 1080 2 PENCE
7.12 g., Copper Plated Steel, 25.91 mm. **Ruler:** Elizabeth II **Subject:** Diamond Wedding **Rev:** Conjoined busts of Elizabeth II and Philip

Date	Mintage	F12	VF20	XF40	MS60	MS63
2007	—	—	—	—	0.50	0.65

KM# 1100 2 PENCE
7.12 g., Copper Plated Steel, 25.91 mm. **Ruler:** Elizabeth II **Obv:** Bust right **Obv. Legend:** ELIZABETH II QUEEN OF GIBRALTAR

Date	Mintage	F12	VF20	XF40	MS60	MS63
2012	—	—	—	—	0.50	0.65

KM# 775 5 PENCE
3.25 g., Copper-Nickel, 18 mm. **Ruler:** Elizabeth II **Obv:** Head with tiara right **Rev:** Barbary Ape left divides denomination **Edge:** Reeded

Date	Mintage	F12	VF20	XF40	MS60	MS63
2001 AB	—	—	—	—	0.60	0.75
2002 AB	—	—	—	—	0.60	0.75
2003 AA	—	—	—	—	0.60	0.75

KM# 1049 5 PENCE
3.25 g., Copper-Nickel, 18 mm. **Ruler:** Elizabeth II **Subject:** Tercentenary 1704-2004 **Obv:** Elizabeth II **Rev:** British Royal Sceptre **Edge:** Reeded

Date	Mintage	F12	VF20	XF40	MS60	MS63
2004	—	—	—	—	—	1.50

KM# 1081 5 PENCE
3.25 g., Copper-Nickel, 18 mm. **Ruler:** Elizabeth II **Obv:** Bust in diadem right **Rev:** Barbary ape seated **Edge:** Reeded

Date	Mintage	F12	VF20	XF40	MS60	MS63
2005	—	—	—	—	0.60	0.75
2006	—	—	—	—	0.60	0.75
2007	—	—	—	—	0.60	0.75
2008	—	—	—	—	0.60	0.75
2009	—	—	—	—	0.60	0.75
2010	—	—	—	—	0.60	0.75
2011	—	—	—	—	0.60	0.75

KM# 1101 5 PENCE
3.25 g., Copper-Nickel, 18 mm. **Ruler:** Elizabeth II **Obv:** Bust right **Obv. Legend:** ELIZABETH II QUEEN OF GIBRALTAR

Date	Mintage	F12	VF20	XF40	MS60	MS63
2012	—	—	—	—	0.60	0.75

KM# 776 10 PENCE
6.50 g., Copper-Nickel, 24.5 mm. **Ruler:** Elizabeth II **Obv:** Head with tiara right, date below **Rev:** Denomination below building **Edge:** Reeded

Date	Mintage	F12	VF20	XF40	MS60	MS63
2001 AC	—	—	—	—	1.00	1.25
2001 AB	—	—	—	—	1.00	1.25
2001 AE	—	—	—	—	1.00	1.25
2001 AA	—	—	—	—	1.00	1.25
2002 AC	—	—	—	—	1.00	1.25
2003 AA	—	—	—	—	1.00	1.25

KM# 1047 10 PENCE
6.50 g., Copper-Nickel, 24.5 mm. **Ruler:** Elizabeth II **Subject:** 300th Anniversary **Obv:** Elizabeth II **Rev:** Three military officers planning Operation Torch 1942 **Edge:** Reeded

Date	Mintage	F12	VF20	XF40	MS60	MS63
2004	—	—	—	—	0.75	1.00

KM# 1082 10 PENCE
6.50 g., Copper-Nickel, 24.5 mm. **Ruler:** Elizabeth II **Subject:** The Great Siege, 1779-1783 **Obv:** Bust in diadem right **Rev:** Cannon left **Edge:** Reeded

Date	Mintage	F12	VF20	XF40	MS60	MS63
2005	—	—	—	—	0.75	1.00
2006	—	—	—	—	0.75	1.00
2007	—	—	—	—	0.75	1.00
2008	—	—	—	—	0.75	1.00
2009	—	—	—	—	0.75	1.00
2010	—	—	—	—	0.75	1.00
2011	—	—	—	—	0.75	1.00

KM# 1102 10 PENCE
6.50 g., Copper-Nickel, 24.5 mm. **Ruler:** Elizabeth II **Obv:** Bust right **Obv. Legend:** ELIZABETH II QUEEN OF GIBRALTAR

Date	Mintage	F12	VF20	XF40	MS60	MS63
2012	—	—	—	—	0.75	1.00

KM# 777 20 PENCE
5.00 g., Copper-Nickel, 21.4 mm. **Ruler:** Elizabeth II **Obv:** Head with tiara right, date below **Rev:** Our Lady of Europa, denomination below and right **Shape:** 7-sided

Date	Mintage	F12	VF20	XF40	MS60	MS63
2001 AA	—	—	—	—	1.50	2.00
2002 AA	—	—	—	—	1.50	2.00
2003 AA	—	—	—	—	1.50	2.00

KM# 1048 20 PENCE
5.00 g., Copper-Nickel, 21.4 mm. **Ruler:** Elizabeth II **Subject:** 300th Anniversary **Obv:** Crowned buat right **Rev:** Neanderthal skull found in Gibraltar in 1848 **Edge:** Plain **Shape:** 7-sided

Date	Mintage	F12	VF20	XF40	MS60	MS63
2004	—	—	—	—	1.00	1.50

KM# 1083 20 PENCE
5.00 g., Copper-Nickel, 21.4 mm. **Ruler:** Elizabeth II **Obv:** Bust in diadem right **Rev:** Keyring with four keys **Shape:** 7-sided

Date	Mintage	F12	VF20	XF40	MS60	MS63
2005	—	—	—	—	1.50	2.00
2006	—	—	—	—	1.50	2.00
2007	—	—	—	—	1.50	2.00
2008	—	—	—	—	1.50	2.00
2009	—	—	—	—	1.50	2.00
2010	—	—	—	—	1.50	2.00
2011	—	—	—	—	1.50	2.00

KM# 1103 20 PENCE
5.00 g., (No Composition), 21.4 mm. **Ruler:** Elizabeth II **Obv:** Bust right **Obv. Legend:** ELIZABETH II QUEEN OF GIBRALTAR

Date	Mintage	F12	VF20	XF40	MS60	MS63
2012 1103	—	—	—	—	1.50	2.00

KM# 778 50 PENCE
8.00 g., Copper-Nickel, 27.3 mm. **Ruler:** Elizabeth II **Obv:** Head with tiara right **Rev:** Dolphins surround denomination **Edge:** Plain **Shape:** 7-sided

Date	Mintage	F12	VF20	XF40	MS60	MS63
2001 AA	—	—	—	—	4.50	5.50
2001 AB	—	—	—	—	4.50	5.50
2003 AB	—	—	—	—	4.50	5.50

KM# 971 50 PENCE
8.00 g., Copper-Nickel, 27.3 mm. **Ruler:** Elizabeth II **Subject:** Christmas **Obv:** Head with tiara right, date below **Rev:** Three wise men **Edge:** Plain **Shape:** 7-sided

Date	Mintage	F12	VF20	XF40	MS60	MS63
2001 BB	30,000	—	—	—	10.00	12.00

KM# 971a 50 PENCE
8.00 g., 0.925 Silver 0.2364 oz. ASW, 27.3 mm. **Ruler:** Elizabeth II **Obv:** Head with tiara right, date below **Rev:** Three wise men **Edge:** Plain **Shape:** 7-sided

Date	Mintage	F12	VF20	XF40	MS60	MS63
2001	5,000	PF63 28.00		PF65 35.00		

KM# 971b 50 PENCE
8.00 g., 0.9167 Gold 0.2343 oz. AGW, 27.3 mm. **Ruler:** Elizabeth II **Obv:** Head with tiara right, date below **Rev:** Three wise men **Edge:** Plain **Shape:** 7-sided

Date	Mintage	F12	VF20	XF40	MS60	MS63
2001	250	PF63 625		PF65 645		

KM# 1026 50 PENCE
8.00 g., Copper-Nickel, 27.3 mm. **Ruler:** Elizabeth II **Subject:** Christmas **Obv:** Head with tiara right, date below **Rev:** Shepherds **Edge:** Plain **Shape:** 7-sided

Date	Mintage	F12	VF20	XF40	MS60	MS63
2002PM BB	30,000	—	—	—	10.00	12.00

KM# 1026a 50 PENCE
8.00 g., 0.925 Silver 0.2364 oz. ASW, 27.3 mm. **Ruler:** Elizabeth II **Subject:** Christmas **Obv:** Head with tiara right, date below **Rev:** Two shepherds **Edge:** Plain **Shape:** 7-sided

Date	Mintage	F12	VF20	XF40	MS60	MS63
2002PM	2,002	PF63 28.00		PF65 35.00		

KM# 1063a 50 PENCE
8.00 g., 0.925 Silver 0.2364 oz. ASW, 27.3 mm. **Ruler:** Elizabeth II **Subject:** Christmas **Rev:** Joseph & Mary **Shape:** 7-sided

Date	Mintage	F12	VF20	XF40	MS60	MS63
2003PM BB	—	—	—	—	12.00	14.00

KM# 1063 50 PENCE
8.00 g., Copper-Nickel, 27.3 mm. **Ruler:** Elizabeth II **Series:** Christmas **Obv:** Head with tiara right, date below **Rev:** Joseph & Mary **Shape:** 7-sided

Date	Mintage	F12	VF20	XF40	MS60	MS63
2003PM BB	—	—	—	—	10.00	12.00

KM# 1050 50 PENCE
8.00 g., Copper-Nickel, 27.3 mm. **Ruler:** Elizabeth II **Subject:** Tercentenary 1704-2004 **Obv:** Elizabeth II **Rev:** HMS Victory sailing past Gibraltar **Edge:** Plain **Shape:** 7-sided

Date	Mintage	F12	VF20	XF40	MS60	MS63
2004	—	—	—	—		3.00

KM# 1066 50 PENCE
8.00 g., Copper-Nickel, 27.3 mm. **Ruler:** Elizabeth II **Subject:** Christmas **Rev:** Santa Claus walking left with sack over shoulder and waving **Shape:** 7-sided

Date	Mintage	F12	VF20	XF40	MS60	MS63
2004	—	—	—	—	10.00	12.00

KM# 1084 50 PENCE
8.00 g., Copper-Nickel, 27.3 mm. **Ruler:** Elizabeth II **Subject:** Glorious 1st of June, 1794 **Rev:** Marines firing from deck of Naval ship **Shape:** 7-sided

Date	Mintage	F12	VF20	XF40	MS60	MS63
2004	—	—	—	—	10.00	12.00

KM# 1085 50 PENCE
8.00 g., Copper-Nickel, 27.3 mm. **Ruler:** Elizabeth II **Subject:** Siege of Sebastopol, 1854 **Rev:** Troops in the Crimea **Shape:** 7-sided

Date	Mintage	F12	VF20	XF40	MS60	MS63
2004	—	—	—	—	10.00	12.00

KM# 1086 50 PENCE
8.00 g., Copper-Nickel, 27.3 mm. **Ruler:** Elizabeth II **Subject:** World War I **Rev:** Troops advancing right **Shape:** 7-sided

Date	Mintage	F12	VF20	XF40	MS60	MS63
2004	—	—	—	—	10.00	12.00

KM# 1087 50 PENCE
8.00 g., Copper-Nickel, 27.3 mm. **Ruler:** Elizabeth II **Subject:** World War II **Rev:** Troops in fox hole **Shape:** 7-sided

Date	Mintage	F12	VF20	XF40	MS60	MS63
2004	—	—	—	—	10.00	12.00

KM# 1088 50 PENCE
8.00 g., Copper-Nickel, 27.3 mm. **Ruler:** Elizabeth II **Subject:** The Falklands, 1982 **Rev:** Troops advancing forward **Shape:** 7-sided

Date	Mintage	F12	VF20	XF40	MS60	MS63
2004	—	—	—	—	10.00	12.00

KM# 1067 50 PENCE
8.00 g., Copper-Nickel, 27.3 mm. **Ruler:** Elizabeth II **Subject:** Christmas **Rev:** Mary and child **Shape:** 7-sided

Date	Mintage	F12	VF20	XF40	MS60	MS63
2005	—	—	—	—	10.00	12.00

KM# 1074 50 PENCE
8.00 g., Copper-Nickel, 27.3 mm. **Ruler:** Elizabeth II **Subject:** Capture of Gibraltar **Rev:** Naval Battle **Shape:** 7-sided

Date	Mintage	F12	VF20	XF40	MS60	MS63
2005	—	—	—	—	7.50	10.00

KM# 1089 50 PENCE
8.00 g., Copper-Nickel, 27.3 mm. **Ruler:** Elizabeth II **Subject:** Capture of Gibraltar, 1704 **Rev:** Naval Battle **Shape:** 7-sided

Date	Mintage	F12	VF20	XF40	MS60	MS63
2006	—	—	—	—	4.50	5.50
2007	—	—	—	—	4.50	5.50
2008	—	—	—	—	4.50	5.50
2009	—	—	—	—	4.50	5.50
2010	—	—	—	—	4.50	5.50
2011	—	—	—	—	4.50	5.50

KM# 1068 50 PENCE
8.00 g., Copper-Nickel, 27.3 mm. **Ruler:** Elizabeth II **Subject:** Christmas **Rev:** Tree **Shape:** 7-sided

Date	Mintage	F12	VF20	XF40	MS60	MS63
2006	—	—	—	—	10.00	12.00

KM# 1069 50 PENCE
8.00 g., Copper-Nickel, 27.3 mm. **Ruler:** Elizabeth II **Subject:** Christmas **Rev:** Santa, large face **Shape:** 7-sided

Date	Mintage	F12	VF20	XF40	MS60	MS63
2007	—	—	—	—	10.00	12.00

KM# 1070 50 PENCE
8.00 g., Copper-Nickel, 27.3 mm. **Ruler:** Elizabeth II **Subject:** Christmas **Shape:** 7-sided

Date	Mintage	F12	VF20	XF40	MS60	MS63
2008	—	—	—	—	10.00	12.00

KM# 1090 50 PENCE
8.00 g., Copper-Nickel, 27.3 mm. **Ruler:** Elizabeth II **Subject:** Our Lady of Europe **Rev:** Madonna and Child seated **Shape:** 7-sided

Date	Mintage	F12	VF20	XF40	MS60	MS63
2008	—	—	—	—	7.50	9.00

KM# 1071 50 PENCE
8.00 g., Copper-Nickel, 27.3 mm. **Ruler:** Elizabeth II **Subject:** Christmas **Shape:** 7-sided

Date	Mintage	F12	VF20	XF40	MS60	MS63
2009	—	—	—	—	10.00	12.00

KM# 1104 50 PENCE
8.00 g., Copper-Nickel, 27.3 mm. **Ruler:** Elizabeth II **Obv:** Bust right **Obv. Legend:** ELIZABETH II QUEEN OF GIBRALTAR

Date	Mintage	F12	VF20	XF40	MS60	MS63
2012	—	—	—	—	4.50	5.50

KM# 988 1/25 CROWN
1.22 g., 0.999 Gold 0.0391 oz. AGW, 13.92 mm. **Ruler:** Elizabeth II **Subject:** Peter Rabbit Centennial **Obv:** Crowned bust right **Rev:** Peter Rabbit **Edge:** Reeded

Date	Mintage	F12	VF20	XF40	MS60	MS63
2002	5,000	PF63 70.00	PF65 75.00			

KM# 988a 1/25 CROWN
1.22 g., 0.999 Platinum 0.0391 oz. APW, 13.92 mm. **Ruler:** Elizabeth II **Subject:** Peter Rabbit Centennial **Obv:** Crowned bust right **Rev:** Peter Rabbit **Edge:** Reeded

Date	Mintage	F12	VF20	XF40	MS60	MS63
2002	3,000	PF63 85.00	PF65 95.00			

KM# 1016 1/25 CROWN
1.24 g., 0.9999 Gold 0.0397 oz. AGW, 13.92 mm. **Ruler:** Elizabeth II **Obv:** Crowned bust right **Rev:** Peter Pan and Tinkerbell flying above city **Edge:** Reeded

Date	Mintage	F12	VF20	XF40	MS60	MS63
2002	10,000	PF63 70.00	PF65 75.00			

KM# 989 1/10 CROWN
3.11 g., 0.999 Gold 0.0992 oz. AGW, 17.95 mm. **Ruler:** Elizabeth II **Subject:** Peter Rabbit Centennial **Obv:** Crowned bust right **Rev:** Peter Rabbit **Edge:** Reeded

Date	Mintage	F12	VF20	XF40	MS60	MS63
2002	5,000	PF63 175	PF65 185			

KM# 989a 1/10 CROWN
3.11 g., 0.999 Platinum 0.0992 oz. APW, 17.95 mm. **Ruler:** Elizabeth II **Subject:** Peter Rabbit Centennial **Obv:** Crowned bust right **Rev:** Peter Rabbit **Edge:** Reeded

Date	Mintage	F12	VF20	XF40	MS60	MS63
2002	2,000	PF63 220	PF65 235			

KM# 1017 1/10 CROWN
3.11 g., 0.9999 Gold 0.0993 oz. AGW, 17.95 mm. **Ruler:** Elizabeth II **Subject:** Peter Pan **Obv:** Crowned bust right **Rev:** Peter Pan and Tinkerbell flying above city **Edge:** Reeded

Date	Mintage	F12	VF20	XF40	MS60	MS63
2002	—	PF63 175	PF65 185			

KM# 902 1/5 CROWN
6.22 g., 0.9999 Gold 0.1987 oz. AGW, 22 mm. **Ruler:** Elizabeth II **Subject:** Queen Mother **Obv:** Bust with tiara right **Rev:** 1953 Coronation scene **Edge:** Reeded

Date	Mintage	F12	VF20	XF40	MS60	MS63
2001	5,000	PF63 350	PF65 375			

KM# 903 1/5 CROWN
6.22 g., 0.9999 Gold 0.1987 oz. AGW, 22 mm. **Ruler:** Elizabeth II **Obv:** Bust with tiara right **Rev:** Queen Mother and Prince Charles in 1954

Date	Mintage	F12	VF20	XF40	MS60	MS63
2001	5,000	PF63 350	PF65 375			

KM# 909 1/5 CROWN
6.22 g., 0.9999 Gold 0.1987 oz. AGW, 22 mm. **Ruler:** Elizabeth II **Series:** Victorian Era - Victoria's Coronation 1838 **Obv:** Bust with tiara right **Rev:** 1838 Coronation scene **Edge:** Reeded

Date	Mintage	F12	VF20	XF40	MS60	MS63
2001	5,000	PF63 350	PF65 375			

KM# 909.1 1/5 CROWN
6.22 g., 0.9999 Gold 0.1987 oz. AGW, 22 mm. **Ruler:** Elizabeth II **Series:** Victorian Era **Obv:** Bust with tiara right **Rev:** 1838 Coronation scene with a tiny emerald set in the field below the 1838 date **Edge:** Reeded

Date	Mintage	F12	VF20	XF40	MS60	MS63
2001	2,001	PF63 350	PF65 375			

KM# 911.1 1/5 CROWN
6.22 g., 0.9999 Gold 0.1987 oz. AGW, 22 mm. **Ruler:** Elizabeth II **Series:** Victorian Era - Empress of India 1876 **Obv:** Bust with tiara right **Rev:** Crowned portrait of Victoria and two elephants **Edge:** Reeded

Date	Mintage	F12	VF20	XF40	MS60	MS63
2001	5,000	PF63 350	PF65 375			

KM# 911.2 1/5 CROWN
6.22 g., 0.9999 Gold 0.1987 oz. AGW, 22 mm. **Ruler:** Elizabeth II **Series:** Victorian Era - Empress of India 1876 **Obv:** Bust with tiara right **Rev:** Tiny ruby set in the field behind Victoria's head **Edge:** Reeded

Date	Mintage	F12	VF20	XF40	MS60	MS63
2001	2,001	PF63 350	PF65 375			

KM# 913.1 1/5 CROWN
6.22 g., 0.9999 Gold 0.1987 oz. AGW, 22 mm. **Ruler:** Elizabeth II **Series:** Victorian Era - Diamond Jubilee 1897 **Obv:** Bust with tiara right **Rev:** Victoria's cameo portrait above naval ships **Edge:** Reeded

Date	Mintage	F12	VF20	XF40	MS60	MS63
2001	5,000	PF63 350	PF65 375			

KM# 913.2 1/5 CROWN
6.22 g., 0.9999 Gold 0.1987 oz. AGW, 22 mm. **Ruler:** Elizabeth II **Series:** Victorian Era - Diamond Jubilee 1897 **Obv:** Bust with tiara right **Rev:** Tiny diamond set at the top of the fourth mast **Edge:** Reeded

Date	Mintage	F12	VF20	XF40	MS60	MS63
2001	2,001	PF63 350	PF65 375			

KM# 915.1 1/5 CROWN
6.22 g., 0.9999 Gold 0.1987 oz. AGW, 22 mm. **Ruler:** Elizabeth II **Series:** Victorian Era - Victoria's Death 1901 **Obv:** Bust with tiara right **Rev:** Victoria's cameo portrait and Osborne Manor **Edge:** Reeded

Date	Mintage	F12	VF20	XF40	MS60	MS63
2001	5,000	PF63 350	PF65 375			

KM# 915.2 1/5 CROWN
6.22 g., 0.9999 Gold 0.1987 oz. AGW, 22 mm. **Ruler:** Elizabeth II **Series:** Victorian Era - Victoria's Death 1901 **Obv:** Bust with tiara right **Rev:** Tiny sapphire set in the field between the towers **Edge:** Reeded

Date	Mintage	F12	VF20	XF40	MS60	MS63
2001	2,001	PF63 350	PF65 375			

KM# 917 1/5 CROWN
6.22 g., 0.9999 Gold 0.1987 oz. AGW, 22 mm. **Ruler:** Elizabeth II **Series:** Victorian Era - Prince Albert and the Great Exhibition 1851 **Obv:** Bust with tiara right **Rev:** Albert's cameo portrait and the exhibit hall **Edge:** Reeded

Date	Mintage	F12	VF20	XF40	MS60	MS63
2001	5,000	PF63 350	PF65 375			

KM# 919 1/5 CROWN
6.22 g., 0.9999 Gold 0.1987 oz. AGW, 22 mm. **Ruler:** Elizabeth II **Series:** Victorian Era - Isambard K. Brunel **Obv:** Bust with tiara right **Rev:** Portrait in top hat and railroad bridge **Edge:** Reeded

Date	Mintage	F12	VF20	XF40	MS60	MS63
2001	5,000	PF63 350	PF65 375			

KM# 921 1/5 CROWN
6.22 g., 0.9999 Gold 0.1987 oz. AGW, 22 mm. **Ruler:** Elizabeth II **Series:** Victorian Era - Charles Dickens **Obv:** Bust with tiara right **Rev:** Portrait and scene from "Oliver Twist **Edge:** Reeded

Date	Mintage	F12	VF20	XF40	MS60	MS63
2001	5,000	PF63 350	PF65 375			

KM# 923 1/5 CROWN
6.22 g., 0.9999 Gold 0.1987 oz. AGW, 22 mm. **Ruler:** Elizabeth II **Series:** Victorian Era - Charles Darwin **Obv:** Bust with tiara right **Rev:** Portrait, ship and a squatting aboriginal figure **Edge:** Reeded

Date	Mintage	F12	VF20	XF40	MS60	MS63
2001	5,000	PF63 350	PF65 375			

KM# 925 1/5 CROWN
6.22 g., 0.9999 Gold 0.1987 oz. AGW, 22 mm. **Ruler:** Elizabeth II **Series:** Mythology of the Solar System **Obv:** Queens portrait **Rev:** Standing goddess with snake basket **Edge:** Reeded

Date	Mintage	F12	VF20	XF40	MS60	MS63
2001	5,000	PF63 350	PF65 375			

KM# 926 1/5 CROWN
Bi-Metallic, 32.25 mm. **Ruler:** Elizabeth II **Series:** Mythology of the Solar System **Obv:** Bust with tiara right **Rev:** Standing goddess with snake basket **Edge:** Reeded

Date	Mintage	F12	VF20	XF40	MS60	MS63
2001 In Proof sets only	999	PF65 500				

KM# 929.1 1/5 CROWN
6.22 g., 0.9999 Gold 0.1987 oz. AGW, 22 mm. **Ruler:** Elizabeth II **Series:** Mythology of the Solar System - Sun **Obv:** Bust with tiara right **Rev:** Helios in chariot and the sun **Edge:** Reeded

Date	Mintage	F12	VF20	XF40	MS60	MS63
2001	5,000	PF63 350	PF65 375			

KM# 929.2 1/5 CROWN
6.22 g., 0.9999 Gold 0.1987 oz. AGW, 22 mm. **Ruler:** Elizabeth II **Series:** Mythology of the Solar System **Obv:** Bust with tiara right **Rev:** Fiery hologram in the sun **Edge:** Reeded

Date	Mintage	F12	VF20	XF40	MS60	MS63
2001 In Proof sets only	999	PF63 350	PF65 375			

KM# 931.1 1/5 CROWN
6.22 g., 0.9999 Gold 0.1987 oz. AGW, 22 mm. **Ruler:** Elizabeth II **Series:** Mythology of the Solar System - Moon **Obv:** Bust with tiara right **Rev:** Goddess Diana and the moon **Edge:** Reeded

Date	Mintage	F12	VF20	XF40	MS60	MS63
2001	5,000	PF63 350	PF65 375			

KM# 931.2 1/5 CROWN
6.22 g., 0.9999 Gold 0.1987 oz. AGW, 22 mm. **Ruler:** Elizabeth II **Series:** Mythology of the Solar System - Moon **Obv:** Bust with tiara right **Rev:** Small pearl set in the moon **Edge:** Reeded

Date	Mintage	F12	VF20	XF40	MS60	MS63
2001 In Proof sets only	999	PF65 450				

KM# 933.1 1/5 CROWN
6.22 g., 0.9999 Gold 0.1987 oz. AGW, 22 mm. **Ruler:** Elizabeth II **Series:** Mythology of the Solar System - Atlas **Obv:** Bust with tiara right **Rev:** Atlas carrying the earth **Edge:** Reeded

Date	Mintage	F12	VF20	XF40	MS60	MS63
2001	5,000	PF63 350	PF65 375			

KM# 933.2 1/5 CROWN
6.22 g., 0.9999 Gold 0.1987 oz. AGW, 22 mm. **Ruler:** Elizabeth II **Series:** Mythology of the Solar System - Atlas **Obv:** Bust with tiara right **Rev:** Tiny diamond set in the earth **Edge:** Reeded

Date	Mintage	F12	VF20	XF40	MS60	MS63
2001 In Proof sets only	999	PF65 450				

KM# 935 1/5 CROWN
6.22 g., 0.9999 Gold 0.1987 oz. AGW, 22 mm. **Ruler:** Elizabeth II **Series:** Mythology of the Solar System - Neptune **Obv:** Bust with tiara right **Rev:** Seated god with trident and ringed planet **Edge:** Reeded

Date	Mintage	F12	VF20	XF40	MS60	MS63
2001	5,000	PF63 350	PF65 375			

KM# 937 1/5 CROWN
6.22 g., 0.9999 Gold 0.1987 oz. AGW, 22 mm. **Ruler:** Elizabeth II **Series:** Mythology of the Solar System - Jupiter **Obv:** Bust with tiara right **Rev:** Seated god with lightning bolts and a planet **Edge:** Reeded

Date	Mintage	F12	VF20	XF40	MS60	MS63
2001	5,000	PF63 350	PF65 375			

KM# 939 1/5 CROWN
6.22 g., 0.9999 Gold 0.1987 oz. AGW, 22 mm. **Ruler:** Elizabeth II **Series:** Mythology of the Solar System - Mars **Obv:** Bust with tiara right **Rev:** Standing Roman solider and a planet **Edge:** Reeded

Date	Mintage	F12	VF20	XF40	MS60	MS63
2001	5,000	PF63 350	PF65 375			

KM# 941 1/5 CROWN
6.22 g., 0.9999 Gold 0.1987 oz. AGW, 22 mm. **Ruler:** Elizabeth II **Series:** Mythology of the Solar System - Mercury **Obv:** Bust with tiara right **Rev:** Seated god with caduceus and a planet **Edge:** Reeded

Date	Mintage	F12	VF20	XF40	MS60	MS63
2001	5,000	PF63 350	PF65 375			

KM# 943 1/5 CROWN
6.22 g., 0.9999 Gold 0.1987 oz. AGW, 22 mm. **Ruler:** Elizabeth II **Series:** Mythology of the Solar System - Uranus **Obv:** Bust with tiara right **Rev:** Seated god with scepter **Edge:** Reeded

Date	Mintage	F12	VF20	XF40	MS60	MS63
2001	5,000	PF63 350	PF65 375			

KM# 945 1/5 CROWN
6.22 g., 0.9999 Gold 0.1987 oz. AGW, 22 mm. **Ruler:** Elizabeth II **Series:** Mythology of the Solar System - Saturn **Obv:** Bust with tiara right **Rev:** Seated god with long handled sickle and a ringed planet **Edge:** Reeded

Date	Mintage	F12	VF20	XF40	MS60	MS63
2001	5,000	PF63 350	PF65 375			

KM# 947 1/5 CROWN
6.22 g., 0.9999 Gold 0.1987 oz. AGW, 22 mm. **Ruler:** Elizabeth II **Series:** Mythology of the Solar System - Pluto **Obv:** Bust with tiara right **Rev:** Seated god with dogs and a planet **Edge:** Reeded

Date	Mintage	F12	VF20	XF40	MS60	MS63
2001	5,000	PF63 350	PF65 375			

KM# 949 1/5 CROWN
6.22 g., 0.9999 Gold 0.1987 oz. AGW, 22 mm. **Ruler:** Elizabeth II **Series:** Mythology of the Solar System - Venus **Obv:** Bust with tiara right **Rev:** Goddess seated on a half shell **Edge:** Reeded

Date	Mintage	F12	VF20	XF40	MS60	MS63
2001	5,000	PF63 350	PF65 375			

KM# 951 1/5 CROWN
6.22 g., 0.9999 Gold 0.1987 oz. AGW, 22 mm. **Ruler:** Elizabeth II **Subject:** Queen's 76th Birthday **Obv:** Bust with tiara right **Rev:** Queen in Order of the Garter robes with a tiny inset diamond **Edge:** Reeded

Date	Mintage	F12	VF20	XF40	MS60	MS63
2001	2,001	PF63 350	PF65 375			

KM# 954 1/5 CROWN
6.22 g., 0.9999 Gold 0.1987 oz. AGW, 22 mm. **Ruler:** Elizabeth II **Series:** Victorian Age Part II - Victoria's Accession to the Throne **Obv:** Bust with tiara right **Rev:** Victoria learning of her accession **Edge:** Reeded

Date	Mintage	F12	VF20	XF40	MS60	MS63
2001	5,000	PF63 350	PF65 375			

KM# 956 1/5 CROWN
6.22 g., 0.9999 Gold 0.1987 oz. AGW, 22 mm. **Ruler:** Elizabeth II **Series:** Victorian Age Part II - Royal Family **Rev:** Victoria and Albert seated with children **Edge:** Reeded

Date	Mintage	F12	VF20	XF40	MS60	MS63
2001	5,000	PF63 350	PF65 375			

KM# 958 1/5 CROWN
6.22 g., 0.9999 Gold 0.1987 oz. AGW, 22 mm. **Ruler:** Elizabeth II **Series:** Victorian Age Part II - Victoria in Scotland **Obv:** Bust with tiara right **Rev:** Victoria on horse and servant **Edge:** Reeded

Date	Mintage	F12	VF20	XF40	MS60	MS63
2001	5,000	PF63 350	PF65 375			

KM# 960 1/5 CROWN
6.22 g., 0.9999 Gold 0.1987 oz. AGW, 22 mm. **Ruler:** Elizabeth II **Series:** Victorian Age Part II **Obv:** Bust with tiara right **Rev:** Portraits of Gladstone and Disaraeli **Edge:** Reeded

Date	Mintage	F12	VF20	XF40	MS60	MS63
2001	5,000	PF63 350	PF65 375			

KM# 962 1/5 CROWN
6.22 g., 0.9999 Gold 0.1987 oz. AGW, 22 mm. **Ruler:** Elizabeth II **Series:** Victorian Age Part II **Obv:** Bust with tiara right **Rev:** Florence Nightingale holding lantern **Edge:** Reeded

Date	Mintage	F12	VF20	XF40	MS60	MS63
2001	5,000	PF63 350	PF65 375			

KM# 964 1/5 CROWN
6.22 g., 0.9999 Gold 0.1987 oz. AGW, 22 mm. **Ruler:** Elizabeth II **Series:** Victorian Age Part II **Obv:** Bust with tiara right **Rev:** Lord Tennyson with the Light Brigade in background **Edge:** Reeded

Date	Mintage	F12	VF20	XF40	MS60	MS63
2001	5,000	PF63 350	PF65 375			

KM# 966 1/5 CROWN
6.22 g., 0.9999 Gold 0.1987 oz. AGW, 22 mm. **Ruler:** Elizabeth II **Series:** Victorian Age Part II **Obv:** Bust with tiara right **Rev:** Stanley meeting Dr. Livingstone **Edge:** Reeded

Date	Mintage	F12	VF20	XF40	MS60	MS63
2001	5,000	PF63 350	PF65 375			

KM# 968 1/5 CROWN
6.22 g., 0.9999 Gold 0.1987 oz. AGW, 22 mm. **Ruler:** Elizabeth II **Series:** Victorian Age Part II **Obv:** Bust with tiara right **Rev:** Bronte sisters **Edge:** Reeded

Date	Mintage	F12	VF20	XF40	MS60	MS63
2001	5,000	PF63 350	PF65 375			

KM# 978 1/5 CROWN
6.22 g., 0.999 Gold 0.1985 oz. AGW, 22 mm. **Ruler:** Elizabeth II **Subject:** Queen Mother's Life **Obv:** Bust right **Rev:** Prince William's christening scene **Edge:** Reeded

Date	Mintage	F12	VF20	XF40	MS60	MS63
2002	5,000	PF63 350	PF65 375			

KM# 980 1/5 CROWN
6.22 g., 0.9999 Gold 0.1987 oz. AGW, 22 mm. **Ruler:** Elizabeth II **Subject:** World Cup Soccer **Obv:** Bust right **Rev:** Two players about to collide **Edge:** Reeded

Date	Mintage	F12	VF20	XF40	MS60	MS63
2002	—	PF63 350	PF65 375			

KM# 982 1/5 CROWN
6.22 g., 0.9999 Gold 0.1987 oz. AGW, 22 mm. **Ruler:** Elizabeth II **Subject:** World Cup Soccer **Obv:** Bust right **Rev:** Two players facing viewer **Edge:** Reeded

Date	Mintage	F12	VF20	XF40	MS60	MS63
2002	—	PF63 350	PF65 375			

KM# 984 1/5 CROWN
6.22 g., 0.9999 Gold 0.1987 oz. AGW, 22 mm. **Ruler:** Elizabeth II **Subject:** World Cup Soccer **Obv:** Bust right **Rev:** Two horizontal players **Edge:** Reeded

Date	Mintage	F12	VF20	XF40	MS60	MS63
2002	—	PF63 350	PF65 375			

KM# 986 1/5 CROWN
6.22 g., 0.9999 Gold 0.1987 oz. AGW, 22 mm. **Ruler:** Elizabeth II **Subject:** World Cup Soccer **Obv:** Bust right **Rev:** Two players moving to the left **Edge:** Reeded

Date	Mintage	F12	VF20	XF40	MS60	MS63
2002	—	PF63 350	PF65 375			

KM# 990 1/5 CROWN
6.22 g., 0.999 Gold 0.1985 oz. AGW, 22 mm. **Ruler:** Elizabeth II **Subject:** Peter Rabbit Centennial **Obv:** Bust right **Rev:** Peter Rabbit **Edge:** Reeded

Date	Mintage	F12	VF20	XF40	MS60	MS63
2002	3,500	PF63 350	PF65 375			

KM# 990a 1/5 CROWN
6.22 g., 0.999 Platinum 0.1985 oz. APW, 22 mm. **Ruler:** Elizabeth II **Subject:** Peter Rabbit Centennial **Obv:** Bust right **Rev:** Peter Rabbit **Edge:** Reeded

Date	Mintage	F12	VF20	XF40	MS60	MS63
2002	1,500	PF65 450				

KM# 993 1/5 CROWN
6.22 g., 0.375 Gold 0.0745 oz. AGW, 22 mm. **Ruler:** Elizabeth II **Subject:** Queen's Golden Jubilee **Obv:** Bust with tiara right **Rev:** Royal couple and tree house **Edge:** Reeded

Date	Mintage	F12	VF20	XF40	MS60	MS63
2002	—	PF63 125	PF65 140			

KM# 993a 1/5 CROWN
6.22 g., 0.9999 Gold 0.1987 oz. AGW, 22 mm. **Ruler:** Elizabeth II **Subject:** Queen's Golden Jubilee **Obv:** Bust with tiara right **Rev:** Royal couple and tree house **Edge:** Reeded

Date	Mintage	F12	VF20	XF40	MS60	MS63
2002	—	PF63 350	PF65 375			

KM# 995 1/5 CROWN
6.22 g., 0.375 Gold 0.0745 oz. AGW, 22 mm. **Ruler:** Elizabeth II **Subject:** Queen's Golden Jubilee **Obv:** Bust with tiara right **Rev:** Royal coach **Edge:** Reeded

Date	Mintage	F12	VF20	XF40	MS60	MS63
2002	—	PF63 125	PF65 140			

KM# 995a 1/5 CROWN
6.22 g., 0.9999 Gold 0.1987 oz. AGW, 22 mm. **Ruler:** Elizabeth II **Subject:** Queen's Golden Jubilee **Obv:** Bust with tiara right **Rev:** Royal coach **Edge:** Reeded

Date	Mintage	F12	VF20	XF40	MS60	MS63
2002	—	PF63 350	PF65 375			

KM# 997 1/5 CROWN
6.22 g., 0.375 Gold 0.0745 oz. AGW, 22 mm. **Ruler:** Elizabeth II **Subject:** Queen's Golden Jubilee **Obv:** Bust with tiara right **Rev:** Queen holding baby **Edge:** Reeded

Date	Mintage	F12	VF20	XF40	MS60	MS63
2002	—	PF63 125	PF65 140			

KM# 997a 1/5 CROWN
6.22 g., 0.9999 Gold 0.1987 oz. AGW, 22 mm. **Ruler:** Elizabeth II **Subject:** Queen's Golden Jubilee **Obv:** Bust with tiara right **Rev:** Queen holding baby **Edge:** Reeded

Date	Mintage	F12	VF20	XF40	MS60	MS63
2002	—	PF63 350	PF65 375			

KM# 999 1/5 CROWN
6.22 g., 0.375 Gold 0.0745 oz. AGW, 22 mm. **Ruler:** Elizabeth II **Subject:** Queen's Golden Jubilee **Obv:** Bust with tiara right **Rev:** Yacht under Tower bridge **Edge:** Reeded

Date	Mintage	F12	VF20	XF40	MS60	MS63
2002	—	PF63 125	PF65 140			

KM# 999a 1/5 CROWN
6.22 g., 0.9999 Gold 0.1987 oz. AGW, 22 mm. **Ruler:** Elizabeth II **Subject:** Queen's Golden Jubilee **Obv:** Bust with tiara right **Rev:** Yacht under Tower bridge **Edge:** Reeded

Date	Mintage	F12	VF20	XF40	MS60	MS63
2002	—	PF63 350	PF65 375			

KM# 1001 1/5 CROWN
6.22 g., 0.9999 Gold 0.1987 oz. AGW, 22 mm. **Ruler:** Elizabeth II **Subject:** Queen's Golden Jubilee **Obv:** Bust with tiara right **Rev:** Crown jewels inset with a tiny diamond, ruby, sapphire and emerald **Edge:** Reeded

Date	Mintage	F12	VF20	XF40	MS60	MS63
2002	—	PF63 350	PF65 375			

KM# 1003 1/5 CROWN
6.22 g., Electrum, 22 mm. **Ruler:** Elizabeth II **Series:** Ancient Coins **Obv:** Bust with tiara right **Rev:** Head of Athena left **Edge:** Reeded **Note:** From a Mysia electrum coin c.520BC.

Date	Mintage	F12	VF20	XF40	MS60	MS63
2002	3,600	PF63 176	PF65 186			

KM# 1005 1/5 CROWN
6.22 g., Electrum, 22 mm. **Ruler:** Elizabeth II **Series:** Ancient Coins **Obv:** Bust with tiara right **Rev:** Head of Hercules right **Edge:** Reeded **Note:** From a Lesbos coin c. 480-450 BC.

Date	Mintage	F12	VF20	XF40	MS60	MS63
2002	3,500	PF63 175	PF65 185			

KM# 1007 1/5 CROWN
6.22 g., 0.999 Electrum 0.1985 oz., 22 mm. **Ruler:** Elizabeth II **Series:** Ancient Coins **Obv:** Bust with tiara right **Rev:** Pegasus **Edge:** Reeded **Note:** From a Lampsakos electrum coin c. 450 BC.

Date	Mintage	F12	VF20	XF40	MS60	MS63
2002	3,500	PF63 175	PF65 185			

KM# 1009 1/5 CROWN
6.22 g., Electrum, 22 mm. **Ruler:** Elizabeth II **Series:** Ancient Coins **Obv:** Bust with tiara right **Rev:** Lion and bull facing **Edge:** Reeded **Note:** From a Kroisos "sic" coin c. 560-546 BC.

Date	Mintage	F12	VF20	XF40	MS60	MS63
2002	3,500	PF63 175	PF65 185			

KM# 1012 1/5 CROWN
6.22 g., 0.9999 Gold 0.1987 oz. AGW, 22 mm. **Ruler:** Elizabeth II **Subject:** Queen Mother **Obv:** Bust with tiara right **Rev:** Queen Mother trout fishing **Edge:** Reeded

Date	Mintage	F12	VF20	XF40	MS60	MS63
2002	—	PF63 350	PF65 375			

KM# 1014 1/5 CROWN
6.22 g., 0.9999 Gold 0.1987 oz. AGW, 22 mm. **Ruler:** Elizabeth II **Subject:** Princess Diana **Obv:** Bust right **Rev:** Diana's portrait **Edge:** Reeded

Date	Mintage	F12	VF20	XF40	MS60	MS63
2002	—	PF63 350	PF65 375			

KM# 1018 1/5 CROWN
6.22 g., 0.9999 Gold 0.1987 oz. AGW, 22 mm. **Ruler:** Elizabeth II **Subject:** Peter Pan **Obv:** Bust right **Rev:** Peter Pan and Tinkerbell flying above city **Edge:** Reeded

Date	Mintage	F12	VF20	XF40	MS60	MS63
2002	—	PF63 350	PF65 375			

KM# 1020 1/5 CROWN
6.22 g., 0.9999 Gold 0.1987 oz. AGW, 22 mm. **Ruler:** Elizabeth II **Subject:** Grand Masonic Lodge **Obv:** Bust right **Rev:** Masonic seal above Gibraltar **Edge:** Reeded

Date	Mintage	F12	VF20	XF40	MS60	MS63
2002	—	PF63 350	PF65 375			

KM# 991 1/2 CROWN
15.55 g., 0.999 Gold 0.4962 oz. AGW, 30 mm. **Ruler:** Elizabeth II **Subject:** Peter Rabbit Centennial **Obv:** Bust right **Rev:** Peter Rabbit **Edge:** Reeded

Date	Mintage	F12	VF20	XF40	MS60	MS63
2002	1,000	PF63 850	PF65 900			

KM# 1002 1/2 CROWN
15.55 g., 0.9999 Gold 0.4967 oz. AGW, 30 mm. **Ruler:** Elizabeth II **Subject:** Queen's Golden Jubilee **Obv:** Bust with tiara right **Rev:** Crown jewels inset with a tiny diamond, ruby, sapphire and emerald **Edge:** Reeded

Date	Mintage	F12	VF20	XF40	MS60	MS63
2002	—	PF63 850	PF65 900			

KM# 1004 1/2 CROWN
15.55 g., Electrum, 32.2 mm. **Ruler:** Elizabeth II **Series:** Ancient Coins **Obv:** Bust with tiara right **Rev:** Head of Athena left **Edge:** Reeded **Note:** From a Mysia electrum coin c. 520 BC.

Date	Mintage	F12	VF20	XF40	MS60	MS63
2002	2,000	PF63 300	PF65 325			

KM# 1006 1/2 CROWN
15.55 g., Electrum, 32.2 mm. **Ruler:** Elizabeth II **Series:** Ancient Coins **Obv:** Bust with tiara right **Rev:** Head of Hercules right **Edge:** Reeded **Note:** From a Lesbos coin c. 480-450 BC.

Date	Mintage	F12	VF20	XF40	MS60	MS63
2002	2,000	PF63 300	PF65 325			

KM# 1008 1/2 CROWN
15.55 g., Gold with Silver, 32.2 mm. **Ruler:** Elizabeth II **Series:** Ancient Coins **Obv:** Bust with tiara right **Rev:** Pegasus **Edge:** Reeded **Note:** From a Lampsakos electrum coin c. 450 BC.

Date	Mintage	F12	VF20	XF40	MS60	MS63
2002	2,000	PF63 300	PF65 325			

KM# 1010 1/2 CROWN
15.55 g., Electrum, 32.2 mm. **Ruler:** Elizabeth II **Series:** Ancient Coins **Obv:** Bust with tiara right **Rev:** Lion and bull facing **Edge:** Reeded **Note:** From a Kroisos [sic] coin c. 560-546 BC.

Date	Mintage	F12	VF20	XF40	MS60	MS63
2002	2,000	PF63 300	PF65 325			

KM# 1056 CROWN
31.10 g., 0.999 Tri-Metallic 0.9925 oz., 38.60 mm. **Ruler:** Elizabeth II **Subject:** 21st Century **Obv:** Crowned bust right **Obv. Legend:** GIBRALTER • ELIZABETH II **Rev:** Helmeted cross at center flanked by satellites, archaic sailing ship below **Rev. Legend:** 21st CENTURY **Edge:** Reeded

Date	Mintage	F12	VF20	XF40	MS60	MS63
2001	2,001	PF65 700				

KM# 904 CROWN
28.28 g., Copper-Nickel, 38.6 mm. **Ruler:** Elizabeth II **Subject:** The Life of Queen Elizabeth - The Queen Mother **Obv:** Bust with tiara right **Rev:** 1953 Coronation scene **Edge:** Reeded

Date	Mintage	F12	VF20	XF40	MS60	MS63
2001	—	—	—	—	10.00	12.00

KM# 904a CROWN
28.28 g., 0.925 Silver 0.8356 oz. ASW, 38.6 mm. **Ruler:** Elizabeth II **Subject:** The Life of Queen Elizabeth - The Queen Mother **Obv:** Bust with tiara right **Rev:** 1953 Coronation scene **Edge:** Reeded

Date	Mintage	F12	VF20	XF40	MS60	MS63
2001	10,000	PF63 45.00	PF65 47.00			

KM# 905 CROWN
28.28 g., Copper-Nickel, 38.6 mm. **Ruler:** Elizabeth II **Subject:** The Life of Queen Elizabeth - The Queen Mother **Obv:** Bust with tiara right **Rev:** Queen Mother with Prince Charles in 1954 **Edge:** Reeded

Date	Mintage	F12	VF20	XF40	MS60	MS63
2001	—	—	—	—	10.00	12.00

KM# 905a CROWN
28.28 g., 0.925 Silver 0.8356 oz. ASW **Ruler:** Elizabeth II **Subject:** The Life of Queen Elizabeth - The Queen Mother **Obv:** Bust with tiara right **Rev:** Queen Mother with Prince Charles in 1954 **Edge:** Reeded

Date	Mintage	F12	VF20	XF40	MS60	MS63
2001	10,000	PF63 45.00	PF65 47.00			

KM# 906 CROWN
28.28 g., Copper-Nickel, 38.6 mm. **Ruler:** Elizabeth II **Subject:** 21st Century **Obv:** Crowned bust right, date below **Rev:** Celtic cross, Viking ship and modern technological items **Edge:** Reeded

Date	Mintage	F12	VF20	XF40	MS60	MS63
2001	—	—	—	—	10.00	12.00

KM# 906a CROWN
31.10 g., 0.999 Silver 0.9926 oz. ASW, 38.6 mm. **Ruler:** Elizabeth II **Subject:** 21st Century **Obv:** Crowned bust right, date below **Rev:** Celtic cross, Viking ship and modern technological items **Edge:** Reeded **Note:** 31.1035 .999 Silver, 1.000 ASW with a gold plated inner ring and a blackened outer ring.

Date	Mintage	F12	VF20	XF40	MS60	MS63
2001	2,001	PF65 75.00				

KM# 906b CROWN
31.10 g., Tri-Metallic **Ruler:** Elizabeth II **Subject:** 21st Century **Obv:** Crowned bust right, date below **Rev:** Celtic cross, Viking ship and modern technological items

Date	Mintage	F12	VF20	XF40	MS60	MS63
2001	999	PF65 750				

KM# 910 CROWN
28.28 g., Copper-Nickel, 38.6 mm. **Ruler:** Elizabeth II **Series:** The Victorian Age **Obv:** Bust with tiara right **Rev:** 1838 Coronation of Queen Victoria **Edge:** Reeded

Date	Mintage	F12	VF20	XF40	MS60	MS63
2001	—	—	—	—	10.00	12.00

KM# 910a CROWN
28.28 g., 0.925 Silver 0.8356 oz. ASW, 38.6 mm. **Ruler:** Elizabeth II **Series:** Victorian Era **Obv:** Bust with tiara right **Rev:** 1838 Coronation scene **Edge:** Reeded

Date	Mintage	F12	VF20	XF40	MS60	MS63
2001	10,000	PF63 45.00	PF65 47.00			

KM# 912 CROWN
Copper-Nickel, 38.6 mm. **Ruler:** Elizabeth II **Series:** Victorian Era - Empress of India 1876 **Obv:** Bust with tiara right **Rev:** Crowned portrait of Victoria and two elephants

Date	Mintage	F12	VF20	XF40	MS60	MS63
2001	—	—	—	—	10.00	12.00

KM# 912a CROWN
28.28 g., 0.925 Silver 0.8356 oz. ASW **Ruler:** Elizabeth II **Series:** The Victorian Age - Empress of India 1876 **Obv:** Bust with tiara right **Rev:** Crowned portrait of Victoria and two elephants

Date	Mintage	F12	VF20	XF40	MS60	MS63
2001	10,000	PF63 45.00	PF65 47.00			

KM# 914 CROWN
Copper-Nickel, 38.6 mm. **Ruler:** Elizabeth II **Series:** Victorian Era - Diamond Jubilee **Obv:** Bust with tiara right **Rev:** Victoria's cameo portrait above naval ships

Date	Mintage	F12	VF20	XF40	MS60	MS63
2001	—	—	—	—	10.00	12.00

KM# 914a CROWN
28.28 g., 0.925 Silver 0.8356 oz. ASW **Ruler:** Elizabeth II **Series:** The Victorian Age - Diamond Jubilee 1897 **Obv:** Bust with tiara right **Rev:** Victoria's cameo above naval ships, Spithead Review

Date	Mintage	F12	VF20	XF40	MS60	MS63
2001	10,000	PF63 45.00	PF65 47.00			

KM# 916 CROWN
Copper-Nickel, 38.6 mm. **Ruler:** Elizabeth II **Series:** The Victorian Age - Victoria's Death 1901 **Obv:** Bust with tiara right **Rev:** Victoria's cameo portrait and Osborne Manor

Date	Mintage	F12	VF20	XF40	MS60	MS63
2001	—	—	—	—	10.00	12.00

KM# 916a CROWN
28.28 g., 0.925 Silver 0.8356 oz. ASW, 38.6 mm. **Ruler:** Elizabeth II **Series:** The Victorian Age - Victoria's Death 1901 **Obv:** Bust with tiara right **Rev:** Victoria's cameo portrait and Osborne Manor

Date	Mintage	F12	VF20	XF40	MS60	MS63
2001	10,000	PF63 45.00	PF65 47.00			

KM# 918 CROWN
Copper-Nickel, 38.6 mm. **Ruler:** Elizabeth II **Series:** The Victorian Age - Prince Albert and the Great Exhibition 1851 **Obv:** Bust with tiara right **Rev:** Albert's cameo portrait and the exhibit hall

Date	Mintage	F12	VF20	XF40	MS60	MS63
2001	5,000	PF63 175				

KM# 918a CROWN
28.28 g., 0.925 Silver 0.8356 oz. ASW, 38.6 mm. **Ruler:**

Elizabeth II **Series:** The Victorian Age - Prince Albert and the Great Exhibition 1851 **Obv:** Bust with tiara right **Rev:** Albert's cameo portrait and the exhibit hall

Date	Mintage	F12	VF20	XF40	MS60	MS63
2001	10,000	PF63 45.00	PF65 47.00			

KM# 920 CROWN
Copper-Nickel, 38.6 mm. **Ruler:** Elizabeth II **Series:** The Victorian Age **Obv:** Bust with tiara right **Rev:** 1/2 bust of Isambard K. Brunel half left in front of railroad bridge

Date	Mintage	F12	VF20	XF40	MS60	MS63
2001	—	—	—	—	10.00	12.00

KM# 920a CROWN
28.28 g., 0.925 Silver 0.8356 oz. ASW, 38.6 mm. **Ruler:** Elizabeth II **Series:** Victorian Era **Obv:** Bust with tiara right **Rev:** 1/2 bust of Isambard K. Brunel half left in front of railroad bridge

Date	Mintage	F12	VF20	XF40	MS60	MS63
2001	10,000	PF63 45.00	PF65 47.00			

KM# 922 CROWN
Copper-Nickel, 38.6 mm. **Ruler:** Elizabeth II **Series:** The Victorian Age **Obv:** Bust with tiara right **Rev:** 1/2 length bust of Charles Dickens half left, scene from "Oliver Twist" in background

Date	Mintage	F12	VF20	XF40	MS60	MS63
2001	—	—	—	—	10.00	12.00

KM# 922a CROWN
28.28 g., 0.925 Silver 0.8356 oz. ASW, 38.6 mm. **Series:** The Victorian Age **Obv:** Bust with tiara right **Rev:** 1/2 length bust of Charles Dickens half left, scene from "Oliver Twist" in background

Date	Mintage	F12	VF20	XF40	MS60	MS63
2001	10,000	PF63 45.00	PF65 47.00			

KM# 924 CROWN
Copper-Nickel, 38.6 mm. **Ruler:** Elizabeth II **Series:** The Victorian Age **Obv:** Bust with tiara right **Rev:** 3/4-length figure of Charles Darwin right, ship and a squatting aboriginal figure

Date	Mintage	F12	VF20	XF40	MS60	MS63
2001	—	—	—	—	10.00	12.00

KM# 924a CROWN
28.28 g., 0.925 Silver 0.8356 oz. ASW, 38.6 mm. **Ruler:** Elizabeth II **Series:** The Victorian Age **Obv:** Bust with tiara right **Rev:** 3/4-length figure of Charles Darwin right, ship and a squatting aboriginal figure

Date	Mintage	F12	VF20	XF40	MS60	MS63
2001	10,000	PF63 45.00	PF65 47.00			

KM# 927 CROWN
28.28 g., Copper-Nickel, 38.6 mm. **Ruler:** Elizabeth II **Series:** Mythology of the Solar System **Obv:** Bust with tiara right **Rev:** Standing goddess with snake basket **Edge:** Reeded

Date	Mintage	F12	VF20	XF40	MS60	MS63
2001	—	—	—	—	10.00	12.00

KM# 927a CROWN
28.28 g., 0.925 Silver 0.8356 oz. ASW, 38.6 mm. **Ruler:** Elizabeth II **Series:** Mythology of the Solar System **Obv:** Bust with tiara right **Rev:** Standing goddess with snake basket **Edge:** Reeded

Date	Mintage	F12	VF20	XF40	MS60	MS63
2001	10,000	PF63 45.00	PF65 47.00			

KM# 928 CROWN
Bi-Metallic, 32.25 mm. **Ruler:** Elizabeth II **Series:** Mythology of the Solar System **Obv:** Bust with tiara right **Rev:** Standing goddess with snake basket **Edge:** Reeded

Date	Mintage	F12	VF20	XF40	MS60	MS63
2001 In Proof sets only	2,001	PF65 150				

KM# 930 CROWN
Copper-Nickel, 38.6 mm. **Ruler:** Elizabeth II **Series:** Mythology of the Solar System - Sun **Obv:** Bust with tiara right **Rev:** Helios in chariot and the sun

Date	Mintage	F12	VF20	XF40	MS60	MS63
2001	—	—	—	—	10.00	12.00

KM# 930a CROWN
28.28 g., 0.925 Silver 0.8356 oz. ASW, 38.6 mm. **Ruler:** Elizabeth II **Series:** Mythology of the Solar System - Sun **Obv:** Bust with tiara right **Rev:** Helios in chariot and the sun

Date	Mintage	F12	VF20	XF40	MS60	MS63
2001	10,000	PF63 45.00	PF65 47.00			

KM# 930a.1 CROWN
28.28 g., 0.925 Silver 0.8356 oz. ASW **Ruler:** Elizabeth II **Series:** Mythology of the Solar System - Sun **Obv:** Bust with tiara right **Rev:** Fiery hologram in the sun

Date	Mintage	F12	VF20	XF40	MS60	MS63
2001	2,001	PF65 90.00				

KM# 932 CROWN
Copper-Nickel, 38.6 mm. **Ruler:** Elizabeth II **Series:** Mythology of the Solar System - Moon **Obv:** Bust with tiara right **Rev:** Goddess Diana and the moon

Date	Mintage	F12	VF20	XF40	MS60	MS63
2001	—	—	—	—	10.00	12.00

KM# 932a CROWN
28.28 g., 0.925 Silver 0.8356 oz. ASW, 38.6 mm. **Ruler:** Elizabeth II **Series:** Mythology of the Solar System - Moon **Obv:** Bust with tiara right **Rev:** Goddess Diana and the moon

Date	Mintage	F12	VF20	XF40	MS60	MS63
2001	10,000	PF63 45.00	PF65 47.00			

KM# 932a.1 CROWN
28.28 g., 0.925 Silver 0.8356 oz. ASW, 38.6 mm. **Ruler:** Elizabeth II **Series:** Mythology of the Solar System - Moon **Obv:** Bust with tiara right **Rev:** Small pearl set in the moon

Date	Mintage	F12	VF20	XF40	MS60	MS63
2001	2,001	PF65 90.00				

KM# 934 CROWN
Copper-Nickel **Ruler:** Elizabeth II **Series:** Mythology of the Solar System - Atlas **Obv:** Bust with tiara right **Rev:** Atlas carrying the earth

Date	Mintage	F12	VF20	XF40	MS60	MS63
2001	—	—	—	—	10.00	12.00

KM# 934a CROWN
28.28 g., 0.925 Silver 0.8356 oz. ASW, 38.6 mm. **Ruler:** Elizabeth II **Series:** Mythology of the Solar System - Atlas **Obv:** Bust with tiara right **Rev:** Atlas carrying the earth

Date	Mintage	F12	VF20	XF40	MS60	MS63
2001	10,000	PF63 45.00	PF65 47.00			

KM# 934a.1 CROWN
28.28 g., 0.925 Silver 0.8356 oz. ASW, 38.6 mm. **Ruler:** Elizabeth II **Series:** Mythology of the Solar System - Atlas **Obv:** Bust with tiara right **Rev:** Fancy diamond set in the earth

Date	Mintage	F12	VF20	XF40	MS60	MS63
2001	2,001	PF65 90.00				

KM# 936 CROWN
Copper-Nickel, 38.6 mm. **Ruler:** Elizabeth II **Series:** Mythology of the Solar System **Obv:** Bust with tiara right **Rev:** Seated Neptune with trident and ringed planet

Date	Mintage	F12	VF20	XF40	MS60	MS63
2001	—	—	—	—	10.00	12.00

KM# 936a CROWN
28.28 g., 0.925 Silver 0.8356 oz. ASW, 38.6 mm. **Ruler:** Elizabeth II **Series:** Mythology of the Solar System **Obv:** Bust with tiara right **Rev:** Seated Neptune with trident and ringed planet

Date	Mintage	F12	VF20	XF40	MS60	MS63
2001	10,000	PF63 45.00	PF65 47.00			

KM# 938 CROWN
Copper-Nickel, 38.6 mm. **Ruler:** Elizabeth II **Series:** Mythology of the Solar System **Obv:** Bust with tiara right **Rev:** Seated Jupiter with lightening bolts and a planet

Date	Mintage	F12	VF20	XF40	MS60	MS63
2001	—	—	—	—	10.00	12.00

KM# 938a CROWN
28.28 g., 0.925 Silver 0.8356 oz. ASW, 38.6 mm. **Ruler:** Elizabeth II **Series:** Mythology of the Solar System **Obv:** Bust with tiara right **Rev:** Seated Jupiter with lightening bolts and a planet

Date	Mintage	F12	VF20	XF40	MS60	MS63
2001	10,000	PF63 45.00	PF65 47.00			

KM# 940 CROWN
Copper-Nickel, 38.6 mm. **Ruler:** Elizabeth II **Series:** Mythology of the Solar System - Mars **Obv:** Bust with tiara right **Rev:** Standing Roman soldier and a planet

Date	Mintage	F12	VF20	XF40	MS60	MS63
2001	—	—	—	—	10.00	12.00

KM# 940a CROWN
28.28 g., 0.925 Silver 0.8356 oz. ASW, 38.6 mm. **Ruler:** Elizabeth II **Series:** Mythology of the Solar System - Mars **Obv:** Bust with tiara right **Rev:** Standing Roman soldier and a planet

Date	Mintage	F12	VF20	XF40	MS60	MS63
2001	10,000	PF63 45.00	PF65 47.00			

KM# 942 CROWN
Copper-Nickel, 38.6 mm. **Ruler:** Elizabeth II **Series:** Mythology of the Solar System **Obv:** Bust with tiara right **Rev:** Seated Mercury with caduceus and a planet

Date	Mintage	F12	VF20	XF40	MS60	MS63
2001	—	—	—	—	10.00	12.00

KM# 942a CROWN
28.28 g., 0.925 Silver 0.8356 oz. ASW, 38.6 mm. **Ruler:** Elizabeth II **Series:** Mythology of the Solar System **Obv:** Bust with tiara right **Rev:** Seated Mercury with caduceus and a planet

Date	Mintage	F12	VF20	XF40	MS60	MS63
2001	10,000	PF63 45.00	PF65 47.00			

KM# 944 CROWN
Copper-Nickel, 38.6 mm. **Ruler:** Elizabeth II **Series:** Mythology of the Solar System **Obv:** Bust with tiara right **Rev:** Seated Uranus with scepter

Date	Mintage	F12	VF20	XF40	MS60	MS63
2001	—	—	—	—	10.00	12.00

KM# 944a CROWN
28.28 g., 0.925 Silver 0.8356 oz. ASW, 38.6 mm. **Ruler:** Elizabeth II **Series:** Mythology of the Solar System **Obv:** Bust with tiara right **Rev:** Seated Uranus with scepter

Date	Mintage	F12	VF20	XF40	MS60	MS63
2001	10,000	PF63 45.00	PF65 47.00			

KM# 946 CROWN
Copper-Nickel, 38.6 mm. **Ruler:** Elizabeth II **Series:** Mythology of the Solar System **Obv:** Bust with tiara right **Rev:** Seated Saturn with long handled sickle and a ringed planet

Date	Mintage	F12	VF20	XF40	MS60	MS63
2001	—	—	—	—	10.00	12.00

KM# 946a CROWN
28.28 g., 0.925 Silver 0.8356 oz. ASW, 38.6 mm. **Ruler:** Elizabeth II **Series:** Mythology of the Solar System **Obv:** Bust with tiara right **Rev:** Seated Saturn with long handled sickle and a ringed planet

Date	Mintage	F12	VF20	XF40	MS60	MS63
2001	10,000	PF63 45.00	PF65 47.00			

KM# 948 CROWN
Copper-Nickel, 38.6 mm. **Ruler:** Elizabeth II **Series:** Mythology of the Solar System **Obv:** Bust with tiara right **Rev:** Seated Pluto with dogs and planet

Date	Mintage	F12	VF20	XF40	MS60	MS63
2001	—	—	—	—	10.00	12.00

KM# 948a CROWN
28.28 g., 0.925 Silver 0.8356 oz. ASW, 38.6 mm. **Ruler:** Elizabeth II **Series:** Mythology of the Solar System **Obv:** Bust with tiara right **Rev:** Seated Pluto with dogs and planet

Date	Mintage	F12	VF20	XF40	MS60	MS63
2001	10,000	PF63 45.00	PF65 47.00			

KM# 950 CROWN
Copper-Nickel, 38.6 mm. **Ruler:** Elizabeth II **Series:** Mythology of the Solar System **Obv:** Bust with tiara right **Rev:** Venus seated on a half shell

Date	Mintage	F12	VF20	XF40	MS60	MS63
2001	—	—	—	—	10.00	12.00

KM# 950a CROWN
28.28 g., 0.925 Silver 0.8356 oz. ASW, 38.6 mm. **Ruler:** Elizabeth II **Series:** Mythology of the Solar System **Obv:** Bust with tiara right **Rev:** Venus seated on a half shell

Date	Mintage	F12	VF20	XF40	MS60	MS63
2001	10,000	PF63 45.00	PF65 47.00			

KM# 952 CROWN
28.28 g., Copper-Nickel, 38.6 mm. **Ruler:** Elizabeth II **Subject:** Queen's 75th Birthday **Obv:** Bust with tiara right **Rev:** Queen in Order of Garter robes **Edge:** Reeded

Date	Mintage	F12	VF20	XF40	MS60	MS63
2001	—	—	—	—	10.00	12.00

KM# 952a CROWN
28.28 g., 0.925 Silver 0.8356 oz. ASW, 38.6 mm. **Ruler:** Elizabeth II **Subject:** Queen's 75th Birthday **Obv:** Bust with tiara right **Rev:** Queen in Order of Garter robes **Edge:** Reeded

Date	Mintage	F12	VF20	XF40	MS60	MS63
2001	10,000	PF63 45.00	PF65 47.00			

KM# 955 CROWN
28.28 g., Copper-Nickel, 38.6 mm. **Ruler:** Elizabeth II **Series:** Victorian Age Part II **Obv:** Bust with tiara right **Rev:** Victoria learning of her accession **Edge:** Reeded

Date	Mintage	F12	VF20	XF40	MS60	MS63
2001	—	—	—	—	10.00	12.00

KM# 955a CROWN
28.28 g., 0.925 Silver 0.8356 oz. ASW, 38.6 mm. **Ruler:** Elizabeth II **Series:** Victorian Age Part II **Obv:** Bust with tiara right **Rev:** Victoria learning of her accession **Edge:** Reeded

Date	Mintage	F12	VF20	XF40	MS60	MS63
2001	10,000	PF63 45.00	PF65 47.00			

KM# 957 CROWN
Copper-Nickel, 38.6 mm. **Ruler:** Elizabeth II **Series:** Victorian Age Part II - Royal Family **Obv:** Bust with tiara right **Rev:** Victoria and Albert seated with children **Edge:** Reeded

Date	Mintage	F12	VF20	XF40	MS60	MS63
2001	—	—	—	—	10.00	12.00

KM# 957a CROWN
28.28 g., 0.925 Silver 0.8356 oz. ASW, 38.6 mm. **Ruler:** Elizabeth II **Series:** Victorian Age Part II - Royal Family **Obv:** Bust with tiara right **Rev:** Victoria and Albert seated with children **Edge:** Reeded

Date	Mintage	F12	VF20	XF40	MS60	MS63
2001	10,000		PF63 45.00	PF65 47.00		

KM# 959 CROWN
Copper-Nickel, 38.6 mm. **Ruler:** Elizabeth II **Series:** Victorian Age Part II - Victoria in Scotland **Obv:** Bust with tiara right **Rev:** Victoria on horse with servant **Edge:** Reeded

Date	Mintage	F12	VF20	XF40	MS60	MS63
2001	2,001	—	—	—	10.00	12.00

KM# 959a CROWN
28.28 g., 0.925 Silver 0.8356 oz. ASW, 38.6 mm. **Ruler:** Elizabeth II **Series:** Victorian Age Part II - Victoria in Scotland **Obv:** Bust with tiara right **Rev:** Victoria on horse with servant **Edge:** Reeded

Date	Mintage	F12	VF20	XF40	MS60	MS63
2001	10,000		PF63 45.00	PF65 47.00		

KM# 961 CROWN
Copper-Nickel, 38.6 mm. **Ruler:** Elizabeth II **Series:** Victorian Age Part II - Gladstone and Disraeli **Obv:** Bust with tiara right **Rev:** Portraits of both politicians **Edge:** Reeded

Date	Mintage	F12	VF20	XF40	MS60	MS63
2001	—	—	—	—	10.00	12.00

KM# 961a CROWN
28.28 g., 0.925 Silver 0.8356 oz. ASW, 38.6 mm. **Ruler:** Elizabeth II **Series:** Victorian Age Part II - Gladstone and Disraeli **Obv:** Bust with tiara right **Rev:** Portraits of both politicians **Edge:** Reeded

Date	Mintage	F12	VF20	XF40	MS60	MS63
2001	10,000		PF63 45.00	PF65 47.00		

KM# 963 CROWN
Copper-Nickel, 38.6 mm. **Ruler:** Elizabeth II **Series:** Victorian Age Part II **Obv:** Bust with tiara right **Rev:** Florence Nightingale holding lantern **Edge:** Reeded

Date	Mintage	F12	VF20	XF40	MS60	MS63
2001	—	—	—	—	10.00	12.00

KM# 963a CROWN
28.28 g., 0.925 Silver 0.8356 oz. ASW, 38.6 mm. **Ruler:** Elizabeth II **Series:** Victorian Age Part II **Obv:** Bust with tiara right **Rev:** Florence Nightingale holding lantern **Edge:** Reeded

Date	Mintage	F12	VF20	XF40	MS60	MS63
2001	10,000		PF63 45.00	PF65 47.00		

KM# 965 CROWN
Copper-Nickel, 38.6 mm. **Ruler:** Elizabeth II **Series:** Victorian Age Part II **Obv:** Bust with tiara right **Rev:** Lord Tennyson with the Light Brigade in background **Edge:** Reeded

Date	Mintage	F12	VF20	XF40	MS60	MS63
2001	—	—	—	—	10.00	12.00

KM# 965a CROWN
28.28 g., 0.925 Silver 0.8356 oz. ASW, 38.6 mm. **Ruler:** Elizabeth II **Series:** Victorian Age Part II **Obv:** Bust with tiara right **Rev:** Lord Tennyson with the Light Brigade in background **Edge:** Reeded

Date	Mintage	F12	VF20	XF40	MS60	MS63
2001	10,000		PF63 45.00	PF65 47.00		

KM# 967 CROWN
Copper-Nickel, 38.6 mm. **Ruler:** Elizabeth II **Series:** Victorian Age Part II **Obv:** Bust with tiara right **Rev:** Stanley meeting Dr. Livingstone **Edge:** Reeded

Date	Mintage	F12	VF20	XF40	MS60	MS63
2001	—	—	—	—	10.00	12.00

KM# 967a CROWN
28.28 g., 0.925 Silver 0.8356 oz. ASW, 38.6 mm. **Ruler:** Elizabeth II **Series:** Victorian Age Part II **Obv:** Bust with tiara right **Rev:** Stanley meeting Dr. Livingstone **Edge:** Reeded

Date	Mintage	F12	VF20	XF40	MS60	MS63
2001	10,000		PF63 45.00	PF65 47.00		

KM# 969 CROWN
Copper-Nickel, 38.6 mm. **Ruler:** Elizabeth II **Series:** Victorian Age Part II **Obv:** Bust with tiara right **Rev:** Bronte sisters **Edge:** Reeded

Date	Mintage	F12	VF20	XF40	MS60	MS63
2001	—	—	—	—	10.00	12.00

KM# 969a CROWN
28.28 g., 0.925 Silver 0.8356 oz. ASW, 38.6 mm. **Ruler:** Elizabeth II **Series:** Victorian Age Part II **Obv:** Bust with tiara right **Rev:** Bronte sisters **Edge:** Reeded

Date	Mintage	F12	VF20	XF40	MS60	MS63
2001	10,000		PF63 45.00	PF65 47.00		

KM# 1058 CROWN
31.10 g., 1.000 Electrum 0.9935 oz. **Ruler:** Elizabeth II **Series:** Ancient Coins **Obv:** Crowned head right **Rev:** Head of Athena left **Note:** From a Mysia electrum coin c. 520 BC.

Date	Mintage	F12	VF20	XF40	MS60	MS63
2002	—	PF65 700				

KM# 1059 CROWN
31.10 g., Electrum **Ruler:** Elizabeth II **Series:** Ancient Coins **Obv:** Crowned bust right **Rev:** Head of Hercules right **Note:** From a Lesbos coin c. 480-450

Date	Mintage	F12	VF20	XF40	MS60	MS63
2002	—	PF65 700				

KM# 1060 CROWN
31.10 g., Electrum **Ruler:** Elizabeth II **Series:** Ancient Coins. **Obv:** Crowned bust right **Rev:** Lion and bull facing **Note:** From a Lampsakos electrum coin c. 450 BC.

Date	Mintage	F12	VF20	XF40	MS60	MS63
2002	—	PF65 700				

KM# 1061 CROWN
31.10 g., Electrum **Ruler:** Elizabeth II **Series:** Ancient Coins **Obv:** Crowned bust right **Rev:** Lion and bull facing **Note:** From a Kroisos [sic] coin c. 560-546 BC.

Date	Mintage	F12	VF20	XF40	MS60	MS63
2002	—	PF65 700				

KM# 1025a CROWN
28.28 g., 0.925 Silver 0.8356 oz. ASW, 38.6 mm. **Ruler:** Elizabeth II **Subject:** Calpe Conference **Obv:** Bust with tiara right **Rev:** Crossed flags and arms **Edge:** Reeded

Date	Mintage	F12	VF20	XF40	MS60	MS63
2002PM	10,000		PF63 45.00	PF65 47.00		

KM# 979 CROWN
28.28 g., Copper-Nickel, 38.6 mm. **Ruler:** Elizabeth II **Subject:** Queen Mother's Life **Obv:** Bust with tiara right **Rev:** Christening of Prince William **Edge:** Reeded

Date	Mintage	F12	VF20	XF40	MS60	MS63
2002	—	—	—	—	10.00	12.00

KM# 979a CROWN
28.28 g., 0.925 Silver 0.8356 oz. ASW, 38.6 mm. **Ruler:** Elizabeth II **Subject:** Queen Mother's Life **Obv:** Bust with tiara right **Rev:** Prince William's christening **Edge:** Reeded

Date	Mintage	F12	VF20	XF40	MS60	MS63
2002	10,000		PF63 45.00	PF65 47.00		

KM# 981 CROWN
28.28 g., Copper-Nickel, 38.6 mm. **Ruler:** Elizabeth II **Subject:** World Cup Soccer **Obv:** Bust with tiara right **Rev:** Two players about to collide **Edge:** Reeded

Date	Mintage	F12	VF20	XF40	MS60	MS63
2002	—	—	—	—	10.00	11.50

KM# 981a CROWN
28.28 g., 0.925 Silver 0.8356 oz. ASW, 38.6 mm. **Ruler:** Elizabeth II **Subject:** World Cup Soccer **Obv:** Bust with tiara right **Rev:** Two players about to collide **Edge:** Reeded

Date	Mintage	F12	VF20	XF40	MS60	MS63
2002	10,000	PF63 45.00	PF65 47.00			

KM# 983 CROWN
28.28 g., Copper-Nickel, 38.6 mm. **Ruler:** Elizabeth II **Subject:** World Cup Soccer **Obv:** Bust with tiara right **Rev:** Two players facing viewer **Edge:** Reeded

Date	Mintage	F12	VF20	XF40	MS60	MS63
2002	—	—	—	—	10.00	11.50

KM# 983a CROWN
28.28 g., 0.925 Silver 0.8356 oz. ASW, 38.6 mm. **Ruler:** Elizabeth II **Subject:** World Cup Soccer **Obv:** Bust with tiara right **Rev:** Two players facing viewer **Edge:** Reeded

Date	Mintage	F12	VF20	XF40	MS60	MS63
2002	10,000	PF63 45.00	PF65 47.00			

KM# 985 CROWN
28.28 g., Copper-Nickel, 38.6 mm. **Ruler:** Elizabeth II **Subject:** World Cup Soccer **Obv:** Bust with tiara right **Rev:** Two horizontal players **Edge:** Reeded

Date	Mintage	F12	VF20	XF40	MS60	MS63
2002	—	—	—	—	10.00	11.50

KM# 985a CROWN
28.28 g., 0.925 Silver 0.8356 oz. ASW, 38.6 mm. **Ruler:** Elizabeth II **Subject:** World Cup Soccer **Obv:** Bust with tiara right **Rev:** Two horizontal players **Edge:** Reeded

Date	Mintage	F12	VF20	XF40	MS60	MS63
2002	10,000	PF63 45.00	PF65 47.00			

KM# 987 CROWN
28.28 g., Copper-Nickel, 38.6 mm. **Ruler:** Elizabeth II **Subject:** World Cup Soccer **Obv:** Bust with tiara right **Rev:** Two players moving to left **Edge:** Reeded

Date	Mintage	F12	VF20	XF40	MS60	MS63
2002	—	—	—	—	10.00	11.50

KM# 987a CROWN
28.28 g., 0.925 Silver 0.8356 oz. ASW, 38.6 mm. **Ruler:** Elizabeth II **Subject:** World Cup Soccer **Obv:** Bust with tiara right **Rev:** Two players moving to left **Edge:** Reeded

Date	Mintage	F12	VF20	XF40	MS60	MS63
2002	10,000	PF63 45.00	PF65 47.00			

KM# 992.1 CROWN
28.28 g., Copper-Nickel, 38.6 mm. **Ruler:** Elizabeth II **Subject:** Peter Rabbit Centennial **Obv:** Bust with tiara right **Rev:** Peter Rabbit **Edge:** Reeded

Date	Mintage	F12	VF20	XF40	MS60	MS63
2002	—	—	—	—	10.00	12.00

KM# 992a CROWN
28.28 g., 0.925 Silver 0.8356 oz. ASW, 38.6 mm. **Ruler:** Elizabeth II **Subject:** Peter Rabbit Centennial **Obv:** Bust with tiara right **Rev:** Peter Rabbit **Edge:** Reeded

Date	Mintage	F12	VF20	XF40	MS60	MS63
2002	10,000	PF63 45.00	PF65 47.00			

KM# 992.2 CROWN
Copper-Nickel **Ruler:** Elizabeth II **Obv:** Bust with tiara right **Rev:** Peter Rabbit in multi-color

Date	Mintage	F12	VF20	XF40	MS60	MS63
2002	—	—	—	—	10.00	12.00

KM# 994 CROWN
28.28 g., Copper-Nickel, 38.6 mm. **Ruler:** Elizabeth II **Subject:** Queen's Golden Jubilee **Obv:** Bust with tiara right **Rev:** Royal couple and tree house **Edge:** Reeded

Date	Mintage	F12	VF20	XF40	MS60	MS63
2002	—	—	—	—	10.00	12.00

KM# 994a CROWN
Yellow Brass, 38.6 mm. **Ruler:** Elizabeth II **Subject:** Queen's Golden Jubilee **Obv:** Bust with tiara right **Rev:** Royal couple and tree house **Edge:** Reeded

Date	Mintage	F12	VF20	XF40	MS60	MS63
2002	15,000	PF63 20.00	PF65 22.00			

KM# 994b CROWN
28.28 g., 0.925 Gold Clad Silver 0.8356 oz., 38.6 mm. **Ruler:** Elizabeth II **Subject:** Queen's Golden Jubilee **Obv:** Bust with tiara right **Rev:** Royal couple and tree house **Edge:** Reeded

Date	Mintage	F12	VF20	XF40	MS60	MS63
2002	10,000	PF65 55.00				

KM# 996 CROWN
28.28 g., Copper-Nickel, 38.6 mm. **Ruler:** Elizabeth II **Subject:** Queen's Golden Jubilee **Obv:** Bust with tiara right **Rev:** Royal coach **Edge:** Reeded

Date	Mintage	F12	VF20	XF40	MS60	MS63
2002	—	—	—	—	10.00	12.00

KM# 996a CROWN
Yellow Brass, 38.6 mm. **Ruler:** Elizabeth II **Subject:** Queen's Golden Jubilee **Obv:** Bust with tiara right **Rev:** Royal coach **Edge:** Reeded

Date	Mintage	F12	VF20	XF40	MS60	MS63
2002	15,000	PF63 20.00	PF65 22.00			

KM# 996b CROWN
28.28 g., 0.925 Gold Clad Silver 0.8356 oz., 38.6 mm. **Ruler:** Elizabeth II **Subject:** Queen's Golden Jubilee **Obv:** Bust with tiara right **Rev:** Royal coach **Edge:** Reeded

Date	Mintage	F12	VF20	XF40	MS60	MS63
2002	10,000	PF65 55.00				

KM# 998 CROWN
28.28 g., Copper-Nickel, 38.6 mm. **Ruler:** Elizabeth II **Subject:** Queen's Golden Jubilee **Obv:** Bust with tiara right **Rev:** Royal couple with baby **Edge:** Reeded

Date	Mintage	F12	VF20	XF40	MS60	MS63
2002	—	—	—	—	10.00	12.00

KM# 998a CROWN
Yellow Brass, 38.6 mm. **Ruler:** Elizabeth II **Subject:** Queen's Golden Jubilee **Obv:** Bust with tiara right **Rev:** Royal couple with baby **Edge:** Reeded

Date	Mintage	F12	VF20	XF40	MS60	MS63
2002	15,000	PF63 20.00	PF65 22.00			

KM# 998b CROWN
28.28 g., 0.925 Gold Clad Silver 0.8356 oz., 38.6 mm. **Ruler:** Elizabeth II **Subject:** Queen's Golden Jubilee **Obv:** Bust with tiara right **Rev:** Royal couple with baby **Edge:** Reeded

Date	Mintage	F12	VF20	XF40	MS60	MS63
2002	1,000	PF65 55.00				

KM# 1000 CROWN
28.28 g., Copper-Nickel, 38.6 mm. **Ruler:** Elizabeth II **Subject:** Queen's Golden Jubilee **Obv:** Bust with tiara right **Rev:** Royal yacht under Tower bridge **Edge:** Reeded

Date	Mintage	F12	VF20	XF40	MS60	MS63
2002	—	—	—	—	10.00	12.00

KM# 1000a CROWN
Yellow Brass, 38.6 mm. **Ruler:** Elizabeth II **Subject:** Queen's Golden Jubilee **Obv:** Bust with tiara right **Rev:** Royal yacht under Tower bridge **Edge:** Reeded

Date	Mintage	F12	VF20	XF40	MS60	MS63
2002	15,000	PF63 20.00	PF65 22.00			

KM# 1000b CROWN
28.28 g., 0.925 Gold Clad Silver 0.8356 oz., 38.6 mm. **Ruler:** Elizabeth II **Subject:** Queen's Golden Jubilee **Obv:** Bust with tiara right **Rev:** Royal yacht under Tower bridge **Edge:** Reeded

Date	Mintage	F12	VF20	XF40	MS60	MS63
2002	10,000	PF65 55.00				

KM# 1013 CROWN
28.28 g., Copper-Nickel, 38.6 mm. **Ruler:** Elizabeth II **Subject:** Death of Queen Mother **Obv:** Bust with tiara right **Rev:** Queen Mother trout fishing **Edge:** Reeded

Date	Mintage	F12	VF20	XF40	MS60	MS63
2002	—	—	—	—	10.00	12.00

KM# 1013a CROWN
28.28 g., 0.925 Silver 0.8356 oz. ASW, 38.6 mm. **Ruler:** Elizabeth II **Subject:** Queen Mother **Obv:** Bust with tiara right **Rev:** Queen Mother trout fishing **Edge:** Reeded **Note:** Obv. and rev. have blackened legends.

Date	Mintage	F12	VF20	XF40	MS60	MS63
2002	—	PF65 175				

KM# 1015 CROWN
28.28 g., Copper-Nickel, 38.6 mm. **Ruler:** Elizabeth II **Subject:** Princess Diana **Obv:** Bust with tiara right **Rev:** Diana's portrait **Edge:** Reeded

Date	Mintage	F12	VF20	XF40	MS60	MS63
2002	—	—	—	—	10.00	12.00

KM# 1015a CROWN
28.28 g., 0.925 Silver 0.8356 oz. ASW, 38.6 mm. **Ruler:** Elizabeth II **Subject:** Princess Diana **Obv:** Bust with tiara right **Rev:** Diana's portrait **Edge:** Reeded

Date	Mintage	F12	VF20	XF40	MS60	MS63
2002	10,000	PF63 45.00	PF65 47.00			

KM# 1019 CROWN
28.28 g., Copper-Nickel, 38.6 mm. **Ruler:** Elizabeth II **Subject:** Peter Pan **Obv:** Bust with tiara right **Rev:** Peter Pan and Tinkerbell flying above city **Edge:** Reeded

Date	Mintage	F12	VF20	XF40	MS60	MS63
2002	—	—	—	—	10.00	12.00

KM# 1019a CROWN
28.28 g., 0.925 Silver 0.8356 oz. ASW, 38.6 mm. **Ruler:** Elizabeth II **Subject:** Peter Pan **Obv:** Bust with tiara right **Rev:** Peter Pan and Tinkerbell flying above city **Edge:** Reeded

Date	Mintage	F12	VF20	XF40	MS60	MS63
2002	10,000	PF63 45.00	PF65 47.00			

KM# 1021 CROWN
28.28 g., Copper-Nickel, 38.6 mm. **Ruler:** Elizabeth II **Subject:** Grand Masonic Lodge **Obv:** Bust with tiara right **Rev:** Masonic seal above Gibraltar **Edge:** Reeded

Date	Mintage	F12	VF20	XF40	MS60	MS63
2002	—	PF63 12.00	PF65 14.00			

KM# 1021a CROWN
28.28 g., 0.925 Silver 0.8356 oz. ASW, 38.6 mm. **Ruler:** Elizabeth II **Subject:** Grand Masonic Lodge **Obv:** Bust with tiara right **Rev:** Masonic seal above Gibraltar **Edge:** Reeded

Date	Mintage	F12	VF20	XF40	MS60	MS63
2002	10,000	PF63 45.00	PF65 47.00			

KM# 1025 CROWN
28.28 g., Copper-Nickel, 38.6 mm. **Ruler:** Elizabeth II **Subject:** Calpe Conference **Obv:** Bust with tiara right **Rev:** Crossed flags and arms **Edge:** Reeded

Date	Mintage	F12	VF20	XF40	MS60	MS63
2002PM	—	—	—	—	10.00	12.00

KM# 1052 CROWN
Copper-Nickel **Ruler:** Elizabeth II **Subject:** 2004 Athens Olympics **Rev:** Horse jumping left

Date	Mintage	F12	VF20	XF40	MS60	MS63
2003	—	—	—	—	10.00	12.00

KM# 1053 CROWN
Copper-Nickel **Ruler:** Elizabeth II **Subject:** 2004 Athens Olympics **Rev:** Javelin thrower

Date	Mintage	F12	VF20	XF40	MS60	MS63
2003	—	—	—	—	10.00	12.00

KM# 1054 CROWN
Copper-Nickel **Ruler:** Elizabeth II **Subject:** 2004 Athens Olympics **Rev:** Field Hockey

Date	Mintage	F12	VF20	XF40	MS60	MS63
2003	—	—	—	—	10.00	12.00

KM# 1055 CROWN
Copper-Nickel **Ruler:** Elizabeth II **Subject:** 2004 Athens Olympics **Rev:** Wrestlers

Date	Mintage	F12	VF20	XF40	MS60	MS63
2003	—	—	—	—	10.00	12.00

KM# 1035a CROWN
28.28 g., 0.925 Silver 0.8356 oz. ASW, 38.6 mm. **Ruler:** Elizabeth II **Subject:** 1700th Anniversary - Death of St. George **Obv:** Bust with tiara right **Rev:** St. George and the dragon **Edge:** Reeded

Date	Mintage	F12	VF20	XF40	MS60	MS63
2003	10,000	PF63 45.00	PF65 47.00			

KM# 1040a CROWN
31.10 g., Tri-Metallic, 38.6 mm. **Ruler:** Elizabeth II **Subject:** Centennial of Powered Flight **Obv:** Queens portrait **Rev:** Stealth bomber within circles of WWI and WWII planes **Edge:** Reeded

Date	Mintage	F12	VF20	XF40	MS60	MS63
2003PM	999	PF65 1,750				

KM# 1035 CROWN
28.28 g., Nickel-Brass, 38.6 mm. **Ruler:** Elizabeth II **Subject:** 1700th Anniversary - Death of St. George **Obv:** Bust with tiara right **Rev:** St. George and the dragon **Edge:** Reeded

Date	Mintage	F12	VF20	XF40	MS60	MS63
2003	—	—	—	—	9.00	10.00

KM# 1039 CROWN
28.30 g., Copper-Nickel, 38.6 mm. **Ruler:** Elizabeth II **Subject:** Peter Rabbit **Obv:** Bust with tiara right **Rev:** Peter Rabbit holding carrot **Edge:** Reeded

Date	Mintage	F12	VF20	XF40	MS60	MS63
2003PM	—	—	—	—	9.00	10.00

KM# 1040 CROWN
28.28 g., Copper-Nickel, 38.6 mm. **Ruler:** Elizabeth II **Subject:** Centennial of Powered Flight **Obv:** Queens portrait **Rev:** Stealth bomber within circles of WWI and WWII planes **Edge:** Reeded

Date	Mintage	F12	VF20	XF40	MS60	MS63
2003PM	—	—	—	—	10.00	12.00

KM# 1041 CROWN
28.28 g., Copper-Nickel, 38.6 mm. **Ruler:** Elizabeth II **Subject:** 50th Anniversary of Coronation **Obv:** Queens portrait **Rev:** Buckingham Palace **Edge:** Reeded

Date	Mintage	F12	VF20	XF40	MS60	MS63
2003PM	—	—	—	—	10.00	12.00

KM# 1094 CROWN
28.28 g., Copper-Nickel, 38.6 mm. **Ruler:** Elizabeth II **Rev:** Battleship Bismark under fire, colored poppy below

Date	Mintage	F12	VF20	XF40	MS60	MS63
2004	—	—	—	—	10.00	12.00

KM# 1075 CROWN
28.28 g., Copper-Nickel, 38.6 mm. **Ruler:** Elizabeth II **Subject:** Trafalgar - First Shot **Rev:** Naval battle scene

Date	Mintage	F12	VF20	XF40	MS60	MS63
2005	—	—	—	—	10.00	12.00

KM# 1076 CROWN
28.28 g., Copper-Nickel, 38.6 mm. **Ruler:** Elizabeth II **Subject:** Trafalgar - Breaking the line **Rev:** Naval battle

Date	Mintage	F12	VF20	XF40	MS60	MS63
2005	—	—	—	—	10.00	12.00

KM# 1077 CROWN
28.28 g., Copper-Nickel, 38.6 mm. **Ruler:** Elizabeth II **Subject:** Trafalgar - Hardy **Rev:** Bust facing

Date	Mintage	F12	VF20	XF40	MS60	MS63
2005	—	—	—	—	10.00	12.00

KM# 1078 CROWN
28.28 g., Copper-Nickel, 38.6 mm. **Ruler:** Elizabeth II **Subject:** Trafalgar - Nelson **Rev:** Bust facing

Date	Mintage	F12	VF20	XF40	MS60	MS63
2005	—	—	—	—	10.00	12.00

KM# 1034 2 CROWN
41.50 g., Bi-Metallic, 50 mm. **Ruler:** Elizabeth II **Subject:** Euro's First Anniversary **Obv:** Crowned bust right within star silhouette **Rev:** Europa riding a bull, stars and star silhouette in background **Edge:** Reeded

Date	Mintage	F12	VF20	XF40	MS60	MS63
2003PM	3,500	PF63 125		PF65 145		

KM# 1034a 2 CROWN
50.00 g., Bi-Metallic, 50 mm. **Ruler:** Elizabeth II **Subject:** 1st Anniversary - Euro **Obv:** Crowned bust right within star silhouette **Rev:** Europa riding the bull, stars and star silhouette in background **Edge:** Reeded

Date	Mintage	F12	VF20	XF40	MS60	MS63
2003PM	2,003	PF65 850				

KM# 1034b 2 CROWN
56.30 g., Bi-Metallic, 50 mm. **Ruler:** Elizabeth II **Subject:** 1st Anniversary - Euro **Obv:** Crowned bust right within star silhouette **Rev:** Europa riding the bull, stars and star silhouette in background **Edge:** Reeded

Date	Mintage	F12	VF20	XF40	MS60	MS63
2003PM	2,003	PF65 900				

KM# 907 5 CROWN
Tri-Metallic, 50 mm. **Ruler:** Elizabeth II **Subject:** 21st Century **Obv:** Crowned bust right, date below **Rev:** Celtic cross, Viking ship and modern technological items **Edge:** Reeded

Date	Mintage	F12	VF20	XF40	MS60	MS63
2001	199	PF63 6,500				

KM# 1042 5 CROWN
155.55 g., 0.999 Silver 4.9639 oz. ASW, 65 mm. **Ruler:** Elizabeth II **Subject:** 50th Anniversary of Coronation **Obv:** Queens portrait **Rev:** Buckingham Palace with tiny .01ct ruby, diamond and sapphire inserts above the main entrance **Edge:** Reeded

Date	Mintage	F12	VF20	XF40	MS60	MS63
2003PM	2,003	PF63 200		PF65 225		

KM# 1045 32 CROWNS
1000.00 g., 0.999 Silver 31.9118 oz. ASW **Ruler:** Elizabeth II **Subject:** Beatrix Potter's Peter Rabbit **Obv:** Bust with tiara right **Rev:** Multicolor Peter Rabbit holding carrot, with blue coat and red slippers

Date	Mintage	F12	VF20	XF40	MS60	MS63
2003	1,000	PF63 1,000		PF65 1,100		

KM# 869 POUND
9.50 g., Nickel-Brass, 22.5 mm. **Ruler:** Elizabeth II **Obv:** Head with tiara right **Rev:** Gibraltar coat of arms - castle and key

Date	Mintage	F12	VF20	XF40	MS60	MS63
2001 AA	—	—	—	—	3.50	4.50
2001 AB	—	—	—	—	3.50	4.50
2002 AC	—	—	—	—	3.50	4.50

KM# 1036 POUND
9.50 g., Nickel-Brass, 22 mm. **Ruler:** Elizabeth II **Subject:** 1700th Anniversary - Death of St. George **Obv:** Bust with tiara right **Rev:** St. George and the dragon **Edge:** Reeded

Date	Mintage	F12	VF20	XF40	MS60	MS63
2003	—	—	—	—	9.00	10.00

KM# 1051 POUND
9.50 g., Nickel-Brass, 22.5 mm. **Ruler:** Elizabeth II **Subject:** Tercentenary 1704-2004 **Obv:** Elizabeth II **Rev:** Old cannon set for a downhill target **Edge:** Reeded

Date	Mintage	F12	VF20	XF40	MS60	MS63
2004PM	—	—	—	—	—	4.00

KM# 1091 POUND
9.50 g., Nickel-Brass, 22.5 mm. **Ruler:** Elizabeth II **Obv:** Bust in diadem right **Rev:** Neanderthal Skull

Date	Mintage	F12	VF20	XF40	MS60	MS63
2005	—	—	—	—	3.50	4.50
2006	—	—	—	—	3.50	4.50
2007	—	—	—	—	3.50	4.50
2008	—	—	—	—	3.50	4.50
2009	—	—	—	—	3.50	4.50
2010	—	—	—	—	3.50	4.50
2011	—	—	—	—	3.50	4.50

KM# 1105 POUND
9.50 g., Nickel-Brass, 27.5 mm. **Ruler:** Elizabeth II **Obv:** Bust right **Obv. Legend:** ELIZABETH II QUEEN OF GIBRALTAR

Date	Mintage	F12	VF20	XF40	MS60	MS63
2012	—	—	—	—	3.50	4.50

KM# 970 2 POUNDS
12.00 g., Bi-Metallic, 28.4 mm. **Ruler:** Elizabeth II **Subject:** Bicentennial of the Union Jack **Obv:** Head with tiara right **Rev:** Standing Britannia flag as a cape **Edge:** Reeded

Date	Mintage	F12	VF20	XF40	MS60	MS63
2001 AA	—				10.00	12.00

KM# 970a 2 POUNDS
12.00 g., 0.999 Bi-Metallic 0.3829 oz., 28.4 mm. **Ruler:** Elizabeth II **Subject:** Bicentennial of the Union Jack **Obv:** Head with tiara right **Rev:** Standing Britannia wearing flag as a cape **Edge:** Reeded

Date	Mintage	F12	VF20	XF40	MS60	MS63
2001	7,500	—		—	35.00	40.00

KM# 1043 2 POUNDS
12.00 g., Bi-Metallic, 28.4 mm. **Ruler:** Elizabeth II **Obv:** Head with tiara right **Rev:** Old cannon **Edge:** Reeded

Date	Mintage	F12	VF20	XF40	MS60	MS63
2003PM	—	—	—	—	10.00	12.00

KM# 1057 2 POUNDS
12.00 g., Bi-Metallic, 28.4 mm. **Ruler:** Elizabeth II **Subject:** Tercentenary 1704-2004 **Obv:** Elizabeth II **Rev:** Naval Battle, capture of Gibraltar **Edge:** Reeded

Date	Mintage	F12	VF20	XF40	MS60	MS63
2004PM	—	—	—	—	10.00	12.00

KM# 1072 2 POUNDS
12.00 g., Bi-Metallic, 28.4 mm. **Ruler:** Elizabeth II **Subject:** Capture of Gibraltar **Rev:** Sea Battle

Date	Mintage	F12	VF20	XF40	MS60	MS63
2004	—	—	—	—	10.00	12.00

KM# 1092 2 POUNDS
12.00 g., Bi-Metallic, 28.4 mm. **Ruler:** Elizabeth II **Subject:** Battle of Trafalgar **Rev:** Two Naval vessels and rock in background

Date	Mintage	F12	VF20	XF40	MS60	MS63
2005	—	—	—	—	10.00	12.00
2006	—	—	—	—	10.00	12.00
2007	—	—	—	—	10.00	12.00
2008	—	—	—	—	10.00	12.00
2009	—	—	—	—	10.00	12.00
2010	—	—	—	—	10.00	12.00
2011	—	—	—	—	10.00	12.00

KM# 1093 2 POUNDS
12.00 g., Bi-Metallic, 28.4 mm. **Ruler:** Elizabeth II **Subject:** Diamond Wedding Anniversary **Obv:** Bust in diadem right **Rev:** Conjoined busts of Elizabeth and Philip

Date	Mintage	F12	VF20	XF40	MS60	MS63
2007					10.00	12.00

KM# 1106 2 POUNDS
12.00 g., Bi-Metallic, 28.4 mm. **Ruler:** Elizabeth II **Obv:** Bust right **Obv. Legend:** ELIZABETH II QUEEN OF GIBRALTAR

Date	Mintage	F12	VF20	XF40	MS60	MS63
2012					10.00	12.00

KM# 953 5 POUNDS
20.00 g., Virenium, 36.1 mm. **Ruler:** Elizabeth II **Subject:** Gibraltar Chronicle 200 Years **Obv:** Head with tiara right **Rev:** Naval battle scene with newspaper in background **Edge:** Reeded

Date	Mintage	F12	VF20	XF40	MS60	MS63
2001					17.00	20.00

KM# 953a 5 POUNDS
23.50 g., 0.925 Silver 0.6944 oz. ASW, 36.1 mm. **Ruler:** Elizabeth II **Subject:** Gibraltar Chronicle 200 Years **Obv:** Head with tiara right **Rev:** Naval battle scene with newspaper in background **Edge:** Reeded

Date	Mintage	F12	VF20	XF40	MS60	MS63
2001	10,000	PF63 50.00	PF65 60.00			

KM# 953b 5 POUNDS
39.83 g., 0.9167 Gold 1.1663 oz. AGW, 36.1 mm. **Ruler:** Elizabeth II **Subject:** Gibraltar Chronicle 200 Years **Obv:** Head with tiara right **Rev:** Naval battle scene with newspaper in background **Edge:** Reeded

Date	Mintage	F12	VF20	XF40	MS60	MS63
2001	850	PF65 2,100				

KM# 1011 5 POUNDS
20.00 g., Virenium, 36.1 mm. **Ruler:** Elizabeth II **Subject:** Queen's Golden Jubilee **Obv:** Head with tiara right **Rev:** Coronation scene **Edge:** Reeded

Date	Mintage	F12	VF20	XF40	MS60	MS63
2002	—	—	—	—	17.00	20.00

KM# 1011a 5 POUNDS
23.50 g., 0.925 Silver 0.6944 oz. ASW, 36.1 mm. **Ruler:** Elizabeth II **Subject:** Queen's Golden Jubilee **Obv:** Head with tiara right **Rev:** Coronation scene **Edge:** Reeded

Date	Mintage	F12	VF20	XF40	MS60	MS63
2002	10,000	PF63 50.00	PF65 60.00			

KM# 1011b 5 POUNDS
39.83 g., 0.9166 Gold 1.1662 oz. AGW, 36.1 mm. **Ruler:** Elizabeth II **Subject:** Queen's Golden Jubilee **Obv:** Head with tiara right **Rev:** Coronation scene **Edge:** Reeded

Date	Mintage	F12	VF20	XF40	MS60	MS63
2002	—	PF65 2,100				

KM# 1064 5 POUNDS
Silver, 38 mm. **Ruler:** Elizabeth II **Subject:** 200th Anniversary, Battle of Trafalgar **Rev:** Two naval vessels **Edge:** Reeded

Date	Mintage	F12	VF20	XF40	MS60	MS63
2005	—	PF63 45.00	PF65 50.00			

KM# 1095 5 POUNDS
Silver, 38.6 mm. **Ruler:** Elizabeth II **Subject:** History fo the RAF - Flypast **Obv:** Bust in crown right **Rev:** Bomber and two planes in flight

Date	Mintage	F12	VF20	XF40	MS60	MS63
2007	—	PF63 45.00	PF65 50.00			

KM# 1096 5 POUNDS
Silver, 38.61 mm. **Ruler:** Elizabeth II **Subject:** History of the RAF - Avro Lancaster **Obv:** Bust in crown right **Rev:** Lancaster bomber flying right

Date	Mintage	F12	VF20	XF40	MS60	MS63
2007	—	PF63 45.00	PF65 50.00			

SOVEREIGN COINAGE

KM# 1037 1/5 SOVEREIGN
1.22 g., 0.9999 Gold 0.039 oz. AGW, 13.92 mm. **Ruler:** Elizabeth II **Subject:** Death of St. George **Obv:** Bust with tiara right **Rev:** St. George and the dragon **Edge:** Reeded

Date	Mintage	F12	VF20	XF40	MS60	MS63
2003	10,000	PF63 75.00	PF65 85.00			

KM# 1038 SOVEREIGN
6.22 g., 0.9999 Gold 0.1987 oz. AGW, 22 mm. **Ruler:** Elizabeth II **Subject:** Death of St. George **Obv:** Bust with tiara right **Rev:** St. George and the dragon **Edge:** Reeded

Date	Mintage	F12	VF20	XF40	MS60	MS63
2003	5,000	PF63 350	PF65 375			

ROYAL COINAGE

KM# 896 1/25 ROYAL
1.24 g., 0.9999 Gold 0.0397 oz. AGW, 13.92 mm. **Ruler:**

Elizabeth II **Subject:** Bullion **Obv:** Bust with tiara right **Rev:** Two cherubs **Edge:** Reeded

Date	Mintage	F12	VF20	XF40	MS60	MS63
2001	—	—	—	—	—	75.00
2001	1,000	PF63 77.50				

KM# 972 1/25 ROYAL
1.24 g., 0.999 Gold 0.0397 oz. AGW, 13.92 mm. **Ruler:** Elizabeth II **Subject:** Cherubs **Obv:** Bust with tiara right **Rev:** Two cherubs shooting arrrows **Edge:** Reeded

Date	Mintage	F12	VF20	XF40	MS60	MS63
2002	—	—	—	—	—	75.00
2002	1,000	PF63 77.50				

KM# 1027 1/25 ROYAL
1.24 g., 0.9999 Gold 0.0397 oz. AGW, 13.92 mm. **Ruler:** Elizabeth II **Obv:** Bust with tiara right **Rev:** Cherub with crossed arms **Edge:** Reeded

Date	Mintage	F12	VF20	XF40	MS60	MS63
2003PM	—	PF63 77.50				
2003PM	—	—	—	—	—	75.00

KM# 897 1/10 ROYAL
3.11 g., 0.9999 Gold 0.0993 oz. AGW, 18 mm. **Ruler:** Elizabeth II **Subject:** Bullion **Obv:** Bust with tiara right **Rev:** Two cherubs **Edge:** Reeded

Date	Mintage	F12	VF20	XF40	MS60	MS63
2001	—	—	—	—	—	175
2001	1,000	PF63 180				

KM# 973 1/10 ROYAL
3.11 g., 0.999 Gold 0.0992 oz. AGW, 17.95 mm. **Ruler:** Elizabeth II **Subject:** Cherubs **Obv:** Bust with tiara right **Rev:** Two cherubs shooting arrows **Edge:** Reeded

Date	Mintage	F12	VF20	XF40	MS60	MS63
2002	1,000	PF63 180				
2002	—	—	—	—	—	175

KM# 1028 1/10 ROYAL
3.11 g., 0.9999 Gold 0.0993 oz. AGW, 17.95 mm. **Ruler:** Elizabeth II **Obv:** Bust with tiara right **Rev:** Cherub with crossed arms **Edge:** Reeded

Date	Mintage	F12	VF20	XF40	MS60	MS63
2003PM	—	—	—	—	—	175
2003PM	—	PF63 180				

KM# 898 1/5 ROYAL
6.22 g., 0.999 Gold 0.1985 oz. AGW, 22 mm. **Ruler:** Elizabeth II **Subject:** Bullion **Obv:** Bust with tiara right **Rev:** Two cherubs **Edge:** Reeded

Date	Mintage	F12	VF20	XF40	MS60	MS63
2001	—	—	—	—	—	350
2001	1,000	PF63 355				

KM# 974 1/5 ROYAL
6.22 g., 0.999 Gold 0.1985 oz. AGW, 22 mm. **Ruler:** Elizabeth II **Obv:** Bust with tiara right **Rev:** Two cherubs shooting arrows **Edge:** Reeded

Date	Mintage	F12	VF20	XF40	MS60	MS63
2002	—	—	—	—	—	350
2002	1,000	PF63 355				

KM# 1029 1/5 ROYAL
6.22 g., 0.9999 Gold 0.1987 oz. AGW, 22 mm. **Ruler:** Elizabeth II **Obv:** Bust with tiara right **Rev:** Cherub with crossed arms **Edge:** Reeded

Date	Mintage	F12	VF20	XF40	MS60	MS63
2003PM	—	—	—	—	—	350
2003PM	—	PF63 355				

KM# 899 1/2 ROYAL
15.55 g., 0.9999 Gold 0.4967 oz. AGW, 30 mm. **Ruler:** Elizabeth II **Subject:** Bullion **Obv:** Bust with tiara right **Rev:** Two cherubs **Edge:** Reeded

Date	Mintage	F12	VF20	XF40	MS60	MS63
2001	—	—	—	—	—	875
2001	1,000	PF63 880				

KM# 975 1/2 ROYAL
15.55 g., 0.999 Gold 0.4963 oz. AGW, 30 mm. **Ruler:** Elizabeth II **Obv:** Bust with tiara right **Rev:** Two cherubs shooting arrows **Edge:** Reeded

Date	Mintage	F12	VF20	XF40	MS60	MS63
2002	—	—	—	—	—	875
2002	1,000	PF63 880				

KM# 1030 1/2 ROYAL
15.55 g., 0.9999 Gold 0.4967 oz. AGW, 30 mm. **Ruler:** Elizabeth II **Obv:** Bust with tiara right **Rev:** Cherub with crossed arms **Edge:** Reeded

Date	Mintage	F12	VF20	XF40	MS60	MS63
2003PM	—	—	—	—	—	875
2003PM	—	PF63 880				

KM# 900 ROYAL
28.28 g., Copper-Nickel, 38.6 mm. **Ruler:** Elizabeth II **Obv:** Bust with tiara right **Rev:** Two cherubs **Edge:** Reeded

Date	Mintage	F12	VF20	XF40	MS60	MS63
2001	—	—	—	—	10.00	12.00

KM# 900a ROYAL
31.10 g., 0.999 Silver 0.9926 oz. ASW **Ruler:** Elizabeth II **Obv:** Bust with tiara right **Rev:** Two cherubs

Date	Mintage	F12	VF20	XF40	MS60	MS63
2001	10,000	PF63 45.00	PF65 47.00			

KM# 901 ROYAL
31.10 g., 0.9999 Gold 0.9935 oz. AGW, 32.7 mm. **Ruler:** Elizabeth II **Subject:** Bullion **Obv:** Bust with tiara right **Rev:** Two cherubs **Edge:** Reeded

Date	Mintage	F12	VF20	XF40	MS60	MS63
2001	—	—	—	—	—	1,750
2001	1,000	PF63 1,800				

KM# 976 ROYAL
28.28 g., Copper-Nickel, 38.6 mm. **Ruler:** Elizabeth II **Obv:** Bust with tiara right **Rev:** Two cherubs shooting arrows **Edge:** Reeded

Date	Mintage	F12	VF20	XF40	MS60	MS63
2002	—	—	—	—	10.00	12.00

KM# 976a ROYAL
31.10 g., 0.999 Silver 0.9926 oz. ASW **Ruler:** Elizabeth II **Obv:** Bust with tiara right **Rev:** Two cherubs shooting arrows **Edge:** Reeded

Date	Mintage	F12	VF20	XF40	MS60	MS63
2002	1,000	PF63 45.00	PF65 47.00			

KM# 977 ROYAL
31.10 g., 0.999 Gold 0.9926 oz. AGW, 32.7 mm. **Ruler:** Elizabeth II **Obv:** Bust with tiara right **Rev:** Two cherubs shooting arrows **Edge:** Reeded

Date	Mintage	F12	VF20	XF40	MS60	MS63
2002	—	—	—	—	—	1,750
2002	1,000	PF63 1,800				

KM# 1031 ROYAL
28.28 g., Copper-Nickel, 38.6 mm. **Ruler:** Elizabeth II **Obv:** Bust with tiara right **Rev:** Cherub with crossed arms **Edge:** Reeded

Date	Mintage	F12	VF20	XF40	MS60	MS63
2003PM	—	—	—	—	10.00	12.00

KM# 1032 ROYAL
31.10 g., 0.9999 Gold 0.9935 oz. AGW, 32.7 mm. **Ruler:** Elizabeth II **Obv:** Bust with tiara right **Rev:** Cherub with crossed arms **Edge:** Reeded

Date	Mintage	F12	VF20	XF40	MS60	MS63
2003PM	—	PF63 1,800				
2003PM	—	—	—	—	—	1,750

KM# 1031a ROYAL
28.28 g., 0.999 Silver 0.9025 oz. ASW, 38.6 mm. **Ruler:** Elizabeth II **Obv:** Bust with tiara right **Rev:** Cherub with crossed arms **Edge:** Reeded

Date	Mintage	F12	VF20	XF40	MS60	MS63
2003PM	10,000	PF63 45.00	PF65 47.00			

PROOF SETS

KM#	Date	Mintage	Identification	Issue Price	Mkt Val
PS29	2001 (5)	1,000	KM#896-899, 901	—	3,300
PS30	2003 (5)	1,000	KM#1027-30, 1032	—	3,300

GREAT BRITAIN

The United Kingdom of Great Britain and Northern Ireland, located off the northwest coast of the European continent, has an area of 94,227 sq. mi. (244,820 sq. km.) and a population of 54 million. Capital: London. The economy is based on industrial activity and trading. Machinery, motor vehicles, chemicals, and textile yarns and fabrics are exported.

By the mid-20th century, most of the territories formerly comprising the British Empire had gained independence, and the empire had evolved into the Commonwealth of Nations, an association of equal and autonomous states, which enjoy special trade interests. The Commonwealth is presently composed of 54 member nations, including the United Kingdom. All recognize the British monarch as head of the Commonwealth. Sixteen continue to recognize the British monarch as Head of State. They are: United Kingdom, Antigua and Barbuda, Australia, Bahamas, Barbados, Belize, Canada, Grenada, Jamaica, New Zealand, Papua New Guinea, St. Christopher & Nevis, Saint Lucia, Saint Vincent and the Grenadines, Solomon Islands, and Tuvalu. Elizabeth II is personally, and separately, the Queen of the sovereign, independent countries just mentioned. There is no other British connection between the several individual, national sovereignties, except that High Commissioners represent them each instead of ambassadors in each other's countries.

RULERS
Elizabeth II, 1952--

MINT MARKS
H - Heaton
KN - King's Norton

KINGDOM
Resumed

PRE-DECIMAL COINAGE

KM# 898 PENNY
0.47 g., 0.925 Silver, 11 mm. **Ruler:** Elizabeth II **Obv:** Laureate bust right **Rev:** Crowned value in sprays divides date within wreath **Edge:** Reeded

Date	Mintage	F12	VF20	XF40	MS60	MS63
2001 Prooflike	1,132	—	—	—	50.00	55.00
2002 Prooflike	1,681	—	—	—	50.00	55.00
2003 Prooflike	1,608	—	—	—	55.00	60.00
2004 Prooflike	1,613	—	—	—	55.00	60.00
2005 Prooflike	1,685	—	—	—	55.00	60.00
2006 Prooflike	1,811	—	—	—	55.00	60.00
2006 Proof	6,394	—	—	—	—	—
2007 Prooflike	1,985	—	—	—	55.00	60.00
2008 Prooflike	1,833	—	—	—	55.00	60.00
2009 Prooflike	1,602	—	—	—	55.00	60.00
2010 Prooflike	1,617	—	—	—	55.00	60.00
2011 Prooflike	—	—	—	—	55.00	60.00
2012 Prooflike	—	—	—	—	55.00	60.00

KM# 898a PENNY
0.9167 Gold AGW, 11 mm. **Ruler:** Elizabeth II **Obv:** Laureate bust right **Rev:** Crowned denomination divides date within wreath

Date	Mintage	F12	VF20	XF40	MS60	MS63
2002	2,002	PF63 1,000				

KM# 899 2 PENCE
0.94 g., 0.925 Silver, 13 mm. **Ruler:** Elizabeth II **Obv:** Laureate bust right **Obv. Legend:** Without BRITT OMN **Rev:** Crowned value in sprays divides date within wreath **Edge:** Reeded

Date	Mintage	F12	VF20	XF40	MS60	MS63
2001 Prooflike	1,132	—	—	—	60.00	70.00
2002 Prooflike	1,681	—	—	—	60.00	70.00
2003 Prooflike	1,608	—	—	—	65.00	75.00
2004 Prooflike	1,613	—	—	—	65.00	75.00
2005 Prooflike	1,685	—	—	—	65.00	75.00
2006 Prooflike	1,811	—	—	—	65.00	75.00
2006 Proof	6,394	—	—	—	—	—
2007 Prooflike	1,822	—	—	—	65.00	75.00
2008 Prooflike	1,999	—	—	—	65.00	75.00
2009 Prooflike	1,602	—	—	—	65.00	75.00
2010 Prooflike	1,617	—	—	—	65.00	75.00
2011 Prooflike	—	—	—	—	65.00	75.00
2012 Prooflike	—	—	—	—	65.00	75.00

KM# 899a 2 PENCE
0.9167 Gold AGW, 13 mm. **Ruler:** Elizabeth II **Series:** Maundy Sets **Obv:** Laureate bust right **Obv. Legend:** Without BRITT OMN **Rev:** Crowned denomination divides date within wreath

Date	Mintage	F12	VF20	XF40	MS60	MS63
2002	2,002	PF63 1,100				

KM# 901 3 PENCE
1.41 g., 0.925 Silver 0.0418 oz. ASW, 16 mm. **Ruler:** Elizabeth II **Obv:** Laureate bust right **Obv. Legend:** without BRITT OMN **Rev:** Crowned value in sprays divides date within wreath **Edge:** Reeded

Date	Mintage	F12	VF20	XF40	MS60	MS63
2001 Prooflike	1,132	—	—	—	65.00	75.00
2002 Prooflike	1,681	—	—	—	65.00	75.00
2003 Prooflike	1,608	—	—	—	70.00	80.00
2004 Prooflike	1,613	—	—	—	70.00	80.00
2005 Prooflike	1,685	—	—	—	70.00	00.00
2006 Prooflike	1,811	—	—	—	70.00	80.00
2006 Proof	6,394	—	—	—	—	—
2007 Prooflike	1,822	—	—	—	70.00	80.00
2008 Prooflike	1,833	—	—	—	70.00	80.00
2009 Prooflike	1,794	—	—	—	70.00	80.00
2010 Prooflike	1,617	—	—	—	70.00	80.00
2011 Prooflike	—	—	—	—	70.00	80.00
2012 Prooflike	—	—	—	—	70.00	80.00

KM# 901a 3 PENCE
0.9167 Gold AGW, 16 mm. **Ruler:** Elizabeth II **Obv:** Laureate bust right **Obv. Legend:** Without RITT OMN **Rev:** Crowned denomination divides date within wreath

Date	Mintage	F12	VF20	XF40	MS60	MS63
2002	2,002	PF63 1,150				

KM# 902 4 PENCE (Groat)
1.89 g., 0.925 Silver 0.0557 oz. ASW, 18 mm. **Ruler:** Elizabeth II **Obv:** Laureate bust right **Obv. Legend:** without BRITT OMN **Rev:** Crowned denomination divides date within wreath **Edge:** Reeded

Date	Mintage	F12	VF20	XF40	MS60	MS63
2001 Prooflike	1,132	—	—	—	65.00	75.00
2002 Prooflike	1,681	—	—	—	65.00	75.00
2003 Prooflike	1,608	—	—	—	65.00	75.00
2004 Prooflike	1,613	—	—	—	65.00	75.00
2005 Prooflike	1,685	—	—	—	65.00	75.00
2006 Prooflike	1,811	—	—	—	65.00	75.00
2006 Proof	6,394	—	—	—	—	—
2007 Prooflike	1,822	—	—	—	65.00	75.00
2008 Prooflike	1,833	—	—	—	65.00	75.00
2009 Prooflike	1,602	—	—	—	65.00	75.00
2010 Prooflike	1,787	—	—	—	65.00	75.00
2011 Prooflike	—	—	—	—	65.00	75.00
2012 Prooflike	—	—	—	—	65.00	75.00

KM# 902a 4 PENCE
0.9167 Gold AGW, 18 mm. **Ruler:** Elizabeth II **Obv:** Laureate bust right **Obv. Legend:** Without BRITT OMN **Rev:** Crowned denomination divides date within wreath

Date	Mintage	F12	VF20	XF40	MS60	MS63
2002	2,002	PF63 1,250				

DECIMAL COINAGE
1971-1981: 100 New Pence = 1 Pound;
1982-present: 100 Pence = 1 Pound

KM# 986 PENNY
3.56 g., Copper Plated Steel, 20.32 mm. **Ruler:** Elizabeth II **Subject:** Badge of Henry VII **Obv:** Head with tiara right **Rev:** Crowned portcullis with chains **Edge:** Plain

Date	Mintage	F12	VF20	XF40	MS60	MS63
2001	928,698,000			0.15	1.75	2.50
2001		PF63 3.25				
2002	601,446,000			0.15	1.75	2.50
2002	60,770	PF63 3.25				
2003	539,436,000			0.15	1.75	2.50
2003	43,513	PF63 3.25				
2004	739,764,000			0.15	1.75	2.50
2004	35,020	PF63 3.25				
2005	536,318,000			0.15	1.75	2.50
2005	40,563	PF63 3.25				
2006	524,605,000			0.15	1.75	2.50
2006	37,689	PF63 3.25				
2007	548,002,000			0.15	1.75	2.50
2007	38,215	PF63 3.25				
2008	180,600,000			0.25	2.50	3.00
2008	36,333	PF63 3.25				

KM# 986b PENNY
3.56 g., 0.925 Silver 0.1052 oz. ASW, 20.3 mm. **Ruler:** Elizabeth II **Obv:** Head with tiara right **Rev:** Crowned portcullis **Edge:** Plain

Date	Mintage	F12	VF20	XF40	MS60	MS63
2008	10,000	PF63 16.50				

KM# 986c PENNY
0.9167 Gold AGW, 20.3 mm. **Ruler:** Elizabeth II **Obv:** Head with tiara right **Rev:** Crowned portcullis

Date	Mintage	F12	VF20	XF40	MS60	MS63
2002	—	PF63 750				
2008	2,008	PF63 550				

KM# 1107 PENNY
3.59 g., Copper Plated Steel, 20.3 mm. **Ruler:** Elizabeth II **Obv:** Head with tiara right **Rev:** Section of the Royal Arms - Lion and Harp

Date	Mintage	F12	VF20	XF40	MS60	MS63
2008	—	PF63 3.50				
2008	507,952,000	—	—	—	—	0.20
2009	556,412,000	—	—	—	—	0.20
2009	—	PF63 3.50				
2010	421,002,000	—	—	—	—	0.20
2010	—	PF63 3.50				
2011	—	—	—	—	—	0.20
2011	—	PF63 3.50				
2012	—	—	—	—	—	0.20
2012	—	PF63 3.50				
2013	—	—	—	—	—	0.20
2013	—	PF63 3.50				

KM# 1107a PENNY
3.56 g., 0.925 Silver 0.1052 oz. ASW, 20.3 mm. **Ruler:** Elizabeth II **Obv:** Head with tiara right **Rev:** Section of the Royal Arms - Lion and Harp

Date	Mintage	F12	VF20	XF40	MS60	MS63
2008	—	PF63 13.50				
2009	—	—	—	—	—	25.00
2009	—	PF63 25.00				
2010	—	—	—	—	—	25.00
2010	3,500	PF63 25.00				
2013	2,013	PF63 25.00				

KM# 1107b PENNY
0.9167 Gold AGW, 20.3 mm. **Ruler:** Elizabeth II **Obv:** Head with tiara right **Rev:** Section of the Royal Arms - Lion and Harp

Date	Mintage	F12	VF20	XF40	MS60	MS63
2008	—	PF63 350				

KM# 1107c PENNY
Platinum APW, 20.3 mm. **Ruler:** Elizabeth II **Obv:** Head with tiara right **Rev:** Section of the Royal Arms - Lion and Harp

Date	Mintage	F12	VF20	XF40	MS60	MS63
2008	—	PF63 600				

KM# 1107a.1 PENNY
3.56 g., 0.925 Silver 0.1052 oz. ASW, 20.3 mm. **Ruler:** Elizabeth II **Obv:** Head with tiara right **Rev:** Section of the Royal Arms - Lion and Harp, gilt

Date	Mintage	F12	VF20	XF40	MS60	MS63
2012	—	PF63 25.00				

KM# 987 2 PENCE
7.14 g., Copper Plated Steel, 25.86 mm. **Ruler:** Elizabeth II **Obv:** Head with tiara right **Rev:** Welsh plumes and crown **Edge:** Plain

Date	Mintage	F12	VF20	XF40	MS60	MS63
2001	551,880,000	—	—	0.15	1.75	2.50
2002	168,556,000	—	—	0.15	1.75	2.50
2003	260,225,000	—	—	0.15	1.75	2.50
2003	43,513	PF63 3.25				
2004	356,396,000	—	—	0.15	1.75	2.50
2004	35,020	PF63 3.25				
2005	280,396,000	—	—	0.15	1.75	2.50
2005	40,563	PF63 3.25				
2006	170,637,000	—	—	0.15	1.75	2.50
2006	37,689	PF63 3.25				
2007	254,500,000	—	—	0.15	1.75	2.50
2007	38,215	PF63 3.25				
2008	10,600,000	—	—	0.25	3.00	3.50

KM# 987a 2 PENCE
Bronze, 25.91 mm. **Ruler:** Elizabeth II **Obv:** Head with tiara right **Rev:** Welsh plumes and crown

Date	Mintage	F12	VF20	XF40	MS60	MS63
2002	60,770	PF63 2.50				
2003	43,513	PF63 2.50				
2004	35,020	PF63 2.50				

KM# 987b 2 PENCE
7.12 g., 0.925 Silver 0.2104 oz. ASW, 25.9 mm. **Ruler:** Elizabeth II **Obv:** Head with tiara right **Rev:** Welsh plumes and crown **Edge:** Plain

Date	Mintage	F12	VF20	XF40	MS60	MS63
2008	10,000	PF63 18.50				

KM# 987c 2 PENCE
0.9167 Gold AGW, 25.91 mm. **Ruler:** Elizabeth II **Subject:** Queen's Golden Jubilee - 1952-2002 **Obv:** Head with tiara right **Rev:** Welsh plumes and crown

Date	Mintage	F12	VF20	XF40	MS60	MS63
2002	—	PF63 850				
2008	2,008	PF63 650				

KM# 1108a 2 PENCE
7.12 g., 0.925 Silver 0.2104 oz. ASW, 25.91 mm. **Ruler:** Elizabeth II **Obv:** Head with tiara right **Rev:** Section of the Royal Arms - Lion

Date	Mintage	F12	VF20	XF40	MS60	MS63
2008	—	PF63 17.50				
2009	—	PF63 17.50				
2010	3,500	PF63 17.50				
2011	—	PF63 25.00				
	Note: Also exists as a Piedfort, P78.					
2013	2,013	PF63 25.00				

KM# 1108 2 PENCE
7.10 g., Copper Plated Steel, 25.86 mm. **Ruler:** Elizabeth II **Obv:** Head with tiara right **Rev:** Section of the Royal Arms - Lion

Date	Mintage	F12	VF20	XF40	MS60	MS63
2008	241,679,000	—	—	0.15	1.75	2.50
2008	36,333	PF63 3.25				
2009	150,400,500	—	—	0.15	1.75	2.50
2009	40,000	PF63 3.25				
2010	38,000,000	—	—	0.15	1.75	2.50
2010	40,000	PF63 3.25				
2011	—	—	—	0.15	1.75	2.50
2011	—	PF63 3.25				
2012	—	—	—	0.15	1.75	2.50
2012	—	PF63 3.25				
2013	—	—	—	0.15	1.75	2.50
2013	—	PF63 3.25				

KM# 1108b 2 PENCE
0.9167 Gold AGW, 25.9 mm. **Ruler:** Elizabeth II **Obv:** Head in tiara right **Rev:** Section of the Royal Arms - Lion

Date	Mintage	F12	VF20	XF40	MS60	MS63
2008	—	PF63 700				

KM# 1108c 2 PENCE
Platinum APW, 25.9 mm. **Ruler:** Elizabeth II **Obv:** Head in tiara right **Rev:** Section of Royal Arms - Lion

Date	Mintage	F12	VF20	XF40	MS60	MS63
2008	—	PF63 1,100				

KM# 1108a.1 2 PENCE
7.12 g., 0.925 Silver 0.2104 oz. ASW, 25.86 mm. **Ruler:** Elizabeth II **Obv:** Head with tiara right **Rev:** Section of the Royal Arms - Lion

Date	Mintage	F12	VF20	XF40	MS60	MS63
2012	—	PF63 17.50				

KM# 988 5 PENCE
3.25 g., Copper-Nickel, 18 mm. **Ruler:** Elizabeth II **Obv:** Head with tiara right **Rev:** Crowned thistle

Date	Mintage	F12	VF20	XF40	MS60	MS63
2001	337,930,000	—	—	0.25	2.00	2.50
2001	45,617	PF63 3.00				
2002	219,258,000	—	—	0.25	2.00	2.50
2002	60,770	PF63 3.00				
2003	333,230,000	—	—	0.25	2.00	2.50
2003	43,513	PF63 3.00				
2004	271,810,000	—	—	0.25	2.00	2.50
2004	35,020	PF63 3.00				
2005	236,212,000	—	—	0.25	2.00	2.50
2005	40,563	PF63 3.00				
2006	317,697,000	—	—	0.25	2.00	2.50
2006	37,689	PF63 3.00				
2007	246,720,000	—	—	0.25	2.00	2.50
2007	38,215	PF63 3.00				
2008	92,880,000	—	—	—	4.50	5.00

KM# 988a 5 PENCE
3.25 g., 0.925 Silver 0.096 oz. ASW, 18 mm. **Ruler:** Elizabeth II **Obv:** Head with tiara right **Rev:** Crowned thistle **Edge:** Reeded

Date	Mintage	F12	VF20	XF40	MS60	MS63
2008	10,000	PF63 22.50				

KM# 988b 5 PENCE
0.9167 Gold AGW, 18 mm. **Ruler:** Elizabeth II **Obv:** Head with tiara right **Rev:** Crowned thistle

Date	Mintage	F12	VF20	XF40	MS60	MS63
2002	—	PF63 450				
2008	—	PF63 400				

KM# 1109a 5 PENCE
3.25 g., 0.925 Silver 0.096 oz. ASW, 18 mm. **Ruler:** Elizabeth II **Obv:** Head in tiara right **Rev:** Section of Royal Arms - Center of shield

Date	Mintage	F12	VF20	XF40	MS60	MS63
2008	—	PF63 20.00				
2009	—	PF63 20.00				
2010	3,500	PF63 20.00				
2011	—	PF63 35.00				

Note: Also exists as a Piedfort, P79.

| 2013 | 2,013 | PF63 35.00 | | | | |

KM# 1109 5 PENCE
3.25 g., Copper-Nickel, 18 mm. **Ruler:** Elizabeth II **Obv:** Head with tiara right **Rev:** Section of the Royal Arms - Center of shield

Date	Mintage	F12	VF20	XF40	MS60	MS63
2008	165,172,000	—	—	0.25	2.00	2.50
2008	36,333	PF63 3.00				
2009	132,960,300	—	—	0.25	2.00	2.50
2009	40,000	PF63 3.00				
2010	180,250,500	—	—	0.25	2.00	2.50
2010	40,000	PF63 3.00				

KM# 1109b 5 PENCE
0.9167 Gold AGW, 18 mm. **Ruler:** Elizabeth II **Obv:** Head in tiara right **Rev:** Section of Royal Arms - Center

Date	Mintage	F12	VF20	XF40	MS60	MS63
2008	—	PF63 500				

KM# 1109c 5 PENCE
Platinum APW, 18 mm. **Ruler:** Elizabeth II **Obv:** Head in tiara right **Rev:** Section of Royal Arms - Center

Date	Mintage	F12	VF20	XF40	MS60	MS63
2008	—	PF63 800				

KM# 1109d 5 PENCE
3.25 g., Nickel Plated Steel, 18 mm. **Ruler:** Elizabeth II **Obv:** Head with tiara right **Rev:** Section of Royal Arms - Center of shield

Date	Mintage	F12	VF20	XF40	MS60	MS63
2011	—	—	—	0.25	2.00	2.50
2011	—	PF63 3.00				
2012	—	—	—	0.25	2.00	2.50

Date	Mintage	F12	VF20	XF40	MS60	MS63
2012	—	PF63 3.00				
2013	—	—	—	0.25	2.00	2.50
2013	—	PF63 3.00				

KM# 1109a.1 5 PENCE
3.25 g., 0.925 Silver 0.096 oz. ASW, 18 mm. **Ruler:** Elizabeth II **Obv:** Head with tiara right **Rev:** Section of the Royal Arms - Center of shield

Date	Mintage	F12	VF20	XF40	MS60	MS63
2012	—	PF63 20.00				

KM# 989 10 PENCE
6.50 g., Copper-Nickel, 24.5 mm. **Ruler:** Elizabeth II **Obv:** Head with tiara right **Rev:** Crowned lion passant left

Date	Mintage	F12	VF20	XF40	MS60	MS63
2001	129,281,000	—	—	0.50	3.50	4.00
2001	45,617	PF63 3.50				
2002	80,934,000	—	—	0.50	3.50	4.00
2002	60,770	PF63 3.50				
2003	88,118,000	—	—	0.50	3.50	4.00
2003	43,513	PF63 3.50				
2004	99,602,000	—	—	0.50	3.50	4.00
2004	35,020	PF63 3.50				
2005	69,604,000	—	—	0.50	3.50	4.00
2005	40,563	PF63 3.50				
2006	118,803,000	—	—	0.50	3.50	4.00
2006	37,689	PF63 3.50				
2007	72,720,000	—	—	0.50	3.50	4.00
2007	38,215	PF63 3.50				
2008	9,720,000	—	—	0.50	3.50	4.00

KM# 989a 10 PENCE
6.50 g., 0.925 Silver 0.1921 oz. ASW, 24.5 mm. **Ruler:** Elizabeth II **Obv:** Head with tiara right **Rev:** Crowned lion prancing left **Edge:** Reeded

Date	Mintage	F12	VF20	XF40	MS60	MS63
2008	10,000	PF63 20.00				

KM# 989b 10 PENCE
0.9167 Gold AGW, 24.5 mm. **Ruler:** Elizabeth II **Obv:** Head with tiara right **Rev:** Crowned lion prancing left

Date	Mintage	F12	VF20	XF40	MS60	MS63
2002	—	PF63 650				
2008	2,008	PF63 550				

KM# 1110a 10 PENCE
6.50 g., 0.925 Silver 0.1921 oz. ASW, 24.5 mm. **Ruler:** Elizabeth II **Obv:** Head with tiara right **Rev:** Section of the Royal Arms - two lions

Date	Mintage	F12	VF20	XF40	MS60	MS63
2008	—	PF63 25.00				
2009 proof	—	PF63 25.00				
2010	3,500	PF63 25.00				
2011	—	PF63 80.00				

Note: Also exists as a Piedfort, P80.

| 2013 | 2,013 | PF63 80.00 | | | | |

KM# 1110 10 PENCE
6.50 g., Copper-Nickel, 24.5 mm. **Ruler:** Elizabeth II **Obv:** Head with tiara right **Rev:** Section of the Royal Arms - two lions

Date	Mintage	F12	VF20	XF40	MS60	MS63
2008	71,447,000	—	—	0.50	3.50	4.00
2008	36,333	PF63 3.50				
2009	84,360,000	—	—	0.50	3.50	4.00
2009	40,000	PF63 3.50				
2010	25,320,500	—	—	0.50	3.50	4.00
2010	40,000	PF63 3.50				

KM# 1110b 10 PENCE
0.9167 Gold AGW, 24.5 mm. **Ruler:** Elizabeth II **Obv:** Head in tiara right **Rev:** Section of the Royal Arms - two lions

Date	Mintage	F12	VF20	XF40	MS60	MS63
2008	—	PF63 950				

KM# 1110c 10 PENCE
Platinum APW, 24.5 mm. **Ruler:** Elizabeth II **Obv:** Head in tiara right **Rev:** Section of Royal Arms - two lions

Date	Mintage	F12	VF20	XF40	MS60	MS63
2008	—	PF63 1,600				

KM# 1110d 10 PENCE
6.50 g., Nickel Plated Steel, 24.5 mm. **Ruler:** Elizabeth II **Obv:** Head with tiara right **Rev:** Section of Royal Arms - two lions

Date	Mintage	F12	VF20	XF40	MS60	MS63
2011	—	—	—	0.50	3.50	4.00
2011	—	PF63 3.50				
2012	—	—	—	0.50	3.50	4.00
2012	—	PF63 3.50				
2013	—	—	—	0.50	3.50	4.00
2013	—	PF63 3.50				

KM# 1110a.1 10 PENCE
6.50 g., 0.925 Silver 0.1921 oz. ASW, 24.5 mm. **Ruler:** Elizabeth II **Obv:** Head with tiara right **Rev:** Section of the Royal Arms - two lions

Date	Mintage	F12	VF20	XF40	MS60	MS63
2012	—	PF63 25.00				

KM# 990 20 PENCE
5.00 g., Copper-Nickel, 21.4 mm. **Ruler:** Elizabeth II **Obv:** Head with tiara right **Rev:** Crowned double rose **Shape:** 7-sided

Date	Mintage	F12	VF20	XF40	MS60	MS63
2001	148,122,500	—	—	0.50	3.50	4.00
2001	45,617	PF63 4.50				
2002	93,360,000	—	—	0.50	3.50	4.00
2002	60,770	PF63 4.50				
2003	153,383,750	—	—	0.50	3.50	4.00
2003	43,513	PF63 4.50				
2004	120,212,500	—	—	0.50	3.50	4.00
2004	35,020	PF63 4.50				
2005	124,488,750	—	—	0.50	3.50	4.00
2005	40,563	PF63 4.50				
2006	114,800,000	—	—	0.50	3.50	4.00
2006	37,689	PF63 4.50				
2007	117,075,000	—	—	0.50	3.50	4.00
2007	38,215	PF63 4.50				
2008	11,900,000	—	—	0.50	3.50	4.00

KM# 990a 20 PENCE
5.00 g., 0.925 Silver 0.1477 oz. ASW, 21.4 mm. **Ruler:** Elizabeth II **Obv:** Head with tiara right **Rev:** Crowned double rose **Edge:** Plain **Shape:** 7-sided

Date	Mintage	F12	VF20	XF40	MS60	MS63
2008	10,000	PF63 22.50				

KM# 990b 20 PENCE
0.9167 Gold AGW, 21.4 mm. **Ruler:** Elizabeth II **Obv:** Head with tiara right **Rev:** Crowned double rose **Shape:** 7-sided

Date	Mintage	F12	VF20	XF40	MS60	MS63
2002	—	PF63 550				
2008	2,008	PF63 500				

KM# 1111a 20 PENCE
5.00 g., 0.925 Silver 0.1477 oz. ASW, 21.4 mm. **Ruler:** Elizabeth II **Obv:** Head in tiara right **Rev:** Section of the Royal Arms - lion's tails **Shape:** 7-sided

Date	Mintage	F12	VF20	XF40	MS60	MS63
2008	—	PF63 35.00				
2009	—	PF63 35.00				
2010	3,500	PF63 35.00				
2011	—	PF63 80.00				

Note: Also exists as a Piedfort, P81.

| 2013 | 2,013 | PF63 80.00 | | | | |

KM# 1111 20 PENCE
5.00 g., Copper-Nickel, 21.4 mm. **Ruler:** Elizabeth II **Obv:** Head with tiara right **Rev:** Section of the Royal Arms - lion's tails **Shape:** 7-sided

Date	Mintage	F12	VF20	XF40	MS60	MS63
2008	115,022,000	—	—	0.50	3.50	4.00
2008	36,333	PF63 4.50				
2009	121,625,300	—	—	0.50	3.50	4.00
2009	40,000	PF63 4.50				
2010	91,700,500	—	—	0.50	3.35	4.00
2010	40,000	PF63 4.50				
2011	—	—	—	5.00	3.50	4.00
2011	—	PF63 4.50				
2012	—	—	—	0.50	3.50	4.00
2012	—	PF63 4.50				
2013	—	—	—	0.50	3.50	4.00
2013	—	PF63 4.50				

KM# 1111b 20 PENCE
0.9167 Gold AGW, 21.4 mm. **Ruler:** Elizabeth II **Obv:** Head in tiara right **Rev:** Section of Royal Arms - lion's tails **Shape:** 7-sided

Date	Mintage	F12	VF20	XF40	MS60	MS63
2008	—	PF63 700				

KM# 1111c 20 PENCE
Platinum APW, 21.4 mm. **Ruler:** Elizabeth II **Obv:** Head in tiara right **Rev:** Section of Royal Arms - lion's tails **Shape:** 7-sided

Date	Mintage	F12	VF20	XF40	MS60	MS63
2008	—	PF63 1,200				

KM# 1122 20 PENCE
5.00 g., Copper-Nickel, 21.4 mm. **Ruler:** Elizabeth II **Obv:** Head right. Obverse of KM#990 **Rev:** Royal Arms part. Reverse of KM#1111 **Note:** Mule.

Date	Mintage	F12	VF20	XF40	MS60	MS63
ND-2008	—	20.00	30.00	40.00		

KM# 1111a.1 20 PENCE
5.00 g., 0.925 Silver 0.1477 oz. ASW, 21.4 mm. **Ruler:** Elizabeth II **Obv:** Head with tiara right **Rev:** Section of Royal Arms - lion's tails

Date	Mintage	F12	VF20	XF40	MS60	MS63
2012	—	PF63 35.00				

KM# 1266 20 PENCE
15.71 g., 0.999 Silver 0.5013 oz. ASW, 27 mm. **Ruler:** Elizabeth II **Obv:** Head with tiara right **Rev:** St. George slaying dragon

Date	Mintage	F12	VF20	XF40	MS60	MS63
2013	250,000	—	—	—	—	40.00

KM# 991 50 PENCE
8.00 g., Copper-Nickel, 27.3 mm. **Ruler:** Elizabeth II **Obv:** Head with tiara right **Rev:** Britannia seated right with shield, spear and lion **Shape:** 7-sided

Date	Mintage	F12	VF20	XF40	MS60	MS63
2001	84,998,500	—	—	1.00	3.50	4.00
2001	45,617	PF63 4.00				
2002	23,907,500	—	—	1.00	3.50	4.00
2002	60,770	PF63 4.00				
2003	23,583,000	—	—	1.00	3.50	4.00
2003	43,513	PF63 4.00				
2004	35,315,500	—	—	1.00	3.50	4.00
2004	35,020	PF63 4.00				
2005	25,363,500	—	—	1.00	3.50	4.00
2005	40,563	PF63 4.00				
2006	24,567,000	—	—	1.00	3.50	4.00
2006	37,689	PF63 4.00				
2007	11,200,000	—	—	1.00	3.50	4.00
2007	38,215	PF63 4.00				
2008	3,500,000	—	—	1.50	5.00	6.00

KM# 991b 50 PENCE
0.9167 Gold AGW, 27.3 mm. **Ruler:** Elizabeth II **Obv:** Head with tiara right **Rev:** Britannia seated right with shield, spear and lion **Shape:** 7-sided

Date	Mintage	F12	VF20	XF40	MS60	MS63
2002	—	PF63 700				
2008	—	PF63 650				

KM# 1036a 50 PENCE
8.00 g., 0.925 Silver 0.2364 oz. ASW, 27.3 mm. **Ruler:** Elizabeth II **Subject:** Woman's Social and Political Union, 100th Anniversary **Obv:** Head with tiara right **Rev:** Standing suffragette chained to railings and holding banner **Edge:** Plain **Shape:** 7-sided

Date	Mintage	F12	VF20	XF40	MS60	MS63
2003	6,267	PF63 45.00				

Note: Also exists as a Piefort, P40.

KM# 1036b 50 PENCE
15.50 g., 0.9166 Gold 0.4538 oz. AGW, 27.3 mm. **Ruler:** Elizabeth II **Subject:** Woman's Social and Political Union, 100th Anniversary **Obv:** Head with tiara right **Rev:** Standing suffragette chained to railings and holding banner **Edge:** Plain **Shape:** 7-sided

Date	Mintage	F12	VF20	XF40	MS60	MS63
2003	942	PF65 800				

KM# 1036 50 PENCE
8.00 g., Copper-Nickel, 27.3 mm. **Ruler:** Elizabeth II **Subject:** Woman's Social and Political Union, 100th Anniversary **Obv:** Head with tiara right **Rev:** Standing suffragette chained to railings and holding banner **Edge:** Plain **Shape:** 7-sided

Date	Mintage	F12	VF20	XF40	MS60	MS63
2003	3,124,030	—	—	1.00	3.50	4.00
2003	35,513	PF63 9.50				

KM# 1047 50 PENCE
8.00 g., Copper-Nickel, 27.3 mm. **Ruler:** Elizabeth II **Subject:** Roger Bannister, 50th Anniversary of the four minute mile **Obv:** Head with tiara right **Rev:** Running legs, stop watch and value **Edge:** Plain

Date	Mintage	F12	VF20	XF40	MS60	MS63
2004	35,020	PF63 7.50				
2004	9,032,500	—	—	1.50	5.00	6.00

KM# 1047a 50 PENCE
8.00 g., 0.925 Silver 0.2364 oz. ASW, 27.3 mm. **Ruler:** Elizabeth II **Subject:** Roger Bannister, 50th Anniversary four minute mile **Obv:** Head with tiara right **Rev:** Running legs, stop watch and value **Shape:** 7-sided

Date	Mintage	F12	VF20	XF40	MS60	MS63
2004	4,924	PF63 50.00				

Note: Also exists as a Piedfort, P43.

KM# 1050 50 PENCE
8.00 g., Copper-Nickel, 27.3 mm. **Ruler:** Elizabeth II **Subject:** Samuel Johnson's Dictonary of the English Language, 250th Anniversary **Obv:** Head with tiara right **Rev:** Dictonary entries for Fifty and Pence **Edge:** Plain **Shape:** 7-sided

Date	Mintage	F12	VF20	XF40	MS60	MS63
2005	40,563	PF63 6.00				
2005	17,649,000	—	—	1.00	3.50	4.00

KM# 1050a 50 PENCE
8.00 g., 0.925 Silver 0.2364 oz. ASW, 27.3 mm. **Ruler:** Elizabeth II **Subject:** Samuel Johnson's Dictonary of the English Language, 250th Anniversary **Obv:** Head with tiara right **Rev:** Dictonary entries for Fifty and Pence **Edge:** Plain **Shape:** 7-sided

Date	Mintage	F12	VF20	XF40	MS60	MS63
2005	4,029	PF63 45.00				

Note: Also exists as a Piedfort, P48.

KM# 1050b 50 PENCE
15.50 g., 0.9167 Gold 0.4539 oz. AGW, 27.3 mm. **Ruler:** Elizabeth II **Subject:** Samuel Johnson's Dictonary of the English Language, 250th Anniversary **Obv:** Head with tiara right **Rev:** Dictonary entries for Fifty and Pence **Edge:** Plain **Shape:** 7-sided

Date	Mintage	F12	VF20	XF40	MS60	MS63
2005	1,000	PF63 800				

KM# 1057a 50 PENCE
8.00 g., 0.925 Silver 0.2364 oz. ASW **Ruler:** Elizabeth II **Subject:** Victoria Cross, 150th Anniversary **Obv:** Head with tiara right **Rev:** Victoria Cross Medal, obverse and reverse views

Date	Mintage	F12	VF20	XF40	MS60	MS63
2006	7,500	PF63 40.00				

Note: Also exists as a Piedfort, P53.

KM# 1058a 50 PENCE
8.00 g., 0.925 Silver 0.2364 oz. ASW, 27.3 mm. **Ruler:** Elizabeth II **Subject:** Victoria Cross, 150th Anniversary **Obv:** Head with tiara right **Rev:** Heroic Act scene of a soldier carring a wounded comrade with outline of the Victoria Cross in the background **Shape:** 7-sided

Date	Mintage	F12	VF20	XF40	MS60	MS63
2006	—	PF63 40.00				

Note: Also exists as a Piedfort, P-54.

KM# 1057 50 PENCE
8.00 g., Copper-Nickel, 27.3 mm. **Ruler:** Elizabeth II **Subject:** Victoria Cross, 150th Anniversary **Obv:** Head with tiara right **Rev:** Victoria Cross Medal, obverse and reverse views **Edge:** Plain **Shape:** 7-sided

Date	Mintage	F12	VF20	XF40	MS60	MS63
2006	12,087,000	—	—	1.50	5.00	6.00
2006	Est. 50000	PF63 7.50				
2007	—	PF63 7.50				

KM# 1058 50 PENCE
8.00 g., Copper-Nickel, 27.3 mm. **Ruler:** Elizabeth II **Subject:** Victoria Cross, 150th Anniversary **Obv:** Head with tiara right **Rev:** Heroic Act scene of a soldier carring a wounded comrade with outline of the Victoria Cross in the background **Edge:** Plain **Shape:** 7-sided

Date	Mintage	F12	VF20	XF40	MS60	MS63
2006	10,000,500	—	—	1.50	5.00	6.00
2006	Est. 50000	PF63 7.50				

KM# 1073 50 PENCE
8.00 g., Copper-Nickel, 27.3 mm. **Ruler:** Elizabeth II **Subject:** Scouting Movement, 100th Anniversary **Obv:** Head with tiara right **Rev:** Fleur-de-lis emblem superimposed on globe **Edge:** Plain **Shape:** Seven sided

Date	Mintage	F12	VF20	XF40	MS60	MS63
2007	Est. 50000	PF63 7.50				
2007	7,710,750	—	—	1.50	5.00	6.00

KM# 1073a 50 PENCE
8.00 g., 0.925 Silver 0.2364 oz. ASW, 27.3 mm. **Ruler:** Elizabeth II **Subject:** Scouting Movement, 100th Anniversary **Obv:** Head with tiara right **Rev:** Fleur-de-lis emblem superimposed on globe **Edge:** Plain **Shape:** 7-sided

Date	Mintage	F12	VF20	XF40	MS60	MS63
2007	10,895	PF63 60.00				

Note: Also exists as a Piedfort, P-59.

KM# 1073b 50 PENCE
15.50 g., 0.9166 Gold 0.4538 oz. AGW, 27.3 mm. **Ruler:** Elizabeth II **Subject:** Scouting Movement, 100th Anniversary **Obv:** Head with tiara right **Rev:** Fleur-de-lis emblem superimposed on globe **Edge:** Plain **Shape:** 7-sided

Date	Mintage	F12	VF20	XF40	MS60	MS63
2007	1,250	PF63 800				

KM# 1112a 50 PENCE
8.00 g., 0.925 Silver 0.2364 oz. ASW, 27.3 mm. **Ruler:** Elizabeth II **Obv:** Head in tiara right **Rev:** Section of Royal Arms - bottom center **Shape:** 7-sided

Date	Mintage	F12	VF20	XF40	MS60	MS63
2008	—	PF63 50.00				

Note: Also exists as a Piedfort, P-97.

2009	—	PF63 50.00				
2010	3,500	PF63 50.00				
2011	—	PF63 50.00				

Note: Also exists as a Piedfort, P-82.

2013	2,013	PF63 50.00				

KM# 1112 50 PENCE
8.00 g., Copper-Nickel, 27.3 mm. **Ruler:** Elizabeth II **Obv:** Head with tiara right **Rev:** Section of the Royal Arms - bottom center **Shape:** 7-sided

Date	Mintage	F12	VF20	XF40	MS60	MS63
2008	22,747,000	—	—	1.00	3.50	4.00
2008	36,333	PF63 7.00				
2009 In sets only					3.50	4.00
2009	40,000	PF63 7.00				
2010 In sets only					3.50	4.00
2010	40,000	PF63 7.00				
2011 In sets only					3.50	4.00
2011	—	PF63 7.00				
2012	—			1.00	3.50	4.00
2012	—	PF63 7.00				
2013	—			1.00	3.50	4.00
2013	—	PF63 7.00				

KM# 1112b 50 PENCE
15.50 g., 0.9167 Gold 0.4539 oz. AGW, 27.3 mm. **Ruler:** Elizabeth II **Obv:** Head in tiara right **Rev:** Section of Royal Arms - bottom center **Shape:** 7-sided

Date	Mintage	F12	VF20	XF40	MS60	MS63
2008	—	PF63 825				
2009	—	PF63 825				

KM# 1112c 50 PENCE
Platinum APW, 27.3 mm. **Ruler:** Elizabeth II **Obv:** Head in tiara right **Rev:** Section of Royal Arms - bottom center **Shape:** 7-sided

Date	Mintage	F12	VF20	XF40	MS60	MS63
2008	—	PF63 1,350				

KM# 1114 50 PENCE
8.00 g., Copper-Nickel, 27.3 mm. **Ruler:** Elizabeth II **Subject:** Royal Botanical Gardens at Kew, 250th Anniversary **Obv:** Head with tiara right **Rev:** Pagoda and vine, 1759-2009 **Edge:** Plain **Shape:** 7-sided

Date	Mintage	F12	VF20	XF40	MS60	MS63
2009	—	PF63 7.50				
2009	10,000	—	—	1.50	6.00	5.00

KM# 1114a 50 PENCE
8.00 g., 0.925 Silver 0.2364 oz. ASW, 27.3 mm. **Ruler:** Elizabeth II **Subject:** Royal Botanical Gardens at Kew, 250th Anniversary **Obv:** Head right **Rev:** Pagoda and vine, 1759 2009 **Edge:** Plain **Shape:** 7-sided

Date	Mintage	F12	VF20	XF40	MS60	MS63
2009	7,500	PF63 50.00				

Note: Also exists as a Piedfort, P98.

KM# 1114b 50 PENCE
15.50 g., 0.916 Gold 0.4535 oz. AGW, 27.3 mm. **Ruler:** Elizabeth II **Subject:** Royal Botanical Gardens at Kew, 250th Anniversary **Obv:** Head right **Rev:** Pagoda and vine, 1759 2009 **Edge:** Plain **Shape:** 7-sided

Date	Mintage	F12	VF20	XF40	MS60	MS63
2009	1,000	PF63 800				

KM# 1150 50 PENCE
8.00 g., Copper-Nickel, 27.3 mm. **Ruler:** Elizabeth II **Subject:** London Olympics, 2012 - Athletics **Obv:** Head with tiara right **Rev:** Youth's drawing of kid going over vault **Edge:** Plain **Shape:** 7-sided

Date	Mintage	F12	VF20	XF40	MS60	MS63
2009	—			1.00	3.50	4.00
2011	900,000			—	2.50	3.50

KM# 1150a 50 PENCE
8.00 g., 0.925 Silver 0.2364 oz. ASW, 27.3 mm. **Ruler:** Elizabeth II **Subject:** London Olympics, 2012 **Obv:** Head with tiara right **Rev:** Youth drawing of high jumper

Date	Mintage	F12	VF20	XF40	MS60	MS63
2009	—	PF63 50.00				

KM# 1165a 50 PENCE
8.00 g., 0.925 Silver 0.2364 oz. ASW, 27.3 mm. **Ruler:** Elizabeth II **Subject:** Girl Guides, 100th Anniversary **Obv:** Head with tiara right **Rev:** Circle of six trifoils **Edge:** Plain **Shape:** 7-sided

Date	Mintage	F12	VF20	XF40	MS60	MS63
2010	—	PF63 50.00				

Note: Also exists as a Piedfort, P99.

KM# 1165 50 PENCE
8.00 g., Copper-Nickel, 27.3 mm. **Ruler:** Elizabeth II **Subject:** Girl Guides, 100th Anniversary **Obv:** Head with tiara right **Rev:** Circle of six trefoils **Edge:** Plain **Shape:** 7-sided

Date	Mintage	F12	VF20	XF40	MS60	MS63
2010	510,090	—	—	1.50	4.00	5.00
2010	—	PF63 10.00				

KM# 1196 50 PENCE
8.00 g., Copper-Nickel, 27.3 mm. **Ruler:** Elizabeth II **Subject:** World Wildlife Fund, 50th Anniversary **Obv:** Head with tiara right **Rev:** Panda in center of animal shaped blocks **Edge:** Plain **Shape:** 7-sided

Date	Mintage	F12	VF20	XF40	MS60	MS63
2011	—	PF63 8.50				
2011	—			1.50	5.00	6.00

KM# 1166 50 PENCE
8.00 g., Copper-Nickel, 27.3 mm. **Ruler:** Elizabeth II **Subject:** 2012 London Olympics - Aquatics **Obv:** Head with tiara right **Edge:** Plain **Shape:** 7-sided

Date	Mintage	F12	VF20	XF40	MS60	MS63
2011	1,000,000	—	—	1.50	5.00	6.00

KM# 1167 50 PENCE
8.00 g., Copper-Nickel, 27.3 mm. **Ruler:** Elizabeth II **Subject:** 2012 London Paralympics - Archery **Obv:** Head with tirara right **Edge:** Plain **Shape:** 7-sided

Date	Mintage	F12	VF20	XF40	MS60	MS63
2011	800,000	—	—	1.50	5.00	6.00

KM# 1168 50 PENCE
8.00 g., Copper-Nickel, 27.3 mm. **Ruler:** Elizabeth II **Subject:** 2012 London Olympics - Canoeing **Obv:** Head with tiara right **Edge:** Plain **Shape:** 7-sided

Date	Mintage	F12	VF20	XF40	MS60	MS63
2011	800,000	—	—	1.50	5.00	6.00

KM# 1169 50 PENCE
8.00 g., Copper-Nickel, 27.3 mm. **Ruler:** Elizabeth II **Subject:** 2012 London Olympics - Cycling **Obv:** Head with tiara right **Rev:** Cycle racing in a Velodrome **Edge:** Plain **Shape:** 7-sided

Date	Mintage	F12	VF20	XF40	MS60	MS63
2011	400,000	—	—	1.50	5.00	6.00

KM# 1170 50 PENCE
8.00 g., Copper-Nickel, 27.3 mm. **Ruler:** Elizabeth II **Subject:** 2012 London Olympics - Gymnastics **Obv:** Head with tiara right **Edge:** Plain **Shape:** 7-sided

Date	Mintage	F12	VF20	XF40	MS60	MS63
2011	900,000	—	—	1.50	5.00	6.00

KM# 1171 50 PENCE
8.00 g., Copper-Nickel, 27.3 mm. **Ruler:** Elizabeth II **Subject:** 2012 London Olympics - Hockey **Obv:** Head with tiara right **Edge:** Plain **Shape:** 7-sided

Date	Mintage	F12	VF20	XF40	MS60	MS63
2011	1,000,000	—	—	1.50	5.00	6.00

KM# 1172 50 PENCE
8.00 g., Copper-Nickel, 27.3 mm. **Ruler:** Elizabeth II **Subject:** 2012 London Olympics - Rowing **Obv:** Head with tiara right **Edge:** Plain **Shape:** 7-sided

Date	Mintage	F12	VF20	XF40	MS60	MS63
2011	700,000	—	—	1.50	5.00	6.00

KM# 1173 50 PENCE
8.00 g., Copper-Nickel, 27.3 mm. **Ruler:** Elizabeth II **Subject:** 2012 London Olympics - Triathlon **Obv:** Head with tiara right **Edge:** Plain **Shape:** 7-sided

Date	Mintage	F12	VF20	XF40	MS60	MS63
2011	1,000,000	—	—	1.50	5.00	6.00

KM# 1174 50 PENCE
8.00 g., Copper-Nickel, 27.3 mm. **Ruler:** Elizabeth II **Subject:** 2012 London Olympics - Badminton **Obv:** Head with tiara right **Edge:** Plain **Shape:** 7-sided

Date	Mintage	F12	VF20	XF40	MS60	MS63
2011	900,000	—	—	1.50	5.00	6.00

KM# 1175 50 PENCE
8.00 g., Copper-Nickel, 27.3 mm. **Ruler:** Elizabeth II **Subject:** 2012 London Olympics - Boxing **Obv:** Head with tiara right **Edge:** Plain **Shape:** 7-sided

Date	Mintage	F12	VF20	XF40	MS60	MS63
2011	800,000	—	—	1.50	5.00	6.00

KM# 1176 50 PENCE
8.00 g., Copper-Nickel, 27.3 mm. **Ruler:** Elizabeth II **Subject:** 2012 London Olympics - Equestrian **Obv:** Head with tiara right **Edge:** Plain **Shape:** 7-sided

Date	Mintage	F12	VF20	XF40	MS60	MS63
2011	—	—	—	1.50	5.00	6.00

KM# 1177 50 PENCE
8.00 g., Copper-Nickel, 27.3 mm. **Ruler:** Elizabeth II **Subject:** 2012 London Olympics - Modern Pentathlon **Obv:** Head with tiara right **Edge:** Plain **Shape:** 7-sided

Date	Mintage	F12	VF20	XF40	MS60	MS63
2011	—	—	—	1.50	5.00	6.00

KM# 1179 50 PENCE
8.00 g., Copper-Nickel, 27.3 mm. **Ruler:** Elizabeth II **Subject:** 2012 London Olympics - Shooting **Obv:** Head with tiara right **Edge:** Plain **Shape:** 7-sided

Date	Mintage	F12	VF20	XF40	MS60	MS63
2011	—	—	—	1.50	5.00	6.00

KM# 1180 50 PENCE
8.00 g., Copper-Nickel, 27.3 mm. **Ruler:** Elizabeth II **Subject:** 2012 London Paralympics - Table Tennis **Obv:** Head with tiara right **Edge:** Plain **Shape:** 7-sided

Date	Mintage	F12	VF20	XF40	MS60	MS63
2011	1,000,000	—	—	1.50	5.00	6.00

KM# 1181 50 PENCE
8.00 g., Copper-Nickel, 27.3 mm. **Ruler:** Elizabeth II **Subject:** 2012 London Olympics - Volleyball **Shape:** 7-sided

Date	Mintage	F12	VF20	XF40	MS60	MS63
2011	1,000,000	—	—	1.50	5.00	6.00

KM# 1182 50 PENCE
8.00 g., Copper-Nickel, 27.3 mm. **Ruler:** Elizabeth II **Subject:** 2012 London Olympics - Canoeing **Shape:** 7-sided

Date	Mintage	F12	VF20	XF40	MS60	MS63
2011	800,000	—	—	1.50	5.00	6.00

KM# 1183 50 PENCE
8.00 g., Copper-Nickel, 27.3 mm. **Ruler:** Elizabeth II **Subject:** 2012 London Paralympics - Goalball **Obv:** Head with tiara right **Edge:** Plain **Shape:** 7-sided

Date	Mintage	F12	VF20	XF40	MS60	MS63
2011	900,000	—	—	1.50	5.00	6.00

KM# 1185 50 PENCE
8.00 g., Copper-Nickel, 27.3 mm. **Ruler:** Elizabeth II **Subject:** 2012 London Olympics - Taekwondo **Obv:** Head with tiara right **Edge:** Plain **Shape:** 7-sided

Date	Mintage	F12	VF20	XF40	MS60	MS63
2011	—	—	—	1.50	5.00	6.00

KM# 1186 50 PENCE
8.00 g., Copper-Nickel, 27.3 mm. **Ruler:** Elizabeth II **Subject:** 2012 London Olympics - Weightlifting **Obv:** Head with tiara right **Edge:** Plain **Shape:** 7-sided

Date	Mintage	F12	VF20	XF40	MS60	MS63
2011	—	—	—	1.50	5.00	6.00

KM# 1187 50 PENCE
8.00 g., Copper-Nickel, 27.3 mm. **Ruler:** Elizabeth II **Subject:** 2012 London Paralympics - Wheelchair Rugby **Obv:** Head with tiara right **Edge:** Plain **Shape:** 7-sided

Date	Mintage	F12	VF20	XF40	MS60	MS63
2011	—	—	—	1.50	5.00	6.00

KM# 1188 50 PENCE
8.00 g., Copper-Nickel, 27.3 mm. **Ruler:** Elizabeth II **Subject:** 2012 Summer Olympics - Wrestling **Obv:** Head with tiara right **Edge:** Plain **Shape:** 7-sided

Date	Mintage	F12	VF20	XF40	MS60	MS63
2011	—	—	—	1.50	5.00	6.00

KM# 1189 50 PENCE
8.00 g., Copper-Nickel, 27.3 mm. **Ruler:** Elizabeth II **Subject:** 2012 London Paralympics - Boccia **Obv:** Head with tiara right **Edge:** Plain **Shape:** 7-sided

Date	Mintage	F12	VF20	XF40	MS60	MS63
2011	900,000	—	—	1.50	5.00	6.00

KM# 1190 50 PENCE
8.00 g., Copper-Nickel, 27.3 mm. **Ruler:** Elizabeth II **Subject:** 2012 London Olympics - Basketball **Obv:** Head with tiara right **Edge:** Plain **Shape:** 7-sided

Date	Mintage	F12	VF20	XF40	MS60	MS63
2011	—	—	—	1.50	5.00	6.00

KM# 1191 50 PENCE
8.00 g., Copper-Nickel, 27.3 mm. **Ruler:** Elizabeth II **Subject:** 2012 London Olympics - Fencing **Obv:** Head with tiara right **Edge:** Plain **Shape:** 7-sided

Date	Mintage	F12	VF20	XF40	MS60	MS63
2011	1,000,000	—	—	1.50	5.00	6.00

KM# 1192 50 PENCE
8.00 g., Copper-Nickel, 27.3 mm. **Ruler:** Elizabeth II **Subject:** 2012 London Olympics - Handball **Obv:** Head with tiara right **Edge:** Plain **Shape:** 7-sided

Date	Mintage	F12	VF20	XF40	MS60	MS63
2011	—	—	—	1.50	5.00	6.00

KM# 1193 50 PENCE
8.00 g., Copper-Nickel, 27.3 mm. **Ruler:** Elizabeth II **Subject:** 2012 London Olympics - Football (Soccer) **Obv:** Head with tiara right **Edge:** Plain **Shape:** 7-sided

Date	Mintage	F12	VF20	XF40	MS60	MS63
2011	—	—	—	1.50	5.00	6.00

KM# 1194 50 PENCE
8.00 g., Copper-Nickel, 27.3 mm. **Ruler:** Elizabeth II **Subject:** 2012 London Olympics - Tennis **Obv:** Head with tiara right **Edge:** Plain **Shape:** 7-sided

Date	Mintage	F12	VF20	XF40	MS60	MS63
2011	—	—	—	1.50	5.00	6.00

KM# 1195 50 PENCE
8.00 g., Copper-Nickel, 27.3 mm. **Ruler:** Elizabeth II **Subject:** London Olympics - Sailing **Obv:** Head with tiara right **Edge:** Plain **Shape:** 7-sided

Date	Mintage	F12	VF20	XF40	MS60	MS63
2011	—	—	—	1.00	5.00	6.00

KM# 1196a 50 PENCE
8.00 g., 0.925 Silver 0.2364 oz. ASW, 27.3 mm. **Ruler:** Elizabeth II **Subject:** World Wildlife Fund, 50th Anniversary **Obv:** Head with tiara right **Rev:** Panda at center, animal shapes as blocks **Edge:** Plain **Shape:** 7-sided

Date	Mintage	F12	VF20	XF40	MS60	MS63
2011	—	PF63 50.00				

Note: Also exists as a Piedfort, P86

KM# 1184 50 PENCE
8.00 g., Copper-Nickel, 24.3 mm. **Ruler:** Elizabeth II **Subject:** 2012 London Olympics - Judo **Obv:** Head with tiara right **Edge:** Plain **Shape:** 7-sided

Date	Mintage	F12	VF20	XF40	MS60	MS63
2011	—	—	—	1.50	5.00	6.00

KM# 1112a.1 50 PENCE
8.00 g., 0.925 Silver 0.2364 oz. ASW, 27.3 mm. **Ruler:** Elizabeth II **Obv:** Head with tiara right **Rev:** Section of Royal Arms - bottom center

Date	Mintage	F12	VF20	XF40	MS60	MS63
2012	—	PF63 50.00				

KM# 1178 50 PENCE
8.00 g., Copper-Nickel, 27.3 mm. **Ruler:** Elizabeth II **Subject:** 2012 London Olympics - Sailing **Obv:** Head with tiara right **Edge:** Plain **Shape:** 7-sided

Date	Mintage	F12	VF20	XF40	MS60	MS63
2012	—	—	—	1.50	5.00	6.00

KM# 1253 50 PENCE
8.00 g., Copper-Nickel, 27.3 mm. **Ruler:** Elizabeth II **Subject:** Benjamin Britten, 100th Anniversary of Birth **Obv:** Head with tiara right **Rev:** Quote from Tennyson: BLOW BUGLE BLOW: SET THE WILD ECHOES FLYING **Shape:** 7-sided

Date	Mintage	F12	VF20	XF40	MS60	MS63
2013	—	—	—	—	3.50	4.00

KM# 1253b 50 PENCE
15.50 g., 0.916 Gold 0.4535 oz. AGW, 27.3 mm. **Ruler:** Elizabeth II **Subject:** Benjamin Britten, 100th Anniversary of Birth **Obv:** Head with tiara right

Date	Mintage	F12	VF20	XF40	MS60	MS63
2013	—	PF63 850				

KM# 1246a 50 PENCE
8.00 g., 0.925 Silver 0.2364 oz. ASW, 27.3 mm. **Ruler:** Elizabeth II **Subject:** Christopher Ironside, 100th Anniversary of Birth **Obv:** Bust with tiara right **Rev:** Royal arms with supporters **Shape:** 7-sided

Date	Mintage	F12	VF20	XF40	MS60	MS63
2013	2,013	PF63 50.00				

KM# 1253a 50 PENCE
8.00 g., 0.925 Silver 0.2364 oz. ASW, 27.3 mm. **Ruler:** Elizabeth II **Subject:** Bnjamin Britten, 100th Anniversary of Birth **Obv:** Head with tiara right **Shape:** 7-sided

Date	Mintage	F12	VF20	XF40	MS60	MS63
2013	—	PF63 40.00				

KM# 1246 50 PENCE
8.00 g., Copper-Nickel, 27.3 mm. **Ruler:** Elizabeth II **Subject:** Christopher Ironside, 100th Anniversary of Birth **Obv:** Head with tiara right **Rev:** Royal Arms **Shape:** 7-sided

Date	Mintage	F12	VF20	XF40	MS60	MS63
2013	—	—	—	—	—	15.00
2013	44,000	PF63 50.00				

KM# 993 POUND
9.50 g., Nickel-Brass, 22.5 mm. **Ruler:** Elizabeth II **Subject:** United Kingdom **Obv:** Head with tiara right **Rev:** Royal Arms with supporters **Edge:** Reeded and lettered **Edge Lettering:** DECUS ET TUTAMEN

Date	Mintage	F12	VF20	XF40	MS60	MS63
2003	61,596,500	—	—	3.00	6.00	7.50
2003	43,513	PF63 7.50				
2008	—	—	—	3.00	6.00	7.50

KM# 993a POUND
9.50 g., 0.925 Silver 0.2807 oz. ASW, 22.5 mm. **Ruler:** Elizabeth II **Subject:** United Kingdom **Obv:** Head with tiara right **Rev:** Royal Arms with supporters **Edge:** Reeded and lettered **Edge Lettering:** DECUS ET TUTAMEN

Date	Mintage	F12	VF20	XF40	MS60	MS63
2003 (2008)	15,830	PF63 45.00				

Note: Also exists as a Piedfort, P41

KM# 1013 POUND
9.50 g., Nickel-Brass, 22.5 mm. **Ruler:** Elizabeth II **Subject:** Northern Ireland **Obv:** Head with tiara right **Rev:** Celtic cross with a pimpernel flower at the center **Edge:** Reeded and lettered **Edge Lettering:** DECUS ET TUTAMEN

Date	Mintage	F12	VF20	XF40	MS60	MS63
2001	63,968,065	—	—	3.00	6.00	7.50
2001	45,617	PF63 7.50				

KM# 1013a POUND
9.50 g., 0.925 Silver 0.2807 oz. ASW, 22.5 mm. **Ruler:** Elizabeth II **Subject:** Northern Ireland **Obv:** Head with tiara right **Rev:** Celtic cross with a pimpernel flower in the center **Edge:** Reeded and lettered **Edge Lettering:** DECUS ET TUTAMEN

Date	Mintage	F12	VF20	XF40	MS60	MS63
2001	25,000	PF63 45.00				

Note: Also exists as a Piedfort, P101

KM# 1030 POUND
9.50 g., Nickel-Brass, 22.5 mm. **Ruler:** Elizabeth II **Subject:** England **Obv:** Head with tiara right **Rev:** Three lions passant left **Edge:** Reeded and lettered **Edge Lettering:** DECUS ET TUTAMEN

Date	Mintage	F12	VF20	XF40	MS60	MS63
2002	60,770	PF63 7.50				
2002	77,818,000	—	—	3.00	6.00	7.00

KM# 1030a POUND
9.50 g., 0.925 Silver 0.2807 oz. ASW, 22.5 mm. **Ruler:** Elizabeth II **Subject:** England **Obv:** Head with tiara right **Rev:** Three lions passant left **Edge:** Reeded and lettered **Edge Lettering:** DECUS ET TUTAMEN

Date	Mintage	F12	VF20	XF40	MS60	MS63
2002	—	PF63 45.00				

Note: Also exists as a Piedfort, P102

KM# 1030b POUND
0.9167 Gold AGW, 22.5 mm. **Ruler:** Elizabeth II **Subject:** England **Obv:** Head with tiara right **Rev:** Three lions left passant left **Edge:** Reeded and lettered **Edge Lettering:** DECUS ET TUTAMEN

Date	Mintage	F12	VF20	XF40	MS60	MS63
2002	—	PF63 850				

KM# 1048a POUND
9.50 g., 0.925 Silver 0.2807 oz. ASW, 22.5 mm. **Ruler:** Elizabeth II **Obv:** Head with tiara right **Rev:** Forth Railway Bridge in Scotland **Edge:** Ornamented and reeded

Date	Mintage	F12	VF20	XF40	MS60	MS63
2004	Est. 20000	PF63 45.00				

Note: Also exists as a Piedfort, P44

KM# 1048b POUND
19.62 g., 0.9166 Gold 0.5744 oz. AGW, 22.5 mm. **Ruler:** Elizabeth II **Obv:** Head with tiara right **Rev:** Forth Railway Bridge in Scotland **Edge:** Reeded and ornamented

Date	Mintage	F12	VF20	XF40	MS60	MS63
2004	Est. 1500	PF63 1,100				

KM# 1048 POUND
9.50 g., Nickel-Brass, 22.5 mm. **Ruler:** Elizabeth II **Obv:** Head with tiara right **Rev:** Forth Rail Bridge in Scotland **Edge:** Reeded and ornamented

Date	Mintage	F12	VF20	XF40	MS60	MS63
2004	39,162,000	—	—	3.50	7.50	9.00
2004	35,020	PF63 9.00				

KM# 1051 POUND
9.50 g., Nickel-Brass, 22.5 mm. **Ruler:** Elizabeth II **Obv:** Head with tiara right **Rev:** Menai Bridge to the Isle of Anglesey

Date	Mintage	F12	VF20	XF40	MS60	MS63
2005	40,563	PF63 10.00	PF65 12.00			
2005	99,429,500	—	—	3.00	6.00	7.50

KM# 1051a POUND
9.50 g., 0.925 Silver 0.2807 oz. ASW, 22.5 mm. **Ruler:** Elizabeth II **Obv:** Head with tiara right **Rev:** Menai Bridge to the Isle of Anglesey **Edge:** Reeded and lettered **Edge Lettering:** PLEIDOL WYF I'M GWLAD

Date	Mintage	F12	VF20	XF40	MS60	MS63
2005	Est. 15000	PF63 45.00				

Note: Also exists as a Piedfort, P50

KM# 1051a.2 POUND
9.50 g., 0.925 Silver 0.2807 oz. ASW, 22.5 mm. **Ruler:** Elizabeth II **Obv:** Elizabeth II **Rev:** Menai Bridge to the Isle of Anglesey **Edge:** Reeded and ornamented

Date	Mintage	F12	VF20	XF40	MS60	MS63
2005	Est. 20000	PF63 45.00				

KM# 1051b POUND
19.62 g., 0.9167 Gold 0.5745 oz. AGW, 22.5 mm. **Ruler:** Elizabeth II **Obv:** Head with tiara right **Rev:** Menai Bridge to the Isle of Anglesey **Edge:** Reeded and lettered **Edge Lettering:** PLEIDOL WYF I'M GWLAD

Date	Mintage	F12	VF20	XF40	MS60	MS63
2005	Est. 1500	PF63 1,000				

KM# 1051b.2 POUND
19.62 g., 0.9166 Gold 0.5744 oz. AGW, 22.5 mm. **Ruler:** Elizabeth II **Obv:** Head with tiara right **Rev:** Menai Bridge to the Isle of Anglesey **Edge:** Reeded and ornamented

Date	Mintage	F12	VF20	XF40	MS60	MS63
2005	Est. 1500	PF63 1,000				

KM# 1059 POUND
9.60 g., Nickel-Brass, 22.5 mm. **Ruler:** Elizabeth II **Obv:** Head with tiara right **Rev:** Egyptian Arch Railway Bridge at Newry **Edge:** Reeded and lettered

Date	Mintage	F12	VF20	XF40	MS60	MS63
2006	37,689	PF63 10.00				
2006	38,938,000	—	—	4.00	8.00	9.00
2007	—	PF63 10.00				

KM# 1059a POUND
9.50 g., 0.925 Silver 0.2807 oz. ASW, 22.5 mm. **Ruler:** Elizabeth II **Obv:** Head with tiara right **Rev:** Egyptian Arch Railway Bridge at Newry **Edge:** Reeded and lettered **Edge Lettering:** DECUS ET TUTAMEN

Date	Mintage	F12	VF20	XF40	MS60	MS63
2006	Est. 20000	PF63 50.00				

Note: Also exists as a Piedfort, P55

KM# 1059a.2 POUND
9.50 g., 0.925 Silver 0.2807 oz. ASW, 22.5 mm. **Ruler:** Elizabeth II **Obv:** Head with tiara right **Rev:** Egyptian Arch Railway Bridge at Newry **Edge:** Reeded and ornamented

Date	Mintage	F12	VF20	XF40	MS60	MS63
2006	Est. 20000	PF63 45.00				

KM# 1059b POUND
19.62 g., 0.9167 Gold 0.5745 oz. AGW, 22.5 mm. **Ruler:** Elizabeth II **Obv:** Head with tiara right **Rev:** Egyptian Arch Railway Bridge at Newry **Edge:** Reeded and lettered **Edge Lettering:** DECUS ET TUTAMEN

Date	Mintage	F12	VF20	XF40	MS60	MS63
2006	—	PF63 1,000				

KM# 1059b.2 POUND
19.62 g., 0.9166 Gold 0.5744 oz. AGW, 22.5 mm. **Ruler:** Elizabeth II **Obv:** Head with tiara right **Rev:** Egyptian Arch Railway Bridge at Newry **Edge:** Reeded and ornamented

Date	Mintage	F12	VF20	XF40	MS60	MS63
2006	Est. 1500	PF63 1,100				

KM# 1074a POUND
9.50 g., 0.925 Silver 0.2807 oz. ASW, 22.5 mm. **Ruler:** Elizabeth II **Obv:** head with tiara right **Rev:** Millennium Bridge at Gateshead **Edge:** Reeded and ornamented

Date	Mintage	F12	VF20	XF40	MS60	MS63
2007	Est. 20000	PF63 45.00				

Note: Also exists as a Piedfort, P60

KM# 1074b POUND
19.62 g., 0.9166 Gold 0.5744 oz. AGW, 22.5 mm. **Ruler:** Elizabeth II **Obv:** Head with tiara right **Rev:** Millennium Bridge at Gateshead **Edge:** Reeded and ornamented

Date	Mintage	F12	VF20	XF40	MS60	MS63
2007	Est. 1500	PF63 1,000				

KM# 1074 POUND
9.50 g., Nickel-Brass, 22.5 mm. **Ruler:** Elizabeth II **Obv:** Head with tiara right **Rev:** Millennium Bridge at Gateshead **Edge:** Reeded and ornamented

Date	Mintage	F12	VF20	XF40	MS60	MS63
2007	26,180,160	—	—	4.00	8.00	9.00
2007	38,215	PF63 10.00				

KM# 1113a POUND
9.50 g., 0.925 Silver 0.2807 oz. ASW, 22.5 mm. **Ruler:** Elizabeth II **Obv:** Head in tiara right **Rev:** Shield of the Royal Arms

Date	Mintage	F12	VF20	XF40	MS60	MS63
2008	5,000	PF63 50.00				
	Note: Also exists as a Piedfort, P103					
2009	50,000	—	—	—	—	50.00
2009	20,000	PF63 60.00				
2010	50,000	—	—	—	—	50.00
2010	20,000	PF63 60.00				

KM# 1113 POUND
9.50 g., Nickel-Brass, 22.5 mm. **Ruler:** Elizabeth II **Obv:** Head with tiara right **Rev:** Shield of the Royal Arms **Edge:** Reeded and lettered **Edge Lettering:** DECUS ET TUTAMEN

Date	Mintage	F12	VF20	XF40	MS60	MS63
2008	43,827,300	—	—	3.00	7.50	6.00
2008	36,333	PF63 7.50				
2009	27,625,600	—	—	4.00	9.00	8.00
2009	40,000	PF63 9.00				
2010	38,505,000	—	—	3.00	7.50	6.00
2010	40,000	PF63 7.50				
2011	—	—	—	3.00	7.50	6.00
2011	—	PF63 7.50				
2012	—	—	—	3.00	7.50	6.00
2012	—	PF63 7.50				
2013	—	—	—	3.00	7.50	6.00
2013	—	PF63 7.50				

KM# 993b POUND
19.60 g., 0.9167 Gold 0.5739 oz. AGW, 22.5 mm. **Ruler:** Elizabeth II **Subject:** United Kingdom **Obv:** Head with tiara right **Rev:** Royal Arms with supporters **Edge Lettering:** DECUS ET TUTAMEN

Date	Mintage	F12	VF20	XF40	MS60	MS63
2008	Est. 2008	PF63 1,100				
2013	100	PF65 1,200				

KM# 1113b POUND
16.62 g., 0.9167 Gold 0.4867 oz. AGW, 22.5 mm. **Ruler:** Elizabeth II **Obv:** Head in tiara right **Rev:** Shield of the Royal Arms

Date	Mintage	F12	VF20	XF40	MS60	MS63
2008	860	PF65 1,100				
2009	1,000	PF63 1,000				
2013	100	PF65 1,250				

KM# 1113c POUND
Platinum APW, 22.5 mm. **Ruler:** Elizabeth II **Obv:** Head in tiara right **Rev:** Shield of the Royal Arms

Date	Mintage	F12	VF20	XF40	MS60	MS63
2008	—	PF63 1,650				

KM# 1158 POUND
9.50 g., Nickel-Brass, 22.5 mm. **Ruler:** Elizabeth II **Obv:** Head with tiara right **Rev:** City of London arms, three smaller arms below **Edge:** Reeded and lettered **Edge Lettering:** DOMINE DIRIGE NOS

Date	Mintage	F12	VF20	XF40	MS60	MS63
2010	—	PF63 10.00	PF65 12.00			
2010	—	—	—	3.00	6.00	7.50

KM# 1158a POUND
9.50 g., 0.925 Silver 0.2807 oz. ASW, 22.5 mm. **Ruler:** Elizabeth II **Obv:** Head with tiara right **Rev:** City of London arms, three smaller arms below

Date	Mintage	F12	VF20	XF40	MS60	MS63
2010	20,000	PF63 60.00				

Note: Also exists as a Piedfort, P75

KM# 1159a POUND
9.50 g., 0.925 Silver 0.2807 oz. ASW, 22.5 mm. **Ruler:** Elizabeth II **Obv:** Head with tiara right **Rev:** City of Belfast arms, three smaller arms below

Date	Mintage	F12	VF20	XF40	MS60	MS63
2010	20,000	PF63 60.00				

Note: Also exists as a Piedfort, P76

KM# 1158b POUND
19.62 g., 0.9167 Gold 0.5745 oz. AGW, 22.5 mm. **Ruler:** Elizabeth II **Obv:** Head with tiara right **Rev:** City of London arms, three smaller arms below

Date	Mintage	F12	VF20	XF40	MS60	MS63
2010	2,500	PF63 1,100				

KM# 1159b POUND
19.62 g., 0.9167 Gold 0.5745 oz. AGW, 22.5 mm. **Ruler:** Elizabeth II **Obv:** Head with tiara right **Rev:** City of Belfast arms, three smaller arms below

Date	Mintage	F12	VF20	XF40	MS60	MS63
2010	2,500	PF63 1,100				

KM# 1159 POUND
9.50 g., Nickel-Brass, 22.5 mm. **Ruler:** Elizabeth II **Obv:** Head with tiara right **Rev:** City of Belfast arms, three smaller arms below **Edge:** Reeded and lettered **Edge Lettering:** PRO TANTO QUID RETRIBUAMUS

Date	Mintage	F12	VF20	XF40	MS60	MS63
2010	—	—	—	3.00	6.00	7.50
2010	—	PF63 10.00	PF65 12.00			

KM# 1197a POUND
9.50 g., 0.925 Silver 0.2807 oz. ASW, 22.5 mm. **Ruler:** Elizabeth II **Obv:** Head with tiara right **Rev:** Edinburgh City arms, three smaller arms below

Date	Mintage	F12	VF20	XF40	MS60	MS63
2011	—	PF63 45.00				

Note: Also exists as a Piedfort, P83

KM# 1197 POUND
9.50 g., Nickel-Brass, 22.5 mm. **Ruler:** Elizabeth II **Obv:** Head with tiara right **Rev:** Edinburgh city arms, three smaller arms below **Edge:** Reeded and lettered **Edge Lettering:** NISI DOMINUS FRUSTRA

Date	Mintage	F12	VF20	XF40	MS60	MS63
2011	—	—	—	3.00	6.00	7.50
2011	—	PF63 10.00 PF65 12.00				

KM# 1198 POUND
9.50 g., Nickel-Brass, 22.5 mm. **Ruler:** Elizabeth II **Obv:** Head with tiara right **Rev:** Cardiff city arms, three smaller arms below **Edge:** Reeded and lettered **Edge Lettering:** DDRAIG GOCH DDYRY CYCHWYN

Date	Mintage	F12	VF20	XF40	MS60	MS63
2011	—	—	—	3.00	6.00	7.50
2011	—	PF63 10.00 PF65 12.00				

KM# 1198a POUND
9.50 g., 0.925 Silver 0.2807 oz. ASW, 22.5 mm. **Ruler:** Elizabeth II **Obv:** Head with tiara right **Rev:** Cardiff city arms, three smaller arms below

Date	Mintage	F12	VF20	XF40	MS60	MS63
2011	—	PF63 45.00				

Note: Also exists as a Piedfort, P84

KM# 1113a.1 POUND
9.50 g., 0.925 Silver 0.2807 oz. ASW, 22.5 mm. **Ruler:** Elizabeth II **Obv:** Head with tiara right **Rev:** Shield of the Royal Arms

Date	Mintage	F12	VF20	XF40	MS60	MS63
2012	—	PF63 60.00				

KM# 1238 POUND
9.50 g., Nickel-Brass, 22.5 mm. **Ruler:** Elizabeth II **Obv:** Head with tiara right **Rev:** Wales flora - Leek and daffodil

Date	Mintage	F12	VF20	XF40	MS60	MS63
2013	—	PF63 10.00 PF65 12.00				
2013	—	—	—	3.00	6.00	7.50

KM# 1237a POUND
9.50 g., 0.925 Silver 0.2807 oz. ASW, 22.5 mm. **Ruler:** Elizabeth II **Obv:** Bust with tiara right **Rev:** England flora - Rose and oak

Date	Mintage	F12	VF20	XF40	MS60	MS63
2013	12,500	PF63 40.00				

KM# 1238a POUND
9.50 g., 0.925 Silver 0.2807 oz. ASW, 22.5 mm. **Ruler:** Elizabeth II **Obv:** Head with tiara right **Rev:** Wales flora - leek and daffodil

Date	Mintage	F12	VF20	XF40	MS60	MS63
2013	12,500	PF63 40.00				

KM# 1237b POUND
19.61 g., 0.9167 Gold 0.5742 oz. AGW, 22.5 mm. **Ruler:** Elizabeth II **Obv:** Head with tiara right **Rev:** England Flora - oak and rose

Date	Mintage	F12	VF20	XF40	MS60	MS63
2013	560	PF65 1,400				

KM# 1237 POUND
9.50 g., Nickel-Brass, 22.5 mm. **Ruler:** Elizabeth II **Obv:** Head with tiara right **Rev:** England flora - Rose and oak

Date	Mintage	F12	VF20	XF40	MS60	MS63
2013	—	—	—	3.00	6.00	7.50
2013	—	PF63 10.00 PF65 12.00				

KM# 1238b POUND
19.61 g., 0.9167 Gold 0.5742 oz. AGW, 22.5 mm. **Ruler:** Elizabeth II **Obv:** Head with tiara right **Rev:** Wales flora - leek and daffodil

Date	Mintage	F12	VF20	XF40	MS60	MS63
2013	560	PF65 1,400				

KM# 1245 POUND
16.62 g., 0.917 Gold 0.4868 oz. AGW, 22.5 mm. **Ruler:** Elizabeth II **Obv:** Head with tiara right **Rev:** Crowned shield of the United Kingdom **Edge Lettering:** DECUS ET TUTAMEN

Date	Mintage	F12	VF20	XF40	MS60	MS63
2013	100	PF63 1,200				

KM# 994 2 POUNDS
12.00 g., Bi-Metallic, 28.4 mm. **Ruler:** Elizabeth II **Subject:** Technology **Obv:** Head with tiara right **Rev:** Symbolic depiction in concentric circles of technological development from the Iron Age to the Internet **Edge Lettering:** STANDING ON THE SHOULDERS OF GIANTS

Date	Mintage	F12	VF20	XF40	MS60	MS63
2001	34,984,750	—		5.00	9.50	12.00
2001	—	PF63 12.00				
2002	13,024,750	—		5.00	9.50	12.00
2002	—	PF63 12.00				
2003	17,531,250	—		5.00	9.50	12.00
2003	43,513	PF63 12.00				
2004	11,981,500	—		5.00	9.50	12.00
2004	35,020	PF63 12.00				
2005	3,837,250	—		5.00	9.50	12.00
2005	40,563	PF63 12.00				
2006	16,715,000	—		5.00	9.50	12.00
2006	—	PF63 12.00				
2007	10,270,000	—		5.00	9.50	12.00
2007	—	PF63 12.00				
2008	30,107,000	—		5.00	9.50	12.00
2008	—	PF63 12.00				
2009	8,775,000	—		5.00	9.50	12.00
2009	—	PF63 12.00				
2010	2,015,000	—		5.00	9.50	12.00
2010	—	PF63 12.00				
2011	—	—		5.00	9.50	12.00
2011	—	PF63 12.00				
2012	—	—		5.00	9.50	12.00
2012	—	PF63 12.00				
2013	—	—		5.00	9.50	12.00
2013	—	PF63 12.00				

KM# 994a 2 POUNDS
12.00 g., 0.925 Silver 0.3546 oz. ASW, 28.35 mm. **Ruler:** Elizabeth II **Subject:** Technology **Obv:** Head with tiara right **Rev:** Symbolic depiction in concentric circles of technological development from the Iron Age to the Internet **Note:** Gold plated silver ring, silver center.

Date	Mintage	F12	VF20	XF40	MS60	MS63
2006	—	PF63 45.00				

KM# 994c 2 POUNDS
15.98 g., 0.9167 Gold 0.4679 oz. AGW, 28.35 mm. **Ruler:** Elizabeth II **Subject:** Technology **Obv:** Head with tiara right **Rev:** Symbolic depiction in concentric circles of technological development from the Iron Age to the Internet

Date	Mintage	F12	VF20	XF40	MS60	MS63
2002	—	PF63 900				

KM# 1014 2 POUNDS
11.97 g., Bi-Metallic, 28.35 mm. **Ruler:** Elizabeth II **Subject:** First Transatlantic Radio Transmission **Obv:** Head with tiara right within circle **Rev:** Symbolic design **Edge:** Reeded and inscribed **Edge Lettering:** WIRELESS BRIDGES THE ATLANTIC... MARCONI... 1901

Date	Mintage	F12	VF20	XF40	MS60	MS63
2001	4,558,000	—	—	5.00	9.50	12.00
2001	—	PF63 14.00 PF65 16.00				

KM# 1014a 2 POUNDS
12.00 g., 0.925 Silver 0.3546 oz. ASW, 28.4 mm. **Ruler:** Elizabeth II **Subject:** First Transatlantic Radio Transmission **Obv:** Head with tiara right within circle **Rev:** Symbolic design **Edge Lettering:** WIRELESS BRIDGES THE ATLANTIC... MARCONI 1901...

Date	Mintage	F12	VF20	XF40	MS60	MS63
2001	11,488	PF63 45.00				

Note: Also exists as a Piefort, P106

KM# 1014b 2 POUNDS
15.97 g., 0.9166 Gold 0.4676 oz. AGW, 28.4 mm. **Ruler:** Elizabeth II **Subject:** First Transatlantic Radio Transmission **Obv:** Head with tiara right **Rev:** Symbolic design

Date	Mintage	F12	VF20	XF40	MS60	MS63
2001	1,658	PF63 900				

KM# 1031a 2 POUNDS
12.00 g., 0.925 Silver 0.3546 oz. ASW, 28.4 mm. **Ruler:** Elizabeth II **Subject:** Commonwealth Games - England **Obv:** Head with tiara right **Rev:** Runner breaking ribbon at finish line **Edge:** Reeded and lettered

Date	Mintage	F12	VF20	XF40	MS60	MS63
2002	10,000	PF63 45.00				

Note: Also exists as a Piefort, P107

KM# 1032a 2 POUNDS
12.00 g., 0.925 Silver 0.3546 oz. ASW, 28.4 mm. **Ruler:** Elizabeth II **Subject:** Commonwealth Games - Scotland **Obv:** Head with tiara right **Rev:** Runner breaking ribbon at finish line **Edge:** Reeded and lettered

Date	Mintage	F12	VF20	XF40	MS60	MS63
2002	10,000	PF63 35.00				

Note: Also exists as a Piefort, P108

KM# 1033a 2 POUNDS
12.00 g., 0.925 Silver 0.3546 oz. ASW, 28.4 mm. **Ruler:** Elizabeth II **Subject:** Commonwealth Games - Wales **Obv:** Head with tiara right **Rev:** Runner breaking ribbon at finish line **Edge:** Reeded and lettered

Date	Mintage	F12	VF20	XF40	MS60	MS63
2002	10,000	PF63 35.00				

Note: Also exists as a Piefort, P109

KM# 1034a 2 POUNDS
12.00 g., 0.925 Silver 0.3546 oz. ASW, 28.4 mm. **Ruler:** Elizabeth II **Subject:** Commonwealth Games - Northern Ireland **Obv:** Head with tiara right **Rev:** Runner breaking ribbon at finish line **Edge:** Reeded and lettered

Date	Mintage	F12	VF20	XF40	MS60	MS63
2002	10,000	PF63 35.00				

Note: Also exists as a Piefort, P110

KM# 1031b 2 POUNDS
15.98 g., 0.916 Gold 0.4676 oz. AGW, 28.4 mm. **Ruler:** Elizabeth II **Subject:** Commonwealth Games - England **Obv:** Head with tiara right **Rev:** Runner breaking ribbon at finish line **Edge:** Reeded and lettered

Date	Mintage	F12	VF20	XF40	MS60	MS63
2002	500	PF65 950				

KM# 1032b 2 POUNDS
15.98 g., 0.916 Gold 0.4676 oz. AGW, 28.4 mm. **Ruler:** Elizabeth II **Subject:** Commonwealth Games - Scotland **Obv:** Head with tiara right **Rev:** Runner breaking ribbon at finish line **Edge:** Reeded and lettered

Date	Mintage	F12	VF20	XF40	MS60	MS63
2002	500	PF65 950				

KM# 1033b 2 POUNDS
15.98 g., 0.916 Gold 0.4676 oz. AGW, 28.4 mm. **Ruler:** Elizabeth II **Subject:** Commonwealth Games - Wales **Obv:** Head with tiara right **Rev:** Runner breaking ribbon at finish line **Edge:** Reeded and lettered

Date	Mintage	F12	VF20	XF40	MS60	MS63
2002	500	PF65 950				

KM# 1034b 2 POUNDS
15.98 g., 0.916 Gold 0.4676 oz. AGW, 28.4 mm. **Ruler:** Elizabeth II **Subject:** Commonwealth Games - Northern Ireland **Obv:** Head with tiara right **Rev:** Runner breaking ribbon at finish line **Edge:** Reeded and lettered

Date	Mintage	F12	VF20	XF40	MS60	MS63
2002	500	PF65 950				

KM# 1031 2 POUNDS
12.00 g., Bi-Metallic, 28.4 mm. **Ruler:** Elizabeth II **Subject:** 17th Commonwealth Games - Manchester, England **Obv:** Head with tiara right **Rev:** Runner breaking ribbon at finish line, national flag of England in circle behind athlete **Edge:** Reeded and lettered **Edge Lettering:** SPIRIT OF FRIENDSHIP MANCHESTER 2002

Date	Mintage	F12	VF20	XF40	MS60	MS63
2002	650,500	—	—	6.00	12.00	15.00
2002	—	PF63 16.00		PF65 18.00		

KM# 1032 2 POUNDS
12.00 g., Bi-Metallic, 28.4 mm. **Ruler:** Elizabeth II **Subject:** 17th Commonwealth Games - Manchester, England **Obv:** Head with tiara right **Rev:** Runner breaking ribbon at finish line, national flag of Scotland in circle behind athlete **Edge:** Reeded and lettered

Date	Mintage	F12	VF20	XF40	MS60	MS63
2002	771,750	—	—	6.00	12.00	15.00
2002	—	PF63 16.00		PF65 18.00		

KM# 1033 2 POUNDS
12.00 g., Bi-Metallic, 28.4 mm. **Ruler:** Elizabeth II **Subject:** 17th Commonwealth Games - Manchester, England **Obv:** Head with tiara right **Rev:** Runner breaking ribbon at finish line, national flag of Wales in circle behind athlete **Edge:** Reeded and lettered **Edge Lettering:** SPIRIT OF FRIENDSHIP MANCHESTER 2002

Date	Mintage	F12	VF20	XF40	MS60	MS63
2002	588,500	—	—	6.00	12.00	15.00
2002	—	PF63 16.00		PF65 18.00		

KM# 1034 2 POUNDS
12.00 g., Bi-Metallic, 28.4 mm. **Ruler:** Elizabeth II **Subject:** 17th Commonwealth Games - Manchester, England **Obv:** Head with tiara right **Rev:** Runner breaking ribbon at finish line, national flag of Northern Ireland in circle behind athlete **Edge:** Reeded and lettered **Edge Lettering:** SPIRIT OF FRIENDSHIP MANCHESTER 2002

Date	Mintage	F12	VF20	XF40	MS60	MS63
2002	485,500	—	—	6.00	12.00	15.00
2002	—	PF63 16.00		PF65 18.00		

KM# 1037 2 POUNDS
12.00 g., Bi-Metallic, 28.4 mm. **Ruler:** Elizabeth II **Subject:** 50th Anniversary of the Discovery of DNA **Obv:** Head with tiara right **Rev:** DNA Double Helix **Edge:** Reeded and inscribed **Edge Lettering:** DEOXYRIBONUCLEIC ACID

Date	Mintage	F12	VF20	XF40	MS60	MS63
ND(2003)	4,299,000	—	—	6.00	12.00	15.00
ND(2003)	43,513	PF63 16.00		PF65 18.00		

KM# 1037a 2 POUNDS
12.00 g., 0.925 Silver 0.3546 oz. ASW, 28.4 mm. **Ruler:** Elizabeth II **Obv:** Head with tiara right **Rev:** DNA Double Helix **Edge:** Reeded and lettered

Date	Mintage	F12	VF20	XF40	MS60	MS63
ND(2003)	11,204	PF63 35.00				

Note: Also exists as a Piefort, P42

KM# 1037b 2 POUNDS
15.98 g., 0.9167 Gold 0.4679 oz. AGW, 28.4 mm. **Ruler:** Elizabeth II **Obv:** Head with tiara right **Rev:** DNA Double Helix **Edge:** Reeded and lettered

Date	Mintage	F12	VF20	XF40	MS60	MS63
ND2003	1,500	PF63 900				

KM# 1049a 2 POUNDS
12.00 g., 0.925 Silver 0.3546 oz. ASW, 28.4 mm. **Ruler:** Elizabeth II **Obv:** Head with tiara right **Rev:** First steam locomotive **Rev. Legend:** 2004 R. TREVITHICK 1804 INVENTION-INDUSTRY-PROGRESS **Edge:** Incuse railway line motif

Date	Mintage	F12	VF20	XF40	MS60	MS63
2004	19,233	PF63 35.00				
2004	1,923	—	—			50.00

Note: Also exists as a Piefort, P45

KM# 1049b 2 POUNDS
15.98 g., 0.9166 Gold 0.4679 oz. AGW, 28.4 mm. **Ruler:** Elizabeth II **Obv:** Head with tiara right **Rev:** First steam locomotive **Rev. Legend:** 2004 R. TREVITHICK 1804 INVENTION-INDUSTRY-PROGRESS **Edge:** Incuse railway line motif

Date	Mintage	F12	VF20	XF40	MS60	MS63
2004	1,500	PF63 900				

KM# 1049 2 POUNDS
12.00 g., Bi-Metallic, 28.4 mm. **Ruler:** Elizabeth II **Subject:** Richard Trevithick, Inventor of the First Steam Locomotive **Obv:** Head with tiara right **Rev:** First steam locomotive **Rev. Legend:** 2004 R. TREVITHICK 1804 INVENTION-INDUSTRY-PROGRESS **Edge:** Incuse railway line motif

Date	Mintage	F12	VF20	XF40	MS60	MS63
2004	5,004,500	—	—	6.00	12.00	15.00
2004	35,020	PF63 16.00		PF65 18.00		

KM# 1052 2 POUNDS
12.00 g., Bi-Metallic, 28.4 mm. **Ruler:** Elizabeth II **Subject:** 400th Anniversary - The Gunpowder Plot **Obv:** Head with tiara right **Rev:** Circular design of Royal scepters, swords and crosiers **Edge:** Reeded and lettered **Edge Lettering:** REMEMBER REMEMBER THE FIFTH OF NOVEMBER

Date	Mintage	F12	VF20	XF40	MS60	MS63
ND-2005	5,140,500	—	—	6.00	12.00	15.00
ND-2005	40,563	PF63 16.00		PF65 18.00		

Note: Also exists as a Piefort, P46

KM# 1056 2 POUNDS
Bi-Metallic, 28.4 mm. **Ruler:** Elizabeth II **Subject:** 60th Anniversary of the End of WW II **Obv:** Head with tiara right **Rev:** St. Paul's Cathedral amid search light beams **Edge:** Reeded and lettered **Edge Lettering:** IN VICTORY MAGNANIMITY IN PEACE GOODWILL

Date	Mintage	F12	VF20	XF40	MS60	MS63
ND (2005)	10,191,000	—	—	6.00	12.00	15.00

KM# 1056a 2 POUNDS
12.00 g., 0.925 Silver 0.3546 oz. ASW, 28.4 mm. **Ruler:** Elizabeth II **Subject:** 60th Anniversary of the End of WWII **Obv:** Crowned head right **Rev:** St. Paul's Cathedral amid search light beams **Edge:** Reeded and lettered **Edge Lettering:** IN VICTORY MAGNANIMITY IN PEACE GOODWILL

Date	Mintage	F12	VF20	XF40	MS60	MS63
ND-2005	21,734	PF63 35.00				

Note: Also exists as a Piefort, P49

KM# 1056b 2 POUNDS
15.97 g., 0.9167 Gold 0.4676 oz. AGW, 28.4 mm. **Ruler:** Elizabeth II **Subject:** 60th Anniversary of the End of WWII **Obv:** Crowned head right **Rev:** St. Paul's Cathedral amid search light beams **Edge:** Reeded and lettered **Edge Lettering:** IN VICTORY MAGNANIMITY IN PEACE GOODWILL

Date	Mintage	F12	VF20	XF40	MS60	MS63
ND-2005	2,924	PF63 900				

KM# 1060a 2 POUNDS
12.00 g., 0.925 Silver 0.3546 oz. ASW, 28.4 mm. **Ruler:** Elizabeth II **Subject:** Brunel's 200th Birthday **Obv:** Head with tiara right **Rev:** Brunel and gears

Date	Mintage	F12	VF20	XF40	MS60	MS63
2006	—	PF63 55.00				

Note: Also exists as a Piefort, P56

KM# 1060 2 POUNDS
12.00 g., Bi-Metallic, 28.4 mm. **Ruler:** Elizabeth II **Subject:** 200th Birthday of Engineer Isambard Kingdom Brunel **Obv:** Head with tiara right **Rev:** Isambard Brunel **Edge Lettering:** 1806-1859 ISAMBARD KINGDOM BRUNEL ENGINEER

Date	Mintage	F12	VF20	XF40	MS60	MS63
2006	7,925,250	—	—	16.00	20.00	
2006	Est. 50000	PF63 22.00	PF65 24.00			

KM# 1061 2 POUNDS
12.00 g., Bi-Metallic, 28.4 mm. **Ruler:** Elizabeth II **Subject:** Engineering Achievements of Isambard Kingdom Brunel **Obv:** Head with tiara right **Rev:** Paddington Station structural supports **Edge Lettering:** SO MANY IRONS IN THE FIRE

Date	Mintage	F12	VF20	XF40	MS60	MS63
2006	7,452,250	—	—	16.00	20.00	
2006	Est. 50000	PF63 22.00	PF65 24.00			

KM# 1060b 2 POUNDS
15.98 g., 0.916 Gold 0.4676 oz. AGW, 28.4 mm. **Ruler:** Elizabeth II **Subject:** Brunel's 200th Birthday **Obv:** Head with tiara right **Rev:** Brunel and gears

Date	Mintage	F12	VF20	XF40	MS60	MS63
2006	—	PF63 900				

KM# 1061a 2 POUNDS
12.00 g., 0.925 Silver 0.3546 oz. ASW, 28.4 mm. **Ruler:** Elizabeth II **Subject:** Brunel's engineering achievements **Obv:** Head with tiara right **Rev:** Archways

Date	Mintage	F12	VF20	XF40	MS60	MS63
2006	—	PF63 55.00				

Note: Also exists as a Piefort, P57

KM# 1061b 2 POUNDS
15.98 g., 0.916 Gold 0.4676 oz. AGW, 28.4 mm. **Ruler:** Elizabeth II **Subject:** Brunel's engineering achievements **Obv:** Head with tiara right **Rev:** Archways

Date	Mintage	F12	VF20	XF40	MS60	MS63
2006	—	PF63 900				

KM# 1075 2 POUNDS
12.00 g., Bi-Metallic, 28.4 mm. **Ruler:** Elizabeth II **Subject:** 200th Anniversary of the Abolition of the Slave Trade **Obv:** Bust right **Rev:** Chain crossing 1807 date **Edge:** Reeded and lettered **Edge Lettering:** AM I NOT A MAN AND A BROTHER

Date	Mintage	F12	VF20	XF40	MS60	MS63
2007	8,445,000	—	—	6.00	12.50	15.00
2007	Est. 50000	PF63 16.00	PF65 18.00			

KM# 1075a 2 POUNDS
12.00 g., 0.925 Silver 0.3546 oz. ASW, 28.4 mm. **Ruler:** Elizabeth II **Subject:** Abolition of the Slave Trade **Obv:** Elizabeth II right **Rev:** Zero in 1807 date as a broken chain link **Edge:** Reeded and lettered **Edge Lettering:** AM I NOT A MAN AND A BROTHER

Date	Mintage	F12	VF20	XF40	MS60	MS63
2007	7,095	PF63 55.00				

Note: Also exists as a Piefort, P61

KM# 1075b 2 POUNDS
15.97 g., 0.9166 Gold 0.4676 oz. AGW, 28.4 mm. **Ruler:** Elizabeth II **Subject:** Abolition of the Slave Trade **Obv:** Head with tiara right **Rev:** Zero in 1807 date as a broken chain link **Edge:** Reeded and lettered **Edge Lettering:** AM I NOT A MAN AND A BROTHER

Date	Mintage	F12	VF20	XF40	MS60	MS63
2007	1,000	PF63 900				

KM# 1076 2 POUNDS
12.00 g., Bi-Metallic, 28.4 mm. **Ruler:** Elizabeth II **Subject:** 300th Anniversary of the Act of Union of England and Scotland **Obv:** Head with tiara right **Rev:** Combination of British and Scottish arms **Edge:** Reeded and lettered **Edge Lettering:** UNITED INTO ONE KINGDOM

Date	Mintage	F12	VF20	XF40	MS60	MS63
2007	7,545,000	—	—	6.00	12.50	15.00
2007	Est. 50000	PF63 16.00	PF65 18.00			

KM# 1076a 2 POUNDS
12.00 g., 0.925 Silver 0.3546 oz. ASW, 28.4 mm. **Ruler:** Elizabeth II **Subject:** 300th Anniv. Union of Scotland and England **Obv:** Head with tiara right **Rev:** Combined English and Scottish arms **Edge:** Reeded and lettered

Date	Mintage	F12	VF20	XF40	MS60	MS63
2007	8,310	PF63 55.00				

Note: Also exists as a Piefort, P62

KM# 1076b 2 POUNDS
15.98 g., 0.9166 Gold 0.4679 oz. AGW, 28.4 mm. **Ruler:** Elizabeth II **Subject:** 300th Anniv. Union of Scotland and England **Obv:** Head with tiara right **Rev:** Combined English and Scottish arms **Edge:** Reeded and lettered

Date	Mintage	F12	VF20	XF40	MS60	MS63
2007	750	PF63 900				

KM# 1106 2 POUNDS
12.00 g., Bi-Metallic, 28.4 mm. **Ruler:** Elizabeth II **Subject:** Beijing - London Olympic Flag handoff **Obv:** Head with tiara right **Rev:** London 2012 Games Flag hand off **Edge Lettering:** I CALL UPON THE YOUTH OF THE WORLD

Date	Mintage	F12	VF20	XF40	MS60	MS63
2008	Est. 250000	PF63 45.00				
2008	918,000	—	—	—	18.00	22.00

KM# 1106a 2 POUNDS
12.00 g., 0.925 Silver 0.3546 oz. ASW, 28.4 mm. **Ruler:** Elizabeth II **Obv:** Head with tiara right **Rev:** Handoff of the Olympic Flag

Date	Mintage	F12	VF20	XF40	MS60	MS63
2008	—	PF63 55.00				

Note: Also exists as a Piefort, P65

KM# 1106b 2 POUNDS
15.98 g., 0.916 Gold 0.4676 oz. AGW, 28.4 mm. **Ruler:** Elizabeth II **Subject:** Countdown to 2010 London Olympics **Obv:** Head right **Rev:** Handoff of the Olympic flag **Edge Lettering:** I CALL UPON THE YOUTH OF THE WORLD

Date	Mintage	F12	VF20	XF40	MS60	MS63
2008	3,000	PF63 875				

KM# 1105 2 POUNDS
12.00 g., Bi-Metallic, 28.4 mm. **Ruler:** Elizabeth II **Subject:** London 1908 - Olympics **Obv:** Head with tiara right **Rev:** Sprint track **Edge:** Lettered and reeded **Edge Lettering:** THE 4TH OLYMPIAD LONDON

Date	Mintage	F12	VF20	XF40	MS60	MS63
2008	910,000	—	—	6.00	15.00	12.50
2008	—	PF63 15.00	PF65 17.00			

KM# 1115 2 POUNDS
12.00 g., Bi-Metallic, 28.4 mm. **Ruler:** Elizabeth II **Subject:** Charles Darwin, 200th Anniversary of Birth **Obv:** Head with tiara right **Rev:** Darwin and ape heads facing **Edge Lettering:** ON THE ORIGIN OF SPECIES 1859

Date	Mintage	F12	VF20	XF40	MS60	MS63
2009	—	PF63 25.00				
2009	3,903,000	—	—	—	16.00	20.00

KM# 1115a 2 POUNDS
12.00 g., 0.925 Silver 0.3546 oz. ASW, 28.4 mm. **Ruler:** Elizabeth II **Subject:** Charles Darwin, 200th Anniversary of Brith **Obv:** Head with tiara right **Rev:** Darwin and ape heads facing

Date	Mintage	F12	VF20	XF40	MS60	MS63
2009	—	PF63 55.00				

Note: Also exists as a Piefort, P66

KM# 1115b 2 POUNDS
15.98 g., 0.916 Gold 0.4676 oz. AGW, 28.4 mm. **Ruler:** Elizabeth II **Subject:** Charles Darwin, 200th Anniversary of Birth **Obv:** Head with tiara right **Rev:** Darwin and ape heads facing

Date	Mintage	F12	VF20	XF40	MS60	MS63
2009	—	PF63 900				

KM# 1116 2 POUNDS
12.00 g., Bi-Metallic, 28.4 mm. **Ruler:** Elizabeth II **Subject:** Robert Burns, 250th Anniversary of Birth **Obv:** Head with tiara right **Rev:** Text **Edge:** Reeded and lettered **Edge Lettering:** SHOULD AULD ACQUAINTANCE BE FORGOT

Date	Mintage	F12	VF20	XF40	MS60	MS63
2009	—	PF63 25.00				
2009	3,253,000	—	—	—	16.00	20.00

KM# 1116a 2 POUNDS
12.00 g., 0.925 Silver 0.3546 oz. ASW, 28.4 mm. **Ruler:** Elizabeth II **Subject:** Robert Burns, 250th Anniversary of Birth **Obv:** Head with tiara right **Rev:** Text

Date	Mintage	F12	VF20	XF40	MS60	MS63
2009	—	PF63 55.00				

Note: Also exists as a Piefort, P

KM# 1116b 2 POUNDS
15.97 g., 0.9167 Gold 0.4676 oz. AGW, 28.4 mm. **Ruler:** Elizabeth II **Subject:** Robert Burns, 250th Anniversary of Birth **Obv:** Head with tiara right **Rev:** Text

Date	Mintage	F12	VF20	XF40	MS60	MS63
2009	1,000	PF63 900				

KM# 1160 2 POUNDS
11.97 g., Bi-Metallic, 28.35 mm. **Ruler:** Elizabeth II **Subject:** Florence Nightingale, 100th Anniversary of Death **Obv:** Head with tiara right **Rev:** Hand taking pulse **Edge Lettering:** 150 YEARS OF NURSING

Date	Mintage	F12	VF20	XF40	MS60	MS63
2010	—	—	—	6.00	12.00	15.00
2010	—	PF63 16.00	PF65 18.00			

KM# 1199 2 POUNDS
11.97 g., Bi-Metallic, 28.4 mm. **Ruler:** Elizabeth II **Subject:** Mary Rose, 500th Anniversary of Birth **Obv:** Head with tiara right **Rev:** H.M.S. Mary Rose under sail **Edge Lettering:** YOUR NOBLEST SHIPPE 1511

Date	Mintage	F12	VF20	XF40	MS60	MS63
2011	—	—	—	6.00	12.00	15.00

KM# 1199b 2 POUNDS
15.98 g., 0.9166 Gold 0.4679 oz. AGW, 28.4 mm. **Ruler:** Elizabeth II **Subject:** Mary Rose, 500th Anniversary **Obv:** Head with tiara right **Rev:** H.M.S. Mary Rose under sail **Edge Lettering:** YOUR NOBLEST SHIPPE 1511

Date	Mintage	F12	VF20	XF40	MS60	MS63
2011	—	PF63 1,600				

KM# 1200 2 POUNDS
11.97 g., Bi-Metallic, 28.4 mm. **Ruler:** Elizabeth II **Subject:** King James Bible, 400th Anniversary **Obv:** Head in tiara right **Rev:** Lead type and printed page of bible text **Edge:** Reeded and lettered **Edge Lettering:** THE AUTHORIZED VERSION

Date	Mintage	F12	VF20	XF40	MS60	MS63
2011	—	—	—	6.00	12.00	15.00
2011	—	PF63 16.00	PF65 18.00			

KM# 1200a 2 POUNDS
12.00 g., 0.925 Silver 0.3546 oz. ASW, 28.4 mm. **Ruler:** Elizabeth II **Subject:** King James Bible, 500th Anniversary **Obv:** Head with tiara right **Rev:** Lead type and printed page

Date	Mintage	F12	VF20	XF40	MS60	MS63
2011	—	PF63 55.00				

Note: Also exists as a Piefort, P88

KM# 994a.1 2 POUNDS
12.00 g., 0.925 Silver 0.3546 oz. ASW, 28.35 mm. **Ruler:** Elizabeth II **Obv:** Head with tiara right **Rev:** Symbolic depictions of technological development

Date	Mintage	F12	VF20	XF40	MS60	MS63
2012	—	PF63 50.00				

KM# 1224 2 POUNDS
12.00 g., Bi-Metallic, 28.4 mm. **Ruler:** Elizabeth II **Rev:** Head of Charles Dickens left

Date	Mintage	F12	VF20	XF40	MS60	MS63
2012	—	—	—	6.00	12.00	15.00

KM# 1224a 2 POUNDS
12.00 g., 0.925 Silver 0.3546 oz. ASW, 28.4 mm. **Ruler:** Elizabeth II **Rev:** Head of Charles Dickens left

Date	Mintage	F12	VF20	XF40	MS60	MS63
2012	—	PF63 35.00				

KM# 1244 2 POUNDS
12.00 g., Bi-Metallic, 28.4 mm. **Ruler:** Elizabeth II **Subject:** Olympic flag handoff to Brazil - Rio, 2016 **Obv:** Head with tiara right **Rev:** UK and Brazil flags **Edge Lettering:** I CALL UPON THE YOUTH OF THE WORLD

Date	Mintage	F12	VF20	XF40	MS60	MS63
2012	—	—	—	6.00	12.50	15.00
2012	—	PF63 16.00	PF65 18.00			

KM# 1244a 2 POUNDS
12.00 g., 0.925 Bi-Metallic 0.3546 oz., 28.4 mm. **Ruler:** Elizabeth II

Date	Mintage	F12	VF20	XF40	MS60	MS63
2012	12,000	PF63 145				

KM# 1244b 2 POUNDS
15.97 g., 0.916 Gold 0.4673 oz. AGW, 28.4 mm. **Ruler:** Elizabeth II

Date	Mintage	F12	VF20	XF40	MS60	MS63
2012	1,200	PF65 2,250				

KM# 1239 2 POUNDS
12.00 g., Bi-Metallic, 28.4 mm. **Ruler:** Elizabeth II **Subject:** London Subway, 125th Anniversary **Obv:** Head with tiara right **Rev:** London Subway train in tube **Edge:** Linear representation of the Tube map

Date	Mintage	F12	VF20	XF40	MS60	MS63
2013	—	—	—	6.00	12.00	15.00
2013	—	PF63 16.00	PF65 18.00			

KM# 1239a 2 POUNDS
12.00 g., 0.925 Silver 0.3546 oz. ASW, 28.4 mm. **Ruler:** Elizabeth II **Obv:** Head with tiara right **Rev:** London Subway in tube **Edge:** Linear representation of the Tube map

Date	Mintage	F12	VF20	XF40	MS60	MS63
2013	12,000	PF63 75.00				

KM# 1239b 2 POUNDS
15.97 g., 0.9167 Gold 0.4676 oz. AGW, 28.4 mm. **Ruler:** Elizabeth II **Obv:** Head with tiara right **Rev:** London Subway train in tube **Edge:** Linear representation of the Tube map

Date	Mintage	F12	VF20	XF40	MS60	MS63
2013	960	PF65 1,600				

KM# 1240 2 POUNDS
12.00 g., Bi-Metallic, 28.4 mm. **Ruler:** Elizabeth II **Subject:** London Subway, 125th Anniversary **Obv:** Head with tiara right **Rev:** Underground logo **Edge Lettering:** MIND THE GAP

Date	Mintage	F12	VF20	XF40	MS60	MS63
2013	—	—	—	6.00	12.00	15.00
2013	—	PF63 16.00	PF65 18.00			

KM# 1240a 2 POUNDS
12.00 g., 0.925 Silver 0.3546 oz. ASW, 28.4 mm. **Ruler:** Elizabeth II **Obv:** Head with tiara right **Rev:** Underground logo **Edge Lettering:** MIND THE GAP

Date	Mintage	F12	VF20	XF40	MS60	MS63
2013	12,000	PF63 75.00				

KM# 1240b 2 POUNDS
15.97 g., 0.9167 Gold 0.4676 oz. AGW, 28.4 mm. **Ruler:** Elizabeth II **Obv:** Head with tiara right **Rev:** London Underground logo **Edge Lettering:** MIND THE GAP

Date	Mintage	F12	VF20	XF40	MS60	MS63
2013	960	PF65 1,600				

KM# 1241 2 POUNDS
12.00 g., Bi-Metallic, 28.4 mm. **Ruler:** Elizabeth II **Subject:** Anniversary of the Spade Guinea coinage of George III **Obv:** Head with tiara right **Rev:** Spade shield crowned **Edge Lettering:** WHAT IS A GUINEA? 'TIS A SPLENDID THING

Date	Mintage	F12	VF20	XF40	MS60	MS63
2013	—	—	—	6.00	12.00	15.00
2013	44,000	PF63 15.00	PF65 18.00			

KM# 1241a 2 POUNDS
12.00 g., 0.925 Silver 0.3546 oz. ASW, 28.4 mm. **Ruler:** Elizabeth II **Obv:** Head with tiara right **Rev:** Spade shield crowned **Edge Lettering:** WHAT IS A GUINEA? 'TIS A SPLENDID THING

Date	Mintage	F12	VF20	XF40	MS60	MS63
2013	2,013	PF63 55.00				

KM# 1015 5 POUNDS
28.28 g., Copper-Nickel, 38.6 mm. **Ruler:** Elizabeth II **Subject:** Centennial of Queen Victoria's death **Obv:** Head with tiara right **Rev:** Young portrait from stamp, within industrial "V **Edge:** Reeded

Date	Mintage	F12	VF20	XF40	MS60	MS63
2001	851,491	—	—	—	15.00	18.00
2001	—	PF63 20.00	PF65 22.00			

KM# 1015a 5 POUNDS
28.28 g., 0.925 Silver 0.8356 oz. ASW, 38.6 mm. **Ruler:** Elizabeth II **Subject:** Centennial of Queen Victoria **Obv:** Head with tiara right **Rev:** Queen Victoria's portrait within "V

Date	Mintage	F12	VF20	XF40	MS60	MS63
2001	—	PF63 50.00				

KM# 1015b 5 POUNDS
39.94 g., 0.9167 Gold 1.1696 oz. AGW **Ruler:** Elizabeth II **Subject:** Centennial of Queen Victoria **Obv:** Head with tiara right **Rev:** Queen Victoria's portrait within "V

Date	Mintage	F12	VF20	XF40	MS60	MS63
2001	1,000	PF63 2,100				

KM# 1024 5 POUNDS
28.28 g., Copper-Nickel, 38.6 mm. **Ruler:** Elizabeth II **Subject:** Queen's Golden Jubilee of Reign **Obv:** Crowned bust in royal garb right **Rev:** Queen on horse right **Edge:** Reeded

Date	Mintage	F12	VF20	XF40	MS60	MS63
2002	3,469,243	—	—	—	15.00	18.00
2002	—	PF63 20.00				

Note: Mintage figure includes KM#1035

KM# 1024a 5 POUNDS
28.28 g., 0.925 Silver 0.8356 oz. ASW, 38.6 mm. **Ruler:** Elizabeth II **Subject:** Queen's Golden Jubilee of Reign **Obv:** Crowned bust in royal garb right **Rev:** Queen on horse **Edge:** Reeded

Date	Mintage	F12	VF20	XF40	MS60	MS63
2002	—	PF63 50.00				

KM# 1024b 5 POUNDS
39.94 g., 0.9167 Gold 1.1696 oz. AGW, 38.6 mm. **Ruler:** Elizabeth II **Subject:** Queen's Golden Jubilee of Reign **Obv:** Crowned bust in royal garb right **Rev:** Queen on horse left **Edge:** Reeded

Date	Mintage	F12	VF20	XF40	MS60	MS63
2002	—	PF63 2,100				

KM# 1035a 5 POUNDS
28.28 g., Silver, 38.6 mm. **Ruler:** Elizabeth II **Subject:** Queen Mother **Obv:** Head with tiara right **Rev:** Queen Mother's portrait in wreath **Edge:** Reeded

Date	Mintage	F12	VF20	XF40	MS60	MS63
ND(2002)				PF63 50.00		

KM# 1035b 5 POUNDS
39.94 g., 0.9167 Gold 1.1696 oz. AGW, 38.6 mm. **Ruler:** Elizabeth II **Subject:** Queen Mother **Obv:** Head with tiara right **Rev:** Queen Mother's portrait in wreath **Edge:** Reeded

Date	Mintage	F12	VF20	XF40	MS60	MS63
ND(2002)	—			PF65 2,150		

KM# 1035 5 POUNDS
28.28 g., Copper-Nickel, 38.6 mm. **Ruler:** Elizabeth II **Subject:** Queen Mother **Obv:** Head with tiara right **Rev:** Queen Mother's portrait in wreath **Edge:** Reeded

Date	Mintage	F12	VF20	XF40	MS60	MS63
ND(2002)	—	—	—		15.00	18.00
ND(2002)	—	PF63 20.00				

Note: Mintage included with KM#1024.

KM# 1038 5 POUNDS
28.28 g., Copper-Nickel, 38.6 mm. **Ruler:** Elizabeth II **Subject:** Queen's Golden Jubilee **Obv:** Queen's stylized portrait **Rev:** Childlike lettering **Edge:** Reeded

Date	Mintage	F12	VF20	XF40	MS60	MS63
2003	1,307,147	—	—		15.00	18.00
2003	43,513	PF63 20.00	PF65 22.00			

KM# 1038a 5 POUNDS
28.28 g., 0.925 Silver 0.8356 oz. ASW, 38.6 mm. **Ruler:** Elizabeth II **Subject:** Queen's Golden Jubilee **Obv:** Stylized Queens portrait **Rev:** Childlike lettering **Edge:** Reeded

Date	Mintage	F12	VF20	XF40	MS60	MS63
2003	28,758	PF63 50.00				

KM# 1038b 5 POUNDS
39.94 g., 0.9166 Gold 1.1694 oz. AGW, 38.6 mm. **Ruler:** Elizabeth II **Subject:** Queen's Golden Jubilee **Obv:** Stylized Queens portrait **Rev:** Childlike lettering **Edge:** Reeded

Date	Mintage	F12	VF20	XF40	MS60	MS63
2003	1,896	PF63 2,100				

KM# 1055 5 POUNDS
28.28 g., Copper-Nickel, 38.6 mm. **Ruler:** Elizabeth II **Subject:** Entente Cordiale **Obv:** Head with tiara right **Rev:** Britannia and Marianne **Edge:** Reeded

Date	Mintage	F12	VF20	XF40	MS60	MS63
2004	1,205,594	—	—		15.00	18.00
2004	51,527	PF63 20.00	PF65 22.00			

KM# 1055a 5 POUNDS
28.28 g., 0.925 Silver 0.8356 oz. ASW, 38.6 mm. **Ruler:** Elizabeth II **Subject:** Entente Cordiale **Obv:** Head with tiara right **Rev:** Britannia and Marianne **Edge:** Reeded

Date	Mintage	F12	VF20	XF40	MS60	MS63
2004	11,295	PF63 50.00				

Note: Also exists as a Piefort, P47

KM# 1055b 5 POUNDS
39.94 g., 0.9167 Gold 1.1696 oz. AGW, 38.6 mm. **Ruler:** Elizabeth II **Subject:** Entente Cordiale **Obv:** Head with tiara right **Rev:** Britannia and Marianne **Edge:** Reeded

Date	Mintage	F12	VF20	XF40	MS60	MS63
2004	926	PF65 2,150				

KM# 1055c 5 POUNDS
94.20 g., 0.9995 Platinum 3.0076 oz. APW, 38.6 mm. **Ruler:** Elizabeth II **Subject:** Entente Cordiale **Obv:** Head with tiara right **Rev:** Britannia and Marianne **Edge:** Reeded

Date	Mintage	F12	VF20	XF40	MS60	MS63
2004	501	PF65 5,700				

KM# 1053 5 POUNDS
28.28 g., Copper-Nickel, 38.6 mm. **Ruler:** Elizabeth II **Subject:** Battle of Trafalgar **Obv:** Head with tiara right **Obv. Legend:** ELIZABETH • II D • G • REG • F • D **Rev:** HMS Victory and HMS Temeraire at Trafalgar **Rev. Legend:** TRAFALGAR **Edge:** Reeded

Date	Mintage	F12	VF20	XF40	MS60	MS63
2005	40,563	PF63 20.00	PF65 22.00			
2005	1,075,516	—	—	—	15.00	18.00

KM# 1053a 5 POUNDS
28.28 g., 0.925 Silver 0.8356 oz. ASW, 38.6 mm. **Ruler:** Elizabeth II **Subject:** Battle of Trafalgar **Obv:** Head with tiara right **Obv. Legend:** ELIZABETH • II D • G • REG • F • D **Rev:** Ships HMS Victory and Temeraire at Trafalgar **Rev. Legend:** TRAFALGAR **Edge:** Reeded

Date	Mintage	F12	VF20	XF40	MS60	MS63
2005	21,448	PF63 50.00				

Note: Also exists as a Piefort, P51

KM# 1053b 5 POUNDS
39.94 g., 0.9167 Gold 1.1696 oz. AGW, 38.6 mm. **Ruler:** Elizabeth II **Subject:** Battle of Trafalgar **Obv:** Head with tiara right **Obv. Legend:** ELIZABETH • II D • G • REG • F • D **Rev:** Ships HMS Victory and Temeraire at Trafalgar **Rev. Legend:** TRAFALGAR **Edge:** Reeded

Date	Mintage	F12	VF20	XF40	MS60	MS63
2005	1,805	PF63 2,000	PF65 2,100			

KM# 1054 5 POUNDS
28.28 g., Copper-Nickel, 38.6 mm. **Ruler:** Elizabeth II **Obv:** Head with tiara right **Obv. Legend:** ELIZABETH • II D • G • REG • F • D **Rev:** Uniformed facing 1/2 bust of Admiral Horatio Nelson **Rev. Legend:** HORATIO NELSON **Edge:** Reeded

Date	Mintage	F12	VF20	XF40	MS60	MS63
2005	40,563	PF63 20.00	PF65 22.00			
2005	—	—	—		15.00	18.00

Note: Mintage included with KM#1053b, 2005.

KM# 1054a 5 POUNDS
28.28 g., 0.925 Silver 0.8356 oz. ASW, 38.6 mm. **Ruler:** Elizabeth II **Obv:** Queen's head with tiara right **Obv. Legend:** ELIZABETH • II D • G • REG • F • D **Rev:** Uniformed facing 1/2 bust of Admiral Horatio Nelson **Rev. Legend:** HORATIO NELSON

Date	Mintage	F12	VF20	XF40	MS60	MS63
2005	12,852	PF63 50.00				

Note: Also exists as a Piefort, P52

KM# 1054b 5 POUNDS
39.94 g., 0.9167 Gold 1.1696 oz. AGW, 38.6 mm. **Ruler:** Elizabeth II **Subject:** Battle of Trafalgar **Obv:** Queen's head with tiara right **Obv. Legend:** ELIZABETH • II D • G • REG • F • D **Rev:** Uniformed facing 1/2 bust of Admiral Horatio Nelson **Rev. Legend:** HORATIO NELSON

Date	Mintage	F12	VF20	XF40	MS60	MS63
2005	1,700	PF63 2,000	PF65 2,100			

KM# 1062 5 POUNDS
28.28 g., Copper-Nickel, 38.6 mm. **Ruler:** Elizabeth II **Obv:** Head with tiara right **Rev:** Three bannered trumpets **Edge:** Reeded

Date	Mintage	F12	VF20	XF40	MS60	MS63
2006	Est. 50000	PF63 30.00	PF65 32.00			
2006	—	—	—		20.00	25.00

KM# 1062a 5 POUNDS
28.28 g., 0.925 Silver 0.8356 oz. ASW **Ruler:** Elizabeth II **Subject:** Queen's 80th Birthday Celebration **Obv:** Queens head right **Obv. Legend:** ELIZABETH • II D • G • REG • F • D **Rev:** Three bannered trumpets **Rev. Legend:** VIVAT REGINA **Edge:** Reeded

Date	Mintage	F12	VF20	XF40	MS60	MS63
2006	—	PF63 50.00				

Note: Also exists as a Piefort, P58

KM# 1062b 5 POUNDS
39.94 g., 0.9167 Gold 1.1696 oz. AGW, 38.6 mm. **Ruler:** Elizabeth II **Subject:** Queen's 80th Birthday Celebration **Obv:** Queen's head with tiara right **Obv. Legend:** ELIZABETH • II D • G • REG • F • D **Rev:** Three bannered trumpets **Rev. Legend:** VIVAT REGINA **Edge:** Reeded

Date	Mintage	F12	VF20	XF40	MS60	MS63
2006	—	PF65 2,150				

KM# 1077 5 POUNDS
28.28 g., Copper-Nickel, 38.6 mm. **Ruler:** Elizabeth II **Subject:** Queen's 60th Wedding Anniversary **Obv:** Conjoined busts of Queen Elizabeth II and Prince Philip **Rev:** Westminster Abbey's North Rose Window **Edge:** Reeded

Date	Mintage	F12	VF20	XF40	MS60	MS63
2007	Est. 50000	PF63 30.00	PF65 32.00			
2007	—	—	—	—	20.00	25.00

KM# 1077a 5 POUNDS
28.28 g., 0.925 Silver 0.8356 oz. ASW, 38.6 mm. **Ruler:** Elizabeth II **Subject:** 60th Wedding Anniversary **Obv:** Conjoined busts of Queen Elizabeth II and Prince Philip **Rev:** Westminster Abbey's North Rose Window **Edge Lettering:** MY STRENGTH AND STAY

Date	Mintage	F12	VF20	XF40	MS60	MS63
ND (2007)	Est. 35000	PF63 50.00				

Note: Also exists as a Piefort, P63

KM# 1077b 5 POUNDS
39.94 g., 0.9167 Gold 1.1696 oz. AGW, 28.4 mm. **Ruler:** Elizabeth II **Subject:** 60th Wedding Anniversary **Obv:** Conjoined busts of Queen Elizabeth II and Prince Philip **Rev:** Westminster Abbey's North Rose Window **Edge Lettering:** MY STRENGTH AND STAY

Date	Mintage	F12	VF20	XF40	MS60	MS63
ND (2007)	—	PF65 2,150				

Note: Also exists as a Piefort, P64

KM# 1103 5 POUNDS
28.28 g., Copper-Nickel, 38.6 mm. **Ruler:** Elizabeth II **Subject:** Charles, Prince of Wales 60th Birthday **Obv:** Head with tiara right **Rev:** Head right of Prince Charles

Date	Mintage	F12	VF20	XF40	MS60	MS63
2008	500,000				18.00	15.00
2008		PF63 20.00	PF65 22.00			

KM# 1103a 5 POUNDS
28.28 g., 0.925 Silver 0.8356 oz. ASW, 38.6 mm. **Ruler:** Elizabeth II **Subject:** Charles, Prince of Wales 60th Birthday **Obv:** Head with tiara right **Rev:** Head right of Prince Charles

Date	Mintage	F12	VF20	XF40	MS60	MS63
2008	10,398	PF63 50.00				

Note: Exists as a Piedfort, P113.

KM# 1104 5 POUNDS
28.28 g., Copper-Nickel, 38.6 mm. **Ruler:** Elizabeth II **Subject:** Elizabeth I Accession 1558-2008 **Obv:** Head with tiara right **Rev:** Bust of Elizabeth I

Date	Mintage	F12	VF20	XF40	MS60	MS63
2008	500,000	—	—	—	15.00	18.00
2008	—	PF63 20.00	PF65 22.00			

KM# 1104a 5 POUNDS
28.28 g., 0.925 Silver 0.8356 oz. ASW, 38.6 mm. **Ruler:** Elizabeth II **Subject:** Elizabeth I Accession 1558-2008 **Obv:** Head with tiara right **Rev:** Bust of Elizabeth I

Date	Mintage	F12	VF20	XF40	MS60	MS63
2008	7,446	PF63 2,100				

Note: Exists as a Piedfort, P67

KM# 1121 5 POUNDS
28.28 g., Copper-Nickel, 38.61 mm. **Ruler:** Elizabeth II **Subject:** Countdown to 2012 London Olympics **Obv:** Bust right **Rev:** Swimmer, stopwatch, 3 in center

Date	Mintage	F12	VF20	XF40	MS60	MS63
2009	—	PF63 30.00				
2009	500,000	—	—	—	20.00	25.00

KM# 1121a 5 POUNDS
28.28 g., 0.925 Silver 0.8356 oz. ASW, 38.61 mm. **Ruler:** Elizabeth II **Subject:** Countdown to the 2010 London Olympics **Obv:** Bust right **Rev:** Swimmer, stopwatch, 3 in center

Date	Mintage	F12	VF20	XF40	MS60	MS63
2009	30,000	PF63 50.00				

KM# 1118 5 POUNDS
28.28 g., Copper-Nickel, 38.6 mm. **Ruler:** Elizabeth II **Obv:** Head with tiara right **Rev:** Henry VIII standing, HR flanking

Date	Mintage	F12	VF20	XF40	MS60	MS63
2009		PF63 40.00				

KM# 1118a 5 POUNDS
28.28 g., 0.925 Silver 0.8356 oz. ASW, 38.6 mm. **Ruler:** Elizabeth II **Obv:** Head with tiara right **Rev:** Henry VIII standing, HR flanking

Date	Mintage	F12	VF20	XF40	MS60	MS63
2009	20,000	PF63 50.00				

Note: Also exists as a Piedfort, P70

KM# 1121b 5 POUNDS
39.94 g., 0.9167 Gold 1.1696 oz. AGW, 38.61 mm. **Ruler:** Elizabeth II **Subject:** Countdown to 2012 London Olympics **Rev:** 3 in large stopwatch, swimmer

Date	Mintage	F12	VF20	XF40	MS60	MS63
2009	—	PF65 2,100				

KM# 1140 5 POUNDS
28.28 g., 0.925 Silver 0.8356 oz. ASW, 38.6 mm. **Ruler:** Elizabeth II **Subject:** London Olympics, 2012 **Obv:** Head with tiara right **Rev:** Angel of the North, blue logo

Date	Mintage	F12	VF20	XF40	MS60	MS63
2009	95,000	PF63 50.00	PF65 55.00			

KM# 1141 5 POUNDS
28.28 g., 0.925 Silver 0.8356 oz. AGW, 38.6 mm. **Ruler:** Elizabeth II **Subject:** London Olympics, 2012 **Obv:** Head with tiara right **Rev:** Big Ben, blue logo

Date	Mintage	F12	VF20	XF40	MS60	MS63
2009	95,000	PF63 50.00	PF65 55.00			

KM# 1141a 5 POUNDS
28.28 g., Copper-Nickel, 38.6 mm. **Ruler:** Elizabeth II **Subject:** London Olympics, 2012 **Obv:** Head in tiara right **Rev:** Big Ben, blue logo

Date	Mintage	F12	VF20	XF40	MS60	MS63
2009	—	PF63 30.00				

KM# 1142 5 POUNDS
28.28 g., 0.925 Silver 0.8356 oz. ASW, 38.6 mm. **Ruler:** Elizabeth II **Subject:** London Olympics, 2012 **Obv:** Head with tiara right **Rev:** Flying Scotsman, blue logo

Date	Mintage	F12	VF20	XF40	MS60	MS63
2009	95,000	PF63 50.00	PF65 55.00			

KM# 1143 5 POUNDS
28.28 g., 0.925 Silver 0.8356 oz. ASW, 38.6 mm. **Ruler:** Elizabeth II **Subject:** London Olympics, 2012 **Obv:** Head with tiara right **Rev:** Globe Theatre, blue logo

Date	Mintage	F12	VF20	XF40	MS60	MS63
2009	95,000	PF63 50.00	PF65 55.00			

KM# 1144 5 POUNDS
28.28 g., 0.925 Silver 0.8356 oz. ASW, 38.6 mm. **Ruler:** Elizabeth II **Subject:** London Olympics, 2012 **Obv:** Head with tiara right **Rev:** Man in leg braces, Issac Newton quote, blue logo

Date	Mintage	F12	VF20	XF40	MS60	MS63
2009	95,000	PF63 50.00	PF65 55.00			

KM# 1145 5 POUNDS
28.28 g., 0.925 Silver 0.8356 oz. ASW, 38.6 mm. **Ruler:** Elizabeth II **Series:** London Olympics, 2012 **Obv:** Head with tiara right **Rev:** Stonehenge, blue logo

Date	Mintage	F12	VF20	XF40	MS60	MS63
2009	95,000	PF63 50.00	PF65 55.00			

KM# 1139 5 POUNDS
28.28 g., Copper-Nickel, 38.6 mm. **Ruler:** Elizabeth II **Obv:** Head with tiara right **Rev:** Runners and stopwatch, 2 in center

Date	Mintage	F12	VF20	XF40	MS60	MS63
2010	—	PF63 30.00	PF65 32.00			
2010	500,000				20.00	25.00

KM# 1139a 5 POUNDS
28.28 g., 0.925 Silver 0.8356 oz. ASW, 38.6 mm. **Ruler:** Elizabeth II **Obv:** Head with tiara right **Rev:** Runners and stopwatch, 2 in center

Date	Mintage	F12	VF20	XF40	MS60	MS63
2010		PF63 50.00				

KM# 1139b 5 POUNDS
39.94 g., 0.9167 Gold 1.1696 oz. AGW, 38.61 mm. **Ruler:** Elizabeth II **Subject:** Countdown to the 2012 London Olympics **Obv:** Head with tiara right **Rev:** Runners and stopwatch, 2 in center

Date	Mintage	F12	VF20	XF40	MS60	MS63
2010	—	PF65 2,100				

KM# 1146 5 POUNDS
28.28 g., 0.925 Silver 0.8356 oz. ASW, 38.6 mm. **Ruler:** Elizabeth II **Subject:** London Olympics, 2012 **Obv:** Head with tiara right **Rev:** Churchill figure and quote, blue logo

Date	Mintage	F12	VF20	XF40	MS60	MS63
2010	95,000	PF63 50.00	PF65 55.00			

KM# 1146a 5 POUNDS
28.28 g., Copper-Nickel, 38.6 mm. **Ruler:** Elizabeth II **Subject:** London Olympics, 2012 **Obv:** Head with tiara right **Rev:** Churchill figure and quote, blue logo

Date	Mintage	F12	VF20	XF40	MS60	MS63
2010	—	PF63 40.00				

KM# 1147 5 POUNDS
28.28 g., 0.925 Silver 0.8356 oz. ASW, 38.6 mm. **Ruler:** Elizabeth II **Subject:** London Olympics, 2012 **Obv:** Head with tiara right **Rev:** Unity, flora, blue logo

Date	Mintage	F12	VF20	XF40	MS60	MS63
2010	95,000	PF63 50.00	PF65 55.00			

KM# 1148 5 POUNDS
28.28 g., 0.999 Silver 0.9025 oz. ASW, 38.6 mm. **Ruler:** Elizabeth II **Subject:** London Olympics, 2012 **Obv:** Head with tiara right **Rev:** Buckingham Palace and the Mall, blue logo

Date	Mintage	F12	VF20	XF40	MS60	MS63
2010	95,000	PF63 50.00	PF65 55.00			

KM# 1148a 5 POUNDS
28.28 g., Copper-Nickel, 38.6 mm. **Ruler:** Elizabeth II **Subject:** London Olympics, 2012 **Obv:** Head with tiara right **Rev:** Buckingham Palace and the Mall, blue logo

Date	Mintage	F12	VF20	XF40	MS60	MS63
2010	—	PF63 40.00				

KM# 1149 5 POUNDS
28.28 g., 0.925 Silver 0.8356 oz. ASW, 38.6 mm. **Ruler:** Elizabeth II **Subject:** London Olympics, 2012 **Obv:** Head with tiara right **Rev:** Musical instruments, blue logo

Date	Mintage	F12	VF20	XF40	MS60	MS63
2010	95,000	PF63 50.00	PF65 55.00			

KM# 1151 5 POUNDS
28.28 g., Copper-Nickel, 38.6 mm. **Ruler:** Elizabeth II **Subject:** Restoration of the Monarchy, 1660 **Obv:** Head with tiara right

Date	Mintage	F12	VF20	XF40	MS60	MS63
2010	—	—	—	—	20.00	25.00

KM# 1151a 5 POUNDS
28.28 g., 0.925 Silver 0.8356 oz. ASW, 38.6 mm. **Ruler:** Elizabeth II **Subject:** Restoration of the Monarchy, 1660 **Obv:** Head with tiara right

Date	Mintage	F12	VF20	XF40	MS60	MS63
2010		PF63 50.00				

Note: Also exists as a Piedfort, P114

KM# 1151b 5 POUNDS
39.94 g., 0.9167 Gold 1.1696 oz. AGW, 38.61 mm. **Ruler:** Elizabeth II **Subject:** Restoration of the Monarchy, 1660 **Obv:** Head with tiara right **Rev:** Crown above wreath

Date	Mintage	F12	VF20	XF40	MS60	MS63
2010	—	PF65 2,100				

KM# 1152 5 POUNDS
28.28 g., 0.925 Silver 0.8356 oz. ASW, 38.6 mm. **Ruler:** Elizabeth II **Subject:** London Olympics, 2012 **Obv:** Head with tiara right **Rev:** Giants Causeway, orange logo

Date	Mintage	F12	VF20	XF40	MS60	MS63
2010	95,000	PF63 50.00	PF65 55.00			

KM# 1153 5 POUNDS
28.28 g., 0.925 Silver 0.8356 oz. ASW, 38.6 mm. **Ruler:** Elizabeth II **Subject:** London Olympics, 2012 **Obv:** Head with tiara right **Rev:** Coastline, orange logo

Date	Mintage	F12	VF20	XF40	MS60	MS63
2010	95,000	PF63 50.00	PF65 55.00			

KM# 1154 5 POUNDS
28.28 g., 0.925 Silver 0.8356 oz. ASW, 38.6 mm. **Ruler:** Elizabeth II **Subject:** London Olympics, 2012 **Obv:** Head with tiara right **Rev:** River Thames, orange logo

Date	Mintage	F12	VF20	XF40	MS60	MS63
2010	95,000	PF63 50.00	PF65 55.00			

KM# 1155 5 POUNDS
28.28 g., 0.925 Silver 0.8356 oz. ASW, 38.6 mm. **Ruler:** Elizabeth II **Subject:** London Olympics, 2012 **Obv:** Head with tiara right **Rev:** British flora -oak leaves and acorn, orange logo

Date	Mintage	F12	VF20	XF40	MS60	MS63
2010	95,000	PF63 50.00	PF65 55.00			

KM# 1156 5 POUNDS
28.28 g., 0.925 Silver 0.8356 oz. ASW, 38.6 mm. **Ruler:** Elizabeth II **Subject:** London Olympics, 2012 **Obv:** Head with tiara right **Rev:** Owl, orange logo

Date	Mintage	F12	VF20	XF40	MS60	MS63
2010	95,000	**PF63** 50.00	**PF65** 55.00			

KM# 1157 5 POUNDS
28.28 g., 0.925 Silver 0.8356 oz. ASW, 38.6 mm. **Ruler:** Elizabeth II **Subject:** London Olympics, 2012 **Obv:** Head with tiara right **Rev:** Weather vane, orange logo

Date	Mintage	F12	VF20	XF40	MS60	MS63
2010	95,000	**PF63** 50.00	**PF65** 55.00			

KM# 1260 5 POUNDS
28.28 g., 0.925 Silver 0.8356 oz. ASW, 38.6 mm. **Ruler:** Elizabeth II **Subject:** 2012 Summer Olympics, London **Obv:** Head with tiara right **Rev:** Beefeaters

Date	Mintage	F12	VF20	XF40	MS60	MS63
2010	—	**PF63** 50.00				

KM# 1261 5 POUNDS
28.28 g., 0.925 Silver 0.8356 oz. ASW, 38.6 mm. **Ruler:** Elizabeth II **Subject:** 2012 Summer Olympics, London **Obv:** Head with tiara right **Rev:** Rabbit

Date	Mintage	F12	VF20	XF40	MS60	MS63
2013 (2010)	—	**PF63** 50.00				

KM# 1201 5 POUNDS
28.28 g., Copper-Nickel, 38.6 mm. **Ruler:** Elizabeth II **Subject:** Prince Philip's 90th Birthday **Obv:** Head with tiara right **Rev:** Large head of Prince Philip in profile right

Date	Mintage	F12	VF20	XF40	MS60	MS63
2011	—	**PF63** 30.00	**PF65** 32.00			
2011	—	—	—	—	20.00	25.00

KM# 1201a 5 POUNDS
28.28 g., 0.925 Silver 0.8356 oz. ASW, 38.6 mm. **Ruler:** Elizabeth II **Subject:** Prince Philip, 90th Birthday

Date	Mintage	F12	VF20	XF40	MS60	MS63
2011	—	**PF63** 50.00				

Note: Also exists as a Piedfort, P89

KM# 1201b 5 POUNDS
39.94 g., 0.9167 Gold 1.1696 oz. AGW, 38.61 mm. **Ruler:** Elizabeth II **Subject:** Prince Philip's 90th Birthday **Obv:** Head with tiara right **Rev:** Large head of Prince Philip in profile right

Date	Mintage	F12	VF20	XF40	MS60	MS63
2011	—	**PF65** 2,100				

KM# 1202 5 POUNDS
28.28 g., Copper-Nickel, 38.6 mm. **Ruler:** Elizabeth II **Subject:** Countdown to London Olympics, 2012 **Obv:** Head with tiara right **Rev:** 1 between wheels of cyclist traveling left

Date	Mintage	F12	VF20	XF40	MS60	MS63
2011	—	**PF63** 30.00	**PF65** 32.00			
2011	—	—	—	—	20.00	25.00

KM# 1202a 5 POUNDS
28.28 g., 0.925 Silver 0.8356 oz. ASW, 38.6 mm. **Ruler:** Elizabeth II **Subject:** Countdown to London Olympics, 2012 **Obv:** Head with tiara right **Rev:** 1 between wheels of cyclist traveling left

Date	Mintage	F12	VF20	XF40	MS60	MS63
2011	—	**PF63** 50.00				

KM# 1203 5 POUNDS
28.28 g., Copper-Nickel, 38.6 mm. **Ruler:** Elizabeth II **Subject:** Royal Wedding - William and Katherine **Rev:** Heads facing

Date	Mintage	F12	VF20	XF40	MS60	MS63
2011	—	—	—	—	20.00	25.00

KM# 1203a 5 POUNDS
28.28 g., 0.925 Silver 0.8356 oz. ASW, 38.6 mm. **Ruler:** Elizabeth II **Subject:** Royal Wedding - William and Catherine

Date	Mintage	F12	VF20	XF40	MS60	MS63
2011	—	**PF63** 50.00				

KM# 1216 5 POUNDS
28.28 g., Copper-Nickel, 38.61 mm. **Ruler:** Elizabeth II **Subject:** Elizabeth's 60th anniversary of reign **Obv:** Bust with tiara in robes of the Garter, right **Rev:** Young head portrait right

Date	Mintage	F12	VF20	XF40	MS60	MS63
2012	—	**PF63** 25.00				

KM# 1242a 5 POUNDS
28.28 g., 0.925 Silver 0.8356 oz. ASW, 38.61 mm. **Ruler:** Elizabeth II **Subject:** Elizabeth's coronation, 60th Anniversary **Obv:** Head with tiara right **Rev:** State Crown

Date	Mintage	F12	VF20	XF40	MS60	MS63
2013	60,000	**PF63** 125				

KM# 1242b 5 POUNDS
28.28 g., 0.999 Silver 0.9025 oz. ASW, 38.61 mm. **Ruler:** Elizabeth II **Subject:** Elizabeth's coronation, 60th Anniversary **Obv:** Head with tiara right **Rev:** State Crown

Date	Mintage	F12	VF20	XF40	MS60	MS63
2013	12,500	**PF63** 150				

KM# 1242c 5 POUNDS
39.94 g., 0.9167 Gold 1.1696 oz. AGW, 38.61 mm. **Ruler:** Elizabeth II **Subject:** Elizabeth's coronation, 60th Anniversary **Obv:** Head with tiara right **Rev:** State Crown

Date	Mintage	F12	VF20	XF40	MS60	MS63
2013	2,060	**PF65** 3,500				

KM# 1242d 5 POUNDS
94.20 g., 0.9995 Platinum 3.0076 oz. APW, 38.61 mm. **Ruler:** Elizabeth II **Subject:** Elizabeth's coronation, 60th Anniversary **Obv:** Head with tiara right **Rev:** State Crown

Date	Mintage	F12	VF20	XF40	MS60	MS63
2013	150	**PF65** 9,000				

KM# 1242 5 POUNDS
28.28 g., Copper-Nickel, 38.61 mm. **Ruler:** Elizabeth II **Subject:** Elizabeth's coronation, 60th Anniversary **Obv:** Head with tiara right **Rev:** State Crown

Date	Mintage	F12	VF20	XF40	MS60	MS63
2013	—	—	—	—	25.00	
2013	44,000	**PF63** 35.00	**PF65** 37.00			

KM# 1247 5 POUNDS
28.28 g., 0.925 Silver 0.8356 oz. ASW, 38.61 mm. **Ruler:** Elizabeth II **Obv:** Young Head Portrait **Rev:** Royal Arms

Date	Mintage	F12	VF20	XF40	MS60	MS63
2013	Est. 5000	**PF63** 150				

KM# 1247a 5 POUNDS
39.95 g., 0.9167 Gold 1.1698 oz. AGW, 38.61 mm. **Ruler:** Elizabeth II **Obv:** Young bust right **Rev:** Royal Arms

Date	Mintage	F12	VF20	XF40	MS60	MS63
2013	Est. 500	**PF65** 3,000				

KM# 1248 5 POUNDS
28.28 g., 0.925 Silver 0.8356 oz. ASW, 38.61 mm. **Ruler:**
Elizabeth II **Obv:** Bust right by Arnold Machin **Rev:** Royal Arms

Date	Mintage	F12	VF20	XF40	MS60	MS63
2013	Est. 5000	PF63 150				

KM# 1248a 5 POUNDS
39.95 g., 0.9167 Gold 1.1698 oz. AGW, 38.61 mm. **Ruler:**
Elizabeth II **Obv:** Bust with tiara right **Rev:** Royal Arms

Date	Mintage	F12	VF20	XF40	MS60	MS63
2013	Est. 500	PF65 3,000				

KM# 1249 5 POUNDS
28.28 g., 0.925 Silver 0.8356 oz. ASW, 38.61 mm. **Ruler:**
Elizabeth II **Obv:** Head with crown right **Rev:** Royal Arms

Date	Mintage	F12	VF20	XF40	MS60	MS63
2013	—	PF63 150				

KM# 1249a 5 POUNDS
39.95 g., 0.9167 Gold 1.1698 oz. AGW, 38.61 mm. **Ruler:**
Elizabeth II **Obv:** Head with crown right **Rev:** Royal Arms

Date	Mintage	F12	VF20	XF40	MS60	MS63
2013	—	PF65 3,000				

KM# 1250 5 POUNDS
28.28 g., 0.925 Silver 0.8356 oz. ASW, 38.61 mm. **Ruler:**
Elizabeth II **Obv:** Head with tiara right **Rev:** Royal Arms

Date	Mintage	F12	VF20	XF40	MS60	MS63
2013	Est. 5000	PF63 150				

KM# 1250a 5 POUNDS
39.94 g., 0.9167 Gold 1.1696 oz. AGW, 38.61 mm. **Ruler:**
Elizabeth II **Obv:** Head with tiara right **Rev:** Royal Arms

Date	Mintage	F12	VF20	XF40	MS60	MS63
2013	Est. 500	PF65 3,000				

KM# 1251 5 POUNDS
28.28 g., 0.925 Silver 0.8356 oz. ASW, 38.61 mm. **Ruler:**
Elizabeth II **Subject:** Birth of HRH George Alexander Louis,
son of William and Katherine **Obv:** Head in tiara right **Rev:** St.
George slaying dragon

Date	Mintage	F12	VF20	XF40	MS60	MS63
2013	10,000	PF63 185				

KM# 1259 5 POUNDS
28.28 g., Copper-Nickel, 38.61 mm. **Ruler:** Elizabeth II
Subject: Christening of Prince George

Date	Mintage	F12	VF20	XF40	MS60	MS63
2013	—	—	—	—	—	25.00

KM# 1227 10 POUNDS
155.50 g., 0.999 Silver 4.9623 oz. ASW **Ruler:** Elizabeth II
Obv: Head with tiara right **Rev:** Pegasus right

Date	Mintage	F12	VF20	XF40	MS60	MS63
2012	—	PF63 225				

KM# 1227a 10 POUNDS
155.50 g., 0.999 Gold 4.9623 oz. AGW **Ruler:** Elizabeth II **Obv:**
Head with tiara right **Rev:** Pegasus right

Date	Mintage	F12	VF20	XF40	MS60	MS63
2012	—	PF65 9,500				

KM# 1264 10 POUNDS
155.60 g., Silver, 65 mm. **Ruler:** Elizabeth II **Rev:** Coronation
insignia and Westminster Abbey

Date	Mintage	F12	VF20	XF40	MS60	MS63
2013	Est. 1953	PF63 525				

KM# 1163 25 POUNDS
8.51 g., 0.9167 Gold 0.2492 oz. AGW, 22 mm. **Ruler:** Elizabeth
II **Subject:** London Olympics, 2012 **Obv:** Head with tiara right
Rev: Mercury and cyclists

Date	Mintage	F12	VF20	XF40	MS60	MS63
2010	20,000	PF63 800				

KM# 1164 25 POUNDS
8.51 g., 0.9167 Gold 0.2492 oz. AGW, 22 mm. **Ruler:** Elizabeth
II **Subject:** London Olympics, 2012 **Obv:** Head with tiara right
Rev: Diana and cyclists

Date	Mintage	F12	VF20	XF40	MS60	MS63
2010	20,000	PF63 800				

KM# 1218 25 POUNDS
8.51 g., 0.9167 Gold 0.2492 oz. AGW, 22 mm. **Ruler:** Elizabeth
II **Subject:** London Olympics, 2012 **Obv:** Head with tiara right
Rev: Juno

Date	Mintage	F12	VF20	XF40	MS60	MS63
2011	—	PF63 800				

KM# 1219 25 POUNDS
8.51 g., 0.9167 Gold 0.2492 oz. AGW, 22 mm. **Ruler:** Elizabeth
II **Obv:** Head with tiara right **Rev:** Apollo

Date	Mintage	F12	VF20	XF40	MS60	MS63
2011	—	PF63 800				

KM# 1221 25 POUNDS
8.51 g., 0.9167 Gold 0.2492 oz. AGW, 22 mm. **Ruler:** Elizabeth
II **Obv:** Head with tiara right **Rev:** Minervia

Date	Mintage	F12	VF20	XF40	MS60	MS63
2012	—	PF63 800				

KM# 1222 25 POUNDS
8.51 g., 0.9167 Gold 0.2492 oz. AGW, 22 mm. **Ruler:** Elizabeth
II **Obv:** Head with tiara right **Rev:** Vulcan

Date	Mintage	F12	VF20	XF40	MS60	MS63
2012	—	PF63 800				

KM# 1162 100 POUNDS
32.69 g., 0.9167 Gold 0.9573 oz. AGW, 32.7 mm. **Ruler:**
Elizabeth II **Subject:** London Olympics, 2012 **Obv:** Head with
tiara right **Rev:** Neptune and sailing

Date	Mintage	F12	VF20	XF40	MS60	MS63
2010	7,500	PF63 1,850				

KM# 1220 100 POUNDS
32.69 g., 0.9167 Gold 0.9573 oz. AGW, 32.7 mm. **Ruler:**
Elizabeth II **Obv:** Head with tiara right **Rev:** Jupiter

Date	Mintage	F12	VF20	XF40	MS60	MS63
2011	—	PF63 1,850				

KM# 1223 100 POUNDS
32.69 g., 0.9167 Gold 0.9573 oz. AGW, 32.7 mm. **Ruler:**
Elizabeth II **Obv:** Head with tiara right **Rev:** Mars

Date	Mintage	F12	VF20	XF40	MS60	MS63
2012	—	PF63 1,850				

KM# 1235 500 POUNDS
1000.00 g., 0.9999 Silver 31.9406 oz. ASW **Ruler:** Elizabeth II
Subject: London Olympics, 2012 **Rev:** Ring of Penants around
central legend

Date	Mintage	F12	VF20	XF40	MS60	MS63
2012	2,012	PF63 1,500				

KM# 1243 500 POUNDS
1000.00 g., 0.9999 Silver 31.9406 oz. ASW **Ruler:** Elizabeth II
Subject: Elizabeth II, 60th Anniversary of reign **Obv:** Bust with
tiara and in robes of the Garter right **Rev:** Royal Arms crowned
and supported within wreath

Date	Mintage	F12	VF20	XF40	MS60	MS63
2012	—	PF63 1,300				

KM# 1265 500 POUNDS
1000.00 g., 0.999 Gold 31.9118 oz. AGW, 100 mm. **Ruler:**
Elizabeth II **Rev:** Coronation insignia on roses and laurel

Date	Mintage	F12	VF20	XF40	MS60	MS63
2013	Est. 400	PF63 2,600				

KM# 1236 1000 POUNDS
1000.00 g., 0.999 Gold 31.9118 oz. AGW **Ruler:** Elizabeth II

Rev: Weight bar bell and wreath

Date	Mintage	F12	VF20	XF40	MS60	MS63
2012	60	PF63 58,000				

KM# 1263 1000 POUNDS
1000.00 g., 0.999 Gold 31.9118 oz. AGW, 100 mm. **Ruler:**
Elizabeth II **Obv:** Bust in robes of the Garter **Rev:** Shield before
Buckingham palace

Date	Mintage	F12	VF20	XF40	MS60	MS63
2012	Est. 60	PF63 55,000				

SOVEREIGN COINAGE

KM# 1117 1/4 SOVEREIGN
2.00 g., 0.917 Gold 0.0586 oz. AGW, 13.5 mm. **Ruler:** Elizabeth
II **Obv:** Head with tiara right **Rev:** St. George slaying dragon

Date	Mintage	F12	VF20	XF40	MS60	MS63
2009	50,000	—	—	—	—	115
2009	25,000	PF63 135				
2010	250,000	—	—	—	—	115
2010	25,000	PF63 135				
2011	—	—	—	—	—	115
2011	15,000	PF63 135				
2013	—	—	—	—	—	115
2013	5,645	PF63 135				

KM# 1205 1/4 SOVEREIGN
2.00 g., 0.917 Gold 0.0586 oz. AGW, 13.5 mm. **Ruler:** Elizabeth
II **Obv:** Head with tiara right **Rev:** St. George spearing dragon
head

Date	Mintage	F12	VF20	XF40	MS60	MS63
2012	—	PF63 135				

KM# 1001 1/2 SOVEREIGN
3.99 g., 0.917 Gold 0.1169 oz. AGW **Ruler:** Elizabeth II **Obv:**
Head with tiara right **Rev:** St. George slaying the dragon

Date	Mintage	F12	VF20	XF40	MS60	MS63
2001	94,763	—	—	—	—	BV
2001	10,000	PF63 BV+5%				
2002	61,347	—	—	—	—	BV
2003	47,818	—	—	—	—	BV
2003	14,750	PF63 BV+5%				
2004	34,924	—	—	—	—	BV
2006	30,299	—	—	—	—	BV
2006	8,500	PF63 BV+5%				
2007	75,000	—	—	—	—	BV
2007	7,500	PF63 BV+5%				
2008	75,000	—	—	—	—	BV
2008	7,500	PF63 BV+5%				

KM# 1025 1/2 SOVEREIGN
3.99 g., 0.917 Gold 0.1168 oz. AGW, 19.3 mm. **Ruler:**
Elizabeth II **Subject:** Queen Elizabeth II's Golden Jubilee **Obv:**
Head with tiara right **Rev:** Crowned arms within wreath, date
below **Edge:** Reeded

Date	Mintage	F12	VF20	XF40	MS60	MS63
2002	61,347	—	—	—	—	BV+10%
2002	10,000	PF63 BV+25%				

KM# 1064 1/2 SOVEREIGN
3.99 g., 0.9167 Gold 0.117 oz. AGW, 19.3 mm. **Ruler:** Elizabeth
II **Obv:** Head with tiara right **Rev:** Knight fighting dragon with
sword **Edge:** Reeded

Date	Mintage	F12	VF20	XF40	MS60	MS63
2005	30,299	—	—	—	—	BV
2005	5,011	PF63 BV+15%				

KM# 1001.1 1/2 SOVEREIGN
3.99 g., 0.917 Gold 0.1169 oz. AGW **Ruler:** Elizabeth II **Obv:**
Head with tiara right **Rev:** St. George slaying the dragon

Date	Mintage	F12	VF20	XF40	MS60	MS63
2009	50,000	—	—	—	—	BV+5%
2009	6,000	PF63 BV+15%				
2010	250,000	—	—	—	—	BV+5%
2010	7,000	PF63 BV+15%				
2011	—	—	—	—	—	BV+5%
2011	—	PF63 BV+15%				
2013	—	—	—	—	—	BV+5%
2013	4,795	PF63 BV+15%				

KM# 1206 1/2 SOVEREIGN
3.99 g., 0.917 Gold 0.1169 oz. AGW, 19.3 mm. **Ruler:** Elizabeth
II **Obv:** Head with tiara right **Rev:** St. George spearing dragon
head

Date	Mintage	F12	VF20	XF40	MS60	MS63
2012	—	PF63 BV+15%				

KM# 1002 SOVEREIGN
7.99 g., 0.917 Gold 0.234 oz. AGW **Ruler:** Elizabeth II **Obv:**
Head with tiara right **Rev:** St. George slaying the dragon

Date	Mintage	F12	VF20	XF40	MS60	MS63
2001	49,462	—	—	—	—	BV
2001	15,000	PF63 425				
2002	75,264	—	—	—	—	BV
2003	43,230	—	—	—	—	BV
2003	19,750	PF63 425				
2004	30,688	—	—	—	—	BV
2006	45,542	—	—	—	—	BV
2006	16,000	PF63 425				
2007	75,000	—	—	—	—	BV
2007	12,500	PF63 425				
2008	75,000	—	—	—	—	BV
2008	12,500	PF63 425				

KM# 1026 SOVEREIGN
7.98 g., 0.9167 Gold 0.2337 oz. AGW, 22 mm. **Ruler:** Elizabeth
II **Subject:** Queen Elizabeth II's Golden Jubilee **Obv:** Head with
tiara right **Rev:** Crowned arms within wreath, date below **Edge:**
Reeded

Date	Mintage	F12	VF20	XF40	MS60	MS63
2002	75,264	—	—	—	—	BV
2002	20,500	PF63 425				

KM# 1065 SOVEREIGN
7.99 g., 0.9176 Gold 0.2341 oz. AGW, 22.05 mm. **Ruler:**
Elizabeth II **Obv:** Head with tiara right **Rev:** Knight fighting
dragon with sword **Edge:** Reeded

Date	Mintage	F12	VF20	XF40	MS60	MS63
2005	17,500	PF63 425				
2005	45,542	—	—	—	—	BV

KM# 1002.1 SOVEREIGN
7.98 g., 0.917 Gold 0.2338 oz. AGW **Ruler:** Elizabeth II **Obv:**
Head with tiara right **Rev:** St. George slaying the dragon

Date	Mintage	F12	VF20	XF40	MS60	MS63
2009	75,000	—	—	—	—	BV+5%
2009	12,500	PF63 425				
2010	250,000	—	—	—	—	BV+5%
2010	12,500	PF63 425				
2011	—	—	—	—	—	BV+5%
2011	12,500	PF63 425				
2013	—	—	—	—	—	BV+5%
2013	10,295	PF63 425				

KM# 1207 SOVEREIGN
7.99 g., 0.917 Gold 0.234 oz. AGW, 22 mm. **Ruler:** Elizabeth
II **Obv:** Head with tiara right **Rev:** St. George spearing dragon
head

Date	Mintage	F12	VF20	XF40	MS60	MS63
2012	—	PF63 425				

KM# 1027 2 POUNDS
15.97 g., 0.9167 Gold 0.4676 oz. AGW, 28.4 mm. **Ruler:** Elizabeth II **Subject:** Queen Elizabeth II's Golden Jubilee **Obv:** Head with tiara right **Rev:** Crowned arms within wreath, date below **Edge:** Reeded

Date	Mintage	F12	VF20	XF40	MS60	MS63
2002	8,000	PF63 850				

KM# 1066 2 POUNDS
15.98 g., 0.9167 Gold 0.4678 oz. AGW, 28.4 mm. **Ruler:** Elizabeth II **Obv:** Head with tiara right **Rev:** Knight fighting dragon with sword **Edge:** Reeded

Date	Mintage	F12	VF20	XF40	MS60	MS63
2005	5,000	PF63 850				

KM# 1072 2 POUNDS
15.97 g., 0.9167 Gold 0.4676 oz. AGW, 28.4 mm. **Ruler:** Elizabeth II **Obv:** Head with tiara right **Rev:** St. George slaying the Dragon **Edge:** Reeded

Date	Mintage	F12	VF20	XF40	MS60	MS63
2006	3,500	PF63 850				
2007	2,500	PF63 875				
2008	2,500	PF63 875				

KM# 1072.1 2 POUNDS
15.97 g., 0.917 Gold 0.4678 oz. AGW **Ruler:** Elizabeth II **Obv:** Head with tiara right **Rev:** St. George slaying the dragon

Date	Mintage	F12	VF20	XF40	MS60	MS63
2009	2,500	PF63 875				
2010	2,750	PF63 875				
2011	2,950	PF63 875				
2013	1,895	PF63 875				

KM# 1208 2 POUNDS
15.97 g., 0.9167 Gold 0.4676 oz. AGW, 28.4 mm. **Ruler:** Elizabeth II **Obv:** Head with tiara right **Rev:** St. George spearing dragon's head

Date	Mintage	F12	VF20	XF40	MS60	MS63
2012	—	PF63 875				

KM# 1003 5 POUNDS
39.94 g., 0.917 Gold 1.1699 oz. AGW, 36 mm. **Ruler:** Elizabeth II **Obv:** Head with tiara right **Rev:** St. George slaying dragon **Edge:** Reeded

Date	Mintage	F12	VF20	XF40	MS60	MS63
2001 (u)	1,000	—	—	—	—	2,100
2001	1,000	PF63 2,250				
2003	812	—	—	—	—	2,100
2003	2,250	PF63 2,150				
2004	1,000	—	—	—	—	2,100
2004 Proof	1,750	—	—	—	—	—
2006	1,000	—	—	—	—	2,100
2006	1,750	PF63 2,150				
2007	768	—	—	—	—	2,100
2007	1,750	—	—	—	—	2,100
2008	750	—	—	—	—	2,100
2008	1,750	PF63 2,150				

KM# 1028 5 POUNDS
39.94 g., 0.9167 Gold 1.1696 oz. AGW, 36 mm. **Ruler:** Elizabeth II **Subject:** Queen Elizabeth II's Golden Jubilee **Obv:** Head with

tiara right **Rev:** Crowned arms within wreath **Edge:** Reeded

Date	Mintage	F12	VF20	XF40	MS60	MS63
2002	1,370	—	—	—	—	2,100
2002	3,000	PF63 2,150				

KM# 1067 5 POUNDS
39.94 g., 0.9167 Gold 1.1696 oz. AGW, 36 mm. **Ruler:** Elizabeth II **Obv:** Head with tiara right **Rev:** Knight fighting dragon with sword **Edge:** Reeded

Date	Mintage	F12	VF20	XF40	MS60	MS63
2005	936	—	—	—	—	2,100
2005	2,500	PF63 2,150				

KM# 1003.1 5 POUNDS
39.94 g., 0.917 Gold 1.1699 oz. AGW **Ruler:** Elizabeth II **Obv:** Head with tiara right **Rev:** St. George slaying the dragon

Date	Mintage	F12	VF20	XF40	MS60	MS63
2009	1,000	—	—	—	—	2,100
2009	1,750	PF63 2,150				
2010	1,000	—	—	—	—	2,100
2010	2,000	PF63 2,150				
2011	—	PF63 2,150				
2013	1,000	PF63 2,150				

KM# 1209 5 POUNDS
39.94 g., 0.9167 Gold 1.1696 oz. AGW, 36 mm. **Ruler:** Elizabeth II **Obv:** Head with tiara right **Rev:** St. George spearing dragon's head

Date	Mintage	F12	VF20	XF40	MS60	MS63
2012	—	PF63 2,250				

BULLION COINAGE
Until 1990, .917 Gold was commonly alloyed with copper by the British Royal Mint. Starting in 2013 the bullion coins have been struck at .999 fine.

All proof issues have designers name as P. Nathan. The uncirculated issues use only Nathan.

KM# 1254 10 PENCE
1.58 g., 0.999 Silver 0.0504 oz. ASW, 12 mm. **Ruler:** Elizabeth II **Obv:** Head with tiara right **Rev:** Britannia seated with owl and trident

Date	Mintage	F12	VF20	XF40	MS60	MS63
2013	12,000	PF63 15.00				

KM# 1079 20 PENCE
3.24 g., 0.9584 Silver 0.0992 oz. ASW, 16.5 mm. **Ruler:** Elizabeth II **Obv:** Head with tiara right **Rev:** Britannia standing **Edge:** Reeded

Date	Mintage	F12	VF20	XF40	MS60	MS63
2002	—	PF63 25.00				
2004	—	PF63 25.00				
2006	—	PF63 25.00				
2012	—	PF63 25.00				

KM# 1016 20 PENCE
3.24 g., 0.9584 Silver 0.0992 oz. ASW, 16.5 mm. **Ruler:** Elizabeth II **Subject:** Britannia Bullion **Obv:** Head with tiara right **Rev:** Una and Lion **Edge:** Reeded

Date	Mintage	F12	VF20	XF40	MS60	MS63
2001	15,000	PF63 25.00				

KM# 1044 20 PENCE
3.24 g., 0.9584 Silver 0.0992 oz. ASW, 16.5 mm. **Ruler:** Elizabeth II **Obv:** Head with tiara right **Rev:** Britannia portrait behind wavy lines **Edge:** Reeded

Date	Mintage	F12	VF20	XF40	MS60	MS63
2003	5,848	PF63 35.00				

KM# 1085 20 PENCE
3.24 g., 0.9584 Silver 0.0992 oz. ASW, 16.5 mm. **Ruler:** Elizabeth II **Obv:** Head with tiara right **Rev:** Britannia seated with shield left **Edge:** Reeded

Date	Mintage	F12	VF20	XF40	MS60	MS63
2005	3,273	PF63 25.00				

KM# 1088 20 PENCE
3.24 g., 0.9584 Silver 0.0992 oz. ASW, 16.5 mm. **Ruler:** Elizabeth II **Obv:** Head with tiara right **Rev:** Britannia seated with reclining lion right **Edge:** Reeded

Date	Mintage	F12	VF20	XF40	MS60	MS63
2007	3,401	PF63 25.00				

KM# 1095 20 PENCE
3.24 g., 0.9584 Silver 0.0992 oz. ASW, 16.5 mm. **Ruler:** Elizabeth II **Obv:** Head with tiara right **Rev:** Britannia standing facing left with trident, flowing garment, shield **Edge:** Reeded

Date	Mintage	F12	VF20	XF40	MS60	MS63
2008	5,000	PF63 35.00				

KM# 1123 20 PENCE
3.24 g., 0.958 Silver 0.0992 oz. ASW, 16.5 mm. **Ruler:** Elizabeth II **Obv:** Head right **Rev:** Britania in chariot right

Date	Mintage	F12	VF20	XF40	MS60	MS63
2009	6,000	PF63 35.00				

KM# 1131 20 PENCE
3.24 g., 0.958 Silver 0.0992 oz. ASW, 16.5 mm. **Ruler:** Elizabeth II **Obv:** Head right **Rev:** Britannia bust right

Date	Mintage	F12	VF20	XF40	MS60	MS63
2010	8,000	PF63 35.00				

KM# 1262 20 PENCE
3.24 g., 0.958 Silver 0.0992 oz. ASW, 16.5 mm. **Ruler:** Elizabeth II **Obv:** Head with tiara right **Rev:** Britannia seated behind Union Jack veil

Date	Mintage	F12	VF20	XF40	MS60	MS63
2011 Proof	—	—	—	—	—	—

KM# 1255 20 PENCE
3.15 g., 0.999 Silver 0.1005 oz. ASW, 16.5 mm. **Ruler:** Elizabeth II **Obv:** Head with tiara right **Rev:** Britannia seated with owl and trident

Date	Mintage	F12	VF20	XF40	MS60	MS63
2013	12,000	PF63 25.00				

KM# 1080 50 PENCE
8.11 g., 0.9584 Silver 0.2483 oz. ASW, 22 mm. **Ruler:** Elizabeth II **Obv:** Head with tiara right **Rev:** Britannia standing **Edge:** Reeded

Date	Mintage	F12	VF20	XF40	MS60	MS63
2002	—	PF63 35.00				
2004	—	PF63 35.00				
2006	—	PF63 35.00				
2012	—	PF63 35.00				

KM# 1017 50 PENCE
8.11 g., 0.9584 Silver 0.2483 oz. ASW, 27.3 mm. **Ruler:** Elizabeth II **Subject:** Britannia Bullion **Obv:** Head with tiara right **Rev:** Una and Lion **Edge:** Reeded

Date	Mintage	F12	VF20	XF40	MS60	MS63
2001	5,000	PF63 35.00				

KM# 1045 50 PENCE
8.11 g., 0.9584 Silver 0.2483 oz. ASW, 22 mm. **Ruler:** Elizabeth II **Obv:** Head with tiara right **Rev:** Britannia portrait behind wavy lines **Edge:** Reeded

Date	Mintage	F12	VF20	XF40	MS60	MS63
2003	3,669	PF63 35.00				

KM# 1086 50 PENCE
8.11 g., 0.9584 Silver 0.2483 oz. ASW, 22 mm. **Ruler:** Elizabeth II **Obv:** Head with tiara right **Rev:** Britannia seated with shield left **Edge:** Reeded

Date	Mintage	F12	VF20	XF40	MS60	MS63
2005	2,360	PF63 35.00				

KM# 1089 50 PENCE
8.11 g., 0.9584 Silver 0.2483 oz. ASW, 22 mm. **Ruler:** Elizabeth II **Obv:** Head with tiara right **Rev:** Britannia seated with reclining lion right **Edge:** Reeded

Date	Mintage	F12	VF20	XF40	MS60	MS63
2007	2,500	PF63 35.00				

KM# 1096 50 PENCE
8.11 g., 0.9584 Silver 0.2483 oz. ASW, 22 mm. **Ruler:** Elizabeth II **Obv:** Head with tiara right **Rev:** Britannia standing facing left with trident, flowing garment, shield **Edge:** Reeded

Date	Mintage	F12	VF20	XF40	MS60	MS63
2008	2,500	PF63 45.00				

KM# 1124 50 PENCE
8.11 g., 0.958 Silver 0.2482 oz. ASW, 22 mm. **Ruler:** Elizabeth II **Obv:** Head right **Rev:** Britannia in chariot right

Date	Mintage	F12	VF20	XF40	MS60	MS63
2009	2,500	PF63 50.00				

KM# 1132 50 PENCE
8.11 g., 0.958 Silver 0.2482 oz. ASW, 22 mm. **Ruler:** Elizabeth II **Obv:** Head right **Rev:** Britannia bust right

Date	Mintage	F12	VF20	XF40	MS60	MS63
2010	3,500	PF63 50.00				

KM# 1228 50 PENCE
8.11 g., 0.9584 Silver 0.2483 oz. ASW, 22 mm. **Ruler:** Elizabeth II **Obv:** Head with tiara right **Rev:** Britannia seated behind Union Jack veil

Date	Mintage	F12	VF20	XF40	MS60	MS63
2011	—	PF63 50.00				

KM# 1080a 50 PENCE
7.78 g., 0.999 Silver 0.2481 oz. ASW, 22 mm. **Ruler:** Elizabeth II **Obv:** Head with tiara right **Rev:** Britannia standing **Edge Lettering:** SS GAIRSOPPA **Note:** Struck from recovered silver from WWII era shipwreck

Date	Mintage	F12	VF20	XF40	MS60	MS63
2013	Est. 500000	—	—	—	—	20.00

KM# 1256 50 PENCE
7.78 g., 0.999 Silver 0.2481 oz. ASW, 22 mm. **Ruler:** Elizabeth II **Obv:** Head with tiara right **Rev:** Britannia seated with owl and trident

Date	Mintage	F12	VF20	XF40	MS60	MS63
2013	4,500	PF63 35.00				

KM# 1081 POUND
16.22 g., 0.9584 Silver 0.4966 oz. ASW, 27 mm. **Ruler:** Elizabeth II **Obv:** Head with tiara right **Rev:** Britannia standing **Edge:** Reeded

Date	Mintage	F12	VF20	XF40	MS60	MS63
2002	—	PF63 50.00				
2004	—	PF63 50.00				
2006	—	PF63 50.00				
2012	2,012	PF63 115				

KM# 1084 POUND
16.22 g., 0.9584 Silver 0.4966 oz. ASW, 27 mm. **Ruler:** Elizabeth II **Obv:** Head with tiara right **Rev:** Britannia in chariot right **Edge:** Reeded

Date	Mintage	F12	VF20	XF40	MS60	MS63
2012	2,012	PF63 60.00				

KM# 1018 POUND
16.22 g., 0.9584 Silver 0.4966 oz. ASW, 27 mm. **Ruler:** Elizabeth II **Obv:** Head with tiara right **Rev:** Una and Lion **Edge:** Reeded

Date	Mintage	F12	VF20	XF40	MS60	MS63
2001	5,000	PF63 50.00				
2012	2,012	PF63 115				

KM# 1046 POUND
16.22 g., 0.9584 Silver 0.4966 oz. ASW, 27 mm. **Ruler:** Elizabeth II **Obv:** Head with tiara right **Rev:** Britannia portrait behind wavy lines **Edge:** Reeded

Date	Mintage	F12	VF20	XF40	MS60	MS63
2003	3,669	PF63 50.00				
2012	2,012	PF63 115				

KM# 1087 POUND
16.22 g., 0.9504 Silver 0.4966 oz. ASW, 27 mm. **Ruler:** Elizabeth II **Obv:** Head with tiara right **Rev:** Britannia seated with shield left **Edge:** Reeded

Date	Mintage	F12	VF20	XF40	MS60	MS63
2005	2,360	PF63 70.00				
2012	2,012	PF63 115				

KM# 1090 POUND
16.22 g., 0.9584 Silver 0.4966 oz. ASW, 27 mm. **Ruler:** Elizabeth II **Obv:** Head with tiara right **Rev:** Britannia seated with reclining lion right **Edge:** Reeded

Date	Mintage	F12	VF20	XF40	MS60	MS63
2007	2,500	PF63 70.00				
2012	2,012	PF63 115				

KM# 1097 POUND
16.22 g., 0.9584 Silver 0.4966 oz. ASW, 27 mm. **Ruler:** Elizabeth II **Obv:** Head with tiara right **Rev:** Britannia standing facing left with trident, flowing garment, shield **Edge:** Reeded

Date	Mintage	F12	VF20	XF40	MS60	MS63
2008	2,500	PF63 70.00				
2012	2,012	PF63 115				

KM# 1125 POUND
16.22 g., 0.958 Silver 0.4964 oz. ASW, 27 mm. **Ruler:** Elizabeth II **Obv:** Head right **Rev:** Britannia in chariot right

Date	Mintage	F12	VF20	XF40	MS60	MS63
2009	2,500	PF63 70.00				
2012	2,012	PF63 115				

KM# 1133 POUND
16.22 g., 0.958 Silver 0.4964 oz. ASW, 27 mm. **Ruler:** Elizabeth II **Obv:** Head right **Rev:** Britannia bust right

Date	Mintage	F12	VF20	XF40	MS60	MS63
2010	3,500	PF63 70.00				
2012	2,012	PF63 115				

KM# 1229 POUND
16.22 g., 0.9584 Silver 0.4966 oz. ASW, 27 mm. **Ruler:** Elizabeth II **Obv:** Head with tiara right **Rev:** Britannia seated behind Union Jack veil

Date	Mintage	F12	VF20	XF40	MS60	MS63
2011	—	PF63 60.00				
2012	2,012	PF63 115				

KM# 1257 POUND
15.71 g., 0.999 Silver 0.5013 oz. ASW, 27 mm. **Ruler:** Elizabeth II **Obv:** Head with tiara right **Rev:** Britannia seated with owl and trident

Date	Mintage	F12	VF20	XF40	MS60	MS63
2013	4,500	PF63 40.00				

KM# 1269 POUND
1.57 g., 0.999 Gold 0.050 oz. AGW, 12 mm. **Ruler:** Elizabeth II **Obv:** Head with tiara right **Rev:** Britannia seated left with owl

Date	Mintage	F12	VF20	XF40	MS60	MS63
2013	Est. 5750	PF63 95.00				

KM# 1029 2 POUNDS
32.54 g., 0.958 Silver 0.9958 oz. ASW, 40 mm. **Ruler:** Elizabeth II **Obv:** Head with tiara right **Rev:** Standing Britannia **Edge:** Reeded

Date	Mintage	F12	VF20	XF40	MS60	MS63
2002	36,543	—	—	—	—	38.00
2002	—	PF63 60.00				
2004	100,000	—	—	—	—	38.00
2004	2,174	PF63 60.00				
2006	100,000	—	—	—	—	38.00
2006	2,529	PF63 60.00				
2012	—	—	—	—	—	38.00
2012	—	PF63 60.00				
2013	—	—	—	—	—	38.00
2013	—	PF63 60.00				

KM# 1000 2 POUNDS
32.54 g., 0.958 Silver 0.9958 oz. ASW, 40 mm. **Ruler:** Elizabeth II **Obv:** Head with tiara right **Rev:** Britannia in chariot **Edge:** Reeded

Date	Mintage	F12	VF20	XF40	MS60	MS63
2009	—	—	—	—	—	40.00
2009	—	PF63 60.00				

KM# 1019 2 POUNDS
32.45 g., 0.9584 Silver 0.9935 oz. ASW, 40 mm. **Ruler:** Elizabeth II **Subject:** Britannia Bullion **Obv:** Head with tiara right **Rev:** Una and Lion **Edge:** Reeded

Date	Mintage	F12	VF20	XF40	MS60	MS63
2001	44,816	—	—	—	38.00	42.00
2001	3,047	PF63 65.00				

KM# 1039 2 POUNDS
32.45 g., 0.958 Silver 0.993 oz. ASW, 40 mm. **Ruler:** Elizabeth II **Subject:** Britannia Bullion **Obv:** Head with tiara right **Rev:** Britannia portrait behind wavy puzzle-like lines **Edge:** Reeded

Date	Mintage	F12	VF20	XF40	MS60	MS63
2003	73,271	—	—	—	—	38.00
2003	2,016	PF63 65.00				

KM# 1039a 2 POUNDS
32.45 g., 0.958 Silver 0.993 oz. ASW, 40 mm. **Ruler:** Elizabeth II **Obv:** Head with tiara right **Rev:** Britannia head gilt **Edge:** Reeded

Date	Mintage	F12	VF20	XF40	MS60	MS63
2006	3,000	PF63 100				

KM# 1063 2 POUNDS
32.45 g., 0.958 Silver 0.993 oz. ASW, 40 mm. **Ruler:** Elizabeth II **Obv:** Head with tiara right **Rev:** Seated Britannia **Edge:** Reeded

Date	Mintage	F12	VF20	XF40	MS60	MS63
2005	100,000	—	—	—	—	38.00
2005	1,539	PF63 70.00				

KM# 1063a 2 POUNDS
32.45 g., 0.958 Silver 0.993 oz. ASW, 40 mm. **Ruler:** Elizabeth

II **Obv:** Head with tiara right **Rev:** Britannia seated, gilt **Edge:** Reeded

Date	Mintage	F12	VF20	XF40	MS60	MS63
2006	3,000	PF63 100				

KM# 1029a 2 POUNDS
32.45 g., 0.958 Silver 0.993 oz. ASW, 40 mm. **Ruler:** Elizabeth II **Obv:** Head with tiara right **Rev:** Britannia standing with shield, gilt **Edge:** Reeded

Date	Mintage	F12	VF20	XF40	MS60	MS63
2006	3,000	PF63 100				

KM# 1000a 2 POUNDS
32.45 g., 0.958 Silver 0.993 oz. ASW, 40 mm. **Ruler:** Elizabeth II **Obv:** Head with tiara right **Rev:** Britannia in chariot, gilt **Edge:** Reeded

Date	Mintage	F12	VF20	XF40	MS60	MS63
2006	3,000	PF63 100				

KM# 1019a 2 POUNDS
32.45 g., 0.958 Silver 0.993 oz. ASW, 40 mm. **Ruler:** Elizabeth II **Subject:** Golden Silhouette Britannias **Obv:** Head with tiara right **Rev:** Gold plated Britannia and Lion **Edge:** Reeded

Date	Mintage	F12	VF20	XF40	MS60	MS63
2006	3,000	PF63 100				

KM# 1078 2 POUNDS
32.45 g., 0.958 Silver 0.993 oz. ASW, 40 mm. **Ruler:** Elizabeth II **Subject:** Britannia series **Obv:** Elizabeth II **Rev:** Seated, bareheaded Britannia with a recumbent lion at her feet **Edge:** Reeded

Date	Mintage	F12	VF20	XF40	MS60	MS63
2007	100,000	—	—	—	—	40.00
2007	2,500	PF63 65.00				

KM# 1098 2 POUNDS
32.45 g., 0.9584 Silver 0.9935 oz. ASW, 40 mm. **Ruler:** Elizabeth II **Obv:** Head with tiara right **Rev:** Britannia standing facing left with trident, flowing garment, shield **Edge:** Reeded

Date	Mintage	F12	VF20	XF40	MS60	MS63
2008		—	—	—	—	40.00
2008		PF63 80.00				

KM# 1134 2 POUNDS
32.45 g., 0.958 Silver 0.993 oz. ASW, 40 mm. **Ruler:** Elizabeth II **Obv:** Head right **Rev:** Britannia bust right

Date	Mintage	F12	VF20	XF40	MS60	MS63
2010		—	—	—	—	38.00
2010	8,000	PF63 90.00				

KM# 1230 2 POUNDS
32.54 g., 0.958 Silver 0.9958 oz. ASW, 40 mm. **Ruler:** Elizabeth II **Obv:** Head with tiara right **Rev:** Britannia seated behind Union Jack veil

Date	Mintage	F12	VF20	XF40	MS60	MS63
2011		—	—	—	—	40.00
2011	—	PF63 80.00				

KM# 1258 2 POUNDS
31.21 g., 0.999 Silver 0.996 oz. ASW, 38.61 mm. **Ruler:** Elizabeth II **Obv:** Head with tiara right **Rev:** Britannia seated with owl and trident

Date	Mintage	F12	VF20	XF40	MS60	MS63
2013	8,500	PF63 65.00				

KM# 1267 2 POUNDS
31.21 g., 0.9999 Silver 0.9969 oz. ASW, 38.61 mm. **Ruler:** Elizabeth II **Obv:** Head with tiara right **Rev:** Standing Britannia **Edge:** Reeded

Date	Mintage	F12	VF20	XF40	MS60	MS63
2013		—	—	—	—	45.00
2013	—	PF63 60.00				
2014		—	—	—	—	
2014	—	PF63 60.00				40.00

KM# 1008 10 POUNDS
3.41 g., 0.9167 Gold 0.0999 oz. AGW, 16.5 mm. **Ruler:** Elizabeth II **Obv:** Head with tiara right **Rev:** Britannia standing **Edge:** Reeded

Date	Mintage	F12	VF20	XF40	MS60	MS63
2002		—	—	—	—	BV+16%
2002	1,500	PF63 210				
2004	929	PF63 225				
2006	700	PF63 225				

KM# 1020 10 POUNDS
3.41 g., 0.9167 Gold 0.0999 oz. AGW, 16.5 mm. **Ruler:** Elizabeth II **Subject:** Britannia Bullion **Obv:** Head with tiara right **Rev:** Stylized "Britannia and the Lion **Edge:** Reeded

Date	Mintage	F12	VF20	XF40	MS60	MS63
2001	1,100	—	—	—	—	BV+16%
2001	1,557	PF63 210				

KM# 1040 10 POUNDS
3.41 g., 0.9167 Gold 0.0999 oz. AGW, 16.5 mm. **Ruler:** Elizabeth II **Obv:** Head with tiara right **Rev:** Britannia portrait behind wavy lines **Edge:** Reeded

Date	Mintage	F12	VF20	XF40	MS60	MS63
2003	—	—	—	—	—	BV+16%
2003	4,000	PF63 210				

KM# 1068 10 POUNDS
3.41 g., 0.9167 Gold 0.0999 oz. AGW, 16.5 mm. **Ruler:** Elizabeth II **Obv:** Head with tiara right **Rev:** Seated Britannia **Edge:** Reeded

Date	Mintage	F12	VF20	XF40	MS60	MS63
2005	1,225	PF63 210				

KM# 1091 10 POUNDS
3.41 g., 0.9167 Gold 0.0999 oz. AGW, 16.5 mm. **Ruler:** Elizabeth II **Obv:** Head with tiara right **Rev:** Britannia seated with reclining lion right **Edge:** Reeded

Date	Mintage	F12	VF20	XF40	MS60	MS63
2007	—	PF63 BV+16%				
2007	893	PF63 225				

KM# 1091a 10 POUNDS
3.11 g., 0.9999 Platinum 0.0993 oz. APW, 16.5 mm. **Ruler:** Elizabeth II **Obv:** Head with tiara right **Rev:** Britannia seated with reclining lion right **Edge:** Reeded

Date	Mintage	F12	VF20	XF40	MS60	MS63
2007	691	PF63 300				

KM# 1099 10 POUNDS
3.41 g., 0.9167 Gold 0.0999 oz. AGW, 16.5 mm. **Ruler:** Elizabeth II **Obv:** Head with tiara right **Rev:** Britannia standing facing left with trident, flowing garment, shield **Edge:** Reeded

Date	Mintage	F12	VF20	XF40	MS60	MS63
2000	—	PF63 210				

KM# 1099a 10 POUNDS
3.11 g., 0.9999 Platinum 0.0993 oz. APW, 16.5 mm. **Ruler:** Elizabeth II **Obv:** Head with tiara right **Rev:** Britannia standing facing left with trident, flowing garment, shield **Edge:** Reeded

Date	Mintage	F12	VF20	XF40	MS60	MS63
2008	—	PF63 300				

KM# 1127 10 POUNDS
3.41 g., 0.916 Gold 0.0998 oz. AGW, 16.5 mm. **Ruler:** Elizabeth II **Obv:** Head right **Rev:** Britannia in chariot right

Date	Mintage	F12	VF20	XF40	MS60	MS63
2009	2,000	PF63 210				

KM# 1135 10 POUNDS
3.41 g., 0.916 Gold 0.0998 oz. AGW, 16.5 mm. **Ruler:** Elizabeth II **Obv:** Head right **Rev:** Britannia bust right

Date	Mintage	F12	VF20	XF40	MS60	MS63
2010	750	PF63 225				

KM# 1231 10 POUNDS
3.41 g., 0.9167 Gold 0.0999 oz. AGW, 22 mm. **Ruler:** Elizabeth II **Obv:** Head with tiara right **Rev:** Britannia seated behind Union Jack veil

Date	Mintage	F12	VF20	XF40	MS60	MS63
2011	—	PF63 210				

KM# 1268 10 POUNDS
157.25 g., 0.999 Silver 5.0181 oz. ASW, 65 mm. **Ruler:** Elizabeth II **Obv:** Head with tiara right **Rev:** Britannia seated left with owl

Date	Mintage	F12	VF20	XF40	MS60	MS63
2013	Est. 1150	PF63 400				

KM# 1270 10 POUNDS
3.13 g., 0.999 Gold 0.100 oz. AGW, 16.5 mm. **Ruler:** Elizabeth II **Obv:** Head with tiara right **Rev:** Britannia seated left with owl

Date	Mintage	F12	VF20	XF40	MS60	MS63
2013	Est. 1125	PF63 190				

KM# 1009 25 POUNDS
8.51 g., 0.9167 Gold 0.2492 oz. AGW, 22 mm. **Ruler:** Elizabeth II **Obv:** Head with tiara right **Rev:** Britannia standing **Edge:** Reeded

Date	Mintage	F12	VF20	XF40	MS60	MS63
2002	—	PF63 465				
2004	750	PF63 465				
2006	1,000	PF63 465				

KM# 1021 25 POUNDS
8.51 g., 0.9167 Gold 0.2492 oz. AGW, 22 mm. **Ruler:** Elizabeth II **Subject:** Britannia Bullion **Obv:** Head with tiara right **Rev:** Stylized "Britannia and the Lion **Edge:** Reeded

Date	Mintage	F12	VF20	XF40	MS60	MS63
2001	1,100	—	—	—	BV+25%	—
2001	1,500	PF63 450				
2006	—	PF63 450				

KM# 1041 25 POUNDS
8.51 g., 0.9167 Gold 0.2492 oz. AGW, 22 mm. **Ruler:** Elizabeth II **Obv:** Head with tiara right **Rev:** Britannia portrait behind wavy lines **Edge:** Reeded

Date	Mintage	F12	VF20	XF40	MS60	MS63
2003	609	PF63 465				
2006	—	PF63 465				

KM# 1069 25 POUNDS
8.51 g., 0.9167 Gold 0.2492 oz. AGW, 22 mm. **Ruler:** Elizabeth II **Obv:** Head with tiara right **Rev:** Seated Britannia **Edge:** Reeded

Date	Mintage	F12	VF20	XF40	MS60	MS63
2005	750	PF63 465				
2006	—	PF63 465				

KM# 1204 25 POUNDS
8.51 g., 0.9167 Gold 0.2492 oz. AGW **Ruler:** Elizabeth II **Rev:** Standing Britannia in horse drawn chariot

Date	Mintage	F12	VF20	XF40	MS60	MS63
2006	—	PF63 465				
2009	—	PF63 465				

KM# 1092a 25 POUNDS
0.9999 Platinum APW, 22 mm. **Ruler:** Elizabeth II **Obv:** Head with tiara right **Rev:** Britannia seated with reclining lion right **Edge:** Reeded

Date	Mintage	F12	VF20	XF40	MS60	MS63
2007	—	PF63 650				

KM# 1092 25 POUNDS
8.51 g., 0.9167 Gold 0.2492 oz. AGW, 22 mm. **Ruler:** Elizabeth II **Obv:** Head with tiara right **Rev:** Britannia seated with reclining lion right **Edge:** Reeded

Date	Mintage	F12	VF20	XF40	MS60	MS63
2007	—	—	—	—	—	BV+25%
2007	1,000	PF63 465				

KM# 1100 25 POUNDS
8.51 g., 0.9167 Gold 0.2492 oz. AGW, 22 mm. **Ruler:** Elizabeth II **Obv:** Head with tiara right **Rev:** Britannia standing facing left with trident, flowing garment, shield **Edge:** Reeded

Date	Mintage	F12	VF20	XF40	MS60	MS63
2008	1,000	PF63 465				

KM# 1100a 25 POUNDS
0.9999 Platinum APW, 22 mm. **Ruler:** Elizabeth II **Obv:** Head with tiara right **Rev:** Britannia standing facing left with trident, flowing garment, shield **Edge:** Reeded

Date	Mintage	F12	VF20	XF40	MS60	MS63
2008	—	PF63 650				

KM# 1128 25 POUNDS
8.51 g., 0.916 Gold 0.249 oz. AGW, 22 mm. **Ruler:** Elizabeth II **Obv:** Head right **Rev:** Britannia in chariot right

Date	Mintage	F12	VF20	XF40	MS60	MS63
2009	2,250	PF63 450				

KM# 1136 25 POUNDS
8.51 g., 0.916 Gold 0.249 oz. AGW, 22 mm. **Ruler:** Elizabeth II **Obv:** Head right **Rev:** Britannia bust right

Date	Mintage	F12	VF20	XF40	MS60	MS63
2010	3,000	PF63 450				

KM# 1232 25 POUNDS
8.51 g., 0.9167 Gold 0.2492 oz. AGW, 22 mm. **Ruler:** Elizabeth II **Obv:** Head with tiara right **Rev:** Britannia seated behind Union Jack veil

Date	Mintage	F12	VF20	XF40	MS60	MS63
2011	—	PF63 450				

KM# 1271 25 POUNDS
7.81 g., 0.9999 Gold 0.2496 oz. AGW, 22 mm. **Ruler:** Elizabeth II **Obv:** Head with tiara right **Rev:** Britannia seated left with owl

Date	Mintage	F12	VF20	XF40	MS60	MS63
2013	Est. 875	PF63 450				

KM# 1010 50 POUNDS
17.03 g., 0.9167 Gold 0.4987 oz. AGW, 27 mm. **Ruler:** Elizabeth II **Obv:** Head with tiara right **Rev:** Britannia standing **Edge:** Reeded

Date	Mintage	F12	VF20	XF40	MS60	MS63
2002	1,000	PF63 BV+10%				
2004	—	PF63 BV+15%				
2006	—	PF63 BV+15%				

KM# 1022 50 POUNDS
17.02 g., 0.9167 Gold 0.4984 oz. AGW, 27 mm. **Ruler:** Elizabeth II **Subject:** Britannia Bullion **Obv:** Head with tiara right **Rev:** Stylized "Britannia and the Lion **Edge:** Reeded

Date	Mintage	F12	VF20	XF40	MS60	MS63
2001	600	—	—	—	BV+25%	—
2001	1,000	PF63 BV+10%				

KM# 1042 50 POUNDS
17.02 g., 0.9167 Gold 0.4984 oz. AGW, 27 mm. **Ruler:** Elizabeth II **Obv:** Head with tiara right **Rev:** Britannia portrait behind wavy lines **Edge:** Reeded

Date	Mintage	F12	VF20	XF40	MS60	MS63
2003	—	—	—	—	BV+15%	—
2003	2,500	PF63 BV+5%				

KM# 1070 50 POUNDS
17.03 g., 0.9167 Gold 0.4987 oz. AGW, 27 mm. **Ruler:** Elizabeth II **Obv:** Head with tiara right **Rev:** Seated Britannia **Edge:** Reeded

Date	Mintage	F12	VF20	XF40	MS60	MS63
2005	2,000	PF63 BV+5%				

KM# 1093a 50 POUNDS
0.9999 Platinum APW, 27 mm. **Ruler:** Elizabeth II **Obv:** Head with tiara right **Rev:** Britannia seated with reclining lion right **Edge:** Reeded

Date	Mintage	F12	VF20	XF40	MS60	MS63
2007	—	PF63 1,500				

KM# 1093 50 POUNDS
17.03 g., 0.9167 Gold 0.4985 oz. AGW, 27 mm. **Ruler:** Elizabeth II **Obv:** Head with tiara right **Rev:** Britannia seated with reclining lion right **Edge:** Reeded

Date	Mintage	F12	VF20	XF40	MS60	MS63
2007	—	—	—	—	—	BV+15%
2007	—	PF63 BV+10%				

KM# 1101 50 POUNDS
17.03 g., 0.9167 Gold 0.4985 oz. AGW, 27 mm. **Ruler:** Elizabeth II **Obv:** Head with tiara right **Rev:** Britannia standing facing left with trident, flowing garment, shield **Edge:** Reeded

Date	Mintage	F12	VF20	XF40	MS60	MS63
2008	—	PF63 BV+10%				

KM# 1101a 50 POUNDS
0.9999 Platinum APW, 27 mm. **Ruler:** Elizabeth II **Obv:** Head with tiara right **Rev:** Britannia standing facing left with trident, flowing garment, shield **Edge:** Reeded

Date	Mintage	F12	VF20	XF40	MS60	MS63
2008	—	PF63 1,500				

KM# 1129 50 POUNDS
17.03 g., 0.916 Gold 0.4982 oz. AGW, 27 mm. **Ruler:** Elizabeth II **Obv:** Head right **Rev:** Britania in chariot right

Date	Mintage	F12	VF20	XF40	MS60	MS63
2009	1,250	PF63 BV+10%				
2009	—	—	—	—	—	BV+15%

KM# 1137 50 POUNDS
17.02 g., 0.916 Gold 0.498 oz. AGW, 27 mm. **Ruler:** Elizabeth II **Obv:** Head right **Rev:** Britannia bust right

Date	Mintage	F12	VF20	XF40	MS60	MS63
2010	1,250	PF63 BV+10%				

KM# 1233 50 POUNDS
17.02 g., 0.9167 Gold 0.4984 oz. AGW, 27 mm. **Ruler:** Elizabeth II

Date	Mintage	F12	VF20	XF40	MS60	MS63
2011	—	PF63 1,500				

KM# 1272 50 POUNDS

15.61 g., 0.9999 Gold 0.4985 oz. AGW, 27 mm. **Ruler:** Elizabeth II **Obv:** Head with tiara right **Rev:** Britannia seated left with owl

Date	Mintage	F12	VF20	XF40	MS60	MS63
2013	Est. 525	PF63 900				

KM# 1011 100 POUNDS

34.05 g., 0.9167 Gold 0.9971 oz. AGW, 32.7 mm. **Ruler:** Elizabeth II **Obv:** Head with tiara right **Rev:** Britannia standing **Edge:** Reeded

Date	Mintage	F12	VF20	XF40	MS60	MS63
2002	1,000	PF63 BV+5%				
2004	—	—	—	—	—	BV+15%
2004	—	PF63 BV+5%				
2006	—	PF63 BV+5%				
2012	—	PF63 BV+5%				

KM# 1023 100 POUNDS

34.05 g., 0.9167 Gold 0.9971 oz. AGW, 32.7 mm. **Ruler:** Elizabeth II **Subject:** Britannia Bullion **Obv:** Head with tiara right **Rev:** Stylized "Britannia and the Lion **Edge:** Reeded

Date	Mintage	F12	VF20	XF40	MS60	MS63
2001	900	—	—	—	—	BV+15%
2001	1,000	PF63 BV+5%				

KM# 1043 100 POUNDS

34.05 g., 0.9167 Gold 0.9971 oz. AGW, 32.7 mm. **Ruler:** Elizabeth II **Obv:** Head with tiara right **Rev:** Britannia portrait behind wavy lines **Edge:** Reeded

Date	Mintage	F12	VF20	XF40	MS60	MS63
2003	—	—	—	—	—	BV+15%
2003	1,500	PF63 BV+5%				

KM# 1071 100 POUNDS

34.05 g., 0.9167 Gold 0.9971 oz. AGW, 32.7 mm. **Ruler:** Elizabeth II **Obv:** Head with tiara right **Rev:** Seated Britannia **Edge:** Reeded

Date	Mintage	F12	VF20	XF40	MS60	MS63
2005	1,500	PF63 BV+5%				

KM# 1094 100 POUNDS

34.05 g., 0.9167 Gold 0.9971 oz. AGW, 32.7 mm. **Ruler:** Elizabeth II **Obv:** Head with tiara right **Rev:** Britannia seated with reclining lion right **Edge:** Reeded

Date	Mintage	F12	VF20	XF40	MS60	MS63
2007	—	—	—	—	—	BV+15%
2007	—	PF63 BV+5%				

KM# 1094a 100 POUNDS

0.9999 Platinum APW, 32.7 mm. **Ruler:** Elizabeth II **Obv:** Head with tiara right **Rev:** Britannia seated with reclining lion right **Edge:** Reeded

Date	Mintage	F12	VF20	XF40	MS60	MS63
2007	—	PF63 2,900				

KM# 1102 100 POUNDS

34.05 g., 0.9167 Gold 0.9971 oz. AGW, 32.7 mm. **Ruler:** Elizabeth II **Obv:** Head with tiara right **Rev:** Britannia standing facing left with trident, flowing garment, shield **Edge:** Reeded

Date	Mintage	F12	VF20	XF40	MS60	MS63
2008	—	—	—	—	—	BV+15%
2008	—	PF63 BV+5%				

Date	Mintage	F12	VF20	XF40	MS60	MS63
2013	—	—	—	—	—	BV+15%
2013	—	PF63 BV+5%				

KM# 1102a 100 POUNDS

0.9999 Platinum APW, 32.7 mm. **Ruler:** Elizabeth II **Obv:** Head with tiara right **Rev:** Britannia standing facing left with trident, flowing garment, shield **Edge:** Reeded

Date	Mintage	F12	VF20	XF40	MS60	MS63
2008	—	PF63 2,900				

KM# 1130 100 POUNDS

32.69 g., 0.916 Gold 0.9565 oz. AGW, 32.6 mm. **Ruler:** Elizabeth II **Obv:** Head right **Rev:** Britannia in chariot right

Date	Mintage	F12	VF20	XF40	MS60	MS63
2009	—	—	—	—	—	BV+15%
2009	1,250	PF63 BV+5%				

KM# 1138 100 POUNDS

34.05 g., 0.916 Gold 0.9963 oz. AGW, 32.7 mm. **Ruler:** Elizabeth II **Obv:** Head right **Rev:** Britannia bust right

Date	Mintage	F12	VF20	XF40	MS60	MS63
2010	—	—	—	—	—	BV+15%
2010	1,250	PF63 BV+5%				

KM# 1234 100 POUNDS

34.05 g., 0.9167 Gold 0.9971 oz. AGW, 32.7 mm. **Ruler:** Elizabeth II **Obv:** Head with tiara right **Rev:** Britannia seated behind Union Jack veil

Date	Mintage	F12	VF20	XF40	MS60	MS63
2011	—	PF63 BV+5%				

KM# 1011a 100 POUNDS

31.11 g., 0.999 Gold 0.9926 oz. AGW, 32.7 mm. **Ruler:** Elizabeth II **Obv:** Head with tiara right **Rev:** Britannia standing **Edge:** Reeded

Date	Mintage	F12	VF20	XF40	MS60	MS63
2013	—	—	—	—	—	BV+15%
2013	—	PF63 BV+5%				

KM# 1266 100 POUNDS

31.21 g., 0.9999 Gold 0.9969 oz. AGW, 38.61 mm. **Ruler:** Elizabeth II **Obv:** Head with tiara right **Rev:** Britannia standing

Date	Mintage	F12	VF20	XF40	MS60	MS63
2013	—	PF63 BV+15%				

KM# 1273 100 POUNDS

31.21 g., 0.9999 Gold 0.9969 oz. AGW, 38.61 mm. **Ruler:** Elizabeth II **Obv:** Head with tiara right **Rev:** Britannia seated left with owl

Date	Mintage	F12	VF20	XF40	MS60	MS63
2013	Est. 400	PF63 1,800				

KM# 1274 500 POUNDS

156.29 g., 0.9999 Gold 4.992 oz. AGW **Ruler:** Elizabeth II **Obv:** Head with tiara right **Rev:** Britannia seated left with owl

Date	Mintage	F12	VF20	XF40	MS60	MS63
2013	Est. 100	PF63 8,500				

PIEDFORT

KM#	Date	Mintage	Identification	Mkt Val
P101	2001	8,464	Pound 0.925 Silver KM#1013a	115
P106	2001	6,759	2 Pounds 0.925 Silver KM#1014a	115
P102	2002	6,599	Pound 0.925 Silver KM#1030a	115
P107	2002	—	2 Pounds 0.925 Silver KM#1031a	125
P108	2002	—	2 Pounds 0.925 Silver KM#1032a	125
P109	2002	—	2 Pounds 0.925 Silver KM#1033a	125
P110	2002	—	2 Pounds 0.925 Silver Piedfort w/ color. KM#1034a.	125
P40	2003	6,795	50 Pence 0.925 Silver KM#1036a	110
		Note: Also exists as a Piefort, P1004a.		
P41	2003	9,871	Pound 0.925 Silver KM#993a	115
P42	ND2003	8,728	2 Pounds 0.925 Silver KM#1037a.	95.00
P43	2004	4,054	50 Pence 0.925 Silver KM#1047a.	110
P44	2004	7,013	Pound 0.925 Silver KM#1048a.	115
P45	2004	5,303	2 Pounds 0.925 Silver KM#1049a.	125
P47	2004	2,500	5 Pounds 0.925 Silver KM#1055a.	150
P46	ND2005	4,585	2 Pounds 0.925 Silver KM#1052a.	95.00
P48	2005	3,808	50 Pence 0.925 Silver KM#1050a.	110
P49	ND2005	4,798	2 Pounds 0.925 Silver KM#1056a.	95.00
P50	2005	6,007	Pound 0.925 Silver KM#1051a.	115
P51	2005	—	5 Pounds 0.925 Silver KM#1053a.	150
P52	2005	—	5 Pounds 0.925 Silver KM#1054a.	150
P53	2006	3,532	50 Pence 0.925 Silver KM#1057a.	110
P54	2006	3,415	50 Pence 0.925 Silver KM#1058a.	110
P55	2006	7,500	Pound 0.925 Silver KM#1051a.	125
P56	2006	3,199	2 Pounds 0.925 Silver KM#1060a.	115
P57	2006	3,018	2 Pounds 0.925 Silver KM#1061a.	115
P58	2006	5,000	5 Pounds 0.925 Silver KM#1062a.	150
P59	2007	1,555	50 Pence 0.925 Silver KM#1073a.	135
P60	2007	5,739	Pound 0.925 Silver KM#1074a.	95.00
P61	2007	4,000	2 Pounds 0.925 Silver KM#1075a.	115
P62	2007	3,990	2 Pounds 0.925 Silver KM#1076a.	115
P63	2007	2,000	5 Pounds 0.925 Silver KM#1077a.	150
P64	2007	250	5 Pounds 0.9995 Platinum	7,500
P65	2008	—	2 Pounds 0.925 Silver KM#1106a.	115
P67	2008	—	5 Pounds 0.925 Silver KM#1104.	150
P68	2008	—	5 Pounds 0.925 Silver KM#1103.	150
P97	2008	—	50 Pence Silver KM#1112a	125
P103	2008	8,000	Pound 0.925 Silver KM#1113a	125
P113	2008	5,000	5 Pounds 0.925 Silver KM#1103a	150
P66	2009	3,500	2 Pounds 0.925 Silver KM#1115a.	115
P70	2009	4,009	5 Pounds 0.925 Silver KM#1118a.	180
P98	2009	—	50 Pence Silver KM#1114a	125
P111	2009	3,500	2 Pounds Silver	115
P75	2010	3,000	Pound 0.925 Silver KM#1158a.	110
P76	2010	5,000	Pound 0.925 Silver	110
P99	2010	—	50 Pence 0.925 Silver KM#1165a	125
P114	2010	—	5 Pounds 0.925 Silver KM#1151a	160
P77	2011	—	Penny 0.925 Silver KM#1107a.	15.00
P78	2011	—	2 Pence 0.925 Silver KM#1108a.	25.00
P79	2011	—	5 Pence 0.925 Silver KM#1109a.	35.00
P80	2011	—	10 Pence 0.925 Silver KM#1110a.	80.00
P81	2011	—	20 Pence 0.925 Silver KM#1111a.	80.00
P82	2011	—	50 Pence 0.925 Silver KM#1112a.	125
P83	2011	—	Pound 0.925 Silver KM#1113a.	115
P84	2011	—	Pound 0.925 Silver KM#1197a.	115
P85	2011	—	Pound 0.925 Silver KM#1198a.	115
P86	2011	—	50 Pence 0.925 Silver KM#1196a.	125
P87	2011	—	2 Pounds 0.925 Silver KM#1199a.	115
P88	2011	—	2 Pounds 0.925 Silver KM#1200a.	115
P89	2011	—	5 Pounds 0.925 Silver KM#1201a.	150

MAUNDY SETS

KM#	Date	Mintage	Identification	Issue Price	Mkt Val
MDS260	2001 (4)	1,132	KM#898-899, 901-902.	—	300
MDS261	2002 (4)	1,681	KM#898-899, 901-902.	—	300
MDS262	2003 (4)	1,608	KM#898-899, 901-902.	—	325
MDS263	2004 (4)	1,613	KM#898-899, 901-902.	—	325
MDS264	2005 (4)	1,685	KM#898-899, 901-902.	—	325
MDS265	2006 (4)	1,811	KM#898-899, 901-902.	—	325
MDS266	2007 (4)	1,822	KM#898-899, 901-902.	—	325
MDS267	2008 (4)	1,833	KM#898-899, 901-902.	—	325
MDS268	2009 (4)	1,602	KM#898-899, 901-902.	—	325
MDS269	2010 (4)	1,617	KM#898-899, 901-902.	—	325
MDS270	2011 (4)	—	KM#898-899, 901-902.	—	325

MINT SETS

KM#	Date	Mintage	Identification	Issue Price	Mkt Val
MS129	2001 (9)	57,741	KM#986-991, 994, 1013-1015	22.50	25.00
MS130	2001 (9)	—	KM#986-991, 994, 1013-1014	27.50	25.00
MS131	2001 (9)	—	KM#986-991, 994, 1013-1014	27.50	25.00
MS132	2002 (8)	60,539	KM#986-991, 994, 1030	22.50	20.00
MS133	2002 (8)	—	KM#986-991, 994, 1030	27.50	20.00

MS134	2002 (8)	— KM#986-991, 994, 1030	27.50	20.00
MS135	2003 (10)	62,741 KM#986-991, 993, 994, 1036-1037	22.50	35.00
MS136	2003 (10)	7,130 KM#986-991, 993, 994, 1036-1037	27.50	30.00
MS137	2003 (10)	43,128 KM#986-991, 993, 994, 1036-1037	27.50	30.00
MS138	2005 (10)	51,776 KM#986-991, 994, 1050-1052	26.50	30.00
MS139	2005 (10)	29,924 KM#986-991, 994, 1050-1052	36.50	35.00
MS140	2005 (3)	— KM#1050-1052	16.25	17.50
MS141	2005 (2)	— KM#1053-1054	36.00	35.00
MS142	2006 (10)	74,231 KM#986-990, 1057-1061, BV set	30.00	60.00
MS143	2006 (10)	25,878 KM#986-990, 1057-1061	38.50	60.00
MS144	2007 (6)	— KM#986-991	—	10.00
MSA135	2004 (10)	46,032 KM#986-991, 994, 1047-1049	—	35.00
MSB135	2004 (10)	4,214 KM#986-991, 994, 1047-1049, 1055	—	35.00
MSC135	2004 (10)	34,371 KM#986-991, 994, 1047-1049, 1055	—	35.00

PROOF SETS

KM#	Date	Mintage Identification	Issue Price	Mkt Val
PS116	2001 (3)	1,500 KM#1001-1002, 1014a	795	525
PS117	2001 (4)	1,000 KM#1001-1003,1014a	1,645	2,250
PS118	2001 (4)	5,000 KM#1016-1019	—	175
PS119	2001 (4)	1,000 KM#1020-1023	1,595	3,200
PS120	2002 (3)	5,000 KM#1025-1027	795	1,275
PS121	2002 (4)	3,000 KM#1025-1028	1,645	3,000
PS122	2002 (4)	3,358 KM#1031-1034; Standard Set	34.95	35.00
PS123	2002 (4)	673 KM#1031-1034; Display Set	44.95	40.00
PS124	2002 (4)	2,553 KM#1031a-1034a; Display Set	120	150
PS125	2002 (4)	315 KM#1031b-1034b; Display Set	1,675	3,000
PS126	2002 (4)	1,000 KM#1008-1011	1,600	3,200
PS127	2001 (10)	10,000 KM#986-991, 994, 1013-1015	115	80.00
PS128	2001 (10)	30,000 KM#986-991, 994, 1013-1015	72.50	80.00
PS129	2001 (10)	28,244 KM#986-991, 994, 1013-1015	50.00	65.00
PS130	2001 (10)	1,351 KM#986-991, 994, 1013-1015	65.00	65.00
PS131	2002 (9)	5,000 KM#986-991, 994, 1024, 1030	100	60.00
PS132	2002 (9)	30,000 KM#986-991, 994, 1024, 1030	70.00	55.00
PS133	2002 (9)	30,884 KM#986-991, 994, 1024, 1030	48.00	55.00
PS134	2002 (9)	1,544 KM#986-991, 994, 1024, 1030	62.40	55.00
PS135	2003 (11)	5,000 KM#986-991, 993, 994, 1036-1038	100	85.00
PS136	2003 (11)	14,863 KM#986-991, 993, 994, 1036-1038	72.00	80.00
PS137	2003 (11)	23,650 KM#986-991, 993, 994, 1036-1038	50.00	80.00
PS138	2005 (12)	4,290 KM#986-991, 994, 1050-1054	145	95.00
PS139	2005 (12)	14,899 KM#986-991, 994, 1050-1054	80.00	95.00
PS140	2005 (12)	21,374 KM#986-991, 994, 1050-1054, Standard Proof Set	60.00	95.00
PS141	2005 (3)	417 KM#1068-1070	850	1,350
PS142	2005 (4)	1,439 KM#1068-1071	1,895	2,850
PS143	2005 (4)	2,500 KM#1064-1066	820	1,100
PS144	2005 (4)	2,500 KM#1064-1067	1,925	2,600
PS145	2005 (2)	— P39, P40	—	175
PS146	2006 (13)	5,000 KM#986-991, 994, 1057-1062	—	140
PS147	2006 (13)	15,000 KM#986-991, 994, 1057-1062	82.50	140
PS148	2006 (13)	17,689 KM#986-991, 994, 1057-1062	65.00	140
PS149	2006 (5)	3,000 KM#1000a, 1012a, 1018a, 1039, 1063a	475	525
PS150	2006 (3)	1,750 KM#1001, 1002, 1072	1,015	1,150
PS151	2006 (4)	1,750 KM#1001-1003, 1072	2,091	2,650
PS152	2007 (13)	18,215 KM#986-991, 994, 1057-1062	65.00	140
PS153	2007 (4)	1,750 KM#1001-1003, 1072	—	2,850
PS154	2007 (3)	750 KM#1001-1002, 1072	—	1,200
PS155	2007 (2)	5,000 KM#1001-1002	—	550
PS156	2007 (5)	3,000 KM#P33, P35-P38	450	500
PS160	2002 (4)	— KM#1029, 1079-1081	—	175
PS161	2003 (4)	1,250 KM#1040-1043	—	2,800
PS162	2004 (4)	— KM#1029, 1079-1081	—	175

KM#	Date	Mintage Identification	Issue Price	Mkt Val
PS163	2004 (4)	973 KM#1008-1011	—	3,000
PS164	2005 (4)	2,360 KM#1063, 1085-1087	—	185
PS165	2006 (4)	— KM#1029, 1079-1081	—	175
PS166	2006 (4)	— KM#1008-1011	—	2,900
PS167	2007 (4)	— KM#1078, 1088-1090	—	185
PS168	2007 (4)	— KM#1091-1094	—	2,950
PS169	2007 (4)	— KM#1091a-1094a	—	5,850
PS170	2008 (4)	— KM#1095-1098	—	225
PS171	2008 (4)	— KM#1099-1102	—	3,000
PS172	2008 (4)	— KM#1099a-1102a	—	5,850
PSA119	2001 (3)	1,500 KM#1001, 1002, 1014b	—	525
PSA135	2002 (13)	— KM#898a, 899a, 901a, 902a, 986c, 987c, 988b, 989b, 990b, 991b, 1030b, 994c, 1024b	—	11,250
PSA138	2003 (4)	3,669 KM#1039, 1044-1046	—	180
PSB119	2001 (4)	1,000 KM#1001, 1002, 1014b, 1015b	—	2,700
PSB138	2004 (11)	4,101 KM#986-991, 994, 1047-1049, 1055	—	80.00
PSC138	2004 (11)	12,968 KM#986-991, 994, 1047-1049, 1055	—	80.00
PSD138	2004 (11)	17,951 KM#986-991, 994, 1047-1049, 1055	—	80.00

GREECE

The Hellenic (Greek) Republic is situated in southeastern Europe on the southern tip of the Balkan Peninsula. The republic includes many islands, the most important of which are Crete and the Ionian Islands. Greece (including islands) has an area of 50,944 sq. mi. (131,940 sq. km.) and a population of 10.3 million. Capital: Athens. Greece is still largely agricultural. Tobacco, cotton, fruit and wool are exported.

MONETARY SYSTEM
100 Euro Cent = 1 Euro

REPUBLIC

EURO COINAGE

The Greek Euro coinage series contains the denomination in Lepta as well.European Union Issues

KM# 181 EURO CENT
2.27 g., Copper Plated Steel, 16.2 mm. **Obv:** Ancient Athenian trireme **Rev:** Denomination and globe **Edge:** Plain

Date	Mintage	F12	VF20	XF40	MS60	MS63
2002	101,000,000	—	—	—	0.35	—
2002 F in star	15,000,000	—	—	—	1.25	—
2003	35,200,000	—	—	—	0.35	—
2004	50,000,000	—	—	—	0.35	—
2005	15,000,000	—	—	—	0.35	—
2006	45,000,000	—	—	—	0.35	—
2007	60,000,000	—	—	—	0.35	—
2008	24,000,000	—	—	—	0.35	—
2009	50,000,000	—	—	—	0.35	—
2010	27,000,000	—	—	—	0.35	—
2011	35,000,000	—	—	—	0.35	—
2011 Proof, In sets only	2,500	PF63 15.00				
2012	48,000,000	—	—	—	0.35	—
2012 Proof, In sets only	2,500	PF63 15.00				

KM# 182 2 EURO CENT
3.03 g., Copper Plated Steel, 18.7 mm. **Obv:** Corvette sailing ship **Rev:** Denomination and globe **Edge:** Grooved

Date	Mintage	F12	VF20	XF40	MS60	MS63
2002	176,000,000	—	—	—	0.50	—
2002 F in star	18,000,000	—	—	—	1.00	—
2003	10,000,000	—	—	—	0.50	—
2004	25,000,000	—	—	—	0.50	—
2005	15,000,000	—	—	—	0.50	—
2006	45,000,000	—	—	—	0.50	—

Date	Mintage	F12	VF20	XF40	MS60	MS63
2007	25,000,103	—	—	—	0.50	—
2008	68,000,000	—	—	—	0.50	—
2009	16,000,000	—	—	—	0.50	—
2010	32,000,000	—	—	—	0.50	—
2011	47,000,000	—	—	—	0.50	—
2011	2,500	PF63 15.00				
2012	34,000,000	—	—	—	0.50	—
2012 Proof, In sets only	2,500	PF63 15.00				

KM# 183 5 EURO CENT
3.86 g., Copper Plated Steel, 21.2 mm. **Obv:** Freighter **Rev:** Denomination and globe **Edge:** Plain

Date	Mintage	F12	VF20	XF40	MS60	MS63
2002	211,000,000	—	—	—	1.00	—
2002 F in star	90,000,000	—	—	—	1.25	—
2003	750,000	—	—	—	1.00	—
2004	250,000	—	—	—	1.00	—
2005	1,000,000	—	—	—	1.00	—
2006	50,000,000	—	—	—	1.00	—
2007	55,005,598	—	—	—	1.00	—
2008	50,000,000	—	—	—	1.00	—
2009	38,000,000	—	—	—	1.00	—
2010	5,000,000	—	—	—	1.00	—
2011	2,500	PF63 15.00				
2011	34,000,000	—	—	—	1.00	—
2012	1,000,000	—	—	—	1.00	—
2012	2,500	PF63 15.00				

KM# 184 10 EURO CENT
4.07 g., Brass, 19.7 mm. **Obv:** Bust of Rhgas Feriaou's half right **Rev:** Denomination and map **Edge:** Reeded

Date	Mintage	F12	VF20	XF40	MS60	MS63
2002	138,000,000	—	—	—	1.25	—
2002 F in star	100,000,000	—	—	—	2.00	—
2003	600,000	—	—	—	1.25	—
2004	10,000,000	—	—	—	1.25	—
2005	25,000,000	—	—	—	1.25	—
2006	45,000,000	—	—	—	1.25	—

KM# 211 10 EURO CENT
4.07 g., Brass, 19.25 mm. **Obv:** Bust of Rhgas Feriaou's half right **Rev:** Relief map of Western Europe, stars, lines and value **Edge:** Reeded

Date	Mintage	F12	VF20	XF40	MS60	MS63
2007	63,000,000	—	—	—	1.25	1.50
2008	40,000,000	—	—	—	1.25	1.50
2009	46,000,000	—	—	—	1.25	1.50
2010	5,000,000	—	—	—	1.25	1.50
2011	36,000,000	—	—	—	1.25	1.50
2011	2,500	PF63 15.00				
2012	1,000,000	—	—	—	1.25	1.50
2012	2,500	PF63 15.00				

KM# 185 20 EURO CENT
5.73 g., Brass, 22.25 mm. **Obv:** Bust of John Kapodistrias half right **Rev:** Denomination and map **Edge:** Notched

Date	Mintage	F12	VF20	XF40	MS60	MS63
2002	209,000,000	—	—	—	1.25	—
2002 E in star	120,000,000	—	—	—	2.25	—
2003	800,000	—	—	—	1.25	—
2004	500,000	—	—	—	1.25	—
2005	1,000,000	—	—	—	1.25	—
2006	1,000,000	—	—	—	1.25	—

KM# 212 20 EURO CENT
5.73 g., Brass, 22.1 mm. **Obv:** Bust of John Kapodistrias' half right **Rev:** Relief map of Western Europe, stars, lines and value **Edge:** Notched

Date	Mintage	F12	VF20	XF40	MS60	MS63
2007	1,000,000	—	—	—	1.25	—
2008	20,000,000	—	—	—	1.25	—
2009	24,000,000	—	—	—	1.25	—
2010	12,000,000	—	—	—	1.25	—
2011	965,000	—	—	—	1.25	—
2011	2,500	PF63 20.00				
2012	1,000,000	—	—	—	1.25	—
2012	2,500	PF63 20.00				

KM# 186 50 EURO CENT
7.81 g., Brass, 24.2 mm. **Obv:** Bust of El. Venizelos half left **Rev:** Denomination and map **Edge:** Reeded

Date	Mintage	F12	VF20	XF40	MS60	MS63
2002	93,000,000	—	—	—	1.50	—
2002 F in star	70,000,000	—	—	—	2.50	—
2003	700,000	—	—	—	1.50	—
2004	500,000	—	—	—	1.50	—
2005	1,000,000	—	—	—	1.50	—
2006	1,000,000	—	—	—	1.50	—

KM# 213 50 EURO CENT
7.81 g., Brass, 24.2 mm. **Obv:** Bust of El. Venizelos half left **Rev:** Relief map of Western Europe, stars, lines and value **Edge:** Reeded

Date	Mintage	F12	VF20	XF40	MS60	MS63
2007	1,000,000	—	—	—	1.00	1.50
2008	10,000,000	—	—	—	1.00	1.50
2009	7,000,000	—	—	—	1.00	1.50
2010	6,000,000	—	—	—	1.00	1.50
2011	7,000,000	—	—	—	1.00	1.50
2011	2,500	PF63 25.00				
2012	1,000,000	—	—	—	1.00	1.50
2012	2,500	PF63 25.00				

KM# 187 EURO
7.50 g., Bi-Metallic, 23.25 mm. **Obv:** Ancient Athenian coin design **Rev:** Denomination and map **Edge:** Segmented reeding

Date	Mintage	F12	VF20	XF40	MS60	MS63
2002	61,500,000	—	—	—	4.00	—
2002 S in star	50,000,000	—	—	—	6.00	—
2003	11,000,000	—	—	—	7.50	—
2004	10,000,000	—	—	—	5.00	—
2005	10,000,000	—	—	—	5.00	—
2006	10,000,000	—	—	—	5.00	—

KM# 214 EURO
7.50 g., Bi-Metallic, 23.25 mm. **Obv:** Ancient Athenian coin

---

design **Rev:** Relief map of Western Europe, stars, lines and value **Edge:** Segmented reeding

Date	Mintage	F12	VF20	XF40	MS60	MS63
2007	24,000,000	—	—	—	3.00	4.00
2008	4,000,000	—	—	—	3.00	4.00
2009	18,000,000	—	—	—	3.00	4.00
2010	11,000,000	—	—	—	3.00	4.00
2011	965,000	—	—	—	3.00	4.00
2011	2,500	PF63 40.00				
2012	1,000,000	—	—	—	3.00	4.00
2012	2,500	PF63 40.00				

KM# 188 2 EURO
8.50 g., Bi-Metallic, 25.75 mm. **Obv:** Europa seated on a bull **Rev:** Denomination and map **Edge:** Reeded with Greek legend and stars

Date	Mintage	F12	VF20	XF40	MS60	MS63
2002	75,400,000	—	—	—	4.00	—
2002 S in star	70,000,000	—	—	—	6.50	—
2003	550,000	—	—	—	20.00	—
2004 In sets only	30,000	—	—	—	50.00	—
2005	1,000,000	—	—	—	4.00	—
2006	1,000,000	—	—	—	4.00	—

KM# 209 2 EURO
8.50 g., Bi-Metallic, 25.75 mm. **Subject:** 2004 Olympics **Obv:** Discus thrower **Rev:** Denomination and map **Edge:** Reeded with Greek legend and stars

Date	Mintage	F12	VF20	XF40	MS60	MS63
2004	49,500,000	—	—	—	4.00	6.00
2004 Prooflike	500,000	—	—	—	—	15.00

KM# 215 2 EURO
8.50 g., Bi-Metallic, 25.75 mm. **Obv:** Europa seated on a bull **Rev:** Relief map of Western Europe, stars, lines and value **Edge:** Reeded with Greek legend and stars

Date	Mintage	F12	VF20	XF40	MS60	MS63
2007 In sets only	15,000	—	—	—	—	25.00
2008	2,000,000	—	—	—	3.00	10.00
2009	982,000	—	—	—	3.00	5.00
2010	2,000,000	—	—	—	3.00	5.00
2011	—	—	—	—	3.00	5.00
2011	2,500	PF63 50.00				
2012	2,500	PF63 50.00				
2012	2,000,000	—	—	—	3.00	5.00

KM# 216 2 EURO
8.50 g., Bi-Metallic, 25.75 mm. **Subject:** 50th Anniversary - Treaty of Rome **Obv:** Open treaty book **Rev:** Large value at left, modified outline of Europe at right **Edge:** Reeded with Greek legend and stars

Date	Mintage	F12	VF20	XF40	MS60	MS63
2007	4,000,000	—	—	—	—	9.00

KM# 227 2 EURO
8.50 g., Bi-Metallic, 25.75 mm. **Subject:** European Monetary Union, 10th Anniversary **Obv:** Stick figure and Euro symbol **Edge:** Reeded with Greek legend and stars

Date	Mintage	F12	VF20	XF40	MS60	MS63
2009	4,000,000	—	—	—	—	7.00

KM# 236 2 EURO
8.50 g., Bi-Metallic, 25.75 mm. **Subject:** Battle of Marathon, 2500th Anniversary **Obv:** Ancient Greek Warrior holding javelin running **Edge:** Reeded with Greek legend and stars

Date	Mintage	F12	VF20	XF40	MS60	MS63
2010	3,500,000	—	—	—	4.00	9.00

KM# 239 2 EURO
8.50 g., Bi-Metallic, 25.75 mm. **Subject:** Special Olympics - Athens **Obv:** Figure standing in spiral, laureal weath at left

Date	Mintage	F12	VF20	XF40	MS60	MS63
2011	1,000,000	—	—	—	6.00	7.50

KM# 245 2 EURO
8.50 g., Bi-Metallic, 25.75 mm. **Subject:** Euro coinage, 10th Anniversary **Obv:** Euro symbol on globe at center, child-like rendering around

Date	Mintage	F12	VF20	XF40	MS60	MS63
2012 Special Unc.	5,000	—	—	—	—	15.00
2012	1,000,000	—	—	—	6.00	8.00
2012 Proof, In sets only	2,500	PF63 50.00				

KM# 252 2 EURO
8.50 g., Bi-Metallic, 25.75 mm. **Obv:** Plato, head left

Date	Mintage	F12	VF20	XF40	MS60	MS63
2013	750,000	—	—	—	4.00	6.00

KM# 253 2 EURO
8.50 g., Bi-Metallic, 25.75 mm. **Subject:** 1913 Revolution **Obv:** Man with flag

Date	Mintage	F12	VF20	XF40	MS60	MS63
2013	750,000	—	—	—	4.00	6.00

KM# 190 10 EURO
34.00 g., 0.925 Silver 1.0046 oz. ASW, 40 mm. **Subject:** Olympics **Obv:** Olympic rings in wreath above value within circle of stars **Rev:** Ancient and modern runners **Edge:** Plain **Note:** Olympics

Date	Mintage	F12	VF20	XF40	MS60	MS63
ND (2003)	68,000	PF63 60.00				

KM# 191 10 EURO
34.00 g., 0.925 Silver 1.0046 oz. ASW, 40 mm. **Subject:** Olympics **Obv:** Olympic rings in wreath above value within circle of stars **Rev:** Ancient and modern discus throwers **Edge:** Plain

Date	Mintage	F12	VF20	XF40	MS60	MS63
ND(2003)	68,000	PF63 60.00				

KM# 193 10 EURO
34.00 g., 0.925 Silver 1.0046 oz. ASW, 40 mm. **Subject:** Olympics **Obv:** Olympic rings in wreath above value within circle of stars **Rev:** Ancient and modern javelin throwers **Edge:** Plain

Date	Mintage	F12	VF20	XF40	MS60	MS63
ND(2003)	68,000	PF63 60.00				

KM# 194 10 EURO
34.00 g., 0.925 Silver 1.0046 oz. ASW, 40 mm. **Subject:** Olympics **Obv:** Olympic rings in wreath above value within circle of stars **Rev:** Ancient and modern long jumpers **Edge:** Plain

Date	Mintage	F12	VF20	XF40	MS60	MS63
ND(2003)	68,000	PF63 60.00				

KM# 196 10 EURO
34.00 g., 0.925 Silver 1.0046 oz. ASW, 40 mm. **Subject:** Olympics **Obv:** Olympic rings in wreath above value within circle of stars **Rev:** Ancient and modern relay runners **Edge:** Plain

Date	Mintage	F12	VF20	XF40	MS60	MS63
ND(2003)	68,000	PF63 60.00				

KM# 197 10 EURO
34.00 g., 0.925 Silver 1.0046 oz. ASW, 40 mm. **Subject:** Olympics **Obv:** Olympic rings in wreath above value within circle of stars **Rev:** Ancient and modern horsemen **Edge:** Plain

Date	Mintage	F12	VF20	XF40	MS60	MS63
ND(2003)	68,000	PF63 60.00				

KM# 199 10 EURO
34.00 g., 0.925 Silver 1.0046 oz. ASW, 40 mm. **Subject:** Olympics **Obv:** Olympic rings in wreath above value within circle of stars **Rev:** Modern ribbon dancer and two ancient female acrobats **Edge:** Plain

Date	Mintage	F12	VF20	XF40	MS60	MS63
ND(2003)	68,000	PF63 60.00				

KM# 200 10 EURO
34.00 g., 0.925 Silver 1.0046 oz. ASW, 40 mm. **Subject:** Olympics **Obv:** Olympic rings in wreath above value within a circle of stars **Rev:** Ancient and modern female swimmers **Edge:** Plain

Date	Mintage	F12	VF20	XF40	MS60	MS63
ND(2003)	68,000	PF63 60.00				

KM# 208 10 EURO
9.75 g., 0.925 Silver 0.2881 oz. ASW, 28.25 mm. **Subject:** Greek Presidency of E. U. **Obv:** National arms in wreath above value **Rev:** Stylized document design **Edge:** Notched

Date	Mintage	F12	VF20	XF40	MS60	MS63
2003	50,000	PF63 80.00				

KM# 202 10 EURO
34.00 g., 0.925 Silver 1.0046 oz. ASW, 40 mm. **Subject:** Olympics **Obv:** Olympic rings in wreath above value within circle of stars **Rev:** Ancient and modern weight lifters **Edge:** Plain

Date	Mintage	F12	VF20	XF40	MS60	MS63
ND(2004)	68,000	PF63 60.00				

KM# 203 10 EURO
34.00 g., 0.925 Silver 1.0046 oz. ASW, 40 mm. **Subject:** Olympics **Obv:** Olympic rings in wreath above value within circle of stars **Rev:** Ancient and modern wrestlers **Edge:** Plain

Date	Mintage	F12	VF20	XF40	MS60	MS63
ND(2004)	68,000	PF63 60.00				

KM# 205 10 EURO
34.00 g., 0.925 Silver 1.0046 oz. ASW, 40 mm. **Subject:** Olympics **Obv:** Olympic rings in wreath above value within circle of stars **Rev:** Ancient and modern handball players **Edge:** Plain

Date	Mintage	F12	VF20	XF40	MS60	MS63
ND(2004)	68,000	PF63 60.00				

KM# 206 10 EURO
34.00 g., 0.925 Silver 1.0046 oz. ASW, 40 mm. **Subject:** Olympics **Obv:** Olympic rings in wreath above value within circle of stars **Rev:** Ancient and modern soccer players **Edge:** Plain

Date	Mintage	F12	VF20	XF40	MS60	MS63
ND(2004)	68,000	PF63 60.00				

KM# 230 10 EURO
34.00 g., 0.925 Silver 1.0046 oz. ASW, 40 mm. **Obv:** Wreath **Rev:** Torch runner and map of Australia

Date	Mintage	F12	VF20	XF40	MS60	MS63
2004	10,000	PF63 100	PF65 115			

KM# 231 10 EURO
34.00 g., 0.925 Silver 1.0046 oz. ASW, 40 mm. **Rev:** Torch runner and map of Asia

Date	Mintage	F12	VF20	XF40	MS60	MS63
2004	10,000	PF63 100	PF65 115			

KM# 232 10 EURO
34.00 g., 0.925 Silver 1.0046 oz. ASW, 40 mm. **Rev:** Torch runner and map of Africa

Date	Mintage	F12	VF20	XF40	MS60	MS63
2004	10,000	PF63 100	PF65 115			

KM# 233 10 EURO
34.00 g., 0.925 Silver 1.0046 oz. ASW, 40 mm. **Rev:** Torch runner and map of North and South America

Date	Mintage	F12	VF20	XF40	MS60	MS63
2004	10,000	PF63 100	PF65 115			

KM# 217 10 EURO
9.75 g., 0.925 Silver 0.2881 oz. ASW **Subject:** Olympic National Park **Obv:** National arms above stylized flowers **Rev:** Four Titans above flowers in camp

Date	Mintage	F12	VF20	XF40	MS60	MS63
2005	25,000	PF63 45.00				

KM# 218 10 EURO
9.75 g., 0.925 Silver 0.2881 oz. ASW, 28.25 mm. **Subject:** PATRA - European Capitol of Culture - Achaia **Obv:** National arms at upper right, stylized bridge below **Rev:** PATRA logo **Edge:** Plain

Date	Mintage	F12	VF20	XF40	MS60	MS63
2006	—	PF63 50.00				

KM# 219 10 EURO
34.00 g., 0.925 Silver 1.0046 oz. ASW, 40 mm. **Obv:** National arms above stylized flowers **Rev:** Outline of Greece at left, statue of Zeus, flowers at right **Edge:** Plain

Date	Mintage	F12	VF20	XF40	MS60	MS63
2006	5,000	PF63 55.00				

KM# 220 10 EURO
34.00 g., 0.925 Silver 1.0046 oz. ASW, 40 mm. **Subject:** National Parks - Mount Olympus - International Biosphere Reserve **Obv:** National arms above stylized flowers **Rev:** Archaeological outline of Dion City above landscape **Edge:** Plain

Date	Mintage	F12	VF20	XF40	MS60	MS63
2006	5,000	PF63 55.00				

KM# 221 10 EURO
34.00 g., 0.925 Silver 1.0046 oz. ASW, 40 mm. **Subject:** National Parks - Arkoudorema River in Southern Pindos - Valia Kalda **Obv:** National arms on stylized tree **Rev:** Outlined map at upper left, bird perched on stalk, flowers at center right **Edge:** Plain

Date	Mintage	F12	VF20	XF40	MS60	MS63
2007	5,000	PF63 60.00				

KM# 222 10 EURO
34.00 g., 0.925 Silver 1.0046 oz. ASW, 40 mm. **Subject:** National Parks - Valia Kalda - Southern Pindos **Obv:** National arms on stylized tree **Rev:** Tree line **Edge:** Plain

Date	Mintage	F12	VF20	XF40	MS60	MS63
2007	5,000	PF63 60.00				

KM# 223 10 EURO
9.75 g., 0.925 Silver 0.2881 oz. ASW, 28.25 mm. **Subject:** 30th Anniversary Death of Maria Callas, Operatic Soprano **Obv:** National arms above denomination, facsimile signature below, music scores in background **Rev:** Bust of Maria Callas right **Edge:** Plain **Shape:** Spanish Flower

Date	Mintage	F12	VF20	XF40	MS60	MS63
2007	5,000	PF63 50.00				

KM# 224 10 EURO
9.75 g., 0.925 Silver 0.2881 oz. ASW, 28.25 mm. **Subject:** 50th Anniversary death of Nikos Kazantzakis, Author **Obv:** National arms above denomination, facsimile signature below **Rev:** Head of N. Kazantzakis facing 3/4 left **Edge:** Plain **Shape:** Spanish Flower

Date	Mintage	F12	VF20	XF40	MS60	MS63
2007	5,000	PF63 50.00				

KM# 225 10 EURO
9.75 g., 0.925 Silver 0.2881 oz. ASW, 28.25 mm. **Subject:** Acropolis Museum **Obv:** Panoramic view of the Acropolis **Rev:** Pediment sculpture

Date	Mintage	F12	VF20	XF40	MS60	MS63
2008	10,000					50.00

KM# 226 10 EURO
9.75 g., 0.925 Silver 0.2881 oz. ASW, 28.25 mm. **Subject:** Yannis Ritsas

Date	Mintage	F12	VF20	XF40	MS60	MS63
2009	—	PF63 50.00				

KM# 228 10 EURO
9.75 g., 0.925 Silver 0.2881 oz. ASW, 28.25 mm. **Subject:** International Year of Astronomy

Date	Mintage	F12	VF20	XF40	MS60	MS63
2009	—	PF63 45.00				

KM# 237 10 EURO
34.00 g., 0.925 Silver 1.0046 oz. ASW, 40 mm. **Subject:** Sofia Vempo, 100th Anniversary of Birth **Obv:** Sofia Vempo portrait **Rev:** Stave, national emblem and value **Shape:** Spanish flower

Date	Mintage	F12	VF20	XF40	MS60	MS63
2010	5,000	PF63 65.00				

KM# 238 10 EURO
9.75 g., 0.925 Silver 0.2881 oz. ASW, 28.25 mm. **Subject:** International Year of Biodiversity **Obv:** Various species of Biodiversity **Rev:** Nature's species, national emblem and value **Shape:** Spanish flower

Date	Mintage	F12	VF20	XF40	MS60	MS63
2010	5,000	PF63 50.00				

KM# 242 10 EURO
34.10 g., 0.925 Silver 1.0076 oz. ASW, 40 mm. **Subject:** Special Olympics, Highlight **Obv:** Highlight from an event during the games **Rev:** Stylized elements from the XIII Special Olympics emblem in Athens, National Arms, value below

Date	Mintage	F12	VF20	XF40	MS60	MS63
2011	2,000	PF63 130				

KM# 243 10 EURO
34.10 g., 0.925 Silver 1.0076 oz. ASW, 40 mm. **Subject:** Special Olympics, Torch-bearer **Obv:** Torch-bearer **Rev:** Stylized elements from the XIII Special Olympics emblem in Athens, National Arms, value below

Date	Mintage	F12	VF20	XF40	MS60	MS63
2011	2,000	PF63 130				

KM# 240 10 EURO
9.75 g., 0.925 Silver 0.2881 oz. ASW, 28.25 mm. **Subject:** XIII Special Olympics, Special Olympics Founder Declaration **Obv:** Declaration over the Acropolis of Athens, Radiant Sun **Rev:** Special Olympics emblem, National arms below value **Shape:** 5 double edge notches

Date	Mintage	F12	VF20	XF40	MS60	MS63
(2011)	—	—	—	—	—	—
2011 Proof, In sets only	7,500	PF63 40.00				

KM# 241 10 EURO
9.75 g., 0.925 Silver 0.2881 oz. ASW, 28.25 mm. **Subject:** XIII Special Olympics, Athletes in Union **Obv:** Stylized athletes around a radiant sun and olive branch **Rev:** Panathenaikon Stadium below the National Arms and value **Shape:** 5 double edge notches

Date	Mintage	F12	VF20	XF40	MS60	MS63
2011						
2011 Proof, in sets only	7,500	PF63 40.00				

KM# 246 10 EURO
9.75 g., 0.925 Silver 0.2881 oz. ASW, 28.25 mm. **Subject:** Dr. George N. Papanicolaou **Obv:** Dr. Papanicolaou and a microscope **Rev:** Shaped human cells around the national emblem and value **Shape:** 5 double edge notches

Date	Mintage	F12	VF20	XF40	MS60	MS63
2012 Prooflike, In sets only	10,000	—	—	—	—	60.00

KM# 247 10 EURO
34.10 g., 0.925 Silver 1.0076 oz. ASW, 40 mm. **Subject:** Greek Culture" - Poet: Aeschylus **Obv:** Aeschylus (524-455 B.C.) portrait. **Rev:** Ancient lyrics, national emblem, value and date

Date	Mintage	F12	VF20	XF40	MS60	MS63
2012	5,000	PF63 120				

KM# 248 10 EURO
34.10 g., 0.925 Silver 1.0076 oz. ASW, 40 mm. **Subject:** Greek Culture" - Socrates **Obv:** Socrates (469-399 B.C.) portrait facing left **Rev:** Ancient sayings, national emblem, value and date

Date	Mintage	F12	VF20	XF40	MS60	MS63
2012	5,000	PF63 120				

KM# 254 10 EURO
34.00 g., 0.925 Silver 1.0046 oz. ASW, 40 mm. **Subject:** Pythagoras of Samos

Date	Mintage	F12	VF20	XF40	MS60	MS63
2013	1,000	—	—	—	—	110

KM# 255 10 EURO
34.00 g., 0.925 Silver 1.0046 oz. ASW, 40 mm. **Subject:** Sophocles

Date	Mintage	F12	VF20	XF40	MS60	MS63
2013	1,000	PF63 110				

KM# 210 20 EURO
24.00 g., 0.925 Silver 0.7092 oz. ASW, 37 mm. **Subject:** Bank of Greece 75th Anniversary **Obv:** Value **Rev:** Flag

Date	Mintage	F12	VF20	XF40	MS60	MS63
2003	15,000	PF63 170				

KM# 251 50 EURO
1.00 g., 0.9999 Gold 0.0319 oz. AGW, 14 mm. **Subject:** Ancient Pella (Macedonia), Northern Greece. **Obv:** Wave and geometric pattern, ornaments of a stone slab table (Hellenistic era) found in Pella, capital of ancient Macedonia **Rev:** Wave shaped ornament of a stove slab table (Hellensitic era) found in Pella, capital of ancient Macedonia, Pella, and the national arms of Greece, value below

Date	Mintage	F12	VF20	XF40	MS60	MS63
2012	4,000	PF63 95.00				

KM# 192 100 EURO
10.00 g., 0.9999 Gold 0.3194 oz. AGW, 25 mm. **Subject:** Olympics **Obv:** Olympic rings in wreath above value within circle of stars **Rev:** Knossos Palace **Edge:** Plain

Date	Mintage	F12	VF20	XF40	MS60	MS63
ND(2003)	28,000	PF63 525	PF65 575			

KM# 195 100 EURO
10.00 g., 0.9999 Gold 0.3194 oz. AGW, 25 mm. **Subject:** Olympics **Obv:** Olympic rings in wreath above value within circle of stars **Rev:** Krypte archway **Edge:** Plain

Date	Mintage	F12	VF20	XF40	MS60	MS63
ND(2003)	28,000	PF63 525	PF65 575			

KM# 198 100 EURO
10.00 g., 0.9999 Gold 0.3194 oz. AGW, 25 mm. **Subject:** Olympics **Obv:** Olympic rings in wreath above value within circle of stars **Rev:** Panathenean Stadium **Edge:** Plain

Date	Mintage	F12	VF20	XF40	MS60	MS63
ND(2003)	28,000	PF63 525	PF65 575			

KM# 201 100 EURO
10.00 g., 0.9999 Gold 0.3194 oz. AGW, 25 mm. **Subject:** Olympics **Obv:** Olympic rings in wreath above value within circle of stars **Rev:** Zappeion Mansion **Edge:** Plain

Date	Mintage	F12	VF20	XF40	MS60	MS63
ND(2003)	28,000	PF63 525	PF65 575			

KM# 204 100 EURO
10.00 g., 0.9999 Gold 0.3194 oz. AGW, 25 mm. **Subject:** Olympics **Obv:** Olympic rings in wreath above value within circle of stars **Rev:** Acropolis **Edge:** Plain

Date	Mintage	F12	VF20	XF40	MS60	MS63
ND(2004)	28,000	PF63 525	PF65 575			

KM# 207 100 EURO
10.00 g., 0.9999 Gold 0.3194 oz. AGW, 25 mm. **Subject:** Olympics **Obv:** Olympic rings in wreath above value within circle of stars **Rev:** Academy of Athens **Edge:** Plain

Date	Mintage	F12	VF20	XF40	MS60	MS63
ND(2004)	28,000	PF63 525	PF65 575			

KM# 234 100 EURO
10.00 g., 0.999 Gold 0.3191 oz. AGW, 25 mm. **Rev:** Classical female handing torch to kneeling runner

Date	Mintage	F12	VF20	XF40	MS60	MS63
2004	10,000	PF63 550	PF65 600			

KM# 235 100 EURO
10.00 g., 0.999 Gold 0.3191 oz. AGW, 25 mm. **Rev:** Torch runner and flag

Date	Mintage	F12	VF20	XF40	MS60	MS63
2004	10,000	PF63 550	PF65 600			

KM# 244 100 EURO
7.99 g., 0.9166 Gold 0.2339 oz. AGW, 22.1 mm. **Subject:** Special Olympics' Athletes in Union **Obv:** Stylized Athletes around a radiant sun and olive branch **Rev:** Panathenaikon Stadium below the National Arms and value

Date	Mintage	F12	VF20	XF40	MS60	MS63
2011	1,000	PF63 1,250	PF65 1,350			

KM# 249 100 EURO
7.99 g., 0.9166 Gold 0.2339 oz. AGW, 22.1 mm. **Subject:** Liberation of Thessaloniki, 100th Anniversary **Obv:** Golden round ornament with rosette (480 B.C.) from an ancient tomb, flag of modern Greece background. **Rev:** The White Tower (symbol of Thewsaloniki) with the National Arms engraved and value, shaped laurels above

Date	Mintage	F12	VF20	XF40	MS60	MS63
2012	1,500	PF63 750	PF65 800			

KM# 250 100 EURO
7.99 g., 0.916 Gold 0.2337 oz. AGW, 22.1 mm. **Subject:** Balkan Wars outbreak, 100th Anniversary **Obv:** Admiral Parlos Kountouriotis bust, the flag of Greece on the background **Rev:** The battleship "Averoph", national arms above left and value below

Date	Mintage	F12	VF20	XF40	MS60	MS63
2012	1,500	PF63 750	PF65 800			

KM# 229 200 EURO
31.11 g., 0.999 Gold 0.9926 oz. AGW, 37 mm. **Subject:** Bank of Greece, 75th Anniversary

Date	Mintage	F12	VF20	XF40	MS60	MS63
2003	1,000	PF65 3,500				

MINT SETS

KM#	Date	Mintage	Identification	Issue Price	Mkt Val
MS6	2002 (8)	50,000	KM#181-188	—	30.00
MS7	2002F (8)	5,000	KM#181-188	—	300
MS8	2003 (8)	—	KM#181-188	—	40.00
MS9	2003 (9)	—	KM#181-188, 208	—	80.00
MS11	2004 (8)	20,000	KM#181-188	—	65.00
MS12	2005 (8)	25,000	KM#181-188	—	35.00
MS13	2005 (9)	25,000	KM#181-188, 220	—	70.00
MS14	2006 (9)	25,000	KM#181-188 (2005), 220	28.00	70.00
MS15	2006 (9)	25,000	KM#181-188, 218	50.00	70.00
MS16	2007 (8)	15,000	KM#181-183, 211-215	—	50.00
MS17	2007 (9)	15,000	KM#181-183, 211-215, 224	50.00	75.00
MS18	2007 (9)	15,000	KM#181-183, 211-215, 223	50.00	95.00
MS19	2008 (8)	15,000	KM#181-183, 211-215	28.00	40.00
MS20	2008 (9)	10,000	KM#181-183, 211-215, 225	45.00	55.00
MS21	2009 (8)	7,500	KM#181-183, 211-215	28.00	45.00
MS22	2009 (9)	5,000	KM#181-183, 211-215, 226	45.00	55.00
MS23	2009 (9)	5,000	KM#181-183, 211-215, 228	45.00	55.00
MS24	2010 (8)	7,500	KM#181-183, 211-215	28.00	30.00
MS25	2010 (8)	7,500	KM#181-183, 214, 236	28.00	30.00
MS26	2010 (9)	5,000	KM#181-183, 211-215, 237	45.00	80.00
MS27	2010 (9)	5,000	KM#181-183, 211-215, 238	45.00	75.00
MS28	2011 (8)	15,000	KM#181-183, 211-215	28.00	40.00
MS29	2011 (9)	5,000	KM#181-183, 211-215, 239	28.00	45.00
MS30	2011 (9)	7,500	KM#181-183, 211-215, 240	45.00	70.00
MS31	2011 (9)	7,500	KM#181-183, 211-215, 241	45.00	70.00
MS32	2012 (9)	10,000	KM#181-183, 211-215, 246, Dr. George Papanicolaou	45.00	65.00
MS33	2012 (8)	20,000	KM#181-183, 211-215. Santorini, the Island of Lava	28.00	40.00

PROOF SETS

KM#	Date	Mintage	Identification	Issue Price	Mkt Val
PS6	2011 (8)	2,500	KM#181-183, 211-215	115	300
PS7	2012 (9)	2,500	KM#181-183, 211-215, 245		250

GUATEMALA

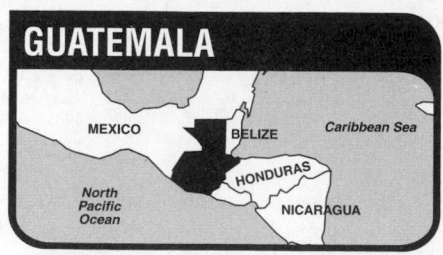

The Republic of Guatemala, the northernmost of the five Central American republics, has an area of 42,042 sq. mi. (108,890 sq. km.) and a population of 10.7 million. Capital: Guatemala City. The economy of Guatemala is heavily dependent on agriculture, however, the country is rich in nickel resources which are being developed. Coffee, cotton and bananas are exported.

Guatemala, once the site of an ancient Mayan civilization, was conquered by Pedro de Alvarado, the resourceful lieutenant of Cortes who undertook the conquest from Mexico. Cruel but strategically skillful, he progressed rapidly along the Pacific coastal lowlands to the highland plain of Quetzaltenango where the decisive battle for Guatemala was fought. After routing the Indian forces, he established the city of Guatemala in 1524. The Spanish Captaincy-General of Guatemala included all Central America but Panama. Guatemala declared its independence of Spain in 1821 and was absorbed into the Mexican empire of Augustin Iturbide (1822-23). From 1823 to 1839 Guatemala was a constituent state of the Central American Republic. Upon dissolution of that confederation, Guatemala proclaimed itself an independent republic. Like El Salvador, Guatemala suffered from internal strife between right-wing, US-backed military government and leftist indigenous peoples from ca. 1954 to ca. 1997.

MINT MARKS
(L) – London, Royal Mint

REPUBLIC
REFORM COINAGE
100 Centavos = 1 Quetzal

KM# 282 CENTAVO (Un)
0.80 g., Aluminum, 19 mm. **Subject:** Fray Bartolome de las Casas **Obv:** National arms **Rev:** Bust left **Edge:** Plain **Note:** 7-sided interior field

Date	Mintage	F12	VF20	XF40	MS60	MS63
2007	—	—	—	0.15	0.25	0.35

KM# 276.6 5 CENTAVOS
1.60 g., Copper-Nickel, 16 mm. **Obv:** National arms, smaller sized emblem, no dots by date **Obv. Legend:** REPUBLICA DE GUATEMALA 1997 **Rev:** Kapok tree center, value at right, ground below **Edge:** Reeded **Note:** Varieties exist.

Date	Mintage	F12	VF20	XF40	MS60	MS63
2006	—	—	—	0.15	0.30	0.50
2008	—	—	—	0.15	0.30	0.50
2009	—	—	—	0.15	0.30	0.50
2010	—	—	—	0.15	0.30	0.50

KM# 277.6 10 CENTAVOS
3.20 g., Copper-Nickel, 21 mm. **Obv:** National arms, small letters in legend **Obv. Legend:** REPUBLICA DE GUATEMALA **Rev:** Monolith **Rev. Legend:** MONOLITO DE QUIRIGUA **Edge:** Reeded **Note:** Varieties exist.

Date	Mintage	F12	VF20	XF40	MS60	MS63
2006	—	—	0.15	0.25	0.75	1.00
2008	—	—	0.15	0.25	0.75	1.00
2009	—	—	0.15	0.25	0.75	1.00

KM# 283 50 CENTAVOS
5.50 g., Nickel-Brass, 26.5 mm. **Obv:** National arms **Rev:** Whitenun orchid (lycaste skinneri var. alba orchidaceae) **Edge:** Reeded

Date	Mintage	F12	VF20	XF40	MS60	MS63
2001	—	—	—	0.50	1.00	1.25
2007	—	—	—	0.50	1.00	1.25

KM# 284 QUETZAL

11.00 g., Nickel-Brass, 29 mm. **Obv:** National arms **Obv. Legend:** REPUBLIC OF GUATEMALA **Rev:** PAZ above stylized dove **Rev. Legend:** Paz Firme y Duradera 29 de Diciembre de 1996 **Edge:** Reeded

Date	Mintage	F12	VF20	XF40	MS60	MS63
2001 Thick letters	—	—	—	0.25	1.00	1.50
2006 Thin letters	—	—	—	0.25	1.00	1.50
2008	—	—	—	0.25	1.00	1.50
2011 Thin letters	—	—	—	0.25	1.00	1.50

KM# 287 QUETZAL

31.10 g., 0.9999 Silver 0.9935 oz. ASW, 30 mm. **Subject:** Canonization of Brother Pedro Betancourt **Obv:** National arms **Rev:** Standing monk **Edge:** Plain

Date	Mintage	F12	VF20	XF40	MS60	MS63
ND(2002)	6,000	PF60 30.00	PF63 45.00	PF65 60.00		

KM# 288 QUETZAL

31.10 g., 0.999 Silver 0.9926 oz. ASW, 40 mm. **Subject:** Discovery of the Americas **Obv:** Shields around inner circle holding arms with date below **Rev:** Native peoples in canoe with fish

Date	Mintage	F12	VF20	XF40	MS60	MS63
2002		PF60 30.00	PF63 45.00	PF65 60.00		

KM# 289 QUETZAL

27.00 g., 0.925 Silver 0.7978 oz. ASW, 40 mm. **Obv:** Arms at center surrounded by odler arms **Rev:** Ancient temple

Date	Mintage	F12	VF20	XF40	MS60	MS63
2005		PF60 30.00	PF63 45.00	PF65 60.00		

KM# 290 QUETZAL

27.00 g., 0.925 Silver 0.7978 oz. ASW, 40 mm. **Obv:** Arms surrounded by older arms **Rev:** Female dancer and figures

Date	Mintage	F12	VF20	XF40	MS60	MS63
2007	—	PF60 30.00	PF63 45.00	PF65 60.00		

KM# 291 QUETZAL

27.00 g., 0.925 Silver 0.7978 oz. ASW, 40 mm. **Subject:** Ibero-American series

Date	Mintage	F12	VF20	XF40	MS60	MS63
2010	—	PF60 30.00	PF63 45.00	PF65 60.00		

GUERNSEY

The Bailiwick of Guernsey, a British crown dependency located in the English Channel 30 miles (48 km.) west of Normandy, France, has an area of 30 sq. mi. (194 sq. km.) (including the isles of Alderney, Jethou, Herm, Brechou, and Sark), and a population of 54,000. Capital: St. Peter Port. Agriculture and cattle breeding are the main occupations.

Guernsey is administered by its own laws and customs. Unless the island is mentioned specifically, acts passed by the British Parliament are not applicable to Guernsey. During World War II, German troops occupied the island from June 30, 1940 till May 9, 1945.

RULER
British

MONETARY SYSTEM
100 Pence = 1 Pound

BRITISH DEPENDENCY
DECIMAL COINAGE

KM# 89 PENNY

3.56 g., Copper Plated Steel, 20.32 mm. **Ruler:** Elizabeth II **Obv:** Head with tiara right **Rev:** Edible crab **Edge:** Plain

Date	Mintage	F12	VF20	XF40	MS60	MS63
2003	1,302,600	—	—	—	0.35	1.00
2006	1,731,000	—	—	—	0.35	0.75
2012	—	—	—	—	0.35	0.75

KM# 96 2 PENCE

7.12 g., Copper Plated Steel, 25.91 mm. **Ruler:** Elizabeth II **Obv:** Head with tiara, shield at left **Rev:** Guernsey cows **Edge:** Plain

Date	Mintage	F12	VF20	XF40	MS60	MS63
2003	662,600	—	—	—	0.50	1.00
2006	1,322,000	—	—	—	0.50	1.00
2011	—	—	—	—	0.50	1.00
2012	—	—	—	—	0.50	1.00

KM# 97 5 PENCE

3.25 g., Copper-Nickel, 18 mm. **Ruler:** Elizabeth II **Obv:** Head with tiara right **Rev:** Sailboat **Edge:** Reeded

Date	Mintage	F12	VF20	XF40	MS60	MS63
2003	292,600	—	—	—	0.45	0.65
2006	1,217,000	—	—	—	0.45	0.65
2010	—	—	—	—	0.45	0.65

KM# 97a 5 PENCE

3.25 g., Nickel Plated Steel, 18 mm. **Ruler:** Elizabeth II **Obv:** Head with tiara right **Rev:** Sailboat **Edge:** Reeded

Date	Mintage	F12	VF20	XF40	MS60	MS63
2012	—	—	—	—	0.45	0.65

KM# 149 10 PENCE

6.50 g., Copper-Nickel, 24.5 mm. **Ruler:** Elizabeth II **Obv:** Crowned head right **Rev:** Tomato plant **Edge:** Reeded

Date	Mintage	F12	VF20	XF40	MS60	MS63
2003	32,600	—	—	—	0.60	0.85
2006	26,000	—	—	—	0.60	0.85

KM# 149a 10 PENCE

6.50 g., Nickel Plated Steel, 24.5 mm. **Ruler:** Elizabeth II **Obv:** Head with tiara right **Rev:** Tomato plant **Edge:** Reeded

Date	Mintage	F12	VF20	XF40	MS60	MS63
2012	—	—	—	—	0.60	0.85

KM# 90 20 PENCE

5.00 g., Copper-Nickel, 21.4 mm. **Ruler:** Elizabeth II **Obv:** Head with tiara right, small arms at left **Rev:** Island map within cogwheel **Shape:** 7-sided

Date	Mintage	F12	VF20	XF40	MS60	MS63
2003	732,600	—	—	—	0.90	1.25
2006	16,250	—	—	—	0.90	1.25
2009	—	—	—	—	0.90	1.25
2012	—	—	—	—	0.90	1.25

KM# 145 50 PENCE

8.00 g., Copper-Nickel, 27.3 mm. **Ruler:** Elizabeth II **Subject:**

Coronation Jubilee **Obv:** Head with tiara right **Rev:** Queen on horseback **Edge:** Plain **Shape:** 7-sided

Date	Mintage	F12	VF20	XF40	MS60	MS63
2003	—	—	—	—	1.50	2.50

KM# 146 50 PENCE

8.00 g., Copper-Nickel, 27.3 mm. **Ruler:** Elizabeth II **Subject:** Coronation Jubilee **Obv:** Head with tiara right **Rev:** Queen on throne **Edge:** Plain **Shape:** 7-sided

Date	Mintage	F12	VF20	XF40	MS60	MS63
2003	—	—	—	—	1.50	2.50

KM# 147 50 PENCE

8.00 g., Copper-Nickel, 27.3 mm. **Ruler:** Elizabeth II **Subject:** Coronation Jubilee **Obv:** Head with tiara right **Rev:** Crown **Edge:** Plain **Shape:** 7-sided

Date	Mintage	F12	VF20	XF40	MS60	MS63
2003	—	—	—	—	1.50	2.50

KM# 148 50 PENCE

8.00 g., Copper-Nickel, 27.3 mm. **Ruler:** Elizabeth II **Subject:** Coronation Jubilee **Obv:** Head with tiara right **Rev:** Crowned ERII monogram **Edge:** Plain **Shape:** 7-sided

Date	Mintage	F12	VF20	XF40	MS60	MS63
2003	—	—	—	—	1.50	2.50

KM# 156 50 PENCE

8.00 g., Copper-Nickel, 27.3 mm. **Ruler:** Elizabeth II **Obv:** Head with tiara right **Rev:** Crossed flowers **Edge:** Plain **Shape:** 7-sided

Date	Mintage	F12	VF20	XF40	MS60	MS63
2003	—	—	—	—	1.75	2.75
2006	19,000	—	—	—	1.75	2.75
2008	—	—	—	—	1.75	2.75
2012	—	—	—	—	1.75	2.75

KM# 145a 50 PENCE

8.10 g., 0.925 Silver 0.2393 oz. ASW, 27.3 mm. **Ruler:** Elizabeth II **Subject:** Coronation Jubilee **Obv:** Head with tiara right **Rev:** Queen on horseback **Edge:** Plain **Shape:** 7-sided

Date	Mintage	F12	VF20	XF40	MS60	MS63
2003		PF65 25.00				

KM# 146a 50 PENCE

8.10 g., 0.925 Silver 0.2393 oz. ASW, 27.3 mm. **Ruler:** Elizabeth II **Subject:** Coronation Jubilee **Obv:** Head with tiara right **Rev:** Queen on throne **Edge:** Plain **Shape:** 7-sided

Date	Mintage	F12	VF20	XF40	MS60	MS63
2003		PF65 25.00				

KM# 147a 50 PENCE

8.10 g., 0.925 Silver 0.2393 oz. ASW, 27.3 mm. **Ruler:** Elizabeth II **Subject:** Coronation Jubilee **Obv:** Head with tiara right **Rev:** Crown **Edge:** Plain **Shape:** 7-sided

Date	Mintage	F12	VF20	XF40	MS60	MS63
2003	—	PF65 25.00				

KM# 148a 50 PENCE

8.10 g., 0.925 Silver 0.2393 oz. ASW, 27.3 mm. **Ruler:** Elizabeth II **Subject:** Coronation Jubilee **Obv:** Head with tiara right **Rev:** Crowned ERII monogram **Edge:** Plain **Shape:** 7-sided

Date	Mintage	F12	VF20	XF40	MS60	MS63
2003	—	PF65 25.00				

KM# 110 POUND
9.50 g., Nickel-Brass, 22.5 mm. **Ruler:** Elizabeth II **Subject:** Circulation Type **Obv:** Head with tiara right **Rev:** Denomination **Edge:** Reeded

Date	Mintage	F12	VF20	XF40	MS60	MS63
2001	175,000	—	—	—	2.50	3.50
2003	46,600	—	—	—	2.50	3.50
2006	11,000	—	—	—	2.50	3.50
2012	—	—	—	—	2.50	3.50

KM# 111 POUND
9.50 g., 0.925 Silver 0.2807 oz. ASW, 22.5 mm. **Ruler:** Elizabeth II **Subject:** Elizabeth II, 75th Birthday **Obv:** Head with tiara right **Rev:** Queen's portrait in wreath **Edge:** Reeded

Date	Mintage	F12	VF20	XF40	MS60	MS63
2001	50,000	PF63 22.00	PF65 27.00			

KM# 142 POUND
30.93 g., 0.925 Silver 0.9139 oz. ASW, 38.6 mm. **Ruler:** Elizabeth II **Obv:** Head with tiara right **Rev:** 1/2-bust of William, Duke of Normandy holding sword at left **Edge:** Reeded

Date	Mintage	F12	VF20	XF40	MS60	MS63
2002	—	—	—	—	40.00	50.00

KM# 83 2 POUNDS
12.00 g., Bi-Metallic, 28.4 mm. **Ruler:** Elizabeth II **Obv:** Head with tiara right **Rev:** Latent image arms on cross **Edge:** BAILIWICK OF GUERNSEY

Date	Mintage	F12	VF20	XF40	MS60	MS63
2003	19,600	—	—	—	8.50	10.00
2006	9,500	—	—	—	8.50	10.00

KM# 106 5 POUNDS
28.28 g., Copper-Nickel, 38.6 mm. **Ruler:** Elizabeth II **Subject:** Queen Victoria Centennial **Obv:** Head with tiara right **Rev:** Bust of Queen Victoria left **Edge:** Reeded

Date	Mintage	F12	VF20	XF40	MS60	MS63
2001	12,754	—	—	—	7.50	8.50
2001	30,000	PF63 18.00	PF65 20.00			

KM# 106a 5 POUNDS
28.28 g., 0.925 Silver 0.8356 oz. ASW, 38.6 mm. **Ruler:** Elizabeth II **Subject:** Queen Victoria 1837-1901 **Obv:** Head with tiara right **Rev:** Bust of Queen Victoria left **Edge:** Reeded

Date	Mintage	F12	VF20	XF40	MS60	MS63
2001	10,000	PF63 40.00	PF65 50.00			

KM# 108 5 POUNDS
28.28 g., Copper-Nickel, 38.6 mm. **Ruler:** Elizabeth II **Subject:** Queen Elizabeth's 75th Birthday **Obv:** Head with tiara right **Rev:** Queen's portrait in wreath **Edge:** Reeded

Date	Mintage	F12	VF20	XF40	MS60	MS63
2001	14,000	—	—	—	6.00	7.00

KM# 108a 5 POUNDS
28.28 g., 0.925 Silver 0.8356 oz. ASW, 38.6 mm. **Ruler:** Elizabeth II **Subject:** Queen's 75th Birthday **Obv:** Head with tiara right **Rev:** Queen's portrait in wreath **Edge:** Reeded

Date	Mintage	F12	VF20	XF40	MS60	MS63
2001	20,000	PF63 45.00	PF65 55.00			

KM# 114 5 POUNDS
28.28 g., Copper-Nickel, 38.6 mm. **Ruler:** Elizabeth II **Subject:** 19th Century Monarchy **Obv:** Head with tiara right **Rev:** Four portraits **Edge:** Reeded

Date	Mintage	F12	VF20	XF40	MS60	MS63
2001	5,700	—	—	—	11.50	12.50

KM# 114a 5 POUNDS
28.28 g., 0.925 Silver 0.8356 oz. ASW, 38.6 mm. **Ruler:** Elizabeth II **Obv:** Head with tiara right **Rev:** Four portraits **Edge:** Reeded

Date	Mintage	F12	VF20	XF40	MS60	MS63
2001	10,000	PF63 45.00	PF65 55.00			

KM# 106b 5 POUNDS
39.94 g., 0.917 Gold 1.1699 oz. AGW, 38.61 mm. **Ruler:** Elizabeth II **Subject:** Queen Victoria 1837-1901 **Obv:** Head with tiara right **Rev:** Queen Victoria's portrait **Edge:** Reeded

Date	Mintage	F12	VF20	XF40	MS60	MS63
2001	300	PF65 2,250				

KM# 108b 5 POUNDS
39.94 g., 0.917 Gold 1.1699 oz. AGW, 38.61 mm. **Ruler:** Elizabeth II **Subject:** Queen's 75th Birthday **Obv:** Head with tiara right **Rev:** Queen's portrait in wreath **Edge:** Reeded

Date	Mintage	F12	VF20	XF40	MS60	MS63
2001	250	PF65 2,150				

KM# 114b 5 POUNDS
39.94 g., 0.9166 Gold 1.1694 oz. AGW, 38.6 mm. **Ruler:** Elizabeth II **Subject:** 19th Century Monarchy **Obv:** Head with tiara right **Rev:** Four royal portraits **Edge:** Reeded

Date	Mintage	F12	VF20	XF40	MS60	MS63
2001	200	PF65 2,200				

KM# 119a 5 POUNDS
28.28 g., Base Metal Gilt, 38.6 mm. **Ruler:** Elizabeth II **Subject:** Golden Jubilee **Obv:** Head with tiara right **Rev:** Queen in coach **Edge:** Reeded

Date	Mintage	F12	VF20	XF40	MS60	MS63
2002	50,000	—	—	—	15.00	16.50

KM# 129a 5 POUNDS
28.28 g., 0.925 Silver 0.8356 oz. ASW, 38.6 mm. **Ruler:** Elizabeth II **Subject:** The Duke of Wellington **Obv:** Head with tiara right **Rev:** Portrait with multicolor mounted dragoons in background **Edge:** Reeded

Date	Mintage	F12	VF20	XF40	MS60	MS63
2002	15,000	PF63 40.00	PF65 50.00			

KM# 121a 5 POUNDS
28.28 g., 0.925 Silver 0.8356 oz. ASW, 38.6 mm. **Ruler:** Elizabeth II **Subject:** Queen's Golden Jubilee **Obv:** Head with tiara right **Rev:** Trooping the Colors scene **Edge:** Reeded

Date	Mintage	F12	VF20	XF40	MS60	MS63
2002	—	PF63 40.00	PF65 50.00			

KM# 122a 5 POUNDS
28.28 g., 0.925 Silver 0.8356 oz. ASW, 38.61 mm. **Ruler:** Elizabeth II **Subject:** Princess Diana **Obv:** Head with tiara right **Rev:** World and children behind Diana's cameo portrait **Edge:** Reeded

Date	Mintage	F12	VF20	XF40	MS60	MS63
2002	20,000	PF63 35.00	PF65 45.00			

KM# 124a 5 POUNDS
28.28 g., 0.925 Silver 0.8356 oz. ASW, 38.6 mm. **Ruler:** Elizabeth II **Subject:** 18th Century British Monarchy **Obv:** Head with tiara right **Rev:** Five royal portraits **Edge:** Reeded

Date	Mintage	F12	VF20	XF40	MS60	MS63
2002	10,000	PF63 40.00	PF65 50.00			

KM# 127a 5 POUNDS
28.28 g., 0.925 Silver 0.8356 oz. ASW, 38.6 mm. **Ruler:** Elizabeth II **Subject:** Queen Mother **Obv:** Head with tiara right **Rev:** The late Queen Mother's portrait **Edge:** Reeded

Date	Mintage	F12	VF20	XF40	MS60	MS63
2002	15,000	PF63 40.00	PF65 50.00			

KM# 119 5 POUNDS
27.71 g., Copper-Nickel, 38.6 mm. **Ruler:** Elizabeth II **Subject:** The Golden Jubilee **Obv:** Head with tiara right **Rev:** The queen in her coach **Edge:** Reeded

Date	Mintage	F12	VF20	XF40	MS60	MS63
2002	9,250	—	—	—	16.50	18.00

KM# 119b 5 POUNDS
28.28 g., 0.925 Silver 0.8356 oz. ASW, 38.6 mm. **Ruler:** Elizabeth II **Subject:** Queen's Golden Jubilee **Obv:** Head with tiara right **Rev:** Queen in her coach **Edge:** Reeded **Note:** Prev. KM#119a.

Date	Mintage	F12	VF20	XF40	MS60	MS63
2002	—	PF63 40.00	PF65 50.00			

KM# 119c 5 POUNDS
39.94 g., 0.9166 Gold 1.1694 oz. AGW, 38.6 mm. **Ruler:** Elizabeth II **Subject:** Golden Jubilee **Obv:** Head with tiara right **Rev:** Queen in coach **Edge:** Reeded

Date	Mintage	F12	VF20	XF40	MS60	MS63
2002	250	PF65 2,200				

KM# 121 5 POUNDS
27.71 g., Copper-Nickel, 38.6 mm. **Ruler:** Elizabeth II **Subject:** Queen's Golden Jubilee **Obv:** Head with tiara right **Rev:** Trooping the Colors scene **Edge:** Reeded

Date	Mintage	F12	VF20	XF40	MS60	MS63
2002	2,000	—	—	—	17.50	20.00

KM# 121b 5 POUNDS
39.94 g., 0.9166 Gold 1.1694 oz. AGW, 38.6 mm. **Ruler:** Elizabeth II **Subject:** Golden Jubilee **Obv:** Head with tiara right **Rev:** Trooping the Colors scene **Edge:** Reeded

Date	Mintage	F12	VF20	XF40	MS60	MS63
2002	250	PF65 2,200				

KM# 122 5 POUNDS
28.28 g., Copper-Nickel, 38.6 mm. **Ruler:** Elizabeth II **Subject:** Princess Diana **Obv:** Head with tiara right **Rev:** World and children behind cameo portrait of Diana **Edge:** Reeded

Date	Mintage	F12	VF20	XF40	MS60	MS63
2002	4,231	—	—	—	13.50	15.00

KM# 122b 5 POUNDS
39.94 g., 0.9167 Gold 1.1696 oz. AGW, 38.61 mm. **Ruler:** Elizabeth II **Subject:** Princess Diana **Obv:** Head with tiara right **Rev:** World and children behind Diana's cameo portrait **Edge:** Reeded

Date	Mintage	F12	VF20	XF40	MS60	MS63
2002	100	PF65 2,250				

KM# 124 5 POUNDS
28.28 g., Copper-Nickel, 38.6 mm. **Ruler:** Elizabeth II **Subject:** 18th Century British Monarchy **Obv:** Head with tiara right **Rev:** Five royal portraits **Edge:** Reeded

Date	Mintage	F12	VF20	XF40	MS60	MS63
2002	1,300	—	—	—	15.00	16.50

KM# 124b 5 POUNDS
39.94 g., 0.9100 Gold 1.1094 oz. AGW, 38.0 mm. **Ruler:** Elizabeth II **Subject:** 18th Century British Monarchy **Obv:** Head with tiara right **Rev:** Five royal portraits **Edge:** Reeded

Date	Mintage	F12	VF20	XF40	MS60	MS63
2002	200	PF65 2,200				

KM# 127b 5 POUNDS
39.94 g., 0.9166 Gold 1.1694 oz. AGW, 38.6 mm. **Ruler:** Elizabeth II **Subject:** Queen Mother **Obv:** Head with tiara right **Rev:** Queen Mother's portrait **Edge:** Reeded

Date	Mintage	F12	VF20	XF40	MS60	MS63
2002	250	PF65 2,200				

KM# 129 5 POUNDS
28.28 g., Copper-Nickel, 38.6 mm. **Ruler:** Elizabeth II **Subject:** The Duke of Wellington **Obv:** Head with tiara right **Rev:** Portrait with mounted dragoons in background **Edge:** Reeded

Date	Mintage	F12	VF20	XF40	MS60	MS63
2002	675	—	—	—	22.50	25.00

KM# 129b 5 POUNDS
39.94 g., 0.9166 Gold 1.1694 oz. AGW, 38.6 mm. **Ruler:** Elizabeth II **Subject:** Duke of Wellington **Obv:** Head with tiara right **Rev:** Wellington's portrait with multicolor cavalry scene **Edge:** Reeded

Date	Mintage	F12	VF20	XF40	MS60	MS63
2002	200	PF65 2,200				

KM# 127 5 POUNDS
28.28 g., Copper-Nickel, 38.6 mm. **Ruler:** Elizabeth II **Subject:** Queen Mother **Obv:** Head with tiara right **Rev:** The late Queen Mother's portrait **Edge:** Reeded

Date	Mintage	F12	VF20	XF40	MS60	MS63
2002	1,750	—	—	—	15.00	16.50
2002	1,680	PF63 18.00	PF65 20.00			

KM# 143 5 POUNDS
28.28 g., Copper-Nickel, 38.6 mm. **Ruler:** Elizabeth II **Obv:** Head with tiara right **Rev:** Prince William wearing sweater **Edge:** Reeded

Date	Mintage	F12	VF20	XF40	MS60	MS63
2003	3,700	—	—	—	17.50	20.00

KM# 158 5 POUNDS
28.28 g., Copper-Nickel, 38.7 mm. **Ruler:** Elizabeth II **Subject:** Golden Hind **Obv:** Head with tiara right **Rev:** The Golden Hind ship **Edge:** Reeded

Date	Mintage	F12	VF20	XF40	MS60	MS63
2003	300	—	—	—	—	25.00

KM# 159 5 POUNDS
Copper-Nickel **Ruler:** Elizabeth II **Subject:** 17th Century Monarchs **Obv:** Head with tiara right

Date	Mintage	F12	VF20	XF40	MS60	MS63
2003	500	—	—	—	—	22.50

KM# 160 5 POUNDS
Copper-Nickel **Ruler:** Elizabeth II **Subject:** Royal Navy - H. Nelson **Obv:** Head with tiara right

Date	Mintage	F12	VF20	XF40	MS60	MS63
2003	550	—	—	—	—	22.50

KM# 143a 5 POUNDS
28.28 g., 0.925 Silver 0.8356 oz. ASW, 38.6 mm. **Ruler:** Elizabeth II **Obv:** Head with tiara right **Rev:** Prince William wearing sweater **Edge:** Reeded

Date	Mintage	F12	VF20	XF40	MS60	MS63
2003	5,000	PF63 40.00	PF65 50.00			

KM# 143b 5 POUNDS
39.94 g., 0.9166 Gold 1.1694 oz. AGW, 38.6 mm. **Ruler:** Elizabeth II **Obv:** Head with tiara right **Rev:** Prince William wearing sweater **Edge:** Reeded

Date	Mintage	F12	VF20	XF40	MS60	MS63
2003	200	PF65 2,200				

KM# 160a 5 POUNDS
28.32 g., Nickel-Brass, 38 mm. **Ruler:** Elizabeth II **Subject:** History of the Royal Navy **Rev:** Two naval vessels and Horatio Nelson, flag in color

Date	Mintage	F12	VF20	XF40	MS60	MS63
2003	—	PF63 35.00	PF65 40.00			

KM# 160b 5 POUNDS
39.94 g., 0.917 Gold 1.1699 oz. AGW, 38.61 mm. **Ruler:** Elizabeth II **Subject:** History of the Navy - Horatio Nelson

Date	Mintage	F12	VF20	XF40	MS60	MS63
2003	—	PF65 2,150				

KM# 150 5 POUNDS
28.28 g., Copper-Nickel, 38.6 mm. **Ruler:** Elizabeth II **Subject:** D-Day **Obv:** Head with tiara right **Rev:** British troops storming ashore **Edge:** Reeded

Date	Mintage	F12	VF20	XF40	MS60	MS63
2004	65,611	—	—	—	15.00	16.50

KM# 154 5 POUNDS
28.28 g., 0.925 Silver 0.8356 oz. ASW, 38.6 mm. **Ruler:** Elizabeth II **Subject:** D-Day **Obv:** Head with tiara right **Rev:** British soldier advancing to left **Edge:** Reeded

Date	Mintage	F12	VF20	XF40	MS60	MS63
2004	10,000	PF63 75.00	PF65 85.00			

KM# 161 5 POUNDS
Copper-Nickel **Ruler:** Elizabeth II **Subject:** 16th Century Monarchs **Obv:** Head with tiara right

Date	Mintage	F12	VF20	XF40	MS60	MS63
2004	500	—	—	—	—	22.50

KM# 162 5 POUNDS
Copper-Nickel **Ruler:** Elizabeth II **Subject:** Mallard Locomotive **Obv:** Head with tiara right

Date	Mintage	F12	VF20	XF40	MS60	MS63
2004	2,193	—	—	—	—	17.50

KM# 163 5 POUNDS
Copper-Nickel **Ruler:** Elizabeth II **Subject:** City of Truro Train **Obv:** Head with tiara right

Date	Mintage	F12	VF20	XF40	MS60	MS63
2004	500	—	—	—	—	22.50

KM# 164 5 POUNDS
Copper-Nickel **Ruler:** Elizabeth II **Subject:** The Boat Train **Obv:** Head with tiara right

Date	Mintage	F12	VF20	XF40	MS60	MS63
2004	250	—	—	—	—	25.00

KM# 165 5 POUNDS
Copper-Nickel **Ruler:** Elizabeth II **Subject:** Train Spotter **Obv:** Head with tiara right

Date	Mintage	F12	VF20	XF40	MS60	MS63
2004	300	—	—	—	—	25.00

KM# 166 5 POUNDS
Copper-Nickel **Ruler:** Elizabeth II **Subject:** Royal Navy - Henry VIII **Obv:** Head with tiara right

Date	Mintage	F12	VF20	XF40	MS60	MS63
2004	300	—	—	—	—	25.00

KM# 167 5 POUNDS
Copper-Nickel **Ruler:** Elizabeth II **Subject:** Royal Navy - Invincible **Obv:** Head with tiara right

Date	Mintage	F12	VF20	XF40	MS60	MS63
2004	300	—	—	—	—	25.00

KM# 176 5 POUNDS
28.32 g., Silver, 38 mm. **Ruler:** Elizabeth II **Subject:** History of the Royal Navy **Rev:** HMS Invincible, flag in color

Date	Mintage	F12	VF20	XF40	MS60	MS63
2004	—	PF63 45.00	PF65 50.00			

KM# 154a 5 POUNDS
39.94 g., 0.9167 Gold 1.1696 oz. AGW, 38.6 mm. **Ruler:** Elizabeth II **Subject:** D-Day **Obv:** Head with tiara right **Rev:** British soldier advancing to left **Edge:** Reeded

Date	Mintage	F12	VF20	XF40	MS60	MS63
2004	500	PF65 2,100				

KM# 155a 5 POUNDS
28.28 g., 0.925 Silver 0.8356 oz. ASW, 38.6 mm. **Ruler:** Elizabeth II **Obv:** Head with tiara right **Rev:** Sgt. Luke O'Conner, first army Victoria Cross winner, above Battle of Alma scene with multicolor flag **Edge:** Reeded

Date	Mintage	F12	VF20	XF40	MS60	MS63
2004	10,000	PF63 75.00	PF65 85.00			

KM# 155b 5 POUNDS
39.94 g., 0.9166 Gold 1.1694 oz. AGW, 38.6 mm. **Ruler:** Elizabeth II **Obv:** Head with tiara right **Rev:** Sgt. Luke O'Connor, first army Victoria Cross winner, above Battle of Alma scene with multicolor flag **Edge:** Reeded

Date	Mintage	F12	VF20	XF40	MS60	MS63
2004	500	PF65 2,100				

KM# 130a 5 POUNDS
28.28 g., 0.925 Silver 0.8356 oz. ASW, 38.61 mm. **Ruler:** Elizabeth II **Subject:** Steam Locomotives **Rev:** Tower switchman at leavers

Date	Mintage	F12	VF20	XF40	MS60	MS63
2004	Est. 10000	PF63 50.00	PF65 60.00			

KM# 133a 5 POUNDS
28.28 g., 0.925 Silver 0.8356 oz. ASW, 38.61 mm. **Ruler:** Elizabeth II **Subject:** Steam Locomotives **Rev:** Two locomotives side-by-side view of tender being refilled with water, and fireman shoveling coal

Date	Mintage	F12	VF20	XF40	MS60	MS63
2004	Est. 10000	PF63 50.00	PF65 60.00			

KM# 155 5 POUNDS
28.28 g., Copper-Nickel, 38.6 mm. **Ruler:** Elizabeth II **Subject:** 150th Anniversary of the Crimean War **Obv:** Head with tiara right **Rev:** Sgt. Luke O'Connor, first army Victoria Cross winner, above Battle of Alma scene with multicolor flag **Edge:** Reeded

Date	Mintage	F12	VF20	XF40	MS60	MS63
2004 plain	—	—	—	—	25.00	27.50
2004 partial color	1,060	—	—	—	25.00	27.50

KM# 130 5 POUNDS
28.28 g., Copper-Nickel, 38.61 mm. **Ruler:** Elizabeth II **Subject:** Steam Locomotives **Rev:** Tower switchman at leavers

Date	Mintage	F12	VF20	XF40	MS60	MS63
2004	—	—	—	—	—	25.00

KM# 133 5 POUNDS
28.28 g., Copper-Nickel, 38.61 mm. **Ruler:** Elizabeth II **Subject:** Steam Locomotives **Rev:** Two locomotives side-by-side view of tender being refilled with water, and fireman shoveling coal

Date	Mintage	F12	VF20	XF40	MS60	MS63
2004	—	—	—	—	—	25.00

KM# 168a 5 POUNDS
28.28 g., 0.925 Silver 0.8356 oz. ASW, 38.6 mm. **Ruler:** Elizabeth II **Subject:** End of WWII **Obv:** Head with tiara right **Rev:** Churchill and George VI **Edge:** Reeded

Date	Mintage	F12	VF20	XF40	MS60	MS63
2005	5,000	PF63 75.00	PF65 85.00			

KM# 168b 5 POUNDS
39.94 g., 0.9167 Gold 1.1696 oz. AGW, 38.6 mm. **Ruler:** Elizabeth II **Subject:** End of WWII **Obv:** Head with tiara right **Rev:** Churchill and George VI **Edge:** Reeded

Date	Mintage	F12	VF20	XF40	MS60	MS63
2005	150	PF65 2,250				

KM# 169a 5 POUNDS
39.94 g., 0.9167 Gold 1.1696 oz. AGW, 38.6 mm. **Ruler:** Elizabeth II **Subject:** WWII Liberation **Obv:** Head with tiara right **Rev:** Soldiers and waving crowd **Edge:** Reeded

Date	Mintage	F12	VF20	XF40	MS60	MS63
2005	150	PF65 2,250				

KM# 189a 5 POUNDS
28.28 g., 0.925 Silver 0.8356 oz. ASW, 38.61 mm. **Ruler:** Elizabeth II **Subject:** Battle of Trafalgar, 200th Anniversary **Rev:** H.M.S. Victory

Date	Mintage	F12	VF20	XF40	MS60	MS63
2005	—	PF63 50.00	PF65 60.00			

KM# 186a 5 POUNDS
28.28 g., 0.925 Silver 0.8356 oz. ASW, 38.61 mm. **Ruler:** Elizabeth II **Subject:** Royal Navy - Sir John Jellicoe **Rev:** Flag in color

Date	Mintage	F12	VF20	XF40	MS60	MS63
2005	Est. 15000	PF63 50.00	PF65 60.00			

KM# 186 5 POUNDS
28.28 g., Copper-Nickel, 38.61 mm. **Ruler:** Elizabeth II **Subject:** Royal Navy - Sir John Jellicoe

Date	Mintage	F12	VF20	XF40	MS60	MS63
2005	—	—	—	—	—	17.50

KM# 187 5 POUNDS
28.28 g., Copper-Nickel, 38.61 mm. **Ruler:** Elizabeth II **Subject:** Royal Navy **Rev:** H.M.S. Ark Royal

Date	Mintage	F12	VF20	XF40	MS60	MS63
2005	—	—	—	—	—	17.50

KM# 187a 5 POUNDS
28.28 g., 0.925 Silver 0.8356 oz. ASW, 38.61 mm. **Ruler:** Elizabeth II **Subject:** Royal Navy **Rev:** H.M.S. Ark Royal, flag in color

Date	Mintage	F12	VF20	XF40	MS60	MS63
2005	Est. 15000	PF63 50.00	PF65 60.00			

KM# 189 5 POUNDS
28.28 g., Copper-Nickel, 38.61 mm. **Ruler:** Elizabeth II **Subject:** Battle of Trafalgar, 200th Anniversary **Rev:** H.M.S. Victory

Date	Mintage	F12	VF20	XF40	MS60	MS63
2005	—	—	—	—	—	17.50

KM# 189b 5 POUNDS
39.94 g., 0.917 Gold 1.1699 oz. AGW, 38.61 mm. **Ruler:** Elizabeth II **Subject:** Battle of Trafalgar, 200th Anniversary **Rev:** H.M.S. Victory

Date	Mintage	F12	VF20	XF40	MS60	MS63
2005	—	PF65 2,250				

KM# 170 5 POUNDS
28.28 g., 0.925 Silver 0.8356 oz. ASW, 38.6 mm. **Ruler:** Elizabeth II **Subject:** Queen's 80th Birthday **Obv:** Head with tiara right - gilt **Obv. Legend:** ELIZABETH II BAILIWICK OF GUERNSEY **Rev:** Bust at left looking upwards, tower and florals at upper right

Date	Mintage	F12	VF20	XF40	MS60	MS63
2006	—	PF63 40.00	PF65 45.00			

KM# 173 5 POUNDS
28.28 g., 0.925 Silver 0.8356 oz. ASW, 22 mm. **Ruler:** Elizabeth II **Subject:** FIFA - XVIII World Football Championship - Germany 2006 **Rev:** Wembley Stadium

Date	Mintage	F12	VF20	XF40	MS60	MS63
2006	50,000	PF63 55.00	PF65 65.00			

KM# 191a 5 POUNDS
28.28 g., 0.925 Silver 0.8356 oz. ASW, 38.61 mm. **Ruler:** Elizabeth II **Rev:** Horatio Nelson

Date	Mintage	F12	VF20	XF40	MS60	MS63
2006	25,000	PF63 50.00	PF65 60.00			

KM# 192a 5 POUNDS
28.28 g., 0.925 Silver 0.8356 oz. ASW, 38.61 mm. **Ruler:** Elizabeth II **Rev:** Isambard Kingdom Brunel

Date	Mintage	F12	VF20	XF40	MS60	MS63
2006	25,000	PF63 50.00	PF65 60.00			

KM# 195a 5 POUNDS
28.28 g., 0.925 Silver 0.8356 oz. ASW, 38.61 mm. **Ruler:** Elizabeth II **Subject:** Elizabeth II, 80th Birthday **Rev:** Elizabeth II and Queen Mother, gilt

Date	Mintage	F12	VF20	XF40	MS60	MS63
2006	25,000	PF63 50.00	PF65 60.00			

KM# 196a 5 POUNDS
39.94 g., 0.917 Gold 1.1699 oz. AGW, 8.61 mm. **Ruler:** Elizabeth II **Subject:** Elizabeth II, 80th Birthday **Rev:** Elizabeth II portrait by Mary Gillick

Date	Mintage	F12	VF20	XF40	MS60	MS63
2006	—	PF65 2,250				

KM# 197a 5 POUNDS
28.28 g., 0.925 Silver 0.8356 oz. ASW, 38.61 mm. **Ruler:** Elizabeth II **Subject:** Victoria Cross, 150th Anniversary **Rev:** Herbert Wallace le Patourel

Date	Mintage	F12	VF20	XF40	MS60	MS63
2006	Est. 30000	PF63 50.00	PF65 60.00			

KM# 130b 5 POUNDS
28.28 g., 0.925 Silver 0.8356 oz. ASW, 38.61 mm. **Ruler:** Elizabeth II **Subject:** Steam Locomotives **Rev:** Tower Switchmen at leavers

Date	Mintage	F12	VF20	XF40	MS60	MS63
2006	25,000	PF63 50.00	PF65 60.00			

KM# 133b 5 POUNDS
28.28 g., 0.925 Silver 0.8356 oz. ASW, 38.61 mm. **Ruler:** Elizabeth II **Subject:** Steam Locomotives **Rev:** Two locomotives side-by-side view of tender being refilled with water, and fireman shoveling coal

Date	Mintage	F12	VF20	XF40	MS60	MS63
2006	Est. 25000	PF63 50.00	PF65 60.00			

KM# 191 5 POUNDS
28.28 g., Copper-Nickel, 38.61 mm. **Ruler:** Elizabeth II **Rev:** Horatio Nelson

Date	Mintage	F12	VF20	XF40	MS60	MS63
2006	—	—	—	—	—	15.00

KM# 192 5 POUNDS
28.28 g., Copper-Nickel, 38.61 mm. **Ruler:** Elizabeth II **Rev:** Isambard Kingdom Brunel

Date	Mintage	F12	VF20	XF40	MS60	MS63
2006	—	—	—	—	—	15.00

KM# 193 5 POUNDS
28.28 g., 0.925 Silver 0.8356 oz. ASW, 38.61 mm. **Ruler:** Elizabeth II **Rev:** Robert Falcon Scott

Date	Mintage	F12	VF20	XF40	MS60	MS63
2006	25,000	PF63 50.00	PF65 60.00			

KM# 194 5 POUNDS
28.28 g., 0.925 Silver 0.8356 oz. ASW, 38.61 mm. **Ruler:** Elizabeth II **Rev:** Queen Victoria

Date	Mintage	F12	VF20	XF40	MS60	MS63
2006	25,000	PF63 50.00		PF65 60.00		

KM# 195 5 POUNDS
28.28 g., Copper-Nickel, 38.61 mm. **Ruler:** Elizabeth II **Subject:** Elizabeth II, 80th Birthday **Rev:** Elizabeth II and Queen Mother

Date	Mintage	F12	VF20	XF40	MS60	MS63
2006	—					15.00

KM# 196 5 POUNDS
28.28 g., 0.925 Silver 0.8356 oz. ASW, 38.61 mm. **Ruler:** Elizabeth II **Subject:** Elizabeth II, 80th Birthday **Rev:** Elizabeth II portrait by Mary Gillick

Date	Mintage	F12	VF20	XF40	MS60	MS63
2006	—	PF63 50.00		PF65 60.00		

KM# 197 5 POUNDS
28.28 g., Copper-Nickel, 38.61 mm. **Ruler:** Elizabeth II **Subject:** Victoria Cross, 150th Anniversary **Rev:** Herbert Wallace le Patourel

Date	Mintage	F12	VF20	XF40	MS60	MS63
2006	—					15.00

KM# 198 5 POUNDS
28.28 g., 0.925 Silver 0.8356 oz. ASW, 38.61 mm. **Ruler:** Elizabeth II **Subject:** Victoria Cross, 150th Anniversary **Rev:** Victor Buller Turner

Date	Mintage	F12	VF20	XF40	MS60	MS63
2006	Est. 30000	PF63 50.00		PF65 60.00		

KM# 199 5 POUNDS
28.28 g., 0.925 Silver 0.8356 oz. ASW, 38.61 mm. **Ruler:** Elizabeth II **Subject:** Victoria Cross, 150th Anniversary **Rev:** William Leefe Robinson

Date	Mintage	F12	VF20	XF40	MS60	MS63
2006	30,000	PF63 50.00		PF65 60.00		

KM# 200 5 POUNDS
28.28 g., 0.925 Silver 0.8356 oz. ASW, 38.61 mm. **Ruler:** Elizabeth II **Subject:** Victoria Cross, 150th Anniversary **Rev:** Gerard Roope

Date	Mintage	F12	VF20	XF40	MS60	MS63
2006	Est. 30000	PF63 50.00		PF65 60.00		

KM# 201 5 POUNDS
28.28 g., 0.925 Silver 0.8356 oz. ASW, 38.61 mm. **Ruler:** Elizabeth II **Subject:** Victoria Cross, 150th Anniversary **Rev:** Robert Henry Cain

Date	Mintage	F12	VF20	XF40	MS60	MS63
2006	Est. 30000	PF63 50.00		PF65 60.00		

KM# 202 5 POUNDS
28.28 g., 0.925 Silver 0.8356 oz. ASW, 38.61 mm. **Ruler:** Elizabeth II **Subject:** Victoria Cross, 150th Anniversary **Rev:** Eugene Esmonde

Date	Mintage	F12	VF20	XF40	MS60	MS63
2006	Est. 30000	PF63 50.00		PF65 60.00		

KM# 207a 5 POUNDS
28.28 g., 0.925 Silver 0.8356 oz. ASW, 38.61 mm. **Ruler:** Elizabeth II **Subject:** Elizabeth II and Prince Philip, 60th Wedding Anniversary **Rev:** Busts

Date	Mintage	F12	VF20	XF40	MS60	MS63
2007	—	PF63 45.00		PF65 55.00		

KM# 208a 5 POUNDS
28.28 g., 0.925 Silver 0.8356 oz. ASW, 38.61 mm. **Ruler:** Elizabeth II **Subject:** Elizabeth II and Prince Philip, 60th Wedding Anniversary **Rev:** Honeymoon

Date	Mintage	F12	VF20	XF40	MS60	MS63
2007	—	PF63 45.00		PF65 55.00		

KM# 210a 5 POUNDS
28.28 g., 0.925 Silver 0.8356 oz. ASW, 38.61 mm. **Ruler:** Elizabeth II **Subject:** Elizabeth II and Prince Philip, 60th Wedding Anniversary **Rev:** Wedding scene

Date	Mintage	F12	VF20	XF40	MS60	MS63
2007	—	PF63 45.00		PF65 55.00		

KM# 203 5 POUNDS
28.28 g., 0.925 Silver 0.8356 oz. ASW, 38.61 mm. **Ruler:** Elizabeth II **Rev:** Sir Alexander Fleming

Date	Mintage	F12	VF20	XF40	MS60	MS63
2007	25,000	PF63 45.00		PF65 55.00		

KM# 204 5 POUNDS
28.28 g., 0.925 Silver 0.8356 oz. ASW, 38.61 mm. **Ruler:** Elizabeth II **Rev:** Montgomery

Date	Mintage	F12	VF20	XF40	MS60	MS63
2007	Est. 25000	PF63 45.00		PF65 55.00		

KM# 205 5 POUNDS
28.28 g., 0.925 Silver 0.8356 oz. ASW, 38.61 mm. **Ruler:** Elizabeth II **Rev:** Oliver Cromwell

Date	Mintage	F12	VF20	XF40	MS60	MS63
2007	Est. 25000	PF63 45.00		PF65 55.00		

KM# 206 5 POUNDS
28.28 g., 0.925 Silver 0.8356 oz. ASW, 38.61 mm. **Ruler:** Elizabeth II **Rev:** Alexander Graham Bell

Date	Mintage	F12	VF20	XF40	MS60	MS63
2007	—	PF63 45.00		PF65 55.00		

KM# 207 5 POUNDS
28.28 g., Copper-Nickel, 38.61 mm. **Ruler:** Elizabeth II **Subject:** Elizabeth II and Prince Philip, 60th Wedding Anniversary **Rev:** Busts

Date	Mintage	F12	VF20	XF40	MS60	MS63
2007	—					15.00

KM# 208 5 POUNDS
28.28 g., Copper-Nickel, 38.61 mm. **Ruler:** Elizabeth II **Subject:** Elizabeth II and Prince Philip, 60th Wedding Anniversary **Rev:** Honeymoon

Date	Mintage	F12	VF20	XF40	MS60	MS63
2007	—					15.00

KM# 209 5 POUNDS
28.28 g., Copper-Nickel, 38.61 mm. **Ruler:** Elizabeth II **Subject:** Elizabeth II and Prince Philip, 60th Wedding Anniversary **Rev:** Bouquet

Date	Mintage	F12	VF20	XF40	MS60	MS63
2007	—					15.00

KM# 209a 5 POUNDS
28.28 g., 0.925 Silver 0.8356 oz. ASW, 38.61 mm. **Ruler:** Elizabeth II **Subject:** Elizabeth II and Prince Philip, 60th Wedding Anniversary **Rev:** Bouquet

Date	Mintage	F12	VF20	XF40	MS60	MS63
2007	—	PF63 45.00		PF65 55.00		

KM# 210 5 POUNDS
28.28 g., Copper-Nickel 0.8356 oz., 38.61 mm. **Ruler:** Elizabeth II **Subject:** Elizabeth II and Prince Philip, 60th Wedding Anniversary **Rev:** Wedding scene

Date	Mintage	F12	VF20	XF40	MS60	MS63
2007	—					15.00

KM# 179a 5 POUNDS
28.28 g., 0.925 Silver 0.8356 oz. ASW, 38.61 mm. **Ruler:** Elizabeth II **Subject:** Royal Air Force, 90th Anniversary **Rev:** Air battle

Date	Mintage	F12	VF20	XF40	MS60	MS63
2008	Est. 25000	PF63 45.00		PF65 55.00		

KM# 211a 5 POUNDS
28.28 g., 0.925 Silver 0.8356 oz. ASW, 38.61 mm. **Ruler:** Elizabeth II **Subject:** Royal Air Force, 90th Anniversary **Rev:** Lancaster bomber

Date	Mintage	F12	VF20	XF40	MS60	MS63
2008	Est. 25000	PF63 45.00		PF65 55.00		

KM# 217 5 POUNDS
28.28 g., 0.925 Silver 0.8356 oz. ASW, 38.61 mm. **Ruler:** Elizabeth II **Subject:** Royal Air Force, 90th Anniversary **Rev:** Gulf War

Date	Mintage	F12	VF20	XF40	MS60	MS63
2008	Est. 25000	PF63 45.00		PF65 55.00		

KM# 179 5 POUNDS
28.28 g., Copper-Nickel, 38.61 mm. **Ruler:** Elizabeth II **Subject:** Royal Air Force, 90th Anniversary **Obv:** Head with tiara right **Rev:** Air battle

Date	Mintage	F12	VF20	XF40	MS60	MS63
2008	—					15.00

KM# 211 5 POUNDS
28.28 g., Copper-Nickel, 38.61 mm. **Ruler:** Elizabeth II **Subject:** Royal Air Force, 90th Anniversary **Rev:** Lancaster bomber

Date	Mintage	F12	VF20	XF40	MS60	MS63
2008	—					15.00

KM# 212 5 POUNDS
28.28 g., 0.925 Silver 0.8356 oz. ASW, 38.61 mm. **Ruler:** Elizabeth II **Subject:** Royal Air Force, 90th Anniversary **Rev:** Founding of the Air Force, 1918

Date	Mintage	F12	VF20	XF40	MS60	MS63
2008	Est. 25000	PF63 45.00		PF65 55.00		

KM# 213 5 POUNDS
28.28 g., 0.925 Silver 0.8356 oz. ASW, 38.61 mm. **Ruler:** Elizabeth II **Subject:** Royal Air Force, 90th Anniversary **Rev:** Berlin Airlift, 1949

Date	Mintage	F12	VF20	XF40	MS60	MS63
2008	Est. 25000	PF63 45.00		PF65 55.00		

KM# 214 5 POUNDS
28.28 g., 0.925 Silver 0.8356 oz. ASW, 38.61 mm. **Ruler:** Elizabeth II **Subject:** Royal Air Force, 90th Anniversary **Rev:** Monarchy

Date	Mintage	F12	VF20	XF40	MS60	MS63
2008	Est. 25000	PF63 45.00		PF65 55.00		

KM# 215 5 POUNDS
28.28 g., 0.925 Silver 0.8356 oz. ASW, 38.61 mm. **Ruler:** Elizabeth II **Subject:** Royal Air Force, 90th Anniversary **Rev:** Schneider Trophy

Date	Mintage	F12	VF20	XF40	MS60	MS63
2008	Est. 25000	PF63 45.00		PF65 55.00		

KM# 216 5 POUNDS
28.28 g., 0.925 Silver 0.8356 oz. ASW, 38.61 mm. **Ruler:** Elizabeth II **Subject:** Royal Air Force, 90th Anniversary **Rev:** Falkland Islands War, 1982

Date	Mintage	F12	VF20	XF40	MS60	MS63
2008	—	PF63 45.00		PF65 55.00		

KM# 219a 5 POUNDS
28.28 g., 0.925 Silver 0.8356 oz. ASW, 38.61 mm. **Ruler:** Elizabeth II **Subject:** British Warships **Rev:** H.M.S. Daring, destroyer

Date	Mintage	F12	VF20	XF40	MS60	MS63
2009	Est. 25000	PF63 45.00		PF65 55.00		

KM# 220a 5 POUNDS
28.28 g., 0.925 Silver 0.8356 oz. ASW, 38.61 mm. **Ruler:** Elizabeth II **Subject:** British Warships **Rev:** H.M.S. Mary Rose, 1511

Date	Mintage	F12	VF20	XF40	MS60	MS63
2009	25,000	PF63 45.00		PF65 55.00		

KM# 222a 5 POUNDS
28.28 g., 0.925 Silver 0.8356 oz. ASW, 38.61 mm. **Ruler:** Elizabeth II **Subject:** British Aircraft Carrier, 100th Anniversary **Rev:** H.M.S. Royal Ark VI and fighter aircraft

Date	Mintage	F12	VF20	XF40	MS60	MS63
2009	—	PF63 45.00		PF65 55.00		

KM# 223a 5 POUNDS
28.28 g., 0.925 Silver 0.8356 oz. ASW, 38.61 mm. **Ruler:** Elizabeth II **Subject:** Apollo 11 moon landing, 40th Anniversary **Rev:** Lunar module Eagle and moon

Date	Mintage	F12	VF20	XF40	MS60	MS63
2009	—	PF63 45.00		PF65 55.00		

KM# 219 5 POUNDS
28.28 g., Copper-Nickel, 38.61 mm. **Ruler:** Elizabeth II **Subject:** British Warships **Rev:** H.M.S. Daring, destroyer

Date	Mintage	F12	VF20	XF40	MS60	MS63
2009	—					15.00

KM# 220 5 POUNDS
28.28 g., Copper-Nickel, 38.61 mm. **Ruler:** Elizabeth II **Subject:** British Warships **Rev:** H.M.S. Mary Rose, 1511

Date	Mintage	F12	VF20	XF40	MS60	MS63
2009	—					15.00

KM# 222 5 POUNDS
28.28 g., Copper-Nickel, 38.61 mm. **Ruler:** Elizabeth II **Subject:** British Aircraft carriers, 100th Anniversary **Rev:** H.M.S. Ark Royal IV with combat aircraft

Date	Mintage	F12	VF20	XF40	MS60	MS63
2009	—					15.00

KM# 223 5 POUNDS
28.28 g., 0.925 Copper-Nickel 0.8356 oz., 38.61 mm. **Ruler:** Elizabeth II **Subject:** Apollo 11 moon landing, 40th Anniversary **Rev:** Lunar Module Eagle and moon in color

Date	Mintage	F12	VF20	XF40	MS60	MS63
2009	—					15.00

KM# 226a 5 POUNDS
28.28 g., 0.925 Silver 0.8356 oz. ASW, 38.61 mm. **Ruler:** Elizabeth II **Subject:** Royal Wedding **Rev:** Prince William and Catherine Middleton

Date	Mintage	F12	VF20	XF40	MS60	MS63
2011	—	PF63 45.00		PF65 55.00		

KM# 225 5 POUNDS
28.28 g., Copper-Nickel, 38.61 mm. **Ruler:** Elizabeth II **Subject:** Decimalization, 40th Anniversary **Rev:** Coins in color

Date	Mintage	F12	VF20	XF40	MS60	MS63
2011	—	PF63 15.00		PF65 17.50		

KM# 226 5 POUNDS
28.28 g., Copper-Nickel, 38.61 mm. **Ruler:** Elizabeth II **Subject:** Royal Wedding **Rev:** Prince William and Catherine Middleton

Date	Mintage	F12	VF20	XF40	MS60	MS63
2011	—					15.00

KM# 227 5 POUNDS
28.28 g., Copper-Nickel, 38.61 mm. **Ruler:** Elizabeth II **Subject:** Prince Philip, 90th Birthday

Date	Mintage	F12	VF20	XF40	MS60	MS63
2011	—					20.00

KM# 228 5 POUNDS
28.28 g., Brass, 38.61 mm. **Ruler:** Elizabeth II **Subject:** Royal British Legion, 90th Anniversary **Rev:** Poppies in color on the battlefield of the Somme

Date	Mintage	F12	VF20	XF40	MS60	MS63
2011	Est. 19500	—	—			35.00

KM# 116 10 POUNDS
141.75 g., 0.999 Silver 4.5235 oz. ASW, 65 mm. **Ruler:** Elizabeth II **Subject:** 19th Century Monarchy **Obv:** Head with tiara right **Rev:** Four portraits **Edge:** Reeded

Date	Mintage	F12	VF20	XF40	MS60	MS63
2001	950	PF63 200		PF65 225		

KM# 126 10 POUNDS
155.52 g., 0.999 Silver 4.9628 oz. ASW, 65 mm. **Ruler:** Elizabeth II **Subject:** British Monarchy 18th Century **Obv:** Head with tiara right **Rev:** Five royal portraits **Edge:** Reeded

Date	Mintage	F12	VF20	XF40	MS60	MS63
2002	950	PF63 200		PF65 225		

KM# 125 10 POUNDS
155.50 g., 0.925 Silver 4.5947 oz. ASW, 65 mm. **Ruler:** Elizabeth II **Subject:** British Monarchs, 1700 years

Date	Mintage	F12	VF20	XF40	MS60	MS63
2003	Est. 950	PF63 225		PF65 275		

KM# 151 10 POUNDS
155.52 g., 0.925 Silver 4.5952 oz. ASW, 65 mm. **Ruler:** Elizabeth II **Subject:** D-Day **Obv:** Head with tiara right **Rev:** British troops storming ashore **Edge:** Reeded

Date	Mintage	F12	VF20	XF40	MS60	MS63
2004	1,944	PF63 375	PF65 400			

KM# 175 10 POUNDS
155.50 g., 0.925 Silver 4.5947 oz. ASW, 65 mm. **Ruler:** Elizabeth II **Subject:** British monarch of the 1500s **Rev:** Five portraits

Date	Mintage	F12	VF20	XF40	MS60	MS63
2004	—	PF63 250	PF65 275			

KM# 180 10 POUNDS
155.50 g., 0.917 Gold 4.555 oz. AGW, 65 mm. **Ruler:** Elizabeth II **Subject:** Crimea, 150th Anniversary

Date	Mintage	F12	VF20	XF40	MS60	MS63
2004	—	PF65 11,000				

KM# 184a 10 POUNDS
155.50 g., 0.917 Gold 4.555 oz. AGW, 65 mm. **Ruler:** Elizabeth II **Subject:** Return of the Islanders

Date	Mintage	F12	VF20	XF40	MS60	MS63
2005	—	PF65 11,000				

KM# 182 10 POUNDS
155.50 g., 0.925 Silver 4.5947 oz. ASW, 65 mm. **Ruler:** Elizabeth II **Subject:** End of WWII, 60th Anniversary

Date	Mintage	F12	VF20	XF40	MS60	MS63
2005	—	PF63 250	PF65 280			

KM# 182a 10 POUNDS
155.50 g., 0.917 Gold 4.555 oz. AGW, 65 mm. **Ruler:** Elizabeth II **Subject:** End of WWII, 60th Anniversary

Date	Mintage	F12	VF20	XF40	MS60	MS63
2005	—	PF65 11,000				

KM# 182b 10 POUNDS
155.50 g., 0.9995 Platinum 4.9648 oz. APW, 65 mm. **Ruler:** Elizabeth II **Subject:** End of WWII, 60th Anniversary

Date	Mintage	F12	VF20	XF40	MS60	MS63
2005	—	PF65 11,000				

KM# 184 10 POUNDS
155.50 g., 0.925 Silver 4.5947 oz. ASW, 65 mm. **Ruler:** Elizabeth II **Subject:** Return of the Islanders

Date	Mintage	F12	VF20	XF40	MS60	MS63
2005	—	PF63 270	PF65 300			

KM# 190 10 POUNDS
155.50 g., 0.917 Gold 4.555 oz. AGW, 65 mm. **Ruler:** Elizabeth II **Subject:** Battle of Trafalgar, 200th Anniversary **Rev:** H.M.S. Victory

Date	Mintage	F12	VF20	XF40	MS60	MS63
2005	—	PF65 9,500				

KM# 224a 10 POUNDS
155.50 g., 0.917 Gold 4.555 oz. AGW, 65 mm. **Ruler:** Elizabeth II **Subject:** Apollo 11 moon landing, 40th Anniversary **Rev:** Lunar module Eagle and moon scape

Date	Mintage	F12	VF20	XF40	MS60	MS63
2009	—	PF65 9,000				

KM# 224 10 POUNDS
155.50 g., 0.999 Silver 4.9623 oz. ASW, 65 mm. **Ruler:** Elizabeth II **Subject:** Apollo 11 moon landing, 40th Anniversary **Rev:** Lunar module Eagle and moon

Date	Mintage	F12	VF20	XF40	MS60	MS63
2009	—	PF63 245	PF65 275			

KM# 107 25 POUNDS
7.81 g., 0.917 Gold 0.2288 oz. AGW, 22 mm. **Ruler:** Elizabeth II **Subject:** Queen Victoria Centennial **Obv:** Head with tiara right **Rev:** Queen Victoria's portrait **Edge:** Reeded

Date	Mintage	F12	VF20	XF40	MS60	MS63
2001	2,500	PF63 425	PF65 450			

KM# 112 25 POUNDS
7.81 g., 0.917 Gold 0.2288 oz. AGW, 22 mm. **Ruler:** Elizabeth II **Subject:** Queen's 75th Birthday **Obv:** Head with tiara right **Rev:** Queen's portrait in wreath **Edge:** Reeded

Date	Mintage	F12	VF20	XF40	MS60	MS63
2001	5,000	PF63 400	PF65 425			

KM# 123 25 POUNDS
7.98 g., 0.9167 Gold 0.2337 oz. AGW, 22.05 mm. **Ruler:** Elizabeth II **Subject:** Princess Diana **Obv:** Head with tiara right **Rev:** Diana's cameo portrait in wreath **Edge:** Reeded

Date	Mintage	F12	VF20	XF40	MS60	MS63
2002	2,500	PF63 425	PF65 450			

KM# 131 25 POUNDS
7.81 g., 0.9166 Gold 0.2287 oz. AGW, 22 mm. **Ruler:** Elizabeth II **Subject:** The Duke of Wellington **Obv:** Head with tiara right **Rev:** Portrait with mounted dragoons in the background **Edge:** Reeded

Date	Mintage	F12	VF20	XF40	MS60	MS63
2002	2,500	PF63 400	PF65 425			

KM# 139 25 POUNDS
7.98 g., 0.9166 Gold 0.2337 oz. AGW, 22 mm. **Ruler:** Elizabeth II **Subject:** Golden Jubilee **Obv:** Head with tiara right **Rev:** Queen in coach **Edge:** Reeded

Date	Mintage	F12	VF20	XF40	MS60	MS63
2002	5,000	PF63 420	PF65 445			

KM# 140 25 POUNDS
7.98 g., 0.9166 Gold 0.2337 oz. AGW, 22 mm. **Ruler:** Elizabeth II **Subject:** Queen Mother **Obv:** Head with tiara right **Rev:** Queen Mother's portrait **Edge:** Reeded

Date	Mintage	F12	VF20	XF40	MS60	MS63
2002	2,500	PF63 425	PF65 450			

KM# 141 25 POUNDS
7.98 g., 0.9166 Gold 0.2337 oz. AGW, 22 mm. **Ruler:** Elizabeth II **Subject:** Golden Jubilee **Obv:** Head with tiara right **Rev:** Trooping the Colors scene **Edge:** Reeded

Date	Mintage	F12	VF20	XF40	MS60	MS63
2003	5,000	PF63 420	PF65 445			

KM# 128 25 POUNDS
7.98 g., 0.917 Gold 0.2338 oz. AGW, 22 mm. **Ruler:** Elizabeth II **Subject:** Royal Navy - Golden Hind and Sir Francis Drake

Date	Mintage	F12	VF20	XF40	MS60	MS63
2003	—	PF63 475	PF65 525			

KM# 152 25 POUNDS
7.98 g., 0.9167 Gold 0.2337 oz. AGW, 22 mm. **Ruler:** Elizabeth II **Subject:** D-Day **Obv:** Head with tiara right **Rev:** Advancing British soldier **Edge:** Reeded

Date	Mintage	F12	VF20	XF40	MS60	MS63
2004	500	PF63 450	PF65 475			

KM# 144 25 POUNDS
7.98 g., 0.917 Gold 0.2338 oz. AGW, 22 mm. **Ruler:** Elizabeth II **Subject:** Steam Locomotives **Rev:** Mallard Locomotive

Date	Mintage	F12	VF20	XF40	MS60	MS63
2004	Est. 2500	PF63 475	PF65 525			

KM# 172 25 POUNDS
7.98 g., 0.917 Gold 0.2338 oz. AGW, 22 mm. **Ruler:** Elizabeth II **Subject:** Steam Locomotives **Rev:** City of Truro locomotive

Date	Mintage	F12	VF20	XF40	MS60	MS63
2004	Est. 2500	PF63 475	PF65 525			

KM# 181 25 POUNDS
7.98 g., 0.917 Gold 0.2338 oz. AGW, 22 mm. **Ruler:** Elizabeth II **Subject:** Crimea, 150th Anniversary

Date	Mintage	F12	VF20	XF40	MS60	MS63
2004	—	PF63 475	PF65 525			

KM# 183 25 POUNDS
7.98 g., 0.917 Gold 0.2338 oz. AGW, 22 mm. **Ruler:** Elizabeth II **Subject:** End of WWII, 60th Anniversary

Date	Mintage	F12	VF20	XF40	MS60	MS63
2005	—	PF63 475	PF65 525			

KM# 185 25 POUNDS
7.98 g., 0.917 Gold 0.2338 oz. AGW, 22 mm. **Ruler:** Elizabeth II **Rev:** Return of the Islanders

Date	Mintage	F12	VF20	XF40	MS60	MS63
2005	—	PF63 475	PF65 525			

KM# 188 25 POUNDS
7.98 g., 0.917 Gold 0.2338 oz. AGW, 22 mm. **Ruler:** Elizabeth II **Subject:** Royal Navy **Rev:** H.M.S. Ark Royal

Date	Mintage	F12	VF20	XF40	MS60	MS63
2005	—	PF63 475	PF65 525			

KM# 174 25 POUNDS
7.98 g., 0.9166 Gold 0.2337 oz. AGW, 22 mm. **Ruler:** Elizabeth II **Subject:** FIFA - XVIII World Football Championship - Germany 2006 **Rev:** Wembley Stadium

Date	Mintage	F12	VF20	XF40	MS60	MS63
2006	2,500	PF63 420	PF65 445			

KM# 218 25 POUNDS
7.98 g., 0.917 Gold 0.2338 oz. AGW, 22 mm. **Ruler:** Elizabeth II **Subject:** Royal Air Force, 90th Anniversary **Rev:** Lancaster

Date	Mintage	F12	VF20	XF40	MS60	MS63
2008	—	PF63 450	PF65 475			

KM# 221 25 POUNDS
7.98 g., 0.917 Gold 0.2338 oz. AGW, 22 mm. **Ruler:** Elizabeth II **Subject:** British Warships **Rev:** H.M.S. Mary Rose, 1511

Date	Mintage	F12	VF20	XF40	MS60	MS63
2009	Est. 995	PF63 450	PF65 475			

KM# 177 50 POUNDS
1000.00 g., 0.916 Silver 29.2605 oz. ASW, 100 mm. **Ruler:** Elizabeth II **Subject:** Coronation, 50th Anniversary **Rev:** Buckingham Palace

Date	Mintage	F12	VF20	XF40	MS60	MS63
2003	Est. 999	PF63 950	PF65 1,100			

KM# 153 50 POUNDS
1000.00 g., 0.925 Silver 29.548 oz. ASW, 100 mm. **Ruler:** Elizabeth II **Subject:** D-Day **Obv:** Head with tiara right **Rev:** British troops storming ashore **Edge:** Reeded

Date	Mintage	F12	VF20	XF40	MS60	MS63
2004	600	PF63 1,100	PF65 1,300			

KM# 178 50 POUNDS
7.98 g., 0.916 Gold 0.2335 oz. AGW, 22.05 mm. **Ruler:** Elizabeth II **Subject:** Royal Air Force, 90th Anniversary **Rev:** Pilots scrambling to planes, some in the sky **Edge:** Reeded

Date	Mintage	F12	VF20	XF40	MS60	MS63
2008	—	PF63 450	PF65 475			

PIEDFORT

KM#	Date	Mintage	Identification	Mkt Val
P3	2002	100	5 Pounds 0.9166 Gold Queen's portrait Queen in coach	4,250

MINT SETS

KM#	Date	Mintage	Identification	Issue Price	Mkt Val
MS10	2003 (8)	—	KM#83, 89-90, 96-97, 110, 148-49		22.50
MS11	2004 (1)	—	Guernsey KM#155, Alderney KM#43, Jersey KM#126, 150th Anniversary of the Crimean War		80.00

GUINEA

The Republic of Guinea, situated on the Atlantic Coast of Africa between Sierra Leone and Guinea-Bissau, has an area of 94,964 sq. mi. (245,860 sq. km.) and a population of 6.4 million. Capital: Conakry. Although Guinea contains one-third of the world's reserves of bauxite and significant deposits of iron ore, gold and diamonds, the economy is still dependent on agriculture, aluminum, bananas, copra and coffee are exported.

The coast of Guinea was known to Portuguese navigators of the 15th century but was seldom visited by European traders of the 16th-18th centuries because of its dangerous coastal waters. French penetration of the area began in the mid-19th century with the entering into of protectorate treaties with several of the coastal chiefs. After a long struggle with Guinea's native leader Samory Toure, France secured the area and until 1890 administered it as a part of Senegal. In 1895 the colony (Guinee Francais) became an autonomous part of the federation of French West Africa. The inhabitants were extended French citizenship in 1946 when the colony became an overseas territory of the French Union. Guinea became an independent republic on Oct. 2, 1958, when it declined to enter the new French Community.

MONETARY SYSTEM
100 Centimes = 1 Franc

REPUBLIC

REFORM COINAGE

KM# 65 2000 FRANCS
22.20 g., 0.900 Silver 0.6382 oz. ASW, 37 mm. **Obv:** National Arms **Rev:** Map and female figure

Date	Mintage	F12	VF20	XF40	MS60	MS63
2002	500	PF65 120				

GUYANA

VENEZUELA
SURINAME
North Atlantic Ocean
COLOMBIA
FRENCH GUIANA
BRAZIL

The Cooperative Republic of Guyana, is situated on the northeast coast of South America, has an area of 83,000 sq. mi. (214,970 sq. km.) and a population of 729,000. Capital: Georgetown. The economy is basically agrarian. Sugar, rice and bauxite are exported.

The original area of Essequibo and Demerary, which included present-day Suriname, French Guiana, and parts of Brazil and Venezuela was sighted by Columbus in 1498. Guyana became a republic on Feb. 23, 1970. It is a member of the Commonwealth of Nations. The president is the Chief of State. The prime minister is the Head of Government. Guyana is a member of the Caribbean Community and Common Market (CARICOM).

REPUBLIC
DECIMAL COINAGE

KM# 50 DOLLAR
2.40 g., Copper Plated Steel, 17 mm. **Obv:** Helmeted and supported arms **Rev:** Hand gathering rice **Edge:** Reeded

Date	Mintage	F12	VF20	XF40	MS60	MS63
2001	—	—	—	—	0.50	0.65
2002	—	—	—	—	0.50	0.65
2005	—	—	—	—	0.50	0.65
2008	—	—	—	—	0.50	0.65
2011	—	—	—	—	0.50	0.65

KM# 51 5 DOLLARS
3.78 g., Copper Plated Steel, 20.5 mm. **Obv:** Helmeted and supported arms **Rev:** Sugar cane **Edge:** Reeded

Date	Mintage	F12	VF20	XF40	MS60	MS63
2002	—	—	—	0.35	0.75	1.00
2005	—	—	—	0.35	0.75	1.00
2008	—	—	—	0.35	0.75	1.00
2009	—	—	—	0.35	0.75	1.00

KM# 52 10 DOLLARS
5.00 g., Nickel Plated Steel, 23 mm. **Obv:** Helmeted and supported arms **Rev:** Gold mining scene **Edge:** Reeded **Shape:** 7-sided **Note:** Slightly different die for each date.

Date	Mintage	F12	VF20	XF40	MS60	MS63
2007	—	—	—	0.75	1.25	1.50
2009	—	—	—	0.75	1.25	1.50

KM# 54 1000 DOLLARS
28.28 g., 0.925 Silver 0.8356 oz. ASW, 38.6 mm. **Subject:** Bank of Guyana, 40th Anniversary **Obv:** Arms **Rev:** Bank building, partially gilt

Date	Mintage	F12	VF20	XF40	MS60	MS63
2005	1,000	PF65 85.00				

KM# 54a 1000 DOLLARS
28.28 g., Copper-Nickel, 38.61 mm. **Subject:** Central Bank, 40th Anniversary **Obv:** Supported arms **Rev:** Building

Date	Mintage	F12	VF20	XF40	MS60	MS63
2005	—	—	—	—	—	50.00

KM# 55 2000 DOLLARS
28.28 g., 0.925 Silver 0.8356 oz. ASW, 38.61 mm. **Obv:** National Arms **Rev:** National soccer stadium

Date	Mintage	F12	VF20	XF40	MS60	MS63
2007	Est. 4000	PF63 80.00	PF65 90.00			

KM# 56 2000 DOLLARS
25.00 g., Copper-Nickel, 39 mm. **Obv:** National Arms **Rev:** Face design

Date	Mintage	F12	VF20	XF40	MS60	MS63
2008	—	—	—	—	—	75.00

HAITI

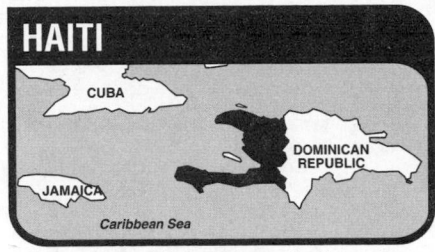

CUBA
DOMINICAN REPUBLIC
JAMAICA
Caribbean Sea

The Republic of Haiti, which occupies the western one-third of the island of Hispaniola in the Caribbean Sea between Puerto Rico and Cuba, has an area of 10,714 sq. mi. (27,750 sq. km.) and a population of 6.5 million. Capital: Port-au-Prince. The economy is based on agriculture; but light manufacturing and tourism are increasingly important. Coffee, bauxite, sugar, essential oils and handicrafts are exported.

The French language is used on Haitian coins although it is spoken by only about 10% of the populace. A form of Creole is the language of the Haitians.

MONETARY SYSTEM
100 Centimes = 1 Gourde

REPUBLIC
DECIMAL COINAGE

KM# 155 GOURDE
6.30 g., Brass Plated Steel, 23 mm. **Obv:** Citadelle de Roi Christophe **Shape:** 7-sided

Date	Mintage	F12	VF20	XF40	MS60	MS63
2003	—	—	—	—	1.75	2.00
2009	—	—	—	—	1.75	2.00

KM# 156 5 GOURDES
9.20 g., Brass Plated Steel, 28 mm. **Obv:** Four portraits in circle of Haitian statesmen top: Gen. Tonsaint Louverture, Left: Henri Christophe, Right: Jean Jacques Dessalines, Bottom: Alexandre Petion, date below **Rev:** National arms **Shape:** 7-sided

Date	Mintage	F12	VF20	XF40	MS60	MS63
2007	—	—	—	—	2.75	3.00

HONDURAS

MEXICO
BELIZE
Caribbean Sea
North Pacific Ocean
GUATEMALA
NICARAGUA
EL SALVADOR

The Republic of Honduras, situated in Central America alongside El Salvador, between Nicaragua and Guatemala, has an area of 43,277 sq. mi. (112,090 sq. km.) and a population of 5.6 million. Capital: Tegucigalpa. Agriculture, mining (gold and silver), and logging are the major economic activities, with increasing tourism and emerging petroleum resource discoveries. Precious metals, bananas, timber and coffee are exported.

From 1933 to 1940 General Tiburcio Carias Andino was dictator president of the Republic. Since 1990 democratic practices have become more consistent.

MONETARY SYSTEM
100 Centavos = 1 Lempira

REPUBLIC
REFORM COINAGE

KM# 72.4 5 CENTAVOS
3.20 g., Brass, 21 mm. **Obv:** National arms **Rev:** Value in circle within sprays **Edge:** Plain

Date	Mintage	F12	VF20	XF40	MS60	MS63
2002	—	—	—	0.10	0.25	0.35
2003	—	—	—	0.10	0.25	0.35
2005	—	—	—	0.10	0.25	0.35
2006	—	—	—	0.10	0.25	0.35
2007	—	—	—	0.10	0.25	0.35

KM# 76.3 10 CENTAVOS
6.00 g., Brass, 26 mm. **Obv:** National arms, without clouds behind pyramid **Rev:** Denomination within circle, wreath surrounds **Edge:** Plain

Date	Mintage	F12	VF20	XF40	MS60	MS63
2002	—	—	—	0.20	0.45	0.65
2003	—	—	—	0.20	0.45	0.65
2005	—	—	—	0.20	0.45	0.65
2006	—	—	—	0.20	0.45	0.65
2007	—	—	—	0.20	0.45	0.65

KM# 76.4 10 CENTAVOS
6.00 g., Brass, 26 mm. **Obv:** National arms, slightly larger legend, large date **Rev:** Value in circle within wreath **Edge:** Plain

Date	Mintage	F12	VF20	XF40	MS60	MS63
2006	—	—	—	0.15	0.35	0.45
2007	—	—	—	0.15	0.35	0.45
2010	—	—	—	0.15	0.35	0.45

KM# 83a.2 20 CENTAVOS
2.00 g., Nickel Plated Steel, 18 mm. **Obv:** National arms, without clouds **Rev:** Chief Lempira head left within circle **Edge:** Reeded

Date	Mintage	F12	VF20	XF40	MS60	MS63
2007	—	—	—	0.20	0.60	1.00
2010	—	—	—	0.20	0.60	1.00

KM# 84a.2 50 CENTAVOS
5.00 g., Nickel Plated Steel, 24 mm. **Obv:** National arms above date **Rev:** Chief Lempira head left within circle **Edge:** Reeded

Date	Mintage	F12	VF20	XF40	MS60	MS63
2005	—	—	0.15	0.35	0.90	1.25
2007	—	—	0.15	0.35	0.90	1.25

KM# 91 10 LEMPIRAS
27.00 g., 0.925 Silver 0.7978 oz. ASW, 40 mm. **Obv:** State arms **Rev:** Bust of Jose Trinidad Cabanas Fiallos, president 1852-1855

Date	Mintage	F12	VF20	XF40	MS60	MS63
2005	—	PF60 90.00	PF63 100	PF65 120		

HONG KONG

Hong Kong, a former British colony, reverted to control of the People's Republic of China on July 1, 1997 as a Special Administrative Region. It is situated at the mouth of the Canton or Pearl River 90 miles (145 km.) southeast of Canton, has an area of 403 sq. mi. (1,040 sq. km.) and an estimated population of 6.3 million. Capital: Victoria. The free port of Hong Kong, the commercial center of the Far East, is a trans-shipment point for goods destined for China and the countries of the Pacific Rim. Light manufacturing and tourism are important components of the economy.

SPECIAL ADMINISTRATION REGION (S.A.R.)

DECIMAL COINAGE

KM# 80 50 DOLLARS
35.43 g., 0.925 Silver 1.0469 oz. ASW, 40 mm. **Series:** Five Blessings **Obv:** Bauhinia flower **Rev:** Jade Ju-I

Date	Mintage	F12	VF20	XF40	MS60	MS63
2002	60,000	PF63 75.00	PF65 95.00			

KM# 81 50 DOLLARS
35.43 g., 0.925 Silver 1.0469 oz. ASW, 40 mm. **Series:** Five Blessings **Obv:** Bauhinia flower **Rev:** Fish

Date	Mintage	F12	VF20	XF40	MS60	MS63
2002	60,000	PF63 75.00	PF65 95.00			

KM# 82 50 DOLLARS
35.25 g., 0.925 Silver 1.0416 oz. ASW, 40 mm. **Series:** Five Blessings **Obv:** Bauhinia flower **Rev:** Horses

Date	Mintage	F12	VF20	XF40	MS60	MS63
2002	60,000	PF63 75.00	PF65 95.00			

KM# 83 50 DOLLARS
35.34 g., 0.925 Silver 1.0442 oz. ASW, 40 mm. **Series:** Five Blessings **Obv:** Bauhinia flower **Rev:** Peony flower

Date	Mintage	F12	VF20	XF40	MS60	MS63
2002	60,000	PF63 75.00	PF65 95.00			

KM# 84 50 DOLLARS
35.14 g., 0.925 Silver 1.0383 oz. ASW, 40 mm. **Series:** Five Blessings **Obv:** Bauhinia flower **Rev:** Windmills

Date	Mintage	F12	VF20	XF40	MS60	MS63
2002	60,000	PF63 75.00	PF65 95.00			

PROOF SETS

KM#	Date	Mintage	Identification	Issue Price	Mkt Val
PS8	2002 (5)	60,000	KM#80-84 plus 7.8g, .9999, AGW .2508, 25mm gold medal	370	625

HUNGARY

Hungary, located in central Europe, has an area of 35,929 sq. mi. (93,030 sq. km.) and a population of 10.7 million. Capital: Budapest. The economy is based on agriculture, bauxite and a rapidly expanding industrial sector. Machinery, chemicals, iron and steel, and fruits and vegetables are exported.

MINT MARKS
BP - Budapest

MONETARY SYSTEM
Commencing 1946
100 Filler = 1 Forint

SECOND REPUBLIC

DECIMAL COINAGE

KM# 692 FORINT
2.05 g., Nickel-Brass, 16.5 mm. **Obv:** Crowned shield **Rev:** Denomination

Date	Mintage	F12	VF20	XF40	MS60	MS63
2001BP	65,007,000	—		—	0.10	0.25
2001BP	3,000	PF60 3.75				
2002BP	70,007,000	—		—	0.10	0.25
2002BP	3,000	PF60 3.75				
2003BP	75,008,000	—		—	0.10	0.25
2003BP	7,000	PF60 3.50				
2004BP	96,008,000	—		—	0.10	0.25
2004BP	7,000	PF60 3.50				
2005BP	80,008,000	—		—	0.10	0.25
2005BP	7,000	PF60 3.50				
2006BP	67,008,000	—		—	0.10	0.25
2006BP	7,000	PF60 3.50				
2007BP	85,013,010	—		—	0.10	0.25
2007BP	7,000	PF60 3.50				
2008BP In sets only	8,010					3.50
2008BP	7,000	PF60 3.50				

KM# 693 2 FORINT
3.10 g., Copper-Nickel, 19.2 mm. **Obv:** Native flower: Colchicum Hungaricum **Rev:** Denomination **Edge:** Reeded

Date	Mintage	F12	VF20	XF40	MS60	MS63
2001BP	50,007,000	—		—	0.20	0.35
2001BP	—	PF60 4.25				
2002BP	60,007,000	—		—	0.20	0.35
2002BP	3,000	PF60 4.25				
2003BP	7,008,000	—		—	0.20	0.35
2003BP	7,000	PF60 4.00				
2004BP	88,008,000	—		—	0.20	0.35
2004BP	7,000	PF60 4.00				
2005BP	72,008,000	—		—	0.20	0.35
2005BP	7,000	PF60 4.00				
2006BP	54,008,000	—		—	0.20	0.35
2006BP	7,000	PF60 4.00				
2007BP	82,013,010	—		—	0.20	0.35
2007BP	7,000	PF60 4.00				
2008BP In sets only	8,010					4.00
2009BP	7,000	PF60 4.00				

KM# 694 5 FORINT
4.20 g., Nickel-Brass, 21.2 mm. **Obv:** Great White Egret **Rev:** Denomination

Date	Mintage	F12	VF20	XF40	MS60	MS63
2001BP	18,007,000	—		—	1.00	1.50
2001BP	—	PF60 5.00				
2002BP	11,007,000	—		—	1.00	1.50
2002BP	3,000	PF60 5.00				
2003BP	15,008,000	—		—	1.00	1.50
2003BP	7,000	PF60 4.50				
2004BP	40,008,000	—		—	1.00	1.50
2004BP	7,000	PF60 4.50				
2005BP	16,008,000	—		—	1.00	1.50
2005BP	7,000	PF60 4.50				
2006BP	21,008,000	—		—	1.00	1.50
2006BP	7,000	PF60 4.50				
2007BP	33,008,000	—		—	1.00	1.50
2007BP	7,000	PF60 4.50				
2008BP	34,038,005	—		—	1.00	1.50
2008BP	7,000	PF60 4.50				
2009BP	5,980,015	—		—	1.00	1.50
2009BP	7,000	PF60 4.50				
2010BP	45,015,520	—		—	1.00	1.50
2010BP	7,000	PF60 4.50				
2011BP In sets only	9,000					1.50
2011BP	7,000	PF60 4.50				
2012BP		—		—	1.00	1.50

KM# 847 5 FORINT
4.20 g., Nickel-Brass, 21.2 mm. **Obv:** Great White Egret **Obv. Legend:** MAGYARORSZAG **Rev:** Denomination

Date	Mintage	F12	VF20	XF40	MS60	MS63
2012BP	10,000,000	—		—	1.00	1.50
2012BP	4,000	PF65 2.50				
2013BP	—	—		—	1.00	1.50
2013BP	—	PF65 2.50				

KM# 695 10 FORINT
6.10 g., Copper-Nickel, 24.8 mm. **Obv:** Crowned shield **Rev:** Denomination **Edge:** Segmented reeding

Date	Mintage	F12	VF20	XF40	MS60	MS63
2001BP	12,007,000	—		—	1.00	2.50
2001BP	—	PF60 5.50				
2002BP	5,007,000	—		—	1.00	2.50
2002BP	3,000	PF60 5.50				
2003BP	1,008,000	—		—	1.00	2.50
2003BP	7,000	PF60 5.00				
2004BP	19,008,000	—		—	1.00	2.50
2004BP	7,000	PF60 5.00				
2005BP	8,981,000	—		—	1.00	2.50
2005BP	7,000	PF60 5.00				
2006BP	15,008,000	—		—	1.00	2.50
2006BP	7,000	PF60 5.00				
2007	25,008,000	—		—	1.00	2.50
2007	7,000	PF60 5.00				
2008	14,003,005	—		—	1.00	2.50
2008	7,000	PF60 5.00				
2009	2,015,015	—		—	1.00	2.50
2009	7,000	PF60 5.00				
2010	15,020	—		—	1.00	2.50
2010	7,000	PF60 5.00				
2011 In sets only	9,000					2.50
2011	7,000	PF60 5.00				

KM# 779 10 FORINT
6.10 g., Copper-Nickel, 24.8 mm. **Obv:** Attila Jozsef **Rev:** Value **Edge:** Segmented reeding

Date	Mintage	F12	VF20	XF40	MS60	MS63
2005BP	20,000	—	—	—	2.50	3.00
2005BP	7,000	PF65 3.50				

KM# 848 10 FORINT
6.10 g., Copper-Nickel, 24.8 mm. **Obv:** Crowned shield **Obv. Legend:** MAGYARORSZAG **Rev:** Denomination **Edge:** Segmented reeding

Date	Mintage	F12	VF20	XF40	MS60	MS63
2012BP	10,000,000	—	—	—	1.00	2.50
2012BP	4,000	PF65 5.00				
2013BP	—	—	—	—	1.00	2.50
2013BP	—	PF65 5.00				

KM# 696 20 FORINT
6.90 g., Nickel-Brass, 26.3 mm. **Obv:** Hungarian Iris **Rev:** Denomination **Edge:** Reeded

Date	Mintage	F12	VF20	XF40	MS60	MS63
2001BP	7,000	—	—	—	—	2.00
2001BP	3,000	PF60 4.50				
2002BP	7,000	—	—	—	—	2.00
2002BP	3,000	PF60 4.50				
2003BP	8,000	—	—	—	—	2.00
2003BP	7,000	PF60 4.00				
2004BP	7,008,000	—	—	—	1.50	2.00
2004BP	7,000	PF60 4.00				
2005BP	11,008,000	—	—	—	1.50	2.00
2005BP	7,000	PF60 4.00				
2006BP	14,008,000	—	—	—	1.50	2.00
2006BP	7,000	PF60 4.00				
2007DP	18,008,010	—	—	—	1.50	2.00
2007BP	7,000	PF60 4.00				
2008BP	9,020,505	—	—	—	1.50	2.00
2008BP	7,000	PF60 4.00				
2009BP	4,997,515	—	—	—	1.50	2.00
2009BP	7,000	PF60 4.00				
2010BP	14,020	—	—	—	—	2.00
2010BP	7,000	PF60 4.00				
2011BP	9,000	—	—	—	—	2.00
2011BP	7,000	PF60 4.00				

KM# 768 20 FORINT
6.90 g., Nickel-Brass, 26.3 mm. **Obv:** Ferenc Deak **Rev:** Denomination **Edge:** Reeded

Date	Mintage	F12	VF20	XF40	MS60	MS63
2003BP	993,000	—	—	—	1.50	2.00
2003BP	7,000	PF65 4.00				

KM# 849 20 FORINT
6.90 g., Nickel-Brass, 26.3 mm. **Obv:** Hungarian Iris **Obv. Legend:** MAGYARORSZAG **Rev:** Denomination **Edge:** Reeded

Date	Mintage	F12	VF20	XF40	MS60	MS63
2012BP	10,000,000	—	—	—	1.50	2.50
2012BP	4,000	PF65 5.00				
2013BP	—	—	—	—	1.50	2.50
2013BP	—	PF65 5.00				

KM# 697 50 FORINT
7.60 g., Copper-Nickel, 27.5 mm. **Obv:** Saker falcon **Rev:** Denomination

Date	Mintage	F12	VF20	XF40	MS60	MS63
2001BP	15,007,000	—	—	—	3.00	4.00
2001BP	—	PF60 6.00				
2002BP	7,000	—	—	—	—	3.50

Date	Mintage	F12	VF20	XF40	MS60	MS63
2002BP	3,000	PF60 5.50				
2003BP	7,008,000	—	—	—	3.00	3.50
2003BP	7,000	PF60 5.00				
2004BP	8,000	—	—	—	—	3.50
2004BP	7,000	PF60 5.00				
2005BP	9,007,000	—	—	—	3.00	3.50
2005BP	8,000	PF60 5.00				
2006BP	5,008,000	—	—	—	3.00	3.50
2006BP	7,000	PF60 5.00				
2007BP	13,008,000	—	—	—	3.00	3.50
2007BP	7,000	PF60 5.00				
2008BP	6,032,010	—	—	—	3.00	3.50
2008BP	7,000	PF60 5.00				
2009BP	1,986,010	—	—	—	3.00	3.50
2009BP	7,000	PF60 5.00				
2010BP	14,020	—	—	—	—	3.50
2010BP	7,000	PF60 5.00				
2011BP	9,000	—	—	—	—	3.50
2011BP	7,000	PF60 5.00				

KM# 773 50 FORINT
7.70 g., Copper-Nickel, 27.5 mm. **Obv:** National arms above Euro Union star circle **Rev:** Denomination **Edge:** Plain

Date	Mintage	F12	VF20	XF40	MS60	MS63
2004BP	993,000	—	—	—	3.00	3.50
2004BP	7,000	PF65 6.00				

KM# 780 50 FORINT
7.70 g., Copper-Nickel, 27.4 mm. **Subject:** International Childrens Safety Service **Obv:** Stylized crying child **Rev:** Denomination **Edge:** Plain

Date	Mintage	F12	VF20	XF40	MS60	MS63
2005BP	2,000,000	—	—	—	3.00	3.50

KM# 788 50 FORINT
7.70 g., Copper-Nickel, 27.4 mm. **Obv:** Hungarian Red Cross 125th Anniversary seal above date and country name **Rev:** Value **Edge:** Plain

Date	Mintage	F12	VF20	XF40	MS60	MS63
2006BP	2,000,000	—	—	—	3.00	3.50

KM# 789 50 FORINT
7.70 g., Copper-Nickel, 27.4 mm. **Subject:** 1956 Revolution **Obv:** Holed flag with Parliament building in background **Rev:** Value **Edge:** Plain

Date	Mintage	F12	VF20	XF40	MS60	MS63
2006BP	2,000,000	—	—	—	3.00	3.50

KM# 805 50 FORINT
7.70 g., Copper-Nickel, 27.4 mm. **Subject:** Celebrating 50 years of the Treaty of Rome **Obv:** Book logo **Rev:** Value

Date	Mintage	F12	VF20	XF40	MS60	MS63
2007	2,000,000	—	—	—	1.50	2.00
2007	5,000	PF65 3.50				

KM# 850 50 FORINT
7.60 g., Copper-Nickel, 27.5 mm. **Obv:** Saker falcon **Obv. Legend:** MAGYARORSZAG **Rev:** Denomination

Date	Mintage	F12	VF20	XF40	MS60	MS63
2012BP	—	—	—	—	3.00	3.50
2012BP	4,000	PF65 7.00				
2013BP	—	—	—	—	3.00	3.50
2013BP	—	PF65 7.00				

KM# 721 100 FORINT
8.00 g., Bi-Metallic, 23.8 mm. **Obv:** Crowned shield **Rev:** Denomination **Edge:** Reeded

Date	Mintage	F12	VF20	XF40	MS60	MS63
2001BP	7,000	—	—	—	—	5.00
2001BP	3,000	PF60 8.00				
2002BP	7,000	—	—	—	—	5.00
2002BP	3,000	PF60 8.00				
2003BP	8,000	—	—	—	—	5.00
2003BP	7,000	PF60 7.50				
2004BP	4,008,000	—	—	—	3.50	5.00
2004BP	7,000	PF60 7.50				
2005BP	8,000	—	—	—	—	5.00
2005BP	7,000	PF60 7.50				
2006BP	8,000	—	—	—	—	5.00
2006BP	7,000	PF60 7.50				
2007BP	7,008,010	—	—	—	3.50	5.00
2007BP	7,000	PF60 7.50				
2008BP	7,008,010	—	—	—	3.50	5.00
2008BP	7,000	PF60 7.50				
2009BP	11,210	—	—	—	—	5.00
2009BP	7,000	PF60 7.50				
2010BP	14,020	—	—	—	—	5.00
2010BP	7,000	PF60 7.50				
2011BP	9,000	—	—	—	—	5.00
2011BP	7,000	PF60 7.50				

KM# 760 100 FORINT
8.00 g., Bi-Metallic, 23.8 mm. **Subject:** Lajos Kossuth **Obv:** Head right within circle **Rev:** Denomination within circle **Edge:** Reeded

Date	Mintage	F12	VF20	XF40	MS60	MS63
2002BP	997,000	—	—	—	2.00	2.50
2002BP	3,000	PF65 5.00				

KM# 851 100 FORINT
8.00 g., Bi-Metallic, 23.6 mm. **Obv:** Crowned shield **Obv. Legend:** MAGYARORSZAG **Rev:** Denomination

Date	Mintage	F12	VF20	XF40	MS60	MS63
2012BP	—	—	—	—	3.50	5.00
2012BP	4,000	PF63 7.00	PF65 10.00			
2013BP	—	—	—	—	3.50	5.00
2013BP	—	PF63 7.00	PF65 10.00			

KM# 844 100 FORINT
10.00 g., Copper-Nickel, 30 mm. **Subject:** Hungarian Scout Association, 100th Anniversary **Obv:** Hungarian Scout emblem at right **Rev:** Scout in uniform blowing bugle towards left **Shape:** 12-sided

Date	Mintage	F12	VF20	XF40	MS60	MS63
2012BP	5,000	—	—	—	—	20.00
2012BP	10,000	PF63 22.00	PF65 25.00			

KM# 754 200 FORINT
9.40 g., Brass, 29.2 mm. **Subject:** Childrens Literature: Ludas Matyi **Obv:** Denomination **Rev:** Man holding a goose **Edge:** Plain

Date	Mintage	F12	VF20	XF40	MS60	MS63
2001BP	12,000	—	—	—	7.50	9.50
2001BP	5,000	PF63 15.00	PF65 18.00			

KM# 755 200 FORINT
Brass, 29.2 mm. **Subject:** Childrens Literature: Janos Vitez **Obv:** Denomination **Rev:** Soldier riding a flying bird **Edge:** Plain

Date	Mintage	F12	VF20	XF40	MS60	MS63
2001BP	12,000	—	—	—	7.50	9.50
2001BP	5,000	PF63 15.00	PF65 18.00			

KM# 756 200 FORINT
Brass, 29.2 mm. **Subject:** Childrens Literature: Toldi **Obv:** Denomination **Rev:** Knight kicking a boat off the shore **Edge:** Plain

Date	Mintage	F12	VF20	XF40	MS60	MS63
2001BP	12,000	—	—	—	7.50	9.50
2001BP	5,000	PF63 15.00	PF65 18.00			

KM# 757 200 FORINT
Brass, 29.2 mm. **Subject:** Childrens Literature: A Pal Utcai Fiuk **Obv:** Denomination **Rev:** Two men and cordwood **Edge:** Plain

Date	Mintage	F12	VF20	XF40	MS60	MS63
2001	12,000	—	—	—	7.50	9.50
2001	5,000	PF63 15.00	PF65 18.00			

KM# 826 200 FORINT
9.00 g., Bi-Metallic, 28.3 mm. **Obv:** Suspension Bridge over the Danube **Rev:** Value **Edge:** Segmented reeding

Date	Mintage	F12	VF20	XF40	MS60	MS63
2009BP	71,010,010	—	—	—	4.00	5.00
2009BP Proof	7,000					
2010BP	25,014,020	—	—	—	4.00	5.00
2010BP Proof	7,000					
2011BP	30,009,000	—	—	—	4.00	5.00
2011BP Proof	7,000					

KM# 852 200 FORINT
9.00 g., Bi-Metallic, 28.3 mm. **Obv:** Suspension Bridge over the Danube **Obv. Legend:** MAGYARORSZAG **Rev:** Denomination **Edge:** Segmented reeding

Date	Mintage	F12	VF20	XF40	MS60	MS63
2012BP	—	—	—	—	4.00	5.00
2012BP	4,000	PF63 7.00	PF65 10.00			
2013BP	—	—	—	—	4.00	5.00
2013BP	—	PF63 7.00	PF65 10.00			

KM# 765 500 FORINT
13.80 g., Copper-Nickel, 28.4x28.4 mm. **Subject:** Rubik's Cube **Obv:** Inscription on Rubik's Cube design **Rev:** Rubik's Cube with inscription **Edge:** Plain **Shape:** Square

Date	Mintage	F12	VF20	XF40	MS60	MS63
2002BP	5,000	—	—	—	20.00	25.00
2002BP	5,000	PF65 50.00				

KM# 764 500 FORINT
13.90 g., Copper-Nickel, 28.4x28.4 mm. **Subject:** Farkas Kempelen's Chess Machine **Obv:** Denomination, letters A-H and numbers 1-8 repeated along edges **Rev:** Robotic human form chess playing machine built in 1769 **Edge:** Plain **Shape:** Square

Date	Mintage	F12	VF20	XF40	MS60	MS63
2002BP	5,000	—	—	—	22.00	27.00
2002BP	5,000	PF65 55.00				

KM# 781 500 FORINT
14.00 g., Copper-Nickel, 28.4x28.4 mm. **Obv:** Old wheel **Rev:** First Hungarian Post Office motor vehicle **Edge:** Plain **Shape:** Square **Note:** 28.43 x 28.43mm

Date	Mintage	F12	VF20	XF40	MS60	MS63
2005BP	5,000	—	—	—	17.00	22.00
2005BP	10,000	PF63 32.00	PF65 35.00			

KM# 766 1000 FORINT
Bronze **Obv:** Denomination and satellite dish **Rev:** Mercury

Date	Mintage	F12	VF20	XF40	MS60	MS63
2002	15,000	—	—	—	15.00	16.50

KM# 787 1000 FORINT
13.81 g., Copper-Nickel, 28.3 mm. **Obv:** Value and partial front view of antique automobile **Rev:** Model T Ford **Edge:** Plain **Shape:** Square

Date	Mintage	F12	VF20	XF40	MS60	MS63
2006BP	10,000	—	—	—	17.00	20.00
2006BP	10,000	PF63 28.00	PF65 30.00			

KM# 797 1000 FORINT
14.00 g., Copper-Nickel, 28.43 x 28.43 mm. **Subject:** 125th Anniversary - Birth of János Adorján **Obv:** Early two cylinder aircraft motor with propeller **Obv. Legend:** MAGYAR / KOZTARSASAG **Rev:** Early monoplane **Rev. Legend:** ADORJAN JANOS / AZ ELSO SIKERES MAGYAR / REPULOGEP TERVEZOJE **Edge:** Plain **Shape:** Square

Date	Mintage	F12	VF20	XF40	MS60	MS63
2007BP	10,000	—	—	—	17.00	20.00
2007BP	10,000	PF63 28.00	PF65 30.00			

KM# 809 1000 FORINT
14.00 g., Copper-Nickel, 28.43 x 28.43 mm. **Subject:** Telephone Herald **Edge:** Plain **Shape:** Square

Date	Mintage	F12	VF20	XF40	MS60	MS63
2008	10,000	—	—	—	17.00	20.00
2008	15,000	PF63 25.00	PF65 27.00			

KM# 813 1000 FORINT
14.00 g., Copper-Nickel, 28.4 x 28.4 mm. **Subject:** Donat Banki, 150th Anniversary of Birth **Obv:** Denomination view of crossflow turbine **Rev:** Portrait facing in suit **Shape:** Square

Date	Mintage	F12	VF20	XF40	MS60	MS63
2009BP	10,000	—	—	—	16.00	18.00
2009BP	10,000	PF63 22.00	PF65 25.00			

KM# 818 1000 FORINT
14.00 g., Copper-Nickel, 28.4 x 28.4 mm. **Subject:** Laszlo Jozsef Biro, Inventor of the ball point pen **Obv:** Ball point pen schematic **Rev:** Bust facing **Shape:** Square

Date	Mintage	F12	VF20	XF40	MS60	MS63
2010BP	10,000	—	—	—	17.00	20.00
2010BP	10,000	PF63 25.00	PF65 28.00			

KM# 829 1000 FORINT
14.00 g., Copper-Nickel, 28.43x28.43 mm. **Subject:** Anyos Jedlik, principals of the dynamo, 1861 **Obv:** Dynamo **Rev:** Jedlik portrait

Date	Mintage	F12	VF20	XF40	MS60	MS63
2011BP	10,000	—	—	—	15.00	18.00
2011BP	10,000	PF63 22.00	PF65 25.00			

KM# 840 1000 FORINT
14.00 g., Copper-Nickel, 28.43x28.43 mm. **Subject:** Masat-1 satellite launch **Obv:** Land-based antenna **Rev:** Satellite above Eastern Europe map, Hungary highlighted

Date	Mintage	F12	VF20	XF40	MS60	MS63
2012BP	5,000	—	—	—		25.00
2012BP	5,000	PF65 25.00				

KM# 752 3000 FORINT
31.46 g., 0.925 Silver 0.9296 oz. ASW, 38.5 mm. **Subject:** Hungarian Silver Coinage Millennium **Obv:** Denomination in ornamental frame **Rev:** Thaler design circa 1500 portraying Ladislaus I (1077-95) with the title of saint **Edge:** Reeding over "1001-2001 **Edge Lettering:** BP • NX • KB • HX • GY • F • AF • MM • C +

Date	Mintage	F12	VF20	XF40	MS60	MS63
2001BP	5,000	—	—	—	40.00	45.00
2001BP	5,000	PF65 50.00				

KM# 759 3000 FORINT
31.80 g., 0.925 Silver 0.9396 oz. ASW, 38.7 mm. **Subject:** Centennial of First Hungarian Film "The Dance **Obv:** Denomination **Rev:** Two dancers on film **Edge:** Reeded

Date	Mintage	F12	VF20	XF40	MS60	MS63
2001BP	3,500	—	—	—	42.00	47.50
2001BP	3,500	PF65 55.00				

KM# 762 3000 FORINT
31.46 g., 0.925 Silver 0.9296 oz. ASW, 38.5 mm. **Subject:** 200th Anniversary - National Library **Obv:** Small coat of arms in ornate frame **Rev:** Interior view of library **Edge:** Reeded

Date	Mintage	F12	VF20	XF40	MS60	MS63
2002BP	3,000	—	—	—	40.00	45.00
2002BP	3,000	PF65 50.00				

KM# 763 3000 FORINT
31.46 g., 0.925 Silver 0.9296 oz. ASW, 38.5 mm. **Subject:** Janos Bolyai's publication of his "Appendix **Obv:** Circular graph **Rev:** Signature above 7-line inscription, name and dates **Edge:** Reeded

Date	Mintage	F12	VF20	XF40	MS60	MS63
2002BP	3,000	—	—	—	40.00	45.00
2002BP	3,000	PF65 50.00				

KM# 767 3000 FORINT
31.46 g., 0.925 Silver 0.9296 oz. ASW **Subject:** 100th Anniversary - Birth of Kovacs Margit (1902-1977) **Obv:** Denomination **Rev:** The "Trumpet of Judgement Day

Date	Mintage	F12	VF20	XF40	MS60	MS63
2002	4,000	—	—	—	40.00	45.00
2002	—	PF65 55.00				

KM# 761 3000 FORINT
31.33 g., 0.925 Silver 0.9257 oz. ASW, 38.6 mm. **Subject:** Hortobagy National Park **Obv:** Landscape, denomination **Rev:** Hungarian Grey Longhorn bull

Date	Mintage	F12	VF20	XF40	MS60	MS63
2002BP	5,000	—	—	—	25.00	35.00
2002BP	5,000	PF65 50.00				

KM# 817 3000 FORINT
10.00 g., 0.925 Silver 0.2955 oz. ASW **Subject:** Ferenc Kazinczy, 250th Anniversary of Birth **Obv:** Quill pen and rolled document **Rev:** Bust facing

Date	Mintage	F12	VF20	XF40	MS60	MS63
2009	5,000	—	—	—	17.00	20.00
2009	5,000	PF65 40.00				

KM# 828 3000 FORINT
10.00 g., 0.925 Silver 0.2955 oz. ASW, 30 mm. **Subject:** Hungary's EU Council Presidency, 2011 **Obv:** Crowned shield within grometic design **Rev:** Skyline view below EU star circle

Date	Mintage	F12	VF20	XF40	MS60	MS63
2011BP	3,000	—	—	—		30.00
2011BP	5,000	PF65 45.00				

KM# 842 3000 FORINT
24.00 g., 0.925 Silver 0.7092 oz. ASW, 30 mm. **Subject:** XXX Summer Olympics, London **Obv:** Two kayak paddles **Rev:** Three kayakers advancing right

Date	Mintage	F12	VF20	XF40	MS60	MS63
2012BP	3,000	—	—	—		45.00
2012BP	5,000	PF65 50.00				

KM# 845 3000 FORINT
10.00 g., 0.925 Silver 0.2955 oz. ASW, 30x25 mm. **Subject:** Albert Szent-Gyorgyi, Nobel prize winner **Obv:** Paprika, value at upper right **Rev:** Szent-Gyorgyi bust at left **Shape:** Horizontal oval

Date	Mintage	F12	VF20	XF40	MS60	MS63
2012BP	2,000	—	—	—		45.00
2012BP	5,000	PF65 50.00				

KM# 846 3000 FORINT
20.00 g., 0.925 Silver 0.591 oz. ASW, 34 mm. **Subject:** Sandor Popovics, 150th Anniversary of Birth **Obv:** Architectural statuary group **Rev:** Popovics bust

Date	Mintage	F12	VF20	XF40	MS60	MS63
2012BP	2,000	—	—	—	—	45.00
2012BP	4,000	PF65 50.00				

KM# 837 3000 FORINT
20.00 g., 0.925 Silver 0.591 oz. ASW, 34 mm. **Subject:** Imre Madach's The Tragedy of Man, 150th Anniversary **Obv:** Bust at left, large value **Rev:** Two figures standing on hilltop, guardian in background

Date	Mintage	F12	VF20	XF40	MS60	MS63
2012BP	2,000	—	—	—	—	45.00
2012BP	4,000	PF65 50.00				

KM# 853 3000 FORINT
Silver **Subject:** Traditional dance **Obv:** Tulip **Rev:** Family dancing

Date	Mintage	F12	VF20	XF40	MS60	MS63
2013	—	PF65 50.00				

KM# 854 3000 FORINT
12.50 g., 0.925 Silver 0.3693 oz. ASW, 30x25 mm. **Subject:** Albert Szenj-Gyorgyi Nobel in Physiology 1937 **Shape:** Horizontal oval

Date	Mintage	F12	VF20	XF40	MS60	MS63
2012BP	2,000	—	—	—	—	30.00
2012BP	5,000	PF65 40.00				

KM# 856 3000 FORINT
10.00 g., 0.925 Silver 0.2955 oz. ASW, 30x25 mm. **Subject:** Wigner Jeno, Nobel Prize 1963 **Shape:** Oval

Date	Mintage	F12	VF20	XF40	MS60	MS63
2013	—	—	—	—	—	45.00

KM# 751 4000 FORINT
31.46 g., 0.925 Silver 0.9296 oz. ASW, 26.4 x 39.6 mm. **Subject:** Godollo Artist Colony Centennial **Obv:** Denomination **Rev:** Sisters" stained glass window design **Edge:** Plain **Shape:** Vertical rectangle

Date	Mintage	F12	VF20	XF40	MS60	MS63
2001BP	4,000	—	—	—	40.00	45.00
2001BP	4,000	PF65 50.00				

KM# 769 5000 FORINT
31.46 g., 0.925 Silver 0.9296 oz. ASW, 38.6 mm. **Subject:** Budapest Philharmonic Orchestra **Obv:** Crowned arms in wreath **Rev:** Four coin-like portraits of Erkel, Dohnanyi, Bartók and Kodaly **Edge:** Reeded

Date	Mintage	F12	VF20	XF40	MS60	MS63
2003BP	4,000	—	—	—	37.50	42.50
2003BP	4,000	PF65 50.00				

KM# 770 5000 FORINT
31.46 g., 0.925 Silver 0.9296 oz. ASW, 38.6 mm. **Subject:** Janos Neumann, 100th Anniversary of Birth **Obv:** Denomination and binary number date **Rev:** Portrait and building **Edge:** Reeded

Date	Mintage	F12	VF20	XF40	MS60	MS63
2003BP	3,000	—	—	—	40.00	45.00
2003BP	3,000	PF65 75.00				

KM# 771 5000 FORINT
31.46 g., 0.925 Silver 0.9296 oz. ASW, 38.6 mm. **Subject:** Rakoczi's War of Liberation **Obv:** Transylvanian ducat design above country name, value and date **Rev:** Kuruc cavalryman with sword and trumpet **Edge:** Reeded

Date	Mintage	F12	VF20	XF40	MS60	MS63
2003BP	3,000	—	—	—	45.00	50.00
2003BP	3,000	PF65 65.00				

KM# 772 5000 FORINT
31.46 g., 0.925 Silver 0.9296 oz. ASW, 38.6 mm. **Subject:** World Heritage in Hungary - Holloko **Obv:** Holloko castle ruins above country name, value and date **Rev:** Village view behind woman in folk costume **Edge:** Reeded

Date	Mintage	F12	VF20	XF40	MS60	MS63
2003BP	5,000	—	—	—	42.50	45.00
2003BP	5,000	PF65 60.00				

KM# 776 5000 FORINT
31.46 g., 0.925 Silver 0.9296 oz. ASW, 38.6 mm. **Obv:** Value and country name above Euro Union stars **Rev:** Mythical stag seen through an ornate window **Edge:** Reeded

Date	Mintage	F12	VF20	XF40	MS60	MS63
2004BP	10,000	PF63 50.00 PF65 55.00				

KM# 774 5000 FORINT
31.46 g., 0.925 Silver 0.9296 oz. ASW, 38.6 mm. **Obv:** Value **Rev:** Two Olympic boxers **Edge:** Reeded

Date	Mintage	F12	VF20	XF40	MS60	MS63
2004BP	3,000	—	—	—	45.00	47.50
2004BP	9,000	PF65 55.00				

KM# 775 5000 FORINT
31.46 g., 0.925 Silver 0.9296 oz. ASW, 38.6 mm. **Obv:** Solomon Tower" above value **Rev:** Visegrad Castle with the Solomon Tower **Edge:** Reeded

Date	Mintage	F12	VF20	XF40	MS60	MS63
2004BP	4,000	—	—	—	45.00	50.00
2004BP	4,000	PF65 60.00				

KM# 778 5000 FORINT
31.46 g., 0.925 Silver 0.9296 oz. ASW, 38.6 mm. **Subject:** Ancient Christian Necropolis at Pecs **Obv:** Value and ancient artifact **Rev:** Interior view of tomb **Edge:** Reeded

Date	Mintage	F12	VF20	XF40	MS60	MS63
2004BP	5,000	—	—	—	40.00	45.00
2004BP	5,000	PF65 50.00				

KM# 782 5000 FORINT
31.46 g., 0.925 Silver 0.9296 oz. ASW, 38.6 mm. **Obv:** Bat flying above value **Rev:** Interior cave view **Edge:** Reeded

Date	Mintage	F12	VF20	XF40	MS60	MS63
2005BP	5,000	—	—	—	45.00	50.00
2005BP	5,000	PF65 55.00				

KM# 783 5000 FORINT
31.46 g., 0.925 Silver 0.9296 oz. ASW, 38.6 mm. **Obv:** Hungarian National Bank building **Rev:** Ignac Alpar and life dates **Edge:** Reeded

Date	Mintage	F12	VF20	XF40	MS60	MS63
ND (2005)BP	3,000	—	—	—	45.00	50.00
ND (2005)BP	3,000	PF65 60.00				

KM# 784 5000 FORINT
31.46 g., 0.925 Silver 0.9296 oz. ASW, 38.6 mm. **Obv:** Knight on horse with lance **Rev:** Diosgyor Castle **Edge:** Reeded

Date	Mintage	F12	VF20	XF40	MS60	MS63
2005BP	4,000	—	—	—	45.00	50.00
2005BP	4,000	PF65 60.00				

KM# 785 5000 FORINT
31.46 g., 0.925 Silver 0.9296 oz. ASW, 38.6 mm. **Obv:** Large building above value **Rev:** Karoli Gaspar Reformed (Calvinist) University seal **Edge:** Reeded

Date	Mintage	F12	VF20	XF40	MS60	MS63
2005BP	3,000	—	—	—	45.00	50.00
2005BP	3,000	PF65 60.00				

KM# 786 5000 FORINT
31.46 g., 0.925 Silver 0.9296 oz. ASW, 38.6 mm. **Obv:** Coin design of a Transylvanian KM-10 thaler reverse dated 1605 **Rev:** Stephan Bocskai (1557-1606) **Edge:** Reeded

Date	Mintage	F12	VF20	XF40	MS60	MS63
2005BP	3,000	—	—	—	45.00	50.00
2005BP	3,000	PF65 55.00				

KM# 790 5000 FORINT
31.46 g., 0.925 Silver 0.9296 oz. ASW, 38.61 mm. **Series:** Masterpieces of Ecclesiastical Architecture **Obv:** View of interior of dome **Obv. Legend:** MAGYAR KÖZTÁRSASÁG **Rev:** Basilica facade **Rev. Legend:** ESZTERGOMI BAZILIKA

Date	Mintage	F12	VF20	XF40	MS60	MS63
2006BP	2,500	—	—	—	50.00	55.00
2006BP	3,500	PF65 65.00				

KM# 791 5000 FORINT
31.46 g., 0.925 Silver 0.9296 oz. ASW, 38.61 mm. **Subject:** 125th Anniversary - Birth of Béla Bartók **Obv:** Transylvanian woodcarving **Obv. Legend:** MAGYAR KÖZTÁRSASÁG **Rev:** Bust of Bartók right, Euro star behind **Edge:** Reeded and lettered **Edge Lettering:** Bartók Béla repeated three times

Date	Mintage	F12	VF20	XF40	MS60	MS63
2006BP	25,000	PF63 40.00	PF65 45.00			

KM# 792 5000 FORINT
31.46 g., 0.925 Silver 0.9296 oz. ASW, 38.61 mm. **Series:** Heritage Sites **Obv:** Great White Egret in flight **Obv. Legend:** MAGYAR - KÖZTÁRSASÁG **Rev:** Landscape, Schneeberg Mountain above Esterházy palace facade

Date	Mintage	F12	VF20	XF40	MS60	MS63
2006BP	5,000	—	—	—	42.50	47.50
2006BP	5,000	PF65 55.00				

KM# 793 5000 FORINT
31.46 g., 0.925 Silver 0.9296 oz. ASW, 38.61 mm. **Series:** Hungarian Castles **Subject:** Hungarian Castles **Obv:** Portrait of Ilona Zrinyi **Obv. Legend:** MAGYAR KÖZTÁRSASÁG **Rev:** Munkács Castle

Date	Mintage	F12	VF20	XF40	MS60	MS63
2006BP	4,000	—	—	—	42.50	47.50
2006BP	4,000	PF65 55.00				

KM# 794 5000 FORINT
31.46 g., 0.925 Silver 0.9296 oz. ASW, 38.61 mm. **Subject:** 500th Anniversary - Victory in Nándorfehévár **Obv:** Decorative sword hilt **Obv. Legend:** MAGYAR KÖZTÁRSASÁG **Rev:** János Hunyadi in armor at left, John Capistrano in monk's garb at right **Rev. Inscription:** NÁNDORFEHÉRVÁRI / DIADAL

Date	Mintage	F12	VF20	XF40	MS60	MS63
2006BP	2,500	—	—	—	45.00	50.00
2006BP	3,500	PF65 60.00				

KM# 795 5000 FORINT
31.46 g., 0.925 Silver 0.9296 oz. ASW, 38.61 mm. **Subject:** 50th Anniversary - Hungarian Revolution **Obv:** 1956 repeated in stone blocks at right **Obv. Legend:** MAGYAR KÖZTÁRSASÁG **Rev:** 1956 repeated in stone blocks at left, freedom fighter's flag at center **Rev. Legend:** MAGYAR FORRADALOM ÉS SZABADSÁGHARC

Date	Mintage	F12	VF20	XF40	MS60	MS63
2006BP	5,000	—	—	—	42.50	47.50
2006BP	5,000	PF65 55.00				

KM# 798 5000 FORINT
31.46 g., 0.925 Silver 0.9296 oz. ASW, 38.61 mm. **Series:** Hungarian Castles **Obv:** Walled tower **Obv. Inscription:** MAGYAR / KÖZTÁRSASÁG **Rev:** Gyula castle **Rev. Inscription:** GYULAI / VÁR

Date	Mintage	F12	VF20	XF40	MS60	MS63
2007BP	4,000	—	—	—	55.00	60.00
2007BP	4,000	PF65 75.00				

KM# 799 5000 FORINT
31.46 g., 0.925 Silver 0.9296 oz. ASW, 38.61 mm. **Subject:** 200th Anniversary - Birth of Count Lajos Batthyány **Obv:** Seal dated 1848 with crowned arms above Batthyány's autograph **Obv. Legend:** MAGYAR KÖZTÁRSASÁG **Rev:** 1/2 length figure of Batthyány facing **Rev. Legend:** BATTHYÁNY LAJOS

Date	Mintage	F12	VF20	XF40	MS60	MS63
2007BP	20,000	PF63 40.00	PF65 45.00			

KM# 800 5000 FORINT

31.46 g., 0.925 Silver 0.9296 oz. ASW, 38.61 mm. **Subject:** 125th Anniversary - Birth of Zoltán Kodály **Obv:** Gramaphone **Obv. Legend:** MAGYAR KÖZTÁRSASÁG **Rev:** Bust of Kodály facing 3/4 right

Date	Mintage	F12	VF20	XF40	MS60	MS63
2007BP	4,000	—	—	—	42.50	47.50
2007BP	6,000	PF65 50.00				

KM# 802 5000 FORINT

31.46 g., 0.925 Silver 0.9296 oz. ASW, 38.61 mm. **Subject:** 800th Anniversary - Birth of St. Elizabeth **Obv:** Stylized image of St. Elizabeth feeding the hungry **Obv. Inscription:** Magyar / Köztárszág **Rev:** 3/4 length figure of St. Elizabeth seated facing holding roses and bread rolls in her lap

Date	Mintage	F12	VF20	XF40	MS60	MS63
2007BP	4,000	—	—	—	52.50	55.00
2007BP	4,000	PF65 65.00				

KM# 804 5000 FORINT

31.46 g., 0.925 Silver 0.9296 oz. ASW, 38.61 mm. **Subject:** Great Reformed Church - Debrecen **Obv:** Church interior **Obv. Legend:** MAGYAR KOZTARSASAG **Rev:** Church facade **Rev. Legend:** DEBRECENI REFORMATUS NAGYTEMPLOM **Edge:** Plain **Shape:** 12-sided

Date	Mintage	F12	VF20	XF40	MS60	MS63
2007BP	4,000	—	—	—	42.50	47.50
2007BP	6,000	PF65 50.00				

KM# 811 5000 FORINT

31.46 g., 0.925 Silver 0.9296 oz. ASW, 38.6 mm. **Subject:** Europa heritage site Tokaj Wine Region **Obv:** Value within grape wreath **Rev:** Tokaj Hill and TV tower **Edge:** Reeded

Date	Mintage	F12	VF20	XF40	MS60	MS63
2008BP	5,000	—	—	—	—	48.00
2008BP	15,000	PF63 50.00	PF65 55.00			

KM# 806 5000 FORINT

31.46 g., 0.925 Silver 0.9296 oz. ASW, 38.61 mm. **Obv:** Grape wreath rim with denomination, legend & mintmark inside **Rev:** Tokaj hill, TV tower, grapefield with a village & church **Edge:** Milled

Date	Mintage	F12	VF20	XF40	MS60	MS63
2008	5,000	—	—	—	—	48.00
2008	15,000	PF63 50.00	PF65 55.00			

KM# 807 5000 FORINT

31.46 g., 0.925 Silver 0.9296 oz. ASW, 38.61 mm. **Subject:** Castle of the Siklós **Obv:** Castle, tower, Franciscan monastery & church **Rev:** Castle of the Siklós

Date	Mintage	F12	VF20	XF40	MS60	MS63
2008	4,000	—	—	—	—	45.00
2008	6,000	PF65 50.00				

KM# 808 5000 FORINT

31.46 g., 0.925 Silver 0.9296 oz. ASW, 38.61 mm. **Subject:** 29th Summer Olympics **Obv:** Coat of arms over water **Rev:** Water polo player **Edge:** Milled

Date	Mintage	F12	VF20	XF40	MS60	MS63
2008	4,000	—	—	—	—	40.00
2008	14,000	PF63 42.00	PF65 45.00			

KM# 810 5000 FORINT

31.46 g., 0.925 Silver 0.9296 oz. ASW, 38.61 mm. **Subject:** Centenery birth of Ede Teller **Obv:** Diagram of Deuterium-tritium fusion reaction **Rev:** Portrait Ede Teller

Date	Mintage	F12	VF20	XF40	MS60	MS63
2008	4,000	—	—	—	—	45.00
2008	6,000	PF65 55.00				

KM# 827 5000 FORINT

31.46 g., 0.925 Silver 0.9296 oz. ASW, 38.6 mm. **Subject:** John Calvin, 500th Anniversary

Date	Mintage	F12	VF20	XF40	MS60	MS63
2009BP	—	PF65 75.00				

KM# 812 5000 FORINT

31.46 g., 0.925 Silver 0.9296 oz. ASW **Subject:** Miklós Badnóti, 100th Anniversary of Birth **Obv:** Value **Rev:** Bust in suit facing

Date	Mintage	F12	VF20	XF40	MS60	MS63
2009	4,000	—	—	—	—	50.00
2009	4,000	PF65 65.00				

KM# 814 5000 FORINT

31.46 g., 0.925 Silver 0.9296 oz. ASW, 38.6 mm. **Subject:** Dohany Street Synagogue, 150th Anniversary **Obv:** Stained glass window **Rev:** Synagogue facade **Shape:** 12-sided

Date	Mintage	F12	VF20	XF40	MS60	MS63
2009BP	4,000	—	—	—	—	50.00
2009BP	4,000	PF65 65.00				

KM# 815 5000 FORINT

31.46 g., 0.925 Silver 0.9296 oz. ASW, 38.61 mm. **Subject:** Budapest - World Heritage Site **Obv:** Street scene **Rev:** Panoramic view of Danube and Parliament

Date	Mintage	F12	VF20	XF40	MS60	MS63
2009	5,000	—	—	—	—	50.00
2009	5,000	PF65 60.00				

KM# 819 5000 FORINT

31.46 g., 0.925 Silver 0.9296 oz. ASW, 38.61 mm. **Subject:** Kosztolanyi Dezso, 125th Anniversary of Birth **Obv:** Architectural element of stone **Rev:** Portrait

Date	Mintage	F12	VF20	XF40	MS60	MS63
2010BP	3,000	—	—	—	40.00	45.00
2010BP	5,000	PF65 55.00				

KM# 820 5000 FORINT

31.46 g., 0.925 Silver 0.9296 oz. ASW, 39.6x26.4 mm. **Subject:** Orseg National Park **Obv:** Butterfly **Rev:** Traditional rural buildings **Shape:** Rectangle

Date	Mintage	F12	VF20	XF40	MS60	MS63
2010BP	3,000	—	—	—	40.00	45.00
2010BP	5,000	PF65 55.00				

KM# 821 5000 FORINT
31.46 g., 0.925 Silver 0.9296 oz. ASW, 38.61 mm. **Subject:** European Watersports Championships **Obv:** Value and waves **Rev:** Swimmer with butterfly stroke

Date	Mintage	F12	VF20	XF40	MS60	MS63
2010BP	4,000	—	—	—	40.00	45.00
2010BP	6,000	PF65 50.00				

KM# 822 5000 FORINT
0.50 g., 0.999 Gold AGW, 11 mm. **Subject:** Ferenc Erkel - 200th Anniversary of Birth **Obv:** Denomination **Rev:** Large bust facing

Date	Mintage	F12	VF20	XF40	MS60	MS63
2010BP	10,000	PF63 45.00	PF65 50.00			

KM# 823 5000 FORINT
31.46 g., 0.925 Silver 0.9296 oz. ASW, 38.61 mm. **Subject:** Ferenc Erkel, 200th Anniversary of Birth **Obv:** House **Rev:** Bust facing, signature below

Date	Mintage	F12	VF20	XF40	MS60	MS63
2010BP	5,000	PF65 55.00				

KM# 830 5000 FORINT
31.46 g., 0.925 Silver 0.9296 oz. ASW, 38.61 mm. **Subject:** Busojaras Carnival in Mohacs **Obv:** Standing figure in carnival costume **Rev:** Horned demon face

Date	Mintage	F12	VF20	XF40	MS60	MS63
2011BP	3,000	—	—	—	—	45.00
2011BP	5,000	PF65 65.00				

KM# 831 5000 FORINT
31.46 g., 0.925 Silver 0.9296 oz. ASW, 38.61 mm. **Subject:** Árpád Tóth, 125th Anniversary of Birth **Obv:** Handwritten poem at center **Rev:** Tóth bust

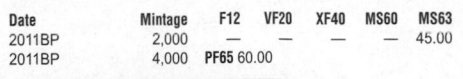

Date	Mintage	F12	VF20	XF40	MS60	MS63
2011BP	2,000					45.00
2011BP	4,000	PF65 60.00				

KM# 832 5000 FORINT
31.46 g., 0.925 Silver 0.9296 oz. ASW, 39.6x26.4 mm. **Subject:** Duna-Drava National Park **Obv:** Riverside scene **Rev:** Bird in flight

Date	Mintage	F12	VF20	XF40	MS60	MS63
2011BP	3,000	—	—	—	—	45.00
2011BP	5,000	PF65 55.00				

KM# 833 5000 FORINT
31.46 g., 0.925 Silver 0.9296 oz. ASW, 38.61 mm. **Subject:** Deak-Ter Evangelistic Church, Budapest **Obv:** Altar detail **Rev:** Church exterior **Shape:** Scalloped

Date	Mintage	F12	VF20	XF40	MS60	MS63
2011BP	3,000	—	—	—	—	45.00
2011BP	5,000	PF65 55.00				

KM# 834 5000 FORINT
31.46 g., 0.925 Silver 0.9296 oz. ASW, 38.61 mm. **Subject:** István Bibó, 100 Anniversary of Birth **Obv:** Value and legend **Rev:** Bibó seated, writing at table

Date	Mintage	F12	VF20	XF40	MS60	MS63
2011BP	6,000	PF65 60.00				

KM# 835 5000 FORINT
0.50 g., 0.999 Gold AGW, 11 mm. **Subject:** Adam Clark, 200th Anniversary of Birth **Obv:** Large value **Rev:** Large portrait

Date	Mintage	F12	VF20	XF40	MS60	MS63
2011BP Prooflike	10,000	—	—	—	—	75.00

KM# 843 5000 FORINT
0.50 g., 0.999 Gold AGW, 11 mm. **Subject:** XXX Summer Olympics, London **Obv:** Paddle in water **Rev:** Canoeist advancing front

Date	Mintage	F12	VF20	XF40	MS60	MS63
2012BP Prooflike	10,000	—	—	—	—	75.00

KM# 838 5000 FORINT
31.46 g., 0.925 Silver 0.9296 oz. ASW, 38.61 mm. **Subject:** Jozsef Remenyi, 125th Anniversary of Birth **Obv:** Kneeling nude female with vase on shoulder **Rev:** Remenyi profile left

Date	Mintage	F12	VF20	XF40	MS60	MS63
2012BP	6,000	PF65 50.00				

KM# 839 5000 FORINT
31.46 g., 0.925 Silver 0.9296 oz. ASW, 38.61 mm. **Subject:** István Örkény, 100th Anniversary of Birth **Obv:** Text forming rectangle at center **Rev:** Large portrait

Date	Mintage	F12	VF20	XF40	MS60	MS63
2012BP	2,000	—	—	—	—	45.00
2012BP	4,000	PF65 60.00				

KM# 841 10000 FORINT (Tizezer)
13.96 g., 0.986 Gold 0.4398 oz. AGW, 20 mm. **Subject:** Charles I florin **Obv:** Old coin: Fleur-dis-lis at center **Rev:** Old coin: St. John standing

Date	Mintage	F12	VF20	XF40	MS60	MS63
2012BP	5,000	PF65 800				

Note: A piefort of this type exists with edge lettering

KM# 855 5000 FORINT
20.00 g., 0.925 Silver 0.591 oz. ASW, 38.61 mm. **Subject:** Sandor Weöres, 100th Anniversary of Birth

Date	Mintage	F12	VF20	XF40	MS60	MS63
2013	—	PF65 50.00				

KM# 753 20000 FORINT
6.98 g., 0.986 Gold 0.2199 oz. AGW, 22 mm. **Subject:** Hungarian Coinage Millennium **Obv:** Denomination **Rev:** Hammered coinage minting scene above old coin design **Edge:** Plain

Date	Mintage	F12	VF20	XF40	MS60	MS63
2001BP	3,000	PF65 425				

KM# 777 50000 FORINT
13.96 g., 0.986 Gold 0.4398 oz. AGW, 25 mm. **Obv:** Value and country name above Euro Union stars **Rev:** Mythical stag seen through ornate window **Edge:** Reeded

Date	Mintage	F12	VF20	XF40	MS60	MS63
2004BP	7,000	PF63 750	PF65 800			

KM# 803 50000 FORINT
10.00 g., 0.986 Gold 0.315 oz. AGW, 25 mm. **Subject:** 550th Anniversary - Enthronement of Matthias Hunyadi **Obv:** Raven holding a ring in its beak **Rev:** Portrait of Mátyás Hunyadi based on a marble relief **Edge:** Smooth

Date	Mintage	F12	VF20	XF40	MS60	MS63
2008	5,000	PF65 600				

KM# 816 50000 FORINT
10.00 g., 0.986 Gold 0.315 oz. AGW, 25 mm. **Subject:** Ferenc Kazinczy, 250th Anniversary of Birth **Obv:** Value and classical facade **Rev:** Bust at left

Date	Mintage	F12	VF20	XF40	MS60	MS63
2009	5,000	PF65 600				

KM# 825 50000 FORINT
6.98 g., 0.986 Gold 0.2199 oz. AGW, 22 mm. **Subject:** St. Stephen and St. Emeric **Obv:** Medieval document **Rev:** St. Stephen and prince standing

Date	Mintage	F12	VF20	XF40	MS60	MS63
2010BP	5,000	PF65 425				

KM# 836 50000 FORINT
6.98 g., 0.986 Gold 0.2199 oz. AGW, 22 mm. **Subject:** Franz Liszt, 200th Anniversary of Birth **Obv:** Open piano case above musical score **Rev:** Bust right **Edge:** Plain

Date	Mintage	F12	VF20	XF40	MS60	MS63
2011BP	5,000	PF65 450				

Note: A piefort exists with edge lettering

KM# 758 100000 FORINT
31.10 g., 0.986 Gold 0.9797 oz. AGW, 37 mm. **Subject:** Saint Stephen **Obv:** Angels crowning coat of arms **Rev:** King seated on throne **Edge:** Reeded

Date	Mintage	F12	VF20	XF40	MS60	MS63
2001BP	3,000	PF65 1,750				

KM# 796 100000 FORINT
20.95 g., 0.986 Gold 0.6597 oz. AGW, 38.61 mm. **Subject:** 50th Anniversary - Hungarian Revolution **Obv:** 1956 repeated in cut out stone **Rev:** 1956 repeated in cut out stone with two freedom fighter's flags

Date	Mintage	F12	VF20	XF40	MS60	MS63
2006BP	5,000	PF65 1,250				

KM# 824 500,000 FORINT
62.84 g., 0.986 Gold 1.9792 oz. AGW, 46 mm. **Subject:** St. Stephen and St. Emeric **Obv:** Medieval document **Rev:** King and prince standing **Note:** 18 Ducats

Date	Mintage	F12	VF20	XF40	MS60	MS63
2010BP	500	PF65 3,750				

PIEDFORT

KM#	Date	Mintage	Identification	Mkt Val
P27	2011BP	1,500	50000 Forint 0.986 Gold KM#836.	800
P28	2012BP	1,500	10000 Forint 0.986 Gold KM#341	900

MINT SETS

KM#	Date	Mintage	Identification	Issue Price	Mkt Val
MS32	2001 (7)	—	KM#692-697, 721	—	16.50
MS33	2002 (8)	—	KM#692, 693, 694, 695, 696, 697, 721, 760	—	18.00
MS34	2003 (8)	—	KM#692, 693, 694, 695, 696, 697, 721, 768	—	17.50
MS35	2004 (8)	—	KM#692, 693, 694, 695, 696, 697, 721, 773	—	19.00
MS36	2005 (8)	—	KM#692-697, 721, 779	—	20.00
MS37	2006 (7)	—	KM#692-697, 721, plus silver 1946 KM532	—	17.50
MS38	2009 (6)	—	KM#694-697, 721, 826	—	20.00
MS39	2010 (6)	—	KM#694-697, 721, 826	—	20.00
MS40	2011 (6)	—	KM#694-697, 721, 826	—	20.00
MS41	2012 (6)	—	KM#847-852	—	20.00

PROOF SETS

KM#	Date	Mintage	Identification	Issue Price	Mkt Val
PS28	2001 (7)	—	KM#692-697, 721	35.00	37.50
PS29	2002 (8)	—	KM#692-697, 721, 760	—	42.50
PS30	2003 (8)	—	KM#692-697, 721, 768	—	40.00
PS31	2004 (8)	—	KM#692-697, 721, 773	—	40.00
PS32	2005 (8)	7,000	KM#692-697, 721, 779	—	37.50
PS33	2006 (7)	—	KM#692-697, 721	—	35.00
PS34	2007 (8)	—	KM#692-697, 721, 805	—	40.00
PS35	2008 (7)	—	KM#692-697, 721	—	35.00
PS36	2012 (6)	4,000	KM#847-852	—	40.00
PS37	2009 (6)	—	KM#694-697, 721, 826	—	28.00
PS38	2010 (6)	—	KM#694-697, 721, 826	—	28.00
PS39	2011 (6)	—	KM#694-697, 721, 826	—	28.00
PS40	2012 (6)	—	KM#847-852	—	40.00

ICELAND

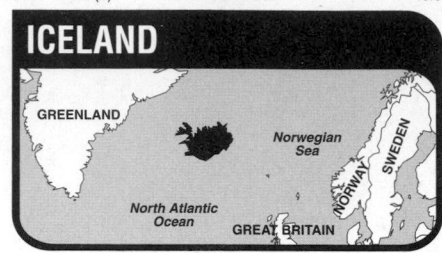

Iceland, an island of recent volcanic origin in the North Atlantic east of Greenland and immediately south of the Arctic Circle, has an area of 39,768 sq. mi. (103,000 sq. km.) and a population of just over 300,000. Capital: Reykjavik. Fishing is the chief industry and accounts for a little less than 60 percent of the exports.

REPUBLIC

REFORM COINAGE

100 Old Kronur = 1 New Krona

KM# 27a KRÓNA
4.00 g., Nickel Plated Steel, 21.5 mm. **Obv:** Giant facing **Rev:** Cod **Edge:** Reeded

Date	Mintage	F12	VF20	XF40	MS60	MS63
2003	5,144,000	—	—	—	0.85	1.70
2005	5,000,000	—	—	—	0.85	1.70
2006	10,000,000	—	—	—	0.85	1.70
2007	10,000,000	—	—	—	0.85	1.70
2011	5,000,000	—	—	—	0.85	1.70

KM# 28a 5 KRÓNUR
5.60 g., Nickel Plated Steel, 24.5 mm. **Obv:** Quartered design of Eagle, dragon, bull and giant **Rev:** Two dolphins leaping left **Edge:** Reeded

Date	Mintage	F12	VF20	XF40	MS60	MS63
2005	2,000,000	—	—	—	2.25	3.25
2006	2,000,000	—	—	—	2.25	3.25
2007	10,000,000	—	—	—	2.25	3.25
2008	1,900,000	—	—	—	2.25	3.25

KM# 29.1a 10 KRÓNUR
7.00 g., Nickel Plated Steel, 27.5 mm. **Obv:** Quartered design of Eagle, dragon, bull and giant **Rev:** Four capelins left **Edge:** Reeded

Date	Mintage	F12	VF20	XF40	MS60	MS63
2004	2,000,000	—	—	—	1.85	2.75
2005	4,505,000	—	—	—	1.85	2.75
2006	7,800,000	—	—	—	1.85	2.75
2008	1,520,000	—	—	—	2.00	3.00

KM# 31 50 KRÓNUR
8.25 g., Nickel-Brass, 23 mm. **Obv:** Quartered design of eagle, dragon, bull and giant **Rev:** Crab **Edge:** Reeded

Date	Mintage	F12	VF20	XF40	MS60	MS63
2001	2,000,000	—	—	—	4.25	5.00
2005	2,000,000	—	—	—	4.25	5.00

KM# 35 100 KRÓNUR
8.50 g., Nickel-Brass, 25.5 mm. **Obv:** Quartered design of Eagle, dragon, bull and giant **Rev:** Lumpfish left **Edge:** Reeded

Date	Mintage	F12	VF20	XF40	MS60	MS63
2001	2,140,000	—	—	—	6.50	7.75
2004	2,400,000	—	—	—	6.50	7.75
2006	2,000,000	—	—	—	6.50	7.75
2007	3,000,000	—	—	—	6.50	7.75
2011	3,000,000	—	—	—	6.50	7.75

INDIA - REPUBLIC

The Republic of India, a subcontinent jutting southward from the mainland of Asia, has an area of 1,269,346 sq. mi. (3,287,590 sq. km.) and a population of over 900 million, second only to that of the People's Republic of China. Capital: New Delhi. India's economy is based on agriculture and industrial activity. Engineering goods, cotton apparel and fabrics, handicrafts, tea, iron and steel are exported.

The Republic of India is a member of the Common-wealth of Nations. The president is the Chief of State. The prime minister is the Head of Government.

MINT MARKS
(Mint marks usually appear directly below the date.)
B - Mumbai (Bombay), proof issues only
(B) - Mumbai (Bombay), diamond
(C) - Calcutta, no mint mark
(H) - Hyderabad, star (1963--)
M - Mumbai (Bombay), proof only after 1996
(N) - Noida, dot
(T) - Taegu (Korea), star below first or last date digit

REPUBLIC
DECIMAL COINAGE

KM# 54 25 PAISE
2.82 g., Stainless Steel, 19 mm. **Obv:** Small Lion capitol of Ashoka Pillar above value **Rev:** Rhinoceros left **Edge:** Plain **Note:** Varieties of date size exist.

Date	Mintage	F12	VF20	XF40	MS60	MS63
2001(B)	—	—	1.00	3.00	4.00	7.00
2001(C)	—	—	1.00	3.00	4.00	7.00
2001(H)	—	—	1.00	3.00	4.00	7.00
2002(B)	—	—	1.00	3.00	4.00	7.00
2002(C)	—	—	1.00	3.00	4.00	7.00
2002(H)	—	—	1.00	3.00	4.00	7.00

KM# 69 50 PAISE
3.80 g., Stainless Steel, 22 mm. **Subject:** Parliament Building in New Delhi **Obv:** Denomination **Rev:** Building

Date	Mintage	F12	VF20	XF40	MS60	MS63
2001(B)	—	—	1.00	1.50	2.00	4.00
2001(C)	—	—	1.00	1.50	2.00	4.00
2001(H)	—	—	1.00	1.50	2.00	4.00
2001(N)	—	—	1.00	1.50	2.00	4.00
2002(B)	—	—	1.00	1.50	2.00	4.00
2002(C)	—	—	1.00	1.50	2.00	4.00
2002(H)	—	—	1.00	1.50	2.00	4.00
2002(N)	—	—	1.00	1.50	2.00	4.00
2003(B)	—	—	4.00	5.00	6.00	10.00

Date	Mintage	F12	VF20	XF40	MS60	MS63
2007(C)	—	—	6.00	7.00	8.00	10.00
2007(N)	—	—	6.00	7.00	8.00	10.00

KM# 374 50 PAISE
3.80 g., Stainless Steel, 23 mm. **Obv:** Lion capitol of Ashoka Pillar **Rev:** Clenched fist and value

Date	Mintage	F12	VF20	XF40	MS60	MS63
2008(B)	—	—	0.30	0.60	1.00	1.50
2008(C)	—	—	0.30	0.60	1.00	1.50
2008(H)	—	—	0.30	0.60	1.00	1.50
2008(N)	—	—	0.30	0.60	1.00	1.50
2009(B)	—	—	0.30	0.60	1.00	1.50
2009(C)	—	—	0.30	0.60	1.00	1.50
2010(C)	—	—	1.00	1.50	2.00	3.00

KM# 398 50 PAISE
Stainless Steel, 19 mm. **Obv:** Lion capitol of Ashoka Pillar **Rev:** Value flanked by flora **Edge:** Reeded

Date	Mintage	F12	VF20	XF40	MS60	MS63
2011(B)	—	—	—	1.00	3.00	—
2011(H)	—	—	—	0.50	1.50	—
2013H	—	—	—	0.50	1.50	—
2013C	—	—	—	0.50	1.50	—

KM# 92.2 RUPEE
4.90 g., Stainless Steel, 25 mm. **Obv:** Lion capitol of Ashoka Pillar **Rev:** Denomination and date, grain ears flank **Edge:** Plain **Note:** Mint mark varieties exist.

Date	Mintage	F12	VF20	XF40	MS60	MS63
2001(B)	—	—	0.50	1.00	1.50	—
2001(C)	—	—	0.50	1.00	1.50	—
2001(K)	—	—	0.50	1.00	1.50	—
2001(N)	—	—	0.50	1.00	1.50	—
2001(H)	—	—	0.50	1.00	1.50	—

Note: Small and large mint mark exist, doubled left or right of wheat stalks

Date	Mintage	F12	VF20	XF40	MS60	MS63
2002(B)	—	—	0.50	1.00	1.50	—
2002(N)	—	—	0.50	1.00	1.50	—
2002(C)	—	—	0.50	1.00	1.50	—
2002(H)	—	—	0.50	1.00	1.50	—
2003(B)	—	—	0.50	1.00	1.50	—
2003(C)	—	—	0.50	1.00	1.50	—
2003(H)	—	—	0.50	1.00	1.50	—
2004(B)	—	—	1.50	2.00	3.00	—
2004(C)	—	—	1.50	2.00	3.00	—
2004(H)	—	—	1.50	2.00	3.00	—
2004(N)	—	—	1.50	2.00	3.00	—

KM# 313 RUPEE
4.95 g., Stainless Steel, 25 mm. **Subject:** 100th Anniversary - Birth of Jaya Prakash Narayan **Obv:** Lion capitol of Ashoka Pillar **Rev:** Bust of Jaya Prakash Narayan slightly left **Edge:** Plain

Date	Mintage	F12	VF20	XF40	MS60	MS63
2002	—	—	30.00	40.00	50.00	—

Note: B without mint mark

Date	Mintage	F12	VF20	XF40	MS60	MS63
2002(B)	—	—	4.00	5.00	6.00	—
2002(B)	—	PF63 40.00				
2002(H)	—	—	2.00	3.00	4.00	—

KM# 314 RUPEE
4.95 g., Stainless Steel, 25 mm. **Subject:** Maharana Pratap **Obv:** Lion capitol of Ashoka Pillar **Rev:** Bust left in national costume **Edge:** Plain

Date	Mintage	F12	VF20	XF40	MS60	MS63
2003(B)	—	—	4.00	7.00	10.00	—
2003(B)	—	PF63 60.00				
2003(H)	—	—	2.00	3.00	7.00	—

KM# 316 RUPEE
4.85 g., Stainless Steel, 25 mm. **Obv:** Lion capitol of Ashoka Pillar **Rev:** 3/4 length military figure Veer Durgadass with spear left **Edge:** Plain **Note:** Weak strike typical for 2003(H)

Date	Mintage	F12	VF20	XF40	MS60	MS63
2003(B)	—	PF63 40.00				
2003(H)	—	—	1.00	2.00	6.00	—

KM# 322 RUPEE
4.95 g., Stainless Steel, 24.8 mm. **Obv:** Lion capitol of Ashoka Pillar at left, value at right **Rev:** Cross dividing four dots **Edge:** Plain

Date	Mintage	F12	VF20	XF40	MS60	MS63
2004(B)	—	—	10.00	20.00	30.00	—
2005(C)	—	—	0.50	2.00	3.00	—
2005(B)	—	—	0.50	1.00	1.50	—
2005(H)	—	—	0.50	1.00	1.50	—
2005(N)	—	—	0.50	1.00	1.50	—
2006(N)	—	—	4.00	6.00	10.00	—

KM# 321 RUPEE
5.00 g., Stainless Steel, 24.9 mm. **Subject:** 150th Anniversary of the Indian Postal Service **Obv:** Lion capitol of Ashoka Pillar above value **Rev:** Partial postage stamp design **Edge:** Grooved

Date	Mintage	F12	VF20	XF40	MS60	MS63
2004(C)	—	—	6.00	8.00	10.00	—
2004(C)	—	PF63 50.00				
2004(C) Proof, restrike	—	PF63 40.00				

KM# 331 RUPEE
4.90 g., Stainless Steel, 25 mm. **Subject:** Bharata Natyam Dance Expressions **Obv:** Lion capitol of Ashoka Pillar **Rev:** Gesture of hand with thumb up **Edge:** Plain

Date	Mintage	F12	VF20	XF40	MS60	MS63
2007(C)	—	—	0.50	1.00	1.50	—
2007(H)	—	—	0.50	1.00	1.50	—
2007(N)	—	—	0.50	1.00	1.50	—
2008(B)	—	—	0.50	1.00	1.50	—
2008(C)	—	—	0.50	1.00	1.50	—
2008(Hy)	—	—	0.50	1.00	1.50	—
2008(N)	—	—	0.50	1.00	1.50	—
2009(B)	—	—	0.50	1.00	1.50	—
2009(C)	—	—	0.50	1.00	1.50	—
2009(Hy)	—	—	0.50	1.00	1.50	—
2009(N)	—	—	0.50	1.00	1.50	—
2010(B)	—	—	0.50	1.00	1.50	—
2010(H)	—	—	0.50	1.00	1.50	—
2010(N)	—	—	0.50	1.00	1.50	—
2011(C)	—	—	1.00	1.50	2.00	—
2011(H)	—	—	1.00	1.50	2.00	—
2011(N)	—	—	1.00	1.50	2.00	—

KM# 385 RUPEE

4.95 g., Stainless Steel, 24.8 mm. **Subject:** Reserve Bank of India, 75th Anniversary **Obv:** Lion capitol of Ashoka Pillar above value **Rev:** Lion advancing left, palm tree in background

Date	Mintage	F12	VF20	XF40	MS60	MS63
2010(B)	—	PF63 20.00				
2010(H)	—		1.00	1.50	2.00	—

KM# 394 RUPEE

4.95 g., Stainless Steel, 22 mm. **Obv:** Lion capitol of Ashoka Pillar **Rev:** New Rupee symbol above value

Date	Mintage	F12	VF20	XF40	MS60	MS63
2011(B)	—	—	—	—	0.40	—
2011(C)	—	—	—	—	0.40	—
2011(H)	—	—	—	—	0.40	—
2011(N)	—	—	—	—	0.40	—
2012(B)	—	—	—	—	0.40	—
2012(C)	—	—	—	—	0.40	—
2012(H)	—	—	—	—	0.40	—
2012(N)	—	—	—	—	0.40	—

KM# 121.3 2 RUPEES

6.00 g., Copper-Nickel, 26 mm. **Subject:** National Integration **Obv:** Type A Lion capitol of Ashoka Pillar **Rev:** Flag on map **Edge:** Plain **Shape:** 11-sided **Note:** Reduced size, non magnetic.

Date	Mintage	F12	VF20	XF40	MS60	MS63
2001(B)	—	—	1.00	1.50	2.00	—
2001(C)	—	—	1.00	1.50	2.00	—
2002(C)	—	—	1.00	1.50	2.00	—
2003(C)	—	—	1.00	1.50	2.00	—
2003(H)	—	—	1.00	1.50	2.00	—
2003(N)	—	—	1.00	1.50	2.00	—

KM# 121.5 2 RUPEES

6.06 g., Copper-Nickel, 26 mm. **Subject:** National Integration **Obv:** Type C Lion capitol of Ashoka Pillar **Rev:** Flag on map **Edge:** Plain **Note:** 11-sided

Date	Mintage	F12	VF20	XF40	MS60	MS63
2001(B)	—	—	0.60	0.80	1.20	—
2001(C)	—	—	0.60	0.80	1.20	—
2001(H)	—	—	0.60	0.80	1.20	—
2002(B)	—	—	0.60	0.80	1.20	—
2002(C)	—	—	0.60	0.80	1.20	—
2002(H)	—	—	0.60	0.80	1.20	—
2002(N)	—	—	0.60	0.80	1.20	—
2003(B)	—	—	0.60	0.80	1.20	—
2003(C)	—	—	0.60	0.80	1.20	—
2003(H)	—	—	0.60	0.80	1.20	—
2004(B)	—	—	1.00	1.50	2.00	—
2004(C)	—	—	4.00	20.00	40.00	—
2004(H)	—	—	2.00	3.00	4.00	—

KM# 303 2 RUPEES

6.24 g., Copper-Nickel, 25.7 mm. **Subject:** 100th Anniversary - Birth of Dr. Syama P. Mookerjee **Obv:** Type B Lion capitol of Ashoka Pillar above denomination **Rev:** Bust of Dr. Mookerjee right **Edge:** Plain

Date	Mintage	F12	VF20	XF40	MS60	MS63
2001(C)	—	—	5.00	8.00	10.00	—
2001(C)	—	PF63 40.00				
2001(H)	—	—	1.00	1.50	2.00	—
2001(N)	—	—	1.00	1.50	2.00	—

KM# 305 2 RUPEES

6.10 g., Copper-Nickel, 25.7 mm. **Subject:** Sant Tukaram **Obv:** Lion capitol of Ashoka Pillar above value **Rev:** Seated musician **Shape:** 11-sided

Date	Mintage	F12	VF20	XF40	MS60	MS63
2002(B)	—		1.00	2.50	4.00	—
2002(C)	—		4.00	5.00	6.00	—
2002(C)	—	PF63 60.00				
2002(H)	—		1.00	1.50	2.00	—
2002(N)	—		4.00	7.00	10.00	—

KM# 307 2 RUPEES

6.05 g., Copper-Nickel **Subject:** 150th Anniversary - Indian Railways **Obv:** Lion capitol of Ashoka Pillar above value **Rev:** Cartoon elephant holding railroad lantern **Edge:** Plain **Shape:** 11-sided **Note:** Generally poor strike quality.

Date	Mintage	F12	VF20	XF40	MS60	MS63
2003(B)	—	—	1.50	2.50	4.00	—
2003(C)	—	—	1.50	2.50	4.00	—
2003(C)	—	PF63 40.00				
2003(C) Proof, restrike	—	PF63 30.00				
2003(H)	—	—	1.00	1.50	2.00	—
2003(N)	—	—	4.00	7.00	10.00	—

KM# 334 2 RUPEES

6.00 g., Copper-Nickel, 26 mm. **Subject:** 150th Anniversary - Telecommunications **Obv:** Lion capitol of Ashoka Pillar **Rev:** Cartoon bird standing holding cell phone **Edge:** Plain **Shape:** 11-sided

Date	Mintage	F12	VF20	XF40	MS60	MS63
2004(C)	—	PF63 60.00				
Note: Issued only as part of a set.						
2004(C) Proof, restrike	—	PF63 50.00				

KM# 326 2 RUPEES

5.80 g., Stainless Steel **Obv:** Lion capitol of Ashoka Pillar at left and value at right **Rev:** Cross with U-shaped arms and dots **Edge:** Plain **Note:** Size varies 26.75 - 27.07 mm

Date	Mintage	F12	VF20	XF40	MS60	MS63
2005(B)	—		0.40	0.60	1.00	—
2005(C)	—		0.40	0.60	1.00	—
2005(C) Reverse same as 2007 Calcutta	—		10.00	20.00	30.00	—
2005(H)	—		0.40	0.60	1.00	—
2005(N)	—		0.40	0.60	1.00	—
2006(B) small date	—		0.40	0.60	1.00	—
2006(B) large date	—		0.40	0.60	1.00	—
2006(H)	—		0.40	0.60	1.00	—
2006(N)	—		0.40	0.60	1.00	—
2007(B)	—		0.40	0.60	1.00	—
2007(C)	—		0.40	0.60	1.00	—
2007(C) Reverse same as 2005 Calcutta	—		6.00	12.00	20.00	—
2007(H)	—		0.40	0.60	1.00	—
2007(N)	—		1.00	1.50	2.00	—

KM# 327 2 RUPEES

5.80 g., Stainless Steel, 27 mm. **Obv:** Lion capitol of Ashoka Pillar at center **Obv. Inscription:** INDIA in Hindi and English **Rev:** Hasta Mudra - hand gesture from the dance Bharata Natyam **Edge:** Plain

Date	Mintage	F12	VF20	XF40	MS60	MS63
2007(B)	—		0.40	0.60	1.00	—
2007(C)	—		0.40	0.60	1.00	—
2007(H)	—		0.40	0.60	1.00	—
2007(N)	—		0.40	0.60	1.00	—
2008(B)	—		0.40	0.60	1.00	—
2008(C)	—		0.40	0.60	1.00	—
2008(H)	—		0.40	0.60	1.00	—
2008(N)	—		0.40	0.60	1.00	—
2009(B)	—		0.40	0.60	1.00	—
2009(C)	—		0.40	0.60	1.00	—
2009(N)	—		0.40	0.60	1.00	—
2010(B)	—		0.40	0.60	1.00	—
2010(C)	—		0.40	0.60	1.00	—
2010(H)	—		0.40	0.60	1.00	—
2011(H)	—		0.40	0.60	1.00	—
2011(N)	—		0.40	0.60	1.00	—

KM# 350 2 RUPEES

6.00 g., Stainless Steel, 26.9 mm. **Subject:** 75th Anniversary Indian Air Force **Obv:** Lion capitol of Ashoka Pillar at left and value at right **Rev:** Planes in flight **Edge:** Plain **Shape:** 11-sided

Date	Mintage	F12	VF20	XF40	MS60	MS63
2007(C)	—	—		6.00	8.00	10.00
2007(C)	—	PF63 40.00				

KM# 375 2 RUPEES

5.80 g., Stainless Steel, 27 mm. **Subject:** Natya Mudra **Obv:** Lion capitol of Ashoka Pillar **Rev:** Hasta Mudra - hand gesture from the dance Bharata Natyam **Note:** Issued in Mule only

Date	Mintage	F12	VF20	XF40	MS60	MS63
2008(N)	—	—	200	350	500	—

KM# 368 2 RUPEES

5.80 g., Stainless Steel, 27 mm. **Subject:** Louis Braille, 200th Anniversary of Birth **Obv:** Lion capitol of Ashoka Pillar **Rev:** Facing portrait above Braille text

Date	Mintage	F12	VF20	XF40	MS60	MS63
2009(B)	—	—	1.00	1.50	2.00	—
2009(C)	—	—	1.00	1.50	2.00	—
2009(C) Packaged	—				—	5.00
2009(C)	—	PF63 20.00				
2009(C) Proof, packaged	—	PF63 7.00				
2009(Hy) Packaged	—				—	5.00

KM# 386 2 RUPEES

5.80 g., Stainless Steel, 27 mm. **Subject:** Reserve Bank of India, 75th Anniversary **Obv:** Lion capitol of Ashoka Pillar **Rev:** Lion advancing left, palm tree in background

Date	Mintage	F12	VF20	XF40	MS60	MS63
2010(B)	—	PF63 20.00				
2010(C)	—	—	1.00	1.50	3.50	—

KM# 401 2 RUPEES
5.75 g., Stainless Steel, 25 mm. **Subject:** 19th Commonwealth Games

Date	Mintage	F12	VF20	XF40	MS60	MS63
2010(B)	—	—	—	—	3.00	—
2010(C)	—	—	—	—	1.25	—
2010(C)	—	PF63 5.00				
2010(Hy)	—	—	—	—	3.00	—
2010(Hy) Packaged	—	—	—	—	—	4.00
2010(N)	—	—	—	—	1.25	—

KM# 395 2 RUPEES
4.85 g., Stainless Steel, 25 mm. **Obv:** Lion capitol of Ashoka Pillar **Rev:** New Rupee symbol above value **Edge:** Reeded **Note:** The spacing in the reeding is different at some mints.

Date	Mintage	F12	VF20	XF40	MS60	MS63
2011(B)	—	—	0.40	0.60	1.00	—
2011(C)	—	—	0.40	0.60	1.00	—
2011(H)	—	—	0.40	0.60	1.00	—
2011(N)	—	—	0.40	0.60	1.00	—
2012(B)	—	—	0.40	0.60	1.00	—
2012(H)	—	—	0.40	0.60	1.00	—

KM# 154.2 5 RUPEES
8.91 g., Copper-Nickel, 23 mm. **Obv:** Lion capitol of Ashoka Pillar **Rev:** Denomination flanked by flowers **Edge:** Reeded

Date	Mintage	F12	VF20	XF40	MS60	MS63
2001(C)	—	—	10.00	19.00	20.00	—
2002(C)	—	—	10.00	19.00	20.00	—
2003(C)	—	—	10.00	19.00	20.00	—

KM# 154.1 5 RUPEES
9.30 g., Copper-Nickel, 23.4 mm. **Obv:** Lion capitol of Ashoka Pillar, Type I **Rev:** Denomination flanked by flowers **Edge:** Security **Note:** (C) - Calcutta mint has issued 2 distinctly different security edge varieties every year 1992-2003 with large dots and thick center line, w/small dots and narrow center line.

Date	Mintage	F12	VF20	XF40	MS60	MS63
2001(N)	—	—	1.00	1.50	2.00	—
2001(C) Plain 1	—	—	1.00	1.50	2.00	—
2001(C) Serif 1	—	—	1.00	1.50	2.00	—
2001(H)	—	—	1.00	1.50	2.00	—
2001(N)	—	—	1.00	1.50	2.00	—
2002(C)	—	—	1.00	1.50	2.00	—
2002(H)	—	—	1.00	1.50	2.00	—
2002(N)	—	—	1.00	1.50	2.00	—
2003(C)	—	—	1.00	1.50	2.00	—
2003(H)	—	—	1.00	1.50	2.00	—
2003(N)	—	—	1.00	1.50	2.00	—
2004(C)	—	—	10.00	15.00	20.00	—
2004(H)	—	—	2.00	3.00	4.00	—
2004(N)	—	—	1.00	1.50	2.00	—
2005(B)	—	—	1.00	1.50	2.00	—

KM# 154.4 5 RUPEES
9.30 g., Copper-Nickel, 23.4 mm. **Obv:** Lion capitol of Ashoka Pillar, Type II, Small Lion **Rev:** Denomination flanked by flowers **Edge:** Security

Date	Mintage	F12	VF20	XF40	MS60	MS63
2001(B)	—	—	1.00	1.50	2.00	—
2002(B)	—	—	1.00	1.50	2.00	—
2003(B)	—	—	1.00	1.50	2.00	—
2004(B)	—	—	1.00	1.50	2.00	—

KM# 304 5 RUPEES
9.07 g., Copper-Nickel, 23.19 mm. **Subject:** 2600th Anniversary Birth of Bhagwan Mahavir **Obv:** Lion capitol of Ashoka Pillar above denomination **Rev:** Swastika above hand in irregular frame **Edge:** Security

Date	Mintage	F12	VF20	XF40	MS60	MS63
2001(B)	—	—	2.00	6.00	10.00	—
2001(B)	—	PF63 70.00				
2001(N)	—	—	2.00	6.00	10.00	—

KM# A308 5 RUPEES
Copper-Nickel, 23.1 mm. **Subject:** Dadabhai Naroji **Obv:** Lion capital of Ashoka Pillar above denomination **Rev:** Bust of Naroji 3/4 right **Edge:** Security

Date	Mintage	F12	VF20	XF40	MS60	MS63
ND-2003(C)	—	—	10.00	15.00	20.00	—
ND-2003(C) Reeded Edge	—	—	10.00	18.00	30.00	—

KM# 308 5 RUPEES
8.92 g., Copper-Nickel, 23.1 mm. **Subject:** Dadabhai Naroji **Obv:** Lion capitol of Ashoka Pillar above value **Rev:** Bust of Naroji 3/4 right **Edge:** Security

Date	Mintage	F12	VF20	XF40	MS60	MS63
ND(2003)(B)	—	—	2.50	4.50	6.50	—
ND-2003(C)	—	—	2.00	4.00	6.00	—
ND-2003(H)	—	—	2.00	4.00	6.00	—

KM# 317.1 5 RUPEES
8.80 g., Copper-Nickel, 23.1 mm. **Obv:** Lion capitol of Ashoka Pillar **Rev:** K. Kamaraj bust 3/4 left, dates below **Edge:** Security

Date	Mintage	F12	VF20	XF40	MS60	MS63
ND-2003(B)	—	—	2.00	7.00	11.00	—
ND-2003(B)	—	PF63 40.00				
ND-2003(B) Proof, restrike	—	PF63 30.00				
ND-2003(H)	—	—	2.00	4.00	6.00	—

KM# 317.2 5 RUPEES
8.80 g., Copper-Nickel, 23.1 mm. **Obv:** Lion capitol of Ashoka Pillar **Rev:** K. Kamaraj bust 3/4 left, dates below **Edge:** Reeded

Date	Mintage	F12	VF20	XF40	MS60	MS63
ND (2003)(H)	—	—	10.00	15.00	20.00	—

KM# 329a 5 RUPEES
6.03 g., Stainless Steel, 23 mm. **Obv:** Lion capital of Ashoka Pillar, value below **Rev:** Shastri bust 3/4 left **Rev. Legend:** LALBAHADUR SHASTRI BIRTH CENTENARY **Edge:** Security

Date	Mintage	F12	VF20	XF40	MS60	MS63
2004(C)	—	—	6.00	12.00	20.00	—

KM# 329 5 RUPEES
9.07 g., Copper-Nickel, 23.1 mm. **Obv:** Lion capitol of Ashoka Pillar, value below **Rev:** Shastri bust 3/4 left **Rev. Legend:** LALBAHADUR SHASTRI BIRTH CENTENARY **Edge:** Security

Date	Mintage	F12	VF20	XF40	MS60	MS63
ND-2004(C)	—	—	4.00	10.00	20.00	—
ND-2004(C)	—	PF63 40.00				

KM# 325a 5 RUPEES
6.03 g., Stainless Steel, 23 mm. **Subject:** 75th Anniversary Dandi March **Obv:** Lion capital of Ashoka Pillar **Rev:** Ghandi leading marchers **Edge:** Security

Date	Mintage	F12	VF20	XF40	MS60	MS63
ND-2005(B)	—	—	2.00	3.00	4.00	—

KM# 325 5 RUPEES
8.85 g., Copper-Nickel, 23 mm. **Subject:** 75th Anniversary Dandi March **Obv:** Lion capitol of Ashoka Pillar **Rev:** Ghandi leading marchers **Edge:** Security type

Date	Mintage	F12	VF20	XF40	MS60	MS63
ND-2005(B)	—	—	50.00	75.00	100	—
ND-2005(B)	—	PF63 125				
ND-2005(B) Proof, restrike	—	PF63 100				

KM# A365 5 RUPEES
6.03 g., Stainless Steel, 23 mm. **Subject:** Dandi March, 75th Anniversary **Note:** New design

Date	Mintage	F12	VF20	XF40	MS60	MS63
2005(B)	—	—	1.00	1.50	2.00	—

KM# 324a 5 RUPEES
6.00 g., Stainless Steel **Subject:** Mahatma Basveshwara

Date	Mintage	F12	VF20	XF40	MS60	MS63
ND-2006(B)	—	—	—	—	4.00	—

KM# 324 5 RUPEES
8.85 g., Copper-Nickel, 23 mm. **Obv:** Lion capitol of Ashoka Pillar **Rev:** Mahatma Basaveshwara bust 3/4 left **Edge:** Security

Date	Mintage	F12	VF20	XF40	MS60	MS63
ND-2006(B)	—	—	4.00	6.00	10.00	—
ND-2006(B)	—	PF63 15.00				
ND-2006(B) Proof, packaged	—	PF63 10.00				

KM# A324 5 RUPEES
6.03 g., Stainless Steel, 23 mm. **Obv:** Lion capital of Ashoka Pillar **Rev:** Mahatma Basaveshwara bust 3/4 left **Edge:** Security

Date	Mintage	F12	VF20	XF40	MS60	MS63
ND-2006(B)	—	—	6.00	8.00	10.00	—

KM# 355a 5 RUPEES
6.03 g., Stainless Steel, 22.9 mm. **Subject:** Jagadguru Shree Narayan Guru **Obv:** Lion capitol of Ashoka Pilar **Rev:** Bust facing

Date	Mintage	F12	VF20	XF40	MS60	MS63
ND-2006(B)	—	—	—	—	6.00	—

KM# 354 5 RUPEES
6.03 g., Stainless Steel, 22.8 mm. **Subject:** O.N.G.C., 50th Anniversary **Obv:** Lion capitol of Ashoka Pillar, value below

Date	Mintage	F12	VF20	XF40	MS60	MS63
ND-2006(C)	—	—	—	—	2.00	—
ND-2006(C)	—	PF63 20.00				
ND-2006(H)	—	—	—	—	2.00	—

KM# 355 5 RUPEES
9.50 g., Copper-Nickel, 23.1 mm. **Subject:** Jagathguru Sree Narayana Gurudev **Obv:** Lion capitol of Ashoka Pillar **Rev:** Bust facing

Date	Mintage	F12	VF20	XF40	MS60	MS63
ND-2006(B)	—	—	4.00	6.00	10.00	—
ND-2006(B)	—	PF63 40.00				

KM# 357 5 RUPEES

6.03 g., Stainless Steel, 22.9 mm. **Subject:** State Bank of India, 200th Anniversary **Obv:** Lion capitol of Ashoka Pillar, value below **Edge:** Security

Date	Mintage	F12	VF20	XF40	MS60	MS63
ND-2006(C)	—	—	—	—	2.00	—
ND-2006(C)	—	PF63	10.00			
ND-2006(H)	—	—	—	—	2.00	—
ND-2006(C) Proof, restrike	—	PF63	7.50			

KM# 409 5 RUPEES

Nickel-Brass, 23 mm. **Subject:** Kuka Movement, 150th Anniversary **Note:** Issued in 2013.

Date	Mintage	F12	VF20	XF40	MS60	MS63
1857-2007	—	—	—	—	1.00	3.00

KM# A330 5 RUPEES

6.03 g., Stainless Steel, 23 mm. **Subject:** Information Technology **Obv:** Lion capitol of Ashoka Pillar **Rev:** Waves below value **Edge:** Security **Note:** Mule, Obv of 50 Paisa

Date	Mintage	F12	VF20	XF40	MS60	MS63
2008(C)	—	—	60.00	80.00	100	—

KM# 330 5 RUPEES

6.03 g., Stainless Steel, 23 mm. **Subject:** Information Technology **Obv:** Lion capitol of Ashoka Pillar **Rev:** Waves below value **Edge:** Security

Date	Mintage	F12	VF20	XF40	MS60	MS63
2007(B)	—	—	—	1.00	4.00	—
2007(C)	—	—	—	1.00	4.00	—
2007(H)	—	—	—	1.00	4.00	—
2008(B)	—	—	—	1.00	4.00	—
2008(C)	—	—	—	1.00	4.00	—
2008(H)	—	—	—	1.00	4.00	—

KM# 356 5 RUPEES

6.03 g., Copper-Nickel, 22.9 mm. **Subject:** Lokmanya Bal Gangadhar Tilak, 150th Anniversary

Date	Mintage	F12	VF20	XF40	MS60	MS63
2007(B)	—	PF63	20.00			
2007(N)	—	—	—	—	100	—

Note: Withdrawn.

KM# 360.1 5 RUPEES

6.03 g., Stainless Steel, 23 mm. **Subject:** Khadi and Village Industries Commission, 50th Anniversary **Rev:** Ghandi seated facing

Date	Mintage	F12	VF20	XF40	MS60	MS63
2007(B)	—	—	—	—	10.00	—

KM# 360.1a 5 RUPEES

9.50 g., Copper-Nickel, 23 mm. **Rev:** Ghandi seated facing

Date	Mintage	F12	VF20	XF40	MS60	MS63
2007(B)	—	—	—	—	100	—
2007(B)	—	PF63	60.00			

KM# 360.2 5 RUPEES

6.03 g., Stainless Steel, 23 mm. **Rev:** Ghandi seated facing **Note:** Mint mark "M" in between 2007

Date	Mintage	F12	VF20	XF40	MS60	MS63
2007(B)	—	—	—	—	12.00	—

KM# 359 5 RUPEES

6.03 g., Stainless Steel, 22.9 mm. **Subject:** First War of Independence **Obv:** Lion capitol of Ashoka Pillar, value below

Date	Mintage	F12	VF20	XF40	MS60	MS63
ND-2007(B)	—	—	—	—	4.00	—
ND-2007(B)	—	PF63	20.00			
ND-2007(B)	—	PF63	10.00			
Proof, restrike						

KM# 390 5 RUPEES

6.03 g., Stainless Steel, 22.9 mm. **Obv:** Lion capitol of Ashoka Pillar **Rev:** Cross

Date	Mintage	F12	VF20	XF40	MS60	MS63
2007(C)	—	—	—	—	20.00	—

KM# 403.2 5 RUPEES

Nickel-Brass, 23 mm. **Subject:** Comptroller & Auditgeneral of India, 150th Anniversary **Obv:** Lion capital of Ashoka Pillar **Rev:** Logo **Note:** The date on coin is 2007 but issued in 2012

Date	Mintage	F12	VF20	XF40	MS60	MS63
2007(C)	—	PF63	40.00			
2007(H)	—	—	—	—	1.00	—

KM# 406 5 RUPEES

6.00 g., Stainless Steel, 23 mm. **Subject:** Shaheed Bhagat Singh, 100th Anniversary of Birth **Obv:** Lion capital of Ashoka Pillar **Rev:** Bust facing wearing hat **Note:** Dated 2007, but released in 2012.

Date	Mintage	F12	VF20	XF40	MS60	MS63
1907-2007(C)	—	PF63	40.00			
1907-2007(H)	—	—	—	2.00	6.50	—
1907-2007(H)	—	—	—	2.00	6.50	—
1907-2007(Hy) Packaged	—	—	—	—	—	6.00

KM# 365 5 RUPEES

6.03 g., Nickel-Brass, 23 mm. **Subject:** St. Alphonsa, 100th Anniversary **Obv:** Lion capitol of Ashoka Pillar **Rev:** Bust facing in habit

Date	Mintage	F12	VF20	XF40	MS60	MS63
2009(B)	—	—	—	—	3.00	—
2009(B) Packaged	—	—	—	—	—	6.00
2009(B)	—	PF63	40.00			
2009(C)	—	—	—	—	4.00	—
2009(H)	—	—	—	—	4.50	—

KM# 367 5 RUPEES

6.03 g., Nickel-Brass, 23 mm. **Subject:** C. N. Annadurai, 100th Anniversary of Birth **Obv:** Lion capitol of Ashoka Pillar **Rev:** Portrait, signature below

Date	Mintage	F12	VF20	XF40	MS60	MS63
2009(B)	—	—	—	—	3.00	—
2009(C)	—	—	—	—	2.00	—
2009(C)	—	PF63	30.00			
2009(H)	—	—	—	—	6.00	—

KM# 376 5 RUPEES

6.03 g., Nickel-Brass, 23 mm. **Subject:** 60th Anniversary of Commonwealth **Obv:** Lion capitol of Ashoka Pillar **Rev:** Building

Date	Mintage	F12	VF20	XF40	MS60	MS63
2009(B)	—	—	—	—	3.00	—
2009(B)	—	PF63	30.00			
2009(C)	—	—	—	—	2.00	—
2009(H)	—	—	—	—	4.00	—

KM# 373 5 RUPEES

6.00 g., Nickel-Brass, 23 mm. **Obv:** Lion capitol of Ashoka Pillar **Rev:** Value flanked by flowers

Date	Mintage	F12	VF20	XF40	MS60	MS63
2009(B)	—	—	—	—	1.00	—
2009(C)	—	—	—	—	1.00	—
2009(H)	—	—	—	—	1.00	—
2010(B)	—	—	—	—	1.00	—
2010(C)	—	—	—	—	1.00	—
2010(H)	—	—	—	—	1.00	—
2010(N)	—	—	—	—	2.00	—

KM# 392 5 RUPEES

6.03 g., Nickel-Brass, 23 mm. **Subject:** Dr. Rajendra Prasad **Obv:** Lion capitol of Ashoka Pillar

Date	Mintage	F12	VF20	XF40	MS60	MS63
2009(B)	—	—	—	2.50	4.00	—
2009(C)	—	—	—	—	2.00	—
2009(Hy)	—	PF63	30.00			
2009(Hy)	—	—	—	—	2.00	—
2009(Hy) Packaged	—	—	—	—	—	5.00
2009(N)	—	—	—	—	2.00	—

KM# 413 5 RUPEES

6.00 g., Nickel-Brass, 23 mm. **Subject:** Perarignar Anna, 100th Anniversary of Birth

Date	Mintage	F12	VF20	XF40	MS60	MS63
2009(B)	—	—	—	—	—	4.00
2009(C)	—	—	—	—	—	4.00
2009(H)	—	—	—	—	—	4.00
2009	—	PF63	30.00			

KM# 377 5 RUPEES

6.00 g., Nickel-Brass, 23 mm. **Obv:** Lion capitol of Ashoka Pillar **Rev:** C. Subramaniam facing **Edge:** Reeded

Date	Mintage	F12	VF20	XF40	MS60	MS63
2010	—	—	—	—	3.00	—
Note: (B)without mint mark						
2010(B)	—	PF63	30.00			
2010(C)	—	—	—	—	3.00	—
2010(Hy)	—	—	—	—	1.00	—
2010(Hy) Packaged	—	—	—	—	—	5.50
2010(N)	—	—	—	—	1.00	—

KM# 378 5 RUPEES
6.00 g., Nickel-Brass, 23 mm. **Subject:** Brihadeeswarar Temple, 1000th Anniversary **Obv:** Lion capitol of Ashoka Pillar **Rev:** Statue of King Raja Rajan I before temple **Edge:** Reeded

Date	Mintage	F12	VF20	XF40	MS60	MS63
2010(B)	—	—	—	—	1.00	—
2010(B)		PF63 30.00				
2010(C)	—	—	—	—	2.00	—
2010(Hy)	—	—	—	—	1.00	—
2010(Hy) Packaged	—	—	—	—	—	5.50
2010(N)	—	—	—	—	1.00	—

KM# 379 5 RUPEES
6.00 g., Nickel-Brass, 23 mm. **Subject:** Income Tax, 150th Anniversary **Obv:** Lion capitol of Ashoka Pillar **Rev:** Chanakya portrait at right **Edge:** Reeded

Date	Mintage	F12	VF20	XF40	MS60	MS63
2010(B)	—	—	—	1.00	4.00	—
2010(C)	—	—	—	1.00	4.00	—
2010(C)		—	PF63 20.00			
2010(Hy)	—	—	—	1.00	4.00	—
2010(Hy) Packaged	—	—	—	—	—	5.50

KM# 381 5 RUPEES
6.03 g., Nickel-Brass, 23 mm. **Subject:** Mother Theresa, 100th Anniversary of Birth **Obv:** Lion capitol of Ashoka Pillar **Rev:** Bust facing

Date	Mintage	F12	VF20	XF40	MS60	MS63
2010(B)	—	—	—	—	3.00	—
2010(C)	—	—	—	—	4.00	—
2010(C)		PF63 30.00				
2010(Hy)	—	—	—	—	4.00	—
2010(Hy) Packaged	—	—	—	—	—	5.50
2010(N)	—	—	—	—	4.00	—

KM# 387 5 RUPEES
6.03 g., Nickel-Brass, 23 mm. **Subject:** Reserve Bank of India, 75th Anniversary **Obv:** Lion capitol of Ashoka Pillar **Rev:** Lion advancing left, palm tree in background

Date	Mintage	F12	VF20	XF40	MS60	MS63
2010(B)	—	—	0.75	1.00	2.00	—
2010(B)		—	PF63 30.00			

KM# A391 5 RUPEES
6.00 g., Nickel-Brass **Subject:** XIX Commonwealth Game Delhi 2010 **Obv:** Lion capital of Ashoka Pillar, KM#399.1 **Rev:** Logo of Commonwealth Games **Note:** Mule, without Denomination

Date	Mintage	F12	VF20	XF40	MS60	MS63
2010(C)	—	—	50.00	100	200	—

KM# 391 5 RUPEES
6.00 g., Nickel-Brass, 23 mm. **Subject:** 19th Commonwealth Games Delhi 2010 **Obv:** Lion capital of Ashoka Pillar **Rev:** Logo of commonwealth

Date	Mintage	F12	VF20	XF40	MS60	MS63
2010(B)	—	—	—	3.00	4.00	—
2010(C)	—	—	—	—	2.00	—
2010(C)		PF63 30.00				
2010(Hy)	—	—	—	—	2.00	—
2010(Hy) Packaged	—	—	—	—	—	5.50
2010(N)	—	—	—	—	2.00	—

KM# 403.1 5 RUPEES
Nickel-Brass, 23 mm. **Subject:** Comptroller & Auditgeneral of India, 150th Anniversary **Obv:** Lion capital of Ashoka Pillar **Rev:** Logo

Date	Mintage	F12	VF20	XF40	MS60	MS63
2010(B)	—	—	—	2.50	4.00	—
2010(C)	—	—	—	2.50	4.00	—
2010(C)		—	PF63 30.00			
2010(H)	—	—	—	2.50	4.00	—
2010(N)	—	—	—	2.50	4.00	—

KM# 396 5 RUPEES
6.00 g., Nickel-Brass, 23 mm. **Subject:** Indian Council of Medical Research, 100th Anniversary **Obv:** Lion capitol of Ashoka Pillar **Rev:** Anniversary Logo

Date	Mintage	F12	VF20	XF40	MS60	MS63
2011(B)	—	—	—	1.00	4.00	—
2011(B)		—	PF63 30.00			
2011(C)	—	—	—	1.00	4.00	—
2011(H)	—	—	—	1.00	4.00	—
2011(N)	—	—	—	1.00	4.00	—

KM# 397 5 RUPEES
Nickel-Brass, 23 mm. **Subject:** Civil Aviation, 100th Anniversary **Obv:** Lion capitol of Ashoka Pillar **Rev:** Aircraft above 100

Date	Mintage	F12	VF20	XF40	MS60	MS63
2011(B)	—	—	—	1.00	4.00	—
2011(B)		—	PF63 40.00			
2011(C)	—	—	—	1.00	4.00	—
2011(H)	—	—	—	1.00	4.00	—
2011(N)	—	—	—	1.00	4.00	—

KM# 399.2 5 RUPEES
Nickel-Brass, 23 mm. **Obv:** Lion capital of Ashoka Pillar **Rev:** New rupee value flanked by flora **Edge:** Reeded **Note:** Type 2

Date	Mintage	F12	VF20	XF40	MS60	MS63
2011(B)	—	—	—	—	10.00	—

KM# 399.3 5 RUPEES
Nickel-Brass, 23 mm. **Obv:** Lion capitol of Ashoka Pillar **Rev:** New rupee value flanked by flora **Edge:** Reeded

Date	Mintage	F12	VF20	XF40	MS60	MS63
2011(C)	—	—	—	—	10.00	—
2012(C)	—	—	—	—	10.00	—

KM# 393 5 RUPEES
6.00 g., Nickel-Brass, 23 mm. **Subject:** Rabindranath Tagore, 150th Anniversary of Birth **Obv:** Lion capitol of Ashoka Pillar **Rev:** Bust facing **Edge:** Reeded

Date	Mintage	F12	VF20	XF40	MS60	MS63
2011(B)	—	—	—	4.00	5.00	—
2011(C)	—	—	—	3.00	4.00	—
2011(C)		—	PF63 40.00			
2011(C) Proof, packaged		—	PF63 4.00			
2011(Hy)	—	—	—	2.00	4.00	—
2011(Hy) Packaged	—	—	—	—	—	5.50
2011(N)	—	—	—	2.00	4.00	—

KM# 399.1 5 RUPEES
6.00 g., Nickel-Brass, 23 mm. **Obv:** Lion capitol of Ashoka Pillar **Rev:** New rupee value flanked by flora **Edge:** Reeded **Note:** Type I

Date	Mintage	F12	VF20	XF40	MS60	MS63
2011(C)	—	—	—	—	1.00	—
2011(H)	—	—	—	—	1.00	—
2011(N)	—	—	—	—	1.00	—
2012(B)	—	—	—	—	1.00	—
2012(C)	—	—	—	—	1.00	—
2012(H)	—	—	—	—	1.00	—
2012(N)	—	—	—	—	1.00	—

KM# 405 5 RUPEES
6.00 g., Nickel-Brass, 23 mm. **Subject:** Madan Mohan Malaviya, 150th Anniversary of Birth **Obv:** Lion capital of Ashoka Pillar **Rev:** Bust facing **Note:** Released in 2013.

Date	Mintage	F12	VF20	XF40	MS60	MS63
2011(B)	—	—	—	—	4.00	5.00

KM# 404 5 RUPEES
6.00 g., Nickel-Brass, 23 mm. **Subject:** Indian Parliament, 60th Anniversary **Obv:** Lion capital of Ashoka Pillar **Rev:** Building at center

Date	Mintage	F12	VF20	XF40	MS60	MS63
2012(B)	—	—	0.50	2.00	4.00	—
2012(H)	—	—	0.50	2.00	4.00	—

KM# 425 5 RUPEES
6.00 g., Nickel-Brass, 23 mm. **Subject:** Madan Mohan Malviya, 150 Anniversary of Birth

Date	Mintage	F12	VF20	XF40	MS60	MS63
2012	—	—	—	—	4.00	5.00

KM# 423 5 RUPEES
6.00 g., Nickel-Brass, 23 mm. **Subject:** Swami Vivekanad, 150th Anniversary of Birth

Date	Mintage	F12	VF20	XF40	MS60	MS63
2013	—	—	—	—	4.00	5.00

KM# 427 5 RUPEES
6.00 g., Stainless Steel, 23 mm. **Subject:** Jamsetji Nusserwanji Tata, 175th Anniversary of Birth

Date	Mintage	F12	VF20	XF40	MS60	MS63
2014	—	—	—	—	4.00	5.00

KM# 309 10 RUPEES
12.50 g., Copper-Nickel, 31 mm. **Subject:** 100th Anniversary Birth of Dr. Syama P. Mookerjee **Obv:** Lion capitol of Ashoka Pillar **Rev:** Bust of Dr. Mookerjee 1/2 right **Edge:** Reeded

Date	Mintage	F12	VF20	XF40	MS60	MS63
2001(C)	—	—	—	200	250	—
2001(C)		—	PF63 350			

KM# 344 10 RUPEES
12.50 g., Copper-Nickel, 31 mm. **Subject:** 100th Anniversary Birth of Jaya Prakash Narayan **Obv:** Lion capitol of Ashoka Pillar **Rev:** Bust of Jaya Prakash Narayan slightly left **Edge:** Reeded

Date	Mintage	F12	VF20	XF40	MS60	MS63
2002(B)	—	—	—	80.00	110	—
2002(B)		—	PF63 175			

KM# 347 10 RUPEES
12.50 g., Copper-Nickel, 31 mm. **Subject:** Sant Tukaram **Obv:** Lion capitol of Ashoka Pillar **Edge:** Reeded

Date	Mintage	F12	VF20	XF40	MS60	MS63
2002(C)	—	—	—	250	350	—
2002(C)		—	PF63 500			

KM# 319 10 RUPEES
12.50 g., Copper-Nickel, 31 mm. **Obv:** Lion capitol of Ashoka Pillar **Rev:** Bust of Maharana Pratap left

Date	Mintage	F12	VF20	XF40	MS60	MS63
2003(B)	—	—	—	80.00	100	—
2003(B)		—	PF63 150			

KM# 332 10 RUPEES
12.50 g., Copper-Nickel, 31 mm. **Obv:** Lion capitol of Ashoka Pillar **Rev:** 3/4 length military figure Veer Durgadass with spear left **Edge:** Reeded

Date	Mintage	F12	VF20	XF40	MS60	MS63
2003(B)	—	—	—	50.00	70.00	
2003(B)	—	PF63 100				

KM# 353 10 RUPEES
7.70 g., Bi-Metallic, 27 mm. **Subject:** Unity in Diversity **Obv:** Asoka Pillar **Rev:** Four heads sharing a common body

Date	Mintage	F12	VF20	XF40	MS60	MS63
2005(N)	—	—	—	—	9.00	—
2006(N)	—	—	—	—	4.00	—
2007(N)	—	—	—	—	6.00	—

Note: Poor strike quality

KM# 363 10 RUPEES
7.70 g., Bi-Metallic, 27 mm. **Subject:** Connectivity and Information Technology **Obv:** Lion capitol of Ashoka Pillar **Rev:** Large 10, wide rays above

Date	Mintage	F12	VF20	XF40	MS60	MS63
2008(N)	—	—	—	—	2.00	—
2009(N)	—	—	—	—	4.00	—
2010(B)	—	—	—	—	16.50	—
2010(N)	—	—	—	—	2.00	—

KM# 371 10 RUPEES
7.70 g., Bi-Metallic, 27 mm. **Subject:** Tercentenary of Gurta-Gaddi of Shri Guru Granth Sahibji **Obv:** Lion capitol of Ashoka Pillar and value

Date	Mintage	F12	VF20	XF40	MS60	MS63
2008(Hy) Packaged	—	—	—	—	—	7.00
2008(M) Packaged	—	—	—	—	—	7.00
2008(M)	—	PF63 20.00				

KM# 372 10 RUPEES
7.70 g., Bi-Metallic, 27 mm. **Subject:** Dr. Homi Bhabha - 100th Anniversary of Birth **Obv:** Lion capitol of Ashoka Pillar and value **Rev:** Portrait

Date	Mintage	F12	VF20	XF40	MS60	MS63
2009(B)	—	—	—	—	9.00	—
2009(B)	—	PF63 20.00				
2009(N)	—	—	—	—	2.00	—

KM# 388 10 RUPEES
8.00 g., Bi-Metallic, 27 mm. **Subject:** Reserve Bank of India, 75th Anniversary **Obv:** Lion capitol of Ashoka Pillar **Rev:** Lion advancing left, palm tree in background

Date	Mintage	F12	VF20	XF40	MS60	MS63
2010(B)	—	—	—	2.00	6.00	
2010(B)	—	PF63 20.00				
2010(N)	—	—	—	4.00	7.00	

KM# 400 10 RUPEES
Bi-Metallic, 27 mm. **Obv:** Lion capitol of Ashoka Pillar **Rev:** New rupee symbol above value

Date	Mintage	F12	VF20	XF40	MS60	MS63
2011(B)	—	—	—	—	6.00	—
2011(C)	—	—	—	—	6.00	—
2011(H)	—	—	—	—	6.00	—
2011(N)	—	—	—	—	6.00	—
2012(B)	—	—	—	—	4.00	—
2012(C)	—	—	—	—	3.00	—
2012(H)	—	—	—	—	3.00	—
2012(N)	—	—	—	—	2.00	—

KM# 407 10 RUPEES
8.00 g., Bi-Metallic, 27 mm. **Subject:** Indian Parliament, 60th Anniversary **Obv:** Lion capital of Ashoka Pillar, value below **Rev:** Parliament Building

Date	Mintage	F12	VF20	XF40	MS60	MS63
2012(B)	—	—	—	4.00	6.00	—
2012(N)	—	—	—	4.00	6.00	—

KM# 310 50 RUPEES
30.00 g., Copper-Nickel, 39 mm. **Subject:** 100th Anniversary Birth of Dr. Syama P. Mookerjee **Obv:** Lion capitol of Ashoka Pillar **Rev:** Bust of Dr. Mookerjee 1/2 right **Edge:** Reeded

Date	Mintage	F12	VF20	XF40	MS60	MS63
2001(C)	—	—	—	300	340	—
2001(C)	—	PF63 450				

KM# 348 50 RUPEES
30.00 g., Copper-Nickel, 39 mm. **Subject:** Sant Tukaram **Obv:** Lion capitol of Ashoka Pillar **Edge:** Reeded

Date	Mintage	F12	VF20	XF40	MS60	MS63
2002(C)	—	—	—	300	340	—
2002(C)	—	PF63 450				

KM# 352 50 RUPEES
30.00 g., Copper-Nickel, 39 mm. **Subject:** O.N.G.C., 50th Anniversary

Date	Mintage	F12	VF20	XF40	MS60	MS63
2006	—	—	—	—	20.00	30.00
2006	—	PF63 50.00				

KM# 361 50 RUPEES
30.00 g., Copper-Nickel, 39 mm. **Subject:** Khadi & Village Industries Commission, 50th Anniversary

Date	Mintage	F12	VF20	XF40	MS60	MS63
2007	—	—	—	—	—	50.00
2007	—	PF63 100				

KM# 408 60 RUPEES
Silver **Subject:** 60th Anniversary of Indian Parliament **Obv:** Lion capital of Ashoka Pillar

Date	Mintage	F12	VF20	XF40	MS60	MS63
2012	—	PF63 50.00				

KM# 389 75 RUPEES
35.00 g., 0.500 Silver 0.559 oz. ASW, 42 mm. **Subject:** Reserve Bank of India, 75th Anniversary **Obv:** Lion capitol of Ashoka Pillar **Rev:** Lion advancing left, palm tree in background

Date	Mintage	F12	VF20	XF40	MS60	MS63
2010(B)	—	—	—	—	50.00	55.00
2010B	—	PF63 85.00				
2010(C)	—	—	—	—	50.00	55.00
2010(N)	—	—	—	—	50.00	55.00

KM# 311 100 RUPEES
35.00 g., 0.500 Silver 0.559 oz. ASW, 44 mm. **Subject:** 10th Anniversary Dr, Syama P. Mookerjee **Obv:** Lion capitol of Ashoka Pillar **Rev:** Bust of Dr. Mookerjee 1/2 right **Edge:** Reeded

Date	Mintage	F12	VF20	XF40	MS60	MS63
2001(C)	—	—	—	325	400	—
2001(C)	—	PF63 500				

KM# 312 100 RUPEES
35.00 g., 0.500 Silver 0.559 oz. ASW, 44 mm. **Subject:** 2600th Anniversary Birth of Bhagwan Mahavir **Obv:** Lion capitol of Ashoka Pillar **Rev:** Swastika above hand in irregular frame **Edge:** Reeded

Date	Mintage	F12	VF20	XF40	MS60	MS63
2001(B)	—	—	—	350	400	—
2001(B)	—	PF63 500				

KM# 345 100 RUPEES
35.00 g., 0.500 Silver 0.559 oz. ASW, 44 mm. **Subject:** 100th Anniversary Birth of Jaya Prakash Narayan **Obv:** Lion capitol of Ashoka Pillar **Rev:** Bust of Jaya Prakash Narayan slightly left **Edge:** Reeded

Date	Mintage	F12	VF20	XF40	MS60	MS63
2002(B)	—	—	—	200	—	250
2002(B)	—	PF63 325				

KM# 349 100 RUPEES
35.00 g., 0.500 Silver 0.559 oz. ASW, 44 mm. **Subject:** Sant Tukaram **Obv:** Lion capitol of Ashoka Pillar **Edge:** Reeded

Date	Mintage	F12	VF20	XF40	MS60	MS63
2002(C)	—	—	—	400	—	450
2002(C)	—	PF63 60.00				

KM# 318 100 RUPEES
35.00 g., 0.500 Silver 0.559 oz. ASW, 44 mm. **Obv:** Lion capitol of Ashoka Pillar **Rev:** K. Kamaraj above life dates **Edge:** Reeded

Date	Mintage	F12	VF20	XF40	MS60	MS63
ND-2003(B)	—		—	80.00	120	—
ND-2003(B)	—	PF63 150				
ND-2003(B) Proof, restrike	—	PF63 80.00				

KM# 320 100 RUPEES
35.00 g., 0.500 Silver 0.559 oz. ASW, 44 mm. **Obv:** Lion capitol of Ashoka Pillar **Rev:** Bust of Maharana Pratap left **Edge:** Reeded

Date	Mintage	F12	VF20	XF40	MS60	MS63
2003(B)	—	—		120	140	—
2003(B)	—	PF63 225				

KM# 333 100 RUPEES
35.00 g., 0.500 Silver 0.559 oz. ASW, 44 mm. **Obv:** Lion capitol of Ashoka Pillar **Rev:** 3/4 length military figure Veer Durgadass with spear left **Edge:** Reeded

Date	Mintage	F12	VF20	XF40	MS60	MS63
2003(B)	—	—		60.00	80.00	—
2003(B)	—	PF63 120				

KM# 340 100 RUPEES
35.00 g., 0.500 Silver 0.559 oz. ASW, 44 mm. **Subject:** 150th Anniversary Indian Railways **Obv:** Lion capitol of Ashoka Pillar **Rev:** Cartoon elephant holding railroad lantern **Edge:** Reeded

Date	Mintage	F12	VF20	XF40	MS60	MS63
2003(C)	—	—		60.00	80.00	—
2003(C)	—	PF63 120				
2003(C) Proof, restrike	—	PF63 80.00				

KM# 335 100 RUPEES
35.00 g., 0.500 Silver 0.559 oz. ASW, 44 mm. **Subject:** 150th Anniversary Telecommunications **Obv:** Lion capitol of Ashoka Pillar **Rev:** Cartoon bird standing holding cell phone **Edge:** Reeded

Date	Mintage	F12	VF20	XF40	MS60	MS63
2004(B)	—	—		60.00	100	—
2004(B)	—	PF63 120				
2004(B) Proof, restrike	—	PF63 80.00				

KM# 337 100 RUPEES
35.00 g., 0.500 Silver 0.559 oz. ASW, 44 mm. **Subject:** 100th Anniversary Birth of Lal Bahadur Shasti **Obv:** Lion capitol of Ashoka Pillar **Rev:** Bust of Lal Bahadur Shastri 3/4 left **Edge:** Reeded

Date	Mintage	F12	VF20	XF40	MS60	MS63
ND-2004(C)	—	—		60.00	80.00	—
ND-2004(C)	—	PF63 120				

KM# 343 100 RUPEES
35.00 g., 0.500 Silver 0.559 oz. ASW, 44 mm. **Subject:** Indian Postal Service, 150th Anniversary **Obv:** Lion capitol of Ashoka Pillar **Rev:** Perforation corner of a postage stamp **Edge:** Reeded

Date	Mintage	F12	VF20	XF40	MS60	MS63
2004(C)	—	—		60.00	80.00	—
2004(C)	—	PF63 120				
2004(C) Proof, restrike	—	PF63 80.00				

KM# 338 100 RUPEES
35.00 g., 0.500 Silver 0.559 oz. ASW, 44 mm. **Subject:** 75th Anniversary Dandi March **Obv:** Lion capitol of Ashoka Pillar **Rev:** Chandi leading marchers **Edge:** Reeded

Date	Mintage	F12	VF20	XF40	MS60	MS63
ND-2005(B)	—	—		50.00	60.00	—
ND-2005(B)	—	PF63 80.00				
ND-2005(B) Proof, restrike	—	PF63 75.00				

KM# 339 100 RUPEES
35.00 g., 0.500 Silver 0.559 oz. ASW, 44 mm. **Obv:** Lion capitol of Ashoka Pillar **Rev:** Bust of Mahatma Basaveshwara slightly left **Edge:** Reeded

Date	Mintage	F12	VF20	XF40	MS60	MS63
ND-2006B	—	—		50.00	60.00	—
ND-2006B	—	PF63 80.00				

KM# 358 100 RUPEES
35.00 g., 0.500 Silver 0.559 oz. ASW, 44 mm. **Subject:** State Bank of India, 200th Anniversary

Date	Mintage	F12	VF20	XF40	MS60	MS63
2006	—	—		—	—	65.00
2006(C)	—	PF63 90.00				
2006(C) Proof, restrike	—	PF63 75.00				

KM# 364 100 RUPEES
35.00 g., 0.500 Silver 0.559 oz. ASW, 44 mm. **Subject:** Jagatguru Shree Narayan Gurudev

Date	Mintage	F12	VF20	XF40	MS60	MS63
2006	—	—		—	40.00	50.00
2006	—	PF63 100				

KM# 410 100 RUPEES
35.00 g., 0.500 Silver 0.559 oz. ASW, 44 mm. **Subject:** Kuka Movement, 150th Anniversary **Note:** Issued in 2012.

Date	Mintage	F12	VF20	XF40	MS60	MS63
1857-2007	—	PF63 55.00				

KM# 351 100 RUPEES
35.00 g., 0.500 Silver 0.559 oz. ASW, 44 mm. **Subject:** 75th Anniversary Indian Air Force **Obv:** Lion capitol of Ashoka Pillar **Edge:** Reeded

Date	Mintage	F12	VF20	XF40	MS60	MS63
2007(C)	—	—	—	50.00	60.00	—
2007(C)	—	PF63 80.00				

KM# 366 100 RUPEES
35.00 g., 0.500 Silver 0.559 oz. ASW, 44 mm. **Subject:** Lokmanya Bal Gangadhar Tilak, 150th Anniversary

Date	Mintage	F12	VF20	XF40	MS60	MS63
2007	—	—	—	—	—	50.00
2007	—	PF63 100				

KM# 384 100 RUPEES
35.00 g., 0.500 Silver 0.559 oz. ASW, 44 mm. **Subject:** First War of Independence, 150th Anniversary

Date	Mintage	F12	VF20	XF40	MS60	MS63
2007	—	—	—	—	—	50.00
2007	—	PF63 90.00				
2007 Proof, restrike	—	PF63 70.00				

KM# 370 100 RUPEES
35.00 g., 0.500 Silver 0.559 oz. ASW, 44 mm. **Subject:** Gur-Ta Gaddi, 300th Anniversary

Date	Mintage	F12	VF20	XF40	MS60	MS63
2008	—	—	—	—	—	75.00
2008	—	PF63 100				

KM# 369 100 RUPEES
35.00 g., 0.500 Silver 0.559 oz. ASW, 44 mm. **Subject:** Louis Braille, 200th Anniversary of Birth **Obv:** Lion capitol of Ashoka Pillar

Date	Mintage	F12	VF20	XF40	MS60	MS63
2009	—	—	—	50.00	60.00	—
2009	—	PF63 80.00				

KM# 383 100 RUPEES
35.00 g., 0.500 Silver 0.559 oz. ASW, 44 mm. **Subject:** Homi Bhamba **Obv:** Lion capitol of Ashoka Pillar

Date	Mintage	F12	VF20	XF40	MS60	MS63
2009	—	—	—	50.00	60.00	—
2009	—	PF63 80.00				

KM# 411 100 RUPEES
35.00 g., 0.500 Silver 0.559 oz. ASW, 44 mm. **Subject:** Saint Alphanso, 100th Anniversary of Birth

Date	Mintage	F12	VF20	XF40	MS60	MS63
2009	—	—	—	—	—	50.00
2009	—	PF63 75.00				

KM# 412 100 RUPEES
35.00 g., 0.500 Silver 0.559 oz. ASW, 44 mm. **Subject:** Perarignar Anna, 100th Anniversary

Date	Mintage	F12	VF20	XF40	MS60	MS63
2009	—	—	—	—	—	50.00
2009	—	PF63 75.00				

KM# 414 100 RUPEES
35.00 g., 0.500 Silver 0.559 oz. ASW, 44 mm. **Subject:** Commonwealth, 60th Anniversary

Date	Mintage	F12	VF20	XF40	MS60	MS63
2009	—	—	—	—	—	50.00
2009	—	PF63 75.00				

KM# 382 100 RUPEES
35.00 g., 0.500 Silver 0.559 oz. ASW, 44 mm. **Subject:** Mother Theresa, 100th Anniversary of birth **Obv:** Lion capitol of Ashoka Pillar **Rev:** Bust facing

Date	Mintage	F12	VF20	XF40	MS60	MS63
2010	—	—	—	50.00	60.00	—
2010	—	PF63 80.00				

KM# 415 100 RUPEES
35.00 g., 0.500 Silver 0.559 oz. ASW, 44 mm. **Subject:** Dr. Rajendra Prasad, 125th Anniversary of Birth

Date	Mintage	F12	VF20	XF40	MS60	MS63
2010	—	—	—	—	—	50.00
2010	—	PF63 75.00				

KM# 417 100 RUPEES
35.00 g., 0.500 Silver 0.559 oz. ASW, 44 mm. **Subject:** 19th Commonwealth Games, Delhi

Date	Mintage	F12	VF20	XF40	MS60	MS63
2010	—	—	—	—	—	50.00
2010	—	PF63 75.00				

KM# 418 100 RUPEES
35.00 g., 0.500 Silver 0.559 oz. ASW, 44 mm. **Subject:** C. Subramaniam, 100th Anniversary of Birth

Date	Mintage	F12	VF20	XF40	MS60	MS63
2010	—	—	—	—	—	40.00
2010		PF63 70.00				

KM# 420 100 RUPEES
35.00 g., 0.500 Silver 0.559 oz. ASW, 44 mm. **Subject:** Civil Aviation, 100th Anniversary

Date	Mintage	F12	VF20	XF40	MS60	MS63
2011	—	—	—	—	—	50.00
2011		PF63 70.00				

KM# 421 100 RUPEES
35.00 g., 0.500 Silver 0.559 oz. ASW, 44 mm. **Subject:** Council of Medical Research, 100th Anniversary

Date	Mintage	F12	VF20	XF40	MS60	MS63
2011	—	—	—	—	—	50.00
2011		PF63 70.00				

KM# 428 100 RUPEES
35.00 g., 0.500 Silver 0.559 oz. ASW, 44 mm. **Subject:** Jamsetji Nusserwanji Tata, 175th Anniversary of Birth

Date	Mintage	F12	VF20	XF40	MS60	MS63
2014	—	—	—	—	—	50.00

KM# 380 150 RUPEES
35.00 g., 0.500 Silver 0.559 oz. ASW, 44 mm. **Subject:** Income Tax, 150th Anniversary **Obv:** Lion capitol of Ashoka Pillar **Rev:** Chanakya portrait at right

Date	Mintage	F12	VF20	XF40	MS60	MS63
2010(C)	—	—	—	50.00	60.00	—
2010(C)		PF63 80.00				

KM# 416 150 RUPEES
35.00 g., 0.500 Silver 0.559 oz. ASW, 44 mm. **Subject:** Rabindranth Tagore, 150th Anniversary of Birth

Date	Mintage	F12	VF20	XF40	MS60	MS63
2010	—	—	—	—	—	50.00
2010		PF63 80.00				

KM# 419 150 RUPEES
35.00 g., 0.500 Silver 0.559 oz. ASW, 44 mm. **Subject:** Comptroller & Auditor General, 150th Anniversary

Date	Mintage	F12	VF20	XF40	MS60	MS63
2011	—	—	—	—	—	40.00
2011		PF63 75.00				

KM# 426 150 RUPEES
35.00 g., 0.5626 Silver 0.629 oz. ASW, 44 mm. **Subject:** Madan Mohan Malviya, 150th Anniversary of Birth

Date	Mintage	F12	VF20	XF40	MS60	MS63
2012	—	—	—	—	—	50.00

KM# 424 150 RUPEES
0.50 g., 0.562 Silver ASW, 44 mm. **Subject:** Swami Vivekanad, 150th Anniversary of Birth

Date	Mintage	F12	VF20	XF40	MS60	MS63
2013	—	—	—	—	—	50.00

KM# 422 1000 RUPEES
35.00 g., 0.500 Silver 0.559 oz. ASW, 44 mm. **Subject:** Brihadeeswarar Temple, 1000th Anniversary

Date	Mintage	F12	VF20	XF40	MS60	MS63
2010	—	—	—	—	—	75.00
2010		PF63 90.00				

MINT SETS

KM#	Date	Mintage	Identification	Issue Price	Mkt Val
KM81	2008 (2)	—	KM#370, 371	—	100
MS60	2002 (3)	—	KM#347, 348, 349	—	780
MS61	2001 (3)	—	KM#309, 310, 311.	—	750
MS62	2001 (2)	—	KM#304, 312	—	325
MS63	2002 (3)	—	KM#313, 344, 345	—	275
MS64	2003 (3)	—	KM#314, 319, 320	—	200
MS66	2003 (3)	—	KM#316, 332, 333	—	150
MS66A	2003 (2)	—	KM#307, 340	—	80.00
MS67	2004 (2)	—	KM#321, 343	—	110
MS67A	2004 (2)	—	KM#321, 343	—	80.00
MS68	2003 (2)	—	KM#317.1, 318	—	130
MS68A	2003 (2)	—	KM#317.1, 318	—	125
MS69	2004 (2)	—	KM#334, 335	—	110
MS69A	2004 (2)	—	KM#334, 335	—	100
MS70	2005 (2)	—	KM#325, 338	—	150
MS70A	2005 (2)	—	KM#325, 338	—	125
MS71	2005 (2)	—	KM#329, 337	—	120
MS72	2006 (2)	—	KM#357, 358	—	90.00
MS72A	2006 (2)	—	KM#357, 358	—	80.00
MS73	2006 (2)	—	KM#324, 339	—	120
MS74	2006 (2)	—	KM#352, 354	—	30.00
MS75	2006 (2)	—	KM#355, 364	—	120
MS76	2007 (2)	—	KM#356, 366	—	120
MS77	2007 (2)	—	KM#350, 351	—	85.00
MS78	2007 (2)	—	KM#361, 362	—	120
MS79	2007 (2)	—	KM#359, 384	—	120
MS79A	2007 (2)	—	KM#359, 384	—	100
MS80	2007 (2)	—	MK#402, 406	—	100
MS80A	2007 (2)	—	KM#402, 406	—	110
MS81	2008 (2)	—	KM#370, 371	—	100
MS81A	2008 (2)	—	KM#370, 371	—	100
MS82	2009 (2)	—	KM#368, 369	—	70.00
MS83	2009 (2)	—	KM#365, 411	—	100
MS84	2009 (2)	—	KM#412, 413	—	100
MS85	2009 (2)	—	KM#372, 383	—	100
MS86	2009 (2)	—	KM#376, 414	—	100
MS87	2010 (2)	—	KM#392, 415	—	100
MS88	2010 (2)	—	MS#393, 416	—	100
MS89	2010 (5)	—	KM#385-389	—	100
MS90	2010 (3)	—	KM#391, 401, 417	—	90.00
MS91	2010 (2)	—	KM#381, 382	—	70.00
MS91A	2010 (2)	—	KM#381, 382	—	70.00
MS92	2010 (2)	—	KM#377, 418	—	70.00
MS92A	2010 (2)	—	KM#377, 418	—	90.00
MS93	2011 (5)	—	KM#394, 395, 398, 399.1, 400	—	11.00
MS94	2011 (2)	—	KM#379, 380	—	100
MS95	2011 (2)	—	KM#403.1, 419	—	90.00
MS96	2011 (2)	—	KM#397, 420	—	100
MS97	2011 (2)	—	KM#396, 421	—	100
MS98	2010 (2)	—	KM#378, 422, released 2011	—	90.00

PROOF SETS

KM#	Date	Mintage	Identification	Issue Price	Mkt Val
PS69	2002(C) (4)	—	KM#346-349	—	1,200
PS70	2001 (4)	—	KM#303, 309, 310, 311	—	1,200
PS71	2001 (2)	—	KM#304, 312	—	480
PS72	2002B (3)	—	KM#313, 344, 345	—	400
PS73	2003 (3)	—	KM#314, 319, 320	—	320
PS74	2003B (3)	—	KM#316, 332, 333	—	210
PS75	2003(C) (2)	—	KM#307, 340	—	180
PS76	2003 (2)	—	KM#307, 340	—	120
PS77	2004 (2)	—	KM#321, 343	—	140
PS78	2004 (2)	—	KM#324, 343	—	80.00
PS79	ND(2003) (2)	—	KM#317.1, 318	—	150
PS80	2004 (2)	—	KM#317.1, 318	—	150
PS81	2004 (2)	—	KM#317.1, 318	—	170
PS82	2004B (2)	—	KM#334, 335	—	150
PS83	2005 (2)	—	KM#3334, 335	—	140
PS84	2005B (2)	—	KM#325, 338	—	150
PS85	2005 (2)	—	KM#325, 338	—	140
PS86	2005 (2)	—	KM#325, 338	—	175
PS87	2004(C) (2)	—	KM#336, 337	—	160
PS88	2006 (2)	—	KM#357, 358	—	110
PS89	2006 (2)	—	KM#357, 358	—	90.00
PS90	2006B (2)	—	KM#324, 339	—	150
PS91	2006 (2)	—	KM#352, 354	—	352
PS92	2006 (2)	—	KM#355, 364	—	150
PS93	2007 (2)	—	KM#356, 366	—	150
PS94	2007 (2)	—	KM#350, 351	—	100
PS95	2007 (2)	—	KM#361, 362	—	150
PS96	2007 (2)	—	KM#359, 384	—	150
PS97	2007 (2)	—	KM#359, 384	—	140
PS98	2007 (2)	—	KM#402, 406	—	135
PS99	2007 (2)	—	KM#402, 406	—	140
PS100	2008 (2)	—	KM#370, 371	—	150
PS101	2008 (2)	—	KM#370, 371	—	140
PS102	2009 (2)	—	KM#368, 369	—	140
PS103	2009 (2)	—	KM#365, 411	—	150
PS104	2009 (2)	—	KM#412, 413	—	140
PS105	2009 (2)	—	KM#372, 383	—	150
PS106	2009 (2)	—	KM#376, 414	—	150
PS107	2010 (2)	—	KM#392, 415	—	135
PS108	2010 (2)	—	KM#393, 416	—	150
PS109	2010 (5)	—	KM#385, 386, 387, 388, 389	—	140
PS110	2010 (3)	—	KM#391, 401, 417	—	135
PS111	2010 (2)	—	KM#381, 382	—	110
PS112	2010 (2)	—	KM#381, 382	—	80.00
PS113	2010 (2)	—	KM#381, 382	—	80.00
PS114	2010 (2)	—	KM#377, 418	—	140
PS115	2010 (2)	—	KM#377, 418	—	155
PS116	2011 (2)	—	KM#379, 380	—	140
PS117	2011 (2)	—	KM#403.1, 419	—	135
PS118	2011 (2)	—	KM#397, 420	—	135
PS119	2011 (2)	—	KM#396, 421	—	135
PS120	2010 (2)	—	KM#378, 422	—	110
PS121	2010 (2)	—	KM#378, 422	—	150
PS122	2010 (2)	—	KM#378, 422	—	180

INDONESIA

The Republic of Indonesia, the world's largest archipelago, extends for more than 3,000 miles (4,827 km.) along the equator from the mainland of southeast Asia to Australia. The 17,508 islands comprising the archipelago have a combined area of 788,425 sq. mi. (1,919,440 sq. km.) and a population of 205 million, including East Timor. On August 30, 1999, the Timorese majority voted for independence. The Inter FET (International Forces for East Timor) is now in charge of controlling the chaotic situation. Capitol: Jakarta. Petroleum, timber, rubber, and coffee are exported.

Modern coinage issued by the Republic of Indonesia includes separate series for West Irian and for the Riau Archipelago, an area of small islands between Singapore and Sumatra.

MONETARY SYSTEM
100 Sen = 1 Rupiah

REPUBLIC
STANDARD COINAGE

KM# 60 50 RUPIAH
1.35 g., Aluminum, 19.95 mm. **Obv:** National emblem **Rev:** Black-naped Oriole **Edge:** Plain

Date	Mintage	F12	VF20	XF40	MS60	MS63
2001	—	—	—	—	0.30	1.00
2002	—	—	—	—	0.30	1.00

KM# 61 100 RUPIAH
1.79 g., Aluminum, 23 mm. **Obv:** National emblem **Rev:** Palm Cockatoo **Edge:** Plain

Date	Mintage	F12	VF20	XF40	MS60	MS63
2001	—	—	—	—	0.75	1.25
2002	—	—	—	—	0.75	1.25
2003	—	—	—	—	0.75	1.25
2004	—	—	—	—	0.75	1.25
2005	—	—	—	—	0.75	1.25

KM# 66 200 RUPIAH
2.40 g., Aluminum, 25 mm. **Obv:** National arms **Rev:** Balinese starling bird above value **Edge:** Plain

Date	Mintage	F12	VF20	XF40	MS60	MS63
2003	—	—	—	—	1.00	1.50

Note: The typeface of the date often makes 2003 look like 2008

KM# 59 500 RUPIAH
5.35 g., Aluminum-Bronze, 24 mm. **Obv:** National emblem **Rev:** Jasmine above denomination

Date	Mintage	F12	VF20	XF40	MS60	MS63
2001	—	—	—	—	1.75	2.25
2002	—	—	—	—	1.75	2.25
2003	—	—	—	—	1.75	2.25

KM# 67 500 RUPIAH
3.05 g., Aluminum, 27.2 mm. **Obv:** National arms **Rev:** Jasmine flower above value **Edge:** Segmented reeding

Date	Mintage	F12	VF20	XF40	MS60	MS63
2003	—	—	—	—	2.00	2.50

Note: The typeface of the date often makes 2003 look like 2008.

KM# 70 1000 RUPIAH
4.50 g., Nickel Plated Steel, 24 mm. **Obv:** National arms above value **Rev:** Angklung - a traditional bamboo musical instrument; West Java Provincial's Governor office in Bandung in background **Rev. Legend:** ANGKLUNG / date

Date	Mintage	F12	VF20	XF40	MS60	MS63
2010	—	—	—	—	0.75	1.00

KM# 64 25000 RUPIAH
28.28 g., 0.925 Silver 0.8356 oz. ASW, 38.6 mm. **Subject:** Centennial of Sukarno's Birth **Obv:** National arms **Rev:** Uniformed bust of Sukarno **Edge:** Reeded

Date	Mintage	F12	VF20	XF40	MS60	MS63
2001	500	PF63 120		PF65 150		

KM# 68 25000 RUPIAH
28.28 g., 0.925 Silver 0.8356 oz. ASW, 38.61 mm. **Subject:** Mohammas Hatta, vice-president (1945-1956) **Obv:** National Arms **Rev:** Bust facing

Date	Mintage	F12	VF20	XF40	MS60	MS63
2002	2,000	PF63 120		PF65 150		

KM# 65 500,000 RUPIAH
15.00 g., 0.999 Gold 0.4787 oz. AGW, 28.2 mm. **Subject:** Centennial of Sukarno's Birth **Obv:** National arms **Rev:** Head left **Edge:** Reeded

Date	Mintage	F12	VF20	XF40	MS60	MS63
2001	500	PF63 1,000		PF65 1,100		

KM# 69 500,000 RUPIAH
15.00 g., 0.999 Gold 0.4787 oz. AGW, 28.2 mm. **Subject:** Mohammad Hatta, vice-president (1945-1956) **Obv:** National Arms **Rev:** Bust facing

Date	Mintage	F12	VF20	XF40	MS60	MS63
2002	2,000	PF63 850		PF65 875		

IRAN

The Islamic Republic of Iran, located between the Caspian Sea and the Persian Gulf in southwestern Asia, has an area of 636,296 sq. mi. (1,648,000 sq. km.) and a population of 59.7 million. Capital: Tehran. Although predominantly an agricultural state, Iran depends heavily on oil for foreign exchange. Crude oil, carpets and agricultural products are exported.

On March 22, 1935 the Kingdom of Persia became the Kingdom of Iran. In 1979 the monarchy was toppled and an Islamic Republic proclaimed.

TITLES

دار الخلافة

Dar al-Khilafat

RULERS
Islamic Republic, SH1358-/1979-AD

MINT NAME

طهران

Tehran

تفليس

Tiflis

MINT MARKS
H - Heaton (Birmingham)
L - Leningrad (St. Petersburg)

COIN DATING
Iranian coins were dated according to the Moslem lunar calendar until March 21, 1925 (AD), when dating was switched to a new calendar based on the solar year, indicated by the notation SH. The monarchial calendar system was adopted in 1976 = MS2535 and was abandoned in 1978 = MS2537. The previously used solar year calendar was restored at that time.

MONETARY SYSTEM
20 Shahis = 1 Rial (100 Dinars)

ISLAMIC REPUBLIC
MILLED COINAGE

KM# 1260 50 RIALS
Copper-Nickel, 26 mm. **Subject:** Shrine of Hazrat Masumah **Obv:** Value and date **Rev:** Shrine within beaded circle **Edge:** Reeded

Date	Mintage	F12	VF20	XF40	MS60	MS63
SH1380 (2001)	—	—	2.50	3.50	5.00	—
SH1382 (2003)	—	—	2.50	3.50	5.00	—

KM# 1266 50 RIALS
3.51 g., Aluminum-Bronze, 20.1 mm. **Obv:** Value and date **Rev:** Hazrat Masumah Shrine **Edge:** Reeded **Mint:** Tehran

Date	Mintage	F12	VF20	XF40	MS60	MS63
SH1382(2003)	—	—	—	—	50.00	—
SH1383(2004)	—	—	—	—	2.50	—
SH1384(2005)	—	—	—	—	2.50	—
SH1385(2006)	—	—	—	—	2.50	—

KM# 1261.2 100 RIALS
Copper-Nickel, 29 mm. **Obv:** Value and date **Rev:** Shrine within designed border **Note:** Thick denomination and numerals

Date	Mintage	F12	VF20	XF40	MS60	MS63
SH1380 (2001)	—	—	—	—	6.50	—
SH1382 (2003)	—	—	—	—	6.50	—

KM# 1267 100 RIALS
4.62 g., Aluminum-Bronze, 22.9 mm. **Obv:** Value, date divides wreath below **Rev:** Imam Reza Shrine **Edge:** Reeded **Mint:** Tehran

Date	Mintage	F12	VF20	XF40	MS60	MS63
SH1382(2003)	—	—	—	—	50.00	—
SH1383(2004)	—	—	—	—	3.50	—
SH1384(2005)	—	—	—	—	3.50	—
SH1385(2006)	—	—	—	—	3.50	—

KM# 1262 250 RIALS
10.70 g., Bi-Metallic, 28.3 mm. **Obv:** Value within circle, inscription and date divide wreath **Rev:** Stylized flower within circle and wreath

Date	Mintage	F12	VF20	XF40	MS60	MS63
SH1381 (2002)	—	—	—	—	7.50	—
SH1382 (2003)	—	—	—	—	7.50	—

KM# 1268 250 RIALS
5.50 g., Copper-Nickel, 24.6 mm. **Obv:** Value, date below divides sprays **Rev:** Stylized flower within sprays **Edge:** Plain **Mint:** Tehran

Date	Mintage	F12	VF20	XF40	MS60	MS63
SH1382(2003)	—	—	—	—	50.00	—
SH1383(2004)	—	—	—	—	4.50	—
SH1384(2005)	—	—	—	—	4.50	—
SH1385(2006)	—	—	—	—	4.50	—

KM# 1282 250 RIALS
5.00 g., Aluminum-Bronze, 24 mm. **Obv:** Value, date below divides sprays **Rev:** Stylized flower within sprays **Mint:** Tehran

Date	Mintage	F12	VF20	XF40	MS60	MS63
SH1386(2007)	—	—	—	—	0.75	1.75

KM# 1269 500 RIALS
8.91 g., Bi-Metallic, 27.1 mm. **Obv:** Value **Rev:** Bird and flowers **Edge:** Reeded **Mint:** Tehran

Date	Mintage	F12	VF20	XF40	MS60	MS63
SH1382(2003)	—	—	—	—	50.00	—
SH1383(2004)	—	—	—	—	6.00	—
SH1384(2005)	—	—	—	—	6.00	—
SH1385(2006)	—	—	—	—	6.00	—
SH1386 (2007)	—	—	—	—	—	6.00

KM# 1283 500 RIALS
6.35 g., Aluminum-Bronze, 25.5 mm. **Obv:** Value in ornamental circle **Rev:** Bird and flowers **Mint:** Tehran

Date	Mintage	F12	VF20	XF40	MS60	MS63
SH1386(2007)	—	—	—	—	1.50	3.00

REFORM COINAGE

KM# 1287 1000 DINARS
4.60 g., Aluminum-Bronze, 23 mm. **Subject:** Shah Cheragh **Obv:** Value **Rev:** Shah Cheragh shrine

Date	Mintage	F12	VF20	XF40	MS60	MS63
SH1391 (2012)	—	—	—	—	2.25	4.50

KM# 1288 2000 DINARS
6.80 g., Copper-Nickel, 26.3 mm. **Subject:** Master plan **Obv:** Value **Rev:** Stylized star

Date	Mintage	F12	VF20	XF40	MS60	MS63
SH1391 (2012)	—	—	—	—	—	8.00

KM# 1289 5000 DINARS
10.00 g., Copper-Nickel, 29.4 mm. **Obv:** Value **Rev:** Mosque

Date	Mintage	F12	VF20	XF40	MS60	MS63
SH1392 (2013)	—	—	—	—	—	10.00

KM# 1270 250 RIALS
2.80 g., Aluminum-Bronze, 18.5 mm. **Rev:** Feyziyeh School

Date	Mintage	F12	VF20	XF40	MS60	MS63
AH1387 (2008)	—	—	—	—	0.55	1.00
SH1388 (2009)	—	—	—	—	0.55	1.00
SH1389 (2010)	—	—	—	—	0.55	1.00
SH1390 (2011)	—	—	—	—	0.55	1.00

KM# 1271 500 RIALS
3.90 g., Copper-Nickel, 20.6 mm. **Rev:** Saadi Tomb

Date	Mintage	F12	VF20	XF40	MS60	MS63
SH1387 (2008)	—	—	—	—	—	6.00
SH1387 (2009)	—	—	—	—	—	6.00
SH1389 (2010)	—	—	—	—	—	6.00
1390 (2011)	—	—	—	—	—	6.00

KM# 1281 500 RIALS
3.90 g., Copper-Nickel, 20.6 mm. **Subject:** Freedom of Khorramshahr **Obv:** Value in wreath **Rev:** Stylized flower

Date	Mintage	F12	VF20	XF40	MS60	MS63
SH1390 (2011)	—	—	—	—	2.00	5.00

KM# 1285 500 RIALS
3.50 g., Aluminum-Bronze, 20.3 mm. **Obv:** Vlaue **Rev:** Dove shaped tulip **Mint:** Tehran

Date	Mintage	F12	VF20	XF40	MS60	MS63
AH1390 (2011)	50,000,000	—	—	—	—	1.50	3.00

KM# 1272 1000 RIALS
5.80 g., Aluminum-Brass, 23.7 mm. **Rev:** Khajou Bridge in Isfahan

Date	Mintage	F12	VF20	XF40	MS60	MS63
SH1387 (2008)	—	—	—	—	—	12.00
SH1388 (2009)	—	—	—	—	—	12.00
SH1389 (2010)	—	—	—	—	—	12.00

KM# 1274 1000 RIALS
5.80 g., Copper-Nickel, 23.7 mm. **Subject:** Eid al-Ghadeer **Rev:** Ali in star

Date	Mintage	F12	VF20	XF40	MS60	MS63
SH1389(2010)	—	—	—	—	—	6.00

KM# 1275 1000 RIALS
5.80 g., Brass, 23.7 mm. **Subject:** Eid al-Adha **Rev:** Kaaba Cubus

Date	Mintage	F12	VF20	XF40	MS60	MS63
SH1389(2010)	—	—	—	—	—	6.00

KM# 1284 1000 RIALS
5.80 g., Aluminum-Bronze, 23.7 mm. **Subject:** National Statistical Office, 75th Anniversary **Obv:** Mountain above value **Rev:** Tile motif **Mint:** Tehran

Date	Mintage	F12	VF20	XF40	MS60	MS63
AH1389 (2010)	—	—	—	—	—	2.25	4.50

KM# 1286 1000 RIALS
4.60 g., Aluminum-Bronze, 23 mm. **Subject:** 15 Shaaban **Obv:** Value **Rev:** Dafoldills **Mint:** Tehran

Date	Mintage	F12	VF20	XF40	MS60	MS63
AH1390 (2011)	60,000,000	—	—	—	—	2.25	4.50

KM# 1276 2000 RIALS
6.80 g., Copper-Nickel, 23.7 mm. **Subject:** Central Bank of the Islamic Republic of Iran, 50th Anniversary

Date	Mintage	F12	VF20	XF40	MS60	MS63
SH1389(2010)	—	—	—	—	—	8.00

KM# 1278 2000 RIALS
Copper-Nickel **Obv:** Value **Rev:** Mosque

Date	Mintage	F12	VF20	XF40	MS60	MS63
SH1389 (2010)	—	—	—	—	—	8.00

KM# 1277 5000 RIALS
10.20 g., Copper-Nickel, 29.4 mm. **Subject:** Central Bank, 50th Anniversary **Obv:** Value **Rev:** Commemorative calligraphy

Date	Mintage	F12	VF20	XF40	MS60	MS63
SH1389(2010)	—	—	—	—	—	10.00

KM# 1279 5000 RIALS
10.20 g., Copper-Nickel, 29.4 mm. **Obv:** Value **Rev:** Calligraphy

Date	Mintage	F12	VF20	XF40	MS60	MS63
SH1389 (2010)	—	—	—	—	—	10.00

KM# 1280 5000 RIALS
12.00 g., Aluminum-Bronze, 28.5 mm. **Subject:** Muslim Week **Obv:** Value **Rev:** Two roses

Date	Mintage	F12	VF20	XF40	MS60	MS63
SH1389 (2010)	—	—	—	—	—	10.00

KM# 1290
Aluminum-Bronze **Obv:** Value **Rev:** Mosque

Date	Mintage	F12	VF20	XF40	MS60	MS63
SH1389 (2010)	—	—	—	—	—	

BULLION COINAGE
Issued by the National Bank of Iran

KM# 1250.2 1/2 AZADI
4.07 g., 0.900 Gold 0.117 oz. AGW **Obv:** Legend larger **Obv. Legend:** Spring of Freedom

Date	Mintage	F12	VF20	XF40	MS60	MS63
SH1381 (2002)	—	—	—	—	215	—
SH1383 (2004)	—	—	—	—	215	—

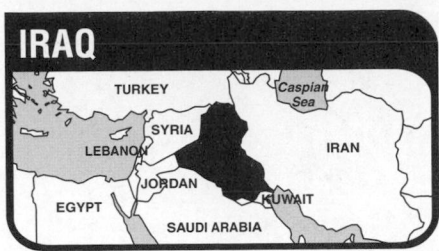

IRAQ

The Republic of Iraq, historically known as Mesopotamia, is located in the Near East and is bordered by Kuwait, Iran, Turkey, Syria, Jordan and Saudi Arabia. It has an area of 167,925 sq. mi. (434,920 sq. km.) and a population of 19 million. Capital: Baghdad. The economy of Iraq is based on agriculture and petroleum. Crude oil accounted for 94 percent of the exports before the war with Iran began in 1980.

Mesopotamia was the site of a number of flourishing civilizations of antiquity - Sumeria, Assyria, Babylonia, Parthia, Persia and the Biblical cities of Ur, Ninevehand and Babylon. Desired because of its favored location, which embraced the fertile alluvial plains of the Tigris and Euphrates Rivers, Mesopotamia - 'land between the rivers'- was conquered by Cyrus the Great of Persia, Alexander of Macedonia and by Arabs who made the legendary city of Baghdad the capital of the ruling caliphate. Suleiman the Magnificent conquered Mesopotamia for Turkey in 1534, and it formed part of the Ottoman Empire until 1623, and from 1638 to 1917. Great Britain, given a League of Nations mandate over the territory in 1920, recognized Iraq as a kingdom in 1922. Iraq became an independent constitutional monarchy presided over by the Hashemite family, direct descendants of the prophet Mohammed, in 1932. In 1958, the army-led revolution of July 14 overthrew the monarchy and proclaimed a republic.

MONETARY SYSTEM

Falus, Fulus   Fals, Fils   Falsan

50 Fils = 1 Dirham
200 Fils = 1 Riyal
1000 Fils = 1 Dinar (Pound)

REPUBLIC
DECIMAL COINAGE

KM# 175 25 DINARS
2.50 g., Copper Plated Steel, 17.4 mm. **Obv:** Value **Rev:** Map **Edge:** Plain

Date	Mintage	F12	VF20	XF40	MS60	MS63
AH1425-2004	—	—	—	0.30	0.75	1.00

KM# 176 50 DINARS
4.34 g., Brass Plated Steel, 22 mm. **Obv:** Value and legend **Rev:** Map **Edge:** Plain

Date	Mintage	F12	VF20	XF40	MS60	MS63
AH1425-2004	—	—	—	0.50	1.00	1.50

KM# 177 100 DINARS
4.30 g., Stainless Steel, 22 mm. **Obv:** Value **Rev:** Map **Edge:** Reeded

Date	Mintage	F12	VF20	XF40	MS60	MS63
AH1425-2004	—	—	—	0.80	1.00	1.50

Date	Mintage	F12	VF20	XF40	MS60	MS63
2007	10,000	PF63 18.00				
2008	45,990,533	—	—	—	1.25	—
2009	4,279,307	—	—	—	1.25	—
2009	5,000	PF63 18.00				
2010	1,027,059	—	—	—	1.25	—
2010	5,000	PF63 18.00				
2011	1,201,428	—	—	—	1.25	—
2011	5,000	PF63 18.00				
2012	—	—	—	—	1.25	—
2012	5,000	PF63 18.00				
2013	—	—	—	—	1.25	—
2014	—	—	—	—	1.25	—

IRELAND REPUBLIC

Ireland, which occupies five-sixths of the island of Ireland located in the Atlantic Ocean west of Great Britain, has an area of 27,136 sq. mi. (70,280 sq. km.) and a population of 4.3 million. Capital: Dublin. Agriculture and dairy farming are the principal industries. Meat, livestock, dairy products and textiles are exported.

REPUBLIC

EURO COINAGE
European Union Issues

KM# 32 EURO CENT
2.27 g., Copper Plated Steel, 16.25 mm. **Obv:** Harp **Rev:** Denomination and globe **Edge:** Plain

Date	Mintage	F12	VF20	XF40	MS60	MS63
2002	404,339,788	—	—	—	0.35	—
2003	67,902,182	—	—	—	0.35	—
2004	174,833,634	—	—	—	0.35	—
2005	126,964,391	—	—	—	0.35	—
2006	105,413,273	—	—	—	0.35	—
2006	5,000	PF63 15.00				
2007	18,515,843	—	—	—	0.35	—
2007	10,000	PF63 12.00				
2008	59,002,134	—	—	—	0.35	—
2009	42,109,347	—	—	—	0.35	—
2009	5,000	PF63 12.00				
2010	4,946,711	—	—	—	0.35	—
2010	5,000	PF63 12.00				
2011	23,261,567	—	—	—	0.35	—
2011	5,000	PF63 12.00				
2012	—	—	—	—	0.35	—
2012	5,000	PF63 12.00				
2013	—	—	—	—	0.35	—
2014	—	—	—	—	0.35	—

KM# 33 2 EURO CENT
3.00 g., Copper Plated Steel, 18.75 mm. **Obv:** Harp **Rev:** Denomination and globe **Edge:** Plain with groove

Date	Mintage	F12	VF20	XF40	MS60	MS63
2002	354,643,386	—	—	—	0.50	—
2003	177,290,034	—	—	—	0.50	—
2004	143,004,694	—	—	—	0.50	—
2005	72,544,884	—	—	—	0.50	—
2006	26,568,597	—	—	—	0.50	—
2006	5,000	PF63 15.00				
2007	84,291,248	—	—	—	0.50	—
2007	10,000	PF63 12.00				
2008	42,116,152	—	—	—	0.50	—
2009	7,284,499	—	—	—	0.50	—
2009	5,000	PF63 12.00				
2010	3,496,511	—	—	—	0.50	—
2010	5,000	PF63 12.00				
2011	4,813,844	—	—	—	0.50	—
2011	5,000	PF63 12.00				
2012	—	—	—	—	0.50	—
2012	5,000	PF63 12.00				
2013	—	—	—	—	0.50	—
2014	—	—	—	—	0.50	—

KM# 34 5 EURO CENT
4.00 g., Copper Plated Steel, 19.60 mm. **Obv:** Harp **Rev:** Denomination and globe **Edge:** Plain

Date	Mintage	F12	VF20	XF40	MS60	MS63
2002	456,270,848	—	—	—	0.75	—
2003	48,352,370	—	—	—	0.75	—
2004	80,354,322	—	—	—	0.75	—
2005	56,454,380	—	—	—	0.75	—
2006	88,003,370	—	—	—	0.75	—
2006	5,000	PF63 18.00				
2007	36,225,742	—	—	—	0.75	—
2007	10,000	PF63 15.00				
2008	61,844,008	—	—	—	0.75	—
2009	10,333,341	—	—	—	0.75	—
2009	5,000	PF63 15.00				
2010	1,023,881	—	—	—	0.75	—
2010	5,000	PF63 15.00				
2011	1,024,637	—	—	—	0.75	—
2011	5,000	PF63 15.00				
2012	—	—	—	—	0.75	—
2012	5,000	PF63 15.00				
2013	—	—	—	—	0.75	—
2014	—	—	—	—	0.75	—

KM# 35 10 EURO CENT
4.07 g., Brass, 19.75 mm. **Obv:** Harp **Rev:** Denomination and map **Edge:** Reeded

Date	Mintage	F12	VF20	XF40	MS60	MS63
2002	275,913,000	—	—	—	1.00	—
2003	133,815,907	—	—	—	1.00	—
2004	36,732,778	—	—	—	1.00	—
2005	4,652,786	—	—	—	1.00	—
2006	9,208,411	—	—	—	1.00	—
2006	5,000	PF63 18.00				

KM# 47 10 EURO CENT
4.07 g., Brass, 19.75 mm. **Obv:** Harp **Rev:** Relief map of Western Europe, stars, lines and value **Edge:** Reeded

Date	Mintage	F12	VF20	XF40	MS60	MS63
2007	54,434,307	—	—	—	1.00	—
2007	10,000	PF63 15.00				
2008	53,997,990	—	—	—	1.00	—
2009	10,850,328	—	—	—	1.00	—
2009	5,000	PF63 15.00				
2010	1,078,313	—	—	—	1.00	—
2010	5,000	PF63 15.00				
2011	1,030,118	—	—	—	1.00	—
2011	5,000	PF63 15.00				
2012	—	—	—	—	1.00	—
2012	5,000	PF63 15.00				
2013	—	—	—	—	1.00	—
2014	—	—	—	—	1.00	—

KM# 36 20 EURO CENT
5.73 g., Brass, 22.25 mm. **Obv:** Harp **Rev:** Denomination and map **Edge:** Notched

Date	Mintage	F12	VF20	XF40	MS60	MS63
2002	234,575,562	—	—	—	1.25	—
2003	57,142,221	—	—	—	1.25	—
2004	32,421,447	—	—	—	1.25	—
2005	40,439,062	—	—	—	1.25	—
2006	10,357,229	—	—	—	1.25	—
2006	5,000	PF63 20.00				

KM# 48 20 EURO CENT
5.73 g., Brass, 22.25 mm. **Obv:** Harp **Rev:** Relief map of Western Europe, stars, lines and value **Edge:** Notched

Date	Mintage	F12	VF20	XF40	MS60	MS63
2007	12,953,789	—	—	—	1.25	

KM# 37 50 EURO CENT
7.81 g., Brass, 24.25 mm. **Obv:** Harp **Rev:** Denomination and map **Edge:** Reeded

Date	Mintage	F12	VF20	XF40	MS60	MS63
2002	144,144,592	—	—	—	1.50	—
2003	11,811,926	—	—	—	1.50	—
2004	6,748,912	—	—	—	1.50	—
2005	17,253,568	—	—	—	1.50	—
2006	966,138	—	—	—	1.50	—
2006 Proof	5,000					

KM# 49 50 EURO CENT
7.81 g., Brass, 24.25 mm. **Obv:** Harp **Rev:** Relief map of Western Europe, stars, lines and value **Edge:** Reeded

Date	Mintage	F12	VF20	XF40	MS60	MS63
2007	4,991,002	—	—	—	1.50	—
2007	10,000	PF63 20.00				
2008	1,122,371	—	—	—	1.50	—
2009	1,876,011	—	—	—	1.50	—
2009	5,000	PF63 20.00				
2010	1,173,242	—	—	—	1.50	—
2010	5,000	PF63 20.00				
2011	1,096,961	—	—	—	1.50	—
2011	5,000	PF63 20.00				
2012	—	—	—	—	1.50	—
2012	5,000	PF63 20.00				
2013	—	—	—	—	1.50	—
2014 0	—	—	—	—	1.50	—

KM# 38 EURO
7.50 g., Bi-Metallic, 23.25 mm. **Obv:** Harp **Rev:** Denomination and map **Edge:** Reeded and plain sections

Date	Mintage	F12	VF20	XF40	MS60	MS63
2002	135,139,737	—	—	—	2.75	—
2003	2,520,000	—	—	—	2.75	—
2004	1,632,990	—	—	—	2.75	—
2005	6,769,777	—	—	—	2.75	—
2006	4,023,722	—	—	—	2.75	—
2006	5,000	PF63 25.00				

KM# 50 EURO
7.50 g., Bi-Metallic, 23.25 mm. **Obv:** Harp **Rev:** Relief map of Western Europe, stars, lines and value **Edge:** Reeded and plain sections

Date	Mintage	F12	VF20	XF40	MS60	MS63
2007	1,850,049	—	—	—	2.75	—
2007	10,000	PF63 22.00				
2008	2,609,757	—	—	—	2.75	—

Date	Mintage	F12	VF20	XF40	MS60	MS63
2009	3,314,828	—	—	—	2.75	—
2009	5,000	PF63 22.00				
2010	1,082,716	—	—	—	2.75	—
2010	5,000	PF63 22.00				
2011	1,104,965	—	—	—	2.75	—
2011	5,000	PF63 22.00				
2012	—	—	—	—	2.75	—
2012	5,000	PF63 22.00				
2013	—	—	—	—	2.75	—
2014	—	—	—	—	2.75	—

KM# 39 2 EURO
8.52 g., Bi-Metallic, 25.7 mm. **Obv:** Harp **Rev:** Denomination and map **Edge:** Reeded with 2's and stars

Date	Mintage	F12	VF20	XF40	MS60	MS63
2002	90,548,166	—	—	—	4.00	—
2003	2,631,076	—	—	—	4.00	—
2004	3,738,186	—	—	—	4.00	—
2005	11,982,981	—	—	—	4.00	—
2006	3,860,519	—	—	—	4.00	—
2006	5,000	PF63 28.00				

KM# 51 2 EURO
8.52 g., Bi-Metallic, 25.7 mm. **Obv:** Harp **Rev:** Relief map of Western Europe, stars, lines and value **Edge:** Reeded with 2's and stars

Date	Mintage	F12	VF20	XF40	MS60	MS63
2007	7,595,260	—	—	—	4.00	—
2007	10,000	PF63 25.00				
2008	5,792,003	—	—	—	4.00	—
2009	30,063	—	—	—	4.00	—
2009	5,000	PF63 25.00				
2010	1,448,746	—	—	—	4.00	—
2010	5,000	PF63 25.00				
2011	1,053,271	—	—	—	4.00	—
2011	5,000	PF63 25.00				
2012	—	—	—	—	4.00	—
2012	5,000	PF63 25.00				
2013	—	—	—	—	4.00	—
2014	—	—	—	—	4.00	—

KM# 53 2 EURO
8.45 g., Bi-Metallic, 25.72 mm. **Subject:** 50th Anniversary Treaty of Rome **Obv:** Open treaty book **Rev:** Large value at left, modified outline of Europe at right **Edge:** Reeded with stars and 2's

Date	Mintage	F12	VF20	XF40	MS60	MS63
2007	4,605,112	—	—	—	5.00	10.00
2007 Special Unc.	35,000	—	—	—	—	20.00
2007	10,000	PF63 25.00				

KM# 62 2 EURO
8.52 g., Bi-Metallic, 25.72 mm. **Subject:** EMU, 10th Anniversary

Date	Mintage	F12	VF20	XF40	MS60	MS63
2009	5,000,000	—	—	—	8.00	10.00
2009	7,000	PF63 115				

KM# 71 2 EURO
8.50 g., Bi-Metallic, 25.75 mm. **Subject:** Euro Coinage, 10th Anniversary **Obv:** Euro symbol on globe at center, child-like rendering around

Date	Mintage	F12	VF20	XF40	MS60	MS63
2012	3,000,000	—	—	—	6.00	8.00
2012	—	PF63 25.00				

KM# 40 5 EURO
14.19 g., Copper-Nickel, 28.4 mm. **Subject:** Special Olympics **Obv:** Harp **Rev:** Multicolor games logo **Edge:** Reeded

Date	Mintage	F12	VF20	XF40	MS60	MS63
2003	35,000	—	—	—	15.00	18.00
2003	25,000	PF63 25.00	PF65 28.00			

KM# 56 5 EURO
8.52 g., 0.925 Silver 0.2517 oz. ASW, 28 mm. **Subject:** International Polar Year **Obv:** Harp within wreath **Rev:** Ernest Shackleton, Tom Crean and The Endurance in distance **Edge:** Reeded

Date	Mintage	F12	VF20	XF40	MS60	MS63
2008	5,000	PF63 85.00	PF65 95.00			

KM# 41 10 EURO
28.28 g., 0.925 Silver 0.8356 oz. ASW, 38.61 mm. **Subject:** Special Olympics **Obv:** Gold highlighted harp, 2003, Eire **Rev:** Gold highlighted games logo **Edge:** Reeded

Date	Mintage	F12	VF20	XF40	MS60	MS63
2003	30,000	PF63 50.00	PF65 60.00			

KM# 42 10 EURO
28.28 g., 0.925 Silver 0.8356 oz. ASW, 38.61 mm. **Subject:** EU Presidency **Obv:** 2004, Eire, Harp **Rev:** Stylized Celtic swan **Edge:** Reeded

Date	Mintage	F12	VF20	XF40	MS60	MS63
2004	50,000	PF63 45.00	PF65 55.00			

KM# 44 10 EURO
28.28 g., 0.925 Silver 0.8356 oz. ASW, 38.6 mm. **Subject:** Sir

William R. Hamilton **Obv:** Eire, 2005, Harp **Rev:** Triangle in circle of Greek letters used as math symbols **Edge:** Reeded

Date	Mintage	F12	VF20	XF40	MS60	MS63
2005	30,000	PF63 55.00	PF65 65.00			

KM# 45 10 EURO
28.28 g., 0.925 Silver 0.8356 oz. ASW, 38.61 mm. **Subject:** Samuel Beckett 1906-1989 **Obv:** 2006, Eire, Harp **Rev:** Face, value and play scene **Edge:** Reeded

Date	Mintage	F12	VF20	XF40	MS60	MS63
2006	35,000	PF63 50.00	PF65 60.00			

KM# 58 10 EURO
28.28 g., 0.925 Silver 0.8356 oz. ASW, 38.6 mm. **Subject:** European Culture - Ireland **Obv:** Irish Harp **Rev:** Celtic design

Date	Mintage	F12	VF20	XF40	MS60	MS63
2007	35,000	PF63 55.00	PF65 65.00			

KM# 54 10 EURO
28.28 g., 0.925 Silver 0.8356 oz. ASW, 38.61 mm. **Subject:** Skellig Michael Island **Rev:** Birds and 12 stars above island **Rev. Legend:** SCEILIG MHICHIL

Date	Mintage	F12	VF20	XF40	MS60	MS63
2008	25,000	PF63 65.00	PF65 75.00			

KM# 60 10 EURO
28.28 g., 0.925 Silver 0.8356 oz. ASW, 38.61 mm. **Subject:** First currency, 80th Anniversary **Obv:** Irish harp **Rev:** Ploughman design

Date	Mintage	F12	VF20	XF40	MS60	MS63
2009	15,000	PF63 55.00	PF65 65.00			

KM# 65 10 EURO
28.28 g., 0.925 Silver 0.8356 oz. ASW, 38.61 mm. **Subject:** The President's Award - Gaisce

Date	Mintage	F12	VF20	XF40	MS60	MS63
2010	8,000	PF63 65.00	PF65 75.00			

KM# 67 10 EURO
28.28 g., 0.925 Silver 0.8356 oz. ASW, 38.61 mm. **Subject:** St. Brendan the Navigator **Rev:** Medieval ship

Date	Mintage	F12	VF20	XF40	MS60	MS63
2011	15,000	**PF63** 60.00	**PF65** 70.00			

KM# 70 10 EURO
28.28 g., 0.925 Silver 0.8356 oz. ASW, 38.61 mm. **Subject:** Jack B. Yates

Date	Mintage	F12	VF20	XF40	MS60	MS63
2012	12,000	**PF63** 60.00	**PF65** 70.00			

KM# 75 10 EURO
28.28 g., 0.925 Silver 0.8356 oz. ASW, 38.61 mm. **Subject:** Micahel Collins **Rev:** Bust facing

Date	Mintage	F12	VF20	XF40	MS60	MS63
2012	14,000	**PF63** 70.00	**PF65** 80.00			

KM# 78 10 EURO
28.28 g., 0.925 Silver 0.8356 oz. ASW, 38.61 mm. **Subject:** J.F. Kennedy, 50th Anniversary of Visit

Date	Mintage	F12	VF20	XF40	MS60	MS63
2013	25,000	**PF63** 60.00	**PF65** 70.00			

KM# 80 10 EURO
28.28 g., 0.925 Silver 0.8356 oz. ASW, 38.61 mm. **Subject:** James Joyce James Joyce

Date	Mintage	F12	VF20	XF40	MS60	MS63
2013	10,000	**PF63** 65.00	**PF65** 75.00			

KM# 81 10 EURO
28.28 g., 0.925 Silver 0.8356 oz. ASW, 38.61 mm. **Subject:** John McCormack

Date	Mintage	F12	VF20	XF40	MS60	MS63
2014	10,000	**PF63** 65.00	**PF65** 75.00			

KM# 52 15 EURO
28.28 g., 0.925 Silver 0.8356 oz. ASW, 37 mm. **Obv:** Stylized clover with date and harp **Rev:** Ivan Mestroviae's Seated Woman with Harp design **Edge:** Plain **Note:** Illustration reduced.

Date	Mintage	F12	VF20	XF40	MS60	MS63
2007	10,000	**PF63** 85.00	**PF65** 100			

Note: 8,000 were sold in a single coin case. 1,000 were sold in a two coin set with the corresponding Croatian coin, as an Ireland set. An additional 1,000 were sold with the corresponding Croatian coin as a Croatia set. coins in both sets were the same but the packaging was different.

KM# 63 15 EURO
28.28 g., 0.925 Silver 0.8356 oz. ASW, 38.61 mm. **Subject:** Gaelic Athletics, 125 years

Date	Mintage	F12	VF20	XF40	MS60	MS63
2009	10,000	**PF63** 75.00	**PF65** 85.00			

KM# 64 15 EURO
28.28 g., 0.925 Silver 0.8356 oz. ASW, 38.61 mm. **Rev:** Foal and mare

Date	Mintage	F12	VF20	XF40	MS60	MS63
2010	15,000	**PF63** 75.00	**PF65** 85.00			

KM# 68 15 EURO
28.28 g., 0.925 Silver 0.8356 oz. ASW, 38.61 mm. **Rev:** Salmon

Date	Mintage	F12	VF20	XF40	MS60	MS63
2011	12,000	**PF63** 75.00	**PF65** 85.00			

KM# 72 15 EURO
28.28 g., 0.925 Silver 0.8356 oz. ASW, 38.61 mm. **Rev:** Wolfhounds

Date	Mintage	F12	VF20	XF40	MS60	MS63
2012	8,000	**PF63** 75.00	**PF65** 85.00			

KM# 77 15 EURO
28.28 g., 0.925 Silver 0.8356 oz. ASW, 38.61 mm. **Subject:** Dublin Lockout, 100th Anniversary

Date	Mintage	F12	VF20	XF40	MS60	MS63
2013	10,000	**PF63** 75.00	**PF65** 85.00			

KM# 46 20 EURO
1.24 g., 0.999 Gold 0.0396 oz. AGW, 14 mm. **Subject:** Samuel Beckett 1906-1989 **Obv:** 2006, Eire, Harp **Rev:** Face, value and play **Edge:** Reeded

Date	Mintage	F12	VF20	XF40	MS60	MS63
2006	20,000	**PF63** 75.00	**PF65** 85.00			

KM# 59 20 EURO
1.24 g., 0.999 Gold 0.0397 oz. AGW, 14 mm. **Subject:** European Culture - Ireland **Obv:** Map **Rev:** Celtic design

Date	Mintage	F12	VF20	XF40	MS60	MS63
2007	25,000	**PF63** 95.00	**PF65** 110			

KM# 55 20 EURO
1.24 g., 0.999 Gold 0.0397 oz. AGW, 14 mm. **Subject:** Skellig Michael Island **Rev:** Birds and 12 stars above island **Rev. Legend:** SCEILIG MHICHIL

Date	Mintage	F12	VF20	XF40	MS60	MS63
2008	15,000	**PF63** 90.00	**PF65** 100			

KM# 61 20 EURO
1.24 g., 0.999 Gold 0.0397 oz. AGW, 14 mm. **Subject:** First currency, 80th Anniversary

Date	Mintage	F12	VF20	XF40	MS60	MS63
2009	15,000	**PF63** 80.00	**PF65** 90.00			

KM# 66 20 EURO
1.24 g., 0.999 Gold 0.0396 oz. AGW, 14 mm. **Subject:** The President's Award - Gaisce

Date	Mintage	F12	VF20	XF40	MS60	MS63
2010	6,000	**PF63** 90.00	**PF65** 100			

KM# 69 20 EURO
0.50 g., 0.999 Gold AGW, 11 mm. **Rev:** Celtic Cross

Date	Mintage	F12	VF20	XF40	MS60	MS63
2011	12,000	**PF63** 45.00	**PF65** 50.00			

KM# 73 20 EURO
0.50 g., 0.999 Gold AGW, 11 mm. **Obv:** Irish Monastic Art **Rev:** Book of Kells

Date	Mintage	F12	VF20	XF40	MS60	MS63
2012	12,000	**PF63** 55.00	**PF65** 65.00			

KM# 74 20 EURO
0.50 g., 0.999 Gold AGW **Rev:** Michael Collins

Date	Mintage	F12	VF20	XF40	MS60	MS63
2012	18,000	**PF63** 55.00	**PF65** 65.00			

KM# 76 20 EURO
0.50 g., 0.999 Gold AGW, 11 mm. **Subject:** Medieval Irish Architecture **Rev:** Rock of Cashel architectural elements

Date	Mintage	F12	VF20	XF40	MS60	MS63
2013	10,000	**PF63** 55.00	**PF65** 65.00			

KM# 79 20 EURO
1.00 g., 0.999 Gold 0.0319 oz. AGW, 13.92 mm. **Subject:** J.F. Kennedy, 50th Anniversary of Visit

Date	Mintage	F12	VF20	XF40	MS60	MS63
2013	—	**PF63** 55.00	**PF65** 65.00			

KM# 57 100 EURO
15.55 g., 0.999 Gold 0.4962 oz. AGW, 28 mm. **Subject:** International Polar Year **Obv:** Harp within wreath **Rev:** Ernest Shackleton, Tom Crean and The Endurance in distance **Edge:** Reeded

Date	Mintage	F12	VF20	XF40	MS60	MS63
2008	2,000	**PF65** 950				

MINT SETS

KM#	Date	Mintage	Identification	Issue Price	Mkt Val
MS10	2002 (8)	20,000	KM#32-39	16.00	200
MS11	2003 (8)	30,000	KM#32-39	20.00	65.00
MS12	2003 (9)	35,000	KM#32-40	25.00	90.00
MS13	2004 (8)	40,000	KM#32-39	25.00	45.00
MS14	2005 (8)	50,000	KM#32-39	29.00	40.00
MS15	2006 (8)	40,000	KM#32-39	26.00	40.00
MS16	2006 (8)	—	KM#32-39	35.00	42.50
MS17	2006 (8)	—	KM#32-39	35.00	42.50
MS18	2007 (8)	20,000	KM#32-34, 47-51 Aran Islands	29.00	30.00
MS19	2007 (8)	—	KM#32-34, 47-51 Boy Baby Set	—	30.00
MS20	2007 (8)	—	KM#32-34, 47-51 Girl Baby Set	—	30.00
MS21	2007 (9)	20,000	KM#32-34, 47-51, 53	—	30.00
MS22	2008 (8)	30,000	KM#32-34, 47-51 Newgrange	—	30.00
MS23	2008 (8)	—	KM#32-34, 47-51 Boy Baby Set	—	30.00
MS24	2008 (8)	—	KM#32-34, 47-51 Girl Baby Set	—	30.00
MS25	2009 (8)	25,000	KM#32-34, 47-51 GAA 125th Anniversary	—	30.00
MS26	2009 (8)	—	KM#32-34, 47-51 Boy Baby Set	—	30.00
MS27	2009 (8)	—	KM#32-34, 47-51 Girl Baby Set	—	30.00
MS28	2010 (8)	20,000	KM#32-34, 47-51 Horse	45.00	45.00
MS29	2010 (8)	—	KM#32-34, 47-51 Baby Set	45.00	45.00
MS30	2011 (8)	20,000	KM#32-34, 47-51	—	45.00
MS31	2012 (8)	—	KM#32-34, 47-51	—	45.00

PROOF SETS

KM#	Date	Mintage	Identification	Issue Price	Mkt Val
PS6	2006 (8)	5,000	KM#32-39	125	165
PS7	2006 (2)	—	KM#45, 46	—	135
PS8	2007 (9)	10,000	KM#32-34, 47-51, 53	—	165
PS9	2007 (2)	—	KM#58-59	—	150
PS10	2008 (2)	—	KM#54-55	—	165
PS11	2008 (2)	—	KM#56-57	—	950
PS12	2009 (9)	—	KM#32-34, 47-51, 58 GAA 125th Anniversary	—	200
PS13	2009 (9)	5,000	KM#32-34, 47-51, 61.	—	225
PS14	2009 (2)	5,000	KM#60, 61. Ploughman Bank Note	—	160
PS15	2010 (2)	—	KM#65-66	—	150
PS16	2010 (8)	5,000	KM#32-34, 47-51	—	200
PS17	2011 (8)	5,000	KM#32-34, 47-51	—	200
PS18	2012 (9)	5,000	KM#32-34, 47-51, 71	—	125
PS19	2012 (4)	6,000	KM#74, 75	—	150

ISLE OF MAN

The Isle of Man, a dependency of the British Crown located in the Irish Sea equidistant from Ireland, Scotland and England, has an area of 227 sq. mi. (588 sq. km.) and a population of 68,000. Capital: Douglas. Agriculture, dairy farming, fishing and tourism are the chief industries.

MINT MARK
PM - Pobjoy Mint

BRITISH DEPENDENCY

DECIMAL COINAGE
100 Pence = 1 Pound

KM# 1036 PENNY
3.56 g., Copper Plated Steel, 20.32 mm. **Ruler:** Elizabeth II **Obv:** Head with tiara right with small triskeles dividing legend **Rev:** Ruins **Edge:** Plain

Date	Mintage	F12	VF20	XF40	MS60	MS63
2001PM AA	—	—	—	—	0.25	0.45
2001PM AC	—	—	—	—	0.25	0.45
2002PM AA	—	—	—	—	0.25	0.45
2002PM AE	—	—	—	—	0.25	0.45
2003PM AA	—	—	—	—	0.25	0.45
2003PM AE	—	—	—	—	0.25	0.45

KM# 1253 PENNY
3.56 g., Copper Plated Steel, 20.3 mm. **Ruler:** Elizabeth II **Obv:** Head with tiara right **Rev:** Santon War Memorial

Date	Mintage	F12	VF20	XF40	MS60	MS63
2004PM AA	—	—	—	—	0.25	0.45
2004PM AB	—	—	—	—	0.25	0.45
2005PM AA	—	—	—	—	0.25	0.45
2005PM AB	—	—	—	—	0.25	0.45
2006PM AA	—	—	—	—	0.25	0.45
2006PM AB	—	—	—	—	0.25	0.45
2007PM AA	—	—	—	—	0.25	0.45
2007PM AB	—	—	—	—	0.25	0.45
2007PM BA	—	—	—	—	0.25	0.45
2008PM AA	—	—	—	—	0.25	0.45
2009PM AA	—	—	—	—	0.25	0.45
2010PM AA	—	—	—	—	0.25	0.45
2011PM AA	—	—	—	—	0.25	0.45
2012PM AA	—	—	—	—	0.25	0.45
2013PM AA	—	—	—	—	—	0.45

KM# 1037 2 PENCE
7.12 g., Copper Plated Steel, 25.9 mm. **Ruler:** Elizabeth II **Obv:** Head with tiara right **Rev:** Sailboat **Edge:** Plain

Date	Mintage	F12	VF20	XF40	MS60	MS63
2001PM AA	—	—	—	—	0.40	0.60
2001PM AB	—	—	—	—	0.40	0.60
2001PM AC	—	—	—	—	0.40	0.60
2002PM AA	—	—	—	—	0.40	0.60
2002PM AB	—	—	—	—	0.40	0.60
2002PM AC	—	—	—	—	0.40	0.60
2002PM AF	—	—	—	—	0.40	0.60
2003PM AA	—	—	—	—	0.40	0.60
2003PM AF	—	—	—	—	0.40	0.60

KM# 1254 2 PENCE
7.12 g., Copper Plated Steel, 25.9 mm. **Ruler:** Elizabeth II **Obv:** Head with tiara right **Rev:** Albert Tower

Date	Mintage	F12	VF20	XF40	MS60	MS63
2004PM AA	—	—	—	—	0.40	0.60
2004PM AB	—	—	—	—	0.40	0.60
2005PM AA	—	—	—	—	0.40	0.60
2005PM AB	—	—	—	—	0.40	0.60
2006PM AA	—	—	—	—	0.40	0.60
2006PM AB	—	—	—	—	0.40	0.60
2007PM AA	—	—	—	—	0.40	0.60
2007PM AB	—	—	—	—	0.40	0.60
2007PM BA	—	—	—	—	0.40	0.60
2008PM AA	—	—	—	—	0.40	0.60
2009PM AA	—	—	—	—	0.40	0.60
2010PM AA	—	—	—	—	0.40	0.60
2011PM AA	—	—	—	—	0.40	0.60
2012PM AA	—	—	—	—	0.40	0.60
2013PM AA	—	—	—	—	—	0.60

KM# 1038 5 PENCE
3.25 g., Copper-Nickel, 18 mm. **Ruler:** Elizabeth II **Obv:** Head with tiara right **Rev:** Gaut's Cross **Edge:** Reeded

Date	Mintage	F12	VF20	XF40	MS60	MS63
2001PM AA	—	—	—	—	0.75	1.00
2002PM AA	—	—	—	—	0.75	1.00
2002PM AC	—	—	—	—	0.75	1.00
2002PM AD	—	—	—	—	0.75	1.00
2002PM AE	—	—	—	—	0.75	1.00
2003PM AA	—	—	—	—	0.75	1.00
2003PM AB	—	—	—	—	0.75	1.00
2003PM AD	—	—	—	—	0.75	1.00

KM# 1255 5 PENCE
3.25 g., Copper-Nickel, 18 mm. **Ruler:** Elizabeth II **Obv:** Head with tiara right **Rev:** Tower of Refuge **Edge:** Reeded

Date	Mintage	F12	VF20	XF40	MS60	MS63
2004PM AA	—	—	—	—	0.75	1.00
2004PM AB	—	—	—	—	0.75	1.00
2005PM AA	—	—	—	—	0.75	1.00
2005PM AB	—	—	—	—	0.75	1.00
2006PM AA	—	—	—	—	0.75	1.00
2006PM AB	—	—	—	—	0.75	1.00
2007PM AA	—	—	—	—	0.75	1.00
2007PM AB	—	—	—	—	0.75	1.00
2008PM AA	—	—	—	—	0.75	1.00
2009PM AA	—	—	—	—	0.75	1.00
2010PM AA	—	—	—	—	0.75	1.00
2011PM AA	—	—	—	—	0.75	1.00
2012PM AA	—	—	—	—	0.75	1.00
2013PM AA	—	—	—	—	—	1.00

KM# 1039 10 PENCE
6.50 g., Copper-Nickel, 24.5 mm. **Ruler:** Elizabeth II **Obv:** Head with tiara right **Rev:** Cathedral **Edge:** Reeded

Date	Mintage	F12	VF20	XF40	MS60	MS63
2001PM AA	—	—	—	—	1.00	1.50
2002PM AA	—	—	—	—	1.00	1.50
2003PM AA	—	—	—	—	1.00	1.50

KM# 1256 10 PENCE
6.50 g., Copper-Nickel, 24.5 mm. **Ruler:** Elizabeth II **Obv:** Head with tiara right **Rev:** Chicken Rock Lighthouse **Edge:** Reeded

Date	Mintage	F12	VF20	XF40	MS60	MS63
2004PM AA	—	—	—	—	1.00	1.50
2004PM AB	—	—	—	—	1.00	1.50
2005PM AA	—	—	—	—	1.00	1.50
2005PM AB	—	—	—	—	1.00	1.50
2006PM AA	—	—	—	—	1.00	1.50
2006PM AB	—	—	—	—	1.00	1.50
2007PM AA	—	—	—	—	1.00	1.50
2007PM AB	—	—	—	—	1.00	1.50
2008PM AA	—	—	—	—	1.00	1.50

Date	Mintage	F12	VF20	XF40	MS60	MS63
2009PM AA	—	—	—	—	1.00	1.50
2010PM AA	—	—	—	—	1.00	1.50
2011PM AA	—	—	—	—	1.00	1.50
2012PM AA	—	—	—	—	1.00	1.50
2013PM AA	—	—	—	—	—	1.50

KM# 1040 20 PENCE
5.00 g., Copper-Nickel, 21.4 mm. **Ruler:** Elizabeth II **Subject:** Rushen Abbey **Obv:** Head with tiara right **Rev:** Monk writing **Edge:** Plain **Shape:** 7-sided

Date	Mintage	F12	VF20	XF40	MS60	MS63
2001PM AA	—	—	—	—	1.50	2.00
2001PM AB	—	—	—	—	1.50	2.00
2002PM AA	—	—	—	—	1.50	2.00
2002PM AB	—	—	—	—	1.50	2.00
2002PM AC	—	—	—	—	1.50	2.00
2003PM AA	—	—	—	—	1.50	2.00
2003PM BA	—	—	—	—	1.50	2.00

KM# 1257 20 PENCE
5.00 g., Copper-Nickel, 21.4 mm. **Ruler:** Elizabeth II **Obv:** Head with tiara right **Rev:** Castle Rushen Clock **Edge:** Plain **Shape:** 7-sided

Date	Mintage	F12	VF20	XF40	MS60	MS63
2004PM AA	—	—	—	—	1.50	2.00
2004PM AB	—	—	—	—	1.50	2.00
2005PM AA	—	—	—	—	1.50	2.00
2005PM AB	—	—	—	—	1.50	2.00
2006PM AA	—	—	—	—	1.50	2.00
2006PM AB	—	—	—	—	1.50	2.00
2007PM AA	—	—	—	—	1.50	2.00
2007PM AB	—	—	—	—	1.50	2.00
2008PM AA	—	—	—	—	1.50	2.00
2009PM AA	—	—	—	—	1.50	2.00
2010PM AA	—	—	—	—	1.50	2.00
2011PM AA	—	—	—	—	1.50	2.00
2012PM AA	—	—	—	—	1.50	2.00
2013PM AA	—	—	—	—	—	2.00

KM# 1041 50 PENCE
8.00 g., Copper-Nickel, 27.3 mm. **Ruler:** Elizabeth II **Obv:** Head with tiara right **Rev:** Stylized crucifix **Edge:** Plain **Shape:** 7-sided

Date	Mintage	F12	VF20	XF40	MS60	MS63
2001PM AA	—	—	—	—	2.25	2.75
2002PM AA	—	—	—	—	2.25	2.75
2003PM AA	—	—	—	—	2.25	2.75

KM# 1105 50 PENCE
8.00 g., Copper-Nickel, 27.3 mm. **Ruler:** Elizabeth II **Subject:** Christmas **Obv:** Head with tiara right **Rev:** Postman and children **Edge:** Plain **Shape:** 7-sided

Date	Mintage	F12	VF20	XF40	MS60	MS63
2001PM BB	30,000	—	—	—	4.50	6.00

KM# 1105a 50 PENCE
8.00 g., 0.925 Silver 0.2364 oz. ASW, 27.3 mm. **Ruler:** Elizabeth II **Obv:** Head with tiara right **Rev:** Postman and children **Edge:** Plain **Shape:** 7-sided

Date	Mintage	F12	VF20	XF40	MS60	MS63
2001PM	5,000	PF65 35.00				

KM# 1105b 50 PENCE
8.00 g., 0.9167 Gold 0.2343 oz. AGW, 27.3 mm. **Ruler:** Elizabeth II **Obv:** Head with tiara right **Rev:** Postman and children **Edge:** Plain **Shape:** 7-sided

Date	Mintage	F12	VF20	XF40	MS60	MS63
2001PM	250	PF65 450				

KM# 1160 50 PENCE
8.00 g., Copper-Nickel, 27.3 mm. **Ruler:** Elizabeth II **Subject:** Christmas **Obv:** Head with tiara right **Rev:** Scrooge in bed **Edge:** Plain **Shape:** 7-sided

Date	Mintage	F12	VF20	XF40	MS60	MS63
2002BB (2002) PM	30,000	—	—	—	4.50	6.00

KM# 1160a 50 PENCE
8.00 g., 0.925 Silver 0.2364 oz. ASW, 27.3 mm. **Ruler:** Elizabeth II **Subject:** Christmas **Obv:** Head with tiara right **Rev:** Scrooge in bed **Edge:** Plain **Shape:** 7-sided

Date	Mintage	F12	VF20	XF40	MS60	MS63
2002PM	5,000	PF65 35.00				

KM# 1160b 50 PENCE
8.00 g., 0.9167 Gold 0.2343 oz. AGW, 27.3 mm. **Ruler:** Elizabeth II **Subject:** Christmas **Obv:** Head with tiara right **Rev:** Scrooge in bed **Edge:** Plain **Shape:** 7-sided

Date	Mintage	F12	VF20	XF40	MS60	MS63
2002PM	250	PF65 450				

KM# 1183 50 PENCE
8.00 g., Copper-Nickel, 27.3 mm. **Ruler:** Elizabeth II **Obv:** Head with tiara right **Rev:** The Snowman and James **Edge:** Plain **Shape:** 7-sided

Date	Mintage	F12	VF20	XF40	MS60	MS63
2003PM BB	10,000	—	—	—	6.50	8.00
2008PM	—	—	—	—	6.50	8.00

KM# 1183a 50 PENCE
8.00 g., 0.925 Silver 0.2364 oz. ASW, 27.3 mm. **Ruler:** Elizabeth II **Subject:** Christmas **Obv:** Head with tiara right **Rev:** The Snowman and James **Edge:** Plain **Shape:** 7-sided

Date	Mintage	F12	VF20	XF40	MS60	MS63
2003PM	3,000	PF65 35.00				

KM# 1183b 50 PENCE
8.00 g., 0.9167 Gold 0.2343 oz. AGW, 27.3 mm. **Ruler:** Elizabeth II **Obv:** Head with tiara right **Rev:** The Snowman and James **Edge:** Plain **Shape:** 7-sided

Date	Mintage	F12	VF20	XF40	MS60	MS63
2003PM	100	PF65 475				

KM# 1258 50 PENCE
8.00 g., Copper-Nickel, 27.3 mm. **Ruler:** Elizabeth II **Obv:** Head with tiara right **Rev:** Milner's Tower **Edge:** Plain **Shape:** 7-sided

Date	Mintage	F12	VF20	XF40	MS60	MS63
2004PM AA	—	—	—	—	2.25	2.75
2004PM AB	—	—	—	—	2.25	2.75
2005PM AA	—	—	—	—	2.25	2.75
2005PM AB	—	—	—	—	2.25	2.75
2006PM AA	—	—	—	—	2.25	2.75
2006PM AB	—	—	—	—	2.25	2.75
2007PM AA	—	—	—	—	2.25	2.75
2007PM AB	—	—	—	—	2.25	2.75
2008PM AA	—	—	—	—	2.25	2.75
2009PM AA	—	—	—	—	2.25	2.75
2010PM AA	—	—	—	—	2.25	2.75
2011PM AA	—	—	—	—	2.25	2.75
2012PM AA	—	—	—	—	2.25	2.75
2013PM AA	—	—	—	—	—	2.75

KM# 1293 50 PENCE
8.00 g., Copper-Nickel, 27.3 mm. **Ruler:** Elizabeth II **Obv:** Queen's new portrait **Rev:** Tourist Trophy Races **Shape:** 7-sided

Date	Mintage	F12	VF20	XF40	MS60	MS63
2004PM AA	—	—	—	—	6.00	7.00
2007PM AA	—	—	—	—	6.00	7.00

KM# 1262 50 PENCE
8.00 g., Copper-Nickel, 27.3 mm. **Ruler:** Elizabeth II **Subject:** Christmas **Obv:** Head with tiara right **Rev:** Laxey Wheel **Edge:** Plain **Shape:** 7-sided

Date	Mintage	F12	VF20	XF40	MS60	MS63
2004PM AA	—	—	—	—	6.00	7.00
2004PM BA	30,000	—	—	—	6.00	7.00

KM# 1262a 50 PENCE
9.19 g., 0.925 Silver 0.2714 oz. ASW, 27.3 mm. **Ruler:** Elizabeth II **Subject:** Christmas **Obv:** Head with tiara right **Rev:** Laxey Wheel **Edge:** Plain **Shape:** 7-sided

Date	Mintage	F12	VF20	XF40	MS60	MS63
2004PM	5,000	PF65 35.00				

KM# 1262b 50 PENCE
15.41 g., 0.9167 Gold 0.4512 oz. AGW, 27.3 mm. **Ruler:** Elizabeth II **Subject:** Christmas **Obv:** Head with tiara right **Rev:** Laxey Wheel **Edge:** Plain **Shape:** 7-sided

Date	Mintage	F12	VF20	XF40	MS60	MS63
2004PM	250	PF65 850				

KM# 1294 50 PENCE
8.00 g., Copper-Nickel, 27.3 mm. **Ruler:** Elizabeth II **Obv:** Queen's new portrait **Rev:** Partridge in a pear tree **Shape:** 7-sided

Date	Mintage	F12	VF20	XF40	MS60	MS63
2005	—	—	—	—	6.50	8.00

KM# 1320.1 50 PENCE
8.00 g., Copper-Nickel, 27.3 mm. **Ruler:** Elizabeth II **Series:** 12 Days of Christmas **Obv:** Head with tiara right **Obv. Legend:** ISLE OF MAN - ELIZABETH II **Rev:** Partridge in a Pear Tree **Rev. Legend:** CHRISTMAS **Edge:** Plain **Shape:** 7-sided

Date	Mintage	F12	VF20	XF40	MS60	MS63
2005PM AA	30,000	—	—	—	—	16.00

KM# 1320.2 50 PENCE
8.00 g., Copper-Nickel, 27.3 mm. **Ruler:** Elizabeth II **Series:** 12 Days of Christmas **Obv:** Head with tiara right **Obv. Legend:** ISLE OF MAN - ELIZABETH II **Rev:** Partidge in a Pear Tree multicolor **Rev. Legend:** CHRISTMAS **Edge:** Plain **Shape:** 7-sided

Date	Mintage	F12	VF20	XF40	MS60	MS63
2005PM	Inc. above	—	—	—	—	20.00

KM# 1320.1a 50 PENCE
9.18 g., 0.925 Silver 0.2713 oz. ASW, 27.3 mm. **Ruler:** Elizabeth II **Series:** 12 Days of Christmas **Obv:** Head with tiara right **Obv. Legend:** ISLE OF MAN - ELIZABETH II **Rev:** Partridge in a Pear Tree **Rev. Legend:** CHRISTMAS **Edge:** Plain **Shape:** 7-sided

Date	Mintage	F12	VF20	XF40	MS60	MS63
2005PM	—	PF65 35.00				

KM# 1320.2a 50 PENCE
8.00 g., 0.925 Silver 0.2364 oz. ASW, 27.3 mm. **Ruler:** Elizabeth II **Series:** 12 Days of Christmas **Obv:** Head with tiara right **Obv. Legend:** ISLE OF MAN - ELIZABETH II **Rev:** Partridge in a Pear Tree multicolor **Rev. Legend:** CHRISTMAS **Edge:** Plain **Shape:** 7-sided

Date	Mintage	F12	VF20	XF40	MS60	MS63
2005PM	—	PF65 35.00				

KM# 1320b 50 PENCE
0.9167 Gold AGW, 27.3 mm. **Ruler:** Elizabeth II **Series:** 12 Days of Christmas **Obv:** Head with tiara right **Obv. Legend:** ISLE OF MAN - ELIZABETH II **Rev:** Partridge in a Pear Tree **Rev. Legend:** CHRISTMAS **Edge:** Plain **Shape:** 7-sided

Date	Mintage	F12	VF20	XF40	MS60	MS63
2005PM	—	PF65 850				

KM# 1321.1 50 PENCE
8.00 g., Copper-Nickel, 27.3 mm. **Ruler:** Elizabeth II **Series:** 12 Days of Christmas **Obv:** Head with tiara right **Obv. Legend:** ISLE OF MAN - ELIZABETH II **Rev:** Two Turtle Doves **Rev. Legend:** CHRISTMAS **Edge:** Plain **Shape:** 7-sided

Date	Mintage	F12	VF20	XF40	MS60	MS63
2006PM AA	—	—	—	—	6.00	7.00

KM# 1321.2 50 PENCE
8.00 g., Copper-Nickel, 27.3 mm. **Ruler:** Elizabeth II **Series:** 12 Days of Christmas **Obv:** Head with tiara right **Obv. Legend:** ISLE OF MAN - ELIZABETH II **Rev:** 2 Turtle Doves multicolor **Rev. Legend:** CHRISTMAS **Edge:** Plain **Shape:** 7-sided

Date	Mintage	F12	VF20	XF40	MS60	MS63
2006PM	—	—	—	—	8.00	10.00

KM# 1321.1a 50 PENCE
0.925 Silver, 27.3 mm. **Ruler:** Elizabeth II **Series:** 12 Days of Christmas **Obv:** Head with tiara right **Obv. Legend:** ISLE OF MAN - ELIZABETH II **Rev:** Two Turtle Doves **Rev. Legend:** CHRISTMAS **Edge:** Plain **Shape:** 7-sided

Date	Mintage	F12	VF20	XF40	MS60	MS63
2006PM	—	PF65 35.00				

KM# 1321.2a 50 PENCE
0.925 Silver, 27.3 mm. **Ruler:** Elizabeth II **Series:** 12 Days of Christmas **Obv:** Head with tiara right **Obv. Legend:** ISLE OF MAN - ELIZABETH II **Rev:** 2 Turtle Doves multicolor **Rev. Legend:** CHRISTMAS **Edge:** Plain **Shape:** 7-sided

Date	Mintage	F12	VF20	XF40	MS60	MS63
2006PM	—	PF65 40.00				

KM# 1321b 50 PENCE
0.9167 Gold AGW, 27.3 mm. **Ruler:** Elizabeth II **Series:** 12 Days of Christmas **Obv:** Head with tiara right **Obv. Legend:** ISLE OF MAN - ELIZABETH II **Rev:** 2 Turtle Doves **Rev. Legend:** CHRISTMAS **Edge:** Plain **Shape:** 7-sided

Date	Mintage	F12	VF20	XF40	MS60	MS63
2006PM	—	PF65 850				

KM# 1322.1 50 PENCE
8.00 g., Copper-Nickel, 27.3 mm. **Ruler:** Elizabeth II **Series:** 12 Days of Christmas **Obv:** Head with tiara right **Obv. Legend:** ISLE OF MAN - ELIZABETH II **Rev:** 3 French Hens **Rev. Legend:** CHRISTMAS **Edge:** Plain **Shape:** 7-sided

Date	Mintage	F12	VF20	XF40	MS60	MS63
2007PM AA	—	—	—	—	6.00	7.00

KM# 1322.2 50 PENCE
8.00 g., Copper-Nickel, 27.3 mm. **Ruler:** Elizabeth II **Series:** 12 Days of Christmas **Obv:** Head with tiara right **Obv. Legend:** ISLE OF MAN - ELIZABETH II **Rev:** 3 French Hens multicolor **Rev. Legend:** CHRISTMAS **Edge:** Plain **Shape:** 7-sided

Date	Mintage	F12	VF20	XF40	MS60	MS63
2007PM	—	—	—	—	8.00	10.00

KM# 1322.1a 50 PENCE
0.925 Silver, 27.3 mm. **Ruler:** Elizabeth II **Series:** 12 Days of Christmas **Obv:** Head with tiara right **Obv. Legend:** ISLE OF MAN - ELIZABETH II **Rev:** 3 French Hens **Rev. Legend:** CHRISTMAS **Edge:** Plain **Shape:** 7-sided

Date	Mintage	F12	VF20	XF40	MS60	MS63
2007PM	—	PF65 35.00				

KM# 1322.2a 50 PENCE
0.925 Silver, 27.3 mm. **Ruler:** Elizabeth II **Series:** 12 Days of Christmas **Obv:** Head with tiara right **Obv. Legend:** ISLE OF MAN - ELIZABETH II **Rev:** 3 French Hens multicolor **Rev. Legend:** CHRISTMAS **Edge:** Plain **Shape:** 7-sided

Date	Mintage	F12	VF20	XF40	MS60	MS63
2007PM	—	PF65 40.00				

KM# 1322b 50 PENCE
0.9167 Gold AGW, 27.3 mm. **Ruler:** Elizabeth II **Series:** 12 Days of Christmas **Obv:** Head with tiara right **Obv. Legend:** ISLE OF MAN - ELIZABETH II **Rev:** 3 French Hens **Rev. Legend:** CHRISTMAS **Edge:** Plain **Shape:** 7-sided

Date	Mintage	F12	VF20	XF40	MS60	MS63
2007PM	250	PF65 850				

KM# 1425 50 PENCE
8.00 g., Copper-Nickel, 27.3 mm. **Ruler:** Elizabeth II **Subject:** TT Centennial **Obv:** Head with tiara right **Rev:** Two motorcyclists within wreath **Shape:** 7-sided

Date	Mintage	F12	VF20	XF40	MS60	MS63
2007PM	—	—	—	—	8.00	10.00

KM# 1487a 50 PENCE
8.00 g., 0.925 Silver 0.2364 oz. ASW, 27.3 mm. **Ruler:** Elizabeth II **Subject:** Christmas **Rev:** 4 Calling birds **Shape:** 7-sided

Date	Mintage	F12	VF20	XF40	MS60	MS63
2008PM	—	PF65 25.00				

KM# 1393.1 50 PENCE
8.00 g., Copper-Nickel, 27.3 mm. **Ruler:** Elizabeth II **Subject:** Christmas **Rev:** Snowman **Shape:** 7-sided

Date	Mintage	F12	VF20	XF40	MS60	MS63
2008PM	—	—	—	—	10.00	12.00

KM# 1393.2 50 PENCE
8.00 g., Copper-Nickel, 27.3 mm. **Ruler:** Elizabeth II **Subject:** Christmas **Rev:** Snowman, multicolored **Shape:** 7-sided

Date	Mintage	F12	VF20	XF40	MS60	MS63
2008PM	—	—	—	—	10.00	12.00

KM# 1487 50 PENCE
8.00 g., Copper-Nickel, 27.3 mm. **Ruler:** Elizabeth II **Subject:** Christmas **Rev:** 4 Calling Birds **Shape:** 7-sided

Date	Mintage	F12	VF20	XF40	MS60	MS63
2008PM	—	—	—	—	—	9.00

KM# 1487b 50 PENCE
8.00 g., 0.9167 Gold 0.2343 oz. AGW, 27.3 mm. **Ruler:** Elizabeth II **Subject:** Christmas **Rev:** 4 Calling birds **Shape:** 7-sided

Date	Mintage	F12	VF20	XF40	MS60	MS63
2008PM	—	PF65 500				

KM# 1372 50 PENCE
8.00 g., Copper-Nickel, 27.3 mm. **Ruler:** Elizabeth II **Subject:** Honda, 50th Anniversary TT **Shape:** 7-sided

Date	Mintage	F12	VF20	XF40	MS60	MS63
2009PM AA	—	—	—	—	—	9.00

KM# 1431a 50 PENCE
8.00 g., 0.925 Silver 0.2364 oz. ASW, 27.3 mm. **Ruler:** Elizabeth II **Subject:** Fifth day of Christmas **Rev:** Five golden rings **Shape:** 7-sided

Date	Mintage	F12	VF20	XF40	MS60	MS63
2009PM	5,000	PF65 20.00				

KM# 1433.1a 50 PENCE
8.00 g., 0.925 Silver 0.2364 oz. ASW, 27.3 mm. **Ruler:** Elizabeth II **Subject:** Christmas **Rev:** Six geese a laying **Shape:** 7-sided

Date	Mintage	F12	VF20	XF40	MS60	MS63
2009PM	5,000	PF65 15.00				

KM# 1431 50 PENCE
8.00 g., Copper-Nickel, 27.3 mm. **Ruler:** Elizabeth II **Subject:** Fifth day of Christmas **Rev:** Five rings **Shape:** 7-sided

Date	Mintage	F12	VF20	XF40	MS60	MS63
2009PM	30,000	—	—	—	—	10.00

KM# 1431b 50 PENCE
8.00 g., 0.9167 Gold 0.2343 oz. AGW, 27.3 mm. **Ruler:** Elizabeth II **Subject:** Fifth day of Christmas **Rev:** Five golden rings **Shape:** 7-sided

Date	Mintage	F12	VF20	XF40	MS60	MS63
2009PM	250	PF65 500				

KM# 1433.1 50 PENCE
8.00 g., Copper-Nickel, 27.3 mm. **Ruler:** Elizabeth II **Rev:** Six Geese a laying **Shape:** 7-sided

Date	Mintage	F12	VF20	XF40	MS60	MS63
2010PM	30,000	—	—	—	—	10.00

KM# 1433.1b 50 PENCE
8.00 g., 0.9167 Gold 0.2343 oz. AGW, 27.3 mm. **Ruler:** Elizabeth II **Subject:** Christmas **Rev:** Six geese a laying **Shape:** 7-sided

Date	Mintage	F12	VF20	XF40	MS60	MS63
2010PM	—	PF65 500				

KM# 1433.2 50 PENCE
8.00 g., Copper-Nickel, 27.3 mm. **Ruler:** Elizabeth II **Subject:** Christmas **Rev:** Six geese a laying in color **Shape:** 7-sided

Date	Mintage	F12	VF20	XF40	MS60	MS63
2010PM	—	—	—	—	—	12.00

KM# 1469 50 PENCE
8.00 g., Copper-Nickel, 27.3 mm. **Ruler:** Elizabeth II **Subject:** Isle of Man TT race **Rev:** Suzuki driver left **Shape:** 7-sided

Date	Mintage	F12	VF20	XF40	MS60	MS63
2010PM	—	—	—	—	—	9.00

KM# 1453.1a 50 PENCE
8.00 g., 0.925 Silver 0.2364 oz. ASW, 27.3 mm. **Ruler:** Elizabeth II **Subject:** Christmas **Rev:** Santa Claus **Shape:** 7-sided

Date	Mintage	F12	VF20	XF40	MS60	MS63
2011PM	5,000	PF65 25.00				

KM# 1454a 50 PENCE
8.00 g., 0.925 Silver 0.2364 oz. ASW, 27.3 mm. **Ruler:** Elizabeth II **Subject:** Isle of Man Tourist Trophy race **Rev:** Yamaha motorcycle and racer **Shape:** 7-sided

Date	Mintage	F12	VF20	XF40	MS60	MS63
2011PM	5,000	PF65 25.00				

KM# 1453.1 50 PENCE
8.00 g., Copper-Nickel, 27.3 mm. **Ruler:** Elizabeth II **Subject:** Christmas **Rev:** Santa Claus **Shape:** 7-sided

Date	Mintage	F12	VF20	XF40	MS60	MS63
2011PM	30,000	—	—	—	—	10.00

KM# 1453.1b 50 PENCE
8.00 g., 0.9167 Gold 0.2343 oz. AGW, 27.3 mm. **Ruler:** Elizabeth II **Subject:** Christmas **Rev:** Santa Claus **Shape:** 7-sided

Date	Mintage	F12	VF20	XF40	MS60	MS63
2011PM proof	250	PF65 500				

KM# 1453.2 50 PENCE
8.00 g., Copper-Nickel, 27.3 mm. **Ruler:** Elizabeth II **Subject:** Christmas **Rev:** Santa Claus in color **Shape:** 7-sided

Date	Mintage	F12	VF20	XF40	MS60	MS63
2011PM	—	—	—	—	—	12.00

KM# 1454 50 PENCE
8.00 g., Copper-Nickel, 27.3 mm. **Ruler:** Elizabeth II **Subject:** Isle of Man Tourist Trophy race **Rev:** Yamaha motorcycle and racer **Shape:** 7-sided

Date	Mintage	F12	VF20	XF40	MS60	MS63
2011PM	—	—	—	—	—	10.00

KM# 1488 50 PENCE
8.00 g., Copper-Nickel, 27.3 mm. **Ruler:** Elizabeth II **Subject:** Diamond Jubilee

Date	Mintage	F12	VF20	XF40	MS60	MS63
2012PM	—	—	—	—	—	6.50

KM# 1491a 50 PENCE
0.925 Silver, 27.3 mm. **Ruler:** Elizabeth II **Subject:** Mark Cavendish **Shape:** 7-sided

Date	Mintage	F12	VF20	XF40	MS60	MS63
2012PM	—	PF65 25.00				

KM# 1492a 50 PENCE
0.925 Silver, 27.3 mm. **Ruler:** Elizabeth II **Subject:** Enduro Motorcucle Sport - Dave Knight **Shape:** 7-Sided

Date	Mintage	F12	VF20	XF40	MS60	MS63
2012PM	—	PF65 25.00				

KM# 1490.1 50 PENCE
8.00 g., Copper-Nickel, 27.3 mm. **Ruler:** Elizabeth II **Subject:**

Christmas **Rev:** Angel in flight

Date	Mintage	F12	VF20	XF40	MS60	MS63
2012PM	Est. 30000	—	—	—	—	10.00

KM# 1490.2 50 PENCE
8.00 g., Copper-Nickel, 27.3 mm. **Ruler:** Elizabeth II **Subject:** Christmas **Rev:** Angel in color **Shape:** 7-sided

Date	Mintage	F12	VF20	XF40	MS60	MS63
2012PM	—	—	—	—	—	10.00

KM# 1490a 50 PENCE
0.925 Silver, 27.3 mm. **Ruler:** Elizabeth II **Rev:** Angel in flight **Shape:** 7-sided

Date	Mintage	F12	VF20	XF40	MS60	MS63
2012PM	—	PF65 25.00				

KM# 1490b 50 PENCE
0.917 Gold AGW, 27.3 mm. **Ruler:** Elizabeth II **Rev:** Angel in flight **Shape:** 7-sided

Date	Mintage	F12	VF20	XF40	MS60	MS63
2012PM	250	PF65 450				

KM# 1491 50 PENCE
8.00 g., 0.925 Copper-Nickel 0.2364 oz., 27.3 mm. **Ruler:** Elizabeth II **Subject:** Mark Cavendish **Shape:** 7-sided

Date	Mintage	F12	VF20	XF40	MS60	MS63
2012PM	—	—	—	—	—	10.00

KM# 1492 50 PENCE
8.00 g., 0.925 Copper-Nickel 0.2364 oz., 27.3 mm. **Ruler:** Elizabeth II **Subject:** Enduro Motorcycle Sport - Dave Knight **Shape:** 7-sided

Date	Mintage	F12	VF20	XF40	MS60	MS63
2012PM	Est. 5000	—	—	—	—	10.00

KM# 1941a 50 PENCE
0.925 Silver, 27.3 mm. **Ruler:** Elizabeth II **Subject:** Mark Cavendish **Shape:** 7-sided

Date	Mintage	F12	VF20	XF40	MS60	MS63
2013PM	—	PF65 25.00				

KM# 1128 60 PENCE
Bi-Metallic, 38.6 mm. **Ruler:** Elizabeth II **Subject:** Euro Currency Converter **Obv:** Head with tiara right **Rev:** Rotating map with cut out arrow revealing the Euro equivalent of the country's currency to which the arrow is pointed **Edge:** Reeded

Date	Mintage	F12	VF20	XF40	MS60	MS63
2002	15,000	—	—	—	20.00	22.50

KM# 1042 POUND
9.50 g., Nickel-Brass, 22.5 mm. **Ruler:** Elizabeth II **Subject:** Millennium Bells **Obv:** Head with tiara right **Rev:** Triskeles and three bells **Edge:** Segmented reeding

Date	Mintage	F12	VF20	XF40	MS60	MS63
2001PM AA	—	—	—	—	4.00	5.00
2002PM AA	—	—	—	—	4.00	5.00
2003PM AA	—	—	—	—	4.00	5.00
2003PM BA	—	—	—	—	4.00	5.00

KM# 1259 POUND
9.50 g., Nickel-Brass, 22.5 mm. **Ruler:** Elizabeth II **Obv:** Head with tiara right **Rev:** St. John's Chapel **Edge:** Segmented reeding

Date	Mintage	F12	VF20	XF40	MS60	MS63
2004PM	—	—	—	—	4.00	5.00
2004PM AA	—	—	—	—	4.00	5.00
2004PM AB	—	—	—	—	4.00	5.00
2004PM AC	—	—	—	—	4.00	5.00
2005PM AA	—	—	—	—	4.00	5.00
2005PM AB	—	—	—	—	4.00	5.00
2006PM AA	—	—	—	—	4.00	5.00
2006PM AB	—	—	—	—	4.00	5.00
2007PM AA	—	—	—	—	4.00	5.00
2007PM BA	—	—	—	—	4.00	5.00
2007PM AB	—	—	—	—	4.00	5.00
2008PM AA	—	—	—	—	4.00	5.00
2008PM BA	—	—	—	—	4.00	5.00
2009PM AA	—	—	—	—	4.00	5.00
2010PM AA	—	—	—	—	4.00	5.00
2011PM AA	—	—	—	—	4.00	5.00
2012PM AA	—	—	—	—	4.00	5.00
2013PM AA	—	—	—	—	—	5.00

KM# 1043 2 POUNDS
12.00 g., Bi-Metallic, 28.4 mm. **Ruler:** Elizabeth II **Subject:** Thorwald's Cross **Obv:** Head with tiara right within beaded circle **Rev:** Ancient drawing within circle **Edge:** Reeded

Date	Mintage	F12	VF20	XF40	MS60	MS63
2001PM AA	—	—	—	—	6.50	7.50
2002PM AA	—	—	—	—	6.50	7.50
2003PM AA	—	—	—	—	6.50	7.50
2003PM AB	—	—	—	—	6.50	7.50

KM# 1260 2 POUNDS
12.00 g., Bi-Metallic, 28.4 mm. **Ruler:** Elizabeth II **Obv:** Head with tiara right **Rev:** Round Tower of Peel Castle **Edge:** Reeded

Date	Mintage	F12	VF20	XF40	MS60	MS63
2004PM AA	—	—	—	—	6.50	7.50
2005PM AA	—	—	—	—	6.50	7.50
2006PM AA	—	—	—	—	6.50	7.50
2007PM AA	—	—	—	—	6.50	7.50
2007PM AB	—	—	—	—	6.50	7.50
2008PM AA	—	—	—	—	6.50	7.50
2009PM AA	—	—	—	—	6.50	7.50
2010PM AA	—	—	—	—	6.50	7.50
2011PM AA	—	—	—	—	6.50	7.50
2012PM AA	—	—	—	—	6.50	7.50

KM# 1476 2 POUNDS
12.00 g., Bi-Metallic, 28.4 mm. **Ruler:** Elizabeth II **Obv:** Head with tiara right **Rev:** Tosha the cat, games mascot and games logo

Date	Mintage	F12	VF20	XF40	MS60	MS63
2011PM	—	—	—	—	6.00	7.50

KM# 1044 5 POUNDS
20.10 g., Virenium, 36.5 mm. **Ruler:** Elizabeth II **Subject:** St. Patrick's Hymn **Obv:** Head with tiara right **Rev:** Stylized cross design **Edge:** Segmented reeding

Date	Mintage	F12	VF20	XF40	MS60	MS63
2001PM AA	—	—	—	—	15.00	16.50
2002PM AA	—	—	—	—	15.00	16.50
2003PM AA	—	—	—	—	15.00	16.50

KM# 1261 5 POUNDS
20.10 g., Virenium, 36 mm. **Ruler:** Elizabeth II **Obv:** Head with tiara right **Rev:** Laxey Wheel **Edge:** Reeded

Date	Mintage	F12	VF20	XF40	MS60	MS63
2004PM AA	—	—	—	—	15.00	16.50
2005PM AA	—	—	—	—	15.00	16.50
2006PM AA	—	—	—	—	15.00	16.50
2007PM AA	—	—	—	—	15.00	16.50
2007PM AB	—	—	—	—	15.00	16.50
2008PM AA	—	—	—	—	15.00	16.50
2009PM AA	—	—	—	—	15.00	16.50
2010PM AA	—	—	—	—	15.00	16.50
2011PM AA	—	—	—	—	15.00	16.50
2012PM AA	—	—	—	—	15.00	16.50

KM# 1494a CROWN
28.28 g., Silver, 38.6 mm. **Ruler:** Elizabeth II **Subject:** St. Patrick

Date	Mintage	F12	VF20	XF40	MS60	MS63
2013	Est. 10000	PF63 45.00		PF65 50.00		

KM# 1494 CROWN
28.28 g., Copper-Nickel, 38.60 mm. **Ruler:** Elizabeth II **Subject:** St. Patrick

Date	Mintage	F12	VF20	XF40	MS60	MS63
2013	—	—	—	—	—	10.00

CROWN SERIES

(M) MATTE - Normal circulation strike
(U) SPECIAL UNCIRCULATED - Polished or prooflike in appearance, slightly frosted features.
(P) PROOF - The highest quality obtainable having mirror-like fields and frosted features.

KM# 1472 1/64 CROWN
0.49 g., 0.9999 Gold AGW **Ruler:** Elizabeth II **Obv:** Bust in tiara right **Rev:** Buckingham Palace

Date	Mintage	F12	VF20	XF40	MS60	MS63
2010PM	—	PF65 50.00				

KM# 1129 1/32 CROWN
1.00 g., 0.972 Gold 0.031 oz. AGW, 9.8 mm. **Ruler:** Elizabeth II **Subject:** Queen's Golden Jubilee **Obv:** Head with tiara right **Rev:** Seated crowned Queen holding sceptre at her coronation **Edge:** Plain

Date	Mintage	F12	VF20	XF40	MS60	MS63
2002 Prooflike	—	—	—	—	—	60.00

KM# 1058 1/25 CROWN
1.24 g., 0.9999 Gold 0.0397 oz. AGW, 13.92 mm. **Ruler:** Elizabeth II **Subject:** Year of the Snake **Obv:** Bust with tiara right **Rev:** Snake **Edge:** Reeded

Date	Mintage	F12	VF20	XF40	MS60	MS63
2001	20,000	PF65 75.00				

KM# 1086 1/25 CROWN
1.24 g., 0.9999 Gold 0.0397 oz. AGW, 13.9 mm. **Ruler:** Elizabeth II **Subject:** Harry Potter **Obv:** Bust with tiara right **Rev:** Boy with magic wand **Edge:** Reeded

Date	Mintage	F12	VF20	XF40	MS60	MS63
2001	10,000	PF65 75.00				

KM# 1088 1/25 CROWN
1.24 g., 0.9999 Gold 0.0397 oz. AGW, 13.9 mm. **Ruler:** Elizabeth II **Series:** Harry Potter **Subject:** Journey to Hogwarts School **Obv:** Bust with tiara right **Rev:** Boat full of children going to Hogwarts School **Edge:** Reeded

Date	Mintage	F12	VF20	XF40	MS60	MS63
2001	10,000	PF65 75.00				

KM# 1090 1/25 CROWN
1.24 g., 0.9999 Gold 0.0397 oz. AGW, 13.9 mm. **Ruler:** Elizabeth II **Series:** Harry Potter **Subject:** First Quidditch Match **Obv:** Bust with tiara right **Rev:** Harry flying a broom **Edge:** Reeded

Date	Mintage	F12	VF20	XF40	MS60	MS63
2001	10,000	PF65 75.00				

KM# 1092 1/25 CROWN
1.24 g., 0.9999 Gold 0.0397 oz. AGW, 13.9 mm. **Ruler:** Elizabeth II **Series:** Harry Potter **Subject:** Birth of Norbert **Obv:** Bust with tiara right **Edge:** Reeded

Date	Mintage	F12	VF20	XF40	MS60	MS63
2001	10,000	PF65 75.00				

KM# 1094 1/25 CROWN
1.24 g., 0.9999 Gold 0.0397 oz. AGW, 13.9 mm. **Ruler:** Elizabeth II **Series:** Harry Potter **Subject:** School **Obv:** Bust with tiara right **Rev:** Harry in Potions class **Edge:** Reeded

Date	Mintage	F12	VF20	XF40	MS60	MS63
2001	10,000	PF65 75.00				

KM# 1096 1/25 CROWN
1.24 g., 0.9999 Gold 0.0397 oz. AGW, 13.9 mm. **Ruler:** Elizabeth II **Series:** Harry Potter **Subject:** Keys **Obv:** Bust with tiara right **Rev:** Harry chasing the golden snitch **Edge:** Reeded

Date	Mintage	F12	VF20	XF40	MS60	MS63
2001	10,000	PF65 75.00				

KM# 1067a 1/25 CROWN
1.24 g., 0.9995 Platinum 0.0397 oz. APW, 13.9 mm. **Ruler:** Elizabeth II **Subject:** Somali Kittens **Obv:** Head with tiara right **Rev:** Two kittens **Edge:** Reeded

Date	Mintage	F12	VF20	XF40	MS60	MS63
2001	—				—	80.00

KM# 1067 1/25 CROWN
1.24 g., 0.9999 Gold 0.0397 oz. AGW, 13.9 mm. **Ruler:** Elizabeth II **Subject:** Somali Kittens **Obv:** Head with tiara right **Rev:** Two kittens **Edge:** Reeded

Date	Mintage	F12	VF20	XF40	MS60	MS63
2001	—			—		72.50
2001	1,000	PF63 75.00	PF65 78.00			

KM# 1098 1/25 CROWN
1.24 g., 0.9999 Gold 0.0397 oz. AGW, 13.9 mm. **Ruler:** Elizabeth II **Subject:** Year of the Horse **Obv:** Bust with tiara right **Rev:** Two horses **Edge:** Reeded

Date	Mintage	F12	VF20	XF40	MS60	MS63
2002	20,000	PF65 75.00				

KM# 1143 1/25 CROWN
1.24 g., 0.9999 Gold 0.0397 oz. AGW, 13.92 mm. **Ruler:** Elizabeth II **Subject:** Harry Potter **Obv:** Bust with tiara right **Rev:** Tom Riddle twirling Harry's magic wand **Edge:** Reeded

Date	Mintage	F12	VF20	XF40	MS60	MS63
2002PM	10,000	PF65 75.00				

KM# 1145 1/25 CROWN
1.24 g., 0.9999 Gold 0.0397 oz. AGW, 13.92 mm. **Ruler:** Elizabeth II **Subject:** Harry Potter Series **Obv:** Bust with tiara right **Rev:** Harry and friends making Polyjuice potion **Edge:** Reeded

Date	Mintage	F12	VF20	XF40	MS60	MS63
2002PM	10,000	PF65 75.00				

KM# 1147 1/25 CROWN
1.24 g., 0.9999 Gold 0.0397 oz. AGW, 13.92 mm. **Ruler:** Elizabeth II **Subject:** Harry Potter **Obv:** Bust with tiara right **Rev:** Harry arrives at the Burrow in a flying car **Edge:** Reeded

Date	Mintage	F12	VF20	XF40	MS60	MS63
2002PM	10,000	PF65 75.00				

KM# 1149 1/25 CROWN
1.24 g., 0.9999 Gold 0.0397 oz. AGW, 13.92 mm. **Ruler:** Elizabeth II **Subject:** Harry Potter Series **Obv:** Bust with tiara right **Rev:** Harry retrieves Gryffindor sword from snake **Edge:** Reeded

Date	Mintage	F12	VF20	XF40	MS60	MS63
2002PM	10,000	PF65 75.00				

KM# 1151 1/25 CROWN
1.22 g., 0.9999 Gold 0.0391 oz. AGW, 13.92 mm. **Ruler:** Elizabeth II **Series:** Harry Potter **Obv:** Bust with tiara right **Rev:** Harry and Ron encounter the spider Aragog **Edge:** Reeded

Date	Mintage	F12	VF20	XF40	MS60	MS63
2002PM	10,000	PF65 75.00				

KM# 1153 1/25 CROWN
1.24 g., 0.9999 Gold 0.0397 oz. AGW, 13.92 mm. **Ruler:** Elizabeth II **Series:** Harry Potter **Obv:** Bust with tiara right **Rev:** Harry in hospital **Edge:** Reeded

Date	Mintage	F12	VF20	XF40	MS60	MS63
2002PM	10,000	PF65 75.00				

KM# 1107a 1/25 CROWN
1.24 g., 0.999 Platinum 0.0397 oz. APW, 13.92 mm. **Ruler:** Elizabeth II **Subject:** Bengal Cat **Obv:** Head with tiara right **Rev:** Cat and kitten **Edge:** Reeded

Date	Mintage	F12	VF20	XF40	MS60	MS63
2002	—	PF65 90.00				

KM# 1107 1/25 CROWN
1.24 g., 0.999 Gold 0.0397 oz. AGW, 13.92 mm. **Ruler:** Elizabeth II **Subject:** Bengal Cat **Obv:** Head with tiara right **Rev:** Cat and kitten **Edge:** Reeded

Date	Mintage	F12	VF20	XF40	MS60	MS63
2002	—				—	80.00
2002	1,000	PF65 85.00				

KM# 1167 1/25 CROWN
1.24 g., 0.9999 Gold 0.0397 oz. AGW, 13.9 mm. **Ruler:** Elizabeth II **Subject:** Year of the Goat **Obv:** Head with tiara right **Rev:** Three goats **Edge:** Reeded

Date	Mintage	F12	VF20	XF40	MS60	MS63
2003PM	20,000	PF65 75.00				

KM# 1186 1/25 CROWN
1.24 g., 0.9999 Gold 0.0397 oz. AGW, 13.9 mm. **Ruler:** Elizabeth II **Subject:** Lord of the Rings **Obv:** Bust with tiara right **Rev:** Frodo Baggins with short sword **Edge:** Reeded

Date	Mintage	F12	VF20	XF40	MS60	MS63
2003PM	6,000	PF65 75.00				

KM# 1161a 1/25 CROWN
1.24 g., 0.9995 Platinum 0.0397 oz. APW, 13.92 mm. **Ruler:** Elizabeth II **Subject:** Cat **Obv:** Head with tiara right **Rev:** Two Balinese kittens **Edge:** Reeded

Date	Mintage	F12	VF20	XF40	MS60	MS63
2003PM	—	PF65 85.00				

KM# 1161 1/25 CROWN
1.24 g., 0.9999 Gold 0.0397 oz. AGW, 13.92 mm. **Ruler:** Elizabeth II **Subject:** Cat **Obv:** Head with tiara right **Rev:** Two Balinese kittens **Edge:** Reeded

Date	Mintage	F12	VF20	XF40	MS60	MS63
2003PM	—					72.50
2003PM	—	PF63 75.00	PF65 78.00			

KM# 1203 1/25 CROWN
1.24 g., 0.9999 Gold 0.0397 oz. AGW, 14 mm. **Ruler:** Elizabeth II **Obv:** Bust with tiara right **Rev:** Harry Potter and patron fighting off a spectre **Edge:** Reeded

Date	Mintage	F12	VF20	XF40	MS60	MS63
2004PM	2,500	PF65 75.00				

KM# 1205 1/25 CROWN
1.24 g., 0.9999 Gold 0.0397 oz. AGW, 14 mm. **Ruler:** Elizabeth II **Obv:** Bust with tiara right **Rev:** Harry Potter in the shrieking shack **Edge:** Reeded

Date	Mintage	F12	VF20	XF40	MS60	MS63
2004PM	2,500	PF65 75.00				

KM# 1207 1/25 CROWN
1.24 g., 0.9999 Gold 0.0397 oz. AGW, 14 mm. **Ruler:** Elizabeth II **Obv:** Bust with tiara right **Rev:** Harry Potter and Professor Dumbledore **Edge:** Reeded

Date	Mintage	F12	VF20	XF40	MS60	MS63
2004PM	2,500	PF65 75.00				

KM# 1209 1/25 CROWN
1.24 g., 0.9999 Gold 0.0397 oz. AGW, 14 mm. **Ruler:** Elizabeth II **Obv:** Bust with tiara right **Rev:** Sirius Black on flying griffin **Edge:** Reeded

Date	Mintage	F12	VF20	XF40	MS60	MS63
2004PM	2,500	PF65 75.00				

KM# 1211 1/25 CROWN
1.24 g., 0.9999 Gold 0.0397 oz. AGW, 14 mm. **Ruler:** Elizabeth II **Obv:** Head with tiara right **Rev:** Three Olympic Swimmers **Edge:** Reeded

Date	Mintage	F12	VF20	XF40	MS60	MS63
2004PM	5,000	PF65 75.00				

KM# 1213 1/25 CROWN
1.24 g., 0.9999 Gold 0.0397 oz. AGW, 14 mm. **Ruler:** Elizabeth II **Obv:** Head with tiara right **Rev:** Three Olympic Cyclists **Edge:** Reeded

Date	Mintage	F12	VF20	XF40	MS60	MS63
2004PM	5,000	PF65 75.00				

KM# 1215 1/25 CROWN
1.24 g., 0.9999 Gold 0.0397 oz. AGW, 14 mm. **Ruler:** Elizabeth II **Obv:** Head with tiara right **Rev:** Three Olympic Runners **Edge:** Reeded

Date	Mintage	F12	VF20	XF40	MS60	MS63
2004PM	5,000	PF65 75.00				

KM# 1217 1/25 CROWN
1.24 g., 0.9999 Gold 0.0397 oz. AGW, 14 mm. **Ruler:** Elizabeth II **Obv:** Head with tiara right **Rev:** Three Olympic Sail Boarders **Edge:** Reeded

Date	Mintage	F12	VF20	XF40	MS60	MS63
2004PM	5,000	PF65 75.00				

KM# 1240 1/25 CROWN
1.24 g., 0.9999 Gold 0.0397 oz. AGW, 14 mm. **Ruler:** Elizabeth II **Obv:** Head with tiara right **Rev:** Monkey **Edge:** Reeded

Date	Mintage	F12	VF20	XF40	MS60	MS63
2004PM	20,000	PF65 75.00				

KM# 1247 1/25 CROWN
1.24 g., 0.9999 Gold 0.0397 oz. AGW, 14 mm. **Ruler:** Elizabeth

II **Obv:** Head with tiara right **Rev:** Two Tonkinese cats **Edge:** Reeded

Date	Mintage	F12	VF20	XF40	MS60	MS63
2004PM	—				—	80.00
2004PM	1,000	PF65 85.00				

KM# 1269 1/25 CROWN
1.24 g., 0.9999 Gold 0.0397 oz. AGW, 13.92 mm. **Ruler:** Elizabeth II **Obv:** Bust with tiara right **Rev:** Himalayan cat and two kittens **Edge:** Reeded

Date	Mintage	F12	VF20	XF40	MS60	MS63
2005PM	—	PF65 75.00				

KM# 1269a 1/25 CROWN
1.24 g., 0.995 Platinum 0.0395 oz. APW, 13.92 mm. **Ruler:** Elizabeth II **Obv:** Bust with tiara right **Rev:** Himalayan cat and two kittens **Edge:** Reeded

Date	Mintage	F12	VF20	XF40	MS60	MS63
2005PM	—	PF65 85.00				

KM# 1340 1/25 CROWN
1.24 g., 0.9999 Gold 0.0397 oz. AGW, 13.92 mm. **Ruler:** Elizabeth II **Obv:** Bust with tiara right **Rev:** Three Exotic Shorthair cats sitting facing **Edge:** Reeded

Date	Mintage	F12	VF20	XF40	MS60	MS63
2006PM	—				—	80.00

KM# 1308 1/25 CROWN
1.24 g., 0.9999 Gold 0.0397 oz. AGW, 13.92 mm. **Ruler:** Elizabeth II **Subject:** 100th Anniversary of Scouting **Obv:** Bust with tiara right **Obv. Legend:** ELIZABETH II - ISLE OF MAN **Rev:** 3/4 length figure of Robert Baden-Powell standing facing 3/4 left, Fleur-de-lys below, images of scouting at left and right **Rev. Legend:** CENTENARY OF SCOUTING **Edge:** Reeded

Date	Mintage	F12	VF20	XF40	MS60	MS63
2007PM	—	PF65 75.00				

KM# 1314 1/25 CROWN
1.24 g., 0.9999 Gold 0.0396 oz. AGW, 13.92 mm. **Ruler:** Elizabeth II **Obv:** Bust with tiara right **Obv. Legend:** ELIZABETH II - ISLE OF MAN **Rev:** Two swans facing **Edge:** Reeded

Date	Mintage	F12	VF20	XF40	MS60	MS63
2007	10,000	PF65 75.00				

KM# 1343 1/25 CROWN
1.24 g., 0.9999 Gold 0.0397 oz. AGW, 13.92 mm. **Ruler:** Elizabeth II **Obv:** Bust with tiara right **Obv. Legend:** ELIZABETH II - ISLE OF MAN **Rev:** Ragdoll cat with two kittens sitting facing **Edge:** Reeded

Date	Mintage	F12	VF20	XF40	MS60	MS63
2007PM	—				—	80.00

KM# 1349 1/25 CROWN
1.24 g., 0.9999 Gold 0.0397 oz. AGW, 13.92 mm. **Ruler:** Elizabeth II **Subject:** The Tale of Peter Rabbit **Obv:** Bust with tiara right **Obv. Legend:** ELIZABETH II - ISLE OF MAN **Rev:** Peter walking with friends **Edge:** Reeded

Date	Mintage	F12	VF20	XF40	MS60	MS63
2007PM	—				—	72.50

KM# 1387 1/25 CROWN
1.24 g., 0.995 Platinum 0.0394 oz. APW, 13.92 mm. **Ruler:** Elizabeth II **Obv:** Bust right **Rev:** Chinchilla cat and kitten

Date	Mintage	F12	VF20	XF40	MS60	MS63
2009	—					85.00

KM# 1383 1/25 CROWN
1.24 g., 0.9999 Gold 0.0396 oz. AGW, 13.92 mm. **Ruler:** Elizabeth II **Obv:** Bust right **Rev:** Chinchilla cat and kitten

Date	Mintage	F12	VF20	XF40	MS60	MS63
2009	—					80.00
2009	1,000	PF63 85.00	PF65 90.00			

KM# 1473 1/25 CROWN
1.24 g., 0.999 Gold 0.0396 oz. AGW, 13.92 mm. **Ruler:** Elizabeth II **Subject:** George F. Handel, 325th Anniversary of Birth **Obv:** Bust in tiara right **Rev:** Handel bust, music score in background

Date	Mintage	F12	VF20	XF40	MS60	MS63
2010PM	—	PF65 100				

KM# 1435 1/25 CROWN
1.24 g., 0.9999 Gold 0.0396 oz. AGW, 13.92 mm. **Ruler:** Elizabeth II **Subject:** Turkish Angora cat

Date	Mintage	F12	VF20	XF40	MS60	MS63
2011PM	1,000	PF63 105	PF65 115			
2011PM	—	—	—	—	—	100

KM# 1059 1/10 CROWN
3.11 g., 0.9999 Gold 0.0993 oz. AGW, 17.95 mm. **Ruler:** Elizabeth II **Subject:** Year of the Snake **Obv:** Bust with tiara right **Rev:** Snake **Edge:** Reeded

Date	Mintage	F12	VF20	XF40	MS60	MS63
2001	15,000	PF65 180				

KM# 1328 1/10 CROWN
3.11 g., 0.999 Gold 0.0992 oz. AGW, 18 mm. **Ruler:** Elizabeth II **Subject:** Harry Potter **Obv:** Bust right **Rev:** Boy with magic wand **Edge:** Reeded

Date	Mintage	F12	VF20	XF40	MS60	MS63
2001	7,500	PF63 175	PF65 180			

KM# 1329 1/10 CROWN
3.11 g., 0.999 Gold 0.0992 oz. AGW, 18 mm. **Ruler:** Elizabeth II **Subject:** Harry Potter - Journey to Hogwarts **Obv:** Bust right **Rev:** Boat full of children going to Hogwarts School **Edge:** Reeded

Date	Mintage	F12	VF20	XF40	MS60	MS63
2001	7,500	PF63 175	PF65 180			

KM# 1330 1/10 CROWN
3.11 g., 0.999 Gold 0.0992 oz. AGW, 18 mm. **Ruler:** Elizabeth II **Subject:** Harry Potter **Obv:** Bust right **Rev:** Harry flying on a broomstick **Edge:** Reeded

Date	Mintage	F12	VF20	XF40	MS60	MS63
2001	7,500	PF63 175	PF65 180			

KM# 1331 1/10 CROWN
3.11 g., 0.999 Gold 0.0992 oz. AGW, 18 mm. **Ruler:** Elizabeth II **Subject:** Harry Potter **Obv:** Bust right **Rev:** Birth of Norbert the dragon **Edge:** Reeded

Date	Mintage	F12	VF20	XF40	MS60	MS63
2001	7,500	PF63 175	PF65 180			

KM# 1332 1/10 CROWN
3.11 g., 0.999 Gold 0.0992 oz. AGW, 18 mm. **Ruler:** Elizabeth II **Subject:** Harry Potter **Obv:** Bust right **Rev:** Harry in Potions class **Edge:** Reeded

Date	Mintage	F12	VF20	XF40	MS60	MS63
2001	7,500	PF63 175	PF65 180			

KM# 1333 1/10 CROWN
3.11 g., 0.999 Gold 0.0992 oz. AGW, 18 mm. **Ruler:** Elizabeth II **Subject:** Harry Potter **Obv:** Bust right **Rev:** Harry chasing a snitch **Edge:** Reeded

Date	Mintage	F12	VF20	XF40	MS60	MS63
2001	7,500	PF63 175	PF65 180			

KM# 1068a 1/10 CROWN
3.11 g., 0.9995 Platinum 0.0993 oz. APW, 18 mm. **Ruler:** Elizabeth II **Obv:** Head with tiara right **Rev:** Somali kittens **Edge:** Reeded

Date	Mintage	F12	VF20	XF40	MS60	MS63
2001	—	PF65 200				

KM# 1068 1/10 CROWN
3.11 g., 0.9999 Gold 0.0993 oz. AGW, 18 mm. **Ruler:** Elizabeth II **Obv:** Head with tiara right **Rev:** Somali kittens **Edge:** Reeded

Date	Mintage	F12	VF20	XF40	MS60	MS63
2001	—	—	—	—	—	175
2001	1,000	PF63 180	PF65 185			

KM# 1099 1/10 CROWN
3.11 g., 0.9999 Gold 0.0993 oz. AGW, 17.95 mm. **Ruler:** Elizabeth II **Subject:** Year of the Horse **Obv:** Bust with tiara right **Rev:** Two horses **Edge:** Reeded

Date	Mintage	F12	VF20	XF40	MS60	MS63
2002	15,000	PF65 180				

KM# 1155 1/10 CROWN
3.11 g., 0.999 Gold 0.0992 oz. AGW, 17.95 mm. **Ruler:** Elizabeth II **Subject:** Queen's Golden Jubilee **Obv:** Queen's portrait **Rev:** Queen on horse **Edge:** Reeded

Date	Mintage	F12	VF20	XF40	MS60	MS63
2002PM	500	PF65 180				

KM# 1108 1/10 CROWN
3.11 g., 0.999 Gold 0.0992 oz. AGW, 17.95 mm. **Ruler:** Elizabeth II **Subject:** Bengal Cat **Obv:** Head with tiara right **Rev:** Cat and kitten **Edge:** Reeded

Date	Mintage	VG8	F12	VF20	XF40	MS60
2002	—	—	—	—	—	185
2002	—	PF65 190				

KM# 1108a 1/10 CROWN
3.11 g., 0.999 Platinum 0.0992 oz. APW, 17.95 mm. **Ruler:** Elizabeth II **Subject:** Bengal Cat **Obv:** Head with tiara right **Rev:** Cat and kitten **Edge:** Reeded

Date	Mintage	F12	VF20	XF40	MS60	MS63
2002	—	—	—	—	—	195

KM# 1168 1/10 CROWN
3.11 g., 0.9999 Gold 0.0993 oz. AGW, 17.95 mm. **Ruler:** Elizabeth II **Subject:** Year of the Goat **Obv:** Bust with tiara right **Rev:** Three goats **Edge:** Reeded

Date	Mintage	F12	VF20	XF40	MS60	MS63
2003PM	—	PF65 180				

KM# 1187 1/10 CROWN
3.11 g., 0.9999 Gold 0.0993 oz. AGW, 18 mm. **Ruler:** Elizabeth II **Subject:** Lord of the Rings **Obv:** Bust with tiara right **Rev:** Aragorn with broad sword **Edge:** Reeded

Date	Mintage	F12	VF20	XF40	MS60	MS63
2003PM	4,500	PF65 180				

KM# 1162a 1/10 CROWN
3.11 g., 0.9995 Platinum 0.0993 oz. APW, 17.95 mm. **Ruler:** Elizabeth II **Subject:** Cat **Obv:** Head with tiara right **Rev:** Two Balinese kittens **Edge:** Reeded

Date	Mintage	F12	VF20	XF40	MS60	MS63
2003PM	—	—	—	—	—	190

KM# 1162 1/10 CROWN
3.11 g., 0.9999 Gold 0.0993 oz. AGW, 17.95 mm. **Ruler:** Elizabeth II **Subject:** Cat **Obv:** Head with tiara right **Rev:** Two Balinese kittens **Edge:** Reeded

Date	Mintage	F12	VF20	XF40	MS60	MS63
2003PM	—	—	—	—	—	175
2003PM	—	PF63 180	PF65 185			

KM# 1241 1/10 CROWN
3.11 g., 0.9999 Gold 0.0993 oz. AGW, 18 mm. **Ruler:** Elizabeth II **Obv:** Head with tiara right **Rev:** Monkey **Edge:** Reeded

Date	Mintage	F12	VF20	XF40	MS60	MS63
2004PM	15,000	PF65 180				

KM# 1248 1/10 CROWN
3.11 g., 0.9999 Gold 0.0993 oz. AGW, 18 mm. **Ruler:** Elizabeth II **Obv:** Head with tiara right **Rev:** Two Tonkinese cats **Edge:** Reeded

Date	Mintage	F12	VF20	XF40	MS60	MS63
2004PM	—	—	—	—	—	185
2004PM	1,000	PF63 190	PF65 195			

KM# 1270 1/10 CROWN
3.11 g., 0.9999 Gold 0.0993 oz. AGW, 18 mm. **Ruler:** Elizabeth II **Obv:** Bust with tiara right **Rev:** Himalayan cat and two kittens **Edge:** Reeded

Date	Mintage	F12	VF20	XF40	MS60	MS63
2005PM	—	PF65 190				

KM# 1270a 1/10 CROWN
3.11 g., 0.995 Platinum 0.0988 oz. APW, 18 mm. **Ruler:** Elizabeth II **Obv:** Queen Elizabeth II **Rev:** Himalayan cat and two kittens **Edge:** Reeded

Date	Mintage	F12	VF20	XF40	MS60	MS63
2005PM	—	PF65 200				

KM# 1341 1/10 CROWN
3.11 g., 0.9999 Gold 0.0993 oz. AGW, 18 mm. **Ruler:** Elizabeth II **Obv:** Bust with tiara right **Rev:** Three Exotic Shorthair cats sitting facing **Edge:** Reeded

Date	Mintage	F12	VF20	XF40	MS60	MS63
2006PM	—	—	—	—	—	180

KM# 1344 1/10 CROWN
3.11 g., 0.9999 Gold 0.0993 oz. AGW, 18 mm. **Ruler:** Elizabeth II **Obv:** Bust with tiara right **Obv. Legend:** ELIZABETH II - ISLE OF MAN **Rev:** Ragdoll cat with two kittens sitting facing **Edge:** Reeded

Date	Mintage	F12	VF20	XF40	MS60	MS63
2007PM	—	—	—	—	—	185

KM# 1350 1/10 CROWN
3.11 g., 0.9999 Gold 0.0993 oz. AGW, 18 mm. **Ruler:** Elizabeth II **Subject:** The Tale of Peter Rabbit **Obv:** Bust with tiara right **Obv. Legend:** ELIZABETH II - ISLE OF MAN **Rev:** Peter walking with friends **Edge:** Reeded

Date	Mintage	F12	VF20	XF40	MS60	MS63
2007PM	—	—	—	—	—	175

KM# 1382 1/10 CROWN
3.11 g., 0.9999 Gold 0.0993 oz. AGW, 18 mm. **Ruler:** Elizabeth II **Obv:** Bust right **Rev:** Chinchilla cat and kitten

Date	Mintage	F12	VF20	XF40	MS60	MS63
2009	—	—	—	—	—	185
2009	1,000	PF63 190	PF65 195			

KM# 1386 1/10 CROWN
3.11 g., 0.995 Platinum 0.0988 oz. APW, 18 mm. **Ruler:** Elizabeth II **Obv:** Bust right **Rev:** Chinchilla cat and kitten

Date	Mintage	F12	VF20	XF40	MS60	MS63
2009	—	—	—	—	—	190

KM# 1436 1/10 CROWN
3.11 g., 0.9999 Gold 0.0993 oz. AGW, 18 mm. **Ruler:** Elizabeth II **Subject:** Turkish Angora Cat

Date	Mintage	F12	VF20	XF40	MS60	MS63
2011PM	1,000	PF63 230	PF65 240			
2011PM	—	—	—	—	—	225

KM# 1060 1/5 CROWN
6.22 g., 0.9999 Gold 0.1987 oz. AGW, 22 mm. **Ruler:** Elizabeth II **Subject:** Year of the Snake **Obv:** Bust with tiara right **Rev:** Snake **Edge:** Reeded

Date	Mintage	F12	VF20	XF40	MS60	MS63
2001	12,000	PF65 355				

KM# 1074 1/5 CROWN
6.22 g., 0.9999 Gold 0.1987 oz. AGW, 22 mm. **Ruler:** Elizabeth II **Subject:** Queen Mother **Obv:** Head with tiara right **Rev:** 1948 Silver wedding anniversary **Edge:** Reeded

Date	Mintage	F12	VF20	XF40	MS60	MS63
2001	5,000	PF63 355	PF65 360			

KM# 1075 1/5 CROWN
6.22 g., 0.9999 Gold 0.1987 oz. AGW, 22 mm. **Ruler:** Elizabeth II **Subject:** Queen Mother **Obv:** Head with tiara right **Rev:** 1948 holding baby Prince Charles **Edge:** Reeded

Date	Mintage	F12	VF20	XF40	MS60	MS63
2001	5,000	PF63 355	PF65 360			

KM# 1078 1/5 CROWN
6.22 g., 0.9999 Gold 0.1987 oz. AGW, 22 mm. **Ruler:** Elizabeth II **Subject:** Martin Frobisher **Obv:** Head with tiara right **Rev:** Portrait, ship and map **Edge:** Reeded

Date	Mintage	F12	VF20	XF40	MS60	MS63
2001	5,000	PF63 355	PF65 360			

KM# 1079 1/5 CROWN
6.22 g., 0.9999 Gold 0.1987 oz. AGW, 22 mm. **Ruler:** Elizabeth II **Subject:** Ronald Amundsen **Obv:** Head with tiara right **Rev:** Portrait, ship and dirigible **Edge:** Reeded

Date	Mintage	F12	VF20	XF40	MS60	MS63
2001	5,000	PF63 355	PF65 360			

KM# 1082 1/5 CROWN
6.22 g., 0.9999 Gold 0.1987 oz. AGW, 22 mm. **Ruler:** Elizabeth II **Subject:** Queen's 75th Birthday **Obv:** Head with tiara right **Rev:** Flower bouquet with a tiny diamond mounted on the bow of the ribbon **Edge:** Reeded

Date	Mintage	F12	VF20	XF40	MS60	MS63
2001	2,000	PF63 355	PF65 360			

KM# 1334 1/5 CROWN
6.15 g., 0.999 Gold 0.1963 oz. AGW, 22 mm. **Ruler:** Elizabeth II **Subject:** Harry Potter **Obv:** Bust right **Rev:** Harry with magic wand **Edge:** Reeded

Date	Mintage	F12	VF20	XF40	MS60	MS63
2001	5,000	PF63 355	PF65 360			

KM# 1335 1/5 CROWN
6.15 g., 0.999 Gold 0.1963 oz. AGW, 22 mm. **Ruler:** Elizabeth II **Subject:** Harry Potter - Journey to Hogwarts School **Obv:** Bust right **Rev:** Boat full of children going to Hogwarts School **Edge:** Reeded

Date	Mintage	F12	VF20	XF40	MS60	MS63
2001	5,000	PF63 355	PF65 360			

KM# 1336 1/5 CROWN
6.15 g., 0.999 Gold 0.1963 oz. AGW, 22 mm. **Ruler:** Elizabeth II **Subject:** Harry Potter - First Quidditch Match **Obv:** Bust right **Rev:** Harry flying a broom in a quidditch match **Edge:** Reeded

Date	Mintage	F12	VF20	XF40	MS60	MS63
2001	5,000	PF63 355	PF65 360			

KM# 1337 1/5 CROWN
6.15 g., 0.999 Gold 0.1963 oz. AGW, 22 mm. **Ruler:** Elizabeth II **Subject:** Harry Potter **Obv:** Bust right **Rev:** Birth of Norbert, the dragon **Edge:** Reeded

Date	Mintage	F12	VF20	XF40	MS60	MS63
2001	5,000	PF63 355	PF65 360			

KM# 1338 1/5 CROWN
6.15 g., 0.999 Gold 0.1963 oz. AGW, 22 mm. **Ruler:** Elizabeth II **Subject:** Harry Potter **Obv:** Bust right **Rev:** Harry in Potions class **Edge:** Reeded

Date	Mintage	F12	VF20	XF40	MS60	MS63
2001	5,000	PF63 355	PF65 360			

KM# 1339 1/5 CROWN
6.15 g., 0.999 Gold 0.1963 oz. AGW, 22 mm. **Ruler:** Elizabeth

II **Subject:** Harry Potter **Obv:** Bust right **Rev:** Harry chasing a jeweled snitch **Edge:** Reeded

Date	Mintage	F12	VF20	XF40	MS60	MS63
2001	5,000	PF63 355		PF65 360		

KM# 1069a 1/5 CROWN
6.22 g., 0.9995 Platinum 0.1986 oz. APW, 22 mm. **Ruler:** Elizabeth II **Obv:** Head with tiara right **Rev:** Somali kittens **Edge:** Reeded

Date	Mintage	F12	VF20	XF40	MS60	MS63
2001	—	—	—	—	—	400

KM# 1069 1/5 CROWN
6.22 g., 0.9999 Gold 0.1987 oz. AGW, 22 mm. **Ruler:** Elizabeth II **Obv:** Head with tiara right **Rev:** Two Somali kittens **Edge:** Reeded

Date	Mintage	F12	VF20	XF40	MS60	MS63
2001	—	—	—	—	—	350
2001	1,000	PF63 355		PF65 360		

KM# 1117 1/5 CROWN
6.22 g., 0.999 Gold 0.1985 oz. AGW, 22 mm. **Ruler:** Elizabeth II **Subject:** Queen Mother's Love of Horses **Obv:** Bust with tiara right **Rev:** Queen Mother and horse **Edge:** Reeded

Date	Mintage	F12	VF20	XF40	MS60	MS63
2002	5,000	PF63 355		PF65 360		

KM# 1156 1/5 CROWN
6.22 g., 0.999 Gold 0.1985 oz. AGW, 22 mm. **Ruler:** Elizabeth II **Subject:** Queen's Golden Jubilee **Obv:** Queen's portrait **Rev:** Queen on horse **Edge:** Reeded

Date	Mintage	F12	VF20	XF40	MS60	MS63
2002PM	500	PF65 355				

KM# 1109 1/5 CROWN
6.22 g., 0.999 Gold 0.1985 oz. AGW, 22 mm. **Ruler:** Elizabeth II **Subject:** Bengal Cat **Obv:** Head with tiara right **Rev:** Cat and kitten **Edge:** Reeded

Date	Mintage	VG8	F12	VF20	XF40	MS60
2002	—	—	—	—	—	
2002	1,000	PF63 385		PF65 400		

KM# 1109a 1/5 CROWN
6.22 g., 0.999 Platinum 0.1985 oz. APW, 22 mm. **Ruler:** Elizabeth II **Subject:** Bengal Cat **Obv:** Head with tiara right **Rev:** Cat and kitten **Edge:** Reeded

Date	Mintage	F12	VF20	XF40	MS60	MS63
2002	—	—	—	—	—	400

KM# 1100 1/5 CROWN
6.22 g., 0.9999 Gold 0.1987 oz. AGW, 22 mm. **Ruler:** Elizabeth II **Subject:** Year of the Horse **Obv:** Bust with tiara right **Rev:** Two horses **Edge:** Reeded

Date	Mintage	F12	VF20	XF40	MS60	MS63
2002	12,000	PF65 355				

KM# 1113 1/5 CROWN
6.22 g., 0.999 Gold 0.1985 oz. AGW, 22 mm. **Ruler:** Elizabeth II **Subject:** Olympics - Salt Lake City **Obv:** Bust with tiara right **Rev:** Skier, torch and flag **Edge:** Reeded

Date	Mintage	F12	VF20	XF40	MS60	MS63
2002	5,000	PF63 355		PF65 360		

KM# 1114 1/5 CROWN
6.22 g., 0.999 Gold 0.1985 oz. AGW, 22 mm. **Ruler:** Elizabeth II **Subject:** Olympics - Salt Lake City **Obv:** Bust with tiara right **Rev:** Bobsled, torch and stadium **Edge:** Reeded

Date	Mintage	F12	VF20	XF40	MS60	MS63
2002	5,000	PF63 355		PF65 360		

KM# 1120 1/5 CROWN
6.22 g., 0.999 Gold 0.1985 oz. AGW, 22 mm. **Ruler:** Elizabeth II **Subject:** World Cup 2002 Japan - Korea **Obv:** Bust with tiara right **Rev:** Player running right **Edge:** Reeded

Date	Mintage	F12	VF20	XF40	MS60	MS63
2002	5,000	PF63 355		PF65 360		

KM# 1122 1/5 CROWN
6.22 g., 0.999 Gold 0.1985 oz. AGW, 22 mm. **Ruler:** Elizabeth II **Subject:** World Cup 2002 Japan - Korea **Obv:** Bust with tiara right **Rev:** Player kicking to right **Edge:** Reeded

Date	Mintage	F12	VF20	XF40	MS60	MS63
2002	5,000	PF63 355		PF65 360		

KM# 1124 1/5 CROWN
6.22 g., 0.999 Gold 0.1985 oz. AGW, 22 mm. **Ruler:** Elizabeth II **Subject:** World Cup 2002 Japan - Korea **Obv:** Head with tiara right **Rev:** Player kicking to left **Edge:** Reeded

Date	Mintage	F12	VF20	XF40	MS60	MS63
2002	5,000	PF63 355		PF65 360		

KM# 1126 1/5 CROWN
6.22 g., 0.999 Gold 0.1985 oz. AGW, 22 mm. **Ruler:** Elizabeth II **Subject:** World Cup 2002 Japan - Korea **Obv:** Head with tiara right **Rev:** Player running to left **Edge:** Reeded

Date	Mintage	F12	VF20	XF40	MS60	MS63
2002	5,000	PF63 355		PF65 360		

KM# 1130 1/5 CROWN
6.22 g., 0.375 Gold 0.0745 oz. AGW, 22 mm. **Ruler:** Elizabeth II **Subject:** Elizabeth II's Golden Jubilee **Obv:** Bust with tiara right **Rev:** Seated crowned Queen holding scepter at her coronation **Edge:** Reeded

Date	Mintage	F12	VF20	XF40	MS60	MS63
2002	2,002	PF65 140				

KM# 1132 1/5 CROWN
6.22 g., 0.375 Gold 0.0745 oz. AGW, 22 mm. **Ruler:** Elizabeth II **Subject:** Elizabeth II's Golden Jubilee **Obv:** Bust with tiara right **Rev:** Queen on horse **Edge:** Reeded

Date	Mintage	F12	VF20	XF40	MS60	MS63
2002	2,002	PF65 140				

KM# 1134 1/5 CROWN
6.22 g., 0.375 Gold 0.0745 oz. AGW, 22 mm. **Ruler:** Elizabeth II **Subject:** Elizabeth II's Golden Jubilee **Obv:** Head with tiara right **Rev:** Queen with dog **Edge:** Reeded

Date	Mintage	F12	VF20	XF40	MS60	MS63
2002	2,002	PF65 140				

KM# 1136 1/5 CROWN
6.22 g., 0.375 Gold 0.0745 oz. AGW, 22 mm. **Ruler:** Elizabeth II **Subject:** Elizabeth II's Golden Jubilee **Obv:** Bust with tiara right **Rev:** Queen at war memorial **Edge:** Reeded

Date	Mintage	F12	VF20	XF40	MS60	MS63
2002	2,002	PF65 140				

KM# 1138 1/5 CROWN
6.22 g., 0.999 Gold 0.1985 oz. AGW, 22 mm. **Ruler:** Elizabeth II **Subject:** Queen Mother **Obv:** Bust with tiara right **Rev:** Queen Mother and Castle May **Edge:** Reeded

Date	Mintage	F12	VF20	XF40	MS60	MS63
2002	5,000	PF63 355		PF65 360		

KM# 1140 1/5 CROWN
6.22 g., 0.9999 Gold 0.1987 oz. AGW, 22 mm. **Ruler:** Elizabeth II **Subject:** Princess Diana **Obv:** Bust with tiara right **Rev:** Diana's portrait **Edge:** Reeded

Date	Mintage	F12	VF20	XF40	MS60	MS63
2002	—	PF63 355		PF65 360		

KM# 1169 1/5 CROWN
6.22 g., 0.9999 Gold 0.1987 oz. AGW, 22 mm. **Ruler:** Elizabeth II **Subject:** Year of the Goat **Obv:** Bust with tiara right **Rev:** Three goats **Edge:** Reeded

Date	Mintage	F12	VF20	XF40	MS60	MS63
2003PM	—	PF65 355				

KM# 1175 1/5 CROWN
6.22 g., 0.9999 Gold 0.1987 oz. AGW, 22 mm. **Ruler:** Elizabeth II **Subject:** Olympics **Obv:** Bust with tiara right **Rev:** Swimmers **Edge:** Reeded

Date	Mintage	F12	VF20	XF40	MS60	MS63
2003PM	5,000	PF63 355		PF65 360		

KM# 1177 1/5 CROWN
6.22 g., 0.9999 Gold 0.1987 oz. AGW, 22 mm. **Ruler:** Elizabeth II **Subject:** Olympics **Obv:** Bust with tiara right **Rev:** Runners **Edge:** Reeded

Date	Mintage	F12	VF20	XF40	MS60	MS63
2003PM	5,000	PF63 355		PF65 360		

KM# 1179 1/5 CROWN
6.22 g., 0.9999 Gold 0.1987 oz. AGW, 22 mm. **Ruler:** Elizabeth II **Subject:** Olympics **Obv:** Bust with tiara right **Rev:** Bicyclists **Edge:** Reeded

Date	Mintage	F12	VF20	XF40	MS60	MS63
2003PM	5,000	PF63 355		PF65 360		

KM# 1181 1/5 CROWN
6.22 g., 0.9999 Gold 0.1987 oz. AGW, 22 mm. **Ruler:** Elizabeth II **Subject:** Olympics **Obv:** Head with tiara right **Rev:** Sail Boarders **Edge:** Reeded

Date	Mintage	F12	VF20	XF40	MS60	MS63
2003PM	—	PF63 355		PF65 360		

KM# 1188 1/5 CROWN
6.22 g., 0.9999 Gold 0.1987 oz. AGW, 22 mm. **Ruler:** Elizabeth

II **Subject:** Lord of the Rings **Obv:** Bust with tiara right **Rev:** Legolas with bow and arrow **Edge:** Reeded

Date	Mintage	F12	VF20	XF40	MS60	MS63
2003PM	3,500	PF65 355				

KM# 1163a 1/5 CROWN
6.22 g., 0.9995 Platinum 0.1986 oz. APW, 22 mm. **Ruler:** Elizabeth II **Subject:** Cat **Obv:** Head with tiara right **Rev:** Two Balinese kittens **Edge:** Reeded

Date	Mintage	F12	VF20	XF40	MS60	MS63
2003PM	—	—	—	—	—	385

KM# 1163 1/5 CROWN
6.22 g., 0.9999 Gold 0.1987 oz. AGW, 22 mm. **Ruler:** Elizabeth II **Subject:** Cat **Obv:** Head with tiara right **Rev:** Two Balinese kittens **Edge:** Reeded

Date	Mintage	F12	VF20	XF40	MS60	MS63
2003PM	—	—	—	—	—	350
2003PM	—	PF63 355		PF65 360		

KM# 1198 1/5 CROWN
6.22 g., 0.999 Palladium 0.1985 oz. APW, 22 mm. **Ruler:** Elizabeth II **Subject:** Palladium Bicentennial **Obv:** Head with tiara right **Rev:** Athena **Edge:** Reeded

Date	Mintage	F12	VF20	XF40	MS60	MS63
2004PM	999	PF65 175				

KM# 1223 1/5 CROWN
6.22 g., 0.9999 Gold 0.1987 oz. AGW, 22 mm. **Ruler:** Elizabeth II **Obv:** Bust with tiara right **Rev:** D-Day Invasion Plan Map **Edge:** Reeded

Date	Mintage	F12	VF20	XF40	MS60	MS63
2004PM	5,000	PF63 355		PF65 360		

KM# 1225 1/5 CROWN
6.22 g., 0.9999 Gold 0.1987 oz. AGW, 22 mm. **Ruler:** Elizabeth II **Obv:** Bust with tiara right **Rev:** Victoria Cross and battle scene **Edge:** Reeded

Date	Mintage	F12	VF20	XF40	MS60	MS63
2004PM	5,000	PF63 355		PF65 360		

KM# 1227 1/5 CROWN
6.22 g., 0.9999 Gold 0.1987 oz. AGW, 22 mm. **Ruler:** Elizabeth II **Obv:** Bust with tiara right **Rev:** Silver Star and battle scene **Edge:** Reeded

Date	Mintage	F12	VF20	XF40	MS60	MS63
2004PM	5,000	PF63 355		PF65 360		

KM# 1229 1/5 CROWN
6.22 g., 0.9999 Gold 0.1987 oz. AGW, 22 mm. **Ruler:** Elizabeth II **Obv:** Bust with tiara right **Rev:** George Cross and rescue scene **Edge:** Reeded

Date	Mintage	F12	VF20	XF40	MS60	MS63
2004PM	5,000	PF63 355		PF65 360		

KM# 1231 1/5 CROWN
6.22 g., 0.9999 Gold 0.1987 oz. AGW, 22 mm. **Ruler:** Elizabeth II **Obv:** Bust with tiara right **Rev:** White Rose of Finland Medal and battle scene **Edge:** Reeded

Date	Mintage	F12	VF20	XF40	MS60	MS63
2004PM	5,000	PF63 355		PF65 360		

KM# 1233 1/5 CROWN
6.22 g., 0.9999 Gold 0.1987 oz. AGW, 22 mm. **Ruler:** Elizabeth II **Obv:** Bust with tiara right **Rev:** The Norwegian War Medal and naval battle scene **Edge:** Reeded

Date	Mintage	F12	VF20	XF40	MS60	MS63
2004PM	5,000	PF63 355		PF65 360		

KM# 1235 1/5 CROWN
6.22 g., 0.9999 Gold 0.1987 oz. AGW, 22 mm. **Ruler:** Elizabeth II **Obv:** Bust with tiara right **Rev:** French Croix de Guerre and Partisan battle scene **Edge:** Reeded

Date	Mintage	F12	VF20	XF40	MS60	MS63
2004PM	5,000	PF63 355		PF65 360		

KM# 1249.1 1/5 CROWN
6.22 g., 0.9999 Gold 0.1987 oz. AGW, 22 mm. **Ruler:** Elizabeth II **Obv:** Head with tiara right **Rev:** Two Tonkinese cats **Edge:** Reeded

Date	Mintage	F12	VF20	XF40	MS60	MS63
2004PM	1,000	PF63 375		PF65 380		
2004PM	—	—	—	—	—	370

KM# 1249.2 1/5 CROWN
6.22 g., 0.9999 Gold 0.1987 oz. AGW, 22 mm. **Ruler:** Elizabeth II **Obv:** Head with tiara right **Rev:** Two multicolor Tonkinese cats **Edge:** Reeded

Date	Mintage	F12	VF20	XF40	MS60	MS63
2004PM	—	PF63 375		PF65 380		

KM# 1271.1 1/5 CROWN
6.22 g., 0.9999 Gold 0.1987 oz. AGW, 22 mm. **Ruler:** Elizabeth II **Rev:** Two cats, colored

Date	Mintage	F12	VF20	XF40	MS60	MS63
2004	—					

KM# 1271 1/5 CROWN
6.22 g., 0.9999 Gold 0.1987 oz. AGW, 22 mm. **Ruler:** Elizabeth II **Obv:** Bust with tiara right **Rev:** Himalayan cat and two kittens **Edge:** Reeded

Date	Mintage	F12	VF20	XF40	MS60	MS63
2005PM	—	PF65 375				

KM# 1271a 1/5 CROWN
6.22 g., 0.995 Platinum 0.1977 oz. APW, 22 mm. **Ruler:** Elizabeth II **Obv:** Bust with tiara right **Rev:** Himalayan cat and two kittens **Edge:** Reeded

Date	Mintage	F12	VF20	XF40	MS60	MS63
2005PM	—				PF65 390	

KM# 1295 1/5 CROWN
6.22 g., 0.9999 Gold 0.1987 oz. AGW, 22 mm. **Ruler:** Elizabeth II **Subject:** Battles that Changed the World **Obv:** Elizabeth II **Rev:** Trojan War scene **Edge:** Reeded

Date	Mintage	F12	VF20	XF40	MS60	MS63
2006PM	5,000	PF63 355			PF65 360	

KM# 1297 1/5 CROWN
6.22 g., 0.9999 Gold 0.1987 oz. AGW, 22 mm. **Ruler:** Elizabeth II **Subject:** Battles that Changed the World **Obv:** Elizabeth II **Rev:** Battle of Arbela scene **Edge:** Reeded

Date	Mintage	F12	VF20	XF40	MS60	MS63
2006PM	5,000	PF63 355			PF65 360	

KM# 1299 1/5 CROWN
6.22 g., 0.9999 Gold 0.1987 oz. AGW, 22 mm. **Ruler:** Elizabeth II **Subject:** Battles that Changed the World **Obv:** Elizabeth II **Rev:** Battle of Thapsus scene **Edge:** Reeded

Date	Mintage	F12	VF20	XF40	MS60	MS63
2006PM	5,000	PF63 355			PF65 360	

KM# 1301 1/5 CROWN
6.22 g., 0.9999 Gold 0.1987 oz. AGW, 22 mm. **Ruler:** Elizabeth II **Subject:** Battles that Changed the World **Obv:** Elizabeth II **Rev:** Battle of Cologne scene **Edge:** Reeded

Date	Mintage	F12	VF20	XF40	MS60	MS63
2006PM	5,000	PF63 355			PF65 360	

KM# 1303 1/5 CROWN
6.22 g., 0.9999 Gold 0.1987 oz. AGW, 22 mm. **Ruler:** Elizabeth II **Subject:** Battles that Changed the World **Obv:** Elizabeth II **Rev:** Siege of Valencia scene **Edge:** Reeded

Date	Mintage	F12	VF20	XF40	MS60	MS63
2006PM	5,000	PF63 355			PF65 360	

KM# 1305 1/5 CROWN
6.22 g., 0.9999 Gold 0.1987 oz. AGW, 22 mm. **Ruler:** Elizabeth II **Subject:** Battles that Changed the World **Obv:** Elizabeth II **Rev:** Battle of Agincourt scene **Edge:** Reeded

Date	Mintage	F12	VF20	XF40	MS60	MS63
2006PM	5,000	PF63 355			PF65 360	

KM# 1342 1/5 CROWN
6.22 g., 0.9999 Gold 0.1987 oz. AGW, 22 mm. **Ruler:** Elizabeth II **Obv:** Bust with tiara right **Rev:** Three Exotic Shorthair cats sitting facing **Edge:** Reeded

Date	Mintage	F12	VF20	XF40	MS60	MS63
2006PM	—				PF65 375	

KM# 1309 1/5 CROWN
6.22 g., 0.9999 Gold 0.1987 oz. AGW, 22 mm. **Ruler:** Elizabeth II **Subject:** 100th Anniversary of Scouting **Obv:** Bust with tiara right **Obv. Legend:** ELIZABETH II - ISLE OF MAN **Rev:** 3/4 length figure of Robert Baden-Powell standing facing 3/4 left, Fleur-de-lys below, images of scouting at left and right **Rev. Legend:** CENTENARY OF SCOUTING **Edge:** Reeded

Date	Mintage	F12	VF20	XF40	MS60	MS63
2007	—	PF63 355			PF65 360	

KM# 1345 1/5 CROWN
6.22 g., 0.9999 Gold 0.1987 oz. AGW, 22 mm. **Ruler:** Elizabeth II **Obv:** Bust with tiara right **Obv. Legend:** ELIZABETH II - ISLE OF MAN **Rev:** Ragdoll cat with two kittens sitting facing **Edge:** Reeded

Date	Mintage	F12	VF20	XF40	MS60	MS63
2007PM	—	—	—	—	—	350

KM# 1351.1 1/5 CROWN
6.22 g., 0.9999 Gold 0.1987 oz. AGW **Ruler:** Elizabeth II **Subject:** The Tale of Peter Rabbit **Obv:** Bust with tiara right **Obv. Legend:** ELIZABETH II - ISLE OF MAN **Rev:** Peter walking with friends **Edge:** Reeded

Date	Mintage	F12	VF20	XF40	MS60	MS63
2007PM	—	—	—	—	—	350

KM# 1351.2 1/5 CROWN
6.22 g., 0.9999 Gold 0.1987 oz. AGW **Ruler:** Elizabeth II **Subject:** The Tale of Peter Rabbit **Obv:** Bust with tiara right **Obv. Legend:** ELIZABETH II - ISLE OF MAN **Rev:** Peter walking with friends **Edge:** Reeded

Date	Mintage	F12	VF20	XF40	MS60	MS63
2007PM	—	—	—	—	—	350

KM# 1352 1/5 CROWN
6.22 g., 0.9999 Gold 0.1987 oz. AGW, 22 mm. **Ruler:** Elizabeth II **Subject:** Prince Charles 60th Birthday **Obv:** Bust with tiara right **Obv. Legend:** ELIZABETH II - ISLE OF MAN **Rev:** Heads of Charles, Princes William and Henry right **Edge:** Reeded

Date	Mintage	F12	VF20	XF40	MS60	MS63
2008PM	5,000	PF63 355			PF65 360	

KM# 1375 1/5 CROWN
6.22 g., 0.9999 Gold 0.1987 oz. AGW, 22 mm. **Ruler:** Elizabeth II **Subject:** Terra Cotta Army **Obv:** Bust right **Rev:** Making of the Soldier

Date	Mintage	F12	VF20	XF40	MS60	MS63
2009	5,000	PF63 355			PF65 360	

KM# 1377 1/5 CROWN
6.22 g., 0.9999 Gold 0.1987 oz. AGW, 22 mm. **Ruler:** Elizabeth II **Subject:** Terra Cotta Army **Obv:** Bust right **Rev:** Making of the Horse

Date	Mintage	F12	VF20	XF40	MS60	MS63
2009	5,000	PF63 355			PF65 360	

KM# 1381 1/5 CROWN
6.22 g., 0.9999 Gold 0.1987 oz. AGW **Ruler:** Elizabeth II **Obv:** Bust right **Rev:** Chinchilla cat and kitten

Date	Mintage	F12	VF20	XF40	MS60	MS63
2009	—	—	—	—	—	370
2009	1,000	PF63 375			PF65 380	

KM# 1437 1/5 CROWN
6.22 g., 0.9999 Gold 0.1987 oz. AGW, 22 mm. **Ruler:** Elizabeth II **Subject:** Turkish Angora Cat

Date	Mintage	F12	VF20	XF40	MS60	MS63
2011PM	1,000	PF63 410		PF65 425		
2011PM	—	—	—	—	—	400

KM# 1385 1/4 CROWN
6.22 g., 0.995 Platinum 0.1977 oz. APW, 22 mm. **Ruler:** Elizabeth II **Series:** Bust right **Obv:** Chinchilla cat and kitten

Date	Mintage	F12	VF20	XF40	MS60	MS63
2009	—	—	—	—	—	385

KM# 1061 1/2 CROWN
15.55 g., 0.9999 Gold 0.4967 oz. AGW, 30 mm. **Ruler:** Elizabeth II **Subject:** Year of the Snake **Obv:** Bust with tiara right **Rev:** Snake **Edge:** Reeded

Date	Mintage	F12	VF20	XF40	MS60	MS63
2001	6,000	PF65 875				

KM# 1071 1/2 CROWN
15.55 g., 0.9995 Platinum 0.4965 oz. APW, 27 mm. **Ruler:** Elizabeth II **Obv:** Head with tiara right **Rev:** Two Somali kittens **Edge:** Reeded

Date	Mintage	F12	VF20	XF40	MS60	MS63
2001	—	—	—	—	—	950

KM# 1070 1/2 CROWN
15.55 g., 0.9999 Gold 0.4967 oz. AGW, 30 mm. **Ruler:** Elizabeth II **Obv:** Head with tiara right **Rev:** Two Somali kittens **Edge:** Reeded

Date	Mintage	F12	VF20	XF40	MS60	MS63
2001	—	—	—	—	—	870
2001	1,000	PF63 875			PF65 880	

KM# 1157 1/2 CROWN
15.55 g., 0.999 Gold 0.4963 oz. AGW, 30 mm. **Ruler:** Elizabeth II **Subject:** Queen's Golden Jubilee **Obv:** Queen's portrait **Rev:** Queen on horse **Edge:** Reeded

Date	Mintage	F12	VF20	XF40	MS60	MS63
2002PM	500	PF65 875				

KM# 1101 1/2 CROWN
15.55 g., 0.9999 Gold 0.4967 oz. AGW, 30 mm. **Ruler:** Elizabeth II **Subject:** Year of the Horse **Obv:** Bust with tiara right **Rev:** Two horses **Edge:** Reeded

Date	Mintage	F12	VF20	XF40	MS60	MS63
2002	6,000	PF65 875				

KM# 1110 1/2 CROWN
15.55 g., 0.999 Gold 0.4963 oz. AGW, 30 mm. **Ruler:** Elizabeth II **Subject:** Bengal Cat **Obv:** Head with tiara right **Rev:** Cat and kitten **Edge:** Reeded

Date	Mintage	VG8	F12	VF20	XF40	MS60
2002	—	—	—	—	—	
2002	1,000	PF65 900				

KM# 1110a 1/2 CROWN
6.22 g., 0.999 Platinum 0.1985 oz. APW, 30 mm. **Ruler:** Elizabeth II **Subject:** Bengal Cat **Obv:** Head with tiara right **Rev:** Cat and kitten **Edge:** Reeded

Date	Mintage	F12	VF20	XF40	MS60	MS63
2002	—	—	—	—	—	390

KM# 1170 1/2 CROWN
15.55 g., 0.9999 Gold 0.4967 oz. AGW, 30 mm. **Ruler:** Elizabeth II **Subject:** Year of the Goat **Obv:** Bust with tiara right **Rev:** Three goats **Edge:** Reeded

Date	Mintage	F12	VF20	XF40	MS60	MS63
2003PM	—	PF65 875				

KM# 1189 1/2 CROWN
15.55 g., 0.9999 Gold 0.4967 oz. AGW, 30 mm. **Ruler:** Elizabeth II **Subject:** Lord of the Rings **Obv:** Bust with tiara right **Rev:** Gimli with two battle axes **Edge:** Reeded

Date	Mintage	F12	VF20	XF40	MS60	MS63
2003PM	1,000	PF65 875				

KM# 1164a 1/2 CROWN
15.55 g., 0.9995 Platinum 0.4965 oz. APW, 30 mm. **Ruler:** Elizabeth II **Subject:** Cat **Obv:** Head with tiara right **Rev:** Two Balinese kittens **Edge:** Reeded

Date	Mintage	F12	VF20	XF40	MS60	MS63
2003PM	—	—	—	—	—	950

KM# 1164 1/2 CROWN
15.55 g., 0.9999 Gold 0.4967 oz. AGW, 30 mm. **Ruler:** Elizabeth II **Subject:** Cat **Obv:** Head with tiara right **Rev:** Two Balinese kittens **Edge:** Reeded

Date	Mintage	F12	VF20	XF40	MS60	MS63
2003PM	—	—	—	—	—	870
2003PM	—	PF63 875			PF65 880	

KM# 1199 1/2 CROWN
15.55 g., 0.999 Bi-Metallic 0.4962 oz., 30 mm. **Ruler:** Elizabeth II **Subject:** Palladium Bicentennial **Obv:** Bust with tiara right **Rev:** Athena **Edge:** Reeded

Date	Mintage	F12	VF20	XF40	MS60	MS63
2004PM	500	PF65 1,050				

KM# 1243 1/2 CROWN
15.55 g., 0.9999 Gold 0.4967 oz. AGW, 30 mm. **Ruler:** Elizabeth II **Obv:** Head with tiara right **Rev:** Monkey **Edge:** Reeded

Date	Mintage	F12	VF20	XF40	MS60	MS63
2004PM	6,000	PF65 875				

KM# 1250 1/2 CROWN
15.55 g., 0.9999 Gold 0.4967 oz. AGW, 30 mm. **Ruler:** Elizabeth II **Obv:** Head with tiara right **Rev:** Two Tonkinese cats **Edge:** Reeded

Date	Mintage	F12	VF20	XF40	MS60	MS63
2004PM	—	—	—	—	—	890
2004PM	1,000	PF63 900			PF65 910	

KM# 1272 1/2 CROWN
15.55 g., 0.9999 Gold 0.4967 oz. AGW, 27 mm. **Ruler:** Elizabeth II **Obv:** Bust with tiara right **Rev:** Himalayan cat and two kittens **Edge:** Reeded

Date	Mintage	F12	VF20	XF40	MS60	MS63
2005PM	—	PF65 900				

KM# 1272a 1/2 CROWN
15.55 g., 0.995 Platinum 0.4943 oz. APW, 27 mm. **Ruler:** Elizabeth II **Obv:** Bust with tiara right **Rev:** Himalayan cat and two kittens **Edge:** Reeded

Date	Mintage	F12	VF20	XF40	MS60	MS63
2005PM	—	—	—	—	—	950
2005PM	—	PF63 960		PF65 970		

KM# 1346 1/2 CROWN
15.55 g., 0.9999 Gold 0.4967 oz. AGW **Ruler:** Elizabeth II **Obv:** Bust with tiara right **Obv. Legend:** ELIZABETH II - ISLE OF MAN **Rev:** Ragdoll cat with two kittens sitting facing **Edge:** Reeded

Date	Mintage	F12	VF20	XF40	MS60	MS63
2007PM	—	—	—	—	—	900

KM# 1396 1/2 CROWN
6.22 g., 0.9999 Gold 0.1987 oz. AGW, 30x20 mm. **Ruler:** Elizabeth II **Rev:** Tut's golden mask

Date	Mintage	F12	VF20	XF40	MS60	MS63
2008PM	—	—	—	—	—	355

KM# 1399 1/2 CROWN
6.22 g., 0.9999 Gold 0.1987 oz. AGW **Ruler:** Elizabeth II **Obv:** Bust with tiara right in Egyptian motif **Rev:** Statue standing **Shape:** Triangle

Date	Mintage	F12	VF20	XF40	MS60	MS63
2008PM	—	PF63 355		PF65 360		

KM# 1400 1/2 CROWN
6.22 g., 0.9999 Gold 0.1987 oz. AGW **Ruler:** Elizabeth II **Obv:** Bust with tiara right in Egyptian motif **Rev:** Statue standing, vile of sand above **Shape:** Triangle

Date	Mintage	F12	VF20	XF40	MS60	MS63
2008PM	—	PF63 355		PF65 360		

KM# 1384 1/2 CROWN
15.55 g., 0.995 Platinum 0.4942 oz. APW, 27 mm. **Ruler:** Elizabeth II **Obv:** Bust right **Rev:** Chinchilla cat and kitten

Date	Mintage	F12	VF20	XF40	MS60	MS63
2009	—	—	—	—	—	950

KM# 1380 1/2 CROWN
15.55 g., 0.9999 Gold 0.4967 oz. AGW, 30 mm. **Ruler:** Elizabeth II **Obv:** Bust right **Rev:** Chinchilla cat and kitten

Date	Mintage	F12	VF20	XF40	MS60	MS63
2009	—	—	—	—	—	890
2009	1,000	PF63 900		PF65 910		

KM# 1474 1/2 CROWN
Titanium **Ruler:** Elizabeth II **Subject:** George F. Handel, 325th Anniversary of Birth **Obv:** Bust in tiara right **Rev:** Fireworks above river barges **Note:** Blue in color.

Date	Mintage	F12	VF20	XF40	MS60	MS63
2010PM	—	PF65 125				

KM# 1438 1/2 CROWN
15.55 g., 0.9999 Gold 0.4967 oz. AGW, 30 mm. **Ruler:** Elizabeth II **Subject:** Turkish Angora Cat

Date	Mintage	F12	VF20	XF40	MS60	MS63
2011PM	1,000	PF63 960		PF65 975		
2011PM	—					950

KM# 1447 1/2 CROWN
12.00 g., 0.999 Silver 0.3829 oz. ASW, 38.6 mm. **Ruler:** Elizabeth II **Subject:** Olympics, London **Rev:** Horse jumper

Date	Mintage	F12	VF20	XF40	MS60	MS63
2012PM	10,000	PF63 20.00		PF65 22.00		

KM# 1448 1/2 CROWN
12.00 g., 0.999 Silver 0.3829 oz. ASW, 38.6 mm. **Ruler:** Elizabeth II **Subject:** Olympics, London **Rev:** Track Cyclist, road cyclist in background

Date	Mintage	F12	VF20	XF40	MS60	MS63
2012PM	10,000	PF63 20.00		PF65 22.00		

KM# 1449 1/2 CROWN
12.00 g., 0.999 Silver 0.3829 oz. ASW, 38.6 mm. **Ruler:** Elizabeth II **Subject:** Olympics, London **Rev:** Swimmer, two divers in background

Date	Mintage	F12	VF20	XF40	MS60	MS63
2012PM	10,000	PF63 20.00		PF65 22.00		

KM# 1450 1/2 CROWN
12.00 g., 0.999 Silver 0.3829 oz. ASW, 38.6 mm. **Ruler:** Elizabeth II **Subject:** Olympics, London **Rev:** Canoeist, two rowers in background

Date	Mintage	F12	VF20	XF40	MS60	MS63
2012PM	10,000	PF63 20.00		PF65 22.00		

KM# 1451 1/2 CROWN
12.00 g., 0.999 Silver 0.3829 oz. ASW, 38.6 mm. **Ruler:** Elizabeth II **Subject:** Olympics, London **Rev:** Judo players, two boxers in background

Date	Mintage	F12	VF20	XF40	MS60	MS63
2012PM	10,000	PF63 20.00		PF65 22.00		

KM# 1452 1/2 CROWN
12.00 g., 0.999 Silver 0.3829 oz. ASW, 38.6 mm. **Ruler:** Elizabeth II **Subject:** Olympics, London **Rev:** Table tennis, Lawn tennis in background

Date	Mintage	F12	VF20	XF40	MS60	MS63
2012PM	10,000	PF63 20.00		PF65 22.00		

KM# 1457 1/2 CROWN
12.00 g., 0.999 Silver 0.3829 oz. ASW, 38.6 mm. **Ruler:** Elizabeth II **Subject:** European Football Championships 2012 **Rev:** Player heading a football, Statue of Liberty in Lviv and Neptune's fountain in Gdansk

Date	Mintage	F12	VF20	XF40	MS60	MS63
2012PM	10,000	PF63 20.00		PF65 22.00		

KM# 1458 1/2 CROWN
12.00 g., 0.999 Silver 0.3829 oz. ASW, 38.6 mm. **Ruler:** Elizabeth II **Subject:** European Football Championships 2012 **Rev:** Player passing the ball, Motherland statue in Kiev and King Sigismund's statue in Warsaw in background

Date	Mintage	F12	VF20	XF40	MS60	MS63
2012PM	10,000	PF63 20.00		PF65 22.00		

KM# 1459 1/2 CROWN
12.00 g., 0.999 Silver 0.3829 oz. ASW, 38.6 mm. **Ruler:** Elizabeth II **Subject:** European Football Championships 2012 **Rev:** Footballer shooting, Cathedral of the Transfiguration in Donetsk and the Raclawice Panorama in Wroclaw in background

Date	Mintage	F12	VF20	XF40	MS60	MS63
2012PM	10,000	PF63 20.00		PF65 22.00		

KM# 1460 1/2 CROWN
12.00 g., 0.999 Silver 0.3829 oz. ASW, 38.6 mm. **Ruler:** Elizabeth II **Subject:** European Football Championships 2012 **Rev:** Two footballers tackling, Cathedral of the Annunciation in Kharkiv and the Cathedral in Poznan in background

Date	Mintage	F12	VF20	XF40	MS60	MS63
2012PM	10,000	PF63 20.00		PF65 22.00		

KM# 1062 CROWN
28.28 g., Copper-Nickel, 38.6 mm. **Ruler:** Elizabeth II **Subject:** Year of the Snake **Obv:** Bust with tiara right **Rev:** Snake **Edge:** Reeded

Date	Mintage	F12	VF20	XF40	MS60	MS63
2001	—	—	—	—	10.00	15.00

KM# 1076 CROWN
28.28 g., Copper-Nickel, 38.6 mm. **Ruler:** Elizabeth II **Subject:** Queen Mother **Obv:** Bust with tiara right **Rev:** 1948 Silver wedding anniversary **Edge:** Reeded

Date	Mintage	F12	VF20	XF40	MS60	MS63
2001	—	—	—	—	10.00	12.00

KM# 1077 CROWN
Copper-Nickel, 38.6 mm. **Ruler:** Elizabeth II **Subject:** Queen Mother **Obv:** Bust with tiara right **Rev:** 1948 holding baby Prince Charles **Edge:** Reeded

Date	Mintage	F12	VF20	XF40	MS60	MS63
2001	—	—	—	—	10.00	12.00

KM# 1080 CROWN
Copper-Nickel, 38.6 mm. **Ruler:** Elizabeth II **Subject:** Martin Frobisher **Obv:** Bust with tiara right **Rev:** Bust at left, ship at right and map below **Edge:** Reeded

Date	Mintage	F12	VF20	XF40	MS60	MS63
2001	—	—	—	—	10.00	12.00

KM# 1081 CROWN
Copper-Nickel, 38.6 mm. **Ruler:** Elizabeth II **Subject:** Roald Amundsen **Obv:** Bust with tiara right **Rev:** Bust at right, ship at center, dirigible above at left **Edge:** Reeded

Date	Mintage	F12	VF20	XF40	MS60	MS63
2001	—	—	—	—	10.00	12.00

KM# 1083 CROWN
28.28 g., Copper-Nickel, 38.6 mm. **Ruler:** Elizabeth II **Subject:** Queen's 75th Birthday **Obv:** Bust with tiara right **Rev:** Flower bouquet **Edge:** Reeded

Date	Mintage	F12	VF20	XF40	MS60	MS63
2001	—	—	—	—	14.00	16.00

KM# 1085 CROWN
28.28 g., Copper-Nickel, 38.6 mm. **Ruler:** Elizabeth II **Subject:** Joey Dunlop (1952-2000) **Obv:** Bust with tiara right **Rev:** Motorcycle racer **Edge:** Reeded

Date	Mintage	F12	VF20	XF40	MS60	MS63
2001 Black finish	—	—	—	—	10.00	12.00

KM# 1087 CROWN
28.28 g., Copper-Nickel, 38.6 mm. **Ruler:** Elizabeth II **Series:** Harry Potter **Obv:** Bust with tiara right **Rev:** Harry with magic wand **Edge:** Reeded

Date	Mintage	F12	VF20	XF40	MS60	MS63
2001	—	—	—	—	10.00	12.00

KM# 1089 CROWN
28.28 g., Copper-Nickel, 38.6 mm. **Ruler:** Elizabeth II **Series:** Harry Potter **Subject:** Journey to Hogwart's **Obv:** Bust with tiara right **Rev:** Boat full of children going to Hogwart's **Edge:** Reeded

Date	Mintage	F12	VF20	XF40	MS60	MS63
2001	—	—	—	—	10.00	12.00

KM# 1091 CROWN
Copper-Nickel **Ruler:** Elizabeth II **Series:** Harry Potter **Subject:** First Quidditch Match **Obv:** Bust with tiara right **Rev:** Harry flying his Nimbus 2000

Date	Mintage	F12	VF20	XF40	MS60	MS63
2001	—	—	—	—	10.00	12.00

KM# 1093 CROWN
Copper-Nickel **Ruler:** Elizabeth II **Series:** Harry Potter **Subject:** Birth of Norbert **Obv:** Bust with tiara right **Rev:** Hagrid and children watching Norbert hatch

Date	Mintage	F12	VF20	XF40	MS60	MS63
2001	—	—	—	—	10.00	14.00

KM# 1095 CROWN
Copper-Nickel **Ruler:** Elizabeth II **Series:** Harry Potter **Subject:** School **Obv:** Bust with tiara right **Rev:** Harry in Potions class

Date	Mintage	F12	VF20	XF40	MS60	MS63
2001	—	—	—	—	10.00	12.00

KM# 1097 CROWN
Copper-Nickel, 38.72 mm. **Ruler:** Elizabeth II **Series:** Harry Potter **Obv:** Bust with tiara right **Rev:** Harry catching the golden snitch **Edge:** Reeded

Date	Mintage	F12	VF20	XF40	MS60	MS63
2001	—	—	—	—	10.00	12.00

KM# 1062a CROWN
28.28 g., 0.925 Silver 0.8356 oz. ASW, 38.6 mm. **Ruler:** Elizabeth II **Subject:** Year of the Snake **Obv:** Head with tiara right **Rev:** Snake **Edge:** Reeded

Date	Mintage	F12	VF20	XF40	MS60	MS63
2001	30,000	PF63 42.00		PF65 47.00		

KM# 1076a CROWN
28.28 g., 0.925 Silver 0.8356 oz. ASW, 38.6 mm. **Ruler:** Elizabeth II **Subject:** Queen Mother **Obv:** Bust with tiara right **Rev:** 1948 Silver wedding anniversary **Edge:** Reeded

Date	Mintage	F12	VF20	XF40	MS60	MS63
2001	10,000	PF63 42.00		PF65 47.00		

KM# 1077a CROWN
28.28 g., 0.925 Silver 0.8356 oz. ASW, 38.6 mm. **Ruler:** Elizabeth II **Subject:** Queen Mother **Obv:** Head with tiara right **Rev:** 1948 holding baby Prince Charles **Edge:** Reeded

Date	Mintage	F12	VF20	XF40	MS60	MS63
2001	10,000	PF63 42.00		PF65 47.00		

KM# 1080a CROWN
28.28 g., 0.925 Silver 0.8356 oz. ASW, 38.6 mm. **Ruler:** Elizabeth II **Subject:** Martin Frobisher **Obv:** Bust of Queen Elizabeth II right **Edge:** Reeded

Date	Mintage	F12	VF20	XF40	MS60	MS63
2001	10,000	PF63 42.00		PF65 47.00		

KM# 1081a CROWN
28.28 g., 0.925 Silver 0.8356 oz. ASW, 38.6 mm. **Ruler:** Elizabeth II **Subject:** Roald Amundsen **Obv:** Bust with tiara right **Rev:** Bust at right, ship at center, dirigible at upper left **Edge:** Reeded

Date	Mintage	F12	VF20	XF40	MS60	MS63
2001	10,000	PF63 42.00		PF65 47.00		

KM# 1083a CROWN
28.28 g., 0.925 Silver 0.8356 oz. ASW, 38.6 mm. **Ruler:** Elizabeth II **Subject:** Queen's 75th Birthday **Obv:** Bust with tiara right **Rev:** Flower bouquet **Edge:** Reeded

Date	Mintage	F12	VF20	XF40	MS60	MS63
2001	10,000	PF63 45.00		PF65 50.00		

KM# 1085a CROWN
28.28 g., 0.925 Silver 0.8356 oz. ASW, 38.6 mm. **Ruler:** Elizabeth II **Subject:** Joey Dunlop (1952-2000) **Obv:** Bust with tiara right **Rev:** Motorcycle racer **Edge:** Reeded

Date	Mintage	F12	VF20	XF40	MS60	MS63
2001	10,000	PF63 42.00		PF65 47.00		

KM# 1087a CROWN
28.28 g., 0.925 Silver 0.8356 oz. ASW, 38.6 mm. **Ruler:** Elizabeth II **Series:** Harry Potter **Obv:** Bust with tiara right **Rev:** Harry with magic wand **Edge:** Reeded

Date	Mintage	F12	VF20	XF40	MS60	MS63
2001	15,000	PF63 42.00		PF65 47.00		

KM# 1089a CROWN
28.28 g., 0.925 Silver 0.8356 oz. ASW, 38.6 mm. **Ruler:** Elizabeth II **Series:** Harry Potter **Obv:** Bust with tiara right **Rev:** Boat full of children going to Hogwart's **Edge:** Reeded

Date	Mintage	F12	VF20	XF40	MS60	MS63
2001	15,000	PF63 42.00		PF65 47.00		

KM# 1091a CROWN
28.28 g., 0.925 Silver 0.8356 oz. ASW **Ruler:** Elizabeth II **Series:** Harry Potter **Subject:** First Quidditch Match **Obv:** Bust with tiara right **Rev:** Harry flying his Nimbus 2000

Date	Mintage	F12	VF20	XF40	MS60	MS63
2001	15,000	PF63 42.00		PF65 47.00		

KM# 1093a CROWN
28.28 g., 0.925 Silver 0.8356 oz. ASW **Ruler:** Elizabeth II **Series:** Harry Potter **Subject:** Birth of Norbert **Obv:** Bust with tiara right **Rev:** Hagrid and children watching Norbert hatch

Date	Mintage	F12	VF20	XF40	MS60	MS63
2001	15,000	PF63 42.00		PF65 47.00		

KM# 1095a CROWN
28.28 g., 0.925 Silver 0.8356 oz. ASW **Ruler:** Elizabeth II **Series:** Harry Potter **Subject:** School **Obv:** Bust with tiara right **Rev:** Harry in Potions class

Date	Mintage	F12	VF20	XF40	MS60	MS63
2001	15,000	PF63 42.00		PF65 47.00		

KM# 1097a CROWN
28.28 g., 0.925 Silver 0.8356 oz. ASW, 38.71 mm. **Ruler:** Elizabeth II **Series:** Harry Potter **Obv:** Bust with tiara right **Rev:** Harry catching the golden snitch **Edge:** Reeded

Date	Mintage	F12	VF20	XF40	MS60	MS63
2001	15,000	PF63 42.00		PF65 47.00		

KM# 1073 CROWN
31.10 g., 0.9999 Gold 0.9935 oz. AGW, 32.7 mm. **Ruler:** Elizabeth II **Subject:** Somali Kittens **Obv:** Bust with tiara right **Rev:** Two kittens **Edge:** Reeded

Date	Mintage	F12	VF20	XF40	MS60	MS63
2001	—					1,825
2001	1,000	PF63 1,850	PF65 1,875			

KM# 1072a CROWN
31.10 g., 0.999 Silver 0.9926 oz. ASW, 38.6 mm. **Ruler:** Elizabeth II **Subject:** Somali Kittens **Obv:** Bust with tiara right **Rev:** Two kittens **Edge:** Reeded

Date	Mintage	F12	VF20	XF40	MS60	MS63
2001	50,000	PF63 42.00	PF65 47.00			

KM# 1063 CROWN
31.10 g., 0.9999 Gold 0.9935 oz. AGW, 32.7 mm. **Ruler:** Elizabeth II **Subject:** Year of the Snake **Obv:** Bust with tiara right **Rev:** Snake **Edge:** Reeded

Date	Mintage	F12	VF20	XF40	MS60	MS63
2001	—					1,800
2001	2,000	PF63 1,825	PF65 1,850			

KM# 1072 CROWN
28.28 g., Copper-Nickel, 38.6 mm. **Ruler:** Elizabeth II **Subject:** Somali Kittens **Obv:** Bust with tiara right **Rev:** Two kittens **Edge:** Reeded

Date	Mintage	F12	VF20	XF40	MS60	MS63
2001	—			—	11.00	15.00

KM# 1102 CROWN
28.28 g., Copper-Nickel, 38.6 mm. **Ruler:** Elizabeth II **Subject:** Year of the Horse **Obv:** Bust with tiara right **Rev:** Two horses **Edge:** Reeded

Date	Mintage	F12	VF20	XF40	MS60	MS63
2002	—			—	12.00	15.00

KM# 1102a CROWN
28.28 g., 0.925 Silver 0.8356 oz. ASW, 38.6 mm. **Ruler:** Elizabeth II **Subject:** Year of the Horse **Obv:** Bust with tiara right **Rev:** Two horses **Edge:** Reeded

Date	Mintage	F12	VF20	XF40	MS60	MS63
2002	30,000	PF63 42.00	PF65 47.00			

KM# 1103 CROWN
31.10 g., 0.9999 Gold 0.9934 oz. AGW **Ruler:** Elizabeth II **Subject:** Year of the Horse **Obv:** Bust with tiara right

Date	Mintage	F12	VF20	XF40	MS60	MS63
2002	2,000	PF65 1,800				

KM# 1111 CROWN
28.28 g., Copper-Nickel, 38.6 mm. **Ruler:** Elizabeth II **Subject:** Bengal Cat **Obv:** Bust with tiara right **Rev:** Cat and kitten **Edge:** Reeded

Date	Mintage	F12	VF20	XF40	MS60	MS63
2002	—			—	12.50	14.00

KM# 1111a CROWN
31.10 g., 0.999 Silver 0.9926 oz. ASW, 38.6 mm. **Ruler:** Elizabeth II **Subject:** Bengal Cat **Obv:** Bust with tiara right **Rev:** Cat and kitten **Edge:** Reeded

Date	Mintage	F12	VF20	XF40	MS60	MS63
2002	10,000	PF65 70.00				

KM# 1112 CROWN
31.10 g., 0.999 Gold 0.9926 oz. AGW, 33 mm. **Ruler:** Elizabeth II **Subject:** Bengal Cat **Obv:** Bust with tiara right **Rev:** Cat and kitten **Edge:** Reeded

Date	Mintage	F12	VF20	XF40	MS60	MS63
2002	—					1,800
2002	1,000	PF63 1,825	PF65 1,850			

KM# 1115 CROWN
28.28 g., Copper-Nickel, 38.6 mm. **Ruler:** Elizabeth II **Subject:** Olympics - Salt Lake City **Obv:** Bust with tiara right **Rev:** Skier, torch and flag **Edge:** Reeded

Date	Mintage	F12	VF20	XF40	MS60	MS63
2002	—			—	10.00	12.00

KM# 1115a CROWN
28.28 g., 0.925 Silver 0.8356 oz. ASW, 38.6 mm. **Ruler:** Elizabeth II **Subject:** Olympics - Salt Lake City **Obv:** Bust with tiara right **Rev:** Skier, torch and flag **Edge:** Reeded

Date	Mintage	F12	VF20	XF40	MS60	MS63
2002	10,000	PF63 42.00	PF65 47.00			

KM# 1116 CROWN
28.28 g., Copper-Nickel, 38.6 mm. **Ruler:** Elizabeth II **Subject:** Olympics - Salt Lake City **Obv:** Bust with tiara right **Rev:** Bobsled, torch and stadium **Edge:** Reeded

Date	Mintage	F12	VF20	XF40	MS60	MS63
2002	—			—	10.00	12.00

KM# 1116a CROWN
28.28 g., 0.925 Silver 0.8356 oz. ASW, 38.6 mm. **Ruler:** Elizabeth II **Subject:** Olympics - Salt Lake City **Obv:** Bust with tiara right **Rev:** Bobsled, torch and stadium **Edge:** Reeded

Date	Mintage	F12	VF20	XF40	MS60	MS63
2002	10,000	PF63 42.00	PF65 47.00			

KM# 1118 CROWN
28.28 g., Copper-Nickel, 38.6 mm. **Ruler:** Elizabeth II **Subject:** Queen Mother's Love of Horses **Obv:** Bust with tiara right **Rev:** Queen Mother and horse **Edge:** Reeded

Date	Mintage	F12	VF20	XF40	MS60	MS63
2002	—			—	10.00	12.00

KM# 1118a CROWN
28.28 g., 0.925 Silver 0.8356 oz. ASW, 38.6 mm. **Ruler:** Elizabeth II **Subject:** Queen Mother's Love of Horses **Obv:** Bust with tiara right **Rev:** Queen Mother and horse **Edge:** Reeded

Date	Mintage	F12	VF20	XF40	MS60	MS63
2002	10,000	PF63 42.00	PF65 47.00			

KM# 1119 CROWN
35.00 g., 0.750 Gold 0.8385 oz. AGW, 38.6 mm. **Ruler:** Elizabeth II **Subject:** Golden Jubilee **Obv:** Bust with tiara right **Rev:** Queen Elizabeth II's young laureate bust right **Edge:** Reeded **Note:** Red Gold center in a White Gold inner ring within a Yellow Gold outer ring.

Date	Mintage	F12	VF20	XF40	MS60	MS63
2002	999	PF65 1,550				

KM# 1121 CROWN
28.28 g., Copper-Nickel, 38.6 mm. **Ruler:** Elizabeth II **Subject:** World Cup 2002 Japan - Korea **Obv:** Bust with tiara right **Rev:** Player running right **Edge:** Reeded

Date	Mintage	F12	VF20	XF40	MS60	MS63
2002	—			—	10.00	12.00

KM# 1121a CROWN
28.28 g., 0.925 Silver 0.8356 oz. ASW, 38.6 mm. **Ruler:** Elizabeth II **Subject:** World Cup 2002 Japan - Korea **Obv:** Bust with tiara right **Rev:** Player running right **Edge:** Reeded

Date	Mintage	F12	VF20	XF40	MS60	MS63
2002	10,000	PF63 42.00	PF65 47.00			

KM# 1123 CROWN
28.28 g., Copper-Nickel, 38.6 mm. **Ruler:** Elizabeth II **Subject:** World Cup 2002 Japan - Korea **Obv:** Bust with tiara right **Rev:** Player kicking to right **Edge:** Reeded

Date	Mintage	F12	VF20	XF40	MS60	MS63
2002	—	—	—	—	10.00	12.00

KM# 1123a CROWN
28.28 g., 0.925 Silver 0.8356 oz. ASW, 38.6 mm. **Ruler:** Elizabeth II **Subject:** World Cup 2002 Japan - Korea **Obv:** Bust with tiara right **Rev:** Player kicking to right **Edge:** Reeded

Date	Mintage	F12	VF20	XF40	MS60	MS63
2002	10,000	PF63 42.00	PF65 47.00			

KM# 1125 CROWN
28.28 g., Copper-Nickel, 38.6 mm. **Ruler:** Elizabeth II **Subject:** World Cup 2002 Japan - Korea **Obv:** Bust with tiara right **Rev:** Player kicking to left **Edge:** Reeded

Date	Mintage	F12	VF20	XF40	MS60	MS63
2002	—	—	—	—	10.00	12.00

KM# 1125a CROWN
28.28 g., 0.925 Silver 0.8356 oz. ASW, 38.6 mm. **Ruler:** Elizabeth II **Subject:** World Cup 2002 Japan - Korea **Obv:** Bust with tiara right **Rev:** Player kicking to left **Edge:** Reeded

Date	Mintage	F12	VF20	XF40	MS60	MS63
2002	10,000	PF63 42.00	PF65 47.00			

KM# 1127 CROWN
28.28 g., Copper-Nickel, 38.6 mm. **Ruler:** Elizabeth II **Subject:** World Cup 2002 Japan - Korea **Obv:** Bust with tiara right **Rev:** Player running to left **Edge:** Reeded

Date	Mintage	F12	VF20	XF40	MS60	MS63
2002	—	—	—	—	10.00	12.00

KM# 1127a CROWN
28.28 g., 0.925 Silver 0.8356 oz. ASW, 38.6 mm. **Ruler:** Elizabeth II **Subject:** World Cup 2002 Japan - Korea **Obv:** Bust with tiara right **Rev:** Player running to left **Edge:** Reeded

Date	Mintage	F12	VF20	XF40	MS60	MS63
2002	10,000	PF63 42.00	PF65 47.00			

KM# 1131 CROWN
28.28 g., Copper-Nickel, 38.6 mm. **Ruler:** Elizabeth II **Subject:** Queen Elizabeth II's Golden Jubilee **Obv:** Bust with tiara right **Rev:** Seated crowned Queen holding scepter at her coronation **Edge:** Reeded

Date	Mintage	F12	VF20	XF40	MS60	MS63
2002	—	—	—	—	10.00	12.00

KM# 1131a CROWN
28.28 g., Gold Color Base Metal, 38.6 mm. **Ruler:** Elizabeth II **Subject:** Queen Elizabeth II's Golden Jubilee **Obv:** Bust with tiara right **Rev:** Seated crowned Queen holding scepter at her coronation **Edge:** Reeded

Date	Mintage	F12	VF20	XF40	MS60	MS63
2002	15,000	—	—	—	10.00	12.00

KM# 1131b CROWN
28.28 g., 0.925 Gold Clad Silver 0.8356 oz., 38.6 mm. **Ruler:** Elizabeth II **Subject:** Queen Elizabeth II's Golden Jubilee **Obv:** Bust with tiara right **Rev:** Seated crowned Queen holding scepter at her coronation **Edge:** Reeded

Date	Mintage	F12	VF20	XF40	MS60	MS63
2002	10,000	PF63 42.00	PF65 47.00			

KM# 1133 CROWN
28.28 g., Copper-Nickel, 38.6 mm. **Ruler:** Elizabeth II **Subject:** Queen Elizabeth II's Golden Jubilee **Obv:** Bust with tiara right **Rev:** Queen on horse **Edge:** Reeded

Date	Mintage	F12	VF20	XF40	MS60	MS63
2002	—	—	—	—	10.00	12.00

KM# 1133a CROWN
28.28 g., Gold Color Base Metal, 38.6 mm. **Ruler:** Elizabeth II **Subject:** Queen Elizabeth II's Golden Jubilee **Obv:** Bust with tiara right **Rev:** Queen on horse **Edge:** Reeded

Date	Mintage	F12	VF20	XF40	MS60	MS63
2002	15,000	—	—	—	10.00	12.00

KM# 1133b CROWN
28.28 g., 0.925 Gold Clad Silver 0.8356 oz., 38.6 mm. **Ruler:** Elizabeth II **Subject:** Queen Elizabeth II's Golden Jubilee **Obv:** Bust with tiara right **Rev:** Queen on horse half left **Edge:** Reeded

Date	Mintage	F12	VF20	XF40	MS60	MS63
2002	10,000	PF63 42.00	PF65 47.00			

KM# 1135 CROWN
28.28 g., Copper-Nickel, 38.6 mm. **Ruler:** Elizabeth II **Subject:** Queen Elizabeth II's Golden Jubilee **Obv:** Bust with tiara right **Rev:** Queen with her pet Corgi **Edge:** Reeded

Date	Mintage	F12	VF20	XF40	MS60	MS63
2002	—	—	—	—	10.00	12.00

KM# 1135a CROWN
28.28 g., Gold Color Base Metal, 38.6 mm. **Ruler:** Elizabeth II **Subject:** Queen Elizabeth II's Golden Jubilee **Obv:** Bust with tiara right **Rev:** Seated Queen with her pet Corgi **Edge:** Reeded

Date	Mintage	F12	VF20	XF40	MS60	MS63
2002	15,000	—	—	—	10.00	12.00

KM# 1135b CROWN
28.28 g., 0.925 Gold Clad Silver 0.8356 oz., 38.6 mm. **Ruler:** Elizabeth II **Subject:** Queen Elizabeth II's Golden Jubilee **Obv:** Bust with tiara right **Rev:** Queen with her pet Corgi **Edge:** Reeded

Date	Mintage	F12	VF20	XF40	MS60	MS63
2002	10,000	PF63 42.00	PF65 47.00			

KM# 1137 CROWN
28.28 g., Copper-Nickel, 38.6 mm. **Ruler:** Elizabeth II **Subject:** Queen Elizabeth II's Golden Jubilee **Obv:** Bust with tiara right **Rev:** Queen at war memorial **Edge:** Reeded

Date	Mintage	F12	VF20	XF40	MS60	MS63
2002	—	—	—	—	10.00	12.00

KM# 1137a CROWN
28.28 g., Gold Color Base Metal, 38.6 mm. **Ruler:** Elizabeth II **Subject:** Queen Elizabeth II's Golden Jubilee **Obv:** Bust with tiara right **Rev:** Queen at war memorial **Edge:** Reeded

Date	Mintage	F12	VF20	XF40	MS60	MS63
2002	15,000	—	—	—	10.00	12.00

KM# 1137b CROWN
28.28 g., Gold Clad Silver, 38.6 mm. **Ruler:** Elizabeth II **Subject:** Queen Elizabeth II's Golden Jubilee **Obv:** Bust with tiara right **Rev:** Queen at war memorial **Edge:** Reeded

Date	Mintage	F12	VF20	XF40	MS60	MS63
2002	10,000	PF63 42.00	PF65 47.00			

KM# 1139 CROWN
Copper-Nickel, 38.6 mm. **Ruler:** Elizabeth II **Subject:** Queen Mother **Obv:** Bust with tiara right **Rev:** Queen Mother and Castle May **Edge:** Reeded

Date	Mintage	F12	VF20	XF40	MS60	MS63
2002	—	—	—	—	10.00	12.00

KM# 1139a CROWN
28.28 g., 0.925 Silver 0.8356 oz. ASW, 38.6 mm. **Ruler:** Elizabeth II **Obv:** Head with tiara right with blackened legends **Rev:** Queen Mother standing at left in front of Castle May with blackened legends

Date	Mintage	F12	VF20	XF40	MS60	MS63
2002	10,000	PF63 42.00	PF65 47.00			

KM# 1141 CROWN
28.28 g., Copper-Nickel, 38.6 mm. **Ruler:** Elizabeth II **Subject:** Princess Diana **Obv:** Bust with tiara right **Rev:** Diana's bust facing **Edge:** Reeded

Date	Mintage	F12	VF20	XF40	MS60	MS63
2002	—	—	—	—	10.00	12.00

KM# 1141a CROWN
28.28 g., 0.925 Silver 0.8356 oz. ASW, 38.6 mm. **Ruler:** Elizabeth II **Subject:** Princess Diana **Obv:** Bust with tiara right **Rev:** Diana facing **Edge:** Reeded

Date	Mintage	F12	VF20	XF40	MS60	MS63
2002	10,000	PF63 42.00	PF65 47.00			

KM# 1144 CROWN
28.28 g., Copper-Nickel, 38.6 mm. **Ruler:** Elizabeth II **Series:** Harry Potter **Obv:** Bust with tiara right **Rev:** Tom Riddle twirling Harry's magic wand **Edge:** Reeded

Date	Mintage	F12	VF20	XF40	MS60	MS63
2002PM	—	—	—	—	10.00	12.00

KM# 1144a CROWN
28.28 g., 0.925 Silver 0.8356 oz. ASW, 28.6 mm. **Ruler:** Elizabeth II **Series:** Harry Potter **Obv:** Bust with tiara right **Rev:** Tom Riddle twirling Harry's magic wand **Edge:** Reeded

Date	Mintage	F12	VF20	XF40	MS60	MS63
2002PM	15,000	PF63 45.00	PF65 50.00			

KM# 1146 CROWN
28.28 g., Copper-Nickel, 38.6 mm. **Ruler:** Elizabeth II **Series:** Harry Potter **Obv:** Bust with tiara right **Rev:** Harry and friends making Polyjuice potion **Edge:** Reeded

Date	Mintage	F12	VF20	XF40	MS60	MS63
2002PM	—	—	—	—	10.00	12.00

KM# 1146a CROWN
28.28 g., 0.925 Silver 0.8356 oz. ASW, 38.6 mm. **Ruler:** Elizabeth II **Series:** Harry Potter **Obv:** Bust with tiara right **Rev:** Harry Potter and friends making Polyjuice potion **Edge:** Reeded

Date	Mintage	F12	VF20	XF40	MS60	MS63
2002PM	15,000	PF63 45.00	PF65 50.00			

KM# 1148 CROWN
28.28 g., Copper-Nickel, 38.6 mm. **Ruler:** Elizabeth II **Series:** Harry Potter **Obv:** Bust with tiara right **Rev:** Harry arrives at the Burrow in a flying car **Edge:** Reeded

Date	Mintage	F12	VF20	XF40	MS60	MS63
2002PM	—	—	—	—	10.00	12.00

KM# 1148a CROWN
28.28 g., 0.925 Silver 0.8356 oz. ASW, 38.6 mm. **Ruler:** Elizabeth II **Series:** Harry Potter **Obv:** Bust with tiara right **Rev:** Harry arrives at the Burrow in a flying car **Edge:** Reeded

Date	Mintage	F12	VF20	XF40	MS60	MS63
2002PM	15,000	PF63 45.00	PF65 50.00			

KM# 1150 CROWN
28.28 g., Copper-Nickel, 38.6 mm. **Ruler:** Elizabeth II **Series:** Harry Potter **Obv:** Bust with tiara right **Rev:** Harry retrieves Gryffindor sword from sorting hat **Edge:** Reeded

Date	Mintage	F12	VF20	XF40	MS60	MS63
2002PM	—	—	—	—	10.00	12.00

KM# 1150a CROWN
28.28 g., 0.925 Silver 0.8356 oz. ASW, 38.6 mm. **Ruler:** Elizabeth II **Series:** Harry Potter **Obv:** Bust with tiara right **Rev:** Harry retrieves Gryffindor sword from sorting hat **Edge:** Reeded

Date	Mintage	F12	VF20	XF40	MS60	MS63
2002PM	15,000	PF63 45.00	PF65 50.00			

KM# 1152 CROWN
28.28 g., Copper-Nickel, 38.6 mm. **Ruler:** Elizabeth II **Series:** Harry Potter **Obv:** Bust with tiara right **Rev:** Harry and Ron encounter the spider Aragog **Edge:** Reeded

Date	Mintage	F12	VF20	XF40	MS60	MS63
2002PM	—	—	—	—	10.00	12.00

KM# 1152a CROWN
28.28 g., 0.925 Silver 0.8356 oz. ASW, 38.6 mm. **Ruler:** Elizabeth II **Series:** Harry Potter **Obv:** Bust with tiara right **Rev:** Harry and Ron encounter the spider Aragog **Edge:** Reeded

Date	Mintage	F12	VF20	XF40	MS60	MS63
2002PM	15,000	PF63 45.00	PF65 50.00			

KM# 1154 CROWN
28.28 g., Copper-Nickel, 38.6 mm. **Ruler:** Elizabeth II **Series:** Harry Potter **Obv:** Bust with tiara right **Rev:** Harry in hospital with Dobby **Edge:** Reeded

Date	Mintage	F12	VF20	XF40	MS60	MS63
2002PM	—	—	—	—	10.00	12.00

KM# 1154a CROWN
28.28 g., 0.925 Silver 0.8356 oz. ASW, 38.6 mm. **Ruler:** Elizabeth II **Series:** Harry Potter **Obv:** Bust with tiara right **Rev:** Harry in hospital with Dobby **Edge:** Reeded

Date	Mintage	F12	VF20	XF40	MS60	MS63
2002PM	15,000	PF63 45.00	PF65 50.00			

KM# 1165 CROWN
28.28 g., Copper-Nickel, 38.6 mm. **Ruler:** Elizabeth II **Subject:** Cat **Obv:** Bust with tiara right **Rev:** Two Balinese kittens **Edge:** Reeded

Date	Mintage	F12	VF20	XF40	MS60	MS63
2003PM	—	—	—	—	12.00	14.00

KM# 1171 CROWN
28.28 g., Copper-Nickel, 38.6 mm. **Ruler:** Elizabeth II **Subject:** Year of the Goat **Obv:** Bust with tiara right **Rev:** Three goats **Edge:** Reeded

Date	Mintage	F12	VF20	XF40	MS60	MS63
2003PM	—	—	—	—	12.00	14.00

KM# 1172 CROWN
31.10 g., 0.9999 Gold 0.9935 oz. AGW, 32.7 mm. **Ruler:** Elizabeth II **Subject:** Year of the Goat **Obv:** Bust with tiara right **Rev:** Three goats **Edge:** Reeded

Date	Mintage	F12	VF20	XF40	MS60	MS63
2003PM	2,000	PF65 1,850				

KM# 1174 CROWN
28.53 g., Copper-Nickel, 38.6 mm. **Ruler:** Elizabeth II **Obv:** Bust with tiara right **Rev:** The Star of India sailing ship **Edge:** Reeded

Date	Mintage	F12	VF20	XF40	MS60	MS63
2003PM	—	—	—	—	10.00	12.00

KM# 1176 CROWN
28.28 g., Copper-Nickel, 38.6 mm. **Ruler:** Elizabeth II **Subject:** Olympics **Obv:** Bust with tiara right **Rev:** Swimmers **Edge:** Reeded

Date	Mintage	F12	VF20	XF40	MS60	MS63
2003PM	—	—	—	—	10.00	12.00

KM# 1178 CROWN
28.28 g., Copper-Nickel, 38.6 mm. **Ruler:** Elizabeth II **Subject:** Olympics **Obv:** Bust with tiara right **Rev:** Runners **Edge:** Reeded

Date	Mintage	F12	VF20	XF40	MS60	MS63
2003PM	—	—	—	—	10.00	12.00

KM# 1180 CROWN
28.28 g., Copper-Nickel, 38.6 mm. **Ruler:** Elizabeth II **Subject:** Olympics **Obv:** Bust with tiara right **Rev:** Bicyclists **Edge:** Reeded

Date	Mintage	F12	VF20	XF40	MS60	MS63
2003PM	—	—	—	—	10.00	12.00

KM# 1182 CROWN
28.28 g., Copper-Nickel, 38.6 mm. **Ruler:** Elizabeth II **Subject:** Olympics **Obv:** Bust with tiara right **Rev:** Sail Boarders **Edge:** Reeded

Date	Mintage	F12	VF20	XF40	MS60	MS63
2003PM	—	—	—	—	10.00	12.00

KM# 1185 CROWN
28.28 g., Copper-Nickel, 38.6 mm. **Ruler:** Elizabeth II **Obv:** Bust with tiara right **Rev:** Lord of the Rings characters **Edge:** Reeded

Date	Mintage	F12	VF20	XF40	MS60	MS63
2003PM	100,000	—	—	—	12.50	14.50

KM# 1190 CROWN
31.10 g., 0.9999 Gold 0.9935 oz. AGW, 32.7 mm. **Ruler:** Elizabeth II **Subject:** Lord of the Rings **Obv:** Bust with tiara right **Rev:** Man on horse **Edge:** Reeded

Date	Mintage	F12	VF20	XF40	MS60	MS63
2003PM	1,000	PF65 1,850				

KM# 1191 CROWN
28.28 g., 0.925 Silver 0.8356 oz. ASW, 38.6 mm. **Ruler:** Elizabeth II **Subject:** Lord of the Rings **Obv:** Bust with tiara right **Rev:** Man with short sword **Edge:** Reeded

Date	Mintage	F12	VF20	XF40	MS60	MS63
2003PM	5,000	PF65 47.50				

KM# 1192 CROWN
28.28 g., 0.925 Silver 0.8356 oz. ASW, 38.6 mm. **Ruler:** Elizabeth II **Subject:** Lord of the Rings **Obv:** Bust with tiara right **Rev:** Aragorn with broadsword **Edge:** Reeded

Date	Mintage	F12	VF20	XF40	MS60	MS63
2003PM	5,000	PF65 47.50				

KM# 1193 CROWN
28.28 g., 0.925 Silver 0.8356 oz. ASW, 38.6 mm. **Ruler:** Elizabeth II **Subject:** Lord of the Rings **Obv:** Bust with tiara right **Rev:** Legolas **Edge:** Reeded

Date	Mintage	F12	VF20	XF40	MS60	MS63
2003PM	5,000	PF65 47.50				

KM# 1194 CROWN
28.28 g., 0.925 Silver 0.8356 oz. ASW, 38.6 mm. **Ruler:** Elizabeth II **Subject:** Lord of the Rings **Obv:** Bust with tiara right **Rev:** Gimli with two battle axes **Edge:** Reeded

Date	Mintage	F12	VF20	XF40	MS60	MS63
2003PM	5,000	PF65 47.50				

KM# 1195 CROWN
28.28 g., 0.925 Silver 0.8356 oz. ASW, 38.6 mm. **Ruler:** Elizabeth II **Subject:** Lord of the Rings **Obv:** Bust with tiara right **Rev:** Man on horse **Edge:** Reeded

Date	Mintage	F12	VF20	XF40	MS60	MS63
2003PM	5,000	PF65 47.50				

KM# 1196 CROWN
28.44 g., Copper-Nickel, 38.6 mm. **Ruler:** Elizabeth II **Obv:** Bust with tiara right **Rev:** Four pre-1918 airplanes **Edge:** Reeded

Date	Mintage	F12	VF20	XF40	MS60	MS63
2003PM	—	—	—	—	10.00	12.00

KM# 1197 CROWN
28.44 g., Copper-Nickel, 38.6 mm. **Obv:** Bust with tiara right **Rev:** Propeller plain, Zeppelin and two jet airliners **Edge:** Reeded

Date	Mintage	F12	VF20	XF40	MS60	MS63
2003PM	—	—	—	—	10.00	12.00

KM# 1165a CROWN
31.10 g., 0.999 Silver 0.9926 oz. ASW, 38.6 mm. **Ruler:** Elizabeth II **Subject:** Cat **Obv:** Head with tiara right **Rev:** Two Balinese kittens **Edge:** Reeded

Date	Mintage	F12	VF20	XF40	MS60	MS63
2003PM	50,000	PF65 70.00				

KM# 1171a CROWN
28.28 g., 0.925 Silver 0.8356 oz. ASW, 38.6 mm. **Ruler:** Elizabeth II **Subject:** Year of the Goat **Obv:** Bust with tiara right **Rev:** Three goats **Edge:** Reeded

Date	Mintage	F12	VF20	XF40	MS60	MS63
2003PM	—	PF63 42.00	PF65 47.00			

KM# 1176a CROWN
28.28 g., 0.925 Silver 0.8356 oz. ASW, 38.6 mm. **Ruler:** Elizabeth II **Subject:** Olympics **Obv:** Bust with tiara right **Rev:** Swimmers **Edge:** Reeded

Date	Mintage	F12	VF20	XF40	MS60	MS63
2003PM	10,000	PF63 42.00	PF65 47.00			

KM# 1178a CROWN
28.28 g., 0.925 Silver 0.8356 oz. ASW, 38.6 mm. **Ruler:** Elizabeth II **Subject:** Olympics **Obv:** Bust with tiara right **Rev:** Runners **Edge:** Reeded

Date	Mintage	F12	VF20	XF40	MS60	MS63
2003PM	10,000	PF63 42.00	PF65 47.00			

KM# 1180a CROWN
28.28 g., 0.925 Silver 0.8356 oz. ASW, 38.6 mm. **Ruler:** Elizabeth II **Subject:** Olympics **Obv:** Bust with tiara right **Rev:** Bicyclists **Edge:** Reeded

Date	Mintage	F12	VF20	XF40	MS60	MS63
2003PM	10,000	PF63 42.00	PF65 47.00			

KM# 1182a CROWN
28.28 g., 0.925 Silver 0.8356 oz. ASW, 38.6 mm. **Ruler:** Elizabeth II **Subject:** Olympics **Obv:** Bust with tiara right **Rev:** Sail Boarders **Edge:** Reeded

Date	Mintage	F12	VF20	XF40	MS60	MS63
2003PM	10,000	PF63 42.00	PF65 47.00			

KM# 1185a CROWN
28.28 g., 0.925 Silver 0.8356 oz. ASW, 38.6 mm. **Ruler:** Elizabeth II **Obv:** Bust with tiara right **Rev:** Lord of the Rings characters **Edge:** Reeded

Date	Mintage	F12	VF20	XF40	MS60	MS63
2003PM	10,000	PF63 45.00	PF65 50.00			

KM# 1166 CROWN
31.10 g., 0.9999 Gold 0.9935 oz. AGW, 32.7 mm. **Ruler:** Elizabeth II **Subject:** Cat **Obv:** Head with tiara right **Rev:** Two Balinese kittens **Edge:** Reeded

Date	Mintage	F12	VF20	XF40	MS60	MS63
2003PM	—	—	—	—	—	1,800
2003PM	—	PF63 1,825	PF65 1,850			

KM# 1201 CROWN
28.28 g., Copper-Nickel, 38.6 mm. **Ruler:** Elizabeth II **Obv:** Bust with tiara right **Rev:** European Union map within hand held rope circle **Edge:** Reeded

Date	Mintage	F12	VF20	XF40	MS60	MS63
2004PM	—	—	—	—	10.00	12.00

KM# 1202 CROWN
28.28 g., Copper-Nickel, 38.6 mm. **Ruler:** Elizabeth II **Obv:** Bust with tiara right **Rev:** Harry Potter and patron fighting off a Deventer **Edge:** Reeded

Date	Mintage	F12	VF20	XF40	MS60	MS63
2004PM	—	—	—	—	15.00	17.00

KM# 1204 CROWN
28.28 g., Copper-Nickel, 38.6 mm. **Ruler:** Elizabeth II **Obv:** Bust with tiara right **Rev:** Harry Potter in the shrieking shed **Edge:** Reeded

Date	Mintage	F12	VF20	XF40	MS60	MS63
2004PM	—	—	—	—	15.00	17.00

KM# 1206 CROWN
28.28 g., Copper-Nickel, 38.6 mm. **Ruler:** Elizabeth II **Obv:** Bust with tiara right **Rev:** Harry Potter and Professor Dumbledore **Edge:** Reeded

Date	Mintage	F12	VF20	XF40	MS60	MS63
2004PM	—	—	—	—	15.00	17.00

KM# 1208 CROWN
28.28 g., Copper-Nickel, 38.6 mm. **Ruler:** Elizabeth II **Obv:** Bust with tiara right **Rev:** Sirius Black on flying griffin **Edge:** Reeded

Date	Mintage	F12	VF20	XF40	MS60	MS63
2004PM	—	—	—	—	15.00	17.00

KM# 1210 CROWN
28.28 g., Copper-Nickel, 38.6 mm. **Ruler:** Elizabeth II **Obv:** Bust with tiara right **Rev:** Three Olympic Swimmers **Edge:** Reeded

Date	Mintage	F12	VF20	XF40	MS60	MS63
2004PM	—	—	—	—	10.00	12.00

KM# 1212 CROWN
28.28 g., Copper-Nickel, 38.6 mm. **Ruler:** Elizabeth II **Obv:** Bust with tiara right **Rev:** Three Olympic Cyclists **Edge:** Reeded

Date	Mintage	F12	VF20	XF40	MS60	MS63
2004PM	—	—	—	—	10.00	12.00

KM# 1214 CROWN
28.28 g., Copper-Nickel, 38.6 mm. **Ruler:** Elizabeth II **Obv:** Bust with tiara right **Rev:** Three Olympic Runners **Edge:** Reeded

Date	Mintage	F12	VF20	XF40	MS60	MS63
2004PM	—	—	—	—	10.00	12.00

KM# 1216 CROWN
28.28 g., Copper-Nickel, 38.6 mm. **Ruler:** Elizabeth II **Obv:** Bust with tiara right **Rev:** Three Olympic Sail Boarders **Edge:** Reeded

Date	Mintage	F12	VF20	XF40	MS60	MS63
2004PM	—	—	—	—	10.00	12.00

KM# 1218 CROWN
28.28 g., Copper-Nickel, 38.6 mm. **Ruler:** Elizabeth II **Obv:** Bust with tiara right **Rev:** Ocean Liner Queen Mary 2 **Edge:** Reeded

Date	Mintage	F12	VF20	XF40	MS60	MS63
2004PM	—	—	—	—	15.00	17.00

KM# 1220 CROWN
28.28 g., Copper-Nickel, 38.6 mm. **Ruler:** Elizabeth II **Obv:** Bust with tiara right **Rev:** Lt. Quillan portrait above Battle of Trafalgar scene **Edge:** Reeded

Date	Mintage	F12	VF20	XF40	MS60	MS63
2004PM	—	—	—	—	15.00	17.00

KM# 1221 CROWN
28.28 g., Copper-Nickel, 38.6 mm. **Ruler:** Elizabeth II **Obv:** Bust with tiara right **Rev:** Napoleon and Nelson portraits above Battle of Trafalgar scene **Edge:** Reeded

Date	Mintage	F12	VF20	XF40	MS60	MS63
2004PM	—	—	—	—	15.00	17.00

KM# 1222 CROWN
28.28 g., Copper-Nickel, 38.6 mm. **Ruler:** Elizabeth II **Obv:** Bust with tiara right **Rev:** D-Day Invasion Plan Map **Edge:** Reeded

Date	Mintage	F12	VF20	XF40	MS60	MS63
2004PM	—	—	—	—	15.00	17.00

KM# 1224 CROWN
28.28 g., Copper-Nickel, 38.6 mm. **Ruler:** Elizabeth II **Obv:** Bust with tiara right **Rev:** Victoria Cross and battle scene **Edge:** Reeded

Date	Mintage	F12	VF20	XF40	MS60	MS63
2004PM	—	—	—	—	15.00	17.00

KM# 1226 CROWN
28.28 g., Copper-Nickel, 38.6 mm. **Ruler:** Elizabeth II **Obv:** Bust with tiara right **Rev:** Silver Star and battle scene **Edge:** Reeded

Date	Mintage	F12	VF20	XF40	MS60	MS63
2004PM	—	—	—	—	15.00	17.00

KM# 1228 CROWN
28.28 g., Copper-Nickel, 38.6 mm. **Ruler:** Elizabeth II **Obv:** Bust with tiara right **Rev:** George Cross and rescue scene **Edge:** Reeded

Date	Mintage	F12	VF20	XF40	MS60	MS63
2004PM	—	—	—	—	15.00	17.00

KM# 1230 CROWN
28.28 g., Copper-Nickel, 38.6 mm. **Ruler:** Elizabeth II **Obv:** Bust with tiara right **Rev:** White Rose of Finland Medal and battle scene **Edge:** Reeded

Date	Mintage	F12	VF20	XF40	MS60	MS63
2004PM	—	—	—	—	15.00	17.00

KM# 1232 CROWN
28.28 g., Copper-Nickel, 38.6 mm. **Ruler:** Elizabeth II **Obv:** Bust with tiara right **Rev:** The Norwegian War Medal and naval battle scene **Edge:** Reeded

Date	Mintage	F12	VF20	XF40	MS60	MS63
2004PM	—	—	—	—	15.00	17.00

KM# 1234 CROWN
28.28 g., Copper-Nickel, 38.6 mm. **Ruler:** Elizabeth II **Obv:** Bust with tiara right **Rev:** French Croix de Guerre and partisan battle scene **Edge:** Reeded

Date	Mintage	F12	VF20	XF40	MS60	MS63
2004PM	—	—	—	—	15.00	17.00

KM# 1236 CROWN
28.28 g., Copper-Nickel, 38.6 mm. **Ruler:** Elizabeth II **Obv:** Bust with tiara right **Rev:** Multicolor cartoon soccer player **Edge:** Reeded

Date	Mintage	F12	VF20	XF40	MS60	MS63
2004PM	—	—	—	—	10.00	12.00

KM# 1237 CROWN
28.28 g., Copper-Nickel, 38.6 mm. **Ruler:** Elizabeth II **Obv:** Bust with tiara right **Rev:** Soccer ball in flight **Edge:** Reeded

Date	Mintage	F12	VF20	XF40	MS60	MS63
2004PM	—	—	—	—	10.00	12.00

KM# 1238 CROWN
28.28 g., Copper-Nickel, 38.6 mm. **Ruler:** Elizabeth II **Obv:** Bust with tiara right **Rev:** Gibbon monkey **Edge:** Reeded

Date	Mintage	F12	VF20	XF40	MS60	MS63
2004PM	—	—	—	—	10.00	15.00

KM# 1239 CROWN
31.10 g., 0.9999 Gold 0.9935 oz. AGW, 32.7 mm. **Ruler:** Elizabeth II **Obv:** Bust with tiara right **Rev:** Monkey **Edge:** Reeded

Date	Mintage	F12	VF20	XF40	MS60	MS63
2004PM	2,000	PF65 1,850				

KM# 1242 CROWN
6.22 g., 0.9999 Gold 0.1987 oz. AGW, 22 mm. **Ruler:** Elizabeth II **Obv:** Bust with tiara right **Rev:** Monkey **Edge:** Reeded

Date	Mintage	F12	VF20	XF40	MS60	MS63
2004PM	12,000	PF65 375				

KM# 1245 CROWN
28.28 g., Copper-Nickel, 38.6 mm. **Ruler:** Elizabeth II **Subject:** Lord of the Rings **Obv:** Bust with tiara right **Rev:** Nine characters **Edge:** Reeded

Date	Mintage	F12	VF20	XF40	MS60	MS63
2004PM	100,000	—	—	—	15.00	17.00

KM# 1246.1 CROWN
28.28 g., Copper-Nickel, 38.6 mm. **Ruler:** Elizabeth II **Obv:** Head with tiara right **Rev:** Pair of Tonkinese cats **Edge:** Reeded

Date	Mintage	F12	VF20	XF40	MS60	MS63
2004PM	—	—	—	—	14.00	16.00

KM# 1246.2 CROWN
28.28 g., Copper-Nickel **Ruler:** Elizabeth II **Obv:** Head with tiara right **Rev:** Two multicolor Tonkinese cats **Edge:** Reeded

Date	Mintage	F12	VF20	XF40	MS60	MS63
2004PM	—	—	—	—	14.00	16.00

KM# 1201a CROWN
28.28 g., 0.925 Silver 0.8356 oz. ASW, 38.6 mm. **Ruler:** Elizabeth II **Obv:** Bust with tiara right **Rev:** European Union map within a hand held rope circle **Edge:** Reeded

Date	Mintage	F12	VF20	XF40	MS60	MS63
2004PM	10,000	PF63 45.00	PF65 50.00			

KM# 1202a CROWN
28.28 g., 0.925 Silver 0.8356 oz. ASW, 38.6 mm. **Ruler:** Elizabeth II **Obv:** Bust with tiara right **Rev:** Harry Potter and patron fighting off a Deventer **Edge:** Reeded

Date	Mintage	F12	VF20	XF40	MS60	MS63
2004PM	10,000	PF63 45.00	PF65 50.00			

KM# 1204a CROWN
28.28 g., 0.925 Silver 0.8356 oz. ASW, 38.6 mm. **Ruler:** Elizabeth II **Obv:** Bust with tiara right **Rev:** Harry Potter in the shrieking shack **Edge:** Reeded

Date	Mintage	F12	VF20	XF40	MS60	MS63
2004PM	10,000	PF63 45.00	PF65 50.00			

KM# 1206a CROWN
28.28 g., 0.925 Silver 0.8356 oz. ASW, 38.6 mm. **Ruler:** Elizabeth II **Obv:** Bust with tiara right **Rev:** Harry Potter and Professor Dumbledore **Edge:** Reeded

Date	Mintage	F12	VF20	XF40	MS60	MS63
2004PM	10,000	PF63 45.00	PF65 50.00			

KM# 1208a CROWN
28.28 g., 0.925 Silver 0.8356 oz. ASW, 38.6 mm. **Ruler:** Elizabeth II **Obv:** Bust with tiara right **Rev:** Sirius Black on flying griffin **Edge:** Reeded

Date	Mintage	F12	VF20	XF40	MS60	MS63
2004PM	10,000	PF63 45.00	PF65 50.00			

KM# 1210a CROWN
28.28 g., 0.925 Silver 0.8356 oz. ASW, 38.6 mm. **Ruler:** Elizabeth II **Obv:** Bust with tiara right **Rev:** Three Olympic Swimmers **Edge:** Reeded

Date	Mintage	F12	VF20	XF40	MS60	MS63
2004PM	10,000	PF63 45.00	PF65 50.00			

KM# 1212a CROWN
28.28 g., 0.925 Silver 0.8356 oz. ASW, 38.6 mm. **Ruler:** Elizabeth II **Obv:** Bust with tiara right **Rev:** Three Olympic Cyclists **Edge:** Reeded

Date	Mintage	F12	VF20	XF40	MS60	MS63
2004PM	10,000	PF63 45.00	PF65 50.00			

KM# 1214a CROWN
28.28 g., 0.925 Silver 0.8356 oz. ASW, 38.6 mm. **Ruler:** Elizabeth II **Obv:** Bust with tiara right **Rev:** Three Olympic Runners **Edge:** Reeded

Date	Mintage	F12	VF20	XF40	MS60	MS63
2004PM	10,000	PF63 45.00	PF65 50.00			

KM# 1216a CROWN
28.28 g., 0.925 Silver 0.8356 oz. ASW, 38.6 mm. **Ruler:** Elizabeth II **Obv:** Bust with tiara right **Rev:** Three Olympic Sail Boarders **Edge:** Reeded

Date	Mintage	F12	VF20	XF40	MS60	MS63
2004PM	10,000	PF63 45.00	PF65 50.00			

KM# 1220a CROWN
28.28 g., 0.925 Silver 0.8356 oz. ASW, 38.6 mm. **Ruler:** Elizabeth II **Obv:** Bust with tiara right **Rev:** Lt. Quillan portrait above Battle of Trafalgar scene **Edge:** Reeded

Date	Mintage	F12	VF20	XF40	MS60	MS63
2004PM	10,000	PF63 45.00	PF65 50.00			

KM# 1221a CROWN
28.28 g., 0.999 Silver 0.9025 oz. ASW, 38.6 mm. **Ruler:** Elizabeth II **Obv:** Bust with tiara right **Rev:** Napoleon and Nelson portraits above Battle of Trafalgar scene **Edge:** Reeded

Date	Mintage	F12	VF20	XF40	MS60	MS63
2004PM	10,000	PF63 45.00	PF65 50.00			

KM# 1222a CROWN
28.28 g., 0.925 Silver 0.8356 oz. ASW, 38.6 mm. **Ruler:** Elizabeth II **Obv:** Bust with tiara right **Rev:** D-Day Invasion Plan Map **Edge:** Reeded

Date	Mintage	F12	VF20	XF40	MS60	MS63
2004PM	10,000	PF63 45.00	PF65 50.00			

KM# 1224a CROWN
28.28 g., 0.925 Silver 0.8356 oz. ASW, 38.6 mm. **Ruler:** Elizabeth II **Obv:** Bust with tiara right **Rev:** Victoria Cross and battle scene **Edge:** Reeded

Date	Mintage	F12	VF20	XF40	MS60	MS63
2004PM	10,000	PF63 45.00	PF65 50.00			

KM# 1226a CROWN
28.28 g., 0.925 Silver 0.8356 oz. ASW, 38.6 mm. **Ruler:** Elizabeth II **Obv:** Bust with tiara right **Rev:** Silver Star and battle scene **Edge:** Reeded

Date	Mintage	F12	VF20	XF40	MS60	MS63
2004PM	10,000	PF63 45.00	PF65 50.00			

KM# 1228a CROWN
28.28 g., 0.925 Silver 0.8356 oz. ASW, 38.6 mm. **Ruler:** Elizabeth II **Obv:** Bust with tiara right **Rev:** George Cross and rescue scene **Edge:** Reeded

Date	Mintage	F12	VF20	XF40	MS60	MS63
2004PM	10,000	PF63 45.00	PF65 50.00			

KM# 1230a CROWN
28.28 g., 0.925 Silver 0.8356 oz. ASW, 38.6 mm. **Ruler:** Elizabeth II **Obv:** Bust with tiara right **Rev:** White Rose of Finland Medal and battle scene **Edge:** Reeded

Date	Mintage	F12	VF20	XF40	MS60	MS63
2004PM	10,000	PF63 45.00	PF65 50.00			

KM# 1232a CROWN
28.28 g., 0.925 Silver 0.8356 oz. ASW, 38.6 mm. **Ruler:** Elizabeth II **Obv:** Bust with tiara right **Rev:** The Norwegian War Medal and a naval battle scene **Edge:** Reeded

Date	Mintage	F12	VF20	XF40	MS60	MS63
2004PM	10,000	PF63 45.00	PF65 50.00			

KM# 1234a CROWN
28.28 g., 0.925 Silver 0.8356 oz. ASW, 38.6 mm. **Ruler:** Elizabeth II **Obv:** Bust with tiara right **Rev:** French Croix de Guerre and partisan battle scene **Edge:** Reeded

Date	Mintage	F12	VF20	XF40	MS60	MS63
2004PM	10,000	PF63 45.00	PF65 50.00			

KM# 1236a CROWN
28.28 g., 0.925 Silver 0.8356 oz. ASW, 38.6 mm. **Ruler:** Elizabeth II **Obv:** Bust with tiara right **Rev:** Multicolor cartoon soccer player **Edge:** Reeded

Date	Mintage	F12	VF20	XF40	MS60	MS63
2004PM	7,500	PF63 45.00	PF65 50.00			

KM# 1237a CROWN
28.28 g., 0.925 Silver 0.8356 oz. ASW, 38.6 mm. **Ruler:** Elizabeth II **Obv:** Bust with tiara right **Rev:** Soccer ball in flight **Edge:** Reeded

Date	Mintage	F12	VF20	XF40	MS60	MS63
2004PM	7,500	PF63 45.00	PF65 50.00			

KM# 1238a CROWN
28.28 g., 0.925 Silver 0.8356 oz. ASW, 38.6 mm. **Ruler:** Elizabeth II **Obv:** Bust with tiara right **Rev:** Monkey **Edge:** Reeded

Date	Mintage	F12	VF20	XF40	MS60	MS63
2004PM	30,000	PF63 45.00	PF65 50.00			

KM# 1245a CROWN
28.28 g., 0.925 Silver 0.8356 oz. ASW, 38.6 mm. **Ruler:** Elizabeth II **Subject:** Lord of the Rings **Obv:** Bust with tiara right **Rev:** Nine characters **Edge:** Reeded

Date	Mintage	F12	VF20	XF40	MS60	MS63
2004PM	10,000	PF63 45.00	PF65 50.00			

KM# 1246a.1 CROWN
31.10 g., 0.999 Silver 0.9926 oz. ASW, 38.6 mm. **Ruler:** Elizabeth II **Obv:** Head with tiara right **Rev:** Two Tonkinese cats **Edge:** Reeded

Date	Mintage	F12	VF20	XF40	MS60	MS63
2004PM	50,000	PF63 65.00	PF65 70.00			

KM# 1246a.2 CROWN
31.10 g., 0.999 Silver 0.9926 oz. ASW, 38.6 mm. **Ruler:** Elizabeth II **Obv:** Head with tiara right **Rev:** Two multicolor Tonkinese cats **Edge:** Reeded

Date	Mintage	F12	VF20	XF40	MS60	MS63
2004PM	—	PF63 70.00	PF65 75.00			

KM# 1251 CROWN
31.10 g., 0.9999 Gold 0.9935 oz. AGW, 32.7 mm. **Ruler:** Elizabeth II **Obv:** Head with tiara right **Rev:** Two Tonkinese cats **Edge:** Reeded

Date	Mintage	F12	VF20	XF40	MS60	MS63
2004PM	—	—	—	—	—	1,800
2004PM	1,000	PF63	1,825	PF65	1,850	

KM# 1266 CROWN
28.33 g., Copper-Nickel, 38.7 mm. **Ruler:** Elizabeth II **Obv:** Bust with tiara right **Rev:** Himalayan cat with two kittens **Edge:** Reeded

Date	Mintage	F12	VF20	XF40	MS60	MS63
2005PM	—	—	—	—	12.00	14.00

KM# 1268 CROWN
31.10 g., 0.9999 Gold 0.9934 oz. AGW, 32.7 mm. **Ruler:** Elizabeth II **Obv:** Bust with tiara right **Rev:** Himalayan cat and two kittens **Edge:** Reeded

Date	Mintage	F12	VF20	XF40	MS60	MS63
2005PM	—	PF65	1,050			

KM# 1273 CROWN
28.28 g., Copper-Nickel, 38.6 mm. **Ruler:** Elizabeth II **Obv:** Bust with tiara right **Rev:** Harry Potter and the Hungarian Horn Tail, Tri-Wizard Tournament feat **Edge:** Reeded

Date	Mintage	F12	VF20	XF40	MS60	MS63
2005PM	—	—	—	—	15.00	17.00

KM# 1274 CROWN
28.28 g., Copper-Nickel, 38.6 mm. **Ruler:** Elizabeth II **Subject:** 60th Anniversary - End of WW II **Obv:** Bust with tiara right **Rev:** Sir Winston Churchill

Date	Mintage	F12	VF20	XF40	MS60	MS63
2005	—	—	—	—	10.00	12.00

KM# 1275 CROWN
28.28 g., Copper-Nickel, 38.6 mm. **Ruler:** Elizabeth II **Subject:** 400th Anniversary - Gunpowder plot **Obv:** Bust with tiara right **Rev:** Tower of London, Beefeaters

Date	Mintage	F12	VF20	XF40	MS60	MS63
2005	—	—	—	—	10.00	12.00

KM# 1276 CROWN
28.28 g., Copper-Nickel, 38.6 mm. **Ruler:** Elizabeth II **Obv:** Bust with tiara right **Rev:** Harry Potter and Tri-Wizard Tournament feat - Underwater retrieval

Date	Mintage	F12	VF20	XF40	MS60	MS63
2005	—	—	—	—	10.00	12.00

KM# 1277 CROWN
28.28 g., Copper-Nickel, 38.6 mm. **Ruler:** Elizabeth II **Obv:** Bust with tiara right **Rev:** Harry Potter and pensive

Date	Mintage	F12	VF20	XF40	MS60	MS63
2005	—	—	—	—	10.00	12.00

KM# 1278 CROWN
28.28 g., Copper-Nickel, 38.6 mm. **Ruler:** Elizabeth II **Obv:** Bust with tiara right **Rev:** Harry Potter and portkey

Date	Mintage	F12	VF20	XF40	MS60	MS63
2005	—	—	—	—	10.00	12.00

KM# 1279 CROWN
28.28 g., Copper-Nickel, 38.6 mm. **Ruler:** Elizabeth II **Subject:** The Battle of Cape St. Vincent **Obv:** Bust with tiara right **Rev:** Naval battle scene

Date	Mintage	F12	VF20	XF40	MS60	MS63
2005	—	—	—	—	10.00	12.00

KM# 1280 CROWN
28.28 g., Copper-Nickel, 38.6 mm. **Ruler:** Elizabeth II **Subject:** Nelson Funeral Procession **Obv:** Bust with tiara right **Rev:** Thames and Greenwich view

Date	Mintage	F12	VF20	XF40	MS60	MS63
2005	—	—	—	—	10.00	12.00

KM# 1281 CROWN
Copper-Nickel **Ruler:** Elizabeth II **Subject:** Battle of the Nile **Obv:** Bust with tiara right **Rev:** Naval battle

Date	Mintage	F12	VF20	XF40	MS60	MS63
2005	—	—	—	—	10.00	12.00

KM# 1282 CROWN
28.28 g., Copper-Nickel, 38.6 mm. **Ruler:** Elizabeth II **Subject:** Norway Independence **Obv:** Bust with tiara right **Rev:** Three swords

Date	Mintage	F12	VF20	XF40	MS60	MS63
2005	—	—	—	—	10.00	12.00

KM# 1283 CROWN
28.28 g., Copper-Nickel, 38.6 mm. **Ruler:** Elizabeth II **Subject:** Nelson - Trafalgar 200th Anniversary **Rev:** Nelson portrait

Date	Mintage	F12	VF20	XF40	MS60	MS63
2005	—	—	—	—	10.00	12.00

KM# 1284 CROWN
28.28 g., Copper-Nickel, 38.6 mm. **Ruler:** Elizabeth II **Subject:** Battle of Trafalgar **Rev:** Naval battle scene

Date	Mintage	F12	VF20	XF40	MS60	MS63
2005	—	—	—	—	10.00	12.00

KM# 1285 CROWN
28.28 g., Copper-Nickel, 38.6 mm. **Ruler:** Elizabeth II **Subject:** Steam Packet - King Orry III **Obv:** Bust with tiara right **Rev:** Ship view

Date	Mintage	F12	VF20	XF40	MS60	MS63
2005	—	—	—	—	10.00	12.00

KM# 1286 CROWN
28.28 g., Copper-Nickel, 38.6 mm. **Ruler:** Elizabeth II **Subject:** Isle of Man Steam Packet Company - 175th Anniversary **Obv:** Bust with tiara right **Rev:** Modern and early ferry

Date	Mintage	F12	VF20	XF40	MS60	MS63
2005	—	—	—	—	10.00	12.00

KM# 1287 CROWN
28.28 g., Copper-Nickel, 38.6 mm. **Ruler:** Elizabeth II **Rev:** Motorcycle right

Date	Mintage	F12	VF20	XF40	MS60	MS63
2005	—	—	—	—	10.00	12.00

KM# 1288 CROWN
28.28 g., Copper-Nickel, 38.6 mm. **Ruler:** Elizabeth II **Rev:** Motorcycle forward

Date	Mintage	F12	VF20	XF40	MS60	MS63
2005	—	—	—	—	10.00	12.00

KM# 1289 CROWN
28.28 g., Copper-Nickel, 38.6 mm. **Ruler:** Elizabeth II **Subject:** Ugly Duckling story **Obv:** Bust with tiara right **Rev:** Farm animals

Date	Mintage	F12	VF20	XF40	MS60	MS63
2005	—	—	—	—	12.00	14.00

KM# 1291 CROWN
28.28 g., Copper-Nickel, 38.6 mm. **Ruler:** Elizabeth II **Subject:** Trafalgar - 200th Anniversary **Obv:** Bust with tiara right **Rev:** Nelson at Battle of Copenhagen

Date	Mintage	F12	VF20	XF40	MS60	MS63
2005	—	—	—	—	10.00	12.00

KM# 1266a CROWN
31.10 g., 0.999 Silver 0.9926 oz. ASW, 38.6 mm. **Ruler:** Elizabeth II **Obv:** Bust with tiara right **Rev:** Himalayan cat and two kittens **Edge:** Reeded

Date	Mintage	F12	VF20	XF40	MS60	MS63
2005PM	50,000	PF63 65.00	PF65 70.00			

KM# 1428 CROWN
28.28 g., Copper-Nickel, 38.6 mm. **Ruler:** Elizabeth II **Subject:** Trafalgar, 200th Anniversary **Rev:** Quillian portrait above naval battle scene

Date	Mintage	F12	VF20	XF40	MS60	MS63
2005PM	—	—	—	—	10.00	12.00

KM# 1429 CROWN
28.28 g., Copper-Nickel, 38.6 mm. **Ruler:** Elizabeth II **Subject:** Trafalgar, 200th Anniversary **Rev:** Napoleon and Nelson portraits above Naval battle scene

Date	Mintage	F12	VF20	XF40	MS60	MS63
2005PM	—	—	—	—	10.00	12.00

KM# 1296 CROWN
28.28 g., Copper-Nickel, 38.6 mm. **Ruler:** Elizabeth II **Subject:** Battles that Changed the World **Obv:** Elizabeth II **Rev:** Trojan War scene **Edge:** Reeded

Date	Mintage	F12	VF20	XF40	MS60	MS63
2006PM	—	—	—	—	10.00	12.00

KM# 1298 CROWN
28.28 g., Copper-Nickel, 38.6 mm. **Ruler:** Elizabeth II **Subject:** Battles that Changed the World **Obv:** Elizabeth II **Rev:** Battle of Arbela scene **Edge:** Reeded

Date	Mintage	F12	VF20	XF40	MS60	MS63
2006PM	—	—	—	—	10.00	12.00

KM# 1300 CROWN

28.28 g., Copper-Nickel, 38.6 mm. **Ruler:** Elizabeth II **Subject:** Battles that Changed the World **Obv:** Elizabeth II **Rev:** Battle of Thapsus scene **Edge:** Reeded

Date	Mintage	F12	VF20	XF40	MS60	MS63
2006PM	—	—	—	—	10.00	12.00

KM# 1302 CROWN

28.28 g., Copper-Nickel, 38.6 mm. **Ruler:** Elizabeth II **Subject:** Battles that Changed the World **Obv:** Elizabeth II **Rev:** Battle of Cologne scene **Edge:** Reeded

Date	Mintage	F12	VF20	XF40	MS60	MS63
2006PM	—	—	—	—	10.00	12.00

KM# 1304 CROWN

28.28 g., Copper-Nickel, 38.6 mm. **Ruler:** Elizabeth II **Subject:** Battles that Changed the World **Obv:** Elizabeth II **Rev:** Siege of Valencia scene **Edge:** Reeded

Date	Mintage	F12	VF20	XF40	MS60	MS63
2006PM	—	—	—	—	10.00	12.00

KM# 1306 CROWN

28.28 g., Copper-Nickel, 38.6 mm. **Ruler:** Elizabeth II **Subject:** Battles that Changed the World **Obv:** Elizabeth II **Rev:** Battle of Agincourt scene **Edge:** Reeded

Date	Mintage	F12	VF20	XF40	MS60	MS63
2006PM	—	—	—	—	10.00	12.00

KM# 1323.1 CROWN

28.28 g., Copper-Nickel, 38.60 mm. **Ruler:** Elizabeth II **Subject:** Hans Christian Anderson's Fairy Tales **Obv:** Bust with tiarra right **Obv. Legend:** ELIZABETH II - ISLE OF MAN **Rev:** Three bears startling Goldilocks in bed **Rev. Legend:** Goldilocks and the Three Bears **Edge:** Reeded

Date	Mintage	F12	VF20	XF40	MS60	MS63
2006PM	—	—	—	—	—	35.00

KM# 1296a CROWN

28.28 g., 0.925 Silver 0.8356 oz. ASW, 38.6 mm. **Ruler:** Elizabeth II **Subject:** Battles that Changed the World **Obv:** Elizabeth II **Rev:** Trojan War scene **Edge:** Reeded

Date	Mintage	F12	VF20	XF40	MS60	MS63
2006PM	10,000	PF63 42.00		PF65 47.00		

KM# 1298a CROWN

28.28 g., 0.925 Silver 0.8356 oz. ASW, 38.6 mm. **Ruler:** Elizabeth II **Subject:** Battles that Changed the World **Obv:** Elizabeth II **Rev:** Battle of Arbela scene **Edge:** Reeded

Date	Mintage	F12	VF20	XF40	M3G0	M3G3
2006PM	10,000	PF63 42.00		PF65 47.00		

KM# 1300a CROWN

28.28 g., 0.925 Silver 0.8356 oz. ASW, 38.6 mm. **Ruler:** Elizabeth II **Subject:** Battles that Changed the World **Obv:** Elizabeth II **Rev:** Battle of Thapsus scene **Edge:** Reeded

Date	Mintage	F12	VF20	XF40	MS60	MS63
2006PM	10,000	PF63 42.00		PF65 47.00		

KM# 1302a CROWN

28.28 g., 0.925 Silver 0.8356 oz. ASW, 38.6 mm. **Ruler:** Elizabeth II **Subject:** Battles that Changed the World **Obv:** Elizabeth II **Rev:** Battle of Cologne scene **Edge:** Reeded

Date	Mintage	F12	VF20	XF40	MS60	MS63
2006PM	10,000	PF63 42.00		PF65 47.00		

KM# 1304a CROWN

28.28 g., 0.925 Silver 0.8356 oz. ASW, 38.6 mm. **Ruler:** Elizabeth II **Subject:** Battles that Changed the World **Obv:** Elizabeth II **Rev:** Siege of Valencia scene **Edge:** Reeded

Date	Mintage	F12	VF20	XF40	MS60	MS63
2006PM	10,000	PF63 42.00		PF65 47.00		

KM# 1306a CROWN

28.28 g., 0.925 Silver 0.8356 oz. ASW, 38.6 mm. **Ruler:** Elizabeth II **Subject:** Battles that Changed the World **Obv:** Elizabeth II **Rev:** Battle of Agincourt scene **Edge:** Reeded

Date	Mintage	F12	VF20	XF40	MS60	MS63
2006PM	10,000	PF63 42.00		PF65 47.00		

KM# 1290a CROWN

28.28 g., Copper-Nickel, 38.6 mm. **Ruler:** Elizabeth II **Obv:** Bust with tiara right **Rev:** Three Exotic Shorthair cats sitting facing **Edge:** Reeded

Date	Mintage	F12	VF20	XF40	MS60	MS63
2006PM	—	—	—	—	12.00	14.00

KM# 1290b CROWN

28.28 g., 0.925 Silver 0.8356 oz. ASW, 38.6 mm. **Ruler:** Elizabeth II **Obv:** Bust with tiara right **Rev:** Three Exotic Shorthair cats sitting facing **Edge:** Reeded

Date	Mintage	F12	VF20	XF40	MS60	MS63
2006PM	—	—	—	—	—	70.00

KM# 1290c CROWN

31.10 g., 0.9999 Gold 0.9934 oz. AGW **Ruler:** Elizabeth II **Obv:** Bust with tiara right **Rev:** Three Exotic Shorthair cats sitting facing, multicolor **Edge:** Reeded

Date	Mintage	F12	VF20	XF40	MS60	MS63
2006PM	—	—	—	—	—	1,825

KM# 1423.1 CROWN

28.28 g., Copper-Nickel, 38.6 mm. **Ruler:** Elizabeth II **Subject:** Concord, 30th Anniversary of transatlantic service **Obv:** Bust with tiara right **Rev:** Concord in flight, buildings below

Date	Mintage	F12	VF20	XF40	MS60	MS63
2006PM	—	PF65 30.00				

KM# 1423.2 CROWN

28.28 g., Copper-Nickel, 38.6 mm. **Ruler:** Elizabeth II **Subject:** Concorde, 30th Anniversary of transatlantic service **Obv:** Bust with tiara right **Rev:** Concorde in flight, multicolor

Date	Mintage	F12	VF20	XF40	MS60	MS63
2006PM	—	PF65 50.00				

KM# 1323.2 CROWN

28.28 g., Copper-Nickel, 38.60 mm. **Ruler:** Elizabeth II **Subject:** Hans Christian Anderson's Fairy Tales **Obv:** Bust with tiara right **Obv. Legend:** ELIZABETH II - ISLE OF MAN **Rev:** Three bears startling Goldilocks in bed multicolor **Rev. Legend:** Goldilocks and the Three Bears **Edge:** Reeded

Date	Mintage	F12	VF20	XF40	MS60	MS63
2006PM	—	—	—	—	—	40.00

KM# 1323.1a CROWN

28.28 g., 0.925 Silver 0.8356 oz. ASW, 38.60 mm. **Ruler:** Elizabeth II **Subject:** Hans Christian Anderson's Fairy Tales **Obv:** Bust with tiara right **Obv. Legend:** ELIZABETH II - ISLE OF MAN **Rev:** Three bears startling Goldilocks in bed **Rev. Legend:** Goldilocks and the Three Bears **Edge:** Reeded

Date	Mintage	F12	VF20	XF40	MS60	MS63
2006PM	—	PF65 80.00				

KM# 1323.2a CROWN

28.28 g., 0.925 Silver 0.8356 oz. ASW, 38.60 mm. **Ruler:** Elizabeth II **Subject:** Hans Christian Anderson's Fairy Tales **Obv:** Bust with tiara right **Obv. Legend:** ELIZABETH II - ISLE OF MAN **Rev:** Three bears startling Goldilocks in bed multicolor **Rev. Legend:** Goldilocks and the Three Bears **Edge:** Reeded

Date	Mintage	F12	VF20	XF40	MS60	MS63
2006PM	—	PF65 100				

KM# 1310 CROWN
28.28 g., Copper-Nickel, 38.6 mm. **Ruler:** Elizabeth II **Subject:** 100th Anniversary of Scouting **Obv:** Bust with tiara right **Obv. Legend:** ELIZABETH II - ISLE OF MAN **Rev:** 3/4 length figure of Robert Baden-Powell standing facing 3/4 left, Fleur-de-lys below, images of scouting at left and right **Rev. Legend:** CENTENARY OF SCOUTING **Edge:** Reeded

Date	Mintage	F12	VF20	XF40	MS60	MS63
2007	—	—	—	—	17.00	20.00

KM# 1311 CROWN
28.28 g., 0.9167 Silver 0.8281 oz. ASW **Ruler:** Elizabeth II **Subject:** 100th Anniversary of Scouting **Obv:** Bust with tiara right **Obv. Legend:** ELIZABETH II - ISLE OF MAN **Rev:** 3/4 length figure of Robert Baden-Powell standing facing 3/4 left, Fleur-de-lys below, images of scouting at left and right **Rev. Legend:** CENTENARY OF SCOUTING **Edge:** Reeded

Date	Mintage	F12	VF20	XF40	MS60	MS63
2007	—	PF65 50.00				

KM# 1312 CROWN
0.750 Gold AGW **Ruler:** Elizabeth II **Subject:** Diamond Wedding Anniversary **Obv:** Bust with tiara right **Obv. Legend:** ELIZABETH II - ISLE OF MAN **Rev:** Crowned pair of doves surrounded by a leek, thistle, rose and shamrock **Edge:** Reeded

Date	Mintage	F12	VF20	XF40	MS60	MS63
2007	—	PF65 2,000				

KM# 1313 CROWN
28.28 g., Copper-Nickel, 38.60 mm. **Ruler:** Elizabeth II **Obv:** Bust with tiara right **Obv. Legend:** ELIZABETH II - ISLE OF MAN **Rev:** Two swans facing **Edge:** Reeded

Date	Mintage	F12	VF20	XF40	MS60	MS63
2007	—	—	—	—	15.00	18.00

KM# 1315 CROWN
28.28 g., 0.9167 Silver 0.8281 oz. ASW, 38.60 mm. **Ruler:** Elizabeth II **Obv:** Bust with tiara right **Obv. Legend:** ELIZABETH II - ISLE OF MAN **Rev:** Two swans facing **Edge:** Reeded

Date	Mintage	F12	VF20	XF40	MS60	MS63
2007	10,000	PF65 50.00				

KM# 1316 CROWN
28.28 g., Copper-Nickel, 38.6 mm. **Ruler:** Elizabeth II **Subject:** Diamond Wedding Anniversary **Obv:** Conjoined busts with Philip right **Obv. Legend:** ELIZABETH II - ISLE OF MAN **Rev:** Bridal bouquet of white orchids **Rev. Legend:** Diamond Wedding of H.M. Queen Elizabeth II & H.R.H. Prince Philip **Edge:** Reeded

Date	Mintage	F12	VF20	XF40	MS60	MS63
2007	—	—	—	—	15.00	18.00

KM# 1317 CROWN
28.28 g., Copper-Nickel **Ruler:** Elizabeth II **Subject:** Diamond Wedding Anniversary **Obv:** Conjoined busts with Philip right **Obv. Legend:** ELIZABETH II - ISLE OF MAN **Rev:** Westminster Abbey **Rev. Legend:** Diamond Wedding of H.M. Queen Elizabeth II & H.R.H. Prince Philip **Edge:** Reeded

Date	Mintage	F12	VF20	XF40	MS60	MS63
2007	—	—	—	—	15.00	18.00

KM# 1318 CROWN
28.28 g., Copper-Nickel, 38.6 mm. **Ruler:** Elizabeth II **Subject:** Diamond Wedding Anniversary **Obv:** Conjoined busts with Philip right **Obv. Legend:** ELIZABETH II - ISLE OF MAN **Rev:** Royal Family of five standing facing **Rev. Legend:** Diamond Wedding of H.M. Queen Elizabeth II & H.R.H. Prince Philip **Edge:** Reeded

Date	Mintage	F12	VF20	XF40	MS60	MS63
2007	—	—	—	—	15.00	18.00

KM# 1319 CROWN
28.28 g., Copper-Nickel, 38.6 mm. **Ruler:** Elizabeth II **Subject:** Diamond Wedding Anniversary **Obv:** Conjoined busts with Philip right **Obv. Legend:** ELIZABETH II - ISLE OF MAN **Rev:** Bride and groom standing facing **Rev. Legend:** Diamond Wedding of H.M. Queen Elizabeth II & H.R.H. Prince Philip **Edge:** Reeded

Date	Mintage	F12	VF20	XF40	MS60	MS63
2007	—	—	—	—	15.00	18.00

KM# 1347 CROWN
31.10 g., 0.9999 Gold 0.9934 oz. AGW **Ruler:** Elizabeth II **Obv:** Bust with tiara right **Obv. Legend:** ELIZABETH II - ISLE OF MAN **Rev:** Ragdoll cat with two kittens sitting facing **Edge:** Reeded

Date	Mintage	F12	VF20	XF40	MS60	MS63
2007PM	—	—	—	—	—	1,825

KM# 1348.1 CROWN
Copper-Nickel **Ruler:** Elizabeth II **Subject:** The Tale of Peter Rabbit **Obv:** Bust with tiara right **Obv. Legend:** ELIZABETH II - ISLE OF MAN **Rev:** Peter walking with friends **Edge:** Reeded

Date	Mintage	F12	VF20	XF40	MS60	MS63
2007PM	—	—	—	—	—	30.00

KM# 1348.2 CROWN
Copper-Nickel **Ruler:** Elizabeth II **Subject:** The Tale of Peter Rabbit **Obv:** Bust with tiara right **Obv. Legend:** ELIZABETH II - ISLE OF MAN **Rev:** Peter walking with friends, multicolor **Edge:** Reeded

Date	Mintage	F12	VF20	XF40	MS60	MS63
2007PM	—	—	—	—	—	35.00

KM# 1316a CROWN
28.28 g., 0.9167 Silver 0.8281 oz. ASW **Ruler:** Elizabeth II **Subject:** Diamond Wedding Anniversary **Obv:** Conjoined busts with Philip right **Obv. Legend:** ELIZABETH II - ISLE OF MAN **Rev:** Bridal bouquet of white orchids **Rev. Legend:** Diamond Wedding of H.M. Queen Elizabeth II & H.R.H. Prince Philip **Edge:** Reeded

Date	Mintage	F12	VF20	XF40	MS60	MS63
2007	—	PF63 45.00	PF65 50.00			

KM# 1317a CROWN
28.28 g., 0.9167 Silver 0.8281 oz. ASW **Ruler:** Elizabeth II **Subject:** Diamond Wedding Anniversary **Obv:** Conjoined busts with Philip right **Obv. Legend:** ELIZABETH II - ISLE OF MAN **Rev:** Westminster Abbey **Rev. Legend:** Diamond Wedding of H.M. Queen Elizabeth II & H.R.H. Prince Philip **Edge:** Reeded

Date	Mintage	F12	VF20	XF40	MS60	MS63
2007	—	PF63 45.00	PF65 50.00			

KM# 1318a CROWN
28.28 g., 0.9167 Silver 0.8281 oz. ASW, 38.6 mm. **Ruler:** Elizabeth II **Subject:** Diamond Wedding Anniversary **Obv:** Conjoined busts with Philip right **Obv. Legend:** ELIZABETH II - ISLE OF MAN **Rev:** Royal Family of five standing facing **Rev. Legend:** Diamond Wedding of H.M. Queen Elizabeth II & H.R.H. Prince Philip **Edge:** Reeded

Date	Mintage	F12	VF20	XF40	MS60	MS63
2007	—	PF63 45.00	PF65 50.00			

KM# 1319a CROWN
28.28 g., 0.9167 Silver 0.8281 oz. ASW, 38.6 mm. **Ruler:** Elizabeth II **Subject:** Diamond Wedding Anniversary **Obv:** Conjoined busts with Philip right **Obv. Legend:** ELIZABETH II - ISLE OF MAN **Rev:** Bride and groom standing facing **Rev. Legend:** Diamond Wedding of H.M. Queen Elizabeth II & H.R.H. Prince Philip **Edge:** Reeded

Date	Mintage	F12	VF20	XF40	MS60	MS63
2007	—	PF63 45.00	PF65 50.00			

KM# 1348.1a CROWN
0.925 Silver **Ruler:** Elizabeth II **Subject:** The Tale of Peter Rabbit **Obv:** Bust with tiara right **Obv. Legend:** ELIZABETH II - ISLE OF MAN **Rev:** Peter walking with friends **Edge:** Reeded

Date	Mintage	F12	VF20	XF40	MS60	MS63
2007PM	—	PF63 45.00	PF65 50.00			

KM# 1348.2a CROWN
0.925 Silver **Ruler:** Elizabeth II **Subject:** The Tale of Peter Rabbit **Obv:** Bust with tiara right **Obv. Legend:** ELIZABETH II - ISLE OF MAN **Rev:** Peter walking with friends, multicolor **Edge:** Reeded

Date	Mintage	F12	VF20	XF40	MS60	MS63
2007PM	—	PF65 75.00				

KM# 1324.1 CROWN
28.28 g., Copper-Nickel, 38.60 mm. **Ruler:** Elizabeth II **Subject:** Hans Christian Anderson's Fairy Tales **Obv:** Bust with tiara right **Obv. Legend:** ELIZABETH II - ISLE OF MAN **Rev:** Prince awakening Sleeping Beauty, castle in background **Rev. Legend:** Sleeping Beauty **Edge:** Reeded

Date	Mintage	F12	VF20	XF40	MS60	MS63
2007PM	—	—	—	—	—	25.00

KM# 1325.1 CROWN
28.28 g., Copper-Nickel, 38.60 mm. **Ruler:** Elizabeth II **Subject:** Hans Christian Anderson's Fairy Tales **Obv:** Bust with tiara right **Obv. Legend:** ELIZABETH II - ISLE OF MAN **Rev:** Wolf at right trying to blow pig's house down, two pigs fleeing above in background **Rev. Legend:** Three Little Pigs **Edge:** Reeded

Date	Mintage	F12	VF20	XF40	MS60	MS63
2007PM	—	—	—	—	—	35.00

KM# 1325.2 CROWN
28.28 g., Copper-Nickel, 38.60 mm. **Ruler:** Elizabeth II **Subject:** Hans Christian Anderson's Fairy Tales **Obv:** Bust with tiara right **Obv. Legend:** ELIZABETH II - ISLE OF MAN **Rev:** Wolf at right trying to blow pig's house down, two pigs fleeing above in background multicolor **Rev. Legend:** Three Little Pigs **Edge:** Reeded

Date	Mintage	F12	VF20	XF40	MS60	MS63
2007PM	—	—	—	—	—	40.00

KM# 1325.1a CROWN
28.28 g., 0.925 Silver 0.8356 oz. ASW, 38.60 mm. **Ruler:** Elizabeth II **Subject:** Hans Christian Anderson's Fairy Tales **Obv:** Bust with tiara right **Obv. Legend:** ELIZABETH II - ISLE OF MAN **Rev:** Wolf at right trying to blow pig's house down, two pigs fleeing above in background **Rev. Legend:** Three Little Pigs **Edge:** Reeded

Date	Mintage	F12	VF20	XF40	MS60	MS63
2007PM	—	PF63 45.00	PF65 50.00			

KM# 1325.2a CROWN
28.28 g., 0.925 Silver 0.8356 oz. ASW, 38.60 mm. **Ruler:** Elizabeth II **Subject:** Hans Christian Anderson's Fairy Tales **Obv:** Bust with tiara right **Obv. Legend:** ELIZABETH II - ISLE OF MAN **Rev:** Wolf at right trying to blow pig's house down, two pigs fleeing above in background multicolor **Rev. Legend:** Three Little Pigs **Edge:** Reeded

Date	Mintage	F12	VF20	XF40	MS60	MS63
2007PM	—	PF65 75.00				

KM# 1307.1 CROWN
28.28 g., Copper-Nickel, 38.6 mm. **Ruler:** Elizabeth II **Rev:** Ragdoll cat and kittens

Date	Mintage	F12	VF20	XF40	MS60	MS63
2007	—	—	—	—	15.00	18.00

KM# 1307.2 CROWN
28.28 g., Copper-Nickel, 38.6 mm. **Ruler:** Elizabeth II **Rev:** Three cats, multicolor

Date	Mintage	F12	VF20	XF40	MS60	MS63
2007PM	—	—	—	—	—	25.00

KM# 1324.1a CROWN
28.28 g., 0.925 Silver 0.8356 oz. ASW, 38.60 mm. **Ruler:** Elizabeth II **Subject:** Hans Christian Anderson's Fairy Tales **Obv:** Bust with tiara right **Obv. Legend:** ELIZABETH II - ISLE OF MAN **Rev:** Prince wakening Sleeping Beauty, castle in background **Rev. Legend:** Sleeping Beauty **Edge:** Reeded

Date	Mintage	F12	VF20	XF40	MS60	MS63
2007PM	—	PF63 45.00	PF65 50.00			

KM# 1324.2 CROWN
28.28 g., Copper-Nickel, 38.60 mm. **Ruler:** Elizabeth II **Subject:** Hans Christian Anderson's Fairy Tales **Obv:** Bust with tiara right **Obv. Legend:** ELIZABET II - ISLE OF MAN **Rev:** Prince awakening Sleeping Beauty, castle in background multicolor **Rev. Legend:** Sleeping Beauty **Edge:** Reeded

Date	Mintage	F12	VF20	XF40	MS60	MS63
2007PM	—	—	—	—	—	25.00

KM# 1324.2a CROWN
28.28 g., 0.925 Silver 0.8356 oz. ASW, 38.60 mm. **Ruler:** Elizabeth II **Subject:** Hans Christian Anderson's Fairy Tales **Obv:** Bust with tiara right **Obv. Legend:** ELIZABETH II - ISLE OF MAN **Rev:** Prince awakening Sleeping Beauty, castle in background multicolor **Rev. Legend:** Sleeping Beauty **Edge:** Reeded

Date	Mintage	F12	VF20	XF40	MS60	MS63
2007PM	—	PF63 45.00	PF65 50.00			

KM# 1418 CROWN
28.28 g., Copper-Nickel, 38.6 mm. **Ruler:** Elizabeth II **Subject:** TT Centennial **Obv:** Bust with tiara right **Rev:** Motorcyclist left

Date	Mintage	F12	VF20	XF40	MS60	MS63
2007PM	—	—	—	—	15.00	17.00

KM# 1419 CROWN
28.28 g., Copper-Nickel, 38.6 mm. **Ruler:** Elizabeth II **Subject:** TT Centennial **Obv:** Bust with tiara right **Rev:** Motorcyclists Dunlop

Date	Mintage	F12	VF20	XF40	MS60	MS63
2007PM	—	—	—	—	15.00	17.00

KM# 1420 CROWN
28.28 g., Copper-Nickel, 38.6 mm. **Ruler:** Elizabeth II **Subject:** TT Centennial **Obv:** Bust with tiara right **Rev:** Motorcyclists Woods

Date	Mintage	F12	VF20	XF40	MS60	MS63
2007PM	—	—	—	—	15.00	17.00

KM# 1421 CROWN
28.28 g., Copper-Nickel, 38.6 mm. **Ruler:** Elizabeth II **Subject:** TT Centennial **Obv:** Bust with tiara right **Rev:** Motorcyclists Haliwood

Date	Mintage	F12	VF20	XF40	MS60	MS63
2007PM	—	—	—	—	15.00	17.00

KM# 1422 CROWN
28.28 g., Copper-Nickel, 38.6 mm. **Ruler:** Elizabeth II **Subject:** TT Centennial **Obv:** Bust with tiara right **Rev:** Motorcyclists Colier

Date	Mintage	F12	VF20	XF40	MS60	MS63
2007PM	—	—	—	—	15.00	17.00

KM# 1353 CROWN
28.28 g., Copper-Nickel, 38.6 mm. **Ruler:** Elizabeth II **Subject:** Prince Charles 60th Birthday **Obv:** Bust with tiara right **Obv. Legend:** ELIZABETH II - ISLE OF MAN **Rev:** Heads of Charles, Princes William and Henry right **Edge:** Reeded

Date	Mintage	F12	VF20	XF40	MS60	MS63
2008PM	—	—	—	—	10.00	12.00

KM# 1353a CROWN
28.28 g., 0.925 Silver 0.8356 oz. ASW, 38.6 mm. **Ruler:** Elizabeth II **Subject:** Prince Charles 60th Birthday **Obv:** Bust with tiara right **Obv. Legend:** ELIZABETH II - ISLE OF MAN **Rev:** Heads of Charles, Princes William and Henry right **Edge:** Reeded

Date	Mintage	F12	VF20	XF40	MS60	MS63
2008PM	10,000	PF63 45.00		PF65 50.00		

KM# 1394 CROWN
28.28 g., Copper-Nickel, 38.6 mm. **Ruler:** Elizabeth II **Rev:** Snowman and James

Date	Mintage	F12	VF20	XF40	MS60	MS63
2008PM AA	—	—	—	—	—	20.00

KM# 1397 CROWN
0.925 Silver, 56.2x40 mm. **Ruler:** Elizabeth II **Obv:** Bust with tiara right within Egyptian motif **Rev:** Seated figure and attendant **Shape:** Triangle

Date	Mintage	F12	VF20	XF40	MS60	MS63
2008PM	2,500	PF65 75.00				

KM# 1398 CROWN
0.925 Silver, 56.2x40 mm. **Ruler:** Elizabeth II **Obv:** Bust right in Tiaria within Egyptian motif **Rev:** Statue standing **Shape:** Triangle

Date	Mintage	F12	VF20	XF40	MS60	MS63
2008PM	2,500	PF65 75.00				

KM# 1401 CROWN
28.28 g., 0.925 Silver 0.8356 oz. ASW, 38.6 mm. **Ruler:** Elizabeth II **Obv:** Bust with tiara right, multicolor band around **Rev:** Seated figures, multicolor band

Date	Mintage	F12	VF20	XF40	MS60	MS63
2008PM	—	PF65 65.00				

KM# 1403 CROWN
28.28 g., Copper-Nickel, 38.6 mm. **Ruler:** Elizabeth II **Subject:** Bejing Olympics **Obv:** Bust with tiara right **Rev:** Torch runner and Great Wall of China

Date	Mintage	F12	VF20	XF40	MS60	MS63
2008PM	—	PF63 22.00		PF65 25.00		

KM# 1404 CROWN
28.28 g., Copper-Nickel, 38.6 mm. **Ruler:** Elizabeth II **Obv:** Bust wiht tiara right **Rev:** Paddington Bear

Date	Mintage	F12	VF20	XF40	MS60	MS63
2008PM	—	PF63 22.00		PF65 25.00		

KM# 1405 CROWN
31.10 g., 0.999 Silver 0.9926 oz. ASW, 56.2x40.7 mm. **Ruler:** Elizabeth II **Obv:** Bust with tiara right **Rev:** Three figures standing, vile of sand above **Shape:** Triangle

Date	Mintage	F12	VF20	XF40	MS60	MS63
2008PM	3,000	**PF65** 75.00				

KM# 1424 CROWN
28.28 g., Copper-Nickel, 38.6 mm. **Ruler:** Elizabeth II **Obv:** Bust with tiara right **Rev:** Two cats seated

Date	Mintage	F12	VF20	XF40	MS60	MS63
2008PM	—				15.00	17.00

KM# 1424a CROWN
31.11 g., 0.999 Silver 0.9926 oz. ASW, 38.6 mm. **Ruler:** Elizabeth II **Obv:** Bust with tiara right **Rev:** Two cats seated

Date	Mintage	F12	VF20	XF40	MS60	MS63
2008PM	—	**PF65** 70.00				

KM# 1373 CROWN
28.28 g., Copper-Nickel, 38.6 mm. **Ruler:** Elizabeth II **Rev:** Berlin Wall and Brandenburg Gate statue group

Date	Mintage	F12	VF20	XF40	MS60	MS63
2009	—	—	—	—	15.00	18.00

KM# 1374 CROWN
28.28 g., Copper-Nickel, 38.6 mm. **Ruler:** Elizabeth II **Subject:** Terra Cotta Army **Obv:** Bust right **Rev:** Making of the Soldier

Date	Mintage	F12	VF20	XF40	MS60	MS63
2009	—	—	—	—	12.00	15.00

KM# 1376 CROWN
28.28 g., 0.925 Copper-Nickel 0.8356 oz., 38.6 mm. **Ruler:** Elizabeth II **Subject:** Terra Cotta Army **Obv:** Bust right **Rev:** Making of the Horse

Date	Mintage	F12	VF20	XF40	MS60	MS63
2009	—	—	—	—	12.00	15.00

KM# 1388 CROWN
31.11 g., 0.9999 Gold 0.9935 oz. AGW, 45x31.1 mm. **Ruler:** Elizabeth II **Subject:** Howard Carter, 70th Anniversary of Death **Obv:** Bust right **Rev:** Pharoah and Anubis carving, encased with sand **Shape:** Triangle

Date	Mintage	F12	VF20	XF40	MS60	MS63
2009	250	**PF65** 1,850				

KM# 1389 CROWN
31.10 g., 0.999 Silver 0.9926 oz. ASW, 56.2x40.7 mm. **Ruler:** Elizabeth II **Subject:** Howard Carter, 70th Anniversary of death **Obv:** Bust right **Rev:** Pharoah and Anubis, encased with sand **Shape:** Triangle

Date	Mintage	F12	VF20	XF40	MS60	MS63
2009	3,000	**PF65** 125				

KM# 1391 CROWN
28.28 g., Copper-Nickel, 38.6 mm. **Ruler:** Elizabeth II **Obv:** Bust right **Rev:** Henry VIII and portraits of wives

Date	Mintage	F12	VF20	XF40	MS60	MS63
2009	—	—	—	—	15.00	18.00

KM# 1392 CROWN
28.28 g., Copper-Nickel, 38.6 mm. **Ruler:** Elizabeth II **Subject:** FIFA World Cup - South Africa **Obv:** Bust right **Rev:** Two soccer players

Date	Mintage	F12	VF20	XF40	MS60	MS63
2009	—	—	—	—	15.00	18.00

KM# 1373a CROWN
28.28 g., 0.925 Silver 0.8356 oz. ASW, 38.6 mm. **Ruler:** Elizabeth II **Rev:** Berlin Wall and Brandenberg Gate

Date	Mintage	F12	VF20	XF40	MS60	MS63
2009	10,000	**PF63** 35.00	**PF65** 40.00			

KM# 1374a CROWN
28.28 g., 0.925 Silver 0.8356 oz. ASW, 38.6 mm. **Ruler:** Elizabeth II **Subject:** Terra Cotta Army **Obv:** Bust right **Rev:** Making of the Soldier

Date	Mintage	F12	VF20	XF40	MS60	MS63
2009	10,000	**PF63** 35.00	**PF65** 40.00			

KM# 1376a CROWN
28.28 g., 0.925 Silver 0.8356 oz. ASW, 38.6 mm. **Ruler:** Elizabeth II **Subject:** Terra Cotta Army **Obv:** Bust right **Rev:** Making of the Horse

Date	Mintage	F12	VF20	XF40	MS60	MS63
2009	10,000	**PF63** 35.00	**PF65** 40.00			

KM# 1391a CROWN
28.28 g., 0.925 Silver 0.8356 oz. ASW, 38.6 mm. **Ruler:** Elizabeth II **Obv:** Bust right **Rev:** Henry VIII

Date	Mintage	F12	VF20	XF40	MS60	MS63
2009	10,000	**PF63** 35.00	**PF65** 40.00			

KM# 1392a CROWN
28.28 g., 0.925 Silver 0.8356 oz. ASW, 38.6 mm. **Ruler:** Elizabeth II **Subject:** FIFA World Cup - South Africa **Obv:** Bust right

Date	Mintage	F12	VF20	XF40	MS60	MS63
2009	10,000	**PF63** 35.00	**PF65** 40.00			

KM# 1409a CROWN
28.28 g., 0.925 Silver 0.8356 oz. ASW, 38.6 mm. **Ruler:** Elizabeth II **Subject:** Olympics, London **Rev:** Two female runners by St. Paul's Cathedral

Date	Mintage	F12	VF20	XF40	MS60	MS63
2009PM	10,000	**PF63** 45.00	**PF65** 50.00			

KM# 1378.1 CROWN
28.28 g., Copper-Nickel, 38.6 mm. **Ruler:** Elizabeth II **Obv:** Bust right **Rev:** Chinchilla cat and kitten

Date	Mintage	F12	VF20	XF40	MS60	MS63
2009	—	—	—	—	15.00	18.00

KM# 1390.1a CROWN
28.28 g., 0.925 Silver 0.8356 oz. ASW, 38.6 mm. **Ruler:** Elizabeth II **Subject:** Corcorde test flight, 40th Anniversary **Obv:** Bust right **Rev:** Concorde and five world landmarks

Date	Mintage	F12	VF20	XF40	MS60	MS63
2009	10,000	**PF63** 35.00	**PF65** 40.00			

KM# 1406a CROWN
28.28 g., 0.925 Silver 0.8356 oz. ASW, 38.6 mm. **Ruler:** Elizabeth II **Series:** Olympics, London **Rev:** Three cyclists speeding past Buckingham Palace

Date	Mintage	F12	VF20	XF40	MS60	MS63
2009PM	10,000	**PF63** 45.00	**PF65** 50.00			

KM# 1407a CROWN
28.28 g., 0.925 Silver 0.8356 oz. ASW, 38.6 mm. **Ruler:** Elizabeth II **Subject:** Olympics, London **Rev:** Skull of 4 rowers on Thames

Date	Mintage	F12	VF20	XF40	MS60	MS63
2009PM	10,000	**PF63** 45.00	**PF65** 50.00			

KM# 1408a CROWN
28.28 g., 0.925 Silver 0.8356 oz. ASW, 38.6 mm. **Ruler:** Elizabeth II **Subject:** Olympics, London **Rev:** Swimmer in the Thames, Tower of London in background

Date	Mintage	F12	VF20	XF40	MS60	MS63
2009PM	10,000	**PF63** 45.00	**PF65** 50.00			

KM# 1410a CROWN
28.28 g., 0.925 Silver 0.8356 oz. ASW, 38.6 mm. **Ruler:** Elizabeth II **Subject:** Olympics, London **Rev:** Sailing on the Thames, Tower Bridge in background

Date	Mintage	F12	VF20	XF40	MS60	MS63
2009PM	10,000	**PF63** 45.00	**PF65** 50.00			

KM# 1411a CROWN
28.28 g., 0.925 Silver 0.8356 oz. ASW, 38.6 mm. **Ruler:** Elizabeth II **Subject:** Olympics, London **Rev:** Boxers with London architecture in background

Date	Mintage	F12	VF20	XF40	MS60	MS63
2009PM	10,000	**PF63** 45.00	**PF65** 50.00			

KM# 1379 CROWN
31.11 g., 0.9999 Gold 0.9935 oz. AGW, 32.7 mm. **Ruler:** Elizabeth II **Obv:** Bust right **Rev:** Chinchilla cat and kitten

Date	Mintage	F12	VF20	XF40	MS60	MS63
2009						1,800
2009	1,000	**PF63** 1,825	**PF65** 1,850			

KM# 1378.1a CROWN
31.11 g., 0.999 Silver 0.9926 oz. ASW, 38.6 mm. **Ruler:** Elizabeth II **Obv:** Bust with tiara right **Rev:** Two cats

Date	Mintage	F12	VF20	XF40	MS60	MS63
2009PM	—	PF65 70.00				

KM# 1378.2 CROWN
28.28 g., Copper-Nickel, 38.6 mm. **Ruler:** Elizabeth II **Obv:** Bust right **Rev:** Multicolor chinchilla cat and kitten

Date	Mintage	F12	VF20	XF40	MS60	MS63
2009	—	—	—	—	—	25.00

KM# 1378.2a CROWN
31.11 g., 0.999 Silver 0.9926 oz. ASW, 38.6 mm. **Ruler:** Elizabeth II **Obv:** Bust with tiara right **Rev:** Two cats, multicolor

Date	Mintage	F12	VF20	XF40	MS60	MS63
2009PM	—	PF65 80.00				

KM# 1390.1 CROWN
28.28 g., Copper-Nickel, 38.6 mm. **Ruler:** Elizabeth II **Subject:** Concorde test flight, 40th Anniversary **Obv:** Bust right **Rev:** Concorde and five world landmarks

Date	Mintage	F12	VF20	XF40	MS60	MS63
2009	—	—	—	—	15.00	18.00

KM# 1390.2 CROWN
28.28 g., Copper-Nickel, 38.6 mm. **Ruler:** Elizabeth II **Subject:** 40th Anniversary of test flight **Rev:** Concorde in color

Date	Mintage	F12	VF20	XF40	MS60	MS63
2009PM	—	—	—	—	—	25.00

KM# 1406 CROWN
28.28 g., Copper-Nickel, 38.6 mm. **Ruler:** Elizabeth II **Series:** London Olympics 2012 **Obv:** Bust wiht tiara right **Rev:** Three cyclists before Buckingham Palace

Date	Mintage	F12	VF20	XF40	MS60	MS63
2009PM	—	PF63 22.00	PF65 25.00			

KM# 1407 CROWN
28.28 g., Copper-Nickel, 38.6 mm. **Ruler:** Elizabeth II **Subject:** London Olympics, 2012 **Obv:** Bust with tiara right **Rev:** Rowers before Big Ben and Parliament

Date	Mintage	F12	VF20	XF40	MS60	MS63
2009PM	—	PF63 22.00	PF65 25.00			

KM# 1408 CROWN
28.28 g., Copper-Nickel, 38.6 mm. **Ruler:** Elizabeth II **Subject:** London Olympics, 2012 **Obv:** Bust with tiara right **Rev:** Swimmer before Tower of London

Date	Mintage	F12	VF20	XF40	MS60	MS63
2009PM	—	PF63 22.00	PF65 25.00			

KM# 1409 CROWN
28.28 g., Copper-Nickel, 38.6 mm. **Ruler:** Elizabeth II **Subject:** London Olympics, 2012 **Obv:** Bust with tiara right **Rev:** Two runners before St. Paul's Cathedral

Date	Mintage	F12	VF20	XF40	MS60	MS63
2009PM	—	PF63 22.00	PF65 25.00			

KM# 1410 CROWN
28.28 g., Copper-Nickel, 38.6 mm. **Ruler:** Elizabeth II **Subject:** London Olympics, 2012 **Obv:** Bust with tiara right **Rev:** Two sailboats before Tower Bridge

Date	Mintage	F12	VF20	XF40	MS60	MS63
2009PM	—	PF63 22.00	PF65 25.00			

KM# 1411 CROWN
28.28 g., Copper-Nickel, 38.6 mm. **Ruler:** Elizabeth II **Subject:** London Olympics, 2012 **Obv:** Bust with tiara right **Rev:** Two boxers before London Wheel and skyline

Date	Mintage	F12	VF20	XF40	MS60	MS63
2009PM	—	PF63 22.00	PF65 25.00			

KM# 1412 CROWN
28.28 g., Copper-Nickel, 38.6 mm. **Ruler:** Elizabeth II **Subject:** Vancouver Olympics, 2010 **Obv:** Bust with tiara right **Rev:** Torch at center of four sports, hockey, sled, figure skating and bobsled

Date	Mintage	F12	VF20	XF40	MS60	MS63
2009PM	—	PF63 22.00	PF65 25.00			

KM# 1413 CROWN
28.28 g., Copper-Nickel, 38.6 mm. **Ruler:** Elizabeth II **Subject:** Vancouver Olympics, 2010 **Obv:** Bust with tiara right **Rev:** Torch at center of four sports, ski jump, snoboardiong, biathlon and Salom

Date	Mintage	F12	VF20	XF40	MS60	MS63
2009PM	—	PF63 22.00	PF65 25.00			

KM# 1414 CROWN
28.28 g., Copper-Nickel, 38.6 mm. **Ruler:** Elizabeth II **Subject:**
Bee Gee's 50th Anniversary **Obv:** Bust with tiara right **Rev:**
Band name at center

Date	Mintage	F12	VF20	XF40	MS60	MS63
2009PM	—	PF63 22.00	PF65 25.00			

KM# 1415 CROWN
28.28 g., Copper-Nickel, 38.6 mm. **Ruler:** Elizabeth II **Subject:**
First man on the Moon, 40th Anniversary **Obv:** Bust with tiara
right **Rev:** Man in space suit with American Flag on moon

Date	Mintage	F12	VF20	XF40	MS60	MS63
2009PM	—	PF63 22.00	PF65 25.00			

KM# 1465 CROWN
31.10 g., 0.9999 Gold 0.9934 oz. AGW, 45x32.1 mm. **Ruler:**
Elizabeth II **Subject:** Howard Carter, 70th Anniversary of Death
Shape: Triangle

Date	Mintage	F12	VF20	XF40	MS60	MS63
2009PM	250	PF65 1,850				

KM# 1426a CROWN
31.11 g., 0.999 Silver 0.9926 oz. ASW, 38.6 mm. **Ruler:**
Elizabeth II **Obv:** Bust with tiara right **Rev:** Cat standing right

Date	Mintage	F12	VF20	XF40	MS60	MS63
2010PM	—	PF65 70.00				

KM# 1417 CROWN
0.999 Silver **Ruler:** Elizabeth II **Obv:** Bust with tiara right within
ornimentation **Rev:** Kubla Kahn standing **Shape:** Vertical
rectangle

Date	Mintage	F12	VF20	XF40	MS60	MS63
2010PM	—	PF65 50.00				

KM# 1426 CROWN
28.28 g., Copper-Nickel, 38.6 mm. **Ruler:** Elizabeth II **Obv:**
Bust with tiara right **Rev:** Abyssinian Cat standing right over
kitten **Edge:** Reeded

Date	Mintage	F12	VF20	XF40	MS60	MS63
2010PM	—	—	—	—	15.00	17.00

KM# 1471 CROWN
28.28 g., Copper-Nickel, 38.6 mm. **Ruler:** Elizabeth II **Obv:**
Bust in tiara right **Rev:** Buckingham Palace

Date	Mintage	F12	VF20	XF40	MS60	MS63
2010PM	—	—	—	—	—	10.00

KM# 1471a CROWN
28.28 g., 0.925 Silver 0.8356 oz. ASW, 38.6 mm. **Ruler:**
Elizabeth II **Obv:** Bust in tiara right **Rev:** Buckingham Palace

Date	Mintage	F12	VF20	XF40	MS60	MS63
2010PM	—	PF63 45.00	PF65 50.00			
2010PM	—	PF63 50.00	PF65 55.00			

Note: Script WK privy mark for engagement

KM# 1439 CROWN
31.11 g., 0.9999 Gold 0.9935 oz. AGW, 32.7 mm. **Ruler:**
Elizabeth II **Subject:** Turkish Angora Cat

Date	Mintage	F12	VF20	XF40	MS60	MS63
2011PM	1,000	PF63 1,875	PF65 1,900			
2011PM	—	—	—	—	1,850	

KM# 1440a.1 CROWN
31.11 g., 0.999 Silver 0.9926 oz. ASW, 38.6 mm. **Ruler:**
Elizabeth II **Subject:** Turkish Angora Cat

Date	Mintage	F12	VF20	XF40	MS60	MS63
2011PM	10,000	PF65 70.00				

KM# 1455a CROWN
28.28 g., 0.925 Silver 0.8356 oz. ASW, 38.6 mm. **Ruler:**
Elizabeth II **Subject:** Isle of Man Tourist Trophy race **Rev:** Two
racers and map of the Isle of Man

Date	Mintage	F12	VF20	XF40	MS60	MS63
2011PM	10,000	PF63 45.00	PF65 50.00			

KM# 1478a CROWN
28.28 g., 0.925 Silver 0.8356 oz. ASW, 38.6 mm. **Ruler:**
Elizabeth II **Subject:** Royal Wedding **Rev:** Busts left of
Catherine Middleton in large hat and Prince William

Date	Mintage	F12	VF20	XF40	MS60	MS63
2011PM	10,000	PF63 45.00	PF65 50.00			

KM# 1485a CROWN
28.28 g., 0.925 Silver 0.8356 oz. ASW, 38.6 mm. **Ruler:**
Elizabeth II **Subject:** Year of the Rabbit **Rev:** Beatrix Potter's
Peter Rabbit

Date	Mintage	F12	VF20	XF40	MS60	MS63
2011PM	10,000	PF63 45.00	PF65 50.00			

KM# 1440 CROWN
28.28 g., Copper-Nickel, 38.6 mm. **Ruler:** Elizabeth II **Subject:**
Turkish Angora Cat

Date	Mintage	F12	VF20	XF40	MS60	MS63
2011PM	—	—	—	—	—	10.00

KM# 1440a.2 CROWN
31.11 g., 0.999 Silver 0.9926 oz. ASW, 38.6 mm. **Ruler:**
Elizabeth II **Rev:** Two cats in color

Date	Mintage	F12	VF20	XF40	MS60	MS63
2011PM	—	—	—	—	—	75.00

KM# 1455 CROWN
28.28 g., Copper-Nickel, 38.6 mm. **Ruler:** Elizabeth II **Subject:**
Isle of Man Tourist Trophy race **Rev:** Two racers and outline
map of the Isle of Man

Date	Mintage	F12	VF20	XF40	MS60	MS63
2011PM	—	—	—	—	—	10.00

KM# 1456 CROWN
31.10 g., 0.9999 Gold 0.9934 oz. AGW, 32.7 mm. **Ruler:**
Elizabeth II **Subject:** Donatello's Chellini Madonna **Rev:** Mary
and child in very high relief

Date	Mintage	F12	VF20	XF40	MS60	MS63
2011PM	999	PF65 1,850				

KM# 1477 CROWN
28.28 g., Copper-Nickel, 38.6 mm. **Ruler:** Elizabeth II **Rev:**
Busts right of Elizabeth II and Prince Philip, flags flanking, royal
shield below

Date	Mintage	F12	VF20	XF40	MS60	MS63
2011PM	—	—	—	—	—	10.00

KM# 1477a CROWN
28.28 g., 0.925 Silver 0.8356 oz. ASW, 38.6 mm. **Ruler:**
Elizabeth II **Rev:** Busts right of Elizabeth II and Prince Philip,
flags flanking, royal shield below

Date	Mintage	F12	VF20	XF40	MS60	MS63
2011PM	10,000	PF63 45.00	PF65 50.00			

KM# 1478 CROWN
28.28 g., Copper-Nickel, 38.6 mm. **Ruler:** Elizabeth II **Subject:**
Royal Wedding **Rev:** Busts left of Catherine Middleton in large
hat and Prince William

Date	Mintage	F12	VF20	XF40	MS60	MS63
2011PM	—	—	—	—	—	10.00

KM# 1485 CROWN
28.28 g., Copper-Nickel, 38.6 mm. **Ruler:** Elizabeth II **Subject:** Year of the Rabbit **Rev:** Image of Beatrix Potter's Peter Rabbit

Date	Mintage	F12	VF20	XF40	MS60	MS63
2011PM	—	—	—	—	—	10.00

KM# 1441a CROWN
28.28 g., 0.925 Silver 0.8356 oz. ASW, 38.6 mm. **Ruler:** Elizabeth II **Subject:** Olympics, London **Rev:** Horse jumping

Date	Mintage	F12	VF20	XF40	MS60	MS63
2012PM	10,000	PF63 45.00	PF65 50.00			

KM# 1442a CROWN
28.28 g., 0.925 Silver 0.8356 oz. ASW, 38.6 mm. **Ruler:** Elizabeth II **Subject:** Olympics, London **Rev:** Track Cyclist

Date	Mintage	F12	VF20	XF40	MS60	MS63
2012PM	10,000	PF63 45.00	PF65 50.00			

KM# 1443a CROWN
28.28 g., 0.925 Silver 0.8356 oz. ASW, 38.6 mm. **Ruler:** Elizabeth II **Subject:** Olympics, London **Rev:** Swimmer, divers in background

Date	Mintage	F12	VF20	XF40	MS60	MS63
2012PM	10,000	PF63 45.00	PF65 50.00			

KM# 1444a CROWN
28.28 g., 0.925 Silver 0.8356 oz. ASW, 38.6 mm. **Ruler:** Elizabeth II **Subject:** Olympics, London **Rev:** Canoeist, two rowers in background

Date	Mintage	F12	VF20	XF40	MS60	MS63
2012PM	10,000	PF63 45.00	PF65 50.00			

KM# 1445a CROWN
28.28 g., 0.925 Silver 0.8356 oz. ASW, 38.6 mm. **Ruler:** Elizabeth II **Subject:** Olympics, London **Rev:** Judo players, two boxers in background

Date	Mintage	F12	VF20	XF40	MS60	MS63
2012PM	10,000	PF63 45.00	PF65 50.00			

KM# 1446a CROWN
28.28 g., 0.925 Silver 0.8356 oz. ASW, 38.6 mm. **Ruler:** Elizabeth II **Subject:** Olympics, London **Rev:** Table tennis players, Lawn tennis players in background

Date	Mintage	F12	VF20	XF40	MS60	MS63
2012PM	10,000	PF63 45.00	PF65 50.00			

KM# 1461a CROWN
28.28 g., 0.925 Silver 0.8356 oz. ASW, 38.6 mm. **Ruler:** Elizabeth II **Subject:** European Football Championships 2012 **Rev:** Footballer heading ball, Sitting Statue of Liberty in Lviv and Neptune's fountain in Gdansk in background

Date	Mintage	F12	VF20	XF40	MS60	MS63
2012PM	10,000	PF63 45.00	PF65 50.00			

KM# 1462a CROWN
28.28 g., 0.925 Silver 0.8356 oz. ASW, 38.6 mm. **Ruler:** Elizabeth II **Subject:** European Football Championships 2012 **Rev:** Player passing the ball, Motherland Statue in Kiev and King Sigismund's statue in Warsaw in background

Date	Mintage	F12	VF20	XF40	MS60	MS63
2012PM	10,000	PF63 45.00	PF65 50.00			

KM# 1463a CROWN
28.28 g., 0.925 Silver 0.8356 oz. ASW, 38.6 mm. **Ruler:** Elizabeth II **Subject:** European Football Championships 2012 **Rev:** Footballer shooting, Cathedral of the Transfiguration in Donetsk and the Raclawice Panorama in Wroclaw in background

Date	Mintage	F12	VF20	XF40	MS60	MS63
2012PM	10,000	PF63 45.00	PF65 50.00			

KM# 1464a CROWN
28.28 g., 0.925 Silver 0.8356 oz. ASW, 38.6 mm. **Ruler:** Elizabeth II **Subject:** European Football Championships 2012 **Rev:** Two footballers tackling, Catheral of the annunciation in Kharkiv and the Cathedral in Poznan in background

Date	Mintage	F12	VF20	XF40	MS60	MS63
2012PM	10,000	PF63 45.00	PF65 50.00			

KM# 1480a CROWN
28.28 g., 0.925 Silver 0.8356 oz. ASW, 38.6 mm. **Ruler:** Elizabeth II **Obv:** Conjoined busts right **Rev:** Elizabeth II at coronation with sceptre, orb and state crown

Date	Mintage	F12	VF20	XF40	MS60	MS63
2012PM	10,000	PF63 45.00	PF65 50.00			

KM# 1481a CROWN
28.28 g., 0.925 Silver 0.8356 oz. ASW, 38.6 mm. **Ruler:** Elizabeth II **Obv:** Conjoined busts right **Rev:** Elizabeth, the Queen Mother

Date	Mintage	F12	VF20	XF40	MS60	MS63
2012PM	10,000	PF63 45.00	PF65 50.00			

KM# 1482a CROWN
28.28 g., 0.925 Silver 0.8356 oz. ASW, 38.6 mm. **Ruler:** Elizabeth II **Obv:** Conjoined busts right **Rev:** Passengers boarding Titanic

Date	Mintage	F12	VF20	XF40	MS60	MS63
2012PM	10,000	PF63 50.00	PF65 55.00			

KM# 1483a CROWN
28.28 g., 0.925 Silver 0.8356 oz. ASW, 38.6 mm. **Ruler:** Elizabeth II **Obv:** Conjoined busts right **Rev:** Titanic sailing into icefield

Date	Mintage	F12	VF20	XF40	MS60	MS63
2012PM	10,000	PF63 45.00	PF65 50.00			

KM# 1441 CROWN
28.28 g., Copper-Nickel, 38.6 mm. **Ruler:** Elizabeth II **Subject:** Olympics, London **Rev:** Horse Jumping

Date	Mintage	F12	VF20	XF40	MS60	MS63
2012PM	—	—	—	—	—	10.00

KM# 1442 CROWN
28.28 g., Copper-Nickel, 38.6 mm. **Ruler:** Elizabeth II **Subject:** Olympics, London **Rev:** Track cyclist

Date	Mintage	F12	VF20	XF40	MS60	MS63
2012PM	—	—	—	—	—	10.00

KM# 1443 CROWN
28.28 g., Copper-Nickel, 38.6 mm. **Ruler:** Elizabeth II **Subject:** Olympics, London **Rev:** Swimmer with divers in background

Date	Mintage	F12	VF20	XF40	MS60	MS63
2012PM	—	—	—	—	—	10.00

KM# 1444 CROWN
28.28 g., Copper-Nickel, 38.6 mm. **Ruler:** Elizabeth II **Subject:** Olympics, London **Rev:** Canoeist, two rowers in background

Date	Mintage	F12	VF20	XF40	MS60	MS63
2012PM	—	—	—	—	—	10.00

KM# 1445 CROWN
28.28 g., Copper-Nickel, 38.6 mm. **Ruler:** Elizabeth II **Subject:** Olympics, London **Rev:** Judo players, two boxers in background

Date	Mintage	F12	VF20	XF40	MS60	MS63
2012PM	—	—	—	—	—	10.00

KM# 1446 CROWN
28.28 g., Copper-Nickel, 38.6 mm. **Ruler:** Elizabeth II **Subject:** Olympics, London **Rev:** Table tennis players, Lawn Tennis players in background

Date	Mintage	F12	VF20	XF40	MS60	MS63
2012PM	—	—	—	—	—	10.00

KM# 1461 CROWN
28.28 g., Copper-Nickel, 38.6 mm. **Ruler:** Elizabeth II **Subject:** European Football Championships 2012 **Obv:** Player heading a football, Sitting Statue of Liberty in Lviv and Neptune's fountain in Gdansk in background

Date	Mintage	F12	VF20	XF40	MS60	MS63
2012PM	—	—	—	—	—	10.00

KM# 1462 CROWN
28.28 g., Copper-Nickel, 38.6 mm. **Ruler:** Elizabeth II **Subject:** European Football Championships 2012 **Rev:** Player passing ball, Motherland Statue in Kiev and King Sigismund's statue in Warsaw

Date	Mintage	F12	VF20	XF40	MS60	MS63
2012PM	—	—	—	—	—	10.00

KM# 1463 CROWN
28.28 g., Copper-Nickel, 38.6 mm. **Ruler:** Elizabeth II **Subject:** European Football Championships 2012 **Rev:** Footballer shooting, Cathedral of the Transfiguration in Donetsk and the Raclawice Panorama in Wroclaw in background

Date	Mintage	F12	VF20	XF40	MS60	MS63
2012PM	—	—	—	—	—	10.00

KM# 1464 CROWN
28.28 g., Copper-Nickel, 38.6 mm. **Ruler:** Elizabeth II **Subject:** European Football Championships 2012 **Rev:** Two footballers tackling, Cathedral of the Annunciation in Kharkiv and the Cathedral in Poznan in background

Date	Mintage	F12	VF20	XF40	MS60	MS63
2012PM	—	—	—	—	—	10.00

KM# 1480 CROWN
28.28 g., Copper-Nickel, 38.6 mm. **Ruler:** Elizabeth II **Obv:** Conjoined busts right **Rev:** Elizabeth II at coronation with scepter, orb and state crown

Date	Mintage	F12	VF20	XF40	MS60	MS63
2012PM	—	—	—	—	—	10.00

KM# 1481 CROWN
28.28 g., Copper-Nickel, 38.6 mm. **Ruler:** Elizabeth II **Obv:** Conjoined busts right **Rev:** Elizabeth II during 2010 visit to Canada

Date	Mintage	F12	VF20	XF40	MS60	MS63
2012PM	—	—	—	—	—	10.00

KM# 1482 CROWN
28.28 g., Copper-Nickel, 38.6 mm. **Ruler:** Elizabeth II **Obv:** Conjoined busts right **Rev:** Passengers boarding Titanic

Date	Mintage	F12	VF20	XF40	MS60	MS63
2012PM	—	—	—	—	—	10.00

KM# 1483 CROWN
28.28 g., Copper-Nickel, 38.6 mm. **Ruler:** Elizabeth II **Obv:** Conjoined busts right **Rev:** Titanic sailing into icefield

Date	Mintage	F12	VF20	XF40	MS60	MS63
2012PM	—	—	—	—	—	10.00

KM# 1489 CROWN
Copper-Nickel, 38.8 mm. **Ruler:** Elizabeth II **Obv:** Two busts right

Date	Mintage	F12	VF20	XF40	MS60	MS63
2012PM Proof	—	—	—	—	—	10.00

KM# 1200 2 CROWNS
62.20 g., 0.999 Palladium 1.9849 oz. APW, 40 mm. **Ruler:** Elizabeth II **Subject:** Discovery of Palladium Bicentennial **Obv:** Bust with tiara right **Rev:** Pallas Athena left **Edge:** Reeded

Date	Mintage	F12	VF20	XF40	MS60	MS63
2004PM	300	PF65 1,650				

KM# 1402 2 CROWNS
0.925 Silver, 40 mm. **Ruler:** Elizabeth II **Obv:** Bust with tiara right **Rev:** Seven Wonders of the World, multicolor central item

Date	Mintage	F12	VF20	XF40	MS60	MS63
2008PM	—	PF65 100				

KM# 1064 5 CROWN
155.52 g., 0.9999 Gold 4.9673 oz. AGW, 65 mm. **Ruler:** Elizabeth II **Subject:** Year of the Snake **Obv:** Bust with tiara right **Rev:** Snake **Edge:** Reeded

Date	Mintage	F12	VF20	XF40	MS60	MS63
2001	250	PF60 7,500	PF63 8,500	PF65 9,500		

KM# 1104 5 CROWN
155.51 g., 0.9999 Gold 4.9671 oz. AGW, 65 mm. **Ruler:** Elizabeth II **Subject:** Year of the Horse **Obv:** Bust with tiara right **Rev:** Two horses **Edge:** Reeded

Date	Mintage	F12	VF20	XF40	MS60	MS63
2002	250	PF60 7,500	PF63 8,500	PF65 9,500		

KM# 1173 5 CROWN
155.51 g., 0.9999 Gold 4.9671 oz. AGW, 65 mm. **Ruler:** Elizabeth II **Subject:** Year of the Goat **Obv:** Bust with tiara right **Rev:** Three goats **Edge:** Reeded

Date	Mintage	F12	VF20	XF40	MS60	MS63
2003PM	250	PF60 7,500	PF63 8,500	PF65 9,500		

KM# 1244 5 CROWN
155.52 g., 0.9999 Gold 4.9673 oz. AGW, 65 mm. **Ruler:** Elizabeth II **Obv:** Bust with tiara right **Rev:** Monkey **Edge:** Reeded

Date	Mintage	F12	VF20	XF40	MS60	MS63
2004PM	250	PF60 7,500	PF63 8,500	PF65 9,500		

KM# 1219 64 CROWNS
2000.00 g., 0.999 Silver 63.8237 oz. ASW, 140 mm. **Ruler:** Elizabeth II **Obv:** Bust with tiara right **Rev:** Ocean Liner Queen Mary 2 **Edge:** Reeded

Date	Mintage	F12	VF20	XF40	MS60	MS63
2004PM	500	PF65 2,350				

KM# 1142 100 CROWNS
3000.00 g., 0.9999 Silver 95.8218 oz. ASW, 130 mm. **Ruler:** Elizabeth II **Subject:** Queen's Golden Jubilee **Obv:** Bust with tiara right **Rev:** Queen on horse **Edge:** Reeded **Note:** Illustration reduced.

Date	Mintage	F12	VF20	XF40	MS60	MS63
2002	—	PF65 3,500				

KM# 1184 130 CROWNS
4000.00 g., 0.999 Silver 127.6473 oz. ASW, 130 mm. **Ruler:** Elizabeth II **Obv:** Bust with tiara right **Rev:** Gold clad cameo portrait of Elizabeth I with a .035ct ruby inset on her forehead all within a circle of portraits **Edge:** Reeded

Date	Mintage	F12	VF20	XF40	MS60	MS63
2003PM	500	PF65 4,700				

SILVER BULLION COINAGE
Angel Series

KM# 1475 ANGEL
31.11 g., 0.999 Silver 0.9926 oz. ASW **Ruler:** Elizabeth II **Subject:** 15th Anniversary of the Angel **Obv:** Bust in tiara right **Rev:** St. Michael slaying dragon

Date	Mintage	F12	VF20	XF40	MS60	MS63
2010PM	—	PF65 50.00				

Note: Privy mark: 15

SILVER BULLION COINAGE
Nobel Series

KM# 1484 NOBLE
31.11 g., 0.9999 Silver 0.9935 oz. ASW, 38.6 mm. **Ruler:** Elizabeth II **Obv:** Bust with tiara right **Rev:** Viking ship

Date	Mintage	F12	VF20	XF40	MS60	MS63
2011PM Prooflike	—				—	50.00

GOLD BULLION COINAGE
Angel Issues

KM# 1479 1/64 ANGEL
0.49 g., 0.9999 Gold AGW **Ruler:** Elizabeth II **Rev:** St. Michael slaying dragon

Date	Mintage	F12	VF20	XF40	MS60	MS63
2011PM	—	PF65 50.00				

Note: Privy mark: Wedding bells and date

KM# 393 1/20 ANGEL
1.56 g., 0.9999 Gold 0.0497 oz. AGW, 18 mm. **Ruler:** Elizabeth II **Obv:** Crowned bust right **Rev:** Archangel Michael slaying dragon right

Date	Mintage	F12	VF20	XF40	MS60	MS63
2001	—	—	—	—	—	90.00
2001	—	PF60 90.00				
2001	—	PF60 95.00				
Note: Privy mark: 3 Kings						
2002	—	—	—	—	—	90.00
2002	—	PF60 90.00				
2002	—	PF60 95.00				
Note: Privy mark: Candy cane						
2003	—	—	—	—	—	90.00
2003	—	PF60 90.00				
2003	—	PF60 95.00				
Note: Privy mark: Candy						
2004	—	—	—	—	—	90.00
2004	—	PF60 90.00				
2004	—	PF60 95.00				
Note: Privy mark: Partridge in a Pear Tree						
2005	—	—	—	—	—	90.00
2005	—	PF60 90.00				
2005	—	PF60 95.00				
Note: Privy mark: 2 Turtle doves						
2006	—	—	—	—	—	90.00
2006	—	PF60 90.00				
2006	—	PF60 95.00				
Note: Privy mark: 3 French hens						
2007	—	—	—	—	—	90.00
2007	—	PF60 90.00				
2007	—	PF60 95.00				

Note: Privy mark: 4 Calling birds

KM# 1106 1/20 ANGEL
1.56 g., 0.9999 Gold 0.0497 oz. AGW, 18 mm. **Ruler:** Elizabeth II **Obv:** Bust with tiara right **Rev:** St. Michael slaying dragon, three crown privy mark at right **Edge:** Reeded

Date	Mintage	F12	VF20	XF40	MS60	MS63
2001 (3c)	1,000	PF65 95.00				
2002	—	PF65 95.00				

Note: With candy cane privy mark

KM# 1252 1/20 ANGEL
1.56 g., 0.9999 Gold 0.0497 oz. AGW, 18 mm. **Ruler:** Elizabeth II **Obv:** Bust with tiara right **Rev:** St. Michael and Christmas privy mark **Edge:** Reeded

Date	Mintage	F12	VF20	XF40	MS60	MS63
2004PM	1,000	PF65 95.00				

KM# 1430 1/20 ANGEL
1.55 g., 0.9999 Gold 0.0495 oz. AGW, 18 mm. **Ruler:** Elizabeth II **Rev:** St. Michael slaying the dragon

Date	Mintage	F12	VF20	XF40	MS60	MS63
2009PM Six Geese a laying privy mark	1,000	PF65 125				
2010PM Seven swans a swimming privy mark	1,000	PF65 125				
2011PM Eight maids a milking privy mark	1,000	PF65 125				

KM# 394 1/10 ANGEL
3.11 g., 0.9999 Gold 0.0993 oz. AGW, 23 mm. **Ruler:** Elizabeth II **Obv:** Crowned bust right **Rev:** Archangel Michael

Date	Mintage	F12	VF20	XF40	MS60	MS63
2001	—	PF60 180				
2001	—	—	—	—	—	175
2002	—	—	—	—	—	175
2002	—	PF60 180				
2003	—	—	—	—	—	175
2003	—	PF60 180				
2004	—	—	—	—	—	175

KM# 395 1/4 ANGEL
7.78 g., 0.9999 Gold 0.2484 oz. AGW **Ruler:** Elizabeth II **Obv:** Crowned bust right **Rev:** Archangel Michael slaying dragon

Date	Mintage	F12	VF20	XF40	MS60	MS63
2004	—	PF60 180				
2005	—	—	—	—	—	175
2005	—	PF60 180				

KM# 395 1/4 ANGEL
7.78 g., 0.9999 Gold 0.2484 oz. AGW **Ruler:** Elizabeth II **Obv:** Crowned bust right **Rev:** Archangel Michael slaying dragon

Date	Mintage	F12	VF20	XF40	MS60	MS63
2001	—	—	—	—	—	450
2001	—	PF60 455				
2002	—	PF60 455				
2002	—	—	—	—	—	450
2003	—	PF60 455				
2003	—	—	—	—	—	450
2004	—	—	—	—	—	450
2004	—	PF60 455				
2005	—	—	—	—	—	450
2005	—	PF60 455				

KM# 397 ANGEL
31.10 g., 0.9999 Gold 0.9935 oz. AGW **Ruler:** Elizabeth II **Obv:** Crowned bust right **Rev:** Archangel Michael slaying dragon right

Date	Mintage	F12	VF20	XF40	MS60	MS63
2001	—	—	—	—	—	1,725
2001	—	PF60 1,750				
2002	—	PF60 1,750				
2002	—	—	—	—	—	1,725
2003	—	—	—	—	—	1,725
2003	—	PF60 1,750				
2004	—	PF60 1,750				
2004	—	—	—	—	—	1,725
2005	—	PF60 1,750				
2005	—	—	—	—	—	1,725
2006	500	PF60 1,750				
2006	—	—	—	—	—	1,725
2007	—	PF60 1,750				
2007	—	—	—	—	—	1,725

KM# 397.1 ANGEL
31.10 g., 0.999 Gold 0.9926 oz. AGW **Ruler:** Elizabeth II **Obv:** Crowned bust right **Rev:** Archangel Michael slaying dragon right

Date	Mintage	F12	VF20	XF40	MS60	MS63
2006 Proof, High Relief	Est. 1000	PF60 1,725				
2007 Proof, High Relief	Est. 1000	PF60 1,725				

KM# 1466 ANGEL
31.11 g., 0.9999 Gold 0.9935 oz. AGW, 33 mm. **Ruler:** Elizabeth II **Obv:** Bust in tiara right **Rev:** St. Michael slaying dragon

Date	Mintage	F12	VF20	XF40	MS60	MS63
2008PM	—	—	—	—	—	1,850
2008PM	—	PF63 1,860 PF65 1,875				

KM# 1467 ANGEL
31.11 g., 0.9999 Gold 0.9935 oz. AGW, 33 mm. **Ruler:** Elizabeth II **Obv:** Bust with tiara right **Rev:** St. Michael lunging right with spear

Date	Mintage	F12	VF20	XF40	MS60	MS63
2009PM	—	PF63 1,860 PF65 1,875				

KM# 1468 ANGEL
31.11 g., 0.9999 Gold 0.9935 oz. AGW, 33 mm. **Ruler:** Elizabeth II **Obv:** Bust with tiara right **Rev:** Dragon receiving spear wound

Date	Mintage	F12	VF20	XF40	MS60	MS63
2009PM			PF63 1,860	PF65 1,875		

BI-METALLIC BULLION COINAGE

KM# 1486 NOBLE
39.10 g., Bi-Metallic, 36.7 mm. **Ruler:** Elizabeth II **Rev:** Viking ship, 15 in left field

Date	Mintage	F12	VF20	XF40	MS60	MS63
2009PM	3,000	PF65 1,900				

MINT SETS

KM#	Date	Mintage	Identification	Issue Price	Mkt Val
MS30	2001 (8)	—	KM#1036-1043	—	22.50
MS31	2001 (9)	—	KM#1036-1044	—	40.00
MS32	2002 (8)	—	KM#1036-1043	—	22.50
MS33	2002 (9)	—	KM#1036-1044	—	40.00
MS34	2003 (8)	—	KM#1036-1043	—	22.50
MS35	2003 (9)	—	KM#1036-1044	—	40.00
MS36	2004 (8)	—	KM#1253-1260	—	25.00
MS37	2004 (9)	—	KM#1253-1261	—	40.00
MS38	2005 (8)	—	KM#1253-1260	—	22.50
MS39	2005 (9)	—	KM#1253-1261	—	40.00
MS40	2006 (8)	—	MS#1253-1260	35.00	25.00
MS41	2006 (9)	—	KM1253-1261	42.50	40.00
MS42	2007 (8)	—	KM1253-1260	35.00	22.50
MS43	2007 (9)	—	KM1253-1261	42.50	40.00

PROOF SETS

KM#	Date	Mintage	Identification	Issue Price	Mkt Val
PS59	2001 (5)	1,000	KM#1067-1070, 1073	—	3,350
PS60	2003 (3)	—	KM#1186, 1187, 1188	—	650
PS61	2003 (5)	—	KM#1186, 1187, 1188, 1189, 1190 w/ gold ring	—	3,300
PS62	2003 (5)	—	KM#1191-1195 w/ gold-plated silver ring	—	245
PS63	2004 (5)	1,000	KM#1247, 1248, 1249.1, 1250, 1251	—	3,375

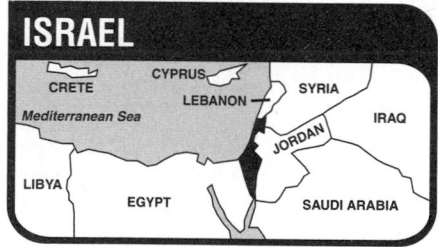

ISRAEL

The state of Israel, a Middle Eastern republic at the eastern end of the Mediterranean Sea, bounded by Lebanon on the north, Syria on the northeast, Jordan on the east, and Egypt on the southwest, has an area of 9,000sq. mi. (20,770 sq. km.) and a population of 6 million. Capital: Jerusalem. Finished diamonds, chemicals, citrus, textiles, minerals, electronic and transportation equipment are exported.

HEBREW COIN DATING

Israeli coins are dated according to the Christian year (AD). The JE New Year falls in September or during the first few days of October. In the case of dual-dated coins, with some exceptions, the JE date is 3,760 years greater than the AD date. Thus, for example, JE5735 is equivalent to AD1975. Exceptions are almost all of the Hanukka (Festival of Lights) commemorative coins because Hanukka falls early in the JE year and late in the AD year (late November or December) and certain other commemorative coins issued early in the JE year. In the case of the dual-dated Hanukka coins (other than the JE5720 coin) and certain others, the difference is 3,761 years. However, for ease of reference, except in the case of such dual-dated coins, the AD date given is always 3,760 years greater than the JE date (including the Hanukka coins bearing only a JE date). In the case of Hanukka mint sets, however, where the packaging gives an AD date that differs from the JE date by 3,761 years, the AD date on the packaging is indicated by the issued date in brackets.

Israel's coins carry Hebrew dating formed from a combination of the 22 consonant letters of the Hebrew alphabet and read from right to left. The Jewish calendar dates back more than 5700 years; but five millenniums are assumed in the dating

of coins (until 1981). Thus, the year 5735 (1975AD) appears as 735, with the first two characters from the right indicating the number of years in hundreds; tav (400), plus shin (300). The next is lamedh (30), followed by a separation mark which has the appearance of double quotation marks, then heh (5).

The separation mark - generally similar to a single quotation mark through 5718 (1958 AD), and like a double quotation mark thereafter - serves the purpose of indicating that the letters form a number, not a word, and on some issues can be confused with the character yodh (10), which in a stylized rendering can appear similar, although slightly larger and thicker. The separation mark does not appear in either form on a few commemorative issues.

The Star of David is not a mintmark. It appears only on some coins sold by the Israel Government Coins and Medals Corporation Ltd., which is owned by the Israel government, and is a division of the Prime Minister's office and sole distributor to collectors. The Star of David was first used in 1971 on the science coin to signify that it was minted in Jerusalem, but was later used by different mint facilities.

AD DATE		JEWISH ERA
2001	התשס"א	5761
2002	התשס"ב	5762
2003	התשס"ג	5763
2004	התשס"ד	5764
2005	התשס"ה	5765
2006	התשס"ו	5766
2007	התשס"ז	5767
2008	התשס"ח	5768
2009	התשס"ט	5769
2010	התש"ע	5770
2011	התשע"א	5771
2012	התשע"ב	5772
2013	התשע"ג	5773
2014	התשע"ד	5774
2015	התשע"ה	5775

MINT MARKS

מ

(m) - Mem
(o) - Ottawa
(s) - San Francisco
None - Jerusalem

REPUBLIC

REFORM COINAGE
100 Agorot = 1 New Sheqel
1,000 Sheqalim = 1 New Sheqel;
September 4, 1985-present

KM# 157 5 AGOROT
3.00 g., Aluminum-Bronze, 19.5 mm. **Obv:** Ancient coin **Rev:** Value within lined square **Edge:** Plain

Date	Mintage	F12	VF20	XF40	MS60	MS63
JE5761 (2001)(dj)	6,144,000	—	—	—	0.15	—
JE5762 (2002)(dj)	6,144,000	—	—	—	0.15	—
JE5764 (2004)		—	—	—	0.15	—
JE5765 (2005)		—	—	—	0.15	—
JE5766 (2006)		—	—	—	0.15	—
JE5767 (2007)		—	—	—	0.15	—

KM# 172 5 AGOROT
3.00 g., Aluminum-Bronze, 19.5 mm. **Subject:** Hanukka **Obv:** Ancient coin **Rev:** Value within lined square **Note:** JE5754-5768 coins contain the Star of David mint mark; the JE5747-5753 coins do not.

Date	Mintage	F12	VF20	XF40	MS60	MS63
JE5761 (2001)(u)	4,000	—	—	—	2.50	—
In sets only						
JE5762 (2002)(u)	4,000	—	—	—	2.50	—
In sets only						
JE5763 (2003)(u)	3,000	—	—	—	3.00	—
In sets only						

Date	Mintage	F12	VF20	XF40	MS60	MS63
JE5764 (2004)(u)	3,000	—	—	—	3.00	—
In sets only						
JE5765 (2005)(u)	2,500	—	—	—	3.00	—
In sets only						
JE5766 (2006)(u)	3,000	—	—	—	3.00	—
In sets only						
JE5767 (2007)(u)	3,000	—	—	—	3.00	—
In sets only						
JE5768 (2008)(u)	3,000	—	—	—	3.00	—
In sets only						

KM# 158 10 AGOROT
4.00 g., Aluminum-Bronze, 22 mm. **Obv:** Menorah **Rev:** Value within lined square **Edge:** Plain

Date	Mintage	F12	VF20	XF40	MS60	MS63
JE5761 (2001)(dj)	46,140,000	—	—	—	0.20	—
Note: Sides of central part of zero are rounded.						
JE5761 (2001)(so)	32,256,000	—	—	—	0.20	—
Note: Sides of central part of zero are straight.						
JE5762 (2002)(w)	4,608,000	—	—	—	0.20	—
JE5763 (2003)(dj)	22,980,000	—	—	—	0.20	—
JE5764 (2004)		—	—	—	0.20	—
JE5765 (2005)		—	—	—	0.20	—
JE5766 (2006)		—	—	—	0.20	—
JE5767 (2007)(dj)		—	—	—	0.20	—
JE5768 (2008)(dj)		—	—	—	0.20	—
JE5769 (2009)(dj)		—	—	—	0.20	—
JE5770 (2010)(dj)		—	—	—	0.20	—
JE5771 (2011)(dj)		—	—	—	0.20	—
JE5772 (2012)(dj)		—	—	—	0.20	—
(2013)		—	—	—	0.20	—

KM# 173 10 AGOROT
4.00 g., Aluminum-Bronze, 22 mm. **Subject:** Hanukka **Obv:** Menorah **Rev:** Value within lined square **Edge:** Plain **Note:** JE5754-5770 have the Star of David mint mark, JE5747-5753 coins do not.

Date	Mintage	F12	VF20	XF40	MS60	MS63
JE5761 (2001)(u)	4,000	—	—	—	3.00	—
In sets only						
JE5762 (2002)(u)	4,000	—	—	—	3.00	—
In sets only						
JE5763 (2003)(u)	3,000	—	—	—	3.00	—
In sets only						
JE5764 (2004)(u)	3,000	—	—	—	3.00	—
In sets only						
JE5765 (2005)(u)	2,500	—	—	—	3.00	—
In sets only						
JE5766 (2006)(u)	3,000	—	—	—	3.00	—
In sets only						
JE5767 (2007)(u)	3,000	—	—	—	3.00	—
In sets only						
JE5768 (2008)(u)	3,000	—	—	—	3.00	—
In sets only						
JE5769 (2009)(u)	1,800	—	—	—	3.50	—
In sets only						
JE5770 (2010)(u)	1,800	—	—	—	3.50	—
In sets only						

KM# 159 1/2 NEW SHEQEL
6.50 g., Aluminum-Bronze, 26 mm. **Obv:** Value **Rev:** Lyre **Edge:** Plain

Date	Mintage	F12	VF20	XF40	MS60	MS63
JE5762 (2002)(so)	2,880,000	—	—	—	0.75	—
JE5762 (2002)(v)	5,760,000	—	—	—	0.75	—
Note: Length of fraction line is 4 or 4.5 mm. but which mint produced which coin is not known.						
JE5763 (2003)		—	—	—	0.75	—
JE5764 (2004)(so)	2,640,000	—	—	—	0.75	—
JE5765 (2005)		—	—	—	0.75	—
JE5766 (2006)		—	—	—	0.75	—
JE5767 (2007)		—	—	—	0.75	—
JE5768 (2008)(dj)		—	—	—	0.75	—
JE5769 (2009)(dj)		—	—	—	0.60	—
JE5770 (2010)(dj)		—	—	—	0.60	—
JE5771 (2011)(v)		—	—	—	0.60	—
JE5772 (2012)(dj)		—	—	—	0.50	—

KM# 174 1/2 NEW SHEQEL
6.50 g., Aluminum-Bronze, 26 mm. **Subject:** Hanukka **Obv:** Value **Rev:** Lyre **Note:** Coins dated JE5754-5770 have the Star of David mint mark; the coins dated JE5747-5753 do not.

Date	Mintage	F12	VF20	XF40	MS60	MS63
JE5761 (2001)(u)	4,000	—	—	—	3.50	—
In sets only						
JE5762 (2002)(u)	4,000	—	—	—	3.50	—
In sets only						
JE5763 (2003)(u)	3,000	—	—	—	3.50	—
In sets only						

Date	Mintage	F12	VF20	XF40	MS60	MS63
JE5764 (2004)(u)	3,000	—	—	—	—	3.50
In sets only						
JE5765 (2005)(u)	2,500	—	—	—	—	3.50
In sets only						
JE5766 (2006)(u)	3,000	—	—	—	—	3.50
In sets only						
JE5767 (2007)(u)	3,000	—	—	—	—	3.50
In sets only						
JE5768 (2008)(u)	3,000	—	—	—	—	3.50
In sets only						
JE5769 (2009)(u)	1,800	—	—	—	—	3.50
In sets only						
JE5770 (2010)(u)	1,800	—	—	—	—	3.50
In sets only						

KM# 354 1/2 NEW SHEQEL
6.50 g., Aluminum-Bronze, 26 mm. **Subject:** Hanukka **Obv:** Denomination **Rev:** Curacao Hanukka lamp **Edge:** Plain **Shape:** 12-sided **Note:** Struck for sets only

Date	Mintage	F12	VF20	XF40	MS60	MS63
JE5761 (2001)(u)	4,000	—	—	—	—	11.00

KM# 355 1/2 NEW SHEQEL
6.50 g., Aluminum-Bronze, 26 mm. **Obv:** Value **Rev:** Yemenite Hanukka Lamp **Edge:** Twelve plain sections **Note:** Struck for sets only

Date	Mintage	F12	VF20	XF40	MS60	MS63
JE5762 (2002)(u)	4,000	—	—	—	—	11.00

KM# 389 1/2 NEW SHEQEL
6.50 g., Aluminum-Bronze, 26 mm. **Obv:** Value **Rev:** Polish Hanukka Lamp **Edge:** Plain **Shape:** 12-sided **Note:** Struck for sets only

Date	Mintage	F12	VF20	XF40	MS60	MS63
JE5763 (2003)(u)	3,000	—	—	—	—	12.00
Note: Even though not a proof, the coin has a mem						

KM# 390 1/2 NEW SHEQEL
6.50 g., Aluminum-Bronze, 26 mm. **Obv:** Value **Rev:** Iraqi Hanukka Lamp **Edge:** Plain **Shape:** 12-sided **Note:** Struck for sets only

Date	Mintage	F12	VF20	XF40	MS60	MS63
JE5764 (2004)(u)	3,000	—	—	—	—	12.00

KM# 391 1/2 NEW SHEQEL
6.50 g., Aluminum-Bronze, 26 mm. **Obv:** Value **Rev:** Syrian Hanukka Lamp **Edge:** Plain **Shape:** 12-sided **Note:** Struck for sets only

Date	Mintage	F12	VF20	XF40	MS60	MS63
JF5765 (2005)(u)	2,500	—	—	—	—	12.00

KM# 415 1/2 NEW SHEQEL
6.50 g., Aluminum-Bronze, 26 mm. **Obv:** Value and mini-Hanukka Lamp **Rev:** Dutch Hanukka Lamp **Edge:** Plain **Shape:** 12-sided **Note:** Struck for sets only

Date	Mintage	F12	VF20	XF40	MS60	MS63
JE5766 (2006)(u)	3,000	—	—	—	—	12.00

KM# 422 1/2 NEW SHEQEL
6.50 g., Aluminum-Bronze, 26 mm. **Obv:** Value and mini-Hanukka Lamp **Rev:** Corfu (Greek) Hanukka Lamp **Edge:** Plain **Shape:** 12-sided **Note:** Struck for sets only

Date	Mintage	F12	VF20	XF40	MS60	MS63
JE5767 (2007)(u)	3,000	—	—	—	—	12.00

KM# 434 1/2 NEW SHEQEL
6.50 g., Aluminum-Bronze, 26 mm. **Subject:** Hanukka **Obv:** Value, date, inscriptions and menorah **Rev:** Egyptian Hanukka lamp **Shape:** 12-sided **Note:** Struck for sets only

Date	Mintage	F12	VF20	XF40	MS60	MS63
JE5768 (2008)(u)	3,000	—	—	—	—	12.00

KM# 436 1/2 NEW SHEQEL
6.50 g., Aluminum-Bronze, 26 mm. **Subject:** Hanukka **Obv:** Value, date, inscriptions and menorah **Rev:** Prague Hanukka Lamp **Shape:** 12-sided **Note:** Struck for sets only

Date	Mintage	F12	VF20	XF40	MS60	MS63
JE5769 (2009)(u)	1,800	—	—	—	—	12.00

KM# 466 1/2 NEW SHEQEL
6.50 g., Aluminum-Bronze, 26 mm. **Subject:** Hanukka **Obv:** Value, date, inscriptions and menorah **Rev:** Algerian Hanukka Lamp **Edge:** Plain **Note:** Struck for sets only

Date	Mintage	F12	VF20	XF40	MS60	MS63
JE5770 (2010)(u)	1,800	—	—	—	—	12.00

KM# 163 NEW SHEQEL
4.00 g., Copper-Nickel, 18 mm. **Subject:** Hanukka **Obv:** Value **Rev:** Lily, state emblem and ancient Hebrew inscription. **Note:** Coins dated JE5754-5769 have the Star of David mint mark; the JE5746-5753 coins do not.

Date	Mintage	F12	VF20	XF40	MS60	MS63
JE5761 (2001)(u)	4,000	—	—	—	—	4.00
Note: In sets only						
JE5770 (2010) (2001)	1,800	—	—	—	—	4.00
JE5762 (2002)(u)	4,000	—	—	—	—	4.00
Note: In sets only						
JE5763 (2003)(u)	3,000	—	—	—	—	4.00
Note: In sets only						
JE5764 (2004)(u)	3,000	—	—	—	—	4.00
Note: In sets only						
JE5765 (2005)(u)	2,500					

Date	Mintage	F12	VF20	XF40	MS60	MS63
Note: In sets only						
JE5766 (2006)(u)	3,000	—	—	—	—	4.00
Note: In sets only						
JE5767 (2007)(u)	3,000	—	—	—	—	4.00
Note: In sets only						
JE5769 (2009)(u)	1,800	—	—	—	—	4.00
Note: In sets only						
JE5770 (2010)(u)	1,800	—	—	—	—	4.00
Note: In sets only						

KM# 163a NEW SHEQEL
4.00 g., Copper-Nickel, 18 mm. **Subject:** Hanukka **Obv:** Value, small menorah, country name in Hebrew, English and Arabic and inscription "HANUKKA" in Hebrew and English **Rev:** Lily, state emblem, ancient Hebrew inscription and Star of David mintmark **Note:** Non-magnetic.

Date	Mintage	F12	VF20	XF40	MS60	MS63
JE5768 (2008) (u)	3,000	—	—	—	—	4.00
Note: In sets only.						

KM# 160a NEW SHEQEL
3.45 g., Nickel Plated Steel, 17.97 mm. **Obv:** Value **Rev:** Lily, state emblem and ancient Hebrew inscription **Edge:** Plain

Date	Mintage	F12	VF20	XF40	MS60	MS63
JE5761 (2001)(h)	9,648,000	—	—	—	—	1.00
JE5762 (2002)(h)	18,816,000	—	—	—	—	1.00
JE5763 (2003)(v)	10,198,500	—	—	—	—	1.00
JE5765 (2005)		—	—	—	—	1.00
JE5766 (2006)		—	—	—	—	1.00
Note: Coin alignment error exists. Value: $100 in Unc, $50 in XF.						
JE5767 (2007) (2006)		—	—	—	—	1.00
JE5769 (2009)		—	—	—	—	1.00
JE5771 (2011)(h and v)		—	—	—	—	0.75
JE5772 (2012)		—	—	—	—	0.75
JE (2013)		—	—	—	—	0.75

KM# 163b NEW SHEQEL
3.50 g., Nickel Bonded Steel, 18 mm. **Subject:** Hanukka **Obv:** Value, small menorah, country name in Hebrew, English and Arabic and inscription "HANUKKA" in Hebrew and English **Rev:** Lily, state emblem, ancient Hebrew inscription and Star of David mintmark **Edge:** Plain

Date	Mintage	F12	VF20	XF40	MS60	MS63
JE5761 (2001)(u)	4,000	—	—	—	—	4.00
Note: In sets only						
JE5762 (2002)(u)	4,000	—	—	—	—	4.00
Note: In sets only						
JE5763 (2003)(u)	3,000	—	—	—	—	4.00
Note: In sets only						
JE5764 (2004)(u)	3,000	—	—	—	—	4.00
Note: In sets only						
JE5765 (2005)(u)	2,500	—	—	—	—	4.00
Note: In sets only						
JE5766 (2006)(u)	3,000	—	—	—	—	4.00
Note: In sets only						
JE5767 (2007)(u)	3,000	—	—	—	—	4.00
Note: In sets only						
JE5769 (2009)(u)	1,800	—	—	—	—	4.00
Note: In sets only						
JE5770 (2010)(u)	1,800	—	—	—	—	4.00
Note: In sets only						

KM# 344 NEW SHEQEL
14.40 g., 0.925 Silver 0.4255 oz. ASW, 30 mm. **Series:** Independence Day **Subject:** Education **Obv:** Denomination **Rev:** Pomegranate full of symbols - Hebrew 'ABC-123', etc. **Edge:** Plain

Date	Mintage	F12	VF20	XF40	MS60	MS63
JE5761-2001(u) Prooflike	1,653	—	—	—	—	30.00

KM# 351 NEW SHEQEL
14.40 g., 0.925 Silver 0.4255 oz. ASW, 30 mm. **Series:** Art and Culture in Israel **Subject:** Music **Obv:** National arms and denomination **Rev:** Musical instruments **Edge:** Plain

Date	Mintage	F12	VF20	XF40	MS60	MS63
JE5761-2001(u) Prooflike	1,182	—	—	—	—	35.00

KM# 356 NEW SHEQEL
14.40 g., 0.925 Silver 0.4255 oz. ASW, 30 mm. **Series:** Independence Day **Subject:** Volunteering **Obv:** Denomination **Rev:** Heart in hands **Edge:** Plain

Date	Mintage	F12	VF20	XF40	MS60	MS63
JE5762-2002(o) Prooflike	1,364	—	—	—	—	30.00

KM# 359 NEW SHEQEL
14.40 g., 0.925 Silver 0.4255 oz. ASW, 30 mm. **Series:** Biblical Art **Subject:** Tower of Babel **Obv:** National arms in spiral inscription **Rev:** Tower of Hebrew verses **Edge:** Plain

Date	Mintage	F12	VF20	XF40	MS60	MS63
JE5762 (2002)(o) Prooflike	1,312	—	—	—	—	55.00

KM# 371 NEW SHEQEL
14.40 g., 0.925 Silver 0.4255 oz. ASW, 30 mm. **Series:** Independence Day **Subject:** Space Exploration **Obv:** Ofeq" satellite in orbit **Rev:** Shavit" rocket **Edge Lettering:** Hebrew: "In memory of Ilan Ramon and his colleagues in the Columbia

Date	Mintage	F12	VF20	XF40	MS60	MS63
JE5763-2003(v) Prooflike	1,233	—	—	—	—	40.00

KM# 374 NEW SHEQEL
14.40 g., 0.925 Silver 0.4255 oz. ASW, 30 mm. **Series:** Biblical Art **Subject:** Jacob and Rachel **Obv:** Value **Rev:** Jacob and Rachel floating in air **Edge:** Plain

Date	Mintage	F12	VF20	XF40	MS60	MS63
JE5763-2003(u) Prooflike	1,661	—	—	—	—	55.00

KM# 377 NEW SHEQEL
14.40 g., 0.925 Silver 0.4255 oz. ASW, 30 mm. **Series:** Art and Culture in Israel **Subject:** Architecture and design **Obv:** Value **Rev:** Architecture and design **Edge:** Plain **Note:** With enamel.

Date	Mintage	F12	VF20	XF40	MS60	MS63
JE5764-2004(u) Prooflike	930	—	—	—	—	35.00

KM# 380 NEW SHEQEL
14.40 g., 0.925 Silver 0.4255 oz. ASW, 30 mm. **Series:** Independence Day **Subject:** Children of Israel **Obv:** Value **Rev:** Parent and child **Edge:** Plain

Date	Mintage	F12	VF20	XF40	MS60	MS63
JE5764-2004(u)	1,446	—	—	—	—	35.00
Prooflike						

KM# 383 NEW SHEQEL
14.40 g., 0.925 Silver 0.4255 oz. ASW, 30 mm. **Subject:** 2004 Summer Olympics **Obv:** Four windsurfers, value and national arms **Rev:** Eight windsurfers **Edge:** Plain

Date	Mintage	F12	VF20	XF40	MS60	MS63
JE5764-2004(v)	2,800	—	—	—	—	40.00
Prooflike						

KM# 386 NEW SHEQEL
14.40 g., 0.925 Silver 0.4255 oz. ASW, 30 mm. **Series:** Biblical Art **Subject:** Burning Bush **Obv:** Burning twig and value **Rev:** Burning Bush **Edge:** Plain

Date	Mintage	F12	VF20	XF40	MS60	MS63
JE5764-2004(v)	1,274	—	—	—	—	55.00
Prooflike						

KM# 405.1 NEW SHEQEL
1.24 g., 0.999 Gold 0.0397 oz. AGW, 13.92 mm. **Series:** Biblical Art **Subject:** Jacob and Rachel **Obv:** Value **Rev:** Jacob and Rachel floating in air **Edge:** Reeded

Date	Mintage	F12	VF20	XF40	MS60	MS63
JE5764 (2004)(u)	6,057	PF65 150				

KM# 405.2 NEW SHEQEL
1.24 g., 0.999 Gold 0.0397 oz. AGW, 13.92 mm. **Series:** Biblical Art **Subject:** Jacob and Rachel **Obv:** Value **Rev:** Jacob and Rachel floating in air. Arabic legend Israel is mispelled **Edge:** Reeded

Date	Mintage	F12	VF20	XF40	MS60	MS63
JE5764 (2004)(u)	682	PF65 200				

KM# 406 NEW SHEQEL
14.40 g., 0.925 Silver 0.4255 oz. ASW, 30 mm. **Subject:** FIFA 2006 World Cup **Obv:** Value and soccer ball **Rev:** Map and soccer ball **Edge:** Plain

Date	Mintage	F12	VF20	XF40	MS60	MS63
JE5764-2004(u)	Est. 1200	—	—	—	—	40.00
Prooflike						

Date	Mintage	F12	VF20	XF40	MS60	MS63
Note: Issued in 2006						

KM# 396 NEW SHEQEL
14.40 g., 0.925 Silver 0.4255 oz. ASW, 30 mm. **Subject:** Einstein's Relativity Theory **Obv:** Concentric circles above equation **Rev:** Value above signature

Date	Mintage	F12	VF20	XF40	MS60	MS63
JE5765-2005(v)	1,100	—	—	—	—	48.00
Prooflike						

KM# 399 NEW SHEQEL
14.40 g., 0.925 Silver 0.4255 oz. ASW, 30 mm. **Series:** Biblical Art **Subject:** Moses and the Ten Commandments **Obv:** Ten Commandments and value **Rev:** Moses and the Ten Commandments

Date	Mintage	F12	VF20	XF40	MS60	MS63
JE5765-2005(u)	1,400	—	—	—	—	55.00
Prooflike						

KM# 402 NEW SHEQEL
14.40 g., 0.925 Silver 0.4255 oz. ASW, 30 mm. **Series:** Independence Day **Subject:** Israel 57th Anniversary The Golden Years **Obv:** Value and olive branch **Rev:** Twisted olive tree

Date	Mintage	F12	VF20	XF40	MS60	MS63
JE5765-2005(u)	1,100	—	—	—	—	40.00
Prooflike						

KM# 412 NEW SHEQEL
14.40 g., 0.925 Silver 0.4255 oz. ASW, 30 mm. **Series:** Art and Culture in Israel **Subject:** Naomi Shemer **Obv:** Value **Rev:** Portrait of Naomi Shemer **Edge:** Plain

Date	Mintage	F12	VF20	XF40	MS60	MS63
JE5765-2005(u)	1,100	—	—	—	—	35.00
Prooflike						

KM# 409 NEW SHEQEL
14.40 g., 0.925 Silver 0.4255 oz. ASW, 30 mm. **Series:** Biblical Art **Subject:** Abraham and the Three Angels **Obv:** Value and stars **Rev:** Abraham and the three angels **Edge:** Reeded

Date	Mintage	F12	VF20	XF40	MS60	MS63
JE5766-2006(ig)	1,075	—	—	—	—	55.00
Prooflike						

KM# 416 NEW SHEQEL
14.40 g., 0.925 Silver 0.4255 oz. ASW, 30 mm. **Series:** Independence Day **Subject:** Higher Education in Israel **Obv:** Value and design **Rev:** Symbols of Science, Humanities, Technology and Mathematics **Edge:** Plain

Date	Mintage	F12	VF20	XF40	MS60	MS63
JE5766-2006(ig)	737	—	—	—	—	45.00
Prooflike						

KM# 419 NEW SHEQEL
14.40 g., 0.925 Silver 0.4255 oz. ASW, 30 mm. **Series:** UNESCO World Heritage Sites in Israel **Subject:** White City of Tel Aviv **Obv:** Value and Bauhaus building **Rev:** Fall of Bauhaus style building and UNESCO symbol **Edge:** Plain

Date	Mintage	F12	VF20	XF40	MS60	MS63
JE5766-2006(ig)	844	—	—	—	—	50.00
Prooflike						

KM# 423 NEW SHEQEL
14.40 g., 0.925 Silver 0.4255 oz. ASW, 30 mm. **Series:** Independence Day **Subject:** Performing Arts in Israel **Obv:** Value, state emblem and inscriptions **Rev:** Stylized actor, dancer and musician and inscription in Hebrew, English and Arabic, Performing Arts in Israel **Edge:** Plain

Date	Mintage	F12	VF20	XF40	MS60	MS63
JE5767-2007(ig)	765	—	—	—	—	50.00
Prooflike						

KM# 426 NEW SHEQEL
14.40 g., 0.925 Silver 0.4255 oz. ASW, 30 mm. **Subject:** 2008 Olympics - Judo **Obv:** Value, state emblem, judo belt and inscriptions **Rev:** 2 judo athletes and inscriptions in Hebrew, English and Arabic **Edge:** Plain

Date	Mintage	F12	VF20	XF40	MS60	MS63
JE5767-2007(u)	1,160	—	—	—	—	50.00
Prooflike						

KM# 429 NEW SHEQEL
14.40 g., 0.925 Silver 0.4255 oz. ASW, 30 mm. **Series:** Biblical Art **Subject:** Isaiah, Wolf with the Lamb **Obv:** Value, state emblem and inscriptions in Hebrew, English and Arabic **Obv. Inscription:** And the Wolf shall dwell with the Lamb **Rev:** Wolf and lamb lying together under a tree **Edge:** Plain

Date	Mintage	F12	VF20	XF40	MS60	MS63
JE5767-2007(v)	1,363	—	—	—	—	55.00
Prooflike						

KM# 437 NEW SHEQEL
1.24 g., 0.999 Gold 0.0397 oz. AGW, 13.92 mm. **Series:** Biblical Art **Subject:** Abraham and the Angels **Obv:** Value, state emblem and Moses in Hebrew, English and Arabic **Rev:** Abraham greeting three angels **Edge:** Reeded

Date	Mintage	F12	VF20	XF40	MS60	MS63
JE5767-2007(v)	1,500	PF65 150				

KM# 438 NEW SHEQEL
1.24 g., 0.999 Gold 0.0397 oz. AGW, 13.92 mm. **Series:** Biblical Art **Subject:** Moses and the Ten Commandments **Obv:** Value, state emblem and Moses in Hebrew **Rev:** Moses holding the Ten Commandments **Edge:** Reeded

Date	Mintage	F12	VF20	XF40	MS60	MS63
JE5767-2007	2,467	PF65 150				

KM# 439 NEW SHEQEL
14.40 g., 0.925 Silver 0.4255 oz. ASW, 30 mm. **Series:** Israeli Nobel Prize Laureates **Subject:** Shmuel Yosef Agnon **Obv:** Value, state emblem, outline of Agnon **Rev:** Portrait of Agnon **Edge:** Plain

Date	Mintage	F12	VF20	XF40	MS60	MS63
JE5768-2008(ig)	666	—	—	—	—	60.00
Prooflike						

KM# 440 NEW SHEQEL
1.24 g., 0.999 Gold 0.0397 oz. AGW, 13.92 mm. **Series:** Biblical Art **Subject:** Isaiah, Wolf with the Lamb **Obv:** Value, state emblem, and inscriptions **Rev:** Wolf and lamb lying under tree **Edge:** Reeded

Date	Mintage	F12	VF20	XF40	MS60	MS63
JE5768-2008(v)	3,302	PF65 150				

KM# 441 NEW SHEQEL
14.40 g., 0.925 Silver 0.4255 oz. ASW, 30 mm. **Series:** Independence Day **Subject:** Israel's Sixtieth Anniversary **Obv:** Value, state emblem and inscriptions including "Independence Day **Rev:** 60" the zero is shaped like a pomegranite and a dove

Date	Mintage	F12	VF20	XF40	MS60	MS63
JE5768-2008(v)	1,800	—	—	—	—	60.00
Prooflike						

KM# 442 NEW SHEQEL
14.40 g., 0.925 Silver 0.4255 oz. ASW, 30 mm. **Subject:** Israel Defense Forces Reserves **Obv:** Triangle, state emblem and inscription **Rev:** Teddy bear pendant over soldier's ID tag

Date	Mintage	F12	VF20	XF40	MS60	MS63
JE5768-2008(ig)	492	—	—	—	—	60.00
Prooflike						

KM# 444 NEW SHEQEL
14.40 g., 0.925 Silver 0.4255 oz. ASW, 30 mm. **Series:** Biblical Art **Subject:** Parting of the Red Sea **Obv:** Value, state emblem and inscriptions **Rev:** Israelites passing through the Red Sea

Date	Mintage	F12	VF20	XF40	MS60	MS63
JE5769-2008(v)	Est. 987	—	—	—	—	60.00
Prooflike						

KM# 453 NEW SHEQEL
14.40 g., 0.925 Silver 0.4255 oz. ASW, 30 mm. **Series:** UNESCO World Heritage Sites in Israel **Subject:** Masada **Obv:** Value, state emblem, image of Masada **Rev:** View of Masada, UNESCO emblem, World Heritage Site emblem **Edge:** Plain

Date	Mintage	F12	VF20	XF40	MS60	MS63
JE5769 (2009)(u)	Est. 783	—	—	—	—	60.00
Prooflike						

KM# 456 NEW SHEQEL
14.40 g., 0.925 Silver 0.4255 oz. ASW, 30 mm. **Series:** Independence Day **Subject:** Israel's Sixty-first Anniversary Birds of Israel **Obv:** Value, state emblem, finch **Rev:** Three birds, hoopoe, warbler and finch **Edge:** Plain

Date	Mintage	F12	VF20	XF40	MS60	MS63
JE5769 (2009)(u)	Est. 790	—	—	—	—	60.00
Prooflike						

KM# 459 NEW SHEQEL
14.40 g., 0.925 Silver 0.4255 oz. ASW, 30 mm. **Subject:** 2010 FIFA World Cup South Africa **Obv:** Soccer Player, ball, outline of globe, value, state emblem **Rev:** Soccer ball with design **Edge:** Plain

Date	Mintage	F12	VF20	XF40	MS60	MS63
JE5769 (2009)(u)	771	—	—	—	—	60.00
Prooflike						

KM# 462 NEW SHEQEL
1.24 g., 0.999 Gold 0.0397 oz. AGW, 13.92 mm. **Series:** Biblical Art **Subject:** Samson and the Lion **Obv:** Small stylized palm tree, value, state emblem **Rev:** Stylized Samson wrestling a lion and small stylized palm tree **Edge:** Reeded

Date	Mintage	F12	VF20	XF40	MS60	MS63
JE5769 (2009)(u)	Est. 5000	PF65 125				

KM# 463 NEW SHEQEL
14.40 g., 0.925 Silver 0.4255 oz. ASW, 30 mm. **Series:** Biblical Art **Subject:** Samson and the Lion **Obv:** Small stylized palm tree, value, state emblem **Rev:** Stylized Samson wrestling a lion and small stylized palm tree **Edge:** Plain

Date	Mintage	F12	VF20	XF40	MS60	MS63
JE5769 (2009)(u)	Est. 1800	—	—	—	—	60.00
Prooflike						

KM# 468 NEW SHEQEL
14.40 g., 0.925 Silver 0.4255 oz. ASW, 30 mm. **Series:** UNESCO World Heritage Sites in Israel **Subject:** Old Akko (Acre) **Obv:** Fortress of Akko as seen agains backdrop of Mediterranean Sea, state emblem, value UNESCO logo **Rev:** Ancient fortress walls, Khan-el-Undan caravanserale and its clock tower, underground Crussader Knights' hall, White Mosque and other buildings **Edge:** Plain

Date	Mintage	F12	VF20	XF40	MS60	MS63
JE5770 (2010)(h)	Est. 1800	—	—	—	—	60.00
Prooflike						

KM# 471 NEW SHEQEL
14.40 g., 0.925 Silver 0.4255 oz. ASW, 30 mm. **Series:** Independence Day **Subject:** Israeli National Trail 62nd Anniversary **Obv:** Trail forming stylized 62, state emblem **Rev:** Map of Isreal highlighting trail, boot, flowers **Edge:** Plain

Date	Mintage	F12	VF20	XF40	MS60	MS63
JE5770-2010(h)	Est. 1800	—	—	—	—	60.00
Prooflike						

KM# 474 NEW SHEQEL
1.24 g., 0.999 Gold 0.0397 oz. AGW, 13.92 mm. **Series:** Biblical Art **Subject:** Jonah in the Whale **Obv:** Small image of Jonah, value, state emblem **Rev:** Stylized Jonah in belly of

whale **Edge:** Reeded

Date	Mintage	F12	VF20	XF40	MS60	MS63
JE5770-2010(v)		PF65 140				

KM# 475 NEW SHEQEL
14.40 g., 0.925 Silver 0.4255 oz. ASW, 30 mm. **Series:** Biblical Art **Subject:** Jonah in the Whale **Obv:** Small image of Jonah, value, state emblem **Rev:** Stylized Jonah in belly of whale **Edge:** Plain

Date	Mintage	F12	VF20	XF40	MS60	MS63
JE5770-2010(v)	Est. 1800	—	—	—	—	70.00
Prooflike						

KM# 478 NEW SHEQEL
14.40 g., 0.925 Silver 0.4255 oz. ASW, 30 mm. **Series:** Israeli Nobel Prize Laureates **Subject:** Menachem Begin **Obv:** Menachem Begin, Jimmy Carter and Anwar Sadat in triple handshake on White House lawn **Rev:** Portrait of Begin **Edge:** Plain

Date	Mintage	F12	VF20	XF40	MS60	MS63
JE5771-2010(u)	Est. 2800	—	—	—	—	65.00
Prooflike						

KM# 481 NEW SHEQEL
14.40 g., 0.925 Silver 0.4255 oz. ASW, 30 mm. **Series:** Independence Day **Subject:** Independence day sixty-third anniversary, Dead Sea **Obv:** Image of Dead Sea region, ibex and legend "DEAD SEA" in Hebrew, English and Arabic **Rev:** Value, mirror image of value, state emblem, dates, country name in Hebrew, English and Arabic and legend "INDEPENDENCE DAY" in Hebrew and English

Date	Mintage	F12	VF20	XF40	MS60	MS63
JE5771-2011(u)	Est. 1800	—	—	—	—	75.00
Prooflike						

KM# 484 NEW SHEQEL
14.40 g., 0.925 Silver 0.4255 oz. ASW, 30 mm. **Subject:** 2012 London Olympics, Gymnastics **Obv:** Stlyized gymnast holding a ribbon in the shape of the Star of David and legends "THE OLYMPIC DELEGATION OF ISRAEL 2012" and "gymnastics" in Hebrew, English and Arabic **Rev:** Ribbon representation of Israeli flag, statem emblem, value, dates, country name in Hebrew, English and Arabic and inscription

Date	Mintage	F12	VF20	XF40	MS60	MS63
JE5771-2011(u)	Est. 1800	PF65 75.00				
Prooflike						

KM# 487 NEW SHEQEL
14.40 g., 0.925 Silver 0.4255 oz. ASW, 30 mm. **Series:** Biblical Art **Subject:** Elijah in the Whirlwind **Obv:** State emblem, dates, country name in Hebrew, English and Arabic and inscription "ELIJAH WENT UP BY A WHIRLWIND INTO HEAVEN" in Hebrew, English and Arabic **Rev:** Stylized Elijah ascending to heaven in a horse-drawn chariot of fire in a whirlwind with Elijah below

Date	Mintage	F12	VF20	XF40	MS60	MS63
JE5771-2011(v)	Est. 1800	—	—	—	—	75.00
Prooflike						

KM# 488 NEW SHEQEL
1.24 g., 0.999 Gold 0.0397 oz. AGW, 13.92 mm. **Series:** Biblical Art **Subject:** Elijah in the Whirlwind **Obv:** State emblem dates, country name in Hebrew, English Arabic **Rev:** Stylized Elijah ascending to heaven in a horse-drawn chariot of fire **Edge:** Reeded

Date	Mintage	F12	VF20	XF40	MS60	MS63
JE5771-2011(v)	Est. 5000	PF65 125				

KM# 492 NEW SHEQEL
14.40 g., 0.925 Silver 0.4255 oz. ASW, 30 mm. **Subject:** Tel Megiddo, UNESCO Heritage site

Date	Mintage	F12	VF20	XF40	MS60	MS63
JE5772-2012(u)	Est. 1,800	—	—	—	—	70.00
Prooflike						

KM# 495 NEW SHEQEL
14.40 g., 0.925 Silver 0.4255 oz. ASW, 30 mm. **Subject:** Yitzhak Rabin **Rev:** Bust left

Date	Mintage	F12	VF20	XF40	MS60	MS63
JE5772-2012 (2011)(u)	Est. 1,800	—	—	—	—	70.00
Prooflike						

KM# 501 NEW SHEQEL
14.40 g., 0.925 Silver 0.4255 oz. ASW, 30 mm. **Subject:** Biblical Art - Daniel and the lion's den **Obv:** State emblem **Rev:** Daniel with two lions **Edge:** Plain

Date	Mintage	F12	VF20	XF40	MS60	MS63
2012	—	—	—	—	—	60.00

KM# 504 NEW SHEQEL
14.40 g., 0.925 Silver 0.4255 oz. ASW, 30 mm. **Subject:** Eilat - Coral reef **Obv:** State emblem and two tropical sea fish **Rev:** Dolphin and tropical fish in coral reef **Edge:** Plain

Date	Mintage	F12	VF20	XF40	MS60	MS63
2012	—	—	—	—	—	60.00

KM# 498 NEW SHEQEL
14.40 g., 0.925 Silver 0.4255 oz. ASW, 30 mm. **Subject:** Independence, 60th Anniversary

Date	Mintage	F12	VF20	XF40	MS60	MS63
2013	—	PF65 60.00				

KM# 508 NEW SHEQEL
14.40 g., 0.925 Silver 0.4255 oz. ASW, 30 mm. **Subject:** Yad Vashem, 60th Anniversary **Obv:** State emblem and star of David **Rev:** Large Star of David and a Concentration Camp uniform **Edge:** Plain

Date	Mintage	F12	VF20	XF40	MS60	MS63
2013	—	—	—	—	—	60.00

KM# 352 2 NEW SHEQALIM
28.80 g., 0.925 Silver 0.851 oz. ASW, 38.7 mm. **Series:** Art and Culture in Israel **Subject:** Music **Obv:** National arms and denomination **Rev:** Musical instruments **Edge:** Reeded

Date	Mintage	F12	VF20	XF40	MS60	MS63
JE5761-2001(u)	1,747	PF65 55.00				

KM# 349 2 NEW SHEQALIM
28.80 g., 0.925 Silver 0.851 oz. ASW, 38.7 mm. **Series:** Wildlife **Subject:** Wild goat and acacia tree **Obv:** Acacia tree **Rev:** Ibex **Edge:** Reeded

Date	Mintage	F12	VF20	XF40	MS60	MS63
JE5761-2000 (2001)(u)	2,000	PF65 60.00				

KM# 345 2 NEW SHEQALIM
28.80 g., 0.925 Silver 0.851 oz. ASW, 38.7 mm. **Series:** Independence Day **Subject:** Education **Obv:** Denomination **Rev:** Pomegranate full of symbols **Edge:** Reeded

Date	Mintage	F12	VF20	XF40	MS60	MS63
JE5761-2001(u)	1,847	PF65 70.00				

KM# 357 2 NEW SHEQALIM
28.80 g., 0.925 Silver 0.851 oz. ASW, 38.7 mm. **Series:** Independence Day **Subject:** Volunteering **Obv:** Denomination **Rev:** Heart in hands **Edge:** Reeded

Date	Mintage	F12	VF20	XF40	MS60	MS63
JE5762-2002(o)	1,426	PF65 48.00				

KM# 360 2 NEW SHEQALIM
28.80 g., 0.925 Silver 0.851 oz. ASW, 38.7 mm. **Series:** Biblical Art **Subject:** Tower of Babel **Obv:** National arms in spiral inscription **Rev:** Tower of Hebrew verses **Edge:** Reeded

Date	Mintage	F12	VF20	XF40	MS60	MS63
JE5762-2002(o)	1,295	PF65 100				

KM# 372 2 NEW SHEQALIM
28.80 g., 0.925 Silver 0.851 oz. ASW, 38.7 mm. **Subject:** Space Exploration **Obv:** Amos" satellite in orbit **Rev:** Shavit" rocket **Edge Lettering:** Hebrew: "In memory of Ilan Ramon and his colleagues in the Columbia

Date	Mintage	F12	VF20	XF40	MS60	MS63
JE5763-2003(v)	1,249	PF65 60.00				

KM# 375 2 NEW SHEQALIM
28.80 g., 0.925 Silver 0.851 oz. ASW, 38.7 mm. **Series:** Biblical Art **Subject:** Jacob and Rachel **Obv:** Value **Rev:** Figures floating in air above flower and sheep **Edge:** Reeded

Date	Mintage	F12	VF20	XF40	MS60	MS63
JE5763-2003(u)	1,377	PF65 100				

KM# 378 2 NEW SHEQALIM
28.80 g., 0.925 Silver 0.851 oz. ASW, 38.7 mm. **Series:** Art and Culture in Israel **Subject:** Architecture and design **Obv:** Value and enameled shapes **Rev:** Architectural design **Edge:** Reeded

Date	Mintage	F12	VF20	XF40	MS60	MS63
JE5764-2004(u)	1,084	PF65 60.00				

KM# 381 2 NEW SHEQALIM
28.80 g., 0.925 Silver 0.851 oz. ASW, 38.7 mm. **Series:** Independence Day **Subject:** Children of Israel **Obv:** Value and stylized human shapes **Rev:** Stylized parent and child **Edge:** Reeded

Date	Mintage	F12	VF20	XF40	MS60	MS63
JE5764-2004(u)	1,182	PF65 50.00				

KM# 384 2 NEW SHEQALIM
28.80 g., 0.925 Silver 0.851 oz. ASW, 38.7 mm. **Subject:** 2004 Summer Olympics **Obv:** Four windsurfers, value and national arms **Rev:** Eight windsurfers **Edge:** Reeded

Date	Mintage	F12	VF20	XF40	MS60	MS63
JE5764-2004(v)	2,800	PF65 60.00				

KM# 387 2 NEW SHEQALIM
28.80 g., 0.925 Silver 0.851 oz. ASW, 38.7 mm. **Series:** Biblical Art **Subject:** Burning Bush **Obv:** Burning twig and value **Rev:** Burning Bush **Edge:** Reeded

Date	Mintage	F12	VF20	XF40	MS60	MS63
JE5764-2004(v)	1,354	PF65 100				

KM# 407 2 NEW SHEQALIM
28.80 g., 0.925 Silver 0.851 oz. ASW, 38.7 mm. **Subject:** FIFA 2006 World Cup **Obv:** Value and soccer ball **Rev:** Map and soccer ball **Edge:** Reeded

Date	Mintage	F12	VF20	XF40	MS60	MS63
JE5764-2004(u)	Est. 5000	**PF65** 60.00				

Note: Issued in 2006

KM# 397 2 NEW SHEQALIM
28.80 g., 0.925 Silver 0.851 oz. ASW, 38.7 mm. **Subject:** Einstein's Relativity Theory **Obv:** Concentric circles above equation **Rev:** Value above signature

Date	Mintage	F12	VF20	XF40	MS60	MS63
JE5765-2005(v)	1,600	**PF65** 85.00				

KM# 400 2 NEW SHEQALIM
28.80 g., 0.925 Silver 0.851 oz. ASW, 38.7 mm. **Series:** Biblical Art **Subject:** Moses and the Ten Commandments **Obv:** Ten Commandments and value **Rev:** Moses and Ten Commandments

Date	Mintage	F12	VF20	XF40	MS60	MS63
JE5765-2005(u)	1,400	**PF65** 100				

KM# 403 2 NEW SHEQALIM
28.80 g., 0.925 Silver 0.851 oz. ASW, 38.7 mm. **Series:** Independence Day **Subject:** Israel 57th Anniversary - The Golden Years **Obv:** Value and olive branch **Rev:** Twisted olive tree **Edge:** Reeded

Date	Mintage	F12	VF20	XF40	MS60	MS63
JE5765-2005(u)	1,100	**PF65** 50.00				

KM# 413 2 NEW SHEQALIM
28.80 g., 0.925 Silver 0.851 oz. ASW, 38.7 mm. **Series:** Art and Culture in Israel **Subject:** Naomi Shemer **Obv:** Value **Rev:** Portrait of Naomi Shemer **Edge:** Reeded

Date	Mintage	F12	VF20	XF40	MS60	MS63
JE5765-2005(u)	1,100	**PF65** 60.00				

KM# 410 2 NEW SHEQALIM
28.80 g., 0.925 Silver 0.851 oz. ASW, 38.7 mm. **Series:** Biblical Art **Subject:** Abraham and the Three Angels **Obv:** Value and stars **Rev:** Abraham and the three angels **Edge:** Reeded

Date	Mintage	F12	VF20	XF40	MS60	MS63
JE5766-2006(ig)	967	**PF65** 110				

KM# 417 2 NEW SHEQALIM
28.80 g., 0.925 Silver 0.851 oz. ASW, 38.7 mm. **Series:** Independence Day **Subject:** Higher Education in Israel **Obv:** Value and design **Rev:** Symbols of Science, Humanities, Technology and Mathematics **Edge:** Reeded

Date	Mintage	F12	VF20	XF40	MS60	MS63
JE5766-2006(ig)	846	**PF65** 60.00				

KM# 420 2 NEW SHEQALIM
28.80 g., 0.925 Silver 0.851 oz. ASW, 38.7 mm. **Series:** UNESCO World Heritage Sites in Israel **Subject:** White City of Tel Aviv **Obv:** Value and Bauhaus building **Rev:** Fall of Bauhaus building and UNESCO symbol **Edge:** Reeded

Date	Mintage	F12	VF20	XF40	MS60	MS63
JE5766-2006(ig)	837	**PF65** 75.00				

KM# 424 2 NEW SHEQALIM
28.80 g., 0.925 Silver 0.851 oz. ASW, 38.7 mm. **Series:** Independence Day **Subject:** Performing Arts in Israel **Obv:** Value, state emblem and inscriptions **Rev:** Stylized actor, dancer and musician and inscription in Hebrew, English and Arabiv **Edge:** Reeded

Date	Mintage	F12	VF20	XF40	MS60	MS63
JE5767-2007(ig)	756	**PF65** 75.00				

KM# 427 2 NEW SHEQALIM
28.80 g., 0.925 Silver 0.851 oz. ASW, 38.7 mm. **Subject:** 2008 Olympics - Judo **Obv:** Value, state emblem, judo belt and inscriptions **Rev:** 2 judo athletes and inscriptions **Edge:** Reeded

Date	Mintage	F12	VF20	XF40	MS60	MS63
JE5767-2007(u)	5,211	**PF65** 75.00				

KM# 430 2 NEW SHEQALIM
28.80 g., 0.925 Silver 0.851 oz. ASW, 38.7 mm. **Series:** Biblical Art **Subject:** Isaiah, Wolf with the Lamb **Obv:** Value, state emblem and inscriptions in Hebrew, English and Arabic **Obv. Inscription:** And the Wolf shall dwell with the Lamb **Rev:** Wolf and lamb lying together under a tree **Edge:** Reeded

Date	Mintage	F12	VF20	XF40	MS60	MS63
JE5767-2007(v)	1,734	**PF65** 100				

KM# 432 2 NEW SHEQALIM
5.70 g., Nickel Plated Steel, 21.6 mm. **Subject:** Hanukka **Obv:** Value, date, inscriptions and menorah **Rev:** Double cornucopiae (horns of plenty) draped in ribbons and filled with fruit and grain including a pomegranate **Edge:** Plain with 4 notches

Date	Mintage	F12	VF20	XF40	MS60	MS63
JE5768 (2008)(u)	3,000				5.00	
	Note: In sets only					
JE5769 (2009)(u)	1,800				5.00	
	Note: In sets only					
JE5770 (2010)(u)	1,800				5.00	
	Note: In sets only					

KM# 433 2 NEW SHEQALIM
5.70 g., Nickel Plated Steel, 21.6 mm. **Obv:** Value, date and inscriptions **Rev:** Double cornucopiae (horns of plenty) draped in ribbons and filled with fruit and grain including a pomegranate **Edge:** Plain with 4 notches

Date	Mintage	F12	VF20	XF40	MS60	MS63
JE5768 (2008)(u)	Est. 26000000	—	—	—	1.25	—
JE5769 (2009)(u)		—	—	—	1.25	—
JE5770 (2010)(u)		—	—	—	1.25	—
JE5771 (2011)(v)		—	—	—	1.25	—

KM# 445 2 NEW SHEQALIM
28.80 g., 0.925 Silver 0.851 oz. ASW, 38.7 mm. **Series:** Israeli Nobel Prize Laureates **Subject:** Shmuel Yosef Agnon **Obv:** Value, state emblem and outline of Agnon **Rev:** Portrait of Agnon **Edge:** Reeded

Date	Mintage	F12	VF20	XF40	MS60	MS63
JE5768-2008(ig)	666	**PF65** 90.00				

KM# 446 2 NEW SHEQALIM
28.80 g., 0.925 Silver 0.851 oz. ASW, 38.7 mm. **Series:** Independence Day **Subject:** Israel's 60th Anniversary **Obv:** Value, state emblem and inscription "Independence Day" **Rev:** 60" the zero is shaped like a pomegranate and a dove

Date	Mintage	F12	VF20	XF40	MS60	MS63
JE5768-2008(v)	1,800	**PF65** 110				

KM# 447 2 NEW SHEQALIM
28.80 g., 0.925 Silver 0.851 oz. ASW, 38.7 mm. **Subject:** Israel Defense Forces Reserves **Obv:** Triangle, state emblem and inscription **Rev:** Teddy bear pendant over a soldier's ID tag **Edge:** Reeded

Date	Mintage	F12	VF20	XF40	MS60	MS63
JE5768-2008(ig)	481	**PF65** 95.00				

KM# 443 2 NEW SHEQALIM
1.24 g., 0.999 Gold 0.0397 oz. AGW, 13.92 mm. **Series:** Biblical Art **Subject:** Parting of the Red Sea **Obv:** Value, state emblem and inscriptions **Rev:** Israelites passing through the Red Sea **Edge:** Reeded

Date	Mintage	F12	VF20	XF40	MS60	MS63
JE5769-2008(v)	1,896	**PF65** 125				

KM# 448 2 NEW SHEQALIM
28.80 g., 0.925 Silver 0.851 oz. ASW, 38.7 mm. **Series:** Biblical Art **Subject:** Parting of the Red Sea **Obv:** Value, state emblem and inscriptions **Rev:** Israelites passing through the Red Sea **Edge:** Reeded

Date	Mintage	F12	VF20	XF40	MS60	MS63
JE5769-2008(v)	1,800	**PF65** 100				

KM# 454 2 NEW SHEQALIM
28.80 g., 0.925 Silver 0.851 oz. ASW, 38.7 mm. **Series:** UNESCO World Heritage Sites in Israel **Subject:** Masada **Obv:** Value, state emblem, image of Masada **Rev:** View of Masada, UNESCO emblem, World Heritage Site emblem **Edge:** Reeded

Date	Mintage	F12	VF20	XF40	MS60	MS63
JE5769 (2009)(u)	Est. 1037	**PF65** 90.00				

KM# 457 2 NEW SHEQALIM

28.80 g., 0.925 Silver 0.851 oz. ASW, 38.7 mm. **Series:** Independence Day **Subject:** Israel's Sixty-first Anniversary- Birds of Israel **Obv:** Value, state emblem, hoopoe **Rev:** Three birds, hoopoe, warbler and finch **Edge:** Reeded

Date	Mintage	F12	VF20	XF40	MS60	MS63
JE5769 (2009)(u)	2,800	PF65 110				

KM# 460 2 NEW SHEQALIM

28.80 g., 0.925 Silver 0.851 oz. ASW, 38.7 mm. **Subject:** 2010 FIFA World Cup South Africa **Obv:** Soccer Player, ball, outline of globe **Rev:** Soccer player with design **Edge:** Reeded

Date	Mintage	F12	VF20	XF40	MS60	MS63
JE5769 (2009)(u)	Est. 5000	PF65 90.00				

KM# 464 2 NEW SHEQALIM

28.80 g., 0.925 Silver 0.851 oz. ASW, 38.7 mm. **Series:** Biblical Art **Subject:** Samson and the Lion **Obv:** Small stylized palm tree, value, state emblem **Rev:** Stylized Samson wrestling with a lion and small stylized palm tree **Edge:** Reeded

Date	Mintage	F12	VF20	XF40	MS60	MS63
JE5769 (2009)(u)	—	PF65 100				

KM# 469 2 NEW SHEQALIM

28.80 g., 0.925 Silver 0.851 oz. ASW, 38.7 mm. **Series:** UNESCO World Heritage Sites in Israel **Subject:** Old Akko (Acre) **Obv:** Fortress of Akko as seen against backdrop of Mediterranean Sea, state emblem, value **Rev:** Ancient fortress walls, Khan-el-Umdan caravanseraie and its clock tower, underground Crusader Knights' Hall, White Mosque and other buildings **Edge:** Reeded

Date	Mintage	F12	VF20	XF40	MS60	MS63
JE5770 (2010)(h)	Est. 2800	PF65 90.00				

KM# 472 2 NEW SHEQALIM

28.80 g., 0.925 Silver 0.851 oz. ASW, 38.7 mm. **Series:** Independence Day **Subject:** Israel National Trail **Obv:** Trail forming stylized 62, state emblem **Rev:** Map of Israel highlighting national trail, boot, flowers **Edge:** Reeded

Date	Mintage	F12	VF20	XF40	MS60	MS63
JE5770-2010(h)	Est. 1800	PF65 90.00				

KM# 476 2 NEW SHEQALIM

28.80 g., 0.925 Silver 0.851 oz. ASW, 38.7 mm. **Series:** Biblical Art **Subject:** Jonah in the Whale **Obv:** Small image of Jonah, value, state emblem **Rev:** Stylized Jonah in belly of whale **Edge:** Reeded

Date	Mintage	F12	VF20	XF40	MS60	MS63
JE5770-2010(v)	Est. 2800	PF65 120				

KM# 479 2 NEW SHEQALIM

28.80 g., 0.925 Silver 0.851 oz. ASW, 38.7 mm. **Series:** Israeli Nobel Pize Laureates **Subject:** Menachem Begin **Obv:** Menachem Begin, Jimmy Carter and Anwar Sadat in triple handshake on White House lawn, state emblem **Rev:** Portrait of Menachem Begin **Edge:** Reeded

Date	Mintage	F12	VF20	XF40	MS60	MS63
JE5771-2010(u)	—	PF65 120				

KM# 482 2 NEW SHEQALIM

28.80 g., 0.925 Silver 0.851 oz. ASW, 38.7 mm. **Series:** Independence Day **Subject:** Israel's sixty-third anniversary, Dead Sea **Obv:** Image of Dead Sea region, ibex and legend "DEAD SEA" in Hebrew, English and Arabic **Rev:** Value, mirror image of value, state emblem, dates, country name in Hebrew, English and Arabic and legend "INDEPENDENCE DAY" in Hebrew and English **Edge:** Reeded

Date	Mintage	F12	VF20	XF40	MS60	MS63
JE5771-2011	—	PF65 120				

KM# 485 2 NEW SHEQALIM

28.80 g., 0.925 Silver 0.851 oz. ASW, 38.7 mm. **Subject:** 2012 London Olympics, Gymnastics **Obv:** Stylized gymnast holding a ribbon in the shape of the Star of David and legends "THE OLYMPIC DELEGATION OF ISRAEL 2012" and "gymnastics" in Hebrew, English and Arabic **Rev:** Ribbon representation of Israeli flag, state emblem, value, dates, country name in Hebrew, English and Arabic and inscription **Edge:** Reeded

Date	Mintage	F12	VF20	XF40	MS60	MS63
JE5771-2011(u)	Est. 5000	PF65 120				

KM# 489 2 NEW SHEQALIM

28.80 g., 0.925 Silver 0.851 oz. ASW, 38.7 mm. **Series:** Biblical Art **Subject:** Elijah caught up in the firestorm **Obv:** State emblem, dates, country name in Hebrew, English and Arabic and inscription "ELIJAH WENT UP BY A WHIRLWIND INTO HEAVEN" in Hebrew, English and Arabic **Rev:** Stylized Elijah ascending to heaven in a horse-drawn chariot of fire in a whirlwind with Elisha below **Edge:** Reeded

Date	Mintage	F12	VF20	XF40	MS60	MS63
JE5771-2011(v)	Est. 2800	PF65 120				

KM# 496 2 NEW SHEQALIM

28.28 g., 0.925 Silver 0.8356 oz. ASW, 38.7 mm. **Subject:** Yitzhak Rabin **Rev:** Bust left **Edge:** Reeded

Date	Mintage	F12	VF20	XF40	MS60	MS63
JE5772-2011(u)	Est. 2800	PF65 110				

KM# 493 2 NEW SHEQALIM

28.80 g., 0.925 Silver 0.851 oz. ASW, 38.7 mm. **Subject:** Tel Megiddo, UNESCO Heritage site **Edge:** Reeded

Date	Mintage	F12	VF20	XF40	MS60	MS63
JE5772-2012(u)	Est. 2800	PF65 110				

KM# 502 2 NEW SHEQALIM

28.28 g., 0.925 Silver 0.8356 oz. ASW **Subject:** Biblical Arts - Daniel and the lion's den **Obv:** State emblem **Rev:** Daniel and two lions

Date	Mintage	F12	VF20	XF40	MS60	MS63
2012	—	PF65 120				

KM# 505 2 NEW SHEQALIM

28.28 g., 0.925 Silver 0.8356 oz. ASW, 38.7 mm. **Subject:** Eilat - Coral reef **Obv:** State emblem and two tropical fish **Rev:** Dolphin and tropical fish in coral reef **Edge:** Reeded

Date	Mintage	F12	VF20	XF40	MS60	MS63
2013 (2012)	—	PF65 120				

KM# 499 2 NEW SHEQALIM

28.28 g., 0.925 Silver 0.8356 oz. ASW, 38.7 mm. **Subject:** Independence, 60th Anniversary

Date	Mintage	F12	VF20	XF40	MS60	MS63
2013	—	PF65 100				

KM# 509 2 NEW SHEQALIM

28.28 g., 0.925 Silver 0.8356 oz. ASW, 38.7 mm. **Subject:** Yad Vashem, 60th Anniversary **Obv:** State emblem and Star of David **Rev:** Large Star of David and a Concentration Camp uniform **Edge:** Reeded

Date	Mintage	F12	VF20	XF40	MS60	MS63
2013	—					120

KM# 207 5 NEW SHEQALIM

8.20 g., Copper-Nickel, 24 mm. **Obv:** Value **Rev:** Ancient column capitol **Edge:** Plain **Shape:** 12-sided

Date	Mintage	F12	VF20	XF40	MS60	MS63
JE5762 (2002)(wg)	4,464,000	—	—	—	3.75	—
	Note: The JE5762 coins are practically round.					
JE5765 (2005)		—	—	—	3.00	—
JE5766 (2006)		—	—	—	3.00	—
JE5768 (2008)(dj)		—	—	—	3.00	—
JE5769 (2009)(dj)		—	—	—	3.00	—
JE5771 (2011)(dj)		—	—	—	3.00	—
JE5772 (2012)(dj)		—	—	—	3.00	—
5773 (2013)		—	PF65 3.00			

KM# 217 5 NEW SHEQALIM

8.20 g., Copper-Nickel, 24 mm. **Obv:** Value, small menorah and inscription Hanukka **Rev:** Ancient column capitol **Edge:** Plain **Shape:** 12-sided **Note:** Coins dated JE5754-5770 have the Star of David mint mark; the JE5751-5753 coins do not.

Date	Mintage	F12	VF20	XF40	MS60	MS63
JE5762 (2002)(u)	4,000	—	—	—	7.00	—
Note: In sets only						
JE5763 (2003)(u)	3,000	—	—	—	8.00	—
Note: In sets only						
JE5764 (2004)(u)	3,000	—	—	—	8.00	—
Note: In sets only						
JE5765 (2005)(u)	2,500	—	—	—	8.00	—
Note: In sets only						
JE5766 (2006)(u)	3,000	—	—	—	8.00	—
Note: In sets only						
JE5767 (2007)(u)	3,000	—	—	—	8.00	—
Note: In sets only						
JE5768 (2008)(u)	3,000	—	—	—	8.00	—
Note: In sets only						
JE5769 (2009)(u)	1,800	—	—	—	8.00	—
Note: In sets only						
JE5770 (2010)(u)	1,800	—	—	—	8.00	—
Note: In sets only						

KM# 408 5 NEW SHEQALIM

7.78 g., 0.999 Gold 0.2482 oz. AGW, 27 mm. **Subject:** FIFA 2006 World Cup **Obv:** Value and soccer ball **Rev:** Map and soccer ball **Edge:** Reeded **Note:** Issued in 2006

Date	Mintage	F12	VF20	XF40	MS60	MS63
JE5764-2004(u)	—	PF65 500				

KM# 461 5 NEW SHEQALIM

7.77 g., 0.999 Gold 0.248 oz. AGW, 27 mm. **Subject:** 2010 FIFA World Cup South Africa **Obv:** Soccer Player, ball, outline of globe **Rev:** Soccer ball with design **Edge:** Reeded

Date	Mintage	F12	VF20	XF40	MS60	MS63
JE5769 (2009)(u)	391	PF65 550				

KM# 270 10 NEW SHEQALIM

7.00 g., Bi-Metallic, 23 mm. **Obv:** Value, vertical lines and text within circle **Rev:** Palm tree and baskets within half beaded circle **Edge:** Reeded

Date	Mintage	F12	VF20	XF40	MS60	MS63
JE5762 (2002)(h)	4,749,000	—	—	—	5.00	—
JE5765 (2005)		—	—	—	5.00	—
Note: Coin alignment error exists. Value: $200 in Unc, $100 in XF.						
JE5766 (2006)		—	—	—	5.00	—
JE5769 (2009)		—	—	—	5.00	—
JE5770 (2010)		—	—	—	5.00	—
JE5771 (2011)(h)		—	—	—	5.00	—
JE5772 (2012)(v)		—	—	—	5.00	—
JE5773 (2013)		—	—	—	5.00	—

KM# 315 10 NEW SHEQALIM

7.00 g., Bi-Metallic, 23 mm. **Subject:** Hanukka **Obv:** Value, text and menorah within circle and vertical lines **Rev:** Palm tree and baskets within half beaded circle **Edge:** Reeded

Date	Mintage	F12	VF20	XF40	MS60	MS63
JE5761 (2001)(u)	4,000	—	—	—	9.00	—
Note: In sets only						
JE5762 (2002)(u)	4,000	—	—	—	9.00	—
Note: In sets only						
JE5763 (2003)(u)	3,000	—	—	—	10.00	—
Note: In sets only						
JE5764 (2004)(u)	3,000	—	—	—	10.00	—
Note: In sets only						
JE5765 (2005)(u)	2,500	—	—	—	10.00	—
Note: In sets only						
JE5766 (2006)(u)	3,000	—	—	—	10.00	—
Note: In sets only						
JE5767 (2007)(u)	3,000	—	—	—	10.00	—
Note: In sets only						
JE5768 (2008)(u)	3,000	—	—	—	10.00	—
Note: In sets only						
JE5769 (2009)(u)	1,800	—	—	—	10.00	—
Note: In sets only						
JE5770 (2010)(u)	1,800	—	—	—	10.00	—
Note: In sets only						

KM# 346 10 NEW SHEQALIM

16.96 g., 0.917 Gold 0.4968 oz. AGW, 30 mm. **Series:** Independence Day **Subject:** Education **Obv:** Value **Rev:** Pomegranate full of symbols - Hebrew for 'ABC - 123', etc. **Edge:** Reeded

Date	Mintage	F12	VF20	XF40	MS60	MS63
JE5761-2001(u)	660	PF65 1,100				

KM# 353 10 NEW SHEQALIM

16.96 g., 0.917 Gold 0.4968 oz. AGW, 30 mm. **Series:** Art and Culture in Israel **Subject:** Music **Obv:** National arms and value **Rev:** Musical instruments **Edge:** Reeded

Date	Mintage	F12	VF20	XF40	MS60	MS63
JE5761-2001(u)	766	PF65 1,000				

KM# 358 10 NEW SHEQALIM

16.96 g., 0.9166 Gold 0.4966 oz. AGW, 30 mm. **Series:** Independence Day **Subject:** Volunteering **Obv:** Value **Rev:** Heart in hands **Edge:** Reeded

Date	Mintage	F12	VF20	XF40	MS60	MS63
JE5762-2002(o)	617	PF65 1,100				

KM# 361 10 NEW SHEQALIM

16.96 g., 0.917 Gold 0.4968 oz. AGW, 30 mm. **Series:** Biblical Art **Subject:** Tower of Babel **Obv:** National arms in spiral inscription **Rev:** Tower of Hebrew verses **Edge:** Reeded

Date	Mintage	F12	VF20	XF40	MS60	MS63
JE5762-2002(o)	750	PF65 1,150				

KM# 373 10 NEW SHEQALIM

16.96 g., 0.917 Gold 0.4968 oz. AGW, 30 mm. **Series:** Independence Day **Subject:** Space Exploration **Obv:** Eros" satellite in orbit **Rev:** Shavit" rocket **Edge Lettering:** Hebrew: In memory of Ilan Ramon and his colleagues in the Columbia

Date	Mintage	F12	VF20	XF40	MS60	MS63
JE5763-2003(v)	573	PF65 1,125				

KM# 376 10 NEW SHEQALIM

16.96 g., 0.917 Gold 0.4968 oz. AGW, 30 mm. **Series:** Biblical Art **Subject:** Jacob and Rachel **Obv:** Value **Rev:** Jacob and Rachel floating in air above tree and sheep **Edge:** Reeded

Date	Mintage	F12	VF20	XF40	MS60	MS63
JE5763-2003(u)	686	PF65 1,150				

KM# 379 10 NEW SHEQALIM

16.96 g., 0.917 Gold 0.4968 oz. AGW, 30 mm. **Series:** Art and Culture in Israel **Subject:** Architecture and Design **Obv:** Value **Rev:** Architectural design **Edge:** Reeded

Date	Mintage	F12	VF20	XF40	MS60	MS63
JE5764-2004(u)	555	PF65 1,100				

KM# 382 10 NEW SHEQALIM

16.96 g., 0.917 Gold 0.4968 oz. AGW, 30 mm. **Series:** Independence Day **Subject:** Children of Israel **Obv:** Value **Rev:** Stylized parent and child **Edge:** Reeded

Date	Mintage	F12	VF20	XF40	MS60	MS63
JE5764-2004(u)	539	PF65 1,100				

KM# 385 10 NEW SHEQALIM

16.96 g., 0.917 Gold 0.4968 oz. AGW, 30 mm. **Subject:** 2004 Summer Olympics **Obv:** Four windsurfers, value and national arms **Rev:** Eight windsurfers **Edge:** Reeded

Date	Mintage	F12	VF20	XF40	MS60	MS63
JE5764-2004(v)	540	PF65 1,100				

KM# 388 10 NEW SHEQALIM

16.96 g., 0.917 Gold 0.4968 oz. AGW, 30 mm. **Series:** Biblical Art **Subject:** Burning Bush **Obv:** Burning twig and value **Rev:** Burning Bush **Edge:** Reeded

Date	Mintage	F12	VF20	XF40	MS60	MS63
JE5764-2004(v)	555	PF65 1,150				

KM# 398 10 NEW SHEQALIM

16.96 g., 0.9166 Gold 0.4966 oz. AGW, 30 mm. **Subject:** Einstein's Relativity Theory **Obv:** Concentric circles above equation **Rev:** Value above signature **Edge:** Reeded

Date	Mintage	F12	VF20	XF40	MS60	MS63
JE5765-2005(v)	555	PF65 1,200				

KM# 401 10 NEW SHEQALIM

16.96 g., 0.9166 Gold 0.4966 oz. AGW, 30 mm. **Series:** Biblical Art **Subject:** Moses and the Ten Commandments **Obv:** The Ten Commandments and value **Rev:** Moses and the Ten Commandments **Edge:** Reeded

Date	Mintage	F12	VF20	XF40	MS60	MS63
JE5765-2005(u)	555	PF65 1,150				

KM# 404 10 NEW SHEQALIM

16.96 g., 0.9166 Gold 0.4966 oz. AGW, 30 mm. **Series:** Independence Day **Subject:** Israel 57th Anniversary - Golden years **Obv:** Value and olive branch **Rev:** Twisted olive tree **Edge:** Reeded

Date	Mintage	F12	VF20	XF40	MS60	MS63
JE5765-2005(u)	485	PF65 1,100				

KM# 414 10 NEW SHEQALIM

16.96 g., 0.917 Gold 0.4968 oz. AGW, 30 mm. **Series:** Art and Culture in Israel **Subject:** Naomi Shemer **Obv:** Value **Rev:** Portrait of Naomi Shemer **Edge:** Reeded

Date	Mintage	F12	VF20	XF40	MS60	MS63
JE5765-2005(u)	455	PF65 1,150				

KM# 411 10 NEW SHEQALIM

16.96 g., 0.917 Gold 0.4968 oz. AGW, 30 mm. **Series:** Biblical Art **Subject:** Abraham and the Three Angels **Obv:** Value and stars **Rev:** Abraham and the three angels **Edge:** Reeded

Date	Mintage	F12	VF20	XF40	MS60	MS63
JE5766-2006(ig)	555	PF65 1,150				

KM# 418 10 NEW SHEQALIM

16.96 g., 0.917 Gold 0.4968 oz. AGW, 30 mm. **Series:** Independence Day **Subject:** Higher Education in Israel **Obv:** Value and design **Rev:** Symbols of Science, Humanities, Technology and Mathematics **Edge:** Reeded

Date	Mintage	F12	VF20	XF40	MS60	MS63
JE5766-2006(ig)	444	PF65 1,100				

KM# 421 10 NEW SHEQALIM
16.96 g., 0.917 Gold 0.4968 oz. AGW, 30 mm. **Series:** UNESCO World Heritage Sites in Israel **Subject:** White City of Tel Aviv **Obv:** Value and Bauhaus building **Rev:** Face of Bauhaus building and UNESCO symbol **Edge:** Reeded

Date	Mintage	F12	VF20	XF40	MS60	MS63
JE5766-2006(ig)	383	PF65 1,150				

KM# 425 10 NEW SHEQALIM
16.96 g., 0.917 Gold 0.4968 oz. AGW, 30 mm. **Series:** Independence Day **Subject:** Performing Arts in Israel **Obv:** Value, state emblem and inscriptions **Rev:** Stylized actor, dancer and musician and inscription in Hebrew, English and Arabic, "Performing Arts in Israel **Edge:** Reeded

Date	Mintage	F12	VF20	XF40	MS60	MS63
JE5767-2007(ig)	332	PF65 1,200				

KM# 428 10 NEW SHEQALIM
16.96 g., 0.917 Gold 0.4968 oz. AGW, 30 mm. **Subject:** 2008 Olympics - Judo **Obv:** Value, state emblem, judo belt and inscriptions **Rev:** 2 judo athletes and inscriptions in Hebrew, English and Arabic **Edge:** Reeded

Date	Mintage	F12	VF20	XF40	MS60	MS63
JE5767 (2007)(u)	548	PF65 1,050				

KM# 431 10 NEW SHEQALIM
16.96 g., 0.917 Gold 0.4968 oz. AGW, 30 mm. **Series:** Biblical Art **Subject:** Isaiah, Wolf with the Lamb **Obv:** Value, state emblem and inscriptions in Hebrew, English and Arabic. **Obv. Inscription:** And the Wolf shall dwell with the Lamb **Rev:** Wolf and lamb lying together under a tree **Edge:** Reeded

Date	Mintage	F12	VF20	XF40	MS60	MS63
JE5767-2007(v)	553	PF65 1,150				

KM# 452 10 NEW SHEQALIM
16.96 g., 0.917 Gold 0.4968 oz. AGW, 30 mm. **Series:** Biblical Art **Subject:** Parting of the Red Sea **Obv:** Value, state emblem

and inscriptions **Rev:** Israelites passing through the Red Sea **Edge:** Reeded

Date	Mintage	F12	VF20	XF40	MS60	MS63
JE5769-2008(v)	Est. 491	PF65 1,150				

KM# 449 10 NEW SHEQALIM
16.96 g., 0.917 Gold 0.4968 oz. AGW, 30 mm. **Series:** Israeli Nobel Prize Laureates **Subject:** Shmuel Yosef Agnon **Obv:** Value, state emblem and outline of Agnon **Rev:** Portrait of Agnon **Edge:** Reeded

Date	Mintage	F12	VF20	XF40	MS60	MS63
JE5768-2008(ig)	322	PF65 1,200				

KM# 450 10 NEW SHEQALIM
16.96 g., 0.917 Gold 0.4968 oz. AGW, 30 mm. **Series:** Independence Day **Subject:** Israel's 60th Anniversary **Obv:** Value, state emblem and inscription "Independence Day **Rev:** 60" the zero is shaped like a pomegranite and a dove **Edge:** Reeded

Date	Mintage	F12	VF20	XF40	MS60	MS63
JE5768-2008(v)	444	PF65 1,100				

KM# 451 10 NEW SHEQALIM
16.96 g., 0.917 Gold 0.4968 oz. AGW, 30 mm. **Subject:** Israel Defense Force Reserves **Obv:** Value over a triangle, state emblem and inscriptions **Rev:** Teddy bear pendant over a soldier's ID tag **Edge:** Reeded

Date	Mintage	F12	VF20	XF40	MS60	MS63
JE5768-2008	262	PF65 1,200				

KM# 455 10 NEW SHEQALIM
16.96 g., 0.917 Gold 0.4968 oz. AGW, 30 mm. **Series:** UNESCO World Heritage Sites in Israel **Subject:** Masada **Obv:** Value, state emblem, image of Masada, UNESCO emblem, World Heritage Site Emblem **Rev:** View of Masada, UNESCO emblem, World Heritage Site Emblem **Edge:** Reeded

Date	Mintage	F12	VF20	XF40	MS60	MS63
JE5769 (2009)(u)	Est. 548	PF65 1,150				

KM# 458 10 NEW SHEQALIM
16.96 g., 0.917 Gold 0.4968 oz. AGW, 30 mm. **Series:** Independence Day **Subject:** Israel's Sixty-first Anniversary Birds of Israel **Obv:** Value, state emblem, warbler **Rev:** Three birds, hoopoe, warbler and finch **Edge:** Reeded

Date	Mintage	F12	VF20	XF40	MS60	MS63
JE5769 (2009)(u)	Est. 445	PF65 1,200				

KM# 465 10 NEW SHEQALIM
16.96 g., 0.917 Gold 0.4968 oz. AGW, 30 mm. **Series:** Biblical Art **Subject:** Samson and the Lion **Obv:** Small stylized palm tree, value, state emblem **Rev:** Stylized Samson wrestling a lion, stylized palm tree **Edge:** Reeded

Date	Mintage	F12	VF20	XF40	MS60	MS63
JE5769 (2009)(u)	—	PF65 1,150				

KM# 470 10 NEW SHEQALIM
16.96 g., 0.917 Gold 0.4968 oz. AGW, 30 mm. **Series:** UNESCO World Heritage Sites in Israel **Subject:** Old Akko (Acre) **Obv:** Fortress of Akko as seen against backdrop of Mediterranean Sea, state emblem, value **Rev:** Ancient fortress walls, Khan-el-Umdan caravanseraie and its clock tower, underground Crusader Knights' hall, White Mosque and other buildings **Edge:** Reeded

Date	Mintage	F12	VF20	XF40	MS60	MS63
JE5770 (2010)(h)	Est. 555	PF65 1,150				

KM# 473 10 NEW SHEQALIM
16.95 g., 0.917 Gold 0.4965 oz. AGW, 30 mm. **Series:** Independence Day **Subject:** Israel National Trail **Obv:** Trail forming stylized 62, state emblem **Rev:** Map of Israel highlighting trail, boot, flowers **Edge:** Reeded

Date	Mintage	F12	VF20	XF40	MS60	MS63
JE5770-2010(h)	Est. 555	PF65 1,150				

KM# 477 10 NEW SHEQALIM
16.96 g., 0.917 Gold 0.4968 oz. AGW, 30 mm. **Series:** Biblical Art **Subject:** Jonah in the Whale **Obv:** Small image of Jonah, value, state emblem **Rev:** Stylized Jonah in belly of whale **Edge:** Reeded

Date	Mintage	F12	VF20	XF40	MS60	MS63
JE5770-2010	Est. 555	PF65 1,200				

KM# 480 10 NEW SHEQALIM
16.96 g., 0.917 Gold 0.4968 oz. AGW, 30 mm. **Series:** Israeli Nobel Prize Laureates **Subject:** Menachem Begin **Obv:** Menachem Begin, Jimmy Carter adn Anwar Sadat in triple handshake on White House lawn, state emblem **Rev:** Portrait of Menachem Begin **Edge:** Reeded

Date	Mintage	F12	VF20	XF40	MS60	MS63
JE5771-2010(u)	Est. 888	PF65 1,200				

KM# 483 10 NEW SHEQALIM
16.96 g., 0.917 Gold 0.4968 oz. AGW, 30 mm. **Series:** Independence Day **Subject:** Israel's sixty-third anniversary, Dead Sea **Obv:** Image of Dead Sea region, ibex and legend "DEAD SEA" in Hebrew, English and Arabic **Rev:** Value, mirror image of value, state emblem, dates, country name in Hebrew. **Rev. Legend:** "INDEPENDENCE DAY" in Hebrew and English **Edge:** Reeded

Date	Mintage	F12	VF20	XF40	MS60	MS63
JE5771-2011(u)	Est. 555	PF65 1,200				

KM# 486 10 NEW SHEQALIM
16.96 g., 0.917 Gold 0.4968 oz. AGW, 30 mm. **Subject:** 2012 London Olympics, Gymnastics **Obv:** Stylized gymnast holding a ribbon in the shape of the Star of David and legends "THE OLYMPIC DELEGATION OF ISRAEL 2012" and "gymnastics" in Hebrew, English and Arabic **Rev:** Ribbon representation of Israeli flag, state emblem, value, dates, country name in Hebrew, English and Arabic and inscription **Edge:** Reeded

Date	Mintage	F12	VF20	XF40	MS60	MS63
JE5771-2011(u)	Est. 555	PF65 1,200				

KM# 490 10 NEW SHEQALIM
16.96 g., 0.917 Gold 0.4968 oz. AGW, 30 mm. **Series:** Biblical Art **Subject:** Elijah in the Whirlwind **Obv:** State emblem, dates, country name in Hebrew, English and Arabic and inscription "ELIJAH WENT UP BY A WHIRLWIND INTO HEAVEN" in Hebrew, English and Arabic **Rev:** Stylized Elijah ascending to heaven in a horse-drawn chariot of fire in a whirlwind with Elisha below **Edge:** Reeded

Date	Mintage	F12	VF20	XF40	MS60	MS63
JE5771-2011(v)	Est. 555	PF65 1,200				

KM# 497 10 NEW SHEQALIM
16.90 g., 0.917 Gold 0.495 oz. AGW, 30 mm. **Subject:** Yitzhak Rabin **Rev:** Bust left **Edge:** Reeded

Date	Mintage	F12	VF20	XF40	MS60	MS63
JE5772-2011	Est. 888	PF65 1,100				

KM# 494 10 NEW SHEQALIM
16.96 g., 0.917 Gold 0.4968 oz. AGW, 30 mm. **Subject:** Tel Megiddo, UNESCO Heritage site **Edge:** Reeded

Date	Mintage	F12	VF20	XF40	MS60	MS63
JE5772-2012(u)	Est. 555	PF65 1,100				

KM# 503 10 NEW SHEQALIM
16.96 g., 0.917 Gold 0.4968 oz. AGW, 30 mm. **Subject:** Biblical art - Daniel and the lion's den **Obv:** State emblem **Rev:** Daniel and two lions **Edge:** Reeded

Date	Mintage	F12	VF20	XF40	MS60	MS63
2012		PF65 1,100				

KM# 506 10 NEW SHEQALIM
16.96 g., 0.917 Gold 0.4968 oz. AGW, 30 mm. **Subject:** Eilat - Coral reef **Obv:** State emblem and two tropical fish **Rev:** Dolphin and tropical fish in coral reef **Edge:** Reeded

Date	Mintage	F12	VF20	XF40	MS60	MS63
2012		PF65 1,100				

KM# 500 10 NEW SHEQALIM
16.90 g., 0.917 Gold 0.495 oz. AGW, 30 mm. **Subject:** Independence, 60th Anniversary

Date	Mintage	F12	VF20	XF40	MS60	MS63
2013		PF65 1,200				

KM# 510 10 NEW SHEQALIM
16.96 g., 0.917 Gold 0.4968 oz. AGW, 30 mm. **Subject:** Yad Vashem, 60th Anniversary **Obv:** State emblem, Star of David **Rev:** Large Star of David and a Concentration Camp uniform **Edge:** Reeded

Date	Mintage	F12	VF20	XF40	MS60	MS63
2013		PF65 1,100				

BULLION COINAGE

KM# 467 20 NEW SHEQALIM
31.10 g., 0.999 Gold 0.9925 oz. AGW, 32 mm. **Series:** Jerusalem of Gold **Subject:** Tower of David **Obv:** State emblem above lion of Megiddo and country name in Hebrew, English and Arabic **Rev:** Tower of David near the Jaffa Gate in Jerusalem **Edge:** Plain

Date	Mintage	F12	VF20	XF40	MS60	MS63
JE5770 (2010)(u)	3,600	—	—	—	BV+20%	

KM# 491 20 NEW SHEQALIM
31.10 g., 0.999 Gold 0.9925 oz. AGW, 32 mm. **Series:** Jerusalem of Gold **Subject:** Western Wall of the Temple **Obv:** State emblem above lion of Megiddo **Rev:** Sestern wall of the Temple, dates and legends "JERUSALEM" in Hebrew, English and Arabic and "1 OZ FINE GOLD .9999" in English and Hebrew

Date	Mintage	F12	VF20	XF40	MS60	MS63
JE5771 (2011)(u)	Est. 3600	—	—	—	BV+20%	

KM# 507 20 NEW SHEQALIM
31.11 g., 0.999 Gold 0.9926 oz. AGW, 32 mm. **Rev:** Menorah and the Knesset building **Edge:** Plain

Date	Mintage	F12	VF20	XF40	MS60	MS63
2012		—	—	—	BV+20%	

KM# 511 20 NEW SHEQALIM
31.10 g., 0.999 Gold 0.9925 oz. AGW, 32 mm. **Rev:** Shrine of the Book in the Israel Museum **Edge:** Plain

Date	Mintage	F12	VF20	XF40	MS60	MS63
2013		—	—	—	BV+20%	

MINT SETS

KM#	Date	Mintage	Identification	Issue Price	Mkt Val
MS86	JE5761 (2001) (7)	4,000	KM#163b, 172-174, 217, 315, 354 (plastic case) 350th Anniversary of the Jewish Community of Curacao	24.00	37.00
MS88	JE5762 (2002) (7)	4,000	KM#163b, 172-174, 217, 315, 355 (plastic case) Yemenite Jewry (issued 2001)	27.00	40.00

KM#	Date	Mintage	Identification	Issue Price	Mkt Val
MS89	JE5761-5762 (2001-2002) (9)	3,000	KM#157, 158, 160a (JE5761), 157-159, 160a, 207, 270 (JE5762) plus Twin Towers medal (folder) Israel - New York	—	30.00
MS91	JE5763 (2003) (7)	3,000	KM#163b, 172-174, 217, 315, 389 (plastic case) The March of the Living into Poland (issued 2002)	30.00	42.00
MS93	JE5764 (2004) (7)	3,000	KM#163b, 172-174, 217, 315, 390 (plastic case) Iraqi Jewry (issued 2003)	—	40.00
MS94	JE5761-5763 (2001-2003) (6)	3,000	KM#157-159, 160a, 207, 270 (various dates) (folder) Bank of Israel Jubilee; (given or sold to Bank of Israel employees and VIP guests, not to the general public; issued 2004)	—	45.00
MS96	JE5765 (2005) (7)	2,500	KM#163b, 172-174, 217, 315, 391 (plastic case) Syrian Jewry (issued 2004)	—	42.00
MS97	JE5764-5765 (2004-2005) (6)	3,000	KM#158, 159 (JE5764), 157, 160a, 207, 270 (JE5765) (folder) Israel Today	37.00	35.00
MS98	JE5766 (2006) (7)	2,700	KM#163b, 172-174, 217, 315, 415 (folder) Dutch Jewry (issued 2005)	45.00	45.00
MS99	JE5766 (2006) (7)	300	KM#163b, 172-174, 217, 315, 415 (plastic case) Dutch Jewry (issued 2005)	—	45.00
MS100	JE5766 (2006) (6)	2,000	KM#157-159, 160a, 207, 270 (folder) To the North With Love	37.00	35.00
MS101	JE5767 (2007) (7)	3,000	KM#163b, 172-174, 217, 315, 422 (folder) Greek Jewry (issued 2006)	43.00	42.00
MS102	JE5768 (2008) (8)	3,000	KM#163a, 172-174, 217, 315, 432, 434 (folder) Egyptian Jewry (issued 2007)	43.00	45.00
MS103	JE5767-5768 (2007-2008) (8)	1,000	KM#157-159, 160a (JE5767), 158, 159, 207, 433 (JE5768) (folder) The Negev Shall Blossom	37.00	46.00
MS104	JE5769 (2009) (7)	1,800	KM#163b, 173, 174, 217, 315, 432, 436 (folder) Glorious Prague (issued 2008)	43.00	45.00
MS105	JE5770 (2010) (7)	1,800	KM#163b, 173, 174, 217, 315, 432, 466 (folder) Jews of Algeria	43.00	45.00
MS106	JE5766-5770 (2006-10) (7)	—	KM#270 (JE5766), 160a (JE5767), 207 (JE5768), 158, 433 (JE5769), 159 (JE5770) (folder) 2010 coin set, Type I	29.95	30.00
MS107	JE5769-5770 (2009-10) (6)	—	KM#160a, 207, 433 (JE5769), 158, 159, 270 (JE5770) (folder) 2010 coin set, Type II	29.95	30.00
MS108	JE5770-5771 (2010-2011) (5)	—	KM#433 (JE5770), 158, 159, 160a, 207, 270 (JE5771) The Western Wall, 2011 Uncirculated Coin Set	36.00	36.00

MINT SETS NON-STANDARD METALS

KM#	Date	Mintage	Identification	Issue Price	Mkt Val
MS85	JE5761 (2001) (7)	4,000	KM#163b, 172-174, 217, 315, 354 (folder) 350th Anniversary of the Jewish Community of Curacao (issued 2000)	32.00	38.00
MS87	JE5762 (2002) (7)	4,000	KM#163b, 172-174, 217, 315, 355 (folder) Yemenite Jewry (issued 2001)	32.00	40.00
MS90	JE6763 (2003) (7)	3,000	KM#163b, 172-174, 217, 315, 389 (folder) The March of the Living into Poland (issued 2002)	33.00	39.00
MS92	JE5764 (2004) (7)	3,000	KM#163b, 172-174, 217, 315, 390 (folder) Iraqi Jewry (issued 2003)	39.00	40.00
MS95	JE5765 (2005) (7)	2,500	KM#163b, 172-174, 217, 315, 391 (folder) Syrian Jewry (issued 2004)	39.00	40.00

PIEFORT PROOF SETS (PPS)

KM#	Date	Mintage	Identification	Issue Price	Mkt Val
PPS24	JE5760 (2000) (h) & (u) (8)	4,000	KM#P121-P128 (plastic case)	—	45.00

ITALY

The Italian Republic, a 700-mile-long peninsula extending into the heart of the Mediterranean Sea, has an area of 116,304 sq. mi. (301,230 sq. km.) and a population of 60 million. Capital: Rome. The economy centers around agriculture, manufacturing, forestry and fishing. Machinery, textiles, clothing and motor vehicles are exported.

MINT
R - Rome

REPUBLIC

DECIMAL COINAGE

KM# 91 LIRA
0.62 g., Aluminum, 17 mm. **Obv:** Balance scales **Rev:** Cornucopia, value and date **Note:** The 1968-1969 and 1982-2001 dates were issued in sets only.

Date	Mintage	F12	VF20	XF40	MS60	MS63
2001R	100,000	—	—	—	10.00	—
2001R	10,000	PF60 70.00				

KM# 219 LIRA
11.00 g., 0.835 Silver 0.2934 oz. ASW, 29 mm. **Subject:** History of the Lira - Lira of 1946 (KM#87) **Obv:** Head with laureate left within circle **Rev:** Apple on branch within circle flanked by sprigs **Edge:** Reeded **Note:** This is a Lira Series reproducing an old coin design in the center of each coin.

Date	Mintage	F12	VF20	XF40	MS60	MS63
2001R	50,000	—	—	—	40.00	—
2001R	6,100	PF63 100				

KM# 220 LIRA
6.00 g., 0.835 Silver 0.160 oz. ASW, 24 mm. **Subject:** History of the Lira - Lira of 1951 (KM#91) **Obv:** Balance scale within circle **Rev:** Value and cornucopia within circle **Edge:** Reeded **Note:** This is a Lira Series reproducing an old coin design in the center of each coin.

Date	Mintage	F12	VF20	XF40	MS60	MS63
2001R	50,000	—	—	—	40.00	—
2001R	6,100	PF63 100				

KM# 87a LIRA
8.00 g., 0.900 Gold 0.230 oz. AGW, 21.6 mm. **Obv:** Ceres **Rev:** Orange on branch **Edge:** Plain **Note:** Official Restrike

Date	Mintage	F12	VF20	XF40	MS60	MS63
1946 (2006)R	1,999	PF63 750				

KM# 91a LIRA
4.00 g., 0.900 Gold 0.115 oz. AGW, 17.2 mm. **Obv:** Balance scale **Rev:** Cornucopia, date and value **Edge:** Plain **Note:** Official Restrike

Date	Mintage	F12	VF20	XF40	MS60	MS63
1951 (2006)R	1,999	PF63 400				

KM# 94 2 LIRE
0.80 g., Aluminum, 18 mm. **Obv:** Honey bee **Rev:** Olive branch and value **Edge:** Reeded **Note:** The 1968-1969 and 1982-2001 dates were issued in sets only.

Date	Mintage	F12	VF20	XF40	MS60	MS63
2001R	100,000	—	—	—	10.00	—
2001R	10,000	PF60 70.00				

KM# 88a 2 LIRE
11.00 g., 0.900 Gold 0.3162 oz. AGW, 24.1 mm. **Obv:** Farmer plowing field **Rev:** Wheat ear **Edge:** Plain **Note:** Official Restrike

Date	Mintage	F12	VF20	XF40	MS60	MS63
1946 (2006)R	1,999	PF63 900				

KM# 94a 2 LIRE
5.00 g., 0.900 Gold 0.1437 oz. AGW, 18.3 mm. **Obv:** Honey bee **Rev:** Olive branch **Edge:** Reeded **Note:** Official Restrike

Date	Mintage	F12	VF20	XF40	MS60	MS63
1953 (2006)R	1,999	PF63 550				

KM# 92 5 LIRE
1.04 g., Aluminum, 20.12 mm. **Obv:** Rudder **Rev:** Dolphin and value **Edge:** Plain

Date	Mintage	F12	VF20	XF40	MS60	MS63
2001R	100,000	—	—	—	12.00	—
2001R	10,000	PF60 25.00				

KM# 89a 5 LIRE
16.00 g., 0.900 Gold 0.460 oz. AGW, 26.7 mm. **Obv:** Italia with torch **Rev:** Bunch of grapes **Edge:** Reeded **Note:** Official Restrike

Date	Mintage	F12	VF20	XF40	MS60	MS63
1946 (2006)R	1,999	PF63 1,200				

KM# 92a 5 LIRE
6.00 g., 0.900 Gold 0.1725 oz. AGW, 20.2 mm. **Obv:** Rudder **Rev:** Dolphin and value **Edge:** Plain **Note:** Official Restrike

Date	Mintage	F12	VF20	XF40	MS60	MS63
1951 (2006)R	1,999	PF63 650				

KM# 93 10 LIRE
1.60 g., Aluminum, 23.25 mm. **Obv:** Plow **Rev:** Value within wheat ears **Edge:** Plain

Date	Mintage	F12	VF20	XF40	MS60	MS63
2001R	100,000	—	—	—	12.00	—
2001R	10,000	PF60 30.00				

KM# 90a 10 LIRE
19.00 g., 0.900 Gold 0.5462 oz. AGW, 29 mm. **Obv:** Pegasus **Rev:** Olive branch **Edge:** Lettered **Edge Lettering:** REPVBBLICA ITALIANA **Note:** Official Restrike

Date	Mintage	F12	VF20	XF40	MS60	MS63
1946 (2006)R	1,999	PF63 1,400				

KM# 93a 10 LIRE
10.00 g., 0.900 Gold 0.2875 oz. AGW, 23.3 mm. **Obv:** Plow **Rev:** Value within wheat ears **Edge:** Plain **Note:** Official Restrike

Date	Mintage	F12	VF20	XF40	MS60	MS63
1951 (2006)R	1,999	PF63 800				

KM# 97.2 20 LIRE
3.60 g., Aluminum-Bronze, 21.25 mm. **Obv:** Wheat sprigs within head left **Rev:** Oak leaves divide value and date **Edge:** Plain

Date	Mintage	F12	VF20	XF40	MS60	MS63
2001R	100,000	—	—	—	10.00	—
2001R	10,000	PF60 25.00				

KM# 97.1a 20 LIRE
8.00 g., 0.900 Gold 0.230 oz. AGW, 21.3 mm. **Obv:** Head laureate left **Rev:** Oak leaves divides date and value **Edge:** Reeded **Note:** Official Restrike

Date	Mintage	F12	VF20	XF40	MS60	MS63
1957 (2006)R	1,999	PF63 800				

KM# 183 50 LIRE
4.50 g., Copper-Nickel, 19 mm. **Obv:** Turreted head left **Rev:** Large value within wreath of produce

Date	Mintage	F12	VF20	XF40	MS60	MS63
2001R	100,000	—	—	—	10.00	—
2001R	10,000	PF60 20.00				

KM# 95.1a 50 LIRE
14.00 g., 0.900 Gold 0.4025 oz. AGW, 24.8 mm. **Obv:** Italia **Rev:** Vulcan **Edge:** Reeded **Note:** Official Restrike

Date	Mintage	F12	VF20	XF40	MS60	MS63
1954 (2006)R	1,999	PF63 1,000				

KM# 183a 50 LIRE
9.00 g., 0.900 Gold 0.2587 oz. AGW, 19.2 mm. **Obv:** Roma **Rev:** Value within wreath **Edge:** Plain **Note:** Official Restrike

Date	Mintage	F12	VF20	XF40	MS60	MS63
1996 (2006)R	1,999	PF63 700				

KM# 159 100 LIRE
4.50 g., Copper-Nickel, 22 mm. **Obv:** Turreted head left **Rev:** Large value within circle flanked by sprigs **Edge:** Segmented reeding

Date	Mintage	F12	VF20	XF40	MS60	MS63
2001R	100,000	—	—	—	12.00	—
2001R	10,000	PF60 20.00				

KM# 96.1a 100 LIRE
18.00 g., 0.900 Gold 0.5175 oz. AGW, 27.8 mm. **Obv:** Ancient athlete **Rev:** Minerva standing **Edge:** Reeded **Note:** Official Restrike

Date	Mintage	F12	VF20	XF40	MS60	MS63
1955 (2006)R	1,999	PF63 1,300				

KM# 159a 100 LIRE
9.00 g., 0.900 Gold 0.2587 oz. AGW, 22 mm. **Obv:** Turreted head left **Rev:** Large value within circle flanked by sprigs **Edge:** Segmented reeding **Note:** Official Restrike

Date	Mintage	F12	VF20	XF40	MS60	MS63
1993 (2006)R	1,999	PF63 700				

KM# 105 200 LIRE
5.00 g., Aluminum-Bronze, 24 mm. **Obv:** Head right **Rev:** Value within gear **Edge:** Reeded

Date	Mintage	F12	VF20	XF40	MS60	MS63
2001R	100,000	—	—	—	12.00	—
2001R	10,000	PF60 30.00				

KM# 105a 200 LIRE
11.00 g., 0.900 Gold 0.3162 oz. AGW, 24 mm. **Obv:** Head right **Rev:** Value within gear **Edge:** Reeded **Note:** Official Restrike

Date	Mintage	F12	VF20	XF40	MS60	MS63
1977 (2006)R	1,999	PF63 900				

KM# 98 500 LIRE
11.00 g., 0.835 Silver 0.2934 oz. ASW, 29.3 mm. **Obv:** Columbus' ships **Rev:** Bust left within wreath **Edge:** Dates in raised lettering

Date	Mintage	F12	VF20	XF40	MS60	MS63
2001R	100,000	—	—	—	30.00	—
2001R	10,000	PF60 160				

KM# 111 500 LIRE
6.80 g., Bi-Metallic, 25.8 mm. **Obv:** Head left within circle **Rev:** Plaza within circle flanked by sprigs **Edge:** Segmented reeding

Date	Mintage	F12	VF20	XF40	MS60	MS63
2001R	100,000	—	—	—	12.00	—
2001R	10,000	PF60 30.00				

KM# 98a 500 LIRE
18.00 g., 0.900 Gold 0.5175 oz. AGW, 29 mm. **Obv:** Columbus' ships **Rev:** Bust left within wreath **Edge:** Lettered **Edge Lettering:** REPVBBLICA ITALIANA *** 1958*** **Note:** Official Restrike

Date	Mintage	F12	VF20	XF40	MS60	MS63
1958 (2006)R	1,999	PF63 1,300				

KM# 99a 500 LIRE
18.00 g., 0.900 Gold 0.5175 oz. AGW, 29 mm. **Obv:** Seated Italia **Rev:** Lady **Edge:** Lettered **Edge Lettering:** 1 CENTENARIO VNITA'D'ITALIA * 1861-1961* **Note:** Official Restrike

Date	Mintage	F12	VF20	XF40	MS60	MS63
1961 (2006)R	1,999	PF63 1,300				

KM# 100a 500 LIRE
18.00 g., 0.900 Gold 0.5175 oz. AGW, 29 mm. **Obv:** Dante **Rev:** Hell **Edge:** Lettered **Edge Lettering:** 7 CENTENARIO DELLA NASCITA DI DANTE **Note:** Official Restrike

Date	Mintage	F12	VF20	XF40	MS60	MS63
1965 (2006)R	1,999	PF63 1,300				

KM# 111a 500 LIRE
14.00 g., Bi-Metallic, 25.8 mm. **Obv:** Head left within circle **Rev:** Plaza within circle flanked by sprigs **Edge:** Segmented reeding **Note:** Official Restrike

Date	Mintage	F12	VF20	XF40	MS60	MS63
1982 (2006)R	1,999	PF63 1,000				

KM# 194 1000 LIRE
8.80 g., Bi-Metallic, 27 mm. **Subject:** European Union **Obv:** Head left within circle **Rev:** Corrected map with United Germany within globe design **Edge:** Segmented reeding

Date	Mintage	F12	VF20	XF40	MS60	MS63
2001R	100,000	—	—	—	10.00	—
2001R	10,000	PF60 40.00				

KM# 236 1000 LIRE
14.60 g., 0.835 Silver 0.3894 oz. ASW, 31.4 mm. **Obv:** Giuseppe Verdi **Rev:** Building

Date	Mintage	F12	VF20	XF40	MS60	MS63
2001R	115,000	—	—	—	50.00	—
2001R	10,000	PF63 80.00				

KM# 101a 1000 LIRE
24.00 g., 0.900 Gold 0.690 oz. AGW, 31.2 mm. **Obv:** Concordia **Rev:** Geometric shape above value **Edge Lettering:** REPVBBLICA ITALIANA **Note:** Official restrike.

Date	Mintage	F12	VF20	XF40	MS60	MS63
1970 (2006)R	1,999	PF63 1,500				

KM# 190a 1000 LIRE
17.00 g., 0.900 Gold 0.4887 oz. AGW, 27 mm. **Obv:** Roma **Rev:** European map **Edge:** Segmented reeding **Note:** Official Restrike

Date	Mintage	F12	VF20	XF40	MS60	MS63
1997 (2006)R	1,999	PF63 1,250				

KM# 234 50000 LIRE
7.50 g., 0.900 Gold 0.2156 oz. AGW, 20 mm. **Subject:** 250th Anniversary - Palace of Caserta **Obv:** Front view of palace **Rev:** Fountain, date and denomination

Date	Mintage	F12	VF20	XF40	MS60	MS63
2001R	6,200	PF63 800				

KM# 233 100000 LIRE
15.00 g., 0.900 Gold 0.4312 oz. AGW, 25 mm. **Subject:** 700th Anniversary - Pulpit at the Church of St. Andrea a Pistoia **Obv:** Full pulpit **Rev:** Enlarged detail of the pulpit

Date	Mintage	F12	VF20	XF40	MS60	MS63
2001R	4,500	PF63 1,400				

EURO COINAGE
European Union Issues

KM# 210 EURO CENT
2.30 g., Copper Plated Steel, 16.25 mm. **Obv:** Castle del Monte **Rev:** Value and globe **Edge:** Plain

Date	Mintage	F12	VF20	XF40	MS60	MS63
2002R	1,348,899,500	—	—	—	0.25	—
2003R	9,629,000	—	—	—	0.35	—
2003R	12,000	PF63 10.00				
2004R	100,000,000	—	—	—	0.25	—
2004R	12,000	PF63 7.00				
2005R	180,000,000	—	—	—	0.25	—
2005R	12,000	PF63 5.00				
2006R	159,000,000	—	—	—	0.25	—
2006R	12,000	PF63 5.00				
2007R	215,000,000	—	—	—	0.25	—
2007R	12,000	PF63 5.00				
2008R	180,000,000	—	—	—	0.25	—
2008R	5,000	PF63 5.00				
2009R	174,951,500	—	—	—	0.25	—
2009R	5,500	PF63 5.00				
2010R	42,000,000	—	—	—	0.25	—
2010R	5,000	PF63 5.00				
2011R	134,000,000	—	—	—	0.25	—
2011R	5,000	PF63 5.00				
2012R	217,959,500	—	—	—	0.25	—
2012R	—	PF63 5.00				
2013R	—	—	—	—	0.25	—
2013R	—	PF63 5.00				

KM# 211 2 EURO CENT
3.06 g., Copper Plated Steel, 18.75 mm. **Obv:** Observation tower in Turin **Rev:** Value and globe **Edge:** Grooved

Date	Mintage	F12	VF20	XF40	MS60	MS63
2002R	1,099,166,250	—	—	—	0.25	—
2003R	21,817,000	—	—	—	0.25	—
2003R	12,000	PF63 10.00				
2004R	120,000,000	—	—	—	0.25	—
2004R	12,000	PF63 7.00				
2005R	120,000,000	—	—	—	0.25	—
2005R	12,000	PF63 5.00				
2006R	196,000,000	—	—	—	0.25	—
2006R	12,000	PF63 5.00				
2007R	140,000,000	—	—	—	0.25	—
2007R	12,000	PF63 5.00				
2008R	135,000,000	—	—	—	0.25	—
2008R	5,000	PF63 5.00				
2009R	184,951,500	—	—	—	0.25	—
2009R	5,500	PF63 5.00				
2010R	115,000,000	—	—	—	0.25	—
2010R	5,000	PF63 5.00				
2011R	109,000,000	—	—	—	0.25	—
2011R	5,000	PF63 5.00				
2012R	79,959,500	—	—	—	0.25	—
2012R	—	PF63 5.00				
2013R	—	—	—	—	0.25	—
2013R	—	PF63 5.00				

KM# 212 5 EURO CENT
3.92 g., Copper Plated Steel, 21.25 mm. **Obv:** Colosseum **Rev:** Value and globe **Edge:** Plain

Date	Mintage	F12	VF20	XF40	MS60	MS63
2002R	1,341,742,204	—	—	—	0.25	—
2003R	1,960,000	—	—	—	10.00	—
2003R	12,000	PF63 20.00				
2004R	10,000,000	—	—	—	0.25	—
2004R	12,000	PF63 8.00				
2005R	70,000,000	—	—	—	0.25	—
2005R	12,000	PF63 6.00				
2006R	119,000,000	—	—	—	0.25	—
2006R	12,000	PF63 6.00				
2007R	85,000,000	—	—	—	0.25	—
2007R	12,000	PF63 6.00				
2008R	90,000,000	—	—	—	0.25	—
2008R	5,000	PF63 6.00				
2009R	84,955,000	—	—	—	0.25	—
2009R	5,500	PF63 6.00				
2010R	32,000,000	—	—	—	0.25	—
2010R	5,000	PF63 6.00				
2011R	37,000,000	—	—	—	0.25	—
2011R	5,000	PF63 6.00				
2012R	75,959,500	—	—	—	0.25	—
2012R	—	PF63 6.00				
2013R	—	—	—	—	0.25	—
2013R	—	PF63 6.00				

KM# 213 10 EURO CENT
4.10 g., Brass, 19.75 mm. **Obv:** Venus by Botticelli **Rev:** Value and map **Edge:** Reeded

Date	Mintage	F12	VF20	XF40	MS60	MS63
2002R	1,142,383,000	—	—	—	0.25	—
	Note: Three varieties in size of the obverse designer's name					
2003R	29,976,000	—	—	—	0.25	—
2003R	12,000	PF63 15.00				
2004R	5,000,000	—	—	—	5.00	—
2004R	12,000	PF63 10.00				
2005R	100,000,000	—	—	—	0.25	—
2005R	12,000	PF63 7.00				
2006R	180,000,000	—	—	—	0.25	—
2006R	12,000	PF63 7.00				
2007R	105,000,000	—	—	—	0.25	—
2007R	12,000	PF63 7.00				

KM# 247 10 EURO CENT
4.10 g., Brass, 19.75 mm. **Obv:** Venus by Botticelli **Rev:** Relief Map of Western Europe, stars, lines and value **Edge:** Reeded

Date	Mintage	F12	VF20	XF40	MS60	MS63
2008R	104,955,000	—	—	—	0.25	0.35
2008R	5,000	PF63 7.00				
2009R	105,951,500	—	—	—	0.25	—
2009R	5,500	PF63 7.00				
2010R	57,000,000	—	—	—	0.25	—
2010R	5,000	PF63 7.00				
2011R	76,000,000	—	—	—	0.25	—
2011R	5,000	PF63 7.00				
2012R	99,959,500	—	—	—	0.25	—
2012R	—	PF63 7.00				
2013R	—	—	—	—	0.25	—
2013R	—	PF63 7.00				

KM# 214 20 EURO CENT
5.74 g., Brass, 22.25 mm. **Obv:** Futuristic sculpture by Boccioni **Rev:** Value and map **Edge:** Notched

Date	Mintage	F12	VF20	XF40	MS60	MS63
2002R	1,411,836,000	—	—	—	0.30	—
2003R	26,155,000	—	—	—	0.30	—
2003R	12,000	PF63 16.00				
2004R	5,000,000	—	—	—	0.30	—
2004R	12,000	PF63 14.00				
2005R	5,000,000	—	—	—	0.30	—
2005R	12,000	PF63 8.00				
2006R	5,000,000	—	—	—	0.30	—
2006R	12,000	PF63 8.00				
2007R	5,000,000	—	—	—	0.30	—
2007R	12,000	PF63 8.00				

KM# 248 20 EURO CENT
5.74 g., Brass, 22.25 mm. **Obv:** Futuristic sculpture **Rev:** Relief map of Western Europe, stars, lines and value **Edge:** Notched

Date	Mintage	F12	VF20	XF40	MS60	MS63
2008R	4,955,000	—	—	—	0.30	—
2008R	5,000	PF63 8.00				
2009R	59,951,500	—	—	—	0.30	—
2009R	5,500	PF63 8.00				
2010R	23,000,000	—	—	—	0.30	—
2010R	5,000	PF63 8.00				
2011R	67,000,000	—	—	—	0.30	—
2011R	5,000	PF63 8.00				
2012R	4,959,500	—	—	—	0.30	—
2012R	—	PF63 8.00				
2013R	—	—	—	—	0.30	—
2013R	—	PF63 8.00				

KM# 215 50 EURO CENT
7.80 g., Brass, 24.25 mm. **Obv:** Sculpture of Marcus Aurelius on horseback **Rev:** Value and map **Edge:** Reeded

Date	Mintage	F12	VF20	XF40	MS60	MS63
2002R	1,136,718,000	—	—	—	0.80	—
2003R	44,825,000	—	—	—	1.00	—
2003R	12,000	PF63 18.00				
2004R	5,000,000	—	—	—	1.00	—
2004R	12,000	PF63 16.00				
2005R	5,000,000	—	—	—	1.00	—
2005R	12,000	PF63 10.00				
2006R	5,000,000	—	—	—	1.00	—
2006R	12,000	PF63 10.00				
2007R	5,000,000	—	—	—	1.00	—
2007R	12,000	PF63 10.00				

KM# 249 50 EURO CENT
7.80 g., Brass, 24.25 mm. **Obv:** Sculpture of Marcus Aurelius on horseback **Rev:** Relief map of Western Europe, stars, lines and value **Edge:** Reeded

Date	Mintage	F12	VF20	XF40	MS60	MS63
2008R	4,955,000	—	—	—	1.00	—
2008R	5,000	PF63 10.00				
2009R	2,451,500	—	—	—	1.00	—
2009R	5,500	PF63 10.00				
2010R	9,000,000	—	—	—	1.00	—
2010R	5,000	PF63 10.00				
2011R	5,000,000	—	—	—	1.00	—
2011R	5,000	PF63 10.00				
2012R	4,959,500	—	—	—	1.00	—
2012R	—	PF63 10.00				
2013R	—	—	—	—	1.00	—
2013R	—	PF63 10.00				

KM# 216 EURO

7.50 g., Bi-Metallic, 23.25 mm. **Obv:** Male figure drawing by Leonardo da Vinci within circle of stars **Rev:** Value and map within circle **Edge:** Segmented reeding

Date	Mintage	F12	VF20	XF40	MS60	MS63
2002R	966,025,300	—	—	—	1.50	—
Note: A variety exists which lacks the artist's signature						
2003R	66,474,000	—	—	—	1.50	—
2003R	12,000	PF63 20.00				
2004R	5,000,000	—	—	—	1.50	—
2004R	12,000	PF63 18.00				
2005R	5,000,000	—	—	—	1.50	—
2005R	12,000	PF63 15.00				
2006R	108,000,000	—	—	—	1.50	—
2006R	12,000	PF63 15.00				
2007R	135,000,000	—	—	—	1.50	—
2007R	12,000	PF63 15.00				

KM# 250 EURO

7.50 g., Bi-Metallic, 23.25 mm. **Obv:** Male figure drawing by Leonardo da Vinci **Rev:** Relief map of Western Europe, stars, lines and value **Edge:** Segmented reeding

Date	Mintage	F12	VF20	XF40	MS60	MS63
2008R	134,955,000	—	—	—	1.50	—
2008R	5,000	PF63 15.00				
2009R	144,951,500	—	—	—	1.50	—
2009R	5,500	PF63 15.00				
2010R	50,000,000	—	—	—	1.50	—
2010R	5,000	PF63 15.00				
2011R	88,000,000	—	—	—	1.50	—
2011R	5,000	PF63 15.00				
2012R	4,959,500	—	—	—	1.50	—
2012R	—	PF63 15.00				
2013R	—	—	—	—	1.50	—
2013R	—	PF63 15.00				

KM# 217 2 EURO

8.50 g., Bi-Metallic, 25.75 mm. **Obv:** Bust of Dante Aligheri left **Rev:** Value and map within circle **Edge:** Reeded **Edge Lettering:** 2's and stars

Date	Mintage	F12	VF20	XF40	MS60	MS63
2002R	463,702,000	—	—	—	3.00	—
2003R	36,160,000	—	—	—	3.00	—
2003R	12,000	PF63 25.00				
2004R	7,000,000	—	—	—	3.00	—
2004R	12,000	PF63 22.00				
2005R	62,000,000	—	—	—	3.00	—
2005R	12,000	PF63 20.00				
2006R	10,000,000	—	—	—	3.00	—
2006R	12,000	PF63 20.00				
2007R	5,000,000	—	—	—	3.00	—
2007R	12,000	PF63 20.00				

KM# 237 2 EURO

8.50 g., Bi-Metallic, 25.75 mm. **Obv:** World Food Program globe within circle **Rev:** Value and map within circle **Edge:** Reeded and lettered **Edge Lettering:** 2's and stars

Date	Mintage	F12	VF20	XF40	MS60	MS63
2004R	16,000,000	—	—	—	3.00	—

KM# 245 2 EURO

8.50 g., Bi-Metallic, 25.75 mm. **Subject:** European Constitution **Obv:** Europa holding an open book while sitting on a bull within circle **Rev:** Value and map within circle **Edge:** Reeding over stars and 2's

Date	Mintage	F12	VF20	XF40	MS60	MS63
2005R	18,000,000	—	—	—	3.00	—

KM# 246 2 EURO

8.50 g., Bi-Metallic, 25.75 mm. **Subject:** Torino Winter Olympics **Obv:** Skier and other designs within circle **Rev:** Value and map within circle **Edge:** Reeded with stars and 2's

Date	Mintage	F12	VF20	XF40	MS60	MS63
2006R	40,000,000	—	—	—	3.00	—

KM# 311 2 EURO

8.50 g., Bi-Metallic, 25.75 mm. **Subject:** Treaty of Rome, 50th Anniversary **Obv:** Open treaty

Date	Mintage	F12	VF20	XF40	MS60	MS63
2007R	5,000,000	—	—	—	3.00	—

KM# 251 2 EURO

8.50 g., Bi-Metallic, 25.75 mm. **Obv:** Bust of Dante Aligheri **Rev:** Relief map of Western Europe, stars, lines and value **Edge:** Reeded **Edge Lettering:** 2's and stars

Date	Mintage	F12	VF20	XF40	MS60	MS63
2008R	5,000	PF63 10.00				
2008R	2,455,000	—	—	—	3.00	—
2009R	1,951,500	—	—	—	3.00	—
2009R	5,500	PF63 10.00				
2010R	6,000,000	—	—	—	3.00	—
2010R	5,000	PF63 10.00				
2011R	20,000,000	—	—	—	3.00	—
2011R	5,000	PF63 10.00				
2012R	26,959,500	—	—	—	3.00	—
2012R	—	PF63 10.00				
2013R	—	—	—	—	3.00	—
2013R	—	PF63 10.00				

KM# 301 2 EURO

8.50 g., Bi-Metallic, 25.75 mm. **Subject:** Declaration of Rights **Obv:** Nude male and female figures

Date	Mintage	F12	VF20	XF40	MS60	MS63
2008R	5,000,000	—	—	—	3.00	—

KM# 310 2 EURO

8.50 g., Bi-Metallic, 25.75 mm. **Subject:** Louis Braille **Obv:** Hand reading book in braille font

Date	Mintage	F12	VF20	XF40	MS60	MS63
2009R	2,000,000	—	—	—	6.00	—

KM# 312 2 EURO

8.50 g., Bi-Metallic, 25.75 mm. **Subject:** European Monetary Union, 10th Anniversary **Obv:** Stick figure and Euro symbol

Date	Mintage	F12	VF20	XF40	MS60	MS63
2009R	2,000,000	—	—	—	6.00	—
2009R	5,500	PF63 25.00				

KM# 328 2 EURO

8.50 g., Bi-Metallic, 25.75 mm. **Subject:** Camillo Benso Count of Cavour **Obv:** Bust 3/4 right

Date	Mintage	F12	VF20	XF40	MS60	MS63
2010R	4,000,000	—	—	—	5.00	—
2010R Special Unc.	16,000	—	—	—	—	15.00
2010R	5,000	PF63 25.00				

KM# 338 2 EURO

8.50 g., Bi-Metallic, 25.75 mm. **Subject:** Italian Unification, 150th Anniversary **Obv:** Three banners

Date	Mintage	F12	VF20	XF40	MS60	MS63
2011R	10,000,000	—	—	—	3.00	—
2011R Special Unc.	20,000	—	—	—	—	15.00
2011R	5,000	PF63 25.00				

KM# 350 2 EURO

8.50 g., Bi-Metallic, 25.75 mm. **Subject:** Eurocoinage, 10th Anniversary **Obv:** Euro symbol on globe at center, child-like drawings around

Date	Mintage	F12	VF20	XF40	MS60	MS63
2012R	15,000,000	—	—	—	5.00	—

KM# 355 2 EURO

8.50 g., Bi-Metallic, 25.75 mm. **Subject:** Giovanni Pascoli, 100th Anniversary of Death **Obv:** Giovanni Pascoli bust **Edge:** Reeded with 2's and stars

Date	Mintage	F12	VF20	XF40	MS60	MS63
2012R	15,000,000	—	—	—	5.00	—
2012 Special Unc	—	—	—	—	—	15.00

KM# 357 2 EURO

8.50 g., Bi-Metallic, 25.75 mm. **Obv:** Giuseppe Verdi bust facing

Date	Mintage	F12	VF20	XF40	MS60	MS63
2013	10,000,000	—	—	—	—	5.00

KM# 358 2 EURO

8.50 g., Bi-Metallic, 25.75 mm. **Obv:** Giovanni Boccaccio head facing

Date	Mintage	F12	VF20	XF40	MS60	MS63
2013	—	—	—	—	—	6.00

KM# 367 2 EURO

8.50 g., Bi-Metallic, 25.75 mm. **Subject:** Carabinieri, 150th Anniversary

Date	Mintage	F12	VF20	XF40	MS60	MS63
2014	—	—	—	—	—	5.00

KM# 302 5 EURO
18.00 g., 0.925 Silver 0.5319 oz. ASW, 32 mm. **Subject:** Antonia Meucci - 200th Birthday

Date	Mintage	F12	VF20	XF40	MS60	MS63
2003R Proof	—	—	—	—	—	40.00

KM# 252 5 EURO
18.00 g., 0.925 Silver 0.5319 oz. ASW, 32 mm. **Subject:** People in Europe

Date	Mintage	F12	VF20	XF40	MS60	MS63
2003R	8,000	PF63 60.00				
2003R	25,000	PF63 40.00				

KM# 253 5 EURO
18.00 g., 0.925 Silver 0.5319 oz. ASW, 32 mm. **Subject:** Work in Europe

Date	Mintage	F12	VF20	XF40	MS60	MS63
2003R	12,000	PF63 65.00				
2003R	50,000	—	—	—	35.00	—

KM# 239 5 EURO
18.00 g., 0.925 Silver 0.5319 oz. ASW, 32 mm. **Subject:** Madam Butterfly **Obv:** La Scala Opera House, where Madam Butterfly was first performed there in 1904 **Rev:** Geisha

Date	Mintage	F12	VF20	XF40	MS60	MS63
2004R	12,000	PF63 40.00				
2004R	30,000	—	—	—	35.00	—

KM# 254 5 EURO
18.00 g., 0.925 Silver 0.5319 oz. ASW, 32 mm. **Subject:** 50th Anniversary of Italian Television

Date	Mintage	F12	VF20	XF40	MS60	MS63
2004R	15,000	PF63 80.00				
2004R	40,000	—	—	—	40.00	—

KM# 238 5 EURO
18.00 g., 0.925 Silver 0.5319 oz. ASW, 32 mm. **Subject:** World Cup Soccer - Germany 2006 **Obv:** Santa Croce Square in Florence **Rev:** Soccer ball and world globe design

Date	Mintage	F12	VF20	XF40	MS60	MS63
2004R	35,000	PF63 90.00				

KM# 255 5 EURO
18.00 g., 0.925 Silver 0.5319 oz. ASW, 32 mm. **Subject:** 85th Birthday of Federico Fellini

Date	Mintage	F12	VF20	XF40	MS60	MS63
2005R	22,000	PF63 140				
2005R	35,000	—	—	—	65.00	—

KM# 256 5 EURO
18.00 g., 0.925 Silver 0.5319 oz. ASW, 32 mm. **Subject:** 2006 Olympic Winter Games Torino Ski Jump

Date	Mintage	F12	VF20	XF40	MS60	MS63
2005R	35,000	PF63 55.00				

KM# 257 5 EURO
18.00 g., 0.925 Silver 0.5319 oz. ASW, 32 mm. **Subject:** 2006 Olympic Winter Games Cross Country Skiing

Date	Mintage	F12	VF20	XF40	MS60	MS63
2005R	35,000	PF63 55.00				

KM# 266 5 EURO
18.00 g., 0.925 Silver 0.5319 oz. ASW, 32 mm. **Subject:** 2006 Olympic Games Torino Figure Skating

Date	Mintage	F12	VF20	XF40	MS60	MS63
2005	35,000	PF63 55.00				

KM# 282 5 EURO
18.00 g., 0.925 Silver 0.5319 oz. ASW, 32 mm. **Subject:** FIFA World Cup 12

Date	Mintage	F12	VF20	XF40	MS60	MS63
2006R	25,000	PF63 65.00				

KM# 294 5 EURO
18.00 g., 0.925 Silver 0.5319 oz. ASW, 32 mm. **Subject:** Arturo Toscani - 50th Aniversary Death

Date	Mintage	F12	VF20	XF40	MS60	MS63
2007R	7,000	—	—	—	50.00	—

KM# 291 5 EURO
18.00 g., 0.925 Silver 0.5319 oz. ASW, 32 mm. **Subject:** Kyoto Agreement - 5th Anniversary **Obv:** Allegorical representation of nature rebelling against pollution **Rev:** Allegorical representation of clear air with a spiral of vital energy

Date	Mintage	F12	VF20	XF40	MS60	MS63
2007R Special Unc	20,000	—	—	—	50.00	—
2007R	7,000	PF63 85.00				

KM# 292 5 EURO
18.00 g., 0.925 Silver 0.5319 oz. ASW, 32 mm. **Subject:** Giuseppe Garibaldi - 200th Anniversary Birth **Obv:** Portrait facing **Rev:** Harbor Lympia in Nice

Date	Mintage	F12	VF20	XF40	MS60	MS63
2007R Special Unc.	8,000	—	—	—	120	—

KM# 293 5 EURO
18.00 g., 0.925 Silver 0.5319 oz. ASW, 32 mm. **Subject:** Aitero Spinelini 100th Birthday **Obv:** Bust 3/4 facing **Rev:** Representation of Ventotene island and Parliament hemicycle

Date	Mintage	F12	VF20	XF40	MS60	MS63
2007R Special Unc.	7,000	—	—	—	120	—

KM# 323 5 EURO
18.00 g., 0.925 Silver 0.5319 oz. ASW, 32 mm. **Subject:** Arturo Toscanini. 50th Death Anniversary **Obv:** Profile left **Rev:** Hand with baton, and musical instruments

Date	Mintage	F12	VF20	XF40	MS60	MS63
2007R Special Unc.	7,000	—	—	—	125	—

KM# 281 5 EURO
18.00 g., 0.925 Silver 0.5319 oz. ASW, 32 mm. **Subject:** Italian Republic - 60th Anniversary

Date	Mintage	F12	VF20	XF40	MS60	MS63
2008R	—	—	—	—	—	65.00

KM# 303 5 EURO
18.00 g., 0.925 Silver 0.5319 oz. ASW, 32 mm. **Subject:** Anna Magnani, 100th Anniversary of Birth

Date	Mintage	F12	VF20	XF40	MS60	MS63
(2008)	9,000	PF63 75.00				

KM# 304 5 EURO
18.00 g., 0.925 Silver 0.5319 oz. ASW, 32 mm. **Subject:** Italian Constitution - 60th Anniversary

Date	Mintage	F12	VF20	XF40	MS60	MS63
2008	9,000	—	—	—	—	65.00

KM# 325 5 EURO
18.00 g., 0.925 Silver 0.5319 oz. ASW, 32 mm. **Series:** IFAD, 30th Anniversary

Date	Mintage	F12	VF20	XF40	MS60	MS63
2008R	20,000	—	—	—	60.00	—
2008R	5,000	PF63 130				

KM# 326 5 EURO
18.00 g., 0.925 Silver 0.5319 oz. ASW, 32 mm. **Subject:** Antonio Meucci **Obv:** Bust 3/4 facing right

Date	Mintage	F12	VF20	XF40	MS60	MS63
2008R	9,000	PF63 75.00				

KM# 313 5 EURO
18.00 g., 0.925 Silver 0.5319 oz. ASW, 32 mm. **Subject:** Giro d'Italy - Cycling Race Centennial **Obv:** Two cyclists **Rev:** Bicycle and map of Italy

Date	Mintage	F12	VF20	XF40	MS60	MS63
2009R Special Unc.	14,000	—	—	—	60.00	—

KM# 314 5 EURO
18.00 g., 0.925 Silver 0.5319 oz. ASW, 32 mm. **Subject:** World Aquatics Championships **Obv:** River God reclining **Rev:** Two swimmers

Date	Mintage	F12	VF20	XF40	MS60	MS63
2009R	21,000	—	—	—	50.00	—
2009R	7,500	—	—	—	—	—

KM# 315 5 EURO
18.00 g., 0.925 Silver 0.5319 oz. ASW, 32 mm. **Subject:** Herculaneum Discovery, 300th Anniversary **Obv:** Four dogs nipping at horse **Rev:** Marble relief of nymph drawing water with a horn

Date	Mintage	F12	VF20	XF40	MS60	MS63
2009R	9,000	—	—	—	55.00	—

KM# 327 5 EURO
18.00 g., 0.925 Silver 0.5319 oz. ASW, 32 mm. **Subject:** FINA, 13th Anniversary **Obv:** Sculpture Allegory of the Tiber River **Rev:** Swimmer Mosaics decorating the Foro Italico

Date	Mintage	F12	VF20	XF40	MS60	MS63
2009R	21,000	—	—	—	65.00	—
2009R	5,500	PF63 110				

KM# 329 5 EURO
18.00 g., 0.925 Silver 0.5319 oz. ASW, 32 mm. **Subject:** Alfa Romeo 100th Anniversary **Obv:** Two Automobiles: 24HP in back, new Giulietta in front **Rev:** Company logo

Date	Mintage	F12	VF20	XF40	MS60	MS63
2010R	17,000	—	—	—	65.00	—
2010R	5,500	PF63 110				

KM# 330 5 EURO
18.00 g., 0.925 Silver 0.5319 oz. ASW, 32 mm. **Subject:** Confindustria 100th Anniversary **Obv:** Female head left, mechanical gears within spiral at right **Rev:** Linear eagle and 100 logo

Date	Mintage	F12	VF20	XF40	MS60	MS63
2010R	7,500	—	—	—	65.00	—

KM# 331 5 EURO
18.00 g., 0.925 Silver 0.5319 oz. ASW, 32 mm. **Subject:** Santa Chiara in Naples **Obv:** Church facade **Rev:** Cloister interior

Date	Mintage	F12	VF20	XF40	MS60	MS63
2010R	7,500	PF63 80.00				

KM# 341 5 EURO
18.00 g., 0.925 Silver 0.5319 oz. ASW, 32 mm. **Subject:** Italian unification, 150th Anniversary

Date	Mintage	F12	VF20	XF40	MS60	MS63
2011R	5,000	PF63 100				
2011R	18,000	—	—	—	65.00	—

KM# 343 5 EURO
18.00 g., 0.925 Silver 0.5319 oz. ASW, 32 mm. **Subject:** Italian Council of State, 180th Anniversary

Date	Mintage	F12	VF20	XF40	MS60	MS63
2011R	7,000	PF63 85.00				

KM# 344 5 EURO
18.00 g., 0.925 Silver 0.5319 oz. ASW, 32 mm. **Subject:** Historical Building of the Italian Mint, 100th Anniversary

Date	Mintage	F12	VF20	XF40	MS60	MS63
2011R	7,000	—	—	—	70.00	—

KM# 345 5 EURO
18.00 g., 0.925 Silver 0.5319 oz. ASW, 32 mm. **Subject:** Art in Italy - Anagini

Date	Mintage	F12	VF20	XF40	MS60	MS63
2011R	7,000	PF63 85.00				

KM# 353 5 EURO
18.00 g., 0.925 Silver 0.5319 oz. ASW, 32 mm. **Subject:** Italian Monetary Unification, 150th Anniversary **Obv:** Italia head in vertical oval **Rev:** Alegory and fruits

Date	Mintage	F12	VF20	XF40	MS60	MS63
2012R	7,000	—	—	—	70.00	—

KM# 359 5 EURO
18.00 g., 0.925 (No Composition) 0.5319 oz., 32 mm. **Subject:** Gabriele D'Annunzio, 150th Anniversary of Birth **Obv:** Bust right **Rev:** Winged angel holding wreath above head

Date	Mintage	F12	VF20	XF40	MS60	MS63
2013 Anticipated but not issued	—	—	—	—	—	—

KM# 360 5 EURO
18.00 g., 0.925 Silver 0.5319 oz. ASW, 32 mm. **Subject:** Giuseppe Gioachino Belli, 150th Anniversary of Death **Obv:** Bust facing **Rev:** Temple of Hercules and Basilica of Santa Maria in Cosmedin

Date	Mintage	F12	VF20	XF40	MS60	MS63
2013	—	—	—	—	—	65.00

KM# 361 5 EURO
18.00 g., 0.925 Silver 0.5319 oz. ASW, 18 mm. **Obv:** Temple of Hera in Salinas **Rev:** Statue of Perseus and Medusa

Date	Mintage	F12	VF20	XF40	MS60	MS63
2013	—	PF63 75.00				

KM# 362 5 EURO
18.00 g., 0.925 Silver 0.5319 oz. ASW, 32 mm. **Obv:** Mosaic from Hadrian's villa **Rev:** Hadrian's villa in Tivoli

Date	Mintage	F12	VF20	XF40	MS60	MS63
2013	—	PF63 75.00				

KM# 258 10 EURO
22.00 g., 0.925 Silver 0.6501 oz. ASW, 34 mm. **Subject:** People In Europe

Date	Mintage	F12	VF20	XF40	MS60	MS63
2003	25,000	—	—	—	40.00	—
2003R	8,000	PF63 60.00				

KM# 259 10 EURO
22.00 g., 0.925 Silver 0.6501 oz. ASW, 34 mm. **Subject:** Italian Presidency of E.U.

Date	Mintage	F12	VF20	XF40	MS60	MS63
2003R	40,000	—	—	—	50.00	—
2003R	8,000	PF63 140				

KM# 240 10 EURO
22.00 g., 0.925 Silver 0.6501 oz. ASW, 34 mm. **Subject:** City of Genoa **Obv:** Sculpture and art works **Rev:** Tower and harbor map

Date	Mintage	F12	VF20	XF40	MS60	MS63
2004R	10,500	PF63 110				
2004R	20,000	—	—	—	60.00	—

KM# 241 10 EURO
22.00 g., 0.925 Silver 0.6501 oz. ASW, 34 mm. **Subject:** Giacomo Puccini **Obv:** Puccini wearing hat **Rev:** Stage, music and quill

Date	Mintage	F12	VF20	XF40	MS60	MS63
2004R	8,000	PF63 60.00				
2004R	13,500	—	—	—	40.00	—

KM# 260 10 EURO
22.00 g., 0.925 Silver 0.6501 oz. ASW, 34 mm. **Subject:** 2006 Olympic Winter Games Torino Alpine Skiing

Date	Mintage	F12	VF20	XF40	MS60	MS63
2005R	40,000	PF63 80.00				

KM# 261 10 EURO
22.00 g., 0.925 Silver 0.6501 oz. ASW, 34 mm. **Subject:** 2006 Olympic Winter Games Torino Ice Hockey

Date	Mintage	F12	VF20	XF40	MS60	MS63
2005R	35,000	PF63 80.00				

KM# 262 10 EURO
22.00 g., 0.925 Silver 0.6501 oz. ASW, 34 mm. **Subject:** 2006 Olympic Winter Games Torino Speed Skating

Date	Mintage	F12	VF20	XF40	MS60	MS63
2005R	35,000	PF63 80.00				

KM# 268 10 EURO
22.00 g., 0.925 Silver 0.6501 oz. ASW, 34 mm. **Subject:** 60th Anniversary UN "ONU

Date	Mintage	F12	VF20	XF40	MS60	MS63
2005	25,000	—	—	—	65.00	—

KM# 271 10 EURO
22.00 g., 0.925 Silver 0.6501 oz. ASW, 34 mm. **Subject:** Peace and Freedom In Europe

Date	Mintage	F12	VF20	XF40	MS60	MS63
2005	22,000	PF63 100				

KM# 283 10 EURO
22.00 g., 0.925 Silver 0.6501 oz. ASW, 34 mm. **Subject:** FIFA World Cup - Germany

Date	Mintage	F12	VF20	XF40	MS60	MS63
2006R	20,000	—	—	—	65.00	—

KM# 284 10 EURO
22.00 g., 0.925 Silver 0.6501 oz. ASW **Subject:** Andre Martenga - 500th Anniversary

Date	Mintage	F12	VF20	XF40	MS60	MS63
2006R	8,000	PF63 150				

KM# 285 10 EURO
22.00 g., 0.925 Silver 0.6501 oz. ASW, 34 mm. **Subject:** Leonardo da Vinci

Date	Mintage	F12	VF20	XF40	MS60	MS63
2006R	25,000	PF63 85.00				

KM# 286 10 EURO
22.00 g., 0.925 Silver 0.6501 oz. ASW, 34 mm. **Subject:** UNICEF 60th Anniversary

Date	Mintage	F12	VF20	XF40	MS60	MS63
2006R	15,000	—	—	—	70.00	—

KM# 295 10 EURO
22.00 g., 0.925 Silver 0.6501 oz. ASW, 34 mm. **Subject:** Treaty of Rome, 50th Anniversary

Date	Mintage	F12	VF20	XF40	MS60	MS63
2007R	20,504	PF63 100				

KM# 296 10 EURO
22.00 g., 0.925 Silver 0.6501 oz. ASW, 34 mm. **Subject:** Antonia Canova - 250th Anniversary Birth **Obv:** Portrait facing **Rev:** Sculpture Eros and Psyche

Date	Mintage	F12	VF20	XF40	MS60	MS63
2007R	8,000	PF63 100				

KM# 297 10 EURO
22.00 g., 0.925 Silver 0.6501 oz. ASW, 34 mm. **Subject:** Mint of Rome's School of Medallic Art - 100th Anniversary **Obv:** Sculptor designing medal, from a medal by Giuseppe Romagnoli **Rev:** School logo

Date	Mintage	F12	VF20	XF40	MS60	MS63
2007R	8,000	PF63 65.00				

KM# 324 10 EURO
22.00 g., 0.925 Silver 0.6501 oz. ASW, 34 mm. **Subject:** Treaty of Rome, 50th Anniversary **Obv:** Pavement pattern from Capitol Square in Rome **Rev:** Steps leading up to Capitol

Date	Mintage	F12	VF20	XF40	MS60	MS63
2008R	22,000	PF63 85.00				

KM# 305 10 EURO
22.00 g., 0.925 Silver 0.6501 oz. ASW, 34 mm. **Subject:** Andrea Palladio - 500th Birthday

Date	Mintage	F12	VF20	XF40	MS60	MS63
2008	16,000	PF63 90.00				

KM# 306 10 EURO
22.00 g., 0.925 Silver 0.6501 oz. ASW, 34 mm. **Subject:** University of Perugia - 700th Anniversary

Date	Mintage	F12	VF20	XF40	MS60	MS63
2008	9,000	PF63 90.00				

KM# 316 10 EURO
22.00 g., 0.925 Silver 0.6501 oz. ASW, 34 mm. **Subject:** International Year of Astronomy **Obv:** Head right, astrolabe at left **Rev:** Galilei's telescope, details of an astrolabe and sky

Date	Mintage	F12	VF20	XF40	MS60	MS63
2009R	9,000	PF63 80.00				

KM# 317 10 EURO
22.00 g., 0.925 Silver 0.6501 oz. ASW, 34 mm. **Subject:** Guglielmo Maroni's Nobel Prize in Physics **Obv:** Bust and yacht Elettra **Rev:** Radio receiver and antenna and radio waves

Date	Mintage	F12	VF20	XF40	MS60	MS63
2009R	18,000	PF63 85.00				

KM# 318 10 EURO
22.00 g., 0.925 Silver 0.6501 oz. ASW, 34 mm. **Subject:** Annibale Carracci, 400th Anniversary **Obv:** 1/2 length figure standing **Rev:** Historical cart

Date	Mintage	F12	VF20	XF40	MS60	MS63
2009R	9,000	PF63 80.00				

KM# 319 10 EURO
22.00 g., 0.925 Silver 0.6501 oz. ASW, 34 mm. **Subject:** Futurist movement, 100th Anniversary **Obv:** Building design **Rev:** Round sculpture

Date	Mintage	F12	VF20	XF40	MS60	MS63
2009R	9,000	PF63 85.00				

KM# 337 10 EURO
22.00 g., 0.925 Silver 0.6501 oz. ASW, 34 mm. **Subject:** L'Aquila Earthquake, reconstruction

Date	Mintage	F12	VF20	XF40	MS60	MS63
2009R	5,000	PF63 130				

KM# 332 10 EURO
22.00 g., 0.925 Silver 0.6501 oz. ASW, 34 mm. **Subject:** Caravaggio 400th Death Anniversary **Obv:** Bust 3/4 facing left, basket of fruit below **Rev:** Medussa head painting detail

Date	Mintage	F12	VF20	XF40	MS60	MS63
2010R	7,500	PF63 85.00				

KM# 333 10 EURO
22.00 g., 0.925 Silver 0.6501 oz. ASW, 34 mm. **Subject:** Giorgione, 500th Death Anniverdary **Obv:** Bust 3/4 left **Rev:** Detail from the painting "La Tempesta"

Date	Mintage	F12	VF20	XF40	MS60	MS63
2010R	7,500	PF63 85.00				

KM# 334 10 EURO
22.00 g., 0.925 Silver 0.6501 oz. ASW, 34 mm. **Subject:** Arts of Italy, Aquileia **Obv:** Basilica and architechtural floorplan **Rev:** Interpertation from the "Tabula Peuntigeriana

Date	Mintage	F12	VF20	XF40	MS60	MS63
2010R	7,500	PF63 85.00				

KM# 339 10 EURO
22.00 g., 0.925 Silver 0.6501 oz. ASW, 34 mm. **Subject:** Amerigo Vespucci

Date	Mintage	F12	VF20	XF40	MS60	MS63
2011R	7,000	PF63 95.00				

KM# 340 10 EURO
22.00 g., 0.925 Silver 0.6501 oz. ASW, 34 mm. **Subject:** Alcide de Gasperi, 130th Anniversary of Birth

Date	Mintage	F12	VF20	XF40	MS60	MS63
2011R	7,000	PF63 95.00				

KM# 342 10 EURO
22.00 g., 0.925 Silver 0.6501 oz. ASW, 34 mm. **Subject:** Giorgio Vasari, 500th Anniversary of Birth

Date	Mintage	F12	VF20	XF40	MS60	MS63
2011R	7,000	PF63 95.00				

KM# 346 10 EURO
22.00 g., 0.925 Silver 0.6501 oz. ASW, 34 mm. **Subject:** Art in Italy - Torino

Date	Mintage	F12	VF20	XF40	MS60	MS63
2011R	7,000	PF63 95.00				

KM# 349 10 EURO
22.00 g., 0.925 Silver 0.6501 oz. ASW, 34 mm. **Subject:** Bari **Obv:** St. Nicolas Church

Date	Mintage	F12	VF20	XF40	MS60	MS63
2011R	7,000	PF63 95.00				

KM# 354 10 EURO
22.00 g., 0.925 Silver 0.6501 oz. ASW, 34 mm. **Subject:** Francesco Guardi, 300th anniversary of Birth **Obv:** Venice from the lagoon **Rev:** Guardi bust

Date	Mintage	F12	VF20	XF40	MS60	MS63
2012R	7,000	PF63 100				

KM# 356 10 EURO
22.00 g., 0.925 Silver 0,6501 oz. ASW, 34 mm. **Obv:** Bust right, signature below **Rev:** Head of David statue at left, Holy Year Door at right

Date	Mintage	F12	VF20	XF40	MS60	MS63
2012R	9,000	PF63 100				

KM# 363 10 EURO
22.00 g., 0.925 Silver 0.6501 oz. ASW, 34 mm. **Obv:** Half-length figure left, seated, hand holding head **Rev:** Stone figure from theater scene

Date	Mintage	F12	VF20	XF40	MS60	MS63
2013	—	PF63 85.00				

KM# 364 10 EURO
22.00 g., 0.925 Silver 0.6501 oz. ASW **Obv:** Fenis castle **Rev:** Fresco of St. George slaying dragon

Date	Mintage	F12	VF20	XF40	MS60	MS63
2013	—	PF63 85.00				

KM# 368 10 EURO
22.00 g., 0.925 Silver 0.6501 oz. ASW, 34 mm. **Subject:** Gioachino Rossini

Date	Mintage	F12	VF20	XF40	MS60	MS63
2014	—	PF63 85.00				

KM# 263 20 EURO
6.45 g., 0.900 Gold 0.1854 oz. AGW, 21 mm. **Subject:** Arts in Europe - Italy

Date	Mintage	F12	VF20	XF40	MS60	MS63
2003R	6,000	PF63 550				

KM# 242 20 EURO
6.45 g., 0.900 Gold 0.1854 oz. AGW, 21 mm. **Obv:** Arts In Europe: Belgium **Rev:** Flying bird obscuring a man's face

Date	Mintage	F12	VF20	XF40	MS60	MS63
2004R	6,000	PF63 550				

KM# 243 20 EURO
6.45 g., 0.900 Gold 0.1854 oz. AGW, 21 mm. **Subject:** World Cup Soccer - Germany 2006 **Obv:** Mascot **Rev:** Soccer ball and world globe

Date	Mintage	F12	VF20	XF40	MS60	MS63
2004R	7,500	PF63 550				

KM# 265 20 EURO
6.45 g., 0.900 Gold 0.1854 oz. AGW, 21 mm. **Subject:** 2006 Olympic Winter Games Torino Porte Palatine Gate

Date	Mintage	F12	VF20	XF40	MS60	MS63
2005R	10,000	PF63 500				

KM# 267 20 EURO
6.45 g., 0.900 Gold 0.1854 oz. AGW, 21 mm. **Subject:** 2006 Olympic Games Torino Madama Palace

Date	Mintage	F12	VF20	XF40	MS60	MS63
2005R	10,000	PF63 500				

KM# 269 20 EURO
6.45 g., 0.900 Gold 0.1854 oz. AGW, 21 mm. **Subject:** 2006 Olympic Games Torino Stupinigi Palace

Date	Mintage	F12	VF20	XF40	MS60	MS63
2005R	10,000	PF63 500				

KM# 272 20 EURO
6.45 g., 0.900 Gold 0.1854 oz. AGW, 21 mm. **Subject:** Art In Europe - Finland **Obv:** Sailing ship

Date	Mintage	F12	VF20	XF40	MS60	MS63
2005R	5,000	PF63 550				

KM# 287 20 EURO
6.45 g., 0.900 Gold 0.1854 oz. AGW, 21 mm. **Subject:** FIFA World Cup

Date	Mintage	F12	VF20	XF40	MS60	MS63
2006R	4,350	PF63 550				

KM# 288 20 EURO
6.45 g., 0.900 Gold 0.1854 oz. AGW, 21 mm. **Subject:** European Arts - Germany

Date	Mintage	F12	VF20	XF40	MS60	MS63
2006R	3,100	PF63 600				

KM# 298 20 EURO
6.45 g., 0.900 Gold 0.1854 oz. AGW, 21 mm. **Subject:** Treaty of Rome - 50th Anniversary **Obv:** Pavement pattern in Capital Square in Rome **Rev:** Steps leading to Capital Building

Date	Mintage	F12	VF20	XF40	MS60	MS63
2007R	4,000	PF63 550				

KM# 299 20 EURO
6.45 g., 0.900 Gold 0.1854 oz. AGW, 21 mm. **Subject:** European Art - Ireland **Obv:** Sailing ship **Rev:** Tara Brooch

Date	Mintage	F12	VF20	XF40	MS60	MS63
2007R	3,500	PF63 600				

KM# 307 20 EURO
6.45 g., 0.900 Gold 0.1854 oz. AGW, 21 mm. **Subject:** Andrea Palladio - 500th Birthday **Obv:** Head left **Rev:** Building façade and floorplans

Date	Mintage	F12	VF20	XF40	MS60	MS63
2008R	5,500	PF63 550				

KM# 308 20 EURO
6.45 g., 0.900 Gold 0.1854 oz. AGW, 21 mm. **Subject:** Arts in Europe - Netherlands **Obv:** Sailing ship

Date	Mintage	F12	VF20	XF40	MS60	MS63
2008R	2,011	PF63 550				

KM# 320 20 EURO
6.45 g., 0.900 Gold 0.1854 oz. AGW, 21 mm. **Subject:** Guglielmo Marconi, 100th Anniversary of Nobel in Physics **Obv:** Bust and yacht Elettra **Rev:** Radio receiver with antenna and radio waves

Date	Mintage	F12	VF20	XF40	MS60	MS63
2009R	5,000	PF63 550				

KM# 321 20 EURO
6.45 g., 0.900 Gold 0.1854 oz. AGW, 21 mm. **Subject:** Arts in Europe - Great Britain **Obv:** Sailing ship **Rev:** Venus by Edward B. Jones

Date	Mintage	F12	VF20	XF40	MS60	MS63
2009R	3,000	PF63 550				

KM# 335 20 EURO
6.45 g., 0.900 Gold 0.1854 oz. AGW, 21 mm. **Subject:** Arts of Europe - Sweden **Obv:** Sailing ship **Rev:** Viking Helmet

Date	Mintage	F12	VF20	XF40	MS60	MS63
2010R	2,000	PF63 650				

KM# 347 20 EURO
6.45 g., 0.900 Gold 0.1854 oz. AGW, 21 mm. **Subject:** Flora in art

Date	Mintage	F12	VF20	XF40	MS60	MS63
2011R	1,500	PF63 650				

KM# 352 20 EURO
6.45 g., 0.900 Gold 0.1855 oz. AGW, 21 mm. **Subject:** Flora in Art - Middle ages **Obv:** Face at center of triskles **Rev:** Two peacocks face-to-face

Date	Mintage	F12	VF20	XF40	MS60	MS63
2012R	1,500	PF63 650				

KM# 365 20 EURO
6.45 g., 0.900 Gold 0.1855 oz. AGW, 21 mm. **Obv:** Lis from Florence's state emblem **Rev:** Female head by Botticelli

Date	Mintage	F12	VF20	XF40	MS60	MS63
2013	—	PF63 550				

KM# 369 20 EURO
6.45 g., 0.900 Gold 0.1854 oz. AGW, 21 mm. **Subject:** Baroque art **Rev:** Female statue

Date	Mintage	F12	VF20	XF40	MS60	MS63
2013	—	PF63 550				

KM# 264 50 EURO
16.13 g., 0.900 Gold 0.4637 oz. AGW, 28 mm. **Subject:** Arts in Europe - Austria

Date	Mintage	F12	VF20	XF40	MS60	MS63
2003R	6,000	PF63 1,200				

KM# 244 50 EURO
16.13 g., 0.900 Gold 0.4637 oz. AGW, 28 mm. **Obv:** Arts In Europe: Denmark **Rev:** Angel carrying away two children

Date	Mintage	F12	VF20	XF40	MS60	MS63
2004R	6,000	PF63 1,200				

KM# 270 50 EURO
16.13 g., 0.900 Gold 0.4637 oz. AGW, 28 mm. **Subject:** 2006 Olympic Games Torino Emanuele Filiberto

Date	Mintage	F12	VF20	XF40	MS60	MS63
2005R	6,000	PF63 1,200				

KM# 273 50 EURO
16.13 g., 0.900 Gold 0.4637 oz. AGW, 28 mm. **Subject:** Art In Europe - France

Date	Mintage	F12	VF20	XF40	MS60	MS63
2005R	5,000	PF63 1,200				

KM# 274 50 EURO
16.13 g., 0.900 Gold 0.4637 oz. AGW, 28 mm. **Subject:** 2006 Olympic Games Torino Olympic Torch

Date	Mintage	F12	VF20	XF40	MS60	MS63
2006R	5,000	PF63 1,200				

KM# 289 50 EURO
16.13 g., 0.900 Gold 0.4637 oz. AGW, 28 mm. **Subject:** European Arts - Greece

Date	Mintage	F12	VF20	XF40	MS60	MS63
2006R	1,792	PF63 1,200				

KM# 300 50 EURO
16.13 g., 0.900 Gold 0.4637 oz. AGW, 28 mm. **Subject:** European Art - Norway **Obv:** Sailing ship **Rev:** Painting "The Scream" by Edvard Munch

Date	Mintage	F12	VF20	XF40	MS60	MS63
2007R	2,000	PF63 1,250				

KM# 309 50 EURO
16.13 g., 0.900 Gold 0.4637 oz. AGW, 28 mm. **Subject:** Arts in Europe - Portugal

Date	Mintage	F12	VF20	XF40	MS60	MS63
2008R	2,000	PF63 1,250				

KM# 322 50 EURO
16.13 g., 0.900 Gold 0.4637 oz. AGW, 28 mm. **Subject:** Arts in Europe - Spain **Obv:** Sailing ship **Rev:** Sagrada Familia of Antoni Gaudí

Date	Mintage	F12	VF20	XF40	MS60	MS63
2009R	2,000	PF63 1,250				

KM# 336 50 EURO
16.13 g., 0.900 Gold 0.4637 oz. AGW, 28 mm. **Subject:** Arts of Europe - Hungary **Obv:** Sailing ship **Rev:** Detail of painting "Rozsi Szinyei Merse" by Pal Szinyel Merse

Date	Mintage	F12	VF20	XF40	MS60	MS63
2010R	1,500	PF63 1,300				

KM# 348 50 EURO
16.13 g., 0.900 Gold 0.4637 oz. AGW, 28 mm. **Subject:** Fauna in art

Date	Mintage	F12	VF20	XF40	MS60	MS63
2011R	1,000	PF63 1,800				

KM# 351 50 EURO
16.13 g., 0.900 Gold 0.4637 oz. AGW, 28 mm. **Subject:** Fauna in Art - Middle ages **Obv:** Stylized animal's head facing **Rev:** Statue of lions confronted

Date	Mintage	F12	VF20	XF40	MS60	MS63
2012R	—	PF63 1,600				

KM# 366 50 EURO
16.13 g., 0.900 Gold 0.4637 oz. AGW, 28 mm. **Obv:** Lion statue by Bardi **Rev:** Gianfrancesco Gonzaga of Mantua on horseback by Pisanello

Date	Mintage	F12	VF20	XF40	MS60	MS63
2013	—	PF63 1,300				

MINT SETS

KM#	Date	Mintage	Identification	Issue Price	Mkt Val
MS39	2001 (12)	125,200	KM#91-94, 97.2, 98, 105, 111, 159, 183, 194, 236	—	70.00
MS40	2002 (8)	50,000	KM#210-217	—	25.00
MS41	2003 (8)	50,000	KM#210-217	—	45.00
MS42	2003 (9)	50,000	KM#210-217, 253	—	70.00
MS43	2004 (8)	40,000	KM#210-217	—	35.00
MS44	2004 (9)	40,000	KM#210-217, 254	—	75.00

MS45	2005 (8)	35,000	KM#210-217	—	45.00
MS46	2005 (9)	35,000	KM#210-217, 255	—	100
MS47	2006 (8)	25,000	KM#210-217	—	40.00
MS48	2007 (8)	20,000	KM#210-217	—	60.00
MS49	2008 (8)	20,000	KM#210-216, 301	—	50.00
MS50	2008 (9)	22,000	KM#210-217, 281	—	100
MS51	2009 (9)	22,000	KM#210-212; 247-251	—	50.00
MS52	2010 (9)	21,000	KM#210-212; 247-251	—	60.00

PROOF SETS

KM#	Date	Mintage	Identification	Issue Price	Mkt Val
PS25	2001 (12)	10,000	KM#91-94, 97.2, 98, 105, 111, 159, 183, 194, 236	—	470
PS26	2003 (9)	12,000	KM#210-217, 253	—	180
PS27	2004 (9)	15,000	KM#210-217, 254	—	100
PS28	2005 (9)	12,000	KM#210-217, 255	—	140
PS29	2006 (9)	10,000	KM#210-217	—	150
PS30	2007 (9)	7,000	KM#210-217	—	160
PS31	2008 (9)	5,000	KM#210-212, 247-251, 325	—	200
PS32	2009 (10)	5,500	KM#210-212, 247-251, 312, 327	—	200
PS33	2010 (10)	5,000	KM#210-212, 247-251, 328, 329	—	200
PS34	2011 (10)	5,000	KM#210-212, 247-251, 338, 341	—	200

IVORY COAST

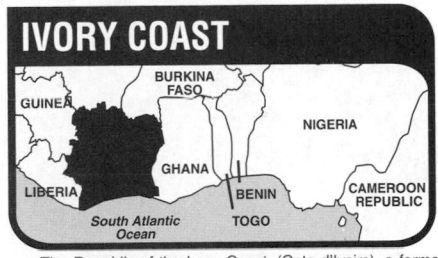

The Republic of the Ivory Coast, (Cote d'Ivoire), a former French Overseas territory located on the south side of the African bulge between Liberia and Ghana, has an area of 124,504 sq. mi. (322,463 sq. km.) and a population of 11.8 million. Capital: Yamoussoukro. The predominantly agricultural economy is one of Africa's most prosperous. Coffee, tropical woods, cocoa, and bananas are exported.

REPUBLIC
DECIMAL COINAGE

KM# 9 1000 CFA FRANCS
20.00 g., 0.925 Silver 0.591 oz. ASW, 38.61 mm. **Rev:** Sabre-Tooth Tiger

Date	Mintage	F12	VF20	XF40	MS60	MS63
2011 Proof	Est. 1000	—	—	—	—	—

KM# 10 100 FRANCS
25.00 g., Silver Plated Copper-Nickel, 38.61 mm. **Subject:** The Big Five **Obv:** Coat of Arms **Rev:** Elephants in color

Date	Mintage	F12	VF20	XF40	MS60	MS63
2010	2,500	PF63 40.00	PF65 45.00			

KM# 11 100 FRANCS
27.00 g., Silver Plated Copper-Nickel, 38.61 mm. **Subject:** The Big Five **Obv:** Coat of Arms **Rev:** Leopard in color

Date	Mintage	F12	VF20	XF40	MS60	MS63
Proof (2010)	1,000	PF63 40.00	PF65 45.00			

KM# 6 1000 FRANCS
25.00 g., 0.925 Silver 0.7387 oz. ASW, 38.6 mm. **Obv:** National arms **Rev:** Mamouth and embedded tooth fragment

Date	Mintage	F12	VF20	XF40	MS60	MS63
2010	2,500	PF63 75.00	PF65 85.00			

KM# 8 1000 FRANCS
25.00 g., 0.925 Silver 0.7387 oz. ASW, 38.61 mm. **Obv:** National arms **Rev:** Map of Africa with montage of animals, blue field

Date	Mintage	F12	VF20	XF40	MS60	MS63
2010	2,500	PF63 75.00	PF65 85.00			

KM# 12 1000 FRANCS
25.00 g., 0.999 Silver 0.7978 oz. ASW, 38.61 mm. **Obv:** Coat of Arms **Rev:** Lord Ganesha in color

Date	Mintage	F12	VF20	XF40	MS60	MS63
2013	1,001	PF63 75.00	PF65 85.00			

KM# 13 1500 FRANCS
1.00 g., 0.917 Gold 0.0293 oz. AGW, 16 mm. **Subject:** Eurosoccer 2008 **Obv:** Coat of Arms **Rev:** Football stadium

Date	Mintage	F12	VF20	XF40	MS60	MS63
2007	—	PF63 125	PF65 135			

KM# 7 1500 FRANCS
273.00 g., 0.925 Silver 8.0666 oz. ASW, 50 mm. **Subject:** Qibia Compass **Obv:** National arms **Rev:** Legend and design around center disc for compass spoon

Date	Mintage	F12	VF20	XF40	MS60	MS63
2010 Antique patina	—	—	—	—	500	—

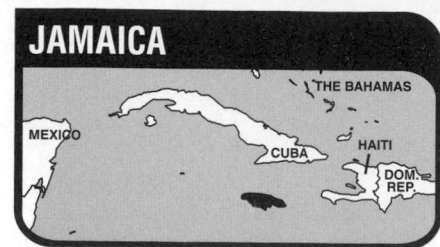

JAMAICA

Jamaica is situated in the Caribbean Sea 90 miles south of Cuba, has an area of 4,244 sq. mi. (10,990 sq. km.) and a population of 2.1 million. Capital: Kingston. The economy is founded chiefly on mining, tourism and agriculture. Aluminum, bauxite, sugar, rum and molasses are exported.

Jamaica is a member of the Commonwealth of Nations. Elizabeth II is the Head of State, as Queen of Jamaica.

MONETARY SYSTEM
100 Cents = 1 Dollar

COMMONWEALTH
DECIMAL COINAGE

KM# 64 CENT
1.22 g., Aluminum, 21.08 mm. **Ruler:** Elizabeth II **Series:** F.A.O. **Obv:** National arms, country named spaced beyond supporters **Obv. Legend:** JAMAICA **Rev:** Ackee fruit above value **Edge:** Plain **Shape:** 12-sided

Date	Mintage	F12	VF20	XF40	MS60	MS63
2002	—	—	—	0.25	0.50	0.75
2002	500	PF60 1.00				

KM# 146.2 10 CENTS
2.40 g., Copper Plated Steel, 17 mm. **Ruler:** Elizabeth II **Series:** National Heroes **Subject:** Paul Bogle **Obv:** National arms **Obv. Legend:** JAMAICA **Rev:** Bust facing **Edge:** Plain **Note:** Reduced size.

Date	Mintage	F12	VF20	XF40	MS60	MS63
2002	—	—	—	0.25	0.50	0.75
2002	500	PF60 2.00				
2003	—	—	—	0.25	0.50	0.75
2008	—	—	—	0.25	0.50	0.75

KM# 167 25 CENTS
3.60 g., Copper Plated Steel, 20 mm. **Ruler:** Elizabeth II **Series:** National Heroes **Subject:** Marcus Garvey **Obv:** National arms **Obv. Legend:** JAMAICA **Rev:** Head 1/4 right **Edge:** Plain

Date	Mintage	F12	VF20	XF40	MS60	MS63
2002	—	—	—	0.25	0.50	0.75
2002	500	PF60 3.00				
2003	—	—	—	0.25	0.50	0.75

KM# 164 DOLLAR
2.91 g., Nickel Plated Steel, 18.5 mm. **Ruler:** Elizabeth II **Series:** National Heroes **Subject:** Sir Alexander Bustamante **Obv:** National arms **Obv. Legend:** JAMAICA **Rev:** Bust facing **Edge:** Plain **Shape:** 7-sided

Date	Mintage	F12	VF20	XF40	MS60	MS63
2002	—	—	—	0.40	1.00	1.50
2002	500	PF60 4.00				
2003	—	—	—	0.40	1.00	1.50
2005	—	—	—	0.40	1.00	1.50
2006	—	—	—	0.40	1.00	1.50
2008	—	—	—	0.40	1.00	1.50

KM# 189 DOLLAR
2.90 g., Nickel Plated Steel, 18.5 mm. **Ruler:** Elizabeth II **Rev:** Sir Alexander Bustamante

Date	Mintage	F12	VF20	XF40	MS60	MS63
2008	—	—	—	—	1.00	1.50
2009	—	—	—	—	1.00	1.50

KM# 163 5 DOLLARS
4.30 g., Nickel Plated Steel, 21.5 mm. **Ruler:** Elizabeth II **Series:** National Heroes **Subject:** Norman Manley **Obv:** National arms **Obv. Legend:** JAMAICA **Rev:** Head left **Edge:** Reeded

Date	Mintage	F12	VF20	XF40	MS60	MS63
2002	—	—	—	1.50	2.50	3.50
2002	500	PF60 5.00				
2006	—	—	—	1.50	2.50	3.50

KM# 181 10 DOLLARS
5.94 g., Nickel Plated Steel **Ruler:** Elizabeth II **Series:** National Heroes **Subject:** George William Gordon **Obv:** National arms **Obv. Legend:** JAMAICA / TEN DOLLARS - (date) **Rev:** Bust facing **Edge:** Plain **Shape:** Scalloped **Note:** Diameter varies: 24-24.6.

Date	Mintage	F12	VF20	XF40	MS60	MS63
2002	—	—	—	1.50	3.00	4.00

Date	Mintage	F12	VF20	XF40	MS60	MS63
2002	500	PF60 9.00				
2005	—	—	—	1.50	3.00	4.00

KM# 197 10 DOLLARS
28.28 g., 0.925 Silver 0.8356 oz. ASW, 38.61 mm. **Ruler:** Elizabeth II **Subject:** UNICEF, 55th Anniversary

Date	Mintage	F12	VF20	XF40	MS60	MS63
2001	—	PF65 125				

KM# 190 10 DOLLARS
6.00 g., Nickel Plated Steel, 24.5 mm. **Ruler:** Elizabeth II **Obv:** Arms **Obv. Legend:** JAMAICA / TEN DOLLARS (date) **Rev:** George William Gordon

Date	Mintage	F12	VF20	XF40	MS60	MS63
2008	—	—	—	—	6.00	7.50
2009	—	—	—	—	6.00	7.50

KM# 182 20 DOLLARS
7.80 g., Bi-Metallic, 23 mm. **Ruler:** Elizabeth II **Series:** National Heroes **Subject:** Marcus Garvey **Obv:** Value above national arms within circle **Obv. Legend:** JAMAICA **Rev:** Head 1/4 right within circle **Edge:** Segmented reeding

Date	Mintage	F12	VF20	XF40	MS60	MS63
2001	—	—	—	1.50	3.00	4.00
2002	—	—	—	1.50	3.00	4.00
2002	500	PF60 15.00				

KM# 186 25 DOLLARS
28.28 g., 0.925 Silver 0.8356 oz. ASW, 38.6 mm. **Ruler:** Elizabeth II **Subject:** UNICEF **Obv:** Arms with supporters **Rev:** Two boys above "Pals **Edge:** Reeded

Date	Mintage	F12	VF20	XF40	MS60	MS63
2001	—	PF63 65.00	PF65 75.00			

KM# 185 25 DOLLARS
28.28 g., 0.925 Silver 0.8356 oz. ASW, 38.6 mm. **Ruler:** Elizabeth II **Subject:** IAAF World Junior Championships **Obv:** Arms with supporters and value **Rev:** Female runner **Edge:** Reeded

Date	Mintage	F12	VF20	XF40	MS60	MS63
2002	5,500	PF63 60.00	PF65 70.00			

KM# 198 25 DOLLARS
28.28 g., 0.925 Silver 0.8356 oz. ASW, 38.61 mm. **Subject:** Diamond Jubilee of Queen Elizabeth II - St. Edward's Crown

Date	Mintage	F12	VF20	XF40	MS60	MS63
2011	Est. 10000	PF63 65.00	PF65 75.00			

KM# 199 25 DOLLARS
28.28 g., 0.925 Silver 0.8356 oz. ASW, 38.61 mm. **Ruler:** Elizabeth II **Obv:** National arms **Rev:** Crown and trumpets

Date	Mintage	F12	VF20	XF40	MS60	MS63
2011	—	PF65 100				

KM# 184 50 DOLLARS
28.45 g., 0.925 Silver 0.8406 oz. ASW, 38.6 mm. **Ruler:** Elizabeth II **Subject:** Millennium **Obv:** Arms with supporters **Rev:** Family within radiant sun **Edge:** Reeded

Date	Mintage	F12	VF20	XF40	MS60	MS63
ND-2002	5,000	PF63 65.00	PF65 75.00			

PROOF SETS

KM#	Date	Mintage	Identification	Issue Price	Mkt Val
PS33	2002 (8)	500	KM#64, 146.2, 163, 164, 167, 181, 182, 185	99.00	110

JAPAN

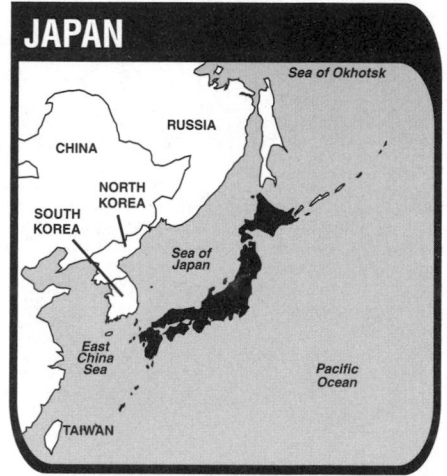

Japan, a constitutional monarchy situated off the east coast of Asia, has an area of 145,809 sq. mi. (377,835 sq. km.) and a population of 123.2 million. Capital: Tokyo. Japan, one of the major industrial nations of the world, exports machinery, motor vehicles, electronics and chemicals.

Japanese coinage of concern to this catalog includes those issued for the Ryukyu Islands (also called Liuchu), a chain of islands extending southwest from Japan toward Taiwan (Formosa), before the Japanese government converted the islands into a prefecture under the name Okinawa. Many of the provinces of Japan issued their own definitive coinage under the Shogunate.

RULERS

Emperors

Akihito (Heisei), 1989-

Years 1 -

NOTE: The personal name of the emperor is followed by the name that he chose for his regnal era.

MONETARY UNITS

Yen

円 or 圓 or 圓

EMPIRE
REFORM COINAGE

Y# 95.2 YEN
1.00 g., Aluminum, 20 mm. **Ruler:** Akihito **Obv:** Sprouting branch divides authority and value **Rev:** Value within circles above date **Edge:** Plain

Date	Mintage	F12	VF20	XF40	MS60	MS63
Yr.13(2001)	7,786,000	—	—	0.70	1.25	1.50
Yr.13(2001)	238,000	PF60 3.00				
Yr.14(2002)	9,428,000	—	—	0.70	1.25	1.50
Yr.14(2002)	239,000	PF60 5.00				
Yr.15(2003)	117,131,000	—	—	—	—	0.50
Yr.15(2003)	275,000	PF60 3.00				
Yr.16(2004)	52,620,000	—	—	—	—	0.50
Yr.16(2004)	283,000	PF60 3.00				
Yr.17(2005)	29,771,000	—	—	—	—	0.50

Date	Mintage	F12	VF20	XF40	MS60	MS63
Yr.17(2005)	258,000	PF60 3.00				
Yr.18(2006)	129,347,000			—	—	0.25
Yr.18(2006)	247,000	PF60 3.00				
Yr.19(2007)	223,702,200			—	—	0.25
Yr.19(2007)	201,800	PF60 4.00				
Yr.20(2008)	134,642,800			—	—	0.25
Yr.20(2008)	168,200	PF60 4.00				
Yr.21(2009)	47,871,000			—	—	0.25
Yr.21(2009)	132,000	PF60 4.00				
Yr.22(2010)	7,775,000			—	0.40	0.50
Yr.22(2010)	130,000	PF60 5.00				
Yr.23(2011)	348,000			—	3.50	5.00
Yr.23(2011)	108,000	PF60 10.00				
Yr.24(2012)	556,000			—	3.50	5.00
Yr.24(2012)	103,000	PF60 9.00				
Yr.25(2013)	554,000			—	3.50	5.00
Yr.25(2013)	—	PF60 5.00				

Y# 96.2 5 YEN
3.75 g., Brass, 22 mm. **Ruler:** Akihito **Obv:** Hole in center flanked by a seed leaf with authority on top and date below **Rev:** Gear design around center hole with bending rice stalk above value in horizontal lines below

Date	Mintage	F12	VF20	XF40	MS60	MS63
Yr.13(2001)	77,787,000			—	0.20	0.35
Yr.13(2001)	238,000	PF60 3.50				
Yr.14(2002)	143,423,000			—	0.20	0.35
Yr.14(2002)	239,000	PF60 3.50				
Yr.15(2003)	102,031,000			—	0.20	0.35
Yr.15(2003)		PF60 3.50				
Yr.16(2004)	70,620,000			—	0.20	0.35
Yr.16(2004)	283,000	PF60 3.50				
Yr.17(2005)	15,771,000			0.50	0.75	1.00
Yr.17(2005)	258,000	PF60 6.00				
Yr.18(2006)	9,347,000			0.75	1.25	1.50
Yr.18(2006)	247,000	PF60 8.00				
Yr.19(2007)	9,702,200			0.75	1.25	1.50
Yr.19(2007)	201,800	PF60 8.00				
Yr.20(2008)	9,642,800			0.75	1.25	1.50
Yr.20(2008)	168,200	PF60 8.00				
Yr.21(2009)	3,871,000			0.50	1.25	1.50
Yr.21(2009)	132,000	PF80 8.00				
Yr.22(2010)	380,000			3.00	4.00	6.00
Yr.22(2010)	130,000	PF60 12.00				
Yr.23(2011)	348,000			3.00	4.00	6.00
Yr.23(2011)	108,000	PF60 12.00				
Yr.24 (2012)	556,000			2.00	3.00	4.00
Yr.24 (2012)	103,000	PF60 12.00				
Yr.25 (2013)	—			1.25	1.75	2.00
Yr.25 (2013)	—	PF60 8.00				

Y# 97.2 10 YEN
4.50 g., Bronze, 23.5 mm. **Ruler:** Akihito **Obv:** Temple divides authority and value **Rev:** Value within wreath

Date	Mintage	F12	VF20	XF40	MS60	MS63
Yr.13(2001)	541,786,000			—	0.35	0.45
Yr.13(2001)	238,000	PF60 10.00				
Yr.14(2002)	445,428,000			—	0.35	0.45
Yr.14(2002)	239,000	PF60 10.00				
Yr.15(2003)	551,131,000			—	0.35	0.45
Yr.15(2003)	275,000	PF60 10.00				
Yr.16(2004)	592,620,000			—	0.35	0.45
Yr.16(2004)	283,000	PF60 10.00				
Yr.17(2005)	503,771,000			—	0.35	0.45
Yr.17(2005)	258,000	PF60 10.00				
Yr.18(2006)	440,347,000			—	0.35	0.45
Yr.18(2006)	247,000	PF60 10.00				
Yr.19(2007)	388,702,200			—	0.35	0.45
Yr.19(2007)	201,800	PF60 10.00				
Yr.20(2008)	362,642,800			—	0.35	0.45
Yr.20(2008)	168,200	PF60 10.00				
Yr.21(2009)	337,871,000			—	0.35	0.45
Yr.21(2009)	132,000	PF60 10.00				
Yr.22(2010)	328,775,000			—	0.35	0.45
Yr.22(2010)	130,000	PF60 10.00				
Yr.23(2011)	255,828,000			—	0.35	0.45
Yr.23(2011)	108,000	PF60 10.00				
Yr.24(2012)	279,108,000			—	0.35	0.45
Yr.24(2012)	103,000	PF60 10.00				
Yr.25 (2013)	—			—	0.35	0.45
Yr.25 (2013)	—	PF60 10.00				

Y# 101.2 50 YEN
4.00 g., Copper-Nickel, 21 mm. **Ruler:** Akihito **Obv:** Center hole flanked by chrysanthemums, authority at top and value below **Rev:** Value above hole in center **Edge:** Reeded

Date	Mintage	F12	VF20	XF40	MS60	MS63
Yr.13(2001)	7,786,000			—	2.00	3.00
Yr.13(2001)	238,000	PF60 10.00				
Yr.14(2002)	11,428,000			—	2.00	3.00
Yr.14(2002)	239,000	PF60 10.00				
Yr.15(2003)	10,131,000			—	2.00	3.00
Yr.15(2003)	275,000	PF60 10.00				
Yr.16(2004)	9,620,000			—	2.00	3.00
Yr.16(2004)	283,000	PF60 10.00				
Yr.17(2005)	9,771,000			—	2.00	3.00
Yr.17(2005)	258,000	PF60 10.00				
Yr.18(2006)	10,347,000			—	2.00	3.00
Yr.18(2006)	247,000	PF60 10.00				

Date	Mintage	F12	VF20	XF40	MS60	MS63
Yr.19(2007)	9,702,200			—	2.00	3.00
Yr.19(2007)	201,800	PF60 10.00				
Yr.20(2008)	8,642,800			—	2.00	3.00
Yr.20(2008)	168,200	PF60 10.00				
Yr.21(2009)	4,871,000			—	2.50	4.00
Yr.21(2009)	132,000	PF60 10.00				
Yr.22(2010)	380,000			5.00	6.00	7.00
Yr.22(2010)	130,000	PF60 15.00				
Yr.23(2011)	348,000			5.00	6.00	7.00
Yr.23(2011)	108,000	PF60 15.00				
Yr.24(2012)	556,000			4.00	5.00	6.00
Yr.24(2012)	103,000	PF60 15.00				
Yr.25(2013)	—			—	—	4.00
Yr.25(2013)	—	PF60 15.00				

Y# 98.2 100 YEN
4.80 g., Copper-Nickel, 22.6 mm. **Ruler:** Akihito **Obv:** Cherry blossoms **Rev:** Large numeral 100, date in western numerals **Edge:** Reeded

Date	Mintage	F12	VF20	XF40	MS60	MS63
Yr.13(2001)	7,786,000			—	5.00	7.50
Yr.13(2001)	238,000	PF60 12.00				
Yr.14(2002)	10,428,000			—	4.00	5.00
Yr.14(2002)	239,000	PF60 12.00				
Yr.15(2003)	98,131,000			—	2.00	2.50
Yr.15(2003)	275,000	PF60 12.00				
Yr.16(2004)	204,620,000			—	2.00	2.50
Yr.16(2004)	283,000	PF60 15.00				
Yr.17(2005)	299,771,000			—	2.00	2.50
Yr.17(2005)	258,000	PF60 15.00				
Yr.18(2006)	216,347,000			—	1.75	2.00
Yr.18(2006)	247,000	PF60 15.00				
Yr.19(2007)	129,702,200			—	1.75	2.00
Yr.19(2007)	201,800	PF60 15.00				
Yr.20(2008)	93,642,800			—	1.75	2.00
Yr.20(2008)	168,200	PF60 18.00				
Yr.21(2009)	114,871,000			—	1.75	2.00
Yr.21(2009)	132,000	PF60 18.00				
Yr.22(2010)	67,775,000			—	1.75	2.00
Yr.22(2010)	130,000	PF60 18.00				
Yr.23(2011)	178,828,000			—	1.75	2.00
Yr.23(2011)	108,000	PF80 18.00				
Yr.24(2012)	402,108,000			—	1.75	2.00
Yr.24(2012)	103,000	PF60 18.00				
Yr.25 (2013)	—			—	1.75	2.00
Yr.25 (2013)	—	PF60 18.00				

Y# 125 500 YEN
7.00 g., Nickel-Brass, 26.5 mm. **Ruler:** Akihito **Obv:** Pawlownia flower and highlighted legends **Rev:** Value with latent zeros **Edge:** Slanted reeding

Date	Mintage	F12	VF20	XF40	MS60	MS63
Yr.13(2001)	607,813,000			—	7.00	9.00
Yr.13(2001)	238,000	PF60 22.00				
Yr.14(2002)	504,422,000			—	7.00	9.00
Yr.14(2002)	239,000	PF60 22.00				
Yr.15(2003)	438,130,000			—	7.00	9.00
Yr.15(2003)	275,000	PF60 22.00				
Yr.16(2004)	356,620,000			—	7.00	9.00
Yr.16(2004)	283,000	PF60 22.00				
Yr.17(2005)	344,772,000			—	7.00	9.00
Yr.17(2005)	258,000	PF60 22.00				
Yr.18(2006)	381,346,000			—	7.00	9.00
Yr.18(2006)	247,000	PF60 22.00				
Yr.19(2007)	409,701,200			—	7.00	9.00
Yr.19(2007)	201,800	PF60 30.00				
Yr.20(2008)	432,642,800			—	7.00	9.00
Yr.20(2008)	168,200	PF60 30.00				
Yr.21(2009)	342,871,000			—	7.00	9.00
Yr.21(2009)	132,000	PF60 30.00				
Yr.22(2010)	130,000			—	7.00	9.00
Yr.22(2010)	406,775,000	PF60 30.00				
Yr.23(2011)	301,828,000			—	7.00	9.00
Yr.23(2011)	108,000	PF60 30.00				
Yr.24(2012)	267,108,000			—	7.00	9.00
Yr.24(2012)	103,000	PF60 30.00				
Yr.25(2013)	—			—	7.00	9.00
Yr.25(2013)	—	PF60 30.00				

Y# 126 500 YEN
7.00 g., Copper-Nickel-Zinc, 26.5 mm. **Ruler:** Akihito **Subject:** World Cup Soccer - Europe & Africa **Obv:** Four players and map background **Rev:** Games logo within shooting star wreath **Edge:** Reeded

Date	Mintage	VG8	F12	VF20	XF40	MS63
Yr.14(2002)	10,000,000	—	—	—	7.50	10.00

Y# 127 500 YEN
7.00 g., Copper-Nickel-Zinc, 26.5 mm. **Ruler:** Akihito **Subject:** World Cup Soccer - Asia & Oceania **Obv:** Three players and map background **Rev:** Games logo within shooting star wreath **Edge:** Reeded

Date	Mintage	VG8	F12	VF20	XF40	MS63
Yr. 14(2002)	10,000,000	—	—	—	7.50	10.00

Y# 128 500 YEN
7.00 g., Copper-Nickel-Zinc, 26.5 mm. **Ruler:** Akihito **Subject:** World Cup Soccer - North & South America **Obv:** Four players and map background **Rev:** Games logo **Edge:** Reeded

Date	Mintage	VG8	F12	VF20	XF40	MS63
Yr. 14 (2002)	10,000,000	—	—	—	7.50	10.00

Y# 133 500 YEN
7.00 g., Copper-Nickel-Zinc, 26.5 mm. **Ruler:** Akihito **Subject:** Expo 2005 - Aichi, Japan **Obv:** Pacific map an globe **Rev:** Circular Expo logo

Date	Mintage	VG8	F12	VF20	XF40	MS63
Yr. 17(2005)	8,241,000	—	—	—	7.50	10.00

Y# 134 500 YEN
15.60 g., 0.999 Silver 0.4978 oz. ASW, 28 mm. **Ruler:** Akihito **Subject:** Chubu International Airport **Obv:** Aircraft wing in flight over airport **Rev:** Aircraft silhouettes over maps

Date	Mintage	F12	VF20	XF40	MS60	MS63
Yr. 17(2005)	50,000	PF65 85.00				

Y# 137 500 YEN
7.00 g., Copper-Nickel-Zinc, 26.5 mm. **Ruler:** Akihito **Subject:** 50th Anniversary of Japanese Antarctic Research **Obv:** Ship and two dogs **Rev:** Map of Antarctica **Edge:** Helical ridges

Date	Mintage	F12	VF20	XF40	MS60	MS63
Yr.19(2007)	6,600,000	—	—	9.00	10.00	12.00

Y# 139 500 YEN

7.00 g., Copper-Nickel-Zinc, 26.5 mm. **Ruler:** Akihito **Subject:** Centenary of Japanese immigration to Brazil/Japan-Brazil year of exchange **Obv:** Ship **Rev:** Crossed sprigs of cherry and coffee **Note:** Prev. #Y143.

Date	Mintage	F12	VF20	XF40	MS60	MS63
Yr. 20 (2008)	4,800,000	—	—	11.00	13.00	15.00

Y# 145 500 YEN

7.10 g., Bi-Metallic, 26.5 mm. **Ruler:** Akihito **Subject:** Local Autonomy - Shimane Prefecture **Obv:** Bell shaped bronze vessel, artifact from Kamoiwakura **Rev:** Cash coin

Date	Mintage	F12	VF20	XF40	MS60	MS63
Yr.20(2008)	1,940,000	—	—	8.00	15.00	17.50
Yr.20(2008)	30,000	PF63 45.00		PF65 50.00		

Y# 141 500 YEN

7.10 g., Bi-Metallic, 26.5 mm. **Ruler:** Akihito **Subject:** Local Autonomy - Hokkaido Prefecture **Obv:** Lake Toya and the former Hokkaido Government Building

Date	Mintage	F12	VF20	XF40	MS60	MS63
Yr.20(2008)	2,070,000	—	—	8.00	15.00	17.50
Yr.20(2008)	30,000	PF63 45.00		PF65 50.00		

Y# 143 500 YEN

7.10 g., Bi-Metallic, 26.5 mm. **Ruler:** Akihito **Subject:** Local Autonomy - Kyoto Prefecture **Obv:** Scene from an antique illustrated version of the Tale of Genji **Rev:** Cash coin

Date	Mintage	F12	VF20	XF40	MS60	MS63
Yr.20(2008)	2,020,000	—	—	8.00	15.00	17.50
Yr20(2008)	30,000	PF63 45.00		PF65 50.00		

Y# 157 500 YEN

7.00 g., Nickel-Brass, 26.5 mm. **Ruler:** Akihito **Subject:** 20th Anniversary of Emperor's Enthronement **Obv:** Imperial chrysthantem crest **Rev:** Chrysthantem blosums

Date	Mintage	F12	VF20	XF40	MS60	MS63
Yr.21(2009)	50,000	PF63 25.00		PF65 30.00		
Yr.21(2009)	9,950,000	—	—	8.00	10.00	12.50

Y# 147 500 YEN

7.10 g., Bi-Metallic, 26.5 mm. **Ruler:** Akihito **Subject:** Local Autonomy - Nagano Prefecture **Obv:** Zenkoji Temple and ox

Date	Mintage	F12	VF20	XF40	MS60	MS63
Yr.21(2009)	1,800,000	—	—	8.00	15.00	17.50
Yr.21(2009)	30,000	PF63 45.00		PF65 50.00		

Y# 149 500 YEN

7.10 g., Bi-Metallic, 26.5 mm. **Ruler:** Akihito **Subject:** Local Autonomy - Niigata Prefecture **Obv:** Two Japanese crested ibises and rice terrace

Date	Mintage	F12	VF20	XF40	MS60	MS63
Yr.21(2009)	1,800,000	—	—	8.00	15.00	17.50
Yr.21(2009)	30,000	PF63 45.00		PF65 50.00		

Y# 153 500 YEN

7.10 g., Bi-Metallic, 26.5 mm. **Ruler:** Akihito **Subject:** Local Autonomy - Ibaraki Prefecture **Obv:** Kairakuen Garden and plum tree **Rev:** Cast Japanese coin

Date	Mintage	F12	VF20	XF40	MS60	MS63
Yr.21(2009)	1,840,000	—	—	8.00	15.00	17.50
Yr.21(2009)	30,000	PF63 45.00		PF65 50.00		

Y# 155 500 YEN

7.10 g., Bi-Metallic, 26.5 mm. **Ruler:** Akihito **Subject:** Local Autonomy - Nara Prefecture **Obv:** Kentoshi-sen, ship of the Japanese envoy to China in Tang Dynasty **Rev:** Cast Japanese coin

Date	Mintage	F12	VF20	XF40	MS60	MS63
Yr.21(2009)	1,770,000	—	—	8.00	15.00	17.50
Yr.21(2009)	30,000	PF63 45.00		PF65 50.00		

Y# 169 500 YEN

7.10 g., Bi-Metallic, 26.5 mm. **Ruler:** Akihito **Subject:** Local Autonomy commemorative - Saga Prefecture **Obv:** OKUMA Shigenobu and Saga Nishiki fabric **Rev:** Legend for 47 prefectures coin program, and ancient coin design reading "local autonomy

Date	Mintage	F12	VF20	XF40	MS60	MS63
Yr.22 (2010)	30,000	PF63 45.00		PF65 50.00		
Yr.22 (2010)	1,880,000	—	—	8.00	15.00	17.50

Y# 163 500 YEN

7.10 g., Bi-Metallic, 26.5 mm. **Ruler:** Akihito **Subject:** Local Autonomy commemorative - Fukui Prefecture **Obv:** Fukuiraptor (foreground) and Fukuisaurus **Rev:** Legend for 47 prefectures coin program, and ancient coin design reading "local autonomy

Date	Mintage	F12	VF20	XF40	MS60	MS63
Yr.22(2010)	30,000	PF63 45.00		PF65 50.00		
Yr.22(2010)	1,800,000	—	—	8.00	15.00	17.50

Y# 165 500 YEN

7.10 g., Bi-Metallic, 26.5 mm. **Ruler:** Akihito **Subject:** Local Autonomy commemorative - Aichi Prefecture **Obv:** Prefectural capitol building and rabbit-ear iris **Rev:** Legend for 47 prefectures coin program, and ancient coin design reading "local autonomy

Date	Mintage	F12	VF20	XF40	MS60	MS63
Yr.22 (2010)	30,000	PF63 45.00		PF65 50.00		
Yr.22 (2010)	1,920,000	—	—	8.00	15.00	17.50

Y# 167 500 YEN

7.10 g., Bi-Metallic, 26.5 mm. **Ruler:** Akihito **Subject:** Local Autonomy commemorative - Aomori Prefecture **Obv:** Jomon period structure and figurines **Rev:** Legend for 47 prefectures coin program and ancient coin design reading "local autonomy

Date	Mintage	F12	VF20	XF40	MS60	MS63
Yr.22 (2010)	30,000	PF63 45.00		PF65 50.00		
Yr.22 (2010)	1,870,000	—	—	8.00	15.00	17.50

Y# 159 500 YEN

7.10 g., Bi-Metallic, 26.5 mm. **Ruler:** Akihito **Subject:** Local Autonomy commemorative - Kochi Prefecture **Obv:** SAKAMOTO Ryoma **Rev:** Legend for 47 prefectures coin program, and ancient coin design reading "local autonomy

Date	Mintage	F12	VF20	XF40	MS60	MS63
Yr.22(2010)	1,930,000	—	—	8.00	15.00	17.50
Yr.22(2010)	30,000	PF63 45.00		PF65 50.00		

Y# 161 500 YEN

7.10 g., Bi-Metallic, 26.5 mm. **Ruler:** Akihito **Subject:** Local Autonomy commemorative - Gifu Prefecture **Obv:** Shirakawa village and Chinese milk vetch **Rev:** Legend for 47 prefectures coin program, and ancient coin design reading "local autonomy

Date	Mintage	F12	VF20	XF40	MS60	MS63
Yr.22(2010)	1,830,000	—	—	8.00	15.00	17.50
Yr.22(2010)	30,000	PF63 45.00		PF65 50.00		

Y# 171 500 YEN

7.10 g., Bi-Metallic, 26.5 mm. **Ruler:** Akihito **Subject:** Local Autonomy commemorative - Toyama Prefecture **Obv:** Owara Kaze-no-bon Festival dancers **Rev:** Legend for 47 prefectures coin program and ancient coin design reading "local autonomy

Date	Mintage	F12	VF20	XF40	MS60	MS63
Yr. 23 (2011)	1,770,000	—	—	8.00	15.00	17.50
Yr. 23 (2011)	30,000	PF63 45.00		PF65 50.00		

Y# 173 500 YEN
7.10 g., Bi-Metallic, 26.5 mm. **Ruler:** Akihito **Subject:** Local Autonomy commemorative - Tottori Prefecture **Obv:** Nageiredo Hall at Mitokusan Sanbutsuji Temple **Rev:** Legend for 47 prefectures coin program and ancient coin design reading "local autonomy

Date	Mintage	F12	VF20	XF40	MS60	MS63
Yr. 23 (2011)	1,740,000	—	—	8.00	15.00	17.50
Yr. 23 (2011)	30,000	PF63 45.00	PF65 50.00			

Y# 175 500 YEN
7.10 g., Bi-Metallic, 26.5 mm. **Ruler:** Akihito **Subject:** Local Autonomy commemorative - Kumamoto Prefecture **Obv:** Kumamoto Castle **Rev:** Legend for 47 prefectures con program and ancient coin design reading "local autonomy

Date	Mintage	F12	VF20	XF40	MS60	MS63
Yr. 23 (2011)	1,840,000	—	—	8.00	15.00	17.50
Yr. 23 (2011)	30,000	PF63 45.00	PF65 50.00			

Y# 177 500 YEN
7.10 g., Bi-Metallic, 26.5 mm. **Ruler:** Akihito **Subject:** Local Autonomy - Shiga Prefecture **Obv:** Biwa catfish and Round Crucian carp

Date	Mintage	F12	VF20	XF40	MS60	MS63
Yr. 23 (2011)	1,740,000	—	—	8.00	15.00	17.50
Yr. 23 (2011)	30,000	PF63 45.00	PF65 50.00			

Y# 179 500 YEN
7.10 g., Bi-Metallic, 26.5 mm. **Ruler:** Akihito **Subject:** Local Autonomy - Iwate Prefecture **Obv:** Water Poetry Party at Môtsû-ji

Date	Mintage	F12	VF20	XF40	MS60	MS63
Yr. 23 (2011)	1,760,000	—	—	8.00	15.00	17.50
Yr. 23 (2011)	30,000	PF63 45.00	PF65 50.00			

Y# 181 500 YEN
7.10 g., Bi-Metallic, 26.5 mm. **Ruler:** Akihito **Subject:** Local Autonomy - Akita Prefecture **Obv:** Nobu Shirase (explorer) and Kanto festival

Date	Mintage	F12	VF20	XF40	MS60	MS63
Yr. 23 (2011)	1,710,000	—	—	8.00	15.00	17.50
Yr. 23 (2011)	30,000	PF63 45.00	PF65 50.00			

Y# 183 500 YEN
7.10 g., Bi-Metallic, 26.5 mm. **Ruler:** Akihito **Subject:** Local Autonomy - Okinawa Prefecture **Rev:** Naha Giant Tug-of-war and Eisa folk dance

Date	Mintage	F12	VF20	XF40	MS60	MS63
Yr.24(2012)	30,000	PF63 45.00	PF65 50.00			
Yr.24(2012)	1,780,000	—	—	8.00	15.00	17.50

Y# 187 500 YEN
7.10 g., Bi-Metallic, 26.5 mm. **Ruler:** Akihito **Subject:** Local Autonomy - Miyazaki Prefecture **Rev:** Miyazaki Prefectural Government Building

Date	Mintage	F12	VF20	XF40	MS60	MS63
Yr.24(2012)	30,000	PF63 45.00	PF65 50.00			
Yr.24(2012)	1,710,000	—	—	8.00	15.00	17.50

Y# 189 500 YEN
7.10 g., Bi-Metallic, 26.5 mm. **Ruler:** Akihito **Subject:** Local Autonomy - Tochigi Prefecture **Obv:** Sleeping cat in flora **Rev:** Ancient cash

Date	Mintage	F12	VF20	XF40	MS60	MS63
Yr. 24 (2012)	1,770,000	—	—	8.00	15.00	17.50
Yr. 24 (2012)	30,000	PF63 45.00	PF65 50.00			

Y# 191 500 YEN
7.10 g., Bi-Metallic, 26.5 mm. **Ruler:** Akihito **Subject:** Hyogo **Obv:** Two black beak storks **Rev:** Ancient cast coin

Date	Mintage	F12	VF20	XF40	MS60	MS63
Yr. 24 (2012)	1,770,000	—	—	8.00	15.00	17.50
Yr.24(2012)	30,000	PF63 45.00	PF65 50.00			

Y# 193 500 YEN
7.10 g., Bi-Metallic, 26.5 mm. **Ruler:** Akihito **Subject:** Oita **Obv:** Buddha statue **Rev:** Ancient cash coin

Date	Mintage	F12	VF20	XF40	MS60	MS63
Yr.24(2012)	176,000	—	—	8.00	15.00	17.50
Yr.24(2012)	30,000	PF63 45.00	PF65 50.00			

Y# 185 500 YEN
7.10 g., Bi-Metallic, 26.5 mm. **Ruler:** Akihito **Subject:** Local Autonomy - Kanagawa Prefecture **Rev:** Great Buddah of Kamakura

Date	Mintage	F12	VF20	XF40	MS60	MS63
Yr.24(2012)	Est. 30000	PF63 45.00	PF65 50.00			
Yr.24(2012)		—	8.00	15.00	17.50	

Y# 196 500 YEN
Bi-Metallic, 26.5 mm. **Ruler:** Akihito **Subject:** Miyagi Prefecture **Obv:** Tassles in the wind **Rev:** Historical coin design

Date	Mintage	F12	VF20	XF40	MS60	MS63
yr.25 (2013)	30,000	PF63 45.00	PF65 50.00			
yr.25 (2013)	1,670,000	—	—	8.00	15.00	17.50

Y# 198 500 YEN
7.
7.1 g., Bi-Metallic, 26.5 mm. **Ruler:** Akihito **Subject:** Hiroshima Prefecture

Date	Mintage	F12	VF20	XF40	MS60	MS63
yr.25 (2013)	30,000	PF63 45.00	PF65 50.00			
yr.25 (2013)	1,670,000	—	—	8.00	15.00	17.50

Y# 202 500 YEN
7.10 g., Bi-Metallic, 26.5 mm. **Ruler:** Akihito **Subject:** Yamanashl Prefecture

Date	Mintage	F12	VF20	XF40	MS60	MS63
yr. 25 (2013)	30,000	PF63 45.00	PF65 50.00			
yr. 25 (2013)	1,640,000	—	—	8.00	15.00	17.50

Y# 200 500 YEN
7.10 g., Bi-Metallic, 26.5 mm. **Ruler:** Akihito **Subject:** Gunma Prefecture

Date	Mintage	F12	VF20	XF40	MS60	MS63
yr. 25 (2013)	1,690,000	—	—	8.00	15.00	17.50
yr. 25 (2013)	30,000	PF63 45.00	PF65 50.00			

Y# 204 500 YEN
7.10 g., Bi-Metallic, 26.5 mm. **Ruler:** Akihito **Subject:** Shizuoka Prefecture

Date	Mintage	F12	VF20	XF40	MS60	MS63
yr. 25 (2013)	1,670,000	—	—	8.00	15.00	17.50
yr. 25 (2013)	30,000	PF63 45.00	PF65 50.00			

Y# 206 500 YEN
7.10 g., Bi-Metallic, 26.5 mm. **Ruler:** Akihito **Subject:** Okayama Prefecture

Date	Mintage	F12	VF20	XF40	MS60	MS63
yr. 25 (2013)	1,630,000	—	—	8.00	15.00	17.50
yr. 25 (2013)	30,000	PF63 45.00	PF65 50.00			

Y# 208 500 YEN
7.10 g., Bi-Metallic, 26.5 mm. **Ruler:** Akihito **Subject:** Kagoshima Prefecture

Date	Mintage	F12	VF20	XF40	MS60	MS63
yr. 25 (2013)	1,630,000	—	—	8.00	15.00	17.50
yr. 25 (2013)	30,000	PF63 45.00	PF65 50.00			

Y# 129 1000 YEN
31.10 g., 0.999 Silver 0.9925 oz. ASW, 40 mm. **Ruler:** Akihito **Subject:** World Cup Soccer **Obv:** Trophy within flower sprigs **Rev:** Games logo flanked by players **Edge:** Reeded

Date	Mintage	F12	VF20	XF40	MS60	MS63
Yr. 14 (2002)	100,000	PF65 200				

Y# 131 1000 YEN
31.10 g., 0.999 Silver 0.9925 oz. ASW, 40 mm. **Ruler:** Akihito **Subject:** 5th Winter Asian Games, Aomori **Obv:** Skier and skater **Rev:** Three red apples and multicolor games logo

Date	Mintage	VG8	F12	VF20	XF40	MS63
Yr.15 (2003)	50,000	PF65 625				

Y# 132 1000 YEN

31.10 g., 0.999 Silver 0.9925 oz. ASW, 40 mm. **Ruler:** Akihito
Subject: 50th Anniversary of the reversion of the Amami Islands
Obv: Lily and bird in multicolor enamel **Rev:** Map of the Amami-shoto

Date	Mintage	F12	VF20	XF40	MS60	MS63
Yr. 15 (2003)	50,000	PF65 220				

Y# 135 1000 YEN

31.10 g., 0.999 Silver 0.9925 oz. ASW, 40 mm. **Ruler:** Akihito
Subject: Expo 2005 **Obv:** Blue and white enamel Pacific map in wreath **Rev:** Expo logo

Date	Mintage	F12	VF20	XF40	MS60	MS63
Yr. 16 (2004)	70,000	PF65 165				

Y# 138 1000 YEN

31.10 g., 1.000 Silver 0.9935 oz. ASW, 40 mm. **Ruler:** Akihito
Subject: 50th Anniversary of Japan's Entry into the United Nations **Obv:** Globe and plum blossom wreath (enameled blue, pink and green) **Rev:** UN emblem

Date	Mintage	F12	VF20	XF40	MS60	MS63
Yr.18(2006)	70,000	PF65 165				

Y# 140 1000 YEN

31.10 g., 0.999 Silver 0.9925 oz. ASW, 40 mm. **Ruler:** Akihito
Obv: Dual multicolor rainbows **Obv. Inscription:** SKILLS / 2007 **Rev:** Mount Fuji **Rev. Legend:** International Skills Festival for All, Japan **Edge:** Helical ridges **Note:** Prev. #Y142.

Date	Mintage	F12	VF20	XF40	MS60	MS63
Yr.19(2007)	80,000	PF65 75.00				

Y# 142 1000 YEN

31.10 g., 0.999 Silver 0.9925 oz. ASW, 40 mm. **Ruler:** Akihito
Subject: Local Autonomy - Hokkaido Prefecture **Obv:** Lake Toya and two multicolor red-crowned cranes in flight **Rev:** Snowflakes, cherry blossoms and crescent

Date	Mintage	F12	VF20	XF40	MS60	MS63
Yr.20(2008)	100,000	PF65 135				

Y# 144 1000 YEN

31.10 g., 0.999 Silver 0.9925 oz. ASW, 40 mm. **Ruler:** Akihito
Subject: Local Autonomy - Kyoto Prefecture **Obv:** Multicolor scene from an antique illustrated version of the Tale of Genji **Rev:** Snowflakes, cherry blossoms and crescent **Edge:** Reeded

Date	Mintage	F12	VF20	XF40	MS60	MS63
Yr.20(2008)	100,000	PF65 120				

Y# 146 1000 YEN

31.10 g., 0.999 Silver 0.9925 oz. ASW, 40 mm. **Ruler:** Akihito
Subject: Local Autonomy - Shimane Prefecture **Obv:** Multicolor peony flowers and Otoriosame chogin coin **Rev:** Snowflakes, cherry blossoms and crescent **Edge:** Reeded

Date	Mintage	F12	VF20	XF40	MS60	MS63
Yr.20(2008)	100,000	PF65 115				

Y# 154 1000 YEN

31.10 g., 0.999 Silver 0.9925 oz. ASW **Ruler:** Akihito **Subject:** Local Autonomy - Ibaraki Prefecture **Obv:** Multicolor H-II launch vehicle and Mt. Tsukuba **Rev:** Snowflakes, cherry blossoms and crescent **Edge:** Reeded

Date	Mintage	F12	VF20	XF40	MS60	MS63
Yr.21(2008)	100,000	PF65 100				

Y# 156 1000 YEN

31.10 g., 0.999 Silver 0.9925 oz. ASW **Ruler:** Akihito **Subject:** Local Autonomy - Nara Prefecture **Obv:** Daigokuden Audience Hall in multicolor, cherry blossoms and Kemari (ancient ball players) **Rev:** Snowflakes, cherry blossoms and crescent **Edge:** Reeded

Date	Mintage	F12	VF20	XF40	MS60	MS63
Yr.21(2008)	100,000	PF65 115				

Y# 148 1000 YEN

31.10 g., 0.999 Silver 0.9925 oz. ASW, 40 mm. **Ruler:** Akihito
Subject: Local Autonomy - Nagano Prefecture **Obv:** Multicolor Japan Alps and Kamikochi **Rev:** Snowflakes, cherry blossoms and crescent **Edge:** Reeded

Date	Mintage	F12	VF20	XF40	MS60	MS63
Yr.21(2009)	100,000	PF65 115				

Y# 150 1000 YEN

31.10 g., 0.999 Silver 0.9925 oz. ASW, 40 mm. **Ruler:** Akihito
Subject: Local Autonomy - Niigata Prefecture **Obv:** Two Japanese crested ibis and Sado Island **Rev:** Snowflakes, cherry blossoms and crescent **Edge:** Reeded

Date	Mintage	F12	VF20	XF40	MS60	MS63
Yr.21(2009)	100,000	PF65 100				

Y# 160 1000 YEN

31.10 g., 0.999 Silver 0.9925 oz. ASW, 40 mm. **Ruler:** Akihito
Subject: Local Autonomy commemorative - Kochi Prefecture **Obv:** SAKAMOTO Ryoma and Katsurahama Beach **Rev:** Snowflakes, cherry blossoms and crescent **Rev. Legend:** Local Autonomy 60 Years **Edge:** Reeded

Date	Mintage	F12	VF20	XF40	MS60	MS63
Yr.22(2010)	100,000	PF65 130				
Proof; colorized						

Y# 162 1000 YEN

31.10 g., 0.999 Silver 0.9925 oz. ASW, 40 mm. **Ruler:** Akihito
Subject: Local Autonomy commemorative - Gifu Prefecture **Obv:** Cormorant fishing on the Nagara River **Rev:** Snowflakes, cherry blossoms, and crescent moon with legend **Rev. Legend:** Local Autonomy 60 Years **Edge:** Reeded

Date	Mintage	F12	VF20	XF40	MS60	MS63
Yr.22(2010) Proof; colorized	100,000	PF65 130				

Y# 164 1000 YEN

31.10 g., 0.999 Silver 0.9925 oz. ASW, 40 mm. **Ruler:** Akihito
Subject: Local Autonomy commemorative - Fukui Prefecture **Obv:** Fukuiraptor and Tojinbo Cliffs **Rev:** Snowflakes, cherry blossoms, and crescent moon with legend **Rev. Legend:** Local Autonomy 60 Years **Edge:** Reeded

Date	Mintage	F12	VF20	XF40	MS60	MS63
Yr.22(2010) Proof; colorized	100,000	PF65 130				

Y# 166 1000 YEN
31.10 g., 1.000 Silver 0.9935 oz. ASW, 40 mm. **Ruler:** Akihito **Subject:** Local Autonomy commemorative - Aichi Prefecture **Obv:** Golden dolphin, rabbit-ear iris and the Atsumi Peninsula **Rev:** Snowflakes, cherry blossoms and crescent moon with legend reading "local autonomy 60 years **Edge:** Reeded

Date	Mintage	F12	VF20	XF40	MS60	MS63
Yr.22 (2010)	100,000	PF65 130				

Y# 168 1000 YEN
31.10 g., 1.000 Silver 0.9935 oz. ASW, 40 mm. **Ruler:** Akihito **Subject:** Local Autonomy commemorative - Aomori Prefecture **Obv:** Traditional parade floats and apples **Rev:** Snowflakes, cherry blossoms and crescent moon with legend reading "local autonomy 60 years **Edge:** Reeded

Date	Mintage	F12	VF20	XF40	MS60	MS63
Yr.22 (2010)	100,000	PF65 130				

Y# 170 1000 YEN
31.10 g., 1.000 Silver 0.9935 oz. ASW, 40 mm. **Ruler:** Akihito **Subject:** Local Autonomy commemorative - Saga Prefecture **Obv:** OKUMA Shigenobu and Imari - Arita ware **Rev:** Snowflakes, cherry blossoms and crescent moon with legend reading "local autonomy 60 years **Edge:** Reeded

Date	Mintage	F12	VF20	XF40	MS60	MS63
Yr.22 (2010)	100,000	PF65 130				

Y# 172 1000 YEN
31.11 g., 1.000 Silver 0.9936 oz. ASW, 40 mm. **Ruler:** Akihito **Subject:** Local Autonomy commemorative - Toyama Prefecture **Obv:** Tateyama mountain range rising from the sea **Rev:** Snowflakes, cherry blossoms and crescent moon with legend reading "local autonomy 60 years **Edge:** Reeded

Date	Mintage	F12	VF20	XF40	MS60	MS63
Yr. 23 (2011)	100,000	PF65 130				

Y# 174 1000 YEN
31.10 g., 1.000 Silver 0.9935 oz. ASW, 40 mm. **Ruler:** Akihito **Subject:** Local Autonomy commemorative - Tottori Prefecture **Obv:** Tottori Sand Dunes and San'in Kaigan Coast **Rev:** Snowflakes, cherry blossoms and crescent moon with legend reading "local autonomy 60 years **Edge:** Reeded

Date	Mintage	F12	VF20	XF40	MS60	MS63
Yr. 23 (2011)	100,000	PF65 130				

Y# 176 1000 YEN
31.10 g., 1.000 Silver 0.9935 oz. ASW, 40 mm. **Ruler:** Akihito **Subject:** Local Autonomy commemorative - Kumamoto Prefecture **Obv:** Mount Aso **Rev:** Snowflakes, cherry blossoms and crescent moon with legend reading "local autonomy 60 years **Edge:** Reeded

Date	Mintage	F12	VF20	XF40	MS60	MS63
Yr. 23 (2011)	100,000	PF65 130				

Y# 178 1000 YEN
31.11 g., 0.999 Silver 0.9926 oz. ASW, 40 mm. **Ruler:** Akihito **Subject:** Local Autonomy - Shiga Prefecture **Obv:** Lake Biwa, family of little grebe birds and Ukimido temple **Edge:** Reeded

Date	Mintage	F12	VF20	XF40	MS60	MS63
Yr. 23 (2011)	100,000	PF65 115				

Y# 180 1000 YEN
31.11 g., 0.999 Silver 0.9926 oz. ASW, 40 mm. **Ruler:** Akihito **Subject:** Local Autonomy - Iwate Prefecture **Obv:** Konjikodo, the golden hall of Chuson-ji Temple, lotus and Pure Land Garden of Motsu-ji temple **Edge:** Reeded

Date	Mintage	F12	VF20	XF40	MS60	MS63
Yr. 23 (2011)	100,000	PF65 110				

Y# 182 1000 YEN
31.11 g., 0.999 Silver 0.9926 oz. ASW, 40 mm. **Ruler:** Akihito **Subject:** Local Autonomy - Akita Prefecture **Obv:** Nobu Shirase, Antartic explorer, Namahage folk ritual **Edge:** Reeded

Date	Mintage	F12	VF20	XF40	MS60	MS63
Yr. 23 (2011)	100,000	PF65 110				

Y# 184 1000 YEN
31.10 g., 0.999 Silver 0.9925 oz. ASW, 40 mm. **Ruler:** Akihito **Subject:** Local Autonomy - Okinawa Prefecture **Obv:** State Hall in Suri and Kumidori dancer **Edge:** Reeded

Date	Mintage	F12	VF20	XF40	MS60	MS63
Yr.24(2012)	100,000	PF65 100				

Y# 186 1000 YEN
31.10 g., 0.999 Silver 0.9925 oz. ASW, 40 mm. **Ruler:** Akihito **Subject:** Local Autonomy - Kanagawa Prefecture **Obv:** Tsurugaoka Hachimangu Shrine and horseback archery - Yabusame **Edge:** Reeded

Date	Mintage	F12	VF20	XF40	MS60	MS63
Yr.24(2012)	100,000	PF65 100				

Y# 188 1000 YEN
31.10 g., 0.999 Silver 0.9925 oz. ASW, 40 mm. **Ruler:** Akihito **Subject:** Local Autonomy - Miyazaki Prefecture **Obv:** Miyazaki Prefectural Government Building and Takachiho Yokagura dancer **Edge:** Reeded

Date	Mintage	F12	VF20	XF40	MS60	MS63
Yr.24(2012)	100,000	PF65 100				

Y# 190 1000 YEN
31.13 g., 0.999 Silver 0.9934 oz. ASW, 40 mm. **Ruler:** Akihito **Subject:** Tochigi **Obv:** Tokugawa Ieyasu Mausoleum in Nikko in color **Rev:** Crescent moon, flora and snowflake

Date	Mintage	F12	VF20	XF40	MS60	MS63
Yr.24 (2012)	100,000	PF65 95.00				

Y# 192 1000 YEN
31.13 g., 0.999 Silver 0.9934 oz. ASW, 40 mm. **Ruler:** Akihito **Subject:** Hyogo **Obv:** Black beaked stork in flight over Himeji temple **Rev:** Crescent moon, flora and snowflake

Date	Mintage	F12	VF20	XF40	MS60	MS63
Yr. 24 (2012)	100,000	PF65 95.00				

Y# 194 1000 YEN

31.13 g., 0.999 Silver 0.9934 oz. ASW, 40 mm. **Ruler:** Akihito **Subject:** Oita **Obv:** Sumo wreestler Akiyoski Sadaji, and Usa shrine **Rev:** Crescent moon, flora and snowflake

Date	Mintage	F12	VF20	XF40	MS60	MS63
Yr.24 (2012)	100,000	PF65 95.00				

Y# 195 1000 YEN

31.13 g., 0.999 Silver 0.9934 oz. ASW, 40 mm. **Ruler:** Akihito **Subject:** International Monatary Fund Meeting, Toyko **Obv:** Mt. Fuji and traditional pesants in color **Rev:** Pan-Pacific map

Date	Mintage	F12	VF20	XF40	MS60	MS63
Yr.24 (2012)	50,000	PF65 95.00				

Y# 197 1000 YEN

31.10 g., Silver, 40 mm. **Ruler:** Akihito **Subject:** Miyagi Prefecture

Date	Mintage	F12	VF20	XF40	MS60	MS63
yr.25 (2013)	100,000	PF65 100				

Y# 199 1000 YEN

31.10 g., Silver, 40 mm. **Ruler:** Akihito **Subject:** Hiroshima Prefecture

Date	Mintage	F12	VF20	XF40	MS60	MS63
yr. 25 (2013)	100,000	PF65 100				

Y# 201 1000 YEN

31.10 g., Silver, 40 mm. **Ruler:** Akihito **Subject:** Gunma Prefecture

Date	Mintage	F12	VF20	XF40	MS60	MS63
yr. 25 (2013)	100,000	PF65 100				

Y# 203 1000 YEN

31.10 g., Silver, 40 mm. **Ruler:** Akihito **Subject:** Yamanashi Prefecture

Date	Mintage	F12	VF20	XF40	MS60	MS63
yr. 25 (2013)	100,000	PF65 100				

Y# 205 1000 YEN

31.10 g., Silver, 40 mm. **Ruler:** Akihito **Subject:** Shizuoka Prefecture

Date	Mintage	F12	VF20	XF40	MS60	MS63
yr. 25 (2013)	100,000	PF65 100				

Y# 207 1000 YEN

31.10 g., Silver, 40 mm. **Ruler:** Akihito **Subject:** Okayama Prefecture

Date	Mintage	F12	VF20	XF40	MS60	MS63
yr. 25 (2013)	100,000	PF65 100				

Y# 209 1000 YEN

31.10 g., Silver, 40 mm. **Ruler:** Akihito **Subject:** Kagoshima Prefecture

Date	Mintage	F12	VF20	XF40	MS60	MS63
yr. 25 (2013)	—	PF65 100				

Y# 130 10000 YEN

15.60 g., 0.999 Gold 0.4978 oz. AGW, 26 mm. **Ruler:** Akihito **Subject:** World Cup Soccer **Obv:** Two soccer players **Rev:** Games logo **Edge:** Reeded

Date	Mintage	F12	VF20	XF40	MS60	MS63
Yr.14(2002)	100,000	PF65 950				

Y# 136 10000 YEN

15.60 g., 0.999 Gold 0.4978 oz. AGW, 26 mm. **Ruler:** Akihito **Subject:** Expo 2005 **Obv:** Two owls on globe **Rev:** Expo logo

Date	Mintage	F12	VF20	XF40	MS60	MS63
Yr. 16(2004)	70,000	PF65 950				

Y# 158 10000 YEN

20.00 g., 0.999 Gold 0.6382 oz. AGW, 28 mm. **Ruler:** Akihito **Subject:** 20th Anniversary of Emperor's enthronment **Obv:** Imperial christaniumn crest **Rev:** Phoenix, an auspicious cloud, Niju-bashi bridge

Date	Mintage	F12	VF20	XF40	MS60	MS63
Yr.21(2009)	100,000	PF65 1,050				

MINT SETS

KM#	Date	Mintage	Identification	Issue Price	Mkt Val
MS125	2001 (6)	8,000	Y#95.2-98.2, 101.2, 125	16.00	30.00
MS126	2001 (6)	85,000	Y#95.2-98.2, 101.2, 125	17.00	30.00
MS127	2001 (6)	10,000	Y#95.2-98.2, 101.2, 125	17.00	33.00
MS128	2001 (6)	10,000	Y#95.2-98.2, 101.2, 125	17.00	30.00
MS129	2001 (6)	5,000	Y#95.2-98.2, 101.2, 125	17.00	30.00
MS130	2001 (6)	8,000	Y#95.2-98.2, 101.2, 125	17.00	30.00
MS131	2001 (6)	5,000	Y#95.2-98.2, 101.2, 125	17.00	33.00
MS132	2001 (6)	5,000	Y#95.2-98.2, 101.2, 125	17.00	40.00
MS133	2001 (6)	193,600	Y#95.2-98.2, 101.2, 125	17.00	27.00
MS134	2001 (6)	190,300	Y#95.2-98.2, 101.2, 125	17.00	27.00
MS135	2001 (6)	8,300	Y#95.2-98.2, 101.2, 125	18.00	33.00
MS136	2001 (1)	4,000	Y#125	8.00	10.00
MS137	2001 (6)	224,000	Y#95.2-98.2, 101.2, 125	15.00	27.00
MS138	2001 (6)	7,300	Y#95.2-98.2, 101.2, 125	17.00	30.00
MS139	2001 (2)	5,000	Y#96.2, 125	8.50	13.00
MS140	2001 (6)	128,700	Y#95.2-98.2, 101.2, 125	17.00	27.00
MS141	2002 (1)	3,000	Y#125	7.50	10.00
MSA141	2002 (3)	50,000	Y#126-128	26.00	35.00
MS142	2002 (6)	7,000	Y#95.2-98.2, 102.2, 125	18.00	27.00
MS143	2002 (2)	4,000	Y#96.2, 125.	8.50	13.00
MS144	2002 (6)	6,000	Y#95.2-98.2, 101.2, 125	17.00	23.00
MS145	2002 (6)	4,000	Y#95.2-98.2, 101.2, 125	16.00	33.00
MS146	2002 (6)	80,000	Y#95.2-98.2, 101.2, 125	16.00	20.00
MS147	2002 (6)	10,000	Y#95.2-98.2, 101.2, 125	16.00	23.00
MS148	2002 (6)	10,000	Y#95.2-98.2, 101.2, 125	16.00	20.00
MS149	2002 (6)	6,000	Y#95.2-98.2, 101.2, 125	16.00	23.00
MS150	2002 (6)	194,000	Y#95.2-98.2, 101.2, 125	19.00	20.00
MS151	2002 (6)	6,000	Y#95.2-98.2, 101.2, 125	16.00	23.00
MS152	2002 (6)	3,000	Y#395.2-98.2, 101.2, 125	16.00	120
MS153	2002 (6)	2,000	Y#395.2-98.2, 101.2, 125	25.00	40.00
MS154	2002 (6)	214,800	Y#395.2-98.2, 101.2, 125	15.00	20.00
MS155	2003 (6)	8,000	Y#95.2-98.2, 101.2, 125	17.00	20.00
MS156	2003 (6)	7,000	Y#95.2-98.2, 101.2, 125	18.00	20.00
MS157	2003 (6)	3,000	Y#95.2-98.2, 101.2, 125	25.00	27.00
MS158	2003 (6)	6,000	Y#95.2-98.2, 101.2, 125	16.00	30.00
MS159	2003 (6)	80,000	Y#95.2-98.2, 101.2, 125	16.00	20.00
MS160	2003 (6)	10,000	Y#95.2-98.2, 101.2, 125	16.00	20.00
MS161	2003 (6)	10,000	Y#95.2-98.2, 101.2, 125	16.00	20.00
MS162	2003 (6)	6,000	Y#95.2-98.2, 101.2, 125	16.00	20.00
MS163	2003 (6)	235,000	Y#95.2-98.2, 101.2, 125	16.00	20.00
MS164	2003 (6)	130,000	Y#95.2-98.2, 101.2, 125	19.00	17.00
MS165	2003 (6)	5,000	Y#95.2-98.2, 101.2, 125	17.00	30.00
MS166	2003 (6)	5,000	Y#95.2-98.2, 101.2, 125	17.00	27.00
MS167	2003 (6)	5,000	Y#95.2-98.2, 101.2, 125	17.00	23.00
MS168	2003 (6)	205,000	Y#95.2-98.2, 101.2, 125	17.00	16.00
MS169	2003 (6)	100,000	Y#95.2-98.2, 101.2, 125	22.00	27.00
MS170	2003 (6)	100,000	Y#95.2-98.2, 101.2, 126	22.00	16.00
MS171	2003 (6)	5,000	Y#95.2-98.2, 101.2, 126	22.00	200
MS172	2004 (6)	8,000	Y#95.2-98.2, 101.2, 125	19.00	20.00
MS173	2004 (6)	5,000	Y#95.2-98.2, 101.2, 125	20.00	22.00
MS174	2004 (6)	5,000	Y#95.2-98.2, 101.2, 125	28.50	27.00
MS175	2004 (6)	4,000	Y#95.2-98.2, 101.2, 125	18.00	53.00
MS176	2004 (6)	70,000	Y#95.2-98.2, 101.2, 125	18.00	20.00
MS177	2004 (6)	10,000	Y#95.2-98.2, 101.2, 125	18.00	20.00
MS178	2004 (6)	10,000	Y#95.2-98.2, 101.2, 125	18.00	20.00
MS179	2004 (6)	6,000	Y#95.2-98.2, 101.2, 125	18.00	20.00
MS180	2004 (6)	100,000	Y#95.2-98.2, 101.2, 125	19.00	20.00
MS181	2004 (6)	122,500	Y#95.2-98.2, 101.2, 125	20.00	20.00
MS182	2004 (6)	5,000	Y#95.2-98.2, 101.2, 125	18.00	23.00
MS183	2004 (6)	189,000	Y#95.2-98.2, 101.2, 125	16.00	17.00
MS184	2004 (6)	5,000	Y#95.2-98.2, 101.2, 125	17.00	23.00
MS185	2004 (6)	226,000	Y#95.2-98.2, 101.2, 125	22.00	23.00
MS186	2004 (6)	5,000	Y#95.2-98.2, 101.2, 125	17.00	33.00
MS187	2004 (6)	44,000	Y#95.2-98.2, 101.2, 125	21.00	17.00
MS188	2004 (6)	38,500	Y#95.2-98.2, 101.2, 125	21.00	17.00
MS189	2005 (6)	200,000	Y#95.2-98.2, 101.2, 133	22.00	23.00
MSA189	2005 (6)	1,000	Y#95.2-98.2, 101.2, 125	—	—
MS190	2005 (6)	8,000	Y#95.2-98.2, 101.2, 125	17.00	16.00
MS191	2005 (6)	5,000	Y#95.2-98.2, 101.2, 125	19.00	20.00
MS192	2005 (6)	2,000	Y#95.2-98.2, 101.2, 125	27.50	27.00
MS193	2005 (6)	5,000	Y#95.2-98.2, 101.2, 125	17.00	33.00
MS194	2005 (6)	60,000	Y#95.2-98.2, 101.2, 125	17.00	23.00
MS195	2005 (6)	10,000	Y#95.2-98.2, 101.2, 125	17.00	20.00
MS196	2005 (6)	10,000	Y#95.2-98.2, 101.2, 125	17.00	20.00
MS197	2005 (6)	5,000	Y#95.2-98.2, 101.2, 125	17.00	23.00
MS198	2005 (6)	126,500	Y#95.2-98.2, 101.2, 125	18.00	20.00
MS199	2005 (6)	104,500	Y#95.2-98.2, 101.2, 125	19.00	20.00
MS200	2005 (6)	5,000	Y#95.2-98.2, 101.2, 125	18.00	23.00
MS201	2005 (6)	5,000	Y#95.2-98.2, 101.2, 125	17.00	23.00
MS202	2005 (6)	182,000	Y#95.2-98.2, 101.2, 125	17.00	30.00
MS203	2005 (6)	141,000	Y#95.2-98.2, 101.2, 125	16.00	18.00
MS204	2005 (6)	75,800	Y#95.2-98.2, 101.2, 125	18.00	20.00
MS205	2005 (6)	5,000	Y#95.2-98.2, 101.2, 125	17.00	40.00
MS206	2005 (6)	83,600	Y#95.2-98.2, 101.2, 125	21.00	20.00
MS207	2005 (6)	56,600	Y#95.2-98.2, 101.2, 125	21.00	20.00
MS208	2006 (6)	5,000	Y#95.2-98.2, 101.2, 125	17.00	17.50
MS209	2006 (6)	9,000	Y#95.2-98.2, 101.2, 125	18.00	18.00
MS210	2006 (6)	5,000	Y#95.2-98.2, 101.2, 125	19.00	20.00
MS211	2006 (6)	189,400	Y#95.2-98.2, 101.2, 125	16.00	17.00
MS212	2006 (6)	66,000	Y#95.2-98.2, 101.2, 125	18.00	18.00
MS213	2006 (6)	60,000	Y#95.2-98.2, 101.2, 125	17.00	17.50
MS214	2006 (6)	8,000	Y#95.2-98.2, 101.2, 125	17.00	17.50
MS215	2006 (6)	8,000	Y#95.2-98.2, 101.2, 125	17.00	18.50
MS216	2006 (6)	85,500	Y#95.2-98.2, 101.2, 125	19.00	20.00
MS217	2006 (6)	4,000	Y#95.2-98.2, 101.2, 125	17.00	18.50
MS218	2006 (6)	4,000	Y#95.2-98.2, 101.2, 125	17.00	17.50
MS219	2006 (6)	105,200	Y#95.2-98.2, 101.2, 125	22.00	22.50
MS220	2006 (6)	3,500	Y#95.2-98.2, 101.2, 125	17.00	17.50
MS221	2006 (6)	4,000	Y#95.2-98.2, 101.2, 125	17.00	50.00
MS222	2006 (6)	49,600	Y#95.2-98.2, 101.2, 125	21.00	27.00
MS223	2006 (6)	56,600	Y#95.2-98.2, 101.2, 125	21.00	27.00
MS224	2007 (6)	180,000	Y#95.2-98.2, 101.2, 137	23.00	30.00
MS225	2007 (6)	4,000	Y#95.2-98.2, 101.2, 125	17.00	18.00
MS226	2007 (6)	8,000	Y#95.2-98.2, 101.2, 125	18.00	20.00
MS227	2007 (6)	5,700	Y#95.2-98.2, 101.2, 125	19.00	20.00
MS228	2007 (6)	150,000	Y#95.2-98.2, 101.2, 125	16.00	18.00
MS229	2007 (6)	82,200	Y#95.2-98.2, 101.2, 125	22.00	25.00
MS230	2007 (6)	7,000	Y#95.2-98.2, 101.2, 125	18.00	20.00
MS231	2007 (6)	60,000	Y#95.2-98.2, 101.2, 125	17.00	18.00
MS232	2007 (6)	6,000	Y#95.2-98.2, 101.2, 125	17.00	18.00
MS233	2007 (6)	4,000	Y#95.2-98.2, 101.2, 125	17.00	18.00
MS234	2007 (6)	76,500	Y#95.2-98.2, 101.2, 125	22.00	25.00
MS235	2007 (6)	2,720	Y#95.2-98.2, 101.2, 125	17.00	18.00
MS236	2007 (6)	4,000	Y#95.2-98.2, 101.2, 125	17.00	18.00
MS237	2007 (6)	69,000	Y#95.2-98.2, 101.2, 125	19.00	20.00
MS238	2007 (6)	4,000	Y#95.2-98.2, 101.2, 125	17.00	18.00
MS239	2007 (6)	45,200	Y#95.2-98.2, 101.2, 125	21.00	22.00
MS240	2007 (6)	36,500	Y#95.2-98.2, 101.2, 125	21.00	22.00
MS241	2007 (6)	74,500	Y#95.2-98.2, 101.2, 125	18.00	20.00
MS242	2008 (6)	4,000	Y#95.2-98.2, 101.2, 125, Mint exhibition in Miyazaki	18.00	20.00
MS243	2008 (6)	15,100	Y#95.2-98.2, 101.2, 125, "Japan Coin Set"	19.00	20.00
MS244	2008 (6)	7,500	Y#95.2-98.2, 101.2, 125, "Anniversary" folder	20.00	20.00
MS245	2008 (6)	154,022	Y#95.2-98.2, 101.2, 125, Mint Bureau Box	17.00	20.00
MS246	2008 (6)	4,500	Y#95.2-98.2, 101.2, 125, Hiroshima Flower Tour	18.00	20.00

KM#	Date	Mintage	Identification	Issue Price	Mkt Val
MS247	2008 (6)	60,000	Y95.2-98.2, 101.2, 125, Osaka cherry blossoms	18.00	20.00
MS248	2008 (6)	5,500	Y95.2-98.2, 101.2, 125, 19th Tokyo International Coin Convention	18.00	20.00
MS249	2008 (6)	4,000	Y25.2-98.2, 101.2, 125, G8 Finance Ministers' meeting, Osaka	18.00	18.00
MS250	2008 (6)	3,500	Y95.2-98.2, 101.2, 125, Sixth Osaka Coin Show.	18.00	20.00
MS251	2008 (6)	4,000	Y95.2-98.2, 101.2, 125, Kobe Coin and Stamp Exposition.	18.00	18.00
MS252	2008 (6)	142,000	Y95.2-98.2, 101.2, 125, Japan-Brazil Year of Exchange and Centenary of Japanese Immigration to Brazil	24.00	25.00
MS253	2008 (6)	100,000	Y95.2-98.2, 101.2, 125, Children's song coin set, Red Dragonfly.	23.00	25.00
MS254	2008 (6)	4,000	Y95.2-98.2, 101.2, 125	20.00	20.00
MS255	2009 (6)	3,950	Y95.2-Y98.2, 101.2, 125	20.00	21.00
MS256	2009 (6)	11,500	Y95.2-Y98.2, 101.2, 125	21.00	22.00
MS257	2009 (6)	7,650	Y95.2-Y98.2, 101.2, 125	22.00	22.00
MS258	2009 (6)	4,500	Y95.2-Y98.2, 101.2, 125	20.00	20.00
MS259	2009 (6)	60,000	Y95.2-Y98.2, 101.2, 125	20.00	20.00
MS260	2009 (6)	5,500	Y95.2-Y98.2, 101.2, 125	20.00	20.00
MS261	2009 (6)	152,637	Y95.2-Y98.2, 101.2, 125	19.00	20.00
MS262	2009 (6)	4,850	Y95.2-Y98.2, 101.2, 125	20.00	20.00
MS263	2009 (6)	4,000	Y95.2-Y98.2, 101.2, 125	20.00	20.00
MS264	2009 (6)	5,300	Y95.2-Y98.2, 101.2, 125	20.00	20.00
MS265	2009 (6)	4,000	Y95.2-Y98.2, 101.2, 125	20.00	20.00
MS266	2009 (6)	7,413	Y95.2-98.2, 101.2, 125	19.00	20.00
MS267	2009 (6)	70,000	Y95.2-98.2, 101.2, 125	25.00	25.00
MS268	2009 (6)	4,000	Y95.2-98.2, 101.2, 125	20.00	20.00
MS269	2010 (6)	152,500	Y95.2-98.2, 101.2, 125	19.00	25.00
MS270	2010 (6)	7,900	Y95.2-98.2, 101.2, 125	20.00	20.00
MS271	2010 (6)	10,500	Y95.2-98.2, 101.2, 125	20.00	21.00
MS272	2010 (6)	4,748	Y95.2-98.2, 101.2, 125	22.00	22.00
MS273	2010 (6)	4,748	Y95.2-98.2, 101.2, 125	20.00	20.00
MS274	2010 (6)	5,000	Y95.2-98.2, 101.2, 125	20.00	20.00
MS275	2010 (6)	60,000	Y95.2-98.2, 101.2, 125	20.00	20.00
MS276	2010 (6)	6,000	Y95.2-90.2, 101.2, 125	20.00	20.00
MS277	2010 (6)	4,000	Y95.2-98.2, 101.2, 125	20.00	20.00
MS278	2010 (6)	4,572	Y95.2-98.2, 101.2, 125	20.00	20.00
MS279	2010 (6)	4,267	Y95.2-98.2, 101.2, 125	20.00	20.00
MS280	2010 (6)	42,300	Y95.2-98.2, 101.2, 125	22.00	22.00
MS281	2010 (6)	8,012	Y95.2-98.2, 101.2, 125	20.00	20.00
MS282	2010 (6)	58,001	Y95.2-98.2, 101.2, 125	26.00	28.00

PIEFORT PROOF SETS (PPS)

KM#	Date	Mintage	Identification	Issue Price	Mkt Val
PS85	2010 (6)	20,000	Y95.2-98.2, 101.2, 125	144	150

PROOF SETS

KM#	Date	Mintage	Identification	Issue Price	Mkt Val
PS32	2001 (6)	138,000	Y#95.2-98.2, 101.2, 125	62.50	47.00
PS33	2001 (6)	100,000	Y95.2-98.2, 101.2, 125	62.50	53.00
PS34	2002 (6)	141,000	Y#95.2-98.2, 101.2, 125	62.50	53.00
PS35	2002 (6)	3,000	Y#95.2-98.2, 101.2, 125	62.50	100
PS36	2002 (6)	95,000	Y#95.2-98.2, 101.2, 125	62.50	53.00
PS38	2002 (2)	50,000	Y#129, 130	385	550
PS39	2003 (6)	98,400	Y#95.2-98.2, 101.2, 125	67.50	53.00
PSA39	2003 (6)	6,600	Y95.2-98.2, 101.2, 125	66.00	100
PS40	2003 (6)	90,000	Y95.2-98.2, 101.2, 125	115	100
PSA40	2003 (6)	6,600	Y95.2-98.2, 101.2, 125	66.00	100
PS41	2003 (6)	5,000	Y95.2-98.2, 101.2, 125	67.50	100
PS42	2003 (6)	70,000	Y#95.2-90.2, 101.2, 125	125	120
PS43	2003 (6)	5,000	Y95.2-98.2, 101.2, 125	67.50	165
PS44	2004 (6)	94,900	Y#95.2-98.2, 101.2, 125	71.00	60.00
PS45	2004 (6)	13,100	Y95.2-98.2, 101.2, 125	70.00	100
PS46	2004 (6)	60,000	Y95.2-98.2, 101.2, 125	120	145
PS47	2004 (6)	60,000	Y95.2-98.2, 101.2, 125	71.00	60.00
PS48	2004 (6)	50,000	Y95.2-98.2, 101.2, 125	120	150
PS49	2004 (6)	5,000	Y95.2-98.2, 101.2, 125	71.00	100
PS50	2004 (2)	35,000	Y#135-136	425	500
PS51	2005 (6)	76,700	Y95.2-98.2, 101.2, 125	71.00	65.00
PS52	2005 (6)	10,000	Y95.2-98.2, 101.2, 125	70.00	100
PS53	2005 (6)	60,000	Y95.2-98.2, 101.2, 125	125	170
PS54	2005 (6)	34,000	Y95.2-98.2, 101.2, 125	125	170
PS55	2005 (6)	30,000	Y95.2-98.2, 101.2, 125	125	100
PS56	2005 (6)	47,300	Y95.2-98.2, 101.2, 125	71.00	65.00
PS57	2006 (6)	63,400	Y95.2-98.2, 101.2, 125	71.00	65.00
PS58	2006 (6)	8,700	Y95.2-98.2, 101.2, 125	70.00	65.00
PS59	2006 (6)	35,000	Y95.2-98.2, 101.2, 125	125	125

KM#	Date	Mintage	Identification	Issue Price	Mkt Val
PS60	2006 (6)	46,000	Y#95.2-98.2, 101.2, 125	128	145
PS61	2006 (6)	49,900	Y#95.2-98.2, 101.2, 125	125	120
PS62	2006 (6)	4,000	Y#95.2-98.2, 101.2, 125	71.00	150
PS63	2006 (6)	40,000	Y#95.2-98.2, 101.2, 125	125	150
PS64	2007 (6)	53,200	Y#95.2-98.2, 101.2, 125	71.00	75.00
PS65	2007 (6)	7,000	Y#95.2-98.2, 101.2, 125	70.00	75.00
PS66	2007 (6)	35,000	Y#95.2-98.2, 101.2, 125	125	125
PS67	2007 (6)	40,100	Y#95.2-98.2, 101.2, 125	125	125
PS68	2007 (6)	33,500	Y#95.2-98.2, 101.2, 125	125	125
PS69	2007 (6)	3,000	Y#95.2-98.2, 101.2, 125	71.00	75.00
PS70	2007 (6)	30,000	Y#95.2-98.2, 101.2, 125	125	120
PS71	2008 (6)	55,200	Y95.2-95.2, 101.2, 125	75.00	75.00
PS72	2008 (6)	6,000	Y95.2-98.2, 101.2, 125	73.50	75.00
PS73	2008 (6)	27,000	Y95.2-98.2, 101.2, 125	130	130
PS74	2008 (6)	44,000	Y95.2-98.2, 101.2, 125	130	110
PS75	2008 (6)	33,000	Y95.2-98.2, 101.2, 125	100	100
PS76	2008 (6)	3,000	Y95.2-Y98.2, 101.2, 125	79.00	75.00
PS77	2009 (6)	48,400	Y95.2-Y98.2, 101.2, 125	79.00	70.00
PS78	2009 (6)	5,600	Y95.2-Y98.2, 101.2, 125	77.50	80.00
PS79	2009 (6)	25,000	Y95.2-Y98.2, 101.2, 125	136	135
PS80	2009 (6)	25,000	Y95.2-Y98.2, 101.2, 125	136	135
PS81	2009 (6)	30,000	Y95.2-Y98.2, 101.2, 125	136	135
PS82	2009 (6)	3,000	Y95.2-98.2, 101.2, 125	83.00	85.00
PS83	2010 (6)	41,687	Y95.2-98.2, 101.2, 125	83.00	80.00
PS84	2010 (6)	20,000	Y95.2-98.2, 101.2, 125	144	150
PS86	2010 (6)	20,000	Y95.2-98.2, 101.2, 125	111	115
PS87	2010 (6)	20,000	Y95.2-98.2, 101.2, 125	144	150

JERSEY

The Bailiwick of Jersey, a British Crown dependency located in the English Channel 12 miles (19 km.) west of Normandy, France, has an area of 45 sq. mi. (117 sq. km.) and a population of 74,000. Capital: St. Helier. The economy is based on agriculture and cattle breeding – the importation of cattle is prohibited to protect the purity of the island's world-famous strain of milk cows.

The island together with the Bailiwick of Guernsey, is the only part of the Dutchy of Normandy belonging to the British Crown, has been a possession of Britain since the Norman conquest of 1066. Jersey is administered by its own laws and customs. Unless the island is mentioned specifically, acts passed by the British Parliament are not applicable to Jersey. During WW II, German troops occupied the island from 1940 to 1945.

RULER
British

MINT MARK
H - Heaton, Birmingham

BRITISH DEPENDENCY

DECIMAL COINAGE

100 New Pence = 1 Pound

KM# 103 PENNY
3.56 g., Copper Plated Steel, 20.3 mm. **Ruler:** Elizabeth II **Obv:** Crowned head right **Rev:** Le Hoeq Watchtower, St. Clement **Edge:** Plain

Date	Mintage	F12	VF20	XF40	MS60	MS63
2002	1,520,000	—	—	0.15	0.65	—
2003	1,575,000	—	—	0.15	0.65	—
2005	—	—	—	0.15	0.65	—
2006	585,000	—	—	0.15	0.65	—
2008	4,800,000	—	—	0.15	0.65	—
2012	—	—	—	—	—	—

KM# 104 2 PENCE
7.12 g., Copper Plated Steel, 25.91 mm. **Ruler:** Elizabeth II **Obv:** Head with tiara right **Rev:** L'Hermitage, St. Helier **Edge:** Plain

Date	Mintage	F12	VF20	XF40	MS60	MS63
2002	1,259,000	—	—	0.20	0.65	—
2003	10,000	—	—	0.20	0.65	—
2005	400,000	—	—	0.20	0.65	—
2006	1,200,000	—	—	0.20	0.65	—
2008	2,459,000	—	—	0.20	0.65	—
2013 (2012)	—	—	—	—	0.65	—

KM# 105 5 PENCE
3.25 g., Copper-Nickel, 18 mm. **Ruler:** Elizabeth II **Obv:** Head with tiara right **Rev:** Seymour Tower, Grouville, L'Avathigon **Edge:** Reeded

Date	Mintage	F12	VF20	XF40	MS60	MS63
2002	1,200,000	—	—	0.20	0.65	—
2003	1,005,000	—	—	0.20	0.65	—
2006	1,200,000	—	—	0.20	0.65	—
2008	3,600,000	—	—	0.20	0.65	—
2012	—	—	—	—	—	0.65

KM# 106 10 PENCE
6.50 g., Copper-Nickel, 24.5 mm. **Ruler:** Elizabeth II **Obv:** Head with tiara right **Rev:** La Hougne Bie, Faldouet, St. Martin

Date	Mintage	F12	VF20	XF40	MS60	MS63
2002	500,000	—	—	—	1.25	1.50
2003	10,000	—	—	—	1.25	1.50
2005	—	—	—	—	1.25	1.50
2006	—	—	—	—	1.25	1.50
2007	630,000	—	—	—	1.25	1.50
2010	—	—	—	—	1.25	1.50
2012	—	—	—	—	—	1.50

KM# 107 20 PENCE
5.00 g., Copper-Nickel, 21.4 mm. **Ruler:** Elizabeth II **Obv:** Head with tiara right

Date	Mintage	F12	VF20	XF40	MS60	MS63
2002	975,500	—	—	—	1.00	1.25
2003	10,000	—	—	—	1.00	1.25
2005	500,000	—	—	—	1.00	1.25
2006	500,000	—	—	—	1.00	1.25
2007	780,000	—	—	—	1.00	1.25
2009	1,500,000	—	—	—	1.00	1.25
2012	—	—	—	—	—	1.25

KM# 108 50 PENCE
8.00 g., Copper-Nickel, 27.3 mm. **Ruler:** Elizabeth II **Obv:** Crowned bust right **Rev:** Gothic gate arch **Edge:** Plain **Shape:** 7-sided

Date	Mintage	F12	VF20	XF40	MS60	MS63
2003	10,000	—	—	1.00	2.50	3.00
2005	200,000	—	—	1.00	2.50	3.00
2006	300,000	—	—	1.00	2.50	3.00
2009	480,000	—	—	1.00	2.50	3.00

KM# 123a 50 PENCE
8.00 g., 0.925 Silver 0.2364 oz. ASW, 27.3 mm. **Ruler:** Elizabeth II **Subject:** Coronation, 50th Anniversary **Obv:** Crowned head right **Rev:** Archbishop crowning Queen **Edge:** Plain **Shape:** 7-sided

Date	Mintage	F12	VF20	XF40	MS60	MS63
2003	15,000	PF63 22.00	PF65 25.00			

KM# 148a 50 PENCE
8.00 g., 0.925 Silver 0.2364 oz. ASW, 27.3 mm. **Ruler:** Elizabeth II **Subject:** Coronation, 50th Anniversary **Rev:** Regalia in quatrilobe **Shape:** 7-sided

Date	Mintage	F12	VF20	XF40	MS60	MS63
2003	15,000	PF63 22.00	PF65 25.00			

KM# 150a 50 PENCE
8.00 g., 0.925 Silver 0.2364 oz. ASW, 27.3 mm. **Ruler:** Elizabeth II **Subject:** Coronation, 50th Anniversary **Rev:** Crown, sceptre and shield **Shape:** 7-sided

Date	Mintage	F12	VF20	XF40	MS60	MS63
2003	15,000	PF63 22.00	PF65 25.00			

KM# 123 50 PENCE
8.00 g., Copper-Nickel, 27.3 mm. **Ruler:** Elizabeth II **Subject:** Coronation, 50th Anniversary **Obv:** Crowned head right **Rev:** Archbishop crowning Queen **Edge:** Plain **Shape:** 7-sided

Date	Mintage	F12	VF20	XF40	MS60	MS63
2003	10,000	—	—	—	2.50	3.00

KM# 148 50 PENCE
8.00 g., Copper-Nickel, 27.3 mm. **Ruler:** Elizabeth II **Subject:** Coronation, 50th Anniversary **Rev:** Regalia in quatrilobe **Shape:** 7-sided

Date	Mintage	F12	VF20	XF40	MS60	MS63
2003	—	—	—	—	2.50	3.50

KM# 149 50 PENCE
8.00 g., Copper-Nickel, 27.3 mm. **Ruler:** Elizabeth II **Subject:** Coronation, 50th Anniversary **Rev:** Queen facing, seated on throne **Shape:** 7-sided

Date	Mintage	F12	VF20	XF40	MS60	MS63
2003	10,000	—	—	—	2.50	3.50

KM# 149a 50 PENCE
8.00 g., 0.925 Silver 0.2364 oz. ASW, 27.3 mm. **Ruler:** Elizabeth II **Subject:** Coronation, 50th Anniversary **Rev:** Queen facing, seated on throne **Shape:** 7-sided

Date	Mintage	F12	VF20	XF40	MS60	MS63
2003	15,000	PF63 22.00		PF65 25.00		

KM# 150 50 PENCE
8.00 g., Copper-Nickel, 27.3 mm. **Ruler:** Elizabeth II **Subject:** Coronation, 50th Anniversary **Rev:** Crown, scepter and shield **Shape:** 7-sided

Date	Mintage	F12	VF20	XF40	MS60	MS63
2003	10,000	—	—	—	2.50	3.50

KM# 101 POUND
9.50 g., Nickel-Brass, 22.5 mm. **Ruler:** Elizabeth II **Obv:** Head with tiara right **Rev:** Schooner, Resolute **Edge Lettering:** CAESAREA INSULA

Date	Mintage	F12	VF20	XF40	MS60	MS63
2003	10,000	—	—	—	4.00	4.50
2005	200,000	—	—	—	4.00	4.50
2006	93,000	—	—	—	4.00	4.50

KM# 160 POUND
1.24 g., 0.999 Gold 0.0396 oz. AGW, 13.92 mm. **Ruler:** Elizabeth II **Subject:** Trafalgar, 200th Anniversary

Date	Mintage	F12	VF20	XF40	MS60	MS63
2005	—	PF65 100				

KM# 173 POUND
1.24 g., 0.999 Gold 0.0396 oz. AGW, 13.92 mm. **Ruler:**

Elizabeth II Subject: Princess Diana

Date	Mintage	F12	VF20	XF40	MS60	MS63
2007	—	PF65 100				

KM# 102 2 POUNDS
12.00 g., Bi-Metallic, 28.4 mm. **Ruler:** Elizabeth II **Obv:** Head with tiara right **Rev:** Latent image value within circle of assorted shields **Edge Lettering:** CAESAREA INSULA

Date	Mintage	F12	VF20	XF40	MS60	MS63
2002	—	—	—	—	10.00	12.00
2003	10,000	—	—	—	10.00	12.00
2006	3,500	—	—	—	10.00	12.00

KM# 111b 5 POUNDS
39.94 g., 0.9167 Gold 1.1696 oz. AGW, 38.6 mm. **Ruler:** Elizabeth II **Subject:** Princess Diana **Obv:** Crowned head right **Rev:** Diana's cameo above people **Edge:** Reeded

Date	Mintage	F12	VF20	XF40	MS60	MS63
2002	100	PF65 2,150				

KM# 113b 5 POUNDS
39.94 g., 0.9166 Gold 1.1694 oz. AGW, 38.6 mm. **Ruler:** Elizabeth II **Subject:** Queen Mother **Obv:** Crowned head right **Rev:** Queen Mother's bust right, (circa 1918) **Rev. Legend:** HER MAJESTY QUEEN ELIZABETH THE QUEEN MOTHER **Edge:** Reeded

Date	Mintage	F12	VF20	XF40	MS60	MS63
2002	250	PF65 2,100				

KM# 115b 5 POUNDS
39.94 g., 0.9166 Gold 1.1694 oz. AGW, 38.6 mm. **Ruler:** Elizabeth II **Subject:** Golden Jubilee **Obv:** Crowned head right **Rev:** Abbey procession scene **Edge:** Reeded

Date	Mintage	F12	VF20	XF40	MS60	MS63
2002	100	PF65 2,150				

KM# 111 5 POUNDS
28.28 g., Copper-Nickel, 38.6 mm. **Ruler:** Elizabeth II **Subject:** Princess Diana **Obv:** Crowned head right **Rev:** Diana's cameo above people **Edge:** Reeded

Date	Mintage	F12	VF20	XF40	MS60	MS63
2002	—	—	—	—	13.50	15.00

KM# 113 5 POUNDS
28.28 g., Copper-Nickel, 38.6 mm. **Ruler:** Elizabeth II **Subject:** Queen Mother **Obv:** Crowned head right **Rev:** Queen Mother's bust right (circa 1918) **Rev. Legend:** HER MAJESTY QUEEN ELIZABETH THE QUEEN MOTHER **Edge:** Reeded

Date	Mintage	F12	VF20	XF40	MS60	MS63
2002	—	—	—	—	13.50	15.00

KM# 115 5 POUNDS
28.28 g., Copper-Nickel, 38.6 mm. **Ruler:** Elizabeth II **Subject:** Golden Jubilee **Obv:** Crowned head right **Rev:** Abbey procession scene **Edge:** Reeded

Date	Mintage	F12	VF20	XF40	MS60	MS63
2002	—	—	—	—	13.50	15.00

KM# 117 5 POUNDS
28.28 g., Copper-Nickel, 38.6 mm. **Ruler:** Elizabeth II **Subject:** Duke of Wellington **Obv:** Crowned head right **Rev:** Wellington's portrait with multicolor infantry scene **Edge:** Reeded

Date	Mintage	F12	VF20	XF40	MS60	MS63
2002	—	—	—	—	13.50	15.00

KM# 111a 5 POUNDS
28.28 g., 0.925 Silver 0.8356 oz. ASW, 38.6 mm. **Ruler:** Elizabeth II **Subject:** Princess Diana **Obv:** Crowned head right **Rev:** Diana's cameo above people **Edge:** Reeded

Date	Mintage	F12	VF20	XF40	MS60	MS63
2002	20,000	PF63 40.00		PF65 45.00		

KM# 113a 5 POUNDS
28.28 g., 0.925 Silver 0.8356 oz. ASW, 38.6 mm. **Ruler:** Elizabeth II **Subject:** Queen Mother **Obv:** Crowned head right **Rev:** Queen Mother's bust right, (circa 1918) **Rev. Legend:** HER MAJESTY QUEEN ELIZABETH THE QUEEN MOTHER **Edge:** Reeded

Date	Mintage	F12	VF20	XF40	MS60	MS63
2002	15,000	PF63 45.00		PF65 50.00		

KM# 115a 5 POUNDS
28.28 g., 0.925 Silver 0.8356 oz. ASW, 38.6 mm. **Ruler:** Elizabeth II **Subject:** Golden Jubilee **Obv:** Crowned head right **Rev:** Abbey procession scene **Edge:** Reeded

Date	Mintage	F12	VF20	XF40	MS60	MS63
2002	20,000	PF63 45.00		PF65 50.00		

KM# 117a 5 POUNDS
28.28 g., 0.925 Silver 0.8356 oz. ASW, 38.6 mm. **Ruler:** Elizabeth II **Subject:** Duke of Wellington **Obv:** Crowned head right **Rev:** Wellington's portrait with multicolor infantry scene **Edge:** Reeded

Date	Mintage	F12	VF20	XF40	MS60	MS63
2002	15,000	PF63 45.00		PF65 50.00		

KM# 117b 5 POUNDS
39.94 g., 0.9166 Gold 1.1694 oz. AGW, 38.6 mm. **Ruler:** Elizabeth II **Subject:** Duke of Wellington **Obv:** Crowned head right **Rev:** Wellington's portrait with multicolor infantry scene **Edge:** Reeded

Date	Mintage	F12	VF20	XF40	MS60	MS63
2002	200	PF65 2,100				

KM# 119 5 POUNDS
28.28 g., Copper-Nickel, 38.6 mm. **Ruler:** Elizabeth II **Subject:** Golden Jubilee **Obv:** Crowned head right **Rev:** Honor guard and memorial **Edge:** Reeded

Date	Mintage	F12	VF20	XF40	MS60	MS63
2003	—	—	—	—	13.50	15.00

KM# 121 5 POUNDS
28.28 g., Copper-Nickel, 38.6 mm. **Ruler:** Elizabeth II **Obv:** Crowned head right **Rev:** Bust of Prince William facing and crowned arms with supporters **Edge:** Reeded

Date	Mintage	F12	VF20	XF40	MS60	MS63
2003	—	—	—	—	16.50	18.00

KM# 119a 5 POUNDS
28.28 g., 0.925 Silver 0.8356 oz. ASW, 38.6 mm. **Ruler:** Elizabeth II **Subject:** Golden Jubilee **Obv:** Crowned head right **Rev:** Honor guard and monument **Edge:** Reeded

Date	Mintage	F12	VF20	XF40	MS60	MS63
2003	20,000	PF63 45.00		PF65 50.00		

KM# 119b 5 POUNDS
39.94 g., 0.9166 Gold 1.1694 oz. AGW, 38.6 mm. **Ruler:** Elizabeth II **Subject:** Golden Jubilee **Obv:** Crowned head right **Rev:** Honor guard and monument **Edge:** Reeded

Date	Mintage	F12	VF20	XF40	MS60	MS63
2003	250	PF65 2,100				

KM# 121a 5 POUNDS
28.28 g., 0.925 Silver 0.8356 oz. ASW, 38.6 mm. **Ruler:** Elizabeth II **Obv:** Crowned head right **Rev:** Bust of Prince William facing and crowned arms with supporters **Edge:** Reeded

Date	Mintage	F12	VF20	XF40	MS60	MS63
2003	5,000	PF63 42.00		PF65 47.00		

KM# 121b 5 POUNDS
39.94 g., 0.9166 Gold 1.1694 oz. AGW, 38.6 mm. **Ruler:** Elizabeth II **Obv:** Crowned head right **Rev:** Bust of Prince William facing and crowned arms with supporters **Edge:** Reeded

Date	Mintage	F12	VF20	XF40	MS60	MS63
2003	200	PF65 2,100				

KM# 130a 5 POUNDS
28.28 g., 0.925 Silver 0.8356 oz. ASW, 38.6 mm. **Ruler:** Elizabeth II **Subject:** Drake **Obv:** Crowned head right **Rev:** Naval leader Sir Francis Drake

Date	Mintage	F12	VF20	XF40	MS60	MS63
2003	—	PF63 65.00	PF65 75.00			

KM# 131a 5 POUNDS
28.28 g., 0.925 Silver 0.8356 oz. ASW, 38.6 mm. **Ruler:** Elizabeth II **Subject:** Sovereign Of The Seas **Obv:** Crowned head right **Rev:** The Sovereign of the Seas ship

Date	Mintage	F12	VF20	XF40	MS60	MS63
2003	—	PF63 65.00	PF65 75.00			

KM# 132a 5 POUNDS
28.28 g., 0.925 Silver 0.8356 oz. ASW, 38.6 mm. **Ruler:** Elizabeth II **Subject:** John Fisher **Obv:** Crowned head right **Rev:** WWI Naval leader Sir John Fisher

Date	Mintage	F12	VF20	XF40	MS60	MS63
2003	—	PF63 65.00	PF65 75.00			

KM# 133a 5 POUNDS
28.28 g., 0.925 Silver 0.8356 oz. ASW, 38.6 mm. **Ruler:** Elizabeth II **Subject:** HMS Victory **Obv:** Crowned head right **Rev:** Nelson's flag ship HMS Victory, multicolor flag at top

Date	Mintage	F12	VF20	XF40	MS60	MS63
2004 (2003)	—	PF63 65.00	PF65 75.00			

KM# 134 5 POUNDS
28.28 g., Copper-Nickel, 38.6 mm. **Ruler:** Elizabeth II **Obv:** Crowned head right **Rev:** WWII Admiral Andrew B. Cunningham

Date	Mintage	F12	VF20	XF40	MS60	MS63
2003	—	—	—	—	—	15.00

KM# 134a 5 POUNDS
28.28 g., 0.925 Silver 0.8356 oz. ASW, 38.6 mm. **Ruler:** Elizabeth II **Subject:** Cunningham **Obv:** Crowned head right **Rev:** WWII Admiral Andrew B. Cunningham

Date	Mintage	F12	VF20	XF40	MS60	MS63
2003	—	PF63 65.00	PF65 75.00			

KM# 135a 5 POUNDS
28.28 g., 0.925 Silver 0.8356 oz. ASW, 38.6 mm. **Ruler:** Elizabeth II **Subject:** Conqueror **Obv:** Crowned head right **Rev:** Submarine HMS Conqueror

Date	Mintage	F12	VF20	XF40	MS60	MS63
2003	—	PF63 65.00	PF65 75.00			

KM# 144a 5 POUNDS
28.28 g., 0.925 Silver 0.8356 oz. ASW, 38.61 mm. **Ruler:** Elizabeth II **Subject:** History of the Royal Navy **Obv:** Head left with tiarra **Obv. Legend:** ELIZABETH II BAILIWICK - OF JERSEY **Rev:** Five heads of King Alfred the Great, Sir Francis Drake, Admirals Horatio Nelson, John Fisher and John Woodward at five ships, colored flag at top **Edge:** Reeded

Date	Mintage	F12	VF20	XF40	MS60	MS63
2003	—	PF63 65.00	PF65 75.00			

KM# 130 5 POUNDS
28.28 g., Copper-Nickel, 38.6 mm. **Ruler:** Elizabeth II **Subject:** Sir Francis Drake **Obv:** Crowned head right

Date	Mintage	F12	VF20	XF40	MS60	MS63
2003	—	—	—	—	—	15.00

KM# 131 5 POUNDS
28.28 g., Copper-Nickel, 38.6 mm. **Ruler:** Elizabeth II **Subject:** Sovereign of the Seas **Obv:** Crowned head right **Rev:** Sailing ship

Date	Mintage	F12	VF20	XF40	MS60	MS63
2003	—	—	—	—	—	15.00

KM# 132 5 POUNDS
28.28 g., Copper-Nickel, 38.6 mm. **Ruler:** Elizabeth II **Obv:** Crowned head right **Rev:** WWI naval leader Sir John Fisher

Date	Mintage	F12	VF20	XF40	MS60	MS63
2003	—	—	—	—	—	15.00

KM# 133 5 POUNDS
28.28 g., Copper-Nickel, 38.6 mm. **Ruler:** Elizabeth II **Subject:** HMS Victory **Obv:** Crowned head right **Rev:** Nelson's flagship HMS Victory

Date	Mintage	F12	VF20	XF40	MS60	MS63
2003	—	—	—	—	—	15.00

KM# 135 5 POUNDS
28.28 g., Copper-Nickel, 38.6 mm. **Ruler:** Elizabeth II **Subject:** HMS Conqueror **Obv:** Crowned head right **Rev:** Submarine HMS Conqueror

Date	Mintage	F12	VF20	XF40	MS60	MS63
2003	—	—	—	—	—	15.00

KM# 144 5 POUNDS
28.28 g., Copper-Nickel, 38.6 mm. **Ruler:** Elizabeth II **Subject:** History of the Royal Navy **Rev:** Five heads, four ships and a sub

Date	Mintage	F12	VF20	XF40	MS60	MS63
2003	—	—	—	—	—	15.00

KM# 139a 5 POUNDS
28.28 g., 0.925 Silver 0.8356 oz. ASW, 38.6 mm. **Ruler:** Elizabeth II **Subject:** Driver and Fireman **Obv:** Crowned head right **Rev:** Familiar image from the Golden Age of Steam: the driver and fireman

Date	Mintage	F12	VF20	XF40	MS60	MS63
2004	—	PF63 65.00	PF65 75.00			

KM# 124a 5 POUNDS
28.28 g., 0.925 Silver 0.8356 oz. ASW, 38.6 mm. **Ruler:** Elizabeth II **Obv:** Crowned head right **Rev:** British Horsa gliders in flight

Date	Mintage	F12	VF20	XF40	MS60	MS63
2004	10,000	PF63 75.00	PF65 85.00			

KM# 126a 5 POUNDS
28.28 g., 0.925 Silver 0.8356 oz. ASW, 38.6 mm. **Ruler:**

KM# 136a 5 POUNDS
Elizabeth II **Obv:** Crowned head right **Rev:** Charge of the Light Brigade scene with one blue uniform behind the Earl of Cardigan **Edge:** Reeded

Date	Mintage	F12	VF20	XF40	MS60	MS63
2004	10,000	PF63 75.00	PF65 85.00			

KM# 136a 5 POUNDS
28.28 g., 0.925 Silver 0.8356 oz. ASW, 38.6 mm. **Ruler:** Elizabeth II **Subject:** Coronation **Obv:** Crowned head right **Rev:** The Pacific Class Coronation

Date	Mintage	F12	VF20	XF40	MS60	MS63
2004	—	PF63 65.00	PF65 75.00			

KM# 137a 5 POUNDS
28.28 g., 0.925 Silver 0.8356 oz. ASW, 38.6 mm. **Ruler:** Elizabeth II **Subject:** Flying Scotsman **Obv:** Crowned head right **Rev:** Famous Flying Scotsman Locomotive, designed by Sir Nigel Gresley

Date	Mintage	F12	VF20	XF40	MS60	MS63
2004	—	PF63 65.00	PF65 75.00			

KM# 138a 5 POUNDS
28.28 g., 0.925 Silver 0.8356 oz. ASW, 38.6 mm. **Ruler:** Elizabeth II **Subject:** Golden Arrow **Obv:** Crowned head right **Rev:** The Golden Arrow, which ran from London to Dover en route to Paris

Date	Mintage	F12	VF20	XF40	MS60	MS63
2004	—	PF63 65.00	PF65 75.00			

KM# 140a 5 POUNDS
28.28 g., 0.925 Silver 0.8356 oz. ASW, 38.6 mm. **Ruler:** Elizabeth II **Subject:** Tunnel **Obv:** Crowned head right **Rev:** Steam locomotive exiting from tunnel

Date	Mintage	F12	VF20	XF40	MS60	MS63
2004	—	PF63 65.00	PF65 75.00			

KM# 141a 5 POUNDS
28.28 g., 0.925 Silver 0.8356 oz. ASW, 38.6 mm. **Ruler:** Elizabeth II **Subject:** Evening Star **Obv:** Crowned head right **Rev:** The Evening Star - representing the last British Rail Steam Locomotive

Date	Mintage	F12	VF20	XF40	MS60	MS63
2004	—	PF63 65.00	PF65 75.00			

KM# 124 5 POUNDS
28.28 g., Copper-Nickel, 38.6 mm. **Ruler:** Elizabeth II **Obv:** Crowned head right **Rev:** British Horsa gliders in flight **Edge:** Reeded **Note:** D-Day

Date	Mintage	F12	VF20	XF40	MS60	MS63
2004	—	—	—	—	15.00	17.00

KM# 124b 5 POUNDS
39.94 g., 0.9167 Gold 1.1696 oz. AGW, 38.6 mm. **Ruler:** Elizabeth II **Obv:** Crowned head right **Rev:** British Horsa gliders in flight

Date	Mintage	F12	VF20	XF40	MS60	MS63
2004	500	PF65 2,100				

KM# 126 5 POUNDS
28.28 g., Copper-Nickel, 38.6 mm. **Ruler:** Elizabeth II **Subject:** 150th Anniversary of the Crimean War **Obv:** Crowned head right **Rev:** Charge of the Light Brigade scene with one blue uniform behind the Earl of Cardigan **Edge:** Reeded

Date	Mintage	F12	VF20	XF40	MS60	MS63
2004 plain	—	—	—	—	25.00	27.50

KM# 126b 5 POUNDS
39.94 g., 0.9166 Gold 1.1694 oz. AGW, 38.6 mm. **Ruler:** Elizabeth II **Obv:** Crowned head right **Rev:** Charge of the Light Brigade scene with one blue uniform behind the Earl of Cardigan **Edge:** Reeded

Date	Mintage	F12	VF20	XF40	MS60	MS63
2004	500	PF65 2,100				

KM# 136 5 POUNDS
28.28 g., Copper-Nickel, 38.6 mm. **Ruler:** Elizabeth II **Subject:** Steam Locomotive - Coronation **Obv:** Crowned head right **Rev:** The Pacific class (4-6-2) Coronation

Date	Mintage	F12	VF20	XF40	MS60	MS63
2004	—	—	—	—	—	15.00

KM# 137 5 POUNDS
28.28 g., Copper-Nickel, 38.6 mm. **Ruler:** Elizabeth II **Subject:** Steam Locomotive - Flying Scotsman **Obv:** Crowned head right **Rev:** Sir Nigel Gresley's Flying Scotsman

Date	Mintage	F12	VF20	XF40	MS60	MS63
2004	—	—	—	—	—	15.00

KM# 138 5 POUNDS
28.28 g., Copper-Nickel, 38.6 mm. **Ruler:** Elizabeth II **Subject:** Steam Locomotive - The Golden Arrow **Obv:** Crowned head right **Rev:** The Golden Arrow, London-Dover to Paris service

Date	Mintage	F12	VF20	XF40	MS60	MS63
2004	—	—	—	—	—	15.00

KM# 139 5 POUNDS
28.28 g., Copper-Nickel, 38.6 mm. **Ruler:** Elizabeth II **Subject:** Steam Locomotive driver and fireman **Obv:** Crowned head right **Rev:** Driver and Fireman

Date	Mintage	F12	VF20	XF40	MS60	MS63
2004	—	—	—	—	—	15.00

KM# 140 5 POUNDS
28.28 g., Copper-Nickel, 38.6 mm. **Ruler:** Elizabeth II **Subject:** Tunnel **Obv:** Crowned head right **Rev:** Steam locomotive exiting tunnel

Date	Mintage	F12	VF20	XF40	MS60	MS63
2004	—	—	—	—	—	15.00

KM# 141 5 POUNDS
28.28 g., Copper-Nickel, 38.6 mm. **Ruler:** Elizabeth II **Subject:** The Evening Star **Obv:** Crowned head right **Rev:** The Evening Star, representing the last British Steam Locomotive

Date	Mintage	F12	VF20	XF40	MS60	MS63
2004	—	—	—	—	—	15.00

KM# 129a 5 POUNDS
39.94 g., 0.9167 Gold 1.1696 oz. AGW, 38.6 mm. **Ruler:** Elizabeth II **Subject:** WWII Liberation **Obv:** Crowned head right **Rev:** Returning evacuees **Edge:** Reeded

Date	Mintage	F12	VF20	XF40	MS60	MS63
2005	150	PF65 2,150				

KM# 127a 5 POUNDS
28.28 g., 0.925 Silver 0.8356 oz. ASW, 38.6 mm. **Ruler:** Elizabeth II **Subject:** Nelson Trafalger **Obv:** Crowned head right **Rev:** 200th Anniversary of the Battle of Trafalgar, image of Nelson with a gilded ship in the background

Date	Mintage	F12	VF20	XF40	MS60	MS63
2005	—	PF63 65.00	PF65 75.00			

KM# 128a 5 POUNDS
28.28 g., 0.925 Silver 0.8356 oz. ASW, 38.6 mm. **Ruler:** Elizabeth II **Subject:** WWII Liberation **Obv:** Crowned head right **Rev:** Big Ben Tower **Edge:** Reeded

Date	Mintage	F12	VF20	XF40	MS60	MS63
2005	5,000	PF63 75.00	PF65 85.00			

KM# 127 5 POUNDS
28.28 g., Copper-Nickel, 38.61 mm. **Ruler:** Elizabeth II **Subject:** Battle of Trafalgar **Obv:** Crowned head right

Date	Mintage	F12	VF20	XF40	MS60	MS63
2005	—	—	—	—	7.50	10.00

KM# 128 5 POUNDS
28.28 g., Copper-Nickel, 38.61 mm. **Ruler:** Elizabeth II **Subject:** 60th Anniversary - End of WW II **Obv:** Crowned head right **Rev:** Big Ben Tower

Date	Mintage	F12	VF20	XF40	MS60	MS63
2005	—	—	—	—	7.50	10.00

KM# 128b 5 POUNDS
39.94 g., 0.9167 Gold 1.1696 oz. AGW, 38.6 mm. **Ruler:** Elizabeth II **Subject:** WWII Liberation **Obv:** Crowned head right **Rev:** Big Ben Tower **Edge:** Reeded

Date	Mintage	F12	VF20	XF40	MS60	MS63
2005	150	PF65 2,150				

KM# 129 5 POUNDS
28.28 g., Copper-Nickel, 38.61 mm. **Ruler:** Elizabeth II **Subject:** WW II Liberation **Obv:** Crowned head right **Rev:** Returning evacuees **Edge:** Reeded

Date	Mintage	F12	VF20	XF40	MS60	MS63
2005	—	—	—	—	7.50	10.00

KM# 164 5 POUNDS
28.28 g., 0.925 Silver 0.8356 oz. ASW, 38.61 mm. **Ruler:** Elizabeth II **Subject:** Charles Robert Darwin

Date	Mintage	F12	VF20	XF40	MS60	MS63
2005	—	PF63 55.00	PF65 60.00			

KM# 145a 5 POUNDS
28.28 g., 0.925 Silver 0.8356 oz. ASW, 38.61 mm. **Ruler:** Elizabeth II **Subject:** Elizabeth II, 80th Birthday **Rev:** Bobby Moor and Wembley's Royal Box

Date	Mintage	F12	VF20	XF40	MS60	MS63
2006	—	PF63 55.00	PF65 60.00			

KM# 167a 5 POUNDS
28.28 g., 0.925 Silver 0.8356 oz. ASW, 38.61 mm. **Ruler:** Elizabeth II **Subject:** Guy Penrose Gibson, Victoria Cross

Date	Mintage	F12	VF20	XF40	MS60	MS63
2006	Est. 30000	PF63 45.00	PF65 50.00			

KM# 142 5 POUNDS
28.28 g., 0.925 Silver 0.8356 oz. ASW, 38.6 mm. **Ruler:** Elizabeth II **Subject:** Queen's 80th Birthday **Obv:** Head with tiara right - gilt **Obv. Legend:** ELIZABETH II BAILIWICK - OF JERSEY **Rev:** Queen horseback facing

Date	Mintage	F12	VF20	XF40	MS60	MS63
2006	—	PF63 40.00	PF65 45.00			

KM# 145 5 POUNDS
28.28 g., Copper-Nickel, 38.61 mm. **Ruler:** Elizabeth II **Subject:** Elizabeth II's 80th Birthday **Rev:** Bobby Moore and Wembley's Royal Box

Date	Mintage	F12	VF20	XF40	MS60	MS63
2006	—	—	—	—	—	15.00

KM# 142a 5 POUNDS
28.28 g., 0.925 Silver 0.8356 oz. ASW, 38.6 mm. **Ruler:** Elizabeth II **Subject:** Elizabeth II's 80th Birthday **Obv:** Head with tiara right **Obv. Legend:** ELIZABETH II BAILIWICK - OF JERSEY **Rev:** Queen on horseback **Edge:** Reeded

Date	Mintage	F12	VF20	XF40	MS60	MS63
2006	—	PF63 40.00	PF65 45.00			

KM# 163 5 POUNDS
28.28 g., 0.925 Silver 0.8356 oz. ASW **Ruler:** Elizabeth II **Subject:** Sir Winston Churchill

Date	Mintage	F12	VF20	XF40	MS60	MS63
2006	Est. 25000	PF63 55.00	PF65 60.00			

KM# 165 5 POUNDS
28.28 g., 0.925 Silver 0.8356 oz. ASW, 38.61 mm. **Ruler:** Elizabeth II **Subject:** Robert (Bobby) Moore, soccerplayer

Date	Mintage	F12	VF20	XF40	MS60	MS63
2006	Est. 25000	PF63 55.00	PF65 60.00			

KM# 166 5 POUNDS
28.28 g., 0.925 Silver 0.8356 oz. ASW, 38.61 mm. **Ruler:** Elizabeth II **Subject:** Florence Nightingale

Date	Mintage	F12	VF20	XF40	MS60	MS63
2006	25,000	PF63 55.00	PF65 60.00			

KM# 167 5 POUNDS
28.28 g., Copper-Nickel, 38.61 mm. **Ruler:** Elizabeth II **Subject:** Guy Penrose Gibson, Victoria Cross

Date	Mintage	F12	VF20	XF40	MS60	MS63
2006	—	—	—	—	—	15.00

KM# 168 5 POUNDS
28.28 g., 0.925 Silver 0.8356 oz. ASW, 38.61 mm. **Ruler:** Elizabeth II **Subject:** Nicholson

Date	Mintage	F12	VF20	XF40	MS60	MS63
2006	—	PF63 45.00	PF65 50.00			

KM# 169 5 POUNDS
28.28 g., 0.925 Silver 0.8356 oz. ASW, 38.61 mm. **Ruler:** Elizabeth II **Subject:** Hook, Char and Bro

Date	Mintage	F12	VF20	XF40	MS60	MS63
2006	—	PF63 45.00	PF65 50.00			

KM# 170 5 POUNDS
28.28 g., 0.925 Silver 0.8356 oz. ASW, 38.61 mm. **Ruler:** Elizabeth II **Subject:** First Lanc Fusiliers

Date	Mintage	F12	VF20	XF40	MS60	MS63
2006	—	PF63 45.00	PF65 50.00			

KM# 171 5 POUNDS
28.28 g., 0.925 Silver 0.8356 oz. ASW, 38.61 mm. **Ruler:** Elizabeth II **Subject:** Noel Godfrey Chavasse

Date	Mintage	F12	VF20	XF40	MS60	MS63
2006	—	PF63 45.00	PF65 50.00			

KM# 172 5 POUNDS
28.28 g., 0.925 Silver 0.8356 oz. ASW, 38.61 mm. **Ruler:** Elizabeth II **Subject:** David MacKay

Date	Mintage	F12	VF20	XF40	MS60	MS63
2006	—	PF63 45.00	PF65 50.00			

KM# 179a 5 POUNDS
28.28 g., 0.925 Silver 0.8356 oz. ASW, 38.61 mm. **Ruler:** Elizabeth II **Subject:** Elizabeth II and Prince Philip, 60th Wedding Anniversary **Rev:** Westminster Abbey

Date	Mintage	F12	VF20	XF40	MS60	MS63
2007	—	PF63 55.00	PF65 60.00			

KM# 178a 5 POUNDS
28.28 g., 0.925 Silver 0.8356 oz. ASW, 38.61 mm. **Ruler:** Elizabeth II **Subject:** Elizabeth II and Prince Philip, 60th Wedding Anniversary **Rev:** Elizabeth and Philip, 1947

Date	Mintage	F12	VF20	XF40	MS60	MS63
2007	—	PF63 55.00	PF65 60.00			

KM# 180a 5 POUNDS
28.28 g., 0.925 Silver 0.8356 oz. ASW, 38.61 mm. **Ruler:** Elizabeth II **Subject:** Elizabeth II and Prince Philip, 60th Wedding Anniversary **Rev:** Wedding cake

Date	Mintage	F12	VF20	XF40	MS60	MS63
2007	—	PF63 55.00	PF65 60.00			

KM# 181a 5 POUNDS
28.28 g., 0.925 Silver 0.8356 oz. ASW, 38.61 mm. **Ruler:** Elizabeth II **Subject:** Elizabeth II and Prince Philip, 60th Wedding Anniversary **Rev:** Elizabeth and Philip, 2007

Date	Mintage	F12	VF20	XF40	MS60	MS63
2007	—	PF63 55.00	PF65 60.00			

KM# 174 5 POUNDS
28.28 g., 0.925 Silver 0.8356 oz. ASW, 38.61 mm. **Ruler:** Elizabeth II **Subject:** Elizabeth, the Queen Mother

Date	Mintage	F12	VF20	XF40	MS60	MS63
2007	Est. 2500	PF63 55.00	PF65 60.00			

KM# 175 5 POUNDS
28.28 g., 0.925 Silver 0.8356 oz. ASW, 38.61 mm. **Ruler:** Elizabeth II **Subject:** Henry VIII

Date	Mintage	F12	VF20	XF40	MS60	MS63
2007	Est. 25000	PF63 55.00	PF65 60.00			

KM# 176 5 POUNDS
28.28 g., 0.925 Silver 0.8356 oz. ASW, 38.61 mm. **Ruler:** Elizabeth II **Subject:** Diana, Princess of Wales

Date	Mintage	F12	VF20	XF40	MS60	MS63
2007	Est. 25000	PF63 55.00	PF65 60.00			

KM# 177 5 POUNDS
28.28 g., 0.925 Silver 0.8356 oz. ASW, 38.61 mm. **Ruler:** Elizabeth II **Subject:** Christopher Wren

Date	Mintage	F12	VF20	XF40	MS60	MS63
2007	Est. 25000	PF63 55.00	PF65 60.00			

KM# 178 5 POUNDS
28.28 g., Copper-Nickel, 38.61 mm. **Ruler:** Elizabeth II **Subject:** Elizabeth II and Prince Philip, 60th Wedding Anniversary **Rev:** Elizabeth and Philip, 1947

Date	Mintage	F12	VF20	XF40	MS60	MS63
2007	—	—	—	—	—	15.00

KM# 179 5 POUNDS
28.28 g., Copper-Nickel, 38.61 mm. **Ruler:** Elizabeth II **Subject:** Elizabeth II and Prince Philip, 60th Wedding Anniversary **Rev:** Westminster Abbey

Date	Mintage	F12	VF20	XF40	MS60	MS63
2007	—	—	—	—	—	15.00

KM# 180 5 POUNDS
28.28 g., Copper-Nickel, 38.61 mm. **Ruler:** Elizabeth II **Subject:** Elizabeth II and Prince Philip, 60th Wedding Anniversary **Rev:** Wedding cake

Date	Mintage	F12	VF20	XF40	MS60	MS63
2007	—	—	—	—	—	15.00

KM# 181 5 POUNDS
28.28 g., Copper-Nickel, 38.61 mm. **Ruler:** Elizabeth II **Subject:** Elizabeth II and Prince Philip, 60th Wedding Anniversary **Rev:** Elizabeth and Prince Philip, 2007

Date	Mintage	F12	VF20	XF40	MS60	MS63
2007	—	—	—	—	—	15.00

KM# 182a 5 POUNDS
26.00 g., Brass, 38.61 mm. **Ruler:** Elizabeth II **Subject:** Royal Air Force **Rev:** Barnes Wallis, Roy Chadwick, Guy Penrose Gibson

Date	Mintage	F12	VF20	XF40	MS60	MS63
2008	Est. 25000	PF63 25.00		PF65 30.00		

KM# 182b 5 POUNDS
28.28 g., 0.925 Silver 0.8356 oz. ASW, 38.61 mm. **Ruler:** Elizabeth II **Subject:** Royal Air Force **Rev:** Barnes Wallis, Roy Chadwick, Guy Penrose Gibson

Date	Mintage	F12	VF20	XF40	MS60	MS63
2008	Est. 25000	PF63 55.00		PF65 60.00		

KM# 183a 5 POUNDS
28.28 g., 0.925 Silver 0.8356 oz. ASW, 38.61 mm. **Ruler:** Elizabeth II **Subject:** Royal Air Force **Rev:** Reginald Joseph Mitchell, Spitfire

Date	Mintage	F12	VF20	XF40	MS60	MS63
2008	—	PF63 55.00		PF65 60.00		

KM# 186a 5 POUNDS
28.28 g., 0.925 Silver 0.8356 oz. ASW, 38.61 mm. **Ruler:** Elizabeth II **Subject:** Royal Air Force **Rev:** Hugh Trenchard, founder of the British Air Force

Date	Mintage	F12	VF20	XF40	MS60	MS63
2008	—	PF63 55.00		PF65 60.00		

KM# 193.1 5 POUNDS
Copper-Nickel, 38.61 mm. **Ruler:** Elizabeth II **Obv:** Head in tiara right **Rev:** Sundial motif **Shape:** Number 8

Date	Mintage	F12	VF20	XF40	MS60	MS63
2008	—	—	—	—	—	18.00

KM# 182 5 POUNDS
28.28 g., Copper-Nickel, 38.61 mm. **Ruler:** Elizabeth II **Subject:** Royal Air Force **Rev:** Barnes Wallis, Roy Chadwick, Guy Penrose Gibson

Date	Mintage	F12	VF20	XF40	MS60	MS63
2008	—	—	—	—	—	15.00

KM# 183 5 POUNDS
28.28 g., Copper-Nickel, 38.61 mm. **Ruler:** Elizabeth II **Subject:** Royal Air Force **Rev:** Reginald Joseph Mitchell, Spitfire

Date	Mintage	F12	VF20	XF40	MS60	MS63
2008	—	—	—	—	—	15.00

KM# 184 5 POUNDS
28.28 g., Copper-Nickel, 38.61 mm. **Ruler:** Elizabeth II **Subject:** Royal Air Force **Rev:** Battle of Britain

Date	Mintage	F12	VF20	XF40	MS60	MS63
2008	—	—	—	—	—	15.00

KM# 185 5 POUNDS
28.28 g., Copper-Nickel, 38.61 mm. **Ruler:** Elizabeth II **Subject:** Royal Air Force **Rev:** Frank Whittle

Date	Mintage	F12	VF20	XF40	MS60	MS63
2008	—	—	—	—	—	15.00

KM# 186 5 POUNDS
28.28 g., Copper-Nickel, 38.61 mm. **Ruler:** Elizabeth II **Subject:** Royal Air Force **Rev:** Hugh Trenchard, founder of the British Air Force

Date	Mintage	F12	VF20	XF40	MS60	MS63
2008	—	—	—	—	—	15.00

KM# 187 5 POUNDS
28.28 g., Copper-Nickel, 38.61 mm. **Ruler:** Elizabeth II **Subject:** British Air Force

Date	Mintage	F12	VF20	XF40	MS60	MS63
2008	—	—	—	—	—	15.00

KM# 188 5 POUNDS
28.28 g., Copper-Nickel, 38.61 mm. **Ruler:** Elizabeth II **Subject:** Royal Air Force

Date	Mintage	F12	VF20	XF40	MS60	MS63
2008	—	—	—	—	—	15.00

KM# 189 5 POUNDS
28.28 g., Copper-Nickel, 38.61 mm. **Ruler:** Elizabeth II **Subject:** Royal Air Force

Date	Mintage	F12	VF20	XF40	MS60	MS63
2008						

KM# 190 5 POUNDS
28.28 g., Copper-Nickel, 38.61 mm. **Ruler:** Elizabeth II **Subject:** Royal Air Force

Date	Mintage	F12	VF20	XF40	MS60	MS63
2008	—	—	—	—	—	15.00

KM# 191 5 POUNDS
28.28 g., Copper-Nickel, 38.61 mm. **Ruler:** Elizabeth II **Subject:** Royal Air Force

Date	Mintage	F12	VF20	XF40	MS60	MS63
2008	—	—	—	—	—	15.00

KM# 193.2 5 POUNDS
Copper-Nickel, 38.61 mm. **Ruler:** Elizabeth II **Subject:** End of World War I **Obv:** Head in tiara right **Rev:** Sundial motif in color **Shape:** Number 8

Date	Mintage	F12	VF20	XF40	MS60	MS63
2008	—	—	—	—	—	25.00

KM# 193a 5 POUNDS
28.00 g., 0.925 Silver 0.8273 oz. ASW, 38.61 mm. **Ruler:** Elizabeth II **Subject:** End of World War I **Obv:** Head with tiara right **Rev:** Sundial motif **Shape:** Number 8

Date	Mintage	F12	VF20	XF40	MS60	MS63
2008	9,500	PF63 55.00		PF65 60.00		

KM# 193b 5 POUNDS
28.00 g., 0.916 Gold 0.8193 oz. AGW, 38.61 mm. **Ruler:** Elizabeth II **Subject:** End of World War I **Obv:** Head with tiara right **Rev:** Sundial motif **Shape:** Numeral 8

Date	Mintage	F12	VF20	XF40	MS60	MS63
2008	Est. 450	PF65 1,500				

KM# 194 5 POUNDS
Silver **Ruler:** Elizabeth II **Rev:** St. George slaying the dragon

Date	Mintage	F12	VF20	XF40	MS60	MS63
2008	—	—	—	—	—	—

KM# 146 5 POUNDS
28.28 g., 0.925 Silver 0.8356 oz. ASW, 38.6 mm. **Ruler:** Elizabeth II **Subject:** Battle of Agincourt, 1415 **Obv:** Head right **Rev:** Archers and horsemen

Date	Mintage	F12	VF20	XF40	MS60	MS63
2009	2,500	PF63 50.00		PF65 55.00		

KM# 147 5 POUNDS
155.50 g., 0.925 Silver 4.5947 oz. ASW, 65 mm. **Ruler:** Elizabeth II **Obv:** Head right **Rev:** St. George slaying dragon, partially gilt

Date	Mintage	F12	VF20	XF40	MS60	MS63
2009	450	PF65 350				

KM# 195a 5 POUNDS
28.28 g., 0.925 Silver 0.8356 oz. ASW, 38.61 mm. **Ruler:** Elizabeth II **Subject:** Henry VIII, 500th Anniversary of reign

Date	Mintage	F12	VF20	XF40	MS60	MS63
2009	—	PF63 55.00		PF65 60.00		

KM# 211a 5 POUNDS
28.28 g., 0.925 Silver 0.8356 oz. ASW, 38.61 mm. **Ruler:** Elizabeth II **Subject:** James Cook

Date	Mintage	F12	VF20	XF40	MS60	MS63
2009	—	PF63 55.00		PF65 60.00		

KM# 212a 5 POUNDS
28.28 g., 0.925 Silver 0.8356 oz. ASW, 38.61 mm. **Ruler:** Elizabeth II **Subject:** Robert F. Scott

Date	Mintage	F12	VF20	XF40	MS60	MS63
2009	—	PF63 55.00		PF65 60.00		

KM# 213a 5 POUNDS
28.28 g., 0.925 Silver 0.8356 oz. ASW, 38.61 mm. **Ruler:** Elizabeth II **Subject:** Naval Airforce

Date	Mintage	F12	VF20	XF40	MS60	MS63
2009	—	PF63 55.00		PF65 60.00		

KM# 214a 5 POUNDS
28.28 g., 0.925 Copper-Nickel 0.8356 oz., 38.61 mm. **Ruler:** Elizabeth II **Subject:** Falkland War

Date	Mintage	F12	VF20	XF40	MS60	MS63
2009	—	PF63 55.00		PF65 60.00		

KM# 216 5 POUNDS
28.28 g., 0.925 Silver 0.8356 oz. ASW, 38.61 mm. **Ruler:** Elizabeth II **Subject:** H.M.S. Ark Royal

Date	Mintage	F12	VF20	XF40	MS60	MS63
2009	—	PF63 55.00		PF65 60.00		

KM# 195 5 POUNDS
28.28 g., Copper-Nickel, 38.61 mm. **Ruler:** Elizabeth II **Subject:** Henry VIII, 500th Anniversary of reign

Date	Mintage	F12	VF20	XF40	MS60	MS63
2009	—	—	—	—	—	15.00

KM# 195b 5 POUNDS
39.94 g., 0.916 Gold 1.1687 oz. AGW, 38.91 mm. **Ruler:** Elizabeth II **Subject:** Henry VIII, 500th Anniversary of reign

Date	Mintage	F12	VF20	XF40	MS60	MS63
2009	—	PF65 2,150				

KM# 197 5 POUNDS
28.28 g., 0.925 Silver 0.8356 oz. ASW, 38.61 mm. **Ruler:** Elizabeth II **Subject:** British Battles - Agincourt

Date	Mintage	F12	VF20	XF40	MS60	MS63
2009	25,000	PF63 55.00		PF65 60.00		

KM# 198 5 POUNDS
28.28 g., 0.925 Silver 0.8356 oz. ASW, 38.61 mm. **Ruler:** Elizabeth II **Subject:** British Battles - Somme

Date	Mintage	F12	VF20	XF40	MS60	MS63
2009	Est. 25000	PF63 55.00		PF65 60.00		

KM# 199 5 POUNDS
28.28 g., 0.925 Silver 0.8356 oz. ASW, 38.61 mm. **Ruler:** Elizabeth II **Subject:** British Battles - Normandie

Date	Mintage	F12	VF20	XF40	MS60	MS63
2009	Est. 25000	PF63 55.00		PF65 60.00		

KM# 200 5 POUNDS
28.28 g., 0.925 Silver 0.8356 oz. ASW, 38.61 mm. **Ruler:** Elizabeth II **Subject:** British Battles - El Alamein

Date	Mintage	F12	VF20	XF40	MS60	MS63
2009	Est. 25000	PF63 55.00		PF65 60.00		

KM# 201 5 POUNDS
28.28 g., 0.925 Silver 0.8356 oz. ASW, 38.61 mm. **Ruler:** Elizabeth II **Subject:** British Battles - Hastings

Date	Mintage	F12	VF20	XF40	MS60	MS63
2009	Est. 25000	PF63 55.00		PF65 60.00		

KM# 202 5 POUNDS
28.28 g., 0.925 Silver 0.8356 oz. ASW, 38.61 mm. **Ruler:** Elizabeth II **Subject:** British Battles - Bosworth

Date	Mintage	F12	VF20	XF40	MS60	MS63
2009	Est. 25000	PF63 55.00		PF65 60.00		

KM# 203 5 POUNDS
28.28 g., 0.925 Silver 0.8356 oz. ASW, 38.61 mm. **Ruler:** Elizabeth II **Subject:** British Battles - Naseby

Date	Mintage	F12	VF20	XF40	MS60	MS63
2009	Est. 25000	PF63 55.00		PF65 60.00		

KM# 204 5 POUNDS
28.28 g., 0.925 Silver 0.8356 oz. ASW, 38.61 mm. **Ruler:** Elizabeth II **Subject:** British Battles - Culloden

Date	Mintage	F12	VF20	XF40	MS60	MS63
2009	Est. 25000	PF63 55.00		PF65 60.00		

KM# 205 5 POUNDS
28.28 g., 0.925 Silver 0.8356 oz. ASW, 38.61 mm. **Ruler:** Elizabeth II **Subject:** British Battles - Waterloo

Date	Mintage	F12	VF20	XF40	MS60	MS63
2009	—	PF63 55.00		PF65 60.00		

KM# 206 5 POUNDS
28.28 g., 0.925 Silver 0.8356 oz. ASW, 38.61 mm. **Ruler:** Elizabeth II **Subject:** British Battles - Alma

Date	Mintage	F12	VF20	XF40	MS60	MS63
2009	Est. 25000	PF63 55.00		PF65 60.00		

KM# 207 5 POUNDS
28.28 g., 0.925 Silver 0.8356 oz. ASW, 38.61 mm. **Ruler:** Elizabeth II **Subject:** British Battles - Rorkes Drift

Date	Mintage	F12	VF20	XF40	MS60	MS63
2009	Est. 25000	PF63 55.00		PF65 60.00		

KM# 208 5 POUNDS
28.28 g., 0.925 Silver 0.8356 oz. ASW, 38.61 mm. **Ruler:** Elizabeth II **Subject:** British Battles - Mafeking

Date	Mintage	F12	VF20	XF40	MS60	MS63
2009	Est. 25000	PF63 55.00		PF65 60.00		

KM# 211 5 POUNDS
28.28 g., Copper-Nickel, 38.61 mm. **Ruler:** Elizabeth II **Subject:** James Cook

Date	Mintage	F12	VF20	XF40	MS60	MS63
2009	—	—	—	—	—	15.00

KM# 212 5 POUNDS
28.28 g., Copper-Nickel, 38.61 mm. **Ruler:** Elizabeth II **Subject:** Robert F. Scott

Date	Mintage	F12	VF20	XF40	MS60	MS63
2009	—	—	—	—	—	15.00

KM# 213 5 POUNDS
28.28 g., Copper-Nickel, 38.61 mm. **Ruler:** Elizabeth II **Subject:** Naval Airforce

Date	Mintage	F12	VF20	XF40	MS60	MS63
2009	—	—	—	—	—	15.00

KM# 214 5 POUNDS
28.28 g., Copper-Nickel, 38.61 mm. **Ruler:** Elizabeth II **Subject:** Falkland War

Date	Mintage	F12	VF20	XF40	MS60	MS63
2009	—	—	—	—	—	15.00

KM# 215 5 POUNDS
28.28 g., Copper-Nickel, 38.61 mm. **Ruler:** Elizabeth II **Subject:** H.M.S. Ark Royal

Date	Mintage	F12	VF20	XF40	MS60	MS63
2009	—	—	—	—	—	15.00

KM# 217 5 POUNDS
28.28 g., 0.925 Silver 0.8356 oz. ASW, 38.6 mm. **Ruler:** Elizabeth II **Obv:** Head with tiara right **Rev:** Katherine Middleton and Prince William facing

Date	Mintage	F12	VF20	XF40	MS60	MS63
2011	—	PF63 75.00		PF65 85.00		

KM# 143 10 POUNDS
155.50 g., 0.925 Silver 4.5947 oz. ASW, 65 mm. **Ruler:** Elizabeth II **Subject:** 50th Anniversary of Coronation **Obv:** Queens silver portrait on gold plated fields **Rev:** Crown and scepter above arms, gold plated

Date	Mintage	F12	VF20	XF40	MS60	MS63
2003	2,000	—	—	—	135	150

KM# 154 10 POUNDS
155.50 g., 0.916 Gold 4.550 oz. AGW, 65 mm. **Ruler:** Elizabeth II **Subject:** Crimean War, 150th anniversary **Rev:** Light Brigade, Earl of Cardigan

Date	Mintage	F12	VF20	XF40	MS60	MS63
2004	—	PF65 8,500				

KM# 159 10 POUNDS
155.50 g., 0.925 Silver 4.5947 oz. ASW, 65 mm. **Ruler:** Elizabeth II **Subject:** End of World War II, 60th Anniversary **Rev:** Parlament buildings

Date	Mintage	F12	VF20	XF40	MS60	MS63
2005	—	PF63 175	PF65 200			

KM# 161 10 POUNDS
155.50 g., 0.916 Gold 4.550 oz. AGW, 65 mm. **Ruler:** Elizabeth II **Subject:** Trafalgar, 200th Anniversary

Date	Mintage	F12	VF20	XF40	MS60	MS63
2005	—	PF65 8,500				

KM# 192 10 POUNDS
155.50 g., 0.925 Silver 4.5947 oz. ASW, 65 mm. **Ruler:** Elizabeth II **Subject:** Royal Air Force **Rev:** Reginald Joseph Mitchell, founder of the Royal Air Force

Date	Mintage	F12	VF20	XF40	MS60	MS63
2008	Est. 1943	PF65 200				

KM# 112 25 POUNDS
7.98 g., 0.9167 Gold 0.2337 oz. AGW, 22.05 mm. **Ruler:** Elizabeth II **Subject:** Princess Diana **Obv:** Crowned head right **Rev:** Diana's portrait **Edge:** Reeded

Date	Mintage	F12	VF20	XF40	MS60	MS63
2002	2,500	PF63 425	PF65 450			

KM# 114 25 POUNDS
7.98 g., 0.9166 Gold 0.2337 oz. AGW, 22 mm. **Ruler:** Elizabeth II **Subject:** Queen Mother **Obv:** Crowned head right **Rev:** Queen Mother's portrait circa 1918 **Edge:** Reeded

Date	Mintage	F12	VF20	XF40	MS60	MS63
2002	2,500	PF63 425	PF65 450			

KM# 116 25 POUNDS
7.98 g., 0.9166 Gold 0.2337 oz. AGW, 22 mm. **Ruler:** Elizabeth II **Subject:** Golden Jubilee **Obv:** Crowned head right **Rev:** Abbey procession scene **Edge:** Reeded

Date	Mintage	F12	VF20	XF40	MS60	MS63
2002	2,500	PF63 425	PF65 450			

KM# 118 25 POUNDS
7.98 g., 0.9166 Gold 0.2337 oz. AGW, 22 mm. **Ruler:** Elizabeth II **Subject:** Duke of Wellington **Obv:** Crowned head right **Rev:** Wellington's portrait with infantry scene **Edge:** Reeded

Date	Mintage	F12	VF20	XF40	MS60	MS63
2002	2,500	PF63 425	PF65 450			

KM# 151 25 POUNDS
7.98 g., 0.916 Gold 0.2335 oz. AGW, 22.05 mm. **Ruler:** Elizabeth II **Rev:** Multipe portraits of Alfred, Drake, Nelson, Fisher and Woodward and the Mary Rose, Visctory, Warspite, Ark Royal and Conqueror

Date	Mintage	F12	VF20	XF40	MS60	MS63
2003	—	PF63 425	PF65 450			

KM# 120 25 POUNDS
7.98 g., 0.9166 Gold 0.2337 oz. AGW, 22 mm. **Ruler:** Elizabeth II **Subject:** Golden Jubilee **Obv:** Crowned head right **Rev:** Honor guard and monument **Edge:** Reeded

Date	Mintage	F12	VF20	XF40	MS60	MS63
2003	5,000	PF63 425	PF65 450			

KM# 155 25 POUNDS
7.98 g., 0.916 Gold 0.2335 oz. AGW, 22.05 mm. **Ruler:** Elizabeth II **Subject:** Crimean War, 150th anniversary **Rev:** Light Brigade, Earl of Cardigan

Date	Mintage	F12	VF20	XF40	MS60	MS63
2004	—	PF63 425	PF65 450			

KM# 125 25 POUNDS
7.98 g., 0.9167 Gold 0.2337 oz. AGW, 22 mm. **Ruler:** Elizabeth II **Subject:** D-Day **Obv:** Crowned head right **Rev:** British Horsa gliders in flight **Edge:** Reeded

Date	Mintage	F12	VF20	XF40	MS60	MS63
2004	500	PF63 425	PF65 450			

KM# 152 25 POUNDS
7.98 g., 0.916 Gold 0.2335 oz. AGW, 22.05 mm. **Ruler:** Elizabeth II **Rev:** Locomotive 6220 Coronation, and LMSR Pacific

Date	Mintage	F12	VF20	XF40	MS60	MS63
2004	Est. 2500	PF63 425	PF65 450			

KM# 153 25 POUNDS
7.98 g., 0.916 Gold 0.2335 oz. AGW, 22.05 mm. **Ruler:** Elizabeth II **Rev:** British Railway's locomotive 92229 Evening Star

Date	Mintage	F12	VF20	XF40	MS60	MS63
2004	Est. 2500	PF63 425	PF65 450			

KM# 156 25 POUNDS
7.98 g., 0.916 Gold 0.2335 oz. AGW, 22.05 mm. **Ruler:** Elizabeth II **Subject:** Royal Navy **Rev:** H.M.S. Vicotry

Date	Mintage	F12	VF20	XF40	MS60	MS63
2004	—	PF63 425	PF65 450			

KM# 157 25 POUNDS
7.98 g., 0.916 Gold 0.2335 oz. AGW, 22.05 mm. **Ruler:** Elizabeth II **Subject:** Royal Navy **Rev:** Admiral Andrew B. Cunningham

Date	Mintage	F12	VF20	XF40	MS60	MS63
2004	—	PF63 425	PF65 450			

KM# 158 25 POUNDS
7.98 g., 0.916 Gold 0.2335 oz. AGW, 22.05 mm. **Ruler:** Elizabeth II **Subject:** Royal Navy **Rev:** Submarine H.M.S. Conqueror

Date	Mintage	F12	VF20	XF40	MS60	MS63
2004	—	PF63 425	PF65 450			

KM# 162 25 POUNDS
7.98 g., 0.916 Gold 0.2335 oz. AGW, 22.05 mm. **Ruler:** Elizabeth II **Subject:** Trafalgar, 200th Anniversary

Date	Mintage	F12	VF20	XF40	MS60	MS63
2005	—	PF63 425	PF65 450			

KM# 196 25 POUNDS
7.98 g., 0.916 Gold 0.2335 oz. AGW, 22.05 mm. **Ruler:** Elizabeth II **Subject:** Henry VIII, 500th Anniversary of reign

Date	Mintage	F12	VF20	XF40	MS60	MS63
2009	Est. 995	PF63 425	PF65 450			

KM# 209 25 POUNDS
7.98 g., 0.916 Gold 0.2335 oz. AGW, 22.05 mm. **Ruler:** Elizabeth II **Subject:** British Battles - Agincourt

Date	Mintage	F12	VF20	XF40	MS60	MS63
2009	Est. 995	PF63 425	PF65 450			

KM# 210 25 POUNDS
7.98 g., 0.916 Gold 0.2335 oz. AGW, 22.05 mm. **Ruler:** Elizabeth II **Subject:** British Battles - Somme

Date	Mintage	F12	VF20	XF40	MS60	MS63
2009	Est. 995	PF63 425	PF65 450			

KM# 122 50 POUNDS
1000.00 g., 0.925 Silver 29.548 oz. ASW, 100 mm. **Ruler:** Elizabeth II **Obv:** Crowned head right **Rev:** Bust facing and crowned arms with supporters **Edge:** Reeded

Date	Mintage	F12	VF20	XF40	MS60	MS63
2003	500	PF63 1,000	PF65 1,150			

PIEDFORT

P# 4 5 POUNDS
56.56 g., 0.925 Silver 1.6712 oz. ASW **Ruler:** Elizabeth II **Note:** KM#195a but with enamel

	Date	Mintage	Identification				Mkt Val
4	2009	Est. 450	5 Pounds 0.925 Silver KM#195a but with enamel				125
P3	2002	100	5 Pounds 0.9166 Gold Queen's portrait Abbey procession scene Underweight piefort				1,900

MINT SETS

KM#	Date	Mintage	Identification	Issue Price	Mkt Val
MS7	2004 (1)	—	Jersey KM#126, Guernsey KM#155, Alderney KM#43, 150th Anniversary of the Crimean War	—	100

JORDAN

The Hashemite Kingdom of Jordan, a constitutional monarchy in southwest Asia, has an area of 37,738 sq. mi.(91,880 sq. km.) and a population of 3.5 million. Capital: Amman. Agriculture and tourism comprise Jordan's economic base. Chief exports are phosphates, tomatoes and oranges.

RULER
Abdullah Ibn Al-Hussein, 1999-

MONETARY SYSTEM
100 Piastres = 1 Dinar

KINGDOM
DECIMAL COINAGE

KM# 78.1 QIRSH (Piastre)
5.47 g., Copper Plated Steel, 25 mm. **Ruler:** Abdullah II **Obv:** King Abdullah II **Rev:** Christian date left, Islamic date right **Edge:** Plain

Date	Mintage	F12	VF20	XF40	MS60	MS63
AH1430-2009	—	—	—	—	1.00	1.50
AH1432-2011	—	—	—	—	1.00	1.50

KM# 78.2 QIRSH (Piastre)
5.47 g., Copper Plated Steel, 24.9 mm. **Ruler:** Abdullah **Obv:** King Abdullah II **Rev:** Islamic date left, Christian date right **Edge:** Plain

Date	Mintage	F12	VF20	XF40	MS60	MS63
AH1430-2009	—	—	—	—	7.50	10.00

KM# 73 5 PIASTRES
5.00 g., Copper Plated Steel, 25.8 mm. **Ruler:** Abdullah II **Obv:** Bust right **Rev:** Value to left within lines below date with written value at lower right **Edge:** Milled

Date	Mintage	F12	VF20	XF40	MS60	MS63
AH1427-2006	—	—	—	—	1.50	2.00
AH1429-2008	—	—	—	—	1.50	2.00
AH1430-2009	—	—	—	—	1.50	2.00
AH1433-2012	—	—	—	—	1.50	2.00

KM# 74 10 PIASTRES
8.00 g., Nickel Plated Steel, 28 mm. **Ruler:** Abdullah II **Obv:** Bust right **Rev:** Value at left within lines below date with written value at lower right **Edge:** Milled

Date	Mintage	F12	VF20	XF40	MS60	MS63
AH1425-2004	—	—	—	—	1.75	3.50
AH1427-2006	—	—	—	—	1.75	3.50
AH1429-2008	—	—	—	—	1.75	3.50
AH1430-2009	—	—	—	—	1.75	3.50
AH1433-2012	—	—	—	—	1.75	3.50

KM# 83 1/4 DINAR
7.40 g., Nickel-Brass, 26.5 mm. **Ruler:** Abdullah II **Obv:** Bust right **Edge:** Plain **Shape:** 7-sided

Date	Mintage	F12	VF20	XF40	MS60	MS63
AH1425-2004	—	—	—	—	2.00	3.00
AH1427-2006	—	—	—	—	2.00	3.00
AH1429-2008	—	—	—	—	2.00	3.00
AH1430-2009	—	—	—	—	2.00	3.00

KM# 79 1/2 DINAR
9.67 g., Bi-Metallic, 29 mm. **Ruler:** Abdullah II **Obv:** Bust right within circle **Rev:** Value in center of circled wreath **Edge:** Plain **Shape:** 7-sided

Date	Mintage	F12	VF20	XF40	MS60	MS63
AH1427-2006	—	—	—	—	3.00	4.00
AH1429-2008	—	—	—	—	3.00	4.00
AH1430-2009	—	—	—	—	3.00	4.00

KM# 75 3 DINARS
28.50 g., Brass, 40 mm. **Ruler:** Abdullah II **Subject:** Amman: Arabic Culture Capital **Obv:** Bust right **Rev:** Building **Edge:** Milled

Date	Mintage	F12	VF20	XF40	MS60	MS63
AH1423//2002	2,000	—	—	—	130	150

Note: Only 500 sold to collectors. Rest were taken by Amman municipality as official gifts

KM# 86 5 DINARS
120.00 g., Bronze, 60 mm. **Ruler:** Abdullah **Subject:** Selection of Petra as one of the new Seven Wonders of the World **Obv:** King Abdullah II and Queen Rania **Rev:** Petra **Edge:** Milled

Date	Mintage	F12	VF20	XF40	MS60	MS63
AH1428-2008	500	PF63 160				

KM# 84 10 DINARS
120.00 g., 0.999 Silver 3.8294 oz. ASW, 60 mm. **Ruler:** Abdullah **Subject:** 60th Anniversary of Jordan's Independence **Obv:** King Abdullah I and Independence speech **Rev:** The National Assembly building **Edge:** Milled

Date	Mintage	F12	VF20	XF40	MS60	MS63
2006	250	PF63 350				

Note: Issued primarily for use as official state gifts

KM# 88 10 DINARS
31.11 g., 0.999 Silver 0.9926 oz. ASW, 40 mm. **Ruler:** Abdullah II **Subject:** Accession, 10th Anniversary **Obv:** Bust facing **Rev:** Crowned and mantled shield

Date	Mintage	F12	VF20	XF40	MS60	MS63
2009	2,250	PF63 150				

KM# 87 20 DINARS
120.00 g., 0.999 Silver 3.8294 oz. ASW, 60 mm. **Ruler:** Abdullah **Subject:** Selection of Petra as one of the new Seven Wonders of the World **Obv:** King Abdullah II and Queen Rania **Rev:** Petra **Edge:** Milled

Date	Mintage	F12	VF20	XF40	MS60	MS63
AH1428-2008	500	PF63 350				

KM# 89 50 DINARS
16.96 g., 0.999 Gold 0.5412 oz. AGW, 30 mm. **Ruler:** Abdullah II **Subject:** Accession, 10th Anniversary **Obv:** Bust **Rev:** Arms

Date	Mintage	F12	VF20	XF40	MS60	MS63
2009	1,750	PF63 975				

KM# 85 60 DINARS
72.75 g., 0.917 Gold 2.131 oz. AGW, 40 mm. **Ruler:** Abdullah **Subject:** 60th Anniversary of Jordan's Independence **Obv:** King Abdullah II **Rev:** Treasury in Petra **Edge:** Milled

Date	Mintage	F12	VF20	XF40	MS60	MS63
2006	250	PF63 3,750				

Note: Issued primarily for use as official state gifts

MINT SETS

KM#	Date	Mintage	Identification	Issue Price	Mkt Val
MS4	2000-2004 (5)	—	KM#73-74, 78.1, 79, 83, mixed dates	—	20.00

PROOF SETS

KM#	Date	Mintage	Identification	Issue Price	Mkt Val
PS14	2006 (2)	250	KM#84-85	—	3,500
PS15	2008 (2)	—	KM#86-87	—	425

KAZAKHSTAN

The Republic of Kazakhstan (formerly Kazakhstan S.S.R.) is bordered to the west by the Caspian Sea and Russia, to the north by Russia, in the east by the Peoples Republic of China and in the south by Uzbekistan and Kirghizia. It has an area of 1,049,155 sq. mi. (2,717,300 sq. km.) and a population of 16.7 million. Capital: Astana. Rich in mineral resources including coal, tungsten, copper, lead, zinc and manganese with huge oil and natural gas reserves. Agriculture is very important, (it previously represented 20 percent of the total arable acreage of the combined U.S.S.R.) Non-ferrous metallurgy, heavy engineering and chemical industries are leaders in its economy.

MONETARY SYSTEM
100 Tyin = 1 Tenge

REPUBLIC

DECIMAL COINAGE

KM# 23 TENGE
1.60 g., Nickel-Brass, 15 mm. **Obv:** National emblem **Rev:** Value flanked by designs **Edge:** Plain

Date	Mintage	F12	VF20	XF40	MS60	MS63
2002	—	—	—	—	0.50	0.85
2004	—	—	—	—	0.50	0.85
2005	—	—	—	—	0.50	0.85
2011	—	—	—	—	0.50	0.85
2012	—	—	—	—	0.50	0.85

KM# 64 2 TENGE
1.82 g., Nickel-Brass, 16 mm. **Obv:** National emblem **Rev:** Value flanked by designs **Edge:** Plain

Date	Mintage	F12	VF20	XF40	MS60	MS63
2005	—	—	—	—	0.65	1.20
2006	—	—	—	—	0.65	1.20

KM# 24 5 TENGE
2.20 g., Nickel-Brass, 17.3 mm. **Obv:** National emblem **Rev:** Value flanked by designs

Date	Mintage	F12	VF20	XF40	MS60	MS63
2002	—	—	—	—	0.50	0.85
2004	—	—	—	—	0.50	0.85
2005	—	—	—	—	0.50	0.85
2006	—	—	—	—	0.50	0.85
2010	—	—	—	—	0.50	0.85
2011	—	—	—	—	0.50	0.85
2012	—	—	—	—	0.50	0.85

KM# 25 10 TENGE
2.80 g., Nickel-Brass, 19.6 mm. **Obv:** National emblem **Rev:** Value above design

Date	Mintage	F12	VF20	XF40	MS60	MS63
2002	—	—	—	—	0.75	1.25
2004	—	—	—	—	0.75	1.25
2005	—	—	—	—	0.75	1.25
2006	—	—	—	—	0.75	1.25
2010	—	—	—	—	0.75	1.25
2011	—	—	—	—	0.75	1.25
2012	—	—	—	—	0.75	1.25

KM# 26 20 TENGE
2.90 g., Copper-Nickel-Zinc, 18.3 mm. **Obv:** National emblem **Rev:** Value above design **Edge:** Segmented reeding **Edge Lettering:** * CTO TENGE * Y 3 TENGE

Date	Mintage	F12	VF20	XF40	MS60	MS63
2002	—	—	—	—	1.00	1.75
2004	—	—	—	—	1.00	1.75
2006	—	—	—	—	1.00	1.75
2010	—	—	—	—	1.00	1.75
2011	—	—	—	—	1.00	1.75
2012	—	—	—	—	1.00	1.75

KM# 27 50 TENGE
4.70 g., Copper-Nickel-Zinc, 23 mm. **Obv:** National emblem **Rev:** Value above design

Date	Mintage	F12	VF20	XF40	MS60	MS63
2002	—	—	—	—	2.00	3.50

KM# 40 50 TENGE
11.50 g., Copper-Nickel, 31 mm. **Obv:** Eagle superimposed on ornate 10 **Edge:** Reeded and plain sections

Date	Mintage	F12	VF20	XF40	MS60	MS63
2001	—	—	—	—	4.00	6.50

KM# 41 50 TENGE
11.20 g., Copper-Nickel, 31.1 mm. **Subject:** Gabiden Mustafin **Obv:** National emblem above value **Rev:** Bust 1/4 left **Edge:** Segmented reeding

Date	Mintage	F12	VF20	XF40	MS60	MS63
ND(2002)	—	—	—	—	4.00	6.50

KM# 69 50 TENGE
Copper-Nickel, 31 mm. **Subject:** Gabit Mosrepov **Obv:** Symbol and value **Rev:** Bust facing

Date	Mintage	F12	VF20	XF40	MS60	MS63
2002	—	—	—	—	4.00	6.50

KM# 70 50 TENGE
Copper-Nickel, 31 mm. **Subject:** 200th Anniversary of Makhambet Utemisov **Obv:** Symbol and value

Date	Mintage	F12	VF20	XF40	MS60	MS63
2003	—	—	—	—	7.00	10.00

KM# 54 50 TENGE
11.50 g., Copper-Nickel, 31.1 mm. **Obv:** National emblem above value **Rev:** Painter Abylichan Kasteev (1904-1973) **Edge:** Reeded and plain sections

Date	Mintage	F12	VF20	XF40	MS60	MS63
2004	—	—	—	—	7.00	10.00

KM# 65 50 TENGE
11.50 g., Copper-Nickel, 31.1 mm. **Subject:** Alken Margulan **Obv:** National emblem above value **Rev:** Bust facing **Edge:** Segmented reeding

Date	Mintage	F12	VF20	XF40	MS60	MS63
2004	—	—	—	—	7.00	10.00

KM# 58 50 TENGE
11.50 g., Copper-Nickel, 31.1 mm. **Subject:** 10th Anniversary of the Constitution **Obv:** National emblem above value **Rev:** National emblem within circle above book **Edge:** Segmented reeding

Date	Mintage	F12	VF20	XF40	MS60	MS63
2005	—	—	—	—	7.00	10.00

KM# 71 50 TENGE
10.95 g., Copper-Nickel, 31 mm. **Subject:** 60 Years Victory WWII **Obv:** Symbol and value

Date	Mintage	F12	VF20	XF40	MS60	MS63
2005	—	—	—	—	7.00	10.00

KM# 73 50 TENGE
11.37 g., Copper-Nickel, 31 mm. **Obv:** Human figure and solar system **Rev:** Astronaut and solar system **Edge:** Segmented reeding

Date	Mintage	F12	VF20	XF40	MS60	MS63
2006	50,000	—	—	—	7.00	10.00

KM# 74 50 TENGE
11.37 g., Copper-Nickel, 31 mm. **Obv:** National arms on tapestry **Rev:** Woman with baby in cradle **Edge:** Segmented reeding

Date	Mintage	F12	VF20	XF40	MS60	MS63
2006	—	—	—	—	7.00	10.00

KM# 75 50 TENGE
11.37 g., Copper-Nickel, 31 mm. **Obv:** National arms **Rev:** Altai Snowcock **Edge:** Segmented reeding

Date	Mintage	F12	VF20	XF40	MS60	MS63
2006	50,000	—	—	—	7.00	10.00

KM# 77 50 TENGE
11.37 g., Copper-Nickel, 31 mm. **Obv:** National arms **Rev:** Altyn Kyran Order Breast Star **Edge:** Segmented reeding

Date	Mintage	F12	VF20	XF40	MS60	MS63
2006	50,000	—	—	—	7.00	10.00

KM# 78 50 TENGE
11.37 g., Copper-Nickel, 31 mm. **Obv:** National arms **Rev:** Zhubanov bust and music score **Edge:** Segmented reeding

Date	Mintage	F12	VF20	XF40	MS60	MS63
2006	50,000	—	—	—	7.00	10.00

KM# 79 50 TENGE
11.22 g., Copper-Nickel, 31 mm. **Subject:** 20th Anniversary **Obv:** National arms above value **Rev:** Happy woman **Edge:** Segmented reeding

Date	Mintage	F12	VF20	XF40	MS60	MS63
1986-2006	—	—	—	—	7.00	10.00

KM# 80 50 TENGE
10.89 g., Copper-Nickel, 31.10 mm. **Subject:** 50th Anniversary Launch of Sputnik I **Obv:** Stylized view of solar system **Obv. Legend:** REPUBLIC OF KAZAKHSTAN **Rev:** Sputnik I in space, earth in background **Rev. Legend:** THE FIRST SPACE SATELLITE OF THE EARTH **Edge:** Segmented reeding

Date	Mintage	F12	VF20	XF40	MS60	MS63
1957-2007	—				7.00	10.00

KM# 81 50 TENGE
11.11 g., Copper-Nickel, 31 mm. **Obv:** National arms, value below **Obv. Legend:** КАЗАКСТАН.... **Rev:** Eurasian Spoonbill standing left **Rev. Legend:** ... • PLATALEA LEUCORODIA **Edge:** Segmented reeding

Date	Mintage	F12	VF20	XF40	MS60	MS63
2007	—	—	—	—	7.00	10.00

KM# 164 50 TENGE
11.37 g., Copper-Nickel, 31 mm. **Obv:** National arms on tapestry **Rev:** Child and two men

Date	Mintage	F12	VF20	XF40	MS60	MS63
2007	—				7.00	10.00

KM# 165 50 TENGE
11.37 g., Copper-Nickel, 31 mm. **Obv:** National arms above value **Rev:** Otan badge

Date	Mintage	F12	VF20	XF40	MS60	MS63
2007	—				7.00	10.00

KM# 86 50 TENGE
Copper-Nickel, 31 mm. **Obv:** National Arms

Date	Mintage	F12	VF20	XF40	MS60	MS63
2008 Prooflike	—					12.00

KM# 169 50 TENGE
11.37 g., Copper-Nickel, 31 mm. **Obv:** National arms on tapersry background **Rev:** Two horsemen

Date	Mintage	F12	VF20	XF40	MS60	MS63
2008	—				7.00	10.00

KM# 170 50 TENGE
11.37 g., Copper-Nickel, 31 mm. **Obv:** National arms above vlaue **Rev:** Dank Order Star

Date	Mintage	F12	VF20	XF40	MS60	MS63
2008	—				7.00	10.00

KM# 171 50 TENGE
11.37 g., Copper-Nickel, 31 mm. **Obv:** National arms **Rev:** Aibyn Order Star

Date	Mintage	F12	VF20	XF40	MS60	MS63
2008	—				7.00	10.00

KM# 172 50 TENGE
11.37 g., Copper-Nickel, 31 mm. **Subject:** Astana capital, 10th Anniversary **Obv:** National arms **Rev:** Architecture

Date	Mintage	F12	VF20	XF40	MS60	MS63
2008	—	—	—	—	7.00	10.00

KM# 201 50 TENGE
11.37 g., Copper-Nickel, 31 mm. **Obv:** National emblem **Rev:** Building views

Date	Mintage	F12	VF20	XF40	MS60	MS63
2008	50,000	—	—	—	7.00	10.00

KM# 202 50 TENGE
11.37 g., Copper-Nickel, 31 mm. **Obv:** Human figure and solar system **Rev:** Spaceship Vostok

Date	Mintage	F12	VF20	XF40	MS60	MS63
2008	50,000	—	—	—	7.00	10.00

KM# 132 50 TENGE
Copper-Nickel, 31 mm. **Subject:** Betashar **Obv:** Arms **Rev:** Two figures standing

Date	Mintage	F12	VF20	XF40	MS60	MS63
2009	50,000				7.00	10.00

KM# 135 50 TENGE
0.50 g., 0.999 Gold AGW, 11 mm. **Obv:** Value **Rev:** Cat head sculpture

Date	Mintage	F12	VF20	XF40	MS60	MS63
2009	14,000	PF63 40.00	PF65 50.00			

KM# 140 50 TENGE
Copper-Nickel, 31 mm. **Obv:** Arms **Rev:** Parassat medal insignia

Date	Mintage	F12	VF20	XF40	MS60	MS63
2009	50,000	—	—	—	7.00	10.00

KM# 141 50 TENGE
Copper-Nickel **Obv:** Arms **Rev:** Porcupine advancing right **Shape:** 31

Date	Mintage	F12	VF20	XF40	MS60	MS63
2009	50,000	—	—	—	7.00	15.00

KM# 144 50 TENGE
Copper-Nickel, 31 mm. **Obv:** Man standing in solar system **Rev:** Apollo-Soyoz space craft

Date	Mintage	F12	VF20	XF40	MS60	MS63
2009	50,000	—	—	—	7.00	10.00

KM# 145 50 TENGE
Copper-Nickel, 31 mm. **Obv:** Arms **Rev:** Star of the Order of Dostyk

Date	Mintage	F12	VF20	XF40	MS60	MS63
2009	50,000	—	—	—	7.00	10.00

KM# 146 50 TENGE
Copper-Nickel, 31 mm. **Subject:** T. Bassenov, 100th Anniversary of Birth **Obv:** Arms **Rev:** Bust at right, architectural column

Date	Mintage	F12	VF20	XF40	MS60	MS63
2009	50,000	—	—	—	7.00	10.00

KM# 152 50 TENGE
0.50 g., 0.999 Gold AGW, 11 mm. **Subject:** Ahalavlinky Treasure **Obv:** Value **Rev:** Historical jewelry design

Date	Mintage	F12	VF20	XF40	MS60	MS63
2009	14,000	PF63 35.00	PF65 45.00			

KM# 174 50 TENGE
Copper-Nickel, 31 mm. **Subject:** Moon Exploration, 40th Anniversary **Obv:** Figure standing within solar system design **Rev:** Lunar Rover vehicle

Date	Mintage	F12	VF20	XF40	MS60	MS63
2010	—	—	—	—	7.00	10.00

KM# 175 50 TENGE
Copper-Nickel, 31 mm. **Subject:** Great Victory, 65th Anniversary **Obv:** National Emblem, value below **Rev:** Order star, 1945 above

Date	Mintage	F12	VF20	XF40	MS60	MS63
2010	—	—	—	—	7.00	10.00

KM# 224 50 TENGE
Copper-Nickel, 31 mm. **Obv:** Arms **Rev:** Star of the Order of Kormet

Date	Mintage	F12	VF20	XF40	MS60	MS63
2010	—	—	—	—	—	10.00

KM# 239 50 TENGE
11.37 g., Copper-Nickel, 31 mm. **Rev:** Curly head pelican

Date	Mintage	F12	VF20	XF40	MS60	MS63
2010 Proof	50,000	—	—	—	—	8.00

KM# 240 50 TENGE
11.37 g., Copper-Nickel, 31 mm. **Subject:** Qurmet Civilian Award

Date	Mintage	F12	VF20	XF40	MS60	MS63
2010	50,000	—	—	—	—	8.00

KM# 241 50 TENGE
11.37 g., Copper-Nickel, 31 mm. **Rev:** Horseman with Yerts Cross

Date	Mintage	F12	VF20	XF40	MS60	MS63
2010	50,000	—	—	—	—	8.00

KM# 206 50 TENGE
Copper-Nickel, 31 mm. **Subject:** Aktobe **Rev:** Griffin seal

Date	Mintage	F12	VF20	XF40	MS60	MS63
2011		—	—	—	2.25	7.50

KM# 207 50 TENGE
4.71 g., Copper-Nickel, 31 mm. **Subject:** Aitys **Obv:** National arms **Rev:** Celebration

Date	Mintage	F12	VF20	XF40	MS60	MS63
2011	50,000	—	—	—	2.25	7.50

KM# 208 50 TENGE
4.71 g., Copper-Nickel, 31 mm. **Subject:** Ust Kamenogorsk **Obv:** Shield **Rev:** Value

Date	Mintage	F12	VF20	XF40	MS60	MS63
2011	50,000	—	—	—	2.25	7.50

KM# 209 50 TENGE
4.71 g., Copper-Nickel **Subject:** Karaganda **Obv:** Shield **Rev:** Value

Date	Mintage	F12	VF20	XF40	MS60	MS63
2011	50,000	—	—	—	2.25	7.50

KM# 210 50 TENGE
Copper-Nickel, 31 mm. **Subject:** Independence, 20th Anniversary **Obv:** Arms **Rev:** Anniversary logo

Date	Mintage	F12	VF20	XF40	MS60	MS63
2011		—	—	—	5.00	10.00

KM# 253 50 TENGE
11.37 g., Copper-Nickel, 31 mm. **Subject:** Manned space flight, 50th Anniversary **Rev:** Juri A. Gagarin

Date	Mintage	F12	VF20	XF40	MS60	MS63
2011	50,000	—	—	—	—	8.00

KM# 256 50 TENGE
11.37 g., Copper-Nickel, 31 mm. **Rev:** Hawk

Date	Mintage	F12	VF20	XF40	MS60	MS63
2011	50,000	—	—	—	—	8.00

KM# 39 100 TENGE
6.23 g., Bi-Metallic, 24.4 mm. **Obv:** National emblem **Rev:** Value within lined circle flanked by designs **Edge:** Reeding over incuse value

Date	Mintage	F12	VF20	XF40	MS60	MS63
2002	—	—	—	—	3.50	5.50
2004	—	—	—	—	3.50	5.50
2005	—	—	—	—	3.50	5.50
2006	—	—	—	—	3.50	5.50
2007	—	—	—	—	3.50	5.50

KM# 49 100 TENGE
6.40 g., Bi-Metallic, 24.5 mm. **Obv:** Stylized chicken **Rev:** Value within lined circle flanked by designs **Edge:** Reeded and lettered

Date	Mintage	F12	VF20	XF40	MS60	MS63
2003	100,000	—	—	—	4.00	6.50

KM# 50 100 TENGE
6.40 g., Bi-Metallic, 24.5 mm. **Obv:** Stylized panther **Rev:** Value within lined circle flanked by designs **Edge:** Reeded and lettered

Date	Mintage	F12	VF20	XF40	MS60	MS63
2003	100,000	—	—	—	4.00	6.50

KM# 51 100 TENGE
6.40 g., Bi-Metallic, 24.5 mm. **Obv:** Stylized wolf's head **Rev:** Value within lined circle flanked by designs **Edge:** Reeded and lettered

Date	Mintage	F12	VF20	XF40	MS60	MS63
2003	100,000	—	—	—	4.00	6.50

KM# 52 100 TENGE
6.40 g., Bi-Metallic, 24.5 mm. **Obv:** Stylized sheep's head **Rev:** Value within lined circle flanked by designs **Edge:** Reeded and lettered

Date	Mintage	F12	VF20	XF40	MS60	MS63
2003	100,000	—	—	—	4.00	6.50

KM# 116 100 TENGE
31.10 g., 0.925 Silver 0.9189 oz. ASW, 37 mm. **Subject:** Olympics **Obv:** Arms and stylized stadium **Rev:** Two cyclists

Date	Mintage	F12	VF20	XF40	MS60	MS63
2004	—	PF65 55.00				

KM# 119 100 TENGE
31.10 g., 0.925 Silver 0.9189 oz. ASW, 37 mm. **Subject:** FIFA World Cup, Germany **Obv:** Arms and stylized stadium **Rev:** Two soccer players and large ball

Date	Mintage	F12	VF20	XF40	MS60	MS63
2004	—	PF65 55.00				

KM# 120 100 TENGE
1.24 g., 0.999 Gold 0.0396 oz. AGW, 13.92 mm. **Subject:** King Kroisos **Obv:** Arms **Rev:** Head left, coin, temple

Date	Mintage	F12	VF20	XF40	MS60	MS63
2004	—	PF63 75.00	PF65 85.00			

KM# 121 100 TENGE
1.24 g., 0.999 Gold 0.0396 oz. AGW, 13.92 mm. **Subject:** King Midas **Rev:** King Midas reclining on bench

Date	Mintage	F12	VF20	XF40	MS60	MS63
2004	—	PF63 75.00	PF65 85.00			

KM# 122 100 TENGE
1.24 g., 0.999 Gold 0.0396 oz. AGW, 13.92 mm. **Subject:** Ancient Turkestan **Obv:** Arms **Rev:** Camel caravan and building

Date	Mintage	F12	VF20	XF40	MS60	MS63
2004	—	PF63 75.00	PF65 85.00			

KM# 188 100 TENGE
1.24 g., 0.999 Gold 0.0396 oz. AGW, 13.92 mm. **Rev:** Marco Polo

Date	Mintage	F12	VF20	XF40	MS60	MS63
2004	15,000	PF63 85.00	PF65 100			

KM# 57 100 TENGE
6.40 g., Bi-Metallic, 24.5 mm. **Subject:** 60th Anniversary of the UN **Obv:** UN logo as part of the number 60 **Rev:** Value within lined circle flanked by designs **Edge:** Reeded and lettered

Date	Mintage	F12	VF20	XF40	MS60	MS63
2005	—	—	—	—	5.00	7.50

KM# 191 100 TENGE
31.11 g., 0.925 Silver 0.9191 oz. ASW, 38.61 mm. **Subject:** Torino Winter Olympics **Rev:** Three stone cross-country skiers

Date	Mintage	F12	VF20	XF40	MS60	MS63
2005	10,000	PF63 50.00	PF65 60.00			

KM# 95 100 TENGE
31.11 g., 0.925 Silver 0.9189 oz. ASW, 38.61 mm. **Subject:** Baiturramman Mosque **Rev:** Mosque and reflecting pool

Date	Mintage	F12	VF20	XF40	MS60	MS63
2006 (2008) (2006)	6,000	PF65 80.00				

KM# 98 100 TENGE
31.11 g., 0.925 Silver 0.9191 oz. ASW, 38.61 mm. **Subject:** Zahir Mosque **Rev:** Mosque

Date	Mintage	F12	VF20	XF40	MS60	MS63
2006	6,000	PF65 80.00				

KM# 195 100 TENGE
31.11 g., 0.925 Silver 0.9191 oz. ASW, 38.61 mm. **Subject:** Olympics 2008 **Obv:** National emblem in stadium **Rev:** Boxers

Date	Mintage	F12	VF20	XF40	MS60	MS63
2006	4,000	PF65 75.00				

KM# 200 100 TENGE
1.24 g., 0.999 Gold 0.0396 oz. AGW, 13.92 mm. **Obv:** National emblem **Rev:** Decoration

Date	Mintage	F12	VF20	XF40	MS60	MS63
2006	18,000	PF63 85.00	PF65 100			

KM# 166 100 TENGE
31.10 g., 0.925 Silver 0.9189 oz. ASW, 37 mm. **Subject:** Olympics - Pentathlon **Obv:** National arms and stylized stadium **Rev:** Five sports

Date	Mintage	F12	VF20	XF40	MS60	MS63
2007	—	PF65 55.00				

KM# 96 100 TENGE
31.11 g., 0.925 Silver 0.9191 oz. ASW, 38.61 mm. **Subject:** Faisal Mosque, Islamabad **Rev:** Mosque

Date	Mintage	F12	VF20	XF40	MS60	MS63
2006 (2008)	6,000	PF65 80.00				

KM# 97 100 TENGE
31.11 g., 0.925 Silver 0.9191 oz. ASW, 38.61 mm. **Subject:**

Hodja Akhmed Yassavi Mausoleum Turkestan **Rev:** Mausoleum

Date	Mintage	F12	VF20	XF40	MS60	MS63
2006 (2008)	6,000	PF65 80.00				

KM# 110 100 TENGE
31.11 g., 0.925 Silver 0.9191 oz. ASW, 38.61 mm. **Subject:** Chingis Khan **Rev:** Khan on horseback facing

Date	Mintage	F12	VF20	XF40	MS60	MS63
2008	13,000	PF63 55.00	PF65 65.00			

KM# 125 100 TENGE
31.11 g., 0.925 Silver 0.9191 oz. ASW, 38.61 mm. **Subject:** Attila the Hun **Rev:** Medallic Profile right

Date	Mintage	F12	VF20	XF40	MS60	MS63
2009	13,000	PF63 65.00	PF65 75.00			

KM# 126 100 TENGE
31.11 g., 0.925 Silver 0.9191 oz. ASW, 38.61 mm. **Subject:** 2010 Olympics **Rev:** Ski jumper over Vancouver skyline

Date	Mintage	F12	VF20	XF40	MS60	MS63
2009	12,000	PF63 45.00	PF65 55.00			

KM# 134 100 TENGE
31.10 g., 0.925 Silver 0.9189 oz. ASW **Obv:** Arms **Rev:** Western Lynx head facing, partially gilt

Date	Mintage	F12	VF20	XF40	MS60	MS63
2009	13,000	PF63 45.00	PF65 55.00			

KM# 136 100 TENGE
1.24 g., 0.999 Gold 0.0396 oz. AGW, 13.92 mm. **Obv:** Value **Rev:** Cat head sculpture

Date	Mintage	F12	VF20	XF40	MS60	MS63
2009	9,500	PF63 75.00	PF65 85.00			

KM# 147 100 TENGE
31.10 g., 0.925 Silver 0.9189 oz. ASW, 38.6 mm. **Obv:** Arms
Rev: Tiger advancing right

Date	Mintage	F12	VF20	XF40	MS60	MS63
2009	13,000	PF63 55.00	PF65 65.00			

KM# 151 100 TENGE
31.10 g., 0.999 Silver 0.9925 oz. ASW, 38.61 mm. **Subject:**
World Cup, South Africa **Obv:** Arms and stadium **Rev:** Soccer
Player, gilt ball

Date	Mintage	F12	VF20	XF40	MS60	MS63
2009	—	PF65 50.00				

KM# 153 100 TENGE
1.24 g., 0.999 Gold 0.0396 oz. AGW, 13.92 mm. **Subject:**
Zhalavlinky Treasure **Obv:** Arms **Rev:** Historic jewelery design

Date	Mintage	F12	VF20	XF40	MS60	MS63
2009	9,500	PF63 75.00	PF65 85.00			

KM# 220 100 TENGE
1.24 g., 0.999 Gold 0.0396 oz. AGW, 13.92 mm. **Rev:** Two
lions on rock

Date	Mintage	F12	VF20	XF40	MS60	MS63
2009	—	PF63 110	PF65 125			

KM# 227 100 TENGE
1.24 g., 0.999 Gold 0.0396 oz. AGW, 13.92 mm. **Subject:** Snow
Leopard

Date	Mintage	F12	VF20	XF40	MS60	MS63
2009	Est. 9500	PF63 75.00	PF65 85.00			

KM# 228 100 TENGE
31.10 g., 0.925 Silver 0.9189 oz. ASW, 38.61 mm. **Subject:**
Snow Leopard

Date	Mintage	F12	VF20	XF40	MS60	MS63
2009	Est. 7000	PF65 55.00				

KM# 176 100 TENGE
31.10 g., 0.925 Silver 0.9189 oz. ASW, 38.61 mm. **Obv:** State
Emblem, gilt horsemen at right **Rev:** Queen Tomris

Date	Mintage	F12	VF20	XF40	MS60	MS63
2010	—	PF65 70.00				

KM# 245 100 TENGE
1.24 g., 0.999 Gold 0.0396 oz. AGW, 13.92 mm. **Subject:**
Asian Winter Games in Astana and Almaty **Obv:** Fir in the Sky
Mountains **Rev:** Games logo

Date	Mintage	F12	VF20	XF40	MS60	MS63
2010	8,000	PF65 90.00				

KM# 248 100 TENGE
31.10 g., 0.925 Silver 0.9189 oz. ASW, 38.61 mm. **Subject:**
XXX Summer Olympics - London **Rev:** Wrestlers

Date	Mintage	F12	VF20	XF40	MS60	MS63
2010	12,000	PF63 55.00	PF65 65.00			

KM# 249 100 TENGE
31.10 g., 0.925 Silver 0.9189 oz. ASW, 38.61 mm. **Subject:**
XXX Summer Olympics - London **Rev:** Weightlifter

Date	Mintage	F12	VF20	XF40	MS60	MS63
2010	12,000	PF63 55.00	PF65 65.00			

KM# 211 100 TENGE
31.11 g., 0.925 Silver 0.9191 oz. ASW, 38.61 mm. **Subject:**
Olympics, 2014 **Rev:** Speed Skating

Date	Mintage	F12	VF20	XF40	MS60	MS63
2011	—	PF65 75.00				

KM# 234 100 TENGE
31.11 g., 0.925 Silver 0.9191 oz. ASW, 38.61 mm. **Subject:**
Sultan Baybars **Obv:** Sultan on horseback at left, National Arms
gilt at right **Rev:** Sultan on horseback

Date	Mintage	F12	VF20	XF40	MS60	MS63
2012	—	PF65 75.00				

KM# 263 100 TENGE
24.00 g., 0.925 Silver 0.7092 oz. ASW, 37 mm. **Subject:** 2016
Olympics - Pole Vault

Date	Mintage	F12	VF20	XF40	MS60	MS63
2013	Est. 8000	PF63 65.00	PF65 75.00			

KM# 226 100 TENGE
31.10 g., 0.925 Silver 0.9189 oz. ASW, 38.61 mm. **Subject:**
Sotchi Olympic Games - Skating

Date	Mintage	F12	VF20	XF40	MS60	MS63
2014	Est. 8000	PF63 45.00	PF65 55.00			

KM# 237 200 TENGE
62.20 g., 0.9999 Gold 1.9867 oz. AGW, 38.61 mm. **Rev:** Irbis

Date	Mintage	VG8	F12	VF20	XF40	MS60
2010						

KM# 66 500 TENGE
24.00 g., 0.925 Silver 0.7092 oz. ASW, 37 mm. **Obv:** Man
seated under tree playing stringed instrument **Rev:** Stringed
instrument, musical notes

Date	Mintage	F12	VF20	XF40	MS60	MS63
2001	—	PF65 50.00				

KM# 37 500 TENGE
23.90 g., 0.925 Silver 0.7062 oz. ASW, 37 mm. **Subject:** Wildlife
Obv: Value **Rev:** Female Saiga with two calves **Edge:** Plain

Date	Mintage	F12	VF20	XF40	MS60	MS63
2001	3,000	PF65 90.00				

KM# 38 500 TENGE
23.81 g., 0.925 Silver 0.7035 oz. ASW, 36.9 mm. **Subject:** 10
Years of Independence **Obv:** Monument and flag **Rev:** National
emblem within design above value **Edge:** Plain

Date	Mintage	F12	VF20	XF40	MS60	MS63
2001	—	PF65 125				

KM# 55 500 TENGE
24.00 g., 0.925 Silver 0.7092 oz. ASW, 37 mm. **Obv:** Value
Rev: Altai Mountain petroglyph **Edge:** Plain

Date	Mintage	F12	VF20	XF40	MS60	MS63
2001	3,000	PF65 175				

KM# 112 500 TENGE
24.00 g., 0.925 Silver 0.7092 oz. ASW **Subject:** Applied art,
stringed instrument **Obv:** Man seated under tree **Rev:** Stringed
instrument and notes

Date	Mintage	F12	VF20	XF40	MS60	MS63
2001	—	PF65 42.00				

KM# 42 500 TENGE
23.90 g., 0.925 Silver 0.7062 oz. ASW, 37 mm. **Subject:**
Music **Obv:** Musician and value divided by tree **Rev:** Musical
instruments **Edge:** Plain

Date	Mintage	F12	VF20	XF40	MS60	MS63
2002	—	PF65 165				

KM# 43 500 TENGE
23.90 g., 0.925 Silver 0.7062 oz. ASW, 37 mm. **Subject:**
Prehistoric Art **Obv:** Value **Rev:** Prehistoric cave art **Edge:**
Plain

Date	Mintage	F12	VF20	XF40	MS60	MS63
2002	3,000	PF65 140				

KM# 44 500 TENGE
23.90 g., 0.925 Silver 0.7062 oz. ASW, 37 mm. **Subject:** Bighorn Sheep **Obv:** Value **Rev:** Kazakhstan Argali Ram **Edge:** Plain

Date	Mintage	F12	VF20	XF40	MS60	MS63
2002	3,000	PF65 120				

KM# 113 500 TENGE
24.00 g., 0.925 Silver 0.7092 oz. ASW, 37 mm. **Subject:** Petroglyph **Obv:** Value on traditional weave pattern **Rev:** Horse petroglyph

Date	Mintage	F12	VF20	XF40	MS60	MS63
2002	—	PF65 60.00				

KM# 183 500 TENGE
24.00 g., 0.925 Silver 0.7092 oz. ASW, 36. mm. **Obv:** Large value within brick arch design **Rev:** Byzantine church and floor plan

Date	Mintage	F12	VF20	XF40	MS60	MS63
2002	3,000	PF65 75.00				

KM# 53 500 TENGE
24.00 g., 0.925 Silver 0.7092 oz. ASW, 37 mm. **Obv:** Value **Rev:** Great Bustard bird standing on ground **Edge:** Plain

Date	Mintage	F12	VF20	XF40	MS60	MS63
2003	3,000	PF65 75.00				

KM# 56 500 TENGE
24.00 g., 0.925 Silver 0.7092 oz. ASW, 37 mm. **Subject:** Applied Arts **Obv:** Folk Dancer **Rev:** Cultural artifacts **Edge:** Plain

Date	Mintage	F12	VF20	XF40	MS60	MS63
2003	3,000	PF65 80.00				

KM# 184 500 TENGE
24.00 g., 0.925 Silver 0.7092 oz. ASW **Rev:** Warriors in a cave

Date	Mintage	F12	VF20	XF40	MS60	MS63
2003	3,000	PF65 75.00				

KM# 185 500 TENGE
24.00 g., 0.925 Silver 0.7092 oz. ASW, 36 mm. **Obv:** Intricate tile design **Rev:** View of Kecensci Mausoleum

Date	Mintage	F12	VF20	XF40	MS60	MS63
2003	3,000	PF65 75.00				

KM# 59 500 TENGE
31.10 g., 0.925 Bi-Metallic 0.9189 oz., 38.6 mm. **Subject:** Denga **Obv:** Black square holed coin design above value **Rev:** Black square holed coin design and metal content statement **Edge:** Reeded

Date	Mintage	F12	VF20	XF40	MS60	MS63
2004	5,000	PF65 90.00				

KM# 117 500 TENGE
31.10 g., 0.925 Silver 0.9189 oz. ASW, 38.6 mm. **Obv:** Three riders **Rev:** Golden deer ornament **Shape:** 12-sided

Date	Mintage	F12	VF20	XF40	MS60	MS63
2004	—	PF65 100				

KM# 186 500 TENGE
24.00 g., 0.925 Silver 0.7092 oz. ASW **Rev:** Saker Falcon

Date	Mintage	F12	VF20	XF40	MS60	MS63
2004	3,000	PF65 75.00				

KM# 187 500 TENGE
24.00 g., 0.925 Silver 0.7092 oz. ASW, 37 mm. **Rev:** Cave painting of a Shaman in Tamgaly

Date	Mintage	F12	VF20	XF40	MS60	MS63
2004	3,000	PF65 75.00				

KM# 189 500 TENGE
24.00 g., 0.925 Sllver 0.7092 oz. ASW, 36 mm. **Obv:** Tree of Life **Rev:** Three stone figures

Date	Mintage	F12	VF20	XF40	MS60	MS63
2004	3,000	PF65 75.00				

KM# 190 500 TENGE
24.00 g., 0.925 Silver 0.7092 oz. ASW, 36 mm. **Obv:** Woman in national costume playing the zither **Rev:** Zither and musical notes

Date	Mintage	F12	VF20	XF40	MS60	MS63
2004	3,000	PF65 75.00				

KM# 60 500 TENGE
24.00 g., 0.925 Silver 0.7092 oz. ASW, 37 mm. **Obv:** Value **Rev:** Prehistoric art horseman **Edge:** Plain

Date	Mintage	F12	VF20	XF40	MS60	MS63
2005	3,000	PF65 70.00				

KM# 61 500 TENGE
24.00 g., 0.925 Silver 0.7092 oz. ASW, 37 mm. **Obv:** Value **Rev:** Two Goitered Gazelles **Edge:** Plain

Date	Mintage	F12	VF20	XF40	MS60	MS63
2005	3,000	PF65 70.00				

KM# 62 500 TENGE
31.10 g., 0.925 Silver 0.9189 oz. ASW, 38.6 mm. **Obv:** Horse race and value **Rev:** Gold plated tiger **Edge:** Plain **Shape:** 12-sided

Date	Mintage	F12	VF20	XF40	MS60	MS63
2005	5,000	PF66 120				

KM# 63 500 TENGE
31.10 g., 0.925 Bi-Metallic 0.9189 oz., 38.6 mm. **Subject:** Drakhma" coin **Obv:** Old coin design **Rev:** Old coin design **Edge:** Reeded

Date	Mintage	F12	VF20	XF40	MS60	MS63
2005	5,000	PF65 65.00				

KM# 72 500 TENGE
31.10 g., 0.925 Silver 0.9189 oz. ASW, 38.6 mm. **Obv:** Horse race and value **Rev:** Gold plated rider **Edge:** Plain

Date	Mintage	F12	VF20	XF40	MS60	MS63
2005	5,000	PF65 100				

KM# 124 500 TENGE
24.00 g., 0.925 Silver 0.7092 oz. ASW, 37 mm. **Subject:** Zhoshi Khan Mausoleum **Rev:** 3/4 view of building facade

Date	Mintage	F12	VF20	XF40	MS60	MS63
2005	—	PF65 50.00				

KM# 192 500 TENGE
24.00 g., 0.925 Silver 0.7092 oz. ASW, 36 mm. **Obv:** Man seated with stringed musical instrument **Rev:** two string musical instruments, musical notes at right

Date	Mintage	F12	VF20	XF40	MS60	MS63
2005	3,000	PF65 75.00				

KM# 193 500 TENGE
7.78 g., 0.999 Gold 0.2483 oz. AGW, 25 mm. **Obv:** State shield **Rev:** head of a dhole

Date	Mintage	F12	VF20	XF40	MS60	MS63
2005	—	PF65 750				

KM# 162 500 TENGE
0.999 Gold AGW **Obv:** Archway **Rev:** Al-Baram Mosque in Mecca

Date	Mintage	F12	VF20	XF40	MS60	MS63
2006	—	PF65 500				

KM# 163 500 TENGE
0.999 Gold AGW **Obv:** Archway **Rev:** Al-Nabawi Mosque in Medina

Date	Mintage	F12	VF20	XF40	MS60	MS63
2006	—	PF65 500				

KM# 76 500 TENGE
31.10 g., 0.925 Silver 0.9189 oz. ASW **Series:** Flora **Rev:** Tulopa Regeli in multicolor

Date	Mintage	F12	VF20	XF40	MS60	MS63
2006	—	PF65 150				

KM# 83 500 TENGE
24.00 g., 0.925 Silver 0.7092 oz. ASW, 38.7 mm. **Obv:** Value at center **Rev:** Tetraogallus Altalcus, Altai Snowcock

Date	Mintage	F12	VF20	XF40	MS60	MS63
2006	3,000	PF65 100				

KM# 84 500 TENGE
31.10 g., 0.925 Bi-Metallic 0.9189 oz., 38.6 mm. **Subject:** Dirkhem" coin **Obv:** Old coin design **Rev:** Old coin design **Edge:** Reeded

Date	Mintage	F12	VF20	XF40	MS60	MS63
2006	5,000	PF65 65.00				

KM# 194 500 TENGE
24.00 g., 0.925 Silver 0.7092 oz. ASW **Rev:** Triumph cars

Date	Mintage	F12	VF20	XF40	MS60	MS63
2006	3,000	PF65 75.00				

KM# 196 500 TENGE
31.11 g., 0.925 Silver 0.9191 oz. ASW, 38.61 mm. **Obv:** National emblem **Rev:** Figure seated at loom

Date	Mintage	F12	VF20	XF40	MS60	MS63
2006	4,000	PF65 75.00				

KM# 197 500 TENGE
31.11 g., 0.925 Silver 0.9191 oz. ASW, 38.61 mm. **Obv:** State emblem **Rev:** Central Mosque in Almati

Date	Mintage	F12	VF20	XF40	MS60	MS63
2006	4,000	PF65 75.00				

KM# 198 500 TENGE
31.11 g., 0.925 Silver 0.9191 oz. ASW, 38.61 mm. **Rev:** female with apples, a drawing by Sidorkin

Date	Mintage	F12	VF20	XF40	MS60	MS63
2006	4,000	PF65 75.00				

KM# 199 500 TENGE
41.00 g., Bi-Metallic, 38.61 mm. **Obv:** Figure standing within solar system **Rev:** Spaceman and orbits of planets

Date	Mintage	F12	VF20	XF40	MS60	MS63
2006	4,000	PF65 135				

KM# 168 500 TENGE
7.77 g., 0.999 Gold 0.248 oz. AGW, 25 mm. **Obv:** Arms **Rev:** Lynx, crystal eyes **Rev. Legend:** FELIS LYNX

Date	Mintage	F12	VF20	XF40	MS60	MS63
2007	—	PF65 475				

KM# 82 500 TENGE
41.40 g., Bi-Metallic, 38.61 mm. **Subject:** 50th Anniversary Launch of Sputnik I **Obv:** Stylized view of our solar system, multicolor **Obv. Legend:** REPUBLIC OF KAZAKHSTAN **Rev:** Sputnik I in space, earth in background, multicolor **Rev. Legend:** THE FIRST SPACE SATELLITE OF THE EARTH **Edge:** Reeded

Date	Mintage	F12	VF20	XF40	MS60	MS63
ND(2007)	4,000	PF65 100				

KM# 85 500 TENGE
31.10 g., 0.925 Bi-Metallic 0.9189 oz., 38.6 mm. **Subject:** Otyrar" coin **Obv:** Old coin design **Rev:** Old coin design **Edge:** Reeded

Date	Mintage	F12	VF20	XF40	MS60	MS63
2007	4,000	PF65 75.00				

KM# 87 500 TENGE
24.00 g., 0.925 Silver 0.7092 oz. ASW, 38.6 mm. **Obv:** Value **Rev:** Terekin Valley - noble deer petraglyph

Date	Mintage	F12	VF20	XF40	MS60	MS63
2007	3,000	PF65 90.00				

KM# 88 500 TENGE
31.10 g., 0.925 Silver 0.9189 oz. ASW **Subject:** Movement series - myth **Obv:** Value within square **Rev:** Design

Date	Mintage	F12	VF20	XF40	MS60	MS63
2007	4,000	PF65 80.00				

KM# 89 500 TENGE
31.10 g., 0.925 Silver 0.9189 oz. ASW, 38.6 mm. **Subject:** Gold of the Romans **Obv:** Four horseman **Rev:** Gilt Roman seal ring **Shape:** 12-sided

Date	Mintage	F12	VF20	XF40	MS60	MS63
2007	5,000	PF65 100				

KM# 90 500 TENGE
31.10 g., 0.925 Silver 0.9189 oz. ASW, 38.6 mm. **Obv:** State emblem **Rev:** Church

Date	Mintage	F12	VF20	XF40	MS60	MS63
2007	4,000	PF65 75.00				

KM# 91 500 TENGE
31.10 g., 0.925 Silver 0.9189 oz. ASW, 38.6 mm. **Obv:** State emblem **Rev:** Traditional family

Date	Mintage	F12	VF20	XF40	MS60	MS63
2007	4,000	PF65 70.00				

KM# 92 500 TENGE
31.10 g., 0.925 Silver 0.9189 oz. ASW, 38.6 mm. **Obv:** Leaves **Rev:** Tree growth rings, multicolor seeds

Date	Mintage	F12	VF20	XF40	MS60	MS63
2007	4,000	PF65 75.00				

KM# 93 500 TENGE
24.00 g., 0.925 Silver 0.7092 oz. ASW, 38.6 mm. **Subject:** Spoon billed duck **Obv:** Value **Rev:** Duck in reeds

Date	Mintage	F12	VF20	XF40	MS60	MS63
2007	3,000	PF65 85.00				

KM# 167 500 TENGE
7.78 g., 0.999 Gold 0.2483 oz. AGW, 25 mm. **Subject:** Olympics, high jump **Obv:** Arms and stylized stadium **Rev:** Female high jump

Date	Mintage	F12	VF20	XF40	MS60	MS63
2007	—	PF65 460				

KM# 94 500 TENGE
31.11 g., 0.925 Silver 0.9191 oz. ASW, 38.6 mm. **Subject:** National currency, 15th Anniversary **Obv:** Three coin designs

Date	Mintage	F12	VF20	XF40	MS60	MS63
2008	5,000	PF65 75.00				

KM# 99 500 TENGE
31.11 g., 0.925 Silver 0.9191 oz. ASW, 38.61 mm. **Subject:** Eurasic Capitals - Astana **Rev:** Skyline montage

Date	Mintage	F12	VF20	XF40	MS60	MS63
2008	5,000	PF65 75.00				

KM# 100 500 TENGE
24.00 g., 0.925 Silver 0.7092 oz. ASW, 38.61 mm. **Subject:** Tien Shan - Brown Bear **Rev:** Bear seated

Date	Mintage	F12	VF20	XF40	MS60	MS63
2008	3,000	PF65 85.00				

KM# 101 500 TENGE
31.11 g., 0.925 Silver 0.9191 oz. ASW, 38.61 mm. **Subject:** Nomad Gold **Rev:** Diadem fragment **Shape:** 12-sided

Date	Mintage	F12	VF20	XF40	MS60	MS63
2008	5,000	PF65 115				

KM# 102 500 TENGE
31.11 g., 0.925 Silver 0.9191 oz. ASW, 38.61 mm. **Subject:** Kalmykov **Rev:** Fantasy scene

Date	Mintage	F12	VF20	XF40	MS60	MS63
2008	4,000	PF65 80.00				

KM# 103 500 TENGE
31.11 g., 0.925 Silver 0.9191 oz. ASW, 38.61 mm. **Subject:** Kyz Kuu **Rev:** Two horseback riders

Date	Mintage	F12	VF20	XF40	MS60	MS63
2008	4,000	PF65 80.00				

KM# 104 500 TENGE
31.11 g., 0.925 Silver 0.9191 oz. ASW, 38.61 mm. **Subject:** Linum Olgae **Rev:** Flowers

Date	Mintage	F12	VF20	XF40	MS60	MS63
2008	4,000	PF65 100				

KM# 106 500 TENGE
24.00 g., 0.925 Silver 0.7092 oz. ASW, 38.6x28.8 mm. **Subject:** Papilio Alexanor **Rev:** Two butterflies **Shape:** oval

Date	Mintage	F12	VF20	XF40	MS60	MS63
2008	4,000	PF65 115				

KM# 107 500 TENGE
31.11 g., 0.925 Silver 0.9191 oz. ASW, 38.61 mm. **Subject:** Saraichik Coin **Rev:** Coin of the 14th Century

Date	Mintage	F12	VF20	XF40	MS60	MS63
2008	5,000	PF65 75.00				

KM# 108 500 TENGE
41.40 g., Bi-Metallic, 38.61 mm. **Subject:** Vostok **Rev:** Space
ship

Date	Mintage	F12	VF20	XF40	MS60	MS63
2008	4,000	PF65 110				

KM# 109 500 TENGE
31.11 g., 0.925 Silver 0.9191 oz. ASW, 38.61 mm. **Subject:**
Zharkent Mosque **Rev:** Mosque

Date	Mintage	F12	VF20	XF40	MS60	MS63
2008	400	PF65 145				

KM# 118 500 TENGE
24.00 g., 0.925 Silver 0.7092 oz. ASW, 37 mm. **Subject:**
Kazakhstan Railroads, 100th Anniversary **Obv:** Arms **Rev:**
Modern train and Steam locomotive, country route map in
background

Date	Mintage	F12	VF20	XF40	MS60	MS63
2008	—	PF65 55.00				

KM# 131 500 TENGE
31.11 g., 0.925 Silver 0.9191 oz. ASW, 38.61 mm. **Subject:**
Almaty Aport **Rev:** Apple tree branch and flower

Date	Mintage	F12	VF20	XF40	MS60	MS63
2009	4,000	PF65 80.00				

KM# 149 500 TENGE
31.11 g., 0.925 Silver 0.9191 oz. ASW, 38.61 mm. **Subject:**
Balkhash Tiger **Rev:** Tiger on the hunt

Date	Mintage	F12	VF20	XF40	MS60	MS63
2009	5,000	PF65 75.00				

KM# 133 500 TENGE
31.11 g., 0.999 Silver 0.9926 oz. ASW, 38.61 mm. **Subject:**
Betashar **Rev:** Two figures standing

Date	Mintage	F12	VF20	XF40	MS60	MS63
2009	4,000	PF65 75.00				

KM# 139 500 TENGE
31.11 g., 0.925 Silver 0.9191 oz. ASW, 38.6 mm. **Subject:** Nur-
Astana Mosque **Rev:** Mosque

Date	Mintage	F12	VF20	XF40	MS60	MS63
2009	4,000	PF65 75.00				

KM# 142 500 TENGE
24.00 g., 0.925 Silver 0.7092 oz. ASW, 38.61 mm. **Rev:**
Porcupine left with quills raised

Date	Mintage	F12	VF20	XF40	MS60	MS63
2009	3,000	PF65 90.00				

KM# 143 500 TENGE
31.11 g., 0.999 Silver 0.9926 oz. ASW, 38.61 mm. **Rev:** Satir
head facing **Shape:** 12-sided

Date	Mintage	F12	VF20	XF40	MS60	MS63
2009	5,000	PF65 100				

KM# 130 500 TENGE
41.40 g., Bi-Metallic, 38.61 mm. **Subject:** Apollo - Soyuz
Missions **Rev:** Spacecraft docked in orbit above the earth

Date	Mintage	F12	VF20	XF40	MS60	MS63
2009	4,000	PF65 115				

KM# 137 500 TENGE
31.11 g., 0.925 Silver 0.9191 oz. ASW, 38.61 mm. **Subject:**
Coin of Almaty **Rev:** 13th Century coin

Date	Mintage	F12	VF20	XF40	MS60	MS63
2009	4,000	PF65 100				

KM# 127 500 TENGE
7.78 g., 0.999 Gold 0.2483 oz. AGW, 25 mm. **Subject:**
Olympics - Biathlon **Obv:** Arms and stylized stadium **Rev:**
Biathlon, 2 cross country skiers and shooter

Date	Mintage	F12	VF20	XF40	MS60	MS63
2009	5,000	PF65 445				

KM# 128 500 TENGE
31.10 g., 0.999 Silver 0.9925 oz. ASW, 38.6 mm. **Subject:**
Almaty Aport **Obv:** Value and leaves **Rev:** Apples and flower

Date	Mintage	F12	VF20	XF40	MS60	MS63
2009	4,000	PF65 65.00				

KM# 129 500 TENGE
31.10 g., 0.925 Silver 0.9189 oz. ASW, 36.6 mm. **Subject:**
Eurasian Economic Community **Obv:** Arms **Rev:** Alpamys Batyr

Date	Mintage	F12	VF20	XF40	MS60	MS63
2009	5,000	PF65 55.00				

KM# 138 500 TENGE
24.00 g., 0.925 Silver 0.7092 oz. ASW, 28.61x28.81 mm.
Subject: Flamingo **Obv:** Partial butterfly **Rev:** Pair of flamings standing in holographic water **Shape:** Vertical oval

Date	Mintage	F12	VF20	XF40	MS60	MS63
2009	4,000	PF65 80.00				

KM# 148 500 TENGE
7.78 g., 0.999 Gold 0.2483 oz. AGW, 21.87 mm. **Rev:** Tiger walking right

Date	Mintage	F12	VF20	XF40	MS60	MS63
2009	3,000	PF65 450				

KM# 150 500 TENGE
7.78 g., 0.999 Gold 0.2483 oz. AGW, 25 mm. **Subject:** Uncia **Obv:** Arms **Rev:** Snow Leopard head left

Date	Mintage	F12	VF20	XF40	MS60	MS63
2009	5,000	PF65 445				

KM# 225 500 TENGE
7.78 g., 0.999 Gold 0.2483 oz. AGW, 25 mm. **Subject:** Biathlon Gold with 3 Diamonds

Date	Mintage	F12	VF20	XF40	MS60	MS63
2012 (2009)	Est. 5000	PF65 550				

KM# 230 500 TENGE
31.10 g., 0.999 Gold 0.9925 oz. AGW, 32 mm. **Subject:** Snow Leopard

Date	Mintage	F12	VF20	XF40	MS60	MS63
2009	Est. 1500	PF65 2,150				

KM# 231 500 TENGE
7.78 g., 0.999 Gold 0.2483 oz. AGW, 25 mm. **Subject:** Snow Leopard with 2 Diamonds

Date	Mintage	F12	VF20	XF40	MS60	MS63
2009	Est. 5000	PF65 550				

KM# 179 500 TENGE
31.10 g., 0.925 Silver 0.9189 oz. ASW, 38.6 mm. **Obv:** Three horsemen **Rev:** Buckle, gilt pair of seated raindeer **Shape:** 12-sided

Date	Mintage	F12	VF20	XF40	MS60	MS63
2010	5,000	PF65 85.00				

KM# 177 500 TENGE
31.10 g., 0.925 Silver 0.9189 oz. ASW **Obv:** Outline of three pelicans **Rev:** Pelecanus Crispus, pelican standing

Date	Mintage	F12	VF20	XF40	MS60	MS63
2010	5,000	PF65 75.00				

KM# 178 500 TENGE
31.10 g., 0.925 Silver 0.9189 oz. ASW, 38.6 mm. **Subject:** Otau Koteru **Obv:** National Emblem **Rev:** Horseman and large ceremonial umbrella

Date	Mintage	F12	VF20	XF40	MS60	MS63
2010	5,000	PF65 90.00				

KM# 180 500 TENGE
31.10 g., 0.925 Silver 0.9189 oz. ASW **Subject:** Flora **Rev:** Papaver Pavoninum in color

Date	Mintage	F12	VF20	XF40	MS60	MS63
2010	4,000	PF65 90.00				

KM# 181 500 TENGE
3.11 g., 0.999 Gold 0.0992 oz. AGW, 16 mm. **Obv:** Archway **Rev:** Dome of the Rock, Jerusalem

Date	Mintage	F12	VF20	XF40	MS60	MS63
2010	—	PF65 200				

KM# 182 500 TENGE
31.10 g., 0.925 Silver 0.9189 oz. ASW **Rev:** Musical instrument

Date	Mintage	F12	VF20	XF40	MS60	MS63
2010	—	PF65 75.00				

KM# 238 500 TENGE
155.50 g., 0.999 Gold 4.9623 oz. AGW **Rev:** Irbis

Date	Mintage	VG8	F12	VF20	XF40	MS60
2010	—	—	—	—	—	—

KM# 242 500 TENGE
26.80 g., 0.925 Silver 0.7919 oz. ASW, 38.61 mm. **Subject:** 40th anniversary of Lunar rover **Obv:** Man within universe **Rev:** Moon vehicle

Date	Mintage	G4	VG8	F12	VF20	XF40
2010	—	PF65 135				

KM# 243 500 TENGE
24.00 g., 0.925 Silver 0.7092 oz. ASW, 38.61x28.81 mm. **Subject:** Flora and Fauna **Rev:** Phrynocephalus mystaceus - Agamidae **Shape:** Oval

Date	Mintage	F12	VF20	XF40	MS60	MS63
2010	4,000	PF65 75.00				

KM# 244 500 TENGE
31.10 g., 0.925 Silver 0.9189 oz. ASW, 38.61 mm. **Subject:** Asia Winter Games in Astana and Almaty **Obv:** Drawing of Sun Gog Tengi in Mountains **Rev:** Games logo in kinegram

Date	Mintage	F12	VF20	XF40	MS60	MS63
2010	13,000	PF63 65.00	PF65 75.00			

KM# 250 500 TENGE
31.10 g., 0.925 Silver 0.9189 oz. ASW, 38.61 mm. **Subject:** Euroasian Economic Community, 10th Anniversary

Date	Mintage	F12	VF20	XF40	MS60	MS63
2010	5,000	PF65 65.00				

KM# 251 500 TENGE
3.11 g., 0.999 Gold 0.0992 oz. AGW, 16 mm. **Subject:** Mosques **Rev:** Ka'aba in Mecca

Date	Mintage	F12	VF20	XF40	MS60	MS63
2010	3,000	PF65 200				

KM# 252 500 TENGE
3.11 g., 0.999 Gold 0.0992 oz. AGW, 16 mm. **Subject:** Mosques **Rev:** Masjid Sultan in Singapore

Date	Mintage	F12	VF20	XF40	MS60	MS63
2010	3,000	PF65 200				

KM# 205 500 TENGE
24.00 g., 0.925 Silver 0.7092 oz. ASW, 38.61 mm. **Obv:** Stylized hawk at right **Rev:** Hawk on branch

Date	Mintage	F12	VF20	XF40	MS60	MS63
2011	—	PF65 85.00				

KM# 212 500 TENGE
31.11 g., 0.925 Silver 0.9191 oz. ASW, 38.61 mm. **Subject:** Independence, 20th Anniversary **Obv:** Map **Rev:** Architecture

Date	Mintage	F12	VF20	XF40	MS60	MS63
2011	—	PF65 75.00				

KM# 213 500 TENGE
31.11 g., 0.925 Silver 0.9191 oz. ASW, 38.61 mm. **Subject:** Issyk Chieftain **Rev:** Standing figure, gilt **Shape:** 8-sided

Date	Mintage	F12	VF20	XF40	MS60	MS63
2011	—	PF65 100				

KM# 214 500 TENGE
24.00 g., 0.925 Silver 0.7092 oz. ASW, 38.61x28.8 mm. **Subject:** Sturgen **Shape:** Oval

Date	Mintage	F12	VF20	XF40	MS60	MS63
2011	5,000	PF65 75.00				

KM# 215 500 TENGE
31.10 g., 0.925 Silver 0.9189 oz. ASW, 38.61 mm. **Subject:** Aldar Rose **Obv:** Arms **Rev:** Figure riding donkey

Date	Mintage	F12	VF20	XF40	MS60	MS63
2011	—	PF65 75.00				

KM# 217 500 TENGE
31.11 g., 0.925 Silver 0.9191 oz. ASW, 38.61 mm. **Subject:** Gold of the Nomads - Elk's head **Rev:** Artistic elk's head gilt **Shape:** 12-sided

Date	Mintage	F12	VF20	XF40	MS60	MS63
2011	—	PF65 100				

KM# 218 500 TENGE
40.70 g., Bi-Metallic, 38.61 mm. **Obv:** Stylized view of solar system, man standing at center **Rev:** First astronaut at right, spacecraft at left

Date	Mintage	F12	VF20	XF40	MS60	MS63
2011	—	PF65 100				

KM# 219 500 TENGE
31.11 g., 0.925 Silver 0.9191 oz. ASW, 38.61 mm. **Subject:** Year of the Rabbit **Obv:** Zodiac constelations of the Milky Way **Rev:** Rabbit in center of 12-year sysle of animals **Shape:** 12-sided

Date	Mintage	F12	VF20	XF40	MS60	MS63
2011	—	PF65 100				

KM# 221 500 TENGE
7.77 g., 0.999 Gold 0.248 oz. AGW, 25 mm. **Rev:** Eagle owl head, crystal eye

Date	Mintage	F12	VF20	XF40	MS60	MS63
2011	—	PF65 550				

KM# 232 500 TENGE
7.78 g., 0.999 Gold 0.2483 oz. AGW, 25 mm. **Subject:** Eagle Owl

Date	Mintage	F12	VF20	XF40	MS60	MS63
2011	Est. 5000	PF65 550				

KM# 254 500 TENGE
31.10 g., 0.925 Silver 0.9189 oz. ASW, 38.61 mm. **Subject:** Shanghai Cooperation Organization, 10th Anniversary **Obv:** National arms **Rev:** Logo

Date	Mintage	F12	VF20	XF40	MS60	MS63
2011	4,000	PF65 65.00				

KM# 255 500 TENGE
7.78 g., 0.999 Gold 0.2483 oz. AGW, 21.87 mm. **Subject:** Year of the Rabbit **Obv:** Constellations **Rev:** Rabbit in center of Zodiac

Date	Mintage	F12	VF20	XF40	MS60	MS63
2011	3,000	PF65 550				

KM# 257 500 TENGE
3.11 g., 0.999 Gold 0.0992 oz. AGW, 16 mm. **Subject:** Mosques **Obv:** Archway **Rev:** Alabaster Mosque of Mohammed Ali in Cairo

Date	Mintage	F12	VF20	XF40	MS60	MS63
2011	3,000	PF65 250				

KM# 258 500 TENGE
3.11 g., 0.999 Gold 0.0992 oz. AGW **Subject:** Mosques **Obv:** Archway **Rev:** Sultan Omar Ali Saifuddien mosque in Brunei

Date	Mintage	F12	VF20	XF40	MS60	MS63
2011	3,000	PF65 250				

KM# 259 500 TENGE
3.11 g., 0.999 Gold 0.0992 oz. AGW **Subject:** Mosques **Obv:** Archway **Rev:** Taj ul Masajid Mosque in Bhopal **Shape:** 16

Date	Mintage	F12	VF20	XF40	MS60	MS63
2011	3,000	PF65 250				

KM# 260 500 TENGE
7.78 g., 0.999 Gold 0.2483 oz. AGW **Rev:** Abu Nasir Muhammad bin Muhammad al Farabi, 1 Tenge bank note

Date	Mintage	F12	VF20	XF40	MS60	MS63
2011	4,000	PF65 550				

KM# 222 500 TENGE
31.10 g., 0.999 Silver 0.9925 oz. ASW, 38.6 mm. **Subject:** Kolobuk **Rev:** Fairy tale characters

Date	Mintage	F12	VF20	XF40	MS60	MS63
2012	—	PF65 75.00				

KM# 223 500 TENGE
0.93 g., 31.105 Silver, 38.61 mm. **Obv:** Soviet and Kazakhstan arms **Rev:** Portrait of D. Kunaev facing **Shape:** 8-sided

Date	Mintage	F12	VF20	XF40	MS60	MS63
2012	—	PF65 75.00				

KM# 233 500 TENGE
31.11 g., 0.925 Silver 0.9191 oz. ASW, 38.61 mm. **Subject:** Security: 20th Anniversary **Obv:** National arms **Rev:** Four-pronged device in circle

Date	Mintage	F12	VF20	XF40	MS60	MS63
2012	—	PF65 75.00				

KM# 235 500 TENGE
8.00 g., Bi-Metallic, 31 mm. **Subject:** Mir

Date	Mintage	F12	VF20	XF40	MS60	MS63
2012	—	PF65 100				

KM# 236 500 TENGE
7.78 g., 0.999 Gold 0.2483 oz. AGW, 21.87 mm. **Obv:** Year of the Dragon **Shape:** 12-Sided

Date	Mintage	F12	VF20	XF40	MS60	MS63
2012	—	PF65 675				

KM# 68 1000 TENGE
7.78 g., 0.999 Gold 0.2483 oz. AGW, 20 mm. **Obv:** Two winged ibexes **Rev:** Ancient warrior **Edge:** Reeded

Date	Mintage	F12	VF20	XF40	MS60	MS63
2001	—	PF65 445				

KM# 114 1000 TENGE
67.25 g., 0.925 Silver 1.9871 oz. ASW, 50 mm. **Subject:** National Currency, 10th Anniversary **Obv:** Flag, multicolor **Rev:** Coin and bank note designs

Date	Mintage	F12	VF20	XF40	MS60	MS63
2003	—	PF65 150				

KM# 115 1000 TENGE
67.25 g., 0.925 Silver 1.9871 oz. ASW, 50 mm. **Subject:** National Currency, 10th Anniversary **Obv:** Arms, gilt and blue enamel **Rev:** Coin montage

Date	Mintage	F12	VF20	XF40	MS60	MS63
2003	—	PF65 170				

KM# 67 5000 TENGE
1000.00 g., 0.925 Silver 29.548 oz. ASW, 100 mm. **Subject:** 10th Anniversary of Independence **Obv:** National arms above value **Rev:** Monument statue

Date	Mintage	F12	VF20	XF40	MS60	MS63
2001	—	PF65 1,150				

KM# 173 5000 TENGE
1000.00 g., 0.925 Silver 29.548 oz. ASW, 100 mm. **Subject:** Astana capitol, 10th anniversary **Obv:** National arms **Rev:** Architectural elements

Date	Mintage	F12	VF20	XF40	MS60	MS63
2008	—	PF65 1,250				

KM# 229 5000 TENGE
1000.00 g., 0.925 Silver 29.548 oz. ASW, 100 mm. **Subject:** Snow Leopard

Date	Mintage	F12	VF20	XF40	MS60	MS63
2009	Est. 700	PF65 1,150				

KM# 245 5000 TENGE
1000.00 g., 0.925 Silver 29.548 oz. ASW, 100 mm. **Subject:** Asian Winter games in Astana and Almaty **Obv:** Fir in the Sky mountains **Rev:** Games logo

Date	Mintage	F12	VF20	XF40	MS60	MS63
2010	225	PF65 1,350				

Note: Proof

KM# 105 50000 TENGE
1000.00 g., 0.9999 Gold 31.9406 oz. AGW, 100 mm. **Subject:** National Currency, 15th Anniversary **Rev:** Coin and bank note montage

Date	Mintage	F12	VF20	XF40	MS60	MS63
2008	100	PF65 60,000				

KM# 247 50000 TENGE
1000.00 g., 0.999 Gold 31.9118 oz. AGW, 100 mm. **Subject:** Asian Winter Games in Astana and Almaty **Obv:** Sun god and snowflakes **Rev:** Games logo

Date	Mintage	F12	VF20	XF40	MS60	MS63
2010	145	PF65 65,000				

KM# 216 50000 TENGE
1000.00 g., 0.999 Gold 31.9118 oz. AGW, 100 mm. **Subject:** Independence, 20th Anniversary **Obv:** Map and national arms **Rev:** Architecture montage

Date	Mintage	F12	VF20	XF40	MS60	MS63
2011	—	PF65 60,000				

BULLION COINAGE

KM# 161 TENGE
31.11 g., 0.999 Silver 0.9926 oz. ASW, 38.61 mm. **Obv:** Arms **Rev:** Snow Leopard standing right on rock

Date	Mintage	F12	VF20	XF40	MS60	MS63
2009	—	—	—	—	—	65.00

KM# 160 2 TENGE
64.21 g., 0.999 Silver 2.0491 oz. ASW, 50 mm. **Obv:** Arms **Rev:** Snow Leopard standing right on rock

Date	Mintage	F12	VF20	XF40	MS60	MS63
2009	—	—	—	—	—	125

KM# 159 5 TENGE
155.00 g., 0.999 Silver 4.9463 oz. ASW, 65 mm. **Obv:** Arms **Rev:** Snow Leopard standing right on rock

Date	Mintage	F12	VF20	XF40	MS60	MS63
2009	—	—	—	—	—	250

KM# 157 10 TENGE
3.11 g., 0.999 Gold 0.0992 oz. AGW **Obv:** Arms **Rev:** Snow Leopard standing right on rock

Date	Mintage	F12	VF20	XF40	MS60	MS63
2009	—	—	—	—	—	225

KM# 158 10 TENGE
311.05 g., 0.999 Silver 9.9262 oz. ASW **Obv:** Arms **Rev:** Snow Leopard standing right on rock

Date	Mintage	F12	VF20	XF40	MS60	MS63
2009	—	—	—	—	—	550

KM# 156 20 TENGE
7.78 g., 0.999 Gold 0.2483 oz. AGW **Obv:** Arms **Rev:** Snow Leopard standing right on rock

Date	Mintage	F12	VF20	XF40	MS60	MS63
2009	—	—	—	—	—	450

KM# 155 50 TENGE
15.55 g., 0.999 Gold 0.4962 oz. AGW, 25 mm. **Obv:** Arms **Rev:** Snow Leopard standing right on rock

Date	Mintage	F12	VF20	XF40	MS60	MS63
2009	—	—	—	—	—	900

KM# 154 100 TENGE
31.11 g., 0.999 Gold 0.9926 oz. AGW, 32 mm. **Obv:** Arms **Rev:** Snow Leopard standing right on rock

Date	Mintage	F12	VF20	XF40	MS60	MS63
2009	—	—	—	—	—	1,750

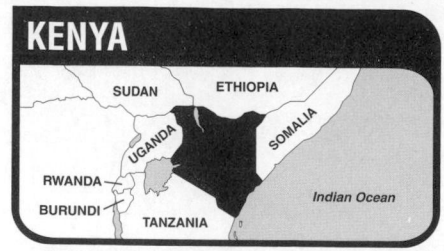

KENYA

The Republic of Kenya, located on the east coast of Central Africa, has an area of 224,961 sq. mi (582,650 sq. km.) and a population of 20.1 million. Capital: Nairobi. The predominantly agricultural country exports coffee, tea and petroleum products.

Independence was attained on Dec. 12, 1963. Kenya became a republic in 1964. It is a member of the Commonwealth of Nations. The president is Chief of State and Head of Government.

MONETARY SYSTEM
100 Cents = 1 Shilling

REPUBLIC

STANDARD COINAGE

KM# 39 5 CENTS
Copper Clad Steel **Subject:** First President **Obv:** National arms **Rev:** Bust of Mzee Jomo Kenyatta left **Note:** Initially a planned issue, abandoned prior to release for circulation.

Date	Mintage	F12	VF20	XF40	MS60	MS63
2005	—	—	—	—	—	—

KM# 40 10 CENTS
Copper Clad Steel **Subject:** First President **Obv:** National arms **Rev:** Bust of Mzee Jomo Kenyatta left **Note:** Initially a planned issue, abandoned prior to release for circulation.

Date	Mintage	F12	VF20	XF40	MS60	MS63
2005	—	—	—	—	—	—

KM# 41 50 CENTS
4.50 g., Nickel Plated Steel, 21.9 mm. **Subject:** First President **Obv:** National arms, value **Rev:** Bust of Mwee Jomo Kenyatta left

Date	Mintage	F12	VF20	XF40	MS60	MS63
2005	—	—	—	—	0.60	0.80
2009	—	—	—	—	0.60	0.80

KM# 34 SHILLING
5.46 g., Nickel Plated Steel, 23.9 mm. **Subject:** First President **Obv:** Value above national arms **Rev:** Bust of President Mzee Jomo Kenyata left **Edge:** Segmented reeding

Date	Mintage	F12	VF20	XF40	MS60	MS63
2005	—	—	—	—	0.80	1.20
2009	—	—	—	—	0.80	1.20
2010	—	—	—	—	0.80	1.20

KM# 37.1 5 SHILLINGS
3.75 g., Bi-Metallic, 19.5 mm. **Subject:** First President **Obv:** Value above national arms **Obv. Legend:** REPUBLIC OF KENYA **Rev:** Bust of President Mzee Jomo Kenyatta left **Edge:** Reeded

Date	Mintage	F12	VF20	XF40	MS60	MS63
2005	—	—	—	0.60	1.50	2.00
2009	—	—	—	0.60	1.50	2.00

KM# 37.2 5 SHILLINGS
3.75 g., Bi-Metallic, 19.5 mm. **Obv:** Value above national arms **Rev:** Bust of President Mzee Jomo Kenyatta **Edge:** Reeded **Note:** Larger numeral and smaller shield.

Date	Mintage	F12	VF20	XF40	MS60	MS63
2010	—	—	—	0.60	1.00	2.00

KM# 35.1 10 SHILLINGS
5.00 g., Bi-Metallic, 23 mm. **Subject:** First President **Obv:** Value above national arms **Obv. Legend:** REPUBLIC OF KENYA **Rev:** Bust of President Mzee Jomo Kenyatta left **Edge:** Reeded

Date	Mintage	F12	VF20	XF40	MS60	MS63
2005	—	—	—	0.90	2.25	3.00
2009	—	—	—	0.90	2.25	3.00

KM# 35.2 10 SHILLINGS
5.00 g., Bi-Metallic, 23 mm. **Obv:** Value above national arms **Rev:** Bust of President Mzee Jomo Kenyatta left **Edge:** Reeded **Note:** Larger value and smaller shield.

Date	Mintage	F12	VF20	XF40	MS60	MS63
2010	—	—	—	0.90	2.25	3.00

KM# 36.1 20 SHILLINGS
9.00 g., Bi-Metallic, 26 mm. **Subject:** First President **Obv:** Large value above national arms **Obv. Legend:** REPUBLIC OF KENYA **Rev:** Bust of President Mzee Jomo Kenyatta left **Edge:** Segmented reeding

Date	Mintage	F12	VF20	XF40	MS60	MS63
2005	—	—	—	1.20	3.00	4.00
2009	—	—	—	1.20	3.00	4.00

KM# 36.2 20 SHILLINGS
9.00 g., Bi-Metallic, 26 mm. **Obv:** Value above shield **Rev:** Bust of President Mzee Jomo Kenyatta **Note:** Larger value and smaller shield than 36.1.

Date	Mintage	F12	VF20	XF40	MS60	MS63
2010	—	—	—	—	3.00	4.00

KM# 33 40 SHILLINGS
11.00 g., Bi-Metallic, 27.5 mm. **Obv:** Bust of H. E. Mwai Kibaki facing **Rev:** National arms, value below **Edge:** Reeded and lettered **Edge Lettering:** 40 YEARS OF INDEPENDENCE **Note:** Issued December 11, 2003.

Date	Mintage	F12	VF20	XF40	MS60	MS63
ND(2003)	—	—	—	—	6.00	7.50

KM# 38 1000 SHILLINGS
28.28 g., 0.925 Silver 0.8356 oz. ASW, 38.61 mm. **Subject:** 40th Anniversary Independence **Obv:** National arms **Rev:** Bust of President H. E. Mwai Kibaki facing

Date	Mintage	F12	VF20	XF40	MS60	MS63
1963-2003	—	PF63 55.00		PF65 65.00		

KM# 43 5000 SHILLINGS
39.94 g., 0.9167 Gold 1.1696 oz. AGW, 27.5 mm. **Obv:** National arms **Rev:** H.E. Mwai Kibaki, 3rd president **Edge:** Reeded

Date	Mintage	F12	VF20	XF40	MS60	MS63
1963-2003	—	PF63 2,000		PF65 2,200		

KIRIBATI

The Republic of Kiribati (formerly the Gilbert Islands), consists of 30 coral atolls and islands spread over more than one million sq. mi. (2,590,000 sq. km.) of the southwest Pacific Ocean, has an area of 332 sq. mi. (717 sq. km.) and a population of 64,200. Capital: Bairiki, on Tarawa. In addition to the Gilbert Islands proper, Kiribati includes Ocean Island, the Central and Southern Line Islands, and the Phoenix Islands, though possession of Canton and Enderbury of the Phoenix Islands is disputed with the United States. Most families engage in subsistence fishing. Copra and phosphates are exported, mostly to Australia and New Zealand.

Kiribati is a member of the Commonwealth of Nations. The President is the Head of State and Head of Government.

MONETARY SYSTEM
100 Cents = 1 Dollar

REPUBLIC

DECIMAL COINAGE

KM# 40 5 CENTS
4.24 g., Brass, 22.9 mm. **Obv:** National arms **Rev:** Gorilla **Edge:** Reeded

Date	Mintage	F12	VF20	XF40	MS60	MS63
2003	—	—	—	—	1.00	1.50

KM# 60 DOLLAR
26.00 g., Silver Plated Copper, 38.61 mm. **Subject:** London Olympics, 2012 **Obv:** Shield **Rev:** Weightlifter and sunrise

Date	Mintage	F12	VF20	XF40	MS60	MS63
2011	Est. 10000	PF63 18.00		PF65 20.00		

KM# 62 DOLLAR
0.50 g., 0.999 Gold AGW, 11 mm. **Obv:** Shield **Rev:** Mary, Child Jesus and Joseph, in manger with cattle

Date	Mintage	F12	VF20	XF40	MS60	MS63
2011	—	PF65 55.00				

KM# 68 DOLLAR
0.50 g., 0.585 Gold AGW, 11 mm. **Obv:** Shield **Rev:** Mother and child

Date	Mintage	F12	VF20	XF40	MS60	MS63
2012	—	PF65 215				

KM# 78 DOLLAR
0.50 g., 0.585 Gold AGW, 11 mm. **Subject:** Holy Family

Date	Mintage	F12	VF20	XF40	MS60	MS63
2013	Est. 5000	PF63 45.00	PF65 50.00			

KM# 69 5 DOLLARS
12.00 g., 0.925 Silver 0.3546 oz. ASW, 38.61 mm. **Obv:** Shield **Rev:** Santa in sled in color

Date	Mintage	F12	VF20	XF40	MS60	MS63
2012	—	PF65 50.00				

KM# 70 5 DOLLARS
12.00 g., 0.925 Silver 0.3546 oz. ASW, 38.61 mm. **Obv:** Shield **Rev:** Rudolph gilt, crystal red nose

Date	Mintage	F12	VF20	XF40	MS60	MS63
2012	Est. 7500	PF63 50.00	PF65 55.00			

KM# 74 5 DOLLARS
20.00 g., 0.925 Silver 0.591 oz. ASW, 38.61 mm. **Subject:** Rudolph the red-nose reindeer

Date	Mintage	F12	VF20	XF40	MS60	MS63
2013	Est. 5000	PF63 65.00	PF65 75.00			

KM# 75 5 DOLLARS
20.00 g., 0.925 Silver 0.591 oz. ASW, 38.61 mm. **Subject:** Jingle Bells

Date	Mintage	F12	VF20	XF40	MS60	MS63
2013	Est. 5000	PF63 65.00	PF65 75.00			

KM# 54 10 DOLLARS
1.25 g., 0.999 Gold 0.0399 oz. AGW, 13.92 mm. **Obv:** Shield **Rev:** Angel with horn

Date	Mintage	F12	VF20	XF40	MS60	MS63
2005	Est. 15000	PF63 75.00	PF65 85.00			

KM# 55 10 DOLLARS
1.24 g., 0.999 Gold 0.0396 oz. AGW, 13.92 mm. **Obv:** Shield **Rev:** Angel

Date	Mintage	F12	VF20	XF40	MS60	MS63
2006	Est. 15000	PF63 75.00	PF65 85.00			

KM# 58 10 DOLLARS
31.11 g., 0.999 Silver 0.9926 oz. ASW, 38.61 mm. **Obv:** Shield **Rev:** The Magi

Date	Mintage	F12	VF20	XF40	MS60	MS63
2011	10,000	PF63 45.00	PF65 50.00			

KM# 59 10 DOLLARS
28.28 g., 0.925 Silver 0.8356 oz. ASW, 38.61 mm. **Subject:** London Olympics, 2012 **Obv:** Shield **Rev:** Weightlifting and sunrise

Date	Mintage	F12	VF20	XF40	MS60	MS63
2011	Est. 10000	PF63 35.00	PF65 40.00			

KM# 61 10 DOLLARS
28.28 g., 0.925 Silver 0.8356 oz. ASW, 38.61 mm. **Subject:** Ships and explorers **Obv:** Shield **Rev:** Mayflower, 1620

Date	Mintage	F12	VF20	XF40	MS60	MS63
2011	Est. 5000	PF65 45.00				

KM# 63 10 DOLLARS
28.28 g., 0.925 Silver 0.8356 oz. ASW, 38.61 mm. **Subject:** Elizabeth II 60th Anniversary of reign, 90th Birthday of Prince Philip **Obv:** Shield **Rev:** Prince Philip at right, Philip and Elizabeth at right

Date	Mintage	F12	VF20	XF40	MS60	MS63
2011	10,000	PF63 35.00	PF65 40.00			

KM# 65 10 DOLLARS
1.24 g., 0.999 Gold 0.0396 oz. AGW, 13.92 mm. **Obv:** Shield **Rev:** Joseph, Jesus and Mary, in manger, with cattle

Date	Mintage	F12	VF20	XF40	MS60	MS63
2011	Est. 7500	PF63 75.00	PF65 85.00			

KM# 66 10 DOLLARS
12.00 g., 0.925 Silver 0.3546 oz. ASW, 38.61 mm. **Obv:** Shield **Rev:** Water Scene - Dark blue sky

Date	Mintage	F12	VF20	XF40	MS60	MS63
2012	Est. 5000	PF63 55.00	PF65 65.00			

KM# 71 10 DOLLARS
20.00 g., 0.925 Silver 0.591 oz. ASW, 38.61 mm. **Subject:** 2016 Olympics - Sailing

Date	Mintage	F12	VF20	XF40	MS60	MS63
2013	Est. 10000	PF63 65.00	PF65 75.00			

KM# 72 10 DOLLARS
10.00 g., 0.500 Silver 0.1597 oz. ASW, 25 mm. **Subject:** ANZAC Day - Trumpet

Date	Mintage	F12	VF20	XF40	MS60	MS63
2013	Est. 150000	PF63 40.00	PF65 50.00			

KM# 73 10 DOLLARS
10.00 g., 0.500 Silver 0.1597 oz. ASW, 25 mm. **Subject:** ANZAC Day - Rifle

Date	Mintage	F12	VF20	XF40	MS60	MS63
2013	Est. 150000	PF63 40.00	PF65 50.00			

KM# 67 20 DOLLARS
62.21 g., 0.925 Silver 1.8382 oz. ASW, 55 mm. **Obv:** Shield **Rev:** Christmas tree cut out, gilt highlights

Date	Mintage	F12	VF20	XF40	MS60	MS63
2012	Est. 999	PF65 200				

KM# 76 20 DOLLARS
62.20 g., 0.925 Silver 1.8379 oz. ASW, 55 mm. **Subject:** Christmas Bells

Date	Mintage	F12	VF20	XF40	MS60	MS63
2013	Est. 999	PF65 125				

KM# 53 50 DOLLARS
3.11 g., 0.999 Gold 0.0992 oz. AGW, 18.5 mm. **Obv:** Shield **Rev:** Jesus and Mary riding donkey, Joseph walking beside

Date	Mintage	F12	VF20	XF40	MS60	MS63
2005	1,500	PF65 185				

KM# 56 50 DOLLARS
3.11 g., 0.999 Gold 0.0992 oz. AGW, 18.5 mm. **Obv:** Shield **Rev:** Holy family in manger

Date	Mintage	F12	VF20	XF40	MS60	MS63
2006	1,500	PF65 185				

KM# 64 50 DOLLARS
7.77 g., 0.999 Gold 0.248 oz. AGW, 25 mm. **Obv:** Shield **Rev:** Angel, facing hands in prayer

Date	Mintage	F12	VF20	XF40	MS60	MS63
2011	Est. 1500	PF65 475				

KM# 77 150 DOLLARS
0.50 g., 0.999 Gold AGW, 11 mm. **Subject:** Holy Family

Date	Mintage	F12	VF20	XF40	MS60	MS63
2013	Est. 5000			PF63 45.00	PF65 50.00	

KM# 52 200 DOLLARS
31.11 g., 0.999 Gold 0.9926 oz. AGW, 40 mm. **Obv:** Shield **Rev:** The Holy Family - Joseph, Mary and Jesus

Date	Mintage	F12	VF20	XF40	MS60	MS63
2005	500			PF65 1,800		

KM# 57 200 DOLLARS
31.11 g., 0.999 Gold 0.9926 oz. AGW, 40 mm. **Obv:** Shield **Rev:** Holy Family and shepards in manger

Date	Mintage	F12	VF20	XF40	MS60	MS63
2006	500			PF65 1,800		

NORTH KOREA

The Democratic Peoples Republic of Korea, situated in northeastern Asia on the northern half of the Korean peninsula between the Peoples Republic of China and the Republic of Korea, has an area of 46,540 sq. mi. (120,540 sq. km.) and a population of 20 million. Capital: Pyongyang. The economy is based on heavy industry and agriculture. Metals, minerals and farm produce are exported.

MONETARY SYSTEM
100 Chon = 1 Won

MINT
Pyongyang

DATING
In the year 2001 the North Korean adopted the "Juche" dating system which is based on the birth year of Kim Il Sung, founder of North Korea. He was born in 1911. "Quel" refers to month and "Quil" refers to day. 9 Quel 3 Quil refers to September 3rd. The western dates on these coins follow the "Juche" date in parenthesis.

PEOPLES REPUBLIC
DECIMAL COINAGE

KM# 183 1/2 CHON
2.16 g., Aluminum, 27.02 mm. **Obv:** State arms **Rev:** Horse **Edge:** Plain

Date	Mintage	F12	VF20	XF40	MS60	MS63
2002	—			—	1.25	1.50

KM# 184 1/2 CHON
2.16 g., Aluminum, 27.02 mm. **Obv:** State arms **Rev:** Orangutan **Edge:** Plain

Date	Mintage	F12	VF20	XF40	MS60	MS63
2002	—			—	1.25	1.50

KM# 185 1/2 CHON
2.16 g., Aluminum, 27.02 mm. **Obv:** State arms **Rev:** Leopard **Edge:** Plain

Date	Mintage	F12	VF20	XF40	MS60	MS63
2002	—			—	1.25	1.50

KM# 186 1/2 CHON
2.16 g., Aluminum, 27.02 mm. **Obv:** State arms **Rev:** Two giraffes **Edge:** Plain

Date	Mintage	F12	VF20	XF40	MS60	MS63
2002	—			—	1.25	1.50

KM# 187 1/2 CHON
2.16 g., Aluminum, 27.02 mm. **Obv:** State arms **Rev:** Helmeted guineafowl **Edge:** Plain

Date	Mintage	F12	VF20	XF40	MS60	MS63
2002	—			—	1.25	1.50

KM# 188 1/2 CHON
2.16 g., Aluminum, 27.02 mm. **Obv:** State arms **Rev:** Mamushi pit viper **Edge:** Plain

Date	Mintage	F12	VF20	XF40	MS60	MS63
2002	—			—	1.25	1.50

KM# 189 1/2 CHON
2.16 g., Aluminum, 27.02 mm. **Obv:** State arms **Rev:** Bighorn sheep **Edge:** Plain

Date	Mintage	F12	VF20	XF40	MS60	MS63
2002	—			—	1.25	1.50

KM# 190 1/2 CHON
2.16 g., Aluminum, 27.02 mm. **Obv:** State arms **Rev:** Hippopotamus **Edge:** Plain

Date	Mintage	F12	VF20	XF40	MS60	MS63
2002	—			—	1.25	1.50

KM# 191 1/2 CHON
2.16 g., Aluminum, 27.02 mm. **Subject:** FAO **Obv:** State arms **Rev:** Ancient ship **Edge:** Plain

Date	Mintage	F12	VF20	XF40	MS60	MS63
2002	—			—	1.25	1.50

KM# 192 1/2 CHON
2.16 g., Aluminum, 27.02 mm. **Subject:** FAO **Obv:** State arms **Rev:** Archaic ship **Edge:** Plain

Date	Mintage	F12	VF20	XF40	MS60	MS63
2002	—			—	1.25	1.50

KM# 193 1/2 CHON
2.16 g., Aluminum, 27.02 mm. **Subject:** FAO **Obv:** State arms **Rev:** Modern train **Edge:** Plain

Date	Mintage	F12	VF20	XF40	MS60	MS63
2002	—			—	1.25	1.50

KM# 194 1/2 CHON
2.16 g., Aluminum, 27.02 mm. **Subject:** FAO **Obv:** State arms **Rev:** Jet airliner **Edge:** Plain

Date	Mintage	F12	VF20	XF40	MS60	MS63
2002	—			—	1.25	1.50

KM# 195 CHON
4.63 g., Brass, 21.7 mm. **Subject:** FAO **Obv:** State arms **Rev:** Antique steam locomotive **Edge:** Plain

Date	Mintage	F12	VF20	XF40	MS60	MS63
2002	—			—	1.50	1.75

KM# 196 CHON
4.63 g., Brass, 21.7 mm. **Subject:** FAO **Obv:** State arms **Rev:** Antique automobile **Edge:** Plain

Date	Mintage	F12	VF20	XF40	MS60	MS63
2002	—			—	1.50	1.75

KM# 197 2 CHON
6.04 g., Copper-Nickel, 24.2 mm. **Subject:** FAO **Obv:** State arms **Rev:** Antique touring car **Edge:** Plain

Date	Mintage	F12	VF20	XF40	MS60	MS63
2002	—			—	2.00	2.50

KM# 499 50 CHON
Aluminum, 27 mm. **Rev:** Two bicyclists

Date	Mintage	F12	VF20	XF40	MS60	MS63
2001 Proof, rare	—	—	—	—	—	—

KM# 162.2 WON
7.00 g., Aluminum, 40 mm. **Obv:** State arms, date above value **Rev:** Radiant Korean map and landmarks **Edge:** Plain

Date	Mintage	F12	VF20	XF40	MS60	MS63
2001	—	PF65 15.00				

KM# 351 WON
7.00 g., Aluminum, 40 mm. **Obv:** State arms, date and value below **Rev:** North Korean Arch of Triumph **Edge:** Plain

Date	Mintage	F12	VF20	XF40	MS60	MS63
2001	—	PF65 12.00				

KM# 352 WON
28.60 g., Brass, 40.1 mm. **Obv:** State arms, value below **Rev:** North Korean Arch of Triumph **Edge:** Plain

Date	Mintage	F12	VF20	XF40	MS60	MS63
2001	—	PF65 15.00				

KM# 353 WON
0.45 g., Aluminum, 40 mm. **Obv:** State arms, value below **Rev:** N. Korean landmarks and tourists above ship **Edge:** Plain

Date	Mintage	F12	VF20	XF40	MS60	MS63
2001	—	PF65 12.00				

KM# 354 WON
27.63 g., Brass, 40 mm. **Obv:** State arms, date and value below **Rev:** N. Korean landmarks and tourists above ship **Edge:** Plain

Date	Mintage	F12	VF20	XF40	MS60	MS63
2001	—	PF65 15.00				

KM# 355 WON
6.75 g., Aluminum, 40 mm. **Obv:** State arms, value below **Rev:** Temple of Heaven above Hong Kong city view below **Edge:** Plain

Date	Mintage	F12	VF20	XF40	MS60	MS63
ND (2001)	—	PF65 12.00				

KM# 356 WON
28.10 g., Brass, 40 mm. **Obv:** State arms, date and value below **Rev:** Temple of Heaven above, Hong Kong city view below **Edge:** Plain

Date	Mintage	F12	VF20	XF40	MS60	MS63
2001	—	PF65 15.00				

KM# 358 WON
6.75 g., Aluminum, 40 mm. **Obv:** State arms **Rev:** Old fort **Edge:** Plain

Date	Mintage	F12	VF20	XF40	MS60	MS63
2001	—	PF65 12.00				

KM# 359 WON
7.00 g., Aluminum, 40.1 mm. **Obv:** State arms **Rev:** Old couple above dates 1945-2000 **Edge:** Plain

Date	Mintage	F12	VF20	XF40	MS60	MS63
2001	—	PF65 12.00				

KM# 360 WON
27.80 g., Brass, 40.1 mm. **Obv:** State arms **Rev:** Blue Dragon **Edge:** Plain

Date	Mintage	F12	VF20	XF40	MS60	MS63
2001	—	PF65 20.00				

KM# 361 WON
7.00 g., Aluminum, 40.1 mm. **Obv:** State arms **Rev:** Head of Deng Zio Ping 3/4 left, 1904-1997 flanking, sprigs below **Edge:** Plain

Date	Mintage	F12	VF20	XF40	MS60	MS63
2001	—	PF65 12.00				

KM# 362 WON
7.00 g., Aluminum, 40.1 mm. **Obv:** State arms **Rev:** Children flying a kite **Edge:** Plain

Date	Mintage	F12	VF20	XF40	MS60	MS63
2001	—	PF65 15.00				

KM# 363 WON
7.00 g., Aluminum, 40.1 mm. **Obv:** State arms **Rev:** Children on seesaw **Edge:** Plain

Date	Mintage	F12	VF20	XF40	MS60	MS63
2001	—	PF65 15.00				

KM# 364 WON
7.00 g., Aluminum, 40.1 mm. **Obv:** State arms **Rev:** Children wrestling **Edge:** Plain

Date	Mintage	F12	VF20	XF40	MS60	MS63
2001	—	PF65 15.00				

KM# 365 WON
7.00 g., Aluminum, 40.1 mm. **Obv:** State arms **Rev:** Girl on swing **Edge:** Plain

Date	Mintage	F12	VF20	XF40	MS60	MS63
2001	—	PF65 15.00				

KM# 366 WON
7.00 g., Aluminum, 40.1 mm. **Obv:** State arms **Rev:** Girls jumping rope **Edge:** Plain

Date	Mintage	F12	VF20	XF40	MS60	MS63
2001	—	PF65 15.00				

KM# 367 WON
8.70 g., Aluminum, 40.4 mm. **Obv:** State arms **Rev:** Kumdang-2 Injection" in center square on leaves **Edge:** Plain

Date	Mintage	F12	VF20	XF40	MS60	MS63
2001	—	PF65 15.00				

KM# 368 WON
27.61 g., Brass, 40.2 mm. **Obv:** State arms **Rev:** Bust of Kim Il-Sung, 1912-1994 flanking, sprigs below **Edge:** Plain

Date	Mintage	F12	VF20	XF40	MS60	MS63
JU90-2001	—	PF65 17.50				

KM# 369 WON
6.55 g., Aluminum, 40.4 mm. **Obv:** State arms **Rev:** Train at left, couple below jet plane at right **Edge:** Plain

Date	Mintage	F12	VF20	XF40	MS60	MS63
2001	—	PF65 15.00				

KM# 370 WON
27.56 g., Brass, 40.1 mm. **Obv:** State arms **Rev:** Train at left, couple below jet plane at right **Edge:** Plain

Date	Mintage	F12	VF20	XF40	MS60	MS63
2001	—	PF65 17.50				

KM# 371 WON
5.05 g., Aluminum, 35 mm. **Obv:** State arms **Rev:** Hong Kong city view **Edge:** Plain

Date	Mintage	F12	VF20	XF40	MS60	MS63
2001	—	PF65 10.00				

KM# 372 WON
6.40 g., Aluminum, 40 mm. **Obv:** State arms **Rev:** Bust with beard facing flanked by text **Edge:** Plain

Date	Mintage	F12	VF20	XF40	MS60	MS63
2001	—	PF65 12.00				

KM# 373 WON
6.90 g., Aluminum, 40 mm. **Subject:** 1996 Olympics **Obv:** State arms **Rev:** Two green gymnasts and multicolor flame **Edge:** Plain

Date	Mintage	F12	VF20	XF40	MS60	MS63
2001	—	PF65 15.00				

KM# 374 WON
7.00 g., Aluminum, 40 mm. **Obv:** State arms **Rev:** Taedong Gatehouse **Edge:** Plain

Date	Mintage	F12	VF20	XF40	MS60	MS63
2001	—	PF65 15.00				

KM# 375 WON
8.50 g., Aluminum, 40.2 mm. **Obv:** State arms **Rev:** Logo above Baektn Mountain volcano crater **Edge:** Plain

Date	Mintage	F12	VF20	XF40	MS60	MS63
JU90-2001	—	PF65 10.00				

KM# 376 WON
7.10 g., Aluminum, 40.1 mm. **Subject:** 1996 Olympics **Obv:** State arms **Rev:** Horse jumping **Edge:** Plain

Date	Mintage	F12	VF20	XF40	MS60	MS63
2001	—	PF65 15.00				

KM# 377 WON
7.00 g., Aluminum, 40.1 mm. **Subject:** 1996 Olympics **Obv:** State arms **Rev:** Four runners **Edge:** Plain

Date	Mintage	F12	VF20	XF40	MS60	MS63
2001	—	PF65 15.00				

KM# 378 WON
6.84 g., Aluminum, 40.1 mm. **Obv:** State arms **Rev:** Monument flanked by multicolor flags and flowers **Edge:** Plain

Date	Mintage	F12	VF20	XF40	MS60	MS63
2001	—	PF65 12.00				

KM# 379 WON
6.60 g., Aluminum, 40.1 mm. **Obv:** State arms **Rev:** Olympic diver **Edge:** Plain

Date	Mintage	F12	VF20	XF40	MS60	MS63
2001	—	PF65 15.00				

KM# 380 WON
6.91 g., Aluminum, 40.1 mm. **Obv:** State arms **Rev:** Olympic handball player **Edge:** Plain

Date	Mintage	F12	VF20	XF40	MS60	MS63
2001	—	PF65 15.00				

KM# 381 WON
7.11 g., Aluminum, 40.2 mm. **Obv:** State arms **Rev:** Olympic high bar gymnast **Edge:** Plain

Date	Mintage	F12	VF20	XF40	MS60	MS63
2001	—	PF65 15.00				

KM# 382 WON
6.50 g., Aluminum, 40.1 mm. **Obv:** State arms **Rev:** Olympic archer **Edge:** Plain

Date	Mintage	F12	VF20	XF40	MS60	MS63
2001	—	PF65 15.00				

KM# 383 WON
7.10 g., Aluminum, 40.1 mm. **Obv:** State arms **Rev:** Olympic hurdler **Edge:** Plain

Date	Mintage	F12	VF20	XF40	MS60	MS63
2001	—	PF65 15.00				

KM# 384 WON
7.15 g., Aluminum, 40.1 mm. **Obv:** State arms **Rev:** Kim Il Sung's birthplace side view **Edge:** Plain

Date	Mintage	F12	VF20	XF40	MS60	MS63
JU90-2001	—	PF65 15.00				

KM# 385 WON
7.00 g., Aluminum, 40.1 mm. **Obv:** State arms **Rev:** Mt.
Kumgang Fairy playing flute **Edge:** Plain

Date	Mintage	F12	VF20	XF40	MS60	MS63
2001	—	PF65 12.00				

KM# 452 WON
27.44 g., Brass, 40 mm. **Obv:** State arms **Rev:** Early sailing ship
Rev. Legend: • HISTORY OF SEAFARING • MERCHANTMAN
- THE DPR KOREA . KORYO PERIOD . 918-1392 **Edge:** Plain

Date	Mintage	F12	VF20	XF40	MS60	MS63
2001	—	PF65 9.00				

KM# 505 WON
28.00 g., Brass **Obv:** National arms **Rev:** Rainbow lori

Date	Mintage	F12	VF20	XF40	MS60	MS63
2001	—	PF65 8.50				

KM# 238a WON
7.14 g., Aluminum, 40.1 mm. **Obv:** State arms **Rev:** Tiger and
cub **Edge:** Plain

Date	Mintage	F12	VF20	XF40	MS60	MS63
2001	—	PF65 17.00				

KM# 294a WON
6.75 g., Aluminum, 40 mm. **Obv:** State arms **Rev:** Antique
ceramics **Edge:** Plain

Date	Mintage	F12	VF20	XF40	MS60	MS63
2001	—	PF65 15.00				

KM# 358a WON
28.10 g., Brass, 40 mm. **Obv:** State arms **Rev:** Old fort **Edge:**
Plain

Date	Mintage	F12	VF20	XF40	MS60	MS63
2001	—	PF65 15.00				

KM# 359a WON
27.80 g., Brass, 40.1 mm. **Obv:** State arms **Rev:** Old couple
above dates 1945-2000 **Edge:** Plain

Date	Mintage	F12	VF20	XF40	MS60	MS63
2001	—	PF65 15.00				

KM# 361a WON
27.80 g., Brass, 40.1 mm. **Obv:** State arms **Rev:** Head 3/4 left
divides dates(1904-1997) flanked by sprigs **Edge:** Plain

Date	Mintage	F12	VF20	XF40	MS60	MS63
2001	—	PF65 15.00				

KM# 362a WON
27.80 g., Brass, 40.1 mm. **Obv:** State arms **Rev:** Children
flying a kite **Edge:** Plain

Date	Mintage	F12	VF20	XF40	MS60	MS63
2001	—	PF65 17.50				

KM# 363a WON
27.80 g., Brass, 40.1 mm. **Obv:** State arms **Rev:** Children on
seesaw **Edge:** Plain

Date	Mintage	F12	VF20	XF40	MS60	MS63
2001	—	PF65 17.50				

KM# 364a WON
27.80 g., Brass, 40.1 mm. **Obv:** State arms **Rev:** Children
wrestling **Edge:** Plain

Date	Mintage	F12	VF20	XF40	MS60	MS63
2001	—	PF65 17.50				

KM# 365a WON
27.80 g., Brass, 40.1 mm. **Obv:** State arms **Rev:** Girl on swing
Edge: Plain

Date	Mintage	F12	VF20	XF40	MS60	MS63
2001	—	PF65 17.50				

KM# 366a WON
27.80 g., Brass, 40.1 mm. **Obv:** State arms **Rev:** Girls jumping
rope **Edge:** Plain

Date	Mintage	F12	VF20	XF40	MS60	MS63
2001	—	PF65 17.50				

KM# 367a WON
26.54 g., Brass, 40.2 mm. **Obv:** State arms **Rev:** Kumdang-2
Injection" in center square on leaves **Edge:** Plain

Date	Mintage	F12	VF20	XF40	MS60	MS63
2001	—	PF65 17.50				

KM# 372a WON
27.70 g., Brass, 40 mm. **Obv:** State arms **Rev:** Bust with beard
facing flanked by text **Edge:** Plain

Date	Mintage	F12	VF20	XF40	MS60	MS63
2001	—	PF65 15.00				

KM# 381a WON
28.82 g., Brass, 40.1 mm. **Obv:** State arms **Rev:** Olympic high
bar gymnast **Edge:** Plain

Date	Mintage	F12	VF20	XF40	MS60	MS63
2001	—	PF65 17.50				

KM# 382a WON
27.41 g., Brass, 40.2 mm. **Obv:** State arms **Rev:** Olympic
archer **Edge:** Plain

Date	Mintage	F12	VF20	XF40	MS60	MS63
2001	—	PF65 17.50				

KM# 383a WON
28.00 g., Brass, 40.1 mm. **Obv:** State arms **Rev:** Olympic
hurdler **Edge:** Plain

Date	Mintage	F12	VF20	XF40	MS60	MS63
2001	—	PF65 17.50				

KM# 385a WON
28.16 g., Brass, 40.2 mm. **Obv:** State arms **Rev:** Mt. Kumgang
Fairy playing flute **Edge:** Plain

Date	Mintage	F12	VF20	XF40	MS60	MS63
2001	—	PF65 15.00				

KM# 159 WON
17.00 g., Copper-Nickel, 35 mm. **Subject:** First Nobel Prize
Winner in Physics - Wilhelm C. Roentgen **Obv:** State arms
Rev: Bust 3/4 right at left with same person seated in lab at
right **Edge:** Plain

Date	Mintage	F12	VF20	XF40	MS60	MS63
ND-2001	2,000	PF65 100				

KM# 158 WON
17.00 g., Copper-Nickel, 35 mm. **Subject:** First Nobel Prize
Winner in Literature - Sully Prudhomme **Obv:** State arms **Rev:**
Half length seated bust left flanked by shelves and books **Edge:**
Plain

Date	Mintage	F12	VF20	XF40	MS60	MS63
ND-2001	2,000	PF65 100				

KM# 160a WON
17.00 g., Copper-Nickel, 35 mm. **Subject:** Wildlife **Obv:** State
arms **Rev:** Two nesting Japanese Ibis birds **Edge:** Plain

Date	Mintage	F12	VF20	XF40	MS60	MS63
JU2001	200	PF65 100				

KM# 160b WON
5.35 g., Aluminum, 35.1 mm. **Obv:** State arms **Rev:** Two nest
building Japanese Ibis birds **Edge:** Plain

Date	Mintage	F12	VF20	XF40	MS60	MS63
JU90-2001	—	PF65 15.00				

KM# 207a WON
16.05 g., Brass, 35 mm. **Obv:** State arms **Rev:** Two Longtail
Gorals **Edge:** Plain

Date	Mintage	F12	VF20	XF40	MS60	MS63
JU90-2001	—	PF65 12.50				

KM# 236a WON
7.00 g., Aluminum, 40 mm. **Obv:** State arms **Rev:** Hyonmu
Edge: Plain

Date	Mintage	F12	VF20	XF40	MS60	MS63
2001	—	PF65 17.50				

KM# 157 WON
6.70 g., Aluminum, 40 mm. **Subject:** Seafaring Ships **Obv:**
State arms **Rev:** Cruise ship below stylized head left profile
Edge: Plain

Date	Mintage	F12	VF20	XF40	MS60	MS63
JU90-2001	—	PF65 10.00				

KM# 157a WON
29.05 g., Brass, 40.2 mm. **Obv:** State arms **Rev:** Cruise ship
below stylized head profile left **Edge:** Plain

Date	Mintage	F12	VF20	XF40	MS60	MS63
2001	—	PF65 17.50				

KM# 458 WON
5.00 g., Aluminum, 35 mm. **Obv:** National arms, Country name
Rev: Krugenstern

Date	Mintage	F12	VF20	XF40	MS60	MS63
2001	—	PF65 7.00				

KM# 158a WON
5.00 g., Aluminum, 35 mm. **Subject:** Nobel prize in literature,
Sully Prudhomme

Date	Mintage	F12	VF20	XF40	MS60	MS63
2001	—	PF65 6.00				

KM# 158b WON
16.20 g., Brass, 35 mm. **Subject:** First Nobel Prize Winner in
Literature - Sully Prudhomme **Obv:** State arms **Rev:** Half length
seated bust left flanked by shelves and books **Edge:** Plain

Date	Mintage	F12	VF20	XF40	MS60	MS63
ND-2001	—	PF65 10.00				

KM# 159a WON
5.00 g., Aluminum, 35 mm. **Subject:** Nobel in Physics, Wilhelm
C. Rontgen

Date	Mintage	F12	VF20	XF40	MS60	MS63
2001	—	PF65 6.00				

KM# 159b WON
16.20 g., Brass, 35 mm. **Subject:** First Nobel Prize in Physics
- Wiliam C. Rontgen **Obv:** State arms **Rev:** Bust 3/4 right at left
with same person seated in lab at right **Edge:** Plain

Date	Mintage	F12	VF20	XF40	MS60	MS63
ND-2001	—	PF65 10.00				

KM# 160 WON
16.20 g., Brass, 35 mm. **Subject:** Nipponia Nippon **Obv:** State
arms **Rev:** Two nest building Japanese ibis **Edge:** Plain

Date	Mintage	F12	VF20	XF40	MS60	MS63
JU90-2001	—	PF65 15.00				

KM# 202 WON
17.00 g., Copper-Nickel, 35 mm. **Subject:** School Ships **Obv:**
State arms **Rev:** SS Krusenstern **Edge:** Plain

Date	Mintage	F12	VF20	XF40	MS60	MS63
ND-2001	200	PF65 100				

KM# 204 WON
17.00 g., Copper-Nickel, 35 mm. **Subject:** Wildlife **Obv:** State arms **Rev:** Two standing Japanese Ibis birds **Edge:** Plain

Date	Mintage	F12	VF20	XF40	MS60	MS63
JU90-2001	100	PF65 150				

KM# 207 WON
17.00 g., Copper-Nickel, 35 mm. **Subject:** Wildlife **Obv:** State arms **Rev:** Two Korean Longtail Gorals **Edge:** Plain

Date	Mintage	F12	VF20	XF40	MS60	MS63
JU90-2001	200	PF65 100				

KM# 207b WON
5.35 g., Aluminum, 35.1 mm. **Obv:** State arms **Rev:** Two Longtail Gorals **Edge:** Plain

Date	Mintage	F12	VF20	XF40	MS60	MS63
JU90-2001	—	PF65 10.00				

KM# 209 WON
17.00 g., Copper-Nickel, 35 mm. **Subject:** First Nobel Prize Winner in Medicine - Emil A. von Behring **Obv:** State arms **Rev:** Lab beaker divides half length figures facing each other **Edge:** Plain

Date	Mintage	F12	VF20	XF40	MS60	MS63
ND-2001	2,000	PF65 100				

KM# 209b WON
16.00 g., Brass, 35 mm. **Subject:** Nobel prize in Medicine, Emil von Behring

Date	Mintage	F12	VF20	XF40	MS60	MS63
2001	—	PF65 7.00				

KM# 209a WON
5.00 g., Aluminum, 35 mm. **Subject:** Nobel prize in Medicine, Emil von Behring

Date	Mintage	F12	VF20	XF40	MS60	MS63
2001	—	PF65 6.00				

KM# 210 WON
17.00 g., Copper-Nickel, 35 mm. **Subject:** First Nobel Prize Winner in Peace - Henri Dunant **Obv:** State arms **Rev:** Bust facing at left, war wounded at right **Edge:** Plain

Date	Mintage	F12	VF20	XF40	MS60	MS63
ND-2001	2,000	PF65 100				

KM# 210a WON
5.00 g., Aluminum, 35 mm. **Subject:** Nobel Peace Prize, Jean H. Dunant

Date	Mintage	F12	VF20	XF40	MS60	MS63
2001	—	PF65 6.00				

KM# 210b WON
5.00 g., Aluminum, 35 mm. **Subject:** Nobel Peace prize, Jean H. Dunant

Date	Mintage	F12	VF20	XF40	MS60	MS63
2001	—	PF65 7.00				

KM# 211 WON
17.00 g., Copper-Nickel, 35 mm. **Subject:** First Nobel Prize Winner in Chemistry - Jacobus Van't Hoff **Obv:** State arms **Rev:** Standing figures in lab scene **Edge:** Plain

Date	Mintage	F12	VF20	XF40	MS60	MS63
ND-2001	2,000	PF65 100				

KM# 211a WON
5.00 g., Aluminum, 35 mm. **Subject:** Nobel in Chemistry, Jacob van't Hoff

Date	Mintage	F12	VF20	XF40	MS60	MS63
2001	—	PF65 6.00				

KM# 211b WON
16.00 g., Brass, 35 mm. **Subject:** Nobel prize in Chemistry, Jabob van't Hoff

Date	Mintage	F12	VF20	XF40	MS60	MS63
2001	—	PF65 7.00				

KM# 212 WON
17.00 g., Copper-Nickel, 35 mm. **Subject:** First Nobel Prize Winner in Peace - Frederic Passy **Obv:** State arms **Rev:** Head left at right with allegorical scene at left **Edge:** Plain

Date	Mintage	F12	VF20	XF40	MS60	MS63
ND-2001	2,000	PF65 100				

KM# 212a WON
5.00 g., Aluminum, 35 mm. **Subject:** Nobel Peace Prize, Frederic Passy

Date	Mintage	F12	VF20	XF40	MS60	MS63
2001	—	PF65 6.00				

KM# 212b WON
16.00 g., Brass, 35 mm. **Subject:** Nobel Peace Prize, Frederic Passy

Date	Mintage	F12	VF20	XF40	MS60	MS63
2001	—	PF65 7.00				

KM# 232 WON
28.11 g., Brass, 40 mm. **Obv:** State arms **Rev:** White-bellied woodpecker **Edge:** Plain

Date	Mintage	F12	VF20	XF40	MS60	MS63
2001	—	PF65 27.50				

KM# 233 WON
28.11 g., Brass, 40 mm. **Obv:** State arms **Rev:** Black grouse **Edge:** Plain

Date	Mintage	F12	VF20	XF40	MS60	MS63
2001	—	PF65 27.50				

KM# 234 WON
28.11 g., Brass, 40 mm. **Obv:** State arms **Rev:** Sand grouse **Edge:** Plain

Date	Mintage	F12	VF20	XF40	MS60	MS63
2001	—	PF65 27.50				

KM# 235 WON
28.11 g., Brass, 40 mm. **Obv:** State arms **Rev:** Fairy Pitta bird **Edge:** Plain

Date	Mintage	F12	VF20	XF40	MS60	MS63
2001	—	PF65 27.50				

KM# 236 WON
28.11 g., Brass, 40 mm. **Obv:** State arms **Rev:** Mythical "Hyonmu **Edge:** Plain

Date	Mintage	F12	VF20	XF40	MS60	MS63
2001	—	PF65 27.50				

KM# 237 WON
28.11 g., Brass, 40 mm. **Obv:** State arms **Rev:** Blue Dragon
Edge: Plain

Date	Mintage	F12	VF20	XF40	MS60	MS63
2001	—	PF65 27.50				

KM# 238 WON
28.11 g., Brass, 40 mm. **Obv:** State arms **Rev:** Two tigers
Edge: Plain

Date	Mintage	F12	VF20	XF40	MS60	MS63
2001	—	PF65 27.50				

KM# 239 WON
28.11 g., Brass, 40 mm. **Obv:** State arms **Rev:** Brontosaurus
Edge: Plain

Date	Mintage	F12	VF20	XF40	MS60	MS63
2001	—	PF65 27.50				

KM# 247 WON
26.95 g., Brass, 40 mm. **Obv:** State arms **Rev:** Soldier
watching an air raid on a Yalu River bridge **Edge:** Plain

Date	Mintage	F12	VF20	XF40	MS60	MS63
2001	—	PF65 20.00				

KM# 248 WON
7.00 g., Aluminum, 40 mm. **Obv:** State arms **Rev:** Multicolor
rabbit and hearts **Edge:** Plain **Note:** Year of the Rabbit

Date	Mintage	F12	VF20	XF40	MS60	MS63
2001	—	PF65 20.00				

KM# 290 WON
28.20 g., Brass, 40.1 mm. **Obv:** State arms **Rev:** Bust of Kim
Johg-Il facing above flower sprigs **Edge:** Plain

Date	Mintage	F12	VF20	XF40	MS60	MS63
JU90-2001	—	PF65 20.00				

KM# 291 WON
28.20 g., Brass, 40.1 mm. **Obv:** State arms **Rev:** Bust of Kim
Jung-Suk facing, 1917-1949 flanking, flower sprigs below **Edge:**
Plain

Date	Mintage	F12	VF20	XF40	MS60	MS63
JU90-2001	—	PF65 20.00				

KM# 293 WON
28.20 g., Brass, 40.2 mm. **Obv:** State arms **Rev:** Olympic
runners **Edge:** Crude reeding

Date	Mintage	F12	VF20	XF40	MS60	MS63
2001	—	PF65 20.00				

KM# 294 WON
28.20 g., Brass, 40.2 mm. **Obv:** State arms **Rev:** Antique
porcelain objects **Edge:** Plain

Date	Mintage	F12	VF20	XF40	MS60	MS63
2001	—	PF65 20.00				

KM# 310 WON
Aluminum **Obv:** State arms **Rev:** Tomb of King Tongmyong

Date	Mintage	F12	VF20	XF40	MS60	MS63
2001	—	PF65 12.00				

KM# 458a WON
16.00 g., Brass, 35 mm. **Subject:** Tall ships **Obv:** Arms **Rev:**
Krugenstern

Date	Mintage	F12	VF20	XF40	MS60	MS63
2001	—	PF65 8.00				

KM# 459 WON
Brass, 35 mm. **Subject:** Return of Hong Kong **Obv:** Arms **Rev:**
Architecture

Date	Mintage	F12	VF20	XF40	MS60	MS63
2001	—	PF65 6.50				

KM# 460 WON
Brass, 35 mm. **Subject:** Return of Hong Kong **Obv:** Skyline
Rev: Dragon boat

Date	Mintage	F12	VF20	XF40	MS60	MS63
2001	—	PF65 12.00				

KM# 461 WON
6.00 g., Aluminum, 38 mm. **Obv:** National arms, Central Bank
name **Rev:** Speed skater

Date	Mintage	F12	VF20	XF40	MS60	MS63
2001 Proof	—	—	—	—	—	—

KM# 461a WON
25.00 g., Brass **Subject:** 2002 Olympics **Obv:** Arms **Rev:**
Speedskater

Date	Mintage	F12	VF20	XF40	MS60	MS63
2001	—	PF65 10.00				

KM# 462 WON
Aluminum, 40 mm. **Subject:** Tae Kwon do **Obv:** Arms **Rev:**
Two sportsmen

Date	Mintage	F12	VF20	XF40	MS60	MS63
2001	—	PF65 8.00				

KM# 462a WON
28.00 g., Brass, 40 mm. **Obv:** National arms, Country name
Rev: Two Taekwondo players

Date	Mintage	F12	VF20	XF40	MS60	MS63
2001	—	PF65 7.00				

KM# 463 WON
Aluminum, 40 mm. **Obv:** Arms **Rev:** Multicolor flowers

Date	Mintage	F12	VF20	XF40	MS60	MS63
2001	—	PF65 8.00				

KM# 464 WON
Aluminum, 40 mm. **Obv:** Arms **Rev:** Woodpecker on branch
(Dryocopus Javensis)

Date	Mintage	F12	VF20	XF40	MS60	MS63
2001	—	PF65 8.00				

KM# 465 WON
Aluminum, 35 mm. **Obv:** Arms **Rev:** Zhou Enlai portrait facing

Date	Mintage	F12	VF20	XF40	MS60	MS63
2001	—	PF65 8.00				

KM# 466 WON
Aluminum, 40 mm. **Obv:** Arms **Rev:** Buddha seated, facing

Date	Mintage	F12	VF20	XF40	MS60	MS63
2001	—	PF65 7.00				

KM# 467 WON
Brass **Obv:** Arms **Rev:** Buddha seated, facing

Date	Mintage	F12	VF20	XF40	MS60	MS63
2001	—	PF65 10.00				

KM# 468 WON
Brass **Obv:** Arms **Rev:** Couple embracing, 1945-2000

Date	Mintage	F12	VF20	XF40	MS60	MS63
ND-2001	—	PF65 10.00				

KM# 504 WON
7.00 g., Aluminum, 40 mm. **Obv:** National arms **Rev:** Rainbow
lori in color

Date	Mintage	F12	VF20	XF40	MS60	MS63
2001	—	PF65 8.50				

KM# 506 WON
7.00 g., Aluminum **Rev:** Mandarian Ducks in color

Date	Mintage	F12	VF20	XF40	MS60	MS63
2001	—	PF65 8.50				

KM# 507 WON
Brass **Rev:** Mandarin Ducks

Date	Mintage	F12	VF20	XF40	MS60	MS63
2001	—	PF65 9.00				

KM# 535 WON
7.00 g., Aluminum, 40 mm. **Obv:** National arms **Rev:** Power in teh frowing area of Kaeseong in color

Date	Mintage	F12	VF20	XF40	MS60	MS63
2001 Proof	—	—	—	—	—	—

KM# 539 WON
7.00 g., Aluminum, 40 mm. **Obv:** National arms **Rev:** Panda seated in color, eating

Date	Mintage	F12	VF20	XF40	MS60	MS63
2001	—	PF65 7.50				

KM# 541 WON
7.00 g., Aluminum, 40 mm. **Obv:** National arms **Rev:** Two pandas in color

Date	Mintage	F12	VF20	XF40	MS60	MS63
2001	—	PF65 7.50				

KM# 542 WON
28.00 g., Brass **Obv:** National arms, name of the Central Bank **Rev:** Two pandas

Date	Mintage	F12	VF20	XF40	MS60	MS63
2001	—	PF65 8.00				

KM# 548 WON
7.00 g., Aluminum, 40 mm. **Obv:** National arms, name of the Central Bank **Rev:** Rainbow lori in color

Date	Mintage	F12	VF20	XF40	MS60	MS63
2001	—	PF65 7.50				

KM# 549 WON
7.00 g., Aluminum, 40 mm. **Obv:** National arms, name of the Central Bank **Rev:** Manderin duck in color

Date	Mintage	F12	VF20	XF40	MS60	MS63
2001	—	PF65 7.50				

KM# 556 WON
Brass **Rev:** Show jumper

Date	Mintage	F12	VF20	XF40	MS60	MS63
2001	—	PF65 8.00				

KM# 557 WON
7.00 g., Aluminum, 40 mm. **Obv:** National arms, name of the Central Bank **Rev:** Rythem dancers and logo in color

Date	Mintage	F12	VF20	XF40	MS60	MS63
2001	—	PF65 7.50				

KM# 558 WON
7.00 g., Aluminum, 40 mm. **Obv:** National arms, name of the Central Bank **Rev:** Chinese Peony

Date	Mintage	F12	VF20	XF40	MS60	MS63
2001	—	PF65 7.50				

KM# 559 WON
7.00 g., Aluminum, 40 mm. **Obv:** National arms, name of the Central Bank **Rev:** Panda seated in color eating

Date	Mintage	F12	VF20	XF40	MS60	MS63
2001	—	PF65 7.50				

KM# 560 WON
Brass, 28 mm. **Obv:** National arms, name of the Central Bank **Rev:** Panda seated eating

Date	Mintage	F12	VF20	XF40	MS60	MS63
2001	—	PF65 8.00				

KM# 561 WON
28.00 g., Brass, 40 mm. **Obv:** National arms, name of the Central Bank **Rev:** Soldiers attack bridge over the Yalu river at Dandong (1951)

Date	Mintage	F12	VF20	XF40	MS60	MS63
2001	—	PF65 7.50				

KM# 562 WON
28.00 g., Brass, 40 mm. **Obv:** National arms **Rev:** Soldiers attack bridge over the Yalu river at Dandong (1951)

Date	Mintage	F12	VF20	XF40	MS60	MS63
2001	—	PF65 7.50				

KM# 563 WON
28.00 g., Brass, 40 mm. **Obv:** National arms, name of the Central Bank **Rev:** Tower of Friendship in Pyeongyang with North Korean and P.R.C. flags

Date	Mintage	F12	VF20	XF40	MS60	MS63
2001	—	PF65 8.00				

KM# 568 WON
7.00 g., Aluminum, 40 mm. **Obv:** National arms **Rev:** Rocket and satelite

Date	Mintage	F12	VF20	XF40	MS60	MS63
2001	—	PF65 6.50				

KM# 568a WON
28.00 g., Brass, 40 mm. **Obv:** National arms **Rev:** Rocket and satellite

Date	Mintage	F12	VF20	XF40	MS60	MS63
2001	—	PF65 7.50				

KM# 572 WON
28.00 g., Brass, 40 mm. **Obv:** National arms, country name **Rev:** Dragon rising

Date	Mintage	F12	VF20	XF40	MS60	MS63
2001	—	PF65 7.50				

KM# 573 WON
28.00 g., Brass, 40 mm. **Obv:** National arms, name of the Central Bank **Rev:** Dragon rising

Date	Mintage	F12	VF20	XF40	MS60	MS63
2001	—	PF65 7.50				

KM# 574 WON
Brass **Obv:** National arms, country name **Rev:** Two girls on the seasaw

Date	Mintage	F12	VF20	XF40	MS60	MS63
2001	—	PF65 7.50				

KM# 575 WON
Brass **Obv:** National arms, Central Bank name **Rev:** Two girls on the seasaw

Date	Mintage	F12	VF20	XF40	MS60	MS63
2001	—	PF65 7.50				

KM# 576 WON
Brass **Obv:** National arms, country name **Rev:** Korean struggle

Date	Mintage	F12	VF20	XF40	MS60	MS63
2001	—	PF65 7.50				

KM# 577 WON
Brass **Obv:** National arms, Central Bank name **Rev:** Korean struggle

Date	Mintage	F12	VF20	XF40	MS60	MS63
2001	—	PF65 7.50				

KM# 578 WON
Brass **Obv:** National arms, country name **Rev:** Child on swing

Date	Mintage	F12	VF20	XF40	MS60	MS63
2001	—	PF65 7.50				

KM# 579 WON
Brass **Obv:** National arms, Central Bank name **Rev:** Child on swing

Date	Mintage	F12	VF20	XF40	MS60	MS63
2001	—	PF65 7.50				

KM# 580 WON
Brass **Obv:** National arms, country name **Rev:** Children skipping

Date	Mintage	F12	VF20	XF40	MS60	MS63
2001	—	PF65 7.50				

KM# 581 WON
28.00 g., Brass, 40 mm. **Obv:** National arms, Central Bank name **Rev:** Children skipping

Date	Mintage	F12	VF20	XF40	MS60	MS63
2001	—	PF65 7.50				

KM# 608 WON
7.00 g., Aluminum, 40 mm. **Obv:** National arms, Central Bank name **Rev:** Rabbit in color

Date	Mintage	F12	VF20	XF40	MS60	MS63
2001	—	PF65 7.50				

KM# 609 WON
28.00 g., Brass, 40 mm. **Obv:** National arms, country name **Rev:** Rabbit

Date	Mintage	F12	VF20	XF40	MS60	MS63
2001	—	PF65 7.50				

KM# 616 WON
7.00 g., Aluminum, 40 mm. **Obv:** National arms, Central Bank name **Rev:** White bellied woodpecker

Date	Mintage	F12	VF20	XF40	MS60	MS63
2001	—	PF65 6.00				

KM# 617 WON
7.00 g., Aluminum, 40 mm. **Obv:** National arms, Country name **Rev:** Black grouse

Date	Mintage	F12	VF20	XF40	MS60	MS63
2001	—	PF65 6.00				

KM# 618 WON
7.00 g., Aluminum, 40 mm. **Obv:** National arms, Country name **Rev:** Sand grouse

Date	Mintage	F12	VF20	XF40	MS60	MS63
2001	—	PF65 6.00				

KM# 619 WON
7.00 g., Aluminum, 40 mm. **Obv:** National arms, Country name **Rev:** Indian Pitta bird

Date	Mintage	F12	VF20	XF40	MS60	MS63
2001	—	PF65 6.00				

KM# 636 WON
28.00 g., Brass, 40 mm. **Obv:** National arms, Country name **Rev:** Two siberian tigers

Date	Mintage	F12	VF20	XF40	MS60	MS63
2001	—	PF65 7.00				

KM# 641 WON
7.00 g., Aluminum, 40 mm. **Obv:** National arms, Country name **Rev:** Gojumong, first king

Date	Mintage	F12	VF20	XF40	MS60	MS63
2001	—	PF65 6.00				

KM# 642 WON
28.00 g., Brass, 40 mm. **Obv:** National arms, Country name **Rev:** Gojumong, 1st king

Date	Mintage	F12	VF20	XF40	MS60	MS63
2001	—	PF65 7.00				

KM# 643 WON
28.00 g., Brass, 40 mm. **Obv:** National arms, Central Bank name **Rev:** Gojumong, 1st king

Date	Mintage	F12	VF20	XF40	MS60	MS63
2001	—	PF65 7.00				

KM# 644 WON
7.00 g., Aluminum, 40 mm. **Obv:** National arms, Country name **Rev:** Buddha figure as Myogilsand as rock relief in inner diamond mountain

Date	Mintage	F12	VF20	XF40	MS60	MS63
2001	—	PF65 6.00				

KM# 645 WON
28.00 g., Brass, 40 mm. **Obv:** National arms, Country name **Rev:** Buddha figure Myogilsang as rock relief in inner diamond mountain

Date	Mintage	F12	VF20	XF40	MS60	MS63
2001	—	PF65 7.00				

KM# 646 WON
Aluminum **Obv:** Dragon and country name **Rev:** King Gojoseon

Date	Mintage	F12	VF20	XF40	MS60	MS63
2001	—	PF65 6.00				

KM# 647 WON
28.00 g., Brass, 40 mm. **Obv:** Dragon and country name **Rev:** King Gojoseon

Date	Mintage	F12	VF20	XF40	MS60	MS63
2001	—	PF65 7.00				

KM# 648 WON
28.00 g., Brass, 40 mm. **Obv:** Dragon, Central Bank name **Rev:** King Gojoseon

Date	Mintage	F12	VF20	XF40	MS60	MS63
2001	—	PF65 7.00				

KM# 663 WON
7.00 g., Aluminum, 40 mm. **Obv:** National arms, Central Bank name **Rev:** Map of Korea in circle

Date	Mintage	F12	VF20	XF40	MS60	MS63
2001	—	PF65 6.00				

KM# 664 WON
28.00 g., Brass, 40 mm. **Obv:** National arms, Country name **Rev:** Map of Korea in circle

Date	Mintage	F12	VF20	XF40	MS60	MS63
2001	—	PF65 7.00				

KM# 666 WON
28.00 g., Brass, 40 mm. **Obv:** National arms, Country name **Rev:** First married couple to see again after the 1945 seperation

Date	Mintage	F12	VF20	XF40	MS60	MS63
2001	—	PF65 7.00				

KM# 670 WON
28.00 g., Brass, 40 mm. **Obv:** National arms, Central Bank name **Rev:** Kim Jeongil and Kim Daejung embrace

Date	Mintage	F12	VF20	XF40	MS60	MS63
2001	—	PF65 7.00				

KM# 671 WON
28.00 g., Brass, 40 mm. **Obv:** National arms, Central bank name **Rev:** Picture pose of Kim Jeongil and Kim Daejung

Date	Mintage	F12	VF20	XF40	MS60	MS63
2001	—	PF65 7.00				

KM# 672 WON
28.00 g., Brass, 40 mm. **Obv:** National arms, Central Bank name **Rev:** Kim Jeongil and Kim Daejung sign joint agreement

Date	Mintage	F12	VF20	XF40	MS60	MS63
2001	—	PF65 7.00				

KM# 674 WON
28.00 g., Brass, 40 mm. **Subject:** Sydney Olympics, 2000 **Obv:** National arms, Country name **Rev:** Archer

Date	Mintage	F12	VF20	XF40	MS60	MS63
2001	—	PF65 7.00				

KM# 675 WON
28.00 g., Brass, 40 mm. **Obv:** National arms, Country name **Rev:** Handball player

Date	Mintage	F12	VF20	XF40	MS60	MS63
2001	—	PF65 7.00				

KM# 676 WON
7.00 g., Aluminum, 40 mm. **Obv:** National arms, Country name **Rev:** Korean ringer

Date	Mintage	F12	VF20	XF40	MS60	MS63
2001	—	PF65 6.00				

KM# 677 WON
28.00 g., Brass, 40 mm. **Subject:** Sydney Olympics **Obv:** National arms, Country name **Rev:** Korean ringer

Date	Mintage	F12	VF20	XF40	MS60	MS63
2001	—	PF65 7.00				

KM# 691 WON
28.00 g., Brass, 40 mm. **Subject:** Kim Ilseong's 90th birthday **Obv:** National arms, Central Bank name **Rev:** Kim Ilseong

Date	Mintage	F12	VF20	XF40	MS60	MS63
2001	—	PF65 7.00				

KM# 692 WON
28.00 g., Brass, 40 mm. **Obv:** National arms, Central Bank name **Rev:** Kim Jeongil

Date	Mintage	F12	VF20	XF40	MS60	MS63
2001	—	PF65 7.00				

KM# 693 WON
28.00 g., Brass, 40 mm. **Obv:** National arms, Central Bank name **Rev:** Kim Jeongsuk

Date	Mintage	F12	VF20	XF40	MS60	MS63
2001	—	PF65 7.00				

KM# 698 WON
7.00 g., Aluminum, 40 mm. **Obv:** National arms, Country name **Rev:** House where Kim Ilseong was born

Date	Mintage	F12	VF20	XF40	MS60	MS63
2001	—	PF65 6.00				

KM# 699 WON
28.00 g., Brass, 40 mm. **Obv:** National arms, Country name **Rev:** House were Kim Ilseong was born

Date	Mintage	F12	VF20	XF40	MS60	MS63
2001	—	PF65 7.00				

KM# 700 WON
28.00 g., Brass, 40 mm. **Obv:** National arms, Central Bank name **Rev:** House where Kim Ilseong was born

Date	Mintage	F12	VF20	XF40	MS60	MS63
2001	—	PF65 7.00				

KM# 701 WON
28.00 g., Brass, 40 mm. **Obv:** National arms **Rev:** Mountain hut

Date	Mintage	F12	VF20	XF40	MS60	MS63
2001 Proof						

KM# 702 WON
7.00 g., Aluminum, 40 mm. **Obv:** National arms **Rev:** House where Kim Jeongsuk was born

Date	Mintage	F12	VF20	XF40	MS60	MS63
2001 Proof						

KM# 703 WON
28.00 g., Brass, 40 mm. **Obv:** National arms **Rev:** House where Kim Jeongsuk was born

Date	Mintage	F12	VF20	XF40	MS60	MS63
2001 Proof						

KM# 706 WON
7.00 g., Aluminum, 40 mm. **Obv:** National arms, Country name **Rev:** East gate of Pyeongyang

Date	Mintage	F12	VF20	XF40	MS60	MS63
2001	—	PF65 6.00				

KM# 707 WON
28.00 g., Brass, 40 mm. **Obv:** National arms, Country name **Rev:** East gate of Pyeongyang

Date	Mintage	F12	VF20	XF40	MS60	MS63
2001	—	PF65 7.00				

KM# 708 WON
28.00 g., Brass, 40 mm. **Obv:** National arms, Central Bank name **Rev:** East gate of Pyeongyang

Date	Mintage	F12	VF20	XF40	MS60	MS63
2001	—	PF65 7.00				

KM# 709 WON
7.00 g., Aluminum, 40 mm. **Obv:** National arms, Country name **Rev:** North gate of Pyeongyang reconstructed

Date	Mintage	F12	VF20	XF40	MS60	MS63
2001	—	PF65 6.00				

KM# 710 WON
28.00 g., Brass, 40 mm. **Obv:** National arms, Country name **Rev:** North gate of Pyeongyang reconstructed

Date	Mintage	F12	VF20	XF40	MS60	MS63
2001	—	PF65 7.00				

KM# 711 WON
28.00 g., Brass, 40 mm. **Obv:** National arms, Central Bank name **Rev:** North gate of Pyeongyang reconstructed

Date	Mintage	F12	VF20	XF40	MS60	MS63
2001	—	PF65 7.00				

KM# 712 WON
28.00 g., Brass, 40 mm. **Obv:** National arms, Country name with date **Rev:** Celadon pottery

Date	Mintage	F12	VF20	XF40	MS60	MS63
2001	—	PF65 7.00				

KM# 713 WON
28.00 g., Brass, 40 mm. **Obv:** National arms, Country name **Rev:** Celadon pottery

Date	Mintage	F12	VF20	XF40	MS60	MS63
2001	—	PF65 7.00				

KM# 714 WON
28.00 g., Brass, 40 mm. **Obv:** National arms, Central bank name **Rev:** Celadon pottery

Date	Mintage	F12	VF20	XF40	MS60	MS63
2001	—	PF65 7.00				

KM# 719 WON
28.00 g., Brass, 40 mm. **Obv:** National arms, Central Bank name **Rev:** Ginsing plant

Date	Mintage	F12	VF20	XF40	MS60	MS63
2001	—	PF65 7.00				

KM# 721 WON
7.00 g., Aluminum, 40 mm. **Obv:** National arms, Central Bank name **Rev:** Fairwell to the steam railway, 1945 and again in 2001

Date	Mintage	F12	VF20	XF40	MS60	MS63
2001	—	PF65 6.00				

KM# 722 WON
28.00 g., Brass, 40 mm. **Obv:** National arms, Central Bank name **Rev:** Fairwell to the steam train, 1945, and then again, 2001

Date	Mintage	F12	VF20	XF40	MS60	MS63
2001	—	PF65 7.00				

KM# 724 WON
7.00 g., Aluminum, 40 mm. **Obv:** National arms. Central Bank name **Rev:** Married couple in front of Pyongyang attractions with national flag and ferryboat

Date	Mintage	F12	VF20	XF40	MS60	MS63
2001	—	PF65 6.00				

KM# 725 WON
28.00 g., Brass, 40 mm. **Obv:** National arms, Country name **Rev:** Married couple in front of Pyongyang attractions with national flag and ferryboat

Date	Mintage	F12	VF20	XF40	MS60	MS63
2001	—	PF65 7.00				

KM# 726 WON
7.00 g., Aluminum, 40 mm. **Obv:** National arms, Central Bank name **Rev:** Ferryboat from Koreans in Japan on the route from Niigata to Wonsan

Date	Mintage	F12	VF20	XF40	MS60	MS63
2001	—	PF65 6.00				

KM# 727 WON
28.00 g., Brass, 40 mm. **Obv:** National arms, Central Bank name **Rev:** Ferryboat from Koreans in Japan on the route from Niigata to Wonsan

Date	Mintage	F12	VF20	XF40	MS60	MS63
2001	—	PF65 7.00				

KM# 728 WON
7.00 g., Aluminum, 40 mm. **Obv:** National arms, Country name **Rev:** Arch of Triumph on Moranbong in Pyeongyang

Date	Mintage	F12	VF20	XF40	MS60	MS63
2001	—	PF65 6.00				

KM# 729 WON
28.00 g., Brass, 40 mm. **Obv:** National arms, Central Bank name **Rev:** Arch of Triumph on Moranbong in Pyeongyang

Date	Mintage	F12	VF20	XF40	MS60	MS63
2001	—	PF65 7.00				

KM# 730 WON
7.00 g., Aluminum, 40 mm. **Obv:** National arms, Central Bank name **Rev:** Chonji crater on the Paektusan

Date	Mintage	F12	VF20	XF40	MS60	MS63
2001	—	PF65 6.00				

KM# 731 WON
28.00 g., Brass, 40 mm. **Obv:** National arms, Central Bank name **Rev:** Chonji crater on the Paektusan

Date	Mintage	F12	VF20	XF40	MS60	MS63
2001	—	PF65 7.00				

KM# 746 WON
28.00 g., Brass, 40 mm. **Obv:** National arms **Rev:** Kim Jeongill in Pudong industrial area of Shanghai

Date	Mintage	F12	VF20	XF40	MS60	MS63
2001 Proof	—	—	—	—	—	—

KM# 718 WON
Aluminum, 40 mm. **Obv:** National arms, Central Bank name **Rev:** Ginsing plant

Date	Mintage	F12	VF20	XF40	MS60	MS63
2001	—	PF65 7.00				

KM# 749 WON
28.00 g., Brass, 40 mm. **Obv:** National arms, Central Bank name **Rev:** Deng Xiaoping between peonies

Date	Mintage	F12	VF20	XF40	MS60	MS63
2001	—	PF65 7.00				

KM# 750 WON
17.00 g., Copper-Nickel, 35 mm. **Obv:** National arms **Rev:** Orca before tourist boat

Date	Mintage	F12	VF20	XF40	MS60	MS63
2001	—	PF65 14.00				

KM# 751 WON
5.00 g., Aluminum, 35 mm. **Obv:** National arms, Central Bank name **Rev:** Orca before tourist boat

Date	Mintage	F12	VF20	XF40	MS60	MS63
2001	—	PF65 6.00				

KM# 751a WON
16.00 g., Brass, 35 mm. **Obv:** National arms, Central Bank name **Rev:** Orca before tourist boat

Date	Mintage	F12	VF20	XF40	MS60	MS63
2001	—	PF65 7.00				

KM# 752 WON
17.00 g., Copper-Nickel, 35 mm. **Obv:** National arms, Country name **Rev:** Humpback whale

Date	Mintage	F12	VF20	XF40	MS60	MS63
2001	—	PF65 14.00				

KM# 753 WON
5.00 g., Aluminum, 35 mm. **Obv:** National arms, Central Bank name **Rev:** Humpback whale

Date	Mintage	F12	VF20	XF40	MS60	MS63
2001	—	PF65 6.00				

KM# 753a WON
16.00 g., Brass, 35 mm. **Obv:** National arms, Central Bank name **Rev:** Humpback whale

Date	Mintage	F12	VF20	XF40	MS60	MS63
2001	—	PF65 7.00				

KM# 754 WON
17.00 g., Copper-Nickel, 35 mm. **Obv:** National arms, Country name **Rev:** Sperm whale

Date	Mintage	F12	VF20	XF40	MS60	MS63
2001	—	PF65 14.00				

KM# 755 WON
5.00 g., Aluminum, 35 mm. **Obv:** National arms, Central Bank name **Rev:** Sperm whale

Date	Mintage	F12	VF20	XF40	MS60	MS63
2001	—	PF65 6.00				

KM# 755a WON
16.00 g., Brass, 35 mm. **Obv:** National arms, Central Bank name **Rev:** Sperm whale

Date	Mintage	F12	VF20	XF40	MS60	MS63
2001	—	PF65 7.00				

KM# 756 WON
17.00 g., Copper-Nickel, 35 mm. **Obv:** National arms, Country name **Rev:** Pilot whale

Date	Mintage	F12	VF20	XF40	MS60	MS63
2001	—	PF65 14.00				

KM# 757 WON
5.00 g., Aluminum, 35 mm. **Obv:** National arms, Central Bank name **Rev:** Pilot whale

Date	Mintage	F12	VF20	XF40	MS60	MS63
2001	—	PF65 6.00				

KM# 757a WON
16.00 g., Brass, 35 mm. **Obv:** National arms, Central Bank name **Rev:** Pilot whale

Date	Mintage	F12	VF20	XF40	MS60	MS63
2001	—	PF65 7.00				

KM# 758 WON
17.00 g., Copper-Nickel, 35 mm. **Obv:** National arms, Country name **Rev:** Northern Right Whale

Date	Mintage	F12	VF20	XF40	MS60	MS63
2001	—	PF65 14.00				

KM# 759 WON
5.00 g., Aluminum, 35 mm. **Obv:** National arms, Central Bank name **Rev:** Northern Right Whale

Date	Mintage	F12	VF20	XF40	MS60	MS63
2001	—	PF65 14.00				

KM# 759a WON
16.00 g., Brass, 35 mm. **Obv:** National arms, Central Bank name **Rev:** Northern Right Whale

Date	Mintage	F12	VF20	XF40	MS60	MS63
2001	—	PF65 10.00				

KM# 760 WON
17.00 g., Copper-Nickel, 35 mm. **Obv:** National arms, Country name **Rev:** Blue whale

Date	Mintage	F12	VF20	XF40	MS60	MS63
2001	—	PF65 14.00				

KM# 761 WON
5.00 g., Aluminum, 35 mm. **Obv:** National arms, Central Bank name **Rev:** Blue Whale

Date	Mintage	F12	VF20	XF40	MS60	MS63
2001	—	PF65 6.00				

KM# 761a WON
16.00 g., Brass, 35 mm. **Obv:** National arms, Central Bank name **Rev:** Blue whale

Date	Mintage	F12	VF20	XF40	MS60	MS63
2001	—	PF65 7.00				

KM# 762 WON
17.00 g., Copper-Nickel, 35 mm. **Obv:** National arms, Country name **Rev:** Bowhead whale

Date	Mintage	F12	VF20	XF40	MS60	MS63
2001	—	PF65 14.00				

KM# 763 WON
5.00 g., Aluminum, 35 mm. **Obv:** National arms, Central Bank name **Rev:** Bowhead whale

Date	Mintage	F12	VF20	XF40	MS60	MS63
2001	—	PF65 6.00				

KM# 763a WON
16.00 g., Brass, 35 mm. **Obv:** National arms, Central Bank name **Rev:** Bowhead whale

Date	Mintage	F12	VF20	XF40	MS60	MS63
2001	—	PF65 7.00				

KM# 764 WON
17.00 g., Copper-Nickel, 35 mm. **Obv:** National arms, Country name **Rev:** Killer whale off the coast

Date	Mintage	F12	VF20	XF40	MS60	MS63
2001	—	PF65 14.00				

KM# 765 WON
5.00 g., Aluminum, 35 mm. **Obv:** Naitonal arms, Central Bank name **Rev:** Killer whale off the coast

Date	Mintage	F12	VF20	XF40	MS60	MS63
2001	—	PF65 6.00				

KM# 765a WON
16.00 g., Brass, 35 mm. **Obv:** National arms, Central Bank name **Rev:** Killer whale off the coast

Date	Mintage	F12	VF20	XF40	MS60	MS63
2001	—	PF65 7.00				

KM# 766 WON
15.00 g., 0.999 Silver 0.4787 oz. ASW, 35 mm. **Obv:** National arms, Country name **Rev:** Northern Right Whale

Date	Mintage	F12	VF20	XF40	MS60	MS63
2001	—	PF65 35.00				

KM# 767 WON
5.00 g., Aluminum, 35 mm. **Obv:** National arms, Country name **Rev:** Chinese dragon boat

Date	Mintage	F12	VF20	XF40	MS60	MS63
2001	—	PF65 6.00				

KM# 767a WON
Brass, 35 mm. **Obv:** National arms, Country name **Rev:** Chinese dragon boat

Date	Mintage	F12	VF20	XF40	MS60	MS63
2001	—	PF65 7.00				

KM# 769 WON
16.00 g., Brass, 35 mm. **Obv:** East gate of Pyeongyang **Rev:** Krusenstern

Date	Mintage	F12	VF20	XF40	MS60	MS63
2001	—	PF65 7.00				

KM# 771 WON
6.00 g., Aluminum, 38 mm. **Obv:** National arms, Central Bank name **Rev:** White-tailed sea eagle

Date	Mintage	F12	VF20	XF40	MS60	MS63
2001	—	PF65 8.00				

KM# 771a WON
25.00 g., Brass, 38 mm. **Obv:** National arms, Central Bank name **Rev:** White-tailed sea eagle

Date	Mintage	F12	VF20	XF40	MS60	MS63
2001 Proof	—	—	—	—	—	—

KM# 772 WON
7.00 g., Aluminum, 40 mm. **Obv:** National arms, Country name **Rev:** Taekwondo kicker

Date	Mintage	F12	VF20	XF40	MS60	MS63
2001	—	PF65 6.00				

KM# 772a WON
28.00 g., Brass, 40 mm. **Obv:** National arms, Country name **Rev:** Taekwondo kicker

Date	Mintage	F12	VF20	XF40	MS60	MS63
2001	—	PF65 7.00				

KM# 773 WON
7.00 g., Aluminum, 40 mm. **Obv:** National arms, Country name **Rev:** Taekwondo kicker

Date	Mintage	F12	VF20	XF40	MS60	MS63
2001 Proof	—	—	—	—	—	—

KM# 774 WON
Aluminum, 40 mm. **Obv:** National arms, Central Bank name **Rev:** Two taekwondo players

Date	Mintage	F12	VF20	XF40	MS60	MS63
2001	—	PF65 6.00				

KM# 305 WON
7.00 g., Aluminum, 40 mm. **Obv:** Arms **Rev:** Tomb of King Kong Min

Date	Mintage	F12	VF20	XF40	MS60	MS63
2002	—	PF65 7.50				

KM# 470 WON
Brass, 35 mm. **Subject:** 2004 Olympics **Obv:** Arms **Rev:** Three Karate Sportsmen

Date	Mintage	F12	VF20	XF40	MS60	MS63
2002	—	PF65 6.50				

KM# 471 WON
Brass **Obv:** Arms **Rev:** Bridge

Date	Mintage	F12	VF20	XF40	MS60	MS63
2002 (91) (2002)	—	PF65 7.50				

KM# 474 WON
Brass **Obv:** Arms **Rev:** Family about to hug

Date	Mintage	F12	VF20	XF40	MS60	MS63
2002	—	PF65 10.00				

KM# 475 WON
Brass, 40 mm. **Obv:** Arms **Rev:** Three people in group hug

Date	Mintage	F12	VF20	XF40	MS60	MS63
2002	—	PF65 10.00				

KM# 476 WON
Brass **Obv:** Arms **Rev:** Four dragons around map of North Korea

Date	Mintage	F12	VF20	XF40	MS60	MS63
2002	—	PF65 10.00				

KM# 305a WON
28.20 g., Brass, 40.2 mm. **Obv:** State arms **Rev:** Tomb of King Kong Min **Edge:** Plain

Date	Mintage	F12	VF20	XF40	MS60	MS63
JU91-2002	—	PF65 20.00				

KM# 306 WON
7.10 g., Aluminum, 40 mm. **Obv:** State arms **Rev:** Two horses within circle of Asian zodiac animals **Edge:** Plain **Note:** Prev. KM#398.

Date	Mintage	F12	VF20	XF40	MS60	MS63
2002	—	PF65 20.00				

KM# 306a WON
28.20 g., Brass, 40.2 mm. **Obv:** State arms **Rev:** Two horses within circle of Asian zodiac animals **Edge:** Plain

Date	Mintage	F12	VF20	XF40	MS60	MS63
2002	—	PF65 20.00				

KM# 308 WON
6.90 g., Aluminum, 40 mm. **Obv:** State arms **Rev:** Arirang dancer with cranes flying above **Edge:** Plain **Note:** Prev. KM#390.

Date	Mintage	F12	VF20	XF40	MS60	MS63
JU91-(2002)	—	PF65 15.00				

KM# 308a WON
28.20 g., Brass, 40.2 mm. **Subject:** Arirang **Obv:** State arms **Rev:** Performers and flying cranes **Edge:** Plain

Date	Mintage	F12	VF20	XF40	MS60	MS63
JU91-(2002)	—	PF65 20.00				

KM# 313 WON
6.70 g., Aluminum, 40 mm. **Obv:** State arms **Rev:** Arirang dancer **Edge:** Plain **Note:** Prev. KM#389.

Date	Mintage	F12	VF20	XF40	MS60	MS63
JU91-(2002)	—	PF65 15.00				

KM# 313a WON
28.20 g., Brass, 40.2 mm. **Subject:** Arirang **Obv:** State arms **Rev:** Dancer with upheld arms **Edge:** Plain

Date	Mintage	F12	VF20	XF40	MS60	MS63
JU91-(2002)	—	PF65 20.00				

KM# 388 WON
7.10 g., Aluminum, 40 mm. **Obv:** State arms **Rev:** Arirang dancer Silhouette **Edge:** Plain

Date	Mintage	F12	VF20	XF40	MS60	MS63
2002	—	PF65 15.00				

KM# 391 WON
7.10 g., Aluminum, 40 mm. **Obv:** State arms **Rev:** Arirang ribbon dancer **Edge:** Plain

Date	Mintage	F12	VF20	XF40	MS60	MS63
JU91-2002	—	PF65 15.00				

KM# 392 WON
7.00 g., Aluminum, 40 mm. **Obv:** State arms **Rev:** May Day Stadium **Edge:** Plain

Date	Mintage	F12	VF20	XF40	MS60	MS63
JU91-2002	—	PF65 12.00				

KM# 392a WON
28.50 g., Brass, 40.1 mm. **Obv:** State arms **Rev:** May Day Stadium **Edge:** Plain

Date	Mintage	F12	VF20	XF40	MS60	MS63
JU91-2002	—	PF65 15.00				

KM# 393 WON
7.10 g., Aluminum, 40 mm. **Obv:** State arms **Rev:** Woman floating above stadium **Edge:** Plain

Date	Mintage	F12	VF20	XF40	MS60	MS63
JU91-2002	—	PF65 15.00				

KM# 393a WON
28.20 g., Brass, 40 mm. **Obv:** State arms **Rev:** Woman floating above stadium **Edge:** Plain

Date	Mintage	F12	VF20	XF40	MS60	MS63
JU91-2002	—	PF65 17.50				

KM# 394 WON
27.50 g., Brass, 40 mm. **Obv:** State arms **Rev:** Ribbon dancer with Korea shaped ribbon **Edge:** Plain

Date	Mintage	F12	VF20	XF40	MS60	MS63
JU91-2002	—	PF65 17.50				

KM# 395 WON
27.50 g., Brass, 40 mm. **Obv:** State arms **Rev:** Dancer in the shape of Korea **Edge:** Plain

Date	Mintage	F12	VF20	XF40	MS60	MS63
JU91-2002	—	PF65 17.50				

KM# 396 WON
7.00 g., Aluminum, 40 mm. **Obv:** State arms **Rev:** Bust with hat facing divides dates(1337-1392) above building foundation **Edge:** Plain

Date	Mintage	F12	VF20	XF40	MS60	MS63
JU91-2002	—	PF65 15.00				

KM# 397 WON
7.00 g., Aluminum, 40 mm. **Obv:** State arms **Rev:** Victorious athletes hugging **Edge:** Plain

Date	Mintage	F12	VF20	XF40	MS60	MS63
JU91-(2002)	—	PF65 10.00				

KM# 397a WON
28.24 g., Brass, 40 mm. **Obv:** State arms **Rev:** Victorious athletes hugging **Edge:** Plain

Date	Mintage	F12	VF20	XF40	MS60	MS63
JU91-(2002)	—	PF65 12.50				

KM# 399 WON
4.86 g., Aluminum, 35 mm. **Obv:** State arms **Rev:** Cantering horse **Edge:** Plain

Date	Mintage	F12	VF20	XF40	MS60	MS63
JU91-(2002)	—	PF65 15.00				

KM# 399a WON
16.93 g., Brass, 35 mm. **Obv:** State arms **Rev:** Cantering horse **Edge:** Plain

Date	Mintage	F12	VF20	XF40	MS60	MS63
JU91-(2002)	—					
	PF65 15.00					

KM# 400 WON
5.10 g., Aluminum, 35 mm. **Obv:** State arms **Rev:** Two wrestlers **Edge:** Plain

Date	Mintage	F12	VF20	XF40	MS60	MS63
JU91-(2002)	—					
	PF65 12.50					

KM# 400a WON
16.50 g., Brass, 35 mm. **Obv:** State arms **Rev:** Two wrestlers **Edge:** Plain

Date	Mintage	F12	VF20	XF40	MS60	MS63
JU91-(2002)	—					
	PF65 15.00					

KM# 310a WON
28.20 g., Brass, 40.2 mm. **Obv:** State arms **Rev:** Tomb of King Tongmyong **Edge:** Plain

Date	Mintage	F12	VF20	XF40	MS60	MS63
JU91-2002	—					
	PF65 15.00					

KM# 786 WON
5.00 g., Aluminum, 35 mm. **Subject:** Year of the Horse **Obv:** National arms, Country name **Rev:** Horse head

Date	Mintage	F12	VF20	XF40	MS60	MS63
2002	—					
	PF65 6.00					

KM# 786a WON
16.00 g., Brass, 35 mm. **Obv:** National arms, Country name **Rev:** Horse head

Date	Mintage	F12	VF20	XF40	MS60	MS63
2002	—					
	PF65 7.00					

KM# 794 WON
7.00 g., Aluminum, 40 mm. **Obv:** National arms **Rev:** Reconstruction of the Mausoleums for King Dangun

Date	Mintage	F12	VF20	XF40	MS60	MS63
2002	—					
	PF65 6.00					

KM# 795 WON
28.00 g., Brass, 40 mm. **Obv:** Naitonal arms, Country name **Rev:** Reconstruction of the mausoleum for King Dangun

Date	Mintage	F12	VF20	XF40	MS60	MS63
2002	—					
	PF65 7.00					

KM# 796 WON
7.00 g., Aluminum, 40 mm. **Obv:** National arms **Rev:** Dongmyeong, 1st King of Goguryeo

Date	Mintage	F12	VF20	XF40	MS60	MS63
2002	—					
	PF65 6.00					

KM# 797 WON
28.00 g., Brass, 40 mm. **Obv:** National arms **Rev:** Dongmyeong, 1st King of Goguryeo

Date	Mintage	F12	VF20	XF40	MS60	MS63
2002	—					
	PF65 7.00					

KM# 798 WON
7.00 g., Aluminum, 40 mm. **Obv:** National arms, Central Bank name **Rev:** Wanggeon, 1st King of Goryeo dynasty

Date	Mintage	F12	VF20	XF40	MS60	MS63
2002	—					
	PF65 6.00					

KM# 799 WON
28.00 g., Brass, 40 mm. **Obv:** National arms, Central Bank name **Rev:** Wanggeon, 1st King of Goryeo dynasty

Date	Mintage	F12	VF20	XF40	MS60	MS63
2002	—					
	PF65 7.00					

KM# 800 WON
7.00 g., Aluminum, 40 mm. **Obv:** National arms **Rev:** Jeon Bongjun

Date	Mintage	F12	VF20	XF40	MS60	MS63
2002	—					
	PF65 6.00					

KM# 801 WON
28.00 g., Brass, 40 mm. **Obv:** National arms, Central Bank name **Rev:** Jeon Bongjun

Date	Mintage	F12	VF20	XF40	MS60	MS63
2002	—					
	PF65 7.00					

KM# 821 WON
7.00 g., Aluminum, 40 mm. **Obv:** National arms **Rev:** Prince Hodong and Princess Nakrang on horseback

Date	Mintage	F12	VF20	XF40	MS60	MS63
2002	—					
	PF65 6.00					

KM# 821a WON
28.00 g., Brass, 40 mm. **Obv:** National arms **Rev:** Prince Hodong and Princess Nakrang on horseback

Date	Mintage	F12	VF20	XF40	MS60	MS63
2002	—					
	PF65 7.00					

KM# 822 WON
7.00 g., Aluminum, 40 mm. **Obv:** National arms **Rev:** Half-length figures of Prince Hodong and Princess Nakrang

Date	Mintage	F12	VF20	XF40	MS60	MS63
2002	—					
	PF65 6.00					

KM# 822a WON
28.00 g., Brass, 40 mm. **Obv:** National arms **Rev:** Half-length figures of Prince Hodong and Princess Nakrang

Date	Mintage	F12	VF20	XF40	MS60	MS63
2002	—					
	PF65 8.00					

KM# 836 WON
4.00 g., Aluminum, 35 mm. **Obv:** National arms, Central Bank and Country name **Rev:** Ariang inscription

Date	Mintage	F12	VF20	XF40	MS60	MS63
2002	Est. 1000	PF65 6.00				

KM# 837 WON
4.00 g., Aluminum, 35 mm. **Obv:** National arms, Central Bank and Country name **Rev:** Three soldiers

Date	Mintage	F12	VF20	XF40	MS60	MS63
2002	—					
	PF65 7.00					

KM# 838 WON
4.00 g., Aluminum, 35 mm. **Obv:** Naitonal arms, Central Bank and Country name **Rev:** Princess fairy paying flute

Date	Mintage	F12	VF20	XF40	MS60	MS63
2002	—					
	PF65 7.00					

KM# 839 WON
4.00 g., Aluminum, 35 mm. **Obv:** National arms, Central Bank and Country name **Rev:** Bronze statue

Date	Mintage	F12	VF20	XF40	MS60	MS63
2002	—					
	PF65 6.00					

KM# 840 WON
4.00 g., Aluminum, 35 mm. **Obv:** National arms, Central Bank and Country name **Rev:** Women in the worship of the Sun

Date	Mintage	F12	VF20	XF40	MS60	MS63
2002	—					
	PF65 6.00					

KM# 841 WON
4.00 g., Aluminum, 35 mm. **Obv:** National arms, Central Bank and Country name **Rev:** Three principals of unification

Date	Mintage	F12	VF20	XF40	MS60	MS63
2002	—					
	PF65 6.00					

KM# 842 WON
4.00 g., Aluminum, 35 mm. **Obv:** National arms, Central Bank and Country name **Rev:** Dancing children

Date	Mintage	F12	VF20	XF40	MS60	MS63
2002	—					
	PF65 6.00					

KM# 843 WON
31.11 g., 0.999 Gold 0.9926 oz. AGW, 35 mm. **Obv:** National arms, Central Bank and Country name **Rev:** Arirang inscription

Date	Mintage	F12	VF20	XF40	MS60	MS63
2002	—					
	PF65 1,600					

KM# 882 WON
Copper-Nickel, 38 mm. **Obv:** National arms, Central Bank name **Rev:** World cup tophy, player and Brandenburg gate

Date	Mintage	F12	VF20	XF40	MS60	MS63
2002	—					
	PF65 14.00					

KM# 882b WON
25.00 g., Brass, 38 mm. **Obv:** National arms, Central Bank name **Rev:** World cup, player and Brandenberg Gate

Date	Mintage	F12	VF20	XF40	MS60	MS63
2002	—					
	PF65 7.00					

KM# 882a WON
6.00 g., Aluminum, 38 mm. **Obv:** National arms, Central Bank name **Rev:** World cup, player and Brandenburg Gate

Date	Mintage	F12	VF20	XF40	MS60	MS63
2002	—					
	PF65 6.00					

KM# 264 WON
7.00 g., Aluminum, 40 mm. **Obv:** National arms **Rev:** Sheep in center of Asian Zodiac animals

Date	Mintage	F12	VF20	XF40	MS60	MS63
2003	—					
	PF65 6.00					

KM# 264a WON
28.47 g., Brass, 40 mm. **Obv:** State arms **Rev:** Sheep within circle of Asian Zodiac animals **Edge:** Plain

Date	Mintage	F12	VF20	XF40	MS60	MS63
2003	—					
	PF65 22.00					

KM# 319 WON
9.62 g., Aluminum, 40 mm. **Obv:** State arms **Rev:** Helmeted head with two antenna-like horns on the helmet **Edge:** Plain

Date	Mintage	F12	VF20	XF40	MS60	MS63
JU92-2003	—					
	PF65 15.00					

KM# 319a WON
28.20 g., Brass, 40.2 mm. **Obv:** State arms **Rev:** Helmeted head with two antenna-like horns on helmet **Edge:** Plain

Date	Mintage	F12	VF20	XF40	MS60	MS63
JU92-2003	—					
	PF65 17.50					

KM# 323 WON
6.94 g., Aluminum, 40 mm. **Obv:** State arms **Rev:** Turtle shaped armoured ship of 1592 **Edge:** Plain

Date	Mintage	F12	VF20	XF40	MS60	MS63
JU92-2003	—	PF65 15.00				

KM# 323a WON
28.10 g., Brass, 40.2 mm. **Obv:** State arms **Rev:** Turtle-shaped armoured ship of 1592 **Edge:** Plain

Date	Mintage	F12	VF20	XF40	MS60	MS63
JU92-2003	—	PF65 20.00				

KM# 403 WON
7.00 g., Aluminum, 40 mm. **Obv:** National arms, Central Bank name **Rev:** Kang Kam-cheo bust facing

Date	Mintage	F12	VF20	XF40	MS60	MS63
2003	—	PF65 7.00				

KM# 403a WON
22.10 g., Brass, 40 mm. **Obv:** State arms **Rev:** Kang Kam-cheo bust facing **Edge:** Plain

Date	Mintage	F12	VF20	XF40	MS60	MS63
JU92-2003	—	PF65 17.50				

KM# 404 WON
9.63 g., Aluminum, 40 mm. **Obv:** State arms **Rev:** Armored bust wearing a horned helmet **Edge:** Plain

Date	Mintage	F12	VF20	XF40	MS60	MS63
JU92-2003	—	PF65 15.00				

KM# 404a WON
22.25 g., Brass, 40 mm. **Obv:** State arms **Rev:** Armored bust wearing a horned helmet **Edge:** Plain

Date	Mintage	F12	VF20	XF40	MS60	MS63
JU92-2003	—	PF65 17.50				

KM# 405 WON
7.00 g., Aluminum, 40 mm. **Obv:** State arms **Rev:** Ram within circle of Asian Zodiac animals

Date	Mintage	F12	VF20	XF40	MS60	MS63
2003	—	PF65 15.00				

KM# 405a WON
28.44 g., Brass, 40 mm. **Obv:** State arms **Rev:** Ram within circle of Asian Zodiac animals **Edge:** Plain

Date	Mintage	F12	VF20	XF40	MS60	MS63
2003	—	PF65 17.50				

KM# 406 WON
10.15 g., Aluminum, 40 mm. **Obv:** State arms **Rev:** Children kicking a shuttlecock **Edge:** Plain

Date	Mintage	F12	VF20	XF40	MS60	MS63
JU92-2003	—	PF65 15.00				

KM# 406a WON
24.63 g., Brass, 40 mm. **Obv:** State arms **Rev:** Children kicking a shuttlecock **Edge:** Plain

Date	Mintage	F12	VF20	XF40	MS60	MS63
JU92-2003	—	PF65 17.50				

KM# 407a WON
23.10 g., Brass, 40 mm. **Obv:** State arms **Rev:** Children playing jacks **Edge:** Plain

Date	Mintage	F12	VF20	XF40	MS60	MS63
JU92-2003	—	PF65 17.50				

KM# 408a WON
24.56 g., Brass, 40 mm. **Obv:** State arms **Rev:** Children spinning tops **Edge:** Plain

Date	Mintage	F12	VF20	XF40	MS60	MS63
JU92-2003	—	PF65 17.50				

KM# 410a WON
24.64 g., Brass, 40 mm. **Obv:** State arms **Rev:** Large dome building **Edge:** Plain

Date	Mintage	F12	VF20	XF40	MS60	MS63
JU92-2003	—	PF65 17.50				

KM# 904 WON
31.11 g., 0.999 Silver 0.9926 oz. ASW, 40 mm. **Subject:** Athens olympics **Obv:** National arms, Central Bank name **Rev:** Wrestlers

Date	Mintage	F12	VF20	XF40	MS60	MS63
2003	Est. 1000	PF65 45.00				

KM# 918 WON
25.00 g., Brass, 38 mm. **Obv:** National arms, Central Bank name **Rev:** Steamship Princess Charlotte of Prussia

Date	Mintage	F12	VF20	XF40	MS60	MS63
2003	Est. 500		PF65 45.00			

KM# 919 WON
25.00 g., Brass, 35 mm. **Obv:** National arms, Central Bank name **Rev:** Ship Queen Maria

Date	Mintage	F12	VF20	XF40	MS60	MS63
2003	—		PF65 45.00			

KM# 920 WON
25.00 g., Brass, 38 mm. **Obv:** National arms **Rev:** Trans-atlantic sail steamship Helena Sloman

Date	Mintage	F12	VF20	XF40	MS60	MS63
2003	—		PF65 45.00			

KM# 924 WON
25.00 g., Brass, 38 mm. **Obv:** National arms, Central Bank name **Rev:** Alder, 1835 steam locomotive

Date	Mintage	F12	VF20	XF40	MS60	MS63
2003	Est. 500		PF65 45.00			

KM# 925 WON
25.00 g., Silver, 38 mm. **Obv:** National arms, Central Bank name **Rev:** Saxonia, 1838 steam locomotive

Date	Mintage	F12	VF20	XF40	MS60	MS63
2003	—		PF65 45.00			

KM# 926 WON
25.00 g., Brass, 38 mm. **Obv:** National arms, Central Bank name **Rev:** Rheingold, 1928 Steam locomotive

Date	Mintage	F12	VF20	XF40	MS60	MS63
2003	—		PF65 45.00			

KM# 930 WON
25.00 g., Brass, 38 mm. **Obv:** National arms, Central Bank name **Rev:** Gorch Fock 1 sailing ship

Date	Mintage	F12	VF20	XF40	MS60	MS63
2003	—		PF65 45.00			

KM# 265 WON
17.70 g., Brass, 23.2 x 40.1 mm. **Obv:** State arms **Rev:** White-tufted-ear Marmoset **Edge:** Plain

Date	Mintage	F12	VF20	XF40	MS60	MS63
2004	—		PF65 27.50			

KM# 266 WON
17.70 g., Brass, 23.2 x 40.1 mm. **Obv:** State arms **Rev:** Cercopjthecus Mitis monkey **Edge:** Plain

Date	Mintage	F12	VF20	XF40	MS60	MS63
2004	—		PF65 27.50			

KM# 267 WON
17.70 g., Brass, 23.2 x 40.1 mm. **Obv:** State arms **Rev:** Two Saguinus Midas monkeys **Edge:** Plain

Date	Mintage	F12	VF20	XF40	MS60	MS63
2004	—		PF65 27.50			

KM# 330 WON
9.92 g., Aluminum, 45 mm. **Obv:** State arms **Rev:** Mountain cabin **Edge:** Plain **Note:** Prev. KM#411.

Date	Mintage	F12	VF20	XF40	MS60	MS63
JU93-2004	—		PF65 15.00			

KM# 330a WON
26.45 g., Brass, 45 mm. **Obv:** State arms **Rev:** Mountain cabin **Edge:** Plain

Date	Mintage	F12	VF20	XF40	MS60	MS63
JU93-2004	—		PF65 20.00			

KM# 331 WON
10.00 g., Aluminum, 45 mm. **Obv:** State arms **Rev:** Kim Il Sung's birthplace, front view **Edge:** Plain **Note:** Prev. KM#412.

Date	Mintage	F12	VF20	XF40	MS60	MS63
JU93-2004	—		PF65 15.00			

KM# 331a WON
26.45 g., Brass, 45 mm. **Obv:** State arms **Rev:** Sung's birth place, front view **Edge:** Plain

Date	Mintage	F12	VF20	XF40	MS60	MS63
JU93-2004	—		PF65 20.00			

KM# 332 WON
10.00 g., Aluminum, 45 mm. **Obv:** State arms **Rev:** Kim Il Sung's birthplace, side view **Edge:** Plain **Note:** Prev. KM#413.

Date	Mintage	F12	VF20	XF40	MS60	MS63
JU93-2004	—		PF65 15.00			

KM# 332a WON
26.45 g., Brass, 45 mm. **Obv:** State arms **Rev:** Sung's birthplace, side view **Edge:** Plain

Date	Mintage	F12	VF20	XF40	MS60	MS63
JU93-2004	—		PF65 20.00			

KM# 333 WON
10.00 g., Aluminum, 45 mm. **Obv:** Naitonal arms, Central Bank name **Rev:** Kim Jeongsuk

Date	Mintage	F12	VF20	XF40	MS60	MS63
2004	—		PF65 8.00			

KM# 333a WON
26.45 g., Brass, 45 mm. **Obv:** State arms **Rev:** Kim Jung Sook facing **Edge:** Plain

Date	Mintage	F12	VF20	XF40	MS60	MS63
JU93-2004	—		PF65 22.50			

KM# 334 WON
10.00 g., Aluminum, 45 mm. **Obv:** National arms, Central Bank name **Rev:** Kim Jeong-il bust facing

Date	Mintage	F12	VF20	XF40	MS60	MS63
2004	—				**PF65** 8.00	

KM# 334a WON
26.45 g., Brass, 45 mm. **Obv:** State arms **Rev:** Kim Jong-il bust facing **Edge:** Plain

Date	Mintage	F12	VF20	XF40	MS60	MS63
JU93-2004	—				**PF65** 22.50	

KM# 335 WON
10.00 g., Aluminum, 45 mm. **Obv:** National arms, Central Bank name **Rev:** Kim Il-seong bust facing

Date	Mintage	F12	VF20	XF40	MS60	MS63
2004	—				**PF65** 8.00	

KM# 335a WON
26.45 g., Brass, 45 mm. **Obv:** State arms **Rev:** Kim Il-seong bust facing **Edge:** Plain

Date	Mintage	F12	VF20	XF40	MS60	MS63
JU93-2004	—				**PF65** 22.50	

KM# 336 WON
10.10 g., Aluminum, 45 mm. **Obv:** State arms **Rev:** Kim Il-sung flower, orchid **Edge:** Plain **Note:** Prev. KM#414.

Date	Mintage	F12	VF20	XF40	MS60	MS63
JU93-2004	—				**PF65** 15.00	

KM# 336a WON
26.45 g., Brass, 45 mm. **Obv:** State arms **Rev:** Kim Il-sung flower, orchid **Edge:** Plain

Date	Mintage	F12	VF20	XF40	MS60	MS63
JU93-2004	—				**PF65** 20.00	

KM# 337 WON
10.10 g., Aluminum, 45 mm. **Obv:** State arms **Rev:** Kim Jong-Il flower, peony **Edge:** Plain **Note:** Prev. KM#415.

Date	Mintage	F12	VF20	XF40	MS60	MS63
JU93-2004	—				**PF65** 15.00	

KM# 337a WON
26.45 g., Brass, 45 mm. **Obv:** State arms **Rev:** Kim Jong-Il flower, peony **Edge:** Plain

Date	Mintage	F12	VF20	XF40	MS60	MS63
JU93-2004	—				**PF65** 20.00	

KM# 338 WON
9.93 g., Aluminum, 45 mm. **Obv:** State arms **Rev:** Jin Dal Lae flower, Rose of Sharon **Edge:** Plain **Note:** Prev. KM#416.

Date	Mintage	F12	VF20	XF40	MS60	MS63
JU93-2004	—				**PF65** 15.00	

KM# 338a WON
26.45 g., Brass, 45 mm. **Obv:** State arms **Rev:** Rose of Sharon flowers **Edge:** Plain

Date	Mintage	F12	VF20	XF40	MS60	MS63
JU93-2004	—				**PF65** 20.00	

KM# 410 WON
20.00 g., Aluminum, 40 mm. **Obv:** National arms, Central bank name **Rev:** Sports hall in Pyeongyang

Date	Mintage	F12	VF20	XF40	MS60	MS63
2004	—				**PF65** 16.00	

KM# 939 WON
7.00 g., Aluminum, 40 mm. **Obv:** National arms, Central Bank arms **Rev:** Monkey in the center of the Zodiac

Date	Mintage	F12	VF20	XF40	MS60	MS63
2004	—				**PF65** 10.00	

KM# 939a WON
28.00 g., Brass, 35 mm. **Obv:** National arms, Central Bank name **Rev:** Monkey in center of Zodiac

Date	Mintage	F12	VF20	XF40	MS60	MS63
2004	—				**PF65** 30.00	

KM# 994 WON
25.00 g., Brass, 38 mm. **Obv:** National arms, Central Bank name **Rev:** Statsraad Lehmkuhl sailing ship

Date	Mintage	F12	VF20	XF40	MS60	MS63
2004	—				**PF65** 45.00	

KM# 995 WON
25.00 g., Brass, 38 mm. **Obv:** Naitonal arms, Central Bank name **Rev:** Henry Hudson's Halve Maen

Date	Mintage	F12	VF20	XF40	MS60	MS63
2004	—				**PF65** 45.00	

KM# 1025a WON
28.00 g., Brass, 40 mm. **Obv:** National arms, Central Bank name **Rev:** General Hong Beomdo

Date	Mintage	F12	VF20	XF40	MS60	MS63
2005	—				**PF65** 20.00	

KM# 1016 WON
7.00 g., Aluminum, 40 mm. **Obv:** National arms, Central Bank name **Rev:** Rooster within Zodiac circle

Date	Mintage	F12	VF20	XF40	MS60	MS63
2005	—				**PF65** 17.50	

KM# 1016a WON
28.00 g., Brass, 40 mm. **Obv:** National arms, Central Bank name **Rev:** Rooster in Zodiac circle

Date	Mintage	F12	VF20	XF40	MS60	MS63
2005	—				**PF65** 20.00	

KM# 1019 WON
28.00 g., 0.999 Brass 0.8935 oz., 40 mm. **Obv:** National arms, Central Bank name **Rev:** Timber and tap in color

Date	Mintage	F12	VF20	XF40	MS60	MS63
2005	—				**PF65** 30.00	

KM# 1020 WON
7.00 g., Aluminum, 40 mm. **Obv:** National arms, Central Bank name **Rev:** Hae Mosu in the sky with the five dragons

Date	Mintage	F12	VF20	XF40	MS60	MS63
2005	—				**PF65** 17.50	

KM# 1020a WON
28.00 g., Brass, 40 mm. **Obv:** National arms, Central Bank name **Rev:** Hae Mosu in flight with the five dragons

Date	Mintage	F12	VF20	XF40	MS60	MS63
2005	—				**PF65** 20.00	

KM# 1024 WON
7.00 g., Aluminum, 40 mm. **Obv:** National arms, Central Bank name **Rev:** Admiral Yi Sunsin and turtle boat

Date	Mintage	F12	VF20	XF40	MS60	MS63
2005	—				**PF65** 10.00	

KM# 1024a WON
28.00 g., Brass, 40 mm. **Obv:** National arms, Central Bank name **Rev:** Admiral Yi Sunsin and turtle boat

Date	Mintage	F12	VF20	XF40	MS60	MS63
2005	—				**PF65** 15.00	

KM# 1025 WON
7.00 g., Aluminum, 40 mm. **Obv:** National arms, Central Bank name **Rev:** General Hong Beomdo

Date	Mintage	F12	VF20	XF40	MS60	MS63
2005	—	PF65 14.00				

KM# 1034 WON
25.00 g., Brass, 40 mm. **Obv:** National arms, Central Bank name **Rev:** Rally in front of the monument ot the three principals of reunification

Date	Mintage	F12	VF20	XF40	MS60	MS63
2005	—	PF65 20.00				

KM# 1035 WON
28.00 g., Brass, 40 mm. **Obv:** National arms, Central Bank name **Rev:** Demonstration on the crater lake

Date	Mintage	F12	VF20	XF40	MS60	MS63
2005	—	PF65 20.00				

KM# 1036 WON
28.00 g., Brass, 40 mm. **Obv:** National arms, Central Bank name **Rev:** Three drum dance

Date	Mintage	F12	VF20	XF40	MS60	MS63
2005	—	PF65 20.00				

KM# 1040 WON
28.00 g., Brass, 40 mm. **Obv:** National arms, Central Bank name **Rev:** Map of Korea, pair of peace doves, rainbow

Date	Mintage	F12	VF20	XF40	MS60	MS63
2005	—	PF65 10.00				

KM# 1043 WON
28.00 g., Brass **Obv:** National arms, Central Bank name **Rev:** Tomb of the Unknown Soldier in Moscow, Russian legend **Edge Lettering:** 40

Date	Mintage	F12	VF20	XF40	MS60	MS63
2005	—	PF65 14.00				

KM# 1044 WON
28.00 g., Brass, 40 mm. **Obv:** National arms, Central Bank name **Rev:** Memorial to mothers in St. Petersburg, Russian legend

Date	Mintage	F12	VF20	XF40	MS60	MS63
2005	—	PF65 14.00				

KM# 1074 WON
6.00 g., Aluminum, 38 mm. **Subject:** Torino Winter Olympics, 2006 **Obv:** National arms, Central Bank name **Rev:** Bobsled

Date	Mintage	F12	VF20	XF40	MS60	MS63
2005	—	PF65 12.00				

KM# 1074a WON
25.00 g., Brass, 38 mm. **Subject:** Torino Winter Olympics, 2006 **Obv:** National arms, Central Bank name **Rev:** Bobsled

Date	Mintage	F12	VF20	XF40	MS60	MS63
2005	—	PF65 30.00				

KM# 1088 WON
28.00 g., Brass, 40 mm. **Obv:** National arms, Central Bank name **Rev:** Dog in color

Date	Mintage	F12	VF20	XF40	MS60	MS63
2006	—	PF65 30.00				

KM# 1089 WON
7.00 g., Aluminum, 40 mm. **Obv:** National arms, Central Bank name **Rev:** Ryuhwa, Mother of King Dongmyeong

Date	Mintage	F12	VF20	XF40	MS60	MS63
2006	—	PF65 10.00				

KM# 1089a WON
28.00 g., Brass, 40 mm. **Obv:** National arms, Central Bank name **Rev:** Ryuhwa, Mother of King Dongmyeong

Date	Mintage	F12	VF20	XF40	MS60	MS63
2006	—	PF65 14.00				

KM# 1109 WON
28.00 g., Brass, 40 mm. **Obv:** National arms, Central Bank name **Rev:** Pig in color

Date	Mintage	F12	VF20	XF40	MS60	MS63
2007	—	PF65 30.00				

KM# 483 WON
Copper-Nickel **Subject:** Uzgn Monument **Obv:** Arms **Rev:** Map and building

Date	Mintage	F12	VF20	XF40	MS60	MS63
2008	—	PF65 15.00				

KM# 781 2 WON
7.00 g., 0.999 Silver 0.2234 oz. ASW, 30 mm. **Obv:** National arms, Central Bank name **Rev:** Panda in color

Date	Mintage	F12	VF20	XF40	MS60	MS63
2001	Est. 5000	PF65 30.00				

KM# 892 2 WON
7.00 g., 0.999 Silver 0.2234 oz. ASW, 30 mm. **Obv:** National arms, Central Bank name **Rev:** Two panda in color

Date	Mintage	F12	VF20	XF40	MS60	MS63
2002	Est. 5000	PF65 30.00				

KM# 249 2 WON
7.00 g., 0.999 Silver 0.2234 oz. ASW, 30 mm. **Obv:** State arms **Rev:** Two multicolor pandas **Edge:** Plain

Date	Mintage	F12	VF20	XF40	MS60	MS63
2003	—	PF65 30.00				

KM# 933 2 WON
7.00 g., 0.999 Silver 0.2234 oz. ASW, 30 mm. **Obv:** National arms, Central Bank name **Rev:** High speed train in Aichi

Date	Mintage	F12	VF20	XF40	MS60	MS63
2003	—	PF65 30.00				

KM# 934 2 WON
7.00 g., 0.999 Silver 0.2234 oz. ASW, 30 mm. **Obv:** National Arms, Central Bank name **Rev:** Two soccer players in color

Date	Mintage	F12	VF20	XF40	MS60	MS63
2003	—	PF65 30.00				

KM# 417 2 WON
24.66 g., Brass, 31.6x45.75 mm. **Obv:** State arms **Rev:** Half length uniformed figure standing in land rover saluting below dates 1904-2004 **Edge:** Plain **Shape:** Rectangle

Date	Mintage	F12	VF20	XF40	MS60	MS63
ND(2004)	—	PF65 25.00				

KM# 969 2 WON
25.00 g., Brass, 40 mm. **Obv:** Dokdo, rocky islands, Central Bank name **Rev:** Map of the Island group

Date	Mintage	F12	VF20	XF40	MS60	MS63
2004	—	PF65 25.00				

KM# 970 2 WON
25.00 g., Brass, 40 mm. **Obv:** Dokdo, rocky islands, Central Bank name **Rev:** Fisher Ahn Yongbok

Date	Mintage	F12	VF20	XF40	MS60	MS63
2004	—	PF65 25.00				

KM# 971 2 WON
25.00 g., Brass, 40 mm. **Obv:** Dokdo, rocky islands, Central Bank name **Rev:** Seodo, western island

Date	Mintage	F12	VF20	XF40	MS60	MS63
2004	—	PF65 25.00				

KM# 972 2 WON
25.00 g., Brass, 40 mm. **Obv:** Dokdo, rocky islands, Central Bank name **Rev:** Eastern island, Dongdo

Date	Mintage	F12	VF20	XF40	MS60	MS63
2004	—	PF65 25.00				

KM# 973 2 WON
25.00 g., Brass, 40 mm. **Obv:** Dokdo, rocky islands, Central Bank name **Rev:** Three brother islands

Date	Mintage	F12	VF20	XF40	MS60	MS63
2004	—	PF65 25.00				

KM# 974 2 WON
25.00 g., Brass, 40 mm. **Obv:** Dokdo, rocky islands, Central Bank name **Rev:** Chicken island

Date	Mintage	F12	VF20	XF40	MS60	MS63
2004	—	PF65 25.00				

KM# 975 2 WON
25.00 g., Brass, 40 mm. **Obv:** Dokdo, rocky islands, Central Bank name **Rev:** Candle island

Date	Mintage	F12	VF20	XF40	MS60	MS63
2004	—	PF65 25.00				

KM# 976 2 WON
25.00 g., Brass, 40 mm. **Obv:** Dokdo, rocky islands, Central Bank name **Rev:** Dome island

Date	Mintage	F12	VF20	XF40	MS60	MS63
2004	—	PF65 25.00				

KM# 1008 2 WON
7.00 g., 0.999 Silver 0.2234 oz. ASW, 30 mm. **Obv:** National arms, Central Bank name **Rev:** Three pandas in color

Date	Mintage	F12	VF20	XF40	MS60	MS63
2004	Est. 5000	PF65 30.00				

KM# 1078 2 WON
7.00 g., Silver, 30 mm. **Obv:** National arms, Central Bank name **Rev:** Panda in color

Date	Mintage	F12	VF20	XF40	MS60	MS63
2005	Est. 5000	PF65 30.00				

KM# 1079 2 WON
7.00 g., 0.999 Silver 0.2234 oz. ASW, 30 mm. **Subject:** Battle of Trafalgar, 200th Anniversary **Obv:** National arms, Central Bank name **Rev:** Horatio Nelson and the H.M.S. Victory, partially gilt

Date	Mintage	F12	VF20	XF40	MS60	MS63
2005	Est. 5000	PF65 30.00				

KM# 1101 2 WON
7.00 g., 0.999 Silver 0.2234 oz. ASW, 30 mm. **Obv:** National arms, Central Bank name **Rev:** Two pandas in color

Date	Mintage	F12	VF20	XF40	MS60	MS63
2006	Est. 5000	PF65 30.00				

KM# 1124 2 WON
7.00 g., 0.999 Silver 0.2234 oz. ASW, 30 mm. **Obv:** National arms, Central Bank name **Rev:** Panda in color

Date	Mintage	F12	VF20	XF40	MS60	MS63
2007	Est. 5000	PF65 30.00				

KM# 339 3 WON
12.55 g., Aluminum, 50.1 mm. **Obv:** Korean map **Rev:** Huh Jun Chosun doctor at left, books at right **Edge:** Plain

Date	Mintage	F12	VF20	XF40	MS60	MS63
JU93-2004	—	PF65 20.00				

KM# 339a 3 WON
40.53 g., Brass, 50.2 mm. **Obv:** Korean map **Rev:** Huh Jun Chosun doctor at left, books at right **Edge:** Plain

Date	Mintage	F12	VF20	XF40	MS60	MS63
JU93-2004	—	PF65 25.00				

KM# 203 5 WON
15.00 g., 0.999 Silver 0.4787 oz. ASW, 35 mm. **Subject:** School Ships **Obv:** State arms **Rev:** SS Krusenstern **Edge:** Plain

Date	Mintage	F12	VF20	XF40	MS60	MS63
ND-2001	500	PF65 75.00				

KM# 205 5 WON
15.00 g., 0.999 Silver 0.4787 oz. ASW, 35 mm. **Subject:**
Wildlife **Obv:** State arms **Rev:** Two standing Japanese Ibis
birds **Edge:** Plain

Date	Mintage	F12	VF20	XF40	MS60	MS63
JU90-2001	100	PF65 200				

KM# 206 5 WON
15.00 g., 0.999 Silver 0.4787 oz. ASW, 35 mm. **Subject:**
Wildlife **Obv:** State arms **Rev:** Two nesting Japanese Ibis birds
Edge: Plain

Date	Mintage	F12	VF20	XF40	MS60	MS63
JU90-2001	3,000	PF65 50.00				

KM# 208 5 WON
15.00 g., 0.999 Silver 0.4787 oz. ASW, 35 mm. **Subject:** Wildlife
Obv: State arms **Rev:** Two Korean Longtail Gorals **Edge:** Plain

Date	Mintage	F12	VF20	XF40	MS60	MS63
JU90-2001	3,000	PF65 50.00				

KM# 219 5 WON
14.96 g., 0.999 Silver 0.4774 oz. ASW, 35 mm. **Obv:** State
arms **Rev:** Dragon ship **Edge:** Plain

Date	Mintage	F12	VF20	XF40	MS60	MS63
2001	—	PF65 35.00				

KM# 226 5 WON
20.00 g., 0.999 Silver 0.6382 oz. ASW, 33.8 mm. **Subject:**
Olympics **Obv:** State arms **Rev:** Hurdler **Edge:** Reeded

Date	Mintage	F12	VF20	XF40	MS60	MS63
2001	—	PF65 35.00				

KM# 240 5 WON
14.94 g., 0.999 Silver 0.4768 oz. ASW, 35 mm. **Obv:** State
arms **Rev:** Orca" (Killer Whale) **Edge:** Plain

Date	Mintage	F12	VF20	XF40	MS60	MS63
2001	—	PF65 60.00				

KM# 241 5 WON
14.92 g., 0.999 Silver 0.4761 oz. ASW, 35 mm. **Obv:** State
arms **Rev:** Orca and Eco-Tourists in boat **Edge:** Plain

Date	Mintage	F12	VF20	XF40	MS60	MS63
2001	—	PF65 60.00				

KM# 242 5 WON
14.87 g., 0.999 Silver 0.4745 oz. ASW, 35 mm. **Obv:** State
arms **Rev:** Pottwal" (Sperm Whale) **Edge:** Plain

Date	Mintage	F12	VF20	XF40	MS60	MS63
2001	—	PF65 60.00				

KM# 243 5 WON
14.95 g., 0.999 Silver 0.4771 oz. ASW, 35 mm. **Obv:** State
arms **Rev:** Buckelwal" (Humpback Whale) **Edge:** Plain

Date	Mintage	F12	VF20	XF40	MS60	MS63
2001	—	PF65 60.00				

KM# 244 5 WON
14.93 g., 0.999 Silver 0.4764 oz. ASW, 35 mm. **Obv:** State arms
Rev: Groenlandwal" (Greenland Right Whale) **Edge:** Plain

Date	Mintage	F12	VF20	XF40	MS60	MS63
2001	—	PF65 60.00				

KM# 245 5 WON
14.95 g., 0.999 Silver 0.4771 oz. ASW, 35 mm. **Obv:** State
arms **Rev:** Blauwal" (Blue Whale) **Edge:** Plain

Date	Mintage	F12	VF20	XF40	MS60	MS63
2001	—	PF65 60.00				

KM# 246 5 WON
14.96 g., 0.999 Silver 0.4774 oz. ASW, 35 mm. **Obv:** State
arms **Rev:** Grindwal" (Pilot Whale) **Edge:** Plain

Date	Mintage	F12	VF20	XF40	MS60	MS63
2001	—	PF65 60.00				

KM# 250 5 WON
14.96 g., 0.999 Silver 0.4774 oz. ASW, 35 mm. **Subject:** Return
of Hong Kong to China **Obv:** State arms **Rev:** City view **Edge:**
Plain

Date	Mintage	F12	VF20	XF40	MS60	MS63
2001	—	PF65 20.00				

KM# 694 5 WON
27.00 g., 0.999 Silver 0.8616 oz. ASW, 40 mm. **Obv:** National
arms, Country name **Rev:** Kim Ilseong

Date	Mintage	F12	VF20	XF40	MS60	MS63
2001	—	PF65 70.00				

KM# 695 5 WON
Silver, 40 mm. **Obv:** National arms, Country name **Rev:** Kim
Jeongil

Date	Mintage	F12	VF20	XF40	MS60	MS63
2001	—	PF65 75.00				

KM# 696 5 WON
27.00 g., 0.999 Silver 0.8616 oz. ASW, 40 mm. **Obv:** National
arms, Central Bank name **Rev:** Kim Jeongsuk

Date	Mintage	F12	VF20	XF40	MS60	MS63
2001	—	PF65 75.00				

KM# 747 5 WON
27.00 g., Silver, 40 mm. **Obv:** National arms, Country name
Rev: Confucius

Date	Mintage	F12	VF20	XF40	MS60	MS63
2001	—	PF65 135				

KM# 770 5 WON
15.00 g., 0.999 Silver 0.4787 oz. ASW, 35 mm. **Obv:** National
arms, Central Bank name **Rev:** Krusenstern

Date	Mintage	F12	VF20	XF40	MS60	MS63
2001	—	PF65 32.00				

KM# 782 5 WON
15.00 g., Silver, 35 mm. **Obv:** National arms, Central Bank
name **Rev:** Two pandas

Date	Mintage	F12	VF20	XF40	MS60	MS63
2001	Est. 5000	PF65 32.00				

KM# 783 5 WON
15.00 g., 0.999 Silver 0.4787 oz. ASW, 35 mm. **Obv:** National
arms, Central Bank name **Rev:** Titanic

Date	Mintage	F12	VF20	XF40	MS60	MS63
2001	Est. 5000	PF65 32.00				

KM# 784 5 WON
Silver Obv: National arms, Central Bank name Rev: Five masted ship, Royal Clipper

Date	Mintage	F12	VF20	XF40	MS60	MS63
2001	—	PF65 32.00				

KM# 785 5 WON
15.00 g., 0.999 Silver 0.4787 oz. ASW, 35 mm. Subject: 2002 Soccer - Korea and Japan Obv: National arms, Central Bank name Rev: Player and stadium

Date	Mintage	F12	VF20	XF40	MS60	MS63
2001	Est. 5000	PF65 32.00				

KM# 251 5 WON
14.90 g., 0.999 Silver 0.4755 oz. ASW, 35 mm. Subject: Year of the Horse Obv: State arms Rev: Cantering horse Edge: Plain

Date	Mintage	F12	VF20	XF40	MS60	MS63
2002	—	PF65 30.00				

KM# 252 5 WON
14.92 g., 0.999 Silver 0.4761 oz. ASW, 35 mm. Subject: Korean Games Obv: State arms Rev: Two wrestlers Edge: Plain

Date	Mintage	F12	VF20	XF40	MS60	MS63
JU91-2002	—	PF65 20.00				

KM# 303 5 WON
15.00 g., 0.999 Silver 0.4787 oz. ASW, 35 mm. Obv: State arms Rev: Janggo dancer Edge: Segmented reeding

Date	Mintage	F12	VF20	XF40	MS60	MS63
JU91-2002	—	PF65 30.00				

KM# 304 5 WON
15.00 g., 0.999 Silver 0.4787 oz. ASW, 35 mm. Obv: State arms Rev: Armored Knight Edge: Segmented reeding

Date	Mintage	F12	VF20	XF40	MS60	MS63
JU91-2002	—	PF65 30.00				

KM# 790 5 WON
15.00 g., 0.999 Silver 0.4787 oz. ASW Obv: National arms, Country name Rev: Horse head Shape: 35

Date	Mintage	F12	VF20	XF40	MS60	MS63
2002	—	PF65 35.00				

KM# 877 5 WON
15.00 g., 0.999 Silver 0.4787 oz. ASW, 35 mm. Obv: National arms, Central Bank name Rev: Map of Korea

Date	Mintage	F12	VF20	XF40	MS60	MS63
2002	—	PF65 45.00				

KM# 878 5 WON
15.00 g., 0.999 Silver 0.4787 oz. ASW, 35 mm. Obv: National arms, Central Bank name Rev: Traditional Korean wedding

Date	Mintage	F12	VF20	XF40	MS60	MS63
2002	—	PF65 35.00				

KM# 879 5 WON
15.00 g., 0.999 Silver 0.4787 oz. ASW, 35 mm. Obv: National arms, Central Bank name Rev: Trasitional wedding procession

Date	Mintage	F12	VF20	XF40	MS60	MS63
2002	—	PF65 35.00				

KM# 893 5 WON
20.00 g., 0.999 Silver 0.6382 oz. ASW, 38 mm. Obv: Naitonal arms, Central Bank name Rev: Asian wild ox

Date	Mintage	F12	VF20	XF40	MS60	MS63
2002	—	PF65 60.00				

KM# 894 5 WON
20.00 g., 0.999 Silver 0.6382 oz. ASW, 38 mm. Obv: National arms, Central Bank name Rev: Two scocer players with flag

Date	Mintage	F12	VF20	XF40	MS60	MS63
2002	Est. 5000	PF65 35.00				

KM# 895 5 WON
20.00 g., 0.999 Silver 0.6382 oz. ASW, 38 mm. Obv: National arms, Central Bank name Rev: Celebrating player in Yokohama stadium

Date	Mintage	F12	VF20	XF40	MS60	MS63
2002	—	PF65 60.00				

KM# 327 5 WON
20.00 g., 0.999 Silver 0.6382 oz. ASW, 35 mm. Obv: State arms Rev: Turtle Boat " of 1592 Edge: Segmented reeding

Date	Mintage	F12	VF20	XF40	MS60	MS63
JU92-2003	—	PF65 35.00				

KM# 328 5 WON
20.00 g., 0.999 Silver 0.6382 oz. ASW, 35 mm. Obv: State arms Rev: Olympic fencers Edge: Segmented reeding

Date	Mintage	F12	VF20	XF40	MS60	MS63
JU92-2003	—	PF65 35.00				

KM# 329 5 WON
20.00 g., 0.999 Silver 0.6382 oz. ASW, 35 mm. Obv: State arms Rev: Three wild horses Edge: Segmented reeding

Date	Mintage	F12	VF20	XF40	MS60	MS63
JU92-2003	—	PF65 35.00				

KM# 900 5 WON
20.00 g., 0.999 Silver 0.6382 oz. ASW, 35 mm. Obv: National arms, Central Bank name Rev: Swan

Date	Mintage	F12	VF20	XF40	MS60	MS63
2003	Est. 1000	PF65 45.00				

KM# 901 5 WON
20.00 g., 0.999 Silver 0.6382 oz. ASW, 35 mm. Obv: National arms, Central Bank name Rev: Pelican

Date	Mintage	F12	VF20	XF40	MS60	MS63
2003	—	PF65 45.00				

KM# 902 5 WON
20.00 g., 0.999 Silver 0.6382 oz. ASW, 35 mm. Obv: National arms, Rev: Stone eagle

Date	Mintage	F12	VF20	XF40	MS60	MS63
2003	—	PF65 45.00				

KM# 903 5 WON
31.11 g., 0.999 Silver 0.9926 oz. ASW, 40 mm. Obv: National arms, Central Bank name Rev: Chinese pangolin and young

Date	Mintage	F12	VF20	XF40	MS60	MS63
2003	Est. 1000	PF65 60.00				

KM# 935 5 WON
15.00 g., 0.999 Silver 0.4787 oz. ASW, 30 mm. Subject: Franz Schubert, 175th anniversary of death Obv: National arms, Central Bank name Rev: Franz Schubert

Date	Mintage	F12	VF20	XF40	MS60	MS63
2003	—	PF65 45.00				

KM# 936 5 WON
20.00 g., 0.999 Silver 0.6382 oz. ASW, 38 mm. Obv: National arms, Central Bank name Rev: Horatio Nelson and H.M.S. Victory

Date	Mintage	F12	VF20	XF40	MS60	MS63
2003	—	PF65 45.00				

KM# 937 5 WON
20.00 g., 0.999 Silver 0.6382 oz. ASW, 38 mm. Obv: National arms, Central Bank name Rev: Leopard

Date	Mintage	F12	VF20	XF40	MS60	MS63
2003	Est. 5000	PF65 40.00				

KM# 1009 5 WON
15.00 g., 0.999 Silver 0.4787 oz. ASW, 35 mm. Obv: National arms, Central Bank name Rev: Red deer in forest glade in color

Date	Mintage	F12	VF20	XF40	MS60	MS63
2004	—	PF65 60.00				

KM# 1010 5 WON
15.00 g., 0.999 Silver 0.4787 oz. ASW, 35 mm. Obv: National arms, Central Bank name Rev: Kingfisher in color

Date	Mintage	F12	VF20	XF40	MS60	MS63
2004	—	PF65 60.00				

KM# 1011 5 WON
31.11 g., 0.999 Silver 0.9926 oz. ASW, 35 mm. Obv: National arms, Central Bank name Rev: Bewick's swan in flight in color

Date	Mintage	F12	VF20	XF40	MS60	MS63
2004	—	PF65 60.00				

KM# 1012 5 WON
15.00 g., 0.999 Silver 0.4787 oz. ASW, 35 mm. Obv: National arms, Central Bank name Rev: Two blue whales and iceberg in color

Date	Mintage	F12	VF20	XF40	MS60	MS63
2004	—	PF65 60.00				

KM# 1013 5 WON
15.00 g., 0.999 Silver 0.4787 oz. ASW, 35 mm. Obv: National arms, Central Bank name Rev: Lion in color

Date	Mintage	F12	VF20	XF40	MS60	MS63
2004	—	PF65 60.00				

KM# 1014 5 WON
20.00 g., 0.999 Silver 0.6382 oz. ASW, 38 mm. Obv: National arms, Central Bank name Rev: Leopard

Date	Mintage	F12	VF20	XF40	MS60	MS63
2004	—	PF65 45.00				

KM# 1015 5 WON
1.15 g., Aluminum, 21 mm. Obv: National arms, Central Bank name Rev: Large numeral 5

Date	Mintage	F12	VF20	XF40	MS60	MS63
2005	—	—	—	—	3.00	5.00

KM# 1080 5 WON
15.00 g., 0.999 Silver 0.4787 oz. ASW, 35 mm. Subject: Tschaikowsky, 165 Birthday Obv: National arms, Central Bank name Rev: Peter Tschaikowsky

Date	Mintage	F12	VF20	XF40	MS60	MS63
2005	—	PF65 45.00				

KM# 1081 5 WON
15.00 g., 0.999 Silver 0.4787 oz. ASW, 35 mm. Obv: National arms, Central Bank name Rev: Squirrel in color

Date	Mintage	F12	VF20	XF40	MS60	MS63
2005	—	PF65 30.00				

KM# 1082 5 WON
15.00 g., 0.999 Silver 0.4787 oz. ASW, 35 mm. Obv: National arms, Central Bank name Rev: Firefox in color

Date	Mintage	F12	VF20	XF40	MS60	MS63
2005	—	PF65 30.00				

KM# 1083 5 WON
20.00 g., 0.999 Silver 0.6382 oz. ASW, 38 mm. Obv: National arms, Central Bank name Rev: Saiga antelope

Date	Mintage	F12	VF20	XF40	MS60	MS63
2005	—	PF65 45.00				

KM# 1084 5 WON
20.00 g., 0.999 Silver 0.6382 oz. ASW, 38 mm. **Obv:** National arms, Central Bank name **Rev:** Malayian Tapir and young

Date	Mintage	F12	VF20	XF40	MS60	MS63
2005	Est. 5000	PF65 45.00				

KM# 1085 5 WON
20.00 g., 0.999 Silver 0.6382 oz. ASW, 38 mm. **Obv:** National arms, Central Bank name **Rev:** Sedov sailing ship

Date	Mintage	F12	VF20	XF40	MS60	MS63
2005	Est. 5000	PF65 45.00				

KM# 1102 5 WON
15.00 g., 0.999 Silver 0.4787 oz. ASW, 35 mm. **Obv:** National arms, Central Bank name **Rev:** Orca whale in color

Date	Mintage	F12	VF20	XF40	MS60	MS63
2006	—	PF65 60.00				

KM# 1103 5 WON
15.00 g., 0.999 Silver 0.4787 oz. ASW, 35 mm. **Obv:** National arms, Central Bank name **Rev:** javanese flying frog in color

Date	Mintage	F12	VF20	XF40	MS60	MS63
2006	—	PF65 60.00				

KM# 1104 5 WON
15.00 g., 0.999 Silver 0.4787 oz. ASW, 35 mm. **Obv:** National arms, Central Bank name **Rev:** Hymalayian Pheasant in color

Date	Mintage	F12	VF20	XF40	MS60	MS63
2006	—	PF65 60.00				

KM# 1105 5 WON
15.00 g., 0.999 Silver 0.4787 oz. ASW, 35 mm. **Obv:** National arms, Central Bank name **Rev:** Karl Marx bust left

Date	Mintage	F12	VF20	XF40	MS60	MS63
2006	—	PF65 45.00				

KM# 1106 5 WON
20.00 g., 0.999 Silver 0.6382 oz. ASW, 38 mm. **Obv:** National arms, Central Bank name **Rev:** Mir sailing ship

Date	Mintage	F12	VF20	XF40	MS60	MS63
2006	Est. 5000	PF65 45.00				

KM# 1107 5 WON
20.00 g., 0.999 Silver 0.6382 oz. ASW, 38 mm. **Subject:** Bejing Summer Olympics, 2008 **Obv:** National arms, Central Bank name **Rev:** Handball player making shot

Date	Mintage	F12	VF20	XF40	MS60	MS63
2006	Est. 5000	PF65 35.00				

KM# 1108 5 WON
20.00 g., 0.999 Silver 0.6382 oz. ASW, 38 mm. **Subject:** Bejing Summer Olympics, 2008 **Obv:** National arms, Central Bank name **Rev:** Archer before target

Date	Mintage	F12	VF20	XF40	MS60	MS63
2006	Est. 5000	PF65 35.00				

KM# 1125 5 WON
15.00 g., 0.999 Silver 0.4787 oz. ASW, 35 mm. **Obv:** National arms, Central Bank name **Rev:** Japanese snow money in color

Date	Mintage	F12	VF20	XF40	MS60	MS63
2007	—	PF65 60.00				

KM# 1126 5 WON
20.00 g., 0.999 Silver 0.6382 oz. ASW, 38 mm. **Obv:** National arms, Central Bank name **Rev:** Siberian musk deer

Date	Mintage	F12	VF20	XF40	MS60	MS63
2007	Est. 5000	PF65 60.00				

KM# 1127 5 WON
20.00 g., 0.999 Silver 0.6382 oz. ASW, 38 mm. **Obv:** National arms, Central Bank name **Rev:** Ming treasure ship

Date	Mintage	F12	VF20	XF40	MS60	MS63
2007	Est. 5000	PF65 45.00				

KM# 220 7 WON
20.00 g., 0.999 Silver 0.6382 oz. ASW, 38 mm. **Subject:** 2002 Olympics **Obv:** State arms **Rev:** Two speed skaters **Edge:** Plain

Date	Mintage	F12	VF20	XF40	MS60	MS63
2001	10,000	PF63 35.00	PF65 40.00			

KM# 221 7 WON
20.00 g., 0.999 Silver 0.6382 oz. ASW, 38 mm. **Subject:** Endangered Wildlife **Obv:** State arms **Rev:** White-tailed sea Eagle **Edge:** Plain

Date	Mintage	F12	VF20	XF40	MS60	MS63
2001	10,000	PF63 30.00	PF65 35.00			

KM# 881 7 WON
20.00 g., 0.999 Silver 0.6382 oz. ASW **Obv:** Naitonal arms, Central Bank name **Rev:** Taekwondo **Shape:** 38

Date	Mintage	F12	VF20	XF40	MS60	MS63
2002		PF65 35.00				

KM# 883 7 WON
20.00 g., 0.999 Silver 0.6382 oz. ASW, 38 mm. **Obv:** National arms, Central Bank name **Rev:** World Cup, player and Brandenburg Gate

Date	Mintage	F12	VF20	XF40	MS60	MS63
2002	—	PF65 30.00				

KM# 921 7 WON
20.00 g., 0.999 Silver 0.6382 oz. ASW, 38 mm. **Obv:** National arms, Central Bank name **Rev:** Steamer Princess Charlotte of Prussia

Date	Mintage	F12	VF20	XF40	MS60	MS63
2003	Est. 500	PF65 70.00				

KM# 922 7 WON
20.00 g., 0.999 Silver 0.6382 oz. ASW, 35 mm. **Obv:** National arms, Central Bank name **Rev:** Steamship Queen Maria

Date	Mintage	F12	VF20	XF40	MS60	MS63
2003	—	PF65 75.00				

KM# 923 7 WON
20.00 g., 0.999 Silver 0.6382 oz. ASW, 38 mm. **Obv:** National arms, Central Bank name **Rev:** Transatlantic sail steamship Helena Sloman

Date	Mintage	F12	VF20	XF40	MS60	MS63
2003	Est. 500	PF65 75.00				

KM# 927 7 WON
20.00 g., 0.999 Silver 0.6382 oz. ASW, 38 mm. **Obv:** National arms, Central Bank name **Rev:** Adler, 1835 steam locomotive

Date	Mintage	F12	VF20	XF40	MS60	MS63
2003	—	PF65 60.00				

KM# 928 7 WON
20.00 g., 0.999 Silver 0.6382 oz. ASW, 38 mm. **Obv:** National arms, Central Bank name **Rev:** Saxonia, 1838 steam locomotive

Date	Mintage	F12	VF20	XF40	MS60	MS63
2003	—	PF65 60.00				

KM# 929 7 WON
20.00 g., 0.999 Silver 0.6382 oz. ASW, 38 mm. **Obv:** National arms, Central Bank name **Rev:** Rheingold, 1928 steam locomotive

Date	Mintage	F12	VF20	XF40	MS60	MS63
2003	—	PF65 60.00				

KM# 931 7 WON
20.00 g., 0.999 Silver 0.6382 oz. ASW, 38 mm. **Obv:** National arms, Central Bank name **Rev:** Gorch Fock I, sailing ship

Date	Mintage	F12	VF20	XF40	MS60	MS63
2003	—	PF65 60.00				

KM# 932 7 WON
20.00 g., 0.999 Silver 0.6382 oz. ASW, 38 mm. **Obv:** National arms, Central Bank name **Rev:** Skier

Date	Mintage	F12	VF20	XF40	MS60	MS63
2003	Est. 5000	PF65 40.00				

KM# 477 7 WON
20.00 g., Bi-Metallic **Obv:** Arms **Rev:** Stadium along river

Date	Mintage	F12	VF20	XF40	MS60	MS63
2004	—	PF65 55.00				

KM# 945 7 WON
20.00 g., Silver, 23x40 mm. **Obv:** East gate of Pyeongyang **Rev:** Mormoset **Shape:** Rectangle

Date	Mintage	F12	VF20	XF40	MS60	MS63
2004	—	PF65 35.00				

KM# 946 7 WON
20.00 g., 0.999 Silver 0.6382 oz. ASW, 23x40 mm. **Obv:** East gate of Pyeongyang **Rev:** Blue monkey **Shape:** Rectangle

Date	Mintage	F12	VF20	XF40	MS60	MS63
2004	—	PF65 35.00				

KM# 947 7 WON
20.00 g., Silver, 23x40 mm. **Obv:** East gate of Pyeongyang **Rev:** Monkies **Shape:** Rectangle

Date	Mintage	F12	VF20	XF40	MS60	MS63
2004	—	PF65 35.00				

KM# 996 7 WON
20.00 g., 0.999 Silver 0.6382 oz. ASW, 38 mm. **Obv:** National arms, Central Bank name **Rev:** Statsraad Lehmkuhl sailing ship

Date	Mintage	F12	VF20	XF40	MS60	MS63
2004	Est. 3000	PF65 60.00				

KM# 997 7 WON
20.00 g., 0.999 Silver 0.6382 oz. ASW, 38 mm. **Obv:** National arms, Central Bank name **Rev:** Henry Hudson's Halve Maen

Date	Mintage	F12	VF20	XF40	MS60	MS63
2004	Est. 3000	PF65 60.00				

KM# 998 7 WON
20.00 g., 0.999 Silver 0.6382 oz. ASW, 38 mm. **Subject:** 1980 Lake PLacid Olympics **Obv:** National arms, Central Bank name **Rev:** Speed skater

Date	Mintage	F12	VF20	XF40	MS60	MS63
2004	Est. 5000	PF65 35.00				

KM# 1071 7 WON
20.00 g., 0.999 Silver 0.6382 oz. ASW, 38 mm. **Subject:** Squaw Valley 1960 Winter Olympics **Obv:** National arms, Central Bank name **Rev:** Ice Dancing

Date	Mintage	F12	VF20	XF40	MS60	MS63
2005	Est. 5000	PF65 45.00				

KM# 1072 7 WON
20.00 g., 0.999 Silver 0.6382 oz. ASW, 38 mm. **Subject:** Calgary Winter Olympics, 1988 **Obv:** National arms, Central Bank name

Date	Mintage	F12	VF20	XF40	MS60	MS63
2005	—	PF65 45.00				

KM# 1073 7 WON
20.00 g., 0.999 Silver 0.6382 oz. ASW, 38 mm. **Subject:** Nagano Winter Olympics, 1998 **Obv:** National arms, Central Bank name **Rev:** Snowboarder

Date	Mintage	F12	VF20	XF40	MS60	MS63
2005	—	PF65 45.00				

KM# 1075 7 WON
20.00 g., 0.999 Silver 0.6382 oz. ASW, 38 mm. **Subject:** Torino Winter Olympics, 2006 **Obv:** National arms, Central Bank name **Rev:** bobsled

Date	Mintage	F12	VF20	XF40	MS60	MS63
2005	—	PF65 45.00				

KM# 1076 7 WON
20.00 g., 0.999 Silver 0.6382 oz. ASW, 38 mm. **Obv:** National arms, Central Bank name **Rev:** Black faced spoonbill

Date	Mintage	F12	VF20	XF40	MS60	MS63
2005	—	PF65 60.00				

KM# 1077 7 WON
20.00 g., 0.999 Silver 0.6382 oz. ASW, 38 mm. **Obv:** National arms, Central Bank name **Rev:** Flying dog

Date	Mintage	F12	VF20	XF40	MS60	MS63
2005	Est. 5000	PF65 60.00				

KM# 152 10 WON
31.00 g., 0.999 Silver 0.9893 oz. ASW, 39.8 mm. **Subject:** Asian Money Fair **Obv:** State arms **Rev:** Two snakes **Edge:** Reeded and plain sections

Date	Mintage	F12	VF20	XF40	MS60	MS63
2001	—	PF65 60.00				

KM# 153 10 WON
31.00 g., 0.999 Silver 0.9893 oz. ASW, 39.8 mm. **Subject:**
Tortoise-Serpent **Obv:** State arms **Rev:** Mythical creature
Edge: Reeded and plain sections

Date	Mintage	F12	VF20	XF40	MS60	MS63
2001	—	PF65 55.00				

KM# 227 10 WON
31.06 g., 0.925 Silver 0.9178 oz. ASW, 39.9 mm. **Subject:**
General Ri Sun Sin **Obv:** State arms **Rev:** Helmeted head 1/4
left **Edge:** Reeded

Date	Mintage	F12	VF20	XF40	MS60	MS63
2001	—	PF65 47.50				

KM# 253 10 WON
31.11 g., 0.999 Silver 0.9928 oz. ASW, 40.2 mm. **Obv:** State
arms **Rev:** Deng Xio Ping head 3/4 left, 1904-1997 flanking,
sprigs below **Edge:** Plain

Date	Mintage	F12	VF20	XF40	MS60	MS63
2001	—	PF65 45.00				

KM# 292 10 WON
31.00 g., 0.999 Silver 0.9893 oz. ASW, 40.2 mm. **Obv:** State
arms **Rev:** Kim Il-Seung bust facing, 1912-1994 flanking, sprigs
below **Edge:** Plain

Date	Mintage	F12	VF20	XF40	MS60	MS63
JU90-2001	—	PF65 45.00				

KM# 295 10 WON
31.00 g., 0.999 Silver 0.9893 oz. ASW, 40.2 mm. **Obv:** State
arms **Rev:** Mountain cabin **Edge:** Plain

Date	Mintage	F12	VF20	XF40	MS60	MS63
JU90-2001	—	PF65 45.00				

KM# 296 10 WON
31.00 g., 0.999 Silver 0.9893 oz. ASW, 40.2 mm. **Obv:** State
arms **Rev:** KUMDANG - 2 INJECTION" in center of leaves
Edge: Plain

Date	Mintage	F12	VF20	XF40	MS60	MS63
2001	—	PF65 50.00				

KM# 297 10 WON
31.00 g., 0.999 Silver 0.9893 oz. ASW, 40.2 mm. **Obv:** State
arms **Rev:** Train scene and a couple below a jet liner **Rev.
Legend:** ...1945 - 2001... **Edge:** Plain

Date	Mintage	F12	VF20	XF40	MS60	MS63
ND-2001	—	PF65 45.00				

KM# 298 10 WON
31.00 g., 0.999 Silver 0.9893 oz. ASW, 40.2 mm. **Obv:** State
arms **Rev:** Cruise ship below stylized head left profile **Edge:**
Plain

Date	Mintage	F12	VF20	XF40	MS60	MS63
JU90-2001	—	PF65 50.00				

KM# 299 10 WON
31.00 g., 0.999 Silver 0.9893 oz. ASW, 40.2 mm. **Obv:** State
arms **Rev:** Old fortress **Edge:** Plain

Date	Mintage	F12	VF20	XF40	MS60	MS63
JU90-2001	—	PF65 47.50				

KM# 300 10 WON
31.00 g., 0.999 Silver 0.9893 oz. ASW, 40.2 mm. **Obv:** State
arms **Rev:** Landmarks, flag and tourist couple above cruise
ship **Edge:** Plain

Date	Mintage	F12	VF20	XF40	MS60	MS63
JU90-2001	—	PF65 45.00				

KM# 301 10 WON
31.00 g., 0.999 Silver 0.9893 oz. ASW, 40.2 mm. **Obv:** State
arms **Rev:** 2 facing half length men shaking hands **Edge:** Plain

Date	Mintage	F12	VF20	XF40	MS60	MS63
JU90-2001	—	PF65 45.00				

KM# 302 10 WON
31.00 g., 0.999 Silver 0.9893 oz. ASW, 40.1 mm. **Obv:** State
arms **Rev:** Great East Gate **Edge:** Plain

Date	Mintage	F12	VF20	XF40	MS60	MS63
JU90-2001	—	PF65 47.50				

KM# 357 10 WON
31.00 g., 0.999 Silver 0.9893 oz. ASW, 40.2 mm. **Obv:** State arms **Rev:** Antique ceramic items **Edge:** Plain

Date	Mintage	F12	VF20	XF40	MS60	MS63
2001	—	PF65 45.00				

KM# 386 10 WON
30.76 g., 0.999 Silver 0.9816 oz. ASW, 40.1 mm. **Obv:** State arms **Rev:** Kim Jung Sook facing flanked by dates (1917-1949) above flower sprigs **Edge:** Plain

Date	Mintage	F12	VF20	XF40	MS60	MS63
JU90-2001	—	PF65 47.50				

KM# 387 10 WON
30.76 g., 0.999 Silver 0.9816 oz. ASW, 40.1 mm. **Obv:** State arms **Rev:** Kim Jung-Il bust facing, sprigs below **Edge:** Plain

Date	Mintage	F12	VF20	XF40	MS60	MS63
JU90-2001	—	PF65 47.50				

KM# 697 10 WON
27.00 g., 0.999 Silver 0.8616 oz. ASW, 40 mm. **Obv:** National arms, value in English **Rev:** Kim Jeongsuk

Date	Mintage	F12	VF20	XF40	MS60	MS63
2001	—	PF65 60.00				

KM# 704 10 WON
31.11 g., Silver, 40 mm. **Obv:** National arms, Country name **Rev:** House where Kim Ilseong was born

Date	Mintage	F12	VF20	XF40	MS60	MS63
2001 Proof	—					

KM# 705 10 WON
31.11 g., 0.999 Silver 0.9926 oz. ASW, 40 mm. **Obv:** National arms, Country name **Rev:** House where Kim Jeongsuk was born

Date	Mintage	F12	VF20	XF40	MS60	MS63
2001 Proof	—					

KM# 732 10 WON
7.00 g., Aluminum, 40 mm. **Obv:** East gate of Pyeongyang **Rev:** Married couple before flag and ferryboat

Date	Mintage	F12	VF20	XF40	MS60	MS63
2001 Proof	—					

KM# 733 10 WON
7.00 g., Aluminum, 40 mm. **Obv:** East gate of Pyeongyang **Rev:** Ferryboat between Korea and Japan

Date	Mintage	F12	VF20	XF40	MS60	MS63
2001 Proof	—					

KM# 734 10 WON
7.00 g., Aluminum, 40 mm. **Obv:** East gate of Pyeongyang **Rev:** Triumphial arch of Moranbong in Pyeongyang

Date	Mintage	F12	VF20	XF40	MS60	MS63
2001 Proof	—					

KM# 735 10 WON
Aluminum, 40 mm. **Obv:** East gate of Pyeongyang **Rev:** Chonji crater in Paektusan

Date	Mintage	F12	VF20	XF40	MS60	MS63
2001 Proof	—					

KM# 740 10 WON
Silver, 40 mm. **Obv:** National arms, Country name **Rev:** Triumphial arch of Moranbong in Pyeongyang

Date	Mintage	F12	VF20	XF40	MS60	MS63
2001 Proof	—					

KM# 741 10 WON
Silver, 40 mm. **Obv:** National arms, Country name **Rev:** Chonji crater in Paektusan

Date	Mintage	F12	VF20	XF40	MS60	MS63
2001 Proof	—					

KM# 775 10 WON
7.00 g., Aluminum, 40 mm. **Obv:** East gate in Pyeongyang **Rev:** Taekwondo player

Date	Mintage	F12	VF20	XF40	MS60	MS63
2001	—	PF65 6.00				

KM# 776 10 WON
7.00 g., Aluminum, 40 mm. **Obv:** National arms, Country name **Rev:** Two taekwondo players

Date	Mintage	F12	VF20	XF40	MS60	MS63
2001	—	PF65 6.00				
2007	—	PF65 6.00				

KM# 779 10 WON
31.11 g., 0.999 Silver 0.9926 oz. ASW, 40 mm. **Obv:** National arms, Central Bank name **Rev:** Taewankdo kicker

Date	Mintage	F12	VF20	XF40	MS60	MS63
2001	—	PF65 60.00				

KM# 780 10 WON
31.11 g., 0.999 Silver 0.9926 oz. ASW, 40 mm. **Obv:** National arms, Central Bank name **Rev:** Two taekwondo players

Date	Mintage	F12	VF20	XF40	MS60	MS63
2001	—	PF65 60.00				

KM# 231 10 WON
31.00 g., 0.999 Silver 0.9893 oz. ASW, 39.9 mm. **Subject:** Kim Ill Sung **Obv:** State arms **Rev:** Bust facing **Edge:** Segmented reeding

Date	Mintage	F12	VF20	XF40	MS60	MS63
JU91-2002	—	PF65 50.00				

KM# 254 10 WON
30.77 g., 0.999 Silver 0.9819 oz. ASW, 40.15 mm. **Obv:** State arms **Rev:** Tangun bust facing and his tomb **Edge:** Plain

Date	Mintage	F12	VF20	XF40	MS60	MS63
JU91-2002	—	PF65 42.50				

KM# 255 10 WON
30.94 g., 0.999 Silver 0.9874 oz. ASW, 40.2 mm. **Subject:** Jongmongju and Sonjukgyo **Obv:** State arms **Rev:** Head with hat facing above building foundation **Edge:** Plain

Date	Mintage	F12	VF20	XF40	MS60	MS63
JU91-2002	—	PF65 42.50				

KM# 307 10 WON
31.00 g., 0.999 Silver 0.9893 oz. ASW, 40.1 mm. **Obv:** State arms **Rev:** Two horses within a circle of Asian Zodiac animals **Edge:** Plain

Date	Mintage	F12	VF20	XF40	MS60	MS63
2002	—	PF65 45.00				

KM# 309 10 WON
31.00 g., 0.999 Silver 0.9893 oz. ASW, 40.2 mm. **Subject:** Arirang **Obv:** State arms **Rev:** Performers and flying cranes **Edge:** Plain

Date	Mintage	F12	VF20	XF40	MS60	MS63
JU91-2002	—	PF65 45.00				

KM# 311 10 WON
31.00 g., 0.999 Silver 0.9893 oz. ASW, 40.2 mm. **Obv:** State arms **Rev:** Tomb of King Tongmyong **Edge:** Plain

Date	Mintage	F12	VF20	XF40	MS60	MS63
JU91-2002	—	PF65 45.00				

KM# 312 10 WON
31.00 g., 0.999 Silver 0.9893 oz. ASW, 40.2 mm. **Obv:** State arms **Rev:** Tomb of King Kong Min **Edge:** Plain

Date	Mintage	F12	VF20	XF40	MS60	MS63
JU91-2002	—	PF65 45.00				

KM# 314 10 WON
31.00 g., 0.999 Silver 0.9893 oz. ASW, 40.2 mm. **Subject:** Arirang **Obv:** State arms **Rev:** Stiyilized dancer **Edge:** Plain

Date	Mintage	F12	VF20	XF40	MS60	MS63
2002	—	PF65 45.00				

KM# 315 10 WON
31.00 g., 0.999 Silver 0.9893 oz. ASW, 40.2 mm. **Obv:** State arms **Rev:** Korean map shaped dancer **Edge:** Plain

Date	Mintage	F12	VF20	XF40	MS60	MS63
JU91-2002	—	PF65 47.50				

KM# 316 10 WON
31.00 g., 0.999 Silver 0.9893 oz. ASW, 40.2 mm. **Obv:** State arms **Rev:** Korean map shaped ribbon dancer **Edge:** Plain

Date	Mintage	F12	VF20	XF40	MS60	MS63
JU91-2002	—	PF65 47.50				

KM# 317 10 WON
31.00 g., 0.999 Silver 0.9893 oz. ASW, 40.2 mm. **Obv:** State arms **Rev:** Victorious athletes hugging **Edge:** Plain

Date	Mintage	F12	VF20	XF40	MS60	MS63
JU91-2002	—	PF65 45.00				

KM# 318 10 WON
31.00 g., 0.999 Silver 0.9893 oz. ASW, 40.2 mm. **Obv:** State arms **Rev:** Woman floating above arena **Edge:** Plain

Date	Mintage	F12	VF20	XF40	MS60	MS63
JU91-2002	—	PF65 45.00				

KM# 401 10 WON
31.00 g., 0.999 Silver 0.9893 oz. ASW, 40.1 mm. **Obv:** State arms **Rev:** Arirang dancer **Edge:** Plain

Date	Mintage	F12	VF20	XF40	MS60	MS63
JU91-2002	—	PF65 45.00				

KM# 402 10 WON
31.00 g., 0.999 Silver 0.9893 oz. ASW, 40.1 mm. **Obv:** State arms **Rev:** Arirang ribbon dancer **Edge:** Plain

Date	Mintage	F12	VF20	XF40	MS60	MS63
JU91-2002	—	PF65 45.00				

KM# 812 10 WON
31.11 g., 0.999 Silver 0.9926 oz. ASW, 40 mm. **Obv:** National arms, Central Bank name **Rev:** Dongmyeong, 1st King of Goguryeo

Date	Mintage	F12	VF20	XF40	MS60	MS63
2002	—	PF65 60.00				

KM# 813 10 WON
31.11 g., 0.999 Silver 0.9926 oz. ASW, 40 mm. **Obv:** National arms, Central Bank name **Rev:** Wanggeon, 1st King of Goryeo dynasty

Date	Mintage	F12	VF20	XF40	MS60	MS63
2002	—	PF65 60.00				

KM# 814 10 WON
31.11 g., 0.999 Silver 0.9926 oz. ASW, 40 mm. **Obv:** National arms, Central Bank name **Rev:** Jeon Bongjun

Date	Mintage	F12	VF20	XF40	MS60	MS63
2002	—	PF65 60.00				

KM# 823 10 WON
31.11 g., 0.999 Silver 0.9926 oz. ASW, 40 mm. **Obv:** National arms **Rev:** Prince Hodong and Princess Nakrang on horseback

Date	Mintage	F12	VF20	XF40	MS60	MS63
2002	—	PF65 60.00				

KM# 824 10 WON
31.11 g., 0.999 Silver 0.9926 oz. ASW, 40 mm. **Obv:** National arms **Rev:** Half-length figures of Prince Hodong and Princess Nakrang

Date	Mintage	F12	VF20	XF40	MS60	MS63
2002	—	PF65 60.00				

KM# 827 10 WON
7.00 g., Aluminum, 40 mm. **Obv:** East gate of Pyeongyang **Rev:** Reconstruction of the Mausoleum of King Dongmyeong

Date	Mintage	F12	VF20	XF40	MS60	MS63
2002	—	PF65 7.00				

KM# 828 10 WON
7.00 g., Aluminum, 40 mm. **Obv:** East gate in Pyeongyang **Rev:** Mausoleum for Gongmin

Date	Mintage	F12	VF20	XF40	MS60	MS63
2002	—	PF65 7.00				

KM# 829 10 WON
7.00 g., Aluminum, 40 mm. **Obv:** East gate in Pyeongyang **Rev:** Stadium

Date	Mintage	F12	VF20	XF40	MS60	MS63
2002	—	PF65 7.00				

KM# 860 10 WON
7.00 g., Aluminum, 40 mm. **Obv:** East gate of Pyeongyang **Rev:** The family

Date	Mintage	F12	VF20	XF40	MS60	MS63
2002	—	PF65 7.00				

KM# 861 10 WON
7.00 g., Aluminum, 40 mm. **Obv:** East gate of Pyeongyang **Rev:** Map of Korea with the four cardinal compass points

Date	Mintage	F12	VF20	XF40	MS60	MS63
2002	—	PF65 7.00				

KM# 862 10 WON
7.00 g., Aluminum, 40 mm. **Obv:** East gate of Pyeongyang **Rev:** Ryhmathic dancing and map of Korea

Date	Mintage	F12	VF20	XF40	MS60	MS63
2002	—	PF65 7.00				

KM# 863 10 WON
7.00 g., Aluminum, 40 mm. **Obv:** East gate of Pyeongyang **Rev:** Drum dancer in form of the map of Korea

Date	Mintage	F12	VF20	XF40	MS60	MS63
2002	—	PF65 7.00				

KM# 864 10 WON
7.00 g., Aluminum, 40 mm. **Obv:** East gate of Pyeongyang **Rev:** Victory celebration of Korean Teammates

Date	Mintage	F12	VF20	XF40	MS60	MS63
2002	—	PF65 7.00				

KM# 865 10 WON
28.00 g., Brass, 40 mm. **Obv:** East gate of Pyeongyang **Rev:** Family

Date	Mintage	F12	VF20	XF40	MS60	MS63
2002	—	PF65 7.00				

KM# 870 10 WON
31.11 g., 0.999 Silver 0.9926 oz. ASW, 40 mm. **Obv:** National arms, Central Bank name **Rev:** Family

Date	Mintage	F12	VF20	XF40	MS60	MS63
2002	—	PF65 60.00				

KM# 871 10 WON
31.11 g., 0.999 Silver 0.9926 oz. ASW, 40 mm. **Obv:** National arms, Central Bank name **Rev:** Map of Korea with the four cardinal points

Date	Mintage	F12	VF20	XF40	MS60	MS63
2002	—	PF65 60.00				

KM# 833 10 WON
31.11 g., 0.999 Silver 0.9926 oz. ASW, 40 mm. **Obv:** National arms, Central Bank name **Rev:** Stadium

Date	Mintage	F12	VF20	XF40	MS60	MS63
2002	—	PF65 60.00				

KM# 884 10 WON
31.11 g., 0.999 Silver 0.9926 oz. ASW, 40 mm. **Subject:** Final issue of the German Mark **Obv:** National arms, Central Bank name **Rev:** Mark coin and Brandenburg Gate in color

Date	Mintage	F12	VF20	XF40	MS60	MS63
2002	Est. 2001	PF65 85.00				

KM# 885 10 WON
31.11 g., 0.999 Silver 0.9926 oz. ASW, 40 mm. **Subject:** Final issue of the Belgian franc **Obv:** National arms, Central Bank name **Rev:** Franc and Axon in Brussels

Date	Mintage	F12	VF20	XF40	MS60	MS63
2002	Est. 2001	PF65 85.00				

KM# 886 10 WON
31.11 g., 0.999 Silver 0.9926 oz. ASW, 40 mm. **Subject:** Final issue of the Greek Drachma **Obv:** National arms, Central Bank name **Rev:** Drachma and Acropolis in color

Date	Mintage	F12	VF20	XF40	MS60	MS63
2002	Est. 2001	PF65 85.00				

KM# 887 10 WON
31.11 g., 0.999 Silver 0.9926 oz. ASW, 40 mm. **Subject:** Final issue of the Austrian schilling **Obv:** National arms, Central bank name **Rev:** Schilling and St. Stephen's in Vienna in color

Date	Mintage	F12	VF20	XF40	MS60	MS63
2002	Est. 2001	PF65 85.00				

KM# 888 10 WON
31.11 g., 0.999 Silver 0.9926 oz. ASW, 40 mm. **Subject:** Final issue of the Netherland Gulden **Obv:** National arms, Central Bank name **Rev:** Gulden and Windmill in color

Date	Mintage	F12	VF20	XF40	MS60	MS63
2002	Est. 2001					PF65 85.00

KM# 889 10 WON
31.11 g., 0.999 Silver 0.9926 oz. ASW, 40 mm. **Subject:** Final issue of the San Marino Lira **Obv:** National arms, Central Bank name **Rev:** Lira and Mount Titano in color

Date	Mintage	F12	VF20	XF40	MS60	MS63
2002	Est. 2001					PF65 85.00

KM# 890 10 WON
31.11 g., 0.999 Silver 0.9926 oz. ASW, 40 mm. **Subject:** Final Vatican Lira **Obv:** National arms, Central Bank name **Rev:** Lira coin and St. Peter's in color

Date	Mintage	F12	VF20	XF40	MS60	MS63
2002	Est. 2001					PF65 85.00

KM# 320 10 WON
31.00 g., 0.999 Silver 0.9893 oz. ASW, 40.2 mm. **Obv:** State arms **Rev:** Helmeted head with two antenna-like horns on helmet **Edge:** Plain

Date	Mintage	F12	VF20	XF40	MS60	MS63
JU92-2003	—					PF65 47.50

KM# 321 10 WON
31.00 g., 0.999 Silver 0.9893 oz. ASW, 40.2 mm. **Obv:** State arms **Rev:** Helmeted head with horns **Edge:** Plain

Date	Mintage	F12	VF20	XF40	MS60	MS63
JU92-2003	—					PF65 47.50

KM# 322 10 WON
31.00 g., 0.999 Silver 0.9893 oz. ASW, 40.2 mm. **Obv:** State arms **Rev:** Armored bust of Kang Kam-cheon facing (948-1031) wearing winged helmet **Edge:** Plain

Date	Mintage	F12	VF20	XF40	MS60	MS63
JU92-2003	—					PF65 47.50

KM# 324 10 WON
31.00 g., 0.999 Silver 0.9893 oz. ASW, 40.2 mm. **Obv:** State arms **Rev:** Turtle-shaped armored ship of 1592 **Edge:** Plain

Date	Mintage	F12	VF20	XF40	MS60	MS63
JU92-2003	—					PF65 45.00

KM# 325 10 WON
31.00 g., 0.999 Silver 0.9893 oz. ASW, 40.2 mm. **Obv:** State arms **Rev:** Children playing jacks **Edge:** Plain

Date	Mintage	F12	VF20	XF40	MS60	MS63
JU92-2003	—					PF65 45.00

KM# 326 10 WON
31.00 g., 0.999 Silver 0.9893 oz. ASW, 40.2 mm. **Obv:** State arms **Rev:** Children kicking a shuttlecock **Edge:** Plain

Date	Mintage	F12	VF20	XF40	MS60	MS63
JU92-2003	—					PF65 45.00

KM# 409 10 WON
30.94 g., 0.999 Silver 0.9874 oz. ASW, 40 mm. **Obv:** State arms **Rev:** Children spinning tops **Edge:** Plain

Date	Mintage	F12	VF20	XF40	MS60	MS63
JU92-2003	—					PF65 45.00

KM# 453 10 WON
31.00 g., 0.999 Silver 0.9893 oz. ASW **Subject:** FIFA World Championship - Germany 2006 **Obv:** National arms **Rev:** Two hands holding up cup in rays at lower right, two smallplayers at left. **Rev. Legend:** WORLD CUP **Rev. Inscription:** FIFA

Date	Mintage	F12	VF20	XF40	MS60	MS63
JU92-2003	—					PF65 60.00

KM# 896 10 WON
7.00 g., Aluminum, 40 mm. **Obv:** East gate of Pyeongand **Rev:** Sheep in center of Zodac

Date	Mintage	F12	VF20	XF40	MS60	MS63
2003	—					PF65 7.00

KM# 898 10 WON
31.11 g., 0.999 Silver 0.9926 oz. ASW, 40 mm. **Obv:** Naitonal arms **Rev:** Sheep at center of Zodiac

Date	Mintage	F12	VF20	XF40	MS60	MS63
2003	—					PF65 60.00

KM# 905 10 WON
31.11 g., 0.999 Silver 0.9926 oz. ASW, 40 mm. **Obv:** National arms, Central Bank name **Rev:** Highway and vehicles, train

Date	Mintage	F12	VF20	XF40	MS60	MS63
2003	Est. 1000					PF65 70.00

KM# 906 10 WON
7.00 g., Aluminum, 40 mm. **Obv:** East gate of Pyeongyang **Rev:** Eulji Mundeok

Date	Mintage	F12	VF20	XF40	MS60	MS63
2003	—					PF65 7.00

KM# 907 10 WON
7.00 g., Aluminum, 40 mm. **Obv:** East gate of Pyrongyang **Rev:** Yeon Gaesomun

Date	Mintage	F12	VF20	XF40	MS60	MS63
2003	—					PF65 7.00

KM# 908 10 WON
7.00 g., Aluminum, 40 mm. **Obv:** East gate of Pyeongyang **Rev:** Gang Gaesomun

Date	Mintage	F12	VF20	XF40	MS60	MS63
2003	—					PF65 7.00

KM# 911 10 WON
28.00 g., Brass, 40 mm. **Obv:** East gate of Pyeongyang **Rev:** Gang Camchan

Date	Mintage	F12	VF20	XF40	MS60	MS63
2003	—					PF65 7.00

KM# 915 10 WON
7.00 g., Aluminum, 40 mm. **Obv:** East gate of Pyeongyang **Rev:** Turtle boat

Date	Mintage	F12	VF20	XF40	MS60	MS63
2003	—					PF65 7.00

KM# 342 10 WON
31.00 g., 0.999 Silver 0.9893 oz. ASW, 40 mm. **Obv:** State arms **Rev:** Domed building **Edge:** Plain

Date	Mintage	F12	VF20	XF40	MS60	MS63
JU93-2004	—					PF65 47.50

KM# 343 10 WON
31.00 g., 0.999 Silver 0.9893 oz. ASW, 40 mm. **Obv:** State arms **Rev:** Pigeon on branch **Edge:** Segmented reeding

Date	Mintage	F12	VF20	XF40	MS60	MS63
JU93-2004	—					PF65 45.00

KM# 344 10 WON
31.00 g., 0.999 Silver 0.9893 oz. ASW, 40 mm. **Obv:** State arms **Rev:** Two Leiothrix birds **Edge:** Segmented reeding

Date	Mintage	F12	VF20	XF40	MS60	MS63
JU93-2004	—					PF65 45.00

KM# 345 10 WON
31.00 g., 0.999 Silver 0.9893 oz. ASW, 40 mm. **Obv:** State arms **Rev:** Two cranes standing in water **Edge:** Segmented reeding

Date	Mintage	F12	VF20	XF40	MS60	MS63
JU93-2004	—					PF65 47.50

KM# 346 10 WON
31.00 g., 0.999 Silver 0.9893 oz. ASW, 40 mm. **Obv:** State arms **Rev:** Curlew bird **Edge:** Segmented reeding

Date	Mintage	F12	VF20	XF40	MS60	MS63
JU93-2004	—	PF65 45.00				

KM# 347 10 WON
31.00 g., 0.999 Silver 0.9893 oz. ASW, 40 mm. **Obv:** State arms **Rev:** Goshawk on branch **Edge:** Segmented reeding

Date	Mintage	F12	VF20	XF40	MS60	MS63
JU93-2004	—	PF65 45.00				

KM# 418 10 WON
31.00 g., 0.999 Silver 0.9893 oz. ASW, 39.7 mm. **Obv:** State arms **Rev:** Ibis standing in water **Edge:** Segmented reeding

Date	Mintage	F12	VF20	XF40	MS60	MS63
JU93-2004	—	PF65 50.00				

KM# 938 10 WON
31.11 g., 0.999 Silver 0.9926 oz. ASW, 40 mm. **Obv:** National arms, Central Bank name **Rev:** Monkey King Sun Wukong from Journey to the West

Date	Mintage	F12	VF20	XF40	MS60	MS63
2004	—	PF65 70.00				

KM# 940 10 WON
31.11 g., 0.999 Silver 0.9926 oz. ASW, 40 mm. **Obv:** National arms, Central Bank name **Rev:** Monkey in center of Zodiac

Date	Mintage	F12	VF20	XF40	MS60	MS63
2004	—	PF65 60.00				

KM# 948 10 WON
Silver, 32x46 mm. **Subject:** Deng Xiaoping, 100th Birth Anniversary **Obv:** National arms **Rev:** Deng Xiaoping saluting **Shape:** Vertical rectangle

Date	Mintage	F12	VF20	XF40	MS60	MS63
2004	—	PF65 60.00				

KM# 951 10 WON
31.11 g., 0.999 Silver 0.9926 oz. ASW, 40 mm. **Obv:** Naitonal arms, Central Bank name **Rev:** Broad throaded bird

Date	Mintage	F12	VF20	XF40	MS60	MS63
2004	—	PF65 45.00				

KM# 952 10 WON
31.11 g., 0.999 Silver 0.9926 oz. ASW, 40 mm. **Obv:** Naitonal arms, Central Bank name **Rev:** Imperial eagle

Date	Mintage	F12	VF20	XF40	MS60	MS63
2004	—	PF65 45.00				

KM# 953 10 WON
31.11 g., 0.999 Silver 0.9926 oz. ASW, 40 mm. **Obv:** National arms, Central Bank name **Rev:** Bittern

Date	Mintage	F12	VF20	XF40	MS60	MS63
2004	—	PF65 45.00				

KM# 954 10 WON
31.11 g., 0.999 Silver 0.9926 oz. ASW, 40 mm. **Obv:** National arms, Central Bank name **Rev:** Pheasant

Date	Mintage	F12	VF20	XF40	MS60	MS63
2004	—	PF65 45.00				

KM# 999 10 WON
31.11 g., 0.999 Silver 0.9926 oz. ASW, 40 mm. **Obv:** National arms, Central Bank name **Rev:** Tallinn castle in color, Estonian Krone

Date	Mintage	F12	VF20	XF40	MS60	MS63
2004	Est. 2004	PF65 85.00				

KM# 1000 10 WON
31.11 g., 0.999 Silver 0.9926 oz. ASW, 40 mm. **Obv:** National arms, Central Bank name **Rev:** Malta's lira and Fort St. Angelo in color

Date	Mintage	F12	VF20	XF40	MS60	MS63
2004	—	PF65 85.00				

KM# 1001 10 WON
31.11 g., 0.999 Silver 0.9926 oz. ASW, 40 mm. **Obv:** National arms, Central Bank name **Rev:** Polish zloty and Danzig Grain Tower in color

Date	Mintage	F12	VF20	XF40	MS60	MS63
2004	—	PF65 85.00				

KM# 1002 10 WON
31.11 g., 0.999 Silver 0.9926 oz. ASW, 40 mm. **Obv:** National arms, Central Bank name **Rev:** Slovakian Korun and Bratislava castle in color

Date	Mintage	F12	VF20	XF40	MS60	MS63
2004	Est. 2004	PF65 85.00				

KM# 1003 10 WON
31.11 g., 0.999 Silver 0.9926 oz. ASW, 40 mm. **Obv:** National arms, Central Bank name **Rev:** Czech Korun and Prague castle in color

Date	Mintage	F12	VF20	XF40	MS60	MS63
2004	Est. 2004	PF65 85.00				

KM# 1004 10 WON
31.11 g., 0.999 Silver 0.9926 oz. ASW, 40 mm. **Obv:** National arms, Central Bank name **Rev:** Hungarian Forint and St. Stephan statue in Budapest castle in color

Date	Mintage	F12	VF20	XF40	MS60	MS63
2004	Est. 2004	PF65 85.00				

KM# 1005 10 WON
31.11 g., 0.999 Silver 0.9926 oz. ASW, 40 mm. **Obv:** National arms, Central Bank name **Rev:** Cypriot Pound and Temple of Apollo

Date	Mintage	F12	VF20	XF40	MS60	MS63
2004	—	PF65 85.00				

KM# 1006 10 WON
31.11 g., 0.999 Silver 0.9926 oz. ASW, 40 mm. **Subject:** Athens olympics **Obv:** National arms, Central Bank name **Rev:** Discus thrower in color

Date	Mintage	F12	VF20	XF40	MS60	MS63
2004	—	PF65 115				

KM# 1007 10 WON
31.11 g., 0.999 Silver 0.9926 oz. ASW, 40 mm. **Obv:** National arms, Central Bank name **Rev:** Gorch Fock II sailing ship in color

Date	Mintage	F12	VF20	XF40	MS60	MS63
2004	Est. 2004	PF65 115				

KM# 420 10 WON
30.91 g., 0.999 Silver 0.9864 oz. ASW, 40 mm. **Subject:** End of WWII 60th Anniversary **Obv:** State arms **Rev:** Multicolor radiant map, doves, rainbow and inscription **Edge:** Plain

Date	Mintage	F12	VF20	XF40	MS60	MS63
JU94-2005	—	PF65 45.00				

KM# 425 10 WON
1.67 g., Aluminum, 23 mm. **Obv:** State arms **Rev:** Value

Date	Mintage	F12	VF20	XF40	MS60	MS63
JU94(2005)	—	—	—	—	1.00	1.25

KM# 1017 10 WON
31.11 g., 0.999 Silver 0.9926 oz. ASW, 40 mm. **Obv:** National arms, Central Bank name **Rev:** Rooster within Zodiac circle

Date	Mintage	F12	VF20	XF40	MS60	MS63
2005	—	PF65 50.00				

KM# 1021 10 WON
7.00 g., Aluminum, 40 mm. **Obv:** East gate in Pyeongyang **Rev:** Hae Mosu in flight with the five dragons

Date	Mintage	F12	VF20	XF40	MS60	MS63
2005	—	PF65 20.00				

KM# 1023 10 WON
31.11 g., 0.999 Silver 0.9926 oz. ASW, 40 mm. **Obv:** National arms, Central Bank name **Rev:** Hae Mosu in flight with the five dragons

Date	Mintage	F12	VF20	XF40	MS60	MS63
2005	—	PF65 50.00				

KM# 1026 10 WON
7.00 g., Aluminum, 40 mm. **Obv:** East gate of Pyeongyang **Rev:** Admiral Yi Sunsin and turtle boat

Date	Mintage	F12	VF20	XF40	MS60	MS63
2005	—	PF65 20.00				

KM# 1027 10 WON
7.00 g., Aluminum, 40 mm. **Obv:** East gate of Pyeongyang **Rev:** General Hong Beomdo

Date	Mintage	F12	VF20	XF40	MS60	MS63
2005	—	PF65 20.00				

KM# 1030 10 WON
31.11 g., 0.999 Silver 0.9926 oz. ASW, 40 mm. **Obv:** National arms, Central Bank name **Rev:** Admiral Yi Sunsin and turtle boat

Date	Mintage	F12	VF20	XF40	MS60	MS63
2005	—	PF65 50.00				

KM# 1031 10 WON
31.11 g., 0.999 Silver 0.9926 oz. ASW, 40 mm. **Obv:** National arms, Central Bank name **Rev:** General Hong Beomdo

Date	Mintage	F12	VF20	XF40	MS60	MS63
2005	—	PF65 85.00				

KM# 1037 10 WON
31.11 g., 0.999 Silver 0.9926 oz. ASW, 40 mm. **Obv:** National arms, Central Bank name **Rev:** March before the monument of the three principals of reunification

Date	Mintage	F12	VF20	XF40	MS60	MS63
2005	—	PF65 50.00				

KM# 1038 10 WON
31.11 g., 0.999 Silver 0.9926 oz. ASW, 40 mm. **Obv:** National arms, Central Bank name **Rev:** Demonstrations before crater lake

Date	Mintage	F12	VF20	XF40	MS60	MS63
2005	—	PF65 50.00				

KM# 1039 10 WON
31.11 g., 0.999 Silver 0.9926 oz. ASW, 40 mm. **Obv:** National arms, Central Bank name **Rev:** Three drum dance

Date	Mintage	F12	VF20	XF40	MS60	MS63
2005	—	PF65 50.00				

KM# 1045 10 WON
31.11 g., 0.999 Silver 0.9926 oz. ASW, 40 mm. **Obv:** National arms, Central Bank name **Rev:** Tomb of the unknown solder in Moscow

Date	Mintage	F12	VF20	XF40	MS60	MS63
2005	—	PF65 85.00				

KM# 1046 10 WON
31.11 g., 0.999 Silver 0.9926 oz. ASW, 40 mm. **Obv:** National arms, Central Bank name **Rev:** Monument to mothers in St. Petersburg, Russian legend

Date	Mintage	F12	VF20	XF40	MS60	MS63
2005	—	PF65 85.00				

KM# 1090 10 WON
7.00 g., Aluminum, 40 mm. **Obv:** East gate of Pyeongyang **Rev:** Ryuhwa, mother of King Dongmyeong

Date	Mintage	F12	VF20	XF40	MS60	MS63
2006	—	PF65 15.00				

KM# 1091 10 WON
31.11 g., 0.999 Silver 0.9926 oz. ASW, 40 mm. **Obv:** National arms, Central Bank name **Rev:** Ryuhwa, mother of King Dongmyeong

Date	Mintage	F12	VF20	XF40	MS60	MS63
2006 proof	—	PF65 50.00				

KM# 496 10 WON
7.00 g., Aluminum, 40 mm. **Rev:** Eastern City Gate in Pyeongyang

Date	Mintage	F12	VF20	XF40	MS60	MS63
2007	—	PF65 7.50				

KM# 501 10 WON
7.00 g., Aluminum, 40 mm. **Obv:** Eastern city gate in Pyeongyang **Rev:** Brontosaurus

Date	Mintage	F12	VF20	XF40	MS60	MS63
2007	—	PF65 6.50				

KM# 508 10 WON
7.00 g., Aluminum, 40 mm. **Obv:** Eastern gate in Pyeongyang **Rev:** Rainbow lori in color

Date	Mintage	F12	VF20	XF40	MS60	MS63
2007	—	PF65 8.50				

KM# 509 10 WON
7.00 g., Aluminum **Obv:** Eastern Gate in Pyeongyang **Rev:** Manderian Duck in color

Date	Mintage	F12	VF20	XF40	MS60	MS63
2007	—	PF65 8.50				

KM# 514 10 WON
7.00 g., Aluminum, 40 mm. **Obv:** East gate in Pyeoongyang **Rev:** Sports gym and emblem in color

Date	Mintage	F12	VF20	XF40	MS60	MS63
2007	—	PF65 8.50				

KM# 536 10 WON
7.00 g., Aluminum, 40 mm. **Obv:** Eastern gate in Pyeongyang **Rev:** Growth in the Kaeseong area

Date	Mintage	F12	VF20	XF40	MS60	MS63
2007	—	PF65 7.50				

KM# 540 10 WON
7.00 g., Aluminum, 40 mm. **Obv:** Eastern gate of Pyeongyang **Rev:** Panda seated eating

Date	Mintage	F12	VF20	XF40	MS60	MS63
2007	—	PF65 7.50				

KM# 543 10 WON
7.00 g., Aluminum, 40 mm. **Obv:** Eastern gate in Pyeongyang **Rev:** Two pandas

Date	Mintage	F12	VF20	XF40	MS60	MS63
2007	—	PF65 7.50				

KM# 569 10 WON
7.00 g., Aluminum, 40 mm. **Obv:** Eastern gate in Pyeongyang **Rev:** Rocket and satellite

Date	Mintage	F12	VF20	XF40	MS60	MS63
2007	—	PF65 6.50				

KM# 582 10 WON
7.00 g., Aluminum, 40 mm. **Obv:** Eastern gate in Pyeongyang **Rev:** Dragon rising

Date	Mintage	F12	VF20	XF40	MS60	MS63
2007	—	PF65 6.00				

KM# 583 10 WON
7.00 g., Aluminum, 40 mm. **Obv:** Eastern gate in Pyeongyang **Rev:** Two girls on seasaw

Date	Mintage	F12	VF20	XF40	MS60	MS63
2007	—	PF65 6.00				

KM# 584 10 WON
7.00 g., Aluminum, 40 mm. **Obv:** Eastern gate in Pyeongyang **Rev:** Korean struggle

Date	Mintage	F12	VF20	XF40	MS60	MS63
2007	—	PF65 6.00				

KM# 585 10 WON
7.00 g., Aluminum, 40 mm. **Obv:** Eastern gate in Pyeongyang **Rev:** Girl on swing

Date	Mintage	F12	VF20	XF40	MS60	MS63
2007	—	PF65 6.00				

KM# 586 10 WON
7.00 g., Aluminum, 40 mm. **Obv:** Eastern gate in Pyeongyang **Rev:** Girls skipping

Date	Mintage	F12	VF20	XF40	MS60	MS63
2007	—	PF65 6.00				

KM# 610 10 WON
7.00 g., Aluminum, 40 mm. **Obv:** Eastern gate in Pyeongyang **Rev:** Rabbit

Date	Mintage	F12	VF20	XF40	MS60	MS63
2007	—	PF65 7.50				

KM# 620 10 WON
7.00 g., Aluminum, 40 mm. **Obv:** Eastern gate in Pyeongyang **Rev:** White bellied woodpecker

Date	Mintage	F12	VF20	XF40	MS60	MS63
2007	—	PF65 6.00				

KM# 621 10 WON
7.00 g., Aluminum, 40 mm. **Obv:** Eastern gate in Pyeongyang **Rev:** Black grouse

Date	Mintage	F12	VF20	XF40	MS60	MS63
2007	—	PF65 6.00				

KM# 622 10 WON
7.00 g., Aluminum, 40 mm. **Obv:** Eastern gate in Pyeongyang **Rev:** Sand Grouse

Date	Mintage	F12	VF20	XF40	MS60	MS63
2007	—	PF65 6.00				

KM# 623 10 WON
7.00 g., Aluminum, 40 mm. **Obv:** Eastern gate in Pyeongyang **Rev:** Indian Pitta bird

Date	Mintage	F12	VF20	XF40	MS60	MS63
2007	—	PF65 6.00				

KM# 632 10 WON
7.00 g., Aluminum, 40 mm. **Obv:** Eastern gate in Pyeongyang **Rev:** Blue dragon right

Date	Mintage	F12	VF20	XF40	MS60	MS63
2007	—	PF65 15.00				

KM# 637 10 WON
7.00 g., Aluminum, 40 mm. **Obv:** Eastern gate in Pyeongyang **Rev:** Two siberian tigers

Date	Mintage	F12	VF20	XF40	MS60	MS63
2007	—	PF65 6.00				

KM# 649 10 WON
Aluminum, 40 mm. **Obv:** Eastern gate in Pyeongyang **Rev:** King Goguryeo

Date	Mintage	F12	VF20	XF40	MS60	MS63
2007	—	PF65 15.00				

KM# 650 10 WON
Aluminum, 40 mm. **Obv:** Eastern gate in Pyeongyang **Rev:** Buddha figure

Date	Mintage	F12	VF20	XF40	MS60	MS63
2007	—	PF65 15.00				

KM# 651 10 WON
Aluminum, 40 mm. **Obv:** Eastern gate in Pyeongyang **Rev:** King Gojoseon

Date	Mintage	F12	VF20	XF40	MS60	MS63
2007	—	PF65 6.00				

KM# 667 10 WON
7.00 g., Aluminum, 40 mm. **Obv:** Eastern gate in Pyeongyang **Rev:** First married couple to see again since the 1945 division

Date	Mintage	F12	VF20	XF40	MS60	MS63
2007	—	PF65 15.00				

KM# 715 10 WON
7.00 g., Aluminum, 40 mm. **Obv:** East gate of Pyeongyang **Rev:** Celadon pottery

Date	Mintage	F12	VF20	XF40	MS60	MS63
2007	—	PF65 6.00				

KM# 802 10 WON
7.00 g., Aluminum, 40 mm. **Obv:** East gate in Pyeongyang **Rev:** Reconstruction of the mausoleum for King Dangun

Date	Mintage	F12	VF20	XF40	MS60	MS63
2007	—	PF65 10.00				

KM# 803 10 WON
7.00 g., Aluminum, 40 mm. **Obv:** East gate in Pyeongyang **Rev:** Dongmyeong, 1st King of Goguryeb

Date	Mintage	F12	VF20	XF40	MS60	MS63
2007	—	PF65 10.00				

KM# 804 10 WON
7.00 g., Aluminum, 40 mm. **Obv:** East gate in Pyeongyang **Rev:** Wanggeon, 1st king of Goryeo dynasty

Date	Mintage	F12	VF20	XF40	MS60	MS63
2007	—	PF65 10.00				

KM# 805 10 WON
7.00 g., Aluminum, 40 mm. **Obv:** East gate in Pyeongyang **Rev:** Jeong Mongju

Date	Mintage	F12	VF20	XF40	MS60	MS63
2007	—	PF65 10.00				

KM# 806 10 WON
7.00 g., Aluminum, 40 mm. **Obv:** East gate in Pyeongyang **Rev:** Jeon Bongjun

Date	Mintage	F12	VF20	XF40	MS60	MS63
2007	—	PF65 10.00				

KM# 850 10 WON
7.00 g., Aluminum, 40 mm. **Obv:** East gate of Pyeongyang **Rev:** Dancer

Date	Mintage	F12	VF20	XF40	MS60	MS63
2007	—	PF65 6.00				

KM# 851 10 WON
7.00 g., Aluminum, 40 mm. **Obv:** East gate of Pyeongyang **Rev:** Dancer

Date	Mintage	F12	VF20	XF40	MS60	MS63
2007	—	PF65 7.00				

KM# 852 10 WON
7.00 g., Aluminum, 40 mm. **Obv:** National arms, Central Bank name **Rev:** Female in national costume

Date	Mintage	F12	VF20	XF40	MS60	MS63
2007	—	PF65 7.00				

KM# 853 10 WON
7.00 g., Aluminum, 40 mm. **Obv:** National arms, Central Bank name **Rev:** Crane dancer

Date	Mintage	F12	VF20	XF40	MS60	MS63
2007	—	PF65 7.00				

KM# 854 10 WON
7.00 g., Aluminum, 40 mm. **Obv:** National arms, Central Bank name **Rev:** Fairy princess

Date	Mintage	F12	VF20	XF40	MS60	MS63
2007	—	PF65 7.00				

KM# 880 10 WON
6.00 g., 0.999 Aluminum 0.1915 oz., 38 mm. **Obv:** East gate of Pyeongyang **Rev:** Taekwondo

Date	Mintage	F12	VF20	XF40	MS60	MS63
2007	—	PF65 6.00				

KM# 736 20 WON
28.00 g., Brass, 40 mm. **Obv:** East gate of Pyeongyang **Rev:** Married couple before Korean flag and ferryboat

Date	Mintage	F12	VF20	XF40	MS60	MS63
2001	—	PF65 20.00				

KM# 737 20 WON
28.00 g., Brass, 40 mm. **Obv:** East gate of Pyeongyang **Rev:** Ferryboat between Korea and Japan

Date	Mintage	F12	VF20	XF40	MS60	MS63
2001	—	PF65 7.00				

KM# 738 20 WON
28.00 g., Brass, 40 mm. **Obv:** East gate in Pyeongyang **Rev:** Triumphial arch of Moranbong in Pyeongyang

Date	Mintage	F12	VF20	XF40	MS60	MS63
2001	—	PF65 20.00				

KM# 739 20 WON
28.00 g., Brass, 40 mm. **Obv:** East gate in Pyeongyang **Rev:** Chonji crater in Paektusan

Date	Mintage	F12	VF20	XF40	MS60	MS63
2001	—	PF65 20.00				

KM# 768 20 WON
16.00 g., Brass, 35 mm. **Obv:** East gate of Pyeongyang **Rev:** Chinese Dragon boat

Date	Mintage	F12	VF20	XF40	MS60	MS63
2001	—	PF65 7.00				

KM# 777 20 WON
28.00 g., Brass, 40 mm. **Obv:** East gate of Pyeongyang **Rev:** Taekwondo kicker

Date	Mintage	F12	VF20	XF40	MS60	MS63
2001	—	PF65 7.00				

KM# 778 20 WON
28.00 g., Brass, 40 mm. **Obv:** East gate of Pyeongyang **Rev:** Two taekwondo players

Date	Mintage	F12	VF20	XF40	MS60	MS63
2001	—	PF65 7.00				

KM# 787 20 WON
16.00 g., Brass, 35 mm. **Obv:** East gate of Pyeongyang **Rev:** Horse head

Date	Mintage	F12	VF20	XF40	MS60	MS63
2002	—	PF65 7.00				

KM# 788 20 WON
16.00 g., Brass, 35 mm. **Obv:** East gate of Pyeongyang **Rev:** Horse right

Date	Mintage	F12	VF20	XF40	MS60	MS63
2002	—	PF65 20.00				

KM# 789 20 WON
28.00 g., Brass, 40 mm. **Obv:** East gate of Pyeongyang **Rev:** Two horses

Date	Mintage	F12	VF20	XF40	MS60	MS63
2002	—	PF65 7.00				

KM# 809 20 WON
28.00 g., Brass, 40 mm. **Obv:** East gate of Pyeongyang **Rev:** Wanggeon, 1st King of Goryeo dynasty

Date	Mintage	F12	VF20	XF40	MS60	MS63
2002	—	PF65 7.00				

KM# 810 20 WON
28.00 g., Brass, 40 mm. **Obv:** East gate of Pyeongyang **Rev:** Jeong Mongju

Date	Mintage	F12	VF20	XF40	MS60	MS63
2002	—	PF65 7.00				

KM# 830 20 WON
28.00 g., Brass, 40 mm. **Obv:** East gate of Pyeongyang **Rev:** Resconstruction of the Mausoleums of King Dongmyeong

Date	Mintage	F12	VF20	XF40	MS60	MS63
2002	—	PF65 7.00				

KM# 831 20 WON
28.00 g., Brass, 40 mm. **Obv:** East gate of Pyeongyang **Rev:** Mausoleum of King Gongmin

Date	Mintage	F12	VF20	XF40	MS60	MS63
2002	—	PF65 7.00				

KM# 832 20 WON
28.00 g., Brass, 40 mm. **Obv:** East gate of Pyeongyang **Rev:** Stadium

Date	Mintage	F12	VF20	XF40	MS60	MS63
2002	—	PF65 7.00				

KM# 866 20 WON
28.00 g., Brass, 40 mm. **Obv:** East gate of Pyeongyang **Rev:** Map of Korea with the four cardinal directions

Date	Mintage	F12	VF20	XF40	MS60	MS63
2002	—	PF65 7.00				

KM# 867 20 WON
28.00 g., Brass, 40 mm. **Obv:** East gate of Pyeongyang **Rev:** Rythem dancers and map of Korea

Date	Mintage	F12	VF20	XF40	MS60	MS63
2002	—	PF65 7.00				

KM# 897 20 WON
28.00 g., Brass, 40 mm. **Obv:** East gate of Pyeongyang **Rev:** Sheep in center of Zodiac

Date	Mintage	F12	VF20	XF40	MS60	MS63
2003	—	PF65 7.00				

KM# 909 20 WON
28.00 g., Brass, 40 mm. **Obv:** East gate of Pyeongyang **Rev:** Eulji Mundeok

Date	Mintage	F12	VF20	XF40	MS60	MS63
2003	—	PF65 7.00				

KM# 910 20 WON
28.00 g., Brass, 40 mm. **Obv:** East gate in Pyeongyang **Rev:** Yeon Gaesomun

Date	Mintage	F12	VF20	XF40	MS60	MS63
2003	—	PF65 7.00				

KM# 916 20 WON
28.00 g., Brass, 40 mm. **Obv:** East gate of Pyeongyang **Rev:** Turtle boat

Date	Mintage	F12	VF20	XF40	MS60	MS63
2003	—	PF65 7.00				

KM# 256 20 WON
42.06 g., 0.999 Silver 1.3422 oz. ASW, 45.1 mm. **Obv:** State arms **Rev:** Rose of sharon flower **Edge:** Plain

Date	Mintage	F12	VF20	XF40	MS60	MS63
JU93-2004	—	PF65 65.00				

KM# 257 20 WON
42.22 g., 0.999 Silver 1.3472 oz. ASW, 45.1 mm. **Obv:** State arms **Rev:** Kim Jong-Il, Peony flower **Edge:** Plain

Date	Mintage	F12	VF20	XF40	MS60	MS63
JU93-2004	—	PF65 65.00				

KM# 258 20 WON
41.92 g., 0.999 Silver 1.3377 oz. ASW, 45.1 mm. **Obv:** State arms **Rev:** Kim Il-seung, Orchid flowers **Edge:** Plain

Date	Mintage	F12	VF20	XF40	MS60	MS63
JU93-2004	—	PF65 65.00				

KM# 259 20 WON
42.00 g., 0.999 Silver 1.3403 oz. ASW, 45.1 mm. **Obv:** State arms **Rev:** Kim Il Sung's birth place, side view **Edge:** Plain

Date	Mintage	F12	VF20	XF40	MS60	MS63
JU93-2004	—	PF65 65.00				

KM# 260 20 WON
41.62 g., 0.999 Silver 1.3282 oz. ASW, 45.1 mm. **Obv:** State arms **Rev:** Mountain cabin **Edge:** Plain

Date	Mintage	F12	VF20	XF40	MS60	MS63
JU93-2004	—	PF65 65.00				

KM# 261 20 WON
41.91 g., 0.999 Silver 1.3374 oz. ASW, 45.1 mm. **Obv:** State arms **Rev:** Kim Il Sung's birth place, front view **Edge:** Plain

Date	Mintage	F12	VF20	XF40	MS60	MS63
JU93-2004	—	PF65 65.00				

KM# 340 20 WON
31.00 g., 0.999 Silver 0.9893 oz. ASW, 39.8 mm. **Obv:** State arms **Rev:** Kim Jong-Il and Vladimir Putin clasping hands **Edge:** Segmented reeding

Date	Mintage	F12	VF20	XF40	MS60	MS63
2004	—	PF65 50.00				

KM# 341 20 WON
31.00 g., 0.999 Silver 0.9893 oz. ASW, 39.8 mm. **Obv:** State arms **Rev:** Bust facing **Edge:** Segmented reeding

Date	Mintage	F12	VF20	XF40	MS60	MS63
2004	—	PF65 50.00				

KM# 419 20 WON
31.00 g., 0.999 Silver 0.9893 oz. ASW, 39.75 mm. **Subject:** Historic Pyongyang Meeting **Obv:** State arms **Rev:** Kim Jong-Il and Kim Dae-Jung clasping hands, English legend **Edge:** Segmented reeding

Date	Mintage	F12	VF20	XF40	MS60	MS63
2004	—	PF65 50.00				

KM# 942 20 WON
19.00 g., Copper, 23x40 mm. **Obv:** East gate of Pyeongyang **Rev:** Marmoset **Shape:** Rectangle

Date	Mintage	F12	VF20	XF40	MS60	MS63
2004	—	PF65 8.00				

KM# 943 20 WON
19.00 g., Copper, 23x40 mm. **Obv:** East gate of Pyeongyang **Rev:** Blue monkey

Date	Mintage	F12	VF20	XF40	MS60	MS63
2004	—	PF65 8.00				

KM# 944 20 WON
19.00 g., Copper, 23x40 mm. **Obv:** East gate of Pyeongyang **Rev:** two monkies

Date	Mintage	F12	VF20	XF40	MS60	MS63
2004	—	PF65 8.00				

KM# 949 20 WON
Brass, 40 mm. **Obv:** East gate of Pyeongyang **Rev:** Sports hall in Pyeongyang

Date	Mintage	F12	VF20	XF40	MS60	MS63
2004	—	PF65 14.00				

KM# 955 20 WON
42.22 g., 0.999 Silver 1.3472 oz. ASW, 45 mm. **Obv:** National arms, Central Bank name **Rev:** Kim Ilseong

Date	Mintage	F12	VF20	XF40	MS60	MS63
2004	—	PF65 70.00				

KM# 956 20 WON
42.22 g., 0.999 Silver 1.3472 oz. ASW, 45 mm. **Obv:** National arms, Central Bank name **Rev:** Kim Jeongil

Date	Mintage	F12	VF20	XF40	MS60	MS63
2004	—	PF65 70.00				

KM# 957 20 WON
42.22 g., 0.999 Silver 1.3472 oz. ASW, 45 mm. **Obv:** Naitonal arms, Central Bank name **Rev:** Kim Jeongsuk

Date	Mintage	F12	VF20	XF40	MS60	MS63
2004	—	PF65 70.00				

KM# 966 20 WON
31.11 g., 0.999 Silver 0.9926 oz. ASW, 40 mm. **Obv:** National arms, Central Bank name **Rev:** Kim Jeongil and Hu Jintao

Date	Mintage	F12	VF20	XF40	MS60	MS63
2004	—	PF65 60.00				

KM# 977 20 WON
31.11 g., 0.999 Silver 0.9926 oz. ASW, 40 mm. **Obv:** Dokdo, rocky islands, Central Bank name **Rev:** Map of the island group

Date	Mintage	F12	VF20	XF40	MS60	MS63
2004	—	PF65 70.00				

KM# 978 20 WON
31.11 g., 0.999 Silver 0.9926 oz. ASW, 40 mm. **Obv:** Dokdo, rocky islands, Central Bank name **Rev:** Fisher Ahn Yongbok

Date	Mintage	F12	VF20	XF40	MS60	MS63
2004	—	PF65 70.00				

KM# 979 20 WON
31.11 g., 0.999 Silver 0.9926 oz. ASW, 40 mm. **Obv:** Dokdo, rocky islands, Central Bank name **Rev:** West island

Date	Mintage	F12	VF20	XF40	MS60	MS63
2004	—	PF65 70.00				

KM# 980 20 WON
31.11 g., 0.999 Silver 0.9926 oz. ASW, 40 mm. **Obv:** Dokdo, rocky islands, Central Bank name **Rev:** East island

Date	Mintage	F12	VF20	XF40	MS60	MS63
2004	—	PF65 70.00				

KM# 981 20 WON
31.11 g., 0.999 Silver 0.9926 oz. ASW, 40 mm. **Obv:** Dokdo, rocky islands, Central Bank name **Rev:** Three brother island

Date	Mintage	F12	VF20	XF40	MS60	MS63
2004	—	PF65 70.00				

KM# 982 20 WON
31.11 g., 0.999 Silver 0.9926 oz. ASW, 40 mm. **Obv:** Dokdo, rocky islands, Central Bank name **Rev:** Chicken island

Date	Mintage	F12	VF20	XF40	MS60	MS63
2004	—	PF65 70.00				

KM# 983 20 WON
31.11 g., 0.999 Silver 0.9926 oz. ASW, 40 mm. **Obv:** Dokdo, rocky islands, Central Bank name **Rev:** Candle island

Date	Mintage	F12	VF20	XF40	MS60	MS63
2004	—	PF65 70.00				

KM# 984 20 WON
31.11 g., 0.999 Silver 0.9926 oz. ASW, 40 mm. **Obv:** Dokdo, rocky islands, Central Bank name **Rev:** Dome island

Date	Mintage	F12	VF20	XF40	MS60	MS63
2004	—	PF65 70.00				

KM# 478 20 WON
27.30 g., Brass, 40 mm. **Obv:** Temple **Rev:** Multicolor rooster right

Date	Mintage	F12	VF20	XF40	MS60	MS63
2005	—	PF65 10.00				

KM# 479 20 WON
31.11 g., 0.999 Silver 0.9926 oz. ASW **Obv:** Arms **Rev:** A puppy, dog's head facing

Date	Mintage	F12	VF20	XF40	MS60	MS63
2005	—	PF65 45.00				

KM# 1022 20 WON
28.00 g., Brass, 40 mm. **Obv:** East gate of Pyeongyang **Rev:** Hae Mosu in flight with the five dragons

Date	Mintage	F12	VF20	XF40	MS60	MS63
2005	—	PF65 20.00				

KM# 1028 20 WON
28.00 g., Brass, 40 mm. **Obv:** East gate of Pyeongyang **Rev:** Admiral Yi Sunsin and turtle boat

Date	Mintage	F12	VF20	XF40	MS60	MS63
2005	—	PF65 12.50				

KM# 1029 20 WON
28.00 g., Brass, 40 mm. **Obv:** East gate of Pyeongyong **Rev:** General Hong Beomdo

Date	Mintage	F12	VF20	XF40	MS60	MS63
2005	—	PF65 12.50				

KM# 1041 20 WON
28.00 g., Brass, 40 mm. **Obv:** East gate of Pyeongyang **Rev:** Map of Korea, pair of peace doves, rainbow

Date	Mintage	F12	VF20	XF40	MS60	MS63
2005	—	PF65 12.50				

KM# 1049 20 WON
31.11 g., 0.999 Silver 0.9926 oz. ASW, 40 mm. **Obv:** National arms, Central Bank name **Rev:** Dongmyeong, 1st king of Goguryeo

Date	Mintage	F12	VF20	XF40	MS60	MS63
2005	—	PF65 65.00				

KM# 1050 20 WON
31.11 g., 0.999 Silver 0.9926 oz. ASW, 40 mm. **Obv:** National arms, Central Bank name **Rev:** Blue dragon, Cheongryong, of the East

Date	Mintage	F12	VF20	XF40	MS60	MS63
2005	—	PF65 45.00				

KM# 1051 20 WON
31.11 g., 0.999 Silver 0.9926 oz. ASW, 40 mm. **Obv:** National arms, Central Bank name **Rev:** Red bird, Jujak, of the South

Date	Mintage	F12	VF20	XF40	MS60	MS63
2005	—	PF65 45.00				

KM# 1052 20 WON
31.11 g., 0.999 Silver 0.9926 oz. ASW, 40 mm. **Obv:** National arms, Central Bank name **Rev:** White tiger, Baekho, of the West

Date	Mintage	F12	VF20	XF40	MS60	MS63
2005	—	PF65 45.00				

KM# 1053 20 WON
31.11 g., 0.999 Silver 0.9926 oz. ASW, 40 mm. **Obv:** National arms, Central Bank name **Rev:** Black snake, Hyeonmu, of the North

Date	Mintage	F12	VF20	XF40	MS60	MS63
2005	—	PF65 45.00				

KM# 1054 20 WON
31.11 g., 0.999 Silver 0.9926 oz. ASW, 40 mm. **Obv:** National arms, Central Bank name **Rev:** Horse and rider

Date	Mintage	F12	VF20	XF40	MS60	MS63
2005	—	PF65 45.00				

KM# 1055 20 WON
31.11 g., 0.999 Silver 0.9926 oz. ASW, 40 mm. **Obv:** National arms, Central Bank name **Rev:** Horse drummers

Date	Mintage	F12	VF20	XF40	MS60	MS63
2005	—	PF65 45.00				

KM# 1056 20 WON
31.11 g., 0.999 Silver 0.9926 oz. ASW, 40 mm. **Obv:** National arms, Central Bank name **Rev:** Bugler to horse

Date	Mintage	F12	VF20	XF40	MS60	MS63
2005	—	PF65 45.00				

KM# 1057 20 WON
31.11 g., 0.999 Silver 0.9926 oz. ASW, 40 mm. **Obv:** National arms, Central Bank name **Rev:** Horseback hunter

Date	Mintage	F12	VF20	XF40	MS60	MS63
2005	—	PF65 45.00				

KM# 1058 20 WON
31.11 g., 0.999 Silver 0.9926 oz. ASW, 40 mm. **Obv:** National arms, Central Bank name **Rev:** Crane and bamboo image by Yi Kyeongyun

Date	Mintage	F12	VF20	XF40	MS60	MS63
2005	—	PF65 65.00				

KM# 1059 20 WON
31.11 g., 0.999 Silver 0.9926 oz. ASW, 40 mm. **Obv:** National arms, Central Bank name **Rev:** Ibis, image by Kim Sik

Date	Mintage	F12	VF20	XF40	MS60	MS63
2005	—	PF65 65.00				

KM# 1060 20 WON
31.11 g., 0.999 Silver 0.9926 oz. ASW, 40 mm. **Obv:** National arms, Central Bank name **Rev:** Pheasant by Jang Seungeop

Date	Mintage	F12	VF20	XF40	MS60	MS63
2005	—	PF65 65.00				

KM# 1061 20 WON
31.11 g., 0.999 Silver 0.9926 oz. ASW, 40 mm. **Obv:** National arms, Central Bank name **Rev:** Fairy princess of the diamond mountain

Date	Mintage	F12	VF20	XF40	MS60	MS63
2005	—	PF65 65.00				

KM# 1062 20 WON
31.11 g., 0.999 Silver 0.9926 oz. ASW, 40 mm. **Obv:** National arms, Central Bank name **Rev:** Big stone in the diamond mountain

Date	Mintage	F12	VF20	XF40	MS60	MS63
2005	—	PF65 65.00				

KM# 1063 20 WON
31.11 g., 0.999 Silver 0.9926 oz. ASW, 40 mm. **Obv:** National arms, Central Bank name **Rev:** Two rabbits

Date	Mintage	F12	VF20	XF40	MS60	MS63
2005	Est. 2000	PF65 45.00				

KM# 1064 20 WON
31.11 g., 0.999 Silver 0.9926 oz. ASW, 40 mm. **Obv:** National arms, Central Bank name **Rev:** Cat

Date	Mintage	F12	VF20	XF40	MS60	MS63
2005	Est. 2000	PF65 45.00				

KM# 1065 20 WON
31.11 g., 0.999 Silver 0.9926 oz. ASW, 40 mm. **Subject:** North-South Railway connection **Obv:** National arms, Central Bank name **Rev:** Map of Korea and railway line

Date	Mintage	F12	VF20	XF40	MS60	MS63
2005	—	PF65 65.00				

KM# 1066 20 WON
31.11 g., 0.999 Silver 0.9926 oz. ASW, 40 mm. **Obv:** National arms, Central Bank name **Rev:** FIFA World Cup trophy

Date	Mintage	F12	VF20	XF40	MS60	MS63
2005	—	PF65 45.00				

KM# 480 20 WON
23.70 g., Brass, 40 mm. **Obv:** Temple **Rev:** Multicolor German shepard

Date	Mintage	F12	VF20	XF40	MS60	MS63
2006	—	PF65 10.00				

KM# 481 20 WON
Brass **Obv:** Arms **Rev:** Bejeweled female head

Date	Mintage	F12	VF20	XF40	MS60	MS63
2006	—	PF65 10.00				

KM# 482 20 WON
27.30 g., Brass, 40 mm. **Obv:** Temple **Rev:** Multicolor pig and pigletts

Date	Mintage	F12	VF20	XF40	MS60	MS63
2007	—	PF65 10.00				

KM# 497 20 WON
28.00 g., Brass, 40 mm. **Rev:** Eastern city gate of Pyeongyang

Date	Mintage	F12	VF20	XF40	MS60	MS63
2007	—	PF65 8.50				

KM# 502 20 WON
28.00 g., Brass, 40 mm. **Obv:** Eastern city gate of Pyeongyang **Rev:** Brontosaurus

Date	Mintage	F12	VF20	XF40	MS60	MS63
2007	—	PF65 8.50				

KM# 570 20 WON
28.00 g., Brass, 40 mm. **Obv:** Eastern gate in Pyeongyang **Rev:** Rocket and satellite

Date	Mintage	F12	VF20	XF40	MS60	MS63
2007	—	PF65 7.50				

KM# 587 20 WON
28.00 g., Brass, 40 mm. **Obv:** Eastern gate in Pyeongyang **Rev:** Dragon rising

Date	Mintage	F12	VF20	XF40	MS60	MS63
2007	—	PF65 7.50				

KM# 588 20 WON
28.00 g., Brass, 40 mm. **Obv:** Eastern gate in Pyeongyang **Rev:** Two girls on seasaw

Date	Mintage	F12	VF20	XF40	MS60	MS63
2007	—	PF65 7.50				

KM# 589 20 WON
28.00 g., Brass, 40 mm. **Obv:** Eastern gate in Pyeongyang **Rev:** Korean struggle

Date	Mintage	F12	VF20	XF40	MS60	MS63
2007	—	PF65 7.50				

KM# 590 20 WON
28.00 g., Brass, 40 mm. **Obv:** Eastern gate in Pyeongyang **Rev:** Girl on swing

Date	Mintage	F12	VF20	XF40	MS60	MS63
2007	—	PF65 7.50				

KM# 591 20 WON
28.00 g., Brass, 40 mm. **Obv:** Eastern gate in Pyeongyang **Rev:** Children Skipping

Date	Mintage	F12	VF20	XF40	MS60	MS63
2007	—	PF65 7.50				

KM# 624 20 WON
28.00 g., Brass, 40 mm. **Obv:** Eastern gate in Pyeongyang **Rev:** White bellied woodpecker

Date	Mintage	F12	VF20	XF40	MS60	MS63
2007	—	PF65 7.00				

KM# 625 20 WON
28.00 g., Brass, 40 mm. **Obv:** Eastern gate in Pyeongyang **Rev:** Black grouse

Date	Mintage	F12	VF20	XF40	MS60	MS63
2007	—	PF65 7.00				

KM# 626 20 WON
28.00 g., Brass, 40 mm. **Obv:** Eastern gate in Pyeongyang **Rev:** Sand Grouse

Date	Mintage	F12	VF20	XF40	MS60	MS63
2007	—	PF65 7.00				

KM# 627 20 WON
28.00 g., Brass, 40 mm. **Obv:** Eastern gate in Pyeongyang **Rev:** Indian Pitta bird

Date	Mintage	F12	VF20	XF40	MS60	MS63
2007	—	PF65 7.00				

KM# 633 20 WON
28.00 g., Brass, 40 mm. **Obv:** Eastern gate in Pyeongyang **Rev:** Blue dragon right

Date	Mintage	F12	VF20	XF40	MS60	MS63
2007	—	PF65 7.00				

KM# 638 20 WON
28.00 g., Brass, 40 mm. **Obv:** Eastern gate in Pyeongyang **Rev:** Two siberian tigers

Date	Mintage	F12	VF20	XF40	MS60	MS63
2007	—	PF65 7.00				

KM# 652 20 WON
28.00 g., Brass, 40 mm. **Obv:** Eastern gate in Pyeongyang **Rev:** Dongmyeong, King of Goguryeo

Date	Mintage	F12	VF20	XF40	MS60	MS63
2007	—	PF65 7.00				

KM# 653 20 WON
28.00 g., Brass, 40 mm. **Obv:** Eastern gate in Pyeongyang **Rev:** Buddha figure

Date	Mintage	F12	VF20	XF40	MS60	MS63
2007	—	PF65 7.00				

KM# 654 20 WON
28.00 g., Brass, 40 mm. **Obv:** Eastern gate in Pyeongyang **Rev:** Dangun, King of Gojoseon

Date	Mintage	F12	VF20	XF40	MS60	MS63
2007	—	PF65 7.00				

KM# 668 20 WON
28.00 g., Brass, 40 mm. **Obv:** Eastern gate in Pyeongyang **Rev:** First married couple to meet again after the 1945 division

Date	Mintage	F12	VF20	XF40	MS60	MS63
2007	—	PF65 7.00				

KM# 690 20 WON
28.00 g., Brass, 40 mm. **Obv:** East gate of Pyeongyang **Rev:** Hyonmu

Date	Mintage	F12	VF20	XF40	MS60	MS63
2007	—	PF65 7.00				

KM# 716 20 WON
28.00 g., Brass, 40 mm. **Obv:** East gate of Pyeongyang **Rev:** Celadon pottery

Date	Mintage	F12	VF20	XF40	MS60	MS63
2007	—	PF65 7.00				

KM# 807 20 WON
28.00 g., Brass, 40 mm. **Obv:** East gate in Pyeongyang **Rev:** Reconstruction of the mausoleum of King Dangun

Date	Mintage	F12	VF20	XF40	MS60	MS63
2007	—	PF65 7.00				

KM# 808 20 WON
28.00 g., Brass, 40 mm. **Obv:** East gate of Pyeongyang **Rev:** Dongmyeong, 1st King of Goguryeo

Date	Mintage	F12	VF20	XF40	MS60	MS63
2007	—	PF65 7.00				

KM# 811 20 WON
28.00 g., Brass, 40 mm. **Obv:** East gate of Pyeongyang **Rev:** Jeon Bongjun

Date	Mintage	F12	VF20	XF40	MS60	MS63
2007	—	PF65 7.00				

KM# 855 20 WON
28.00 g., Brass, 40 mm. **Obv:** East gate of Pyeongyang **Rev:** Dancer

Date	Mintage	F12	VF20	XF40	MS60	MS63
2007	—	PF65 7.00				

KM# 856 20 WON
28.00 g., Brass, 40 mm. **Obv:** East gate of Pyeongyang **Rev:** Dancer

Date	Mintage	F12	VF20	XF40	MS60	MS63
2007	—	PF65 7.00				

KM# 857 20 WON
28.00 g., Brass, 40 mm. **Obv:** East gate of Pyeongyang **Rev:** Woman in national costume

Date	Mintage	F12	VF20	XF40	MS60	MS63
2007	—	PF65 7.00				

KM# 858 20 WON
28.00 g., Brass, 40 mm. **Obv:** East gate of Pyeongyang **Rev:** Crane dancer

Date	Mintage	F12	VF20	XF40	MS60	MS63
2007	—	PF65 7.00				

KM# 859 20 WON
28.00 g., Brass, 40 mm. **Obv:** East gate of Pyeongyang **Rev:** Fairy princess

Date	Mintage	F12	VF20	XF40	MS60	MS63
2007	—	PF65 7.00				

KM# 868 20 WON
28.00 g., Brass, 40 mm. **Obv:** East gate of Pyeongyang **Rev:** Drum dancers in shape of Korean map

Date	Mintage	F12	VF20	XF40	MS60	MS63
2007	—	PF65 7.00				

KM# 869 20 WON
28.00 g., Brass, 40 mm. **Obv:** East gate of Pyeongyang **Rev:** Korean team victory celebration

Date	Mintage	F12	VF20	XF40	MS60	MS63
2007	—	PF65 7.00				

KM# 1128 20 WON
28.00 g., Brass, 40 mm. **Obv:** National arms, Central Bank name **Rev:** Hoopoe

Date	Mintage	F12	VF20	XF40	MS60	MS63
2007	—	PF65 17.50				

KM# 1129 20 WON
28.00 g., Brass, 40 mm. **Obv:** National arms, Central Bank name **Rev:** Ural owl

Date	Mintage	F12	VF20	XF40	MS60	MS63
2007	Est. 2000	PF65 17.50				

KM# 1130 20 WON
28.00 g., Brass, 40 mm. **Obv:** National arms, Central Bank name **Rev:** Eagle

Date	Mintage	F12	VF20	XF40	MS60	MS63
2007	Est. 2000	PF65 17.50				

KM# 1131 20 WON
28.00 g., Brass, 40 mm. **Obv:** National arms, Central Bank name **Rev:** White rhino

Date	Mintage	F12	VF20	XF40	MS60	MS63
2007	Est. 2000	PF65 17.50				

KM# 1132 20 WON
28.00 g., Brass, 40 mm. **Obv:** National arms, Central Bank name **Rev:** African elephant family

Date	Mintage	F12	VF20	XF40	MS60	MS63
2007	Est. 2000	PF65 17.50				

KM# 1133 20 WON
28.00 g., Brass, 40 mm. **Obv:** National arms, Central Bank name **Rev:** Lion family

Date	Mintage	F12	VF20	XF40	MS60	MS63
2007	Est. 2000	PF65 17.50				

KM# 1134 20 WON
28.00 g., Brass, 40 mm. **Obv:** National arms, Central Bank name **Rev:** Cape Buffalo

Date	Mintage	F12	VF20	XF40	MS60	MS63
2007	Est. 2000	PF65 17.50				

KM# 1135 20 WON
28.00 g., Brass **Obv:** National arms, Central Bank name **Rev:** Marine turtle

Date	Mintage	F12	VF20	XF40	MS60	MS63
2007	Est. 2000	PF65 17.50				

KM# 1136 20 WON
28.00 g., Brass, 40 mm. **Obv:** National arms, Central Bank name **Rev:** Penguin

Date	Mintage	F12	VF20	XF40	MS60	MS63
2007	Est. 2000	PF65 17.50				

KM# 1137 20 WON
28.00 g., Brass, 40 mm. **Obv:** National arms, Central Bank name **Rev:** Emu

Date	Mintage	F12	VF20	XF40	MS60	MS63
2007	—	PF65 17.50				

KM# 1138 20 WON
28.00 g., Brass, 40 mm. **Obv:** National arms, Central Bank name **Rev:** Eagle owl

Date	Mintage	F12	VF20	XF40	MS60	MS63
2007	Est. 2000	PF65 17.50				

KM# 1139 20 WON
28.00 g., Brass, 40 mm. **Obv:** National arms, Central Bank name **Rev:** Lemur

Date	Mintage	F12	VF20	XF40	MS60	MS63
2007	Est. 2000	PF65 17.50				

KM# 1140 20 WON
28.00 g., Brass, 40 mm. **Obv:** National arms, Central Bank name **Rev:** Lion

Date	Mintage	F12	VF20	XF40	MS60	MS63
2007	Est. 2000	PF65 17.50				

KM# 1141 20 WON
28.00 g., Brass, 40 mm. **Obv:** National arms, Central Bank name **Rev:** Two Arfican elephants

Date	Mintage	F12	VF20	XF40	MS60	MS63
2007	—	PF65 17.50				

KM# 484 20 WON
27.30 g., Brass, 40 mm. **Obv:** Temple **Rev:** Multicolor goat left

Date	Mintage	F12	VF20	XF40	MS60	MS63
2008	—	PF65 10.00				

KM# 485 20 WON
27.30 g., Brass, 40 mm. **Obv:** Temple **Rev:** Multicolor snake and flowers

Date	Mintage	F12	VF20	XF40	MS60	MS63
2008	—	PF65 10.00				

KM# 486 20 WON
27.30 g., Brass, 40 mm. **Obv:** Temple **Rev:** Multicolor, two rabbits

Date	Mintage	F12	VF20	XF40	MS60	MS63
2008	—	PF65 10.00				

KM# 487 20 WON
27.30 g., Brass, 40 mm. **Obv:** Temple **Rev:** Multicolor two white rats

Date	Mintage	F12	VF20	XF40	MS60	MS63
2008	—	PF65 10.00				

KM# 488 20 WON
27.30 g., Brass, 40 mm. **Obv:** Temple **Rev:** Multicolor monkey seated on branch

Date	Mintage	F12	VF20	XF40	MS60	MS63
2008	—	PF65 10.00				

KM# 489 20 WON
27.30 g., Brass, 40 mm. **Obv:** Temple **Rev:** Multicolor tiger

Date	Mintage	F12	VF20	XF40	MS60	MS63
2008	—	PF65 10.00				

KM# 490 20 WON
27.30 g., Brass, 40 mm. **Obv:** Temple **Rev:** Multicolor horse prancing right

Date	Mintage	F12	VF20	XF40	MS60	MS63
2008	—	PF65 10.00				

KM# 491 20 WON
27.30 g., Brass, 40 mm. **Obv:** Temple **Rev:** Multicolor two oxen

Date	Mintage	F12	VF20	XF40	MS60	MS63
2009	—	PF65 10.00				

KM# 495 20 WON
Aluminum, 45 mm. **Obv:** Raised Pagoda in ornamental loop **Rev:** Tiger with color inlay **Edge:** Plain

Date	Mintage	F12	VF20	XF40	MS60	MS63
2010	—		—	—	—	20.00

KM# 891 50 WON
155.00 g., 0.999 Silver 4.9463 oz. ASW, 65 mm. **Obv:** National arms, Central Bank name **Rev:** Orca whale

Date	Mintage	F12	VF20	XF40	MS60	MS63
2002	Est. 500	PF65 400				

KM# 815 50 WON
1.24 g., 0.999 Gold 0.0396 oz. AGW, 14 mm. **Obv:** Naitonal arms, Central Bank name **Rev:** Wanggeon, 1st King of Goryeo Dynasty

Date	Mintage	F12	VF20	XF40	MS60	MS63
2003	Est. 20000	PF63 75.00	PF65 90.00			

KM# 262 50 WON
70.00 g., 0.999 Silver 2.2338 oz. ASW, 50 mm. **Obv:** Korean map **Rev:** Huh Jun Chosun doctor at left, books at right **Edge:** Plain

Date	Mintage	F12	VF20	XF40	MS60	MS63
JU93-2004	—	PF65 100				

KM# 426 50 WON
2.01 g., Aluminum, 25 mm. **Obv:** State arms **Rev:** Value

Date	Mintage	F12	VF20	XF40	MS60	MS63
JU94-2005	—	—	—	—	1.20	1.50

KM# 427 100 WON
2.27 g., Aluminum, 27 mm. **Obv:** State arms **Rev:** Value

Date	Mintage	F12	VF20	XF40	MS60	MS63
JU94-2005	—	—	—	—	1.35	1.75

KM# 445 200 WON
5.19 g., 0.999 Silver 0.1656 oz. ASW, 30.00 mm. **Series:** Endangered Wildlife **Obv:** Fortress Gate **Rev:** Polar Bear standing facing **Rev. Legend:** URSUS MARITIMUS **Edge:** Plain

Date	Mintage	F12	VF20	XF40	MS60	MS63
2007	5,000	PF65 15.00				

KM# 1110 200 WON
25.00 g., Brass, 38 mm. **Subject:** Railways in Russia, 170th Anniversary **Obv:** East gate of Pyeongyang **Rev:** Steam train

Date	Mintage	F12	VF20	XF40	MS60	MS63
2007	Est. 200	PF65 70.00				

KM# 1111 200 WON
25.00 g., Brass, 35 mm. **Obv:** East gate of Pyeongyang **Rev:** Constantine Eduardovic and Sputnik

Date	Mintage	F12	VF20	XF40	MS60	MS63
2007	—	PF65 25.00				

KM# 1086 250 WON
26.96 g., 0.900 Silver 0.7751 oz. ASW **Obv:** Old coins and Central Bank name

Date	Mintage	F12	VF20	XF40	MS60	MS63
2005	Est. 1000	—	—	—	—	25.00

KM# 835 400 WON
20.00 g., 0.999 Gold 0.6382 oz. AGW, 35 mm. **Obv:** National arms, Central Bank name **Rev:** Korean folk games, wrestling

Date	Mintage	F12	VF20	XF40	MS60	MS63
2002	—	PF65 1,200				

KM# 441 500 WON
12.00 g., 0.999 Silver 0.3829 oz. ASW, 38.00 mm. **Subject:** 170th Anniversary First Public Railway St. Petersburg - Zarskoje Selo **Obv:** Fortress Gate **Rev:** First train arriving **Edge:** Plain

Date	Mintage	F12	VF20	XF40	MS60	MS63
ND(2007)	5,000	PF65 70.00				

KM# 447 500 WON
12.00 g., 0.999 Silver 0.3829 oz. ASW, 38.00 mm. **Subject:** 150th Anniversay Birth of Ziolkowski and 50th Anniversary Launch of Sputnik I **Obv:** Fortress Gate **Rev:** Bust of Ziolkowski facing 3/4 right at lower left, Sputnik circling earth at upper right **Edge:** Plain

Date	Mintage	F12	VF20	XF40	MS60	MS63
ND(2007)	5,000	PF65 65.00				

KM# 1112 500 WON
12.00 g., Silver, 38 mm. **Obv:** East gate of Pyeongyong **Rev:** Great Wall and Temple of Heaven in Bejing

Date	Mintage	F12	VF20	XF40	MS60	MS63
2007	—	PF65 35.00				

KM# 1113 500 WON
12.00 g., 0.999 Silver 0.3829 oz. ASW, 38 mm. **Subject:** Bejing Olympics, 2008 **Obv:** East gate of Pyeongyong **Rev:** Fencing

Date	Mintage	F12	VF20	XF40	MS60	MS63
2007	Est. 5000	PF65 35.00				

KM# 1114 500 WON
12.00 g., 0.999 Silver 0.3829 oz. ASW, 38 mm. **Subject:** Bejing Olympics, 2008 **Obv:** East gate of Pyeongyong **Rev:** Boxing

Date	Mintage	F12	VF20	XF40	MS60	MS63
2007	—	PF65 35.00				

KM# 1115 500 WON
12.00 g., 0.999 Silver 0.3829 oz. ASW, 38 mm. **Obv:** East gate of Pyeongyong **Rev:** Swimming

Date	Mintage	F12	VF20	XF40	MS60	MS63
2007	—	PF65 35.00				

KM# 1116 500 WON
12.00 g., 0.999 Silver 0.3829 oz. ASW, 38 mm. **Subject:** Bejing Olympics, 2008 **Obv:** East gate of Pyeongyong **Rev:** Weightlifting

Date	Mintage	F12	VF20	XF40	MS60	MS63
2007	—	PF65 35.00				

KM# 1117 500 WON
12.00 g., 0.999 Silver 0.3829 oz. ASW, 38 mm. **Subject:** Bejing Olympics, 2008 **Obv:** East gate of Pyeongyong **Rev:** Baseball

Date	Mintage	F12	VF20	XF40	MS60	MS63
2007	Est. 5000	PF65 35.00				

KM# 1118 500 WON
12.00 g., 0.999 Silver 0.3829 oz. ASW, 38 mm. **Subject:** Bejing Olympics, 2008 **Obv:** East gate of Pyeongyong **Rev:** Wrestlers

Date	Mintage	F12	VF20	XF40	MS60	MS63
2007	—	PF65 35.00				

KM# 1119 500 WON
12.00 g., 0.999 Silver 0.3829 oz. ASW, 38 mm. **Subject:** Bejing Olympics, 2008 **Obv:** East gate of Pyeongyong **Rev:** Gymnast

Date	Mintage	F12	VF20	XF40	MS60	MS63
2007	—	PF65 35.00				

KM# 1120 500 WON
12.00 g., 0.999 Silver 0.3829 oz. ASW, 28 mm. **Subject:** Bejing Olympics, 2008 **Obv:** East gate of Pyeongyong **Rev:** Kayakers

Date	Mintage	F12	VF20	XF40	MS60	MS63
2007	Est. 5000	PF65 35.00				

KM# 1121 500 WON
12.00 g., 0.999 Silver 0.3829 oz. ASW, 38 mm. **Subject:** Bejing Olympics, 2008 **Obv:** East gate of Pyeongyong **Rev:** Hurdler

Date	Mintage	F12	VF20	XF40	MS60	MS63
2007	Est. 5000	PF65 35.00				

KM# 1122 500 WON
12.00 g., 0.999 Silver 0.3829 oz. ASW, 38 mm. **Subject:** Bejing Olympics, 2008 **Obv:** East gate of Pyeongyong **Rev:** Taekwondo

Date	Mintage	F12	VF20	XF40	MS60	MS63
2007	Est. 5000	PF65 35.00				

KM# 1123 500 WON
12.00 g., 0.999 Silver 0.3829 oz. ASW, 38 mm. **Subject:** Bejing Olympics, 2008 **Obv:** East gate of Pyeongyong **Rev:** Olympic Sport

Date	Mintage	F12	VF20	XF40	MS60	MS63
2007	Est. 5000	PF65 35.00				

KM# 443 500 WON
12.00 g., 0.999 Silver 0.3829 oz. ASW, 38.00 mm. **Subject:** Lunar Year of the Rat **Obv:** Fortress Gate **Rev:** Two rats within circle of Lunar figures **Edge:** Plain

Date	Mintage	F12	VF20	XF40	MS60	MS63
2008	—	—	—	—	—	50.00
2008	5,000	PF65 70.00				

KM# 1178 500 WON
12.00 g., 0.999 Silver 0.3829 oz. ASW, 38 mm. **Subject:** Bejing Summer Olympics, 2008 **Obv:** East gate of Pyeongyang **Rev:** Great Wall, Temple of Heaven and Soccer player

Date	Mintage	F12	VF20	XF40	MS60	MS63
2008	Est. 5000	PF65 35.00				

KM# 1179 500 WON
12.00 g., 0.999 Silver 0.3829 oz. ASW, 38 mm. **Subject:** Bejing Summer Olympics, 2008 **Obv:** East gate of Pyeongyang **Rev:** Hockey player

Date	Mintage	F12	VF20	XF40	MS60	MS63
2008	—	PF65 35.00				

KM# 1180 500 WON
12.00 g., 0.999 Silver 0.3829 oz. ASW, 38 mm. **Subject:** Bejing Summer Olympics, 2008 **Obv:** East gate of Pyeongyang **Rev:** Basketball player

Date	Mintage	F12	VF20	XF40	MS60	MS63
2008	—	PF65 35.00				

KM# 1181 500 WON
12.00 g., 0.999 Silver 0.3829 oz. ASW, 38 mm. **Subject:** Bejing Summer Olympics, 2008 **Obv:** East gate of Pyeongyang **Rev:** Archer

Date	Mintage	F12	VF20	XF40	MS60	MS63
2008	Est. 5000	PF65 35.00				

KM# 1182 500 WON
12.00 g., 0.999 Silver 0.3829 oz. ASW, 38 mm. **Subject:** Bejing Summer Olympics, 2008 **Obv:** East gate of Pyeongyang **Rev:** Volleyball

Date	Mintage	F12	VF20	XF40	MS60	MS63
2008	Est. 5000	PF65 35.00				

KM# 1183 500 WON
12.00 g., 0.999 Silver 0.3829 oz. ASW, 38 mm. **Subject:** Bejing Summer Olympics, 2008 **Obv:** East gate of Pyeongyang **Rev:** Table tennis

Date	Mintage	F12	VF20	XF40	MS60	MS63
2008	—	PF65 35.00				

KM# 1184 500 WON
12.00 g., 0.999 Silver 0.3829 oz. ASW, 38 mm. **Subject:** Bejing Summer Olympics, 2008 **Obv:** East gate of Pyeongyang **Rev:** Rowers

Date	Mintage	F12	VF20	XF40	MS60	MS63
2008	Est. 5000	PF65 35.00				

KM# 717 700 WON
31.11 g., 0.999 Gold 0.9926 oz. AGW **Obv:** National arms **Rev:** Caledon pottery

Date	Mintage	F12	VF20	XF40	MS60	MS63
2001	—	PF65 1,800				

KM# 720 700 WON
31.11 g., 0.999 Gold 0.9926 oz. AGW, 40 mm. **Obv:** National arms, Central Bank name **Rev:** Ginsing plant

Date	Mintage	F12	VF20	XF40	MS60	MS63
2001	—	PF65 1,800				

KM# 723 700 WON
31.11 g., 0.999 Gold 0.9926 oz. AGW, 40 mm. **Obv:** National arms **Rev:** End of the steam train in 1945 and again in 2001

Date	Mintage	F12	VF20	XF40	MS60	MS63
2001	—	PF65 1,800				

KM# 742 700 WON
31.11 g., 0.999 Gold 0.9926 oz. AGW, 40 mm. **Obv:** National arms, Central Bank name **Rev:** Ferryboat, married couple and flag

Date	Mintage	F12	VF20	XF40	MS60	MS63
2001	—	PF65 1,800				

KM# 743 700 WON
31.11 g., 0.9999 Gold 0.9935 oz. AGW, 40 mm. **Obv:** National arms, Central Bank name **Rev:** Ferryboat between Korea and Japan

Date	Mintage	F12	VF20	XF40	MS60	MS63
2001	—	PF65 1,800				

KM# 744 700 WON
31.11 g., 0.999 Gold 0.9926 oz. AGW, 40 mm. **Obv:** National arms, Central Bank name **Rev:** Triumphial arch of Moranbong in Pyeongyang

Date	Mintage	F12	VF20	XF40	MS60	MS63
2001	—	PF65 1,800				

KM# 745 700 WON
31.11 g., 0.999 Gold 0.9926 oz. AGW, 40 mm. **Obv:** National arms, Central Bank name **Rev:** Chonji crater in Paektusan

Date	Mintage	F12	VF20	XF40	MS60	MS63
2001	—	PF65 1,800				

KM# 748 700 WON
31.11 g., 0.999 Gold 0.9926 oz. AGW, 40 mm. **Obv:** National arms, Central Bank name **Rev:** Kim Jeongil and Jiang Zemin clasping hands

Date	Mintage	F12	VF20	XF40	MS60	MS63
2001	—	PF65 1,800				

KM# 503 700 WON
31.11 g., 0.999 Gold 0.9926 oz. AGW, 40 mm. **Obv:** National arms **Rev:** Brontosaurus

Date	Mintage	F12	VF20	XF40	MS60	MS63
2002	—	PF65 1,800				

KM# 537 700 WON
31.11 g., 0.999 Gold 0.9926 oz. AGW **Obv:** National arms **Rev:** Zhou Enlai, president of the P.R.C.

Date	Mintage	F12	VF20	XF40	MS60	MS63
2002	—	PF65 1,800				

KM# 612 700 WON
31.11 g., 0.999 Gold 0.9926 oz. AGW **Obv:** National arms **Rev:** Chinese Junk at sail

Date	Mintage	F12	VF20	XF40	MS60	MS63
2002	—	PF65 1,800				

KM# 634 700 WON
31.11 g., 0.999 Gold 0.9926 oz. AGW **Obv:** National arms, Central Bank name **Rev:** Blue dragon right

Date	Mintage	F12	VF20	XF40	MS60	MS63
2002	—	PF65 1,800				

KM# 640 700 WON
31.11 g., 0.999 Gold 0.9926 oz. AGW **Obv:** National arms, Country name **Rev:** Two siberian tigers

Date	Mintage	F12	VF20	XF40	MS60	MS63
2002	—	PF65 1,800				

KM# 655 700 WON
31.11 g., 0.999 Gold 0.9926 oz. AGW, 40 mm. **Obv:** National arms, Central Bank name **Rev:** Dongmyeong, King of Goguryeo

Date	Mintage	F12	VF20	XF40	MS60	MS63
2002	—	PF65 1,800				

KM# 656 700 WON
31.11 g., 0.999 Gold 0.9926 oz. AGW, 40 mm. **Obv:** National arms, Central Bank name **Rev:** Buddha figure

Date	Mintage	F12	VF20	XF40	MS60	MS63
2002	—	PF65 1,800				

KM# 657 700 WON
31.11 g., 0.999 Gold 0.9926 oz. AGW, 40 mm. **Obv:** National arms, Central Bank name **Rev:** Dangun, King of Gojoseon

Date	Mintage	F12	VF20	XF40	MS60	MS63
2002	—	PF65 1,800				

KM# 791 700 WON
31.11 g., 0.999 Gold 0.9926 oz. AGW, 35 mm. **Obv:** National arms **Rev:** Horse head

Date	Mintage	F12	VF20	XF40	MS60	MS63
2002	—	PF65 1,800				

KM# 792 700 WON
31.11 g., 0.999 Gold 0.9926 oz. AGW, 35 mm. **Obv:** National arms **Rev:** Horse to the right

Date	Mintage	F12	VF20	XF40	MS60	MS63
2002	—	PF65 1,800				

KM# 793 700 WON
31.11 g., 0.999 Gold 0.9926 oz. AGW, 35 mm. **Obv:** National arms **Rev:** Two horses in center of the Zodiac

Date	Mintage	F12	VF20	XF40	MS60	MS63
2002	—	PF65 1,800				

KM# 816 700 WON
31.11 g., 0.999 Gold 0.9926 oz. AGW, 40 mm. **Obv:** National arms, Central Bank name **Rev:** Reconstruction of the Mousoleum for King Dangun

Date	Mintage	F12	VF20	XF40	MS60	MS63
2002	—	PF65 1,800				

KM# 817 700 WON
31.11 g., 0.999 Gold 0.9926 oz. AGW, 40 mm. **Obv:** National arms, Central Bank name **Rev:** Dongmyeong, 1st King of Goguryeo

Date	Mintage	F12	VF20	XF40	MS60	MS63
2002	—	PF65 1,800				

KM# 818 700 WON
31.11 g., 0.999 Gold 0.9926 oz. AGW, 40 mm. **Obv:** National arms, Central Bank name **Rev:** Wanggeon, 1st King of Boryeo Dynasty

Date	Mintage	F12	VF20	XF40	MS60	MS63
2002	—	PF65 1,800				

KM# 819 700 WON
31.11 g., 0.999 Gold 0.9926 oz. AGW, 40 mm. **Obv:** National arms, Central Bank name **Rev:** Jeong Mongju

Date	Mintage	F12	VF20	XF40	MS60	MS63
2002	—	PF65 1,800				

KM# 820 700 WON
31.11 g., 0.999 Gold 0.9926 oz. AGW, 40 mm. **Obv:** National arms, Central Bank name **Rev:** Jeon Bongjun

Date	Mintage	F12	VF20	XF40	MS60	MS63
2002	—	PF65 1,800				

KM# 825 700 WON
31.11 g., 0.999 Gold 0.9926 oz. AGW, 40 mm. **Obv:** National arms **Rev:** Prince Hodong and Princess Nakrang on horseback

Date	Mintage	F12	VF20	XF40	MS60	MS63
2002	—	PF65 1,800				

KM# 826 700 WON
31.11 g., 0.999 Gold 0.9926 oz. AGW, 40 mm. **Obv:** National arms **Rev:** Half-length figures of Prince Hodong and Princess Nakrang

Date	Mintage	F12	VF20	XF40	MS60	MS63
2002	—	PF65 1,800				

KM# 834 700 WON
31.11 g., 0.999 Gold 0.9926 oz. AGW, 35 mm. **Obv:** National Arms, Central Bank name **Rev:** Bust of Kim Ilseong

Date	Mintage	F12	VF20	XF40	MS60	MS63
2002	—	PF65 1,800				

KM# 844 700 WON
31.11 g., 0.999 Gold 0.9926 oz. AGW, 35 mm. **Obv:** National arms, Central Bank and Country name **Rev:** The soldiers

Date	Mintage	F12	VF20	XF40	MS60	MS63
2002	—	PF65 1,800				

KM# 845 700 WON
31.11 g., 0.999 Gold 0.9926 oz. AGW, 35 mm. **Obv:** National arms, Central Bank and Country name **Rev:** Fairy princess

Date	Mintage	F12	VF20	XF40	MS60	MS63
2002	—	PF65 1,800				

KM# 846 700 WON
31.11 g., 0.999 Gold 0.9926 oz. AGW, 35 mm. **Obv:** National arms, Central Bank and Country name **Rev:** Bronze statue

Date	Mintage	F12	VF20	XF40	MS60	MS63
2002	—	PF65 1,800				

KM# 847 700 WON
31.11 g., 0.999 Gold 0.9926 oz. AGW, 35 mm. **Obv:** National arms, Central Bank and Country name **Rev:** Female worshipers of the sun

Date	Mintage	F12	VF20	XF40	MS60	MS63
2002	—	PF65 1,800				

KM# 848 700 WON
31.11 g., 0.999 Gold 0.9926 oz. AGW, 35 mm. **Obv:** National arms, Central Bank and Country name **Rev:** Trhee prinicpals of re-unification

Date	Mintage	F12	VF20	XF40	MS60	MS63
2002	—	PF65 1,800				

KM# 849 700 WON
31.11 g., 0.999 Gold 0.9926 oz. AGW, 35 mm. **Obv:** National arms, Central Bank and Country name **Rev:** Dancing children

Date	Mintage	F12	VF20	XF40	MS60	MS63
2002	—	PF65 1,800				

KM# 872 700 WON
31.11 g., 0.999 Gold 0.9926 oz. AGW, 40 mm. **Obv:** National arms, Central bank name **Rev:** Family

Date	Mintage	F12	VF20	XF40	MS60	MS63
2002	—	PF65 1,800				

KM# 873 700 WON
31.11 g., 0.999 Gold 0.9926 oz. AGW, 40 mm. **Obv:** National arms, Central Bank name **Rev:** Map of Korea with four cardinal compass points

Date	Mintage	F12	VF20	XF40	MS60	MS63
2002	—	PF65 1,800				

KM# 874 700 WON
31.11 g., 0.999 Gold 0.9926 oz. AGW, 40 mm. **Obv:** Naitonal arms, Central Bank name **Rev:** Rythem dancer and map of Korea

Date	Mintage	F12	VF20	XF40	MS60	MS63
2002	—	PF65 1,800				

KM# 875 700 WON
31.11 g., 0.999 Gold 0.9926 oz. AGW, 40 mm. **Obv:** National arms, Central Bank name **Rev:** Drum dancers and map of Korea

Date	Mintage	F12	VF20	XF40	MS60	MS63
2002	—	PF65 1,800				

KM# 876 700 WON
31.11 g., 0.999 Gold 0.9926 oz. AGW, 40 mm. **Obv:** National arms, Central Bank name **Rev:** Korean team victory celebration

Date	Mintage	F12	VF20	XF40	MS60	MS63
2002	—	PF65 1,800				

KM# 899 700 WON
31.11 g., 0.999 Gold 0.9926 oz. AGW, 40 mm. **Obv:** East gate of Pyeongyang **Rev:** Sheep at center of Zodiac

Date	Mintage	F12	VF20	XF40	MS60	MS63
2003	—	PF65 1,800				

KM# 912 700 WON
31.11 g., 0.999 Gold 0.9926 oz. AGW, 40 mm. **Obv:** National arms, Central Bank name **Rev:** Eulji Mundeok

Date	Mintage	F12	VF20	XF40	MS60	MS63
2003	—	PF65 1,800				

KM# 913 700 WON
31.11 g., 0.999 Gold 0.9926 oz. AGW, 40 mm. **Obv:** National arms, Central Bank name **Rev:** Yeon Gaesomun

Date	Mintage	F12	VF20	XF40	MS60	MS63
2003	—	PF65 1,800				

KM# 914 700 WON
31.11 g., 0.999 Gold 0.9926 oz. AGW, 40 mm. **Obv:** National arms, Central Bank name **Rev:** Gang Camchan

Date	Mintage	F12	VF20	XF40	MS60	MS63
2003	—	PF65 1,800				

KM# 917 700 WON
31.11 g., 0.999 Gold 0.9926 oz. AGW, 40 mm. **Obv:** National arms, Central Bank name **Rev:** Turtle boat

Date	Mintage	F12	VF20	XF40	MS60	MS63
2003	—	PF65 1,800				

KM# 941 700 WON
31.11 g., 0.999 Gold 0.9926 oz. AGW, 40 mm. **Obv:** Naitonal arms, Central Bank name **Rev:** Monkey at center of Zodiac

Date	Mintage	F12	VF20	XF40	MS60	MS63
2004	—	PF65 1,800				

KM# 1018 700 WON
31.11 g., 0.999 Gold 0.9926 oz. AGW, 40 mm. **Obv:** National arms, Central Bank name **Rev:** Rooster within Zodiac circle

Date	Mintage	F12	VF20	XF40	MS60	MS63
2005	—	PF65 1,800				

KM# 1032 700 WON
31.11 g., 0.999 Gold 0.9926 oz. AGW, 40 mm. **Obv:** National arms, Central Bank name **Rev:** Admiral Yi Sunsin and turtle boat

Date	Mintage	F12	VF20	XF40	MS60	MS63
2005	—	PF65 1,800				

KM# 1033 700 WON
31.11 g., 0.999 Gold 0.9926 oz. AGW, 40 mm. **Obv:** National arms, Central Bank name **Rev:** General Hong Beomdo

Date	Mintage	F12	VF20	XF40	MS60	MS63
2005	—	PF65 1,800				

KM# 1042 700 WON
31.11 g., 0.999 Gold 0.9926 oz. AGW, 40 mm. **Obv:** National arms, Central Bank name **Rev:** Map of Korea, two peace doves, rainbow

Date	Mintage	F12	VF20	XF40	MS60	MS63
2005	—	PF65 1,800				

KM# 1047 700 WON
31.11 g., 0.999 Gold 0.9926 oz. AGW, 40 mm. **Obv:** National arms, Central Bank name **Rev:** Tomb of the unknown soldier in Moscow, Russian legend

Date	Mintage	F12	VF20	XF40	MS60	MS63
2005	—	PF65 1,800				

KM# 1048 700 WON
31.11 g., 0.999 Gold 0.9926 oz. AGW, 40 mm. **Obv:** National arms, Central Bank name **Rev:** Memorial to mothers in St. Petersburg

Date	Mintage	F12	VF20	XF40	MS60	MS63
2005	—	PF65 1,800				

KM# 428 700 WON
15.55 g., 0.999 Silver 0.4962 oz. ASW, 30.00 mm. **Series:** European Union Euro Commemoratives **Obv:** National arms **Rev:** Schleswig-Holstein City gate in relief in tiger's-eye **Edge:** Plain

Date	Mintage	F12	VF20	XF40	MS60	MS63
2006	3,000	PF65 70.00				

KM# 429 700 WON
15.55 g., 0.999 Silver 0.4962 oz. ASW, 30.00 mm. **Series:** European Union Euro Commemoratives **Obv:** National arms **Rev:** Vatican in relief in tiger's-eye **Edge:** Plain

Date	Mintage	F12	VF20	XF40	MS60	MS63
2006	3,000	PF65 70.00				

KM# 430 700 WON
15.55 g., 0.999 Silver 0.4962 oz. ASW, 30.00 mm. **Series:** European Union Euro Commemoratives **Obv:** National arms **Rev:** Male Olympic statue - discus - Athens in relief in tiger's-eye **Edge:** Plain

Date	Mintage	F12	VF20	XF40	MS60	MS63
2006	3,000	PF65 70.00				

KM# 431 700 WON
15.55 g., 0.999 Silver 0.4962 oz. ASW, 30.00 mm. **Series:** European Union Euro Commemoratives **Obv:** National arms **Rev:** 50th Anniversary Austrian States Treaty in relief in tiger's-eye **Edge:** Plain

Date	Mintage	F12	VF20	XF40	MS60	MS63
2006	3,000	PF65 70.00				

KM# 432 700 WON
15.55 g., 0.999 Silver 0.4962 oz. ASW, 30.00 mm. **Series:** European Union Euro Commemoratives **Obv:** National arms **Rev:** Don Quixote in relief in tiger's-eye **Edge:** Plain

Date	Mintage	F12	VF20	XF40	MS60	MS63
2006	3,000	PF65 70.00				

KM# 433 700 WON
15.55 g., 0.999 Silver 0.4962 oz. ASW, 30.00 mm. **Series:** European Union Euro Commemoratives **Obv:** National arms **Rev:** Head of Henri, Grand Duke of Luxembourg at left facing right, crowned H at right in relief in tiger's-eye **Edge:** Plain

Date	Mintage	F12	VF20	XF40	MS60	MS63
2006	3,000	PF65 70.00				

KM# 434 700 WON
15.55 g., 0.999 Silver 0.4962 oz. ASW, 30 mm. **Series:** European Union Euro Commemoratives **Obv:** National arms **Rev:** Italian FAO logo in relief in tiger's-eye **Edge:** Plain

Date	Mintage	F12	VF20	XF40	MS60	MS63
2006	3,000	PF65 70.00				

KM# 435 700 WON
15.55 g., 0.999 Silver 0.4962 oz. ASW, 30 mm. **Series:** European Union Euro Commemoratives **Obv:** National arms **Rev:** Finland - stylized flower in relief in tiger's-eye **Edge:** Plain

Date	Mintage	F12	VF20	XF40	MS60	MS63
2006	3,000	PF65 70.00				

KM# 436 700 WON
15.55 g., 0.999 Silver 0.4962 oz. ASW, 30 mm. **Series:** European Union Euro Commemoratives **Obv:** National arms **Rev:** Conjoined heads of Grand Duke Henri of Luxembourg and King Albert of Belgium left in tiger's-eye **Edge:** Plain

Date	Mintage	F12	VF20	XF40	MS60	MS63
2006	3,000	PF65 70.00				

KM# 437 700 WON
15.55 g., 0.999 Silver 0.4962 oz. ASW, 30 mm. **Series:** European Union Euro Commemoratives **Obv:** National arms **Rev:** San Marino - bust of Bartolomeo Borghesi slightly right in relief in tiger's-eye **Edge:** Plain

Date	Mintage	F12	VF20	XF40	MS60	MS63
2006	3,000	PF65 70.00				

KM# 438 700 WON
15.55 g., 0.999 Silver 0.4962 oz. ASW, 30 mm. **Series:** European Union Euro Commemoratives **Obv:** National arms **Rev:** Vatican - World Youth Day in Cologne **Edge:** Plain

Date	Mintage	F12	VF20	XF40	MS60	MS63
2006	3,000	PF65 70.00				

KM# 439 700 WON
15.55 g., 0.999 Silver 0.4962 oz. ASW, 30 mm. **Series:** European Union Euro Commemoratives **Obv:** National arms **Rev:** San Marino - Year of Physics design in relief in tiger's-eye **Edge:** Plain

Date	Mintage	F12	VF20	XF40	MS60	MS63
2006	3,000	PF65 70.00				

KM# 958 1000 WON
42.22 g., 0.999 Gold 1.3472 oz. AGW, 45 mm. **Obv:** National arms, Central Bank name **Rev:** Kim Ilseong

Date	Mintage	F12	VF20	XF40	MS60	MS63
2004		PF65 2,450				

KM# 959 1000 WON
42.22 g., 0.999 Gold 1.3472 oz. AGW, 45 mm. **Obv:** National arms, Central Bank name **Rev:** Kim Jeongil

Date	Mintage	F12	VF20	XF40	MS60	MS63
2004		PF65 2,500				

KM# 960 1000 WON
42.22 g., 0.999 Gold 1.3472 oz. AGW, 45 mm. **Obv:** National arms, Central Bank name **Rev:** Kim Jeongsuk

Date	Mintage	F12	VF20	XF40	MS60	MS63
2004		PF65 2,500				

KM# 961 1000 WON
42.22 g., 0.999 Gold 1.3472 oz. AGW, 45 mm. **Obv:** National arms, Central Bank name **Rev:** Kim Ilseong's birthplace

Date	Mintage	F12	VF20	XF40	MS60	MS63
2004		PF65 2,500				

KM# 962 1000 WON
42.22 g., 0.999 Gold 1.3472 oz. AGW, 45 mm. **Obv:** National arms, Central Bank name **Rev:** Mountain cottage of Kim Jeongil

Date	Mintage	F12	VF20	XF40	MS60	MS63
2004		PF65 2,500				

KM# 963 1000 WON
42.22 g., 0.999 Gold 1.3472 oz. AGW, 45 mm. **Obv:** National arms, Central Bank name **Rev:** House where Kim Jeongsuk was born

Date	Mintage	F12	VF20	XF40	MS60	MS63
2004		PF65 2,500				

KM# 1097 1000 WON
20.00 g., 0.999 Silver 0.6382 oz. ASW, 38 mm. **Subject:** Lake Placid Winter Olympics, 1936 **Obv:** National arms, Central Bank name **Rev:** Bobsled

Date	Mintage	F12	VF20	XF40	MS60	MS63
2006	Est. 5000	PF65 45.00				

KM# 1098 1000 WON
20.00 g., 0.999 Silver 0.6382 oz. ASW, 38 mm. **Subject:** Sarajevo Winter Olympics, 1984 **Obv:** National arms, Central Bank name **Rev:** Ice Hockey player

Date	Mintage	F12	VF20	XF40	MS60	MS63
2006	Est. 5000	PF65 45.00				

KM# 1099 1000 WON
20.00 g., 0.999 Silver 0.6382 oz. ASW, 38 mm. **Obv:** National arms, Central Bank name **Rev:** Soccer player and Brazil flag and map

Date	Mintage	F12	VF20	XF40	MS60	MS63
2006	Est. 5000	PF65 45.00				

KM# 1100 1000 WON
20.00 g., 0.999 Silver 0.6382 oz. ASW, 38 mm. **Subject:** Bejing Summer Olympics, 2008 **Obv:** National arms, Central Bank name **Rev:** Gymnast on pommel horse

Date	Mintage	F12	VF20	XF40	MS60	MS63
2006	—	PF65 35.00				

KM# 440 1000 WON
20.00 g., 0.999 Silver 0.6382 oz. ASW, 38 mm. **Obv:** National arms **Rev:** Arctic animals with map of North Pole in background **Rev. Legend:** INTERNATIONAL POLAR YEAR / ARCTIC ANIMALS **Edge:** Plain

Date	Mintage	F12	VF20	XF40	MS60	MS63
ND(2007)	—	PF65 85.00				

KM# 446 1000 WON
20.00 g., 0.999 Silver 0.6382 oz. ASW, 38 mm. **Series:** Endangered Wildlife **Obv:** Fortress Gate **Rev:** Polar Bear standing facing **Rev. Legend:** URSUS MAITIMUS **Edge:** Plain

Date	Mintage	F12	VF20	XF40	MS60	MS63
2007	5,000	PF65 70.00				

KM# 1186 1000 WON
20.00 g., 0.999 Silver 0.6382 oz. ASW, 38 mm. **Subject:** Vancouver Winter Olympics, 2010 **Obv:** East gate of Pyeongyang **Rev:** Nordic Combine and triumphial arch

Date	Mintage	F12	VF20	XF40	MS60	MS63
2008	—	PF65 45.00				

KM# 1187 1000 WON
20.00 g., 0.999 Silver 0.6382 oz. ASW, 38 mm. **Subject:** Wold Cup Soccer, South Africa, 2010 **Obv:** East gate of Pyeongyang **Rev:** Soccer foul play

Date	Mintage	F12	VF20	XF40	MS60	MS63
2008	—	PF65 35.00				

KM# 993 1500 WON
70.00 g., 0.999 Gold 2.2338 oz. AGW, 50 mm. **Obv:** Map of Korea, Central Bank name **Rev:** Court physician Heo Jun

Date	Mintage	F12	VF20	XF40	MS60	MS63
2004	—	PF65 4,000				

KM# 1067 1500 WON
31.11 g., 0.999 Silver 0.9926 oz. ASW, 40 mm. **Obv:** Trumpeter, Central Bank name **Rev:** Triumphial arch in Pyeongyang

Date	Mintage	F12	VF20	XF40	MS60	MS63
2005	—	PF65 115				

KM# 1069 1500 WON
31.11 g., 0.999 Silver 0.9926 oz. ASW, 40 mm. **Subject:** Worker's Party, 60th Anniversary **Obv:** National arms, Central Bank name **Rev:** Party emblem

Date	Mintage	F12	VF20	XF40	MS60	MS63
2005	—	PF65 115				

KM# 1070 1500 WON
31.11 g., 0.999 Gold 0.9926 oz. AGW, 40 mm. **Subject:** Worker's Party, 60th Anniversary **Obv:** National arms, Central Bank name **Rev:** Party emblem

Date	Mintage	F12	VF20	XF40	MS60	MS63
2005	—	PF65 1,800				

KM# 1092 1500 WON
31.11 g., 0.999 Silver 0.9926 oz. ASW, 40 mm. **Obv:** National arms, Central Bank name **Rev:** Two dogs

Date	Mintage	F12	VF20	XF40	MS60	MS63
2006	—	PF65 60.00				

KM# 1093 1500 WON
31.11 g., 0.999 Silver 0.9926 oz. ASW, 40 mm. **Obv:** National arms, Central Bank name **Rev:** Bronze staue of flying horse

Date	Mintage	F12	VF20	XF40	MS60	MS63
2006	—	PF65 115				

KM# 1094 1500 WON
31.11 g., 0.999 Silver 0.9926 oz. ASW, 40 mm. **Obv:** National arms, Central Bank name **Rev:** Triumphial arch

Date	Mintage	F12	VF20	XF40	MS60	MS63
2006	—	PF65 115				

KM# 1142 1500 WON
31.11 g., 0.999 Silver 0.9926 oz. ASW, 40 mm. **Obv:** National arms, Central Bank name **Rev:** Hoopoe

Date	Mintage	F12	VF20	XF40	MS60	MS63
2007	Est. 500	PF65 60.00				

KM# 1143 1500 WON
31.11 g., 0.999 Silver 0.9926 oz. ASW, 40 mm. **Obv:** National arms, Central Bank name **Rev:** Ural owl

Date	Mintage	F12	VF20	XF40	MS60	MS63
2007	Est. 500	PF65 100				

KM# 1144 1500 WON
31.11 g., 0.9926 Silver 0.9926 oz. ASW, 40 mm. **Obv:** National arms, Central Bank name **Rev:** Eagle

Date	Mintage	F12	VF20	XF40	MS60	MS63
2007	—	PF65 60.00				

KM# 1145 1500 WON
31.11 g., 0.9926 Silver 0.9926 oz. ASW, 40 mm. **Obv:** National arms, Central Bank name **Rev:** White Rhino

Date	Mintage	F12	VF20	XF40	MS60	MS63
2007	—	PF65 60.00				

KM# 1146 1500 WON
31.11 g., 0.999 Silver 0.9926 oz. ASW, 40 mm. **Obv:** National arms, Central Bank name **Rev:** African elephant family

Date	Mintage	F12	VF20	XF40	MS60	MS63
2007	Est. 500	PF65 60.00				

KM# 1147 1500 WON
31.11 g., 0.999 Silver 0.9926 oz. ASW, 40 mm. **Obv:** National arms, Central Bank name **Rev:** Lion family

Date	Mintage	F12	VF20	XF40	MS60	MS63
2007	Est. 500	PF65 60.00				

KM# 1148 1500 WON
31.11 g., 0.999 Silver 0.9926 oz. ASW, 40 mm. **Obv:** National arms, Central Bank name **Rev:** Cape buffalo

Date	Mintage	F12	VF20	XF40	MS60	MS63
2007	Est. 500	PF65 60.00				

KM# 1149 1500 WON
31.11 g., 0.999 Silver 0.9926 oz. ASW, 40 mm. **Obv:** National arms, Central Bank name **Rev:** Marine turtle

Date	Mintage	F12	VF20	XF40	MS60	MS63
2007	Est. 500	PF65 60.00				

KM# 1150 1500 WON
31.11 g., 0.999 Silver 0.9926 oz. ASW, 40 mm. **Obv:** National arms, Central Bank name **Rev:** Penguin

Date	Mintage	F12	VF20	XF40	MS60	MS63
2007	Est. 500	PF65 60.00				

KM# 1151 1500 WON
31.11 g., 0.999 Silver 0.9926 oz. ASW, 40 mm. **Obv:** National arms, Central Bank name **Rev:** Emu

Date	Mintage	F12	VF20	XF40	MS60	MS63
2007	Est. 500	PF65 60.00				

KM# 1152 1500 WON
31.11 g., 0.999 Silver 0.9926 oz. ASW, 40 mm. **Obv:** National arms, Central Bank name **Rev:** Eagle owl

Date	Mintage	F12	VF20	XF40	MS60	MS63
2007	Est. 500	PF65 60.00				

KM# 1153 1500 WON
31.11 g., 0.999 Silver 0.9926 oz. ASW, 40 mm. **Obv:** National arms, Central Bank name **Rev:** Lemur

Date	Mintage	F12	VF20	XF40	MS60	MS63
2007	—	PF65 60.00				

KM# 1154 1500 WON
31.11 g., 0.999 Silver 0.9926 oz. ASW, 40 mm. **Obv:** National arms, Central Bank name **Rev:** Lion

Date	Mintage	F12	VF20	XF40	MS60	MS63
2007	Est. 500	PF65 60.00				

KM# 1155 1500 WON
31.11 g., 0.999 Silver 0.9926 oz. ASW, 40 mm. **Obv:** National arms, Central Bank name **Rev:** Two African elephants

Date	Mintage	F12	VF20	XF40	MS60	MS63
2007	Est. 500	PF65 60.00				

KM# 1176 1500 WON
31.11 g., 0.999 Silver 0.9926 oz. ASW, 40 mm. **Subject:** Nationhood, 60th Anniversary **Obv:** National arms, Central Bank name **Rev:** National flag, star above

Date	Mintage	F12	VF20	XF40	MS60	MS63
2008	—	PF65 115				

KM# 1185 1500 WON
31.11 g., 0.9926 Silver 0.9926 oz. ASW, 40 mm. **Subject:** Bejing Summer Olympics, 2008 **Obv:** East gate of Pyeongyang **Rev:** Ancient ring gymnast

Date	Mintage	F12	VF20	XF40	MS60	MS63
2008	Est. 5000	PF65 60.00				

KM# 950 2000 WON
31.11 g., 0.999 Bi-Metallic 0.9926 oz., 40 mm. **Obv:** National arms, Central Bank name **Rev:** Sports hall in Pyeongyang

Date	Mintage	F12	VF20	XF40	MS60	MS63
2004	—	PF65 2,200				

KM# 964 2000 WON
31.11 g., 0.999 Gold 0.9926 oz. AGW, 35 mm. **Subject:** 10th Anniversary of the takeover **Obv:** National arms, Central Bank name **Rev:** Kim Jeongil

Date	Mintage	F12	VF20	XF40	MS60	MS63
2004	—	PF65 2,100				

KM# 965 2000 WON
31.11 g., 0.999 Gold 0.9926 oz. AGW, 35 mm. **Obv:** National arms, Central Bank name **Rev:** Kim Jeongil and Kim Daejung

Date	Mintage	F12	VF20	XF40	MS60	MS63
2004	—	PF65 2,000				

KM# 967 2000 WON
31.11 g., 0.999 Gold 0.9926 oz. AGW, 35 mm. **Obv:** National arms, Central Bank name **Rev:** Kim Jeongil and Hu Jintao

Date	Mintage	F12	VF20	XF40	MS60	MS63
2004	—	PF65 2,000				

KM# 968 2000 WON
31.11 g., 0.999 Gold 0.9926 oz. AGW, 35 mm. **Obv:** National arms, Central Bank name **Rev:** Kim Jeongil and Vladimir Putin

Date	Mintage	F12	VF20	XF40	MS60	MS63
2004	—	PF65 2,100				

KM# 985 2000 WON
31.11 g., 0.999 Gold 0.9926 oz. AGW, 40 mm. **Obv:** Dokdo, rocky islands, Central Bank name **Rev:** Island group map

Date	Mintage	F12	VF20	XF40	MS60	MS63
2004	—	PF65 2,000				

KM# 986 2000 WON
31.11 g., 0.999 Gold 0.9926 oz. AGW, 40 mm. **Obv:** Dokdo, rocky islands, Central Bank name **Rev:** Fisher Ahn Yongbok

Date	Mintage	F12	VF20	XF40	MS60	MS63
2004	—	PF65 2,100				

KM# 987 2000 WON
31.11 g., 0.999 Gold 0.9926 oz. AGW, 40 mm. **Obv:** Dokdo, rocky islands, Central Bank name **Rev:** West Island

Date	Mintage	F12	VF20	XF40	MS60	MS63
2004	—	PF65 2,100				

KM# 988 2000 WON
31.11 g., 0.999 Gold 0.9926 oz. AGW, 40 mm. **Obv:** Dokdo, rocky islands, Central Bank name **Rev:** East island

Date	Mintage	F12	VF20	XF40	MS60	MS63
2004	—	PF65 2,100				

KM# 989 2000 WON
31.11 g., 0.999 Gold 0.9926 oz. AGW, 40 mm. **Obv:** Dokdo, rocky islands, Central Bank name **Rev:** Three brothers islands

Date	Mintage	F12	VF20	XF40	MS60	MS63
2004	—	PF65 2,100				

KM# 990 2000 WON
31.11 g., 0.999 Gold 0.9926 oz. AGW, 40 mm. **Obv:** Dokdo, rocky islands, Central Bank name **Rev:** Chicken island

Date	Mintage	F12	VF20	XF40	MS60	MS63
2004	—	PF65 2,100				

KM# 991 2000 WON
31.11 g., 0.999 Gold 0.9926 oz. AGW, 40 mm. **Obv:** Dokdo, rocky islands, Central Bank name **Rev:** Candle island

Date	Mintage	F12	VF20	XF40	MS60	MS63
2004	—	PF65 2,100				

KM# 1087 2500 WON
33.33 g., 0.900 Gold 0.9582 oz. AGW **Obv:** Old coins and Central Bank name

Date	Mintage	F12	VF20	XF40	MS60	MS63
2005	Est. 200	—	—	—	—	2,050

KM# 1290 3000 WON
62.21 g., 0.999 Silver 1.9852 oz. ASW **Subject:** Stone Lamp **Obv:** Temple **Rev:** Stone Lamp

Date	Mintage	F12	VF20	XF40	MS60	MS63
2012 Proof	—	—	—	—	—	—

KM# 442 15000 WON
7.78 g., 0.999 Gold 0.2483 oz. AGW, 26 mm. **Subject:** 170th Anniversary First Public Railway St. Petersburg - Zarskoje Selo **Obv:** Fortress Gate **Rev:** First train arriving **Edge:** Plain

Date	Mintage	F12	VF20	XF40	MS60	MS63
ND(2007)	2,000	PF65 550				

KM# 448 15000 WON
7.78 g., 0.999 Gold 0.2483 oz. AGW, 26 mm. **Subject:** 150th Anniversary Birth of Ziolkowski and 50th Anniversary Launch of Sputnik I **Obv:** Fortress Gate **Rev:** Bust of Ziolkowski facing 3/4 right at lower left, Sputnik circling earth at top right **Edge:** Plain

Date	Mintage	F12	VF20	XF40	MS60	MS63
ND(2007)	2,000	PF65 550				

KM# 444 15000 WON
7.78 g., 0.999 Gold 0.2483 oz. AGW, 26 mm. **Subject:** Lunar Year of the Rat **Obv:** Fortress Gate **Rev:** Two rats within circle of Lunar figures **Edge:** Plain

Date	Mintage	F12	VF20	XF40	MS60	MS63
2008	2,000	PF65 550				

KM# 1068 60000 WON
31.11 g., 0.999 Gold 0.9926 oz. AGW, 35 mm. **Obv:** Trumpeter, Central Bank name **Rev:** Triumphia arch in Pyeongyang

Date	Mintage	F12	VF20	XF40	MS60	MS63
2005	—	PF65 1,800				

KM# 1095 60000 WON
31.11 g., 0.999 Gold 0.9926 oz. AGW, 35 mm. **Obv:** National arms, Central Bank name **Rev:** Bronze statue of flying horse

Date	Mintage	F12	VF20	XF40	MS60	MS63
2006	—	PF65 2,100				

KM# 1096 60000 WON
31.11 g., 0.999 Gold 0.9926 oz. AGW, 35 mm. **Obv:** National arms, Central Bank name **Rev:** Triumphial arch

Date	Mintage	F12	VF20	XF40	MS60	MS63
2006	—	PF65 2,100				

KM# 1156 60000 WON
31.11 g., 0.999 Gold 0.9926 oz. AGW, 35 mm. **Obv:** National arms, Central Bank name **Rev:** Hoopoe

Date	Mintage	F12	VF20	XF40	MS60	MS63
2007	Est. 500	PF65 2,100				

KM# 1157 60000 WON
31.11 g., 0.999 Gold 0.9926 oz. AGW, 35 mm. **Obv:** National arms, Central Bank name **Rev:** Ural owl

Date	Mintage	F12	VF20	XF40	MS60	MS63
2007	Est. 500	PF65 2,100				

KM# 1158 60000 WON
31.11 g., 0.999 Gold 0.9926 oz. AGW, 35 mm. **Obv:** National arms, Central Bank name **Rev:** Eagle

Date	Mintage	F12	VF20	XF40	MS60	MS63
2007	Est. 500	PF65 2,100				

KM# 1159 60000 WON
31.11 g., 0.999 Gold 0.9926 oz. AGW, 35 mm. **Obv:** National arms, Central Bank name **Rev:** White rhino

Date	Mintage	F12	VF20	XF40	MS60	MS63
2007	Est. 500	PF65 2,100				

KM# 1160 60000 WON
31.11 g., 0.999 Gold 0.9926 oz. AGW, 35 mm. **Obv:** National arms, Central Bank name **Rev:** African elephant family

Date	Mintage	F12	VF20	XF40	MS60	MS63
2007	Est. 500	PF65 2,100				

KM# 1161 60000 WON
31.11 g., 0.999 Gold 0.9926 oz. AGW, 35 mm. **Obv:** National arms, Central Bank name **Rev:** Lion family

Date	Mintage	F12	VF20	XF40	MS60	MS63
2007	Est. 500	PF65 2,100				

KM# 1162 60000 WON
31.11 g., 0.999 Gold 0.9926 oz. AGW, 35 mm. **Obv:** National arms, Central Bank name **Rev:** Cape buffalo

Date	Mintage	F12	VF20	XF40	MS60	MS63
2007	—	PF65 2,100				

KM# 1163 60000 WON
31.11 g., 0.999 Gold 0.9926 oz. AGW, 35 mm. **Obv:** National arms, Central Bank name **Rev:** Marine turtle

Date	Mintage	F12	VF20	XF40	MS60	MS63
2007	—	PF65 2,100				

KM# 1164 60000 WON
31.11 g., 0.999 Gold 0.9926 oz. AGW, 35 mm. **Obv:** National arms, Central Bank name **Rev:** Penguin

Date	Mintage	F12	VF20	XF40	MS60	MS63
2007	Est. 500	PF65 2,100				

KM# 1165 60000 WON
31.11 g., 0.999 Gold 0.9926 oz. AGW, 35 mm. **Obv:** National arms, Central Bank name **Rev:** Emu

Date	Mintage	F12	VF20	XF40	MS60	MS63
2007	Est. 500	PF65 2,100				

KM# 1166 60000 WON
31.11 g., 0.999 Gold 0.9926 oz. AGW, 35 mm. **Obv:** National arms, Central Bank name **Rev:** Eagle owl

Date	Mintage	F12	VF20	XF40	MS60	MS63
2007	Est. 500	PF65 2,100				

KM# 1167 60000 WON
31.11 g., 0.999 Gold 0.9926 oz. AGW, 35 mm. **Obv:** National arms, Central Bank name **Rev:** Lemur

Date	Mintage	F12	VF20	XF40	MS60	MS63
2007	—	PF65 2,100				

KM# 1168 60000 WON
31.11 g., 0.999 Gold 0.9926 oz. AGW, 35 mm. **Obv:** National arms, Central Bank name **Rev:** Lion

Date	Mintage	F12	VF20	XF40	MS60	MS63
2007	—	PF65 2,100				

KM# 1169 60000 WON
31.11 g., 0.999 Gold 0.9926 oz. AGW, 35 mm. **Obv:** National arms, Central Bank name **Rev:** Two African elephants

Date	Mintage	F12	VF20	XF40	MS60	MS63
2007	—	PF65 2,100				

KM# 1177 60000 WON
31.11 g., 0.999 Gold 0.9926 oz. AGW, 35 mm. **Subject:** Nationhood, 60th Anniversary **Obv:** National arms, Central Bank name **Rev:** National flag, star above

Date	Mintage	F12	VF20	XF40	MS60	MS63
2008	—	PF65 2,100				

REFORM COINAGE
100 (Old) Won = 1 (new) Won

KM# 1170 CHON
Aluminum, 18 mm. **Obv:** National arms, Central Bank name

Date	Mintage	F12	VF20	XF40	MS60	MS63
2008	—	—	—	—	3.00	5.00

KM# 1171 5 CHON
Aluminum, 19 mm. **Obv:** National arms, Central Bank name **Rev:** Magnolia

Date	Mintage	F12	VF20	XF40	MS60	MS63
2008	—	—	—	—	3.00	5.00

KM# 1172 10 CHON
1.00 g., Aluminum, 20 mm. **Obv:** National arms, Central Bank name **Rev:** Rhododendron

Date	Mintage	F12	VF20	XF40	MS60	MS63
2002	—				1.00	1.75

KM# 1173 50 CHON
1.50 g., Aluminum, 22 mm. **Obv:** National arms, Central Bank name **Rev:** Begonia

Date	Mintage	F12	VF20	XF40	MS60	MS63
2002	—				1.00	2.00

KM# 1174 WON
1.80 g., Aluminum, 24 mm. **Obv:** National arms, Central Bank name **Rev:** Beognia

Date	Mintage	F12	VF20	XF40	MS60	MS63
2002	—		—		1.50	2.50

KM# 1188 2 WON
7.00 g., 0.999 Silver 0.2234 oz. ASW, 30 mm. **Obv:** National arms, Central Bank name **Rev:** Panda in color

Date	Mintage	F12	VF20	XF40	MS60	MS63
2008	Est. 5000	PF65 30.00				

KM# 1217 2 WON
7.00 g., 0.999 Silver 0.2234 oz. ASW, 30 mm. **Obv:** National arms, Central Bank name **Rev:** Panda in color

Date	Mintage	F12	VF20	XF40	MS60	MS63
2009	Est. 5000	PF65 30.00				

KM# 1220 2 WON
7.00 g., 0.999 Silver 0.2234 oz. ASW, 30 mm. **Obv:** National arms, Central Bank name **Rev:** Corwn gate of the Dresden Zwingers

Date	Mintage	F12	VF20	XF40	MS60	MS63
2009	—	PF65 30.00				

KM# 1221 2 WON
7.00 g., 0.999 Silver 0.2234 oz. ASW, 30 mm. **Obv:** National arms, Central Bank name **Rev:** Acropolis in Athens

Date	Mintage	F12	VF20	XF40	MS60	MS63
2009	—	PF65 30.00				

KM# 1222 2 WON
7.00 g., 0.999 Silver 0.2234 oz. ASW, 30 mm. **Obv:** National arms, Central Bank name **Rev:** Sydney Opera House

Date	Mintage	F12	VF20	XF40	MS60	MS63
2009	—	PF65 30.00				

KM# 1223 2 WON
7.00 g., 0.999 Silver 0.2234 oz. ASW, 30 mm. **Obv:** National arms, Central Bank name **Rev:** Angkor Wat temple complex

Date	Mintage	F12	VF20	XF40	MS60	MS63
2009	—	PF65 30.00				

KM# 1224 2 WON
7.00 g., 0.999 Silver 0.2234 oz. ASW, 30 mm. **Obv:** National arms, Central Bank name **Rev:** Minakshi and Sundareshwara temples in Madurai

Date	Mintage	F12	VF20	XF40	MS60	MS63
2009	—	PF65 30.00				

KM# 1225 2 WON
7.00 g., 0.999 Silver 0.2234 oz. ASW, 30 mm. **Obv:** National arms, Central Bank name **Rev:** Kremlin in Moscow

Date	Mintage	F12	VF20	XF40	MS60	MS63
2009	—	PF65 30.00				

KM# 1226 2 WON
7.00 g., 0.999 Silver 0.2234 oz. ASW, 30 mm. **Obv:** National arms, Central Bank name **Rev:** Abu Simbel

Date	Mintage	F12	VF20	XF40	MS60	MS63
2009	—	PF65 30.00				

KM# 1227 2 WON
7.00 g., 0.999 Silver 0.2234 oz. ASW, 30 mm. **Obv:** National arms, Central Bank name **Rev:** Eiffel Tower in Paris

Date	Mintage	F12	VF20	XF40	MS60	MS63
2009	—	PF65 30.00				

KM# 1228 2 WON
7.00 g., 0.999 Silver 0.2234 oz. ASW, 30 mm. **Obv:** National arms, Central Bank name **Rev:** Dalai Lama's Palace in Lhasa

Date	Mintage	F12	VF20	XF40	MS60	MS63
2009	—	PF65 30.00				

KM# 1229 2 WON
7.00 g., 0.999 Silver 0.2234 oz. ASW, 30 mm. **Obv:** National arms, Central Bank name **Rev:** Terracotta warriors of King Qin Shihuangdi in China

Date	Mintage	F12	VF20	XF40	MS60	MS63
2009	—	PF65 30.00				

KM# 1230 2 WON
7.00 g., 0.999 Silver 0.2234 oz. ASW, 30 mm. **Obv:** National arms, Central Bank name **Rev:** Palace at Versailles

Date	Mintage	F12	VF20	XF40	MS60	MS63
2009	—	PF65 30.00				

KM# 1231 2 WON
7.00 g., 0.999 Silver 0.2234 oz. ASW, 30 mm. **Obv:** National arms, Central Bank name **Rev:** Aachen Cathedral

Date	Mintage	F12	VF20	XF40	MS60	MS63
2010	—	PF65 30.00				

KM# 1232 2 WON
7.00 g., 0.999 Silver 0.2234 oz. ASW, 30 mm. **Obv:** National arms, Central Bank name **Rev:** Leaning Tower of Pisa

Date	Mintage	F12	VF20	XF40	MS60	MS63
2010	—	PF65 30.00				

KM# 1233 2 WON
7.00 g., 0.999 Silver 0.2234 oz. ASW, 30 mm. **Obv:** National arms, Central Bank name **Rev:** Chapel in Luzern

Date	Mintage	F12	VF20	XF40	MS60	MS63
2010	—	PF65 30.00				

KM# 1272 2 WON
7.00 g., 0.999 Silver 0.2234 oz. ASW, 30 mm. **Obv:** National arms, Central Bank name **Rev:** Three pandas in color

Date	Mintage	F12	VF20	XF40	MS60	MS63
2010	Est. 5000	PF65 30.00				

KM# 1276 2 WON
7.00 g., 0.999 Silver 0.2234 oz. ASW, 30 mm. **Obv:** National arms, Central Bank name **Rev:** Great Mosque of Cordoba

Date	Mintage	F12	VF20	XF40	MS60	MS63
2010	—	PF65 30.00				

KM# 1277 2 WON
7.00 g., 0.999 Silver 0.2234 oz. ASW, 30 mm. **Obv:** National arms, Central Bank name **Rev:** Cathedral of Santiago de Compostela

Date	Mintage	F12	VF20	XF40	MS60	MS63
2010	—	PF65 30.00				

KM# 1278 2 WON
7.00 g., 0.999 Silver 0.2234 oz. ASW, 30 mm. **Obv:** National arms, Central Bank name **Rev:** Timbuktu

Date	Mintage	F12	VF20	XF40	MS60	MS63
2010	—	PF65 30.00				

KM# 1279 2 WON
7.00 g., 0.999 Silver 0.2234 oz. ASW, 30 mm. **Obv:** National arms, Central Bank name **Rev:** London's Big Ben clock tower

Date	Mintage	F12	VF20	XF40	MS60	MS63
2010	—	PF65 30.00				

KM# 1280 2 WON
7.00 g., 0.999 Silver 0.2234 oz. ASW, 30 mm. **Obv:** National arms, Central Bank name **Rev:** Prague castle

Date	Mintage	F12	VF20	XF40	MS60	MS63
2010	—	PF65 30.00				

KM# 1281 2 WON
7.00 g., 0.999 Silver 0.2234 oz. ASW, 30 mm. **Obv:** National arms, Central Bank name **Rev:** Teoihuacan pyramid

Date	Mintage	F12	VF20	XF40	MS60	MS63
2010	—	PF65 30.00				

KM# 1282 2 WON
7.00 g., 0.999 Silver 0.2234 oz. ASW, 30 mm. **Obv:** National arms, Central Bank name **Rev:** Forbidden city

Date	Mintage	F12	VF20	XF40	MS60	MS63
2010	—	PF65 30.00				

KM# 1189 5 WON
20.00 g., 0.999 Silver 0.6382 oz. ASW, 38 mm. **Obv:** National arms, Central Bank name **Rev:** Sailing ship Grand Duchess Elizabeth

Date	Mintage	F12	VF20	XF40	MS60	MS63
2008	Est. 5000	PF65 45.00				

KM# 1191 5 WON
20.00 g., 0.999 Silver 0.6382 oz. ASW, 38 mm. **Obv:** National arms, Central Bank name **Rev:** Four-masted schooner Elizabeth Bandi and three-masted bark Seute Deern

Date	Mintage	F12	VF20	XF40	MS60	MS63
2008	Est. 5000	PF65 45.00				

KM# 1219 5 WON
20.00 g., 0.999 Silver 0.6382 oz. ASW, 38 mm. **Obv:** National arms, Central Bank name **Rev:** U.S.C.G. Barque Eagle

Date	Mintage	F12	VF20	XF40	MS60	MS63
2008	—	PF65 45.00				

KM# 1190 5 WON
20.00 g., 0.999 Silver 0.6382 oz. ASW, 38 mm. **Obv:** National arms, Central Bank name **Rev:** Three-masted sailing ship Passat

Date	Mintage	F12	VF20	XF40	MS60	MS63
2009	Est. 5000	PF65 45.00				

KM# 1192 5 WON
20.00 g., 0.999 Silver 0.6382 oz. ASW, 38 mm. **Obv:** National arms, Central Bank name **Rev:** Sail training ship Deutschland

Date	Mintage	F12	VF20	XF40	MS60	MS63
2009	Est. 5000	PF65 45.00				

KM# 1193 5 WON
20.00 g., 0.999 Silver 0.6382 oz. ASW, 38 mm. **Obv:** National Bank name **Rev:** Three-masted sailing ship Gorch Fock II

Date	Mintage	F12	VF20	XF40	MS60	MS63
2009	Est. 5000	PF65 45.00				

KM# 1218 5 WON
20.00 g., 0.999 Silver 0.6382 oz. ASW, 38 mm. **Obv:** National arms, Central Bank name **Rev:** Sailing ship Dar Mlodziezy

Date	Mintage	F12	VF20	XF40	MS60	MS63
2009	—	PF65 45.00				

KM# 1273 5 WON
20.00 g., 0.999 Silver 0.6382 oz. ASW, 38 mm. **Obv:** National arms, Central Bank name **Rev:** Philippine hood eagle

Date	Mintage	F12	VF20	XF40	MS60	MS63
2010	—	PF65 60.00				

KM# 1274 5 WON
20.00 g., 0.999 Silver 0.6382 oz. ASW, 38 mm. **Obv:** National arms, Central Bank name **Rev:** Tibetian ox

Date	Mintage	F12	VF20	XF40	MS60	MS63
2010	—	PF65 60.00				

KM# 1196.1 10 WON
1.00 g., 0.916 Gold 0.0293 oz. AGW, 16 mm. **Obv:** National arms, Central Bank name **Rev:** Alexander von Humboldt **Rev. Legend:** ...Humoldt **Note:** Error spelling of ship's name

Date	Mintage	F12	VF20	XF40	MS60	MS63
2008	401	—	—	—	80.00	90.00

KM# 1194 10 WON
1.00 g., 0.916 Gold 0.0293 oz. AGW, 16 mm. **Obv:** National arms, Central Bank name **Rev:** Rickmer Rickmers

Date	Mintage	F12	VF20	XF40	MS60	MS63
2008	7,500	—	—	—	65.00	75.00

KM# 1195 10 WON
1.00 g., 0.916 Gold 0.0293 oz. AGW, 16 mm. **Obv:** National arms, Central Bank name **Rev:** Prussen

Date	Mintage	F12	VF20	XF40	MS60	MS63
2008	Est. 7500	—	—	—	65.00	75.00

KM# 1196.2 10 WON
1.00 g., 0.916 Gold 0.0293 oz. AGW, 16 mm. **Obv:** National arms, Central Bank name **Rev:** Alexander von Humbolt **Rev. Legend:** ...Humboldt **Note:** Ship's name corrected.

Date	Mintage	F12	VF20	XF40	MS60	MS63
2008	7,100	—	—	—	65.00	75.00

KM# 1197 10 WON
1.00 g., 0.916 Gold 0.0293 oz. AGW, 16 mm. **Obv:** National arms, Central Bank name **Rev:** Grand Duchess Elizabeth

Date	Mintage	F12	VF20	XF40	MS60	MS63
2008	Est. 7500	—	—	—	65.00	75.00

KM# 1198 10 WON
1.00 g., 0.916 Gold 0.0293 oz. AGW, 16 mm. **Obv:** National arms, Central Bank name **Rev:** Three masted training ship Passat

Date	Mintage	F12	VF20	XF40	MS60	MS63
2008	7,500	—	—	—	65.00	75.00

KM# 1199 10 WON
1.00 g., 0.916 Gold 0.0293 oz. AGW, 16 mm. **Obv:** National arms, Central Bank name **Rev:** Four-masted schoner Elizabeth Bandi and three-masted bark Seute Deern

Date	Mintage	F12	VF20	XF40	MS60	MS63
2008	7,500	—	—	—	65.00	75.00

KM# 1200 10 WON
1.00 g., 0.916 Gold 0.0293 oz. AGW, 16 mm. **Obv:** National arms, Central Bank name **Rev:** Sail training ship Deutschland

Date	Mintage	F12	VF20	XF40	MS60	MS63
2008	Est. 7500	—	—	—	65.00	75.00

KM# 1201 10 WON
1.00 g., 0.916 Gold 0.0293 oz. AGW, 16 mm. **Obv:** National arms, Central Bank name **Rev:** Three-masted barque Gorch Fock II

Date	Mintage	F12	VF20	XF40	MS60	MS63
2008	Est. 7500	—	—	—	65.00	75.00

KM# 1235 10 WON
0.50 g., 0.999 Gold AGW, 11 mm. **Obv:** National arms, Central Bank name **Rev:** Alhambra in Granada

Date	Mintage	F12	VF20	XF40	MS60	MS63
2009	—	PF65 45.00				

KM# 1234 10 WON
0.50 g., 0.999 Gold AGW, 11 mm. **Obv:** National arms, Central Bank name **Rev:** Cathedral of the Holy Family in Barcelona

Date	Mintage	F12	VF20	XF40	MS60	MS63
2009	—	PF65 45.00				

KM# 1236 10 WON
1.00 g., 0.999 Gold 0.0319 oz. AGW, 14 mm. **Obv:** National arms, Central Bank name **Rev:** Crown tower in Dresden Zwigers

Date	Mintage	F12	VF20	XF40	MS60	MS63
2009	—	PF65 75.00				

KM# 1237 10 WON
1.00 g., 0.999 Gold 0.0319 oz. AGW, 14 mm. **Obv:** National arms, Central Bank name **Rev:** Acropolis in Athens

Date	Mintage	F12	VF20	XF40	MS60	MS63
2009	—	PF65 75.00				

KM# 1238 10 WON
1.00 g., 0.999 Silver 0.0319 oz. ASW, 14 mm. **Obv:** National arms, Central Bank name **Rev:** Sydney Opera House

Date	Mintage	F12	VF20	XF40	MS60	MS63
2009	—	PF65 75.00				

KM# 1239 10 WON
1.00 g., 0.999 Gold 0.0319 oz. AGW, 14 mm. **Obv:** National arms, Central Bank name **Rev:** Angkor Wat temple complex

Date	Mintage	F12	VF20	XF40	MS60	MS63
2009	—	PF65 75.00				

KM# 1240 10 WON
1.00 g., 0.999 Gold 0.0319 oz. AGW, 14 mm. **Obv:** National arms, Central Bank name **Rev:** Minaksji and Sundareshwara Temples in Madurai

Date	Mintage	F12	VF20	XF40	MS60	MS63
2009	—	PF65 75.00				

KM# 1241 10 WON
1.00 g., 0.999 Gold 0.0319 oz. AGW, 14 mm. **Obv:** National arms, Central Bank name **Rev:** Kremlin in Moscow

Date	Mintage	F12	VF20	XF40	MS60	MS63
2009	—	PF65 75.00				

KM# 1242 10 WON
1.00 g., 0.999 Gold 0.0319 oz. AGW, 14 mm. **Obv:** National arms, Central Bank name **Rev:** Abu Simbel

Date	Mintage	F12	VF20	XF40	MS60	MS63
2009	—	PF65 75.00				

KM# 1243 10 WON
1.00 g., 0.999 Gold 0.0319 oz. ACW, 14 mm. **Obv:** National arms, Central Bank name **Rev:** Eiffel Tower in Paris

Date	Mintage	F12	VF20	XF40	MS60	MS63
2009	—	PF65 75.00				

KM# 1244 10 WON
1.00 g., 0.999 Gold 0.0319 oz. AGW, 14 mm. **Obv:** National arms, Central Bank name **Rev:** Dali Lama's Palace in Lhasa

Date	Mintage	F12	VF20	XF40	MS60	MS63
2009	—	PF65 75.00				

KM# 1245 10 WON
1.00 g., 0.999 Gold 0.0319 oz. AGW, 14 mm. **Obv:** National arms, Central Bank name **Rev:** Terra Cotta Warriors

Date	Mintage	F12	VF20	XF40	MS60	MS63
2009	—	PF65 75.00				

KM# 1246 10 WON
1.00 g., 0.999 Gold 0.0319 oz. AGW, 14 mm. **Obv:** National arms, Central Bank name **Rev:** Palace in Versalles

Date	Mintage	F12	VF20	XF40	MS60	MS63
2009	—	PF65 75.00				

KM# 1247 10 WON
1.00 g., 0.999 Gold 0.0319 oz. AGW, 14 mm. **Obv:** National arms, Central Bank name **Rev:** Aachen Cathedral

Date	Mintage	F12	VF20	XF40	MS60	MS63
2009	—	PF65 75.00				

KM# 1248 10 WON
1.00 g., 0.999 Gold 0.0319 oz. AGW, 14 mm. **Obv:** National arms, Central Bank name **Rev:** Leaning tower of Pisa

Date	Mintage	F12	VF20	XF40	MS60	MS63
2009	—	PF65 75.00				

KM# 1249 10 WON
1.00 g., 0.999 Gold 0.0319 oz. AGW, 14 mm. **Obv:** National arms, Central Bank name **Rev:** Chapel in Luzern

Date	Mintage	F12	VF20	XF40	MS60	MS63
2009	—	PF65 75.00				

KM# 1262 10 WON
Brass, 40 mm. **Obv:** National arms, Central Bank name **Rev:** South tower in Kaeseong

Date	Mintage	F12	VF20	XF40	MS60	MS63
2010	—	PF65 7.00				

KM# 1263 10 WON
Brass, 40 mm. **Obv:** National arms, Central Bank name **Rev:** Mausoleum of King Wanggeon

Date	Mintage	F12	VF20	XF40	MS60	MS63
2010	—	PF65 7.00				

KM# 1264 10 WON
Brass, 40 mm. **Obv:** National arms, Central Bank name **Rev:** Birthplace of Pyochung

Date	Mintage	F12	VF20	XF40	MS60	MS63
2010	—	PF65 7.00				

KM# 1265 10 WON
Brass, 40 mm. **Obv:** National arms, Central Bank name **Rev:** Stone pagoda of Hyunhwa in Seongkyunkwan

Date	Mintage	F12	VF20	XF40	MS60	MS63
2010	—	PF65 7.00				

KM# 1266 10 WON
Brass, 40 mm. **Obv:** National arms, Central Bank name **Rev:** Seongkyunkwan

Date	Mintage	F12	VF20	XF40	MS60	MS63
2010	—	PF65 7.00				

KM# 1267 10 WON
Brass, 40 mm. **Obv:** National arms, Central Bank name **Rev:** Anhwa Temple

Date	Mintage	F12	VF20	XF40	MS60	MS63
2010	—	PF65 7.00				

KM# 1268 10 WON
Brass, 40 mm. **Obv:** National arms, Central Bank name **Rev:** Nahanjun in Anhwa Temple

Date	Mintage	F12	VF20	XF40	MS60	MS63
2010	—	PF65 7.00				

KM# 1269 10 WON
Brass, 40 mm. **Obv:** National arms, Central Bank name **Rev:** Turned wheel in Yungtong Temple

Date	Mintage	F12	VF20	XF40	MS60	MS63
2010	—	PF65 7.00				

KM# 1270 10 WON
Brass, 40 mm. **Obv:** National arms, Central Bank name **Rev:** Shrine in Sungyang Sowon

Date	Mintage	F12	VF20	XF40	MS60	MS63
2010	—	PF65 7.00				

KM# 1271 10 WON
Brass, 40 mm. **Obv:** National arms, Central Bank name **Rev:** Waterfall in Pakyeon

Date	Mintage	F12	VF20	XF40	MS60	MS63
2010	—	PF65 7.00				

KM# 1275 10 WON
0.50 g., 0.999 Gold AGW, 11 mm. **Obv:** National arms, Central Bank name **Rev:** Ernesto "Che" Guevara

Date	Mintage	F12	VF20	XF40	MS60	MS63
2010	—	PF65 50.00				

KM# 1283 10 WON
1.00 g., 0.999 Gold 0.0319 oz. AGW, 14 mm. **Obv:** National arms, Central Bank name **Rev:** Grand Mosque in Cordoba

Date	Mintage	F12	VF20	XF40	MS60	MS63
2010	—	PF65 75.00				

KM# 1284 10 WON
1.00 g., 0.999 Gold 0.0319 oz. AGW, 14 mm. **Obv:** National arms, Central Bank name **Rev:** Cathedral of Santiago de Compostela

Date	Mintage	F12	VF20	XF40	MS60	MS63
2010	—	PF65 75.00				

KM# 1285 10 WON
1.00 g., 0.999 Gold 0.0319 oz. AGW, 14 mm. **Obv:** National arms, Central Bank name **Rev:** Timbuktu

Date	Mintage	F12	VF20	XF40	MS60	MS63
2010	—	PF65 75.00				

KM# 1286 10 WON
1.00 g., 0.999 Gold 0.0319 oz. AGW, 14 mm. **Obv:** National arms, Central Bank name **Rev:** London's Big Ben tower

Date	Mintage	F12	VF20	XF40	MS60	MS63
2010	—	PF65 75.00				

KM# 1287 10 WON
1.00 g., 0.999 Gold 0.0319 oz. AGW, 14 mm. **Obv:** National arms, Central Bank name **Rev:** Prague castle

Date	Mintage	F12	VF20	XF40	MS60	MS63
2010	—	PF65 75.00				

KM# 1288 10 WON
1.00 g., 0.999 Gold 0.0319 oz. AGW, 14 mm. **Obv:** National arms, Central Bank name **Rev:** Teotihuacan pyramid

Date	Mintage	F12	VF20	XF40	MS60	MS63
2010	—	PF65 75.00				

KM# 1289 10 WON
1.00 g., 0.999 Gold 0.0319 oz. AGW, 14 mm. **Obv:** National arms, Central Bank name **Rev:** Forbidden City

Date	Mintage	F12	VF20	XF40	MS60	MS63
2010	—	PF65 75.00				

KM# 1175 20 WON
28.00 g., Brass, 40 mm. **Obv:** East gate of Pyeongyang **Rev:** Dragon in color

Date	Mintage	F12	VF20	XF40	MS60	MS63
2008	—	PF65 7.50				

KM# 1202 20 WON
Brass, 30 mm. **Obv:** East gate of Pyeongyang **Rev:** Rat in color

Date	Mintage	F12	VF20	XF40	MS60	MS63
2009	—	PF65 6.00				

KM# 1203 20 WON
Brass, 30 mm. **Obv:** East gate of Pyeongyang **Rev:** Ox in color

Date	Mintage	F12	VF20	XF40	MS60	MS63
2009	—	PF65 6.00				

KM# 1204 20 WON
Brass, 30 mm. **Obv:** East gate of Pyeongyang **Rev:** Tiger in color

Date	Mintage	F12	VF20	XF40	MS60	MS63
2009	—	PF65 6.00				

KM# 1205 20 WON
Brass, 30 mm. **Obv:** East gate of Pyeongyang **Rev:** Rabbit in color

Date	Mintage	F12	VF20	XF40	MS60	MS63
2009	—	PF65 6.00				

KM# 1206 20 WON
Brass, 30 mm. **Obv:** East gate of Pyeongyang **Rev:** Dragon in color

Date	Mintage	F12	VF20	XF40	MS60	MS63
2009	—	PF65 6.00				

KM# 1207 20 WON
Brass, 30 mm. **Obv:** East gate of Pyeongyang **Rev:** Snake in color

Date	Mintage	F12	VF20	XF40	MS60	MS63
2009	—	PF65 6.00				

KM# 1208 20 WON
Brass, 30 mm. **Obv:** East gate of Pyeongyang **Rev:** Horse in color

Date	Mintage	F12	VF20	XF40	MS60	MS63
2009	—	PF65 6.00				

KM# 1209 20 WON
Brass, 30 mm. **Obv:** East gate of Pyeongyang **Rev:** Goat in color

Date	Mintage	F12	VF20	XF40	MS60	MS63
2009	—	PF65 6.00				

KM# 1210 20 WON
Brass, 30 mm. **Obv:** East gate of Pyeongyang **Rev:** Monkey in color

Date	Mintage	F12	VF20	XF40	MS60	MS63
2009			PF65 6.00			

KM# 1211 20 WON
Brass, 30 mm. **Obv:** East gate of Pyeongyang **Rev:** Rooster in color

Date	Mintage	F12	VF20	XF40	MS60	MS63
2009			PF65 6.00			

KM# 1212 20 WON
Brass, 30 mm. **Obv:** East gate of Pyeongyang **Rev:** Dog in color

Date	Mintage	F12	VF20	XF40	MS60	MS63
2009			PF65 6.00			

KM# 1213 20 WON
Brass, 30 mm. **Obv:** East gate of Pyeongyang **Rev:** Pin in color

Date	Mintage	F12	VF20	XF40	MS60	MS63
2009			PF65 6.00			

KM# 492 20 WON
Aluminum, 45 mm. **Obv:** Raised Pagoda in ornamental loop **Rev:** Hippopotamus with color inlay **Rev. Legend:** Hippopotamus amphibius **Edge:** Plain

Date	Mintage	F12	VF20	XF40	MS60	MS63
2010	—	—	—	—	—	20.00

KM# 493 20 WON
Aluminum, 45 mm. **Obv:** Raised Pagoda with ornamental loop **Rev:** Rabbit with color inlay **Edge:** Plain

Date	Mintage	F12	VF20	XF40	MS60	MS63
2010	—	—	—	—	—	20.00

KM# 494 20 WON
Aluminum, 45 mm. **Obv:** Raised Pagoda in ornamental loop **Rev:** Deer with color inlay **Edge:** Plain

Date	Mintage	F12	VF20	XF40	MS60	MS63
2010	—	—	—	—	—	20.00

KM# 1250 20 WON
Brass, 45 mm. **Obv:** East gate in Pyeongyang **Rev:** Rat in center of Zodiac

Date	Mintage	F12	VF20	XF40	MS60	MS63
2010 Proof						7.00

KM# 1251 20 WON
Brass, 45 mm. **Obv:** East gate in Pyeongyang **Rev:** Buffalo at center of Zodiac

Date	Mintage	F12	VF20	XF40	MS60	MS63
2010			PF65 7.00			

KM# 1252 20 WON
Brass, 45 mm. **Obv:** East gate in Pyeongyang **Rev:** Tiger at center of Zodiac

Date	Mintage	F12	VF20	XF40	MS60	MS63
2010			PF65 7.00			

KM# 1253 20 WON
Brass, 45 mm. **Obv:** East gate in Pyeongyang **Rev:** Rabbit in center of Zodiac

Date	Mintage	F12	VF20	XF40	MS60	MS63
2010			PF65 7.00			

KM# 1254 20 WON
Brass, 45 mm. **Obv:** East gate in Pyeongyang **Rev:** Dragon at center of Zodiac

Date	Mintage	F12	VF20	XF40	MS60	MS63
2010			PF65 7.00			

KM# 1255 20 WON
Brass, 45 mm. **Obv:** East gate in Pyeongyang **Rev:** Snake in center of Zodiac

Date	Mintage	F12	VF20	XF40	MS60	MS63
2010			PF65 7.00			

KM# 1256 20 WON
Brass, 45 mm. **Obv:** East gate in Pyeongyang **Rev:** Horse in center of Zodiac

Date	Mintage	F12	VF20	XF40	MS60	MS63
2010			PF65 7.00			

KM# 1257 20 WON
Brass, 45 mm. **Obv:** East gate in Pyeongyang **Rev:** Goat in center of Zodiac

Date	Mintage	F12	VF20	XF40	MS60	MS63
2010			PF65 7.00			

KM# 1258 20 WON
Brass, 45 mm. **Obv:** East gate in Pyeongyang **Rev:** Monkey in center of Zodiac

Date	Mintage	F12	VF20	XF40	MS60	MS63
2010			PF65 7.00			

KM# 1259 20 WON
Brass, 45 mm. **Obv:** East gate in Pyeongyang **Rev:** Rooster in center of Zodiac

Date	Mintage	F12	VF20	XF40	MS60	MS63
2010			PF65 7.00			

KM# 1260 20 WON
Brass, 45 mm. **Obv:** East gate in Pyeongyang **Rev:** Dog in center of Zodiac

Date	Mintage	F12	VF20	XF40	MS60	MS63
2010			PF65 7.00			

KM# 1261 20 WON
Brass, 45 mm. **Obv:** East gate in Pyeongyang **Rev:** Pig in center of Zodiac

Date	Mintage	F12	VF20	XF40	MS60	MS63
2010			PF65 7.00			

KM# 1214 350 WON
6.20 g., 0.999 Silver 0.1979 oz. ASW, 35 mm. **Obv:** East gate of Pyeongyang **Rev:** Chinese Junk, Marco Polo

Date	Mintage	F12	VF20	XF40	MS60	MS63
2009	—		PF65 25.00			

KM# 1215 350 WON
6.20 g., 0.999 Silver 0.1979 oz. ASW, 35 mm. **Obv:** East gate of Pyeongyang **Rev:** Viking ship and map of the Atlantic, Leif Eriksson

Date	Mintage	F12	VF20	XF40	MS60	MS63
2009	Est. 5000		PF65 25.00			

KM# 1216 1000 WON
20.00 g., 0.999 Silver 0.6382 oz. ASW, 38 mm. **Subject:** World Cup Soccer, South Africa, 2010 **Obv:** East gate of Pyeongyang **Rev:** Two soccer players

Date	Mintage	F12	VF20	XF40	MS60	MS63
2009	Est. 10000	PF63 27.00		PF65 35.00		

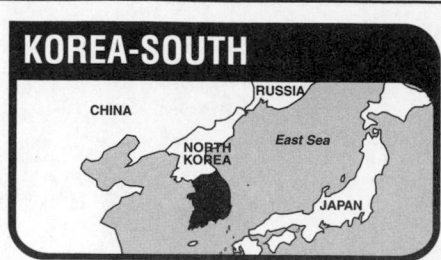

KOREA-SOUTH

The Republic of Korea, situated in northeastern Asia on the southern half of the Korean peninsula between North Korea and the Korean Strait, has an area of 38,025 sq. mi. (98,480 sq. km.) and a population of 42.5 million. Capital: Seoul. The economy is based on agriculture and light and medium industry. Some of the world's largest oil tankers are built here. Automobiles, plywood, electronics, and textile products are exported.
NOTE: For earlier coinage see Korea.

MINT
KOMSCO - Korea Minting and Security Printing Corporation

REPUBLIC
REFORM COINAGE
10 Hwan = 1 Won

KM# 31 WON
0.73 g., Aluminum, 17.2 mm. **Obv:** Rose of Sharon **Rev:** Value and date

Date	Mintage	F12	VF20	XF40	MS60	MS63
2001	130,000	—	—	—	0.15	0.25
2002	122,000	—	—	—	0.15	0.25
2003	20,000	—	—	—	0.15	0.25
2004	25,500	—	—	—	0.15	0.25
2005	38,000	—	—	—	0.15	0.25
2006	53,000	—	—	—	0.15	0.25
2007	53,000	—	—	—	0.15	0.25
2008		—	—	—	0.15	0.25
2009		—	—	—	0.15	0.25
2010		—	—	—	0.15	0.25
2011		—	—	—	0.15	0.25
2012		—	—	—	0.15	0.25

KM# 32 5 WON
2.95 g., Brass, 20.4 mm. **Obv:** Iron-clad turtle boat **Rev:** Value and date **Edge:** Plain

Date	Mintage	F12	VF20	XF40	MS60	MS63
2001	130,000	—		0.10	0.20	0.30
2002	120,000	—		0.10	0.20	0.30
2003	20,000	—		0.10	0.20	0.30
2004	25,500	—		0.10	0.20	0.30
2005	38,000	—		0.10	0.20	0.30
2006	53,000	—		0.10	0.20	0.30
2007	53,000	—		0.10	0.20	0.30
2008		—		0.10	0.20	0.30
2009		—		0.10	0.20	0.30
2010		—		0.10	0.20	0.30
2011		—		0.10	0.20	0.30
2012		—		0.10	0.20	0.30

KM# 33.2 10 WON
4.06 g., Brass **Obv:** Pagoda at Pul Guk Temple **Rev:** Thicker value below date

Date	Mintage	F12	VF20	XF40	MS60	MS63
2001	345,000,000	—	—	—	0.35	0.50
2002	100,000,000	—	—	—	0.35	0.50
2003	128,000,000	—	—	—	0.35	0.50
2004	135,000,000	—	—	—	0.35	0.50
2005	250,000,000	—	—	—	0.35	0.50

KM# 103 10 WON
1.22 g., Copper Clad Aluminum, 18 mm. **Obv:** Pagoda at Pul Guk Temple **Rev:** Value below date **Edge:** Plain **Note:** Prev. KM #106.

Date	Mintage	F12	VF20	XF40	MS60	MS63
2006	40,800,000	—	—	0.10	0.20	0.25
2007	210,000,000	—	—	0.10	0.20	0.25
2008		—	—	0.10	0.20	0.25
2009		—	—	0.10	0.20	0.25
2010		—	—	0.10	0.20	0.25
2011		—	—	0.10	0.20	0.25
2012		—	—	0.10	0.20	0.25
2013		—	—	0.10	0.20	0.25

KM# 33.2a 10 WON
1.22 g., Aluminum-Bronze, 18 mm. **Obv:** Pagoda at Pul Guk Temple **Rev:** Value below date

Date	Mintage	F12	VF20	XF40	MS60	MS63
2006	109,200,000	—	—	—	0.10	0.35
2007		—	—	—	0.10	0.35
2008		—	—	—	0.10	0.35
2009		—	—	—	0.10	0.35

KM# 34 50 WON
4.16 g., Copper-Nickel-Zinc, 21.6 mm. **Series:** F.A.O. **Obv:** Text below sagging oat sprig **Rev:** Value and date **Edge:** Reeded
Note: Die varieties exist.

Date	Mintage	F12	VF20	XF40	MS60	MS63
2001	102,000,000	—	—	0.10	0.35	1.00
2002	100,000,000	—	—	0.10	0.35	0.50
2003	169,000,000	—	—	0.10	0.35	0.50
2004	100,000,000	—	—	0.10	0.45	1.00
2005	90,000,000	—	—	0.10	0.35	0.50
2006	120,000,000	—	—	0.10	0.35	0.50
2007	50,000,000	—	—	0.10	0.35	0.50
2008	—	—	—	0.10	0.35	0.50
2009	—	—	—	0.10	0.35	0.50
2010	—	—	—	0.10	0.35	0.50
2011	—	—	—	0.10	0.35	0.50
2012	—	—	—	0.10	0.35	0.50

KM# 35.2 100 WON
5.42 g., Copper-Nickel, 24 mm. **Obv:** Admiral Yi-Sun-Sin, large bust with hat facing **Rev:** Value and date **Edge:** Reeded

Date	Mintage	F12	VF20	XF40	MS60	MS63
2001	470,000,000	—	0.25	0.50	1.00	3.00
2002	490,000,000	—	0.15	0.25	0.55	1.00
2003	415,000,000	—	0.15	0.25	0.55	1.00
2004	250,000,000	—	0.15	0.25	0.55	1.00
2005	205,000,000	—	0.15	0.25	0.55	1.00
2006	310,000,000	—	0.15	0.25	0.55	0.75
2007	240,000,000	—	0.15	0.25	0.55	0.75
2008	—	—	0.15	0.25	0.55	0.75
2009	—	—	0.15	0.25	0.55	0.75
2010	—	—	0.15	0.25	0.55	0.75
2011	—	—	0.15	0.25	0.55	0.75
2012	—	—	0.15	0.25	0.55	0.75

KM# 27 500 WON
7.70 g., Copper-Nickel, 26.5 mm. **Obv:** Manchurian crane **Rev:** Value and date **Edge:** Reeded

Date	Mintage	F12	VF20	XF40	MS60	MS63
2001	113,000,000	—	—	1.00	2.50	5.00
2002	110,000,000	—	—	1.00	2.50	5.00
2003	122,000,000	—	—	1.00	2.50	5.00
2004	45,000,000	—	—	1.00	2.50	5.00
2005	105,000,000	—	—	1.00	2.50	5.00
2006	170,000,000	—	—	1.00	2.50	5.00
2007	70,000,000	—	—	1.00	2.50	5.00
2008	—	—	—	1.00	2.50	5.00
2009	—	—	—	1.00	2.50	5.00
2010	—	—	—	1.00	2.50	5.00
2011	—	—	—	1.00	2.50	5.00
2012	—	—	—	1.00	2.50	5.00

KM# 89 1000 WON
12.00 g., Brass, 32 mm. **Series:** World Cup Soccer **Obv:** FIFA World Cup logo **Rev:** Mascot soccer player **Edge:** Reeded

Date	Mintage	F12	VF20	XF40	MS60	MS63
2001	102,000	—	—	—	10.00	12.00

KM# 112 1000 WON
12.00 g., Aluminum-Bronze, 32 mm. **Rev:** Soccer player

Date	Mintage	F12	VF20	XF40	MS60	MS63
2002	102,002	—	—	—	—	12.50

KM# 127 1000 WON
10.10 g., Tri-Metallic, 28.2 mm **Subject:** Expo 2012 **Obv:** Mascots Yeony and Suny **Rev:** Expo logo

Date	Mintage	F12	VF20	XF40	MS60	MS63
2012	137,512	—	—	—	—	20.00

KM# 115 2000 WON
26.00 g., Copper, 40 mm. **Subject:** 14th Asian Games, Busan **Rev:** Bird sanctuary

Date	Mintage	F12	VF20	XF40	MS60	MS63
2002	—	PF60 20.00	PF63 15.00			

KM# 116 2000 WON
26.00 g., Copper-Nickel, 40 mm. **Rev:** Torch and sport images

Date	Mintage	F12	VF20	XF40	MS60	MS63
2002	—	PF60 30.00	PF63 25.00			

KM# 124 5000 WON
15.50 g., 0.999 Silver 0.4946 oz. ASW, 32 mm. **Subject:** Expo 2012 **Obv:** Korean Pavilion with latent image **Rev:** Expo logo in color

Date	Mintage	F12	VF20	XF40	MS60	MS63
2012	20,000	PF60 45.00	PF63 35.00			

KM# 125 5000 WON
15.50 g., 0.999 Silver 0.4946 oz. ASW, 32 mm. **Subject:** Expo 2012 **Obv:** Theme Pavilion and latent image **Rev:** Expo logo in color

Date	Mintage	F12	VF20	XF40	MS60	MS63
2012	20,000	PF60 40.00	PF63 30.00			

KM# 90 10000 WON
31.10 g., 0.999 Silver 0.9926 oz. ASW, 35 mm. **Series:** World Cup Soccer **Subject:** Gwangju Stadium **Obv:** Multicolor soccer logo **Rev:** Player heading the ball **Edge:** Reeded

Date	Mintage	F12	VF20	XF40	MS60	MS63
2001	37,000	PF60 50.00	PF63 40.00			

KM# 91 10000 WON
31.10 g., 0.999 Silver 0.9926 oz. ASW, 35 mm. **Series:** World Sup Soccer **Subject:** Busan Stadium **Obv:** Multicolor soccer logo **Rev:** Player kicking the ball **Edge:** Reeded

Date	Mintage	F12	VF20	XF40	MS60	MS63
2001	37,000	PF60 50.00	PF63 40.00			

KM# 92 10000 WON
31.10 g., 0.999 Silver 0.9926 oz. ASW, 35 mm. **Series:** World Cup Soccer **Subject:** Daegu Stadium **Obv:** Multicolor soccer logo **Rev:** Player controlling the ball **Edge:** Reeded

Date	Mintage	F12	VF20	XF40	MS60	MS63
2001	37,000	PF60 50.00	PF63 40.00			

KM# 93 10000 WON
31.10 g., 0.999 Silver 0.9926 oz. ASW, 35 mm. **Series:** World Cup Soccer **Subject:** Suwon Stadium **Obv:** Multicolor soccer logo **Rev:** Player kicking the ball **Edge:** Reeded

Date	Mintage	F12	VF20	XF40	MS60	MS63
2001	37,000	PF60 50.00	PF63 40.00			

KM# 98 10000 WON
31.10 g., 0.999 Silver 0.9926 oz. ASW, 35 mm. **Obv:** Multi-color FIFA World Cup logo **Rev:** Player "Heading" ball **Edge:** Reeded

Date	Mintage	F12	VF20	XF40	MS60	MS63
2002	—	PF60 50.00	PF63 45.00			

KM# 99 10000 WON
31.10 g., 0.999 Silver 0.9926 oz. ASW, 35 mm. **Obv:** Multi-color FIFA World Cup logo **Rev:** Goalie catching ball **Edge:** Reeded

Date	Mintage	F12	VF20	XF40	MS60	MS63
2002	—	PF60 50.00	PF63 45.00			

KM# 100 10000 WON
31.10 g., 0.999 Silver 0.9926 oz. ASW, 35 mm. **Obv:** Multi-color FIFA World Cup logo **Rev:** Player's leg kicking ball **Edge:** Reeded

Date	Mintage	F12	VF20	XF40	MS60	MS63
2002	—	PF60 50.00	PF63 45.00			

KM# 101 10000 WON
31.10 g., 0.999 Silver 0.9926 oz. ASW, 35 mm. Obv: Multi-color FIFA World Cup logo Rev: Two players' legs and ball Edge: Reeded

Date	Mintage	F12	VF20	XF40	MS60	MS63
2002	—	PF60 50.00	PF63 45.00			

KM# 118 10000 WON
Silver, 38.61 g. Subject: 14th Asian Games, Busan Obv: Multicolor games logo Rev: Two dancers

Date	Mintage	F12	VF20	XF40	MS60	MS63
2002	—	PF60 90.00	PF63 80.00			

KM# 117 10000 WON
31.11 g., 0.999 Silver 0.9926 oz. ASW, 40 mm. Rev: Stadium, mascott at top

Date	Mintage	F12	VF20	XF40	MS60	MS63
2005	—	PF60 90.00	PF63 80.00			

KM# 126 10000 WON
31.11 g., 0.999 Silver 0.9926 oz. ASW, 40 mm. Subject: Expo 2012 Obv: Exposition's Sky Tower and sea image Rev: Expo logo in color

Date	Mintage	F12	VF20	XF40	MS60	MS63
2012	20,000	PF60 60.00	PF63 50.00			

KM# 128 15000 WON
7.77 g., 0.999 Gold 0.248 oz. AGW, 22 mm. Subject: Expo 2012 Obv: The Big-O maine stage Rev: Expo logo

Date	Mintage	F12	VF20	XF40	MS60	MS63
2012	10,000	PF60 500	PF63 425			

KM# 94 20000 WON
15.55 g., 0.999 Gold 0.4963 oz. AGW, 28 mm. Series: World Cup Soccer Obv: Soccer logo Rev: World Cup soccer trophy Edge: Reeded

Date	Mintage	F12	VF20	XF40	MS60	MS63
2001	20,000	PF60 900	PF63 850			

KM# 113 20000 WON
15.55 g., 0.999 Gold 0.4962 oz. AGW, 28 mm. Rev: World Cup venues on map

Date	Mintage	F12	VF20	XF40	MS60	MS63
2002	19,502	PF60 925	PF63 875			

KM# 119 20000 WON
15.55 g., 0.999 Gold 0.4962 oz. AGW Subject: 14th Asian Games, Busan Obv: Games logo Rev: Crown

Date	Mintage	F12	VF20	XF40	MS60	MS63
2002	—	PF60 925	PF63 875			

KM# 97 20000 WON
20.70 g., Silver, 35 mm. Obv: Blue circle with APEC, 2005 Korea at bottom at upper center, Vista Pacific Economic Cooperation and value below Rev: APEC on World map at upper center, building below with Korean words below it

Date	Mintage	F12	VF20	XF40	MS60	MS63
2005	10,000	PF60 65.00	PF63 55.00			

KM# 102 20000 WON
20.70 g., 0.999 Silver 0.6606 oz. ASW Subject: 60th Anniversary of Independence Obv: Adult hand reaching out towards child's hand Note: Prev. KM #103.

Date	Mintage	F12	VF20	XF40	MS60	MS63
2005	10,000	PF60 65.00	PF63 55.00			

KM# 104 20000 WON
19.00 g., 0.999 Silver 0.6063 oz. ASW Subject: 560th Year of Hangeul - Alphabet Obv: Early alphabet characters Obv. Legend: THE BANK OF KOREA Rev: Modern alphabet characters Shape: Round with square center hole

Date	Mintage	F12	VF20	XF40	MS60	MS63
2006	—	PF60 75.00	PF63 65.00			

KM# 105 20000 WON
19.00 g., 0.999 Silver 0.6063 oz. ASW, 33.00 mm. Series: Traditional Folk Dance Subject: Talchum - Mask Dances Obv: Mask at center surrounded by 6 other masks Obv. Legend: THE BANK OF KOREA Rev: Mask dancer at left center Edge: Plain Shape: 12-sided Note: Prev. KM #102.

Date	Mintage	F12	VF20	XF40	MS60	MS63
2007	50,000	PF60 75.00	PF63 65.00			

KM# 106 20000 WON
19.00 g., 0.999 Silver 0.6063 oz. ASW, 33 mm. Subject: Mask dance Rev: Ganggangsullae ("Circle dance") Shape: 12-sided

Date	Mintage	F12	VF20	XF40	MS60	MS63
2008	50,000	PF60 75.00	PF63 65.00			

KM# 108 20000 WON
19.00 g., 0.900 Silver 0.5462 oz. ASW, 33 mm. Subject: Mask dance Rev: Youngsan Juldarigi (Tug of War)

Date	Mintage	F12	VF20	XF40	MS60	MS63
2009	50,000	PF60 75.00	PF63 65.00			

KM# 109 20000 WON
19.00 g., 0.999 Silver 0.6063 oz. ASW, 33 mm. Subject: Traditional Folk Games - Yeongsan Juldarigi (Tug of war)

Date	Mintage	F12	VF20	XF40	MS60	MS63
2009	50,000	PF60 55.00	PF63 45.00			

KM# 129 20000 WON
15.55 g., 0.999 Gold 0.4962 oz. AGW, 28 mm. Subject: Expo 2012 Obv: International Pavilion Rev: Expo logo

Date	Mintage	F12	VF20	XF40	MS60	MS63
2012	6,000	PF60 950	PF63 900			

KM# 95 30000 WON
31.10 g., 0.999 Gold 0.9926 oz. AGW, 35 mm. Series: World Cup Soccer Obv: Soccer logo Rev: Nude soccer player flanked by other players Edge: Reeded

Date	Mintage	F12	VF20	XF40	MS60	MS63
2001	12,000	PF60 1,775	PF63 1,675			

KM# 114 30000 WON
31.11 g., 0.999 Gold 0.9926 oz. AGW, 35 mm. Obv: World Cup soccer trophy Rev: Stadium, fireworks, soccer ball

Date	Mintage	F12	VF20	XF40	MS60	MS63
2002	12,002	PF60 1,800	PF63 1,700			

KM# 120 30000 WON
31.11 g., 0.999 Gold 0.9926 oz. AGW, 35 mm. Subject: 14th Asian Games, Busan Obv: Games logo Rev: Many hands reaching upwards

Date	Mintage	F12	VF20	XF40	MS60	MS63
2002	—	PF60 1,850	PF63 1,750			

KM# 107 30000 WON
Silver Subject: Flag, 60th Anniversary Obv: Flag Rev: Multicolor 60 logo

Date	Mintage	F12	VF20	XF40	MS60	MS63
2008	—	PF60 75.00	PF63 65.00			

KM# 110 30000 WON
19.00 g., 0.999 Silver 0.6063 oz. ASW, 33 mm. Subject: UNESCO World Heritage Site - Jongmyo Shrine Obv: Main Hall of the Jongmyo Shrine Rev: Scene of the Royal Ancestral Ritual in the shrine Edge: Reeded

Date	Mintage	F12	VF20	XF40	MS60	MS63
2010	50,000	PF60 60.00	PF63 50.00			

KM# 111 30000 WON
19.00 g., 0.999 Silver 0.6063 oz. ASW, 33 mm. Subject: G-20 Summit in Seoul Obv: Gwang-Hwa-Mun restored on Independence Day Rev: Multicolor lantern in national colors Edge: Reeded

Date	Mintage	F12	VF20	XF40	MS60	MS63
2010	50,000	PF60 55.00	PF63 45.00			

KM# 121 50000 WON
19.00 g., 0.999 Silver 0.6063 oz. ASW, 33 mm. Subject: Jeju Volcanic Island and Lava Tubes - UNESCO World Heritage Site Obv: Volcano Crater Rev: Lava tubes

Date	Mintage	F12	VF20	XF40	MS60	MS63
2011	30,000	PF60 55.00	PF63 45.00			

KM# 122 50000 WON
19.00 g., 0.999 Silver 0.6063 oz. ASW, 33 mm. Subject: International Association of Athletics Federations Championships Obv: High Jumping athlete Rev: Athlete running thru finish line tape in color

Date	Mintage	F12	VF20	XF40	MS60	MS63
2011	30,000	PF60 100	PF63 90.00			

KM# 123 50000 WON
19.00 g., 0.999 Silver 0.6063 oz. ASW, 33 mm. **Subject:** Nuclear Security Summit **Obv:** Five hands raising up globe **Rev:** Summit logo in color

Date	Mintage	F12	VF20	XF40	MS60	MS63
2012	20,000	PF60 40.00	PF63 30.00			

KM# 130 50000 WON
19.00 g., 0.999 Silver 0.6063 oz. ASW, 33 mm. **Subject:** UNESCO World Heritage Site - Seokguram Grotto and Bulguksa Temple

Date	Mintage	F12	VF20	XF40	MS60	MS63
2012	—	PF60 70.00	PF63 60.00			

KM# 131 50000 WON
19.00 g., 0.999 Silver 0.6063 oz. ASW, 33 mm. **Subject:** World Conservation Congress **Rev:** Logo in color

Date	Mintage	F12	VF20	XF40	MS60	MS63
2012	20,000	PF60 85.00	PF63 75.00			

MINT SETS

KM#	Date	Mintage Identification	Issue Price	Mkt Val
MS8	2001 (7)	— KM#27, 31, 32, 33.2, 34, 35.2, 89	10.00	22.50

PROOF SETS

KM#	Date	Mintage Identification	Issue Price	Mkt Val
PS10	2001 (6)	2,002 KM#90-95	—	2,500

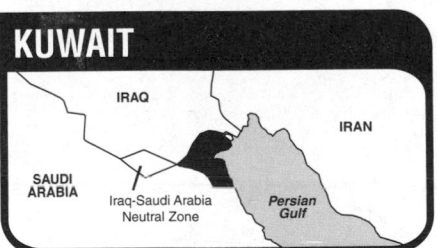

KUWAIT

The State of Kuwait, a constitutional monarchy located on the Arabian Peninsula at the northwestern corner of the Persian Gulf, has an area of 6,880 sq. mi. (17,820 sq. km.) and a population of 1.7 million. Capital: Kuwait. Petroleum, the basis of the economy, provides 95 percent of the exports.

RULERS

Al Sabah Dynasty

Jabir Ibn Ahmad, 1977-2006
Sabah Al Ahmad Al Sabah, 2006-

MONETARY SYSTEM
1000 Fils = 1 Dinar

SOVEREIGN EMIRATE
MODERN COINAGE

KM# 9a FILS
2.41 g., 0.925 Silver 0.0712 oz. ASW, 17 mm. **Ruler:** Jabir Ibn Ahmad **Obv:** Value within circle **Rev:** Ship with sails

Date	Mintage	F12	VF20	XF40	MS60	MS63
AH1429-2008	—	PF63 65.00				

KM# 9c FILS
2.41 g., 0.925 Silver Gilt 0.0712 oz., 17 mm. **Obv:** Value within circle **Rev:** Dhow, dates below

Date	Mintage	F12	VF20	XF40	MS60	MS63
AH1429-2008	—	PF60 75.00				

KM# 10 5 FILS
2.50 g., Nickel-Brass, 19.5 mm. **Ruler:** Jabir Ibn Ahmad **Obv:** Value within circle **Rev:** Dhow, dates below

Date	Mintage	F12	VF20	XF40	MS60	MS63
AH1422-2001	—	—	0.10	0.20	0.40	—
AH1424-2003	—	—	0.10	0.20	0.40	—
AH1426-2005	—	—	0.10	0.20	0.40	—
AH1427-2006	—	—	0.10	0.20	0.40	—
AH1427-2007	—	—	0.10	0.20	0.40	—
AH1428-2008	—	—	0.10	0.20	0.40	—
AH1429-2008	—	—	0.10	0.20	0.40	—
AH1430-2009	—	—	0.10	0.20	0.40	—
AH1431-2010	—	—	0.10	0.20	0.40	—

KM# 10a 5 FILS
3.01 g., 0.925 Silver 0.0889 oz. ASW, 19.5 mm. **Ruler:** Jabir Ibn Ahmad **Obv:** Value within circle **Rev:** Ship with sails

Date	Mintage	F12	VF20	XF40	MS60	MS63
AH1429-2008	—	PF63 70.00				

KM# 10c 5 FILS
3.01 g., 0.925 Silver Gilt 0.0889 oz., 19.5 mm. **Obv:** Value in circle **Rev:** Dhow, dates below

Date	Mintage	F12	VF20	XF40	MS60	MS63
AH1429-2008	—	PF60 80.00				

KM# 11 10 FILS
3.75 g., Nickel-Brass, 21 mm. **Ruler:** Jabir Ibn Ahmad **Obv:** Value within circle **Rev:** Dhow, dates below

Date	Mintage	F12	VF20	XF40	MS60	MS63
AH1422-2001	—	—	—	0.25	0.75	—
AH1424-2003	—	—	—	0.25	0.75	—
AH1426-2005	—	—	—	0.25	0.75	—
AH1427-2006	—	—	—	0.25	0.75	—
AH1428-2007	—	—	—	0.25	0.75	—
AH1429-2008	—	—	—	0.25	0.75	—
AH1430-2009	—	—	—	0.25	0.75	—
AH1431-2010	—	—	—	0.25	0.75	—

KM# 11a 10 FILS
4.35 g., 0.925 Silver 0.1285 oz. ASW, 21 mm. **Ruler:** Jabir Ibn Ahmad **Obv:** Value within circle **Rev:** Ship with sails

Date	Mintage	F12	VF20	XF40	MS60	MS63
AH1429-2008	—	PF63 75.00				

KM# 11c 10 FILS
4.35 g., 0.925 Silver Gilt 0.1285 oz., 21 mm. **Obv:** Value within circle **Rev:** Dhow, dates below

Date	Mintage	F12	VF20	XF40	MS60	MS63
AH1429-2008	—	PF60 85.00				

KM# 12 20 FILS
3.00 g., Copper-Nickel, 20 mm. **Ruler:** Jabir Ibn Ahmad **Obv:** Value within circle **Rev:** Dhow, dates below **Edge:** Reeded **Note:** Varieties exist.

Date	Mintage	F12	VF20	XF40	MS60	MS63
AH1422-2001	—	—	0.20	0.45	2.00	—
AH1423-2002	—	—	0.20	0.45	2.00	—
AH1424-2002	—	—	0.20	0.45	2.00	—
AH1424-2003	—	—	0.20	0.45	2.00	—
AH1426-2005	—	—	0.20	0.45	2.00	—
AH1427-2006	—	—	0.20	0.45	2.00	—
AH1428-2007	—	—	0.20	0.45	2.00	—
AH1429-2008	—	—	0.20	0.45	2.00	—
AH1430-2009	—	—	0.20	0.45	2.00	—
AH1431-2010	—	—	0.20	0.45	2.00	—

KM# 12a 20 FILS
3.37 g., 0.925 Silver 0.0996 oz. ASW, 20 mm. **Ruler:** Jabir Ibn Ahmad **Obv:** Value within circle **Rev:** Dhow, dates below

Date	Mintage	F12	VF20	XF40	MS60	MS63
AH1429-2008	—	PF63 80.00				

KM# 12c 20 FILS
Stainless Steel, 20 mm. **Ruler:** Jabir Ibn Ahmad **Obv:** Value **Rev:** Dhow, dates below

Date	Mintage	F12	VF20	XF40	MS60	MS63
AH1422-2001	—	—	0.20	0.35	1.00	—
AH1424-2003	—	—	0.20	0.35	1.00	—
AH1426-2005	—	—	0.20	0.35	1.00	—

KM# 12d 20 FILS
3.37 g., 0.925 Silver Gilt 0.0996 oz., 20 mm. **Obv:** Value within circle **Rev:** Dhow, dates below

Date	Mintage	F12	VF20	XF40	MS60	MS63
1429-2008	—	PF60 90.00				

KM# 13 50 FILS
4.50 g., Copper-Nickel, 23 mm. **Ruler:** Jabir Ibn Ahmad **Obv:** Value within circle **Rev:** Dhow, dates below **Edge:** Reeded

Date	Mintage	F12	VF20	XF40	MS60	MS63
AH1422-2001	—	—	0.25	0.35	1.25	—
AH1424-2003	—	—	0.25	0.35	1.00	—
AH1426-2005	—	—	0.25	0.35	1.00	—
AH1427-2006	—	—	0.25	0.35	1.00	—
AH1428-2007	—	—	0.25	0.35	1.00	—
AH1429-2008	—	—	0.25	0.35	1.00	—
AH1430-2009	—	—	0.25	0.35	1.00	—
AH1431-2010	—	—	0.25	0.35	1.00	—
AH1432-2011	—	—	0.25	0.35	1.00	—

KM# 13a 50 FILS
5.07 g., 0.925 Silver 0.1498 oz. ASW, 23 mm. **Ruler:** Jabir Ibn Ahmad **Obv:** Value within circle **Rev:** Ship with sails

Date	Mintage	F12	VF20	XF40	MS60	MS63
AH1429-2008	—	PF63 85.00				

KM# 13c 50 FILS
5.07 g., 0.925 Silver Gilt 0.1498 oz., 23 mm. **Obv:** Value within circle **Rev:** Dhow, dates below

Date	Mintage	F12	VF20	XF40	MS60	MS63
1429-2008	—	PF60 100				

KM# 14 100 FILS
6.50 g., Copper-Nickel, 26 mm. **Ruler:** Jabir Ibn Ahmad **Obv:** Value within circle **Rev:** Dhow, dates below **Edge:** Reeded

Date	Mintage	F12	VF20	XF40	MS60	MS63
AH1424-2003	—	—	0.50	0.75	1.50	—
AH1426-2005	—	—	0.50	0.75	1.50	—
AH1427-2006	—	—	0.50	0.75	1.50	—
AH1428-2007	—	—	0.50	0.75	1.50	—
AH1429-2008	—	—	0.50	0.75	1.50	—
AH1430-2009	—	—	0.50	0.75	1.50	—
AH1431-2010	—	—	0.50	0.75	1.50	—

KM# 14a 100 FILS
7.34 g., 0.925 Silver 0.2169 oz. ASW, 26 mm. **Ruler:** Jabir Ibn Ahmad **Obv:** Value within circle **Rev:** Ship with sails

Date	Mintage	F12	VF20	XF40	MS60	MS63
AH1429-2008	—	PF63 90.00				

KM# 14c 100 FILS
7.34 g., 0.925 Silver Gilt 0.2169 oz., 26 mm. **Obv:** Value within circle **Rev:** Dhow, dates below

Date	Mintage	F12	VF20	XF40	MS60	MS63
1429-2008	—	PF60 110				

PROOF SETS

KM#	Date	Mintage Identification	Issue Price	Mkt Val
PS5	2008 (6)	— KM#9a-14a	—	475
PS6	2008 (6)	— KM#9c-11c, 12d, 13c-14c	—	500

KYRGYZSTAN

The Kyrgyz Republic, (formerly Kirghiz S.S.R., a Union Republic of the U.S.S.R.), is an independent state since Aug. 31, 1991, a member of the United Nations and of the C.I.S. It was the last state of the Union Republics to declare its sovereignty. Capital: Bishkek (formerly Frunze).

MONETARY SYSTEM
100 Tiyin = 1 Som

REPUBLIC
STANDARD COINAGE

KM# 11 TIYIN
1.00 g., Aluminum-Bronze, 13.98 mm. **Obv:** National arms **Rev:** Flower at left of value **Edge:** Reeded **Note:** Prev. KM #8.

Date	Mintage	F12	VF20	XF40	MS60	MS63
2008 In sets only	95,000	—	—	—	—	1.25

KM# 12 10 TIYIN
1.30 g., Brass Plated Steel, 15 mm. **Obv:** National arms **Rev:** Flower at left of value **Edge:** Plain **Note:** Prev. KM #9.

Date	Mintage	F12	VF20	XF40	MS60	MS63
2008	—	—	—	—	0.85	1.50

KM# 13 50 TIYIN
1.80 g., Brass Plated Steel, 17 mm. **Obv:** National arms **Rev:** Flower at left of value **Edge:** Plain **Note:** Prev. KM #10.

Date	Mintage	F12	VF20	XF40	MS60	MS63
2008	—	—	—	—	1.25	2.00

KM# 14 SOM
2.50 g., Nickel Plated Steel, 19 mm. **Obv:** National arms **Rev:** Symbol at left of denomination **Edge:** Reeded **Note:** Prev. KM #11.

Date	Mintage	F12	VF20	XF40	MS60	MS63
2008	—	—	—	—	1.50	2.25

KM# 19 SOM
12.00 g., Copper-Nickel, 30 mm. **Series:** Great Silk Road **Subject:** Tashrabat **Obv:** Arms **Rev:** Fortress

Date	Mintage	F12	VF20	XF40	MS60	MS63
2008 Prooflike	5,000	—	—	—	10.00	15.00

KM# 21 SOM
12.00 g., Copper-Nickel, 30 mm. **Subject:** Uzgen Architectural Complex **Obv:** Arms **Rev:** Tower and building - map above

Date	Mintage	F12	VF20	XF40	MS60	MS63
2008 Prooflike	5,000	—	—	—	10.00	15.00

KM# 35 SOM
12.00 g., Copper-Nickel, 30 mm. **Series:** Great Silk Road **Subject:** Burana Tower **Rev:** Tower and map

Date	Mintage	F12	VF20	XF40	MS60	MS63
2008 Prooflike	5,000	—	—	—	10.00	15.00

KM# 31 SOM
12.00 g., Copper-Nickel, 30 mm. **Series:** Great Silk Road **Subject:** Suilaman Mountain

Date	Mintage	F12	VF20	XF40	MS60	MS63
2009 Prooflike	5,000	—	—	—	10.00	15.00

KM# 33 SOM
12.00 g., Copper-Nickel, 30 mm. **Series:** Great Silk Road **Subject:** Lake Issykkul

Date	Mintage	F12	VF20	XF40	MS60	MS63
2009 Prooflike	5,000	—	—	—	10.00	15.00

KM# 45 SOM
12.00 g., Copper-Nickel, 30 mm. **Subject:** Pobeda Peak **Obv:** National arms above stylized peaks **Rev:** Mountian range

Date	Mintage	F12	VF20	XF40	MS60	MS63
2011	5,000	—	—	—	—	25.00

KM# 47 SOM
12.00 g., Copper-Nickel, 30 mm. **Obv:** National arms **Rev:** Khan-Tengri Peak

Date	Mintage	F12	VF20	XF40	MS60	MS63
2011	5,000	—	—	—	—	25.00

KM# 51 SOM
12.00 g., Copper-Nickel, 30 mm. **Subject:** Saimaluu-Tash **Obv:** Rock carvings **Rev:** Rock drawings

Date	Mintage	F12	VF20	XF40	MS60	MS63
2013	5,000	—	—	—	—	25.00

KM# 55 SOM
28.28 g., 0.925 Silver 0.8356 oz. ASW, 38.6 mm. **Subject:** Saimaluu-Tash **Obv:** Rock carvings **Rev:** Rock drawings

Date	Mintage	F12	VF20	XF40	MS60	MS63
2013	3,000	PF65 110				

KM# 15 3 SOM
3.20 g., Nickel Plated Steel, 21 mm. **Obv:** National arms **Rev:** Symbol above right of denomination **Edge:** Reeded **Note:** Prev. KM #12.

Date	Mintage	F12	VF20	XF40	MS60	MS63
2008	—	—	—	—	1.25	2.00

KM# 16 5 SOM
4.20 g., Nickel Plated Steel, 23 mm. **Obv:** National arms **Rev:** Symbol at right of value **Edge:** Reeded **Note:** Prev. KM #13.

Date	Mintage	F12	VF20	XF40	MS60	MS63
2008	—	—	—	—	1.50	2.50

KM# 52 5 SOM
14.35 g., Copper-Nickel, 33 mm. **Obv:** National arms and traditional musical instruments **Rev:** Man with Komuz

Date	Mintage	F12	VF20	XF40	MS60	MS63
2012	3,000	—	—	—	—	25.00

KM# 4 10 SOM
28.28 g., 0.925 Silver 0.8356 oz. ASW, 38.6 mm. **Subject:** Tenth Anniversary of Republic **Obv:** National arms within circle **Rev:** Value and Khan Tengri mountain **Edge:** Reeded **Note:** Prev. KM #3.

Date	Mintage	F12	VF20	XF40	MS60	MS63
2001	1,000	PF65 175				

KM# 5 10 SOM
28.28 g., 0.925 Silver 0.8356 oz. ASW, 38.6 mm. **Subject:**
International Year of the mountains **Obv:** National arms **Rev:**
Edelweiss flower and mountain **Edge:** Reeded **Note:** Prev. KM
#4.

Date	Mintage	F12	VF20	XF40	MS60	MS63
2002	1,000	**PF65** 125				

KM# 6 10 SOM
28.28 g., 0.925 Silver 0.8356 oz. ASW, 38.6 mm. **Subject:**
International Year of the Mountains **Obv:** National arms **Rev:**
Argali Ram head and mountain **Edge:** Reeded **Note:** Prev. KM
#5.

Date	Mintage	F12	VF20	XF40	MS60	MS63
2002	1,000	**PF65** 125				

KM# 36 10 SOM
28.28 g., 0.925 Silver 0.8356 oz. ASW, 38.6 mm. **Subject:**
Som, 10th Anniversary **Obv:** National arms **Rev:** Som coin
designs, some gilt

Date	Mintage	F12	VF20	XF40	MS60	MS63
2003 (2002)	—	**PF65** 150				

KM# 7 10 SOM
28.28 g., 0.925 Silver 0.8356 oz. ASW, 38.6 mm. **Subject:**
Genesis of the Kyrgyz Statehood **Obv:** Arms **Rev:** Classical
designs

Date	Mintage	F12	VF20	XF40	MS60	MS63
2003	1,000	**PF65** 250				

KM# 8 10 SOM
28.28 g., 0.925 Silver 0.8356 oz. ASW, 38.6 mm. **Subject:** 60
Years of Great Victory **Rev:** Figure of a mother, eternal light,
Victory Memorial complex **Note:** Prev. KM #6.

Date	Mintage	F12	VF20	XF40	MS60	MS63
2005	1,000	**PF65** 110				

KM# 9 10 SOM
28.28 g., 0.825 Silver 0.7453 oz. ASW, 38.6 mm. **Series:** Great
Silk Road **Subject:** Tashrabat **Note:** Prev. KM #7.

Date	Mintage	F12	VF20	XF40	MS60	MS63
2005	1,500	**PF65** 100				

KM# 10 10 SOM
28.28 g., 0.925 Silver 0.8356 oz. ASW, 38.6 mm. **Subject:**
Shanghai Cooperation **Obv:** Arms **Rev:** Multicolor logo of the
Shanghai Cooperation Organization

Date	Mintage	F12	VF20	XF40	MS60	MS63
2007	1,000	**PF65** 180				

KM# 22 10 SOM
28.28 g., 0.925 Silver 0.8356 oz. ASW, 38.6 mm. **Series:** Great
Silk Road **Subject:** Uzgen Architectural Complex

Date	Mintage	F12	VF20	XF40	MS60	MS63
2007	1,500	**PF65** 120				

KM# 18 10 SOM
28.28 g., 0.925 Silver 0.8356 oz. ASW, 38.6 mm. **Series:** Great
Silk Road **Subject:** Burana Tower **Rev:** Buildings with partial
gilting

Date	Mintage	F12	VF20	XF40	MS60	MS63
2008	1,500	**PF65** 110				

KM# 23 10 SOM
28.28 g., 0.925 Silver 0.8356 oz. ASW, 38.6 mm. **Series:**
Capitals of the Eurasia Economic Community **Subject:** City
of Bishkek **Obv:** National emblem **Rev:** Horseman statue,
multicolor logo

Date	Mintage	F12	VF20	XF40	MS60	MS63
2008	2,500	**PF65** 90.00				

KM# 24 10 SOM
28.28 g., 0.925 Silver 0.8356 oz. ASW, 38.6 mm. **Rev:**
Chynqyz Aytmatov

Date	Mintage	F12	VF20	XF40	MS60	MS63
2009	2,000	**PF65** 75.00				

KM# 25 10 SOM
28.28 g., 0.925 Silver 0.8356 oz. ASW, 38.6 mm. **Series:**
Chinqiz Aitmatov's work's **Rev:** Jamila

Date	Mintage	F12	VF20	XF40	MS60	MS63
2009	3,000	**PF65** 75.00				

KM# 26 10 SOM
28.28 g., 0.925 Silver 0.8356 oz. ASW, 38.6 mm. **Series:** Chingiz Aitmatov's works **Rev:** Duishen

Date	Mintage	F12	VF20	XF40	MS60	MS63
2009	3,000	PF65 75.00				

KM# 27 10 SOM
28.28 g., 0.925 Silver 0.8356 oz. ASW, 38.6 mm. **Series:** Chinqiz Aitmatov's works **Rev:** Mother field

Date	Mintage	F12	VF20	XF40	MS60	MS63
2009	3,000	PF65 75.00				

KM# 28 10 SOM
28.28 g., 0.925 Silver 0.8356 oz. ASW, 38.5 mm. **Series:** Chinqiz Aitmatov's works **Rev:** Farewell, Gulsary!

Date	Mintage	F12	VF20	XF40	MS60	MS63
2009	3,000	PF65 75.00				

KM# 29 10 SOM
28.28 g., 0.925 Silver 0.8356 oz. ASW, 38.5 mm. **Series:** Chinqiz Aitmatov's works **Rev:** The white ship

Date	Mintage	F12	VF20	XF40	MS60	MS63
2009	3,000	PF65 75.00				

KM# 32 10 SOM
28.28 g., 0.925 Silver 0.8356 oz. ASW, 38.6 mm. **Series:** Great Silk Road **Subject:** Suliman Mountain

Date	Mintage	F12	VF20	XF40	MS60	MS63
2009	1,500	PF65 110				

KM# 34 10 SOM
28.28 g., 0.925 Silver 0.8356 oz. ASW, 38.6 mm. **Series:** Great Silk Road **Subject:** Lake Issykkul

Date	Mintage	F12	VF20	XF40	MS60	MS63
2009	1,500	PF65 110				

KM# 38 10 SOM
31.10 g., 0.925 Silver 0.9189 oz. ASW, 38.6 mm. **Obv:** National arms at top of repeating motif **Rev:** Eagle in flight right, multicolor logo below

Date	Mintage	F12	VF20	XF40	MS60	MS63
2009	3,000	PF65 90.00				

KM# 41 10 SOM
31.10 g., 0.925 Silver 0.9189 oz. ASW, 38.6 mm. **Obv:** National emblem and linear design **Rev:** Two people riding deer, as in a cave painting; multicolor logo below

Date	Mintage	F12	VF20	XF40	MS60	MS63
2009	3,000	PF65 95.00				

KM# 43 10 SOM
5.40 g., Nickel Plated Steel, 24.5 mm. **Obv:** National Arms **Rev:** Symbol above value

Date	Mintage	F12	VF20	XF40	MS60	MS63
2009	—	—	—	—	4.50	6.00

KM# 39 10 SOM
31.10 g., 0.925 Silver 0.9189 oz. ASW, 38.6 mm. **Obv:** National Arms, multicolor design **Rev:** Frame construction of a Yurta

Date	Mintage	F12	VF20	XF40	MS60	MS63
2010	3,000	PF65 75.00				

KM# 40 10 SOM
31.10 g., 0.925 Silver 0.9189 oz. ASW, 38.6 mm. **Subject:**

EurAsEC 10th Anniversary **Obv:** National arms and globe **Rev:** Five world sites, multicolor logo at center

Date	Mintage	F12	VF20	XF40	MS60	MS63
2010	2,000	PF65 75.00				

KM# 44 10 SOM
28.28 g., Silver, 38.6 mm. **Subject:** Independence, 20th Anniversary **Obv:** National arms **Rev:** Colored flag above map with Manas on horseback right **Edge:** Reeded

Date	Mintage	F12	VF20	XF40	MS60	MS63
2011	2,000	PF65 75.00				

KM# 46 10 SOM
28.28 g., 0.925 Silver 0.8356 oz. ASW, 38.6 mm. **Subject:** Pobeda Peak **Obv:** National arms above stylized mountains **Rev:** Mountian range **Edge:** Reeded

Date	Mintage	F12	VF20	XF40	MS60	MS63
2011	3,000	PF65 75.00				

KM# 48 10 SOM
31.10 g., 0.925 Silver 0.9189 oz. ASW, 38.6 mm. **Subject:** Great Silk Road **Obv:** National arms above caravan riding right **Rev:** Skyline views and Silk Road map of Eurasia, color logo at top **Edge:** Reeded

Date	Mintage	F12	VF20	XF40	MS60	MS63
2011	Est. 2000	PF65 75.00				

KM# 49 10 SOM
33.94 g., 0.925 Silver 1.0029 oz. ASW, 38.6 mm. **Subject:** World of our Children **Obv:** National arms and six flowers **Rev:** Child's drawing in color of sun, girl and medow **Edge:** Reeded

Date	Mintage	F12	VF20	XF40	MS60	MS63
2011	—	PF65 75.00				

KM# 50 10 SOM
28.28 g., 0.925 Silver 0.8356 oz. ASW, 38.6 mm. **Subject:** Kumranjan Datka, 200th Anniversary **Obv:** Arms, horseman below **Rev:** Female head wearing turban, facing

Date	Mintage	F12	VF20	XF40	MS60	MS63
2012	—	PF65 110				

KM# 53 10 SOM
28.28 g., 0.925 Silver 0.8356 oz. ASW, 38.6 mm. **Obv:** Arms, stylized animals below **Rev:** Resting leopard, crystal inserts

Date	Mintage	F12	VF20	XF40	MS60	MS63
2012	3,000	PF65 110				

KM# 54 10 SOM
28.28 g., 0.925 Silver 0.8356 oz. ASW, 38.6 mm. **Obv:** Arms, stylized animals below **Rev:** Gazelle, crystal inserts

Date	Mintage	F12	VF20	XF40	MS60	MS63
2012	3,000	PF65 110				

KM# 37 100 SOM
6.22 g., 0.999 Gold 0.1985 oz. AGW, 22 mm. **Rev:** Two horsemen

Date	Mintage	F12	VF20	XF40	MS60	MS63
2008	—	PF65 375				

KM# 42 100 SOM
31.10 g., 0.925 Silver 0.9189 oz. ASW, 38.61 mm. **Rev:** Panthera Tigris, gilt tiger

Date	Mintage	F12	VF20	XF40	MS60	MS63
2009	13,000	PF63 85.00	PF65 100			

MINT SETS

KM#	Date	Mintage	Identification	Issue Price	Mkt Val
MS1	2008 (6)	—	KM#11-16	—	30.00

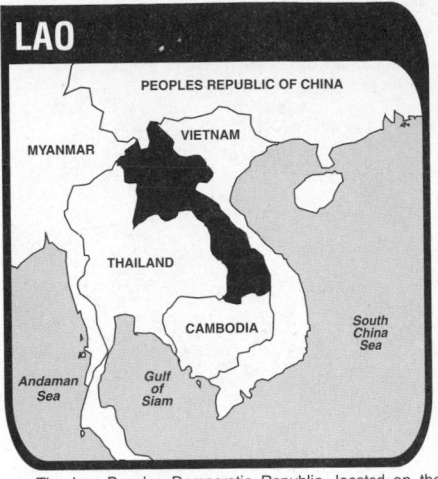

LAO

The Lao Peoples Democratic Republic, located on the Indo-Chinese Peninsula between the Socialist Republic of Vietnam and the Kingdom of Thailand, has an area of 91,428 sq. mi. (236,800 km.) and a population of 3.6 million. Capital Vientiane. Agriculture employs 95 per cent of the people. Tin, lumber and coffee are exported.

MONETARY SYSTEM
100 Att = 1 Kip

PEOPLES DEMOCRATIC REPUBLIC

KM# 159 500 KIP
0.50 g., 0.999 Gold AGW, 11 mm. **Obv:** National emblem **Rev:** Peacock

Date	Mintage	F12	VF20	XF40	MS60	MS63
2008	15,000	PF63 50.00	PF65 60.00			

KM# 160 500 KIP
0.50 g., 0.999 Gold AGW, 11 mm. **Obv:** National emblem **Rev:** Victory Gate, Patouxai

Date	Mintage	F12	VF20	XF40	MS60	MS63
2008	10,000	PF63 50.00	PF65 60.00			

KM# 151 500 KIP
0.50 g., 0.999 Gold AGW, 11 mm. **Rev:** Lion's head

Date	Mintage	F12	VF20	XF40	MS60	MS63
2009	—	PF65 50.00				

KM# 152 500 KIP
0.50 g., 0.999 Gold AGW, 11 mm. **Subject:** Year of the Tiger **Rev:** Tiger

Date	Mintage	F12	VF20	XF40	MS60	MS63
2010	Est. 5000	PF65 50.00				

KM# 162 500 KIP
0.50 g., 0.999 Gold AGW, 11 mm. **Obv:** National emblem **Rev:** Buddha seated in archway

Date	Mintage	F12	VF20	XF40	MS60	MS63
2010	—	PF65 60.00				

KM# 165 500 KIP
0.50 g., 0.999 Gold AGW, 11 mm. **Subject:** Year of the Rabbit **Obv:** National emblem **Rev:** Rabbit seated upright right, head looking left

Date	Mintage	F12	VF20	XF40	MS60	MS63
2011	Est. 5000	PF65 50.00				

KM# 168 500 KIP
0.50 g., 0.585 Gold AGW, 11 mm. **Subject:** Golden Pha - That Luang

Date	Mintage	F12	VF20	XF40	MS60	MS63
2012	Est. 5000	PF65 70.00				

KM# 85 1000 KIP
31.50 g., 0.999 Silver 1.0052 oz. ASW, 38.5 mm. **Subject:** Olympics **Obv:** State emblem **Rev:** Freestyle skier **Edge:** Reeded

Date	Mintage	F12	VF20	XF40	MS60	MS63
2001	—	PF63 45.00	PF65 50.00			

KM# 96 1000 KIP
31.45 g., 0.999 Silver 1.0036 oz. ASW, 38.5 mm. **Obv:** State emblem **Rev:** Soccer player **Edge:** Reeded

Date	Mintage	F12	VF20	XF40	MS60	MS63
2001	—	PF65 50.00				

KM# 122 1000 KIP
1.24 g., 0.999 Gold 0.0396 oz. AGW, 13.92 mm. **Rev:** Tiger head

Date	Mintage	F12	VF20	XF40	MS60	MS63
2003	Est. 15000	PF63 75.00	PF65 90.00			

KM# 126 1000 KIP
Silver **Subject:** Beijing olympics, 2008 **Rev:** Torch relay between Parthenon in Athens and Temple of Heaven in Beijing

Date	Mintage	F12	VF20	XF40	MS60	MS63
2004	—	PF65 35.00				

KM# 136 1000 KIP
1.24 g., 0.999 Gold 0.0396 oz. AGW, 13.92 mm. **Rev:** Wat Phu Champasak

Date	Mintage	F12	VF20	XF40	MS60	MS63
2005	—	PF65 90.00				

KM# 161 1000 KIP
1.24 g., 0.999 Gold 0.0396 oz. AGW, 13.92 mm. **Subject:** Rennes le Chateau **Obv:** National emblem **Rev:** Town gate and menorah

Date	Mintage	F12	VF20	XF40	MS60	MS63
2007	Est. 15000	PF63 75.00	PF65 85.00			

KM# 150 1000 KIP
28.28 g., 0.925 Silver 0.8356 oz. ASW, 38.61 mm. **Subject:** Qinghai - Tibet Railway **Obv:** National emblem **Rev:** Train and map of the railroad from Zining to Lhasa

Date	Mintage	F12	VF20	XF40	MS60	MS63
2008	—	PF65 75.00				

KM# 157 1000 KIP
28.28 g., 0.925 Silver 0.8356 oz. ASW, 38.61 mm. **Subject:** Beijing to London Olympic transfer **Obv:** National emblem **Rev:** Temple of Heaven, Tower Bridge and athlete

Date	Mintage	F12	VF20	XF40	MS60	MS63
2008	Est. 10000	PF63 65.00	PF65 75.00			

KM# 104 1000 KIP
36.47 g., 0.925 Silver 1.0776 oz. ASW, 38.6 mm. **Subject:** Terra Cotta Warriors **Obv:** Arms **Rev:** Gilt warrior standing, background warriors face right **Note:** Central gilt warrior is detachable and stands upright.

Date	Mintage	F12	VF20	XF40	MS60	MS63
2009	5,000	PF63 85.00	PF65 100			

KM# 105 1000 KIP
36.47 g., 0.925 Silver 1.0776 oz. ASW, 38.61 mm. **Subject:** Terra Cotta Warrior **Obv:** Arms **Rev:** Gilt standing warrior, warriors in background facing **Note:** Central gilt warrior is detachable and stands upright.

Date	Mintage	F12	VF20	XF40	MS60	MS63
2009	5,000	PF63 85.00	PF65 100			

KM# 106 1000 KIP
36.47 g., 0.925 Silver 1.0776 oz. ASW, 38.6 mm. **Subject:** Terra Cotta Warrior **Obv:** Arms **Rev:** Archer kneeling **Note:** Central gilt warrior is detachable and stands upright.

Date	Mintage	F12	VF20	XF40	MS60	MS63
2009	1,000	PF63 85.00	PF65 100			

KM# 107 1000 KIP
36.47 g., 0.925 Silver 1.0776 oz. ASW **Subject:** Terra Cotta Warrior **Obv:** Arms **Rev:** Gilt horse **Note:** Central gilt warrior is detachable and stands upright.

Date	Mintage	F12	VF20	XF40	MS60	MS63
2009	1,000	PF63 85.00	PF65 100			

KM# 153 1000 KIP
28.28 g., 0.925 Silver 0.8356 oz. ASW, 38.61 mm. **Subject:** World Cup 2010 in South Africa **Rev:** Sculpture of soccer players

Date	Mintage	F12	VF20	XF40	MS60	MS63
2010	—	PF65 60.00				

KM# 163 1000 KIP
1.00 g., 0.999 Gold 0.0319 oz. AGW, 13.92 mm. **Obv:** National emblem **Rev:** Buddha Park, stone staute head

Date	Mintage	F12	VF20	XF40	MS60	MS63
2010	Est. 10000	PF63 65.00	PF65 75.00			

KM# 167 1000 KIP
28.35 g., 0.999 Silver 0.9047 oz. ASW, 40 mm. **Subject:** Lunar Series - Year of the Dragon, Colorized

Date	Mintage	F12	VF20	XF40	MS60	MS63
2012	Est. 8888	PF65 90.00				

KM# 164 2000 KIP
62.21 g., 0.999 Silver 1.9852 oz. ASW, 55 mm. **Subject:** Year of the Rabbit **Obv:** Naitonal emblem **Rev:** Rabbit and jade inlay

Date	Mintage	F12	VF20	XF40	MS60	MS63
2011	Est. 2888	PF65 200				

KM# 155 2000 KIP
62.20 g., 0.999 Silver 1.9849 oz. ASW, 55 mm. **Subject:** Year of the Dragon **Obv:** National arms **Rev:** Dragon with jade ring

Date	Mintage	F12	VF20	XF40	MS60	MS63
2012	2,888	PF65 140				

KM# 166 2000 KIP
56.70 g., 0.999 Silver 1.8094 oz. ASW, 55 mm. **Subject:** Lunar Series - Year of the Dragon

Date	Mintage	F12	VF20	XF40	MS60	MS63
2012	Est. 2888	PF65 225				

KM# 169 2000 KIP
62.20 g., 0.999 (No Composition) 1.9849 oz., 55 mm. **Subject:** Year of the Horse **Rev:** Gilt horse prancing left within jade insert

Date	Mintage	F12	VF20	XF40	MS60	MS63
2014	2,888	PF65 225				

KM# 119 5000 KIP
0.30 g., 0.999 Gold AGW, 7 mm. **Rev:** Cichlasoma fish

Date	Mintage	F12	VF20	XF40	MS60	MS63
2003	—	—	—	—	—	50.00

KM# 124 5000 KIP
0.30 g., 0.999 Gold AGW, 7 mm. **Rev:** Rhino

Date	Mintage	F12	VF20	XF40	MS60	MS63
2004	—	—	—	—	—	50.00

KM# 127 5000 KIP
37.00 g., Gold Plated Bronze, 45 mm. **Rev:** Majextic rooster as a laser engraving

Date	Mintage	F12	VF20	XF40	MS60	MS63
2005	Est. 28000	—	—	—	—	35.00

KM# 129 5000 KIP
0.30 g., 0.999 Gold AGW, 7 mm. **Rev:** Majestic rooster in pose

Date	Mintage	F12	VF20	XF40	MS60	MS63
2005	—	PF65 50.00				

KM# 139 5000 KIP
0.30 g., 0.999 Gold AGW, 7 mm. **Subject:** Year of the Dog **Rev:** Dog with kinegram background

Date	Mintage	F12	VF20	XF40	MS60	MS63
2006	—	—	—	—	—	50.00

KM# 158 5000 KIP
7.77 g., 0.583 Gold 0.1447 oz. AGW, 25 mm. **Subject:** Beijing to London Olympic transfer **Obv:** National emblem **Rev:** Temple of Heaven, Tower Bridge and athlete

Date	Mintage	F12	VF20	XF40	MS60	MS63
2008	Est. 1000	PF65 450				

KM# 170 50000 KIP
31.11 g., 0.999 Silver 0.9926 oz. ASW **Subject:** That Luang Vietrane elephants, 450th Anniversary

Date	Mintage	F12	VF20	XF40	MS60	MS63
2010	10,000	PF63 140	PF65 150			

KM# 113 10000 KIP
1.24 g., 0.999 Gold 0.0396 oz. AGW, 13.92 mm. **Rev:** Two redshank dress apes

Date	Mintage	F12	VF20	XF40	MS60	MS63
2001	—	PF65 90.00				

KM# 114 10000 KIP
1.24 g., 0.999 Gold 0.0396 oz. AGW, 13.92 mm. **Rev:** Horse drawing in color by Xu Beihong

Date	Mintage	F12	VF20	XF40	MS60	MS63
2002	—	—	—	—	—	90.00

KM# 120 10000 KIP
1.24 g., 0.999 Gold 0.0396 oz. AGW, 13.92 mm. **Rev:** Cichlasoma fish

Date	Mintage	F12	VF20	XF40	MS60	MS63
2003	—	—	—	—	—	90.00

KM# 125 10000 KIP
1.24 g., 0.999 Gold 0.0396 oz. AGW, 13.92 mm. **Rev:** Black crested gibbon

Date	Mintage	F12	VF20	XF40	MS60	MS63
2004	—	—	—	—	—	80.00

KM# 130 10000 KIP
1.24 g., 0.999 Gold 0.0396 oz. AGW, 13.92 mm. **Obv:** National Arms **Rev:** Majestic rooster right

Date	Mintage	F12	VF20	XF40	MS60	MS63
2005	—	—	—	—	—	80.00

KM# 133 10000 KIP
1.24 g., 0.999 Gold 0.0396 oz. AGW, 13.92 mm. **Obv:** National arms **Rev:** Mazu seated, waves in background

Date	Mintage	F12	VF20	XF40	MS60	MS63
2005	Est. 6888	PF63 75.00	PF65 90.00			

KM# 140 10000 KIP
1.24 g., 0.999 Gold 0.0396 oz. AGW, 13.92 mm. **Subject:** Year of the Dog **Rev:** Don seated

Date	Mintage	F12	VF20	XF40	MS60	MS63
2006	—	—	—	—	—	90.00

KM# 142 10000 KIP
1.24 g., 0.999 Gold 0.0396 oz. AGW, 13.92 mm. **Rev:** Mazu standing

Date	Mintage	F12	VF20	XF40	MS60	MS63
2006	—	—	—	—	—	90.00

KM# 146 10000 KIP
1.24 g., 0.999 Gold 0.0396 oz. AGW **Rev:** Buddha in meditation **Shape:** 13.92

Date	Mintage	F12	VF20	XF40	MS60	MS63
2006	Est. 6888	PF63 75.00	PF65 90.00			

KM# 149 10000 KIP
1.24 g., 0.999 Gold 0.0396 oz. AGW, 13.92 mm. **Subject:** Year of the Pig **Obv:** National arms **Rev:** Pig

Date	Mintage	F12	VF20	XF40	MS60	MS63
2007	—	—	—	—	—	90.00

KM# 154 10000 KIP
1.00 g., 0.999 Gold 0.0319 oz. AGW, 13.92 mm. **Subject:** World Cup Soccer, South Africa **Rev:** Sculpture of soccer players

Date	Mintage	F12	VF20	XF40	MS60	MS63
2010	—	PF65 90.00				

KM# 86 15000 KIP
20.00 g., 0.925 Silver 0.591 oz. ASW, 38.7 mm. **Subject:** Year of the Horse **Obv:** State emblem **Rev:** Multicolor horse **Edge:** Reeded

Date	Mintage	F12	VF20	XF40	MS60	MS63
2002	9,500	PF63 45.00	PF65 50.00			

KM# 87 15000 KIP
20.00 g., 0.925 Silver 0.591 oz. ASW, 38.7 mm. **Subject:** Year of the Horse **Obv:** State emblem **Rev:** Horse with multicolor holographic background **Edge:** Reeded

Date	Mintage	F12	VF20	XF40	MS60	MS63
2002	9,500	PF63 50.00	PF65 55.00			

KM# 116 15000 KIP
20.00 g., 0.925 Silver 0.591 oz. ASW **Obv:** National arms **Rev:** Shoulder-spot cichlid in color

Date	Mintage	F12	VF20	XF40	MS60	MS63
2003	Est. 2300	PF65 60.00				

KM# 117 15000 KIP
20.00 g., 0.925 Silver 0.591 oz. ASW, 38 mm. **Rev:** Chilasoma flower horn fish swimming left

Date	Mintage	F12	VF20	XF40	MS60	MS63
2003	—	PF65 60.00				

KM# 118 15000 KIP
20.00 g., 0.925 Silver 0.591 oz. ASW, 38 mm. **Rev:** Fish in color kinegram

Date	Mintage	F12	VF20	XF40	MS60	MS63
2003	—	PF65 60.00				

KM# 94 15000 KIP
20.00 g., 0.999 Silver 0.6382 oz. ASW, 38.7 mm. **Obv:** State emblem **Rev:** Multicolor Golden Monkey **Edge:** Reeded

Date	Mintage	F12	VF20	XF40	MS60	MS63
2004	2,300	PF65 55.00				

KM# 123 15000 KIP
20.00 g., 0.999 Silver 0.6382 oz. ASW **Rev:** Black crested gibbon

Date	Mintage	F12	VF20	XF40	MS60	MS63
2004	Est. 3800	PF65 60.00				

KM# 128 15000 KIP
20.00 g., 0.999 Silver 0.6382 oz. ASW **Rev:** Majestic Rooster with kinegram background

Date	Mintage	F12	VF20	XF40	MS60	MS63
2005	Est. 3800	PF65 60.00				

KM# 132 15000 KIP
20.00 g., 0.925 Silver 0.591 oz. ASW, 38 mm. **Obv:** National arms **Rev:** Mazu seated, waves in background

Date	Mintage	F12	VF20	XF40	MS60	MS63
2005	Est. 6888	PF63 50.00	PF65 60.00			

KM# 98 15000 KIP
Silver, 38.7 mm. **Issuer:** Bank of Lao PDR **Obv:** National arms **Obv. Legend:** THE LAO PEOPLE'S DEMOCRATIC REPUBLIC **Rev:** Statue of Mazu with stylized Phoenix at left and right **Rev. Legend:** GODDESS OF THE SEA **Edge:** Reeded

Date	Mintage	F12	VF20	XF40	MS60	MS63
2006	6,888	PF63 60.00	PF65 65.00			

KM# 137 15000 KIP
20.00 g., 0.999 Silver 0.6382 oz. ASW, 38 mm. **Subject:** Year of the Dog **Rev:** Three dogs

Date	Mintage	F12	VF20	XF40	MS60	MS63
2006	—	PF65 60.00				

KM# 138 15000 KIP
Silver **Subject:** Year of the Dog **Rev:** Dog with kinegram background

Date	Mintage	F12	VF20	XF40	MS60	MS63
2006	—	PF65 60.00				

KM# 145 15000 KIP
20.00 g., 0.925 Silver 0.591 oz. ASW, 38 mm. **Rev:** Buddha head facing

Date	Mintage	F12	VF20	XF40	MS60	MS63
2006	Est. 6888	PF63 50.00	PF65 60.00			

KM# 148 15000 KIP
20.00 g., 0.999 Silver 0.6382 oz. ASW, 38 mm. **Subject:** Year of the Pig **Obv:** National arms **Rev:** Pig with kinegram background

Date	Mintage	F12	VF20	XF40	MS60	MS63
2007	—	PF65 60.00				

KM# 115 50000 KIP
7.78 g., 0.999 Gold 0.2483 oz. AGW, 22 mm. **Obv:** National arms **Rev:** Horse advancing right

Date	Mintage	F12	VF20	XF40	MS60	MS63
2002	—	—	—	—	—	475

KM# 88 60000 KIP
155.52 g., 0.925 Silver 4.5952 oz. ASW, 65 mm. **Subject:** Year of the Horse **Obv:** State emblem **Rev:** Multicolor horse **Edge:** Reeded

Date	Mintage	F12	VF20	XF40	MS60	MS63
2002	1,000	PF65 225				

KM# 89 100000 KIP
15.55 g., 0.9999 Gold 0.4967 oz. AGW, 27 mm. **Subject:** Year of the Horse **Obv:** State emblem **Rev:** Horse **Edge:** Reeded

Date	Mintage	F12	VF20	XF40	MS60	MS63
2002	2,000	PF65 925				

KM# 121 100000 KIP
15.55 g., 0.999 Gold 0.4962 oz. AGW, 27 mm. **Rev:** Cichlasoma fish left

Date	Mintage	F12	VF20	XF40	MS60	MS63
2003	Est. 888	PF65 950				

KM# 95 100000 KIP
15.55 g., 0.999 Gold 0.4963 oz. AGW, 27 mm. **Obv:** State emblem **Rev:** Black Gibbon on holographic background **Edge:** Reeded

Date	Mintage	F12	VF20	XF40	MS60	MS63
2004	888	PF65 950				

KM# 131 100000 KIP
15.55 g., 0.999 Gold 0.4962 oz. AGW, 27 mm. **Rev:** Majestic rooster right , kinegram background

Date	Mintage	F12	VF20	XF40	MS60	MS63
2005	Est. 888	PF65 950				

KM# 134 100000 KIP
15.55 g., 0.999 Gold 0.4962 oz. AGW **Rev:** Mazu seated, waves in background

Date	Mintage	F12	VF20	XF40	MS60	MS63
2005	688	PF65 950				

KM# 141 100000 KIP
15.55 g., 0.999 Gold 0.4962 oz. AGW **Subject:** Year of the Dog

Date	Mintage	F12	VF20	XF40	MS60	MS63
2006	Est. 888	PF65 950				

KM# 143 100000 KIP
15.55 g., 0.999 Gold 0.4962 oz. AGW, 27 mm. **Rev:** Mazu half lenght left

Date	Mintage	F12	VF20	XF40	MS60	MS63
2006	—	PF65 950				

KM# 147 100000 KIP
15.55 g., 0.999 Gold 0.4962 oz. AGW, 27 mm. **Rev:** Buddha in meditation

Date	Mintage	F12	VF20	XF40	MS60	MS63
2006	Est. 688	PF65 950				

KM# 103 100000 KIP
7.78 g., 0.999 Gold 0.2481 oz. AGW, 27 mm. **Subject:** President Print Souphanouvong, 100th Anniversary of Birth **Obv:** Bust facing **Rev:** Presidential Palace

Date	Mintage	F12	VF20	XF40	MS60	MS63
ND (2009)	1,000	PF65 475				

KM# 102 100000 KIP
38.50 g., 0.925 Silver 1.1376 oz. ASW, 36.5 mm. **Subject:** President Print Souphanouvong, 100th Anniversary of Birth **Obv:** Bust facing **Rev:** Presidential Palace

Date	Mintage	F12	VF20	XF40	MS60	MS63
ND (2009)	1,000	PF65 100				

KM# 90 1000000 KIP
155.52 g., 0.9999 Gold 4.9673 oz. AGW, 55 mm. **Subject:** Year of the Horse **Obv:** State emblem **Rev:** Horse with multicolor holographic background **Edge:** Reeded

Date	Mintage	F12	VF20	XF40	MS60	MS63
2002	500	PF65 9,250				

KM# 135 1000000 KIP
155.50 g., 0.999 Gold 4.9623 oz. AGW **Rev:** Mazu seated, waves in background

Date	Mintage	F12	VF20	XF40	MS60	MS63
2005	99	PF65 9,750				

KM# 99 1000000 KIP
155.52 g., 0.9999 Gold 4.9672 oz. AGW, 55.0 mm. **Issuer:** Bank of Lao PDR **Obv:** National arms **Obv. Legend:** THE LAO PEOPLE'S DEMOCRATIC REPUBLIC **Rev:** Multi-latent color bust of Lord Buddha "Fo Guang Pu Zhao" facing with diamond insert in forehead **Edge:** Reeded

Date	Mintage	F12	VF20	XF40	MS60	MS63
2006	99	PF65 9,750				

KM# 144 1000000 KIP
155.50 g., 0.999 Gold 4.9623 oz. AGW **Rev:** Mazu standing

Date	Mintage	F12	VF20	XF40	MS60	MS63
2006	—	PF65 9,750				

PROOF SETS

KM#	Date	Mintage	Identification	Issue Price	Mkt Val
PS7	2000-2001 (3)	3,500	KM#74-76	138	200
PS8	2000-2001 (3)	500	KM#74-76	213	300
PS9	2000-2001 (2)	800	KM#78, 83	—	1,100

LATVIA

The Republic of Latvia, the central Baltic state in east Europe, has an area of 24,749 sq. mi. (43,601 sq. km.) and a population of *2.6 million. Capital: Riga. Livestock raising and manufacturing are the chief industries. Butter, bacon, fertilizers and telephone equipment are exported.

MONETARY SYSTEM
100 Santimu = 1 Lats

MODERN REPUBLIC
1991-present
STANDARD COINAGE

KM# 15 SANTIMS
1.60 g., Copper Clad Steel, 15.65 mm. **Obv:** National arms **Rev:** Value flanked by diamonds below lined arch **Edge:** Plain

Date	Mintage	F12	VF20	XF40	MS60	MS63
2003	30,000,000	—	—	0.10	0.30	0.50
2005	20,000,000	—	—	0.10	0.30	0.50
2007	25,000,000	—	—	0.10	0.30	0.50
2008	75,000,000	—	—	0.10	0.30	0.50

KM# 21 2 SANTIMI
1.90 g., Copper Clad Steel, 17 mm. **Obv:** National arms **Rev:** Lined arch above value flanked by diamonds **Edge:** Plain

Date	Mintage	F12	VF20	XF40	MS60	MS63
2006	18,000,000	—	—	0.20	0.50	0.75
2007	30,000,000	—	—	0.20	0.50	0.75
2009	50,000,000	—	—	0.20	0.50	0.75

KM# 16 5 SANTIMI
2.50 g., Nickel-Brass, 18.5 mm. **Obv:** National arms **Obv. Legend:** LATVIJAS REPUBLIKA **Rev:** Lined arch above value flanked by diamonds **Edge:** Plain

Date	Mintage	F12	VF20	XF40	MS60	MS63
2006	8,000,000	—	—	0.30	0.75	1.00
2007	15,000,000	—	—	0.30	0.75	1.00
2009	10,000,000	—	—	0.30	0.75	1.00

KM# 17 10 SANTIMU
3.25 g., Nickel-Brass, 19.9 mm. **Obv:** National arms **Rev:** Lined arch above value flanked by diamonds **Edge:** Plain

Date	Mintage	F12	VF20	XF40	MS60	MS63
2008	15,000,000	—	—	0.50	1.00	1.50

KM# 22.1 20 SANTIMU
4.00 g., Nickel-Brass, 21.5 mm. **Obv:** National arms **Rev:** Lined arch above value flanked by diamonds **Edge:** Plain **Note:** 1.5mm thick.

Date	Mintage	F12	VF20	XF40	MS60	MS63
2007	7,000,000	—	—	0.50	1.00	2.00
2009	10,000,000	—	—	0.50	1.00	2.00

KM# 13 50 SANTIMU
3.50 g., Copper-Nickel, 18.8 mm. **Obv:** National arms **Rev:** Triple sprig above value **Edge:** Reeded

Date	Mintage	F12	VF20	XF40	MS60	MS63
2007	4,000,000	—	—	2.00	3.00	4.00
2009	5,000,000	—	—	2.00	3.00	4.00

KM# 70 100 SANTIMU
31.47 g., 0.925 Silver 0.9299 oz. ASW, 38.6 mm. **Obv:** Baron von Muenchausen with chain of birds around a dog with a lantern hanging from its tail. **Rev:** Baron von Muenchausen and dog hunting a circle of animals **Edge Lettering:** LATVIJAS BANKA LATVIJAS REPUBLIKA

Date	Mintage	F12	VF20	XF40	MS60	MS63
2005	Est. 5000	PF65 150				

KM# 12 LATS
4.80 g., Copper-Nickel, 21.75 mm. **Obv:** Arms with supporters **Rev:** Salmon above value **Edge Lettering:** LATVIJAS BANKA • LATVIJAS BANKA

Date	Mintage	F12	VF20	XF40	MS60	MS63
2007	7,000,000	—	—	2.00	4.00	7.00
2008	25,000,000	—	—	2.00	4.00	7.00

KM# 49 LATS
31.47 g., 0.925 Silver 0.9299 oz. ASW, 38.6 mm. **Subject:** Hanseatic City of Cesis **Obv:** City arms **Rev:** Sailing ship above, inverted walled city view below **Edge Lettering:** LATVIJAS REPUBLIKA • LATVIJAS BANKA

Date	Mintage	F12	VF20	XF40	MS60	MS63
2001	Est. 15000	PF63 55.00	PF65 75.00			

KM# 50 LATS
31.47 g., 0.925 Silver 0.9299 oz. ASW. **Series:** Ice Hockey **Obv:** Arms with supporters **Rev:** Hockey player

Date	Mintage	F12	VF20	XF40	MS60	MS63
2001	Est. 15000	PF65 90.00				

KM# 51 LATS
31.47 g., 0.925 Silver 0.9299 oz. ASW, 38.6 mm. **Subject:** Heaven **Obv:** Stylized design **Rev:** Stylized woman holding sun **Edge:** Plain

Date	Mintage	F12	VF20	XF40	MS60	MS63
2001	—	PF65 125				

KM# 54 LATS
4.80 g., Copper-Nickel, 21.75 mm. **Obv:** Arms with supporters **Rev:** Nesting stork above value **Edge Lettering:** LATVIJAS BANKA • LATVIJAS BANKA

Date	Mintage	F12	VF20	XF40	MS60	MS63
2001	250,000	—	—	7.00	12.00	15.00

KM# 52 LATS
31.47 g., 0.925 Silver 0.9299 oz. ASW, 38.6 mm. **Subject:** Destiny **Obv:** Stylized design **Rev:** Apple tree and landscape **Edge:** Plain

Date	Mintage	F12	VF20	XF40	MS60	MS63
2002	Est. 5000	PF65 150				

KM# 53 LATS
31.47 g., 0.925 Silver 0.9299 oz. ASW, 38.6 mm. **Subject:** Hanseatic City of Kuldiga **Obv:** City arms **Rev:** City view and ships **Edge:** Lettered

Date	Mintage	F12	VF20	XF40	MS60	MS63
2002	Est. 15000	PF63 65.00	PF65 75.00			

KM# 55 LATS

31.47 g., 0.925 Silver 0.9299 oz. ASW, 38.6 mm. **Subject:** National Library **Obv:** Country name and diamonds pattern **Rev:** Library building sketch and diamonds design **Edge Lettering:** GAISMU SAUCA • GAISMA AUSA

Date	Mintage	F12	VF20	XF40	MS60	MS63
2002	Est. 5000		PF63 65.00	PF65 75.00		

KM# 56 LATS

15.00 g., 0.925 Silver 0.4432 oz. ASW, 28 mm. **Subject:** Coin of Fortune **Obv:** Totally gold plated sun above country name **Rev:** Waning moon, date and value **Edge:** Plain

Date	Mintage	F12	VF20	XF40	MS60	MS63
2002	Est. 5000	PF65 250				

KM# 57 LATS

31.47 g., 0.925 Silver 0.9299 oz. ASW, 38.6 mm. **Subject:** Olympics 2004 **Obv:** Arms with supporters **Rev:** Ancient wrestlers **Edge Lettering:** LATVIJAS BANKA • LATVIJAS BANKA

Date	Mintage	F12	VF20	XF40	MS60	MS63
2002	Est. 26000		PF63 60.00	PF65 70.00		

KM# 60 LATS

31.47 g., 0.925 Silver 0.9299 oz. ASW, 38.6 mm. **Subject:** Courland **Obv:** Crowned arms above partially built ship **Rev:** Hemp weighing scene with Iron foundry and brick wall in background **Edge Lettering:** LATVIJAS REPUBLIKA • LATVIJAS BANKA

Date	Mintage	F12	VF20	XF40	MS60	MS63
2003	Est. 5000	PF65 80.00				

KM# 71 LATS

31.47 g., 0.925 Silver 0.9299 oz. ASW, 38.6 mm. **Subject:** Vidzeme **Obv:** Crowned arms above horse drawn wagon **Rev:** Two men sawing wood **Edge Lettering:** LATVIJAS BANKA • LATVIJAS REPUBLIKA

Date	Mintage	F12	VF20	XF40	MS60	MS63
ND (2003)		PF65 75.00				
2004		PF65 75.00				

KM# 72 LATS

31.47 g., 0.925 Silver 0.9299 oz. ASW, 38.6 mm. **Subject:** Latgale **Obv:** Madonna and Child above landscape **Rev:** Man sowing seeds and an angel **Edge Lettering:** LATVIJAS BANKA • LATVIJAS REPUBLIKA

Date	Mintage	F12	VF20	XF40	MS60	MS63
ND (2003)	—	PF65 75.00				
2004	Est. 5000	PF65 75.00				

KM# 75 LATS

31.47 g., 0.925 Silver 0.9299 oz. ASW, 38.61 mm. **Subject:** Hanseatic City of Valmiera **Obv:** Coat of arms **Rev:** St. Simanis Church with VALMIERA and reflection of sailing ship **Edge:** LATVIJAS REPUBLIKA • LATVIJAS BANKA

Date	Mintage	F12	VF20	XF40	MS60	MS63
2003	Est. 15000		PF63 55.00	PF65 65.00		

KM# 58 LATS

4.80 g., Copper-Nickel, 21.75 mm. **Obv:** Arms with supporters **Rev:** Ant above value **Edge Lettering:** LATVIJAS BANKA • LATVIJAS BANKA

Date	Mintage	F12	VF20	XF40	MS60	MS63
2003	250,000	—	5.00	6.50	8.00	

KM# 64 LATS

31.47 g., 0.925 Silver 0.9299 oz. ASW, 38.6 mm. **Subject:** Latvian European Union Membership **Obv:** Arms with supporters **Rev:** P.S. LATVIJA-ES 2004 above value **Edge Lettering:** LATVIJAS BANKA • LATVIJAS BANKA

Date	Mintage	F12	VF20	XF40	MS60	MS63
2004	Est. 15000		PF63 75.00	PF65 85.00		

KM# 61 LATS

4.80 g., Copper-Nickel, 21.75 mm. **Obv:** Arms with supporters **Rev:** Spriditis with shovel above value **Edge Lettering:**

LATVIJAS BANKA • LATVIJAS BANKA

Date	Mintage	F12	VF20	XF40	MS60	MS63
2004	500,000			3.00	4.00	6.00

KM# 62 LATS

17.15 g., Bi-Metallic, 34 mm. **Subject:** Coin of Time **Obv:** Heraldic Rose **Rev:** Clock dial in center, rings of hours, minutes, months and days around **Edge:** Plain

Date	Mintage	F12	VF20	XF40	MS60	MS63
2004	Est. 5000					450

KM# 63 LATS

31.47 g., 0.925 Silver 0.9299 oz. ASW, 38.6 mm. **Obv:** Arms with supporters **Rev:** World Cup Soccer player **Edge Lettering:** LATVIJA three times

Date	Mintage	F12	VF20	XF40	MS60	MS63
2004	Est. 50000		PF63 60.00	PF65 70.00		

KM# 67 LATS

4.80 g., Copper-Nickel, 21.75 mm. **Obv:** National arms **Obv. Legend:** LATVIJAS REPUBLIKA **Rev:** Mushroom above value **Edge Lettering:** LATVIJAS BANKA • LATVIJAS BANKA

Date	Mintage	F12	VF20	XF40	MS60	MS63
2004	500,000	—	—	3.00	4.00	6.00

KM# 65 LATS

4.80 g., Copper-Nickel, 21.75 mm. **Obv:** Arms with supporters **Rev:** Weathercock (from the spire of Riga's St. Peter Church) above value **Edge Lettering:** LATVIJAS BANKA • LATVIJAS BANKA

Date	Mintage	F12	VF20	XF40	MS60	MS63
2005	500,000	—	—	3.00	6.00	8.00

KM# 68 LATS

31.47 g., 0.925 Silver 0.9299 oz. ASW, 38.6 mm. **Subject:**

Janis Plieksans "Rainis **Obv:** Mountains and value **Rev:** Laser picture of Rainis the mountain climbing poet, dramatist and patriot. **Edge Lettering:** LATVIJAS BANKA • LATVIJAS REPUBLIKA

Date	Mintage	F12	VF20	XF40	MS60	MS63
2005	Est. 5000	PF65 55.00				

KM# 69 LATS
31.47 g., 0.925 Silver 0.9299 oz. ASW, 38.6 mm. **Obv:** National arms **Rev:** Bobsled **Edge Lettering:** LATVIJA (three times)

Date	Mintage	F12	VF20	XF40	MS60	MS63
2005	Est. 15000	PF65 50.00				

KM# 76 LATS
31.47 g., 0.925 Silver 0.9299 oz. ASW, 38.61 mm. **Subject:** Ice Hockey World Championship **Obv:** Large coat of arms, date below **Rev:** Two hockey players viewed from above, RIGA 2006 on either side with hockey puck in center **Edge Lettering:** LATVIJA (three times)

Date	Mintage	F12	VF20	XF40	MS60	MS63
2005		PF65 65.00				

KM# 77 LATS
31.47 g., 0.925 Silver 0.9299 oz. ASW, 38.61 mm. **Subject:** Hanseatic City of Koknese **Obv:** Coat of arms **Rev:** Koknese castle on top with moon and sun on sides, reflection of Hanseatic Castle and ship on bottom **Edge Lettering:** LATVIJAS REPUBLIKA • LATVIJAS BANKA

Date	Mintage	F12	VF20	XF40	MS60	MS63
2005	Est. 15000	PF63 55.00	PF65 75.00			

KM# 81 LATS
1.24 g., 0.9999 Gold 0.0397 oz. AGW, 13.92 mm. **Subject:** Art Nouveau **Obv:** Ribbon design **Obv. Legend:** RIGAS / LATVIJAS REPUBLIKA **Rev:** Stone face **Edge:** Reeded

Date	Mintage	F12	VF20	XF40	MS60	MS63
2005	Est. 20000	PF65 100				

KM# 66 LATS
4.80 g., Copper-Nickel, 21.75 mm. **Obv:** National arms **Obv. Legend:** LATVIJAS REPUBLIKA **Rev:** Pretzel above value **Edge Lettering:** LATVIJAS BANKA • LATVIJAS BANKA

Date	Mintage	F12	VF20	XF40	MS60	MS63
2005	500,000	—	—	3.00	4.00	6.00

KM# 73 LATS
4.80 g., Copper-Nickel, 21.75 mm. **Subject:** Summer Solstice

Obv: National arms **Rev:** Head wearing Ligo wreath above value **Edge Lettering:** LATVIJAS BANKA • LATVIJAS BANKA

Date	Mintage	F12	VF20	XF40	MS60	MS63
2006	500,000	—	—	3.00	4.00	6.00

KM# 74 LATS
4.80 g., Copper-Nickel, 21.75 mm. **Obv:** National arms **Rev:** Pine cone above value **Edge Lettering:** LATVIJAS BANKA • LATVIJAS BANKA

Date	Mintage	F12	VF20	XF40	MS60	MS63
2006	1,000,000	—	—	3.00	5.00	6.00

KM# 78 LATS
31.47 g., 0.925 Silver 0.9299 oz. ASW, 38.61 mm. **Subject:** The Barricades of January 1991 **Obv:** Stylized bonfire flames **Obv. Legend:** janvāris 1991 **Rev:** Latvian mythological hero with raised sword against the background of concrete block barricades, rising sun behind **Edge Lettering:** LATVIJAS BANKA (twice)

Date	Mintage	F12	VF20	XF40	MS60	MS63
2006	Est. 5000	PF65 65.00				

KM# 79 LATS
31.47 g., 0.925 Silver 0.9299 oz. ASW, 38.61 mm. **Subject:** Krisjanis Barons **Obv:** Starry sky on left with value on right side **Rev:** Portrait of Barons on right side and starry sky on left **Edge Lettering:** LATVIJAS BANKA • LATVIJAS REPUBLIKA

Date	Mintage	F12	VF20	XF40	MS60	MS63
2006	Est. 5000	PF65 65.00				

KM# 80 LATS
31.47 g., 0.925 Silver 0.9299 oz. ASW, 38.61 mm. **Subject:** Krishjanis Valdemars **Obv:** Seagul flying above water on left, value on right **Rev:** Portrait of Valdemars on right with sea on left **Edge Lettering:** LATVIJAS BANKA • LATVIJAS REPUBLIKA

Date	Mintage	F12	VF20	XF40	MS60	MS63
2006	—	PF65 65.00				

KM# 82 LATS
31.47 g., 0.925 Silver 0.9299 oz. ASW, 38.61 mm. **Subject:** Fight for Freedom **Obv:** Outline of Latvia with three stars above **Obv. Inscription:** LATVIJAS REPUBLIKA **Rev:** Two crossed swords outlined against the sun **Rev. Inscription:** NO ZOBENA SAULE LECA **Edge:** Plain

Date	Mintage	F12	VF20	XF40	MS60	MS63
2006	Est. 5000	PF65 65.00				

KM# 83 LATS
31.47 g., 0.925 Silver 0.9299 oz. ASW, 38.61 mm. **Subject:** Hanseatic City of Straupe **Obv:** Coat of arms, date and value below **Obv. Inscription:** ROOP / 1 LATS **Rev:** Lielstraupe castle church top, reflection of Hanseatic ship with trees on both sides on bottom **Edge Lettering:** LATVIJAS REPUBLIKA • LATVIJAS BANKA

Date	Mintage	F12	VF20	XF40	MS60	MS63
2006	Est. 15000	PF65 55.00				

KM# 84 LATS
27.00 g., 0.999 Silver 0.8616 oz. ASW, 38.61 mm. **Subject:** Coin of Digits **Obv:** Arabic O at center against an oriental background **Rev:** Roman I at center **Shape:** 7-sided

Date	Mintage	F12	VF20	XF40	MS60	MS63
2006	2,007	PF65 550				

KM# 85 LATS
4.80 g., Copper-Nickel, 21.75 mm. **Obv:** National arms **Obv. Legend:** LATVIJAS REPUBLIKA **Rev:** Snowman **Edge Lettering:** LATVIJAS BANKA • LATVIJAS BANKA

Date	Mintage	F12	VF20	XF40	MS60	MS63
2007	1,000,000	—	—	3.00	4.00	6.00

KM# 86 LATS
4.80 g., Copper-Nickel, 21.75 mm. **Obv:** National arms **Obv. Legend:** LATVIJAS REPUBLIKA **Rev:** Medieval owl figurine **Edge Lettering:** LATVIJAS BANKA • LATVIJAS BANKA

Date	Mintage	F12	VF20	XF40	MS60	MS63
2007	1,000,000	—	—	2.00	5.00	7.00

KM# 87 LATS
31.47 g., 0.925 Silver 0.9299 oz. ASW, 38.6 mm. **Subject:** Foreign Rulers **Obv:** Fragment of a large coat of arms **Rev:** Large coat of arms broken into fragments **Edge:** Plain

Date	Mintage	F12	VF20	XF40	MS60	MS63
2007	—	PF65 65.00				

KM# 88 LATS
31.47 g., 0.925 Silver 0.9299 oz. ASW, 38.6 mm. **Subject:** Rebirth of the State **Obv:** Large coat of arms **Rev:** Sun with its rays forming the red-white-red flag of the Republic **Edge:** Plain

Date	Mintage	F12	VF20	XF40	MS60	MS63
2007	Est. 5000	PF65 65.00				

KM# 89 LATS
31.47 g., 0.925 Silver 0.9299 oz. ASW, 38.6 mm. **Subject:** Sigulda **Obv:** Horse and sword within pendant **Rev:** Gauja Valley with the Turaida Castle and Sigulda Castle **Edge Lettering:** LATVIJAS REPUBLIKA • LATVIJAS BANKA

Date	Mintage	F12	VF20	XF40	MS60	MS63
2007	Est. 5000	PF65 55.00				

KM# 90 LATS
17.15 g., Bi-Metallic, 34 mm. **Subject:** Coin of Time II **Obv:** Heraldic rose at center **Rev:** Outer ring signs of the zodiac, inner circle different evolutionary stages of the plant world **Edge:** Plain

Date	Mintage	F12	VF20	XF40	MS60	MS63
2007	7,000	—	—	—	—	175

KM# 91 LATS
1.24 g., 0.999 Gold 0.0397 oz. AGW, 13.92 mm. **Obv:** Small coat of arms **Rev:** Logo of the publishing house Zelta abele **Edge:** Reeded

Date	Mintage	F12	VF20	XF40	MS60	MS63
2007	Est. 15000	PF63 95.00	PF65 125			

KM# 97 LATS
31.47 g., 0.925 Silver 0.9299 oz. ASW, 38.6 mm. **Subject:** Coin of life **Obv:** Mother holding gilt wrapped child **Rev:** Golden heart-shaped leaves **Edge:** Plain

Date	Mintage	F12	VF20	XF40	MS60	MS63
2007	5,000	PF65 185				

KM# 98 LATS
22.00 g., 0.925 Silver 0.6501 oz. ASW, 35 mm. **Subject:** Lucky Coin **Obv:** Cat pearched on rooftop peak **Rev:** Chimney-sweep with ladder and rope coil with bruch and weight. **Edge Lettering:** LATVIJAS BANKA • LATVIJAS BANKA

Date	Mintage	F12	VF20	XF40	MS60	MS63
2008	5,000	PF65 65.00				

KM# 99 LATS
31.47 g., 0.925 Silver 0.9299 oz. ASW, 38.6 mm. **Subject:** 90th Anniversary of Statehood **Obv:** First Arms of the Republic **Rev:** Two children holding multicolor flag **Edge Lettering:** LATVIJAS BANKA (twice)

Date	Mintage	F12	VF20	XF40	MS60	MS63
2008	5,000	PF65 95.00				

KM# 93a LATS
31.47 g., 0.925 Silver 0.9299 oz. ASW, 38.61 mm. **Obv:** Woman walking holding wheat **Rev:** Man walking holding flowers **Edge Lettering:** DZIESMAI SODIEN LIELA DIENA

Date	Mintage	F12	VF20	XF40	MS60	MS63
2008	10,000	PF65 75.00				

KM# 92 LATS
4.80 g., Copper-Nickel, 21.75 mm. **Obv:** National arms **Obv. Legend:** LATVIJAS REPUBLIKA **Rev:** Water Lily **Edge Lettering:** LATVIJAS BANKA • LATVIJAS BANKA

Date	Mintage	F12	VF20	XF40	MS60	MS63
2008	1,000,000	—	—	3.00	4.00	6.00

KM# 93 LATS
12.40 g., Copper-Nickel, 30 mm. **Obv:** Woman walking holding wheat **Rev:** Man walking holding flowers **Edge Lettering:** DZIESMAI SODIEN LIELA DIENA

Date	Mintage	F12	VF20	XF40	MS60	MS63
2008	30,000	—	—	7.00	9.00	

KM# 94 LATS
31.47 g., 0.925 Silver 0.9299 oz. ASW, 38.61 mm. **Subject:** Hanseatic City of Limbazi **Obv:** Hanseatic city seal with coat of arms **Rev:** Limbazi Castle ruins and St. Johns Church with reflection of Hanseatic Ship on lower half **Edge Lettering:** LATVIJAS REPUBLIKA • LATVIJAS BANKA

Date	Mintage	F12	VF20	XF40	MS60	MS63
2008	15,000	PF65 65.00				

KM# 95 LATS
31.47 g., 0.925 Silver 0.9299 oz. ASW, 38.6 mm. **Subject:** Basketball **Obv:** Three stars and stylized basket ball design **Rev:** Two basketball players and a jump shot **Edge Lettering:** LATVIJAS BANKA • LATVIJAS REPUBLIKA

Date	Mintage	F12	VF20	XF40	MS60	MS63
2008	5,000	PF65 80.00				

KM# 107 LATS
4.80 g., Copper-Nickel, 21.75 mm. **Obv:** National arms **Rev:** Chimney sweep standing with brush and ladder **Edge Lettering:** LATVIJAS BANKA • LATVIJAS BANKA

Date	Mintage	F12	VF20	XF40	MS60	MS63
2008	1,000,000	—	—	—	5.00	6.00

KM# 101 LATS
4.80 g., Copper-Nickel, 21.75 mm. **Obv:** National Arms **Rev:** Namejs ring **Edge Lettering:** LATVIJAS BANKA • LATVIJAS BANKA

Date	Mintage	F12	VF20	XF40	MS60	MS63
2009	1,000,000	—	—	3.00	5.00	6.00

KM# 100 LATS
20.00 g., 0.925 Silver 0.591 oz. ASW, 34 mm. **Subject:** Children's drawing contest - My Dream Coin **Obv:** State Arms **Rev:** Piglet right **Edge Lettering:** LATVIJAS BANKA • LATVIJAS BANKA

Date	Mintage	F12	VF20	XF40	MS60	MS63
2009	5,000	PF65 70.00				

KM# 102 LATS
31.47 g., 0.925 Silver 0.9299 oz. ASW, 38.6 mm. **Subject:** Time of the Land-Surveyors, Novel's 130th Anniversary **Obv:** Brali Kaudzites standing **Rev:** Six figures form novel, forming spokes of wheel **Edge Lettering:** LATVIJAS REPUBLICA • LATVIJAS BANKA

Date	Mintage	F12	VF20	XF40	MS60	MS63
2009	7,000	PF65 60.00				

KM# 103 LATS
31.47 g., 0.925 Silver 0.9299 oz. ASW, 38.6 mm. **Subject:** University of Latvia **Obv:** Oak tree within wreath, partially minted photo image **Rev:** Owl standing on open book, University building in background **Edge Lettering:** VIVAT • CRESCAT • FLOREAT

Date	Mintage	F12	VF20	XF40	MS60	MS63
2009	7,000	PF65 70.00				

KM# 104 LATS
26.00 g., 0.925 Silver 0.7682 oz. ASW, 32x32 mm. **Subject:** Coin of Water **Obv:** Water droplets **Rev:** Snowflake crystal **Edge:** Plain **Shape:** Square

Date	Mintage	F12	VF20	XF40	MS60	MS63
2009	7,000	PF65 125				

KM# 105 LATS
22.00 g., 0.925 Silver 0.6501 oz. ASW, 35 mm. **Subject:** Christmas Tree, 500th Anniversary **Obv:** Three children in folktale costumes **Rev:** Man walking with cut tree in moonlight, squirrel jumping from tree **Edge Lettering:** LATVIJAS BANKA • LATVIJAS REPUBLIKA

Date	Mintage	F12	VF20	XF40	MS60	MS63
2009	20,000	PF65 60.00				

KM# 106 LATS
4.80 g., Copper-Nickel, 21.75 mm. **Obv:** National Arms **Rev:** Christmas tree, heart as ornament **Edge Lettering:** LATVIJAS BANKA • LATVIJAS BANKA

Date	Mintage	F12	VF20	XF40	MS60	MS63
2009	1,000,000	—	—	—	4.00	6.00

KM# 108 LATS
4.80 g., Copper-Nickel, 21.75 mm. **Obv:** National arms **Rev:** Toad **Edge Lettering:** LATVIJAS BANKA • LATVIJAS BANKA

Date	Mintage	F12	VF20	XF40	MS60	MS63
2010	1,000,000	—	—	—	4.00	5.00

KM# 109 LATS
20.70 g., 0.925 Silver 0.6116 oz. ASW, 35 mm. **Subject:** Amber Coin **Obv:** Amber stone on seashore **Rev:** Eye with amber as pupil **Edge:** Plain

Date	Mintage	F12	VF20	XF40	MS60	MS63
2010	7,000	PF65 150				

KM# 110 LATS
12.40 g., Copper-Nickel, 30 mm. **Subject:** The Latvian ABC Book **Obv:** Cock **Rev:** Teacher with students **Edge Lettering:** LATVIJAS BANKA • LATVIJAS REPUBLIKA

Date	Mintage	F12	VF20	XF40	MS60	MS63
2010	10,000	—	—	—	—	10.00

KM# 111 LATS
31.47 g., 0.925 Silver 0.9299 oz. ASW, 38.61 mm. **Subject:** Latvian ABC Book **Obv:** Cock **Rev:** Teacher and students **Edge Lettering:** LATVIJAS BANKA • LATVIJAS REPUBLIKA

Date	Mintage	F12	VF20	XF40	MS60	MS63
2010	5,000	PF65 80.00				

KM# 112 LATS
31.47 g., 0.925 Silver 0.9299 oz. ASW, 38.61 mm. **Subject:** Duke Jacob, 400th Anniversary of birth **Obv:** Bust right, value at bottom **Rev:** Arms **Edge Lettering:** LATVIJAS REPUBLIKA • LATVIJAS BANKA

Date	Mintage	F12	VF20	XF40	MS60	MS63
2010	5,000	PF65 70.00				

KM# 113 LATS
31.47 g., 0.925 Silver 0.9299 oz. ASW, 38.61 mm. **Subject:** Declaration of Independence, 20th Anniversary **Obv:** Three small buds, red in color **Rev:** Elderly female with yoke of oppression **Edge Lettering:** LATVIJAS BANKA (twice)

Date	Mintage	F12	VF20	XF40	MS60	MS63
2010	7,000	PF65 60.00				

KM# 114 LATS
17.15 g., Bi-Metallic, 34 mm. **Subject:** Coin of Time III **Obv:** Heraldic Rose **Rev:** Forests, fields, rocks and water in center, eight lunar phases around **Edge:** Plain

Date	Mintage	F12	VF20	XF40	MS60	MS63
2010	7,000	—	—	—	—	100

KM# 117 LATS
4.80 g., Copper-Nickel, 21.75 mm. **Obv:** National arms **Rev:** Horseshoe with open end upwards **Edge Lettering:** LATVIJAS BANKA • LATVIJAS BANKA

Date	Mintage	F12	VF20	XF40	MS60	MS63
2010	500,000	—	—	—	5.00	6.00

KM# 118 LATS
4.80 g., Copper-Nickel, 21.75 mm. **Obv:** Naitonal arms **Rev:** Horseshoe with open end downwards **Edge Lettering:** LATVIJAS BANKA • LATVIJAS BANKA

Date	Mintage	F12	VF20	XF40	MS60	MS63
2010	500,000	—	—	—	5.00	6.00

KM# 119 LATS
4.80 g., Copper-Nickel, 21.75 mm. **Obv:** National arms **Rev:** Beer stein **Edge Lettering:** LATVIJAS BANKA • LATVIJAS BANKA

Date	Mintage	F12	VF20	XF40	MS60	MS63
2011	1,000,000	—	—	—	5.00	6.00

KM# 120 LATS
26.00 g., 0.925 Silver 0.7682 oz. ASW, 32x32 mm. **Subject:** Aleksandris Caks **Obv:** Window, glass with imprints of lips and leaves **Rev:** Cobble-stone paving, leave with lips imprint

Date	Mintage	F12	VF20	XF40	MS60	MS63
2011	7,000	PF65 85.00				

KM# 121 LATS
31.47 g., 0.925 Silver 0.9299 oz. ASW, 38.61 mm. **Subject:** Rundale Palace **Obv:** Arms of Earl Ernst Johann von Biron **Rev:** Ariel view of the palace and gardens

Date	Mintage	F12	VF20	XF40	MS60	MS63
2011	5,000	PF63 45.00	PF65 65.00			

KM# 122 LATS
31.47 g., 0.925 Silver 0.9299 oz. ASW, 38.61 mm. **Subject:** Hansa Cities - Riga **Obv:** Riga arms, gothic ornaments flanking **Rev:** Riga city view at top, Hanseatic ship inverted below

Date	Mintage	F12	VF20	XF40	MS60	MS63
2011	15,000	PF63 45.00	PF65 65.00			

KM# 123 LATS
22.00 g., 0.925 Silver 0.6501 oz. ASW, 35 mm. **Subject:** Riga Cathedral **Obv:** Angel at left **Rev:** Cross at left, cathedral exterior at right

Date	Mintage	F12	VF20	XF40	MS60	MS63
2011	5,000	PF65 70.00				

KM# 124 LATS
12.50 g., 0.925 Silver 0.3693 oz. ASW, 28 mm. **Subject:** Riga coinage, 800th Anniversary **Obv:** Pfennig of Bishop Albert (1198-1229) - Bishop in mitre **Rev:** Pfennig of Bishop Albert on frosted surface

Date	Mintage	F12	VF20	XF40	MS60	MS63
2011	5,000	PF65 55.00				

KM# 125 LATS
22.00 g., 0.925 Silver 0.6501 oz. ASW, 35 mm. **Subject:** Railways in Latvia, 50th Anniversary **Obv:** Steam locomotive's drive wheel **Rev:** Steam locomotive profile

Date	Mintage	F12	VF20	XF40	MS60	MS63
2011	5,000	PF65 60.00				

KM# 126 LATS
Bi-Metallic, 35 mm. **Subject:** Granite Stone **Obv:** Country name at top, denomination at bottom **Rev:** National folk ornamentation

Date	Mintage	F12	VF20	XF40	MS60	MS63
2011	7,000	PF65 75.00				

KM# 127 LATS
4.80 g., Copper-Nickel, 21.75 mm. **Obv:** National arms with supporters **Rev:** Gingerbread heart **Edge Lettering:** LATVIJAS BANKA • LATVIJAS BANKA

Date	Mintage	F12	VF20	XF40	MS60	MS63
2011	1,000,000			—	5.00	6.00

KM# 128 LATS
22.00 g., 0.925 Silver 0.6501 oz. ASW, 35 mm. **Subject:** Latvia's participation in the 2012 London Olympics **Obv:** Three Latvian runners right **Rev:** Three ancient Greek runners right

Date	Mintage	F12	VF20	XF40	MS60	MS63
2012	5,000	PF65 65.00				

KM# 129 LATS
22.00 g., 0.925 Silver 0.6501 oz. ASW, 35 mm. **Subject:** Riga Zoo, 100th Anniversary **Obv:** Zoo entrance gate and exotic animals **Rev:** Seven animal figures **Edge Lettering:** LATVIJAS BANKA • LATVIJAS REPUBLIKA • 2012

Date	Mintage	F12	VF20	XF40	MS60	MS63
2012	5,000	PF65 75.00				

KM# 131 LATS
26.00 g., 0.925 Silver 0.7682 oz. ASW, 32x32 mm. **Subject:** Riga Technical University, 150th Anniversary **Obv:** Curved guage and mm scale **Rev:** Town view, gilt dividers and drafting triangle **Note:** Two-part.

Date	Mintage	F12	VF20	XF40	MS60	MS63
2012	3,000	PF65 175				

KM# 132 LATS
22.00 g., 0.925 Silver 0.6501 oz. ASW, 35 mm. **Subject:** K. Zale **Obv:** Head left **Rev:** Sculpture: Dying Horseman I **Edge Lettering:** LATVIJAS BANKA • LATVIJAS REPUBLIKA • 2012

Date	Mintage	F12	VF20	XF40	MS60	MS63
2012	7,000	PF65 65.00				

KM# 133 LATS
22.00 g., 0.925 Silver 0.6501 oz. ASW, 35 mm. **Subject:** Latvian National Traditions

Date	Mintage	F12	VF20	XF40	MS60	MS63
2012	5,000	PF65 65.00				

KM# 134 LATS
22.00 g., 0.925 Silver 0.6501 oz. ASW, 35 mm. **Subject:** K. Blaumanis

Date	Mintage	F12	VF20	XF40	MS60	MS63
2012	3,000	PF65 70.00				

KM# 135 LATS
4.80 g., Copper-Nickel, 21.75 mm. **Subject:** Hedgehog **Obv:** National arms **Rev:** Hedgehog **Edge Lettering:** LATVIJAS BANKA • LATVIJAS BANKA

Date	Mintage	F12	VF20	XF40	MS60	MS63
2012	1,000,000		—		4.00	5.00

KM# 136 LATS
4.80 g., Copper-Nickel, 21.75 mm. **Subject:** Christmas Bells **Obv:** National arms **Rev:** Christmas bells **Edge Lettering:** LATVIJAS BANKA • LATVIJAS BANKA

Date	Mintage	F12	VF20	XF40	MS60	MS63
2012	1,000,000	—		—	4.00	5.00

KM# 137 LATS
22.00 g., 0.925 Silver 0.6501 oz. ASW, 35 mm. **Subject:** Rudolfs Blaumanis - 150th Anniversary of Birth **Obv:** Horse in the woods **Rev:** Portrait and writing

Date	Mintage	F12	VF20	XF40	MS60	MS63
2013	Est. 7000	PF65 30.00				

KM# 139 LATS
22.00 g., 0.925 Silver 0.6501 oz. ASW, 35 mm. **Obv:** bird holding basket with baby **Rev:** Mouse pulling a cart **Edge:** Lettered

Date	Mintage	F12	VF20	XF40	MS60	MS63
2013	—	PF65 25.00				

KM# 140 LATS
22.00 g., 0.925 Silver 0.6501 oz. ASW, 35 mm. **Subject:** Richard Wagner, 100th Anniversary of Birth **Obv:** Profile left, horn flowing into flower **Rev:** Ship in stormy seas **Edge:** Lettered

Date	Mintage	F12	VF20	XF40	MS60	MS63
2013	—	PF65 25.00				

KM# 141 LATS
22.00 g., 0.925 Silver 0.6501 oz. ASW, 35 mm. **Subject:** Jazeps Vitols, 150th Anniversary of Birth **Obv:** Profile bust left **Rev:** Group of five rays of light **Edge:** Lettered

Date	Mintage	F12	VF20	XF40	MS60	MS63
2013	—	PF65 25.00				

KM# 142 LATS
4.80 g., Copper-Nickel, 21.75 mm. **Obv:** National Arms **Rev:** Kokle, folk instrument

Date	Mintage	F12	VF20	XF40	MS60	MS63
2013	—	—	—	—	4.00	5.00

KM# 143 LATS
16.40 g., 0.925 Silver 0.4846 oz. ASW, 30 mm. **Subject:** Last Lats

Date	Mintage	F12	VF20	XF40	MS60	MS63
2013	5,000	PF65 45.00				

KM# 144 LATS
1.24 g., 0.9999 Gold 0.0397 oz. AGW, 13.92 mm. **Subject:** Oh Holy Listene **Obv:** Acanthus leaf design from the side décor of altar of the Lestene church **Rev:** Head of an angel from the altar of the Lestene church

Date	Mintage	F12	VF20	XF40	MS60	MS63
2013	5,000	PF65 85.00				

KM# 38 2 LATI
9.50 g., Bi-Metallic, 26.3 mm. **Obv:** Arms with supporters within circle **Rev:** Cow above value within circle **Edge Lettering:** LATVIJAS BANKA

Date	Mintage	F12	VF20	XF40	MS60	MS63
2003 In sets only	30,000	—	—	—	—	12.00
2009	2,000,000	—	—	7.00	8.00	9.00

KM# 59 5 LATI
1.24 g., 0.9999 Gold 0.0397 oz. AGW, 13.92 mm. **Obv:** Bust right **Rev:** Arms with supporters above value **Edge:** Reeded **Note:** Remake of the popular KM-9 design

Date	Mintage	F12	VF20	XF40	MS60	MS63
2003	Est. 20000	PF65 125				

KM# 130 5 LATI
25.00 g., 0.925 Silver 0.7387 oz. ASW, 37 mm. **Subject:** Bank of Latvia and national currency, 90th Anniversary **Obv:** Female head in national costume right **Rev:** National arms **Edge Lettering:** DIEVS SVETI LATVIJS

Date	Mintage	F12	VF20	XF40	MS60	MS63
2012	Est. 10000	PF65 125				

KM# 138 20 LATU
11.00 g., 0.925 Silver 0.325 oz. ASW, 21.75 mm. **Subject:** 20th Anniversary of the return of Lats coinage **Obv:** National arms **Rev:** Salmon **Edge:** Lettered

Date	Mintage	F12	VF20	XF40	MS60	MS63
2013	—	PF65 15.00				

KM# 96 20 LATI
10.00 g., 0.999 Gold 0.3191 oz. AGW, 22 mm. **Obv:** Woman's head covered with scarf **Rev:** Vessel with a milk bottle, apple, jug of milk, bread & knife on table

Date	Mintage	F12	VF20	XF40	MS60	MS63
2008	5,000	—	—	—	—	750

EURO COINAGE

KM# 150 EURO CENT
2.30 g., Copper Plated Steel, 16.25 mm. **Obv:** National shield, three stars above **Rev:** Value and globe **Edge:** Plain

Date	Mintage	F12	VF20	XF40	MS60	MS63
2014	—	—	—	—	0.25	0.35

KM# 151 2 EURO CENT
3.06 g., Copper Plated Steel, 18.75 mm. **Obv:** National shield, three stars above **Rev:** Value and globe

Date	Mintage	F12	VF20	XF40	MS60	MS63
2014	—	—	—	—	0.25	0.35

KM# 152 5 EURO CENT
3.92 g., Copper Plated Steel, 21.25 mm. **Obv:** National shield, three stars above **Rev:** Value and globe

Date	Mintage	F12	VF20	XF40	MS60	MS63
2014	—	—	—	—	0.25	0.35

KM# 153 10 EURO CENT
4.10 g., Brass, 19.75 mm. **Obv:** National arms **Rev:** Relief map of Western Europe; stars, lines and value **Edge:** Reeded

Date	Mintage	F12	VF20	XF40	MS60	MS63
2014	—	—	—	—	0.75	1.00

KM# 154 20 EURO CENT
5.74 g., Brass, 22.25 mm. **Obv:** National arms **Rev:** Relief map of Western Europe; stars, lines and value **Edge:** Notched

Date	Mintage	F12	VF20	XF40	MS60	MS63
2014	—	—	—	—	0.75	1.00

KM# 155 50 EURO CENT
7.80 g., Brass, 24.25 mm. **Obv:** National arms **Rev:** Relief map of Western Europe; stars, lines and value

Date	Mintage	F12	VF20	XF40	MS60	MS63
2014	—	—	—	—	0.75	1.00

KM# 156 EURO
7.50 g., Bi-Metallic, 23.25 mm. **Obv:** Female head in national costume right **Rev:** Value and map; stars and lines **Edge:** Segmented reeding

Date	Mintage	F12	VF20	XF40	MS60	MS63
2014	—	—	—	—	1.75	2.50

KM# 157 2 EURO
8.50 g., Bi-Metallic, 25.75 mm. **Obv:** Female head in national costume right **Rev:** Value and map, stars and lines. **Edge Lettering:** 2's and stars

Date	Mintage	F12	VF20	XF40	MS60	MS63
2014	—	—	—	—	4.00	5.00

LEBANON

The Lebanese Republic, situated on the eastern shore of the Mediterranean Sea between Syria and Israel, has an area of 4,015 sq. mi. (10,400 sq. km.) and a population of 3.5 million. Capital: Beirut. The economy is based on agriculture, trade and tourism. Fruit, other foodstuffs and textiles are exported.

MONETARY SYSTEM
100 Piastres = 1 Livre (Pound)

REPUBLIC
STANDARD COINAGE

KM# 41 LIVRE
28.28 g., Silver **Subject:** Amin Maalouf to French Academy **Obv:** Cypress tree

Date	Mintage	F12	VF20	XF40	MS60	MS63
2012 proof	Est. 1000	—	—	—	—	550

KM# 40 25 LIVRES
2.82 g., Nickel Plated Steel, 20.5 mm. **Obv:** Large value on cedar tree **Rev:** Value within square design **Rev. Legend:** BANQUE DU LIBAN **Edge:** Plain

Date	Mintage	F12	VF20	XF40	MS60	MS63
2002(c)	—	—	—	0.30	0.80	1.20
2009(v)	—	—	—	0.30	0.80	1.20

KM# 37a 50 LIVRES
Nickel, 18.35 mm. **Obv:** Cedar tree with Arabic value superimposed. Arabic legend above, date below. **Rev:** Value in center.

Date	Mintage	F12	VF20	XF40	MS60	MS63
2006	—	—	—	0.50	1.20	1.80

KM# 38 100 LIVRES
4.00 g., Brass, 22.5 mm. **Obv:** Arabic legend above large value on cedar tree **Rev:** Stylized flag above large value "100 **Rev. Legend:** BANQUE DU LIBAN **Edge:** Plain

Date	Mintage	F12	VF20	XF40	MS60	MS63
2006(c)	—	—	—	0.65	1.50	2.00

KM# 38a 100 LIVRES
4.05 g., Stainless Steel, 22.48 mm. **Obv:** Arabic legend above large value on cedar tree **Rev:** Stylized flag above large value "100 **Rev. Legend:** BANQUE DU LIBAN **Edge:** Plain

Date	Mintage	F12	VF20	XF40	MS60	MS63
2003(c)	—	—	—	0.60	1.50	2.00

KM# 38b 100 LIVRES
4.07 g., Copper Plated Steel, 22.49 mm. **Obv:** Arabic legend above large value on cedar tree **Rev:** Stylized flag above large value "100 **Rev. Legend:** BANQUE DU LIBAN **Edge:** Plain

Date	Mintage	F12	VF20	XF40	MS60	MS63
2006	—	—	—	0.60	1.50	2.00
2009	—	—	—	0.60	1.50	2.00

KM# 36 250 LIVRES
5.00 g., Aluminum-Bronze, 23.5 mm. **Obv:** Arabic legend above large value on cedar tree **Rev:** Large 250 within eliptical border design **Edge:** Reeded

Date	Mintage	F12	VF20	XF40	MS60	MS63
2003(c)	—	—	—	0.75	1.85	2.50
2006(a)	—	—	—	0.75	1.85	2.50
2009(v)	—	—	—	0.75	1.85	2.50
2012	—	—	—	0.75	1.85	2.50

KM# 36a 250 LIVRES
5.00 g., Aluminum-Bronze, 23.5 mm. **Obv:** Arabic legend above rhodium plated large value on cedar tree **Rev:** Large 250 within elliptical border design **Edge:** Reeded

Date	Mintage	F12	VF20	XF40	MS60	MS63
2012	—	—	—	—	—	1.85

KM# 36a 250 LIVRES
5.00 g., Aluminum-Bronze, 23.5 mm. **Obv:** Arabic legend above rhodium plated large value and cedar tree **Rev:** Large 250 within elliptical border design **Edge:** Reeded

Date	Mintage	F12	VF20	XF40	MS60	MS63
2012	100,000	—	—	—	—	15.00

KM# 39 500 LIVRES
6.06 g., Nickel Plated Steel, 24.5 mm. **Obv:** Arabic legend above large value on cedar tree **Rev:** Large value "500", thick segmented circular border **Rev. Legend:** BANQUE DU LIBAN **Edge:** Plain

Date	Mintage	F12	VF20	XF40	MS60	MS63
2003(c)	—	—	—	0.90	2.25	3.00
2006(a)	—	—	—	0.90	2.25	3.00
2009(v)	—	—	—	0.90	2.25	3.00
2012	—	—	—	0.90	2.25	

KM# 39a 500 LIVRES
6.06 g., Stainless Steel, 24.5 mm. **Obv:** Arabic legend above large value on cedar tree **Rev:** Large value 500 , thick segmented circular border

Date	Mintage	F12	VF20	XF40	MS60	MS63
2012	—	—	—	—	2.25	3.00

LESOTHO

The Kingdom of Lesotho, a constitutional monarchy located within the east-central part of the Republic of South Africa, has an area of 11,720 sq. mi. (30,350 sq. km.) and a population of 1.5 million. Capital: Maseru. The economy is based on subsistence agriculture and livestock raising. Wool, mohair, and cattle are exported.

Lesotho (formerly Basutoland) was sparsely populated until the end of the 16th century. Between the 16th and 19th centuries an influx of refugees from tribal wars led to the development of a distinct Basotho group. During the reign of tribal chief Mashoeshoe I (1823-70), a series of wars with the Orange Free State resulted in the loss of large areas of territory to South Africa. Mashoeshoe appealed to the British for help, and Basutoland was constituted a native state under British protection. In 1871 it was annexed to Cape Colony, but was restored to direct control by the Crown in 1884. From 1884 to 1959 legislative and executive authority was vested in a British High Commissioner. The constitution of 1959 recognized the expressed wish of the people for independence, which was attained on Oct.4, 1966.

Lesotho is a member of the Commonwealth of Nations.

The king is Head of State.

RULERS
Moshoeshoe II, 1966-1990
Letsie III, 1990-1995
Moshoeshoe II, 1995-

MONETARY SYSTEM
100 Licente/Lisente = 1 Maloti/Loti

KINGDOM
STANDARD COINAGE

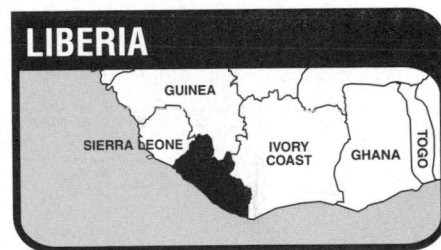

KM# 62 5 LICENTE (Lisente)
1.64 g., Brass Plated Steel, 15 mm. **Ruler:** Letsie III **Obv:** Arms with supporters **Rev:** Two pine trees among grass, hills and value

Date	Mintage	F12	VF20	XF40	MS60	MS63
2006	—	—	—	0.35	0.75	1.00

KM# 63 10 LICENTE (Lisente)
1.96 g., Brass Plated Steel, 16 mm. **Ruler:** Moshoeshoe II **Obv:** Arms with supporters **Rev:** Angora goat

Date	Mintage	F12	VF20	XF40	MS60	MS63
2010	—	—	—	—	1.00	1.50

KM# 66 LOTI
3.88 g., Nickel Plated Steel, 21 mm. **Ruler:** Letsie III **Obv:** Native seated right **Rev:** Value at left of arms with supporters

Date	Mintage	F12	VF20	XF40	MS60	MS63
2010	—	—	—	—	1.50	2.00

KM# 59 5 MALOTI
6.37 g., Nickel Plated Steel, 25 mm. **Ruler:** Moshoeshoe II **Obv:** Arms with supporters **Rev:** Wheat sprigs and value

Date	Mintage	F12	VF20	XF40	MS60	MS63
2010	—	—	—	—	4.50	5.00

KM# 73 25 MALOTI
Silver **Ruler:** Moshoeshoe II **Subject:** Central Bank, 25th Anniversary

Date	Mintage	F12	VF20	XF40	MS60	MS63
2005	—	PF63 65.00	PF65 75.00			

LIBERIA

The Republic of Liberia, located on the southern side of the West African bulge between Sierra Leone and Ivory Coast, has an area of 38,250 sq. mi. (111,370 sq. km) and a population of 2.2 million. Capital: Monrovia. The major industries are agriculture, mining and lumbering. Iron ore, diamonds, rubber, coffee and coca are exported.

MINT MARKS
PM - Pobjoy Mint

MONETARY SYSTEM
100 Cents = 1 Dollar

REPUBLIC
STANDARD COINAGE

KM# 618 5 CENTS
5.02 g., Copper-Nickel, 23.8 mm. **Obv:** National arms **Rev:** Chimpanzee family **Edge:** Plain

Date	Mintage	F12	VF20	XF40	MS60	MS63
2003	—	—	—	—	1.50	2.00

KM# 1033 DOLLAR
Silver ASW, 50 mm. **Subject:** Euro Currency **Obv:** Europa on a bull and map **Rev:** French coin

Date	Mintage	F12	VF20	XF40	MS60	MS63
2002	—	PF63 25.00	PF65 30.00			

KM# 1034 DOLLAR
Silver ASW, 50 mm. **Subject:** Euro Currency **Obv:** Europa on a bull and map **Rev:** Belgian coin

Date	Mintage	F12	VF20	XF40	MS60	MS63
2002				PF63 25.00	PF65 30.00	

KM# 1035 DOLLAR
Silver ASW, 50 mm. **Subject:** Euro currency **Obv:** Europa on a bull and map **Rev:** Irish coin

Date	Mintage	F12	VF20	XF40	MS60	MS63
2002				PF63 25.00	PF65 30.00	

KM# 1036 DOLLAR
Copper-Nickel, 25 mm. **Obv:** National arms **Rev:** Ordination of a priest

Date	Mintage	F12	VF20	XF40	MS60	MS63
2005		—	—	—	—	15.00

KM# 1037 DOLLAR
15.57 g., 0.999 Silver 0.4969 oz. ASW, 33.02 mm. **Subject:** Merry Christmas & Happy New Year **Obv:** National arms **Rev:** Angel

Date	Mintage	F12	VF20	XF40	MS60	MS63
2009	5,000			PF63 30.00	PF65 35.00	

KM# 1003 2 DOLLARS
15.55 g., 0.999 Silver 0.4962 oz. ASW, 38.6 mm. **Obv:** National arms **Rev:** Santa in sleigh in color

Date	Mintage	F12	VF20	XF40	MS60	MS63
2011	—			PF65 45.00		

KM# 1004 2 DOLLARS
15.55 g., 0.999 Silver 0.4962 oz. ASW, 38.6 mm. **Obv:** National arms **Rev:** Christmas toys in color

Date	Mintage	F12	VF20	XF40	MS60	MS63
2011	—			PF65 45.00		

KM# 1005 2 DOLLARS
15.55 g., 0.999 Silver 0.4962 oz. ASW, 38.6 mm. **Obv:** National arms **Rev:** Christmas Angel in color

Date	Mintage	F12	VF20	XF40	MS60	MS63
2011	—			PF65 45.00		

KM# 1006 2 DOLLARS
15.55 g., 0.999 Silver 0.4962 oz. ASW, 38.6 mm. **Obv:** National arms **Rev:** Christmas - Drummer in color

Date	Mintage	F12	VF20	XF40	MS60	MS63
2011	—			PF65 45.00		

KM# 1007 2 DOLLARS
15.55 g., 0.999 Silver 0.4962 oz. ASW, 38.6 mm. **Obv:** National arms **Rev:** Christmas - bells in color

Date	Mintage	F12	VF20	XF40	MS60	MS63
2011	—			PF65 45.00		

KM# 1008 2 DOLLARS
15.55 g., 0.999 Silver 0.4962 oz. ASW, 38.6 mm. **Obv:** National arms **Rev:** Christmas Nutcracker in color

Date	Mintage	F12	VF20	XF40	MS60	MS63
2011	—			PF65 45.00		

KM# 568 5 DOLLARS
14.63 g., Copper-Nickel, 33.1 mm. **Subject:** Battle of Gettysburg **Obv:** National arms **Rev:** Cannon and crossed flags divides busts facing **Edge:** Reeded **Note:** This also exists in an obverse denominated type for $2,000. Also see KM828.

Date	Mintage	F12	VF20	XF40	MS60	MS63
2001B	—		—	—	12.00	14.00

KM# 651 5 DOLLARS
14.56 g., Copper-Nickel, 38 mm. **Obv:** National arms **Rev:** Japanese "Zero" flying over Pearl Harbor **Edge:** Reeded

Date	Mintage	F12	VF20	XF40	MS60	MS63
2001					10.00	12.00

KM# 494 5 DOLLARS
8.50 g., 0.9999 Silver 0.2715 oz. ASW, 30 mm. **Subject:** Soccer **Obv:** National arms **Rev:** Soccer player divides circle **Edge:** Reeded

Date	Mintage	F12	VF20	XF40	MS60	MS63
2002	3,000			PF63 20.00	PF65 25.00	

KM# 829 5 DOLLARS
14.94 g., Copper-Nickel, 32.9 mm. **Subject:** 12th Anniversary Columbia Space Shuttle **Obv:** National arms **Rev:** Astronaut, space shuttle **Edge:** Reeded

Date	Mintage	F12	VF20	XF40	MS60	MS63
2003	—		—	—	8.00	10.00

KM# 831 5 DOLLARS
15.55 g., 0.999 Niobium 0.4962 oz., 38 mm. **Series:** From ancient to Modern Sports **Obv:** National arms **Rev:** Discus throwers **Edge:** Plain

Date	Mintage	F12	VF20	XF40	MS60	MS63
2004	2,004	—	—	—	—	30.00

KM# 832 5 DOLLARS
15.55 g., 0.999 Niobium 0.4962 oz., 38 mm. **Series:** From Ancient to Modern Sports **Obv:** National arms **Rev:** Javelin throwers **Edge:** Plain

Date	Mintage	F12	VF20	XF40	MS60	MS63
2004	2,004	—	—	—	—	30.00

KM# 833 5 DOLLARS
15.55 g., 0.999 Niobium 0.4962 oz., 38 mm. **Series:** From ancient to Modern Sports **Obv:** National arms **Rev:** Broad jumpers **Edge:** Plain

Date	Mintage	F12	VF20	XF40	MS60	MS63
2004	2,004	—	—	—	—	30.00

KM# 834 5 DOLLARS
15.55 g., 0.999 Niobium 0.4962 oz., 38 mm. **Series:** From Ancient to Modern Sports **Obv:** National arms **Rev:** Runners **Edge:** Plain

Date	Mintage	F12	VF20	XF40	MS60	MS63
2004	2,004	—	—	—	—	30.00

KM# 835 5 DOLLARS
15.55 g., 0.999 Niobium 0.4962 oz., 38 mm. **Series:** From Ancient to Modern Sports **Obv:** National arms **Rev:** Wrestlers **Edge:** Plain

Date	Mintage	F12	VF20	XF40	MS60	MS63
2004	2,004	—	—	—	—	30.00

KM# 664 5 DOLLARS
6.40 g., Bi-Metallic, 25.7 mm. **Obv:** National arms **Rev:** Pope and cathedral within circle **Edge:** Reeded

Date	Mintage	F12	VF20	XF40	MS60	MS63
2005	—		—	—	12.00	14.00

KM# 809 5 DOLLARS
25.95 g., Silver Plated Copper-Nickel, 39.97 mm. **Subject:** Papal visits to Africa **Obv:** National arms **Rev:** 1/2 length multicolor figure of Pope John Paul II at center left, outlined map of Africa at center right in background **Edge:** Reeded

Date	Mintage	F12	VF20	XF40	MS60	MS63
2005	—	PF65 35.00				

KM# 810 5 DOLLARS
25.72 g., Silver, 39.92 mm. **Obv:** National arms **Rev:** St. Peter's square in background, multicolor bust of Pope Benedict XVI in oval frame at upper right **Edge:** Reeded

Date	Mintage	F12	VF20	XF40	MS60	MS63
2005	—	PF65 40.00				

KM# 865 5 DOLLARS
7.78 g., Niobium, 35 mm. **Subject:** 10th Anniversary of the Euro - San Marino **Rev:** Castle

Date	Mintage	F12	VF20	XF40	MS60	MS63
2006	10,000	PF65 50.00				

KM# 866 5 DOLLARS
7.78 g., Niobium, 35 mm. **Subject:** 10th Anniversary of the Euro - Slovakia **Rev:** Bratislava Castle

Date	Mintage	F12	VF20	XF40	MS60	MS63
2006	10,000	PF65 50.00				

KM# 867 5 DOLLARS
7.78 g., Niobium, 35 mm. **Subject:** 10th Anniversary of the Euro - Latvia **Rev:** Old Buildings

Date	Mintage	F12	VF20	XF40	MS60	MS63
2006	10,000	PF65 50.00				

KM# 868 5 DOLLARS
7.78 g., Niobium, 35 mm. **Subject:** 10th Anniversary of the Euro - Monaco **Rev:** Ariel view of Principality

Date	Mintage	F12	VF20	XF40	MS60	MS63
2006	10,000	PF65 50.00				

KM# 869 5 DOLLARS
7.78 g., Niobium, 35 mm. **Subject:** 10th Anniversary of the Euro - Slovenia **Rev:** Hill-top buildings

Date	Mintage	F12	VF20	XF40	MS60	MS63
2006	10,000	PF65 50.00				

KM# 724 5 DOLLARS
26.30 g., Silver Plated Bronze, 38.6 mm. **Obv:** National arms **Rev:** Multicolor Pope John Paul II with cross **Edge:** Reeded

Date	Mintage	F12	VF20	XF40	MS60	MS63
2007	—	PF65 30.00				

KM# 733 5 DOLLARS
27.00 g., Copper-Nickel, 38.61 mm. **Subject:** The Black Madonna of Czestochowa **Obv:** Arms **Obv. Legend:** REPUBLIC OF LIBERIA **Rev:** 1/2 length figure of Madonna facing with child

Date	Mintage	F12	VF20	XF40	MS60	MS63
2007	1,000	PF65 40.00				

KM# 1022 5 DOLLARS
28.28 g., 0.999 Silver 0.9025 oz. ASW, 38.6 mm. **Obv:** National arms **Rev:** Christ at center, apostles in 12 segments around

Date	Mintage	F12	VF20	XF40	MS60	MS63
2008	—	PF63 32.00	PF65 37.00			

KM# 1024 5 DOLLARS
28.28 g., 0.999 Silver 0.9025 oz. ASW, 38.6 mm. **Subject:** Tanks of WWII **Obv:** National arms **Rev:** T-34 in color applique

Date	Mintage	F12	VF20	XF40	MS60	MS63
2008	—	PF65 32.00				

KM# 1025 5 DOLLARS
28.28 g., 0.999 Silver 0.9025 oz. ASW, 38.6 mm. **Subject:** Tanks of WWII **Obv:** National arms **Rev:** Mark IV Churchill

Date	Mintage	F12	VF20	XF40	MS60	MS63
2008	—	PF65 32.00				

KM# 1026 5 DOLLARS
28.28 g., 0.999 Silver 0.9025 oz. ASW, 38.6 mm. **Subject:** Tanks of WWII **Obv:** National arms **Rev:** M4 Sherman

Date	Mintage	F12	VF20	XF40	MS60	MS63
2008	—	PF65 32.00				

KM# 1027 5 DOLLARS
28.28 g., 0.999 Silver 0.9025 oz. ASW, 38.6 mm. **Subject:** Tanks of WWII **Obv:** National arms **Rev:** VI Tiger

Date	Mintage	F12	VF20	XF40	MS60	MS63
2008	—	PF65 32.00				

KM# 1028 5 DOLLARS
28.28 g., 0.999 Silver 0.9025 oz. ASW, 38.6 mm. **Subject:** Tanks of WWII **Obv:** National arms **Rev:** Type 95

Date	Mintage	F12	VF20	XF40	MS60	MS63
2008	—	PF65 32.00				

KM# 958 5 DOLLARS
31.11 g., Copper-Nickel **Rev:** Martin van Buren multicolor applique

Date	Mintage	F12	VF20	XF40	MS60	MS63
2009	—	—	—	—	—	5.00

KM# 951 5 DOLLARS
31.11 g., Copper-Nickel **Rev:** George Washington multicolor applique

Date	Mintage	F12	VF20	XF40	MS60	MS63
2009	—	—	—	—	—	5.00

KM# 952 5 DOLLARS
31.11 g., Copper-Nickel **Rev:** John Adams multicolor applique

Date	Mintage	F12	VF20	XF40	MS60	MS63
2009	—	—	—	—	—	5.00

KM# 953 5 DOLLARS
31.11 g., Copper-Nickel **Rev:** Thomas Jefferson multicolor applique

Date	Mintage	F12	VF20	XF40	MS60	MS63
2009	—	—	—	—	—	5.00

KM# 954 5 DOLLARS
31.11 g., Copper-Nickel **Rev:** James Madison multicolor applique

Date	Mintage	F12	VF20	XF40	MS60	MS63
2009	—	—	—	—	—	5.00

KM# 955 5 DOLLARS
31.11 g., Copper-Nickel **Rev:** James Monroe multicolor applique

Date	Mintage	F12	VF20	XF40	MS60	MS63
2009	—	—	—	—	—	5.00

KM# 956 5 DOLLARS
31.11 g., Copper-Nickel **Rev:** John Quincey Adams multicolor applique

Date	Mintage	F12	VF20	XF40	MS60	MS63
2009	—	—	—	—	—	5.00

KM# 957 5 DOLLARS
31.11 g., Copper-Nickel **Rev:** Andrew Jackson multicolor applique

Date	Mintage	F12	VF20	XF40	MS60	MS63
2009	—	—	—	—	—	5.00

KM# 959 5 DOLLARS
31.11 g., Copper-Nickel **Rev:** William Henry Harrison multicolor applique

Date	Mintage	F12	VF20	XF40	MS60	MS63
2009	—	—	—	—	—	5.00

KM# 960 5 DOLLARS
31.11 g., Copper-Nickel **Rev:** John Tyler multicolor applique

Date	Mintage	F12	VF20	XF40	MS60	MS63
2009	—	—	—	—	—	5.00

KM# 961 5 DOLLARS
31.11 g., Copper-Nickel **Rev:** James K. Polk multicolor applique

Date	Mintage	F12	VF20	XF40	MS60	MS63
2009	—					5.00

KM# 962 5 DOLLARS
31.11 g., Copper-Nickel **Rev:** Zachary Taylor multicolor applique

Date	Mintage	F12	VF20	XF40	MS60	MS63
2009	—					5.00

KM# 963 5 DOLLARS
31.11 g., Copper-Nickel **Rev:** Millard Filmore multicolor applique

Date	Mintage	F12	VF20	XF40	MS60	MS63
2009	—					5.00

KM# 964 5 DOLLARS
31.11 g., Copper-Nickel **Rev:** Franklin Pierce multicolor applique

Date	Mintage	F12	VF20	XF40	MS60	MS63
2009	—					5.00

KM# 965 5 DOLLARS
31.11 g., Copper-Nickel **Rev:** James Buchanan multicolor applique

Date	Mintage	F12	VF20	XF40	MS60	MS63
2009	—				→	5.00

KM# 966 5 DOLLARS
31.11 g., Copper-Nickel **Rev:** Abraham Lincoln multicolor applique

Date	Mintage	F12	VF20	XF40	MS60	MS63
2009	—					5.00
2009	—					5.00

KM# 967 5 DOLLARS
31.11 g., Copper-Nickel **Rev:** Andrew Johnson multicolor applique

Date	Mintage	F12	VF20	XF40	MS60	MS63
2009	—					5.00

KM# 968 5 DOLLARS
31.11 g., Copper-Nickel **Rev:** Ulysses S. Grant multicolor applique

Date	Mintage	F12	VF20	XF40	MS60	MS63
2009	—					5.00

KM# 969 5 DOLLARS
31.11 g., Copper-Nickel **Rev:** Rutherford B. Hayes multicolor applique

Date	Mintage	F12	VF20	XF40	MS60	MS63
2009	—					5.00

KM# 970 5 DOLLARS
31.11 g., Copper-Nickel **Rev:** James A. Garfield multicolor applique

Date	Mintage	F12	VF20	XF40	MS60	MS63
2009	—					5.00

KM# 971 5 DOLLARS
31.11 g., Copper-Nickel **Rev:** Chester Arthur multicolor underprint

Date	Mintage	F12	VF20	XF40	MS60	MS63
2009	—					5.00

KM# 972 5 DOLLARS
31.11 g., Copper-Nickel **Rev:** Grover Cleveland multicolor applique

Date	Mintage	F12	VF20	XF40	MS60	MS63
2009	—					5.00

KM# 973 5 DOLLARS
31.11 g., Copper-Nickel **Rev:** Benjamin Harrison multicolor applique

Date	Mintage	F12	VF20	XF40	MS60	MS63
2009	—					5.00

KM# 974 5 DOLLARS
31.11 g., Copper-Nickel **Rev:** William McKinley multicolor applique

Date	Mintage	F12	VF20	XF40	MS60	MS63
2009	—					5.00

KM# 975 5 DOLLARS
31.11 g., Copper-Nickel **Rev:** Theodore Roosevelt multicolor applique

Date	Mintage	F12	VF20	XF40	MS60	MS63
2009	—					5.00

KM# 976 5 DOLLARS
31.11 g., Copper-Nickel **Rev:** William Howard Taft multicolor applique

Date	Mintage	F12	VF20	XF40	MS60	MS63
2009	—					5.00

KM# 977 5 DOLLARS
31.11 g., Copper-Nickel **Rev:** Woodrow Wilson multicolor applique

Date	Mintage	F12	VF20	XF40	MS60	MS63
2009	—					5.00

KM# 978 5 DOLLARS
31.11 g., Copper-Nickel **Rev:** Warren G. Harding multicolor applique

Date	Mintage	F12	VF20	XF40	MS60	MS63
2009	—					5.00

KM# 979 5 DOLLARS
31.11 g., Copper-Nickel **Rev:** Calvin Collidge multicolor applique

Date	Mintage	F12	VF20	XF40	MS60	MS63
2009	—					5.00

KM# 980 5 DOLLARS
31.11 g., Copper-Nickel **Rev:** Herbert Hoover multicolor applique

Date	Mintage	F12	VF20	XF40	MS60	MS63
2009	—					5.00

KM# 981 5 DOLLARS
31.11 g., Copper-Nickel **Rev:** Franklin D. Roosevelt multicolor applique

Date	Mintage	F12	VF20	XF40	MS60	MS63
2009	—					5.00

KM# 982 5 DOLLARS
31.11 g., Copper-Nickel **Rev:** Harry S Truman multicolor applique

Date	Mintage	F12	VF20	XF40	MS60	MS63
2009	—					5.00

KM# 983 5 DOLLARS
31.11 g., Copper-Nickel **Rev:** Swight D. Eisenhower multicolor applique

Date	Mintage	F12	VF20	XF40	MS60	MS63
2009	—					5.00

KM# 984 5 DOLLARS
31.11 g., Copper-Nickel **Rev:** John F. Kennedy multicolor applique

Date	Mintage	F12	VF20	XF40	MS60	MS63
2009	—					5.00

KM# 985 5 DOLLARS
31.11 g., Copper-Nickel **Rev:** Lyndon B. Johnson multicolor applique

Date	Mintage	F12	VF20	XF40	MS60	MS63
2009	—					5.00

KM# 986 5 DOLLARS
31.11 g., Copper-Nickel **Rev:** Richard M. Nixon multicolor applique

Date	Mintage	F12	VF20	XF40	MS60	MS63
2009	—					5.00

KM# 987 5 DOLLARS
31.11 g., Copper-Nickel **Rev:** Gerald R. Ford multicolor applique

Date	Mintage	F12	VF20	XF40	MS60	MS63
2009	—					5.00

KM# 988 5 DOLLARS
31.11 g., Copper-Nickel **Rev:** Jimmy Carter multicolor applique

Date	Mintage	F12	VF20	XF40	MS60	MS63
2009	—					5.00

KM# 989 5 DOLLARS
31.11 g., Copper-Nickel **Rev:** Ronald Reagan multicolor applique

Date	Mintage	F12	VF20	XF40	MS60	MS63
2009	—					5.00

KM# 990 5 DOLLARS
31.11 g., Copper-Nickel **Rev:** George H. W. Bush multicolor applique

Date	Mintage	F12	VF20	XF40	MS60	MS63
2009	—					5.00

KM# 991 5 DOLLARS
31.11 g., Copper-Nickel **Rev:** Bill Clinton multicolor applique

Date	Mintage	F12	VF20	XF40	MS60	MS63
2009	—					5.00

KM# 992 5 DOLLARS
31.11 g., Copper-Nickel **Rev:** George W. Bush multicolor applique

Date	Mintage	F12	VF20	XF40	MS60	MS63
2009	—					5.00

KM# 993 5 DOLLARS
31.11 g., Copper-Nickel **Rev:** Barack Obama multicolor applique

Date	Mintage	F12	VF20	XF40	MS60	MS63
2009	—					5.00

KM# 1023 5 DOLLARS
28.28 g., 0.999 Silver 0.9025 oz. ASW, 38.6 mm. **Obv:** National arms **Rev:** Saint standing at center, 12 segments of artibutes around

Date	Mintage	F12	VF20	XF40	MS60	MS63
2009	—	PF63 32.00		PF65 37.00		

KM# 997 5 DOLLARS
28.28 g., 0.999 Silver 0.9025 oz. ASW, 38.6 mm. **Obv:** National arms **Rev:** Kremlin - Tsar Canon, gilt shield

Date	Mintage	F12	VF20	XF40	MS60	MS63
2011	—	PF65 90.00				

KM# 998 5 DOLLARS
28.28 g., 0.999 Silver 0.9025 oz. ASW, 38.6 mm. **Obv:** National arms **Rev:** Kremlin - Tsar bell, gilt shield

Date	Mintage	F12	VF20	XF40	MS60	MS63
2011	—	PF65 90.00				

KM# 999 5 DOLLARS
28.28 g., 0.999 Silver 0.9025 oz. ASW, 38.6 mm. **Obv:** National arms **Rev:** Kremlin - Golden Cap, gilt shield

Date	Mintage	F12	VF20	XF40	MS60	MS63
2011	—	PF65 90.00				

KM# 1000 5 DOLLARS
28.28 g., 0.999 Silver 0.9025 oz. ASW, 38.6 mm. **Obv:** National arms **Rev:** Kremlin - Palace, gilt shield

Date	Mintage	F12	VF20	XF40	MS60	MS63
2011	—	PF65 90.00				

KM# 1001 5 DOLLARS
28.28 g., 0.999 Silver 0.9025 oz. ASW, 38.6 mm. **Obv:** National arms **Rev:** Kremlin - Uspenski Cathedral, gilt shield

Date	Mintage	F12	VF20	XF40	MS60	MS63
2011	—	PF65 90.00				

KM# 1002 5 DOLLARS
28.28 g., 0.999 Silver 0.9025 oz. ASW, 38.6 mm. **Obv:** National arms **Rev:** Kremlin - Spasski tower, gilt shield

Date	Mintage	F12	VF20	XF40	MS60	MS63
2011	—	PF65 90.00				

KM# 1010 5 DOLLARS
20.00 g., 0.999 Silver 0.6382 oz. ASW, 38.6 mm. **Subject:** Trains **Obv:** National arms **Rev:** Adler in color

Date	Mintage	F12	VF20	XF40	MS60	MS63
2011	—	PF65 70.00				

KM# 1011 5 DOLLARS
20.00 g., 0.999 Silver 0.6382 oz. ASW, 38.6 mm. **Subject:** Trains **Obv:** National arms **Rev:** KKSTB 310.23

Date	Mintage	F12	VF20	XF40	MS60	MS63
2011	—	PF65 70.00				

KM# 1012 5 DOLLARS
20.00 g., 0.999 Silver 0.6382 oz. ASW, 38.6 mm. **Subject:** Trains **Obv:** National arms **Rev:** Mallard locomotive in color

Date	Mintage	F12	VF20	XF40	MS60	MS63
2011	—	PF65 70.00				

KM# 1013 5 DOLLARS
20.00 g., 0.999 Silver 0.6382 oz. ASW, 38.6 mm. **Subject:** Trains **Obv:** National arms **Rev:** Flying Scottsman locomotive in color

Date	Mintage	F12	VF20	XF40	MS60	MS63
2011	—	PF65 70.00				

KM# 1014 5 DOLLARS
20.00 g., 0.999 Silver 0.6382 oz. ASW, 38.6 mm. **Subject:** Trains **Obv:** National arms **Rev:** Trans-Siberian Express in color

Date	Mintage	F12	VF20	XF40	MS60	MS63
2011	—	PF65 70.00				

KM# 1015 5 DOLLARS
20.00 g., 0.999 Silver 0.6382 oz. ASW, 38.6 mm. **Subject:** Trains **Obv:** National arms **Rev:** Blue Train in color

Date	Mintage	F12	VF20	XF40	MS60	MS63
2011	—	PF65 70.00				

KM# 843 10 DOLLARS
0.73 g., 0.999 Gold AGW, 11 mm. **Obv:** Arms **Rev:** John F. Kennedy head left

Date	Mintage	F12	VF20	XF40	MS60	MS63
2006	20,000	PF63 55.00 PF65 60.00				

KM# 491 10 DOLLARS
25.25 g., 0.925 Silver 0.7461 oz. ASW, 36.8 mm. **Subject:** Illusion **Obv:** National arms **Rev:** Stylized head with glasses facing **Edge:** Plain **Shape:** 10-sided

Date	Mintage	F12	VF20	XF40	MS60	MS63
2001	5,000	PF63 32.50 PF65 37.50				

KM# 513 10 DOLLARS
28.50 g., Copper-Nickel, 38.6 mm. **Series:** Moments of Freedom **Subject:** Hungarian Revolution of 1848 **Obv:** National arms **Rev:** Multicolor heroic scene **Edge:** Reeded

Date	Mintage	F12	VF20	XF40	MS60	MS63
2001	9,999	PF65 12.00				

KM# 777 10 DOLLARS
14.55 g., Copper-Nickel, 32 mm. **Subject:** 43rd President of USA **Obv:** National arms **Obv. Legend:** REPUBLIC OF LIBERIA **Rev:** George W. Bush, flag in background

Date	Mintage	F12	VF20	XF40	MS60	MS63
2001	—	PF65 12.00				

KM# 822 10 DOLLARS
1.24 g., Gold AGW, 13.68 mm. **Obv:** National arms **Rev:** Bust of Marlene Dietrich facing **Edge:** Reeded

Date	Mintage	F12	VF20	XF40	MS60	MS63
2001	—	PF65 75.00				

KM# 493 10 DOLLARS
770.00 g., Copper, 100 mm. **Subject:** Wreck of the Princess Louisa **Obv:** National arms **Rev:** Sailing ship **Edge:** Reeded **Note:** Illustration reduced. With an encased glass shard recovered from the wreck site of the Princess Louisa.

Date	Mintage	F12	VF20	XF40	MS60	MS63
2001	2,000	—	—	—	225	—

KM# 510 10 DOLLARS
33.24 g., Copper Gilt, 40.1 mm. **Obv:** National arms **Rev:** Multicolor holographic bald eagle **Edge:** Reeded

Date	Mintage	F12	VF20	XF40	MS60	MS63
2001	20,000	—	—	—	—	35.00

KM# 537 10 DOLLARS
28.50 g., Copper-Nickel, 38.6 mm. **Subject:** Moments of Freedom **Obv:** National arms **Rev:** Multicolor Buddha, spelled "Budha" on the coin **Edge:** Reeded

Date	Mintage	F12	VF20	XF40	MS60	MS63
2001	—	PF65 12.00				

KM# 538 10 DOLLARS
28.50 g., Copper-Nickel, 38.6 mm. **Subject:** Moments of Freedom **Obv:** National arms **Rev:** Multicolor Battle of Marathon scene **Edge:** Reeded

Date	Mintage	F12	VF20	XF40	MS60	MS63
2001	—	PF65 12.00				

KM# 539 10 DOLLARS
28.50 g., Copper-Nickel, 38.6 mm. **Series:** Moments of Freedom **Obv:** National arms **Rev:** Multicolor founding of Liberia design **Edge:** Reeded

Date	Mintage	F12	VF20	XF40	MS60	MS63
2001	—	PF65 12.00				

KM# 540 10 DOLLARS
28.50 g., Copper-Nickel, 38.6 mm. **Series:** Moments of Freedom **Obv:** National arms **Rev:** Multicolor portrait of Constantine I **Edge:** Reeded

Date	Mintage	F12	VF20	XF40	MS60	MS63
2001	—	PF65 12.00				

KM# 541 10 DOLLARS
28.50 g., Copper-Nickel, 38.6 mm. **Series:** Moments of Freedom **Obv:** National arms **Rev:** Multicolor William Tell statue **Edge:** Reeded

Date	Mintage	F12	VF20	XF40	MS60	MS63
2001	—	PF65 12.00				

KM# 542 10 DOLLARS
28.50 g., Copper-Nickel, 38.6 mm. **Series:** Moments of Freedom **Obv:** National arms **Rev:** Multicolor bust facing **Edge:** Reeded

Date	Mintage	F12	VF20	XF40	MS60	MS63
2001	—	PF65 12.00				

KM# 543 10 DOLLARS
28.50 g., Copper-Nickel, 38.6 mm. **Series:** Moments of Freedom **Obv:** National arms **Rev:** Multicolor head with headdress and battle scene **Edge:** Reeded

Date	Mintage	F12	VF20	XF40	MS60	MS63
2001	—	PF65 12.00				

KM# 544 10 DOLLARS
28.50 g., Copper-Nickel, 38.6 mm. **Series:** Moments of Freedom **Obv:** National arms **Rev:** Multicolor Brandenburg Gate scene **Edge:** Reeded

Date	Mintage	F12	VF20	XF40	MS60	MS63
2001	—	PF65 12.00				

KM# 545 10 DOLLARS
28.50 g., Copper-Nickel, 38.6 mm. **Series:** Moments of Freedom **Obv:** National arms **Rev:** Multicolor half length figure facing **Edge:** Reeded

Date	Mintage	F12	VF20	XF40	MS60	MS63
2001	—	PF65 12.00				

KM# 546 10 DOLLARS
28.50 g., Copper-Nickel, 38.6 mm. **Series:** Moments of Freedom **Obv:** National arms **Rev:** Multicolor Sitting Bull portrait **Edge:** Reeded

Date	Mintage	F12	VF20	XF40	MS60	MS63
2001	—	PF65 12.00				

KM# 547 10 DOLLARS
28.50 g., Copper-Nickel, 38.6 mm. **Series:** Moments of Freedom **Obv:** National arms **Rev:** Multicolor Declaration of Independence scene **Edge:** Reeded

Date	Mintage	F12	VF20	XF40	MS60	MS63
2001	—	PF65 12.00				

KM# 548 10 DOLLARS
28.50 g., Copper-Nickel, 38.6 mm. **Series:** Moments of Freedom **Obv:** National arms **Rev:** Multicolor allegorical woman **Edge:** Reeded

Date	Mintage	F12	VF20	XF40	MS60	MS63
2001	—	PF65 12.00				

KM# 549 10 DOLLARS
28.50 g., Copper-Nickel, 38.6 mm. **Series:** Moments of Freedom **Obv:** National arms **Rev:** Multicolor bust of Gandhi looking down **Edge:** Reeded

Date	Mintage	F12	VF20	XF40	MS60	MS63
2001	—	PF65 12.00				

KM# 550 10 DOLLARS
28.50 g., Copper-Nickel, 38.6 mm. **Series:** Moments of Freedom **Obv:** National arms **Rev:** Multicolor picture of a soldier at the moment he is shot in battle **Edge:** Reeded

Date	Mintage	F12	VF20	XF40	MS60	MS63
2001	—	PF65 12.00				

KM# 551 10 DOLLARS
28.50 g., Copper-Nickel, 38.6 mm. **Series:** Moments of Freedom **Obv:** National arms **Rev:** Multicolor inmates behind wire fence scene **Edge:** Reeded

Date	Mintage	F12	VF20	XF40	MS60	MS63
2001	—	PF65 12.00				

KM# 552 10 DOLLARS
28.50 g., Copper-Nickel, 38.6 mm. **Series:** Moments of Freedom **Obv:** National arms **Rev:** Multicolor Iwo Jima flag raising scene **Edge:** Reeded

Date	Mintage	F12	VF20	XF40	MS60	MS63
2001	—	PF65 12.00				

KM# 553 10 DOLLARS
28.50 g., Copper-Nickel, 38.6 mm. **Series:** Moments of Freedom **Obv:** National arms **Rev:** Multicolor UN logo and dove **Edge:** Reeded

Date	Mintage	F12	VF20	XF40	MS60	MS63
2001	—	PF65 12.00				

KM# 554 10 DOLLARS
28.50 g., Copper-Nickel, 38.6 mm. **Series:** Moments of Freedom **Obv:** National arms **Rev:** Multicolor Solzhenitsyn portrait **Edge:** Reeded

Date	Mintage	F12	VF20	XF40	MS60	MS63
2001	—	PF65 12.00				

KM# 555 10 DOLLARS
28.50 g., Copper-Nickel, 38.6 mm. **Series:** Moments of Freedom **Obv:** National arms **Rev:** Multicolor Spartacus and troops **Edge:** Reeded

Date	Mintage	F12	VF20	XF40	MS60	MS63
2001	—	PF65 12.00				

KM# 556 10 DOLLARS
28.50 g., Copper-Nickel, 38.6 mm. **Series:** Moments of Freedom **Obv:** National arms **Rev:** Multicolor Soviet tank in Prague **Edge:** Reeded

Date	Mintage	F12	VF20	XF40	MS60	MS63
2001	—	PF65 12.00				

KM# 557 10 DOLLARS
28.50 g., Copper-Nickel, 38.6 mm. **Series:** Moments of Freedom **Obv:** National arms **Rev:** Multicolor Bastille scene **Edge:** Reeded

Date	Mintage	F12	VF20	XF40	MS60	MS63
2001	—	PF65 12.00				

KM# 558 10 DOLLARS
28.50 g., Copper-Nickel, 38.6 mm. **Series:** Moments of Freedom **Obv:** National arms **Rev:** Multicolor Nelson Mandela and fist **Edge:** Reeded

Date	Mintage	F12	VF20	XF40	MS60	MS63
2001	—	PF65 12.00				

KM# 559 10 DOLLARS
28.50 g., Copper-Nickel, 38.6 mm. **Series:** Moments of Freedom **Obv:** National arms **Rev:** Multicolor circuit board and world globe **Edge:** Reeded

Date	Mintage	F12	VF20	XF40	MS60	MS63
2001	—	PF65 12.00				

KM# 994 10 DOLLARS
0.999 Gold AGW, 12 mm. **Obv:** National Arms **Rev:** Franklin, Jefferson, Adams and Declaration of Independence

Date	Mintage	F12	VF20	XF40	MS60	MS63
2001	—	PF65 70.00				

KM# 654 10 DOLLARS
15.33 g., Copper-Nickel, 33.2 mm. **Obv:** National arms **Rev:** GEORGE W. BUSH..." No value at bottom **Edge:** Reeded

Date	Mintage	F12	VF20	XF40	MS60	MS63
2002	—	—	—	—	10.00	

KM# 705 10 DOLLARS
31.10 g., 0.999 Silver 0.9926 oz. ASW, 38.6 mm. **Subject:** 2002 World Football Championship - Japan - South Korea **Obv:** National arms **Rev:** Pagoda superimposed on a soccer ball, legend around **Edge:** Reeded

Date	Mintage	F12	VF20	XF40	MS60	MS63
2002	—	PF65 45.00				

KM# 806 10 DOLLARS
14.30 g., Copper-Nickel, 33.11 mm. **Obv:** National arms **Rev:** Bust of President Bush facing at left, soldier standing at right facing, flag in background **Rev. Legend:** America's Fight For Freedom **Edge:** Reeded

Date	Mintage	F12	VF20	XF40	MS60	MS63
2002	—	—	—	—	10.00	12.00

KM# 1016 10 DOLLARS
Copper-Nickel **Obv:** National arms **Rev:** San Francisco cablecar hologram

Date	Mintage	F12	VF20	XF40	MS60	MS63
2002	—	PF63 30.00	PF65 35.00			

KM# 602 10 DOLLARS
25.00 g., 0.925 Silver 0.7387 oz. ASW, 38.6 mm. **Obv:** National arms **Rev:** Icarus and Daedalus in flight **Edge:** Reeded

Date	Mintage	F12	VF20	XF40	MS60	MS63
2003	—	PF63 30.00	PF65 35.00			

KM# 603 10 DOLLARS
25.00 g., 0.925 Silver 0.7387 oz. ASW, 38.6 mm. **Obv:** National arms **Rev:** First parachute **Edge:** Reeded

Date	Mintage	F12	VF20	XF40	MS60	MS63
2003	—	PF63 30.00	PF65 35.00			

KM# 604 10 DOLLARS
25.00 g., 0.925 Silver 0.7387 oz. ASW, 38.6 mm. **Obv:** National arms **Rev:** Montgolfier ballon **Edge:** Reeded

Date	Mintage	F12	VF20	XF40	MS60	MS63
2003	—	PF63 30.00	PF65 35.00			

KM# 605 10 DOLLARS
25.00 g., 0.925 Silver 0.7387 oz. ASW, 38.6 mm. **Obv:** National arms **Rev:** Otto v. Lillenthal **Edge:** Reeded

Date	Mintage	F12	VF20	XF40	MS60	MS63
2003	—	PF63 30.00	PF65 35.00			

KM# 606 10 DOLLARS
25.00 g., 0.925 Silver 0.7387 oz. ASW, 38.6 mm. **Obv:** National arms **Rev:** Wright Brothers **Edge:** Reeded

Date	Mintage	F12	VF20	XF40	MS60	MS63
2003	—	PF63 30.00	PF65 35.00			

KM# 607 10 DOLLARS
25.00 g., 0.925 Silver 0.7387 oz. ASW, 38.6 mm. **Obv:** National arms **Rev:** Mach 1- Bell X **Edge:** Reeded

Date	Mintage	F12	VF20	XF40	MS60	MS63
2003	—	PF63 30.00	PF65 35.00			

KM# 608 10 DOLLARS
25.00 g., 0.925 Silver 0.7387 oz. ASW, 38.6 mm. **Obv:** National arms **Rev:** The Concorde **Edge:** Reeded

Date	Mintage	F12	VF20	XF40	MS60	MS63
2003	—	PF63 30.00	PF65 35.00			

KM# 708 10 DOLLARS
25.10 g., 0.925 Silver 0.7417 oz. ASW, 38.6 mm. **Obv:** National arms **Rev:** Clipper ship "Flying Cloud **Edge:** Reeded

Date	Mintage	F12	VF20	XF40	MS60	MS63
2003	—	PF65 35.00				

KM# 807 10 DOLLARS
26.30 g., Copper-Nickel, 40.36 mm. **Subject:** America's First Ladies **Obv:** National arms **Rev:** Bust of Jacqueline Kennedy facing, small oval portrait of President John F. Kennedy at right **Edge:** Reeded

Date	Mintage	F12	VF20	XF40	MS60	MS63
2003	—	PF65 15.00				

KM# 824 10 DOLLARS
14.60 g., Copper-Nickel, 33 mm. **Subject:** Abraham Lincoln **Obv:** National arms **Rev:** Bust facing at left, Lincoln Memorial in background **Edge:** Reeded

Date	Mintage	F12	VF20	XF40	MS60	MS63
2003	20,000	PF65 12.00				

KM# 1030 10 DOLLARS
Silver **Subject:** Hapag 1848 Deutschland **Rev:** Sailing ship left

Date	Mintage	F12	VF20	XF40	MS60	MS63
2003	—	PF65 50.00				

KM# 611 10 DOLLARS

62.21 g., 0.999 Silver 1.9851 oz. ASW, 50 mm. **Obv:** National arms left of window design with Tiffany Glass inlay **Rev:** Window design with Tiffany Glass inlay **Edge:** Plain

Date	Mintage	F12	VF20	XF40	MS60	MS63
2004	999	—	—	—	—	200

KM# 823 10 DOLLARS

1.23 g., Gold AGW, 13.88 mm. **Subject:** 2006 World Football championship Gernany **Obv:** National arms **Rev:** Football at lower left, stadium at center **Rev. Legend:** DEUTSCHLAND 2006 **Edge:** Reeded

Date	Mintage	F12	VF20	XF40	MS60	MS63
2004	—	PF65 75.00				

KM# 740 10 DOLLARS

20.00 g., 0.999 Silver 0.6382 oz. ASW, 38.00 mm. **Series:** Endangered Wildlife **Obv:** National arms **Obv. Legend:** REPUBLIC OF LIBERIA **Rev:** Gilt Siberian Tiger with diamonds inset in eyes **Rev. Legend:** RUSSIA **Edge:** Plain

Date	Mintage	F12	VF20	XF40	MS60	MS63
2004	5,000	PF65 115				

KM# 741 10 DOLLARS

20.00 g., 0.999 Silver 0.6382 oz. ASW, 38.00 mm. **Series:** Endangered Wildlife **Obv:** National arms **Obv. Legend:** REPUBLIC OF LIBERIA **Rev:** Two gilt Hyacinth Macaws perched on branch with diamond insets in eyes **Rev. Legend:** BRAZIL **Edge:** Plain

Date	Mintage	F12	VF20	XF40	MS60	MS63
2004	5,000	PF65 115				

KM# 742 10 DOLLARS

20.00 g., 0.999 Silver 0.6382 oz. ASW, 38.00 mm. **Series:** Endangered Wildlife **Obv:** National arms **Obv. Legend:** REPUBLIC OF LIBERIA **Rev:** Gilt young Giant Panda seated eating bamboo shoots **Rev. Legend:** CHINA **Edge:** Plain

Date	Mintage	F12	VF20	XF40	MS60	MS63
2004	5,000	PF65 115				

KM# 743 10 DOLLARS

20.00 g., 0.999 Silver 0.6382 oz. ASW, 38.00 mm. **Subject:** Endangered Wildlife **Obv:** National arms **Obv. Legend:** REPUBLIC OF LIBERIA **Rev:** Two gilt Bald Eagles. one perched at left, one alighting at center right **Rev. Legend:** USA **Edge:** Plain

Date	Mintage	F12	VF20	XF40	MS60	MS63
2004	5,000	PF65 115				

KM# 744 10 DOLLARS

20.00 g., 0.999 Silver 0.6382 oz. ASW, 38 mm. **Series:** Endangered Wildlife **Obv:** National arms **Obv. Legend:** REPUBLIC OF LIBERIA **Rev:** Gilt Puma standing with diamonds inset in eyes **Rev. Legend:** MEXICO **Edge:** Plain

Date	Mintage	F12	VF20	XF40	MS60	MS63
2004	5,000	PF65 115				

KM# 745 10 DOLLARS

20.00 g., 0.999 Silver 0.6382 oz. ASW, 38 mm. **Series:** Endangered Wildlife **Obv:** National arms **Obv. Legend:** REPUBLIC OF LIBERIA **Rev:** Gilt Red-ruffed Lemur on branch with diamonds inset in eyes **Rev. Legend:** MADAGASCAR **Edge:** Plain

Date	Mintage	F12	VF20	XF40	MS60	MS63
2004	5,000	PF65 115				

KM# 746 10 DOLLARS

20.00 g., 0.999 Silver 0.6382 oz. ASW, 38 mm. **Series:** Endangered Wildlife **Obv:** National arms **Obv. Legend:** REPUBLIC OF LIBERIA **Rev:** Two gilt Andean Condors, one lifting off at center, one perched at right **Rev. Legend:** CHILE **Edge:** Plain

Date	Mintage	F12	VF20	XF40	MS60	MS63
2004	5,000	PF65 115				

KM# 747 10 DOLLARS

20.00 g., 0.999 Silver 0.6382 oz. ASW, 38 mm. **Series:** Endangered Wildlife **Obv:** Natlonal arms **Obv. Legend:** REPUBLIC OF LIBERIA **Rev:** Two gilt Yellow-eyed Penguins standing facing with diamonds inset in eyes **Rev. Legend:** NEW ZEALAND **Edge:** Plain

Date	Mintage	F12	VF20	XF40	MS60	MS63
2004	5,000	PF65 115				

KM# 748 10 DOLLARS

20.00 g., 0.999 Silver 0.6382 oz. ASW, 38 mm. **Series:** Endangered Wildlife **Obv:** National arms **Obv. Legend:** REPUBLIC OF LIBERIA **Rev:** Gilt African lion standing facing with diamonds inset in eyes **Rev. Legend:** SOUTH AFRICA **Edge:** Plain

Date	Mintage	F12	VF20	XF40	MS60	MS63
2004	5,000	PF65 115				

KM# 749 10 DOLLARS

20.00 g., 0.999 Silver 0.6382 oz. ASW, 38 mm. **Series:** Endangered Wildlife **Obv:** National arms **Obv. Legend:** REPUBLIC OF LIBERIA **Rev:** Two gilt perched Kookaburras with diamonds inset in eyes **Rev. Legend:** AUSTRALIA **Edge:** Plain

Date	Mintage	F12	VF20	XF40	MS60	MS63
2004	5,000	PF65 115				

KM# 750 10 DOLLARS

20.00 g., 0.999 Silver 0.6382 oz. ASW, 38 mm. **Series:** Endangered Wildlife **Obv:** National arms **Obv. Legend:** REPUBLIC OF LIBERIA **Rev:** Gilt Polar Bear standing facing with diamonds inset in eyes **Rev. Legend:** CANADA **Edge:** Plain

Date	Mintage	F12	VF20	XF40	MS60	MS63
2004	5,000	PF65 115				

KM# 751 10 DOLLARS

20.00 g., 0.999 Silver 0.6382 oz. ASW **Series:** Endangered Wildlife **Obv:** National arms **Obv. Legend:** REPUBLIC OF LIBERIA **Rev:** Gilt perched Blakiston's Fish-owl with diamonds inset in eyes **Rev. Legend:** JAPAN

Date	Mintage	F12	VF20	XF40	MS60	MS63
2004	5,000	PF65 115				

KM# 808 10 DOLLARS

14.58 g., Copper-Nickel, 32.98 mm. **Obv:** National arms **Rev:** Bust of President Ronald Reagon facing, flag in background **Edge:** Reeded

Date	Mintage	F12	VF20	XF40	MS60	MS63
2004	—	—	—	—	8.00	10.00

KM# 830 10 DOLLARS

15.62 g., Copper-Nickel, 33.3 mm. **Obv:** National arms **Rev:** Flag at left, bust of 43rd President George W. Bush facing at right **Edge:** Reeded

Date	Mintage	F12	VF20	XF40	MS60	MS63
2004	—	—	—	—	10.00	12.00

KM# 738 10 DOLLARS

27.19 g., Copper-Nickel, 43 mm. **Subject:** Death of Pope John-Paul II **Edge:** Reeded

Date	Mintage	F12	VF20	XF40	MS60	MS63
2005	—	—	—	—	12.00	14.00

KM# 739.1 10 DOLLARS

25.00 g., 0.925 Silver 0.7387 oz. ASW **Subject:** Death of Pope John-Paul II **Rev:** Silhouette of John-Paul gilt, backgound in Ruthenium

Date	Mintage	F12	VF20	XF40	MS60	MS63
2005	7,500	—	—	—	—	60.00

KM# 739.2 10 DOLLARS

25.00 g., 0.925 Silver 0.7387 oz. ASW **Subject:** Death of Pope John-Paul II **Rev:** Silhouette of John-Paul gilt, blackened background

Date	Mintage	F12	VF20	XF40	MS60	MS63
2005	7,500	—	—	—	—	47.50

KM# 752 10 DOLLARS

20.00 g., 0.999 Silver 0.6382 oz. ASW, 38 mm. **Series:** Endangered Wildlife **Obv:** National arms **Obv. Legend:** REPUBLIC OF LIBERIA **Rev:** Gilt Koala perched on branch with diamonds inset in eyes **Rev. Legend:** AUSTRALIA **Edge:** Plain

Date	Mintage	F12	VF20	XF40	MS60	MS63
2005	5,000	PF65 115				

KM# 753 10 DOLLARS

20.00 g., 0.999 Silver 0.6382 oz. ASW, 38 mm. **Series:** Endangered Wildlife **Obv:** National arms **Obv. Legend:** REPUBLIC OF LIBERIA **Rev:** Two perched gilt Yellow-eared Conures with diamonds inset in eyes **Rev. Legend:** COLOMBIA **Edge:** Plain

Date	Mintage	F12	VF20	XF40	MS60	MS63
2005	5,000	PF65 115				

KM# 754 10 DOLLARS

20.00 g., 0.999 Silver 0.6382 oz. ASW, 38 mm. **Series:** Endangered Wildlife **Obv:** National arms **Obv. Legend:** REPUBLIC OF LIBERIA **Rev:** Gilt Iberian Lynx standing facing with diamonds inset in eyes **Rev. Legend:** SPAIN **Edge:** Plain

Date	Mintage	F12	VF20	XF40	MS60	MS63
2005	5,000	PF65 115				

KM# 755 10 DOLLARS

20.00 g., 0.999 Silver 0.6382 oz. ASW, 38 mm. **Series:** Endangered Wildlife **Obv:** National arms **Obv. Legend:** REPUBLIC OF LIBERIA **Rev:** Two perched gilt Yellow-crested Cockatoos **Rev. Legend:** INDONESIA **Edge:** Plain

Date	Mintage	F12	VF20	XF40	MS60	MS63
2005	5,000	PF65 115				

KM# 756 10 DOLLARS

20.00 g., 0.999 Silver 0.6382 oz. ASW, 38 mm. **Series:** Endangered Wildlife **Obv:** National arms **Obv. Legend:** REPUBLIC OF LIBERIA **Rev:** Gilt Jaguar resting on branch with diamonds inset in eyes **Rev. Legend:** BELIZE **Edge:** Plain

Date	Mintage	F12	VF20	XF40	MS60	MS63
2005	5,000	PF65 115				

KM# 757 10 DOLLARS

20.00 g., 0.999 Silver 0.6382 oz. ASW, 38 mm. **Series:** Endangered Wildlife **Obv:** National arms **Obv. Legend:** REPUBLIC OF LIBERIA **Rev:** Two perched gilt Plate-billed Mountain Toucans with diamonds inset in eyes **Rev. Legend:** ECUADOR **Edge:** Plain

Date	Mintage	F12	VF20	XF40	MS60	MS63
2005	5,000	PF65 115				

KM# 758 10 DOLLARS

20.00 g., 0.999 Silver 0.6382 oz. ASW, 38 mm. **Series:** Endangered Wildlife **Obv:** National arms **Obv. Legend:** REPUBLIC OF LIBERIA **Rev:** Gilt Red Panda resting facing with diamonds inset in eyes **Rev. Legend:** INDIA **Edge:** Plain

Date	Mintage	F12	VF20	XF40	MS60	MS63
2005	5,000	PF65 115				

KM# 759 10 DOLLARS

20.00 g., 0.999 Silver 0.6382 oz. ASW, 38 mm. **Series:** Endangered Wildlife **Obv:** National arms **Obv. Legend:** REPUBLIC OF LIBERIA **Rev:** Two perched gilt Resplendent Quetzals with diamonds inset in eyes **Rev. Legend:** GUATEMALA **Edge:** Plain

Date	Mintage	F12	VF20	XF40	MS60	MS63
2005	5,000	PF65 115				

KM# 760 10 DOLLARS

20.00 g., 0.999 Silver 0.6382 oz. ASW, 38 mm. **Series:** Endangered Wildlife **Obv:** National arms **Obv. Legend:** REPUBLIC OF LIBERIA **Rev:** Gilt Snow Leopard standing left looking back with diamonds inset in eyes **Rev. Legend:** NEPAL **Edge:** Plain

Date	Mintage	F12	VF20	XF40	MS60	MS63
2005	5,000	PF65 115				

KM# 761 10 DOLLARS

20.00 g., 0.999 Silver 0.6382 oz. ASW, 38 mm. **Series:** Endangered Wildlife **Obv:** National arms **Obv. Legend:** REPUBLIC OF LIBERIA **Rev:** Gilt Fossa standing right on branch facing with diamonds inset in eyes **Rev. Legend:** MADAGASCAR **Edge:** Plain

Date	Mintage	F12	VF20	XF40	MS60	MS63
2005	5,000	PF65 115				

KM# 762 10 DOLLARS

20.00 g., 0.999 Silver 0.6382 oz. ASW, 38 mm. **Series:** Endangered Wildlife **Obv:** National arms **Obv. Legend:** REPUBLIC OF LIBERIA **Rev:** Two gilt Chilean Flamingos standing left with diamonds inset in eyes **Rev. Legend:** ARGENTINA **Edge:** Plain

Date	Mintage	F12	VF20	XF40	MS60	MS63
2005	5,000	PF65 115				

KM# 763 10 DOLLARS

20.00 g., 0.999 Silver 0.6382 oz. ASW, 38 mm. **Series:** Endangered Wildlife **Obv:** National arms **Obv. Legend:** REPUBLIC OF LIBERIA **Rev:** Two gilt White-winged ducks, one standing, one swimming right with diamonds inset in eyes **Rev. Legend:** THAILAND **Edge:** Plain

Date	Mintage	F12	VF20	XF40	MS60	MS63
2005	5,000	PF65 115				

KM# 860 10 DOLLARS

25.00 g., 0.925 Silver 0.7387 oz. ASW, 38.6 mm. **Subject:** Poison frogs **Rev:** Green Frog, multicolor

Date	Mintage	F12	VF20	XF40	MS60	MS63
2005	2,500	PF65 50.00				

KM# 861 10 DOLLARS

25.00 g., 0.925 Silver 0.7387 oz. ASW, 38.6 mm. **Subject:** Poison frogs **Rev:** Red frog, multicolor

Date	Mintage	F12	VF20	XF40	MS60	MS63
2005	2,500	PF65 50.00				

KM# 862 10 DOLLARS
25.00 g., 0.925 Silver 0.7387 oz. ASW, 38.6 mm. **Subject:** Poison frogs **Rev:** Blue frog, multicolor

Date	Mintage	F12	VF20	XF40	MS60	MS63
2005	2,500	PF65 50.00				

KM# 864 10 DOLLARS
0.50 g., 0.585 Gold AGW, 11 mm. **Subject:** 25th Anniversary of the Krugerrand **Obv:** Shield **Rev:** Paul Krueger bust left

Date	Mintage	F12	VF20	XF40	MS60	MS63
2005	—	PF65 35.00				

KM# 996 10 DOLLARS
62.20 g., 0.999 Silver 1.9849 oz. ASW, 50 mm. **Subject:** Romanesque Architecture **Rev:** Facade, Tiffany Glass insert

Date	Mintage	F12	VF20	XF40	MS60	MS63
2005 Antique finish	999	—	—	—	125	

KM# 1017 10 DOLLARS
Silver **Subject:** Election of Pope Benedict XVI **Rev:** Pope with outstretched arms, St. Peter's in background

Date	Mintage	F12	VF20	XF40	MS60	MS63
2005	—	PF63 30.00	PF65 35.00			

KM# 1018 10 DOLLARS
Silver **Subject:** Moric Benovsky **Obv:** Naitonal arms **Rev:** Sailing ship right

Date	Mintage	F12	VF20	XF40	MS60	MS63
2005	—	PF63 30.00	PF65 35.00			

KM# 1019 10 DOLLARS
Silver, oval mm. **Obv:** National arms **Rev:** Titanic with recovered coal insert

Date	Mintage	F12	VF20	XF40	MS60	MS63
2005	—	PF63 30.00	PF65 35.00			

KM# 764 10 DOLLARS
20.00 g., 0.999 Silver 0.6382 oz. ASW, 38 mm. **Series:** Endangered Wildlife **Obv:** National arms **Obv. Legend:** REPUBLIC OF LIBERIA **Rev:** Gilt Crested Genet on branch facing with diamonds inset in eyes **Rev. Legend:** CAMEROON **Edge:** Plain

Date	Mintage	F12	VF20	XF40	MS60	MS63
2006	5,000	PF65 115				

KM# 765 10 DOLLARS
20.00 g., 0.999 Silver 0.6382 oz. ASW, 38 mm. **Series:** Endangered Wildlife **Obv:** National arms **Obv. Legend:** REPUBLIC OF LIBERIA **Rev:** Two gilt Dalmatian Pelicans, one swimming, one standing with diamonds inset in eyes **Rev. Legend:** MONTENEGRO **Edge:** Plain

Date	Mintage	F12	VF20	XF40	MS60	MS63
2006	5,000	PF65 115				

KM# 766 10 DOLLARS
20.00 g., 0.999 Silver 0.6382 oz. ASW, 38 mm. **Series:** Endangered Wildlife **Obv:** National arms **Obv. Legend:** REPUBLIC OF LIBERIA **Rev:** Gilt Hairy-bared Dwarf Lemue standing on branch with diamonds inset in eyes **Rev. Legend:** MADAGASCAR **Edge:** Plain

Date	Mintage	F12	VF20	XF40	MS60	MS63
2006	5,000	PF65 115				

KM# 767 10 DOLLARS
20.00 g., 0.999 Silver 0.6382 oz. ASW, 38 mm. **Series:** Endangered Wildlife **Obv:** National arms **Obv. Legend:** REPUBLIC OF LIBERIA **Rev:** Two gilt Visayan Tarictics perched on branches with diamonds inset in eyes **Rev. Legend:** Philippines **Edge:** Plain

Date	Mintage	F12	VF20	XF40	MS60	MS63
2006	5,000	PF65 115				

KM# 768 10 DOLLARS
20.00 g., 0.999 Silver 0.6382 oz. ASW, 38 mm. **Series:** Endangered Wildlife **Obv:** National arms **Obv. Legend:** REPUBLIC OF LIBERIA **Rev:** Two gilt Ethiopian Wolves, one seated, one laying with diamonds inset in eyes **Rev. Legend:** ETHIOPIA **Edge:** Plain

Date	Mintage	F12	VF20	XF40	MS60	MS63
2006	5,000	PF65 115				

KM# 769 10 DOLLARS
20.00 g., 0.999 Silver 0.6382 oz. ASW, 38 mm. **Series:** Endangered Wildlife **Obv:** National arms **Obv. Legend:** REPUBLIC OF LIBERIA **Rev:** Two gilt Kakapos perched on a branch with diamonds inset in eyes **Rev. Legend:** NEW ZEALAND **Edge:** Plain

Date	Mintage	F12	VF20	XF40	MS60	MS63
2006	5,000	PF65 115				

KM# 770 10 DOLLARS
20.00 g., 0.999 Silver 0.6382 oz. ASW, 38 mm. **Series:** Endangered Wildlife **Obv:** National arms **Obv. Legend:** REPUBLIC OF LIBERIA **Rev:** Gilt Spectacled Bear standing with diamonds inset in eyes **Rev. Legend:** BOLIVIA **Edge:** Plain

Date	Mintage	F12	VF20	XF40	MS60	MS63
2006	5,000	PF65 115				

KM# 771 10 DOLLARS
20.00 g., 0.999 Silver 0.6382 oz. ASW, 38 mm. **Series:** Endangered Wildlife **Obv:** National arms **Obv. Legend:** REPUBLIC OF LIBERIA **Rev:** Two gilt Mauritius Kestrels perched on branch with diamonds inset in eyes **Rev. Legend:** MAURITIUS **Edge:** Plain

Date	Mintage	F12	VF20	XF40	MS60	MS63
2006	5,000	PF65 115				

KM# 772 10 DOLLARS
20.00 g., 0.999 Silver 0.6382 oz. ASW, 38 mm. **Series:** Endangered Wildlife **Obv:** National arms **Obv. Legend:** REPUBLIC OF LIBERIA **Rev:** Two gilt Mhorr Gazelles, one standing, one resting with diamonds inset in eyes **Rev. Legend:** MALI **Edge:** Plain

Date	Mintage	F12	VF20	XF40	MS60	MS63
2006	5,000	PF65 115				

KM# 773 10 DOLLARS
20.00 g., 0.999 Silver 0.6382 oz. ASW, 38 mm. **Series:** Endangered Wildlife **Obv:** National arms **Obv. Legend:** REPUBLIC OF LIBERIA **Rev:** Two gilt Blue Lorikeets perched on branches with diamonds inset in eyes **Rev. Legend:** FRENCH POLYNESIA **Edge:** Plain

Date	Mintage	F12	VF20	XF40	MS60	MS63
2006	5,000	PF65 115				

KM# 774 10 DOLLARS
20.00 g., 0.999 Silver 0.6382 oz. ASW, 38 mm. **Series:** Endangered Wildlife **Obv:** National arms **Obv. Legend:** REPUBLIC OF LIBERIA **Rev:** Gilt resting Arabian Leopard with diamonds inset in eyes **Rev. Legend:** SAUDI ARABIA **Edge:** Plain

Date	Mintage	F12	VF20	XF40	MS60	MS63
2006	5,000	PF65 115				

KM# 775 10 DOLLARS
20.00 g., 0.999 Silver 0.6382 oz. ASW, 38 mm. **Series:** Endangered Wildlife **Obv:** National arms **Obv. Legend:** REPUBLIC OF LIBERIA **Rev:** Two gilt Hawaiian Geese standing with diamonds inset in eyes **Rev. Legend:** USA **Edge:** Plain

Date	Mintage	F12	VF20	XF40	MS60	MS63
2006	5,000	PF65 115				

KM# 827 10 DOLLARS
14.60 g., Copper-Nickel, 33 mm. **Subject:** Abraham Lincoln **Obv:** National arms **Rev:** Bust facing 3/4 right **Edge:** Reeded

Date	Mintage	F12	VF20	XF40	MS60	MS63
2006	50,000	PF65 10.00				

KM# 725 10 DOLLARS
3.11 g., 0.999 Gold 0.0992 oz. AGW, 16 mm. **Obv:** National arms **Rev:** Leopard head **Edge:** Reeded

Date	Mintage	F12	VF20	XF40	MS60	MS63
2007	120	PF65 200				

KM# 734 10 DOLLARS
25.00 g., 0.925 Silver 0.7387 oz. ASW, 38.61 mm. **Subject:** The Black Madonna of Czestochowa **Obv:** Arms **Obv. Legend:** REPUBLIC OF LIBERIA **Rev:** 1/2 length figure of Madonna facing with child

Date	Mintage	F12	VF20	XF40	MS60	MS63
2007	1,000	PF65 70.00				

KM# 1009 10 DOLLARS
62.21 g., 0.999 Silver 1.9852 oz. ASW **Obv:** National arms **Rev:** Christmas tree in color

Date	Mintage	F12	VF20	XF40	MS60	MS63
2010	—	PF65 150				

KM# 1029 12 DOLLARS
0.62 g., 0.999 Gold AGW, 10 mm. **Rev:** Christ at center, apostles in 12 segments around

Date	Mintage	F12	VF20	XF40	MS60	MS63
2007	—	PF65 70.00				

KM# 514 20 DOLLARS
31.10 g., 0.999 Silver 0.9926 oz. ASW, 38.2 mm. **Subject:** Bush-Cheney Inauguration **Obv:** White House **Rev:** Conjoined busts right **Edge:** Reeded

Date	Mintage	F12	VF20	XF40	MS60	MS63
2001	—	PF65 45.00				

KM# 643 20 DOLLARS
15.55 g., 0.999 Silver 0.4962 oz. ASW, 30.4 mm. **Obv:** St. Peter's Basilica **Rev:** Bust of Pope facing **Edge:** Reeded

Date	Mintage	F12	VF20	XF40	MS60	MS63
2001S (2001)	—	PF65 28.00				

KM# 650 20 DOLLARS
19.91 g., 0.999 Silver 0.6354 oz. ASW, 40 mm. **Obv:** National arms **Rev:** Bust of Charles Lindbergh facing and Spirit of St. Louis in background **Edge:** Reeded

Date	Mintage	F12	VF20	XF40	MS60	MS63
2001	—	PF65 40.00				

KM# 715 20 DOLLARS
20.00 g., 0.999 Silver 0.6382 oz. ASW, 40.3 mm. **Series:** American History **Obv:** National arms **Rev:** First Continental Congress in prayer **Edge:** Reeded

Date	Mintage	F12	VF20	XF40	MS60	MS63
2001	20,000	PF65 32.00				

KM# 716 20 DOLLARS
20.00 g., 0.999 Silver 0.6382 oz. ASW, 40.3 mm. **Series:** American History **Obv:** National arms **Rev:** U.S. Constitution Ratification, text in stars of folded flag **Edge:** Reeded

Date	Mintage	F12	VF20	XF40	MS60	MS63
2001	20,000	PF65 32.00				

KM# 717 20 DOLLARS
20.00 g., 0.999 Silver 0.6382 oz. ASW, 40.3 mm. **Series:** American History **Obv:** National arms **Rev:** Washington's Inauguration scene **Edge:** Reeded

Date	Mintage	F12	VF20	XF40	MS60	MS63
2001	20,000	PF65 32.00				

KM# 718 20 DOLLARS
20.00 g., 0.925 Silver 0.591 oz. ASW, 40.3 mm. **Series:** American History **Obv:** National arms **Rev:** Appomattox Courthouse surrender scene with Lee and Grant **Edge:** Reeded

Date	Mintage	F12	VF20	XF40	MS60	MS63
2001	20,000	PF65 32.00				

KM# 719 20 DOLLARS
20.00 g., 0.999 Silver 0.6382 oz. ASW, 40.3 mm. **Series:** American History **Obv:** National arms **Rev:** Prohibition, hatchet, barrels and bottles destruction **Edge:** Reeded

Date	Mintage	F12	VF20	XF40	MS60	MS63
2001	20,000	PF65 32.00				

KM# 720 20 DOLLARS
20.00 g., 0.999 Silver 0.6382 oz. ASW, 40.3 mm. **Series:** American History **Obv:** National arms **Rev:** Cuban Missile Crisis, Castro, Khrushchev, Kennedy, missiles and map **Edge:** Reeded

Date	Mintage	F12	VF20	XF40	MS60	MS63
2001	20,000	PF65 32.00				

KM# 721 20 DOLLARS
20.00 g., 0.999 Silver 0.6382 oz. ASW, 40.3 mm. **Series:** American History **Obv:** National arms **Rev:** First Man on Moon, Armstrong and Lander **Edge:** Reeded

Date	Mintage	F12	VF20	XF40	MS60	MS63
2001	20,000	PF65 32.00				

KM# 722 20 DOLLARS
20.00 g., 0.999 Silver 0.6382 oz. ASW, 40.3 mm. **Series:** American History **Obv:** National arms **Rev:** Desert Storm, soldier, helicopter, rocket launcher etc. **Edge:** Reeded

Date	Mintage	F12	VF20	XF40	MS60	MS63
2001	20,000	PF65 32.00				

KM# 616 20 DOLLARS
31.20 g., 0.999 Silver 0.9956 oz. ASW, 38.7 mm. **Obv:** National arms **Rev:** Diamond studded scorpion (Scorpio) **Edge:** Reeded

Date	Mintage	F12	VF20	XF40	MS60	MS63
2002	—	PF65 60.00				

KM# 617 20 DOLLARS
31.20 g., 0.999 Silver 0.9956 oz. ASW, 38.7 mm. **Obv:** National arms **Rev:** Diamond studded archer (Sagittarius) **Edge:** Reeded

Date	Mintage	F12	VF20	XF40	MS60	MS63
2002	—	PF65 60.00				

KM# 825 20 DOLLARS
20.00 g., Silver, 40 mm. **Series:** America's First Ladies **Subject:** Mary Todd Lincoln **Obv:** National arms **Rev:** Bust facing slightly left at center left, oval portrait of Abraham Lincoln at right **Edge:** Reeded

Date	Mintage	F12	VF20	XF40	MS60	MS63
2003	20,000	PF65 32.50				

KM# 826 20 DOLLARS
20.00 g., Silver, 40 mm. **Series:** History of America **Subject:**

Emancipation Proclamation **Obv:** National arms **Rev:** Lincoln seated with seven politicians gathered **Edge:** Reeded

Date	Mintage	F12	VF20	XF40	MS60	MS63
2004	20,000	PF65 37.50				

KM# 1020 20 DOLLARS
Silver **Subject:** U.S. Constitution

Date	Mintage	F12	VF20	XF40	MS60	MS63
2006	—	PF63 30.00	PF65 35.00			

KM# 1021 20 DOLLARS
1.25 g., 0.999 Gold 0.0399 oz. AGW, 14 mm. **Subject:** World Cup Soccer, Germany **Obv:** National arms **Rev:** Soccer player heading ball

Date	Mintage	F12	VF20	XF40	MS60	MS63
2006	—	PF65 80.00				

KM# 634 25 DOLLARS
0.73 g., 0.999 Gold AGW, 11.1 mm. **Obv:** National arms **Rev:** Joan of Arc **Edge:** Reeded

Date	Mintage	F12	VF20	XF40	MS60	MS63
2001	—	PF65 60.00				

KM# 666 25 DOLLARS
1.52 g., Gold AGW, 13.68 mm. **Subject:** Abraham Lincoln **Obv:** National arms **Rev:** Statue of Lincoln seated **Edge:** Reeded

Date	Mintage	F12	VF20	XF40	MS60	MS63
2001	—	PF65 95.00				

KM# 667 25 DOLLARS
0.73 g., 0.999 Gold AGW, 11 mm. **Obv:** National arms **Rev:** Mount Rushmore **Edge:** Reeded

Date	Mintage	F12	VF20	XF40	MS60	MS63
2001	20,000	PF65 65.00				

KM# 995 25 DOLLARS
0.73 g., 0.999 Gold AGW, 11 mm. **Obv:** National Arms **Rev:** Martin Luther King and Washington Monument

Date	Mintage	F12	VF20	XF40	MS60	MS63
2001	—	PF65 70.00				

KM# 669 25 DOLLARS
0.73 g., 0.999 Gold AGW, 11 mm. **Subject:** Abraham Lincoln **Obv:** National arms **Rev:** Bust facing at right, Lincoln Memorial in background **Edge:** Reeded

Date	Mintage	F12	VF20	XF40	MS60	MS63
2002	20,000	PF65 65.00				

KM# 730 25 DOLLARS
0.02 g., 0.999 Gold AGW **Obv:** Shield **Rev:** Map of Germany and stars

Date	Mintage	F12	VF20	XF40	MS60	MS63
2003B	—	PF65 35.00				

KM# 804 25 DOLLARS
1.25 g., 0.999 Gold 0.0399 oz. AGW, 14.5 x 9 mm. **Subject:** R. M. S. Titanic - Expedition 2000 **Obv:** National arms **Obv. Legend:** REPUBLIC OF LIBERIA **Rev:** Titanic with small piece of recovered coal embedded in hull. **Edge:** Reeded **Shape:** Oval

Date	Mintage	F12	VF20	XF40	MS60	MS63
2005	—	PF65 80.00				

KM# 495 50 DOLLARS
907.00 g., 0.999 Silver 28.944 oz. ASW, 100 mm. **Subject:** Wreck of the Princess Louisa **Obv:** National arms and value **Rev:** Ship under sail **Edge:** Reeded **Note:** Each coin has a cob coin recovered from the wreck site encased in a hole with clear resin. Illustration reduced.

Date	Mintage	F12	VF20	XF40	MS60	MS63
2001	500	—	—	—	1,150	

KM# 731 50 DOLLARS
222.08 g., 0.999 Silver 7.087 oz. ASW, 80.04 mm. **Subject:** Japanese Attack on Pearl Harbor **Obv:** National arms **Obv. Legend:** REPUBLIC OF LIBERIA **Rev:** USA flag hologram at upper left, bust of Franklin D. Roosevelt facing above Japanese aircraft attacking ship in harbor **Rev. Legend:** REMEMBERING PEARL HARBOR - DECEMBER 7, 1941

Date	Mintage	F12	VF20	XF40	MS60	MS63
2001	—	PF65 275				

KM# 776 50 DOLLARS
93.30 g., 0.999 Silver 2.9774 oz. ASW, 65.00 mm. **Series:** Endangered Wildlife **Obv:** National arms **Obv. Legend:** REPUBLIC OF LIBERIA **Rev:** Two gilt Cheetahs, one sitting, one resting with diamonds inset in eyes **Rev. Legend:** TANZANIA **Edge:** Plain

Date	Mintage	F12	VF20	XF40	MS60	MS63
2005	999	PF65 450				

KM# 726 50 DOLLARS
62.21 g., 0.999 Silver 1.9851 oz. ASW, 50 mm. **Obv:** National arms **Rev:** Leopard lying across a map of Africa **Edge:** Reeded

Date	Mintage	F12	VF20	XF40	MS60	MS63
2007	500	PF65 125				

KM# 844 100 DOLLARS
1000.00 g., 0.999 Silver 31.9118 oz. ASW **Subject:** Tanks of World War II - T-34

Date	Mintage	F12	VF20	XF40	MS60	MS63
2008	1,000	PF65 1,500				

KM# 845 100 DOLLARS
1000.00 g., 0.999 Silver 31.9118 oz. ASW **Subject:** Tanks of World War II - VI-Tiger

Date	Mintage	F12	VF20	XF40	MS60	MS63
2008	1,000	PF65 1,500				

KM# 846 100 DOLLARS
1000.00 g., 0.999 Silver 31.9118 oz. ASW, 120 mm. **Obv:** Arms
Rev: St. Paul standing, events of his life around

Date	Mintage	F12	VF20	XF40	MS60	MS63
2008	1,000	PF65 2,000				

KM# 847 100 DOLLARS
1000.00 g., 0.999 Silver 31.9118 oz. ASW, 120 mm. **Obv:**
National shield **Rev:** Christ at center, apostles around

Date	Mintage	F12	VF20	XF40	MS60	MS63
2008	1,000	PF65 2,000				

KM# 727 2500 DOLLARS
155.52 g., 0.999 Gold 4.9628 oz. AGW, 60 mm. **Obv:** National
arms **Rev:** Leopard lying across a map of Africa **Edge:** Reeded

Date	Mintage	F12	VF20	XF40	MS60	MS63
2007	48	PF65 9,500				

PATTERNS
Including off metal strikes

KM#	Date	Mintage	Identification	Mkt Val
Pn58	2001	—	10 Dollars Copper-Nickel National arms 9-11" Flag raising scene	250
Pn59	2001	—	20 Dollars Silver Plated Base Metal National arms 9-11" Flag raising scene	150
Pn60	2001	—	100 Dollars Base Metal Gilt National arms 9-11" Flag raising scene	125

LIBYA

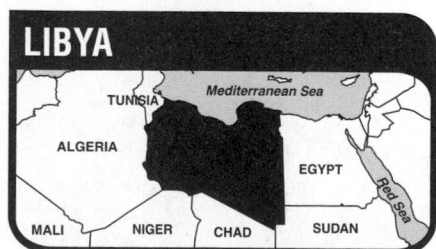

The Socialist People's Libyan Arab Jamahariya, located
on the north-central coast of Africa between Tunisia and
Egypt, has an area of 679,358 sq. mi. (1,759,540 sq. km.) and
a population of 3.9 million. Capital: Tripoli. Crude oil, which
accounts for 90 per cent of the export earnings, is the mainstay
of the economy.

TITLES

المملكة الليبية

al-Mamlaka(t) al-Libiya(t)

الجمهورية الليبية

al-Jomhuriya(t) al-Arabiya(t) al-Libiya(t)

GREAT SOCIALIST PEOPLE'S LIBYAN ARAB JAMAHIRIYA

STANDARD COINAGE
1000 Dirhams = 1 Dinar

KM# 28 50 DIRHAMS
6.25 g., Copper-Nickel, 25 mm. **Obv:** Armored equestrian **Rev:**
Value at center **Shape:** Scalloped

Date	Mintage	F12	VF20	XF40	MS60	MS63
MD1377-2009	—	—	—	2.50	6.00	—

KM# 29 100 DIRHAMS
Copper-Nickel, 27 mm. **Obv:** Armored Equestrian **Rev:** Value
at center

Date	Mintage	F12	VF20	XF40	MS60	MS63
MD1377-2009	—	—	—	4.50	9.00	—

KM# 26 1/4 DINAR
11.15 g., Nickel-Brass, 28 mm. **Obv:** Libyan knight on horse
with gun 1/2 left surrounded by name of Libyan Arab Jamahiriya,
ornamental legend with date **Rev:** Value in Arabic script above
wheat ears in ornamented frame **Edge:** Ten alternating reeded
and plain flat sections **Shape:** 10-sided

Date	Mintage	F12	VF20	XF40	MS60	MS63
MD1369 (2001)	—	—	—	5.00	8.00	10.00

Note: Restruck in 2001-2002

KM# 30 1/4 DINAR
11.50 g., Nickel-Brass, 28 mm. **Obv:** Armored horseman **Rev:**
Value at center **Shape:** 10-sided

Date	Mintage	F12	VF20	XF40	MS60	MS63
MD1377-2009	—	—	—	9.00	12.50	—

KM# 27 1/2 DINAR
11.50 g., Bi-Metallic, 30 mm. **Obv:** Man on horse with gun 1/2
left, ornamental legend with date **Rev:** Value in Arabic script
above wheat ears in ornamented frame **Edge:** Reeded

Date	Mintage	F12	VF20	XF40	MS60	MS63
MD1372 (2004)	—	—	—	—	10.00	12.00

KM# 31 1/2 DINAR
11.50 g., Bi-Metallic, 30 mm. **Obv:** Armored horseman **Rev:**
Value at center **Edge:** Reeded

Date	Mintage	F12	VF20	XF40	MS60	MS63
MD1377-2009	—	—	—	12.50	15.00	—

LIECHTENSTEIN

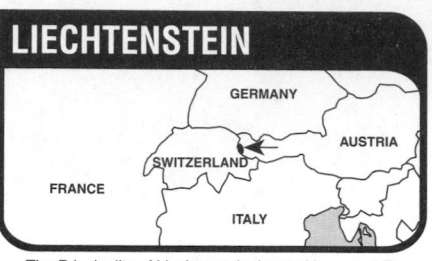

The Principality of Liechtenstein, located in central Europe
on the east bank of the Rhine between Austria and Switzerland,
has an area of 62 sq. mi. (160 sq. km.) and a population of
27,200. Capital: Vaduz. The economy is based on agriculture
and light manufacturing. Canned goods, textiles, ceramics and
precision instruments are exported.

RULERS
Prince Hans Adam II, 1990-

MINT MARKS
B - Bern

PRINCIPALITY

REFORM COINAGE
100 Rappen = 1 Frank

Y# 24 10 FRANKEN
29.95 g., 0.900 Silver 0.861 oz. ASW, 37.3 mm. **Ruler:** Prince
Hans Adam II **Subject:** 200 Years of Sovereignty **Obv:** Vertical
inscription between crowned arms and value **Rev:** Johann I
(1760-1836) **Edge:** Reeded

Date	Mintage	F12	VF20	XF40	MS60	MS63
ND (2006)B	—	PF63 45.00	PF65 55.00			

Y# 25 50 FRANKEN
8.88 g., 0.999 Gold 0.2834 oz. AGW **Ruler:** Prince Hans Adam
II **Subject:** 200th Anniversary of Sovereignty

Date	Mintage	F12	VF20	XF40	MS60	MS63
ND (2006)B	—	PF63 500	PF65 525			

LITHUANIA

The Principality of Liechtenstein, located in central Europe on the east bank of the Rhine between Austria and Switzerland, has an area of 62 sq. mi. (160 sq. km.) and a population of 27,200. Capital: Vaduz. The economy is based on agriculture and light manufacturing. Canned goods, textiles, ceramics and precision instruments are exported.

RULERS
Prince Hans Adam II, 1990-

MINT MARKS
B - Bern

MODERN REPUBLIC
1991-present

REFORM COINAGE
100 Centas = 1 Litas

KM# 106 10 CENTŲ
2.60 g., Nickel-Brass, 17 mm. **Obv:** National arms **Rev:** Value **Edge:** Reeded

Date	Mintage	F12	VF20	XF40	MS60	MS63
2003 Prooflike	10,000	—	—	—	—	4.00
2006	—	—	—	—	—	0.40
2006	2,000	PF63 45.00				
2007	—	—	—	—	—	0.40
2008	—	—	—	—	—	0.40
2008 Prooflike	200	—	—	—	—	5.00
2009	—	—	—	—	—	0.40
2009 Prooflike	500	—	—	—	—	16.00
2010	—	—	—	—	—	0.40
2011 In sets only	4,500	—	—	—	—	0.75
2012 In sets only	4,000	—	—	—	—	0.75
2013 In sets only	7,000	—	—	—	—	0.75

KM# 107 20 CENTŲ
4.80 g., Nickel-Brass, 20.5 mm. **Obv:** National arms **Rev:** Value **Edge:** Reeded

Date	Mintage	F12	VF20	XF40	MS60	MS63
2003 In sets only	—	—	—	—	—	1.50
2003	10,000	PF60 2.00				
2007	—	—	—	—	—	1.00
2008	—	—	—	—	—	1.00
2008 Prooflike	200	—	—	—	—	5.00
2009	—	—	—	—	—	1.00
2009 Prooflike	500	—	—	—	—	3.00
2010	—	—	—	—	—	1.00
2011 In sets only	4,500	—	—	—	—	2.00
2012 In sets only	4,000	—	—	—	—	2.00
2013 In sets only	7,500	—	—	—	—	2.00

KM# 108 50 CENTŲ
6.00 g., Nickel-Brass, 23 mm. **Obv:** National arms **Rev:** Value within designed circle **Edge:** Reeded

Date	Mintage	F12	VF20	XF40	MS60	MS63
2003 In sets only	—	—	—	—	—	4.00
2003	10,000	PF60 2.00				
2008 In sets only	4,000	—	—	—	—	4.00
2008 Prooflike	200	—	—	—	—	30.00
2009 In sets only	5,000	—	—	—	—	10.00
2009 Prooflike	500	—	—	—	—	4.00
2010 In sets only	3,500	—	—	—	—	10.00
2011 In sets only	4,500	—	—	—	—	4.00
2012 In sets only	4,000	—	—	—	—	4.00
2013 In sets only	7,500	—	—	—	—	4.00

KM# 111 LITAS
6.25 g., Copper-Nickel, 22.3 mm. **Obv:** National arms **Rev:** Value within circle above lined designs **Edge:** Reeded

Date	Mintage	F12	VF20	XF40	MS60	MS63
2001	—	—	—	—	1.50	2.00
2002	—	—	—	—	1.50	2.00
2003 In sets only	—	—	—	—	—	5.00
2003	10,000	PF60 8.00				
2008	—	—	—	—	1.50	2.00
2008 Prooflike	200	—	—	—	—	6.00
2009	—	—	—	—	1.50	2.00
2009 Prooflike	500	—	—	—	—	4.00
2010	—	—	—	—	1.50	2.00
2011 In sets only	4,500	—	—	—	—	3.00
2012 In sets only	4,000	—	—	—	—	3.00
2013 In sets only	7,500	—	—	—	—	3.00

KM# 137 LITAS
6.25 g., Copper-Nickel, 22.3 mm. **Subject:** 425th Anniversary - University of Vilnius **Obv:** Knight on horse within rope wreath **Rev:** Building within court yard **Edge:** Segmented reeding

Date	Mintage	F12	VF20	XF40	MS60	MS63
2004	200,000	—	—	—	5.00	8.00

KM# 142 LITAS
6.25 g., Copper-Nickel, 22.3 mm. **Obv:** Knight on horse within circle **Rev:** Palace **Edge:** Segmented reeding

Date	Mintage	F12	VF20	XF40	MS60	MS63
2005	1,000,000	—	—	—	2.00	3.00

KM# 162 LITAS
6.25 g., Copper-Nickel, 22.3 mm. **Subject:** Vilnius - European Culture Capital **Obv:** National Arms **Rev:** Female figure standing at easel **Edge:** Segmented reeding

Date	Mintage	F12	VF20	XF40	MS60	MS63
2009	1,000,000	—	—	—	3.00	4.00

KM# 172 LITAS
6.25 g., Copper-Nickel, 22.3 mm. **Subject:** Battle of Grunwald, 600th Anniversary **Obv:** National arms **Rev:** Long spears attacking each other **Edge:** Segmented reeding

Date	Mintage	F12	VF20	XF40	MS60	MS63
2010	1,000,000	—	—	—	3.00	4.00

KM# 177 LITAS
6.25 g., Copper-Nickel, 22.3 mm. **Subject:** European

Basketball Championship **Obv:** National arms **Rev:** Basketball **Rev. Legend:** EUROPOS KREPSINIO CEMPIONATAS **Edge:** Reeded

Date	Mintage	F12	VF20	XF40	MS60	MS63
2011	1,000,000	—	—	—	3.00	7.00

KM# 182 LITAS
6.25 g., Copper-Nickel, 22.3 mm. **Subject:** Presidency of the EU **Obv:** Stylized map of Europe with stars **Rev:** Stylized Vytis with stars

Date	Mintage	F12	VF20	XF40	MS60	MS63
2013	100,000	—	—	—	3.00	7.00

KM# 112 2 LITAI
7.50 g., Bi-Metallic, 25 mm. **Obv:** National arms within circle **Rev:** Value within circle **Edge:** Segmented reeding

Date	Mintage	F12	VF20	XF40	MS60	MS63
2001	—	—	—	—	3.00	5.00
2002	—	—	—	—	3.00	5.00
2003	10,000	PF60 3.50				
2008	—	—	—	—	2.25	3.00
2008 Prooflike	200	—	—	—	—	30.00
2009	—	—	—	—	3.00	5.00
2009 Prooflike	500	—	—	—	—	25.00
2010	—	—	—	—	3.00	5.00
2011 In sets only	4,500	—	—	—	—	5.00
2012 In sets only	4,000	—	—	—	—	5.00
2013 In sets only	7,500	—	—	—	—	5.00

KM# 183.1 2 LITAI
7.50 g., Bi-Metallic, 25 mm. **Subject:** Resorts - Birstonas **Obv:** National arms **Rev:** Arms of Birstonas

Date	Mintage	F12	VF20	XF40	MS60	MS63
2012	100,000	—	—	—	3.00	5.00

KM# 183.2 2 LITAI
7.50 g., Bi-Metallic, 25 mm. **Subject:** Resorts - Birstonas **Obv:** National arms **Rev:** Arms of Birstonas in color

Date	Mintage	F12	VF20	XF40	MS60	MS63
2012	2,500	PF65 25.00				

KM# 184.1 2 LITAI
7.50 g., Bi-Metallic, 25 mm. **Subject:** Resorts - Druskininkai **Obv:** National arms **Rev:** Arms of Druskininkai

Date	Mintage	F12	VF20	XF40	MS60	MS63
2012	100,000	—	—	—	3.00	5.00

KM# 184.2 2 LITAI
7.50 g., Bi-Metallic, 25 mm. **Subject:** Resorts - Druskininkai **Obv:** National arms **Rev:** Arms of Druskininkai in color

Date	Mintage	F12	VF20	XF40	MS60	MS63
2012	2,500	PF65 25.00				

KM# 185.1 2 LITAI
7.50 g., Bi-Metallic, 25 mm. **Subject:** Resorts - Neringa **Obv:** National arms **Rev:** Arms of Neringa

Date	Mintage	F12	VF20	XF40	MS60	MS63
2012	100,000	—	—	—	3.00	5.00

KM# 185.2 2 LITAI
7.50 g., Bi-Metallic, 25 mm. **Subject:** Resorts - Neringa **Obv:** National arms **Rev:** Arms of Neringa in color

Date	Mintage	F12	VF20	XF40	MS60	MS63
2012	2,500	PF65 25.00				

KM# 186.1 2 LITAI
7.50 g., Bi-Metallic, 25 mm. **Subject:** Resorts - Palanga **Obv:** National arms **Rev:** Arms of Palanga

Date	Mintage	F12	VF20	XF40	MS60	MS63
2012	100,000	—	—	—	3.00	5.00

KM# 186.2 2 LITAI
7.50 g., Bi-Metallic, 25 mm. **Subject:** Resorts - Palanga **Obv:** National arms **Rev:** Arms of Palanga

Date	Mintage	F12	VF20	XF40	MS60	MS63
2012	2,500	PF65 25.00				

KM# 191 2 LITAI
1.24 g., 0.999 Gold 0.0397 oz. AGW, 13.92 mm. **Subject:** Science **Obv:** Vytis **Rev:** Heart surgery

Date	Mintage	F12	VF20	XF40	MS60	MS63
2012	5,000	PF65 50.00				

KM# 187 2 LITAI
7.50 g., Bi-Metallic, 25 mm. **Obv:** National arms **Rev:** Distaff (spinning tool)

Date	Mintage	F12	VF20	XF40	MS60	MS63
2013	100,000	—	—	—	3.00	5.00

KM# 188 2 LITAI
7.50 g., Bi-Metallic **Obv:** National arms **Rev:** Kurenas (traditional wooden boat)

Date	Mintage	F12	VF20	XF40	MS60	MS63
2013	100,000	—	—	—	3.00	5.00

KM# 189 2 LITAI
7.50 g., Bi-Metallic, 25 mm. **Obv:** National arms **Rev:** Puntukas stone

Date	Mintage	F12	VF20	XF40	MS60	MS63
2013	100,000	—	—	—	3.00	5.00

KM# 190 2 LITAI
7.50 g., Bi-Metallic, 25 mm. **Obv:** National arms **Rev:** Stelmuze oak

Date	Mintage	F12	VF20	XF40	MS60	MS63
2013	100,000	—	—	—	3.00	5.00

KM# 113 5 LITAI
10.10 g., Bi-Metallic, 27.5 mm. **Obv:** National arms within circle **Rev:** Value within circle **Edge Lettering:** PENKI LITAI

Date	Mintage	F12	VF20	XF40	MS60	MS63
2003 In sets only	—	—	—	—	—	14.00
2003	10,000	PF63 15.00				
2008 In sets only	3,800	—	—	—	—	15.00
2008 Prooflike	200	—	—	—	—	30.00
2009	—	—	—	—	4.00	6.00
2009 Prooflike	500	—	—	—	—	20.00
2010 In sets only	3,500	—	—	—	—	15.00
2011 In sets only	4,500	—	—	—	—	10.00
2012 In sets only	4,000	—	—	—	—	10.00
2013 In sets only	7,500	—	—	—	—	10.00

KM# 132 5 LITAI
28.28 g., 0.925 Silver 0.8356 oz. ASW, 38.6 mm. **Series:** Endangered Wildlife **Obv:** Knight on horse **Rev:** Barn owl in flight **Edge Lettering:** LIETUVOS BANKAS

Date	Mintage	F12	VF20	XF40	MS60	MS63
2002	3,000	PF65 150				

KM# 131 10 LITŲ
13.15 g., Copper-Nickel, 28.7 mm. **Obv:** Knight on horse on shield within aerial harbor view **Rev:** Shield within city view **Edge Lettering:** KLAIPEDAI - 75 (twice)

Date	Mintage	F12	VF20	XF40	MS60	MS63
2002	5,000	PF63 25.00	PF65 35.00			

KM# 160 10 LITŲ
1.24 g., 0.999 Gold 0.0396 oz. AGW, 13.92 mm. **Obv:** Castle gate **Rev:** Geometric design

Date	Mintage	F12	VF20	XF40	MS60	MS63
2007LMK	7,000	PF63 100	PF65 125			

KM# 169 10 LITŲ
11.40 g., 0.925 Silver 0.3368 oz. ASW, 28.7 mm. **Subject:** Lithuanian Culture - Music **Obv:** Vilnus **Rev:** Two chello and musical notations

Date	Mintage	F12	VF20	XF40	MS60	MS63
2010	10,000	PF63 45.00	PF65 50.00			

KM# 175 10 LITŲ
12.44 g., 0.925 Silver 0.3676 oz. ASW, 28.7 mm. **Subject:** Lithuanian Culture - Theatre **Obv:** State emblem **Rev:** Theatre motif, two half faces **Edge Lettering:** LIETUVOS KULTURA * TEATRAS (twice)

Date	Mintage	F12	VF20	XF40	MS60	MS63
2011	10,000	PF63 45.00	PF65 50.00			

KM# 180 10 LITŲ
Gold AGW **Subject:** Science - Mokslas

Date	Mintage	F12	VF20	XF40	MS60	MS63
2012	—	—	—	—	—	—

KM# 179 10 LITŲ
12.44 g., 0.925 Silver 0.3676 oz. ASW, 28.7 mm. **Subject:** Artist's pallete

Date	Mintage	F12	VF20	XF40	MS60	MS63
2012	4,000	PF63 45.00	PF65 50.00			

KM# 129 50 LITŲ
28.28 g., 0.925 Silver 0.8356 oz. ASW, 38.61 mm. **Subject:** Motiejus Valancius' 200th Birthday **Obv:** Knight on horse within shield above church and landscape **Rev:** Bust facing **Edge Lettering:** LIETUVISKAS ZODIS RASTAS IR TIKEJMAS TAUTOS GYVASTIS

Date	Mintage	F12	VF20	XF40	MS60	MS63
2001	2,000	PF65 200				

KM# 130 50 LITŲ
28.28 g., 0.925 Silver 0.8356 oz. ASW, 38.61 mm. **Subject:** Jonas Basanavicius (1851-1927) **Obv:** Knight on horse **Rev:** Jonas Basanavicius **Edge Lettering:** KAD AUSRAI AUSTANT PRAVISTU IR LIETUVOS DVASIA

Date	Mintage	F12	VF20	XF40	MS60	MS63
2001	—	PF65 200				

KM# 133 50 LITŲ
28.28 g., 0.925 Silver 0.8356 oz. ASW, 38.61 mm. **Series:** Historical Architecture **Obv:** Republic of Lithuania coat of arms **Rev:** Trakai Island Castle **Edge Lettering:** ISTORIJOS IR ARCHITEKTUROS PAMINKLAI

Date	Mintage	F12	VF20	XF40	MS60	MS63
2002	1,500	PF65 200				

KM# 134 50 LITŲ
28.28 g., 0.925 Silver 0.8356 oz. ASW, 38.6 mm. **Obv:** Knight on horse above value **Rev:** Vilnius Cathedral **Edge Lettering:** ISTORIJOS IR ARCHITEKTUROS PAMINKLAI

Date	Mintage	F12	VF20	XF40	MS60	MS63
2003	1,500	PF65 175				

KM# 135 50 LITŲ
28.28 g., 0.925 Silver 0.8356 oz. ASW, 38.6 mm. **Subject:** Olympics **Obv:** Knight on horse above value **Rev:** Stylized cyclists **Edge Lettering:** XXVIII OLIMPIADOS ZAIDYNEMS

Date	Mintage	F12	VF20	XF40	MS60	MS63
2003	2,000	PF65 150				

KM# 138 50 LITŲ
28.28 g., 0.925 Silver 0.8356 oz. ASW, 38.6 mm. **Series:** Historical Architecture **Subject:** 425th Anniversary - University of Vilnius **Obv:** Knight on horse **Rev:** Old university buildings **Edge:** Lettered **Edge Lettering:** ISTORIJOS IR ARCHITEKTUROS PAMINKLAI

Date	Mintage	F12	VF20	XF40	MS60	MS63
2004	2,000	PF65 150				

KM# 139 50 LITŲ
28.28 g., 0.925 Silver 0.8356 oz. ASW, 38.6 mm. **Obv:** Knight on horse **Rev:** Pazaislis Monastery **Edge:** Lettered **Edge Lettering:** ISTORIJOS IR ARCHITEKTUROS PAMINKLAI

Date	Mintage	F12	VF20	XF40	MS60	MS63
2004	1,500	PF65 150				

KM# 140 50 LITŲ
28.28 g., 0.925 Silver 0.8356 oz. ASW, 38.6 mm. **Subject:** First Lithuanian Statute of 1529 **Obv:** Knight on horse **Rev:** Seated and kneeling figures **Edge:** Lettered **Edge Lettering:** BUKIME TEISES VERGAI, KAD GALETUME NAUDOTIS LAISVEMIS

Date	Mintage	F12	VF20	XF40	MS60	MS63
2004	1,000	PF65 200				

KM# 141 50 LITŲ
28.28 g., 0.925 Silver 0.8356 oz. ASW, 38.6 mm. **Subject:** Curonian Spit **Obv:** Knight on horse **Rev:** Shifting sand dunes design **Edge:** Ornamented pattern from Neringa emblem

Date	Mintage	F12	VF20	XF40	MS60	MS63
2004	2,000	PF65 175				

KM# 143 50 LITŲ
28.28 g., 0.925 Silver 0.8356 oz. ASW, 38.61 mm. **Series:** Historical Architecture **Obv:** Denar coin with Knight on horse **Rev:** Kernavé hill fort **Edge Lettering:** ISTORIJOS IR ARCHITEKTUROS PAMINKLAI

Date	Mintage	F12	VF20	XF40	MS60	MS63
2005	2,000	PF65 150				

KM# 147 50 LITŲ
28.28 g., 0.925 Silver 0.8356 oz. ASW, 38.6 mm. **Subject:** 1905 Lithuanian Congress **Obv:** Knight on horse **Rev:** Legend and inscription **Edge:** Ornamented

Date	Mintage	F12	VF20	XF40	MS60	MS63
2005	1,500	PF65 225				

KM# 144 50 LITŲ
28.28 g., 0.925 Silver 0.8356 oz. ASW, 38.6 mm. **Subject:** 150th Anniversary - National Museum **Obv:** Trio of ancient Lithuanian coins **Rev:** Man blowing horn **Edge Lettering:** PRO PUBLICO BONO

Date	Mintage	F12	VF20	XF40	MS60	MS63
2005	1,500	PF65 275				

KM# 145 50 LITŲ
28.28 g., 0.925 Silver 0.8356 oz. ASW, 38.6 mm. **Subject:** Knight on horse and cross **Rev:** Cardinal Vincentas Sladkevicius **Edge Lettering:** LET OUR LIFE BE BUILT ON GOODNESS AND HOPE

Date	Mintage	F12	VF20	XF40	MS60	MS63
2005	2,000	PF65 175				

KM# 148 50 LITŲ
28.28 g., 0.925 Silver 0.8356 oz. ASW, 38.6 mm. **Obv:** National arms on forest background **Rev:** Lynx prowling **Edge:** Stylized lynx paw prints

Date	Mintage	F12	VF20	XF40	MS60	MS63
2006	3,000	PF65 175				

KM# 149 50 LITŲ
28.28 g., 0.925 Silver 0.8356 oz. ASW, 38.6 mm. **Obv:** National arms against castle wall background **Rev:** Medininkai Castle **Edge Lettering:** ISTORIJOS IR ARCHITEKTUROS PAMINKLAI

Date	Mintage	F12	VF20	XF40	MS60	MS63
2006	2,500	PF65 200				

KM# 151 50 LITŲ
28.28 g., 0.925 Silver 0.8356 oz. ASW, 38.61 mm. **Subject:** 1831 Uprising **Obv:** Small national arms above battle scene **Obv. Legend:** LIETUVA **Rev:** Bust of Pliaterytė facing **Rev. Legend:** EMILIJA PLIATERYTĖ **Edge Lettering:** 1831 * SUKILIMAS

Date	Mintage	F12	VF20	XF40	MS60	MS63
2006	2,500	PF65 200				

KM# 152 50 LITŲ
28.28 g., 0.925 Silver 0.8356 oz. ASW, 38.6 mm. **Subject:** XXIX Olympics 2008 - Beijing **Obv:** National arms **Obv. Legend:** LIETUVA **Rev:** Stylized swimmer right **Rev. Legend:** PEKINAS

Date	Mintage	F12	VF20	XF40	MS60	MS63
2007	5,000	PF65 150				

KM# 161 50 LITŲ
28.28 g., 0.925 Silver 0.8356 oz. ASW, 38.6 mm. **Subject:** Panemune Castle **Obv:** Shield and fortress detail **Rev:** Castle towers

Date	Mintage	F12	VF20	XF40	MS60	MS63
2007LMK	5,000	PF65 150				

KM# 153 50 LITŲ
28.28 g., 0.925 Silver 0.8356 oz. ASW, 38.6 mm. **Series:**
European Cultural Heritage **Obv:** National arms surrounded by
seven archaic crosses **Obv. Legend:** LIETUVA **Rev:** Circular
latent image surrounded by seven archaic crosses

Date	Mintage	F12	VF20	XF40	MS60	MS63
2008	10,000	PF63 120	PF65 150			

KM# 155 50 LITŲ
28.28 g., 0.925 Silver 0.8356 oz. ASW, 38.6 mm. **Obv:** National
arms **Obv. Legend:** LIETUVA **Rev:** Partial castle wall, towers
Rev. Legend: KAUNO PILIS

Date	Mintage	F12	VF20	XF40	MS60	MS63
2008	10,000	PF63 120	PF65 150			

KM# 154 50 LITŲ
28.28 g., 0.925 Silver 0.8356 oz. ASW, 38.6 mm. **Subject:**
550th Anniversary Birth of St. Casimer **Obv:** National arms
on shield **Obv. Legend:** LIETUVA **Rev:** St. Casimer standing
holding flowers **Rev. Legend:** SV. KAZIMIERAS

Date	Mintage	F12	VF20	XF40	MS60	MS63
2008	5,000	PF65 175				

KM# 159 50 LITŲ
28.28 g., 0.925 Silver 0.8356 oz. ASW, 38.6 mm. **Subject:**
Lithuania Nature **Obv:** National Arms **Rev:** Bee

Date	Mintage	F12	VF20	XF40	MS60	MS63
2008	10,000	PF63 120	PF65 150			

KM# 163 50 LITŲ
28.28 g., 0.925 Silver 0.8356 oz. ASW, 38.6 mm. **Subject:**
Vilnius - European Culture Capital **Obv:** National Arms **Rev:**
Female figure standing at easel

Date	Mintage	F12	VF20	XF40	MS60	MS63
2009	10,000	PF63 120	PF65 150			

KM# 164 50 LITŲ
28.28 g., 0.925 Silver 0.8356 oz. ASW, 38.6 mm. **Subject:**
Tytuvenai **Obv:** National Arms in Shield **Rev:** Tytuvenai Church
facade at left

Date	Mintage	F12	VF20	XF40	MS60	MS63
2009	10,000	PF63 120	PF65 150			

KM# 165 50 LITŲ
28.28 g., 0.925 Silver 0.8356 oz. ASW, 38.6 mm. **Subject:**
Nature, Naktiziede **Obv:** Knight on horseback left **Rev:** Flowers

Date	Mintage	F12	VF20	XF40	MS60	MS63
2009LMK	—	PF63 120	PF65 150			

KM# 170 50 LITŲ
28.28 g., 0.925 Silver 0.8356 oz. ASW, 38.61 mm. **Subject:**
Biržai Castle **Obv:** Viltus in shield **Rev:** Castle view and ariel
plan

Date	Mintage	F12	VF20	XF40	MS60	MS63
2010	10,000	PF63 75.00	PF65 85.00			

KM# 171 50 LITŲ
28.28 g., 0.925 Silver 0.8356 oz. ASW, 38.61 mm. **Obv:** Vilnus
Rev: Misgurnus Fossilis - European Weather Loach **Edge
Lettering:** LIETUVOS GAMTA

Date	Mintage	F12	VF20	XF40	MS60	MS63
2010	10,000	PF63 75.00	PF65 85.00			

KM# 176 50 LITŲ
3.10 g., 0.9999 Gold 0.099 oz. AGW, 16.25 mm. **Subject:**
European Basketball Championship **Obv:** State emblem
Rev: Basketball **Rev. Legend:** EUROPOS KREPSINIO
CEMPIONATAS **Edge:** Reeded

Date	Mintage	F12	VF20	XF40	MS60	MS63
2011	5,000	PF63 500	PF65 550			

KM# 174 50 LITŲ
28.28 g., 0.925 Silver 0.8356 oz. ASW, 38.61 mm. **Subject:**
Gabriele Petkevicaite-Bite, 150th Anniversary of Birth **Obv:**
State emblem **Rev:** Portrait **Edge Lettering:** AD ASTRA
(repeated 3 times)

Date	Mintage	F12	VF20	XF40	MS60	MS63
2011	10,000	PF63 85.00	PF65 100			

KM# 178 50 LITŲ
28.28 g., 0.925 Silver 0.8356 oz. ASW, 38.61 mm. **Rev:** Balinis
Vezlys - Emysorbicularis - Turtle **Edge Lettering:** LIETUVOS
GAMTA

Date	Mintage	F12	VF20	XF40	MS60	MS63
2012 Proof	—					

KM# 181 50 LITŲ
Silver ASW **Subject:** Battle of Grunwald

Date	Mintage	F12	VF20	XF40	MS60	MS63
2012						

KM# 192 50 LITŲ
28.28 g., 0.925 Silver 0.8356 oz. ASW, 38.61 mm. **Subject:**
Maironis, 150th Anniversary of Birth **Obv:** Vytis **Rev:** Maironis
and text

Date	Mintage	F12	VF20	XF40	MS60	MS63
2012	3,000	PF65 100				

KM# 193 50 LITŲ
28.28 g., 0.925 Silver 0.8356 oz. ASW, 38.61 mm. **Obv:** Vytis
Rev: Dionizas Poska's "Baubliai"

Date	Mintage	F12	VF20	XF40	MS60	MS63
2012	4,000	PF65 100				

KM# 194 50 LITŲ
28.28 g., 0.925 Silver 0.8356 oz. ASW, 38.61 mm. **Obv:** Vytis
Rev: Christening of Samogitia

Date	Mintage	F12	VF20	XF40	MS60	MS63
2013	3,000	PF65 100				

KM# 195 50 LITŲ
28.28 g., 0.925 Silver 0.8356 oz. ASW, 38.61 mm. **Subject:** Sajudis demonstration, 125th Anniversary **Obv:** Vytis

Date	Mintage	F12	VF20	XF40	MS60	MS63
2013	4,000	PF65 100				

KM# 196 50 LITŲ
28.28 g., 0.925 Silver 0.8356 oz. ASW, 38.61 mm. **Subject:** Presidency of the EU Council **Obv:** Stylized map of Europe with stars **Rev:** Vytis with stars

Date	Mintage	F12	VF20	XF40	MS60	MS63
2013	4,000	PF65 100				

KM# 197 50 LITŲ
28.28 g., 0.925 Silver 0.8356 oz. ASW, 38.61 mm. **Subject:** Uprising of 1863-64 **Obv:** Three shields **Rev:** Swords

Date	Mintage	F12	VF20	XF40	MS60	MS63
2013	3,000	PF65 100				

KM# 158 100 LITŲ
7.78 g., 0.999 Gold 0.2483 oz. AGW, 22.3 mm. **Subject:** Use of the Name Lithuania Millenium **Obv:** Linear National Arms **Rev:** Circular Legend

Date	Mintage	F12	VF20	XF40	MS60	MS63
2007	5,000	PF65 600				

KM# 156 100 LITŲ
7.78 g., 0.9999 Gold 0.2485 oz. AGW, 22.3 mm. **Subject:** Millennium of name "Lithuania **Obv:** Stylized national arms **Obv. Legend:** LIETUVA **Rev:** Partial parchment **Rev. Legend:** LIETUVOS DIDZIOJI KUNIGAIKSTYSTS

Date	Mintage	F12	VF20	XF40	MS60	MS63
2008	10,000	PF63 500 PF65 550				

KM# 166 100 LITŲ
7.78 g., 0.999 Gold 0.2483 oz. AGW, 22.3 mm. **Subject:** 1000th Anniversary of Name Lithuania **Obv:** Linear knight **Rev:** Timeline

Date	Mintage	F12	VF20	XF40	MS60	MS63
2009LMK	10,000	PF63 500 PF65 550				

KM# 198 100 LITŲ
56.56 g., 0.925 Gold 1.6712 oz. AGW **Subject:** First map, 400th Anniversary **Shape:** Square

Date	Mintage	F12	VF20	XF40	MS60	MS63
2013	4,000	PF65 200				

KM# 136 200 LITŲ
15.00 g., Bi-Metallic, 27 mm. **Subject:** 750th Anniversary - King Mindaugas **Obv:** Knight on horse **Obv. Legend:** LIETUVA **Rev:** Seated King **Rev. Legend:** MINDAUGO KARUNAVIMAS **Edge Lettering:** LIETUVOS KARALYSTE 1253

Date	Mintage	F12	VF20	XF40	MS60	MS63
2003	2,000	PF65 1,050				

KM# 146 500 LITŲ
31.10 g., 0.9999 Gold 0.9934 oz. AGW, 32.5 mm. **Obv:** Knight on horse **Rev:** Palace **Edge:** Plain

Date	Mintage	F12	VF20	XF40	MS60	MS63
2005	1,000	PF65 1,500				

KM# 173 500 LITŲ
31.10 g., 0.999 Gold 0.9925 oz. AGW, 32.5 mm. **Subject:** Battle of Grunwald **Obv:** Shield around seated king **Rev:** Knights on horseback, warriors on foot

Date	Mintage	F12	VF20	XF40	MS60	MS63
2010	1,000	PF65 1,500				

MINT SETS

KM#	Date	Mintage	Identification	Issue Price	Mkt Val
MS4	2003 (6)	10,000	KM#106-108, 111-113	7.50	35.00
MS5	2008 (9)	4,000	KM#85-87 (dated 1991), 106-108, 111-113	30.00	30.00
MS6	2009 (9)	5,000	KM#85-87, 106-108, 111-113	—	30.00
MS7	2010 (7)	3,500	KM#106-108, 111-113 plus medal	—	35.00
MS8	2011 (7)	4,500	KM#106-108, 111-113 plus medal	—	25.00
MS9	2012 (7)	4,000	KM#106-108, 111-113 plus medal	—	25.00
MS10	2013 (7)	3,500	KM#106-108, 111-113 plus medal. Victorious battles of the Grand Duchy of Lithuania.	—	25.00
MS11	2013 (7)	3,500	KM#106-108, 111-113 plus medal. Transatlantic flight anniversary.	—	25.00

PROOF-LIKE SETS (PL)

KM#	Date	Mintage	Identification	Issue Price	Mkt Val
PL1	2008 (6)	200	KM#106-108, 111-113	—	115
PL2	2009 (6)	500	KM#106-108, 111-113	—	75.00

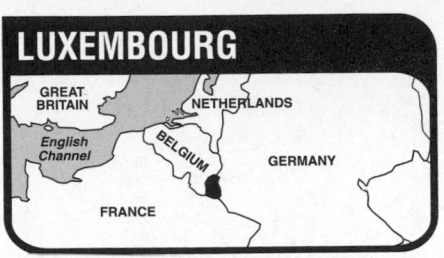

LUXEMBOURG

The Grand Duchy of Luxembourg is located in western Europe between Belgium, Germany and France, has an area of 1,103 sq. mi. (2,586 sq. km.) and a population of 377,100. Capital: Luxembourg. The economy is based on steel.

RULER
Henri, 2000-

MINT MARK
SA - Paris
(b) - Brussels, privy marks only
H – Gunzburg
(n) – lion - Namur
(u) - Utrecht, privy marks only

GRAND DUCHY

EURO COINAGE
European Economic Community Issues

KM# 75 EURO CENT
2.30 g., Copper Plated Steel, 16.25 mm. **Ruler:** Henri **Obv:** Head right **Rev:** Value and globe **Edge:** Plain

Date	Mintage	F12	VF20	XF40	MS60	MS63
2002(u)	34,557,500	—	—	—	0.35	0.50
2002(u)	1,500	PF63 3.00				
2003(u)	1,500,000	—	—	—	0.50	0.75
2003(u)	1,500	PF63 3.00				
2004(u)	21,001,000	—	—	—	0.35	0.50
2004(u)	1,500	PF63 3.00				
2005(u)	7,000,000	—	—	—	0.35	0.50
2005(u)	1,500	PF63 3.00				
2006(u)	4,000,000	—	—	—	0.35	0.50
2006(u)	2,000	PF63 4.00				
2007(a)	6,000,000	—	—	—	0.35	0.50
2007(a)	2,500	PF63 4.00				
2008(a)	10,000,000	—	—	—	0.35	0.50
2008(a)	2,500	PF63 4.00				
2009(a)	4,000,000	—	—	—	0.35	0.50
2009(a)	2,500	PF63 4.00				
2010(u)	6,000,000	—	—	—	0.35	0.50
2010(u)	1,500	PF63 4.00				
2011(u)	7,600,000	—	—	—	0.35	0.50
2011(u)	1,500	PF63 4.00				
2012(u)	9,200,000	—	—	—	0.35	0.50
2012(u)		PF63 4.00				
2013		—	—	—	0.35	0.50
2013		PF63 4.00				
2014		—	—	—	0.35	0.50
2014		PF63 4.00				

KM# 76 2 EURO CENT
3.06 g., Copper Plated Steel, 18.75 mm. **Ruler:** Henri **Obv:** Head right **Rev:** Value and globe **Edge:** Grooved

Date	Mintage	F12	VF20	XF40	MS60	MS63
2002(u)	35,917,500	—	—	—	0.50	0.75
2002(u)	1,500	PF63 5.00				
2003(u)	1,500,000	—	—	—	0.65	0.85
2003(u)	1,500	PF63 5.00				
2004(u)	20,001,000	—	—	—	0.50	0.75
2004(u)	1,500	PF63 5.00				
2005(u)	13,000,000	—	—	—	0.50	0.75
2005(u)	1,500	PF63 5.00				
2006(u)	4,000,000	—	—	—	0.50	0.75
2006(u)	2,000	PF63 6.00				
2007(a)	8,000,000	—	—	—	0.50	0.75
2007(a)	2,500	PF63 6.00				
2008(a)	12,000,000	—	—	—	0.50	0.75
2008(a)	2,500	PF63 6.00				
2009(a)	3,000,000	—	—	—	0.50	0.75
2009(a)	2,500	PF63 6.00				
2010(u)	8,000,000	—	—	—	0.50	0.75
2010(u)	1,500	PF63 6.00				

Date	Mintage	F12	VF20	XF40	MS60	MS63
2011(u)	6,200,000	—			0.50	0.75
2011(u)	1,500	PF63 6.00				
2012(u)	7,200,000	—			0.50	0.75
2012(u)	—	PF63 6.00				
2013	—				0.50	0.75
2013	—	PF63 6.00				
2014	—				0.50	0.75
2014	—	PF63 6.00				

KM# 77 5 EURO CENT
3.92 g., Copper Plated Steel, 21.25 mm. **Ruler:** Henri **Obv:** Head right **Rev:** Value and globe **Edge:** Plain

Date	Mintage	F12	VF20	XF40	MS60	MS63
2002(u)	28,917,500	—	—	—	0.75	1.00
2002(u)	1,500	PF63 7.00				
2003(u)	4,500,000	—		—	1.00	1.25
2003(u)	1,500	PF63 7.00				
2004(u)	16,001,000	—		—	0.75	1.00
2004(u)	1,500	PF63 7.00				
2005(u)	6,000,000	—		—	0.75	1.00
2005(u)	1,500	PF63 7.00				
2006(u)	5,000,000	—		—	0.75	1.00
2006(u)	2,000	PF63 8.00				
2007(a)	5,000,000	—		—	0.75	1.00
2007(a)	2,500	PF63 9.00				
2008(a)	9,000,000	—		—	0.75	1.00
2008(a)	2,500	PF63 9.00				
2009(u)	6,000,000	—		—	0.75	1.00
2009(u)	2,500	PF63 9.00				
2010(u)	6,000,000	—		—	0.75	1.00
2010(u)	1,500	PF63 9.00				
2011(u)	6,700,000	—		—	0.75	1.00
2011(u)	1,500	PF63 9.00				
2012(u)	5,200,000	—		—	0.75	1.00
2012(u)	—	PF63 9.00				
2013	—	PF63 9.00				
2013	—			—	0.75	1.00
2014	—	PF63 9.00				
2014	—			—	0.75	1.00

KM# 78 10 EURO CENT
4.10 g., Brass, 19.75 mm. **Ruler:** Henri **Obv:** Grand Duke's portrait **Rev:** Value and map **Edge:** Reeded

Date	Mintage	F12	VF20	XF40	MS60	MS63
2002(u)	25,117,500	—	—	—	0.75	—
2002(u)	1,500	PF63 14.00				
2003(u)	1,500,000	—		—	1.00	—
2003(u)	1,500	PF63 14.00				
2004(u)	12,001,000	—		—	0.75	—
2004(u)	1,500	PF63 14.00				
2005(u)	2,000,000	—		—	0.75	—
2005(u)	1,500	PF63 14.00				
2006(u)	4,000,000	—		—	0.75	—
2006(u)	2,000	PF63 14.00				

KM# 89 10 EURO CENT
4.10 g., Brass, 19.75 mm. **Ruler:** Henri **Obv:** Prince's portrait **Rev:** Relief map of Western Europe, stars, lines and value **Edge:** Reeded

Date	Mintage	F12	VF20	XF40	MS60	MS63
2007(a)	5,000,000	—		—	0.75	1.00
2007(a)	2,500	PF63 14.00				
2008(a)	5,000,000	—		—	0.75	1.00
2008(a)	2,500	PF63 14.00				
2009(u)	4,000,000	—		—	0.75	1.00
2009(u)	2,500	PF63 14.00				
2010(u)	4,000,000	—		—	0.75	1.00
2010(u)	1,500	PF63 14.00				
2011(u)	4,800,000	—		—	0.75	1.00
2011(u)	1,500	PF63 14.00				
2012(u)	2,200,000	—		—	0.75	1.00
2012(u)	—	PF63 14.00				
2013	—	PF63 14.00				
2013	—			—	0.75	1.00

Date	Mintage	F12	VF20	XF40	MS60	MS63
2014	—	PF63 14.00				
2014	—	—	—	—	0.75	1.00

KM# 79 20 EURO CENT
5.74 g., Brass, 22.25 mm. **Ruler:** Henri **Obv:** Grand Duke's portrait **Rev:** Value and map **Edge:** Notched

Date	Mintage	F12	VF20	XF40	MS60	MS63
2002(u)	25,717,500	—		—	1.00	—
2002(u)	1,500	PF63 16.00				
2003(u)	1,500,000	—			1.25	—
2003(u)	1,500	PF63 16.00				
2004(u)	14,001,000	—		—	1.00	—
2004(u)	1,500	PF63 16.00				
2005(u)	6,000,000	—		—	1.00	—
2005(u)	1,500	PF63 16.00				
2006(u)	7,000,000	—		—	1.00	—
2006(u)	2,000	PF63 16.00				

KM# 90 20 EURO CENT
5.74 g., Brass, 22.25 mm. **Ruler:** Henri **Obv:** Prince's portrait **Rev:** Relief map of Western Europe, stars, lines and value **Edge:** Notched

Date	Mintage	F12	VF20	XF40	MS60	MS63
2007(a)	8,000,000	—		—	1.00	1.25
2007(a)	2,500	PF63 16.00				
2008(a)	6,000,000	—		—	1.00	1.25
2008(a)	2,500	PF63 16.00				
2009(u)	5,000,000	—		—	1.00	1.25
2009(u)	2,500	PF63 16.00				
2010(u)	8,000,000	—		—	1.00	1.25
2010(u)	1,500	PF63 16.00				
2011(u)	5,300,000	—		—	1.00	1.25
2011(u)	1,500	PF63 16.00				
2012(u)	5,200,000	—		—	1.00	1.25
2012(u)	—	PF63 16.00				
2013	—	PF63 16.00				
2013	—	—	—	—	1.00	1.25
2014	—	PF63 16.00				
2014	—	—	—	—	1.00	1.25

KM# 80 50 EURO CENT
7.80 g., Brass, 24.25 mm. **Ruler:** Henri **Obv:** Grand Duke's portrait **Rev:** Value and map **Edge:** Reeded

Date	Mintage	F12	VF20	XF40	MS60	MS63
2002(u)	21,917,500	—		—	1.25	—
2002(u)	1,500	PF63 18.00				
2003(u)	2,500,000	—		—	1.50	—
2003(u)	1,500	PF63 18.00				
2004(u)	10,001,000	—		—	1.25	—
2004(u)	1,500	PF63 18.00				
2005(u)	3,000,000	—		—	1.25	—
2005(u)	1,500	PF63 18.00				
2006(u)	3,000,000	—		—	1.25	—
2006(u)	2,000	PF63 18.00				

KM# 91 50 EURO CENT
7.80 g., Brass, 24.25 mm. **Ruler:** Henri **Obv:** Prince's portrait **Rev:** Relief map of Western Europe, stars, lines and value **Edge:** Reeded

Date	Mintage	F12	VF20	XF40	MS60	MS63
2007(a)	4,000,000	—		—	1.25	1.50

Date	Mintage	F12	VF20	XF40	MS60	MS63
2007(a)	2,500	PF63 18.00				
2008(a)	4,000,000	—		—	1.25	1.50
2008(a)	2,500	PF63 18.00				
2009(u)	2,000,000	—		—	1.25	1.50
2009(u)	2,500	PF63 18.00				
2010(u)	5,000,000	—		—	1.25	1.50
2010(u)	1,500	PF63 18.00				
2011(u)	3,500,000	—		—	1.25	1.50
2011(u)	1,500	PF63 18.00				
2012(u)	2,600,000	—		—	1.25	1.50
2012(u)	—	PF63 18.00				
2013	—	PF63 18.00				
2013	—	—	—	—	1.25	1.50
2014	—	PF63 18.00				
2014	—	—	—	—	1.25	1.50

KM# 81 EURO
7.50 g., Bi-Metallic, 23.25 mm. **Ruler:** Henri **Obv:** Grand Duke's portrait **Rev:** Value and map within divided circle **Edge:** Segmented reeding

Date	Mintage	F12	VF20	XF40	MS60	MS63
2002(u)	21,318,525	—		—	2.50	—
2002(u)	1,500	PF63 18.00				
2003(u)	1,500,000	—		—	2.75	—
2003(u)	1,500	PF63 18.00				
2004(u)	9,001,000	—		—	2.50	—
2004(u)	1,500	PF63 18.00				
2005(u)	2,000,000	—		—	2.50	—
2005(u)	1,500	PF63 18.00				
2006(u)	1,000,000	—		—	2.50	—
2006(u)	2,000	PF63 18.00				

KM# 92 EURO
7.50 g., Bi-Metallic, 23.25 mm. **Ruler:** Henri **Obv:** Prince's portrait **Rev:** Relief map of Western Europe, stars, lines and value **Edge:** Segmented reeding

Date	Mintage	F12	VF20	XF40	MS60	MS63
2007(a)	480,000	—		—	2.25	2.75
2007(a)	2,500	PF63 24.00				
2008(a)	480,000	—		—	2.25	2.75
2008(a)	2,500	PF63 24.00				
2009(u)	240,000	—		—	2.25	2.75
2009(u)	2,500	PF63 24.00				
2010(u)	1,000,000	—		—	2.25	2.75
2010(u)	1,500	PF63 24.00				
2011(u)	1,520,000	—		—	2.25	2.75
2011(u)	1,500	PF63 24.00				
2012(u)	2,240,000	—		—	2.25	2.75
2012(u)	—	PF63 24.00				
2013	—	PF63 24.00				
2013	—	—	—	—	2.25	2.75
2014	—	PF63 24.00				
2014	—	—	—	—	2.25	2.75

KM# 82 2 EURO
8.50 g., Bi-Metallic, 25.75 mm. **Ruler:** Henri **Obv:** Grand Duke's portrait **Rev:** Value and map within divided circle **Edge:** Reeded with 2's and stars

Date	Mintage	F12	VF20	XF40	MS60	MS63
2002(u)	18,517,500	—		—	3.75	—
2002(u)	1,500	PF63 28.00				
2003(u)	3,500,000	—		—	4.50	—
2003(u)	1,500	PF63 28.00				
2004(u)	7,553,200	—		—	4.00	—
2004(u)	1,500	PF63 28.00				
2005(u)	3,500,000	—		—	4.00	—
2005(u)	1,500	PF63 28.00				
2006(u)	2,000,000	—		—	4.00	—
2006(u)	2,000	PF63 28.00				

KM# 85 2 EURO
8.50 g., Bi-Metallic, 25.75 mm. **Ruler:** Henri **Obv:** Head right and crowned monogram within 1/2 star circle **Rev:** Value and map within divided circle **Edge:** Reeded with 2's and stars

Date	Mintage	F12	VF20	XF40	MS60	MS63
2004(u)	2,447,800	—	—	—	7.00	9.00
2004(u) Special Unc.	10,000	—	—	—	—	50.00
2004(u)	4,000	PF63 50.00				

KM# 87 2 EURO
8.50 g., Bi-Metallic, 25.75 mm. **Ruler:** Henri **Obv:** Conjoined heads right within circle **Rev:** Value and map within divided circle **Edge:** Reeded with 2's and stars

Date	Mintage	F12	VF20	XF40	MS60	MS63
2005	2,720,000	—	—	—	7.00	9.00
2005 Special Unc.	10,000	—	—	—	—	75.00
2005	4,000	PF63 50.00				

KM# 88 2 EURO
8.50 g., Bi-Metallic, 25.75 mm. **Ruler:** Henri **Obv:** Conjoined heads right within circle and star border **Rev:** Value and map within divided circle **Edge:** Reeded with 2's and stars

Date	Mintage	F12	VF20	XF40	MS60	MS63
2006	1,030,000	—	—	—	7.00	9.00
2006 Special Unc.	15,000	—	—	—	—	32.00
2006	4,500	PF63 50.00				

KM# 93 2 EURO
8.50 g., Bi-Metallic, 25.75 mm. **Ruler:** Henri **Obv:** Prince's portrait **Rev:** Relief map of Western Europe, stars, lines and value **Edge:** Reeded with 2's and stars

Date	Mintage	F12	VF20	XF40	MS60	MS63
2007(a)	4,000,000	—	—	—	4.00	5.00
2007(a)	2,500	PF63 28.00				
2008(a)	6,000,000	—	—	—	4.00	5.00
2008(a)	2,500	PF63 28.00				
2009(u)	240,000	—	—	—	6.00	7.50
2009(u)	2,500	PF63 30.00				
2010(u)	3,500,000	—	—	—	4.00	5.00
2010(u)	1,500	PF63 30.00				
2011(u)	2,320,000	—	—	—	4.00	5.00
2011(u)	1,500	PF63 30.00				
2012(u)	3,760,000	—	—	—	4.00	5.00
2012(u)	—	PF63 30.00				
2013	—	PF63 30.00				
2013	—	—	—	—	4.00	5.00
2014	—	PF63 30.00				
2014	—	—	—	—	4.00	5.00

KM# 94 2 EURO
8.50 g., Bi-Metallic, 25.75 mm. **Ruler:** Henri **Subject:** 50th Anniversary Treaty of Rome **Obv:** Open treaty book with latent image on left hand page **Obv. Legend:** LÊTZEBUERG **Rev:** Large value at left, modified outline of Europe at right **Edge:** Reeded with 2's and stars

Date	Mintage	F12	VF20	XF40	MS60	MS63
2007(a)	2,026,000	—	—	—	6.50	9.00
2007(a) Special Unc.	15,000	—	—	—	—	25.00
2007(a)	5,000	PF63 30.00				

KM# 95 2 EURO
8.50 g., Bi-Metallic, 25.75 mm. **Ruler:** Henri **Obv:** Palace in background at left, head 3/4 left at right **Obv. Legend:** LETZEBUERG **Rev:** Large value at left, modified outline of Europe at right **Edge:** Reeded with 2's and stars

Date	Mintage	F12	VF20	XF40	MS60	MS63
2007(a)	1,011,000	—	—	—	6.50	9.00
2007(a) Special Unc.	15,000	—	—	—	—	25.00
2007(a)	5,000	PF63 40.00				

KM# 96 2 EURO
8.50 g., Bi-Metallic, 25.75 mm. **Ruler:** Henri **Obv:** Head at left, Chateau de Berg at right **Obv. Legend:** LETZEBUERG **Rev:** Large value at left, modified outline of Europe at right **Edge:** Reeded with 2's and stars

Date	Mintage	F12	VF20	XF40	MS60	MS63
2008(a)	1,000,000	—	—	4.00	5.00	6.25
2008(a) Special Unc.	15,000	—	—	—	—	30.00
2008(a)	5,000	PF63 15.00				

KM# 106 2 EURO
8.50 g., Bi-Metallic, 25.75 mm. **Ruler:** Henri **Subject:** 90th Anniversary of Grand Duchess Charlotte **Obv:** Conjoined busts of Charlotte and Henri **Edge:** Reeded with 2's and stars

Date	Mintage	F12	VF20	XF40	MS60	MS63
2009	822,500	—	—	—	7.00	9.00
2009 Special Unc.	10,000	—	—	—	—	30.00
2009	2,500	PF63 15.00				

KM# 107 2 EURO
8.50 g., Bi-Metallic, 25.75 mm. **Ruler:** Henri **Subject:** European Monetary Union - 10th Anniversary **Obv:** Alternating stick figure with Euro emblem design or Head of Grand-Duke **Edge:** Reeded with 2's and stars

Date	Mintage	F12	VF20	XF40	MS60	MS63
2009	812,500	—	—	—	5.00	6.00
2009 Special Unc.	10,000	—	—	—	—	30.00
2009	2,500	PF63 15.00				

KM# 115 2 EURO
8.50 g., Bi-Metallic, 25.75 mm. **Ruler:** Henri **Obv:** Henry head facing, crowned shield **Rev:** Large value at left, modified outline mape of Europe at right **Edge:** Reeded with 2's and stars

Date	Mintage	F12	VF20	XF40	MS60	MS63
2010(a) Special Unc.	7,500	—	—	—	—	30.00
2010(a)	500,000	—	—	—	6.50	9.00
2010(a)	1,500	PF63 20.00				

KM# 116 2 EURO
8.50 g., Bi-Metallic, 25.75 mm. **Ruler:** Henri **Subject:** Jean of Luxembourg - Nassau, 50th Anniversary of his appointment as Grand Duke **Obv:** Conjoined head left of Charlotte, Jean and Henri **Edge:** Reeded with 2's and stars

Date	Mintage	F12	VF20	XF40	MS60	MS63
2011 Special Unc.	7,500	—	—	—	—	30.00
2011	707,500	—	—	—	7.00	9.00
2011	1,500	PF63 15.00				

KM# 119 2 EURO
8.50 g., Bi-Metallic, 25.75 mm. **Ruler:** Henri **Subject:** Euro coinage, 10th Anniversary **Obv:** Euro symbol on globe, child-like rendering around

Date	Mintage	F12	VF20	XF40	MS60	MS63
2012	1,400,000	—	—	—	6.00	8.00

KM# 120 2 EURO
8.50 g., Bi-Metallic, 25.75 mm. **Subject:** Royal Wedding **Obv:** Three portraits

Date	Mintage	F12	VF20	XF40	MS60	MS63
2012	—	—	—	—	—	8.00

KM# 121 2 EURO
8.50 g., Bi-Metallic, 25.75 mm. **Subject:** 100th anniversary of the death of William IV

Date	Mintage	F12	VF20	XF40	MS60	MS63
2012	—	—	—	—	—	8.00

KM# 125 2 EURO
8.50 g., Bi-Metallic, 25.75 mm. **Ruler:** Henri **Obv:** National anthem at left, profile at right

Date	Mintage	F12	VF20	XF40	MS60	MS63
2013	722,000	—	—	—	4.00	5.00
2013 Special Unc.	—	—	—	—	—	30.00
2013	—	PF63 20.00				

KM# 129 2 EURO
Bi-Metallic, 25.75 mm. **Ruler:** Henri **Subject:** 175th Anniversary

Date	Mintage	F12	VF20	XF40	MS60	MS63
2014	—	—	—	—	6.50	9.00

KM# 84 5 EURO
6.22 g., 0.999 Gold 0.1985 oz. AGW, 20 mm. **Ruler:** Henri **Subject:** European Central Bank **Obv:** Grand Duke Henri **Rev:** Building

Date	Mintage	F12	VF20	XF40	MS60	MS63
2003(u)	20,000	PF63 350	PF65 375			

KM# 108 5 EURO
16.60 g., Bi-Metallic, 34 mm. **Ruler:** Henri **Subject:** Vianden Castle **Obv:** Head right **Rev:** Castle view

Date	Mintage	F12	VF20	XF40	MS60	MS63
2009	7,500	—	—	—	—	150

KM# 109 5 EURO
Bi-Metallic, 34 mm. **Ruler:** Henri **Subject:** Common Kestrel **Obv:** Head right **Rev:** Bird

Date	Mintage	F12	VF20	XF40	MS60	MS63
2009	3,000	PF63 60.00	PF65 70.00			

KM# 111 5 EURO
16.60 g., Bi-Metallic, 34 mm. **Ruler:** Henri **Subject:** Chateau d'Esch-Sur-Sûre **Obv:** Head right **Rev:** Chateau view

Date	Mintage	F12	VF20	XF40	MS60	MS63
2010 Prooflike	3,000	—	—	—	—	100

KM# 112 5 EURO
Bi-Metallic, 34 mm. **Ruler:** Henri **Subject:** Flora and Fauna - Arnica Montana **Obv:** Head right **Rev:** Flowers

Date	Mintage	F12	VF20	XF40	MS60	MS63
2010	3,000	PF63 50.00	PF65 60.00			

KM# 117 5 EURO
16.60 g., Bi-Metallic, 34 mm. **Ruler:** Henri **Subject:** Mersch Castle **Obv:** Head right **Rev:** Castle vie

Date	Mintage	F12	VF20	XF40	MS60	MS63
2011 Prooflike	3,000	—	—	—	—	100

KM# 124 5 EURO
15.00 g., Bi-Metallic, 34 mm. **Ruler:** Henri **Rev:** Ophrys orchid

Date	Mintage	F12	VF20	XF40	MS60	MS63
2012	3,000	PF63 120				

KM# 126 5 EURO
16.60 g., Bi-Metallic, 34 mm. **Ruler:** Henri **Obv:** Profile right **Rev:** Beaufort castle

Date	Mintage	F12	VF20	XF40	MS60	MS63
2013	3,000	PF63 135				

KM# 127 5 EURO
16.00 g., Bi-Metallic, 34 mm. **Ruler:** Henri **Rev:** European honey bee flower

Date	Mintage	F12	VF20	XF40	MS60	MS63
2013	3,000	PF63 120				

KM# 113 700 EURO CENTS
20.00 g., 0.925 Silver 0.591 oz. ASW, 34 mm. **Ruler:** Henri **Subject:** 700th Anniversary - Marriage of John of Luxembourg

Date	Mintage	F12	VF20	XF40	MS60	MS63
2010	3,000	PF63 75.00	PF65 85.00			

KM# 97 10 EURO
3.11 g., 0.999 Gold 0.0992 oz. AGW, 25.71 mm. **Ruler:** Henri **Subject:** Culture **Obv:** Head right **Rev:** Hellenic sculpture head

Date	Mintage	F12	VF20	XF40	MS60	MS63
2004	5,000	PF63 175	PF65 200			

KM# 99 10 EURO
8.00 g., Bi-Metallic, 26 mm. **Ruler:** Henri **Subject:** State Bank 150th Anniversary **Obv:** Head right **Rev:** Bank Plaza

Date	Mintage	F12	VF20	XF40	MS60	MS63
2006	7,500	—	—	—	—	150

KM# 101 10 EURO
3.11 g., 0.999 Gold 0.0992 oz. AGW, 16 mm. **Ruler:** Henri **Obv:** Head right **Rev:** Wild pig of Titelberg

Date	Mintage	F12	VF20	XF40	MS60	MS63
2006	5,000	PF63 175	PF65 200			

KM# 104 10 EURO
10.37 g., 0.999 Gold 0.3309 oz. AGW, 23 mm. **Ruler:** Henri **Subject:** Banque Central - 10th Anniversary **Obv:** Head right **Rev:** Old and new bank buildings

Date	Mintage	F12	VF20	XF40	MS60	MS63
2008	1,250	PF63 575	PF65 600			

KM# 110 10 EURO
3.11 g., 0.999 Gold 0.0992 oz. AGW, 16 mm. **Ruler:** Henri **Subject:** Deer of Orval's Refuge **Obv:** Head right **Rev:** Stag seated, flower in background

Date	Mintage	F12	VF20	XF40	MS60	MS63
2009	3,000	PF63 175	PF65 200			

KM# 114 10 EURO
13.50 g., Bi-Metallic, 34 mm. **Ruler:** Henri **Subject:** Schengen Accord, 25th Anniversary **Obv:** Head right **Rev:** Building

Date	Mintage	F12	VF20	XF40	MS60	MS63
2010 Prooflike	3,000	—	—	—	—	125

KM# 118 10 EURO
16.15 g., Bi-Metallic, 34 mm. **Ruler:** Henri **Subject:** Flora and Fauna - Otter

Date	Mintage	F12	VF20	XF40	MS60	MS63
2011	3,000	PF63 50.00	PF65 60.00			

KM# 122 10 EURO
3.11 g., 0.999 Gold 0.0992 oz. AGW, 16 mm. **Ruler:** Henri **Obv:** Profile right **Rev:** Renert the fox

Date	Mintage	F12	VF20	XF40	MS60	MS63
2011	3,000	PF63 225				

KM# 128 10 EURO
3.11 g., 0.999 Gold 0.0992 oz. AGW, 16 mm. **Ruler:** Henri **Rev:** Golden Frau statue

Date	Mintage	F12	VF20	XF40	MS60	MS63
2013	3,000	PF63 220				

KM# 102 20 EURO
13.50 g., Bi-Metallic, 34 mm. **Ruler:** Henri **Obv:** Three heads facing **Rev:** Council D'Etat building

Date	Mintage	F12	VF20	XF40	MS60	MS63
2006	4,000	—	—	—	—	120

KM# 83 25 EURO
22.85 g., 0.925 Silver 0.6752 oz. ASW, 37 mm. **Ruler:** Henri **Subject:** European Court System **Obv:** Grand Duke Henri **Rev:** Sword scale on law book

Date	Mintage	F12	VF20	XF40	MS60	MS63
2002(u)	20,000	PF63 80.00	PF65 100			

KM# 86 25 EURO
22.85 g., 0.925 Silver 0.6752 oz. ASW, 37 mm. **Ruler:** Henri **Subject:** European Parliament **Obv:** Grand Duke Henri **Rev:** Parliament

Date	Mintage	F12	VF20	XF40	MS60	MS63
2004(u)	20,000	PF63 80.00	PF65 100			

KM# 98 25 EURO
22.85 g., 0.925 Silver 0.6737 oz. ASW, 37 mm. **Ruler:** Henri **Subject:** EU Presidency **Obv:** Head right **Rev:** Conseil de l'Union building in Brussels

Date	Mintage	F12	VF20	XF40	MS60	MS63
2005	10,000	PF63 80.00	PF65 100			

KM# 100 25 EURO
22.80 g., 0.925 Silver 0.6737 oz. ASW, 37 mm. **Ruler:** Henri **Obv:** Head right **Rev:** European Commission building "Berlaymont" in Brussels

Date	Mintage	F12	VF20	XF40	MS60	MS63
2006	5,000	PF63 85.00	PF65 110			

KM# 103 25 EURO
22.85 g., 0.925 Silver 0.6752 oz. ASW, 37 mm. **Ruler:** Henri **Subject:** European Court of Auditors 30th Anniversary

Date	Mintage	F12	VF20	XF40	MS60	MS63
2007	3,000	PF63 80.00	PF65 100			

KM# 105 25 EURO
22.85 g., 0.925 Silver 0.6752 oz. ASW, 37 mm. **Ruler:** Henri **Subject:** European Investment Bank

Date	Mintage	F12	VF20	XF40	MS60	MS63
2008	4,000	PF63 275				

KM# 123 5 EURO
16.60 g., Bi-Metallic, 34 mm. **Ruler:** Henri **Obv:** Profile right **Rev:** Bourscheid castle

Date	Mintage	F12	VF20	XF40	MS60	MS63
2012	3,000	PF63 135				

MINT SETS

KM#	Date	Mintage	Identification	Issue Price	Mkt Val
MS7	2002 (8)	35,000	KM#75-82	—	20.00
MS8	2002 (8)	—	KM#75-82	—	20.00
MS9	2003 (8)	50,000	KM#75-82, Adolph Brucke	—	30.00
MS10	2003 (8)	3,500	KM#75-82 plus stamps	—	75.00
MS11	2004 (8)	40,000	KM#75-82	—	50.00
MS12	2004 (8)	6,400	KM#75-82 plus stamps	—	50.00
MS13	2004 (8)	500	KM#75-82, Grand Duke	—	—
MS14	2004 (8)	500	KM#75-82, Ducal Palace	—	—
MS15	2005 (9)	20,000	KM#75-82, 87	40.00	65.00
MS16	2005 (8)	6,500	KM#75-82 plus stamps	—	55.00
MS17	2005 (8)	2,000	KM#75-82, Women and Myth, signed by Gastauer	—	75.00
MS18	2006 (9)	15,000	KM#75-82, 88	40.00	65.00
MS19	2006 (8)	2,000	KM#75-82 plus stamps	—	75.00
MS20	2007 (9)	11,000	KM#75-78, 89-93, 94	37.50	50.00
MS21	2008 (9)	10,000	KM#75-77, 89-93, 96	37.50	40.00
MS22	2009 (9)	10,000	KM#75-77, 89-93, 106	37.50	40.00
MS23	2010 (9)	7,500	KM#75-77, 89-93, 115	37.50	40.00
MS24	2011 (9)	7,500	KM#75-77, 89-93, 116	37.50	40.00

PROOF SETS

KM#	Date	Mintage	Identification	Issue Price	Mkt Val
PS2	2002 (8)	1,500	KM#75-82	100	300
PS3	2003 (8)	1,500	KM#75-82	100	300
PS4	2004 (9)	1,500	KM#75-82, 85	105	300
PS5	2005 (9)	1,500	KM#75-82, 87	105	250
PS6	2006 (9)	2,000	KM#75-82, 88	120	200
PS7	2007 (10)	2,500	KM#75-77, 89-95	125	200
PS8	2008 (9)	2,500	KM#75-77, 89-93, 96	125	250
PS9	2004-2008 (6)	2,500	KM#85, 87, 88, 94, 95, 96	105	200
PS10	2009 (10)	2,000	KM#75-77, 89-93, 106, 107	125	250
PS11	2010 (9)	2,500	KM#75-77, 89-93, 115	125	250
PS12	2011 (9)	1,500	KM#75-77, 89-93, 116	125	200

MACAU

The Province of Macau, a Portuguese overseas province located in the South China Sea 40 miles southwest of Hong Kong, consists of the peninsula of Macau and the islands of Taipa and Coloane. It has an area of 6.2 sq. mi.(16 sq. km.) and a population of 500,000. Capital: Macau. Macau's economy is based on light industry, commerce, tourism, fishing, and gold trading - Macau is one of the entirely free markets for gold in the world. Cement, textiles, fireworks, vegetable oils, and metal products are exported.

In 1987, Portugal and China agreed that Macau would become a Chinese Territory in 1999. In December of 1999, Macau became a special administrative zone of China.

MINT MARKS
(p) - Pobjoy Mint
(s) - Singapore Mint

Pobjoy Mint   Singapore Mint

SPECIAL ADMINISTRATIVE REGION (S.A.R.)

STANDARD COINAGE
100 Avos = 1 Pataca

KM# 70 10 AVOS
1.38 g., Brass, 17 mm. **Obv:** MACAU written at center with date below **Rev:** Crowned lion dance scene above value flanked by mint marks

Date	Mintage	F12	VF20	XF40	MS60	MS63
2005	—	—	—	—	0.75	1.25
2007	—	—	—	—	0.75	1.25

KM# 72 50 AVOS
4.59 g., Brass, 23 mm. **Obv:** MACAU written across center of globe with date below **Rev:** The dragon dance led by a man

Date	Mintage	F12	VF20	XF40	MS60	MS63
2003	—	—	—	—	1.50	2.50
2005	—	—	—	—	1.50	2.50

KM# 57 PATACA
9.18 g., Copper-Nickel, 25.98 mm. **Obv:** MACAU written across center of globe with date below **Rev:** Guia Fortress and Chapel of Our Lady of Guia **Edge:** Reeded

Date	Mintage	F12	VF20	XF40	MS60	MS63
2003	—	—	—	0.60	1.50	2.00
2005	—	—	—	0.60	1.50	2.00
2007	—	—	—	—	1.50	2.00

KM# 56 5 PATACAS
10.10 g., Copper-Nickel, **Obv:** MACAU written across center of globe with date below **Rev:** Chinese junk, ruins of St. Paul's Cathedral in background **Edge:** Plain **Shape:** 12-sided

Date	Mintage	F12	VF20	XF40	MS60	MS63
2003	—	—	—	—	6.50	10.00
2005	—	—	—	—	6.50	10.00
2007	—	—	—	—	6.50	10.00

KM# 153 10 PATACAS
0.30 g., 0.999 Gold AGW, 7 mm. **Obv:** A Ma statue **Rev:** Lotus flower

Date	Mintage	F12	VF20	XF40	MS60	MS63
2009	Est. 5000	PF63 22.00	PF65 25.00			

KM# 165 10 PATACAS
31.11 g., 0.999 Silver 0.9926 oz. ASW, 40.7 mm. **Subject:** Year of the Snake **Obv:** Snake, color at right **Rev:** Ruins of St. Pauls

Date	Mintage	F12	VF20	XF40	MS60	MS63
2013	Est. 6000	PF63 75.00	PF65 85.00			

KM# 142 20 PATACAS
31.11 g., 0.999 Silver 0.9926 oz. ASW, 40.7 mm. **Subject:** Year of the Rat **Obv:** A Ma Temple **Rev:** Rat, multicolor flowers at right

Date	Mintage	F12	VF20	XF40	MS60	MS63
2008	6,000	PF65 130				

KM# 145 20 PATACAS
31.11 g., 0.999 Silver 0.9926 oz. ASW, 40.7 mm. **Subject:** Year of the Ox **Obv:** Moorish Barracks **Rev:** Ox, multicolor flowers at right

Date	Mintage	F12	VF20	XF40	MS60	MS63
2009	—	PF65 60.00				

KM# 151 20 PATACAS
31.11 g., 0.999 Silver 0.9926 oz. ASW, 40.7 mm. **Obv:** A Ma statue **Rev:** Lotus flower

Date	Mintage	F12	VF20	XF40	MS60	MS63
2009	Est. 5600	PF63 65.00	PF65 75.00			

KM# 156 20 PATACAS
31.11 g., 0.999 Silver 0.9926 oz. ASW, 40.7 mm. **Subject:** Year of the Tiger **Rev:** Tiger in color

Date	Mintage	F12	VF20	XF40	MS60	MS63
2010	Est. 6000	PF63 65.00	PF65 75.00			

KM# 159 20 PATACAS
31.11 g., 0.999 Silver 0.9926 oz. ASW, 40.7 mm. **Obv:** Rabbit in color **Rev:** Dom Pedro V theater

Date	Mintage	F12	VF20	XF40	MS60	MS63
2011	—	PF65 75.00				

KM# 162 20 PATACAS
28.28 g., 0.925 Silver 0.8356 oz. ASW, 40.7 mm. **Subject:** Year of the Dragon **Obv:** Dragon in color

Date	Mintage	F12	VF20	XF40	MS60	MS63
2012	—	PF65 150				

KM# 128 50 PATACAS
28.28 g., 0.925 Silver 0.8356 oz. ASW **Subject:** 1st World Championship Grand Prix **Rev:** Two race cars - gilt

Date	Mintage	F12	VF20	XF40	MS60	MS63
2003	5,000	PF65 75.00				

KM# 154 50 PATACAS
1.24 g., 0.999 Gold 0.0396 oz. AGW, 13.92 mm. **Obv:** A Ma statue **Rev:** Lotus flower

Date	Mintage	F12	VF20	XF40	MS60	MS63
2009	Est. 5000	PF63 75.00	PF65 90.00			

KM# 102 100 PATACAS
28.28 g., 0.925 Silver 0.8356 oz. ASW **Subject:** Year of the Snake **Obv:** Church façade **Rev:** Snake

Date	Mintage	F12	VF20	XF40	MS60	MS63
2001	4,000	PF65 55.00				

KM# 107 100 PATACAS
28.28 g., 0.925 Silver 0.8356 oz. ASW, 38.6 mm. **Subject:** Year of the Horse **Obv:** Church façade flanked by stars **Rev:** Horse above value **Edge:** Reeded

Date	Mintage	F12	VF20	XF40	MS60	MS63
2002	—	PF65 45.00				

KM# 130 100 PATACAS
28.28 g., 0.925 Silver 0.8356 oz. ASW **Series:** Lunar **Subject:** Year of the Monkey

Date	Mintage	F12	VF20	XF40	MS60	MS63
2004	4,000	PF65 75.00				
2004	1,000	—			—	60.00

KM# 122 100 PATACAS
28.28 g., 0.925 Silver 0.8356 oz. ASW **Subject:** 5th Anniversary Return of Macao to China

Date	Mintage	F12	VF20	XF40	MS60	MS63
2004	10,000	PF63 50.00	PF65 60.00			

KM# 134 100 PATACAS
28.28 g., 0.925 Silver 0.8356 oz. ASW **Series:** Lunar **Subject:** Year of the Rooster **Rev:** Stylized rooster walking left

Date	Mintage	F12	VF20	XF40	MS60	MS63
2005	—	PF65 90.00				

KM# 137 100 PATACAS
28.28 g., 0.925 Silver 0.8356 oz. ASW **Subject:** IV East Asian Games - FRIENDSHIP

Date	Mintage	F12	VF20	XF40	MS60	MS63
2005	6,000	PF63 65.00	PF65 75.00			

KM# 139 100 PATACAS
28.28 g., 0.925 Silver 0.8356 oz. ASW **Series:** Lunar **Subject:** Year of the Dog **Rev:** Stylized dog standing left

Date	Mintage	F12	VF20	XF40	MS60	MS63
2006	—	PF65 90.00				

KM# 148 100 PATACAS
31.11 g., 0.925 Silver 0.9191 oz. ASW, 40 mm. **Subject:** Year of the Pig **Rev:** Pig in color

Date	Mintage	F12	VF20	XF40	MS60	MS63
2007	Est. 15000	PF63 75.00	PF65 90.00			

KM# 143 100 PATACAS
155.50 g., 0.999 Silver 4.9623 oz. ASW, 65 mm. **Subject:** Year of the Rat **Obv:** A Ma Temple **Rev:** Rat, multicolor flowers at right **Note:** Illustration reduced.

Date	Mintage	F12	VF20	XF40	MS60	MS63
2008	500	PF65 250				

KM# 146 100 PATACAS
155.50 g., 0.999 Silver 4.9623 oz. ASW, 65 mm. **Subject:** Year of the Ox **Obv:** Moorish Barracks **Rev:** Ox, multicolor flowers at right **Note:** Illustration reduced.

Date	Mintage	F12	VF20	XF40	MS60	MS63
2009	500	PF65 250				

KM# 152 100 PATACAS
155.50 g., 0.999 Silver 4.9623 oz. ASW, 65 mm. **Obv:** A Ma statue **Rev:** Lotus flower

Date	Mintage	F12	VF20	XF40	MS60	MS63
2009	Est. 1000	PF65 275				

KM# 157 100 PATACAS
155.50 g., 0.999 Silver 4.9623 oz. ASW, 65 mm. **Subject:** Year of the Tiger **Rev:** Tiger in color

Date	Mintage	F12	VF20	XF40	MS60	MS63
2010	—	PF65 450				

KM# 160 100 PATACAS
155.50 g., 0.999 Silver 4.9623 oz. ASW, 65 mm. **Subject:** Year of the Rabbit **Obv:** Rabbit in color **Rev:** Dom Pedro V theater

Date	Mintage	F12	VF20	XF40	MS60	MS63
2011	500	PF65 400				

KM# 163 100 PATACAS
155.50 g., 0.999 Silver 4.9623 oz. ASW, 65 mm. **Subject:** Year of the Dragon **Obv:** Dragon in color

Date	Mintage	F12	VF20	XF40	MS60	MS63
2012	—	PF65 750				

KM# 166 100 PATACAS
155.52 g., 0.950 Silver 4.7195 oz. ASW, 65 mm. **Subject:** Year of the Snake **Obv:** Snake at right - color **Rev:** Ruins of St. Pauls

Date	Mintage	F12	VF20	XF40	MS60	MS63
2013	—	PF65 540				

KM# 123 200 PATACAS
28.28 g., 0.925 Silver 0.8356 oz. ASW **Subject:** 5th Anniversary Return of Macao to China

Date	Mintage	F12	VF20	XF40	MS60	MS63
2004	10,000	PF63 65.00	PF65 75.00			

KM# 138 200 PATACAS
28.28 g., 0.925 Silver 0.8356 oz. ASW **Subject:** IV East Asian Games **Rev:** U-N-I-T-Y in blocks at left - bottom. logo at upper right

Date	Mintage	F12	VF20	XF40	MS60	MS63
2005	6,000	PF65 120				

KM# 103 250 PATACAS
3.99 g., 0.9167 Gold 0.1168 oz. AGW **Subject:** Year of the Snake **Obv:** Church façade **Rev:** Snake

Date	Mintage	F12	VF20	XF40	MS60	MS63
2001	2,500	PF65 240				

KM# 108 250 PATACAS
3.99 g., 0.9167 Gold 0.1168 oz. AGW, 19.3 mm. **Subject:** Year of the Horse **Obv:** Church of St. Paul façade **Rev:** Horse above value **Edge:** Reeded

Date	Mintage	F12	VF20	XF40	MS60	MS63
2002	2,500	PF65 240				

KM# 119 250 PATACAS
3.99 g., 0.9167 Gold 0.1168 oz. AGW, 19.3 mm. **Subject:** Year of the Goat **Obv:** Church façade **Rev:** Goat above value **Edge:** Reeded

Date	Mintage	F12	VF20	XF40	MS60	MS63
2003	2,500	PF65 240				

KM# 131 250 PATACAS
3.99 g., 0.9167 Gold 0.1168 oz. AGW **Series:** Lunar **Subject:** Year of the Monkey

Date	Mintage	F12	VF20	XF40	MS60	MS63
2004	2,500	PF65 280				

KM# 135 250 PATACAS
2.83 g., 0.999 Gold 0.0903 oz. AGW **Series:** Lunar **Subject:** Year of the Rooster **Rev:** Stylized rooster walking left

Date	Mintage	F12	VF20	XF40	MS60	MS63
2005	—	PF65 280				

KM# 140 250 PATACAS
3.11 g., 0.999 Gold 0.0992 oz. AGW **Series:** Lunar **Subject:** Year of the Dog **Rev:** Stylized dog standing left - multicolor

Date	Mintage	F12	VF20	XF40	MS60	MS63
2006	—	PF65 280				

KM# 149 250 PATACAS
3.11 g., 0.999 Gold 0.0992 oz. AGW, 18 mm. **Subject:** Year of the Pig **Rev:** Pig in color

Date	Mintage	F12	VF20	XF40	MS60	MS63
2007	—	PF65 220				

KM# 144 250 PATACAS
7.79 g., 0.999 Gold 0.2486 oz. AGW **Subject:** Year of the Rat **Obv:** Temple **Rev:** Rat and multicolor flowers at right

Date	Mintage	F12	VF20	XF40	MS60	MS63
2008	—	PF65 525				

KM# 147 250 PATACAS
7.77 g., 0.999 Gold 0.248 oz. AGW **Subject:** Year of the Ox **Obv:** Moorish Barracks **Rev:** Ox, multicolor flowers at right

Date	Mintage	F12	VF20	XF40	MS60	MS63
2009	—	PF65 550				

KM# 155 250 PATACAS
7.78 g., 0.999 Gold 0.2483 oz. AGW, 22 mm. **Obv:** A Ma statue **Rev:** Lotus flower

Date	Mintage	F12	VF20	XF40	MS60	MS63
2009	Est. 1600	PF65 550				

KM# 158 250 PATACAS
7.78 g., 0.999 Gold 0.2483 oz. AGW, 22 mm. **Subject:** Year of the Tiger **Rev:** Tiger in color

Date	Mintage	F12	VF20	XF40	MS60	MS63
2010	Est. 3000	PF65 700				

KM# 161 250 PATACAS
7.78 g., 0.999 Gold 0.2483 oz. AGW, 22 mm. **Subject:** Year of the Rabbit **Obv:** Rabbit in color **Rev:** Dom Pedro V theater

Date	Mintage	F12	VF20	XF40	MS60	MS63
2011(s)	—	PF65 700				

KM# 167 250 PATACAS
7.77 g., 0.999 Gold 0.248 oz. AGW, 22 mm. **Subject:** Year of the Snake **Obv:** Snake at right, color **Rev:** Ruins of St. Pauls

Date	Mintage	F12	VF20	XF40	MS60	MS63
2013	Est. 3000	PF65 575				

KM# 104 500 PATACAS
7.99 g., 0.9167 Gold 0.234 oz. AGW **Subject:** Year of the Snake **Obv:** Church façade **Rev:** Snake

Date	Mintage	F12	VF20	XF40	MS60	MS63
2001	2,500	PF65 550				

KM# 109 500 PATACAS
7.98 g., 0.9167 Gold 0.2337 oz. AGW, 22.05 mm. **Subject:** Year of the Horse **Obv:** Church façade **Rev:** Horse above value **Edge:** Reeded

Date	Mintage	F12	VF20	XF40	MS60	MS63
2002	2,500	PF65 550				

KM# 120 500 PATACAS
7.98 g., 0.9167 Gold 0.2337 oz. AGW, 22 mm. **Subject:** Year of the Goat **Obv:** Church façade **Rev:** Goat above value **Edge:** Reeded

Date	Mintage	F12	VF20	XF40	MS60	MS63
2003	2,500	PF65 550				

KM# 129 500 PATACAS
7.96 g., 0.9167 Gold 0.2331 oz. AGW **Subject:** 1st World Championship Grand Prix **Rev:** Two race cars

Date	Mintage	F12	VF20	XF40	MS60	MS63
2003	2,000	PF65 550				

KM# 124 500 PATACAS
62.21 g., 0.999 Silver 1.9851 oz. ASW **Subject:** 5th Anniversary Return of Macao to China

Date	Mintage	F12	VF20	XF40	MS60	MS63
2004	1,000	PF65 120				

KM# 132 500 PATACAS
7.98 g., 0.9167 Gold 0.2337 oz. AGW **Series:** Lunar **Subject:** Year of the Monkey

Date	Mintage	F12	VF20	XF40	MS60	MS63
2004	2,500	PF65 525				

KM# 136 500 PATACAS
7.96 g., 0.999 Gold 0.254 oz. AGW **Series:** Lunar **Subject:** Year of the Rooster **Rev:** Stylized rooster walking left

Date	Mintage	F12	VF20	XF40	MS60	MS63
2005	—	PF65 550				

KM# 141 500 PATACAS
7.96 g., 0.999 Gold 0.254 oz. AGW **Series:** Lunar **Subject:** Year of the Dog **Rev:** Stylized dog standing left

Date	Mintage	F12	VF20	XF40	MS60	MS63
2006	—	PF65 550				

KM# 150 500 PATACAS
7.96 g., 0.999 Gold 0.254 oz. AGW, 22 mm. **Subject:** Year of the Pig **Rev:** Pig in color

Date	Mintage	F12	VF20	XF40	MS60	MS63
2007	Est. 4000	PF65 600				

KM# 164 500 PATACAS
7.78 g., 0.999 Gold 0.2483 oz. AGW, 22 mm. **Subject:** Year of the Dragon **Obv:** Dragon in color

Date	Mintage	F12	VF20	XF40	MS60	MS63
2012	—	PF65 950				

KM# 105 1000 PATACAS
16.98 g., 0.9167 Gold 0.4971 oz. AGW **Subject:** Year of the Snake **Obv:** Church façade flanked by stars **Rev:** Snake

Date	Mintage	F12	VF20	XF40	MS60	MS63
2001	4,000	PF65 1,000				

KM# 110 1000 PATACAS
15.97 g., 0.9167 Gold 0.4676 oz. AGW, 28.4 mm. **Subject:** Year of the Horse **Obv:** Church façade **Rev:** Horse above value **Edge:** Reeded

Date	Mintage	F12	VF20	XF40	MS60	MS63
2002	—	PF65 1,000				

KM# 118 1000 PATACAS
28.28 g., 0.925 Silver 0.8356 oz. ASW, 38.6 mm. **Subject:** Year of the Goat **Obv:** Church façade **Rev:** Goat above value **Edge:** Reeded

Date	Mintage	F12	VF20	XF40	MS60	MS63
2003	4,000	PF65 45.00				

KM# 121 1000 PATACAS
15.98 g., 0.917 Gold 0.468 oz. AGW **Subject:** Year of the Goat **Obv:** Church façade flanked by stars **Rev:** Goat above value **Edge:** Reeded

Date	Mintage	F12	VF20	XF40	MS60	MS63
2003	4,000	PF65 1,000				

KM# 133 1000 PATACAS
15.98 g., 0.9167 Gold 0.4679 oz. AGW **Series:** Lunar **Subject:** Year of the Monkey

Date	Mintage	F12	VF20	XF40	MS60	MS63
2004	4,000	PF65 1,000				
2004	500	—	—	—	—	950

KM# 125 1000 PATACAS
155.52 g., 0.999 Silver 4.9628 oz. ASW **Subject:** 5th Anniversary Return of Macao to China

Date	Mintage	F12	VF20	XF40	MS60	MS63
2004	3,000	PF65 310				

KM# 126 2000 PATACAS
155.52 g., 0.999 Silver 4.9628 oz. ASW **Subject:** 5th Anniversary Return of Macao to China

Date	Mintage	F12	VF20	XF40	MS60	MS63
2004	1,500	PF65 300				

PROOF SETS

KM#	Date	Mintage	Identification	Issue Price	Mkt Val
PS16	2001 (3)	2,500	KM#103-105	849	1,800
PS17	2002 (3)	4,000	KM#108-110	849	1,800
PS18	2003 (3)	2,500	KM#119-121	849	1,800
PS19	2004 (4)	—	KM#130-133	—	2,000
PS20	2005 (3)	—	KM#134-136	—	925
PS21	2006 (3)	—	KM#139-141	—	925
PS22	2007 (3)	—	KM#148-150	—	925
PS23	2008 (3)	—	KM#142-144	—	925
PS24	2009 (3)	—	KM#145-147	—	875
PS25	2010 (3)	—	KM#156-158	—	1,225
PS26	2011 (3)	—	KM#159-161	—	1,175
PS27	2012 (3)	—	KM#162-164	—	1,850

MACEDONIA

The Republic of Macedonia is land-locked, and is bordered in the north by Yugoslavia, to the east by Bulgaria, in the south by Greece and to the west by Albania and has an area of 9,781 sq. mi. (25,713 sq. km.) and a population at the 1991 census was 2,038,847, of which the predominating ethnic groups were Macedonians. The capital is Skopje.

On Nov. 20, 1991 parliament promulgated a new constitution, and declared its independence on Nov.20, 1992, but failed to secure EC and US recognition owing to Greek objections to use of the name *Macedonia*. On Dec. 11, 1992, the UN Security Council authorized the expedition of a small peacekeeping force to prevent hostilities spreading into Macedonia.

There is a 120-member single-chamber National Assembly.

REPUBLIC
STANDARD COINAGE

KM# 2 DENAR
5.15 g., Brass, 23.7 mm. **Obv:** Macedonian sheepdog **Obv. Legend:** РЕПУБЛИКА МАКЕДОНИЈА **Rev:** Radiant value **Edge:** Plain

Date	Mintage	F12	VF20	XF40	MS60	MS63
2001	12,874,000	—	0.20	0.35	1.50	4.00
2006	—	—	—	—	1.25	3.75
2008	—	—	—	—	1.25	3.75

KM# 3 2 DENARI
5.15 g., Brass, 23.7 mm. **Obv:** Trout above water **Obv. Legend:** РЕПУБЛИКА МАКЕДОНИЈА **Rev:** Radiant value **Edge:** Plain

Date	Mintage	F12	VF20	XF40	MS60	MS63
2001	11,672,000	—	—	0.50	1.25	3.00
2006	—	—	—	0.50	1.00	2.50
2008	—	—	—	—	1.00	2.50

KM# 4 5 DENARI
7.25 g., Brass, 27.5 mm. **Obv:** European lynx **Obv. Legend:** РЕПУБЛИКА МАКЕДОНИЈА **Rev:** Radiant value **Edge:** Plain

Date	Mintage	F12	VF20	XF40	MS60	MS63
2001	6,921,000	—	0.35	0.75	1.75	3.50
2006	—	—	—	—	1.50	3.00
2008	—	—	—	—	1.50	3.00

KM# 13 10 DENARI
10.00 g., 0.916 Gold 0.2926 oz. AGW, 27 mm. **Subject:** 10th Anniversary of Independence **Obv:** Value in circle within radiant map **Rev:** Grape vine

Date	Mintage	F12	VF20	XF40	MS60	MS63
2001	1,000	—	—	—	550	575

KM# 31 10 DENARI
6.60 g., Copper-Nickel-Zinc, 24.5 mm. **Obv:** Peacock **Rev:** Value within rays

Date	Mintage	F12	VF20	XF40	MS60	MS63
2008	—	—	—	—	—	2.00

KM# 32 50 DENARI
7.70 g., Brass, 26.5 mm. **Obv:** Classical female bust right **Rev:** Value within rays

Date	Mintage	F12	VF20	XF40	MS60	MS63
2008	—	—	—	—	—	2.00

KM# 22 60 DENARI
6.00 g., 0.916 Gold 0.1756 oz. AGW, 23.8 mm. **Subject:** 100th Anniversary - Statehood **Obv:** Monument above value within circle **Rev:** Djorce Petrov

Date	Mintage	F12	VF20	XF40	MS60	MS63
2003	500	—	—	—	375	400

KM# 23 60 DENARI
6.00 g., 0.916 Gold 0.1756 oz. AGW, 23.8 mm. **Subject:** 100th Anniversary - Statehood **Obv:** Monument above value within circle **Rev:** Krste Petkov-Misirkov

Date	Mintage	F12	VF20	XF40	MS60	MS63
2003	500	—	—	—	375	400

KM# 24 60 DENARI
6.00 g., 0.916 Gold 0.1756 oz. AGW, 23.8 mm. **Subject:** 100th Anniversary - Statehood **Obv:** Monument above value within circle **Rev:** Metodije Andonov

Date	Mintage	F12	VF20	XF40	MS60	MS63
2003	500	—	—	—	375	400

KM# 25 60 DENARI
6.00 g., 0.916 Gold 0.1756 oz. AGW, 23.8 mm. **Subject:** 100th Anniversary - Statehood **Obv:** Monument above value within circle **Rev:** Mihailo Apostolski

Date	Mintage	F12	VF20	XF40	MS60	MS63
2003	500	—	—	—	375	400

KM# 26 60 DENARI
6.00 g., 0.916 Gold 0.1756 oz. AGW, 23.8 mm. **Subject:** 100th Anniversary - Statehood **Obv:** Monument above value within circle **Rev:** Blaze Koneski

Date	Mintage	F12	VF20	XF40	MS60	MS63
2003	500	—	—	—	375	400

KM# 21 60 DENARI
8.00 g., 0.916 Gold 0.2341 oz. AGW, 23.8 mm. **Subject:** 50th Anniversary of separation from Greece **Obv:** The Monifest **Rev:** Monastery

Date	Mintage	F12	VF20	XF40	MS60	MS63
2004	500	—	—	—	425	450

KM# 14 100 DENARI
6.00 g., 0.916 Gold 0.1756 oz. AGW, 23.8 mm. **Subject:** 100th Anniversary of Statehood **Obv:** Monument above value within circle **Rev:** Cherry tree cannon divides circle

Date	Mintage	F12	VF20	XF40	MS60	MS63
2003	500	PF63 400				

KM# 15 100 DENARI
6.00 g., 0.916 Gold 0.1756 oz. AGW, 23.8 mm. **Subject:** 100th Anniversary of Statehood - Goce Delcev **Obv:** Monument above value within circle **Rev:** Bust facing within circle

Date	Mintage	F12	VF20	XF40	MS60	MS63
2003	500	PF63 400				

KM# 16 100 DENARI
6.00 g., 0.916 Gold 0.1756 oz. AGW, 23.8 mm. **Subject:** 100th Anniversary of Statehood - Pitu Guli **Obv:** Monument above value within circle **Rev:** Head with hat facing within circle

Date	Mintage	F12	VF20	XF40	MS60	MS63
2003	500	PF63 400				

KM# 17 100 DENARI
6.00 g., 0.916 Gold 0.1756 oz. AGW, 23.8 mm. **Subject:** 100th Anniversary of Statehood - Jane Sandanski **Obv:** Monument above value within circle **Rev:** Head facing within circle

Date	Mintage	F12	VF20	XF40	MS60	MS63
2003	500	PF63 400				

KM# 18 100 DENARI
6.00 g., 0.916 Gold 0.1756 oz. AGW, 23.8 mm. **Subject:** 100th Anniversary of Statehood - Dame Gruev **Obv:** Monument above value within circle **Rev:** Bust left within circle

Date	Mintage	F12	VF20	XF40	MS60	MS63
2003	500	PF63 400				

KM# 19 100 DENARI
6.00 g., 0.916 Gold 0.1756 oz. AGW, 23.8 mm. **Subject:** 100th Anniversary of Statehood - Nikola Karev **Obv:** Monument above value within circle **Rev:** Bust right within circle

Date	Mintage	F12	VF20	XF40	MS60	MS63
2003	500	PF63 400				

KM# 28 100 DENARI
6.00 g., 0.916 Gold 0.1756 oz. AGW **Subject:** 100th Anniversary of Statehood - Djorce Petrov **Obv:** Monument **Rev:** Bust facing

Date	Mintage	F12	VF20	XF40	MS60	MS63
2003	500	PF63 400				

KM# 29 100 DENARI
6.00 g., 0.916 Gold 0.1756 oz. AGW **Subject:** 100th Anniversary of Statehood - Krste Petkov-Misirkov **Obv:** Monument **Rev:** Bust facing

Date	Mintage	F12	VF20	XF40	MS60	MS63
2003	500	PF63 400				

KM# 30 100 DENARI
6.00 g., 0.916 Gold 0.1756 oz. AGW **Subject:** 100th Anniversary of statehood - Metodije Adamov-Cengo **Obv:** Monument **Rev:** Bust facing

Date	Mintage	F12	VF20	XF40	MS60	MS63
2003	500	PF63 400				

KM# 33 100 DENARI
6.00 g., 0.916 Gold 0.1756 oz. AGW, 23.8 mm. **Subject:** 100th Anniversary of Statehood - Mihailo Apostolski **Obv:** Monument **Rev:** Bust facing in field cap

Date	Mintage	F12	VF20	XF40	MS60	MS63
2003	500	PF63 400				

KM# 34 100 DENARI
6.00 g., 0.916 Gold 0.1756 oz. AGW, 23.8 mm. **Subject:** 100th Anniversary of Statehood - Blaze Koneski **Obv:** Monument **Rev:** Bust facing, wearing glasses

Date	Mintage	F12	VF20	XF40	MS60	MS63
2003	500	PF63 400				

PATTERNS
(Including off-metal strikes)

KM#	Date	Mintage	Identification	Mkt Val
Pn2	2003	50	100 Denari 0.926 Silver KM#15.	150
Pn3	2003	50	100 Denari 0.925 Silver KM#16.	150
Pn4	2003	50	100 Denari 0.925 Silver KM#17.	150
Pn5	2003	50	100 Denari 0.925 Silver KM#18.	150
Pn6	2003	50	100 Denari 0.925 Silver KM#19.	150
Pn7	2003	50	100 Denari 0.925 Silver	150
Pn8	2003	50	100 Denari 0.925 Silver KM#29.	150
Pn9	2003	50	100 Denari 0.925 Silver KM#30.	150
Pn10	2003	50	100 Denari 0.925 Silver KM#33.	150
Pn11	2003	50	100 Denari 0.925 Silver	100
Pn1	2003	50	100 Denari 0.925 Silver KM#14	150

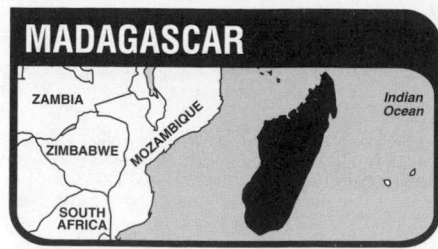

MADAGASCAR

The Republic of Madagascar, an independent member of the French Community located in the Indian Ocean 250 miles (402 km.) off the southeast coast of Africa, has an area of 226,656 sq. mi. (587,040 sq. km.) and a population of 10 million. Capital: Antananarivo. The economy is primarily agricultural; large bauxite deposits are being developed. Coffee, vanilla, graphite, and rice are exported.

MONETARY SYSTEM
100 Centimes = 1 Franc

MINT MARKS
(a) - Paris, privy marks only
SA - Pretoria

MALAGASY REPUBLIC
STANDARD COINAGE
1 Ariary = 100 Iraimbilanja

KM# 8 FRANC
2.40 g., Stainless Steel **Obv:** Poinsettia **Rev:** Value within horns of ox head above sprigs

Date	Mintage	F12	VF20	XF40	MS60	MS63
2002(a)	—	0.15	0.20	0.40	1.45	—

MADAGASIKARA REPUBLIC

KM# 28 10 FRANCS (2 Ariary)
4.34 g., Bronze (Red to Yellow), 21.9 mm. **Obv:** Monkey **Obv. Legend:** BANKY FOIBEN'I MADAGASIKARA **Rev:** Value within steer horns flanked by sprigs **Edge:** Plain

Date	Mintage	F12	VF20	XF40	MS60	MS63
2003	—	—	1.00	2.50	3.50	

KM# 29 ARIARY
4.93 g., Stainless Steel, 22 mm. **Obv:** Flower **Obv. Legend:** BANKY FOIBEN'I MADAGASIKARA **Rev:** Value within steer horns above sprigs **Edge:** Plain

Date	Mintage	F12	VF20	XF40	MS60	MS63
2004(a)	—	—	0.90	2.25	3.00	

KM# 30 2 ARIARY
3.23 g., Copper Plated Steel, 21 mm. **Obv:** Plant **Obv. Legend:** BANKY FOIBEN'I MADAGASIKARA **Rev:** Value within steer horns flanked by sprigs **Edge:** Reeded

Date	Mintage	F12	VF20	XF40	MS60	MS63
2003	—	—	0.90	2.25	3.00	

KM# 25.2 50 ARIARY
10.15 g., Stainless Steel, 30 mm. **Obv:** Star above value within sprays **Rev:** Avenue of the Baobabs **Rev. Inscription:** Motto C **Edge:** Plain **Shape:** 11-sided

Date	Mintage	F12	VF20	XF40	MS60	MS63
2005	—			2.40	6.00	—

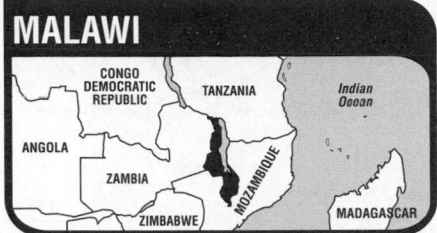

MALAWI

The Republic of Malawi (formerly Nyasaland), located in southeastern Africa to the west of Lake Malawi (Nyasa), has an area of 45,745 sq. mi. (118,480 sq. km.) and a population of 7 million. Capital: Lilongwe. The economy is predominantly agricultural. Tobacco, tea, peanuts and cotton are exported.

REPUBLIC

DECIMAL COINAGE
100 Tambala = 1 Kwacha

KM# 33a TAMBALA
Copper Plated Steel, 17.3 mm. **Obv:** Arms with supporters **Rev:** 2 Talapia fish **Edge:** Plain

Date	Mintage	F12	VF20	XF40	MS60	MS63
2003	—				1.00	1.50

KM# 34a 2 TAMBALA
Copper Plated Steel, 20.3 mm. **Obv:** Arms with supporters **Rev:** Paradise whydah bird divides date and value, designer's initials "P.V. **Edge:** Plain

Date	Mintage	F12	VF20	XF40	MS60	MS63
2003	—				1.00	1.50

KM# 32.2 5 TAMBALA
Nickel Plated Steel, 19.35 mm. **Obv:** Arms with supporters **Rev:** Purple heron, value, designer's initials "P.V.

Date	Mintage	F12	VF20	XF40	MS60	MS63
2003	—				2.50	3.00

KM# 27 10 TAMBALA
5.62 g., Nickel Plated Steel, 23.6 mm. **Obv:** Bust right **Rev:** Bundled corn cobs divide date and value

Date	Mintage	F12	VF20	XF40	MS60	MS63
2003	—				2.25	3.00

KM# 29 20 TAMBALA
7.52 g., Nickel Clad Steel, 26.5 mm. **Obv:** Bust right **Rev:** Elephants

Date	Mintage	F12	VF20	XF40	MS60	MS63
2003	—				3.75	4.50

KM# 30 50 TAMBALA
4.40 g., Brass Plated Steel, 22 mm. **Obv:** Bust right **Rev:** Arms with supporters **Shape:** 7-sided

Date	Mintage	F12	VF20	XF40	MS60	MS63
2003	—				4.50	5.00
2004	—				4.50	5.00

KM# 66 50 TAMBALA
4.40 g., Brass Plated Steel, 22 mm. **Obv:** State arms and supporters with country name below **Rev:** Zebras with date above and value below **Shape:** 7-sided

Date	Mintage	F12	VF20	XF40	MS60	MS63
2004	—				4.50	5.00

KM# 28 KWACHA
9.00 g., Brass Plated Steel, 26 mm. **Obv:** Bust right **Rev:** Fish eagle

Date	Mintage	F12	VF20	XF40	MS60	MS63
2003	—				7.00	10.00

KM# 65 KWACHA
9.50 g., Brass Plated Steel, 26 mm. **Obv:** State arms, country name **Rev:** Fish eagle, date

Date	Mintage	F12	VF20	XF40	MS60	MS63
2004	—				2.50	3.50

KM# 201 KWACHA
31.11 g., 0.999 Silver 0.9926 oz. ASW, 47x27 mm. **Rev:** Impalla

Date	Mintage	F12	VF20	XF40	MS60	MS63
2009 Proof	100					
	Note: Individually numbered					

KM# 202 KWACHA
0.62 g., 0.999 Gold AGW, 11 mm. **Rev:** Impalla

Date	Mintage	F12	VF20	XF40	MS60	MS63
2009	100	PF65 50.00				

KM# 203 KWACHA
3.11 g., 0.999 Gold 0.0992 oz. AGW, 18 mm. **Rev:** Impalla

Date	Mintage	F12	VF20	XF40	MS60	MS63
2009	100	PF65 250				

KM# 204 KWACHA
7.78 g., 0.999 Gold 0.2483 oz. AGW, 25 mm. **Rev:** Impalla

Date	Mintage	F12	VF20	XF40	MS60	MS63
2009	100	PF65 550				

KM# 205 KWACHA
15.55 g., 0.999 Gold 0.4962 oz. AGW, 30 mm. **Rev:** Impalla

Date	Mintage	F12	VF20	XF40	MS60	MS63
2009	100	PF65 1,150				

KM# 212 KWACHA
3.00 g., Stainless Steel, 20 mm. **Obv:** National arms, MALAWI below **Rev:** Flying eagle with date above and value below **Edge:** Reeded

Date	Mintage	F12	VF20	XF40	MS60	MS63
2012	—			—	1.25	2.00

KM# 59 5 KWACHA
Brass, 45x27.5 mm. **Obv:** National arms, date and value **Rev:** USS Coral Sea aircraft carrier **Edge:** Plain

Date	Mintage	F12	VF20	XF40	MS60	MS63
2005	—	PF63 20.00	PF65 22.50			

KM# 62 5 KWACHA
Brass, 45x27.5 mm. **Obv:** National arms, date and value **Rev:** Ship USSR Molotov **Edge:** Plain

Date	Mintage	F12	VF20	XF40	MS60	MS63
2005	—	PF63 20.00	PF65 22.50			

KM# 63 5 KWACHA
Brass, 45x27.5 mm. **Obv:** National arms, date and value **Rev:** Ship USS Missouri **Edge:** Plain

Date	Mintage	F12	VF20	XF40	MS60	MS63
2005	—	PF63 20.00	PF65 22.50			

KM# 64 5 KWACHA
Brass, 45x27.5 mm. **Obv:** National arms, date and value **Rev:** Ship HMS Hood **Edge:** Plain

Date	Mintage	F12	VF20	XF40	MS60	MS63
2005	—	PF63 20.00	PF65 22.50			

KM# 98 5 KWACHA
29.10 g., Copper-Nickel, 38.7 mm. **Obv:** Arms **Rev:** Pope John Paul II holding child

Date	Mintage	F12	VF20	XF40	MS60	MS63
2005	—	PF63 22.00	PF65 25.00			

KM# 44 5 KWACHA
22.00 g., Silver Plated Copper-Nickel, 40 mm. **Subject:** Asian Zodiac Animals **Obv:** Queen Elizabeth II above Zambian arms **Rev:** Multicolor stylized rat **Edge:** Reeded

Date	Mintage	F12	VF20	XF40	MS60	MS63
2005 Prooflike	835	—	—	—	—	17.50

KM# 45 5 KWACHA
22.00 g., Silver Plated Copper-Nickel, 40 mm. **Subject:** Asian Zodiac Animals **Obv:** Queen Elizabeth II above Zambian arms **Rev:** Multicolor stylized ox **Edge:** Reeded

Date	Mintage	F12	VF20	XF40	MS60	MS63
2005 Prooflike	835	—	—	—	—	17.50

KM# 46 5 KWACHA

22.00 g., Silver Plated Copper-Nickel, 40 mm. **Subject:** Asian Zodiac Animals **Obv:** Queen Elizabeth II above Zambian arms **Rev:** Multicolor stylized tiger **Edge:** Reeded

Date	Mintage	F12	VF20	XF40	MS60	MS63
2005 Prooflike	835	—	—	—	—	17.50

KM# 47 5 KWACHA

22.00 g., Silver Plated Copper-Nickel, 40 mm. **Subject:** Asian Zodiac Animals **Obv:** Queen Elizabeth II above Zambian arms **Rev:** Multicolor stylized rabbit **Edge:** Reeded

Date	Mintage	F12	VF20	XF40	MS60	MS63
2005 Prooflike	835	—	—	—	—	17.50

KM# 48 5 KWACHA

22.00 g., Silver Plated Copper-Nickel, 40 mm. **Subject:** Asian Zodiac Animals **Obv:** Queen Elizabeth II above Zambian arms **Rev:** Multicolor stylized dragon **Edge:** Reeded

Date	Mintage	F12	VF20	XF40	MS60	MS63
2005 Prooflike	835	—	—	—	—	17.50

KM# 49 5 KWACHA

22.00 g., Silver Plated Copper-Nickel, 40 mm. **Subject:** Asian Zodiac Animals **Obv:** Queen Elizabeth II above Zambian arms **Rev:** Multicolor stylized snake **Edge:** Reeded

Date	Mintage	F12	VF20	XF40	MS60	MS63
2005 Prooflike	835	—	—	—	—	17.50

KM# 50 5 KWACHA

22.00 g., Silver Plated Copper-Nickel, 40 mm. **Subject:** Asian Zodiac Animals **Obv:** Queen Elizabeth II above Zambian arms **Rev:** Multicolor stylized horse **Edge:** Reeded

Date	Mintage	F12	VF20	XF40	MS60	MS63
2005 Prooflike	835	—	—	—	—	17.50

KM# 51 5 KWACHA

22.00 g., Silver Plated Copper-Nickel, 40 mm. **Subject:** Asian Zodiac Animals **Obv:** Queen Elizabeth II above Zambian arms **Rev:** Multicolor stylized goat **Edge:** Reeded

Date	Mintage	F12	VF20	XF40	MS60	MS63
2005 Prooflike	835	—	—	—	—	17.50

KM# 52 5 KWACHA

22.00 g., Silver Plated Copper-Nickel, 40 mm. **Subject:** Asian Zodiac Animals **Obv:** Queen Elizabeth II above Zambian arms **Rev:** Multicolor stylized monkey **Edge:** Reeded

Date	Mintage	F12	VF20	XF40	MS60	MS63
2005 Prooflike	835	—	—	—	—	17.50

KM# 53 5 KWACHA

22.00 g., Silver Plated Copper-Nickel, 40 mm. **Subject:** Asian Zodiac Animals **Obv:** Queen Elizabeth II above Zambian arms **Rev:** Multicolor stylized rooster **Edge:** Reeded

Date	Mintage	F12	VF20	XF40	MS60	MS63
2005 Prooflike	835	—	—	—	—	17.50

KM# 54 5 KWACHA

22.00 g., Silver Plated Copper-Nickel, 40 mm. **Subject:** Asian Zodiac Animals **Obv:** Queen Elizabeth II above Zambian arms **Rev:** Multicolor stylized dog **Edge:** Reeded

Date	Mintage	F12	VF20	XF40	MS60	MS63
2005 Prooflike	835	—	—	—	—	17.50

KM# 55 5 KWACHA

22.00 g., Silver Plated Copper-Nickel, 40 mm. **Subject:** Asian Zodiac Animals **Obv:** Queen Elizabeth II above Zambian arms **Rev:** Multicolor stylized pig **Edge:** Reeded

Date	Mintage	F12	VF20	XF40	MS60	MS63
2005 Prooflike	835	—	—	—	—	17.50

KM# 57 5 KWACHA

10.25 g., Bi-Metallic, 27 mm. **Obv:** State arms and supporters with country name below **Obv. Legend:** MALAWI **Rev:** Fisherman at work with date above and value below **Edge:** Reeded

Date	Mintage	F12	VF20	XF40	MS60	MS63
2006	—	—	—	—	3.50	5.00

KM# 159 5 KWACHA

28.28 g., 0.925 Silver 0.8356 oz. ASW, 38.61 mm. **Subject:** Journey through Africa **Obv:** National arms **Rev:** Lion

Date	Mintage	F12	VF20	XF40	MS60	MS63
2006	Est. 15000	PF63 50.00			PF65 60.00	

KM# 160 5 KWACHA

28.28 g., 0.925 Silver 0.8356 oz. ASW, 38.61 mm. **Subject:** Journey through Africa **Obv:** National arms **Rev:** African elephant

Date	Mintage	F12	VF20	XF40	MS60	MS63
2006	Est. 15000	PF63 50.00			PF65 60.00	

KM# 161 5 KWACHA

28.28 g., 0.925 Silver 0.8356 oz. ASW, 38.61 mm. **Subject:** Journey through Africa **Obv:** National Arms **Rev:** Lake Malawi

Date	Mintage	F12	VF20	XF40	MS60	MS63
2006	Est. 15000	PF63 50.00			PF65 60.00	

KM# 162 5 KWACHA

28.28 g., 0.925 Silver 0.8356 oz. ASW, 38.61 mm. **Subject:** Journey through Africa **Obv:** National arms **Rev:** Sahara lizard

Date	Mintage	F12	VF20	XF40	MS60	MS63
2006	Est. 15000	PF63 50.00			PF65 60.00	

KM# 163 5 KWACHA

28.28 g., 0.925 Silver 0.8356 oz. ASW, 38.61 mm. **Subject:** Journey through Arfica **Obv:** National arms **Rev:** Mt. Kilimanjaro

Date	Mintage	F12	VF20	XF40	MS60	MS63
2006	Est. 15000	PF63 50.00			PF65 60.00	

KM# 164 5 KWACHA

28.28 g., 0.925 Silver 0.8356 oz. ASW, 38.61 mm. **Subject:** Journey through Africa **Obv:** National arms **Rev:** Tribal life

Date	Mintage	F12	VF20	XF40	MS60	MS63
2006	Est. 15000	PF63 50.00			PF65 60.00	

KM# 165 5 KWACHA
28.28 g., 0.925 Silver 0.8356 oz. ASW, 38.61 mm. **Rev:** Safari in color

Date	Mintage	F12	VF20	XF40	MS60	MS63
2006	Est. 15000	PF63 50.00	PF65 60.00			

KM# 166 5 KWACHA
31.11 g., 0.925 Silver 0.9191 oz. ASW, 38.61 mm. **Rev:** Victoria Falls in color

Date	Mintage	F12	VF20	XF40	MS60	MS63
2006	Est. 15000	PF63 50.00	PF65 60.00			

KM# 167 5 KWACHA
28.28 g., 0.925 Silver 0.8356 oz. ASW, 38.61 mm. **Rev:** Table top mountain in Cape town

Date	Mintage	F12	VF20	XF40	MS60	MS63
2006	Est. 15000	PF63 50.00	PF65 60.00			

KM# 168 5 KWACHA
28.28 g., 0.925 Silver 0.8356 oz. ASW, 38.61 mm. **Rev:** Nile in color

Date	Mintage	F12	VF20	XF40	MS60	MS63
2006	Est. 15000	PF63 50.00	PF65 60.00			

KM# 169 5 KWACHA
28.28 g., 0.925 Silver 0.8356 oz. ASW, 38.61 mm. **Rev:** Pyramids in color

Date	Mintage	F12	VF20	XF40	MS60	MS63
2006	Est. 15000	PF63 50.00	PF65 60.00			

KM# 170 5 KWACHA
28.28 g., 0.925 Silver 0.8356 oz. ASW, 38.61 mm. **Rev:** Great Sphinx in color

Date	Mintage	F12	VF20	XF40	MS60	MS63
2006	Est. 15000	PF63 50.00	PF65 60.00			

KM# 196 5 KWACHA
27.00 g., Copper-Nickel, 40 mm. **Subject:** 2000th Anniversary of the ambush in the forest against the legions of Varus **Rev:** Centopah of Marcus Caelius and the 18th Legion

Date	Mintage	F12	VF20	XF40	MS60	MS63
2009	—	—	—	—	—	20.00

KM# 197 5 KWACHA
20.00 g., Silver Plated Copper, 40 mm. **Rev:** Battleship Bismarck in color

Date	Mintage	F12	VF20	XF40	MS60	MS63
2009	Est. 5000	—	—	—	—	30.00

KM# 198 5 KWACHA
20.00 g., Silver Plated Copper, 40 mm. **Rev:** Ship Tirpitz in color

Date	Mintage	F12	VF20	XF40	MS60	MS63
2009	Est. 5000	—	—	—	—	30.00

KM# 199 5 KWACHA
20.00 g., Silver Plated Copper, 40 mm. **Rev:** Ship Gneisenau in color

Date	Mintage	F12	VF20	XF40	MS60	MS63
2009	Est. 5000	—	—	—	—	30.00

KM# 200 5 KWACHA
20.00 g., Silver Plated Copper, 40 mm. **Rev:** Ship Scharnhorst in color

Date	Mintage	F12	VF20	XF40	MS60	MS63
2009	Est. 5000	—	—	—	—	30.00

KM# 195 5 KWACHA
27.00 g., Copper-Nickel, 40 mm. **Subject:** 2000th Anniversary of the ambush in the forest against the legions of Varus **Rev:** Arminius

Date	Mintage	F12	VF20	XF40	MS60	MS63
2009	Est. 5000	—	—	—	—	20.00

KM# 207 5 KWACHA
30.70 g., Silver, 38.6 mm. **Subject:** John Paul II, 10th Anniversary of visits to Kazakistan and Armenia **Obv:** National arms **Rev:** John Paul II

Date	Mintage	F12	VF20	XF40	MS60	MS63
2011	1,000	PF65 75.00				

KM# 213 5 KWACHA
4.50 g., Iron, 22 mm. **Obv:** National arms, MALAWI below **Rev:** Standing heron, date above, value below

Date	Mintage	F12	VF20	XF40	MS60	MS63
2012	—	—	—	—	2.50	4.00

KM# 39 10 KWACHA
29.10 g., Copper-Nickel, 38.7 mm. **Subject:** Soccer World Championship **Obv:** Arms with supporters **Rev:** Soccer players **Edge:** Reeded

Date	Mintage	F12	VF20	XF40	MS60	MS63
2002	—	PF65 50.00				

KM# 117 10 KWACHA
Silver **Rev:** U.S.S. Nimitz

Date	Mintage	F12	VF20	XF40	MS60	MS63
2002	—	PF65 40.00				

KM# 42 10 KWACHA
19.74 g., 0.999 Silver 0.6299 oz. ASW, 29.9 mm. **Subject:** XXVII Olympic Games - Athens 2004 **Obv:** Arms with supporters divides date **Obv. Legend:** REPUBLIC OF MALAWI **Rev:** Two rowers within circle flanked by sprigs **Edge:** Reeded

Date	Mintage	F12	VF20	XF40	MS60	MS63
2003	—	PF65 40.00				

KM# 80 10 KWACHA
24.00 g., 0.999 Silver 0.7659 oz. ASW, 38.5 mm. **Obv:** Arms **Rev:** Pope John Paul II in mitre and vestments

Date	Mintage	F12	VF20	XF40	MS60	MS63
2003	—	PF65 30.00				

KM# 102 10 KWACHA
19.30 g., Silver, 38 mm. **Subject:** Antelopes of Africa **Obv:** National arms **Rev:** Eland

Date	Mintage	F12	VF20	XF40	MS60	MS63
2003	—	PF63 22.00	PF65 25.00			

KM# 103 10 KWACHA
19.30 g., Silver, 38 mm. **Subject:** Antelopes of Africa **Obv:** National Arms **Rev:** Nyala

Date	Mintage	F12	VF20	XF40	MS60	MS63
2003	—	PF63 22.00	PF65 25.00			

KM# 104 10 KWACHA
19.30 g., Silver, 38 mm. **Subject:** Antelopes of Africa **Obv:** National Arms **Rev:** Springbok

Date	Mintage	F12	VF20	XF40	MS60	MS63
2003	—	PF63 22.00	PF65 25.00			

KM# 105 10 KWACHA
19.30 g., Silver, 38 mm. **Subject:** Antelopes of Africa **Obv:** National Arms **Rev:** Kudu

Date	Mintage	F12	VF20	XF40	MS60	MS63
2003	—	PF63 22.00	PF65 25.00			

KM# 106 10 KWACHA
19.30 g., Silver, 38 mm. **Subject:** Antelopes of Africa **Obv:** National Arms **Rev:** Sable pair

Date	Mintage	F12	VF20	XF40	MS60	MS63
2003	—	PF63 22.00	PF65 25.00			

KM# 107 10 KWACHA
Bronze **Obv:** National Arms **Rev:** John Paul II in mitre and vestments

Date	Mintage	F12	VF20	XF40	MS60	MS63
2003	—	PF65 7.50				

KM# 118 10 KWACHA
Silver **Subject:** Elizabeth, the Queen Mother, First anniversary of death

Date	Mintage	F12	VF20	XF40	MS60	MS63
2003	—	PF65 30.00				

KM# 119 10 KWACHA
0.925 Silver, 38.6 mm. **Rev:** Trans-Siberian Railway

Date	Mintage	F12	VF20	XF40	MS60	MS63
2003	—	PF63 35.00	PF65 45.00			

KM# 120 10 KWACHA
Silver **Subject:** Los Angeles Olympics, 1984 **Rev:** Ribbon dancer

Date	Mintage	F12	VF20	XF40	MS60	MS63
2003	—	PF63 35.00	PF65 45.00			

KM# 60 10 KWACHA
29.15 g., Copper-Nickel, 38.7 mm. **Subject:** Endangered Wildlife **Obv:** National arms **Rev:** Multicolor Zebra and colt **Edge:** Reeded

Date	Mintage	F12	VF20	XF40	MS60	MS63
2004	—	PF65 17.00				

KM# 61 10 KWACHA
29.15 g., Copper-Nickel, 38.7 mm. **Subject:** Endangered Wildlife **Obv:** National arms **Rev:** Multicolor Leopard with cub **Edge:** Reeded

Date	Mintage	F12	VF20	XF40	MS60	MS63
2004	—	PF65 17.00				

KM# 84 10 KWACHA
29.14 g., Copper-Nickel, 38.7 mm. **Obv:** National arms **Rev:** Multicolor elephant and calf **Edge:** Reeded

Date	Mintage	F12	VF20	XF40	MS60	MS63
2004	—	PF65 17.00				

KM# 86 10 KWACHA
29.15 g., Copper-Nickel, 38.7 mm. **Subject:** Endangered Wildlife **Obv:** National arms **Rev:** Multicolor Lion and cub **Edge:** Reeded

Date	Mintage	F12	VF20	XF40	MS60	MS63
2004	—	PF65 17.00				

KM# 89 10 KWACHA
29.15 g., Copper-Nickel, 38.7 mm. **Obv:** National arms **Rev:**
Multicolor Deer and fawn **Edge:** Reeded

Date	Mintage	F12	VF20	XF40	MS60	MS63
2004	—	PF65 17.00				

KM# 90 10 KWACHA
29.15 g., Copper-Nickel, 38.7 mm. **Obv:** National arms **Rev:**
Multicolor Giraffe and her calf **Edge:** Reeded

Date	Mintage	F12	VF20	XF40	MS60	MS63
2004	—	PF65 17.00				

KM# 81 10 KWACHA
Copper-Nickel **Obv:** Arms **Rev:** Chevrotain advancing left

Date	Mintage	F12	VF20	XF40	MS60	MS63
2005	—	PF65 17.00				

KM# 82 10 KWACHA
Copper-Nickel **Obv:** Arms **Rev:** Lemur on branch

Date	Mintage	F12	VF20	XF40	MS60	MS63
2005	—	PF65 17.00				

KM# 83 10 KWACHA
Copper-Nickel **Obv:** Arms **Rev:** Pigmy Hippo

Date	Mintage	F12	VF20	XF40	MS60	MS63
2005	—	PF65 17.00				

KM# 88 10 KWACHA
Copper-Nickel **Obv:** Arms **Rev:** Oryx in photo insert

Date	Mintage	F12	VF20	XF40	MS60	MS63
2005	—	—	—	—	—	20.00

KM# 71 10 KWACHA
23.50 g., Silver Plated Copper-Nickel, 39 mm. **Subject:**
Endangered wildlife **Obv:** National arms **Rev:** Tree pangolin
(Manis Tricuspis)

Date	Mintage	F12	VF20	XF40	MS60	MS63
2005	—	PF65 17.00				

KM# 87 10 KWACHA
Copper-Nickel **Obv:** Arms **Rev:** Monkies in photo insert

Date	Mintage	F12	VF20	XF40	MS60	MS63
2005	—	PF65 17.50				

KM# 130 10 KWACHA
24.50 g., Silver Plated Brass, 38.6 mm. **Obv:** State shield **Rev:**
Crocodile

Date	Mintage	F12	VF20	XF40	MS60	MS63
2005	Est. 1000	PF65 15.00				

KM# 131 10 KWACHA
24.50 g., Silver Plated Brass, 38.6 mm. **Rev:** Pygmy
Chimpanzie

Date	Mintage	F12	VF20	XF40	MS60	MS63
2005	—	PF65 15.00				

KM# 132 10 KWACHA
24.50 g., Silver Plated Brass, 38.6 mm. **Rev:** Corner

Date	Mintage	F12	VF20	XF40	MS60	MS63
2005	1,000	PF65 15.00				

KM# 58 10 KWACHA
15.10 g., Bi-Metallic, 28 mm. **Obv:** State arms and supporters
with country name below **Obv. Legend:** MALAWI **Rev:** Farm
worker harvesting **Edge:** Coarse reeding

Date	Mintage	F12	VF20	XF40	MS60	MS63
2006	—	—	—	—	4.50	6.00

KM# 157 10 KWACHA
Silver Plated **Subject:** World Cup Soccer 2006 **Obv:** National
arms **Rev:** Soccer player in the stadium

Date	Mintage	F12	VF20	XF40	MS60	MS63
2006	—	PF65 15.00				

KM# 158 10 KWACHA
28.28 g., 0.925 Silver 0.8356 oz. ASW, 38.6 mm. **Subject:**
Elizabeth II, 80th Birthday **Obv:** National arms **Rev:** Elizabeth II

Date	Mintage	F12	VF20	XF40	MS60	MS63
2006	—	PF65 37.50				

KM# 99 10 KWACHA
0.999 Silver, 20x40 mm. **Obv:** Arms **Rev:** deRutter painting
of ships

Date	Mintage	F12	VF20	XF40	MS60	MS63
2007	—	PF65 45.00				

KM# 100 10 KWACHA
Silver, 38.6 mm **Obv:** Arms **Rev:** Puccini colorized

Date	Mintage	F12	VF20	XF40	MS60	MS63
2007	—	PF65 40.00				

KM# 185 10 KWACHA
Silver Plated Copper-Nickel, 45x30 mm. **Obv:** State arms **Rev:**
Treaty of Rome anniversary in color

Date	Mintage	F12	VF20	XF40	MS60	MS63
2007	—	PF65 15.00				

KM# 186 10 KWACHA
Silver Plated Copper-Nickel, 45x30 mm. **Rev:** Mother Theresa
in color

Date	Mintage	F12	VF20	XF40	MS60	MS63
2007	—	PF65 15.00				

KM# 187 10 KWACHA
Silver Plated Copper-Nickel, 45x30 mm. **Rev:** Verdespaleis
Centennial

Date	Mintage	F12	VF20	XF40	MS60	MS63
2007	—	PF65 15.00				

KM# 188 10 KWACHA
Silver Plated Copper-Nickel, 45x30 mm. **Rev:** Ship painting of
Michiel de Ruyter

Date	Mintage	F12	VF20	XF40	MS60	MS63
2007	—	PF65 15.00				

KM# 189 10 KWACHA
Silver Plated Copper-Nickel, 45x30 mm. **Rev:** Tulips in color

Date	Mintage	F12	VF20	XF40	MS60	MS63
2007	—	PF65 15.00				

KM# 190 10 KWACHA
Silver Plated Copper-Nickel **Rev:** 60th Anniversary, treaty of
Rome, color

Date	Mintage	F12	VF20	XF40	MS60	MS63
2007	—	PF65 15.00				

KM# 191 10 KWACHA
Silver Plated Copper-Nickel **Rev:** Love and Psyche, in color

Date	Mintage	F12	VF20	XF40	MS60	MS63
2007	—	PF65 15.00				

KM# 192 10 KWACHA
Silver Plated Copper-Nickel **Rev:** Giuseppe Garibaldi in color

Date	Mintage	F12	VF20	XF40	MS60	MS63
2007	—	PF65 15.00				

KM# 110 10 KWACHA
62.20 g., 0.999 Silver 1.9849 oz. ASW, 42x42 mm. **Rev:** Lion
with two crystal eyes

Date	Mintage	F12	VF20	XF40	MS60	MS63
2009	2,500	PF65 135				

KM# 91 10 KWACHA
23.50 g., Silver Plated Copper-Nickel, 39 mm. **Subject:**
Endangered Frogs - Blue Poison Arrowfrog **Rev:** Multicolor
blue frog right

Date	Mintage	F12	VF20	XF40	MS60	MS63
2010	—	PF65 24.00				

KM# 92 10 KWACHA
23.50 g., Silver Plated Copper-Nickel, 39 mm. **Subject:**
Endangered Frogs - Dyeing Poison Arrow frog **Rev:** Multicolor
blue frog left

Date	Mintage	F12	VF20	XF40	MS60	MS63
2010	—	PF65 24.00				

KM# 93 10 KWACHA
23.50 g., Silver Plated Copper-Nickel, 39 mm. **Subject:**
Endangered Frogs - Darwin Frog **Rev:** Multicolor green frog
right

Date	Mintage	F12	VF20	XF40	MS60	MS63
2010	—	PF65 24.00				

KM# 94 10 KWACHA
23.50 g., Silver Plated Copper-Nickel, 39 mm. **Subject:** Endangered Frogs - Panamanian Spotted frog **Rev:** Multicolor orange and black frog

Date	Mintage	F12	VF20	XF40	MS60	MS63
2010	—	PF65 24.00				

KM# 95 10 KWACHA
23.50 g., Silver Plated Copper-Nickel, 39 mm. **Subject:** Endangered Frogs - Purple frog **Rev:** Multicolor purple frog left

Date	Mintage	F12	VF20	XF40	MS60	MS63
2010	—	PF65 24.00				

KM# 96 10 KWACHA
23.50 g., Silver Plated Copper-Nickel, 39 mm. **Subject:** Endangered Frogs - Carnileri Harlequin **Rev:** Multicolor red frog left

Date	Mintage	F12	VF20	XF40	MS60	MS63
2010	—	PF65 24.00				

KM# 97 10 KWACHA
23.50 g., Silver Plated Copper-Nickel, 39 mm. **Subject:** Endangered Frogs - Tree frog **Rev:** Multicolor tree frog

Date	Mintage	F12	VF20	XF40	MS60	MS63
2010	—	PF65 24.00				

KM# 214 10 KWACHA
5.70 g., Iron, 22 mm. **Obv:** National arms, MALAWI below **Rev:** Elephant and calf walking right

Date	Mintage	F12	VF20	XF40	MS60	MS63
2012	—	—	—	—	4.00	6.00

KM# 184 15 KWACHA
20.00 g., 0.999 Silver 0.6382 oz. ASW, 38 mm. **Rev:** Brandenburg gate in color, map of Germany

Date	Mintage	F12	VF20	XF40	MS60	MS63
2006	Est. 1000	PF65 90.00				

KM# 56 20 KWACHA
31.10 g., 0.999 Silver 0.9925 oz. ASW, 38.6 mm. **Series:** The Big Five **Obv:** National arms **Rev:** Two water buffalo on green malachite center insert **Edge:** Plain

Date	Mintage	F12	VF20	XF40	MS60	MS63
2004	3,000	PF63 50.00	PF65 55.00			

KM# 67 20 KWACHA
31.10 g., 0.999 Silver 0.9925 oz. ASW, 38.6 mm. **Series:** The Big Five **Obv:** National arms **Rev:** Elephant family on Haematite (blood stone) center insert **Edge:** Plain

Date	Mintage	F12	VF20	XF40	MS60	MS63
2004	3,000	PF63 50.00	PF65 55.00			

KM# 68 20 KWACHA
31.10 g., 0.999 Silver 0.9925 oz. ASW, 38.6 mm. **Series:** The Big Five **Obv:** National arms **Rev:** Leopard family on hawk or falcon-eye center insert **Edge:** Plain

Date	Mintage	F12	VF20	XF40	MS60	MS63
2004	3,000	PF63 50.00	PF65 55.00			

KM# 69 20 KWACHA
31.10 g., 0.999 Silver 0.9925 oz. ASW, 38.6 mm. **Series:** The Big Five **Obv:** National arms **Rev:** Lion family on tiger-eye center insert **Edge:** Plain

Date	Mintage	F12	VF20	XF40	MS60	MS63
2004	3,000	PF63 50.00	PF65 55.00			

KM# 70 20 KWACHA
31.10 g., 0.999 Silver 0.9925 oz. ASW, 38.6 mm. **Series:** The Big Five **Obv:** National arms **Rev:** Rhinoceros family on heliotrope center insert **Edge:** Plain

Date	Mintage	F12	VF20	XF40	MS60	MS63
2004	3,000	PF63 50.00	PF65 55.00			

KM# 133 20 KWACHA
Acrylic, 65 mm. **Subject:** Year of the Dog

Date	Mintage	F12	VF20	XF40	MS60	MS63
2006	Est. 2000	—	—	—	—	75.00

KM# 134 20 KWACHA
31.11 g., 0.999 Silver 0.9926 oz. ASW, 31x25 mm. **Subject:** Year of the Rat **Obv:** Temple of Heaven

Date	Mintage	F12	VF20	XF40	MS60	MS63
2006	Est. 2000	PF63 65.00	PF65 75.00			

KM# 135 20 KWACHA
31.11 g., 0.999 Silver 0.9926 oz. ASW, 31x25 mm. **Subject:** Year of the Ox **Obv:** Temple of Heaven

Date	Mintage	F12	VF20	XF40	MS60	MS63
2006	Est. 2000	PF63 65.00	PF65 75.00			

KM# 136 20 KWACHA
31.11 g., 0.999 Silver 0.9926 oz. ASW, 31x25 mm. **Subject:** Year of the Tiger **Obv:** Temple of Heaven

Date	Mintage	F12	VF20	XF40	MS60	MS63
2006	—	PF63 65.00	PF65 75.00			

KM# 137 20 KWACHA
31.11 g., 0.999 Silver 0.9926 oz. ASW, 31x25 mm. **Subject:** Year of the Hare **Obv:** Temple of Heaven

Date	Mintage	F12	VF20	XF40	MS60	MS63
2006	—	PF63 65.00	PF65 75.00			

KM# 138 20 KWACHA
31.11 g., 0.999 Silver 0.9926 oz. ASW, 31x25 mm. **Subject:** Year of the dragon **Obv:** Temple of Heaven

Date	Mintage	F12	VF20	XF40	MS60	MS63
2006	Est. 2000	PF63 65.00	PF65 75.00			

KM# 139 20 KWACHA
31.11 g., 0.999 Silver 0.9926 oz. ASW, 31x25 mm. **Subject:** Year of the Snake **Obv:** Temple of Heaven

Date	Mintage	F12	VF20	XF40	MS60	MS63
2006	Est. 2000	PF63 65.00	PF65 75.00			

KM# 140 20 KWACHA
31.11 g., 0.999 Silver 0.9926 oz. ASW, 31x25 mm. **Subject:** Year of the Horse **Obv:** Temple of Heaven

Date	Mintage	F12	VF20	XF40	MS60	MS63
2006	Est. 2000	PF63 65.00	PF65 75.00			

KM# 141 20 KWACHA
31.11 g., 0.999 Silver 0.9926 oz. ASW, 31x25 mm. **Subject:** Year of the goat **Obv:** Temple of Heaven

Date	Mintage	F12	VF20	XF40	MS60	MS63
2006	Est. 2000	PF63 65.00	PF65 75.00			

KM# 142 20 KWACHA
31.11 g., 0.999 Silver 0.9926 oz. ASW, 31x25 mm. **Subject:** Year of the monkey **Obv:** Temple of Heaven

Date	Mintage	F12	VF20	XF40	MS60	MS63
2006	Est. 2000	PF63 65.00	PF65 75.00			

KM# 143 20 KWACHA
31.11 g., 0.999 Silver 0.9926 oz. ASW, 31x25 mm. **Subject:** Year of the Rooster **Obv:** Temple of Heaven

Date	Mintage	F12	VF20	XF40	MS60	MS63
2006	Est. 2000	PF63 65.00	PF65 75.00			

KM# 144 20 KWACHA
31.11 g., 0.999 Silver 0.9926 oz. ASW, 31x25 mm. **Subject:** Year of the Dog **Obv:** Temple of Heaven

Date	Mintage	F12	VF20	XF40	MS60	MS63
2006	Est. 2000	PF63 65.00	PF65 75.00			

KM# 145 20 KWACHA
31.11 g., 0.999 Silver 0.9926 oz. ASW, 31x25 mm. **Subject:** Year of the pig **Obv:** Temple of Heaven

Date	Mintage	F12	VF20	XF40	MS60	MS63
2006	Est. 2000	PF63 65.00	PF65 75.00			

KM# 147 20 KWACHA
31.11 g., 0.999 Silver 0.9926 oz. ASW **Rev:** Sitting panda, city view of Moscow and flag in color

Date	Mintage	F12	VF20	XF40	MS60	MS63
2006	Est. 5000	PF65 60.00				

KM# 148 20 KWACHA
31.11 g., 0.999 Silver 0.9926 oz. ASW **Rev:** Sitting panda, city view of Osaka and flag in color

Date	Mintage	F12	VF20	XF40	MS60	MS63
2006	Est. 5000	PF65 60.00				

KM# 149 20 KWACHA
31.11 g., 0.999 Silver 0.9926 oz. ASW **Rev:** Sitting panda, city view of Paris and flag in color

Date	Mintage	F12	VF20	XF40	MS60	MS63
2006	Est. 5000	PF65 60.00				

KM# 150 20 KWACHA
31.11 g., 0.999 Silver 0.9926 oz. ASW **Rev:** Sitting panda, city view of Mexico City and flag in color

Date	Mintage	F12	VF20	XF40	MS60	MS63
2006	—	PF65 60.00				

KM# 151 20 KWACHA
31.11 g., 0.999 Silver 0.9926 oz. ASW **Rev:** Sitting panda, city view of Madrid and flag in color

Date	Mintage	F12	VF20	XF40	MS60	MS63
2006	Est. 5000	PF65 60.00				

KM# 152 20 KWACHA
31.11 g., 0.999 Silver 0.9926 oz. ASW **Rev:** Panda on rock, city view of Pyeongyang and flag in color

Date	Mintage	F12	VF20	XF40	MS60	MS63
2006	5,000	PF65 60.00				

KM# 153 20 KWACHA
31.11 g., 0.999 Silver 0.9926 oz. ASW

Date	Mintage	F12	VF20	XF40	MS60	MS63
2006	Est. 5000	PF65 60.00				

KM# 154 20 KWACHA
31.11 g., 0.999 Silver 0.9926 oz. ASW **Rev:** Panda on rock, city view of Berlin and flag in color

Date	Mintage	F12	VF20	XF40	MS60	MS63
2006	—	PF65 60.00				

KM# 155 20 KWACHA
31.11 g., 0.999 Silver 0.9926 oz. ASW **Rev:** Panda on rock, city view of London and flag in color

Date	Mintage	F12	VF20	XF40	MS60	MS63
2006	5,000	PF65 60.00				

KM# 156 20 KWACHA
31.11 g., 0.999 Silver 0.9926 oz. ASW **Rev:** Panda on rock, city view of Hong Kong and flag in color

Date	Mintage	F12	VF20	XF40	MS60	MS63
2006	Est. 5000	PF65 60.00				

KM# 74 20 KWACHA
0.50 g., 0.999 Gold AGW **Subject:** Springbok, 40 years, first design

Date	Mintage	F12	VF20	XF40	MS60	MS63
2007	—	PF63 65.00	PF65 70.00			

KM# 75 20 KWACHA
0.50 g., 0.999 Gold AGW **Subject:** Springbok, 40th Anniversary, second desgin

Date	Mintage	F12	VF20	XF40	MS60	MS63
2007	—	PF63 65.00	PF65 70.00			

KM# 76 20 KWACHA
0.50 g., 0.999 Gold AGW **Subject:** Springbok, 40th Anniversary, third design

Date	Mintage	F12	VF20	XF40	MS60	MS63
2007	—	PF63 65.00	PF65 70.00			

KM# 111 20 KWACHA
28.28 g., 0.925 Silver 0.8356 oz. ASW, 38.61 mm. **Subject:** Biosphere Reserves **Obv:** National Arms **Rev:** Goat on hillside, multicolor flower

Date	Mintage	F12	VF20	XF40	MS60	MS63
2010	8,000	PF65 60.00				

KM# 208 20 KWACHA
50.00 g., Silver Plated Base Metal, 65 mm. **Obv:** John Paul
II and St. Peter's **Rev:** John Paul II hand raised in benidiction

Date	Mintage	F12	VF20	XF40	MS60	MS63
2011	2,000	PF65 100				

KM# 209 20 KWACHA
28.28 g., 0.925 Silver 0.8356 oz. ASW, 38.61 mm. **Obv:**
National arms **Rev:** Bison Zubr and grass in color

Date	Mintage	F12	VF20	XF40	MS60	MS63
2011	5,000	PF65 150				

KM# 210 20 KWACHA
28.28 g., 0.925 Silver 0.8356 oz. ASW, 28x40 mm. **Rev:**
Elephant hunt in color **Shape:** Vertical rectangle

Date	Mintage	F12	VF20	XF40	MS60	MS63
2011	3,000	PF65 150				

KM# 211 20 KWACHA
28.28 g., 0.925 Silver 0.8356 oz. ASW, 28x40 mm. **Rev:** Duck
hunt in color **Shape:** Vertical rectangle

Date	Mintage	F12	VF20	XF40	MS60	MS63
2011	—	PF65 150				

KM# 77 40 KWACHA
1.00 g., 0.999 Gold 0.0319 oz. AGW **Rev:** Springbok

Date	Mintage	F12	VF20	XF40	MS60	MS63
2008	—	PF65 100				

KM# 78 40 KWACHA
1.00 g., 0.999 Palladium 0.0319 oz. APW **Rev:** Springbok

Date	Mintage	F12	VF20	XF40	MS60	MS63
2008	—	PF65 75.00				

KM# 79 40 KWACHA
1.00 g., 0.999 Platinum 0.0319 oz. APW **Rev:** Springbok

Date	Mintage	F12	VF20	XF40	MS60	MS63
2008	—	PF65 125				

KM# 43 50 KWACHA
141.21 g., Bronze, 65 mm. **Subject:** Republic of China **Obv:**
Large building above value within circle **Rev:** Conjoined busts
facing within circle **Edge:** Reeded **Note:** Illustration reduced.

Date	Mintage	F12	VF20	XF40	MS60	MS63
2004	1,000	PF63 85.00	PF65 100			

KM# 108 50 KWACHA
Silver **Obv:** National Arms **Rev:** Soccer ball in flight from
Germany to South Africa

Date	Mintage	F12	VF20	XF40	MS60	MS63
2006	—	PF65 45.00				

KM# 109 50 KWACHA
Silver **Obv:** National Arms **Rev:** Two female hurdlers

Date	Mintage	F12	VF20	XF40	MS60	MS63
2008	—	PF65 45.00				

KM# 193 50 KWACHA
27.00 g., Silver Plated Brass, 38.6 mm. **Rev:** Springbock

Date	Mintage	F12	VF20	XF40	MS60	MS63
2008	Est. 4444	—	—	—	—	70.00

KM# 194 50 KWACHA
1.00 g., 0.999 Silver 0.0319 oz. ASW, 8.5x15 mm. **Rev:**
Springbock

Date	Mintage	F12	VF20	XF40	MS60	MS63
2008	Est. 5000	PF65 14.00				

KM# 85 50 KWACHA
62.21 g., 0.999 Silver 1.9852 oz. ASW, 42x42 mm. **Obv:** Arms
Rev: White lion with crystal inserts in eyes **Shape:** Square

Date	Mintage	F12	VF20	XF40	MS60	MS63
2009	2,500	PF65 175				

KM# 215 50 KWACHA
31.31 g., 0.999 Silver 0.9992 oz. ASW, 40 mm. **Obv:** National
arms **Rev:** Gazelle

Date	Mintage	F12	VF20	XF40	MS60	MS63
2010	—	PF65 65.00				

KM# 146 75 KWACHA
4.00 g., 0.999 Gold 0.1276 oz. AGW, 20 mm. **Obv:** Temple of
Mazu **Rev:** Mazu, goddess of protection

Date	Mintage	F12	VF20	XF40	MS60	MS63
2006	Est. 3000	PF63 225	PF65 275			

KM# 171 100 KWACHA
Gold AGW **Subject:** 2008 Bejing Olympics **Rev:** Two hurdlers

Date	Mintage	F12	VF20	XF40	MS60	MS63
2006 Proof	—	—	—	—	—	—

KM# 216 100 KWACHA
62.21 g., 0.999 Gold 1.9852 oz. AGW, 44x44 mm. **Obv:**
National arms **Rev:** White lion with crystal inserts in eyes
Shape: Square

Date	Mintage	F12	VF20	XF40	MS60	MS63
2009	99	PF65 2,700				

PATTERNS
Including off metal strikes

KM#	Date	Mintage	Identification	Mkt Val
Pn2	2002	—	10 Kwacha Copper-Nickel National arms Alexander the Great	—
Pn3	2002	—	10 Kwacha Copper-Nickel National arms Olympic torch under two world globes	—
Pn4	2002	—	10 Kwacha Copper-Nickel National arms MILLENNIUM" above Mona Lisa like portrait	—
Pn5	2003	—	10 Kwacha Silver Plated National arms Trans-Siberian Express train	—
Pn6	2003	—	10 Kwacha Silver Plated National arms Blesbok antelope	—
Pn7	2003	—	10 Kwacha Copper-Nickel National arms Eland antelope	—
Pn8	2003	—	10 Kwacha Copper-Nickel National arms Kudu antelope	—
Pn9	2003	—	10 Kwacha Silver Plated Nyala antelope	—
Pn15	ND (2004)	—	10 Kwacha Silver Plated National arms Multicolor pair of birds with chick	15.00

MALAYSIA

The independent limited constitutional monarchy of Malaysia, which occupies the southern part of the Malay Peninsula in Southeast Asia and the northern part of the island of Borneo, has an area of 127,316 sq. mi. (329,750 sq. km.) and a population of 15.4 million. Capital: Kuala Lumpur. The economy is based on agriculture, mining and forestry. Rubber, tin, timber and palm oil are exported.

Malaysia came into being on Sept. 16, 1963, as a federation of Malaya (Johore, Kelantan, Kedah, Perlis, Trengganu, Negri-Sembilan, Pahang, Perak, Selangor, Penang, Malacca), Singapore, Sabah (British North Borneo) and Sarawak. Following two serious racial riots involving Malays and Chinese, Singapore withdrew from the federation on Aug. 9, 1965. Malaysia is a member of the Commonwealth of Nations.

MINT MARK
FM - Franklin Mint, U.S.A.

CONSTITUTIONAL MONARCHY

STANDARD COINAGE

100 Sen = 1 Ringgit (Dollar)

KM# 49 SEN
1.80 g., Bronze Clad Steel, 17.66 mm. **Obv:** Value divides date below flower blossom **Obv. Legend:** BANK NEGARA MALAYSIA **Rev:** Drum **Edge:** Plain

Date	Mintage	F12	VF20	XF40	MS60	MS63
2001	213,645,000	—	—	—	0.15	0.25
2002	185,220,000	—	—	—	0.15	0.25
2003	235,350,000	—	—	—	0.15	0.25
2004	227,700,000	—	—	—	0.15	0.25
2005	437,400,000	—	—	—	0.15	0.25
2006	328,050,000	—	—	—	0.15	0.25
2007		—	—	—	0.15	0.25

KM# 50 5 SEN
1.40 g., Copper-Nickel, 16.25 mm. **Obv:** Value divides date below flower blossom **Obv. Legend:** BANK NEGARA MALAYSIA **Rev:** Top with string **Edge:** Reeded

Date	Mintage	F12	VF20	XF40	MS60	MS63
2001	94,617,472	—	—	—	0.15	0.25
2002	85,316,000	—	—	—	0.15	0.25
2003	75,690,000	—	—	—	0.15	0.25
2004	11,520,000	—	—	—	0.15	0.25
2005	119,520,000	—	—	—	0.15	0.25
2006	87,120,000	—	—	—	0.15	0.25
2007	97,200,338	—	—	—	0.15	0.25
2008	91,440,000	—	—	—	0.15	0.25
2009	125,172,842	—	—	—	0.15	0.25
2010		—	—	—	0.15	0.25
2011		—	—	—	0.15	0.25

KM# 201 5 SEN
1.72 g., Stainless Steel, 17.78 mm. **Obv:** Flower, date and value **Obv. Legend:** BANK NEGARA MALAYSIA **Rev:** Geometric pattern

Date	Mintage	F12	VF20	XF40	MS60	MS63
2011	—	—	—	—	0.15	0.25
2012	—	—	—	—	0.15	0.25
2013	—	—	—	—	0.15	0.25

KM# 51 10 SEN
2.82 g., Copper-Nickel, 19.4 mm. **Obv:** Value divides date below flower blossom **Obv. Legend:** BANK NEGARA MALAYSIA **Rev:** Ceremonial table **Edge:** Reeded

Date	Mintage	F12	VF20	XF40	MS60	MS63
2001	313,422,000	—	—	—	0.25	0.40
2002	290,451,948	—	—	—	0.25	0.40
2003	8,640,000	—	—	—	0.25	0.40
2004	170,640,000	—	—	—	0.25	0.40
2005	316,800,000	—	—	—	0.25	0.40
2006	304,560,000	—	—	—	0.25	0.40
2007	237,967,970	—	—	—	0.25	0.40
2008	241,560,000	—	—	—	0.25	0.40
2009	336,150,800	—	—	—	0.25	0.40
2010	—	—	—	—	0.25	0.40
2011	—	—	—	—	0.25	0.40

KM# 202 10 SEN
2.98 g., Stainless Steel, 18.8 mm. **Obv:** Flower, date and value **Obv. Legend:** BANK NEGARA MALAYSIA **Rev:** Star-like geometric pattern **Edge:** Reeded

Date	Mintage	F12	VF20	XF40	MS60	MS63
2011	—	—	—	—	0.25	0.40
2012	—	—	—	—	0.25	0.40
2013	—	—	—	—	0.25	0.40

KM# 52 20 SEN
5.66 g., Copper-Nickel, 23.6 mm. **Obv:** Value divides date below flower blossom **Obv. Legend:** BANK NEGARA MALAYSIA **Rev:** Basket with food and utensils **Edge:** Reeded

Date	Mintage	F12	VF20	XF40	MS60	MS63
2001	278,802,000	—	—	—	0.35	0.50
2002	131,279,881	—	—	—	0.35	0.50
2003		—	—	—	0.35	0.50
2004	96,840,000	—	—	—	0.35	0.50
2005	209,700,000	—	—	—	0.35	0.50
Note: Obverse varieties exist with thick or thin lettering						
2006	155,880,000	—	—	—	0.35	0.50
2007	212,897,236	—	—	—	0.35	0.50
2008	19,764,000	—	—	—	0.35	0.50
2009		—	—	—	0.35	0.50
2010		—	—	—	0.35	0.50
2011		—	—	—	0.35	0.50

KM# 203 20 SEN
4.18 g., Nickel-Brass, 20.6 mm. **Obv:** Flower, date and value **Obv. Legend:** BANK NEGARA MALAYSIA **Rev:** flowers on patterned background

Date	Mintage	F12	VF20	XF40	MS60	MS63
2011	—	—	—	—	0.35	0.50
2012	—	—	—	—	0.35	0.50
2013	—	—	—	—	0.35	0.50

KM# 77 25 SEN
9.14 g., Brass, 30 mm. **Series:** Endangered Species **Obv:** Logo left, value right **Rev:** Sumatran Rhinoceros **Edge:** Reeded

Date	Mintage	F12	VF20	XF40	MS60	MS63
2003	100,000	—	—	—	—	5.00

KM# 78 25 SEN
9.14 g., Brass, 30 mm. **Series:** Endangered Species **Obv:** Logo left, value right **Rev:** Elephant **Edge:** Reeded

Date	Mintage	F12	VF20	XF40	MS60	MS63
2003	100,000	—	—	—	—	8.00

KM# 79 25 SEN
9.14 g., Brass, 30 mm. **Series:** Endangered Species **Obv:** Logo left, value right **Rev:** Orangutan **Edge:** Reeded

Date	Mintage	F12	VF20	XF40	MS60	MS63
2003	100,000	—	—	—	—	5.00

KM# 80 25 SEN
9.14 g., Brass, 30 mm. **Series:** Endangered Species **Obv:** Logo left, value right **Rev:** Sumatran Tiger **Edge:** Reeded

Date	Mintage	F12	VF20	XF40	MS60	MS63
2003	100,000	—	—	—	—	5.00

KM# 81 25 SEN
9.14 g., Brass, 30 mm. **Series:** Endangered Species **Obv:** Logo left, value right **Rev:** Slow Loris on branch **Edge:** Reeded

Date	Mintage	F12	VF20	XF40	MS60	MS63
2003	100,000	—	—	—	—	5.00

KM# 82 25 SEN
9.14 g., Brass, 30 mm. **Series:** Endangered Species **Obv:** Logo left, value right **Rev:** Barking Deer **Edge:** Reeded

Date	Mintage	F12	VF20	XF40	MS60	MS63
2003	100,000	—	—	—	—	5.00

KM# 83 25 SEN
9.14 g., Brass, 30 mm. **Series:** Endangered Species **Obv:** Logo left, value right **Rev:** Malayan Tapir **Edge:** Reeded

Date	Mintage	F12	VF20	XF40	MS60	MS63
2003	100,000	—	—	—	—	5.00

KM# 84 25 SEN

9.14 g., Brass, 30 mm. **Series:** Endangered Species **Obv:** Logo left, value right **Rev:** Serow **Edge:** Reeded

Date	Mintage	F12	VF20	XF40	MS60	MS63
2003	100,000	—	—	—	—	5.00

KM# 85 25 SEN

9.14 g., Brass, 30 mm. **Series:** Endangered Species **Obv:** Logo left, value right **Rev:** Sambar Deer **Edge:** Reeded

Date	Mintage	F12	VF20	XF40	MS60	MS63
2003	100,000	—	—	—	—	5.00

KM# 86 25 SEN

9.14 g., Brass, 30 mm. **Series:** Endangered Species **Obv:** Logo left, value right **Rev:** Seated Proboscis Monkey flanked by sprigs **Edge:** Reeded

Date	Mintage	F12	VF20	XF40	MS60	MS63
2003	100,000	—	—	—	—	5.00

KM# 87 25 SEN

9.14 g., Brass, 30 mm. **Series:** Endangered Species **Obv:** Logo left, value right **Rev:** Gaur **Edge:** Reeded

Date	Mintage	F12	VF20	XF40	MS60	MS63
2003	100,000	—	—	—	—	5.00

KM# 88 25 SEN

9.14 g., Brass, 30 mm. **Series:** Endangered Species **Obv:** Logo left, value right **Rev:** Clouded Leopard **Edge:** Reeded

Date	Mintage	F12	VF20	XF40	MS60	MS63
2003	100,000	—	—	—	—	5.00

KM# 89 25 SEN

9.14 g., Brass, 30 mm. **Series:** Endangered Species **Obv:** Logo left, value right **Obv. Legend:** BANK NEGARA MALAYSIA - SIRI HAIWAN TERANCAM **Rev:** Straw-headed Bulbul bird (Barau-Barau) **Edge:** Reeded

Date	Mintage	F12	VF20	XF40	MS60	MS63
2005	—	—	—	—	—	5.00

KM# 90 25 SEN

9.14 g., Brass, 30 mm. **Series:** Endangered Species **Obv:** Logo left, value right **Obv. Legend:** BANK NEGARA MALAYSIA - SIRI HAIWAN TERANCAM **Rev:** Great Argus Pheasant (Kuang Raya) **Edge:** Reeded

Date	Mintage	F12	VF20	XF40	MS60	MS63
2005	40,000	—	—	—	—	5.00

KM# 91 25 SEN

9.14 g., Brass, 30 mm. **Series:** Endangered Species **Obv:** Logo left, value right **Obv. Legend:** BANK NEGARA MALAYSIA - SIRI HAIWAN TERANCAM **Rev:** White-collared Kingfisher (Pekaka Sungai) **Edge:** Reeded

Date	Mintage	F12	VF20	XF40	MS60	MS63
2005	40,000	—	—	—	—	5.00

KM# 92 25 SEN

9.14 g., Brass, 30 mm. **Series:** Endangered Species **Obv:** Logo left, value right **Obv. Legend:** BANK NEGARA MALAYSIA - SIRI HAIWAN TERANCAM **Rev:** White-bellied Sea Eagle (Lang Siput) perched on branch **Edge:** Reeded

Date	Mintage	F12	VF20	XF40	MS60	MS63
2005	40,000	—	—	—	—	5.00

KM# 93 25 SEN

9.16 g., Brass, 30 mm. **Series:** Endangered Species **Obv:** Logo left, value right **Obv. Legend:** BANK NEGARA MALAYSIA - SIRI HAIWAN TERANCAM **Rev:** Asian Fairy Bluebird (Dendang Gajah) **Edge:** Reeded

Date	Mintage	F12	VF20	XF40	MS60	MS63
2005	40,000	—	—	—	—	5.00

KM# 94 25 SEN

9.16 g., Brass, 30 mm. **Series:** Endangered Species **Obv:** Logo left, value right **Obv. Legend:** BANK NEGARA MALAYSIA - SIRI HAIWAN TERANCAM **Rev:** Rhinoceros Hornbill bird (Enggang Badak) **Edge:** Reeded

Date	Mintage	F12	VF20	XF40	MS60	MS63
2005	40,000	—	—	—	—	5.00

KM# 95 25 SEN

9.16 g., Brass, 30 mm. **Series:** Endangered Species **Obv:** Logo left, value right **Obv. Legend:** BANK NEGARA MALAYSIA - SIRI HAIWAN TERANCAM **Rev:** Nicobar Pigeon (Merpati Emas) **Edge:** Reeded

Date	Mintage	F12	VF20	XF40	MS60	MS63
2005	40,000	—	—	—	—	5.00

KM# 96 25 SEN

9.16 g., Brass, 30 mm. **Series:** Endangered Species **Obv:** Logo left, value right **Obv. Legend:** BANK NEGARA MALAYSIA - SIRI HAIWAN TERANCAM **Rev:** Two Crested Wood Partridges (Siul Berjambul) **Edge:** Reeded

Date	Mintage	F12	VF20	XF40	MS60	MS63
2005	40,000	—	—	—	—	5.00

KM# 97 25 SEN

9.16 g., Brass, 30 mm. **Series:** Endangered Species **Obv:** Logo left, value right **Obv. Legend:** BANK NEGARA MALAYSIA - SIRI HAIWAN TERANCAM **Rev:** Black and Red Broadbill bird (Takau Rakit) **Edge:** Reeded

Date	Mintage	F12	VF20	XF40	MS60	MS63
2005	40,000	—	—	—	—	5.00

KM# 98 25 SEN

9.16 g., Brass, 30 mm. **Series:** Endangered Species **Obv:** Logo left, value right **Obv. Legend:** BANK NEGARA MALAYSIA - SIRI HAIWAN TERANCAM **Rev:** Green Imperial Pigeon (Pergam Besar) on branch **Edge:** Reeded

Date	Mintage	F12	VF20	XF40	MS60	MS63
2005	40,000	—	—	—	—	5.00

KM# 99 25 SEN

9.16 g., Brass, 30 mm. **Series:** Endangered Species **Obv:** Logo left, value right **Obv. Legend:** BANK NEGARA MALAYSIA - SIRI HAIWAN TERANCAM **Rev:** Great Egret (Bangau Besar) **Edge:** Reeded

Date	Mintage	F12	VF20	XF40	MS60	MS63
2005	40,000	—	—	—	—	5.00

KM# 100 25 SEN

9.16 g., Brass, 30 mm. **Series:** Endangered Species **Obv:** Logo left, value right **Obv. Legend:** BANK NEGARA MALAYSIA - SIRI HAIWAN TERANCAM **Rev:** Brown Shrike (Tirjup Tanah) on branch **Edge:** Reeded

Date	Mintage	F12	VF20	XF40	MS60	MS63
2005	40,000	—	—	—	—	5.00

KM# 101 25 SEN

Brass, 34 mm. **Series:** Endangered Species **Obv:** Logo and value **Obv. Legend:** BANK NEGARA MALAYSIA - SIRI HAIWAN TERANCAM **Rev:** Olive Ridley Turtle (Pengu Lipas)

Date	Mintage	F12	VF20	XF40	MS60	MS63
2006	40,000	—	—	—	—	5.00

KM# 102 25 SEN

Brass, 34 mm. **Series:** Endangered Species **Obv:** Logo and value **Obv. Legend:** BANK NEGARA MALAYSIA - SIRI HAIWAN TERANCAM **Rev:** Leatherback turtle (Penyu Belimbing)

Date	Mintage	F12	VF20	XF40	MS60	MS63
2006	40,000	—	—	—	—	5.00

KM# 103 25 SEN

Brass, 34 mm. **Series:** Endangered Species **Obv:** Logo and value **Obv. Legend:** BANK NEGARA MALAYSIA - SIRI HAIWAN TERANCAM **Rev:** Green turtle (Penyu Agar)

Date	Mintage	F12	VF20	XF40	MS60	MS63
2006	40,000	—	—	—	—	5.00

KM# 104 25 SEN

Brass, 34 mm. **Series:** Endangered Species **Obv:** Logo and value **Obv. Legend:** BANK NEGARA MALAYSIA - SIRI HAIWAN TERANCAM **Rev:** Hawksbill turtle (Penyu Karah)

Date	Mintage	F12	VF20	XF40	MS60	MS63
2006	40,000	—	—	—	—	5.00

KM# 105 25 SEN
15.50 g., Brass, 34 mm. **Series:** Endangered Species **Obv:** Logo and value **Obv. Legend:** BANK NEGARA MALAYSIA - SIRI HAIWAN TERANCAM **Rev:** Dugong **Edge:** Reeded

Date	Mintage	F12	VF20	XF40	MS60	MS63
2006	40,000	—	—	—	—	8.00

KM# 106 25 SEN
15.50 g., Brass, 34 mm. **Series:** Endangered Species **Obv:** Logo and value **Obv. Legend:** BANK NEGARA MALAYSIA - SIRI HAIWAN TERANCAM **Rev:** Whale Shark (Jerung Paus) **Edge:** Reeded

Date	Mintage	F12	VF20	XF40	MS60	MS63
2006	40,000	—	—	—	—	5.00

KM# 107 25 SEN
15.50 g., Brass, 34 mm. **Series:** Endangered Species **Obv:** Logo and value **Obv. Legend:** BANK NEGARA MALAYSIA - SIRI HAIWAN TERANCAM **Rev:** Irraddy Dolphin (Lumba-Lumba Empesut) **Edge:** Reeded

Date	Mintage	F12	VF20	XF40	MS60	MS63
2006	40,000	—	—	—	—	5.00

KM# 108 25 SEN
15.50 g., Brass, 34 mm. **Series:** Endangered Species **Obv:** Logo and value **Obv. Legend:** BANK NEGARA MALAYSIA - SIRI HAIWAN TERANCAM **Rev:** Bottlenose Dolphin (Lumba Lumba) **Edge:** Reeded

Date	Mintage	F12	VF20	XF40	MS60	MS63
2006	40,000	—	—	—	—	5.00

KM# 109 25 SEN
15.50 g., Brass, 34 mm. **Series:** Endangered Species **Obv:** Logo and value **Obv. Legend:** BANK NEGARA MALAYSIA - SIRI HAIWAN TERANCAM **Rev:** Siamese Crocodile (Buaya Siam) **Edge:** Reeded

Date	Mintage	F12	VF20	XF40	MS60	MS63
2006	40,000	—	—	—	—	5.00

KM# 110 25 SEN
15.50 g., Brass, 34 mm. **Series:** Endangered Species **Obv:** Logo and value **Obv. Legend:** BANK NEGARA MALAYSIA - SIRI HAIWAN TERANCAM **Rev:** Indopacific Crocodile (Buaya Tembaga) **Edge:** Reeded

Date	Mintage	F12	VF20	XF40	MS60	MS63
2006	40,000	—	—	—	—	5.00

KM# 111 25 SEN
15.50 g., Brass, 34 mm. **Series:** Endangered Species **Obv:** Logo and value **Obv. Legend:** BANK NEGARA MALAYSIA - SIRI HAIWAN TERANCAM **Rev:** Malayan Gharial (Buaya Julong) **Edge:** Reeded

Date	Mintage	F12	VF20	XF40	MS60	MS63
2006	40,000	—	—	—	—	5.00

KM# 112 25 SEN
15.50 g., Brass, 34 mm. **Series:** Endangered Species **Obv:** Logo and value **Obv. Legend:** BANK NEGARA MALAYSIA - SIRI HAIWAN TERANCAM **Rev:** Painted Terrapin turtle (Tuntung Laut) **Edge:** Reeded

Date	Mintage	F12	VF20	XF40	MS60	MS63
2006	40,000	—	—	—	—	5.00

KM# 53 50 SEN
9.33 g., Copper-Nickel, 27.75 mm. **Obv:** Value divides date below flower blossom **Obv. Legend:** BANK NEGARA MALAYSIA **Rev:** Ceremonial kite **Edge Lettering:** BANK NEGARA MALAYSIA (twice)

Date	Mintage	F12	VF20	XF40	MS60	MS63
2001	67,371,000	—	—	—	0.65	0.85
2002	61,928,000	—	—	—	0.65	0.85
2003	32,580,000	—	—	—	0.65	0.85
2004	37,890,000	—	—	—	0.65	0.85
2005	691,680,006	—	—	—	0.65	0.85
2006	19,480,006	—	—	—	0.65	0.85
2007	—	—	—	—	0.65	0.85
2008	61,380,000	—	—	—	0.65	0.85
2009	94,691,783	—	—	—	0.65	0.85
2010	—	—	—	—	0.65	0.85
2011	—	—	—	—	0.65	0.85

KM# 204 50 SEN
5.66 g., Nickel-Brass Plated Copper, 22.65 mm. **Obv:** Flower, date and value **Obv. Legend:** BANK NEGARA MALAYSIA **Rev:** Vine on patterned circle **Edge:** Notched

Date	Mintage	F12	VF20	XF40	MS60	MS63
2011	—	—	—	—	0.65	0.85
2012	—	—	—	—	0.65	0.85
2013	—	—	—	—	0.65	0.85

KM# 71 RINGGIT
16.80 g., Copper-Nickel, 33.7 mm. **Subject:** XXI SEA Games **Obv:** Games logo **Rev:** Cartoon mascot **Edge:** Reeded

Date	Mintage	F12	VF20	XF40	MS60	MS63
2001	200,000	—	—	—	5.00	6.00

KM# 74 RINGGIT
16.80 g., Copper-Nickel, 33.7 mm. **Subject:** Coronation of Agong XII **Obv:** Head with headdress facing **Rev:** Arms with supporters within sprigs **Edge:** Reeded **Note:** Prev. KM#72.

Date	Mintage	F12	VF20	XF40	MS60	MS63
ND(2002)	100,000	—	—	—	6.00	7.00

KM# 165 RINGGIT
10.40 g., Copper Plated Zinc, 26 mm. **Subject:** 10th Men's Hockey World Cup **Obv:** Logo **Obv. Legend:** BANK NEGARA MALAYSIA **Rev:** 2 stylized players **Rev. Legend:** KEJOHANAN HOKI LELAKI PIALA DUNIA **Edge:** Reeded

Date	Mintage	F12	VF20	XF40	MS60	MS63
2002	100,000	—	—	—	—	12.00

KM# 168 RINGGIT
Brass **Subject:** 45th National Day **Obv:** Buildings, tower, metro liner **Obv. Legend:** BANK NEGARA MALAYSIA **Rev:** Stylized waving flag **Rev. Legend:** 45 TAHUN MERDEKA

Date	Mintage	F12	VF20	XF40	MS60	MS63
2002	10,000	—	—	—	—	10.00

KM# 171 RINGGIT
Brass **Subject:** XIII NAM Summit **Obv:** Modern building, plaza **Obv. Legend:** MALAYSIA - BANK NEGARA MALAYSIA **Rev:** Stylized dove in rays **Rev. Legend:** XIII CONFERENCE OF HEADS OF STATE OR GOVERNMENT OF THE NON-ALIGNED MOVEMENT

Date	Mintage	F12	VF20	XF40	MS60	MS63
2003	9,400	PF63 8.00	PF65 10.00			

KM# 174 RINGGIT
Brass **Subject:** LIMA - 7th Bi-annual Langkawi Island Trade Fair **Obv:** Jet fighter plane above naval missile corvette **Obv. Legend:** BANK NEGARA MALAYSIA **Rev:** Logo **Rev. Legend:** LANGKAWI INTERNATIONAL MARITIME & AEROSPACE

Date	Mintage	F12	VF20	XF40	MS60	MS63
2003	25,000	—	—	—	—	10.00

KM# 177 RINGGIT
Brass **Subject:** 10th Session Islamic Summit Conference **Obv:** Circular Arabic text **Obv. Legend:** BANK NEGARA MALAYSIA **Rev:** Symmetrical design **Rev. Legend:** PERSIDANGAN KETUA-KETUA NEGARASLAM

Date	Mintage	F12	VF20	XF40	MS60	MS63
2003	25,000	—	—	—	—	10.00

KM# 200 RINGGIT
8.15 g., Bi-Metallic, 26.5 mm. **Subject:** 46th Anniversary of Independence **Rev:** Group of four people

Date	Mintage	F12	VF20	XF40	MS60	MS63
2003	—	—	—	—	—	10.00

KM# 114 RINGGIT
Copper-Nickel **Subject:** Century of Tunku Abdul Rahman **Obv:** National arms **Obv. Legend:** BANK NEGARA MALAYSIA - BAPA KEMERDEKAAN **Rev:** 3/4 length figure of Tunku Abdul Rahman left with right hand raised **Rev. Legend:** Y. T. M. TUNKU ABDUL RAHMAN PUTRA AL-HAJ

Date	Mintage	F12	VF20	XF40	MS60	MS63
2005	25,000	—	—	—	—	10.00

KM# 132 RINGGIT
Brass **Subject:** 30th Annual Meeting Islamic Development Bank **Obv:** Circular Arabic text **Obv. Legend:** BANK NEGARA MALYSIA - MESYUARAT TAHUNAN BANK PEMBANCUNAN ISLAM KE - 30 **Rev:** Logo

Date	Mintage	F12	VF20	XF40	MS60	MS63
2005	20,000	—	—	—	—	10.00

KM# 135 RINGGIT
Copper-Nickel **Subject:** 11th ASEAN Summit **Obv:** Twin towers center right **Obv. Legend:** BANK NEGARA MALAYSIA - SIDANG KEMUNCAK ASEAN KE-11 **Rev:** Logo

Date	Mintage	F12	VF20	XF40	MS60	MS63
2005	20,000	—	—	—	—	8.00

KM# 138 RINGGIT
Bi-Metallic **Subject:** Songket - The Regal Heritage **Obv:** Stylized flower - Bunga Ketola **Obv. Legend:** BANK NEGARA MALAYSIA **Rev:** Floral pattern below inscription

Date	Mintage	F12	VF20	XF40	MS60	MS63
2005	20,000	—	—	—	—	8.00

KM# 141 RINGGIT
Brass **Subject:** 50th Anniversary Mara Technology University **Obv:** Large "50" with horizontal lines in background **Obv. Legend:** BANK NEGARA MALAYSIA - JUBLI EMAS UITM **Rev:** Logo **Rev. Legend:** Universiti Teknologi Mara

Date	Mintage	F12	VF20	XF40	MS60	MS63
ND-2006	12,050	—	—	—	—	8.00

KM# 144 RINGGIT
Brass **Subject:** 50th Anniversary P. Felda **Obv:** 1/2 length figure of Felda 3/4 right **Obv. Legend:** BANK NEGARA MALYSIA **Rev:** Two opposed hands holding symbol **Rev. Legend:** MENEMPA KEJAYAAN

Date	Mintage	F12	VF20	XF40	MS60	MS63
2006	10,000	—	—	—	—	8.00

KM# 147 RINGGIT
Subject: 9th Malaysian Plan **Obv:** Bust 3/4 right **Obv. Legend:** BANK NEGARA MALAYSIA - CEMERLANG GEMILANG TERBILANg **Rev:** Globe logo **Rev. Legend:** RANCANGAN MALAYSIA KE SEMBILAN

Date	Mintage	F12	VF20	XF40	MS60	MS63
2006	10,000	—	—	—	—	8.00

KM# 162 RINGGIT
Brass **Subject:** 200th Anniversary Malaysian Police Force **Obv:** Police badge **Obv. Legend:** BANK NEGARA MALAYSIA **Rev:** Two hands clasped in sprays

Date	Mintage	F12	VF20	XF40	MS60	MS63
2007	20,000	—	—	—	—	7.00

KM# 182 RINGGIT
8.80 g., Aluminum-Bronze, 30 mm. **Subject:** Installation of Agong XIII **Obv:** National arms within wreath **Rev:** Facing portrait

Date	Mintage	F12	VF20	XF40	MS60	MS63
2007	10,000	—	—	—	—	10.00
2007 Proof	600	—	—	—	—	

KM# 185 RINGGIT
8.80 g., Aluminum-Bronze, 30 mm. **Subject:** Independence, 50th Anniversary **Obv:** National Arms **Rev:** 50 above city skyline

Date	Mintage	F12	VF20	XF40	MS60	MS63
2007	10,000	—	—	—	—	10.00
2007 Proof	2,000	—	—	—	—	

KM# 188 RINGGIT
8.80 g., Aluminum-Bronze, 30 mm. **Subject:** Royal Malaysian Air Force, 50th Anniversary **Obv:** Air Force insignia **Rev:** Old and modern plane

Date	Mintage	F12	VF20	XF40	MS60	MS63
2008 Proof	350	—	—	—	—	
2008	10,000	—	—	—	—	10.00

KM# 191 RINGGIT
8.80 g., Aluminum-Bronze, 30 mm. **Subject:** St. John's Ambulance, 100th Anniversary **Obv:** St. John's insignia in wreath above valye **Rev:** Cliernt being loaded into ambulance

Date	Mintage	F12	VF20	XF40	MS60	MS63
2008	10,000	—	—	—	—	10.00
2008 Proof	350	—	—	—	—	

KM# 155 RINGGIT
8.80 g., Brass, 30 mm. **Subject:** Bank Negara Malaysia, 50th Anniversary **Obv:** Bank logo **Rev:** 14-pointed star

Date	Mintage	F12	VF20	XF40	MS60	MS63
2009	13,700	—	—	—	—	10.00
2009 Proof	3,300	—	—	—	—	

KM# 159 RINGGIT
8.00 g., Brass, 30 mm. **Subject:** Parliament, 50th Anniversary **Obv:** National Arms and 2 maces **Rev:** Parliament Building

Date	Mintage	F12	VF20	XF40	MS60	MS63
2009	10,000	—	—	—	—	10.00
2009 Proof	450	—	—	—	—	

KM# 194 RINGGIT
8.80 g., Aluminum-Bronze, 30 mm. **Subject:** International Year of Astronomy **Obv:** Adult and Child looking to the heavens **Rev:** Langkawi National Observatory

Date	Mintage	F12	VF20	XF40	MS60	MS63
2009	10,000	—	—	—	—	10.00
2009 Proof	350	—	—	—	—	

KM# 197 RINGGIT
8.80 g., Aluminum-Bronze, 30 mm. **Subject:** Royal Malaysian Navy, 75th Anniversary **Obv:** Submarine **Rev:** Navy insignia

Date	Mintage	F12	VF20	XF40	MS60	MS63
2009	10,000	—	—	—	—	10.00
2009 Proof	450	—	—	—	—	

KM# 209 RINGGIT
8.80 g., Nordic Gold, 30 mm. **Subject:** Girl Guides

Date	Mintage	F12	VF20	XF40	MS60	MS63
2012	Est. 15000	—	—	—	—	12.00

KM# 72 10 RINGGIT
21.70 g., 0.925 Silver 0.6412 oz. ASW, 35.7 mm. **Subject:** XXI SEA Games **Obv:** Games logo **Rev:** Cartoon mascot **Edge:** Reeded

Date	Mintage	F12	VF20	XF40	MS60	MS63
2001	3,000	PF65 70.00				

KM# 75 10 RINGGIT
21.70 g., 0.925 Silver 0.6412 oz. ASW, 35.7 mm. **Subject:** Coronation of Agong XII **Obv:** Head with headdress facing **Rev:** Arms with supporters within sprigs **Edge:** Reeded

Date	Mintage	F12	VF20	XF40	MS60	MS63
ND(2002)	10,000	PF63 100	PF65 120			

KM# 166 10 RINGGIT
16.80 g., 0.925 Silver 0.4964 oz. ASW, 32 mm. **Subject:** 10th Men's Hockey World Cup **Obv:** Official logo of the World Cup games **Obv. Legend:** BANK NEGARA MALAYSIA **Rev:** 2 stylized players in front of the Kuala Lumpur skyline **Rev. Legend:** KEJOHANAN HOKI LELAKI PIALA

Date	Mintage	F12	VF20	XF40	MS60	MS63
2002	3,000	PF63 140	PF65 160			

KM# 169 10 RINGGIT
0.925 Silver **Subject:** 45th National Day **Obv:** Buildings, tower, metro liner **Obv. Legend:** BANK NEGARA MALAYSIA **Rev:** Stylized waving flag **Rev. Legend:** 45 TAHUN MERDEKA

Date	Mintage	F12	VF20	XF40	MS60	MS63
2002	1,800	PF63 110	PF65 125			

KM# 172 10 RINGGIT
0.925 Silver **Subject:** XIII NAM Summit **Obv:** Modern building, plaza **Obv. Legend:** MALAYSIA - BANK NEGARA MALAYSIA **Rev:** Stylized dove in rays **Rev. Legend:** XIII CONFERENCE OF HEADS OF STATE OR GOVERNMENT OF THE NON-ALIGNED MOVEMENT

Date	Mintage	F12	VF20	XF40	MS60	MS63
2003	2,400	PF63 110	PF65 125			

KM# 175 10 RINGGIT
0.925 Silver **Subject:** LIMA - 7th bi-annual Langkawi Island Trade Fair **Obv:** Jet fighter plane above naval missile corvette **Obv. Legend:** BANK NEGARA MALAYSIA **Rev. Legend:** LANGKAWI INTERNATIONAL MARITIME & SPACE

Date	Mintage	F12	VF20	XF40	MS60	MS63
2003	—	PF63 100	PF65 120			

KM# 178 10 RINGGIT
0.925 Silver **Subject:** 10th Session Islamic Summit Conference **Obv:** Circular Arabic Text **Obv. Legend:** BANK NEGARA MALAYSIA **Rev. Legend:** PERSIDANGAN KETUA - KETUA NEGARA ISLAM

Date	Mintage	F12	VF20	XF40	MS60	MS63
2003	300	PF65 120				

KM# 115 10 RINGGIT
0.925 Silver **Subject:** Century of Tunku Abdul Rahman **Obv:** National arms **Obv. Legend:** BANK NEGARA MALAYSIA - BAPA KEMERDEKAAN **Rev:** 3/4 length figure of Tunku Abdul Rahman left with right hand raised **Rev. Legend:** Y. T. M. TUNKU ABDUL RAHMAN PUTRA AL-HAJ

Date	Mintage	F12	VF20	XF40	MS60	MS63
2005	200	PF65 120				

KM# 136 10 RINGGIT
21.70 g., Silver, 35.7 mm. **Subject:** 11th ASEAN Summit **Obv:** Twin towers center right **Obv. Legend:** BANK NEGARA MALAYSIA - SIDANG KEMUNCAK ASEAN KE-11 **Rev:** Logo

Date	Mintage	F12	VF20	XF40	MS60	MS63
2005	250	PF65 120				

KM# 139 10 RINGGIT
21.70 g., Silver, 35.7 mm. **Subject:** Songket - The Regal Heritage **Obv:** Uniform pattern - Bunga Bintang **Obv. Legend:** BANK NEGARA MALAYSIA **Rev:** Floral pattern below inscription

Date	Mintage	F12	VF20	XF40	MS60	MS63
2005	250	PF65 120				

KM# 142 10 RINGGIT
21.70 g., Silver, 35.7 mm. **Subject:** 50th Anniversary Mara Technology Universit **Obv:** Large "50" with horizontal lines in background **Obv. Legend:** BANK NEGARA MALAYSIA - JUBLI EMAS UITM **Rev:** Logo **Rev. Legend:** Universiti Teknologi Mara

Date	Mintage	F12	VF20	XF40	MS60	MS63
ND-2006	500	PF65 110				

KM# 145 10 RINGGIT
31.11 g., Silver, 40 mm. **Subject:** 50th Anniversary P. Felda **Obv:** Outlined map of South East Asia above logo **Obv. Legend:** BANK NEGARA MALAYSIA **Rev:** Monument at left, Felda with 4 others at right **Rev. Legend:** MENEMPA KEJAYAAN

Date	Mintage	F12	VF20	XF40	MS60	MS63
2006	300	PF65 110				

KM# 148 10 RINGGIT
21.00 g., Silver, 35.7 mm. **Subject:** 9th Malaysian Plan **Obv:** Bust 3/4 right **Obv. Legend:** BANK NEGARA MALAYSIA - CEMERLANG GEMILANG TERBILANG **Rev:** Globe logo **Rev. Legend:** RANCANGAN MALAYSIA KE SEMBILAN

Date	Mintage	F12	VF20	XF40	MS60	MS63
2006	300	PF65 110				

KM# 163 10 RINGGIT
21.00 g., Silver, 35.70 mm. **Subject:** 200th Anniversary Malaysian Police Force **Obv:** Police badge **Obv. Legend:** BANK NEGARA MALAYSIA **Rev:** Two hands clasped in sprays

Date	Mintage	F12	VF20	XF40	MS60	MS63
2007	500	PF65 110				

KM# 183 10 RINGGIT
21.00 g., 0.925 Silver 0.6205 oz. ASW, 35.7 mm. **Subject:** Installation of Agong XIII **Obv:** National arms in wreath **Rev:** Portrait facing

Date	Mintage	F12	VF20	XF40	MS60	MS63
2007	200	PF65 100				

KM# 186 10 RINGGIT
21.00 g., 0.925 Silver 0.6205 oz. ASW, 35.7 mm. **Subject:** Independence, 50th Anniversary **Obv:** National Arms **Rev:** 50 above city skyline

Date	Mintage	F12	VF20	XF40	MS60	MS63
2007	200	PF65 110				

KM# 189 10 RINGGIT
21.00 g., 0.925 Silver 0.6205 oz. ASW, 35.7 mm. **Subject:** Royal Malaysian Air Force, 50th Anniversary **Obv:** Air Force insignia **Rev:** Old and new plane

Date	Mintage	F12	VF20	XF40	MS60	MS63
2008	350	PF65 100				

KM# 192 10 RINGGIT
21.00 g., 0.925 Silver 0.6205 oz. ASW, 35.7 mm. **Subject:** St. John's Ambulance **Obv:** St. John's emblem in wreath above vlaue **Rev:** Client being loaded into ambulance

Date	Mintage	F12	VF20	XF40	MS60	MS63
2008	350	PF65 100				

KM# 156 10 RINGGIT
21.00 g., 0.925 Silver 0.6205 oz. ASW, 35.7 mm. **Subject:** Bank Negara Malaysia, 50th Anniversary **Obv:** Bank logo **Rev:** 14-pointed star

Date	Mintage	F12	VF20	XF40	MS60	MS63
2009	400	PF65 100				

KM# 160 10 RINGGIT
21.00 g., 0.925 Silver 0.6205 oz. ASW, 35.7 mm. **Subject:** Parliament, 50th Anniversary **Obv:** National Arms and 2 maces **Rev:** Parliament Building

Date	Mintage	F12	VF20	XF40	MS60	MS63
2009	300	PF65 120				

KM# 195 10 RINGGIT
21.00 g., 0.925 Silver 0.6205 oz. ASW, 35.7 mm. **Subject:** International Year of Astronomy **Obv:** Adult and child looking to the heavens **Rev:** Langkawi Naitonal Observatory

Date	Mintage	F12	VF20	XF40	MS60	MS63
2009	350	PF65 120				

KM# 198 10 RINGGIT
21.00 g., 0.925 Silver 0.6205 oz. ASW, 35.7 mm. **Subject:** Royal Malaysian navy, 75th Anniversary **Obv:** Submarine **Rev:** Navy insignia

Date	Mintage	F12	VF20	XF40	MS60	MS63
2009	300	PF65 120				

KM# 206 10 RINGGIT
Silver **Rev:** Belia flower

Date	Mintage	F12	VF20	XF40	MS60	MS63
2011	—	PF65 125				

KM# 207 10 RINGGIT
0.999 Silver **Rev:** Wanita flower

Date	Mintage	F12	VF20	XF40	MS60	MS63
2011	—	PF65 125				

KM# 208 10 RINGGIT
31.00 g., 0.925 Silver 0.916 oz. ASW, 35.7 mm. **Subject:** Girl Guides

Date	Mintage	F12	VF20	XF40	MS60	MS63
2012	Est. 600	PF65 55.00				

KM# 133 20 RINGGIT
31.10 g., Silver, 40 mm. **Subject:** 30th Annual Meeting Islamic Development Bank **Obv:** Mosque **Obv. Legend:** BANK NEGARA MALAYSIA **Rev:** Logo

Date	Mintage	F12	VF20	XF40	MS60	MS63
2005	1,000	PF65 100				

KM# 157 50 RINGGIT
10.07 g., 0.999 Gold 0.3214 oz. AGW, 25 mm. **Subject:** Bank Negara Malaysia, 50th Anniversary **Obv:** Bank logo **Rev:** 14-pointed star

Date	Mintage	F12	VF20	XF40	MS60	MS63
2009	300	PF65 1,000				

KM# 73 100 RINGGIT
8.60 g., 0.916 Gold 0.2516 oz. AGW, 22 mm. **Subject:** XXI SEA Games **Obv:** Games logo **Rev:** Cartoon mascot **Edge:** Reeded

Date	Mintage	F12	VF20	XF40	MS60	MS63
2001	500	PF65 800				

KM# 76 100 RINGGIT
8.60 g., 0.916 Gold 0.2516 oz. AGW, 22 mm. **Subject:** Coronation of Agong XII **Obv:** Head with headdress facing **Rev:** Arms with supporters within sprigs **Edge:** Reeded

Date	Mintage	F12	VF20	XF40	MS60	MS63
ND(2002)	300	PF65 900				

KM# 167 100 RINGGIT
9.00 g., 0.900 Gold 0.2587 oz. AGW, 22 mm. **Subject:** 10th Men's Hockey World Cup **Obv:** Logo **Obv. Legend:** BANK NEGARA MALAYSIA **Rev:** 2 stylized players in front of Kuala Lumpur skyline **Rev. Legend:** KEJOHANAN HOKI LELAKI PIALA

Date	Mintage	F12	VF20	XF40	MS60	MS63
2002	1,000	PF63 600	PF65 700			

KM# 170 100 RINGGIT
8.60 g., 0.9999 Gold 0.2747 oz. AGW **Subject:** 45th National Day **Obv:** Buildings, tower, metro liner **Obv. Legend:** BANK NEGARA MALAYSIA **Rev:** Stylized waving flag **Rev. Legend:** 45 TAHUN MERDEKA

Date	Mintage	F12	VF20	XF40	MS60	MS63
2002	300	PF65 900				

KM# 173 100 RINGGIT
8.60 g., 0.9999 Gold 0.2747 oz. AGW, 22 mm. **Subject:** XIII NAM Summit **Obv:** Modern building, plaza **Obv. Legend:** MALAYSIA - BANK NEGARA MALAYSIA **Rev:** Stylized dove in rays **Rev. Legend:** XIII CONFERENCE OF HEADS OF STATE OR GOVERNMENT OF THE NON-ALIGNED MOVEMENT

Date	Mintage	F12	VF20	XF40	MS60	MS63
2003	300	PF65 900				

KM# 176 100 RINGGIT
8.60 g., 0.9999 Gold 0.2747 oz. AGW, 22 mm. **Subject:** LIMA - 7th bi-annual Langkawi Island Trade Fair **Obv:** Jet fighter plane above naval missile corvette **Obv. Legend:** BANK NEGARA MALAYSIA **Rev:** Logo **Rev. Legend:** LANGKAWI INTERNATIONAL MARITIME & AEROSPACE

Date	Mintage	F12	VF20	XF40	MS60	MS63
2003	50	PF65 1,400				

KM# 179 100 RINGGIT
8.60 g., 0.9999 Gold 0.2747 oz. AGW, 22 mm. **Obv:** Circular Arabic text **Obv. Legend:** BANK NEGARA MALAYSIA **Rev:** Symmetrical design **Rev. Legend:** PERSIDANGAN KETUA - KETUA NEGARA ISLAM

Date	Mintage	F12	VF20	XF40	MS60	MS63
2003	200	PF65 900				

KM# 116 100 RINGGIT
0.9999 Gold AGW **Subject:** Century of Tunku Abdul Rahman **Obv:** National arms **Obv. Legend:** BANK NEGARA MALAYSIA - BAPA KEMERDEKAAN **Rev:** 3/4 length figure of Tunku Abdul Rahman left with right hand raised **Rev. Legend:** Y. T. M. TUNKU ABDUL RAHMAN PUTRA AL-HAJ

Date	Mintage	F12	VF20	XF40	MS60	MS63
2005	100	PF65 900				

KM# 137 100 RINGGIT
8.60 g., Gold AGW, 22 mm. **Subject:** 11th ASEAN Summit **Obv:** Twin towers center right **Obv. Legend:** BANK NEGARA MALAYSIA - SIDANG KEMUNCAK ASEAN KE-11 **Rev:** Logo

Date	Mintage	F12	VF20	XF40	MS60	MS63
2005	200	PF65 900				

KM# 140 100 RINGGIT
8.60 g., Gold AGW, 22 mm. **Subject:** Songket - The Regal Heritage **Obv:** Uniform pattern - Tampur Kesemak **Obv. Legend:** BANK NEGARA MALAYSIA **Rev:** Floral pattern below inscription

Date	Mintage	F12	VF20	XF40	MS60	MS63
2005	150	PF65 900				

KM# 143 100 RINGGIT
8.60 g., Gold AGW, 22 mm. **Subject:** 50th Anniversary Mara Technology University **Obv:** Large "50" with horizontal lines in background **Obv. Legend:** BANK NEGARA MALAYSIA - JUBLI EMAS UITM **Rev:** Logo **Rev. Legend:** Universiti Teknologi Mara

Date	Mintage	F12	VF20	XF40	MS60	MS63
ND-2006	300	PF65 900				

KM# 146 100 RINGGIT
9.00 g., Gold AGW, 22 mm. **Subject:** 50th Anniversary P. Felda **Obv:** 1/2 length figure of Felda 3/4 right **Obv. Legend:** BANK NEGARA MALAYSIA **Rev:** Stylized palm tree at left, rubber tree trunk at right **Rev. Legend:** MENEMPA KEJAYAAN

Date	Mintage	F12	VF20	XF40	MS60	MS63
2006	200	PF65 900				

KM# 149 100 RINGGIT
7.96 g., Gold AGW, 22 mm. **Subject:** 9th Malaysian Plan **Obv:** Bust 3/4 right **Obv. Legend:** BANK NEGARA MALAYSIA - CEMERLANG GEMILANG TERBILANG **Rev:** Globe logo **Rev. Legend:** RANCANGAN MALAYSIA KE SEMBILAN

Date	Mintage	F12	VF20	XF40	MS60	MS63
2006	500	PF65 900				

KM# 164 100 RINGGIT
7.96 g., Gold AGW, 22 mm. **Subject:** 200th Anniversary Malaysian Police Force **Obv:** Police badge **Obv. Legend:** BANK NEGARA MALAYSIA **Rev:** Two hands clasped in sprays

Date	Mintage	F12	VF20	XF40	MS60	MS63
2007	500	PF65 900				

KM# 184 100 RINGGIT
7.96 g., 0.9999 Gold 0.2542 oz. AGW, 22 mm. **Subject:** Installation of the King **Obv:** National Arms within wreath **Rev:** Facing portrait

Date	Mintage	F12	VF20	XF40	MS60	MS63
2007	100	PF65 900				

KM# 187 100 RINGGIT
7.96 g., 0.9999 Gold 0.2542 oz. AGW, 22 mm. **Subject:** Independence, 50th Anniversary **Obv:** National Arms **Rev:** 50 above city skyline

Date	Mintage	F12	VF20	XF40	MS60	MS63
2007	100	PF65 900				

KM# 190 100 RINGGIT
7.96 g., 0.9999 Gold 0.2542 oz. AGW, 22 mm. **Subject:** Royal Malaysian Air Force, 50th Anniversary **Obv:** Royal Airforce insignia **Rev:** Old and new plane

Date	Mintage	F12	VF20	XF40	MS60	MS63
2008	100	PF65 900				

KM# 193 100 RINGGIT
7.96 g., 0.9999 Gold 0.2542 oz. AGW, 22 mm. **Subject:** St. John's Ambulance, 100th Anniversary **Obv:** St. John's insignia in wreath above value **Rev:** Client being loaded into ambulance

Date	Mintage	F12	VF20	XF40	MS60	MS63
2008	100	PF65 900				

KM# 158 100 RINGGIT
7.96 g., 0.999 Gold 0.254 oz. AGW, 22 mm. **Subject:** Bank Negara Malaysia, 50th Anniversary **Obv:** Bank logo **Rev:** 14-pointed star

Date	Mintage	F12	VF20	XF40	MS60	MS63
2009	300	PF65 1,000				

KM# 180 100 RINGGIT
7.96 g., 0.9999 Gold 0.2542 oz. AGW, 22 mm. **Subject:** Parliament, 50th Anniversary **Obv:** National arms above mace and sceptre **Rev:** Parliament buildings, sunburst

Date	Mintage	F12	VF20	XF40	MS60	MS63
2009	100	PF65 800				

KM# 196 100 RINGGIT
7.96 g., 0.9999 Gold 0.2542 oz. AGW, 22 mm. **Subject:** International Year of Astronomy **Obv:** Adult and child looking to the ehavens **Rev:** Langkawi National Observatory

Date	Mintage	F12	VF20	XF40	MS60	MS63
2009	100	PF65 900				

KM# 199 100 RINGGIT
7.96 g., 0.9999 Gold 0.2542 oz. AGW, 22 mm. **Subject:** Royal Malaysian Navy, 75th Anniversary **Obv:** Submarine **Rev:** Navy insignia

Date	Mintage	F12	VF20	XF40	MS60	MS63
2009	100	PF65 900				

KM# 134 200 RINGGIT
15.55 g., Gold AGW, 28 mm. **Subject:** 30th Annual Meeting Islamic Development Bank **Obv:** Mosque in rays **Obv. Legend:** BANK NEGARA MALAYSIA **Rev:** Logo

Date	Mintage	F12	VF20	XF40	MS60	MS63
2005	500	PF65 600				

PROOF SETS

KM#	Date	Mintage	Identification	Issue Price	Mkt Val
PS19	2003 (2)	300	KM#171, 172	—	150
PS20	2003 (3)	300	KM#171-173	—	1,200
PS21	2003 (2)	300	KM#174, 175	—	200
PS22	2003 (3)	100	KM#174-176	—	1,800
PS23	2003 (2)	500	KM#177, 178	—	150
PS24	2003 (3)	250	KM#177-179	—	1,100
PS25	2005 (2)	300	KM#114, 115	—	150
PS26	2005 (3)	100	KM#114-116	—	1,400
PS27	2005 (2)	1,000	KM#132, 133	—	150
PS28	2005 (3)	500	KM#132-134	—	1,200
PS29	2005 (2)	200	KM#135, 136	—	150
PS30	2005 (3)	150	KM#135-137	—	1,200
PS31	2006 (2)	150	KM#138, 139	—	150
PS32	2005 (3)	150	KM#138-140	—	1,200
PS33	2006 (2)	300	KM#141, 142	—	150
PS34	2006 (3)	300	KM#141-143	—	1,200
PS35	2006 (2)	500	KM#144, 145	—	150
PS36	2006 (3)	500	KM#144-146	—	1,100
PS37	2006 (2)	300	KM#147, 148	—	150
PS38	2006 (3)	500	KM#147-149	—	1,000
PS39	2007 (2)	200	KM#162, 163	—	150
PS40	2007 (3)	200	KM#162-164	—	1,000

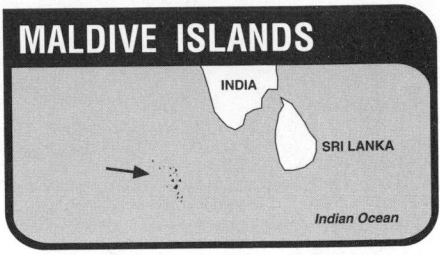

MALDIVE ISLANDS

The Republic of Maldives, an archipelago of 2,000 coral islets in the northern Indian Ocean 417 miles (671 km.) west of Ceylon, has an area of 116 sq. mi. (298 sq. km.) and a population of 189,000. Capital: Male. Fishing employs 95% of the male work force. Dried fish, copra and coir yarn are exported.

The Maldive Islands were visited by Arab traders and converted to Islam in 1153. After being harassed in the 16th and 17th centuries by Mopla pirates of the Malabar coast and Portuguese raiders, the Maldivians voluntarily placed themselves under the suzerainty of Ceylon. In 1887 the islands became an internally self-governing British protectorate and a nominal dependency of Ceylon. Traditionally a sultanate, the Maldives became a republic in 1953 but restored the sultanate in 1954. The Sultanate of the Maldive Islands attained complete internal and external autonomy on July 26, 1965, and on Nov. 11, 1968, again became a republic. The Maldives is a member of the Commonwealth of Nations.

MONETARY SYSTEM
100 Lari = 1 Rupee (Rufiyaa)

2ND REPUBLIC
STANDARD COINAGE
100 Laari = 1 Rufiyaa

KM# 68 LAARI
0.46 g., Aluminum, 15 mm. **Obv:** Value **Rev:** Palm tree within circle **Edge:** Plain

Date	Mintage	F12	VF20	XF40	MS60	MS63
AH1423-2002	—	—	—	0.10	0.15	0.20
AH1433-2012	—	—	—	0.10	0.15	0.20

KM# 70 10 LAARI
1.95 g., Aluminum, 23.11 mm. **Obv:** Value **Rev:** Maldivian sailing ship - Odi **Shape:** Scalloped

Date	Mintage	F12	VF20	XF40	MS60	MS63
AH1422-2001	—	—	—	0.10	0.20	0.30

KM# 71a 25 LAARI
Brass Plated Steel, 20.2 mm. **Obv:** Value **Rev:** Mosque and minaret at Male

Date	Mintage	F12	VF20	XF40	MS60	MS63
AH1429-2008	—	—	—	—	0.15	0.45

KM# 72a 50 LAARI
Brass Plated Steel, 23.6 mm. **Obv:** Value **Rev:** Loggerhead sea turtle

Date	Mintage	F12	VF20	XF40	MS60	MS63
AH1429-2008	—	—	—	—	1.50	2.50

KM# 73b RUFIYAA
6.54 g., Nickel Plated Steel, 25.8 mm. **Obv:** Value **Obv. Legend:** REPUBLIC OF MALDIVES **Rev:** National arms **Edge:** Reeded

Date	Mintage	F12	VF20	XF40	MS60	MS63
AH1428-2007	—	—	—	0.50	2.00	3.00

KM# 105 RUFIYAA
26.00 g., Silver Plated Copper, 38.61 mm. **Subject:** London Olympics **Obv:** National emblem **Rev:** Soccer

Date	Mintage	F12	VF20	XF40	MS60	MS63
2011	Est. 10000	PF63 22.00	PF65 25.00			

KM# 88 2 RUFIYAA
11.70 g., Nickel-Brass, 25.5 mm. **Obv:** Value **Rev:** Pacific triton sea shell **Edge:** Reeded and lettered **Edge Lettering:** REPUBLIC OF MALDIVES

Date	Mintage	F12	VF20	XF40	MS60	MS63
AH1428-2007	—	—	—	2.25	5.50	7.50

KM# 103 10 RUFIYAA
6.22 g., 0.999 Gold 0.1985 oz. AGW, 35 mm. **Subject:** Ships and Explorers **Obv:** National emblem **Rev:** Cutty Sark and map

Date	Mintage	F12	VF20	XF40	MS60	MS63
2011	Est. 5000	PF63 475	PF65 550			

KM# 104 20 RUFIYAA
28.28 g., 0.925 Silver 0.8356 oz. ASW, 38.61 mm. **Subject:** London Olympics **Obv:** National emblem **Rev:** Soccer

Date	Mintage	F12	VF20	XF40	MS60	MS63
2011	—	PF63 35.00	PF65 45.00			

KM# 107 20 RUFIYAA
0.50 g., 0.999 Gold AGW, 11 mm. **Obv:** National emblem **Rev:** Two Anemonefish left

Date	Mintage	F12	VF20	XF40	MS60	MS63
2011	Est. 5000	PF63 50.00	PF65 55.00			

KM# 109 20 RUFIYAA
28.28 g., 0.925 Silver 0.8356 oz. ASW, 38.61 mm. **Subject:** Elizabeth II, 60th Anniversary of reign **Obv:** National emblem **Rev:** Windsor castle

Date	Mintage	F12	VF20	XF40	MS60	MS63
2011	10,000	PF63 35.00	PF65 45.00			

KM# 113 20 RUFIYAA
28.28 g., 0.925 Silver 0.8356 oz. ASW, 38.61 mm. **Obv:** National emblem **Rev:** Windsor Castle, Elizabeth II and Philip

Date	Mintage	F12	VF20	XF40	MS60	MS63
2011	—	PF63 85.00	PF65 100			

KM# 110 20 RUFIYAA
20.00 g., 0.925 Silver 0.591 oz. ASW, 38.61 mm. **Subject:** 2014 FIFA World Cup, Brazil **Obv:** National emblem **Rev:** Soccer field and ball in color

Date	Mintage	F12	VF20	XF40	MS60	MS63
2012	Est. 10000	PF63 35.00	PF65 45.00			

KM# 111 20 RUFIYAA
0.50 g., 0.585 Gold AGW, 11 mm. **Obv:** National emblem **Rev:** Picasso Triggerfish

Date	Mintage	F12	VF20	XF40	MS60	MS63
2012	Est. 5000	PF63 30.00	PF65 35.00			

KM# 112 20 RUFIYAA
20.00 g., 0.925 Silver 0.591 oz. ASW, 38.61 mm. **Subject:** 2016 Olympics - Beach Volleyball

Date	Mintage	F12	VF20	XF40	MS60	MS63
2013	Est. 10000	PF63 65.00	PF65 75.00			

KM# 108 50 RUFIYAA
1.24 g., 0.999 Gold 0.0396 oz. AGW, 13.92 mm. **Obv:** National emblem **Rev:** Two anemonefish left

Date	Mintage	F12	VF20	XF40	MS60	MS63
2011	Est. 5000	PF63 75.00	PF65 85.00			

KM# 106 500 RUFIYAA
7.78 g., 0.585 Gold 0.1454 oz. AGW, 25 mm. **Subject:** London Olympics **Obv:** National emblem **Rev:** Soccer players

Date	Mintage	F12	VF20	XF40	MS60	MS63
2011	Est. 1000	PF65 300				

MALTA

The Republic of Malta, an independent parliamentary democracy, is situated in the Mediterranean Sea between Sicily and North Africa. With the islands of Gozo and Comino, Malta has an area of 124 sq. mi. (320 sq. km.) and a population of 386,000.Capital: Valletta. Malta has no proven mineral resources, agriculture insufficient to its needs, and a small, but expanding, manufacturing facility. Clothing, textile yarns and fabrics, and knitted wear are exported.

Malta became a republic on Dec. 13, 1974, but remained a member of the Commonwealth of Nations. The president is Chief of State. The prime minister is the Head of Government. Malta is also a member of the European Union since May 2004.

REPUBLIC

DECIMAL COINAGE
10 Mils = 1 Cent; 100 Cents = 1 Pound

KM# 5 2 MILS
0.95 g., Aluminum, 20.3 mm. **Obv:** Maltese cross **Rev:** Value within 3/4 wreath **Shape:** Scalloped

Date	Mintage	F12	VF20	XF40	MS60	MS63
2005 In sets only	—	—	—	—	—	4.00
2006 In sets only	—	—	—	—	—	4.00
2007 In sets only	—	—	—	—	—	4.00

REFORM COINAGE
1982 - Present;
10 Mils = 1 Cent; 100 Cents = 1 Lira

KM# 93 CENT
2.81 g., Nickel-Brass, 18.51 mm. **Obv:** Crowned shield within sprigs **Rev:** Common Weasel (ballottra) below value **Edge:** Plain

Date	Mintage	F12	VF20	XF40	MS60	MS63
2001	—	—	0.40	0.50	1.00	—
2002 In sets only	—	—	—	—	1.00	—
2004	—	—	0.40	0.50	0.75	—
2005 In sets only	—	—	—	—	1.00	—
2006 In sets only	—	—	—	—	1.00	—
2007 In sets only	—	—	—	—	1.00	—

KM# 94 2 CENTS
2.26 g., Copper-Nickel, 17.78 mm. **Obv:** Crowned shield within sprigs **Rev:** Zebbuga branch and value **Edge:** Reeded

Date	Mintage	F12	VF20	XF40	MS60	MS63
2002	—	—	0.75	1.00	1.25	—
2004	—	—	0.75	1.00	1.25	—
2005	—	—	—	—	1.25	—
2006 In sets only	—	—	—	—	1.25	—
2007 In sets only	—	—	—	—	1.25	—

KM# 95 5 CENTS
3.51 g., Copper-Nickel, 19.78 mm. **Obv:** Crowned shield within sprigs **Rev:** Freshwater Crab (il-Qobru) and value **Edge:** Reeded

Date	Mintage	F12	VF20	XF40	MS60	MS63
2001	—	—	0.75	1.00	1.25	2.00
2005 In sets only	—	—	—	—	—	2.00
2006 In sets only	—	—	—	—	—	2.00
2007 In sets only	—	—	—	—	—	2.00

KM# 96 10 CENTS
5.01 g., Copper-Nickel, 21.78 mm. **Obv:** Crowned shield within sprigs **Rev:** Lampuka and value **Edge:** Reeded

Date	Mintage	F12	VF20	XF40	MS60	MS63
2005	—	—	1.25	1.50	2.00	—
2006 In sets only	—	—	—	—	2.00	—
2007 In sets only	—	—	—	—	2.00	—

KM# 97 25 CENTS
6.19 g., Copper-Nickel, 24.95 mm. **Obv:** Crowned shield within sprigs **Rev:** Ghirlanda flower and value

Date	Mintage	F12	VF20	XF40	MS60	MS63
2001	—	—	2.25	2.50	3.00	—
2005	—	—	2.25	2.50	3.00	—
2006 In sets only	—	—	—	—	3.00	—
2007 In sets only	—	—	—	—	3.00	—

KM# 98 50 CENTS
8.00 g., Copper-Nickel, 27 mm. **Obv:** Crowned shield within sprigs **Rev:** Tulliera plant and value **Edge Lettering:** BANK CENTRALI TA' MALTA

Date	Mintage	F12	VF20	XF40	MS60	MS63
2001	—	—	2.50	5.00	10.00	—
2005 In sets only	—	—	—	—	10.00	—
2006 In sets only	—	—	—	—	10.00	—
2007 In sets only	—	—	—	—	10.00	—

KM# 99 LIRA

13.00 g., Nickel, 29.82 mm. **Obv:** Crowned shield within sprigs **Rev:** Merill bird and value **Edge Lettering:** BANK CENTRALI TA' MALTA

Date	Mintage	F12	VF20	XF40	MS60	MS63
2005	—	—	—	4.50	6.50	12.00
2006 In sets only	—	—	—	—	—	12.00
2007 In sets only	—	—	—	—	—	12.00

KM# 117 5 LIRI

28.28 g., 0.925 Silver 0.8356 oz. ASW, 38.6 mm. **Obv:** Crowned shield within sprigs **Rev:** Enrico Mizzi right **Edge:** Reeded

Date	Mintage	F12	VF20	XF40	MS60	MS63
2001	2,000	PF65 80.00				

KM# 118 5 LIRI

28.28 g., 0.925 Silver 0.8356 oz. ASW, 38.6 mm. **Obv:** Crowned shield within sprigs **Rev:** Nicolo Isouard left **Edge:** Reeded

Date	Mintage	F12	VF20	XF40	MS60	MS63
2002	2,000	PF65 80.00				

KM# 120 5 LIRI

28.28 g., 0.925 Silver 0.8356 oz. ASW, 38.6 mm. **Obv:** Crowned shield within sprigs **Rev:** Sir Adriano Dingli as Grand Commander of the St. Michael and George Order **Edge:** Reeded

Date	Mintage	F12	VF20	XF40	MS60	MS63
2003	2,000	PF65 80.00				

KM# 121 5 LIRI

28.28 g., 0.925 Silver 0.8356 oz. ASW, 38.6 mm. **Obv:** Crowned shield within sprigs **Rev:** Painter Giuseppe Cali with palette **Edge:** Reeded

Date	Mintage	F12	VF20	XF40	MS60	MS63
2004	2,000	PF65 120				

KM# 138 5 LIRI

Silver, 39 mm. **Subject:** Zammit **Edge:** Reeded

Date	Mintage	F12	VF20	XF40	MS60	MS63
2006	—	PF63 70.00		PF65 75.00		

KM# 123 5 LIRI

28.28 g., 0.925 Silver 0.8356 oz. ASW, 38.61 mm. **Subject:** 450th Anniversary of Jean de la Valete appointed Grand master **Rev:** de la Vallete standing facing left, city of Valletta map at lower left

Date	Mintage	F12	VF20	XF40	MS60	MS63
ND(2007)	25,000	PF63 65.00		PF65 75.00		

KM# 119 10 LIRI

1.24 g., 0.999 Gold 0.0396 oz. AGW, 13.92 mm. **Obv:** Crowned shield within sprigs **Rev:** Xprunara sailboat **Edge:** Reeded

Date	Mintage	F12	VF20	XF40	MS60	MS63
2002 Prooflike Est. 25000		—	—	—	—	130

KM# 122 25 LIRI

3.99 g., 0.9167 Gold 0.117 oz. AGW, 19.3 mm. **Subject:** Accession to the European Union **Obv:** Crowned shield within sprigs **Rev:** Maltese flag under European Union star circle **Edge:** Reeded

Date	Mintage	F12	VF20	XF40	MS60	MS63
2004	6,000	PF65 290				

KM# 124 25 LIRI

6.50 g., 0.920 Gold 0.191 oz. AGW, 21 mm. **Subject:** 450th Anniversary Jean de la Valette Appointed as Grand Master **Rev:** de la Valette standing facing left, city of Valletta map at lower left

Date	Mintage	F12	VF20	XF40	MS60	MS63
ND(2007)	2,500	PF65 375				

EURO COINAGE

KM# 125 EURO CENT

2.30 g., Copper Plated Steel, 16.25 mm. **Obv:** Doorway **Rev:** Denomination and globe **Edge:** Plain

Date	Mintage	F12	VF20	XF40	MS60	MS63
2008	14,960,000	—	—	—	—	1.00
2008	40,000	PF60 5.00				
2009 In sets only	40,000	—	—	—	—	1.50
2010 In sets only	30,000	—	—	—	—	1.50
2011 In sets only	50,000	—	—	—	—	1.50
2012 In sets only	50,000	—	—	—	—	1.50

KM# 126 2 EURO CENT

3.06 g., Copper Plated Steel, 18.75 mm. **Obv:** Doorway **Rev:** Denomination and globe **Edge:** Grooved

Date	Mintage	F12	VF20	XF40	MS60	MS63
2008	35,960,000	—	—	—	—	0.70
2008	40,000	PF60 5.00				
2009 In sets only	40,000	—	—	—	—	2.00
2010 In sets only	30,000	—	—	—	—	2.00
2011 In sets only	50,000	—	—	—	—	2.00
2012 In sets only	50,000	—	—	—	—	2.00

KM# 127 5 EURO CENT

3.92 g., Copper Plated Steel, 21.25 mm. **Obv:** Doorway **Rev:** Denomination and globe

Date	Mintage	F12	VF20	XF40	MS60	MS63
2008	33,960,000	—	—	—	—	0.70
2008	40,000	PF60 5.00				
2009 In sets only	40,000	—	—	—	—	2.50
2010 In sets only	30,000	—	—	—	—	2.50
2011 In sets only	50,000	—	—	—	—	2.50
2012 In sets only	50,000	—	—	—	—	2.50

KM# 128 10 EURO CENT

4.10 g., Brass, 19.75 mm. **Obv:** Crowned shield within wreath **Rev:** Value and relief map of Europe **Edge:** Notched

Date	Mintage	F12	VF20	XF40	MS60	MS63
2008	40,960,000	—	—	—	—	1.00
2008	40,000	PF60 7.50				
2009 In sets only	40,000	—	—	—	—	3.00
2010 In sets only	30,000	—	—	—	—	3.00
2011 In sets only	50,000	—	—	—	—	3.00
2012 In sets only	50,000	—	—	—	—	3.00

KM# 129 20 EURO CENT

5.75 g., Brass, 22.25 mm. **Obv:** Crowned shield within wreath **Rev:** Denomination and Map of Western Europe **Edge:** Notched

Date	Mintage	F12	VF20	XF40	MS60	MS63
2008	39,960,000	—	—	—	—	1.50
2008	40,000	PF60 7.50				
2009 In sets only	40,000	—	—	—	—	4.00
2010 In sets only	30,000	—	—	—	—	4.00
2011 In sets only	50,000	—	—	—	—	4.00
2012 In sets only	50,000	—	—	—	—	4.00

KM# 130 50 EURO CENT

7.80 g., Brass, 24.25 mm. **Obv:** Crowned shield within wreath **Rev:** Relief map of Western Europe **Edge:** Reeded

Date	Mintage	F12	VF20	XF40	MS60	MS63
2008	14,960,000	—	—	—	—	2.00
2008	40,000	PF60 7.50				
2009 In sets only	40,000	—	—	—	—	5.00
2010 In sets only	30,000	—	—	—	—	5.00
2011 In sets only	50,000	—	—	—	—	5.00
2012 In sets only	50,000	—	—	—	—	5.00

KM# 131 EURO

7.50 g., Bi-Metallic, 23.25 mm. **Obv:** Maltese Cross **Rev:** Value and relief map of Europe **Edge:** Segmented reeding

Date	Mintage	F12	VF20	XF40	MS60	MS63
2008	13,960,000	—	—	—	—	4.00
2008	40,000	PF60 15.00				
2009 In sets only	40,000	—	—	—	—	5.00
2010 In sets only	30,000	—	—	—	—	5.00
2011 In sets only	50,000	—	—	—	—	5.00
2012 In sets only	50,000	—	—	—	—	5.00

KM# 132 2 EURO

8.50 g., Bi-Metallic, 25.75 mm. **Obv:** Maltese Cross **Rev:** Value and Relief Map of Western Europe **Edge:** Reeded with 2s and Maltese Crosses

Date	Mintage	F12	VF20	XF40	MS60	MS63
2008	9,960,000	—	—	—	—	6.00
2008	40,000	PF63 25.00				
2009 In sets only	40,000	—	—	—	—	8.00
2010	10,000,000	—	—	—	—	8.00
2011 In sets only	50,000	—	—	—	—	8.00
2012 In sets only	50,000	—	—	—	—	8.00

KM# 134 2 EURO

8.50 g., Bi-Metallic, 25.75 mm. **Subject:** E.M.U., 10th Anniversary **Obv:** Stick figure and large E symbol **Rev:** Value and relief map of Western Europe **Edge:** Segmented reeding

Date	Mintage	F12	VF20	XF40	MS60	MS63
2009	7,000,000	—	—	—	—	6.00

KM# 144 2 EURO

8.50 g., Bi-Metallic, 25.75 mm. **Subject:** First Elected Representatives of 1849 **Obv:** Hand placing ballot in slot

Date	Mintage	F12	VF20	XF40	MS60	MS63
2011 Special Unc.	50,000	—	—	—	—	15.00
2011	375,000	—	—	—	6.00	8.00
2011	5,000	PF63 25.00				

KM# 139 2 EURO

8.50 g., Bi-Metallic, 25.75 mm. **Subject:** Euro Coinage, 10th Anniversary **Obv:** Euro symbol on globe, child-like rendering around

Date	Mintage	F12	VF20	XF40	MS60	MS63
2012	—	PF63 25.00				
2012	7,000,000	—	—	—	6.00	8.00

KM# 145 2 EURO

8.50 g., Bi-Metallic, 25.75 mm. **Subject:** Majority representation **Obv:** Jubilee crowd at Governor's Palace in Valletta

Date	Mintage	F12	VF20	XF40	MS60	MS63
2012	430,000	—	—	—	—	15.00

KM# 136 10 EURO
28.28 g., 0.925 Silver 0.8356 oz. ASW, 38.6 mm. **Subject:** Auberge de Castille **Rev:** Building tower

Date	Mintage	F12	VF20	XF40	MS60	MS63
2008	18,000	PF63 55.00	PF65 60.00			

KM# 133 10 EURO
28.28 g., 0.925 Silver 0.8356 oz. ASW, 38.6 mm. **Rev:** La Castellania, Merchant's Street, Valletta

Date	Mintage	F12	VF20	XF40	MS60	MS63
2009	15,000	PF63 55.00	PF65 60.00			

KM# 140 10 EURO
28.28 g., 0.925 Silver 0.8356 oz. ASW, 38.61 mm. **Subject:** Valetta - Auberge d'Italie **Obv:** Crowned shield **Rev:** Archetectural detail

Date	Mintage	F12	VF20	XF40	MS60	MS63
2010	12,500	PF63 60.00	PF65 65.00			

KM# 142 10 EURO
28.28 g., 0.925 Silver 0.8356 oz. ASW, 38.61 mm. **Subject:** Phoenicians in Malta **Obv:** Crowned shield **Rev:** Ancient Phoenician boat

Date	Mintage	F12	VF20	XF40	MS60	MS63
2011	10,000	PF63 70.00	PF65 75.00			

KM# 147 10 EURO
28.28 g., 0.925 Silver 0.8356 oz. ASW, 38.6 mm. **Subject:** Composer of National Amthem **Rev:** Portrait looking left

Date	Mintage	F12	VF20	XF40	MS60	MS63
2013	—	PF63 60.00	PF65 65.00			

KM# 148 10 EURO
28.28 g., 0.925 Silver 0.8356 oz. ASW, 38.6 mm. **Subject:** Sir Paul Boffa, Prime Minister **Obv:** Crowned shield **Rev:** Bust facing

Date	Mintage	F12	VF20	XF40	MS60	MS63
2013	—	PF63 55.00	PF65 60.00			

KM# 137 50 EURO
6.50 g., 0.916 Gold 0.1902 oz. AGW, 21 mm. **Subject:** Auberge de Castille **Rev:** Building tower

Date	Mintage	F12	VF20	XF40	MS60	MS63
2008	3,000	PF65 375				

KM# 135 50 EURO
6.50 g., 0.916 Gold 0.1902 oz. AGW, 21 mm. **Rev:** La Castellania, Merchant's Street, Valletta

Date	Mintage	F12	VF20	XF40	MS60	MS63
2009	3,000	PF65 375				

KM# 141 50 EURO
6.50 g., 0.916 Gold 0.1902 oz. AGW, 21 mm. **Subject:** Valetta - Auberge d'Italie **Obv:** Crowned shield **Rev:** Archetectural detail

Date	Mintage	F12	VF20	XF40	MS60	MS63
2010	3,000	PF65 400				

KM# 143 50 EURO
6.50 g., 0.916 Gold 0.1902 oz. AGW, 21 mm. **Subject:** Phoenicians in Malta **Obv:** Crowned shield **Rev:** Ancient Phoenician boat

Date	Mintage	F12	VF20	XF40	MS60	MS63
2011	2,000	PF65 385				

KM# 146 50 EURO
6.50 g., 0.916 Gold 0.1902 oz. AGW, 21 mm. **Subject:** Antonio Sciortino **Obv:** National arms **Rev:** Three figures

Date	Mintage	F12	VF20	XF40	MS60	MS63
2012	—	PF65 400				

MINT SETS

KM#	Date	Mintage	Identification	Issue Price	Mkt Val
MS26	2005 (8)	—	KM#5, 93-99	—	35.00
MS27	2006 (8)	—	KM#5, 93-99	—	37.50
MS28	2007 (8)	—	KM#5, 93-99	—	45.00
MS29	2008 (8)	40,000	KM#125-132, wooden box	—	70.00
MS30	2008 (8)	30,000	KM#125-132, Malta Post and Lombard Bank card	—	45.00

PROOF SETS

KM#	Date	Mintage	Identification	Issue Price	Mkt Val
PS12	2008 (9)	40,000	KM#125-132, plus ingot	—	80.00

MAURITANIA

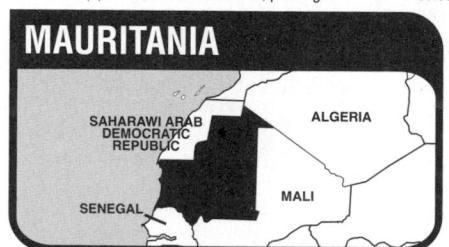

The Islamic Republic of Mauritania, located in northwest Africa bounded by Western Sahara, Mali, Algeria, Senegal and the Atlantic Ocean, has an area of 397,955 sq. mi.(1,030,700 sq. km.) and a population of 1.9 million. Capital: Nouakchott. The economy centers on herding, agriculture, fishing and mining. Iron ore, copper concentrates and fish products are exported.

On June 28, 1973, in a move designed to emphasize its non-alignment with France, Mauritania converted its currency from the old French-supported C.F.A. franc unit to a new unit called the Ouguiya.

MONETARY SYSTEM
5 Khoums = 1 Ouguiya

REPUBLIC
STANDARD COINAGE

KM# 6 OUGUIYA
3.60 g., Aluminum-Bronze, 21 mm. **Obv:** National emblem divides date above value **Obv. Legend:** BANQUE CENTRALE DE MAURITANIE **Rev:** Star and crescent divide sprigs with legend below value, all within circle **Edge:** Reeded

Date	Mintage	F12	VF20	XF40	MS60	MS63
AH1423//2003	—	—	—	0.50	1.25	2.00

KM# 10 OUGUIYA
3.60 g., Steel, 21 mm. **Obv:** National arms **Rev:** Star and crescent

Date	Mintage	F12	VF20	XF40	MS60	MS63
AH1430//2009	—	—	—	0.50	1.25	2.00

KM# 3 5 OUGUIYA
5.88 g., Aluminum-Bronze, 25 mm. **Obv:** National emblem divides date above value **Obv. Legend:** BANQUE CENTRALE DE MAURITANIE **Rev:** Star and crescent divide sprigs below value within circle **Edge:** Plain

Date	Mintage	F12	VF20	XF40	MS60	MS63
AH1423//2003	—	—	—	1.75	3.50	5.00
AH1425//2004	—	—	—	1.75	3.50	5.00

KM# 3a 5 OUGUIYA
6.00 g., Copper Plated Steel, 25 mm. **Obv:** National emblem divides date above value **Obv. Legend:** BANQUE CENTRALE DE MAURITANIE **Rev:** Star and crescent divides sprigs below value within circle **Edge:** Plain

Date	Mintage	F12	VF20	XF40	MS60	MS63
AH1425//2004	—	—	—	1.00	2.00	3.00
AH1426//2005	—	—	—	1.00	2.00	3.00
AH1430//2009	—	—	—	1.00	2.00	3.00
AH1434//2013	—	—	—	1.00	2.00	3.00

KM# 4 10 OUGUIYA
6.00 g., Copper-Nickel, 25 mm. **Obv:** National emblem divides date above value **Obv. Legend:** BANQUE CENTRALE DE MAURITANIE **Rev:** Crescent and star divide sprigs within circle **Edge:** Reeded

Date	Mintage	F12	VF20	XF40	MS60	MS63
AH1423//2003	—	—	—	2.00	4.00	5.50
AH1425//2004	—	—	—	2.00	4.00	5.50

KM# 4a 10 OUGUIYA
5.80 g., Nickel Plated Steel, 24.5 mm. **Obv:** National emblem divides date above value **Obv. Legend:** BANQUE CENTRALE DE MAURITANIE **Rev:** Crescent and star divide sprigs within circle **Edge:** Reeded

Date	Mintage	F12	VF20	XF40	MS60	MS63
AH1425//2004	—	—	—	1.25	3.00	4.50
AH1426//2005	—	—	—	1.25	3.00	4.50
AH1430//2009	—	—	—	1.25	3.00	4.50
AH1434//2013	—	—	—	1.25	3.00	4.50

KM# 5 20 OUGUIYA
8.00 g., Copper-Nickel, 28 mm. **Obv:** National emblem divides date above value **Obv. Legend:** BANQUE CENTRALE DE MAURITANIE **Rev:** Star and crescent divide sprigs below value within circle **Edge:** Reeded

Date	Mintage	F12	VF20	XF40	MS60	MS63
AH1423//2003	—	—	—	3.00	6.00	8.00
AH1425//2004	—	—	—	3.00	6.00	8.00

KM# 5a 20 OUGUIYA
7.80 g., Nickel Plated Steel, 28 mm. **Obv:** National emblem divides date above value **Obv. Legend:** BANQUE CENTRALE DE MAURITANIE **Rev:** Star and crescent divide sprigs below value within circle **Edge:** Reeded

Date	Mintage	F12	VF20	XF40	MS60	MS63
AH1425//2004	—	—	—	2.00	4.00	6.00
AH1426//2005	—	—	—	2.00	4.00	6.00
AH1430//2009	—	—	—	2.00	4.00	6.00

KM# 8 20 OUGUIYA
Bi-Metallic **Obv:** Value within wreath **Rev:** National arms above value

Date	Mintage	F12	VF20	XF40	MS60	MS63
2009	—	—	—	—	6.00	7.50
2010	—	—	—	—	6.00	7.50

KM# 9 50 OUGUIYA
Bi-Metallic **Obv:** Value above wreath **Rev:** National arms above value

Date	Mintage	F12	VF20	XF40	MS60	MS63
2010	—	—	—	—	5.00	7.50

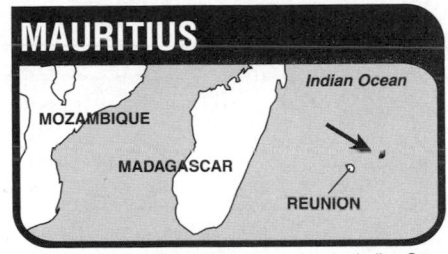

MAURITIUS

Indian Ocean

MOZAMBIQUE

MADAGASCAR

REUNION

The Republic of Mauritius, is located in the Indian Ocean 500 miles (805 km.) east of Madagascar, has an area of 790 sq. mi. (1,860 sq. km.) and a population of 1 million. Capital: Port Louis. Sugar provides 90 percent of the export revenue.

Mauritius became independent on March 12, 1968. It is a member of the Commonwealth of Nations.

MONETARY SYSTEM
100 Cents = 1 Rupee

REPUBLIC
STANDARD COINAGE

KM# 52 5 CENTS
3.00 g., Copper Plated Steel **Obv:** Value within beaded circle **Rev:** Bust of Sir Seewoosagur Ramgoolam 3/4 right

Date	Mintage	F12	VF20	XF40	MS60	MS63
2003	—	—	—	0.10	0.35	0.50
2004	—	—	—	0.10	0.35	0.50
2005	—	—	—	0.10	0.35	0.50
2007	—	—	—	0.10	0.35	0.50
2010	—	—	—	0.10	0.35	0.50
2012	—	—	—	0.10	0.35	0.50

KM# 53 20 CENTS
3.00 g., Nickel Plated Steel, 19 mm. **Obv:** Value within beaded circle **Rev:** Bust of Sir Seewoosagur Ramgoolam 3/4 right

Date	Mintage	F12	VF20	XF40	MS60	MS63
2001	—	—	—	0.20	0.50	0.75
2003	—	—	—	0.20	0.50	0.75
2004	—	—	—	0.20	0.50	0.75
2005	—	—	—	0.20	0.50	0.75
2007	—	—	—	0.20	0.50	0.75
2010	—	—	—	0.20	0.50	0.75
2012	—	—	—	0.20	0.50	0.75

KM# 54 1/2 RUPEE
5.90 g., Nickel Plated Steel, 23.6 mm. **Obv:** Stag left **Rev:** Bust of Sir Seewoosagur Ramgoolam 3/4 right

Date	Mintage	F12	VF20	XF40	MS60	MS63
2002	—	—	—	0.60	1.50	2.00
2003	—	—	—	0.60	1.50	2.00
2004	—	—	—	0.60	1.50	2.00
2005	—	—	—	0.60	1.50	2.00
2007	—	—	—	0.60	1.50	2.00
2009	—	—	—	0.60	1.50	2.00
2010	—	—	—	0.60	1.50	2.00

KM# 55 RUPEE
7.50 g., Copper-Nickel, 26.6 mm. **Obv:** Shield divides date above value **Rev:** Bust of Sir Seewoosagur Ramgoolam 3/4 right **Edge:** Reeded

Date	Mintage	F12	VF20	XF40	MS60	MS63
2002	—	—	—	0.65	1.65	2.75
2004	—	—	—	0.65	1.65	2.75
2005	—	—	—	0.65	1.65	2.75
2007	—	—	—	0.65	1.65	2.75
2008	—	—	—	0.65	1.65	2.75
2009	—	—	—	0.65	1.65	2.75
2010	—	—	—	0.65	1.65	2.75

KM# 55a RUPEE
Nickel Plated Steel, 26.6 mm. **Obv:** Shield **Rev:** Sir Seewoosagur Ramgoolam 3/4 right

Date	Mintage	F12	VF20	XF40	MS60	MS63
2012	—	—	—	—	1.65	2.75

KM# 56 5 RUPEES
12.40 g., Copper-Nickel, 31 mm. **Obv:** Value within palm trees **Rev:** Bust of Sir Seewoosagur Ramgoolam 3/4 right

Date	Mintage	F12	VF20	XF40	MS60	MS63
2009	—	—	—	—	3.00	5.00
2010	—	—	—	—	3.00	5.00
2012	—	—	—	—	3.00	5.00

KM# 66 20 RUPEES
10.10 g., Bi-Metallic, 27.96 mm. **Obv:** Bank of Mauritius tower **Rev:** Bust of Sir Seewoosagur Ramgoolam KT 3/4 right **Edge:** Reeded

Date	Mintage	F12	VF20	XF40	MS60	MS63
2007	—	—	—	2.00	5.00	7.00

KM# 65 100 RUPEES
36.67 g., 0.925 Silver 1.0806 oz ASW, 43.9 mm. **Obv:** National arms, date below **Obv. Legend:** MAURITIUS ONE HUNDRED RUPEES **Rev:** Bust of Gandhi 3/4 right **Rev. Legend:** MAHATMA GANDHI CENTENARY OF ARRIVAL IN MAURITIUS **Edge:** Reeded

Date	Mintage	F12	VF20	XF40	MS60	MS63
2001	—	PF63 100	PF65 125			

KM# 67 1500 RUPEES
7.78 g., 0.999 Platinum 0.2483 oz. APW, 25 mm. **Subject:** Sir Seewoosagur Ramgoolan **Obv:** Portrait **Rev:** State House **Edge:** Plain

Date	Mintage	F12	VF20	XF40	MS60	MS63
2009	—	PF63 450	PF65 500			

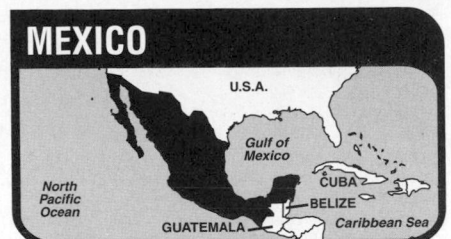

MEXICO

U.S.A.

Gulf of Mexico

North Pacific Ocean

CUBA

GUATEMALA   BELIZE

Caribbean Sea

The United Mexican States, located immediately south of the United States has an area of 759,529 sq. mi. (1,967,183 sq. km.) and an estimated population of 100 million. Capital: Mexico City. The economy is based on agriculture, manufacturing and mining. Oil, cotton, silver, coffee, and shrimp are exported.

UNITED STATES
REFORM COINAGE
1 New Peso = 1000 Old Pesos; 100 centavos = 1 New Peso; 100 Centavos = 1 Peso

KM# 546 5 CENTAVOS
1.58 g., Stainless Steel, 15.5 mm. **Obv:** National arms **Rev:** Large value **Edge:** Plain

Date	Mintage	F12	VF20	XF40	MS60	MS63
2001Mo	34,811,000	—	—	0.15	0.20	0.50
2002Mo	14,901,000	—	—	0.20	0.75	1.00

KM# 547 10 CENTAVOS
2.08 g., Stainless Steel, 17 mm. **Obv:** National arms, eagle left **Rev:** Large value

Date	Mintage	F12	VF20	XF40	MS60	MS63
2001Mo	618,061,000	—	—	0.20	0.25	0.30
2002Mo	463,968,000	—	—	0.20	0.25	0.30
2003Mo	378,938,000	—	—	0.20	0.25	0.30
2004Mo	393,705,000	—	—	0.20	0.25	0.30
2005Mo	488,594,000	—	—	0.20	0.25	0.30
2006Mo	473,261,000	—	—	0.20	0.25	0.30
2007Mo	498,735,000	—	—	0.20	0.25	0.30
2008Mo	433,951,000	—	—	0.20	0.25	0.30
2009Mo	90,968,000	—	—	0.20	0.25	0.30

KM# 934 10 CENTAVOS
1.75 g., Stainless Steel, 14 mm. **Obv:** National arms **Rev:** Large value **Edge:** Grooved

Date	Mintage	F12	VF20	XF40	MS60	MS63
2009Mo	343,772,000	—	—	—	0.10	0.25
2010Mo	453,849,000	—	—	—	0.10	0.25
2011Mo	463,960,000	—	—	—	0.10	0.25
2012Mo	419,017,000	—	—	—	0.10	0.25
2013Mo	Est. 400000000	—	—	—	0.10	0.25

KM# 548 20 CENTAVOS
3.04 g., Aluminum-Bronze, 19.5 mm. **Obv:** National arms, eagle left **Rev:** Value and date within 3/4 wreath **Shape:** 12-sided

Date	Mintage	F12	VF20	XF40	MS60	MS63
2001Mo	234,360,000	—	—	0.25	0.35	0.40
2002Mo	229,256,000	—	—	0.25	0.35	0.40
2003Mo	149,518,000	—	—	0.25	0.35	0.40
2004Mo	174,351,000	—	—	0.25	0.35	0.40
2005Mo	204,426,000	—	—	0.25	0.35	0.40
2006Mo	234,263,000	—	—	0.25	0.35	0.40
2007Mo	234,301,000	—	—	0.25	0.35	0.40
2008Mo	214,313,000	—	—	0.25	0.35	0.40
2009Mo	41,167,000	—	—	0.25	0.35	0.40

KM# 935 20 CENTAVOS
2.26 g., Stainless Steel, 15.3 mm. **Obv:** National arms **Rev:** Value and date within wreath **Edge:** Segmented reeding

Date	Mintage	F12	VF20	XF40	MS60	MS63
2009Mo	164,362,000	—	—	—	0.25	0.35
2010Mo	224,359,000	—	—	—	0.25	0.35
2011Mo	239,362,000	—	—	—	0.25	0.35
2012Mo	209,434,000	—	—	—	0.25	0.35
2013Mo	Est. 195000000	—	—	—	0.25	0.35

KM# 549 50 CENTAVOS
4.39 g., Aluminum-Bronze, 22 mm. **Obv:** National arms, eagle left **Rev:** Value and date within 1/2 designed wreath **Shape:** 12-sided

Date	Mintage	F12	VF20	XF40	MS60	MS63
2001Mo	199,006,000	—	—	0.45	0.75	1.00
2002Mo	94,552,000	—	—	0.45	0.75	1.00
2003Mo	124,522,000	—	—	0.45	0.75	1.00

Date	Mintage	F12	VF20	XF40	MS60	MS63
2004Mo	154,434,000	—	—	0.45	0.75	1.00
2005Mo	179,296,000	—	—	0.45	0.75	1.00
2006Mo	234,142,000	—	—	0.45	0.75	1.00
2007Mo	253,634,000	—	—	0.45	0.75	1.00
2008Mo	249,279,000	—	—	0.45	0.75	1.00
2009Mo	90,602,000	—	—	0.45	0.75	1.00

KM# 936 50 CENTAVOS

3.10 g., Stainless Steel, 17 mm. **Obv:** National arms **Rev:** Value and date within wreath **Edge:** Reeded

Date	Mintage	F12	VF20	XF40	MS60	MS63
2009Mo	19,910,000	—	—	—	0.75	1.00
2010Mo	114,567,000	—	—	—	0.75	1.00
2011Mo	194,480,000	—	—	—	0.75	1.00
2012Mo	359,183,000	—	—	—	0.60	0.75
2013Mo	Est. 360000000	—	—	—	0.60	0.75

KM# 603 PESO

3.95 g., Bi-Metallic, 21 mm. **Obv:** National arms, eagle left within circle **Rev:** Value and date within circle **Note:** Similar to KM#550 but without N.

Date	Mintage	F12	VF20	XF40	MS60	MS63
2001Mo	208,576,000	—	—	—	1.25	2.75
2002Mo	119,514,000	—	—	—	1.25	2.75
2003Mo	169,320,000	—	—	—	1.25	2.75
2004Mo	208,611,000	—	—	—	1.25	2.75
2005Mo	253,923,000	—	—	—	1.25	2.75
2006Mo	289,834,000	—	—	—	1.25	2.75
2007Mo	368,408,000	—	—	—	1.25	2.75
2008Mo	363,878,000	—	—	—	1.25	2.75
2009Mo	239,229,000	—	—	—	1.25	2.75
2010Mo	209,313,000	—	—	—	0.75	1.25
2011Mo	199,283,000	—	—	—	0.75	1.00
2012Mo	383,908,000	—	—	—	0.75	1.00
2013Mo	Est. 265000000	—	—	—	0.75	1.00

KM# 604 2 PESOS

5.19 g., Bi-Metallic, 23 mm. **Obv:** National arms, eagle left within circle **Rev:** Value and date within center circle of assorted emblems **Note:** Similar to KM#551, but denomination without N.

Date	Mintage	F12	VF20	XF40	MS60	MS63
2001Mo	74,563,000	—	—	—	2.35	4.00
2002Mo	74,547,000	—	—	—	2.35	4.00
2003Mo	39,814,000	—	—	—	2.35	4.00
2004Mo	89,496,000	—	—	—	2.35	4.00
2005Mo	94,532,000	—	—	—	2.35	4.00
2006Mo	144,123,000	—	—	—	2.35	4.00
2007Mo	129,422,000	—	—	—	2.35	4.00
2008Mo	134,235,000	—	—	—	2.35	4.00
2009Mo	64,650,000	—	—	—	2.35	4.00
2010Mo	34,878,000	—	—	—	1.00	1.50
2011Mo	114,522,000	—	—	—	1.00	1.50
2012Mo	134,445,000	—	—	—	1.00	1.25
2013Mo	Est. 105,000,000	—	—	—	1.00	1.25

KM# 605 5 PESOS

7.07 g., Bi-Metallic, 25.5 mm. **Obv:** National arms, eagle left within circle **Rev:** Value within circle **Note:** Similar to KM#552 but denomination without N.

Date	Mintage	F12	VF20	XF40	MS60	MS63
2001Mo	79,169,000	—	—	2.00	3.50	8.00
2002Mo	34,754,000	—	—	2.00	3.50	6.00
2003Mo	54,676,000	—	—	2.00	3.50	6.00
2004Mo	89,518,000	—	—	2.00	3.50	6.00
2005Mo	94,482,000	—	—	2.00	3.50	6.00
2006Mo	89,447,000	—	—	2.00	3.50	6.00
2007Mo	123,382,000	—	—	2.00	3.50	6.00
2008Mo	9,939,000	—	—	2.50	4.00	6.00
2009Mo	9,898,000	—	—	2.50	4.00	6.00
2010Mo	6,929,000	—	—	2.50	3.00	3.50

Date	Mintage	F12	VF20	XF40	MS60	MS63
2011Mo	209,214,000	—	—	1.00	2.00	2.50
2012Mo	159,398,000	—	—	—	2.00	2.50
2013Mo	Est. 130,000,000	—	—	—	2.00	2.50

KM# 651 5 PESOS

31.10 g., 0.999 Silver 0.9926 oz. ASW, 40 mm. **Series:** Endangered Wildlife - Manatee **Obv:** National arms in center of past and present arms **Rev:** Manatee, value and date **Edge:** Reeded

Date	Mintage	F12	VF20	XF40	MS60	MS63
2001Mo	30,000	—	—	—	45.00	—

KM# 653 5 PESOS

31.10 g., 0.999 Silver 0.9926 oz. ASW, 40 mm. **Series:** Endangered Wildlife **Subject:** Harpy Eagle (Aguila Arpia) **Obv:** National arms in center of past and present arms **Rev:** Crowned Harpy Eagle perched on branch, value and date

Date	Mintage	F12	VF20	XF40	MS60	MS63
2001Mo	30,000	—	—	—	45.00	—

KM# 654 5 PESOS

31.10 g., 0.999 Silver 0.9926 oz. ASW, 40 mm. **Series:** Endangered Wildlife **Subject:** Black Bear (Oso Negro) **Obv:** National arms in center of past and present arms **Rev:** Black bear, value and date

Date	Mintage	F12	VF20	XF40	MS60	MS63
2001Mo	30,000	—	—	—	45.00	—

KM# 658 5 PESOS

31.10 g., 0.999 Silver 0.9926 oz. ASW, 40 mm. **Series:** Endangered Wildlife - Jaguar **Obv:** National arms in center of past and present arms **Rev:** Jaguar, value and date

Date	Mintage	F12	VF20	XF40	MS60	MS63
2001Mo	30,000	—	—	—	45.00	—

KM# 659 5 PESOS

31.10 g., 0.999 Silver 0.9926 oz. ASW, 40 mm. **Series:** Endangered Wildlife - Prairie Dog **Obv:** National arms in center of past and present arms **Rev:** Prairie dog, value and date

Date	Mintage	F12	VF20	XF40	MS60	MS63
2001Mo	30,000	—	—	—	45.00	—

KM# 660 5 PESOS

31.10 g., 0.999 Silver 0.9926 oz. ASW, 40 mm. **Series:** Endangered Wildlife - Volcano Rabbit **Obv:** National arms in center of past and present arms **Rev:** Volcano rabbit, value and date

Date	Mintage	F12	VF20	XF40	MS60	MS63
2001Mo	30,000	—	—	—	45.00	—

KM# 678 5 PESOS

27.00 g., 0.925 Silver 0.7978 oz. ASW, 40 mm. **Series:** Ibero-America **Subject:** Acapulco Galleon **Obv:** National arms in center of past and present arms **Rev:** Spanish galleon with Pacific Ocean background and trading scene in foreground **Edge:** Reeded

Date	Mintage	F12	VF20	XF40	MS60	MS63
2003Mo	17,015	PF63 60.00				

KM# 765 5 PESOS

31.10 g., 0.919 Silver 0.919 oz. ASW, 40 mm. **Series:** Ibero-America **Subject:** Palacio de Bellas Artes **Obv:** Mexican Eagle and Snake **Rev:** Palace of Fine Arts **Edge:** Reeded

Date	Mintage	F12	VF20	XF40	MS60	MS63
2005Mo	8,005	PF63 90.00				

KM# 769 5 PESOS

15.55 g., 0.999 Silver 0.4963 oz. ASW, 33 mm. **Subject:** Monetary Reform of 1905 **Obv:** Mexican Eagle and Snake **Rev:** Cap and rays coin design

Date	Mintage	F12	VF20	XF40	MS60	MS63
2005Mo	1,505	PF63 40.00				

KM# 770 5 PESOS

31.10 g., 0.999 Silver 0.9926 oz. ASW, 40 mm. **Subject:** World Cup Soccer **Obv:** Mexican Eagle and Snake **Rev:** Mayan Pelota player and soccer ball

Date	Mintage	F12	VF20	XF40	MS60	MS63
2006Mo	40,005	PF63 90.00				

KM# 805 5 PESOS
31.11 g., 0.925 Silver 0.9191 oz. ASW, 40 mm. **Series:** Ibero-America **Obv:** Eagle on cactus within shields **Rev:** Mayan ball game

Date	Mintage	F12	VF20	XF40	MS60	MS63
2008Mo	8,013	PF63 75.00				

KM# 900.2 5 PESOS
7.07 g., Bi-Metallic, 25.5 mm. **Series:** Mexican Independence 200th Anniversary **Subject:** Francisco Primode Verdad y Ramos **Obv:** National arms - Eagle left **Rev:** Francisco Primode Verdad y Ramos bust right **Note:** No pellets at 4 and 7 o'clock in legend.

Date	Mintage	F12	VF20	XF40	MS60	MS63
2008Mo	Inc. above	—	—	—	10.00	15.00

KM# 894 5 PESOS
7.07 g., Bi-Metallic, 25.5 mm. **Series:** Mexican Independence, 200th Anniversary **Subject:** Ignacio Rayon **Obv:** National Arms - Eagle left **Rev:** Ignacio Rayon bust left

Date	Mintage	F12	VF20	XF40	MS60	MS63
2008Mo	9,934,397	—	—	0.75	1.50	—
2008Mo Prooflike	4,267	—	—	—	—	7.50

KM# 895 5 PESOS
7.07 g., Bi-Metallic, 25.5 mm. **Series:** Mexican Revolution 100th Anniversary **Subject:** Alvaro Obregon **Obv:** National Arms - Eagle left **Rev:** Alvaro Obregon bust 3/4 facing left

Date	Mintage	F12	VF20	XF40	MS60	MS63
2008Mo	9,948,722	—	—	0.75	1.50	—
2008Mo Prooflike	4,727	—	—	—	—	7.50

KM# 896 5 PESOS
7.07 g., Bi-Metallic, 25.5 mm. **Series:** Mexican Independence 200th Anniversary **Subject:** Carlos Maria de Bustamante **Obv:** National Arms - Eagle left **Rev:** Carlos Maria de Bustamante bust left

Date	Mintage	F12	VF20	XF40	MS60	MS63
2008Mo	9,941,302	—	—	0.75	1.50	—
2008Mo Prooflike	4,852	—	—	—	—	7.50

KM# 897 5 PESOS
7.07 g., Bi-Metallic, 25.5 mm. **Series:** Mexican Revolution 100th Anniversary **Subject:** Jose Vasconcelos **Obv:** National Arms - Eagle left **Rev:** Jose Vasconcelos bust left

Date	Mintage	F12	VF20	XF40	MS60	MS63
2008Mo	9,939,839	—	—	0.75	1.50	—
2008Mo Prooflike	4,767	—	—	—	—	7.50

KM# 898 5 PESOS
7.07 g., Bi-Metallic, 25.5 mm. **Series:** Mexican Independence

---

200th Anniversary **Subject:** Francisco Xavier Mina **Obv:** National Arms - Eagle left **Rev:** Francisco Mina bust 3/4 facing left

Date	Mintage	F12	VF20	XF40	MS60	MS63
2008Mo	9,914,938	—	—	0.75	1.50	—
2008Mo Prooflike	4,523	—	—	—	—	7.50

KM# 899 5 PESOS
7.07 g., Bi-Metallic, 25.5 mm. **Series:** Mexican Revolution 100th Anniversary **Subject:** Francisco Villa **Obv:** National Arms - Eagle left **Rev:** Francisco Villa on horseback left

Date	Mintage	F12	VF20	XF40	MS60	MS63
2008Mo	9,917,084	—	—	0.75	1.50	—
2008Mo Prooflike	4,866	—	—	—	—	7.50

KM# 900.1 5 PESOS
7.07 g., Bi-Metallic, 25.5 mm. **Series:** Mexican Independence 200th Anniversary **Subject:** Francisco Primo de Verdad y Ramos **Obv:** National Arms - Eagle left **Rev:** Francisco Primode Verdad y Ramos bust right **Note:** Pellets at 4 and 7 o'clock in legend.

Date	Mintage	F12	VF20	XF40	MS60	MS63
2008Mo	9,937,000	—	—	0.75	1.50	—
2008Mo Prooflike	4,279	—	—	—	—	7.50

KM# 901 5 PESOS
7.07 g., Bi-Metallic, 25.5 mm. **Series:** Mexican Revolution 100th Anniversary **Subject:** Heriberto Jara **Obv:** National Arms - Eagle left **Rev:** Heriberto Jara bust 3/4 facing left

Date	Mintage	F12	VF20	XF40	MS60	MS63
2008Mo	9,936,333	—	—	0.75	1.50	—
2008Mo Prooflike	4,870	—	—	—	—	7.50

KM# 902 5 PESOS
7.07 g., Bi-Metallic, 25.5 mm. **Series:** Mexican Independence 200th Anniversary **Subject:** Mariano Matamoros **Obv:** National Arms - Eagle left **Rev:** Mariano Matamoros bust 3/4 facing right

Date	Mintage	F12	VF20	XF40	MS60	MS63
2008Mo	9,947,802	—	—	0.75	1.50	—
2008Mo Prooflike	4,820	—	—	—	—	7.50

KM# 903 5 PESOS
7.07 g., Bi-Metallic, 25.5 mm. **Series:** Mexican Revolution 100th Anniversary **Subject:** Ricardo Magon **Obv:** National Arms - Eagle left **Rev:** Ricardo Magon bust right

Date	Mintage	F12	VF20	XF40	MS60	MS63
2008Mo	9,940,278	—	—	0.75	1.50	—
2008Mo Prooflike	4,690	—	—	—	—	7.50

KM# 904 5 PESOS
7.07 g., Bi-Metallic, 25.5 mm. **Series:** Mexican Independence 200th Anniversary **Subject:** Miguel Ramos Arizpe **Obv:** National Arms - Eagle left **Rev:** Miguel Ramos Arizpe bust right

Date	Mintage	F12	VF20	XF40	MS60	MS63
2008Mo	9,927,433	—	—	0.75	1.50	—
2008Mo Prooflike	4,863	—	—	—	—	7.50

KM# 905 5 PESOS
7.07 g., Bi-Metallic, 25.5 mm. **Series:** Mexican Revolution 100th Anniversary **Subject:** Francisco J. Mugica **Obv:** National arms, eagle left **Rev:** Francisco J. Mugica bust 3/4 facing left

Date	Mintage	F12	VF20	XF40	MS60	MS63
2008Mo	9,926,537	—	—	0.75	1.50	—
2008Mo Prooflike	4,588	—	—	—	—	7.50

KM# 906 5 PESOS
7.07 g., Bi-Metallic, 25.5 mm. **Series:** Mexican Independence 200th Anniversary **Subject:** Hormenegildo Galeana **Obv:** National Arms, eagle left **Rev:** Hermenegildo Galeana bust 3/4 facing left

Date	Mintage	F12	VF20	XF40	MS60	MS63
2008Mo	9,935,901	—	—	0.75	1.50	—
2008Mo Prooflike	4,966	—	—	—	—	7.50

KM# 907 5 PESOS
7.07 g., Bi-Metallic, 25.5 mm. **Series:** Mexican Revolution, 100th Anniversary **Subject:** Filomeno Mata **Obv:** National arms, eagle left **Rev:** Filomeno Mata bust facing left

Date	Mintage	F12	VF20	XF40	MS60	MS63
2009Mo	9,935,689	—	—	0.75	1.50	—
2009Mo Prooflike	4,920	—	—	—	—	7.50

KM# 908 5 PESOS
7.07 g., Bi-Metallic, 25.5 mm. **Series:** Mexican Independence 200th Anniversary **Subject:** Jose Maria Cos **Obv:** National arms, eagle left. **Rev:** Jose Maria Cos bust right

Date	Mintage	F12	VF20	XF40	MS60	MS63
2009Mo	9,935,040	—	—	0.75	1.50	—
2009Mo Prooflike	4,950	—	—	—	—	7.50

KM# 909 5 PESOS
7.07 g., Bi-Metallic, 25.5 mm. **Series:** Mexican Revolution 100th Anniversary **Subject:** Carmen Serdan **Obv:** National Amrs, Eagle left **Rev:** Carmen Serdan bust facing slightly right

Date	Mintage	F12	VF20	XF40	MS60	MS63
2009Mo	7,160,841	—	—	0.75	1.50	—
2009Mo Prooflike	4,787	—	—	—	—	7.50

KM# 910 5 PESOS
7.07 g., Bi-Metallic, 25.5 mm. **Series:** Mexican Independence, 200th Anniversary **Subject:** Pedro Moreno **Obv:** National arms, eagle left **Rev:** Pedro Moreno bust 3/4 right

Date	Mintage	F12	VF20	XF40	MS60	MS63
2009Mo	6,942,480	—	—	0.75	1.50	—
2009Mo Prooflike	4,940	—	—	—	—	7.50

KM# 911 5 PESOS
7.07 g., Bi-Metallic, 25.5 mm. **Series:** Mexican Revolution 100th Anniversary **Subject:** Andres Molina Enriquez **Obv:** National arms, eagle left **Rev:** Andres Molina Enriquez, bust 3/4 right

Date	Mintage	F12	VF20	XF40	MS60	MS63
2009Mo	6,942,763	—	—	0.75	1.50	—
2009Mo Prooflike	4,666	—	—	—	—	7.50

KM# 912 5 PESOS
7.07 g., Bi-Metallic, 25.5 mm. **Series:** Mexican Independence, 200th Anniversary **Subject:** Agustin de Iturbide **Obv:** National arms, eagle left **Rev:** Agustin de Iturbide bust left

Date	Mintage	F12	VF20	XF40	MS60	MS63
2009Mo	6,944,222	—	—	0.75	1.50	—
2009Mo Prooflike	4,838	—	—	—	—	7.50

KM# 913 5 PESOS
7.07 g., Bi-Metallic, 25.5 mm. **Series:** Mexican Revolution 100th Anniversary **Subject:** Luis Cabrera **Obv:** National Arms, eagle left **Rev:** Luis Cabrera bust 3/4 facing left

Date	Mintage	F12	VF20	XF40	MS60	MS63
2009Mo	6,902,593	—	—	0.75	1.50	—
2009Mo Prooflike	4,656	—	—	—	—	7.50

KM# 914 5 PESOS
7.07 g., Bi-Metallic, 25.5 mm. **Series:** Mexican Independence 200th Anniversary **Subject:** Nicolas Bravo **Obv:** National Arms, Eagle left **Rev:** Nicolas Bravo bust 3/4 facing left

Date	Mintage	F12	VF20	XF40	MS60	MS63
2009Mo	6,930,174	—	—	0.75	0.50	—
2009Mo Prooflike	4,780	—	—	—	—	7.50

KM# 915 5 PESOS
7.07 g., Bi-Metallic, 25.5 mm. **Series:** Mexican Revolution 100th Anniversary **Subject:** Eulalio Gutierrez **Obv:** National Arms, eagle left **Rev:** Eulalio Gutierrez bust 3/4 right

Date	Mintage	F12	VF20	XF40	MS60	MS63
2009Mo	6,908,760	—	—	0.75	1.50	—
2009Mo Prooflike	4,862	—	—	—	—	7.50

KM# 916 5 PESOS
7.07 g., Bi-Metallic, 25.5 mm. **Series:** Mexican Independence 200th Anniversary **Subject:** Servando Teresa de Mier **Obv:** National Arms, eagle left **Rev:** Servando Teresa de Mier bust left

Date	Mintage	F12	VF20	XF40	MS60	MS63
2009Mo	6,937,421	—	—	0.75	1.50	—
2009Mo Prooflike	4,675	—	—	—	—	7.50

KM# 917 5 PESOS
7.07 g., Bi-Metallic, 25.5 mm. **Series:** Mexican Revolution 100th Anniversary **Subject:** Otilio Montano **Obv:** National Arms, eagle left **Rev:** Otilio Montano bust left

Date	Mintage	F12	VF20	XF40	MS60	MS63
2009Mo	6,890,052	—	—	0.75	1.50	—
2009Mo Prooflike	4,923	—	—	—	—	7.50

KM# 918 5 PESOS
7.07 g., Bi-Metallic, 25.5 mm. **Series:** Mexican Revolution 100th Anniversary **Subject:** Belisario Dominguez **Obv:** National Arms, eagle left **Rev:** Belisario Dominguez bust 3/4 left

Date	Mintage	F12	VF20	XF40	MS60	MS63
2009Mo	6,926,606	—	—	0.75	1.50	—
2009Mo Prooflike	4,773	—	—	—	—	7.50

KM# 919 5 PESOS
7.07 g., Bi-Metallic, 25.5 mm. **Series:** Mexican Independence 200th Anniversary **Subject:** Leona Vicario **Obv:** National Arms, eagle left **Rev:** Leona Vicario bust left

Date	Mintage	F12	VF20	XF40	MS60	MS63
2009Mo	6,937,872	—	—	0.75	1.50	—
2009Mo Prooflike	4,730	—	—	—	—	7.50

KM# 944 5 PESOS
27.01 g., 0.925 Silver 0.7979 oz. ASW, 40 mm. **Series:** Ibero-American **Subject:** Ibero-American Historical Coins **Obv:** National arms (eagle and snake facing left), legend **Obv. Legend:** ESTADOS UNIDOS MEXICANOS **Rev:** Mexican Cabillito Peso, legend **Rev. Legend:** MONEDAS HISTORICAS IBEROAMERICANAS

Date	Mintage	F12	VF20	XF40	MS60	MS63
2010Mo	8,000	PF63 70.00				

KM# 920 5 PESOS
7.07 g., Bi-Metallic, 25.5 mm. **Series:** Mexican Independence 200th Anniversary **Subject:** Miguel Hidalgo y Costilla **Obv:** National Arms, eagle left **Rev:** Miguel Hidalgo y Costilla bust

Date	Mintage	F12	VF20	XF40	MS60	MS63
2010Mo	6,932,486	—	—	0.75	1.50	—
2010Mo Prooflike	4,763	—	—	—	—	7.50

KM# 922 5 PESOS
7.07 g., Bi-Metallic, 25.5 mm. **Series:** Mexican Revolution 100th Anniversary **Subject:** Francisco I. Madero **Rev:** Francisco I. Madero head facing 1/4 left

Date	Mintage	F12	VF20	XF40	MS60	MS63
2010Mo	6,930,998	—	—	0.75	1.50	—
2010Mo Prooflike	4,750	—	—	—	—	7.50

KM# 923 5 PESOS
7.07 g., Bi-Metallic, 25.5 mm. **Series:** Mexican Independence 200th Anniversary **Subject:** Jose Maria Morelos y Pavon **Rev:** Jose Maria Morelos y Pavon head facing 1/2 right

Date	Mintage	F12	VF20	XF40	MS60	MS63
2010Mo	6,927,961	—	—	0.75	1.50	—
2010Mo Prooflike	4,725	—	—	—	—	7.50

KM# 924 5 PESOS
7.07 g., Bi-Metallic, 25.5 mm. **Series:** Mexican Revolution 100th Anniversary **Subject:** Emiliano Zapata **Rev:** Emiliano Zapata head 1/4 facing left

Date	Mintage	F12	VF20	XF40	MS60	MS63
2010Mo	6,921,306	—	—	0.75	1.50	—
2010Mo Prooflike	4,810	—	—	—	—	7.50

KM# 925 5 PESOS

7.07 g., Bi-Metallic, 25.5 mm. **Series:** Mexican Independence 200th Anniversary **Subject:** Vicente Guerrero **Rev:** Vicente Guerrero head facing 1/4 left

Date	Mintage	F12	VF20	XF40	MS60	MS63
2010Mo	6,929,709	—	—	0.75	1.50	—
2010Mo Prooflike	4,716	—	—	—	—	7.50

KM# 926 5 PESOS

7.07 g., Bi-Metallic, 25.5 mm. **Series:** Mexican Revolution 100th Anniversary **Subject:** Venustiano Carranza **Rev:** Venustiano Carranza head 1/4 facing left

Date	Mintage	F12	VF20	XF40	MS60	MS63
2010Mo	6,936,993	—	—	0.75	1.50	—
2010Mo Prooflike	4,837	—	—	—	—	7.50

KM# 927 5 PESOS

7.07 g., Bi-Metallic, 25.5 mm. **Series:** Mexican Independence 200th Anniversary **Subject:** Ignacio Allende **Rev:** Ignacio Allende head facing 1/2 left

Date	Mintage	F12	VF20	XF40	MS60	MS63
2010Mo	6,939,957	—	—	0.75	1.50	—
2010Mo Prooflike	4,752	—	—	—	—	7.50

KM# 928 5 PESOS

7.07 g., Bi-Metallic, 25.5 mm. **Series:** Mexican Revolution 100th Anniversary **Subject:** La Soldadera **Rev:** Female soldier's head facing 1/4 left

Date	Mintage	F12	VF20	XF40	MS60	MS63
2010Mo	6,936,336	—	—	0.75	1.50	—
2010Mo Prooflike	4,730	—	—	—	—	7.50

KM# 929 5 PESOS

7.07 g., Bi-Metallic, 25.5 mm. **Series:** Mexican Indpendence 200th Anniversary **Subject:** Guadalupe Victoria **Rev:** Guadalupe Victoria head 1/4 facing left

Date	Mintage	F12	VF20	XF40	MS60	MS63
2010Mo	6,934,638	—	—	0.75	1.50	—
2010Mo Prooflike	4,767	—	—	—	—	7.50

KM# 930 5 PESOS

7.07 g., Bi-Metallic, 25.5 mm. **Series:** Mexican Revolution 100th Anniversary **Subject:** Jose Mario Pino Suarez **Rev:** Jose Mario Pino Suarez head

Date	Mintage	F12	VF20	XF40	MS60	MS63
2010Mo	6,930,255	—	—	0.75	1.50	—
2010Mo Prooflike	4,752	—	—	—	—	7.50

KM# 931 5 PESOS

7.07 g., Bi-Metallic, 25.5 mm. **Series:** Mexican Independence 200th Anniversary **Subject:** Josefa Ortiz de Dominguez **Rev:** Josefa Ortiz de Dominguez head right

Date	Mintage	F12	VF20	XF40	MS60	MS63
2010Mo	6,936,400	—	—	0.75	1.50	—
2010Mo Prooflike	4,743	—	—	—	—	7.50

KM# 945 5 PESOS

31.10 g., 0.999 Silver 0.9925 oz. ASW, 40 mm. **Subject:** Chichen Itza, the Nunnery **Obv:** National arms (eagle and snake facing left), legend **Obv. Legend:** ESTADOS UNIDOS MEXICANOS **Rev:** Nunnery of Chichen Itza, legend

Date	Mintage	F12	VF20	XF40	MS60	MS63
ND-2011Mo	10,000	PF63 90.00				

KM# 946 5 PESOS

31.10 g., 0.999 Silver 0.9925 oz. ASW, 40 mm. **Subject:** Chichen Itza, the Observatory **Obv:** National arms (eagle and snake facing left) legend **Obv. Legend:** ESTADOS UNIDOS MEXICANOS **Rev:** Observatory of Chichen Itza, legend **Rev. Legend:** OBSRVATORIO

Date	Mintage	F12	VF20	XF40	MS60	MS63
ND-2011	10,000	PF63 90.00				

KM# 947 5 PESOS

31.10 g., 0.999 Silver 0.9926 oz. ASW, 40 mm. **Subject:** Chichen Itza, the Observatory **Obv:** National Arms (eagle and snake facing left) legend **Obv. Legend:** ESTADOS UNIDOS MEXICANOS **Rev:** Observatory of Chichen Itza, legend **Rev. Legend:** CHICHEN ITZA, OBSRVATORIO

Date	Mintage	F12	VF20	XF40	MS60	MS63
ND-2011Mo	3,000	PF63 80.00				

KM# 962 5 PESOS

27.00 g., 0.925 Silver 0.7978 oz. ASW, 40 mm. **Subject:** Ibero-American Series **Obv:** National arms within circle of other national arms **Rev:** Horse Peso

Date	Mintage	F12	VF20	XF40	MS60	MS63
2011Mo	8,000	PF63 80.00				

KM# 616 10 PESOS

10.33 g., Bi-Metallic, 28 mm. **Obv:** National arms **Obv. Legend:** ESTADOS UNIDOS MEXICANOS **Rev:** Aztec design of Tonatiuh with the Fire Mask

Date	Mintage	F12	VF20	XF40	MS60	MS63
2002Mo	44,721,000	—	—	2.50	4.00	8.00
2004Mo	74,739,000	—	—	2.50	4.00	8.00
2005Mo	64,616,000	—	—	2.50	4.00	8.00
2006Mo	84,575,000	—	—	2.50	4.00	8.00
2007Mo	89,678,000	—	—	2.50	4.00	8.00
2008Mo	64,744,000	—	—	2.50	4.00	8.00
2009Mo	54,812,000	—	—	2.00	3.00	6.00
2010Mo	54,822,000	—	—	2.00	3.00	6.00
2011Mo	69,731,000	—	—	—	3.00	6.00
2012Mo	89,732,000	—	—	—	3.00	6.00
2013Mo	Est. 45,000,000	—	—	—	2.50	3.00

KM# 636 10 PESOS

10.33 g., Bi-Metallic, 28 mm. **Series:** Millennium **Obv:** National arms **Obv. Legend:** ESTADOS UNIDOS MEXICANOS **Rev:** Aztec carving **Edge Lettering:** ANO (year) repeated 3 times

Date	Mintage	F12	VF20	XF40	MS60	MS63
2001Mo	44,768,000	—	—	3.00	4.00	8.00

KM# 679 10 PESOS

31.10 g., 0.999 Silver 0.9926 oz. ASW, 39.9 mm. **Series:** First **Subject:** 180th Anniversary of Federation **Obv:** National arms **Obv. Legend:** ESTADOS UNIDOS MEXICANOS **Rev:** State Arms **Rev. Legend:** ESTADO DE ZACATECAS **Edge:** Reeded

Date	Mintage	F12	VF20	XF40	MS60	MS63
2003Mo	10,000	PF63 70.00				

KM# 680 10 PESOS

31.10 g., 0.999 Silver 0.9926 oz. ASW, 39.9 mm. **Series:** First **Subject:** 180th Anniversary of Federation **Obv:** National arms **Obv. Legend:** ESTADO UNIDOS MEXICANOS **Rev:** State arms **Rev. Legend:** ESTADO DE YUCATÁN **Edge:** Reeded

Date	Mintage	F12	VF20	XF40	MS60	MS63
2003Mo	10,000	PF63 60.00				

KM# 681 10 PESOS

31.10 g., 0.999 Silver 0.9926 oz. ASW, 39.9 mm. **Series:** First **Subject:** 180th Anniversary of Federation **Obv:** National arms **Obv. Legend:** ESTADOS UNIDOS MEXICANOS **Rev:** State arms **Rev. Legend:** ESTADO DE VERACRUZ-LLAVE **Edge:** Reeded

Date	Mintage	F12	VF20	XF40	MS60	MS63
2003Mo	10,000	PF63 60.00				

KM# 682 10 PESOS

31.10 g., 0.999 Silver 0.9926 oz. ASW, 39.9 mm. **Series:** First **Subject:** 180th Anniversary of Frederation **Obv:** National arms **Obv. Legend:** ESTADOS UNIDOS MEXICANOS **Rev:** State arms **Rev. Legend:** ESTADO DE TLAXCALA **Edge:** Reeded

Date	Mintage	F12	VF20	XF40	MS60	MS63
2003Mo	10,000	PF63 60.00				

KM# 683 10 PESOS

31.10 g., 0.999 Silver 0.9926 oz. ASW, 39.9 mm. **Series:** First **Subject:** 180th Anniversary of Federation **Obv:** National arms **Obv. Legend:** ESTADOS UNIDOS MEXICANOS **Rev:** State arms **Rev. Legend:** ESTADO DE TAMAULIPAS **Edge:** Reeded

Date	Mintage	F12	VF20	XF40	MS60	MS63
2004Mo	10,000	PF63 60.00				

KM# 684 10 PESOS

31.10 g., 0.999 Silver 0.9926 oz. ASW, 39.9 mm. **Series:** First **Subject:** 180th Anniversary of Federation **Obv:** National arms **Obv. Legend:** ESTADOS UNIDOS DE MEXICANOS **Rev:** State arms **Rev. Legend:** ESTADO DE TABASCO **Edge:** Reeded

Date	Mintage	F12	VF20	XF40	MS60	MS63
2004Mo	10,000	PF63 60.00				

KM# 685 10 PESOS

31.10 g., 0.999 Silver 0.9926 oz. ASW, 39.9 mm. **Series:** First **Subject:** 180th Anniversary of Federation **Obv:** National arms **Obv. Legend:** ESTADOS UNIDOS MEXICANOS **Rev:** State arms **Rev. Legend:** ESTADO DE SONORA **Edge:** Reeded **Note:** Mexican States: Sonora

Date	Mintage	F12	VF20	XF40	MS60	MS63
2004Mo	10,000	PF63 60.00				

KM# 686 10 PESOS

31.10 g., 0.999 Silver 0.9926 oz. ASW, 39.9 mm. **Series:** First **Subject:** 180th Anniversary of Federation **Obv:** National arms **Obv. Legend:** ESTADOS UNIDOS DE MEXICANOS **Rev:** State arms **Rev. Legend:** ESTADO DE SINALOA **Edge:** Reeded **Note:** Mexican States: Sinaloa

Date	Mintage	F12	VF20	XF40	MS60	MS63
2004Mo	10,000	PF63 60.00				

KM# 687 10 PESOS

31.10 g., 0.999 Silver 0.9926 oz. ASW, 39.9 mm. **Series:** First **Subject:** 180th Anniversary of Federation **Obv:** National arms **Obv. Legend:** ESTADOS UNIDOS MEXICANOS **Rev:** State arms **Rev. Legend:** ESTADO DE SAN LUIS POTOSÍ **Edge:** Reeded

Date	Mintage	F12	VF20	XF40	MS60	MS63
2004Mo	10,000	PF63 60.00				

KM# 735 10 PESOS

31.10 g., 0.999 Silver 0.9926 oz. ASW, 39.9 mm. **Series:** First **Subject:** 180th Anniversary of Federation **Obv:** National arms **Obv. Legend:** ESTADOS UNIDOS MEXICANOS **Rev:** State arms **Rev. Legend:** ESTADO DE QUINTANA ROO

Date	Mintage	F12	VF20	XF40	MS60	MS63
2004Mo	10,000	PF63 60.00				

KM# 733 10 PESOS

31.10 g., 0.999 Silver 0.9926 oz. ASW, 39.9 mm. **Series:** First **Subject:** 180th Anniversary of Federation **Obv:** National arms **Obv. Legend:** ESTADOS UNIDOS MEXICANOS **Rev:** State arms **Rev. Legend:** ESTADO DE QUERÉTARO ARTEAGA **Edge:** Reeded

Date	Mintage	F12	VF20	XF40	MS60	MS63
2004Mo	10,000	PF63 60.00				

KM# 737 10 PESOS

31.10 g., 0.999 Silver 0.9926 oz. ASW, 39.9 mm. **Series:** First **Subject:** 180th Anniversary of Federation **Obv:** National arms **Obv. Legend:** ESTADOS UNIDOS MEXICANOS **Rev:** State arms **Rev. Legend:** ESTADO DE PUEBLA **Edge:** Reeded

Date	Mintage	F12	VF20	XF40	MS60	MS63
2004Mo	10,000	PF63 60.00				

KM# 739 10 PESOS

31.10 g., 0.999 Bi-Metallic 0.9926 oz., 39.9 mm. **Series:** First **Subject:** 180th Anniversary of Federation **Obv:** National arms **Obv. Legend:** ESTADOS UNIDOS MEXICANOS **Rev:** State arms **Rev. Legend:** ESTADO DE OAXACA **Edge:** Reeded

Date	Mintage	F12	VF20	XF40	MS60	MS63
2004Mo	10,000	PF63 60.00				

KM# 741 10 PESOS

31.10 g., 0.999 Silver 0.9926 oz. ASW, 39.9 mm. **Series:** First **Subject:** 180th Anniversary of Federation **Obv:** National arms **Obv. Legend:** ESTADOS UNIDOS MEXICANOS **Rev:** State arms **Rev. Legend:** ESTADO DE NUEVO LEÓN **Edge:** Reeded

Date	Mintage	F12	VF20	XF40	MS60	MS63
2004Mo	10,000	PF63 60.00				

KM# 743 10 PESOS

31.10 g., 0.999 Silver 0.9926 oz. ASW, 39.9 mm. **Series:** First **Subject:** 180th Anniversary of Federation **Obv:** National arms **Obv. Legend:** ESTADOS UNIDOS MEXICANOS **Rev:** State arms **Rev. Legend:** ESTADO DE NAYARIT **Edge:** Reeded

Date	Mintage	F12	VF20	XF40	MS60	MS63
2004Mo	10,000	PF63 60.00				

KM# 745 10 PESOS

31.10 g., 0.999 Silver 0.9926 oz. ASW, 39.9 mm. **Series:** First **Subject:** 180th Anniversary of Federation **Obv:** National arms **Obv. Legend:** ESTADOS UNIDOS MEXICANOS **Rev:** State arms **Rev. Legend:** ESTADO DE MORELOS **Edge:** Reeded

Date	Mintage	F12	VF20	XF40	MS60	MS63
2004Mo	10,000	PF63 60.00				

KM# 796 10 PESOS
31.10 g., 0.999 Silver 0.9926 oz. ASW, 39.9 mm. **Series:** First **Subject:** 180th Anniversary of Federation **Obv:** National arms **Obv. Legend:** ESTADOS UNIDOS MEXICANOS **Rev:** State arms **Rev. Legend:** ESTADO DE MICHOACÁN DE OCAMPO **Edge:** Reeded

Date	Mintage	F12	VF20	XF40	MS60	MS63
2004Mo	10,000	PF63 60.00				

KM# 747 10 PESOS
31.10 g., 0.999 Silver 0.9926 oz. ASW, 39.9 mm. **Series:** First **Subject:** 180th Anniversary of Federation **Obv:** National arms **Obv. Legend:** ESTADOS UNIDOS MEXICANOS **Rev:** State arms **Rev. Legend:** ESTADO DE MÉXICO **Edge:** Reeded

Date	Mintage	F12	VF20	XF40	MS60	MS63
2004Mo	10,000	PF63 60.00				

KM# 749 10 PESOS
31.10 g., 0.999 Silver 0.9926 oz. ASW, 39.9 mm. **Series:** First **Subject:** 180th Anniversary of Federation **Obv:** National arms **Obv. Legend:** ESTADOS UNIDOS MEXICANOS **Rev:** State arms **Rev. Legend:** ESTADO DE JALISCO **Edge:** Reeded

Date	Mintage	F12	VF20	XF40	MS60	MS63
2004Mo	10,000	PF63 60.00				

KM# 961 10 PESOS
31.10 g., 0.999 Silver 0.9925 oz. ASW, 40 mm. **Subject:** National University, 75th Anniversary

Date	Mintage	F12	VF20	XF40	MS60	MS63
2010 (2004)	—	PF63 100				

KM# 766 10 PESOS
31.10 g., 0.999 Silver 0.9926 oz. ASW, 40 mm. **Subject:** Cervantes Festival **Obv:** Mexican Eagle and Snake **Rev:** Don Quixote **Edge:** Reeded

Date	Mintage	F12	VF20	XF40	MS60	MS63
2005Mo	1,205	PF63 75.00				

KM# 768 10 PESOS
31.10 g., 0.999 Silver 0.9926 oz. ASW, 40 mm. **Subject:** 470th Anniversary - Mexico City Mint **Obv:** Mexican Eagle and Snake **Rev:** Antique coin press

Date	Mintage	F12	VF20	XF40	MS60	MS63
2005Mo	2,005	PF63 55.00				

KM# 711 10 PESOS
31.10 g., 0.999 Silver 0.9926 oz. ASW, 39.9 mm. **Series:** First **Subject:** 180th Anniversary of Federation **Obv:** National arms **Obv. Legend:** ESTADOS UNIDOS MEXICANOS **Rev:** State arms **Rev. Legend:** ESTADO DE HIDALGO **Edge:** Reeded

Date	Mintage	F12	VF20	XF40	MS60	MS63
2005Mo	10,000	PF63 60.00				

KM# 710 10 PESOS
31.10 g., 0.999 Silver 0.9926 oz. ASW, 39.9 mm. **Series:** First **Subject:** 180th Anniversary of Federation **Obv:** National arms **Obv. Legend:** ESTADOS UNIDOS MEXICANOS **Rev:** State arms **Rev. Legend:** ESTADO DE GUERRERO **Edge:** Reeded

Date	Mintage	F12	VF20	XF40	MS60	MS63
2005Mo	10,000	PF63 60.00				

KM# 709 10 PESOS
31.10 g., 0.999 Silver 0.9926 oz. ASW, 39.9 mm. **Series:** First **Subject:** 180th Anniversary of Federation **Obv:** National arms **Obv. Legend:** ESTADOS UNIDOS MEXICANOS **Rev:** State arms **Rev. Legend:** ESTADO DE GUANAJUATO **Edge:** Reeded

Date	Mintage	F12	VF20	XF40	MS60	MS63
2005Mo	10,000	PF63 60.00				

KM# 708 10 PESOS
31.10 g., 0.999 Silver 0.9926 oz. ASW, 39.9 mm. **Series:** First **Subject:** 180th Anniversary of Federation **Obv:** National arms **Obv. Legend:** ESTADOS UNIDOS MEXICANOS **Rev:** State arms **Rev. Legend:** ESTADO DE DURANGO **Edge:** Reeded

Date	Mintage	F12	VF20	XF40	MS60	MS63
2005Mo	10,000	PF63 60.00				

KM# 707 10 PESOS
31.10 g., 0.999 Silver 0.9926 oz. ASW, 39.9 mm. **Series:** First **Subject:** 180th Anniversary of Federation **Obv:** National arms **Obv. Legend:** ESTADOS UNIDOS MEXICANOS **Rev:** Federal District arms **Rev. Legend:** DISTRITO FEDERAL **Edge:** Reeded

Date	Mintage	F12	VF20	XF40	MS60	MS63
2005Mo	10,000	PF63 60.00				

KM# 753 10 PESOS
31.10 g., 0.999 Silver 0.9926 oz. ASW, 39.9 mm. **Series:** First **Subject:** 180th Anniversary of Federation **Obv:** National arms **Obv. Legend:** ESTADOS UNIDOS MEXICANOS **Rev:** State arms **Rev. Legend:** ESTADO DE CHIHUAHUA **Edge:** Reeded

Date	Mintage	F12	VF20	XF40	MS60	MS63
2005Mo	10,000	PF63 60.00				

KM# 706 10 PESOS
31.10 g., 0.999 Silver 0.9926 oz. ASW, 39.9 mm. **Series:** First **Subject:** 180th Anniversary of Federation **Obv:** National arms **Obv. Legend:** ESTADOS UNIDOS MEXICANOS **Rev:** State arms **Rev. Legend:** ESTADO DE CHIAPAS **Edge:** Reeded

Date	Mintage	F12	VF20	XF40	MS60	MS63
2005Mo	10,000	PF63 60.00				

KM# 728 10 PESOS
31.10 g., 0.999 Silver 0.9926 oz. ASW, 39.9 mm. **Series:** First **Subject:** 180th Anniversary of Federation **Obv:** National arms **Obv. Legend:** ESTADOS UNIDOS MEXICANOS **Rev:** State arms **Rev. Legend:** ESTADO DE COLIMA **Edge:** Reeded

Date	Mintage	F12	VF20	XF40	MS60	MS63
2005Mo	10,000	PF63 60.00				

KM# 751 10 PESOS
31.10 g., 0.999 Silver 0.9926 oz. ASW, 39.9 mm. **Series:** First
Subject: 180th Anniversary of Federation **Obv:** National arms
Obv. Legend: ESTADOS UNIDOS MEXICANOS **Rev:** State
arms **Rev. Legend:** ESTADO DE COAHUILA DE ZARAGOZA
Edge: Reeded

Date	Mintage	F12	VF20	XF40	MS60	MS63
2005Mo	10,000	PF63 60.00				

KM# 726 10 PESOS
31.10 g., 0.999 Silver 0.9926 oz. ASW, 39.9 mm. **Series:** First
Subject: 180th Anniversary of Federation **Obv:** National arms
Obv. Legend: ESTADOS UNIDOS MEXICANOS **Rev:** State
arms **Rev. Legend:** ESTADO DE CAMPECHE **Edge:** Reeded

Date	Mintage	F12	VF20	XF40	MS60	MS63
2005Mo	10,000	PF63 60.00				

KM# 724 10 PESOS
31.10 g., 0.999 Silver 0.9926 oz. ASW, 39.9 mm. **Series:** First
Subject: 180th Anniversary of Federation **Obv:** National arms
Obv. Legend: ESTADOS UNIDOS MEXICANOS **Rev:** State
arms **Rev. Legend:** ESTADO DE BAJA CALIFORNIA SUR
Edge: Reeded

Date	Mintage	F12	VF20	XF40	MS60	MS63
2005Mo	10,000	PF63 60.00				

KM# 722 10 PESOS
31.10 g., 0.999 Silver 0.9926 oz. ASW, 39.9 mm. **Series:** First
Subject: 180th Anniversary of Federation **Obv:** National arms
Obv. Legend: ESTADOS UNIDOS MEXICANOS **Rev:** State
arms **Rev. Legend:** ESTADO DE BAJA CALIFORNIA **Edge:**
Reeded

Date	Mintage	F12	VF20	XF40	MS60	MS63
2005Mo	10,000	PF63 60.00				

KM# 720 10 PESOS
31.10 g., 0.999 Silver 0.9926 oz. ASW, 39.9 mm. **Series:** First
Subject: 180th Anniversary of Federation **Obv:** National arms
Obv. Legend: ESTADOS UNIDOS MEXICANOS **Rev:** State
arms **Rev. Legend:** ESTADO DE AGUASCALIENTES **Edge:**
Reeded

Date	Mintage	F12	VF20	XF40	MS60	MS63
2005Mo	10,000	PF63 60.00				

KM# 718 10 PESOS
31.10 g., 0.999 Silver 0.9926 oz. ASW, 40 mm. **Series:**
Second **Obv:** National arms **Obv. Legend:** ESTADOS UNIDOS
MEXICANOS **Rev:** Facade of the San Marcos garden above
sculpture of national emblem at left, San Antonio Temple at right
Rev. Legend: AGUASCALIENTES **Edge:** Reeded

Date	Mintage	F12	VF20	XF40	MS60	MS63
2005Mo	6,000	PF63 65.00				

KM# 757 10 PESOS
31.10 g., 0.999 Silver 0.9926 oz. ASW, 40 mm. **Series:**
Second **Obv:** National arms **Obv. Legend:** ESTADOS UNIDOS
MEXICANOS **Rev:** Rams head, mountain outline in background
Rev. Legend: BAJA CALIFORNIA - GOBIERNO DEL ESTADO
Edge: Reeded

Date	Mintage	F12	VF20	XF40	MS60	MS63
2005Mo	6,000	PF63 65.00				

KM# 755 10 PESOS
31.10 g., 0.999 Silver 0.9926 oz. ASW, 40 mm. **Obv:** National
arms **Rev:** Baja California del Norte arms

Date	Mintage	F12	VF20	XF40	MS60	MS63
2005Mo	—	PF63 75.00				

KM# 763 10 PESOS
31.10 g., 0.999 Silver 0.9926 oz. ASW, 40 mm. **Obv:** National
arms **Rev:** Benito Juarez **Edge:** Reeded

Date	Mintage	F12	VF20	XF40	MS60	MS63
2006Mo	—	PF63 75.00				

KM# 761 10 PESOS
31.10 g., 0.999 Silver 0.9926 oz. ASW, 40 mm. **Series:**
Second **Obv:** National arms **Obv. Legend:** ESTADOS UNIDOS
MEXICANOS **Rev:** Outlined map of peninsula at center, cave
painting of deer behind, cactus at right **Rev. Legend:** ESTADO
DE BAJA CALIFORNIA SUR **Edge:** Reeded

Date	Mintage	F12	VF20	XF40	MS60	MS63
2006Mo	6,000	PF63 65.00				

KM# 759 10 PESOS
31.10 g., 0.999 Silver 0.9926 oz. ASW, 40 mm. **Series:**
Second **Obv:** National arms **Obv. Legend:** ESTADOS UNIDOS
MEXICANOS **Rev:** Jade mask - Calakmul, Campeche **Rev.
Legend:** ESTADO DE CAMPECHE **Edge:** Reeded

Date	Mintage	F12	VF20	XF40	MS60	MS63
2006Mo	6,000	PF63 65.00				

KM# 780 10 PESOS
31.10 g., 0.999 Silver 0.9926 oz. ASW, 40 mm. **Series:**
Second **Obv:** National arms **Obv. Legend:** ESTADOS UNIDOS
MEXICANOS **Rev:** Outlined map with turtle, mine cart above
grapes at center, Friendship dam above Christ of the Nodas
at left, chimneys above crucibles and bell tower of Santiago's
cathedral at right **Rev. Inscription:** COAHUILA DE ZARAGOZA
Edge: Reeded

Date	Mintage	F12	VF20	XF40	MS60	MS63
2006Mo	6,000	PF63 65.00				

KM# 776 10 PESOS
31.10 g., 0.999 Silver 0.9926 oz. ASW, 40 mm. **Series:**
Second **Obv:** National arms **Obv. Legend:** ESTADOS UNIDOS
MEXICANOS **Rev:** State arms at lower center, Nevado de
Colima and Volcan de Fuego volcanos in background **Rev.
Legend:** Colima **Rev. Inscription:** GENEROSO **Edge:** Reeded

Date	Mintage	F12	VF20	XF40	MS60	MS63
2006Mo	6,000	PF63 65.00				

KM# 772 10 PESOS
31.10 g., 0.999 Silver 0.9926 oz. ASW, 40 mm. **Series:** Second **Obv:** National arms **Obv. Legend:** ESTADOS UNIDOS MEXICANOS **Rev:** Head of Pakal, ancient Mayan king, Palenque **Rev. Legend:** ESTADO DE CHIAPAS - CABEZA MAYA DEL REY PAKAL, PALENQUE **Edge:** Reeded

Date	Mintage	F12	VF20	XF40	MS60	MS63
2006Mo	6,000	PF63 65.00				

KM# 774 10 PESOS
31.10 g., 0.999 Silver 0.9926 oz. ASW, 40 mm. **Series:** Second **Obv:** National arms **Obv. Legend:** ESTADOS UNIDOS MEXICANOS **Rev:** Angel of Liberty **Rev. Legend:** MÉXICO - ANGEL DE LA LIBERTAD, CHIHUAHUA **Edge:** Reeded

Date	Mintage	F12	VF20	XF40	MS60	MS63
2006Mo	6,000	PF63 65.00				

KM# 778 10 PESOS
31.10 g., 0.999 Silver 0.9926 oz. ASW, 40 mm. **Series:** Second **Obv:** National arms **Obv. Legend:** ESTADOS UNIDOS MEXICANOS **Rev:** National Palace **Rev. Legend:** DISTRITO FEDERAL - ANTIGUO AYUNTAMIENTO **Edge:** Reeded

Date	Mintage	F12	VF20	XF40	MS60	MS63
2006Mo	6,000	PF63 65.00				

KM# 786 10 PESOS
31.10 g., 0.999 Silver 0.9926 oz. ASW, 40 mm. **Series:** Second **Obv:** National arms **Obv. Legend:** ESTADOS UNIDOS MEXICANOS **Rev:** Tree **Rev. Legend:** PRIMERA RESERVA NACIONAL FORESTAL - DURANGO **Edge:** Reeded

Date	Mintage	F12	VF20	XF40	MS60	MS63
2006Mo	6,000	PF63 65.00				

KM# 788 10 PESOS
31.10 g., 0.999 Silver 0.9926 oz. ASW, 40 mm. **Series:** Second **Obv:** National arms **Obv. Legend:** ESTADOS UNIDOS MEXICANOS **Rev:** State arms at center, statue of Miguel Hidalgo at left, monument to Pípila at lower right **Rev. Inscription:** Guanajuato **Edge:** Reeded

Date	Mintage	F12	VF20	XF40	MS60	MS63
2006Mo	6,000	PF63 65.00				

KM# 790 10 PESOS
31.10 g., 0.999 Silver 0.9926 oz. ASW, 40 mm. **Series:** Second **Obv:** National arms **Obv. Legend:** ESTADOS UNIDOS MEXICANOS **Rev:** Stylized portrait of Vicente Guerrero at left, church of Taxco at upper center, Acapulco's la Quebrada with diver above Christmas Eve flower and mask **Rev. Legend:** GUERRERO **Edge:** Reeded

Date	Mintage	F12	VF20	XF40	MS60	MS63
2006Mo	6,000	PF63 65.00				

KM# 792 10 PESOS
31.10 g., 0.999 Silver 0.9926 oz. ASW, 40 mm. **Series:** Second **Obv:** National arms **Obv. Legend:** ESTADOS UNIDOS MEXICANOS **Rev:** Monument of Pachuca Hidalgo **Rev. Inscription:** RELOJ / MONUMENTAL / DE / PACHUCA / HIDALGO - La / Bella / Airosa **Edge:** Reeded

Date	Mintage	F12	VF20	XF40	MS60	MS63
2006Mo	6,000	PF63 65.00				

KM# 794 10 PESOS
31.10 g., 0.999 Silver 0.9926 oz. ASW, 40 mm. **Series:** Second **Obv:** National arms **Obv. Legend:** ESTADOS UNIDOS MEXICANOS **Rev:** Hospicio Cabañas orphanage **Rev. Legend:** ESTADO DE JALISCCO **Edge:** Reeded

Date	Mintage	F12	VF20	XF40	MS60	MS63
2006Mo	6,000	PF63 65.00				

KM# 830 10 PESOS
31.10 g., 0.999 Silver 0.9926 oz. ASW, 40 mm. **Series:** Second **Obv:** National arms **Obv. Legend:** ESTADOS UNIDOS MEXICANOS **Rev:** Pyramid de la Loona (Moon) **Rev. Legend:** ESTADO DE MÉXICO **Edge:** Reeded

Date	Mintage	F12	VF20	XF40	MS60	MS63
2006Mo	6,000	PF63 65.00				

KM# 831 10 PESOS
31.10 g., 0.999 Silver 0.9926 oz. ASW, 40 mm. **Series:** Second **Obv:** National arms **Obv. Legend:** ESTADOS UNIDOS MEXICANOS **Rev:** Four Monarch butterflies **Rev. Legend:** ESTADO DE MICHOACÁN **Edge:** Reeded

Date	Mintage	F12	VF20	XF40	MS60	MS63
2006Mo	6,000	PF63 65.00				

KM# 832 10 PESOS
31.10 g., 0.999 Silver 0.9926 oz. ASW, 40 mm. **Series:** Second **Obv:** National arms **Obv. Legend:** ESTADOS UNIDOS MEXICANOS **Rev:** 1/2 length figure of Chinelo (local dancer) at right, Palacio de Cortes in background **Rev. Inscription:** ESTADO DE / MORELOS **Edge:** Reeded

Date	Mintage	F12	VF20	XF40	MS60	MS63
2006Mo	6,000	PF63 65.00				

KM# 833 10 PESOS
31.10 g., 0.999 Silver 0.9926 oz. ASW, 40 mm. **Series:** Second **Obv:** National arms **Obv. Legend:** ESTADOS UNIDOS MEXICANOS **Rev:** Isle de Mexcaltitlán **Rev. Legend:** ESTADO DE NAYARIT **Edge:** Reeded

Date	Mintage	F12	VF20	XF40	MS60	MS63
2007Mo	6,000	PF63 65.00				

KM# 834 10 PESOS

31.10 g., 0.999 Silver 0.9926 oz. ASW, 40 mm. **Series:** Second **Obv:** National arms **Obv. Legend:** ESTADOS UNIDOS MEXICANOS **Rev:** Old foundry in Pargue Fundidora (public park) at right, Cerro de la Silla (Saddle Hill) in background **Rev. Legend:** ESTADO DE NUEVO LEÓN **Edge:** Reeded

Date	Mintage	F12	VF20	XF40	MS60	MS63
2007Mo	6,000	**PF63** 65.00				

KM# 835 10 PESOS

31.10 g., 0.999 Silver 0.9926 oz. ASW, 40 mm. **Series:** Second **Obv:** National arms **Obv. Legend:** ESTADOS UNIDOS MEXICANOS **Rev:** Teatro Macedonio Alcala (theater) **Rev. Legend:** OAXACA **Edge:** Reeded

Date	Mintage	F12	VF20	XF40	MS60	MS63
2007Mo	6,000	**PF63** 65.00				

KM# 836 10 PESOS

31.10 g., 0.999 Silver 0.9926 oz. ASW, 40 mm. **Series:** Second **Obv:** National arms **Obv. Legend:** ESTADOS UNIDOS MEXICANOS **Rev:** Talavera porcelain dish **Rev. Legend:** ESTADO DE PUEBLA **Edge:** Reeded

Date	Mintage	F12	VF20	XF40	MS60	MS63
2007Mo	6,000	**PF63** 65.00				

KM# 837 10 PESOS

31.10 g., 0.999 Silver 0.9926 oz. ASW, 40 mm. **Series:** Second **Obv:** National arms **Obv. Legend:** ESTADOS UNIDOS MEXICANOS **Rev:** Mask at left, rays above state arms at center, Mayan ruins at right **Rev. Legend:** QUINTANA ROO **Edge:** Reeded

Date	Mintage	F12	VF20	XF40	MS60	MS63
2007Mo	6,000	**PF63** 65.00				

KM# 838 10 PESOS

31.10 g., 0.999 Silver 0.9926 oz. ASW, 40 mm. **Series:** Second **Obv:** National arms **Obv. Legend:** ESTADOS UNIDOS MEXICANOS **Rev:** Acqueduct of Querétaro at left, church of Santa Rosa de Viterbo at right **Rev. Legend:** ESTADO DE QUERÉTARO ARTEAGA **Edge:** Reeded

Date	Mintage	F12	VF20	XF40	MS60	MS63
2007Mo	6,000	**PF63** 65.00				

KM# 839 10 PESOS

31.10 g., Silver, 40 mm. **Series:** Second **Obv:** National arms **Obv. Legend:** ESTADOS UNIDOS MEXICANOS **Rev:** Facade of Caja Real **Rev. Legend:** • SAN LUIS POTOSÍ • **Edge:** Reeded

Date	Mintage	F12	VF20	XF40	MS60	MS63
2007Mo	6,000	**PF63** 65.00				

KM# 840 10 PESOS

31.10 g., 0.999 Silver 0.9926 oz. ASW, 40 mm. **Series:** Second **Obv:** National arms **Obv. Legend:** ESTADOS UNIDOS MEXICANOS **Rev:** Shield on pile of cactus fruits **Rev. Legend:** ESTADO DE SINALOA - LUGAR DE PITAHAYAS **Edge:** Reeded

Date	Mintage	F12	VF20	XF40	MS60	MS63
2007Mo	6,000	**PF63** 65.00				

KM# 841 10 PESOS

31.10 g., 0.999 Silver 0.9926 oz. ASW, 40 mm. **Series:** Second **Obv:** National arms **Obv. Legend:** ESTADOS UNIDOS MEXICANOS **Rev:** Local in Dance of the Deer at left, cactus at right, mountains in background **Rev. Legend:** ESTADO DE SONORA **Edge:** Reeded

Date	Mintage	F12	VF20	XF40	MS60	MS63
2007Mo	6,000	**PF63** 65.00				

KM# 842 10 PESOS

31.10 g., 0.999 Silver 0.9926 oz. ASW, 40 mm. **Series:** Second **Obv:** National arms **Obv. Legend:** ESTADOS UNIDOS MEXICANOS **Rev:** Fuente de los Pescadores (fisherman fountain) at lower left, giant head from the Olmec-pre-Hispanic culture at right, Planetario Tabasco in background **Rev. Legend:** TABASCO **Edge:** Reeded

Date	Mintage	F12	VF20	XF40	MS60	MS63
2007Mo	6,000	**PF63** 65.00				

KM# 843 10 PESOS

31.10 g., 0.999 Silver 0.9926 oz. ASW, 40 mm. **Series:** Second **Obv:** National arms **Obv. Legend:** ESTADOS UNIDOS MEXICANOS **Rev:** Ridge - Cerro Del Bernal, Gonzáles **Rev. Legend:** TAMAULIPAS **Edge:** Reeded

Date	Mintage	F12	VF20	XF40	MS60	MS63
2007Mo	6,000	**PF63** 65.00				

KM# 844 10 PESOS

31.10 g., 0.999 Silver 0.9926 oz. ASW, 40 mm. **Series:** Second **Obv:** National arms **Obv. Legend:** ESTADOS UNIDOS MEXICANOS **Rev:** Basilica de Ocotlán at left, state arms above Capilla Abierta, Plaza de Toros Ranchero Aguilar below, Exconvento de San Francisco at right **Rev. Legend:** ESTADO DE TLAXCALA **Edge:** Reeded

Date	Mintage	F12	VF20	XF40	MS60	MS63
2007Mo	6,000	**PF63** 65.00				

KM# 845 10 PESOS

31.10 g., 0.999 Silver 0.9926 oz. ASW, 40 mm. **Series:** Second **Obv:** National arms **Obv. Legend:** ESTADOS UNIDOS MEXICANOS **Rev:** Pyramid of El Tajín **Rev. Legend:** • VERACRUZ • • • DE IGNACIO DE LA LLAVE • **Edge:** Reeded

Date	Mintage	F12	VF20	XF40	MS60	MS63
2007Mo	6,000	**PF63** 65.00				

KM# 846 10 PESOS
31.10 g., 0.999 Silver 0.9926 oz. ASW, 40 mm. **Series:** Second **Obv:** National arms **Obv. Legend:** ESTADOS UNIDOS MEXICANOS **Rev:** Stylized pyramid of Chichén-Itzá **Rev. Legend:** Castillo de Chichén Itzá **Rev. Inscription:** YUCATÁN **Edge:** Reeded

Date	Mintage	F12	VF20	XF40	MS60	MS63
2007Mo	6,000	PF63 65.00				

KM# 847 10 PESOS
31.10 g., 0.999 Silver 0.9926 oz. ASW, 40 mm. **Series:** Second **Obv:** National arms **Obv. Legend:** ESTADOS UNIDOS MEXICANOS **Rev:** Cable car above Monumento al Minero at left, Cathedral de Zacatecas at center right **Rev. Legend:** Zacatecas **Edge:** Reeded

Date	Mintage	F12	VF20	XF40	MS60	MS63
2007Mo	6,000	PF63 65.00				

KM# 937 10 PESOS
62.20 g., 0.999 Silver 1.9849 oz. ASW, 48 mm. **Series:** Mexican Revolution 100th Anniversary **Subject:** Revolutionary woman **Obv:** National arms (eagle and snake facing left) and legend **Obv. Legend:** ESTRADOS UNIDOS MEXICANOS **Rev:** Adelita on a railroad car, denomination and legend **Rev. Legend:** REVOLUCION MEXICANA

Date	Mintage	F12	VF20	XF40	MS60	MS63
2010Mo	20,000	PF63 120				

KM# 938 10 PESOS
62.20 g., 0.999 Silver 1.9849 oz. ASW, 48 mm. **Series:** Mexican Revolution 100th Anniversary **Subject:** Railroad **Obv:** National arms (eagle and snake facing left) and legend **Obv. Legend:** ESTADOS UNIDOS MEXICANOS **Rev:** Four seated armed revolutionaries on locomotive **Rev. Legend:** REVOLUCION MEXICANA

Date	Mintage	F12	VF20	XF40	MS60	MS63
2010Mo	20,000	PF63 120				

KM# 942 10 PESOS
31.10 g., 0.999 Silver 0.9925 oz. ASW, 40 mm. **Subject:** 100th Anniversary of the National Autonomous University of Mexico **Obv:** National arms (eagle and snake facing left) and legend **Obv. Legend:** ESTADOS UNIDOS MEXICANOS **Rev:** University buildings, sculpture and legend **Rev. Legend:** UNIVERSIDAD NACIONAL AUTONOMIA DE MEXICO

Date	Mintage	F12	VF20	XF40	MS60	MS63
2010Mo Prooflike	5,000	—				60.00

KM# 948 10 PESOS
62.20 g., 0.999 Silver 1.9849 oz. ASW, 65 mm. **Subject:** Chichen Itza, Temple of Warriors **Obv:** National arms (eagle and snake facing left), legend **Obv. Legend:** ESTADOS UNIDOS MEXICANOS **Rev:** Temple of Warriors of Chichen Itza **Rev. Legend:** CHICHEN ITZA, TEMPLO DE LOS GUERROS

Date	Mintage	F12	VF20	XF40	MS60	MS63
ND-2011Mo	3,000	PF63 150				

KM# 956 10 PESOS
10.33 g., Bi-Metallic, 28 mm. **Subject:** Battle of Puebla 150th Anniversary **Obv:** National arms (eagle and snake facing left) and legend **Obv. Legend:** ESTADOS UNIDOS MEXICANOS **Rev:** Head of General Zaragoza facing left, legends **Rev. Legend:** 150 ANNIVERSARIO DE LA BATALLA DE PUEBLA, 5 DE MAYO **Edge:** Reeded

Date	Mintage	F12	VF20	XF40	MS60	MS63
2012Mo	29,871,000	—		—	2.00	2.50

KM# 637 20 PESOS
Bi-Metallic, 32 mm. **Subject:** Xiuhtecuhtli **Obv:** National arms, eagle left within circle **Rev:** Aztec with torch within spiked circle

Date	Mintage	F12	VF20	XF40	MS60	MS63
2001Mo	2,478,000	—	2.50	3.50	16.00	18.00

KM# 638 20 PESOS
Bi-Metallic, 32 mm. **Subject:** Octavio Paz **Obv:** National arms, eagle left within circle **Rev:** Head 1/4 right within circle

Date	Mintage	F12	VF20	XF40	MS60	MS63
2001Mo	2,515,000	—	2.50	3.50	16.00	18.50

KM# 704 20 PESOS
62.40 g., 0.999 Silver 1.9913 oz. ASW, 48.1 mm. **Subject:** 400th Anniversary of Don Quijote de la Manchia **Obv:** National arms **Rev:** Skeletal figure horseback with spear galloping right **Edge:** Plain

Date	Mintage	F12	VF20	XF40	MS60	MS63
ND-2005Mo	3,605	PF63 85.00				

KM# 767 20 PESOS
62.40 g., 0.999 Silver 1.9913 oz. ASW, 48 mm. **Subject:** 80th Anniversary - Bank of Mexico **Obv:** National arms **Rev:** 100 Peso banknote design of 1925

Date	Mintage	F12	VF20	XF40	MS60	MS63
2005Mo	—					80.00
2005Mo	3,005	PF63 90.00				

KM# 939 20 PESOS
62.20 g., 0.999 Silver 1.9849 oz. ASW, 48 mm. **Series:** Mexican Independence 200th Anniversary **Subject:** Dolores Parrish Church **Obv:** National arms (eagle and snake facing left) and legend **Obv. Legend:** ESTADOS UNIDOS MEXICANOS **Rev:** Dolores Parrish church, Independence Bell **Rev. Legend:** Bicentenario de la Independencia de Mexico

Date	Mintage	F12	VF20	XF40	MS60	MS63
2010Mo	15,000	PF63 100				

KM# 940 20 PESOS
62.21 g., 0.999 Silver 1.9851 oz. ASW, 48 mm. **Series:** Mexican Independence 200th Anniversary **Subject:** Miguel Hidalgo y Costilla and Jose maria Morelos y Pavon **Obv:** National arms (eagle and snake facing left) and legend **Obv. Legend:** ESTADDOS UNIDOS MEXICANOS **Rev:** Miguel Hidalgo y Costilla and Jose Maria Morelos y Pavon, denomination and legend **Rev. Legend:** BICENTENARIO DE LA INDEPENDENCIA

Date	Mintage	F12	VF20	XF40	MS60	MS63
2010Mo	15,000	PF63 100				

KM# 943 20 PESOS
15.95 g., Bi-Metallic, 32 mm. **Subject:** 20th Anniversary of Octavio Paz **Obv:** National arms (eagle and snake facing left) and legend **Obv. Legend:** ESTADOS UNIDOS MEXICANOS **Rev:** Bust of Octavio Paz facing right and Legend **Rev. Legend:** Premio Nobel de Lieteratura **Edge:** Segmented reeding

Date	Mintage	F12	VF20	XF40	MS60	MS63
2010Mo	4,954,000	—		—	3.50	4.00
Note: Minted in 2011						

KM# 949 20 PESOS
155.15 g., 0.999 Silver 4.9511 oz. ASW, 65 mm. **Subject:** Chichen Itza, Pyramid of Kukulcan **Obv:** National arms (eagle and snake facing left), legend **Obv. Legend:** ESTADOS UNIDOS MEXICANOS **Rev:** Pyramid of Kukulcan of Chichen Itza, legends **Rev. Legend:** CHICHEN ITZA, PIRAMID DE KUKULCAN

Date	Mintage	F12	VF20	XF40	MS60	MS63
ND-2011Mo	3,000	PF63 260				

KM# 969 20 PESOS
15.95 g., Bi-Metallic, 32 mm. **Subject:** Armed Forces, 100th Anniversary **Obv:** National arms **Rev:** Silhouette of soldier with a helmet **Edge:** Segmented reeding

Date	Mintage	F12	VF20	XF40	MS60	MS63
2013Mo	Est. 5000000	—		—	3.50	4.00

KM# 970 20 PESOS
15.95 g., Bi-Metallic, 32 mm. **Subject:** Belisario Dominguez Palencia, 150th Anniversary of Birth and 100th Anniversary of Death **Obv:** National arms **Rev:** Bust 1/4 right **Edge:** Segmented reeding

Date	Mintage	F12	VF20	XF40	MS60	MS63
2013Mo	Est. 1000000	—		—	4.50	5.00

KM# 688 100 PESOS
33.94 g., Bi-Metallic, 39.04 mm. **Series:** First **Subject:** 180th Anniversary of Federation **Obv:** National arms **Obv. Legend:** ESTADOS UNIDOS MEXICANOS **Rev:** State arms **Rev. Legend:** ESTADO DE ZACATECAS **Edge:** Segmented reeding

Date	Mintage	F12	VF20	XF40	MS60	MS63
2003Mo	244,900	—	—	—	40.00	50.00

KM# 696 100 PESOS
29.17 g., Bi-Metallic, 34.5 mm. **Series:** First **Subject:** 180th Anniversary of Federation **Obv:** National arms **Obv. Legend:** ESTADOS UNIDOS MEXICANOS **Rev:** State arms **Rev. Legend:** ESTADO DE ZACATECAS **Edge:** Segmented reeding

Date	Mintage	F12	VF20	XF40	MS60	MS63
2003Mo	1,000	PF65 1,200				

KM# 689 100 PESOS
33.94 g., Bi-Metallic, 39.04 mm. **Series:** First **Subject:** 180th Anniversary of Federation **Obv:** National arms **Obv. Legend:** ESTADOS UNIDOS MEXICANOS **Rev:** State arms **Rev. Legend:** ESTADO DE YUCATÁN **Edge:** Segmented reeding

Date	Mintage	F12	VF20	XF40	MS60	MS63
2003Mo	235,763	—	—	—	40.00	50.00

KM# 697 100 PESOS
29.17 g., Bi-Metallic, 34.5 mm. **Series:** First **Subject:** 180th Anniversary of Federation **Obv:** National arms **Obv. Legend:** ESTADOS UNIDOS MEXICANOS **Rev:** State arms **Rev. Legend:** ESTADO DE YUCATÁN **Edge:** Segmented reeding

Date	Mintage	F12	VF20	XF40	MS60	MS63
2003Mo	1,000	**PF65** 1,200				

KM# 690 100 PESOS
33.94 g., Bi-Metallic, 39.04 mm. **Series:** First **Subject:** 180th Anniversary of Federation **Obv:** National arms **Obv. Legend:** ESTADOS UNIDOS MEXICANOS **Rev:** State arms **Rev. Legend:** ESTADO DE VERACRUZ-LLAVE **Edge:** Segmented reeding

Date	Mintage	F12	VF20	XF40	MS60	MS63
2003Mo	248,810	—	—	—	40.00	50.00

KM# 698 100 PESOS
29.17 g., Bi-Metallic, 34.5 mm. **Series:** First **Subject:** 180th Anniversary of Federation **Obv:** National arms **Obv. Legend:** ESTADOS UNIDOS MEXICANOS **Rev:** State arms **Rev. Legend:** ESTADO DE VERACRUZ-LLAVE **Edge:** Segmented reeding

Date	Mintage	F12	VF20	XF40	MS60	MS63
2003Mo	1,000	**PF65** 1,200				

KM# 691 100 PESOS
33.94 g., Bi-Metallic, 39.9 mm. **Series:** First **Subject:** 180th Anniversary of Federation **Obv:** National arms **Obv. Legend:** ESTADOS UNIDOS MEXICANOS **Rev:** State arms **Rev. Legend:** ESTADO DE TLAXCALA **Edge:** Segmented reeding

Date	Mintage	F12	VF20	XF40	MS60	MS63
2003Mo	248,976	—	—	—	35.00	40.00

KM# 699 100 PESOS
29.17 g., Bi-Metallic, 34.5 mm. **Series:** First **Subject:** 180th Anniversary of Federation **Obv:** National arms **Obv. Legend:** ESTADOS UNIDOS MEXICANOS **Rev:** State arms **Rev. Legend:** ESTADO DE TLAXCALA **Edge:** Segmented reeding

Date	Mintage	F12	VF20	XF40	MS60	MS63
2003Mo	1,000	**PF65** 1,200				

KM# 692 100 PESOS
33.94 g., Bi-Metallic, 39.04 mm. **Series:** First **Subject:** 180th Anniversary of Federation **Obv:** National arms **Obv. Legend:** ESTADOS UNIDOS MEXICANOS **Rev:** State arms **Rev. Legend:** ESTADO DE TAMAULIPAS **Edge:** Segmented reeding

Date	Mintage	F12	VF20	XF40	MS60	MS63
2004Mo	249,398	—	—	—	35.00	40.00

KM# 700 100 PESOS
29.17 g., Bi-Metallic, 34.5 mm. **Series:** First **Subject:** 180th Anniversary of Federation **Obv:** National arms **Obv. Legend:** ESTADOS UNIDOS MEXICANOS **Rev:** State arms **Rev. Legend:** ESTADO DE TAMAULIPAS **Edge:** Segmented reeding

Date	Mintage	F12	VF20	XF40	MS60	MS63
2004Mo	1,000	**PF65** 1,200				

KM# 693 100 PESOS
33.94 g., Bi-Metallic, 39.04 mm. **Series:** First **Subject:** 180th Anniversary of Federation **Obv:** National arms **Obv. Legend:** ESTADOS UNIDOS MEXICANOS **Rev:** State arms **Rev. Legend:** ESTADO DE TABASCO **Edge:** Segmented reeding

Date	Mintage	F12	VF20	XF40	MS60	MS63
2004Mo	249,318	—	—	—	35.00	40.00

KM# 701 100 PESOS
29.17 g., Bi-Metallic, 34.5 mm. **Series:** First **Subject:** 180th Anniversary of Federation **Obv:** National arms **Obv. Legend:** ESTADOS UNIDOS MEXICANOS **Rev:** State arms **Rev. Legend:** ESTADO DE TABASCO **Edge:** Segmented reeding

Date	Mintage	F12	VF20	XF40	MS60	MS63
2004Mo	1,000	**PF65** 1,200				

KM# 694 100 PESOS
33.94 g., Bi-Metallic, 39.04 mm. **Series:** First **Subject:** 180th Anniversary of Federation **Obv:** National arms **Obv. Legend:** ESTADOS UNIDOS MEXICANOS **Rev:** State arms **Rev. Legend:** ESTADO DE SONORA **Edge:** Segmented reeding

Date	Mintage	F12	VF20	XF40	MS60	MS63
2004Mo	249,300	—	—	—	35.00	40.00

KM# 702 100 PESOS
29.17 g., Bi-Metallic, 34.5 mm. **Series:** First **Subject:** 180th Anniversary of Federation **Obv:** National arms **Obv. Legend:** ESTADOS UNIDOS MEXICANOS **Rev:** State arms **Rev. Legend:** ESTADO DE SONORA **Edge:** Segmented reeding

Date	Mintage	F12	VF20	XF40	MS60	MS63
2004Mo	1,000	**PF65** 1,200				

KM# 695 100 PESOS
33.94 g., Bi-Metallic, 39.04 mm. **Series:** First **Subject:** 180th Anniversary of Federation **Obv:** National arms **Obv. Legend:** ESTADOS UNIDOS MEXICANOS **Rev:** State arms **Rev. Legend:** ESTADO DE SINALOA **Edge:** Segmented reeding

Date	Mintage	F12	VF20	XF40	MS60	MS63
2004Mo	244,722	—	—	—	35.00	40.00

KM# 703 100 PESOS
29.17 g., Bi-Metallic, 34.5 mm. **Series:** First **Subject:** 180th Anniversary of Federation **Obv:** National arms **Obv. Legend:** ESTADOS UNIDOS MEXICANOS **Rev:** State arms **Rev. Legend:** ESTADO DE SINALOA **Edge:** Segmented reeding

Date	Mintage	F12	VF20	XF40	MS60	MS63
2004Mo	1,000	**PF65** 1,200				

KM# 803 100 PESOS
33.94 g., Bi-Metallic, 39.04 mm. **Series:** First **Subject:** 180th Anniversary of Federation **Obv:** National arms **Obv. Legend:** ESTADOS UNIDOS MEXICANOS **Rev:** State arms **Rev. Legend:** ESTADO DE SAN LUIS POTOSÍ **Edge:** Segmented reeding

Date	Mintage	F12	VF20	XF40	MS60	MS63
2004Mo	249,662	—	—	—	35.00	40.00

KM# 806 100 PESOS
29.17 g., Bi-Metallic, 34.5 mm. **Series:** First **Subject:** 180th Anniversary of Federation **Obv:** National arms **Obv. Legend:** ESTADOS UNIDOS MEXICANOS **Rev:** State arms **Rev. Legend:** ESTADO DE SAN LUIS POTOSÍ **Edge:** Segmented reeding

Date	Mintage	F12	VF20	XF40	MS60	MS63
2004Mo	1,000	**PF65** 1,200				

KM# 736 100 PESOS
33.94 g., Bi-Metallic, 39.04 mm. **Series:** First **Subject:** 180th Anniversary of Federation **Obv:** National arms **Obv. Legend:** ESTADOS UNIDOS MEXICANOS **Rev:** State arms **Rev. Legend:** ESTADO DE QUINTANA ROO **Edge:** Segmented reeding

Date	Mintage	F12	VF20	XF40	MS60	MS63
2004Mo	249,134	—	—	—	35.00	40.00

KM# 807 100 PESOS
29.17 g., Bi-Metallic, 34.5 mm. **Series:** First **Subject:** 180th Anniversary of Federation **Obv:** National arms **Obv. Legend:** ESTADOS UNIDOS MEXICANOS **Rev:** State arms **Rev. Legend:** ESTADO DE QUINTANA ROO **Edge:** Segmented reeding

Date	Mintage	F12	VF20	XF40	MS60	MS63
2004Mo	1,000	**PF65** 1,200				

KM# 734 100 PESOS
33.94 g., Bi-Metallic, 39.04 mm. **Series:** First **Subject:** 180th Anniversary of Federation **Obv:** National arms **Obv. Legend:** ESTADOS UNIDOS MEXICANOS **Rev:** State arms **Rev. Legend:** ESTADO DE QUERÉTARO ARTEAGA **Edge:** Segmented reeding

Date	Mintage	F12	VF20	XF40	MS60	MS63
2004Mo	249,263	—	—	—	35.00	40.00

KM# 808 100 PESOS
29.17 g., Bi-Metallic, 34.5 mm. **Series:** First **Subject:** 180th Anniversary of Federation **Obv:** National arms **Obv. Legend:** ESTADOS UNIDOS MEXICANOS **Rev:** State arms **Rev. Legend:** ESTADO DE QUERÉTARO ARTEAGA **Edge:** Segmented reeding

Date	Mintage	F12	VF20	XF40	MS60	MS63
2004Mo	1,000	PF65 1,200				

KM# 742 100 PESOS
33.94 g., Bi-Metallic, 39.04 mm. **Series:** First **Subject:** 180th Anniversary of Federation **Obv:** National arms **Obv. Legend:** ESTADOS UNIDOS MEXICANOS **Rev:** State arms **Rev. Legend:** ESTADO DE NUEVO LEÓN **Edge:** Segmented reeding

Date	Mintage	F12	VF20	XF40	MS60	MS63
2004Mo	249,199	—	—	—	35.00	40.00

KM# 811 100 PESOS
29.17 g., Bi-Metallic, 34.5 mm. **Series:** First **Subject:** 180th Anniversary of Federation **Obv:** National arms **Obv. Legend:** ESTADOS UNIDOS MEXICANOS **Rev:** State arms **Rev. Legend:** ESTADO DE NUEVO LEÓN **Edge:** Segmented reeding

Date	Mintage	F12	VF20	XF40	MS60	MS63
2004Mo	1,000	PF65 1,200				

KM# 804 100 PESOS
33.94 g., Bi-Metallic, 39.04 mm. **Series:** First **Subject:** 180th Anniversary of Federation **Obv:** National arms **Obv. Legend:** ESTADOS UNIDOS MEXICANOS **Rev:** State arms **Rev. Legend:** ESTADO DE MICHOACÁN DE OCAMPO **Edge:** Segmented reeding

Date	Mintage	F12	VF20	XF40	MS60	MS63
2004Mo	249,492	—	—	—	35.00	40.00

KM# 814 100 PESOS
29.17 g., Bi-Metallic, 34.5 mm. **Series:** First **Subject:** 180th Anniversary of Federation **Obv:** National arms **Obv. Legend:** ESTADOS UNIDOS MEXICANOS **Rev:** State arms **Rev. Legend:** ESTADO DE MICHOACÁN DE OCAMPO **Edge:** Segmented reeding

Date	Mintage	F12	VF20	XF40	MS60	MS63
2004Mo	1,000	PF65 1,200				

KM# 738 100 PESOS
33.94 g., Bi-Metallic, 39.04 mm. **Series:** First **Subject:** 180th Anniversary of Federation **Obv:** National arms **Obv. Legend:** ESTADOS UNIDOS MEXICANOS **Rev:** State arms **Rev. Legend:** ESTADO DE PUEBLA **Edge:** Segmented reeding

Date	Mintage	F12	VF20	XF40	MS60	MS63
2004Mo	248,850	—	—	—	35.00	40.00

KM# 809 100 PESOS
Bi-Metallic, 34.5 mm. **Series:** First **Subject:** 180th Anniversary of Federation **Obv:** National arms **Obv. Legend:** ESTADOS UNIDOS MEXICANOS **Rev:** State arms **Rev. Legend:** ESTADO DE PUEBLA **Edge:** Segmented reeding

Date	Mintage	F12	VF20	XF40	MS60	MS63
2004Mo	1,000	PF65 1,200				

KM# 744 100 PESOS
33.94 g., Bi-Metallic, 39.04 mm. **Series:** First **Subject:** 180th Anniversary of Federation **Obv:** National arms **Obv. Legend:** ESTADOS UNIDOS MEXICANOS **Rev:** State arms **Rev. Legend:** ESTADO DE NAYARIT **Edge:** Segmented reeding

Date	Mintage	F12	VF20	XF40	MS60	MS63
2004Mo	248,305	—	—	—	35.00	40.00

KM# 812 100 PESOS
29.17 g., Bi-Metallic, 34.5 mm. **Series:** First **Subject:** 180th Anniversary of Federation **Obv:** National arms **Obv. Legend:** ESTADOS UNIDOS MEXICANOS **Rev:** State arms **Rev. Legend:** ESTADO DE NAYARIT **Edge:** Segmented reeding

Date	Mintage	F12	VF20	XF40	MS60	MS63
2004Mo	1,000	PF65 1,200				

KM# 748 100 PESOS
33.94 g., Bi-Metallic, 39.04 mm. **Series:** First **Subject:** 180th Anniversary of Federation **Obv:** National arms **Obv. Legend:** ESTADOS UNIDOS MEXICANOS **Rev:** State arms **Rev. Legend:** ESTADO DE MÉXICO **Edge:** Segmented reeding

Date	Mintage	F12	VF20	XF40	MS60	MS63
2004Mo	249,800	—	—	—	35.00	40.00

KM# 815 100 PESOS
29.17 g., Bi-Metallic, 34.5 mm. **Series:** First **Subject:** 180th Anniversary of Federation **Obv:** National arms **Obv. Legend:** ESTADOS UNIDOS MEXICANOS **Rev:** State arms **Rev. Legend:** ESTADO DE MÉXICO **Edge:** Segmented reeding

Date	Mintage	F12	VF20	XF40	MS60	MS63
2004Mo	1,000	PF65 1,200				

KM# 740 100 PESOS
33.94 g., Bi-Metallic, 39.04 mm. **Series:** First **Subject:** 180th Anniversary of Federation **Obv:** National arms **Obv. Legend:** ESTADOS UNIDOS MEXICANOS **Rev:** State arms **Rev. Legend:** ESTADO DE OAXACA **Edge:** Segmented reeding

Date	Mintage	F12	VF20	XF40	MS60	MS63
2004Mo	249,589	—	—	—	35.00	40.00

KM# 810 100 PESOS
29.17 g., Bi-Metallic, 34.5 mm. **Series:** First **Subject:** 180th Anniversary of Federation **Obv:** National arms **Obv. Legend:** ESTADOS UNIDOS MEXICANOS **Rev:** State arms **Rev. Legend:** ESTADO DE OAXACA **Edge:** Segmented reeding

Date	Mintage	F12	VF20	XF40	MS60	MS63
2004Mo	1,000	PF65 1,200				

KM# 746 100 PESOS
33.94 g., Bi-Metallic, 39.04 mm. **Series:** First **Subject:** 180th Anniversary of Federation **Obv:** National arms **Obv. Legend:** ESTADOS UNIDOS MEXICANOS **Rev:** State arms **Rev. Legend:** ESTADO DE MORELOS **Edge:** Segmented reeding

Date	Mintage	F12	VF20	XF40	MS60	MS63
2004Mo	249,260	—	—	—	35.00	40.00

KM# 813 100 PESOS
29.17 g., Bi-Metallic, 34.5 mm. **Series:** First **Subject:** 180th Anniversary of Federation **Obv:** National arms **Obv. Legend:** ESTADOS UNIDOS MEXICANOS **Rev:** State arms **Rev. Legend:** ESTADO DE MORELOS **Edge:** Segmented reeding

Date	Mintage	F12	VF20	XF40	MS60	MS63
2004Mo	1,000	PF65 1,200				

KM# 750 100 PESOS
33.94 g., Bi-Metallic, 39.04 mm. **Series:** First **Subject:** 180th Anniversary of Federation **Obv:** National arms **Obv. Legend:** ESTADOS UNIDOS MEXICANOS **Rev:** State arms **Rev. Legend:** ESTADO DE JALISCO **Edge:** Segmented reeding

Date	Mintage	F12	VF20	XF40	MS60	MS63
2004Mo	249,115	—	—	—	35.00	40.00

KM# 816 100 PESOS
29.17 g., Bi-Metallic, 34.5 mm. **Series:** First **Subject:** 180th Anniversary of Federation **Obv:** National arms **Obv. Legend:** ESTADOS UNIDOS MEXICANOS **Rev:** State arms **Rev. Legend:** ESTADO DE JALISCO **Edge:** Segmented reeding

Date	Mintage	F12	VF20	XF40	MS60	MS63
2004Mo	1,000	PF65 1,200				

KM# 705 100 PESOS

33.74 g., Bi-Metallic, 39 mm. **Subject:** 400th Anniversary of Don Quijote de la Manchia **Obv:** National arms **Obv. Legend:** ESTADOS UNIDOS MEXICANOS **Rev:** Skeletal figure on horseback with spear galloping right **Edge:** Segmented reeding

Date	Mintage	F12	VF20	XF40	MS60	MS63
2005Mo	726,833	—	—	—	25.00	32.00
2005Mo Prooflike	3,761	—	—	—	—	75.00
2006Mo	5,201	**PF63** 60.00				

KM# 730 100 PESOS

33.83 g., Bi-Metallic, 39.9 mm. **Subject:** Monetary Reform Centennial **Obv:** National arms **Rev:** Radiant Liberty Cap divides date above value within circle **Edge:** Segmented reeding

Date	Mintage	F12	VF20	XF40	MS60	MS63
2005Mo	49,716	—	—	—	40.00	45.00
2005Mo	—	**PF63** 75.00				

KM# 731 100 PESOS

33.83 g., Bi-Metallic, 39.9 mm. **Subject:** Mexico City Mint's 470th Anniversary **Obv:** National arms **Rev:** Screw press, value and date within circle **Edge:** Segmented reeding

Date	Mintage	F12	VF20	XF40	MS60	MS63
2005Mo	49,895	—	—	—	40.00	45.00
2005Mo	—	**PF63** 95.00				

KM# 732 100 PESOS

33.83 g., Bi-Metallic, 39.9 mm. **Subject:** Bank of Mexico's 80th Anniversary **Obv:** National arms **Rev:** Back design of the 1925 hundred peso note **Edge:** Segmented reeding

Date	Mintage	F12	VF20	XF40	MS60	MS63
2005Mo	49,712	—	—	—	40.00	45.00
2005Mo	—	**PF63** 95.00				

KM# 717 100 PESOS

33.94 g., Bi-Metallic, 39.04 mm. **Series:** First **Subject:** 180th Anniversary of Federation **Obv:** National arms **Obv. Legend:** ESTADOS UNIDOS MEXICANOS **Rev:** State arms **Rev. Legend:** ESTADO DE HIDALGO **Edge:** Segmented reeding

Date	Mintage	F12	VF20	XF40	MS60	MS63
2005Mo	249,820	—	—	—	35.00	40.00

KM# 817 100 PESOS

29.17 g., Bi-Metallic, 34.5 mm. **Series:** First **Subject:** 180th Anniversary of Federation **Obv:** National arms **Obv. Legend:** ESTADOS UNIDOS MEXICANOS **Rev:** State arms **Rev. Legend:** ESTADO DE HIDALGO **Edge:** Segmented reeding

Date	Mintage	F12	VF20	XF40	MS60	MS63
2005Mo	1,000	**PF65** 1,200				

KM# 716 100 PESOS

33.94 g., Bi-Metallic, 39.04 mm. **Series:** First **Subject:** 180th Anniversary of Federation **Obv:** National arms **Obv. Legend:** ESTADOS UNIDOS MEXICANOS **Rev:** State arms **Rev. Legend:** ESTADO DE GUERRERO **Edge:** Segmented reeding

Date	Mintage	F12	VF20	XF40	MS60	MS63
2005Mo	248,850	—	—	—	35.00	40.00

KM# 818 100 PESOS

29.17 g., Bi-Metallic, 34.5 mm. **Series:** First **Subject:** 180th Anniversary of Federation **Obv:** National arms **Obv. Legend:** ESTADOS UNIDOS MEXICANOS **Rev:** State arms **Rev. Legend:** ESTADO DE GUERRERO **Edge:** Segmented reeding

Date	Mintage	F12	VF20	XF40	MS60	MS63
2005Mo	1,000	**PF65** 1,200				

KM# 715 100 PESOS

33.94 g., Bi-Metallic, 39.04 mm. **Series:** First **Subject:** 180th Anniversary of Federation **Obv:** National arms **Obv. Legend:** ESTADOS UNIDOS MEXICANOS **Rev:** State arms **Rev. Legend:** ESTADO DE GUANAJUATO **Edge:** Segmented reeding

Date	Mintage	F12	VF20	XF40	MS60	MS63
2005Mo	249,489	—	—	—	35.00	40.00

KM# 819 100 PESOS

29.17 g., Bi-Metallic, 34.5 mm. **Series:** First **Subject:** 180th Anniversary of Federation **Obv:** National arms **Obv. Legend:** ESTADOS UNIDOS MEXICANOS **Rev:** State arms **Rev. Legend:** ESTADO DE GUANAJUATO **Edge:** Segmented reeding

Date	Mintage	F12	VF20	XF40	MS60	MS63
2005Mo	1,000	**PF65** 1,200				

KM# 714 100 PESOS

33.94 g., Bi-Metallic, 39.04 mm. **Series:** First **Subject:** 180th Anniversary of Federation **Obv:** National arms **Obv. Legend:** ESTADOS UNIDOS MEXICANOS **Rev:** State arms **Rev. Legend:** ESTADO DE DURANGO **Edge:** Segmented reeding

Date	Mintage	F12	VF20	XF40	MS60	MS63
2005Mo	249,774	—	—	—	35.00	40.00

KM# 820 100 PESOS

29.17 g., Bi-Metallic, 34.5 mm. **Series:** First **Subject:** 180th Anniversary of Federation **Obv:** National arms **Obv. Legend:** ESTADOS UNIDOS MEXICANOS **Rev:** State arms **Rev. Legend:** ESTADO DE DURANGO **Edge:** Segmented reeding

Date	Mintage	F12	VF20	XF40	MS60	MS63
2005Mo	1,000	**PF65** 1,200				

KM# 713 100 PESOS

33.94 g., Bi-Metallic, 39.04 mm. **Series:** First **Subject:** 180th Anniversary of Federation **Obv:** National arms **Obv. Legend:** ESTADOS UNIDOS MEXICANOS **Rev:** Federal District arms **Rev. Legend:** DISTRITO FEDERAL **Edge:** Segmented reeding

Date	Mintage	F12	VF20	XF40	MS60	MS63
2005Mo	249,461	—	—	—	35.00	40.00

KM# 821 100 PESOS

29.17 g., Bi-Metallic, 34.5 mm. **Series:** First **Subject:** 180th Anniversary of Federation **Obv:** National arms **Obv. Legend:** ESTADOS UNIDOS MEXICANOS **Rev:** Federal District arms **Rev. Legend:** DISTRITO FEDERAL **Edge:** Segmented reeding

Date	Mintage	F12	VF20	XF40	MS60	MS63
2005Mo	1,000	**PF65** 1,200				

KM# 754 100 PESOS

33.94 g., Bi-Metallic, 39.04 mm. **Series:** First **Subject:** 180th Anniversary of Federation **Obv:** National arms **Obv. Legend:** ESTADOS UNIDOS MEXICANOS **Rev:** State arms **Rev. Legend:** ESTADO DE CHIHUAHUA **Edge:** Segmented reeding

Date	Mintage	F12	VF20	XF40	MS60	MS63
2005Mo	249,102	—	—	—	35.00	40.00

KM# 822 100 PESOS

29.17 g., Bi-Metallic, 34.5 mm. **Series:** First **Subject:** 180th Anniversary of Federation **Obv:** National arms **Obv. Legend:** ESTADOS UNIDOS MEXICANOS **Rev:** State arms **Rev. Legend:** ESTADO DE CHIHUAHUA **Edge:** Segmented reeding

Date	Mintage	F12	VF20	XF40	MS60	MS63
2005Mo	1,000	**PF65** 1,200				

KM# 712 100 PESOS
33.94 g., Bi-Metallic, 39.04 mm. **Series:** First **Subject:** 180th Anniversary of Federation **Obv:** National arms **Obv. Legend:** ESTADOS UNIDOS MEXICANOS **Rev:** State arms **Rev. Legend:** ESTADO DE CHIAPAS **Edge:** Segmented reeding

Date	Mintage	F12	VF20	XF40	MS60	MS63
2005Mo	249,417	—	—	—	35.00	40.00

KM# 823 100 PESOS
29.17 g., Bi-Metallic, 34.5 mm. **Series:** First **Subject:** 180th Anniversary of Federation **Obv:** National arms **Obv. Legend:** ESTADOS UNIDOS MEXICANOS **Rev:** State arms **Rev. Legend:** ESTADO DE CHIAPAS **Edge:** Segmented reeding

Date	Mintage	F12	VF20	XF40	MS60	MS63
2005Mo	1,000	PF65 1,200				

KM# 727 100 PESOS
33.94 g., Bi-Metallic, 39.04 mm. **Series:** First **Subject:** 180th Anniversary of Federation **Obv:** National arms **Obv. Legend:** ESTADOS UNIDOS MEXICANOS **Rev:** State arms **Rev. Legend:** ESTADO DE CAMPECHE **Edge:** Segmented reeding

Date	Mintage	F12	VF20	XF40	MS60	MS63
2005Mo	249,040	—	—	—	35.00	40.00

KM# 826 100 PESOS
29.17 g., Bi-Metallic, 34.5 mm. **Series:** First **Subject:** 180th Anniversary of Federation **Obv:** National arms **Obv. Legend:** ESTADOS UNIDOS MEXICANOS **Rev:** State arms **Rev. Legend:** ESTADO DE CAMPECHE **Edge:** Segmented reeding

Date	Mintage	F12	VF20	XF40	MS60	MS63
2005Mo	1,000	PF65 1,200				

KM# 721 100 PESOS
33.94 g., Bi-Metallic, 39.04 mm. **Series:** First **Subject:** 180th Anniversary of Federation **Obv:** National arms **Obv. Legend:** ESTADOS UNIDOS MEXICANOS **Rev:** Estados de Aguascalientes state arms **Rev. Legend:** ESTADO DE AGUASCALIENTES **Edge:** Segmented reeding

Date	Mintage	F12	VF20	XF40	MS60	MS63
2005Mo	248,410	—	—	—	35.00	40.00

KM# 829 100 PESOS
29.17 g., Bi-Metallic, 34.5 mm. **Series:** First **Subject:** 180th Anniversary of Federation **Obv:** National arms **Obv. Legend:** ESTADOS UNIDOS MEXICANOS **Rev:** State arms **Rev. Legend:** ESTADO DE AGUASCALIENTES **Edge:** Segmented reeding

Date	Mintage	F12	VF20	XF40	MS60	MS63
2005Mo	1,000	PF65 1,200				

KM# 729 100 PESOS
33.83 g., Bi-Metallic, 39.04 mm. **Series:** First **Subject:** 180th Anniversary of Federation **Obv:** National arms **Obv. Legend:** ESTADOS UNIDOS MEXICANOS **Rev:** State arms **Rev. Legend:** ESTADO DE COLIMA **Edge:** Segmented reeding

Date	Mintage	F12	VF20	XF40	MS60	MS63
2005Mo	248,850	—	—	—	35.00	40.00

KM# 824 100 PESOS
29.17 g., Bi-Metallic, 34.5 mm. **Series:** First **Subject:** 180th Anniversary of Federation **Obv:** National arms **Obv. Legend:** ESTADOS UNIDOS MEXICANOS **Rev:** State arms **Rev. Legend:** ESTADO DE COLIMA **Edge:** Segmented reeding

Date	Mintage	F12	VF20	XF40	MS60	MS63
2005Mo	1,000	PF65 1,200				

KM# 725 100 PESOS
33.94 g., Bi-Metallic, 39.04 mm. **Series:** First **Subject:** 180th Anniversary of Federation **Obv:** National arms **Obv. Legend:** ESTADOS UNIDOS MEXICANOS **Rev:** State arms **Rev. Legend:** ESTADO DE BAJA CALIFORNIA SUR **Edge:** Segmented reeding

Date	Mintage	F12	VF20	XF40	MS60	MS63
2005Mo	249,585	—	—	—	35.00	40.00

KM# 827 100 PESOS
29.17 g., Bi-Metallic, 34.5 mm. **Series:** First **Subject:** 180th Anniversary of Federation **Obv:** National arms **Obv. Legend:** ESTADOS UNIDOS MEXICANOS **Rev:** State arms **Rev. Legend:** ESTADO DE BAJA CALIFORNIA SUR **Edge:** Segmented reeding

Date	Mintage	F12	VF20	XF40	MS60	MS63
2005Mo	1,000	PF65 1,200				

KM# 719 100 PESOS
33.83 g., Bi-Metallic, 39.04 mm. **Series:** Second **Obv:** National arms **Obv. Legend:** ESTADOS UNIDOS MEXICANOS **Rev:** Facade of the San Marcos garden above sculpture of national emblem at left, San Antonio Temple at right **Rev. Legend:** AGUASCALIENTES **Edge:** Segmented reeding

Date	Mintage	F12	VF20	XF40	MS60	MS63
2005Mo	149,705	—	—	—	25.00	30.00

KM# 862 100 PESOS
29.17 g., Bi-Metallic, 34.5 mm. **Series:** Second **Obv:** National arms **Obv. Legend:** ESTADOS UNIDOS MEXICANOS **Rev:** Facade of the San Marcos garden above sculpture of national emblem at left, San Antonio temple at right **Rev. Legend:** AGUASCALIENTES **Edge:** Segmented reeding

Date	Mintage	F12	VF20	XF40	MS60	MS63
2005Mo	600	PF65 1,200				

KM# 752 100 PESOS
33.94 g., Bi-Metallic, 39.04 mm. **Series:** First **Subject:** 180th Anniversary of Federation **Obv:** National arms **Obv. Legend:** ESTADOS UNIDOS MEXICANOS **Rev:** State arms **Rev. Legend:** ESTADO DE COAHUILA DE ZARAGOZA **Edge:** Segmented reeding

Date	Mintage	F12	VF20	XF40	MS60	MS63
2005Mo	247,991	—	—	—	35.00	40.00

KM# 825 100 PESOS
29.17 g., Bi-Metallic, 34.5 mm. **Series:** First **Subject:** 180th Anniversary of Federation **Obv:** National arms **Obv. Legend:** ESTADOS UNIDOS MEXICANOS **Rev:** State arms **Rev. Legend:** ESTADO DE COAHUILA DE ZARAGOZA **Edge:** Segmented reeding

Date	Mintage	F12	VF20	XF40	MS60	MS63
2005Mo	1,000	PF65 1,200				

KM# 723 100 PESOS
33.94 g., Bi-Metallic, 39.04 mm. **Series:** First **Subject:** 180th Anniversary of Federation **Obv:** National arms **Obv. Legend:** ESTADOS UNIDOS MEXICANOS **Rev:** State arms **Rev. Legend:** ESTADO DE BAJA CALIFORNIA **Edge:** Segmented reeding

Date	Mintage	F12	VF20	XF40	MS60	MS63
2005Mo	249,263	—	—	—	35.00	40.00

KM# 828 100 PESOS
29.17 g., Bi-Metallic, 34.5 mm. **Series:** First **Subject:** 180th Anniversary of Federation **Obv:** National arms **Obv. Legend:** ESTADOS UNIDOS MEXICANOS **Rev:** State arms **Rev. Legend:** ESTADO DE BAJA CALIFORNIA **Edge:** Segmented reeding

Date	Mintage	F12	VF20	XF40	MS60	MS63
2005Mo	1,000	PF65 1,200				

KM# 758 100 PESOS
33.94 g., Bi-Metallic, 39.04 mm. **Series:** Second **Obv:** National arms **Obv. Legend:** ESTADOS UNIDOS MEXICANOS **Rev:** Ram's head and value within circle **Rev. Legend:** BAJA CALIFORNIA - GOBIERNO DEL ESTADO **Edge:** Segmented reeding

Date	Mintage	F12	VF20	XF40	MS60	MS63
2005Mo	149,771	—	—	—	25.00	30.00

KM# 863 100 PESOS
29.17 g., Bi-Metallic, 34.5 mm. **Series:** Second **Obv:** National arms **Obv. Legend:** ESTTADOS UNIDOS MEXICANOS **Rev:** Ram's head, mountain outline in background **Rev. Legend:** BAJA CALIFORNIA - GOBIERNO DEL ESTADO **Edge:** Segmented reeding

Date	Mintage	F12	VF20	XF40	MS60	MS63
2005Mo	600	PF65 1,200				

KM# 762 100 PESOS
33.94 g., Bi-Metallic, 39.04 mm. **Series:** Second **Obv:** National arms **Obv. Legend:** ESTADOS UNIDOS MEXICANOS **Rev:** Outlined map of peninsula at center, cave painting of deer behind, cactus at right **Rev. Legend:** ESTADO DE BAJA CALIFORNIA SUR **Edge:** Segmented reeding

Date	Mintage	F12	VF20	XF40	MS60	MS63
2005Mo	149,152	—	—	—	25.00	30.00

KM# 764 100 PESOS
33.70 g., Bi-Metallic **Subject:** 200th Anniversary Birth of Benito Juarez Garcia **Obv:** National arms **Rev:** Bust 1/4 left within circle

Date	Mintage	F12	VF20	XF40	MS60	MS63
2006Mo	49,913	—	—	—	40.00	45.00

KM# 864 100 PESOS
29.17 g., Bi-Metallic, 34.5 mm. **Series:** Second **Obv:** National arms **Obv. Legend:** ESTADOS UNIDOS MEXICANOS **Rev:** Outlined map of peninsula at center, cave painting of deer behind, cactus at right **Rev. Legend:** ESTADO DE BAJA CALIFORNIA SUR **Edge:** Segmented reeding

Date	Mintage	F12	VF20	XF40	MS60	MS63
2006Mo	600	PF65 1,200				

KM# 760 100 PESOS
33.94 g., Bi-Metallic, 39.04 mm. **Series:** Second **Subject:** Estado de Campeche **Obv:** National arms **Obv. Legend:** ESTADOS UNIDOS MEXICANOS **Rev:** Jade mask - Calakmul, Campeche **Rev. Legend:** ESTADO DE CAMPECHE **Edge:** Segmented reeding

Date	Mintage	F12	VF20	XF40	MS60	MS63
2006Mo	149,803	—	—	—	25.00	30.00

KM# 865 100 PESOS
29.17 g., Bi-Metallic, 34.5 mm. **Series:** Second **Obv:** National arms **Obv. Legend:** ESTADOS UNIDOS MEXICANOS **Rev:** Jade mask - Calakmul, Campeche **Rev. Legend:** ESTADO DE CAMPECHE **Edge:** Segmented reeding

Date	Mintage	F12	VF20	XF40	MS60	MS63
2006Mo	600	PF65 1,200				

KM# 781 100 PESOS
33.70 g., Bi-Metallic, 39.04 mm. **Series:** Second **Obv:** National arms **Obv. Legend:** ESTADOS UNIDOS MEXICANOS **Rev:** Outlined map with turtle, mine cart above grapes at center, Friendship Dam above Christ of the Nodas at left, chimneys above crucibles and bell tower of Santiago's cathedral at right **Rev. Legend:** COAHUILA DE ZARAGOZA **Edge:** Segmented reeding

Date	Mintage	F12	VF20	XF40	MS60	MS63
2006Mo	149,560	—	—	—	25.00	30.00

KM# 866 100 PESOS
29.17 g., Bi-Metallic, 34.5 mm. **Series:** Second **Obv:** National arms **Obv. Legend:** ESTADOS UNIDOS MEXICANOS **Rev:** Outlined map with turtle, mine cart above grapes at center, Friendship dam above Christ of the Nodas at left, chimneys above crucibles and bell tower of Santiago's cathedral at right **Rev. Inscription:** COAHUILA DE ZARAGOZA **Edge:** Segmented reeding

Date	Mintage	F12	VF20	XF40	MS60	MS63
2006Mo	600	PF65 1,200				

KM# 777 100 PESOS
33.94 g., Bi-Metallic, 39.04 mm. **Series:** Second **Obv:** National arms **Obv. Legend:** ESTADOS UNIDOS MEXICANOS **Rev:** State arms at lower center, Nevado de Colima and Volcan de Fuego volcanos in background **Rev. Legend:** Colima **Rev. Inscription:** GENEROSO **Edge:** Segmented reeding

Date	Mintage	F12	VF20	XF40	MS60	MS63
2006Mo	149,041	—	—	—	25.00	30.00

KM# 867 100 PESOS
29.17 g., Bi-Metallic, 34.5 mm. **Series:** Second **Obv:** National arms **Obv. Legend:** ESTADOS UNIDOS MEXICANOS **Rev:** State arms at lower center, Nevado de Colima and Volcan de Fuego volcanos in background **Rev. Legend:** Colima **Rev. Inscription:** GENEROSO **Edge:** Segmented reeding

Date	Mintage	F12	VF20	XF40	MS60	MS63
2006Mo	600	PF65 1,200				

KM# 773 100 PESOS
33.94 g., Bi-Metallic, 39.04 mm. **Series:** Second **Obv:** National arms **Obv. Legend:** ESTADOS UNIDOS MEXICANOS **Rev:** Head of Pakal, ancient Mayan king, Palenque **Rev. Legend:** ESTADO DE CHIAPAS - CABEZA MAYA DEL REY PAKAL, PALENQUE **Edge:** Segmented reeding

Date	Mintage	F12	VF20	XF40	MS60	MS63
2006Mo	149,491	—	—	—	25.00	30.00

KM# 868 100 PESOS
29.17 g., Bi-Metallic, 34.5 mm. **Series:** Second **Obv:** National arms **Obv. Legend:** ESTADOS UNIDOS MEXICANOS **Rev:** Head of Pakal, ancient Mayan king, Palenque **Rev. Legend:** ESTADO DE CHIAPAS - CABEZA MAYA DEL REY PAKAL, PALENQUE **Edge:** Segmented reeding

Date	Mintage	F12	VF20	XF40	MS60	MS63
2006Mo	600	PF65 1,200				

KM# 775 100 PESOS
33.94 g., Bi-Metallic, 39.04 mm. **Series:** Second **Obv:** National arms **Obv. Legend:** ESTADOS UNIDOS MEXICANOS **Rev:** Angel of Liberty **Rev. Legend:** MÉXICO - ANGEL DE LA LIBERTAD, CHIHUAHUA **Edge:** Segmented reeding

Date	Mintage	F12	VF20	XF40	MS60	MS63
2006Mo	149,557	—	—	—	25.00	30.00

KM# 869 100 PESOS
29.17 g., Bi-Metallic, 34.5 mm. **Series:** Second **Obv:** National arms **Obv. Legend:** ESTADOS UNIDOS MEXICANOS **Rev:** Angel of Liberty **Rev. Legend:** MÉXICO - ANGEL DE LA LIBERTAD, CHIHUAHUA **Edge:** Segmented reeding

Date	Mintage	F12	VF20	XF40	MS60	MS63
2006Mo	600	PF65 1,200				

KM# 779 100 PESOS
33.94 g., Bi-Metallic, 39.04 mm. **Series:** Second **Obv:** National arms **Obv. Legend:** ESTADOS UNIDOS MEXICANOS **Rev:** National Palace **Rev. Legend:** DISTRITO FEDERAL - ANTIGUO AYUNTAMIENTO **Edge:** Segmented reeding

Date	Mintage	F12	VF20	XF40	MS60	MS63
2006Mo	149,525	—	—	—	25.00	30.00

KM# 870 100 PESOS
29.17 g., Bi-Metallic, 34.5 mm. **Series:** Second **Obv:** National arms **Obv. Legend:** ESTADOS UNIDOS MEXICANOS **Rev:** National palace **Rev. Legend:** DISTRITO FEDERAL - ANTIGUO AYUNTAMIENTO **Edge:** Segmented reeding

Date	Mintage	F12	VF20	XF40	MS60	MS63
2006Mo	600	PF65 1,200				

KM# 787 100 PESOS
33.94 g., Bi-Metallic, 39.04 mm. **Series:** Second **Obv:** National arms **Obv. Legend:** ESTADOS UNIDOS MEXICANOS **Rev:** Tree **Rev. Legend:** PRIMERA RESERVA NACIONAL FORESTAL - DURANGO **Edge:** Segmented reeding

Date	Mintage	F12	VF20	XF40	MS60	MS63
2006Mo	149,034	—	—	—	25.00	30.00

KM# 871 100 PESOS
29.17 g., Bi-Metallic, 34.5 mm. **Series:** Second **Obv:** National arms **Obv. Legend:** ESYADOS UNIDOS MEXICANOS **Rev:** Tree **Rev. Legend:** PRIMERA RESERVA NACIONAL RORESTAL - DURANGO **Edge:** Segmented reeding

Date	Mintage	F12	VF20	XF40	MS60	MS63
2006Mo	600	**PF65** 1,200				

KM# 789 100 PESOS
33.94 g., Bi-Metallic, 39.04 mm. **Series:** Second **Obv:** National arms **Obv. Legend:** ESTADOS UNIDOS MEXICANOS **Rev:** State arms at center, statue of Miguel Hidalgo at left, monument to Pipla at lower right **Rev. Inscription:** Guanajuato **Edge:** Segmented reeding

Date	Mintage	F12	VF20	XF40	MS60	MS63
2006Mo	149,921	—	—	—	25.00	30.00

KM# 872 100 PESOS
29.17 g., Bi-Metallic, 34.50 mm. **Series:** Second **Obv:** National arms **Obv. Legend:** ESTADOS UNIDOS MEXICANOS **Rev:** State arms at lower center, statue of Miguel Hidalgo at left, monument to Pipila at lower right **Rev. Inscription:** Guanajauto **Edge:** Segmented reeding

Date	Mintage	F12	VF20	XF40	MS60	MS63
2006Mo	600	**PF65** 1,200				

KM# 791 100 PESOS
33.94 g., Bi-Metallic, 39.04 mm. **Series:** Second **Obv:** National arms **Obv. Legend:** ESTADOS UNIDOS MEXICANOS **Rev:** Stylized portrait of Vicente Guerrero at left, church of Taxco at upper center, Acapulco's la Quebrada with diver above Christmas Eve flower and mask **Rev. Legend:** GUERRERO **Edge:** Segmented reeding

Date	Mintage	F12	VF20	XF40	MS60	MS63
2006Mo	149,675	—	—	—	25.00	30.00

KM# 873 100 PESOS
29.17 g., Bi-Metallic, 34.5 mm. **Series:** Second **Obv:** National arms **Obv. Legend:** ESTADOS UNIDOS MEXICANOS **Rev:** Stylized portrait of Vicente Guerrero at left, church of Taxco at upper center, Acapulco's la Quebrada with diver over Christmas Eve flower and mask **Rev. Legend:** GUERRERO **Edge:** Segmented reeding

Date	Mintage	F12	VF20	XF40	MS60	MS63
2006Mo	600	**PF65** 1,200				

KM# 793 100 PESOS
33.94 g., Bi-Metallic, 39.04 mm. **Series:** Second **Obv:** National arms **Obv. Legend:** ESTADOS UNIDOS MEXICANOS **Rev:** Monument of Pachuca Hidalgo **Rev. Inscription:** RELOJ / MONUMENTAL / DE / PACHUCA / HIDALGO - La / Bella / Airosa **Edge:** Segmented reeding

Date	Mintage	F12	VF20	XF40	MS60	MS63
2006Mo	149,273	—	—	—	25.00	30.00

KM# 874 100 PESOS
29.17 g., Bi-Metallic, 34.5 mm. **Series:** Second **Obv:** National arms **Obv. Legend:** ESTADOS UNIDOS MEXICANOS **Rev:** Monument of Pachuca Hidalgo **Rev. Inscription:** RELOJ / MONUMENTAL / DE / PACHUCA / HIDALGO **Edge:** Segmented reeding

Date	Mintage	F12	VF20	XF40	MS60	MS63
2006Mo	600	**PF65** 1,200				

KM# 795 100 PESOS
33.94 g., Bi-Metallic, 39.04 mm. **Series:** Second **Obv:** National arms **Obv. Legend:** ESTADOS UNIDOS MEXICANOS **Rev:** Hospicio Cabañas orphanage **Rev. Legend:** ESTADO DE JALISCO **Edge:** Segmented reeding

Date	Mintage	F12	VF20	XF40	MS60	MS63
2006Mo	149,750	—	—	—	25.00	30.00

KM# 875 100 PESOS
29.17 g., Bi-Metallic, 34.5 mm. **Series:** Second **Obv:** National arms **Obv. Legend:** ESTADOS UNIDOS MEXICANOS **Rev:** Hospicio Cabañas orphanage **Rev. Legend:** ESTADO DE JALISCO **Edge:** Segmented reeding

Date	Mintage	F12	VF20	XF40	MS60	MS63
2006Mo	600	**PF65** 1,200				

KM# 802 100 PESOS
33.94 g., Bi-Metallic, 39.04 mm. **Series:** Second **Obv:** National arms **Obv. Legend:** ESTADOS UNIDOS MEXICANOS **Rev:** Pyramid de la Loona (moon) **Rev. Legend:** ESTADO DE MÉXICO **Edge:** Segmented reeding

Date	Mintage	F12	VF20	XF40	MS60	MS63
2006Mo	149,377	—	—	—	25.00	30.00

KM# 876 100 PESOS
29.17 g., Bi-Metallic, 34.5 mm. **Series:** Second **Obv:** National arms **Obv. Legend:** ESTADOS UNIDOS MEXICANOS **Rev:** Pyramid de la Looona (moon) **Rev. Legend:** ESTADO DE MÉXICO **Edge:** Segmented reeding

Date	Mintage	F12	VF20	XF40	MS60	MS63
2006Mo	600	**PF65** 1,200				

KM# 785 100 PESOS
33.94 g., Bi-Metallic, 39.04 mm. **Series:** Second **Obv:** National arms **Obv. Legend:** ESTADOS UNIDOS MEXICANOS **Rev:** Four Monarch butterflies **Rev. Legend:** ESTADO DE MICHOACÁN **Edge:** Segmented reeding

Date	Mintage	F12	VF20	XF40	MS60	MS63
2006Mo	149,730	—	—	—	25.00	30.00

KM# 877 100 PESOS
29.17 g., Bi-Metallic, 34.5 mm. **Series:** Second **Obv:** National arms **Obv. Legend:** ESTADOS UNIDOS MEXICANOS **Rev:** Four Monarch butterflies **Rev. Legend:** ESTADO DE MICHOACÁN **Edge:** Segmented reeding

Date	Mintage	F12	VF20	XF40	MS60	MS63
2006Mo	600	**PF65** 1,200				

KM# 800 100 PESOS
33.94 g., Bi-Metallic, 39.04 mm. **Series:** Second **Obv:** National arms **Obv. Legend:** ESTADOS UNIDOS MEXICANOS **Rev:** 1/2 length figure of Chinelo (local dancer) at right, Palacio de Cortes in background **Rev. Inscription:** ESTADO DE / MORELOS **Edge:** Segmented reeding

Date	Mintage	F12	VF20	XF40	MS60	MS63
2006Mo	149,648	—	—	—	25.00	30.00

KM# 878 100 PESOS
29.17 g., Bi-Metallic, 34.5 mm. **Series:** Second **Obv:** National arms **Obv. Legend:** ESTADOS UNIDOS MEXICANOS **Rev:** 1/2 length figure of Chinelo (local dancer) at right, Palacio de Cortes in background **Rev. Inscription:** ESTADO DE / MORELOS **Edge:** Segmented reeding

Date	Mintage	F12	VF20	XF40	MS60	MS63
2006Mo	600	**PF65** 1,200				

KM# 798 100 PESOS
33.94 g., 33.825 Bi-Metallic 36.6721 oz., 39.04 mm. **Series:** Second **Obv:** National arms **Obv. Legend:** ESTADOS UNIDOS MEXICANOS **Rev:** Isle de Mexcaltitlán **Rev. Legend:** ESTADO DE NAYARIT **Edge:** Segmented reeding

Date	Mintage	F12	VF20	XF40	MS60	MS63
2007Mo	149,560	—	—	—	25.00	30.00

KM# 879 100 PESOS
29.17 g., Bi-Metallic, 34.5 mm. **Series:** Second **Obv:** National arms **Obv. Legend:** ESTADOS UNIDOS MEXICANOS **Rev:** Isle de Mexcaltitlán **Rev. Legend:** ESTADO DE NAYARIT **Edge:** Segmented reeding

Date	Mintage	F12	VF20	XF40	MS60	MS63
2007Mo	600	**PF65** 1,200				

KM# 848 100 PESOS
33.94 g., Bi-Metallic, 39.04 mm. **Series:** Second **Obv:** National arms **Obv. Legend:** ESTADOS UNIDOS MEXICANOE **Rev:** Old foundry in Parque Fundidora (public park) at right, Cerro de la Silla (Saddle Hill) in background **Rev. Legend:** ESTADO DE NUEVO LÉON **Edge:** Segmented reeding

Date	Mintage	F12	VF20	XF40	MS60	MS63
2007Mo	149,425	—	—	—	25.00	30.00

KM# 880 100 PESOS
29.17 g., Bi-Metallic, 34.5 mm. **Series:** Second **Obv:** National arms **Obv. Legend:** ESTADOS UNIDOS MEXICANOS **Rev:** Old foundry in Parque Fundidora (public park) at right, Cerro de la Silla (Saddle hill) in background **Rev. Legend:** ESTADO DE NUEVO LEÓN **Edge:** Segmented reeding

Date	Mintage	F12	VF20	XF40	MS60	MS63
2007Mo	600	**PF65** 1,200				

KM# 849 100 PESOS
33.94 g., Bi-Metallic, 39.04 mm. **Series:** Second **Obv:** National

arms **Obv. Legend:** ESTADOS UNIDOS MEXICANOS **Rev:** Teatro Macedonio Alcala (theater) **Rev. Legend:** OAXACA **Edge:** Segmented reeding

Date	Mintage	F12	VF20	XF40	MS60	MS63
2007Mo	149,892	—	—	—	25.00	30.00

KM# 881 100 PESOS
29.17 g., Bi-Metallic, 34.50 mm. **Series:** Second **Obv:** National arms **Obv. Legend:** ESTADOS UNIDOS MEXICANOS **Rev:** Teatro Macedonio Alcala (theater) **Rev. Legend:** OAXACA **Edge:** Segmented reeding

Date	Mintage	F12	VF20	XF40	MS60	MS63
2007Mo	600	**PF65** 1,200				

KM# 850 100 PESOS
33.94 g., Bi-Metallic, 39.04 mm. **Series:** Second **Obv:** National arms **Obv. Legend:** ESTADOS UNIDOS MEXICANOS **Rev:** Talavera porcelain dish **Rev. Legend:** ESTADO DE PUEBLA **Edge:** Segmented reeding

Date	Mintage	F12	VF20	XF40	MS60	MS63
2007Mo	149,474	—	—	—	25.00	30.00

KM# 882 100 PESOS
29.17 g., Bi-Metallic, 34.5 mm. **Series:** Second **Obv:** National arms **Obv. Legend:** ESTADOS UNIDOS MEXICANOS **Rev:** Talavera porcelain dish **Rev. Legend:** ESTADO DE PUEBLA **Edge:** Segmented reeding

Date	Mintage	F12	VF20	XF40	MS60	MS63
2007Mo	600	**PF65** 1,200				

KM# 851 100 PESOS
33.94 g., Bi-Metallic, 39.04 mm. **Series:** Second **Obv:** National arms **Obv. Legend:** ESTADOS UNIDOS MEXICANOS **Rev:** Mask at left, rays above state arms at center, Mayan ruins at right **Rev. Legend:** QUINTANA ROO **Edge:** Segmented reeding

Date	Mintage	F12	VF20	XF40	MS60	MS63
2007Mo	149,582	—	—	—	25.00	30.00

KM# 883 100 PESOS
29.17 g., Bi-Metallic, 34.5 mm. **Series:** Second **Obv:** National arms **Obv. Legend:** ESTADOS UNIDOS MEXICANOS **Rev:** Mask at left, rays above state arms at center, Mayan ruins at right **Rev. Legend:** QUINTANA ROO **Edge:** Segmented reeding

Date	Mintage	F12	VF20	XF40	MS60	MS63
2007Mo	600	**PF65** 1,200				

KM# 852 100 PESOS
33.94 g., Bi-Metallic, 39.04 mm. **Series:** Second **Obv:** National arms **Obv. Legend:** ESTADOS UNIDOS MEXICANOS **Rev:** Aqueduct of Querétaro at left, church of Santa Rosa de Viterbo at right **Rev. Legend:** ESTADO DE QUERÉTARO ARTEAGA **Edge:** Segmented reeding

Date	Mintage	F12	VF20	XF40	MS60	MS63
2007Mo	149,127	—	—	—	25.00	30.00

KM# 884 100 PESOS
29.17 g., Bi-Metallic, 34.5 mm. **Series:** Second **Obv:** National arms **Obv. Legend:** ESTADOS UNIDOS MEXICANOS **Rev:** Aqueduct of Querétaro at left, church of Santa Rosa de Viterbo at right **Rev. Legend:** ESTADO DE QUERÉTARO ARTEAGA **Edge:** Segmented reeding

Date	Mintage	F12	VF20	XF40	MS60	MS63
2007Mo	600	**PF65** 1,200				

KM# 853 100 PESOS
33.94 g., Bi-Metallic, 39.04 mm. **Series:** Second **Obv:** National arms **Obv. Legend:** ESTADOS UNIDOS MEXICANOS **Rev:** Facade of Caja Real **Rev. Legend:** • SAN LUIS POTOSÍ • **Edge:** Segmented reeding

Date	Mintage	F12	VF20	XF40	MS60	MS63
2007Mo	148,750	—	—	—	25.00	30.00

KM# 885 100 PESOS
29.17 g., Bi-Metallic, 34.5 mm. **Series:** Second **Obv:** National arms **Obv. Legend:** ESTADOS UNIDOS MEXICANOS **Rev:** Facade of Caja Real **Rev. Legend:** • SAN LUIS POTOSÍ • **Edge:** Segmented reeding

Date	Mintage	F12	VF20	XF40	MS60	MS63
2007Mo	600	**PF65** 1,200				

KM# 854 100 PESOS
33.94 g., Bi-Metallic, 39.04 mm. **Series:** Second **Obv:** National arms **Obv. Legend:** ESTADOS UNIDOS MEXICANOS **Rev:** Shield on pile of cactus fruits **Rev. Legend:** ESTADO DE SINALOA - LUGAR DE PITAHAYAS **Edge:** Segmented reeding

Date	Mintage	F12	VF20	XF40	MS60	MS63
2007Mo	149,032	—	—	—	25.00	30.00

KM# 886 100 PESOS
29.17 g., Bi-Metallic, 34.5 mm. **Series:** Second **Obv:** National arms **Obv. Legend:** ESTADOS UNIDOS MEXICANOS **Rev:** Shield on pile of cactus fruits **Rev. Legend:** ESTADO DE SINALOA - LUGAR DE PITAHAYES **Edge:** Segmented reeding

Date	Mintage	F12	VF20	XF40	MS60	MS63
2007Mo	600	**PF65** 1,200				

KM# 855 100 PESOS
33.94 g., Bi-Metallic, 39.04 mm. **Series:** Second **Obv:** National arms **Obv. Legend:** ESTADOS UNIDOS MEXICANOS **Rev:** Local in Dance of the Deer at left, cactus at right, mountains in background **Rev. Legend:** ESTADO DE SONORA **Edge:** Segmented reeding

Date	Mintage	F12	VF20	XF40	MS60	MS63
2007Mo	149,891	—	—	—	25.00	30.00

KM# 887 100 PESOS
29.17 g., Bi-Metallic, 34.5 mm. **Series:** Second **Obv:** National arms **Obv. Legend:** ESTADOS UNIDOS MEXICANOS **Rev:** Local in Dance of the Deer at left, cactus at right, mountains in background **Rev. Legend:** ESTADO DE SONORA **Edge:** Segmented reeding

Date	Mintage	F12	VF20	XF40	MS60	MS63
2007Mo	600	**PF65** 1,200				

KM# 856 100 PESOS
33.94 g., Bi-Metallic, 39.04 mm. **Series:** Second **Obv:** National arms **Obv. Legend:** ESTADOS UNIDOS MEXICANOS **Rev:** Fuente de los Pescadores (fisherman fountain) at lower left, giant head from the Olmec-pre-Hispanic culture at right, Planetario Tabasco in background **Rev. Legend:** TABASCO **Edge:** Segmented reeding

Date	Mintage	F12	VF20	XF40	MS60	MS63
2007Mo	149,715	—	—	—	25.00	30.00

KM# 888 100 PESOS
29.17 g., Bi-Metallic, 34.5 mm. **Series:** Second **Obv:** National arms **Obv. Legend:** ESTADOS UNIDOS MEXICANOS **Rev:** Fuente de los Pescadores (fisherman fountain) at lower left, giant head from the Olmec-pre-Hispanic culture at right, Planetario Tabasco in background **Rev. Legend:** TABASCO **Edge:** Segmented reeding

Date	Mintage	F12	VF20	XF40	MS60	MS63
2007Mo	600	**PF65** 1,200				

KM# 857 100 PESOS
33.94 g., Bi-Metallic, 39.04 mm. **Series:** Second **Obv:** National arms **Obv. Legend:** ESTADOS UNIDOS MEXICANOS **Rev:** Ridge - Cerro Del Bermal, Gonzáles **Rev. Legend:** TAMAULIPAS **Edge:** Segmented reeding

Date	Mintage	F12	VF20	XF40	MS60	MS63
2007Mo	149,776	—	—	—	25.00	30.00

KM# 889 100 PESOS
29.17 g., Bi-Metallic, 34.5 mm. **Series:** Second **Obv:** National arms **Obv. Legend:** ESTADOS DE MEXICANOS **Rev:** Ridge - Cerro Del Bemal, Gonzáles **Rev. Legend:** TAMAULIPAS **Edge:** Segmented reeding

Date	Mintage	F12	VF20	XF40	MS60	MS63
2007Mo	600	**PF65** 1,200				

KM# 858 100 PESOS
33.94 g., Bi-Metallic, 39.04 mm. **Series:** Second **Obv:** National arms **Obv. Legend:** ESTADOS UNIDOS MEXICANOS **Rev:** Basilica de Ocotlán at left, state arms above Capilla Abierta, Plaza de Toros Ranchero Aguilar below, Exconvento de San Francisco at right **Rev. Legend:** ESTADO DE TLAXCALA **Edge:** Segmented reeding

Date	Mintage	F12	VF20	XF40	MS60	MS63
2007Mo	149,465	—	—	—	25.00	30.00

KM# 890 100 PESOS
29.17 g., Bi-Metallic, 34.5 mm. **Series:** Second **Obv:** National arms **Obv. Legend:** ESTADOS UNIDOS MEXICANOS **Rev:** Basilica de Ocotlán at left, state arms above Capilla Abierta, Plaza de Toros Ranchero Aguilar below, Exconvento de San Francisco at right **Rev. Legend:** ESTADO DE TLAXCALA **Edge:** Segmented reeding

Date	Mintage	F12	VF20	XF40	MS60	MS63
2007Mo	600	PF65 1,200				

KM# 859 100 PESOS
33.94 g., Bi-Metallic, 39.04 mm. **Series:** Second **Obv:** National arms **Obv. Legend:** ESTADOS UNIDOS MEXICANOS **Rev:** Pyramid of El Tajín **Rev. Legend:** • VERACRUZ • • • DE IGNACIO DE LA LLAVE • **Edge:** Segmented reeding

Date	Mintage	F12	VF20	XF40	MS60	MS63
2007Mo	149,703	—	—	—	25.00	30.00

KM# 891 100 PESOS
29.17 g., Bi-Metallic, 34.5 mm. **Series:** Second **Obv:** National arms **Obv. Legend:** ESTADOS UNIDOS MEXICANOS **Rev:** Pyramid of El Tajín **Rev. Legend:** • VERACRUZ • • • DE IGNACIO DE LA LLAVE • **Edge:** Segmented reeding

Date	Mintage	F12	VF20	XF40	MS60	MS63
2007Mo	600	PF65 1,200				

KM# 860 100 PESOS
33.94 g., Bi-Metallic, 39.04 mm. **Series:** Second **Obv:** National arms **Obv. Legend:** ESTADOS UNIDOS MEXICANOS **Rev:** Stylized pyramid of Chichén Itzá **Rev. Legend:** Castillo de Chichén Itzá **Edge:** Segmented reeding

Date	Mintage	F12	VF20	XF40	MS60	MS63
2007Mo	149,579	—	—	—	25.00	30.00

KM# 892 100 PESOS
29.17 g., Bi-Metallic, 34.5 mm. **Series:** Second **Obv:** National arms **Obv. Legend:** ESTADOS UNIDOS MEXICANOS **Rev:** Stylized pyramid of Chichén-Itzá **Rev. Inscription:** YUCATÁN **Edge:** Segmented reeding

Date	Mintage	F12	VF20	XF40	MS60	MS63
2007Mo	600	PF65 1,200				

KM# 861 100 PESOS
33.94 g., Bi-Metallic, 39.04 mm. **Series:** Second **Obv:** National arms **Obv. Legend:** ESTADOS UNIDOS MEXICANOS **Rev:** Cable car above Monumento al Minero at left, Cathedral de Zacatecas at center right **Rev. Legend:** ZACATECAS **Edge:** Segmented reeding

Date	Mintage	F12	VF20	XF40	MS60	MS63
2007Mo	148,833	—	—	—	25.00	30.00

KM# 893 100 PESOS
29.17 g., Bi-Metallic, 34.5 mm. **Series:** Second **Obv:** National arms **Obv. Legend:** ESTADOS UNIDOS MEXICANOS **Rev:** Cable car above Monumento al Minero at left, Cathedral de Zacatecas at center right **Rev. Legend:** Zacatecas **Edge:** Segmented reeding

Date	Mintage	F12	VF20	XF40	MS60	MS63
2007Mo	600	PF65 1,200				

KM# 950 100 PESOS
33.96 g., Bi-Metallic, 39 mm. **Series:** Numismatic Heritage of Mexico **Subject:** 1732 Pillar Dollar **Obv:** National arms (eagle and snake facing left) and legend **Obv. Legend:** ESTADOS UNIDOS MEXICANOS **Rev:** Obverse of 1732 Pillar Dollar, legend **Rev. Legend:** HERENCIA NUMISMATICA DE MEXICO **Edge:** Segmented reeding

Date	Mintage	F12	VF20	XF40	MS60	MS63
2011Mo Prooflike	8,000	—	—	—	—	40.00

KM# 951 100 PESOS
33.97 g., Bi-Metallic, 39 mm. **Series:** Numismatic Heritage of Mexico **Subject:** 1783 Coin with bust of Carlos III **Obv:** National arms (eagle and snake facing left), legend **Obv. Legend:** ESTADOS UNIDOS MEXICANOS **Rev:** Obverse of 1783 coin with bust of Carlos III **Rev. Legend:** HERENCIA NUMISMATICA DE MEXICO **Edge:** Segmented reeding

Date	Mintage	F12	VF20	XF40	MS60	MS63
2011Mo Prooflike	8,000	—	—	—	—	40.00

KM# 952 100 PESOS
33.97 g., Bi-Metallic, 39 mm. **Series:** Numismatic heritage of Mexico **Subject:** SUD 8 Reales **Obv:** National arms (eagle and snake facing left), legend **Obv. Legend:** ESTADOS UNIDOS MEXICANOS **Rev:** Obverse of SUD 8 Rales, legend **Rev. Legend:** HERENCIA NUMISMATICA DE MEXICO **Edge:** Segmented reeding

Date	Mintage	F12	VF20	XF40	MS60	MS63
2011Mo Prooflike	8,000	—	—	—	—	40.00

KM# 953 100 PESOS
33.97 g., Bi-Metallic, 39 mm. **Series:** Numismatic Heritage of Mexico **Subject:** 1824DO 8 Reales **Obv:** National arms (eagle and snake facing left), legend **Obv. Legend:** ESTADOS UNIDOS MEXICANOS **Rev:** Reverse of 1824Do * reales, legend **Rev. Legend:** HERENCIA NUMISMATICA DE MEXICO **Edge:** Segmented reeding

Date	Mintage	F12	VF20	XF40	MS60	MS63
2011Mo Prooflike	8,000	—	—	—	—	40.00

KM# 954 100 PESOS
33.97 g., Bi-Metallic, 39 mm. **Series:** Numismatic Heritage of Mexico **Subject:** 1913 Parral Bolita Peso **Obv:** National arms (eagle and snake facing left) and legend **Obv. Legend:** ESTADOS UNIDOS MEXICANOS **Rev:** Obverse of 1913 Parral Bolita Peso, legend **Rev. Legend:** HERENCIA NUMISMATICA DE MEXICO **Edge:** Segmented reeding

Date	Mintage	F12	VF20	XF40	MS60	MS63
2011Mo Prooflike	8,000	—	—	—	—	40.00

KM# 955 100 PESOS
33.97 g., Bi-Metallic, 39 mm. **Series:** Numismatic Heritage of Mexico **Subject:** 1910 Caballito Peso **Obv:** National arms (eagle and snake facing left) and legend **Obv. Legend:** ESTADOS UNIDOS MEXICANOS **Rev:** Reverse of 1910 Caballito Peso, legend **Rev. Legend:** HERENCIA NUMISMATICA DE MEXICO **Edge:** Segmented reeding

Date	Mintage	F12	VF20	XF40	MS60	MS63
2011Mo Prooflike	8,000	—	—	—	—	40.00

KM# 963 100 PESOS
33.97 g., Bi-Metallic, 39 mm. **Subject:** Numismatic Heritage of Mexico **Obv:** National arms **Rev:** Obverse of 1804Mo 8 Reale coin with chopmarks **Edge:** Segmented reeding

Date	Mintage	F12	VF20	XF40	MS60	MS63
2012Mo Prooflike	8,000	—	—	—	—	40.00

KM# 964 100 PESOS
Bi-Metallic, 39 mm. **Subject:** Numismatic Heritage of Mexico **Obv:** National arms **Rev:** 1608Mo 8 Reales Cob coin of Philip III **Edge:** Segmented reeding

Date	Mintage	F12	VF20	XF40	MS60	MS63
2012Mo Prooflike	8,000	—	—	—	—	40.00

KM# 965 100 PESOS
33.97 g., Bi-Metallic, 39 mm. **Subject:** Numismatic Heritage of Mexico **Obv:** National arms **Rev:** 1811Zs 8 Reale Royalist Provisional Coin **Edge:** Segmented reeding

Date	Mintage	F12	VF20	XF40	MS60	MS63
2012Mo Prooflike	8,000	—	—	—	—	40.00

KM# 966 100 PFSOS
33.97 g., Bi-Metallic, 39 mm. **Subject:** Numismatic Heritage of Mexico **Obv:** National arms **Rev:** 1866Mo 1 Peso coin **Edge:** Segmented reeding

Date	Mintage	F12	VF20	XF40	MS60	MS63
2012Mo Prooflike	8,000	—	—	—	—	40.00

KM# 967 100 PESOS
33.97 g., Bi-Metallic, 39 mm. **Subject:** Numismatic Heritage of Mexico **Obv:** National arms **Rev:** 1828Mo 8 Escudo coin **Edge:** Segmented reeding

Date	Mintage	F12	VF20	XF40	MS60	MS63
2012Mo Prooflike	8,000	—	—	—	—	40.00

KM# 968 100 PESOS
33.97 g., Bi-Metallic, 39 mm. **Subject:** Numismatic Heritage of Mexico **Obv:** National arms **Rev:** 1950Mo 5 Peso Southeast Railway Inauguration coin **Edge:** Segmented reeding

Date	Mintage	F12	VF20	XF40	MS60	MS63
2012Mo Prooflike	8,000	—	—	—	—	40.00

KM# 971 100 PESOS
33.97 g., Bi-Metallic, 39 mm. **Subject:** Numismatic Heritage of Mexico **Obv:** National arms **Rev:** 1915Gro. 2 Peso Zapatista coin from Suriana **Edge:** Segmented reeding

Date	Mintage	F12	VF20	XF40	MS60	MS63
2013Mo Prooflike	—	—	—	—	—	40.00

KM# 972 100 PESOS
33.97 g., Bi-Metallic, 39 mm. **Subject:** Numismatic Heritage of Mexico **Obv:** National arms **Rev:** Early MoR Charles and Joanna 3 Reale coin **Edge:** Segmented reeding

Date	Mintage	F12	VF20	XF40	MS60	MS63
2013Mo Prooflike	—	—	—	—	—	40.00

KM# 973 100 PESOS
33.97 g., Bi-Metallic, 39 mm. **Subject:** Numismatic Heritage of Mexico **Obv:** National arms **Rev:** Zs 1 Peso Scale of Justice coin

Date	Mintage	F12	VF20	XF40	MS60	MS63
2013Mo Prooflike	—	—	—	—	—	40.00

KM# 974 100 PESOS
33.97 g., Bi-Metallic, 39 mm. **Subject:** Numismatic Heritage of Mexico **Obv:** National arms **Rev:** Ca M.M. 8 Reale Republican coin with counterstamp **Edge:** Segmented reeding

Date	Mintage	F12	VF20	XF40	MS60	MS63
2013Mo Prooflike	—	—	—	—	—	40.00

KM# 975 100 PESOS
33.97 g., Bi-Metallic, 39 mm. **Subject:** Numismatic Heritage of Mexico **Obv:** National arms **Rev:** 1811 8 Reale insurgent coin of the Supreme American Governing Board **Edge:** Segmented reeding

Date	Mintage	F12	VF20	XF40	MS60	MS63
2013Mo Prooflike	—	—	—	—	—	40.00

KM# 976 100 PESOS
33.97 g., Bi-Metallic, 39 mm. **Subject:** Numismatic Heritage of Mexico **Obv:** National arms **Rev:** 1822Mo 8 Escudo **Edge:** Segmented reeding

Date	Mintage	F12	VF20	XF40	MS60	MS63
2013Mo Prooflike	—	—	—	—	—	40.00

KM# 941 200 PESOS
1000.00 g., 0.999 Gold 31.9118 oz. AGW, 90 mm. **Series:** Mexican Independence 200th Anniversary **Subject:** Winged Victory **Obv:** National arms (eagle and snake facing left), legend **Obv. Legend:** ESTADOS UNIDOS MEXICANOS **Rev:** Winged Victory, legend **Rev. Legend:** BICENTENARIO **Edge Lettering:** Independencia y Libertad

Date	Mintage	F12	VF20	XF40	MS60	MS63
2010Mo	200	PF65 50,000				

KM# 932 200 PESOS
41.67 g., 0.900 Gold 1.1979 oz. AGW, 37 mm. **Series:** Mexico Independence 200th Anniversary **Subject:** Winged Victory **Obv:** National arms **Obv. Legend:** Bicentenario **Rev:** Winged Victory **Edge Lettering:** Independence y Liberted

Date	Mintage	F12	VF20	XF40	MS60	MS63
2010Mo	50,000	—	—	—	1,800	
2010Mo	5,000	PF65 2,000				

KM# 771 50000 PESOS
7.77 g., 0.999 Gold 0.248 oz. AGW, 23 mm. **Subject:** World Cup Soccer **Obv:** Mexican Eagle and Snake **Rev:** Kneeling Mayan Pelota player and soccer ball

Date	Mintage	F12	VF20	XF40	MS60	MS63
2006Mo	9,505	PF63 600				

SILVER BULLION COINAGE
Libertad Series

KM# 921 100 PESOS
1000.00 g., 0.999 Silver 31.9118 oz. ASW, 110 mm. **Obv:** National arms in center of past and present arms **Rev:** Aztec Calendar **Edge:** Plain

Date	Mintage	F12	VF20	XF40	MS60	MS63
2007Mo Prooflike	303	—	—	—	—	2,000
2008Mo Prooflike	1,000	—	—	—	—	1,800
2009Mo Prooflike	1,500	—	—	—	—	1,500
2010Mo Prooflike	1,500	—	—	—	—	1,500

Date	Mintage	F12	VF20	XF40	MS60	MS63
2011Mo Prooflike	1,500	—	—	—	—	1,500
2012Mo Prooflike	1,500	—	—	—	—	1,800
2013Mo Prooflike	500	—	—	—	—	1,500

KM# 609 1/20 ONZA (1/20 Troy Ounce of Silver)
1.56 g., 0.999 Silver 0.0496 oz. ASW, 16 mm. **Obv:** National arms, eagle left **Rev:** Winged Victory

Date	Mintage	F12	VF20	XF40	MS60	MS63
2001Mo	4,500	—	—	—	—	25.00
2001Mo	1,500	PF63 30.00				
2002Mo	50,000	—	—	—	—	16.00
2002Mo	2,800	PF63 25.00				
2003Mo	30,000	—	—	—	—	16.00
2003Mo	4,400	PF63 25.00				
2004Mo	30,000	—	—	—	—	16.00
2004Mo	2,700	PF63 25.00				
2005Mo	15,000	—	—	—	—	16.00
2005Mo	2,600	PF63 25.00				
2006Mo	20,000	—	—	—	—	16.00
2006Mo	3,300	PF63 25.00				
2007Mo	3,500	—	—	—	—	16.00
2007Mo	4,000	PF63 25.00				
2008Mo	7,000	—	—	—	—	16.00
2008Mo	3,300	PF63 25.00				
2009Mo	10,000	—	—	—	—	10.00
2009Mo	5,000	PF63 12.00				
2010Mo	12,000	—	—	—	—	10.00
2010Mo	10,000	PF63 12.00				
2011Mo	15,000	—	—	—	—	10.00
2011Mo	10,000	PF63 12.00				
2013Mo	13,500	—	—	—	—	8.00
2013Mo	4,200	PF63 12.00				

KM# 610 1/10 ONZA (1/10 Troy Ounce of Silver)
3.11 g., 0.999 Silver 0.0993 oz. ASW, 20 mm. **Obv:** National arms, eagle left **Rev:** Winged Victory

Date	Mintage	F12	VF20	XF40	MS60	MS63
2001Mo	25,000	—	—	—	—	27.50
2001Mo	1,500	PF63 36.00				
2002Mo	35,000	—	—	—	—	20.00
2002Mo	2,800	PF63 30.00				
2003Mo	20,000	—	—	—	—	20.00
2003Mo	4,900	PF63 30.00				
2004Mo	15,000	—	—	—	—	20.00
2004Mo	2,500	PF63 30.00				
2005Mo	9,277	—	—	—	—	20.00
2005Mo	3,000	PF63 27.50				
2006Mo	15,000	—	—	—	—	20.00
2006Mo	3,000	PF63 27.50				
2007Mo	3,500	—	—	—	—	20.00
2007Mo	4,000	PF63 27.50				
2008Mo	10,000	—	—	—	—	20.00
2008Mo	5,000	PF63 27.50				
2009Mo	10,000	—	—	—	—	20.00
2009Mo	5,000	PF63 27.50				
2010Mo	12,000	—	—	—	—	12.00
2010Mo	10,000	PF63 15.00				
2011Mo	15,000	—	—	—	—	12.00
2011Mo	10,000	PF63 15.00				
2012Mo	3,300	—	—	—	—	15.00
2013Mo	18,900	—	—	—	—	10.00
2013Mo	4,100	PF63 15.00				

KM# 611 1/4 ONZA (1/4 Troy Ounce of Silver)
7.78 g., 0.999 Silver 0.2481 oz. ASW, 27 mm. **Obv:** National arms, eagle left **Rev:** Winged Victory

Date	Mintage	F12	VF20	XF40	MS60	MS63
2001Mo	25,000	—	—	—	—	36.00
2001Mo	1,000	PF63 44.00				
2002Mo	35,000	—	—	—	—	27.50
2002Mo	2,800	PF63 40.00				
2003Mo	22,000	—	—	—	—	27.50
2003Mo	3,900	PF63 40.00				

Date	Mintage	F12	VF20	XF40	MS60	MS63
2004Mo	15,000	—	—	—	—	27.50
2004Mo	2,500	PF63 40.00				
2005Mo	15,000	—	—	—	—	27.50
2005Mo	2,400	PF63 37.00				
2006Mo	15,000	—	—	—	—	25.00
2006Mo	2,900	PF63 37.00				
2007Mo	3,500	—	—	—	—	25.00
2007Mo	3,000	PF63 37.00				
2008Mo	9,000	—	—	—	—	25.00
2008Mo	2,900	PF63 37.00				
2009Mo	10,000	—	—	—	—	25.00
2009Mo	3,000	PF63 37.00				
2010Mo	15,500	—	—	—	—	25.00
2010Mo	5,000	PF63 37.00				
2011Mo	15,500	—	—	—	—	25.00
2011Mo	5,000	PF63 37.00				
2012Mo	16,700	—	—	—	—	25.00
2013Mo	9,600	—	—	—	—	12.00
2013Mo	3,200	PF63 30.00				

KM# 612 1/2 ONZA (1/2 Troy Ounce of Silver)
15.55 g., 0.999 Silver 0.4963 oz. ASW, 33 mm. **Obv:** National arms, eagle left **Rev:** Winged Victory

Date	Mintage	F12	VF20	XF40	MS60	MS63
2001Mo	20,000	—	—	—	—	45.00
2001Mo	1,000	PF63 60.00				
2002Mo	35,000	—	—	—	—	37.00
2002Mo	2,800	PF63 50.00				
2003Mo	28,000	—	—	—	—	37.00
2003Mo	3,400	PF63 50.00				
2004Mo	20,000	—	—	—	—	37.00
2004Mo	2,500	PF63 50.00				
2005Mo	10,000	—	—	—	—	37.00
2005Mo	2,800	PF63 45.00				
2006Mo	15,000	—	—	—	—	37.00
2006Mo	2,900	PF63 45.00				
2007Mo	3,500	—	—	—	—	37.00
2007Mo	1,500	PF63 45.00				
2008Mo	9,000	—	—	—	—	37.00
2008Mo	2,500	PF63 45.00				
2009Mo	10,000	—	—	—	—	37.00
2009Mo	3,000	PF63 45.00				
2010Mo	20,000	—	—	—	—	37.00
2010Mo	5,000	PF63 45.00				
2011Mo	30,000	—	—	—	—	37.00
2011Mo	5,000	PF63 45.00				
2012Mo	17,000	—	—	—	—	37.00
2013Mo	24,500	—	—	—	—	20.00
2013Mo Proof	3,000	—	—	—	—	—

KM# 639 ONZA (Troy Ounce of Silver)
31.10 g., 0.999 Silver 0.9925 oz. ASW, 40 mm. **Subject:** Libertad **Obv:** National arms, eagle left within center of past and present arms **Rev:** Winged Victory **Edge:** Reeded

Date	Mintage	F12	VF20	XF40	MS60	MS63
2001Mo	725,000	—	—	—	—	55.00
2001Mo	2,000	PF63 140				
2002Mo	854,000	—	—	—	—	55.00
2002Mo	3,800	PF63 150				
2003Mo	805,000	—	—	—	—	60.00
2003Mo	5,400	PF63 130				
2004Mo	450,000	—	—	—	—	50.00
2004Mo	3,000	PF63 130				
2005Mo	698,281	—	—	—	—	50.00
2005Mo	3,300	PF63 150				
2006Mo	300,000	—	—	—	—	50.00
2006Mo	4,000	PF63 140				
2007Mo	200,000	—	—	—	—	100
2007Mo	5,800	PF63 150				

Date	Mintage	F12	VF20	XF40	MS60	MS63
2008Mo	950,000	—	—	—	—	60.00
2008Mo	11,000	PF63 150				
2009Mo	1,650,000	—	—	—	—	40.00
2009Mo	10,000	PF63 100				
2010Mo	1,000,000	—	—	—	—	50.00
2010Mo	10,000	PF63 140				
2011Mo	1,200,000	—	—	—	—	30.00
2011Mo	10,000	PF63 80.00				
2012Mo	746,400	—	—	—	—	30.00
2012Mo	4,200	PF63 80.00				
2013Mo	777,100	—	—	—	—	80.00
2013Mo	9,100	PF63 40.00				

KM# 614 2 ONZAS (2 Troy Ounces of Silver)
62.21 g., 0.999 Silver 1.9851 oz. ASW, 48 mm. **Subject:** Libertad **Obv:** National arms, eagle left within center of past and present arms **Rev:** Winged Victory **Edge:** Reeded

Date	Mintage	F12	VF20	XF40	MS60	MS63
2001Mo	6,700	—	—	—	—	120
2001Mo	500	PF63 300				
2002Mo	8,700	—	—	—	—	110
2002Mo	1,000	PF63 225				
2003Mo	9,500	—	—	—	—	110
2003Mo	800	PF63 225				
2004Mo	8,000	—	—	—	—	100
2004Mo	1,000	PF63 175				
2005Mo	3,549	—	—	—	—	100
2005Mo	600	PF63 500				
2006Mo	5,800	—	—	—	—	100
2006Mo	1,100	PF63 175				
2007Mo	8,000	—	—	—	—	100
2007Mo	500	PF63 250				
2008Mo	17,000	—	—	—	—	110
2008Mo	1,000	PF63 170				
2009Mo	46,000	—	—	—	—	90.00
2009Mo	6,200	PF63 100				
2010Mo	14,000	—	—	—	—	75.00
2010Mo	1,300	PF63 120				
2011Mo	14,000	—	—	—	—	110
2011Mo	1,000	PF63 140				
2012Mo	18,600	—	—	—	—	70.00
2013Mo	17,400	—	—	—	—	60.00
2013Mo	1,300	PF63 110				

KM# 615 5 ONZAS (5 Troy Ounces of Silver)
155.52 g., 0.999 Silver 4.9628 oz. ASW, 65 mm. **Subject:** Libertad **Obv:** National arms, eagle left within center of past and present arms **Rev:** Winged Victory **Edge:** Reeded **Note:** Illustration reduced.

Date	Mintage	F12	VF20	XF40	MS60	MS63
2001Mo	4,000	—	—	—	—	190
2001Mo	600	PF63 325				
2002Mo	5,200	—	—	—	—	190
2002Mo	1,000	PF63 325				
2003Mo	6,000	—	—	—	—	180
2003Mo	1,500	PF63 250				
2004Mo	3,923	—	—	—	—	180
2004Mo	800	PF63 225				
2005Mo	2,401	—	—	—	—	205
2005Mo	1,000	PF63 225				
2006Mo	3,000	—	—	—	—	180
2006Mo	700	PF63 265				
2007Mo	3,000	—	—	—	—	180
2007Mo	500	PF63 205				
2008Mo	9,000	—	—	—	—	205
2008Mo	900	PF63 270				
2009Mo	21,000	—	—	—	—	250
2009Mo	5,000	PF63 270				
2010Mo	9,500	—	—	—	—	220
2010Mo	2,000	PF63 230				
2011Mo	10,000	—	—	—	—	220
2011Mo	2,000	PF63 230				
2012Mo	9,500	—	—	—	—	220
2013Mo	10,400	—	—	—	—	150
2013Mo	1,600	PF63 220				

KM# 677 KILO (32.15 Troy Ounces of Silver)

999.98 g., 0.999 Silver 31.9111 oz. ASW, 110 mm. **Subject:** Collector Bullion **Obv:** National arms in center of past and present arms **Rev:** Winged Victory **Edge:** Reeded

Date	Mintage	F12	VF20	XF40	MS60	MS63
2001Mo Prooflike	—	—	—	—	—	2,200
2002Mo Prooflike	1,820	—	—	—	—	1,750
2003Mo Prooflike	1,514	—	—	—	—	1,650
2004Mo Prooflike	1,501	—	—	—	—	1,800
2005Mo Prooflike	500	—	—	—	—	1,750
2006Mo Prooflike	874	—	—	—	—	1,650
2007Mo Prooflike	700	—	—	—	—	1,650
2008Mo	2,003	—	—	—	—	1,200
2008Mo Prooflike	1,700	—	—	—	—	1,500
2009Mo	4,000	—	—	—	—	1,200
2009Mo Prooflike	1,700	—	—	—	—	1,500
2010Mo	4,000	—	—	—	—	1,200
2010Mo Prooflike	1,500	—	—	—	—	1,500
2011Mo	6,000	—	—	—	—	1,200
2011Mo Prooflike	1,000	—	—	—	—	1,500
2012Mo Prooflike	500	—	—	—	—	1,500
2013 (2012)Mo	2,300	—	—	—	—	1,200
2013Mo Prooflike	400	—	—	—	—	1,500

GOLD BULLION COINAGE

KM# 957 1.25 GRAMS

1.67 g., 0.0402 Gold 0.0021 oz. AGW, 13 mm. **Series:** Cultural Fusion **Subject:** Architecture **Obv:** National arms (eagle and snake facing left) and legend **Obv. Legend:** ESTADOS UNIDOS MEXICANOS **Rev:** Heads in profile, mail, woman with a plume **Rev. Legend:** FUSIÓN CULTURAL and 1.25 g DE ORO PURO LEY 0.750

Date	Mintage	F12	VF20	XF40	MS60	MS63
2011Mo	2,000	PF63 110				

KM# 958 1.25 GRAMS

1.67 g., 0.750 Gold 0.0399 oz. AGW, 13 mm. **Series:** Cultural fusion **Subject:** Architecture **Obv:** Natioan arms (eagle and snake facing left) and legond **Obv. Legend:** ESTADOS UNIDOS MEXICANOS **Rev:** Pyramid, aquedect, church dome and cacao fruit **Rev. Legend:** FUSIÓN CULTURAL and 1.25 g DE ORO PURO LEY 0.750

Date	Mintage	F12	VF20	XF40	MS60	MS63
2011Mo	2,000	PF63 110				

KM# 959 1.25 GRAMS

1.67 g., 0.750 Gold 0.0399 oz. AGW, 13 mm. **Series:** Cultural Fusion **Subject:** Cacao **Obv:** National arms (eagle and snake facing left) and legend **Obv. Legend:** ESTADOS UNIDOS MEXICANOS **Rev:** Aztec scuplture of a man carrying a cacao husk, legend **Rev. Legend:** XOCOLATL PARA EL MUNDS, EL CACAO and 1.25 g DE ORO PURO LEY

Date	Mintage	F12	VF20	XF40	MS60	MS63
2011Mo 2000	—	PF63 110				

KM# 960 1.25 GRAMS

1.67 g., 0.750 Gold 0.0399 oz. AGW, 13 mm. **Series:** Cultural Fusion **Subject:** Merchandise **Obv:** National arms (eagle and snake facing left) and legend **Obv. Legend:** ESTADOS UNIDOS MEXICANOS **Rev:** Allegory of Mesoamerican and Spanish cultural fusion. **Rev. Legend:** FUSIÓN CULTURAL and 1.25 g DE ORO PURO LEY

Date	Mintage	F12	VF20	XF40	MS60	MS63
2011Mo	2,000	PF63 110				

KM# 671 1/20 ONZA (1/20 Ounce of Pure Gold)

1.56 g., 0.999 Gold 0.0496 oz. AGW, 13 mm. **Obv:** National arms, eagle left **Rev:** Winged Victory **Edge:** Reeded **Note:** Design similar to KM#609. Value estimates do not include the high taxes and surcharges added to the issue prices by the Mexican Government.

Date	Mintage	F12	VF20	XF40	MS60	MS63
2002Mo	5,000	—	—	—	—	BV+30%
2003Mo	800	—	—	—	—	BV+32%

Date	Mintage	F12	VF20	XF40	MS60	MS63
2004Mo	4,000	—	—	—	—	BV+30%
2005Mo	3,200	—	—	—	—	BV+30%
2005Mo	400	PF63 BV+35%				
2006Mo	3,000	—	—	—	—	BV+30%
2006Mo	520	PF63 BV+35%				
2007Mo	500	PF63 BV+35%				
2007Mo	1,200	—	—	—	—	BV+30%
2008Mo	500	PF63 BV+35%				
2008Mo	800	—	—	—	—	BV+30%
2009Mo	2,000	—	—	—	—	BV+30%
2009Mo	600	PF63 BV+35%				
2010Mo	1,500	—	—	—	—	BV+30%
2010Mo	600	PF63 BV+35%				
2011Mo	2,500	—	—	—	—	BV+30%
2011Mo	1,100	PF63 BV+35%				
2013Mo	300	PF63 BV+35%				
2013Mo	650	—	—	—	—	BV+30%

KM# 672 1/10 ONZA (1/10 Ounce of Pure Gold)

3.11 g., 0.999 Gold 0.0993 oz. AGW, 16 mm. **Obv:** National arms, eagle left **Rev:** Winged Victory **Edge:** Reeded **Note:** Design similar to KM#610. Value estimates do not include the high taxes and surcharges added to the issue prices by the Mexican Government.

Date	Mintage	F12	VF20	XF40	MS60	MS63
2002Mo	5,000	—	—	—	—	BV+20%
2003Mo	300	—	—	—	—	BV+22%
2004Mo	2,000	—	—	—	—	BV+20%
2005Mo	500	—	—	—	—	BV+20%
2005Mo	400	PF63 BV+22%				
2006Mo	2,500	—	—	—	—	BV+20%
2006Mo	520	PF63 BV+22%				
2007Mo	1,200	—	—	—	—	BV+20%
2007Mo	500	PF63 BV+22%				
2008Mo	2,500	—	—	—	—	BV+20%
2008Mo	500	PF63 BV+22%				
2009Mo	9,000	—	—	—	—	BV+20%
2009Mo	600	PF63 BV+22%				
2010Mo	4,500	—	—	—	—	BV+20%
2010Mo	600	PF63 BV+22%				
2011Mo	6,500	—	—	—	—	BV+20%
2011Mo	1,100	PF63 BV+22%				
2013Mo	300	PF63 BV+22%				
2013Mo	2,150	—	—	—	—	BV+20%

KM# 673 1/4 ONZA (1/4 Ounce of Pure Gold)

7.78 g., 0.999 Gold 0.2481 oz. AGW, 23 mm. **Obv:** National arms, eagle left **Rev:** Winged Victory **Edge:** Reeded **Note:** Design similar to KM#611. Value estimates do not include the high taxes and surcharges added to the issue prices by the Mexican Government.

Date	Mintage	F12	VF20	XF40	MS60	MS63
2002Mo	5,000	—	—	—	—	BV+12%
2003Mo	300	—	—	—	—	BV+14%
2004Mo	1,500	—	—	—	—	BV+12%
2004Mo	1,000	PF63 BV+15%				
2005Mo	500	—	—	—	—	BV+14%
2005Mo	2,600	PF63 BV+15%				
2006Mo	1,500	—	—	—	—	BV+12%
2006Mo	2,120	PF63 BV+15%				
2007Mo	500	—	—	—	—	BV+14%
2007Mo	1,500	PF63 BV+15%				
2008Mo	800	—	—	—	—	BV+14%
2008Mo	800	PF63 BV+15%				
2009Mo	3,000	—	—	—	—	BV+12%
2000Mo	1,700	PF63 BV+15%				
2010Mo	1,500	—	—	—	—	BV+12%
2010Mo	1,000	PF63 BV+15%				
2011Mo	1,500	—	—	—	—	BV+12%
2011Mo	2,000	PF63 BV+15%				
2013Mo	600	PF63 BV+15%				
2013Mo	500	—	—	—	—	BV+12%

KM# 674 1/2 ONZA (1/2 Ounce of Pure Gold)

15.55 g., 0.999 Gold 0.4963 oz. AGW, 29 mm. **Obv:** National arms, eagle left **Rev:** Winged Victory **Edge:** Reeded **Note:** Design similar to KM#612. Value estimates do not include the high taxes and surcharges added to the issue prices by the Mexican Government.

Date	Mintage	F12	VF20	XF40	MS60	MS63
2002Mo	5,000	—	—	—	—	BV+8%
2003Mo	300	—	—	—	—	BV+10%
2004Mo	500	—	—	—	—	BV+8%
2005Mo	500	—	—	—	—	BV+10%
2005Mo	400	PF63 BV+12%				
2006Mo	500	—	—	—	—	BV+10%
2006Mo	520	PF63 BV+12%				
2007Mo	500	—	—	—	—	BV+10%
2007Mo	500	PF63 BV+12%				
2008Mo	300	—	—	—	—	BV+10%
2008Mo	500	PF63 BV+12%				
2009Mo	3,000	—	—	—	—	BV+8%
2009Mo	600	PF63 BV+12%				
2010Mo	1,500	—	—	—	—	BV+8%
2010Mo	600	PF63 BV+12%				
2011Mo	1,500	—	—	—	—	BV+8%
2011Mo	1,100	PF63 BV+12%				
2013Mo	300	PF63 BV+12%				
2013Mo	500	—	—	—	—	BV+8%

KM# 675 ONZA (Ounce of Pure Gold)

31.10 g., 0.999 Gold 0.9926 oz. AGW, 34.5 mm. **Obv:** National arms, eagle left **Rev:** Winged Victory **Edge:** Reeded **Note:** Design similar to KM#639. Value estimates do not include the high taxes and surcharges added to the issue prices by the Mexican Government.

Date	Mintage	F12	VF20	XF40	MS60	MS63
2002Mo	15,000	—	—	—	—	BV+3%
2003Mo	500	—	—	—	—	BV+4%
2004Mo	3,000	—	—	—	—	BV+3%
2005Mo	3,000	—	—	—	—	BV+3%
2005Mo	250	PF63 BV+5%				
2006Mo	4,000	—	—	—	—	BV+3%
2006Mo	520	PF63 BV+5%				
2007Mo	2,500	—	—	—	—	BV+3%
2007Mo	500	PF63 BV+5%				
2008Mo	800	—	—	—	—	BV+3%
2008Mo	500	PF63 BV+5%				
2009Mo	6,200	—	—	—	—	BV+3%
2009Mo	600	PF63 BV+5%				
2010Mo	4,000	—	—	—	—	BV+3%
2010Mo	600	PF63 BV+5%				
2011Mo	3,000	—	—	—	—	BV+3%
2011Mo	1,100	PF63 BV+5%				
2012Mo	3,000	—	—	—	—	BV+3%
2013Mo	400	PF63 BV+5%				
2013Mo	2,350	—	—	—	—	BV+3%

BANK SETS

KM#	Date	Mintage	Identification	Issue Price	Mkt Val
BS38	2001 (10)	—	KM#546-549, 603-605, 636-638	—	65.00
BS39	2002 (8)	—	KM#546-549, 603-605, 616	—	30.00
BS40	2003 (6)	—	KM#547-549, 603-605	—	30.00

The Republic of Moldova (formerly the Moldavian S.S.R.) is bordered in the north, east and south by the Ukraine and on the west by Romania. It has an area of 13,000 sq.mi. (33,700 sq.km.) and a population of 4.4 million. The capital is Chisinau. Agricultural products are mainly cereals, grapes, tobacco, sugar beets and fruits. Food processing, clothing, building materials and agricultural machinery manufacturing dominate industry.

MONETARY SYSTEM
100 Bani = 1 Leu

REPUBLIC
DECIMAL COINAGE

KM# 1 BAN

0.67 g., Aluminum, 14.5 mm. **Obv:** National arms **Rev:** Value divides date above monogram **Edge:** Plain

Date	Mintage	F12	VF20	XF40	MS60	MS63
2004	—	—	—	—	0.25	0.50
2006	—	—	—	—	0.25	0.50

KM# 2 5 BANI

0.75 g., Aluminum, 16 mm. **Obv:** National arms **Rev:** Monogram divides sprigs below value and date **Edge:** Plain

Date	Mintage	F12	VF20	XF40	MS60	MS63
2001	—	—	—	—	0.35	0.50
2002	—	—	—	—	0.35	0.50
2003	—	—	—	—	0.35	0.50
2004	—	—	—	—	0.35	0.50
2005	—	—	—	—	0.35	0.50
2006	—	—	—	—	0.35	0.50
2008	—	—	—	—	0.35	0.50
2010	—	—	—	—	0.35	0.50
2011	—	—	—	—	0.35	0.50
2012	—	—	—	—	0.35	0.50
2013	—	—	—	—	0.35	0.50

KM# 7 10 BANI

0.85 g., Aluminum, 16.6 mm. **Obv:** National arms **Rev:** Value, date and monogram **Edge:** Plain

Date	Mintage	F12	VF20	XF40	MS60	MS63
2001	—	—	—	—	0.40	0.60
2002	—	—	—	—	0.40	0.60
2003	—	—	—	—	0.40	0.60
2004	—	—	—	—	0.40	0.60
2005	—	—	—	—	0.40	0.60
2006	—	—	—	—	0.40	0.60
2008	—	—	—	—	0.40	0.60
2010	—	—	—	—	0.40	0.60
2011	—	—	—	—	0.40	0.60
2013	—	—	—	—	0.40	0.60

KM# 3 25 BANI

0.95 g., Aluminum, 17.5 mm. **Obv:** National arms **Rev:** Monogram divides sprigs below value and date **Edge:** Plain

Date	Mintage	F12	VF20	XF40	MS60	MS63
2001	—	—	—	0.20	0.50	0.75
2002	—	—	—	0.20	0.50	0.75
2003	—	—	—	0.20	0.50	0.75
2004	—	—	—	0.20	0.50	0.75
2005	—	—	—	0.20	0.50	0.75
2006	—	—	—	0.20	0.50	0.75
2008	—	—	—	0.20	0.50	0.75
2010	—	—	—	0.20	0.50	0.75
2011	—	—	—	0.20	0.50	0.75
2012	—	—	—	0.20	0.50	0.75
2013	—	—	—	0.20	0.50	0.75

KM# 10 50 BANI

3.10 g., Brass Clad Steel, 19 mm. **Obv:** National arms **Rev:** Value and date within grapevine **Edge:** Reeded

Date	Mintage	F12	VF20	XF40	MS60	MS63
2003	—	—	—	—	1.50	2.00
2005	—	—	—	—	1.50	2.00
2008	—	—	—	—	1.50	2.00

KM# 12 10 LEI

13.50 g., 0.925 Silver 0.3989 oz. ASW, 24.5 mm. **Obv:** National arms above value **Rev:** European wildcat within circle **Edge:** Plain

Date	Mintage	F12	VF20	XF40	MS60	MS63
2001	1,000	PF63 60.00	PF65 65.00			

KM# 13 10 LEI

13.50 g., 0.925 Silver 0.3989 oz. ASW, 24.5 mm. **Obv:** National arms above value **Rev:** Green Woodpecker on tree within circle **Edge:** Plain

Date	Mintage	F12	VF20	XF40	MS60	MS63
2001	1,000	PF63 55.00	PF65 60.00			

KM# 19 10 LEI

13.45 g., 0.925 Silver 0.3974 oz. ASW, 24.5 mm. **Obv:** National arms above value **Rev:** European Mink within circle **Edge:** Plain

Date	Mintage	F12	VF20	XF40	MS60	MS63
2003	500	PF65 65.00				

KM# 20 10 LEI

13.45 g., 0.925 Silver 0.3974 oz. ASW, 24.5 mm. **Obv:** National arms above value **Rev:** Black Storks within circle **Edge:** Plain

Date	Mintage	F12	VF20	XF40	MS60	MS63
2003	500	PF65 65.00				

KM# 25 10 LEI

25.00 g., Nickel Plated Brass, 30 mm. **Subject:** Wine Holiday **Obv:** National arms above value **Rev:** Wine grapes, goblet and flask **Edge:** Plain

Date	Mintage	F12	VF20	XF40	MS60	MS63
2003	—	PF65 12.50				

KM# 22 10 LEI

13.50 g., 0.925 Silver 0.3989 oz. ASW, 24.5 mm. **Obv:** National arms above value **Rev:** Pine Marten within circle **Edge:** Plain

Date	Mintage	F12	VF20	XF40	MS60	MS63
2004	500	PF65 65.00				

KM# 29 10 LEI

25.00 g., Nickel Plated Brass, 30 mm. **Subject:** European Women's Chess Championship **Obv:** Arms, date at top, value at bottom **Obv. Legend:** REPUBLICA - 2005 - MOLDOVA **Rev:** 2 chess figures on board at left, map at right **Rev. Inscription:** 2005 CHISINAU **Edge:** Plain

Date	Mintage	F12	VF20	XF40	MS60	MS63
2005	—	PF65 12.50				

KM# 30 10 LEI

13.50 g., 0.925 Silver 0.3989 oz. ASW, 24.5 mm. **Obv:** Arms, value below **Obv. Legend:** REPUBLICA MOLDOVA **Rev:** Imperial eagle on branch, legend follows the coin circumference **Edge:** Plain

Date	Mintage	F12	VF20	XF40	MS60	MS63
2005	500	PF65 65.00				

KM# 33 10 LEI

13.50 g., 0.925 Silver 0.3989 oz. ASW, 24.5 mm. **Obv:** Arms, value below **Obv. Legend:** REPUBLICA - 2006 - MOLDOVA **Rev:** Bird in grass, legend around circumference using Latin name **Edge:** Plain

Date	Mintage	F12	VF20	XF40	MS60	MS63
2006	500	PF65 65.00				

KM# 38 10 LEI

13.50 g., 0.925 Silver 0.3989 oz. ASW, 24.5 mm. **Rev:** Common ground squirrel

Date	Mintage	F12	VF20	XF40	MS60	MS63
2006	500	PF65 65.00				

KM# 43 10 LEI

13.50 g., 0.925 Silver 0.3989 oz. ASW, 24.5 mm. **Rev:** White water lilly

Date	Mintage	F12	VF20	XF40	MS60	MS63
2008	500	PF65 60.00				

KM# 47 20 LEI

13.50 g., 0.925 Silver 0.3989 oz. ASW, 22 mm. **Subject:** Assumption of the Virgin Mary

Date	Mintage	F12	VF20	XF40	MS60	MS63
2009	1,000	PF63 35.00	PF65 40.00			

KM# 17 50 LEI

16.50 g., 0.925 Silver 0.4875 oz. ASW, 30 mm. **Obv:** National arms above value **Rev:** Constantin Brancusi and building **Edge:** Plain

Date	Mintage	F12	VF20	XF40	MS60	MS63
2001	1,000	PF63 60.00	PF65 65.00			

KM# 18 50 LEI

16.50 g., 0.925 Silver 0.4875 oz. ASW, 30 mm. **Obv:** National arms above value **Rev:** Vasile Alecsandri with book and landscape **Edge:** Plain

Date	Mintage	F12	VF20	XF40	MS60	MS63
2001	1,000	PF63 60.00	PF65 65.00			

KM# 36 50 LEI

16.50 g., 0.925 Silver 0.4875 oz. ASW, 30 mm. **Subject:** Vazile Alecsandri, 180th Anniversary **Obv:** Arms **Rev:** Bust and landscape

Date	Mintage	F12	VF20	XF40	MS60	MS63
2001	1,000	PF63 40.00	PF65 45.00			

KM# 14 50 LEI
16.55 g., 0.925 Silver 0.489 oz. ASW, 29.9 mm. **Subject:** Effigy of Miron Costin **Obv:** National arms above value **Rev:** Bust with hat 1/4 right flanked by dates and books **Edge:** Plain

Date	Mintage	F12	VF20	XF40	MS60	MS63
2003	500	PF65 165				

KM# 21 50 LEI
16.50 g., 0.925 Silver 0.4875 oz. ASW, 29.8 mm. **Subject:** Effigy of Dimitrie Cantemir **Obv:** National arms above value **Rev:** Bust facing flanked by dates and scroll **Edge:** Plain

Date	Mintage	F12	VF20	XF40	MS60	MS63
2003	500	PF65 165				

KM# 23 50 LEI
16.50 g., 0.925 Silver 0.4875 oz. ASW, 30 mm. **Obv:** National arms above value **Rev:** Bust of Bishop facing holding scepter **Edge:** Plain

Date	Mintage	F12	VF20	XF40	MS60	MS63
2004	500	PF65 90.00				

KM# 31 50 LEI
16.50 g., 0.925 Silver 0.4875 oz. ASW, 30 mm. **Subject:** 415th Anniversary - Birth of Grigore Ureche **Obv:** Arms, date divides legend at top, value below, **Obv. Legend:** REPUBLICA MOLDOVA **Rev:** Bust faces right, scroll with feather pen at right, inscription on scroll **Rev. Legend:** GRIGORE URECHE **Rev. Inscription:** Letopisetul Tarii Moldovei **Edge:** Plain

Date	Mintage	F12	VF20	XF40	MS60	MS63
2005	—	PF65 120				

KM# 34 50 LEI
16.50 g., 0.925 Silver 0.4875 oz. ASW, 30 mm. **Subject:** 200th Anniversary - Birth of Alexandru Donici **Obv:** Arms, date divides legend above, value below **Obv. Legend:** REPUBLICA MOLDOVA **Rev:** Bust of Donici facing, life dates on ribbon below **Rev. Legend:** ALEXANDRU DONICI

Date	Mintage	F12	VF20	XF40	MS60	MS63
2006	—	PF65 120				

KM# 40 50 LEI
16.50 g., 0.925 Silver 0.4875 oz. ASW, 30 mm. **Subject:** Metropolitian Varilaam **Rev:** Bust 3/4 right

Date	Mintage	F12	VF20	XF40	MS60	MS63
2007	500	PF65 120				

KM# 41 50 LEI
16.50 g., 0.925 Silver 0.4875 oz. ASW, 30 mm. **Subject:** Pottery Tradition **Rev:** Hand modeling clay vessel on pottery wheel

Date	Mintage	F12	VF20	XF40	MS60	MS63
2007	500	PF65 60.00				

KM# 44 50 LEI
16.50 g., 0.925 Silver 0.4875 oz. ASW, 30 mm. **Subject:** Oak tree in Stefan **Rev:** Oak tree

Date	Mintage	F12	VF20	XF40	MS60	MS63
2008	500	PF65 75.00				

KM# 45 50 LEI
16.50 g., 0.925 Silver 0.4875 oz. ASW, 30 mm. **Subject:** Cooper Trade **Rev:** Barrell maker

Date	Mintage	F12	VF20	XF40	MS60	MS63
2008	500	PF65 55.00				

KM# 48 50 LEI
16.50 g., 0.925 Silver 0.4075 oz. ASW, 30 mm. **Subject:** Geodezic arc of Struve **Rev:** Map

Date	Mintage	F12	VF20	XF40	MS60	MS63
2009	500	PF65 75.00				

KM# 49 50 LEI
16.50 g., 0.925 Silver 0.4875 oz. ASW, 30 mm. **Subject:** Rule of Vasile Lupu **Rev:** Open book and coat-of-arms

Date	Mintage	F12	VF20	XF40	MS60	MS63
2009	500	PF65 75.00				

KM# 50 50 LEI
16.50 g., 0.925 Silver 0.4875 oz. ASW, 30 mm. **Subject:** Traditional weaving **Rev:** Woman seated at weaving frame

Date	Mintage	F12	VF20	XF40	MS60	MS63
2009	500	PF65 70.00				

KM# 53 50 LEI
16.50 g., 0.999 Silver 0.5265 oz. ASW, 30 mm. **Subject:** Traditional Musical Instruments **Obv:** National arms **Rev:** Violin, bagpipe, pan pipe and flute

Date	Mintage	F12	VF20	XF40	MS60	MS63
2010	500	PF65 40.00				

KM# 54 50 LEI
16.50 g., 0.999 Silver 0.5265 oz. ASW, 30 mm. **Obv:** National arms **Rev:** Archeological complex of Old Orhei

Date	Mintage	F12	VF20	XF40	MS60	MS63
2010	500	PF65 45.00				

KM# 55 50 LEI
13.00 g., 0.999 Silver 0.4149 oz. ASW, 28 mm. **Subject:** Maria Cebotari, 100th Anniversary of Birth **Obv:** National arms **Rev:** Cebotari bust left

Date	Mintage	F12	VF20	XF40	MS60	MS63
2010	500	PF65 45.00				

KM# 56 50 LEI
13.00 g., 0.999 Silver 0.4149 oz. ASW, 28 mm. **Subject:** Doina and Ion Aldea-Teodorovici **Obv:** National arms **Rev:** Conjoined busts right

Date	Mintage	F12	VF20	XF40	MS60	MS63
2010	500	PF65 45.00				

KM# 58 50 LEI
16.50 g., 0.999 Silver 0.5265 oz. ASW, 30 mm. **Subject:** Moldovan Football, 100th Anniversary **Obv:** National Arms **Rev:** Soccer player

Date	Mintage	F12	VF20	XF40	MS60	MS63
2010	300	PF65 45.00				

KM# 59 50 LEI
16.50 g., 0.999 Silver 0.5265 oz. ASW, 30 mm. **Subject:** Annunciation Church in Chisinau, 200th Anniversary **Obv:** National Arms **Rev:** Church façade

Date	Mintage	F12	VF20	XF40	MS60	MS63
2010	500	PF65 45.00				

KM# 60 50 LEI
13.00 g., 0.999 Silver 0.4149 oz. ASW, 28 mm. **Subject:** Grigore Vieru **Obv:** National Arms **Rev:** Profile bust right

Date	Mintage	F12	VF20	XF40	MS60	MS63
2010	500	PF65 45.00				

KM# 65 50 LEI
13.00 g., 0.999 Silver 0.4149 oz. ASW, 28 mm. **Subject:** Bogdan Petriceicu Hasdeu **Obv:** National arms **Rev:** Bust **Edge:** Reeded

Date	Mintage	F12	VF20	XF40	MS60	MS63
2011	500	PF65 50.00				

KM# 67 50 LEI
13.00 g., 0.999 Silver 0.4149 oz. ASW, 28 mm. **Subject:** Alexandru Bernardazzi, 180th Anniversary of Birth **Obv:** National arms **Rev:** Portrait **Edge:** Reeded

Date	Mintage	F12	VF20	XF40	MS60	MS63
2011	500	PF65 50.00				

KM# 68 50 LEI
16.50 g., 0.999 Silver 0.5265 oz. ASW, 30 mm. **Obv:** National arms **Rev:** Spoonbill standing left, oval background **Edge:** Reeded

Date	Mintage	F12	VF20	XF40	MS60	MS63
2011	500	PF65 50.00				

KM# 69 50 LEI
16.50 g., 0.999 Silver 0.5265 oz. ASW, 30 mm. **Subject:** Holiday Traditions **Obv:** National arms **Rev:** Carolers **Edge:** Reeded

Date	Mintage	F12	VF20	XF40	MS60	MS63
2011	1,000	PF63 45.00	PF65 50.00			

KM# 70 50 LEI
16.50 g., 0.999 Silver 0.5265 oz. ASW, 30 mm. **Subject:** Stefan Cel Mare, 555th Anniversary of Accession **Rev:** Half-length bust facing right

Date	Mintage	F12	VF20	XF40	MS60	MS63
2012	—	PF63 45.00	PF65 50.00			

KM# 71 50 LEI
16.50 g., 0.999 Silver 0.5265 oz. ASW, 30 mm. **Subject:** London Olympics **Rev:** Runner breaking tape at finish line

Date	Mintage	F12	VF20	XF40	MS60	MS63
2012	—	PF63 45.00	PF65 50.00			

KM# 72 50 LEI
16.50 g., 0.999 Silver 0.5265 oz. ASW, 30 mm. **Subject:** Ivo Creanga, 175th Anniversary of Birth

Date	Mintage	F12	VF20	XF40	MS60	MS63
2012	—	PF63 45.00	PF65 50.00			

KM# 73 50 LEI
16.50 g., 0.999 Silver 0.5265 oz. ASW, 30 mm. **Subject:** Soroka Fortress

Date	Mintage	F12	VF20	XF40	MS60	MS63
2012	—	PF63 45.00	PF65 50.00			

KM# 74 50 LEI
16.50 g., 0.999 Silver 0.5265 oz. ASW, 30 mm. **Subject:** Mid-Summer's Day **Obv:** Arms **Rev:** Female head with wheat wreath

Date	Mintage	F12	VF20	XF40	MS60	MS63
2012	—	PF63 45.00	PF65 50.00			

KM# 16 100 LEI
31.10 g., 0.925 Silver 0.9189 oz. ASW, 37 mm. **Subject:** 10th Anniversary of Independence **Obv:** National arms above value **Rev:** Arch monument within circle above value and sprigs **Edge:** Plain

Date	Mintage	F12	VF20	XF40	MS60	MS63
2001	1,000	PF63 200	PF65 220			

KM# 26 100 LEI
7.80 g., 0.9999 Gold 0.2491 oz. AGW, 24 mm. **Obv:** National arms above value **Rev:** King Stephan the Great (1456-1504) **Edge:** Plain

Date	Mintage	F12	VF20	XF40	MS60	MS63
2004	—	PF65 450				

KM# 32 100 LEI
31.10 g., 0.925 Silver 0.9189 oz. ASW, 37 mm. **Subject:** Burebista - King of Dacians **Obv:** Arms, date divides legend at top, value below **Obv. Legend:** REPUBLICA MOLDOVA **Rev:** Bust of Burebista at left, battle scene of Geto-Dacians with Romans at right **Rev. Legend:** BUREBISTA REGELE DACILOR **Edge:** Plain

Date	Mintage	F12	VF20	XF40	MS60	MS63
2005	500	PF65 300				

KM# 35 100 LEI
31.10 g., 0.925 Silver 0.9189 oz. ASW, 37 mm. **Subject:** 15th Anniversary - Independence Proclamation of the Republic of Moldova **Obv:** Arms, date divides legend above, value below **Obv. Legend:** REPUBLICA MOLDOVA **Rev:** Map of Moldova within stars in inner circle, legend around **Rev. Legend:** PROCLAMAREA INDEPENDENTEI / 1991-2006 **Edge:** Plain

Date	Mintage	F12	VF20	XF40	MS60	MS63
2006	500	PF65 500				

KM# 39 100 LEI
31.11 g., 0.925 Silver 0.9191 oz. ASW, 37 mm. **Subject:** National Bank, 15th Anniversary **Rev:** Bank building

Date	Mintage	F12	VF20	XF40	MS60	MS63
2006	500	PF65 140				

KM# 42 100 LEI
31.11 g., 0.925 Silver 0.9191 oz. ASW, 37 mm. **Subject:** Petru Rares **Rev:** Bust 3/4 right

Date	Mintage	F12	VF20	XF40	MS60	MS63
2007	500	PF65 450				

KM# 37 100 LEI
7.78 g., 0.999 Gold 0.2483 oz. AGW, 24 mm. **Subject:** Dimitrie Cantemir

Date	Mintage	F12	VF20	XF40	MS60	MS63
2008	Est. 1000	PF63 575	PF65 600			

KM# 46 100 LEI
31.10 g., 0.925 Silver 0.9189 oz. ASW, 37 mm. **Subject:** Antioh Cantemir **Rev:** Half-length figure standing 3/4 left

Date	Mintage	F12	VF20	XF40	MS60	MS63
2008	1,000	PF63 95.00	PF65 100			

KM# 52 100 LEI
15.50 g., 0.999 Gold 0.4946 oz. AGW, 28 mm. **Subject:** Dimitrie Cantemir **Obv:** National Arms **Rev:** Cantemir seated at desk

Date	Mintage	F12	VF20	XF40	MS60	MS63
2008	300	PF65 950				

KM# 51 100 LEI
22.50 g., 0.925 Silver 0.6648 oz. ASW, 34 mm. **Subject:** Moldovan Chronicals, 15-18 Centuries **Rev:** Man seated writing

Date	Mintage	F12	VF20	XF40	MS60	MS63
2009	1,000	PF63 85.00	PF65 90.00			

KM# 57 100 LEI
15.50 g., 0.999 Gold 0.4946 oz. AGW, 28 mm. **Subject:** Doina and Ion Aldea-Teodorovici **Obv:** National arms **Rev:** Conjoined busts right

Date	Mintage	F12	VF20	XF40	MS60	MS63
2010	300	PF65 950				

KM# 61 100 LEI
15.50 g., 0.999 Gold 0.4946 oz. AGW, 28 mm. **Subject:** Grigore Vieru **Obv:** National Arms **Rev:** Profile bust left

Date	Mintage	F12	VF20	XF40	MS60	MS63
2010	300	PF65 950				

KM# 62 100 LEI
31.10 g., 0.999 Silver 0.9925 oz. ASW, 37 mm. **Subject:** National Bank of Moldova, 20th Anniversary **Obv:** National arms **Rev:** National Bank logo **Edge:** Reeded

Date	Mintage	F12	VF20	XF40	MS60	MS63
2011	500	PF65 80.00				

KM# 63 100 LEI
31.10 g., 0.999 Silver 0.9925 oz. ASW, 37 mm. **Subject:** Independence, 20th Anniversary **Obv:** National arms **Rev:** Father and son holding Moldovian flag **Edge:** Reeded

Date	Mintage	F12	VF20	XF40	MS60	MS63
2011	1,000	PF63 70.00	PF65 75.00			

KM# 64 100 LEI
31.10 g., 0.999 Silver 0.9925 oz. ASW, 37 mm. **Subject:** Chisinau, 575th Anniversary of Founding of the City **Obv:** National arms **Rev:** Mazarachi Hill **Edge:** Reeded

Date	Mintage	F12	VF20	XF40	MS60	MS63
2011	1,000	PF63 70.00	PF65 75.00			

KM# 66 100 LEI
7.80 g., 0.999 Gold 0.2489 oz. AGW, 24 mm. **Subject:** Bogdan Petriceicu Hasdeu **Obv:** National arms **Rev:** Bust **Edge:** Reeded

Date	Mintage	F12	VF20	XF40	MS60	MS63
2011	300	PF65 475				

MONACO

The Principality of Monaco, located on the Mediterranean coast nine miles from Nice, has an area of 0.58 sq. mi. (1.9 sq. km.) and a population of 26,000. Capital: Monaco-Ville. The economy is based on tourism and the manufacture of cosmetics, gourmet foods and highly specialized electronics. Monaco also derives its revenue from a tobacco monopoly and the sale of postage stamps for philatelic purpose. Gambling in Monte Carlo accounts for only a small fraction of the country's revenue.

RULERS
Rainier III, 1949-2005
Albert II, 2005-

MINT PRIVY MARKS
(a) - Paris (privy marks only)
Horseshoe - 2001 and 2002
Heart – 2002-2003
French Horn with starfish in water – 2003-
(p) - Thunderbolt - Poissy

MONETARY SYSTEM
100 Euro Cents = 1 Euro

PRINCIPALITY
EURO COINAGE

KM# 167 EURO CENT
2.30 g., Copper Plated Steel, 16.25 mm. **Ruler:** Rainier III **Obv:** Crowned arms **Rev:** Value and globe **Edge:** Plain

Date	Mintage	F12	VF20	XF40	MS60	MS63
2001(a)	327,200	—	—	—	20.00	35.00
2001(a)	3,500	PF63 75.00				
2002(a) In sets only	40,000	—	—	—	—	75.00
2003(a)		—	—	—	—	10.00
2004(a)	14,999	PF63 25.00				
2005(a)	35,000	PF63 50.00				

KM# 188 EURO CENT
2.30 g., Copper Plated Steel, 16.25 mm. **Ruler:** Albert II **Obv:** Crowned arms within circle of stars **Rev:** Value and globe

Date	Mintage	F12	VF20	XF40	MS60	MS63
2006	11,180	PF63 30.00				
2007		—	—	—	—	30.00
2009 In sets only	8,020	—	—	—	—	30.00

KM# 168 2 EURO CENT
3.06 g., Copper Plated Steel, 18.75 mm. **Ruler:** Rainier III **Obv:** Crowned arms **Rev:** Value and globe **Edge:** Grooved

Date	Mintage	F12	VF20	XF40	MS60	MS63
2001(a)	393,400	—	—	—	15.00	30.00
2001(a)	3,500	PF63 85.00				
2002(a) In sets only	40,000	—	—	—	—	85.00
2003(a)		—	—	—	—	10.00
2004(a)	14,999	PF63 35.00				
2005(a)	35,000	PF63 50.00				

KM# 189 2 EURO CENT
3.06 g., Copper Plated Steel, 18.75 mm. **Ruler:** Albert II **Obv:** Crowned arms within circle of stars **Rev:** Value and globe **Edge:** Grooved

Date	Mintage	F12	VF20	XF40	MS60	MS63
2006	11,260	PF63 25.00				
2007	—	—	—	—	—	25.00
2009 In sets only	8,020	—	—	—	—	25.00

KM# 169 5 EURO CENT

3.92 g., Copper Plated Steel, 21.25 mm. **Ruler:** Rainier III **Obv:** Crowned arms **Rev:** Value and globe **Edge:** Plain

Date	Mintage	F12	VF20	XF40	MS60	MS63
2001(a)	320,000	—	—	—	20.00	35.00
2001(a)	3,500	PF63 95.00				
2002(a) In sets only	40,000	—	—	—	—	85.00
2003(a)	—	—	—	—	—	15.00
2004(a)	14,999	PF63 45.00				
2005(a)	35,000	PF63 55.00				

KM# 190 5 EURO CENT

3.92 g., Copper Plated Steel, 21.25 mm. **Ruler:** Albert II **Obv:** Crowned arms within circle of stars **Rev:** Value and globe

Date	Mintage	F12	VF20	XF40	MS60	MS63
2006	11,180	PF63 30.00				
2007	—	—	—	—	—	30.00
2009 In sets only	8,020	—	—	—	—	30.00
2011 In sets only	7,000	—	—	—	—	30.00

KM# 170 10 EURO CENT

4.10 g., Brass, 19.75 mm. **Ruler:** Rainier III **Obv:** Knight on horse **Rev:** Value and map **Edge:** Reeded

Date	Mintage	F12	VF20	XF40	MS60	MS63
2001(a)	320,000	—	—	—	15.00	25.00
2001(a)	3,500	PF63 110				
2002(a)	407,200	—	—	—	8.00	12.00
2003(a)	100,800	—	—	—	12.00	16.00
2004(a)	14,999	PF63 50.00				

KM# 181 10 EURO CENT

4.10 g., Brass, 19.75 mm. **Ruler:** Albert II **Obv:** Crowned AA monogram **Rev:** Relief map of Western Europe, stars, lines and value **Edge:** Reeded

Date	Mintage	F12	VF20	XF40	MS60	MS63
2006(a)	11,180	PF63 50.00				

KM# 191 10 EURO CENT

4.10 g., Brass, 19.75 mm. **Ruler:** Albert II **Obv:** Crowned AA monogram **Rev:** Relief map of western Europe, stars, lines and value **Edge:** Reeded

Date	Mintage	F12	VF20	XF40	MS60	MS63
2007(a)	—	—	—	—	—	30.00
2009(a) In sets only	8,020	—	—	—	—	30.00
2011(a) In sets only	7,000	—	—	—	—	30.00

KM# 171 20 EURO CENT

5.74 g., Brass, 22.25 mm. **Ruler:** Rainier III **Obv:** Knight on horse **Rev:** Value and map **Edge:** Notched

Date	Mintage	F12	VF20	XF40	MS60	MS63
2001(a)	386,400	—	—	—	15.00	20.00
2001(a)	3,500	PF63 120				
2002(a)	376,000	—	—	—	12.00	16.00
2003(a)	100,000	—	—	—	12.00	16.00
2004(a)	14,999	PF63 60.00				

KM# 182 20 EURO CENT

5.74 g., Brass, 22.25 mm. **Ruler:** Albert II **Obv:** Crowned AA monogram **Rev:** Relief map of Western Europe, stars, lines and value **Edge:** Notched

Date	Mintage	F12	VF20	XF40	MS60	MS63
2006(a)	11,180	PF63 60.00				

KM# 192 20 EURO CENT

5.74 g., Brass, 22.25 mm. **Ruler:** Albert II **Obv:** Crowned AA monogram **Rev:** Relief map of western Europe, stars, lines and value **Edge:** Notched

Date	Mintage	F12	VF20	XF40	MS60	MS63
2007(a)	—	—	—	—	—	30.00
2009(a) In sets only	8,020	—	—	—	—	30.00
2011(a) In sets only	7,000	—	—	—	—	30.00

KM# 172 50 EURO CENT

7.80 g., Brass, 24.25 mm. **Ruler:** Rainier III **Obv:** Knight on horse **Rev:** Value and map **Edge:** Reeded

Date	Mintage	F12	VF20	XF40	MS60	MS63
2001 (a)	320,000	—	—	—	15.00	30.00
2001 (a)	3,500	PF63 130				
2002 (a)	364,000	—	—	—	8.00	12.00
2003 (a)	100,000	—	—	—	12.00	16.00
2004 (a)	14,999	PF63 65.00				

KM# 183 50 EURO CENT

7.80 g., Brass, 24.25 mm. **Ruler:** Albert II **Obv:** Crowned AA monogram **Rev:** Relief map of Western Europe, stars, lines and value **Edge:** Reeded

Date	Mintage	F12	VF20	XF40	MS60	MS63
2006(a)	11,180	PF63 65.00				

KM# 193 50 EURO CENT

7.80 g., Brass, 24.25 mm. **Ruler:** Albert II **Obv:** Crowned AA monogram **Rev:** Relief map of western Europe, stars, lines and values **Edge:** Reeded

Date	Mintage	F12	VF20	XF40	MS60	MS63
2007(a)	—	—	—	—	—	30.00
2009(a) In sets only	8,020	—	—	—	—	30.00
2011(a) In sets only	7,000	—	—	—	—	30.00

KM# 173 EURO

7.50 g., Bi-Metallic, 23.25 mm. **Ruler:** Rainier III **Obv:** Conjoined heads of Prince Ranier and Crown Prince Albert right within circle **Rev:** Value and map **Edge:** Segmented reeding

Date	Mintage	F12	VF20	XF40	MS60	MS63
2001(a)	991,100	—	—	—	10.00	12.00
2001(a)	3,500	PF63 145				
2002(a)	512,500	—	—	—	11.00	14.00
2003(a)	135,000	—	—	—	13.50	18.50
2004(a)	14,999	PF63 75.00				

KM# 184 EURO

7.50 g., Bi-Metallic, 23.25 mm. **Ruler:** Albert II **Obv:** Head right of Prince Albert **Rev:** Relief map of Western Europe, stars, lines and value **Edge:** Segmented reeding

Date	Mintage	F12	VF20	XF40	MS60	MS63
2006(a)	11,180	PF63 75.00				

KM# 194 EURO

7.50 g., Bi-Metallic, 23.25 mm. **Ruler:** Albert II **Obv:** Head right **Rev:** Relief map of western Europe, stars, lines and value **Edge:** Segmented reeding

Date	Mintage	F12	VF20	XF40	MS60	MS63
2007(a)	100,000	—	—	—	—	18.00
2009(a) In sets only	8,020	—	—	—	—	30.00
2011(a) In sets only	7,000	—	—	—	—	30.00

KM# 174 2 EURO

8.50 g., Bi-Metallic, 25.75 mm. **Ruler:** Rainier III **Obv:** Head right within circle flanked by stars **Rev:** Value and map **Edge:** Reeded with 2s and stars

Date	Mintage	F12	VF20	XF40	MS60	MS63
2001(a)	919,800	—	—	—	14.00	25.00
2001(a)	3,500	PF63 165				
2002(a)	496,000	—	—	—	15.00	18.00
2003(a)	228,000	—	—	—	17.50	22.50
2004(a)	14,999	PF63 100				

KM# 185 2 EURO

8.50 g., Bi-Metallic, 25.75 mm. **Ruler:** Albert II **Obv:** Prince Albert's head right **Rev:** Relief map of Western Europe, stars, lines and value **Edge:** Reeded with 2's and stars

Date	Mintage	F12	VF20	XF40	MS60	MS63
2006(a)	11,180	PF63 130				

KM# 186 2 EURO

8.50 g., Bi-Metallic, 25.75 mm. **Ruler:** Albert II **Subject:** Princess Grace, 25th Anniversary of Death **Obv:** Head of Princess Grace left **Rev:** Relief map of Western Europe, stars, lines and value **Edge:** Reeded with 2s and stars

Date	Mintage	F12	VF20	XF40	MS60	MS63
2007(a)	20,000	—	—	—	850	1,250

KM# 195 2 EURO

8.50 g., Bi-Metallic, 25.75 mm. **Ruler:** Albert II **Obv:** Head right **Rev:** Relief map of western Europe, stars, lines and values **Edge:** Reeded with 2's and stars

Date	Mintage	F12	VF20	XF40	MS60	MS63
2007(a)	—	—	—	—	65.00	—
2009(a)	250,000	—	—	—	35.00	—
2009(a) In sets only	8,000	—	—	—	—	150
2010(a)	25,000	PF63 300				
2011(a)	1,039,052	—	—	—	35.00	150
2012(a)	—	—	—	—	35.00	150

KM# 196 2 EURO

8.50 g., Bi-Metallic, 25.75 mm. **Ruler:** Albert II **Subject:** Royal Wedding of Prince Albert II and Princess Charlène **Obv:** Conjoined heads left

Date	Mintage	F12	VF20	XF40	MS60	MS63
2011A	147,877	—	—	—	—	75.00

KM# 199 2 EURO
8.50 g., Bi-Metallic **Ruler:** Albert II **Subject:** 500th Anniversary **Obv:** Lucien I bust left

Date	Mintage	F12	VF20	XF40	MS60	MS63
2012(a)	100,000	—	—	—	—	75.00

KM# 180 5 EURO
12.00 g., 0.900 Silver 0.345 oz. ASW, 29 mm. **Ruler:** Rainier III **Obv:** Bust right **Rev:** Saint standing

Date	Mintage	F12	VF20	XF40	MS60	MS63
2004 (a)	14,999	PF63 150				

KM# 197 5 EURO
12.00 g., 0.900 Silver 0.345 oz. ASW, 29 mm. **Ruler:** Albert II **Subject:** Prince Albert II, 50th Birthday **Obv:** Bust right **Rev:** Crowned and mantled arms

Date	Mintage	F12	VF20	XF40	MS60	MS63
2008(a) Prooflike	9,000	—	—	—	—	185

KM# 178 10 EURO
25.00 g., 0.925 Silver 0.7387 oz. ASW, 37 mm. **Ruler:** Rainier III **Obv:** Conjoined busts of Prince Ranier and Crown Prince Albert right **Rev:** Arms

Date	Mintage	F12	VF20	XF40	MS60	MS63
2003(a)	4,000	PF63 450	PF65 475			

KM# 187 10 EURO
3.22 g., 0.900 Gold 0.0926 oz. AGW **Ruler:** Albert II **Subject:** Death of Rainier III **Obv:** Principality arms **Rev:** Head of Rainier III right

Date	Mintage	F12	VF20	XF40	MS60	MS63
2005(a)	3,313	PF63 500	PF65 550			

KM# 177 20 EURO
18.00 g., 0.925 Gold 0.5319 oz. AGW, 32 mm. **Ruler:** Rainier III **Obv:** Bust right **Rev:** Arms

Date	Mintage	F12	VF20	XF40	MS60	MS63
2002(a)	10,000	PF63 1,000	PF65 1,100			

KM# 198 20 EURO
6.45 g., 0.900 Gold 0.1854 oz. AGW, 21 mm. **Ruler:** Albert II **Subject:** Prince Albert II, 50th Birthday **Obv:** Bust right **Rev:** Crowned and mantled arms

Date	Mintage	F12	VF20	XF40	MS60	MS63
2008(a)	3,000	PF63 550	PF65 600			

KM# 179 100 EURO
29.00 g., 0.900 Gold 0.8337 oz. AGW **Ruler:** Rainier III **Obv:** Bust right **Rev:** Knight on horse

Date	Mintage	F12	VF20	XF40	MS60	MS63
2003(a)	1,000	PF63 3,000	PF65 3,250			

MINT SETS

KM#	Date	Mintage	Identification	Issue Price	Mkt Val
MS1	2001 (8)	20,000	KM#167-174, exercise caution, privately packaged and deceptively false sets exist	35.00	250
MS2	2002 (8)	40,000	KM#167-174, exercise caution, privately packaged and deceptively false sets exist	35.00	350
MS3	2009 (8)	8,000	KM#188-195	—	600

PROOF SETS

KM#	Date	Mintage	Identification	Issue Price	Mkt Val
PS1	2001 (8)	3,500	KM#167-174	—	1,100
PS2	2004 (9)	14,999	KM#167-174, 180	—	700
PS3	2005 (3)	35,000	KM#167-169	—	160
PS4	2006 (8)	11,180	KM#181-185, 188-190	—	475

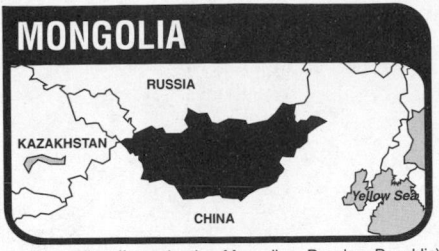

MONGOLIA

Mongolia, (formerly the Mongolian Peoples Republic) a landlocked country in central Asia between Russia and the People's Republic of China, has an area of 604,250 sq. mi. (1,565,000 sq. km.) and a population of 2.26 million. Capital: Ulaan Baator. Animal herds and flocks are the chief economic asset. Wool, cattle, butter, meat and hides are exported.

For earlier issues see Russia - Tannu Tuva.

MONETARY SYSTEM
100 Mongo = 1 Tugrik

STATE
DECIMAL COINAGE

KM# 302 100 TUGRIK
Silver **Subject:** XXVI Summer Olympics, Atlanta **Obv:** Arms **Rev:** 1904 St. Louis World's Fair Program Cover

Date	Mintage	F12	VF20	XF40	MS60	MS63
2002	—	PF65 25.00				

KM# 254 100 TUGRIK
25.00 g., 0.925 Silver 0.7387 oz. ASW **Obv:** Arms **Rev:** Yin-Yang symbol

Date	Mintage	F12	VF20	XF40	MS60	MS63
2007	—	PF65 30.00				

KM# 306 100 TUGRIK
26.00 g., 0.925 Silver 0.7682 oz. ASW, 38.5 mm. **Subject:** Wonders of the World **Obv:** National emblem **Rev:** Rome's Colosseum

Date	Mintage	F12	VF20	XF40	MS60	MS63
2008 Prooflike	—	—	—	—	—	35.00

KM# 307 100 TUGRIK
26.40 g., 0.925 Silver 0.7801 oz. ASW, 38.5 mm. **Subject:** Wonders of the World **Obv:** National Emblem **Rev:** Chichen Itza pyramid

Date	Mintage	F12	VF20	XF40	MS60	MS63
2008 Prooflike	—	—	—	—	—	35.00

KM# 308 100 TUGRIK
25.00 g., 0.925 Silver 0.7387 oz. ASW **Obv:** National emblem **Rev:** Treasury at Petra

Date	Mintage	F12	VF20	XF40	MS60	MS63
2008	—	PF65 75.00				

KM# 317 100 TUGRIK
25.00 g., 0.925 Silver 0.7387 oz. ASW, 38.6 mm. **Subject:** Machu Picchu

Date	Mintage	F12	VF20	XF40	MS60	MS63
2008	—	PF65 50.00				

KM# 321 100 TUGRIK
26.40 g., 0.925 Silver 0.7801 oz. ASW, 38.6 mm. **Subject:** Taj Mahal

Date	Mintage	F12	VF20	XF40	MS60	MS63
2008	—	PF65 50.00				

KM# 282 250 TUGRIK
15.50 g., 0.925 Silver 0.458 oz. ASW, 33 mm. **Subject:** Zodiac - Capricorn **Rev:** Seated goat left, partially gilt

Date	Mintage	F12	VF20	XF40	MS60	MS63
2007	7,000	—	—	—	—	25.00

KM# 283 250 TUGRIK
15.50 g., 0.925 Silver 0.458 oz. ASW, 33 mm. **Subject:** Zodiac - Aquarius **Rev:** Man pouring water, partially gilt

Date	Mintage	F12	VF20	XF40	MS60	MS63
2007	7,000	—	—	—	—	25.00

KM# 284 250 TUGRIK
15.50 g., 0.925 Silver 0.458 oz. ASW, 33 mm. **Subject:** Zodiac - Pisces **Rev:** Two fish partially gilt

Date	Mintage	F12	VF20	XF40	MS60	MS63
2007	7,000	—	—	—	—	25.00

KM# 285 250 TUGRIK
15.50 g., 0.925 Silver 0.458 oz. ASW, 33 mm. **Subject:** Zodiac - Aries **Rev:** Ram seated partially gilt

Date	Mintage	F12	VF20	XF40	MS60	MS63
2007	7,000	—	—	—	—	25.00

KM# 286 250 TUGRIK
15.50 g., 0.925 Silver 0.458 oz. ASW, 33 mm. **Subject:** Zodiac - Taurus **Rev:** Bull, partially gilt

Date	Mintage	F12	VF20	XF40	MS60	MS63
2007	7,000	—	—	—	—	25.00

KM# 287 250 TUGRIK
15.50 g., 0.925 Silver 0.458 oz. ASW, 33 mm. **Subject:** Zodiac - Gemini **Rev:** Twins, partially gilt

Date	Mintage	F12	VF20	XF40	MS60	MS63
2007	7,000	—	—	—	—	25.00

KM# 288 250 TUGRIK
15.50 g., 0.925 Silver 0.458 oz. ASW, 33 mm. **Subject:** Zodiac - Cancer **Rev:** Crab - partially gilt

Date	Mintage	F12	VF20	XF40	MS60	MS63
2007	7,000	—	—	—	—	25.00

KM# 289 250 TUGRIK
15.50 g., 0.925 Silver 0.458 oz. ASW, 33 mm. **Subject:** Zodiac - Leo **Rev:** Lion walking left, partially gilt

Date	Mintage	F12	VF20	XF40	MS60	MS63
2007	7,000	—	—	—	—	25.00

KM# 290 250 TUGRIK
15.50 g., 0.925 Silver 0.458 oz. ASW, 33 mm. **Subject:** Zodiac - Virgo **Rev:** Female, partially gilt

Date	Mintage	F12	VF20	XF40	MS60	MS63
2007	7,000	—	—	—	—	25.00

KM# 291 250 TUGRIK
15.50 g., 0.925 Silver 0.458 oz. ASW, 33 mm. **Subject:** Zodiac - Libra **Rev:** Scales, partially gilt

Date	Mintage	F12	VF20	XF40	MS60	MS63
2007	7,000	—	—	—	—	25.00

KM# 292 250 TUGRIK
15.50 g., 0.925 Silver 0.458 oz. ASW, 33 mm. **Subject:** Zodiac - Scorpio **Rev:** Scorpion, partially gilt

Date	Mintage	F12	VF20	XF40	MS60	MS63
2007	7,000	—	—	—	—	25.00

KM# 293 250 TUGRIK
15.50 g., 0.925 Silver 0.458 oz. ASW, 33 mm. **Subject:** Zodiac - Sagittarius **Rev:** Centar, partailly gilt

Date	Mintage	F12	VF20	XF40	MS60	MS63
2007	7,000	—	—	—	—	25.00

KM# 300 250 TUGRIK
15.50 g., 0.999 Silver 0.4946 oz. ASW, 33 mm. **Subject:** Moscow Waterworks **Rev:** Building in multicolor, aqueduct in background

Date	Mintage	F12	VF20	XF40	MS60	MS63
2007	1,000	—	—	—	—	45.00

KM# 301 250 TUGRIK
15.50 g., 0.999 Silver 0.4946 oz. ASW, 33 mm. **Subject:** Moscow Metro **Rev:** Subway train, multicolor

Date	Mintage	F12	VF20	XF40	MS60	MS63
2007	1,000	—	—	—	—	45.00

KM# 270 250 TUGRIK
15.55 g., 0.925 Silver 0.4595 oz. ASW, 37 mm. **Subject:** Baby Boy **Obv:** Arms **Rev:** Baby seated on flower, multicolor **Shape:** Heart

Date	Mintage	F12	VF20	XF40	MS60	MS63
2008	2,500	PF65 40.00				

KM# 271 250 TUGRIK
15.55 g., 0.925 Silver 0.4595 oz. ASW, 37 mm. **Subject:** Baby Girl **Obv:** Arms **Rev:** Baby Girl on flower **Shape:** Heart

Date	Mintage	F12	VF20	XF40	MS60	MS63
2008	2,500	PF65 40.00				

KM# 189 500 TUGRIK
25.00 g., 0.925 Silver 0.7387 oz. ASW, 38.7 mm. **Obv:** National emblem above value **Rev:** Protoceratops Andrewsi **Edge:** Reeded

Date	Mintage	F12	VF20	XF40	MS60	MS63
2001	2,500	PF63 42.00		PF65 45.00		

KM# 190 500 TUGRIK
25.00 g., 0.925 Silver 0.7387 oz. ASW **Obv:** National emblem above value **Rev:** Velociraptor Mongoliensis

Date	Mintage	F12	VF20	XF40	MS60	MS63
2001	2,500	PF63 42.00		PF65 45.00		

KM# 191 500 TUGRIK
25.00 g., 0.925 Silver 0.7387 oz. ASW **Series:** Olympics **Obv:** National emblem above value **Rev:** Speed skater

Date	Mintage	F12	VF20	XF40	MS60	MS63
2001	15,000	PF63 30.00	PF65 35.00			

KM# 192 500 TUGRIK
25.00 g., 0.925 Silver 0.7387 oz. ASW **Series:** Olympics **Obv:** National emblem above value **Rev:** Cross-country skiers

Date	Mintage	F12	VF20	XF40	MS60	MS63
2001	20,000	PF63 28.00	PF65 32.00			

KM# 195 500 TUGRIK
Copper-Nickel, 22.1 mm. **Subject:** Sukhe-Bataar **Obv:** National emblem and value **Rev:** Crowned head facing **Edge:** Plain

Date	Mintage	F12	VF20	XF40	MS60	MS63
2001	—				2.50	3.00

KM# 238 500 TUGRIK
20.00 g., 0.925 Silver 0.591 oz. ASW **Subject:** Gobi Desert Brown Bear **Obv:** Arms **Rev:** Bear standing on rock in stream

Date	Mintage	F12	VF20	XF40	MS60	MS63
2001	—	PF65 28.00				

KM# 239a 500 TUGRIK
31.11 g., 0.999 Silver 0.9926 oz. ASW **Subject:** Year of the Snake **Obv:** Arms **Rev:** Snake, gilt

Date	Mintage	F12	VF20	XF40	MS60	MS63
2001	—	PF65 75.00				

KM# 239 500 TUGRIK
31.11 g., 0.999 Silver 0.9926 oz. ASW, 38.5 mm. **Subject:** Year of the Snake **Rev:** Snake

Date	Mintage	F12	VF20	XF40	MS60	MS63
2001	—	PF65 65.00				

KM# 241 500 TUGRIK
31.11 g., 0.999 Silver 0.9926 oz. ASW, 38.5 mm. **Subject:** Year of the Horse **Obv:** Arms **Rev:** Horse

Date	Mintage	F12	VF20	XF40	MS60	MS63
2002	—	PF65 65.00				

KM# 241a 500 TUGRIK
31.11 g., 0.999 Silver 0.9926 oz. ASW, 38.5 mm. **Subject:** Year of the Horse **Rev:** Horse, gilt

Date	Mintage	F12	VF20	XF40	MS60	MS63
2002	—	PF65 75.00				

KM# 200 500 TUGRIK
25.57 g., 0.925 Silver 0.7555 oz. ASW, 38.5 mm. **Subject:** Marco Polo, Homeward **Obv:** National emblem above value **Rev:** Five-masted sailing junk **Edge:** Reeded

Date	Mintage	F12	VF20	XF40	MS60	MS63
2003	5,000	PF65 45.00				

KM# 204 500 TUGRIK
25.00 g., 0.925 Silver 0.7387 oz. ASW, 38 mm. **Obv:** National emblem above value **Rev:** Wolf within full moon **Edge:** Reeded

Date	Mintage	F12	VF20	XF40	MS60	MS63
2003	10,000	PF65 90.00				

KM# 205 500 TUGRIK
25.00 g., 0.925 Silver 0.7387 oz. ASW, 38.6 mm. **Obv:** National emblem above value **Rev:** Medallion divides busts **Edge:** Reeded

Date	Mintage	F12	VF20	XF40	MS60	MS63
2003	5,000	PF65 65.00				

KM# 206 500 TUGRIK
1.24 g., 0.9999 Gold 0.0397 oz. AGW, 13.92 mm. **Obv:** National emblem above value **Rev:** Five masted sailing junk **Edge:** Reeded

Date	Mintage	F12	VF20	XF40	MS60	MS63
2003	25,000	PF63 75.00	PF65 85.00			

KM# 207 500 TUGRIK
1.24 g., 0.9999 Gold 0.0397 oz. AGW, 13.92 mm. **Obv:** National emblem above value **Rev:** Medallion divides busts **Edge:** Reeded

Date	Mintage	F12	VF20	XF40	MS60	MS63
2003	25,000	PF63 75.00	PF65 85.00			

KM# 229a 500 TUGRIK
31.11 g., 0.999 Silver 0.9926 oz. ASW, 38.5 mm. **Subject:** Year of the Ram **Obv:** Arms **Rev:** Ram standing left, gilt

Date	Mintage	F12	VF20	XF40	MS60	MS63
2003	—	PF65 75.00				

KM# 229 500 TUGRIK
31.11 g., 0.999 Silver 0.9926 oz. ASW **Obv:** Arms above legend **Rev:** Ram standing left

Date	Mintage	F12	VF20	XF40	MS60	MS63
2003	—					65.00

KM# 208 500 TUGRIK
25.00 g., 0.925 Silver 0.7387 oz. ASW, 38 mm. **Obv:** National emblem above value **Rev:** Holographic Osprey catching fish **Edge:** Reeded

Date	Mintage	F12	VF20	XF40	MS60	MS63
2004	5,000	PF65 45.00				

KM# 218 500 TUGRIK
31.24 g., 0.999 Silver 0.9969 oz. ASW, 38.59 mm. **Series:** Chinese Lunar **Subject:** Year of the Monkey **Obv:** National emblem **Rev:** Monkey seated on branch - gilt, border of scampering monkeys **Edge:** Reeded

Date	Mintage	F12	VF20	XF40	MS60	MS63
ND-2004	20,000	PF65 45.00				

KM# 244a 500 TUGRIK
31.11 g., 0.999 Silver 0.9926 oz. ASW, 38.5 mm. **Subject:** Year of the Monkey **Obv:** Arms **Rev:** Monkey, gilt

Date	Mintage	F12	VF20	XF40	MS60	MS63
2004	—	PF65 75.00				

KM# 219 500 TUGRIK
1.24 g., 0.9999 Gold 0.0396 oz. AGW **Series:** Chinese Lunar **Subject:** Year of the Monkey **Obv:** National emblem **Rev:** Monkey seated on branch

Date	Mintage	F12	VF20	XF40	MS60	MS63
ND-2004	—	PF63 70.00	PF65 80.00			

KM# 244 500 TUGRIK
31.11 g., 0.999 Silver 0.9926 oz. ASW, 38.5 mm. **Subject:** Year of the Monkey **Obv:** Arms **Rev:** Monkey

Date	Mintage	F12	VF20	XF40	MS60	MS63
2004	—	PF65 65.00				

KM# 318 500 TUGRIK
25.00 g., 0.925 Silver 0.7387 oz. ASW, 38.6 mm. **Subject:**
Osprey

Date	Mintage	F12	VF20	XF40	MS60	MS63
2004	Est. 5000	PF65 45.00				

KM# 209 500 TUGRIK
24.93 g., 0.925 Bi-Metallic 0.7366 oz., 30 mm. **Obv:** National
emblem above value, niobium leopard in oval center **Rev:**
Snow Leopard **Edge:** Reeded **Shape:** Oval

Date	Mintage	F12	VF20	XF40	MS60	MS63
2005	5,000	PF65 95.00				

KM# 210 500 TUGRIK
31.10 g., 0.999 Silver 0.9926 oz. ASW, 35x35 mm. **Obv:** Bronze
plated horse and rider on antiqued silver with national emblem
and value **Rev:** Bronze plated horse and rider on antiqued
silver above date **Edge:** Reeded **Shape:** Square

Date	Mintage	F12	VF20	XF40	MS60	MS63
2005	2,500	—	—	—	70.00	75.00

KM# 304 500 TUGRIK
31.10 g., 0.999 Silver 0.9925 oz. ASW, 38.5 mm. **Obv:** National
emblem **Rev:** Sumo Wrestler Yokozuna Ounomatsu in color

Date	Mintage	F12	VF20	XF40	MS60	MS63
2005	—	PF65 125				

KM# 210a 500 TUGRIK
31.10 g., 0.999 Silver 0.9926 oz. ASW, 35x35 mm. **Obv:** Gold
plated horse and rider with national emblem and value **Rev:**
Gold plated horse and rider above date **Edge:** Reeded

Date	Mintage	F12	VF20	XF40	MS60	MS63
2005	2,500	PF65 85.00				

KM# 246a 500 TUGRIK
31.11 g., 0.999 Silver 0.9926 oz. ASW, 38.5 mm. **Subject:** Year
of the Rooster **Obv:** Arms **Rev:** Rooster, gilt

Date	Mintage	F12	VF20	XF40	MS60	MS63
2005	—	PF65 80.00				

KM# 246 500 TUGRIK
31.11 g., 0.999 Silver 0.9926 oz. ASW, 38.5 mm. **Subject:** Year
of the Rooster **Obv:** Arms **Rev:** Rooster standing right

Date	Mintage	F12	VF20	XF40	MS60	MS63
2005	—	PF65 70.00				

KM# 319 500 TUGRIK
25.00 g., 0.925 Silver 0.7387 oz. ASW, 38.6 mm. **Subject:**
Shiranui **Rev:** Classical wrestler in color

Date	Mintage	F12	VF20	XF40	MS60	MS63
2005	—	PF65 100				

KM# 320 500 TUGRIK
25.00 g., 0.925 Silver 0.7387 oz. ASW, 38.6 mm. **Subject:**
Tanikaze **Rev:** Classical wrestler in color

Date	Mintage	F12	VF20	XF40	MS60	MS63
2005	—	PF65 100				

KM# 251a 500 TUGRIK
31.11 g., 0.999 Silver 0.9926 oz. ASW, 38.5 mm. **Subject:** Year
of the Dog **Obv:** Arms **Rev:** Dog standing, gilt

Date	Mintage	F12	VF20	XF40	MS60	MS63
2006	—	PF65 70.00				

KM# 230 500 TUGRIK
25.00 g., 0.925 Silver 0.7387 oz. ASW **Rev:** Swan with crystal
insert

Date	Mintage	F12	VF20	XF40	MS60	MS63
2006	—	PF65 95.00				

KM# 231 500 TUGRIK
25.00 g., 0.925 Silver 0.7387 oz. ASW **Rev:** Gobi bear head
with crystal inserts

Date	Mintage	F12	VF20	XF40	MS60	MS63
2006	—	PF65 150				

KM# 248 500 TUGRIK
25.00 g., 0.925 Silver 0.7387 oz. ASW **Subject:** Long Eared
Jerboa **Obv:** Arms **Rev:** Long eared jerboa, crystal eyes
Shape: 38.6

Date	Mintage	F12	VF20	XF40	MS60	MS63
2006	2,500	PF65 145				

KM# 249 500 TUGRIK
25.00 g., 0.925 Silver 0.7387 oz. ASW, 38.6 mm. **Obv:** Arms
Rev: Scorpion, crystal tail point

Date	Mintage	F12	VF20	XF40	MS60	MS63
2006	2,500	PF65 185				

KM# 250 500 TUGRIK
25.00 g., 0.925 Silver 0.7387 oz. ASW, 38.6 mm. **Rev:** Tiger,
head facing, crystal eyes

Date	Mintage	F12	VF20	XF40	MS60	MS63
2006	2,500	PF65 135				

KM# 251 500 TUGRIK
31.11 g., 0.999 Silver 0.9926 oz. ASW, 38.5 mm. **Subject:** Year
of the Dog **Obv:** Arms **Rev:** Dog standing

Date	Mintage	F12	VF20	XF40	MS60	MS63
2006	—	PF65 60.00				

KM# 260 500 TUGRIK
25.00 g., 0.925 Silver 0.7387 oz. ASW, 38.6 mm. **Subject:**
Great Mongolian State, 800th Anniversary **Obv:** Arms **Rev:**
Chinggis Khan and black pennant

Date	Mintage	F12	VF20	XF40	MS60	MS63
2006	2,500	PF65 75.00				

KM# 261 500 TUGRIK
25.00 g., 0.925 Silver 0.7387 oz. ASW, 38.61 mm. **Subject:**
Great Mongolian State, 800th Anniversary **Obv:** Arms **Rev:**
Nine white pennants

Date	Mintage	F12	VF20	XF40	MS60	MS63
2006	2,500	PF65 75.00				

KM# 316 500 TUGRIK
25.00 g., 0.925 Silver 0.7387 oz. ASW, 38.5 mm. **Subject:** Ice
skating

Date	Mintage	F12	VF20	XF40	MS60	MS63
2006	—	PF63 45.00	PF65 50.00			

KM# 212 500 TUGRIK
31.11 g., 0.999 Silver 0.9926 oz. ASW, 38 mm. **Obv:** Arms and
value **Rev:** Wolverine head facing with diamonds in eyes **Rev.
Inscription:** WILDLIFE PROTECTION GULO GULO

Date	Mintage	F12	VF20	XF40	MS60	MS63
2007	—					1,350

KM# 322 500 TUGRIK
31.11 g., 0.999 Silver 0.9926 oz. ASW, 38.6 mm. **Subject:** Year
of the Pig

Date	Mintage	F12	VF20	XF40	MS60	MS63
2007	—	PF65 80.00				

KM# 265 500 TUGRIK
31.11 g., 0.999 Silver 0.9926 oz. ASW, 38.61 mm. **Subject:**
Society Space exploration **Obv:** Arms **Rev:** Sputnik, rocket,
three figures

Date	Mintage	F12	VF20	XF40	MS60	MS63
2007	1,000	PF65 75.00				

KM# 266 500 TUGRIK
31.11 g., 0.999 Silver 0.9926 oz. ASW, 38.61 mm. **Subject:**
Soviet Space Exploration **Rev:** Laika, first dog in space

Date	Mintage	F12	VF20	XF40	MS60	MS63
2007	500	PF65 85.00				

KM# 267 500 TUGRIK
31.11 g., 0.999 Silver 0.9926 oz. ASW, 38.61 mm. **Subject:**
Soviet Space Exploration **Obv:** Arms **Rev:** Sputnik

Date	Mintage	F12	VF20	XF40	MS60	MS63
2007	500	PF65 85.00				

KM# 268 500 TUGRIK
31.11 g., 0.999 Silver 0.9926 oz. ASW, 38.61 mm. **Subject:**
Soviet Space Exploration **Obv:** Arms **Rev:** Yuri Gagarian

Date	Mintage	F12	VF20	XF40	MS60	MS63
2007	500	PF65 85.00				

KM# 269 500 TUGRIK
31.11 g., 0.999 Silver 0.9926 oz. ASW, 38.61 mm. **Subject:**
Soviet Space Exploration **Obv:** Arms **Rev:** Mir space station

Date	Mintage	F12	VF20	XF40	MS60	MS63
2007	1,000	PF65 85.00				

KM# 322a 500 TUGRIK
31.11 g., 0.999 Silver 0.9926 oz. ASW, 38.6 mm. **Subject:** Year
of the Pig

Date	Mintage	F12	VF20	XF40	MS60	MS63
2007	—	PF65 100				

KM# 325 500 TUGRIK
25.00 g., 0.925 Silver 0.7387 oz. ASW, 38.6 mm. **Rev:** John F. Kennedy at microphone

Date	Mintage	F12	VF20	XF40	MS60	MS63
2007	—	PF65 125				

KM# 213 500 TUGRIK
31.10 g., 0.999 Silver 0.9925 oz. ASW, 39mm mm. **Subject:** Year of the Rat **Obv:** National emblem, value below **Rev:** Three rats in grass **Edge:** Reeded

Date	Mintage	F12	VF20	XF40	MS60	MS63
2008	20,000	—	—	—	—	45.00

KM# 222 500 TUGRIK
25.00 g., 0.925 Silver 0.7387 oz. ASW, 38.61 mm. **Subject:** Wonders of the World **Obv:** Arms **Rev:** Multicolor Chichen Itza

Date	Mintage	F12	VF20	XF40	MS60	MS63
2008	2,500	—	—	—	—	75.00

KM# 223 500 TUGRIK
25.00 g., 0.925 Silver 0.7387 oz. ASW, 38.6 mm. **Subject:** Wonders of the World **Obv:** Arms **Rev:** Multicolor Treasury at Petra

Date	Mintage	F12	VF20	XF40	MS60	MS63
2008	2,500	—	—	—	—	95.00

KM# 224 500 TUGRIK
25.00 g., 0.925 Silver 0.7387 oz. ASW, 38.61 mm. **Subject:** Wonders of the World **Obv:** Arms **Rev:** Multicolor Taj Mahal

Date	Mintage	F12	VF20	XF40	MS60	MS63
2008	2,500	—	—	—	—	75.00

KM# 225 500 TUGRIK
25.00 g., 0.925 Silver 0.7387 oz. ASW, 38.61 mm. **Subject:** Wonders of the World **Obv:** Arms **Rev:** Multicolor Machu Picchu

Date	Mintage	F12	VF20	XF40	MS60	MS63
2008	2,500	—	—	—	—	85.00

KM# 226 500 TUGRIK
25.00 g., 0.925 Silver 0.7387 oz. ASW, 38.61 mm. **Subject:** Wonders of the World **Obv:** Arms **Rev:** Multicolor Great Wall of China

Date	Mintage	F12	VF20	XF40	MS60	MS63
2008	2,500	—	—	—	—	85.00

KM# 227 500 TUGRIK
25.00 g., 0.925 Silver 0.7387 oz. ASW, 38.61 mm. **Subject:** Wonders of the World **Obv:** Arms **Rev:** Multicolor Colosseum in Rome

Date	Mintage	F12	VF20	XF40	MS60	MS63
2008	2,500	—	—	—	—	75.00

KM# 228 500 TUGRIK
25.00 g., 0.925 Silver 0.7387 oz. ASW, 38.61 mm. **Subject:** Wonders of the World **Obv:** Arms **Rev:** Multicolor Christ the Redeemer statue in Rio

Date	Mintage	F12	VF20	XF40	MS60	MS63
2008	2,500	—	—	—	—	65.00

KM# 255 500 TUGRIK
25.00 g., 0.925 Silver 0.7387 oz. ASW, 38.6 mm. **Subject:** Frederic Chopin **Obv:** Arms **Rev:** Bust right, color keyboard vertical in center

Date	Mintage	F12	VF20	XF40	MS60	MS63
2008	1,000	PF65 90.00				

KM# 213a 500 TUGRIK
31.10 g., 0.999 Silver 0.9925 oz. ASW, 39.0 mm. **Subject:** Year of the Rat **Obv:** National emblem, value below **Rev:** Three gilt rats in grass **Edge:** Reeded

Date	Mintage	F12	VF20	XF40	MS60	MS63
2008	5,000	PF65 60.00				

KM# 256 500 TUGRIK
31.11 g., 0.999 Silver 0.9926 oz. ASW, 38.6 mm. **Subject:** Year of the Rat **Obv:** Arms **Rev:** Two mice

Date	Mintage	F12	VF20	XF40	MS60	MS63
2008	—	PF65 55.00				

KM# 256a 500 TUGRIK
31.11 g., 0.999 Silver 0.9926 oz. ASW, 38.6 mm. **Subject:** Year of the Rat **Obv:** Arms **Rev:** Two mice, gilt

Date	Mintage	F12	VF20	XF40	MS60	MS63
2008	—	PF65 65.00				

KM# 272 500 TUGRIK
25.00 g., 0.925 Silver 0.7387 oz. ASW, 38.6 mm. **Series:** Mongolian Olympians, Baatarjav **Obv:** Arms

Date	Mintage	F12	VF20	XF40	MS60	MS63
2008	2,500	PF65 45.00				

KM# 273 500 TUGRIK
25.00 g., 0.925 Silver 0.7387 oz. ASW, 38.61 mm. **Subject:** Mongolian Olympians - Badar-Uugan

Date	Mintage	F12	VF20	XF40	MS60	MS63
2008	2,500	PF65 45.00				

KM# 274 500 TUGRIK
25.00 g., 0.999 Silver 0.7978 oz. ASW, 38.61 mm. **Subject:** Mongolian Olympians - Serdamba

Date	Mintage	F12	VF20	XF40	MS60	MS63
2008	2,500	PF65 45.00				

KM# 275 500 TUGRIK
25.00 g., 0.925 Silver 0.7387 oz. ASW, 38.61 mm. **Subject:**
Mongolian Olympians - Tuvshinbayar

Date	Mintage	F12	VF20	XF40	MS60	MS63
2008	2,500	PF65 45.00				

KM# 276 500 TUGRIK
25.00 g., 0.925 Silver 0.7387 oz. ASW, 38.61 mm. **Subject:**
Mongolian Olympians - Gundegmaa

Date	Mintage	F12	VF20	XF40	MS60	MS63
2008	2,500	PF65 45.00				

KM# 279 500 TUGRIK
0.50 g., 0.999 Gold AGW, 11 mm **Subject:** Mongolian Olympic
Sports - Archery

Date	Mintage	F12	VF20	XF40	MS60	MS63
2008 Proof	15,000	—	—	—	—	50.00

KM# 280 500 TUGRIK
25.00 g., 0.925 Silver 0.7387 oz. ASW, 38.61 mm. **Obv:** Arms
Rev: Two snow leopards, multicolor

Date	Mintage	F12	VF20	XF40	MS60	MS63
2008	2,500	PF65 75.00				

KM# 281 500 TUGRIK
25.00 g., 0.925 Silver 0.7387 oz. ASW, 38.61 mm. **Obv:** Arms
Rev: The Almas, multicolor changing insert

Date	Mintage	F12	VF20	XF40	MS60	MS63
2008	2,500	PF65 55.00				

KM# 305 500 TUGRIK
25.00 g., 0.925 Silver 0.7387 oz. ASW, 38.61 mm. **Subject:**
Frederic Chopin **Obv:** National emblem **Rev:** Piano keys in
color, bust at right

Date	Mintage	F12	VF20	XF40	MS60	MS63
2008		PF65 75.00				

KM# 312 500 TUGRIK
31.11 g., 0.999 Silver 0.9926 oz. ASW, 38.61 mm. **Subject:**
Year of the Rat **Rev:** Mouse in multicolor

Date	Mintage	F12	VF20	XF40	MS60	MS63
2008		PF65 65.00				

KM# 258 500 TUGRIK
31.11 g., 0.999 Silver 0.9926 oz. ASW, 38.6 mm. **Subject:** Year
of the Ox **Obv:** Arms **Rev:** Ox

Date	Mintage	F12	VF20	XF40	MS60	MS63
2009		PF65 60.00				

KM# 258a 500 TUGRIK
31.11 g., 0.999 Silver 0.9926 oz. ASW, 38.6 mm. **Subject:** Year
of the Ox **Obv:** Arms **Rev:** Ox, gilt

Date	Mintage	F12	VF20	XF40	MS60	MS63
2009		PF65 70.00				

KM# 309 500 TUGRIK
31.10 g., 0.925 Silver 0.9189 oz. ASW, 38.6 mm. **Subject:**
Endangered Wildlife **Obv:** National Emblem **Rev:** Owl's head
facing (Strix Uralensis) crystal insert eyes

Date	Mintage	F12	VF20	XF40	MS60	MS63
2011 Antique finish	2,500	—	—	—	—	650

KM# 310 500 TUGRIK
0.50 g., 0.999 Gold AGW, 11 mm. **Subject:** Endangered
Wildlife **Obv:** National emblem **Rev:** Ural Owl (Strix Uralersis)
standing left

Date	Mintage	F12	VF20	XF40	MS60	MS63
2011 Proof	15,000	—	—	—	—	65.00

KM# 314 500 TUGRIK
25.00 g., 0.925 Silver 0.7387 oz. ASW, 38.61 mm. **Subject:**
Joint Societ - mongolian space flight, 30th Anniversary

Date	Mintage	F12	VF20	XF40	MS60	MS63
2011	—	PF65 70.00				

KM# 315 500 TUGRIK
25.00 g., 0.925 Silver 0.7387 oz. ASW, 38.61 mm. **Rev:** Saiga
Tatarica in color

Date	Mintage	F12	VF20	XF40	MS60	MS63
2011	2,500	PF65 70.00				

KM# 324 500 TUGRIK
31.11 g., 0.999 Silver 0.9926 oz. ASW, 38.61 mm. **Rev:** Baby
hedgehog with crystal eyes

Date	Mintage	F12	VF20	XF40	MS60	MS63
2012 Antique patina	—	—	—	—	—	450

KM# 326 500 TUGRIK
(No Composition) **Obv:** National emblem **Rev:** Argali sheep
with crystal eyes

Date	Mintage	F12	VF20	XF40	MS60	MS63
2013 Antique patina	—	—	—	—	—	350

KM# 199 1000 TUGRIK
31.11 g., 0.925 Silver 0.9192 oz. ASW, 38.6 mm. **Obv:** National
emblem above value **Obv. Inscription:** Denomination spelled
"TOGROG **Rev:** Head facing **Edge:** Reeded

Date	Mintage	F12	VF20	XF40	MS60	MS63
2002	17,000	—	—	—	42.00	45.00

KM# 303 1000 TUGRIK
Copper-Nickel, 38 mm. **Obv:** National emblem **Rev:** Two soccer players

Date	Mintage	F12	VF20	XF40	MS60	MS63
2003 Prooflike	2,000	—	—	—	—	10.00

KM# 233 1000 TUGRIK
Gold AGW **Rev:** Snow leopard

Date	Mintage	F12	VF20	XF40	MS60	MS63
2005	—	PF63 85.00	PF65 95.00			

KM# 253 1000 TUGRIK
1.24 g., 0.999 Gold 0.0396 oz. AGW **Subject:** Mozart **Obv:** Arms **Rev:** Portrait and profile heads above building

Date	Mintage	F12	VF20	XF40	MS60	MS63
2006	—	PF63 70.00	PF65 80.00			

KM# 262 1000 TUGRIK
1.24 g., 0.999 Gold 0.0396 oz. AGW, 13.92 mm. **Obv:** Arms **Rev:** Scorpion

Date	Mintage	F12	VF20	XF40	MS60	MS63
2006	25,000	PF63 85.00	PF65 95.00			

KM# 263 1000 TUGRIK
1.24 g., 0.999 Silver 0.0396 oz. ASW, 13.9 mm. **Obv:** Arms **Rev:** Long-eared Jerboa

Date	Mintage	F12	VF20	XF40	MS60	MS63
2006	—	PF63 85.00	PF65 95.00			

KM# 264 1000 TUGRIK
1.24 g., 0.999 Gold 0.0396 oz. AGW, 13.9 mm. **Obv:** Arms **Rev:** Gobi Bear

Date	Mintage	F12	VF20	XF40	MS60	MS63
2006	25,000	PF63 85.00	PF65 95.00			

KM# 294 1000 TUGRIK
62.20 g., 0.999 Silver 1.9849 oz. ASW, 50 mm. **Rev:** Tsarina Catherina multicolor

Date	Mintage	F12	VF20	XF40	MS60	MS63
2007	500	PF65 165				

KM# 295 1000 TUGRIK
62.20 g., 0.999 Silver 1.9849 oz. ASW, 50 mm. **Rev:** Tsar Nicholas I, multicolor

Date	Mintage	F12	VF20	XF40	MS60	MS63
2007	500	PF65 165				

KM# 296 1000 TUGRIK
62.20 g., 0.999 Silver 1.9849 oz. ASW, 50 mm. **Rev:** Tsar Nicholas II

Date	Mintage	F12	VF20	XF40	MS60	MS63
2007	500	PF65 165				

KM# 297 1000 TUGRIK
62.20 g., 0.999 Silver 1.9849 oz. ASW, 50 mm. **Rev:** Tsar Ivan IV, multicolor

Date	Mintage	F12	VF20	XF40	MS60	MS63
2007	500	PF65 165				

KM# 298 1000 TUGRIK
62.20 g., 0.999 Silver 1.9849 oz. ASW, 50 mm. **Rev:** Tsar Peter I, multicolor

Date	Mintage	F12	VF20	XF40	MS60	MS63
2007	500	PF65 165				

KM# 299 1000 TUGRIK
62.20 g., 0.999 Silver 1.9849 oz. ASW, 50 mm. **Rev:** Tsar Yuri

Date	Mintage	F12	VF20	XF40	MS60	MS63
2007	500	PF65 165				

KM# 214 1000 TUGRIK
1.24 g., 0.999 Gold 0.0396 oz. AGW, 14.0 mm. **Subject:** Year of the Rat **Obv:** National emblem, value below **Edge:** Reeded

Date	Mintage	F12	VF20	XF40	MS60	MS63
2008	10,000	PF63 65.00	PF65 75.00			

KM# 277 1000 TUGRIK
1.24 g., 0.999 Gold 0.0396 oz. AGW, 13.92 mm. **Subject:** Mongolian Olympic Sports - Boxing **Rev:** Two fighters in the ring

Date	Mintage	F12	VF20	XF40	MS60	MS63
2008	15,000	PF63 75.00	PF65 85.00			

KM# 278 1000 TUGRIK
1.24 g., 0.999 Gold 0.0396 oz. AGW, 13.92 mm. **Subject:** Mongolian Olympic Sports - Judo **Rev:** Judo athlete getting fliped

Date	Mintage	F12	VF20	XF40	MS60	MS63
2008	15,000	PF63 75.00	PF65 85.00			

KM# 311 1000 TUGRIK
1.24 g., 0.999 Gold 0.0396 oz. AGW, 13.92 mm. **Subject:** Frederic Chopin **Obv:** National Emblem **Rev:** Piano keyboard vertical at left, bust at right

Date	Mintage	F12	VF20	XF40	MS60	MS63
2011	—	PF65 100				

KM# 240 2500 TUGRIK
7.77 g., 0.999 Gold 0.248 oz. AGW **Subject:** Year of the Snake **Obv:** Arms **Rev:** Snake

Date	Mintage	F12	VF20	XF40	MS60	MS63
2001	2,000	PF65 500				

KM# 242 2500 TUGRIK
7.70 g., 0.999 Gold 0.2457 oz. AGW **Subject:** Year of the Horse **Obv:** Arms **Rev:** Year of the Horse

Date	Mintage	F12	VF20	XF40	MS60	MS63
2002	—	PF65 500				

KM# 243 2500 TUGRIK
155.50 g., 0.999 Silver 4.9623 oz. ASW, 65 mm. **Subject:** Year of the Ram **Obv:** Arms **Rev:** Ram standing left, gilt

Date	Mintage	F12	VF20	XF40	MS60	MS63
2003	4,000	PF65 325				

KM# 220 2500 TUGRIK
7.78 g., 0.9999 Gold 0.2485 oz. AGW **Series:** Chinese Lunar **Subject:** Year of the Monkey **Obv:** National emblem **Rev:** Monkey seated on branch **Edge:** Reeded

Date	Mintage	F12	VF20	XF40	MS60	MS63
ND-2004	2,000	PF65 525				

KM# 245 2500 TUGRIK
155.50 g., 0.999 Silver 4.9623 oz. ASW, 65 mm. **Subject:** Year of the Monkey **Obv:** Arms **Rev:** Monkey, gilt

Date	Mintage	F12	VF20	XF40	MS60	MS63
2004	4,000	PF65 325				

KM# 247 2500 TUGRIK
155.50 g., 0.999 Silver 4.9623 oz. ASW, 65 mm. **Subject:** Year
of the Rooster **Obv:** Arms **Rev:** Rooster, gilt

Date	Mintage	F12	VF20	XF40	MS60	MS63
2005	4,000	PF65 325				

KM# 252 2500 TUGRIK
155.50 g., 0.999 Silver 4.9623 oz. ASW, 65 mm. **Subject:** Year
of the Dog **Obv:** Arms **Rev:** Dog standing, gilt

Date	Mintage	F12	VF20	XF40	MS60	MS63
2006	—	PF65 325				

KM# 257 2500 TUGRIK
155.50 g., 0.999 Silver 4.9623 oz. ASW, 65 mm. **Subject:** Year
of the Rat **Obv:** Arms **Rev:** Two mice, gilt

Date	Mintage	F12	VF20	XF40	MS60	MS63
2008	—	PF65 325				

KM# 259 2500 TUGRIK
155.50 g., 0.999 Silver 4.9623 oz. ASW, 65 mm. **Subject:** Year
of the Ox **Obv:** Arms **Rev:** Ox, gilt

Date	Mintage	F12	VF20	XF40	MS60	MS63
2009	—	PF65 325				

KM# 198 5000 TUGRIK
155.50 g., 0.999 Silver 4.9623 oz. ASW, 40x90 mm. **Subject:**
Year of the Horse **Obv:** National emblem above value to left
of Palace Museum **Rev:** Five multicolor running horses **Edge:**
Plain **Note:** Round-cornered rectangle. Photo reduced.

Date	Mintage	F12	VF20	XF40	MS60	MS63
2002	—	PF65 350				

KM# 232 5000 TUGRIK
155.50 g., 0.999 Silver 4.9623 oz. ASW, 40x90 mm. **Rev:**
Three sumo wrestlers, multicolor **Shape:** Rectangle **Note:**
Illustration reduced.

Date	Mintage	F12	VF20	XF40	MS60	MS63
2005	—	PF65 400				

KM# 221 100000 TUGRIK
3000.00 g., 0.999 Silver 95.7355 oz. ASW **Series:** Chinese
Lunar **Subject:** Year of the Monkey **Obv:** National emblem
Rev: Monkey seated on branch

Date	Mintage	F12	VF20	XF40	MS60	MS63
ND-2004	—	PF65 3,750				

KM# 215 100000 TUGRIK
3000.00 g., 0.999 Silver 95.7355 oz. ASW, 130.0 mm. **Subject:**
Year of the Rat **Obv:** National emblem, value below **Rev:** Three
rats in grass **Edge:** Reeded **Note:** Serial number on edge.

Date	Mintage	F12	VF20	XF40	MS60	MS63
2008	500	PF65 3,750				

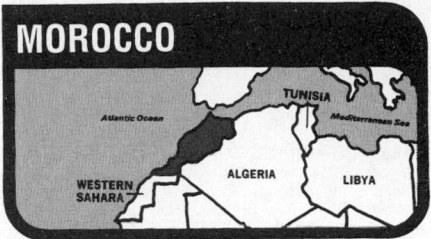

MOROCCO

The Kingdom of Morocco, situated on the northwest
corner of Africa, has an area of 432,620 sq. mi. (710,850 sq.
km.) and a population of 36 million. Capital: Rabat. The economy
is essentially agricultural. Phosphates, fresh and preserved
vegetables, canned fish, and raw materials are exported.

KINGDOM
REFORM COINAGE
100 Santimat = 1 Dirham

Y# 112 5 SANTIMAT
2.00 g., Aluminum-Bronze, 17.5 mm. **Ruler:** Mohammed VI
Obv: Crowned arms with supporters **Rev:** Value, flower and
dates **Edge:** Plain

Date	Mintage	F12	VF20	XF40	MS60	MS63
AH1423-2002	—	—	—	—	0.50	1.00

Y# 158 5 SANTIMAT
Brass Plated Iron **Ruler:** Mohammed VI **Rev:** National arms

Date	Mintage	F12	VF20	XF40	MS60	MS63
2011	—	—	—	—	—	0.70

Y# 114 10 SANTIMAT
3.00 g., Aluminum-Bronze, 20 mm. **Ruler:** Mohammed VI **Obv:**
Crowned arms with supporters **Rev:** Value, design of "sport and
solidarity **Edge:** Reeded

Date	Mintage	F12	VF20	XF40	MS60	MS63
AH1423-2002	—	—	—	—	1.00	2.00

Y# 136 10 SANTIMAT
3.00 g., Brass Plated Steel, 20 mm. **Ruler:** Mohammed VI
Rev: Bee and flower

Date	Mintage	F12	VF20	XF40	MS60	MS63
AH1432-2011	—	—	—	—	1.00	2.00
AH1433-2012	—	—	—	—	1.00	3.00
AH1434-2013	—	—	—	—	1.00	3.00

Y# 115 20 SANTIMAT
4.00 g., Aluminum-Bronze, 23 mm. **Ruler:** Mohammed VI **Obv:**
Crowned arms with supporters **Rev:** Value, design of "tourist
and craftsmen trade **Edge:** Reeded

Date	Mintage	F12	VF20	XF40	MS60	MS63
AH1423-2002	—	—	—	—	1.50	3.00

Y# 137 20 SANTIMAT
4.00 g., Brass Plated Steel, 23 mm. **Ruler:** Mohammed VI

Rev: Lotus flower and globe **Edge:** Reeded

Date	Mintage	F12	VF20	XF40	MS60	MS63
AH1432-2011	—	—	—	—	1.50	3.00
AH1433-2012	—	—	—	—	1.50	3.00
AH1434-2013	—	—	—	—	1.50	3.00

Y# 116 1/2 DIRHAM
4.00 g., Copper-Nickel, 21 mm. **Ruler:** Mohammed VI **Obv:**
Crowned arms with supporters **Rev:** Value, design theme
"telecommunications and new technologies **Edge:** Reeded

Date	Mintage	F12	VF20	XF40	MS60	MS63
AH1423-2002	—	—	—	—	2.00	3.00

Y# 138 1/2 DIRHAM
4.00 g., Nickel Plated Steel, 21 mm. **Ruler:** Mohammed VI
Obv: Crowned national arms with supporters **Rev:** Two fish
and large value **Edge:** Reeded

Date	Mintage	F12	VF20	XF40	MS60	MS63
AH1432-2011	—	—	—	—	3.00	5.00
AH1433-2012	—	—	—	—	3.00	5.00
AH1434-2013	—	—	—	—	3.00	5.00

Y# 117 DIRHAM
6.00 g., Copper-Nickel, 24 mm. **Ruler:** Mohammed VI **Obv:**
Head 3/4 left **Rev:** Crowned arms with supporters above value
Edge: Reeded

Date	Mintage	F12	VF20	XF40	MS60	MS63
AH1423-2002	—	—	—	—	3.00	5.00

Y# 139 DIRHAM
6.00 g., Nickel Plated Steel, 24 mm. **Ruler:** Mohammed VI
Obv: Head left **Rev:** Crowned national arms with supporters,
value below **Edge:** Reeded

Date	Mintage	F12	VF20	XF40	MS60	MS63
AH1432-2011	—	—	—	—	3.50	5.00
AH1433-2012	—	—	—	—	3.50	5.00
AH1434-2013	—	—	—	—	3.50	5.00

Y# 149 25 CENTIMES
0.70 g., Aluminum, 17 mm. **Ruler:** Mohammed VI **Subject:**
F.A.O. **Obv:** National arms **Rev:** Tuna in net

Date	Mintage	F12	VF20	XF40	MS60	MS63
2002	—	—	—	—	—	—

Y# 118 2 DIRHAMS
7.00 g., Copper-Nickel, 26 mm. **Ruler:** Mohammed VI **Obv:**
Head 3/4 left within octagon shape **Rev:** Crowned arms with
supporters above value within octagon shape **Edge:** Reeded

Date	Mintage	F12	VF20	XF40	MS60	MS63
AH1423-2002	—	—	—	—	4.00	6.00

Y# 109 5 DIRHAMS
7.50 g., Bi-Metallic, 25 mm. **Ruler:** Mohammed VI **Obv:** Head
3/4 left **Rev:** Crowned arms with supporters above value **Edge:**
Segmented reeding

Date	Mintage	F12	VF20	XF40	MS60	MS63
AH1423-2002	—	—	—	—	6.00	9.00

Y# 140 5 DIRHAMS
7.50 g., Bi-Metallic, 25 mm. **Ruler:** Mohammed VI **Obv:** Head left **Rev:** Hassan II Mosque in Casablanca **Edge:** Segmented reeding

Date	Mintage	F12	VF20	XF40	MS60	MS63
AH1432-2011	—				6.00	9.00

Y# 110 10 DIRHAMS
9.00 g., Bi-Metallic, 26.9 mm. **Ruler:** Mohammed VI **Obv:** Head 3/4 left **Rev:** Crowned arms with supporters above value **Edge:** Reeded

Date	Mintage	F12	VF20	XF40	MS60	MS63
AH1423-2002	—				10.00	15.00

Y# 141 10 DIRHAMS
9.00 g., Bi-Metallic, 27 mm. **Ruler:** Mohammed VI **Obv:** Head left **Rev:** Boumalne-du-Dades Fortress, palm tree at left, large value at right

Date	Mintage	F12	VF20	XF40	MS60	MS63
AH1432-2011	—				10.00	15.00

Y# 148 100 DIRHAMS
25.00 g., 0.900 Gold 0.7187 oz. AGW, 37 mm. **Ruler:** Mohammed VI **Subject:** Mohammed VI, 38th Birthday **Rev:** National arms

Date	Mintage	F12	VF20	XF40	MS60	MS63
2001		PF65 1,500				

Y# 160 100 DIRHAMS
12.00 g., Bi-Metallic, 28.4 mm. **Ruler:** Mohammed VI **Subject:** UNESCO sites in Rabat **Rev:** Hassan tower and Mohammed V's mausoleum

Date	Mintage	F12	VF20	XF40	MS60	MS63
AH1433-2012	—	PF65 30.00				

Y# 161 100 DIRHAMS
12.00 g., Bi-Metallic, 28.4 mm. **Ruler:** Mohammed VI **Subject:** UNESCO sites in Rabat **Rev:** Chellah door

Date	Mintage	F12	VF20	XF40	MS60	MS63
AH1433-2012	—	PF65 30.00				

Y# 162 100 DIRHAMS
12.00 g., Bi-Metallic, 28.4 mm. **Ruler:** Mohammed VI **Subject:** UNESCO sites in Rabat **Rev:** Udayas Kasbah

Date	Mintage	F12	VF20	XF40	MS60	MS63
AH1433-2012	—	PF65 30.00				

Y# 95 250 DIRHAMS
25.00 g., 0.925 Silver 0.7387 oz. ASW, 37 mm. **Ruler:** Mohammed VI **Subject:** World Children's Day **Obv:** Head 3/4 left **Rev:** Children standing on open book within globe **Edge:** Reeded

Date	Mintage	F12	VF20	XF40	MS60	MS63
AH1422-2001	—	PF65 100				
AH1422-2001	—				60.00	80.00

Y# 107 250 DIRHAMS
25.00 g., 0.925 Silver 0.7387 oz. ASW, 37 mm. **Ruler:** Mohammed VI **Subject:** Inauguration of Mohammed VI 2nd Anniversary **Obv:** Head 3/4 left **Rev:** Crowned arms with supporters above value **Edge:** Reeded

Date	Mintage	F12	VF20	XF40	MS60	MS63
AH1422-2001	—				55.00	70.00

Y# 95a 250 DIRHAMS
25.00 g., 0.9999 Gold 0.7985 oz. AGW, 37 mm. **Ruler:** Mohammed VI **Subject:** World Children's Day **Obv:** Head 3/4 left **Rev:** Two children standing on an open book within globe **Edge:** Reeded **Note:** Prev. Y#95.

Date	Mintage	F12	VF20	XF40	MS60	MS63
AH1422-2001	2,800	PF63 1,400	PF65 1,500			

Y# 108 250 DIRHAMS
25.00 g., 0.925 Silver 0.7387 oz. ASW, 37 mm. **Ruler:** Mohammed VI **Subject:** Mohammed VI's Inauguration 3rd Anniversary **Obv:** Head 3/4 left **Rev:** Crowned arms with supporters above value **Edge:** Reeded **Note:** Slightly different legend of Y-107

Date	Mintage	F12	VF20	XF40	MS60	MS63
AH1423-2002	—	PF65 100				
AH1423-2002	—				60.00	80.00

Y# 113 250 DIRHAMS
25.00 g., 0.925 Silver 0.7387 oz. ASW, 37 mm. **Ruler:** Mohammed VI **Subject:** Marriage of King Mohammed VI, July 12, 2002 **Obv:** Head 3/4 left **Rev:** Crown above radiant flowers **Edge:** Reeded

Date	Mintage	F12	VF20	XF40	MS60	MS63
ND (2002)	—	PF65 100				

Y# 111 250 DIRHAMS
25.00 g., 0.925 Silver 0.7387 oz. ASW, 37 mm. **Ruler:** Mohammed VI **Subject:** Mohammed VI's Inauguration 4th Anniversary **Obv:** Head 3/4 left **Rev:** Crowned arms with supporters above value **Edge:** Reeded **Note:** Virtually identical to Y-107 and Y-108.

Date	Mintage	F12	VF20	XF40	MS60	MS63
AH1424-2003	—				60.00	80.00

Y# 119 250 DIRHAMS
25.00 g., 0.925 Silver 0.7387 oz. ASW, 37 mm. **Ruler:** Mohammed VI **Subject:** Birth of Crown Prince Moulay Al Hassan **Obv:** Head 3/4 left **Rev:** Crowned arms with supporters above value

Date	Mintage	F12	VF20	XF40	MS60	MS63
ND-2003	—	PF65 100				

Y# 120 250 DIRHAMS
25.00 g., 0.925 Silver 0.7387 oz. ASW, 37 mm. **Ruler:** Mohammed VI **Subject:** 50th Anniversary - Kingdom **Obv:** Conjoined heads right **Rev:** Crowned arms with supporters above value

Date	Mintage	F12	VF20	XF40	MS60	MS63
AH1424-2003	—	PF65 100				
AH1424-2003	—				60.00	80.00

Y# 151 250 DIRHAMS
25.00 g., 0.925 Silver 0.7387 oz. ASW, 37 mm. **Ruler:** Mohammed VI **Subject:** International day of People with Disabilities **Rev:** Family on globe

Date	Mintage	F12	VF20	XF40	MS60	MS63
2003						70.00
2003	—	PF65 100				

Y# 121 250 DIRHAMS
25.00 g., 0.925 Silver 0.7387 oz. ASW, 37 mm. **Ruler:** Mohammed VI **Subject:** Year of Handicapped Persons **Obv:** Head 3/4 left **Rev:** Stylized figures

Date	Mintage	F12	VF20	XF40	MS60	MS63
AH1425-2004	—				60.00	80.00

Y# 122 250 DIRHAMS
25.00 g., 0.925 Silver 0.7387 oz. ASW, 37 mm. **Ruler:** Mohammed VI **Subject:** 5th Anniversary of Mohammed VI's Reign **Obv:** Head 3/4 left, national arms **Rev:** Crowned arms with supporters above value **Edge:** Reeded **Note:** Vitually identical to Y-107, 108 and 111.

Date	Mintage	F12	VF20	XF40	MS60	MS63
AH1425-2004	—				60.00	80.00

Y# 123 250 DIRHAMS
25.00 g., 0.925 Silver 0.7387 oz. ASW, 37 mm. **Ruler:** Mohammed VI **Subject:** 30th Anniversary - Green March **Obv:** Head 3/4 left **Rev:** Men marching left with flags aloft

Date	Mintage	F12	VF20	XF40	MS60	MS63
AH1426-2005	—				60.00	80.00

Y# 124 250 DIRHAMS
25.00 g., 0.925 Silver 0.7387 oz. ASW, 37 mm. **Ruler:** Mohammed VI **Subject:** 6th Anniversary of Mohammed VI's Reign **Obv:** Head 3/4 left **Rev:** Crowned arms with supporters above value **Edge:** Reeded **Note:** Virtually identical to Y-107, 108, 111 and 122

Date	Mintage	F12	VF20	XF40	MS60	MS63
AH1426-2005	—				60.00	80.00

Y# 125 250 DIRHAMS
25.00 g., 0.925 Silver 0.7387 oz. ASW, 37 mm. **Ruler:** Mohammed VI **Subject:** 6th Anniversary of Mohammed VI's Reign **Obv:** Head 3/4 left **Rev:** Crowned arms with supporters above value **Edge:** Reeded **Note:** Virtually identical to Y-107, 108, 111 and 122

Date	Mintage	F12	VF20	XF40	MS60	MS63
AH1427-2006	—				60.00	80.00

Y# 126 250 DIRHAMS
25.00 g., 0.925 Silver 0.7387 oz. ASW, 37 mm. **Ruler:** Mohammed VI **Subject:** 8th Anniversary of Mohammed VI's reign **Obv:** Head 3/4 left **Rev:** Corwned arms with supporters, value below **Edge:** Reeded

Date	Mintage	F12	VF20	XF40	MS60	MS63
AH1428/2007	—				60.00	80.00

Y# 153 250 DIRHAMS
25.00 g., 0.925 Silver 0.7387 oz. ASW **Ruler:** Mohammed VI **Subject:** Birth of Princess Lalla Khaduija **Rev:** National arms

Date	Mintage	F12	VF20	XF40	MS60	MS63
2007						70.00
2007	—	PF65 100				

Y# 127 250 DIRHAMS
25.00 g., 0.925 Silver 0.7387 oz. ASW, 37 mm. **Ruler:** Mohammed VI **Subject:** 9th Anniversary of Mohammed VI's reign **Obv:** Head 3/4 left **Rev:** Crowned arms with supporters above value **Edge:** Reeded

Date	Mintage	F12	VF20	XF40	MS60	MS63
AH1429-2008	1,000	PF65 125				

Y# 128 250 DIRHAMS
25.00 g., 0.925 Silver 0.7387 oz. ASW, 37 mm. **Ruler:** Mohammed VI **Subject:** 12 Centuries of Monarchy

Date	Mintage	F12	VF20	XF40	MS60	MS63
AH1429-2008	5,000	PF63 70.00	PF65 80.00			

Y# 133 250 DIRHAMS
6.45 g., 0.900 Gold 0.1854 oz. AGW, 21 mm. **Ruler:** Mohammed VI **Subject:** 12 Centuries of Monarchy

Date	Mintage	F12	VF20	XF40	MS60	MS63
AH1429-2008	3,000	PF63 325	PF65 350			

Y# 129 250 DIRHAMS
25.00 g., 0.925 Silver 0.7387 oz. ASW, 37 mm. **Ruler:** Mohammed VI **Subject:** 10th Anniversary of Mohammed VI's reign **Obv:** Head 3/4 left **Rev:** Crowned arms with supporters above value **Edge:** Reeded

Date	Mintage	F12	VF20	XF40	MS60	MS63
AH1430-2009	1,500	PF65 100				

Y# 130 250 DIRHAMS
25.00 g., 0.925 Silver 0.7387 oz. ASW, 37 mm. **Ruler:** Mohammed VI **Subject:** Bank al Maghrib, 50th Anniversary **Obv:** Head 3/4 left

Date	Mintage	F12	VF20	XF40	MS60	MS63
AH1430-2009	—	PF65 120				

Y# 131 250 DIRHAMS
25.00 g., 0.925 Silver 0.7387 oz. ASW, 37 mm. **Ruler:** Mohammed VI **Subject:** 11th Anniversary of Mohammed VI's reign **Obv:** Head 3/4 left **Rev:** Crowned arms with supporters above value **Edge:** Reeded

Date	Mintage	F12	VF20	XF40	MS60	MS63
AH1431-2010	1,500	PF65 100				

Y# 132 250 DIRHAMS
25.00 g., 0.925 Silver 0.7387 oz. ASW, 37 mm. **Ruler:** Mohammed VI **Subject:** Green March, 35th Anniversary **Edge:** Reeded

Date	Mintage	F12	VF20	XF40	MS60	MS63
AH1431-2010	1,000	PF65 125				

Y# 142 250 DIRHAMS
28.28 g., 0.925 Silver 0.8356 oz. ASW, 38.61 mm. **Ruler:** Mohammed VI **Subject:** 12th Anniversary of Enthronement **Obv:** Head left **Rev:** Royal Palace of Rabat

Date	Mintage	F12	VF20	XF40	MS60	MS63
2012	—	PF65 150				

Y# 157 250 DIRHAMS
28.28 g., 0.925 Silver 0.8356 oz. ASW, 38.61 mm. **Ruler:** Mohammed VI **Subject:** Moroccan Phosphate Co., 90th Anniversary **Rev:** Phosphate mining and agriculture

Date	Mintage	F12	VF20	XF40	MS60	MS63
2010	3,000	PF63 90.00	PF65 100			

Y# 159 250 DIRHAMS
Silver ASW **Ruler:** Mohammed VI **Subject:** Mohammed VI, Coronation, 12th Anniversary **Rev:** Palace

Date	Mintage	F12	VF20	XF40	MS60	MS63
2011	—	PF65 150				

Y# 163 250 DIRHAMS
28.28 g., 0.925 Silver 0.8356 oz. ASW, 38.61 mm. **Ruler:** Mohammed VI **Subject:** Dar As-Sikkah, 25th Anniversary **Edge:** Reeded

Date	Mintage	F12	VF20	XF40	MS60	MS63
AH1433-2012	1,000	PF65 125				

Y# 164 250 DIRHAMS
28.28 g., 0.925 Silver 0.8356 oz. ASW, 38.61 mm. **Ruler:** Mohammed VI **Subject:** Mohammed VI, 13th Anniversary of reign **Edge Lettering:** Reeded

Date	Mintage	F12	VF20	XF40	MS60	MS63
AH1433-2012	1,000	PF65 125				

Y# 165 250 DIRHAMS
28.28 g., 0.925 Silver 0.8356 oz. ASW, 38.61 mm. **Ruler:** Mohammed VI **Subject:** UNESCO sites in Rabat **Edge:** Reeded

Date	Mintage	F12	VF20	XF40	MS60	MS63
AH1433-2012	1,000	PF65 125				

Y# 166 250 DIRHAMS
28.28 g., 0.925 Silver 0.8356 oz. ASW, 38.61 mm. **Ruler:** Mohammed VI **Subject:** Mohammed VI, 50th Birthday **Edge:** Reeded

Date	Mintage	F12	VF20	XF40	MS60	MS63
AH1434-2013	1,000	PF65 125				

Y# 135 500 DIRHAMS
Bi-Metallic **Ruler:** Mohammed VI **Obv:** Head left **Rev:** Building **Note:** Silver and gold similar to Y#130.

Date	Mintage	F12	VF20	XF40	MS60	MS63
AH1430-2009	—	PF65 1,650				

Y# 150 1000 DIRHAMS
25.00 g., 0.9999 Gold 0.7985 oz. AGW, 37 mm. **Ruler:** Mohammed VI **Subject:** Mohammed VI, 40th Birthday **Rev:** National arms

Date	Mintage	F12	VF20	XF40	MS60	MS63
2003	—	PF65 1,500				

Y# 152 1000 DIRHAMS
25.00 g., 0.9999 Gold 0.7985 oz. AGW, 37 mm. **Ruler:** Mohammed VI **Subject:** Mohammed VI, 41st Birthday **Rev:** National arms

Date	Mintage	F12	VF20	XF40	MS60	MS63
2004	—	PF65 1,500				

Y# 154 1000 DIRHAMS
Gold AGW **Ruler:** Mohammed VI **Subject:** Bank al Maghrib, 50th Anniversary **Rev:** Central Bank Building

Date	Mintage	F12	VF20	XF40	MS60	MS63
2009	—	PF65 2,600				

Y# 155 1000 DIRHAMS
Gold AGW **Ruler:** Mohammed VI **Subject:** Mohammed VI, Coronation 10th Anniversary

Date	Mintage	F12	VF20	XF40	MS60	MS63
2009	—	PF65 2,600				

Y# 156 1000 DIRHAMS
Gold AGW **Ruler:** Mohammed VI **Subject:** Mohammed VI, 46th Birthday

Date	Mintage	F12	VF20	XF40	MS60	MS63
2009	—	PF65 2,600				

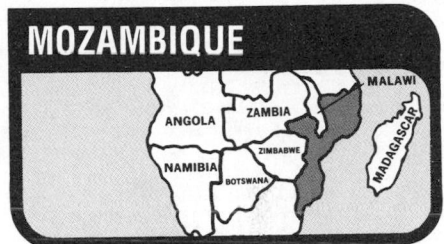

MOZAMBIQUE

The Republic of Mozambique, a former overseas province of Portugal, stretches for 1,430 miles (2,301 km.) along the southeast coast of Africa, has an area of 302,330 sq. mi. (801,590 sq. km.) and a population of 14.1 million, 99 % of whom are native Africans of the Bantu tribes. Capital: Maputo. Agriculture is the chief industry. Cashew nuts, cotton, sugar, copra and tea are exported.

Mozambique became a member of the Commonwealth of Nations in November 1995. The President is Head of State; the Prime Minister is Head of Government.

REPUBLIC

REFORM COINAGE
100 Centavos = 1 Metical; 1994

KM# 130 1000 METICAIS
25.71 g., 0.980 Silver 0.8048 oz. ASW, 38.5 mm. **Subject:** Pedro De Covilha, 1498 **Obv:** National arms within circle **Rev:** Sailing ship within circle **Edge:** Reeded

Date	Mintage	F12	VF20	XF40	MS60	MS63
2003	—	PF60 35.00	PF63 40.00	PF65 45.00		

KM# 141 1000 METICAIS
Silver, 38.6 mm. **Obv:** National arms **Rev:** Vasco de Gamma

Date	Mintage	F12	VF20	XF40	MS60	MS63
2004	—	PF60 35.00	PF63 40.00	PF65 45.00		

KM# 142 1000 METICAIS
Silver, 38.6 mm. **Obv:** National arms **Rev:** David Livingstone and map of Africa

Date	Mintage	F12	VF20	XF40	MS60	MS63
2004	—	PF60 35.00	PF63 40.00	PF65 45.00		

KM# 131 10000 METICAIS
8.04 g., Bi-Metallic, 26.6 mm. **Obv:** National arms within circle **Rev:** Rhino within circle **Edge:** Segmented reeding

Date	Mintage	F12	VF20	XF40	MS60	MS63
2003	—	—	—	1.50	4.00	9.00

REFORM COINAGE
(New) Metical = 1,000 Meticals; 2005

KM# 132 CENTAVO
2.00 g., Copper Plated Steel, 15 mm. **Obv:** Bank logo, date **Obv. Legend:** BANCO DE MOÇAMBIQUE **Rev:** Rhinoceros standing left, value **Edge:** Plain

Date	Mintage	F12	VF20	XF40	MS60	MS63
2006	—	—	—	—	0.15	0.25

KM# 133 5 CENTAVOS
2.30 g., Copper Plated Steel, 19 mm. **Obv:** Bank logo, date **Obv. Legend:** BANCO DE MOÇAMBIQUE **Rev:** Cheetah standing left, value **Edge:** Reeded

Date	Mintage	F12	VF20	XF40	MS60	MS63
2006	—	—	—	0.10	0.25	0.35

KM# 134 10 CENTAVOS
3.06 g., Brass Plated Steel, 17 mm. **Obv:** Bank logo, date **Legend:** BANCO DE MOÇAMBIQUE **Rev:** Farmer cultivating with tractor, value **Edge:** Reeded

Date	Mintage	F12	VF20	XF40	MS60	MS63
2006	—	—	—	0.15	0.35	0.50

KM# 135 20 CENTAVOS
4.10 g., Brass Plated Steel, 20 mm. **Obv:** Bank logo, date **Obv. Legend:** BANCO DE MOÇAMBIQUE **Rev:** Cotton plant, value **Edge:** Reeded

Date	Mintage	F12	VF20	XF40	MS60	MS63
2006	—	—	—	0.20	0.50	0.75

KM# 136 50 CENTAVOS
5.74 g., Brass Plated Steel, 23 mm. **Obv:** Bank logo, date **Obv. Legend:** BANCO DE MOÇAMBIQUE **Rev:** Giant Kingfisher perched on branch, value **Edge:** Reeded

Date	Mintage	F12	VF20	XF40	MS60	MS63
2006	—	—	—	0.50	1.25	1.75

KM# 137 METICAL
5.30 g., Nickel Plated Steel, 21 mm. **Obv:** Bank logo, date **Obv. Legend:** BANCO DE MOÇAMBIQUE **Rev:** Young woman seated left writing, value **Edge:** Plain **Shape:** 7-sided

Date	Mintage	F12	VF20	XF40	MS60	MS63
2006	—	—	—	0.45	1.10	1.50

KM# 138 2 METICAIS
6.00 g., Nickel Plated Steel, 24 mm. **Obv:** Bank logo, date **Obv. Legend:** BANCO DE MOÇAMBIQUE **Rev:** Coelacanth fish, value **Edge:** Segmented reeding

Date	Mintage	F12	VF20	XF40	MS60	MS63
2006	—	—	—	0.75	1.80	2.50

KM# 139 5 METICAIS
6.50 g., Nickel Plated Steel, 27 mm. **Obv:** Bank logo, date **Obv. Legend:** BANCO DE MOÇAMBIQUE **Rev:** Timbila (similar to a xylophone), value **Edge:** Reeded

Date	Mintage	F12	VF20	XF40	MS60	MS63
2006	—	—	—	1.20	3.00	4.00

KM# 140 10 METICAIS
7.50 g., Bi-Metallic, 25 mm. **Obv:** Bank logo **Obv. Legend:** BANCO · DE · MOCAMBIQUE **Rev:** Modern bank building, value below **Edge:** Reeded

Date	Mintage	F12	VF20	XF40	MS60	MS63
2006	—	—	—	1.50	3.75	5.00

NAGORNO-KARABAKH

Nagorno-Karabakh, an ethnically Armenian enclave inside Azerbaijan (pop., 1991 est.: 193,000), SW region. It occupies an area of 1,700 sq mi (4,400 square km) on the NE flank of the Karabakh Mountain Range, with the capital city of Stepanakert.

Russia annexed the area from Persia in 1813, and in 1923 it was established as an autonomous province of the Azerbaijan S.S.R. In 1988 the region's ethnic Armenian majority demonstrated against Azerbaijani rule, and in 1991, after the breakup of the U.S.S.R. brought independence to Armenia and Azerbaijan, war broke out between the two ethnic groups. On January 8, 1992 the leaders of Nagorno-Karabakh declared independence as the Republic of Mountainous Karabakh (RMK). Since 1994, following a cease-fire, ethnic Armenians have held Karabakh, though officially it remains part of Azerbaijan. Karabakh remains sovereign, but the political and military condition is volatile and tensions frequently flare into skirmishes.

Its marvelous nature and geographic situation, have all facilitated Karabakh to be a center of science, poetry and, especially, of the musical culture of Azerbaijan.

MONETARY SYSTEM
100 Luma = 1 Dram

REPUBLIC
STANDARD COINAGE

KM# 6 50 LUMA
0.95 g., Aluminum, 19.8 mm. **Obv:** National arms **Rev:** Horse cantering left **Edge:** Plain

Date	Mintage	F12	VF20	XF40	MS60	MS63
2004	—	—	—	—	1.00	1.25

KM# 7 50 LUMA
0.95 g., Aluminum, 19.8 mm. **Obv:** National arms **Rev:** Gazelle **Edge:** Plain

Date	Mintage	F12	VF20	XF40	MS60	MS63
2004	—	—	—	—	1.00	1.25

KM# 8 DRAM
1.13 g., Aluminum, 21.7 mm. **Obv:** National arms **Rev:** Pheasant **Edge:** Plain

Date	Mintage	F12	VF20	XF40	MS60	MS63
2004	—	—	—	—	1.00	1.25

KM# 9 DRAM
1.12 g., Aluminum, 21.7 mm. **Obv:** National arms **Rev:** 1/2-length Saint facing **Edge:** Plain

Date	Mintage	F12	VF20	XF40	MS60	MS63
2004	—	—	—	—	1.00	1.25

KM# 10 DRAM
1.13 g., Aluminum, 21.7 mm. **Obv:** National arms **Rev:** Cheetah facing **Edge:** Plain

Date	Mintage	F12	VF20	XF40	MS60	MS63
2004	—	—	—	—	1.00	1.25

KM# 11 5 DRAMS
4.40 g., Brass, 21.8 mm. **Obv:** National arms **Rev:** Church **Edge:** Plain

Date	Mintage	F12	VF20	XF40	MS60	MS63
2004	—	—	—	—	1.25	1.50

KM# 12 5 DRAMS
4.50 g., Brass, 21.8 mm. **Obv:** National arms **Rev:** Monument faces **Edge:** Plain

Date	Mintage	F12	VF20	XF40	MS60	MS63
2004	—	—	—	—	1.25	1.50

KM# 23 1000 DRAMS
31.43 g., 0.999 Silver 1.003 oz. ASW, 38.9 mm. **Obv:** National arms **Rev:** Archer **Edge:** Plain

Date	Mintage	F12	VF20	XF40	MS60	MS63
2003	—	PF63 75.00	PF65 120			

KM# 24 1000 DRAMS
31.33 g., 0.999 Silver 0.9998 oz. ASW, 38.39 mm. **Series:** Armenian architectural sculpture **Obv:** National arms **Rev:** Church of the Holy Cross at Aghthamar, Turkey **Edge:** Plain

Date	Mintage	F12	VF20	XF40	MS60	MS63
2003	—	PF63 75.00	PF65 120			

KM# 19 1000 DRAMS
31.37 g., 0.999 Silver 1.0011 oz. ASW, 38.9 mm. **Obv:** National arms **Rev:** Leopard head facing **Edge:** Plain

Date	Mintage	F12	VF20	XF40	MS60	MS63
2004	—	PF63 75.00	PF65 120			

KM# 19a 1000 DRAMS
31.37 g., 0.999 Silver Gilt 1.0011 oz., 38.9 mm. **Obv:** National arms **Rev:** Leopard head facing **Edge:** Plain

Date	Mintage	F12	VF20	XF40	MS60	MS63
2004	—	PF63 75.00	PF65 120			

KM# 20 1000 DRAMS
31.37 g., 0.999 Silver 1.0011 oz. ASW, 38.9 mm. **Obv:** National arms **Rev:** Standing Brown Bear **Edge:** Plain

Date	Mintage	F12	VF20	XF40	MS60	MS63
2004	—	PF63 75.00	PF65 120			

KM# 20a 1000 DRAMS
31.37 g., 0.999 Silver Gilt 1.0011 oz., 38.9 mm. **Obv:** National arms **Rev:** Standing Brown Bear **Edge:** Plain

Date	Mintage	F12	VF20	XF40	MS60	MS63
2004	—	PF63 85.00	PF65 140			

KM# 21 1000 DRAMS
31.37 g., 0.999 Silver 1.0011 oz. ASW, 38.9 mm. **Obv:** National arms **Rev:** Eagle head within circle **Edge:** Plain

Date	Mintage	F12	VF20	XF40	MS60	MS63
2004	—	PF63 75.00	PF65 120			

KM# 21a 1000 DRAMS
31.37 g., 0.999 Silver Gilt 1.0011 oz., 38.9 mm. **Obv:** National arms **Rev:** Eagle head within circle **Edge:** Plain

Date	Mintage	F12	VF20	XF40	MS60	MS63
2004	—	PF63 85.00	PF65 140			

KM# 22 1000 DRAMS
31.12 g., 0.999 Silver 0.9931 oz. ASW, 38.9 mm. **Obv:** National arms **Rev:** 1918 Genocide Victims Monument **Edge:** Plain

Date	Mintage	F12	VF20	XF40	MS60	MS63
2004	—	PF63 65.00	PF65 100			

KM# 25 1000 DRAMS
31.30 g., 0.999 Silver 0.9988 oz. ASW, 38.92 mm. **Obv:** National arms **Rev:** Bust of Kevork Chavoush 3/4 left **Edge:** Plain

Date	Mintage	F12	VF20	XF40	MS60	MS63
2004	—	PF63 75.00	PF65 120			

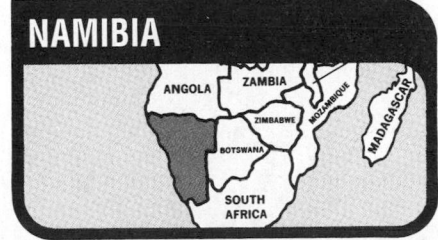

NAMIBIA

The Republic of Namibia, once the German colonial territory of German South West Africa, and later South West Africa, is situated on the Atlantic coast of southern Africa, bounded on the north by Angola, on the east by Botswana, and on the south by South Africa. It has an area of 318,261 sq. mi. (824,290 sq. km.) and a population of *1.4 million. Capital: Windhoek. Diamonds, copper, lead, zinc, and cattle are exported.

On June 17, 1985 the Transitional Government of National Unity was installed. Negotiations were held in 1988 between Angola, Cuba, and South Africa reaching a peaceful settlement on Aug. 5, 1988. By April 1989 Cuban troops were to withdraw from Angola and South African troops from Namibia. The Transitional Government resigned on Feb. 28, 1988 for the upcoming elections of the constituent assembly in Nov. 1989. Independence was finally achieved on March 12, 1990 within the Commonwealth of Nations. The President is the Head of State; the Prime Minister is Head of Government.

MONETARY SYSTEM
100 Cents = 1 Namibia Dollar

REPUBLIC
DECIMAL COINAGE

KM# 1 5 CENTS
2.20 g., Nickel Plated Steel, 17 mm. **Obv:** National arms **Rev:** Value left, aloe plant within 3/4 sun design

Date	Mintage	F12	VF20	XF40	MS60	MS63
2002	—	—	—	0.20	0.50	0.75
2007	—	—	—	0.20	0.50	0.75
2009	—	—	—	0.20	0.50	0.75
2012	—	—	—	0.20	0.50	0.75

KM# 2 10 CENTS
3.40 g., Nickel Plated Steel, 21.5 mm. **Obv:** National arms **Rev:** Camelthorn tree right, partial sun design left, value below

Date	Mintage	F12	VF20	XF40	MS60	MS63
2002	—	—	—	0.35	1.00	1.25
2009	—	—	—	0.35	1.00	1.25
2012	—	—	—	0.35	1.00	1.25

KM# 3 50 CENTS
4.43 g., Nickel Plated Steel, 24 mm. **Obv:** National arms **Rev:** Quiver tree right, partial sun design upper left, value below

Date	Mintage	F12	VF20	XF40	MS60	MS63
2008	—	—	—	—	1.75	2.00
2010	—	—	—	—	1.75	2.00

KM# 4 DOLLAR
5.00 g., Brass, 22.4 mm. **Obv:** National arms **Rev:** Value divides Bateleur eagle at right, partial sun design at left

Date	Mintage	F12	VF20	XF40	MS60	MS63
2002	—	—	—	1.25	3.50	6.00
2006	—	—	—	1.25	3.50	6.00
2008	—	—	—	1.25	3.50	6.00
2010	—	—	—	1.25	3.50	6.00

KM# 5 5 DOLLARS
6.22 g., Brass, 24.9 mm. **Obv:** National arms **Rev:** Partial sun design at top, value at center, African fish eagle below

Date	Mintage	F12	VF20	XF40	MS60	MS63
2012	—	—	—	4.00	7.50	10.00

KM# 21 10 DOLLARS
Bi-Metallic, 30 mm. **Subject:** Bank of Namibia, 20th Anniversary **Obv:** National arms **Rev:** Dr. Sam Nujoma bust facing **Edge:** Segmented reeding

Date	Mintage	F12	VF20	XF40	MS60	MS63
2010	—	—	—	—	4.50	7.50

KM# 23 10 DOLLARS
1.13 g., 0.999 Gold 0.0362 oz. AGW, 13.92 mm. **Series:** 20th Anniversary of the Bank of Namibia

Date	Mintage	F12	VF20	XF40	MS60	MS63
2010	—	PF63 85.00	PF65 95.00			

KM# 22 20 DOLLARS
28.28 g., 0.925 Silver 0.8356 oz. ASW, 38.61 mm. **Subject:** 20th Anniversary of the Bank of Namibia

Date	Mintage	F12	VF20	XF40	MS60	MS63
2010	Est. 2000	PF63 70.00	PF65 80.00			

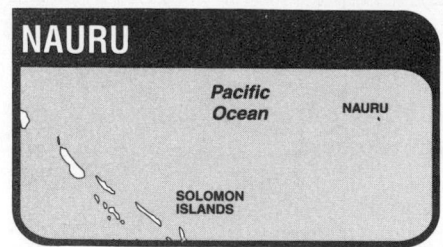

NAURU

Pacific Ocean   NAURU

SOLOMON ISLANDS

The Republic of Nauru, formerly Pleasant Island, is an island republic in the western Pacific Ocean west of the Gilbert Islands. It has an area of 8-1/2 sq. mi. and a population of 7,254. It is known for its phosphate deposits. Nauru is a special member of the Commonwealth of Nations.

RULER
British, until 1968

MONETARY SYSTEM
100 Cents = 1 (Australian) Dollar

REPUBLIC

DECIMAL COINAGE

KM# 38 DOLLAR
27.00 g., Silver Plated Copper, 38.6 mm. **Subject:** Guardian Angel **Obv:** Arms **Rev:** Angel standing, swarovski crystals in hair

Date	Mintage	F12	VF20	XF40	MS60	MS63
2009	10,000	PF63 35.00	PF65 50.00			

KM# 45 5 DOLLARS
Silver, 39 mm. **Subject:** Elizabeth II and Prince Philip, 60th Wedding Anniversary **Obv:** National arms **Rev:** Wedding portraits

Date	Mintage	F12	VF20	XF40	MS60	MS63
2007	—	PF65 45.00				

KM# 46 5 DOLLARS
Silver, 39 mm. **Subject:** Elizabeth II and Prince Philip, 60th Wedding anniversary **Obv:** National arms **Rev:** Engagement photo

Date	Mintage	F12	VF20	XF40	MS60	MS63
2007	—	PF65 45.00				

KM# 36 5 DOLLARS
0.50 g., 0.999 Gold AGW, 11 mm. **Subject:** Kaiser Wilhelm **Obv:** Arms **Rev:** Bust right

Date	Mintage	F12	VF20	XF40	MS60	MS63
2008	—	PF63 45.00	PF65 65.00			

KM# 37 5 DOLLARS
0.50 g., 0.999 Gold AGW, 11 mm. **Subject:** Christmas **Obv:** Arms **Rev:** Bells ringing

Date	Mintage	F12	VF20	XF40	MS60	MS63
2008	—	PF63 45.00	PF65 65.00			

KM# 80 5 DOLLARS
28.28 g., 0.925 Silver 0.8356 oz. ASW, 38.61 mm. **Subject:** Royal Air Force, 90th Anniversary **Rev:** De Havilland Tiger Moth and Avro Anson

Date	Mintage	F12	VF20	XF40	MS60	MS63
2008	—	PF65 60.00				

KM# 39 5 DOLLARS
0.50 g., 0.999 Gold AGW **Subject:** Christmas **Issuer:** 11 **Obv:** Arms **Rev:** Teddy bear seated

Date	Mintage	F12	VF20	XF40	MS60	MS63
2009	—	PF63 45.00	PF65 65.00			

KM# 84 5 DOLLARS
0.50 g., 0.999 Gold AGW, 11 mm. **Subject:** Investor coins of the World - Vreneli

Date	Mintage	F12	VF20	XF40	MS60	MS63
2010	Est. 10000	PF63 45.00	PF65 65.00			

KM# 85 5 DOLLARS
0.50 g., 0.999 Gold AGW, 11 mm. **Subject:** Investor gold coins of the world - Franz Joseph I

Date	Mintage	F12	VF20	XF40	MS60	MS63
2010	Est. 10000	PF63 45.00	PF65 65.00			

KM# 86 5 DOLLARS
0.50 g., 0.999 Gold AGW, 11 mm. **Subject:** Investor coins of the World - French rooster

Date	Mintage	F12	VF20	XF40	MS60	MS63
2010	Est. 5000	PF63 45.00	PF65 65.00			

KM# 18 10 DOLLARS
31.10 g., 0.999 Silver 0.9925 oz. ASW **Subject:** Discontinuation of the German Mark **Obv:** National arms **Obv. Legend:** BANK OF NAURU

Date	Mintage	F12	VF20	XF40	MS60	MS63
2001	—	PF65 150				

KM# 13 10 DOLLARS
31.25 g., 0.999 Silver 0.9972 oz. ASW, 72 mm. **Subject:** First Euro Coinage **Obv:** National arms, matte finish **Rev:** Denomination, inscription and partially gold-plated 1 Euro reverse coin design, Proof finish **Edge:** Plain **Shape:** Like a map

Date	Mintage	F12	VF20	XF40	MS60	MS63
2002	—	PF65 150				

KM# 14 10 DOLLARS
34.60 g., 0.925 Silver 1.0224 oz. ASW, 38.5 mm. **Subject:** Brandenburg Gate **Obv:** National arms **Rev:** Brandenburg Gate **Edge:** Plain **Note:** Gold color 1mm thick

Date	Mintage	F12	VF20	XF40	MS60	MS63
2002 Proof/Matte	—	PF65 150				

KM# 15 10 DOLLARS
31.10 g., 0.999 Silver 0.9925 oz. ASW, 40 mm. **Series:** Save the Whales **Obv:** National arms **Obv. Legend:** BANK OF NAURU **Rev:** Blue Whale on mother-of-pearl insert **Edge:** Plain

Date	Mintage	F12	VF20	XF40	MS60	MS63
2002	2,000	PF65 95.00				

KM# 50 10 DOLLARS
31.11 g., 0.999 Silver 0.9926 oz. ASW, 40 mm. **Rev:** Coloseum in color

Date	Mintage	F12	VF20	XF40	MS60	MS63
2002	2,001	PF65 80.00				

KM# 51 10 DOLLARS
22.22 g., 0.999 Silver 0.7091 oz. ASW, 35x45 mm. **Subject:** Indroduction of Euro **Shape:** Irregular

Date	Mintage	F12	VF20	XF40	MS60	MS63
2002	2,500	**PF65** 55.00				

KM# 19 10 DOLLARS
31.10 g., 0.999 Silver 0.9925 oz. ASW **Subject:** European Union - Mark and Euro **Obv:** National arms **Obv. Legend:** BANK OF NAURU

Date	Mintage	F12	VF20	XF40	MS60	MS63
2003	5,000	**PF65** 100				

KM# 20 10 DOLLARS
1.24 g., 0.999 Gold 0.0396 oz. AGW, 13.92 mm. **Subject:** First Anniversary of the Euro **Obv:** National arms **Obv. Legend:** BANK OF NAURU **Rev:** Euro symbol **Edge:** Reeded

Date	Mintage	F12	VF20	XF40	MS60	MS63
2003	—	**PF65** 85.00				

KM# 21 10 DOLLARS
1.24 g., 0.999 Gold 0.0396 oz. AGW **Subject:** Treasure of Priamos in Troja **Obv:** National arms **Obv. Legend:** BANK OF NAURU

Date	Mintage	F12	VF20	XF40	MS60	MS63
2003	—	**PF63** 75.00 **PF65** 95.00				

KM# 22 10 DOLLARS
1.24 g., 0.999 Gold 0.0396 oz. AGW **Subject:** Treasure of Nibelungen **Obv:** National arms **Obv. Legend:** BANK OF NAURU

Date	Mintage	F12	VF20	XF40	MS60	MS63
2003	—	**PF63** 75.00 **PF65** 95.00				

KM# 23 10 DOLLARS
30.95 g., Silver **Subject:** European Monuments **Obv:** National arms **Obv. Legend:** BANK OF NAURU **Rev. Legend:** GERMANY - DEUTSCHER REICHSTAG **Edge:** Plain

Date	Mintage	F12	VF20	XF40	MS60	MS63
2003 Proof/ Matte	—	**PF65** 150				

KM# 52 10 DOLLARS
31.10 g., 0.925 Silver 0.9189 oz. ASW, 38.61 mm. **Subject:** Euro, 1st Anniversary **Rev:** Euro currency symbol

Date	Mintage	F12	VF20	XF40	MS60	MS63
2003	5,000	**PF65** 85.00				

KM# 53 10 DOLLARS
31.10 g., 0.925 Silver 0.9189 oz. ASW, 38.61 mm. **Rev:** St. Peter's Basilica

Date	Mintage	F12	VF20	XF40	MS60	MS63
2003	Est. 7500	—	—	—	—	75.00

KM# 54 10 DOLLARS
31.10 g., 0.925 Silver 0.9189 oz. ASW, 38.61 mm. **Rev:** Church in Dresden

Date	Mintage	F12	VF20	XF40	MS60	MS63
2004	—	—	—	—	—	75.00

KM# 55 10 DOLLARS
31.10 g., 0.999 Silver 0.9925 oz. ASW, 38.61 mm. **Rev:** Colesum in Rome

Date	Mintage	F12	VF20	XF40	MS60	MS63
2004	7,500	—	—	—	—	75.00

KM# 56 10 DOLLARS
31.10 g., 0.925 Silver 0.9189 oz. ASW, 38.61 mm. **Rev:** Royal Palace in Monaco

Date	Mintage	F12	VF20	XF40	MS60	MS63
2004	7,500	—	—	—	—	75.00

KM# 24 10 DOLLARS
Silver **Series:** European Monuments **Subject:** Palazzo Pubblico in San Marino **Obv:** National arms **Obv. Legend:** BANK OF NAURU **Edge:** Plain

Date	Mintage	F12	VF20	XF40	MS60	MS63
2005 Proof/Matte	—	**PF65** 150				

KM# 25 10 DOLLARS
1.24 g., 0.999 Gold 0.0396 oz. AGW **Subject:** East Gothic stylized eagle broach from Domagnano, Italy in National Museum in Nuremburg **Obv:** National arms **Obv. Legend:** BANK OF NAURU

Date	Mintage	F12	VF20	XF40	MS60	MS63
2005	25,000	**PF63** 75.00 **PF65** 95.00				

KM# 35 10 DOLLARS
31.11 g., 0.999 Silver 0.9926 oz. ASW **Subject:** German Railways, 150th Anniversary **Obv:** National Arms **Rev:** Baureihi "01

Date	Mintage	F12	VF20	XF40	MS60	MS63
2005	—	**PF65** 60.00				

KM# 40 10 DOLLARS
1.24 g., 0.999 Gold 0.0396 oz. AGW, 13.92 mm. **Obv:** National Arms **Rev:** Ludwig Erhard

Date	Mintage	F12	VF20	XF40	MS60	MS63
2005	—	**PF63** 75.00 **PF65** 95.00				

KM# 26 10 DOLLARS
1.24 g., 0.999 Gold 0.0396 oz. AGW **Subject:** Angela Dorothea Merkel, Chancellor of Germany **Obv:** National arms **Obv. Legend:** BANK OF NAURU

Date	Mintage	F12	VF20	XF40	MS60	MS63
2005	—	**PF63** 75.00 **PF65** 95.00				

KM# 41 10 DOLLARS
31.10 g., 0.999 Silver 0.9925 oz. ASW, 38.61 mm. **Rev:** Tower Bridge, gilt

Date	Mintage	F12	VF20	XF40	MS60	MS63
2005	2,000	**PF65** 200				

KM# 43 10 DOLLARS
31.11 g., 0.999 Silver 0.9926 oz. ASW, 38.6 mm. **Rev:** St. Stephens Church, Vienna partially gilt

Date	Mintage	F12	VF20	XF40	MS60	MS63
2005	2,000	**PF65** 50.00				

KM# 57 10 DOLLARS
31.10 g., 0.925 Silver 0.9189 oz. ASW, 38.61 mm. **Rev:** St. Basil's Cathedral, Moscow

Date	Mintage	F12	VF20	XF40	MS60	MS63
2005 Proof	7,500	—	—	—	—	75.00

KM# 58 10 DOLLARS
1.24 g., 0.999 Gold 0.0396 oz. AGW, 13.92 mm. **Subject:** Konrad Adenauer

Date	Mintage	F12	VF20	XF40	MS60	MS63
2005	—	**PF63** 70.00 **PF65** 90.00				

KM# 59 10 DOLLARS
1.24 g., 0.999 Gold 0.0396 oz. AGW, 13.92 mm. **Subject:** Kurt Georg Kiesinger

Date	Mintage	F12	VF20	XF40	MS60	MS63
2005	—	**PF63** 70.00 **PF65** 90.00				

KM# 60 10 DOLLARS
1.24 g., 0.999 Gold 0.0396 oz. AGW, 13.92 mm. **Subject:** Willy Brandt

Date	Mintage	F12	VF20	XF40	MS60	MS63
2005	—	**PF63** 70.00 **PF65** 90.00				

KM# 61 10 DOLLARS
1.24 g., 0.999 Gold 0.0396 oz. AGW, 13.92 mm. **Subject:** Helmut Schmidt

Date	Mintage	F12	VF20	XF40	MS60	MS63
2005	—	**PF63** 70.00 **PF65** 90.00				

KM# 62 10 DOLLARS
1.24 g., 0.999 Gold 0.0396 oz. AGW, 13.92 mm. **Subject:** Helmut Kohl

Date	Mintage	F12	VF20	XF40	MS60	MS63
2005	—	**PF63** 70.00 **PF65** 90.00				

KM# 63 10 DOLLARS
1.24 g., 0.999 Gold 0.0396 oz. AGW, 13.92 mm. **Subject:** Gerhard Schröder

Date	Mintage	F12	VF20	XF40	MS60	MS63
2005	—	**PF63** 70.00 **PF65** 90.00				

KM# 27 10 DOLLARS
1.24 g., 0.999 Gold 0.0396 oz. AGW **Subject:** Konrad Adenauer at 1949 demonstration **Obv:** National arms **Obv. Legend:** BANK OF NAURU

Date	Mintage	F12	VF20	XF40	MS60	MS63
2006	15,000	**PF63** 75.00 **PF65** 95.00				

KM# 28 10 DOLLARS
1.24 g., 0.999 Gold 0.0396 oz. AGW **Subject:** Volkswagen **Obv:** National arms **Obv. Legend:** BANK OF NAURU

Date	Mintage	F12	VF20	XF40	MS60	MS63
2006	—	**PF63** 75.00 **PF65** 95.00				

KM# 29 10 DOLLARS
1.24 g., 0.999 Gold 0.0396 oz. AGW **Subject:** Conrad Schumann in Berlin 1961 **Obv:** National arms **Obv. Legend:** BANK OF NAURU

Date	Mintage	F12	VF20	XF40	MS60	MS63
2006	—	**PF63** 75.00 **PF65** 95.00				

KM# 30 10 DOLLARS
1.24 g., 0.999 Gold 0.0396 oz. AGW **Subject:** Olympic Stadium in Munich 1972 **Obv:** National arms **Obv. Legend:** BANK OF NAURU

Date	Mintage	F12	VF20	XF40	MS60	MS63
2006	—	**PF63** 75.00 **PF65** 95.00				

KM# 31 10 DOLLARS
1.24 g., 0.999 Gold 0.0396 oz. AGW **Subject:** Independent Activists 1980 **Obv:** National arms **Obv. Legend:** BANK OF NAURU

Date	Mintage	F12	VF20	XF40	MS60	MS63
2006	—	**PF63** 75.00 **PF65** 95.00				

KM# 32 10 DOLLARS
1.24 g., 0.999 Gold 0.0396 oz. ACW **Subject:** Brandenburg Gate in Berlin 1990 **Obv:** National arms **Obv. Legend:** BANK OF NAURU

Date	Mintage	F12	VF20	XF40	MS60	MS63
2006	—	**PF63** 75.00 **PF65** 95.00				

KM# 33 10 DOLLARS
1.24 g., 0.999 Gold 0.0396 oz. AGW **Subject:** European Union 2002 **Obv:** National arms **Obv. Legend:** BANK OF NAURU

Date	Mintage	F12	VF20	XF40	MS60	MS63
2006	—	**PF63** 75.00 **PF65** 95.00				

KM# 34 10 DOLLARS
1.24 g., 0.999 Gold 0.0396 oz. AGW **Subject:** Johannes Rau, German President, 1999-2004 **Obv:** National arms **Obv. Legend:** BANK OF NAURU

Date	Mintage	F12	VF20	XF40	MS60	MS63
2006	—	**PF63** 75.00 **PF65** 95.00				

KM# 42 10 DOLLARS
31.10 g., 0.999 Silver 0.9925 oz. ASW, 38.61 mm. **Rev:** Tower of Pisa, gilt

Date	Mintage	F12	VF20	XF40	MS60	MS63
2006	2,000	**PF65** 200				

KM# 64 10 DOLLARS
1.24 g., 0.999 Gold 0.0396 oz. AGW, 13.92 mm. **Subject:** Theodor Heuss

Date	Mintage	F12	VF20	XF40	MS60	MS63
2006	Est. 10000	**PF63** 70.00 **PF65** 90.00				

KM# 65 10 DOLLARS
1.24 g., 0.999 Gold 0.0396 oz. AGW, 13.92 mm. **Subject:** Heinrich Lübke

Date	Mintage	F12	VF20	XF40	MS60	MS63
2006	Est. 10000	**PF63** 70.00 **PF65** 90.00				

KM# 66 10 DOLLARS
1.24 g., 0.999 Gold 0.0396 oz. AGW, 13.92 mm. **Subject:** Gustav Heinemann

Date	Mintage	F12	VF20	XF40	MS60	MS63
2006	Est. 10000	**PF63** 70.00 **PF65** 90.00				

KM# 67 10 DOLLARS
1.24 g., 0.999 Gold 0.0396 oz. AGW, 13.92 mm. **Subject:** Walter Scheel

Date	Mintage	F12	VF20	XF40	MS60	MS63
2006	Est.1000	**PF63** 70.00 **PF65** 90.00				

KM# 68 10 DOLLARS
1.24 g., 0.999 Gold 0.0396 oz. AGW, 13.92 mm. **Subject:** Karl Carstens

Date	Mintage	F12	VF20	XF40	MS60	MS63
2006	Est. 10000	**PF63** 70.00 **PF65** 90.00				

KM# 69 10 DOLLARS
1.24 g., 0.999 Gold 0.0396 oz. AGW, 13.92 mm. **Subject:** Richard Freiherr von Weizsäcker

Date	Mintage	F12	VF20	XF40	MS60	MS63
2006	Est. 10000	**PF63** 70.00 **PF65** 90.00				

KM# 70 10 DOLLARS

1.24 g., 0.999 Gold 0.0396 oz. AGW, 13.92 mm. **Subject:** Roman Herzog

Date	Mintage	F12	VF20	XF40	MS60	MS63
2006	Est. 10000	PF63 70.00	PF65 90.00			

KM# 71 10 DOLLARS
1.24 g., 0.999 Gold 0.0396 oz. AGW, 13.92 mm. **Subject:** Horst Köhler

Date	Mintage	F12	VF20	XF40	MS60	MS63
2006	Est. 10000	PF63 70.00	PF65 90.00			

KM# 72 10 DOLLARS
31.11 g., 0.925 Silver 0.9191 oz. ASW, 38.61 mm. **Rev:** Cathedral Santiago de Compostela

Date	Mintage	F12	VF20	XF40	MS60	MS63
2006	Est. 5000	—	—	—	—	70.00

KM# 73 10 DOLLARS
31.11 g., 0.925 Silver 0.9191 oz. ASW, 38.61 mm. **Rev:** Mt. St. Michel

Date	Mintage	F12	VF20	XF40	MS60	MS63
2006	Est. 5000	—	—	—	—	70.00

KM# 74 10 DOLLARS
31.11 g., 0.925 Silver 0.9191 oz. ASW, 38.61 mm. **Rev:** Axon in Brussels

Date	Mintage	F12	VF20	XF40	MS60	MS63
2006	Est. 5000	—	—	—	—	70.00

KM# 75 10 DOLLARS
28.28 g., 0.925 Silver 0.8356 oz. ASW, 38.61 mm. **Subject:** World Cup Football **Rev:** Brandenburg Gate

Date	Mintage	F12	VF20	XF40	MS60	MS63
2007	—	PF65 55.00				

KM# 76 10 DOLLARS
1.24 g., 0.999 Gold 0.0396 oz. AGW, 13.92 mm. **Rev:** Micronesia

Date	Mintage	F12	VF20	XF40	MS60	MS63
2007	—	PF65 80.00				

KM# 77 10 DOLLARS
28.28 g., 0.925 Silver 0.8356 oz. ASW, 38.61 mm. **Subject:** Sylt to Hamburg Steam Train

Date	Mintage	F12	VF20	XF40	MS60	MS63
2007	Est. 5000	PF65 70.00				

KM# 79 10 DOLLARS
28.28 g., 0.925 Silver 0.8356 oz. ASW, 38.61 mm. **Rev:** Suspended subway

Date	Mintage	F12	VF20	XF40	MS60	MS63
2008	—	PF65 70.00				

KM# 81 10 DOLLARS
31.10 g., 0.999 Silver 0.9925 oz. ASW, 38.61 mm. **Rev:** Santa Claus in color

Date	Mintage	F12	VF20	XF40	MS60	MS63
2008	Est. 15000	—	—	—	—	85.00

KM# 82 10 DOLLARS
0.925 Silver **Subject:** Worldcup Soccer in South Africa

Date	Mintage	F12	VF20	XF40	MS60	MS63
2009	Est. 10000	PF65 60.00				

KM# 83 10 DOLLARS
1.00 g., 0.999 Gold 0.0319 oz. AGW, 13.92 mm. **Subject:** World Cup Soccer in South Africa **Rev:** Mascott leopard Zakumi

Date	Mintage	F12	VF20	XF40	MS60	MS63
2009	Est. 5000	PF65 70.00				

KM# 87 10 DOLLARS
28.28 g., 0.925 Silver 0.8356 oz. ASW, 38.61 mm. **Rev:** German Railways Locomotive 18201

Date	Mintage	F12	VF20	XF40	MS60	MS63
2010	—	PF65 70.00				

KM# 88 10 DOLLARS
0.925 Silver, 34 mm. **Rev:** Leipzig-Dresden Railway's locomotive Saxonia

Date	Mintage	F12	VF20	XF40	MS60	MS63
2010	Est. 10000	PF65 40.00				

KM# 47 10 DOLLARS
Silver, 39 mm. **Subject:** WWII AZNAC troops **Obv:** Head in tiaria right, National arms at right **Rev:** Flag and Bugler

Date	Mintage	F12	VF20	XF40	MS60	MS63
2011	—	PF65 40.00				

NEPAL

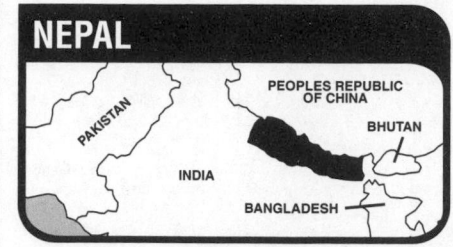

The Kingdom of Nepal, the world's only surviving Hindu kingdom, is a landlocked country occupying the southern slopes of the Himalayas. It has an area of 56,136 sq. mi. (140,800 sq. km.) and a population of 27 million. Capital: Kathmandu. Nepal has deposits of coal, copper, iron and cobalt, but they are largely unexploited. Agriculture is the principal economic activity. Rice, timber and jute are exported, with tourism being the other major foreign exchange earner.

On June 2, 2001 tragedy struck the royal family when Crown Prince Dipendra used an assault rifle to kill his father, mother and other members of the royal family as the result of a dispute over his current lady friend. He died 48 hours later, as King, from self inflicted gunshot wounds. Gyanendra began his second reign as King (his first was a short time as a toddler, 1950-51).

DATING

Bikram Samvat Era (VS)

From 1888AD most copper coins were dated in the Bikram Samvat (VS) era. To convert take VS date - 57 =AD date. Coins with this era have VS before the year in the listing. With the exception of a few gold coins struck in 1890 & 1892, silver and gold coins only changed to the VS era in 1911AD, but now this era is used for all coins struck in Nepal.

RULERS

SHAH DYNASTY

ज्ञानेन्दबीर विक्रम

Gyanendra Bir Bikram
VS2058-/2001AD

NUMERALS

Nepal has used more variations of numerals on their coins than any other nation. The most common are illustrated in the numeral chart in the introduction. The chart below illustrates some variations encompassing the last four centuries.

1	2	3	4	5	6	7	8	9	0

NUMERICS

One — एक

Two — दुइ

Ten — दसा

Twenty-five — पचीसा

Fifty — पचासा

Hundred — सय

DENOMINATIONS

रुपैयाँ

Rupee

Legend on reverse

श्री श्री श्री गोरपनाथ

Shri Shri Shri Gorakhanatha in 8 petals

KINGDOM

KM# 1173 10 PAISA
Aluminum, 17 mm. **Ruler:** Gyanendra Bir Bikram **Obv:** Royal crown **Edge:** Plain

Date	Mintage	F12	VF20	XF40	MS60	MS63
VS2058 (2001)	—	—	—	—	1.00	1.50

KM# 1148 25 PAISA
Aluminum, 20 mm. **Ruler:** Gyanendra Bir Bikram **Obv:** Royal crown **Edge:** Plain

Date	Mintage	F12	VF20	XF40	MS60	MS63
VS2058 (2001)	—	—	—	—	0.50	0.75
VS2059 (2002)	—	—	—	—	0.50	0.75
VS2060 (2003)	—	—	—	—	0.50	0.75

KM# 1149 50 PAISA
Aluminum, 22.5 mm. **Ruler:** Gyanendra Bir Bikram **Obv:** Royal crown **Rev:** Swayambhunath **Edge:** Plain

Date	Mintage	F12	VF20	XF40	MS60	MS63
VS2058 (2001)	—	—	—	—	0.50	0.75
VS2059 (2002)	—	—	—	—	0.50	0.75

KM# 1179 50 PAISA
1.41 g., Aluminum, 22.5 mm. **Ruler:** Gyanendra Bir Bikram **Obv:** Crown above crossed flags **Rev:** Swayambhunath **Edge:** Plain

Date	Mintage	F12	VF20	XF40	MS60	MS63
VS2060 (2003)	—	—	—	—	0.40	0.50
VS2061 (2004)	—	—	—	—	0.40	0.50

KM# 1150.1 RUPEE
Brass Plated Steel **Ruler:** Gyanendra Bir Bikram **Rev:** Large (8.5mm) temple, medium '1' (4.5mm) **Edge:** Reeded **Note:** Non-magnetic.

Date	Mintage	F12	VF20	XF40	MS60	MS63
VS2058 (2001)	—	—	—	—	1.00	1.50

KM# 1150.2 RUPEE
Brass Plated Steel **Ruler:** Gyanendra Bir Bikram **Obv:** Traditional design **Rev:** Small (7mm high) temple, small (4mm) "1 **Edge:** Plain **Note:** Magnetic.

Date	Mintage	F12	VF20	XF40	MS60	MS63
VS2058 (2001)	—	—	—	—	1.00	1.50
VS2059 (2002)	—	—	—	—	1.00	1.50
VS2060 (2003)	—	—	—	—	1.00	1.50

KM# 1150.3 RUPEE
3.96 g., Brass, 20 mm. **Ruler:** Gyanendra Bir Bikram **Obv:** Traditional design **Rev:** Small (6.5mm high) temple, small (4mm) "1 **Edge:** Plain

Date	Mintage	F12	VF20	XF40	MS60	MS63
VS2058 (2001)	—	—	—	—	0.50	0.75

KM# 1150.4 RUPEE
3.96 g., Brass Plated Steel, 20 mm. **Ruler:** Gyanendra Bir Bikram **Obv:** Traditional design **Rev:** Small (7mm high) temple, large (4.5mm) "1 **Note:** Magnetic.

Date	Mintage	F12	VF20	XF40	MS60	MS63
VS2059 (2002)	—	—	—	—	1.00	1.50
VS2060 (2003)	—	—	—	—	1.00	1.50

KM# 1180 RUPEE
3.96 g., Brass Plated Steel, 20 mm. **Ruler:** Gyanendra Bir

Bikram **Obv:** Traditional design **Rev:** Wagheshwari Temple **Edge:** Plain **Note:** "1" in denomination of a different style.

Date	Mintage	F12	VF20	XF40	MS60	MS63
VS2061 (2004)	—	—	—	—	0.75	1.00

KM# 1181 RUPEE
3.94 g., Brass Plated Steel, 19.95 mm. **Ruler:** Gyanendra Bir Bikram **Obv:** Traditional design **Rev:** Sri Talbarahi Temple with outline mountain scene behind **Edge:** Plain

Date	Mintage	F12	VF20	XF40	MS60	MS63
VS2062(2005)	—	—	—	0.50	1.20	1.60

KM# 1170 2 RUPEES
4.94 g., Brass, 25 mm. **Ruler:** Gyanendra Bir Bikram **Obv:** Traditional square design **Rev:** People with flag celebrating 50 Years of Democracy **Edge:** Plain

Date	Mintage	F12	VF20	XF40	MS60	MS63
VS2058(2001)	—	—	—	—	0.50	0.75

KM# 1151.2 2 RUPEES
Brass, 25 mm. **Ruler:** Gyanendra Bir Bikram **Obv:** Traditional design **Rev:** Three domed building **Edge:** Plain

Date	Mintage	F12	VF20	XF40	MS60	MS63
VS2058 (2001)	—	—	—	—	1.50	2.00
VS2059 (2002)	—	—	—	—	1.50	2.00
VS2060 (2003)	—	—	—	—	1.50	2.00

KM# 1151.1 2 RUPEES
5.07 g., Brass Plated Steel, 25 mm. **Ruler:** Gyanendra Bir Bikram **Obv:** Traditional design **Rev:** Three domed building **Edge:** Plain **Note:** Edge varieties exist. Prev. KM#1151. Magnetic.

Date	Mintage	F12	VF20	XF40	MS60	MS63
VS2060 (2003)	—	—	—	—	1.50	2.00

KM# 1151.1a 2 RUPEES
6.70 g., Silver, 25 mm. **Ruler:** Gyanendra Bir Bikram **Obv:** Traditional design **Rev:** Three domed building **Edge:** Plain

Date	Mintage	F12	VF20	XF40	MS60	MS63
VS2060(2003)	—	—	—	—	100	

KM# 1159 25 RUPEE
8.36 g., Copper-Nickel, 29.1 mm. **Ruler:** Gyanendra Bir Bikram **Obv:** Crowned bust right **Rev:** Traditional design **Edge:** Plain

Date	Mintage	F12	VF20	XF40	MS60	MS63
VS2058 (2001)	—	—	—	—	4.00	5.00
VS2059 (2002)	—	—	—	—	4.00	5.00

KM# 1164 25 RUPEE
8.60 g., Copper-Nickel, 29.1 mm. **Ruler:** Gyanendra Bir Bikram **Subject:** Silver Jubilee **Obv:** Traditional design **Rev:** Stylized face design **Edge:** Plain

Date	Mintage	F12	VF20	XF40	MS60	MS63
VS2060 (2003)	—	—	—	—	4.00	5.00

KM# 1183 25 RUPEE
8.55 g., Copper-Nickel, 29.1 mm. **Ruler:** Gyanendra Bir Bikram **Subject:** World Hindu Federation **Obv:** Traditional design **Edge:** Plain

Date	Mintage	F12	VF20	XF40	MS60	MS63
VS2062 (2005)	—	—	—	—	4.00	5.00

KM# 1160 50 RUPEE
20.10 g., Brass, 37.7 mm. **Ruler:** Gyanendra Bir Bikram **Subject:** 50th Anniversary of Scouting in Nepal **Obv:** Traditional design **Rev:** Scouting emblem within beaded wreath **Edge:** Plain

Date	Mintage	F12	VF20	XF40	MS60	MS63
VS2058 (2001)	—	—	—	—	9.00	10.00

KM# 1182 50 RUPEE
8.60 g., Copper-Nickel, 29 mm. **Ruler:** Gyanendra Bir Bikram **Subject:** Golden Jubilee of Supreme Court **Obv:** Traditional design **Rev:** Supreme Court building **Edge:** Plain

Date	Mintage	F12	VF20	XF40	MS60	MS63
VS2063 (2006)	—	—	—	—	6.00	9.00

KM# 1157 100 RUPEE
20.00 g., Brass, 38.7 mm. **Ruler:** Gyanendra Bir Bikram **Subject:** Buddha **Obv:** Traditional design **Rev:** Seated Buddha teaching five seated monks **Edge:** Reeded

Date	Mintage	F12	VF20	XF40	MS60	MS63
VS2058 (2001)	30,000	—	—	10.00	12.00	

KM# 1161 200 RUPEE
18.10 g., 0.500 Silver 0.2891 oz. ASW, 29.6 mm. **Ruler:** Gyanendra Bir Bikram **Subject:** 50th Anniversary of the Nepal Chamber of Commerce **Obv:** Traditional design **Rev:** Swastika within rotary gear **Edge:** Plain

Date	Mintage	F12	VF20	XF40	MS60	MS63
VS2059 (2002)	—	—	—	—	20.00	25.00

KM# 1162 200 RUPEE
18.10 g., 0.500 Silver 0.2891 oz. ASW, 29.6 mm. **Ruler:** Gyanendra Bir Bikram **Subject:** 50th Anniversary of Civil Service **Obv:** Traditional design **Rev:** Crown above flags and value **Edge:** Plain

Date	Mintage	F12	VF20	XF40	MS60	MS63
VS2059 (2002)	—	—	—	—	20.00	25.00

KM# 1171 250 RUPEE
18.00 g., 0.500 Silver 0.2875 oz. ASW, 29 mm. **Ruler:** Gyanendra Bir Bikram **Subject:** 2600th Anniversary of Bhagawan Mahavir **Obv:** Traditional design **Rev:** Haloed head above value **Edge:** Plain

Date	Mintage	F12	VF20	XF40	MS60	MS63
VS2058 (2001)	—	—	—	—	25.00	30.00

KM# 1176 250 RUPEE
17.83 g., 0.500 Silver 0.2848 oz. ASW, 31.6 mm. **Ruler:** Gyanendra Bir Bikram **Subject:** Marwadi, non-profit making organization **Obv:** Traditional design **Rev:** Swastika within circle **Edge:** Reeded

Date	Mintage	F12	VF20	XF40	MS60	MS63
VS2060 (2003)	—	—	—	—	25.00	30.00

KM# 1184 250 RUPEE
18.00 g., Silver, 32 mm. **Ruler:** Gyanendra Bir Bikram **Subject:** 400th Anniversary of Guru Granth Sahib **Obv:** Traditional design **Rev:** Holy Book of Sikhs **Edge:** Reeded

Date	Mintage	F12	VF20	XF40	MS60	MS63
VS2061 (2004)	—	—	—	—	25.00	30.00

KM# 1174 300 RUPEE
22.50 g., 0.500 Silver 0.3594 oz. ASW, 31.8 mm. **Ruler:** Gyanendra Bir Bikram **Subject:** Economic Growth Through Export **Obv:** Traditional design **Rev:** Two joined hands in front of globe **Edge:** Reeded

Date	Mintage	F12	VF20	XF40	MS60	MS63
VS2060 (2003)	—	—	—	—	22.00	28.00

KM# 1163 500 RUPEE
23.34 g., 0.900 Silver 0.671 oz. ASW, 32 mm. **Ruler:** Gyanendra Bir Bikram **Subject:** 50th Anniversary of the Conquest of Mt. Everest **Obv:** Traditional design **Rev:** Mountain and map above value **Edge:** Reeded

Date	Mintage	F12	VF20	XF40	MS60	MS63
VS2000 (2003)	—	—	—	—	30.00	35.00

KM# 1177 500 RUPEE
23.00 g., 0.900 Silver 0.6612 oz. ASW, 31.7 mm. **Ruler:** Gyanendra Bir Bikram **Subject:** Management Education 50th Anniversary **Obv:** Traditional design **Rev:** Six point star outline **Edge:** Reeded

Date	Mintage	F12	VF20	XF40	MS60	MS63
VS2060 (2003)	—	—	—	—	30.00	35.00

KM# 1185 500 RUPEE
20.10 g., Silver, 32 mm. **Ruler:** Gyanendra Bir Bikram **Subject:** 50th Anniversary of Nepal-United Nations **Obv:** Traditional design **Rev:** Head of the late King Mahendra Bir Birkam **Edge:** Reeded

Date	Mintage	F12	VF20	XF40	MS60	MS63
VS2062 (2006)	—	—	—	—	25.00	30.00

KM# 1175 1000 RUPEE
35.00 g., Silver, 40 mm. **Ruler:** Gyanendra Bir Bikram **Subject:** 100 Years - Rotary Club **Edge:** Reeded

Date	Mintage	F12	VF20	XF40	MS60	MS63
VS2062 (2005)	—	—	—	—	45.00	50.00

KM# 1178 1000 RUPEE
35.20 g., 0.500 Silver 0.5622 oz. ASW, 40 mm. **Ruler:** Gyanendra Bir Bikram **Subject:** Rastriya Bank 50th Anniversary **Obv:** Traditional square design **Rev:** Bank seal above value **Edge:** Reeded

Date	Mintage	F12	VF20	XF40	MS60	MS63
VS2062 (2005)	—	—	—	—	27.00	32.00

KM# 1158 1500 RUPEE
20.00 g., 0.925 Silver 0.591 oz. ASW, 38.7 mm. **Ruler:** Gyanendra Bir Bikram **Subject:** Buddha **Obv:** Traditional design **Rev:** Seated Buddha teaching five seated monks **Edge:** Reeded

Date	Mintage	F12	VF20	XF40	MS60	MS63
VS2058 (2001)	15,000	PF60 30.00	PF63 35.00			

KM# 1172 2000 RUPEE
31.20 g., 0.720 Silver 0.7176 oz. ASW, 40 mm. **Ruler:** Gyanendra Bir Bikram **Subject:** Gyanendra's Accession to the Throne **Obv:** Crowned bust right **Rev:** Upright sword above value in circular design **Edge:** Reeded

Date	Mintage	F12	VF20	XF40	MS60	MS63
VS2058 (2001)	—	—	—	—	40.00	45.00

KM# 1201 2000 RUPEE
31.11 g., 0.999 Silver 0.9926 oz. ASW, 40 mm. **Ruler:** Gyanendra Bir Bikram **Subject:** Conquest of Mt. Everest 50th Anniversary **Rev:** Sir Edmond Hillary and Tenzing Norgay at Summit

Date	Mintage	F12	VF20	XF40	MS60	MS63
VS2060 (2003)	8,000	PF60 70.00	PF63 80.00			

KM# 1191 2000 RUPEE
31.20 g., 0.925 Silver 0.9219 oz. ASW, 38.61 mm. **Ruler:** Gyanendra Bir Bikram **Subject:** 2006 FIFA World Cup - Germany **Obv:** Traditional design

Date	Mintage	F12	VF20	XF40	MS60	MS63
VS2063 (2006)	—	—	—	—	45.00	50.00

ASARFI GOLD COINAGE

Fractional designations are approximate for this series. Actual Gold Weight (AGW) is used to identify each type.
(Asarphi)

KM# 1200 ASARPHI
7.77 g., 0.9999 Gold 0.2482 oz. AGW, 22 mm. **Ruler:** Gyanendra Bir Bikram **Subject:** Conquest of Mt. Everest **Rev:** Sir Edward Hillary and Tenzing Norgay at Summit

Date	Mintage	F12	VF20	XF40	MS60	MS63
VS2060 (2003)	2,000	—	—	—	800	

KM# 1153 0.3G ASARPHI
0.30 g., 0.9999 Gold AGW, 7 mm. **Ruler:** Gyanendra Bir Bikram **Subject:** Buddha **Obv:** Traditional design **Rev:** Seated Buddha **Edge:** Plain

Date	Mintage	VG8	F12	VF20	XF40	MS63
VS2058 (2001)	30,000	—	—	—	—	25.00

KM# 1154 1/25-OZ. ASARFI
1.24 g., 0.9999 Gold 0.0397 oz. AGW, 13.92 mm. **Ruler:** Gyanendra Bir Bikram **Subject:** Buddha **Obv:** Traditional design **Rev:** Seated Buddha **Edge:** Reeded

Date	Mintage	VG8	F12	VF20	XF40	MS63
VS2058 (2001)	25,000	—	—	—	—	75.00

KM# 1155 1/10-OZ. ASARFI
3.11 g., 0.9999 Gold 0.0993 oz. AGW, 17.95 mm. **Ruler:** Gyanendra Bir Bikram **Subject:** Buddha **Obv:** Traditional design **Rev:** Seated Buddha **Edge:** Reeded

Date	Mintage	VG8	F12	VF20	XF40	MS63
VS2058 (2001)	15,000	—	—	—	—	185

KM# 1156 1/2-OZ. ASARFI
15.55 g., 0.9999 Gold 0.4967 oz. AGW, 27 mm. **Ruler:** Gyanendra Bir Bikram **Subject:** Buddha **Obv:** Traditional design **Rev:** Seated Buddha **Edge:** Reeded

Date	Mintage	VG8	F12	VF20	XF40	MS63
VS2058 (2001)	2,500	PF63 900				

DEMOCRATIC REPUBLIC

KM# 1204 RUPEE
Brass Plated Steel, 19 mm. **Obv:** Mt. Everest within square **Rev:** Map of Nepal

Date	Mintage	F12	VF20	XF40	MS60	MS63
VS2064 (2008)	—	—	—	—	2.00	3.50

KM# 1188 2 RUPEES
5.00 g., Brass Plated Steel, 24.93 mm. **Obv:** Mount Everest within square **Rev:** Farmer plowing with water buffalos **Edge:** Plain

Date	Mintage	F12	VF20	XF40	MS60	MS63
VS2063(2006)	—	—	—	1.50	2.75	3.50

KM# 1186 25 RUPEE
8.50 g., Copper-Nickel, 29 mm. **Subject:** 125th Anniversary - First Nepal Postal Stamp Issue **Obv:** Features image of legendary 1 Anna stamp **Rev:** Traditional mailman on the reverse

Date	Mintage	F12	VF20	XF40	MS60	MS63
VS2063 (2006)	—	—	—	—	7.00	9.00
VS2064 (2006)	—	—	—	—	7.00	9.00

KM# 1189 50 RUPEE
8.60 g., Copper-Nickel, 29 mm. **Subject:** 250th Anniversary Hindu festival "Kimari Jatra **Obv:** Kumari Temple at Durbar Square in Kathmandu **Rev:** Bust of Goddess Kumari facing **Edge:** Plain

Date	Mintage	F12	VF20	XF40	MS60	MS63
VS2064 (2006)	—	—	—	—	8.00	10.00

KM# 1208 50 RUPEE
Silver ASW **Subject:** National Numismatic Museum

Date	Mintage	F12	VF20	XF40	MS60	MS63
2012	—	—	—	—	—	9.00

KM# 1206 50 RUPEE
8.60 g., Copper-Nickel, 29 mm. **Subject:** International year of Cooperation **Rev:** Stick figures holding large square

Date	Mintage	F12	VF20	XF40	MS60	MS63
VS2069 (2012)	—	—	—	—	—	10.00

KM# 1190 500 RUPEE
14.19 g., 0.500 Silver 0.2266 oz. ASW, 32 mm. **Subject:** 250th Anniversary Hindu festival "Kimari Jatra **Obv:** Kumari Temple at Durbar Square in Kathmandu **Rev:** Bust of Goddess Kumari facing **Edge:** Reeded

Date	Mintage	F12	VF20	XF40	MS60	MS63
VS2064 (2007)	—	—	—	—	25.00	30.00

KM# 1207 1000 RUPEE
35.20 g., 0.500 Silver 0.5622 oz. ASW, 40 mm. **Subject:** International year of Cooperation **Rev:** Stick figures holding up large   square

Date	Mintage	F12	VF20	XF40	MS60	MS63
VS2069 (2012)	—	PF63 27.50				

MINT SETS

KM#	Date	Mintage	Identification	Issue Price	Mkt Val
MSA19	1996, 1995, 2011 (3)	—	KM#709.2 (1996); 711 (1995); 737 (2011)	—	8.00

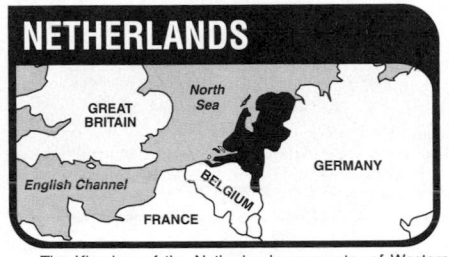

NETHERLANDS

The Kingdom of the Netherlands, a country of Western Europe fronting on the North Sea and bordered by Belgium and Germany, has an area of 15,770 sq. mi. (41,500 sq. km.) and a population of 16.4 million. Capital: Amsterdam, but the seat of government is at The Hague. The economy is based on dairy farming and a variety of industrial activities. Chemicals, yarns and fabrics, and meat products are exported.

NOTE: Excepting the World War II issues struck at U.S. mints, all of the modern coins were struck at the Utrecht Mint (or at the annex in the Birmingham Mint, 1980-2000) and bear the caduceus mint mark of that facility. They also bear the mintmasters' marks.

The BES-islands (Bonaire, St. Eustatius and Saba) have been added to the Netherlands as special municipalities on Oct. 10, 2010. On these islands the U.S. dollar has been the official currency.

RULERS
KINGDOM OF THE NETHERLANDS
Beatrix, 1980-2013
Willam-Alexander 2013-

MINT PRIVY MARKS
Utrecht

Date	Privy Mark
1806-present	Caduceus

MINTMASTERS' PRIVY MARKS
Utrecht Mint

Date	Privy Mark
2001	Wine Tendril w/grapes
2002	Wine tendril w/grapes and star
2003	Sails of a clipper

NOTE: A star adjoining the privy mark indicates that the piece was struck at the beginning of the term of office of a successor. (The star was used only if the successor had not chosen his own mark yet.)
NOTE: Since October 1999, the Dutch Mint has taken the title of Royal Dutch Mint.

MONETARY SYSTEM
Until January 29, 2002
100 Cents = 1 Gulden
Since January 1, 2002
100 Euro Cents = 1 Euro

KINGDOM
DECIMAL COINAGE

KM# 202 5 CENTS
3.50 g., Bronze, 21 mm. **Ruler:** Beatrix **Obv:** Head left with vertical inscription **Rev:** Value within vertical lines **Edge:** Plain

Date	Mintage	F12	VF20	XF40	MS60	MS63
2001	15,815,000	—	—	—	—	0.70
2001	17,000	PF63 4.00				

KM# 203 10 CENTS
1.50 g., Nickel, 15 mm. **Ruler:** Beatrix **Obv:** Head left with vertical inscription **Rev:** Value and vertical lines **Edge:** Reeded

Date	Mintage	F12	VF20	XF40	MS60	MS63
2001	25,600,000	—	—	—	0.45	0.75
2001	17,000	PF63 4.00				

KM# 204 25 CENTS
3.00 g., Nickel, 19 mm. **Ruler:** Beatrix **Obv:** Head left with vertical inscription **Obv. Inscription:** Beatrix/Konincin Der/ Nederlanden **Rev:** Value within vertical and horizontal lines **Edge:** Reeded

Date	Mintage	F12	VF20	XF40	MS60	MS63
2001	11,515,000	—	—	—	0.30	1.00
2001	17,000	PF63 5.00				

KM# 205 GULDEN
6.00 g., Nickel, 25 mm. **Ruler:** Beatrix **Obv:** Head left with vertical inscription **Rev:** Value within vertical and horizontal lines **Edge Lettering:** GOD * ZIJ * MET * ONS *

Date	Mintage	F12	VF20	XF40	MS60	MS63
2001	6,414,500	—	—	—	—	1.25
2001	17,000	PF63 5.00				

KM# 205a GULDEN
7.10 g., 0.925 Silver 0.2098 oz. ASW **Ruler:** Beatrix **Obv:** Head left with vertical inscription **Rev:** Value within vertical and horizontal lines **Edge Lettering:** GOD*ZIJ*MET*OMS*

Date	Mintage	F12	VF20	XF40	MS60	MS63
2001 Prooflike	200,000	—	—	—	—	15.00

KM# 233 GULDEN
6.00 g., Nickel, 25 mm. **Ruler:** Beatrix **Obv:** Head left within inscription **Rev:** Child art design **Edge Lettering:** GOD * ZIJ * MET * ONS *

Date	Mintage	F12	VF20	XF40	MS60	MS63
2001	16,009,000	—	—	—	—	4.00
2001 Prooflike	32,000	—	—	—	—	6.00

KM# 233a GULDEN
7.10 g., 0.925 Silver 0.2098 oz. ASW, 25 mm. **Ruler:** Beatrix **Obv:** Head left within inscription **Rev:** Child art design **Edge Lettering:** GOD * ZIJ * MET * ONS *

Date	Mintage	F12	VF20	XF40	MS60	MS63
2001 Prooflike	360	—	—	—	—	3,300

Note: Given as gifts to workers at the mint

KM# 233b GULDEN
13.20 g., 0.999 Gold 0.4212 oz. AGW, 25 mm. **Ruler:** Beatrix **Obv:** Head left within inscription **Rev:** Child art design **Note:** 98 of 100 pieces melted down, with 2 known in museum collections.

Date	Mintage	F12	VF20	XF40	MS60	MS63
2001 Prooflike; Rare	100	—	—	—	—	—

KM# 205b GULDEN
13.20 g., 0.999 Gold 0.4212 oz. AGW **Ruler:** Beatrix **Obv:** Head left with vertical inscription **Rev:** Value within vertical and horizontal lines **Edge Lettering:** GOD*ZIJ*MET*ONS* **Note:** Prev. KM#205a.

Date	Mintage	F12	VF20	XF40	MS60	MS63
2001 Prooflike	25,500	—	—	—	—	700

Note: Mintage includes KM#205c.

KM# 205c GULDEN
13.20 g., 0.999 Gold 0.4212 oz. AGW **Ruler:** Beatrix **Obv:** Head left with vertical inscription **Rev:** Value within vertical and horizontal lines **Edge:** Plain, missing lettering

Date	Mintage	F12	VF20	XF40	MS60	MS63
2001 Prooflike	Est. 500	—	—	—	—	1,800

KM# 206 2-1/2 GULDEN
10.00 g., Nickel, 29 mm. **Ruler:** Beatrix **Obv:** Head left with vertical inscription **Rev:** Value within horizontal, vertical and diagonal lines **Edge Lettering:** GOD * ZIJ * MET * ONS *

Date	Mintage	F12	VF20	XF40	MS60	MS63
2001	315,000	—	—	—	4.00	6.00
2001	17,000	PF63 7.50				

KM# 210 5 GULDEN

9.25 g., Bronze Clad Nickel, 23.5 mm. **Ruler:** Beatrix **Obv:** Head left with vertical inscription **Rev:** Value within horizontal, vertical and diagonal lines **Edge:** GOD * ZIJ * MET * ONS *

Date	Mintage	F12	VF20	XF40	MS60	MS63
2001	115,000	—	—	—	5.00	10.00
2001	17,000	PF63 7.00				

EURO COINAGE
European Union Issues

KM# 234 EURO CENT
2.30 g., Copper Plated Steel, 16.2 mm. **Ruler:** Beatrix **Obv:** Head left among stars **Rev:** Value and globe **Edge:** Plain

Date	Mintage	F12	VF20	XF40	MS60	MS63
2001	179,800,000	—	—	—	0.35	0.50
2001 Proof	16,500	—	—	—	3.00	1.25
2002	600,000	—	—	—	3.00	1.25
2002	16,500	PF63 5.00				
2003	5,866,000	—	—	—	0.50	0.75
2003	13,000	PF63 4.00				
2004	11,396,000	—	—	—	0.50	0.75
2004	5,000	PF63 4.00				
2005	545,000	—	—	—	1.50	2.00
2005	5,000	PF63 4.00				
2006	378,000	—	—	—	1.50	2.00
2006	3,500	PF63 4.00				
2007	332,000	—	—	—	1.50	2.00
2007	10,000	PF63 3.50				
2008	413,000	—	—	—	1.50	2.00
2008	10,000	PF63 3.50				
2009	335,000	—	—	—	1.50	2.00
2009	75,000	PF63 3.50				
2010	235,000	—	—	—	1.50	2.00
2010	5,000	PF63 3.50				
2011	50,000,000	—	—	—	1.50	2.00
2011	330,000	—	—	—	1.50	2.00
2011	5,000	PF63 3.50				
2012		—	—	—	1.50	2.00
2012	5,000	PF63 3.50				
2013		—	—	—	1.50	2.00
2013	5,000	PF63 3.50				

KM# 344 EURO CENT
2.30 g., Copper Plated Steel, 16.3 mm. **Ruler:** Willem-Alexander **Obv:** Head right **Rev:** Value and globe

Date	Mintage	F12	VF20	XF40	MS60	MS63
2014		—	—	—	1.50	2.00

KM# 235 2 EURO CENT
3.06 g., Copper Plated Steel, 18.7 mm. **Ruler:** Beatrix **Obv:** Head left among stars **Rev:** Value and globe **Edge:** Grooved

Date	Mintage	F12	VF20	XF40	MS60	MS63
2001	142,100,000	—	—	—	0.50	0.75
2001 Proof	16,500					
2002	52,224,000	—	—	—	0.75	1.00
2002 Proof	16,500					
2003	150,750,000	—	—	—	0.50	0.75
2003 Proof	13,000					
2004	115,622,000	—	—	—	0.50	0.75
2004	5,000	PF63 4.00				
2005	595,000	—	—	—	1.50	2.00
2005	5,000	PF63 4.00				
2006	378,000	—	—	—	1.50	2.00
2006	3,500	PF63 4.00				
2007	338,000	—	—	—	1.50	2.00
2007	10,000	PF63 3.50				
2008	413,000	—	—	—	1.50	2.00
2008	10,000	PF63 3.50				
2009	335,000	—	—	—	1.50	2.00
2009	75,000	PF63 3.50				
2010	235,000	—	—	—	1.50	2.00
2010	5,000	PF63 3.50				
2011	330,000	—	—	—	1.50	2.00
2011	5,000	PF63 3.50				
2012		—	—	—	1.50	2.00
2012	5,000	PF63 3.50				
2013		—	—	—	1.50	2.00
2013	5,000	PF63 3.50				

KM# 345 2 EURO CENT
3.06 g., Copper Plated Steel, 18.7 mm. **Ruler:** Willem-Alexander **Obv:** Head right **Rev:** Value and globe

Date	Mintage	F12	VF20	XF40	MS60	MS63
2014		—	—	—	1.50	2.00

KM# 236 5 EURO CENT

3.92 g., Copper Plated Steel, 21.25 mm. **Ruler:** Beatrix **Obv:** Head left among stars **Rev:** Value and globe **Edge:** Plain

Date	Mintage	F12	VF20	XF40	MS60	MS63
2001	206,400,000	—	—	—	0.50	0.75
2001 Proof	16,500	—	—	—	—	—
2002	700,000	—	—	—	1.75	3.50
2002 Proof	16,500	—	—	—	—	—
2003	874,000	—	—	—	1.50	5.00
2003 Proof	13,000	—	—	—	—	—
2004	306,000	—	—	—	2.00	2.50
2004	5,000	PF63 4.00				
2005	80,605,000	—	—	—	1.00	1.25
2005	5,000	PF63 4.00				
2006	60,318,000	—	—	—	1.00	1.25
2006	3,500	PF63 4.00				
2007	75,764,000	—	—	—	1.00	1.25
2007	10,000	PF63 3.50				
2008	50,413,000	—	—	—	1.00	1.25
2008	10,000	PF63 3.50				
2009	70,335,000	—	—	—	1.00	1.25
2009	75,000	PF63 3.50				
2010	70,235,000	—	—	—	1.00	1.25
2010	5,000	PF63 3.50				
2011	40,100,000	—	—	—	1.00	1.25
2011	5,000	PF63 3.50				
2012	—	—	—	—	1.00	1.25
2012	5,000	PF63 3.50				
2013	—	—	—	—	1.00	1.25
2013	5,000	PF63 3.50				

KM# 346 5 EURO CENT

Copper Plated Steel, 21.25 mm. **Ruler:** Willem-Alexander **Obv:** Head right **Rev:** Value and globe

Date	Mintage	F12	VF20	XF40	MS60	MS63
2014	—	—	—	—	1.00	1.25

KM# 237 10 EURO CENT

4.10 g., Brass, 19.7 mm. **Ruler:** Beatrix **Obv:** Head left among stars **Rev:** Value and map

Date	Mintage	F12	VF20	XF40	MS60	MS63
2001	194,200,000	—	—	—	0.75	1.00
2001 Proof	16,500	—	—	—	—	—
2002	600,000	—	—	—	1.50	5.00
2002 Proof	16,500	—	—	—	—	—
2003	818,000	—	—	—	1.50	2.00
2003 Proof	13,000	—	—	—	—	—
2004	262,000	—	—	—	2.00	2.50
2004	5,000	PF63 6.00				
2005	510,000	—	—	—	1.75	2.00
2005	5,000	PF63 6.00				
2006	393,000	—	—	—	1.75	2.50
2006	3,500	PF63 6.00				

KM# 268 10 EURO CENT

4.10 g., Brass, 19.7 mm. **Ruler:** Beatrix **Obv:** Head of Queen Beatrix left **Rev:** Relief map of Western Europe, stars, lines and value

Date	Mintage	F12	VF20	XF40	MS60	MS63
2007	292,000	—	—	—	1.75	2.50
2007	10,000	PF63 5.00				
2008	363,000	—	—	—	1.75	2.75
2008	10,000	PF63 5.00				
2009	285,000	—	—	—	1.75	2.50
2009	7,500	PF63 5.00				
2010	202,000	—	—	—	1.75	2.50
2010	5,000	PF63 5.00				
2011	220,000	—	—	—	1.75	2.50
2011	5,000	PF63 5.00				
2012	—	—	—	—	1.75	2.50
2012	5,000	PF63 5.00				
2013	—	—	—	—	1.75	2.50
2013	5,000	PF63 5.00				

KM# 347 10 EURO CENT

4.10 g., Brass, 19.7 mm. **Ruler:** Willem-Alexander **Obv:** Head

---

right **Rev:** Relief map of Western Europe, stars, lines and value

Date	Mintage	F12	VF20	XF40	MS60	MS63
2014	—	—	—	—	1.75	2.50

KM# 238 20 EURO CENT

5.74 g., Brass, 22.2 mm. **Ruler:** Beatrix **Obv:** Head left among stars **Rev:** Value and map **Edge:** Notched

Date	Mintage	F12	VF20	XF40	MS60	MS63
2001	92,300,000	—	—	—	1.00	1.25
2001 Proof	16,500	—	—	—	—	—
2002	50,691,000	—	—	—	1.00	1.25
2002 Proof	16,500	—	—	—	—	—
2003	57,821,000	—	—	—	1.00	1.25
2003 Proof	13,000	—	—	—	—	—
2004	20,430,000	—	—	—	1.00	1.50
2004	5,000	PF63 8.00				
2005	510,000	—	—	—	2.00	3.00
2005	5,000	PF63 8.00				
2006	393,000	—	—	—	2.00	3.00
2006	3,500	PF63 8.00				

KM# 269 20 EURO CENT

5.70 g., Brass, 22.2 mm. **Ruler:** Beatrix **Obv:** Head of Queen Beatrix left **Rev:** Relief map of Western Europe, stars, lines and value **Edge:** Notched

Date	Mintage	F12	VF20	XF40	MS60	MS63
2007	510,000	—	—	—	2.00	3.00
2007	10,000	PF63 7.00				
2008	293,000	—	—	—	2.50	3.00
2008	10,000	PF63 7.00				
2009	363,000	—	—	—	2.00	3.00
2009	7,500	PF63 7.00				
2010	285,000	—	—	—	2.50	3.00
2010	5,000	PF63 7.00				
2011	202,000	—	—	—	2.50	3.00
2011	5,000	PF63 7.00				
2012	—	—	—	—	2.50	3.00
2012	5,000	PF63 7.00				
2013	—	—	—	—	2.50	3.00
2013	5,000	PF63 7.00				

KM# 348 20 EURO CENT

5.70 g., Brass, 22.2 mm. **Ruler:** Willem-Alexander **Obv:** Head right **Rev:** Relief map of Western Europe, stars, lines and value

Date	Mintage	F12	VF20	XF40	MS60	MS63
2014	—	—	—	—	2.50	3.00

KM# 239 50 EURO CENT

7.80 g., Brass, 24.2 mm. **Ruler:** Beatrix **Obv:** Head left among stars **Rev:** Value and map **Edge:** Notched

Date	Mintage	F12	VF20	XF40	MS60	MS63
2001	87,000,000	—	—	—	1.25	1.50
2001 Proof	16,500	—	—	—	—	—
2002	80,160,000	—	—	—	1.25	1.50
2002 Proof	16,500	—	—	—	—	—
2003	810,000	—	—	—	2.00	2.50
2003 Proof	13,000	—	—	—	—	—
2004	269,000	—	—	—	2.25	3.00
2004	5,000	PF63 10.00				
2005	510,000	—	—	—	2.00	2.50
2005	5,964	PF63 10.00				
2006	363,000	—	—	—	2.00	2.50
2006	3,500	PF63 10.00				

KM# 270 50 EURO CENT

7.80 g., Brass, 24.2 mm. **Ruler:** Beatrix **Obv:** Head of Quen Beatrix left **Rev:** Relief map of Western Europe, stars, lines and value **Edge:** Notched

Date	Mintage	F12	VF20	XF40	MS60	MS63
2006	—	—	—	—	—	2.75
2007	293,000	—	—	—	2.00	2.75
2007	10,000	PF63 9.00				
2008	263,000	—	—	—	2.00	2.75
2008	10,000	PF63 9.00				
2009	285,000	—	—	—	2.00	2.75
2009	7,500	PF63 9.00				
2010	202,000	—	—	—	2.00	2.75
2010	5,000	PF63 9.00				
2011	220,000	—	—	—	2.00	2.75
2011	5,000	PF63 9.00				
2012	—	—	—	—	2.00	2.75
2012	5,000	PF63 9.00				
2013	—	—	—	—	2.00	2.75
2013	5,000	PF63 9.00				

KM# 349 50 EURO CENT

7.80 g., Brass, 24.2 mm. **Ruler:** Willem-Alexander **Obv:** Head right **Rev:** Relief map of Western Europe, stars, lines and value

Date	Mintage	F12	VF20	XF40	MS60	MS63
2014	—	—	—	—	2.00	2.75

KM# 240 EURO

7.50 g., Bi-Metallic, 23.2 mm. **Ruler:** Beatrix **Obv:** Half head left within 1/2 circle and star border, name within vertical lines **Rev:** Value and map within circle **Edge:** Segmented reeding

Date	Mintage	F12	VF20	XF40	MS60	MS63
2001	67,200,000	—	—	—	2.50	3.00
2001 Proof	16,500	—	—	—	—	—
2002	22,560,000	—	—	—	2.50	3.00
2002 Proof	16,500	—	—	—	—	—
2003	950,000	—	—	—	3.50	4.00
2003 Proof	13,000	—	—	—	—	—
2004	235,000	—	—	—	5.00	6.00
2004	5,000	PF63 15.00				
2005	332,000	—	—	—	4.00	5.00
2005	5,964	PF63 15.00				
2006	393,000	—	—	—	4.00	5.00
2006	3,500	PF63 15.00				

KM# 271 EURO

7.50 g., Bi-Metallic, 23.25 mm. **Ruler:** Beatrix **Obv:** Queen's profile left **Rev:** Relief map of Western Europe, stars, lines and value **Edge:** Segmented reeding

Date	Mintage	F12	VF20	XF40	MS60	MS63
2007	224,000	—	—	—	3.50	4.00
2007	10,000	PF63 14.50				
2008	288,000	—	—	—	3.50	4.00
2008	10,000	PF63 14.50				
2009	185,000	—	—	—	3.50	4.00
2009	7,500	PF63 14.50				
2010	166,000	—	—	—	3.50	4.00
2010	5,000	PF63 14.50				
2011	220,000	—	—	—	3.50	4.00
2011	5,000	PF63 14.50				
2012	—	—	—	—	3.50	4.00
2012	5,000	PF63 14.50				
2013	—	—	—	—	3.50	4.00
2013	5,000	PF63 14.50				

KM# 350 EURO

7.50 g., Bi-Metallic, 23.25 mm. **Ruler:** Willem-Alexander **Obv:** Head right **Rev:** Relief map of Western Europe, stars, lines and value **Edge:** Segmented reeding

Date	Mintage	F12	VF20	XF40	MS60	MS63
2014	—	—	—	—	3.50	4.00

KM# 241 2 EURO
8.50 g., Bi-Metallic, 25.75 mm. **Ruler:** Beatrix **Obv:** Profile left within 1/2 circle and star border, name within vertical lines **Rev:** Value and map within circle **Edge Lettering:** GOD * ZIJ * MET * ONS *

Date	Mintage	F12	VF20	XF40	MS60	MS63
2001	116,400,000	—	—	—	4.00	4.50
2001 Proof	16,500	—	—	—	—	—
2002	36,432,000	—	—	—	4.50	12.00
2002 Proof	16,500	—	—	—	—	—
2003	749,000	—	—	—	5.50	8.00
2003 Proof	13,000	—	—	—	—	—
2004	245,000	—	—	—	7.00	12.00
2004	5,000	PF63 18.00				
2005	332,000	—	—	—	6.00	8.00
2005	5,964	PF63 18.00				
2006	341,000	—	—	—	6.00	10.00
2006	3,500	PF63 18.00				

KM# 272 2 EURO
8.50 g., Bi-Metallic, 25.75 mm. **Ruler:** Beatrix **Obv:** Queen's profile left **Rev:** Relief map of Western Europe, stars, lines and value **Edge Lettering:** GOD * ZIJ * MET * ONS *

Date	Mintage	F12	VF20	XF40	MS60	MS63
2007	345,000	—	—	—	6.00	8.00
2007	10,000	PF63 17.50				
2008	288,000	—	—	—	6.00	8.00
2008	10,000	PF63 17.50				
2009	225,000	—	—	—	6.00	8.00
2009	7,500	PF63 17.50				
2010	166,000	—	—	—	6.00	8.00
2010	5,000	PF63 17.50				
2011	220,000	—	—	—	6.00	8.00
2011	5,000	PF63 17.50				
2012	—	—	—	—	6.00	8.00
2012	5,000	PF63 17.50				
2013	—	—	—	—	6.00	8.00
2013	5,000	PF63 17.50				

KM# 273 2 EURO
8.50 g., Bi-Metallic, 25.75 mm. **Ruler:** Beatrix **Subject:** 50th Anniversary Treaty of Rome **Obv:** Open treaty book **Rev:** Large value at left, modified outline of Europe at right **Edge Lettering:** GOD * ZU * MET * ONS * **Note:** 15,000 BU coins are in a Benelux set

Date	Mintage	F12	VF20	XF40	MS60	MS63
2007	6,333,000	—	—	—	6.00	15.00
2007	10,000	PF63 22.00				

KM# 282 2 EURO
8.50 g., Bi-Metallic, 25.75 mm. **Ruler:** Beatrix **Subject:** European Monetary Union, 10th Anniversary **Rev:** Stick figure and euro symbol **Edge Lettering:** *GOD *ZIJ *MET *ONS

Date	Mintage	F12	VF20	XF40	MS60	MS63
2009	5,300,000	—	—	—	4.50	15.00
2009 Proof from set	7,500	PF63 60.00				
2009 Proof in box	2,000	PF63 160				

KM# 303 2 EURO
8.50 g., Bi-Metallic, 25.75 mm. **Ruler:** Beatrix **Obv:** Beatrix at

left, Erasmus writing at right

Date	Mintage	F12	VF20	XF40	MS60	MS63
2011	4,003,000	—	—	—	4.50	30.00
2011 Proof from set	5,000	PF63 50.00				
2011 Proof in box	2,000	PF63 140				

KM# 315 2 EURO
8.50 g., Bi-Metallic, 25.75 mm. **Ruler:** Beatrix **Subject:** 10 years of euro-coins **Obv:** Euro symbol on globe, child-like images around

Date	Mintage	F12	VF20	XF40	MS60	MS63
2012	3,500,000	—	—	—	4.50	
2012 Special Unc.	15,000	—	—	—	—	15.00
2012	—	PF63 25.00				

KM# 324a 2 EURO
8.50 g., Bi-Metallic, 25.75 mm. **Ruler:** Willem-Alexander **Subject:** Kingdom, 200th Anniversary **Obv:** Ribbon portrait of seven Dutch rulers, Willem-Alexander's head in orange ribbon; stars in red, white and blue

Date	Mintage	F12	VF20	XF40	MS60	MS63
2013	1,500	PF63 75.00				

KM# 324 2 EURO
8.50 g., Bi-Metallic, 25.75 mm. **Ruler:** Willem-Alexander **Subject:** Kingdom, 200th Anniversary **Obv:** Ribbon portrait of seven Dutch rulers **Edge:** Reeded and lettered **Edge Lettering:** GOD * ZIJ * MET * ONS *

Date	Mintage	F12	VF20	XF40	MS60	MS63
2013	20,000,000	—	—	—	4.50	15.00
2013 BU card	—	—	—	—	—	15.00
2013	3,500	PF63 50.00				

KM# 332 2 EURO
8.50 g., Bi-Metallic, 25.75 mm. **Ruler:** Willem-Alexander **Subject:** Abdication of Queen Beatrix **Obv:** Beatrix and Willem-Alexander heads left **Edge:** Reeded and lettered **Edge Lettering:** GOD * ZIJ * MET * ONS *

Date	Mintage	F12	VF20	XF40	MS60	MS63
2013	20,000,000	—	—	—	—	4.50
2013 BU in card	25,000	—	—	—	—	15.00
2013	10,000	PF63 50.00				

KM# 351 2 EURO
8.50 g., Bi-Metallic, 25.75 mm. **Ruler:** Willem-Alexander **Obv:** Head right **Rev:** Relief map of Western Europe, stars, lines and value **Edge:** Reeded and lettered **Edge Lettering:** GOD * ZUJ * MET * ONS *

Date	Mintage	F12	VF20	XF40	MS60	MS63
2014	—	—	—	—	6.00	8.00

KM# 245 5 EURO
11.90 g., 0.925 Silver 0.3516 oz. ASW, 29 mm. **Ruler:** Beatrix **Subject:** Vincent Van Gogh **Obv:** Head facing **Rev:** Tilted head facing **Edge Lettering:** GOD * ZIJ * MET * ONS *

Date	Mintage	F12	VF20	XF40	MS60	MS63
ND(2003)	1,000,000	—	—	—	BV	15.00
ND-2003 Prooflike	100,000	—	—	—	—	30.00

KM# 252 5 EURO
11.90 g., 0.925 Silver 0.3516 oz. ASW **Ruler:** Beatrix **Subject:** New EEC member countries **Obv:** Head left **Rev:** Names of old and new member countries **Edge Lettering:** GOD * ZIJ * MET * ONS *

Date	Mintage	F12	VF20	XF40	MS60	MS63
2004	600,000	—	—	—	BV	17.50
2004	55,000	PF63 90.00				

KM# 253 5 EURO
11.90 g., 0.925 Silver 0.3516 oz. ASW **Ruler:** Beatrix **Subject:** 50th Anniversary - End of colonization of Netherlands Antilles **Obv:** Head left **Rev:** Fruit and date within beaded circle **Edge Lettering:** GOD * ZIJ * MET * ONS *

Date	Mintage	F12	VF20	XF40	MS60	MS63
2004	650,000	—	—	—	BV	17.50
2004	26,900	PF63 45.00				

KM# 254 5 EURO
11.91 g., 0.925 Silver 0.3519 oz. ASW, 29 mm. **Ruler:** Beatrix **Subject:** 60th Anniversary of Liberation **Obv:** Queen's image **Rev:** Value and dots **Edge Lettering:** GOD * ZIJ * MET * ONS *

Date	Mintage	F12	VF20	XF40	MS60	MS63
2005	630,000	—	—	—	BV	17.50
2005	40,000	PF63 40.00				

KM# 255 5 EURO
11.90 g., 0.925 Silver 0.3516 oz. ASW, 29 mm. **Ruler:** Beatrix **Obv:** Queen's silhouette centered on a world globe **Rev:** Value above Australia on a world globe **Edge Lettering:** GOD * ZIJ * MET * ONS *

Date	Mintage	F12	VF20	XF40	MS60	MS63
2006	500,000	—	—	—	BV	17.50
2006	22,500	PF63 45.00				

KM# 266 5 EURO
11.90 g., 0.925 Silver 0.3516 oz. ASW, 28.9 mm. **Ruler:** Beatrix **Obv:** Queen Beatrix **Rev:** Rembrandt **Edge Lettering:** GOD * Z IJ * MET * ONS *

Date	Mintage	F12	VF20	XF40	MS60	MS63
ND(2006)	655,000	—	—	—	BV	17.50
ND-2006	35,000	PF63 35.00				

KM# 267 5 EURO
11.90 g., 0.925 Silver 0.3516 oz. ASW, 29 mm. **Ruler:** Beatrix **Subject:** Tax Service, 200th Anniversary **Obv:** Queen's portrait **Rev:** Circles with dates 1806-2006 **Edge Lettering:** GOD * ZIJ * MET * ONS *

Date	Mintage	F12	VF20	XF40	MS60	MS63
2006	359,189	—	—	—	BV	17.50
2006 Prooflike	40,000	—	—	—	—	25.00
2006	15,000	PF63 60.00				

KM# 277 5 EURO
11.90 g., 0.925 Silver 0.3516 oz. ASW, 29 mm. **Ruler:** Beatrix **Subject:** Admiral M.A. de Ruyter, 400th Anniversary of Birth **Obv:** Queen's head 1/4 left **Rev:** deRuyter's head 1/4 right **Edge Lettering:** GOD * ZIJ * MET * ONS *

Date	Mintage	F12	VF20	XF40	MS60	MS63
2007	520,500	—	—	—	BV	17.50
2007	17,500	PF63 40.00				

KM# 280 5 EURO
15.50 g., 0.925 Silver 0.458 oz. ASW, 33 mm. **Ruler:** Beatrix **Subject:** Architecture **Obv:** Portrait facing in names of famous architects **Rev:** Books around map of the Netherlands **Edge Lettering:** GOD * ZIJ * MET * ONS *

Date	Mintage	F12	VF20	XF40	MS60	MS63
2008	24,505	PF63 40.00				

KM# 279 5 EURO
10.50 g., Silver Plated Copper, 29 mm. **Ruler:** Beatrix **Subject:**

Architecture **Obv:** Portrait facing in names of famous Architects **Rev:** Architecture books around map of the Netherlands

Date	Mintage	F12	VF20	XF40	MS60	MS63
2008	350,000	—	—	—	10.00	15.00

KM# 284 5 EURO
15.50 g., 0.925 Silver 0.458 oz. ASW, 33 mm. **Ruler:** Beatrix **Subject:** Manhattan 400th Anniversary **Obv:** Bottom tip of Manhattan Island today **Rev:** Bottom tip of Manhattan Island in 1609 **Edge Lettering:** GOD * ZIJ * MET * ONS *

Date	Mintage	F12	VF20	XF40	MS60	MS63
2009	20,000	PF63 55.00				

KM# 283 5 EURO
10.50 g., Silver Plated Copper, 29 mm. **Ruler:** Beatrix **Subject:** Manhattan 400th Anniversary **Obv:** Tip of Manhattan Island today **Rev:** Tip of Manhattan Island in 1609

Date	Mintage	F12	VF20	XF40	MS60	MS63
2009	303,209	—	—	—	10.00	15.00

KM# 290 5 EURO
15.50 g., 0.925 Silver 0.458 oz. ASW, 33 mm. **Ruler:** Beatrix **Subject:** Netherlands-Japanese Friendship **Obv:** Guilder design of 1982 with Queen **Rev:** Value and date **Edge Lettering:** GOD * ZIJ * MET * ONS *

Date	Mintage	F12	VF20	XF40	MS60	MS63
2009	45,000	PF63 40.00				

KM# 289 5 EURO
10.50 g., Silver Plated Copper, 29 mm. **Ruler:** Beatrix **Subject:** Netherlands-Japanese Friendship **Obv:** Guilder design of 1982 with Queen **Rev:** Value and date

Date	Mintage	F12	VF20	XF40	MS60	MS63
2009	343,859	—	—	—	8.00	10.00

KM# 298 5 EURO
11.90 g., 0.925 Silver 0.3516 oz. ASW, 33 mm. **Ruler:** Beatrix **Subject:** Max Havelaar, 150th Anniversary **Obv:** Queen **Rev:** Ink pen, words in spiral, figures walking around edge **Edge Lettering:** GOD * ZIJ * MET * ONS *

Date	Mintage	F12	VF20	XF40	MS60	MS63
2010	15,000	PF63 50.00				

KM# 297 5 EURO
10.50 g., Silver Plated Copper, 29 mm. **Ruler:** Beatrix **Subject:** Max Havelaar, 150th Anniversary of Birth **Obv:** Queen **Rev:** Ink pen, words in spiral, figures walking around edge **Edge Lettering:** GOD * ZIJ * MET * ONS *

Date	Mintage	F12	VF20	XF40	MS60	MS63
2010	275,010	—	—	—	9.00	12.00

KM# 301 5 EURO
15.50 g., 0.925 Silver 0.458 oz. ASW, 33 mm. **Ruler:** Beatrix **Subject:** Waterland **Obv:** Queen's bust facing, and reflected in water **Rev:** Map of the Netherlands, partly below sea level

Date	Mintage	F12	VF20	XF40	MS60	MS63
2010	17,500	PF63 45.00				

KM# 300 5 EURO
10.50 g., Silver Plated Copper, 29 mm. **Ruler:** Beatrix **Subject:** Waterland **Obv:** Queens bust facing and reflected in water **Rev:** Map of the Netherlands, partly below sea level

Date	Mintage	F12	VF20	XF40	MS60	MS63
2010	227,500	—	—	—	—	10.00

KM# 304 5 EURO
15.50 g., 0.925 Silver 0.458 oz. ASW, 33 mm. **Ruler:** Beatrix **Subject:** World Wildlife Fund, 50th Anniversary **Obv:** Profile left at center of tree leaves **Rev:** Value at center of root system **Edge Lettering:** GOD * ZIJ * MET * ONS *

Date	Mintage	F12	VF20	XF40	MS60	MS63
2011	17,500	PF63 40.00				

KM# 305 5 EURO
10.50 g., Silver Plated Copper, 29 mm. **Ruler:** Beatrix **Subject:** World Wildlife Fund, 50th Anniversary **Obv:** Profile head at center of tree leaves **Rev:** Value at center of root system **Edge Lettering:** GOD * ZIJ * MET * ONS *

Date	Mintage	F12	VF20	XF40	MS60	MS63
2011	250,000	PF63 10.00				

KM# 308 5 EURO
15.50 g., 0.925 Silver 0.458 oz. ASW, 33 mm. **Ruler:** Beatrix **Subject:** Mint building, 100th Anniversary. **Obv:** Bust facing **Rev:** Screw press and a QR-code which is to scan with a mobile telephone **Edge Lettering:** GOD * ZIJ * MET * ONS *

Date	Mintage	F12	VF20	XF40	MS60	MS63
2011	17,500	PF63 40.00				

KM# 307 5 EURO
10.50 g., Silver Plated Copper, 29 mm. **Ruler:** Beatrix **Subject:** Mint building, 100th Anniversary. **Obv:** Bust facing **Rev:** Screw press and a QR-code which is to scan with a **Edge Lettering:** GOD * ZIJ * MET * ONS *

Date	Mintage	F12	VF20	XF40	MS60	MS63
2011	71,618	—	—	—	—	15.00

KM# 308a 5 EURO
Gold AGW, 33 mm. **Ruler:** Beatrix **Subject:** Mint building, 100th Anniversary **Obv:** Bust facing **Rev:** Screw press and a QR-code whcih is to be scanned with a mobile telephone **Edge Lettering:** GOD * ZIJ * MET * ONS * **Note:** Off-metal strike made as presentation item to designer Juan José Sánchez Castaño by the mint director, as the coin won the Coin-of-the-Year award.

Date	Mintage	F12	VF20	XF40	MS60	MS63
2011 Proof	1	—	—	—	—	—

KM# 310 5 EURO
Silver Plated Copper, 29 mm. **Ruler:** Beatrix **Subject:** Painting **Obv:** Queen looking at city view painting **Rev:** Window **Edge Lettering:** GOD * ZIJ * MET * ONS *

Date	Mintage	F12	VF20	XF40	MS60	MS63
2011	230,000	—	—	—	10.00	12.00

KM# 311 5 EURO
15.50 g., 0.925 Silver 0.458 oz. ASW, 33 mm. **Ruler:** Beatrix **Subject:** Painting **Obv:** Queen looking at city view painting **Rev:** Window **Edge Lettering:** GOD * ZIJ * MET * ONS *

Date	Mintage	F12	VF20	XF40	MS60	MS63
2011	250,000	—	—	—	—	30.00
2011	12,500	PF63 40.00				

KM# 316 5 EURO
10.50 g., Silver Plated Copper, 29 mm. **Ruler:** Beatrix **Subject:** 400 years of diplomatic relations Netherlands-Turkey **Edge Lettering:** GOD * ZIJ * MET * ONS *

Date	Mintage	F12	VF20	XF40	MS60	MS63
2012	250,000	—	—	—	10.00	15.00

KM# 317 5 EURO
15.50 g., 0.925 Silver 0.458 oz. ASW, 33 mm. **Ruler:** Beatrix **Subject:** 400 years of diplomatic relations Netherlands-Turkey **Edge Lettering:** GOD * ZIJ * MET * ONS *

Date	Mintage	F12	VF20	XF40	MS60	MS63
2012	12,500	PF63 45.00				

KM# 317.1 5 EURO
15.50 g., 0.925 Silver 0.458 oz. ASW, 33 mm. **Ruler:** Beatrix **Subject:** Netherlands-Turkey diplomatic relations, 400th Anniversary **Rev:** Tulip colored orange

Date	Mintage	F12	VF20	XF40	MS60	MS63
2012	750	PF65 250				

KM# 317.2 5 EURO
15.50 g., 0.925 Silver 0.458 oz. ASW, 33 mm. **Ruler:** Beatrix **Rev:** Tulip in red

Date	Mintage	F12	VF20	XF40	MS60	MS63
2012	750	PF65 250				

KM# 317.3 5 EURO
15.50 g., 0.925 Silver 0.458 oz. ASW, 33 mm. **Ruler:** Beatrix **Rev:** Tulip in white

Date	Mintage	F12	VF20	XF40	MS60	MS63
2012	750	PF65 250				

KM# 317.4 5 EURO
15.50 g., 0.925 Silver 0.458 oz. ASW, 33 mm. **Ruler:** Beatrix **Rev:** Tulip in blue

Date	Mintage	F12	VF20	XF40	MS60	MS63
2012	750	PF65 250				

KM# 321 5 EURO
10.50 g., Silver Plated Copper, 29 mm. **Subject:** Amsterdam Canals **Rev:** Hemisphere map with Amsterdam canal map

Date	Mintage	F12	VF20	XF40	MS60	MS63
2012	218,014	—	—	—	—	10.00
2012 BU in card	10,000	—	—	—	—	25.00

KM# 322 5 EURO
15.50 g., 0.925 Silver 0.458 oz. ASW, 33 mm. **Subject:** Amsterdam Canal **Rev:** Hemisphere map and map of Amsterdam Canals

Date	Mintage	F12	VF20	XF40	MS60	MS63
2012	12,500	PF63 60.00				

KM# 327 5 EURO
10.50 g., Silver Plated Copper, 29 mm. **Ruler:** Beatrix **Subject:** Sculpture

Date	Mintage	F12	VF20	XF40	MS60	MS63
2012	218,013	—	—	—	—	10.00
2012 BU in card	10,000	—	—	—	—	20.00

KM# 328 5 EURO
15.50 g., 0.925 Silver 0.458 oz. ASW, 33 mm. **Ruler:** Beatrix **Subject:** Sculpture

Date	Mintage	F12	VF20	XF40	MS60	MS63
2012	12,500	PF63 50.00				

KM# 325 5 EURO
15.50 g., 0.925 Silver 0.458 oz. ASW, 33 mm. **Ruler:** Willem-Alexander **Subject:** Peace treaty of Utrecht **Obv:** Head of Queen in front of building with 35 feather pens **Rev:** Feathers drawing a globe

Date	Mintage	F12	VF20	XF40	MS60	MS63
2013	220,000	—	—	—	—	10.00
2013 BU in card	10,000	—	—	—	—	25.00

KM# 326 5 EURO
15.50 g., 0.925 Silver 0.458 oz. ASW, 33 mm. **Ruler:** Beatrix **Subject:** Peace treaty of Utrecht

Date	Mintage	F12	VF20	XF40	MS60	MS63
2013	6,500	PF63 60.00				

KM# 333 5 EURO
10.50 g., Silver Plated Copper, 29 mm. **Ruler:** Willem-Alexander **Subject:** Peace Palace in the Hague, 100th Anniversary **Obv:** Head right **Rev:** Two people looking at the Peace Palace

Date	Mintage	F12	VF20	XF40	MS60	MS63
2013	220,000	—	—	—	—	10.00
2013 BU in card	10,000	—	—	—	—	20.00

KM# 334 5 EURO
15.50 g., 0.925 Silver 0.458 oz. ASW, 33 mm. **Ruler:** Willem-Alexander **Subject:** Peace Palace at the Hague, 100th Anniversary **Obv:** Head right **Rev:** Two people looking at the Peace Palace

Date	Mintage	F12	VF20	XF40	MS60	MS63
2013	12,500	PF63 60.00				

KM# 336 5 EURO
10.50 g., Silver Plated Copper, 29 mm. **Ruler:** Willem-Alexander **Subject:** Rietveld Schroder **Obv:** Head right on Atlantic hemisphere in fingerprint **Rev:** House on Eastern hemisphere fingerprint

Date	Mintage	F12	VF20	XF40	MS60	MS63
2013	250,000	—	—	—	—	10.00
2013 BU on card	—	—	—	—	—	25.00

KM# 337 5 EURO
15.50 g., 0.925 Silver 0.458 oz. ASW, 33 mm. **Ruler:** Willem-Alexander **Subject:** Rietveld Schroder house **Obv:** Head right on Atlantic hemisphere in fingerprint **Rev:** House on Eastern hemisphere in fingerprint

Date	Mintage	F12	VF20	XF40	MS60	MS63
2013	12,500	PF63 60.00				

KM# 244 10 EURO
6.72 g., 0.900 Gold 0.1932 oz. AGW, 22.5 mm. **Ruler:** Beatrix **Subject:** Crown Prince's Wedding **Obv:** Head left **Rev:** Two facing silhouettes **Edge:** Reeded

Date	Mintage	F12	VF20	XF40	MS60	MS63
2002 Prooflike	33,000	—	—	—	—	400

KM# 243 10 EURO
17.80 g., 0.925 Silver 0.526 oz. ASW, 33 mm. **Ruler:** Beatrix **Subject:** Wedding of Willem-Alexander and Maxima **Obv:** Queen's head left **Rev:** Conjoined busts left **Edge Lettering:** GOD * ZIJ * MET * ONS *

Date	Mintage	F12	VF20	XF40	MS60	MS63
2002	990,800	—	—	—	BV	40.00
2002	80,000	PF63 55.00				

KM# 246 10 EURO
6.72 g., 0.900 Gold 0.1932 oz. AGW, 22.5 mm. **Ruler:** Beatrix **Subject:** Vincent Van Gogh **Obv:** Head facing **Rev:** Tilted head facing **Edge:** Reeded

Date	Mintage	F12	VF20	XF40	MS60	MS63
ND(2003) Prooflike	20,000	—	—	—	—	400

KM# 248 10 EURO
17.80 g., 0.925 Silver 0.526 oz. ASW, 33 mm. **Ruler:** Beatrix **Obv:** Head left **Rev:** Multi-views of Prince Willem-Alexander, Princess Catherina-Amalia and Princess Maxima **Edge Lettering:** GOD * ZIJ * MET * ONS *

Date	Mintage	F12	VF20	XF40	MS60	MS63
2004	1,000,000	—	—	—	BV	25.00
2004	50,000	PF63 40.00				

KM# 247 10 EURO
6.72 g., 0.900 Gold 0.1932 oz. AGW, 22.5 mm. **Ruler:** Beatrix **Subject:** New EEC members **Obv:** Head left **Rev:** Value and legend **Edge:** Reeded

Date	Mintage	F12	VF20	XF40	MS60	MS63
2004	6,000	PF63 700				

KM# 251 10 EURO
6.72 g., 0.900 Gold 0.1932 oz. AGW, 22.5 mm. **Ruler:** Beatrix **Subject:** 50 Years of Domestic Autonomy, 1954-2004 (for Netherlands Antilles) **Obv:** Small head left **Rev:** Fruit and date within beaded circle **Edge:** Reeded

Date	Mintage	F12	VF20	XF40	MS60	MS63
2004	3,800	PF63 600				

KM# 261 10 EURO
17.80 g., 0.925 Silver 0.526 oz. ASW, 33 mm. **Ruler:** Beatrix **Subject:** Silver Jubilee of Reign **Obv:** Queen's photo **Rev:** Queen taking oath photo **Edge Lettering:** GOD * ZIJ * MET * ONS *

Date	Mintage	F12	VF20	XF40	MS60	MS63
2005	1,000,000	—	—	—	BV	25.00
2005	59,754	PF63 40.00				

KM# 264 10 EURO
6.72 g., 0.900 Gold 0.1932 oz. AGW, 22.5 mm. **Ruler:** Beatrix **Subject:** 60th Anniversary of Liberation **Obv:** Queen and dots **Rev:** Value and dots **Edge:** Reeded

Date	Mintage	F12	VF20	XF40	MS60	MS63
2005	6,000	PF63 600				

KM# 292 10 EURO
6.72 g., 0.900 Gold 0.1932 oz. AGW, 22.5 mm. **Ruler:** Beatrix **Series:** Tax Services, 200th Anniversary **Obv:** Queen's portrait **Rev:** Florin of 1807 **Edge:** Reeded

Date	Mintage	F12	VF20	XF40	MS60	MS63
2006	5,500	PF63 600				

KM# 293 10 EURO
6.72 g., 0.900 Gold 0.1932 oz. AGW, 22.5 mm. **Ruler:** Beatrix **Subject:** Netherlands-Australian Friendship, 400th Anniversary **Obv:** Queens portrait within lines of a globe **Rev:** Australia, value and dates **Edge:** Reeded

Date	Mintage	F12	VF20	XF40	MS60	MS63
2006	3,500	PF63 800				

KM# 294 10 EURO
6.72 g., 0.900 Gold 0.1932 oz. AGW, 22.5 mm. **Ruler:** Beatrix **Subject:** Rembrandt, 400th Anniversary of Birth **Obv:** Queen's portrait **Rev:** Self-portrait **Edge:** Reeded

Date	Mintage	F12	VF20	XF40	MS60	MS63
2006	8,500	PF63 400				

KM# 278 10 EURO
6.72 g., 0.900 Gold 0.1932 oz. AGW, 22.5 mm. **Ruler:** Beatrix **Subject:** Admiral M.A. de Ruyter, 400th Birthday **Obv:** Head 1/4 left **Rev:** Head 1/4 right **Edge:** Reeded

Date	Mintage	F12	VF20	XF40	MS60	MS63
2007	7,000	PF63 400				

KM# 281 10 EURO
6.72 g., 0.900 Gold 0.1932 oz. AGW, 22.5 mm. **Ruler:** Beatrix **Subject:** Architecture **Obv:** Portrait facing in names of famous architects **Rev:** Architecture books around map of the Netherlands **Edge:** Reeded

Date	Mintage	F12	VF20	XF40	MS60	MS63
2008	8,000	PF63 400				

KM# 285 10 EURO
6.72 g., 0.900 Gold 0.1932 oz. AGW, 22.5 mm. **Ruler:** Beatrix **Subject:** Dutch settlement of Manhattan, NY 400th Anniversary **Obv:** Bottom tip of Manhattan Island today **Rev:** Bottom tip of Manhattan Island in 1609 **Edge:** Reeded

Date	Mintage	F12	VF20	XF40	MS60	MS63
2009	6,500	PF63 400				

KM# 291 10 EURO
6.72 g., 0.900 Gold 0.1932 oz. AGW, 22.5 mm. **Ruler:** Beatrix **Subject:** Netherlands-Japanese Friendship **Obv:** Guilder design of 1982 with Queen **Rev:** Value and date **Edge:** Reeded

Date	Mintage	F12	VF20	XF40	MS60	MS63
2009	5,418	PF63 400				

KM# 299 10 EURO
6.72 g., 0.900 Gold 0.1932 oz. AGW, 22.5 mm. **Ruler:** Beatrix **Subject:** Max Havelaar, 150th Anniversary of Birth **Rev:** Ink pen, words in spiral, figures walking around edge **Edge:** Reeded

Date	Mintage	F12	VF20	XF40	MS60	MS63
2010	4,699	PF63 400				

KM# 302 10 EURO
6.72 g., 0.900 Gold 0.1932 oz. AGW, 22.5 mm. **Ruler:** Beatrix **Subject:** Waterland **Obv:** Bust of Queen facing and reflected in water **Rev:** Map of the Netherlands, partly under sea level

Date	Mintage	F12	VF20	XF40	MS60	MS63
2010	4,500	PF63 400				

KM# 306 10 EURO
6.72 g., 0.900 Gold 0.1932 oz. AGW, 22.5 mm. **Ruler:** Beatrix **Subject:** World Wildlife Fund, 50th Anniversary **Obv:** Profile left at center of tree leaves **Rev:** Value at center of root system **Edge:** Reeded

Date	Mintage	F12	VF20	XF40	MS60	MS63
2011	4,000	PF63 400				

KM# 309 10 EURO
6.75 g., 0.900 Gold 0.1941 oz. AGW, 22.5 mm. **Ruler:** Beatrix **Obv:** Head facing **Rev:** Screw press and a QR-code which is to scan with a mobile telephone **Edge:** Reeded

Date	Mintage	F12	VF20	XF40	MS60	MS63
2011	4,000	PF63 400				

KM# 312 10 EURO
6.72 g., 0.900 Gold 0.1932 oz. AGW, 22.5 mm. **Ruler:** Beatrix **Subject:** Painting **Obv:** Queen looking at city view painting **Rev:** Window **Edge:** Reeded

Date	Mintage	F12	VF20	XF40	MS60	MS63
2011	3,500	PF63 400				

KM# 318 10 EURO
6.72 g., 0.900 Gold 0.1932 oz. AGW, 22.5 mm. **Ruler:** Beatrix **Subject:** 400 years of diplomatic relations Netherlands-Turkey **Edge:** Reeded

Date	Mintage	F12	VF20	XF40	MS60	MS63
2012	—	PF63 400				

KM# 323 10 EURO
6.72 g., 0.900 Gold 0.1932 oz. AGW, 22.5 mm. **Ruler:** Beatrix **Subject:** Amsterdam Canals **Obv:** Hemisphere map with fingerprint design **Rev:** Hemisphere map and map of Amsterdam canals

Date	Mintage	F12	VF20	XF40	MS60	MS63
2012	2,000	PF63 500				

KM# 329 10 EURO
6.72 g., 0.900 Gold 0.1932 oz. AGW, 22.5 mm. **Ruler:** Beatrix **Subject:** Sculpture **Obv:** Head facing **Edge:** Reeded

Date	Mintage	F12	VF20	XF40	MS60	MS63
2012	2,000	PF63 500				

KM# 330 10 EURO
6.72 g., 0.900 Gold 0.1932 oz. AGW, 22.5 mm. **Ruler:** Beatrix **Subject:** Peace treaty of Utrecht **Obv:** Head of Queen in front of building with 35 featherpens **Rev:** Feathers drawing a globe and in center, shield of Utrecht **Edge:** Reeded

Date	Mintage	F12	VF20	XF40	MS60	MS63
2013	2,000	PF63 500				

KM# 335 10 EURO
6.72 g., 0.900 Gold 0.1932 oz. AGW, 22.5 mm. **Ruler:** Willem-Alexander **Subject:** Peace Palace in the Hague, 100th Anniversary

Date	Mintage	F12	VF20	XF40	MS60	MS63
2013	2,000	PF63 500				

KM# 338 10 EURO
6.72 g., 0.900 Gold 0.1932 oz. AGW, 22.5 mm. **Ruler:** Willem-Alexander **Subject:** Rietveld Schroder house **Obv:** Head right on Atlantic hemisphere in fingerprint **Rev:** House on Eastern hemisphere in fingerprint

Date	Mintage	F12	VF20	XF40	MS60	MS63
2013	2,000	PF63 500				

KM# 340 10 EURO
15.50 g., 0.900 Silver 0.4456 oz. ASW, 38 mm. **Ruler:** Willem-Alexander **Rev:** Crowd looking toward King

Date	Mintage	F12	VF20	XF40	MS60	MS63
2013	12,500	PF63 70.00				

KM# 339 10 EURO
15.50 g., Silver Plated Copper, 33 mm. **Ruler:** Willem-Alexander **Rev:** Crowd looking toward King

Date	Mintage	F12	VF20	XF40	MS60	MS63
2013	400,000	—	—	—	—	20.00
2013 BU in card	10,000	—	—	—	—	35.00

KM# 249 20 EURO
8.50 g., 0.900 Gold 0.2444 oz. AGW, 25 mm. **Ruler:** Beatrix **Subject:** Birth of Crown-Princess - Catharina-Amalia - July 12, 2003 **Obv:** Bust left **Rev:** Holographic images: left, Princess Maxima; front, Princess Catharina-Amalia; right, Prince Willem-Alexander **Edge:** Reeded

Date	Mintage	F12	VF20	XF40	MS60	MS63
2004	5,345	PF63 530				

KM# 262 20 EURO
8.50 g., 0.900 Gold 0.2444 oz. AGW, 25 mm. **Ruler:** Beatrix **Subject:** Silver Jubilee of Reign **Obv:** Queen's photo **Rev:** Queen taking oath photo **Edge:** Reeded

Date	Mintage	F12	VF20	XF40	MS60	MS63
2005	5,001	PF63 530				

KM# 341 20 EURO
8.50 g., 0.900 Gold 0.2444 oz. AGW, 25 mm. **Ruler:** Willem-Alexander **Rev:** Crowd looking toward king

Date	Mintage	F12	VF20	XF40	MS60	MS63
2013	2,500	PF63 700				

KM# 250 50 EURO
13.44 g., 0.900 Gold 0.3864 oz. AGW, 27 mm. **Ruler:** Beatrix **Subject:** Birth of Crown-Princess - Catharina-Amalia - July 12, 2003 **Obv:** Bust left **Rev:** Holographic images: left, Princess Maxima; front, Princess Catharina-Amalia; right, Prince Willem-Alexander **Edge:** Reeded

Date	Mintage	F12	VF20	XF40	MS60	MS63
2004	3,500	PF63 775				

KM# 263 50 EURO
13.44 g., 0.900 Gold 0.3864 oz. AGW, 27 mm. **Ruler:** Beatrix **Subject:** Silver Jubilee of Reign **Obv:** Queen's photo **Rev:** Queen taking oath photo **Edge:** Reeded

Date	Mintage	F12	VF20	XF40	MS60	MS63
2005	3,500	PF63 775				

KM# 342 50 EURO
13.44 g., 0.900 Gold 0.3864 oz. AGW, 27 mm. **Ruler:** Willem-Alexander **Rev:** Crowd looking toward king

Date	Mintage	F12	VF20	XF40	MS60	MS63
2013	1,000	PF63 1,000				

TRADE COINAGE

KM# 190.2 DUCAT
3.49 g., 0.983 Gold 0.1097 oz. AGW **Ruler:** Beatrix **Obv:** Knight divides date with larger letters in legend **Rev:** Inscription within decorated square

Date	Mintage	F12	VF20	XF40	MS60	MS63
2001	—	PF65 250				
2002	—	PF65 250				
2003	3,800	PF65 250				
2004	2,120	PF65 450				
2005	2,243	PF65 200				
2006	2,097	PF65 300				
2007	2,250	PF65 250				
2008	3,260	PF65 250				
2009	2,750	PF65 250				
2010	1,870	PF65 250				
2011	—	PF65 250				
2012	—	PF65 250				

KM# 211 2 DUCAT
6.99 g., 0.983 Gold 0.2194 oz. AGW, 26 mm. **Ruler:** Beatrix **Obv:** Knight divides date within beaded circle **Rev:** Inscription within decorated square

Date	Mintage	F12	VF20	XF40	MS60	MS63
2002B	6,650	PF65 475				
2003B	4,500	PF65 475				
2004B	2,015	PF65 475				
2005B	3,500	PF65 475				
2006B	1,800	PF65 550				
2007B	2,000	PF65 475				
2008B	2,100	PF65 475				
2009B	2,000	PF65 475				
2010B	2,000	PF65 475				
2011B	1,640	PF65 500				
2012B	—	PF65 500				

SILVER BULLION COINAGE

KM# 242 SILVER DUCAT
28.25 g., 0.873 Silver 0.7878 oz. ASW, 40 mm. **Ruler:** Beatrix **Obv:** Crowned shield **Rev:** Armored knight with sword divides date and circle, shield in front **Edge:** Reeded **Note:** Utrecht coin design circa 1659 based on KM#48.

Date	Mintage	F12	VF20	XF40	MS60	MS63
2001B	9,000	PF65 40.00				

KM# 256 SILVER DUCAT
28.25 g., 0.873 Silver 0.7878 oz. ASW, 40 mm. **Ruler:** Beatrix **Obv:** Crowned shield **Rev:** Armored knight with Gelderland arms **Edge:** Reeded

Date	Mintage	F12	VF20	XF40	MS60	MS63
2002B	9,400	PF65 40.00				

KM# 257 SILVER DUCAT
28.25 g., 0.873 Silver 0.7878 oz. ASW, 40 mm. **Ruler:** Beatrix **Obv:** Crowned shield **Rev:** Armored knight with sword holding arms of Holland **Edge:** Reeded

Date	Mintage	F12	VF20	XF40	MS60	MS63
2003B	4,100	PF65 50.00				

KM# 258 SILVER DUCAT
28.25 g., 0.873 Silver 0.7878 oz. ASW, 40 mm. **Ruler:** Beatrix **Obv:** Crowned shield **Rev:** Armored knight holding sword with Zeeland arms **Edge:** Reeded

Date	Mintage	F12	VF20	XF40	MS60	MS63
2004B	4,109	PF65 50.00				

KM# 259 SILVER DUCAT
28.25 g., 0.873 Silver 0.7878 oz. ASW, 40 mm. **Ruler:** Beatrix **Obv:** Crowned shield **Rev:** Armored knight holding sword with Friesland arms **Edge:** Reeded

Date	Mintage	F12	VF20	XF40	MS60	MS63
2005B	4,000	PF65 50.00				

KM# 260 SILVER DUCAT
28.25 g., 0.873 Silver 0.7878 oz. ASW, 40 mm. **Ruler:** Beatrix **Obv:** Crowned shield **Rev:** Armored knight holding sword with Groningen arms **Edge:** Reeded

Date	Mintage	F12	VF20	XF40	MS60	MS63
2006B	4,000	PF65 50.00				

KM# 275 SILVER DUCAT
28.25 g., 0.873 Silver 0.7878 oz. ASW, 40 mm. **Ruler:** Beatrix **Obv:** Crowned shield **Rev:** Armored knight holding sword with Overyssel arms **Edge:** Reeded

Date	Mintage	F12	VF20	XF40	MS60	MS63
2007	3,500	PF65 45.00				

KM# 295 SILVER DUCAT
28.25 g., 0.873 Silver 0.7878 oz. ASW, 40 mm. **Ruler:** Beatrix **Subject:** Northern Brabant **Obv:** Crowned shield **Rev:** John I, Count of Brabant standing with shield **Edge:** Reeded

Date	Mintage	F12	VF20	XF40	MS60	MS63
2008	3,000	PF65 50.00				

KM# 286 SILVER DUCAT
28.25 g., 0.873 Silver 0.7878 oz. ASW, 40 mm. **Ruler:** Beatrix **Rev:** Jan I standing with sword and Gelderland arms

Date	Mintage	F12	VF20	XF40	MS60	MS63
2009	3,000	PF65 50.00				

KM# 296 SILVER DUCAT
28.25 g., 0.873 Silver 0.7878 oz. ASW, 40 mm. **Ruler:** Beatrix
Subject: Limburg **Obv:** Crowned shield **Rev:** Philip II of Montmorency, Count of Horne, standing **Edge:** Reeded

Date	Mintage	F12	VF20	XF40	MS60	MS63
2009	3,500	PF65 50.00				

KM# 287 SILVER DUCAT
28.25 g., 0.875 Silver 0.7896 oz. ASW, 40 mm. **Ruler:** Beatrix
Obv: William of Orange standing with Zuid-Holland arms **Edge:** Reeded

Date	Mintage	F12	VF20	XF40	MS60	MS63
2010	2,850	PF65 50.00				

KM# 288 SILVER DUCAT
28.25 g., 0.875 Silver 0.7896 oz. ASW, 40 mm. **Ruler:** Beatrix
Obv: Frederik Hendrik standing with Gelderland arms **Edge:** Reeded

Date	Mintage	F12	VF20	XF40	MS60	MS63
2010	3,100	PF65 50.00				

KM# 313 SILVER DUCAT
28.25 g., 0.873 Silver 0.7878 oz. ASW, 40 mm. **Ruler:** Beatrix
Obv: Crowned shield **Rev:** Floris V **Edge:** Reeded

Date	Mintage	F12	VF20	XF40	MS60	MS63
2011	—	PF65 50.00				

KM# 314 SILVER DUCAT
28.25 g., 0.875 Silver 0.7896 oz. ASW, 40 mm. **Ruler:** Beatrix
Subject: Zeeland **Obv:** Crowned shield **Rev:** Michiel de Ruyter with shield of Zeeland **Edge:** Reeded

Date	Mintage	F12	VF20	XF40	MS60	MS63
2011	—	PF65 50.00				

KM# 319 SILVER DUCAT
28.25 g., 0.875 Silver 0.7896 oz. ASW, 40 mm. **Ruler:** Beatrix
Subject: Utrecht **Obv:** Crowned shield **Rev:** Stadtholder Willem III with shield of Utrecht **Edge:** Reeded

Date	Mintage	F12	VF20	XF40	MS60	MS63
2012	—	PF65 60.00				

KM# 320 SILVER DUCAT
28.25 g., 0.875 Silver 0.7896 oz. ASW, 40 mm. **Ruler:** Beatrix
Subject: Friesland **Obv:** Crowned shield **Rev:** Willem Lodewijk van Nassau - Dillenbrug with shield of Friesland **Edge:** Reeded

Date	Mintage	F12	VF20	XF40	MS60	MS63
2012	—	PF65 60.00				

KM# 331 SILVER DUCAT
28.25 g., 0.875 Silver 0.7896 oz. ASW, 40 mm. **Ruler:** Beatrix
Subject: Overijssel

Date	Mintage	F12	VF20	XF40	MS60	MS63
2013	—	PF65 60.00				

KM# 343 SILVER DUCAT
28.25 g., 0.875 Silver 0.7896 oz. ASW, 40 mm. **Ruler:** Willem-Alexander **Subject:** Groningen **Edge:** Reeded

Date	Mintage	F12	VF20	XF40	MS60	MS63
2013	—	PF65 60.00				

KM# 352 SILVER DUCAT
28.25 g., 0.875 Silver 0.7896 oz. ASW, 40 mm. **Ruler:** Willem-Alexander **Subject:** Friesland **Edge:** Reeded

Date	Mintage	F12	VF20	XF40	MS60	MS63
2014	—	PF65 60.00				

PATTERNS
Including off metal strikes

KM#	Date	Mintage	Identification	Mkt Val
Pn164	2001	—	Gulden Nickel Medal rotation	—
Pn165	2001	—	2 Euro Cent Nickel	100
Pn166	2001	—	Euro Brass KM240	150

MINT SETS

KM#	Date	Mintage	Identification	Issue Price	Mkt Val
MS4	2001 (6)	85,000	KM#202-206, 210	12.00	25.00
MS5	2001 (8)	68,000	KM#234-241	15.00	15.00
MS6	2002 (8)	105,000	KM#234-241	15.00	30.00
MS7	2002 (8)	59,500	KM#234-241	15.00	30.00
MS8	2002 (8)	25,000	KM#234-241 plus bear medal	15.50	30.00
MS9	2002 (8)	10,000	KM#234-241 plus medal	15.50	35.00
MS10	2002 (8)	3,500	KM#234-241 plus medal	20.00	110
MS11	2002 (8)	2,002	KM#234-241 plus medal	22.00	150
MS12	2002 (8)	10,000	KM#234-241 plus medal	22.00	30.00
MS13	2002 (8)	10,000	KM#234-241 plus medal	22.00	30.00
MS14	2002 (9)	10,000	KM#234-241 plus medal	22.00	30.00
MS15	2002 (8)	10,000	KM#234-241 plus medal	22.00	30.00
MS16	2002 (8)	3,000	KM#234-241 plus medal	30.00	40.00
MS17	2002 (1)	9,200	KM#243 plus stamp	30.00	55.00
MS17A	2002 (8)	2,500	KM#234-241	20.00	40.00
MS18	2002 (8)	1,000	KM#234-241 plus medal	99.00	60.00
MS19	2003 (8)	75,000	KM#234-241	15.50	25.00
MS20	2003 (8)	15,000	KM#234-241	20.00	40.00
MS21	2003 (8)	10,000	KM#234-241	15.50	25.00
MS22	2003 (8)	10,000	KM#234-241 plus medal	22.00	25.00
MS23	2003 (8)	10,000	KM#234-241 plus medal	42.00	45.00
MS24	2003 (7)	2,003	KM#234-241 plus medal	25.00	100
MS25	2003 (8)	1,000	KM#234-241 plus bi-color medal	—	25.00
MS26	2003 (7)	100	KM#234-241 plus silver medal	70.00	50.00
MS27	2003 (8)	25	KM#234-241 plus golden medal	400	250
MS28	2003 (8)	25,000	KM#234-241 plus bear medal	20.00	25.00
MS29	2003 (8)	15,000	KM#234-241 plus medal	20.00	25.00
MS30	2003 (8)	1,000	KM#234-241	—	25.00
MS31	2003 (8)	150	KM#234-241 plus silver medal	70.00	50.00
MS32	2003 (8)	50	KM#234-241 plus golden medal	400	275
MS33	2003 (8)	3,500	KM#234-241 plus medal	20.00	60.00
MS34	2003 (8)	1,000	KM#234-241	20.00	100
MS35	2003 (8)	15,000	KM234-241	—	35.00
MS36	2003 (8)	20,000	KM#234-241 plus silver medal	22.00	25.00
MS37	2003 (16)	10,000	KM#234-241 and Luxembourg KM#75-81, 40	40.00	45.00
MS38	2003 (40)	10,000	KM#224-231 plus Germany KM#207-214 plus Spain KM#1040-1047 plus Belgium KM#224-231 and Austria KM#3082-3089	85.00	85.00
MS39	2004 (8)	3,500	KM#234-241 plus medal	20.00	60.00
MS40	2004 (8)	10,000	KM#234-241	18.00	30.00
MS41	2004 (9)	20,000	KM#234-241	20.00	30.00
MS42	2004 (8)	1,000	KM#234-241	20.00	110
MS43	2004 (24)	35,000	KM#234-241 and Luxembourg KM#75-81 plus Belgium KM#224-231	60.00	60.00
MS44	2004 (10)	10,000	KM#234-241	25.00	30.00
MS45	2004 (9)	1,500	KM#234-241	30.00	30.00
MS46	2004 (8)	3,500	KM#234-241	20.00	30.00
MS47	2004 (9)	150	KM#234-241	100	100
MS48	2004 (8)	50	KM#234-241	500	500
MS49	2004 (8)	50,000	KM#234-241	18.00	30.00
MS50	2004 (9)	—	KM#234-241	25.00	150
MS51	2005 (9)	3,500	KM#234-241	20.00	60.00
MS52	2005 (9)	—	KM#234-241	25.00	150
MS53	2005 (9)	10,000	KM#234-241	18.00	27.50
MS54	2005 (9)	20,000	KM#234-241	20.00	27.50
MS55	2005 (9)	20,000	KM#234-241	18.00	27.50
MS56	2005 (8)	55,000	KM#234-241	18.00	25.00
MS57	2005 (24)	20,000	KM#234-241, Belgium 224-231, Luxembourg 75-81	60.00	60.00
MS58	2005 (8)	1,000	KM#234-241	25.00	110
MS59	2005 (8)	15,000	KM#234-241	35.00	35.00
MS60	2005 (9)	1,000	KM#234-241	30.00	30.00
MS61	2005 (9)	100	KM#234-241	120	80.00
MS62	2005 (9)	25	KM#234-241	550	300
MS63	2006 (10)	3,500	KM#234-241	20.00	40.00
MS64	2006 (10)	4,000	KM#234-241	250	210
MS65	2006 (10)	500	KM#234-241	900	900
MS66	2006 (8)	45,000	KM#234-241	18.00	30.00
MS67	2006 (9)	2,750	KM#231-241	20.00	30.00
MS68	2006 (9)	100	KM#234-241	—	95.00
MS69	2006 (8)	25	KM#234-241	—	500
MS70	2006 (9)	2,750	KM#234-241	20.00	30.00
MS71	2006 (8)	100	KM#234-241	—	95.00
MS72	2006 (9)	25	KM#234-241	—	500
MS73	2006 (9)	15,000	KM#234-241	65.00	65.00
MS74	2006 (9)	1,050	KM#234-241	22.00	30.00
MS75	2006 (9)	1,500	KM#234-241	30.00	30.00
MS76	2006 (9)	600	KM#234-241	35.00	40.00
MS77	2006 (9)	100	KM#234-241	150	100
MS78	2006 (9)	25	KM#234-241	650	400
MS79	2006 (8)	1,000	KM#234-241	25.00	45.00
MS80	2006 (9)	—	KM#234-241	25.00	120
MS81	2006 (8)	10,000	KM#234-241	25.00	30.00
MS82	2007 (9)	3,500	KM#234-236, 268-272	20.00	40.00
MS83	2007 (9)	100	KM#234-236, 268-272	—	500
MS84	2007 (8)	3,500	KM#234-236, 268-272	—	250
MS85	2007 (8)	500	KM#234-236, 268-272	900	900
MS86	2007 (8)	40,000	KM#234-236, 268-272	18.00	27.50
MS87	2007 (9)	3,000	KM#234-236, 268-272	20.00	27.50
MS88	2007 (9)	100	KM#234-236, 268-272	—	95.00
MS89	2007 (9)	3,000	KM#234-236, 268-272	20.00	27.50
MS90	2007 (9)	100	KM#234-236, 268-272	—	95.00
MS92	2007 (9)	1,050	KM#234-236, 268-272	22.00	27.50
MS93	2007 (9)	1,000	KM#234-236, 268-272	35.00	40.00
MS94	2007 (9)	100	KM#234-236, 268-272	150	150
MS95	2007 (9)	25	KM#234-236, 268-272	650	650
MS96	2007 (8)	1,000	KM#234-236, 268-272	25.00	75.00
MS97	2007 (9)	—	KM#234-236, 268-272	25.00	100
MS98	2007 (8)	5,000	KM#234-236, 268-272	25.00	28.00
MS109	2001 (6)	120,000	KM#202-206, 210 Introduction Euro-coins, no medal	15.00	25.00
MS112	2001 (6)	1,000	KM#202-206, 210 BOLEGO-VOK	—	60.00
MS113	2001 (6)	1,000	KM#202-206, 210 De Akerendam II, with a silver 2 stuiver coin from the wreck	125	145

KM#	Date	Mintage	Identification	MS65	PF65
MS114	2001 (6)	1,000	KM#202-206, 210 United Seven Provinces Groningen	40.00	40.00
MS115	2001 (6)	1,000	KM#202-206, 214 United Seven Provinces Utrecht	40.00	40.00
MS116	2001 (6)	21,000	KM#202-206, 210 Baby set + bear medal	15.50	25.00
MS117	2001 (6)	1,015	KM#202-206, 210 Onderlinge "s-Grdevenhage"	—	70.00
MS121	2001 (8)	68,000	KM#234-241 Charity set, disabled sport	15.00	17.00
MS122	2002 (8)	105,000	KM#234-241 Charity set, blind escort dogs fund	15.00	30.00
MS123	2002 (8)	59,500	KM#234-241 Last FDS-set	15.00	30.00
MS124	2002 (8)	25,000	KM#234-241 Baby set + bear medal	15.50	30.00
MS125	2002 (8)	10,000	KM#234-241 Wedding-set + medal	15.50	35.00
MS126	2002 (8)	3,500	KM#234-241 Queen Beatrix + medal	20.00	110
MS127	2002 (8)	2,002	KM#234-241 10th day of the Mint + medal	22.00	175
MS128	2002 (8)	10,000	KM#234-241 VOC set I + medal	22.00	35.00
MS129	2002 (8)	10,000	KM#234-241 VOC set II + medal	22.00	30.00
MS130	2002 (8)	10,000	KM#234-241 VOC set III + medal	22.00	30.00
MS131	2002 (8)	10,000	KM#234-241 VOC set IV + medal	22.00	30.00
MS132	2002 (8)	3,000	KM#234-241 BVC + medal	30.00	40.00
MS133	2002 (8)	9,200	KM#234-241 10 Euro + poststamp	30.00	30.00
MS134	2002 (8)	2,500	KM#234-241 VVV-Iris gift set	20.00	40.00
MS135	2002 (8)	1,000	KM#234-241 Theo Peters (Christmas) + medal	99.00	90.00
MS136	2003 (8)	75,000	KM#234-241 Charity set, epilepsy fund	15.50	25.00
MS137	2003 (8)	15,000	KM#234-241 Information set Denmark	20.00	40.00
MS138	2003 (8)	10,000	KM#234-241 VVV-Iris gift set	20.00	25.00
MS139	2003 (8)	10,000	KM#234-241 VOC set V + medal	22.00	25.00
MS140	2003 (8)	10,000	KM#234-241 VOC set VI + medal	42.00	45.00
MS141	2003 (8)	2,003	KM#234-241 Day of the mint + medal	25.00	140
MS142	2003 (8)	1,000	KM#234-241 Theo Peters jubilee set + bi-colour medal	—	30.00
MS143	2003 (8)	100	KM#234-241 Theo Peters jubilee set + silver medal	70.00	70.00
MS144	2003 (8)	25	KM#234-241 Theo Peters jubilee set + golden medal	400	410
MS145	2003 (8)	25,000	KM#234-241 Baby set + bear medal	20.00	25.00
MS146	2003 (8)	15,000	KM#234-241 Wedding-set + medal	20.00	25.00
MS147	2003 (8)	1,000	KM#234-241 Theo Peters Christmas set + bi-colour medal	—	30.00
MS148	2003 (8)	150	KM#234-241 Theo Peters Christmas set + silver medal	70.00	70.00
MS149	2003 (8)	50	KM#234-241 Theo Peters Christmas set + golden medal	400	1,000
MS150	2003 (8)	3,500	KM#234-241 Mint masters I + medal	20.00	60.00
MS151	2003 (8)	1,000	KM#234-241 World Money Fair Basel	20.00	130
MS152	2003 (8)	15,000	KM#234-241 Information set Hungaria	20.00	40.00
MS153	2003 (8)	20,000	KM#234-241 Royal birthset of Princess Catharina-Amalia December 7 + silver medal	22.00	25.00
MS154	2003 (8)	10,000	KM#234-241 Benelux set, with Belgium (8) KM#224-231 and Luxembourg (8) KM#75-81	40.00	45.00
MS155	2003 (8)	10,000	KM#234-241 Charles V set + medal, with Germany (8) KM#207-214, Spain (8) KM#1040-1047, Belgium (8) KM#224-231, and Austria (8) KM#3082-3089	85.00	85.00
MS156	2004 (8)	3,500	KM#234-241 Mintmasters II + medal	20.00	60.00
MS157	2004 (8)	10,000	KM#234-241 Wedding-set + medal	18.00	30.00
MS158	2004 (8)	20,000	KM#234-241 Baby set + bear medal	20.00	30.00
MS159	2004 (8)	1,000	KM#234-241 World Money Fair Basel	20.00	110
MS160	2004 (8)	35,000	KM#234-241 Benelux: Belgium, Netherlands + Luxembourg. With silver medal	60.00	60.00
MS161	2004 (8)	10,000	KM#234-241 Queen Juliana-set + silver guilder KM#184 and 30mm silver medal	25.00	30.00
MS162	2004 (8)	1,500	KM#234-241 Theo Peters Christmas set + bi-colour medal	30.00	30.00
MS163	2004 (8)	3,500	KME234-241 VVV-Iris gift set	30.00	25.00
MS164	2004 (8)	150	KM#234-241 Theo Peters Christmas set + silver medal	100	100
MS165	2004 (8)	50	KM#234-241 Theo Peters Christmas set + golden medal	500	500
MS166	2004 (8)	50,000	KM#234-241 Charity set, Fire-burn Centre	18.00	30.00
MS167	2004 (8)	2,004	KM#234-241 Day of the Mint + medal	25.00	150
MS168	2005 (8)	3,500	KM#234-241 Mintmasters III + medal	20.00	60.00
MS169	2005 (8)	2,005	KM#234-241 Day of the Mint + medal	25.00	150
MS170	2005 (8)	10,000	KM#234-241 Wedding-set + medal	18.00	27.50
MS171	2005 (8)	20,000	KM#234-241 Baby set + bear medal	20.00	27.50
MS172	2005 (8)	20,000	KM#234-241 Nijntje-set (Dick Bruna) + medal	18.00	27.50
MS173	2005 (8)	55,000	KM#234-241 Charity set: Princess Beatrix Fonds	18.00	27.50
MS174	2005 (8)	20,000	KM#234-241 Beneluz: Belgium, Netherlands + Luxembourg. With silver medal	60.00	60.00
MS175	2005 (8)	1,000	KM#234-241 World Money Fair Basel	25.00	110
MS176	2005 (8)	15,000	KM#234-241 60th Anniversary Liberation + Canadian 25 ct	35.00	35.00
MS177	2005 (8)	1,000	KM#234-241 Theo Peters Christmas set + bi-colour medal	30.00	30.00
MS178	2005 (8)	100	KM#234-241 Theo Peters Christmas set + silver medal	120	120
MS179	2005 (8)	25	KM#234-241 Theo Peters Christmas set + golden medal	550	550
MS180	2006 (8)	3,500	KM#234-241 Mintmasters IV + medal	20.00	40.00
MS181	2006 (8)	4,000	KM#234-241 5 sets with a Rembrandt silver medal and one set with the Rembrandt 5 euro coin	250	250
MS182	2006 (8)	500	KM#234-241 5 sets with a Rembrandt silver medal and one set with the Rembrandt 10 euro coin	900	900
MS183	2006 (8)	45,000	KM#234-241 Charity set: (Kika)	18.00	30.00
MS184	2006 (8)	2,750	KM#234-241 Baby set boy + bear medal	20.00	30.00
MS185	2006 (8)	100	KM#234-241 Baby set boy + silver medal	—	95.00
MS186	2006 (8)	25	KM#234-241 Baby set boy + gold medal	—	500
MS187	2006 (8)	2,750	KM#234-241 Baby set girl + bear medal	20.00	30.00
MS188	2006 (8)	100	KM#234-241 Baby set girl + silver medal	—	95.00
MS189	2006 (8)	25	KM#234-241 Baby set girl + gold medal	—	500
MS190	2006 (8)	15,000	KM#234-241 Beneluz: Belgium, Netherlands + Luxembourg. With silver medal	65.00	65.00
MS192	2006 (8)	1,050	KM#234-241 Wedding-set + medal	22.00	30.00
MS193	2006 (8)	1,500	KM#234-241 Christmas set Royal Dutch Mint	30.00	30.00
MS194	2006 (8)	600	KM#234-241 Theo Peters Christmas set + bi-colour medal	35.00	40.00
MS195	2006 (8)	100	KM#234-241 Christmas set + silver medal	150	150
MS196	2006 (8)	25	KM#234-241 Christmas set + golden medal	650	650
MS197	2006 (8)	1,000	KM#234-241 Berlin Coin Fair	25.00	45.00
MS198	2006 (8)	2,006	KM#234-241 Day of the Mint + medal	25.00	120
MS199	2006 (8)	10,000	KM#234-241 200 years coins in Kingdom Holland	25.00	30.00
MS200	2006 (8)	3,500	KM#234-236, 268-272 Mintmasters V + medal	20.00	40.00
MS201	2007 (8)	100	KM#234-236, 268-272 Mintmasters V + silver medal	—	600
MS202	2007 (8)	3,500	KM#234-236, 268-272 5 sets Michiel de Ruyter + silver medal and one set with the Michiel de Ruyter 5 euro coin BU	250	250
MS203	2007 (8)	500	KM#234-236, 268-272 5 sets Michiel de Ruyter + silver medal and one set with the Michiel de Ruyter 10 euro coin	900	900
MS204	2007 (8)	40,000	KM#234-236, 268-272 Charity set	18.00	27.50
MS205	2007 (8)	3,000	KM#234-236, 268-272 Baby set boy + bear medal	20.00	27.50
MS206	2007 (8)	100	KM#234-236, 268-272 Baby set boy + silver medal	—	95.00
MS207	2007 (8)	3,000	KM#234-236, 268-272 Baby set girl + bear medal	20.00	27.50
MS208	2007 (8)	100	KM#234-236, 268-272 Baby set girl + silver medal	—	95.00
MS209	2007 (8)	15,000	KM#234-236, 268-272 Benelux: Belgium, Netherlands + Luxembourg. With silver medal + 3x 2 Euro Rome Treaty	75.00	75.00
MS210	2007 (8)	1,050	KM#234-236, 268-272 Wedding-set + medal	22.00	27.50
MS211	2007 (8)	1,000	KM#234-236, 268-272 Christmas set + bi-colour medal	35.00	40.00
MS212	2007 (8)	100	KM#234-236, 268-272 Christmas set + silver medal	150	150
MS213	2007 (8)	25	KM#234-236, 268-272 Christmas set + golden medal	650	650
MS214	2007 (8)	500	KM#234-236, 268-272 Berlin Coin Fair	25.00	90.00
MS215	2007 (8)	2,007	KM#234-236, 268-272 Day of the Mint + medal	25.00	100
MS216	2007 (8)	5,000	KM#234-236, 268-272 200 years of Royal predicate	25.00	28.00
MS217	2008 (8)	3,500	KM#234-236, 268-272 Mintmasters VI + medal	20.00	40.00
MS218	2008 (8)	100	KM#234-236, 268-272 Mintmasters VI + silver medal	20.00	500
MS219	2008 (8)	40,000	KM#234-236, 268-272 National set	20.00	27.50
MS220	2008 (8)	2,500	KM#234-236, 268-272 Baby set boy + bear medal	25.00	27.50
MS221	2008 (8)	100	KM#234-236, 268-272 Baby set boy + silver medal	65.00	65.00
MS222	2008 (8)	2,500	KM#234-236, 268-272 Baby set girl + bear medal	25.00	27.50

ID	Date	Mintage	Identification	Issue	Mkt
MS223	2008 (8)	100	KM#234-236, 268-272 Baby set girl + silver medal	65.00	65.00
MS224	2008 (8)	12,500	KM#234-236, 268-272 Benelux: Belgium, Netherlands + Luxembourg. With silver medal	75.00	75.00
MS225	2008 (8)	1,250	KM#234-236, 268-272 Wedding-set + medal	22.00	27.50
MS226	2008 (8)	500	KM#234-236, 268-272 Christmas set + bi-colour medal	35.00	40.00
MS227	2008 (8)	50	KM#234-236, 268-272 Christmas set + silver medal	130	135
MS228	2008 (8)	25	KM#234-236, 268-272 Christmas set + golden medal	850	850
MS229	2008 (8)	500	KM#234-236, 268-272 Berlin Coin Fair	25.00	75.00
MS230	2008 (8)	2,008	KM#234-236, 268-272 Day of the Mint + medal	25.00	80.00
MS231	2008 (8)	5,000	KM#234-236, 268-272 150 year Queen Emma + silver medal	32.00	35.00
MS232	2008 (8)	500	KM#234-236, 268-272 Theo Peters Jubilation set + bi-colour medal	35.00	40.00
MS233	2008 (8)	50	KM#234-236, 268-272 Theo Peters Jubilation set + silver medal	130	135
MS234	2008 (8)	25	KM#234-236, 268-272 Theo Peters Jubilation set + golden medal	850	850
MS235	2008 (8)	500	KM#234-236, 268-272 5 sets "2 centuries Amsterdam capitol of the Netherlands" + gold plated silver medals and one set with the golden Arctecture 10 euro coin	900	1,000
MS236	2009 (8)	3,500	KM#234-236, 268-272 Mintmasters VII + medal	22.00	40.00
MS237	2009 (8)	100	KM#234-236, 268-272 Mintmasters VII + silver medal	22.00	500
MS238	2009 (8)	35,000	KM#234-236, 268-272 National set	20.00	27.50
MS239	2009 (8)	2,500	KM#234-236, 268-272 Baby set boy + bear medal	25.00	27.50
MS240	2009 (8)	250	KM#234-236, 268-272 Baby set boy + silver medal	65.00	65.00
MS241	2009 (8)	2,500	KM#234-236, 268-272 Baby set girl + bear medal	25.00	27.50
MS242	2009 (8)	250	KM#234-236, 268-272 Baby set girl + silver medal	65.00	65.00
MS243	2009 (8)	12,500	KM#234-236, 268-272 Benelux: Belgium, Netherlands + Luxembourg. With silver medal	75.00	75.00
MS244	2009 (8)	1,250	KM#234-236, 268-272 Wedding-set + medal	22.00	27.50
MS245	2009 (8)	500	KM#234-236, 268-272 Christmas set + bi-colour medal	35.00	40.00
MS246	2009 (8)	500	KM#234-236, 268-272 Berlin Coin Fair	25.00	95.00
MS247	2009 (8)	2,009	KM#234-236, 268-272	25.00	80.00
MS248	2009 (8)	5,000	KM#234-236, 268-272 100 year anniv. Queen Juliana + silver medal	32.00	35.00
MS249	2009 (8)	1,000	KM#234-236, 268-272 Mercedes jubileum (2010)	—	65.00
MS250	2009 (8)	500	KM#234-236, 268-272 Tokyo Coin Fair	—	375
MS251	2010 (8)	3,500	KM#234-236, 268-272 Museum coin treasures 1 + medal	22.00	40.00
MS252	2010 (8)	100	KM#234-236, 268-272 Museum coin treasures 1 + silver medal	22.00	500
MS253	2010 (8)	25,000	KM#234-236, 268-272 National set	20.00	27.50
MS254	2010 (8)	2,000	KM#234-236, 268-272 Baby set boy + bear medal	30.00	30.00
MS255	2010 (8)	250	KM#234-236, 268-272 Baby set boy + silver medal	75.00	75.00
MS256	2010 (8)	2,000	KM#234-236, 268-272 Baby set girl + bear medal	30.00	30.00
MS257	2010 (8)	250	KM#234-236, 268-272 Baby set girl + silver medal	75.00	75.00
MS258	2010 (8)	12,500	KM#234-236, 268-262 Benelux: Belgium, Netherlands + Luxembourg. With silver medal	75.00	75.00
MS259	2010 (8)	1,000	KM#234-236, 268-272 Wedding-set + medal	22.00	27.50
MS260	2010 (8)	500	KM#234-236, 268-272 Christmas set + bi-colour medal	40.00	40.00
MS261	2010 (8)	500	KM#234-236, 268-272 Berlin Coin Fair	25.00	95.00
MS262	2010 (8)	2,010	KM#234-236, 268-272 Day of the Mint + medal	25.00	80.00
MS263	2010 (8)	5,000	KM#234-236, 268-272 30th anniv. Reign Queen Beatrlx + silver medal	40.00	40.00
MS264	2011 (8)	3,500	KM#234-236, 268-272 Museum coin treasures 2 + medal	30.00	40.00
MS265	2011 (8)	100	KM#234-236, 268-272 Museum coin treasures 2 + silver medal	30.00	500
MS266	2011 (8)	25,000	KM#234-236, 268-272 National set	30.00	30.00
MS267	2011 (8)	5,000	KM#234-236, 268-272 Birth set + bear medal	30.00	30.00
MS268	2011 (8)	1,250	KM#234-236, 268-272 Baby set boy + bear medal	30.00	30.00
MS269	2011 (8)	100	KM#234-236, 268-272 Baby set boy + silver medal	80.00	80.00
MS270	2011 (8)	2,000	KM#234-236, 268-272 Baby set girl + bear medal	30.00	30.00
MS271	2011 (8)	100	KM#234-236, 268-272 Baby set girl + silver medal	80.00	80.00
MS272	2011 (8)	10,000	KM#234-236, 268-272 Benelux: Belgium, Netherlands + Luxembourg. With silver medal	75.00	75.00
MS273	2011 (8)	750	KM#234-236, 268-272 Wedding set + medal	30.00	30.00
MS274	2011 (8)	400	KM#234-236, 268-272 Christmas set + bi-colour medal	45.00	45.00
MS275	2011 (9)	400	KM#234-236, 268-272, 298 Christmas set + bi-colour medal	65.00	65.00
MS276	2011 (8)	500	KM#234-236, 268-272 Berlin Coin Fair	25.00	95.00
MS277	2011 (8)	2,011	KM#234-236, 268-272 100th anniv. Bith Prince Bernhard + silver medal	25.00	80.00
MS278	2011 (8)	5,000	KM#234-236, 268-272 100th anniv. Bith Prince Bernhard + silver medal	45.00	45.00
MS279	2012 (8)	—	KM#234-236, 268-272 Museum coin treasures 2 + medal	30.00	40.00
MS280	2012 (8)	—	KM#234-236, 268-272 Museum coin treasures 2 + silver medal	30.00	500
MS281	2012 (8)	—	KM#234-236, 268-272 National set	30.00	30.00
MS282	2012 (8)	—	KM#234-236, 268-272 Birth set + bear medal	30.00	30.00
MS283	2012 (8)	—	KM#234-236, 268-272 Baby set boy + bear medal	30.00	30.00
MS284	2012 (8)	—	KM#234-236, 268-272 Baby set boy + silver medal	80.00	80.00
MS285	2012 (8)	—	KM#234-236, 268-272 Baby set girl + bear medal	30.00	30.00
MS286	2012 (8)	—	KM#234-236, 268-272 Baby set girl + silver medal	80.00	80.00
MS287	2012 (8)	—	KM#234-236, 268-272 Benelux: Belgium Netherlands + Luxembourg. With silver medal	75.00	75.00
MS288	2012 (8)	—	KM#234-236, 268-272 Berlin Coin Fair	25.00	95.00

PROOF SETS

KM#	Date	Mintage	Identification	Issue Price	Mkt Val
PS54	2001 (6)	17,000	KM#202-206, 210	50.00	45.00
PS55	2001 (2)	500	KM#190.2, 242	50.00	220
PS56	2002 (2)	—	KM#190.2, 211	—	650
PS58	2003 (2)	—	KM#190.2, 211	230	650
PS59	2003 (8)	2,000	KM#234-241	85.00	125
PS63	2001 (7)	17,000	KM#202-207, 210 Booklet 5 guilder	50.00	110
PS64	2001 (2)	500	KM#190.2, 242 Gold + silver ducat	—	220
PS65	2002 (2)	—	KM#190.2, 211 Golden ducats	—	650
PS66	2002 (3)	—	KM#190.2, 211, 256 Golden ducats + silver ducat	—	665
PS67	2003 (2)	—	KM#190.2, 211 Golden ducats in wooden box	230	650
PS68	2004 (8)	5,000	KM#234-241 Proof-set in wooden box	60.00	90.00
PS69	2005 (8)	5,000	KM#234-241 Proof-set in wooden box	60.00	90.00
PS70	2005 (2)	2,500	KM#254, 264 60 years of freedom	—	550
PS71	2006 (8)	3,500	KM#234-241, Proof-set in wooden box	—	90.00
PS72	2006 (1)	—	5 Euro KM#255, Australian $5	90.00	110
PS73	2006 (1)	—	5 Euro KM#255, 10 Euro, Australian $5 and $10	—	650
PS74	2007 (9)	10,000	KM#234-236, 268-272, 273	—	90.00
PS75	2008 (8)	10,000	KM#234-236, 268-272	—	65.00
PS76	2003 (8)	2,000	KM#234-241 Frigate-ship "The Netherland" + silver medal and numbered ingot. "Mintmaster Set" in wooden box	125	125
PS77	2004 (8)	1,000	KM#234-241 Value transport over sea during the eighty year of war + silver medal and numbered ingot. "Mintmaster Set" in wooden box	125	125
PS78	2005 (8)	1,000	KM#234-241 Value transport over sea 1650-1750 + silver medal and numbered ingot. "Mintmaster Set" in wooden box	125	125
PS79	2006 (8)	1,500	KM#234-241 Plus silver medal and numbered ingot. "Mintmaster Set" in wooden box	125	125
PS80	2009 (1)	2,000	KM281 EMU	25.00	150
PS81	2009 (9)	7,500	KM234-236, 268-272, 281	—	70.00
PS82	2010 (8)	5,000	KM#234-236, 268-272	—	60.00
PS83	2011 (1)	1,500	KM298 Erasmus	30.00	140
PS84	2011 (9)	5,000	KM#234-236, 268-272, 298	—	100
PS85	2009 (9)	7,500	KM#234-236, 268-272, 281	—	65.00
PS86	2010 (8)	5,000	KM#234-236, 268-272	—	60.00
PS87	2011 (9)	5,000	KM#234-236, 268-272, 298	—	90.00
PS88	2004 (8)	10,000	KM#234-241	—	70.00
PS89	2005 (8)	10,000	KM#234 241	—	70.00

PROOF-LIKE SETS (PL)

KM#	Date	Mintage	Identification	Issue Price	Mkt Val
PL3	2001 (8)	16,500	KM#234-241	50.00	40.00
PL4	2002 (2)	—	KM#243, 244	145	400
PL5	2002 (2)	—	KM#243, 244	145	400
PL6	2002 (8)	15,500	KM#234-241	50.00	40.00
PL7	2003 (8)	10,000	KM#234-241	50.00	40.00
PL12	2001 (8)	16,500	KM#234-241	50.00	40.00

				F12	MS63
PL13	2002 (2)	—	KM#243-244 Wedding set (10 Euro silver and gold) in plastic box	145	400
PL14	2002 (2)	—	KM#243-244 Wedding set in wooden box	145	400
PL15	2002 (8)	16,500	KM#234-241	50.00	40.00
PL16	2003 (8)	16,500	KM#234-241	50.00	40.00

SELECT SETS (FLEUR DE COIN)

KM#	Date	Mintage	Identification	Issue Price	Mkt Val
SS90	2001 (6)	120,000	KM#202-206, 210	15.00	25.00
SS91	2001 (6)	3,400	KM#202-206, 210	17.50	30.00
SS92	2001 (6)	100	KM#202-206, 210	17.50	150
SS93	2001 (6)	1,000	KM#202-206, 210	—	120
SS94	2001 (6)	1,000	KM#202-206, 210, 2 Stuiver coin from the wreck of the De Akerendam II	125	120
SS95	2001 (6)	1,000	KM#202-206, 210	40.00	20.00
SS96	2001 (6)	21,000	KM#202-206, 210	15.50	25.00
SS97	2001 (6)	1,015	KM#202-206, 210	70.00	250

SPECIMEN FDC SETS (FLEUR DE COIN)

KM#	Date	Mintage	Identification	Issue Price	Mkt Val
SS95A	2001 (6)	1,000	KM202-206, 210	40.00	40.00

NETHERLANDS ANTILLES

The Netherlands Antilles, comprises two groups of islands in the West Indies: Aruba (until 1986), Bonaire and Curacao and their dependencies near the Venezuelan coast and St. Eustatius, Saba, and the southern part of St. Martin (*St. Maarten*) southeast of Puerto Rico. The island group has an area of 371 sq. mi. (960 sq. km.) and a population of 225,000. Capital: Willemstad. Chief industries are the refining of crude oil and tourism. Petroleum products and phosphates are exported.

RULERS
Beatrix, 1980-2013
William Alexander, 2013-

Utrecht Mint
(privy marks only)

Date	Privy Mark
2001	Wine Tendril with grapes
2002	Wine tendril with grapes and star
2003	Sails of a clipper

DUTCH ADMINISTRATION
DECIMAL COINAGE

KM# 32 CENT
0.70 g., Aluminum, 14 mm. **Ruler:** Beatrix **Obv:** Orange blossom within circle **Rev:** Value within circle of geometric designed border **Edge:** Reeded

Date	Mintage	F12	VF20	XF40	MS60	MS63
2001(u)	12,806,500	—	—	0.10	0.20	0.50
2002(u) In sets only	6,000	—	—	—	—	2.00
2003(u)	19,604,000	—	—	0.10	0.20	1.50
2004(u) In sets only	7,100	—	—	—	0.60	1.50
2005(u)	22,404,000	—	—	0.10	0.60	1.50
2006(u)	110,000	—	—	0.10	0.60	1.50
2007(u)	5,000	—	—	0.10	0.60	1.50
2008(u)	16,742,000	—	—	0.10	0.60	1.50
2009(u)	2,000	—	—	0.10	0.60	1.50
2010(u)	2,000	—	—	0.10	0.60	1.50
2011(u)	2,000	—	—	0.10	0.60	1.50
2012(u)	8,282,000	—	—	0.10	0.60	1.50

KM# 33 5 CENTS
1.16 g., Aluminum, 16 mm. **Ruler:** Beatrix **Obv:** Orange blossom within circle **Rev:** Value within circle, geometric designed border **Edge:** Reeded

Date	Mintage	F12	VF20	XF40	MS60	MS63
2001	2,006,500	—	—	0.20	0.60	1.25
2002 In sets only	6,000	—	—	—	—	2.50
2003	3,104,000	—	—	0.30	0.60	1.25
2004	2,402,100	—	—	0.30	0.50	1.50
2005	1,609,000	—	—	0.30	0.50	1.50
2006	1,602,000	—	—	0.30	0.50	1.50
2007	2,000	—	—	0.30	0.50	1.50
2008	3,602,000	—	—	0.30	0.50	1.50
2009	1,052,000	—	—	0.30	0.50	1.50
2010	337,000	—	—	0.30	0.50	1.50
2011	2,000	—	—	0.30	0.50	1.50
2012	20,202,000	—	—	0.30	0.50	1.50
2013(u)	2,000	—	—	—	—	3.00

KM# 34 10 CENTS
3.00 g., Nickel Bonded Steel, 18 mm. **Ruler:** Beatrix **Obv:** Orange blossom within circle **Rev:** Value within circle, geometric designed border **Edge:** Reeded

Date	Mintage	F12	VF20	XF40	MS60	MS63
2001 In sets only	11,500	—	—	—	—	3.00
2002 In sets only	6,000	—	—	—	—	3.00
2003	2,104,000	—	—	0.50	1.00	1.75
2004	2,202,100	—	—	0.50	1.00	1.75
2005	1,410,000	—	—	0.50	1.00	1.75
2006	1,402,000	—	—	0.50	1.00	1.75
2007	202,000	—	—	0.50	1.00	1.75
2008	3,872,000	—	—	0.50	1.00	1.75
2009	1,112,000	—	—	0.50	1.00	1.75
2010	2,402,000	—	—	0.50	1.00	1.75
2011	2,000	—	—	—	1.00	2.00
2012	2,452,000	—	—	—	1.00	2.00
(2013)	2,000	—	—	—	—	3.00

KM# 35 25 CENTS
3.50 g., Nickel Bonded Steel, 20.2 mm. **Ruler:** Beatrix **Obv:** Orange blossom within circle **Rev:** Value within circle, geometric designed border **Edge:** Reeded

Date	Mintage	F12	VF20	XF40	MS60	MS63
2001 In sets only	11,500	—	—	—	—	3.00
2002 In sets only	6,000	—	—	—	—	3.00
2003	1,404,000	—	—	0.50	1.25	1.50
2004	1,502,100	—	—	0.50	1.25	1.50
2005	110,000	—	—	0.50	1.25	1.50
2006	102,000	—	—	0.50	1.25	1.50
2007	2,000	—	—	0.50	1.25	1.50
2008	992,000	—	—	0.50	1.25	1.50
2009	2,072,000	—	—	0.50	1.25	1.50
2010	17,988,100	—	—	0.50	1.25	1.50
2011	2,000	—	—	—	1.25	2.00
2012	227,000	—	—	—	1.25	2.00
2013	2,000	—	—	—	—	3.00

KM# 36 50 CENTS
5.00 g., Aureate Steel, 24 mm. **Ruler:** Beatrix **Obv:** Orange blossom within circle, designed border **Rev:** Value within circle of pearls and shell border **Edge:** Plain **Shape:** 4-sided

Date	Mintage	F12	VF20	XF40	MS60	MS63
2001 In sets only	11,500	—	—	—	—	4.00
2002 In sets only	6,000	—	—	—	—	6.00
2003 In sets only	9,000	—	—	—	—	4.00
2004 In sets only	7,100	—	—	—	—	4.00
2005	15,000	—	—	0.75	3.00	4.00
2006 In sets only	2,000	—	—	—	—	6.00
2007	7,000	—	—	0.75	3.00	4.00
2008	7,000	—	—	0.75	3.00	4.00
2009	2,000	—	—	0.75	3.00	6.00
2010	2,000	—	—	0.75	3.00	6.00
2011 In sets only	2,000	—	—	—	3.00	6.00
2012 In sets only	2,000	—	—	—	3.00	6.00
2013 In sets only	2,000	—	—	—	—	6.00

KM# 37 GULDEN
6.00 g., Aureate Steel, 24 mm. **Ruler:** Beatrix **Obv:** Head left **Rev:** Crowned shield divides value above date and ribbon **Edge Lettering:** GOD * ZIJ * MET * ONS *

Date	Mintage	F12	VF20	XF40	MS60	MS63
2001 In sets only	11,500	—	—	—	—	4.00
2002 In sets only	6,000	—	—	—	—	6.00
2003	504,000	—	—	0.75	2.00	4.00
2004 In sets only	7,100	—	—	—	—	6.00
2005	805,000	—	—	0.75	2.00	4.00
2006 In sets only	2,000	—	—	—	—	7.00
2007	7,000	—	—	0.75	3.00	5.00
2008	1,202,000	—	—	0.75	2.00	4.00
2009	857,000	—	—	0.75	2.00	4.00
2010	1,292,000	—	—	0.75	2.00	4.00
2011 In sets only	2,000	—	—	—	—	7.00
2012 In sets only	2,000	—	—	—	3.00	7.00
2013 In sets only	2,000	—	—	—	—	7.00

KM# 38 2-1/2 GULDEN
9.00 g., Aureate Steel, 28 mm. **Ruler:** Beatrix **Obv:** Head left **Rev:** Crowned shield divides value above date and ribbon **Edge Lettering:** GOD * ZIJ * MET * ONS *

Date	Mintage	F12	VF20	XF40	MS60	MS63
2001 In sets only	11,500	—	—	—	—	6.00
2002 In sets only	6,000	—	—	—	—	10.00
2003 In sets only	9,000	—	—	—	—	10.00
2004 In sets only	7,100	—	—	—	—	10.00
2005	15,000	—	—	—	1.00	10.00
2006 In sets only	2,000	—	—	—	1.00	10.00
2007	7,000	—	—	—	1.00	10.00
2008	7,000	—	—	—	1.00	10.00
2009 In sets only	2,000	—	—	—	1.00	10.00
2010 In sets only	2,000	—	—	—	1.00	10.00
2011 In sets only	2,000	—	—	—	—	10.00
2012 In sets only	2,000	—	—	—	—	10.00
2013 In sets only	2,000	—	—	—	—	10.00

KM# 43 5 GULDEN
14.00 g., Aureate Bonded Steel, 26 mm. **Ruler:** Beatrix **Obv:** Head left **Rev:** Crowned shield divides value above date and ribbon **Edge Lettering:** GOD * ZIJ * MET * ONS *

Date	Mintage	F12	VF20	XF40	MS60	MS63
2001 In sets only	9,500	—	—	—	—	10.00
2002 In sets only	6,000	—	—	—	—	10.00
2003 In sets only	7,000	—	—	—	—	10.00
2004	102,100	—	—	2.00	4.00	8.00
2005	11,000	—	—	2.00	5.00	10.00
2006 In sets only	2,000	—	—	—	—	10.00
2007	5,000	—	—	2.00	4.00	10.00
2008	119,000	—	—	2.00	4.00	10.00
2009	227,000	—	—	2.00	4.00	10.00
2010	302,000	—	—	2.00	4.00	10.00
2011 In sets only	2,000	—	—	—	—	10.00
2012 In sets only	2,000	—	—	—	—	10.00
2013 In sets only	2,000	—	—	—	—	10.00

KM# 74.1 5 GULDEN
11.00 g., Aureate Bonded Steel, 26 mm. **Ruler:** Beatrix **Subject:** 50th Anniversary - End To Dutch Colonial Rule **Obv:** Head left **Rev:** Triangular signatures around value **Edge Lettering:** GOD * ZIJ * MET * ONS *

Date	Mintage	F12	VF20	XF40	MS60	MS63
2004	10,000	—	—	7.00	15.00	20.00

KM# 74 5 GULDEN
11.90 g., 0.925 Silver 0.3516 oz. ASW, 29 mm. **Ruler:** Beatrix **Subject:** 50th Anniversary - Charter for the Kingdom of Netherlands including Aruba as third party **Obv:** Head left **Rev:** Triangular design with hands writing signatures around value **Edge Lettering:** GOD * ZIJ * MET * ONS *

Date	Mintage	F12	VF20	XF40	MS60	MS63
2004(u)	4,000	PF63 25.00	PF65 35.00			

KM# 76.1 5 GULDEN
11.00 g., Aureate Bonded Steel, 26 mm. **Ruler:** Beatrix **Subject:** Queen's Silver Jubilee **Obv:** Head left **Rev:** Child art and value **Edge Lettering:** GOD * ZIJ * MET * ONS *

Date	Mintage	F12	VF20	XF40	MS60	MS63
2005	10,000	—	—	7.00	15.00	20.00

KM# 76 5 GULDEN
11.90 g., 0.925 Silver 0.3516 oz. ASW, 29 mm. **Ruler:** Beatrix **Subject:** Queen's Silver Jubilee **Obv:** Head left **Rev:** Child art and value **Edge Lettering:** GOD * ZIJ * MET * ONS *

Date	Mintage	F12	VF20	XF40	MS60	MS63
2005(u)	4,000	PF63 25.00	PF65 35.00			

KM# 80 5 GULDEN
11.90 g., 0.925 Silver 0.3516 oz. ASW, 29 mm. **Ruler:** Beatrix **Subject:** 50 Years Brishopric Willemstad **Obv:** Logo Brishopric **Rev:** Cathedral **Edge Lettering:** GOD * Z'J * MET * ONS *

Date	Mintage	F12	VF20	XF40	MS60	MS63
2008	—	PF63 25.00	PF65 35.00			

KM# 79 5 GULDEN
11.90 g., 0.925 Silver 0.3516 oz. ASW, 29 mm. **Ruler:** Beatrix **Obv:** Antoine Maduro **Rev:** Crowned shield divides value **Edge Lettering:** GOD * ZIJ * MET * ONS *

Date	Mintage	F12	VF20	XF40	MS60	MS63
2009	1,250	PF63 30.00	PF65 40.00			

KM# 85 5 GULDEN
10.40 g., Aureate Bonded Steel, 26 mm. **Ruler:** Beatrix **Subject:** Abdication of Beatrix **Obv:** Value and national arms **Rev:** Beatrix and Willem-Alexander left above Curacao flag in color

Date	Mintage	F12	VF20	XF40	MS60	MS63
2013	11,000	—	—	—	—	15.00

KM# 86 5 GULDEN
10.40 g., Aureate Bonded Steel, 26 mm. **Ruler:** Beatrix **Obv:** Value and national arms **Rev:** Beatrix and Willem-Alexander left above St. Martin flag in color

Date	Mintage	F12	VF20	XF40	MS60	MS63
2013	11,000	—	—	—	—	15.00

KM# 87 5 GULDEN
11.90 g., 0.925 Silver 0.3516 oz. ASW, 29 mm. **Ruler:** Willem-Alexander **Subject:** Welcome to the King **Obv:** Crown with three shield under value **Rev:** Willem-Alexander right

Date	Mintage	F12	VF20	XF40	MS60	MS63
2013	2,000	PF63 55.00	PF65 65.00			

KM# 88 5 GULDEN
11.90 g., 0.925 Silver 0.3516 oz. ASW, 29 mm. **Ruler:** Willem-Alexander **Subject:** End of Slavery, 150th Anniversary **Obv:** Crowned weapon divides 5-G above date **Rev:** Stick figures and one is cutting chain

Date	Mintage	F12	VF20	XF40	MS60	MS63
2013	3,000	PF63 25.00	PF65 35.00			

KM# 89 5 GULDEN
26.50 g., Copper-Nickel-Zinc, 39 mm. **Ruler:** Willem-Alexander **Subject:** Curaçao North Sea Jazz Festival **Obv:** Crowned shield above date **Rev:** Sax player in green and yellow

Date	Mintage	F12	VF20	XF40	MS60	MS63
2013	3,000	PF63 25.00	PF65 35.00			

KM# 49 10 GULDEN
31.10 g., 0.925 Silver 0.919 oz. ASW, 40 mm. **Ruler:** Beatrix **Subject:** Gold Trade Coins: Sulla Aureus **Obv:** Crowned shield divides value above date and ribbon **Rev:** Bust facing with two gold coins at lower left **Edge:** Plain

Date	Mintage	F12	VF20	XF40	MS60	MS63
2001(u)	589	PF65 80.00				

KM# 50 10 GULDEN
31.10 g., 0.925 Silver 0.919 oz. ASW, 40 mm. **Ruler:** Beatrix **Subject:** Gold Trade Coins: Constantin I Solidus **Obv:** Crowned shield divides value above date and ribbon **Rev:** Bust facing with two gold coins at lower right **Edge:** Plain

Date	Mintage	F12	VF20	XF40	MS60	MS63
2001(u)	578	PF65 80.00				

KM# 51 10 GULDEN
31.10 g., 0.925 Silver 0.919 oz. ASW, 40 mm. **Ruler:** Beatrix **Subject:** Gold Trade Coins: Clovis I Tremissis fiorino d'oro **Obv:** Crowned shield divides value above date and ribbon **Rev:** Bust facing with two gold coins **Edge:** Plain

Date	Mintage	F12	VF20	XF40	MS60	MS63
2001(u)	566	PF65 80.00				

KM# 52 10 GULDEN
31.10 g., 0.925 Silver 0.919 oz. ASW, 40 mm. **Ruler:** Beatrix **Subject:** Gold Trade Coins: Cosimo de'Medici Fiorino d'oro **Obv:** Crowned shield divides value above date and ribbon **Rev:** Bust facing with two gold coins **Edge:** Plain

Date	Mintage	F12	VF20	XF40	MS60	MS63
2001(u)	575	PF65 80.00				

KM# 53 10 GULDEN
31.10 g., 0.925 Silver 0.919 oz. ASW, 40 mm. **Ruler:** Beatrix **Subject:** Gold Trade Coins: Dandolo Ducato d'Oro **Obv:** Crowned shield divides value above date and ribbon **Rev:** Bust facing with two gold coins **Edge:** Plain

Date	Mintage	F12	VF20	XF40	MS60	MS63
2001(u)	490	PF65 80.00				

KM# 54 10 GULDEN
31.10 g., 0.925 Silver 0.919 oz. ASW, 40 mm. **Ruler:** Beatrix **Subject:** Gold Trade Coins: Philips IV Ecu d'or la chaise **Obv:** Crowned shield divides value above date and ribbon **Rev:** Bust facing with two gold coins **Edge:** Plain

Date	Mintage	F12	VF20	XF40	MS60	MS63
2001(u)	460	PF65 80.00				

KM# 55 10 GULDEN
31.10 g., 0.925 Silver 0.919 oz. ASW, 40 mm. **Ruler:** Beatrix **Subject:** Gold Trade Coins: Edward III Nobel **Obv:** Crowned shield divides value above date and ribbon **Rev:** Crowned bust facing with two gold coins **Edge:** Plain

Date	Mintage	F12	VF20	XF40	MS60	MS63
2001(u)	575	PF65 80.00				

KM# 56 10 GULDEN
31.10 g., 0.925 Silver 0.919 oz. ASW, 40 mm. **Ruler:** Beatrix **Subject:** Gold Trade Coins: Carolus IV Rhine Gold Guilder **Obv:** Crowned shield divides value above date and ribbon **Rev:** Bust facing with two gold coins **Edge:** Plain

Date	Mintage	F12	VF20	XF40	MS60	MS63
2001(u)	430	PF65 80.00				

KM# 57 10 GULDEN
31.10 g., 0.925 Silver 0.919 oz. ASW, 40 mm. **Ruler:** Beatrix **Subject:** Gold Trade Coins: John II Franc d'or a cheval **Obv:** Crowned shield divides value above date and ribbon **Rev:** Bust facing with two gold coins **Edge:** Plain

Date	Mintage	F12	VF20	XF40	MS60	MS63
2001(u)	464	PF65 80.00				

KM# 58 10 GULDEN
31.10 g., 0.925 Silver 0.919 oz. ASW, 40 mm. **Ruler:** Beatrix **Subject:** Gold Trade Coins: Philip the Good Adriesguilder **Obv:** Crowned shield divides value above date and ribbon **Rev:** Bust facing with two gold coins **Edge:** Plain

Date	Mintage	F12	VF20	XF40	MS60	MS63
2001(u)	250	PF65 120				

KM# 59 10 GULDEN
31.10 g., 0.925 Silver 0.919 oz. ASW, 40 mm. **Ruler:** Beatrix **Subject:** Gold Trade Coins: Louis XI Ecu d'or au soleil **Obv:** Crowned shield divides value above date and ribbon **Rev:** Bust facing with two gold coins **Edge:** Plain

Date	Mintage	F12	VF20	XF40	MS60	MS63
2001(u)	450	PF65 80.00				

KM# 60 10 GULDEN
31.10 g., 0.925 Silver 0.919 oz. ASW, 40 mm. **Ruler:** Beatrix **Subject:** Gold Trade Coins: Elisabeth I Sovereign **Obv:** Crowned shield divides value above date and ribbon **Rev:** Bust facing with two gold coins **Edge:** Plain

Date	Mintage	F12	VF20	XF40	MS60	MS63
2001(u)	450	PF65 80.00				

KM# 61 10 GULDEN
31.10 g., 0.925 Silver 0.919 oz. ASW, 40 mm. **Ruler:** Beatrix **Subject:** Gold Trade Coins: Carolus V Carolus Guilder **Obv:** Crowned shield divides value above date and ribbon **Rev:** Bust facing with two gold coins **Edge:** Plain

Date	Mintage	F12	VF20	XF40	MS60	MS63
2001(u)	440	PF65 80.00				

KM# 62 10 GULDEN
31.10 g., 0.925 Silver 0.919 oz. ASW, 40 mm. **Ruler:** Beatrix **Subject:** Gold Trade Coins: Philips II Real **Obv:** Crowned shield divides value above date and ribbon **Rev:** Bust facing with two gold coins **Edge:** Plain

Date	Mintage	F12	VF20	XF40	MS60	MS63
2001(u)	440	PF65 80.00				

KM# 63 10 GULDEN
31.10 g., 0.925 Silver 0.919 oz. ASW, 40 mm. **Ruler:** Beatrix **Subject:** Gold Trade Coins: Maurits Ducat **Obv:** Crowned shield divides value above date and ribbon **Rev:** Bust facing with two gold coins **Edge:** Plain

Date	Mintage	F12	VF20	XF40	MS60	MS63
2001(u)	443	PF65 80.00				

KM# 64 10 GULDEN
31.10 g., 0.919 Silver 0.919 oz. ASW, 40 mm. **Ruler:** Beatrix **Subject:** Gold Trade Coins: Isabella and Albrecht Double Albertin **Obv:** Crowned shield divides value above date and ribbon **Rev:** Conjoined busts facing with two gold coins **Edge:** Plain

Date	Mintage	F12	VF20	XF40	MS60	MS63
2001(u)	490	PF65 80.00				

KM# 65 10 GULDEN
31.10 g., 0.925 Silver 0.919 oz. ASW, 40 mm. **Ruler:** Beatrix **Subject:** Gold Trade Coins: William III Golden Rider **Obv:** Crowned shield divides value above date and ribbon **Rev:** Bust facing with two gold coins **Edge:** Plain

Date	Mintage	F12	VF20	XF40	MS60	MS63
2001(u)	440	PF65 80.00				

KM# 66 10 GULDEN
31.10 g., 0.925 Silver 0.919 oz. ASW, 40 mm. **Ruler:** Beatrix **Subject:** Gold Trade Coins: Louis XIII Louis d'or **Obv:** Crowned shield divides value above date and ribbon **Rev:** Bust facing with two gold coins **Edge:** Plain

Date	Mintage	F12	VF20	XF40	MS60	MS63
2001(u)	440	PF65 80.00				

KM# 67 10 GULDEN
31.10 g., 0.925 Silver 0.919 oz. ASW, 40 mm. **Ruler:** Beatrix **Subject:** Gold Trade Coins: Catharina the Great Rubel **Obv:** Crowned shield divides value above date and ribbon **Rev:** Crowned laureate bust facing with two gold coins **Edge:** Plain

Date	Mintage	F12	VF20	XF40	MS60	MS63
2001(u)	560	PF65 100				

KM# 68 10 GULDEN
31.10 g., 0.925 Silver 0.919 oz. ASW, 40 mm. **Ruler:** Beatrix **Subject:** Gold Trade Coins: Maria Theresia Double Sovereign **Obv:** Crowned shield divides value above date and ribbon **Rev:** Bust facing with two gold coins **Edge:** Plain

Date	Mintage	F12	VF20	XF40	MS60	MS63
2001(u)	440	PF65 80.00				

KM# 69 10 GULDEN
31.10 g., 0.925 Silver 0.919 oz. ASW, 40 mm. **Ruler:** Beatrix **Subject:** Gold Trade Coins: Napolean Bonaparte 20 Franc **Obv:** Crowned shield divides value above date and ribbon **Rev:** Bust facing with two gold coins **Edge:** Plain

Date	Mintage	F12	VF20	XF40	MS60	MS63
2001(u)	555	PF65 80.00				

KM# 70 10 GULDEN
31.10 g., 0.925 Silver 0.919 oz. ASW, 40 mm. **Ruler:** Beatrix **Series:** Gold Trade Coins: Wilhelmina Golden 10 Guilder **Obv:** Crowned shield divides value above date and ribbon **Rev:** Bust facing with two gold coins **Edge:** Plain

Date	Mintage	F12	VF20	XF40	MS60	MS63
2001(u)	440	PF65 80.00				

KM# 71 10 GULDEN
31.10 g., 0.925 Silver 0.919 oz. ASW, 40 mm. **Ruler:** Beatrix **Subject:** Gold Trade Coins: George III Sovereign **Obv:** Crowned shield divides value above date and ribbon **Rev:** Bust facing with two gold coins **Edge:** Plain

Date	Mintage	F12	VF20	XF40	MS60	MS63
2001(u)	440	PF65 80.00				

KM# 72 10 GULDEN
31.10 g., 0.925 Silver 0.919 oz. ASW, 40 mm. **Ruler:** Beatrix **Subject:** Gold Trade Coins: Albert I Belgium 20 Franc **Obv:** Crowned shield divides value above date and ribbon **Rev:** Bust facing with two gold coins **Edge:** Plain

Date	Mintage	F12	VF20	XF40	MS60	MS63
2001(u)	490	PF65 80.00				

KM# 84 10 GULDEN
17.00 g., 0.925 Silver 0.5023 oz. ASW, 33 mm. **Ruler:** Beatrix **Subject:** Mariage of Willem-Alexander and Maxima **Obv:** Queen's head left **Rev:** Conjoined busts left **Edge Lettering:** GOD * ZIJ * MET * ONS *

Date	Mintage	F12	VF20	XF40	MS60	MS63
2002(u)	1,500	PF63 40.00	PF65 50.00			

KM# 75 10 GULDEN
6.72 g., 0.900 Gold 0.1932 oz. AGW **Ruler:** Beatrix **Subject:** 50th Anniversary - End to Dutch Colonial Rule **Obv:** Head left **Rev:** Triangular signatures around value **Edge:** Reeded

Date	Mintage	F12	VF20	XF40	MS60	MS63
2004	1,000	PF65 400				

KM# 77 10 GULDEN
6.72 g., 0.900 Gold 0.1932 oz. AGW, 22.5 mm. **Ruler:** Beatrix **Subject:** Queen's Silver Jubilee **Obv:** Head left **Rev:** Child art and value **Edge:** Reeded

Date	Mintage	F12	VF20	XF40	MS60	MS63
2005(u)	1,500	PF65 400				

KM# 78 10 GULDEN
1.24 g., 0.999 Gold 0.0397 oz. AGW, 13.92 mm. **Ruler:** Beatrix **Subject:** Year of the dolphin **Obv:** Head left **Obv. Legend:** BEATRIX KONINGIN DER NEDERLANDEN **Rev:** Stylized outlines of birds above dolphins at sunset **Rev. Legend:** NEDERLANDSE ANTILLEN - JAAR VAN DE DOLFIJN **Edge:** Reeded

Date	Mintage	F12	VF20	XF40	MS60	MS63
2007(u)	5,000	PF65 90.00				

KM# 81 10 GULDEN
17.80 g., 0.925 Silver 0.526 oz. ASW, 33 mm. **Ruler:** Beatrix **Subject:** Farewell to the Netherlands Antilles **Obv:** Autonomy monument with five birds **Rev:** Crowned shield divided value **Edge Lettering:** GOD * ZIJ * MET * ONS *

Date	Mintage	F12	VF20	XF40	MS60	MS63
2010(u)	5,000	PF63 40.00	PF65 50.00			

KM# 90 10 GULDEN
3.36 g., 0.900 Gold 0.0967 oz. AGW **Ruler:** Willem-Alexander

Date	Mintage	F12	VF20	XF40	MS60	MS63
2013	750	PF65 150				

KM# 82 25 GULDEN
25.00 g., 0.925 Silver 0.7387 oz. ASW, 38 mm. **Ruler:** Beatrix **Obv:** 175 year Bank of the Netherlands Antilles **Rev:** Sailing ship

Date	Mintage	F12	VF20	XF40	MS60	MS63
2003 Prooflike	1,500	—	—	—	—	50.00

KM# 83 25 GULDEN
25.00 g., 0.925 Silver 0.7387 oz. ASW, 38 mm. **Ruler:** Beatrix **Obv:** 50 years of monument care **Rev:** Folker FXVIII plane over route map **Edge Lettering:** GOD * ZIJ * MET * ONS *

Date	Mintage	F12	VF20	XF40	MS60	MS63
2004	5,000	PF63 45.00	PF65 55.00			

MINT SETS

KM#	Date	Mintage	Identification	Issue Price	Mkt Val
MS22	2001 (8)	6,500	KM#32-38, 43	15.00	20.00
MS23	2002 (8)	6,000	KM#32-38, 43	15.00	25.00
MS24	2003 (8)	4,000	KM#32-38, 43	15.00	25.00
MS25	2004 (8)	2,100	KM32-38, 43	15.00	30.00
MS26	2005 (8)	3,500	KM32-38, 43	17.00	25.00
MS27	2006 (8)	2,000	KM#32-38, 43	20.00	30.00
MS28	2007 (8)	2,000	KM#32-38, 43	20.00	25.00
MS29	2008 (8)	2,000	KM#32-38, 43	21.00	25.00
MS30	2009 (8)	2,000	KM#32-38, 43	27.00	27.00
MS31	2010 (8)	2,000	KM#32-38, 43	28.00	28.00
MS32	2011 (8)	2,000	KM#32-38, 43	28.00	30.00
MS33	2012 (8)	2,000	KM#32-38, 43	28.00	30.00

NEW CALEDONIA

The French Associated State of New Caledonia is a group of about 25 islands in the South Pacific. They are situated about 750 miles (1,207 km.) east of Australia. The territory, which includes the dependencies of Isle des Pins, Loyalty Islands, Isle Huon, Isles Belep, Isles Chesterfield, Isle Walpole, Wallis and Futuna Islands and has a total land area of 7,358 sq. mi.(19,060 sq. km.) and a population of *156,000. Capital: Noumea. The islands are rich in minerals; New Caledonia has some of the world's largest known deposit of nickel. Nickel, nickel castings, coffee and copra are exported.

MINT MARK
Paris, privy marks only

MONETARY SYSTEM
100 Centimes = 1 Franc

FRENCH OVERSEAS TERRITORY
1958-1998

DECIMAL COINAGE

KM# 10 FRANC
1.30 g., Aluminum, 23 mm. **Obv:** Seated figure holding torch, legend added **Obv. Legend:** I. E. O. M. **Rev:** Kagu bird within sprigs below value

Date	Mintage	F12	VF20	XF40	MS60	MS63
2001(a)	100,000	—	—	—	0.50	1.25
2002(a)	1,200,000	—	—	—	0.50	1.25
2003(a)	2,000,000	—	—	—	0.50	1.25
2004(a)	1,200,000	—	—	—	0.50	1.25
2005(a)	700,000	—	—	—	0.50	1.25
2006(a)	1,600,000	—	—	—	0.50	1.25
2007(a)	2,000,000	—	—	—	0.50	1.25
2008(a)	2,800,000	—	—	—	0.50	1.25
2009(a)	—	—	—	—	0.50	1.25
2010(a)	—	—	—	—	0.50	1.25
2011(a)	—	—	—	—	0.50	1.25
2012(a)	—	—	—	—	0.50	1.25

KM# 14 2 FRANCS
2.20 g., Aluminum, 27 mm. **Obv:** Seated figure holding torch, legend added **Obv. Legend:** I. E. O. M. **Rev:** Kagu bird and value within sprigs

Date	Mintage	F12	VF20	XF40	MS60	MS63
2001(a)	800,000	—	—	0.25	0.75	1.50
2002(a)	1,200,000	—	—	0.25	0.75	1.50
2003(a)	2,400,000	—	—	0.20	0.65	1.50
2004(a)	200,000	—	—	0.20	0.65	1.50
2005(a)	530,000	—	—	0.20	0.65	1.50
2006(a)	1,200,000	—	—	0.20	0.65	1.50
2007(a)	600,000	—	—	0.20	0.65	1.50
2008(a)	2,400,000	—	—	0.20	0.65	1.50
2009(a)	—	—	—	0.20	0.65	1.50
2011(a)	—	—	—	0.20	0.65	1.50

KM# 16 5 FRANCS
3.75 g., Aluminum, 31 mm. **Obv:** Seated figure holding torch, legend added **Obv. Legend:** I. E. O. M. **Rev:** Kagu bird and value within sprigs

Date	Mintage	F12	VF20	XF40	MS60	MS63
2001(a)	600,000	—	—	0.50	1.00	2.00
2002(a)	480,000	—	—	0.50	1.00	2.00
2003(a)	700,000	—	—	0.40	1.00	2.00
2004(a)	1,000,000	—	—	0.40	1.00	2.00
2005(a)	360,000	—	—	0.40	1.00	2.00
2006(a)	480,000	—	—	0.40	1.00	2.00
2007(a)	960,000	—	—	0.40	1.00	2.00
2008(a)	1,700,000	—	—	0.40	1.00	2.00
2009(a)	—	—	—	0.40	1.00	2.00
2010(a)	—	—	—	0.40	1.00	2.00
2011(a)	—	—	—	0.40	1.00	2.00

KM# 11 10 FRANCS
6.00 g., Nickel, 24 mm. **Obv:** Liberty head left **Obv. Legend:** I. E. O. M. **Rev:** Sailboat above value

Date	Mintage	F12	VF20	XF40	MS60	MS63
2001(a)	100,000	—	—	0.65	1.25	2.75
2002(a)	200,000	—	—	0.65	1.25	2.75
2003(a)	800,000	—	—	0.65	1.25	2.75
2004(a)	600,000	—	—	0.65	1.25	2.75
2005(a)	64,000	—	—	0.65	1.25	2.75

KM# 12 20 FRANCS
10.00 g., Nickel, 28.5 mm. **Obv:** Liberty head left **Obv. Legend:** I. O. E. M. **Rev:** Three ox heads above value

Date	Mintage	F12	VF20	XF40	MS60	MS63
2001(a)	150,000	—	—	1.00	1.75	3.25
2002(a)	250,000	—	—	1.00	1.75	3.25
2003(a)	250,000	—	—	1.00	1.75	3.25
2004(a)	500,000	—	—	1.00	1.75	3.25
2005(a)	300,000	—	—	1.00	1.75	3.25

KM# 13 50 FRANCS
15.00 g., Nickel, 33 mm. **Obv:** Liberty head left **Obv. Legend:** I. E. O. M. **Rev:** Hut above value in center of palm and pine trees

Date	Mintage	F12	VF20	XF40	MS60	MS63
2001(a)	100,000	—	—	1.25	2.00	4.00
2002(a)	—	—	—	1.25	2.00	4.00
2003(a)	75,000	—	—	1.25	2.00	4.00
2004(a)	150,000	—	—	1.25	2.00	4.00
2005(a)	54,000	—	—	1.25	2.00	4.00

KM# 15 100 FRANCS
10.00 g., Nickel-Bronze, 30 mm. **Obv:** Liberty head left **Rev:** Hut above value in center of palm and pine trees

Date	Mintage	F12	VF20	XF40	MS60	MS63
2001(a)	100,000	—	—	1.50	3.00	5.00
2002(a)	620,000	—	—	1.50	3.00	6.00
2003(a)	500,000	—	—	1.50	3.00	5.00
2004(a)	500,000	—	—	1.50	3.00	5.00
2005(a)	180,000	—	—	1.50	3.00	5.00

FRENCH ASSOCIATED STATE
1998-

KM# 11a 10 FRANCS
6.00 g., Copper-Nickel, 24 mm. **Obv:** Liberty head left **Rev:** Sailboat above value **Edge:** Reeded

Date	Mintage	F12	VF20	XF40	MS60	MS63
2006(a)	60,000	—	—	0.65	1.25	2.75
2007(a)	1,000,000	—	—	0.65	1.25	2.75
2008(a)	1,200,000	—	—	0.65	1.25	2.75
2009(a)	—	—	—	0.65	1.25	2.75
2010(a)	—	—	—	0.65	1.25	2.75
2011(a)	—	—	—	0.65	1.25	2.75

KM# 12a 20 FRANCS
10.00 g., Copper-Nickel, 28.5 mm. **Obv:** Liberty head left **Rev:** Three ox heads above value **Edge:** Reeded

Date	Mintage	F12	VF20	XF40	MS60	MS63
2006(a)	300,000	—	—	1.00	1.75	3.25
2007(a)	800,000	—	—	1.25	1.75	3.25
2008(a)	800,000	—	—	1.25	1.75	3.25
2009(a)	—	—	—	1.25	1.75	3.25
2010(a)	—	—	—	1.25	1.75	3.25
2011(a)	—	—	—	1.25	1.75	3.25

KM# 13a 50 FRANCS
15.00 g., Copper-Nickel **Obv:** Liberty head left **Rev:** Hut in center of palm and pine trees, value below **Edge:** Reeded

Date	Mintage	F12	VF20	XF40	MS60	MS63
2006(a)	75,000	—	—	1.25	2.00	4.00
2007(a)	225,000	—	—	1.25	2.00	4.00
2008(a)	375,000	—	—	1.25	2.00	4.00
2009(a)	—	—	—	1.25	2.00	4.00

KM# 15a 100 FRANCS
10.00 g., Aluminum-Bronze, 30 mm. **Obv:** Liberty head left **Rev:** Hut above value in center of palm and pine trees **Edge:** Reeded

Date	Mintage	F12	VF20	XF40	MS60	MS63
2006(a)	300,000	—	—	1.50	3.00	5.00
2007(a)	800,000	—	—	1.50	3.00	5.00
2008(a)	1,100,000	—	—	1.50	3.00	5.00
2009(a)	—	—	—	1.50	3.00	5.00
2010(a)	—	—	—	1.50	3.00	5.00

MINT SETS

KM#	Date	Mintage	Identification	Issue Price	Mkt Val
MS1	2001 (7)	3,000	KM#10-16	—	25.00
MS2	2002 (7)	5,000	KM#10-16	—	25.00
MS3	2004 (7)	3,000	KM#10-16	—	25.00

NEW ZEALAND

New Zealand, a parliamentary state located in the Southwest Pacific 1,250 miles (2,011 km.) east of Australia, has an area of 103,883 sq. mi. (268,680 sq. km.) and a population of *3.4 million. Capital: Wellington. Wool, meat, dairy products and some manufactured items are exported.

Decimal Currency was introduced in 1967 with special sets commemorating the last issues of pound sterling (1965) and the first of the decimal issues. Since then dollars and sets of coins have been issued nearly every year.

New Zealand is a founding member of the Commonwealth of Nations. Elizabeth II is the Head of State as the Queen of New Zealand; the Prime Minister is the Head of Government.

RULER
British

STATE

DECIMAL COINAGE
100 Cents = 1 Dollar

KM# 116 5 CENTS
2.83 g., Copper-Nickel, 19.43 mm. **Ruler:** Elizabeth II **Obv:** Head with tiara right **Rev:** Value below tuatara **Edge:** Reeded **Note:** Many recalled and melted in 2006.

Date	Mintage	F12	VF20	XF40	MS60	MS63
2001(l)	20,000,000	—	—	0.10	0.50	1.00
2001(c) In sets only	2,910	—	—	—	4.00	5.00
2001(c)	1,364	PF63 3.00				
2002(l)	40,500,000	—	—	0.10	0.50	1.00
2002(c) In sets only	3,000	—	—	—	5.00	6.00
2002(c)	1,500	PF63 3.00				
2003(l)	30,000,000	—	—	—	0.50	1.00
2003(c) In sets only	1,496	—	—	—	5.00	6.00
2003	3,000	PF63 3.00				
2004(l)	15,000,000	—	—	—	2.00	3.00

Note: All but 48,000 melted. Many of these survivors have recently come onto the NZ market in bulk.

Date	Mintage	F12	VF20	XF40	MS60	MS63
2004(c) In sets only	2,800	—	—	—	20.00	30.00
2004(c)	1,750	PF63 3.00				
2005(c) In sets only	3,000	—	—	—	8.00	12.00
2005(c)	2,250	PF63 3.00				
2006(c) In sets only	—	—	—	—	8.00	12.00
2006(c)	—	PF63 3.00				

KM# 117 10 CENTS
5.66 g., Copper-Nickel, 23.62 mm. **Ruler:** Elizabeth II **Obv:** Head with tiara right **Rev:** Value above koruru **Edge:** Reeded **Note:** Many recalled and melted in 2006.

Date	Mintage	F12	VF20	XF40	MS60	MS63
2001(l)	10,000,000	—	—	0.10	0.30	0.50
2001(c) In sets only	2,910	—	—	—	6.00	8.00
2001(c)	1,364	PF63 4.00				
2002(l)	10,000,000	—	—	0.10	0.30	0.50
2002(c)	1,500	PF63 4.00				
2002(c) In sets only	3,000	—	—	—	3.00	5.00
2003(l)	13,000,000	—	—	0.10	0.30	0.50
2003(c) In sets only	3,000	—	—	—	5.00	8.00
2003(l)	1,496	PF63 4.00				
2004(l)	6,500,000	—	—	—	0.30	0.50
2004(c) In sets only	—	—	—	—	5.00	8.00
2004(c)	1,750	PF63 4.00				
2005	2,000,000	—	—	—	30.00	40.00

Note: All but 28,000 melted

Date	Mintage	F12	VF20	XF40	MS60	MS63
2005(c) In sets only	3,000	—	—	—	20.00	30.00
2005(c)	2,250	PF63 4.00				
2006(c) In sets only	3,000	—	—	—	10.00	15.00
2006(c)	2,100	PF63 4.00				

KM# 117a 10 CENTS
3.31 g., Copper Plated Steel, 20.5 mm. **Ruler:** Elizabeth II **Obv:** Head with tiara right **Rev:** Value above koruru **Edge:** Plain

Date	Mintage	F12	VF20	XF40	MS60	MS63
2006(o)	140,200,000	—	—	—	0.20	0.40
2007(o)	15,000,000	—	—	—	—	—
2007(c) In sets only	5,000	—	—	—	—	5.00
2007(c)	3,500	PF63 4.00				
2008(l) In sets only	4,000	—	—	—	—	5.00
2008(l)	3,000	PF63 4.00				
2009(o)	30,000,000	—	—	—	0.20	0.40

Date	Mintage	F12	VF20	XF40	MS60	MS63
2009(w) In sets only	2,000	—	—	—	—	5.00
2009(w)	1,500	PF63 4.00				
2011(o)	10,400,000	—	—	—	2.00	0.40

KM# 234 10 CENTS
3.31 g., Copper Plated Steel, 20.5 mm. **Ruler:** Elizabeth II **Obv:** Head with tiara right **Rev:** Tuatara right **Edge:** Plain

Date	Mintage	F12	VF20	XF40	MS60	MS63
2007(c) In sets only	15,000	—	—	—	0.50	5.00

KM# 117b 10 CENTS
3.73 g., Copper, 20.5 mm. **Ruler:** Elizabeth II **Obv:** Head with tiara right **Rev:** Value above koruru

Date	Mintage	F12	VF20	XF40	MS60	MS63
2010(u)	2,000	—	—	—	—	4.00
2010(u)	1,500	PF63 5.00				
2011(u)	2,000	—	—	—	—	4.00
2011(u)	1,500	PF63 5.00				
2012(u)	2,000	—	—	—	—	4.00
2012(u)	1,500	PF63 5.00				

KM# 117c 10 CENTS
4.37 g., Silver, 20.5 mm. **Ruler:** Elizabeth II **Obv:** Head with tiara right **Rev:** Value above koruru **Edge:** Plain

Date	Mintage	F12	VF20	XF40	MS60	MS63
2011(u)	1,200	PF65 25.00				

KM# 117d 10 CENTS
4.37 g., Silver, 20.5 mm. **Ruler:** Elizabeth II **Obv:** Head with tiara right **Rev:** Value above koruru **Edge:** Plain

Date	Mintage	F12	VF20	XF40	MS60	MS63
2012(u)	1,000	PF65 25.00				

KM# 118 20 CENTS
11.31 g., Copper-Nickel, 28.58 mm. **Ruler:** Elizabeth II **Obv:** Head with tiara right **Rev:** Value below Pukaki **Edge:** Reeded **Note:** Many recalled and melted in 2006.

Date	Mintage	F12	VF20	XF40	MS60	MS63
2001(c)	1,364	PF63 10.00				
2001(c) In sets only	2,910	—	—	—	—	10.00
2002(l)	7,000,000	—	—	0.50	—	—
2002(c) In sets only	3,000	—	—	—	—	8.00
2002(c)	1,500	PF63 10.00				
2003(c) In sets only	3,000	—	—	—	—	8.00
2003(c)	3,000	PF63 10.00				
2004(l)	8,500,000	—	—	0.50	—	—
2004(c) In sets only	2,800	—	—	—	—	10.00
2004(c)	1,750	PF63 10.00				
2005(l)	4,000,000	—	—	—	—	15.00

Note: All but 178,000 melted

Date	Mintage	F12	VF20	XF40	MS60	MS63
2005(c) In sets only	3,000	—	—	—	—	8.00
2005(c)	2,250	PF63 10.00				
2006(c) In sets only	3,000	—	—	—	—	8.00
2006(c)	2,100	PF63 10.00				

KM# 118a 20 CENTS
4.00 g., Nickel Plated Steel, 21.75 mm. **Ruler:** Elizabeth II **Obv:** Head with tiara right **Rev:** Value below Pukaki **Shape:** Scalloped

Date	Mintage	F12	VF20	XF40	MS60	MS63
2006(o)	116,600,000	—	—	—	0.40	0.65
2007(c) In sets only	5,000	—	—	—	—	7.00
2007(c)	4,000	PF63 8.00				
2008(o)	80,000,000	—	—	—	0.40	0.65
2008(l) In sets only	4,000	—	—	—	—	7.00
2008(l)	3,000	PF63 8.00				
2009(w) In sets only	2,000	—	—	—	—	7.00
2009(w)	1,500	PF63 8.00				

KM# 118b 20 CENTS
4.45 g., Copper-Nickel, 21.75 mm. **Ruler:** Elizabeth II **Obv:** Head with tiara right **Rev:** Value below Pukaki **Edge:** Scalloped

Date	Mintage	F12	VF20	XF40	MS60	MS63
2010(u)	2,000	—	—	—	—	7.00

Date	Mintage	F12	VF20	XF40	MS60	MS63
2010(u)	1,500	PF63 8.00				
2011(u)	2,000	—	—	—	—	7.00
2011(u)	1,500	PF63 8.00				
2012(u)	2,000	—	—	—	—	7.00
2012(u)	1,500	PF63 8.00				

KM# 118c 20 CENTS
5.30 g., 0.999 Silver 0.1691 oz. ASW, 21.75 mm. **Ruler:** Elizabeth II **Obv:** Head with tiara right **Rev:** Value below Pukaki **Edge:** Plain

Date	Mintage	F12	VF20	XF40	MS60	MS63
2011(u)	1,200	PF65 30.00				
2012(u)	1,000	PF65 30.00				

KM# 119 50 CENTS
13.61 g., Copper-Nickel, 31.75 mm. **Ruler:** Elizabeth II **Obv:** Head with tiara right **Rev:** H.M.S. Endeavour and value **Edge:** Segmented reeding **Note:** Many recalled and melted in 2006.

Date	Mintage	F12	VF20	XF40	MS60	MS63
2001(l)	5,000,000	—	—	—	1.00	—
2001(c) In sets only	2,910	—	—	—	—	10.00
2001(c)	1,364	PF63 10.00				
2002(l)	3,000,000	—	—	0.50	1.00	—
2002(c) In sets only	3,000	—	—	—	—	8.00
2002(c)	1,500	PF63 10.00				
2003(l)	2,500,000	—	—	0.50	1.00	—
2003(c) In sets only	3,000	—	—	—	—	8.00
2003(c)	1,496	PF63 10.00				
2004(l)	2,000,000	—	—	—	1.00	—
2004(c) In sets only	2,800	—	—	—	—	10.00
2004(c)	1,750	PF63 10.00				
2005(l)	1,000,000	—	—	—	7.50	—

Note: All but 503,800 melted

Date	Mintage	F12	VF20	XF40	MS60	MS63
2005(c) In sets only	3,000	—	—	—	—	8.00
2005(c)	2,250	PF63 10.00				
2006(c) In sets only	3,000	—	—	—	—	8.00
2006(c)	2,100	PF63 10.00				

KM# 135 50 CENTS
13.61 g., Copper-Nickel, 31.75 mm. **Ruler:** Elizabeth II **Subject:** Lord of the Rings **Obv:** Head with tiara right **Rev:** Frodo's head facing to left of vine and value **Edge:** Reeded

Date	Mintage	F12	VF20	XF40	MS60	MS63
2003(l)	41,221	—	—	—	—	15.00

KM# 136 50 CENTS
13.61 g., Copper-Nickel, 31.75 mm. **Ruler:** Elizabeth II **Subject:** Lord of the Rings **Obv:** Head with tiara right **Rev:** Head of Gandalf with hat facing and value **Edge:** Reeded

Date	Mintage	F12	VF20	XF40	MS60	MS63
2003(l)	41,221	—	—	—	—	15.00

KM# 137 50 CENTS
13.61 g., Copper-Nickel, 31.75 mm. **Ruler:** Elizabeth II
Subject: Lord of the Rings **Obv:** Head with tiara right **Rev:** Head of Aragorn facing and value **Edge:** Reeded

Date	Mintage	F12	VF20	XF40	MS60	MS63
2003(I)	41,221	—	—	—	—	15.00

KM# 138 50 CENTS
13.61 g., Copper-Nickel, 31.75 mm. **Ruler:** Elizabeth II
Subject: Lord of the Rings **Obv:** Head with tiara right **Rev:** Head of Gollum facing and value **Edge:** Reeded

Date	Mintage	F12	VF20	XF40	MS60	MS63
2003(I)	38,400	—	—	—	—	15.00

KM# 139 50 CENTS
13.61 g., Copper-Nickel, 31.75 mm. **Ruler:** Elizabeth II
Subject: Lord of the Rings **Obv:** Head with tiara right **Rev:** Saruman, value **Edge:** Reeded

Date	Mintage	F12	VF20	XF40	MS60	MS63
2003(I)	38,400	—	—	—	—	15.00

KM# 140 50 CENTS
13.61 g., Copper-Nickel, 31.75 mm. **Ruler:** Elizabeth II
Subject: Lord of the Rings **Obv:** Head with tiara right **Rev:** Head of Sauron left and value **Edge:** Reeded

Date	Mintage	F12	VF20	XF40	MS60	MS63
2003(I)	38,400	—	—	—	—	15.00

KM# 235 50 CENTS
13.61 g., Copper-Nickel, 31.75 mm. **Ruler:** Elizabeth II **Subject:** Lord of the Rings **Obv:** Head with tiara right **Rev:** Boromir

Date	Mintage	F12	VF20	XF40	MS60	MS63
2003(I)	6,889	—	—	—	—	18.00

KM# 236 50 CENTS
13.61 g., Copper-Nickel, 31.75 mm. **Ruler:** Elizabeth II **Subject:** Lord of the Rings **Obv:** Head with tiara right **Rev:** Gimli

Date	Mintage	F12	VF20	XF40	MS60	MS63
2003(I)	6,889	—	—	—	—	18.00

KM# 237 50 CENTS
13.61 g., Copper-Nickel, 31.75 mm. **Ruler:** Elizabeth II **Subject:** Lord of the Rings **Obv:** Head with tiara right **Rev:** Legolas

Date	Mintage	F12	VF20	XF40	MS60	MS63
2003(I)	6,889	—	—	—	—	18.00

KM# 238 50 CENTS
13.61 g., Copper-Nickel, 31.75 mm. **Ruler:** Elizabeth II **Subject:** Lord of the Rings **Obv:** Head with tiara right **Rev:** Merry

Date	Mintage	F12	VF20	XF40	MS60	MS63
2003(I)	6,889	—	—	—	—	18.00

KM# 239 50 CENTS
13.61 g., Copper-Nickel, 31.75 mm. **Ruler:** Elizabeth II **Subject:** Lord of the Rings **Obv:** Head with tiara right **Rev:** Pippin

Date	Mintage	F12	VF20	XF40	MS60	MS63
2003(I)	6,889	—	—	—	—	18.00

KM# 240 50 CENTS
13.61 g., Copper-Nickel, 31.75 mm. **Ruler:** Elizabeth II **Subject:** Lord of the Rings **Obv:** Head with tiara right **Rev:** Sam

Date	Mintage	F12	VF20	XF40	MS60	MS63
2003(I)	6,889	—	—	—	—	18.00

KM# 241 50 CENTS
13.61 g., Copper-Nickel, 31.75 mm. **Ruler:** Elizabeth II **Subject:** Lord of the Rings **Obv:** Head with tiara right **Rev:** Arwen

Date	Mintage	F12	VF20	XF40	MS60	MS63
2003(I)	4,068	—	—	—	—	20.00

KM# 242 50 CENTS
13.61 g., Copper-Nickel, 31.75 mm. **Ruler:** Elizabeth II **Subject:** Lord of the Rings **Obv:** Head with tiara right **Rev:** Elrond

Date	Mintage	F12	VF20	XF40	MS60	MS63
2003(I)	4,068	—	—	—	—	20.00

KM# 243 50 CENTS
13.61 g., Copper-Nickel, 31.75 mm. **Ruler:** Elizabeth II **Subject:** Lord of the Rings **Obv:** Head with tiara right **Rev:** Eowyn

Date	Mintage	F12	VF20	XF40	MS60	MS63
2003(I)	4,068	—	—	—	—	20.00

KM# 244 50 CENTS
13.61 g., Copper-Nickel, 31.75 mm. **Ruler:** Elizabeth II **Subject:** Lord of the Rings **Obv:** Head with tiara right **Rev:** Galadriel

Date	Mintage	F12	VF20	XF40	MS60	MS63
2003(I)	4,068	—	—	—	—	20.00

KM# 245 50 CENTS
13.61 g., Copper-Nickel, 31.75 mm. **Ruler:** Elizabeth II **Subject:** Lord of the Rings **Obv:** Head with tiara right **Rev:** An Orc

Date	Mintage	F12	VF20	XF40	MS60	MS63
2003(I)	4,068	—	—	—	—	20.00

KM# 246 50 CENTS
13.61 g., Copper-Nickel, 31.75 mm. **Ruler:** Elizabeth II **Subject:** Lord of the Rings **Obv:** Head with tiara right **Rev:** Treebeard

Date	Mintage	F12	VF20	XF40	MS60	MS63
2003(I)	4,068	—	—	—	—	20.00

KM# 119a 50 CENTS
5.00 g., Nickel Plated Steel, 24.75 mm. **Ruler:** Elizabeth II **Obv:** Head with tiara right **Rev:** Ship, H.M.S. Endeavour

Date	Mintage	F12	VF20	XF40	MS60	MS63
2006(o)	70,200,000	—	—	—	0.75	1.00
2007(c) In sets only	5,000	—	—	—	—	8.00
2007(c)	3,500	PF63 10.00				
2008(I) In sets only	4,000	—	—	—	—	8.00
2008(I)	3,000	PF63 10.00				
2009(o)	20,000,000	—	—	—	0.75	1.00
2009(w) In sets only	2,000	—	—	—	—	8.00
2009(w)	1,500	PF63 10.00				

KM# 279 50 CENTS
Aluminum-Bronze, 38.74 mm. **Ruler:** Elizabeth II **Subject:** Narnia **Obv:** Head with tiara right **Rev:** Peter

Date	Mintage	F12	VF20	XF40	MS60	MS63
2006(c)	20,000	—	—	—	—	6.00

KM# 280 50 CENTS
Aluminum-Bronze, 38.74 mm. **Ruler:** Elizabeth II **Subject:** Narnia **Obv:** Head with tiara right **Rev:** Susan

Date	Mintage	F12	VF20	XF40	MS60	MS63
2006(c)	20,000	—	—	—	—	6.00

KM# 281 50 CENTS
Aluminum-Bronze, 38.74 mm. **Ruler:** Elizabeth II **Subject:** Narnia **Obv:** Head with tiara right **Rev:** Edmund

Date	Mintage	F12	VF20	XF40	MS60	MS63
2006(c)	20,000	—	—	—	—	6.00

KM# 282 50 CENTS
Aluminum-Bronze, 38.74 mm. **Ruler:** Elizabeth II **Subject:** Narnia **Obv:** Head with tiara right **Rev:** Lucy

Date	Mintage	F12	VF20	XF40	MS60	MS63
2006(c)	20,000	—	—	—	—	6.00

KM# 283 50 CENTS
Aluminum-Bronze, 38.74 mm. **Ruler:** Elizabeth II **Subject:** Narnia **Obv:** Head with tiara right **Rev:** Mr. Tumnus

Date	Mintage	F12	VF20	XF40	MS60	MS63
2006(c)	20,000	—	—	—	—	6.00

KM# 284 50 CENTS
Aluminum-Bronze, 38.74 mm. **Ruler:** Elizabeth II **Subject:** Narnia **Obv:** Head with tiara right **Rev:** Ginarrbrik

Date	Mintage	F12	VF20	XF40	MS60	MS63
2006(c)	20,000	—	—	—	—	6.00

KM# 119b 50 CENTS
5.60 g., Copper-Nickel, 24.75 mm. **Ruler:** Elizabeth II **Obv:** Head with tiara right **Rev:** Ship, H.M.S. Endeavour

Date	Mintage	F12	VF20	XF40	MS60	MS63
2010(u)	2,000	—	—	—	—	8.00
2010(u)	1,500	PF63 10.00				
2011(u)	2,000	—	—	—	—	8.00
2011(u)	1,500	PF63 10.00				
2012(u)	2,000	—	—	—	—	8.00
2012(u)	1,500	PF63 10.00				

KM# 119c 50 CENTS
6.59 g., 0.999 Silver 0.2103 oz. ASW, 24.75 mm. **Ruler:** Elizabeth II **Obv:** Head with tiara right **Rev:** Ship, H.M.S. Endeavor **Edge:** Plain

Date	Mintage	F12	VF20	XF40	MS60	MS63
2011(u)	1,200	PF65 45.00				
2012(u)	1,000	PF65 45.00				

KM# 120 DOLLAR
8.00 g., Aluminum-Bronze, 23 mm. **Ruler:** Elizabeth II **Obv:** Head with tiara right **Rev:** Kiwi bird within sprigs, value below **Edge:** Segmented reeding

Date	Mintage	F12	VF20	XF40	MS60	MS63
2001(c) In sets only	2,910	—	—	—	—	4.00
2001(c)	1,364	PF63 5.00				
2002(c)	8,000,000	—	—	—	1.00	2.50
2002(c) In sets only	5,000	—	—	—	—	4.00
2002(c)	1,500	PF63 5.00				
2003(I)	4,000,000	—	—	—	1.00	2.50
2003(c) In sets only	5,000	—	—	—	—	4.00
2003(c)	1,750	PF63 5.00				
2004(I)	2,700,000	—	—	—	1.00	2.50
2004(c) In sets only	3,500	—	—	—	—	4.00
2004(c)	2,250	PF63 5.00				
2005(I)	2,000,000	—	—	—	1.00	2.50
2005(c) In sets only	4,000	—	—	—	—	4.00
2005(c)	2,250	PF63 5.00				
2006(c) In sets only	3,000	—	—	—	—	4.00
2006(c)	2,100	PF63 5.00				
2007(c)	5,000	—	—	—	—	4.00
2007(c)	3,500	PF63 5.00				
2008(I)	6,000,000	—	—	—	1.00	2.50
2008(I) In sets only	4,000	—	—	—	—	4.00
2008(I)	3,000	PF63 5.00				
2009(w) In sets only	2,000	—	—	—	—	4.00
2009(w)	1,500	PF63 5.00				
2010(I)	10,000,000	—	—	—	1.00	2.50

KM# 141a DOLLAR
28.28 g., 0.925 Silver 0.8356 oz. ASW, 38.61 mm. **Ruler:** Elizabeth II **Obv:** Head with tiara right **Rev:** Gold-plated ring and edge **Edge:** Reeded

Date	Mintage	F12	VF20	XF40	MS60	MS63
2003(I)	39,244	PF65 70.00				

KM# 141 DOLLAR
28.28 g., Aluminum-Bronze, 38.61 mm. **Ruler:** Elizabeth II **Subject:** Lord of the Rings **Obv:** Head with tiara right **Rev:** Inscribed ring around value **Edge:** Reeded

Date	Mintage	F12	VF20	XF40	MS60	MS63
2003(I)	30,081	—	—	—	—	15.00

Note: Mintage includes 10,454 in sets.

KM# 142 DOLLAR
28.28 g., Aluminum-Bronze, 38.61 mm. **Ruler:** Elizabeth II **Subject:** Lord of the Rings **Obv:** Head with tiara right **Rev:** Head of Frodo looking down above inscription **Edge:** Reeded

Date	Mintage	F12	VF20	XF40	MS60	MS63
2003(I)	10,454	—	—	—	—	10.00

KM# 143 DOLLAR
28.28 g., Aluminum-Bronze, 38.61 mm. **Ruler:** Elizabeth II **Subject:** Lord of the Rings **Obv:** Head with tiara right **Rev:** View of Sauron, value **Edge:** Reeded

Date	Mintage	F12	VF20	XF40	MS60	MS63
2003(I)	10,454	—	—	—	—	10.00

KM# 247 DOLLAR
28.28 g., 0.925 Silver 0.8356 oz. ASW, 38.61 mm. **Ruler:** Elizabeth II **Subject:** Lord of the Rings **Obv:** Head with tiara right **Rev:** Aragorn's Coronation

Date	Mintage	F12	VF20	XF40	MS60	MS63
2003(I)	3,057	PF65 70.00				

KM# 248 DOLLAR
28.28 g., 0.925 Silver 0.8356 oz. ASW, 38.61 mm. **Ruler:** Elizabeth II **Subject:** Lord of the Rings **Obv:** Head with tiara right **Rev:** King Theoden

Date	Mintage	F12	VF20	XF40	MS60	MS63
2003(I)	2,022	PF65 70.00				

KM# 249 DOLLAR
28.28 g., 0.925 Silver 0.8356 oz. ASW, 38.61 mm. **Ruler:** Elizabeth II **Subject:** Lord of the Rings **Obv:** Head with tiara right **Rev:** Flight to the Ford

Date	Mintage	F12	VF20	XF40	MS60	MS63
2003(I)	2,020	PF65 70.00				

KM# 250 DOLLAR
28.28 g., 0.925 Silver 0.8356 oz. ASW, 38.61 mm. **Ruler:** Elizabeth II **Subject:** Lord of the Rings **Obv:** Head with tiara right **Rev:** Mirror of Galadriel

Date	Mintage	F12	VF20	XF40	MS60	MS63
2003(I)	2,036	PF65 70.00				

KM# 251 DOLLAR
28.28 g., 0.925 Silver 0.8356 oz. ASW, 38.61 mm. **Ruler:** Elizabeth II **Subject:** Lord of the Rings **Obv:** Head with tiara right **Rev:** Frodo offering ring to Nazgul

Date	Mintage	F12	VF20	XF40	MS60	MS63
2003(I)	1,784	PF65 70.00				

KM# 252 DOLLAR
28.28 g., 0.925 Silver 0.8356 oz. ASW, 38.61 mm. **Ruler:** Elizabeth II **Subject:** Lord of the Rings **Obv:** Head with tiara right **Rev:** Bridge of Kazad-Dum

Date	Mintage	F12	VF20	XF40	MS60	MS63
2003(I)	952	PF65 70.00				

KM# 253 DOLLAR
28.28 g., 0.925 Silver 0.8356 oz. ASW, 38.61 mm. **Ruler:** Elizabeth II **Subject:** Lord of the Rings **Obv:** Head with tiara right **Rev:** Shelob's Lair

Date	Mintage	F12	VF20	XF40	MS60	MS63
2003(I)	917	PF65 70.00				

KM# 254 DOLLAR
28.28 g., 0.925 Silver 0.8356 oz. ASW, 38.61 mm. **Ruler:** Elizabeth II **Subject:** Lord of the Rings **Obv:** Head with tiara right **Rev:** Taming of Smeagol

Date	Mintage	F12	VF20	XF40	MS60	MS63
2003(I)	1,017	PF65 70.00				

KM# 255 DOLLAR
28.28 g., 0.925 Silver 0.8356 oz. ASW, 38.61 mm. **Ruler:** Elizabeth II **Subject:** Lord of the Rings **Obv:** Head with tiara right **Rev:** Dark Lord's Tower and the Eye

Date	Mintage	F12	VF20	XF40	MS60	MS63
2003(I)	1,002	PF65 70.00				

KM# 256 DOLLAR
28.28 g., 0.925 Silver 0.8356 oz. ASW, 38.61 mm. **Ruler:** Elizabeth II **Subject:** Lord of the Rings **Obv:** Head with tiara right **Rev:** Knife in the Dark

Date	Mintage	F12	VF20	XF40	MS60	MS63
2003(I)	967	PF65 70.00				

KM# 257 DOLLAR
28.28 g., 0.925 Silver 0.8356 oz. ASW, 38.61 mm. **Ruler:** Elizabeth II **Subject:** Lord of the Rings **Obv:** Head with tiara right **Rev:** Gandalf and Saruman

Date	Mintage	F12	VF20	XF40	MS60	MS63
2003(I)	867	PF65 70.00				

KM# 258 DOLLAR
28.28 g., 0.925 Silver 0.8356 oz. ASW, 38.61 mm. **Ruler:** Elizabeth II **Subject:** Lord of the Rings **Obv:** Head with tiara right **Rev:** Council of Elrond

Date	Mintage	F12	VF20	XF40	MS60	MS63
2003(I)	1,204	PF65 70.00				

KM# 259 DOLLAR
28.28 g., 0.925 Silver 0.8356 oz. ASW, 38.61 mm. **Ruler:** Elizabeth II **Subject:** Lord of the Rings **Obv:** Head with tiara right **Rev:** Helm's Deep

Date	Mintage	F12	VF20	XF40	MS60	MS63
2003(I)	967	PF65 70.00				

KM# 260 DOLLAR
28.28 g., 0.925 Silver 0.8356 oz. ASW, 38.61 mm. **Ruler:** Elizabeth II **Subject:** Lord of the Rings **Obv:** Head with tiara right **Rev:** Frodo & Co. at Mt. Doom

Date	Mintage	F12	VF20	XF40	MS60	MS63
2003(I)	917	PF65 70.00				

KM# 261 DOLLAR
28.28 g., 0.925 Silver 0.8356 oz. ASW, 38.61 mm. **Ruler:** Elizabeth II **Subject:** Lord of the Rings **Obv:** Head with tiara right **Rev:** Departure of Boromir

Date	Mintage	F12	VF20	XF40	MS60	MS63
2003(I)	917	PF65 70.00				

KM# 262 DOLLAR
28.28 g., 0.925 Silver 0.8356 oz. ASW, 38.61 mm. **Ruler:** Elizabeth II **Subject:** Lord of the Rings **Obv:** Head with tiara right **Rev:** Meeting of Treebeard

Date	Mintage	F12	VF20	XF40	MS60	MS63
2003(I)	867	PF65 70.00				

KM# 263 DOLLAR
28.28 g., 0.925 Silver 0.8356 oz. ASW, 38.61 mm. **Ruler:** Elizabeth II **Subject:** Lord of the Rings **Obv:** Head with tiara right **Rev:** Battle of Minas Tirith / Pelenor Fields

Date	Mintage	F12	VF20	XF40	MS60	MS63
2003(I)	867	PF65 70.00				

KM# 264 DOLLAR
28.28 g., 0.925 Silver 0.8356 oz. ASW, 38.61 mm. **Ruler:** Elizabeth II **Subject:** Lord of the Rings **Obv:** Head with tiara right **Rev:** Gandalf Reappears

Date	Mintage	F12	VF20	XF40	MS60	MS63
2003(I)	967	PF65 70.00				

KM# 265 DOLLAR
28.28 g., 0.925 Silver 0.8356 oz. ASW, 38.61 mm. **Ruler:** Elizabeth II **Subject:** Lord of the Rings **Obv:** Head with tiara right **Rev:** Army of the Dead

Date	Mintage	F12	VF20	XF40	MS60	MS63
2003(I)	917	PF65 70.00				

KM# 266 DOLLAR
28.28 g., 0.925 Silver 0.8356 oz. ASW, 38.61 mm. **Ruler:** Elizabeth II **Subject:** Lord of the Rings **Obv:** Head with tiara right **Rev:** Travel to the Undying Lands

Date	Mintage	F12	VF20	XF40	MS60	MS63
2003(I)	867	PF65 70.00				

KM# 267 DOLLAR
28.28 g., 0.925 Silver 0.8356 oz. ASW, 38.61 mm. **Ruler:** Elizabeth II **Subject:** Lord of the Rings **Obv:** Head with tiara right **Rev:** Great River

Date	Mintage	F12	VF20	XF40	MS60	MS63
2003(I)	867	PF65 70.00				

KM# 268 DOLLAR
28.28 g., 0.925 Silver 0.8356 oz. ASW, 38.61 mm. **Ruler:** Elizabeth II **Subject:** Lord of the Rings **Obv:** Head with tiara right **Rev:** Death of the Witch King

Date	Mintage	F12	VF20	XF40	MS60	MS63
2003(I)	867	PF65 70.00				

KM# 269 DOLLAR
28.28 g., 0.925 Silver 0.8356 oz. ASW, 38.61 mm. **Ruler:** Elizabeth II **Subject:** Lord of the Rings **Obv:** Head with tiara right **Rev:** March of the Oliphants

Date	Mintage	F12	VF20	XF40	MS60	MS63
2003(I)	867	PF65 70.00				

KM# 152a DOLLAR
31.14 g., 0.999 Silver 0.9936 oz. ASW, 40 mm. **Ruler:** Elizabeth II **Obv:** Crowned head right **Rev:** Little spotted kiwi **Edge:** Reeded

Date	Mintage	F12	VF20	XF40	MS60	MS63
2004(c)	2,000	PF65 50.00				

Note: Includes 500 struck in 2008 for sets.

KM# 152 DOLLAR
28.28 g., Copper-Nickel, 38.6 mm. **Ruler:** Elizabeth II **Obv:** Crowned head right **Rev:** Little spotted kiwi **Edge:** Reeded

Date	Mintage	F12	VF20	XF40	MS60	MS63
2004(c)	2,500	—	—	—	—	45.00

KM# 153a DOLLAR
31.64 g., 0.999 Silver 1.0095 oz. ASW, 38.74 mm. **Ruler:** Elizabeth II **Rev:** Rowi Kiwi

Date	Mintage	F12	VF20	XF40	MS60	MS63
2005(w)	2,700	PF65 80.00				

Note: Mintage includes 500 struck in 2008 for sets.

KM# 156a DOLLAR
28.28 g., 0.925 Silver 0.8356 oz. ASW, 38.61 mm. **Ruler:** Elizabeth II **Series:** Rugby player, Lions crest & New Zealand map **Subject:** Lions Rugby Tour **Obv:** Crowned head right **Edge:** Reeded

Date	Mintage	F12	VF20	XF40	MS60	MS63
2005(I)	5,000	PF65 50.00				

KM# 153 DOLLAR
31.64 g., 0.999 Silver 1.0095 oz. ASW, 40 mm. **Ruler:** Elizabeth II **Obv:** Crowned head right **Rev:** Rowi Kiwi **Edge:** Reeded

Date	Mintage	F12	VF20	XF40	MS60	MS63
2005(w)	4,000	—	—	—	—	45.00

KM# 154 DOLLAR
31.14 g., 0.999 Silver 0.9936 oz. ASW, 40 mm. **Ruler:** Elizabeth II **Subject:** ANZAC **Obv:** Crowned head right **Rev:** Soldiers

seated, multicolor flag in background **Edge:** Reeded

Date	Mintage	F12	VF20	XF40	MS60	MS63
2005(w) P	15,000	PF65 110				

KM# 156 DOLLAR
28.28 g., Aluminum-Bronze, 38.61 mm. **Ruler:** Elizabeth II **Subject:** Lions Rugby Tour **Obv:** Crowned head right **Rev:** Rugby player, Lions crest and New Zealand map

Date	Mintage	F12	VF20	XF40	MS60	MS63
2005(I)	15,000	—	—	—	—	20.00

KM# 157 DOLLAR
Aluminum-Bronze, 38.74 mm. **Ruler:** Elizabeth II **Subject:** ANZAC **Obv:** Crowned head right **Rev:** Soldiers from Chunuk Bair battle with rifles and bayonets **Edge:** Reeded

Date	Mintage	F12	VF20	XF40	MS60	MS63
2005	15,000	PF65 25.00				

KM# 159 DOLLAR
20.00 g., Aluminum-Bronze, 38.74 mm. **Ruler:** Elizabeth II **Subject:** King Kong **Obv:** Crowned head right **Rev:** King Kong **Edge:** Reeded

Date	Mintage	F12	VF20	XF40	MS60	MS63
2005(w)	7,000	—	—	—	—	20.00

KM# 160 DOLLAR
20.00 g., Aluminum-Bronze, 38.74 mm. **Ruler:** Elizabeth II **Subject:** King Kong **Obv:** Crowned head right **Rev:** Multicolored King Kong **Edge:** Reeded

Date	Mintage	F12	VF20	XF40	MS60	MS63
2005(w)	4,000	—	—	—	—	35.00

KM# 161 DOLLAR
20.00 g., Aluminum-Bronze, 38.74 mm. **Ruler:** Elizabeth II **Subject:** King Kong **Obv:** Crowned head right **Rev:** Carl Denham and camera in multicolor **Edge:** Reeded

Date	Mintage	F12	VF20	XF40	MS60	MS63
2005	4,000	—	—	—	—	35.00

KM# 162 DOLLAR
20.00 g., Aluminum-Bronze, 38.74 mm. **Ruler:** Elizabeth II **Subject:** King Kong **Obv:** Crowned head right **Rev:** Ann Darrow and Jack Driscoll multicolored **Edge:** Reeded

Date	Mintage	F12	VF20	XF40	MS60	MS63
2005	4,000	—	—	—	—	35.00

KM# 164 DOLLAR
31.14 g., 0.999 Silver 0.9936 oz. ASW, 40.6 mm. **Ruler:** Elizabeth II **Obv:** Crowned head right **Rev:** King Kong partially gold plated

Date	Mintage	F12	VF20	XF40	MS60	MS63
2005(w)	3,000	PF65 70.00				

KM# 276 DOLLAR
20.00 g., Aluminum-Bronze, 38.74 mm. **Ruler:** Elizabeth II **Subject:** Emblem **Obv:** Head with tiara right **Rev:** Rowi and chick inside patterned ring **Note:** Part of a pair issued with Australia.

Date	Mintage	F12	VF20	XF40	MS60	MS63
2005(w)	20,000	—	—	—	—	25.00

KM# 158 DOLLAR
28.28 g., 0.999 Silver 0.9025 oz. ASW, 38.61 mm. **Ruler:** Elizabeth II **Subject:** FIFA **Obv:** Crowned head right **Rev:** Soccer player, silver fern and map

Date	Mintage	F12	VF20	XF40	MS60	MS63
2006(v)	7,500	PF65 50.00				

KM# 285 DOLLAR
31.10 g., 0.999 Silver 0.9925 oz. ASW, 40 mm. **Ruler:** Elizabeth II **Subject:** Narnia **Obv:** Head with tiara right **Rev:** White Witch

Date	Mintage	F12	VF20	XF40	MS60	MS63
2006(c)	2,000	PF65 70.00				

KM# 286 DOLLAR
20.00 g., Aluminum-Bronze, 38.74 mm. **Ruler:** Elizabeth II **Subject:** Narnia **Obv:** Head with tiara right **Rev:** Asian, lion standing right

Date	Mintage	F12	VF20	XF40	MS60	MS63
2006(c)	8,000	—	—	—	—	20.00

KM# 287 DOLLAR
31.14 g., 0.999 Silver 0.9936 oz. ASW, 40 mm. **Ruler:** Elizabeth II **Subject:** Narnia **Obv:** Head with tiara right **Rev:** Asian

Date	Mintage	F12	VF20	XF40	MS60	MS63
2006(c)	4,320	PF65 70.00				

KM# 288 DOLLAR
31.14 g., 0.999 Silver 0.9936 oz. ASW, 40 mm. **Ruler:** Elizabeth II **Subject:** Narnia **Obv:** Head with tiara right **Rev:** Wardrobe from the Lion, Witch and Wardrobe series

Date	Mintage	F12	VF20	XF40	MS60	MS63
2006(c)	1,000	PF65 70.00				

KM# 289 DOLLAR
20.00 g., Aluminum-Bronze, 38.74 mm. **Ruler:** Elizabeth II **Subject:** Queen's 80th birthday **Obv:** Head with tiara right **Rev:** Heraldic arms

Date	Mintage	F12	VF20	XF40	MS60	MS63
2006	2,000	—	—	—	—	30.00

KM# 290 DOLLAR
31.14 g., 0.999 Silver 0.9936 oz. ASW, 38.74 mm. **Ruler:** Elizabeth II **Subject:** Queen's 80th birthday **Obv:** Head with tiara right **Rev:** Heraldic arms

Date	Mintage	F12	VF20	XF40	MS60	MS63
2006	1,500	PF65 85.00				

KM# 291 DOLLAR
31.14 g., 0.999 Silver 0.9936 oz. ASW, 40 mm. **Ruler:** Elizabeth II **Obv:** Head with tiara right **Rev:** North Island Brown Kiwi **Edge:** Reeded

Date	Mintage	F12	VF20	XF40	MS60	MS63
2006(w)	3,000	—	—	—	—	50.00

KM# 291a DOLLAR
31.14 g., 0.999 Silver 0.9936 oz. ASW, 40 mm. **Ruler:** Elizabeth II **Obv:** Head with tiara right **Rev:** North Island Brown Kiwi **Edge:** Reeded

Date	Mintage	F12	VF20	XF40	MS60	MS63
2006(w)	2,000	PF65 80.00				

Note: Mintage includes 500 struck in 2008 for sets.

KM# 293 DOLLAR
20.00 g., Aluminum-Bronze, 38.74 mm. **Ruler:** Elizabeth II **Subject:** NZ Gold Rushes - West Coast **Obv:** Head with tiara right **Rev:** 1860s miners

Date	Mintage	F12	VF20	XF40	MS60	MS63
2006(w)	1,500	—	—	—	—	35.00

KM# 294 DOLLAR
31.14 g., 0.999 Silver 0.9936 oz. ASW, 40.60 mm. **Ruler:** Elizabeth II **Subject:** NZ Gold Rushes - Thames/Coromandel **Obv:** Head with tiara right **Rev:** Gold panning

Date	Mintage	F12	VF20	XF40	MS60	MS63
2006(w)	1,200	PF65 110				

KM# 232 DOLLAR
31.14 g., 0.999 Silver 0.9936 oz. ASW, 40 mm. **Ruler:** Elizabeth II **Subject:** Aoraki - Mount Cook, Japanese Friendship **Obv:** Head with tiara right **Obv. Legend:** NEW ZEALAND - ELIZABETH II **Rev:** Flowers in bloom, Mount Cook in background multicolor **Note:** Also released in a Japanese proof set.

Date	Mintage	F12	VF20	XF40	MS60	MS63
2007(j)	70,000	PF65 90.00				

KM# 296 DOLLAR
1.24 g., 0.999 Gold 0.0397 oz. AGW, 13.92 mm. **Ruler:** Elizabeth II **Subject:** 50th anniversary of Scott Base **Obv:** Head with tiara right **Rev:** Scott Base, Antarctica and International Polar Year logo

Date	Mintage	F12	VF20	XF40	MS60	MS63
2007(m)	10,000	PF65 100				

KM# 297 DOLLAR
31.14 g., 0.999 Silver 0.9936 oz. ASW, 40 mm. **Ruler:** Elizabeth II **Subject:** 50th anniversary of Scott Base **Obv:** Head with tiara right **Rev:** Scott Base, Antarctica and International Polar Year logo

Date	Mintage	F12	VF20	XF40	MS60	MS63
2007(m)	10,000	PF65 80.00				

KM# 298 DOLLAR
28.28 g., Copper-Nickel, 38.61 mm. **Ruler:** Elizabeth II **Subject:** Scouting centenary **Obv:** Head with tiara right

Date	Mintage	F12	VF20	XF40	MS60	MS63
2007(l)	1,900	—	—	—	—	50.00

KM# 298a DOLLAR
28.28 g., 0.925 Silver 0.8356 oz. ASW, 38.61 mm. **Ruler:** Elizabeth II **Subject:** Scouting centenary **Obv:** Head with tiara right

Date	Mintage	F12	VF20	XF40	MS60	MS63
2007(l)	1,500	PF65 85.00				

KM# 300 DOLLAR
31.14 g., 0.999 Silver 0.9936 oz. ASW, 40 mm. **Ruler:** Elizabeth II **Obv:** Head with tiara right **Rev:** Great Spotted Kiwi **Edge:** Reeded

Date	Mintage	F12	VF20	XF40	MS60	MS63
2007(m)	4,000	—	—	—	—	50.00

KM# 300a DOLLAR
31.14 g., 0.999 Silver 0.9936 oz. ASW, 40 mm. **Ruler:** Elizabeth II **Obv:** Head with tiara right **Rev:** Great Spotted Kiwi **Edge:** Reeded

Date	Mintage	F12	VF20	XF40	MS60	MS63
2007(m)	3,000	PF65 100				

Note: Mintage includes 500 struck in 2008 for sets.

KM# 302 DOLLAR
31.14 g., Copper-Nickel, 40 mm. **Ruler:** Elizabeth II **Subject:** Elizabeth & Philip Diamond Wedding **Obv:** Head with tiara right **Rev:** Royal crests **Edge:** Reeded

Date	Mintage	F12	VF20	XF40	MS60	MS63
2007(m)	1,600	—	—	—	—	32.00

KM# 302a DOLLAR
31.11 g., 0.999 Silver 0.9926 oz. ASW, 40 mm. **Ruler:** Elizabeth II **Subject:** Elizabeth & Philip Diamond Wedding **Obv:** Head with tiara right **Rev:** Royal crests **Edge:** Reeded

Date	Mintage	F12	VF20	XF40	MS60	MS63
2007(m)	1,500	PF65 85.00				

KM# 321 DOLLAR
30.80 g., Brass, 30 mm. **Ruler:** Elizabeth II **Rev:** Sir Edmond Hillary with Mt. Everest **Edge:** Reeded **Note:** Sold in a PNC cover only

Date	Mintage	F12	VF20	XF40	MS60	MS63
2008(w)	4,000	—	—	—	—	20.00

KM# 309 DOLLAR
31.14 g., 0.999 Silver 0.9936 oz. ASW, 40 mm. **Ruler:** Elizabeth II **Obv:** Head with tiara right **Rev:** Haast Tokoeka Kiwi

Date	Mintage	F12	VF20	XF40	MS60	MS63
2008(w)	8,000	—	—	—	—	60.00

KM# 309a DOLLAR
31.14 g., 0.999 Silver 0.9936 oz. ASW, 40 mm. **Ruler:** Elizabeth II **Obv:** Head with tiara right **Rev:** Haast Tokoeka Kiwi

Date	Mintage	F12	VF20	XF40	MS60	MS63
2008(w)	5,000	PF65 85.00				

Note: Includes 500 for 2004-2008 sets.

KM# 311 DOLLAR
31.14 g., 0.999 Silver 0.9936 oz. ASW, 40.6 mm. **Ruler:** Elizabeth II **Subject:** Sir Edmund Hillary **Obv:** Head with tiara right **Rev:** Hillary with Mt. Everest in background

Date	Mintage	F12	VF20	XF40	MS60	MS63
2008(w)	10,000	PF65 90.00				

KM# 323 DOLLAR
31.14 g., 0.999 Silver 0.9936 oz. ASW, 40 mm. **Ruler:** Elizabeth II **Obv:** Bust right **Rev:** Southern Right Whale **Edge:** Reeded

Date	Mintage	F12	VF20	XF40	MS60	MS63
2009(m) Prooflike	11,500	—	—	—	—	70.00

KM# 324 DOLLAR
31.14 g., 0.999 Silver 0.9936 oz. ASW, 40 mm. **Ruler:** Elizabeth II **Rev:** Haast's Eagle

Date	Mintage	F12	VF20	XF40	MS60	MS63
2009(m) Prooflike	11,500	—	—	—	—	80.00

KM# 325 DOLLAR
31.14 g., 0.999 Silver 0.9936 oz. ASW, 40 mm. **Ruler:** Elizabeth II **Rev:** Giant Moa

Date	Mintage	F12	VF20	XF40	MS60	MS63
2009(m) Prooflike	1,500	—	—	—	—	85.00

KM# 326 DOLLAR
31.14 g., 0.999 Silver 0.9936 oz. ASW, 40 mm. **Ruler:** Elizabeth II **Rev:** Colossal squid **Edge:** Reeded

Date	Mintage	F12	VF20	XF40	MS60	MS63
2009(m) Prooflike	1,500	—	—	—	—	85.00

KM# 327 DOLLAR
31.14 g., 0.999 Silver 0.9936 oz. ASW, 40 mm. **Ruler:** Elizabeth II **Rev:** Giant Weta **Edge:** Reeded

Date	Mintage	F12	VF20	XF40	MS60	MS63
2009(m) Prooflike	1,500	—	—	—	—	85.00

KM# 328 DOLLAR
26.45 g., Copper-Nickel-Zinc, 39.19 mm. **Ruler:** Elizabeth II **Subject:** Reserve Bank of New Zealand, 75th Anniversary **Rev:** Tui and Kowhai as on 1940-65 bronze penny

Date	Mintage	F12	VF20	XF40	MS60	MS63
2009(o)	2,000	—	—	—	—	30.00

KM# 322 DOLLAR
28.28 g., Copper-Nickel, 40 mm. **Ruler:** Elizabeth II **Obv:** Head with tiara right **Rev:** Kiwi with map of New Zealand **Edge:** Reeded

Date	Mintage	F12	VF20	XF40	MS60	MS63
2009(m)	10,000	—	—	—	—	50.00

KM# 322a DOLLAR
31.14 g., 0.999 Silver 0.9936 oz. ASW, 40 mm. **Ruler:** Elizabeth II **Subject:** Icons of New Zealand **Rev:** Kiwi with map of New Zealand **Edge:** Reeded

Date	Mintage	F12	VF20	XF40	MS60	MS63
2009(m)	7,500	PF65 80.00				

KM# 120a DOLLAR
8.60 g., Brass **Ruler:** Elizabeth II **Obv:** Head with tiara right **Rev:** Kiwi bird within sprigs, value below **Edge:** Segmented reeding

Date	Mintage	F12	VF20	XF40	MS60	MS63
2010(u)	2,000	—	—	—	—	4.00
2010(u)	1,500	PF63 5.00				
2011(u)	2,000	—	—	—	—	4.00
2011(u)	1,500	PF63 5.00				
2012(u)	2,000	—	—	—	—	4.00
2012(u)	1,500	PF63 5.00				

KM# 331 DOLLAR
31.14 g., 0.999 Silver 0.9936 oz. ASW, 40 mm. **Ruler:** Elizabeth II **Subject:** Icons of New Zealand **Rev:** Kiwi and Southern Cross **Edge:** Reeded

Date	Mintage	F12	VF20	XF40	MS60	MS63
2010(m)	Est. 12500	—	—	—	—	60.00

KM# 331a DOLLAR
31.14 g., 0.999 Silver 0.9936 oz. ASW, 40 mm. **Ruler:** Elizabeth II **Rev:** Kiwi and Southern Cross **Edge:** Reeded

Date	Mintage	F12	VF20	XF40	MS60	MS63
2010(m)	—	PF65 90.00				

KM# 333 DOLLAR
31.14 g., 0.999 Silver 0.9936 oz. ASW, 40 mm. **Ruler:** Elizabeth II **Subject:** 2010 FIFA World Cup **Rev:** Soccer player with stylized NZ koru **Edge:** Reeded

Date	Mintage	F12	VF20	XF40	MS60	MS63
2010(m)	10,000	—	—	—	—	100

Note: Mintage includes 1500 in NZ Post packaging.

KM# 336 DOLLAR
31.11 g., 0.999 Silver 0.9926 oz. ASW, 40 mm. **Ruler:** Elizabeth II **Obv:** Head with tiara right **Rev:** Allosaurus

Date	Mintage	F12	VF20	XF40	MS60	MS63
2010(m) Prooflike	1,500	—	—	—	—	90.00

KM# 337 DOLLAR
31.11 g., 0.999 Silver 0.9926 oz. ASW, 40 mm. **Ruler:** Elizabeth II **Obv:** Head with tiara right **Rev:** Anhanguera

Date	Mintage	F12	VF20	XF40	MS60	MS63
2010(m) Prooflike	1,500	—	—	—	—	90.00

KM# 338 DOLLAR
31.11 g., 0.999 Silver 0.9926 oz. ASW, 40 mm. **Ruler:** Elizabeth II **Obv:** Head with tiara right **Rev:** Mauisaurus

Date	Mintage	F12	VF20	XF40	MS60	MS63
2010(m) Prooflike	1,500	—	—	—	—	90.00

KM# 339 DOLLAR
31.11 g., 0.999 Silver 0.9926 oz. ASW, 40 mm. **Ruler:** Elizabeth II **Obv:** Head with tiara right **Rev:** Moanasaurus

Date	Mintage	F12	VF20	XF40	MS60	MS63
2010(m) Prooflike	1,500	—	—	—	—	90.00

KM# 340 DOLLAR
31.11 g., 0.999 Silver 0.9926 oz. ASW, 40 mm. **Ruler:** Elizabeth II **Obv:** Head with tiara right **Rev:** Titanosaurus

Date	Mintage	F12	VF20	XF40	MS60	MS63
2010(m) Prooflike	1,500	—	—	—	—	90.00

KM# 341 DOLLAR
31.11 g., 0.999 Silver 0.9926 oz. ASW, 40 mm. **Ruler:** Elizabeth II **Obv:** Head with tiara right **Rev:** Multicolor tiki with huia feathers

Date	Mintage	F12	VF20	XF40	MS60	MS63
2010(m)	4,000	PF65 130				

KM# 344 DOLLAR
31.11 g., 0.999 Silver 0.9926 oz. ASW, 40 mm. **Ruler:** Elizabeth II **Obv:** Head with tiara right **Rev:** Black field with repeating fern pattern **Edge:** Reeded

Date	Mintage	F12	VF20	XF40	MS60	MS63
2010(m)	10,000	PF65 100				

KM# 120b DOLLAR
10.73 g., 0.999 Silver 0.3424 oz. ASW, 23 mm. **Ruler:** Elizabeth II **Obv:** Head with tiara right **Rev:** Kiwi bird within sprigs, value

below **Edge:** Segmented reeding

Date	Mintage	F12	VF20	XF40	MS60	MS63
2011(u)	1,200	PF65 50.00				
2012(u)	1,000	PF65 50.00				

KM# 335 DOLLAR
31.14 g., 0.999 Silver 0.9936 oz. ASW, 40 mm. **Ruler:** Elizabeth II **Obv:** Head with tiara right **Rev:** Kiwi and silver fern **Edge:** Reeded

Date	Mintage	F12	VF20	XF40	MS60	MS63
2011(m) Prooflike	10,000	—	—	—	—	65.00

KM# 335a DOLLAR
31.11 g., 0.999 Silver 0.9926 oz. ASW, 40 mm. **Ruler:** Elizabeth II **Obv:** Head in tiara right **Rev:** Kiwi and fern

Date	Mintage	F12	VF20	XF40	MS60	MS63
2011	7,000	PF65 75.00				

KM# 343 DOLLAR
Copper-Nickel, 30 mm. **Ruler:** Elizabeth II **Obv:** Head with tiara right **Rev:** All Black logo with repeating fern pattern in background **Edge:** Reeded

Date	Mintage	F12	VF20	XF40	MS60	MS63
2011(m)	10,000	—	—	—	—	30.00

KM# 345 DOLLAR
31.11 g., 0.999 Silver 0.9926 oz. ASW, 40 mm. **Ruler:** Elizabeth II **Obv:** Head with tiara right **Rev:** All Blacks performing the Haka before a rugby match **Edge Lettering:** KA MATE, KA MATE! KA ORA, KA ORA!

Date	Mintage	F12	VF20	XF40	MS60	MS63
2011(m)	3,000	PF65 140				

KM# 346 DOLLAR
31.11 g., 0.999 Silver 0.9926 oz. ASW, 40 mm. **Ruler:** Elizabeth II **Obv:** Head with tiara right **Rev:** Webb Ellis Cup selectively gold palted **Edge:** Reeded

Date	Mintage	F12	VF20	XF40	MS60	MS63
2011(m)	15,000	PF65 130				

KM# 347 DOLLAR
31.14 g., 0.999 Silver 0.9936 oz. ASW, 38.85 mm. **Ruler:** Elizabeth II **Subject:** 1987 Champions **Obv:** Head with tiara right **Rev:** 1987 All Black player fending off opponent **Edge:** Reeded

Date	Mintage	F12	VF20	XF40	MS60	MS63
2011(w)	2,011	PF65 150				

KM# 350 DOLLAR
31.11 g., 0.999 Silver 0.9926 oz. ASW, 40 mm. **Ruler:** Elizabeth II **Obv:** Head with tiara right **Rev:** Kiwi and kowhai flowers **Edge:** Reeded

Date	Mintage	F12	VF20	XF40	MS60	MS63
2012(m) Prooflike	13,500	—	—	—	—	80.00
2012(m)	5,000	PF65 130				
2013(m)	—	—	—	—	—	80.00
2013(m)	—	PF65 130				

KM# 351 DOLLAR
31.11 g., 0.999 Silver 0.9926 oz. ASW, 38.6 mm. **Ruler:** Elizabeth II **Subject:** Maori Art **Obv:** Head with tiara right **Rev:** Hei matau (neck pendant) **Edge:** Notched

Date	Mintage	F12	VF20	XF40	MS60	MS63
2012(u)	3,000	PF65 140				

KM# 354 DOLLAR
31.11 g., 0.999 Silver 0.9926 oz. ASW, 40 mm. **Ruler:** Elizabeth II **Subject:** 50th years of firendship - New Zealand and Samoa **Rev:** New Zealand and Samoa designs, color background

Date	Mintage	F12	VF20	XF40	MS60	MS63
2012	1,000	PF65 75.00				

KM# 356 DOLLAR
Silver, 40 mm. **Ruler:** Elizabeth II **Subject:** Elizabeth II, 60th Anniversary of reign **Rev:** Elizabeth II delivering Christmas Message, color flora

Date	Mintage	F12	VF20	XF40	MS60	MS63
2012 proof	—	PF65 75.00				

KM# 357 DOLLAR
Silver, 40 mm. **Ruler:** Elizabeth II **Subject:** New Zealand Air Force, 75th Anniversary **Rev:** Pilot and Skyhawk aircraft, "missing man" formation

Date	Mintage	F12	VF20	XF40	MS60	MS63
2012	—	PF65 75.00				

KM# 358 DOLLAR
31.11 g., 0.999 Silver 0.9926 oz. ASW, 40 mm. **Ruler:** Elizabeth II **Subject:** Bilbo Baggins

Date	Mintage	F12	VF20	XF40	MS60	MS63
2012	1,000	PF65 150				

KM# 359 DOLLAR
31.11 g., 0.999 Silver 0.9926 oz. ASW, 40 mm. **Ruler:** Elizabeth II **Subject:** Radagast

Date	Mintage	F12	VF20	XF40	MS60	MS63
2012	1,000	PF65 150				

KM# 360 DOLLAR
31.11 g., 0.999 Silver 0.9926 oz. ASW, 40 mm. **Ruler:** Elizabeth II **Subject:** Elrond

Date	Mintage	F12	VF20	XF40	MS60	MS63
2012	1,000	PF65 150				

KM# 361 DOLLAR
31.11 g., 0.999 Silver 0.9926 oz. ASW, 40 mm. **Ruler:** Elizabeth II **Subject:** Thorin Oakenshield

Date	Mintage	F12	VF20	XF40	MS60	MS63
2012	1,000	PF65 150				

KM# 362 DOLLAR
31.11 g., 0.999 Silver 0.9926 oz. ASW, 40 mm. **Ruler:** Elizabeth II **Subject:** Gandalf

Date	Mintage	F12	VF20	XF40	MS60	MS63
2012	1,000	PF65 150				

KM# 363 DOLLAR
31.11 g., 0.999 Silver 0.9926 oz. ASW, 40 mm. **Ruler:** Elizabeth II **Subject:** Gollum

Date	Mintage	F12	VF20	XF40	MS60	MS63
2012	1,000	PF65 150				

KM# 364 DOLLAR
Aluminum-Bronze **Ruler:** Elizabeth II **Rev:** Bilbo Baggins examining contract with Dwarves

Date	Mintage	F12	VF20	XF40	MS60	MS63
2012	—	PF65 15.00				

KM# 365 DOLLAR
Aluminum-Bronze **Ruler:** Elizabeth II **Subject:** Thorin Oakenshield

Date	Mintage	F12	VF20	XF40	MS60	MS63
2012	—	PF65 15.00				

KM# 366 DOLLAR
Aluminum-Bronze **Ruler:** Elizabeth II **Subject:** Gandalf and Radagast

Date	Mintage	F12	VF20	XF40	MS60	MS63
2012	—	PF65 15.00				

KM# 367 DOLLAR
Aluminum-Bronze **Ruler:** Elizabeth II **Subject:** Three Dwarves

Date	Mintage	F12	VF20	XF40	MS60	MS63
2012	—	PF65 15.00				

KM# 372 DOLLAR
31.11 g., 0.999 Silver 0.9926 oz. ASW, 40 mm. **Ruler:** Elizabeth II **Rev:** Bilbo Baggins, staff in right hand

Date	Mintage	F12	VF20	XF40	MS60	MS63
2012	20,000	PF65 150				

KM# 373 DOLLAR
31.10 g., 0.999 Silver 0.9925 oz. ASW, 40 mm. **Ruler:** Elizabeth II **Subject:** Maori Art - Koru **Obv:** Portrait of Her Majesty Queen Elizabeth II **Rev:** Koru, ferns and God of the Forest

Date	Mintage	F12	VF20	XF40	MS60	MS63
2013	Est. 2000	PF65 75.00				

KM# 121 2 DOLLARS
10.00 g., Aluminum-Bronze, 26.5 mm. **Ruler:** Elizabeth II **Obv:** Head with tiara right **Rev:** White heron (kotuku) above value **Edge:** Reeded with security groove

Date	Mintage	F12	VF20	XF40	MS60	MS63
2001(I)	3,000,000	—	—	—	2.50	5.00
2001(c) In sets only	2,910	—	—	—	—	6.00
2001(c)	2,000	PF63 7.50				
2002(I)	6,000,000	—	—	—	2.50	5.00
2002(c) In sets only	3,000	—	—	—	—	6.00
2002(c)	2,000	PF63 7.50				
2003(I)	6,000,000	—	—	—	2.50	5.00
2003(c) In sets only	3,000	—	—	—	—	6.00
2003(c)	3,000	PF63 7.50				
2004(c) In sets only	2,800	—	—	—	—	5.00
2004	3,500	PF63 7.50				
2005(I)	5,000,000	—	—	—	2.50	5.00
2005(c) In sets only	3,000	—	—	—	—	6.00
2005(c)	3,000	PF63 7.50				
2006(c) In sets only	3,000	—	—	—	—	6.00
2006(c)	2,100	PF63 7.50				
2007(c)	5,000	—	—	—	—	6.00
2007(c)	4,000	PF63 7.50				
2008(I) In sets only	4,000	—	—	—	—	6.00
2008(I)	3,000	PF63 7.50				
2009(w) In sets only	2,000	—	—	—	—	6.00
2009(w)	1,500	PF63 7.50				
2011(I)	8,000,000	—	—	—	2.50	5.00

KM# 121a 2 DOLLARS
11.25 g., Brass, 26.5 mm. **Ruler:** Elizabeth II **Obv:** Head with tiara right **Rev:** White heron (kotuku) above value **Edge:** Reeded with security groove

Date	Mintage	F12	VF20	XF40	MS60	MS63
2010(u)	2,000	—	—	—	—	6.00
2010(u)	1,500	PF63 7.50				
2011(u)	2,000	—	—	—	—	6.00
2011(u)	1,500	PF63 7.50				
2012(u)	2,000	—	—	—	—	6.00
2012(u)	1,500	PF63 7.50				

KM# 121b 2 DOLLARS
14.12 g., 0.999 Silver 0.4506 oz. ASW, 26.5 mm. **Ruler:** Elizabeth II **Obv:** Head with tiara right **Rev:** White heron (kotuku) above value **Edge:** Reeded with security groove

Date	Mintage	F12	VF20	XF40	MS60	MS63
2011(u)	1,200	PF65 75.00				
2012(u)	1,000	PF65 75.00				

KM# 128 5 DOLLARS
28.28 g., Copper-Nickel, 38.6 mm. **Ruler:** Elizabeth II **Subject:** Kereru Bird **Obv:** Head with tiara right **Rev:** Wood Pigeon on branch **Edge:** Reeded

Date	Mintage	F12	VF20	XF40	MS60	MS63
2001(I)	1,500	—	—	—	25.00	—

KM# 149 5 DOLLARS
28.28 g., 0.925 Silver 0.8356 oz. ASW, 38.6 mm. **Ruler:** Elizabeth II **Subject:** Royal Visit (canceled after coin issue) **Obv:** Head with tiara right **Rev:** Queen with flowers and two girls **Edge:** Reeded

Date	Mintage	F12	VF20	XF40	MS60	MS63
2001	2,000	PF65 100				

Note: 200 issued in stamp cover

KM# 128a 5 DOLLARS
28.28 g., 0.999 Silver 0.9025 oz. ASW **Ruler:** Elizabeth II **Obv:** Head with tiara right **Rev:** Pigeon on branch

Date	Mintage	F12	VF20	XF40	MS60	MS63
2001	1,000	PF65 85.00				

KM# 131a 5 DOLLARS
28.28 g., 0.925 Silver 0.8356 oz. ASW, 38.6 mm. **Ruler:** Elizabeth II **Subject:** Architectural Heritage **Obv:** Head with tiara right **Rev:** Auckland Sky Tower **Edge:** Reeded

Date	Mintage	F12	VF20	XF40	MS60	MS63
2002(I)	2,000	PF65 80.00				

Note: 500 pieces were housed in a stamp cover

KM# 145a 5 DOLLARS
27.22 g., 0.999 Silver 0.8687 oz. ASW **Ruler:** Elizabeth II **Obv:** Head with tiara right **Rev:** Two Hector's Dolphins jumping out of the water **Edge:** Reeded

Date	Mintage	F12	VF20	XF40	MS60	MS63
2002(c)	Est. 2000	—	—	—	—	100

Note: 500 in stamp covers

KM# 131 5 DOLLARS
28.28 g., Copper-Nickel, 38.6 mm. **Ruler:** Elizabeth II **Subject:** Architectural Heritage **Obv:** Head with tiara right **Rev:** Auckland Sky Tower **Edge:** Reeded

Date	Mintage	F12	VF20	XF40	MS60	MS63
2002(I)	3,000	—	—	—	12.50	—

Note: 500 pieces were housed in a stamp cover

KM# 145 5 DOLLARS
27.22 g., Copper-Nickel, 38.74 mm. **Ruler:** Elizabeth II **Obv:** Head with tiara right **Rev:** Hector's Dolphins jumping out of the water **Edge:** Reeded

Date	Mintage	F12	VF20	XF40	MS60	MS63
2002(c)	4,000	—	—	—	35.00	—

Note: 500 pieces were housed in a stamp covers

KM# 151 5 DOLLARS
28.28 g., 0.925 Silver Gilt 0.8356 oz., 38.61 mm. **Ruler:** Elizabeth II **Subject:** Queen's Jubilee **Obv:** Gilt head with tiara right **Rev:** Scepter with "Great Star of Africa" at left of vertical band with crowns and shields **Edge:** Reeded

Date	Mintage	F12	VF20	XF40	MS60	MS63
2002(l)	25,000				PF65	80.00

Note: 100 pieces were housed in a stamp cover, value $85

KM# 272 5 DOLLARS
28.28 g., Copper-Nickel, 38.61 mm. **Ruler:** Elizabeth II **Subject:** America's cup

Date	Mintage	F12	VF20	XF40	MS60	MS63
2002(l)	6,000	—	—	—	—	20.00

KM# 272a 5 DOLLARS
28.28 g., 0.925 Silver 0.8356 oz. ASW, 38.61 mm. **Ruler:** Elizabeth II **Subject:** America's Cup **Obv:** Head with tiara right **Rev:** Yachts

Date	Mintage	F12	VF20	XF40	MS60	MS63
2002(l)	4,000				PF65	60.00

Note: Includes 500 in stamp cover, value $60.

KM# 132a 5 DOLLARS
28.28 g., 0.999 Silver 0.9025 oz. ASW, 38.6 mm. **Ruler:** Elizabeth II **Obv:** Head with tiara right **Rev:** Giant Kokopu fish **Edge:** Reeded

Date	Mintage	F12	VF20	XF40	MS60	MS63
2003(c)	1,700				PF65	75.00

Note: Includes 200 issued in a stamp cover

KM# 132 5 DOLLARS
26.70 g., Copper-Nickel, 38.6 mm. **Ruler:** Elizabeth II **Obv:** Head with tiara right **Rev:** Giant Kokopu fish divides circle **Edge:** Reeded

Date	Mintage	F12	VF20	XF40	MS60	MS63
2003(c)	2,400	—	—	—	14.00	27.50

Note: Includes 400 issued in a stamp cover.

KM# 133 5 DOLLARS
26.72 g., Copper-Nickel, 38.6 mm. **Ruler:** Elizabeth II **Subject:** Chatham Island Taiko **Obv:** Head with tiara right **Rev:** Magenta Petrel **Edge:** Reeded

Date	Mintage	F12	VF20	XF40	MS60	MS63
2004(2003)	1,350	—	—	—	—	35.00

KM# 147 5 DOLLARS
28.23 g., 0.925 Silver 0.8341 oz. ASW, 38.6 mm. **Ruler:** Elizabeth II **Subject:** 50th Anniversary of Coronation **Obv:** Gold plated crowned head right **Rev:** Crown above fern and flowers **Edge:** Reeded

Date	Mintage	F12	VF20	XF40	MS60	MS63
2003	25,000				PF65	80.00

Note: Includes 100 issued in a stamp cover

KM# 133a 5 DOLLARS
28.28 g., 0.999 Silver 0.9025 oz. ASW, 38.74 mm. **Ruler:** Elizabeth II **Obv:** Head with tiara right **Rev:** Chatham Island Taiko

Date	Mintage	F12	VF20	XF40	MS60	MS63
2004	1,300				PF65	70.00

KM# 146 5 DOLLARS
27.22 g., Copper-Nickel, 38.74 mm. **Ruler:** Elizabeth II **Obv:** Head with tiara right **Rev:** Fiordland Crested Penguin **Edge:** Reeded

Date	Mintage	F12	VF20	XF40	MS60	MS63
2005(2004)	4,000	—	—	—	25.00	30.00

KM# 146a 5 DOLLARS
27.22 g., 0.999 Silver 0.8686 oz. ASW, 38.74 mm. **Ruler:** Elizabeth II **Obv:** Head with tiara right **Rev:** Fiordland Crested Penguin **Edge:** Reeded

Date	Mintage	F12	VF20	XF40	MS60	MS63
2005	3,500	—	—	—	—	60.00

KM# 148a 5 DOLLARS
28.28 g., 0.999 Silver 0.9025 oz. ASW, 38.74 mm. **Ruler:** Elizabeth II **Obv:** Head with tiara right **Rev:** New Zealand Falcon on tree stump **Edge:** Reeded

Date	Mintage	F12	VF20	XF40	MS60	MS63
2006	2,500				PF65	60.00

KM# 148 5 DOLLARS
27.22 g., Copper-Nickel, 38.74 mm. **Ruler:** Elizabeth II **Obv:** Head with tiara right **Rev:** Falcon on tree stump **Edge:** Reeded

Date	Mintage	F12	VF20	XF40	MS60	MS63
2006	4,000	—	—	—	25.00	30.00

KM# 150a 5 DOLLARS
28.28 g., 0.999 Silver 0.9025 oz. ASW, 38.74 mm. **Ruler:** Elizabeth II **Subject:** Tuatara **Obv:** Head with tiara right **Rev:** Tuatara right **Edge:** Reeded

Date	Mintage	F12	VF20	XF40	MS60	MS63
2007(c)	2,700				PF65	80.00

KM# 150 5 DOLLARS
27.22 g., Copper-Nickel, 38.74 mm. **Ruler:** Elizabeth II **Subject:** Tuatara **Obv:** Head with tiara right **Rev:** Tuatara (Sphenodon punctatus), a lizard-like reptile **Edge:** Reeded

Date	Mintage	F12	VF20	XF40	MS60	MS63
2007(c)	2,200	—	—	—	25.00	30.00

KM# 233a 5 DOLLARS
28.28 g., 0.999 Silver 0.9025 oz. ASW, 38.61 mm. **Ruler:** Elizabeth II **Rev:** Hamilton's frog **Edge:** Reeded

Date	Mintage	F12	VF20	XF40	MS60	MS63
2008(l)	4,000				PF65	90.00

Note: Mintage includes 1500 struck in 2009

KM# 233 5 DOLLARS
28.28 g., Copper-Nickel, 38.6 mm. **Ruler:** Elizabeth II **Subject:** Hamilton's frog **Obv:** Head with tiara right **Obv. Legend:** NEW ZEALAND - ELIZABETH II **Rev:** Frog perched on branch at left center

Date	Mintage	F12	VF20	XF40	MS60	MS63
2008(l)	4,000				35.00	40.00

KM# 329 5 DOLLARS
22.00 g., Copper-Nickel, 38.60 mm. **Ruler:** Elizabeth II **Rev:** Kakapo **Edge:** Reeded

Date	Mintage	F12	VF20	XF40	MS60	MS63
2009(w)	2,000	—	—	—	25.00	30.00

KM# 329a 5 DOLLARS
31.14 g., 0.999 Silver 0.9936 oz. ASW, 38.61 mm. **Ruler:** Elizabeth II **Rev:** Kakapo

Date	Mintage	F12	VF20	XF40	MS60	MS63
2009(w)	4,000				PF65	90.00

KM# 334 5 DOLLARS
31.10 g., Copper-Nickel, 38.7 mm. **Ruler:** Elizabeth II **Series:** Maui's Dolphin, subspecies of the Hector Dolphin **Rev:** Dolphin jumping right **Edge:** Reeded

Date	Mintage	F12	VF20	XF40	MS60	MS63
2010	2,000	—	—	—	—	35.00

KM# 334a 5 DOLLARS
31.11 g., 0.999 Silver 0.9926 oz. ASW, 38.7 mm. **Ruler:** Elizabeth II **Obv:** Head with tiara right **Rev:** Maui's Dolphin **Edge:** Reeded

Date	Mintage	F12	VF20	XF40	MS60	MS63
2010(u)	4,000				PF65	89.00

KM# 348 5 DOLLARS
31.11 g., Copper-Nickel, 38.7 mm. **Ruler:** Elizabeth II **Obv:** Head with tiara right **Rev:** Yellow-eyed Penguin **Edge:** Reeded

Date	Mintage	F12	VF20	XF40	MS60	MS63
2011(u)	2,000	—	—	—	—	35.00

KM# 348a 5 DOLLARS
31.11 g., 0.999 Silver 0.9926 oz. ASW, 38.7 mm. **Ruler:** Elizabeth II **Obv:** Head with tiara right **Rev:** Yellow-eyed Penguin **Edge:** Reeded

Date	Mintage	F12	VF20	XF40	MS60	MS63
2011(u)	4,000				PF65	100

KM# 355 5 DOLLARS
Silver, 40 mm. **Ruler:** Elizabeth II **Rev:** Fairy Tern in flight

Date	Mintage	F12	VF20	XF40	MS60	MS63
2012	—				PF65	65.00

KM# 129 10 DOLLARS
3.89 g., 0.999 Gold 0.1241 oz. AGW, 18 mm. **Ruler:** Elizabeth II **Obv:** Head with tiara right **Rev:** Salvage ship above value **Edge:** Reeded

Date	Mintage	F12	VF20	XF40	MS60	MS63
2001	600	PF65 275				

KM# 130 10 DOLLARS
7.78 g., 0.999 Gold 0.2481 oz. AGW, 22 mm. **Ruler:** Elizabeth II **Obv:** Head with tiara right **Rev:** Ship above value **Edge:** Reeded

Date	Mintage	F12	VF20	XF40	MS60	MS63
2001	600	PF65 525				

KM# 273 10 DOLLARS
Nickel-Brass, 28.4 mm. **Ruler:** Elizabeth II **Subject:** America's Cup **Obv:** Head with tiara right **Rev:** Map, cup and yachts

Date	Mintage	F12	VF20	XF40	MS60	MS63
2002(l)	5,000	—	—	—	—	45.00

KM# 274 10 DOLLARS
15.55 g., 0.999 Gold 0.4963 oz. AGW, 28.4 mm. **Ruler:** Elizabeth II **Subject:** America's Cup **Obv:** Head with tiara right **Rev:** Map, cup and yachts

Date	Mintage	F12	VF20	XF40	MS60	MS63
2002(l)	900	PF65 950				

KM# 144 10 DOLLARS
39.94 g., 0.917 Gold 1.1699 oz. AGW, 38.61 mm. **Ruler:** Elizabeth II **Subject:** Lord of the Rings **Obv:** Head with tiara right **Rev:** The One Ring **Edge:** Reeded

Date	Mintage	F12	VF20	XF40	MS60	MS63
2003(l)	1,198	PF65 2,300				

KM# 270 10 DOLLARS
39.94 g., 0.917 Gold 1.1699 oz. AGW, 38.61 mm. **Ruler:** Elizabeth II **Subject:** Lord of the Rings **Obv:** Head with tiara right **Rev:** Frodo **Edge:** Reeded

Date	Mintage	F12	VF20	XF40	MS60	MS63
2003(l)	142	PF65 2,300				

KM# 271 10 DOLLARS
39.94 g., 0.917 Gold 1.1699 oz. AGW, 38.61 mm. **Ruler:** Elizabeth II **Subject:** Lord of the Rings **Obv:** Head with tiara right **Rev:** Sauron **Edge:** Reeded

Date	Mintage	F12	VF20	XF40	MS60	MS63
2003(l)	142	PF65 2,300				

KM# 275 10 DOLLARS
38.50 g., 0.917 Gold 1.1278 oz. AGW, 38.61 mm. **Ruler:** Elizabeth II **Subject:** Pukaki **Obv:** Head with tiara right **Rev:** Statue of Pukaki **Edge:** Reeded

Date	Mintage	F12	VF20	XF40	MS60	MS63
2004(l)	300	PF65 5,000				
2004(l) NW RB Proof	2	—	—	—	—	—

Note: Initials added for presention to Ngati Whakaue (Maori tribe) and the Reserve Bank.

KM# 165 10 DOLLARS
7.99 g., 0.917 Gold 0.234 oz. AGW, 22.05 mm. **Ruler:** Elizabeth II **Subject:** Lions Rugby Tour **Obv:** Crowned head right **Edge:** Reeded

Date	Mintage	F12	VF20	XF40	MS60	MS63
2005(l)	1,000	PF65 475				

KM# 155 10 DOLLARS
7.78 g., 0.999 Gold 0.2482 oz. AGW, 20.1 mm. **Ruler:** Elizabeth II **Subject:** ANZAC **Obv:** Crowned head right **Rev:** New Zealand soldier playing bugle in front of War Memorial **Edge:** Reeded

Date	Mintage	F12	VF20	XF40	MS60	MS63
2005(w)	1,000	—	—	—	—	500

KM# 295 10 DOLLARS
31.14 g., 0.999 Gold 0.9936 oz. AGW, 34 mm. **Ruler:** Elizabeth II **Subject:** Narnia **Obv:** Head with tiara right **Rev:** Asian

Date	Mintage	F12	VF20	XF40	MS60	MS63
2006	365	PF65 2,100				

KM# 307 10 DOLLARS
7.78 g., 0.999 Gold 0.2482 oz. AGW, 20 mm. **Ruler:** Elizabeth II **Subject:** Queen's 80th birthday **Obv:** Head with tiara right **Rev:** Heraldic arms

Date	Mintage	F12	VF20	XF40	MS60	MS63
2006	500	PF65 550				

KM# 308 10 DOLLARS
15.55 g., 0.999 Gold 0.4964 oz. AGW, 25.10 mm. **Ruler:** Elizabeth II **Subject:** Gold Rushes - Otago **Obv:** Head with tiara right **Rev:** Picks, shovels and nuggets

Date	Mintage	F12	VF20	XF40	MS60	MS63
2006(w)	300	PF65 1,000				

KM# 304 10 DOLLARS
7.78 g., 0.999 Gold 0.2481 oz. AGW, 26 mm. **Ruler:** Elizabeth II **Subject:** Elizabeth & Philip Diamond Wedding Anniversary **Obv:** Head with tiara right **Rev:** Royal crests

Date	Mintage	F12	VF20	XF40	MS60	MS63
2007(m)	300	PF65 550				

KM# 305 10 DOLLARS
31.14 g., 0.917 Gold 0.912 oz. AGW, 38.61 mm. **Ruler:** Elizabeth II **Subject:** Scouting centenary **Obv:** Head with tiara right

Date	Mintage	F12	VF20	XF40	MS60	MS63
2007(l)	150	PF65 1,850				

KM# 306 10 DOLLARS
7.79 g., 0.999 Gold 0.2484 oz. AGW, 20.6 mm. **Ruler:** Elizabeth II **Subject:** Sir Edmund Hilary **Obv:** Head with tiara right **Rev:** Ed Hilary with Mt. Everest in background

Date	Mintage	F12	VF20	XF40	MS60	MS63
2008(w)	1,953	PF65 525				

KM# 330 10 DOLLARS
7.78 g., 0.999 Gold 0.2481 oz. AGW, 26 mm. **Ruler:** Elizabeth II **Subject:** Icons of New Zealand **Rev:** Kiwi and map of New Zealand **Edge:** Reeded

Date	Mintage	F12	VF20	XF40	MS60	MS63
2009(m)	1,500	PF65 575				

KM# 332 10 DOLLARS
7.78 g., 0.999 Gold 0.2481 oz. AGW, 26. mm. **Ruler:** Elizabeth II **Subject:** Icons of New Zealand **Rev:** Kiwi and Southern Cross **Edge:** Reeded

Date	Mintage	F12	VF20	XF40	MS60	MS63
2010(m)	1,800	PF65 575				

KM# 342 10 DOLLARS
31.11 g., 0.999 Gold 0.9926 oz. AGW, 40 mm. **Ruler:** Elizabeth II **Subject:** Maori Art **Obv:** Head with tiara right **Rev:** Tiki with huia feathers

Date	Mintage	F12	VF20	XF40	MS60	MS63
2010(m)	500	PF65 2,650				

KM# 349 10 DOLLARS
7.77 g., 0.999 Gold 0.248 oz. AGW, 26 mm. **Ruler:** Elizabeth II **Obv:** Head with tiara right **Rev:** Kiwi and silver fern **Edge:** Reeded

Date	Mintage	F12	VF20	XF40	MS60	MS63
2011(m)	995	PF65 775				

KM# 352 10 DOLLARS
7.77 g., 0.999 Gold 0.248 oz. AGW, 26 mm. **Ruler:** Elizabeth II **Obv:** Head with tiara right **Rev:** Kiwi and kowhai flowers **Edge:** Reeded

Date	Mintage	F12	VF20	XF40	MS60	MS63
2012(m)	950	PF65 900				

KM# 353 10 DOLLARS
31.11 g., 0.999 Gold 0.9926 oz. AGW, 38.6 mm. **Ruler:** Elizabeth II **Subject:** Maori Art **Obv:** Head with tiara right **Rev:** Hei Matau (neck pendant) **Edge:** Notched

Date	Mintage	F12	VF20	XF40	MS60	MS63
2012(u)	250	PF65 3,950				

KM# 368 10 DOLLARS
31.11 g., 0.999 Gold 0.9926 oz. AGW, 39 mm. **Ruler:** Elizabeth II **Rev:** Bilbo Baggins, staff in his right hand; Hobbit hole door in background

Date	Mintage	F12	VF20	XF40	MS60	MS63
2012	250	PF65 3,700				

KM# 369 10 DOLLARS
31.11 g., 0.999 Gold 0.9926 oz. AGW, 39 mm. **Ruler:** Elizabeth II **Subject:** Gandalf

Date	Mintage	F12	VF20	XF40	MS60	MS63
2012	250	PF65 3,500				

KM# 370 10 DOLLARS
31.11 g., 0.999 Gold 0.9926 oz. AGW, 39 mm. **Ruler:** Elizabeth II **Subject:** Thorin Oakenshield

Date	Mintage	F12	VF20	XF40	MS60	MS63
2012	250	PF65 3,500				

KM# 371 10 DOLLARS
31.11 g., 0.999 Gold 0.9926 oz. AGW, 39 mm. **Ruler:** Elizabeth II **Rev:** Bilbo Baggins, staff in his left hand

Date	Mintage	F12	VF20	XF40	MS60	MS63
2012	1,000	PF65 3,500				

MINT SETS

KM#	Date	Mintage	Identification	Issue Price	Mkt Val
MS50	2001 (7)	2,910	KM#116-121, 128	18.50	60.00
MS51	2002 (7)	3,000	KM#116-121, 145. Hector's dolphin.	18.00	60.00
MS52	2003 (7)	3,000	KM#116-121, 132. Giant Kokopu.	18.00	100
MS53	2003 (6)	34,332	KM#135-140. Lord of the Rings, Light vs. Dark set.	19.95	100

MS54	2003 (9)	2,821	KM#135-137; 235-240. Fellowship of the Ring.	—	175
MS55	2003 (18)	4,068	KM#135-140; 235-246. Lord of the Rings. Character collection.	—	325
MS56	2003 (3)	10,454	KM#141, 142, 143. Lord of the Rings. Battle for the Ring set.	29.95	35.00
MS57	2004 (7)	2,800	KM#116-121, 133. Taiko.	33.00	150
MS58	2005 (7)	3,000	KM#116-121; 146. Crested Penguin.	33.00	120
MS59	2006 (7)	3,000	KM#116-121; 148. Falcon.	33.00	120
MS60	2003-5-6 (7)	5,000	Mixed Set for Change over to smaller size coins. KM#116 (2003); 117-119 (2005); KM#117a-119a (2006).	7.50	70.00
MS61	2007 (6)	5,000	KM#117a-119a; 120-121; 150. Tuatara.	33.00	50.00
MS62	2008 (6)	4,000	KM#117a-119a; 120-121; 233. Hamilton's frog.	37.50	50.00
MS63	2009 (6)	2,000	KM#117a-119a; 120-121; 329. Kakapo.	—	55.00
MS64	2009 (5)	1,500	KM#323-327. Giants of New Zealand.	—	400
MS65	2010 (6)	2,000	KM#117b, 118b, 119b, 120a, 121a, 334. Maui's dolphin.	59.00	65.00
MS66	2010 (5)	1,500	KM#336-340. Ancient Reptiles of New Zealand.	—	450
MS67	2011 (6)	2,000	KM#117b, 118b, 119b, 120a, 121a, 348. Yellow-eyed Penguin.	—	65.00

PROOF SETS

KM#	Date	Mintage	Identification	Issue Price	Mkt Val
PS45	2001 (7)	1,364	KM#116-121, 128a	49.25	170
PS46	2001 (2)	600	KM#129-130	400	800
PS47	2002 (7)	1,500	KM#116-121, 145a	60.00	140
PS48	2003 (6)	810	KM#141a and 5 others.	—	350
PS49	2003 (0)	—	Five coins as per PS48, less 141a	—	—
PS50	2003 (3)	133	KM#144; 270; 271. Lord of the Rings. Gold set.	—	6,900
PS51	2003 (2)	9	KM#270; 271. Lord of the Rings.	—	4,600
PS52	2003 (7)	1,496	KM#116-121, 132a.	60.00	125
PS53	2004 (7)	1,750	KM#116-121, 133a. Chatham Islands Taiko	—	200
PS54	2005 (7)	2,250	KM#116-121; 146a. Crested Penguin.	88.00	165
PS55	2006 (7)	2,100	KM#116-121; 148a. Falcon.	90.00	145
PS56	2006 (3)	1,000	KM#285; 287; 288.	—	225
PS57	2007 (6)	2,200	KM#117a-119a; 120-121; 150a. Tuatara.	88.00	115
PS58	2007 (7)	69,000	KM#232, NZ Aoraki dollar and Japan 95.2; 96.2; 97.2; 98.2; 101.2; 125.	115	110
PS59	2008 (6)	1,441	KM#117a-119a; 120-121; 233a. Hamilton's frog.	94.00	125
PS60	2004-08 (4)	500	KM#152; 153a; 291a; 300a; 309a. Kiwi.	375	450
PS61	2009 (6)	1,041	KM#117a-119a; 120-121; 329a. Kakapo.	—	125
PS62	2010 (6)	1,500	KM#117b, 118b, 119b, 120a, 121a, 334a. Maui's dolphin.	149	125
PS63	2011 (6)	500	KM#117b, 118b, 119b, 120a, 121a, 348a. Yellow-eyed Penguin.	—	135
PS64	2011 (5)	2,011	KM346, 347, plus Australian, British and South African coins.	695	700
PS65	2011 (5)	1,200	KM#117c, 118c, 119c, 120b, 121b.	275	225
PS66	2012 (5)	1,000	KM#117d, 118c, 119c, 120b, 121b.	275	225

NICARAGUA

The Republic of Nicaragua, situated in Central America between Honduras and Costa Rica, has an area of 50,193 sq. mi. (129,494 sq. km.) and a population of *3.7 million. Capital: Managua. Agriculture, mining (gold and silver) and hardwood logging are the principal industries. Cotton, meat, coffee and sugar are exported.

MONETARY SYSTEM
100 Centavos = 1 Cordoba

REPUBLIC
DECIMAL COINAGE

KM# 97 5 CENTAVOS
3.00 g., Copper Plated Steel, 18.5 mm. **Obv:** National arms **Rev:** Value within circle **Edge:** Plain

Date	Mintage	F12	VF20	XF40	MS60	MS63
2002					0.25	0.50

KM# 98 10 CENTAVOS
4.00 g., Brass Plated Steel, 20.5 mm. **Obv:** National arms **Rev:** Value within circle **Edge:** Reeded and plain sections

Date	Mintage	F12	VF20	XF40	MS60	MS63
2002					0.25	0.50

KM# 105 10 CENTAVOS
Aluminum, 20.5 mm. **Obv:** National arms **Rev:** Value at center

Date	Mintage	F12	VF20	XF40	MS60	MS63
2007					0.25	0.50

KM# 99 25 CENTAVOS
5.00 g., Brass Plated Steel, 23.25 mm. **Obv:** National arms **Rev:** Value within circle **Edge:** Segmented reeding

Date	Mintage	F12	VF20	XF40	MS60	MS63
2002					0.25	0.50
2003					0.25	0.50
2003					0.25	0.50

KM# 104 25 CENTAVOS
Brass **Obv:** Arms **Rev:** Value at center **Rev. Legend:** EN DIOS CONFIAMOS

Date	Mintage	F12	VF20	XF40	MS60	MS63
2007					0.25	0.50

KM# 89 CORDOBA
6.20 g., Nickel Clad Steel, 25 mm. **Obv:** National emblem **Rev:** Value above sprigs within circle **Edge:** Reeded

Date	Mintage	F12	VF20	XF40	MS60	MS63
2002					1.00	1.50

KM# 101 CORDOBA
6.25 g., Nickel Clad Steel, 25 mm. **Obv:** National arms **Rev:**

Large value "1 **Rev. Legend:** EN DIOS CONFIAMOS **Edge:** Reeded

Date	Mintage	F12	VF20	XF40	MS60	MS63
2002	—	—	0.35	0.75	1.00	1.50
2007	—	—	0.35	0.75	1.00	1.50
2008	—	—	0.35	0.75	1.00	1.50
2009	—	—	0.35	0.75	1.00	1.50
2010	—	—	0.35	0.75	1.00	1.50

KM# 111 5 CORDOBAS
7.80 g., Nickel Plated Iron, 28 mm. **Obv:** Large value at center **Rev:** Sun over mountains

Date	Mintage	F12	VF20	XF40	MS60	MS63
2012	10,000,000	—	—	—	1.00	1.50

KM# 100 10 CORDOBAS
27.12 g., 0.925 Silver 0.8013 oz. ASW, 40 mm. **Subject:** Ibero-America **Obv:** National arms in circle of arms **Rev:** Sail boat **Edge:** Reeded

Date	Mintage	F12	VF20	XF40	MS60	MS63
2002	—	PF60 30.00		PF63 40.00		PF65 50.00

KM# 106 10 CORDOBAS
27.00 g., 0.925 Silver 0.7978 oz. ASW, 40 mm. **Obv:** National arms within circle of other state arms **Rev:** Leon Cathedral

Date	Mintage	F12	VF20	XF40	MS60	MS63
2005	—	PF60 40.00		PF63 50.00		PF65 60.00

KM# 102 10 CORDOBAS
8.47 g., Brass Plated Steel, 26.5 mm. **Obv:** National arms **Rev:** Value at upper left, circular latent image BCN below, statue of Andrés Castro at right **Edge Lettering:** B C N repeated 4 times

Date	Mintage	F12	VF20	XF40	MS60	MS63
2007	—	—	—	—	1.50	2.50

KM# 107 10 CORDOBAS
27.00 g., 0.925 Silver 0.7978 oz. ASW, 40 mm. **Obv:** National arms within circle of other national arms **Rev:** Baseball batter on field

Date	Mintage	F12	VF20	XF40	MS60	MS63
2007	—	PF60 40.00		PF63 50.00		PF65 60.00

KM# 108 10 CORDOBAS
27.00 g., 0.925 Silver 0.7978 oz. ASW, 40 mm. **Obv:** National arms within circle of other state arms **Rev:** One Cordoba coin of 1912 at center

Date	Mintage	F12	VF20	XF40	MS60	MS63
ND-2010	—	PF60 40.00		PF63 50.00		PF65 60.00

KM# 110a 50 CORDOBAS
31.10 g., 0.999 Silver 0.9925 oz. ASW, 35 mm. **Obv:** National arms **Rev:** Bird and flower in color

Date	Mintage	F12	VF20	XF40	MS60	MS63
2010	—	PF63 45.00		PF65 60.00		

KM# 109 50 CORDOBAS
40.00 g., 0.583 Gold 0.7449 oz. AGW, 40 mm. **Subject:** Central Bank, 50th Anniversary **Obv:** National arms **Rev:** Central Bank building on map of Nicaragua

Date	Mintage	F12	VF20	XF40	MS60	MS63
2010	—	PF65 1,100				

KM# 110 50 CORDOBAS
21.00 g., Copper-Nickel, 35 mm. **Obv:** National arms **Rev:** Bird and flower in color

Date	Mintage	F12	VF20	XF40	MS60	MS63
2010	—	—	—	—	—	15.00

KM# 110b 50 CORDOBAS
31.10 g., 0.999 Gold 0.9925 oz. AGW, 35 mm. **Obv:** National arms **Rev:** Bird and flower in color

Date	Mintage	F12	VF20	XF40	MS60	MS63
2010	—	PF65 1,750				

KM# 112 100 CORDOBAS
31.10 g., 0.900 Silver 0.8941 oz. ASW, 35 mm. **Obv:** Large value in center **Rev:** Sun over mountains

Date	Mintage	F12	VF20	XF40	MS60	MS63
2012	1,000	—	—	—	55.00	65.00

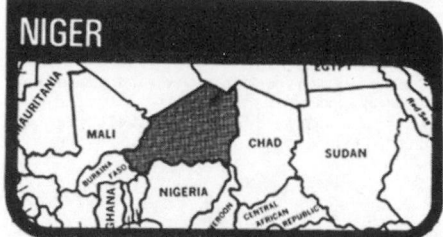

NIGER

The Republic of Niger, located in West Africa's Sahara region 1,000 miles (1,609 km.) from the Mediterranean shore, has an area of 489,191 sq. mi. (1,267,000 sq. km.) and a population of *7.4 million. Capital: Niamey. The economy is based on subsistence agriculture and raising livestock. Peanuts, peanut oil, and livestock are exported.

REPUBLIC
DECIMAL COINAGE

KM# 17 1000 FRANCS
20.00 g., 0.925 Silver 0.591 oz. ASW, 38.61 mm. **Obv:** Shield and flags **Rev:** Mecca pointer and amethyst crystal

Date	Mintage	F12	VF20	XF40	MS60	MS63
2012	1,000	PF63 100				

KM# 18 1000 FRANCS
20.00 g., 0.925 Silver 0.591 oz. ASW, 38.61 mm. **Subject:** African Hippo **Rev:** Hippo in eater with mouth wide open

Date	Mintage	F12	VF20	XF40	MS60	MS63
2012	500	PF65 125				

KM# 19 1000 FRANCS
20.00 g., 0.925 Silver 0.591 oz. ASW, 38.61 mm. **Obv:** Shield and crossed flags **Rev:** Stripped Jackel (Canis adustus) in color

Date	Mintage	F12	VF20	XF40	MS60	MS63
2012	1,000	PF65 125				

KM# 21 1000 FRANCS
Silver ASW **Subject:** The Flert by Mucha

Date	Mintage	F12	VF20	XF40	MS60	MS63
2012	—	PF65 100				

KM# 20 1000 FRANCS
20.00 g., Silver, 38.61 mm. **Subject:** Coyote - Canis Latrans

Date	Mintage	F12	VF20	XF40	MS60	MS63
2013	Est. 1000	PF65 75.00				

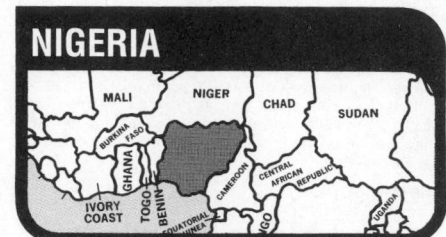

NIGERIA

The Federal Republic of Nigeria, situated on the Atlantic coast of West Africa has an area of 356,669 sq. mi. (923,770 sq. km.). Nigeria is a member of the Commonwealth of Nations. The President is the Head of State and the Head of Government.

FEDERAL REPUBLIC
DECIMAL COINAGE
100 Kobo = 1 Naira

KM# 17 KOBO
4.67 g., Brass, 23.2 mm. **Obv:** Arms with supporters **Rev:** Monkey musicians below value **Edge:** Reeded

Date	Mintage	F12	VF20	XF40	MS60	MS63
2003	—	—	—	—	15.00	20.00

KM# 13.3 50 KOBO
3.50 g., Nickel Clad Steel, 19.44 mm. **Obv:** Arms with supporters **Obv. Legend:** FEDERAL REPUBLIC OF NIGERIA **Rev:** Value at left, corn cob and stalk at right **Edge:** Plain **Note:** Reduced size.

Date	Mintage	F12	VF20	XF40	MS60	MS63
2006	—	—	—	—	1.00	1.35

KM# 18 NAIRA
5.43 g., Bi-Metallic, 21.48 mm. **Obv:** National arms **Obv. Legend:** FEDERAL REPUBLIC OF NIGERIA **Rev:** Small bust of Herbert Macaulay above value **Edge:** Plain

Date	Mintage	F12	VF20	XF40	MS60	MS63
2006	—	—	—	—	2.00	3.00

KM# 19 2 NAIRA
7.48 g., Bi-Metallic, 25.99 mm. **Obv:** National arms **Obv. Legend:** FEDERAL REPUBLIC OF NIGERIA **Rev:** Large value, National Assembly in background **Edge:** Coarse reeding

Date	Mintage	F12	VF20	XF40	MS60	MS63
2006	—	—	—	—	3.00	4.00

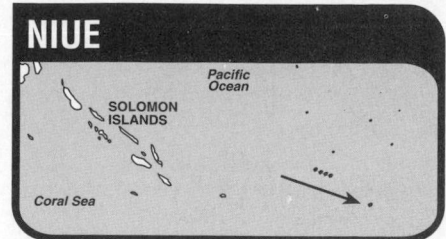

Niue, or Savage Island, a dependent state of New Zealand, ruled by the Queen of England, is located in the Pacific Ocean east of Tonga and southeast of Samoa. The size is 100 sq. mi. (260 sq. km.) with a population of approx. 1,500. Chief village and port is Alofi. Vanilla, noni and taro are exported.

MINT MARK
PM - Pobjoy Mint

NEW ZEALAND DEPENDENT STATE
DECIMAL COINAGE

KM# 193 5 CENTS
4.30 g., Copper Plated Bronze, 19 mm. **Ruler:** Elizabeth II **Obv:** Head right **Rev:** Two whales

Date	Mintage	F12	VF20	XF40	MS60	MS63
2009	—	—	—	—	1.00	2.00
2010	—	—	—	—	1.00	2.00

KM# 194 10 CENTS
5.80 g., Copper Plated Bronze, 22 mm. **Ruler:** Elizabeth II **Obv:** Head right **Rev:** Coconut crab **Edge:** Reeded

Date	Mintage	F12	VF20	XF40	MS60	MS63
2009	—	—	—	—	1.50	2.00
2010	—	—	—	—	1.50	2.00

KM# 195 20 CENTS
7.30 g., Nickel Plated Bronze, 25 mm. **Ruler:** Elizabeth II **Obv:** Head right **Rev:** Two scuba divers and coral

Date	Mintage	F12	VF20	XF40	MS60	MS63
2009	—	—	—	—	2.00	4.00
2010	—	—	—	—	2.00	4.00

KM# 606 50 CENTS
15.55 g., 0.999 Silver 0.4962 oz. ASW, 35 mm. **Ruler:** Elizabeth II **Subject:** Olympics **Rev:** Boxers, ancient and modern

Date	Mintage	F12	VF20	XF40	MS60	MS63
2004-2008 (2004)	—	PF65 40.00				

KM# 607 50 CENTS
15.50 g., 0.999 Silver 0.4946 oz. ASW, 35 mm. **Ruler:** Elizabeth II **Subject:** Olympics **Rev:** Long Jumpers - ancient and modern

Date	Mintage	F12	VF20	XF40	MS60	MS63
2004-2008 (2004)	—	PF65 40.00				

KM# 608 50 CENTS
15.50 g., 0.999 Silver 0.4946 oz. ASW, 35 mm. **Ruler:** Elizabeth II **Subject:** Olympics **Rev:** Shot Put, ancient and modern

Date	Mintage	F12	VF20	XF40	MS60	MS63
2004-2008 (2004)	—	PF65 40.00				

KM# 609 50 CENTS
15.50 g., 0.999 Silver 0.4946 oz. ASW, 35 mm. **Ruler:** Elizabeth II **Subject:** Olympics **Rev:** Archer, ancient and modern

Date	Mintage	F12	VF20	XF40	MS60	MS63
2004-2008 (2004)	—	PF65 40.00				

KM# 610 50 CENTS
15.50 g., 0.999 Silver 0.4946 oz. ASW, 35 mm. **Ruler:** Elizabeth II **Subject:** Olympics **Rev:** Equestrian - ancient and modern views

Date	Mintage	F12	VF20	XF40	MS60	MS63
2004-2008 (2004)	—	PF65 40.00				

KM# 611 50 CENTS
15.50 g., 0.999 Silver 0.4946 oz. ASW, 35 mm. **Ruler:** Elizabeth II **Subject:** Olympics **Rev:** Discus - ancient and modern views

Date	Mintage	F12	VF20	XF40	MS60	MS63
2004-2008 (2004)	—	PF65 40.00				

KM# 612 50 CENTS
15.50 g., 0.999 Silver 0.4946 oz. ASW, 35 mm. **Ruler:** Elizabeth II **Subject:** Olympics **Rev:** Track - ancient and modern views

Date	Mintage	F12	VF20	XF40	MS60	MS63
2004-2008 (2004)	—	PF65 40.00				

KM# 613 50 CENTS
15.50 g., 0.999 Silver 0.4946 oz. ASW, 35 mm. **Ruler:** Elizabeth II **Subject:** Olympics **Rev:** Wrestlers - ancient and modern views

Date	Mintage	F12	VF20	XF40	MS60	MS63
2004-2008 (2004)	—	PF65 40.00				

KM# 614 50 CENTS
15.50 g., 0.999 Silver 0.4946 oz. ASW, 35 mm. **Ruler:** Elizabeth II **Subject:** Olympics **Rev:** Javelin thrower - ancient and modern views

Date	Mintage	F12	VF20	XF40	MS60	MS63
2004-2008 (2004)	—	PF65 40.00				

KM# 615 50 CENTS
15.50 g., 0.999 Silver 0.4946 oz. ASW, 35 mm. **Ruler:** Elizabeth II **Subject:** Olympics **Rev:** Soccer - ancient and modern view

Date	Mintage	F12	VF20	XF40	MS60	MS63
2004-2008 (2004)	—	PF65 40.00				

KM# 616 50 CENTS
15.50 g., 0.999 Silver 0.4946 oz. ASW, 35 mm. **Ruler:** Elizabeth II **Subject:** Olympics **Rev:** Field Hockey - ancient and modern views

Date	Mintage	F12	VF20	XF40	MS60	MS63
2004-2008 (2004)	—	PF65 40.00				

KM# 263 50 CENTS
15.55 g., 0.999 Silver 0.4962 oz. ASW, 35 mm. **Ruler:** Elizabeth II **Series:** Year of the Rooster **Rev:** Multicolor rooster standing right, sunrise

Date	Mintage	F12	VF20	XF40	MS60	MS63
2005	—	PF65 30.00				

KM# 292 50 CENTS
15.55 g., 0.999 Silver 0.4962 oz. ASW, 35 mm. **Ruler:** Elizabeth II **Subject:** Year of the Dog **Rev:** Multicolor dog

Date	Mintage	F12	VF20	XF40	MS60	MS63
2005	—	PF65 35.00				

KM# 189 50 CENTS
15.50 g., 0.999 Silver 0.4946 oz. ASW, 28 mm. **Ruler:** Elizabeth II **Subject:** Year of the Pig **Obv:** Head right **Rev:** Multicolor pig

Date	Mintage	F12	VF20	XF40	MS60	MS63
2007	—	PF65 50.00				

KM# 196 50 CENTS
9.30 g., Nickel Plated Bronze, 28 mm. **Ruler:** Elizabeth II **Obv:** Head right **Rev:** Outrigger canoe **Edge:** Segmented reeding

Date	Mintage	F12	VF20	XF40	MS60	MS63
2009	—	—	—	—	5.00	7.50
2010	—	—	—	—	5.00	7.50

KM# 1105 250 CENTS
3.11 g., 0.999 Gold 0.0992 oz. AGW, 16 mm. **Ruler:** Elizabeth II **Subject:** Family of Rohans: Camille de Rohan

Date	Mintage	F12	VF20	XF40	MS60	MS63
2013	Est. 500	PF65 200				

KM# 1106 250 CENTS
3.11 g., 0.999 Gold 0.0992 oz. AGW, 16 mm. **Ruler:** Elizabeth II **Subject:** Family of Rohans: Henri II de Rohan

Date	Mintage	F12	VF20	XF40	MS60	MS63
2013	Est. 500	PF65 200				

KM# 1107 250 CENTS
3.11 g., 0.999 Gold 0.0992 oz. AGW, 16 mm. **Ruler:** Elizabeth II **Subject:** Family of Rohans: Louis Rene de Rohan

Date	Mintage	F12	VF20	XF40	MS60	MS63
2013	Est. 500	PF65 200				

KM# 1108 250 CENTS
3.11 g., 0.999 Gold 0.0992 oz. AGW, 16 mm. **Ruler:** Elizabeth II **Subject:** Family of Rohans: Marie de Rohan

Date	Mintage	F12	VF20	XF40	MS60	MS63
2013	Est. 500	PF65 200				

KM# 786 2012 CENTS
31.10 g., 0.999 Silver 0.9925 oz. ASW, 30.5x5.5 mm. **Ruler:**
Elizabeth II **Obv:** Queen's head at left, Titanic sailing left **Rev:**
Ship's bell and other items **Shape:** oval

Date	Mintage	F12	VF20	XF40	MS60	MS63
2012	—	PF65 100				

KM# 786a 2012 CENTS
31.10 g., 0.999 Silver 0.9925 oz. ASW, 31.5x5.5 mm. **Ruler:**
Elizabeth II **Obv:** Queen's head at left, Titanic sailing left, sky in color **Rev:** Ship's bell and other items **Shape:** oval

Date	Mintage	F12	VF20	XF40	MS60	MS63
2012	Est. 200	PF65 100				

KM# 462 1/33 DOLLAR
42.50 g., 0.999 Silver 1.3563 oz. ASW, 41.7x40 mm. **Ruler:**
Elizabeth II **Rev:** Sistine Chapel Corner featuring Haman's punishment

Date	Mintage	F12	VF20	XF40	MS60	MS63
2010	500	PF65 75.00				

KM# 463 1/33 DOLLAR
42.50 g., 0.999 Silver 1.3563 oz. ASW, 41.7x40 mm. **Ruler:**
Elizabeth II **Rev:** Sistine Chapel Arch featuring the Prophet Jonah

Date	Mintage	F12	VF20	XF40	MS60	MS63
2010	500	PF65 75.00				

KM# 464 1/33 DOLLAR
42.50 g., 0.999 Silver 1.3563 oz. ASW, 41.7x40 mm. **Ruler:**
Elizabeth II **Rev:** Sistine Chapel Corner Spandrel featuring the Brazen Serpent

Date	Mintage	F12	VF20	XF40	MS60	MS63
2010	500	PF65 75.00				

KM# 465 1/33 DOLLAR
26.80 g., 0.999 Silver 0.8552 oz. ASW, 29x36.1 mm. **Ruler:**
Elizabeth II **Rev:** Sistine Chapel Arch featuring the Prophet Jeremiah

Date	Mintage	F12	VF20	XF40	MS60	MS63
2010	500	PF65 60.00				

KM# 466 1/33 DOLLAR
26.80 g., 0.999 Silver 0.8552 oz. ASW, 29x36.1 mm. **Ruler:**
Elizabeth II **Rev:** Sistine Chapel Arch with Salmon

Date	Mintage	F12	VF20	XF40	MS60	MS63
2010	500	PF65 60.00				

KM# 467 1/33 DOLLAR
26.80 g., 0.999 Silver 0.8552 oz. ASW, 29x36.1 mm. **Ruler:**
Elizabeth II **Rev:** Sistine Chapel Arch with Persian Sibyl

Date	Mintage	F12	VF20	XF40	MS60	MS63
2010	500	PF65 60.00				

KM# 468 1/33 DOLLAR
21.00 g., 0.999 Silver 0.6701 oz. ASW, 23x36.1 mm. **Ruler:**
Elizabeth II **Rev:** Sistine Chapel Arch with Roboam

Date	Mintage	F12	VF20	XF40	MS60	MS63
2010	500	PF65 45.00				

KM# 469 1/33 DOLLAR
26.80 g., 0.999 Silver 0.8552 oz. ASW, 29x36.1 mm. **Ruler:**
Elizabeth II **Rev:** Sistine Chapel Arch with Prophet Ezekiel

Date	Mintage	F12	VF20	XF40	MS60	MS63
2010	500	PF65 60.00				

KM# 470 1/33 DOLLAR
26.80 g., 0.999 Silver 0.8552 oz. ASW, 29x36.1 mm. **Ruler:**
Elizabeth II **Rev:** Sistine Chapel Arch with Ozias

Date	Mintage	F12	VF20	XF40	MS60	MS63
2010	500	PF65 60.00				

KM# 471 1/33 DOLLAR
21.00 g., 0.999 Silver 0.6701 oz. ASW, 23x36.1 mm. **Ruler:**
Elizabeth II **Rev:** Sistine Chapel Arch with Erythraean Sibyl

Date	Mintage	F12	VF20	XF40	MS60	MS63
2010	500	PF65 45.00				

KM# 472 1/33 DOLLAR
26.80 g., 0.999 Silver 0.8552 oz. ASW, 29x36.1 mm. **Ruler:**
Elizabeth II **Rev:** Sistine Chapel Arch with Zorobabel

Date	Mintage	F12	VF20	XF40	MS60	MS63
2010	500	PF65 55.00				

KM# 473 1/33 DOLLAR
21.00 g., 0.999 Silver 0.6701 oz. ASW, 23x36.1 mm. **Ruler:**
Elizabeth II **Rev:** Sistine Chapel Arch with Prophel Joel

Date	Mintage	F12	VF20	XF40	MS60	MS63
2010	500	PF65 45.00				

KM# 474 1/33 DOLLAR
35.50 g., 0.999 Silver 1.1329 oz. ASW, 29x47.8 mm. **Ruler:**
Elizabeth II **Rev:** Sistine Chapel vault depicting Genesis creation story of Separation of Light from Darkness

Date	Mintage	F12	VF20	XF40	MS60	MS63
2010	500	PF65 75.00				

KM# 475 1/33 DOLLAR
35.50 g., 0.999 Silver 1.1329 oz. ASW, 29x47.8 mm. **Ruler:**
Elizabeth II **Rev:** Sistine Chapel vault depicting Genesis story of Creation of Sun and Moon

Date	Mintage	F12	VF20	XF40	MS60	MS63
2010	500	PF65 75.00				

KM# 476 1/33 DOLLAR
35.50 g., 0.999 Silver 1.1329 oz. ASW, 29x47.8 mm. **Ruler:**
Elizabeth II **Rev:** Sistine Chapel vault depicting Genesis creation story of the Separation of Land and Water

Date	Mintage	F12	VF20	XF40	MS60	MS63
2010	500	PF65 75.00				

KM# 477 1/33 DOLLAR
28.00 g., 0.999 Silver 0.8935 oz. ASW, 23x47.8 mm. **Ruler:**
Elizabeth II **Rev:** Sistine Chapel vault depicting Genesis story of the Creation of Adam

Date	Mintage	F12	VF20	XF40	MS60	MS63
2010	500	PF65 60.00				

KM# 478 1/33 DOLLAR
35.50 g., 0.999 Silver 1.1329 oz. ASW, 29x47.8 mm. **Ruler:**
Elizabeth II **Rev:** Sistine Chapel vault depicting the story of the Creation of Eve

Date	Mintage	F12	VF20	XF40	MS60	MS63
2010	500	PF65 75.00				

KM# 479 1/33 DOLLAR
28.00 g., 0.999 Silver 0.8935 oz. ASW, 23x47.8 mm. **Ruler:**
Elizabeth II **Rev:** Sistine Chapel vault depicting the Genesis story of Original Sin

Date	Mintage	F12	VF20	XF40	MS60	MS63
2010	500	PF65 60.00				

KM# 480 1/33 DOLLAR
35.50 g., 0.999 Silver 1.1329 oz. ASW, 29x47.7 mm. **Ruler:**
Elizabeth II **Rev:** Sistine Chapel vault depicting the Genesis story of the Sacrifice of Noah

Date	Mintage	F12	VF20	XF40	MS60	MS63
2010	500	PF65 75.00				

KM# 481 1/33 DOLLAR
28.00 g., 0.999 Silver 0.8935 oz. ASW, 23x47.8 mm. **Ruler:**
Elizabeth II **Rev:** Sistine Chapel vault depicting the Genesis story of the Flood

Date	Mintage	F12	VF20	XF40	MS60	MS63
2010	500	PF65 60.00				

KM# 482 1/33 DOLLAR
35.50 g., 0.999 Silver 1.1329 oz. ASW, 29x47.8 mm. **Ruler:**
Elizabeth II **Rev:** Sistine Chapel vault depicting the Genesis story of the Drunkenness of Noah

Date	Mintage	F12	VF20	XF40	MS60	MS63
2010	500	PF65 75.00				

KM# 483 1/33 DOLLAR
26.80 g., 0.999 Silver 0.8552 oz. ASW, 29x36.1 mm. **Ruler:**
Elizabeth II **Rev:** Sistine Chapel Arch depicting the Libyan Sibyl

Date	Mintage	F12	VF20	XF40	MS60	MS63
2010	500	PF65 60.00				

KM# 484 1/33 DOLLAR
26.80 g., 0.999 Silver 0.8552 oz. ASW, 29x36.1 mm. **Ruler:**
Elizabeth II **Rev:** Sistine Chapel Arch depicting Jesse

Date	Mintage	F12	VF20	XF40	MS60	MS63
2010	500	PF65 60.00				

KM# 485 1/33 DOLLAR
26.80 g., 0.999 Silver 0.8552 oz. ASW, 29x36.1 mm. **Ruler:**
Elizabeth II **Rev:** Sistine Chapel Arch depicting the Prophet Daniel

Date	Mintage	F12	VF20	XF40	MS60	MS63
2010	500	PF65 60.00				

KM# 486 1/33 DOLLAR
21.00 g., 0.999 Silver 0.6701 oz. ASW, 23x36.1 mm. **Ruler:**
Elizabeth II **Rev:** Sistine Chapel Arch depicting Asa

Date	Mintage	F12	VF20	XF40	MS60	MS63
2010	500	PF65 45.00				

KM# 487 1/33 DOLLAR
26.80 g., 0.999 Silver 0.8552 oz. ASW, 29x36.1 mm. **Ruler:**
Elizabeth II **Rev:** Sistine Chapel Arch depicting the Cumaean Sibyl

Date	Mintage	F12	VF20	XF40	MS60	MS63
2010	500	PF65 60.00				

KM# 488 1/33 DOLLAR
21.00 g., 0.999 Silver 0.6701 oz. ASW, 23x36.1 mm. **Ruler:**
Elizabeth II **Rev:** Sistine Chapel Arch depicting Ezxekias

Date	Mintage	F12	VF20	XF40	MS60	MS63
2010	500	PF65 45.00				

KM# 489 1/33 DOLLAR
26.80 g., 0.999 Silver 0.8552 oz. ASW, 29x.36.1 mm. **Ruler:**
Elizabeth II **Rev:** Sistine Chapel Arch depicting the Prophet Isiah

Date	Mintage	F12	VF20	XF40	MS60	MS63
2010	500	PF65 60.00				

KM# 490 1/33 DOLLAR
26.80 g., 0.999 Silver 0.8552 oz. ASW, 29x36.1 mm. **Ruler:**
Elizabeth II **Rev:** Sistine Chapel Arch depicting Josias

Date	Mintage	F12	VF20	XF40	MS60	MS63
2010	500	PF65 60.00				

KM# 491 1/33 DOLLAR
21.00 g., 0.999 Silver 0.6701 oz. ASW, 23x36.1 mm. **Ruler:**
Elizabeth II **Rev:** Sistine Chapel Arch depicting the Delphic Sibyl

Date	Mintage	F12	VF20	XF40	MS60	MS63
2010	500	PF65 45.00				

KM# 492 1/33 DOLLAR
42.50 g., 0.999 Silver 1.3563 oz. ASW, 41.7x40 mm. **Ruler:**
Elizabeth II **Rev:** Sistine Chapel corner spandrel depicting David & Goliath

Date	Mintage	F12	VF20	XF40	MS60	MS63
2010	500	PF65 75.00				

KM# 493 1/33 DOLLAR
42.50 g., 0.999 Silver 1.3563 oz. ASW, 41.7x40 mm. **Ruler:**
Elizabeth II **Rev:** Sistine Chapel Arch vault depicting the Prophet Zechariah

Date	Mintage	F12	VF20	XF40	MS60	MS63
2010	500	PF65 75.00				

KM# 494 1/33 DOLLAR
42.50 g., 0.999 Silver 1.3563 oz. ASW, 41.7x40 mm. **Ruler:**
Elizabeth II **Rev:** Sistine Chapel corner spandrel depicting Judith & Holofornes

Date	Mintage	F12	VF20	XF40	MS60	MS63
2010	500	PF65 75.00				

KM# 526 1/24 DOLLAR
42.50 g., 0.999 Silver 1.3563 oz. ASW, 41.7x40 mm. **Ruler:** Elizabeth II **Obv:** Head with tiara right **Rev:** Partial DaVinci drawing

Date	Mintage	F12	VF20	XF40	MS60	MS63
2011	500	PF65 75.00				

KM# 527 1/24 DOLLAR
42.50 g., 0.999 Silver 1.3563 oz. ASW, 41.7x40 mm. **Ruler:** Elizabeth II **Obv:** Head with tiara right **Rev:** Partial DaVinci drawing

Date	Mintage	F12	VF20	XF40	MS60	MS63
2011	500	PF65 75.00				

KM# 528 1/24 DOLLAR
42.50 g., 0.999 Silver 1.3563 oz. ASW, 41.7x40 mm. **Ruler:** Elizabeth II **Obv:** Head with tiara right **Rev:** Partial DaVinci drawing

Date	Mintage	F12	VF20	XF40	MS60	MS63
2011	500	PF65 75.00				

KM# 529 1/24 DOLLAR
42.50 g., 0.999 Silver 1.3563 oz. ASW, 41.7x40 mm. **Ruler:** Elizabeth II **Obv:** Head with tiara right **Rev:** Partial DaVinci drawing

Date	Mintage	F12	VF20	XF40	MS60	MS63
2011	500	PF65 75.00				

KM# 530 1/24 DOLLAR
42.50 g., 0.999 Silver 1.3563 oz. ASW, 41.7x40 mm. **Ruler:** Elizabeth II **Obv:** Head with tiara right **Rev:** Partial DaVinci drawing

Date	Mintage	F12	VF20	XF40	MS60	MS63
2011	500	PF65 75.00				

KM# 531 1/24 DOLLAR
42.50 g., 0.999 Silver 1.3563 oz. ASW, 41.7x40 mm. **Ruler:** Elizabeth II **Obv:** Head with tiara right **Rev:** Partial DaVinci drawing

Date	Mintage	F12	VF20	XF40	MS60	MS63
2011	500	PF65 75.00				

KM# 534 1/24 DOLLAR
42.50 g., 0.999 Silver 1.3563 oz. ASW, 41.7x40 mm. **Ruler:** Elizabeth II **Obv:** Head with tiara right **Rev:** Partial DaVinci drawing

Date	Mintage	F12	VF20	XF40	MS60	MS63
2011	500	PF65 75.00				

KM# 532 1/24 DOLLAR
42.50 g., 0.999 Silver 1.3563 oz. ASW, 41.7x40 mm. **Ruler:** Elizabeth II **Obv:** Head with tiara right **Rev:** Partial DaVinci drawing

Date	Mintage	F12	VF20	XF40	MS60	MS63
2011	500	PF65 75.00				

KM# 533 1/24 DOLLAR
42.50 g., 0.999 Silver 1.3563 oz. ASW **Ruler:** Elizabeth II **Obv:** Head in tiara right **Rev:** Partial DaVinci drawing

Date	Mintage	F12	VF20	XF40	MS60	MS63
2011	500	PF65 75.00				

KM# 535 1/24 DOLLAR
42.50 g., 0.999 Silver 1.3563 oz. ASW, 41.7x40 mm. **Ruler:** Elizabeth II **Obv:** Head with tiara right **Rev:** Partial DaVinci drawing

Date	Mintage	F12	VF20	XF40	MS60	MS63
2011	500	PF65 75.00				

KM# 536 1/24 DOLLAR
42.50 g., 0.999 Silver 1.3563 oz. ASW, 41.7x40 mm. **Ruler:** Elizabeth II **Obv:** Head in tiara right **Rev:** Partial DaVinci drawing

Date	Mintage	F12	VF20	XF40	MS60	MS63
2011	500	PF65 75.00				

KM# 537 1/24 DOLLAR
42.50 g., 0.999 Silver 1.3563 oz. ASW, 41.7x40 mm. **Ruler:** Elizabeth II **Obv:** Head with tiara right **Rev:** Partial DaVinci drawing

Date	Mintage	F12	VF20	XF40	MS60	MS63
2011	500	PF65 75.00				

KM# 538 1/24 DOLLAR
42.50 g., 0.999 Silver 1.3563 oz. ASW, 41.7x40 mm. **Ruler:** Elizabeth II **Obv:** Head with tiara right **Rev:** Partial DaVinci drawing

Date	Mintage	F12	VF20	XF40	MS60	MS63
2011	500	PF65 75.00				

KM# 539 1/24 DOLLAR
42.50 g., 0.999 Silver 1.3563 oz. ASW, 41.7x40 mm. **Ruler:** Elizabeth II **Obv:** Head with tiara right **Rev:** Partial DaVinci drawing

Date	Mintage	F12	VF20	XF40	MS60	MS63
2011	500	PF65 75.00				

KM# 540 1/24 DOLLAR
42.50 g., 0.999 Silver 1.3563 oz. ASW, 41.7x40 mm. **Ruler:** Elizabeth II **Obv:** Head with tiara right **Rev:** Partial DaVinci drawing

Date	Mintage	F12	VF20	XF40	MS60	MS63
2011	500	PF65 75.00				

KM# 541 1/24 DOLLAR
42.50 g., 0.999 Silver 1.3563 oz. ASW, 41.7x40 mm. **Ruler:** Elizabeth II **Obv:** Head with tiara right **Rev:** Partial DaVinci drawing

Date	Mintage	F12	VF20	XF40	MS60	MS63
2011	500	PF65 75.00				

KM# 542 1/24 DOLLAR
42.50 g., 0.999 Silver 1.3563 oz. ASW, 41.7x40 mm. **Ruler:** Elizabeth II **Obv:** Head with tiara right **Rev:** Partial DaVinci drawing

Date	Mintage	F12	VF20	XF40	MS60	MS63
2011	500	PF65 75.00				

KM# 543 1/24 DOLLAR
42.50 g., 0.999 Silver 1.3563 oz. ASW, 41.7x40 mm. **Ruler:** Elizabeth II **Obv:** Head with tiara right **Rev:** Partial DaVinci drawing

Date	Mintage	F12	VF20	XF40	MS60	MS63
2011	500	PF65 75.00				

KM# 544 1/24 DOLLAR
42.50 g., 0.999 Silver 1.3563 oz. ASW, 41.7x40 mm. **Ruler:** Elizabeth II **Obv:** Head with tiara right **Rev:** Partial DaVinci drawing

Date	Mintage	F12	VF20	XF40	MS60	MS63
2011	500	PF65 75.00				

KM# 545 1/24 DOLLAR
42.50 g., 0.999 Silver 1.3563 oz. ASW, 41.7x40 mm. **Ruler:** Elizabeth II **Obv:** Head with tiara right **Rev:** Partial DaVinci drawing

Date	Mintage	F12	VF20	XF40	MS60	MS63
2011	500	PF65 75.00				

KM# 546 1/24 DOLLAR
42.50 g., 0.999 Silver 1.3563 oz. ASW, 41.7x40 mm. **Ruler:** Elizabeth II **Obv:** Head with tiara right **Rev:** Partial DaVinci drawing

Date	Mintage	F12	VF20	XF40	MS60	MS63
2011	500	PF65 75.00				

KM# 547 1/24 DOLLAR
42.50 g., 0.999 Silver 1.3563 oz. ASW, 41.7x40 mm. **Ruler:** Elizabeth II **Obv:** Head with tiara right **Rev:** Partial DaVinci drawing

Date	Mintage	F12	VF20	XF40	MS60	MS63
2011	500	PF65 75.00				

KM# 548 1/24 DOLLAR
42.50 g., 0.999 Silver 1.3563 oz. ASW, 41.7x40 mm. **Ruler:** Elizabeth II **Obv:** Head with tiara right **Rev:** Partial DaVinci drawing

Date	Mintage	F12	VF20	XF40	MS60	MS63
2011	500	PF65 75.00				

KM# 549 1/24 DOLLAR
42.50 g., 0.999 Silver 1.3563 oz. ASW, 41.7x40 mm. **Ruler:** Elizabeth II **Obv:** Head with tiara right **Rev:** Partial DaVinci drawing

Date	Mintage	F12	VF20	XF40	MS60	MS63
2011	500	PF65 75.00				

KM# 624 1/14 DOLLAR
15.00 g., 0.999 Silver 0.4787 oz. ASW, 29x48 mm. **Ruler:** Elizabeth II **Obv:** Head with tiara right **Rev:** Two scenes from the Passion of Christ **Shape:** Vertical rectangle

Date	Mintage	F12	VF20	XF40	MS60	MS63
2001	250	PF65 45.00				

KM# 625 1/14 DOLLAR
15.00 g., 0.999 Silver 0.4787 oz. ASW, 29x48 mm. **Ruler:** Elizabeth II **Obv:** Head with tiara right **Rev:** Two scenes from the Passion of Christ **Shape:** Vertical rectangle

Date	Mintage	F12	VF20	XF40	MS60	MS63
2011	250	PF65 45.00				

KM# 626 1/14 DOLLAR
15.00 g., 0.999 Silver 0.4787 oz. ASW, 29x48 mm. **Ruler:** Elizabeth II **Obv:** Head in tiara right **Rev:** Two scenes from the Passion of Christ **Shape:** Vertical rectangle

Date	Mintage	F12	VF20	XF40	MS60	MS63
2011	250	PF65 45.00				

KM# 627 1/14 DOLLAR
15.00 g., 0.999 Silver 0.4787 oz. ASW, 36x48 mm. **Ruler:** Elizabeth II **Obv:** Head in tiara right **Rev:** The Cruxifixion of Christ **Shape:** Vertical rectangle

Date	Mintage	F12	VF20	XF40	MS60	MS63
2011	250	PF65 50.00				

KM# 628 1/14 DOLLAR
15.00 g., 0.999 Silver 0.4787 oz. ASW, 29x48 mm. **Ruler:** Elizabeth II **Obv:** Head with tiara right **Rev:** Two scenes form the Passion of Christ **Shape:** Vertical rectangle

Date	Mintage	F12	VF20	XF40	MS60	MS63
2011	250	PF66 45.00				

KM# 629 1/14 DOLLAR
15.00 g., 0.999 Silver 0.4787 oz. ASW, 29x48 mm. **Ruler:** Elizabeth II **Obv:** Head with tiara right **Rev:** Two scenes from the Passion of Christ **Shape:** Vertical rectangle

Date	Mintage	F12	VF20	XF40	MS60	MS63
2011	250	PF65 40.00				

KM# 630 1/14 DOLLAR
15.00 g., 0.999 Silver 0.4787 oz. ASW, 29x48 mm. **Ruler:** Elizabeth II **Obv:** Head with tiara right **Rev:** Two scenes from the Passion of Christ **Shape:** Vertical rectangle

Date	Mintage	F12	VF20	XF40	MS60	MS63
2011	250	PF65 45.00				

KM# 631 1/14 DOLLAR
15.00 g., 0.999 Silver 0.4787 oz. ASW, 29x48 mm. **Ruler:** Elizabeth II **Obv:** Head with tiara right **Rev:** Two scenes from the Passion of Christ **Shape:** Vertical rectangle

Date	Mintage	F12	VF20	XF40	MS60	MS63
2011	250	PF65 45.00				

KM# 632 1/14 DOLLAR
15.00 g., 0.999 Silver 0.4787 oz. ASW, 29x48 mm. **Ruler:** Elizabeth II **Obv:** Head with tiara right **Rev:** Two scenes from the Passion of Christ **Shape:** Vertical rectangle

Date	Mintage	F12	VF20	XF40	MS60	MS63
2011	250	PF65 45.00				

KM# 633 1/14 DOLLAR
15.00 g., 0.999 Silver 0.4787 oz. ASW, 29x48 mm. **Ruler:** Elizabeth II **Obv:** Head with tiara right **Rev:** Two scenes from the Passion of Christ **Shape:** Vertical rectangle

Date	Mintage	F12	VF20	XF40	MS60	MS63
2011	250	PF65 45.00				

KM# 634 1/14 DOLLAR
15.00 g., 0.999 Silver 0.4787 oz. ASW, 36x48 mm. **Ruler:** Elizabeth II **Obv:** Head with tiara right **Rev:** Two scenes from the Passion of Christ **Shape:** Vertical rectangle

Date	Mintage	F12	VF20	XF40	MS60	MS63
2011	250	PF65 50.00				

KM# 635 1/14 DOLLAR
15.00 g., 0.999 Silver 0.4787 oz. ASW, 29x48 mm. **Ruler:** Elizabeth II **Obv:** Head with tiara right **Rev:** Two scenes from the Passion of Christ **Shape:** Vertical rectangle

Date	Mintage	F12	VF20	XF40	MS60	MS63
2011	250	PF65 45.00				

KM# 636 1/14 DOLLAR
15.00 g., 0.999 Silver 0.4787 oz. ASW, 29x48 mm. **Ruler:** Elizabeth II **Obv:** Head with tiara right **Rev:** Two scenes from the Passion of Christ **Shape:** Vertical rectangle

Date	Mintage	F12	VF20	XF40	MS60	MS63
2011	250	PF65 45.00				

KM# 637 1/14 DOLLAR
15.00 g., 0.999 Silver 0.4787 oz. ASW, 29x48 mm. **Ruler:** Elizabeth II **Obv:** Head with tiara right **Rev:** Two scenes from the Passion of Christ **Shape:** Vertical rectangle

Date	Mintage	F12	VF20	XF40	MS60	MS63
2011	250	PF65 45.00				

KM# 574 1/9 DOLLAR
25.40 g., 0.999 Silver 0.8106 oz. ASW, 24x41 mm. **Ruler:** Elizabeth II **Subject:** Fragment of Villa of Mysteries fresco **Shape:** Vertical rectangle

Date	Mintage	F12	VF20	XF40	MS60	MS63
2011	250	PF65 60.00				

KM# 575 1/9 DOLLAR
25.40 g., 0.999 Silver 0.8106 oz. ASW, 24x41 mm. **Ruler:** Elizabeth II **Subject:** Villa of Mysteries Fresco

Date	Mintage	F12	VF20	XF40	MS60	MS63
2011	250	PF65 60.00				

KM# 576 1/9 DOLLAR
33.80 g., 0.999 Silver 1.0786 oz. ASW, 32x41 mm. **Ruler:** Elizabeth II **Subject:** Villa of Mysteries fresco

Date	Mintage	F12	VF20	XF40	MS60	MS63
2011	250	PF65 60.00				

KM# 577 1/9 DOLLAR
33.80 g., 0.999 Silver 1.0786 oz. ASW, 32x41 mm. **Ruler:** Elizabeth II **Subject:** Villa of Mysteries fresco

Date	Mintage	F12	VF20	XF40	MS60	MS63
2011	250	PF65 60.00				

KM# 578 1/9 DOLLAR
50.70 g., 0.999 Silver 1.6179 oz. ASW, 48x41 mm. **Ruler:** Elizabeth II **Subject:** Villa of Mysteries fresco

Date	Mintage	F12	VF20	XF40	MS60	MS63
2011	250	PF65 85.00				

KM# 579 1/9 DOLLAR
50.70 g., 0.999 Silver 1.6179 oz. ASW, 48x41 mm. **Ruler:** Elizabeth II **Subject:** Villa of Mysteries fresco

Date	Mintage	F12	VF20	XF40	MS60	MS63
2011	250	PF65 85.00				

KM# 580 1/9 DOLLAR
33.80 g., 0.999 Silver 1.0786 oz. ASW, 32x41 mm. **Ruler:** Elizabeth II **Subject:** Villa of Mysteries fresco

Date	Mintage	F12	VF20	XF40	MS60	MS63
2011	250	PF65 60.00				

KM# 581 1/9 DOLLAR
50.70 g., 0.999 Silver 1.6179 oz. ASW, 48x41 mm. **Ruler:** Elizabeth II **Subject:** Villa of Mysteries fresco

Date	Mintage	F12	VF20	XF40	MS60	MS63
2011	250	PF65 85.00				

KM# 582 1/9 DOLLAR
50.70 g., 0.999 Silver 1.6179 oz. ASW, 48x41 mm. **Ruler:** Elizabeth II **Subject:** Villa of Mysteries fresco

Date	Mintage	F12	VF20	XF40	MS60	MS63
2011	250	PF65 85.00				

KM# 123 DOLLAR
28.28 g., Copper-Nickel, 38.6 mm. **Ruler:** Elizabeth II **Subject:** Snoopy as an Ace **Obv:** Crowned head right **Rev:** Snoopy flying his dog house **Edge:** Reeded

Date	Mintage	F12	VF20	XF40	MS60	MS63
2001	100,000	—	—	—	3.00	4.50

KM# 128 DOLLAR
28.28 g., Copper-Nickel, 38.6 mm. **Ruler:** Elizabeth II **Series:** Pokemon **Obv:** Crowned shield within sprigs **Rev:** Bulbasaur **Edge:** Reeded

Date	Mintage	F12	VF20	XF40	MS60	MS63
2001	100,000	—	—	—	12.00	14.00

KM# 129 DOLLAR
7.77 g., 0.999 Silver 0.248 oz. ASW, 22 mm. **Ruler:** Elizabeth II **Series:** Pokemon **Obv:** Crowned shield within sprigs **Rev:** Bulbasaur **Edge:** Reeded

Date	Mintage	F12	VF20	XF40	MS60	MS63
2001	20,000	PF65 18.00				

KM# 131 DOLLAR
28.28 g., Copper-Nickel, 38.6 mm. **Ruler:** Elizabeth II **Series:** Pokemon **Obv:** Crowned shield within sprigs **Rev:** Charmander **Edge:** Reeded

Date	Mintage	F12	VF20	XF40	MS60	MS63
2001	100,000	—	—	—	12.00	14.00

KM# 132 DOLLAR
7.77 g., 0.999 Silver 0.248 oz. ASW, 22 mm. **Ruler:** Elizabeth II **Series:** Pokemon **Obv:** Crowned shield within sprigs **Rev:** Charmander **Edge:** Reeded

Date	Mintage	F12	VF20	XF40	MS60	MS63
2001	20,000	PF65 18.00				

KM# 134 DOLLAR
28.28 g., Copper-Nickel, 38.6 mm. **Ruler:** Elizabeth II **Series:** Pokemon **Obv:** Crowned shield within sprigs **Rev:** Meowth **Edge:** Reeded

Date	Mintage	F12	VF20	XF40	MS60	MS63
2001	100,000	—	—	—	12.00	14.00

KM# 135 DOLLAR
7.77 g., 0.999 Silver 0.248 oz. ASW, 22 mm. **Ruler:** Elizabeth II **Series:** Pokemon **Obv:** Crowned shield within sprigs **Rev:** Meowth **Edge:** Reeded

Date	Mintage	F12	VF20	XF40	MS60	MS63
2001	20,000	PF65 18.00				

KM# 137 DOLLAR
28.28 g., Copper-Nickel, 38.6 mm. **Ruler:** Elizabeth II **Series:** Pokemon **Obv:** Crowned shield within sprigs **Rev:** Pikachu **Edge:** Reeded

Date	Mintage	F12	VF20	XF40	MS60	MS63
2001	100,000	—	—	—	12.00	14.00

KM# 138 DOLLAR
7.77 g., 0.999 Silver 0.248 oz. ASW, 22 mm. **Ruler:** Elizabeth II **Series:** Pokemon **Obv:** Crowned shield within sprigs **Rev:** Pikachu **Edge:** Reeded

Date	Mintage	F12	VF20	XF40	MS60	MS63
2001	20,000	PF65 18.00				

KM# 140 DOLLAR
28.28 g., Copper-Nickel, 38.6 mm. **Ruler:** Elizabeth II **Series:** Pokemon **Obv:** Crowned shield within sprigs **Rev:** Squirtle **Edge:** Reeded

Date	Mintage	F12	VF20	XF40	MS60	MS63
2001	100,000	—	—	—	12.00	14.00

KM# 141 DOLLAR
7.77 g., 0.999 Silver 0.248 oz. ASW, 22 mm. **Ruler:** Elizabeth II **Series:** Pokemon **Obv:** Crowned shield within sprigs **Rev:** Squirtle **Edge:** Reeded

Date	Mintage	F12	VF20	XF40	MS60	MS63
2001	20,000	PF65 18.00				

KM# 146 DOLLAR
28.28 g., Copper-Nickel, 38.6 mm. **Ruler:** Elizabeth II **Subject:** Pokemon Series **Obv:** Crowned shield within sprigs **Rev:** Pikachu **Edge:** Reeded

Date	Mintage	F12	VF20	XF40	MS60	MS63
2002PM	100,000	—	—	—	3.00	4.50

KM# 151 DOLLAR
28.28 g., Copper-Nickel, 38.6 mm. **Ruler:** Elizabeth II **Subject:** Pokemon Series **Obv:** Crowned shield within sprigs **Rev:** Pichu **Edge:** Reeded

Date	Mintage	F12	VF20	XF40	MS60	MS63
2002PM	100,000	—	—	—	3.00	4.50

KM# 156 DOLLAR
28.28 g., Copper-Nickel, 38.6 mm. **Ruler:** Elizabeth II **Subject:** Pokemon Series **Obv:** Crowned shield within sprigs **Rev:** Mewtwo **Edge:** Reeded

Date	Mintage	F12	VF20	XF40	MS60	MS63
2002PM	100,000	—	—	—	3.00	4.50

KM# 161 DOLLAR
28.28 g., Copper-Nickel, 38.6 mm. **Ruler:** Elizabeth II **Subject:** Pokemon Series **Obv:** Crowned shield within sprigs **Rev:** Entei **Edge:** Reeded

Date	Mintage	F12	VF20	XF40	MS60	MS63
2002PM	100,000	—	—	—	3.00	4.50

KM# 166 DOLLAR
28.28 g., Copper-Nickel, 38.6 mm. **Ruler:** Elizabeth II **Subject:** Pokemon Series **Obv:** Crowned shield within sprigs **Rev:** Celebi **Edge:** Reeded

Date	Mintage	F12	VF20	XF40	MS60	MS63
2002PM	100,000	—	—	—	3.00	4.50

KM# 186 DOLLAR
31.11 g., 0.999 Silver 0.9926 oz. ASW **Ruler:** Elizabeth II **Subject:** Marshalls of China's Army, 50th Anniversary **Obv:** Head right **Rev:** Multicolor scene of military men

Date	Mintage	F12	VF20	XF40	MS60	MS63
2005	1,000	—	—	—	—	70.00

KM# 187 DOLLAR
31.11 g., 0.999 Silver 0.9926 oz. ASW **Ruler:** Elizabeth II **Subject:** World War II, 60th Anniversary **Obv:** Bust right **Rev:** Multicolor badge

Date	Mintage	F12	VF20	XF40	MS60	MS63
2005	1,000	—	—	—	—	70.00

KM# 188 DOLLAR
31.11 g., 0.999 Silver 0.9926 oz. ASW **Ruler:** Elizabeth II **Series:** Bust right **Obv:** Multicolor image of two astronauts, rocket and map of China

Date	Mintage	F12	VF20	XF40	MS60	MS63
2005	—	PF65 75.00				

KM# 264 DOLLAR
31.10 g., 0.999 Silver 0.9925 oz. ASW, 45 mm. **Ruler:** Elizabeth II **Subject:** Year of the Rooster **Rev:** Multicolor rooster standing right, sunrise

Date	Mintage	F12	VF20	XF40	MS60	MS63
2005	—	PF65 55.00				

KM# 293 DOLLAR
31.11 g., 0.999 Silver 0.9926 oz. ASW, 45 mm. **Ruler:** Elizabeth II **Subject:** Year of the Dog **Rev:** Multicolor dog

Date	Mintage	F12	VF20	XF40	MS60	MS63
2005	—	PF65 60.00				

KM# 262 DOLLAR
Bronze, 38.61 mm. **Ruler:** Elizabeth II **Subject:** Thomas Alva Edison **Rev:** Lightbulb

Date	Mintage	F12	VF20	XF40	MS60	MS63
2005	—	—	—	—	—	30.00

KM# 262a DOLLAR
31.11 g., 0.999 Silver 0.9926 oz. ASW **Ruler:** Elizabeth II **Subject:** Thomas Alva Edison **Rev:** Lightbulb, partially gilt

Date	Mintage	F12	VF20	XF40	MS60	MS63
2005	Est. 2500	PF65 100				

KM# 275 DOLLAR
31.11 g., 0.999 Silver 0.9926 oz. ASW **Ruler:** Elizabeth II **Subject:** 60th Anniversary, China

Date	Mintage	F12	VF20	XF40	MS60	MS63
2005	Est. 1000	PF65 120				

KM# 276 DOLLAR
31.11 g., 0.999 Silver 0.9926 oz. ASW **Ruler:** Elizabeth II **Subject:** Mao Zedong and the Red Army in Beijing

Date	Mintage	F12	VF20	XF40	MS60	MS63
2005	—	PF65 100				

KM# 277 DOLLAR
31.11 g., 0.999 Silver 0.9926 oz. ASW, 45 mm. **Ruler:** Elizabeth II **Subject:** Chinese space achievements **Rev:** Multicolor rocket, flag, map

Date	Mintage	F12	VF20	XF40	MS60	MS63
2005	Est. 5000	PF65 75.00				

KM# 300 DOLLAR
31.11 g., 0.999 Silver 0.9926 oz. ASW, 45 mm. **Ruler:** Elizabeth II **Subject:** Dogs of the World **Rev:** Multicolor Bichon standing before the Louvre

Date	Mintage	F12	VF20	XF40	MS60	MS63
2006	Est 3000	PF65 60.00				

KM# 301 DOLLAR
31.11 g., 0.999 Silver 0.9926 oz. ASW, 45 mm. **Ruler:** Elizabeth II **Subject:** Dogs of the World **Rev:** Multicolor Welsh Corgi before Buckingham Palace

Date	Mintage	F12	VF20	XF40	MS60	MS63
2006	Est. 3000	PF65 60.00				

KM# 302 DOLLAR
31.11 g., 0.999 Silver 0.9926 oz. ASW, 45 mm. **Ruler:** Elizabeth II **Subject:** Dogs of the World **Rev:** Poodle before the Palace at Versailles

Date	Mintage	F12	VF20	XF40	MS60	MS63
2006	Est. 3000	PF65 60.00				

KM# 303 DOLLAR
31.11 g., 0.999 Silver 0.9926 oz. ASW, 45 mm. **Ruler:** Elizabeth II **Subject:** Dogs of the World **Rev:** Bare dog before the Potala Plast

Date	Mintage	F12	VF20	XF40	MS60	MS63
2006	Est. 3000	PF65 60.00				

KM# 304 DOLLAR
31.11 g., 0.999 Silver 0.9926 oz. ASW, 45 mm. **Ruler:** Elizabeth II **Subject:** Dogs of the World **Rev:** Pekineese before the Palastmuseum

Date	Mintage	F12	VF20	XF40	MS60	MS63
2006	Est. 3000	PF65 60.00				

KM# 305 DOLLAR
31.11 g., 0.999 Silver 0.9926 oz. ASW, 45 mm. **Ruler:** Elizabeth II **Subject:** Dogs of the World **Rev:** Malteser before the Schonbrunn

Date	Mintage	F12	VF20	XF40	MS60	MS63
2006	Est. 3000	PF65 60.00				

KM# 306 DOLLAR
31.11 g., 0.999 Silver 0.9926 oz. ASW, 45 mm. **Ruler:** Elizabeth II **Subject:** Dogs of the World **Rev:** Japanese Chin before Emperor's palace in Kyoto

Date	Mintage	F12	VF20	XF40	MS60	MS63
2006	Est. 3000	PF65 60.00				

KM# 307 DOLLAR
31.11 g., 0.999 Silver 0.9926 oz. ASW, 45 mm. **Ruler:** Elizabeth II **Subject:** Dogs of the World **Rev:** King Charles Spaniel before Westminster Abbey

Date	Mintage	F12	VF20	XF40	MS60	MS63
2006	—	PF65 60.00				

KM# 308 DOLLAR
31.11 g., 0.999 Silver 0.9926 oz. ASW, 45 mm. **Ruler:** Elizabeth II **Subject:** Dogs of the World **Rev:** Butterfly dog before the Kings Palace in Madrid

Date	Mintage	F12	VF20	XF40	MS60	MS63
2006	Est. 3000	PF65 60.00				

KM# 309 DOLLAR
31.11 g., 0.999 Silver 0.9926 oz. ASW, 45 mm. **Ruler:** Elizabeth II **Subject:** Olympics **Rev:** Discus thrower

Date	Mintage	F12	VF20	XF40	MS60	MS63
ND (2006)	Est. 2008	PF65 70.00				

KM# 310 DOLLAR
31.11 g., 0.999 Silver 0.9926 oz. ASW, 45 mm. **Ruler:** Elizabeth II **Subject:** Olympics **Rev:** Sprinter

Date	Mintage	F12	VF20	XF40	MS60	MS63
ND (2006)	Est. 2008	PF65 70.00				

KM# 311 DOLLAR
31.11 g., 0.999 Silver 0.9926 oz. ASW, 45 mm. **Ruler:** Elizabeth II **Subject:** Olympics **Rev:** Long Jump

Date	Mintage	F12	VF20	XF40	MS60	MS63
ND (2006)	—	PF65 70.00				

KM# 312 DOLLAR
31.11 g., 0.999 Silver 0.9926 oz. ASW, 45 mm. **Ruler:** Elizabeth II **Subject:** Olympics **Rev:** Javelin Thrower

Date	Mintage	F12	VF20	XF40	MS60	MS63
ND (2006)	Est. 2008	PF65 70.00				

KM# 313 DOLLAR
31.11 g., 0.999 Silver 0.9926 oz. ASW, 45 mm. **Ruler:** Elizabeth II **Subject:** Olympics **Rev:** Weightlifter

Date	Mintage	F12	VF20	XF40	MS60	MS63
ND (2006)	Est. 2008	PF65 70.00				

KM# 314 DOLLAR
31.11 g., 0.999 Silver 0.9926 oz. ASW, 45 mm. **Ruler:** Elizabeth II **Subject:** Olympics **Rev:** Hammer Throw

Date	Mintage	F12	VF20	XF40	MS60	MS63
ND (2006)	Est. 2008	PF65 70.00				

KM# 315 DOLLAR
31.11 g., 0.999 Silver 0.9926 oz. ASW, 45 mm. **Ruler:** Elizabeth II **Subject:** Olympics **Rev:** Archery

Date	Mintage	F12	VF20	XF40	MS60	MS63
ND (2006)	Est. 2008	PF65 70.00				

KM# 316 DOLLAR
31.11 g., 0.999 Silver 0.9926 oz. ASW, 45 mm. **Ruler:** Elizabeth II **Subject:** Olympics **Rev:** Lacrosse player

Date	Mintage	F12	VF20	XF40	MS60	MS63
ND (2006)	Est. 2008	PF65 70.00				

KM# 317 DOLLAR
31.11 g., 0.999 Silver 0.9926 oz. ASW, 45 mm. **Ruler:** Elizabeth II **Subject:** Olympics **Rev:** Soccer player

Date	Mintage	F12	VF20	XF40	MS60	MS63
ND (2006)	Est. 2008	PF65 70.00				

KM# 318 DOLLAR
31.11 g., 0.999 Silver 0.9926 oz. ASW, 45 mm. **Ruler:** Elizabeth II **Subject:** Olympics **Rev:** Boxer

Date	Mintage	F12	VF20	XF40	MS60	MS63
ND (2006)	Est. 2008	PF65 70.00				

KM# 319 DOLLAR
31.11 g., 0.999 Silver 0.9926 oz. ASW, 45 mm. **Ruler:** Elizabeth II **Subject:** Olympics **Rev:** Equestrian

Date	Mintage	F12	VF20	XF40	MS60	MS63
ND (2006)	Est. 2008	PF65 70.00				

KM# 320 DOLLAR
31.11 g., 0.999 Silver 0.9926 oz. ASW, 45 mm. **Ruler:** Elizabeth II **Subject:** Olympics **Rev:** Wrestler

Date	Mintage	F12	VF20	XF40	MS60	MS63
ND (2006)	Est. 2008	PF65 70.00				

KM# 321 DOLLAR
31.11 g., 0.999 Silver 0.9926 oz. ASW, 35x46 mm. **Ruler:** Elizabeth II **Subject:** Life of Christ **Rev:** Radiant Mary **Shape:** Vertical rectangle

Date	Mintage	F12	VF20	XF40	MS60	MS63
2006	Est. 1000	PF65 100				

KM# 322 DOLLAR
31.11 g., 0.999 Silver 0.9926 oz. ASW, 35x46 mm. **Ruler:** Elizabeth II **Subject:** Life of Christ **Rev:** Mary and Child (1483) **Shape:** Vertical rectangle

Date	Mintage	F12	VF20	XF40	MS60	MS63
2006	Est. 1000	PF65 100				

KM# 323 DOLLAR
31.11 g., 0.999 Silver 0.9926 oz. ASW, 35x46 mm. **Ruler:** Elizabeth II **Subject:** Life of Christ **Rev:** Christ in the Jrodan (1478) **Shape:** Vertical rectangle

Date	Mintage	F12	VF20	XF40	MS60	MS63
2006	Est. 1000	PF65 100				

KM# 324 DOLLAR
31.11 g., 0.999 Silver 0.9926 oz. ASW, 35x46 mm. **Ruler:** Elizabeth II **Subject:** Life of Christ **Rev:** Jesus Christ (1481) **Shape:** Vertical rectangle

Date	Mintage	F12	VF20	XF40	MS60	MS63
2006	Est. 1000	**PF65** 100				

KM# 325 DOLLAR
31.11 g., 0.999 Silver 0.9926 oz. ASW, 35x46 mm. **Ruler:** Elizabeth II **Subject:** Life of Christ **Rev:** betrayal of Judas (1303) **Shape:** Vertical rectangle

Date	Mintage	F12	VF20	XF40	MS60	MS63
2006	Est. 1000	**PF65** 100				

KM# 326 DOLLAR
31.11 g., 0.999 Silver 0.9926 oz. ASW, 35x46 mm. **Ruler:** Elizabeth II **Subject:** Life of Christ **Rev:** Stations of the Cross (1517) **Shape:** Vertical rectangle

Date	Mintage	F12	VF20	XF40	MS60	MS63
2006	Est. 1000	**PF65** 100				

KM# 327 DOLLAR
31.11 g., 0.999 Silver 0.9926 oz. ASW, 35x46 mm. **Ruler:** Elizabeth II **Subject:** Life of Christ **Rev:** Jesus on the Cross (1558) **Shape:** Vertical rectangle

Date	Mintage	F12	VF20	XF40	MS60	MS63
2006	Est. 1000	**PF65** 100				

KM# 329 DOLLAR
31.11 g., 0.999 Silver 0.9926 oz. ASW, 35x45 mm. **Ruler:** Elizabeth II **Subject:** Life of Christ **Rev:** Heaven **Shape:** Vertical rectangle

Date	Mintage	F12	VF20	XF40	MS60	MS63
2006	Est. 1000	**PF65** 100				

KM# 331 DOLLAR
28.28 g., 0.925 Silver 0.8356 oz. ASW, 38.61 mm. **Ruler:** Elizabeth II **Subject:** Year of the Pig **Rev:** Pig grazing

Date	Mintage	F12	VF20	XF40	MS60	MS63
2006	Est. 5000	—	—	—	—	55.00

KM# 328 DOLLAR
31.11 g., 0.999 Silver 0.9926 oz. ASW, 35x46 mm. **Ruler:** Elizabeth II **Subject:** Life of Christ **Rev:** Ascension (1520) **Shape:** Vertical rectangle

Date	Mintage	F12	VF20	XF40	MS60	MS63
2006	Est. 1000	**PF65** 100				

KM# 176 DOLLAR
28.28 g., 0.925 Silver 0.8356 oz. ASW **Ruler:** Elizabeth II **Obv:** Tiarra head of Elizabeth II right at left, multicolor Van Gogh's painting "Starry Night" with 3 zircon crystals as stars at center right. **Obv. Inscription:** ELIZABETH II - NIUE ISLAND **Rev:** Van Gogh's painting "Vase with Twelve Sunflowers" at left, self portrait of artist with brush at upper right **Rev. Inscription:** VAN GOGH / Vincent **Edge:** Plain **Shape:** Rectangular, 39.94 x 27.97 mm

Date	Mintage	F12	VF20	XF40	MS60	MS63
2007	10,000	**PF65** 85.00				

KM# 332 DOLLAR
28.28 g., 0.925 Silver 0.8356 oz. ASW **Ruler:** Elizabeth II **Subject:** Year of the Pig **Rev:** Three little pigs dancing, brick house, wolf

Date	Mintage	F12	VF20	XF40	MS60	MS63
2007	—	—	—	—	—	55.00

KM# 334 DOLLAR
28.28 g., 0.925 Silver 0.8356 oz. ASW, 38.61 mm. **Ruler:** Elizabeth II **Rev:** Female advancing left with long dress **Rev. Legend:** Change Flies to the Moon

Date	Mintage	F12	VF20	XF40	MS60	MS63
2007	Est. 5000	—	—	—	—	55.00

KM# 335 DOLLAR
28.28 g., 0.925 Silver 0.8356 oz. ASW, 38.61 mm. **Ruler:** Elizabeth II **Rev:** Man weiding axe against tree **Rev. Legend:** Wu Gang cuts the sweet-scented osmanthus tree

Date	Mintage	F12	VF20	XF40	MS60	MS63
2007	—	—	—	—	—	55.00

KM# 336 DOLLAR
28.28 g., 0.925 Silver 0.8356 oz. ASW, 38.61 mm. **Ruler:** Elizabeth II **Rev:** Group visiting palace **Rev. Legend:** Emperor Mint of Tang Dynasty visit the Moon Palace at Night

Date	Mintage	F12	VF20	XF40	MS60	MS63
2007	Est. 5000	—	—	—	—	65.00

KM# 337 DOLLAR
28.28 g., 0.925 Silver 0.8356 oz. ASW, 38.61 mm. **Ruler:** Elizabeth II **Rev:** Rabbit with mortar and pestile in house yard **Rev. Legend:** The jade rabbit pounds the medicine of immortality

Date	Mintage	F12	VF20	XF40	MS60	MS63
2007 Proof	—	—	—	—	—	55.00

KM# 192 DOLLAR
31.11 g., 0.999 Silver 0.9926 oz. ASW **Ruler:** Elizabeth II **Subject:** Year of the Ox **Obv:** Head right **Rev:** Multicolor ox

Date	Mintage	F12	VF20	XF40	MS60	MS63
2008//2009 (2008)	10,000	**PF65** 75.00				

KM# 212 DOLLAR
Silver **Ruler:** Elizabeth II **Rev:** Ox seated multicolor lotus flower

Date	Mintage	F12	VF20	XF40	MS60	MS63
2008 Antique finish	—	—	—	—	—	55.00

KM# 201 DOLLAR
28.28 g., 0.925 Silver 0.8356 oz. ASW, 38.61 mm. **Ruler:** Elizabeth II **Subject:** Amber Road **Obv:** Roman cart and map, Elizabeth II head at lower left **Rev:** Church, goblet, ancient coin, amber insert **Rev. Legend:** ELBLAG SZLAK BURSZTYNOWY

Date	Mintage	F12	VF20	XF40	MS60	MS63
2008 Antique finish	10,000	—	—	—	—	100

KM# 202 DOLLAR
28.28 g., 0.925 Silver 0.8356 oz. ASW, 38.61 mm. **Ruler:** Elizabeth II **Subject:** Amber Road **Obv:** Roman cart, map, Elizabeth II head at lower left **Rev:** Antonius Pius coins, Nepture statue, mine shaft, amber insert **Rev. Legend:** GDANSK SZLAK BURSZTYNOWY

Date	Mintage	F12	VF20	XF40	MS60	MS63
2008 Antique finish	10,000	—	—	—	—	90.00

KM# 203 DOLLAR
28.28 g., 0.925 Silver 0.8356 oz. ASW, 38.61 mm. **Ruler:** Elizabeth II **Subject:** Amber Road **Obv:** Roman cart, map, Elizabeth II head at lower left **Rev:** Building, statue, amber insert **Rev. Legend:** WROCLAW SZLAK BURSZTYNOWY

Date	Mintage	F12	VF20	XF40	MS60	MS63
2008 Antique finish	10,000	—	—	—	—	100

KM# 204 DOLLAR
28.28 g., 0.999 Silver 0.9025 oz. ASW, 38.61 mm. **Ruler:** Elizabeth II **Subject:** Amber Road **Rev:** Castle, sword, amber insert **Rev. Legend:** SZLAK BURSZTYNOWY KALININGRAD

Date	Mintage	F12	VF20	XF40	MS60	MS63
2008 Antique finish	10,000	—	—	—	—	100

HENRI DE TOULOUSE-LAUTREC

KM# 211 DOLLAR
28.28 g., 0.925 Silver 0.8356 oz. ASW, 28x40 mm. **Ruler:** Elizabeth II **Obv:** Head of Elizabeth II at lower left, Portrait of Lautrec at top right **Rev:** Toulouse-Lautrec and can-can girl

Date	Mintage	F12	VF20	XF40	MS60	MS63
2008	15,000	PF65 100				

KM# 338 DOLLAR
31.11 g., 0.999 Silver 0.9926 oz. ASW, 45 mm. **Ruler:** Elizabeth II **Subject:** Year of the Rat **Rev:** Rat in field, sun rays above

Date	Mintage	F12	VF20	XF40	MS60	MS63
2008	Est. 8000	—	—	—	—	65.00

KM# 339 DOLLAR
31.11 g., 0.999 Silver 0.9926 oz. ASW, 45 mm. **Ruler:** Elizabeth II **Subject:** Year of the Rat **Rev:** Rat left before house

Date	Mintage	F12	VF20	XF40	MS60	MS63
2008	Est. 8000	—	—	—	—	65.00

KM# 340 DOLLAR
31.11 g., 0.999 Silver 0.9926 oz. ASW, 45 mm. **Ruler:** Elizabeth II **Subject:** Year of the Rat **Rev:** Rat standing on hind legs sniffing flora

Date	Mintage	F12	VF20	XF40	MS60	MS63
2008	Est. 8000	—	—	—	—	70.00

KM# 341 DOLLAR
31.11 g., 0.999 Silver 0.9926 oz. ASW, 45 mm. **Ruler:** Elizabeth II **Rev:** Multicolor Happy mouse

Date	Mintage	F12	VF20	XF40	MS60	MS63
2008	—	PF65 60.00				

KM# 342 DOLLAR
31.11 g., 0.999 Silver 0.9926 oz. ASW, 45 mm. **Ruler:** Elizabeth II **Rev:** Multicolor wealthy rat

Date	Mintage	F12	VF20	XF40	MS60	MS63
2008	—	PF65 60.00				

KM# 343 DOLLAR
31.11 g., 0.999 Silver 0.9926 oz. ASW, 45 mm. **Ruler:** Elizabeth II **Rev:** Multicolor happy rat

Date	Mintage	F12	VF20	XF40	MS60	MS63
2008	—	PF65 60.00				

KM# 344 DOLLAR
31.11 g., 0.999 Silver 0.9926 oz. ASW, 45 mm. **Ruler:** Elizabeth II **Rev:** Multicolor successful rat

Date	Mintage	F12	VF20	XF40	MS60	MS63
2008	—	PF65 60.00				

KM# 345 DOLLAR
31.11 g., 0.999 Silver 0.9926 oz. ASW, 45 mm. **Ruler:** Elizabeth II **Rev:** Multicolor rat holding charm

Date	Mintage	F12	VF20	XF40	MS60	MS63
2008	Est. 10000	PF65 60.00				

KM# 346 DOLLAR
3.11 g., 0.999 Gold 0.0992 oz. AGW, 18 mm. **Ruler:** Elizabeth II **Rev:** Rat in garden

Date	Mintage	F12	VF20	XF40	MS60	MS63
2008	Est. 10000	PF65 185				

KM# 347 DOLLAR
28.28 g., 0.925 Silver 0.8356 oz. ASW, 38.61 mm. **Ruler:** Elizabeth II **Rev:** Rat standing infront of multicolor cut cheese wheel

Date	Mintage	F12	VF20	XF40	MS60	MS63
2008	Est. 10000	PF65 50.00				

KM# 348 DOLLAR
28.28 g., 0.925 Silver 0.8356 oz. ASW, 38.61 mm. **Ruler:** Elizabeth II **Rev:** Multicolor dancing mice in garland

Date	Mintage	F12	VF20	XF40	MS60	MS63
2008	—	PF65 50.00				

KM# 197 DOLLAR
17.30 g., Aluminum-Brass, 32 mm. **Ruler:** Elizabeth II **Obv:** Head right **Rev:** Swordfish **Edge:** Reeded

Date	Mintage	F12	VF20	XF40	MS60	MS63
2009	—	—	—	—	7.50	12.50

KM# 231 DOLLAR
31.10 g., 0.999 Silver 0.9926 oz. ASW, 38.6 mm. **Ruler:** Elizabeth II **Subject:** Year of the Tiger **Rev:** Tiger cub in basket playing with ball

Date	Mintage	F12	VF20	XF40	MS60	MS63
2009	6,000	PF65 80.00				

KM# 232 DOLLAR
31.10 g., 0.999 Silver 0.9926 oz. ASW, 38.6 mm. **Ruler:** Elizabeth II **Subject:** Year of the Tiger **Rev:** Tiger advancing left

Date	Mintage	F12	VF20	XF40	MS60	MS63
2009	6,000	PF65 80.00				

KM# 551 DOLLAR
28.28 g., 0.925 Silver 0.8356 oz. ASW, 38.61 mm. **Ruler:** Elizabeth II **Subject:** Father Frost **Rev:** Father and Mrs. Frost standing, multicolor

Date	Mintage	F12	VF20	XF40	MS60	MS63
2009	Est. 6000	PF65 65.00				

KM# 198 DOLLAR
17.30 g., Copper Plated Bronze, 32 mm. **Ruler:** Elizabeth II **Obv:** Head right **Rev:** Taro leaves **Edge:** Reeded

Date	Mintage	F12	VF20	XF40	MS60	MS63
2010	—	—	—	—	7.50	12.50

KM# 234 DOLLAR
28.28 g., 0.925 Silver 0.8356 oz. ASW, 40x40 mm. **Ruler:** Elizabeth II **Obv:** Head right, footprints in field **Rev:** Antilocapra Americana, two antelope running right **Shape:** Square

Date	Mintage	F12	VF20	XF40	MS60	MS63
2010	9,000	PF65 80.00				

KM# 235 DOLLAR
28.28 g., 0.925 Silver 0.8356 oz. ASW, 38.6 mm. **Ruler:** Elizabeth II **Obv:** Head right **Rev:** Lycaena Virgavreae multicolor butterfly

Date	Mintage	F12	VF20	XF40	MS60	MS63
2010	8,000	PF65 80.00				

KM# 236 DOLLAR
14.14 g., 0.925 Silver 0.4178 oz. ASW, 25x28 mm. **Ruler:** Elizabeth II **Obv:** Head right on musical score **Rev:** Chopin bust at left, score **Shape:** Square

Date	Mintage	F12	VF20	XF40	MS60	MS63
2010	6,000	PF65 80.00				

KM# 238 DOLLAR
28.28 g., 0.925 Silver 0.8356 oz. ASW, 36.81 mm. **Ruler:** Elizabeth II **Subject:** Fire **Obv:** Head right, images of early man **Rev:** Volcano and men around fire in multicolor

Date	Mintage	F12	VF20	XF40	MS60	MS63
2010	6,000	PF65 100				

KM# 239 DOLLAR
28.28 g., 0.925 Silver 0.8356 oz. ASW, 40x28 mm. **Ruler:** Elizabeth II **Obv:** Head right, aircraft propeller, wing schematic **Rev:** Greek warrior shield and multicolor Icarus in flight **Shape:** Rectangle

Date	Mintage	F12	VF20	XF40	MS60	MS63
2010	6,000	PF65 100				

KM# 240 DOLLAR
28.28 g., 0.925 Silver 0.8356 oz. ASW, 28x40 mm. **Ruler:** Elizabeth II **Obv:** Head right, propeller, wing schematic **Rev:** Montgolfier brothers and balloon **Shape:** Rectangle

Date	Mintage	F12	VF20	XF40	MS60	MS63
2010	6,000	PF65 75.00				

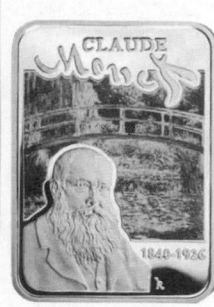

KM# 241 DOLLAR
28.28 g., 0.925 Silver 0.8356 oz. ASW, 40x28 mm. **Ruler:** Elizabeth II **Obv:** Head right, Monet painting **Rev:** Claude Monet portrait and painting **Shape:** Verticle rectangle

Date	Mintage	F12	VF20	XF40	MS60	MS63
2010	15,000	PF65 120				

KM# 242 DOLLAR
28.28 g., 0.925 Silver 0.8356 oz. ASW, 38.61 mm. **Ruler:** Elizabeth II **Obv:** Elizabeth II head at top left, building **Rev:** Napoleon at left, troops in color at right

Date	Mintage	F12	VF20	XF40	MS60	MS63
2010	10,000	PF65 90.00				

KM# 243 DOLLAR
28.28 g., 0.925 Silver 0.8356 oz. ASW, 38.6 mm. **Ruler:** Elizabeth II **Subject:** 65th Anniversary - End of World War II **Obv:** Head right at top, three Soviet medals below **Rev:** Soviet flat, rose and eternal light

Date	Mintage	F12	VF20	XF40	MS60	MS63
2010	7,000	PF65 95.00				

KM# 244 DOLLAR
28.28 g., 0.925 Silver 0.8356 oz. ASW, 38.6 mm. **Ruler:** Elizabeth II **Obv:** Head at left, ship, coins, artifacts **Rev:** Stupsk

Date	Mintage	F12	VF20	XF40	MS60	MS63
2010	8,000	PF65 90.00				

KM# 251 DOLLAR
31.11 g., 0.999 Silver 0.9926 oz. ASW, 38.6 mm. **Ruler:** Elizabeth II **Subject:** Peanuts 60th Anniversary **Rev:** Snoopy as conductor with flowers, Woodstock with red ribbon

Date	Mintage	F12	VF20	XF40	MS60	MS63
2010 Prooflike	3,000	—	—	—	—	80.00

KM# 365 DOLLAR
28.28 g., 0.925 Silver 0.8356 oz. ASW, 38.61 mm. **Ruler:** Elizabeth II **Subject:** WWII, 65th Anniversary **Obv:** Elizabeth II head, WWI medal and two stars below **Rev:** Russian flag and medal ribbon

Date	Mintage	F12	VF20	XF40	MS60	MS63
2010	7,000	PF65 60.00				

KM# 366 DOLLAR
28.28 g., 0.925 Silver 0.8356 oz. ASW, 38.61 mm. **Ruler:** Elizabeth II **Obv:** Enlarged butterfly wing **Rev:** Butterfly - Parnassius Apollo

Date	Mintage	F12	VF20	XF40	MS60	MS63
2010	8,000	PF65 65.00				

KM# 367 DOLLAR
28.28 g., 0.925 Silver 0.8356 oz. ASW, 38.61 mm. **Ruler:** Elizabeth II **Subject:** Amber Route - Stare Hradisko **Rev:** Amber insert, old celtic style coin

Date	Mintage	F12	VF20	XF40	MS60	MS63
2010 Antique finish	10,000—	—	—	—		85.00

KM# 369 DOLLAR
14.14 g., 0.925 Silver 0.4178 oz. ASW, 32 mm. **Ruler:** Elizabeth II **Subject:** Cartoon Characters - Mis Uszatek **Obv:** Elizabeth II head left, movie film **Rev:** Image of rabbits and bear

Date	Mintage	F12	VF20	XF40	MS60	MS63
2010	8,000	PF65 40.00				

KM# 370 DOLLAR
28.28 g., 0.925 Silver 0.8356 oz. ASW **Ruler:** Elizabeth II **Obv:** Elizabeth II head right, Cupid **Rev:** Romeo and Juliet about to kiss

Date	Mintage	F12	VF20	XF40	MS60	MS63
2010	9,000	PF65 60.00				

KM# 392 DOLLAR
14.14 g., 0.925 Silver 0.4178 oz. ASW, 32 mm. **Ruler:** Elizabeth II **Subject:** Cartoon Characters - Wolf and the Hare **Rev:** Wolf and hare characters in multicolor

Date	Mintage	F12	VF20	XF40	MS60	MS63
2010	8,000	PF65 50.00				

KM# 393 DOLLAR
28.28 g., 0.925 Silver 0.8356 oz. ASW, 40x28 mm. **Ruler:** Elizabeth II **Obv:** Queen's head at top left, three airplane views **Rev:** Otto Lilienthal and the glider **Shape:** Rectangle

Date	Mintage	F12	VF20	XF40	MS60	MS63
2010	6,000	PF65 70.00				

KM# 394 DOLLAR
28.28 g., 0.925 Silver 0.8356 oz. ASW, 38.8 mm. **Ruler:** Elizabeth II **Obv:** Queen's head right within star pattern **Rev:** Two portraits of Sitting Bull in multicolor

Date	Mintage	F12	VF20	XF40	MS60	MS63
2010	6,000	PF65 75.00				

KM# 395 DOLLAR
28.28 g., 0.925 Silver 0.8356 oz. ASW, 40x40 mm. **Ruler:** Elizabeth II **Obv:** Head in tiara right within diamond, footprints in background **Rev:** Platypus (Ornithorhynchus anatinus) **Shape:** Square

Date	Mintage	F12	VF20	XF40	MS60	MS63
2010	9,000	PF65 65.00				

KM# 396 DOLLAR
28.28 g., 0.925 Silver 0.8356 oz. ASW, 38.61 mm. **Ruler:** Elizabeth II **Subject:** Amber Route - Carnuntum **Rev:** Arches, ancient coin and statue

Date	Mintage	F12	VF20	XF40	MS60	MS63
2010 Antique patina	10,000	PF65 85.00				

KM# 398 DOLLAR
28.28 g., 0.925 Silver 0.8356 oz. ASW, 38.61 mm. **Ruler:** Elizabeth II **Subject:** Amber Route - Szombathely **Rev:** Cathedral, ancient coin

Date	Mintage	F12	VF20	XF40	MS60	MS63
2010 Antique patina	10,000	PF65 85.00				

KM# 400 DOLLAR

28.28 g., 0.925 Silver 0.8356 oz. ASW, 27x45 mm. **Ruler:** Elizabeth II **Subject:** Milan Cathedral **Obv:** Cathedral's flying buttresses, stained glass colored inset **Rev:** Front facade of cathedral, stained glass colored inset **Shape:** Vertical oval

Date	Mintage	F12	VF20	XF40	MS60	MS63
2010	5,000	PF65 70.00				

KM# 401 DOLLAR

28.28 g., 0.925 Silver 0.8356 oz. ASW, 27x45 mm. **Ruler:** Elizabeth II **Subject:** Cologne Cathedral **Obv:** Cathedral side exterior, stained glass colored inset **Rev:** Cathedral floor plan and facade, stained glass colored inset **Shape:** Vertical oval

Date	Mintage	F12	VF20	XF40	MS60	MS63
2010	5,000	PF65 70.00				

KM# 402 DOLLAR

28.28 g., 0.925 Silver 0.8356 oz. ASW, 27x45 mm. **Ruler:** Elizabeth II **Subject:** Notre Dame Cathedral **Obv:** Cathedral side view, stained glass colored inset **Rev:** Linear cathedral interior view, cathedral facade, stained glass colored inset **Shape:** Vertical oval

Date	Mintage	F12	VF20	XF40	MS60	MS63
2010	5,000	PF65 70.00				

KM# 403 DOLLAR

28.28 g., 0.925 Silver 0.8356 oz. ASW, 28x40 mm. **Ruler:** Elizabeth II **Subject:** Alfons Mucha, 150th Anniversary of Birth **Obv:** Standing Female in multicolor **Rev:** Female portrait and Mucha portrait in multicolor **Shape:** Vertical Rectangle

Date	Mintage	F12	VF20	XF40	MS60	MS63
2010	5,000	PF65 80.00				

KM# 404 DOLLAR

28.28 g., 0.925 Silver 0.8356 oz. ASW, 28x40 mm. **Ruler:** Elizabeth II **Subject:** Carl Brullov **Obv:** Female on horseback in color **Rev:** Two females with grape wreath above, Brullov portrait, Three nuns singing below; all in color **Shape:** Vertical Rectangle

Date	Mintage	F12	VF20	XF40	MS60	MS63
2010	5,000	PF65 75.00				

KM# 406 DOLLAR

28.28 g., 0.925 Silver 0.8356 oz. ASW, 40x40 mm. **Ruler:** Elizabeth II **Obv:** Head with tiara right, in diamond, footprints in background **Rev:** Venus Flytrap in color **Shape:** Square

Date	Mintage	F12	VF20	XF40	MS60	MS63
2010	9,000	PF65 75.00				

KM# 407 DOLLAR

28.28 g., 0.925 Silver 0.8356 oz. ASW, 41 mm. **Ruler:** Elizabeth II **Subject:** Good Luck **Obv:** Head with tiara right, horseshoes below **Rev:** Horseshoes and clover

Date	Mintage	F12	VF20	XF40	MS60	MS63
2010	10,000	PF65 70.00				

KM# 412 DOLLAR

28.28 g., 0.925 Silver 0.8356 oz. ASW, 38.61 mm. **Ruler:** Elizabeth II **Subject:** Siberia **Obv:** Head with tiara right **Rev:** Khanty-Mansiysk

Date	Mintage	F12	VF20	XF40	MS60	MS63
2010 Proof-like	4,000	—	—	—	—	70.00

KM# 413 DOLLAR

28.28 g., 0.925 Silver 0.8356 oz. ASW, 38.61 mm. **Ruler:** Elizabeth II **Subject:** Siberia **Obv:** Head with tiara right **Rev:** Uray

Date	Mintage	F12	VF20	XF40	MS60	MS63
2010 Proof-like	4,000	—	—	—	—	70.00

KM# 414 DOLLAR

28.28 g., 0.925 Silver 0.8356 oz. ASW, 38.61 mm. **Ruler:** Elizabeth II **Subject:** Siberia **Obv:** Head with tiara right **Rev:** Surgut

Date	Mintage	F12	VF20	XF40	MS60	MS63
2010 Proof-like	4,000	—	—	—	—	70.00

KM# 415 DOLLAR

28.28 g., 0.925 Silver 0.8356 oz. ASW, 38.61 mm. **Ruler:** Elizabeth II **Subject:** Siberia **Obv:** Head with tiara right **Rev:** Nizhnevartovsk

Date	Mintage	F12	VF20	XF40	MS60	MS63
2010 Proof-like	4,000	—	—	—	—	70.00

KM# 417 DOLLAR
28.28 g., 0.925 Silver 0.8356 oz. ASW, 38.61 mm. **Ruler:**
Elizabeth II **Subject:** Famous Love Stories - Samson and
Delilah **Obv:** Head with tiara right, Cupid below **Rev:** Portraits
of Samson and Delilah

Date	Mintage	F12	VF20	XF40	MS60	MS63
2010	9,000	PF65 70.00				

KM# 418 DOLLAR
31.10 g., 0.999 Silver 0.9925 oz. ASW, 40 mm. **Ruler:** Elizabeth
II **Subject:** Jaroslawl, 100th Anniversary **Obv:** Head with tiara
right **Rev:** Banner in color

Date	Mintage	F12	VF20	XF40	MS60	MS63
2010	2,000	PF65 75.00				

KM# 419 DOLLAR
31.10 g., 0.999 Silver 0.9925 oz. ASW, 40 mm. **Ruler:** Elizabeth
II **Subject:** Jaroslawl, 1000th Anniversary **Obv:** Head with tiara
right **Rev:** Three church towers in color

Date	Mintage	F12	VF20	XF40	MS60	MS63
2010	9,000	PF65 75.00				

KM# 420 DOLLAR
31.10 g., 0.999 Silver 0.9925 oz. ASW, 40 mm. **Ruler:** Elizabeth
II **Subject:** Jaroslawl, 1000th Anniversary **Obv:** Head in tiara
right **Rev:** Town square in color

Date	Mintage	F12	VF20	XF40	MS60	MS63
2010	9,000	PF65 75.00				

KM# 421 DOLLAR
28.28 g., 0.925 Silver 0.8356 oz. ASW, 36.81 mm. **Ruler:**
Elizabeth II **Subject:** Cultural Achievements **Obv:** Head with
tiara at center **Rev:** Bow and arrows, Bow and firestarting kit

Date	Mintage	F12	VF20	XF40	MS60	MS63
2010	6,000	PF65 80.00				

KM# 422 DOLLAR
28.28 g., 0.925 Silver 0.8356 oz. ASW, 44 mm. **Ruler:**
Elizabeth II **Subject:** Christmas star **Obv:** Head with tiara right,
snowflakes around **Rev:** Children before christmas tree in color
Shape: 7-pointed star

Date	Mintage	F12	VF20	XF40	MS60	MS63
2010	15,000	PF65 95.00				

KM# 426 DOLLAR
28.28 g., 0.925 Silver 0.8356 oz. ASW, 41 mm. **Ruler:** Elizabeth
II **Subject:** Four Leaf Clover **Obv:** Head with titara right, clovers
Rev: four clovers and ripple background

Date	Mintage	F12	VF20	XF40	MS60	MS63
2010	10,000	PF65 70.00				

KM# 427 DOLLAR
28.28 g., 0.925 Silver 0.8356 oz. ASW, 38.61 mm. **Ruler:**
Elizabeth II **Subject:** Veliky Novgorod **Obv:** Head with tiara
right, montage of ship and coins at right **Rev:** Market scene,
Church; city arms below

Date	Mintage	F12	VF20	XF40	MS60	MS63
2010	8,000	PF65 75.00				

KM# 428 DOLLAR
28.28 g., 0.925 Silver 0.8356 oz. ASW, 38.61 mm. **Ruler:**
Elizabeth II **Subject:** Year of the Rabbit **Obv:** Head with tiara
right **Rev:** Rabbit seated in field

Date	Mintage	F12	VF20	XF40	MS60	MS63
2010	3,000	PF65 75.00				

KM# 429 DOLLAR
28.28 g., 0.925 Silver 0.8356 oz. ASW, 38.61 mm. **Ruler:**
Elizabeth II **Subject:** Year of the Rabbit **Obv:** Head with tiara
right **Rev:** Two rabbits holding heart at center

Date	Mintage	F12	VF20	XF40	MS60	MS63
2010	3,000	PF65 75.00				

KM# 432 DOLLAR
28.28 g., 0.925 Silver 0.8356 oz. ASW, 40x28 mm. **Ruler:**
Elizabeth II **Subject:** Francisco Goya **Obv:** Head with tiara
right at left, painting of man and woman at right **Rev:** Goya and
Clothed female reclining **Shape:** Rectangle

Date	Mintage	F12	VF20	XF40	MS60	MS63
2010	10,000	PF65 70.00				

KM# 433 DOLLAR
28.28 g., 0.925 Silver 0.8356 oz. ASW, 38.61 mm. **Ruler:**
Elizabeth II **Subject:** Peter the Great **Obv:** Head with tiara right
above ship and city view **Rev:** Half-length figure holding coins,
map in background

Date	Mintage	F12	VF20	XF40	MS60	MS63
2010	4,000	PF65 75.00				

KM# 434 DOLLAR

28.28 g., 0.925 Silver 0.8356 oz. ASW, 38.61 mm. **Ruler:** Elizabeth II **Subject:** Sea of Love **Obv:** Head in tiara right above sunset at sea with heart at center **Rev:** Two white doves in flight over sea, within heart

Date	Mintage	F12	VF20	XF40	MS60	MS63
2010	7,000	PF65 80.00				

KM# 440 DOLLAR

28.28 g., Coppor Nickel, 38.61 mm. **Ruler:** Elizabeth II **Subject:** Lifetime of Service **Obv:** Head in tiara right **Rev:** Conjoined busts of Elizabeth II and Prince Philip

Date	Mintage	F12	VF20	XF40	MS60	MS63
2010	—	—	—	—	—	20.00

KM# 440a DOLLAR

28.28 g., 0.925 Silver 0.8356 oz. ASW, 38.61 mm. **Ruler:** Elizabeth II **Subject:** Lifetime of Service **Obv:** Head with tiara right **Rev:** Conjoined busts of Elizabeth II and Prince Philip

Date	Mintage	F12	VF20	XF40	MS60	MS63
2010	19,500	PF65 50.00				

KM# 441 DOLLAR

31.10 g., 0.999 Silver 0.9925 oz. ASW, 38.61 mm. **Ruler:** Elizabeth II **Subject:** Slovic mythology - Perun **Rev:** Two warriors, tree in background

Date	Mintage	F12	VF20	XF40	MS60	MS63
2010	1,000	PF65 65.00				

KM# 454 DOLLAR

Silver **Ruler:** Elizabeth II **Subject:** Polish Stadiums **Rev:** Michail Ktzov stadium

Date	Mintage	F12	VF20	XF40	MS60	MS63
2010	—	PF65 75.00				

KM# 455 DOLLAR

Silver **Ruler:** Elizabeth II **Subject:** Polish Stadiums **Rev:** Gdansk

Date	Mintage	F12	VF20	XF40	MS60	MS63
2010	—	PF65 75.00				

KM# 456 DOLLAR

31.10 g., 0.999 Silver 0.9926 oz. ASW, 40 mm. **Ruler:** Elizabeth II **Subject:** Giah Thong - safe conduct pass **Obv:** Head with tiara right **Rev:** Two soldiers below Viet Nam flag

Date	Mintage	F12	VF20	XF40	MS60	MS63
2010 Prooflike	—	—	—	—	—	50.00

KM# 495 DOLLAR

28.28 g., 0.925 Silver 0.8356 oz. ASW, 38.61 mm. **Ruler:** Elizabeth II **Subject:** Zodiac Mucha Paintings **Rev:** Aries

Date	Mintage	F12	VF20	XF40	MS60	MS63
2010	10,000	PF65 65.00				

KM# 496 DOLLAR

28.28 g., 0.925 Silver 0.8356 oz. ASW, 38.61 mm. **Ruler:** Elizabeth II **Subject:** Zodiac Mucha Paintings **Rev:** Taurus

Date	Mintage	F12	VF20	XF40	MS60	MS63
2010	10,000	PF65 65.00				

KM# 497 DOLLAR

28.28 g., 0.925 Silver 0.8356 oz. ASW, 38.61 mm. **Ruler:** Elizabeth II **Subject:** Zodiac Mucha Paintings **Rev:** Gemini

Date	Mintage	F12	VF20	XF40	MS60	MS63
2010	10,000	PF65 65.00				

KM# 498 DOLLAR

28.28 g., 0.925 Silver 0.8356 oz. ASW, 38.61 mm. **Ruler:** Elizabeth II **Subject:** Zodiac Mucha Paintings **Rev:** Cancer

Date	Mintage	F12	VF20	XF40	MS60	MS63
2010	10,000	PF65 65.00				

KM# 499 DOLLAR

28.28 g., 0.925 Silver 0.8356 oz. ASW **Ruler:** Elizabeth II **Subject:** Zodiac Mucha Paintings **Rev:** Leo

Date	Mintage	F12	VF20	XF40	MS60	MS63
2010	10,000	PF65 65.00				

KM# 500 DOLLAR

28.25 g., 0.925 Silver 0.8347 oz. ASW, 38.61 mm. **Ruler:** Elizabeth II **Subject:** Zodiac Mucha Paintings **Rev:** Virgo

Date	Mintage	F12	VF20	XF40	MS60	MS63
2010	10,000	PF65 65.00				

KM# 501 DOLLAR

28.28 g., 0.925 Silver 0.8356 oz. ASW, 38.61 mm. **Ruler:** Elizabeth II **Subject:** Zodiac Mucha Paintings **Rev:** Libra

Date	Mintage	F12	VF20	XF40	MS60	MS63
2010	10,000	PF65 65.00				

KM# 502 DOLLAR

28.28 g., 0.925 Silver 0.8356 oz. ASW, 38.61 mm. **Ruler:** Elizabeth II **Subject:** Zodiac Mucha Paintings **Rev:** Scorpio

Date	Mintage	F12	VF20	XF40	MS60	MS63
2010	10,000	PF65 65.00				

KM# 503 DOLLAR
28.28 g., 0.925 Silver 0.8356 oz. ASW, 38.61 mm. **Ruler:** Elizabeth II **Subject:** Zodiac Mucha Paintings **Rev:** Sagittarius

Date	Mintage	F12	VF20	XF40	MS60	MS63
2010	10,000	PF65 65.00				

KM# 557 DOLLAR
28.28 g., 0.925 Silver 0.8356 oz. ASW, 30x50 mm. **Ruler:** Elizabeth II **Subject:** Westminister Abbey **Obv:** Head with tiara at left, interior view of end windows **Rev:** Exterior view with rose window detail **Shape:** vertical oval

Date	Mintage	F12	VF20	XF40	MS60	MS63
2010	5,000	PF65 100				

KM# 558 DOLLAR
28.28 g., 0.925 Silver 0.8356 oz. ASW, 30x50 mm. **Ruler:** Elizabeth II **Subject:** Stephansdom, Wein **Obv:** Head in tiara at left, view of organ screena dn statue detail **Rev:** Exterior rendering and detail **Shape:** Vertical oval

Date	Mintage	F12	VF20	XF40	MS60	MS63
2010	5,000	PF65 100				

KM# 943 DOLLAR
28.28 g., 0.925 Silver 0.8356 oz. ASW, 36.81 mm. **Ruler:** Elizabeth II **Subject:** Butterflies - Maculinea Arion **Rev:** Blue butterfly

Date	Mintage	F12	VF20	XF40	MS60	MS63
2010 Proof	Est. 8000	—	—	—	—	—

KM# 435 DOLLAR
15.55 g., 0.925 Silver 0.4595 oz. ASW, 35 mm. **Ruler:** Elizabeth II **Subject:** Prehistoric art - Chauvet cave **Rev:** Two figures of cats

Date	Mintage	F12	VF20	XF40	MS60	MS63
2011	1,000	PF65 65.00				

KM# 436 DOLLAR
15.55 g., 0.925 Silver 0.4595 oz. ASW, 35 mm. **Ruler:** Elizabeth II **Subject:** Prehistoric art - Altamira cave **Rev:** Bison artwork

Date	Mintage	F12	VF20	XF40	MS60	MS63
2011	1,000	PF65 65.00				

KM# 437 DOLLAR
15.55 g., 0.925 Silver 0.4595 oz. ASW, 35 mm. **Ruler:** Elizabeth II **Subject:** Prehistoric art - Lascaux cave **Rev:** Horse art

Date	Mintage	F12	VF20	XF40	MS60	MS63
2011	1,000	PF65 65.00				

KM# 438 DOLLAR
15.55 g., 0.925 Silver 0.4595 oz. ASW, 35 mm. **Ruler:** Elizabeth II **Subject:** Prehistoric art - Jabbaren cave **Rev:** Male figure with bow

Date	Mintage	F12	VF20	XF40	MS60	MS63
2011	1,000	PF65 65.00				

KM# 439 DOLLAR
15.55 g., 0.925 Silver 0.4595 oz. ASW, 35 mm. **Ruler:** Elizabeth II **Subject:** Prehistoric art - Tadrart cave **Rev:** Elephant art

Date	Mintage	F12	VF20	XF40	MS60	MS63
2011	1,000	PF65 65.00				

KM# 504 DOLLAR
28.28 g., 0.925 Silver 0.8356 oz. ASW, 38.61 mm. **Ruler:** Elizabeth II **Subject:** Zodiac Mucha Paintings **Rev:** Capricorn

Date	Mintage	F12	VF20	XF40	MS60	MS63
2011	10,000	PF65 65.00				

KM# 505 DOLLAR
28.28 g., 0.925 Silver 0.8356 oz. ASW, 38.61 mm. **Ruler:** Elizabeth II **Subject:** Zodiac Mucha Painting **Rev:** Aquarius

Date	Mintage	F12	VF20	XF40	MS60	MS63
2011	10,000	PF65 65.00				

KM# 506 DOLLAR
28.28 g., 0.925 Silver 0.8356 oz. ASW, 38.61 mm. **Ruler:** Elizabeth II **Subject:** Zodiac Mucha Paintings **Rev:** Pisces

Date	Mintage	F12	VF20	XF40	MS60	MS63
2011	10,000	PF65 65.00				

KM# 508 DOLLAR
Silver **Ruler:** Elizabeth II **Subject:** Russian Cartoons

Date	Mintage	F12	VF20	XF40	MS60	MS63
2011	—	PF65 70.00				

KM# 509 DOLLAR
Silver **Ruler:** Elizabeth II **Subject:** Russian Cartoons

Date	Mintage	F12	VF20	XF40	MS60	MS63
2011	—	PF65 70.00				

KM# 510 DOLLAR
28.28 g., 0.925 Silver 0.8356 oz. ASW, 55.6x41.6 mm. **Ruler:** Elizabeth II **Subject:** Year of the Rabbit **Rev:** Rabbit in the snow **Shape:** Horizontal oval

Date	Mintage	F12	VF20	XF40	MS60	MS63
2011	5,000	PF65 55.00				

KM# 514 DOLLAR
31.11 g., Silver Plated Copper-Nickel, 40 mm. **Ruler:** Elizabeth II **Subject:** Royal Engagement **Obv:** Head with tiara right **Rev:** Prince William and Catherine Middleton facing

Date	Mintage	F12	VF20	XF40	MS60	MS63
2011	10,000	PF65 25.00				

KM# 515 DOLLAR
31.10 g., Silver Plated Copper, 40 mm. **Ruler:** Elizabeth II **Subject:** Diana - A wife, Princess, Mother, Legend

Date	Mintage	F12	VF20	XF40	MS60	MS63
2011	10,000	PF65 20.00				

KM# 516 DOLLAR
31.10 g., Silver Plated Copper, 40 mm. **Ruler:** Elizabeth II
Subject: Diana - Wedding to Charles

Date	Mintage	F12	VF20	XF40	MS60	MS63
2011	10,000	PF65 20.00				

KM# 517 DOLLAR
31.10 g., Silver Plated Copper, 40 mm. **Ruler:** Elizabeth II
Subject: Diana - Engagement to Prince Charles

Date	Mintage	F12	VF20	XF40	MS60	MS63
2011	10,000	PF65 20.00				

KM# 518 DOLLAR
31.10 g., Silver Plated Copper, 40 mm. **Ruler:** Elizabeth II
Subject: Diana - Quote

Date	Mintage	F12	VF20	XF40	MS60	MS63
2011	10,000	PF65 20.00				

KM# 519 DOLLAR
31.10 g., Silver Plated Copper, 40 mm. **Ruler:** Elizabeth II
Subject: Diana - Mother Teresa

Date	Mintage	F12	VF20	XF40	MS60	MS63
2011	10,000	PF65 20.00				

KM# 520 DOLLAR
31.10 g., Silver Plated Copper, 40 mm. **Ruler:** Elizabeth II
Subject: Diana - We will always remember

Date	Mintage	F12	VF20	XF40	MS60	MS63
2011	10,000	PF65 20.00				

KM# 555 DOLLAR
28.28 g., 0.925 Silver 0.8356 oz. ASW, 38.61 mm. **Ruler:**
Elizabeth II **Subject:** Hanseatic Towns - Szezecin **Obv:** Head
with tiara right at left, map and ship **Rev:** Churches and ship at
dock, town shield

Date	Mintage	F12	VF20	XF40	MS60	MS63
2011	Est. 3000	PF65 75.00				

KM# 559 DOLLAR
28.28 g., 0.925 Silver 0.8356 oz. ASW, 38.61 mm. **Ruler:**
Elizabeth II **Subject:** Russian municipalities - Krasnoyarsk
Obv: Head with tiara right **Rev:** Town view

Date	Mintage	F12	VF20	XF40	MS60	MS63
2011	2,000	PF65 85.00				

KM# 560 DOLLAR
28.28 g., 0.925 Silver 0.8356 oz. ASW, 38.61 mm. **Ruler:**
Elizabeth II **Subject:** Russian municipalities - Norilsk **Obv:**
Head with tiara right **Rev:** Town view, shield above

Date	Mintage	F12	VF20	XF40	MS60	MS63
2011	2,000	PF65 85.00				

KM# 561 DOLLAR
28.28 g., 0.925 Silver 0.8356 oz. ASW, 38.61 mm. **Ruler:**
Elizabeth II **Subject:** Russian municipalities - Belgorod **Obv:**
Head with tiara right **Rev:** Statue at center, shield at left, tower
at right

Date	Mintage	F12	VF20	XF40	MS60	MS63
2011	2,000	PF65 85.00				

KM# 562 DOLLAR
28.28 g., 0.925 Silver 0.8356 oz. ASW, 30x50 mm. **Ruler:**
Elizabeth II **Subject:** Russian municipalities - Irkutsk **Obv:**
Head with tiara right **Rev:** Town view **Shape:** Vertical oval

Date	Mintage	F12	VF20	XF40	MS60	MS63
2011	2,000	PF65 85.00				

KM# 571 DOLLAR
28.28 g., 0.925 Silver 0.8356 oz. ASW, 40x40 mm. **Ruler:**
Elizabeth II **Obv:** Head with diadem right, tracks in background
Rev: Flying frog, Rhacophorus reinwardti **Shape:** Square

Date	Mintage	F12	VF20	XF40	MS60	MS63
2011	5,000	PF65 75.00				

KM# 583 DOLLAR
14.14 g., 0.925 Silver 0.4178 oz. ASW, 32 mm. **Ruler:** Elizabeth
II **Subject:** Russian comics - Bolek i Lolek **Rev:** Two western
children on horseback

Date	Mintage	F12	VF20	XF40	MS60	MS63
2011	Est. 4000	PF65 55.00				

KM# 585 DOLLAR
28.28 g., 0.925 Silver 0.8356 oz. ASW, 40x28 mm. **Ruler:**
Elizabeth II **Obv:** Head with tiara right, five girls in painting
Rev: Diego Velazquez and painting of female nude

Date	Mintage	F12	VF20	XF40	MS60	MS63
2011	Est. 5000	PF65 95.00				

KM# 586 DOLLAR
28.28 g., 0.925 Silver 0.8356 oz. ASW, 38.61 mm. **Ruler:**
Elizabeth II **Subject:** Amber Route - Aquileia **Rev:** Statue of
Romulus and Remus and wolf, amber insert

Date	Mintage	F12	VF20	XF40	MS60	MS63
2011 Antique finish	Est. 10000	—	—	—	—	85.00

KM# 617 DOLLAR
28.28 g., 0.925 Silver 0.8356 oz. ASW, 38.61 mm. **Ruler:**
Elizabeth II **Obv:** Bust with tiara right before sailing ship in
ornate frame **Rev:** Yunona and Avos facing each other in color,
ship below

Date	Mintage	F12	VF20	XF40	MS60	MS63
2011	Est. 5000	PF65 75.00				

KM# 618 DOLLAR
28.28 g., 0.925 Silver 0.8356 oz. ASW, 38.61 mm. **Ruler:**
Elizabeth II **Obv:** Head with tiara at left, map and sailing ship
at right, HANSA on ribbon above **Rev:** Town view of the port
of Szczecin

Date	Mintage	F12	VF20	XF40	MS60	MS63
2011	Est. 3000	PF65 75.00				

KM# 619 DOLLAR
28.28 g., 0.925 Silver 0.8356 oz. ASW, 41 mm. **Ruler:** Elizabeth
II **Obv:** Head in tiara at left, elephant in designs **Rev:** Two
elephants at tree, elephant in hologram

Date	Mintage	F12	VF20	XF40	MS60	MS63
2011	Est. 10000	PF65 75.00				

KM# 621 DOLLAR
16.81 g., 0.925 Silver 0.4967 oz. ASW, 36.81 mm. **Ruler:**
Elizabeth II **Obv:** Head with tiara right **Rev:** Chinese dragon
prancing right with ball

Date	Mintage	F12	VF20	XF40	MS60	MS63
2011	Est. 6000	PF65 75.00				

KM# 622 DOLLAR
16.81 g., 0.925 Silver 0.4967 oz. ASW, 36.81 mm. **Ruler:**
Elizabeth II **Obv:** Head with tiara right **Rev:** Child's fantasy
dragon, knight and castle

Date	Mintage	F12	VF20	XF40	MS60	MS63
2011	Est. 6000	PF65 75.00				

KM# 641 DOLLAR

28.28 g., 0.925 Silver 0.8356 oz. ASW, 40x28 mm. **Ruler:** Elizabeth II **Obv:** Portrait at left, painting **Rev:** Portrait at left, painting **Shape:** Horizontal rectangle

Date	Mintage	F12	VF20	XF40	MS60	MS63
2011	5,000	PF65 100				

KM# 647 DOLLAR

31.11 g., 0.999 Silver 0.9926 oz. ASW, 38.61 mm. **Ruler:** Elizabeth II **Subject:** First European to cross the Simpson Desert **Obv:** Head with tiara right **Rev:** Simpson Desert and Ted Colson in 3-D color **Edge:** Reeded

Date	Mintage	F12	VF20	XF40	MS60	MS63
2011	2,000	PF65 75.00				

KM# 652 DOLLAR

28.28 g., 0.925 Silver 0.8356 oz. ASW, 38.61 mm. **Ruler:** Elizabeth II **Subject:** Papilio Machaon **Obv:** Head in tiara right, butterfly wing in background **Rev:** Butterfly in color

Date	Mintage	F12	VF20	XF40	MS60	MS63
2011	Est. 5000	PF65 65.00				

KM# 653 DOLLAR

Silver Plated Copper, 40 mm. **Ruler:** Elizabeth II **Subject:** Star Wars - Obi-Wan Kenobi

Date	Mintage	F12	VF20	XF40	MS60	MS63
2011	—	—	—	—	—	25.00

KM# 654 DOLLAR

Silver Plated Copper, 40 mm. **Ruler:** Elizabeth II **Subject:** Star Wars - Yoda

Date	Mintage	F12	VF20	XF40	MS60	MS63
2011	Est. 50000	—	—	—	—	25.00

KM# 655 DOLLAR

Silver Plated Copper, 40 mm. **Ruler:** Elizabeth II **Subject:** Star Wars - Princess Leia

Date	Mintage	F12	VF20	XF40	MS60	MS63
2011	Est. 50000	—	—	—	—	25.00

KM# 656 DOLLAR

Silver Plated Copper, 40 mm. **Ruler:** Elizabeth II **Subject:** Star Wars - Luke Skywalker

Date	Mintage	F12	VF20	XF40	MS60	MS63
2011	Est. 50000	—	—	—	—	25.00

KM# 657 DOLLAR

Silver Plated Copper, 40 mm. **Ruler:** Elizabeth II **Subject:** Star Wars - C3PO

Date	Mintage	F12	VF20	XF40	MS60	MS63
2011	Est. 50000	—	—	—	—	25.00

KM# 658 DOLLAR

Silver Plated Copper, 40 mm. **Ruler:** Elizabeth II **Subject:** Star Wars - R2-D2

Date	Mintage	F12	VF20	XF40	MS60	MS63
2011	Est. 50000	—	—	—	—	25.00

KM# 659 DOLLAR

Silver Plated Copper, 40 mm. **Ruler:** Elizabeth II **Subject:** Star Wars - Darth Vader

Date	Mintage	F12	VF20	XF40	MS60	MS63
2011	—	—	—	—	—	25.00

KM# 660 DOLLAR

Silver Plated Copper, 40 mm. **Ruler:** Elizabeth II **Subject:** Star Wars - Emperor Palpatine

Date	Mintage	F12	VF20	XF40	MS60	MS63
2011	Est. 50000	—	—	—	—	25.00

KM# 661 DOLLAR

Silver Plated Copper, 40 mm. **Ruler:** Elizabeth II **Subject:** Star Wars - Han Solo

Date	Mintage	F12	VF20	XF40	MS60	MS63
2011	—	—	—	—	—	25.00

KM# 662 DOLLAR

Silver Plated Copper, 40 mm. **Ruler:** Elizabeth II **Subject:** Star Wars - Chewbacca

Date	Mintage	F12	VF20	XF40	MS60	MS63
2011	Est. 50000	—	—	—	—	25.00

KM# 674 DOLLAR
28.28 g., 0.925 Silver 0.8356 oz. ASW, 40x28 mm. **Ruler:** Elizabeth II **Rev:** Orville and Wilbur Wright **Shape:** Rectangle

Date	Mintage	F12	VF20	XF40	MS60	MS63
2011	Est. 6000	PF65 75.00				

KM# 688 DOLLAR
16.81 g., 0.925 Silver 0.4967 oz. ASW, 38.61 mm. **Ruler:** Elizabeth II **Subject:** Amber Route **Rev:** Map of European cities

Date	Mintage	F12	VF20	XF40	MS60	MS63
2011	Est. 15000	PF65 85.00				

KM# 690 DOLLAR
28.28 g., 0.925 Silver 0.8356 oz. ASW, 40.7 mm. **Ruler:** Elizabeth II **Subject:** Lucky-coin - Ladybug **Obv:** Head with tiara right, ladybug and flowers **Rev:** Ladybug and flowers

Date	Mintage	F12	VF20	XF40	MS60	MS63
2011	Est. 10000	PF65 80.00				

KM# 703 DOLLAR
10.00 g., 0.925 Silver 0.2955 oz. ASW, 13x30 mm. **Ruler:** Elizabeth II **Rev:** Amber insert in gilt floral motif **Shape:** Vertical rectangle

Date	Mintage	F12	VF20	XF40	MS60	MS63
2011	Est. 12000	—				50.00

KM# 704 DOLLAR
28.28 g., 0.925 Silver 0.8356 oz. ASW, 30x50 mm. **Ruler:** Elizabeth II **Subject:** Barcerlona Cathedral **Obv:** Cross and interior cathedral view **Rev:** Exterior cathedral view **Shape:** Oval

Date	Mintage	F12	VF20	XF40	MS60	MS63
2011	5,000	PF65 100				

KM# 705 DOLLAR
28.28 g., 0.925 Silver 0.8356 oz. ASW, 30x50 mm. **Ruler:** Elizabeth II **Subject:** Prague's St. Wenceslas Cathedral **Obv:** Cathedral window at top, side exterior view below **Rev:** Cathedral window and ceiling motif **Shape:** Vertical Oval

Date	Mintage	F12	VF20	XF40	MS60	MS63
2011	5,000	PF65 100				

KM# 706 DOLLAR
28.28 g., 0.925 Silver 0.8356 oz. ASW, 30x50 mm. **Ruler:** Elizabeth II **Subject:** Cracow's St. Mary Cathedral **Obv:** Cathedral window and sculpture scene **Rev:** Cathedral Window, exterior view and ceiling rendering **Shape:** Vertical oval

Date	Mintage	F12	VF20	XF40	MS60	MS63
2011	1,500	PF65 100				

KM# 707 DOLLAR
28.28 g., 0.925 Silver 0.8356 oz. ASW, 35x45 mm. **Ruler:** Elizabeth II **Subject:** Love Love Love **Obv:** Queens head within open egg design **Rev:** Two cherubs and heart **Shape:** Vertical oval

Date	Mintage	F12	VF20	XF40	MS60	MS63
2011	7,000	PF65 100				

KM# 709 DOLLAR
16.81 g., 0.925 Silver 0.4967 oz. ASW, 38.61 mm. **Ruler:** Elizabeth II **Obv:** Ancient horsecart **Obv. Legend:** SZLAK BURSZTYNOWY **Rev:** Neptune statue, ancient coin, mine building, amber insert **Rev. Legend:** GDANSK

Date	Mintage	F12	VF20	XF40	MS60	MS63
2011	Est. 12000	PF65 90.00				

KM# 711 DOLLAR
14.14 g., 0.925 Silver 0.4178 oz. ASW, 32 mm. **Ruler:** Elizabeth II **Subject:** Russian Cartoon - Reksio **Rev:** Dog, cat and rooster in color

Date	Mintage	F12	VF20	XF40	MS60	MS63
2011	Est. 6000	PF65 100				

KM# 741 DOLLAR
28.20 g., 0.925 Silver 0.8356 oz ASW **Ruler:** Elizabeth II **Obv:** Head crowned at top, key **Rev:** Cat walking through open door **Shape:** Irregular

Date	Mintage	F12	VF20	XF40	MS60	MS63
2011	7,000	PF65 75.00				

KM# 942 DOLLAR
28.28 g., 0.925 Silver 0.8356 oz. ASW, 38.61 mm. **Ruler:** Elizabeth II **Subject:** Hanseatic Towns: Rostock

Date	Mintage	F12	VF20	XF40	MS60	MS63
2011	Est. 8000	PF65 85.00				

KM# 735 DOLLAR

28.28 g., 0.925 Silver 0.8356 oz. ASW, 38.61 mm. **Ruler:** Elizabeth II **Subject:** Hannibal Barkas **Obv:** Two elephant heads facing each other **Rev:** Hannibal's head left above three war elephants

Date	Mintage	F12	VF20	XF40	MS60	MS63
2012	Est. 5000	PF65 120				

KM# 644 DOLLAR

28.28 g., 0.925 Silver 0.8356 oz. ASW, 35.1x45.1 mm. **Ruler:** Elizabeth II **Subject:** Year of the Dragon **Obv:** Head with crown right **Rev:** Multicolor dragon **Shape:** Vertical oval

Date	Mintage	F12	VF20	XF40	MS60	MS63
2012	5,000	PF65 100				

KM# 645 DOLLAR

28.28 g., 0.925 Silver 0.8356 oz. ASW, 35.1x45.1 mm. **Ruler:** Elizabeth II **Subject:** Year of the Dragon **Obv:** Head with crown right **Rev:** Multicolor juvenile dragon **Shape:** Vertical oval

Date	Mintage	F12	VF20	XF40	MS60	MS63
2012	5,000	PF65 100				

KM# 646 DOLLAR

28.28 g., 0.925 Silver 0.8356 oz. ASW, 45.1x35.1 mm. **Ruler:** Elizabeth II **Subject:** Year of the Dragon **Obv:** Head with crown right **Rev:** Multicolor Love dragon forming heart **Shape:** Horizontal oval

Date	Mintage	F12	VF20	XF40	MS60	MS63
2012	5,000	PF65 100				

KM# 687 DOLLAR

31.11 g., 0.925 Silver 0.9191 oz. ASW, 39 mm. **Ruler:** Elizabeth II **Rev:** Crowned fantasy fish **Shape:** 12-sided

Date	Mintage	F12	VF20	XF40	MS60	MS63
2012	2,000	PF65 80.00				

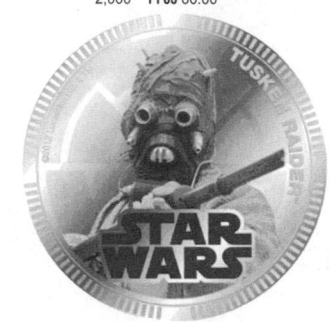

KM# 725 DOLLAR

Nickel Plated Copper, 40.7 mm. **Ruler:** Elizabeth II **Subject:** Star Wars - Tusken Raider

Date	Mintage	F12	VF20	XF40	MS60	MS63
2012	50,000	—	—	—	—	25.00

KM# 726 DOLLAR

Nickel Plated Copper, 40.7 mm. **Ruler:** Elizabeth II **Subject:** Star Wars - Ewok Wicket

Date	Mintage	F12	VF20	XF40	MS60	MS63
2012	50,000	—	—	—	—	25.00

KM# 727 DOLLAR

Silver, 40.7 mm. **Ruler:** Elizabeth II **Subject:** Star Wars - Nien Nunb

Date	Mintage	F12	VF20	XF40	MS60	MS63
2012	50,000	—	—	—	—	25.00

KM# 728 DOLLAR

Nickel Plated Copper, 40.7 mm. **Ruler:** Elizabeth II **Subject:** Star Wars - Lando Calrissian

Date	Mintage	F12	VF20	XF40	MS60	MS63
2012	50,000	—	—	—	—	25.00

KM# 729 DOLLAR

Nickel Plated Copper, 40.7 mm. **Ruler:** Elizabeth II **Subject:** Star Wars - Grand Moff Tarkin

Date	Mintage	F12	VF20	XF40	MS60	MS63
2012	50,000	—	—	—	—	25.00

KM# 730 DOLLAR

Nickel Plated Copper, 40.7 mm. **Ruler:** Elizabeth II **Subject:** Star Wars - Stormtrooper

Date	Mintage	F12	VF20	XF40	MS60	MS63
2012	50,000	—	—	—	—	25.00

KM# 731 DOLLAR

Nickel Plated Copper, 40.7 mm. **Ruler:** Elizabeth II **Subject:** Star Wars - Jabba the Hutt

Date	Mintage	F12	VF20	XF40	MS60	MS63
2012	50,000	—	—	—	—	25.00

KM# 732 DOLLAR

Nickel Plated Copper, 40.7 mm. **Ruler:** Elizabeth II **Subject:** Star Wars - Admiral Ackbar

Date	Mintage	F12	VF20	XF40	MS60	MS63
2012	50,000	—	—	—	—	25.00

KM# 733 DOLLAR
Nickel Plated Copper, 40.7 mm. **Ruler:** Elizabeth II **Subject:** Star Wars - Jawa

Date	Mintage	F12	VF20	XF40	MS60	MS63
2012	50,000	—	—	—	—	25.00

KM# 734 DOLLAR
Nickel Plated Copper, 40.7 mm. **Ruler:** Elizabeth II **Subject:** Star Wars - Boba Fett

Date	Mintage	F12	VF20	XF40	MS60	MS63
2012	50,000	—	—	—	—	25.00

KM# 739 DOLLAR
15.55 g., 0.999 Silver 0.4962 oz. ASW, 36 mm. **Ruler:** Elizabeth II **Subject:** Viet Nam War, 50th Anniversary of Australia's involvement **Rev:** Two soldiers on patrol, on close, helicopter above

Date	Mintage	F12	VF20	XF40	MS60	MS63
2012	2,500	PF65 50.00				

KM# 757 DOLLAR
25.00 g., 0.925 Silver 0.7387 oz. ASW, 40 mm. **Ruler:** Elizabeth II **Subject:** Battle for Australia - Bombing of Darwin **Rev:** Soldier with machine gun post and Japanese plane in sky, ship in distance

Date	Mintage	F12	VF20	XF40	MS60	MS63
2012	Est. 1942	PF65 75.00				

KM# 758 DOLLAR
25.00 g., 0.925 Silver 0.7387 oz. ASW, 40 mm. **Ruler:** Elizabeth II **Subject:** Battle for Australia - Sydney Harbor **Rev:** Sub, ship and pontoon plane with Sydney Harbor bridge

Date	Mintage	F12	VF20	XF40	MS60	MS63
2012	Est. 1942	PF65 100				

KM# 759 DOLLAR
25.00 g., 0.925 Silver 0.7387 oz. ASW, 40 mm. **Ruler:** Elizabeth II **Subject:** Battle for Australia - Kokoda Track **Rev:** Two injured soldiers being protected by third

Date	Mintage	F12	VF20	XF40	MS60	MS63
2012	Est. 1942	PF65 100				

KM# 760 DOLLAR
25.00 g., 0.925 Silver 0.7387 oz. ASW, 40 mm. **Ruler:** Elizabeth II **Subject:** Battle for Australia - Coral Sea **Rev:** Battle ship and planes

Date	Mintage	F12	VF20	XF40	MS60	MS63
2012	Est. 1942	PF65 100				

KM# 761 DOLLAR
25.00 g., 0.925 Silver 0.7387 oz. ASW, 40 mm. **Ruler:** Elizabeth II **Subject:** First car to cross Australia - The Brush **Obv:** Head with crown right **Rev:** Early automobile, color landscape below

Date	Mintage	F12	VF20	XF40	MS60	MS63
2012	Est. 2500	PF65 100				

KM# 763 DOLLAR
28.28 g., 0.925 Silver 0.8356 oz. ASW, 30x50 mm. **Ruler:** Elizabeth II **Rev:** Fisherman and nice trout **Rev. Legend:** BEGINNER'S LUCK **Shape:** Vertical oval

Date	Mintage	F12	VF20	XF40	MS60	MS63
2012	Est. 7000	PF65 120				

KM# 764 DOLLAR
28.28 g., 0.925 Silver 0.8356 oz. ASW, 28x40 mm. **Ruler:** Elizabeth II **Subject:** Ksenia of Petersburg **Rev:** Female saint with cane, church at lower left **Shape:** Vertical rectangle

Date	Mintage	F12	VF20	XF40	MS60	MS63
2012	Est. 7000	PF65 100				

KM# 765 DOLLAR
28.28 g., 0.925 Silver 0.8356 oz. ASW, 38.61 mm. **Ruler:** Elizabeth II **Subject:** Russian Cities - Kuzbas **Rev:** Statue of Worker, gear in background

Date	Mintage	F12	VF20	XF40	MS60	MS63
2012	Est. 4000	PF65 100				

KM# 766 DOLLAR
28.28 g., 0.925 Silver 0.8356 oz. ASW, 38.61 mm. **Ruler:** Elizabeth II **Subject:** Russian Cities - Novosibirsk **Rev:** Church tower, bridge in distance

Date	Mintage	F12	VF20	XF40	MS60	MS63
2012	Est. 2000	PF65 100				

KM# 767 DOLLAR
28.28 g., 0.925 Silver 0.8356 oz. ASW, 38.61 mm. **Ruler:** Elizabeth II **Subject:** Stars Flight **Rev:** International Space Station and Russian stamp

Date	Mintage	F12	VF20	XF40	MS60	MS63
2012	Est. 5000	PF65 100				

KM# 768 DOLLAR
28.28 g., 0.925 Silver 0.8356 oz. ASW, 38.61 mm. **Ruler:** Elizabeth II **Subject:** War of 1812 - Artillery **Rev:** Soldier standing beside cannon

Date	Mintage	F12	VF20	XF40	MS60	MS63
2012	Est. 5000	PF65 100				

KM# 769 DOLLAR
28.28 g., 0.925 Silver 0.8356 oz. ASW, 38.61 mm. **Ruler:** Elizabeth II **Subject:** War of 1812 - Cavalry **Rev:** Horseman with sword

Date	Mintage	F12	VF20	XF40	MS60	MS63
2012	—	PF65 100				

KM# 770 DOLLAR
28.28 g., 0.925 Silver 0.8356 oz. ASW, 38.61 mm. **Ruler:** Elizabeth II **Subject:** War of 1812 - Infantry **Rev:** Soldier with rifle

Date	Mintage	F12	VF20	XF40	MS60	MS63
2012	Est. 5000	PF65 100				

KM# 771 DOLLAR
28.28 g., 0.925 Silver 0.8356 oz. ASW, 38.61 mm. **Ruler:** Elizabeth II **Subject:** War of 1812 - Generals

Date	Mintage	F12	VF20	XF40	MS60	MS63
2012	—	PF65 100				

KM# 772 DOLLAR

27.50 g., Silver Plated Copper-Nickel, 40 mm. **Ruler:** Elizabeth II **Subject:** Benedict XVI's visit to Brazil, 5th Anniversary **Rev:** Statue of Nossa Senhora, image of Benedict

Date	Mintage	F12	VF20	XF40	MS60	MS63
2012	Est. 1000	PF65 25.00				

KM# 773 DOLLAR

16.81 g., 0.925 Silver 0.4967 oz. ASW, 38.61 mm. **Ruler:** Elizabeth II **Subject:** Stare Hradisko **Obv:** Queen's head at left, two horse cart at right **Rev:** Celtic coin image and art, amber insert

Date	Mintage	F12	VF20	XF40	MS60	MS63
2012	Est. 12000	PF65 65.00				

KM# 775 DOLLAR

16.81 g., 0.925 Silver 0.4967 oz. ASW, 29x39 mm. **Ruler:** Elizabeth II **Subject:** Imperial Faberge Eggs - Coronation egg **Rev:** Egg and state coach

Date	Mintage	F12	VF20	XF40	MS60	MS63
2012	Est. 9999	PF65 95.00				

KM# 779 DOLLAR

16.81 g., 0.925 Silver 0.4967 oz. ASW, 38.61 mm. **Ruler:** Elizabeth II **Subject:** Silk Route - Wroclaw **Obv:** Queen's head at left, two horse cart at right **Rev:** Old building at left, statue at right

Date	Mintage	F12	VF20	XF40	MS60	MS63
2012	Est. 12000	PF65 85.00				

KM# 781 DOLLAR

28.28 g., 0.925 Silver 0.8356 oz. ASW, 38.61 mm. **Ruler:** Elizabeth II **Subject:** March 8th, International Woman's Day

Obv: Head with tiara right **Rev:** Flowers, date in Russian

Date	Mintage	F12	VF20	XF40	MS60	MS63
2012	Est. 2000	PF65 75.00				

KM# 787 DOLLAR

0.30 g., 0.999 Gold AGW, 11 mm. **Ruler:** Elizabeth II **Obv:** Head with tiara right **Rev:** Princess Grace of Monaco (Grace Kelly) head left

Date	Mintage	F12	VF20	XF40	MS60	MS63
2012	—	PF65 75.00				

KM# 790 DOLLAR

28.28 g., 0.925 Silver 0.8356 oz. ASW, 28x40 mm. **Ruler:** Elizabeth II **Subject:** Art of Hunting, Fox Hunt **Obv:** Pointer, left **Rev:** Fox, hounds and riders **Shape:** Vertical rectangle

Date	Mintage	F12	VF20	XF40	MS60	MS63
2012	4,000	PF65 120				

KM# 792 DOLLAR

14.14 g., 0.925 Silver 0.4178 oz. ASW, 49.9x32.8x9.15 mm. **Ruler:** Elizabeth II **Subject:** Swallow's Nest **Obv:** Island view **Rev:** Castle atop cliff **Shape:** Irregular

Date	Mintage	F12	VF20	XF40	MS60	MS63
2012	Est. 3000	PF65 100				

KM# 794 DOLLAR

16.81 g., 0.925 Silver 0.4967 oz. ASW, 38.61 mm. **Ruler:** Elizabeth II **Subject:** Szlak Bursztynowy - Szombathely **Rev:** Old coin, building, amber insert

Date	Mintage	F12	VF20	XF40	MS60	MS63
2012	Est. 12000	PF65 75.00				

KM# 800 DOLLAR

28.28 g., 0.925 Silver 0.8356 oz. ASW, 38.61 mm. **Ruler:** Elizabeth II **Rev:** Goliath Birdwing butterfly **Rev. Legend:** ORNITHOPTERA GOLIATH

Date	Mintage	F12	VF20	XF40	MS60	MS63
2012	Est. 8000	PF65 100				

Obv: Head with tiara right **Rev:** Flowers, date in Russian

KM# 804 DOLLAR

14.14 g., 0.925 Silver 0.4178 oz. ASW, 37x30 mm. **Ruler:** Elizabeth II **Subject:** Me **Obv:** Queen's head with tiara right, four baloon hearts **Rev:** Bird facing left **Shape:** Irregular

Date	Mintage	F12	VF20	XF40	MS60	MS63
2012	Est. 10000	PF65 75.00				

KM# 805 DOLLAR

14.14 g., 0.925 Silver 0.4178 oz. ASW, 37x30 mm. **Ruler:** Elizabeth II **Subject:** You **Obv:** Queen's head in tiara at right, three heart baloons **Rev:** Bird facing right **Shape:** Irregular

Date	Mintage	F12	VF20	XF40	MS60	MS63
2012	Est. 10000	PF65 75.00				

KM# 828 DOLLAR

28.28 g., 0.925 Silver 0.8356 oz. ASW, 36.61 mm. **Ruler:** Elizabeth II **Obv:** Crowned ehad right within soccer ball motif **Rev:** Poznan stadium

Date	Mintage	F12	VF20	XF40	MS60	MS63
2012	1,000	PF65 90.00				

KM# 829 DOLLAR

28.28 g., 0.925 Silver 0.8356 oz. ASW, 38.61 mm. **Ruler:** Elizabeth II **Obv:** Head in tiara right within soccer ball motif **Rev:** Wroclaw stadium

Date	Mintage	F12	VF20	XF40	MS60	MS63
2012	1,000	PF65 90.00				

KM# 830 DOLLAR

28.28 g., 0.925 Silver 0.8356 oz. ASW, 38.61 mm. **Ruler:** Elizabeth II **Obv:** Head with tiara right within soccer ball motif **Rev:** Lviv stadium

Date	Mintage	F12	VF20	XF40	MS60	MS63
2012	1,000	PF65 90.00				

KM# 831 DOLLAR
28.28 g., 0.925 Silver 0.8356 oz. ASW, 38.61 mm. **Ruler:**
Elizabeth II **Obv:** Head with tiara right within soccer ball motif
Rev: Kiev stadium

Date	Mintage	F12	VF20	XF40	MS60	MS63
2012	1,000	PF65 90.00				

KM# 832 DOLLAR
28.28 g., 0.925 Silver 0.8356 oz. ASW, 38.61 mm. **Ruler:**
Elizabeth II **Obv:** Head with tiara right within soccer ball motif
Rev: Donetsk stadium

Date	Mintage	F12	VF20	XF40	MS60	MS63
2012	1,000	PF65 90.00				

KM# 833 DOLLAR
28.28 g., 0.925 Silver 0.8356 oz. ASW, 38.61 mm. **Ruler:**
Elizabeth II **Obv:** Head with tiara right within soccer ball motif
Rev: Kharkiv stadium

Date	Mintage	F12	VF20	XF40	MS60	MS63
2012	1,000	PF65 90.00				

KM# 841 DOLLAR
16.81 g., 0.925 Silver 0.4967 oz. ASW, 38.61 mm. **Ruler:**
Elizabeth II **Subject:** Amber Route **Obv:** Head with tiara at
left, cart, map **Rev:** Ruins, statue, coin and amber insert **Rev.**
Legend: CARNUNTUM

Date	Mintage	F12	VF20	XF40	MS60	MS63
2012	12,000	PF65 65.00				

KM# 843 DOLLAR
16.81 g., 0.925 Silver 0.4967 oz. ASW, 38.61 mm. **Ruler:**
Elizabeth II **Subject:** Amber Route **Obv:** Head with tiara at left,
cart, map **Rev:** She-wolf statue, mosaic, coin and amber insert
Rev. Legend: AQUILEIA

Date	Mintage	F12	VF20	XF40	MS60	MS63
2012	12,000	PF65 65.00				

KM# 847 DOLLAR
0.999 Silver **Ruler:** Elizabeth II **Obv:** Crowned head right **Rev:**
Statue of Amore and Psyche **Shape:** Irregular

Date	Mintage	F12	VF20	XF40	MS60	MS63
2012	1,000	PF65 50.00				

KM# 848 DOLLAR
0.999 Silver, 38.61 mm. **Ruler:** Elizabeth II **Obv:** Crowned head
at left **Rev:** Amor and Psyche statue cut out in center

Date	Mintage	F12	VF20	XF40	MS60	MS63
2012	1,000	PF65 50.00				

KM# 852 DOLLAR
28.28 g., 0.925 Silver 0.8356 oz. ASW, 38.61 mm. **Ruler:**
Elizabeth II **Subject:** Russian Municipalties - Tyra **Obv:**
Crowned head right **Rev:** Ancient carving

Date	Mintage	F12	VF20	XF40	MS60	MS63
2012	2,000	PF65 100				

KM# 853 DOLLAR
20.00 g., 0.999 Silver 0.6382 oz. ASW, 40 mm. **Ruler:** Elizabeth
II **Obv:** Crowned head right **Rev:** Vysotsky head at right

Date	Mintage	F12	VF20	XF40	MS60	MS63
2012	5,000	PF65 100				

KM# 854 DOLLAR
28.28 g., 0.925 Silver 0.8356 oz. ASW, 38.61 mm. **Ruler:**
Elizabeth II **Obv:** Crowned head right **Rev:** Alexander Nevski
at right, warriors on horseback at left.

Date	Mintage	F12	VF20	XF40	MS60	MS63
2012	5,000	PF65 100				

KM# 855 DOLLAR
16.81 g., 0.925 Silver 0.4967 oz. ASW, 29x39 mm. **Ruler:**
Elizabeth II **Obv:** Head with tiara right above open egg **Rev:**
Imperial Faberge Egg - Cockerel Egg

Date	Mintage	F12	VF20	XF40	MS60	MS63
2012	Est. 9999	PF65 95.00				

KM# 877 DOLLAR
28.28 g., 0.925 Silver 0.8356 oz. ASW, 41 mm. **Ruler:** Elizabeth
II **Obv:** Head with tiara right above snake insert **Rev:** Two
snakes forming heart shape, snake insert below

Date	Mintage	F12	VF20	XF40	MS60	MS63
2012//2013 (2012)	Est. 10000	PF65 85.00				

KM# 878 DOLLAR
16.81 g., 0.925 Silver 0.4967 oz. ASW, 38.61 mm. **Ruler:**

Elizabeth II **Obv:** Head with tiara right **Rev:** Snake coiled around itself

Date	Mintage	F12	VF20	XF40	MS60	MS63
2012//2013 (2012)	Est. 10000	PF65 50.00				

KM# 879 DOLLAR
28.28 g., 0.925 Silver 0.8356 oz. ASW, 38.61 mm. **Ruler:** Elizabeth II **Obv:** Head with tiara right **Rev:** Two rabbits holding heart

Date	Mintage	F12	VF20	XF40	MS60	MS63
2012	Est. 15000	PF65 100				

KM# 892 DOLLAR
28.28 g., 0.925 Silver 0.8356 oz. ASW, 35 x 45 mm. **Ruler:** Elizabeth II **Subject:** Iverskaya Chapel

Date	Mintage	F12	VF20	XF40	MS60	MS63
2012	Est. 7000	PF65 110				

KM# 893 DOLLAR
28.28 g., 0.925 Silver 0.8356 oz. ASW, 28.61 mm. **Ruler:** Elizabeth II **Subject:** Pskov

Date	Mintage	F12	VF20	XF40	MS60	MS63
2012	Est. 2000	PF65 120				

KM# 894 DOLLAR
28.28 g., 0.925 Silver 0.8356 oz. ASW, 28 x 40 mm. **Ruler:** Elizabeth II **Subject:** Saints of the Cities: John of Kronstadt

Date	Mintage	F12	VF20	XF40	MS60	MS63
2012	Est. 7000	PF65 100				

KM# 895 DOLLAR
28.28 g., 0.925 Silver 0.8356 oz. ASW, 28 x 40 mm. **Ruler:** Elizabeth II **Subject:** Saints of the Cities: St. Matrona

Date	Mintage	F12	VF20	XF40	MS60	MS63
2012	Est. 7000	PF65 100				

KM# 899 DOLLAR
31.10 g., 0.999 Silver 0.9925 oz. ASW, 32 mm. **Ruler:** Elizabeth II **Subject:** Merentibus Silver

Date	Mintage	F12	VF20	XF40	MS60	MS63
2012	Est. 5000	PF65 80.00				

KM# 900 DOLLAR
0.999 Silver **Ruler:** Elizabeth II **Subject:** Durer Codex: Dürer Coat of Arms

Date	Mintage	F12	VF20	XF40	MS60	MS63
2012	Est. 300	PF65 170				

KM# 901 DOLLAR
0.999 Silver **Ruler:** Elizabeth II **Subject:** Durer Codex: Adam & Eve

Date	Mintage	F12	VF20	XF40	MS60	MS63
2012	Est. 300	PF65 170				

KM# 902 DOLLAR
0.999 Silver **Ruler:** Elizabeth II **Subject:** Durer Codex: Melencolia I

Date	Mintage	F12	VF20	XF40	MS60	MS63
2012	Est. 300	PF65 170				

KM# 903 DOLLAR
0.999 Silver **Ruler:** Elizabeth II **Subject:** Durer Codex: The Southern Hemisphere

Date	Mintage	F12	VF20	XF40	MS60	MS63
2012	Est. 300	PF65 170				

KM# 904 DOLLAR
0.999 Silver **Ruler:** Elizabeth II **Subject:** Durer Codex: The Sun of Justice

Date	Mintage	F12	VF20	XF40	MS60	MS63
2012	Est. 300	PF65 170				

KM# 905 DOLLAR
0.999 Silver **Ruler:** Elizabeth II **Subject:** Durer Codex: Praying Hands

Date	Mintage	F12	VF20	XF40	MS60	MS63
2012	Est. 300	PF65 170				

KM# 906 DOLLAR
0.999 Silver **Ruler:** Elizabeth II **Subject:** Durer Codex: Small Triumpal Car

Date	Mintage	F12	VF20	XF40	MS60	MS63
2012	Est. 300	PF65 170				

KM# 907 DOLLAR
0.999 Silver **Ruler:** Elizabeth II **Subject:** Durer Codex: Hercules kills the birds symphalic

Date	Mintage	F12	VF20	XF40	MS60	MS63
2012	Est. 300	PF65 170				

KM# 908 DOLLAR
0.999 Silver **Ruler:** Elizabeth II **Subject:** Durer Codex: Apollo with Solar Disc

Date	Mintage	F12	VF20	XF40	MS60	MS63
2012	Est. 300	PF65 170				

KM# 909 DOLLAR
0.999 Silver **Ruler:** Elizabeth II **Subject:** Durer Codex: Praying Hands

Date	Mintage	F12	VF20	XF40	MS60	MS63
2012	Est. 300	PF65 170				

KM# 910 DOLLAR
0.999 Silver **Ruler:** Elizabeth II **Subject:** Durer Codex: Hands of Christ

Date	Mintage	F12	VF20	XF40	MS60	MS63
2012	Est. 300	PF65 170				

KM# 911 DOLLAR
0.999 Silver **Ruler:** Elizabeth II **Subject:** Durer Codex: Madonna with music making Angel

Date	Mintage	F12	VF20	XF40	MS60	MS63
2012	Est. 300	PF65 170				

KM# 912 DOLLAR
0.999 Silver **Ruler:** Elizabeth II **Subject:** Durer Codex: Nemesis

Date	Mintage	F12	VF20	XF40	MS60	MS63
2012	Est. 300	PF65 170				

KM# 913 DOLLAR
0.999 Silver **Ruler:** Elizabeth II **Subject:** Durer Codex: Praying Hands

Date	Mintage	F12	VF20	XF40	MS60	MS63
2012	Est. 300	PF65 170				

KM# 914 DOLLAR
0.999 Silver **Ruler:** Elizabeth II **Subject:** Durer Codex: Madonna on the Crescent

Date	Mintage	F12	VF20	XF40	MS60	MS63
2012	Est. 300	PF65 170				

KM# 915 DOLLAR
0.999 Silver **Ruler:** Elizabeth II **Subject:** Durer Codex: Rhinoceros

Date	Mintage	F12	VF20	XF40	MS60	MS63
2012	Est. 300	PF65 170				

KM# 916 DOLLAR
0.999 Silver **Ruler:** Elizabeth II **Subject:** Durer Codex: Two Lions

Date	Mintage	F12	VF20	XF40	MS60	MS63
2012	Est. 300	PF65 170				

KM# 917 DOLLAR
0.999 Silver **Ruler:** Elizabeth II **Subject:** Durer Codex: Abduction

Date	Mintage	F12	VF20	XF40	MS60	MS63
2012	Est. 300	PF65 170				

KM# 918 DOLLAR
0.999 Silver **Ruler:** Elizabeth II **Subject:** Durer Codex: Nude Woman with Zodiac

Date	Mintage	F12	VF20	XF40	MS60	MS63
2012	Est. 300	PF65 170				

KM# 919 DOLLAR
0.999 Silver **Ruler:** Elizabeth II **Subject:** Durer Codex: Small Horse

Date	Mintage	F12	VF20	XF40	MS60	MS63
2012	Est. 300	PF65 170				

KM# 920 DOLLAR
0.999 Silver **Ruler:** Elizabeth II **Subject:** Durer Codex: Agony in the garden

Date	Mintage	F12	VF20	XF40	MS60	MS63
2012	Est. 300	PF65 170				

KM# 921 DOLLAR
0.999 Silver **Ruler:** Elizabeth II **Subject:** Durer Codex: Saint George

Date	Mintage	F12	VF20	XF40	MS60	MS63
2012	Est. 300	PF65 170				

KM# 922 DOLLAR
0.999 Silver **Ruler:** Elizabeth II **Subject:** Durer Codex: St. Peter

Date	Mintage	F12	VF20	XF40	MS60	MS63
2012	Est. 300	PF65 170				

KM# 923 DOLLAR
0.999 Silver **Ruler:** Elizabeth II **Subject:** Durer Codex: St. John healing the Cripple

Date	Mintage	F12	VF20	XF40	MS60	MS63
2012	Est. 300	PF65 170				

KM# 925 DOLLAR
31.10 g., 0.925 Gold 0.9189 oz. AGW, 39 mm. **Ruler:** Elizabeth II **Subject:** Team Rubin

Date	Mintage	F12	VF20	XF40	MS60	MS63
2012 Proof-like	Est. 1000	PF65 100				

KM# 926 DOLLAR
31.10 g., 0.925 Silver 0.9189 oz. ASW, 39 mm. **Ruler:** Elizabeth II **Subject:** Team Rubin

Date	Mintage	F12	VF20	XF40	MS60	MS63
2012 Proof-like	Est. 1000	PF65 100				

KM# 927 DOLLAR
31.10 g., 0.925 Silver 0.9189 oz. ASW, 39 mm. **Ruler:** Elizabeth II **Subject:** Team Rubin

Date	Mintage	F12	VF20	XF40	MS60	MS63
2012	Est. 1000	PF65 100				

KM# 933 DOLLAR
13.00 g., 0.999 Silver 0.4149 oz. ASW, 28 mm. **Ruler:** Elizabeth II **Subject:** Ctyrlistek: Pinda

Date	Mintage	F12	VF20	XF40	MS60	MS63
2012	Est. 400	PF65 120				

KM# 934 DOLLAR
13.00 g., 0.999 Silver 0.4149 oz. ASW, 28 mm. **Ruler:** Elizabeth II **Subject:** Ctyrlistek: Myojulin

Date	Mintage	F12	VF20	XF40	MS60	MS63
2012	Est. 400	PF65 120				

KM# 935 DOLLAR
13.00 g., 0.999 Silver 0.4149 oz. ASW, 28 mm. **Ruler:** Elizabeth II **Subject:** Ctyrlistek: Bobik

Date	Mintage	F12	VF20	XF40	MS60	MS63
2012	Est. 400	PF65 120				

KM# 936 DOLLAR
13.00 g., 0.999 Silver 0.4149 oz. ASW, 28 mm. **Ruler:** Elizabeth II **Subject:** Ctyrlistek: Fifinka

Date	Mintage	F12	VF20	XF40	MS60	MS63
2012	Est. 400	PF65 120				

KM# 953 DOLLAR
16.81 g., 0.925 Silver 0.4967 oz. ASW, 39 x 29 mm. **Ruler:** Elizabeth II **Subject:** Imperial Faberge Eggs: Swan Egg

Date	Mintage	F12	VF20	XF40	MS60	MS63
2012	Est. 9999	PF65 95.00				

KM# 954 DOLLAR
28.28 g., 0.925 Silver 0.8356 oz. ASW, 40 x 40 mm. **Ruler:** Elizabeth II **Subject:** Lady With an Ermine

Date	Mintage	F12	VF20	XF40	MS60	MS63
2012	Est. 3000	PF65 120				

KM# 956 DOLLAR
16.81 g., 0.925 Silver 0.4967 oz. ASW, 39 x 29 mm. **Ruler:** Elizabeth II **Subject:** Imperial Faberge Eggs: Moscow Kremlin Egg

Date	Mintage	F12	VF20	XF40	MS60	MS63
2012	Est. 9999	PF65 95.00				

KM# 981 DOLLAR
28.28 g., 0.925 Silver 0.8356 oz. ASW, 40 mm. **Ruler:** Elizabeth II **Subject:** The Horsemen of the Apocalypse: Center coin

Date	Mintage	F12	VF20	XF40	MC60	MS63
2012	Est. 777	PF65 150				

KM# 982 DOLLAR
28.28 g., 0.925 Silver 0.8356 oz. ASW, 40 mm. **Ruler:** Elizabeth II **Subject:** Four Horsemen of the Apocalypse: White Horse

Date	Mintage	F12	VF20	XF40	MS60	MS63
2012	Est. 777	PF65 150				

KM# 983 DOLLAR
28.28 g., 0.925 Silver 0.8356 oz. ASW, 40 mm. **Ruler:** Elizabeth II **Subject:** Four Horsemen of the Apocalypse: Black Horse

Date	Mintage	F12	VF20	XF40	MS60	MS63
2012	Est. 777	PF65 150				

KM# 984 DOLLAR
28.28 g., 0.925 Silver 0.8356 oz. ASW, 40 mm. **Ruler:** Elizabeth II **Subject:** The Horsemen of the Apocalypse: Pale Horse

Date	Mintage	F12	VF20	XF40	MS60	MS63
2012	Est. 777	PF65 150				

KM# 985 DOLLAR
28.28 g., 0.925 Silver 0.8356 oz. ASW, 40 mm. **Ruler:** Elizabeth II **Subject:** Four Horsemen of the Apocalypse: Red Horse

Date	Mintage	F12	VF20	XF40	MS60	MS63
2012	Est. 777	PF65 150				

KM# 1000 DOLLAR
16.81 g., 0.925 Silver 0.4967 oz. ASW, 39 x 29 mm. **Ruler:** Elizabeth II **Subject:** Imperial Faberge Eggs: Bouquet of Lilies

Date	Mintage	F12	VF20	XF40	MS60	MS63
2012	Est. 9999	PF65 95.00				

KM# 1190 DOLLAR
16.81 g., 0.925 Silver 0.4967 oz. ASW, 39 x 29 mm. **Ruler:** Elizabeth II **Subject:** Imperial Faberge Eggs: Rosebud Egg

Date	Mintage	F12	VF20	XF40	MS60	MS63
2012	—	PF65 75.00				

KM# 1247 DOLLAR
28.28 g., 0.925 Silver 0.8356 oz. ASW, 38.61 mm. **Ruler:** Elizabeth II **Subject:** Catherine II

Date	Mintage	F12	VF20	XF40	MS60	MS63
2012	Est. 4000	PF65 125				

KM# 1088 DOLLAR
7.78 g., 0.999 Gold 0.2483 oz. AGW, 22 mm. **Ruler:** Elizabeth II **Subject:** Czech Olympians: Javelin

Date	Mintage	F12	VF20	XF40	MS60	MS63
2013	Est. 200	PF65 125				

KM# 849 DOLLAR
20.50 g., 0.999 Silver 0.6542 oz. ASW, 38.61 mm. **Ruler:** Elizabeth II **Obv:** Crowned head at left, coiled snake at center **Rev:** Coiled snake at center, cobra below

Date	Mintage	F12	VF20	XF40	MS60	MS63
2013	4,000	PF65 120				

KM# 850 DOLLAR
15.50 g., 0.999 Silver 0.4946 oz. ASW, 50 mm. **Ruler:** Elizabeth II **Obv:** Head in tiara right, curles in background **Rev:** Colored snake **Shape:** Ying-Yang

Date	Mintage	F12	VF20	XF40	MS60	MS63
2013	5,000	PF65 55.00				

KM# 851 DOLLAR
15.50 g., 0.925 Silver 0.458 oz. ASW, 50 mm. **Ruler:** Elizabeth II **Obv:** Crowned head right and waves in background **Rev:** Colored snake **Shape:** Ying-Yang

Date	Mintage	F12	VF20	XF40	MS60	MS63
2013	5,000	PF65 55.00				

KM# 861 DOLLAR
7.77 g., 0.999 Silver 0.248 oz. ASW, 22.1x22.1 mm. **Ruler:** Elizabeth II **Obv:** Crowned head right **Rev:** Monopoly board corner square - Go **Shape:** Square

Date	Mintage	F12	VF20	XF40	MS60	MS63
2013	5,000	PF65 40.00				

KM# 862 DOLLAR
7.77 g., 0.999 Silver 0.248 oz. ASW, 22.1x22.1 mm. **Ruler:** Elizabeth II **Obv:** Crowned head right **Rev:** Monopoly board corner square - Free Parking **Shape:** Square

Date	Mintage	F12	VF20	XF40	MS60	MS63
2013	5,000	PF65 40.00				

KM# 863 DOLLAR
7.77 g., 0.999 Silver 0.248 oz. ASW, 22.1x22.1 mm. **Ruler:** Elizabeth II **Obv:** Crowned head right **Rev:** Monopoly board corner square - Go to Jail **Shape:** Square

Date	Mintage	F12	VF20	XF40	MS60	MS63
2013	5,000	PF65 40.00				

KM# 864 DOLLAR
7.77 g., 0.999 Silver 0.248 oz. ASW, 22.1x22.1 mm. **Ruler:** Elizabeth II **Obv:** Crowned head right **Rev:** Monopoly board corner square - Jail **Shape:** Square

Date	Mintage	F12	VF20	XF40	MS60	MS63
2013	5,000	PF65 40.00				

KM# 868 DOLLAR
15.55 g., 0.999 Silver 0.4962 oz. ASW, 36 mm. **Ruler:** Elizabeth II **Obv:** Crowned head right **Rev:** Coral Snake, chinese characters above

Date	Mintage	F12	VF20	XF40	MS60	MS63
2013	8,000	PF65 50.00				

KM# 873 DOLLAR
20.00 g., Silver Plated Copper, 38.61 mm. **Ruler:** Elizabeth II **Obv:** Crowned head right **Rev:** Snake head facing ready to bite

Date	Mintage	F12	VF20	XF40	MS60	MS63
2013 Proof-like	1,500	—	—	—	—	25.00

KM# 874 DOLLAR
28.28 g., 0.925 Silver 0.8356 oz. ASW, 35x45 mm. **Ruler:** Elizabeth II **Obv:** Crowned head right **Rev:** Snake in color, coiled and raised up **Shape:** Vertical oval

Date	Mintage	F12	VF20	XF40	MS60	MS63
2013	3,000	PF65 100				

KM# 875 DOLLAR
28.28 g., 0.925 Silver 0.8356 oz. ASW, 35x45 mm. **Ruler:** Elizabeth II **Obv:** Crowned head right **Rev:** Humorous baby snake in color **Shape:** Vertical oval

Date	Mintage	F12	VF20	XF40	MS60	MS63
2013	7,000	PF65 100				

KM# 876 DOLLAR
28.28 g., 0.925 Silver 0.8356 oz. ASW, 35x45 mm. **Ruler:** Elizabeth II **Obv:** Crowned head right **Rev:** Love snake, coiled up as heart **Shape:** Vertical oval

Date	Mintage	F12	VF20	XF40	MS60	MS63
2013	7,000	PF65 100				

KM# 891 DOLLAR
28.28 g., 0.925 Silver 0.8356 oz. ASW, 35 x 45 mm. **Ruler:** Elizabeth II **Subject:** Love Tree

Date	Mintage	F12	VF20	XF40	MS60	MS63
2013	Est. 7000	PF65 75.00				

KM# 967 DOLLAR
25.50 g., 0.925 Silver 0.7535 oz. ASW, 30 x 40 mm. **Ruler:** Elizabeth II **Subject:** Russian ABCs - Letter B

Date	Mintage	F12	VF20	XF40	MS60	MS63
2013	Est. 5000	PF65 100				

KM# 968 DOLLAR
25.50 g., 0.925 Silver 0.7535 oz. ASW, 30 x 40 mm. **Ruler:** Elizabeth II **Subject:** Russian ABCs: Letter C

Date	Mintage	F12	VF20	XF40	MS60	MS63
2013	—	PF65 100				

KM# 969 DOLLAR
25.50 g., 0.925 Silver 0.7535 oz. ASW, 30 x 40 mm. **Ruler:** Elizabeth II **Subject:** Russian ABCs: Letter A

Date	Mintage	F12	VF20	XF40	MS60	MS63
2013	Est. 5000	PF65 100				

KM# 970 DOLLAR
0.999 Silver, 38.61 mm. **Ruler:** Elizabeth II **Subject:** Pieta - Inside

Date	Mintage	F12	VF20	XF40	MS60	MS63
2013	Est. 1000	PF65 150				

KM# 971 DOLLAR
0.999 Silver, 38.61 mm. **Ruler:** Elizabeth II **Subject:** Pieta - Outside

Date	Mintage	F12	VF20	XF40	MS60	MS63
2013	Est. 1000	PF65 150				

KM# 991 DOLLAR
28.28 g., 0.925 Silver 0.8356 oz. ASW, 38.61 mm. **Ruler:** Elizabeth II **Subject:** Iris Barbata

Date	Mintage	F12	VF20	XF40	MS60	MS63
2013	Est. 7000	PF65 75.00				

KM# 992 DOLLAR
28.28 g., 0.925 Silver 0.8356 oz. ASW **Ruler:** Elizabeth II **Subject:** Iris Florentina

Date	Mintage	F12	VF20	XF40	MS60	MS63
2013	Est. 7000	PF65 75.00				

KM# 993 DOLLAR
28.28 g., 0.925 Silver 0.8356 oz. ASW, 38.61 mm. **Ruler:** Elizabeth II **Subject:** Iris Siberica

Date	Mintage	F12	VF20	XF40	MS60	MS63
2013	Est. 7000	PF65 75.00				

KM# 1001 DOLLAR
42.50 g., 0.999 Silver 1.3563 oz. ASW, 41.7 x 40 mm. **Ruler:** Elizabeth II **Subject:** Divine Comedy - 1 of 24

Date	Mintage	F12	VF20	XF40	MS60	MS63
2013	Est.250	PF65 175				

KM# 1002 DOLLAR
42.50 g., 0.999 Silver 1.3563 oz. ASW, 41.7 x 40 mm. **Ruler:** Elizabeth II **Subject:** Divine Comedy - 2 of 24

Date	Mintage	F12	VF20	XF40	MS60	MS63
2013	Est. 250	PF65 175				

KM# 1003 DOLLAR
42.50 g., 0.999 Silver 1.3563 oz. ASW, 41.7 x 40 mm. **Ruler:** Elizabeth II **Subject:** Divine Comedy - 3 of 24

Date	Mintage	F12	VF20	XF40	MS60	MS63
2013	Est. 250	PF65 175				

KM# 1004 DOLLAR
42.50 g., 0.999 Silver 1.3563 oz. ASW, 41.7 x 40 mm. **Ruler:** Elizabeth II **Subject:** Divine Comedy - 4 of 24

Date	Mintage	F12	VF20	XF40	MS60	MS63
2013	Est. 250	PF65 175				

KM# 1005 DOLLAR
42.50 g., 0.999 Silver 1.3563 oz. ASW, 41.7 x 40 mm. **Ruler:** Elizabeth II **Subject:** Divine Comedy - 5 of 24

Date	Mintage	F12	VF20	XF40	MS60	MS63
2013	Est. 250	PF65 175				

KM# 1006 DOLLAR
42.50 g., 0.999 Silver 1.3563 oz. ASW, 41.7 x 40 mm. **Ruler:** Elizabeth II **Subject:** Divine Comody - 6 of 24

Date	Mintage	F12	VF20	XF40	MS60	MS63
2013	Est. 250	PF65 175				

KM# 1007 DOLLAR
42.50 g., 0.999 Silver 1.3563 oz. ASW, 41.7 x 40 mm. **Ruler:** Elizabeth II **Subject:** Divine Comedy - 7 of 24

Date	Mintage	F12	VF20	XF40	MS60	MS63
2013						

KM# 1008 DOLLAR
42.50 g., 0.999 Silver 1.3563 oz. ASW, 41.7 x 40 mm. **Ruler:** Elizabeth II **Subject:** Divine Comedy - 8 of 24

Date	Mintage	F12	VF20	XF40	MS60	MS63
2013	Est. 250	PF65 175				

KM# 1009 DOLLAR
42.50 g., 0.999 Silver 1.3563 oz. ASW, 41.7 x 40 mm. **Ruler:** Elizabeth II **Subject:** Divine Comedy - 9 of 24

Date	Mintage	F12	VF20	XF40	MS60	MS63
2013	Est. 250	PF65 175				

KM# 1010 DOLLAR
42.50 g., 0.999 Silver 1.3563 oz. ASW, 41.7 x 40 mm. **Ruler:** Elizabeth II **Subject:** Divine Comedy - 10 of 24

Date	Mintage	F12	VF20	XF40	MS60	MS63
2013	Est. 250	PF65 175				

KM# 1011 DOLLAR
42.50 g., 0.999 Silver 1.3563 oz. ASW, 41.7 x 40 mm. **Ruler:** Elizabeth II **Subject:** Divine Comedy - 11 of 24

Date	Mintage	F12	VF20	XF40	MS60	MS63
2013	Est. 250	PF65 175				

KM# 1012 DOLLAR
42.50 g., 0.999 Silver 1.3563 oz. ASW, 41.7 x 40 mm. **Ruler:** Elizabeth II **Subject:** Divine Comedy - 12 of 24

Date	Mintage	F12	VF20	XF40	MS60	MS63
2013	Est. 250	PF65 175				

KM# 1013 DOLLAR
42.50 g., 0.999 Silver 1.3563 oz. ASW, 41.7 x 40 mm. **Ruler:** Elizabeth II **Subject:** Divine Comedy - 13 of 24

Date	Mintage	F12	VF20	XF40	MS60	MS63
2013	Est. 250	PF65 175				

KM# 1014 DOLLAR
42.50 g., 0.999 Silver 1.3563 oz. ASW, 41.7 x 40 mm. **Ruler:** Elizabeth II **Subject:** Divine Comedy - 14 of 24

Date	Mintage	F12	VF20	XF40	MS60	MS63
2013	Est. 250	PF65 175				

KM# 1015 DOLLAR
42.50 g., 0.999 Silver 1.3563 oz. ASW, 41.7 x 40 mm. **Ruler:** Elizabeth II **Subject:** Divine Comedy - 15 of 24

Date	Mintage	F12	VF20	XF40	MS60	MS63
2013	Est. 250	PF65 175				

KM# 1016 DOLLAR
42.50 g., 0.999 Silver 1.3563 oz. ASW, 41.7 x 40 mm. **Ruler:** Elizabeth II **Subject:** Divine Comedy - 16 of 24

Date	Mintage	F12	VF20	XF40	MS60	MS63
2013	Est. 250	PF65 175				

KM# 1017 DOLLAR
42.50 g., 0.999 Silver 1.3563 oz. ASW, 41.7 x 40 mm. **Ruler:** Elizabeth II **Subject:** Divine Comedy - 17 of 24

Date	Mintage	F12	VF20	XF40	MS60	MS63
2013	Est. 250	PF65 175				

KM# 1018 DOLLAR
42.50 g., 0.999 Silver 1.3563 oz. ASW, 41.7 x 40 mm. **Ruler:** Elizabeth II **Subject:** Divine Comedy - 18 of 24

Date	Mintage	F12	VF20	XF40	MS60	MS63
2013	Est. 250	PF65 175				

KM# 1019 DOLLAR
42.50 g., 0.999 Silver 1.3563 oz. ASW, 41.7 x 40 mm. **Ruler:** Elizabeth II **Subject:** Divine Comedy - 19 of 24

Date	Mintage	F12	VF20	XF40	MS60	MS63
2013	Est. 250	PF65 175				

KM# 1020 DOLLAR
42.50 g., 0.999 Silver 1.3563 oz. ASW, 41.7 x 40 mm. **Ruler:** Elizabeth II **Subject:** Divine Comedy - 20 of 24

Date	Mintage	F12	VF20	XF40	MS60	MS63
2013	Est. 250	PF65 175				

KM# 1021 DOLLAR
42.50 g., 0.999 Silver 1.3563 oz. ASW, 41.7 x 40 mm. **Ruler:** Elizabeth II **Subject:** Divine Comedy - 21 of 24

Date	Mintage	F12	VF20	XF40	MS60	MS63
2013	Est. 250	PF65 175				

KM# 1022 DOLLAR
42.50 g., 0.999 Silver 1.3563 oz. ASW, 41.7 x 40 mm. **Ruler:** Elizabeth II **Subject:** Divine Comedy - 22 of 24

Date	Mintage	F12	VF20	XF40	MS60	MS63
2013	Est. 250	PF65 175				

KM# 1023 DOLLAR
42.50 g., 0.999 Silver 1.3563 oz. ASW, 41.7 x 40 mm. **Ruler:** Elizabeth II **Subject:** Divine Comedy - 23 of 24

Date	Mintage	F12	VF20	XF40	MS60	MS63
2013	Est. 250	PF65 175				

KM# 1024 DOLLAR
42.50 g., 0.999 Silver 1.3563 oz. ASW, 41.7 x 40 mm. **Ruler:** Elizabeth II **Subject:** Divine Comedy - 24 of 24

Date	Mintage	F12	VF20	XF40	MS60	MS63
2013	Est. 250	PF65 175				

KM# 1075 DOLLAR
15.55 g., 0.999 Silver 0.4962 oz. ASW **Ruler:** Elizabeth II **Subject:** Australian Soldiers

Date	Mintage	F12	VF20	XF40	MS60	MS63
2013	Est. 2000	PF65 75.00				

KM# 1078 DOLLAR
14.14 g., 0.925 Silver 0.4178 oz. ASW, 32 mm. **Ruler:** Elizabeth II **Subject:** Cartoon Characters: Tom & Jerry

Date	Mintage	F12	VF20	XF40	MS60	MS63
2013	Est. 0000	PF65 75.00				

KM# 1081 DOLLAR
31.10 g., 0.999 Silver 0.9925 oz. ASW, 50 x 27.3 mm. **Ruler:** Elizabeth II **Subject:** In Love - Left

Date	Mintage	F12	VF20	XF40	MS60	MS63
2013	Est. 4444	PF65 80.00				

KM# 1082 DOLLAR
31.10 g., 0.999 Silver 0.9925 oz. ASW, 50 x 27.3 mm. **Ruler:** Elizabeth II **Subject:** In Love - Right

Date	Mintage	F12	VF20	XF40	MS60	MS63
2013	Est. 4444	PF65 80.00				

KM# 1083 DOLLAR
31.10 g., 0.999 Silver 0.9925 oz. ASW, 45 x 31 mm. **Ruler:** Elizabeth II **Subject:** The Orient Express (Engraved) **Obv:** Steam train advancing left **Rev:** Company Logo **Shape:** Horizontal oval

Date	Mintage	F12	VF20	XF40	MS60	MS63
2013	—	PF65 150				

KM# 1083a DOLLAR
31.10 g., 0.999 Silver 0.9925 oz. ASW, 45 x 31 mm. **Ruler:** Elizabeth II **Subject:** Orient Express (Colored) **Obv:** Steam train advancing left **Rev:** Company logo **Shape:** Horizontal oval

Date	Mintage	F12	VF20	XF40	MS60	MS63
2013	Est. 400	PF65 150				

KM# 1084 DOLLAR
16.00 g., 0.999 Silver 0.5106 oz. ASW, 34 mm. **Ruler:** Elizabeth II **Subject:** Czech Olympian Series: Javelin

Date	Mintage	F12	VF20	XF40	MS60	MS63
2013	Est. 500	PF65 125				

KM# 1085 DOLLAR
16.00 g., 0.999 Silver 0.5106 oz. ASW, 34 mm. **Ruler:** Elizabeth II **Subject:** Czech Olympian Series: Running

Date	Mintage	F12	VF20	XF40	MS60	MS63
2013	Est. 500	PF65 125				

KM# 1086 DOLLAR
16.00 g., 0.999 Silver 0.5106 oz. ASW, 34 mm. **Ruler:** Elizabeth II **Subject:** Czech Olympians: Rowing

Date	Mintage	F12	VF20	XF40	MS60	MS63
2013	Est. 500	PF65 125				

KM# 1087 DOLLAR
16.00 g., 0.999 Silver 0.5106 oz. ASW, 34 mm. **Ruler:** Elizabeth II **Subject:** Czech Olympians: Cycling

Date	Mintage	F12	VF20	XF40	MS60	MS63
2013	Est. 500	PF65 125				

KM# 1089 DOLLAR
7.78 g., 0.999 Gold 0.2483 oz. AGW, 22 mm. **Ruler:** Elizabeth II **Subject:** Czech Olympians: Running

Date	Mintage	F12	VF20	XF40	MS60	MS63
2013	—	PF65 125				

KM# 1090 DOLLAR
7.78 g., 0.999 Gold 0.2483 oz. AGW, 22 mm. **Ruler:** Elizabeth II
Subject: Czech Olympians: Rowing

Date	Mintage	F12	VF20	XF40	MS60	MS63
2013	—	PF65 125				

KM# 1091 DOLLAR
7.78 g., 0.999 Gold 0.2483 oz. AGW, 22 mm. **Ruler:** Elizabeth II
Subject: Czech Olympians: Cycling

Date	Mintage	F12	VF20	XF40	MS60	MS63
2013	Est. 200	PF65 125				

KM# 1092 DOLLAR
15.55 g., 0.999 Silver 0.4962 oz. ASW, 36 mm. **Ruler:** Elizabeth II **Subject:** Tooth Fairy

Date	Mintage	F12	VF20	XF40	MS60	MS63
2013	Est. 5000	PF65 45.00				

KM# 1094 DOLLAR
15.55 g., 0.999 Silver 0.4962 oz. ASW, 36 mm. **Ruler:** Elizabeth II **Subject:** Dr. Who - First Doctor, William Hartnell

Date	Mintage	F12	VF20	XF40	MS60	MS63
2013	Est. 4000	PF65 75.00				

KM# 1095 DOLLAR
15.55 g., 0.999 Silver 0.4962 oz. ASW, 36 mm. **Ruler:** Elizabeth II **Subject:** Dr. Who - Second Doctor, Patrick Troughton

Date	Mintage	F12	VF20	XF40	MS60	MS63
2013	Est. 4000	PF65 75.00				

KM# 1096 DOLLAR
15.55 g., 0.999 Silver 0.4962 oz. ASW, 36 mm. **Ruler:** Elizabeth II **Subject:** Dr. Who - Third Doctor, Jon Pertwee

Date	Mintage	F12	VF20	XF40	MS60	MS63
2013	Est. 4000	PF65 75.00				

KM# 1097 DOLLAR
15.55 g., 0.999 Silver 0.4962 oz. ASW, 36 mm. **Ruler:** Elizabeth II **Subject:** Dr. Who - Fourth Doctor, Tom Baker

Date	Mintage	F12	VF20	XF40	MS60	MS63
2013	Est. 4000	PF65 75.00				

KM# 1098 DOLLAR
15.50 g., 0.999 Silver 0.4946 oz. ASW, 36 mm. **Ruler:** Elizabeth II **Subject:** Dr. Who - Fifth Doctor, Peter Davison

Date	Mintage	F12	VF20	XF40	MS60	MS63
2013	Est. 4000	PF65 75.00				

KM# 1099 DOLLAR
15.50 g., 0.999 Silver 0.4946 oz. ASW, 36 mm. **Ruler:** Elizabeth II **Subject:** Dr. Who - Sixth Doctor, Colin Baker

Date	Mintage	F12	VF20	XF40	MS60	MS63
2013	Est. 4000	PF65 75.00				

KM# 1100 DOLLAR
15.50 g., 0.999 Silver 0.4946 oz. ASW, 36 mm. **Ruler:** Elizabeth II **Subject:** Dr. Who - Seventh Doctor, Sylvester McCoy

Date	Mintage	F12	VF20	XF40	MS60	MS63
2013	Est. 4000	PF65 75.00				

KM# 1101 DOLLAR
15.50 g., 0.999 Silver 0.4946 oz. ASW, 36 mm. **Ruler:** Elizabeth II **Subject:** Dr. Who - Eighth Doctor, Paul McGann

Date	Mintage	F12	VF20	XF40	MS60	MS63
2013	Est. 4000	PF65 75.00				

KM# 1102 DOLLAR
15.50 g., 0.999 Silver 0.4946 oz. ASW **Ruler:** Elizabeth II
Subject: Dr. Who - Ninth Doctor, Christopher Eccleston **Shape:** 36

Date	Mintage	F12	VF20	XF40	MS60	MS63
2013	Est. 4000	PF65 75.00				

KM# 1103 DOLLAR
15.50 g., 0.999 Silver 0.4946 oz. ASW, 36 mm. **Ruler:** Elizabeth II **Subject:** Dr. Who - Tenth Doctor, David Tennant

Date	Mintage	F12	VF20	XF40	MS60	MS63
2013	Est. 4000	PF65 75.00				

KM# 1104 DOLLAR
15.50 g., 0.999 Silver 0.4946 oz. ASW, 36 mm. **Ruler:** Elizabeth II **Subject:** Dr. Who - Eleventh Doctor, Matt Smith

Date	Mintage	F12	VF20	XF40	MS60	MS63
2013	Est. 4000	PF65 75.00				

KM# 1109 DOLLAR
16.00 g., 0.999 Silver 0.5106 oz. ASW, 34 mm. **Ruler:** Elizabeth II **Subject:** Family of Rohans: Camille de Rohan

Date	Mintage	F12	VF20	XF40	MS60	MS63
2013	Est. 800	PF65 50.00				

KM# 1110 DOLLAR
16.00 g., 0.999 Silver 0.5106 oz. ASW, 34 mm. **Ruler:** Elizabeth II **Subject:** Family of Rohans: Henri de Rohan

Date	Mintage	F12	VF20	XF40	MS60	MS63
2013	Est. 800	PF65 50.00				

KM# 1111 DOLLAR
16.00 g., 0.999 Silver 0.5106 oz. ASW, 34 mm. **Ruler:** Elizabeth II **Subject:** Family of Rohans: Louis Rene de Rohan

Date	Mintage	F12	VF20	XF40	MS60	MS63
2013	Est. 800	PF65 50.00				

KM# 1112 DOLLAR
16.00 g., 0.999 Silver 0.5106 oz. ASW, 34 mm. **Ruler:** Elizabeth II **Subject:** Family of Rohans: Marie de Rohan

Date	Mintage	F12	VF20	XF40	MS60	MS63
2013	—	PF65 50.00				

KM# 1115 DOLLAR
28.28 g., 0.925 Silver 0.8356 oz. ASW, 35 x 45 mm. **Ruler:** Elizabeth II **Subject:** Jurassic Period: Life on the Ground

Date	Mintage	F12	VF20	XF40	MS60	MS63
2013	Est. 7000	PF65 65.00				

KM# 1116 DOLLAR
28.28 g., 0.925 Silver 0.8356 oz. ASW, 35 x 45 mm. **Ruler:** Elizabeth II **Subject:** Jurassic Period: Life Under Water

Date	Mintage	F12	VF20	XF40	MS60	MS63
2013	Est. 7000	PF65 65.00				

KM# 1119 DOLLAR
14.14 g., 0.925 Silver 0.4178 oz. ASW, 32 mm. **Ruler:** Elizabeth II **Subject:** Cartoon Characters: Scooby Doo

Date	Mintage	F12	VF20	XF40	MS60	MS63
2013	Est. 6000	PF65 75.00				

KM# 1120 DOLLAR
28.28 g., 0.925 Silver 0.8356 oz. ASW, 40 x 28 mm. **Ruler:** Elizabeth II **Subject:** A Russian Beauty

Date	Mintage	F12	VF20	XF40	MS60	MS63
2013	Est. 8888	PF65 80.00				

KM# 1125 DOLLAR
10.00 g., 0.925 Silver 0.2955 oz. ASW, 32 mm. **Ruler:** Elizabeth II **Subject:** Magic Calendar of Happiness - April

Date	Mintage	F12	VF20	XF40	MS60	MS63
2013	Est. 5555	PF65 65.00				

KM# 1127 DOLLAR
28.28 g., 0.925 Silver 0.8356 oz. ASW, 40 x 28 mm. **Ruler:** Elizabeth II **Subject:** Tropical Coral Fish

Date	Mintage	F12	VF20	XF40	MS60	MS63
2013	Est. 8000	PF65 75.00				

KM# 1128 DOLLAR
28.28 g., 0.925 Silver 0.8356 oz. ASW, 40 x 28 mm. **Ruler:** Elizabeth II **Subject:** Royal Gramma

Date	Mintage	F12	VF20	XF40	MS60	MS63
2013	Est. 8000	PF65 75.00				

KM# 1129 DOLLAR
28.28 g., 0.925 Silver 0.8356 oz. ASW, 40 x 28 mm. **Ruler:** Elizabeth II **Subject:** Royal Blue Tang

Date	Mintage	F12	VF20	XF40	MS60	MS63
2013	Est. 8000	PF65 75.00				

KM# 1130 DOLLAR
15.55 g., 0.999 Silver 0.4962 oz. ASW, 36 mm. **Ruler:** Elizabeth II **Series:** Scented Flowers: Kowhai

Date	Mintage	F12	VF20	XF40	MS60	MS63
2013	Est. 8000	PF65 50.00				

KM# 1131 DOLLAR
15.55 g., 0.999 Silver 0.4962 oz. ASW, 36 mm. **Ruler:** Elizabeth II **Subject:** Scented Flowers: Rose

Date	Mintage	F12	VF20	XF40	MS60	MS63
2013	Est. 8000	PF65 50.00				

KM# 1144 DOLLAR
20.00 g., 0.925 Silver 0.591 oz. ASW, 38.61 mm. **Ruler:** Elizabeth II **Subject:** Ghost Ships - Mary Celeste

Date	Mintage	F12	VF20	XF40	MS60	MS63
2013	Est. 1000	PF65 120				

KM# 1148 DOLLAR
28.28 g., 0.925 Silver 0.8356 oz. ASW, 38.61 mm. **Ruler:** Elizabeth II **Subject:** Belgorod

Date	Mintage	F12	VF20	XF40	MS60	MS63
2013	— PF65 85.00					

KM# 1149 DOLLAR
28.28 g., 0.925 Silver 0.8356 oz. ASW, 38.61 mm. **Ruler:** Elizabeth II **Subject:** Murmansk

Date	Mintage	F12	VF20	XF40	MS60	MS63
2013	Est. 2000 PF65 85.00					

KM# 1150 DOLLAR
28.28 g., 0.999 Silver 0.9025 oz. ASW, 28 x 40 mm. **Ruler:** Elizabeth II **Subject:** 10 Kopecks 1860 - First Polish Stamp

Date	Mintage	F12	VF20	XF40	MS60	MS63
2013	— PF65 150					

KM# 1158 DOLLAR
33.63 g., 0.925 Silver 0.9937 oz. ASW, 38.61 mm. **Ruler:** Elizabeth II **Subject:** Day of the Capital Astana

Date	Mintage	F12	VF20	XF40	MS60	MS63
2013 Proof	Est. 3000	—	—	—	—	—

KM# 1159 DOLLAR
33.63 g., 0.925 Silver 0.9937 oz. ASW, 38.61 mm. **Ruler:** Elizabeth II **Subject:** Day of the Constitution

Date	Mintage	F12	VF20	XF40	MS60	MS63
2013 Proof	Est. 3000	—	—	—	—	—

KM# 1160 DOLLAR
10.00 g., 0.925 Silver 0.2955 oz. ASW, 32 mm. **Ruler:** Elizabeth II **Subject:** Magic Calendar of Happiness - May

Date	Mintage	F12	VF20	XF40	MS60	MS63
2013	Est. 5555 PF65 65.00					

KM# 1161 DOLLAR
10.00 g., 0.925 Silver 0.2955 oz. ASW, 32 mm. **Ruler:** Elizabeth II **Subject:** Magic Calendar of Happiness - June

Date	Mintage	F12	VF20	XF40	MS60	MS63
2013	Est. 5555 PF65 65.00					

KM# 1162 DOLLAR
10.00 g., 0.925 Silver 0.2955 oz. ASW, 32 mm. **Ruler:** Elizabeth II **Subject:** Magic Calendar of Happiness - July

Date	Mintage	F12	VF20	XF40	MS60	MS63
2013	— PF65 65.00					

KM# 1164 DOLLAR
33.63 g., 0.925 Silver 0.9937 oz. ASW, 38.61 mm. **Ruler:** Elizabeth II **Subject:** Betashar

Date	Mintage	F12	VF20	XF40	MS60	MS63
2013	Est. 3000 PF65 90.00					

KM# 1170 DOLLAR
28.28 g., 0.925 Silver 0.8356 oz. ASW, 38.61 mm. **Ruler:** Elizabeth II **Subject:** Anna Ioannova - Replicas of the Russian Emperor

Date	Mintage	F12	VF20	XF40	MS60	MS63
2013	Est. 4000 PF65 75.00					

KM# 1185 DOLLAR
15.55 g., 0.999 Silver 0.4962 oz. ASW, 25 x 40 mm. **Ruler:** Elizabeth II **Subject:** Humpback Whale

Date	Mintage	F12	VF20	XF40	MS60	MS63
2013 Proof	—	—	—	—	—	—

KM# 1186 DOLLAR
20.00 g., 0.999 Silver 0.6382 oz ASW, 54 x 32 mm. **Ruler:** Elizabeth II **Subject:** Superbia

Date	Mintage	F12	VF20	XF40	MS60	MS63
2013	1,000 PF65 125					

KM# 1187 DOLLAR
16.81 g., 0.925 Silver 0.4967 oz. ASW, 38.61 mm. **Ruler:** Elizabeth II **Subject:** Treasures of Traditions

Date	Mintage	F12	VF20	XF40	MS60	MS63
2013 Proof	Est. 1000	—	—	—	—	—

KM# 1191 DOLLAR
31.00 g., Copper-Nickel, 41 mm. **Ruler:** Elizabeth II **Subject:** Paavo Nurmi

Date	Mintage	F12	VF20	XF40	MS60	MS63
2013 Proof	Est. 30000	—	—	—	—	—

KM# 1195 DOLLAR
28.28 g., 0.925 Silver 0.8356 oz. ASW, 38.61 mm. **Ruler:** Elizabeth II **Subject:** Orlovsky Trotter

Date	Mintage	F12	VF20	XF40	MS60	MS63
2013	Est. 2000 PF65 95.00					

KM# 1196 DOLLAR
25.00 g., 0.925 Silver 0.7387 oz. ASW, 40 mm. **Ruler:** Elizabeth II **Subject:** Oil Discovery 1953

Date	Mintage	F12	VF20	XF40	MS60	MS63
2013	Est. 4000 PF65 100					

KM# 1197 DOLLAR
33.63 g., 0.925 Silver 0.9937 oz. ASW, 38.61 mm. **Ruler:** Elizabeth II **Subject:** May 1st

Date	Mintage	F12	VF20	XF40	MS60	MS63
2013 Proof	Est. 3000	—	—	—	—	—

KM# 1198 DOLLAR
28.28 g., 0.925 Silver 0.8356 oz. ASW, 40 x 40 mm. **Ruler:** Elizabeth II **Subject:** Madonna Under the Fir Tree

Date	Mintage	F12	VF20	XF40	MS60	MS63
2013	Est. 2000 PF65 125					

KM# 1230 DOLLAR
16.81 g., 0.999 Silver 0.5364 oz. ASW, 39.00 x 29.20 mm. **Ruler:** Elizabeth II **Subject:** Iwan Wigowski

Date	Mintage	F12	VF20	XF40	MS60	MS63
2013	Est. 1555 PF65 40.00					

KM# 1231 DOLLAR
16.81 g., 0.999 Silver 0.5364 oz. ASW, 39.00 x 29.20 mm. **Ruler:** Elizabeth II **Subject:** Piotr Sagajdaczny

Date	Mintage	F12	VF20	XF40	MS60	MS63
2013	Est. 1555 PF65 40.00					

KM# 1232 DOLLAR
16.81 g., 0.999 Silver 0.5364 oz. ASW, 39.00 x 29.20 mm. **Ruler:** Elizabeth II **Subject:** Iwan Mazepa

Date	Mintage	F12	VF20	XF40	MS60	MS63
2013	Est. 1555 PF65 40.00					

KM# 1233 DOLLAR
16.81 g., 0.999 Silver 0.5364 oz. ASW, 39.00 x 29.90 mm. **Ruler:** Elizabeth II **Subject:** Dymitr Wisznewecki

Date	Mintage	F12	VF20	XF40	MS60	MS63
2013	Est. 1555 PF65 40.00					

KM# 1234 DOLLAR
16.81 g., 0.999 Silver 0.5364 oz. ASW, 39.00 x 29.20 mm. **Ruler:** Elizabeth II **Subject:** Bogdon Chmienicki

Date	Mintage	F12	VF20	XF40	MS60	MS63
2013	Est. 1555 PF65 40.00					

KM# 1235 DOLLAR
16.81 g., 0.999 Silver 0.5364 oz. ASW, 39.00 x 29.20 mm. **Ruler:** Elizabeth II **Subject:** Piotr Doroszenko

Date	Mintage	F12	VF20	XF40	MS60	MS63
2013	Est. 1555 PF65 40.00					

KM# 1236 DOLLAR
16.81 g., 0.999 Silver 0.5364 oz. ASW, 39.00 x 29.20 mm. **Ruler:** Elizabeth II **Subject:** Filip Orlik

Date	Mintage	F12	VF20	XF40	MS60	MS63
2013	Est. 1555 PF65 40.00					

KM# 1237 DOLLAR
15.56 g., 0.9999 Gold 0.497 oz. AGW, 28 mm. **Ruler:** Elizabeth II **Subject:** Richard Wagner

Date	Mintage	F12	VF20	XF40	MS60	MS63
2013	Est. 150 PF65 1,250					

KM# 1243 DOLLAR
28.28 g., 0.925 Silver 0.8356 oz. ASW, 38.6 mm. **Ruler:** Elizabeth II **Subject:** 60th Anniversary of the Corronation

Date	Mintage	F12	VF20	XF40	MS60	MS63
2013 Proof	Est. 1500	—	—	—	—	—

KM# 1243a DOLLAR
28.28 g., Copper-Nickel, 38.6 mm. **Ruler:** Elizabeth II **Subject:** 60th Anniversary of the Corronation

Date	Mintage	F12	VF20	XF40	MS60	MS63
2013	—	—	—	—	—	—

KM# 1243b DOLLAR
Brass, 36 mm. **Ruler:** Elizabeth II **Subject:** 60th Anniversary of the Corronation

Date	Mintage	F12	VF20	XF40	MS60	MS63
2013	Est. 3600	—	—	—	—	—

KM# 1245 DOLLAR
20.00 g., 0.925 Silver 0.591 oz. ASW, 38.61 mm. **Ruler:** Elizabeth II **Subject:** 2014 FIFA World Cup Brazil

Date	Mintage	F12	VF20	XF40	MS60	MS63
2013 Proof	Est. 10000	—	—	—	—	—

KM# 1259 DOLLAR
Silver ASW, 38.6 mm. **Ruler:** Elizabeth II **Subject:** Fashion Wedding **Rev:** Bride in Wedding gown

Date	Mintage	F12	VF20	XF40	MS60	MS63
2013	Est. 1000 PF65 75.00					

KM# 1260 DOLLAR
31.11 g., 0.999 Silver 0.9926 oz. ASW, 40 mm. **Ruler:** Elizabeth II **Subject:** Sozunsky Mint, 250th Anniversary

Date	Mintage	F12	VF20	XF40	MS60	MS63
2013	1,000 PF65 75.00					

KM# 1154 DOLLAR
15.55 g., 0.925 Silver 0.4595 oz. ASW, 38.61 mm. **Ruler:** Elizabeth II **Subject:** Fashion - Art

Date	Mintage	F12	VF20	XF40	MS60	MS63
2014	Est. 1000 PF65 65.00					

KM# 1166 DOLLAR
25.00 g., 0.925 Silver 0.7387 oz. ASW, 40 mm. **Ruler:** Elizabeth II **Subject:** Legendary Australian Horses

Date	Mintage	F12	VF20	XF40	MS60	MS63
2014	— PF65 75.00					

KM# 1167 DOLLAR
25.00 g., 0.925 Silver 0.7387 oz. ASW, 40 mm. **Ruler:** Elizabeth II **Subject:** Legendary Australian Horses

Date	Mintage	F12	VF20	XF40	MS60	MS63
2014	— PF65 75.00					

KM# 1168 DOLLAR
25.00 g., 0.925 Silver 0.7387 oz. ASW, 40 mm. **Ruler:** Elizabeth II **Subject:** Legendary Australian Horses

Date	Mintage	F12	VF20	XF40	MS60	MS63
2014	Est. 2000 PF65 75.00					

KM# 1169 DOLLAR
25.00 g., 0.925 Silver 0.7387 oz. ASW, 40 mm. **Ruler:** Elizabeth II **Subject:** Legendary Australian Horses

Date	Mintage	F12	VF20	XF40	MS60	MS63
2014	Est. 2000 PF65 75.00					

KM# 265 2 DOLLARS
62.21 g., 0.999 Silver 1.9852 oz. ASW, 55 mm. **Ruler:** Elizabeth II **Subject:** Year of the Rooster **Rev:** Multicolor rooster standing right, sunrise

Date	Mintage	F12	VF20	XF40	MS60	MS63
2005	— PF65 85.00					

KM# 294 2 DOLLARS
62.20 g., 0.999 Silver 1.9849 oz. ASW, 55 mm. **Ruler:** Elizabeth II **Subject:** Year of the Dog **Rev:** Multicolor dog

Date	Mintage	F12	VF20	XF40	MS60	MS63
2005	— PF65 95.00					

KM# 269 2 DOLLARS
1.24 g., 0.999 Gold 0.0396 oz. AGW, 14 mm. **Ruler:** Elizabeth II **Subject:** Year of the Rooster

Date	Mintage	F12	VF20	XF40	MS60	MS63
2005	— PF65 80.00					

KM# 270 2 DOLLARS
1.56 g., 0.999 Gold 0.0498 oz. AGW, 18 mm. **Ruler:** Elizabeth II **Subject:** Year of the Rooster

Date	Mintage	F12	VF20	XF40	MS60	MS63
2005	— PF65 110					

KM# 271 2 DOLLARS
3.11 g., 0.999 Gold 0.0992 oz. AGW, 18 mm. **Ruler:** Elizabeth II **Subject:** Year of the Rooster

Date	Mintage	F12	VF20	XF40	MS60	MS63
2005	— PF65 185					

KM# 278 2 DOLLARS
3.11 g., 0.999 Gold 0.0992 oz. AGW, 18 mm. **Ruler:** Elizabeth II **Subject:** Chinese space achievements **Rev:** Multicolor rocket, flag, map

Date	Mintage	F12	VF20	XF40	MS60	MS63
2005	— PF65 195					

KM# 279 2 DOLLARS
31.11 g., 0.999 Silver 0.9926 oz. ASW, 35x46 mm. **Ruler:** Elizabeth II **Subject:** Impressionist paintings **Rev:** Multicolor painting of a bridge **Shape:** Vertical rectangle

Date	Mintage	F12	VF20	XF40	MS60	MS63
2005	Est. 2005 PF65 65.00					

KM# 280 2 DOLLARS
31.11 g., 0.999 Silver 0.9926 oz. ASW, 35x46 mm. **Ruler:** Elizabeth II **Subject:** Impressionist paintings **Rev:** Multicolor painting of a female **Shape:** Vertical rectangle

Date	Mintage	F12	VF20	XF40	MS60	MS63
2005	Est. 2005 PF65 65.00					

KM# 281 2 DOLLARS
31.11 g., 0.999 Silver 0.9926 oz. ASW, 35x46 mm. **Ruler:** Elizabeth II **Subject:** Impressionists paintings **Rev:** Multicolor painting of a village **Shape:** Vertical rectangle

Date	Mintage	F12	VF20	XF40	MS60	MS63
2005	Est. 2005 PF65 65.00					

KM# 282 2 DOLLARS
31.11 g., 0.999 Silver 0.9926 oz. ASW, 35x46 mm. **Ruler:** Elizabeth II **Subject:** Impressionists paintings **Rev:** Multicolor painting of a seaside **Shape:** Vertical rectangle

Date	Mintage	F12	VF20	XF40	MS60	MS63
2005	Est. 2005 PF65 65.00					

KM# 283 2 DOLLARS
31.11 g., 0.999 Silver 0.9926 oz. ASW, 35x46 mm. **Ruler:** Elizabeth II **Subject:** Impressionists paintings **Rev:** Multicolor painting of Paris **Shape:** Vertical rectangle

Date	Mintage	F12	VF20	XF40	MS60	MS63
2005	Est. 2005	PF65 65.00				

KM# 284 2 DOLLARS
31.11 g., 0.999 Silver 0.9926 oz. ASW, 35x46 mm. **Ruler:** Elizabeth II **Subject:** Impressionists paintings **Rev:** Multicolor painting of female **Shape:** Vertical rectangle

Date	Mintage	F12	VF20	XF40	MS60	MS63
2005	Est. 2005	PF65 65.00				

KM# 285 2 DOLLARS
31.11 g., 0.999 Silver 0.9926 oz. ASW, 35x46 mm. **Ruler:** Elizabeth II **Subject:** Impressionist paintings **Rev:** Multicolor painting of dancers **Shape:** Vertical rectangle

Date	Mintage	F12	VF20	XF40	MS60	MS63
2005	—	PF65 65.00				

KM# 286 2 DOLLARS
31.11 g., 0.999 Silver 0.9926 oz. ASW, 35x46 mm. **Ruler:** Elizabeth II **Subject:** Impressionists paintings **Rev:** Multicolor painting of Fifer **Shape:** Vertical rectangle

Date	Mintage	F12	VF20	XF40	MS60	MS63
2005	Est. 2005	PF65 65.00				

KM# 287 2 DOLLARS
31.11 g., 0.999 Silver 0.9926 oz. ASW, 35x46 mm. **Ruler:** Elizabeth II **Subject:** Impressionists paintings **Rev:** Multicolor painting of boats **Shape:** Vertical rectangle

Date	Mintage	F12	VF20	XF40	MS60	MS63
2005	Est. 2005	PF65 65.00				

KM# 288 2 DOLLARS
31.11 g., 0.999 Silver 0.9926 oz. ASW, 35x46 mm. **Ruler:** Elizabeth II **Subject:** Impressionists paintings **Obv:** Multicolor painting of Paris scene **Shape:** Vertical rectangle

Date	Mintage	F12	VF20	XF40	MS60	MS63
2005	Est. 2005	PF65 65.00				

KM# 289 2 DOLLARS
31.11 g., 0.999 Silver 0.9926 oz. ASW, 35x46 mm. **Ruler:** Elizabeth II **Subject:** Impressionists paintings **Rev:** Multicolor painting of a maiden **Shape:** Vertical rectangle

Date	Mintage	F12	VF20	XF40	MS60	MS63
2005	Est. 2005	PF65 65.00				

KM# 290 2 DOLLARS
31.11 g., 0.999 Silver 0.9926 oz. ASW, 35x46 mm. **Ruler:** Elizabeth II **Subject:** Impresionists paintings **Rev:** Multicolor painting of an artist **Shape:** Vertical rectangle

Date	Mintage	F12	VF20	XF40	MS60	MS63
2005	Est. 2005	PF65 65.00				

KM# 291 2 DOLLARS
31.11 g., 0.999 Silver 0.9926 oz. ASW, 35x46 mm. **Ruler:** Elizabeth II **Subject:** Impressionists paintings **Rev:** Multicolor painting of Canada **Shape:** Vertical rectangle

Date	Mintage	F12	VF20	XF40	MS60	MS63
2005	Est. 2005	PF65 65.00				

KM# 298 2 DOLLARS
1.56 g., 0.999 Gold 0.0498 oz. AGW, 16 mm. **Ruler:** Elizabeth II **Subject:** Year of the Dog **Rev:** Multicolor dog

Date	Mintage	F12	VF20	XF40	MS60	MS63
2005	—	PF65 95.00				

KM# 299 2 DOLLARS
3.11 g., 0.999 Gold 0.0992 oz. AGW, 18 mm. **Ruler:** Elizabeth II **Subject:** Year of the Dog **Rev:** Multicolor dog

Date	Mintage	F12	VF20	XF40	MS60	MS63
2005	—	PF65 185				

KM# 330 2 DOLLARS
62.20 g., 0.999 Silver 1.9849 oz. ASW, 30x70 mm. **Ruler:** Elizabeth II **Subject:** Life of Christ **Rev:** Last Supper (1495) **Shape:** Vertical rectangle

Date	Mintage	F12	VF20	XF40	MS60	MS63
2006	Est. 1000	PF65 175				

KM# 190 2 DOLLARS
1.50 g., 0.999 Gold 0.0479 oz. AGW **Ruler:** Elizabeth II **Subject:** Year of the Pig **Obv:** Head right **Rev:** Multicolor pig

Date	Mintage	F12	VF20	XF40	MS60	MS63
2007	—	PF65 95.00				

KM# 205 2 DOLLARS
31.11 g., 0.999 Silver 0.9926 oz. ASW, 40.7 mm. **Ruler:** Elizabeth II **Subject:** Peoples Republic of China, 60th Anniversary **Rev:** Dragon and scenes of China in multicolor

Date	Mintage	F12	VF20	XF40	MS60	MS63
2008	6,888	PF65 175				

KM# 185 2 DOLLARS
31.11 g., 0.999 Silver 0.9926 oz. ASW, 40 mm. **Ruler:** Elizabeth II **Subject:** Year of the Ox **Rev:** Gilt ox advancing left

Date	Mintage	F12	VF20	XF40	MS60	MS63
2009	20,000	PF65 185				

KM# 199 2 DOLLARS
25.00 g., 0.925 Silver 0.7387 oz. ASW, 38.6 mm. **Ruler:** Elizabeth II **Rev:** Two spinner dolphins leaping, swarovski crystal chip in eye

Date	Mintage	F12	VF20	XF40	MS60	MS63
2009	2,500	PF65 50.00				

KM# 200 2 DOLLARS
0.50 g., 0.999 Gold AGW, 11 mm. **Ruler:** Elizabeth II **Rev:** Two spinner dolphins leaping out of the water

Date	Mintage	F12	VF20	XF40	MS60	MS63
2009	10,000	PF65 50.00				

KM# 209 2 DOLLARS
1.00 g., 0.900 Gold 0.0287 oz. AGW **Ruler:** Elizabeth II **Subject:** Frederic Chopin **Obv:** Elizabeth II head right **Rev:** Chopin bust and autograph

Date	Mintage	F12	VF20	XF40	MS60	MS63
2009	10,000	PF65 100				

KM# 210 2 DOLLARS
31.11 g., 0.999 Silver 0.9926 oz. ASW, 40.7 mm. **Ruler:**

Elizabeth II **Obv:** Head right **Rev:** Two black swans, multicolor

Date	Mintage	F12	VF20	XF40	MS60	MS63
2009	10,000	PF65 80.00				

KM# 215 2 DOLLARS
31.11 g., 0.999 Silver 0.9926 oz. ASW, 40 mm. **Ruler:** Elizabeth II **Subject:** Russian Ballet **Rev:** Anna Pavlova in multicolor

Date	Mintage	F12	VF20	XF40	MS60	MS63
2009 Prooflike	5,000	—	—	—	—	120

KM# 216 2 DOLLARS
31.10 g., 0.999 Silver 0.9926 oz. ASW, 40.7 mm. **Ruler:** Elizabeth II **Subject:** Russian Ballet **Rev:** Matilda Kshesinskaya in multicolor

Date	Mintage	F12	VF20	XF40	MS60	MS63
2009 Prooflike	10,000	—	—	—	—	100

KM# 217 2 DOLLARS
31.11 g., 0.999 Silver 0.9926 oz. ASW, 40.7 mm. **Ruler:** Elizabeth II **Subject:** Russian Ballet **Rev:** Sergey Lefar in multicolor

Date	Mintage	F12	VF20	XF40	MS60	MS63
2009 Prooflike	10,000	—	—	—	—	100

KM# 218 2 DOLLARS
31.11 g., 0.999 Silver 0.9926 oz. ASW, 40.7 mm. **Ruler:** Elizabeth II **Subject:** Russian Ballet **Rev:** Sergi Daighilev in multicolor

Date	Mintage	F12	VF20	XF40	MS60	MS63
2009 Prooflike	10,000	—	—	—	—	100

KM# 219 2 DOLLARS
31.10 g., 0.999 Silver 0.9926 oz. ASW, 40.7 mm. **Ruler:** Elizabeth II **Subject:** Russian Ballet **Rev:** Vaslav Fomich Nijinsky

Date	Mintage	F12	VF20	XF40	MS60	MS63
2009 Prooflike	10,000	—	—	—	—	100

KM# 220 2 DOLLARS
31.11 g., 0.999 Silver 0.9926 oz. ASW, 40.7 mm. **Ruler:** Elizabeth II **Subject:** Panagyurishte Treasure **Rev:** Vessel in the shape of a female head right

Date	Mintage	F12	VF20	XF40	MS60	MS63
2009	5,000	—	—	—	—	120

KM# 221 2 DOLLARS
31.11 g., 0.999 Silver 0.9926 oz. ASW, 40.7 mm. **Ruler:** Elizabeth II **Subject:** Panagyurishte Treasure **Rev:** Vessel in shape of female head left

Date	Mintage	F12	VF20	XF40	MS60	MS63
2009	5,000	—	—	—	—	120

KM# 222 2 DOLLARS
31.11 g., 0.999 Silver 0.9926 oz. ASW, 40.7 mm. **Ruler:** Elizabeth II **Subject:** Panagyurishte Treasure **Rev:** Vessel in shape of ram's head

Date	Mintage	F12	VF20	XF40	MS60	MS63
2009	5,000	—	—	—	—	120

KM# 223 2 DOLLARS
31.11 g., 0.999 Silver 0.9926 oz. ASW, 40 mm. **Ruler:** Elizabeth II **Subject:** Peoples Republic of China, 60th Anniversary **Rev:** Multicolor background, astronaut, olympic flame and dragon motifs

Date	Mintage	F12	VF20	XF40	MS60	MS63
2009 Prooflike	6,888	—	—	—	—	95.00

KM# 224 2 DOLLARS
31.11 g., 0.999 Silver 0.9926 oz. ASW, 40.7 mm. **Ruler:** Elizabeth II **Series:** Soviet Automobiles **Rev:** GAZ 12 ZIM in multicolor

Date	Mintage	F12	VF20	XF40	MS60	MS63
2009 Prooflike	15,000	—	—	—	—	80.00

KM# 225 2 DOLLARS
31.11 g., 0.999 Silver 0.9926 oz. ASW, 40.7 mm. **Ruler:** Elizabeth II **Subject:** Soviet Automobiles **Rev:** GAZ M290 Pobeda in multicolor

Date	Mintage	F12	VF20	XF40	MS60	MS63
2009 Prooflike	15,000	—	—	—	—	80.00

KM# 226 2 DOLLARS
31.11 g., 0.999 Silver 0.9926 oz. ASW, 40.7 mm. **Ruler:** Elizabeth II **Subject:** Soviet Automobiles **Rev:** GAZ M21 Volga

Date	Mintage	F12	VF20	XF40	MS60	MS63
2009 Prooflike	15,000	—	—	—	—	80.00

KM# 227 2 DOLLARS
31.11 g., 0.999 Silver 0.9926 oz. ASW, 40.7 mm. **Ruler:** Elizabeth II **Subject:** Soviet Automobiles **Rev:** Moskvich 400

Date	Mintage	F12	VF20	XF40	MS60	MS63
2009 Prooflike	15,000	—	—	—	—	80.00

KM# 229 2 DOLLARS
31.11 g., 0.999 Silver 0.9926 oz. ASW, 40 mm. **Ruler:** Elizabeth II **Subject:** Year of the Ox **Rev:** Ox, partially gilt

Date	Mintage	F12	VF20	XF40	MS60	MS63
2009	2,000	PF65 100				

KM# 350 2 DOLLARS
25.00 g., 0.999 Silver 0.7978 oz. ASW, 38.61 mm. **Ruler:** Elizabeth II **Rev:** Partridge in a pear tree

Date	Mintage	F12	VF20	XF40	MS60	MS63
2009	1,500	PF65 70.00				

KM# 351 2 DOLLARS
25.00 g., 0.999 Silver 0.7978 oz. ASW, 38.61 mm. **Ruler:** Elizabeth II **Rev:** Two turtle doves

Date	Mintage	F12	VF20	XF40	MS60	MS63
2009	1,500	PF65 70.00				

KM# 352 2 DOLLARS
25.00 g., 0.999 Silver 0.7978 oz. ASW, 38.61 mm. **Ruler:** Elizabeth II **Rev:** Three French hens

Date	Mintage	F12	VF20	XF40	MS60	MS63
2009	1,500	PF65 70.00				

KM# 353 2 DOLLARS
25.00 g., 0.999 Silver 0.7978 oz. ASW, 38.61 mm. **Ruler:** Elizabeth II **Rev:** Four calling birds

Date	Mintage	F12	VF20	XF40	MS60	MS63
2009	1,500	PF65 70.00				

KM# 354 2 DOLLARS
25.00 g., 0.999 Silver 0.7978 oz. ASW, 38.61 mm. **Ruler:** Elizabeth II **Rev:** Five golden rings

Date	Mintage	F12	VF20	XF40	MS60	MS63
2009	1,500	PF65 70.00				

KM# 355 2 DOLLARS
25.00 g., 0.999 Silver 0.7978 oz. ASW, 38.61 mm. **Ruler:** Elizabeth II **Rev:** Six Geese a-laying

Date	Mintage	F12	VF20	XF40	MS60	MS63
2009	1,500	PF65 70.00				

KM# 356 2 DOLLARS
25.00 g., 0.999 Silver 0.7978 oz. ASW, 38.61 mm. **Ruler:** Elizabeth II **Rev:** Seven swans a-swimming

Date	Mintage	F12	VF20	XF40	MS60	MS63
2009	1,500	PF65 70.00				

KM# 357 2 DOLLARS
25.00 g., 0.999 Silver 0.7978 oz. ASW, 38.61 mm. **Ruler:** Elizabeth II **Rev:** Eight maids a-milking

Date	Mintage	F12	VF20	XF40	MS60	MS63
2009	1,500	PF65 70.00				

KM# 358 2 DOLLARS
25.00 g., 0.999 Silver 0.7978 oz. ASW, 38.61 mm. **Ruler:** Elizabeth II **Rev:** Nine ladies dancing

Date	Mintage	F12	VF20	XF40	MS60	MS63
2009	1,500	PF65 70.00				

KM# 359 2 DOLLARS
25.00 g., 0.999 Silver 0.7978 oz. ASW, 38.61 mm. **Ruler:** Elizabeth II **Rev:** Ten Lords a-leaping

Date	Mintage	F12	VF20	XF40	MS60	MS63
2009	1,500	PF65 70.00				

KM# 360 2 DOLLARS
25.00 g., 0.999 Silver 0.7978 oz. ASW, 38.61 mm. **Ruler:** Elizabeth II **Rev:** Eleven Pipers Piping

Date	Mintage	F12	VF20	XF40	MS60	MS63
2009	1,500	PF65 70.00				

KM# 361 2 DOLLARS
25.00 g., 0.999 Silver 0.7978 oz. ASW, 38.61 mm. **Ruler:** Elizabeth II **Rev:** Twelve drummers drumming

Date	Mintage	F12	VF20	XF40	MS60	MS63
2009	1,500	PF65 70.00				

KM# 362 2 DOLLARS
62.20 g., 0.999 Silver 1.9849 oz. ASW, 63x27 mm. **Ruler:** Elizabeth II **Rev:** Flowers **Shape:** Vertical rectangle

Date	Mintage	F12	VF20	XF40	MS60	MS63
2009	16,888	PF65 110				

KM# 552 2 DOLLARS
Silver **Ruler:** Elizabeth II **Subject:** Russian Cartoons

Date	Mintage	F12	VF20	XF40	MS60	MS63
2009	—	PF65 75.00				

KM# 553 2 DOLLARS
Silver **Ruler:** Elizabeth II **Subject:** Russian Cartoons

Date	Mintage	F12	VF20	XF40	MS60	MS63
2009	—	PF65 75.00				

KM# 206 2 DOLLARS
31.11 g., 0.999 Silver 0.9926 oz. ASW, 40.7 mm. **Ruler:** Elizabeth II **Rev:** Two white swans, red heart in background

Date	Mintage	F12	VF20	XF40	MS60	MS63
2010	20,000	PF65 65.00				

KM# 213 2 DOLLARS
56.60 g., 0.925 Silver 1.6724 oz. ASW, 55.6x41.6 mm. **Ruler:**
Elizabeth II **Subject:** Coronation Egg **Obv:** Open egg - Queen
Elizabeth head right **Rev:** Faberge Egg and coach **Shape:**
Vertical oval

Date	Mintage	F12	VF20	XF40	MS60	MS63
2010	5,000	—	—	—	—	100

KM# 228 2 DOLLARS
31.11 g., 0.999 Silver 0.9926 oz. ASW, 40 mm. **Ruler:** Elizabeth
II **Subject:** Gai Thong Hanh, Safe Conduct Pass **Rev:** Viet
Nam flag and soldiers, partially gilt

Date	Mintage	F12	VF20	XF40	MS60	MS63
2010	5,000	PF65 140				

KM# 233 2 DOLLARS
62.21 g., 0.999 Silver 1.9852 oz. ASW, 40 mm. **Ruler:** Elizabeth
II **Subject:** Year of the Tiger **Rev:** Tiger partially gilt

Date	Mintage	F12	VF20	XF40	MS60	MS63
2010	20,000	PF65 120				

KM# 237 2 DOLLARS
1.00 g., 0.900 Gold 0.0287 oz. AGW, 12 mm. **Ruler:** Elizabeth II
Obv: Head right **Rev:** Copernicus bust 3/4 left

Date	Mintage	F12	VF20	XF40	MS60	MS63
2010	5,000	PF65 75.00				

KM# 245 2 DOLLARS
31.10 g., 0.999 Silver 0.9926 oz. ASW, 40.7 mm. **Ruler:**
Elizabeth II **Subject:** Famous express trains - Trans Siberian
Express **Rev:** Steam train traveling left, multicolor

Date	Mintage	F12	VF20	XF40	MS60	MS63
2010	15,000	PF65 80.00				

KM# 246 2 DOLLARS
31.10 g., 0.999 Silver 0.9926 oz. ASW, 40.7 mm. **Ruler:**
Elizabeth II **Subject:** Famous express trains **Rev:** British
Railways Flying Scotsman locomotive right, multicolor

Date	Mintage	F12	VF20	XF40	MS60	MS63
2010	15,000	PF65 80.00				

KM# 247 2 DOLLARS
31.10 g., 0.999 Silver 0.9926 oz. ASW, 40.7 mm. **Ruler:**
Elizabeth II **Subject:** Famous express trains - Orient Express
Rev: Steam train right, multicolor

Date	Mintage	F12	VF20	XF40	MS60	MS63
2010	15,000	PF65 80.00				

KM# 248 2 DOLLARS
31.10 g., 0.999 Silver 0.9926 oz. ASW, 40.7 mm. **Ruler:**
Elizabeth II **Subject:** Famous express trains - 20th Century
Limited **Rev:** Streamlined steam train left, multicolored

Date	Mintage	F12	VF20	XF40	MS60	MS63
2010	15,000	PF65 80.00				

KM# 252 2 DOLLARS
31.11 g., 0.999 Silver 0.9926 oz. ASW, 38.6 mm. **Ruler:**
Elizabeth II **Subject:** Peanuts 60th Anniversary **Rev:** Charlie
Brown with Snoopy and birthday cake

Date	Mintage	F12	VF20	XF40	MS60	MS63
2010 Prooflike	3,000	—	—	—	—	80.00

KM# 253 2 DOLLARS
31.11 g., 0.999 Silver 0.9926 oz. ASW, 38.6 mm. **Ruler:**
Elizabeth II **Subject:** Peanuts 60th Anniversary **Rev:**
Schroeder and Lucy by piano

Date	Mintage	F12	VF20	XF40	MS60	MS63
2010 Prooflike	3,000	—	—	—	—	80.00

KM# 371 2 DOLLARS
56.56 g., 0.925 Silver 1.6712 oz. ASW, 55.6x41.6 mm. **Ruler:**
Elizabeth II **Subject:** Faberge egg - Lily of the Valley **Obv:**
Elizabeth II head right, open egg **Rev:** Egg on stand **Shape:**
Vertical oval

Date	Mintage	F12	VF20	XF40	MS60	MS63
2010	7,000	PF65 100				

KM# 373 2 DOLLARS
31.11 g., 0.999 Silver 0.9926 oz. ASW, 37.1x31.9 mm. **Ruler:**
Elizabeth II **Subject:** Kiki Lala **Shape:** Heart with ribbon

Date	Mintage	F12	VF20	XF40	MS60	MS63
2010	Est. 3000	PF65 60.00				

KM# 374 2 DOLLARS
31.11 g., 0.999 Silver 0.9926 oz. ASW, 37.1x31.9 mm. **Ruler:**
Elizabeth II **Subject:** My Melo **Shape:** Heart with ribbon

Date	Mintage	F12	VF20	XF40	MS60	MS63
2010	Est. 3000	PF65 60.00				

KM# 381 2 DOLLARS
31.11 g., 0.999 Silver 0.9926 oz. ASW, 40.2 mm. **Ruler:**
Elizabeth II **Subject:** Russian Musicians **Rev:** Viktor Tsoy at
lower right in multicolor

Date	Mintage	F12	VF20	XF40	MS60	MS63
2010	2,000	PF65 65.00				

KM# 382 2 DOLLARS
31.11 g., 0.999 Silver 0.9926 oz. ASW, 40.2 mm. **Ruler:**
Elizabeth II **Subject:** Russian Musicians **Rev:** Vladimir
Vysotsky at lower right in multicolor

Date	Mintage	F12	VF20	XF40	MS60	MS63
2010	2,000	PF65 65.00				

KM# 383 2 DOLLARS
31.11 g., 0.999 Silver 0.9926 oz. ASW **Ruler:** Elizabeth II **Rev:**
Portrait in multicolor

Date	Mintage	F12	VF20	XF40	MS60	MS63
2010	Est. 2000	PF65 65.00				

KM# 384 2 DOLLARS
31.11 g., 0.999 Silver 0.9926 oz. ASW, 38.61 mm. **Ruler:**
Elizabeth II **Subject:** Miffy with friends

Date	Mintage	F12	VF20	XF40	MS60	MS63
2010	Est. 3000	PF65 60.00				

KM# 385 2 DOLLARS
31.11 g., 0.999 Silver 0.9926 oz. ASW, 38.61 mm. **Ruler:**
Elizabeth II **Subject:** Miffy on turtle

Date	Mintage	F12	VF20	XF40	MS60	MS63
2010	—	PF65 60.00				

KM# 386 2 DOLLARS
31.11 g., 0.999 Silver 0.9926 oz. ASW, 38.61 mm. **Ruler:** Elizabeth II **Subject:** Miffy celebration

Date	Mintage	F12	VF20	XF40	MS60	MS63
2010	Est. 3000	PF65 60.00				

KM# 390 2 DOLLARS
31.10 g., 0.999 Silver 0.9926 oz. ASW, 40.7 mm. **Ruler:** Elizabeth II **Subject:** Yamal **Rev:** Child wearing fur coat in multicolor

Date	Mintage	F12	VF20	XF40	MS60	MS63
2010	5,000	PF65 55.00				

KM# 391 2 DOLLARS
31.10 g., 0.999 Silver 0.9926 oz. ASW, 40.7 mm. **Ruler:** Elizabeth II **Subject:** Yamal **Rev:** Gas and Oil exploration in multicolor

Date	Mintage	F12	VF20	XF40	MS60	MS63
2010	5,000	PF65 55.00				

KM# 408 2 DOLLARS
31.10 g., 0.999 Silver 0.9926 oz. ASW, 40.7 mm. **Ruler:** Elizabeth II **Series:** Russian Transport **Obv:** Head with tiara right **Rev:** Bus in multicolor

Date	Mintage	F12	VF20	XF40	MS60	MS63
2010	15,000	PF65 60.00				

KM# 409 2 DOLLARS
31.10 g., 0.999 Silver 0.9926 oz. ASW, 40.7 mm. **Ruler:** Elizabeth II **Subject:** Russian Transport **Obv:** Head with tiara right **Rev:** Trolley Bus in multicolor

Date	Mintage	F12	VF20	XF40	MS60	MS63
2010	15,000	PF65 60.00				

KM# 410 2 DOLLARS
31.10 g., 0.999 Silver 0.9926 oz. ASW, 40.7 mm. **Ruler:** Elizabeth II **Subject:** Russian Transport **Obv:** Head with tiara right **Rev:** Metro in color

Date	Mintage	F12	VF20	XF40	MS60	MS63
2010	15,000	PF65 60.00				

KM# 411 2 DOLLARS
31.10 g., 0.999 Silver 0.9926 oz. ASW, 40.7 mm. **Ruler:** Elizabeth II **Subject:** Russian Transport **Obv:** Head with tiara right **Rev:** Tram in color

Date	Mintage	F12	VF20	XF40	MS60	MS63
2010	15,000	PF65 60.00				

KM# 416 2 DOLLARS
28.28 g., 0.925 Silver 0.8356 oz. ASW, 38.61 mm. **Ruler:** Elizabeth II **Obv:** Head with tiara right **Rev:** Kirovo Chepetsk

Date	Mintage	F12	VF20	XF40	MS60	MS63
2010	2,000	PF65 75.00				

KM# 424 2 DOLLARS
56.56 g., 0.925 Silver 1.6712 oz. ASW, 41.6x55.6 mm. **Ruler:** Elizabeth II **Subject:** Faberge Imperial Eggs - Clover Leaf **Obv:** Head with tiara right above opened egg **Rev:** Egg on stand in color **Shape:** Vertical oval

Date	Mintage	F12	VF20	XF40	MS60	MS63
2010	7,000	PF65 125				

KM# 431 2 DOLLARS
1.00 g., 0.900 Silver 0.0287 oz. ASW, 12 mm. **Ruler:** Elizabeth II **Subject:** Tadeusz Kosciuszko **Obv:** Head with tiara right **Rev:** Head left, signature below

Date	Mintage	F12	VF20	XF40	MS60	MS63
2010	5,000	РГ65 50.00				

KM# 442 2 DOLLARS
25.00 g., 0.925 Silver 0.7387 oz. ASW, 38.61 mm. **Ruler:** Elizabeth II **Subject:** Twelve days of Christmas **Rev:** Partridge in a pear tree

Date	Mintage	F12	VF20	XF40	MS60	MS63
2010	1,500	PF65 60.00				

KM# 443 2 DOLLARS
25.00 g., 0.925 Silver 0.7387 oz. ASW, 38.61 mm. **Ruler:** Elizabeth II **Subject:** Twelve days of Christmas **Rev:** Turtle dove

Date	Mintage	F12	VF20	XF40	MS60	MS63
2010	1,500	PF65 60.00				

KM# 444 2 DOLLARS
25.00 g., 0.925 Silver 0.7387 oz. ASW, 38.61 mm. **Ruler:** Elizabeth II **Subject:** Twelve days of Christmas **Rev:** French hen

Date	Mintage	F12	VF20	XF40	MS60	MS63
2010	1,500	PF65 60.00				

KM# 445 2 DOLLARS
25.00 g., 0.925 Silver 0.7387 oz. ASW **Ruler:** Elizabeth II **Subject:** Twelve days of Christmas **Rev:** Calling bird

Date	Mintage	F12	VF20	XF40	MS60	MS63
2010	1,500	PF65 60.00				

KM# 446 2 DOLLARS
25.00 g., 0.925 Silver 0.7387 oz. ASW, 38.61 mm. **Ruler:** Elizabeth II **Subject:** Twelve days of Christmas **Rev:** Golden rings

Date	Mintage	F12	VF20	XF40	MS60	MS63
2010	1,500	PF65 60.00				

KM# 447 2 DOLLARS
25.00 g., 0.925 Silver 0.7387 oz. ASW, 38.61 mm. **Ruler:** Elizabeth II **Subject:** Twelve days of Christmas **Rev:** Geese a laying

Date	Mintage	F12	VF20	XF40	MS60	MS63
2010	1,500	PF65 60.00				

KM# 448 2 DOLLARS
25.00 g., 0.925 Silver 0.7387 oz. ASW, 38.61 mm. **Ruler:** Elizabeth II **Subject:** Twelve days of Christmas **Rev:** Swans a swimming

Date	Mintage	F12	VF20	XF40	MS60	MS63
2010	1,500	PF65 60.00				

KM# 449 2 DOLLARS
25.00 g., 0.925 Silver 0.7387 oz. ASW, 38.61 mm. **Ruler:** Elizabeth II **Subject:** Twelve days of Christmas **Rev:** Maids a milking

Date	Mintage	F12	VF20	XF40	MS60	MS63
2010	1,500	PF65 60.00				

KM# 450 2 DOLLARS
25.00 g., 0.925 Silver 0.7387 oz. ASW, 38.61 mm. **Ruler:** Elizabeth II **Subject:** Twelve days of Christmas **Rev:** Ladies dancing

Date	Mintage	F12	VF20	XF40	MS60	MS63
2010	1,500	PF65 60.00				

KM# 451 2 DOLLARS
25.00 g., 0.925 Silver 0.7387 oz. ASW, 38.61 mm. **Ruler:** Elizabeth II **Subject:** Twelve days of Christmas **Rev:** Lords a leaping

Date	Mintage	F12	VF20	XF40	MS60	MS63
2010	1,500	PF65 60.00				

KM# 452 2 DOLLARS
25.00 g., 0.925 Silver 0.7387 oz. ASW, 38.61 mm. **Ruler:** Elizabeth II **Subject:** Twelve days of Christmas **Rev:** Pipers piping

Date	Mintage	F12	VF20	XF40	MS60	MS63
2010	1,500	PF65 60.00				

KM# 453 2 DOLLARS
25.00 g., 0.925 Silver 0.7387 oz. ASW, 38.61 mm. **Ruler:** Elizabeth II **Subject:** Twelve days of Christmas **Rev:** Drummers drumming

Date	Mintage	F12	VF20	XF40	MS60	MS63
2010	1,500	PF65 60.00				

KM# 457 2 DOLLARS
31.10 g., 0.999 Silver 0.9926 oz. ASW, 38.61 mm. **Ruler:** Elizabeth II **Subject:** Bulgarian theme roses - Survachka **Rev:** Figure-8 floral arangement

Date	Mintage	F12	VF20	XF40	MS60	MS63
2010	3,000	PF65 55.00				

KM# 458 2 DOLLARS
31.10 g., 0.999 Silver 0.9926 oz. ASW, 38.61 mm. **Ruler:** Elizabeth II **Subject:** Bulgarian rose **Rev:** Top view into colored pink rose, gilt border

Date	Mintage	F12	VF20	XF40	MS60	MS63
2010	6,000	PF65 50.00				

KM# 459 2 DOLLARS
31.10 g., 0.999 Silver 0.9926 oz. ASW, 38.61 mm. **Ruler:** Elizabeth II **Subject:** Bulgarian rose theme - Martenitsa **Rev:** tassle like device

Date	Mintage	F12	VF20	XF40	MS60	MS63
2010	3,000	PF65 55.00				

KM# 460 2 DOLLARS
31.10 g., 0.999 Silver 0.9926 oz. ASW, 38.61 mm. **Ruler:** Elizabeth II **Rev:** Saint Peter icon

Date	Mintage	F12	VF20	XF40	MS60	MS63
2010	2,000	PF65 60.00				

KM# 461 2 DOLLARS
31.10 g., 0.999 Silver 0.9926 oz. ASW, 38.61 mm. **Ruler:** Elizabeth II **Rev:** Saint Paul icon

Date	Mintage	F12	VF20	XF40	MS60	MS63
2010	2,000	PF65 60.00				

KM# 550 2 DOLLARS
Silver, 40 mm. **Ruler:** Elizabeth II **Subject:** Korean War, 60th Anniversary **Rev:** Soldier in multicolor

Date	Mintage	F12	VF20	XF40	MS60	MS63
2010	2,000	PF65 80.00				

KM# 372 2 DOLLARS
31.11 g., 0.999 Silver 0.9926 oz. ASW, 37.1x31.9 mm. **Ruler:** Elizabeth II **Subject:** Hello Kitty **Shape:** Heart with ribbon

Date	Mintage	F12	VF20	XF40	MS60	MS63
2010	Est. 3000	PF65 50.00				

KM# 507 2 DOLLARS
31.10 g., 0.999 Silver 0.9925 oz. ASW, 40.7 mm. **Ruler:** Elizabeth II **Subject:** Love is precious **Rev:** Two pink flamingos within heart

Date	Mintage	F12	VF20	XF40	MS60	MS63
2011	20,000	PF65 50.00				

KM# 521 2 DOLLARS
31.10 g., 0.999 Silver 0.9925 oz. ASW **Ruler:** Elizabeth II **Subject:** The Evangelists - St. Mathew and angel **Rev:** Icon in color

Date	Mintage	F12	VF20	XF40	MS60	MS63
2011	2,000	PF65 60.00				

KM# 522 2 DOLLARS
31.10 g., 0.999 Silver 0.9925 oz. ASW **Ruler:** Elizabeth II **Subject:** The Evangelists - St Mark with lion **Rev:** Icon in color

Date	Mintage	F12	VF20	XF40	MS60	MS63
2011	2,000	PF65 60.00				

KM# 523 2 DOLLARS
31.10 g., 0.999 Silver 0.9925 oz. ASW **Ruler:** Elizabeth II **Subject:** The Evangelists - Luke and oxen **Rev:** Icon in color

Date	Mintage	F12	VF20	XF40	MS60	MS63
2011	2,000	PF65 60.00				

KM# 524 2 DOLLARS
31.10 g., 0.999 Silver 0.9925 oz. ASW **Ruler:** Elizabeth II **Subject:** The Evangelists - John and eagle **Rev:** Icon in color

Date	Mintage	F12	VF20	XF40	MS60	MS63
2011	2,000	PF65 60.00				

KM# 525 2 DOLLARS
31.10 g., 0.999 Silver 0.9925 oz. ASW **Ruler:** Elizabeth II **Subject:** Eternal Love **Rev:** Two white doves within flora and scrolls

Date	Mintage	F12	VF20	XF40	MS60	MS63
2011	5,000	PF65 50.00				

KM# 563 2 DOLLARS
31.11 g., 0.999 Silver 0.9926 oz. ASW **Ruler:** Elizabeth II **Subject:** Pirates of the Caribbean - Blackbeard **Obv:** Head with crown right **Rev:** Blackbeard in multicolor

Date	Mintage	F12	VF20	XF40	MS60	MS63
2011	2,000	PF65 70.00				

KM# 564 2 DOLLARS
31.11 g., 0.999 Silver 0.9926 oz. ASW **Ruler:** Elizabeth II **Series:** Pirates of the Caribbean - Bartholomew Roberts **Obv:** Head with crown right **Rev:** Bartholomew Roberts in multicolor

Date	Mintage	F12	VF20	XF40	MS60	MS63
2011	2,000	PF65 70.00				

KM# 565 2 DOLLARS
31.11 g., 0.999 Silver 0.9926 oz. ASW **Ruler:** Elizabeth II **Subject:** Pirates of the Caribbean - Henry Avery **Obv:** Head with crown right **Rev:** Henry Avery in multicolor

Date	Mintage	F12	VF20	XF40	MS60	MS63
2011	2,000	PF65 70.00				

KM# 566 2 DOLLARS
3.11 g., 0.999 Silver 0.0991 oz. ASW **Ruler:** Elizabeth II **Subject:** Pirates of the Caribbean - Calico Jack **Obv:** Head with crown right **Rev:** Calico Jack and two ladies in multicolor

Date	Mintage	F12	VF20	XF40	MS60	MS63
2011	2,000	PF65 70.00				

KM# 567 2 DOLLARS
31.11 g., 0.999 Silver 0.9926 oz. ASW **Ruler:** Elizabeth II **Subject:** Legends of the Air **Obv:** Head with crown right **Rev:** B-2 Spirit Stealth Bomber in color

Date	Mintage	F12	VF20	XF40	MS60	MS63
2011	2,000	PF65 60.00				

KM# 568 2 DOLLARS
31.11 g., 0.999 Silver 0.9926 oz. ASW **Ruler:** Elizabeth II **Subject:** Legends of the Air **Obv:** Head with crown right **Rev:** F-16 Fighting Falcon

Date	Mintage	F12	VF20	XF40	MS60	MS63
2011	2,000	PF65 60.00				

KM# 569 2 DOLLARS
31.11 g., 0.999 Silver 0.9926 oz. ASW **Ruler:** Elizabeth II **Subject:** Legends of the Air **Obv:** Head with crown right **Rev:** AH-64D Apache Longbow in color

Date	Mintage	F12	VF20	XF40	MS60	MS63
2011	2,000	PF65 60.00				

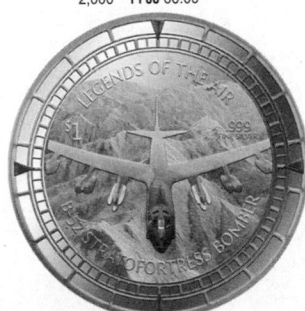

KM# 570 2 DOLLARS
31.11 g., 0.999 Silver 0.9926 oz. ASW **Ruler:** Elizabeth II **Subject:** Legends of the Air **Obv:** Head with crown right **Rev:** B-52 Stratofortress Bomber

Date	Mintage	F12	VF20	XF40	MS60	MS63
2011	2,000	PF65 60.00				

KM# 573 2 DOLLARS
31.11 g., 0.999 Silver 0.9926 oz. ASW, 38.61 mm. **Ruler:** Elizabeth II **Subject:** First crossing of the Simpson Desert, 75th Anniversary **Obv:** Head with crown right **Rev:** Ted Colson in color

Date	Mintage	F12	VF20	XF40	MS60	MS63
2011	2,000	PF65 75.00				

KM# 589 2 DOLLARS
31.10 g., 0.999 Silver 0.9926 oz. ASW, 33x55 mm. **Ruler:** Elizabeth II **Subject:** Kagaya Art Zodiac - Leo

Date	Mintage	F12	VF20	XF40	MS60	MS63
2011	8,000	PF65 80.00				

KM# 590 2 DOLLARS
31.10 g., 0.999 Silver 0.9926 oz. ASW, 33x55 mm. **Ruler:** Elizabeth II **Subject:** Kagaya Art Zodiac - Virgo

Date	Mintage	F12	VF20	XF40	MS60	MS63
2011	8,000	PF65 80.00				

KM# 591 2 DOLLARS
31.10 g., 0.999 Silver 0.9926 oz. ASW, 33x55 mm. **Ruler:** Elizabeth II **Subject:** Kagaya Art Zodiac - Libra **Shape:** Vertical rectangle

Date	Mintage	F12	VF20	XF40	MS60	MS63
2011	8,000	PF65 80.00				

KM# 592 2 DOLLARS
31.10 g., 0.999 Silver 0.9926 oz. ASW, 33x55 mm. **Ruler:**
Elizabeth II **Subject:** Kagaya Art Zodiac - Scorpio **Shape:**
Vertical rectangle

Date	Mintage	F12	VF20	XF40	MS60	MS63
2011	8,000	**PF65** 80.00				

KM# 593 2 DOLLARS
31.10 g., 0.999 Silver 0.9926 oz. ASW, 33x55 mm. **Ruler:**
Elizabeth II **Subject:** Kagaya Art Zodiac - Sagittarius **Shape:**
Vertical rectangle

Date	Mintage	F12	VF20	XF40	MS60	MS63
2011	8,000	**PF65** 80.00				

KM# 601 2 DOLLARS
31.10 g., 0.999 Silver 0.9926 oz. ASW, 40.7 mm. **Ruler:**
Elizabeth II **Subject:** Love Forever **Obv:** Head with crown right
Rev: Two doves in flight, two golden rings, word Forever in
many languages in background

Date	Mintage	F12	VF20	XF40	MS60	MS63
2011	20,000	**PF65** 65.00				

KM# 602 2 DOLLARS
31.10 g., 0.999 Silver 0.9926 oz. ASW, 40.7 mm. **Ruler:**
Elizabeth II **Subject:** Supersonic Transport - TU-144 **Rev:**
Plane color image

Date	Mintage	F12	VF20	XF40	MS60	MS63
2011	8,000	**PF65** 65.00				

KM# 603 2 DOLLARS
31.10 g., 0.999 Silver 0.9926 oz. ASW, 40.7 mm. **Ruler:**
Elizabeth II **Subject:** Supersonic Transport - Concorde **Rev:**
Plane color image

Date	Mintage	F12	VF20	XF40	MS60	MS63
2011	8,000	**PF65** 65.00				

KM# 639 2 DOLLARS
31.14 g., 0.999 Silver 0.9936 oz. ASW, 27x47 mm. **Ruler:**
Elizabeth II **Subject:** Orthodox shrines, Holy Trinity **Obv:** Head
with crown right **Rev:** Five saints seated around table, partially
gilt and colored **Edge:** Plain **Shape:** Vertical rectangle, convex

Date	Mintage	F12	VF20	XF40	MS60	MS63
2011	Est. 3000	**PF65** 100				

KM# 640 2 DOLLARS
31.14 g., 0.999 Silver 0.9936 oz. ASW, 27x47 mm. **Ruler:**
Elizabeth II **Subject:** Orthodox Shrines, Christ Pantokrator
Obv: Head with crown right **Rev:** Christ facing holding gospels,
partially gilt and colored **Edge:** Plain **Shape:** Vertical rectangle,
convex

Date	Mintage	F12	VF20	XF40	MS60	MS63
2011	3,000	**PF65** 100				

KM# 642 2 DOLLARS
31.11 g., 0.999 Silver 0.9926 oz. ASW, 55x33 mm. **Ruler:**
Elizabeth II **Obv:** Head with crown right **Rev:** First man in
space, multicolor **Shape:** rectangle

Date	Mintage	F12	VF20	XF40	MS60	MS63
2011 Proof	5,000	—	—	—		100

KM# 643 2 DOLLARS
31.11 g., 0.999 Silver 0.9926 oz. ASW, 55x33 mm. **Ruler:**
Elizabeth II **Obv:** Head with crown right **Rev:** First space walk

Date	Mintage	F12	VF20	XF40	MS60	MS63
2011	5,000	**PF65** 100				

KM# 663 2 DOLLARS
31.11 g., 0.999 Silver 0.9926 oz. ASW, 40 mm. **Ruler:** Elizabeth
II **Subject:** Star Wars - C3PO and R2D2

Date	Mintage	F12	VF20	XF40	MS60	MS63
2011 Prooflike	Est. 7500	—	—	—	—	120

KM# 664 2 DOLLARS
31.11 g., 0.999 Silver 0.9926 oz. ASW, 40 mm. **Ruler:** Elizabeth
II **Subject:** Star Wars - Darth Vader

Date	Mintage	F12	VF20	XF40	MS60	MS63
2011 Prooflike	Est. 7500	—	—	—	—	120

KM# 665 2 DOLLARS
31.11 g., 0.999 Silver 0.9926 oz. ASW, 40 mm. **Ruler:** Elizabeth
II **Subject:** Star Wars - Emperor Palpatine

Date	Mintage	F12	VF20	XF40	MS60	MS63
2011 Prooflike	Est. 7500	—	—	—	—	120

KM# 666 2 DOLLARS
31.11 g., 0.999 Silver 0.9926 oz. ASW, 40 mm. **Ruler:** Elizabeth II **Subject:** Star Wars - Death Star

Date	Mintage	F12	VF20	XF40	MS60	MS63
2011 Prooflike	Est. 7500	—	—	—	—	120

KM# 667 2 DOLLARS
31.11 g., 0.999 Silver 0.9926 oz. ASW, 40 mm. **Ruler:** Elizabeth II **Subject:** Star Wars - Han Solo and Chewbacca

Date	Mintage	F12	VF20	XF40	MS60	MS63
2011 Prooflike	—	—	—	—	—	120

KM# 668 2 DOLLARS
31.11 g., 0.999 Silver 0.9926 oz. ASW, 40 mm. **Ruler:** Elizabeth II **Subject:** Star Wars - Luke Skywalker and Princess Leia

Date	Mintage	F12	VF20	XF40	MS60	MS63
2011 Prooflike	—	—	—	—	—	120

KM# 669 2 DOLLARS
31.11 g., 0.999 Silver 0.9926 oz. ASW, 40 mm. **Ruler:** Elizabeth II **Series:** Star Wars - Stormtrooper

Date	Mintage	F12	VF20	XF40	MS60	MS63
2011 Prooflike	Est. 7500	—	—	—	—	120

KM# 670 2 DOLLARS
31.11 g., 0.999 Silver 0.9926 oz. ASW, 40 mm. **Ruler:** Elizabeth II **Subject:** Star Wars - Obi-Wan Kenobi and Yoda

Date	Mintage	F12	VF20	XF40	MS60	MS63
2011 Prooflike	Est. 7500	—	—	—	—	120

KM# 671 2 DOLLARS
31.11 g., 0.999 Silver 0.9926 oz. ASW, 40 mm. **Ruler:** Elizabeth II **Subject:** Anne Geddes - Boy

Date	Mintage	F12	VF20	XF40	MS60	MS63
2011 Prooflike	3,000	—	—	—	—	100

KM# 672 2 DOLLARS
31.11 g., 0.999 Silver 0.9926 oz. ASW, 40 mm. **Ruler:** Elizabeth II **Subject:** Anne Geddes - Girl

Date	Mintage	F12	VF20	XF40	MS60	MS63
2011 Prooflike	3,000	—	—	—	—	100

KM# 673 2 DOLLARS
15.55 g., 0.925 Silver 0.4595 oz. ASW, 35 mm. **Ruler:** Elizabeth II **Rev:** Mexican redknee tarantula in color

Date	Mintage	F12	VF20	XF40	MS60	MS63
2011	1,250	—	—	—	—	125

KM# 692 2 DOLLARS
31.11 g., 0.999 Silver 0.9926 oz. ASW, 38.61 mm. **Ruler:** Elizabeth II **Obv:** Head with crown right **Rev:** Virgin Mary with arms outstretched in color **Edge:** Reeded

Date	Mintage	F12	VF20	XF40	MS60	MS63
2011	3,000	PF65 100				

KM# 736 2 DOLLARS
56.56 g., 0.925 Silver 1.6712 oz. ASW, 41.6x55.6 mm. **Ruler:** Elizabeth II **Subject:** Imperial Faberge Egg - Pansy Egg **Obv:** Head right in filigree, open egg below **Rev:** Pansy flowers around closed egg **Shape:** Vertical oval

Date	Mintage	F12	VF20	XF40	MS60	MS63
2011	7,000	PF65 200				

KM# 802 2 DOLLARS
31.10 g., 0.999 Silver 0.9925 oz. ASW, 40.7 mm. **Ruler:** Elizabeth II **Rev:** School children playing with globe

Date	Mintage	F12	VF20	XF40	MS60	MS63
2011	Est. 6000	PF65 100				

KM# 883 2 DOLLARS
10.00 g., 0.925 Silver 0.2955 oz. ASW, 32 mm. **Ruler:** Elizabeth II **Rev:** Earth in color

Date	Mintage	F12	VF20	XF40	MS60	MS63
2011	—	PF65 75.00				

KM# 884 2 DOLLARS
12.00 g., 0.925 Silver 0.3546 oz. ASW, 35x35 mm. **Ruler:** Elizabeth II **Subject:** Elements - Air **Shape:** Irregular

Date	Mintage	F12	VF20	XF40	MS60	MS63
2011	—	PF65 75.00				

KM# 885 2 DOLLARS
12.00 g., 0.925 Silver 0.3546 oz. ASW, 35x35 mm. **Ruler:**
Elizabeth II **Subject:** Elements - Water **Shape:** Irregular

Date	Mintage	F12	VF20	XF40	MS60	MS63
2011	—	PF65 85.00				

KM# 886 2 DOLLARS
12.00 g., 0.925 Silver 0.3546 oz. ASW, 35x35 mm. **Ruler:**
Elizabeth II **Subject:** Elements - Land **Shape:** Irregular

Date	Mintage	F12	VF20	XF40	MS60	MS63
2011	—	PF65 85.00				

KM# 887 2 DOLLARS
12.00 g., 0.925 Silver 0.3546 oz. ASW, 35x35 mm. **Ruler:**
Elizabeth II **Subject:** Elements - Fire **Shape:** Irregular

Date	Mintage	F12	VF20	XF40	MS60	MS63
2011	—	PF65 85.00				

KM# 888 2 DOLLARS
56.56 g., 0.925 Silver 1.6712 oz. ASW, 41.6x56.6 mm. **Ruler:**
Elizabeth II **Subject:** Faberge egg - Dutchess of Marlboro egg
Shape: Vertical oval

Date	Mintage	F12	VF20	XF40	MS60	MS63
2011	—	PF65 100				

KM# 889 2 DOLLARS
31.11 g., 0.999 Silver 0.9926 oz. ASW, 40.7 mm. **Ruler:**
Elizabeth II **Obv:** Crowned head right, eternal flame and wreath
below **Rev:** WWII Russian Victory celebrations in color

Date	Mintage	F12	VF20	XF40	MS60	MS63
2011	5,000	PF65 85.00				

KM# 939 2 DOLLARS
31.10 g., 0.999 Silver 0.9925 oz. ASW, 45 x 31 mm. **Ruler:**
Elizabeth II **Subject:** Family Day

Date	Mintage	F12	VF20	XF40	MS60	MS63
2011 Proof	Est. 8000	—	—	—	—	—

KM# 940 2 DOLLARS
1.00 g., 0.900 Gold 0.0287 oz. AGW, 12 mm. **Ruler:** Elizabeth II
Subject: Adam Michiewicz

Date	Mintage	F12	VF20	XF40	MS60	MS63
2011 Proof	Est. 3000	—	—	—	—	—

KM# 594 2 DOLLARS
31.10 g., 0.999 Silver 0.9926 oz. ASW, 33x55 mm. **Ruler:**
Elizabeth II **Subject:** Kagaya Art Zodiac - Capricorn **Shape:**
Vertical rectangle

Date	Mintage	F12	VF20	XF40	MS60	MS63
2012	8,000	PF65 80.00				

KM# 595 2 DOLLARS
31.10 g., 0.999 Silver 0.9926 oz. ASW, 33x55 mm. **Ruler:**
Elizabeth II **Subject:** Kagaya Art Zodiac - Aquarius **Shape:**
Vertical rectangle

Date	Mintage	F12	VF20	XF40	MS60	MS63
2012	8,000	PF65 80.00				

KM# 596 2 DOLLARS
31.10 g., 0.999 Silver 0.9926 oz. ASW, 33x55 mm. **Ruler:**
Elizabeth II **Subject:** Kagaya Art Zodiac - Pisces **Shape:**
Vertical rectangle

Date	Mintage	F12	VF20	XF40	MS60	MS63
2012	8,000	PF65 80.00				

KM# 597 2 DOLLARS
31.10 g., 0.999 Silver 0.9926 oz. ASW, 33x55 mm. **Ruler:**
Elizabeth II **Subject:** Kagaya Art Zodiac - Aries **Shape:** Vertical
rectangle

Date	Mintage	F12	VF20	XF40	MS60	MS63
2012	8,000	PF65 80.00				

KM# 598 2 DOLLARS
31.10 g., 0.999 Silver 0.9926 oz. ASW, 33x55 mm. **Ruler:** Elizabeth II **Subject:** Kagaya Art Zodiac - Taurus **Shape:** Vertical rectangle

Date	Mintage	F12	VF20	XF40	MS60	MS63
2012	8,000	PF65 80.00				

KM# 599 2 DOLLARS
31.10 g., 0.999 Silver 0.9926 oz. ASW, 33x55 mm. **Ruler:** Elizabeth II **Subject:** Kagaya Art Zodiac - Gemini **Shape:** Vertical rectangle

Date	Mintage	F12	VF20	XF40	MS60	MS63
2012	8,000	PF65 80.00				

KM# 600 2 DOLLARS
31.10 g., 0.999 Silver 0.9926 oz. ASW, 33x55 mm. **Ruler:** Elizabeth II **Subject:** Kagaya Art Zodiac - Cancer **Shape:** Vertical rectangle

Date	Mintage	F12	VF20	XF40	MS60	MS63
2012	8,000	PF65 80.00				

KM# 638 2 DOLLARS
31.11 g., 0.999 Silver 0.9926 oz. ASW, 40.7 mm. **Ruler:** Elizabeth II **Obv:** Head with crown right **Rev:** R.M.S. Titanic sailing right within compass points

Date	Mintage	F12	VF20	XF40	MS60	MS63
2012	2,229	PF65 225				

KM# 675 2 DOLLARS
28.28 g., Copper-Nickel, 38.61 mm. **Ruler:** Elizabeth II **Rev:** Crowned state flowers **Edge:** Reeded

Date	Mintage	F12	VF20	XF40	MS60	MS63
2012	—	—	—	—	—	25.00

KM# 675a 2 DOLLARS
28.28 g., 0.925 Silver 0.8356 oz. ASW, 38.61 mm. **Ruler:** Elizabeth II **Rev:** Crowned state flowers

Date	Mintage	F12	VF20	XF40	MS60	MS63
2012	19,500	PF65 80.00				

KM# 676 2 DOLLARS
31.11 g., 0.999 Silver 0.9926 oz. ASW, 40.7 mm. **Ruler:** Elizabeth II **Rev:** Florida alligator, gilt **Edge:** Reeded

Date	Mintage	F12	VF20	XF40	MS60	MS63
2012	2,500	PF65 80.00				

KM# 677 2 DOLLARS
31.11 g., 0.999 Silver 0.9926 oz. ASW, 40.7 mm. **Ruler:** Elizabeth II **Subject:** Year of the Dragon **Rev:** Dragon

Date	Mintage	F12	VF20	XF40	MS60	MS63
2012	2,500	PF65 80.00				

KM# 691 2 DOLLARS
31.11 g., 0.999 Silver 0.9926 oz. ASW, 27x47 mm. **Ruler:** Elizabeth II **Subject:** Orthodox Shrines **Rev:** Faith, Hope and Charity and their mother, Sofia **Edge:** Plain

Date	Mintage	F12	VF20	XF40	MS60	MS63
2012	3,000	PF65 100				

KM# 693 2 DOLLARS
31.11 g., 0.999 Silver 0.9926 oz. ASW, 38.61 mm. **Ruler:** Elizabeth II **Rev:** Feng Shui - two Koi Carp gilt

Date	Mintage	F12	VF20	XF40	MS60	MS63
2012	10,000	PF65 100				

KM# 694 2 DOLLARS
31.11 g., 0.999 Silver 0.9926 oz. ASW **Ruler:** Elizabeth II **Subject:** Nickelodeon's Sponge Bob **Rev:** Sponge Bob **Shape:** Square

Date	Mintage	F12	VF20	XF40	MS60	MS63
2012	100,000	PF65 75.00				

KM# 695 2 DOLLARS
31.11 g., 0.999 Silver 0.9926 oz. ASW **Ruler:** Elizabeth II **Subject:** Nickelodeon's Sponge Bob **Rev:** Patrick Star **Shape:** Square

Date	Mintage	F12	VF20	XF40	MS60	MS63
2012	100,000	PF65 75.00				

KM# 696 2 DOLLARS
31.11 g., 0.999 Silver 0.9926 oz. ASW **Ruler:** Elizabeth II **Subject:** Nickelodeon's Sponge Bob **Rev:** Sandy Cheeks **Shape:** Square

Date	Mintage	F12	VF20	XF40	MS60	MS63
2012	100,000	PF65 75.00				

KM# 697 2 DOLLARS
31.11 g., 0.999 Silver 0.9926 oz. ASW **Ruler:** Elizabeth II **Subject:** Nickelodeon's Sponge Bob **Rev:** Gary (snail) **Shape:** Square

Date	Mintage	F12	VF20	XF40	MS60	MS63
2012	100,000	PF65 75.00				

KM# 712 2 DOLLARS
31.11 g., 0.999 Silver 0.9926 oz. ASW, 40.7 mm. **Ruler:** Elizabeth II **Rev:** Dragon

Date	Mintage	F12	VF20	XF40	MS60	MS63
2012	50,000	PF65 50.00				

KM# 717 2 DOLLARS
31.11 g., 0.9999 Silver 0.9935 oz. ASW, 40.7 mm. **Ruler:** Elizabeth II **Subject:** Star Wars - Battle Droid

Date	Mintage	F12	VF20	XF40	MS60	MS63
2012 Prooflike	10,000	—	—	—	—	125

KM# 718 2 DOLLARS
31.11 g., 0.999 Silver 0.9926 oz. ASW, 40.7 mm. **Ruler:** Elizabeth II **Subject:** Star Wars - Darth Maul

Date	Mintage	F12	VF20	XF40	MS60	MS63
2012 Prooflike	10,000					125

KM# 719 2 DOLLARS
31.11 g., 0.999 Silver 0.9926 oz. ASW, 40.7 mm. **Ruler:** Elizabeth II **Subject:** Star Wars - young Obi Wan Kenobi

Date	Mintage	F12	VF20	XF40	MS60	MS63
2012 Prooflike	10,000	—	—	—	—	125

KM# 720 2 DOLLARS
31.11 g., 0.999 Silver 0.9926 oz. ASW, 40.7 mm. **Ruler:** Elizabeth II **Subject:** Star Wars - Mace Windu

Date	Mintage	F12	VF20	XF40	MS60	MS63
2012 Prooflike	10,000	—	—	—	—	125

KM# 721 2 DOLLARS
31.11 g., 0.999 Silver 0.9926 oz. ASW, 40.7 mm. **Ruler:** Elizabeth II **Subject:** Star Wars - Yoda

Date	Mintage	F12	VF20	XF40	MS60	MS63
2012 Prooflike	10,000	—	—	—	—	125

KM# 722 2 DOLLARS
31.11 g., 0.999 Silver 0.9926 oz. ASW, 40.7 mm. **Ruler:** Elizabeth II **Subject:** Star Wars - Queen Amidala

Date	Mintage	F12	VF20	XF40	MS60	MS63
2012 Prooflike	10,000	—	—	—	—	125

KM# 723 2 DOLLARS
31.11 g., 0.999 Silver 0.9926 oz. ASW, 40.7 mm. **Ruler:** Elizabeth II **Subject:** Star Wars - Qui-Gon Jinn

Date	Mintage	F12	VF20	XF40	MS60	MS63
2012 Prooflike	10,000	—	—	—	—	125

KM# 724 2 DOLLARS
31.11 g., 0.999 Silver 0.9926 oz. ASW, 40.7 mm. **Ruler:** Elizabeth II **Subject:** Star Wars - young Anakin Skywalker

Date	Mintage	F12	VF20	XF40	MS60	MS63
2012 Prooflike	10,000	—	—	—	—	125

KM# 743 2 DOLLARS
15.55 g., 0.999 Silver 0.4962 oz. ASW, 33 mm. **Ruler:** Elizabeth II **Subject:** Year of the Dragon **Rev:** Dragon with pearl in color

Date	Mintage	F12	VF20	XF40	MS60	MS63
2012	8,000	PF65 50.00				

KM# 744 2 DOLLARS
31.11 g., 0.999 Silver 0.9926 oz. ASW, 45x31 mm. **Ruler:** Elizabeth II **Subject:** Year of the Dragon, Lucky Red dragon **Rev:** Red dragon lying down with rays in background **Shape:** Horizontal oval

Date	Mintage	F12	VF20	XF40	MS60	MS63
2012	4,000	PF65 100				

KM# 745 2 DOLLARS
31.11 g., 0.999 Silver 0.9926 oz. ASW, 45x31 mm. **Ruler:**
Elizabeth II **Subject:** Year of the Dragon - Lucky Blue Dragon
Rev: Blue dragon lying down, rays in background **Shape:**
Horizontal oval

Date	Mintage	F12	VF20	XF40	MS60	MS63
2012	8,000	PF65 100				

KM# 746 2 DOLLARS
31.11 g., 0.999 Silver 0.9926 oz. ASW, 40.7 mm. **Ruler:**
Elizabeth II **Subject:** Year of the Dragon - Lunar Fan Dragon
Rev: Dragon seated left, colored lunar hand fan in background

Date	Mintage	F12	VF20	XF40	MS60	MS63
2012	4,000	PF65 100				

KM# 756 2 DOLLARS
56.56 g., 0.925 Silver 1.6712 oz. ASW, 41.6x55.6 mm. **Ruler:**
Elizabeth II **Subject:** Imperial Faberge Eggs - Bay Tree **Rev:**
Bay tree **Shape:** Vertical oval

Date	Mintage	F12	VF20	XF40	MS60	MS63
2012	Est. 7000	PF65 125				

KM# 762 2 DOLLARS
39.60 g., 0.925 Silver 1.1701 oz. ASW, 48.61 mm. **Ruler:**
Elizabeth II **Subject:** Love Notes **Rev:** Cupid writing on central
tablet

Date	Mintage	F12	VF20	XF40	MS60	MS63
2012	Est. 3000	PF65 100				

KM# 782 2 DOLLARS
31.11 g., 0.999 Silver 0.9926 oz. ASW, 40.7 mm. **Ruler:**
Elizabeth II **Subject:** WWII Nose Art - Yellow Rose

Date	Mintage	F12	VF20	XF40	MS60	MS63
2012	Est. 3000	—	—	—	—	80.00

KM# 783 2 DOLLARS
31.11 g., 0.999 Silver 0.9926 oz. ASW, 40.7 mm. **Ruler:**
Elizabeth II **Subject:** WWII Nose Art - Briefing Time

Date	Mintage	F12	VF20	XF40	MS60	MS63
2012	—	—	—	—	—	80.00

KM# 784 2 DOLLARS
31.11 g., 0.999 Silver 0.9926 oz. ASW, 40.7 mm. **Ruler:**
Elizabeth II **Subject:** WWII Nose Art - Memphis Belle

Date	Mintage	F12	VF20	XF40	MS60	MS63
2012	—	—	—	—	—	80.00

KM# 795 2 DOLLARS
10.00 g., 0.925 Silver 0.2955 oz. ASW, 32 mm. **Ruler:** Elizabeth
II **Subject:** Four seasons, central device **Rev:** Flowers, leaves
and crystal

Date	Mintage	F12	VF20	XF40	MS60	MS63
2012	—	PF65 70.00				

KM# 796 2 DOLLARS
12.00 g., 0.925 Silver 0.3546 oz. ASW, 35x35 mm. **Ruler:**
Elizabeth II **Subject:** Four seasons - Spring **Rev:** Springtime
flora and crystal **Shape:** Irregular

Date	Mintage	F12	VF20	XF40	MS60	MS63
2012	—	PF65 70.00				

KM# 797 2 DOLLARS
12.00 g., 0.925 Silver 0.3546 oz. ASW, 35x35 mm. **Ruler:**
Elizabeth II **Subject:** Four seasons - Summer **Rev:** Summer
flora and crystal **Shape:** Irregular

Date	Mintage	F12	VF20	XF40	MS60	MS63
2012	Est. 9999	PF65 70.00				

KM# 798 2 DOLLARS
12.00 g., 0.925 Silver 0.3546 oz. ASW, 35x35 mm. **Ruler:**
Elizabeth II **Subject:** Four seasons - Autumn **Rev:** Autumn
foilage and crystal **Shape:** Irregular

Date	Mintage	F12	VF20	XF40	MS60	MS63
2012	—	PF65 70.00				

KM# 799 2 DOLLARS
12.00 g., 0.925 Silver 0.3546 oz. ASW, 35x35 mm. **Ruler:**
Elizabeth II **Subject:** Four seasons - Winter **Rev:** Winter
foilage and crystal **Shape:** Irregular

Date	Mintage	F12	VF20	XF40	MS60	MS63
2012	Est. 9999	PF65 70.00				

KM# 803 2 DOLLARS
31.11 g., 0.999 Silver 0.9926 oz. ASW, 40.7 mm. **Ruler:**
Elizabeth II **Rev:** Great White Shark

Date	Mintage	F12	VF20	XF40	MS60	MS63
2012	5,000	PF65 120				

KM# 806 2 DOLLARS
31.11 g., 0.999 Silver 0.9926 oz. ASW, 27x47 mm. **Ruler:** Elizabeth II **Obv:** Crowned head left **Rev:** Katherina icom **Shape:** Vertical rectangle

Date	Mintage	F12	VF20	XF40	MS60	MS63
2012	2,000	PF65 100				

KM# 807 2 DOLLARS
31.11 g., 0.999 Silver 0.9926 oz. ASW, 27x47 mm. **Ruler:** Elizabeth II **Obv:** Crowned head right **Rev:** Rublov - Archangel Michael painting **Shape:** Vertical rectangle

Date	Mintage	F12	VF20	XF40	MS60	MS63
2012	3,000	PF65 100				

KM# 808 2 DOLLARS
31.11 g., 0.999 Silver 0.9926 oz. ASW, 27x47 mm. **Ruler:** Elizabeth II **Obv:** Crowned head right **Rev:** Rubov - Christ painting **Shape:** Vertical rectangle

Date	Mintage	F12	VF20	XF40	MS60	MS63
2012	3,000	PF65 100				

KM# 809 2 DOLLARS
31.11 g., 0.999 Silver 0.9926 oz. ASW, 27x47 mm. **Ruler:** Elizabeth II **Obv:** Crowned head right **Rev:** Rublov - Holy Trinity painting **Shape:** Vertical rectangle

Date	Mintage	F12	VF20	XF40	MS60	MS63
2012	3,000	PF65 100				

KM# 810 2 DOLLARS
31.11 g., 0.999 Silver 0.9926 oz. ASW, 27x47 mm. **Ruler:** Elizabeth II **Obv:** Corwned head right **Rev:** Rublov - Apostle Paul painting **Shape:** Vertical rectangle

Date	Mintage	F12	VF20	XF40	MS60	MS63
2012	3,000	PF65 100				

KM# 811 2 DOLLARS
31.11 g., 0.999 Silver 0.9926 oz. ASW, 27x47 mm. **Ruler:** Elizabeth II **Obv:** Crowned head right **Rev:** Mary and child **Shape:** Vertical rectangle

Date	Mintage	F12	VF20	XF40	MS60	MS63
2012	3,000	PF65 100				

KM# 812 2 DOLLARS
31.11 g., 0.999 Silver 0.9926 oz. ASW, 27x47 mm. **Ruler:** Elizabeth II **Obv:** Crowned head right **Rev:** Christ holding book **Shape:** Vertical rectangle

Date	Mintage	F12	VF20	XF40	MS60	MS63
2012	3,000	PF65 100				

KM# 813 2 DOLLARS
31.11 g., 0.999 Silver 0.9926 oz. ASW, 27x47 mm. **Ruler:** Elizabeth II **Obv:** Crowned head right **Rev:** God the father holding book, angels above **Shape:** Vertical rectangle

Date	Mintage	F12	VF20	XF40	MS60	MS63
2012	3,000	PF65 100				

KM# 814 2 DOLLARS
31.11 g., 0.999 Silver 0.9926 oz. ASW, 38.61 mm. **Ruler:** Elizabeth II **Obv:** Crowned head right **Rev:** Secret Evening, Christ and deciples around table **Edge:** Reeded

Date	Mintage	F12	VF20	XF40	MS60	MS63
2012	2,000	PF65 100				

KM# 818 2 DOLLARS
0.999 Silver **Ruler:** Elizabeth II **Obv:** Crowned head right **Rev:** Saint facing right

Date	Mintage	F12	VF20	XF40	MS60	MS63
2012	500	PF65 100				

KM# 819 2 DOLLARS
0.999 Silver **Ruler:** Elizabeth II **Obv:** Crowned head right **Rev:** Saint standing right

Date	Mintage	F12	VF20	XF40	MS60	MS63
2012	500	PF65 100				

KM# 820 2 DOLLARS
0.999 Silver **Ruler:** Elizabeth II **Obv:** Crowned head right **Rev:** Saint standing right

Date	Mintage	F12	VF20	XF40	MS60	MS63
2012	500	PF65 100				

KM# 821 2 DOLLARS
0.999 Silver **Ruler:** Elizabeth II **Obv:** Crowned head right **Rev:** Saint standing right

Date	Mintage	F12	VF20	XF40	MS60	MS63
2012	500	PF65 100				

KM# 822 2 DOLLARS
0.999 Silver **Ruler:** Elizabeth II **Obv:** Crowned head right **Rev:** Christ facing

Date	Mintage	F12	VF20	XF40	MS60	MS63
2012	500	PF65 150				

KM# 823 2 DOLLARS
0.999 Silver **Ruler:** Elizabeth II **Obv:** Crowned head right **Rev:** Saint standing left

Date	Mintage	F12	VF20	XF40	MS60	MS63
2012	500	PF65 100				

KM# 824 2 DOLLARS
0.999 Silver **Ruler:** Elizabeth II **Obv:** Crowned head right **Rev:** Saint standing left

Date	Mintage	F12	VF20	XF40	MS60	MS63
2012	500	PF65 100				

KM# 825 2 DOLLARS
0.999 Silver **Ruler:** Elizabeth II **Obv:** Crowned head right **Rev:** Saint standing left

Date	Mintage	F12	VF20	XF40	MS60	MS63
2012	500	PF65 100				

KM# 826 2 DOLLARS
0.999 Silver **Ruler:** Elizabeth II **Obv:** Crowned head right **Rev:** Saint standing left

Date	Mintage	F12	VF20	XF40	MS60	MS63
2012	500	PF65 100				

KM# 836 2 DOLLARS
10.00 g., 0.925 Silver 0.2955 oz. ASW, 32 mm. **Ruler:** Elizabeth II **Obv:** Head with tiara right **Rev:** Palace gate

Date	Mintage	F12	VF20	XF40	MS60	MS63
2012	6,999	PF65 70.00				

KM# 837 2 DOLLARS
12.00 g., 0.925 Silver 0.3546 oz. ASW, 35x35 mm. **Ruler:** Elizabeth II **Obv:** Head with tiara right **Rev:** Palace façade **Shape:** Irregular

Date	Mintage	F12	VF20	XF40	MS60	MS63
2012	6,999	PF65 70.00				

KM# 838 2 DOLLARS
12.00 g., 0.925 Silver 0.3546 oz. ASW, 35x35 mm. **Ruler:** Elizabeth II **Obv:** Head with tiara right **Rev:** Tsar bust **Shape:** Iregular

Date	Mintage	F12	VF20	XF40	MS60	MS63
2012	6,999	PF65 70.00				

KM# 839 2 DOLLARS
12.00 g., 0.925 Silver 0.3546 oz. ASW, 35x35 mm. **Ruler:** Elizabeth II **Obv:** Head with tiara right **Rev:** Building view **Shape:** Irregular

Date	Mintage	F12	VF20	XF40	MS60	MS63
2012	6,999	PF65 70.00				

KM# 840 2 DOLLARS
12.00 g., 0.925 Silver 0.3546 oz. ASW, 35x35 mm. **Ruler:** Elizabeth II **Obv:** Head with tiara right **Rev:** Tsarina bust **Shape:** Irregular

Date	Mintage	F12	VF20	XF40	MS60	MS63
2012	6,999	PF65 70.00				

KM# 845 2 DOLLARS
28.28 g., 0.925 Silver 0.8356 oz. ASW, 41 mm. **Ruler:** Elizabeth II **Subject:** Wedding **Obv:** Head with tiara above present, hearts and rings **Rev:** Bridge and groom, rings and bouquet

Date	Mintage	F12	VF20	XF40	MS60	MS63
2012	Est. 15000	PF65 100				

KM# 866 2 DOLLARS
31.11 g., 0.999 Silver 0.9926 oz ASW, 40.7 mm. **Ruler:** Elizabeth II **Subject:** Birds of Prey **Obv:** Crowned head right **Rev:** American Bald Eagle

Date	Mintage	F12	VF20	XF40	MS60	MS63
2012	5,000	PF65 100				

KM# 867 2 DOLLARS
31.11 g., 0.999 Silver 0.9926 oz. ASW, 40.7 mm. **Ruler:** Elizabeth II **Subject:** Birds of Prey **Obv:** Crowned head right **Rev:** Osprey

Date	Mintage	F12	VF20	XF40	MS60	MS63
2012	5,000	PF65 100				

KM# 871 2 DOLLARS
31.11 g., 0.999 Silver 0.9926 oz. ASW, 54x32 mm. **Ruler:** Elizabeth II **Obv:** Crowned head right **Rev:** Blue Iguana head and eye **Shape:** Horizontal oval

Date	Mintage	F12	VF20	XF40	MS60	MS63
2012	1,000	PF65 175				

KM# 872 2 DOLLARS
31.11 g., 0.999 Silver 0.9926 oz. ASW, 45 mm. **Ruler:** Elizabeth II **Obv:** Crowned head right **Rev:** Lotto ball mixer

Date	Mintage	F12	VF20	XF40	MS60	MS63
2012	1,000	PF65 100				

KM# 882 2 DOLLARS
56.56 g., 0.925 Silver 1.6712 oz. ASW, 41.6x55.6 mm. **Ruler:** Elizabeth II **Obv:** Head with tiara right above open egg **Rev:** Imperial Faberge Egg - 100th Anniversary of the Patriotic War of 1812 **Shape:** Vertical oval

Date	Mintage	F12	VF20	XF40	MS60	MS63
2012	Est. 7000	PF65 125				

KM# 896 2 DOLLARS
28.28 g., 0.925 Silver 0.8356 oz. ASW, 44 mm. **Ruler:** Elizabeth II **Subject:** Christmas Star

Date	Mintage	F12	VF20	XF40	MS60	MS63
2012	Est. 7000	PF65 95.00				

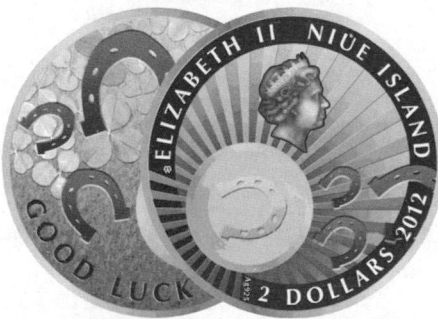

KM# 929 2 DOLLARS
28.28 g., 0.925 Silver 0.8356 oz. ASW, 41 mm. **Ruler:** Elizabeth II **Subject:** Lucky Coin: Horseshoe

Date	Mintage	F12	VF20	XF40	MS60	MS63
2012	Est. 15000	PF65 65.00				

KM# 930 2 DOLLARS
28.28 g., 0.925 Silver 0.8356 oz. ASW, 41 mm. **Ruler:** Elizabeth II **Subject:** Lucky Coin: Elephant

Date	Mintage	F12	VF20	XF40	MS60	MS63
2012	Est. 15000	PF65 65.00				

KM# 931 2 DOLLARS
28.28 g., 0.925 Silver 0.8356 oz. ASW, 41 mm. **Ruler:** Elizabeth II **Subject:** Lucky Coins: Four Leaf Clover

Date	Mintage	F12	VF20	XF40	MS60	MS63
2012	Est. 15000	PF65 65.00				

KM# 932 2 DOLLARS
28.28 g., 0.925 Silver 0.8356 oz. ASW, 41 mm. **Ruler:** Elizabeth II **Subject:** Lucky Coins: Ladybug

Date	Mintage	F12	VF20	XF40	MS60	MS63
2012	Est. 15000	PF65 65.00				

KM# 949 2 DOLLARS
62.20 g., 0.925 Silver 1.8379 oz. ASW, 50 mm. **Ruler:** Elizabeth II **Subject:** Amber Room

Date	Mintage	F12	VF20	XF40	MS60	MS63
2012	Est. 2000	PF65 135				

KM# 957 2 DOLLARS
31.10 g., 0.999 Silver 0.9925 oz. ASW **Ruler:** Elizabeth II **Subject:** Great Horned Owl

Date	Mintage	F12	VF20	XF40	MS60	MS63
2012	Est. 5000	PF65 95.00				

KM# 990 2 DOLLARS
31.10 g., 0.999 Silver 0.9925 oz. ASW, 32 x 45 mm. **Ruler:** Elizabeth II **Subject:** Russian Beauty

Date	Mintage	F12	VF20	XF40	MS60	MS63
2012	Est. 10000	PF65 85.00				

KM# 1070 2 DOLLARS
31.10 g., 0.999 Silver 0.9925 oz. ASW, 40 mm. **Ruler:** Elizabeth II **Subject:** Our Friends: Bengal

Date	Mintage	F12	VF20	XF40	MS60	MS63
2012	Est. 8000	PF65 100				

KM# 1071 2 DOLLARS
31.10 g., 0.999 Silver 0.9925 oz. ASW, 40 mm. **Ruler:** Elizabeth II **Subject:** Our Friends: Kurilian Bobtail

Date	Mintage	F12	VF20	XF40	MS60	MS63
2012	Est. 8000	PF65 100				

KM# 1072 2 DOLLARS
31.10 g., 0.999 Silver 0.9925 oz. ASW, 40 mm. **Ruler:** Elizabeth II **Subject:** Our Friends: Scottish Fold

Date	Mintage	F12	VF20	XF40	MS60	MS63
2012	Est. 8000	PF65 100				

KM# 1077 2 DOLLARS
62.20 g., 0.900 Silver 1.7882 oz. ASW, 50 mm. **Ruler:** Elizabeth II **Subject:** Secrets of Lichtenstein

Date	Mintage	F12	VF20	XF40	MS60	MS63
2012	Est. 999	PF65 225				

KM# 1142 2 DOLLARS
31.10 g., 0.999 Silver 0.9926 oz. ASW, 45.7 x 42.1 mm. **Ruler:** Elizabeth II **Subject:** Christmas Bell **Obv:** Bell - Head with tiara right **Rev:** Three children ice skating with crystal **Shape:** Bell

Date	Mintage	F12	VF20	XF40	MS60	MS63
2012	3,500	PF65 75.00				

KM# 1248 2 DOLLARS
31.11 g., 0.999 Silver 0.9926 oz. ASW, 40.7 mm. **Ruler:** Elizabeth II **Subject:** Robert F. Scott **Rev:** Scott portrait and color background

Date	Mintage	F12	VF20	XF40	MS60	MS63
2012	Est. 5000	PF65 150				

KM# 1249 2 DOLLARS
31.11 g., 0.999 Silver 0.9926 oz. ASW, 40 mm. **Ruler:** Elizabeth II **Subject:** Russian Literature - Lermontov **Obv:** Head with Tiara right

Date	Mintage	F12	VF20	XF40	MS60	MS63
2012	—	PF65 90.00				

KM# 1250 2 DOLLARS
31.11 g., 0.999 Silver 0.9926 oz. ASW, 40 mm. **Ruler:** Elizabeth II **Subject:** Russian Literature - Pushkin **Obv:** Head with tiara right

Date	Mintage	F12	VF20	XF40	MS60	MS63
2012	Est. 8000	PF65 90.00				

KM# 845a 2 DOLLARS
28.28 g., 0.925 Gold Plated Silver 0.8356 oz., 41 mm. **Ruler:** Elizabeth II **Subject:** Wedding Coin

Date	Mintage	F12	VF20	XF40	MS60	MS63
2013	Est. 22222	PF65 90.00				

KM# 857 2 DOLLARS
31.11 g., 0.999 Silver 0.9926 oz. ASW, 40.7 mm. **Ruler:** Elizabeth II **Obv:** Crowned head right **Rev:** Transformers - OPTIMUS PRIME

Date	Mintage	F12	VF20	XF40	MS60	MS63
2013	5,000	PF65 100				

KM# 858 2 DOLLARS
31.11 g., 0.999 Silver 0.9926 oz. ASW, 40.7 mm. **Ruler:** Elizabeth II **Obv:** Crowned head right **Rev:** Transformers - Megatron

Date	Mintage	F12	VF20	XF40	MS60	MS63
2013	5,000	PF65 100				

KM# 859 2 DOLLARS
31.11 g., 0.999 Silver 0.9926 oz. ASW, 30.5x30.5 mm. **Ruler:** Elizabeth II **Obv:** Crowned head right **Rev:** Mr. Monopoly **Shape:** Square

Date	Mintage	F12	VF20	XF40	MS60	MS63
2013	5,000	PF65 125				

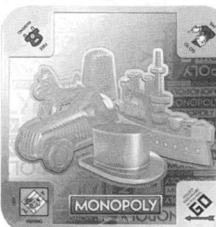

KM# 860 2 DOLLARS
31.11 g., 0.999 Silver 0.9926 oz. ASW, 30.5x30.5 mm. **Ruler:** Elizabeth II **Obv:** Crowned head right **Rev:** Monopoly Game pieces - car, top hat, thimble, dog, battleship **Shape:** Square

Date	Mintage	F12	VF20	XF40	MS60	MS63
2013	5,000	PF65 125				

KM# 870 2 DOLLARS
31.11 g., 0.999 Silver 0.9926 oz. ASW, 45x31 mm. **Ruler:** Elizabeth II **Obv:** Crowned head right **Rev:** Lunar Lucky Snake in color **Shape:** Horizontal oval

Date	Mintage	F12	VF20	XF40	MS60	MS63
2013	8,000	PF65 100				

TWO DOLLARS
2
NIUE ISLAND
2013
ELIZABETH II

Scottsdale Silver
1 TROY OZ
.999 FINE SILVER

KM# 890 2 DOLLARS
31.10 g., 0.999 Silver 0.9925 oz. ASW, 29x50 mm. **Ruler:** Elizabeth II **Subject:** Scottsdale Silver

Date	Mintage	F12	VF20	XF40	MS60	MS63
2013	Est. 350000	PF65 35.00				

KM# 937 2 DOLLARS
28.28 g., Copper-Nickel, 38.61 mm. **Ruler:** Elizabeth II **Subject:** Queen's Home - Buckingham Palace

Date	Mintage	F12	VF20	XF40	MS60	MS63
2013	Est. 75000	PF65 35.00				

KM# 937a 2 DOLLARS
28.28 g., 0.925 Silver 0.8356 oz. ASW, 38.61 mm. **Ruler:** Elizabeth II **Subject:** Queen's Home - Buckingham Palace

Date	Mintage	F12	VF20	XF40	MS60	MS63
2013	Est. 40000	PF65 65.00				

KM# 938 2 DOLLARS
28.28 g., Copper-Nickel, 38.61 mm. **Ruler:** Elizabeth II **Subject:** Queen's Home - Westminster Abbey

Date	Mintage	F12	VF20	XF40	MS60	MS63
2013	Est. 75000	PF65 35.00				

KM# 938a 2 DOLLARS
28.28 g., 0.925 Silver 0.8356 oz. ASW, 38.61 mm. **Ruler:** Elizabeth II **Subject:** Queen's Home - Westminstor Abby

Date	Mintage	F12	VF20	XF40	MS60	MS63
2013	Est. 40000	PF65 65.00				

KM# 951 2 DOLLARS
31.10 g., 0.999 Silver 0.9925 oz. ASW, 40 mm. **Ruler:** Elizabeth II **Subject:** Love is Precious

Date	Mintage	F12	VF20	XF40	MS60	MS63
2013	—	PF65 85.00				

KM# 958 2 DOLLARS
31.10 g., 0.999 Silver 0.9925 oz. ASW **Ruler:** Elizabeth II **Subject:** Feng Shui Horses

Date	Mintage	F12	VF20	XF40	MS60	MS63
2013	Est. 8000	PF65 120				

KM# 962 2 DOLLARS
25.00 g., 0.999 Silver 0.7978 oz. ASW, 38.61 mm. **Ruler:** Elizabeth II **Subject:** Mythologies of the World: The Story of Osiris - Horus

Date	Mintage	F12	VF20	XF40	MS60	MS63
2013	Est. 3000	PF65 115				

KM# 963 2 DOLLARS
25.00 g., 0.999 Silver 0.7978 oz. ASW, 38.61 mm. **Ruler:** Elizabeth II **Subject:** Mythologies of the World: The Story of Osiris - Isis

Date	Mintage	F12	VF20	XF40	MS60	MS63
2013	—	PF65 115				

KM# 964 2 DOLLARS
25.00 g., 0.999 Silver 0.7978 oz. ASW, 38.61 mm. **Ruler:** Elizabeth II **Subject:** Mythologies of the World: The Story of Osiris - Osiris

Date	Mintage	F12	VF20	XF40	MS60	MS63
2013	Est. 3000	PF65 115				

KM# 965 2 DOLLARS
25.00 g., 0.999 Silver 0.7978 oz. ASW, 38.61 mm. **Ruler:** Elizabeth II **Subject:** Mythologies of the World: The Story of Osiris - Nephthys

Date	Mintage	F12	VF20	XF40	MS60	MS63
2013	Est. 3000	PF65 115				

KM# 966 2 DOLLARS
25.00 g., 0.999 Silver 0.7978 oz. ASW, 38.61 mm. **Ruler:** Elizabeth II **Subject:** Mythologies of the World: The Story of Osiris - Set

Date	Mintage	F12	VF20	XF40	MS60	MS63
2013	—	PF65 115				

KM# 986 2 DOLLARS
31.10 g., 0.999 Silver 0.9925 oz. ASW, 40 mm. **Ruler:** Elizabeth II **Subject:** Caucasian Hostage: Three men and car

Date	Mintage	F12	VF20	XF40	MS60	MS63
2013	Est. 8000	PF65 60.00				

KM# 989 2 DOLLARS
31.10 g., 0.999 Silver 0.9925 oz. ASW, 40 mm. **Ruler:** Elizabeth II **Subject:** Love is Precious

Date	Mintage	F12	VF20	XF40	MS60	MS63
2013	—	PF65 60.00				

KM# 994 2 DOLLARS
31.10 g., 0.999 Silver 0.9925 oz. ASW, 40 mm. **Ruler:** Elizabeth II **Subject:** 50th Anniversary of Dr. Who

Date	Mintage	F12	VF20	XF40	MS60	MS63
2013	Est. 10000	PF65 125				

KM# 995 2 DOLLARS
31.10 g., 0.999 Silver 0.9925 oz. ASW, 40 mm. **Ruler:** Elizabeth II **Subject:** Anne Geddes - Protect and Nurture

Date	Mintage	F12	VF20	XF40	MS60	MS63
2013	Est. 5000	PF65 90.00				

ELIZABETH II
NIUE
2 DOLLARS
2013

天下第一
福
1 oz Ag. 999

KM# 996 2 DOLLARS
31.10 g., 0.999 Silver 0.9925 oz. ASW, 27 x 47 mm. **Ruler:** Elizabeth II **Subject:** True Happiness

Date	Mintage	F12	VF20	XF40	MS60	MS63
2013	Est. 9999	PF65 60.00				

KM# 1208 2 DOLLARS
12.00 g., 0.925 Silver 0.3546 oz. ASW, 35 x 35 mm. **Ruler:** Elizabeth II **Subject:** The Monuments of Odessa

Date	Mintage	F12	VF20	XF40	MS60	MS63
2013	Est. 2222	PF65 60.00				

KM# 1093 2 DOLLARS
31.10 g., 0.999 Silver 0.9925 oz. ASW, 40.7 mm. **Ruler:** Elizabeth II **Subject:** Spiderman

Date	Mintage	F12	VF20	XF40	MS60	MS63
2013	Est. 5000	PF65 100				

KM# 1113 2 DOLLARS
31.10 g., 0.999 Silver 0.9925 oz. ASW, 40.7 mm. **Ruler:** Elizabeth II **Series:** Feng Shui Series - Cranes

Date	Mintage	F12	VF20	XF40	MS60	MS63
2013	—	PF65 75.00				

KM# 1117 2 DOLLARS
33.63 g., 0.925 Silver 0.9937 oz. ASW, 38.61 mm. **Ruler:** Elizabeth II **Subject:** Independence of Kazakhstan

Date	Mintage	F12	VF20	XF40	MS60	MS63
2013 Proof	Est. 3000	—	—	—	—	—

KM# 1118 2 DOLLARS
31.10 g., 0.999 Silver 0.9925 oz. ASW, 54 x 32 mm. **Ruler:** Elizabeth II **Subject:** Critically Endangered Species: Croceye

Date	Mintage	F12	VF20	XF40	MS60	MS63
2013	Est. 1000	PF65 150				

KM# 1132 2 DOLLARS
28.28 g., 0.925 Gold Plated Silver 0.8356 oz., 41 mm. **Ruler:** Elizabeth II **Subject:** Lucky Coins - Horseshoe

Date	Mintage	F12	VF20	XF40	MS60	MS63
2013	Est. 22222	PF65 60.00				

KM# 1133 2 DOLLARS
28.28 g., 0.925 Gold Plated Silver 0.8356 oz., 41 mm. **Ruler:** Elizabeth II **Subject:** Lucky Coins - Four Leaf Clover

Date	Mintage	F12	VF20	XF40	MS60	MS63
2013	Est. 22222	PF65 60.00				

KM# 1134 2 DOLLARS
28.28 g., 0.925 Gold Plated Silver 0.8356 oz., 41 mm. **Ruler:** Elizabeth II **Subject:** Lucky Coins - Ladybug

Date	Mintage	F12	VF20	XF40	MS60	MS63
2013	Est. 22222	PF65 60.00				

KM# 1135 2 DOLLARS
28.28 g., 0.925 Gold Plated Silver 0.8356 oz., 41 mm. **Ruler:** Elizabeth II **Subject:** Lucky Coins - Elephant

Date	Mintage	F12	VF20	XF40	MS60	MS63
2013	Est. 22222	PF65 70.00				

KM# 1136 2 DOLLARS
31.10 g., 0.925 Silver 0.9189 oz. ASW, 40 mm. **Ruler:** Elizabeth II **Subject:** Caucasian Hostage: Man, woman and donkey

Date	Mintage	F12	VF20	XF40	MS60	MS63
2013	Est. 8000	PF65 60.00				

KM# 1137 2 DOLLARS
31.10 g., 0.999 Silver 0.9925 oz. ASW, 40 mm. **Ruler:** Elizabeth II **Subject:** Caucasian Hostage: Butler, man and sheep

Date	Mintage	F12	VF20	XF40	MS60	MS63
2013	Est. 8000	PF65 60.00				

KM# 1143 2 DOLLARS
31.10 g., 0.999 Silver 0.9926 oz. ASW, 38.61 mm. **Ruler:** Elizabeth II **Subject:** Fennec Fox

Date	Mintage	F12	VF20	XF40	MS60	MS63
2013	—	PF65 75.00				

KM# 1145 2 DOLLARS
31.10 g., 0.9999 Silver 0.9934 oz. ASW, 40 mm. **Ruler:** Elizabeth II **Subject:** St. Petersburg - Building the Future

Date	Mintage	F12	VF20	XF40	MS60	MS63
2013	—	PF65 120				

KM# 1146 2 DOLLARS
31.10 g., 0.9999 Silver 0.9934 oz. ASW, 40 mm. **Ruler:** Elizabeth II **Subject:** St. Petersburg - Growing Through the Ages

Date	Mintage	F12	VF20	XF40	MS60	MS63
2013	Est. 4000	PF65 120				

KM# 1147 2 DOLLARS
31.10 g., 0.9999 Silver 0.9934 oz. ASW, 40 mm. **Ruler:** Elizabeth II **Subject:** St. Petersburg - White Nights

Date	Mintage	F12	VF20	XF40	MS60	MS63
2013	Est. 4000	PF65 120				

KM# 1151 2 DOLLARS
31.10 g., 0.999 Silver 0.9925 oz. ASW, 52 x 31 mm. **Ruler:** Elizabeth II **Subject:** Pacific Islands

Date	Mintage	F12	VF20	XF40	MS60	MS63
2013 Proof	Est. 3000	—	—	—	—	—

KM# 1152 2 DOLLARS
31.10 g., 0.999 Silver 0.9925 oz. ASW, 40.7 mm. **Ruler:** Elizabeth II **Subject:** Endangered Species - Venerable Collared Lizard

Date	Mintage	F12	VF20	XF40	MS60	MS63
2013	Est. 5000	PF65 85.00				

KM# 1153 2 DOLLARS
31.10 g., 0.999 Silver 0.9925 oz. ASW, 40.7 mm. **Ruler:** Elizabeth II **Subject:** Endangered Species - Grand Cayman Blue Iguana

Date	Mintage	F12	VF20	XF40	MS60	MS63
2013	—	PF65 85.00				

KM# 1157 2 DOLLARS
56.56 g., 0.999 Silver 1.8049 oz. ASW, 41.6 x 56.56 mm. **Ruler:** Elizabeth II **Subject:** Continents - Europe

Date	Mintage	F12	VF20	XF40	MS60	MS63
2013	Est. 2000	PF65 200				

KM# 1165 2 DOLLARS
33.63 g., 0.925 Silver 0.9937 oz. ASW, 38.61 mm. **Ruler:** Elizabeth II **Subject:** Betashar

Date	Mintage	F12	VF20	XF40	MS60	MS63
2013	Est. 3000	PF65 100				

KM# 1173 2 DOLLARS
31.10 g., 0.999 Silver 0.9925 oz. ASW, 40.7 mm. **Ruler:** Elizabeth II **Subject:** 50 Years of Spiderman

Date	Mintage	F12	VF20	XF40	MS60	MS63
2013	Est. 1173	PF65 100				

KM# 1184 2 DOLLARS
31.10 g., 0.999 Silver 0.9925 oz. ASW, 28 x 51 mm. **Ruler:** Elizabeth II **Subject:** Humpback Whale

Date	Mintage	F12	VF20	XF40	MS60	MS63
2013 Proof	—	—	—	—	—	—

KM# 1188 2 DOLLARS
31.10 g., 0.999 Silver 0.9925 oz. ASW, 40.7 mm. **Ruler:** Elizabeth II **Subject:** Real River Monsters - Piranha

Date	Mintage	F12	VF20	XF40	MS60	MS63
2013	Est. 5000	PF65 75.00				

KM# 1192 2 DOLLARS
0.50 g., 0.999 Gold AGW, 11 mm. **Ruler:** Elizabeth II **Subject:** Paavo Nurmi

Date	Mintage	F12	VF20	XF40	MS60	MS63
2013 Proof	Est. 6000	—	—	—	—	—

KM# 1207 2 DOLLARS
10.00 g., 0.925 Silver 0.2955 oz. ASW, 32 mm. **Ruler:** Elizabeth II **Subject:** The Monuments of Odessa

Date	Mintage	F12	VF20	XF40	MS60	MS63
2013	Est. 2222	PF65 60.00				

KM# 1209 2 DOLLARS
12.00 g., 0.925 Silver 0.3546 oz. ASW, 35 x 35 mm. **Ruler:** Elizabeth II **Subject:** The Monuments of Odessa

Date	Mintage	F12	VF20	XF40	MS60	MS63
2013	Est. 2222	PF65 60.00				

KM# 1210 2 DOLLARS
12.00 g., 0.925 Silver 0.3546 oz. ASW, 35 x 35 mm. **Ruler:** Elizabeth II **Subject:** The Monuments of Odessa

Date	Mintage	F12	VF20	XF40	MS60	MS63
2013	—	PF65 60.00				

KM# 1211 2 DOLLARS
12.00 g., 0.925 Silver 0.3546 oz. ASW, 35 x 35 mm. **Ruler:** Elizabeth II **Subject:** The Monuments of Odessa

Date	Mintage	F12	VF20	XF40	MS60	MS63
2013	—	PF65 60.00				

KM# 1229 2 DOLLARS
31.10 g., 0.999 Silver 0.9925 oz. ASW, 40.7 mm. **Ruler:** Elizabeth II **Subject:** Peregrine Falcon

Date	Mintage	F12	VF20	XF40	MS60	MS63
2013	Est. 5000	PF65 80.00				

KM# 1240 2 DOLLARS
28.28 g., 0.925 Silver 0.8356 oz. ASW, 41 mm. **Ruler:** Elizabeth II **Subject:** Lucky Coins - Gold Fish

Date	Mintage	F12	VF20	XF40	MS60	MS63
2013	Est. 15000	PF65 60.00				

KM# 1241 2 DOLLARS
31.10 g., 0.999 Silver 0.9925 oz. ASW, 40 mm. **Ruler:** Elizabeth II **Subject:** T.E. Lawrence

Date	Mintage	F12	VF20	XF40	MS60	MS63
2013	Est. 1888	PF65 65.00				

KM# 1242 2 DOLLARS
56.56 g., 0.925 Silver 1.6712 oz. ASW, 41.6 x 55.6 mm. **Ruler:** Elizabeth II **Subject:** Imperial Faberge Eggs - Kremlin Egg

Date	Mintage	F12	VF20	XF40	MS60	MS63
2013	—	PF65 145				

KM# 1258 2 DOLLARS
31.10 g., 0.999 Silver 0.9926 oz. ASW, 40.7 mm. **Ruler:** Elizabeth II **Obv:** Head with tiara right **Rev:** Giant Coconut Crab in color

Date	Mintage	F12	VF20	XF40	MS60	MS63
2013	—	PF65 75.00				

KM# 1217 2 DOLLARS
80.00 g., 0.999 Silver 2.5529 oz. ASW, 91.55 x 55 mm. **Ruler:** Elizabeth II **Subject:** Giants of Art - The Creation of Adam (1 of 12)

Date	Mintage	F12	VF20	XF40	MS60	MS63
2013	Est. 750	PF65 275				

KM# 785 3 DOLLARS
33.30 g., 0.925 Silver 0.9839 oz. ASW, 38.61 mm. **Ruler:** Elizabeth II **Subject:** Polish Radio, station 3 **Obv:** Head with tiara right **Rev:** Radio microphone and sound arcs

Date	Mintage	F12	VF20	XF40	MS60	MS63
2012	—	PF65 75.00				

KM# 1252 3 DOLLARS
50.00 g., 0.999 Silver 1.5956 oz. ASW, 50 mm. **Ruler:** Elizabeth II **Subject:** Amazing Amazonia **Obv:** Head in tiara right **Rev:** Squirrel Monkey pair in color

Date	Mintage	F12	VF20	XF40	MS60	MS63
2012	—	PF65 300				

KM# 266 5 DOLLARS
155.50 g., 0.999 Silver 4.9623 oz. ASW, 70 mm. **Ruler:** Elizabeth II **Subject:** Year of the Rooster **Rev:** Multicolor rooster standing right, sunrise

Date	Mintage	F12	VF20	XF40	MS60	MS63
2005	—	PF65 225				

KM# 295 5 DOLLARS
155.50 g., 0.999 Silver 4.9623 oz. ASW, 70 mm. **Ruler:** Elizabeth II **Subject:** Year of the Dog **Rev:** Multicolor dog

Date	Mintage	F12	VF20	XF40	MS60	MS63
2005	—	PF65 225				

KM# 272 5 DOLLARS
6.22 g., 0.999 Gold 0.1985 oz. AGW, 25 mm. **Ruler:** Elizabeth II **Subject:** Year of the Rooster

Date	Mintage	F12	VF20	XF40	MS60	MS63
2005	—	PF65 400				

KM# 273 5 DOLLARS
15.55 g., 0.999 Gold 0.4962 oz. AGW, 33 mm. **Ruler:** Elizabeth II **Subject:** Year of the Rooster

Date	Mintage	F12	VF20	XF40	MS60	MS63
2005	—	PF65 950				

KM# 333 5 DOLLARS
15.50 g., 0.917 Gold 0.454 oz. AGW, 27 mm. **Ruler:** Elizabeth II **Subject:** Amber Road - Gdansk **Rev:** Nepture statue, castle, amber insert

Date	Mintage	F12	VF20	XF40	MS60	MS63
2007	—	—	—	—		850

KM# 191 5 DOLLARS
15.50 g., 0.900 Gold 0.4456 oz. AGW, 27 mm. **Ruler:** Elizabeth II **Subject:** Amber road **Obv:** Bust and Roman cart **Rev:** Kaliningrad Castle, Roman coin, Amber insert

Date	Mintage	F12	VF20	XF40	MS60	MS63
2008	2,000	PF65 850				

KM# 230 5 DOLLARS
62.21 g., 0.999 Silver 1.9852 oz. ASW, 50x32 mm. **Ruler:** Elizabeth II **Subject:** Battleship: Tripitz **Shape:** Rectangle

Date	Mintage	F12	VF20	XF40	MS60	MS63
2009	1,000					150

KM# 349 5 DOLLARS
15.50 g., 0.900 Gold 0.4456 oz. AGW, 27 mm. **Ruler:** Elizabeth II **Subject:** Amber Road - Elblag **Rev:** Amber insert

Date	Mintage	F12	VF20	XF40	MS60	MS63
2009	—	PF65 850				

KM# 364 5 DOLLARS
77.70 g., 0.999 Silver 2.4795 oz. ASW, 50x32 mm. **Ruler:** Elizabeth II **Rev:** Battleship Tirpitz sailing left **Shape:** Wavy rectangle

Date	Mintage	F12	VF20	XF40	MS60	MS63
2009	1,000	PF65 175				

KM# 250 5 DOLLARS
0.50 g., 0.999 Gold AGW, 11 mm. **Ruler:** Elizabeth II **Rev:** Ned Kelly

Date	Mintage	F12	VF20	XF40	MS60	MS63
2010	—	PF65 65.00				

KM# 368 5 DOLLARS
15.50 g., 0.900 Gold 0.4456 oz. AGW, 27 mm. **Ruler:** Elizabeth II **Subject:** Amber road - Stare Hradisko **Rev:** Amber insert

Date	Mintage	F12	VF20	XF40	MS60	MS63
2010	2,000	—	—	—	—	850

KM# 376 5 DOLLARS
2.50 g., 0.999 Gold 0.0798 oz. AGW, 14x26.7 mm. **Ruler:** Elizabeth II **Subject:** Kitty **Shape:** Vertical rectangle

Date	Mintage	F12	VF20	XF40	MS60	MS63
2010	—	PF65 175				

KM# 377 5 DOLLARS
2.50 g., 0.999 Gold 0.0798 oz. AGW, 14x26.7 mm. **Ruler:** Elizabeth II **Subject:** Kiki Lala **Shape:** Vertical rectangle

Date	Mintage	F12	VF20	XF40	MS60	MS63
2010	Est. 2000	PF65 175				

KM# 378 5 DOLLARS
2.50 g., 0.999 Gold 0.0798 oz. AGW, 14x26.7 mm. **Ruler:** Elizabeth II **Subject:** My Melo **Shape:** Vertical rectangle

Date	Mintage	F12	VF20	XF40	MS60	MS63
2010	Est. 2000	PF65 175				

KM# 397 5 DOLLARS
15.50 g., 0.900 Gold 0.4456 oz. AGW, 27 mm. **Ruler:** Elizabeth II **Subject:** Amber Road - Carnuntum **Rev:** Arches, ancient coin, statue

Date	Mintage	F12	VF20	XF40	MS60	MS63
2010	2,000	PF65 850				

KM# 399 5 DOLLARS
15.50 g., 0.900 Gold 0.4456 oz. AGW, 27 mm. **Ruler:** Elizabeth II **Subject:** Amber Route - Szombathely **Rev:** Cathedral, ancient coin

Date	Mintage	F12	VF20	XF40	MS60	MS63
2010 Matte finish	2,000	PF65 850				

KM# 423 5 DOLLARS
15.50 g., 0.900 Gold 0.4456 oz. AGW, 27 mm. **Ruler:** Elizabeth II **Subject:** Christmas Star **Obv:** Head with tiara right, snowflakes around **Rev:** Three children and christmas tree, crystal insets

Date	Mintage	F12	VF20	XF40	MS60	MS63
2010	2,000	PF65 850				

KM# 430 5 DOLLARS
15.50 g., 0.900 Gold 0.4456 oz. AGW, 27 mm. **Ruler:** Elizabeth II **Obv:** Head with tiara right, wing enlargement as background **Rev:** Butterfly - Lycaena Virgaureae

Date	Mintage	F12	VF20	XF40	MS60	MS63
2010	1,000	PF65 850				

KM# 513 5 DOLLARS
50.00 g., 0.999 Silver 1.5956 oz. ASW, 35.2x35.2 mm. **Ruler:** Elizabeth II **Subject:** The three kings of 1936 **Obv:** Head with tiara right **Rev:** Busts left of George V, Edward VIII and George VI

Date	Mintage	F12	VF20	XF40	MS60	MS63
2011	2,500	PF65 100				

KM# 587 5 DOLLARS
27.00 g., 0.900 Gold 0.7762 oz. AGW, 27 mm. **Ruler:** Elizabeth II **Subject:** Amber Route - Aquileia **Rev:** Rhomulus and Remus suckling at she-wolf, amber insert

Date	Mintage	F12	VF20	XF40	MS60	MS63
2011	Est. 2000	—	—	—	—	1,500

KM# 620 5 DOLLARS
1.00 g., 0.999 Gold 0.0319 oz. AGW, 12x8 mm. **Ruler:** Elizabeth II **Obv:** Head with crown right **Rev:** Baby tiger, diamond chip and paw print **Shape:** Rectangle

Date	Mintage	F12	VF20	XF40	MS60	MS63
2011	Est. 5000	PF65 100				

KM# 623 5 DOLLARS
8.60 g., 0.900 Gold 0.2472 oz. AGW, 22 mm. **Ruler:** Elizabeth II **Obv:** Head with tiara right **Rev:** Dragon rearing upwards, paw to mouth

Date	Mintage	F12	VF20	XF40	MS60	MS63
2011 Proof	Est. 1000	—	—	—	—	475

KM# 651 5 DOLLARS
25.00 g., 0.999 Silver 0.7978 oz. ASW, 40.6 mm. **Ruler:** Elizabeth II **Obv:** Head with tiara right **Rev:** Tasmanian tiger in lenticular 3-D **Edge:** Reeded

Date	Mintage	F12	VF20	XF40	MS60	MS63
2011	3,000	PF65 75.00				

KM# 689 5 DOLLARS
6.00 g., 0.999 Gold 0.1915 oz. AGW, 21 mm. **Ruler:** Elizabeth II **Subject:** Amber Route **Rev:** Map of European cities

Date	Mintage	F12	VF20	XF40	MS60	MS63
2011	999	PF65 400				

KM# 710 5 DOLLARS
6.00 g., 0.9999 Gold 0.1916 oz. AGW, 21 mm. **Ruler:** Elizabeth II **Obv:** Ancient horsecart **Obv. Legend:** SZLAK BURSZTYNOWY **Rev:** Nepture statue, coin, mine building, amber insert **Rev. Legend:** Gdansk

Date	Mintage	F12	VF20	XF40	MS60	MS63
2011	999	PF65 400				

KM# 941 5 DOLLARS
15.00 g., 0.900 Gold 0.4312 oz. AGW, 27 mm. **Ruler:** Elizabeth II **Subject:** Butterflies: Apollo Gold

Date	Mintage	F12	VF20	XF40	MS60	MS63
2011 Proof	Est. 1000	—	—	—	—	—

KM# 678 5 DOLLARS
40.00 g., 0.999 Silver 1.2765 oz. ASW, 29x47 mm. **Ruler:** Elizabeth II **Subject:** Year of the Dragon

Date	Mintage	F12	VF20	XF40	MS60	MS63
2012	—	PF65 100				

KM# 679 5 DOLLARS
40.00 g., 0.999 Silver 1.2765 oz. ASW, 29x47 mm. **Ruler:** Elizabeth II **Subject:** Year of the Dragon

Date	Mintage	F12	VF20	XF40	MS60	MS63
2012	—	PF65 100				

KM# 680 5 DOLLARS
40.00 g., 0.999 Silver 1.2765 oz. ASW, 29x47 mm. **Ruler:** Elizabeth II **Subject:** Year of the Dragon

Date	Mintage	F12	VF20	XF40	MS60	MS63
2012	—	PF65 100				

KM# 681 5 DOLLARS
40.00 g., 0.999 Silver 1.2765 oz. ASW, 29x47 mm. **Ruler:** Elizabeth II **Subject:** Year of the Dragon

Date	Mintage	F12	VF20	XF40	MS60	MS63
2012	—	PF65 100				

KM# 682 5 DOLLARS
40.00 g., 0.999 Silver 1.2765 oz. ASW, 29x47 mm. **Ruler:** Elizabeth II **Subject:** Year of the Dragon

Date	Mintage	F12	VF20	XF40	MS60	MS63
2012	—	PF65 100				

KM# 683 5 DOLLARS
40.00 g., 0.999 Silver 1.2765 oz. ASW, 29x47 mm. **Ruler:** Elizabeth II **Subject:** Year of the Dragon

Date	Mintage	F12	VF20	XF40	MS60	MS63
2012	—	PF65 100				

KM# 684 5 DOLLARS
40.00 g., 0.999 Silver 1.2765 oz. ASW, 29x47 mm. **Ruler:** Elizabeth II **Subject:** Year of the Dragon

Date	Mintage	F12	VF20	XF40	MS60	MS63
2012	—	PF65 100				

KM# 685 5 DOLLARS
40.00 g., 0.999 Silver 1.2765 oz. ASW, 29x47 mm. **Ruler:** Elizabeth II **Subject:** Year of the Dragon

Date	Mintage	F12	VF20	XF40	MS60	MS63
2012	—	PF65 100				

KM# 686 5 DOLLARS
40.00 g., 0.999 Silver 1.2765 oz. ASW, 29x47 mm. **Ruler:** Elizabeth II **Subject:** Year of the Dragon

Date	Mintage	F12	VF20	XF40	MS60	MS63
2012	—	PF65 100				

KM# 698 5 DOLLARS
0.50 g., 0.999 Gold AGW, 11 mm. **Ruler:** Elizabeth II **Rev:** Ned Kelly standing, name vertically at left **Edge:** Reeded

Date	Mintage	F12	VF20	XF40	MS60	MS63
2012	5,000	PF65 75.00				

KM# 716 5 DOLLARS
1.24 g., 0.9999 Gold 0.0396 oz. AGW, 13.92 mm. **Ruler:** Elizabeth II **Rev:** Dragon

Date	Mintage	F12	VF20	XF40	MS60	MS63
2012	5,000	PF65 125				

KM# 738 5 DOLLARS
155.55 g., 0.999 Silver 4.9639 oz. ASW, 65 mm. **Ruler:** Elizabeth II **Subject:** Vietnam War, 50th Anniversary of Australia's involvement **Rev:** Two soldiers with rifles on patrol, helicopter above

Date	Mintage	F12	VF20	XF40	MS60	MS63
2012	400	PF65 250				

KM# 748 5 DOLLARS
100.00 g., 0.999 Silver 3.1912 oz. ASW, 52.5x118 mm. **Ruler:** Elizabeth II **Subject:** DaVinci's Last Supper **Rev:** Bartholomew **Shape:** Vertical rectangle

Date	Mintage	F12	VF20	XF40	MS60	MS63
2012	750	PF65 150				

KM# 749 5 DOLLARS
100.00 g., 0.999 Silver 3.1912 oz. ASW, 52.5x118 mm. **Ruler:** Elizabeth II **Subject:** DaVinci's Last Supper **Rev:** James Minor and Andrew **Shape:** Vertical rectangle

Date	Mintage	F12	VF20	XF40	MS60	MS63
2012	750	PF65 150				

KM# 750 5 DOLLARS
100.00 g., 0.999 Silver 3.1912 oz. ASW, 52.5x118 mm. **Ruler:** Elizabeth II **Subject:** DaVinci's Last Supper **Rev:** Judas Iscariot, Peter and John **Shape:** Vertical rectangle

Date	Mintage	F12	VF20	XF40	MS60	MS63
2012	750	PF65 150				

KM# 751 5 DOLLARS
100.00 g., 0.999 Silver 3.1912 oz. ASW, 52.5x118 mm. **Ruler:** Elizabeth II **Subject:** DaVinci's Last Supper **Rev:** Jesus **Shape:** Vertical rectangle

Date	Mintage	F12	VF20	XF40	MS60	MS63
2012	750	PF65 150				

KM# 752 5 DOLLARS
100.00 g., 0.999 Silver 3.1912 oz. ASW, 52.5x118 mm. **Ruler:** Elizabeth II **Subject:** DaVinci's Last Supper **Rev:** Thomas, James the Greater, Philip **Shape:** Vertical rectangle

Date	Mintage	F12	VF20	XF40	MS60	MS63
2012	750	PF65 150				

KM# 753 5 DOLLARS
100.00 g., 0.999 Silver 3.1912 oz. ASW, 52.5x118 mm. **Ruler:** Elizabeth II **Subject:** DaVinci's Last Supper **Rev:** Matthew **Shape:** Vertical rectangle

Date	Mintage	F12	VF20	XF40	MS60	MS63
2012	750	PF65 150				

KM# 754 5 DOLLARS
100.00 g., 0.999 Silver 3.1912 oz. ASW, 52.5x118 mm. **Ruler:** Elizabeth II **Subject:** DaVinci's Last Supper **Rev:** Jude Thaddeus and Simon the Zealot **Shape:** Vertical rectangle

Date	Mintage	F12	VF20	XF40	MS60	MS63
2012	750	PF65 150				

KM# 774 5 DOLLARS
6.00 g., 0.9999 Gold 0.1916 oz. AGW, 21 mm. **Ruler:** Elizabeth II **Subject:** Stare Hradisko **Obv:** Queen's head at left, two horse cart at right **Rev:** Celtic coin design and art

Date	Mintage	F12	VF20	XF40	MS60	MS63
2012	999	PF65 400				

KM# 776 5 DOLLARS
6.00 g., 0.900 Gold 0.1725 oz. AGW, 16.7x22.3 mm. **Ruler:** Elizabeth II **Subject:** Imperial Faberge Eggs - Coronation egg **Rev:** Egg and state coach

Date	Mintage	F12	VF20	XF40	MS60	MS63
2012	Est. 777	PF65 425				

KM# 780 5 DOLLARS
6.00 g., 0.9999 Gold 0.1916 oz. AGW, 21 mm. **Ruler:** Elizabeth II **Subject:** Silk Route - Wroclaw **Obv:** Queen's head at left, two horse cart at right **Rev:** Old building at left, statue at right

Date	Mintage	F12	VF20	XF40	MS60	MS63
2012	Est. 999	PF65 400				

KM# 801 5 DOLLARS
6.00 g., 0.999 Gold 0.1915 oz. AGW, 21 mm. **Ruler:** Elizabeth II **Subject:** Szlak Bursztynowy - Szombathely **Rev:** Building, old coins and amber insert

Date	Mintage	F12	VF20	XF40	MS60	MS63
2012	—	PF65 400				

KM# 816 5 DOLLARS
62.21 g., 0.999 Silver 1.9852 oz. ASW, 50 mm. **Ruler:** Elizabeth II **Subject:** Napoleon and 1812, first design **Obv:** Crowned head right **Rev:** Conjoined busts left of Kutusow and Napoleon, Moscow in flames at left, French troops at right **Edge:** Reeded

Date	Mintage	F12	VF20	XF40	MS60	MS63
2012 Antique patina	Est. 500	PF65 150				

KM# 817 5 DOLLARS
62.21 g., 0.999 Silver 1.9852 oz. ASW, 50 mm. **Ruler:** Elizabeth II **Subject:** Napoleon, 2nd design **Obv:** Crowned head right **Rev:** Conjoined busts left of Napoleon and Kutuzov, French soldiers retreating, Cossacks attacking.

Date	Mintage	F12	VF20	XF40	MS60	MS63
2012 Antique patina	Est. 500	PF65 150				

KM# 842 5 DOLLARS
6.00 g., 0.9999 Gold 0.1916 oz. AGW, 21 mm. **Ruler:** Elizabeth II **Obv:** Head with tiara at left, cart, map **Rev:** Ruins, statue, coin and amber insert **Rev. Legend:** CARNUNTUM

Date	Mintage	F12	VF20	XF40	MS60	MS63
2012	999	PF65 400				

KM# 844 5 DOLLARS
6.00 g., 0.9999 Gold 0.1916 oz. AGW, 21 mm. **Ruler:** Elizabeth II **Subject:** Amber Route **Obv:** Head with tiara at left, cart, map **Rev:** She-wold statue, mosaic coin, amber insert **Rev. Legend:** AQUILEIA

Date	Mintage	F12	VF20	XF40	MS60	MS63
2012	999	PF65 400				

KM# 856 5 DOLLARS
6.00 g., 0.900 Gold 0.1725 oz. AGW, 16.7x22.3 mm. **Ruler:** Elizabeth II **Obv:** Head with tiara right above open egg **Rev:** Imperial Faberge Eggs - Cockerel **Shape:** Vertical oval

Date	Mintage	F12	VF20	XF40	MS60	MS63
2012	Est. 777	PF65 425				

KM# 897 5 DOLLARS
20.00 g., 0.999 Silver 0.6382 oz. ASW, 40 mm. **Ruler:** Elizabeth II **Subject:** The Queen's Diamond Jubilee

Date	Mintage	F12	VF20	XF40	MS60	MS63
2012	Est. 2500	PF65 95.00				

KM# 948 5 DOLLARS
1.00 g., 0.9999 Gold 0.0319 oz. AGW, 12 x 8 mm. **Ruler:** Elizabeth II **Subject:** Brilliant Baby Bear: Polar Bear

Date	Mintage	F12	VF20	XF40	MS60	MS63
2012	Est. 3000	PF65 185				

KM# 952 5 DOLLARS
6.00 g., 0.900 Gold 0.1725 oz. AGW, 22.3 x 16.7 mm. **Ruler:** Elizabeth II **Subject:** Imperial Faberge Eggs: Swan Egg

Date	Mintage	F12	VF20	XF40	MS60	MS63
2012	Est. 777	PF65 425				

KM# 955 5 DOLLARS
6.00 g., 0.900 Gold 0.1725 oz. AGW, 22.3 x 16.7 mm. **Ruler:** Elizabeth II **Subject:** Imperial Faberge Eggs: Moscow Kremlin Egg

Date	Mintage	F12	VF20	XF40	MS60	MS63
2012	Est. 777	PF65 425				

KM# 997 5 DOLLARS
6.00 g., 0.900 Gold 0.1725 oz. AGW, 22.3 x 16.7 mm. **Ruler:** Elizabeth II **Subject:** Imperial Faberge Eggs: Rosebud Egg

Date	Mintage	F12	VF20	XF40	MS60	MS63
2012	Est. 777	PF65 425				

KM# 999 5 DOLLARS
6.00 g., 0.900 Gold 0.1725 oz. AGW, 22.3 x 16.7 mm. **Ruler:** Elizabeth II **Subject:** Imperial Faberge Eggs: Bouquet of Lilies Egg

Date	Mintage	F12	VF20	XF40	MS60	MS63
2012	Est. 777	PF65 425				

KM# 974 5 DOLLARS
40.00 g., 0.999 Silver 1.2765 oz. ASW, 36 x 48 mm. **Ruler:** Elizabeth II **Subject:** Vincent Van Gogh Sunflowers 125th Anniversary - 1 of 7

Date	Mintage	F12	VF20	XF40	MS60	MS63
2013	Est. 500	PF65 125				

KM# 975 5 DOLLARS
40.00 g., 0.999 Silver 1.2765 oz. ASW, 36 x 48 mm. **Ruler:** Elizabeth II **Subject:** Vincent Van Gogh's Sunflowers 125th Anniversary - 2 of 7

Date	Mintage	F12	VF20	XF40	MS60	MS63
2013	Est. 500	PF65 125				

KM# 976 5 DOLLARS
40.00 g., 0.999 Silver 1.2765 oz. ASW, 36 x 48 mm. **Ruler:** Elizabeth II **Subject:** Vincent Van Gogh's Sunflowers 125th Anniversary - 3 of 7

Date	Mintage	F12	VF20	XF40	MS60	MS63
2013	Est. 500	PF65 125				

KM# 977 5 DOLLARS
40.00 g., 0.999 Silver 1.2765 oz. ASW, 36 x 48 mm. **Ruler:** Elizabeth II **Subject:** Vincent Van Gogh's Sunflowers 125th Anniversary - 4 of 7

Date	Mintage	F12	VF20	XF40	MS60	MS63
2013	Est. 500	PF65 125				

KM# 978 5 DOLLARS
40.00 g., 0.999 Silver 1.2765 oz. ASW, 36 x 48 mm. **Ruler:** Elizabeth II **Subject:** Vincent Van Gogh's Sunflowers 125th Anniversary - 5 or 7

Date	Mintage	F12	VF20	XF40	MS60	MS63
2013	Est. 500	PF65 125				

KM# 979 5 DOLLARS
40.00 g., 0.999 Silver 1.2765 oz. ASW, 36 x 48 mm. **Ruler:** Elizabeth II **Subject:** Vincent Van Gogh's Sunflowers 125th Anniversary - 6 of 7

Date	Mintage	F12	VF20	XF40	MS60	MS63
2013	Est. 500	PF65 125				

KM# 980 5 DOLLARS
40.00 g., 0.999 Silver 1.2765 oz. ASW, 36 x 48 mm. **Ruler:** Elizabeth II **Subject:** Vincent Van Gogh's Sunflowers 125th Annveriasry - 7 of 7

Date	Mintage	F12	VF20	XF40	MS60	MS63
2013	Est. 500	PF65 125				

KM# 1025 5 DOLLARS
1.00 g., 0.999 Gold 0.0319 oz. AGW, 12 x 8 mm. **Ruler:** Elizabeth II **Subject:** Brilliant Baby Bar - Orangutan

Date	Mintage	F12	VF20	XF40	MS60	MS63
2013	Est. 2000	PF65 185				

KM# 1026 5 DOLLARS
1.00 g., 0.999 Gold 0.0319 oz. AGW, 12 x 8 mm. **Ruler:** Elizabeth II **Subject:** Brilliant Baby Bar - Tiger

Date	Mintage	F12	VF20	XF40	MS60	MS63
2013	Est. 2000	PF65 185				

KM# 1073 5 DOLLARS
5.00 g., 0.999 Gold 0.1596 oz. AGW, 20.7 x 12.25 mm. **Ruler:** Elizabeth II **Subject:** Magic Calendar of Happiness - Spring

Date	Mintage	F12	VF20	XF40	MS60	MS63
2013 Proof	Est. 222	—	—	—	—	—

KM# 1114 5 DOLLARS
62.20 g., 0.999 Silver 1.9849 oz. ASW, 34x70 mm. **Ruler:** Elizabeth II **Subject:** Gods of Ancient Greece - Zeus

Date	Mintage	F12	VF20	XF40	MS60	MS63
2013	Est. 2000	PF65 135				

KM# 1163 5 DOLLARS
5.00 g., 0.999 Gold 0.1596 oz. AGW, 20.7 x 12.25 mm. **Ruler:** Elizabeth II **Subject:** Magic Calendar of Happiness - Summer

Date	Mintage	F12	VF20	XF40	MS60	MS63
2013 Proof	Est. 222					

KM# 1189 5 DOLLARS
6.00 g., 0.900 Gold 0.1725 oz. AGW, 22.3 x 16.7 mm. **Ruler:** Elizabeth II **Subject:** Imperial Faberge Eggs: Rosebud Egg

Date	Mintage	F12	VF20	XF40	MS60	MS63
2013	Est. 777	PF65 425				

KM# 1193 5 DOLLARS
3.11 g., 0.900 Gold 0.0894 oz. AGW, 22.5 mm. **Ruler:** Elizabeth II **Subject:** Paavo Nurmi

Date	Mintage	F12	VF20	XF40	MS60	MS63
2013 Proof	Est. 700	—				

KM# 1205 5 DOLLARS
6.00 g., 0.900 Gold 0.1725 oz. AGW, 22.3 x 16.7 mm. **Ruler:** Elizabeth II **Subject:** Imperial Faberge Eggs - Bouquet of Lilies Egg

Date	Mintage	F12	VF20	XF40	MS60	MS63
2013	Est. 777	PF65 425				

KM# 1218 5 DOLLARS
80.00 g., 0.999 Silver 2.5529 oz. ASW, 91.55 x 55 mm. **Ruler:** Elizabeth II **Subject:** Giants of Art - The Creation of Adam (2 of 12)

Date	Mintage	F12	VF20	XF40	MS60	MS63
2013	Est. 750	PF65 275				

KM# 1219 5 DOLLARS
80.00 g., 0.999 Silver 2.5529 oz. ASW, 91.55 x 55 mm. **Ruler:** Elizabeth II **Subject:** Giants of Art - Creation of Adam (3 of 12)

Date	Mintage	F12	VF20	XF40	MS60	MS63
2013	Est. 750	PF65 275				

KM# 1220 5 DOLLARS
80.00 g., 0.999 Silver 2.5529 oz. ASW, 91.55 x 55 mm. **Ruler:** Elizabeth II **Subject:** Giants of Art - The Creation of Adam (4 of 12)

Date	Mintage	F12	VF20	XF40	MS60	MS63
2013	Est. 750	PF65 275				

KM# 1221 5 DOLLARS
80.00 g., 0.999 Silver 2.5529 oz. ASW, 91.55 x 55 mm. **Ruler:** Elizabeth II **Subject:** Giants of Art - Creation of Adam (5 of 12)

Date	Mintage	F12	VF20	XF40	MS60	MS63
2013	Est. 750	PF65 275				

KM# 1222 5 DOLLARS
80.00 g., 0.999 Silver 2.5529 oz. ASW, 91.55 x 55 mm. **Ruler:** Elizabeth II **Subject:** Giants of Art - Creation of Adam (6 of 12)

Date	Mintage	F12	VF20	XF40	MS60	MS63
2013	Est. 750	PF65 275				

KM# 1223 5 DOLLARS
80.00 g., 0.999 Silver 2.5529 oz. ASW, 91.55 x 55 mm. **Ruler:** Elizabeth II **Subject:** Giants of Art - Creation of Adam (7 of 12)

Date	Mintage	F12	VF20	XF40	MS60	MS63
2013	Est. 750	PF65 275				

KM# 1224 5 DOLLARS
80.00 g., 0.999 Silver 2.5529 oz. ASW, 91.55 x 55 mm. **Ruler:** Elizabeth II **Subject:** Giants of Art - The Creation of Adam (8 of 12)

Date	Mintage	F12	VF20	XF40	MS60	MS63
2013	Est. 750	PF65 275				

KM# 1225 5 DOLLARS
80.00 g., 0.999 Silver 2.5529 oz. ASW, 91.55 x 55 mm. **Ruler:** Elizabeth II **Series:** Giants of Art - The Creation of Adam (9 of 12)

Date	Mintage	F12	VF20	XF40	MS60	MS63
2013	Est. 750	PF65 275				

KM# 1226 5 DOLLARS
80.00 g., 0.999 Silver 2.5529 oz. ASW, 91.55 x 55 mm. **Ruler:** Elizabeth II **Subject:** Giants of Art - The Creation of Adam

Date	Mintage	F12	VF20	XF40	MS60	MS63
2013	Est. 750	PF65 275				

KM# 1227 5 DOLLARS
80.00 g., 0.999 Silver 2.5529 oz. ASW, 91.55 55 mm. **Ruler:** Elizabeth II **Subject:** Giants of Art - Creation of Adam (10 of 12)

Date	Mintage	F12	VF20	XF40	MS60	MS63
2013	Est. 750	PF65 275				

KM# 1228 5 DOLLARS
80.00 g., 0.999 Silver 2.5529 oz. ASW, 91.55 x 55 mm. **Ruler:** Elizabeth II **Subject:** Giants of Art - Creation of Adam (12 of 12)

Date	Mintage	F12	VF20	XF40	MS60	MS63
2013	Est. 750	PF65 275				

KM# 1124 8 DOLLARS
155.50 g., 0.999 Silver 4.9623 oz. ASW, 65 mm. **Ruler:** Elizabeth II **Subject:** 5 oz. Silver Horse

Date	Mintage	F12	VF20	XF40	MS60	MS63
2014	Est. 500	PF65 1,250				

KM# 124 10 DOLLARS
28.28 g., 0.925 Silver 0.8356 oz. ASW, 38.6 mm. **Ruler:** Elizabeth II **Subject:** Snoopy as an Ace **Obv:** Crowned head right **Rev:** Snoopy flying his dog house **Edge:** Reeded

Date	Mintage	F12	VF20	XF40	MS60	MS63
2001	10,000	PF65 35.00				

KM# 130 10 DOLLARS
28.28 g., 0.925 Silver 0.8356 oz. ASW, 38.6 mm. **Ruler:** Elizabeth II **Series:** Pokeman **Obv:** Crowned shield within sprigs **Rev:** Bulbasaur **Edge:** Reeded

Date	Mintage	F12	VF20	XF40	MS60	MS63
2001	10,000	PF65 35.00				

KM# 133 10 DOLLARS
28.28 g., 0.925 Silver 0.8356 oz. ASW, 38.6 mm. **Ruler:** Elizabeth II **Series:** Pokeman **Obv:** Crowned shield within sprigs **Rev:** Charmander **Edge:** Reeded

Date	Mintage	F12	VF20	XF40	MS60	MS63
2001	10,000	PF65 35.00				

KM# 136 10 DOLLARS
28.28 g., 0.925 Silver 0.8356 oz. ASW, 38.6 mm. **Ruler:** Elizabeth II **Series:** Pokeman **Obv:** Crowned shield within sprigs **Rev:** Meowth **Edge:** Reeded

Date	Mintage	F12	VF20	XF40	MS60	MS63
2001	10,000	PF65 35.00				

KM# 139 10 DOLLARS
28.28 g., 0.925 Silver 0.8356 oz. ASW, 38.6 mm. **Ruler:** Elizabeth II **Series:** Pokeman **Obv:** Crowned shield within sprigs **Rev:** Pikachu **Edge:** Reeded

Date	Mintage	F12	VF20	XF40	MS60	MS63
2001	10,000	PF65 35.00				

KM# 142 10 DOLLARS
28.28 g., 0.925 Silver 0.8356 oz. ASW, 38.6 mm. **Ruler:** Elizabeth II **Series:** Pokeman **Obv:** Crowned shield within sprigs **Rev:** Squirtle **Edge:** Reeded

Date	Mintage	F12	VF20	XF40	MS60	MS63
2001	10,000	PF65 35.00				

KM# 147 10 DOLLARS
28.28 g., 0.925 Silver 0.8356 oz. ASW, 38.6 mm. **Ruler:** Elizabeth II **Subject:** Pokémon Series **Obv:** Crowned shield within sprigs **Rev:** Pikachu **Edge:** Reeded

Date	Mintage	F12	VF20	XF40	MS60	MS63
2002PM	10,000	PF65 35.00				

KM# 152 10 DOLLARS
28.28 g., 0.925 Silver 0.8356 oz. ASW, 38.6 mm. **Ruler:** Elizabeth II **Subject:** Pokémon Series **Obv:** Crowned shield within sprigs **Rev:** Pichu **Edge:** Reeded

Date	Mintage	F12	VF20	XF40	MS60	MS63
2002PM	10,000	PF65 35.00				

KM# 157 10 DOLLARS
28.28 g., 0.925 Silver 0.8356 oz. ASW, 38.6 mm. **Ruler:** Elizabeth II **Subject:** Pokémon Series **Obv:** Crowned shield within sprigs **Rev:** Mewtwo **Edge:** Reeded

Date	Mintage	F12	VF20	XF40	MS60	MS63
2002PM	10,000	PF65 35.00				

KM# 162 10 DOLLARS
28.28 g., 0.925 Silver 0.8356 oz. ASW, 38.6 mm. **Ruler:** Elizabeth II **Subject:** Pokémon Series **Obv:** Crowned shield within sprigs **Rev:** Entei **Edge:** Reeded

Date	Mintage	F12	VF20	XF40	MS60	MS63
2002PM	10,000	PF65 35.00				

KM# 167 10 DOLLARS
28.28 g., 0.925 Silver 0.8356 oz. ASW, 38.6 mm. **Ruler:** Elizabeth II **Subject:** Pokémon Series **Obv:** Crowned shield within sprigs **Rev:** Celebi **Edge:** Reeded

Date	Mintage	F12	VF20	XF40	MS60	MS63
2002PM	10,000	PF65 35.00				

KM# 274 10 DOLLARS
31.11 g., 0.999 Gold 0.9926 oz. AGW, 38.6 mm. **Ruler:** Elizabeth II **Subject:** Year of the Rooster

Date	Mintage	F12	VF20	XF40	MS60	MS63
2005	—	PF65 2,000				

KM# 254 10 DOLLARS
155.50 g., 0.999 Silver 4.9623 oz. ASW, 65 mm. **Ruler:** Elizabeth II **Subject:** Peanuts 60th Anniversary **Rev:** Peanut character heads around a central Snoopy

Date	Mintage	F12	VF20	XF40	MS60	MS63
2010 Prooflike	1,000	—	—	—	—	225

KM# 375 10 DOLLARS
100.00 g., 0.999 Silver 3.1912 oz. ASW, 64x54.2 mm. **Ruler:** Elizabeth II **Subject:** Kitty and friends **Shape:** Heart

Date	Mintage	F12	VF20	XF40	MS60	MS63
2010	Est. 1000	PF65 150				

KM# 387 10 DOLLARS
155.50 g., 0.999 Silver 4.9623 oz. ASW, 65 mm. **Ruler:** Elizabeth II **Subject:** Miffy with cake

Date	Mintage	F12	VF20	XF40	MS60	MS63
2010	Est. 1500	PF65 200				

KM# 815 10 DOLLARS
155.55 g., 0.999 Silver 4.9639 oz. ASW, 38.61 mm. **Ruler:** Elizabeth II **Obv:** Crowned head right **Rev:** Secret Evening icon, Christ and deciples around table **Edge:** Reeded

Date	Mintage	F12	VF20	XF40	MS60	MS63
2012	500	PF65 375				

KM# 1074 10 DOLLARS
100.00 g., 0.999 Silver 3.1912 oz. ASW, 35x60 mm. **Ruler:** Elizabeth II **Subject:** Year of the Snake

Date	Mintage	F12	VF20	XF40	MS60	MS63
2013	Est. 6000	PF65 150				

KM# 1181 10 DOLLARS
1.24 g., 0.9999 Gold 0.0396 oz. AGW, 8.5 x 15 mm. **Ruler:** Elizabeth II **Subject:** Humpback Whale

Date	Mintage	F12	VF20	XF40	MS60	MS63
2013 Proof	—	—	—	—	—	—

KM# 1183 10 DOLLARS
155.50 g., 0.999 Silver 4.9623 oz. ASW, 55 x 85 mm. **Ruler:** Elizabeth II **Subject:** Humpback Whale

Date	Mintage	F12	VF20	XF40	MS60	MS63
2013 Proof	—	—	—	—	—	—

KM# 1194 10 DOLLARS
10.00 g., 0.900 Gold 0.2875 oz. AGW, 26 mm. **Ruler:** Elizabeth II **Subject:** Paavo Nurmi

Date	Mintage	F12	VF20	XF40	MS60	MS63
2013 Proof	Est. 200	—	—	—	—	—

KM# 296 15 DOLLARS
500.00 g., 0.999 Silver 15.9559 oz. ASW, 100 mm. **Ruler:** Elizabeth II **Subject:** Year of the Dog **Rev:** Multicolor dog

Date	Mintage	F12	VF20	XF40	MS60	MS63
2005	—	PF65 600				

KM# 267 15 DOLLARS
500.00 g., 0.999 Silver 15.9559 oz. ASW, 100 mm. **Ruler:** Elizabeth II **Subject:** Year of the Rooster **Rev:** Multicolor rooster standing right, sunrise

Date	Mintage	F12	VF20	XF40	MS60	MS63
2005	—	PF65 600				

KM# 898 15 DOLLARS
7.70 g., 0.9999 Gold 0.2459 oz. AGW, 22 mm. **Ruler:** Elizabeth II **Subject:** Merentibus Gold

Date	Mintage	F12	VF20	XF40	MS60	MS63
2012	Est. 2000	PF65 500				

KM# 125 20 DOLLARS
1.24 g., 0.9999 Gold 0.0396 oz. AGW, 13.9 mm. **Ruler:** Elizabeth II **Subject:** Snoopy as an Ace **Obv:** Crowned head right **Rev:** Snoopy flying his dog house **Edge:** Reeded

Date	Mintage	F12	VF20	XF40	MS60	MS63
2001	10,000	PF65 85.00				

KM# 148 20 DOLLARS
1.24 g., 0.9999 Gold 0.0396 oz. AGW, 13.92 mm. **Ruler:** Elizabeth II **Subject:** Pokémon Series **Obv:** Crowned shield within sprigs **Rev:** Pikachu **Edge:** Reeded

Date	Mintage	F12	VF20	XF40	MS60	MS63
2002PM	10,000	PF65 85.00				

KM# 153 20 DOLLARS
1.24 g., 0.9999 Gold 0.0396 oz. AGW, 13.9 mm. **Ruler:** Elizabeth II **Subject:** Pokémon Series **Obv:** Crowned shield within sprigs **Rev:** Pichu **Edge:** Reeded

Date	Mintage	F12	VF20	XF40	MS60	MS63
2002PM	10,000	PF65 85.00				

KM# 158 20 DOLLARS
1.24 g., 0.9999 Gold 0.0396 oz. AGW, 13.92 mm. **Ruler:** Elizabeth II **Subject:** Pokémon Series **Obv:** Crowned shield within sprigs **Rev:** Mewtwo **Edge:** Reeded

Date	Mintage	F12	VF20	XF40	MS60	MS63
2002PM	10,000	PF65 85.00				

KM# 163 20 DOLLARS
1.24 g., 0.9999 Gold 0.0396 oz. AGW, 13.9 mm. **Ruler:** Elizabeth II **Subject:** Pokémon Series **Obv:** Crowned shield within sprigs **Rev:** Entei **Edge:** Reeded

Date	Mintage	F12	VF20	XF40	MS60	MS63
2002PM	10,000	PF65 85.00				

KM# 168 20 DOLLARS
1.24 g., 0.9999 Gold 0.0396 oz. AGW, 13.9 mm. **Ruler:** Elizabeth II **Subject:** Pokémon Series **Obv:** Crowned shield within sprigs **Rev:** Celebi **Edge:** Reeded

Date	Mintage	F12	VF20	XF40	MS60	MS63
2002PM	10,000	PF65 85.00				

KM# 379 20 DOLLARS
0.917 Gold AGW, 13.9x16.7 mm. **Ruler:** Elizabeth II **Subject:** Hello Kitty **Shape:** Face **Note:** Center part to KM#380.

Date	Mintage	F12	VF20	XF40	MS60	MS63
2010	Est. 1000	PF65 475				

KM# 1180 20 DOLLARS
3.11 g., 0.9999 Gold 0.0993 oz. AGW, 14 x 23 mm. **Ruler:** Elizabeth II **Subject:** Humpback Whale

Date	Mintage	F12	VF20	XF40	MS60	MS63
2013 Proof						

KM# 255 25 DOLLARS
15.55 g., 0.999 Gold 0.4962 oz. AGW, 22 mm. **Ruler:** Elizabeth II **Subject:** Peanuts 60th Anniversary **Rev:** Snoopy dancing, Charlie Brown's zig-zag shirt pattern in background

Date	Mintage	F12	VF20	XF40	MS60	MS63
2010 Prooflike	1,000	—	—	—	—	950

KM# 388 25 DOLLARS
7.77 g., 0.999 Gold 0.248 oz. AGW, 22 mm. **Ruler:** Elizabeth II **Subject:** Miffy with key

Date	Mintage	F12	VF20	XF40	MS60	MS63
2010	1,000	PF65 475				

KM# 715 25 DOLLARS
7.78 g., 0.9999 Gold 0.2485 oz. AGW, 22 mm. **Ruler:** Elizabeth II **Rev:** Dragon

Date	Mintage	F12	VF20	XF40	MS60	MS63
2012	2,000	PF65 465				

KM# 846 25 DOLLARS
15.50 g., 0.9999 Gold 0.4951 oz. AGW, 27 mm. **Ruler:** Elizabeth II **Obv:** Head with tiara at left, wreath **Rev:** Stanislaus Augustus head right

Date	Mintage	F12	VF20	XF40	MS60	MS63
2012	8,000	PF65 950				

KM# 268 30 DOLLARS
1000.00 g., 0.999 Silver 31.9118 oz. ASW, 120 mm. **Ruler:** Elizabeth II **Subject:** Year of the Rooster **Rev:** Multicolor rooster standing right, sunrise

Date	Mintage	F12	VF20	XF40	MS60	MS63
2005	—	PF65 1,250				

KM# 297 30 DOLLARS
1000.00 g., 0.999 Silver 31.9118 oz. ASW, 120 mm. **Ruler:** Elizabeth II **Subject:** Year of the Dog **Rev:** Multicolor dog

Date	Mintage	F12	VF20	XF40	MS60	MS63
2005	—	PF65 1,250				

KM# 380 30 DOLLARS
0.917 Gold AGW, 30 mm. **Ruler:** Elizabeth II **Subject:** Bears **Note:** Outer ring for KM#379

Date	Mintage	F12	VF20	XF40	MS60	MS63
2010	Est. 1000	PF65 650				

KM# 742 30 DOLLARS
1000.00 g., 0.999 Silver 31.9118 oz. ASW, 100 mm. **Ruler:** Elizabeth II **Subject:** Year of the Dragon **Rev:** Dragon with pearl in color

Date	Mintage	F12	VF20	XF40	MS60	MS63
2012	250	PF65 1,250				

KM# 788 30 DOLLARS
1000.00 g., 0.999 Silver 31.9118 oz. ASW, 100 mm. **Ruler:** Elizabeth II **Subject:** Russian municipalities - Belgorod **Obv:** Head with crown right **Rev:** Statue, shield and building

Date	Mintage	F12	VF20	XF40	MS60	MS63
2012	—	PF65 1,300				

KM# 869 30 DOLLARS
1000.00 g., 0.999 Silver 31.9118 oz. ASW, 100 mm. **Ruler:** Elizabeth II **Obv:** Crowned head right **Rev:** Coral Snake with chinese character above

Date	Mintage	F12	VF20	XF40	MS60	MS63
2013	300	PF65 1,000				

KM# 126 50 DOLLARS
3.11 g., 0.9999 Gold 0.0993 oz. AGW, 17.9 mm. **Ruler:** Elizabeth II **Subject:** Snoopy as an Ace **Obv:** Crowned head right **Rev:** Snoopy flying his dog house **Edge:** Reeded

Date	Mintage	F12	VF20	XF40	MS60	MS63
2001	7,500	PF65 195				

KM# 149 50 DOLLARS
3.11 g., 0.9999 Gold 0.0993 oz. AGW, 17.9 mm. **Ruler:** Elizabeth II **Subject:** Pokémon Series **Obv:** Crowned shield within sprigs **Rev:** Pikachu **Edge:** Reeded

Date	Mintage	F12	VF20	XF40	MS60	MS63
2002PM	7,500	PF65 195				

KM# 154 50 DOLLARS
3.11 g., 0.9999 Gold 0.0993 oz. AGW, 17.9 mm. **Ruler:** Elizabeth II **Subject:** Pokémon Series **Obv:** Crowned shield within sprigs **Rev:** Pichu **Edge:** Reeded

Date	Mintage	F12	VF20	XF40	MS60	MS63
2002PM	7,500	PF65 195				

KM# 159 50 DOLLARS
3.11 g., 0.9999 Gold 0.0993 oz. AGW, 17.9 mm. **Ruler:** Elizabeth II **Subject:** Pokémon Series **Obv:** Crowned shield within sprigs **Rev:** Mewtwo **Edge:** Reeded

Date	Mintage	F12	VF20	XF40	MS60	MS63
2002PM	7,500	PF65 195				

KM# 164 50 DOLLARS
3.11 g., 0.9999 Gold 0.0993 oz. AGW, 17.9 mm. **Ruler:** Elizabeth II **Subject:** Pokémon Series **Obv:** Crowned shield within sprigs **Rev:** Entei **Edge:** Reeded

Date	Mintage	F12	VF20	XF40	MS60	MS63
2002PM	7,500	PF65 195				

KM# 169 50 DOLLARS
3.11 g., 0.9999 Gold 0.0993 oz. AGW, 17.9 mm. **Ruler:** Elizabeth II **Subject:** Pokémon Series **Obv:** Crowned shield within sprigs **Rev:** Celebi **Edge:** Reeded

Date	Mintage	F12	VF20	XF40	MS60	MS63
2002PM	7,500	PF65 195				

KM# 256 50 DOLLARS
15.55 g., 0.999 Gold 0.4962 oz. AGW, 30 mm. **Ruler:** Elizabeth II **Subject:** Peanuts 60th Anniversary **Rev:** Snoopy as a king

Date	Mintage	F12	VF20	XF40	MS60	MS63
2010 Prooflike	1,000	—	—	—	—	1,000

KM# 389 50 DOLLARS
15.55 g., 0.999 Gold 0.4962 oz. AGW, 30 mm. **Ruler:** Elizabeth II **Subject:** Miffy in flowers

Date	Mintage	F12	VF20	XF40	MS60	MS63
2010	Est. 1000	PF65 950				

KM# 584 50 DOLLARS
250.00 g., 0.999 Silver 7.978 oz. ASW, 67.35x90 mm. **Ruler:** Elizabeth II **Subject:** Russian Royal Family **Obv:** Nicholas II and family standing as Saints in the Othodox Church, head with tiara right below **Rev:** Oval portrait images of the Imperial family **Shape:** Vertical Oval

Date	Mintage	F12	VF20	XF40	MS60	MS63
2011	400	PF65 400				

KM# 702 50 DOLLARS
62.20 g., 0.9999 Gold 1.9867 oz. AGW **Ruler:** Elizabeth II **Rev:** John Wycliff and Jan Hus

Date	Mintage	F12	VF20	XF40	MS60	MS63
2011	Est. 1000	PF65 3,700				

KM# 714 50 DOLLARS
31.11 g., 0.9999 Gold 0.9935 oz. AGW, 32 mm. **Ruler:** Elizabeth II **Rev:** Dragon

Date	Mintage	F12	VF20	XF40	MS60	MS63
2012	2,000	PF65 1,850				

KM# 777 50 DOLLARS
31.10 g., 0.9999 Gold 0.9934 oz. AGW, 29.2x39 mm. **Ruler:** Elizabeth II **Subject:** Imperial Faberge Eggs - Corconation Egg **Rev:** Egg and state coach

Date	Mintage	F12	VF20	XF40	MS60	MS63
2012	Est. 333	PF65 2,000				

KM# 778 50 DOLLARS
250.00 g., 0.999 Silver 7.978 oz. ASW, 67.35x90 mm. **Ruler:** Elizabeth II **Subject:** Imperial Faberge Eggs - Coronation Egg **Rev:** Egg and state coach

Date	Mintage	F12	VF20	XF40	MS60	MS63
2012	Est. 333	PF65 350				

KM# 791 50 DOLLARS
250.00 g., 0.999 Silver 7.978 oz. ASW, 67.35x90 mm. **Ruler:** Elizabeth II **Subject:** Great Ukrainian Hetmans **Obv:** Seven shields around central head of Queen Elizabeth **Rev:** Seven busts around central shield **Shape:** Vertical oval

Date	Mintage	F12	VF20	XF40	MS60	MS63
2012	400	PF65 400				

KM# 793 50 DOLLARS
250.00 g., 0.925 Silver 7.387 oz. ASW, 67.35x90 mm. **Ruler:** Elizabeth II **Subject:** Royal Hunting **Obv:** Saint on horseback **Rev:** Horseman with falcon **Shape:** Vertical oval

Date	Mintage	F12	VF20	XF40	MS60	MS63
2012	Est. 400	PF65 400				

KM# 827 50 DOLLARS
31.11 g., 0.9999 Gold 0.9935 oz. AGW, 32 mm. **Ruler:** Elizabeth II **Obv:** Head in tiara at left, branches **Rev:** Head right of Stanislaus Augustus

Date	Mintage	F12	VF20	XF40	MS60	MS63
2012	Est. 16000	PF65 1,775				

KM# 880 50 DOLLARS

250.00 g., 0.999 Silver 7.978 oz. ASW, 90x67.35 mm. **Ruler:** Elizabeth II **Subject:** Russian Royal Charity **Obv:** Head with tiara at top center, four building façades around **Rev:** Oval portraits at left and right, church at center **Shape:** Horizontal oval

Date	Mintage	F12	VF20	XF40	MS60	MS63
2012	Est. 400	PF65 350				

KM# 972 50 DOLLARS

15.51 g., 0.9999 Gold 0.4954 oz. AGW, 18 x 30 mm. **Ruler:** Elizabeth II **Subject:** The Last Supper

Date	Mintage	F12	VF20	XF40	MS60	MS63
2012	Est. 500	PF65 1,000				

KM# 1079 50 DOLLARS

250.00 g., 0.999 Silver 7.978 oz. ASW, 67.35x90 mm. **Ruler:** Elizabeth II **Subject:** Russian Royal Road

Date	Mintage	F12	VF20	XF40	MS60	MS63
2013	Est. 400	PF65 375				

KM# 1179 50 DOLLARS

7.77 g., 0.999 Gold 0.248 oz. AGW, 14 x 23 mm. **Ruler:** Elizabeth II **Subject:** Humpback Whale

Date	Mintage	F12	VF20	XF40	MS60	MS63
2013 Proof	—	—	—	—	—	—

KM# 1076 50 DOLLARS

186.60 g., 0.999 Silver 5.9547 oz. ASW, 32 x 22.1 mm. **Ruler:** Elizabeth II **Subject:** Fortuna Redux

Date	Mintage	F12	VF20	XF40	MS60	MS63
2014	Est. 2500	PF65 550				

KM# 127 100 DOLLARS

6.22 g., 0.9999 Gold 0.1987 oz. AGW, 22 mm. **Ruler:** Elizabeth II **Subject:** Snoopy as an Ace **Obv:** Crowned head right **Rev:** Snoopy flying his dog house **Edge:** Reeded

Date	Mintage	F12	VF20	XF40	MS60	MS63
2001	5,000	PF65 400				

KM# 150 100 DOLLARS

6.22 g., 0.9999 Gold 0.1987 oz. AGW, 22 mm. **Ruler:** Elizabeth II **Subject:** Pokémon Series **Obv:** Crowned shield within sprigs **Rev:** Pikachu **Edge:** Reeded

Date	Mintage	F12	VF20	XF40	MS60	MS63
2002PM	5,000	PF65 400				

KM# 155 100 DOLLARS

6.22 g., 0.9999 Gold 0.1987 oz. AGW, 22 mm. **Ruler:** Elizabeth II **Subject:** Pokémon Series **Obv:** Crowned shield within sprigs **Rev:** Pichu **Edge:** Reeded

Date	Mintage	F12	VF20	XF40	MS60	MS63
2002PM	5,000	PF65 400				

KM# 160 100 DOLLARS

6.22 g., 0.9999 Gold 0.1987 oz. AGW, 22 mm. **Ruler:** Elizabeth II **Subject:** Pokémon Series **Obv:** Crowned shield within sprigs **Rev:** Mewtwo **Edge:** Reeded

Date	Mintage	F12	VF20	XF40	MS60	MS63
2002PM	5,000	PF65 400				

KM# 165 100 DOLLARS

6.22 g., 0.9999 Gold 0.1987 oz. AGW, 22 mm. **Ruler:** Elizabeth II **Subject:** Pokémon Series **Obv:** Crowned shield within sprigs **Rev:** Entei **Edge:** Reeded

Date	Mintage	F12	VF20	XF40	MS60	MS63
2002PM	5,000	PF65 400				

KM# 170 100 DOLLARS

6.22 g., 0.9999 Gold 0.1987 oz. AGW, 22 mm. **Ruler:** Elizabeth II **Subject:** Pokémon Series **Obv:** Crowned shield within sprigs **Rev:** Celebi **Edge:** reeded

Date	Mintage	F12	VF20	XF40	MS60	MS63
2002PM	5,000	PF65 400				

KM# 425 100 DOLLARS

93.30 g., 0.900 Gold 2.6823 oz. AGW, 41.6x55.6 mm. **Ruler:** Elizabeth II **Subject:** Imperial Faberge Egg - Coronation Egg **Obv:** Head with tiara right above opened egg **Rev:** Coronation egg and coach **Shape:** Vertical oval

Date	Mintage	F12	VF20	XF40	MS60	MS63
2010	222	PF65 5,000				

KM# 511 100 DOLLARS

31.10 g., 0.999 Gold 0.9926 oz. AGW, 38.61 mm. **Ruler:** Elizabeth II **Obv:** Head with tiara right **Rev:** Tasmanian tiger in color

Date	Mintage	F12	VF20	XF40	MS60	MS63
2011	200	PF65 2,000				

KM# 572 100 DOLLARS

93.30 g., 0.900 Gold 2.6823 oz. AGW, 41.6x55.6 mm. **Ruler:** Elizabeth II **Subject:** Imperial Faberge Egg **Obv:** Head with tiara right, open egg below **Rev:** Clover leaf floral egg on stand **Shape:** Vertical oval

Date	Mintage	F12	VF20	XF40	MS60	MS63
2011	222	PF65 5,000				

KM# 648 100 DOLLARS

93.30 g., 0.900 Gold 2.6823 oz. AGW, 41.6x55.6 mm. **Ruler:** Elizabeth II **Subject:** Imperial Easter Egg - Lilly **Obv:** Head with tiara right, open egg below **Rev:** Egg on stand, lillys around

Date	Mintage	F12	VF20	XF40	MS60	MS63
2011	—	PF65 5,000				

KM# 650 100 DOLLARS

50.00 g., 0.999 Silver 1.5956 oz. ASW, 35.2 x 35.2 mm. **Ruler:** Elizabeth II **Obv:** Head with tiara right **Rev:** Three Kings of 1936 - George V, Edward VIII, George VI selectively gilt **Edge:** Reeded **Shape:** Square

Date	Mintage	F12	VF20	XF40	MS60	MS63
2011	1,500	PF65 160				

KM# 701 100 DOLLARS

139.50 g., 0.9999 Gold 4.4557 oz. AGW, 50 mm. **Ruler:** Elizabeth II **Subject:** General Perina, Battle of Britain pilot **Rev:** Perina as pilot

Date	Mintage	F12	VF20	XF40	MS60	MS63
2011	400	PF65 8,500				

KM# 747 100 DOLLARS

400.00 g., 0.9997 Silver 12.7737 oz. ASW, 90 mm. **Ruler:** Elizabeth II **Subject:** Szlak Bursztynowy **Obv:** Queen's head at left, Roman horse cart at right **Rev:** Map of central Europe, amber insert

Date	Mintage	F12	VF20	XF40	MS60	MS63
2011	245	PF65 1,250				

KM# 737 100 DOLLARS
31.11 g., 0.999 Gold 0.9926 oz. AGW, 38.61 mm. **Ruler:** Elizabeth II   **Rev:** Tasmanian Wedge-Tailed Eagle **Edge:** Reeded and numbered

Date	Mintage	F12	VF20	XF40	MS60	MS63
2012	150	PF65 2,000				

KM# 755 100 DOLLARS
93.30 g., 0.900 Gold 2.6823 oz. AGW, 41.6x55.6 mm. **Ruler:** Elizabeth II   **Subject:** Imperial Faberge Eggs - Duchess of Marlborough **Rev:** Serpent at bottom stem of egg **Shape:** Vertical oval

Date	Mintage	F12	VF20	XF40	MS60	MS63
2012	222	PF65 5,000				

KM# 834 100 DOLLARS
93.30 g., 0.900 Gold 2.6823 oz. AGW, 41.6x55.6 mm. **Ruler:** Elizabeth II   **Obv:** Head with tiara above opened egg **Rev:** Imperial Faberge Eggs - Pansy Egg **Shape:** Vertical oval

Date	Mintage	F12	VF20	XF40	MS60	MS63
2012	222	PF65 4,850				

KM# 835 100 DOLLARS
93.30 g., 0.900 Gold 2.6823 oz. AGW, 41.6x55.6 mm. **Ruler:** Elizabeth II   **Obv:** Head in tiara right above opened egg **Rev:** Imperial Faberge Egg - Bay Tree **Shape:** Vertical oval

Date	Mintage	F12	VF20	XF40	MS60	MS63
2012	222	PF65 4,850				

KM# 950 100 DOLLARS
62.20 g., 0.999 Gold 1.9849 oz. AGW, 40 mm. **Ruler:** Elizabeth II   **Subject:** Amber Room

Date	Mintage	F12	VF20	XF40	MS60	MS63
2012	—	PF65 4,500				

KM# 928 100 DOLLARS
31.10 g., 0.9999 Gold 0.9934 oz. AGW, 38.61 mm. **Ruler:** Elizabeth II   **Subject:** Tasmanian Devil

Date	Mintage	F12	VF20	XF40	MS60	MS63
2013	Est. 150	PF65 1,550				

KM# 1126 100 DOLLARS
400.00 g., 0.999 Silver 12.7647 oz. ASW, 90 mm. **Ruler:** Elizabeth II   **Subject:** Magic Year of Happiness

Date	Mintage	F12	VF20	XF40	MS60	MS63
2013	Est. 222	PF65 1,150				

KM# 1156 100 DOLLARS
93.30 g., 0.999 Gold 2.9774 oz. AGW, 41.6 x 55.6 mm. **Ruler:** Elizabeth II   **Subject:** Continents - Europe

Date	Mintage	F12	VF20	XF40	MS60	MS63
2013	Est. 100	PF65 5,000				

KM# 1178 100 DOLLARS
15.55 g., 0.9999 Gold 0.4967 oz. AGW, 25 x 40 mm. **Ruler:** Elizabeth II   **Subject:** Humpback Whale

Date	Mintage	F12	VF20	XF40	MS60	MS63
2013 Proof	—	—	—	—	—	—

KM# 1182 100 DOLLARS
1000.00 g., 0.999 Silver 31.9118 oz. ASW, 90 x 135 mm. **Ruler:** Elizabeth II   **Subject:** Humpback Whale

Date	Mintage	F12	VF20	XF40	MS60	MS63
2013 Proof	—	—	—	—	—	—

KM# 1200 100 DOLLARS
400.00 g., 0.999 Silver 12.7647 oz. ASW, 90 mm. **Ruler:** Elizabeth II   **Subject:** Magic Year of Happiness

Date	Mintage	F12	VF20	XF40	MS60	MS63
2013 Proof	—	—	—	—	—	—

KM# 1201 100 DOLLARS
62.20 g., 0.999 Gold 1.9849 oz. AGW, 40 mm. **Ruler:** Elizabeth II   **Subject:** Holy Grail

Date	Mintage	F12	VF20	XF40	MS60	MS63
2013	Est. 150	PF65 3,750				

KM# 1238 100 DOLLARS
139.50 g., 0.9999 Gold 4.4557 oz. AGW, 50 mm. **Ruler:** Elizabeth II **Subject:** 40 Ducat of Bolivia

Date	Mintage	F12	VF20	XF40	MS60	MS63
2013	Est. 100	PF65 8,500				

KM# 1255 100 DOLLARS
31.11 g., 0.999 Gold 0.9926 oz. AGW, 38.61 mm. **Ruler:** Elizabeth II **Subject:** Tasmanian Devil **Obv:** Head in tiara right

Date	Mintage	F12	VF20	XF40	MS60	MS63
2013	150	PF65 3,750				

KM# 1256 100 DOLLARS
400.00 g., 0.999 Silver 12.7647 oz. ASW, 90 mm. **Ruler:** Elizabeth II **Obv:** Head with tiara right within rays **Rev:** Moon gilt within rays and 12 crystals

Date	Mintage	F12	VF20	XF40	MS60	MS63
2013	—	PF65 800				

KM# 1246 100 DOLLARS
31.10 g., 0.9999 Gold 0.9934 oz. AGW, 38.61 mm. **Ruler:** Elizabeth II **Subject:** Frilled Neck Lizard

Date	Mintage	F12	VF20	XF40	MS60	MS63
2014	Est. 150	PF65 3,750				

KM# 512 200 DOLLARS
62.20 g., 0.999 Gold 1.9849 oz. AGW, 35.2x35.2 mm. **Ruler:** Elizabeth II **Subject:** Three kings of 1935 **Obv:** Head with tiara right **Rev:** Head left of George V, Edward VIII and George VI

Date	Mintage	F12	VF20	XF40	MS60	MS63
2011	75	PF65 5,000				

KM# 713 200 DOLLARS
155.55 g., 0.9999 Gold 4.9684 oz. AGW **Ruler:** Elizabeth II **Rev:** Dragon

Date	Mintage	F12	VF20	XF40	MS60	MS63
2012	100	PF65 9,500				

KM# 740 200 DOLLARS
1000.00 g., 0.999 Silver 31.9118 oz. ASW, 118.2x52.7 mm. **Ruler:** Elizabeth II **Obv:** Head with crown at left **Rev:** Two dragons flanking center ball **Shape:** Horizontal rectangle

Date	Mintage	F12	VF20	XF40	MS60	MS63
2012	1,800	PF65 1,250				

KM# 1174 200 DOLLARS
31.10 g., 0.999 Gold 0.9925 oz. AGW, 40 mm. **Ruler:** Elizabeth II **Subject:** Coronation of HM Queen Elizabeth II

Date	Mintage	F12	VF20	XF40	MS60	MS63
2013 Proof	Est. 200	—	—	—	—	—

KM# 1177 200 DOLLARS
31.10 g., 0.999 Gold 0.9925 oz. AGW, 28 x 51 mm. **Ruler:** Elizabeth II **Subject:** Humpback Whale

Date	Mintage	F12	VF20	XF40	MS60	MS63
2013 Proof	—	—	—	—	—	—

KM# 1244 200 DOLLARS
31.10 g., 0.9999 Gold 0.9934 oz. AGW, 32.7 mm. **Ruler:** Elizabeth II **Subject:** Doctor Who 50th Anniversary

Date	Mintage	F12	VF20	XF40	MS60	MS63
2013	Est. 500	PF65 2,450				

KM# 700 250 DOLLARS
348.50 g., 0.9999 Gold 11.1313 oz. AGW, 65 mm. **Ruler:** Elizabeth II   **Rev:** Jan Amos Komensky seated at desk with globe

Date	Mintage	F12	VF20	XF40	MS60	MS63
2011	Est. 250	PF65 20,000				

KM# 1239 250 DOLLARS
348.60 g., 0.9999 Gold 11.1345 oz. AGW, 65 mm. **Ruler:** Elizabeth II **Subject:** 100 Ducat of Spytihnev

Date	Mintage	F12	VF20	XF40	MS60	MS63
2013 Proof	Est. 50	—	—	—	—	—

KM# 1139 300 DOLLARS
5000.00 g., 0.999 Silver 159.5592 oz. ASW, 180 mm. **Ruler:** Elizabeth II **Subject:** Chairman Mao

Date	Mintage	F12	VF20	XF40	MS60	MS63
2013 Proof	Est. 500	—	—	—	—	—

KM# 973 500 DOLLARS
750.00 g., 0.999 Silver 23.9339 oz. ASW, 100 mm. **Ruler:** Elizabeth II **Subject:** The Last Supper

Date	Mintage	F12	VF20	XF40	MS60	MS63
2012	Est. 199	PF65 2,200				

KM# 1176 500 DOLLARS
155.50 g., 0.9999 Gold 4.9668 oz. AGW, 55 x 85 mm. **Ruler:** Elizabeth II **Subject:** Humpback Whale

Date	Mintage	F12	VF20	XF40	MS60	MS63
2013 Proof	—	—	—	—	—	—

KM# 1175 1000 DOLLARS
1000.00 g., 0.9999 Gold 31.9406 oz. AGW, 90 x 135 mm. **Ruler:** Elizabeth II **Subject:** Humpback Whale

Date	Mintage	F12	VF20	XF40	MS60	MS63
2013 Proof	—	—	—	—	—	—

KM# 405 3000 DOLLARS
500.00 g., 0.9999 Gold 15.9703 oz. AGW, 67.35x90 mm. **Ruler:** Elizabeth II **Subject:** Russian Royal Family **Obv:** Seven figures as Orthodox Saints, Elizabeth head with tiara below **Rev:** Oval portaits of Nicholas II and his family **Shape:** Vertical Oval

Date	Mintage	F12	VF20	XF40	MS60	MS63
2010	23	PF65 29,500				

KM# 588 3000 DOLLARS
500.00 g., 0.9999 Gold 15.9703 oz. AGW, 67.35x90 mm. **Ruler:** Elizabeth II **Subject:** Royal Hunting **Obv:** Russian saint on horseback, head with tiara right below, multicolor **Rev:** Russian figure on horseback with falcon, multicolor

Date	Mintage	F12	VF20	XF40	MS60	MS63
2011	40	PF65 29,500				

KM# 881 3000 DOLLARS
500.00 g., 0.9999 Gold 15.9703 oz. AGW, 90x67.35 mm. **Ruler:** Elizabeth II **Subject:** Russian Royal Charity **Obv:** Head with tiara at top center, four building façades around **Rev:** Vertical oval portraits flanking church **Shape:** Horizontal oval

Date	Mintage	F12	VF20	XF40	MS60	MS63
2012	Est. 30	PF65 29,500				

KM# 1080 3000 DOLLARS
500.00 g., 0.9999 Gold 15.9703 oz. AGW, 90 x 67.35 mm. **Ruler:** Elizabeth II **Subject:** RUssian Royal Road

Date	Mintage	F12	VF20	XF40	MS60	MS63
2013	Est. 35	PF65 29,000				

KM# 699 10000 DOLLARS
1000.00 g., 0.9999 Gold 31.9406 oz. AGW, 85 mm. **Ruler:** Elizabeth II **Rev:** Good Queen Ann seated on throne

Date	Mintage	F12	VF20	XF40	MS60	MS63
2011	Est. 150	PF65 58,500				

KM# 708 10000 DOLLARS
1000.00 g., 0.9999 Gold 31.9406 oz. AGW, 90 mm. **Ruler:** Elizabeth II **Obv:** Ancient horsecart **Obv. Legend:** SZLAK BURSZTYNOWY **Rev:** European map with cities, amber insert

Date	Mintage	F12	VF20	XF40	MS60	MS63
2011	Est. 12	PF65 60,000				

MINT SETS

KM#	Date	Mintage	Identification	Issue Price	Mkt Val
MS1	2009 (5)	20,000	KM#193-197	—	30.00
MS2	2010 (5)	10,000	KM#193-196, 198	—	30.00

NORWAY

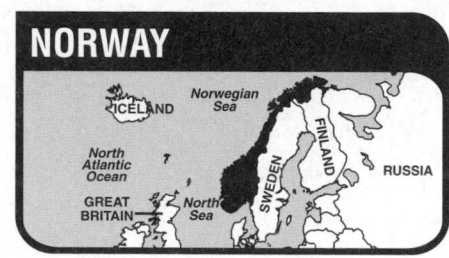

The Kingdom of Norway (*Norge, Noreg*), a constitutional monarchy located in northwestern Europe, has an area of 150,000sq. mi. (324,220 sq. km.), including the island territories of Spitzbergen (Svalbard) and Jan Mayen, and a population of *4.2 million. Capital: Oslo (Christiania). The diversified economic base of Norway includes shipping, fishing, forestry, agriculture, and manufacturing. Nonferrous metals, paper and paperboard, paper pulp, iron, steel and oil are exported.

RULER
Harald V, 1991-

MINT MARK
(h) - Crossed hammers – Kongsberg

MONETARY SYSTEM
100 Ore = 1 Krone

KINGDOM
DECIMAL COINAGE

KM# 460 50 ØRE
3.60 g., Bronze, 18.5 mm. **Ruler:** Harald V **Obv:** Crown **Rev:** Stylized animal and value **Edge:** Plain

Date	Mintage	VG8	F12	VF20	XF40	MS63
2001 without star	16,848,250	—	—	—	—	0.50
2001 with star	13,291,750	—	—	—	1.00	3.00
2001	11,500	PF63 10.00				
2002	28,293,100	—	—	—	—	0.40
2002	11,500	PF63 10.00				
2003	15,522,000	—	—	—	—	0.40
2003	10,800	PF63 10.00				
2004	14,747,500	—	—	—	—	0.40
2004	8,550	PF63 10.00				
2005	4,954,500	—	—	—	—	0.40
2005	8,550	PF63 10.00				
2006	30,218,500	—	—	—	—	0.40
2006	8,500	PF63 10.00				
2007	20,110,500	—	—	—	—	0.40
2007	6,582	PF63 10.00				
2008	19,384,000	—	—	—	—	0.40
2008	7,091	PF63 10.00				
2009	9,897,000	—	—	—	—	0.40
2009	6,310	PF63 10.00				

Date	Mintage	VG8	F12	VF20	XF40	MS63
2010	14,988,000	—	—	—	—	0.40
2010	5,119	PF63 10.00				
2011 11 in date reversed	8,300,000	—	—	—	—	0.40
2011 11 in date corrected	1,666,000	—	—	—	—	0.40
2011	4,142	PF63 10.00				

KM# 462 KRONE
4.35 g., Copper-Nickel, 21 mm. **Ruler:** Harald V **Obv:** Crowned monograms form cross within circle with center hole **Rev:** Bird on vine above center hole date and value below

Date	Mintage	VG8	F12	VF20	XF40	MS63
2001 without star	43,128,650	—	—	—	—	0.65
2001 with star	7,355,350	—	—	—	2.00	4.00
2001	11,500	PF63 10.00				
2002	21,313,000	—	—	—	—	0.65
2002	11,500	PF63 10.00				
2003	24,082,000	—	—	—	—	0.65
2003	10,800	PF63 10.00				
2004	25,142,500	—	—	—	—	0.65
2004	8,550	PF63 10.00				
2005	25,639,500	—	—	—	—	0.65
2005	8,550	PF63 10.00				
2006	63,120,500	—	—	—	—	0.65
2006	8,500	PF63 10.00				
2007	47,101,500	—	—	—	—	0.65
2007	6,582	PF63 10.00				
2008	46,040,000	—	—	—	—	0.65
2008	7,091	PF63 10.00				
2009	50,049,000	—	—	—	—	0.65
2009	6,310	PF63 10.00				
2010	40,021,000	—	—	—	—	0.65
2010	5,119	PF63 10.00				
2011	35,042,000	—	—	—	—	0.50
2011	4,142	PF63 10.00				
2012	19,635,000	—	—	—	—	0.50
2012	3,437	PF63 20.00				

KM# 463 5 KRONER
7.85 g., Copper-Nickel, 26 mm. **Ruler:** Harald V **Subject:** Order of St. Olaf **Obv:** Hole at center of order chain **Rev:** Center hole divides sprigs, value above and date below **Edge:** Reeded

Date	Mintage	VG8	F12	VF20	XF40	MS63
2001	480,000	—	—	—	—	2.50
2001	11,500	PF63 13.00				
2002	3,622,000	—	—	—	—	1.50
2002	11,500	PF63 13.00				
2003	816,000	—	—	—	—	1.50
2003	10,800	PF63 13.00				
2004	494,500	—	—	—	—	1.50
2004	8,550	PF63 14.00				
2005	494,500	—	—	—	—	2.00
2005	8,550	PF63 14.00				
2006	500,500	—	—	—	—	1.50
2006	8,500	PF63 14.00				
2007	9,145,000	—	—	—	—	1.50
2007	6,582	PF63 14.00				
2008	5,495,000	—	—	—	—	1.50
2008	7,091	PF63 14.00				
2009	10,014,000	—	—	—	—	1.50
2009	6,310	PF63 14.00				
2012	1,006,000	—	—	—	—	1.50
2012	3,437	PF63 40.00				

KM# 457 10 KRONER
6.80 g., Nickel-Brass, 24 mm. **Ruler:** Harald V **Obv:** Head right **Rev:** Stylized church rooftop, value and date **Edge:** Segmented reeding

Date	Mintage	VG8	F12	VF20	XF40	MS63
2001 without star	9,854,000	—	—	—	—	3.50
2001 with star	10,000	—	—	—	—	50.00
2001	11,500	PF63 10.00				
2002	1,123,000	—	—	—	—	3.50
2002	11,500	PF63 10.00				
2003	946,000	—	—	—	—	3.50
2003	10,800	PF63 10.00				
2004	494,500	—	—	—	—	4.50
2004	8,550	PF63 10.00				
2005	457,500	—	—	—	—	4.50
2005	8,550	PF63 10.00				
2006	488,500	—	—	—	—	3.50
2006	8,500	PF63 10.00				
2007	467,500	—	—	—	—	3.50
2007	6,582	PF63 10.00				
2008	565,508	—	—	—	—	3.50
2009	469,000	—	—	—	—	3.50
2009	6,310	PF63 10.00				
2012	1,006,000	—	—	—	—	3.00
2012	3,437	PF63 50.00				

KM# 482 10 KRONER
6.80 g., Nickel-Brass, 24 mm. **Ruler:** Harald V **Subject:** Henrik Vergeland **Obv:** Head right **Rev:** Spectacles and vertical signature

Date	Mintage	F12	VF20	XF40	MS60	MS63
2008	4,620,638	—	—	—	3.50	10.00
2008	7,091	PF63 10.00				

KM# 483 10 KRONER
6.80 g., Nickel-Brass, 24 mm. **Ruler:** Harald V **Subject:** Ole Bull 100th Anniversary of Birth **Obv:** Head right **Rev:** Bust and music score **Edge:** Segmented reeding

Date	Mintage	F12	VF20	XF40	MS60	MS63
2010	974,000	—	—	—	3.50	10.00
2010	5,119	PF63 10.00				

KM# 484 10 KRONER
6.80 g., Nickel-Brass, 24 mm. **Ruler:** Harald V **Subject:** Norway's first University, 200th Anniversary **Obv:** Head right **Rev:** Column

Date	Mintage	F12	VF20	XF40	MS60	MS63
2011	2,996,000	—	—	—	3.50	10.00
2011	4,142	PF63 10.00				

KM# 488 10 KRONER
Nickel-Brass **Ruler:** Harald V **Subject:** 100 Years of Women's Suffrage

Date	Mintage	F12	VF20	XF40	MS60	MS63
2013	—	—	—	—	—	3.00

KM# 453 20 KRONER
9.90 g., Nickel-Brass, 27.5 mm. **Ruler:** Harald V **Obv:** Head right **Rev:** Value above 1/2 ancient boat

Date	Mintage	VG8	F12	VF20	XF40	MS63
2001	4,194,000	—	—	—	—	5.00
2001 with star	10,000	—	—	—	—	200
2001	11,500	PF63 25.00				
2002	18,218,000	—	—	—	—	5.00
2003	30,050,000	—	—	—	—	5.00
2003	11,100	PF63 25.00				
2005	544,500	—	—	—	—	5.00
2005	8,550	PF63 25.00				
2007	486,500	—	—	—	—	5.00
2007	6,582	PF63 25.00				
2008	474,000	—	—	—	—	5.00
2008	7,091	PF63 25.00				
2009	467,000	—	—	—	—	5.00
2009	6,310	PF63 25.00				

KM# 471 20 KRONER
9.90 g., Nickel-Brass, 27.5 mm. **Ruler:** Harald V **Subject:** Niels Henrik Abel **Obv:** Head right **Rev:** Pair of glasses, dates and value within mathematical graphs **Edge:** Plain

Date	Mintage	F12	VF20	XF40	MS60	MS63
2002	2,230,000	—	—	—	5.50	12.00
2002	11,500	PF63 25.00				

KM# 478 20 KRONER
9.90 g., Nickel-Brass, 27.5 mm. **Ruler:** Harald V **Subject:** First Norwegian Railroad **Obv:** Head right **Rev:** Railroad track switch and value **Edge:** Plain

Date	Mintage	F12	VF20	XF40	MS60	MS63
2004	490,500	—	—	—	5.50	20.00
2004	8,550	PF63 25.00				

KM# 479 20 KRONER
9.90 g., Nickel-Brass, 27.5 mm. **Ruler:** Harald V **Obv:** Head right **Rev:** Henrik Ibsen caricature walking left, signature **Edge:** Plain

Date	Mintage	F12	VF20	XF40	MS60	MS63
2006	991,500	—	—	—	5.50	12.00
2006	8,500	PF63 10.00				

KM# 469 100 KRONER
33.60 g., 0.925 Silver 0.9928 oz. ASW, 39 mm. **Ruler:** Harald V **Subject:** Nobel Peace Prize Centennial **Obv:** Rampant crowned lion left holding axe **Rev:** Head left **Edge:** Plain

Date	Mintage	F12	VF20	XF40	MS60	MS63
2001	50,000	PF63 200	PF65 225			

KM# 472 100 KRONER
33.80 g., 0.925 Silver 0.9987 oz. ASW, 39 mm. **Ruler:** Harald V **Subject:** 1905 Independence from Sweden **Obv:** Three kings **Rev:** Farm field **Edge:** Plain

Date	Mintage	F12	VF20	XF40	MS60	MS63
2003	65,000	PF63 70.00	PF65 80.00			

KM# 474 100 KRONER
33.80 g., 0.925 Silver 0.9987 oz. ASW, 39 mm. **Ruler:** Harald V **Subject:** 1905 Liberation **Obv:** Three kings **Rev:** Off shore ocean oil well **Edge:** Plain

Date	Mintage	F12	VF20	XF40	MS60	MS63
2004	65,000	PF63 70.00	PF65 80.00			

KM# 476 100 KRONER
33.80 g., 0.925 Silver 0.9987 oz. ASW, 39 mm. **Ruler:** Harald V **Obv:** Three kings **Rev:** Circuit board **Edge:** Plain

Date	Mintage	F12	VF20	XF40	MS60	MS63
2005	72,000	PF63 70.00	PF65 80.00			

KM# 480 200 KRONER
16.85 g., 0.925 Silver 0.4979 oz. ASW, 32 mm. **Ruler:** Harald V **Subject:** Henrik Wergeland, 200th Birth Anniversary **Obv:** Head right **Rev:** Spectacles and signature

Date	Mintage	F12	VF20	XF40	MS60	MS63
2008	40,000	PF63 100	PF65 115			

KM# 481 200 KRONER
16.85 g., 0.925 Silver 0.4979 oz. ASW, 32 mm. **Ruler:** Harald V **Subject:** Knut Hamsun 150th Birth Anniversary **Obv:** Crowned shield **Rev:** Streppled portrait, novel text and signature

Date	Mintage	F12	VF20	XF40	MS60	MS63
2009	40,000	PF63 100	PF65 115			

KM# 485 200 KRONER
16.85 g., 0.925 Silver 0.4979 oz. ASW, 32 mm. **Ruler:** Harald V **Subject:** World Ski Championships, 2011 **Obv:** Head right **Rev:** Different types of skiers

Date	Mintage	F12	VF20	XF40	MS60	MS63
2011	40,000	PF63 100	PF65 115			

KM# 486 200 KRONER
16.85 g., 0.925 Silver 0.4979 oz. ASW, 32 mm. **Ruler:** Harald V **Obv:** Head right **Rev:** Various Athletics, Javelin, track, skating, snowboarding, table tennis.

Date	Mintage	F12	VF20	XF40	MS60	MS63
2011	40,000	PF63 100	PF65 115			

KM# 487 200 KRONER
16.85 g., 0.925 Silver 0.4979 oz. ASW, 32 mm. **Ruler:** Harald V **Subject:** Harold V and Queen Sonia, 75th Birthday **Obv:** Crowned shield **Obv. Legend:** KONGERIKET NORGE **Rev:** Heads 1/4 right of Harold and Sonia **Rev. Legend:** KONG HARALD V DRONNING SONJA 75 AR

Date	Mintage	F12	VF20	XF40	MS60	MS63
2012	40,000	PF63 110	PF65 125			

KM# 470 1500 KRONER
16.96 g., 0.917 Gold 0.4968 oz. AGW, 27 mm. **Ruler:** Harald V **Subject:** Nobel Peace Prize Centennial **Obv:** Head right **Rev:** Reverse design of the prize medal **Edge:** Plain

Date	Mintage	VG8	F12	VF20	XF40	MS63
ND-2001 Matte Proof	7,500	PF65 1,100				

KM# 473 1500 KRONER
16.96 g., 0.917 Gold 0.4968 oz. AGW, 27 mm. **Ruler:** Harald V **Subject:** 1905 Liberation **Obv:** Three kings **Rev:** Various leaf types **Edge:** Plain

Date	Mintage	F12	VF20	XF40	MS60	MS63
2003	10,000	PF65 950				

KM# 475 1500 KRONER
16.96 g., 0.917 Gold 0.4968 oz. AGW, 27 mm. **Ruler:** Harald V **Subject:** 1905 Liberation **Obv:** Three kings **Rev:** Liquid drops on hard surface **Edge:** Plain

Date	Mintage	F12	VF20	XF40	MS60	MS63
2004	10,000	PF65 950				

KM# 477 1500 KRONER
16.96 g., 0.917 Gold 0.4968 oz. AGW, 27 mm. **Ruler:** Harald V **Obv:** Three kings **Rev:** Binary language **Edge:** Plain

Date	Mintage	F12	VF20	XF40	MS60	MS63
2005	10,000	PF65 950				

MINT SETS

KM#	Date	Mintage	Identification	Issue Price	Mkt Val
MS66	2001 (5)	17,000	KM#453, 457, 460, 462, 463. (Uncirculated set, souvenir version, Norwegian text)	20.00	30.00
MS67	2001 (5)	—	KM#453, 457, 460, 462, 463 (Uncirculated Set, Souvenir Version, English text). Mintage included with MS66.	—	30.00
MS68	2001 (5)	30,000	KM#453, 457, 460, 462, 463. Children's (Baby) Set.	18.00	30.00
MS69	2001 (5)	2,000	KM#453, 457, 460, 462, 463 plus medal.	27.00	27.00
MS70	2001 (5)	—	KM#453, 457, 460, 462, 463. Uncirculated set, classic version (hard plastic case)	—	30.00

KM#	Date	Mintage	Identification	Issue Price	Mkt Val
MS71	2002 (5)	55,000	KM#453, 457, 460, 462, 463, Uncirculated set, classic version (hard plastic case)	—	32.00
MS72	2002 (5)	9,893	KM#453, 457, 460, 462, 463 (Uncirculated Set, Souvenir Version, Norwegian text)	—	30.00
MS73	2002 (5)	—	KM#453, 457, 460, 462, 463 (Uncirculated Set, Souvenir Version, English text). Mintage included with MS72.	—	30.00
MS74	2002 (5)	—	KM#453, 457, 460, 462, 463 plus Silver medal Children's (Baby) Set	—	50.00
MS75	2003 (5)	55,000	KM#453, 457, 460, 462, 463, Uncirculated set, classic version (hard plastic case)	—	32.00
MS76	2003 (5)	20,000	KM#453, 457, 460, 462, 463 (Uncirculated Set, Souvenir Version)	—	30.00
MS77	2003 (5)	2,000	KM#453, 457, 460, 462, 463 plus Silver medal Children's (Baby) Set	—	50.00
MS78	2004 (5)	35,000	KM#457, 460, 462, 463, 478, (Uncirculated set, classic version (hard plastic case)	—	28.00
MS79	2004 (5)	6,000	KM#457, 460, 462, 463, 478 (Uncirculated Set, Souvenir Version)	—	30.00
MS80	2004 (5)	2,000	KM#457, 460, 462, 463, 478 plus Silver medal Children's (Baby) Set	—	50.00
MS81	2005 (5)	32,000	KM#453, 457, 460, 462, 463, Uncirculated set, classic version (hard plastic case)	—	25.00
MS82	2005 (5)	6,500	KM#453, 457, 460, 462, 463 (Uncirculated Set, Souvenir Version)	—	35.00
MS83	2005 (5)	—	KM#453, 457, 460, 462, 463 plus Child in Basket Silver medal (Children's (Baby) Set)	—	60.00
MS84	2005 (5)	2,005	KM#453, 457 (proof), 460, 462, 463 plus gilded Silver copy of medal issued for 1905 referendum, all coins minted on June 7, 2005 (Referendum Set)	—	450
MS85	2006 (5)	27,800	KM#457, 460, 462, 463, 479 Uncirculated Set, Classic Version (hard plastic case)	—	28.00
MS86	2006 (5)	5,450	KM#457, 460, 462, 463, 479 Uncirculated Set, Souvenir Version	—	30.00
MS87	2006 (5)	800	KM#457, 460, 462, 463, 479 plus Child in Basket 0.5 oz. 0.999 Silver Medal Children's (Baby) Set	—	65.00
MS88	2006 (5)	2,006	KM#457, 460, 462, 463, 479 plus Gold-plated Silver copy of 1906 King Haakon VII Coronation medal, all coins minted on June 22, 2006 (Coronation Set)	—	375
MS89	2007 (5)	10,000	KM#453, 457, 460, 462, 463 (Brilliant Uncirculated Set)	—	58.00
MS90	2007 (5)	26,135	KM#453, 457, 460, 462, 463 Uncirculated Set, Classic Version (hard plastic case)	—	30.00
MS91	2007 (5)	5,050	KM#453, 457, 460, 462, 463 (Uncirculated Set, Souvenir Version)	—	30.00
MS92	2007 (5)	835	KM#453, 457, 460, 462, 463 plus Child in Basket 0.5 oz. .999 Silver Medal Children's (Baby) Set	—	65.00
MS93	2007 (5)	2,007	KM#453, 457, 460, 462, 463 plus 0.999 Gold-plated 0.925 Silver medal, 32 mm., all coins minted on February 21, 2007 (King Harald V 70th Birthday Set)	—	700
MS94	2008 (5)	2,924	KM#453, 460, 462, 463, 482 (Brilliant Uncirculated Set)	—	58.00
MS95	2008 (5)	26,185	KM#453, 457, 460, 462, 463 Uncirculated Set, Classic Version (hard plastic case)	—	40.00
MS96	2008 (5)	5,000	KM#453, 457, 460, 462, 463 (Uncirculatd Set, Souvenir Version)	—	30.00
MS97	2008 (5)	600	KM#453, 457, 460, 462, 463 plus Child in Basket Silver medal Children's (Baby) Set	—	70.00
MS98	2009 (5)	2,271	KM#453, 457, 460, 462, 463 (Brilliant Uncirculated Set)	—	60.00
MS99	2009 (5)	23,400	KM#453, 457, 460, 462, 463 Uncirculated Set, Classic Version (hard plastic case)	—	30.00
MS100	2009 (5)	4,251	KM#453, 457, 460, 462, 463 (Uncirculated Set, Souvenir Version)	—	30.00
MS101	2009 (5)	675	KM#453, 457, 460, 462, 463 plus Child in Basket Silver medal Children's (Baby) Set	—	65.00
MS102	2010 (3)	1,673	KM#460, 462, 483 (Brilliant Uncirculated Set)	—	60.00
MS103	2010 (3)	21,926	KM#460, 462, 483 Uncirculated Set, Classic Version (hard plastic case)	—	35.00
MS104	2010 (3)	3,823	KM#460, 462, 483 (Uncirculated Set, Souvenir Version)	—	35.00
MS105	2010 (3)	460	KM#460, 462, 483 plus Child in Basket Silver medal (Children's (Baby) Set)	—	65.00
MS106	2011 (3)	1,073	KM#460, 462, 484 (Brilliant Uncirculated Set)	—	58.00
MS107	2011 (3)	18,436	KM#460, 462, 484 plus 325th Anniversary of the Norwegian Mint bimetallic medal (Uncirculated Set, Classic Version (hard plastic case)	—	38.00
MS108	2011 (3)	2,454	KM#460, 462, 484 (Uncirculated Set, Souvenir Version)	—	38.00
MS109	2011 (3)	466	KM#460, 462, 484 plus Child in Basket Silver medal (Children's (Baby) Set)	—	75.00
MS110	2012 (3)	966	KM#457, 462, 463 (Brilliant Uncirculated Set)	—	65.00
MS111	2012 (3)	17,407	KM#457, 462, 463 plus 200th Anniversary of the birth of Peter Christian Asbjørnsen medal (Uncirculated Set, classic Version (hard plastic case)	—	35.00
MS112	2012 (3)	2,208	KM#457, 462, 463 (Uncirculated Set, Souvenir Version)	—	35.00
MS113	2012 (3)	274	KM#457, 462, 463 plus Child in Basket Silver medal (Children's (Baby) Set)	—	75.00

PROOF SETS

KM#	Date	Mintage	Identification	Issue Price	Mkt Val
PS16	2001 (5)	10,000	KM#453, 457, 460, 462, 463 (Classic Proof Set)	—	100
PS17	2001 (5)	1,500	KM#453, 457, 460, 462 463 plus medal (Exclusive Proof Set)	—	300
PS18	2002 (5)	10,000	KM#457, 460, 462, 463, 471 (Classic Proof Set)	—	125
PS19	2002 (5)	1,500	KM#457, 460, 462, 463, 471 plus medal (Exclusive Proof Set)	—	450
PS20	2003 (5)	10,000	KM#453, 457, 460, 462, 463 (Classic Proof Set)	—	100
PS21	2003 (5)	800	KM#453, 457, 460, 462, 463 plus 0.5833 Gold 100th Anniversary of the Birth of King Olav V medal (Exclusive Proof Set)	—	500
PS22	2004 (5)	7,800	KM#457, 460, 462, 463, 478 (Classic Proof Set)	—	100
PS23	2004 (5)	750	KM#457, 460, 462, 463 plus Princess Ingrid Alexandra Gold medal (Exclusive Proof Set)	—	500
PS24	2005 (5)	7,800	KM#453, 457, 460, 462, 463 (Classic Proof Set)	—	100
PS25	2005 (5)	750	KM#453, 457, 460, 462, 463 plus 0.5833 Gold 7th June-9th June-13th August 1905 medal (Exclusive Proof Set)	—	500
PS26	2003-2005 (6)	5,000	KM#472-477	—	3,300
PS27	2006 (5)	8,000	KM#457, 460, 462, 463, 479 (Classic Proof Set)	—	100
PS28	2006 (5)	500	KM#457, 460, 462, 463, 479 plus 3.295 g., 0.999 Platinum, 14.0 mm. medal (Exclusive Proof Set)	—	700
PS29	2007 (5)	6,182	KM#453, 457, 460, 462, 463 (Classic Proof Set)	—	100
PS30	2007 (5)	400	KM#453, 457, 460, 462, 463 plus proof 3.00 g., 0.585 Gold-0.265 Silver-0.150 Palladium, 14.0 mm. medal (Exclusive Proof Set)	—	700
PS31	2008 (5)	6,591	KM#453, 460, 462, 463, 482 (Classic Proof Set)	—	100
PS32	2008 (5)	500	KM#453, 460, 462, 463, 482 plus 3.00 g., 0.585 Gold-0.265 Silver-0.150 Palladium, 14.0 mm. Henrik Wergeland medal (Exclusive Proof Set)	—	700
PS33	2009 (5)	5,910	KM#453, 457, 460, 462, 463 (Classic Proof Set)	—	100
PS34	2009 (6)	400	KM#453, 457, 460, 462, 463, 481 plus 7.70 g., 0.585 Gold, 22.0 mm. 150th Anniversary of Birth of Knut Hamsun medal (Exclusive Proof Set)	—	750
PS35	2010 (3)	4,619	KM#460, 462, 483 plus medal (Classic Proof Set)	—	130
PS36	2010 (3)	500	KM#460, 462, 483 plus 7.70 g., 0.585 Gold, 22.0 mm. Liberation of Norway in 1945 medal (Exclusive Proof Set)	—	750
PS37	2011 (3)	3,642	KM#460, 462, 484 plus 325th Anniversary of the Norwegian Mint gilded medal (Classic Proof Set)	—	130
PS38	2011 (3)	500	KM#460, 462, 484 plus 7.70g., 0.585 Gold, 22.0mm. 100th Anniversary of Roald Amundsen's reaching the South Pole medal (Exclusive Proof Set)	—	850
PS39	2012 (3)	2,937	KM#457, 462, 463 (Classic Proof Set)	—	130
PS40	2012 (3)	500	KM#457, 462, 463 plus 7.70g. 0.585 Gold, 22.0 mm, 200th Anniversary of Birth of P. Chr. Aspjørnsen medal (Exclusive Proof Set)	—	800

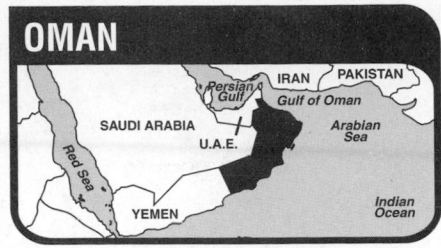

OMAN

The Sultanate of Oman (formerly Muscat and Oman), an independent monarchy located in the southeastern part of the Arabian Peninsula, has an area of 82,030 sq. mi. (212,460 sq. km.) and a population of *1.3 million. Capital: Muscat. The economy is based on agriculture, herding and petroleum. Petroleum products, dates, fish and hides are exported.

RULER:
Qaboos ibn al-Sa'id, AH1390-/1970AD-

SULTANATE

REFORM COINAGE
1972; 1000 Baisa = 1 Omani Rial

KM# 150 5 BAISA
2.65 g., Bronze Clad Steel, 19 mm. **Ruler:** Qabus bin Sa'id **Obv:** National arms **Rev:** Value and dates

Date	Mintage	F12	VF20	XF40	MS60	MS63
AH1429-2008	—			0.20	0.50	0.75

KM# 151 10 BAISA
4.04 g., Bronze Clad Steel, 22.5 mm. **Ruler:** Qabus bin Sa'id **Obv:** National arms **Rev:** Value with both dates

Date	Mintage	F12	VF20	XF40	MS60	MS63
AH1429-2008	—			0.30	0.75	1.00

KM# 152 25 BAISA
3.03 g., Copper-Nickel, 18 mm. **Ruler:** Qabus bin Sa'id **Obv:** National arms **Rev:** Value and both dates **Edge:** Reeded

Date	Mintage	F12	VF20	XF40	MS60	MS63
AH1428-2008	—		0.15	0.35	0.90	1.25
AH1429-2009	—		0.15	0.35	0.90	1.25

KM# 152a 25 BAISA
2.63 g., Nickel Clad Steel, 17.95 mm. **Ruler:** Qabus bin Sa'id **Obv:** National arms **Rev:** Value with both dates **Edge:** Reeded

Date	Mintage	F12	VF20	XF40	MS60	MS63
AH1427-2007	—			0.35	0.90	1.25
AH1428-2008	—			0.35	0.90	1.25
AH1429-2009	—			0.35	0.90	1.25
AH1430-2010	—			0.35	0.90	1.25

KM# 153 50 BAISA
6.40 g., Copper-Nickel, 24 mm. **Ruler:** Qabus bin Sa'id **Obv:** National arms **Rev:** Value with both dates **Edge:** Reeded

Date	Mintage	F12	VF20	XF40	MS60	MS63
AH1429-2008	—		0.25	0.60	1.50	2.00

KM# 153a 50 BAISA
5.57 g., Nickel Clad Steel, 24 mm. **Ruler:** Qabus bin Sa'id **Obv:** National arms **Rev:** Value with both dates **Edge:** Reeded

Date	Mintage	F12	VF20	XF40	MS60	MS63
AH1427-2007	—			0.60	1.50	2.00
AH1428-2008	—			0.60	1.50	2.00
AH1429-2009	—			0.60	1.50	2.00
AH1430-2010	—			0.60	1.50	2.00

KM# 154 OMANI RIAL
28.28 g., 0.925 Silver 0.8356 oz. ASW, 38.6 mm. **Ruler:** Qabus bin Sa'id **Subject:** 31st National Day and Environment Year **Obv:** National arms **Rev:** Multicolor map design

Date	Mintage	F12	VF20	XF40	MS60	MS63
2001	500	—			110	—
2001	105	PF63 150		PF65 170		

KM# 154a OMANI RIAL
37.80 g., 0.916 Gold 1.106 oz. AGW, 38.6 mm. **Ruler:** Qabus bin Sa'id **Subject:** 31st National Day and Environment Year **Obv:** National arms **Rev:** Multicolor map design **Edge:** Reeded

Date	Mintage	F12	VF20	XF40	MS60	MS63
2001	105	PF63 2,200		PF65 2,300		
2001	350	—			2,000	2,100

KM# 156 OMANI RIAL
28.28 g., 0.925 Silver 0.8356 oz. ASW, 38.7 mm. **Ruler:** Qabus bin Sa'id **Series:** Environment Collection **Obv:** National arms **Rev:** Hoopoe bird standing right multicolor

Date	Mintage	F12	VF20	XF40	MS60	MS63
2002	1,000	PF63 90.00		PF65 100		

KM# 157 OMANI RIAL
28.28 g., 0.925 Silver 0.8356 oz. ASW, 38.7 mm. **Ruler:** Qabus bin Sa'id **Series:** Environment Collection **Obv:** National arms **Rev:** Dolphin right multicolor

Date	Mintage	F12	VF20	XF40	MS60	MS63
2002	1,000	PF63 90.00		PF65 100		

KM# 158 OMANI RIAL
28.28 g., 0.925 Silver 0.8356 oz. ASW, 38.7 mm. **Ruler:** Qabus bin Sa'id **Series:** Environment Collection **Obv:** National arms **Rev:** Turtle left multicolor

Date	Mintage	F12	VF20	XF40	MS60	MS63
2002	1,000	PF63 90.00		PF65 100		

KM# 159 OMANI RIAL
28.28 g., 0.925 Silver 0.8356 oz. ASW, 38.7 mm. **Ruler:** Qabus bin Sa'id **Series:** Environment Collection **Obv:** National arms **Rev:** Flower multicolor

Date	Mintage	F12	VF20	XF40	MS60	MS63
2002	1,000	PF63 90.00		PF65 100		

KM# 160 OMANI RIAL
28.28 g., 0.925 Silver 0.8356 oz. ASW, 38.7 mm. **Ruler:** Qabus bin Sa'id **Series:** Environment Collection **Obv:** National arms **Rev:** Ibex standing left multicolor

Date	Mintage	F12	VF20	XF40	MS60	MS63
2002	1,000	PF63 90.00		PF65 100		

KM# 161 OMANI RIAL
28.28 g., 0.925 Silver 0.8356 oz. ASW, 38.7 mm. **Ruler:** Qabus bin Sa'id **Series:** Environment Collection **Obv:** National arms **Rev:** Butterfly multicolor

Date	Mintage	F12	VF20	XF40	MS60	MS63
2002	1,000	PF63 90.00		PF65 100		

KM# 155 OMANI RIAL
28.28 g., 0.925 Silver 0.8356 oz. ASW, 38.6 mm. **Ruler:** Qabus bin Sa'id **Subject:** The Sindibad Voyage, 1980/1981 **Obv:** National arms **Rev:** Sailing ship below map within circle **Edge:** Reeded

Date	Mintage	F12	VF20	XF40	MS60	MS63
2003	—	PF63 80.00	PF65 90.00			

KM# 162 OMANI RIAL
28.28 g., 0.925 Silver 0.8356 oz. ASW, 38.7 mm. **Ruler:** Qabus bin Sa'id **Subject:** Population Census - December, 2003

Date	Mintage	F12	VF20	XF40	MS60	MS63
2003 Rare	—	—	—	—	—	—

KM# 163 OMANI RIAL
28.28 g., 0.925 Silver 0.8356 oz. ASW, 38.7 mm. **Ruler:** Qabus bin Sa'id **Subject:** 35th National Day **Obv:** Oman Map

Date	Mintage	F12	VF20	XF40	MS60	MS63
AH1427-2005	—	—	—	—	100	120

KM# 164 OMANI RIAL
28.28 g., 0.925 Silver 0.8356 oz. ASW, 38.7 mm. **Ruler:** Qabus bin Sa'id **Subject:** 40th Anniversary of First Oil Export from Oman

Date	Mintage	F12	VF20	XF40	MS60	MS63
2007	—	—	—	—	90.00	100

KM# 165 OMANI RIAL
28.28 g., 0.925 Silver 0.8356 oz. ASW, 38.7 mm. **Ruler:** Qabus bin Sa'id **Subject:** 29th GCC Summit held in Muscat in December 2008

Date	Mintage	F12	VF20	XF40	MS60	MS63
2008	—	—	—	—	100	120

KM# 166 OMANI RIAL
28.28 g., 0.925 Silver 0.8356 oz. ASW, 38.7 mm. **Ruler:** Qabus bin Sa'id **Subject:** 19th Arabian Gulf Cup

Date	Mintage	F12	VF20	XF40	MS60	MS63
2008	—	—	—	—	320	

KM# 168 OMANI RIAL
28.28 g., 0.999 Silver 0.9025 oz. ASW **Ruler:** Qabus bin Sa'id **Subject:** Royal Opera House **Rev:** Building exterior

Date	Mintage	F12	VF20	XF40	MS60	MS63
2011	—	PF63 75.00	PF65 85.00			

KM# 169 OMANI RIAL
28.28 g., 0.999 Silver 0.9025 oz. ASW **Ruler:** Qabus bin Sa'id **Subject:** Royal Opera House **Rev:** Violin, Tamboreen in color

Date	Mintage	F12	VF20	XF40	MS60	MS63
2011	—	PF63 75.00	PF65 85.00			

KM# 170 OMANI RIAL
28.28 g., 0.999 Silver 0.9025 oz. ASW **Ruler:** Qabus bin Sa'id **Subject:** Royal Opera House **Rev:** Horns, flute and sax in color

Date	Mintage	F12	VF20	XF40	MS60	MS63
2011	—	PF63 75.00	PF65 85.00			

KM# 171 OMANI RIAL
Silver **Ruler:** Qabus bin Sa'id **Subject:** Royal Opera House **Rev:** Tamboreen, horns and strings in color

Date	Mintage	F12	VF20	XF40	MS60	MS63
2011	—	PF63 75.00	PF65 85.00			

KM# 173 OMANI RIAL
28.28 g., 0.925 Silver 0.8356 oz. ASW, 38.7 mm. **Ruler:** Qabus bin Sa'id **Subject:** National Day, 43th Anniversary **Obv:** Arms **Rev:** Umayyad Dirham

Date	Mintage	F12	VF20	XF40	MS60	MS63
2013	—	PF63 75.00	PF65 85.00			

PAKISTAN

The Islamic Republic of Pakistan, located on the Indian sub-continent between India and Afghanistan, has an area of 310,404 sq. mi. (803,940 sq. km.) and a population of 130 million. Capital: Islamabad. Pakistan is mainly an agricultural land although the industrial base is expanding rapidly. Yarn, textiles, cotton, rice, medical instruments, sports equipment and leather are exported.

TITLE

پاکستان

Pakistan

ISLAMIC REPUBLIC

DECIMAL COINAGE
100 Paisa = 1 Rupee

KM# 62 RUPEE
4.00 g., Bronze, 20 mm. **Obv:** Head of Jinnah facing left **Rev:** Mosque above value **Edge:** Reeded

Date	Mintage	F12	VF20	XF40	MS60	MS63
2001	146,996,000	0.20	0.25	0.35	0.65	0.75
2002	192,252,000	0.20	0.25	0.35	0.65	0.75
2003	217,996,000	0.20	0.25	0.35	0.65	0.75
2004	162,210,000	0.20	0.25	0.35	0.65	0.75
2005	202,330,000	0.20	0.25	0.35	0.65	0.75
2006	113,135,000	0.20	0.25	0.35	0.65	0.75

KM# 67 RUPEE
1.75 g., Aluminum, 20 mm. **Obv:** Head left **Rev:** Mosque

Date	Mintage	F12	VF20	XF40	MS60	MS63
2007	201,670,000	—	—	—	—	2.00
2008	97,953,000	—	—	—	—	2.00
2009	80,280,000	—	—	—	—	2.00
2010	100,000,000	—	—	—	—	2.00
2011	—	—	—	—	—	2.00
2012	—	—	—	—	—	2.00
2013	—	—	—	—	—	2.00

KM# 64 2 RUPEES
5.00 g., Nickel-Brass, 22.5 mm. **Obv:** Crescent, star and date above sprigs **Rev:** Value below mosque and clouds **Edge:** Reeded

Date	Mintage	F12	VF20	XF40	MS60	MS63
2001	85,444,000	0.20	0.30	0.45	0.85	1.00
2002	148,940,000	0.20	0.30	0.45	0.85	1.00
2003	125,220,000	0.20	0.30	0.45	0.85	1.00
2004	105,148,000	0.20	0.30	0.45	0.85	1.00
2005	98,912,000	0.20	0.30	0.45	0.85	1.00
2006	34,432,000	0.20	0.30	0.45	0.85	1.00

KM# 68 2 RUPEES
Aluminum **Obv:** Star and crescent, wheat ears below **Rev:** Mosque

Date	Mintage	F12	VF20	XF40	MS60	MS63
2007	100,848,000	—	—	—	—	2.00
2008	—	—	—	—	—	2.00
2009	100,000,000	—	—	—	—	2.00
2010	5,337,000	—	—	—	—	2.00

Date	Mintage	F12	VF20	XF40	MS60	MS63
2011	—	—	—	—	—	2.00
2012	—	—	—	—	—	2.00
2013	—	—	—	—	—	2.00

KM# 65 5 RUPEES
6.50 g., Copper-Nickel, 24 mm. **Obv:** Cresent, star and date above sprays **Rev:** Value within star design and sprigs **Edge:** Reeded

Date	Mintage	F12	VF20	XF40	MS60	MS63
2001	—	0.50	1.00	1.50	3.00	3.25
2002	35,668,000	0.50	1.00	1.50	3.00	3.25
2003	138,566,000	0.50	1.00	1.50	3.00	3.25
2004	224,228,000	0.50	1.00	1.50	3.00	3.25
2005	148,248,000	0.50	1.00	1.50	3.00	3.25
2006	177,222,000	0.50	1.00	1.50	3.00	3.25

KM# 66 10 RUPEES
7.50 g., Copper-Nickel, 27.5 mm. **Obv:** Cresent, star and date above sprays **Rev. Inscription:** Year of Fatima Jinnah **Edge:** Reeded

Date	Mintage	F12	VF20	XF40	MS60	MS63
2003	200,000	—	—	4.00	6.50	7.50

KM# 69 10 RUPEES
8.25 g., Copper-Nickel, 27.5 mm. **Subject:** Benazir Bhutto **Obv:** Star and crescent, wheat wreath below **Rev:** Bust facing, Urdu script legend above

Date	Mintage	F12	VF20	XF40	MS60	MS63
2007	—	—	—	—	7.50	10.00
2008	300,000	—	—	—	7.50	10.00

KM# 70 10 RUPEES
8.25 g., Copper-Nickel, 27.5 mm. **Subject:** Pakistan - China Friendship, 60 years of Peoples' Republic of China **Obv:** Crescent and star **Rev:** Pakistan and Chinese flags, clasped hands below

Date	Mintage	F12	VF20	XF40	MS60	MS63
2009	100,000	—	—	—	4.50	6.50

KM# 71 20 RUPEES
Copper-Nickel **Subject:** Pakistan-China Friendship, 60th anniversary

Date	Mintage	F12	VF20	XF40	MS60	MS63
2011	—	—	—	—	8.00	15.00

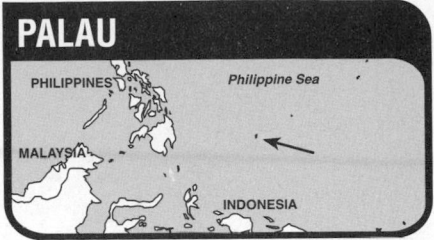

PALAU

The Republic of Palau, a group of about 100 islands and islets, is generally considered a part of the Caroline Islands. It is located about 1,000 miles southeast of Manila and about the same distance southwest of Saipan and has an area of 179 sq. mi. and a population of 12,116. Capital: Koror.

REPUBLIC

MILLED COINAGE

KM# 461 50 DOLLARS
62.20 g., 0.999 Silver 1.9849 oz. ASW, 65 mm. **Subject:** Mask of Tut in gilding

Date	Mintage	F12	VF20	XF40	MS60	MS63
2012	300	PF65 65.00				

KM# 52 DOLLAR
26.86 g., Copper-Nickel, 37.3 mm. **Subject:** Marine Life Protection **Obv:** Mermaid figurehead and value **Rev:** Multicolor jellyfish **Edge:** Reeded

Date	Mintage	F12	VF20	XF40	MS60	MS63
2001	—	PF65 30.00				

KM# 60 DOLLAR
26.80 g., Copper-Nickel, 37.2 mm. **Subject:** Marine Life Protection **Obv:** Seated Mermaid with raised arm above value **Rev:** Two glittering fish **Edge:** Reeded

Date	Mintage	F12	VF20	XF40	MS60	MS63
2001	—	PF65 30.00				

KM# 61 DOLLAR
26.80 g., Copper-Nickel, 37.2 mm. **Subject:** Marine Life

Protection **Obv:** Prone Mermaid above value **Rev:** Two glittering fish **Edge:** Reeded

Date	Mintage	F12	VF20	XF40	MS60	MS63
2001	—	PF65 32.50				

KM# 62 DOLLAR
26.80 g., Copper-Nickel, 37.2 mm. **Subject:** Marine Life Protection **Obv:** Figurehead mermaid and value **Rev:** Moorish-Idol fish **Edge:** Reeded

Date	Mintage	F12	VF20	XF40	MS60	MS63
2001	—	PF65 30.00				

KM# 86 DOLLAR
1.24 g., 0.9999 Gold 0.0397 oz. AGW, 13.94 mm. **Subject:** Marine Life Protection **Obv:** Prone Mermaid **Rev:** Two fish

Date	Mintage	F12	VF20	XF40	MS60	MS63
2001	—	PF65 75.00				

KM# 87 DOLLAR
1.24 g., 0.9999 Gold 0.0397 oz. AGW, 13.94 mm. **Subject:** Marine Life Protection **Obv:** Seated Mermaid with raised arm above value **Rev:** Two glittering fish

Date	Mintage	F12	VF20	XF40	MS60	MS63
2001	—	PF65 65.00				

KM# 88 DOLLAR
1.24 g., 0.9999 Gold 0.0397 oz. AGW, 13.94 mm. **Subject:** Marine Life Protection **Obv:** Figurehead Mermaid and value **Rev:** Moorish Idol fish

Date	Mintage	F12	VF20	XF40	MS60	MS63
2001	—	PF65 75.00				

KM# 89 DOLLAR
1.24 g., 0.9999 Gold 0.0397 oz. AGW, 13.94 mm. **Subject:** Marine Life Protection **Obv:** Figurehead Mermaid and value **Rev:** Moorish Idol fish

Date	Mintage	F12	VF20	XF40	MS60	MS63
2001	—	PF65 75.00				

KM# 253 DOLLAR
1.25 g., 0.999 Gold 0.0399 oz. AGW, 13.9 mm. **Obv:** Mermaid body-surfing wave **Rev:** Blue angelfish

Date	Mintage	F12	VF20	XF40	MS60	MS63
2001	—	PF63 70.00	PF65 75.00			

KM# 254 DOLLAR
1.24 g., 0.999 Gold 0.0396 oz. AGW, 13.9 mm. **Obv:** Large breasted mermaid on beach **Rev:** Emperor Angelfish

Date	Mintage	F12	VF20	XF40	MS60	MS63
2001	—	PF63 70.00	PF65 75.00			

KM# 287 DOLLAR
35.00 g., Copper-Nickel, 50 mm. **Obv:** National Arms **Rev:** Cut card corners, Queens of Hearts, Clubs

Date	Mintage	F12	VF20	XF40	MS60	MS63
ND (2001) Antique finish	—	—	—	—	—	10.00

KM# 288 DOLLAR
35.00 g., Copper-Nickel, 50 mm. **Obv:** National arms **Rev:** Cut card corner, Queen of Spades, diamonds

Date	Mintage	F12	VF20	XF40	MS60	MS63
ND (2001) Antique finish	—	—	—	—	—	10.00

KM# 56 DOLLAR
26.80 g., Copper-Nickel, 37.2 mm. **Subject:** Marine Life Protection **Obv:** Mermaid figurehead and value **Rev:** Multicolor fish scene **Edge:** Reeded

Date	Mintage	F12	VF20	XF40	MS60	MS63
2002	—	PF65 32.50				

KM# 57 DOLLAR
26.80 g., Copper-Nickel, 37.2 mm. **Subject:** Marine Life Protection **Obv:** Mermaid figurehead on approaching ship **Rev:** Multicolor reflective fish scene under an acrylic layer **Edge:** Reeded

Date	Mintage	F12	VF20	XF40	MS60	MS63
2002	—	PF65 37.50				

KM# 63 DOLLAR
26.80 g., Copper-Nickel, 37.2 mm. **Subject:** Marine Life Protection **Obv:** Figurehead mermaid and value **Rev:** Blue Tang Fish **Edge:** Reeded

Date	Mintage	F12	VF20	XF40	MS60	MS63
2002	—	PF65 37.50				

KM# 64 DOLLAR
26.80 g., Copper-Nickel, 37.2 mm. **Subject:** Marine Life Protection **Obv:** Figurehead mermaid and value **Rev:** Multicolor whales **Edge:** Reeded

Date	Mintage	F12	VF20	XF40	MS60	MS63
2002	—	PF65 37.50				

KM# 65 DOLLAR
26.80 g., Copper-Nickel, 37.2 mm. **Subject:** Marine Life Protection **Obv:** Mermaid washing hair and value **Rev:** Multicolor jellyfish **Edge:** Reeded

Date	Mintage	F12	VF20	XF40	MS60	MS63
2002	—	PF65 37.50				

KM# 90 DOLLAR
1.24 g., 0.9999 Gold 0.0397 oz. AGW, 13.94 mm. **Subject:** Marine Life Protection **Obv:** Figurehead Mermaid and value **Rev:** Multicolor whales

Date	Mintage	F12	VF20	XF40	MS60	MS63
2002	—	PF63 70.00 PF65 75.00				

KM# 91 DOLLAR
1.24 g., 0.9999 Gold 0.0397 oz. AGW, 13.94 mm. **Subject:** Marine Life Protection **Obv:** Figurehead Mermaid and value **Rev:** Pufferfish

Date	Mintage	F12	VF20	XF40	MS60	MS63
2002	—	PF63 70.00 PF65 75.00				

KM# 92 DOLLAR
1.24 g., 0.9999 Gold 0.0397 oz. AGW, 13.94 mm. **Subject:** Marine Life Protection **Obv:** Seated Mermaid with both arms raised and value **Rev:** Jellyfish

Date	Mintage	F12	VF20	XF40	MS60	MS63
2002	—	PF63 70.00 PF65 75.00				

KM# 93 DOLLAR
1.24 g., 0.9999 Gold 0.0397 oz. AGW, 13.94 mm. **Subject:** Marine Life Protection **Obv:** Figurehead Mermaid and value **Rev:** Blue Tang Fish

Date	Mintage	F12	VF20	XF40	MS60	MS63
2002	—	PF63 70.00 PF65 75.00				

KM# 94 DOLLAR
1.24 g., 0.9999 Gold 0.0397 oz. AGW, 13.94 mm. **Subject:** Marine Life Protection **Obv:** Figurehead mermaid and value **Rev:** Lionfish

Date	Mintage	F12	VF20	XF40	MS60	MS63
2002	—	PF63 70.00 PF65 75.00				

KM# 66 DOLLAR
26.80 g., Copper-Nickel, 37.2 mm. **Subject:** Marine Life Protection **Obv:** Mermaid under sun and value **Rev:** Orange crab **Edge:** Reeded

Date	Mintage	F12	VF20	XF40	MS60	MS63
2003	—	PF65 37.50				

KM# 67 DOLLAR
26.80 g., Copper-Nickel, 37.2 mm. **Subject:** Marine Life Protection **Obv:** Mermaid riding turtle and value **Rev:** Two glittering fish **Edge:** Reeded

Date	Mintage	F12	VF20	XF40	MS60	MS63
2003	—	PF65 37.50				

KM# 68 DOLLAR
26.80 g., Copper-Nickel, 37.2 mm. **Subject:** Marine Life Protection **Obv:** Seated Mermaid on shell and value **Rev:** Multicolor Orca **Edge:** Reeded

Date	Mintage	F12	VF20	XF40	MS60	MS63
2003	—	PF65 37.50				

KM# 69 DOLLAR
26.80 g., Copper-Nickel, 37.2 mm. **Subject:** Marine Life Protection **Obv:** Mermaid playing shell guitar and value **Rev:** Green fish **Edge:** Reeded

Date	Mintage	F12	VF20	XF40	MS60	MS63
2003	—	PF65 37.50				

KM# 95 DOLLAR
1.24 g., 0.9999 Gold 0.0397 oz. AGW, 13.94 mm. **Subject:** Marine Life Protection **Obv:** Mermaid riding dolphin and value **Rev:** Starfish

Date	Mintage	F12	VF20	XF40	MS60	MS63
2003	—	PF63 70.00	PF65 75.00			

KM# 96 DOLLAR
1.24 g., 0.9999 Gold 0.0397 oz. AGW, 13.94 mm. **Subject:** Marine Life Protection **Obv:** Seated Mermaid on shell and value **Rev:** Multicolor Orca **Edge:** Reeded Proof

Date	Mintage	F12	VF20	XF40	MS60	MS63
2003	—	PF63 70.00	PF65 75.00			

KM# 97 DOLLAR
1.24 g., 0.9999 Gold 0.0397 oz. AGW, 13.94 mm. **Subject:** Marine Life Protection **Obv:** Mermaid under radiant sun and value **Rev:** Crab

Date	Mintage	F12	VF20	XF40	MS60	MS63
2003	—	PF63 70.00	PF65 75.00			

KM# 98 DOLLAR
1.24 g., 0.9999 Gold 0.0397 oz. AGW, 13.94 mm. **Subject:** Marine Life Protection **Obv:** Mermaid riding turtle and value **Rev:** Two glittering fish

Date	Mintage	F12	VF20	XF40	MS60	MS63
2003	—	PF63 70.00	PF65 75.00			

KM# 256 DOLLAR
Copper-Nickel, 38.6 mm. **Obv:** Mermaid on dolphin **Rev:** Red starfish - multicolor

Date	Mintage	F12	VF20	XF40	MS60	MS63
2003	—	—	—	—	—	25.00

KM# 70 DOLLAR
26.80 g., Copper-Nickel, 37.2 mm. **Subject:** Marine Life Protection **Obv:** Seated Mermaid on rock and value **Rev:** School of blue fish **Edge:** Reeded

Date	Mintage	F12	VF20	XF40	MS60	MS63
2004	—	PF65 37.50				

KM# 71 DOLLAR
26.80 g., Copper-Nickel, 37.2 mm. **Subject:** Marine Life Protection **Obv:** Side view of Mermaid facing right and value **Rev:** Clownfish **Edge:** Reeded

Date	Mintage	F12	VF20	XF40	MS60	MS63
2004	—	PF65 37.50				

KM# 72 DOLLAR
26.80 g., Copper-Nickel, 37.2 mm. **Subject:** Marine Life Protection **Obv:** Mermaid flanked by dolphins **Rev:** Multicolor dolphin head **Edge:** Reeded

Date	Mintage	F12	VF20	XF40	MS60	MS63
2004	—	PF65 37.50				

KM# 99 DOLLAR
1.24 g., 0.9999 Gold 0.0397 oz. AGW, 13.94 mm. **Subject:** Marine Life Protection **Obv:** Mermaid under radiant sun and value **Rev:** Clownfish

Date	Mintage	F12	VF20	XF40	MS60	MS63
2004	—	PF63 70.00	PF65 75.00			

KM# 100 DOLLAR
1.24 g., 0.9999 Gold 0.0397 oz. AGW, 13.94 mm. **Subject:** Marine Life Protection **Obv:** Mermaid flanked by dolphins **Rev:** Multicolor dolphin head

Date	Mintage	F12	VF20	XF40	MS60	MS63
2004	—	PF63 70.00	PF65 75.00			

KM# 123 DOLLAR
Copper-Nickel, 37.2 mm. **Subject:** Marine Life Protection **Obv:** Mermaid seated inside a giant conch shell **Rev:** Puffer fish **Edge:** Reeded

Date	Mintage	F12	VF20	XF40	MS60	MS63
2004	—	PF65 35.00				

KM# 124 DOLLAR
Copper-Nickel, 37.2 mm. **Subject:** Marine Life Protection **Obv:** Seated Mermaid **Rev:** Sea turtle **Edge:** Reeded

Date	Mintage	F12	VF20	XF40	MS60	MS63
2004	—	PF65 50.00				

KM# 101 DOLLAR
1.24 g., 0.9999 Gold 0.0397 oz. AGW, 13.94 mm. **Subject:** Marine Life Protection **Obv:** Mermaid sitting in a shell listening to a conch shell **Rev:** Sea Horse

Date	Mintage	F12	VF20	XF40	MS60	MS63
2005	—	PF63 70.00	PF65 75.00			

KM# 139 DOLLAR
26.80 g., Copper-Nickel, 37.2 mm. **Subject:** Marine Life - Protection **Obv:** Mermaid fixing hair, dolphin jumping **Rev:** School of fish

Date	Mintage	F12	VF20	XF40	MS60	MS63
2005	—	—	—	—	—	37.50

KM# 140 DOLLAR
26.80 g., Copper-Nickel, 37.2 mm. **Subject:** Marine Life - Protection **Obv:** Mermaid seated in shell, listening to shell **Rev:** Multicolor sea horse

Date	Mintage	F12	VF20	XF40	MS60	MS63
2005	—				—	37.50

KM# 141 DOLLAR
26.80 g., Copper-Nickel **Subject:** Marine Life - Protection **Obv:** Mermaid and dolphin **Rev:** Multicolor fish scene

Date	Mintage	F12	VF20	XF40	MS60	MS63
2005	—				—	37.50

KM# 255 DOLLAR
Copper-Nickel, 38.6 mm. **Obv:** Mermaid seated on rock **Rev:** Stingray - multicolor

Date	Mintage	F12	VF20	XF40	MS60	MS63
2005	—				—	37.00

KM# 125 DOLLAR
Copper-Nickel, 37.2 mm. **Subject:** Marine Life Protection **Obv:** Mermaid with head tilted back **Rev:** Barracuda

Date	Mintage	F12	VF20	XF40	MS60	MS63
2006	—	PF65 37.50				

KM# 126 DOLLAR
Copper-Nickel, 37.2 mm. **Subject:** Marine Life Protection **Obv:** Two mermaids **Rev:** Parrot fish

Date	Mintage	F12	VF20	XF40	MS60	MS63
2006	—	PF65 50.00				

KM# 127 DOLLAR
Copper-Nickel, 37.2 mm. **Subject:** Marine Life Protection **Obv:** Mermaid swimming downward **Rev:** Hog Fish **Edge:** Reeded

Date	Mintage	F12	VF20	XF40	MS60	MS63
2006	—	PF65 32.50				

KM# 128 DOLLAR
Copper-Nickel, 37.2 mm. **Subject:** Marine Life Protection **Obv:** Seated mermaid with bird perched on outstretched hand **Rev:** Mahi Mahi **Edge:** Reeded

Date	Mintage	F12	VF20	XF40	MS60	MS63
2006	—	PF65 47.50				

KM# 129 DOLLAR
Copper-Nickel, 37.2 mm. **Subject:** Marine Life Protection **Obv:** Mermaid, sailing ship and sun **Rev:** Box Fish **Edge:** Reeded

Date	Mintage	F12	VF20	XF40	MS60	MS63
2006	—	PF65 45.00				

KM# 142 DOLLAR
20.00 g., 0.999 Silver 0.6382 oz. ASW **Obv:** Arms **Rev:** Snowflake with blue crystal **Shape:** 38.6

Date	Mintage	F12	VF20	XF40	MS60	MS63
2006	2,500	PF65 65.00				

KM# 334 DOLLAR
27.00 g., Copper-Nickel, 38.61 mm. **Rev:** Eclectus Parrot head right

Date	Mintage	F12	VF20	XF40	MS60	MS63
2006	Est. 5000	PF65 20.00				

KM# 335 DOLLAR
27.00 g., Copper-Nickel, 38.61 mm. **Rev:** Fruit dove head right

Date	Mintage	F12	VF20	XF40	MS60	MS63
2006	Est. 5000	PF65 20.00				

KM# 336 DOLLAR
27.00 g., Copper-Nickel, 38.61 mm. **Rev:** Rainbow lorikeet head left

Date	Mintage	F12	VF20	XF40	MS60	MS63
2006	Est. 5000	PF65 20.00				

KM# 257 DOLLAR
25.00 g., 0.925 Silver 0.7387 oz. ASW, 38.6 mm. **Obv:** Arms **Rev:** White pearl in shell **Shape:** Heart

Date	Mintage	F12	VF20	XF40	MS60	MS63
2006	500	PF65 125				

KM# 322 DOLLAR
0.50 g., 0.999 Gold AGW, 11.8 mm. **Obv:** National arms **Rev:** Elephant shrew

Date	Mintage	F12	VF20	XF40	MS60	MS63
2006	—	PF63 60.00	PF65 70.00			

KM# 323 DOLLAR
0.50 g., 0.999 Gold AGW, 11.8 mm. **Obv:** National arms **Rev:** Rhino beetle

Date	Mintage	F12	VF20	XF40	MS60	MS63
2006	—	PF63 60.00	PF65 70.00			

KM# 324 DOLLAR
0.50 g., 0.999 Gold AGW, 11.8 mm. **Obv:** National arms **Rev:** Buffalo Weaver

Date	Mintage	F12	VF20	XF40	MS60	MS63
2006	—	PF63 60.00	PF65 70.00			

KM# 325 DOLLAR
0.50 g., 0.999 Gold AGW, 11.8 mm. **Obv:** National arms **Rev:** Ant lion

Date	Mintage	F12	VF20	XF40	MS60	MS63
2006	—	PF63 60.00	PF65 70.00			

KM# 326 DOLLAR
0.50 g., 0.999 Gold AGW, 11.8 mm. **Obv:** National arms **Rev:** Leopard tortoise

Date	Mintage	F12	VF20	XF40	MS60	MS63
2006	—	PF63 60.00	PF65 70.00			

KM# 116 DOLLAR
25.73 g., Silver Plated Bronze, 38.6 mm. **Obv:** National arms **Rev:** Multicolor Pope John Paul II with cross **Edge:** Reeded

Date	Mintage	F12	VF20	XF40	MS60	MS63
2007	—	PF65 37.50				

KM# 118 DOLLAR
27.00 g., Copper-Nickel, 38.61 mm. **Series:** Marine Life Protection **Obv:** Neptune reclining with trident, mermaid at his side **Obv. Legend:** REPUBLIC OF PALAU **Rev:** Multicolor Doctor Fish

Date	Mintage	F12	VF20	XF40	MS60	MS63
2007	5,000	PF65 35.00				

KM# 121 DOLLAR
27.00 g., Copper-Nickel, 38.61 mm. **Obv:** Shield with Neptune holding trident, mermaid reclining at his side, RAINBOW'S / END below **Obv. Legend:** REPUBLIC OF PALAU **Rev:** Red racing car 3/4 left **Rev. Legend:** FERRARI - 60 YEARS ANNIVERSARY

Date	Mintage	F12	VF20	XF40	MS60	MS63
ND-2007	5,000	PF65 35.00				

KM# 144 DOLLAR
27.00 g., 0.925 Silver 0.7978 oz. ASW **Obv:** Shield **Rev:** Multicolor John Paul II waving

Date	Mintage	F12	VF20	XF40	MS60	MS63
2007	—	PF65 45.00				

KM# 145 DOLLAR
1.24 g., 0.999 Gold 0.0397 oz. AGW, 13.92 mm. **Subject:** Marine Life - Protection **Obv:** Neptune and mermaid seated on rocks **Rev:** Tropical fish

Date	Mintage	F12	VF20	XF40	MS60	MS63
2007	—	PF63 70.00	PF65 75.00			

KM# 150 DOLLAR
25.00 g., 0.925 Silver 0.7387 oz. ASW **Subject:** Pacific Wildlife **Obv:** Shield **Rev:** Multicolor seahorse

Date	Mintage	F12	VF20	XF40	MS60	MS63
2007	—	PF65 70.00				

KM# 120 DOLLAR
0.50 g., 0.999 Gold AGW, 11.0 mm. **Obv:** Shield with Neptune holding trident, mermaid reclining at his side, RAINBOW'S / END below **Obv. Legend:** REPUBLIC OF PALAU **Shape:** 4-leaf clover **Note:** Uniface

Date	Mintage	F12	VF20	XF40	MS60	MS63
2007	25,000	PF63 40.00	PF65 50.00			

KM# 258 DOLLAR
25.00 g., 0.999 Silver 0.7978 oz. ASW **Subject:** Pacific Wildlife **Rev:** Seahorse - prism

Date	Mintage	F12	VF20	XF40	MS60	MS63
2007	—	PF65 50.00				

KM# 337 DOLLAR
0.50 g., 0.999 Gold AGW, 11 mm. **Subject:** Christopher Columbus, 500th Anniversary **Rev:** Columbus' flagship, Santa Maria

Date	Mintage	F12	VF20	XF40	MS60	MS63
2007	—	PF63 70.00	PF65 75.00			

KM# 338 DOLLAR
1.24 g., 0.999 Gold 0.0396 oz. AGW, 13.92 mm. **Subject:** Easter, 2007 **Rev:** Christ's Resurrection

Date	Mintage	F12	VF20	XF40	MS60	MS63
2007	Est. 15000	PF63 90.00	PF65 100			

KM# 339 DOLLAR
0.50 g., 0.999 Gold AGW, 11 mm. **Subject:** Deutsche Bundesbank, 50th anniversary **Rev:** Pile of coins

Date	Mintage	F12	VF20	XF40	MS60	MS63
2007	—	PF63 70.00	PF65 75.00			

KM# 154 DOLLAR
26.80 g., Copper-Nickel, 38.61 mm. **Subject:** 150th Anniversary of the Appriations **Obv:** Shield **Rev:** Statue of Our Lady of Lourdes and holy water vile

Date	Mintage	F12	VF20	XF40	MS60	MS63
2008	—	PF65 22.50				

KM# 155 DOLLAR
26.80 g., Copper-Nickel, 37.2 mm. **Subject:** Dealer Button **Obv:** Shield **Rev:** Vegas Chips and cards, Ace of Clubs corner cut

Date	Mintage	F12	VF20	XF40	MS60	MS63
2008	—	—	—	—	—	15.00

KM# 156 DOLLAR
26.80 g., Copper-Nickel, 37.2 mm. **Subject:** Dealer Buttons **Obv:** Shield **Rev:** Vegas Chips and cards, Ace of Diamonds corner cut

Date	Mintage	F12	VF20	XF40	MS60	MS63
2008	—	—	—	—	—	15.00

KM# 157 DOLLAR
26.80 g., Copper-Nickel, 37.2 mm. **Subject:** Dear Buttons **Obv:** Shield **Rev:** Vegas Chips and cards, Ace of Heats corner cut

Date	Mintage	F12	VF20	XF40	MS60	MS63
2008	—	—	—	—	—	15.00

KM# 158 DOLLAR
26.80 g., Copper-Nickel, 37.2 mm. **Obv:** Shield **Rev:** Vegas chips and cards, Ace of Spades corner cut

Date	Mintage	F12	VF20	XF40	MS60	MS63
2008	—				—	15.00

KM# 159 DOLLAR
1.24 g., 0.999 Gold 0.0396 oz. AGW, 13.9 mm. **Subject:** St. Francis of Assisi **Obv:** Shield **Rev:** Bust facing

Date	Mintage	F12	VF20	XF40	MS60	MS63
2008	—	PF63 70.00	PF65 75.00			

KM# 160 DOLLAR
1.24 g., 0.990 Gold 0.0393 oz. AGW, 13.9 mm. **Subject:** St. Francis of Assisi **Obv:** Shield **Rev:** Multicolor bust facing

Date	Mintage	F12	VF20	XF40	MS60	MS63
2008	—				—	80.00

KM# 161 DOLLAR
0.50 g., 0.999 Gold AGW, 11 mm. **Obv:** Shield **Rev:** Multicolor poppy **Shape:** Irregular

Date	Mintage	F12	VF20	XF40	MS60	MS63
2008	—				—	60.00

KM# 162 DOLLAR
0.50 g., 0.999 Gold AGW, 11 mm. **Subject:** Everlasting love **Obv:** Shield **Rev:** Heart **Shape:** Heart

Date	Mintage	F12	VF20	XF40	MS60	MS63
2008	—				—	60.00

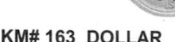

KM# 163 DOLLAR
1.24 g., 0.999 Gold 0.0397 oz. AGW **Subject:** Marine Life-Protection **Obv:** Neptune and mermaid seated on rock **Rev:** Grey reef shark

Date	Mintage	F12	VF20	XF40	MS60	MS63
2008	1,500	PF65 85.00				

KM# 164 DOLLAR
26.80 g., Copper-Nickel, 37.2 mm. **Subject:** Endangered Wildlife **Obv:** Shield **Rev:** Multicolor Tiger shark

Date	Mintage	F12	VF20	XF40	MS60	MS63
2008	—					35.00

KM# 165 DOLLAR
26.80 g., Copper-Nickel, 37.2 mm. **Subject:** Endangered Wildlife **Obv:** Shield **Rev:** Multicolor Hawksbill turtle

Date	Mintage	F12	VF20	XF40	MS60	MS63
2008	—				—	37.50

KM# 166 DOLLAR
26.80 g., Copper-Nickel, 37.2 mm. **Subject:** Endangered Wildlife **Obv:** Shield **Rev:** Multicolored Regal angelfish swimming right

Date	Mintage	F12	VF20	XF40	MS60	MS63
2008	—	PF65 37.50				

KM# 167 DOLLAR
26.80 g., Copper-Nickel, 37.2 mm. **Subject:** Endangered Wildlife **Obv:** Shield **Rev:** Multicolor Spiny lobster

Date	Mintage	F12	VF20	XF40	MS60	MS63
2008	—	PF65 30.00				

KM# 259 DOLLAR
0.50 g., 0.999 Gold AGW, 11 mm. **Subject:** Sitting bull **Obv:** Shield **Rev:** Portrait facing

Date	Mintage	F12	VF20	XF40	MS60	MS63
2008	—	PF63 50.00	PF65 60.00			

KM# 449 DOLLAR
27.00 g., Copper-Nickel, 38.61 mm. **Obv:** National arms **Rev:** Great white shark in color

Date	Mintage	F12	VF20	XF40	MS60	MS63
2008	—	PF65 35.00				

KM# 450 DOLLAR
27.00 g., Copper-Nickel, 38.61 mm. **Subject:** Manfred Albrecht von Richtofen (The Red Baron) **Obv:** National arms **Rev:** Bust in oval below red tri-wing plane

Date	Mintage	F12	VF20	XF40	MS60	MS63
2008	—	PF65 75.00				

KM# 451 DOLLAR
25.00 g., 0.999 Silver 0.7978 oz. ASW, 38.61 mm. **Obv:** National arms **Rev:** Butterfly

Date	Mintage	F12	VF20	XF40	MS60	MS63
2008	—	PF65 80.00				

KM# 177 DOLLAR
1.24 g., 0.999 Gold 0.0397 oz. AGW, 13.9 mm. **Obv:** Shield **Rev:** Madonna and child

Date	Mintage	F12	VF20	XF40	MS60	MS63
ND-2009	25,000	PF63 75.00	PF65 80.00			

KM# 178 DOLLAR
1.24 g., 0.999 Gold 0.0397 oz. AGW, 13.9 mm. **Subject:** FIAA World Cup - South Africa **Obv:** Shield **Rev:** Soccer ball, South African flag and Water Buffalo

Date	Mintage	F12	VF20	XF40	MS60	MS63
2009	—	PF63 70.00	PF65 75.00			

KM# 222 DOLLAR
27.00 g., Silver Plated Copper, 38.6 mm. **Rev:** Lighthouse of Alexandria, multicolor

Date	Mintage	F12	VF20	XF40	MS60	MS63
2009 Prooflike	5,000	—	—		—	20.00

KM# 223 DOLLAR
27.00 g., Silver Plated Copper, 38.6 mm. **Rev:** Zeus statue, multicolor

Date	Mintage	F12	VF20	XF40	MS60	MS63
2009 Prooflike	—				—	20.00

KM# 224 DOLLAR
27.00 g., Silver Plated Copper, 38.6 mm. **Rev:** Hanging Garden of Babylon, multicolor

Date	Mintage	F12	VF20	XF40	MS60	MS63
2009 Prooflike	5,000				—	20.00

KM# 225 DOLLAR
27.00 g., Silver Plated Copper, 38.6 mm. **Rev:** Mausoleum, multicolor

Date	Mintage	F12	VF20	XF40	MS60	MS63
2009 Prooflike	5,000	—	—	—	—	20.00

KM# 226 DOLLAR
27.00 g., Silver Plated Copper, 38.6 mm. **Rev:** Pyramids, multicolor

Date	Mintage	F12	VF20	XF40	MS60	MS63
2009 Prooflike	5,000	—	—	—	—	20.00

KM# 227 DOLLAR
27.00 g., Silver Plated Copper, 38.6 mm. **Rev:** Artemis temple, multicolor

Date	Mintage	F12	VF20	XF40	MS60	MS63
2009 Prooflike	5,000	—	—	—	—	20.00

KM# 228 DOLLAR
27.00 g., Silver Plated Copper, 38.6 mm. **Rev:** Colossus of Rhodes, multicolor

Date	Mintage	F12	VF20	XF40	MS60	MS63
2009 Prooflike	5,000	—	—	—	—	20.00

KM# 229 DOLLAR
27.00 g., Silver Plated Copper, 38.6 mm. **Subject:** Ducati - Casey Stoner **Rev:** Motorcycle left, multicolor

Date	Mintage	F12	VF20	XF40	MS60	MS63
2009 Prooflike	2,008	—	—	—	—	25.00

KM# 230 DOLLAR
27.00 g., Silver Plated Copper, 38.6 mm. **Subject:** Ducati - Troy Bayliss **Rev:** Motorcycle, multicolor

Date	Mintage	F12	VF20	XF40	MS60	MS63
2009 Prooflike	2,008	—	—	—	—	25.00

KM# 233 DOLLAR
27.00 g., Copper-Nickel, 38.6 mm. **Subject:** Marine Life Protection **Obv:** Neptune standing, two mermaids below **Rev:** Lionfish, multicolor

Date	Mintage	F12	VF20	XF40	MS60	MS63
2009 Prooflike	5,000	—	—	—	—	25.00

KM# 234 DOLLAR
1.00 g., 0.999 Gold 0.0319 oz. AGW, 13.9 mm. **Subject:** Marine Life Protection **Rev:** Lionfish

Date	Mintage	F12	VF20	XF40	MS60	MS63
2009	25,000	PF63 60.00	PF65 70.00			

KM# 235 DOLLAR
0.50 g., 0.999 Gold AGW, 11.8 mm. **Subject:** Augustus Aureus **Rev:** Head laureate right

Date	Mintage	F12	VF20	XF40	MS60	MS63
MMIX (2009)	15,000	—	—	—	—	40.00

KM# 236 DOLLAR
0.50 g., 0.999 Gold AGW, 11.8 mm. **Subject:** Germanicus Dupondius **Rev:** General in quadriga right

Date	Mintage	F12	VF20	XF40	MS60	MS63
MMIX (2009)	15,000	—	—	—	—	40.00

KM# 237 DOLLAR
0.50 g., 0.999 Gold AGW, 11.8 mm. **Subject:** Julius Caesar Denarius **Rev:** Head laureate right

Date	Mintage	F12	VF20	XF40	MS60	MS63
MMIX (2009)	15,000	—	—	—	—	40.00

KM# 238 DOLLAR
0.50 g., 0.999 Gold AGW, 11.8 mm. **Subject:** Brutus Denarius **Rev:** Cap flanked by two daggers

Date	Mintage	F12	VF20	XF40	MS60	MS63
MMIX (2009)	15,000	—	—	—	—	40.00

KM# 239 DOLLAR
1.24 g., 0.999 Gold 0.0396 oz. AGW, 13.9 mm. **Subject:** Salesian Order, 150th Anniversary **Rev:** Don Bosco facing

Date	Mintage	F12	VF20	XF40	MS60	MS63
2009	15,000	PF63 65.00	PF65 75.00			

KM# 240 DOLLAR
0.50 g., 0.999 Gold AGW, 11 mm. **Rev:** Pebbled **Shape:** 5-pointed star

Date	Mintage	F12	VF20	XF40	MS60	MS63
ND (2009)	25,000	—	—	—	—	40.00

KM# 241 DOLLAR
1.24 g., 0.999 Gold 0.0396 oz. AGW, 13.9 mm. **Subject:** Fontana de Trevi **Rev:** Trevi fountain and building facade

Date	Mintage	F12	VF20	XF40	MS60	MS63
2009 Proof	15,000	—	—	—	—	75.00

KM# 244 DOLLAR
0.50 g., 0.999 Gold AGW, 11.8 mm. **Subject:** First didrachm **Rev:** Twins sucking at she-wolf

Date	Mintage	F12	VF20	XF40	MS60	MS63
MMIX (2009)	15,000	—	—	—	—	40.00

KM# 245 DOLLAR
0.50 g., 0.999 Gold AGW, 11.8 mm. **Subject:** Claudius aureus **Rev:** Head laureate right

Date	Mintage	F12	VF20	XF40	MS60	MS63
MMIX (2009)	15,000	—	—	—	—	40.00

KM# 246 DOLLAR
0.50 g., 0.999 Gold AGW, 11.8 mm. **Subject:** Tiberius aureus **Rev:** Head laureate right

Date	Mintage	F12	VF20	XF40	MS60	MS63
MMIX (2009)	15,000	—	—	—	—	40.00

KM# 247 DOLLAR
0.50 g., 0.999 Gold AGW, 11.8 mm. **Subject:** Caligula aureus **Rev:** Head laureate right

Date	Mintage	F12	VF20	XF40	MS60	MS63
MMIX (2009)	15,000	—	—	—	—	40.00

KM# 260 DOLLAR
Silver Plated Copper, 30x30 mm. **Subject:** 2000th Anniversary Teutobury Forest Battle **Obv:** Shield **Rev:** Warrior in forest

battle, multicolor **Shape:** Square

Date	Mintage	F12	VF20	XF40	MS60	MS63
MMIX (2009)	2,500	PF65 30.00				

KM# 261 DOLLAR
25.00 g., 0.999 Silver 0.7978 oz. ASW, 38.6 mm. **Subject:** Pacific Wildlife **Obv:** Arms **Rev:** Barn Swallow - prism

Date	Mintage	F12	VF20	XF40	MS60	MS63
2009	2,500	PF65 50.00				

KM# 262 DOLLAR
25.00 g., 0.999 Silver 0.7978 oz. ASW, 38.6 mm. **Subject:** Pacific Wildlife **Obv:** Arms **Rev:** Gecko on rock - prism

Date	Mintage	F12	VF20	XF40	MS60	MS63
2009	2,500	PF65 50.00				

KM# 263 DOLLAR
0.50 g., 0.999 Gold AGW, 11 mm. **Rev:** 4-leaf clover, green

Date	Mintage	F12	VF20	XF40	MS60	MS63
2009	—	—	—	—	—	65.00

KM# 269 DOLLAR
Copper-Nickel, 37.2 mm. **Subject:** Protect Wildlife - Angelfish **Rev:** Angelfish - Prisim

Date	Mintage	F12	VF20	XF40	MS60	MS63
2009	—	—	—	—	—	35.00

KM# 270 DOLLAR
Copper-Nickel, 37.2 mm. **Subject:** Apostles - Peter **Rev:** Multicolor icon image

Date	Mintage	F12	VF20	XF40	MS60	MS63
2009	1,000	PF65 25.00				

KM# 271 DOLLAR
Copper-Nickel, 37.2 mm. **Subject:** Apostles - James Minor **Rev:** Multicolor icon image

Date	Mintage	F12	VF20	XF40	MS60	MS63
2009	1,000	PF65 25.00				

KM# 272 DOLLAR
Copper-Nickel, 37.2 mm. **Subject:** Apostles - John **Rev:** Multicolor icon image

Date	Mintage	F12	VF20	XF40	MS60	MS63
2009	1,000	PF65 25.00				

KM# 273 DOLLAR
Copper-Nickel, 37.2 mm. **Subject:** Apostle - Simon **Rev:** Multicolor icon image

Date	Mintage	F12	VF20	XF40	MS60	MS63
2009	1,000	PF65 25.00				

KM# 274 DOLLAR
Copper-Nickel, 37.2 mm. **Subject:** Apostles - Matthaeus **Rev:** Multicolor icon image

Date	Mintage	F12	VF20	XF40	MS60	MS63
2009	1,000	PF65 25.00				

KM# 275 DOLLAR
Copper-Nickel, 37.2 mm. **Subject:** Apostles - Thomas **Rev:** Multicolor icon image

Date	Mintage	F12	VF20	XF40	MS60	MS63
2009	1,000	PF65 25.00				

KM# 276 DOLLAR
Copper-Nickel, 37.2 mm. **Subject:** Apostles - Judas Thaddaeus **Rev:** Multicolor icon image

Date	Mintage	F12	VF20	XF40	MS60	MS63
2009	1,000	PF65 25.00				

KM# 277 DOLLAR
Copper-Nickel, 37.2 mm. **Subject:** Apostles - Bartholomew **Rev:** Multicolor icon image

Date	Mintage	F12	VF20	XF40	MS60	MS63
2009	1,000	PF65 25.00				

KM# 278 DOLLAR
Copper-Nickel, 37.2 mm. **Subject:** Apostles - Philip **Rev:** Multicolor icon image

Date	Mintage	F12	VF20	XF40	MS60	MS63
2009	1,000	PF65 25.00				

KM# 279 DOLLAR
Copper-Nickel, 37.2 mm. **Subject:** Apostles - John Major **Rev:** Multicolor icon image

Date	Mintage	F12	VF20	XF40	MS60	MS63
2009	1,000	PF65 25.00				

KM# 280 DOLLAR
Copper-Nickel, 37.2 mm. **Subject:** Apostles - Andrew **Rev:** Multicolor icon image

Date	Mintage	F12	VF20	XF40	MS60	MS63
2009	1,000	PF65 25.00				

KM# 281 DOLLAR
Copper-Nickel, 37.2 mm. **Subject:** Apostles - Judas Iscariot **Rev:** Multicolor icon image

Date	Mintage	F12	VF20	XF40	MS60	MS63
2009	1,000	PF65 25.00				

KM# 282 DOLLAR
26.80 g., Copper-Nickel, 37.2 mm. **Subject:** Endangered Wildlife - Orange Lined Tigerfish **Rev:** Multicolor fish left

Date	Mintage	F12	VF20	XF40	MS60	MS63
2009	—	PF65 37.50				

KM# 283 DOLLAR
26.80 g., Copper-Nickel, 37.2 mm. **Subject:** Endangered Wildlife - Blue Grilled Angelfish **Rev:** Multicolor fish

Date	Mintage	F12	VF20	XF40	MS60	MS63
2009	—	PF65 37.50				

KM# 284 DOLLAR
26.80 g., Copper-Nickel, 37.2 mm. **Subject:** Endangered Wildlife - Green Turtle **Rev:** Multicolor turtle

Date	Mintage	F12	VF20	XF40	MS60	MS63
2009	—	PF65 37.50				

KM# 285 DOLLAR
26.80 g., Copper-Nickel, 37.2 mm. **Subject:** Endangered Wildlife - Sailfin Tang fish **Rev:** Multicolor fish right

Date	Mintage	F12	VF20	XF40	MS60	MS63
2009	—	PF65 37.50				

KM# 286 DOLLAR
26.80 g., Copper-Nickel, 37.2 mm. **Subject:** Endangered Wildlife - Clown Trigger fish **Rev:** Multicolor fish left

Date	Mintage	F12	VF20	XF40	MS60	MS63
2009	—	PF65 37.50				

KM# 321 DOLLAR
0.50 g., 0.999 Gold AGW, 11.8 mm. **Obv:** National arms **Rev:** Pamir, sail training vessel

Date	Mintage	F12	VF20	XF40	MS60	MS63
2009	25,000	PF63 60.00	PF65 70.00			

KM# 448 DOLLAR
27.00 g., Copper-Nickel, 38.61 mm. **Obv:** National arms **Rev:** Two spotted fish in color

Date	Mintage	F12	VF20	XF40	MS60	MS63
2009	—	PF65 35.00				

KM# 454 DOLLAR
Silver Plated Copper, 35 x 35 mm. **Subject:** Battle of Teutoburg Forest **Rev:** Roman Legion in color

Date	Mintage	F12	VF20	XF40	MS60	MS63
2009	—	PF65 60.00				

KM# 455 DOLLAR
Silver Plated, 30 x 30 mm. **Subject:** Forest Battle **Obv:** Walhalia Arminius

Date	Mintage	F12	VF20	XF40	MS60	MS63
2009	—	PF65 20.00				

KM# 266 DOLLAR
25.00 g., 0.925 Silver 0.7387 oz. ASW, 30x30 mm. **Subject:** Battle of Grimwald **Rev:** Vyautas and Jagiello busts **Shape:** Square

Date	Mintage	F12	VF20	XF40	MS60	MS63
2010	—	PF65 30.00				

KM# 267 DOLLAR
25.00 g., 0.999 Silver 0.7978 oz. ASW, 30x30 mm. **Subject:** Battle of Grunwald **Rev:** Warrior on horseback in color **Shape:** Square

Date	Mintage	F12	VF20	XF40	MS60	MS63
2010	2,500	PF65 35.00				

KM# 268 DOLLAR
25.00 g., 0.999 Silver 0.7978 oz. ASW, 30x30 mm. **Subject:** Battle of Grunwald **Rev:** Knight kneeling in color **Shape:** Square

Date	Mintage	F12	VF20	XF40	MS60	MS63
2010	2,500	PF65 35.00				

KM# 303 DOLLAR
0.50 g., 0.999 Gold AGW, 11mm mm. **Obv:** National arms **Rev:** Teddy bear **Shape:** Irregular

Date	Mintage	F12	VF20	XF40	MS60	MS63
ND-2010	25,000	—	—	—	—	75.00

KM# 307 DOLLAR
35.00 g., Copper-Nickel, 50 mm. **Subject:** Hold Cards **Obv:** National arms **Rev:** King of Hearts and Clubs

Date	Mintage	F12	VF20	XF40	MS60	MS63
2010 Antique patina	5,000	—	—	—	—	25.00

KM# 308 DOLLAR
35.00 g., Copper-Nickel, 50 mm. **Subject:** Hold Cards **Obv:** National arms **Rev:** King of Spades and Diamonds

Date	Mintage	F12	VF20	XF40	MS60	MS63
2010 Antique patina	5,000	—	—	—	—	25.00

KM# 309 DOLLAR
0.50 g., 0.9999 Gold AGW, 11.8 mm. **Obv:** National arms **Rev:** Nero coin

Date	Mintage	F12	VF20	XF40	MS60	MS63
2010	15,000	—	—	—	—	60.00

KM# 310 DOLLAR
0.50 g., 0.9999 Gold AGW, 11.8 mm. **Obv:** National arms **Rev:** Vespasian coin

Date	Mintage	F12	VF20	XF40	MS60	MS63
2010	15,000	—	—	—	—	60.00

KM# 311 DOLLAR
0.50 g., 0.999 Silver, 11.8 mm. **Obv:** National arms **Rev:** Titus coin

Date	Mintage	F12	VF20	XF40	MS60	MS63
2010	15,000	—	—	—	—	60.00

KM# 312 DOLLAR
0.50 g., 0.9999 Gold AGW, 11.8 mm. **Obv:** National arms **Rev:** Domitian coin

Date	Mintage	F12	VF20	XF40	MS60	MS63
2010	15,000	—	—	—	—	60.00

KM# 313 DOLLAR
27.00 g., Silver Plated Copper, 38.61 mm. **Obv:** Mermaid **Rev:** Hammerhead shark color image

Date	Mintage	F12	VF20	XF40	MS60	MS63
2010 Prooflike	5,000	—	—	—	—	28.00

KM# 315 DOLLAR
1.00 g., 0.9999 Gold 0.0319 oz. AGW, 13.92 mm. **Obv:** Mermaid **Rev:** Hammerhead sharks

Date	Mintage	F12	VF20	XF40	MS60	MS63
2010	25,000	PF63 80.00	PF65 90.00			

KM# 316 DOLLAR
27.00 g., Silver Plated Copper, 35x35 mm. **Obv:** National arms **Rev:** Fernando Alonso and racecar in color

Date	Mintage	F12	VF20	XF40	MS60	MS63
2010 Prooflike	5,000	—	—	—	—	35.00

KM# 317 DOLLAR
0.50 g., 0.9999 Gold AGW, 11 mm. **Obv:** National arms **Rev:** Angel **Shape:** Irregular

Date	Mintage	F12	VF20	XF40	MS60	MS63
ND-2010	15,000	—	—	—	—	50.00

KM# 327 DOLLAR
0.50 g., 0.999 Gold AGW, 11.8 mm. **Obv:** National arms **Rev:** Romulus & Remus

Date	Mintage	F12	VF20	XF40	MS60	MS63
2010	15,000	PF63 40.00	PF65 50.00			

KM# 429 DOLLAR
Copper-Nickel, 38.61 mm. **Obv:** National arms **Rev:** Our Lady of Fatima statue in color at left, Pope benedict XVI at right

Date	Mintage	F12	VF20	XF40	MS60	MS63
2010	—	PF65 25.00				

KM# 445 DOLLAR
1.24 g., 0.999 Gold 0.0396 oz. AGW, 13.92 mm. **Obv:** Naitonal arms **Rev:** Mary, Joseph and Jesus **Rev. Legend:** CHRISTMAS

Date	Mintage	F12	VF20	XF40	MS60	MS63
2010		PF63 80.00	PF65 90.00			

KM# 468 DOLLAR
0.50 g., 0.999 Gold AGW, 11 mm. **Obv:** National arms **Shape:** 5-pointed star

Date	Mintage	F12	VF20	XF40	MS60	MS63
2010	—	—	—	—	—	40.00

KM# 405 DOLLAR
1.24 g., 0.999 Gold 0.0396 oz. AGW, 13.94 mm. **Obv:** Mermaid reclining on rock **Rev:** Anemone fish

Date	Mintage	F12	VF20	XF40	MS60	MS63
2011	—	PF63 80.00	PF65 90.00			

KM# 453 DOLLAR
25.00 g., 0.999 Silver 0.7978 oz. ASW, 38.61 mm. **Obv:** National arms **Rev:** Two striped fish

Date	Mintage	F12	VF20	XF40	MS60	MS63
2011	—	PF65 75.00				

KM# 340 DOLLAR
27.00 g., Silver Plated Copper, 38.61 mm. **Subject:** John Paul II **Rev:** Visions at Fatima

Date	Mintage	F12	VF20	XF40	MS60	MS63
2011 Prooflike	2,500	—	—	—	—	22.00

KM# 341 DOLLAR
27.00 g., Silver Plated Copper, 38.61 mm. **Subject:** John Paul II **Rev:** Election as pope

Date	Mintage	F12	VF20	XF40	MS60	MS63
2011 Prooflike	2,500	—	—	—	—	22.00

KM# 342 DOLLAR
27.00 g., Silver Plated Copper, 38.61 mm. **Subject:** John Paul II **Rev:** Death

Date	Mintage	F12	VF20	XF40	MS60	MS63
2011 Prooflike	2,500	—	—	—	—	22.00

KM# 343 DOLLAR
27.00 g., Silver Plated Copper, 38.61 mm. **Subject:** John Paul II **Rev:** Anouncement as Venerable

Date	Mintage	F12	VF20	XF40	MS60	MS63
2011 Prooflike	2,500	—	—	—	—	22.00

KM# 344 DOLLAR
27.00 g., Silver Plated Copper, 38.61 mm. **Subject:** John Paul II **Rev:** Miracle healing of a Sister

Date	Mintage	F12	VF20	XF40	MS60	MS63
2011 Prooflike	2,500	—	—	—	—	22.00

KM# 345 DOLLAR
27.00 g., Silver Plated Copper, 38.61 mm. **Subject:** John Paul II **Rev:** Benedict VXI's pronouncement

Date	Mintage	F12	VF20	XF40	MS60	MS63
2011 Prooflike	2,500	—	—	—	—	22.00

KM# 346 DOLLAR
27.00 g., Silver Plated Copper, 38.61 mm. **Subject:** John Paul II **Rev:** Opening the cause for sainthood

Date	Mintage	F12	VF20	XF40	MS60	MS63
2011 Prooflike	2,500	—	—	—	—	22.00

KM# 347 DOLLAR
27.00 g., Silver Plated Copper, 38.61 mm. **Subject:** John Paul II **Rev:** Ceremony of Beautification

Date	Mintage	F12	VF20	XF40	MS60	MS63
2011 Prooflike	2,500	—	—	—	—	22.00

KM# 349 DOLLAR
0.50 g., 0.999 Gold AGW, 11.8 mm. **Rev:** Roman Coin - Coliseum

Date	Mintage	F12	VF20	XF40	MS60	MS63
2011	—	PF63 45.00		PF65 55.00		

KM# 350 DOLLAR
0.50 g., 0.999 Gold AGW, 11.8 mm. **Rev:** Roman Coin - Trajain

Date	Mintage	F12	VF20	XF40	MS60	MS63
2011	—	PF63 45.00		PF65 55.00		

KM# 351 DOLLAR
0.50 g., 0.999 Gold AGW, 11.8 mm. **Rev:** Roman Coin - Hadrian

Date	Mintage	F12	VF20	XF40	MS60	MS63
2011	—	PF63 45.00		PF65 55.00		

KM# 352 DOLLAR
0.50 g., 0.999 Gold AGW, 11.8 mm. **Rev:** Roman Coin - Marcus Aurillus

Date	Mintage	F12	VF20	XF40	MS60	MS63
2011	—	PF63 45.00		PF65 55.00		

KM# 370 DOLLAR
0.50 g., 0.999 Gold AGW, 11.8 mm. **Obv:** National arms **Rev:** Diocletian coin

Date	Mintage	F12	VF20	XF40	MS60	MS63
2011	—	—	—	—	—	60.00

KM# 371 DOLLAR
0.50 g., 0.999 Gold AGW, 11.8 mm. **Obv:** National arms **Rev:** Aurelian coin

Date	Mintage	F12	VF20	XF40	MS60	MS63
2011	—	—	—	—	—	60.00

KM# 372 DOLLAR
0.50 g., 0.999 Gold AGW, 11.8 mm. **Obv:** National arms **Rev:** Caracalla coin

Date	Mintage	F12	VF20	XF40	MS60	MS63
2011	—	—	—	—	—	60.00

KM# 373 DOLLAR
0.50 g., 0.999 Gold AGW, 11.8 mm. **Obv:** National arms **Rev:** Septimius Severus coin

Date	Mintage	F12	VF20	XF40	MS60	MS63
2011	—	—	—	—	—	60.00

KM# 406 DOLLAR
27.00 g., Copper-Nickel, 38.6 mm. **Obv:** Mermaid reclining on rock **Rev:** Anemone fish in color

Date	Mintage	F12	VF20	XF40	MS60	MS63
2011	—	—	—	—	—	25.00

KM# 408 DOLLAR
27.00 g., Copper-Nickel, 38.61 mm. **Obv:** National arms **Rev:** Harry Houdini bust at left, top had and wand at right

Date	Mintage	F12	VF20	XF40	MS60	MS63
2011	—	—	—	—	—	25.00

KM# 410 DOLLAR
0.50 g., 0.999 Gold AGW, 11 mm. **Obv:** National arms **Rev:** Golden Butterfly **Shape:** Irregular

Date	Mintage	F12	VF20	XF40	MS60	MS63
ND-2011	—	PF65 85.00				

KM# 452 DOLLAR
25.00 g., 0.999 Silver 0.7978 oz ASW, 38.61 mm. **Obv:** National arms **Rev:** Long nose hawk fish

Date	Mintage	F12	VF20	XF40	MS60	MS63
2011	—	PF65 75.00				

KM# 130 2 DOLLARS
10.00 g., 0.999 Silver 0.3191 oz. ASW, 30 mm. **Obv:** Shield with Neptune holding trident, mermaid reclining at his side **Obv. Legend:** REPUBLIC OF PALAU **Rev:** Red racing car 3/4 right **Rev. Legend:** FERRARI - 60 YEARS ANNIVERSARY

Date	Mintage	F12	VF20	XF40	MS60	MS63
ND-2007	2,500	PF65 45.00				

KM# 131 2 DOLLARS
10.00 g., 0.999 Silver 0.3191 oz. ASW, 30 mm. **Obv:** Shield with Neptune holding trident, mermaid reclining at his side **Obv. Legend:** REPUBLIC OF PALAU **Rev:** Red racing car 3/4 right **Rev. Legend:** FERRARI - 60 YEARS ANNIVERSARY

Date	Mintage	F12	VF20	XF40	MS60	MS63
ND-2007	2,500	PF65 45.00				

KM# 132 2 DOLLARS
10.00 g., 0.999 Silver 0.3191 oz. ASW, 30 mm. **Obv:** Shield with Neptune holding trident, mermaid reclining at his side **Obv. Legend:** REPUBLIC OF PALAU **Rev:** Red racing car front view **Rev. Legend:** FERRARI - 60 YEARS ANNIVERSARY

Date	Mintage	F12	VF20	XF40	MS60	MS63
ND-2007	2,500	PF65 45.00				

KM# 133 2 DOLLARS
10.00 g., 0.999 Silver 0.3191 oz. ASW, 30 mm. **Obv:** Shield with Neptune holding trident, mermaid reclining at his side **Obv. Legend:** REPUBLIC OF PALAU **Rev:** Looking down on red racing car approaching in turn **Rev. Legend:** FERRARI - 60 YEARS ANNIVERSARY

Date	Mintage	F12	VF20	XF40	MS60	MS63
ND-2007	2,500	PF65 45.00				

KM# 134 2 DOLLARS
10.00 g., 0.999 Silver 0.3191 oz. ASW, 30 mm. **Obv:** Shield with Neptune holding trident, reclining mermaid at his side **Obv. Legend:** REPUBLIC OF PALAU **Rev:** Front view of red racing car **Rev. Legend:** FERRARI - 60 YEARS ANNIVERSARY

Date	Mintage	F12	VF20	XF40	MS60	MS63
ND-2007	2,500	PF65 45.00				

KM# 135 2 DOLLARS
10.00 g., 0.999 Silver 0.3191 oz. ASW, 30.0 mm. **Obv:** Shield with Neptune holding trident, mermaid reclining at his side **Obv. Legend:** REPUBLIC OF PALAU **Rev:** Red racing car approaching 3/4 right **Rev. Legend:** FERRARI - 60 YEARS ANNIVERSARY

Date	Mintage	F12	VF20	XF40	MS60	MS63
ND-2007	2,500	PF65 45.00				

KM# 319 2 DOLLARS
15.50 g., 0.925 Silver 0.458 oz. ASW, 35 mm. **Subject:** World of Insects **Obv:** National arms **Rev:** Large color dragon fly - Blue Eye Hawker

Date	Mintage	F12	VF20	XF40	MS60	MS63
2010	1,000	PF65 100				

KM# 375 2 DOLLARS
15.50 g., 0.925 Silver 0.458 oz. ASW, 35 mm. **Subject:** Grasshopper

Date	Mintage	F12	VF20	XF40	MS60	MS63
2010	—	PF65 100				

KM# 353 2 DOLLARS
15.50 g., 0.999 Silver 0.4946 oz. ASW, 35 mm. **Subject:** Bible stories - Creation of the World

Date	Mintage	F12	VF20	XF40	MS60	MS63
2011	1,000	PF65 65.00				

KM# 354 2 DOLLARS
15.50 g., 0.999 Silver 0.4946 oz. ASW, 35 mm. **Subject:** Bible stories - Adam and Eve

Date	Mintage	F12	VF20	XF40	MS60	MS63
2011	1,000	PF65 65.00				

KM# 355 2 DOLLARS
15.50 g., 0.999 Silver 0.4946 oz. ASW, 35 mm. **Subject:** Bible stories - Cain and Abel

Date	Mintage	F12	VF20	XF40	MS60	MS63
2011	1,000	PF65 65.00				

KM# 356 2 DOLLARS
15.50 g., 0.999 Silver 0.4946 oz. ASW, 35 mm. **Subject:** Bible stories - 10 Commandments

Date	Mintage	F12	VF20	XF40	MS60	MS63
2011	1,000	PF65 65.00				

KM# 357 2 DOLLARS
15.57 g., 0.925 Silver 0.4601 oz. ASW, 35 mm. **Obv:** National arms **Rev:** Atelopus Certus, orange frog in color

Date	Mintage	F12	VF20	XF40	MS60	MS63
2011	500	PF65 85.00				

KM# 358 2 DOLLARS
151.57 g., 0.925 Silver 4.4786 oz. ASW, 35 mm. **Obv:** National arms **Rev:** Green frog in color

Date	Mintage	F12	VF20	XF40	MS60	MS63
2011	500	PF65 85.00				

KM# 359 2 DOLLARS
15.57 g., 0.925 Silver 0.4601 oz. ASW, 35 mm. **Obv:** National arms **Rev:** Atelopus Cerus, purple frog in color

Date	Mintage	F12	VF20	XF40	MS60	MS63
2011	500	PF65 85.00				

KM# 360 2 DOLLARS
15.50 g., 0.925 Silver 0.458 oz. ASW, 35 mm. **Rev:** Bombus Latreille - Bumble bee in color

Date	Mintage	F12	VF20	XF40	MS60	MS63
2011	1,000	PF65 100				

KM# 361 2 DOLLARS
15.57 g., 0.925 Silver 0.4601 oz. ASW, 35 mm. **Rev:** John Paul II with cross croizer, doves

Date	Mintage	F12	VF20	XF40	MS60	MS63
2011	1,000	PF65 60.00				

KM# 362 2 DOLLARS
25.00 g., 0.925 Silver 0.7387 oz. ASW, 38.61 mm. **Obv:** National Arms **Rev:** Abu Simbel temple entrance with insert

Date	Mintage	F12	VF20	XF40	MS60	MS63
2011	999	PF65 100				

KM# 363 2 DOLLARS
25.00 g., 0.925 Silver 0.7387 oz. ASW, 41x31 mm. **Subject:** Opera - Carmen **Rev:** Couple kissing in color, two other opera scenes **Shape:** Rectangle

Date	Mintage	F12	VF20	XF40	MS60	MS63
2011	999	PF65 75.00				

KM# 366 2 DOLLARS
25.00 g., 0.925 Silver 0.7387 oz. ASW, 38.61 mm. **Subject:** Princess of the Sea **Rev:** Apricot pearl and shell

Date	Mintage	F12	VF20	XF40	MS60	MS63
2011	2,500	PF65 100				

KM# 409 2 DOLLARS
25.00 g., 0.925 Silver 0.7387 oz. ASW, 38.61 mm. **Obv:** National arms **Rev:** Harry Houdini bust at left, top had and wand at right

Date	Mintage	F12	VF20	XF40	MS60	MS63
2011	—	PF65 60.00				

KM# 442 2 DOLLARS
Silver, 38.61 mm. **Obv:** National arms **Rev:** Giant Prickly Stick Insect in color on flora

Date	Mintage	F12	VF20	XF40	MS60	MS63
2011	—	PF65 100				

KM# 456 2 DOLLARS
15.50 g., 0.925 Silver 0.458 oz. ASW, 35 mm. **Subject:** World of Insects: Bombus Bee

Date	Mintage	F12	VF20	XF40	MS60	MS63
2011 Proof	1,000	—				

KM# 426 2 DOLLARS
15.50 g., Silver, 35 mm. **Obv:** National arms **Rev:** Jansa Gora Monastery, Pope John Paul II, and rose

Date	Mintage	F12	VF20	XF40	MS60	MS63
2012	—	PF65 50.00				

KM# 433 2 DOLLARS
25.00 g., 0.925 Silver 0.7387 oz. ASW, 45x45 mm. **Obv:** National arms **Rev:** Winged heart **Shape:** Heart

Date	Mintage	F12	VF20	XF40	MS60	MS63
2012	—	PF65 55.00				

KM# 467 2 DOLLARS
15.50 g., 0.925 Silver 0.458 oz. ASW, 35 mm. **Subject:** Bible stories - Birth of Jesus

Date	Mintage	F12	VF20	XF40	MS60	MS63
2012	1,000	PF65 100				

KM# 457 2 DOLLARS
15.55 g., Silver, 35 mm. **Subject:** World of Frogs - Litoria Caerulea

Date	Mintage	F12	VF20	XF40	MS60	MS63
2013	Est. 1000	PF65 55.00				

KM# 459 2 DOLLARS
15.55 g., Silver, 35 mm. **Series:** Butterfly

Date	Mintage	F12	VF20	XF40	MS60	MS63
2013	Est. 1000	PF65 55.00				

KM# 460 2 DOLLARS
15.50 g., Silver, 35 mm. **Subject:** 2nd Commandment

Date	Mintage	F12	VF20	XF40	MS60	MS63
2013	Est. 1000	PF65 65.00				

KM# 53 5 DOLLARS
25.00 g., 0.900 Silver 0.7187 oz. ASW, 37.2 mm. **Series:** Marine Life Protection **Obv:** Neptune **Rev:** Multicolor jellyfish **Edge:** Reeded

Date	Mintage	F12	VF20	XF40	MS60	MS63
2001	—	PF65 75.00				

KM# 75 5 DOLLARS
25.00 g., 0.900 Silver 0.7187 oz. ASW, 37.2 mm. **Subject:** Marine Life Protection **Obv:** Neptune behind Polynesian ship and value **Rev:** Moorish-Idol fish **Edge:** Reeded

Date	Mintage	F12	VF20	XF40	MS60	MS63
2001	—	PF65 75.00				

KM# 76 5 DOLLARS
Silver, 37.2 mm. **Subject:** Marine Life Protection **Obv:** Neptune riding seahorse and value **Rev:** Fish **Edge:** Reeded

Date	Mintage	F12	VF20	XF40	MS60	MS63
2001	—	PF65 75.00				

KM# 115 5 DOLLARS
25.00 g., 0.900 Silver 0.7187 oz. ASW, 37.2 mm. **Subject:** Marine Life Protection **Obv:** Neptune waist deep in water above value with mermaid to the left and behind **Rev:** Multicolor iridescent fish scene **Edge:** Reeded

Date	Mintage	F12	VF20	XF40	MS60	MS63
2001	—	PF65 70.00				

KM# 331 5 DOLLARS
25.00 g., 0.900 Silver 0.7187 oz. ASW, 38.61 mm. **Rev:** Angelfish

Date	Mintage	F12	VF20	XF40	MS60	MS63
2001	—	PF65 50.00				

KM# 77 5 DOLLARS
25.00 g., 0.900 Silver 0.7187 oz. ASW, 37.2 mm. **Subject:** Marine Life Protection **Obv:** Neptune in shell boat **Rev:** Blue Tang Fish **Edge:** Reeded

Date	Mintage	F12	VF20	XF40	MS60	MS63
2002	—	PF65 75.00				

KM# 78 5 DOLLARS
25.00 g., 0.900 Silver 0.7187 oz. ASW, 37.2 mm. **Subject:** Marine Life Protection **Obv:** Neptune in sea chariot **Rev:** Multicolor whales **Edge:** Reeded

Date	Mintage	F12	VF20	XF40	MS60	MS63
2002	—	PF65 75.00				

KM# 79 5 DOLLARS
25.00 g., 0.900 Silver 0.7187 oz. ASW, 37.2 mm. **Subject:** Marine Life Protection **Obv:** Zeus and value **Rev:** Multicolor puffer fish **Edge:** Reeded

Date	Mintage	F12	VF20	XF40	MS60	MS63
2002	—	PF65 75.00				

KM# 80 5 DOLLARS
25.00 g., 0.900 Silver 0.7187 oz. ASW, 37.2 mm. **Subject:**

Marine Life Protection **Obv:** Neptune standing behind Polynesian ship **Rev:** Multicolor Jellyfish **Edge:** Reeded

Date	Mintage	F12	VF20	XF40	MS60	MS63
2002	—		PF65 70.00			

KM# 102 5 DOLLARS
25.00 g., 0.900 Silver 0.7187 oz. ASW, 32 mm. **Subject:** Marine Life Protection **Obv:** Neptune in sea chariot with two merhorses **Rev:** Two multicolor reflective fish

Date	Mintage	F12	VF20	XF40	MS60	MS63
2002	—		PF65 60.00			

KM# 332 5 DOLLARS
25.00 g., 0.900 Silver 0.7187 oz. ASW, 38.61 mm. **Rev:** Blowfish

Date	Mintage	F12	VF20	XF40	MS60	MS63
2002	Est. 3000	PF65 55.00				

KM# 103 5 DOLLARS
25.00 g., 0.900 Silver 0.7187 oz. ASW, 32 mm. **Subject:** Marine Life Protection **Obv:** Neptune standing in waves **Rev:** Multicolor starfish

Date	Mintage	F12	VF20	XF40	MS60	MS63
2003	—		PF65 60.00			

KM# 104 5 DOLLARS
25.00 g., 0.900 Silver 0.7187 oz. ASW, 32 mm. **Subject:** Marine Life Protection **Obv:** Neptune standing in sea chariot **Rev:** Two multicolor reflective fish

Date	Mintage	F12	VF20	XF40	MS60	MS63
2003	—		PF65 60.00			

KM# 105 5 DOLLARS
25.00 g., 0.900 Silver 0.7187 oz. ASW, 32 mm. **Subject:** Marine Life Protection **Rev:** Multicolor Orca

Date	Mintage	F12	VF20	XF40	MS60	MS63
2003	—		PF65 60.00			

KM# 106 5 DOLLARS
25.00 g., 0.900 Silver 0.7187 oz. ASW, 32 mm. **Subject:** Marine Life Protection **Obv:** Neptune in sea chariot **Rev:** Multicolor Napoleon Fish

Date	Mintage	F12	VF20	XF40	MS60	MS63
2003	—		PF65 60.00			

KM# 333 5 DOLLARS
25.00 g., 0.900 Silver 0.7187 oz. ASW, 38.61 mm. **Rev:** Crab

Date	Mintage	F12	VF20	XF40	MS60	MS63
2003	Est. 3000	PF65 55.00				

KM# 81 5 DOLLARS
25.00 g., 0.900 Silver 0.7187 oz. ASW, 37.2 mm. **Subject:** Marine Life Protection **Obv:** Neptune with treasure chest **Rev:** Clownfish **Edge:** Reeded

Date	Mintage	F12	VF20	XF40	MS60	MS63
2004	—		PF65 75.00			

KM# 107 5 DOLLARS
25.00 g., 0.900 Silver 0.7187 oz. ASW, 32 mm. **Subject:** Marine Life Protection **Obv:** Neptune seated behind mermaid **Rev:** Multicolor school of sweetlips fish

Date	Mintage	F12	VF20	XF40	MS60	MS63
2004	—		PF65 60.00			

KM# 108 5 DOLLARS
25.00 g., 0.900 Silver 0.7187 oz. ASW, 32 mm. **Subject:** Marine Life Protection **Obv:** Standing Neptune and ship **Rev:** Multicolor Porcupine fish

Date	Mintage	F12	VF20	XF40	MS60	MS63
2004	—		PF65 75.00			

KM# 109 5 DOLLARS
25.00 g., 0.900 Silver 0.7187 oz. ASW, 32 mm. **Subject:** Marine Life Protection **Obv:** Neptune in sea chariot **Rev:** Multicolor Loggerhead turtle

Date	Mintage	F12	VF20	XF40	MS60	MS63
2004	—		PF65 75.00			

KM# 110 5 DOLLARS
25.00 g., 0.900 Silver 0.7187 oz. ASW, 32 mm. **Subject:** Marine Life Protection **Obv:** Neptune and merhorse **Rev:** Multicolor dolphin head

Date	Mintage	F12	VF20	XF40	MS60	MS63
2004	—		PF65 75.00			

KM# 111 5 DOLLARS
25.00 g., 0.900 Silver 0.7187 oz. ASW, 32 mm. **Subject:** Marine Life Protection **Obv:** Neptune flanked by mermaids **Rev:** Multicolor sea horse

Date	Mintage	F12	VF20	XF40	MS60	MS63
2005	—		PF65 75.00			

KM# 113 5 DOLLARS
25.00 g., 0.900 Silver 0.7187 oz. ASW, 32 mm. **Subject:** Marine Life Protection **Obv:** Neptune flanked by mermaids **Rev:** Multicolor fish with ring-like stripes **Edge:** Reeded

Date	Mintage	F12	VF20	XF40	MS60	MS63
2005	—		PF65 75.00			

KM# 114 5 DOLLARS
25.00 g., 0.900 Silver 0.7187 oz. ASW, 32 mm. **Subject:** Marine Life Protection **Obv:** Neptune in shell boat talking to a dolphin **Rev:** Multicolor reef fish scene **Edge:** Reeded

Date	Mintage	F12	VF20	XF40	MS60	MS63
2006	—		PF65 75.00			

KM# 143 5 DOLLARS
25.00 g., 0.925 Silver 0.7387 oz. ASW **Subject:** Nantan Meteroite fall, May 1516 **Obv:** Shield **Rev:** Farmer and oxen plowing field, meteorite insert

Date	Mintage	F12	VF20	XF40	MS60	MS63
2006	2,500	PF65 100				

KM# 185 5 DOLLARS
24.85 g., 0.999 Silver 0.793 oz. ASW, 38.6 mm. **Rev:** Black
pearl oyster

Date	Mintage	F12	VF20	XF40	MS60	MS63
2006	2,500	PF65 300				

KM# 186 5 DOLLARS
25.00 g., 0.999 Silver 0.7978 oz. ASW, 38.61 mm. **Subject:**
Pacific Wildlife **Rev:** Rainbow Lorikeet head left

Date	Mintage	F12	VF20	XF40	MS60	MS63
2006	5,000	PF65 55.00				

KM# 187 5 DOLLARS
25.00 g., 0.999 Silver 0.7978 oz. ASW, 38.61 mm. **Subject:**
Pacific Wildlife **Rev:** Eclectus Parrot head right

Date	Mintage	F12	VF20	XF40	MS60	MS63
2006	5,000	PF65 55.00				

KM# 188 5 DOLLARS
25.00 g., 0.999 Silver 0.7978 oz. ASW, 38.61 mm. **Subject:**
Pacific Wildlife **Rev:** Fruit dove head right

Date	Mintage	F12	VF20	XF40	MS60	MS63
2006	5,000	PF65 55.00				

KM# 189 5 DOLLARS
31.11 g., 0.999 Silver 0.9926 oz. ASW, 38.61 mm. **Subject:**
One ounce of luck **Rev:** Four-leaf clover

Date	Mintage	F12	VF20	XF40	MS60	MS63
2006	5,000	PF65 70.00				

KM# 190 5 DOLLARS
25.00 g., 0.925 Silver 0.7387 oz. ASW, 38.61 mm. **Subject:**
Dream Island **Rev:** Pacific island scene - beach, boat and
sunset

Date	Mintage	F12	VF20	XF40	MS60	MS63
2006	5,000	PF65 50.00				

KM# 443 5 DOLLARS
25.00 g., 0.925 Silver 0.7387 oz. ASW, 38.61 mm. **Obv:**
National arms **Rev:** Volcano, lava in color

Date	Mintage	F12	VF20	XF40	MS60	MS63
2006	—	PF65 100				

KM# 119 5 DOLLARS
25.00 g., 0.900 Silver 0.7187 oz. ASW, 38.61 mm. **Series:**
Marine Life Protection **Obv:** Neptune reclining with trident,
mermaid at his side **Obv. Legend:** REPUBLIC OF PALAU **Rev:**
Multicolor Doctor Fish

Date	Mintage	F12	VF20	XF40	MS60	MS63
2007	1,500	PF65 120				

KM# 122 5 DOLLARS
25.00 g., 0.500 Silver 0.3993 oz. ASW, 38.61 mm. **Obv:** Shield
with Neptune holding trident, mermaid reclining at his side,
RAINBOW'S / End below **Obv. Legend:** REPUBLIC OF PALAU
Rev: Red racing car 3/4 right **Rev. Legend:** FERRARI - 60
YEARS ANNIVERSARY

Date	Mintage	F12	VF20	XF40	MS60	MS63
ND-2007	2,500	PF65 75.00				

KM# 136 5 DOLLARS
25.00 g., 0.925 Silver 0.7387 oz. ASW, 38.61 mm. **Series:**
Pacific Wildlife **Obv:** National arms **Obv. Legend:** REPUBLIC
OF PALAU **Rev:** Saltwater Crocodile with green crystal eye

Date	Mintage	F12	VF20	XF40	MS60	MS63
2007	2,500	PF65 65.00				

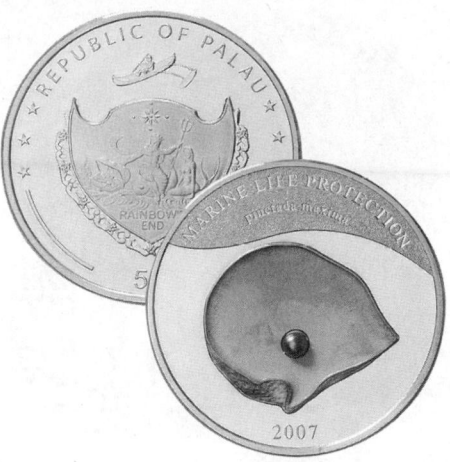

KM# 138 5 DOLLARS
24.70 g., Silver, 38.6 mm. **Series:** Marine Life Protection **Obv:**
National arms with Neptune and mermaid **Rev:** Pearl in oyster
shell - multicolor **Edge:** Reeded

Date	Mintage	F12	VF20	XF40	MS60	MS63
2007	2,500	PF65 185				

KM# 151 5 DOLLARS
25.00 g., 0.925 Silver 0.7387 oz. ASW, 38.6 mm. **Subject:**
Pacific Wildlife **Obv:** Shield **Rev:** Multicolor nautilus shell

Date	Mintage	F12	VF20	XF40	MS60	MS63
2007	—	PF65 70.00				

KM# 152 5 DOLLARS
25.00 g., 0.925 Silver 0.7387 oz. ASW **Subject:** Pacific Wildlife
Obv: Shield **Rev:** Multicolor starfish

Date	Mintage	F12	VF20	XF40	MS60	MS63
2007	—	PF65 70.00				

KM# 153 5 DOLLARS
25.00 g., 0.925 Silver 0.7387 oz. ASW **Subject:** Good heavens!
Obv: Multicolor devil and angel child **Shape:** Heart

Date	Mintage	F12	VF20	XF40	MS60	MS63
2007	2,500	PF65 65.00				

KM# 428 5 DOLLARS
25.00 g., 0.999 Silver 0.7978 oz. ASW, 38.61 mm. **Obv:** Water Vial and National arms **Rev:** Statue of Mary at Lourds, Water Vial

Date	Mintage	F12	VF20	XF40	MS60	MS63
2007	5,000	PF65 100				

KM# 137 5 DOLLARS
24.70 g., 0.925 Silver 0.7298 oz. ASW, 38.5 mm. **Obv:** Outrigger canoe above shield **Obv. Legend:** REPUBLIC OF PALAU **Rev:** Pearl in colorized shell **Rev. Legend:** MARINE LIFE PROTECTION / Pearl of the sea **Edge:** Reeded

Date	Mintage	F12	VF20	XF40	MS60	MS63
2008	2,500	PF65 125				

KM# 168 5 DOLLARS
25.00 g., 0.925 Silver 0.7387 oz. ASW, 30x45 mm. **Obv:** Shield **Rev:** Don Quixote in armor **Shape:** Vertical oval

Date	Mintage	F12	VF20	XF40	MS60	MS63
2008	—	PF65 70.00				

KM# 169 5 DOLLARS
25.00 g., 0.925 Silver 0.7387 oz. ASW, 37.2 mm. **Subject:** Pacific Wildlife **Obv:** Shield **Rev:** Multicolor hologram, blue butterfly (Papilio Pericles)

Date	Mintage	F12	VF20	XF40	MS60	MS63
2008	2,500	PF65 60.00				

KM# 170 5 DOLLARS
25.00 g., 0.925 Silver 0.7387 oz. ASW, 37.2 mm. **Subject:** Pacific Wildlife **Obv:** Shield **Rev:** Multicolor sulphur butterfly (Hebomoia Leucippe)

Date	Mintage	F12	VF20	XF40	MS60	MS63
2008	2,500	PF65 60.00				

KM# 171 5 DOLLARS
25.00 g., 0.925 Silver 0.7387 oz. ASW, 37.2 mm. **Subject:** Pacific Wildlife **Obv:** Shield **Rev:** Multicolor hologram, butterfly

Date	Mintage	F12	VF20	XF40	MS60	MS63
2008	2,500	PF65 60.00				

KM# 172 5 DOLLARS
25.00 g., 0.925 Silver 0.7387 oz. ASW, 38.6 mm. **Subject:** Telescope, 400th Anniversary **Obv:** Shield **Rev:** Hans Lippersheg, lens insert

Date	Mintage	F12	VF20	XF40	MS60	MS63
2008 Matte finish	1,608	—	—	—	—	70.00

KM# 173 5 DOLLARS
25.00 g., 0.925 Silver 0.7387 oz. ASW, 38.6 mm. **Subject:** Telescope, 400th Anniversary **Obv:** Shield **Rev:** The Hubble Telescope, lens insert

Date	Mintage	F12	VF20	XF40	MS60	MS63
2008 Matte finish	1,608	—	—	—	—	70.00

KM# 174 5 DOLLARS
Copper-Nickel, 38.6 mm. **Subject:** Endangered Wildlife **Obv:** Shield **Rev:** Multicolor yellow fish

Date	Mintage	F12	VF20	XF40	MS60	MS63
2008 Proof	—	—	—	—	—	25.00

KM# 175 5 DOLLARS
25.00 g., 0.925 Silver 0.7387 oz. ASW, 38.6 mm. **Subject:** Everything for you **Obv:** Shield **Rev:** Multicolor, outstretched hand, ribbon above **Shape:** Heart

Date	Mintage	F12	VF20	XF40	MS60	MS63
2008	2,500	PF65 100				

KM# 192 5 DOLLARS
25.00 g., 0.925 Silver 0.7387 oz. ASW, 30x45 mm. **Subject:** Illusion Autum Leaves **Rev:** Gilt leaf **Shape:** Oval

Date	Mintage	F12	VF20	XF40	MS60	MS63
2008	2,500	PF65 75.00				

KM# 447 5 DOLLARS
25.00 g., 0.925 Silver 0.7387 oz. ASW, 38.61 mm. **Subject:** 2008 Summer Olympics **Obv:** National arms **Rev:** Kyacker paddeling right

Date	Mintage	F12	VF20	XF40	MS60	MS63
2008	—	PF65 75.00				

KM# 179 5 DOLLARS
25.00 g., 0.925 Silver 0.7387 oz. ASW, 38.61 mm. **Subject:** Scent of Paradise **Obv:** Shield **Rev:** Multicolor open coconut, scented

Date	Mintage	F12	VF20	XF40	MS60	MS63
2009	2,500	—	—	—	—	65.00

KM# 180 5 DOLLARS
25.00 g., 0.925 Silver 0.7387 oz. ASW, 38.5 mm. **Subject:** Jewels of the Sea **Obv:** Shield **Rev:** Multicolor blue oyster with inset pearl

Date	Mintage	F12	VF20	XF40	MS60	MS63
2009	2,500	PF65 150				

KM# 181 5 DOLLARS
25.00 g., 0.925 Silver 0.7387 oz. ASW, 38.5 mm. **Subject:** Louis Braille, 200th Anniversary of Birth **Obv:** Shield **Rev:** Portrait of Braile

Date	Mintage	F12	VF20	XF40	MS60	MS63
2009 Matte finish	2,500	—	—	—	—	45.00

KM# 182 5 DOLLARS
25.00 g., 0.925 Silver 0.7387 oz. ASW **Subject:** Missing you **Obv:** Shield **Rev:** Two angels, multicolor, crystal insert **Shape:** Heart

Date	Mintage	F12	VF20	XF40	MS60	MS63
2009	2,500	PF65 55.00				

KM# 196 5 DOLLARS
25.00 g., 0.925 Silver 0.7387 oz. ASW, 38.61 mm. **Subject:** Pacific Wildlife **Rev:** Angelfish

Date	Mintage	F12	VF20	XF40	MS60	MS63
2009	2,500	PF65 60.00				

KM# 197 5 DOLLARS
25.00 g., 0.925 Silver 0.7387 oz. ASW, 38.61 mm. **Subject:** Pacific Wildlife **Rev:** Barn Swallow

Date	Mintage	F12	VF20	XF40	MS60	MS63
2009	2,500	PF65 60.00				

KM# 198 5 DOLLARS
25.00 g., 0.925 Silver 0.7387 oz. ASW, 38.61 mm. **Subject:** Pacific Wildlife **Rev:** Gecko

Date	Mintage	F12	VF20	XF40	MS60	MS63
2009	2,500	PF65 60.00				

KM# 199 5 DOLLARS
25.00 g., 0.925 Silver 0.7387 oz. ASW, 38.61 mm. **Subject:** Exceptional Animals **Rev:** Bird of Paradise

Date	Mintage	F12	VF20	XF40	MS60	MS63
2009	2,500	PF65 55.00				

KM# 200 5 DOLLARS
25.00 g., 0.925 Silver 0.7387 oz. ASW, 38.61 mm. **Subject:** Exceptional Animals **Rev:** Peacock

Date	Mintage	F12	VF20	XF40	MS60	MS63
2009	2,500	PF65 55.00				

KM# 201 5 DOLLARS
25.00 g., 0.925 Silver 0.7387 oz. ASW, 38.61 mm. **Subject:** Marine Life Protection **Rev:** Lionfish

Date	Mintage	F12	VF20	XF40	MS60	MS63
2009	1,500	PF65 65.00				

KM# 202 5 DOLLARS
25.00 g., 0.999 Silver 0.7978 oz. ASW, 38.61 mm. **Subject:** Fall of the Berlin Wall **Rev:** Brandenburg Gate, half with and half without wall

Date	Mintage	F12	VF20	XF40	MS60	MS63
2009	2,009	PF65 110				

KM# 203 5 DOLLARS
20.00 g., 0.925 Silver 0.591 oz. ASW, 38.61 mm. **Rev:** Sail training vessel Pamir

Date	Mintage	F12	VF20	XF40	MS60	MS63
2009	2,500	PF65 70.00				

KM# 204 5 DOLLARS
25.00 g., 0.925 Silver 0.7387 oz. ASW, 38.61 mm. **Subject:** Wonders of the Ancient World **Rev:** Lighthouse at Alexandria

Date	Mintage	F12	VF20	XF40	MS60	MS63
2009	2,500	PF65 85.00				

KM# 205 5 DOLLARS
25.00 g., 0.925 Silver 0.7387 oz. ASW **Subject:** Wonders of the Ancient World **Rev:** Statue of Zeus

Date	Mintage	F12	VF20	XF40	MS60	MS63
2009	2,500	PF65 85.00				

KM# 206 5 DOLLARS
25.00 g., 0.925 Silver 0.7387 oz. ASW, 38.61 mm. **Subject:** Wonders of the Ancient World **Rev:** Hanging Gardens of Babylon

Date	Mintage	F12	VF20	XF40	MS60	MS63
2009	2,500	PF65 85.00				

KM# 207 5 DOLLARS
25.00 g., 0.925 Silver 0.7387 oz. ASW, 38.61 mm. **Subject:** Wonders of the Ancient World **Rev:** Mausoleum of Halicarnassus

Date	Mintage	F12	VF20	XF40	MS60	MS63
2009	2,500	PF65 85.00				

KM# 208 5 DOLLARS
25.00 g., 0.925 Silver 0.7387 oz. ASW, 38.61 mm. **Subject:**
Wonders of the Ancient World **Rev:** Pyramids of Giza

Date	Mintage	F12	VF20	XF40	MS60	MS63
2009	2,500	PF65 85.00				

KM# 209 5 DOLLARS
25.00 g., 0.925 Silver 0.7387 oz. ASW, 38.61 mm. **Subject:**
Wonders of the Ancient World **Rev:** Temple of Artemis

Date	Mintage	F12	VF20	XF40	MS60	MS63
2009	2,500	PF65 85.00				

KM# 210 5 DOLLARS
25.00 g., 0.925 Silver 0.7387 oz. ASW, 38.61 mm. **Subject:**
Wonders of the Ancient World **Rev:** Colossus of Rhodes

Date	Mintage	F12	VF20	XF40	MS60	MS63
2009	2,500	PF65 85.00				

KM# 211 5 DOLLARS
25.00 g., 0.925 Silver 0.7387 oz. ASW, 38.6 mm. **Subject:**
Flora and Mountains of the Alps **Rev:** Zugspitze and blue flower

Date	Mintage	F12	VF20	XF40	MS60	MS63
2009	2,500	PF65 65.00				

KM# 212 5 DOLLARS
25.00 g., 0.925 Silver 0.7387 oz. ASW, 38.61 mm. **Subject:**
Flora and Mountains of the Alps **Rev:** Grossglockner and white
flower

Date	Mintage	F12	VF20	XF40	MS60	MS63
2009	2,500	PF65 65.00				

KM# 213 5 DOLLARS
25.00 g., 0.925 Silver 0.7387 oz. ASW, 38.61 mm. **Subject:**
Flora and Mountains of the Alps **Rev:** Matterhorn and pink
flower

Date	Mintage	F12	VF20	XF40	MS60	MS63
2009	2,500	PF65 65.00				

KM# 214 5 DOLLARS
25.00 g., 0.925 Silver 0.7387 oz. ASW, 38.61 mm. **Subject:**
Flora and Mountains of the Alps **Rev:** Dachstein and purple
flower

Date	Mintage	F12	VF20	XF40	MS60	MS63
2009	2,500	PF65 65.00				

KM# 215 5 DOLLARS
25.00 g., 0.925 Silver 0.7387 oz. ASW, 38.61 mm. **Subject:**
Flora and Mountains of the Alps **Rev:** Mont Blanc and orange
flower

Date	Mintage	F12	VF20	XF40	MS60	MS63
2009	2,500	PF65 65.00				

KM# 216 5 DOLLARS
25.00 g., 0.925 Silver 0.7387 oz. ASW, 38.61 mm. **Subject:**
Flora and Mountains of the Alps **Rev:** Watzmann and purple
flower

Date	Mintage	F12	VF20	XF40	MS60	MS63
2009	2,500	PF65 65.00				

KM# 217 5 DOLLARS
25.00 g., 0.925 Silver 0.7387 oz. ASW, 38.61 mm. **Subject:**
Flora and Mountains of the Alps **Rev:** Oetscher and yellow
flower

Date	Mintage	F12	VF20	XF40	MS60	MS63
2009	2,500	PF65 65.00				

KM# 218 5 DOLLARS
25.00 g., 0.925 Silver 0.7387 oz. ASW, 38.61 mm. **Subject:**
Flora and Mountains of the Alps **Rev:** Piz Buin and pink flower

Date	Mintage	F12	VF20	XF40	MS60	MS63
2009	2,500	PF65 65.00				

KM# 242 5 DOLLARS
20.00 g., 0.925 Silver 0.591 oz. ASW, 38.6 mm. **Subject:**
Finnish icebreaker Tarmo **Rev:** Ship left in ice pack

Date	Mintage	F12	VF20	XF40	MS60	MS63
2009	2,500	PF65 65.00				

KM# 264 5 DOLLARS
25.00 g., 0.925 Silver 0.7387 oz. ASW, 38.61 mm. **Subject:**
Treasures of the World - Emeralds **Rev:** Mule mine cart and
emerald insert

Date	Mintage	F12	VF20	XF40	MS60	MS63
2009 Antique	2,000	PF65 85.00				

KM# 265 5 DOLLARS
25.00 g., 0.925 Silver 0.7387 oz. ASW, 38.6 mm. **Obv:** Arms
Rev: Our Lady of the Gate of Dawn, partially gilt

Date	Mintage	F12	VF20	XF40	MS60	MS63
2009	1,000	PF65 75.00				

KM# 432 5 DOLLARS

25.00 g., 0.925 Silver 0.7387 oz. ASW, 45x45 mm. **Obv:** National arms **Rev:** Ladybug in color on flora **Rev. Legend:** Good Luck & Prosperity **Shape:** Heart

Date	Mintage	F12	VF20	XF40	MS60	MS63
2009	2,500	PF65 65.00				

KM# 248 5 DOLLARS

25.00 g., 0.925 Silver 0.7387 oz. ASW, 38.6 mm. **Subject:** Marine Life Protection **Rev:** Blue freshwater pearl set within multicolor shell

Date	Mintage	F12	VF20	XF40	MS60	MS63
2010	2,500	PF65 85.00				

KM# 249 5 DOLLARS

25.00 g., 0.925 Silver 0.7387 oz. ASW, 38.6 mm. **Subject:** Scent of Paradise - Sea breeze fragrance **Rev:** Female surfboarder in multicolor wave

Date	Mintage	F12	VF20	XF40	MS60	MS63
2010	2,500	—	—	—	—	65.00

KM# 289 5 DOLLARS

25.00 g., 0.925 Silver 0.7387 oz. ASW, 38.61 mm. **Obv:** National arms **Rev:** St. Basil's Cathedral in color

Date	Mintage	F12	VF20	XF40	MS60	MS63
2010	2,500	PF65 60.00				

KM# 290 5 DOLLARS

25.00 g., 0.925 Silver 0.7387 oz. ASW, 38.61 mm. **Obv:** National arms **Rev:** Statue of Liberty in color

Date	Mintage	F12	VF20	XF40	MS60	MS63
2010	2,500	PF65 60.00				

KM# 291 5 DOLLARS

25.00 g., 0.925 Silver 0.7387 oz. ASW, 38.61 mm. **Obv:** National arms **Rev:** Kiyomizu Temple in color

Date	Mintage	F12	VF20	XF40	MS60	MS63
2010	2,500	PF65 60.00				

KM# 292 5 DOLLARS

25.00 g., 0.925 Silver 0.7387 oz. ASW, 38.61 mm. **Obv:** National arms **Rev:** Neuschwanstein Castle in color

Date	Mintage	F12	VF20	XF40	MS60	MS63
2010	2,500	PF65 60.00				

KM# 293 5 DOLLARS

25.00 g., 0.925 Silver 0.7387 oz. ASW, 38.61 mm. **Obv:** National arms **Rev:** Mt. Everest and Meconopsis betonicifolia in color

Date	Mintage	F12	VF20	XF40	MS60	MS63
2010	250	PF65 60.00				

KM# 294 5 DOLLARS

25.00 g., 0.925 Silver 0.7387 oz. ASW, 38.61 mm. **Obv:** National arms **Rev:** Mt. Kilimanjaro and Protea kilimandscharica in color

Date	Mintage	F12	VF20	XF40	MS60	MS63
2010	2,500	PF65 60.00				

KM# 295 5 DOLLARS

25.00 g., 0.925 Silver 0.7387 oz. ASW, 38.61 mm. **Obv:** National arms **Rev:** Mt. Elbrus and Rhododendron in color

Date	Mintage	F12	VF20	XF40	MS60	MS63
2010	2,500	PF65 60.00				

KM# 296 5 DOLLARS

25.00 g., 0.925 Silver 0.7387 oz. ASW, 38.61 mm. **Obv:** National arms **Rev:** Carstensz Pyramid and Orchidacae in color

Date	Mintage	F12	VF20	XF40	MS60	MS63
2010	2,500	PF65 60.00				

KM# 297 5 DOLLARS

25.00 g., 0.925 Silver 0.7387 oz. ASW, 38.61 mm. **Obv:** National arms **Rev:** Mount McKinley and Anaphalis margaritacea in color

Date	Mintage	F12	VF20	XF40	MS60	MS63
2010	2,500	PF65 60.00				

KM# 298 5 DOLLARS

25.00 g., 0.925 Silver 0.7387 oz. ASW, 38.61 mm. **Obv:** National arms **Rev:** Mt. Aconcagua and Aechmea distichantha in color

Date	Mintage	F12	VF20	XF40	MS60	MS63
2010	2,500	PF65 60.00				

KM# 299 5 DOLLARS
25.00 g., 0.925 Silver 0.7387 oz. ASW, 38.61 mm. **Obv:** National arms **Rev:** Mt. Vinson and Colobanthus quitensis in color

Date	Mintage	F12	VF20	XF40	MS60	MS63
2010	2,500	PF65 60.00				

KM# 300 5 DOLLARS
25.00 g., 0.925 Silver 0.7387 oz. ASW, 38.61 mm. **Obv:** National arms **Rev:** Mt. Elger and Arnica montana in color

Date	Mintage	F12	VF20	XF40	MS60	MS63
2010	2,500	PF65 60.00				

KM# 301 5 DOLLARS
25.00 g., 0.925 Silver 0.7387 oz. ASW, 38.61 mm. **Obv:** National arms **Rev:** Ayers Rock and Calytrix longiflora in color

Date	Mintage	F12	VF20	XF40	MS60	MS63
2010	2,500	PF65 60.00				

KM# 302 5 DOLLARS
25.00 g., 0.925 Silver 0.7387 oz. ASW, 38.61 mm. **Obv:** National arms **Rev:** Mt. Alpspitze and Campanula alpina in color

Date	Mintage	F12	VF20	XF40	MS60	MS63
2010	2,500	PF65 60.00				

KM# 306 5 DOLLARS
25.00 g., 0.925 Silver 0.7387 oz. ASW, 38.61 mm. **Obv:** Naitonal arms **Rev:** Christmas star above winter home scene in color

Date	Mintage	F12	VF20	XF40	MS60	MS63
2010	2,500	PF65 60.00				

KM# 314 5 DOLLARS
25.00 g., 0.925 Silver 0.7387 oz. ASW, 38.61 mm. **Obv:** National arms **Rev:** Hammerhead shark in color image

Date	Mintage	F12	VF20	XF40	MS60	MS63
2010	1,500	PF65 70.00				

KM# 379 5 DOLLARS
25.00 g., 0.925 Silver 0.7387 oz. ASW, 38.61 mm. **Obv:** National arms **Rev:** Acropolis in color

Date	Mintage	F12	VF20	XF40	MS60	MS63
2010	2,500	PF65 50.00				

KM# 388 5 DOLLARS
25.00 g., 0.925 Silver 0.7387 oz. ASW **Obv:** National arms **Rev:** Angkor Wat in color **Shape:** 38.61

Date	Mintage	F12	VF20	XF40	MS60	MS63
2010	2,500	PF65 50.00				

KM# 389 5 DOLLARS
25.00 g., 0.925 Silver 0.7387 oz. ASW, 38.61 mm. **Obv:** National arms **Rev:** Statues of Easter Island in color

Date	Mintage	F12	VF20	XF40	MS60	MS63
2010	2,500	PF65 50.00				

KM# 390 5 DOLLARS
25.00 g., 0.925 Silver 0.7387 oz. ASW, 38.61 mm. **Obv:** National arms **Rev:** Eiffel Tower in color

Date	Mintage	F12	VF20	XF40	MS60	MS63
2010	2,500	PF65 50.00				

KM# 430 5 DOLLARS
25.00 g., 0.925 Silver 0.7387 oz. ASW, 38.61 mm. **Obv:** National arms **Rev:** Gem engraver cutting saphire on wheel

Date	Mintage	F12	VF20	XF40	MS60	MS63
2010 Antique patina	2,000	—	—	—	—	200

KM# 446 5 DOLLARS
25.00 g., 0.925 Silver 0.7387 oz. ASW, 38.61 mm. **Subject:** Mother Theresa of Calcutta, 100th Anniversary of Birth **Obv:** National arms **Rev:** Mother Theresa at left, blue color design of Sister's of Charity order habbit in field

Date	Mintage	F12	VF20	XF40	MS60	MS63
2010	—	PF65 80.00				

KM# 365 5 DOLLARS
25.00 g., 0.925 Silver 0.7387 oz. ASW, 38.61 mm. **Subject:** Cuddley Bear **Rev:** Teddy bear patch

Date	Mintage	F12	VF20	XF40	MS60	MS63
2011	—	PF65 75.00				

KM# 364 5 DOLLARS
25.00 g., 0.999 Silver 0.7978 oz. ASW **Subject:** Treasures of the World **Rev:** Mine scene, ruby insert

Date	Mintage	F12	VF20	XF40	MS60	MS63
2011 Antique patina	2,000	—	—	—	—	200

KM# 374 5 DOLLARS
25.00 g., 0.999 Silver 0.7978 oz. ASW, 30x38 mm. **Subject:** Oyster shell and pearl inset **Shape:** Irregular

Date	Mintage	F12	VF20	XF40	MS60	MS63
2011	2,000	—	—	—	—	450

KM# 376 5 DOLLARS
25.00 g., 0.925 Silver 0.7387 oz. ASW, 38.61 mm. **Obv:** National arms **Rev:** Potala Palace in color

Date	Mintage	F12	VF20	XF40	MS60	MS63
2011	2,500	PF65 50.00				

KM# 377 5 DOLLARS
25.00 g., 0.925 Silver 0.7387 oz. ASW, 38.61 mm. **Obv:** National arms **Rev:** Tower Bridge in color

Date	Mintage	F12	VF20	XF40	MS60	MS63
2011	2,500	PF65 50.00				

KM# 378 5 DOLLARS
25.00 g., 0.925 Silver 0.7387 oz. ASW, 38.61 mm. **Obv:** National arms **Rev:** Temple of Heaven in color

Date	Mintage	F12	VF20	XF40	MS60	MS63
2011	2,500	PF65 50.00				

KM# 380 5 DOLLARS
25.00 g., 0.925 Silver 0.7387 oz. ASW, 38.61 mm. **Obv:** National arms **Rev:** Stonehenge in color

Date	Mintage	F12	VF20	XF40	MS60	MS63
2011	2,500	PF65 50.00				

KM# 381 5 DOLLARS
25.00 g., 0.925 Silver 0.7387 oz. ASW, 38.61 mm. **Obv:** National arms **Rev:** Schonebrunn Palace in color

Date	Mintage	F12	VF20	XF40	MS60	MS63
2011	2,500	PF65 50.00				

KM# 382 5 DOLLARS
25.00 g., 0.925 Silver 0.7387 oz. ASW, 38.61 mm. **Obv:** National arms **Rev:** Chapel Bridge in color

Date	Mintage	F12	VF20	XF40	MS60	MS63
2011	2,500	PF65 50.00				

KM# 383 5 DOLLARS
25.00 g., 0.925 Silver 0.7387 oz. ASW, 38.61 mm. **Obv:** National arms **Rev:** Florence Cathedral

Date	Mintage	F12	VF20	XF40	MS60	MS63
2011	2,500	PF65 50.00				

KM# 384 5 DOLLARS
25.00 g., 0.925 Silver 0.7387 oz. ASW, 38.61 mm. **Obv:** National arms **Rev:** CN Tower in color

Date	Mintage	F12	VF20	XF40	MS60	MS63
2011	2,500	PF65 50.00				

KM# 385 5 DOLLARS
25.00 g., 0.925 Silver 0.7387 oz. ASW, 38.61 mm. **Obv:** National arms **Rev:** Timbuktu in color

Date	Mintage	F12	VF20	XF40	MS60	MS63
2011	2,500	PF65 50.00				

KM# 386 5 DOLLARS
25.00 g., 0.925 Silver 0.7387 oz. ASW, 38.61 mm. **Obv:** National arms **Rev:** Leaning Tower of Pisa in color

Date	Mintage	F12	VF20	XF40	MS60	MS63
2011	2,500	PF65 50.00				

KM# 387 5 DOLLARS
25.00 g., 0.925 Silver 0.7387 oz. ASW, 38.61 mm. **Obv:** National arms **Rev:** Sydney Opera House in color

Date	Mintage	F12	VF20	XF40	MS60	MS63
2011	2,500	PF65 50.00				

KM# 391 5 DOLLARS
25.00 g., 0.925 Silver 0.7387 oz. ASW, 38.61 mm. **Obv:** National arms **Rev:** Mount Rushmore in color

Date	Mintage	F12	VF20	XF40	MS60	MS63
2011	2,500	PF65 50.00				

KM# 392 5 DOLLARS
25.00 g., 0.925 Silver 0.7387 oz. ASW, 38.61 mm. **Obv:** National arms **Rev:** Persepolis - Shiraz in color

Date	Mintage	F12	VF20	XF40	MS60	MS63
2011	2,500	PF65 50.00				

KM# 393 5 DOLLARS
25.00 g., 0.925 Silver 0.7387 oz. ASW, 38.61 mm. **Obv:** National arms **Rev:** Alhambra in color

Date	Mintage	F12	VF20	XF40	MS60	MS63
2011	2,500	PF65 50.00				

KM# 397 5 DOLLARS
25.00 g., 0.925 Silver 0.7387 oz. ASW, 38.61 mm. **Obv:** National arms **Rev:** K-2 and flora in color

Date	Mintage	F12	VF20	XF40	MS60	MS63
2011	2,500	PF65 60.00				

KM# 398 5 DOLLARS
25.00 g., 0.925 Silver 0.7387 oz. ASW, 38.61 mm. **Obv:**
National arms **Rev:** Mount Kenya and flora in color

Date	Mintage	F12	VF20	XF40	MS60	MS63
2011	2,500	PF65 60.00				

KM# 399 5 DOLLARS
25.00 g., 0.925 Silver 0.7387 oz. ASW, 38.61 mm. **Obv:**
National arms **Rev:** Mount Logan and flora in color

Date	Mintage	F12	VF20	XF40	MS60	MS63
2011	2,500	PF65 60.00				

KM# 400 5 DOLLARS
25.00 g., 0.925 Silver 0.7387 oz. ASW, 38.61 mm. **Obv:**
National arms **Rev:** Mount Tyree and flora in color

Date	Mintage	F12	VF20	XF40	MS60	MS63
2011	2,500	PF65 60.00				

KM# 401 5 DOLLARS
25.00 g., 0.925 Silver 0.7387 oz. ASW, 38.61 mm. **Obv:**
National Arms **Rev:** Dyke-Tau and flora in color

Date	Mintage	F12	VF20	XF40	MS60	MS63
2011	2,500	PF65 60.00				

KM# 402 5 DOLLARS
25.00 g., 0.925 Silver 0.7387 oz. ASW, 38.61 mm. **Obv:**
National arms **Rev:** Ojos del Salado and flora in color

Date	Mintage	F12	VF20	XF40	MS60	MS63
2011	2,500	PF65 60.00				

KM# 403 5 DOLLARS
25.00 g., 0.925 Silver 0.7387 oz. ASW, 38.61 mm. **Obv:**
National arms **Rev:** Puncak Trikora and flora in color

Date	Mintage	F12	VF20	XF40	MS60	MS63
2011	2,500	PF65 60.00				

KM# 404 5 DOLLARS
25.00 g., 0.925 Silver 0.7387 oz. ASW, 38.61 mm. **Subject:**
Scent of Paradise **Obv:** National arms **Rev:** Large insence
burner in color

Date	Mintage	F12	VF20	XF40	MS60	MS63
2011	—	PF65 65.00				

KM# 434 5 DOLLARS
Silver Plated Copper, 35x35 mm. **Obv:** National arms **Rev:**
Ferrari FI 2000 in color

Date	Mintage	F12	VF20	XF40	MS60	MS63
2011	—	PF65 40.00				

KM# 435 5 DOLLARS
Silver Plated Copper, 35x35 mm. **Obv:** National arms **Rev:**
Ferrari 500 F-2

Date	Mintage	F12	VF20	XF40	MS60	MS63
2011	—	PF65 40.00				

KM# 436 5 DOLLARS
Silver Plated Copper, 45x45 mm. **Obv:** National arms **Rev:**
Ferrari F-2007

Date	Mintage	F12	VF20	XF40	MS60	MS63
2011	—	PF65 40.00				

KM# 437 5 DOLLARS
Silver Plated Copper, 35x35 mm. **Obv:** National arms **Rev:**
Ferrari 158 F-1

Date	Mintage	F12	VF20	XF40	MS60	MS63
2011	—	PF65 40.00				

KM# 438 5 DOLLARS
Silver Plated Copper, 35x35 mm. **Obv:** National arms **Rev:**
Ferrari 246 F-1

Date	Mintage	F12	VF20	XF40	MS60	MS63
2011	—	PF65 40.00				

KM# 439 5 DOLLARS
Silver Plated Copper, 35x35 mm. **Obv:** National arms **Rev:**
Ferrari D-50

Date	Mintage	F12	VF20	XF40	MS60	MS63
2011	—	PF65 40.00				

KM# 440 5 DOLLARS
Silver Plated Copper, 35x35 mm. **Obv:** National arms **Rev:**
Ferrari 126 C-2

Date	Mintage	F12	VF20	XF40	MS60	MS63
2011	—	PF65 40.00				

KM# 441 5 DOLLARS
Silver Plated Copper, 35x35 mm. **Obv:** National arms **Rev:** Ferrari 312 T

Date	Mintage	F12	VF20	XF40	MS60	MS63
2011	—	PF65 40.00				

KM# 444 5 DOLLARS
25.00 g., 0.925 Silver 0.7387 oz. ASW, 38.61 mm. **Obv:** National arms **Rev:** Pear in white clam shell

Date	Mintage	F12	VF20	XF40	MS60	MS63
2011	—	PF65 125				

KM# 415 5 DOLLARS
25.00 g., 0.925 Silver 0.7387 oz. ASW, 38.61 mm. **Obv:** National arms **Rev:** Brandenburg Gate in color

Date	Mintage	F12	VF20	XF40	MS60	MS63
2012	2,500	PF65 80.00				

KM# 416 5 DOLLARS
25.00 g., 0.925 Silver 0.7387 oz. ASW, 38.61 mm. **Obv:** National arms **Rev:** Itsukushima Shrine in color

Date	Mintage	F12	VF20	XF40	MS60	MS63
2012	2,500	PF65 80.00				

KM# 417 5 DOLLARS
25.00 g., 0.925 Silver 0.7387 oz. ASW, 38.61 mm. **Obv:** National arms **Rev:** Palmyra ruins in color

Date	Mintage	F12	VF20	XF40	MS60	MS63
2012	2,500	PF65 80.00				

KM# 418 5 DOLLARS
25.00 g., 0.925 Silver 0.7387 oz. ASW, 38.61 mm. **Obv:** National arms **Rev:** St. Patrick's Cathedral, Dublin in color

Date	Mintage	F12	VF20	XF40	MS60	MS63
2012	2,500	PF65 80.00				

KM# 419 5 DOLLARS
25.00 g., 0.925 Silver 0.7387 oz. ASW, 38.61 mm. **Obv:** National arms **Rev:** Hagia Sophia in color

Date	Mintage	F12	VF20	XF40	MS60	MS63
2012	2,500	PF65 80.00				

KM# 420 5 DOLLARS
25.00 g., 0.925 Silver 0.7387 oz. ASW, 38.61 mm. **Obv:** National arms **Rev:** Vienna Ferris Wheel in color

Date	Mintage	F12	VF20	XF40	MS60	MS63
2012	2,500	PF65 80.00				

KM# 421 5 DOLLARS
25.00 g., 0.925 Silver 0.7387 oz. ASW, 38.61 mm. **Obv:** National arms **Rev:** Teotihuacan in color

Date	Mintage	F12	VF20	XF40	MS60	MS63
2012	2,500	PF65 80.00				

KM# 422 5 DOLLARS
25.00 g., 0.925 Silver 0.7387 oz. ASW, 38.61 mm. **Obv:** National arms **Rev:** Western Wall in color

Date	Mintage	F12	VF20	XF40	MS60	MS63
2012	2,500	PF65 80.00				

KM# 425 5 DOLLARS
25.00 g., 0.925 Silver 0.7387 oz. ASW, 38.61 mm. **Obv:** National arms **Rev:** Four leaf clover in green

Date	Mintage	F12	VF20	XF40	MS60	MS63
2012	—	PF65 100				

KM# 427 5 DOLLARS
Silver, 20x30 mm. **Obv:** Haliotis oyster shell, National arms **Rev:** Oyster shell with pearl and multicolors **Shape:** Irregular

Date	Mintage	F12	VF20	XF40	MS60	MS63
2012 Matte finish	—	PF65 150				

KM# 466 5 DOLLARS
31.10 g., 0.999 Silver 0.9926 oz. ASW, 38.6 mm. **Rev:** Red Squirrel, crystal insert

Date	Mintage	F12	VF20	XF40	MS60	MS63
125 (2012) Antique Patina	1,000	PF65 100				

KM# 462 5 DOLLARS
20.00 g., Silver, 38.61 mm. **Subject:** Seven Wonders of the World **Rev:** Lighthouse at Alexandria in color

Date	Mintage	F12	VF20	XF40	MS60	MS63
2013	2,500	PF65 65.00				

KM# 463 5 DOLLARS
20.00 g., 0.925 Silver 0.591 oz. ASW, 38.61 mm. **Subject:** Wonders of the World **Obv:** National arms **Rev:** Facade of St. Peter's Basilica in color

Date	Mintage	F12	VF20	XF40	MS60	MS63
2013	Est. 2500	PF65 75.00				

KM# 464 5 DOLLARS
20.00 g., 0.925 Silver 0.591 oz. ASW, 38.61 mm. **Subject:** Seven Wonders of the World **Obv:** National arms **Rev:** Big Ben in color

Date	Mintage	F12	VF20	XF40	MS60	MS63
2013	—	PF65 75.00				

KM# 191 10 DOLLARS
62.21 g., 0.999 Silver 1.9851 oz. ASW, 50 mm. **Subject:** Tiffany
Art **Rev:** Renaissance doorway

Date	Mintage	F12	VF20	XF40	MS60	MS63
2007 Matte Proof	999	PF65 1,200				

KM# 193 10 DOLLARS
62.21 g., 0.999 Silver 1.9852 oz. ASW, 50 mm. **Subject:** Tiffany
Art **Rev:** Mannerism, staircase design

Date	Mintage	F12	VF20	XF40	MS60	MS63
2008 Matte Proof	999	PF65 900				

KM# 194 10 DOLLARS
62.21 g., 0.999 Silver 1.9852 oz. ASW, 42x42 mm. **Subject:**
WWII Battleships **Rev:** Japan's Yamato

Date	Mintage	F12	VF20	XF40	MS60	MS63
2008	1,000	PF65 300				

KM# 195 10 DOLLARS
62.21 g., 0.999 Silver 1.9852 oz. ASW, 42x42 mm. **Subject:**
WWII Battleships **Rev:** USS Missouri, gilt eagle above

Date	Mintage	F12	VF20	XF40	MS60	MS63
2008	1,000	PF65 175				

KM# 184 10 DOLLARS
62.25 g., 0.999 Silver 1.9865 oz. ASW, 42x42 mm. **Subject:**
WWII Battleships **Obv:** Shield **Rev:** Bismarck, gilt Iron Cross
above **Shape:** Square

Date	Mintage	F12	VF20	XF40	MS60	MS63
2009	—	PF65 165				

KM# 219 10 DOLLARS
62.21 g., 0.999 Silver 1.9852 oz. ASW, 50 mm. **Subject:** Tiffany
Art **Rev:** Baroque facade

Date	Mintage	F12	VF20	XF40	MS60	MS63
2009 Matte Proof	—	PF65 600				

KM# 220 10 DOLLARS
62.21 g., 0.999 Silver 1.9852 oz. ASW, 50 mm. **Rev:** Amber
insert

Date	Mintage	F12	VF20	XF40	MS60	MS63
2009 Matte Proof	2,500	PF65 400				

KM# 221 10 DOLLARS
62.21 g., 0.999 Silver 1.9852 oz. ASW, 42x42 mm. **Subject:**
WWII Battleship **Rev:** Britains's HMS Prince of Wales, gilt
Union Jack above

Date	Mintage	F12	VF20	XF40	MS60	MS63
2009	1,000	PF65 145				

KM# 250 10 DOLLARS
62.20 g., 0.999 Silver 1.9849 oz. ASW, 42x42 mm. **Subject:**
Russian Battleship Marat **Rev:** Battleship sailing left

Date	Mintage	F12	VF20	XF40	MS60	MS63
2010	1,000	PF65 80.00				

KM# 252 10 DOLLARS
64.21 g., 0.999 Silver 2.0491 oz. ASW, 50 mm. **Subject:** Tiffany Art - Rococo **Obv:** Arms at lower right, glass insert **Rev:** Cherus at left, glass insert

Date	Mintage	F12	VF20	XF40	MS60	MS63
2010 Antique	999	—	—	—	—	650

KM# 304 10 DOLLARS
62.21 g., 0.925 Silver 1.8382 oz. ASW, 42x42 mm. **Obv:** National arms **Rev:** French Battleship Richelieu, gilt flag at top **Shape:** Square

Date	Mintage	F12	VF20	XF40	MS60	MS63
2010	1,000	PF65 100				

KM# 320 10 DOLLARS
62.20 g., 0.925 Silver 1.8379 oz. ASW, 55 mm. **Subject:** Sagrada Familia **Obv:** National arms **Rev:** Scenes from the Birth of Jesus, insert

Date	Mintage	F12	VF20	XF40	MS60	MS63
2010	2,500	PF65 115				

KM# 369 10 DOLLARS
62.20 g., 0.999 Silver 1.9849 oz. ASW, 42x42 mm. **Rev:** Battleship H.M.A.S. Australia, gilt flag above **Shape:** Square

Date	Mintage	F12	VF20	XF40	MS60	MS63
2011	—	PF65 150				

KM# 318 10 DOLLARS
62.21 g., 0.999 Silver 1.9852 oz. ASW, 50 mm. **Subject:** Tiffany Glass **Obv:** National arms **Rev:** Theater box, red glass insert

Date	Mintage	F12	VF20	XF40	MS60	MS63
2011 Antique patina	999	—	—	—	—	175

KM# 367 10 DOLLARS
62.20 g., 0.999 Silver 1.9849 oz. ASW, 50 mm. **Subject:** Neuschwanstein Castle **Obv:** Exterior of Castle **Rev:** Interior of castle, insert

Date	Mintage	F12	VF20	XF40	MS60	MS63
2011 Antique finish	2,500	—	—	—	375	—

KM# 368 10 DOLLARS
62.20 g., 0.999 Silver 1.9849 oz. ASW, 50 mm. **Subject:** Tiffany Art - Manueline **Rev:** Glass insert

Date	Mintage	F12	VF20	XF40	MS60	MS63
2011 Antique finish	999	—	—	—	650	—

KM# 395 10 DOLLARS
62.21 g., 0.999 Silver 1.9852 oz. ASW, 42x42 mm. **Obv:** National arms **Rev:** RN Vittorio Veneto

Date	Mintage	F12	VF20	XF40	MS60	MS63
2011	1,000	PF65 110				

KM# 411 10 DOLLARS
62.21 g., 0.999 Silver 1.9852 oz. ASW, 42x42 mm. **Subject:** Saint Patrick's Cathedral, New York **Obv:** Interior nave view, window of St. Patrick **Rev:** Exterior cathedral spires, window of St. Patrick

Date	Mintage	F12	VF20	XF40	MS60	MS63
2011 Antique patina	1,000	—	—	—	—	250

KM# 412 10 DOLLARS
62.21 g., 0.999 Silver 1.9852 oz. ASW, 42x42 mm. **Obv:** Santiago de Compostela interior statues, window of St. John the Baptist **Rev:** Santiago de Compostela exterior view

Date	Mintage	F12	VF20	XF40	MS60	MS63
2011 Antique patina	1,000	—	—	—	—	275

KM# 413 10 DOLLARS
62.21 g., 0.999 Silver 1.9852 oz. ASW, 42x42 mm. **Obv:** St. Peter's Bascilica, window of the Holy Spirit **Rev:** St. Peter's Bascilica, window of the Holy Spirit

Date	Mintage	F12	VF20	XF40	MS60	MS63
2011 Antique patina	1,000	—	—	—	—	275

KM# 414 10 DOLLARS
62.21 g., 0.999 Silver 1.9852 oz. ASW, 42x42 mm. **Obv:** Brasilia Cathedral, exterior arches, blue window **Rev:** Brasilia Cathedral, figures, blue window

Date	Mintage	F12	VF20	XF40	MS60	MS63
2011 Antique patina	1,000	—	—	—	—	275

KM# 423 10 DOLLARS
62.21 g., 0.999 Silver 1.9852 oz. ASW, 50 mm. **Subject:** Tiffany Glass, Neoclassicism **Obv:** Archway, green glass insert **Rev:** Alcove, green glass insert

Date	Mintage	F12	VF20	XF40	MS60	MS63
2012 Antique patina	999	—	—	—	—	625

KM# 424 10 DOLLARS
62.21 g., 0.999 Silver 1.9852 oz. ASW, 50 mm. **Obv:** Moscow Kremlin interior room, red glass insert **Rev:** Moscow Kremlin exterior, red glass insert

Date	Mintage	F12	VF20	XF40	MS60	MS63
2012 Antique patina	999	PF65 600				

KM# 458 10 DOLLARS
50.00 g., Silver, 42 x 42 mm. **Subject:** Votive Church Stained Glass

Date	Mintage	F12	VF20	XF40	MS60	MS63
2013	—	PF65 200				

KM# 176 20 DOLLARS
164.00 g., 0.999 Silver 5.2335 oz. ASW, 63 mm. **Obv:** Auto wheel cover **Rev:** Side sillouette of Corvette Z60

Date	Mintage	F12	VF20	XF40	MS60	MS63
2008	—	PF65 275				

KM# 465 20 DOLLARS
15.50 g., 0.925 Silver 0.458 oz. ASW, 35 mm. **Subject:** Biblical stories - Noah

Date	Mintage	F12	VF20	XF40	MS60	MS63
2013	1,000	PF63 85.00				

KM# 183 500 DOLLARS
77.70 g., 0.999 Gold 2.4795 oz. AGW, 42x42 mm. **Obv:** Shield **Rev:** Battleship Bismark

Date	Mintage	F12	VF20	XF40	MS60	MS63
2009	77	PF65 4,500				

KM# 243 500 DOLLARS
77.75 g., 0.999 Gold 2.4811 oz. AGW, 42x42 mm. **Subject:** H.M.S. Prince of Wales **Rev:** Battleship right, Royal Navy flag above

Date	Mintage	F12	VF20	XF40	MS60	MS63
2009	77	PF65 4,500				

KM# 251 500 DOLLARS
77.75 g., 0.999 Gold 2.4811 oz. AGW, 42x42 mm. **Subject:** Battleship Marat **Rev:** Battleship sailing left

Date	Mintage	F12	VF20	XF40	MS60	MS63
2010	77	PF65 4,500				

KM# 305 500 DOLLARS
77.75 g., 0.9999 Gold 2.4834 oz. AGW, 42x42 mm. **Obv:** National arms **Rev:** French battleship Richelieu **Shape:** Square

Date	Mintage	F12	VF20	XF40	MS60	MS63
2010	77	PF65 4,500				

KM# 394 500 DOLLARS
77.75 g., 0.999 Gold 2.4811 oz. AGW, 42x42 mm. **Obv:** National arms **Rev:** H.M.A.S. Australia

Date	Mintage	F12	VF20	XF40	MS60	MS63
2011	77	PF65 4,500				

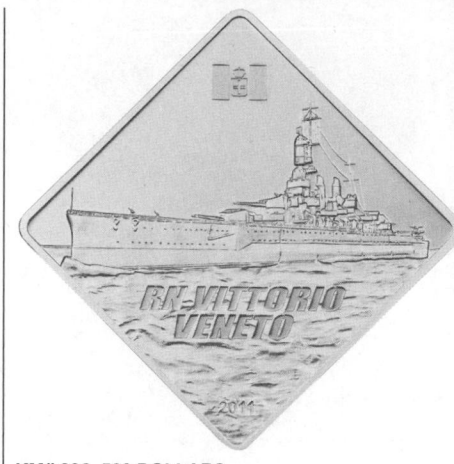

KM# 396 500 DOLLARS
77.70 g., 0.999 Gold 2.4795 oz. AGW, 42x42 mm. **Obv:** National arms **Rev:** RN Vittorio Veneto

Date	Mintage	F12	VF20	XF40	MS60	MS63
2011	77	PF65 4,500				

PROOF SETS

KM#	Date	Mintage	Identification	Issue Price	Mkt Val
PS4	2007 (6)	2,500	KM#130-135	—	375

PANAMA

The Republic of Panama, a Central American country situated between Costa Rica and Colombia, has an area of 29,762 sq. mi. (78,200 sq. km.) and a population of *2.4 million. Capital: Panama City. The Panama Canal is the country's biggest asset; servicing world related transit trade and international commerce. Bananas, refined petroleum, sugar and shrimp are exported.

MONETARY SYSTEM
100 Centesimos = 1 Balboa

REPUBLIC

DECIMAL COINAGE

KM# 125 CENTESIMO
2.50 g., Copper Plated Zinc, 19.05 mm. **Obv:** Written value **Obv. Legend:** REPUBLICA DE PANAMA **Rev:** Native Urraca bust left **Edge:** Plain

Date	Mintage	F12	VF20	XF40	MS60	MS63
2001(c)	160,000,000	—	—	—	0.25	0.50
2008(c)	—	—	—	—	0.25	0.50

KM# 133 5 CENTESIMOS
5.00 g., Copper-Nickel, 21.15 mm. **Subject:** Sara Sotillo **Obv:** National coat of arms **Obv. Legend:** REPUBLICA DE PANAMA **Rev:** Head of Sotillo 3/4 right **Edge:** Plain

Date	Mintage	F12	VF20	XF40	MS60	MS63
2001(c)	8,000,000	—	—	—	0.25	0.75
2008(c)	—	—	—	—	0.25	0.75

KM# 127 1/10 BALBOA
2.27 g., Copper-Nickel Clad Copper, 17.91 mm. **Obv:** National coat of arms **Obv. Legend:** REPUBLICA DE PANAMA **Rev:** Armored bust of Balboa left **Edge:** Reeded

Date	Mintage	F12	VF20	XF40	MS60	MS63
2001(c)	15,000,000	—	—	0.50	0.75	1.00
2008(c)	28,000,000	—	—	0.50	0.75	1.00

KM# 135 25 CENTESIMOS
5.67 g., Copper-Nickel Clad Copper, 24.26 mm. **Obv:** National coat of arms **Obv. Legend:** REPUBLICA DE PANAMA **Rev:** Tower and Spanish ruins **Edge:** Reeded **Note:** Released in 2004

Date	Mintage	F12	VF20	XF40	MS60	MS63
2003(c)	6,000,000	—	—	0.50	2.00	3.00
2003(c)	2,000	PF63 25.00		PF65 30.00		

KM# 136 25 CENTESIMOS
5.67 g., Copper-Nickel Clad Copper, 24.26 mm. **Obv:** National coat of arms **Obv. Legend:** REPUBLICA DE PANAMA **Rev:** King's Bridge **Rev. Legend:** Puente Del Rey **Edge:** Reeded

Date	Mintage	F12	VF20	XF40	MS60	MS63
2005(c)	3,000,000	—	—	—	1.00	1.50
2005(c)	2,000	PF63 20.00		PF65 25.00		

KM# 128 1/4 BALBOA
5.67 g., Copper-Nickel Clad Copper, 24.26 mm. **Obv:** National coat of arms **Obv. Legend:** REPUBLICA DE PANAMA **Rev:** Armored bust of Balboa left **Edge:** Reeded

Date	Mintage	F12	VF20	XF40	MS60	MS63
2001(c)	12,000,000	—	—	0.35	0.75	1.50

KM# 137.1 1/4 BALBOA
5.67 g., Copper-Nickel Clad Copper, 24.26 mm. **Subject:** Breast Cancer Awareness **Obv:** National coat of arms **Obv. Legend:** REPUBLICA DE PANAMA **Rev:** Ribbon **Rev. Legend:** Protegete Mujer **Edge:** Reeded

Date	Mintage	F12	VF20	XF40	MS60	MS63
2008(c)	14,000,000	—	—	—	0.50	1.00

Note: Also available in a laminated Breast Cancer Awareness pink bookmark

KM# 137.2 1/4 BALBOA
5.67 g., Copper-Nickel Clad Copper, 24.26 mm. **Subject:** Breast Cancer Awareness **Obv:** National coat of arms **Obv. Legend:** REPUBLICA DE PANAMA **Rev:** Pink Ribbon **Rev. Legend:** Protegete Mujer **Edge:** Reeded

Date	Mintage	F12	VF20	XF40	MS60	MS63
2008(c) Proof	2,500	PF63 75.00		PF65 80.00		

Note: Pink ribbon proof issued in red plush case with black cardboard sleeve with printed pink ribbon

KM# 138 1/4 BALBOA
5.67 g., Copper-Nickel Clad Copper, 24.26 mm. **Subject:** 50th

---

Anniversary of the Children's Hospital **Obv:** National coat of arms **Obv. Legend:** REPUBLICA DE PANAMA **Rev:** Children's Hospital **Edge:** Reeded

Date	Mintage	F12	VF20	XF40	MS60	MS63
2008	6,000,000	—	—	—	1.00	2.00

KM# 139 50 CENTESIMOS
11.34 g., Copper-Nickel Clad Copper, 30.6 mm. **Subject:** Centenary of the National Bank of Panama **Obv:** National coat of arms **Obv. Legend:** REPUBLICA DE PANAMA **Rev:** BNP Building - Banco Nacional de Panama **Rev. Legend:** BANCO NACIONAL DE PANAMA CENTENARIO **Edge:** Reeded

Date	Mintage	F12	VF20	XF40	MS60	MS63
2009(c)	4,000,000	—	—	—	2.00	3.00

KM# 129 1/2 BALBOA
11.34 g., Copper-Nickel Clad Copper, 30.61 mm. **Obv:** National coat of arms **Obv. Legend:** REPUBLICA DE PANAMA **Rev:** Armored bust of Balboa left **Edge:** Reeded

Date	Mintage	F12	VF20	XF40	MS60	MS63
2001(c)	600,000	—	—	1.00	2.25	4.00
2008(c)	5,800,000	—	—	0.75	1.25	2.00

KM# 140 1/2 BALBOA
11.34 g., Copper-Nickel Clad Copper, 30.61 mm. **Subject:** Convent of the Conception **Obv:** National arms **Rev:** Building ruins **Edge:** Reeded

Date	Mintage	F12	VF20	XF40	MS60	MS63
2010(c)	3,000,000	—	—	—	2.00	3.00

KM# 142 1/2 BALBOA
11.34 g., Copper-Nickel Clad Copper, 30.61 mm. **Obv:** National arms **Obv. Legend:** REPUBLICA DE PANAMA / MEDIO BALBOA **Rev:** Crowned Hapsburg shield **Rev. Legend:** MONEDA DE 1580 / PANAMA VIEJO

Date	Mintage	F12	VF20	XF40	MS60	MS63
2011	3,000,000	—	—	—	2.00	3.00

KM# 143 1/2 BALBOA
11.34 g., Copper-Nickel Clad Copper, 30.61 mm. **Subject:** Casa Reales

Date	Mintage	F12	VF20	XF40	MS60	MS63
2012	—	—	—	—	2.00	3.00

KM# 134 BALBOA
22.68 g., Copper-Nickel Clad Copper, 38.1 mm. **Obv:** Bust of President Mireya Moscoso left, flanked by dates of her presidency **Rev:** Flag and canal scene **Edge:** Reeded

Date	Mintage	F12	VF20	XF40	MS60	MS63
2004(c)	2,000	PF63 50.00		PF65 55.00		
2004(c)	348,000	—	—	1.50	4.50	12.00

KM# 141 BALBOA
7.20 g., Bi-Metallic, 26.5 mm. **Obv:** National arms **Obv. Legend:** REPUBLICA DE PANAMA / date **Rev:** Balboa left **Rev. Legend:** VASCO NUNEZ DE BALBOA / UN BALBOA **Edge Lettering:** PANAMA (reeding) 1 BALBOA (reeding)

Date	Mintage	F12	VF20	XF40	MS60	MS63
2011	40,000,000	—	—	—	1.50	2.00

PAPUA NEW GUINEA

The Independent State of Papua New Guinea occupies the eastern half of the island of New Guinea. It lies north of Australia near the equator and borders on West Irian. The country, which includes nearby Bismark archipelago, Buka and Bougainville, has an area of 178,260 sq. mi. (461,690 sq. km.) and a population of 3.7 million that is divided into more than 1,000 separate tribes, speaking more than 700 mutually unintelligible languages. Capital: Port Moresby. The economy is agricultural, and exports copra, rubber, cocoa, coffee, tea, gold and copper.

Papua New Guinea is a member of the Commonwealth of Nations. Elizabeth II is Head of State, as Queen of Papua New Guinea.

CONSTITUTIONAL MONARCHY
Commonwealth of Nations

STANDARD COINAGE

KM# 1 TOEA
2.00 g., Bronze, 17.65 mm. **Obv:** National emblem **Rev:** Butterfly and value **Edge:** Plain

Date	Mintage	F12	VF20	XF40	MS60	MS63
2001	—	—	—	0.25	1.00	10.00
2002	—	—	—	0.15	1.00	10.00
2004	—	—	—	0.10	1.00	10.00

KM# 2 2 TOEA
4.10 g., Bronze, 21.6 mm. **Obv:** National emblem **Rev:** Lion fish **Edge:** Plain

Date	Mintage	F12	VF20	XF40	MS60	MS63
2001	—	—	—	0.30	0.75	2.50
2002	—	—	—	0.25	0.60	2.00
2004	—	—	—	0.15	0.45	1.25

KM# 3a 5 TOEA
2.55 g., Nickel Plated Steel, 19.53 mm. **Obv:** National emblem **Rev:** Plateless turtle **Edge:** Reeded

Date	Mintage	F12	VF20	XF40	MS60	MS63
2002	—	—	—	0.50	1.25	2.50
2004	—	—	—	0.50	1.25	2.50
2005	—	—	—	0.40	1.00	2.00
2010	—	—	—	0.40	1.00	2.00

KM# 4 10 TOEA
5.65 g., Copper-Nickel, 23.72 mm. **Obv:** National emblem **Rev:** Cuscus and value **Edge:** Reeded

Date	Mintage	F12	VF20	XF40	MS60	MS63
2001	—	—	—	—	1.50	2.00

KM# 4a 10 TOEA
5.16 g., Nickel Plated Steel, 23.72 mm. **Obv:** National emblem **Rev:** Cuscus and value **Edge:** Reeded

Date	Mintage	F12	VF20	XF40	MS60	MS63
2002	—	—	—	0.80	2.00	3.00
2004	—	—	—	0.80	2.00	3.00
2005	—	—	—	6.00	1.50	3.00
2006	—	—	—	0.60	1.50	2.50
2009	—	—	—	0.60	1.50	2.50
2010	—	—	—	0.60	1.50	2.50

KM# 5a 20 TOEA
10.13 g., Nickel Plated Steel, 28.65 mm. **Obv:** National emblem **Rev:** Bennett's Cassowary and value **Edge:** Reeded

Date	Mintage	F12	VF20	XF40	MS60	MS63
2004	—	—	—	0.80	2.00	3.00
2005	—	—	—	0.80	2.00	3.00
2006	—	—	—	0.60	1.50	2.50
2009	—	—	—	0.60	1.50	2.50
2010	—	—	—	0.60	1.50	2.50

KM# 53 50 TOEA
12.10 g., Nickel Plated Steel, 30 mm. **Subject:** St. John's Ambulance, 50th Anniversary **Obv:** National emblem **Rev:** Ambulance corps logo **Shape:** 7-sided

Date	Mintage	F12	VF20	XF40	MS60	MS63
2007	—	—	—	—	4.00	5.00

KM# 54 50 TOEA
12.10 g., Nickel Plated Steel, 30 mm. **Subject:** Bank of Papua New Guinea, 35th Anniversary **Obv:** National emblem **Rev:** Bank logo in colored central applique

Date	Mintage	F12	VF20	XF40	MS60	MS63
2008	—	—	—	—	4.00	5.00

KM# 6a KINA
14.61 g., Nickel Plated Steel, 33.28 mm. **Obv:** Native design **Rev:** Two Salt Water Crocodiles **Edge:** Reeded

Date	Mintage	F12	VF20	XF40	MS60	MS63
2002	—	—	—	1.60	4.00	5.00
2004	—	—	—	1.40	3.50	4.50

KM# 6b KINA
11.13 g., Nickel Plated Steel, 30 mm. **Obv:** Native design **Rev:** Two Salt Water Crocodiles **Edge:** Reeded

Date	Mintage	F12	VF20	XF40	MS60	MS63
2005	—	—	—	1.20	3.00	4.00
2010	—	—	—	1.20	3.00	4.00

KM# 59 KINA
0.50 g., 0.999 Gold AGW, 11 mm. **Subject:** Birdwing Butterfly

Date	Mintage	F12	VF20	XF40	MS60	MS63
2011	Est. 5000	PF63 35.00	PF65 45.00			

KM# 60 KINA
0.50 g., 0.585 Gold AGW, 11 mm. **Subject:** Bird of Paradise

Date	Mintage	F12	VF20	XF40	MS60	MS63
2013	Est. 5000	PF63 50.00	PF65 55.00			

KM# 62 KINA
0.585 Gold AGW, 11 mm. **Subject:** Albert Einstein

Date	Mintage	F12	VF20	XF40	MS60	MS63
2013	Est. 7500	PF63 50.00	PF65 55.00			

KM# 51 2 KINA
12.20 g., Bi-Metallic, 33.3 mm. **Subject:** Bank of Papua New Guinea, 35th Anniversary **Obv:** Bird of Paradise **Rev:** Bank logo **Edge:** Reeded

Date	Mintage	F12	VF20	XF40	MS60	MS63
2008	—	—	—	—	—	5.00

KM# 57 5 KINA
28.28 g., 0.925 Silver 0.8356 oz. ASW, 38.61 mm. **Subject:** Diamond Jubilee of Queen Elizabeth II - Sword of State

Date	Mintage	F12	VF20	XF40	MS60	MS63
2011	Est. 10000	PF63 65.00	PF65 70.00			

KM# 58 5 KINA
1.24 g., 0.999 Gold 0.0396 oz. AGW, 13.92 mm. **Subject:** Bird of Paradise

Date	Mintage	F12	VF20	XF40	MS60	MS63
2011	Est. 5000	PF63 85.00	PF65 95.00			

KM# 56 5 KINA
Silver, 38.61 mm. **Subject:** Belgrave - Gembrook Railway, Victoria, Australia, 50th Anniversary of re-opening **Obv:** Bird of Paradise **Rev:** Steam train and map of Belgrave-Gembrook route

Date	Mintage	F12	VF20	XF40	MS60	MS63
2012	—	PF63 75.00	PF65 85.00			

KM# 61 5 KINA
20.00 g., 0.925 Silver 0.591 oz. ASW, 38.61 mm. **Subject:** 2014 FIFA World Cup - Brazil

Date	Mintage	F12	VF20	XF40	MS60	MS63
2013	Est. 10000	PF63 75.00	PF65 80.00			

KM# 63 5 KINA
0.50 g., 0.999 Gold AGW, 11 mm. **Subject:** Albert Einstein

Date	Mintage	F12	VF20	XF40	MS60	MS63
2013	Est. 7500	PF63 50.00	PF65 55.00			

KM# 64 5 KINA
20.00 g., 0.925 Gold 0.591 oz. AGW, 38.61 mm. **Subject:** 2014 FIFA World Cup - All in one Rhythm

Date	Mintage	F12	VF20	XF40	MS60	MS63
2013	Est. 10000	PF63 75.00	PF65 80.00			

PARAGUAY

The Republic of Paraguay, a landlocked country in the heart of South America surrounded by Argentina, Bolivia and Brazil, has an area of 157,048 sq. mi. (406,750 sq. km.) and a population of *4.5 million, 95 percent of whom are of mixed Spanish and Indian descent. Capital: Asuncion. The country is predominantly agrarian, with no important mineral deposits or oil reserves. Meat, timber, hides, oilseeds, tobacco and cotton account for 70 per-cent of Paraguay's export revenue.

During the Triple Alliance War (1864-1870) in which Paraguay faced Argentina, Brazil and Uruguay, Asuncion's ladies gathered in an Assembly on Feb. 24, 1867 and decided to give up their jewelry in order to help the national defense. The President of the Republic, Francisco Solano Lopez accepted the offering and ordered one twentieth of it be used to mint the first Paraguayan gold coins according to the Decree of the 11th of Sept.1867.

Two dies were made, one by Bouvet, and another by an American, Leonard Charles, while only the die made by Bouvet was eventually used.

MINT MARK
HF – LeLocle (Swiss)

REPUBLIC

REFORM COINAGE
100 Centimos = 1 Guarani

KM# 209 20 CENTIMOS
27.00 g., 0.925 Silver 0.7978 oz. ASW **Subject:** Ibero-American Series **Obv:** National arms in center of other country's arms **Rev:** Ñanduti and value **Edge:** Reeded

Date	Mintage	F12	VF20	XF40	MS60	MS63
2012	—	PF63 100	PF65 110			

KM# 197 GUARANI

27.00 g., 0.925 Silver 0.7978 oz. ASW, 39.7 mm. **Subject:** 50th Anniversary of the Central Bank **Obv:** Naval gunship **Obv. Legend:** REPUBLICA DEL PARAGUAY **Obv. Inscription:** CAÑONERO PARAGUAY **Rev:** Bank building within circle **Rev. Legend:** BANCO CENTRAL DEL PARAGUAY **Edge:** Reeded

Date	Mintage	F12	VF20	XF40	MS60	MS63
2002	3,000	PF63 75.00	PF65 80.00			

KM# 199 GUARANI

26.86 g., 0.925 Silver 0.7937 oz. ASW, 40.03 mm. **Series:** 5th Ibero-America **Subject:** Encounter of the Two Worlds **Obv:** National arms in center with ten national arms in outer circle **Obv. Legend:** REPUBLICA DEL PARAGUAY **Rev:** Native in canoe with outline of South America in background at left, early sailing ship at lower right. **Rev. Legend:** ENCUENTRO DE DOS MUNDOS **Edge:** Reeded

Date	Mintage	F12	VF20	XF40	MS60	MS63
2002	—	PF63 60.00	PF65 65.00			

KM# 200 GUARANI

27.00 g., 0.925 Silver 0.7978 oz. ASW **Subject:** 60th Anniversary of Currency Reform **Obv:** National arms **Obv. Legend:** REPUBLICA DEL PARAGUAY **Rev:** Outline map of Paraguay **Edge:** Reeded

Date	Mintage	F12	VF20	XF40	MS60	MS63
2003	—	PF63 80.00	PF65 90.00			

KM# 201 GUARANI

26.90 g., 0.925 Silver 0.7948 oz. ASW, 40.04 mm. **Subject:** FIFA - XVIII World Football Championship - Germany 2006 **Obv:**

National arms **Obv. Legend:** REPUBLICA DEL PARAGUAY **Rev:** Two opponents after ball **Rev. Legend:** COPA MUNDIAL DE LA FIFA - ALEMANIA **Edge:** Reeded

Date	Mintage	F12	VF20	XF40	MS60	MS63
2003	50,000	PF63 50.00	PF65 60.00			

KM# 202 GUARANI

27.00 g., 0.925 Silver 0.7978 oz. ASW **Subject:** FIFA - XVIII World Football Championship - Germany 2006 **Obv:** National arms **Obv. Legend:** REPUBLICA DEL PARAGUAY **Rev:** Ball in goal **Edge:** Reeded

Date	Mintage	F12	VF20	XF40	MS60	MS63
2004	50,000	PF63 50.00	PF65 60.00			

KM# 204 GUARANI

27.00 g., 0.925 Silver 0.7978 oz. ASW **Series:** 6th Ibero-America **Subject:** Encounter of the Two Worlds **Obv:** National arms in center with ten national arms in outer circle **Obv. Legend:** REPUBLICA DEL PARAGUAY **Rev:** Church of the Most Holy, Trinidad in Yaguarón **Rev. Legend:** ENCUENTRO DE DOS MUNDOS - IGLESIA DE LA SANTISIMA TRINIDAD **Edge:** Reeded

Date	Mintage	F12	VF20	XF40	MS60	MS63
2005	—	PF63 65.00	PF65 75.00			

KM# 205 GUARANI

27.00 g., 0.925 Silver 0.7978 oz. ASW **Subject:** Ibero-American series **Obv:** National arms within circle of other country's arms **Rev:** First coin of Paraguay, 1845 **Edge:** Reeded

Date	Mintage	F12	VF20	XF40	MS60	MS63
2010	—	PF63 100	PF65 110			

KM# 210 GUARANI

27.00 g., 0.925 Silver 0.7978 oz. ASW **Subject:** Currency Reform, 70th Anniversary **Obv:** Guarani Native head 1/4 right **Rev:** Large value within palm and olive leave branch **Edge:** Reeded

Date	Mintage	F12	VF20	XF40	MS60	MS63
2013	700	PF63 100	PF65 110			

KM# 211 GUARANI

6.80 g., 0.999 Gold 0.217 oz. AGW **Subject:** Currency Reform, 70th Anniversary **Obv:** Guarani Native head 1/4 right **Rev:** Large value within palm and olive leaves wreath **Edge:** Reeded

Date	Mintage	F12	VF20	XF40	MS60	MS63
2013	70	PF63 725	PF65 750			

KM# 212 GUARANI

27.000 Silver ASW **Subject:** 2014 FIFA World Cup - Brazil **Obv:** National emblem **Rev:** Soccer player and fans in stands with flags

Date	Mintage	F12	VF20	XF40	MS60	MS63
2013	—	PF63 100	PF65 110			

KM# 191a 50 GUARANIES

Brass Plated Steel **Obv:** Uniformed bust facing **Rev:** Value above river dam **Note:** Magnetic

Date	Mintage	F12	VF20	XF40	MS60	MS63
2005	10,000,000	—	—	—	0.75	1.00

KM# 191b 50 GUARANIES

1.01 g., Aluminum, 18.98 mm. **Obv:** Bust of Major General J.F. Estigarribia facing **Obv. Legend:** REPUBLICA DEL PARAGUAY **Rev:** Acaray River Dam **Rev. Inscription:** REPRESA ACARAY **Edge:** Plain **Note:** Reduced size

Date	Mintage	F12	VF20	XF40	MS60	MS63
2006	25,000,000	—	—	—	1.00	2.00
2008	—	—	—	—	1.00	2.00
2011	—	—	—	—	1.00	2.00
2012	25,000,000	—	—	—	1.00	2.00

KM# 177a 100 GUARANIES

5.45 g., Brass Plated Steel **Obv:** Bust of General Jose E. Dias facing **Obv. Legend:** REPUBLICA DEL PARAGUAY **Rev:** Ruins of Humaita **Rev. Inscription:** RUINAS DE HUMAITA 1865/70 **Note:** Reduced weight and thickness.

Date	Mintage	F12	VF20	XF40	MS60	MS63
2004	15,000,000	—	—	—	1.50	2.00
2005	10,000,000	—	—	—	1.50	2.00

KM# 177b 100 GUARANIES

3.66 g., Nickel-Steel, 20.94 mm. **Obv:** Bust of General Jose E. Dias facing **Obv. Legend:** REPUBLICA DEL PARAGUAY **Rev:** Ruins of Humaita **Rev. Inscription:** RUINAS DE HUMAITA 1865/70 **Edge:** Plain

Date	Mintage	F12	VF20	XF40	MS60	MS63
2006	30,000,000	—	—	—	1.50	2.00
2007	25,000,000	—	—	—	1.50	2.00
2008	—	—	—	—	1.50	2.00
2011	—	—	—	—	1.50	2.00
2012	25,000,000	—	—	—	1.50	2.00

KM# 206 100 GUARANIES

14.70 g., Nordic Gold, 33 mm. **Subject:** Independence, 200th Anniversary **Obv:** Rider on horseback with flag in color **Rev:** Independence House

Date	Mintage	F12	VF20	XF40	MS60	MS63
2011	—	PF63 50.00	PF65 60.00			

KM# 208 100 GUARANIES

6.75 g., 0.999 Gold 0.2154 oz. AGW **Subject:** Independence, 200th Anniversary **Obv:** Rider on horseback with flag in color **Rev:** Independence House

Date	Mintage	F12	VF20	XF40	MS60	MS63
2011	2,000	PF63 775	PF65 800			

KM# 207 150 GUARANIES

27.00 g., 0.925 Silver 0.7978 oz. ASW **Subject:** Independence, 200th Anniversary **Obv:** Rider on horseback with flag in color **Rev:** Independence House

Date	Mintage	F12	VF20	XF40	MS60	MS63
2013 (2011)	3,000	PF63 100	PF65 110			

KM# 195 500 GUARANIES

7.82 g., Brass Plated Steel **Obv:** Head of General Bernardino Caballero facing **Obv. Legend:** REPUBLICA DEL PARAGUAY **Rev:** Bank above value within circle **Rev. Legend:** BANCO CENTRAL DEL PARAGUAY

Date	Mintage	F12	VF20	XF40	MS60	MS63
2002	15,000,000	—	—	—	2.50	3.00
2005	5,000,000	—	—	—	2.50	3.00

KM# 195a 500 GUARANIES

4.80 g., Nickel-Steel, 23 mm. **Obv:** Head of General Bernardino Caballero facing **Obv. Legend:** REPUBLICA DEL PARAGUAY **Rev:** Bank above value in circle **Rev. Legend:** BANCO CENTRAL DEL PARAGUAY **Edge:** Plain

Date	Mintage	F12	VF20	XF40	MS60	MS63
2006	12,000,000	—	—	—	2.00	2.50
2007	25,000,000	—	—	—	2.00	2.50
2008	—	—	—	—	2.00	2.50
2011	—	—	—	—	2.00	2.50
2012	20,000,000	—	—	—	2.00	2.50

KM# 198 MIL (1000) GUARANIES

6.07 g., Nickel-Steel, 25 mm. **Obv:** Bust of Major General Francisco Solano Lopez facing **Obv. Legend:** REPUBLICA DEL PARAGUAY **Rev:** National Heroes Pantheon **Rev. Legend:** BANCO CENTRAL DEL PARAGUAY **Rev. Inscription:** PANTEON NACIONAL / DE LOS HEROES **Edge:** Plain

Date	Mintage	F12	VF20	XF40	MS60	MS63
2006	25,000,000	—	—	—	3.00	4.00
2007	35,000,000	—	—	—	3.00	4.00
2008	—	—	—	—	3.00	4.00

KM# 203 1500 GUARANIES

6.70 g., 0.999 Gold 0.2138 oz. AGW **Subject:** XVIII World Football Championship - Germany 2006 **Obv:** National arms **Obv. Legend:** REPUBLICA DEL PARAGUAY **Rev:** Ball in goal

Date	Mintage	F12	VF20	XF40	MS60	MS63
2004	25,000	PF63 430	PF65 450			

PERU

The Republic of Peru, located on the Pacific coast of South America, has an area of 496,225 sq. mi. (1,285,220 sq. km.) and a population of *21.4 million. Capital: Lima. The diversified economy includes mining, fishing and agriculture. Fishmeal, copper, sugar, zinc and iron ore are exported.

MINT MARKS
L, LIMAE (monogram), Lima (monogram), LIMA = Lima

REPUBLIC
REFORM COINAGE
1991; 1/M Intis = 1 Nuevo Sol;
100 (New) Centimos = 1 Nuevo Sol

KM# 303.4 CENTIMO
1.88 g., Brass, 15.9 mm. **Obv:** National arms, accent mark above "u **Rev:** Without Braille dots, no Chavez **Edge:** Plain **Note:** LIMA monogram is mint mark.

Date	Mintage	F12	VF20	XF40	MS60	MS63
2002LIMA	2,100,000	—	—	—	0.50	0.75
2004LIMA	2,000,000	—	—	—	0.50	0.75
2005LIMA	22,700,000	—	—	—	0.25	0.40
2006LIMA	19,700,000	—	—	—	0.25	0.40

KM# 303.4a CENTIMO
0.82 g., Aluminum, 16 mm. **Obv:** National arms **Rev:** Value flanked by designs **Edge:** Plain **Note:** LIMA monogram is mint mark.

Date	Mintage	F12	VF20	XF40	MS60	MS63
2006LIMA	19,200,000	—	—	—	0.50	0.75
2007LIMA	48,800,000	—	—	—	0.25	0.30
2008LIMA	63,800,000	—	—	—	0.25	0.30
2009LIMA	62,000,000	—	—	—	0.25	0.30
2010LIMA	73,000,000	—	—	—	0.25	0.30
2011LIMA	14,700,000	—	—	—	0.25	0.30

KM# 304.4 5 CENTIMOS
2.69 g., Brass, 18 mm. **Obv:** National arms, accent above "u **Rev:** Value flanked by designs. Without Braille dots, with accent above "e **Edge:** Plain **Note:** LIMA monogram is mint mark.

Date	Mintage	F12	VF20	XF40	MS60	MS63
2002LIMA	3,940,000	—	—	—	0.35	0.50
2005LIMA	8,900,000	—	—	—	0.35	0.50
2006LIMA	11,400,000	—	—	—	0.35	0.50
2007LIMA	12,800,000	—	—	—	0.35	0.50

KM# 304.4a 5 CENTIMOS
1.02 g., Aluminum, 18 mm. **Obv:** National arms **Rev:** Value flanked by native designs **Edge:** Plain **Note:** LIMA monogram is mint mark.

Date	Mintage	F12	VF20	XF40	MS60	MS63
2007LIMA	12,400,000	—	—	—	0.35	0.50
2008LIMA	11,600,000	—	—	—	0.30	0.40
2009LIMA	20,000,000	—	—	—	0.30	0.40
2010LIMA	24,000,000	—	—	—	0.30	0.40
2011LIMA	36,000,000	—	—	—	0.30	0.40
2012LIMA	32,700,000	—	—	—	0.30	0.40
2013LIMA		—	—	—	0.20	0.30

KM# 305.4 10 CENTIMOS
3.50 g., Brass, 20.5 mm. **Obv:** National arms, accent above "u **Rev:** Without braille dots, accent above "e **Edge:** Plain **Note:** LIMA monogram is mint mark.

Date	Mintage	F12	VF20	XF40	MS60	MS63
2001LIMA	50,000,000	—	—	—	0.65	0.85
2002LIMA	37,420,000	—	—	—	0.65	0.85
2003LIMA	56,000,000	—	—	—	0.65	0.85
2004LIMA	27,500,000	—	—	—	0.65	0.85
2005LIMA	39,500,000	—	—	—	0.40	0.50
2006LIMA	54,200,000	—	—	—	0.40	0.50
2007LIMA	64,800,000	—	—	—	0.40	0.50
2008LIMA	79,400,000	—	—	—	0.40	0.50
2009LIMA	63,000,000	—	—	—	0.40	0.50
2010LIMA	82,000,000	—	—	—	0.40	0.50
2011LIMA	94,000,000	—	—	—	0.40	0.50
2012LIMA	112,700,000	—	—	—	0.40	0.50
2013LIMA		—	—	—	0.40	0.50

KM# 306.4 20 CENTIMOS
4.40 g., Brass, 23 mm. **Obv:** National arms, accent above "u **Rev:** Without braille dots, accent above "e **Edge:** Plain **Note:** LIMA monogram is mint mark.

Date	Mintage	F12	VF20	XF40	MS60	MS63
2001LIMA	13,000,000	—	—	—	0.85	1.20
2002LIMA	9,000,000	—	—	—	0.85	1.20
2003LIMA	2,000,000	—	—	—	1.00	1.25
2004LIMA	15,200,000	—	—	—	0.85	1.20
2006LIMA	3,700,000	—	—	—	0.75	1.00
2007LIMA	18,000,000	—	—	—	0.50	0.75
2008LIMA	24,300,000	—	—	—	0.50	0.75
2009LIMA	15,500,000	—	—	—	0.50	0.75
2010LIMA	25,000,000	—	—	—	0.50	0.75
2011LIMA	23,000,000	—	—	—	0.50	0.75
2012LIMA	25,800,000	—	—	—	0.50	0.75
2013LIMA		—	—	—	0.40	0.50

KM# 307.4 50 CENTIMOS
5.45 g., Copper-Nickel-Zinc, 22 mm. **Obv:** National arms, accent above "u **Rev:** Without braille, accent above "e **Edge:** Reeded **Note:** LIMA monogram is mint mark.

Date	Mintage	F12	VF20	XF40	MS60	MS63
2001LIMA	11,000,000	—	—	—	1.00	1.75
2002LIMA	12,000,000	—	—	—	1.50	1.75
2003LIMA	30,000,000	—	—	—	1.50	1.75
2004LIMA	6,000,000	—	—	—	1.50	1.75
2005LIMA	14,600,000	—	—	—	0.75	1.00
2006LIMA	24,200,000	—	—	—	0.75	1.00
2007LIMA	31,200,000	—	—	—	0.75	1.00
2008LIMA	36,200,000	—	—	—	0.75	1.00
2009LIMA	26,700,000	—	—	—	0.75	1.00
2010LIMA	5,180,000	—	—	—	0.75	1.00
2011LIMA	38,000,000	—	—	—	0.75	1.00
2012LIMA	24,900,000	—	—	—	0.75	1.00
2013LIMA		—	—	—	0.75	1.00

KM# 308.4 NUEVO SOL
7.32 g., Copper-Nickel-Zinc, 25.5 mm. **Obv:** National arms, accent above "u **Rev:** Without braille, accent above "e **Edge:** Reeded **Note:** LIMA monogram is mint mark.

Date	Mintage	F12	VF20	XF40	MS60	MS63
2001LIMA	10,000,000	—	—	—	2.50	3.00

Date	Mintage	F12	VF20	XF40	MS60	MS63
2002LIMA	8,000,000	—	—	—	2.50	3.00
2003LIMA	5,000,000	—	—	—	2.50	3.00
2004LIMA	13,900,000	—	—	—	2.50	3.00
2005LIMA	14,600,000	—	—	—	1.50	1.75
2006LIMA	19,700,000	—	—	—	1.50	1.75
2007LIMA	36,700,000	—	—	—	1.25	1.50
2008LIMA	42,800,000	—	—	—	1.25	1.50
2009LIMA	34,330,000	—	—	—	1.25	1.50
2010LIMA	2,000,000	—	—	—	3.00	3.50
2011LIMA	23,000,000	—	—	—	1.25	1.50

KM# 329 NUEVO SOL
33.63 g., 0.925 Silver 0.9936 oz. ASW, 37 mm. **Subject:** 450th Anniversary - San Marcos University **Obv:** National arms **Rev:** University seal and building **Edge:** Reeded **Note:** LIMA monogram is mint mark.

Date	Mintage	F12	VF20	XF40	MS60	MS63
2001LIMA	Est. 5000	—	—	BV	60.00	65.00

KM# 330 NUEVO SOL
33.63 g., 0.925 Silver 0.9936 oz. ASW, 37 mm. **Subject:** 50th Anniversary - Numismatic Society of Peru **Obv:** National arms **Rev:** Stylized design within circle **Edge:** Reeded **Note:** LIMA monogram is mint mark.

Date	Mintage	F12	VF20	XF40	MS60	MS63
2001LIMA	Est. 1000	—	—	BV	60.00	65.00

KM# 331 NUEVO SOL
33.63 g., 0.925 Silver 0.9936 oz. ASW, 37 mm. **Subject:** 200th Anniversary - von Humboldt's visit to Peru **Obv:** National arms **Rev:** Seated figure 1/4 left **Edge:** Reeded **Note:** LIMA monogram is mint mark.

Date	Mintage	F12	VF20	XF40	MS60	MS63
2002LIMA	Est. 1000	—	—	BV	45.00	50.00

KM# 334 NUEVO SOL
27.00 g., 0.925 Silver 0.7978 oz. ASW, 40 mm. **Series:** Ibero-

America **Obv:** National arms in center with ten national arms in outer circle **Obv. Legend:** BANCO CENTRAL DE RESERVA DEL PERÚ **Rev:** Ceramic - Indians in reed boats **Rev. Legend:** PERÚ **Edge:** Reeded

Date	Mintage	F12	VF20	XF40	MS60	MS63
2002(M)	Est. 17000	PF63 50.00	PF65 60.00			

KM# 332 NUEVO SOL
33.63 g., 0.925 Silver 0.9936 oz. ASW, 37 mm. **Subject:** 125th Anniversary of the Inmaculate Jesuitas - Lima College **Obv:** National arms **Rev:** Statue and 3/4 crowned shield **Edge:** Reeded **Note:** LIMA monogram is mint mark.

Date	Mintage	F12	VF20	XF40	MS60	MS63
2003LIMA	Est. 1000	—	—	BV	45.00	50.00

KM# 333 NUEVO SOL
33.63 g., 0.925 Silver 0.9936 oz. ASW, 37 mm. **Subject:** 180th Anniversary of Peru's Congress **Obv:** National arms **Rev:** Statue in front of building **Edge:** Reeded **Note:** LIMA monogram is mint mark.

Date	Mintage	F12	VF20	XF40	MS60	MS63
2003LIMA	Est. 1000	—	—	BV	60.00	65.00

KM# 335 NUEVO SOL
27.00 g., 0.925 Silver 0.7978 oz. ASW, 40 mm. **Subject:** FIFA World Cup Soccer **Obv:** Arms within wreath **Rev:** Action scene beneath globe **Edge:** Reeded

Date	Mintage	F12	VF20	XF40	MS60	MS63
2004(M)	Est. 50000	PF63 60.00	PF65 70.00			

KM# 339 NUEVO SOL
27.00 g., 0.925 Silver 0.7978 oz. ASW, 40 mm. **Series:** Ibero-American **Subject:** Lost city of the Incas **Obv:** National arms in center with ten national arms in outer ring **Obv. Legend:** BANCO CENTRAL DE RESERVA DEL PERÚ **Rev:** Village ruins **Rev. Legend:** MACHU PICCHU . PERÚ **Edge:** Reeded

Date	Mintage	F12	VF20	XF40	MS60	MS63
2005(M)	Est. 17000	PF63 70.00	PF65 80.00			

KM# 356 NUEVO SOL
33.63 g., 0.925 Silver 0.9936 oz. ASW, 37 mm. **Subject:** Lima Regatta Club, 130th Anniversary **Edge:** Reeded

Date	Mintage	F12	VF20	XF40	MS60	MS63
2005LIMA	Est. 1000	—	—	BV	60.00	65.00

KM# 357 NUEVO SOL
27.00 g., 0.925 Silver 0.7978 oz. ASW, 40 mm. **Series:** Ibero-American **Subject:** Volleyball **Rev:** Two volleyball players and net **Edge:** Reeded

Date	Mintage	F12	VF20	XF40	MS60	MS63
2007(M)	Est. 14000	PF63 65.00	PF65 75.00			

KM# 358 NUEVO SOL
33.63 g., 0.925 Silver 0.9936 oz. ASW, 37 mm. **Subject:** Lima-Huancayo Railway, 100th Anniversary **Rev:** Deisel and Steam trains in valley **Edge:** Reeded

Date	Mintage	F12	VF20	XF40	MS60	MS63
2008LIMA	Est. 1000	—	—	BV	45.00	50.00

KM# 359 NUEVO SOL
27.00 g., 0.925 Silver 0.7978 oz. ASW, 40 mm. **Series:** Ibero-American **Subject:** Historical coins of Peru **Edge:** Reeded

Date	Mintage	F12	VF20	XF40	MS60	MS63
2010(M)	Est. 2000	PF63 75.00	PF65 85.00			

KM# 340 NUEVO SOL
7.32 g., Copper-Nickel-Zinc, 25.5 mm. **Series:** Wealth and Pride of Peru **Subject:** Tumi de Oro **Obv:** National arms **Rev:** Tumi de Oro **Edge:** Reeded

Date	Mintage	F12	VF20	XF40	MS60	MS63
2010Lima	10,000,000	—	—	—	2.50	3.00

KM# 341 NUEVO SOL
7.32 g., Copper-Nickel-Zinc, 25.5 mm. **Series:** Wealth and Pride of Peru **Subject:** Sarcophagus of Karajia **Obv:** National arms **Rev:** Sarcophagus of Karajia **Edge:** Reeded

Date	Mintage	F12	VF20	XF40	MS60	MS63
2010LIMA	10,000,000	—	—	—	2.50	3.00

KM# 342 NUEVO SOL
7.32 g., Copper-Nickel-Zinc, 25.5 mm. **Series:** Wealth and Pride of Peru **Obv:** National Arms **Rev:** Estela de Ramondi **Edge:** Reeded

Date	Mintage	F12	VF20	XF40	MS60	MS63
2010LIMA	10,000,000	—	—	—	2.50	3.00

KM# 345 NUEVO SOL
7.30 g., Copper-Nickel-Zinc, 25.5 mm. **Obv:** National arms **Rev:** Chullpas de Sillustani ruins **Edge:** Reeded

Date	Mintage	F12	VF20	XF40	MS60	MS63
2011	10,000,000	—	—	—	2.50	3.00

KM# 346 NUEVO SOL
7.32 g., Copper-Nickel-Zinc, 25.5 mm. **Series:** Wealth and Pride of Peru **Rev:** Monastery of Santa Catalina and plaza **Edge:** Reeded

Date	Mintage	F12	VF20	XF40	MS60	MS63
2011LIMA	10,000,000	—	—	—	2.50	3.00

KM# 360 NUEVO SOL
7.32 g., Copper-Nickel-Zinc, 25.5 mm. **Obv:** National arms **Rev:** Machu Picchu ruins **Edge:** Reeded

Date	Mintage	F12	VF20	XF40	MS60	MS63
2011	10,000,000	—	—	—	2.00	3.00

KM# 361 NUEVO SOL
7.32 g., Copper-Nickel-Zinc, 25.5 mm. **Obv:** National arms **Rev:** Gran Pajaten site

Date	Mintage	F12	VF20	XF40	MS60	MS63
2011	10,000,000	—	—	—	2.00	3.00

KM# 366 NUEVO SOL
7.32 g., Copper-Nickel-Zinc, 25.5 mm. **Obv:** National arms **Rev:** Value within wreath

Date	Mintage	F12	VF20	XF40	MS60	MS63
2012	30,200,000	—	—	—	1.25	1.50
2013		—	—	—	1.25	1.50

KM# 362 NUEVO SOL
7.32 g., Copper-Nickel-Zinc, 25.5 mm. **Subject:** Piedra de Saywite **Obv:** National arms **Rev:** Monolith and animals and geometric designs **Edge:** Reeded

Date	Mintage	F12	VF20	XF40	MS60	MS63
2012	10,000,000	—	—	—	2.00	3.00

KM# 363 NUEVO SOL
7.32 g., Copper-Nickel-Zinc, 25.5 mm. **Subject:** Fortaleza del Real Felipe **Obv:** National arms **Rev:** Fortress ruins **Edge:** Reeded

Date	Mintage	F12	VF20	XF40	MS60	MS63
2012	10,000,000	—	—	—	2.00	3.00

KM# 364 NUEVO SOL
7.32 g., Copper-Nickel-Zinc, 25.5 mm. **Subject:** Templo del Sol Vilcashuaman **Obv:** National arms **Rev:** Temple ruins

Date	Mintage	F12	VF20	XF40	MS60	MS63
2012	10,000,000	—	—	—	2.00	3.00

KM# 365 NUEVO SOL
7.32 g., Copper-Nickel-Zinc, 25.5 mm. **Obv:** National Arms **Rev:** Monolith of Kuntur Wasi **Edge:** Reeded

Date	Mintage	F12	VF20	XF40	MS60	MS63
2012	10,000,000	—	—	—	2.00	3.00

KM# 369 NUEVO SOL
27.00 g., 0.925 Silver 0.7978 oz. ASW, 40 mm. **Subject:** Ibero-American series, 20th Anniversary **Obv:** National arms of Peru in center, Ten arms around **Rev:** Design elements of nine previous coins **Edge:** Reeded

Date	Mintage	F12	VF20	XF40	MS60	MS63
2012(M)	2,000	PF63 50.00	PF65 60.00			

KM# 368 NUEVO SOL
7.32 g., Copper-Nickel-Zinc, 25.5 mm. **Subject:** Textile Art of Paracas **Obv:** National arms **Rev:** Textile with designs

Date	Mintage	F12	VF20	XF40	MS60	MS63
2013LIMA	10,000,000	—	—	—	2.00	2.25

KM# 370 NUEVO SOL
27.00 g., 0.925 Silver 0.7978 oz. ASW, 40 mm. **Subject:** Sol Coinage, 100th Anniversary **Edge Lettering:** Reeded

Date	Mintage	F12	VF20	XF40	MS60	MS63
2013LIMA		—	—	—	—	50.00

KM# 371 NUEVO SOL
7.32 g., Copper-Nickel-Zinc, 25.5 mm. **Subject:** Inca Temple of Huaytara **Obv:** National arms **Rev:** Wall and tower **Edge:** Reeded

Date	Mintage	F12	VF20	XF40	MS60	MS63
2013LIMA	10,000,000	—	—	—	2.00	2.25

KM# 372 NUEVO SOL
7.32 g., Copper-Nickel-Zinc, 25.5 mm. **Subject:** Temple of Kotosh **Obv:** National arms **Rev:** Crossed hands and wall of temple

Date	Mintage	F12	VF20	XF40	MS60	MS63
2013LIMA	10,000,000	—	—	—	2.00	2.25

KM# 373 NUEVO SOL
7.32 g., Copper-Nickel-Zinc, 25.5 mm. **Subject:** Archeological complex of Tunanmarca **Obv:** National arms **Rev:** Ruins of Tunanmarca

Date	Mintage	F12	VF20	XF40	MS60	MS63
2013LIMA	10,000,000	—	—	—	2.00	2.25

KM# 374 NUEVO SOL
7.320 Copper-Nickel-Zinc, 25.5 mm. **Subject:** Anchovy **Obv:** National arms **Rev:** Two anchovies and plant **Edge:** Reeded

Date	Mintage	F12	VF20	XF40	MS60	MS63
2013LIMA	10,000,000	—	—	—	2.00	2.25

KM# 375 NUEVO SOL
7.32 g., Copper-Nickel-Zinc, 25.5 mm. **Subject:** Cocoa Bean **Obv:** National arms **Rev:** Cocoa tree, cocoa pods

Date	Mintage	F12	VF20	XF40	MS60	MS63
2013LIMA	10,000,000	—	—	—	2.00	2.25

KM# 376 NUEVO SOL
7.32 g., Copper-Nickel-Zinc, 25.5 mm. **Obv:** National arms **Rev:** Quinoa plant **Edge:** Reeded

Date	Mintage	F12	VF20	XF40	MS60	MS63
2013LIMA	10,000,000	—	—	—	2.00	2.25

KM# 313 2 NUEVOS SOLES
5.62 g., Bi-Metallic, 22.2 mm. **Obv:** National arms within circle **Rev:** Stylized bird in flight to left of value within circle **Edge:** Plain **Note:** LIMA monogram is mint mark.

Date	Mintage	F12	VF20	XF40	MS60	MS63
2002LIMA	6,000,000	—	—	—	4.00	4.50
2003LIMA	5,000,000	—	—	—	4.00	4.50
2004LIMA	3,000,000	—	—	—	4.50	5.00
2005LIMA	6,000,000	—	—	—	2.00	2.50
2006LIMA	5,100,000	—	—	—	2.00	2.50
2007LIMA	7,000,000	—	—	—	2.00	2.50
2008LIMA	5,800,000	—	—	—	2.00	2.50
2009LIMA	7,000,000	—	—	—	2.00	2.50

KM# 343 2 NUEVOS SOLES
5.62 g., Bi-Metallic, 22.38 mm. **Obv:** National Arms **Rev:** Hummingbird from the Inca Lines, large value at right

Date	Mintage	F12	VF20	XF40	MS60	MS63
2010LIMA	6,235,000	—	—	—	2.00	2.50
2011LIMA	17,000,000	—	—	—	2.00	2.50
2012LIMA	18,730,000	—	—	—	2.00	2.50
(2013)LIMA	—	—	—	—	—	2.00

KM# 316 5 NUEVOS SOLES
6.67 g., Bi-Metallic, 24.32 mm. **Obv:** National arms within circle **Rev:** Stylized bird in flight to left of value within circle **Edge:** Reeded **Note:** LIMA monogram is mint mark.

Date	Mintage	F12	VF20	XF40	MS60	MS63
2001LIMA	5,000,000	—	—	—	5.00	5.50
2002LIMA	2,000,000	—	—	—	5.50	6.00
2005LIMA	6,000,000	—	—	—	4.00	5.00
2006LIMA	5,500,000	—	—	—	4.00	5.00
2007LIMA	6,400,000	—	—	—	4.00	5.00
2008LIMA	9,900,000	—	—	—	3.50	4.00
2009LIMA	10,000,000	—	—	—	3.00	3.50

KM# 344 5 NUEVOS SOLES
6.67 g., Bi-Metallic, 24.38 mm. **Obv:** National Arms **Rev:** Frigate bird from the Nasca lines, large value at right

Date	Mintage	F12	VF20	XF40	MS60	MS63
2010LIMA	6,000,000	—	—	—	4.00	4.50
2011LIMA	15,000,000	—	—	—	3.00	3.50
2012LIMA	14,900,000	—	—	—	3.00	3.50
(2013)LIMA	—	—	—	—	—	3.00

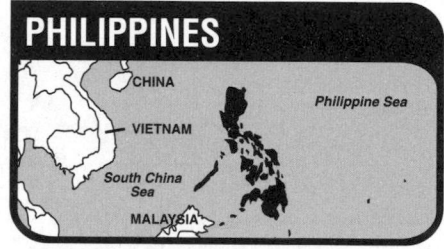

PHILIPPINES

The Republic of the Philippines, an archipelago in the western Pacific 500 miles (805 km.) from the southeast coast of Asia, has an area of 115,830 sq. mi. (300,000 sq. km.) and a population of *64.9 million. Capital: Manila. The economy of the 7,000-island group is based on agriculture, forestry and fishing. Timber, coconut products, sugar and hemp are exported.

MINT MARKS
BSP - Bangko Sentral Pilipinas
M, MA - Manila

REPUBLIC

REFORM COINAGE
100 Sentimos = 1 Piso

KM# 273 SENTIMO
2.00 g., Copper Plated Steel, 15.5 mm. **Obv:** Value and date **Rev:** Central bank seal within circle and gear design, 1993 (date Central Bank was established) below **Rev. Legend:** BANGKO SENTRAL NG PILIPINAS - 1993

Date	Mintage	F12	VF20	XF40	MS60	MS63
2001	—	—	—	—	0.10	0.15
2002	—	—	—	—	0.10	0.15
2004	—	—	—	—	0.10	0.15
2005	—	—	—	—	0.10	0.15
2006	—	—	—	—	0.10	0.15
2007	—	—	—	—	0.10	0.15
2008	—	—	—	—	0.10	0.15
2009	—	—	—	—	0.10	0.15
2011	—	—	—	—	—	0.50

KM# 268 5 SENTIMOS
1.90 g., Copper Plated Steel, 15.5 mm. **Obv:** Numeral value around center hole **Rev:** Hole in center with date, bank and name around border, 1993 (date Central Bank was established) below **Rev. Legend:** BANGKO CENTRAL NG PILIPINAS - 1993 **Edge:** Plain

Date	Mintage	F12	VF20	XF40	MS60	MS63
2001	—	—	—	—	0.20	0.25
2002	—	—	—	—	0.20	0.25
2003	—	—	—	—	0.20	0.25
2004	—	—	—	—	0.50	1.00
2005	—	—	—	—	0.20	0.25
2006	—	—	—	—	0.20	0.25
2007	—	—	—	—	0.20	0.25
2008	—	—	—	—	0.20	0.25
2009	—	—	—	—	0.20	0.25
2010	—	—	—	—	0.20	0.25
2011	—	—	—	—	0.20	0.25
2012	—	—	—	—	0.20	0.25

KM# 270.1 10 SENTIMOS
2.50 g., Copper Plated Steel, 17 mm. **Obv:** Value and date **Rev:** Central Bank seal within circle and gear design, 1993 (date Central Bank was established) below **Rev. Legend:** BANGKO SENTRAL NG PILIPINAS - 1993 **Edge:** Reeded

Date	Mintage	F12	VF20	XF40	MS60	MS63
2001	—	—	—	—	0.10	0.30	0.40
2002	—	—	—	—	0.10	0.30	0.40
2004	—	—	—	0.75	1.50	2.50
2005	—	—	—	—	0.10	0.30	0.40

KM# 270.2 10 SENTIMOS
2.50 g., Copper Plated Steel, 17 mm. **Obv:** Value high on coin, different font, date **Rev:** Central Bank seal within circle and gear design **Rev. Legend:** BANGKO SENTRAL NG PILIPINAS - 1993 **Edge:** Reeded

Date	Mintage	F12	VF20	XF40	MS60	MS63
2006	—	—	—	0.10	0.30	0.40
2007	—	—	—	0.10	0.30	0.40
2008	—	—	—	0.10	0.30	0.40
2009	—	—	—	0.10	0.30	0.40
2010	—	—	—	0.10	0.30	0.40
2011	—	—	—	0.10	0.30	0.40
2012	—	—	—	0.10	0.30	0.40

KM# 271 25 SENTIMOS
3.80 g., Brass, 20 mm. **Obv:** Value and date **Rev:** Central Bank seal within circle and gear design, 1993 (date Central Bank was established) below **Rev. Legend:** BANGKO SENTRAL NG PILIPINAS - 1993 **Edge:** Plain

Date	Mintage	F12	VF20	XF40	MS60	MS63
2001	—	—	0.10	0.25	0.60	0.80
2002	—	—	0.10	0.25	0.60	0.80
2003	—	—	0.10	0.25	0.60	0.80

KM# 271a 25 SENTIMOS
3.60 g., Brass Plated Steel, 20 mm. **Obv:** Value and date **Rev:** Central Bank seal within circle and gear design **Rev. Legend:** BANGKO SENTRAL NG PILIPINAS - 1993 **Edge:** Plain

Date	Mintage	F12	VF20	XF40	MS60	MS63
2004	—	—	—	0.25	2.00	2.50
2005	—	—	—	0.25	1.00	1.25
2006	—	—	—	0.25	1.00	1.25
2007	—	—	—	0.25	1.00	1.25
2008	—	—	—	0.25	0.50	1.00
2009	—	—	—	0.25	0.50	1.00
2010	—	—	—	0.25	0.50	1.00
2011	—	—	—	0.25	0.50	1.00
2012	—	—	—	0.25	0.50	1.00
2013	—	—	—	0.25	0.50	1.00

KM# 269 PISO
6.10 g., Copper-Nickel, 24 mm. **Obv:** Head of Jose Rizal right, value and date **Rev:** Bank seal within circle and gear design, 1993 (date Central Bank was established) below **Rev. Legend:** BANGKO SENTRAL NG PILIPINAS - 1993 **Edge:** Reeded

Date	Mintage	F12	VF20	XF40	MS60	MS63
2001	—	—	0.25	0.50	1.25	1.75
2002	—	—	0.25	0.50	1.25	1.75
2003 Non Magnetic	—	—	—	—	—	11.00

Date	Mintage	F12	VF20	XF40	MS60	MS63
2011	—	—	—	—	0.20	0.25
2012	—	—	—	—	0.20	0.25

KM# 269a PISO
5.40 g., Nickel Plated Steel, 24 mm. **Obv:** Head of Jose Rizal right, value and date **Rev:** Bank seal within circle and gear design **Rev. Legend:** BANGKO SENTRAL NG PILIPINAS - 1993 **Edge:** Reeded

Date	Mintage	F12	VF20	XF40	MS60	MS63
2003	—	—	—	1.00	2.00	3.00
2004	—	—	—	0.45	5.00	7.00
2005	—	—	—	0.45	1.10	1.50
2006	—	—	—	0.45	1.10	1.50
2007	—	—	—	0.45	1.10	1.50
2008	—	—	—	0.45	1.10	1.50
2009	—	—	—	0.45	1.10	1.50
2010	—	—	—	0.45	1.10	1.50
2011	—	—	—	0.45	1.10	1.50
2012	—	—	—	0.45	1.10	1.50

KM# 284 PISO
5.35 g., Nickel Plated Steel, 24 mm. **Subject:** Jose Rizal 150th Birth Anniversary **Edge:** Reeded

Date	Mintage	F12	VF20	XF40	MS60	MS63
2011	10,000,000	—	—	—	1.00	1.50

KM# 272 5 PISO
7.70 g., Nickel-Brass, 27 mm. **Obv:** Head of Emilio Aguinaldo right, value and date within scalloped border **Rev:** Central Bank seal within circle and gear design within scalloped border, 1993 (date Central Bank was established) below **Rev. Legend:** BANGKO SENTRAL NG PILIPINAS - 1993 **Edge:** Plain

Date	Mintage	F12	VF20	XF40	MS60	MS63
2001BSP	—	—	1.00	2.00	3.00	4.50
2002	—	—	0.35	0.70	1.75	3.00
2003	—	—	0.35	0.70	1.75	3.00
2004	—	—	0.50	1.00	5.00	6.00
2005	—	—	0.35	0.70	1.75	3.00
2006	—	—	0.35	0.70	1.75	3.00
2007	—	—	0.35	0.70	1.75	3.00
2008	—	—	0.35	0.70	1.75	3.00
2009	—	—	0.35	0.70	1.75	3.00
2010	—	—	0.35	0.70	1.75	3.00
2011	—	—	0.35	0.70	1.75	3.00
2012	—	—	0.35	0.70	1.75	3.00

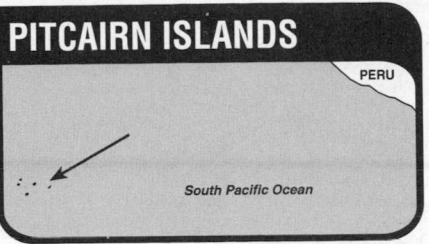

PITCAIRN ISLANDS

PERU

South Pacific Ocean

A small volcanic island, along with the uninhabited islands of Oeno, Henderson, and Ducie, constitute the British Colony of Pitcairn Islands. The main island has an area of about 2 sq. mi. (5 sq. km.) and a population of *68. It is located 1350 miles southeast of Tahiti. The islanders subsist on fishing, garden produce and crops. The sale of postage stamps and carved curios to passing ships brings cash income.

New Zealand currency has been used since July 10, 1967.

BRITISH COLONY
REGULAR COINAGE

KM# 54 5 CENTS
3.40 g., Copper Plated Bronze, 19 mm. **Ruler:** Elizabeth II **Obv:** Head right **Rev:** Anchor from the H.M.A.V. Bounty

Date	Mintage	F12	VF20	XF40	MS60	MS63
2009	20,000	—	—	—	—	2.00
2010	20,000	—	—	—	—	2.00

KM# 55 10 CENTS
4.60 g., Copper Plated Bronze, 22 mm. **Ruler:** Elizabeth II **Obv:** Head right **Rev:** Bell from H.M.A.V. Bounty **Edge:** Reeded

Date	Mintage	F12	VF20	XF40	MS60	MS63
2009	20,000	—	—	—	—	3.00
2010	20,000	—	—	—	—	3.00

KM# 56 20 CENTS
6.50 g., Nickel Plated Bronze, 25 mm. **Ruler:** Elizabeth II **Obv:** Head right **Rev:** Bible from H.M.A.V. Bounty

Date	Mintage	F12	VF20	XF40	MS60	MS63
2009	20,000	—	—	—	—	5.00
2010	20,000	—	—	—	—	5.00

KM# 57 50 CENTS
8.00 g., Copper-Nickel, **Ruler:** Elizabeth II **Obv:** Head right **Rev:** Pitcairn Longboat

Date	Mintage	F12	VF20	XF40	MS60	MS63
2009	—	—	—	—	—	8.00
2010	—	—	—	—	—	8.00

KM# 14 DOLLAR
Copper-Nickel, 38.8 mm. **Ruler:** Elizabeth II **Obv:** Bust facing right **Rev:** Queen Mum, Elizabeth II and Margaret facing **Rev. Legend:** 80th Birthday of H.M. Queen Elizabeth II

Date	Mintage	F12	VF20	XF40	MS60	MS63
2006	—	—	—	—	10.00	12.00

KM# 58 DOLLAR
16.30 g., Aluminum-Brass, 32 mm. **Ruler:** Elizabeth II **Obv:** Head right **Rev:** Cannon from H.A.M.V. Bounty **Edge:** Reeded

Date	Mintage	F12	VF20	XF40	MS60	MS63
2009	20,000	—	—	—	—	10.00
2010	20,000	—	—	—	—	10.00

KM# 45 2 DOLLARS
31.11 g., 0.999 Silver 0.9926 oz. ASW, 40.7 mm. **Ruler:** Elizabeth II **Subject:** Year of the Rat **Rev:** Multicolor rat seated right

Date	Mintage	F12	VF20	XF40	MS60	MS63
2008 Prooflike	30,000	—	—	—	—	85.00

KM# 46 2 DOLLARS
31.11 g., 0.999 Silver 0.9926 oz. ASW, 40.7 mm. **Ruler:** Elizabeth II **Rev:** Multicolor HMAV Bounty under full sail right

Date	Mintage	F12	VF20	XF40	MS60	MS63
2008 Prooflike	5,000	—	—	—	—	75.00

KM# 47 2 DOLLARS
31.11 g., 0.999 Silver 0.9926 oz. ASW, 40.7 mm. **Ruler:** Elizabeth II **Rev:** HMAV Bounty under full sail right

Date	Mintage	F12	VF20	XF40	MS60	MS63
2008	1,500	PF65 85.00				

KM# 278 10 PISO
8.70 g., Bi-Metallic, 26.5 mm. **Obv:** Conjoined heads right within circle **Rev:** Bank seal within circle and gear design, 1993 (date Central Bank was established) below **Rev. Legend:** BANGKO SENTRAL NG PILIPINAS - 1993 **Edge:** Segmented reeding

Date	Mintage	F12	VF20	XF40	MS60	MS63
2001	—	—	0.70	1.40	3.50	5.50
2002	—	—	0.60	1.20	2.00	3.00
2003	—	—	0.60	1.20	3.00	4.00
2004	—	—	0.80	2.00	5.00	8.00
2005	—	—	0.75	1.50	3.75	5.00
2006	—	—	0.60	1.20	3.00	4.00
2007	—	—	0.75	1.50	3.75	5.00
2008	—	—	0.75	1.50	3.75	5.00
2009	—	—	0.75	1.50	3.75	5.00
2010	—	—	0.75	1.50	3.75	5.00
2011	—	—	—	—	7.50	10.00
2012	—	—	0.75	1.50	3.75	5.00

MINT SETS

KM#	Date	Mintage	Identification	Issue Price	Mkt Val
MS39	2005 (7)	—	KM#268-273, 278 plus medal	10.00	15.00
MS40	2006 (7)	—	KM#268-273, 278	10.00	15.00
MS41	2009 (7)	—	KM#268-273, 278	25.00	30.00
MS42	2011 (7)	—	KM#268-273, 278 plus Rizal Medal	25.00	32.00

KM# 59 2 DOLLARS
19.50 g., Aluminum-Brass, 35 mm. **Ruler:** Elizabeth II **Obv:** Head right **Rev:** Helm (wheel) from H.M.A.V. Bounty **Edge:** Seqmented reeding

Date	Mintage	F12	VF20	XF40	MS60	MS63
2009	20,000	—	—	—	—	12.00

KM# 51 2 DOLLARS
31.11 g., 0.999 Silver 0.9926 oz. ASW, 40.7 mm. **Ruler:** Elizabeth II **Rev:** Captain William Bligh partially gilt

Date	Mintage	F12	VF20	XF40	MS60	MS63
2009	1,500	PF65 120				

KM# 67 2 DOLLARS
31.11 g., Silver, 40.7 mm. **Ruler:** Elizabeth II **Rev:** Ox striding right, gilt

Date	Mintage	F12	VF20	XF40	MS60	MS63
2009	15,000	PF65 85.00				

KM# 68 2 DOLLARS
31.11 g., 0.999 Silver 0.9926 oz. ASW, 40.7 mm. **Ruler:** Elizabeth II **Rev:** Ox striding right, color

Date	Mintage	F12	VF20	XF40	MS60	MS63
2009	15,000	PF65 85.00				

KM# 60 2 DOLLARS
Brass, 36 mm. **Ruler:** Elizabeth II **Rev:** H.M.A.V. Bounty at sail **Edge:** Segmented reeding

Date	Mintage	F12	VF20	XF40	MS60	MS63
2010	20,000	—	—	—	—	15.00

KM# 61 2 DOLLARS
15.50 g., 0.925 Silver 0.458 oz. ASW, 35 mm. **Ruler:** Elizabeth II **Subject:** Deep sea fish **Rev:** Black sea devil (Melanocetus Johnsonii) in color

Date	Mintage	F12	VF20	XF40	MS60	MS63
2010	1,000	PF65 95.00				

KM# 62 2 DOLLARS
15.55 g., 0.925 Silver 0.4595 oz. ASW, 35 mm. **Ruler:** Elizabeth II **Subject:** Deep sea fish **Rev:** White spotted jellyfish in color

Date	Mintage	F12	VF20	XF40	MS60	MS63
2010	—	PF65 95.00				

KM# 63 2 DOLLARS
15.55 g., 0.925 Silver 0.4595 oz. ASW, 35 mm. **Ruler:** Elizabeth II **Subject:** Deep sea fish **Rev:** Laternfish (Mychtophios) in color

Date	Mintage	F12	VF20	XF40	MS60	MS63
2010	1,000	PF65 95.00				

KM# 65 2 DOLLARS
31.11 g., 0.999 Silver 0.9926 oz. ASW, 40.7 mm. **Ruler:** Elizabeth II **Rev:** H.M.A.V. Bounty at sail, gilt

Date	Mintage	F12	VF20	XF40	MS60	MS63
2010	3,000	PF65 140				

KM# 66 2 DOLLARS
31.11 g., 0.999 Silver 0.9926 oz. ASW, 40.7 mm. **Ruler:** Elizabeth II **Rev:** Fletcher Christian facing, partially gilt

Date	Mintage	F12	VF20	XF40	MS60	MS63
2010	3,000	PF65 140				

KM# 64 2 DOLLARS
31.11 g., 0.999 Silver 0.9926 oz. ASW, 40.7 mm. **Ruler:** Elizabeth II **Subject:** Alice in Wonderland **Rev:** March Hare within backward clock face

Date	Mintage	F12	VF20	XF40	MS60	MS63
2011	15,000	PF65 85.00				

KM# 69 2 DOLLARS
31.11 g., 0.999 Silver 0.9926 oz. ASW, 40.7 mm. **Ruler:** Elizabeth II **Rev:** Rabbit in snow, multicolor

Date	Mintage	F12	VF20	XF40	MS60	MS63
2011	15,000	PF65 125				

KM# 71 2 DOLLARS
15.50 g., 0.925 Silver 0.458 oz. ASW, 35 mm. **Ruler:** Elizabeth II **Rev:** Cotylorhiza Tuberculata, Jellyfish in color

Date	Mintage	F12	VF20	XF40	MS60	MS63
2011	1,000	PF65 95.00				

KM# 72 2 DOLLARS
15.50 g., 0.925 Silver 0.458 oz. ASW, 35 mm. **Ruler:** Elizabeth II **Rev:** Chrysaora Achlyos, black jellyfish in color

Date	Mintage	F12	VF20	XF40	MS60	MS63
2011	1,000	PF65 95.00				

KM# 73 2 DOLLARS
15.50 g., 0.925 Silver 0.458 oz. ASW, 35 mm. **Ruler:** Elizabeth II
Rev: Anoplogaster Cornuta, Fangtooth fish in color

Date	Mintage	F12	VF20	XF40	MS60	MS63
2011	1,000	PF65 95.00				

KM# 74 2 DOLLARS
15.50 g., 0.925 Silver 0.458 oz. ASW, 35 mm. **Ruler:** Elizabeth II **Rev:** Melanostomias Biseriatus in color

Date	Mintage	F12	VF20	XF40	MS60	MS63
2011	1,000	PF65 95.00				

KM# 75 2 DOLLARS
15.55 g., Silver, 35 mm. **Ruler:** Elizabeth II **Subject:** Deep Sea Fish 5

Date	Mintage	F12	VF20	XF40	MS60	MS63
2013	Est. 1000	PF65 95.00				

KM# 12 5 DOLLARS
31.10 g., 0.999 Silver 0.9925 oz. ASW, 40 mm. **Ruler:** Elizabeth II **Series:** Save the Whales **Obv:** Crowned bust right **Obv. Legend:** ELIZABETH II • PITCAIRN ISLANDS **Rev:** Humpback Whale and date on mother-of-pearl inset **Edge:** Plain

Date	Mintage	F12	VF20	XF40	MS60	MS63
2002	2,000	PF65 95.00				

KM# 50 5 DOLLARS
1.27 g., 0.9999 Gold 0.0406 oz. AGW, 13.92 mm. **Ruler:** Elizabeth II **Obv:** Crowned bust right **Obv. Legend:** Elizabeth II Pitcairn Islands **Rev:** Bounty Bible and ship

Date	Mintage	F12	VF20	XF40	MS60	MS63
2005	—	PF65 90.00				

KM# 48 10 DOLLARS
1.24 g., 0.9999 Gold 0.0397 oz. AGW, 14 mm. **Ruler:** Elizabeth II **Rev:** HMAV Bounty under full sail right

Date	Mintage	F12	VF20	XF40	MS60	MS63
2008	10,000	PF65 165				

KM# 49 25 DOLLARS
7.77 g., 0.999 Gold 0.248 oz. AGW, 22 mm. **Ruler:** Elizabeth II **Rev:** HMAV Bounty under full sail right

Date	Mintage	F12	VF20	XF40	MS60	MS63
2008	1,500	PF65 775				

MINT SETS

KM#	Date	Mintage	Identification	Issue Price	Mkt Val
MS1	2009 (6)	20,000	KM#54; 55; 56; 57; 58; 59	—	45.00
MS2	2010 (6)	20,000	KM#54; 55; 56; 57; 58; 60	—	45.00

The Republic of Poland, located in central Europe, has an area of 120,725 sq. mi. (312,680 sq. km.) and a population of *38.2 million. Capital: Warszawa (Warsaw). The economy is essentially agricultural, but industrial activity provides the products for foreign trade. Machinery, coal, coke, iron, steel and transport equipment are exported.

MINT MARKS
MV, MW, MW-monogram - Warsaw Mint, 1965-
CHI - Valcambi, Switzerland
Other letters appearing with date denote the Mintmaster at the time the coin was struck.
As far back as 1990, production was initiated for the new 1 Grosz - 1 Zlotych coins for a forthcoming monetary reform. It wasn't announced until the Act of July 7, 1994 and was enacted on January 1, 1995.100 Old Zlotych = 1 Grosz; 10,000 Old Zlotych = 1 Zloty

Y# 276 GROSZ
1.64 g., Brass, 15.5 mm. **Obv:** National arms **Obv. Legend:** RZECZPOSPOLITA POLSKA **Rev:** Drooping oak leaf over value **Edge:** Reeded

Date	Mintage	F12	VF20	XF40	MS60	MS63
2001MW	210,000,020	—	—	—	0.10	0.20
2002MW	240,000,000	—	—	—	0.10	0.20
2003MW	250,000,000	—	—	—	0.10	0.20
2004MW	300,000,000	—	—	—	0.10	0.20
2005MW	375,000,000	—	—	—	0.10	0.20
2006MW	184,000,000	—	—	—	0.10	0.20
2007MW	330,000,000	—	—	—	0.10	0.20
2008MW	—	—	—	—	0.10	0.20
2009MW	—	—	—	—	0.10	0.20
2010MW	—	—	—	—	0.10	0.20
2011MW	—	—	—	—	0.10	0.20
2012MW	—	—	—	—	0.10	0.20

Y# 277 2 GROSZE
2.13 g., Brass, 17.5 mm. **Obv:** National arms **Obv. Legend:** RZECZPOSPOLITA POLSKA **Rev:** Drooping oak leaves above value **Edge:** Plain

Date	Mintage	F12	VF20	XF40	MS60	MS63
2001MW	86,100,000	—	—	—	0.15	0.25
2002MW	83,910,000	—	—	—	0.15	0.25
2003MW	80,000,000	—	—	—	0.15	0.25
2004MW	100,000,000	—	—	—	0.15	0.25
2005MW	163,003,250	—	—	—	0.15	0.25
2006MW	105,000,000	—	—	—	0.15	0.25
2007MW	160,000,000	—	—	—	0.15	0.25
2008MW	—	—	—	—	0.15	0.25
2009MW	—	—	—	—	0.15	0.25
2010MW	—	—	—	—	0.15	0.25
2011MW	—	—	—	—	0.15	0.25
2012MW	—	—	—	—	0.15	0.25
2013MW	—	—	—	—	0.15	0.25

Y# 278 5 GROSZY
2.59 g., Brass, 19.5 mm. **Obv:** National arms **Obv. Legend:** RZECZPOSPOLITA POLSKA **Rev:** Value at upper left of oak leaves **Edge:** Segmented reeding

Date	Mintage	F12	VF20	XF40	MS60	MS63
2001MW	67,368,000	—	—	—	0.25	0.45
2002MW	67,200,000	—	—	—	0.25	0.45
2003MW	48,000,000	—	—	—	0.25	0.45
2004MW	62,500,000	—	—	—	0.25	0.45
2005MW	113,000,000	—	—	—	0.25	0.45
2006MW	54,000,000	—	—	—	0.25	0.45
2007MW	116,000,000	—	—	—	0.25	0.45
2008MW	—	—	—	—	0.25	0.45
2009MW	—	—	—	—	0.25	0.45
2010MW	—	—	—	—	0.25	0.45
2011MW	—	—	—	—	0.25	0.45

Date	Mintage	F12	VF20	XF40	MS60	MS63
2012MW	—	—	—	—	0.25	0.45
2013MW	—	—	—	—	0.25	0.45

Y# 279 10 GROSZY
2.55 g., Copper-Nickel, 16.5 mm. **Obv:** National arms **Obv. Legend:** RZECZPOSPOLITA POLSKA **Rev:** Value within wreath

Date	Mintage	F12	VF20	XF40	MS60	MS63
2001MW	62,820,000	—	—	—	0.40	0.60
2002MW	10,500,000	—	—	—	0.40	0.60
2003MW	31,500,000	—	—	—	0.40	0.60
2004MW	70,500,000	—	—	—	0.40	0.60
2005MW	94,000,000	—	—	—	0.40	0.60
2006MW	40,000,000	—	—	—	0.40	0.60
2007MW	100,000,000	—	—	—	0.40	0.60
2008MW	—	—	—	—	0.40	0.60
2009MW	—	—	—	—	0.40	0.60
2010MW	—	—	—	—	0.40	0.60
2011MW	—	—	—	—	0.40	0.60
2012MW	—	—	—	—	0.40	0.60

Y# 280 20 GROSZY
3.22 g., Copper-Nickel, 18.5 mm. **Obv:** National arms **Obv. Legend:** RZECZPOSPOLITA POLSKA **Rev:** Value within artistic design **Edge:** Reeded

Date	Mintage	F12	VF20	XF40	MS60	MS63
2001MW	41,980,001	—	—	—	0.65	0.85
2002MW	10,500,000	—	—	—	0.65	0.85
2003MW	20,400,000	—	—	—	0.65	0.85
2004MW	40,000,025	—	—	—	0.65	0.85
2005MW	37,000,000	—	—	—	0.65	0.85
2006MW	35,000,000	—	—	—	0.65	0.85
2007MW	08,000,000	—	—	—	0.65	0.85
2008MW	—	—	—	—	0.65	0.85
2009MW	—	—	—	—	0.65	0.85
2010MW	—	—	—	—	0.65	0.85
2011MW	—	—	—	—	0.65	0.85
2012MW	—	—	—	—	0.65	0.85

Y# 281 50 GROSZY
3.94 g., Copper-Nickel, 20.5 mm. **Obv:** National arms **Obv. Legend:** RZECZPOSPOLITA POLSKA **Rev:** Value to right of sprig **Edge:** Reeded

Date	Mintage	F12	VF20	XF40	MS60	MS63
2008MW	—	—	—	—	1.00	1.25
2009MW	—	—	—	—	1.00	1.25
2010MW	—	—	—	—	1.00	1.25
2011MW	—	—	—	—	1.00	1.25
2012MW	—	—	—	—	1.00	1.25
2013MW	—	—	—	—	1.00	1.25

Y# 282 ZŁOTY
5.03 g., Copper-Nickel, 23 mm. **Obv:** National arms **Obv. Legend:** RZECZPOSPOLITA POLSKA **Rev:** Value within wreath **Edge:** Segmented reeding

Date	Mintage	F12	VF20	XF40	MS60	MS63
2008MW	—	—	—	—	1.75	2.00
2009MW	—	—	—	—	1.75	2.00
2010MW	—	—	—	—	1.75	2.00
2012MW	—	—	—	—	1.75	2.00
2013MW	—	—	—	—	1.75	2.00

Y# 283 2 ZŁOTE
5.21 g., Bi-Metallic, 21.5 mm. **Obv:** National arms within circle **Obv. Legend:** RZECZPOSPOLITA POLSKA **Rev:** Value flanked by oak leaves **Edge:** Plain

Date	Mintage	F12	VF20	XF40	MS60	MS63
2005MW	5,000,000	—	—	—	4.00	4.50
2006MW	5,000,000	—	—	—	4.00	4.50
2007MW	20,000,000	—	—	—	4.00	4.50

Note: Varieties exist with or without pellets flanking date on obverse.

Date	Mintage	F12	VF20	XF40	MS60	MS63
2008MW	—	—	—	—	4.00	4.50
2009MW	—	—	—	—	4.00	4.50
2010MW	—	—	—	—	4.00	4.50

Y# 408 2 ZŁOTE
8.15 g., Brass, 27 mm. **Subject:** Wieliczka Salt Mine **Obv:** Crowned eagle with wings open **Rev:** Ancient salt miners

Date	Mintage	F12	VF20	XF40	MS60	MS63
2001	500,000	—	—	3.50	7.00	12.00

Y# 410 2 ZŁOTE
8.15 g., Brass, 27 mm. **Subject:** Amber Route **Obv:** Crowned eagle with wings open **Rev:** Ancient Roman coin and map with route marked in stars

Date	Mintage	F12	VF20	XF40	MS60	MS63
2001	500,000	—	—	3.50	7.00	12.00

Y# 412 2 ZŁOTE
8.15 g., Brass, 27 mm. **Subject:** 15 Years of the Constitutional Court **Obv:** Crowned eagle with wings open **Rev:** Crowned eagle head and scale **Edge:** * NBP * eight times

Date	Mintage	F12	VF20	XF40	MS60	MS63
2001MW	500,000	—	—	—	3.00	5.00

Y# 414 2 ZŁOTE
8.15 g., Brass, 27 mm. **Obv:** Crowned eagle with wings open **Rev:** Butterfly **Edge:** * NBP * eight times

Date	Mintage	F12	VF20	XF40	MS60	MS63
2001MW	600,000	—	—	4.00	8.00	15.00

Y# 418 2 ZŁOTE
8.15 g., Brass, 27 mm. **Subject:** Cardinal Stefan Wyszynski **Obv:** Crowned eagle with wings open **Rev:** Bust left wearing mitre **Edge:** NBP" eight times

Date	Mintage	F12	VF20	XF40	MS60	MS63
2001MW	1,200,000	—	—	—	3.00	5.00

Y# 421 2 ZŁOTE
8.15 g., Brass, 27 mm. **Subject:** Michal Siedlecki **Obv:** Crowned eagle with wings open **Rev:** Bust left and art work **Edge:** NBP eight times

Date	Mintage	F12	VF20	XF40	MS60	MS63
2001MW	600,000	—	—	—	3.00	5.00

Y# 422 2 ZŁOTE
8.15 g., Brass, 27 mm. **Subject:** Koledicy **Obv:** Crowned eagle with wings open **Rev:** Christmas celebration scene

Date	Mintage	F12	VF20	XF40	MS60	MS63
2001MW	600,000	—	—	—	3.00	5.00

Y# 423 2 ZŁOTE
8.15 g., Brass, 27 mm. **Subject:** Jan III Sobieski **Obv:** Crowned eagle with wings open **Rev:** Bust facing **Edge Lettering:** * NBP * eight times

Date	Mintage	F12	VF20	XF40	MS60	MS63
2001MW	500,000	—	—	3.50	7.00	12.00

Y# 426 2 ZŁOTE
8.15 g., Brass, 27 mm. **Subject:** Henryk Wieniawski **Obv:** Crowned eagle with wings open **Rev:** Bust left and violin **Edge Lettering:** * NBP * eight times

Date	Mintage	F12	VF20	XF40	MS60	MS63
2001MW	600,000	—	—	—	3.00	5.00

Y# 427 2 ZŁOTE
8.15 g., Brass, 27 mm. **Obv:** Crowned eagle with wings open **Rev:** European Pond Turtles **Edge Lettering:** * NBP * eight times

Date	Mintage	F12	VF20	XF40	MS60	MS63
2002MW	750,000	—	—	3.50	7.00	12.00

Y# 431 2 ZŁOTE
8.15 g., Brass, 27 mm. **Subject:** Bronislaw Malinowski **Obv:** Crowned eagle with wings open **Rev:** Bust facing and Trobriand Islanders **Edge Lettering:** * NBP * eight times

Date	Mintage	F12	VF20	XF40	MS60	MS63
2002MW	680,000	—	—	—	3.50	5.50

Y# 433 2 ZŁOTE
8.15 g., Brass, 27 mm. **Subject:** World Cup Soccer **Obv:** National arms **Rev:** Soccer players **Edge Lettering:** * NBP * eight times

Date	Mintage	F12	VF20	XF40	MS60	MS63
2002MW	1,000,000	—	—	—	3.00	5.00

Y# 439 2 ZŁOTE
8.10 g., Brass, 26.8 mm. **Subject:** August II (1697-1706, 1709-1733) **Obv:** National arms **Rev:** Head facing **Edge Lettering:** * NBP * eight times

Date	Mintage	F12	VF20	XF40	MS60	MS63
2002MW	620,000	—	—	—	4.00	7.00

Y# 440 2 ZŁOTE
8.15 g., Brass, 27 mm. **Subject:** Gen. Wladyslaw Anders **Obv:** Crowned eagle with wings open **Rev:** Uniformed bust facing and cross **Edge Lettering:** * NBP * eight times

Date	Mintage	F12	VF20	XF40	MS60	MS63
2002MW	680,000	—	—	—	3.00	5.00

Y# 443 2 ZŁOTE
8.15 g., Brass, 27 mm. **Subject:** Malbork Castle **Obv:** Crowned eagle with wings open **Rev:** Castle **Edge Lettering:** * NBP * eight times

Date	Mintage	F12	VF20	XF40	MS60	MS63
2002MW	680,000	—	—	—	3.00	5.00

Y# 444 2 ZŁOTE
8.15 g., Brass, 27 mm. **Subject:** Jan Matejko **Obv:** Denomination, crowned eagle and artist's palette **Rev:** Jester behind portrait **Edge Lettering:** * NBP * eight times

Date	Mintage	F12	VF20	XF40	MS60	MS63
2002MW	700,000	—	—	—	3.00	5.00

Y# 445 2 ZŁOTE
8.15 g., Brass, 27 mm. **Subject:** Eels **Obv:** Crowned eagle with wings open **Rev:** Two European eels **Edge Lettering:** * NBP * eight times

Date	Mintage	F12	VF20	XF40	MS60	MS63
2003MW	450,000	—	—	6.00	12.00	20.00

Y# 446 2 ZŁOTE

7.75 g., Brass, 27 mm. **Subject:** Children **Obv:** Children and square design above crowned eagle, date and value **Rev:** Children on square design **Edge Lettering:** * NBP * eight times **Note:** Center hole.

Date	Mintage	F12	VF20	XF40	MS60	MS63
2003MW	2,500,000	—	—	—	4.50	6.50

Y# 447 2 ZŁOTE

8.15 g., Brass, 27 mm. **Subject:** City of Poznan (Posen) **Obv:** Crowned eagle with wings open **Rev:** Clock face and tower flanked by goat heads **Edge Lettering:** * NBP * eight times

Date	Mintage	F12	VF20	XF40	MS60	MS63
2003MW	600,000	—	—	—	5.00	8.00

Y# 451 2 ZŁOTE

8.15 g., Brass, 27 mm. **Subject:** Easter Monday Festival **Obv:** Crowned eagle with wings open **Rev:** Festival scene **Edge Lettering:** * NBP * eight times

Date	Mintage	F12	VF20	XF40	MS60	MS63
2003MW	600,000	—	—	—	4.00	7.00

Y# 455 2 ZŁOTE

8.15 g., Brass, 27 mm. **Subject:** Petroleum and Gas Industry 150th Anniversary **Obv:** Crowned eagle with wings open **Rev:** Portrait and refinery **Edge Lettering:** * NBP * eight times

Date	Mintage	F12	VF20	XF40	MS60	MS63
2003MW	600,000	—	—	—	3.50	5.50

Y# 456 2 ZŁOTE

8.15 g., Brass, 27 mm. **Subject:** General B. S. Maczek **Obv:** Crowned eagle with wings open **Rev:** Military uniformed portrait **Edge Lettering:** * NBP * eight times

Date	Mintage	F12	VF20	XF40	MS60	MS63
2003MW	700,000	—	—	—	3.00	5.00

Y# 465 2 ZŁOTE

8.15 g., Brass, 27 mm. **Subject:** Pope John Paul II **Obv:** Small national arms at lower right with cross in background **Obv. Legend:** RZECZPOSPOLITA POLSKA **Rev:** Pope in prayer at left, cross in background **Edge Lettering:** * NBP * eight times

Date	Mintage	F12	VF20	XF40	MS60	MS63
2003MW	2,000,000	—	—	—	3.00	5.00

Y# 473 2 ZŁOTE

8.15 g., Brass, 27 mm. **Obv:** Crowned eagle with wings open **Rev:** Stanislaus Leszcywski **Edge Lettering:** * NBP * eight times

Date	Mintage	F12	VF20	XF40	MS60	MS63
2003MW	600,000	—	—	—	3.50	5.50

Y# 477 2 ZŁOTE

8.15 g., Brass, 27 mm. **Obv:** Crowned eagle with wings open and artist's palette **Rev:** Self portrait of Jacek Malczewski **Edge Lettering:** * NBP * eight times

Date	Mintage	F12	VF20	XF40	MS60	MS63
2003MW	600,000	—	—	—	3.50	5.50

Y# 479 2 ZŁOTE

8.15 g., Brass, 27 mm. **Subject:** 80th Anniversary of the Modern Zloty Currency **Obv:** Crowned eagle with wings open above value **Rev:** Bust left **Edge Lettering:** * NBP * eight times

Date	Mintage	F12	VF20	XF40	MS60	MS63
2004MW	800,000	—	—	—	3.00	5.00

Y# 481 2 ZŁOTE

8.15 g., Brass, 27 mm. **Subject:** Poland Joining the European Union **Obv:** Crowned eagle with wings open above value **Rev:** Map and stars **Edge Lettering:** * NBP * eight times

Date	Mintage	F12	VF20	XF40	MS60	MS63
2004MW	1,000,000	—	—	—	3.00	5.00

Y# 484 2 ZŁOTE

8.15 g., Brass, 27 mm. **Subject:** Dolnoslaskie (Lower Silesian) District **Obv:** Crowned eagle with wings open on map **Rev:** Silesian eagle on shield **Edge Lettering:** * NBP * eight times

Date	Mintage	F12	VF20	XF40	MS60	MS63
2004MW	700,000	—	—	—	4.00	6.00

Y# 485 2 ZŁOTE

8.15 g., Brass, 27 mm. **Subject:** Kujawsko-Pomorskie District **Obv:** Crowned eagle with wings open **Rev:** Shield with crowned half eagle and griffin **Edge Lettering:** * NBP * eight times

Date	Mintage	F12	VF20	XF40	MS60	MS63
2004MW	750,000	—	—	—	7.00	12.00

Y# 486 2 ZŁOTE

8.15 g., Brass, 27 mm. **Subject:** Lubuskie District **Obv:** Crowned eagle with wings open on map **Rev:** Shield with stag left **Edge Lettering:** * NBP * eight times

Date	Mintage	F12	VF20	XF40	MS60	MS63
2004MW	820,000	—	—	—	3.00	5.00

Y# 487 2 ZŁOTE

8.15 g., Brass, 27 mm. **Subject:** Lodzkie District **Obv:** Crowned eagle with wings open on map **Rev:** Shield with two creatures above an eagle **Edge Lettering:** * NBP * eight times

Date	Mintage	F12	VF20	XF40	MS60	MS63
2004MW	920,000	—	—	—	3.00	5.00

Y# 488 2 ZŁOTE

8.15 g., Brass, 27 mm. **Subject:** Malopolskie District **Obv:** Crowned eagle with wings open on map **Rev:** Shield with crowned eagle **Edge Lettering:** * NBP * eight times

Date	Mintage	F12	VF20	XF40	MS60	MS63
2004MW	920,000	—	—	—	3.00	5.00

Y# 489 2 ZŁOTE

8.15 g., Brass, 27 mm. **Subject:** Mazowieckie District **Obv:** Crowned eagle with wings open on map **Rev:** Eagle on shield **Edge Lettering:** * NBP * eight times

Date	Mintage	F12	VF20	XF40	MS60	MS63
2004MW	920,000	—	—	—	3.00	5.00

Y# 490 2 ZŁOTE

8.15 g., Brass, 27 mm. **Subject:** Podkarpackie District **Obv:** Crowned eagle with wings open on map **Rev:** Shield with iron cross above griffin and lion **Edge Lettering:** * NBP * eight times

Date	Mintage	F12	VF20	XF40	MS60	MS63
2004MW	920,000	—	—	—	3.00	5.00

Y# 491 2 ZŁOTE

8.15 g., Brass, 27 mm. **Subject:** Podlaskie District **Obv:** Crowned eagle with wings open on map **Rev:** Shield with Polish eagle above Lithuanian knight **Edge Lettering:** * NBP * eight times

Date	Mintage	F12	VF20	XF40	MS60	MS63
2004MW	900,000	—	—	—	3.00	5.00

Y# 492 2 ZŁOTE

8.15 g., Brass, 27 mm. **Subject:** Pomorskie District **Obv:** Crowned eagle with wings open on map **Rev:** Griffin on shield **Edge Lettering:** * NBP * eight times

Date	Mintage	F12	VF20	XF40	MS60	MS63
2004MW	900,000	—	—	—	3.00	5.00

Y# 493 2 ZŁOTE

8.15 g., Brass, 27 mm. **Subject:** Slaskie (Silesia) District **Obv:** Crowned eagle with wings open on map **Rev:** Eagle on shield **Edge Lettering:** * NBP * eight times

Date	Mintage	F12	VF20	XF40	MS60	MS63
2004MW	960,000	—	—	—	3.00	5.00

Y# 496 2 ZŁOTE

8.15 g., Brass, 27 mm. **Subject:** Warsaw Uprising 60th Anniversary **Obv:** Crowned eagle with wings open **Rev:** Resistance symbol on brick wall **Edge Lettering:** * NBP * eight times

Date	Mintage	F12	VF20	XF40	MS60	MS63
2004MW	900,000	—	—	—	3.00	5.00

Y# 499 2 ZŁOTE

8.15 g., Brass, 27 mm. **Obv:** Crowned eagle with wings open **Rev:** Gen. Stanislaw F. Sosabowski **Edge Lettering:** * NBP * eight times

Date	Mintage	F12	VF20	XF40	MS60	MS63
2004MW	850,000	—	—	—	3.00	5.00

Y# 501 2 ZŁOTE

8.15 g., Brass, 27 mm. **Subject:** Polish Police 85th Anniversary **Obv:** Crowned eagle with wings open **Rev:** Police badge **Edge Lettering:** * NBP * eight times

Date	Mintage	F12	VF20	XF40	MS60	MS63
2004MW	760,000	—	—	—	3.00	5.00

Y# 503 2 ZŁOTE

8.15 g., Brass, 27 mm. **Subject:** Polish Senate **Obv:** Crowned eagle with wings open **Rev:** Senate eagle and speaker's staff **Edge Lettering:** * NBP * eight times

Date	Mintage	F12	VF20	XF40	MS60	MS63
2004MW	760,000	—	—	—	3.00	5.00

Y# 505 2 ZŁOTE

8.15 g., Brass, 27 mm. **Obv:** Crowned eagle with wings open **Rev:** Aleksander Czekanowski (1833-1876) **Edge Lettering:** * NBP * eight times

Date	Mintage	F12	VF20	XF40	MS60	MS63
2004MW	700,000	—	—	—	3.00	5.00

Y# 507 2 ZŁOTE

8.15 g., Brass, 27 mm. **Obv:** National arms **Obv. Legend:** RZECZPOSPOLITA POLSKA **Rev:** Harvest fest couple in folk costume at left, large group in background at right **Rev. Legend:** DOZYNKI **Edge Lettering:** * NBP * eight times

Date	Mintage	F12	VF20	XF40	MS60	MS63
2004MW	850,000	—	—	—	3.00	5.00

Y# 509 2 ZŁOTE

8.15 g., Brass, 27 mm. **Subject:** Warsaw Fine Arts Academy Centennial **Obv:** Crowned eagle with wings open **Rev:** Painter's hands **Edge Lettering:** * NBP * eight times

Date	Mintage	F12	VF20	XF40	MS60	MS63
2004MW	850,000	—	—	—	3.00	5.00

Y# 516 2 ZŁOTE

8.15 g., Brass, 27 mm. **Subject:** Olympics **Obv:** Crowned eagle with wings open **Rev:** Ancient runners **Edge Lettering:** * NBP * eight times

Date	Mintage	F12	VF20	XF40	MS60	MS63
2004MW	1,000,000	—	—	—	3.00	5.00

Y# 607 2 ZŁOTE

8.15 g., Brass, 27 mm. **Obv:** National arms on outlined map **Obv. Legend:** RZECZPOSPOLITA POLSKA **Rev:** Region arms **Rev. Legend:** WOJEWODZTWO - OPOLSKIE **Edge Lettering:** * NBP * eight times

Date	Mintage	F12	VF20	XF40	MS60	MS63
2004MW	900,000	—	—	—	3.00	5.00

Y# 464 2 ZŁOTE

8.15 g., Brass, 27 mm. **Obv:** Crowned eagle with wings open **Rev:** Harbor Porpoises **Edge Lettering:** * NBP * eight times

Date	Mintage	F12	VF20	XF40	MS60	MS63
2004MW	800,000	—	—	3.50	7.00	12.00

Y# 512 2 ZŁOTE

8.15 g., Brass, 27 mm. **Obv:** Crowned eagle with wings open and artist's palette **Rev:** Stanislaw Wyspianski (1869-1907) **Edge Lettering:** * NBP * eight times

Date	Mintage	F12	VF20	XF40	MS60	MS63
2004MW	900,000	—	—	—	3.00	5.00

Y# 514 2 ZŁOTE

8.15 g., Brass, 27 mm. **Obv:** National arms on outlined map **Rev:** Wojewodztwo-Lubelskie arms with stag on shield **Edge Lettering:** * NBP * eight times

Date	Mintage	F12	VF20	XF40	MS60	MS63
2004MW	820,000	—	—	—	—	7.50

Y# 520 2 ZŁOTE

8.15 g., Brass, 27 mm. **Obv:** National arms **Rev:** Owl perched on nest with owlets **Rev. Legend:** PUCHACZ - Bubo-bubo **Edge Lettering:** * NBP * eight times

Date	Mintage	F12	VF20	XF40	MS60	MS63
2005MW	990,000	—	—	—	4.00	7.00

Y# 521 2 ZŁOTE
8.15 g., Brass, 27 mm. **Obv:** Crowned eagle with wings open **Rev:** Ship within circle **Edge Lettering:** * NBP * eight times

Date	Mintage	F12	VF20	XF40	MS60	MS63
2005MW	920,000	—	—	—	3.50	5.50

Y# 522 2 ZŁOTE
8.15 g., Brass, 26.8 mm. **Subject:** Japan's Aichi Expo **Obv:** Crowned eagle with wings open **Rev:** Two cranes flying over Mt. Fuji with rising sun background **Edge Lettering:** * NBP * eight times

Date	Mintage	F12	VF20	XF40	MS60	MS63
2005MW	1,000,000	—	—	—	3.50	5.50

Y# 524 2 ZŁOTE
8.15 g., Brass, 27 mm. **Subject:** Obrony Jasnej Gory **Obv:** Crowned eagle with wings open **Rev:** Half length figure left and bombarded city scene **Edge Lettering:** * NBP * eight times

Date	Mintage	F12	VF20	XF40	MS60	MS63
2005MW	1,000,000	—	—	—	4.00	6.00

Y# 525 2 ZŁOTE
8.15 g., Brass, 27 mm. **Subject:** Pope John-Paul II **Obv:** National arms **Obv. Legend:** RZECZPOSPOLITA POLSKA **Rev:** Bust right at left, outline of St. Peter's Baslica at center right **Edge Lettering:** * NBP * eight times

Date	Mintage	F12	VF20	XF40	MS60	MS63
2005MW	4,000,000	—	—	—	4.00	6.00

Y# 527 2 ZŁOTE
8.15 g., Brass, 27 mm. **Obv:** Crowned eagle with wings open **Rev:** Bust 1/4 left with horse head and goose at left **Edge Lettering:** * NBP * eight times

Date	Mintage	F12	VF20	XF40	MS60	MS63
2005MW	850,000	—	—	—	3.00	5.00

Y# 528 2 ZŁOTE
8.15 g., Brass, 27 mm. **Obv:** Crowned eagle above wall **Rev:** Kolobrzeg Lighthouse **Edge Lettering:** * NBP * eight times

Date	Mintage	F12	VF20	XF40	MS60	MS63
2005MW	1,100,000	—	—	—	3.00	5.00

Y# 529 2 ZŁOTE
8.15 g., Brass, 27 mm. **Obv:** National arms above gateway **Rev:** Wioclawek Cathedral **Edge Lettering:** * NBP * eight times

Date	Mintage	F12	VF20	XF40	MS60	MS63
2005MW	1,100,000	—	—	—	3.00	5.00

Y# 530 2 ZŁOTE
8.15 g., Brass, 27 mm. **Obv:** National arms **Rev:** Bust of King Stanislaus Poniatowski right **Edge Lettering:** * NBP * eight times

Date	Mintage	F12	VF20	XF40	MS60	MS63
2005MW	990,000	—	—	—	3.00	5.00

Y# 541 2 ZŁOTE
8.15 g., Brass, 27 mm. **Obv:** Eagle, value, palette and paint brushes **Rev:** Painter Tadeusz Makowski **Edge Lettering:** * NBP * eight times

Date	Mintage	F12	VF20	XF40	MS60	MS63
2005MW	900,000	—	—	—	3.00	5.00

Y# 558 2 ZŁOTE
8.15 g., Brass, 27 mm. **Subject:** 60th Anniversary of WWII **Obv:** National arms **Edge Lettering:** * NBP * eight times

Date	Mintage	F12	VF20	XF40	MS60	MS63
2005MW	1,000,000	—	—	—	3.00	5.00

Y# 560 2 ZŁOTE
8.15 g., Brass, 27 mm. **Obv:** National arms on outline map **Obv. Legend:** RZECZPOSPOLITA POLSKA **Rev:** Region arms **Rev. Legend:** WOJEWOZTWO SWIETOKRZYSKIE **Edge Lettering:** * NBP * eight times

Date	Mintage	F12	VF20	XF40	MS60	MS63
2005MW	900,000	—	—	—	3.00	5.00

Y# 562 2 ZŁOTE
8.15 g., Brass, 27 mm. **Obv:** National arms **Rev:** Region Wielkopolskie **Edge Lettering:** * NBP * eight times

Date	Mintage	F12	VF20	XF40	MS60	MS63
2005MW	940,000	—	—	—	3.00	5.00

Y# 563 2 ZŁOTE
8.15 g., Brass, 27 mm. **Obv:** National arms on outlined map **Obv. Legend:** RZECZPOSPOLITA POLSKA **Rev:** Region arms **Rev. Legend:** WOJEWODZTWO ZACHODIOPOMORSKIE **Edge Lettering:** * NBP * eight times

Date	Mintage	F12	VF20	XF40	MS60	MS63
2005	—	—	—	—	3.00	5.00

Y# 564 2 ZŁOTE
8.15 g., Brass, 27 mm. **Obv:** National arms **Rev:** City of Gniezno **Edge Lettering:** * NBP * eight times

Date	Mintage	F12	VF20	XF40	MS60	MS63
2005	1,250,000	—	—	—	3.00	5.00

Y# 565 2 ZŁOTE
8.15 g., Brass, 27 mm. **Obv:** National arms **Rev:** Solidarity **Edge Lettering:** * NBP * eight times

Date	Mintage	F12	VF20	XF40	MS60	MS63
2005MW	1,000,000	—	—	—	3.00	5.00

Y# 608 2 ZŁOTE
8.15 g., Brass, 27 mm. **Subject:** 500th Anniversary Birth of Nikolaja Reja **Obv:** National arms **Obv. Legend:** RZECZPOSPOLITA POLSKA **Rev:** Bust of Reja facing 3/4 right **Edge Lettering:** NBP eight times

Date	Mintage	F12	VF20	XF40	MS60	MS63
2005	850,000	—	—	—	3.00	5.00

Y# 614 2 ZŁOTE
8.15 g., Brass, 27 mm. **Obv:** National arms on outlined map **Obv. Legend:** RZECZPOSPOLITA POLSKA **Rev:** Region arms **Rev. Legend:** WOJEWÓDZTWO WARMINSKO - MAZURSKIE **Edge Lettering:** * NBP * eight times

Date	Mintage	F12	VF20	XF40	MS60	MS63
2005MW	900,000	—	—	—	3.00	5.00

Y# 753 2 ZŁOTE
8.15 g., Brass, 27 mm. **Subject:** Cizsyn **Rev:** Round tower

Date	Mintage	F12	VF20	XF40	MS60	MS63
2005MW	—	—	—	—	3.00	5.00

Y# 532 2 ZŁOTE
8.15 g., Brass, 27 mm. **Obv:** National arms **Rev:** St. John's Night dancer **Edge Lettering:** * NBP * eight times

Date	Mintage	F12	VF20	XF40	MS60	MS63
2006MW	1,000,000	—	—	—	2.50	4.00

Y# 534 2 ZŁOTE
8.15 g., Brass, 27 mm. **Obv:** National arms **Rev:** Alpine Marmot standing **Edge Lettering:** * NBP * eight times

Date	Mintage	F12	VF20	XF40	MS60	MS63
2006MW	1,400,000	—	—	—	3.00	6.00

Y# 543 2 ZŁOTE
8.15 g., Brass, 27 mm. **Obv:** Polish Eagle above castle gate **Rev:** Bochnia church **Edge Lettering:** * NBP * eight times

Date	Mintage	F12	VF20	XF40	MS60	MS63
2006MW	1,100,000	—	—	—	3.00	5.00

Y# 544 2 ZŁOTE
8.15 g., Brass, 27 mm. **Obv:** Polish Eagle above castle gate **Rev:** Chelm church **Edge Lettering:** * NBP * eight times

Date	Mintage	F12	VF20	XF40	MS60	MS63
2006MW	1,100,000	—	—	—	3.00	5.00

Y# 545 2 ZŁOTE
8.15 g., Brass, 27 mm. **Obv:** Polish Eagle above castle gate **Rev:** Chelmno Palace **Edge Lettering:** * NBP * eight times

Date	Mintage	F12	VF20	XF40	MS60	MS63
2006MW	1,100,000	—	—	—	3.00	5.00

Y# 546 2 ZŁOTE
8.15 g., Brass, 27 mm. **Obv:** Polish Eagle above castle gate **Rev:** Elblag tower **Edge Lettering:** * NBP * eight times

Date	Mintage	F12	VF20	XF40	MS60	MS63
2006MW	1,100,000	—	—	—	3.00	5.00

Y# 547 2 ZŁOTE
8.15 g., Brass, 27 mm. **Obv:** Polish Eagle above castle gate **Rev:** Castle **Rev. Legend:** KOSCIOL W. HACZOWIE **Edge Lettering:** * NBP * eight times

Date	Mintage	F12	VF20	XF40	MS60	MS63
2006MW	1,000,000	—	—	—	3.00	5.00

Y# 548 2 ZŁOTE
8.15 g., Brass, 27 mm. **Obv:** National arms above gateway **Rev:** Legnica tower and building **Edge Lettering:** * NBP * eight times

Date	Mintage	F12	VF20	XF40	MS60	MS63
2006MW	1,100,000	—	—	—	3.00	5.00

Y# 549 2 ZŁOTE
8.15 g., Brass, 27 mm. **Obv:** Polish Eagle above castle gate **Rev:** Pszczyna palace **Edge Lettering:** * NBP * eight times

Date	Mintage	F12	VF20	XF40	MS60	MS63
2006MW	1,100,000	—	—	—	3.00	5.00

Y# 550 2 ZŁOTE
8.15 g., Brass, 27 mm. **Obv:** Polish Eagle above castle gate **Rev:** Sandomierz palace **Edge Lettering:** * NBP * eight times

Date	Mintage	F12	VF20	XF40	MS60	MS63
2006MW	1,100,000	—	—	—	3.00	5.00

Y# 566 2 ZŁOTE
8.15 g., Brass, 27 mm. **Obv:** National arms **Rev:** City of Jaroslaw **Edge Lettering:** * NBP * eight times

Date	Mintage	F12	VF20	XF40	MS60	MS63
2006MW	1,200,000	—	—	—	3.00	5.00

Y# 569 2 ZŁOTE
8.15 g., Brass, 27 mm. **Obv:** National arms **Rev:** Castle Zagan **Edge Lettering:** * NBP * eight times

Date	Mintage	F12	VF20	XF40	MS60	MS63
2006MW	1,100,000	—	—	—	3.00	5.00

Y# 570 2 ZŁOTE
815.00 g., Brass, 27 mm. **Obv:** National arms above gateway **Rev:** City of Nysa **Edge Lettering:** * NBP * eight times

Date	Mintage	F12	VF20	XF40	MS60	MS63
2006MW	1,100,000	—	—	—	5.00	3.00

Y# 571 2 ZŁOTE
8.15 g., Brass, 27 mm. **Subject:** 30th Anniversary of June 1976 **Obv:** National arms **Edge Lettering:** * NBP * eight times

Date	Mintage	F12	VF20	XF40	MS60	MS63
2006MW	1,000,000	—	—	—	3.00	5.00

Y# 573 2 ZŁOTE
8.15 g., Brass, 27 mm. **Obv:** Polish eagle above wall **Rev:** Nowy Sacz church **Edge Lettering:** * NBP * eight times

Date	Mintage	F12	VF20	XF40	MS60	MS63
2006MW	1,100,000	—	—	—	3.00	5.00

Y# 574 2 ZŁOTE
8.15 g., Brass, 27 mm. **Subject:** 500th Anniversary of the Publication of the Statute by Laski **Obv:** National arms above value **Rev:** Jan Laski and book **Edge Lettering:** * NBP * eight times

Date	Mintage	F12	VF20	XF40	MS60	MS63
2006MW	1,000,000	—	—	—	3.00	5.00

Y# 575 2 ZŁOTE
8.15 g., Brass, 27 mm. **Subject:** Aleksander Gierymski (painter) **Obv:** Palette, brushes at left, national arms at right **Obv. Legend:** RZECZPOSPOLITA POLSKA **Rev:** Bust of Gierymski facing at left, coastline village in background **Edge Lettering:** * NBP * eight times

Date	Mintage	F12	VF20	XF40	MS60	MS63
2006MW	1,000,000	—	—	—	3.00	5.00

Y# 576 2 ZŁOTE
8.15 g., Brass, 27 mm. **Obv:** National arms **Rev:** Knight on horseback **Edge Lettering:** * NBP * eight times

Date	Mintage	F12	VF20	XF40	MS60	MS63
2006MW	1,000,000	—	—	—	3.00	5.00

Y# 580 2 ZŁOTE
8.15 g., Brass, 27 mm. **Obv:** Polish eagle above wall **Rev:** Kalisz building **Edge Lettering:** * NBP * eight times

Date	Mintage	F12	VF20	XF40	MS60	MS63
2006MW	1,100,000	—	—	—	3.00	5.00

Y# 582 2 ZŁOTE
8.15 g., Brass, 27 mm. **Obv:** National arms **Obv. Legend:** RZECZPOSPOLITA POLSKA **Rev:** Queen's head left as on KM-20, coin design from 1932 **Edge Lettering:** * NBP * eight times

Date	Mintage	F12	VF20	XF40	MS60	MS63
2006MW	1,000,000	—	—	—	3.00	5.00

Y# 605 2 ZŁOTE
8.15 g., Brass, 27 mm. **Obv:** National arms **Obv. Legend:** RZECZPOSPOLITA POLSKA **Rev:** Skier and marksman standing **Rev. Legend:** XX ZIMOWE IGAZYSKA OLIMPIJSKIE - TURYN **Edge Lettering:** * NBP * eight times

Date	Mintage	F12	VF20	XF40	MS60	MS63
2006MW	1,200,000	—	—	—	3.00	5.00

Y# 606 2 ZŁOTE
8.15 g., Brass, 27 mm. **Obv:** National arms **Obv. Legend:** RZECZPOSPOLITA POLSKA **Rev:** Large soccer ball with fancy linked date 2006 **Rev. Legend:** MISTRZOSTWA SWIATA W PltCE NOZNEJ NIEMCY - FIFA **Edge Lettering:** * NBP * eight times

Date	Mintage	F12	VF20	XF40	MS60	MS63
2006MW	1,200,000	—	—	—	3.00	5.00

Y# 609 2 ZŁOTE
8.15 g., Brass, 27 mm. **Subject:** 100th Anniversary - Warsaw School of Economics **Obv:** National arms **Obv. Legend:** RZECZPOSPOLITA POLSKA **Rev:** School facade **Rev. Legend:** SZKOLA CLOWNA HANDLOWA W WARSZAWIE **Rev. Inscription:** Large SGH **Edge Lettering:** * NBP * eight times

Date	Mintage	F12	VF20	XF40	MS60	MS63
2006MW	1,000,000	—	—	—	3.00	5.00

Y# 577 2 ZŁOTE
8.15 g., Brass, 27 mm. **Obv:** Crowned eagle **Rev:** Kwidzyn Castle **Edge Lettering:** * NBP * eight times

Date	Mintage	F12	VF20	XF40	MS60	MS63
2007MW	1,000,000	—	—	—	3.00	5.00

Y# 578 2 ZŁOTE
8.15 g., Brass, 27 mm. **Obv:** Crowned eagle **Rev:** Grey Seal and silhouette **Edge Lettering:** * NBP * eight times

Date	Mintage	F12	VF20	XF40	MS60	MS63
2007MW	1,000,000	—	—	—	4.00	7.00

Y# 586 2 ZŁOTE
8.15 g., Brass, 27 mm. **Subject:** 75th Anniversary Breaking the Enigma Code **Obv:** National arms **Obv. Legend:** RZECZPOSPOLITA POLSKA **Rev:** Enigma machine wheel **Edge Lettering:** * NBP * eight times

Date	Mintage	F12	VF20	XF40	MS60	MS63
2007MW	900,000	—	—	—	3.00	5.00

Y# 590 2 ZŁOTE
8.15 g., Brass, 27 mm. **Obv:** National arms **Obv. Legend:** RZECZPOSPOLITA POLSKA **Rev:** Bust of Domeyko facing **Rev. Legend:** IGNACY DOMEYKO 1802 - 1889 **Edge Lettering:** * NBP * eight times

Date	Mintage	F12	VF20	XF40	MS60	MS63
2007MW	900,000	—	—	—	3.00	5.00

Y# 592 2 ZŁOTE
8.15 g., Brass, 27 mm. **Subject:** History of Zloty **Obv:** Nike at left, obverse of 5 Zlotych, Y#18, national arms below **Obv. Legend:** RZECZPOLPOLITA POLSKA **Rev:** Spray at left of reverse of 5 Zlotych, Y# 18 **Edge Lettering:** * NBP * eight times

Date	Mintage	F12	VF20	XF40	MS60	MS63
2007MW	900,000	—	—	—	3.00	5.00

Y# 594 2 ZŁOTE
8.15 g., Brass, 27 mm. **Subject:** 750th Anniversary Municipality of Krakau **Obv:** National arms **Obv. Legend:** RZECZPOSPOLITA POLSKA **Rev:** Knight standing facing with spear and shield **Edge Lettering:** * NBP * eight times

Date	Mintage	F12	VF20	XF40	MS60	MS63
2007MW	900,000	—	—	—	3.00	5.00

Y# 591 2 ZŁOTE
8.03 g., Brass, 26.77 mm. **Subject:** Konrad Korzeniowski (Joseph Conrad), 100th Anniversary of Death **Obv:** National arms **Obv. Legend:** RZECZPOSPOLITA POLSKA **Rev:** Head of Korzeniowski facing slightly right at left, open book at lower center, sailing ship at right **Edge Lettering:** NBP repeated

Date	Mintage	F12	VF20	XF40	MS60	MS63
2007	—	—	—	—	3.00	4.00

Y# 610 2 ZŁOTE
8.16 g., Brass, 27 mm. **Subject:** Arlic Explorers Antoni B. Dombrowolski and Henryk Arctowski **Obv:** National arms **Obv. Legend:** RZECZPOSPOLITA POLSKA **Rev:** Explorer's bust facing at bottom, sailing ship in background **Edge Lettering:** * NBP * eight times

Date	Mintage	F12	VF20	XF40	MS60	MS63
2007MW	900,000	—	—	—	3.00	5.00

Y# 611 2 ZŁOTE
8.15 g., Brass, 27 mm. **Obv:** National arms **Obv. Legend:** RZECZPOSPOLITA POLSKA **Rev:** Ciezkozbrojny in armor, horseback left **Rev. Legend:** RYCERZ CIEZKOZBROJNY-XV **Edge Lettering:** * NBP * eight times

Date	Mintage	F12	VF20	XF40	MS60	MS63
2007MW	900,000	—	—	—	3.00	5.00

Y# 612 2 ZŁOTE
8.15 g., Brass, 27 mm. **Subject:** 70th Anniversary Death of Szymanowski **Obv:** National arms **Obv. Legend:** RZECZPOSPOLITA POLSKA **Rev:** Bust facing 3/4 right at left, music score in background **Rev. Legend:** ROCZNICA URODZIN KAROLA SYMANOWSKIEGO **Edge Lettering:** * NBP * eight times

Date	Mintage	F12	VF20	XF40	MS60	MS63
2007MW	900,000	—	—	—	3.00	5.00

Y# 613 2 ZŁOTE

8.15 g., Brass, 27 mm. **Obv:** National arms above gateway **Obv. Legend:** RZECZPOSPOLITA POLSKA **Rev:** Buildings **Rev. Legend:** STARGARD - SZCZECINSKI **Edge Lettering:** * NBP * eight times

Date	Mintage	F12	VF20	XF40	MS60	MS63
2007MW	1,000,000	—	—	—	3.00	5.00

Y# 615 2 ZŁOTE

8.15 g., Brass, 27 mm. **Obv:** National arms above gateway **Obv. Legend:** RZECZPOSPOLITA POLSKA **Rev:** Building with branches at left and right **Rev. Legend:** BRZEG **Edge Lettering:** * NBP * eight times

Date	Mintage	F12	VF20	XF40	MS60	MS63
2007MW	1,000,000	—	—	—	3.00	5.00

Y# 616 2 ZŁOTE

8.15 g., Brass, 27 mm. **Obv:** National arms above gateway **Obv. Legend:** RZECZPOSPOLITA POLSKA **Rev:** Church **Rev. Legend:** LOMZA **Edge Lettering:** * NBP alternating normal and inverted 4x

Date	Mintage	F12	VF20	XF40	MS60	MS63
2007MW	1,000,000	—	—	—	3.00	5.00

Y# 617 2 ZŁOTE

8.15 g., Brass, 27 mm. **Obv:** National arms above gateway **Obv. Legend:** RZECZPOSPOLITA POLSKA **Rev:** Church **Rev. Legend:** PLOCK **Edge Lettering:** * NBP * eight times

Date	Mintage	F12	VF20	XF40	MS60	MS63
2007MW	1,000,000	—	—	—	3.00	5.00

Y# 618 2 ZŁOTE

8.15 g., Brass, 27 mm. **Obv:** National arms above gateway **Obv. Legend:** RZECZPOSPOLITA POLSKA **Rev:** Church **Rev. Legend:** PRZEMYSL **Edge Lettering:** * NBP * eight times

Date	Mintage	F12	VF20	XF40	MS60	MS63
2007MW	1,000,000	—	—	—	3.00	5.00

Y# 619 2 ZŁOTE

8.15 g., Brass, 27 mm. **Obv:** National arms above gateway **Obv. Legend:** RZECZPOSPOLITA POLSKA **Rev:** Towered gateway **Rev. Legend:** RACIBÓRZ **Edge Lettering:** * NBP * eight times

Date	Mintage	F12	VF20	XF40	MS60	MS63
2007MW	1,000,000	—	—	—	3.00	5.00

Y# 620 2 ZŁOTE

8.15 g., Brass, 27 mm. **Obv:** National arms above gateway **Obv. Legend:** RZECZPOSPOLITA POLSKA **Rev:** Church **Rev. Legend:** SLUPSK **Edge Lettering:** NBP repeated

Date	Mintage	F12	VF20	XF40	MS60	MS63
2007MW	1,000,000	—	—	—	3.00	5.00

Y# 621 2 ZŁOTE

8.15 g., Brass, 27 mm. **Obv:** National arms above gateway **Obv. Legend:** RZECZPOSPOLITA POLSKA **Rev:** Church **Rev. Legend:** SWIDNICA **Edge Lettering:** * NBP * eight times

Date	Mintage	F12	VF20	XF40	MS60	MS63
2007MW	1,000,000	—	—	—	3.00	5.00

Y# 622 2 ZŁOTE

8.15 g., Brass, 27 mm. **Obv:** National arms **Obv. Legend:** RZECZPOSPOLITA POLSKE **Rev:** Town view **Rev. Legend:** MIASTO SREDNIOWIECZNE - W TORUNIU **Edge Lettering:** * NBP * eight times

Date	Mintage	F12	VF20	XF40	MS60	MS63
2007MW	900,000	—	—	—	3.00	5.00

Y# 623 2 ZŁOTE

8.15 g., Brass, 27 mm. **Obv:** National arms above gateway **Obv. Legend:** RZECZPOSPOLITA POLSKA **Rev:** Church **Rev. Legend:** GORZÓW WIELKOPOLSKI **Edge Lettering:** * NBP * eight times

Date	Mintage	F12	VF20	XF40	MS60	MS63
2007MW	1,000,000	—	—	—	3.00	5.00

Y# 624 2 ZŁOTE

8.15 g., Brass, 27 mm. **Obv:** National arms above gateway **Obv. Legend:** RZECZPOSPOLITA POLSKA **Rev:** Church at lower right, houses to left, fortress in upper background **Rev. Legend:** KLODZKO **Edge Lettering:** * NBP * eight times

Date	Mintage	F12	VF20	XF40	MS60	MS63
2007MW	1,000,000	—	—	—	3.00	5.00

Y# 625 2 ZŁOTE

8.15 g., Brass, 27 mm. **Obv:** National arms above gateway **Obv. Legend:** RZECZPOSPOLITA POLSKE **Rev:** Church **Rev. Legend:** TARNOW **Edge Lettering:** * NBP * eight times

Date	Mintage	F12	VF20	XF40	MS60	MS63
2007MW	1,000,000	—	—	—	3.00	5.00

Y# 626 2 ZŁOTE

8.15 g., Brass, 27 mm. **Subject:** Leon Wyczolkowski **Obv:** Artist's palette, brushes at left, national arms at right **Obv. Legend:** RZECZPOSPOLITA POLSKA **Rev:** Bust facing **Edge Lettering:** * NBP * eight times

Date	Mintage	F12	VF20	XF40	MS60	MS63
2007MW	900,000	—	—	—	3.00	5.00

Y# 627 2 ZŁOTE

8.15 g., Brass, 27 mm. **Obv:** National arms above flags **Obv. Legend:** RZECZPOSPOLITA POLSKA **Rev:** Peregrine Falcon perched on branch **Rev. Legend:** SOKOL WEDROWNY - Falco peregrinus **Edge Lettering:** * NBP * eight times

Date	Mintage	F12	VF20	XF40	MS60	MS63
2008MW	1,600,000	—	—	—	3.00	4.00

Y# 628 2 ZŁOTE

8.15 g., Brass, 27 mm. **Obv:** National arms above gateway **Obv. Legend:** RZECZPOSPOLITA POLSKA **Rev:** National arms ar upper left, Piotrków Tribunal building at lower right **Rev. Legend:** PIOTRKÓW - TRYBUNALSKI **Edge Lettering:** * NBP * eight times

Date	Mintage	F12	VF20	XF40	MS60	MS63
2008MW	1,100,000	—	—	0.90	2.25	3.00

Y# 629 2 ZŁOTE

8.15 g., Brass, 27 mm. **Subject:** 40th Anniversary "Rocznica" March **Obv:** National arms above value **Obv. Legend:** RZECZPOSPOLITA POLSKA **Rev:** University of Warsaw coat of arms above political protest marchers **Edge Lettering:** * NBP * eight times

Date	Mintage	F12	VF20	XF40	MS60	MS63
2008MW	1,400,000	—	—	0.90	2.25	3.00

Y# 630 2 ZŁOTE

8.15 g., Brass, 27 mm. **Obv:** National arms above gateway **Obv. Legend:** RZECZPOSPOLITA POLSKA **Rev:** Building **Rev. Legend:** LOWICZ **Edge Lettering:** * NBP * eight times

Date	Mintage	F12	VF20	XF40	MS60	MS63
2008MW	1,100,000	—	—	0.90	2.25	3.00

Y# 631 2 ZŁOTE

8.15 g., Brass, 27 mm. **Obv:** National arms above gateway **Obv. Legend:** RZECZPOSPOLITA POLSKA **Rev:** Monument **Rev. Legend:** KONIN **Edge Lettering:** * NBP * eight times

Date	Mintage	F12	VF20	XF40	MS60	MS63
2008MW	1,100,000	—	—	0.90	2.25	3.00

Y# 633 2 ZŁOTE

8.15 g., Brass, 27 mm. **Subject:** 65th Anniversary Warsaw Uprising **Obv:** National arms **Obv. Legend:** RZECZPOSPOLITA POLSKA **Rev:** Star of David in barbed wire, female freedom fighter at right. **Rev. Legend:** POWSTANIA W GETCIE WARSZAWSKIM 65. ROCZNICA **Edge Lettering:** * NBP * eight times

Date	Mintage	F12	VF20	XF40	MS60	MS63
2008MW	1,750,000	—	—	—	3.00	5.00

Y# 634 2 ZŁOTE

8.15 g., Brass, 27 mm. **Subject:** Zbigniew Herbert **Obv:** National arms **Obv. Legend:** RZECZPOSPOLITA POLSKA **Rev:** Head of Herbert right **Edge Lettering:** * NBP * eight times

Date	Mintage	F12	VF20	XF40	MS60	MS63
2008MW	1,510,000	—	—	—	3.00	4.00

Y# 638 2 ZŁOTE

8.15 g., Brass, 27 mm. **Subject:** Siberian Exiles **Obv:** National arms **Obv. Legend:** RZECZPOSPOLITA POLSKA **Rev:** Bleak forest **Rev. Inscription:** SYBIRACY **Edge Lettering:** * NBP * eight times

Date	Mintage	F12	VF20	XF40	MS60	MS63
2008MW	1,500,000	—	—	—	3.00	4.00

Y# 641 2 ZŁOTE

8.15 g., Brass, 27 mm. **Subject:** Kazimierz Dolny **Obv:** National arms **Obv. Legend:** RZECZPOSPOLITA POLSKA **Rev:** City view **Edge Lettering:** * NBP * eight times

Date	Mintage	F12	VF20	XF40	MS60	MS63
2008MW	1,380,000	—	—	—	3.00	4.00

Y# 644 2 ZŁOTE

8.15 g., Brass, 27 mm. **Subject:** 29th Olympic Games Beijing 2008 **Obv:** Eagle **Rev:** Two rowers in boat & a square **Edge Lettering:** * NBP * eight times

Date	Mintage	F12	VF20	XF40	MS60	MS63
2008	2,000,000	—	—	—	3.00	4.00

Y# 648 2 ZŁOTE

8.15 g., Brass, 27 mm. **Subject:** Polish Travellers & Explorers **Obv:** Eagle **Rev:** Bust of Bronislaw Pilsudski **Edge Lettering:** * NBP * eight times

Date	Mintage	F12	VF20	XF40	MS60	MS63
2008	1,100,000	—	—	—	3.00	4.00

Y# 650 2 ZŁOTE

8.15 g., Brass, 27 mm. **Subject:** 90th Anniversary of Regaining Freedom **Obv:** Eagle **Rev:** Order of Polonia Restituta **Edge Lettering:** * NBP * eight times

Date	Mintage	F12	VF20	XF40	MS60	MS63
2008	1,200,000	—	—	—	3.00	4.00

Y# 656 2 ZŁOTE

8.15 g., Brass, 27 mm. **Subject:** 450th Anniversary of the Polish Post **Obv:** Eagle **Rev:** Post rider on horse **Edge:** NBP

Date	Mintage	F12	VF20	XF40	MS60	MS63
2008	1,400,000	—	—	—	3.00	4.00

Y# 659 2 ZŁOTE

8.15 g., Brass, 27 mm. **Subject:** 400th Anniversary of Polish settlement in North America **Obv:** Eagle **Rev:** Man blowing glassware **Edge Lettering:** * NBP * eight times

Date	Mintage	F12	VF20	XF40	MS60	MS63
2008	1,200,000	—	—	—	3.00	4.00

Y# 662 2 ZŁOTE

8.15 g., Brass, 27 mm. **Subject:** 90th Anniversary of the Greater Poland Uprising **Obv:** Eagle **Rev:** Bust of Igancy Jan Paderewski, soldiers at bottom **Edge Lettering:** * NBP * eight times

Date	Mintage	F12	VF20	XF40	MS60	MS63
2008	1,100,000	—	—	—	3.00	4.00

Y# 663 2 ZŁOTE

8.15 g., Brass, 27 mm. **Subject:** Belsko - Biala **Obv:** National arms above gateway **Rev:** Building

Date	Mintage	F12	VF20	XF40	MS60	MS63
2008MW	—	—	—	—	3.00	4.00

Y# 670 2 ZŁOTE

8.15 g., Brass, 27 mm. **Subject:** Polish Cavalry **Obv:** National arms above value **Rev:** Hussar Knights, XVII Century

Date	Mintage	F12	VF20	XF40	MS60	MS63
2009MW	1,400,000	—	—	—	3.00	4.00

Y# 673 2 ZŁOTE

8.15 g., Brass, 27 mm. **Subject:** Supreme Chamber of Control, 90th Anniversary **Obv:** National arms above value **Rev:** Building

Date	Mintage	F12	VF20	XF40	MS60	MS63
2009MW	1,200,000	—	—	—	3.00	4.00

Y# 675 2 ZŁOTE

8.15 g., Brass, 27 mm. **Subject:** Central Banking, 180th Anniversary **Obv:** National arms above value **Rev:** Five coins

Date	Mintage	F12	VF20	XF40	MS60	MS63
2009MW	1,300,000	—	—	—	3.00	4.00

Y# 678 2 ZŁOTE
8.15 g., Brass, 27 mm. **Subject:** Green Lizards **Obv:** National arms above value **Rev:** Two green lizards on rocks (lacerta viridis) **Rev. Legend:** JASZCZURKA

Date	Mintage	F12	VF20	XF40	MS60	MS63
2009MW	1,700,000	—	—	—	3.00	4.00

Y# 680 2 ZŁOTE
8.15 g., Brass, 27 mm. **Subject:** General Elections of 1989 **Obv:** National arms above eagle **Rev:** Election notice within wreath

Date	Mintage	F12	VF20	XF40	MS60	MS63
2009MW	1,300,000	—	—	—	3.00	4.00

Y# 684 2 ZŁOTE
8.15 g., Brass, 27 mm. **Subject:** Czeslaw Niemen **Obv:** National arms above value **Rev:** Two dimensional facing portrait

Date	Mintage	F12	VF20	XF40	MS60	MS63
2009MW	1,400,000	—	—	—	3.00	4.00

Y# 687 2 ZŁOTE
8.15 g., Brass, 27 mm. **Subject:** Poets of the Warsaw uprising, 65th Anniversary **Obv:** National arms above eagle

Date	Mintage	F12	VF20	XF40	MS60	MS63
2009MW	1,400,000	—	—	—	3.00	4.00

Y# 690 2 ZŁOTE
8.15 g., Brass, 27 mm. **Subject:** First Cadre March **Obv:** National arms above value **Rev:** Military badge

Date	Mintage	F12	VF20	XF40	MS60	MS63
2009MW	1,000,000	—	—	—	3.00	4.00

Y# 692 2 ZŁOTE
8.15 g., Brass, 27 mm. **Subject:** Liquidation of Lodz Ghetto **Obv:** National arms above value **Rev:** Silhouette of Ghetto

Date	Mintage	F12	VF20	XF40	MS60	MS63
2009MW	1,000,000	—	—	—	3.00	4.00

Y# 694 2 ZŁOTE
8.15 g., Brass, 27 mm. **Subject:** Westerplatte **Obv:** National arms above value **Rev:** Three soldiers and map

Date	Mintage	F12	VF20	XF40	MS60	MS63
2009	1,400,000	—	—	—	3.00	4.00

Y# 697 2 ZŁOTE
8.15 g., Brass, 27 mm. **Subject:** Tatar Mountain Rescue **Obv:** National arms above value **Rev:** Mountain climber

Date	Mintage	F12	VF20	XF40	MS60	MS63
2009MW	1,400,000	—	—	—	3.00	4.00

Y# 700 2 ZŁOTE
8.15 g., Brass, 27 mm. **Subject:** Fr. Jerzy Popieluszko, 25th Anniversary of Murder **Obv:** National arms above value **Rev:** Portrait and candle memorial

Date	Mintage	F12	VF20	XF40	MS60	MS63
2009MW	1,500,000	—	—	—	3.00	4.00

Y# 703 2 ZŁOTE
8.15 g., Brass, 27 mm. **Subject:** Poles saving Jews **Obv:** National arms above value **Rev:** Broken brick wall

Date	Mintage	F12	VF20	XF40	MS60	MS63
2009MW	1,400,000	—	—	—	3.00	4.00

Y# 705 2 ZŁOTE
8.15 g., Brass, 27 mm. **Subject:** Wald Strzeminski **Obv:** Artist palette and National arms **Rev:** Portrait at left

Date	Mintage	F12	VF20	XF40	MS60	MS63
2009MW	1,300,000	—	—	—	3.00	4.00

Y# 707 2 ZŁOTE
8.15 g., Brass, 27 mm. **Subject:** Polish Underground **Obv:** National arms above value **Rev:** Monogram of resistance and map of Poland

Date	Mintage	F12	VF20	XF40	MS60	MS63
2009MW	1,000,000	—	—	—	3.00	4.00

Y# 709 2 ZŁOTE
8.15 g., Brass, 27 mm. **Subject:** Czestochowa **Rev:** Church

Date	Mintage	F12	VF20	XF40	MS60	MS63
2009MW		—	—	—	3.00	4.00

Y# 710 2 ZŁOTE
8.15 g., Brass, 27 mm. **Subject:** Jedrzejow Cistercian Monastery **Rev:** Church

Date	Mintage	F12	VF20	XF40	MS60	MS63
2009MW		—	—	—	3.00	4.00

Y# 711 2 ZŁOTE
8.15 g., Brass, 27 mm. **Subject:** Trzebnica **Rev:** Building

Date	Mintage	F12	VF20	XF40	MS60	MS63
2009MW		—	—	—	3.00	4.00

Y# 712 2 ZŁOTE
8.15 g., Brass, 27 mm. **Subject:** Liberation of Auschwitz **Obv:** National arms above value **Rev:** Three prisoners and camp gate sign

Date	Mintage	F12	VF20	XF40	MS60	MS63
2010MW	1,000,000	—	—	—	3.00	4.00

Y# 715 2 ZŁOTE
8.15 g., Brass, 27 mm. **Subject:** Vancouver Winter Olympics **Obv:** National arms above value **Rev:** Ski jump athlete

Date	Mintage	F12	VF20	XF40	MS60	MS63
2010MW	1,400,000	—	—	—	3.00	4.00

Y# 718 2 ZŁOTE
8.15 g., Brass, 27 mm. **Subject:** Imperial Guard **Obv:** National arms above value **Rev:** Napoleonic era mounted soldier

Date	Mintage	F12	VF20	XF40	MS60	MS63
2010MW	1,400,000	—	—	—	3.00	4.00

Y# 721 2 ZŁOTE
8.15 g., Brass, 27 mm. **Subject:** Katyn Crime **Obv:** National arms above value **Rev:** City name above cap

Date	Mintage	F12	VF20	XF40	MS60	MS63
2010MW	1,000,000	—	—	—	3.00	4.00

Y# 723 2 ZŁOTE
8.15 g., Brass, 27 mm. **Obv:** National arms above value **Rev:** Bat

Date	Mintage	F12	VF20	XF40	MS60	MS63
2010	—	—	—	—	3.00	4.00

Y# 725 2 ZŁOTE
8.15 g., Brass, 27 mm. **Subject:** Polish Scouting Centennial

Date	Mintage	F12	VF20	XF40	MS60	MS63
2010MW	1,100,000	—	—	—	3.00	4.00

Y# 727 2 ZŁOTE
8.15 g., Brass, 27 mm. **Subject:** Popular Music - Krzystof Komeda

Date	Mintage	F12	VF20	XF40	MS60	MS63
2010MW	1,400,000	—	—	—	3.00	4.00

Y# 730 2 ZŁOTE
8.15 g., Brass, 27 mm. **Subject:** Jan Twardowski

Date	Mintage	F12	VF20	XF40	MS60	MS63
2010MW	1,000,000	—	—	—	3.00	4.00

Y# 732 2 ZŁOTE
8.15 g., Brass, 27 mm. **Subject:** Battles of Grunwald and Kluszyn

Date	Mintage	F12	VF20	XF40	MS60	MS63
2010MW	1,400,000	—	—	—	3.00	4.00

Y# 735 2 ZŁOTE
8.15 g., Brass **Subject:** Battle of Warsaw

Date	Mintage	F12	VF20	XF40	MS60	MS63
2010MW	1,200,000	—	—	—	3.00	4.00

Y# 737 2 ZŁOTE
8.15 g., Brass, 27 mm. **Subject:** August of 1980

Date	Mintage	F12	VF20	XF40	MS60	MS63
2010MW	1,400,000	—	—	—	3.00	4.00

Y# 742 2 ZŁOTE
8.15 g., Brass, 27 mm. **Subject:** Polish Explorers - Benedykt Dybowski

Date	Mintage	F12	VF20	XF40	MS60	MS63
2010MW Proof	1,200,000	—	—	—	3.00	4.00

Y# 744 2 ZŁOTE
8.15 g., Brass, 27 mm. **Subject:** City of Krzeszow

Date	Mintage	F12	VF20	XF40	MS60	MS63
2010MW	1,000,000	—	—	—	3.00	4.00

Y# 746 2 ZŁOTE
8.15 g., Brass, 27 mm. **Subject:** Arthur Grottger, painter

Date	Mintage	F12	VF20	XF40	MS60	MS63
2010MW	1,300,000	—	—	—	3.00	4.00

Y# 749 2 ZŁOTE
8.15 g., Brass, 27 mm. **Subject:** City of Kalwaria Zebrzydowska **Obv:** National Arms above value **Rev:** Statue of Saint, Church in background

Date	Mintage	F12	VF20	XF40	MS60	MS63
2010MW	—	—	—	—	3.00	4.00

Y# 751 2 ZŁOTE
8.15 g., Brass, 27 mm. **Subject:** City of Warsaw

Date	Mintage	F12	VF20	XF40	MS60	MS63
2010MW	—	—	—	—	3.00	4.00

Y# 752 2 ZŁOTE
815.00 g., Brass, 27 mm. **Subject:** City of Trzemeszno

Date	Mintage	F12	VF20	XF40	MS60	MS63
2010	—	—	—	—	3.00	4.00

Y# 759 2 ZŁOTE
8.15 g., Brass, 27 mm. **Subject:** City of Gorlice **Obv:** National Arms above value **Rev:** City view

Date	Mintage	F12	VF20	XF40	MS60	MS63
2010	1,000,000	—	—	—	3.00	4.00

Y# 760 2 ZŁOTE
8.15 g., Brass, 27 mm. **Subject:** City of Miechow **Obv:** National Arms above value **Rev:** Building tower

Date	Mintage	F12	VF20	XF40	MS60	MS63
2010	1,000,000	—	—	—	3.00	4.00

Y# 761 2 ZŁOTE
8.15 g., Brass, 27 mm. **Subject:** City of Katowice **Obv:** National Arms above value **Rev:** Town factory view

Date	Mintage	F12	VF20	XF40	MS60	MS63
2010	1,000,000	—	—	—	3.00	4.00

Y# 762 2 ZŁOTE
8.15 g., Brass, 27 mm. **Subject:** Borsuk **Obv:** National Arms above value **Rev:** Eurasian Badgers

Date	Mintage	F12	VF20	XF40	MS60	MS63
2011	1,500,000	—	—	—	3.00	4.00

Y# 764 2 ZŁOTE
8.15 g., Brass, 27 mm. **Subject:** Zofia Stryjenska **Obv:** National arms, value and artist pallet with brushes **Rev:** Portrait facing

Date	Mintage	F12	VF20	XF40	MS60	MS63
2011	1,000,000	—	—	—	3.00	4.00

Y# 767 2 ZŁOTE
8.15 g., Brass, 27 mm. **Subject:** Independent Student's Union, 30th Anniversary

Date	Mintage	F12	VF20	XF40	MS60	MS63
2011MW	800,000	—	—	—	3.00	4.00

Y# 769 2 ZŁOTE
8.15 g., Brass, 27 mm. **Subject:** Smolensk plane crash

Date	Mintage	F12	VF20	XF40	MS60	MS63
2011MW	800,000	—	—	—	3.00	4.00

Y# 772 2 ZŁOTE
8.15 g., Brass, 27 mm. **Subject:** Beatification of Pope John Paul II **Obv:** Eagle **Rev:** Bust within rays

Date	Mintage	F12	VF20	XF40	MS60	MS63
2011MW	1,000,000	—	—	—	3.00	4.00

Y# 777 2 ZŁOTE
8.15 g., Brass, 27 mm. **Subject:** Poland's presidency of the Council of the European Union

Date	Mintage	F12	VF20	XF40	MS60	MS63
2011MW	800,000	—	—	—	3.00	4.00

Y# 780 2 ZŁOTE
8.15 g., Brass, 27 mm. **Subject:** History of the Polish Cavalry - Uhlan

Date	Mintage	F12	VF20	XF40	MS60	MS63
2011MW	1,000,000	—	—	—	3.00	4.00

Y# 783 2 ZŁOTE
8.15 g., Brass, 27 mm. **Subject:** Gdynia

Date	Mintage	F12	VF20	XF40	MS60	MS63
2011MW	800,000	—	—	—	3.00	4.00

Y# 784 2 ZŁOTE
8.15 g., Brass, 27 mm. **Subject:** Warsaw Pilgrimage to the Marian Shrine of Jasna Gora in Czestochowa, 300th Anniversary

Date	Mintage	F12	VF20	XF40	MS60	MS63
2011MW	800,000	—	—	—	3.00	4.00

Y# 785 2 ZŁOTE
8.15 g., Brass, 27 mm. **Subject:** Czeslaw Milosz

Date	Mintage	F12	VF20	XF40	MS60	MS63
2011MW	800,000	—	—	—	3.00	4.00

Y# 788 2 ZŁOTE
8.15 g., Brass, 27 mm. **Subject:** Mlawa

Date	Mintage	F12	VF20	XF40	MS60	MS63
2011MW	800,000	—	—	—	3.00	4.00

Y# 789 2 ZŁOTE
8.15 g., Brass, 27 mm. **Subject:** Ignacy Jan Paderewski

Date	Mintage	F12	VF20	XF40	MS60	MS63
2011MW	800,000	—	—	—	3.00	4.00

Y# 792 2 ZŁOTE
8.15 g., Brass, 27 mm. **Subject:** Silesian Uprising

Date	Mintage	F12	VF20	XF40	MS60	MS63
2011MW	800,000	—	—	—	3.00	4.00

Y# 794 2 ZŁOTE
8.15 g., Brass, 27 mm. **Subject:** Poznan

Date	Mintage	F12	VF20	XF40	MS60	MS63
2011MW	800,000	—	—	—	3.00	4.00

Y# 795 2 ZŁOTE
8.15 g., Brass, 27 mm. **Subject:** Society for the Protection of the Blind, 100th Anniversary

Date	Mintage	F12	VF20	XF40	MS60	MS63
2011MW	800,000	—	—	—	3.00	4.00

Y# 797 2 ZŁOTE
8.15 g., Brass, 27 mm. **Subject:** Ferdynand Ossendowski

Date	Mintage	F12	VF20	XF40	MS60	MS63
2011MW	900,000	—	—	—	3.00	4.00

Y# 799 2 ZŁOTE
8.15 g., Brass, 27 mm. **Subject:** Polonia Warszawa football club

Date	Mintage	F12	VF20	XF40	MS60	MS63
2011MW	800,000	—	—	—	3.00	4.00

Y# 801 2 ZŁOTE
8.15 g., Brass, 27 mm. **Subject:** Jeremi Przybora and Jerzy Wasowski

Date	Mintage	F12	VF20	XF40	MS60	MS63
2011MW	800,000	—	—	—	3.00	4.00

Y# 804 2 ZŁOTE
8.15 g., Brass, 27 mm. **Subject:** Lodz **Rev:** Building and architectural detail

Date	Mintage	F12	VF20	XF40	MS60	MS63
2011MW		—	—	—	3.00	4.00

Y# 805 2 ZŁOTE
8.15 g., Brass, 27 mm. **Subject:** Krakow **Rev:** Church along riverfront

Date	Mintage	F12	VF20	XF40	MS60	MS63
2011MW Proof		—	—	—	3.00	4.00

Y# 806 2 ZŁOTE
8.15 g., Brass, 27 mm. **Subject:** Kalisz **Rev:** Chruch

Date	Mintage	F12	VF20	XF40	MS60	MS63
2011MW	—	—	—	—	3.00	4.00

Y# 809 2 ZŁOTE
8.15 g., Brass, 27 mm. **Subject:** Christmas Charity Orchestra, 20th Anniversary **Rev:** Guitar with love hearts

Date	Mintage	F12	VF20	XF40	MS60	MS63
2012MW	—	—	—	—	3.00	4.00

Y# 811 2 ZŁOTE
8.15 g., Brass, 27 mm. **Subject:** Cooperative banking in Poland, 150th Anniversary **Rev:** Stack of money and coins, wheat ear in center

Date	Mintage	F12	VF20	XF40	MS60	MS63
2012MW	—	—	—	—	3.00	4.00

Y# 813 2 ZŁOTE
8.15 g., Brass, 27 mm. **Subject:** Ulma, Baranek and Kowalski families **Rev:** Mother holding child

Date	Mintage	F12	VF20	XF40	MS60	MS63
2012MW	—	—	—	—	3.00	4.00

Y# 816 2 ZŁOTE
8.15 g., Brass, 27 mm. **Subject:** Polish Radio, 50th Anniversary

Date	Mintage	F12	VF20	XF40	MS60	MS63
2012MW	800,000	—	—	—	3.00	4.00

Y# 817 2 ZŁOTE
8.15 g., Brass, 27 mm. **Subject:** Stefan Banach

Date	Mintage	F12	VF20	XF40	MS60	MS63
2012MW	800,000	—	—	—	3.00	4.00

Y# 820 2 ZŁOTE
8.15 g., Brass, 27 mm. **Subject:** Blyskawica, destroyer

Date	Mintage	F12	VF20	XF40	MS60	MS63
2012MW	800,000	—	—	—	3.00	4.00

Y# 821 2 ZŁOTE
8.15 g., Brass, 27 mm. **Subject:** National Museum in Warsaw, 150th Anniversary

Date	Mintage	F12	VF20	XF40	MS60	MS63
2012	800,000	—	—	—	3.00	4.00

Y# 823 2 ZŁOTE
8.15 g., Brass, 27 mm. **Subject:** European Football Championships

Date	Mintage	F12	VF20	XF40	MS60	MS63
2012MW	1,000,000	—	—	—	3.00	4.00

Y# 832 2 ZŁOTE
8.15 g., Brass, 27 mm. **Subject:** London Olympics, 2012; Polish Team

Date	Mintage	F12	VF20	XF40	MS60	MS63
2012MW	1,000,000	—	—	—	3.00	4.00

Y# 835 2 ZŁOTE
8.15 g., Brass **Subject:** Krzemionki Opatowskie **Shape:** 27

Date	Mintage	F12	VF20	XF40	MS60	MS63
2012MW	800,000	—	—	—	3.00	4.00

Y# 837 2 ZŁOTE
8.15 g., Brass, 27 mm. **Subject:** Orzel, submarine

Date	Mintage	F12	VF20	XF40	MS60	MS63
2012MW	800,000	—	—	—	3.00	4.00

Y# 838 2 ZŁOTE
8.15 g., Brass, 27 mm. **Subject:** Boleslaw Prus

Date	Mintage	F12	VF20	XF40	MS60	MS63
2012MW	8,000,000	—	—	—	3.00	4.00

Y# 841 2 ZŁOTE
8.15 g., Brass, 27 mm. **Subject:** Dragon, light cruiser

Date	Mintage	F12	VF20	XF40	MS60	MS63
2012MW	800,000	—	—	—	3.00	4.00

Y# 842 2 ZŁOTE
8.15 g., Brass, 27 mm. **Subject:** Piotr Michalowski, painter

Date	Mintage	F12	VF20	XF40	MS60	MS63
2012MW	800,000	—	—	—	3.00	4.00

Y# 893 2 ZŁOTE
8.15 g., Brass, 27 mm. **Subject:** Polish Olympic Team, Sochi 2014

Date	Mintage	F12	VF20	XF40	MS60	MS63
2014	800,000	—	—	—	3.00	4.00

Y# 844 2 ZŁOTYCH
8.15 g., Brass, 27 mm. **Obv:** Eagle **Rev:** Destroyer Piorun

Date	Mintage	F12	VF20	XF40	MS60	MS63
2012MW	800,000	—	—	—	—	3.00

Y# 847 2 ZŁOTYCH
8.15 g., Brass, 27 mm. **Subject:** London Olympics, 2012 **Obv:** Eagle **Rev:** Runner motif

Date	Mintage	F12	VF20	XF40	MS60	MS63
2012MW	1,000,000	—	—	—	—	3.00

Y# 848 2 ZŁOTYCH
8.15 g., Brass, 27 mm. **Obv:** Eagle **Rev:** Missile ship - Gdynia

Date	Mintage	F12	VF20	XF40	MS60	MS63
2013MW	800,000	—	—	—	—	3.00

Y# 852 2 ZŁOTYCH
8.15 g., Brass, 27 mm. **Subject:** January 1863 Uprising, 150th Anniversary **Obv:** Eagle **Rev:** Female blessing kneeling soldier, flag in backgorund

Date	Mintage	F12	VF20	XF40	MS60	MS63
2013MW	800,000	—	—	—	—	3.00

Y# 854 2 ZŁOTYCH
8.15 g., Brass, 27 mm. **Subject:** Polish Theatre, 100th Anniversary **Obv:** Eagle **Rev:** Theatre façade

Date	Mintage	F12	VF20	XF40	MS60	MS63
2013MW	800,000	—	—	—	—	3.00

Y# 856 2 ZŁOTYCH
8.15 g., Copper-Aluminum-Nickel, 27 mm. **Subject:** Cyprian Norwid

Date	Mintage	F12	VF20	XF40	MS60	MS63
2013MW	Est. 800000	—	—	—	—	3.00

Y# 859 2 ZŁOTYCH
8.15 g., Copper-Aluminum-Nickel, 27 mm. **Subject:** Polish Ships - Warszawa Guided-Missle Destroyer

Date	Mintage	F12	VF20	XF40	MS60	MS63
2013MW	Est. 800000	—	—	—	—	3.00

Y# 862 2 ZŁOTYCH
8.15 g., Copper-Aluminum-Nickel, 27 mm. **Subject:** Polish Ships - Lublin Class Minelayer - Landing Ship

Date	Mintage	F12	VF20	XF40	MS60	MS63
2013MW	—	—	—	—	—	3.00

Y# 864 2 ZŁOTYCH
8.15 g., Copper-Aluminum-Nickel, 27 mm. **Subject:** Polish Football Clubs - Warta Poznan

Date	Mintage	F12	VF20	XF40	MS60	MS63
2013MW	800,000	—	—	—	—	3.00

Y# 866 2 ZŁOTYCH
8.15 g., Copper-Aluminum-Nickel, 27 mm. **Subject:** Polish Ships - ORP Gen. K. Pulaski Guided-Missile Frigate

Date	Mintage	F12	VF20	XF40	MS60	MS63
2013MW	Est. 800000	—	—	—	—	3.00

Y# 870 2 ZŁOTYCH
8.15 g., Copper-Aluminum-Nickel, 27 mm. **Subject:** Witold Lutoslawski

Date	Mintage	F12	VF20	XF40	MS60	MS63
2013MW	—	—	—	—	—	3.00

Y# 873 2 ZŁOTYCH
8.15 g., Copper-Aluminum-Nickel, 27 mm. **Subject:** 200th Anniversary of the Death of Prince Jozef Poinatowski

Date	Mintage	F12	VF20	XF40	MS60	MS63
2013MW	Est. 800000	—	—	—	—	3.00

Y# 876 2 ZŁOTYCH
8.15 g., Copper-Aluminum-Nickel, 27 mm. **Subject:** 50th Anniversary of the Polish Society for the Mentally Handicapped

Date	Mintage	F12	VF20	XF40	MS60	MS63
2013MW	Est. 800000	—	—	—	—	3.00

Y# 878 2 ZŁOTYCH
8.15 g., Copper-Aluminum-Nickel, 27 mm. **Subject:** Animals of the World - Eukropean Bison

Date	Mintage	F12	VF20	XF40	MS60	MS63
2013MW	Est. 10000000	—	—	—	—	3.00

Y# 880 2 ZŁOTYCH
8.15 g., Copper-Aluminum-Nickel, 27 mm. **Subject:** 200th Anniversary of the Birth of Hipolit Cegielski

Date	Mintage	F12	VF20	XF40	MS60	MS63
2013MW	Est. 800000	—	—	—	—	3.00

Y# 883 2 ZŁOTYCH
8.15 g., Copper-Aluminum-Nickel, 27 mm. **Subject:** History of Polish Popular Music - Agniezka Osiecka

Date	Mintage	F12	VF20	XF40	MS60	MS63
2013MW	Est. 800000	—	—	—	—	3.00

Y# 896 2 ZŁOTYCH
8.15 g., Brass, 27 mm. **Subject:** Konik Horse

Date	Mintage	F12	VF20	XF40	MS60	MS63
2014	800,000	—	—	—	—	3.00

Y# 901 2 ZŁOTYCH
8.15 g., Brass, 27 mm. **Subject:** Jan Karski, 100th Anniversary of Birth

Date	Mintage	F12	VF20	XF40	MS60	MS63
2014	700,000	—	—	—	—	3.00

Y# 851 10 ZŁOTY
14.14 g., 0.925 Silver 0.4178 oz. ASW, 32 mm. **Subject:** January 1893 Uprising, 150th Anniversary **Obv:** Anchor logo, pries and eagle **Rev:** Tri-part sheidl crowned, arms in background

Date	Mintage	F12	VF20	XF40	MS60	MS63
2013MW	28,000	PF63 40.00		PF65 50.00		

Y# 853 10 ZŁOTY
14.00 g., 0.925 Silver 0.4137 oz. ASW, 40x26 mm. **Subject:** Polish Theatre, 100th Anniversary **Obv:** Shield and Eagle **Rev:** Exterior of the theater, open curtain in color **Shape:** Oval

Date	Mintage	F12	VF20	XF40	MS60	MS63
2013MW	28,000	PF63 45.00		PF65 55.00		

Y# 857 10 ZŁOTY
14.14 g., 0.925 Silver 0.4178 oz. ASW, 32 mm. **Subject:** Cyprian Norwid

Date	Mintage	F12	VF20	XF40	MS60	MS63
2013MW	Est. 28000	PF63 42.00		PF65 52.00		

Y# 284 5 ZŁOTYCH
6.54 g., Bi-Metallic, 24 mm. **Obv:** National arms within circle **Obv. Legend:** RZECZPOSPOLITA POLSKA **Rev:** Value within circle flanked by oak leaves

Date	Mintage	F12	VF20	XF40	MS60	MS63
2008MW	—	—	—	—	7.00	8.00
2009MW	—	—	—	—	7.00	8.00
2010MW	—	—	—	—	7.00	8.00

Y# 800 5 ZŁOTYCH
7.07 g., 0.925 Silver 0.2089 oz. ASW, 24 mm. **Subject:** Polonia Warszawa football club

Date	Mintage	F12	VF20	XF40	MS60	MS63
2011MW	50,000				PF63 15.00	PF65 20.00

Y# 863 5 ZŁOTYCH
7.07 g., 0.925 Silver 0.2089 oz. ASW, 24 mm. **Subject:** History of Polish Coin - Denarius of Boleslaw I the Brave

Date	Mintage	F12	VF20	XF40	MS60	MS63
2013MW Proof	—	—	—	—	7.00	8.00

Y# 865 5 ZŁOTYCH
7.07 g., 0.925 Silver 0.2089 oz. ASW, 24 mm. **Subject:** Polish Football CLubs - Warta Poznan

Date	Mintage	F12	VF20	XF40	MS60	MS63
2013MW Proof Est. 40000	—	—	—	—	7.00	8.00

Y# 869 5 ZŁOTYCH
7.07 g., 0.925 Silver 0.2089 oz. ASW, 24 mm. **Subject:** History of Polish Coin - Denarius of Boleslaw II the Bold

Date	Mintage	F12	VF20	XF40	MS60	MS63
2013MW Proof Est. 20000	—	—	—	—	7.00	8.00

Y# 904 5 ZŁOTYCH
6.54 g., Bi-Metallic, 24 mm. **Subject:** Discover Poland

Date	Mintage	F12	VF20	XF40	MS60	MS63
2014	1,200,000	—	—	—	7.00	8.00

Y# 913 5 ZŁOTYCH
6.54 g., Bi-Metallic, 24 mm. **Subject:** Discover Poland

Date	Mintage	F12	VF20	XF40	MS60	MS63
2014	1,200,000	—	—	—	7.00	8.00

Y# 406 10 ZŁOTYCH
14.14 g., 0.925 Silver 0.4178 oz. ASW **Subject:** Year 2001 **Obv:** Crowned eagle with wings open **Rev:** Printed circuit board

Date	Mintage	F12	VF20	XF40	MS60	MS63
2001MW	35,000				PF63 35.00	PF65 55.00

Y# 413 10 ZŁOTYCH
14.14 g., 0.925 Silver 0.4178 oz. ASW, 32 mm. **Subject:** 15 Years of the Constitutional Court **Obv:** Crowned eagle suspended from a judge's neck chain **Rev:** Crowned eagle head and balance scale **Edge Lettering:** TRYBUNAL KONSTYTUCYJNY W SLUZBIE PANSTWA PRAWA

Date	Mintage	F12	VF20	XF40	MS60	MS63
2001MW	25,000				PF63 45.00	PF65 65.00

Y# 419 10 ZŁOTYCH
14.14 g., 0.925 Silver 0.4178 oz. ASW, 32 mm. **Subject:** Cardinal Stefan Wyszynski **Obv:** Crowned eagle with wings open above ribbon **Rev:** Half length figure facing with raised hands **Edge Lettering:** 100 • ROCZNIA URODZIN

Date	Mintage	F12	VF20	XF40	MS60	MS63
2001MW	60,000				PF63 25.00	PF65 30.00

Y# 425 10 ZŁOTYCH
14.21 g., 0.925 Silver 0.4199 oz. ASW, 32 mm. **Subject:** Jan III Sobieski **Obv:** Crowned eagle with wings open **Rev:** 3/4 armored bust facing with army in background **Edge:** Plain

Date	Mintage	F12	VF20	XF40	MS60	MS63
2001MW	24,000				PF63 40.00	PF65 50.00

Y# 458 10 ZŁOTYCH
14.14 g., 0.925 Silver 0.4178 oz. ASW, 32 mm. **Obv:** Crowned eagle with wings open **Rev:** Jan Sobieski, half-length figure in armor standing **Edge:** Plain

Date	Mintage	F12	VF20	XF40	MS60	MS63
2001MW	17,000				PF63 65.00	PF65 85.00

Y# 459 10 ZŁOTYCH
14.14 g., 0.925 Silver 0.4178 oz. ASW, 32 mm. **Obv:** Three violins **Rev:** Henryk Wieniawski **Edge:** Plain

Date	Mintage	F12	VF20	XF40	MS60	MS63
2001MW	28,000				PF63 35.00	PF65 55.00

Y# 460 10 ZŁOTYCH
14.14 g., 0.925 Silver 0.4178 oz. ASW, 32 mm. **Obv:** Crowned eagle with wings open above fish **Rev:** Michal Siedlecki **Edge:** Plain

Date	Mintage	F12	VF20	XF40	MS60	MS63
2001MW	26,000				PF63 30.00	PF65 50.00

Y# 432 10 ZŁOTYCH
14.14 g., 0.925 Silver 0.4178 oz. ASW, 32 mm. **Subject:** Bronislaw Malinowski **Obv:** Small crowned eagle with wings open to right of bust facing **Rev:** Trobriand Islands village scene **Edge Lettering:** etnolog, antropolog kultury

Date	Mintage	F12	VF20	XF40	MS60	MS63
2002MW	—				PF63 25.00	PF65 35.00

Y# 434 10 ZŁOTYCH
14.14 g., 0.925 Silver 0.4178 oz. ASW, 32 mm. **Subject:** World Cup Soccer **Obv:** Crowned eagle with wings open **Rev:** Soccer player **Edge Lettering:** etnolog, antropolog kultury

Date	Mintage	F12	VF20	XF40	MS60	MS63
2002MW	—				PF63 22.00	PF65 27.00

Y# 435 10 ZŁOTYCH
14.14 g., 0.925 Silver 0.4178 oz. ASW, 32 mm. **Subject:** World Cup Soccer **Obv:** Amber soccer ball inset entering goal net **Rev:** Two soccer players with amber soccer ball inset **Edge Lettering:** etnolog, antropolog kultury

Date	Mintage	F12	VF20	XF40	MS60	MS63
2002MW	—				PF63 35.00	PF65 55.00

Y# 437 10 ZŁOTYCH
14.14 g., 0.925 Silver 0.4178 oz. ASW, 32 mm. **Subject:** Pope John Paul II **Obv:** Crowned eagle with wings open within two views of praying Pope **Rev:** Pope facing radiant Holy Door **Edge:** Plain

Date	Mintage	F12	VF20	XF40	MS60	MS63
2002MW	80,000				PF63 25.00	PF65 35.00

Y# 441 10 ZŁOTYCH
14.20 g., 0.925 Silver 0.4196 oz. ASW, 32 mm. **Subject:** Gen. Wladyslaw Anders **Obv:** Crowned eagle with wings open, cross and multicolor flowers **Rev:** Uniformed bust right **Edge:** Plain

Date	Mintage	F12	VF20	XF40	MS60	MS63
2002MW	40,000				PF63 55.00	PF65 75.00

Y# 450 10 ZŁOTYCH
14.14 g., 0.925 Silver 0.4178 oz. ASW, 32 mm. **Subject:** August II (1697-1706, 1709-1735) **Obv:** Crowned eagle with wings open **Rev:** Portrait and Order of the White Eagle **Edge:** Plain

Date	Mintage	F12	VF20	XF40	MS60	MS63
2002MW	30,000	**PF63** 35.00	**PF65** 55.00			

Y# 448 10 ZŁOTYCH
14.14 g., 0.925 Silver 0.4178 oz. ASW, 32 mm. **Subject:** City of Poznan (Posen) **Obv:** Old coin design and arched door **Rev:** Old coin design and city view **Edge:** Plain

Date	Mintage	F12	VF20	XF40	MS60	MS63
2003MW	39,000	**PF63** 35.00	**PF65** 55.00			

Y# 453 10 ZŁOTYCH
14.14 g., 0.925 Silver 0.4178 oz. ASW, 32 mm. **Subject:** Great Orchestra of Christmas Charity **Obv:** Large inscribed heart above crowned eagle with wings open **Rev:** Boy playing flute **Edge:** Plain

Date	Mintage	F12	VF20	XF40	MS60	MS63
2003MW	47,000	**PF63** 35.00	**PF65** 55.00			

Y# 468 10 ZŁOTYCH
14.14 g., 0.925 Silver 0.4178 oz. ASW, 32 mm. **Obv:** Tanks on battlefield **Rev:** General Maczek **Edge:** Plain

Date	Mintage	F12	VF20	XF40	MS60	MS63
2003MW	44,000	**PF63** 25.00	**PF65** 35.00			

Y# 469 10 ZŁOTYCH
14.14 g., 0.925 Silver 0.4178 oz. ASW, 32 mm. **Subject:** Gas and Oil Industry **Obv:** Crowned eagle and highway leading to city view **Rev:** Portrait and refinery **Edge:** Plain

Date	Mintage	F12	VF20	XF40	MS60	MS63
2003MW	43,000	**PF63** 25.00	**PF65** 35.00			

Y# 474 10 ZŁOTYCH
14.14 g., 0.925 Silver 0.4178 oz. ASW, 32 mm. **Obv:** Crowned eagle with wings open **Rev:** Stanislaus I and wife's portrait **Edge:** Plain

Date	Mintage	F12	VF20	XF40	MS60	MS63
2003MW	45,000	**PF63** 25.00	**PF65** 35.00			

Y# 475 10 ZŁOTYCH
14.14 g., 0.925 Silver 0.4178 oz. ASW, 32 mm. **Obv:** Crowned eagle with wings open **Rev:** Half-length figure of Stanislaus I with his wife in background **Edge:** Plain

Date	Mintage	F12	VF20	XF40	MS60	MS63
2003MW	40,000	**PF63** 30.00	**PF65** 40.00			

Y# 480 10 ZŁOTYCH
14.14 g., 0.925 Silver 0.4178 oz. ASW, 32 mm. **Subject:** 80th Anniversary of the Modern Zloty Currency **Obv:** Man wearing glasses behind crowned eagle with wings open **Rev:** Bust left **Edge:** Plain

Date	Mintage	F12	VF20	XF40	MS60	MS63
2004MW	55,000	**PF63** 22.00	**PF65** 32.00			

Y# 482 10 ZŁOTYCH
14.14 g., 0.925 Silver 0.4178 oz. ASW, 32 mm. **Subject:** Poland Joining the European Union **Obv:** Crowned eagle in blue circle with yellow stars **Rev:** Multicolor European Union and Polish flags **Edge:** Plain

Date	Mintage	F12	VF20	XF40	MS60	MS63
2004MW	78,000	**PF63** 25.00	**PF65** 35.00			

Y# 497 10 ZŁOTYCH
14.14 g., 0.925 Silver 0.4178 oz. ASW, 32 mm. **Subject:** Warsaw Uprising 60th Anniversary **Obv:** Crowned eagle and value on resistance symbol **Rev:** Polish soldier wearing captured German helmet **Edge:** Plain

Date	Mintage	F12	VF20	XF40	MS60	MS63
2004MW	92,000	**PF63** 18.00	**PF65** 25.00			

Y# 500 10 ZŁOTYCH
14.14 g., 0.925 Silver 0.4178 oz. ASW, 32 mm. **Obv:** Polish paratrooper badge **Rev:** Gen. Sosabowski and descending paratrooper **Edge:** Plain

Date	Mintage	F12	VF20	XF40	MS60	MS63
2004MW	56,000	**PF63** 18.00	**PF65** 25.00			

Y# 502 10 ZŁOTYCH
14.14 g., 0.925 Silver 0.4178 oz. ASW, 32 mm. **Subject:** Polish Police 85th Anniversary **Obv:** Crowned eagle with wings open **Rev:** Seal partially overlapping police badge **Edge:** Plain

Date	Mintage	F12	VF20	XF40	MS60	MS63
2004MW	65,000	**PF63** 20.00	**PF65** 30.00			

Y# 506 10 ZŁOTYCH
14.14 g., 0.925 Silver 0.4178 oz. ASW, 32 mm. **Obv:** Siberian landscape above crowned eagle and value **Rev:** Aleksander Czekanowski (1833-1876) **Edge:** Plain

Date	Mintage	F12	VF20	XF40	MS60	MS63
2004MW	45,000	**PF63** 18.00	**PF65** 25.00			

Y# 510 10 ZŁOTYCH
14.14 g., 0.925 Silver 0.4178 oz. ASW, 32 mm. **Subject:** Warsaw Fine Arts Academy Centennial **Obv:** Crowned eagle with wings open within city square **Rev:** Art studio, color painting on stand **Edge:** Plain

Date	Mintage	F12	VF20	XF40	MS60	MS63
2004MW	75,000	**PF63** 20.00	**PF65** 30.00			
Antique patina						

Y# 517 10 ZŁOTYCH
14.14 g., 0.925 Silver 0.4178 oz. ASW, 32 mm. **Subject:** Olympics **Obv:** Crowned eagle with wings open and woman **Rev:** Fencers in front of Parthenon **Edge:** Plain

Date	Mintage	F12	VF20	XF40	MS60	MS63
2004MW	70,000	**PF63** 18.00	**PF65** 25.00			

Y# 518 10 ZŁOTYCH
14.14 g., 0.925 Silver 0.4178 oz. ASW, 32 mm. **Subject:** Olympics **Obv:** Crowned eagle with wings open within gold plated center **Rev:** Ancient athlete within gold plated circle **Edge:** Plain

Date	Mintage	F12	VF20	XF40	MS60	MS63
2004MW	90,000	**PF63** 18.00	**PF65** 25.00			

Y# 523 10 ZŁOTYCH
14.23 g., 0.925 Silver 0.4205 oz. ASW, 43.2 x 29.2 mm. **Subject:** Japan's Aichi Expo **Obv:** Monument **Rev:** Two cranes **Edge:** Plain **Shape:** Quarter of circle

Date	Mintage	F12	VF20	XF40	MS60	MS63
2005MW	80,000	**PF63** 25.00	**PF65** 35.00			

Y# 526 10 ZŁOTYCH
14.14 g., 0.925 Silver 0.4178 oz. ASW, 32.1 mm. **Obv:** Crowned eagle with wings open above date and grasping hands **Rev:** Gold plated bust right and church **Edge:** Plain

Date	Mintage	F12	VF20	XF40	MS60	MS63
2005MW	—	**PF63** 20.00	**PF65** 30.00			

Y# 537 10 ZŁOTYCH
14.14 g., 0.925 Silver 0.4178 oz. ASW, 32 mm. **Obv:** Horse drawn carriage **Rev:** Green duck at left and Konstanty Ildefons Galczynski in top hat at right **Edge:** Plain

Date	Mintage	F12	VF20	XF40	MS60	MS63
2005MW	62,000	**PF63** 18.00	**PF65** 25.00			

Y# 539 10 ZŁOTYCH
14.14 g., 0.925 Silver 0.4178 oz. ASW, 32 mm. **Obv:** Baptismal font and Polish eagle **Rev:** Pope John Paul II and St. Peter's Basilica **Edge:** Plain

Date	Mintage	F12	VF20	XF40	MS60	MS63
2005MW	170,000	**PF63** 20.00	**PF65** 30.00			

Y# 552 10 ZŁOTYCH
14.14 g., 0.925 Silver 0.4178 oz. ASW, 32 mm. **Obv:** Crowned eagle above value **Rev:** Stanislaw August Poniatowski and shadow **Edge:** Plain

Date	Mintage	F12	VF20	XF40	MS60	MS63
2005MW	60,000	**PF63** 20.00	**PF65** 30.00			

Y# 553 10 ZŁOTYCH
14.14 g., 0.925 Silver 0.4178 oz. ASW, 32 mm. **Obv:** Crowned eagle above value **Rev:** Stanislaw August Poniatowski and crowned monogram **Edge:** Plain

Date	Mintage	F12	VF20	XF40	MS60	MS63
2005MW	60,000	**PF63** 20.00	**PF65** 30.00			

Y# 554 10 ZŁOTYCH
14.14 g., 0.925 Silver 0.4178 oz. ASW, 32 mm. **Subject:** End of WWII 60th Anniversary **Obv:** Crowned eagle above soldier silhouettes and value **Rev:** City view in ruins above bird with green sprig **Edge:** Plain

Date	Mintage	F12	VF20	XF40	MS60	MS63
2005MW	70,000	**PF63** 22.00	**PF65** 32.00			

Y# 568 10 ZŁOTYCH
14.14 g., 0.925 Silver 0.4178 oz. ASW, 32 mm. **Obv:** Sail ship and obverse design of Y-31 **Rev:** Reverse design of Y-31 on radiant design **Edge:** Lettered

Date	Mintage	F12	VF20	XF40	MS60	MS63
2005MW	61,000	**PF63** 25.00	**PF65** 35.00			

Y# 596 10 ZŁOTYCH
14.18 g., 0.925 Silver 0.419 oz. ASW, 32 mm. **Subject:** 500th Anniversary - Birth of M. Reja **Obv:** National arms in oval, value below **Obv. Legend:** RZECZPOSPOLITA POLSKA **Rev:** Bust of Reja 3/4 right **Rev. Legend:** 500. ROCZNICA URODZIN MIKOLAJA REJA **Edge:** Plain

Date	Mintage	F12	VF20	XF40	MS60	MS63
2005MW	60,000	**PF63** 18.00	**PF65** 25.00			

Y# 556 10 ZŁOTYCH
14.14 g., 0.925 Silver 0.4178 oz. ASW, 32 mm. **Subject:** 2006 Winter Olympics **Obv:** Small national arms at left, figure skating couple at center **Obv. Legend:** RZECZPOSPOLITA POLSKA **Rev:** Female figure skater **Rev. Legend:** XX ZIMOWE IGRZYSKA OLIMPIJSKIE **Edge:** Plain

Date	Mintage	F12	VF20	XF40	MS60	MS63
2006MW	72,000	**PF63** 20.00	**PF65** 30.00			

Y# 599 10 ZŁOTYCH
14.18 g., 0.925 Silver 0.419 oz. ASW, 32 mm. **Series:** History of the Zloty **Obv:** National arms at upper left, 1932 dated 10 Zlotych obverse at lower right, building facade in background **Obv. Legend:** RZECZPOSPOLITA POLSKA **Rev:** Reverse of 1932 dated coin with head of Queen Jadwiga **Rev. Legend:** DZIEJE ZLOTEGO **Edge:** Plain

Date	Mintage	F12	VF20	XF40	MS60	MS63
2006MW	61,000	**PF63** 20.00	**PF65** 30.00			

Y# 555 10 ZŁOTYCH
14.14 g., 0.925 Silver 0.4178 oz. ASW, 32 mm. **Subject:** 2006 Winter Olympics **Obv:** Snow boarder above crowned eagle **Rev:** Snow boarder **Edge:** Plain

Date	Mintage	F12	VF20	XF40	MS60	MS63
2006MW	71,400	**PF63** 20.00	**PF65** 30.00			

Y# 598 10 ZŁOTYCH
14.15 g., 0.925 Silver 0.4181 oz. ASW, 32 mm. **Subject:** 30th Anniversary June 1976 **Obv:** National arms divides denomination, split railroad tracks below **Obv. Legend:** RZECZPOSPOLITA POLSKA **Rev:** 3/4 length woman standing with child, outlined row of shielded forces in background **Rev. Legend:** 30. ROCZNICA - CZERWCA 1976 **Edge:** Plain

Date	Mintage	F12	VF20	XF40	MS60	MS63
2006MW	56,000	**PF63** 20.00	**PF65** 30.00			

Y# 754 10 ZŁOTYCH

14.14 g., Bi-Metallic, 32 mm. **Subject:** World Cup soccer **Obv:** Eagle within net **Rev:** Player kicking ball, sun

Date	Mintage	F12	VF20	XF40	MS60	MS63
2006	—	PF63 20.00	PF65 30.00			

Y# 890 10 ZŁOTYCH

14.14 g., 0.925 Silver 0.4178 oz. ASW **Subject:** 500th Anniversary **Rev:** Coronation scene

Date	Mintage	F12	VF20	XF40	MS60	MS63
2006	—	PF63 18.00	PF65 25.00			

Y# 585 10 ZŁOTYCH

14.14 g., 0.925 Silver 0.4178 oz. ASW, 32 mm. **Obv:** Mountains, Polish Eagle and value **Rev:** Ignacy Domeyko **Edge:** Plain

Date	Mintage	F12	VF20	XF40	MS60	MS63
2007MW	55,000	PF63 18.00	PF65 25.00			

Y# 587 10 ZŁOTYCH

14.14 g., 0.925 Silver 0.4178 oz. ASW, 32 mm. **Subject:** 75th Anniversary - Breaking the Enigma Code **Obv:** Polish Eagle on circuit board **Rev:** Segmented letters **Edge:** Lettered

Date	Mintage	F12	VF20	XF40	MS60	MS63
2007MW	55,000	PF63 35.00	PF65 45.00			

Y# 589 10 ZŁOTYCH

14.14 g., 0.925 Silver 0.4178 oz. ASW, 32 mm. **Obv:** Angel, Polish Eagle and obverse coin design of Y-18 **Rev:** Reverse coin design of Y-18 on wheat ears **Edge:** Plain

Date	Mintage	F12	VF20	XF40	MS60	MS63
2007MW	57,000	PF63 30.00	PF65 40.00			

Y# 595 10 ZŁOTYCH

14.14 g., 0.925 Silver 0.4178 oz. ASW, 32 mm. **Subject:** Municipality of Krakow, 750th Anniversary **Obv:** City gate tower, national arms at lower right **Obv. Legend:** RZECZPOSPOLITA POLSKA **Rev:** Knight with shield standing facing

Date	Mintage	F12	VF20	XF40	MS60	MS63
2007MW	58,000	PF63 20.00	PF65 30.00			

Y# 600 10 ZŁOTYCH

14.10 g., 0.925 Silver 0.4166 oz. ASW, 32 mm. **Subject:** 125th Anniversary - Birth of Szymanowskiego **Obv:** Piano keys at left, national arms on music score at right **Obv. Legend:** RZECZPOSPOLITA POLSKA **Rev:** Bust of Szymanowskiego 3/4 left, music composition at back of head and over upper body, dates as hologram at left **Rev. Legend:** 125. ROCZNICA URODZIN KAROLA SZYMANOWSKIEGO **Edge:** Plain

Date	Mintage	F12	VF20	XF40	MS60	MS63
2007MW	55,000	PF63 18.00	PF65 25.00			

Y# 601 10 ZŁOTYCH

14.30 g., 0.925 Silver 0.4225 oz. ASW, 14 mm. **Subject:** Arctic Explorers **Obv:** Sailing ship at center, national arms at right with denomination below **Obv. Legend:** RZECZPOSPOLITA POLSKA **Rev:** Busts of Henryk Arctowski and Antoni Dobrowolski facing, polar outline map at lower left **Edge:** Plain

Date	Mintage	F12	VF20	XF40	MS60	MS63
2007MW	60,000	PF63 20.00	PF65 30.00			

Y# 602 10 ZŁOTYCH

14.05 g., 0.925 Silver 0.4151 oz. ASW, 31.95 x 22.39 mm. **Obv:** Helmeted national arms, sword and denomination below **Obv. Legend:** RZECZPOSPOLITA - POLSKA **Rev:** Chivalrous knight on horseback jousting right **Rev. Inscription:** RYCERZ - CIEZKOZBROJNY **Edge:** Plain **Shape:** Rectangular

Date	Mintage	F12	VF20	XF40	MS60	MS63
2007MW	57,000	PF63 30.00	PF65 40.00			

Y# 632 10 ZŁOTYCH

14.14 g., 0.925 Silver 0.4178 oz. ASW, 32 mm. **Subject:** 40th Anniversary "Rocznica" March **Obv:** National arms at upper right, manuscript pages fluttering at left **Obv. Legend:** RZECZPOSPOLITA POLSKA **Rev:** Student protesters in front of gates of Warsaw University, military police in silhouette in foreground

Date	Mintage	F12	VF20	XF40	MS60	MS63
2008MW	118,000	PF63 20.00	PF65 30.00			

Y# 635 10 ZŁOTYCH

14.14 g., 0.925 Silver 0.4178 oz. ASW, 32 mm. **Subject:** Zbigniew Herbert **Obv:** Bust of Herbert 3/4 right at left, national arms at lower right **Rev:** Statue of Nike **Edge:** Plain

Date	Mintage	F12	VF20	XF40	MS60	MS63
2008MW	113,000	PF63 20.00	PF65 30.00			

Y# 645 10 ZŁOTYCH

14.40 g., 0.925 Silver 0.4255 oz. ASW, 32 mm. **Subject:** The 29th Olympic Games Beijing 2008 **Obv:** Chinese ornament & dragon **Rev:** Swimmer

Date	Mintage	F12	VF20	XF40	MS60	MS63
2008	140,000	PF63 25.00	PF65 40.00			

Y# 639 10 ZŁOTYCH

14.14 g., 0.925 Silver 0.4178 oz. ASW, 32 mm. **Subject:** Siberian Exiles **Obv:** Small national arms at left, human outlines at right **Obv. Legend:** RZECZPOSPOLITA POLSKA **Rev:** Tree lines with imbedded triangular crystal below **Rev. Inscription:** SYBIRACY **Edge:** Plain

Date	Mintage	F12	VF20	XF40	MS60	MS63
2008MW	135,000	PF63 20.00	PF65 30.00			

Y# 646 10 ZŁOTYCH

14.14 g., 0.925 Silver 0.4178 oz. ASW, 32 mm. **Subject:** The 29th Olympic Games Beijing 2008 **Obv:** Square hole & an eagle **Rev:** Square hole & a windsurfer

Date	Mintage	F12	VF20	XF40	MS60	MS63
2008	150,000	PF63 20.00	PF65 30.00			

Y# 649 10 ZŁOTYCH

14.14 g., 0.925 Silver 0.4178 oz. ASW, 32 mm. **Subject:** Polish Travellers & Explorers **Obv:** Man & woman holding child **Rev:** Bust of Bronislaw Pilsudski

Date	Mintage	F12	VF20	XF40	MS60	MS63
2008	99,000	PF63 22.00	PF65 32.00			

Y# 655 10 ZŁOTYCH

14.14 g., 0.925 Silver 0.4178 oz. ASW, 32 mm. **Subject:** 450th Anniversary of the Polish Post **Obv:** Eagle on top right, post stamp in center with man on horse **Rev:** Post courier

Date		Mintage	F12	VF20	XF40	MS60	MS63
2008		135,000	PF63 25.00	PF65 35.00			

Y# 658 10 ZŁOTYCH

14.14 g., 0.925 Silver 0.4178 oz. ASW, 32 mm. **Subject:** 400th Anniversary - Polish Settlement in North America **Obv:** Man blowing glassware left **Rev:** Man blowing glassware right

Date		Mintage	F12	VF20	XF40	MS60	MS63
2008		126,000	PF63 25.00	PF65 35.00			

Y# 661 10 ZŁOTYCH

14.14 g., 0.925 Silver 0.4178 oz. ASW, 32 mm. **Subject:** 90th Anniversary of the Greater Poland Uprising **Obv:** Eagle at top, Commander riding horse followed by soldiers **Rev:** Rose at left, Bust of Igancy Jan Paderewski at right

Date		Mintage	F12	VF20	XF40	MS60	MS63
2008		107,000	PF63 25.00	PF65 35.00			

Y# 671 10 ZŁOTYCH

14.40 g., 0.925 Silver 0.4255 oz. ASW, 22x32 mm. **Obv:** Eagle, flag and armor **Rev:** Hussar Knights, XVII Century **Shape:** Vertical rectangle

Date		Mintage	F12	VF20	XF40	MS60	MS63
2009		100,000	PF63 20.00	PF65 30.00			

Y# 695 10 ZŁOTYCH

14.14 g., 0.925 Silver 0.4178 oz. ASW, 32 mm. **Subject:** 70th Anniversary of the start of World War II **Obv:** Eagle and map of Nazi and Soviet invasion **Rev:** Planes dropping bombs on Wielun

Date		Mintage	F12	VF20	XF40	MS60	MS63
2009MW		100,000	PF63 25.00	PF65 35.00			

Y# 688 10 ZŁOTYCH

14.14 g., 0.925 Silver 0.4178 oz. ASW, 27 mm. **Subject:** Poets of the Uprising **Obv:** National arms **Rev:** Tadeusz Gajcy portrait

Date		Mintage	F12	VF20	XF40	MS60	MS63
2009MW		100,000	PF63 22.00	PF65 32.00			

Y# 674 10 ZŁOTYCH

14.14 g., 0.925 Silver 0.4178 oz. ASW, 32 mm. **Subject:** Supreme Chamber, 90th Anniversary **Obv:** Building **Rev:** Monogram hologram

Date		Mintage	F12	VF20	XF40	MS60	MS63
2009MW		100,000	PF63 25.00	PF65 35.00			

Y# 676 10 ZŁOTYCH

14.14 g., 0.925 Silver 0.4178 oz. ASW, 32 mm. **Subject:** Central Banking, 180th Anniversary **Obv:** National arms above building **Rev:** Portrait above banknote

Date		Mintage	F12	VF20	XF40	MS60	MS63
2009MW		92,000	PF63 22.00	PF65 32.00			

Y# 681 10 ZŁOTYCH

14.14 g., 0.925 Silver 0.4178 oz. ASW, 32 mm. **Subject:** General Elections of 1989 **Obv:** Eagle **Rev:** Pope John Paul II and Solidarity banner in color

Date		Mintage	F12	VF20	XF40	MS60	MS63
2009MW		100,000	PF63 25.00	PF65 35.00			

Y# 685 10 ZŁOTYCH

14.14 g., 0.925 Silver 0.4178 oz. ASW, 29x29 mm. **Subject:** Czeslaw Niemen **Obv:** National arms and large portrait **Rev:** Female crying **Shape:** Square

Date		Mintage	F12	VF20	XF40	MS60	MS63
2009MW		100,000	PF63 20.00	PF65 30.00			

Y# 686 10 ZŁOTYCH

14.14 g., 0.925 Silver 0.4178 oz. ASW, 32 mm. **Subject:** Cezeslaw Neiman **Obv:** National arms and portrait **Rev:** Abstract painting

Date		Mintage	F12	VF20	XF40	MS60	MS63
2009MW		100,000	PF63 20.00	PF65 30.00			

Y# 689 10 ZŁOTYCH

14.14 g., 0.925 Silver 0.4178 oz. ASW, 32 mm. **Subject:** Poets of the uprising **Obv:** National arms **Rev:** Krzystof Baczynski portrait facing

Date		Mintage	F12	VF20	XF40	MS60	MS63
2009MW		100,000	PF63 22.00	PF65 32.00			

Y# 691 10 ZŁOTYCH

14.14 g., 0.925 Silver 0.4178 oz. ASW, 32 mm. **Subject:** First Cadre Company March **Obv:** National arms and eagle atop stelle monument **Rev:** Troops marching, song and music

Date		Mintage	F12	VF20	XF40	MS60	MS63
2009MW		50,000	PF63 35.00	PF65 45.00			

Y# 698 10 ZŁOTYCH

14.14 g., 0.925 Silver 0.4178 oz. ASW, 32 mm. **Series:** Tatar Rescues, 100th Anniversary **Obv:** National arms and logo colorized **Rev:** Mountains and figure of Karlowicz

Date		Mintage	F12	VF20	XF40	MS60	MS63
2009MW		100,000	PF63 20.00	PF65 30.00			

Y# 701 10 ZŁOTYCH

14.14 g., 0.925 Silver 0.4178 oz. ASW, 32 mm. **Subject:** Fr. Jerzy Popielosko, 25th Anniversary of Murder **Obv:** Rose on monument **Rev:** Statue and tear drop on map of Poland

Date		Mintage	F12	VF20	XF40	MS60	MS63
2009MW		100,000	PF63 22.00	PF65 32.00			

Y# 708 10 ZŁOTYCH
14.14 g., 0.925 Silver 0.4178 oz. ASW, 32 mm. **Subject:** Polish
Underground State **Obv:** National arms and monogram and
cloth flag **Rev:** Figure and cloth flag

Date	Mintage	F12	VF20	XF40	MS60	MS63
2009MW	50,000	PF63 25.00	PF65 35.00			

Y# 713 10 ZŁOTYCH
14.14 g., 0.925 Silver 0.4178 oz. ASW, 32 mm. **Subject:**
Auschwitz liberation **Obv:** National arms, camp sign and barbed
wire fence **Rev:** Prisoner and barbed wire fence

Date	Mintage	F12	VF20	XF40	MS60	MS63
2010MW	80,000	PF63 25.00	PF65 35.00			

Y# 716 10 ZŁOTYCH
14.14 g., 0.925 Silver 0.4178 oz. ASW, 32 mm. **Subject:**
Vancouver Winter Olympics **Obv:** Speedskaters **Rev:** Biathlon

Date	Mintage	F12	VF20	XF40	MS60	MS63
2010MW	80,000	PF63 18.00	PF65 25.00			

Y# 719 10 ZŁOTYCH
14.14 g., 0.925 Silver 0.4178 oz. ASW, 32x22 mm. **Subject:**
Napoleonic Imperial Guard **Obv:** National arms and helmet
Rev: Mounted Napoleonic Guard member **Shape:** Vertical
rectangle

Date	Mintage	F12	VF20	XF40	MS60	MS63
2010MW	100,000	PF63 35.00	PF65 45.00			

Y# 722 10 ZŁOTYCH
14.14 g., 0.925 Silver 0.4178 oz. ASW, 32 mm. **Subject:** Katyn
Crime **Obv:** National emblem and silhouette of a badge **Rev:**
Field of crosses

Date	Mintage	F12	VF20	XF40	MS60	MS63
2010MW Antiqued	80,000	—	—	—	30.00	—

Y# 726 10 ZŁOTYCH
14.14 g., 0.925 Silver 0.4178 oz. ASW, 32 mm. **Subject:** Polish
Scouting Centennial

Date	Mintage	F12	VF20	XF40	MS60	MS63
2010MW	90,000	PF63 18.00	PF65 25.00			

Y# 731 10 ZŁOTYCH
14.14 g., 0.925 Silver 0.4178 oz. ASW, 32 mm. **Subject:** Jan
Twardowski

Date	Mintage	F12	VF20	XF40	MS60	MS63
2010MW	80,000	PF63 18.00	PF65 25.00			

Y# 733 10 ZŁOTYCH
14.14 g., 0.925 Silver 0.4178 oz. ASW, 40x26 mm. **Subject:**
Battles of Grunwald, Kluszyn **Shape:** Oval

Date	Mintage	F12	VF20	XF40	MS60	MS63
2010MW	100,000	PF63 25.00	PF65 35.00			

Y# 738 10 ZŁOTYCH
14.14 g., 0.925 Silver 0.4178 oz. ASW, 32 mm. **Subject:** August
of 1980, 30th Anniversary

Date	Mintage	F12	VF20	XF40	MS60	MS63
2010MW	100,000	PF63 20.00	PF65 30.00			

Y# 743 10 ZŁOTYCH
14.14 g., 0.925 Silver 0.4178 oz. ASW, 32 mm. **Subject:** Polish
Explorers - Benedykt Dybowski

Date	Mintage	F12	VF20	XF40	MS60	MS63
2010MW	100,000	PF63 25.00	PF65 35.00			

Y# 750 10 ZŁOTYCH
14.14 g., 0.925 Silver 0.4178 oz. ASW, 40x26 mm. **Subject:**
Battle of Grunwald **Shape:** Oval

Date	Mintage	F12	VF20	XF40	MS60	MS63
2010MW	100,000	PF63 30.00	PF65 40.00			

Y# 758 10 ZŁOTYCH
14.14 g., 0.925 Silver 0.4178 oz. ASW, 32 mm. **Subject:**
Benedykt Dybowski **Obv:** Books **Rev:** Bust facing, map in
background

Date	Mintage	F12	VF20	XF40	MS60	MS63
2010	60,000	PF63 25.00	PF65 35.00			

Y# 728 10 ZŁOTYCH
14.14 g., 0.925 Silver 0.4178 oz. ASW, 32 mm. **Subject:**
Krzysztof Komeda **Rev:** Komeda and movie film real

Date	Mintage	F12	VF20	XF40	MS60	MS63
2010MW	60,000	PF63 20.00	PF65 30.00			

Y# 729 10 ZŁOTYCH
14.14 g., 0.925 Silver 0.4178 oz. ASW, 28.2x28.2 mm. **Subject:**
Krzysztof Komeda **Shape:** Square

Date	Mintage	F12	VF20	XF40	MS60	MS63
2010MW	60,000	PF63 25.00	PF65 35.00			

Y# 768 10 ZŁOTYCH
14.14 g., 0.925 Silver 0.4178 oz. ASW, 32 mm. **Subject:**
Independent Student's Union, 30th Anniversary

Date	Mintage	F12	VF20	XF40	MS60	MS63
2011MW	50,000	PF63 25.00	PF65 35.00			

Y# 770 10 ZŁOTYCH
14.14 g., 0.925 Silver 0.4178 oz. ASW, 32 mm. **Subject:**
Smolensk plane crash

Date	Mintage	F12	VF20	XF40	MS60	MS63
2011MW	30,000	PF63 35.00	PF65 45.00			

Y# 778 10 ZŁOTYCH
14.14 g., 0.925 Silver 0.4178 oz. ASW, 32 mm. **Subject:**
Poland's presidency of the Council of the European Union

Date	Mintage	F12	VF20	XF40	MS60	MS63
2011MW	50,000	PF63 25.00	PF65 35.00			

Y# 781 10 ZŁOTYCH
14.14 g., 0.925 Silver 0.4178 oz. ASW, 22.4x32 mm. **Subject:**
History of the Polish Cavalry - Ulan of the Second Republic
Obv: Eagle above military items: saddle, rifle, banners, lances
and sword **Rev:** Cavalry officer on horseback **Shape:** Vertical
rectangle

Date	Mintage	F12	VF20	XF40	MS60	MS63
2011MW	50,000	PF63 25.00	PF65 35.00			

Y# 786 10 ZŁOTYCH
14.14 g., 0.925 Silver 0.4178 oz. ASW, 32 mm. **Subject:**
Czeslaw Milosz

Date	Mintage	F12	VF20	XF40	MS60	MS63
2011MW	50,000	PF63 25.00	PF65 35.00			

Y# 790 10 ZŁOTYCH
14.14 g., 0.925 Silver 0.4178 oz. ASW, 32 mm. **Subject:** Ignacy
Jan Paderewski

Date	Mintage	F12	VF20	XF40	MS60	MS63
2011MW	50,000	PF63 22.00	PF65 32.00			

Y# 793 10 ZŁOTYCH
14.14 g., 0.925 Silver 0.4178 oz. ASW, 32 mm. **Subject:**
Silesian Uprising

Date	Mintage	F12	VF20	XF40	MS60	MS63
2011MW	50,000	PF63 20.00	PF65 30.00			

Y# 796 10 ZŁOTYCH
14.14 g., 0.925 Silver 0.4178 oz. ASW, 32 mm. **Subject:**
Society for the Protection of the Blind, 100th Anniversary

Date	Mintage	F12	VF20	XF40	MS60	MS63
2011MW	50,000	PF63 35.00	PF65 45.00			

Y# 798 10 ZŁOTYCH
14.14 g., 0.925 Silver 0.4178 oz. ASW, 32 mm. **Subject:**
Ferdynand Ossendowski

Date	Mintage	F12	VF20	XF40	MS60	MS63
2011MW	50,000	PF63 25.00	PF65 35.00			

Y# 802 10 ZŁOTYCH
14.14 g., 0.925 Silver 0.4178 oz. ASW, 28.2x28.2 mm. **Subject:**
Jeremi Przybora and Jerzy Wasowski **Shape:** Square

Date	Mintage	F12	VF20	XF40	MS60	MS63
2011MW	50,000	PF63 30.00	PF65 40.00			

Y# 803 10 ZŁOTYCH
14.14 g., 0.925 Silver 0.4178 oz. ASW, 32 mm. **Subject:** Jeremi
Przybora and Jerzy Wasowski

Date	Mintage	F12	VF20	XF40	MS60	MS63
2011MW	50,000	PF63 22.00	PF65 32.00			

Y# 810 10 ZŁOTYCH
14.14 g., 0.925 Silver 0.4178 oz. ASW, 28.7x30 mm. **Subject:**
Christmas Charity Orchestra, 20th Anniversary **Obv:** Piano
keyboard **Rev:** Guitar with hearts **Shape:** Heart

Date	Mintage	F12	VF20	XF40	MS60	MS63
2012MW	60,000	PF63 40.00	PF65 50.00			

Y# 812 10 ZŁOTYCH
14.14 g., 0.925 Silver 0.4178 oz. ASW, 32 mm. **Subject:**
Cooperative Banking in Poland, 150th Anniversary **Obv:** Eagle
at left, bank building at right **Rev:** Pile of coin and banknotes at
center, semi-circle of stick figures holding hands at right

Date	Mintage	F12	VF20	XF40	MS60	MS63
2012MW	40,000	PF63 25.00	PF65 35.00			

Y# 818 10 ZŁOTYCH
14.14 g., 0.925 Silver 0.4178 oz. ASW, 32 mm. **Subject:** Stefan
Banach

Date	Mintage	F12	VF20	XF40	MS60	MS63
2012MW	45,000	PF63 25.00	PF65 35.00			

Y# 822 10 ZŁOTYCH
14.14 g., 0.925 Silver 0.4178 oz. ASW, 32 mm. **Subject:**
National Museum in Warsaw, 150th Anniversary

Date	Mintage	F12	VF20	XF40	MS60	MS63
2012MW	45,000	PF63 25.00	PF65 35.00			

Y# 824 10 ZŁOTYCH
33.62 g., 0.925 Silver 0.9934 oz. ASW, 27.3x50 mm. **Subject:**
European Football Championship **Shape:** Yin-Yang **Note:** A

yin-Yang design, with the other half being a Ukraine 10 Hryvnia coin.

Date	Mintage	F12	VF20	XF40	MS60	MS63
2012MW	5,000	PF65 175				

Y# 825 10 ZŁOTYCH
14.14 g., 0.925 Silver 0.4178 oz. ASW, 28.8x28.8 mm. **Subject:** European Football Championship **Note:** Part of a four coin design.

Date	Mintage	F12	VF20	XF40	MS60	MS63
2012MW	15,000	PF65 85.00				

Y# 826 10 ZŁOTYCH
14.14 g., 0.925 Silver 0.4178 oz. ASW, 28.8x28.8 mm. **Subject:** European Football Championship **Note:** Part of a four coin design.

Date	Mintage	F12	VF20	XF40	MS60	MS63
2012MW	15,000	PF65 85.00				

Y# 827 10 ZŁOTYCH
14.14 g., 0.925 Silver 0.4178 oz. ASW, 28.8x28.8 mm. **Subject:** European Football Championships **Note:** Part of a four coin design.

Date	Mintage	F12	VF20	XF40	MS60	MS63
2012MW	15,000	PF65 85.00				

Y# 828 10 ZŁOTYCH
14.14 g., 0.925 Silver 0.4178 oz. ASW, 28.8x28.8 mm. **Subject:** European Football Championships **Note:** Part of a four coin design.

Date	Mintage	F12	VF20	XF40	MS60	MS63
2012MW	15,000	PF65 85.00				

Y# 833 10 ZŁOTYCH
14.14 g., 0.925 Silver 0.4178 oz. ASW, 32 mm. **Subject:** London Olympics, 2012, Polish Team

Date	Mintage	F12	VF20	XF40	MS60	MS63
2012MW	50,000	PF63 25.00	PF65 35.00			

Y# 839 10 ZŁOTYCH
14.14 g., 0.925 Silver 0.4178 oz. ASW, 32 mm. **Subject:** Boleslaw Prus

Date	Mintage	F12	VF20	XF40	MS60	MS63
2012MW	30,000	PF63 30.00	PF65 40.00			

Y# 871 10 ZŁOTYCH
14.14 g., 0.925 Silver 0.4178 oz. ASW, 32 mm. **Subject:** Witold Lutoslawski

Date	Mintage	F12	VF20	XF40	MS60	MS63
2013MW	Est. 28000	PF63 30.00	PF65 40.00			

Y# 874 10 ZŁOTYCH
14.14 g., 0.925 Silver 0.4178 oz. ASW, 32 mm. **Subject:** 200th Anniversary of the Death of Prince Jozef Poniatowski

Date	Mintage	F12	VF20	XF40	MS60	MS63
2013MW	Est. 28000	PF63 30.00	PF65 40.00			

Y# 877 10 ZŁOTYCH
14.14 g., 0.925 Silver 0.4178 oz. ASW, 32 mm. **Subject:** 50th Anniversary of the Polish Society for the Mentally Handicapped

Date	Mintage	F12	VF20	XF40	MS60	MS63
2013MW	Est. 25000	PF63 35.00	PF65 45.00			

Y# 881 10 ZŁOTYCH
14.14 g., 0.925 Silver 0.4178 oz. ASW, 32 mm. **Subject:** 200th Anniversary of the Birth of Hipolit Cegielski

Date	Mintage	F12	VF20	XF40	MS60	MS63
2013MW	Est. 28000	PF63 30.00	PF65 40.00			

Y# 884 10 ZŁOTYCH
14.14 g., 0.925 Silver 0.4178 oz. ASW, 28.2 x 28.2 mm. **Subject:** History of Polish Popular Music - Agnieszka Osiecka

Date	Mintage	F12	VF20	XF40	MS60	MS63
2013MW	Est. 28000	PF63 30.00	PF65 40.00			

Y# 885 10 ZŁOTYCH
14.14 g., 0.925 Silver 0.4178 oz. ASW, 32 mm. **Subject:** History of Polish Popular Music - Agnieszka Osiecka

Date	Mintage	F12	VF20	XF40	MS60	MS63
2013MW	Est. 28000	PF63 30.00	PF65 40.00			

Y# 894 10 ZŁOTYCH
14.14 g., 0.925 Silver 0.4178 oz. ASW, 32 mm. **Subject:** Polish Olympic Team, Sochi 2014

Date	Mintage	F12	VF20	XF40	MS60	MS63
2014	30,000	PF63 25.00	PF65 35.00			

Y# 900 10 ZŁOTYCH
14.14 g., 0.925 Silver 0.4178 oz. ASW, 32 mm. **Subject:** Old Polish Coins - Boleslaw the Wry-Mouthed, denarius

Date	Mintage	F12	VF20	XF40	MS60	MS63
2014	20,000	PF63 40.00	PF65 50.00			

Y# 902 10 ZŁOTYCH
14.14 g., 0.925 Silver 0.4178 oz. ASW, 32 mm. **Subject:** Jan Karski, 100th Anniversary of Birth

Date	Mintage	F12	VF20	XF40	MS60	MS63
2014	30,000	PF63 25.00	PF65 35.00			

Y# 909 10 ZŁOTYCH
14.14 g., 0.925 Silver 0.4178 oz. ASW, 32 mm. **Subject:** Polish Coins - Mieszko the Elder, Bracteate

Date	Mintage	F12	VF20	XF40	MS60	MS63
2014	20,000	PF63 25.00	PF65 35.00			

Y# 910 10 ZŁOTYCH
14.14 g., 0.925 Silver 0.4178 oz. ASW, 32 mm. **Subject:** Stefan Zeromski, 150th Anniversary of Birth

Date	Mintage	F12	VF20	XF40	MS60	MS63
2014	30,000	PF63 25.00	PF65 35.00			

Y# 916 10 ZŁOTYCH
28.28 g., 0.925 Silver 0.8356 oz. ASW, 32 mm. **Subject:** Historical Polish Coins - Leszek I the White - bracteate

Date	Mintage	F12	VF20	XF40	MS60	MS63
2014	20,000	PF63 40.00	PF65 50.00			

Y# 917 10 ZŁOTYCH
14.14 g., 0.925 Silver 0.4178 oz. ASW, 32 mm. **Subject:** Grezegorz Ciechowski, musician

Date	Mintage	F12	VF20	XF40	MS60	MS63
2014	30,000	PF63 30.00	PF65 40.00			

Y# 918 10 ZŁOTYCH
14.14 g., 0.925 Silver 0.4178 oz. ASW, 28.2x28.2 mm. **Subject:** Grzegorz Ciechowski, musician

Date	Mintage	F12	VF20	XF40	MS60	MS63
2014	30,000	PF63 25.00	PF65 35.00			

Y# 409 20 ZŁOTYCH
28.28 g., 0.925 Silver 0.8356 oz. ASW, 38.6 mm. **Subject:** Wieliezce Salt Mine **Obv:** Crowned eagle with wings open in

center of rock **Rev:** Ancient salt miners **Edge:** Plain

Date	Mintage	F12	VF20	XF40	MS60	MS63
2001MW	—	PF65 175				

Y# 411 20 ZŁOTYCH

28.28 g., 0.925 Silver 0.8356 oz. ASW, 38.6 mm. **Subject:** Amber Route **Obv:** Crowned eagle and two ancient Roman silver cups **Rev:** Piece of amber mounted above an ancient Roman coin design and map with the route marked with stars **Edge:** Plain

Date	Mintage	F12	VF20	XF40	MS60	MS63
2001MW	30,000	—	—	—	525	—
Antique finish						

Y# 415 20 ZŁOTYCH

28.28 g., 0.925 Silver 0.8356 oz. ASW, 38.6 mm. **Obv:** Crowned eagle with wings open flanked by flags **Rev:** European Swallowtail Butterfly **Edge:** Plain

Date	Mintage	F12	VF20	XF40	MS60	MS63
2001MW	27,000	PF65 200				

Y# 424 20 ZŁOTYCH

28.77 g., 0.925 Silver 0.8501 oz. ASW, 38.6 mm. **Subject:** Christmas **Obv:** Ornate city view **Rev:** Celebration scene including an attached zirconia star **Edge:** Plain

Date	Mintage	F12	VF20	XF40	MS60	MS63
2001MW	55,000	—	—	—	125	—
Antique patina						

Y# 428 20 ZŁOTYCH

28.28 g., 0.925 Silver 0.8356 oz. ASW, 38.6 mm. **Obv:** Crowned eagle with wings open flanked by flags **Rev:** European Pond Turtles **Edge:** Plain

Date	Mintage	F12	VF20	XF40	MS60	MS63
2002	35,000	PF65 120				

Y# 442 20 ZŁOTYCH

28.05 g., 0.925 Silver 0.8288 oz. ASW, 39.94x27.93 mm. **Subject:** Jan Matejko **Obv:** Seated figure with crowned eagle at lower right **Rev:** Head facing with multicolor artist's palette **Edge:** Plain **Shape:** Rectangle

Date	Mintage	F12	VF20	XF40	MS60	MS63
2002MW	57,000	PF65 135				

Y# 457 20 ZŁOTYCH

28.28 g., 0.925 Silver 0.8356 oz. ASW, 38.6 mm. **Obv:** National arms at lower left, castle complex in background **Rev:** Malborku castle, reddish-brown ceramic applique, **Rev. Legend:** ZAMEK W MALBORKU **Edge:** Plain

Date	Mintage	F12	VF20	XF40	MS60	MS63
2002MW	51,000	—	—	—	70.00	—
Antique patina						

Y# 449 20 ZŁOTYCH

28.47 g., 0.925 Silver 0.8412 oz. ASW, 38.6 mm. **Obv:** Crowned eagle with wings open **Rev:** European Eels and world globe **Edge:** Plain

Date	Mintage	F12	VF20	XF40	MS60	MS63
2003MW	—	PF65 185				

Y# 452 20 ZŁOTYCH

28.28 g., 0.925 Silver 0.8356 oz. ASW, 38.6 mm. **Subject:** Easter Monday Festival **Obv:** Crowned eagle on lace curtain above lamb and multicolor Easter eggs **Rev:** Festival scene **Edge:** Plain

Date	Mintage	F12	VF20	XF40	MS60	MS63
2003MW	44,000	PF65 70.00				

Y# 471 20 ZŁOTYCH

28.28 g., 0.925 Silver 0.8356 oz. ASW, 40 x 40 mm. **Obv:** Standing Pope John Paul II **Rev:** Pope"s portrait **Edge:** Plain **Shape:** Square

Date	Mintage	F12	VF20	XF40	MS60	MS63
2003MW	83,000	PF65 55.00				

Y# 478 20 ZŁOTYCH

28.28 g., 0.925 Silver 0.8356 oz. ASW, 27.93x39.94 mm. **Obv:** Death" allegory closing an old man's eyes, national arms at lower right **Rev:** Self portrait of Jacek Malczewski, palette at lower right multicolor **Edge:** Plain **Shape:** Rectangle

Date	Mintage	F12	VF20	XF40	MS60	MS63
2003MW	64,000	PF65 45.00				

Y# 498 20 ZŁOTYCH

28.28 g., 0.925 Silver 0.8356 oz. ASW, 38.6 mm. **Subject:** Lodz Ghetto (1940-1944) **Obv:** Silhouette on wall **Rev:** Child with a pot **Edge:** Plain

Date	Mintage	F12	VF20	XF40	MS60	MS63
2004MW Matte	64,000	—	—	—	—	40.00

Y# 504 20 ZŁOTYCH

28.28 g., 0.925 Silver 0.8356 oz. ASW, 38.6 mm. **Subject:** Polish Senate **Obv:** Crowned eagle above Senate chamber **Rev:** Senate eagle and speaker's staff **Edge:** Plain

Date	Mintage	F12	VF20	XF40	MS60	MS63
2004MW	67,000	PF65 55.00				

Y# 508 20 ZŁOTYCH

28.28 g., 0.925 Silver 0.8356 oz. ASW, 38.6 mm. **Obv:** Crowned eagle in harvest wreath **Rev:** Harvest fest parade **Edge:** Plain

Date	Mintage	F12	VF20	XF40	MS60	MS63
2004MW	74,000	PF65 40.00				

Y# 513 20 ZŁOTYCH
28.28 g., 0.925 Silver 0.8356 oz. ASW, 40x28 mm. **Obv:** Mother and children **Rev:** Stanislaw Wyspianski (1869-1907) **Edge:** Plain

Date	Mintage	F12	VF20	XF40	MS60	MS63
2004MW	80,000	**PF65** 40.00				

Y# 515 20 ZŁOTYCH
28.28 g., 0.925 Silver 0.8356 oz. ASW, 38.6 mm. **Obv:** National arms **Obv. Legend:** RZECZPOSPOLITA POLSKA **Rev:** 2 Harbor Porpoises **Rev. Legend:** MORSWIN - Phocoena phocoena **Edge:** Plain

Date	Mintage	F12	VF20	XF40	MS60	MS63
2004MW	56,000	**PF65** 120				

Y# 531 20 ZŁOTYCH
28.84 g., 0.925 Silver 0.8522 oz. ASW, 38.6 mm. **Obv:** Polish eagle above value **Rev:** Eagle Owl with nestlings **Edge:** Plain

Date	Mintage	F12	VF20	XF40	MS60	MS63
2005MW	61,000	**PF65** 100				

Y# 542 20 ZŁOTYCH
28.28 g., 0.925 Silver 0.8356 oz. ASW, 28 x 40 mm. **Obv:** Sneak thief stealing from a miser **Rev:** Painter Tadeusz Makowski **Edge:** Plain **Shape:** Rectangular

Date	Mintage	F12	VF20	XF40	MS60	MS63
2005MW	70,000	**PF65** 45.00				

Y# 597 20 ZŁOTYCH
28.50 g., 0.925 Silver 0.8421 oz. ASW, 38.5 mm. **Subject:** 350 Years, Defence of Góry **Obv:** National arms to right of outlined Góry **Obv. Legend:** RZECZPOSPOLITA POLSKA **Obv. Inscription:** Tutaj zawsze / bylismy woini / JAN PAWEL II **Rev:** 1/2 length figure of man at lower right, Góry under bombardment in background **Rev. Legend:** 350 - LECIE OBRONY JASNEJ GÓRY **Edge:** Lettered **Edge Lettering:** CZESTOCHOWA 2005 repeated three times

Date	Mintage	F12	VF20	XF40	MS60	MS63
2005MW	69,000	**PF65** 45.00				

Y# 533 20 ZŁOTYCH
28.84 g., 0.925 Silver 0.8522 oz. ASW, 38.6 mm. **Obv:** Polish eagle above value **Rev:** Multicolor holographic spider web **Edge:** Plain

Date	Mintage	F12	VF20	XF40	MS60	MS63
2006MW	65,000	**PF65** 80.00				

Y# 535 20 ZŁOTYCH
28.84 g., 0.925 Silver 0.8522 oz. ASW, 38.6 mm. **Obv:** Polish eagle above value **Rev:** Alpine Marmot standing **Edge:** Plain

Date	Mintage	F12	VF20	XF40	MS60	MS63
2006MW	60,000	**PF65** 85.00				

Y# 584 20 ZŁOTYCH
28.47 g., 0.925 Silver 0.8412 oz. ASW, 38.6 mm. **Obv:** Polish Eagle on old wood **Rev:** Multi-color wood behind Haczowie church **Edge:** Plain

Date	Mintage	F12	VF20	XF40	MS60	MS63
2006MW	—	**PF65** 45.00				

Y# 604 20 ZŁOTYCH
28.14 g., Silver, 39.95x27.97 mm. **Subject:** Aleksander Gierymski **Obv:** National arms at upper right, painting of elderly woman carrying baskets **Rev:** Bust of Gierymski facing at center, harbor scene at right, painter's palette at lower left multicolor **Edge:** Plain **Shape:** Rectangle

Date	Mintage	F12	VF20	XF40	MS60	MS63
2006MW	66,000	**PF65** 45.00				

Y# 579 20 ZŁOTYCH
28.28 g., 0.925 Silver 0.8356 oz. ASW, 38.6 mm. **Obv:** Crowned eagle **Rev:** Two Grey Seal females and pup with two silhouettes in background **Edge:** Plain

Date	Mintage	F12	VF20	XF40	MS60	MS63
2007MW	58,000	**PF65** 85.00				

Y# 603 20 ZŁOTYCH
28.25 g., 0.925 Silver 0.8347 oz. ASW, 38.5 mm. **Subject:** Medieval Principality of Sredniowieczne in Torin **Obv:** City arms at right, national arms below walled city gate in background **Obv. Legend:** RZECZPOSPOLITA POLSKA **Rev:** City view **Rev. Legend:** MIASTO SREDNIOWIECZNE W TORUNIU **Edge:** Plain

Date	Mintage	F12	VF20	XF40	MS60	MS63
2007MW	58,000	**PF65** 50.00				

Y# 891 20 ZŁOTYCH
28.28 g., 0.925 Silver 0.8356 oz. ASW **Subject:** Leon Cuyczolkowski **Rev:** Portrait facing - color pallet at left

Date	Mintage	F12	VF20	XF40	MS60	MS63
2007	—	**PF65** 45.00				

Y# 636 20 ZŁOTYCH
28.28 g., 0.925 Silver 0.8356 oz. ASW, 38.6 mm. **Subject:** 65th Anniversary Warsaw Ghetto Uprising **Obv:** Small national arms

at left, flames, shattered wall **Obv. Legend:** RZECZPOSPOLITA POLSKA **Rev:** Tree, Star of David, wall in backgound **Rev. Inscription:** 65. ROCZNICA POWSTANIA / W GETCIE WARSZAWSKIM **Edge:** Plain

Date	Mintage	F12	VF20	XF40	MS60	MS63
2008MW	—	PF65 45.00				

Y# 642 20 ZŁOTYCH
28.28 g., 0.925 Silver 0.8356 oz. ASW, 38.61 mm. **Subject:** Kazimierz Dolny **Obv:** Part of a wall and an eagle **Rev:** Houses and a well

Date	Mintage	F12	VF20	XF40	MS60	MS63
2008	125,000	PF65 45.00				

Y# 637 20 ZŁOTYCH
28.28 g., 0.925 Silver 0.8356 oz. ASW, 38.61 mm. **Obv:** National arms **Obv. Legend:** RZECZPOSPOLITA POLSKA **Rev:** Peregrine Falcon by 2 chicks in nest at right **Rev. Legend:** SOKOL WEDROWNY - Falco peregrinus **Edge:** Plain

Date	Mintage	F12	VF20	XF40	MS60	MS63
2008MW	107,000	PF65 55.00				

Y# 651 20 ZŁOTYCH
28.28 g., 0.925 Silver 0.8356 oz. ASW, 38.61 mm. **Subject:** 90th Anniversary of Regaining Freedom **Obv:** War decoration left side, eagle top right **Rev:** 3 generals

Date	Mintage	F12	VF20	XF40	MS60	MS63
2008	110,000	PF65 42.00				

Y# 679 20 ZŁOTYCH
28.28 g., 0.925 Silver 0.8356 oz. ASW, 38.6 mm. **Subject:** Green Lizard **Obv:** National arms above value **Rev:** Two green lizards in nature

Date	Mintage	F12	VF20	XF40	MS60	MS63
2009MW	100,000	PF65 45.00				

Y# 693 20 ZŁOTYCH
28.28 g., 0.925 Silver 0.8356 oz. ASW, 38.6 mm. **Subject:** Liquidation of the Lotz Ghetto **Obv:** New oak sprig amongst broken bricks **Rev:** Oak tree, bare and with leaves, star of David within

Date	Mintage	F12	VF20	XF40	MS60	MS63
2009MW Antiqued	50,000	—	—	—	48.00	

Y# 704 20 ZŁOTYCH
28.28 g., 0.925 Silver 0.8356 oz. ASW, 38.6 mm. **Subject:** Honoring Poles who saved the Jews **Obv:** National arms above broken brick wall **Rev:** Three portraits

Date	Mintage	F12	VF20	XF40	MS60	MS63
2009MW	100,000	PF65 40.00				

Y# 706 20 ZŁOTYCH
28.28 g., 0.925 Silver 0.8356 oz. ASW, 40x28 mm. **Subject:** Wald Strzeminski **Obv:** Portrait and multicolor palette **Rev:** Artwork **Shape:** Rectangle

Date	Mintage	F12	VF20	XF40	MS60	MS63
2009MW	100,000	PF65 45.00				

Y# 724 20 ZŁOTYCH
28.28 g., 0.925 Silver 0.8356 oz. ASW, 38.61 mm. **Subject:** Lesser Horseshoe Bat

Date	Mintage	F12	VF20	XF40	MS60	MS63
2010MW	100,000	PF65 40.00				

Y# 736 20 ZŁOTYCH
28.28 g., 0.925 Silver 0.8356 oz. ASW, 38.6 mm. **Subject:** Battle of Warsaw **Rev:** Battle scene in color

Date	Mintage	F12	VF20	XF40	MS60	MS63
2010MW	100,000	PF65 42.00				

Y# 745 20 ZŁOTYCH
28.28 g., 0.925 Silver 0.8356 oz. ASW, 38.61 mm. **Subject:** Krzeszow

Date	Mintage	F12	VF20	XF40	MS60	MS63
2010MW	80,000	PF65 50.00				

Y# 747 20 ZŁOTYCH
28.28 g., 0.925 Silver 0.8356 oz. ASW, 28x40 mm. **Subject:** Artur Grottger **Shape:** Vertical rectangle

Date	Mintage	F12	VF20	XF40	MS60	MS63
2010MW	100,000	PF65 45.00				

Y# 763 20 ZŁOTYCH
28.28 g., 0.925 Silver 0.8356 oz. ASW, 38.6 mm. **Subject:** Borsuk **Obv:** National Arms above value **Rev:** Eurasian Badgers

Date	Mintage	F12	VF20	XF40	MS60	MS63
2011	80,000	PF65 50.00				

Y# 765 20 ZŁOTYCH
28.28 g., 0.925 Silver 0.8356 oz. ASW, 40x28 mm. **Subject:** Zofia Stryjenska **Obv:** Horseback scene, National Arms at right **Rev:** Portrait with artist pallet with brushes **Shape:** Rectangle

Date	Mintage	F12	VF20	XF40	MS60	MS63
2011	50,000	PF65 50.00				

Y# 771 20 ZŁOTYCH
28.28 g., 0.925 Silver 0.8356 oz. ASW, 38.61 mm. **Subject:** Smolensk plane crash

Date	Mintage	F12	VF20	XF40	MS60	MS63
2011MW	—	PF65 42.00				

Y# 773 20 ZŁOTYCH
14.14 g., 0.925 Silver 0.4178 oz. ASW, 38.61 mm. **Subject:** John Paul II Beautification **Rev:** Pope waving, earth in background in color

Date	Mintage	F12	VF20	XF40	MS60	MS63
2011MW	80,000	PF65 65.00				

Y# 814 20 ZŁOTYCH
28.28 g., 0.925 Silver 0.8356 oz. ASW, 38.61 mm. **Subject:** Ulma, Baranek and Kowalski families **Obv:** Fields and town view **Rev:** Family faces seen thru broken fenceboards

Date	Mintage	F12	VF20	XF40	MS60	MS63
2012MW	40,000	—		—	60.00	—
Antique patina						

Y# 829 20 ZŁOTYCH
28.28 g., 0.925 Silver 0.8356 oz. ASW, 36.2x36.2 mm. **Subject:** European Football Championships

Date	Mintage	F12	VF20	XF40	MS60	MS63
2012MW	35,000	PF65 85.00				

Y# 836 20 ZŁOTYCH
28.28 g., 0.925 Silver 0.8356 oz. ASW, 38.61 mm. **Subject:** Krzemionki Opatowskie

Date	Mintage	F12	VF20	XF40	MS60	MS63
2012MW	45,000	PF65 65.00				

Y# 843 20 ZŁOTYCH
28.28 g., 0.925 Silver 0.8356 oz. ASW, 40x28 mm. **Subject:** Piotr Michalowski, painter **Shape:** Rectangle

Date	Mintage	F12	VF20	XF40	MS60	MS63
2012MW	30,000	PF65 75.00				

Y# 855 20 ZŁOTYCH
31.11 g., 0.999 Silver 0.9926 oz. ASW, 40 mm. **Obv:** Eagle **Rev:** Red-necked Wallaby

Date	Mintage	F12	VF20	XF40	MS60	MS63
2013MW	10,000	PF65 250				

Y# 879 20 ZŁOTYCH
28.28 g., 0.925 Silver 0.8356 oz. ASW, 38.61 mm. **Subject:** Animals of the World - European Bison

Date	Mintage	F12	VF20	XF40	MS60	MS63
2013MW	Est. 35000	PF65 65.00				

Y# 897 20 ZŁOTYCH
28.28 g., 0.925 Silver 0.8356 oz. ASW, 38.61 mm. **Subject:** Konik horse

Date	Mintage	F12	VF20	XF40	MS60	MS63
2014	45,000	PF65 75.00				

Y# 905 20 ZŁOTYCH
31.10 g., 0.925 Silver 0.9189 oz. ASW, 38.61 mm. **Subject:** Turkish-Polish relations, 600th Anniversary

Date	Mintage	F12	VF20	XF40	MS60	MS63
2014	10,000	PF65 50.00				

Y# 906 20 ZŁOTYCH
31.10 g., 0.925 Silver 0.9189 oz. ASW, 38.61 mm. **Subject:** Patriots 1944, Citizens 2014

Date	Mintage	F12	VF20	XF40	MS60	MS63
2014	35,000	PF65 50.00				

Y# 912 20 ZŁOTYCH
28.28 g., 0.925 Silver 0.8356 oz. ASW, 40x28 mm. **Subject:** Jozef Chelmonski, painter **Shape:** Rectangle

Date	Mintage	F12	VF20	XF40	MS60	MS63
2014	30,000	PF65 55.00				

Y# 682 25 ZŁOTYCH
1.00 g., 0.900 Gold 0.0287 oz. AGW, 12 mm. **Subject:** General Elections of 1989 **Obv:** National arms above value **Rev:** Solidarity logo

Date	Mintage	F12	VF20	XF40	MS60	MS63
2009MW	40,000	PF65 65.00				

Y# 740 25 ZŁOTYCH
1.00 g., 0.900 Gold 0.0287 oz. AGW, 12 mm. **Subject:** Constitutional Tribunal

Date	Mintage	F12	VF20	XF40	MS60	MS63
2010MW	10,000	PF65 75.00				

Y# 774 25 ZŁOTYCH
1.00 g., 0.900 Gold 0.0287 oz. AGW, 12 mm. **Subject:** John Paul II Beatification

Date	Mintage	F12	VF20	XF40	MS60	MS63
2011MW	10,000	PF65 75.00				

Y# 739 30 ZŁOTYCH
1.70 g., 0.900 Gold 0.0489 oz. AGW, 16 mm. **Subject:** August of 1980

Date	Mintage	F12	VF20	XF40	MS60	MS63
2010MW	50,000	PF65 100				

Y# 702 37 ZŁOTYCH
1.75 g., 0.900 Gold 0.0503 oz. AGW, 16 mm. **Subject:** Fr. Jorzy Popieluszko, 25th Anniversary of Murder **Obv:** National arms above large 37 **Rev:** Many hands holding crosses

Date	Mintage	F12	VF20	XF40	MS60	MS63
2009MW	60,000	PF65 100				

Y# 860 50 ZŁOTYCH
62.20 g., 0.999 Silver 1.9849 oz. ASW, 45 mm. **Subject:** Treasures of King Stanislaw August - Venceslaus II of Bohemia

Date	Mintage	F12	VF20	XF40	MS60	MS63
2013MW	Est. 5000	—	—	—	—	400

Y# 652 50 ZŁOTYCH
3.13 g., Gold AGW, 18 mm. **Subject:** 90th Annniversary of Regaining Freedom **Obv:** Tomb of the unknown soldier **Rev:** Mounted Commander-In-Chief Jósef Pilsudski

Date	Mintage	F12	VF20	XF40	MS60	MS63
2008	8,800	PF65 125				

Y# 892 50 ZŁOTYCH
3.13 g., Gold AGW, 18 mm. **Subject:** John Paul II Beatification

Date	Mintage	F12	VF20	XF40	MS60	MS63
2011	—	—	—	—	—	—

Y# 850 50 ZŁOTYCH
62.20 g., 0.9999 Silver 1.9867 oz. ASW, 45 mm. **Subject:** King Stanislaw August - Boleslaw I the Brave **Obv:** Long leagend, eagle at bottom **Rev:** Crowned bust right

Date	Mintage	F12	VF20	XF40	MS60	MS63
2013MW	Est. 5000	—	—	—	—	450

Y# 867 50 ZŁOTYCH
62.20 g., 0.999 Silver 1.9849 oz. ASW, 45 mm. **Subject:** Treasures of King Stanislaw August - Wladyslaw the Short

Date	Mintage	F12	VF20	XF40	MS60	MS63
2013MW						375

Y# 898 50 ZŁOTYCH
Silver ASW **Subject:** Stanislaw August - Casimir the Great

Date	Mintage	F12	VF20	XF40	MS60	MS63
2014	5,000	PF65 150				

Y# 907 50 ZŁOTYCH
62.20 g., 0.999 Silver 1.9849 oz. ASW, 45 mm. **Subject:** King Stanislaw August - Louis the Great

Date	Mintage	F12	VF20	XF40	MS60	MS63
2014	5,000	PF65 150				

Y# 914 50 ZŁOTYCH
62.20 g., 0.999 Silver 1.9849 oz. ASW, 45 mm. **Subject:** Stanislaw August - Hedwig

Date	Mintage	F12	VF20	XF40	MS60	MS63
2014	5,000	PF65 150				

Y# 416 100 ZŁOTYCH
8.00 g., 0.900 Gold 0.230 oz. AGW, 21 mm. **Subject:** Wladyslaw I (1320-33) **Obv:** Crowned eagle with wings open **Rev:** Crowned bust facing **Edge:** Plain

Date	Mintage	F12	VF20	XF40	MS60	MS63
2001MW		PF66 876				

Y# 417 100 ZŁOTYCH
8.00 g., 0.900 Gold 0.230 oz. AGW, 21 mm. **Subject:** Boleslaw III (1102-1138) **Obv:** Crowned eagle with wings open **Rev:** Pointed crowned bust facing **Edge:** Plain

Date	Mintage	F12	VF20	XF40	MS60	MS63
2001MW	2,000	PF65 875				

Y# 462 100 ZŁOTYCH
8.00 g., 0.900 Gold 0.230 oz. AGW, 21 mm. **Obv:** Crowned eagle with wings open **Rev:** Jan Sobieski III **Edge:** Plain

Date	Mintage	F12	VF20	XF40	MS60	MS63
2001MV	2,200	PF65 875				

Y# 429 100 ZŁOTYCH
8.00 g., 0.900 Gold 0.230 oz. AGW, 21 mm. **Obv:** Crowned eagle with wings open **Rev:** Crowned bust facing **Edge:** Plain

Date	Mintage	F12	VF20	XF40	MS60	MS63
2002MW	2,400	PF65 875				

Y# 430 100 ZŁOTYCH
8.00 g., 0.900 Gold 0.230 oz. AGW, 21 mm. **Obv:** Crowned eagle with wings open **Rev:** Crowned bust 1/4 left **Edge:** Plain

Date	Mintage	F12	VF20	XF40	MS60	MS63
2002MW	2,200	PF65 875				

Y# 436 100 ZŁOTYCH
8.00 g., 0.900 Gold 0.230 oz. AGW, 21 mm. **Subject:** World Cup Soccer **Obv:** Crowned eagle with wings open and world background **Rev:** Soccer player **Edge:** Plain

Date	Mintage	F12	VF20	XF40	MS60	MS63
2002MW	—	PF65 450				

Y# 454 100 ZŁOTYCH
8.00 g., 0.900 Gold 0.230 oz. AGW, 21 mm. **Obv:** Crowned eagle with wings open **Rev:** Uniformed bust 1/4 left **Edge:** Plain

Date	Mintage	F12	VF20	XF40	MS60	MS63
2003MW	2,000	PF65 1,000				

Y# 466 100 ZŁOTYCH
8.00 g., 0.900 Gold 0.230 oz. AGW, 21 mm. **Subject:** 750th Anniversary - City Charter **Obv:** Door knocker and church **Rev:** Clock face and tower **Edge:** Plain

Date	Mintage	F12	VF20	XF40	MS60	MS63
2003MW	2,100	PF65 750				

Y# 467 100 ZŁOTYCH
8.00 g., 0.900 Gold 0.230 oz. AGW, 21 mm. **Obv:** Crowned eagle with wings open **Rev:** Kazimierz IV (1447-1492) **Edge:** Plain

Date	Mintage	F12	VF20	XF40	MS60	MS63
2003MW	2,300	PF65 750				

Y# 476 100 ZŁOTYCH
8.00 g., 0.900 Gold 0.230 oz. AGW, 21 mm. **Obv:** Crowned eagle with wings open **Rev:** Stanislaus I and eagle **Edge:** Plain

Date	Mintage	F12	VF20	XF40	MS60	MS63
2003MW	2,500	PF65 750				

Y# 494 100 ZŁOTYCH
8.00 g., 0.900 Gold 0.230 oz. AGW, 21 mm. **Obv:** Crowned eagle with wings open **Rev:** King Przemysl II (1295-1296) **Edge:** Plain

Date	Mintage	F12	VF20	XF40	MS60	MS63
2004MW	3,400	PF65 550				

Y# 495 100 ZŁOTYCH
8.00 g., 0.900 Gold 0.230 oz. AGW, 21 mm. **Obv:** Crowned
eagle with wings open **Rev:** King Zygmunt I (1506-1548) **Edge:**
Plain

Date	Mintage	F12	VF20	XF40	MS60	MS63
2004MW	3,400	PF65 550				

Y# 540 100 ZŁOTYCH
8.00 g., 0.900 Gold 0.230 oz. AGW, 21 mm. **Obv:** St. Peters
Basilica dome **Rev:** Pope John Paul II and baptismal font
Edge: Plain

Date	Mintage	F12	VF20	XF40	MS60	MS63
2005MW	18,700	PF65 450				

Y# 581 100 ZŁOTYCH
8.00 g., 0.900 Gold 0.230 oz. AGW, 21 mm. **Obv:** Line of soccer
players on soccer ball surface with Polish eagle in one of the
sections **Rev:** Two soccer players **Edge:** Plain

Date	Mintage	F12	VF20	XF40	MS60	MS63
2006MW	—	PF65 450				

Y# 640 100 ZŁOTYCH
8.00 g., 0.900 Gold 0.230 oz. AGW, 21 mm. **Subject:** Siberian
Exiles **Obv:** Small national arms at left, bleak forest at right **Obv.
Legend:** RZECZPOSPOLITA POLSKA **Rev:** Grieving mother
with child by tree at lower right, building in background at left
Rev. Legend: SYBIRACY

Date	Mintage	F12	VF20	XF40	MS60	MS63
2008MW	12,000	PF65 450				

Y# 657 100 ZŁOTYCH
8.00 g., 0.900 Gold 0.230 oz. AGW, 21 mm. **Subject:** 400th
Anniversary of Polish Settlement in North America **Obv:** Eagle
in center against compass rose. Outline of Europe & North
America. **Rev:** Center compass rose surrounded by 4 men
working

Date	Mintage	F12	VF20	XF40	MS60	MS63
2008	9,500	PF65 450				

Y# 699 100 ZŁOTYCH
8.00 g., 0.900 Gold 0.230 oz. AGW, 21 mm. **Subject:** Tatar
Rescue, 100th Anniversary **Obv:** Figure of Mariusz Zaruski
Rev: Mountains and reszue helicopter image

Date	Mintage	F12	VF20	XF40	MS60	MS63
2009MW	10,000	PF65 450				

Y# 714 100 ZŁOTYCH
8.00 g., 0.900 Gold 0.230 oz. AGW, 21 mm. **Subject:** Auschwitz
liberation **Obv:** Prisoner and railroad track entrance **Rev:**
Buildings

Date	Mintage	F12	VF20	XF40	MS60	MS63
2010MW	8,000	PF65 450				

Y# 741 100 ZŁOTYCH
8.00 g., 0.900 Gold 0.230 oz. AGW, 21 mm. **Subject:**
Constitutional Tribunal

Date	Mintage	F12	VF20	XF40	MS60	MS63
2010MW	5,000	PF65 450				

Y# 766 100 ZŁOTYCH
8.00 g., 0.900 Gold 0.230 oz. AGW, 21 mm. **Subject:** Smolensk
plane crash **Rev:** President Lech Kaczynski and wife Maria

Date	Mintage	F12	VF20	XF40	MS60	MS63
2011	—	PF65 475				

Y# 775 100 ZŁOTYCH
8.00 g., 0.900 Gold 0.230 oz. AGW, 21 mm. **Subject:** John
Paul II Beatification

Date	Mintage	F12	VF20	XF40	MS60	MS63
2011MW	8,000	PF65 450				

Y# 779 100 ZŁOTYCH
8.00 g., 0.900 Gold 0.230 oz. AGW, 21 mm. **Subject:** Poland's
presidency of the Council of the European Union

Date	Mintage	F12	VF20	XF40	MS60	MS63
2011MW	4,000	PF65 500				

Y# 830 100 ZŁOTYCH
8.00 g., 0.900 Gold 0.230 oz. AGW, 21 mm. **Subject:** European
Football Championships

Date	Mintage	F12	VF20	XF40	MS60	MS63
2012MW	4,000	PF65 500				

Y# 407 200 ZŁOTYCH
15.20 g., 0.900 Tri-Metallic 0.437 oz., 27 mm. **Subject:** Year

2001 **Obv:** Crowned eagle with wings open within a swirl **Rev:**
Couple looking into the future **Edge:** Plain

Date	Mintage	F12	VF20	XF40	MS60	MS63
2001MW	—	PF65 900				

Y# 420 200 ZŁOTYCH
15.50 g., 0.900 Gold 0.4456 oz. AGW, 27 mm. **Subject:**
Cardinal Stefan Wyszynski **Obv:** Pillar divides arms and eagle
Rev: Bust left within arch **Edge Lettering:** 100 ROCZNIA
URODZIN

Date	Mintage	F12	VF20	XF40	MS60	MS63
2001MW	4,500	PF65 850				

Y# 463 200 ZŁOTYCH
15.50 g., 0.900 Gold 0.4456 oz. AGW, 27 mm. **Obv:**
Standing violinist **Rev:** Henryk Wieniawski **Edge Lettering:**
XII MIEDZYNARODOWY KONKURS SKRZYPCOWY IM
HENRYKA WIENIAWSKIEGO

Date	Mintage	F12	VF20	XF40	MS60	MS63
2001MW	2,000	PF65 1,150				

Y# 438 200 ZŁOTYCH
15.50 g., 0.900 Gold 0.4456 oz. AGW, 27 mm. **Subject:** Pope
John Paul II **Obv:** Bust left and small eagle with wings open
Rev: Pope facing radiant Holy Door **Edge:** Plain

Date	Mintage	F12	VF20	XF40	MS60	MS63
2002MW	5,000	PF65 1,200				

Y# 470 200 ZŁOTYCH
15.50 g., 0.900 Gold 0.4456 oz. AGW, 27 mm. **Subject:** Gas
and Oil Industry **Obv:** Crowned eagle, oil wells and refinery
Rev: Scientist at work **Edge:** Plain

Date	Mintage	F12	VF20	XF40	MS60	MS63
2003MW	2,100	PF65 1,250				

Y# 472 200 ZŁOTYCH
15.50 g., 0.900 Gold 0.4456 oz. AGW, 27 mm. **Obv:** Standing
Pope John Paul II **Rev:** Seated Pope **Edge:** Plain

Date	Mintage	F12	VF20	XF40	MS60	MS63
2003MW	4,900	PF65 1,300				

Y# 483 200 ZŁOTYCH

15.50 g., 0.900 Gold 0.4456 oz. AGW, 27 mm. **Subject:** Poland Joining the European Union **Obv:** Polish euro coin design elements **Rev:** Polish euro coin design elements **Edge:** Plain

Date	Mintage	F12	VF20	XF40	MS60	MS63
2004MW	4,400	PF65 850				

Y# 511 200 ZŁOTYCH

15.50 g., 0.900 Gold 0.4456 oz. AGW, 27 mm. **Subject:** Warsaw Fine Arts Academy Centennial **Obv:** Campus view **Rev:** Statue and building **Edge:** Plain

Date	Mintage	F12	VF20	XF40	MS60	MS63
2004MW	5,000	PF65 850				

Y# 519 200 ZŁOTYCH

15.50 g., 0.900 Gold 0.4456 oz. AGW, 27 mm. **Subject:** Olympics **Obv:** Woman and crowned eagle **Rev:** Ancient runners painted on pottery **Edge:** Plain

Date	Mintage	F12	VF20	XF40	MS60	MS63
2004MW	6,000	PF65 850				

Y# 536 200 ZŁOTYCH

15.50 g., 0.900 Gold 0.4456 oz. AGW, 27 mm. **Obv:** Chopin **Rev:** Nagoya Castle roof tops and Mt. Fuji **Edge:** Plain **Note:** Aichi Expo Japan

Date	Mintage	F12	VF20	XF40	MS60	MS63
2005MW	4,200	PF65 875				

Y# 538 200 ZŁOTYCH

15.50 g., 0.900 Gold 0.4456 oz. AGW, 27 mm. **Obv:** Horse drawn carriage **Rev:** Konstanty Ildefons Galczynski in top hat **Edge:** Plain

Date	Mintage	F12	VF20	XF40	MS60	MS63
2005MW	3,500	PF65 900				

Y# 886 200 ZŁOTYCH

15.50 g., 0.900 Gold 0.4456 oz. AGW, 27 mm. **Obv:** Solidarity Logo **Rev:** Dove

Date	Mintage	F12	VF20	XF40	MS60	MS63
2005	4,600	PF65 800				

Y# 887 200 ZŁOTYCH

15.50 g., 0.900 Gold 0.4456 oz. AGW **Obv:** Eagle **Rev:** Planes in flight

Date	Mintage	F12	VF20	XF40	MS60	MS63
2005	4,400	PF65 800				

Y# 888 200 ZŁOTYCH

15.50 g., 0.900 Gold 0.4456 oz. AGW **Obv:** Eagle **Rev:** August II bust

Date	Mintage	F12	VF20	XF40	MS60	MS63
2005	—	PF65 800				

Y# 889 200 ZŁOTYCH

15.50 g., 0.900 Gold 0.4456 oz. AGW **Subject:** Mikolaja Reja -500th Anniversary **Obv:** Quill pen

Date	Mintage	F12	VF20	XF40	MS60	MS63
2005	3,600	PF65 800				

Y# 672 200 ZŁOTYCH

15.50 g., 0.900 Gold 0.4456 oz. AGW, 27 mm. **Obv:** Helmet and breastplate **Rev:** Knight of the 15th Century

Date	Mintage	F12	VF20	XF40	MS60	MS63
2007	10,500	PF65 850				

Y# 643 200 ZŁOTYCH

15.50 g., 0.900 Gold 0.4456 oz. AGW, 27 mm. **Subject:** Zbigniew Herbert **Obv:** Eagle and Zbigniew Herbert **Rev:** Mounted statue of Marcus Aurelius

Date	Mintage	F12	VF20	XF40	MS60	MS63
2008	11,200	PF65 850				

Y# 647 200 ZŁOTYCH

15.50 g., 0.900 Gold 0.4456 oz. AGW, 27 mm. **Series:** The 29th Olympic Games Beijing 2008 **Obv:** Two kites and an eagle **Rev:** Female pole vault jumper

Date	Mintage	F12	VF20	XF40	MS60	MS63
2008	—	PF65 850				

Y# 653 200 ZŁOTYCH

15.50 g., 0.900 Gold 0.4456 oz. AGW, 27 mm. **Subject:** 90th Anniversary of Regaining Freedom **Obv:** Tomb of the unknown soldier **Rev:** Mounted Commander-In-Chief Jozef Pilsudski

Date	Mintage	F12	VF20	XF40	MS60	MS63
2008	10,000	PF65 850				

Y# 654 200 ZŁOTYCH

15.50 g., 0.900 Gold 0.4456 oz. AGW, 27 mm. **Subject:** 450 years of the Polish Post **Obv:** Eagle right, bottom against post stamp **Rev:** Horse with rider crossing bridge

Date	Mintage	F12	VF20	XF40	MS60	MS63
2008	11,000	PF65 850				

Y# 660 200 ZŁOTYCH

15.50 g., 0.900 Gold 0.4456 oz. AGW, 27 mm. **Subject:** 90th

Anniversary of the Greater Poland Uprising **Obv:** Eagle at left, eagle at right with chain **Rev:** Charging cavalrymen and German soldiers firing at them

Date	Mintage	F12	VF20	XF40	MS60	MS63
2008	9,400	PF65 850				

Y# 664 200 ZŁOTYCH

15.50 g., 0.900 Gold 0.4456 oz. AGW, 27 mm. **Subject:** Warsaw Ghetto **Obv:** Building on fire, Naitonal arms **Rev:** Face looking out from broken brick wall

Date	Mintage	F12	VF20	XF40	MS60	MS63
2008MW	12,000	PF65 850				

Y# 696 200 ZŁOTYCH

15.15 g., 0.900 Gold 0.4356 oz. AGW, 27 mm. **Obv:** Eagle and statue, flames in background **Rev:** Stefan Starzonski, Warsaw Mayor; Burning of the Clock Tower

Date	Mintage	F12	VF20	XF40	MS60	MS63
2009	10,500	PF65 850				

Y# 677 200 ZŁOTYCH

15.50 g., 0.900 Gold 0.4456 oz. AGW, 27 mm. **Subject:** Central Banking, 180th Anniversary **Obv:** National arms above crowned shield **Rev:** Building and portrait

Date	Mintage	F12	VF20	XF40	MS60	MS63
2009MW	8,500	PF65 850				

Y# 683 200 ZŁOTYCH

15.50 g., 0.900 Gold 0.4456 oz. AGW, 27 mm. **Subject:** General election of 1989 **Obv:** National arms above shipyard scene **Rev:** Lech Walesa silhouette before crowd

Date	Mintage	F12	VF20	XF40	MS60	MS63
2009MW	10,000	PF65 850				

Y# 717 200 ZŁOTYCH

15.50 g., 0.900 Gold 0.4456 oz. AGW, 27 mm. **Subject:** Vancouver Winter Olympics **Obv:** Downhill skiing **Rev:** Cross Country skiing

Date	Mintage	F12	VF20	XF40	MS60	MS63
2010MW	8,000	PF65 850				

Y# 720 200 ZŁOTYCH

15.50 g., 0.900 Gold 0.4456 oz. AGW, 27 mm. **Subject:** Napoleonic Imperial Guard **Obv:** Pile of arms **Rev:** Galloping guardsman

Date	Mintage	F12	VF20	XF40	MS60	MS63
2010MW	10,500	**PF65** 850				

Y# 734 200 ZŁOTYCH

15.50 g., 0.900 Gold 0.4456 oz. AGW, 27 mm. **Subject:** Battles of Grunwald and Kluszyn

Date	Mintage	F12	VF20	XF40	MS60	MS63
2010MW	10,500	**PF65** 850				

Y# 782 200 ZŁOTYCH

15.50 g., 0.900 Gold 0.4456 oz. AGW, 27 mm. **Subject:** Polish Cavalry - Uhlan **Edge Lettering:** 22.4x32

Date	Mintage	F12	VF20	XF40	MS60	MS63
2011MW	5,000	**PF65** 875				

Y# 787 200 ZŁOTYCH

15.50 g., 0.900 Gold 0.4456 oz. AGW, 27 mm. **Subject:** Czeslaw Milosz

Date	Mintage	F12	VF20	XF40	MS60	MS63
2011MW	4,000	**PF65** 875				

Y# 791 200 ZŁOTYCH

15.50 g., 0.900 Gold 0.4456 oz. AGW, 27 mm. **Subject:** Ignacy Jan Paderewski

Date	Mintage	F12	VF20	XF40	MS60	MS63
2011MW	3,000	**PF65** 900				

Y# 819 200 ZŁOTYCH

15.50 g., 0.900 Gold 0.4456 oz. AGW, 27 mm. **Subject:** Stefan Banach

Date	Mintage	F12	VF20	XF40	MS60	MS63
2012MW	4,000	**PF65** 875				

Y# 834 200 ZŁOTYCH

15.50 g., 0.900 Gold 0.4456 oz. AGW, 27 mm. **Subject:** London Olympics, 2012, Polish Team

Date	Mintage	F12	VF20	XF40	MS60	MS63
2012MW	5,000	**PF65** 875				

Y# 840 200 ZŁOTYCH

15.50 g., 0.900 Gold 0.4456 oz. AGW, 27 mm. **Subject:** Boleslaw Prus

Date	Mintage	F12	VF20	XF40	MS60	MS63
2012MW	3,000	**PF65** 900				

Y# 858 200 ZŁOTYCH

15.50 g., 0.900 Gold 0.4456 oz. AGW, 27 mm. **Subject:** Cyprian Norwid

Date	Mintage	F12	VF20	XF40	MS60	MS63
2013MW	Est. 2500	**PF65** 950				

Y# 872 200 ZŁOTYCH

15.50 g., 0.900 Gold 0.4456 oz. AGW, 27 mm. **Subject:** Witold Lutoslawski

Date	Mintage	F12	VF20	XF40	MS60	MS63
2013MW	Est. 2500	**PF65** 850				

Y# 875 200 ZŁOTYCH

15.50 g., 0.900 Gold 0.4456 oz. AGW, 27 mm. **Subject:** 200th Anniversary of the Death of Prince Jozef Poniatowski

Date	Mintage	F12	VF20	XF40	MS60	MS63
2013MW	Est. 3000	**PF65** 850				

Y# 882 200 ZŁOTYCH

15.50 g., 0.900 Gold 0.4456 oz. AGW, 27 mm. **Subject:** 200th Anniversary of the Birth of Hipolit Cegielski

Date	Mintage	F12	VF20	XF40	MS60	MS63
2013MW	Est. 2500	**PF65** 850				

Y# 895 200 ZŁOTYCH

15.50 g., 0.900 Gold 0.4456 oz. AGW, 27 mm. **Subject:** Polish Olympic Team, Sochi 2014

Date	Mintage	F12	VF20	XF40	MS60	MS63
2014	2,500	**PF65** 900				

Y# 903 200 ZŁOTYCH

15.50 g., 0.900 Gold 0.4456 oz. AGW, 27 mm. **Subject:** Jan Karski, 100th Anniversary of Birth

Date	Mintage	F12	VF20	XF40	MS60	MS63
2014	2,500	**PF65** 800				

Y# 911 200 ZŁOTYCH

15.50 g., 0.900 Gold 0.4456 oz. AGW, 27 mm. **Subject:** Stefan Zeromski, 150th Anniversary of Birth

Date	Mintage	F12	VF20	XF40	MS60	MS63
2014	2,500	**PF65** 500				

Y# 831 500 ZŁOTYCH

62.20 g., 0.999 Gold 1.9849 oz. AGW, 40 mm. **Subject:** European Football Championships

Date	Mintage	F12	VF20	XF40	MS60	MS63
2012MW	1,000	**PF65** 3,750				

Y# 849 500 ZŁOTYCH

62.20 g., 0.9999 Gold 1.9867 oz. AGW, 45 mm. **Subject:** King Stanislaw August - Boleslaw I the Brave **Obv:** Long legend and eagle at bottom **Rev:** Crowned bust right

Date	Mintage	F12	VF20	XF40	MS60	MS63
2013MW	Est. 750	—	—	—	—	5,000

Y# 861 500 ZŁOTYCH

62.20 g., 0.9999 Gold 1.9867 oz. AGW, 45 mm. **Subject:** Treasures of King Stanislaw August - Venceslaus II of Bohemia

Date	Mintage	F12	VF20	XF40	MS60	MS63
2013MW	—	—	—	—	—	4,500

Y# 868 500 ZŁOTYCH
62.20 g., 0.9999 Gold 1.9867 oz. AGW, 45 mm. **Subject:** Treasures of King Stanislaw August - Wladyslaw the Short

Date	Mintage	F12	VF20	XF40	MS60	MS63
2013MW	Est. 750	—	—	—	—	4,500

Y# 899 500 ZŁOTYCH
62.20 g., 0.999 Gold 1.9849 oz. AGW, 45 mm. **Subject:** Stanislaw August - Casimir the Great

Date	Mintage	F12	VF20	XF40	MS60	MS63
2014	750	PF65 275				

Y# 908 500 ZŁOTYCH
62.20 g., 0.999 Gold 1.9849 oz. AGW, 45 mm. **Subject:** King Stanislaw August - Louis the Great

Date	Mintage	F12	VF20	XF40	MS60	MS63
2014	750	PF65 2,750				

Y# 915 500 ZŁOTYCH
62.62 g., 0.999 Gold 1.9983 oz. AGW, 45 mm. **Subject:** Stanislaw August - Hedwig

Date	Mintage	F12	VF20	XF40	MS60	MS63
2014	760	PF65 2,750				

Y# 776 1000 ZŁOTYCH
93.30 g., 0.999 Gold 2.9774 oz. AGW, 50 mm. **Subject:** John Paul II Beautification

Date	Mintage	F12	VF20	XF40	MS60	MS63
2011MW	500	PF65 5,750				

GOLD BULLION COINAGE

Y# 292 50 ZŁOTYCH
3.10 g., 0.9999 Gold 0.099 oz. AGW, 18 mm. **Obv:** Crowned eagle with wings open, all within circle **Rev:** Golden eagle

Date	Mintage	F12	VF20	XF40	MS60	MS63
2002	500	—	—	—	BV	220
2004	2,000	—	—	—	BV	200
2006	1,600	—	—	—	BV	200
2007	2,000	—	—	—	BV	200
2008	—	—	—	—	BV	200

Y# 293 100 ZŁOTYCH
7.78 g., 0.9999 Gold 0.2485 oz. AGW, 22 mm. **Obv:** Crowned eagle with wings open, all within circle **Rev:** Golden eagle

Date	Mintage	F12	VF20	XF40	MS60	MS63
2002	800	—	—	—	BV	475
2004	1,000	—	—	—	BV	475
2006	900	—	—	—	BV	475

Date	Mintage	F12	VF20	XF40	MS60	MS63
2007	1,500	—	—	—	BV	475
2008	—	—	—	—	BV	475

Y# 294 200 ZŁOTYCH
15.50 g., 0.900 Gold 0.4456 oz. AGW, 27 mm. **Obv:** Crowned eagle with wings open within beaded circle **Rev:** Golden eagle

Date	Mintage	F12	VF20	XF40	MS60	MS63
2002	1,000	—	—	—	BV	850
2004	1,000	—	—	—	BV	850
2006	900	—	—	—	BV	850
2007	1,500	—	—	—	BV	850
2008	—	—	—	—	BV	850

Y# 295 500 ZŁOTYCH
31.10 g., 0.9999 Gold 0.9935 oz. AGW **Obv:** Crowned eagle with wings open within beaded circle **Rev:** Golden eagle

Date	Mintage	F12	VF20	XF40	MS60	MS63
2002	1,000	—	—	—	BV	1,850
2004	2,500	—	—	—	BV	1,850
2006	600	—	—	—	BV	1,850
2007	2,500	—	—	—	BV	1,850
2008	—	—	—	—	BV	1,850

MINT SETS

KM#	Date	Mintage	Identification	Issue Price	Mkt Val
MS5	2007 (11)	2,000	Y#276-284, 465, 525, mixed date set - 1995-2007	39.95	37.50

PORTUGAL

The Portuguese Republic, located in the western part of the Iberian Peninsula in southwestern Europe, has an area of 35,553 sq. mi. (92,080 sq. km.) and a population of *10.5 million. Capital: Lisbon. Portugal's economy is based on agriculture, tourism, minerals, fisheries and a rapidly expanding industrial sector. Textiles account for 33% of the exports and Portuguese wine is world famous. Portugal has become Europe's number one producer of copper and the world's largest producer of cork.

RULER
Republic, 1910 to date

MONETARY SYSTEM
100 Cents = 1 Euro

REPUBLIC
DECIMAL COINAGE

KM# 631a ESCUDO
4.60 g., 0.9167 Gold 0.1347 oz. AGW, 16 mm. **Subject:** Last Escudo **Obv:** Design above shield with "Au" above top left corner of shield **Rev:** Flower design above value **Edge:** Plain

Date	Mintage	F12	VF20	XF40	MS60	MS63
2001INCM	50,000	—	—	—	235	250
(2001)INCM		PF60 225				

KM# 634.1 20 ESCUDOS
6.90 g., Copper-Nickel, 26.5 mm. **Obv:** Shield divides date with value below **Obv. Legend:** REPUBLICA PORTUGUESA **Rev:** Nautical windrose

Date	Mintage	F12	VF20	XF40	MS60	MS63
2001INCM	Est. 250000	—	—	—	2.75	3.50

KM# 733a 500 ESCUDOS
Gold AGW **Subject:** Porto, European Culture Capital **Obv:** National arms and value **Rev:** Stylized design **Edge:** Reeded

Date	Mintage	F12	VF20	XF40	MS60	MS63
2001INCM	5,000	PF60 550				

KM# 733 500 ESCUDOS
13.96 g., 0.500 Silver 0.223 oz. ASW, 30.1 mm. **Subject:** Porto, European Culture Capital **Obv:** National arms and value **Rev:** Stylized design **Edge:** Reeded

Date	Mintage	F12	VF20	XF40	MS60	MS63
2001INCM		—	—	—	8.50	9.50
2001INCM	10,000	PF60 60.00				

KM# 734 1000 ESCUDOS
26.95 g., 0.500 Silver 0.4304 oz. ASW, 40 mm. **Obv:** National arms and value **Obv. Legend:** REPUBLICA PORTUGUESA 2001 **Rev:** Soccer ball within net **Rev. Legend:** 10º Campeonato Europeu de Futebol - UEFA Euro 2004 Portugal **Edge:** Reeded

Date	Mintage	F12	VF20	XF40	MS60	MS63
2001INCM	50,000	—	—	—	17.50	18.50
2001INCM		PF60 75.00				

EURO COINAGE
European Union Issues

KM# 740 EURO CENT
2.30 g., Copper Plated Steel, 16.25 mm. **Obv:** Royal seal of 1134 with country name and cross **Rev:** Value and globe **Edge:** Plain

Date	Mintage	F12	VF20	XF40	MS60	MS63
2002	278,106,172	—	—	—	0.35	0.50
2002	15,000	PF63 7.00				
2003	50,000	—	—	—	0.35	0.50
2003	15,000	PF63 7.00				
2004	75,000,000	—	—	—	0.35	0.50
2004	15,000	PF63 7.00				
2005	40,000,000	—	—	—	0.35	0.50
2005	10,000	PF63 7.00				
2006	30,000,000	—	—	—	0.35	0.50
2006	3,000	PF63 7.00				
2007	105,000,000	—	—	—	0.35	0.50
2007	2,500	PF63 7.00				
2008	75,000,000	—	—	—	0.35	0.50
2008	3,500	PF63 7.00				
2009	60,000,000	—	—	—	0.35	0.50
2009	4,000	PF63 7.00				
2010	15,000,000	—	—	—	0.35	0.50
2010	4,500	PF63 7.00				
2011	20,000,000	—	—	—	0.35	0.50
2011	4,500	PF63 7.00				
2012	50,000,000	—	—	—	0.35	0.50
2012	4,500	PF63 7.00				
2013	—	—	—	—	0.35	0.50
2013		PF63 7.00				

KM# 741 2 EURO CENT
3.06 g., Copper Plated Steel, 18.75 mm. **Obv:** Royal seal of 1134 with country name and cross **Rev:** Value and globe **Edge:** Grooved

Date	Mintage	F12	VF20	XF40	MS60	MS63
2002	324,376,590	—	—	—	0.50	0.65
2002	15,000	PF63 9.00				
2003	50,000	—	—	—	—	2.50
	Note: In sets only					
2003	15,000	PF63 9.00				
2004	1,000,000	—	—	—	0.50	0.65
2004	15,000	PF63 9.00				
2005	10,000,000	—	—	—	0.50	0.65
2005	10,000	PF63 9.00				
2006	1,000,000	—	—	—	0.50	0.65
2006	3,000	PF63 9.00				
2007	10,000,000	—	—	—	0.50	0.65
2007	2,500	PF63 9.00				

Date	Mintage	F12	VF20	XF40	MS60	MS63
2008	35,000,000	—	—	—	0.50	0.65
2008	3,500	PF63 9.00				
2009	45,000,000	—	—	—	0.50	0.65
2009	4,000	PF63 9.00				
2010	10,000,000	—	—	—	0.50	0.65
2010	4,500	PF63 9.00				
2011	30,000,000	—	—	—	0.50	0.65
2011	4,500	PF63 9.00				
2012	35,000,000	—	—	—	0.50	0.65
2012	4,500	PF63 9.00				
2013	—	—	—	—	0.50	0.65
2013	—	PF63 9.00				

KM# 742 5 EURO CENT
3.92 g., Copper Plated Steel, 21.25 mm. **Obv:** Royal seal of 1134 with country name and cross **Rev:** Value and globe **Edge:** Plain

Date	Mintage	F12	VF20	XF40	MS60	MS63
2002	234,512,047	—	—	—	0.75	1.00
2002	15,000	PF63 10.00				
2003	50,000					4.00
	Note: In sets only					
2003	15,000	PF63 10.00				
2004	40,000,000	—	—	—	0.75	1.00
2004	15,000	PF63 10.00				
2005	30,000,000	—	—	—	0.75	1.00
2005	10,000	PF63 10.00				
2006	20,000,000	—	—	—	0.75	1.00
2006	3,000	PF63 10.00				
2007	25,000,000	—	—	—	0.75	1.00
2007	2,500	PF63 10.00				
2008	25,000,000	—	—	—	0.75	1.00
2008	3,500	PF63 10.00				
2009	25,000,000	—	—	—	0.75	1.00
2009	4,000	PF63 10.00				
2010	5,000,000	—	—	—	0.75	1.00
2010	4,500	PF63 10.00				
2011	25,000,000	—	—	—	0.75	1.00
2011	4,500	PF63 10.00				
2012	15,000,000	—	—	—	0.75	1.00
2012	4,500	PF63 10.00				
2013	—	—	—	—	0.75	1.00
2013	—	PF63 10.00				

KM# 743 10 EURO CENT
4.10 g., Brass, 19.75 mm. **Obv:** Royal seal of 1142, country name in circular design **Rev:** Value and map **Edge:** Reeded

Date	Mintage	F12	VF20	XF40	MS60	MS63
2002	220,289,835	—	—	—	0.75	1.00
2002	15,000	PF63 12.00				
2003	6,332,000	—	—	—	1.00	1.50
2003	15,000	PF63 12.00				
2004	1,000,000	—	—	—	1.50	2.00
2004	15,000	PF63 12.00				
2005	1,000,000	—	—	—	1.50	2.00
2005	10,000	PF63 12.00				
2006	1,000,000	—	—	—	1.50	2.00
2006	3,000	PF63 12.00				
2007	21,500	—	—	—	1.50	2.00
2007	2,500	PF63 12.00				

KM# 763 10 EURO CENT
4.10 g., Brass, 19.75 mm. **Obv:** Royal seal of 1142, country name in circular design **Rev:** Relief map of Western Europe, stars, lines and value **Edge:** Reeded

Date	Mintage	F12	VF20	XF40	MS60	MS63
2008	1,000,000	—	—	—	1.50	2.00
2008	3,500	PF63 12.00				
2009	10,000,000	—	—	—	1.50	2.00
2009	4,000	PF63 12.00				
2010	—	—	—	—	1.50	2.00
2010	4,500	PF63 12.00				
2011	—	—	—	—	1.50	2.00
2011	4,500	PF63 12.00				
2012	—	—	—	—	1.50	2.00

Date	Mintage	F12	VF20	XF40	MS60	MS63
2012	4,500	PF63 12.00				
2013	—	—	—	—	1.50	2.00
2013	—	PF63 12.00				

KM# 744 20 EURO CENT
5.74 g., Brass, 22.25 mm. **Obv:** Royal seal of 1142, country name in circular design **Rev:** Value and map **Edge:** Notched

Date	Mintage	F12	VF20	XF40	MS60	MS63
2002	147,411,038	—	—	—	1.00	1.25
2002	15,000	PF63 14.00				
2003	9,493,600	—	—	—	1.25	1.50
2003	15,000	PF63 14.00				
2004	1,000,000	—	—	—	1.50	2.00
2004	15,000	PF63 14.00				
2005	25,000,000	—	—	—	1.50	2.00
2005	10,000	PF63 14.00				
2006	20,000,000	—	—	—	1.50	2.00
2006	3,000	PF63 14.00				
2007	21,500	—	—	—	1.50	2.00
2007	2,500	PF63 14.00				

KM# 764 20 EURO CENT
5.74 g., Brass, 22.25 mm. **Obv:** Royal seal of 1142, country name in circular design **Rev:** Relief map of Western Europe, stars, lines and value **Edge:** Notched

Date	Mintage	F12	VF20	XF40	MS60	MS63
2008	1,000,000	—	—	—	1.50	2.00
2008	3,500	PF63 14.00				
2009	20,000,000	—	—	—	1.50	2.00
2009	4,000	PF63 14.00				
2010	5,000,000	—	—	—	1.50	2.00
2010	4,500	PF63 14.00				
2011	10,000,000	—	—	—	1.50	2.00
2011	4,500	PF63 14.00				
2012	—	—	—	—	1.50	2.00
2012	4,500	PF63 14.00				
2013	—	—	—	—	1.50	2.00
2013	—	PF63 14.00				

KM# 777 1/4 EURO
1.56 g., 0.999 Gold 0.0498 oz. AGW, 14 mm. **Series:** Portugal Universal **Subject:** King Alfons I, the Conqueror **Obv:** National arms, value **Obv. Legend:** REPÚBLICA PORTUGUESA **Rev:** Stylized 3/4 length armored figure standing facing **Rev. Legend:** D. AFONSO HENRIQUES **Edge:** Reeded **Note:** Each coin is numbered.

Date	Mintage	F12	VF20	XF40	MS60	MS63
2006	30,000	—	—	—	—	145

KM# 826 1/4 EURO
1.56 g., 0.999 Gold 0.0498 oz. AGW, 14 mm. **Subject:** Anthony of Padua

Date	Mintage	F12	VF20	XF40	MS60	MS63
2007	30,000	—	—	—	—	125

KM# 827 1/4 EURO
1.56 g., 0.999 Gold 0.0498 oz. AGW, 14 mm. **Subject:** King Denis

Date	Mintage	F12	VF20	XF40	MS60	MS63
2008	30,000	—	—	—	—	125

KM# 787 1/4 EURO
1.56 g., 0.999 Gold 0.0498 oz. AGW, 14 mm. **Subject:** Vasco da Gama

Date	Mintage	F12	VF20	XF40	MS60	MS63
2009	20,000	—	—	—	125	—

KM# 794 1/4 EURO
1.56 g., 0.999 Gold 0.0498 oz. AGW, 14 mm. **Subject:** Luis Vaz de Camoes

Date	Mintage	F12	VF20	XF40	MS60	MS63
2010	15,000	—	—	—	—	145

KM# 805 1/4 EURO
1.56 g., 0.999 Gold 0.0498 oz. AGW, 14 mm. **Subject:** Fr. António Vieira **Obv:** National arms **Rev:** Linear portrait of Vieira

Date	Mintage	F12	VF20	XF40	MS60	MS63
2011	10,000	—	—	—	—	125

KM# 807 1/4 EURO
1.56 g., 0.999 Gold 0.0498 oz. AGW, 14 mm. **Subject:** Spain and Portugal's accession to the European Union, 25th Anniversary

Date	Mintage	F12	VF20	XF40	MS60	MS63
2011	12,500	—	—	—	—	125

KM# 814 1/4 EURO
1.56 g., 0.999 Gold 0.0498 oz. AGW, 14 mm. **Subject:** Carlos Seixas, composer **Obv:** National arms **Rev:** Head facing, name at left, dates at right

Date	Mintage	F12	VF20	XF40	MS60	MS63
2012	15,000	—	—	—	—	145

KM# 745 50 EURO CENT
7.80 g., Brass, 24.25 mm. **Obv:** Royal seal of 1142, country name in circular design **Rev:** Value and map **Edge:** Reeded

Date	Mintage	F12	VF20	XF40	MS60	MS63
2002	151,947,133	—	—	—	1.50	2.00
2002	15,000	PF63 16.00				
2003	10,353,000	—	—	—	1.50	2.00
2003	15,000	PF63 16.00				
2004	1,000,000	—	—	—	2.50	3.00
2004	15,000	PF63 16.00				
2005	1,000,000	—	—	—	2.50	3.00
2005	10,000	PF63 16.00				
2006	1,000,000	—	—	—	2.50	3.00
2006	3,000	PF63 16.00				
2007	21,500	—	—	—	2.50	3.00
2007	2,500	PF63 16.00				

KM# 765 50 EURO CENT
7.80 g., Brass, 24.25 mm. **Obv:** Royal seal of 1142, country name in circular design **Rev:** Relief map of Western Europe, stars, lines and value **Edge:** Reeded

Date	Mintage	F12	VF20	XF40	MS60	MS63
2008	5,000,000	—	—	—	2.50	3.00
2008	3,500	PF63 16.00				
2009	20,000,000	—	—	—	2.50	3.00
2009	4,000	PF63 16.00				
2010	20,000,000	—	—	—	2.50	3.00
2010	4,500	PF63 16.00				
2011	—	—	—	—	2.50	3.00
2011	4,500	PF63 16.00				
2012	—	—	—	—	2.50	3.00
2012	4,500	PF63 16.00				
2013	—	—	—	—	2.50	3.00
2013	—	PF63 16.00				

KM# 746 EURO
7.50 g., Bi-Metallic, 23.25 mm. **Obv:** Royal seal of 1144, country name in looped design **Rev:** Value and map **Edge:** Segmented reeding

Date	Mintage	F12	VF20	XF40	MS60	MS63
2002	100,228,135	—	—	—	2.00	2.50

Note: Variety in the edge milling, 28 or 29.

Date	Mintage	F12	VF20	XF40	MS60	MS63
2002	15,000	PF63 18.00				
2003	16,206,875	—	—	—	2.00	2.50
2003	15,000	PF63 18.00				
2004	20,000,000	—	—	—	2.00	2.50
2004	15,000	PF63 18.00				
2005	20,000,000	—	—	—	2.00	2.50
2005	10,000	PF63 18.00				
2006	20,000,000	—	—	—	2.00	2.50
2006	3,000	PF63 18.00				
2007	4,935,400	—	—	—	2.00	2.50
2007	2,500	PF63 18.00				

KM# 766 EURO
7.50 g., Bi-Metallic, 23.25 mm. **Obv:** Royal seal of 1144, country name in looped design **Rev:** Relief map of Western Europe, stars, lines and value **Edge:** Segmented reeding

Date	Mintage	F12	VF20	XF40	MS60	MS63
2008	5,000,000	—	—	—	2.75	3.50
2008	3,500	PF63 18.00				
2009	20,000,000	—	—	—	2.75	3.50
2009	4,000	PF63 18.00				
2010	20,000,000	—	—	—	2.75	3.50
2010	4,500	PF63 18.00				
2011	5,000,000	—	—	—	2.75	3.50
2011	4,500	PF63 18.00				
2012	—				2.75	3.50
2012	4,500	PF63 18.00				
2013	—				2.75	3.50
2013	—	PF63 18.00				

KM# 828 1-1/2 EURO
10.00 g., Copper-Nickel, 26.5 mm. **Subject:** Internaitonal Medical Care **Obv:** National Arms **Rev:** AMI logo

Date	Mintage	F12	VF20	XF40	MS60	MS63
2008	300,000	—	—	—	10.00	12.50

KM# 828a 1-1/2 EURO
8.00 g., Copper-Nickel, 26.5 mm. **Subject:** International Medical Assistance **Obv:** National arms **Rev:** AMI logo

Date	Mintage	F12	VF20	XF40	MS60	MS63
2008 Special Unc.	50,000	—	—	—	20.00	25.00

KM# 828b 1-1/2 EURO
10.00 g., 0.925 Silver 0.2955 oz. ASW, 26.5 mm. **Subject:** International Medical Assistance **Obv:** National arms **Rev:** AMI logo

Date	Mintage	F12	VF20	XF40	MS60	MS63
2008	5,000	PF65 60.00				

KM# 788 1-1/2 EURO
10.37 g., 0.999 Gold 0.3309 oz. AGW, 26.5 mm. **Subject:** Numismatics - Marabitino of Sancho II **Obv:** Cross of shields **Rev:** King on horseback

Date	Mintage	F12	VF20	XF40	MS60	MS63
2009	2,500	PF63 650				

KM# 789 1-1/2 EURO
Copper-Nickel, 26.5 mm. **Obv:** Numismatics - Marabitino of Sancho II

Date	Mintage	F12	VF20	XF40	MS60	MS63
2009 Proof	150,000	—	—	—	5.00	6.00

KM# 795 1-1/2 EURO
8.00 g., Copper-Nickel, 26.5 mm. **Subject:** Against Famine

Date	Mintage	F12	VF20	XF40	MS60	MS63
2010	100,000	—	—	—	5.00	6.00
2010INCM Special Unc.	100,000	—	—	—	—	10.00

KM# 795a 1-1/2 EURO
10.00 g., 0.925 Silver 0.2955 oz. ASW, 26.5 mm. **Subject:** Against Famine

Date	Mintage	F12	VF20	XF40	MS60	MS63
2010	5,000	PF65 55.00				

KM# 747 2 EURO
8.50 g., Bi-Metallic, 25.75 mm. **Obv:** Royal seal of 1144, country name in looped design **Rev:** Value and map **Edge:** Reeding over castles and shields

Date	Mintage	F12	VF20	XF40	MS60	MS63
2002	61,930,775	—	—	—	3.50	4.00
2002	15,000	PF63 22.00				
2003	5,979,750	—	—	—	4.25	5.00
2003	15,000	PF63 22.00				
2004	1,000,000	—	—	—	5.50	6.00
2004	15,000	PF63 22.00				
2005	1,000,000	—	—	—	5.50	6.00
2005	10,000	PF63 22.00				
2006	1,000,000	—	—	—	5.50	6.00
2006	3,000	PF63 22.00				
2007	21,500	—	—	—	5.50	6.00
2007	2,500	PF63 22.00				

KM# 771 2 EURO
0.50 g., Bi-Metallic, 25.75 mm. **Subject:** 50th Anniversary Treaty of Rome **Obv:** Open treaty book **Rev:** Large value at left, modified outline of Europe at right **Edge:** Reeded and lettered

Date	Mintage	F12	VF20	XF40	MS60	MS63
2007	1,500,000	—	—	—	4.50	6.00
2007 Prooflike	15,000	—	—	—	—	12.50
2007	5,000	PF63 25.00				

KM# 772 2 EURO
8.50 g., Bi-Metallic, 25.75 mm. **Subject:** European Union President **Obv:** Large tree, small national arms at lower left **Obv. Inscription:** POR / TV / GAL **Rev:** Large value at left, revised map of Europe at right **Edge:** Reeded with repeated symbols

Date	Mintage	F12	VF20	XF40	MS60	MS63
2007	1,250,000	—	—	—	4.50	6.00
2007 Prooflike	15,000	—	—	—	—	12.50
2007	5,000	PF63 25.00				

KM# 767 2 EURO
8.52 g., Bi-Metallic, 25.7 mm. **Obv:** Royal seal of 1144, country name in looped design **Rev:** Relief map of Western Europe, stars, lines and value **Edge:** Reeding over castles and shields

Date	Mintage	F12	VF20	XF40	MS60	MS63
2008 In sets only	—					6.00
2008	3,500	PF63 22.00				
2009 In sets only	—					6.00
2009	4,000	PF63 22.00				
2010	—					6.00
2010	4,500	PF63 22.00				
2011	—					6.00
2011	4,500	PF63 22.00				
2012	—					6.00
2012	4,500	PF63 22.00				
2013	—					6.00
2013	—	PF63 22.00				

KM# 784 2 EURO
8.50 g., Bi-Metallic, 25.75 mm. **Subject:** Declaration of Human Rights, 60th Anniversary **Obv:** Seal above field

Date	Mintage	F12	VF20	XF40	MS60	MS63
2008	1,000,000	—	—	—	4.00	5.00
2008	10,000	PF63 25.00				

KM# 785 2 EURO
8.50 g., Bi-Metallic, 25.75 mm. **Subject:** European Monetary Union, 10th Anniversary **Obv:** Stick figure and Euro symbol

Date	Mintage	F12	VF20	XF40	MS60	MS63
2009	1,250,000	—	—	—	6.00	12.00
2009	15,000	PF63 25.00				

KM# 786 2 EURO
8.50 g., Bi-Metallic, 25.75 mm. **Subject:** Lusofonia Games **Rev:** Figure with long flowing ribbon

Date	Mintage	F12	VF20	XF40	MS60	MS63
2009	1,275,000	—	—	—	—	5.00
2009	10,000	PF63 25.00				

KM# 796 2 EURO
8.50 g., Bi-Metallic, 25.75 mm. **Subject:** Portuguese Republic, 100th Anniversary

Date	Mintage	F12	VF20	XF40	MS60	MS63
2010	10,000	PF63 20.00				
2010	1,265,000	—	—	—	6.00	7.00

KM# 804 2 EURO
8.50 g., Bi-Metallic, 25.75 mm. **Subject:** Fernão Mendes Pinto, 500th Anniversary of Birth **Obv:** Sailing ship right

Date	Mintage	F12	VF20	XF40	MS60	MS63
2011	500,000	—	—	—	6.00	7.00
2011 Special Unc.	12,500	—	—	—	—	9.00
2011	7,500	PF63 25.00				

KM# 812 2 EURO
8.50 g., Bi-Metallic, 25.75 mm. **Subject:** Euro circulation, 10th Anniversary **Obv:** Euro symbol on globe, childlike images around

Date	Mintage	F12	VF20	XF40	MS60	MS63
2012	500,000	—	—	—	6.00	7.00
2012 Special Unc.	10,000	—	—	—	—	9.00
2012	10,000	PF63 25.00				

KM# 813 2 EURO
8.50 g., Bi-Metallic, 25.75 mm. **Subject:** Guimarães, European Cultural Capital **Obv:** Stylized cross and castle

Date	Mintage	F12	VF20	XF40	MS60	MS63
2012	500,000	—	—	—	6.00	7.00
2012 Special Unc.	10,000	—	—	—	—	9.00
2012	10,000	**PF63** 25.00				

KM# 783 2-1/2 EURO
9.85 g., Copper-Nickel, 28 mm. **Obv:** Small national arms on stringed instrument at right **Rev:** Fado musician at lower left **Edge:** Coarse reeding

Date	Mintage	F12	VF20	XF40	MS60	MS63
2008	150,000	—	—	—	6.00	9.00

KM# 783a 2-1/2 EURO
12.00 g., 0.925 Silver 0.3546 oz. ASW, 28 mm. **Obv:** Small national arms on stringed instrument at right **Rev:** Fado musician at lower left

Date	Mintage	F12	VF20	XF40	MS60	MS63
2008	20,000	**PF65** 60.00				

KM# 790 2-1/2 EURO
10.00 g., Copper-Nickel, 28 mm. **Subject:** Bejing Olympics

Date	Mintage	F12	VF20	XF40	MS60	MS63
2008	487,500	—	—	—	6.00	7.00

KM# 790a 2-1/2 EURO
12.00 g., 0.925 Silver 0.3546 oz. ASW, 28 mm. **Subject:** Bejing Olympics

Date	Mintage	F12	VF20	XF40	MS60	MS63
2008	12,500	**PF65** 60.00				

KM# 824 2-1/2 EURO
10.00 g., Copper-Nickel, 28 mm. **Subject:** UNESCO - World Historic Site, Porto **Obv:** National arms **Rev:** Bridge and town view

Date	Mintage	F12	VF20	XF40	MS60	MS63
2008	80,000	—	—	—	10.00	15.00

KM# 824a 2-1/2 EURO
12.00 g., 0.925 Silver 0.3546 oz. ASW, 28 mm. **Subject:** UNESCO Historic Site - Porto **Obv:** National arms **Rev:** Bridge and town view

Date	Mintage	F12	VF20	XF40	MS60	MS63
2008	5,000	**PF65** 60.00				

KM# 825 2-1/2 EURO
10.00 g., Copper-Nickel, 28 mm. **Subject:** UNESCO Historic Site - Wine region of Alto Douro **Obv:** National arms and river **Rev:** Terraced fields

Date	Mintage	F12	VF20	XF40	MS60	MS63
2008	80000	—	—	—	10.00	12.50

KM# 825a 2-1/2 EURO
12.00 g., 0.925 Silver 0.3546 oz. ASW, 28 mm. **Subject:** UNESCO historic sites - Wine region of Alto Douro **Obv:** National arms and river **Rev:** Terraced fields

Date	Mintage	F12	VF20	XF40	MS60	MS63
2008	5,000	**PF65** 60.00				

KM# 792 2-1/2 EURO
Copper-Nickel, 28 mm. **Subject:** UNESCO Heritage Site - Hieronymites Monastery **Obv:** Arched cieling design, National arms **Rev:** Façade detail

Date	Mintage	F12	VF20	XF40	MS60	MS63
2009	150,000	—	—	—	6.00	7.00

KM# 791 2-1/2 EURO
Copper-Nickel, 28 mm. **Subject:** Portugese Literature **Obv:** Portrait of Fernando António Nogueira de Seabra, and text **Rev:** Stylized portrait of Luis Vaz de Camões and lines

Date	Mintage	F12	VF20	XF40	MS60	MS63
2009	150,000	—	—	—	6.00	7.00

KM# 791a 2-1/2 EURO
12.00 g., 0.925 Silver 0.3546 oz. ASW, 28 mm. **Subject:** Portuguese Literature

Date	Mintage	F12	VF20	XF40	MS60	MS63
2009	14,000	**PF65** 60.00				

KM# 791b 2-1/2 EURO
15.55 g., 0.999 Gold 0.4962 oz. AGW, 28 mm. **Subject:** Portuguese Literature

Date	Mintage	F12	VF20	XF40	MS60	MS63
2009	2,500	**PF65** 950				

KM# 792a 2-1/2 EURO
12.00 g., 0.925 Silver 0.3546 oz. ASW, 28 mm. **Subject:** UNESCO World Heritage Site - Hieronymites Monastery **Obv:** Arched ceiling design, National arms **Rev:** Façade detail

Date	Mintage	F12	VF20	XF40	MS60	MS63
2009	5,000	**PF65** 60.00				

KM# 793 2-1/2 EURO
10.00 g., Copper-Nickel, 28 mm. **Obv:** National arms, rope splice below **Rev:** UNESCO World Heritage Site - Belém

Date	Mintage	F12	VF20	XF40	MS60	MS63
2009	150,000	—	—	—	6.00	7.00

KM# 793a 2-1/2 EURO
12.00 g., 0.925 Silver 0.3546 oz. ASW, 28 mm. **Subject:** UNESCO - World Heritage Site - Belém **Obv:** Naitonal arms, rope splice below **Rev:** Fortress

Date	Mintage	F12	VF20	XF40	MS60	MS63
2009	5,000	**PF65** 60.00				

KM# 797 2-1/2 EURO
10.00 g., Copper-Nickel, 28 mm. **Subject:** FIFA Soccer - South Africa

Date	Mintage	F12	VF20	XF40	MS60	MS63
2010INCM	120,000	—	—	—	6.00	7.00

KM# 797a 2-1/2 EURO
12.00 g., 0.925 Silver 0.3546 oz. ASW, 28 mm. **Subject:** FIFA Soccer - South Africa

Date	Mintage	F12	VF20	XF40	MS60	MS63
2010INCM	12,500	**PF65** 55.00				

KM# 798 2-1/2 EURO
10.00 g., Copper-Nickel, 28 mm. **Subject:** Palace Square, Lisbon

Date	Mintage	F12	VF20	XF40	MS60	MS63
2010INCM	120,000	—	—	—	6.00	7.00

KM# 798a 2-1/2 EURO
12.00 g., 0.925 Silver 0.3546 oz. ASW, 28 mm. **Subject:** Palace Square, Lisbon

Date	Mintage	F12	VF20	XF40	MS60	MS63
2010INCM	15,000	**PF65** 55.00				

KM# 798b 2-1/2 EURO
15.55 g., 0.999 Gold 0.4962 oz. AGW, 28 mm. **Subject:** Palace Square, Lisbon

Date	Mintage	F12	VF20	XF40	MS60	MS63
2010INCM	2,500	**PF65** 950				

KM# 800 2-1/2 EURO
10.00 g., Copper-Nickel, 28 mm. **Subject:** Torres Defence Line, 200th Anniversary

Date	Mintage	F12	VF20	XF40	MS60	MS63
2010INCM	—	—	—	—	6.00	7.00

KM# 800a 2-1/2 EURO
12.00 g., 0.925 Silver 0.3546 oz. ASW, 28 mm. **Subject:** Torres Defence Line, 200th Anniversary

Date	Mintage	F12	VF20	XF40	MS60	MS63
2010INCM	—	**PF65** 55.00				

KM# 801 2-1/2 EURO
10.00 g., Copper-Nickel, 28 mm. **Subject:** UNESCO World Cultural Heritage site - Coa Valley

Date	Mintage	F12	VF20	XF40	MS60	MS63
2010INCM	120,000	—	—	—	6.00	7.00

KM# 801a 2-1/2 EURO
12.00 g., 0.925 Silver 0.3546 oz. ASW, 28 mm. **Subject:** UNESCO World Cultural Heritage Site - Coa Valley

Date	Mintage	F12	VF20	XF40	MS60	MS63
2010INCM	5,000	**PF65** 60.00				

KM# 806 2-1/2 EURO
10.00 g., Copper-Nickel, 28 mm. **Subject:** European explorers **Obv:** National arms, tree branch and Chinese characters **Rev:** Two portraits

Date	Mintage	F12	VF20	XF40	MS60	MS63
2011	100,000	—	—	—	—	7.00

KM# 806a 2-1/2 EURO
12.00 g., 0.925 Silver 0.3546 oz. ASW, 28 mm. **Subject:** European explorers **Obv:** National arms, tree branch and Chinese characters **Rev:** Two portraits

Date	Mintage	F12	VF20	XF40	MS60	MS63
2011	—	**PF65** 55.00				

KM# 806b 2-1/2 EURO
15.55 g., 0.999 Gold 0.4962 oz. AGW, 28 mm. **Subject:** European explorers **Obv:** National arms, tree branch, Chinese characters **Rev:** Two portraits

Date	Mintage	F12	VF20	XF40	MS60	MS63
2011	—	**PF65** 950				

KM# 809 2-1/2 EURO
10.00 g., Copper-Nickel, 28 mm. **Subject:** Army College, 100th Anniversary **Obv:** National arms and sword **Rev:** Sword and cadet cap

Date	Mintage	F12	VF20	XF40	MS60	MS63
2011	100,000	—	—	—	—	7.00

KM# 809a 2-1/2 EURO
12.00 g., 0.925 Silver 0.3546 oz. ASW, 28 mm. **Subject:** Army College, 100th Anniversary **Obv:** National arms and sword **Rev:** Sword and cadet cap

Date	Mintage	F12	VF20	XF40	MS60	MS63
2011	—	**PF65** 55.00				

KM# 810 2-1/2 EURO
10.00 g., Copper-Nickel, 28 mm. **Subject:** Pico Island, Azores. Wine growing landscape **Obv:** National arms and tree **Rev:** Grape leaf and vine fields

Date	Mintage	F12	VF20	XF40	MS60	MS63
2011	100,000	—	—	—	—	7.00

KM# 810a 2-1/2 EURO
12.00 g., 0.925 Silver 0.3546 oz. ASW, 28 mm. **Subject:** Pico Island, Azores, Wine growing landscape **Obv:** National arms and tree **Rev:** Wine leaf, wine fields in background

Date	Mintage	F12	VF20	XF40	MS60	MS63
2011	3,000	PF65 55.00				

KM# 815 2-1/2 EURO
10.00 g., Copper-Nickel, 28 mm. **Subject:** José Malhoa **Obv:** Female model at left, national arms at right **Rev:** Malhoa half-length figure with artist pallet and brushes

Date	Mintage	F12	VF20	XF40	MS60	MS63
2012	100,000	—	—	—	—	6.00

KM# 815a 2-1/2 EURO
12.00 g., 0.925 Silver 0.3546 oz. ASW, 28 mm. **Subject:** José Malhoa **Obv:** Female model seated at left, national arms at right **Rev:** Malhoa half-length figure standing with artist pallet and brushes

Date	Mintage	F12	VF20	XF40	MS60	MS63
2012	10,000	PF65 55.00				

KM# 815b 2-1/2 EURO
15.55 g., 0.999 Gold 0.4962 oz. AGW, 28 mm. **Subject:** José Malhoa **Obv:** Female model seated at left, national arms at right **Rev:** Malhoa half-length figure standing wiht artist pallet and brushes

Date	Mintage	F12	VF20	XF40	MS60	MS63
2012	1,500	PF65 950				

KM# 816 2-1/2 EURO
10.00 g., Copper-Nickel, 28 mm. **Subject:** Portugal's participation in 2012 London Olympics **Obv:** National arms and laurel branch **Rev:** Two judo players, geometric pattern

Date	Mintage	F12	VF20	XF40	MS60	MS63
2012	300,000	—	—	—	—	10.00

KM# 816a 2-1/2 EURO
12.00 g., 0.925 Silver 0.3546 oz. ASW, 28 mm. **Subject:** Portugal's participation in 2012 London Olympics **Obv:** National arms and laurel branch **Rev:** Judo players, geometric pattern

Date	Mintage	F12	VF20	XF40	MS60	MS63
2012	5,000	PF65 55.00				

KM# 816b 2-1/2 EURO
Bi-Metallic, 28 mm. **Subject:** Portugal's participation in 2012 London Olympics **Obv:** National arms and laurel branch **Rev:** Judo players and geometric pattern

Date	Mintage	F12	VF20	XF40	MS60	MS63
2012	2,500	PF65 600				

KM# 819 2-1/2 EURO
12.00 g., Copper-Nickel, 28 mm. **Subject:** Guimarães - UNESCO World Heritage site **Obv:** National arms and city plan **Rev:** Linear architectural representations

Date	Mintage	F12	VF20	XF40	MS60	MS63
2012	100,000	—	—	—	—	25.00

KM# 819a 2-1/2 EURO
12.00 g., 0.925 Silver 0.3546 oz. ASW, 28 mm. **Subject:** Guimarães - UNESCO World Heritage site **Obv:** National arms, linear city plan **Rev:** Linear architectural renderings

Date	Mintage	F12	VF20	XF40	MS60	MS63
2012	3,000	PF65 55.00				

KM# 830 2-1/2 EURO
12.00 g., Silver, 28 mm. **Subject:** 100th Anniversary of Lisbon University

Date	Mintage	F12	VF20	XF40	MS60	MS63
2012 Proof	—	—	—	—	—	—

KM# 829 2-1/2 EURO
12.00 g., Silver, 28 mm. **Subject:** Jose Saramago, nobel winner 1998 **Rev:** Portrait at right

Date	Mintage	F12	VF20	XF40	MS60	MS63
2013 Proof	Est. 7500	—	—	—	—	—

KM# 749 5 EURO
14.00 g., 0.500 Silver 0.2236 oz. ASW, 30 mm. **Subject:** 150th Anniversary - First Portuguese Postage Stamp **Obv:** National arms and value within partial stamp design **Rev:** Partial postal stamp design **Edge:** Reeded

Date	Mintage	F12	VF20	XF40	MS60	MS63
2003INCM	300,000	—	—	—	22.50	30.00

KM# 749a 5 EURO
14.00 g., 0.925 Silver 0.4137 oz. ASW, 30 mm. **Obv:** National arms and value within partial stamp design **Rev:** Partial postal stamp design

Date	Mintage	F12	VF20	XF40	MS60	MS63
2003INCM	20,000	—	—	—	—	30.00
2003INCM	20,000	PF65 55.00				

KM# 749b 5 EURO
17.50 g., 0.9166 Gold 0.5124 oz. AGW, 30 mm. **Obv:** National arms and value within partial stamp design **Rev:** Partial postal stamp design

Date	Mintage	F12	VF20	XF40	MS60	MS63
2003INCM	10,000	PF65 1,000				

KM# 754 5 EURO
14.00 g., 0.500 Silver 0.2236 oz. ASW, 30 mm. **Subject:** Convent of Christ **Obv:** National arms above value flanked by designs **Rev:** Ornate convent window **Edge:** Reeded

Date	Mintage	F12	VF20	XF40	MS60	MS63
2004INCM	300,000	—	—	—	30.00	32.50

KM# 754a 5 EURO
14.00 g., 0.925 Silver 0.4137 oz. ASW, 30 mm. **Subject:** Convent of Christ **Obv:** National arms above value flanked by designs **Rev:** Ornate convent window **Edge:** Reeded

Date	Mintage	F12	VF20	XF40	MS60	MS63
2004INCM	10,000	PF65 60.00				

KM# 755 5 EURO
14.00 g., 0.500 Silver 0.2236 oz. ASW, 30 mm. **Subject:** Historic City of Evora **Obv:** National arms and value on city map silhouette **Rev:** Architectural highlights **Edge:** Reeded

Date	Mintage	F12	VF20	XF40	MS60	MS63
2004INCM	300,000	—	—	—	30.00	32.50

KM# 755a 5 EURO
14.00 g., 0.925 Silver 0.4137 oz. ASW, 30 mm. **Subject:** Historic City of Evora **Obv:** National arms and value on city map silhouette **Rev:** Architectural highlights **Edge:** Reeded

Date	Mintage	F12	VF20	XF40	MS60	MS63
2004INCM	10,000	PF65 60.00				

KM# 762 5 EURO
14.00 g., 0.500 Silver 0.2236 oz. ASW, 30 mm. **Subject:** 800th Anniversary Birth of Pope John XXI **Obv:** National arms at lower right with archways in backgound **Obv. Legend:** REPUBLICA PORTUGUESA **Rev:** 1/2 length figure of Pope facing at right with staff dividing dates, small shield at left **Edge:** Reeded

Date	Mintage	F12	VF20	XF40	MS60	MS63
2005INCM	300,000	—	—	—	30.00	32.50

KM# 762a 5 EURO
14.00 g., 0.925 Silver 0.4137 oz. ASW, 30 mm. **Subject:** 800th Anniversary Birth of Pope John XXI **Obv:** National arms at lower right with archways in backgound **Obv. Legend:** REPUBLICA PORTUGUESA **Rev:** 1/2 length figure of Pope facing at right with staff dividing dates, small shield at left **Edge:** Reeded

Date	Mintage	F12	VF20	XF40	MS60	MS63
2005INCM	15,000	PF65 65.00				

-KM# 762b 5 EURO
17.50 g., 0.9167 Gold 0.5125 oz. AGW, 30 mm. **Subject:** 800th Anniversary Birth of Pope John XXI **Obv:** National arms at lower right, archways in background **Obv. Legend:** REPUBLICA PORTUGUESA **Edge:** Reeded

Date	Mintage	F12	VF20	XF40	MS60	MS63
2005INCM	7,500	PF65 1,000				

KM# 760 5 EURO
14.00 g., 0.500 Silver 0.2236 oz. ASW, 30 mm. **Obv:** National arms within circle **Obv. Legend:** REPUBLICA POTUGUESA **Rev:** Angra do Heroismo - Azores Terceira, emblem above **Rev. Legend:** CENTRO HISTÓRICO DE ANGRA DO HEROISMA **Edge:** Reeded

Date	Mintage	F12	VF20	XF40	MS60	MS63
2005	300,000	—	—	—	30.00	32.50

KM# 760a 5 EURO
14.00 g., 0.925 Silver 0.4137 oz. ASW, 30 mm. **Obv:** National arms within circle **Obv. Legend:** REPUBLICA PORTUGUESA **Rev:** Angra do Heroisma - Azores Terceira, emblem above **Rev. Legend:** CENTRO HISTÓRICO DE ANGRA DO HEROISMA **Edge:** Reeded

Date	Mintage	F12	VF20	XF40	MS60	MS63
2005	15,000	PF65 60.00				

KM# 761 5 EURO
14.00 g., 0.500 Silver 0.2236 oz. ASW, 30 mm. **Obv:** Design divides national arms and value **Obv. Legend:** REPUBLICA PORTUGUESA **Rev:** Batalha monastery and emblem **Rev. Legend:** MONTEIRO DA BATALHA **Edge:** Reeded

Date	Mintage	F12	VF20	XF40	MS60	MS63
2005	300,000	—	—	—	30.00	32.50

KM# 761a 5 EURO
14.00 g., 0.925 Silver 0.4137 oz. ASW, 30 mm. **Obv:** Design divides national arms and value **Obv. Legend:** REPUBLICA PORTUGUESA **Rev:** Batalha monastery and emblem **Rev. Legend:** MONTEIRO DA BATALHA **Edge:** Reeded

Date	Mintage	F12	VF20	XF40	MS60	MS63
2005	15,000	PF65 60.00				

KM# 769 5 EURO
14.00 g., 0.500 Silver 0.2236 oz. ASW, 30 mm. **Subject:** UNESCO - Cultural preservation **Obv:** National arms above value **Obv. Legend:** REPUBLICA PORTUGUESA **Rev:** Outlined view **Rev. Legend:** PAISAGEM CULTURAL DE SINTRA **Edge:** Reeded

Date	Mintage	F12	VF20	XF40	MS60	MS63
2006INCM	82,000	—	—	—	30.00	32.50

KM# 769a 5 EURO
14.00 g., 0.925 Silver 0.4137 oz. ASW, 30 mm. **Subject:** UNESCO - Cultural preservation **Obv:** National arms above value **Obv. Legend:** REPUBLICA PORTUGUESA **Rev:** Outlined view **Rev. Legend:** PAISAGEM CULTURAL DE SINTRA **Edge:** Reeded

Date	Mintage	F12	VF20	XF40	MS60	MS63
2006INCM	6,000	PF65 60.00				

KM# 779 5 EURO
14.00 g., 0.500 Silver 0.2236 oz. ASW **Subject:** Alcobaça Monastery **Obv:** National arms **Obv. Legend:** REPÚBLICA PORTUGUESA **Edge:** Reeded

Date	Mintage	F12	VF20	XF40	MS60	MS63
2006INCM	82,000	—	—	—	25.00	27.50

KM# 779a 5 EURO
14.00 g., 0.925 Silver 0.4137 oz. ASW **Subject:** Alcobaça Monestary **Obv:** National arms **Obv. Legend:** REPÚBLICA PORTUGUESA **Edge:** Reeded

Date	Mintage	F12	VF20	XF40	MS60	MS63
2006INCM	6,000	PF65 60.00				

KM# 782 5 EURO
13.95 g., 0.500 Silver 0.2228 oz. ASW, 30 mm. **Series:** UNESCO - World Heritage **Subject:** National Forest Reserve in Madeira Nature Park **Obv:** National arms **Obv. Legend:** REPÚBLICA PORTUGUESA **Rev:** Foliage with small UNESCO World Heritage logo at lower right **Rev. Legend:** FLORESTA LAURISSILVA DA MADEIRA **Edge:** Reeded

Date	Mintage	F12	VF20	XF40	MS60	MS63
2007INCM	75,000	—	—	—	25.00	27.50

KM# 782a 5 EURO
14.00 g., 0.925 Silver 0.4137 oz. ASW, 30 mm. **Series:** UNESCO - World Heritage **Subject:** National Forest Reserve in Madeira Nature Park **Obv:** National arms **Obv. Legend:** REPÚBLICA PORTUGUESA **Rev:** Foliage with small UNESCO World Heritage logo at lower right **Rev. Legend:** FLORESTA LAURISSILVA DA MADEIRA **Edge:** Reeded

Date	Mintage	F12	VF20	XF40	MS60	MS63
2007INCM	6,000	PF65 65.00				

KM# 770 5 EURO
14.00 g., 0.500 Silver 0.2236 oz. ASW, 30 mm. **Subject:** World Scouting Centennial **Obv:** Portuguese Arms, World Scouting emblem **Obv. Legend:** REPUBLICA PORTUGUESA 1907-2007 CENTENARIO DO ESCUTISMO MUNDIAL **Rev:** Linear portrait of Lord Robert Baden-Powell **Rev. Legend:** UM MUNDO UMA PROMESA **Edge:** Reeded

Date	Mintage	F12	VF20	XF40	MS60	MS63
ND(2007)	70,000	—	—	—	25.00	27.50

KM# 770a 5 EURO
14.00 g., 0.925 Silver 0.4137 oz. ASW, 30 mm. **Subject:** World Scouting Centennial **Obv:** National arms, World Scouting emblem **Obv. Legend:** REPUBLICA PORTUGUESA 1907 - 2007 CENTENARIO DO ESCUTISMO MUNDIAL **Rev:** Linear portrait of Lord Robert Baden-Powell **Rev. Legend:** UM MUNDO UMA PROMESA **Edge:** Reeded

Date	Mintage	F12	VF20	XF40	MS60	MS63
ND-2007	10,000	PF65 60.00				

KM# 781 5 EURO
14.04 g., 0.500 Silver 0.2242 oz. ASW, 30 mm. **Subject:** Equal Opportunities **Obv:** Small national arms above moon shaped arc **Obv. Legend:** República Portuguesa **Rev:** Small 3 persons logo above 12 stars along rim **Rev. Legend:** Ano Europeu da Igualdade de Oportunidades para Todos **Edge:** Reeded

Date	Mintage	F12	VF20	XF40	MS60	MS63
2007INCM	70,000	—	—	—	25.00	27.50

KM# 781a 5 EURO
14.00 g., 0.925 Silver 0.4137 oz. ASW, 30 mm. **Subject:** Equal Opportunities **Obv:** Small national arms above moon shaped arc **Obv. Legend:** República Portuguesa **Rev:** Small 3 persons logo above 12 stars along rim **Rev. Legend:** Ano Europeu da Igualdade de Oportunidades para Todos **Edge:** Reeded

Date	Mintage	F12	VF20	XF40	MS60	MS63
2007INCM	7,500	PF65 65.00				

KM# 802 5 EURO
14.00 g., Copper-Nickel, 30 mm. **Subject:** Numismatic Treasurers - Justo of John II

Date	Mintage	F12	VF20	XF40	MS60	MS63
2010INCM	150,000	—	—	—	12.00	15.00

KM# 802a 5 EURO
15.55 g., 0.999 Gold 0.4962 oz. AGW, 30 mm. **Subject:** Numismatic Treasurers - Justo of John II

Date	Mintage	F12	VF20	XF40	MS60	MS63
2010INCM	2,500	PF65 950				

KM# 817 5 EURO
14.00 g., Copper-Nickel, 30 mm. **Subject:** Numismatic Treasurers - João V **Obv:** Bust right **Rev:** Crowned arms

Date	Mintage	F12	VF20	XF40	MS60	MS63
2012L	150,000	—	—	—	—	25.00

KM# 817a 5 EURO
15.55 g., 0.999 Gold 0.4962 oz. AGW, 30 mm. **Subject:** Numismatic Treasurers - João V **Obv:** Bust right **Rev:** Crowned shield

Date	Mintage	F12	VF20	XF40	MS60	MS63
2012		PF65 950				

KM# 811 7.5 EURO
18.50 g., Copper-Nickel, 33 mm. **Subject:** Numismatic Treasurers - Manuel I **Obv:** Short cross **Rev:** National Arms in center of dourble ring legend

Date	Mintage	F12	VF20	XF40	MS60	MS63
2011	100,000	PF63 35.00				

KM# 811a 7.5 EURO
23.33 g., 0.999 Gold 0.7445 oz. AGW, 33 mm. **Subject:** Numismatic Treasurers - Manuel I **Obv:** Short Cross **Rev:** Crowned national shield within double ring legend

Date	Mintage	F12	VF20	XF40	MS60	MS63
2011	—	PF65 1,425				

KM# 750 8 EURO
21.10 g., 0.500 Silver 0.337 oz. ASW, 36 mm. **Obv:** National arms, value and flag-covered globe **Rev:** Flag-covered globe and "Euro 2004" soccer games logo **Edge:** Reeded

Date	Mintage	F12	VF20	XF40	MS60	MS63
2003INCM	1,500,000	—	—	—	35.00	37.50

KM# 750a 8 EURO
31.10 g., 0.925 Silver 0.9189 oz. ASW, 36 mm. **Obv:** National arms, value and flag-covered globe **Rev:** Flag-covered globe and "Euro 2004" soccer games logo

Date	Mintage	F12	VF20	XF40	MS60	MS63
2003INCM Prooflike	30,000	—	—	—	—	100
2003INCM	15,000	PF65 165				

KM# 750b 8 EURO
31.10 g., 0.9166 Gold 0.9106 oz. AGW, 36 mm. **Obv:** National arms, value and flag-covered globe **Rev:** Flag-covered globe and "Euro 2004" soccer games logo

Date	Mintage	F12	VF20	XF40	MS60	MS63
2003INCM	10,000	PF65 1,850				

KM# 751 8 EURO
21.10 g., 0.500 Silver 0.337 oz. ASW, 36 mm. **Obv:** National arms and value below many bubbles **Rev:** Euro 2004" soccer games logo below many hearts **Edge:** Reeded

Date	Mintage	F12	VF20	XF40	MS60	MS63
2003INCM	1,500,000	—	—	—	35.00	37.50

KM# 751a 8 EURO
31.10 g., 0.925 Silver 0.9189 oz. ASW, 36 mm. **Obv:** National arms and value below many bubbles **Rev:** Euro 2004" soccer games logo below many hearts

Date	Mintage	F12	VF20	XF40	MS60	MS63
2003INCM Prooflike	—	—	—	—	—	100
2003INCM	15,000	PF65 165				

KM# 751b 8 EURO
31.10 g., 0.9166 Gold 0.9106 oz. AGW, 36 mm. **Obv:** National arms and value below many bubbles **Rev:** Euro 2004" soccer games logo below many hearts

Date	Mintage	F12	VF20	XF40	MS60	MS63
2003INCM	10,000	PF65 1,850				

KM# 752 8 EURO
21.10 g., 0.500 Silver 0.337 oz. ASW, 36 mm. **Obv:** National arms and value **Rev:** Euro 2004" soccer games logo in center with partial text background **Edge:** Reeded

Date	Mintage	F12	VF20	XF40	MS60	MS63
2003INCM	1,500,000	—	—	—	35.00	37.50

KM# 752a 8 EURO
31.10 g., 0.925 Silver 0.9189 oz. ASW, 36 mm. **Obv:** National arms and value **Rev:** Euro 2004" soccer games logo in center with partial text background

Date	Mintage	F12	VF20	XF40	MS60	MS63
2003INCM Prooflike	—	—	—	—	—	100
2003INCM	15,000	PF65 165				

KM# 752b 8 EURO
31.10 g., 0.9166 Gold 0.9106 oz. AGW, 36 mm. **Obv:** National arms and value **Rev:** Euro 2004" soccer games logo in center with partial text background

Date	Mintage	F12	VF20	XF40	MS60	MS63
2003INCM	10,000	PF65 1,850				

KM# 753 8 EURO
21.22 g., 0.500 Silver 0.3389 oz. ASW, 36 mm. **Subject:** Expansion of the European Union **Obv:** Radiant national arms and value **Rev:** European map **Edge:** Reeded

Date	Mintage	F12	VF20	XF40	MS60	MS63
2004INCM	300,000	—	—	—	25.00	27.50

KM# 753a 8 EURO
31.10 g., 0.925 Silver 0.9189 oz. ASW, 36 mm. **Subject:** Expansion of the European Union **Obv:** Radiant national arms and value **Rev:** European map **Edge:** Reeded

Date	Mintage	F12	VF20	XF40	MS60	MS63
2004INCM	35,000	PF63 50.00	PF65 60.00			

KM# 756 8 EURO
21.00 g., 0.500 Silver 0.3354 oz. ASW, 36 mm. **Subject:** Euro 2004 Soccer **Obv:** National arms **Rev:** Stylized goal keeper **Edge:** Reeded

Date	Mintage	F12	VF20	XF40	MS60	MS63
2004INCM	1,500,000	—	—	—	25.00	27.50

KM# 756a 8 EURO
31.10 g., 0.925 Silver 0.9189 oz. ASW, 36 mm. **Subject:** Euro 2004 Soccer **Obv:** National arms **Rev:** Stylized goal keeper **Edge:** Reeded

Date	Mintage	F12	VF20	XF40	MS60	MS63
2004INCM	30,000	—	—	—	—	80.00

Date	Mintage	F12	VF20	XF40	MS60	MS63
2004INCM	15,000	PF65 150				

KM# 756b 8 EURO
31.10 g., 0.9166 Gold 0.9106 oz. AGW, 36 mm. **Subject:** Euro 2004 Soccer **Obv:** National arms **Rev:** Stylized goal keeper **Edge:** Reeded

Date	Mintage	F12	VF20	XF40	MS60	MS63
2004INCM	10,000	PF65 1,850				

KM# 757 8 EURO
21.00 g., 0.925 Silver 0.6205 oz. ASW, 36 mm. **Subject:** Euro 2004 Soccer **Obv:** National arms **Rev:** Face of player making shot **Edge:** Reeded

Date	Mintage	F12	VF20	XF40	MS60	MS63
2004INCM	1,500,000	—	—	—	25.00	27.50

KM# 757a 8 EURO
31.10 g., 0.925 Silver 0.9189 oz. ASW, 36 mm. **Subject:** Euro 2004 Soccer **Obv:** National arms **Rev:** Face of player making a shot **Edge:** Reeded

Date	Mintage	F12	VF20	XF40	MS60	MS63
2004INCM	15,000	PF65 150				
2004INCM	30,000	—	—	—	—	80.00

KM# 757b 8 EURO
31.10 g., 0.9166 Gold 0.9106 oz. AGW, 36 mm. **Subject:** Euro 2004 Soccer **Obv:** National arms **Rev:** Face of player making a shot **Edge:** Reeded

Date	Mintage	F12	VF20	XF40	MS60	MS63
2004INCM	10,000	PF65 1,850				

KM# 758 8 EURO
21.00 g., 0.500 Silver 0.3354 oz. ASW, 36 mm. **Subject:** Euro 2004 Soccer **Obv:** National arms **Rev:** Symbolic explosion of a goal **Edge:** Reeded

Date	Mintage	F12	VF20	XF40	MS60	MS63
2004INCM	1,500,000	—	—	—	25.00	27.50

KM# 758a 8 EURO
31.10 g., 0.925 Silver 0.9189 oz. ASW, 36 mm. **Subject:** Euro 2004 Soccer **Obv:** National arms **Rev:** Symbolic explosion of a goal **Edge:** Reeded

Date	Mintage	F12	VF20	XF40	MS60	MS63
2004INCM	30,000	—	—	—	—	80.00
2004INCM	15,000	PF65 150				

KM# 758b 8 EURO
31.10 g., 0.9166 Gold 0.9106 oz. AGW, 36 mm. **Subject:** Euro 2004 Soccer **Obv:** National arms **Rev:** Symbolic explosion of a goal **Edge:** Reeded

Date	Mintage	F12	VF20	XF40	MS60	MS63
2004INCM	10,000	PF65 1,850				

KM# 773 8 EURO
21.00 g., 0.500 Silver 0.3354 oz. ASW, 36 mm. **Subject:** 60th Anniversary End of WW II **Obv:** Quill pens horizontal at left center, national arms at lower righr **Obv. Inscription:** REPÚBLICA PORTUGUESA **Rev:** Four quill pens upright, outlined map of Europe in background **Rev. Inscription:** FIM DA II GUERRA MUNDIAL **Edge:** Reeded

Date	Mintage	F12	VF20	XF40	MS60	MS63
2005INCM	300,000	—	—	—	30.00	32.50

KM# 773a 8 EURO
31.10 g., 0.925 Silver 0.9189 oz. ASW, 36 mm. **Subject:** 60th Anniversary End of WW II **Obv:** Quill pens horizontal at left center, national arms at lower right **Obv. Inscription:** REPÚBLICA PORTUGUESA **Rev:** Four quill pens upright, outlined map of Europe in background **Rev. Inscription:** FIM DA II GUERRA MUNDIAL **Edge:** Reeded

Date	Mintage	F12	VF20	XF40	MS60	MS63
2005INCM	35,000	PF63 60.00	PF65 70.00			

KM# 776 8 EURO
20.80 g., 0.500 Silver 0.3322 oz. ASW, 36 mm. **Series:** Famous Europeans **Subject:** Prince Henry the Navigator **Obv:** Small national arms and shield **Obv. Legend:** REPÚBLICA PORTUGUESA **Rev:** Tiny bust 3/4 right **Edge:** Reeded

Date	Mintage	F12	VF20	XF40	MS60	MS63
2006INCM	100,000	—	—	—	30.00	32.50

KM# 776a 8 EURO
31.10 g., 0.925 Silver 0.9189 oz. ASW, 36 mm. **Series:** Famous Europeans **Subject:** Prince Henry the Navigator **Obv:** Small national arms and shield **Obv. Legend:** REPÚBLICA PORTUGUESA **Rev:** Tiny bust 3/4 right **Edge:** Reeded

Date	Mintage	F12	VF20	XF40	MS60	MS63
2006INCM	35,000	PF63 55.00	PF65 65.00			

KM# 778 8 EURO
21.00 g., 0.500 Silver 0.3354 oz. ASW, 36 mm. **Subject:** 150th Anniversary Railroad Lisbon - Carregado **Obv:** National arms on wavy flag **Obv. Legend:** REPÚBLICA PORTUGUESA **Rev. Legend:** 150 ANOS DA PRIMEIRA LINHA FERREA LISBOA CARREGADO **Edge:** Reeded

Date	Mintage	F12	VF20	XF40	MS60	MS63
2006INCM	100,000	—	—	—	32.50	35.00

KM# 778a 8 EURO
31.10 g., 0.925 Silver 0.9189 oz. ASW, 36 mm. **Subject:** 150th Anniversary Railroad Lisbon - Carregado **Obv:** National srms on wavy flag **Obv. Legend:** REPÚBLICA PORTUGUESA **Rev. Legend:** 150 ANOSDA PRIMEIRA LINHA FERREA LISBOA CARREGADO **Edge:** Reeded

Date	Mintage	F12	VF20	XF40	MS60	MS63
2006INCM	35,000	PF63 65.00	PF65 75.00			

KM# 822 8 EURO
21.00 g., 0.500 Silver 0.3354 oz. ASW, 36 mm. **Subject:** Early flying inventions - the Passarola of Bartolomeu de Gusmão **Obv:** Large value and small national arms **Rev:** Schematic of flying machine

Date	Mintage	F12	VF20	XF40	MS60	MS63
2007	70,000	—	—	—	20.00	25.00

KM# 822a 8 EURO
31.11 g., 0.925 Silver 0.9191 oz. ASW, 36 mm. **Subject:** Early flying inventions - the Passarola of Bartolomeu de Gusmão **Obv:** Large value, small national arms **Rev:** Schematic of early flying machine

Date	Mintage	F12	VF20	XF40	MS60	MS63
2007	25,000	PF65 65.00				

KM# 748 10 EURO
27.00 g., 0.500 Silver 0.4312 oz. ASW, 40 mm. **Subject:** Nautica **Obv:** National arms within circle of assorted shields **Rev:** Sailing ship and sextant **Edge:** Reeded

Date	Mintage	F12	VF20	XF40	MS60	MS63
2003INCM	350,000	—	—	—	22.50	25.00

KM# 748a 10 EURO
27.00 g., 0.925 Silver 0.7978 oz. ASW, 40 mm. **Obv:** National arms within circle of assorted shields **Rev:** Sailing ship and sextant **Edge:** Reeded

Date	Mintage	F12	VF20	XF40	MS60	MS63
2003INCM	10,000	PF65 70.00				

KM# 759 10 EURO
27.00 g., 0.500 Silver 0.4312 oz. ASW, 40 mm. **Subject:** Olympics **Obv:** National arms above stylized value **Rev:** Stylized sail above Olympic rings **Edge:** Reeded

Date	Mintage	F12	VF20	XF40	MS60	MS63
2004INCM	350,000	—	—	—	25.00	27.50

KM# 759a 10 EURO
27.00 g., 0.925 Silver 0.7978 oz. ASW, 40 mm. **Subject:** Olympics **Obv:** National arms above stylized value **Rev:** Stylized sail above Olympic rings **Edge:** Reeded

Date	Mintage	F12	VF20	XF40	MS60	MS63
2004INCM	15,000	PF65 65.00				

KM# 768 10 EURO
27.00 g., 0.500 Silver 0.4312 oz. ASW, 40 mm. **Subject:** Arquitectura e Monumentos - Sé do Porto **Obv:** National arms above value in circle of multi-national coats of arms **Rev:** Church facade **Edge:** Reeded

Date	Mintage	F12	VF20	XF40	MS60	MS63
2005INCM	—	—	—	—	—	30.00
2005INCM	300,000	PF63 75.00				

KM# 820 10 EURO
27.00 g., 0.500 Silver 0.4312 oz. ASW, 40 mm. **Subject:** Iberoamerican series - Architecture **Rev:** Façade of the Cathedral Sé de Porto

Date	Mintage	F12	VF20	XF40	MS60	MS63
2005	30,000	—	—	—	30.00	35.00

KM# 820a 10 EURO
27.00 g., 0.925 Silver 0.7978 oz. ASW, 40 mm. **Subject:** Iberoamerican Series - Architecture **Rev:** Façade of Cathedral of Sé do Porto

Date	Mintage	F12	VF20	XF40	MS60	MS63
2005	12,000	PF65 115				

KM# 774 10 EURO
27.00 g., 0.500 Silver 0.4312 oz. ASW, 40 mm. **Subject:** XVIII World Championship Football Games - Germany 2006 **Obv:** National arms above stadium **Obv. Legend:** REPÚBLICA PORTUGUESA **Rev:** Circular legend above sticks representing stadium fans **Rev. Legend:** CAMPEONATO DO MUNDO DE FUTEBOL FIFA ALEMANHA 2006 **Edge:** Reeded

Date	Mintage	F12	VF20	XF40	MS60	MS63
2006INCM	100,000	—	—	—	37.50	40.00

KM# 774a 10 EURO
27.00 g., 0.925 Silver 0.7978 oz. ASW, 40 mm. **Subject:** XVIII World Championship Football Games - Germany 2006 **Obv:** National arms above stadium **Obv. Inscription:** REPÚBLICA PORTUGUESA **Rev:** Circular legend above sticks representing stadium fans **Edge:** Reeded

Date	Mintage	F12	VF20	XF40	MS60	MS63
2006INCM	25,000	PF63 75.00	PF65 85.00			

KM# 775 10 EURO
27.00 g., 0.500 Silver 0.4312 oz. ASW, 40 mm. **Subject:** 20th Anniversary of Spain and Portugal's membership in the European Union **Obv:** National arms **Obv. Legend:** REPÚBLICA PORTUGUESA **Rev:** Viaduct, outlined map of Europe above **Rev. Legend:** ADESÃO AS COMUNIDADES EUROPIAS **Edge:** Reeded

Date	Mintage	F12	VF20	XF40	MS60	MS63
2006INCM	100,000	—	—	—	27.50	30.00

KM# 775a 10 EURO
27.00 g., 0.925 Silver 0.7978 oz. ASW, 40 mm. **Subject:** 20th Anniversary of Spain and Portugal's membership in European Union **Obv:** National arms **Obv. Legend:** REPÚBLICA PORTUGUESA **Rev:** Viaduct, outlined map of Europe above **Rev. Legend:** ADESÃO AS COMUNIDADES EUROPIAS **Edge:** Reeded

Date	Mintage	F12	VF20	XF40	MS60	MS63
2006INCM	25,000	PF63 60.00	PF65 70.00			

KM# 821 10 EURO
27.00 g., 0.500 Silver 0.4312 oz. ASW, 40 mm. **Subject:** Iberoamerican Series - Olympics **Rev:** Warrior running, two modern runners

Date	Mintage	F12	VF20	XF40	MS60	MS63
2007	100,000	—	—	—	25.00	30.00

KM# 821a 10 EURO
27.00 g., 0.925 Silver 0.7978 oz. ASW, 40 mm. **Subject:** Iberoamerican Series - Olympics **Rev:** Ancient warrior running, two modern runners

Date	Mintage	F12	VF20	XF40	MS60	MS63
2007	12,000	PF65 115				

KM# 823 10 EURO
27.00 g., 0.500 Silver 0.4312 oz. ASW, 40 mm. **Subject:** Sailing World Cup - Cascais **Obv:** National arms and stylized sails and waves **Rev:** Stylized sails and waves

Date	Mintage	F12	VF20	XF40	MS60	MS63
2007	70,000	—	—	—	25.00	30.00

KM# 823a 10 EURO
27.00 g., 0.925 Silver 0.7978 oz. ASW, 40 mm. **Subject:** World Sailing Championships - Cascais **Obv:** National arms and stylized sails and waves **Rev:** Stylized sails and waves

Date	Mintage	F12	VF20	XF40	MS60	MS63
2007	7,500	PF65 75.00				

KM# 803 10 EURO
27.00 g., 0.925 Silver 0.7978 oz. ASW, 40 mm. **Subject:** The Escudo

Date	Mintage	F12	VF20	XF40	MS60	MS63
2010INCM	100,000	—	—	—	32.50	35.00

KM# 803a 10 EURO
27.00 g., 0.500 Silver 0.4312 oz. ASW, 40 mm. **Subject:** The Escudo

Date	Mintage	F12	VF20	XF40	MS60	MS63
2010INCM	12,000	PF65 85.00				

KM# 808 10 EURO
27.00 g., Copper-Nickel, 40 mm. **Subject:** Spain and Portugal's accession to the European Union, 25th Anniversary

Date	Mintage	F12	VF20	XF40	MS60	MS63
2011	100,000	—	—	—	—	7.00

KM# 808a 10 EURO
27.00 g., 0.925 Silver 0.7978 oz. ASW, 40 mm. **Subject:** Spain and Portugal's accession to the European Union, 25th Anniversary

Date	Mintage	F12	VF20	XF40	MS60	MS63
2011	6,000	PF65 55.00				

KM# 818 10 EURO
27.00 g., Copper-Nickel, 40 mm. **Subject:** Ibero-American series, 20th Anniversary **Obv:** National arms in center of other countries arms **Rev:** Stylized sails

Date	Mintage	F12	VF20	XF40	MS60	MS63
2012	100,000	—	—	—	—	25.00

KM# 818a 10 EURO
27.00 g., 0.925 Silver 0.7978 oz. ASW, 40 mm. **Subject:** Ibero-American series, 20th Anniversary **Obv:** National arms at center of other national arms **Rev:** Stylized sails

Date	Mintage	F12	VF20	XF40	MS60	MS63
2012	10,000	PF65 55.00				

MINT SETS

KM#	Date	Mintage	Identification	Issue Price	Mkt Val
MS32	2002 (8)	50,000	KM#740-747	—	50.00
MS33	2003 (8)	50,000	KM#740-747	—	50.00
MS34	2004 (8)	50,000	KM#740-747	—	45.00
MS35	2005 (8)	30,000	KM#740-747	—	45.00
MS36	2006 (8)	12,500	KM#740-747	—	45.00

PROOF SETS

KM#	Date	Mintage	Identification	Issue Price	Mkt Val
PS45	2002 (8)	15,000	KM#740-747	—	100
PS46	2003 (8)	15,000	kM#740-747	—	100
PS47	2004 (8)	15,000	KM#740-747	—	100
PS48	2005 (8)	10,000	KM#740-747	—	100
PS49	2006 (8)	3,000	KM#740-747	—	100
PS50	2007 (8)	2,500	KM#740-747	—	300
PS51	2008 (8)	3,500	KM#740-742, 763-767	—	150
PS52	2009 (8)	4,000	KM#740-742, 763-767	—	150
PS53	2010 (8)	4,500	KM#740-742, 763-767	—	100
PS54	2011 (8)	3,500	KM#740-742, 763-767	—	100

QATAR

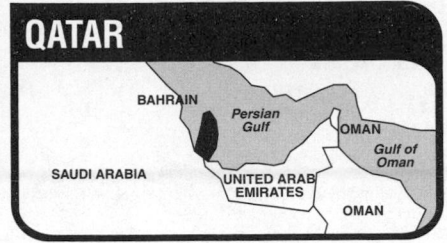

The State of Qatar, an emirate in the Persian Gulf between Bahrain and Trucial Oman, has an area of 4,247 sq. mi. (11,000 sq. km.) and a population of *469,000. Capital: Doha. Oil is the chief industry and export.

TITLES

دولة قطر

Daulat Qatar

RULER

Al-Thani Dynasty

Hamad bin Khalifah, 1995-

MONETARY SYSTEM

100 Dirhem = 1 Riyal

STATE

STANDARD COINAGE

KM# 69 DIRHAM
Copper Plated Silver, 15 mm. **Ruler:** Hamad bin Khalifa **Obv:** National Arms **Rev:** Value

Date	Mintage	F12	VF20	XF40	MS60	MS63
AH1429-2008	—	—	—	—	6.00	8.00

KM# 12 5 DIRHAMS
3.75 g., Bronze, 21.9 mm. **Ruler:** Hamad bin Khalifa **Obv:** National arms **Rev:** Value **Edge:** Plain

Date	Mintage	F12	VF20	XF40	MS60	MS63
AH1427-2006	—	—	—	0.35	0.90	1.25

KM# 13 10 DIRHAMS
7.50 g., Bronze, 27 mm. **Ruler:** Hamad bin Khalifa **Obv:** National arms **Rev:** Value **Edge:** Plain

Date	Mintage	F12	VF20	XF40	MS60	MS63
AH1427-2006	—	—	—	0.60	1.50	2.00

KM# 8 25 DIRHAMS
3.50 g., Copper-Nickel, 20 mm. **Ruler:** Hamad bin Khalifa **Obv:** National arms **Rev:** Value **Rev. Legend:** STATE OF QATAR **Edge:** Reeded

Date	Mintage	F12	VF20	XF40	MS60	MS63
AH1424-2003	—	—	0.30	0.65	1.50	2.50

KM# 14 25 DIRHAMS
3.50 g., Copper-Nickel, 20 mm. **Ruler:** Hamad bin Khalifa **Obv:** National arms **Rev:** Value **Edge:** Reeded

Date	Mintage	F12	VF20	XF40	MS60	MS63
AH1427-2006	—	—	—	0.75	1.85	2.50
AH1429-2008	—	—	—	0.75	1.85	2.50
AH1433-2012	—	—	—	0.75	1.85	2.50

KM# 14a 25 DIRHAMS
Nickel Plated Steel, 20 mm. **Ruler:** Hamad bin Khalifa **Obv:** National Arms **Rev:** Value

Date	Mintage	F12	VF20	XF40	MS60	MS63
AH1429-2008	—	—	—	—	1.50	3.00

KM# 9 50 DIRHAMS
6.50 g., Copper-Nickel, 25 mm. **Ruler:** Hamad bin Khalifa **Obv:** National arms **Rev:** Value **Edge:** Reeded

Date	Mintage	F12	VF20	XF40	MS60	MS63
AH1424-2003	—	—	—	—	2.00	3.00

KM# 15 50 DIRHAMS
6.50 g., Copper-Nickel, 25 mm. **Ruler:** Hamad bin Khalifa **Obv:** National arms **Rev:** Value **Edge:** Reeded

Date	Mintage	F12	VF20	XF40	MS60	MS63
AH1427-2006	—	—	—	0.80	2.00	2.75
AH1429-2008	—	—	—	0.80	2.00	2.75
AH1433-2012	—	—	—	0.80	2.00	2.75

KM# 15a 50 DIRHAMS
6.50 g., Nickel Plated Steel, 25 mm. **Ruler:** Hamad bin Khalifa **Obv:** National Arms **Rev:** Value

Date	Mintage	F12	VF20	XF40	MS60	MS63
AH1429-2008	—	—	—	—	2.25	4.50

KM# 16 RIYAL
Aluminum-Bronze **Ruler:** Hamad bin Khalifa **Subject:** 15th Asian Games **Obv:** Arms above value **Rev:** Multicolor Fox on Bicycle, cartoon character

Date	Mintage	F12	VF20	XF40	MS60	MS63
2006	—	—	—	—	—	25.00

KM# 34 RIYAL
Aluminum-Bronze, 38.74 mm. **Ruler:** Hamad bin Khalifa **Subject:** 15th Asian Games **Obv:** Arms **Rev:** Multicolor mascot with flag

Date	Mintage	F12	VF20	XF40	MS60	MS63
2006	25,000	—	—	—	—	25.00

KM# 35 RIYAL
Aluminum-Bronze, 38.74 mm. **Ruler:** Hamad bin Khalifa **Subject:** 15th Asian Games **Obv:** Arms **Rev:** Multicolor mascot kicking soccer ball

Date	Mintage	F12	VF20	XF40	MS60	MS63
2006	25,000	—	—	—	—	25.00

KM# 36 RIYAL
Aluminum-Bronze, 38.74 mm. **Ruler:** Hamad bin Khalifa **Subject:** 15th Asian Games **Obv:** Arms **Rev:** Three multicolor torches

Date	Mintage	F12	VF20	XF40	MS60	MS63
2006	25,000	—	—	—	—	25.00

KM# 37 RIYAL
Aluminum-Bronze, 38.74 mm. **Ruler:** Hamad bin Khalifa **Subject:** 15th Asian Games **Obv:** Arms **Rev:** Two figures with linked arms

Date	Mintage	F12	VF20	XF40	MS60	MS63
2006	25,000	—	—	—	—	25.00

KM# 38 RIYAL
Aluminum-Bronze, 38.74 mm. **Ruler:** Hamad bin Khalifa **Subject:** 15th Asian Games **Obv:** Arms **Rev:** Figure with outstretched arms

Date	Mintage	F12	VF20	XF40	MS60	MS63
2006	25,000	—	—	—	—	25.00

KM# 25 10 RIYALS
31.10 g., 0.999 Silver 0.9926 oz. ASW, 40.5 mm. **Ruler:** Hamad bin Khalifa **Subject:** 15th Asian Games **Obv:** Arms **Rev:** Runner trailing green color

Date	Mintage	F12	VF20	XF40	MS60	MS63
2006	25,000	PF63 110				

KM# 26 10 RIYALS
31.10 g., 0.999 Silver 0.9926 oz. ASW, 40.5 mm. **Ruler:** Hamad bin Khalifa **Subject:** 15th Asian Games **Obv:** Arms **Rev:** Cyclist trailing red color

Date	Mintage	F12	VF20	XF40	MS60	MS63
2006	25,000	PF63 110				

KM# 27 10 RIYALS
31.10 g., 0.999 Silver 0.9926 oz. ASW, 40.5 mm. **Ruler:** Hamad bin Khalifa **Subject:** 15th Asian Games **Obv:** Arms **Rev:** Soccer player legs on green color

Date	Mintage	F12	VF20	XF40	MS60	MS63
2006	25,000	PF63 110				

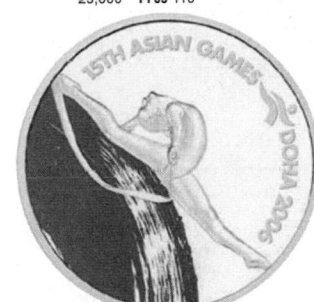

KM# 28 10 RIYALS
31.10 g., 0.999 Silver 0.9926 oz. ASW, 40.5 mm. **Ruler:** Hamad bin Khalifa **Subject:** 15th Asian Games **Obv:** Arms **Rev:** Ribbon dancer trailing red color

Date	Mintage	F12	VF20	XF40	MS60	MS63
2006	25,000	PF63 110				

KM# 29 10 RIYALS
31.10 g., 0.999 Silver 0.9926 oz. ASW, 40.5 mm. **Ruler:** Hamad bin Khalifa **Subject:** 15th Asian Games **Obv:** Arms **Rev:** Karate contestants and dark yellow color

Date	Mintage	F12	VF20	XF40	MS60	MS63
2006	25,000	PF63 110				

KM# 30 10 RIYALS
31.10 g., 0.999 Silver 0.9926 oz. ASW, 40.5 mm. **Ruler:** Hamad bin Khalifa **Subject:** 15th Asian Games **Obv:** Arms **Rev:** Swimmer in aqua colored water

Date	Mintage	F12	VF20	XF40	MS60	MS63
2006	25,000	PF63 110				

KM# 31 10 RIYALS
31.10 g., 0.999 Silver 0.9926 oz. ASW, 40.5 mm. **Ruler:** Hamad bin Khalifa **Subject:** 15th Asian Games **Obv:** Arms **Rev:** Table tennis player and orange-brownish color

Date	Mintage	F12	VF20	XF40	MS60	MS63
2006	25,000	PF63 110				

KM# 32 10 RIYALS
31.10 g., 0.999 Silver 0.9926 oz. ASW, 40.5 mm. **Ruler:** Hamad bin Khalifa **Subject:** 15th Asian Games **Obv:** Arms **Rev:** Tennis player and aqua color

Date	Mintage	F12	VF20	XF40	MS60	MS63
2006	25,000	PF63 110				

KM# 33 10 RIYALS
31.10 g., 0.999 Silver 0.9926 oz. ASW, 40.5 mm. **Ruler:** Hamad bin Khalifa **Subject:** 15th Asian Games **Obv:** Arms **Rev:** Volleyball player trailing purple color

Date	Mintage	F12	VF20	XF40	MS60	MS63
2006	25,000	PF63 110				

KM# 40 100 RIYALS
24.00 g., 0.925 Silver 0.7092 oz. ASW, 37 mm. **Ruler:** Hamad bin Khalifa **Subject:** Yousif al Sharif **Obv:** Wing desing **Rev:** Male bust

Date	Mintage	F12	VF20	XF40	MS60	MS63
2002 Proof	—	—	—	—	—	—

KM# 42 100 RIYALS
100.00 g., 0.999 Silver 3.1912 oz. ASW, 80 mm. **Ruler:** Hamad bin Khalifa **Subject:** Doha Cultural festival

Date	Mintage	F12	VF20	XF40	MS60	MS63
2003 Proof	—	—	—	—	—	—

KM# 17 100 RIYALS
Gold AGW **Ruler:** Hamad bin Khalifa **Subject:** 15th Asian Games **Obv:** Arms above value **Rev:** Games mascot Fox on Bicycle cartoon character

Date	Mintage	F12	VF20	XF40	MS60	MS63
2006	Est. 10000	PF63 550				

KM# 18 100 RIYALS
17.00 g., 0.920 Gold 0.4996 oz. AGW, 31 mm. **Ruler:** Hamad bin Khalifa **Obv:** Arms **Rev:** Central Bank building **Edge:** Reeded

Date	Mintage	F12	VF20	XF40	MS60	MS63
2006	300	PF65 1,500				

KM# 19 100 RIYALS
10.00 g., 0.9999 Gold 0.3194 oz. AGW, 24.5 mm. **Ruler:** Hamad bin Khalifa **Subject:** 15th Asian Games **Obv:** Arms **Rev:** Khalifa Stadium **Edge:** Reeded

Date	Mintage	F12	VF20	XF40	MS60	MS63
2006	—	PF63 650				

KM# 20 100 RIYALS
10.00 g., 0.9999 Gold 0.3194 oz. AGW, 24.5 mm. **Ruler:** Hamad bin Khalifa **Subject:** 15th Asian Games **Obv:** Arms **Rev:** Two oryxes head-butting **Edge:** Reeded

Date	Mintage	F12	VF20	XF40	MS60	MS63
2006	—	PF63 650				

KM# 21 100 RIYALS
10.00 g., 0.9999 Gold 0.3194 oz. AGW, 24.5 mm. **Ruler:** Hamad bin Khalifa **Subject:** 15th Asian Games **Obv:** Arms **Rev:** Falcon bust **Edge:** Reeded

Date	Mintage	F12	VF20	XF40	MS60	MS63
2006	—	PF63 650				

KM# 22 100 RIYALS
10.00 g., 0.9999 Gold 0.3194 oz. AGW, 24.5 mm. **Ruler:** Hamad bin Khalifa **Subject:** 15th Asian Games **Obv:** Arms **Rev:** Coffee pot **Edge:** Reeded

Date	Mintage	F12	VF20	XF40	MS60	MS63
2006	—	PF63 650				

KM# 23 100 RIYALS
10.00 g., 0.9999 Gold 0.3194 oz. AGW, 24.5 mm. **Ruler:** Hamad bin Khalifa **Subject:** 15th Asian Games **Obv:** Arms **Rev:** Radiant sun **Edge:** Reeded

Date	Mintage	F12	VF20	XF40	MS60	MS63
2006	—	PF63 650				

KM# 76 100 RIYALS
22.24 g., 0.925 Silver 0.6571 oz. ASW, 37 mm. **Ruler:** Hamad bin Khalifa **Subject:** 2008 Arab States Stamp Exhibition **Obv:** National Arms **Rev:** Two profiles right

Date	Mintage	F12	VF20	XF40	MS60	MS63
2008	1,000	PF63 90.00				

KM# 77 100 RIYALS
22.24 g., 0.925 Silver 0.6571 oz. ASW, 37 mm. **Ruler:** Hamad bin Khalifa **Subject:** Central Municipal Council, 10th Anniversary **Obv:** National Arms in color **Rev:** Democracy House in color

Date	Mintage	F12	VF20	XF40	MS60	MS63
2009 Proof	—	—	—	—	—	—

KM# 78 100 RIYALS
Silver **Ruler:** Hamad bin Khalifa **Subject:** 10th Gulf Cooperation Council Banking Conference

Date	Mintage	F12	VF20	XF40	MS60	MS63
2011	—	PF63 60.00				

KM# 47 200 RIYALS
Gold AGW **Ruler:** Hamad bin Khalifa **Subject:** al Wabra Wildlife Preservation, 50th Anniversary **Rev:** Blue headed macaw

Date	Mintage	F12	VF20	XF40	MS60	MS63
2003 Proof	240					

KM# 67 200 RIYALS
0.999 Silver, 40 mm. **Ruler:** Hamad bin Khalifa **Subject:** Doha Cultural Festival **Obv:** Wing emblem **Rev:** Four men seated under archway

Date	Mintage	F12	VF20	XF40	MS60	MS63
2004 Proof	—	—	—	—	—	—

KM# 79 200 RIYALS
Silver **Ruler:** Hamad bin Khalifa **Subject:** 10th Gulf Cooperation Council Banking Conference

Date	Mintage	F12	VF20	XF40	MS60	MS63
2011	—	PF63 225	PF65 250			

KM# 11 250 RIYALS
Silver **Ruler:** Hamad bin Khalifa **Subject:** 4th WTO Conference **Obv:** National arms **Rev:** WTO logo, value, date, and legend in English and Islamic

Date	Mintage	F12	VF20	XF40	MS60	MS63
AH1422 (2001)	1,000	PF63 650				

KM# 41 250 RIYALS
31.00 g., 0.999 Gold 0.9893 oz. AGW, 37 mm. **Ruler:** Hamad bin Khalifa **Subject:** Yousif al Sharif **Obv:** Wing design **Rev:** Male bust

Date	Mintage	F12	VF20	XF40	MS60	MS63
2002 Proof	—	—	—	—	—	—

KM# 55 250 RIYALS
120.00 g., 0.999 Silver 3.8294 oz. ASW, 60 mm. **Ruler:** Hamad bin Khalifa **Subject:** al Wabra Wildlife Preservation, 50th Anniversary **Rev:** Dama gazelle

Date	Mintage	F12	VF20	XF40	MS60	MS63
2003	1,800	PF63 250				

KM# 43 250 RIYALS
100.00 g., 0.999 Silver 3.1912 oz. ASW, 80 mm. **Ruler:** Hamad bin Khalifa **Subject:** Doha Cultural festival

Date	Mintage	F12	VF20	XF40	MS60	MS63
2003	1,000	PF63 250				

KM# 44 250 RIYALS
120.00 g., 0.999 Silver 3.8294 oz. ASW, 60 mm. **Ruler:** Hamad bin Khalifa **Subject:** al Wabra Wildlife Preservation, 50th Anniversary **Rev:** Blue headed macaw in color

Date	Mintage	F12	VF20	XF40	MS60	MS63
2003	1,800	PF63 250				

KM# 45 250 RIYALS
120.00 g., 0.999 Silver 3.8294 oz. ASW, 60 mm. **Ruler:** Hamad bin Khalifa **Subject:** al Wabra Wildlife Preservation, 50th Anniversary **Rev:** bird in color

Date	Mintage	F12	VF20	XF40	MS60	MS63
2003	1,800	PF63 250				

KM# 46 250 RIYALS
120.00 g., 0.999 Silver 3.8294 oz. ASW, 60 mm. **Ruler:** Hamad bin Khalifa **Subject:** al Wabra Wildlife Preservation, 50th Anniversary **Rev:** Macaw in color

Date	Mintage	F12	VF20	XF40	MS60	MS63
2003	1,800	PF63 250				

KM# 53 250 RIYALS
120.00 g., 0.999 Silver 3.8294 oz. ASW, 60 mm. **Ruler:** Hamad bin Khalifa **Subject:** al Wabra Wildlife Preservation, 50th Anniversary **Rev:** Gazelle

Date	Mintage	F12	VF20	XF40	MS60	MS63
2003	1,800	PF63 250				

KM# 54 250 RIYALS
120.00 g., 0.999 Silver 3.8294 oz. ASW, 60 mm. **Ruler:** Hamad bin Khalifa **Subject:** al Wabra Wildlife Preservation, 50th Anniversary **Rev:** Sommering gazelle

Date	Mintage	F12	VF20	XF40	MS60	MS63
2003	1,800	PF63 250				

KM# 56 250 RIYALS
120.00 g., 0.999 Silver 3.8294 oz. ASW, 60 mm. **Ruler:** Hamad bin Khalifa **Subject:** al Wabra Wildlife Preservation, 50th Anniversary **Rev:** Stilt gazelle

Date	Mintage	F12	VF20	XF40	MS60	MS63
2003	1,800	PF63 250				

KM# 65 250 RIYALS
120.00 g., 0.999 Silver 3.8294 oz. ASW, 60 mm. **Ruler:** Hamad bin Khalifa **Subject:** National Council for Culture, Arts and Heritage, 5th Anniversary **Obv:** Bust 1/4 left **Rev:** Text and emblem

Date	Mintage	F12	VF20	XF40	MS60	MS63
2003	1,000	PF63 300				

KM# 70 250 RIYALS
120.00 g., 0.999 Silver 3.8294 oz. ASW, 60 mm. **Ruler:** Hamad bin Khalifa **Subject:** National Council for Culture, Arts and Heritage

Date	Mintage	F12	VF20	XF40	MS60	MS63
2006	—	PF63 250				

KM# 39 300 RIYALS
1000.00 g., 0.999 Silver 31.9118 oz. ASW, 100.0 mm. **Ruler:** Hamad bin Khalifa **Obv:** National arms **Obv. Legend:** STATE OF QATAR **Rev:** Sports montage around game's logo **Rev. Inscription:** 15TH ASIAN GAMES / DOHA 2006 **Edge:** Plain

Date	Mintage	F12	VF20	XF40	MS60	MS63
2006	5,000	PF63 1,250				

KM# 68 1000 RIYALS
0.999 Gold AGW, 40 mm. **Ruler:** Hamad bin Khalifa **Subject:** Doha Coultural Festival **Obv:** Wing design **Rev:** Four men seated under archway

Date	Mintage	F12	VF20	XF40	MS60	MS63
2004 Proof	—	—	—	—	—	—

KM# 48 2000 RIYALS
Gold AGW **Ruler:** Hamad bin Khalifa **Subject:** al Wabra Wildlife Preservation, 50th Anniversary **Rev:** bird

Date	Mintage	F12	VF20	XF40	MS60	MS63
2003 Proof	240	—	—	—	—	—

KM# 72 2000 RIYALS
40.64 g., 0.925 Silver 1.2008 oz. ASW, 50 mm. **Ruler:** Hamad bin Khalifa **Subject:** National Day **Obv:** National Arms in color **Rev:** State of Qatar, National arms in color

Date	Mintage	F12	VF20	XF40	MS60	MS63
2007	500	PF65 900				

KM# 73 2000 RIYALS
40.64 g., 0.925 Silver 1.2008 oz. ASW, 50 mm. **Ruler:** Hamad bin Khalifa **Subject:** National Day **Obv:** National Arms in color **Rev:** Qatar Central Bank, National arms in color

Date	Mintage	F12	VF20	XF40	MS60	MS63
2007	500	PF65 900				

KM# 49 5000 RIYALS
Gold AGW **Ruler:** Hamad bin Khalifa **Subject:** al Wabra Wildlife Preservation, 50th Anniversary **Rev:** macaw

Date	Mintage	F12	VF20	XF40	MS60	MS63
2003 Proof	240	—	—	—	—	—

KM# 57 5000 RIYALS
Gold AGW **Ruler:** Hamad bin Khalifa **Subject:** al Wabra Wildlife Preservation, 50th Anniversary **Rev:** Gazelle

Date	Mintage	F12	VF20	XF40	MS60	MS63
2003 Proof	240	—	—	—	—	—

KM# 58 5000 RIYALS
Gold AGW **Ruler:** Hamad bin Khalifa **Subject:** al Wabra Wildlife Preservation, 50th Anniversary **Rev:** Sommering Gazelle

Date	Mintage	F12	VF20	XF40	MS60	MS63
2003 Proof	240	—	—	—	—	—

KM# 59 5000 RIYALS
Gold AGW **Ruler:** Hamad bin Khalifa **Subject:** al Wabra Wildlife Preservation, 50th Anniversary **Rev:** Dama Gazelle

Date	Mintage	F12	VF20	XF40	MS60	MS63
2003 Proof	240	—	—	—	—	—

KM# 60 5000 RIYALS
Gold AGW **Ruler:** Hamad bin Khalifa **Subject:** al Wabra Wildlife Preservation, 50th Anniversary **Rev:** Stilt Gazelle

Date	Mintage	F12	VF20	XF40	MS60	MS63
2003 Proof	240	—	—	—	—	—

KM# 66 5000 RIYALS
160.00 g., 0.999 Gold 5.1059 oz. AGW, 60 mm. **Ruler:** Hamad bin Khalifa **Subject:** National Council for Culture, Arts and Heritage, 5th Anniversary **Obv:** Bust 1/4 left **Rev:** Text and emblem

Date	Mintage	F12	VF20	XF40	MS60	MS63
2003 Proof	500	—	—	—	—	9,750

KM# 71 5000 RIYALS
160.00 g., 0.999 Gold 5.1059 oz. AGW, 60 mm. **Ruler:** Hamad bin Khalifa **Subject:** National Council for Culture, Arts and Heritage

Date	Mintage	F12	VF20	XF40	MS60	MS63
2006 Proof	—	—	—	—	—	—

KM# 50 10000 RIYALS
Platinum APW **Ruler:** Hamad bin Khalifa **Subject:** al Wabra Wildlife Preservation, 50th Anniversary **Rev:** Blue headed macaw

Date	Mintage	F12	VF20	XF40	MS60	MS63
2003 Proof	120	—	—	—	—	—

KM# 51 10000 RIYALS
Platinum APW **Ruler:** Hamad bin Khalifa **Subject:** al Wabra Wildlife Preservation, 50th Anniversary **Rev:** bird

Date	Mintage	F12	VF20	XF40	MS60	MS63
2003 Proof	120	—	—	—	—	—

KM# 52 10000 RIYALS
Platinum APW **Ruler:** Hamad bin Khalifa **Subject:** al Wabra Wildlife Preservation, 50th Anniversary **Rev:** Macaw

Date	Mintage	F12	VF20	XF40	MS60	MS63
2003 Proof	120	—	—	—	—	—

KM# 61 10000 RIYALS
Platinum APW **Ruler:** Hamad bin Khalifa **Subject:** al Wabra Wildlife Preservation, 50th Anniversary **Rev:** Gazelle

Date	Mintage	F12	VF20	XF40	MS60	MS63
2003 Proof	120	—	—	—	—	—

KM# 62 10000 RIYALS
Platinum APW **Ruler:** Hamad bin Khalifa **Subject:** al Wabra Wildlife Preservation, 50th Anniversary **Rev:** Sommering gazelle

Date	Mintage	F12	VF20	XF40	MS60	MS63
2003 Proof	120	—	—	—	—	—

KM# 63 10000 RIYALS
Platinum APW **Ruler:** Hamad bin Khalifa **Subject:** al Wabra Wildlife Preservation, 50th Anniversary **Rev:** Dama gazelle

Date	Mintage	F12	VF20	XF40	MS60	MS63
2003 Proof	120	—	—	—	—	—

KM# 64 10000 RIYALS
Platinum APW **Ruler:** Hamad bin Khalifa **Subject:** al Wabra Wildlife Preservation, 50th Anniversary **Rev:** Stilt gazelle

Date	Mintage	F12	VF20	XF40	MS60	MS63
2003 Proof	120	—	—	—	—	—

KM# 24 10000 RIYALS
1000.00 g., 0.9999 Gold 31.9406 oz. AGW, 75.3 mm. **Ruler:** Hamad bin Khalifa **Subject:** 15th Asian Games **Obv:** Arms **Rev:** Radiant sun **Edge:** Reeded **Note:** Illustration reduced.

Date	Mintage	F12	VF20	XF40	MS60	MS63
2006	—	PF65 57,500				

KM# 74 10000 RIYALS
70.16 g., 0.916 Gold 2.0529 oz. AGW, 50 mm. **Ruler:** Hamad bin Khalifa **Subject:** National Day **Obv:** National Arms **Rev:** State of Qatar, National Arms

Date	Mintage	F12	VF20	XF40	MS60	MS63
2007	500	PF65 4,500				

KM# 75 10000 RIYALS
70.16 g., 0.916 Gold 2.0529 oz. AGW, 50 mm. **Ruler:** Hamad bin Khalifa **Subject:** National Day **Obv:** National Arms **Rev:** Qatar Central Bank, National Arms

Date	Mintage	F12	VF20	XF40	MS60	MS63
2007	500	PF65 4,500				

ROMANIA

Romania (formerly the Socialist Republic of Romania), a country in southeast Europe, has an area of 91,699 sq. mi. (237,500 sq. km.) and a population of 23.2 million. Capital: Bucharest. Machinery, foodstuffs, raw minerals and petroleum products are exported. Heavy industry and oil have become increasingly important to the economy since 1959. Romania joined the European Union in January 2007.

MONETARY SYSTEM
100 Bani = 1 Leu

REPUBLIC
STANDARD COINAGE

KM# 115 LEU
2.52 g., Copper Plated Steel, 19 mm. **Obv:** Value flanked by sprigs **Rev:** Shield divides date

Date	Mintage	F12	VF20	XF40	MS60	MS63
2002	1,500	PF63 5.00				
2003	2,000	PF63 5.00				
2004	2,000	PF63 5.00				
2005	—				1.00	
2005	—	PF63 6.00				
2006	1,000	PF63 6.00				

KM# 114 5 LEI
3.30 g., Nickel Plated Steel, 21 mm. **Obv:** Value flanked by oak leaves **Rev:** Shield divides date **Edge:** Plain

Date	Mintage	F12	VF20	XF40	MS60	MS63
2002	1,500	PF63 5.00				
2003	2,000	PF63 5.00				
2004	—	PF63 5.00				
2005	—	PF63 5.00				

KM# 116 10 LEI
4.70 g., Nickel Clad Steel, 23 mm. **Obv:** Value within sprigs **Rev:** Shield divides date **Edge:** Plain

Date	Mintage	F12	VF20	XF40	MS60	MS63
2002	1,500	PF63 6.00				
2003	2,000	PF63 6.00				

KM# 109 20 LEI
5.00 g., Brass Clad Steel, 24 mm. **Obv:** Crowned bust of Prince Stefan Cel Mare facing, flanked by dots **Rev:** Value and date within half sprigs and dots **Edge:** Plain **Note:** Date varieties exist.

Date	Mintage	F12	VF20	XF40	MS60	MS63
2002	1,500	PF63 7.50				
2003	2,000	PF63 7.50				

KM# 110 50 LEI
5.90 g., Brass Clad Steel, 26 mm. **Obv:** Bust left flanked by dots **Rev:** Sprig divides date and value **Edge:** Plain

Date	Mintage	F12	VF20	XF40	MS60	MS63
2002	1,500	PF63 8.00				
2003	2,000	PF63 8.00				

KM# 159 50 LEI
15.55 g., 0.999 Silver 0.4963 oz. ASW, 31.1 mm. **Series:** Romanian Aviation **Obv:** AVIONUL VUIA 1 - 1906 airplane **Rev:** Traian Vuia **Edge:** Plain **Shape:** Octagonal

Date	Mintage	F12	VF20	XF40	MS60	MS63
2001	500	PF63 165				

KM# 160 50 LEI
15.55 g., 0.999 Silver 0.4963 oz. ASW, 31.1 mm. **Series:** Romanian Aviation **Obv:** Avionul Coanda 1910, world's first (?) jet airplane **Rev:** Portrait of Henri Coanda **Edge:** Plain **Shape:** Octagonal

Date	Mintage	F12	VF20	XF40	MS60	MS63
2001	500	PF63 165				

KM# 161 50 LEI
15.55 g., 0.999 Silver 0.4963 oz. ASW, 27 mm. **Series:** Romanian Aviation **Obv:** IAR CV-11 airplane **Rev:** Elie Carafoli **Edge:** Plain **Shape:** Octagonal

Date	Mintage	F12	VF20	XF40	MS60	MS63
2001	500	PF63 165				

KM# 167 50 LEI
15.55 g., 0.999 Silver 0.4963 oz. ASW, 29.5 mm. **Subject:** National Parks: Retezat **Obv:** National arms in triangular design **Rev:** Chamois **Edge:** Plain **Shape:** Rounded triangle

Date	Mintage	F12	VF20	XF40	MS60	MS63
2002 (2003)	500	PF63 200				

KM# 168 50 LEI
15.55 g., 0.999 Silver 0.4963 oz. ASW, 29.5 mm. **Subject:** National Parks: Pietrosul Mare **Obv:** National arms in triangular design **Rev:** Eagle **Edge:** Plain **Shape:** Rounded triangle

Date	Mintage	F12	VF20	XF40	MS60	MS63
2002 (2003)	500	PF63 200				

KM# 169 50 LEI
15.55 g., 0.999 Silver 0.4963 oz. ASW, 29.5 mm. **Subject:** National Parks: Piatra Craiului **Obv:** National arms in triangular design **Rev:** Lynx **Edge:** Plain **Shape:** Rounded triangle

Date	Mintage	F12	VF20	XF40	MS60	MS63
2002 (2003)	500	PF63 200				

KM# 186 50 LEI
15.55 g., 0.999 Silver 0.4963 oz. ASW, 27 mm. **Subject:** Birds **Obv:** Stylized water drop **Rev:** Dalmatian Pelicans within circle **Edge:** Plain

Date	Mintage	F12	VF20	XF40	MS60	MS63
2003	500	PF63 100				

KM# 187 50 LEI
15.55 g., 0.999 Silver 0.4963 oz. ASW, 27 mm. **Subject:** Birds **Obv:** Stylized water drop **Rev:** Great Egret within circle **Edge:** Plain

Date	Mintage	F12	VF20	XF40	MS60	MS63
2003	500	PF63 100				

KM# 188 50 LEI
15.55 g., 0.999 Silver 0.4963 oz. ASW, 27 mm. **Subject:** Birds **Obv:** Stylized water drop **Rev:** Common Kingfisher within circle **Edge:** Plain

Date	Mintage	F12	VF20	XF40	MS60	MS63
2003	500	PF63 100				

KM# 111 100 LEI
8.75 g., Nickel Plated Steel, 29 mm. **Obv:** Bust with headdress 1/4 right **Rev:** Value within sprigs **Edge Lettering:** ROMANIA

Date	Mintage	F12	VF20	XF40	MS60	MS63
2002	1,500	PF63 8.00				
2003	2,000	PF63 8.00				
2004	2,000	PF63 8.00				
2005	—	—	—	—	2.50	—
2005	2,000	PF63 9.00				
2006	1,000	PF63 9.00				

KM# 165 100 LEI
1.22 g., 0.999 Gold 0.0391 oz. AGW, 13.9 mm. **Subject:** History of Gold - "The Apahida Eagle" **Obv:** National arms in ornamental circle above value **Edge:** Plain

Date	Mintage	F12	VF20	XF40	MS60	MS63
2003	2,000	PF63 125				

KM# 198 100 LEI
1.24 g., 0.999 Gold 0.0397 oz. AGW, 13.93 mm. **Obv:** National arms in wreath **Obv. Legend:** ROMANIA **Edge:** Reeded

Date	Mintage	F12	VF20	XF40	MS60	MS63
2003	—	PF65 100				

KM# 166 100 LEI
1.22 g., 0.999 Gold 0.0391 oz. AGW, 14 mm. **Subject:** History of Gold - Engolpion **Obv:** National arms and country name above two stylized birds and value **Rev:** Jeweled double headed eagle pendant

Date	Mintage	F12	VF20	XF40	MS60	MS63
2004	1,000	PF63 165				

KM# 145 500 LEI
3.70 g., Aluminum, 25 mm. **Obv:** Shield within sprigs **Rev:** Value within 3/4 wreath **Edge:** Lettered **Edge Lettering:** ROMANIA (three times)

Date	Mintage	F12	VF20	XF40	MS60	MS63
2001	—	—	—	0.75	2.00	—
2002	1,500	PF63 7.00				
2003	2,000	PF63 7.00				
2004	2,000	PF63 7.00				
2005	—	—	—	—	3.00	—
2005	1,000	PF63 8.00				
2006	—	—	—	—	3.00	—
2006	—	PF63 8.00				

KM# 170 500 LEI
6.22 g., 0.999 Gold 0.1985 oz. AGW, 11.75 mm. **Subject:** History of Gold - Treasure of Pietroasa **Rev:** "Big Clip" of Pietroasa

Date	Mintage	F12	VF20	XF40	MS60	MS63
(2001)	250	—	—	—	—	700

KM# 171 500 LEI
6.22 g., 0.999 Gold 0.1985 oz. AGW, 11.75 mm. **Subject:** History of Gold - Treasure of Pietroasa **Rev:** "Medium Clip" of Pietroasa

Date	Mintage	F12	VF20	XF40	MS60	MS63
2001	250	—	—	—	—	700

KM# 172 500 LEI
6.22 g., 0.999 Gold 0.1985 oz. AGW, 11.75 mm. **Subject:** History of Gold - Treasure of Pietroasa **Rev:** 12-sided golden bowl

Date	Mintage	F12	VF20	XF40	MS60	MS63
2001	250	—	—	—	—	700

KM# 173 500 LEI
6.22 g., 0.999 Gold 0.1985 oz. AGW, 11.75 mm. **Subject:** History of Gold - Treasure of Pietroasa **Rev:** Pitcher

Date	Mintage	F12	VF20	XF40	MS60	MS63
2001	250	—	—	—	—	700

KM# 176 500 LEI
6.22 g., 0.999 Gold 0.1985 oz. AGW, 23.2 mm. **Subject:** Christian Monuments **Rev:** Mogoşoaia Palace **Shape:** Square

Date	Mintage	F12	VF20	XF40	MS60	MS63
2001	250	—	—	—	—	550

KM# 174 500 LEI
6.22 g., 0.999 Gold 0.1985 oz. AGW, 23.2 mm. **Subject:** Christian Monuments **Rev:** Bistritza Monastery

Date	Mintage	F12	VF20	XF40	MS60	MS63
2002	250	—	—	—	—	550

KM# 175 500 LEI
6.22 g., 0.999 Gold 0.1985 oz. AGW, 23.2 mm. **Subject:** Christian Monuments **Rev:** Colţea Church

Date	Mintage	F12	VF20	XF40	MS60	MS63
2002	250	—	—	—	—	550

KM# 177 500 LEI
31.10 g., 0.999 Silver 0.9926 oz. ASW, 37 mm. **Subject:** 150th Anniversary - Birth of Ciprian Porumbescu, Composer **Obv:** Partial piano and violin left of National arms and value **Rev:** Portrait and musical score **Edge:** Plain

Date	Mintage	F12	VF20	XF40	MS60	MS63
2003	500	PF63 160				

KM# 178 500 LEI
31.10 g., 0.999 Silver 0.9926 oz. ASW, 37 mm. **Subject:** 500th Anniversary - Establishment of Bishopric of Ramnic **Obv:** National arms and value above inscription **Rev:** Bishopric's coat-of-arms **Edge:** Plain

Date	Mintage	F12	VF20	XF40	MS60	MS63
2003	500	PF63 160				

KM# 179 500 LEI
31.10 g., 0.999 Silver 0.9926 oz. ASW, 37 mm. **Subject:** Romanian Numismatic Society Centennial **Obv:** Cornucopia pouring forth coins, value below **Rev:** Minerva and torch

Rev. Legend: CENTENARUL SOCIETATII NUMISMATICE ROMANE, 1903-2003 **Edge:** Plain

Date	Mintage	F12	VF20	XF40	MS60	MS63
2003	1,000	PF63 150				

KM# 163 500 LEI
31.10 g., 0.999 Silver 0.9926 oz. ASW, 37 mm. **Subject:** Christian Feudal Art Monuments **Obv:** National arms, date and value at left, belfry tower of church at right **Rev:** Cotroceni Monastery church **Edge:** Plain **Shape:** 10-sided

Date	Mintage	F12	VF20	XF40	MS60	MS63
2004	500	PF63 150				

KM# 164 500 LEI
31.10 g., 0.999 Silver 0.9926 oz. ASW, 37 mm. **Subject:** Christian Feudal Art Monuments **Obv:** National arms, bell and value **Rev:** St. Trei Ierarhi church in Iasi **Edge:** Plain **Shape:** 10-sided

Date	Mintage	F12	VF20	XF40	MS60	MS63
2004	500	PF63 150				

KM# 180 500 LEI
31.10 g., 0.999 Silver 0.9926 oz. ASW, 37 mm. **Subject:** 140th Anniversary - University of Bucharest **Obv:** Vertical inscription divides National arms, value and date at left. University emblem at right **Obv. Inscription:** ROMANIA **Rev:** Cameo at right and crowned arms at left above University Building **Rev. Inscription:** Upper: UNIVERSITATEA DIN BUCURESTI / 140 DE ANI; Lower: INTEMEIATA LA 1864 DE / AL IOAN CUZA **Edge:** Plain

Date	Mintage	F12	VF20	XF40	MS60	MS63
2004	500	PF63 180				

KM# 193 500 LEI
31.10 g., 0.999 Silver 0.9926 oz. ASW, 37 mm. **Subject:** 150th Anniversary - Birth of Anghel Saligny **Obv:** Arms at left above Cernavoda bridge, inscription, date, and value below **Obv. Inscription:** PODUL DE LA CERNAVODA **Rev:** Bust of bridge builder Anghel Saligny half right, life dates at right, his signature below at left **Edge:** Plain

Date	Mintage	F12	VF20	XF40	MS60	MS63
2004	500	PF65 350				

KM# 218 500 LEI
31.11 g., 0.999 Gold 0.9926 oz. AGW, 35 mm. **Subject:** Union of the Principalities of Moldavia and Wallachia, 150th Anniversary

Date	Mintage	F12	VF20	XF40	MS60	MS63
2009	250	PF65 1,900				

KM# 153 1000 LEI
2.00 g., Aluminum, 22 mm. **Subject:** Constantin Brancoveanu **Obv:** Value above shield within lined circle **Rev:** Bust with headdress facing **Edge:** Plain with serrated sections

Date	Mintage	VG8	F12	VF20	XF40	MS60
2001	—			—	0.25	2.50
2002	—			—	0.25	2.50
2002	1,500	PF63 12.00				
2003	—			—	0.25	2.50
2003	2,000	PF63 12.00				
2004	—			—	0.25	2.50
2004	2,000	PF63 12.00				
2005	—			—	0.25	2.50
2005	—	PF63 13.00				
2006	—	PF63 13.00				

KM# 156 1000 LEI
15.55 g., 0.999 Gold 0.4963 oz. AGW, 27 mm. **Subject:** 1900th Anniversary of the First Roman-Dacian War **Obv:** Traian's column and shield **Rev:** Monument divides cameos **Edge:** Plain

Date	Mintage	VG8	F12	VF20	XF40	MS60
2001	500	PF63 950				

KM# 181 2000 LEI
25.00 g., Bi-Metallic, 35 mm. **Subject:** Ion Heliade Radulescu (1802-1872) **Obv:** Lyre at left, national arms at right in divided circle design **Rev:** Ion Heliade Radulescu above signature **Edge:** Reeded

Date	Mintage	F12	VF20	XF40	MS60	MS63
2002	500	PF63 1,000				

KM# 158 5000 LEI
2.50 g., Aluminum, 24 mm. **Obv:** Value and country name **Rev:** Sprig divides date and shield **Edge:** Plain **Shape:** 12-sided

Date	Mintage	F12	VF20	XF40	MS60	MS63
2001	—			—	0.50	—
2002	1,500	PF63 15.00				
2002	—			—	0.50	—
2003	—			—	0.25	—
2003	2,000	PF63 15.00				
2004	2,000	PF63 16.00				
2004	—			—	0.25	—
2005	—			—	0.25	—
2005	2,000	PF63 17.00				
2006	1,000	PF63 17.00				

KM# 162 5000 LEI
31.10 g., 0.999 Gold 0.9926 oz. AGW, 35 mm. **Subject:** Constantin Brancusi 125th Anniversary of Birth **Obv:** National arms, value and sculpture **Rev:** Bearded portrait and signature **Edge:** Plain

Date	Mintage	F12	VF20	XF40	MS60	MS63
2001	500	PF63 2,250				

KM# 183 5000 LEI
31.10 g., 0.999 Gold 0.9926 oz. AGW, 35 mm. **Subject:** Ion Luca Caragiale, playright (1852-1912) **Obv:** National arms, value and masks of Comedy and Tragedy **Rev:** Portrait **Edge:** Plain

Date	Mintage	F12	VF20	XF40	MS60	MS63
2002	250	PF63 2,500				

KM# 184 5000 LEI
31.10 g., 0.999 Gold 0.9926 oz. AGW, 35 mm. **Subject:** Bran Castle (1378-2003) **Obv:** Two coats of arms on shield above value **Rev:** Castle view **Edge:** Plain

Date	Mintage	F12	VF20	XF40	MS60	MS63
2003	250	PF63 2,000				

KM# 185 5000 LEI
31.10 g., 0.999 Gold 0.9926 oz. AGW, 35 mm. **Subject:** Stephen the Great **Obv:** National arms, value above coin design in wall **Rev:** Portrait of Stephan and Putna Monastery

Date	Mintage	F12	VF20	XF40	MS60	MS63
2004	250	PF63 2,000				

REFORM COINAGE - 2005
10,000 Old Leu = 1 New Leu

KM# 189 BAN
2.40 g., Brass Plated Steel, 16.8 mm. **Subject:** Monetary Reform of 2005 **Obv:** National arms flanked by stars **Rev:** Value **Edge:** Plain

Date	Mintage	F12	VF20	XF40	MS60	MS63
2005	—			—	0.30	0.50
2005	—	PF63 2.50				
2006	—			—	0.30	0.50
2006	—	PF63 2.50				
2007	—			—	0.30	0.50
2007	—	PF63 2.50				
2008	—			—	0.30	0.50
2008	—	PF63 2.50				
2009	—			—	0.30	0.50
2009	—	PF63 2.50				
2010	—			—	0.30	0.50
2010	—	PF63 2.50				
2011	—			—	0.30	0.50
2011	—	PF63 2.50				
2012	—			—	0.30	0.50
2013	—			—	0.30	0.50

KM# 190 5 BANI
2.80 g., Copper Plated Steel, 18.25 mm. **Subject:** Monetary Reform of 2005 **Obv:** National arms flanked by stars **Obv. Legend:** ROMANIA **Rev:** Value **Edge:** Reeded

Date	Mintage	F12	VF20	XF40	MS60	MS63
2005	—			—	0.50	0.75
2005	—	PF63 5.00				
2006	—			—	0.50	0.75
2006	—	PF63 5.00				
2007	—			—	0.50	0.75
2007	—	PF63 5.00				
2008	—			—	0.50	0.75
2008	—	PF63 5.00				
2009	—			—	0.50	0.75
2009	—	PF63 5.00				
2010	—			—	0.50	0.75
2010	—	PF63 5.00				
2011	—			—	0.50	0.75

Date	Mintage	F12	VF20	XF40	MS60	MS63
2011	—	PF63 5.00				
2012	—			—	0.50	0.75

KM# 191 10 BANI
4.00 g., Nickel Plated Steel, 20.4 mm. **Subject:** Monetary Reform of 2005 **Obv:** National arms flanked by stars **Obv. Legend:** ROMANIA **Rev:** Value **Edge:** Segmented reeding

Date	Mintage	F12	VF20	XF40	MS60	MS63
2005	—			—	0.65	0.85
2005	—	PF63 7.00				
2006	—			—	0.60	0.80
2006	—	PF63 7.00				
2007	—			—	0.50	0.75
2007	—	PF63 7.00				
2008	—			—	0.50	0.70
2008	—	PF63 7.00				
2009	—			—	0.50	0.70
2009	—	PF63 7.00				
2010	—			—	0.50	0.70
2010	—	PF63 7.00				
2011	—			—	0.50	0.70
2011	—	PF63 7.00				
2012	—			—	0.50	0.70

KM# 192 50 BANI
6.10 g., Nickel-Brass, 23.75 mm. **Subject:** Monetary Reform of 2005 **Obv:** National arms flanked by stars **Obv. Legend:** ROMANIA **Rev:** Value **Edge:** Lettered **Edge Lettering:** ROMANIA twice

Date	Mintage	F12	VF20	XF40	MS60	MS63
2005	—			—	0.85	1.00
2005	—	PF63 10.00				
2006	—			—	0.75	0.85
2006	—	PF63 10.00				
2007	—			—	0.65	0.75
2007	—	PF63 10.00				
2008	—			—	0.65	0.75
2008	—	PF63 10.00				
2009	—			—	0.65	0.75
2009	—	PF63 10.00				
2010	—			—	0.65	0.75
2010	—	PF63 10.00				
2011	—			—	0.65	0.75
2011	—	PF63 10.00				
2012	—			—	0.65	0.75

KM# 259 50 BANI
6.10 g., Nickel-Brass, 23.75 mm. **Subject:** Aurel Vlaicu

Date	Mintage	F12	VF20	XF40	MS60	MS63
2010	5,000,000	—	—	—	0.65	1.00

Note: Medal rotation

Date	Mintage	F12	VF20	XF40	MS60	MS63
2010	1,000	PF65 150				

Note: Medal rotation

| 2010 | 5,000 | PF65 25.00 | | | | |

Note: Coin rotation

| 2011 Proof | 1,000 | | | | | |

Note: Medal rotation

KM# 260 50 BANI
6.10 g., Nickel-Brass, 23.75 mm. **Subject:** Mircea the old

Date	Mintage	F12	VF20	XF40	MS60	MS63
2011	—			—	0.65	0.75

KM# 287 50 BANI
6.05 g., Aluminum-Bronze **Subject:** Neagoe Basarab

Date	Mintage	F12	VF20	XF40	MS60	MS63
2012	—			—	—	2.00

KM# 209 LEU
23.50 g., Copper Plated Tombac, 37 mm. **Subject:** 140th Anniversary Founding Romanian Academy **Edge:** Plain

Date	Mintage	F12	VF20	XF40	MS60	MS63
2006	35	PF65 750				

Date	Mintage	F12	VF20	XF40	MS60	MS63
2011	—	PF63 5.00				
2012	—			—	0.50	0.75

KM# 220 LEU
23.50 g., Copper Plated Tombac, 37 mm. **Subject:** Centennial - Birth of Mircea Eliade **Obv:** Shield and value **Rev:** Portrait facing **Edge:** Reeded

Date	Mintage	F12	VF20	XF40	MS60	MS63
2007	250	PF65 150				

KM# 223 LEU
23.50 g., Copper Plated Tombac, 37 mm. **Subject:** Dimitrie Cantemir, (Prince of Moldavia 1673-1723), Scientist **Edge:** Reeded

Date	Mintage	F12	VF20	XF40	MS60	MS63
2007	250	PF65 150				

KM# 226 LEU
23.50 g., Copper Plated Tombac, 37 mm. **Subject:** Stephan the Great **Edge:** Reeded

Date	Mintage	F12	VF20	XF40	MS60	MS63
2007	250	PF65 150				

KM# 199 LEU
23.50 g., Copper Plated Tombac, 37 mm. **Subject:** 130th Anniversary of Proclamation of Independence **Obv:** Shield and "The Smardan Assault" painting by Nicolae Grigorescu **Rev:** Meeting of the Parliament

Date	Mintage	F12	VF20	XF40	MS60	MS63
2007	130	PF65 250				

KM# 258 LEU
23.50 g., Copper Plated Tombac, 37 mm. **Subject:** Bucharest, 550th Anniversary **Obv:** Vlad □epe□ **Rev:** Buildings

Date	Mintage	F12	VF20	XF40	MS60	MS63
2009	250	PF65 150				

KM# 234 LEU
23.50 g., Copper Plated Tombac, 37 mm. **Subject:** Nicolae Balcescu, 190th Anniversary of Birth

Date	Mintage	F12	VF20	XF40	MS60	MS63
2009	1,000	PF65 75.00				

KM# 261 LEU
23.50 g., Copper Plated Tombac, 37 mm. **Subject:** Central Bank, 130th Anniversary

Date	Mintage	F12	VF20	XF40	MS60	MS63
2010	1,500	PF65 65.00				

KM# 208 5 LEI
31.10 g., 0.999 Silver 0.9925 oz. ASW, 37 mm. **Subject:** 100th Anniversary - Birth of Grigore Vasiliu-Birlic **Edge:** Plain

Date	Mintage	F12	VF20	XF40	MS60	MS63
2005	150	PF65 1,200				

KM# 210 5 LEI
31.10 g., 0.999 Silver 0.9925 oz. ASW, 37 mm. **Subject:** 140th Anniversary Founding Romanian Academy **Edge:** Plain

Date	Mintage	F12	VF20	XF40	MS60	MS63
2006	500	PF65 300				

KM# 212 5 LEI
31.10 g., 0.999 Silver 0.9925 oz. ASW, 37 mm. **Subject:** Christian Feudal Art - "Wooden Church from Ieud-Deal **Obv:** Fragment of mural in Ieud Church depicting Isaac, Abraham and Jacob at top, inscription, value and date in lower half **Obv. Inscription:** ROMANIA **Rev:** Front view of Ieud Church against frosted background **Rev. Inscription:** BISERICA DE LEMN IEUD DEAL **Edge:** Plain

Date	Mintage	F12	VF20	XF40	MS60	MS63
2006	500	PF65 170				

KM# 213 5 LEI
31.10 g., 0.999 Silver 0.9926 oz. ASW, 37 mm. **Subject:** 150th Anniversary - Establishment of the European Commission of the Danube **Edge:** Plain

Date	Mintage	F12	VF20	XF40	MS60	MS63
2006	500	PF65 170				

KM# 216 5 LEI
31.10 g., 0.999 Silver 0.9926 oz. ASW, 37 mm. **Subject:** Church fron Densus **Obv:** Christ icon on pillar at left, national shield at right **Rev:** Church at left, arch at right

Date	Mintage	F12	VF20	XF40	MS60	MS63
2006	500	PF65 160				

KM# 217 5 LEI
31.10 g., 0.999 Silver 0.9926 oz. ASW, 37 mm. **Subject:** Sibiu - European Capital of Culture **Obv:** 2 city towers in Sibiu at left, fortress wall connecting them, Potter's Tower in background, coat of arms at right **Obv. Inscription:** ROMANIA **Rev:** City of Sibiu's logo at bottom, 2 line inscription at left, 3 line inscription at right, 4 famous edifices at center **Rev. Inscription:** SIBIU / 2007 and CAPITALA / CULTURALA / EUROPEANA **Edge:** Plain

Date	Mintage	F12	VF20	XF40	MS60	MS63
2007	500	PF65 400				

KM# 221 5 LEI
15.55 g., 0.999 Silver 0.4962 oz. ASW, 30 mm. **Subject:** Centennial - Birth of Mircea Eliade **Obv:** Shield and value **Rev:** Portrait facing **Edge:** Reeded

Date	Mintage	F12	VF20	XF40	MS60	MS63
2007	250	PF65 300				

KM# 224 5 LEI
15.55 g., 0.999 Silver 0.4962 oz. ASW, 30 mm. **Subject:** Dimitrie Cantemir, (Prince of Moldavia 1673-1723), Scientist **Edge:** Reeded

Date	Mintage	F12	VF20	XF40	MS60	MS63
2007	250	PF65 300				

KM# 227 5 LEI
15.50 g., 0.999 Silver 0.4946 oz. ASW, 30 mm. **Subject:** Stephan the Great **Edge:** Reeded

Date	Mintage	F12	VF20	XF40	MS60	MS63
2007	250	PF65 300				

KM# 200 5 LEI
15.55 g., 0.999 Silver 0.4962 oz. ASW, 30 mm. **Subject:** 130th Anniversary of Proclamation of Independence **Obv:** Shield and "The Smardan Assault" painting by Nicolae Grigorescu **Rev:** Meeting of the Parliament

Date	Mintage	F12	VF20	XF40	MS60	MS63
2007	130	PF65 500				

KM# 242 5 LEI
15.55 g., 0.999 Silver 0.4962 oz. ASW, 30 mm. **Subject:** Ovidivs Naso **Rev:** Half-length figure

Date	Mintage	F12	VF20	XF40	MS60	MS63
2008	500	PF65 170				

KM# 207 10 LEI
1.22 g., 0.999 Gold 0.0391 oz. AGW, 13.92 mm. **Subject:** History of Gold - The Persinari Hoard **Edge:** Reeded

Date	Mintage	F12	VF20	XF40	MS60	MS63
2005	1,000	PF65 200				

KM# 203 10 LEI
1.22 g., 0.999 Gold 0.0391 oz. AGW, 13.92 mm. **Subject:** Histoy of Gold - The Cucuteni Báiceni Hoard **Obv:** Romania's Coat of Arms with denomination **Rev:** Cheekpiece of the gold helmet in the Cucuteni-Baiceni hoard **Edge:** Reeded

Date	Mintage	F12	VF20	XF40	MS60	MS63
2006	500	PF65 250				

KM# 229 10 LEI
31.10 g., 0.999 Silver 0.9926 oz. ASW, 37 mm. **Subject:** 50th Anniversary - Treaty of Rome **Edge:** Reeded

Date	Mintage	F12	VF20	XF40	MS60	MS63
2007	500	PF65 400				

KM# 240 10 LEI
31.11 g., 0.999 Silver 0.9926 oz. ASW, 37 mm. **Subject:** Petroleum Industry, 150th Anniversary **Rev:** Oil derrick and pump

Date	Mintage	F12	VF20	XF40	MS60	MS63
2007	500	PF65 150				

KM# 241 10 LEI
31.11 g., 0.999 Silver 0.9926 oz. ASW, 37 mm. **Subject:** Snagov Monastery **Rev:** Building and bust

Date	Mintage	F12	VF20	XF40	MS60	MS63
2007	500	PF65 170				

KM# 230 10 LEI
31.10 g., 0.999 Silver 0.9925 oz. ASW, 37 mm. **Subject:** 150th Anniversary of First Postage Stamp **Rev:** Cap de Bour" (bull's

head) stamp **Edge:** Reeded

Date	Mintage	F12	VF20	XF40	MS60	MS63
2008	1,000	PF65 175				

KM# 231 10 LEI
31.10 g., 0.999 Silver 0.9926 oz. ASW, 37 mm. **Subject:** 80th Anniversary Romanian Broadcasting Co. **Obv:** Radio Romania, years 1928 and 2008, coat of arms **Rev:** Radio set from 30's, logo of Radio Romania, headphones **Edge:** Reeded

Date	Mintage	F12	VF20	XF40	MS60	MS63
2008	500	PF65 300				

KM# 232 10 LEI
1.24 g., 0.999 Gold 0.0397 oz. AGW, 13.92 mm. **Subject:** Hoard of Hinova **Obv:** Romanian Coat of Arms, necklace parts **Rev:** Necklace parts, four bell shaped necklace parts, muff **Edge:** Reeded

Date	Mintage	F12	VF20	XF40	MS60	MS63
2008	500	PF65 135				

KM# 244 10 LEI
31.11 g., 0.999 Silver 0.9926 oz. ASW, 37 mm. **Subject:** Costin Kiritescu **Rev:** Bust facing

Date	Mintage	F12	VF20	XF40	MS60	MS63
2008	500	PF65 170				

KM# 245 10 LEI
31.11 g., 0.999 Silver 0.9926 oz. ASW, 37 mm. **Subject:** First printed book in Walachia, 500th Anniversary **Rev:** Building and printers at press

Date	Mintage	F12	VF20	XF40	MS60	MS63
2008	500	PF65 170				

KM# 246 10 LEI
31.11 g., 0.999 Silver 0.9926 oz. ASW, 37 mm. **Subject:** Simon Barnutiu **Rev:** Bust facing

Date	Mintage	F12	VF20	XF40	MS60	MS63
2008	500	PF65 150				

KM# 247 10 LEI
31.11 g., 0.999 Silver 0.9926 oz. ASW, 37 mm. **Subject:** Cozia Monastery **Rev:** Church building

Date	Mintage	F12	VF20	XF40	MS60	MS63
2008	500	PF65 165				

KM# 248 10 LEI
31.11 g., 0.999 Silver 0.9926 oz. ASW, 37 mm. **Subject:** Sambata des Sus Monastery **Rev:** Church building

Date	Mintage	F12	VF20	XF40	MS60	MS63
2008	500	PF65 165				

KM# 249 10 LEI
31.11 g., 0.999 Silver 0.9926 oz. ASW, 37 mm. **Subject:** Voroneţ Monastery **Rev:** Church building

Date	Mintage	F12	VF20	XF40	MS60	MS63
2008	500	PF65 165				

KM# 236 10 LEI
31.11 g., 0.999 Silver 0.9926 oz. ASW, 37 mm. **Subject:** Nicolae Balcescu, 190th Anniversary of Birth

Date	Mintage	F12	VF20	XF40	MS60	MS63
2009	1,000	PF65 85.00				

KM# 250 10 LEI
31.11 g., 0.999 Silver 0.9926 oz. ASW, 37 mm. **Subject:** European Monitary Union, 10th Anniversary **Rev:** Stick figure and Euro symbol

Date	Mintage	F12	VF20	XF40	MS60	MS63
2009	1,000	PF65 150				

KM# 251 10 LEI
31.11 g., 0.999 Silver 0.9926 oz. ASW, 37 mm. **Subject:** Alexander Macedonski **Rev:** Bust left

Date	Mintage	F12	VF20	XF40	MS60	MS63
2009	500	PF65 150				

KM# 252 10 LEI
31.11 g., 0.999 Silver 0.9926 oz. ASW, 37 mm. **Subject:** Walachia's establishment as an Archdiocese, 650th Anniversary **Rev:** Archbishop and Cathedral

Date	Mintage	F12	VF20	XF40	MS60	MS63
2009	500	PF65 170				

KM# 253 10 LEI
31.11 g., 0.999 Silver 0.9926 oz. ASW, 37 mm. **Subject:** Statistical Office, 150th Anniversary **Rev:** Two busts and document

Date	Mintage	F12	VF20	XF40	MS60	MS63
2009	500	PF65 150				

KM# 254 10 LEI
31.11 g., 0.999 Silver 0.9926 oz. ASW, 37 mm. **Subject:** Bucharest - Giurgiu Railway, 150th Anniversary **Rev:** Steam train

Date	Mintage	F12	VF20	XF40	MS60	MS63
2009	500	PF65 170				

KM# 255 10 LEI
31.11 g., 0.999 Silver 0.9926 oz. ASW, 37 mm. **Subject:** Bucharest, 550th Anniversary **Rev:** Architectural elements

Date	Mintage	F12	VF20	XF40	MS60	MS63
2009	500	PF65 160				

KM# 256 10 LEI
31.11 g., 0.999 Silver 0.9926 oz. ASW, 37 mm. **Subject:** Constanta Harbor, 100th Anniversary **Rev:** Ship and buildings

Date	Mintage	F12	VF20	XF40	MS60	MS63
2009	500	PF65 160				

KM# 257 10 LEI
31.11 g., 0.999 Silver 0.9926 oz. ASW, 37 mm. **Subject:** Tropaeum Traiani, 1900th Anniversary **Rev:** Ancient Roman building, Emperor Trajan

Date	Mintage	F12	VF20	XF40	MS60	MS63
2009	500	PF65 150				

KM# 238 10 LEI
1.24 g., 0.999 Gold 0.0396 oz. AGW, 13.92 mm. **Subject:** History of Gold **Rev:** Gold collar from the Gepids hoard

Date	Mintage	F12	VF20	XF40	MS60	MS63
2010	500	PF65 90.00				

KM# 262 10 LEI
31.11 g., 0.999 Silver 0.9926 oz. ASW **Subject:** Central Bank, 130th Anniversary **Shape:** 37

Date	Mintage	F12	VF20	XF40	MS60	MS63
2010	3,000	PF65 75.00				

KM# 266 10 LEI
31.11 g., 0.999 Silver 0.9926 oz. ASW, 37 mm. **Subject:** Romanian Orthodox Church Patriarchs **Rev:** Miron Cristea

Date	Mintage	F12	VF20	XF40	MS60	MS63
2010	1,000	PF65 75.00				

KM# 267 10 LEI
31.11 g., 0.999 Silver 0.9926 oz. ASW, 37 mm. **Subject:** Romanian Orthodox Church Patriarchs **Rev:** Nicodim Munteanu

Date	Mintage	F12	VF20	XF40	MS60	MS63
2010	1,000	PF65 75.00				

KM# 268 10 LEI
31.11 g., 0.999 Silver 0.9926 oz. ASW, 37 mm. **Subject:** Romanian Orthodox Church Patriarchs **Rev:** Justinian Marina

Date	Mintage	F12	VF20	XF40	MS60	MS63
2010	1,000	PF65 75.00				

KM# 269 10 LEI
31.11 g., 0.999 Silver 0.9926 oz. ASW, 37 mm. **Subject:** Romanian Orthodox Church Patriarchs **Rev:** Justin Moisescu

Date	Mintage	F12	VF20	XF40	MS60	MS63
2010	1,000	PF65 75.00				

KM# 270 10 LEI
31.11 g., 0.999 Silver 0.9926 oz. ASW, 37 mm. **Subject:** Romanian Orthodox Church Patriarchs **Rev:** Teoctist Arapasu

Date	Mintage	F12	VF20	XF40	MS60	MS63
2010	1,000	PF65 75.00				

KM# 271 10 LEI
31.11 g., 0.999 Silver 0.9926 oz. ASW, 37 mm. **Subject:** Hariclea Darclee **Obv:** Opera House

Date	Mintage	F12	VF20	XF40	MS60	MS63
2010	1,000	PF65 75.00				

KM# 272 10 LEI
31.11 g., 0.999 Silver 0.9926 oz. ASW, 37 mm. **Subject:** August Treboniu Laurian, 200th Anniversary of Birth **Obv:** She-wolf and twins

Date	Mintage	F12	VF20	XF40	MS60	MS63
2010	1,000	PF65 75.00				

KM# 273 10 LEI
31.11 g., 0.999 Silver 0.9926 oz. ASW, 37 mm. **Subject:** Stefan Ciobotaraşu, 100th Anniversary of Birth **Obv:** Movie Theater

Date	Mintage	F12	VF20	XF40	MS60	MS63
2010	1,000	PF65 75.00				

KM# 274 10 LEI
31.11 g., 0.999 Silver 0.9926 oz. ASW, 37 mm. **Obv:** Turboprop aircraft, 1910 **Rev:** Henri Coanda

Date	Mintage	F12	VF20	XF40	MS60	MS63
2010	1,000	PF65 75.00				

KM# 276 10 LEI
31.11 g., 0.999 Silver 0.9926 oz. ASW, 37 mm. **Subject:** Grigore Alexandrescu, 200th Anniversary of Birth

Date	Mintage	F12	VF20	XF40	MS60	MS63
2010	1,000	PF65 75.00				

KM# 277 10 LEI
1.24 g., 0.999 Gold 0.0396 oz. AGW, 13.92 mm. **Subject:** History of Gold - Church of Sfantul Nicolae

Date	Mintage	F12	VF20	XF40	MS60	MS63
2011	500	PF65 90.00				

KM# 279 10 LEI
31.11 g., 0.999 Silver 0.9926 oz. ASW, 37 mm. **Subject:** Letterpress printing in Romanian language, 450th Anniversary

Date	Mintage	F12	VF20	XF40	MS60	MS63
2011	500	PF65 140				

KM# 280 10 LEI
31.11 g., 0.999 Silver 0.9926 oz. ASW, 37 mm. **Subject:** George Bacovia, 130th Anniversary of Birth

Date	Mintage	F12	VF20	XF40	MS60	MS63
2011	500	PF65 140				

KM# 281 10 LEI
31.11 g., 0.999 Silver 0.9926 oz. ASW, 37 mm. **Subject:** Nicolae Milescu, 375th Anniversary of Birth

Date	Mintage	F12	VF20	XF40	MS60	MS63
2011	500	PF65 140				

KM# 282 10 LEI
31.11 g., 0.999 Silver 0.9926 oz. ASW, 37 mm. **Subject:** ASTRA, 150th Anniversary **Obv:** Andrei Saguna **Rev:** Timotei Cipariu, George Baritiu, Ioan Puscariu

Date	Mintage	F12	VF20	XF40	MS60	MS63
2011	500	PF65 140				

KM# 283 10 LEI
31.11 g., 0.999 Silver 0.9926 oz. ASW, 37 mm. **Subject:** Romanian Military, 150th Anniversary **Obv:** Alexandru Ioan Cuza **Rev:** Mounted officer before infantry

Date	Mintage	F12	VF20	XF40	MS60	MS63
2011	500	PF65 140				

KM# 285 10 LEI
1.24 g., 0.999 Gold 0.0396 oz. AGW, 13.92 mm. **Subject:** History of Gold - Chain with cross

Date	Mintage	F12	VF20	XF40	MS60	MS63
2011	500	PF65 90.00				

KM# 286 10 LEI
31.11 g., 0.999 Silver 0.9926 oz. ASW, 37 mm. **Subject:** Euro, 10th Anniversary **Obv:** Building and map of Romania **Rev:** Euro as world currency

Date	Mintage	F12	VF20	XF40	MS60	MS63
2012	500	PF65 150				

KM# 211 50 LEI
6.45 g., 0.900 Gold 0.1854 oz. AGW, 21 mm. **Subject:** 140th Anniversary Founding Romanian Academy **Edge:** Plain

Date	Mintage	F12	VF20	XF40	MS60	MS63
2006	35	PF65 3,000				

KM# 222 100 LEI
6.45 g., 0.900 Gold 0.1854 oz. AGW, 21 mm. **Subject:** Centennial - Birth of Mircea Eliade **Obv:** Shield and value **Rev:** Portrait facing **Edge:** Reeded

Date	Mintage	F12	VF20	XF40	MS60	MS63
2007	250	PF65 900				

KM# 225 100 LEI
6.45 g., 0.900 Gold 0.1854 oz. AGW, 21 mm. **Subject:** Dimitrie Cantemir, (Prince of Moldavia 1710-1711), Scientist **Edge:** Reeded

Date	Mintage	F12	VF20	XF40	MS60	MS63
2007	250	PF65 900				

KM# 228 100 LEI
6.45 g., 0.900 Gold 0.1855 oz. AGW, 21 mm. **Subject:** 550th Anniversary - Ascension Prince Stephan the Great into Moldavia **Edge:** Reeded

Date	Mintage	F12	VF20	XF40	MS60	MS63
2007	250	PF65 900				

KM# 201 100 LEI
6.45 g., 0.900 Gold 0.1855 oz. AGW, 21 mm. **Subject:** 130th Anniversary of Proclamation of Independence **Obv:** Shield and "The Smardan Assault" painting by Nicole Grigorescu **Rev:** Meeting of the Parliament

Date	Mintage	F12	VF20	XF40	MS60	MS63
2007	130	PF65 1,500				

KM# 235 100 LEI
6.45 g., 0.999 Gold 0.2059 oz. AGW, 21 mm. **Subject:** Battles of Marasti, Marasesti, Oituz 90th Anniversary **Obv:** Mausoleum of Marasesti **Rev:** Group of soldiers at Battle of Marasti

Date	Mintage	F12	VF20	XF40	MS60	MS63
2007	250	PF65 550				

KM# 264 100 LEI
6.45 g., 0.900 Gold 0.1854 oz. AGW, 21 mm. **Subject:** Eugeniu Carada, 100th Anniversary of Death

Date	Mintage	F12	VF20	XF40	MS60	MS63
2010	500	PF65 450				

KM# 275 100 LEI
6.45 g., 0.999 Gold 0.2058 oz. AGW, 21 mm. **Subject:** Maria Alexandria Victoria, 135th Anniversary of Birth

Date	Mintage	F12	VF20	XF40	MS60	MS63
2010	1,000	PF65 500				

KM# 284 100 LEI
6.45 g., 0.999 Gold 0.2058 oz. AGW, 21 mm. **Subject:** Wallachian uprising, 190th Anniversary **Rev:** Tudor Vladimirescu

Date	Mintage	F12	VF20	XF40	MS60	MS63
2011	500	PF65 500				

KM# 263 200 LEI
15.55 g., 0.999 Gold 0.4962 oz. AGW, 27 mm. **Subject:** Central Bank, 130th Anniversary

Date	Mintage	F12	VF20	XF40	MS60	MS63
2010	1,500	PF65 950				

KM# 265 200 LEI
15.55 g., 0.999 Gold 0.4962 oz. AGW, 27 mm. **Subject:** Romanian Orthodox Church

Date	Mintage	F12	VF20	XF40	MS60	MS63
2010	1,000	PF65 1,000				

KM# 278 200 LEI
15.55 g., 0.999 Gold 0.4962 oz. AGW, 27 mm. **Subject:** Cozia Monastery

Date	Mintage	F12	VF20	XF40	MS60	MS63
2011	250	PF65 1,300				

KM# 194 500 LEI
31.10 g., 0.999 Silver 0.9926 oz. ASW, 37 mm. **Subject:** 125th Anniversary - National Bank **Obv:** National arms and coin design of 5 Lei dated 1880 **Rev:** Bank building **Edge:** Plain

Date	Mintage	F12	VF20	XF40	MS60	MS63
2005	—	PF65 1,000				

KM# 206 500 LEI
31.10 g., 0.999 Gold 0.9925 oz. AGW, 35 mm. **Subject:** 50th Anniversary - Death of George Enescu **Edge:** Plain

Date	Mintage	F12	VF20	XF40	MS60	MS63
2005	250	PF65 2,250				

KM# 214 500 LEI
31.10 g., 0.999 Gold 0.9926 oz. AGW, 35 mm. **Subject:** 350th Anniversary - Establishment of the Patriarchal Cathedral **Edge:** Plain

Date	Mintage	F12	VF20	XF40	MS60	MS63
2006	250	PF65 3,000				

KM# 204 500 LEI
31.10 g., 0.999 Gold 0.9926 oz. AGW, 35 mm. **Subject:** Romania's Accession to European Union, January 1 2007 **Obv:** Romania's Coat of Arms surrounded by 12 stars of European Union **Rev:** Map of the European Union including Romania **Edge:** Plain

Date	Mintage	F12	VF20	XF40	MS60	MS63
2007	250	PF65 3,000				

KM# 205 500 LEI
31.10 g., 0.999 Gold 0.9926 oz. AGW, 35 mm. **Subject:** Nicolae Balcescu (1819-1852) **Obv:** Romania's Coat of Arms and **Obv. Inscription:** Justice and Brotherhood **Rev:** Portrait of Nicolae Balcescu **Edge:** Plain

Date	Mintage	F12	VF20	XF40	MS60	MS63
2007	250	PF65 2,250				

KM# 215 500 LEI
31.11 g., 0.999 Gold 0.9926 oz. AGW, 35 mm. **Subject:** Statehood, 90th Anniversary **Obv:** Shield **Rev:** Crown

Date	Mintage	F12	VF20	XF40	MS60	MS63
2008	3,000	PF65 1,850				

KM# 219 500 LEI
31.11 g., 0.999 Gold 0.9926 oz. AGW, 35 mm. **Subject:** Carol I, 170th Anniversary of Birth

Date	Mintage	F12	VF20	XF40	MS60	MS63
2009	250	PF65 1,850				

KM# 233 500 LEI
31.11 g., 0.999 Gold 0.9926 oz. AGW, 35 mm. **Subject:** Bucharest, 550th Anniversary

Date	Mintage	F12	VF20	XF40	MS60	MS63
2009	—	PF65 1,850				

KM# 237 500 LEI
31.11 g., 0.999 Gold 0.9926 oz. AGW, 35 mm. **Subject:** Nicolae Balcescu, 190th Anniversary of Birth

Date	Mintage	F12	VF20	XF40	MS60	MS63
2009	—	PF65 1,850				

KM# 239 500 LEI
31.11 g., 0.999 Gold 0.9926 oz. AGW, 35 mm. **Subject:** Mihai Eminescu, 160th Anniversary of Birth

Date	Mintage	F12	VF20	XF40	MS60	MS63
2010	—	PF65 1,850				

MINT SETS

KM#	Date	Mintage	Identification	Issue Price	Mkt Val
MS4	2006 (4)	—	KM189-192, plus medal	—	75.00
MS5	2007 (4)	1,000	KM189-192, plus medal	—	60.00
MS6	2005 (4)	—	KM#189-192	—	50.00

PROOF SETS

KM#	Date	Mintage	Identification	Issue Price	Mkt Val
PS4	2001 (3)	500	KM#159, 160, 161	80.00	525
PS5	2002 (9)	1,500	KM#109-111, 114-116, 145, 153, 158	20.00	75.00
PS6	2003 (9)	2,000	KM#109-111, 114-116, 145, 153, 158	20.00	75.00
PS7	2003 (3)	500	KM#186, 187, 188	—	325
PS8	2004 (2)	500	KM#163, 164	—	325
PS9	2005 (10)	—	KM#111, 115, 145, 153, 158, 189-192 plus medal	—	80.00
PS10	2006 (10)	—	KM#111, 115, 145, 153, 158, 189-192	—	80.00
PS11	2006 (3)	—	KM#209, 210, 211	—	4,050
PS12	2007 (3)	—	KM#220, 221, 222	—	1,350
PS13	2007 (3)	—	KM#223, 224, 225	—	1,350
PS14	2007 (3)	—	KM#226, 227, 228	—	1,350
PS15	2007 (5)	—	KM#189-192 plus Silver 75th Anniversary of Rodna Mountains National Park medal	—	50.00
PS17	2008 (4)	—	KM#189-192 plus silver medal Antipa Museum	—	50.00
PSA8	2004 (5)	—	KM#111, 115, 145, 153, 158	—	50.00

The Russia Federation, formerly the central power of the Union of Soviet Socialist Republics and now of the Commonwealth of Independent States occupies the northern part of Asia and the eastern part of Europe, has an area of 17,075,400 sq. km. Capital: Moscow. Exports include iron and steel, crude oil, timber, and nonferrous metals.

In the fall of 1991, events moved swiftly in the Soviet Union. Estonia, Latvia and Lithuania won their independence and were recognized by Moscow, Sept. 6. The Commonwealth of Independent States was formed Dec. 8, 1991 in Mensk by Belarus, Russia and Ukraine. It was expanded at a summit Dec. 21, 1991 to include 11 of the 12 remaining republics (excluding Georgia) of the old U.S.S.R.

RUSSIAN FEDERATION
REFORM COINAGE
1,000 Old Roubles = 1 New RoubleJanuary 1, 1998

Y# 600 KOPEK
1.50 g., Copper-Nickel Plated Steel, 15.5 mm. **Obv:** St. George **Obv. Legend:** БАНК РОССИИ **Rev:** Value above vine sprig **Edge:** Plain

Date	Mintage	F12	VF20	XF40	MS60	MS63
2001M	—	—	—	—	0.30	0.40
2001СП	—	—	—	—	0.30	0.40
2002M	—	—	—	—	0.30	0.40
2002СП	—	—	—	—	0.30	0.40
2003M	—	—	—	—	0.30	0.40
2003СП	—	—	—	—	0.30	0.40
2004M	—	—	—	—	0.30	0.40
2004СП	—	—	—	—	0.30	0.40
2005M	—	—	—	—	0.30	0.40
2005СП	—	—	—	—	0.30	0.40
2006M	—	—	—	—	0.30	0.40
2006СП	—	—	—	—	0.30	0.40
2007M	—	—	—	—	0.30	0.40
2007СП	—	—	—	—	0.30	0.40
2008M	—	—	—	—	0.30	0.40
2008СП	—	—	—	—	0.30	0.40
2009M	—	—	—	—	1.00	2.00
2009СП	—	—	—	—	1.00	2.00

Y# 601 5 KOPEKS
2.60 g., Copper-Nickel Clad Steel, 18.5 mm. **Obv:** St. George

Obv. Legend: БАНК РОССИИ **Rev:** Value above vine sprig
Edge: Plain

Date	Mintage	F12	VF20	XF40	MS60	MS63
2001М	—	—	—	—	0.40	0.60
2001СП	—	—	—	—	0.40	0.60
2002	—	—	80.00	95.00	120	—
2002М	—	—	—	—	0.40	0.60
2002СП	—	—	—	—	0.40	0.60
2003	—	—	10.00	15.00	25.00	—
2003М	—	—	—	—	0.35	0.50
2003СП	—	—	—	—	0.35	0.50
2004М	—	—	—	—	0.35	0.50
2004СП	—	—	—	—	0.35	0.50
2005М	—	—	—	—	0.35	0.50
2005СП	—	—	—	—	0.35	0.50
2006М	—	—	—	—	0.35	0.50
2006СП	—	—	—	—	0.35	0.50
2007М	—	—	—	—	0.35	0.50
2007СП	—	—	—	—	0.35	0.50
2008М	—	—	—	—	0.35	0.50
2008СП	—	—	—	—	0.35	0.50
2009М	—	—	—	—	1.00	2.00
2009СП	—	—	—	—	1.00	2.00

Y# 602 10 KOPEKS
1.95 g., Brass, 17.5 mm. **Obv:** St. George horseback right slaying dragon **Rev:** Value above vine sprig **Edge:** Reeded

Date	Mintage	F12	VF20	XF40	MS60	MS63
2001М	—	—	—	—	0.50	0.80
2001СП	—	—	—	—	0.50	0.80
2002М	—	—	—	—	0.50	0.80
2002СП	—	—	—	—	0.50	0.80
2003М	—	—	—	—	0.50	0.80
2003СП	—	—	—	—	0.50	0.80
2004М	—	—	—	—	0.50	0.80
2004СП	—	—	—	—	0.50	0.80
2005М	—	—	—	—	0.50	0.80
2005СП	—	—	—	—	0.50	0.80
2006М	—	—	—	—	0.50	0.80
2006СП	—	—	—	—	0.50	0.80

Y# 602a 10 KOPEKS
1.85 g., Tombac Plated Steel, 17.5 mm. **Obv:** St. George on horseback slaying dragon to right **Obv. Legend:** БАНК РОССИИ **Rev:** Denomination above vine sprig **Edge:** Plain

Date	Mintage	F12	VF20	XF40	MS60	MS63
2006М	—	—	—	—	0.50	0.80
2006СП	—	—	—	—	0.50	0.80
2007М	—	—	—	—	0.50	0.80
2007СП	—	—	—	—	0.50	0.80
2008М	—	—	—	—	0.50	0.80
2008СП	—	—	—	—	0.50	0.80
2009М	—	—	—	—	0.50	0.80
2009СП	—	—	—	—	0.50	0.80
2010М	—	—	—	—	0.50	0.80
2010СП	—	—	—	—	0.50	0.80
2011М	—	—	—	—	0.50	0.80
2012М	—	—	—	—	0.50	0.80

Y# 603 50 KOPEKS
2.90 g., Brass, 19.5 mm. **Obv:** St. George on horseback slaying dragon right **Rev:** Value above vine sprig **Edge:** Reeded

Date	Mintage	F12	VF20	XF40	MS60	MS63
2001M Rare	—	—	—	5,000	—	—
2002М	—	—	—	—	1.50	3.00
2002СП	—	—	—	—	1.50	3.00
2003М	—	—	—	—	0.80	1.00
2003СП	—	—	—	—	0.80	1.00
2004М	—	—	—	—	0.80	1.00
2004СП	—	—	—	—	0.80	1.00
2005М	—	—	—	—	0.80	1.00
2005СП	—	—	—	—	0.80	1.00
2006М	—	—	—	—	0.80	1.00
2006СП	—	—	—	—	0.80	1.00

Y# 603a 50 KOPEKS
2.75 g., Brass Clad Steel, 19.5 mm. **Obv:** St. George on horseback slaying dragon right **Rev:** Value above vine sprig **Edge:** Plain

Date	Mintage	F12	VF20	XF40	MS60	MS63
2006М	—	—	—	—	0.80	1.00
2006СП	—	—	—	—	0.80	1.00
2007М	—	—	—	—	0.80	1.00
2007СП	—	—	—	—	0.80	1.00
2008М	—	—	—	—	0.80	1.00
2008СП	—	—	—	—	0.80	1.00
2009М	—	—	—	—	0.80	1.00
2009СП	—	—	—	—	0.80	1.00
2010М	—	—	—	—	0.80	1.00
2010СП	—	—	—	—	0.80	1.00
2011М	—	—	—	—	0.80	1.00
2012М	—	—	—	—	0.80	1.00

Y# 604 ROUBLE
3.25 g., Copper-Nickel-Zinc, 20.5 mm. **Obv:** Double-headed eagle **Rev:** Value **Edge:** Reeded

Date	Mintage	F12	VF20	XF40	MS60	MS63
2001M Rare						

Y# 731 ROUBLE
3.21 g., Copper-Nickel, 20.7 mm. **Obv:** Double-headed eagle **Rev:** Stylized design above hologram **Edge:** Reeded

Date	Mintage	F12	VF20	XF40	MS60	MS63
2001СПМД	100,000,000	—	—	—	1.50	2.00

Y# 732 ROUBLE
17.43 g., 0.900 Silver 0.5011 oz. ASW, 32.8 mm. **Subject:** Sturgeon **Obv:** Double-headed eagle within beaded circle **Rev:** Sakhalin sturgeon and other fish **Edge:** Reeded

Date	Mintage	F12	VF20	XF40	MS60	MS63
2001	7,500	PF65 60.00				

Y# 745 ROUBLE
17.40 g., 0.900 Silver 0.5002 oz. ASW, 32.8 mm. **Obv:** Double-headed eagle within beaded circle **Rev:** Altai argalia sheep **Edge:** Reeded

Date	Mintage	F12	VF20	XF40	MS60	MS63
2001(sp)	7,500	PF65 65.00				

Y# 746 ROUBLE
17.40 g., 0.900 Silver 0.5002 oz. ASW, 32.8 mm. **Obv:** Double-headed eagle within beaded circle **Rev:** Beavers **Edge:** Reeded

Date	Mintage	F12	VF20	XF40	MS60	MS63
2001(sp)	7,500	PF65 65.00				

Y# 758 ROUBLE
17.44 g., 0.900 Silver 0.5014 oz. ASW, 33 mm. **Obv:** Double-headed eagle within beaded circle **Rev:** Chinese Goral **Edge:** Reeded

Date	Mintage	F12	VF20	XF40	MS60	MS63
2002(sp)	10,000	PF65 50.00				

Y# 759 ROUBLE
17.44 g., 0.900 Silver 0.5014 oz. ASW, 33 mm. **Obv:** Double-headed eagle within beaded circle **Rev:** Sei Whale **Edge:** Reeded

Date	Mintage	F12	VF20	XF40	MS60	MS63
2002(sp)	10,000	PF65 50.00				

Y# 760 ROUBLE
17.44 g., 0.900 Silver 0.5014 oz. ASW, 33 mm. **Subject:** Golden Eagle **Obv:** Double-headed eagle within beaded circle **Rev:** Golden Eagle with nestling **Edge:** Reeded

Date	Mintage	F12	VF20	XF40	MS60	MS63
2002(sp)	10,000	PF65 50.00				

Y# 833 ROUBLE
3.25 g., Copper-Nickel-Zinc, 20.5 mm. **Obv:** Two headed eagle above curved bank name and date, denomination above **Rev:** Value and flower **Edge:** Reeded

Date	Mintage	F12	VF20	XF40	MS60	MS63
2002(m) Mint sets only	15,000	—	—	—	—	—
2002(sp) Mint sets only	15,000	—	—	—	—	—
2003(sp)	15,000	—	—	300	400	500
2005(m)	—	—	—	—	2.00	3.00
2005(sp)	—	—	—	—	2.00	3.00
2006(m)	—	—	—	—	2.00	3.00
2006(sp)	—	—	—	—	2.00	3.00
2007(m)	—	—	—	—	2.00	3.00
2007(sp)	—	—	—	—	2.00	3.00
2008(m)	—	—	—	—	2.00	3.00
2008(sp)	—	—	—	—	2.00	3.00
2009(m)	—	—	—	—	2.00	3.00
2009(sp)	—	—	—	—	2.00	3.00

Y# A834 ROUBLE
7.78 g., 0.925 Silver 0.2299 oz. ASW, 25 mm. **Subject:** St. Petersburg **Obv:** Double-headed eagle within beaded circle **Rev:** Angel on steeple of Cathedral in fortress

Date	Mintage	F12	VF20	XF40	MS60	MS63
2002	5,000	PF65 25.00				

Y# 770 ROUBLE
8.53 g., 0.925 Silver 0.252 oz. ASW, 25 mm. **Subject:** Ministry of Education **Obv:** Double-headed eagle within beaded circle **Rev:** Seedling within open book **Edge:** Reeded

Date	Mintage	F12	VF20	XF40	MS60	MS63
2002(m)	3,000	PF65 50.00				

Y# 771 ROUBLE
8.53 g., 0.925 Silver 0.252 oz. ASW, 25 mm. **Subject:** Ministry of Finances **Obv:** Double-headed eagle within beaded circle **Rev:** Caduceus in monogram **Edge:** Reeded

Date	Mintage	F12	VF20	XF40	MS60	MS63
2002(sp)	3,000	PF65 50.00				

Y# 772 ROUBLE
8.53 g., 0.925 Silver 0.252 oz. ASW, 25 mm. **Subject:** Ministry of Economic Development **Obv:** Double-headed eagle within beaded circle **Rev:** Crowned double-headed eagle with cornucopia and caduceus **Edge:** Reeded

Date	Mintage	F12	VF20	XF40	MS60	MS63
2002(sp)	3,000	PF65 50.00				

Y# 773 ROUBLE
8.53 g., 0.925 Silver 0.252 oz. ASW, 25 mm. **Subject:** Ministry of Foreign Affairs **Obv:** Double-headed eagle within beaded circle **Rev:** Crowned two-headed eagle above crossed sprigs **Edge:** Reeded

Date	Mintage	F12	VF20	XF40	MS60	MS63
2002(sp)	3,000	PF65 50.00				

Y# 774 ROUBLE
8.53 g., 0.925 Silver 0.252 oz. ASW, 25 mm. **Subject:** Ministry of Internal Affairs **Obv:** Double-headed eagle within beaded circle **Rev:** Crowned two-headed eagle with round breast **Edge:** Reeded

Date	Mintage	F12	VF20	XF40	MS60	MS63
2002(sp)	3,000	PF65 50.00				

Y# 775 ROUBLE
8.53 g., 0.925 Silver 0.252 oz. ASW, 25 mm. **Subject:** Ministry of Justice **Obv:** Double-headed eagle within beaded circle **Rev:** Crowned double-headed eagle with column on breast shield **Edge:** Reeded

Date	Mintage	F12	VF20	XF40	MS60	MS63
2002(sp)	3,000	PF65 50.00				

Y# 776 ROUBLE
8.53 g., 0.925 Silver 0.252 oz. ASW, 25 mm. **Subject:** Russian Armed Forces **Obv:** Double-headed eagle within beaded circle **Rev:** Double-headed eagle with crowned top pointed breast shield **Edge:** Reeded

Date	Mintage	F12	VF20	XF40	MS60	MS63
2002(m)	3,000	PF65 50.00				

Y# 835 ROUBLE
7.78 g., 0.925 Silver 0.2299 oz. ASW, 25 mm. **Subject:** St. Petersburg **Obv:** Double-headed eagle within beaded circle **Rev:** Sphinx

Date	Mintage	F12	VF20	XF40	MS60	MS63
2002	5,000	PF65 25.00				

Y# 836 ROUBLE
7.78 g., 0.925 Silver 0.2299 oz. ASW, 25 mm. **Subject:** St. Petersburg **Obv:** Double-headed eagle within beaded circle **Rev:** Small ship

Date	Mintage	F12	VF20	XF40	MS60	MS63
2002	5,000	PF65 25.00				

Y# 837 ROUBLE
7.78 g., 0.925 Silver 0.2299 oz. ASW, 25 mm. **Subject:** St. Petersburg **Obv:** Double-headed eagle within beaded circle **Rev:** Lion

Date	Mintage	F12	VF20	XF40	MS60	MS63
2002	5,000	PF65 25.00				

Y# 838 ROUBLE
7.78 g., 0.925 Silver 0.2299 oz. ASW, 25 mm. **Subject:** St. Petersburg **Obv:** Double-headed eagle within beaded circle **Rev:** Horse sculpture

Date	Mintage	F12	VF20	XF40	MS60	MS63
2002	5,000	PF65 25.00				

Y# 839 ROUBLE
7.78 g., 0.925 Silver 0.2299 oz. ASW, 25 mm. **Subject:** St. Petersburg **Obv:** Double-headed eagle within beaded circle **Rev:** Griffin

Date	Mintage	F12	VF20	XF40	MS60	MS63
2002	5,000	PF65 25.00				

Y# 814 ROUBLE
17.40 g., 0.900 Silver 0.5002 oz. ASW, 32.8 mm. **Obv:** Double-headed eagle within beaded circle **Rev:** Arctic foxes **Edge:** Reeded

Date	Mintage	F12	VF20	XF40	MS60	MS63
2003(sp)	10,000	PF65 35.00				

Y# 815 ROUBLE
17.40 g., 0.900 Silver 0.5002 oz. ASW, 32.8 mm. **Obv:** Double-headed eagle within beaded circle **Rev:** Chinese Softshell turtle **Edge:** Reeded

Date	Mintage	F12	VF20	XF40	MS60	MS63
2003(sp)	10,000	PF65 40.00				

Y# 816 ROUBLE
17.40 g., 0.900 Silver 0.5002 oz. ASW, 32.8 mm. **Obv:** Double-headed eagle within beaded circle **Rev:** Pygmy Cormorant drying its wings **Edge:** Reeded

Date	Mintage	F12	VF20	XF40	MS60	MS63
2003(sp)	10,000	PF65 35.00				

Y# 828 ROUBLE
17.28 g., 0.900 Silver 0.4968 oz. ASW, 33 mm. **Obv:** Two headed eagle within beaded circle **Rev:** Amur Forest Cat on branch **Edge:** Reeded

Date	Mintage	F12	VF20	XF40	MS60	MS63
2004(sp)	10,000	PF65 35.00				

Y# 1029 ROUBLE
16.80 g., 0.925 Silver 0.4964 oz. ASW, 32.8 mm. **Subject:** The Great Bustard

Date	Mintage	F12	VF20	XF40	MS60	MS63
2004	—	PF65 35.00				

Y# 881 ROUBLE
17.28 g., 0.500 Silver 0.276 oz. ASW, 32.8 mm. **Obv:** Double-headed eagle within beaded circle **Rev:** Rush Toad **Edge:** Reeded

Date	Mintage	F12	VF20	XF40	MS60	MS63
2004 (2005)	—	PF65 60.00				

Y# 882 ROUBLE
16.81 g., 0.4999 Silver 0.2684 oz. ASW, 32.8 mm. **Obv:** Double-headed eagle within beaded circle **Rev:** Two Marbled Murrelet sea birds **Edge:** Reeded

Date	Mintage	F12	VF20	XF40	MS60	MS63
2005	—	PF65 35.00				

Y# 883 ROUBLE
16.81 g., 0.4999 Silver 0.2684 oz. ASW, 32.8 mm. **Obv:** Double-headed eagle within beaded circle **Rev:** Asiatic Wild Dog **Edge:** Reeded

Date	Mintage	F12	VF20	XF40	MS60	MS63
2005	—	PF65 35.00				

Y# 884 ROUBLE
16.81 g., 0.4999 Silver 0.2684 oz. ASW, 32.8 mm. **Obv:** Double-headed eagle within beaded circle **Rev:** Volkhov Whitefish **Edge:** Reeded

Date	Mintage	F12	VF20	XF40	MS60	MS63
2005	—	PF65 35.00				

Y# 916 ROUBLE
8.53 g., 0.925 Silver 0.252 oz. ASW, 25 mm. **Obv:** Double-headed eagle **Rev:** Russian Navy Emblem **Edge:** Reeded

Date	Mintage	F12	VF20	XF40	MS60	MS63
2005	10,000	PF65 25.00				

Y# 917 ROUBLE
8.53 g., 0.925 Silver 0.252 oz. ASW, 25 mm. **Obv:** Double-headed eagle **Rev:** Russian Marine circa 1705 **Edge:** Reeded

Date	Mintage	F12	VF20	XF40	MS60	MS63
2005	10,000	PF65 25.00				

Y# 918 ROUBLE
8.53 g., 0.925 Silver 0.252 oz. ASW, 25 mm. **Obv:** Double-headed eagle **Rev:** Russian Marine circa 2005 **Edge:** Reeded

Date	Mintage	F12	VF20	XF40	MS60	MS63
2005	10,000	PF65 25.00				

Y# 981 ROUBLE
15.55 g., 0.925 Silver 0.4595 oz. ASW, 33 mm. **Obv:** Double headed eagle **Rev:** Mongolian Gazelle **Edge:** Reeded

Date	Mintage	F12	VF20	XF40	MS60	MS63
2006	—	PF65 65.00				

Y# 1058 ROUBLE
33.90 g., 0.925 Silver 1.0017 oz. ASW, 39 mm. **Subject:** Swan Goose

Date	Mintage	F12	VF20	XF40	MS60	MS63
2006	—	PF65 45.00				

Y# 1059 ROUBLE
33.90 g., 0.925 Silver 1.0017 oz. ASW, 39 mm. **Subject:** Ussury Clawed Newt

Date	Mintage	F12	VF20	XF40	MS60	MS63
2006	—	PF65 45.00				

Y# 1069 ROUBLE
7.78 g., 0.925 Silver 0.2299 oz. ASW, 22.6 mm. **Subject:** Airborne Troops

Date	Mintage	F12	VF20	XF40	MS60	MS63
2006	—	PF65 25.00				

Y# 1070 ROUBLE
7.78 g., 0.925 Silver 0.2299 oz. ASW, 22.6 mm. **Subject:** Airborne Troops

Date	Mintage	F12	VF20	XF40	MS60	MS63
2006	—	PF65 25.00				

Y# 1071 ROUBLE
7.78 g., 0.925 Silver 0.2299 oz. ASW, 22.6 mm. **Subject:** Airborne Troops

Date	Mintage	F12	VF20	XF40	MS60	MS63
2006	—	PF65 25.00				

Y# 1072 ROUBLE
7.78 g., 0.925 Silver 0.2299 oz. ASW, 22.6 mm. **Subject:** Submarine Forces

Date	Mintage	F12	VF20	XF40	MS60	MS63
2006	—	PF65 25.00				

Y# 1073 ROUBLE
7.78 g., 0.925 Silver 0.2299 oz. ASW, 22.6 mm. **Subject:** Submarine Forces

Date	Mintage	F12	VF20	XF40	MS60	MS63
2006	—	PF65 25.00				

Y# 1074 ROUBLE
7.78 g., 0.925 Silver 0.2299 oz. ASW, 22.6 mm. **Subject:** Submarine Forces

Date	Mintage	F12	VF20	XF40	MS60	MS63
2006	—	PF65 25.00				

Y# 961 ROUBLE
15.55 g., 0.925 Silver 0.4595 oz. ASW, 33 mm. **Obv:** Double headed eagle **Rev:** Red banded snake **Edge:** Reeded

Date	Mintage	F12	VF20	XF40	MS60	MS63
2007	—	PF65 35.00				

Y# 962 ROUBLE
15.55 g., 0.925 Silver 0.4595 oz. ASW, 33 mm. **Obv:** Double headed eagle **Rev:** Pallid Harrier in flight

Date	Mintage	F12	VF20	XF40	MS60	MS63
2007	—	PF65 65.00				

Y# 1109 ROUBLE
33.90 g., 0.925 Silver 1.0017 oz. ASW, 39 mm. **Subject:** Ringed seal

Date	Mintage	F12	VF20	XF40	MS60	MS63
2007	—	PF65 45.00				

Y# 1110 ROUBLE
7.78 g., 0.925 Silver 0.2299 oz. ASW, 33 mm. **Subject:** Space Force

Date	Mintage	F12	VF20	XF40	MS60	MS63
2007	—	PF65 30.00				

Y# 1112 ROUBLE
33.90 g., 0.925 Silver 1.0017 oz. ASW, 3 mm. **Subject:** Space Force

Date	Mintage	F12	VF20	XF40	MS60	MS63
2007	—	PF65 40.00				

Y# 1111 ROUBLE
7.78 g., 0.925 Silver 0.2299 oz. ASW, 33 mm. **Subject:** Space Force

Date	Mintage	F12	VF20	XF40	MS60	MS63
2007	—	PF65 30.00				

Y# 833a ROUBLE
3.00 g., Nickel Plated Steel, 20.5 mm. **Obv:** Two headed eagle above curved bank name and date, denomination above **Rev:** Value and flower

Date	Mintage	F12	VF20	XF40	MS60	MS63
2009ММД	—	—	—	—	0.75	1.50
2009СПМД	—	—	—	—	0.75	1.50
2010ММД	—	—	—	—	0.75	1.50
2010СПМД	—	—	—	—	2.00	3.00
2011ММД	—	—	—	—	0.75	1.50
2012ММД	—	—	—	—	0.75	1.50

Y# 1204 ROUBLE
16.80 g., 0.925 Silver 0.4964 oz. ASW, 33 mm. **Subject:** Air Force

Date	Mintage	F12	VF20	XF40	MS60	MS63
2009	—	PF65 30.00				

Y# 1205 ROUBLE
16.80 g., 0.925 Silver 0.4964 oz. ASW, 33 mm. **Subject:** Air Force

Date	Mintage	F12	VF20	XF40	MS60	MS63
2009	—	PF65 30.00				

Y# 1206 ROUBLE
16.80 g., 0.925 Silver 0.4964 oz. ASW, 33 mm. **Subject:** Air Force

Date	Mintage	F12	VF20	XF40	MS60	MS63
2009	—	PF65 30.00				

Y# 1244 ROUBLE
7.78 g., 0.925 Silver 0.2299 oz. ASW, 33 mm. **Subject:** Armored Forces **Rev:** Crowned eagle emblem

Date	Mintage	F12	VF20	XF40	MS60	MS63
2010	—	PF65 30.00				

Y# 1245 ROUBLE
7.78 g., 0.925 Silver 0.2299 oz. ASW, 33 mm. **Subject:** Armored Force **Rev:** Tank advancing left

Date	Mintage	F12	VF20	XF40	MS60	MS63
2010	—	PF65 30.00				

Y# 1246 ROUBLE
7.78 g., 0.925 Silver 0.2299 oz. ASW, 33 mm. **Subject:** Armored Force **Rev:** Tank advancing right

Date	Mintage	F12	VF20	XF40	MS60	MS63
2010	—	PF65 30.00				

Y# 1253 ROUBLE
7.78 g., 0.925 Silver 0.2299 oz. ASW, 22.6 mm. **Subject:** Russian Aviation

Date	Mintage	F12	VF20	XF40	MS60	MS63
2010	—	PF65 30.00				

Y# 1254 ROUBLE
7.78 g., 0.925 Silver 0.2299 oz. ASW, 33 mm. **Subject:** Russian Aviation

Date	Mintage	F12	VF20	XF40	MS60	MS63
2010	—	PF65 30.00				

Y# 1302 ROUBLE
7.78 g., 0.925 Silver 0.2299 oz. ASW, 25 mm. **Subject:** Russian Aviation **Rev:** TU-144 flying right, color tracer

Date	Mintage	F12	VF20	XF40	MS60	MS63
2011	5,000	PF65 30.00				

Y# 1303 ROUBLE
7.78 g., 0.925 Silver 0.2299 oz. ASW, 25 mm. **Subject:** Russian Aviation **Rev:** U-2 biplane in flight left, color tracer

Date	Mintage	F12	VF20	XF40	MS60	MS63
2011	5,000	PF65 30.00				

Y# 1310 ROUBLE
7.78 g., 0.925 Silver 0.2299 oz. ASW, 25 mm. **Subject:** Strategis Missile Forces **Rev:** Emblem with crowned double ehadded caglo

Date	Mintage	F12	VF20	XF40	MS60	MS63
2011	5,000	PF65 30.00				

Y# 1311 ROUBLE
7.78 g., 0.925 Silver 0.2299 oz. ASW, 25 mm. **Subject:** Strategic Missile Forces **Rev:** Mobile missile system

Date	Mintage	F12	VF20	XF40	MS60	MS63
2011	5,000	PF65 30.00				

Y# 1312 ROUBLE
7.78 g., 0.925 Silver 0.2299 oz. ASW, 25 mm. **Subject:** Strategic Missile Forces **Rev:** Missile system against mountian background

Date	Mintage	F12	VF20	XF40	MS60	MS63
2011	5,000	PF65 30.00				

Y# 1355 ROUBLE
7.78 g., 0.925 Silver 0.2299 oz. ASW, 25 mm. **Subject:** Russian Aviation, I-16

Date	Mintage	F12	VF20	XF40	MS60	MS63
2012	5,000	PF65 30.00				

Y# 1356 ROUBLE
7.78 g., 0.925 Silver 0.2299 oz. ASW, 25 mm. **Subject:** Russian Aviation, IL-76

Date	Mintage	F12	VF20	XF40	MS60	MS63
2012	5,000	PF65 30.00				

Y# 1375 ROUBLE
8.53 g., 0.925 Silver 0.252 oz. ASW, 25 mm. **Subject:** Court of Arbitration

Date	Mintage	F12	VF20	XF40	MS60	MS63
2012	3,000	PF65 35.00				

Y# 1428 ROUBLE
8.53 g., 0.925 Silver 0.252 oz. ASW, 25 mm. **Subject:** Russian Aviation **Rev:** Tu-160 in flight right

Date	Mintage	F12	VF20	XF40	MS60	MS63
2013СПМД	5,000	PF65 30.00				

Y# 1429 ROUBLE
8.53 g., 0.925 Silver 0.252 oz. ASW, 25 mm. **Subject:** Russian aviation **Rev:** АНТ-25 plane in flight

Date	Mintage	F12	VF20	XF40	MS60	MS63
2013СПМД	5,000	PF65 40.00				

Y# 605 2 ROUBLES
5.10 g., Copper-Nickel-Zinc, 23 mm. **Obv:** Double-headed eagle **Rev:** Value and vine sprig **Edge:** Segmented reeding

Date	Mintage	F12	VF20	XF40	MS60	MS63
2001M Rare	—	—	—	—	—	—

Y# 730 2 ROUBLES
17.00 g., 0.925 Silver 0.5023 oz. ASW, 33 mm. **Subject:** V.I. Dal **Obv:** Double-headed eagle **Rev:** Portrait, book, signature, figures **Edge:** Reeded

Date	Mintage	F12	VF20	XF40	MS60	MS63
2001(m)	7,500	PF65 80.00				

Y# 675 2 ROUBLES
5.10 g., Copper-Nickel, 23 mm. **Subject:** Yuri Gagarin **Obv:** Value and date to left of vine sprig **Rev:** Uniformed bust facing **Edge:** Segmented reeding

Date	Mintage	F12	VF20	XF40	MS60	MS63
2001	—	—	100	125	175	—
2001ММД	10,000,000	—	—	—	2.00	4.00
2001СПМД	10,000,000	—	—	—	2.00	4.00

Y# 1002 2 ROUBLES
16.81 g., 0.925 Silver 0.4967 oz. ASW, 33 mm. **Subject:** V. I. Dal. 200th Anniversary of birth

Date	Mintage	F12	VF20	XF40	MS60	MS63
2001	—	PF65 30.00				

Y# 742 2 ROUBLES
17.00 g., 0.925 Silver 0.5023 oz. ASW, 33 mm. **Subject:** Zodiac Signs **Obv:** Double-headed eagle within beaded circle **Rev:**
Leo **Edge:** Reeded

Date	Mintage	F12	VF20	XF40	MS60	MS63
2002(m)	—	PF63 45.00	PF65 55.00			

Y# 747 2 ROUBLES
17.00 g., 0.925 Silver 0.5023 oz. ASW, 33 mm. **Subject:** Zodiac Signs **Obv:** Double-headed eagle within beaded circle **Rev:** Virgo and stars **Edge:** Reeded

Date	Mintage	F12	VF20	XF40	MS60	MS63
2002(m)	20,000	PF63 45.00	PF65 55.00			

Y# 761 2 ROUBLES
17.00 g., 0.925 Silver 0.5023 oz. ASW, 33 mm. **Subject:** Zodiac Signs **Obv:** Double-headed eagle within beaded circle **Rev:** Capricorn **Edge:** Reeded

Date	Mintage	F12	VF20	XF40	MS60	MS63
2002(sp)	20,000	PF63 45.00	PF65 55.00			

Y# 762 2 ROUBLES
17.00 g., 0.925 Silver 0.5023 oz. ASW, 33 mm. **Subject:** Zodiac Signs **Obv:** Double-headed eagle within beaded circle **Rev:** Sagittarius **Edge:** Reeded

Date	Mintage	F12	VF20	XF40	MS60	MS63
2002(sp)	20,000	PF63 45.00	PF65 55.00			

Y# 766 2 ROUBLES
17.00 g., 0.925 Silver 0.5023 oz. ASW, 33 mm. **Subject:** Zodiac Signs **Obv:** Double-headed eagle within beaded circle **Rev:** Scorpion **Edge:** Reeded

Date	Mintage	F12	VF20	XF40	MS60	MS63
2002(m)	20,000	PF63 45.00	PF65 55.00			

Y# 768 2 ROUBLES
17.00 g., 0.925 Silver 0.5023 oz. ASW, 33 mm. **Subject:** Zodiac Signs **Obv:** Double-headed eagle **Rev:** Balance scale **Edge:** Reeded

Date	Mintage	F12	VF20	XF40	MS60	MS63
2002(sp)	20,000	PF63 45.00	PF65 55.00			

Y# 793 2 ROUBLES
17.00 g., 0.925 Silver 0.5023 oz. ASW, 33 mm. **Subject:** L.P. Orlova **Obv:** Double-headed eagle **Rev:** Head facing **Edge:** Reeded

Date	Mintage	F12	VF20	XF40	MS60	MS63
2002(m)	10,000	PF65 40.00				

Y# 834 2 ROUBLES
5.10 g., Copper-Nickel-Zinc, 23 mm. **Obv:** Two headed eagle above curved bank name and date, denomination above **Rev:** Value and flower **Edge:** Segmented reeding

Date	Mintage	F12	VF20	XF40	MS60	MS63
2002ММД Mint sets only	15,000					
2002СПМД Mint sets only	15,000					
2003ММД	15,000	—	—	300	400	500
2006ММД	—	—	—	—	4.00	5.00
2006СПМД	—	—	—	—	4.00	5.00
2007ММД	—	—	—	—	4.00	5.00
2007СПМД	—	—	—	—	4.00	5.00
2008ММД	—	—	—	—	4.00	5.00
2008СПМД	—	—	—	—	4.00	5.00
2009ММД	—	—	—	—	4.00	5.00
2009СПМД	—	—	—	—	4.00	5.00

Y# 803 2 ROUBLES
17.10 g., 0.925 Silver 0.5053 oz. ASW, 32.8 mm. **Subject:** Zodiac signs **Obv:** Double-headed eagle within beaded circle **Rev:** Pisces **Edge:** Reeded

Date	Mintage	F12	VF20	XF40	MS60	MS63
2003(sp)	20,000	PF63 45.00	PF65 55.00			

Y# 804 2 ROUBLES
17.10 g., 0.925 Silver 0.5053 oz. ASW, 32.8 mm. **Subject:** Zodiac signs **Obv:** Double-headed eagle within beaded circle **Rev:** Aquarius **Edge:** Reeded

Date	Mintage	F12	VF20	XF40	MS60	MS63
2003(m)	20,000	PF63 45.00	PF65 55.00			

Y# 820 2 ROUBLES
17.00 g., 0.925 Silver 0.5023 oz. ASW, 33 mm. **Subject:** Zodiac signs **Obv:** Double-headed eagle within beaded circle **Rev:** Cancer Crayfish **Edge:** Reeded

Date	Mintage	F12	VF20	XF40	MS60	MS63
2003(sp)	20,000	PF63 45.00	PF65 55.00			

Y# 840 2 ROUBLES
16.81 g., 0.925 Silver 0.4967 oz. ASW, 33 mm. **Rev:** Guil Yarovsky

Date	Mintage	F12	VF20	XF40	MS60	MS63
2003(m)	10,000	PF65 40.00				

Y# 841 2 ROUBLES
16.81 g., 0.925 Silver 0.4967 oz. ASW, 33 mm. **Rev:** Fedor Tyutchev

Date	Mintage	F12	VF20	XF40	MS60	MS63
2003(sp)	10,000	PF65 40.00				

Y# 844 2 ROUBLES
17.00 g., 0.925 Silver 0.5023 oz. ASW, 33 mm. **Subject:** Zodiac Signs **Obv:** Double-headed eagle within beaded circle **Rev:** Aries

Date	Mintage	F12	VF20	XF40	MS60	MS63
2003	20,000	PF63 45.00	PF65 55.00			

Y# 845 2 ROUBLES
17.00 g., 0.925 Silver 0.5023 oz. ASW, 33 mm. **Subject:** Zodiac Signs **Obv:** Double-headed eagle within beaded circle **Rev:** Taurus

Date	Mintage	F12	VF20	XF40	MS60	MS63
2003	20,000	PF63 45.00	PF65 55.00			

Y# 846 2 ROUBLES
17.00 g., 0.925 Silver 0.5023 oz. ASW, 33 mm. **Subject:** Zodiac Signs **Obv:** Double-headed eagle within beaded circle **Rev:** Gemini

Date	Mintage	F12	VF20	XF40	MS60	MS63
2003	20,000	PF63 45.00	PF65 55.00			

Y# 842 2 ROUBLES
16.81 g., 0.925 Silver 0.4967 oz. ASW, 33 mm. **Rev:** V. P. Tchkalov

Date	Mintage	F12	VF20	XF40	MS60	MS63
2004(m)	7,000	PF65 50.00				

Y# 843 2 ROUBLES
16.81 g., 0.925 Silver 0.4967 oz. ASW, 33 mm. **Rev:** Mikhail Glinka

Date	Mintage	F12	VF20	XF40	MS60	MS63
2004(m)	7,000	PF65 50.00				

Y# 1021 2 ROUBLES
16.80 g., 0.925 Silver 0.4964 oz. ASW, 33 mm. **Subject:** Sini Rerikh, 100th Anniversary of Birth

Date	Mintage	F12	VF20	XF40	MS60	MS63
2004	—	PF65 60.00				

Y# 897 2 ROUBLES
17.00 g., 0.925 Silver 0.5023 oz. ASW, 33 mm. **Obv:** Double-headed eagle **Rev:** Gemini twins **Edge:** Reeded

Date	Mintage	F12	VF20	XF40	MS60	MS63
2005	20,000	PF63 45.00	PF65 55.00			

Y# 899 2 ROUBLES
17.00 g., 0.925 Silver 0.5023 oz. ASW, 33 mm. **Obv:** Double-headed eagle **Rev:** Cancer Crayfish **Edge:** Reeded

Date	Mintage	F12	VF20	XF40	MS60	MS63
2005	20,000	PF63 45.00	PF65 55.00			

Y# 901 2 ROUBLES
17.00 g., 0.925 Silver 0.5023 oz. ASW, 33 mm. **Obv:** Double-headed eagle **Rev:** Leo lion **Edge:** Reeded

Date	Mintage	F12	VF20	XF40	MS60	MS63
2005	20,000	PF63 45.00	PF65 55.00			

Y# 905 2 ROUBLES
17.00 g., 0.925 Silver 0.5023 oz. ASW, 33 mm. **Obv:** Double-headed eagle **Rev:** Mikhail Sholokhov with pen in hand **Edge:** Reeded

Date	Mintage	F12	VF20	XF40	MS60	MS63
2005	10,000	PF65 40.00				

Y# 909 2 ROUBLES
17.00 g., 0.925 Silver 0.5023 oz. ASW, 33 mm. **Obv:** Double-headed eagle **Rev:** Peter Klodt viewing man and horse statue **Edge:** Reeded

Date	Mintage	F12	VF20	XF40	MS60	MS63
2005	10,000	PF65 40.00				

Y# 914 2 ROUBLES
17.00 g., 0.925 Silver 0.5023 oz. ASW, 33 mm. **Obv:** Double-headed eagle **Rev:** Virgo standing lady **Edge:** Reeded

Date	Mintage	F12	VF20	XF40	MS60	MS63
2005	20,000	PF63 45.00	PF65 55.00			

Y# 919 2 ROUBLES
17.00 g., 0.925 Silver 0.5023 oz. ASW, 33 mm. **Obv:** Double-headed eagle **Rev:** Libra - 2 stylized birds forming a balance scale **Edge:** Reeded

Date	Mintage	F12	VF20	XF40	MS60	MS63
2005	20,000	PF63 45.00	PF65 55.00			

Y# 921 2 ROUBLES
17.00 g., 0.925 Silver 0.5023 oz. ASW, 33 mm. **Obv:** Double-headed eagle **Rev:** Scorpio scorpion **Edge:** Reeded

Date	Mintage	F12	VF20	XF40	MS60	MS63
2005	20,000	PF63 45.00	PF65 55.00			

Y# 926 2 ROUBLES
17.00 g., 0.925 Silver 0.5023 oz. ASW, 33 mm. **Obv:** Double-headed eagle **Rev:** Sagittarius the archer **Edge:** Reeded

Date	Mintage	F12	VF20	XF40	MS60	MS63
2005	20,000	PF63 45.00	PF65 55.00			

Y# 928 2 ROUBLES
17.00 g., 0.925 Silver 0.5023 oz. ASW, 33 mm. **Obv:** Double-headed eagle **Rev:** Capricorn as half goat and fish **Edge:** Reeded

Date	Mintage	F12	VF20	XF40	MS60	MS63
2005	20,000	PF63 45.00	PF65 55.00			

Y# 930 2 ROUBLES
17.00 g., 0.925 Silver 0.5023 oz. ASW, 33 mm. **Obv:** Double-headed eagle **Rev:** Pisces as catfish and sturgeon **Edge:** Reeded

Date	Mintage	F12	VF20	XF40	MS60	MS63
2005	20,000	PF63 45.00	PF65 55.00			

Y# 932 2 ROUBLES
17.00 g., 0.925 Silver 0.5023 oz. ASW, 33 mm. **Obv:** Double-headed eagle **Rev:** Aries ram **Edge:** Reeded

Date	Mintage	F12	VF20	XF40	MS60	MS63
2005	20,000	PF63 45.00	PF65 55.00			

Y# 934 2 ROUBLES
17.00 g., 0.925 Silver 0.5023 oz. ASW, 33 mm. **Obv:** Double-headed eagle **Rev:** Taurus bull **Edge:** Reeded

Date	Mintage	F12	VF20	XF40	MS60	MS63
2005	20,000	PF63 45.00	PF65 55.00			

Y# 936 2 ROUBLES
17.00 g., 0.925 Silver 0.5023 oz. ASW, 33 mm. **Obv:** Double-headed eagle **Rev:** Aquarius water carrier **Edge:** Reeded

Date	Mintage	F12	VF20	XF40	MS60	MS63
2005	20,000	PF63 45.00	PF65 55.00			

Y# 1054 2 ROUBLES
16.80 g., 0.925 Silver 0.4964 oz. ASW, 33 mm. **Subject:** O. K. Antonov, 100th Anniversary of Birth

Date	Mintage	F12	VF20	XF40	MS60	MS63
2006	—	PF65 50.00				

Y# 1055 2 ROUBLES
16.80 g., 0.925 Silver 0.4964 oz. ASW, 33 mm. **Subject:** M. A. Vrubel, 150th Anniversary of Birth

Date	Mintage	F12	VF20	XF40	MS60	MS63
2006	—	PF65 50.00				

Y# 1056 2 ROUBLES
16.80 g., 0.925 Silver 0.4964 oz. ASW, 33 mm. **Subject:** A. A. Ivanov, 200th Anniversary of Birth

Date	Mintage	F12	VF20	XF40	MS60	MS63
2006	—	PF65 50.00				

Y# 1057 2 ROUBLES
16.80 g., 0.925 Silver 0.4964 oz. ASW, 33 mm. **Subject:** D. D. Shostakovich, 100th Anniversary of Birth

Date	Mintage	F12	VF20	XF40	MS60	MS63
2006	—	PF65 50.00				

Y# 967 2 ROUBLES
17.00 g., 0.925 Silver 0.5023 oz. ASW, 33.0 mm. **Subject:** 100th Anniversary Birth of Gerasimov **Obv:** Two-headed eagle **Rev:** Gerasimov recreating a man's face **Rev. Legend:** M. M. ГЕРАСИМОВ

Date	Mintage	F12	VF20	XF40	MS60	MS63
2007(m)	10,000	PF65 45.00				

Y# 968 2 ROUBLES
17.00 g., 0.925 Silver 0.5023 oz. ASW, 33.0 mm. **Subject:** 150th Anniversary Birth of Tsiolkovsky **Rev:** Bust of Tsiolkovsky 3/4 right at left, scheme of two flight vehicles with earth in background at upper right **Rev. Legend:** К. Э. ЦИОЛКОВСКИЙ **Edge:** Reeded

Date	Mintage	F12	VF20	XF40	MS60	MS63
2007(m)	10,000	PF65 45.00				

Y# 1104 2 ROUBLES
16.80 g., 0.925 Silver 0.4964 oz. ASW, 33 mm. **Subject:** S.P. Korolyov, 100th Anniversary of Birth

Date	Mintage	F12	VF20	XF40	MS60	MS63
2007	—	PF65 50.00				

Y# 1105 2 ROUBLES
16.80 g., 0.925 Silver 0.4964 oz. ASW, 33 mm. **Subject:** V.M. Bekhterev, 150th Anniversary of Birth

Date	Mintage	F12	VF20	XF40	MS60	MS63
2007	—	PF65 50.00				

Y# 1106 2 ROUBLES
16.80 g., 0.925 Silver 0.4964 oz. ASW, 33 mm. **Subject:** L. Euler, 300th Anniversary of Birth

Date	Mintage	F12	VF20	XF40	MS60	MS63
2007	—	PF65 50.00				

Y# 1107 2 ROUBLES
16.80 g., 0.925 Silver 0.4964 oz. ASW, 33 mm. **Subject:** V. P. Soloviev - Sedoy, 100th Anniversary of Birth

Date	Mintage	F12	VF20	XF40	MS60	MS63
2007	—	PF65 50.00				

Y# 979 2 ROUBLES
15.55 g., 0.925 Silver 0.4595 oz. ASW, 33 mm. **Obv:** Double headed eagle **Rev:** Black caped marmot **Edge:** Reeded

Date	Mintage	F12	VF20	XF40	MS60	MS63
2008	—	PF65 45.00				

Y# 980 2 ROUBLES
15.55 g., 0.925 Silver 0.4595 oz. ASW, 33 mm. **Obv:** Double headed eagle **Rev:** Shemaya fish **Edge:** Reeded

Date	Mintage	F12	VF20	XF40	MS60	MS63
2008	—	PF65 50.00				

Y# 1131 2 ROUBLES
16.80 g., 0.925 Silver 0.4964 oz. ASW, 33 mm. **Subject:** L. D. Landau, 100th Anniversary of Birth

Date	Mintage	F12	VF20	XF40	MS60	MS63
2008	—	PF65 70.00				

Y# 1132 2 ROUBLES
16.80 g., 0.925 Silver 0.4964 oz. ASW, 33 mm. **Subject:** V. P. Glushko, 100th Anniversary of Birth

Date	Mintage	F12	VF20	XF40	MS60	MS63
2008	—	PF65 55.00				

Y# 1133 2 ROUBLES
16.80 g., 0.925 Silver 0.4964 oz. ASW, 33 mm. **Subject:** D. F. Oistrakh, 100th Anniversary of Birth

Date	Mintage	F12	VF20	XF40	MS60	MS63
2008	—	PF65 55.00				

Y# 1134 2 ROUBLES
16.80 g., 0.925 Silver 0.4964 oz. ASW, 33 mm. **Subject:** I. M. Frank, 100th Anniversary of Birth

Date	Mintage	F12	VF20	XF40	MS60	MS63
2008	—	PF65 55.00				

Y# 1135 2 ROUBLES
16.80 g., 0.925 Silver 0.4964 oz. ASW, 33 mm. **Subject:** N. N. Nosoc, 100th Anniversary of Birth

Date	Mintage	F12	VF20	XF40	MS60	MS63
2008	—	PF65 55.00				

Y# 1136 2 ROUBLES
16.80 g., 0.925 Silver 0.4964 oz. ASW, 33 mm. **Subject:** V. I. Nemirovich, 100th Anniversary of Birth

Date	Mintage	F12	VF20	XF40	MS60	MS63
2008	—	PF65 50.00				

Y# 1137 2 ROUBLES
16.80 g., 0.925 Silver 0.4964 oz. ASW, 33 mm. **Subject:** E. V. Vuchetich, 100th Anniversary of Birth

Date	Mintage	F12	VF20	XF40	MS60	MS63
2008	—	PF65 50.00				

Y# 1146 2 ROUBLES
16.80 g., 0.925 Silver 0.4964 oz. ASW, 33 mm. **Subject:** Emperor Dragon Fly

Date	Mintage	F12	VF20	XF40	MS60	MS63
2008	—	PF65 45.00				

Y# 834a 2 ROUBLES
5.00 g., Nickel Plated Steel, 23 mm. **Obv:** Two headed eagle above curved bank name and date, denomination above **Rev:** Value and flower **Edge:** Segmented reeding

Date	Mintage	F12	VF20	XF40	MS60	MS63
2009ММД	—	—	—	—	0.50	1.00
2009СПМД	—	—	—	—	0.50	1.00
2010ММД	—	—	—	—	0.50	1.00
2010СПМД	—	—	—	—	0.50	1.00
2011ММД	—	—	—	—	0.50	1.00
2012ММД	—	—	—	—	0.50	1.00

Y# 1158 2 ROUBLES
16.80 g., 0.925 Silver 0.4964 oz. ASW, 33 mm. **Subject:** D. I. Mendeleyev, 175th Anniversary of Birth

Date	Mintage	F12	VF20	XF40	MS60	MS63
2009	—	PF65 50.00				

Y# 1190 2 ROUBLES
16.80 g., 0.925 Silver 0.4964 oz. ASW, 33 mm. **Subject:** A. V. Koltsov, 200th Anniversary of Birth

Date	Mintage	F12	VF20	XF40	MS60	MS63
2009	—	PF65 50.00				

Y# 1191 2 ROUBLES
16.80 g., 0.925 Silver 0.4964 oz. ASW, 33 mm. **Subject:** A. N. Voronikhin, 250th Anniversary of Birth

Date	Mintage	F12	VF20	XF40	MS60	MS63
2009	—	PF65 60.00				

Y# 1192 2 ROUBLES
16.80 g., 0.925 Silver 0.4964 oz. ASW, 33 mm. **Subject:** G. S. Ulanova, 100th Anniversary of Birth

Date	Mintage	F12	VF20	XF40	MS60	MS63
2009	—	PF65 60.00				

Y# 1193 2 ROUBLES
16.80 g., 0.925 Silver 0.4964 oz. ASW, 33 mm. **Subject:** L. I. Yashin, Soccer player

Date	Mintage	F12	VF20	XF40	MS60	MS63
2009	—	PF65 100				

Y# 1194 2 ROUBLES
16.80 g., 0.925 Silver 0.4964 oz. ASW, 33 mm. **Subject:** E. I. Beskov, Soccer player

Date	Mintage	F12	VF20	XF40	MS60	MS63
2009	—	PF65 100				

Y# 1195 2 ROUBLES
16.80 g., 0.925 Silver 0.4964 oz. ASW, 33 mm. **Subject:** E. A. Stresov, Soccer player

Date	Mintage	F12	VF20	XF40	MS60	MS63
2009	—	PF65 100				

Y# 1196 2 ROUBLES
16.80 g., 0.925 Silver 0.4964 oz. ASW, 33 mm. **Subject:** V. M. Bobrov, Hockey player

Date	Mintage	F12	VF20	XF40	MS60	MS63
2009	—	PF65 125				

Y# 1197 2 ROUBLES
16.80 g., 0.925 Silver 0.4964 oz. ASW, 33 mm. **Subject:** A. N. Maltzev, Hockey player

Date	Mintage	F12	VF20	XF40	MS60	MS63
2009	—	PF65 125				

Y# 1198 2 ROUBLES
16.80 g., 0.925 Silver 0.4964 oz. ASW, 33 mm. **Subject:** V. B. Kharlamov, Hockey player

Date	Mintage	F12	VF20	XF40	MS60	MS63
2009	—	PF65 125				

Y# 1216 2 ROUBLES
16.80 g., 0.925 Silver 0.4964 oz. ASW, 33 mm. **Subject:** N. I. Pirogov, 200th Anniversary of Birth

Date	Mintage	F12	VF20	XF40	MS60	MS63
2010	—	PF65 65.00				

Y# 1217 2 ROUBLES
16.80 g., 0.925 Silver 0.4964 oz. ASW, 33 mm. **Subject:** I. I. Levitan, 150th Anniversary of Birth

Date	Mintage	F12	VF20	XF40	MS60	MS63
2010	—	PF65 100				

Y# 1218 2 ROUBLES
16.80 g., 0.925 Silver 0.4964 oz. ASW, 33 mm. **Subject:** G. S. Ulanova, 100th Anniversary of Birth

Date	Mintage	F12	VF20	XF40	MS60	MS63
2010	—	PF65 55.00				

Y# 1248 2 ROUBLES
16.80 g., 0.925 Silver 0.4964 oz. ASW, 33 mm. **Subject:** Sika Deer

Date	Mintage	F12	VF20	XF40	MS60	MS63
2010	—	PF65 45.00				

Y# 1249 2 ROUBLES
16.80 g., 0.925 Silver 0.4964 oz. ASW, 33 mm. **Subject:** Short tailed albatross

Date	Mintage	F12	VF20	XF40	MS60	MS63
2010	—	PF65 45.00				

Y# 1250 2 ROUBLES
16.80 g., 0.925 Silver 0.4964 oz. ASW, 33 mm. **Subject:** Gjursa

Date	Mintage	F12	VF20	XF40	MS60	MS63
2010	—	PF65 45.00				

Y# 1307 2 ROUBLES
20.35 g., 0.925 Silver 0.6013 oz. ASW, 33 mm. **Subject:** Year of Russian Culture and Language in Italy **Obv:** St. George slaying dragon **Rev:** St. Nicholas church in Bari

Date	Mintage	F12	VF20	XF40	MS60	MS63
2011	10,000	PF65 60.00				

Y# 1319 2 ROUBLES
15.55 g., 0.925 Silver 0.4595 oz. ASW, 33 mm. **Subject:** M.M. Botvinnik **Rev:** Chess player and board

Date	Mintage	F12	VF20	XF40	MS60	MS63
2011	3,000	PF65 100				

Y# 1320 2 ROUBLES
15.55 g., 0.925 Silver 0.4595 oz. ASW, 33 mm. **Subject:** A.I. Raykin **Rev:** Portrait left **Edge:** Reeded

Date	Mintage	F12	VF20	XF40	MS60	MS63
2011	3,000	PF65 125				

Y# 1325 2 ROUBLES
16.81 g., 0.925 Silver 0.4967 oz. ASW, 33 mm. **Subject:** I.A. Goncharov, 200th Anniversary of Birth **Rev:** Half-length figure seated reading

Date	Mintage	F12	VF20	XF40	MS60	MS63
2012	5,000	PF65 60.00				

Y# 1326 2 ROUBLES
16.81 g., 0.925 Silver 0.4967 oz. ASW, 33 mm. **Subject:** P.A. Stolypin, 150th Anniversary of Birth **Rev:** Half-length figure standing in cap and with hands behind back

Date	Mintage	F12	VF20	XF40	MS60	MS63
2012	5,000	PF65 60.00				

Y# 1327 2 ROUBLES
16.81 g., 0.925 Silver 0.5364 oz. ASW, 33 mm **Subject:** M.V. Nesterov, 150th Anniversary of Birth

Date	Mintage	F12	VF20	XF40	MS60	MS63
2012	3,000	PF65 60.00				

Y# 1328 2 ROUBLES
16.81 g., 0.925 Silver 0.4967 oz. ASW, 33 mm. **Subject:** I.N. Kramskoy, 175th Anniversary of Birth **Rev:** Portrait painting in color

Date	Mintage	F12	VF20	XF40	MS60	MS63
2012	5,000	PF65 60.00				

Y# 1329 2 ROUBLES
16.81 g., 0.925 Silver 0.4967 oz. ASW, 33 mm. **Subject:** A.I. Vasilyev, 270th Anniversary of Birth

Date	Mintage	F12	VF20	XF40	MS60	MS63
2012	5,000	PF65 60.00				

Y# 1357 2 ROUBLES
16.80 g., 0.925 Silver 0.4964 oz. ASW, 33 mm. **Subject:** Alpine Weasel

Date	Mintage	F12	VF20	XF40	MS60	MS63
2012	5,000	PF65 55.00				

Y# 1358 2 ROUBLES
16.80 g., 0.925 Silver 0.4964 oz. ASW, 33 mm. **Subject:** Yellow-billed Loon

Date	Mintage	F12	VF20	XF40	MS60	MS63
2012	5,000	PF65 55.00				

Y# 1359 2 ROUBLES
16.80 g., 0.925 Silver 0.4964 oz. ASW, 33 mm. **Subject:** Emerald Rosalia Beetle

Date	Mintage	F12	VF20	XF40	MS60	MS63
2012	5,000	PF65 55.00				

Y# 1361 2 ROUBLES
16.80 g., 0.925 Silver 0.4964 oz. ASW, 33 mm. **Subject:** M.G. Isakova, skater

Date	Mintage	F12	VF20	XF40	MS60	MS63
2012	3,000	PF65 60.00				

Y# 1362 2 ROUBLES
16.80 g., 0.925 Silver 0.4964 oz. ASW, 33 mm. **Subject:** L.P. Skoblikova, skater

Date	Mintage	F12	VF20	XF40	MS60	MS63
2012	3,000	PF65 60.00				

Y# 1363 2 ROUBLES
16.80 g., 0.925 Silver 0.4964 oz. ASW, 33 mm. **Subject:** E.R. Grishin, skater

Date	Mintage	F12	VF20	XF40	MS60	MS63
2012	3,000	PF65 60.00				

Y# 1391 2 ROUBLES
5.00 g., Nickel Plated Steel, 23 mm. **Subject:** War of 1812, 200th Anniversary

Date	Mintage	F12	VF20	XF40	MS60	MS63
2012	5,000,000	—	—	—	1.00	2.00

Y# 1392 2 ROUBLES
Nickel Plated Steel, 23 mm. **Subject:** General Field-Marshal M.I. Kutuzov

Date	Mintage	F12	VF20	XF40	MS60	MS63
2012ММД	5,000,000	—	—	—	1.00	2.00

Y# 1393 2 ROUBLES
Nickel Plated Steel, 23 mm. **Subject:** General Field Marshal M.B. Barklay de Tolly

Date	Mintage	F12	VF20	XF40	MS60	MS63
2012ММД	5,000,000	—	—	—	1.00	2.00

Y# 1394 2 ROUBLES
Nickel Plated Steel, 23 mm. **Subject:** Infantry General P.I. Bagration

Date	Mintage	F12	VF20	XF40	MS60	MS63
2012ММД	5,000,000	—	—	—	1.00	2.00

Y# 1395 2 ROUBLES
Nickel Plated Steel, 23 mm. **Subject:** Calvary General L.L. Benningsen

Date	Mintage	F12	VF20	XF40	MS60	MS63
2012ММД	5,000,000	—	—	—	1.00	2.00

Y# 1396 2 ROUBLES
Nickel Plated Steel, 23 mm. **Subject:** General Field-Marshal P.H. Witgenstein

Date	Mintage	F12	VF20	XF40	MS60	MS63
2012ММД	5,000,000	—	—	—	1.00	2.00

Y# 1397 2 ROUBLES
Nickel Plated Steel, 23 mm. **Subject:** Lieutenant General D.V. Davidov

Date	Mintage	F12	VF20	XF40	MS60	MS63
2012ММД	5,000,000	—	—	—	1.00	2.00

Y# 1398 2 ROUBLES
Nickel Plated Steel, 23 mm. **Subject:** Infantry General, D.S. Dohkturov

Date	Mintage	F12	VF20	XF40	MS60	MS63
2012ММД	5,000,000	—	—	—	1.00	2.00

Y# 1399 2 ROUBLES

Nickel Plated Steel, 23 mm. **Subject:** Staff Captain N.A. Durova

Date	Mintage	F12	VF20	XF40	MS60	MS63
2012ММД	5,000,000	—	—	—	1.00	2.00

Y# 1400 2 ROUBLES

Nickel Plated Steel, 23 mm. **Subject:** Infantry General A.P. Yermolov

Date	Mintage	F12	VF20	XF40	MS60	MS63
2012ММД	5,000,000	—	—	—	1.00	2.00

Y# 1401 2 ROUBLES

Nickel Plated Steel, 23 mm. **Subject:** Kozhina Vasilisa, organizer of the partisan movement

Date	Mintage	F12	VF20	XF40	MS60	MS63
2012ММД	5,000,000	—	—	—	1.00	2.00

Y# 1402 2 ROUBLES

Nickel Plated Steel, 23 mm. **Subject:** Major General A.I. Kutaisov

Date	Mintage	F12	VF20	XF40	MS60	MS63
2012ММД	5,000,000	—	—	—	1.00	2.00

Y# 1403 2 ROUBLES

Nickel Plated Steel, 23 mm. **Subject:** Infantry General M.A. Miloradovich

Date	Mintage	F12	VF20	XF40	MS60	MS63
2012ММД	5,000,000	—	—	—	1.00	2.00

Y# 1404 2 ROUBLES

Nickel Plated Steel, 23 mm. **Subject:** Infantry General A.I. Osterman-Tolstoi

Date	Mintage	F12	VF20	XF40	MS60	MS63
2012ММД	5,000,000	—	—	—	1.00	2.00

Y# 1405 2 ROUBLES

Nickel Plated Steel, 23 mm. **Subject:** Calvary General N.N. Rayevsky

Date	Mintage	F12	VF20	XF40	MS60	MS63
2012ММД	5,000,000	—	—	—	1.00	2.00

Y# 1406 2 ROUBLES

Nickel Plated Steel, 23 mm. **Subject:** Calvary General M.I. Platov

Date	Mintage	F12	VF20	XF40	MS60	MS63
2012ММД	5,000,000	—	—	—	1.00	2.00

Y# 1407 2 ROUBLES

Nickel Plated Steel, 23 mm. **Subject:** Tsar Alexander I

Date	Mintage	F12	VF20	XF40	MS60	MS63
2012ММД	5,000,000	—	—	—	1.00	2.00

Y# 1427 2 ROUBLES

17.00 g., 0.925 Silver 0.5023 oz. ASW, 33 mm. **Subject:** V.S.Chernomyrdin, 75th Anniversary of Birth **Rev:** Bust left **Edge:** Reeded

Date	Mintage	F12	VF20	XF40	MS60	MS63
2013ММД	5,000	PF65 50.00				

Y# 1419 2 ROUBLES

17.00 g., 0.925 Silver 0.5023 oz. ASW, 33 mm. **Subject:** A.S. Dargomyzhsky, 200th Anniversary of Birth **Rev:** Water nymph and water-mill at left, Dargomyzhsky portrait at right **Edge:** Reeded

Date	Mintage	F12	VF20	XF40	MS60	MS63
2013ММД	5,000	PF65 50.00				

Y# 1426 2 ROUBLES

17.00 g., 0.925 Silver 0.5023 oz. ASW, 33 mm. **Subject:** V.I. Vernadsky, 150th Anniversary of Birth **Rev:** Bust at center, lattice sphere and stars in background **Edge:** Reeded

Date	Mintage	F12	VF20	XF40	MS60	MS63
2013СПМД	5,000	PF65 50.00				

Y# 1431 2 ROUBLES

17.00 g., 0.925 Silver 0.5023 oz. ASW, 33 mm. **Subject:** A.I. Pokryshkin, 100th Anniversary of Birth **Rev:** Bust at left, plane at right **Edge:** Reeded

Date	Mintage	F12	VF20	XF40	MS60	MS63
2013ММД	5,000	PF65 50.00				

Y# 677 3 ROUBLES

34.88 g., 0.900 Silver 1.0028 oz. ASW, 39 mm. **Subject:** 225 Years - Bolshoi Theater **Obv:** Double-headed eagle **Rev:** Standing figures facing **Edge:** Reeded

Date	Mintage	F12	VF20	XF40	MS60	MS63
2001	7,500	PF65 75.00				

Y# 680 3 ROUBLES

34.88 g., 0.900 Silver 1.0028 oz. ASW, 39 mm. **Subject:** 40th Anniversary of Manned Space Flight - Yuri Gagarin **Obv:** Double-headed eagle **Rev:** Uniformed bust holding dove **Edge:** Reeded

Date	Mintage	F12	VF20	XF40	MS60	MS63
2001	7,500	PF65 125				

Y# 682 3 ROUBLES

34.88 g., 0.900 Silver 1.0028 oz. ASW, 39 mm. **Subject:** Siberian Exploration **Obv:** Double-headed eagle **Rev:** Men riding horses, deer and sleds **Edge:** Reeded

Date	Mintage	F12	VF20	XF40	MS60	MS63
2001	5,000	PF65 100				

Y# 733 3 ROUBLES

34.88 g., 0.900 Silver 1.0028 oz. ASW, 39 mm. **Subject:** 200th Anniversary of Navigation School **Obv:** Double-headed eagle **Rev:** Navigational tools and building **Edge:** Reeded

Date	Mintage	F12	VF20	XF40	MS60	MS63
2001	5,000	PF65 80.00				

Y# 734 3 ROUBLES

34.88 g., 0.900 Silver 1.0028 oz. ASW, 39 mm. **Subject:** First Moscow Savings Bank **Obv:** Double-headed eagle **Rev:** Beehive above building within circle **Edge:** Reeded

Date	Mintage	F12	VF20	XF40	MS60	MS63
2001	17,500	PF63 50.00 PF65 60.00				

Y# 735 3 ROUBLES

34.88 g., 0.900 Silver 1.0028 oz. ASW, 39 mm. **Subject:** State Labor Savings Bank **Obv:** Double-headed eagle **Rev:** Dam, passbook and tractor **Edge:** Reeded

Date	Mintage	F12	VF20	XF40	MS60	MS63
2001	17,500	PF63 50.00 PF65 60.00				

Y# 736 3 ROUBLES
34.88 g., 0.900 Silver 1.0028 oz. ASW, 39 mm. **Subject:**
Savings Bank of the Russian Federation **Obv:** Double-headed
eagle **Rev:** Chevrons above building **Edge:** Reeded

Date	Mintage	F12	VF20	XF40	MS60	MS63
2001	17,500	**PF63** 50.00		**PF65** 60.00		

Y# 737 3 ROUBLES
34.88 g., 0.900 Silver 1.0028 oz. ASW, 39 mm. **Subject:** 10th
Anniversary - Commonwealth of Independent States **Obv:**
Double-headed eagle **Rev:** Hologram below logo **Edge:**
Reeded

Date	Mintage	F12	VF20	XF40	MS60	MS63
2001	7,500	**PF63** 55.00		**PF65** 65.00		

Y# 738 3 ROUBLES
34.88 g., 0.900 Silver 1.0028 oz. ASW, 39 mm. **Subject:**
Olympics **Obv:** Double-headed eagle **Rev:** Cross-country
skiers **Edge:** Reeded

Date	Mintage	F12	VF20	XF40	MS60	MS63
2002	25,000	**PF63** 45.00		**PF65** 55.00		

Y# 744 3 ROUBLES
34.88 g., 0.900 Silver 1.0028 oz. ASW, 39 mm. **Subject:** St.
John's Nunnery, St. Petersburg **Obv:** Double-headed eagle
Rev: Nunnery and cameo **Edge:** Reeded

Date	Mintage	F12	VF20	XF40	MS60	MS63
2002	—	**PF63** 225		**PF65** 250		

Y# 755 3 ROUBLES
34.88 g., 0.900 Silver 1.0028 oz. ASW, 39 mm. **Subject:**
Admiral Nakhimov **Obv:** Double-headed eagle **Rev:** Monument,
Admiral with cannon and naval battle scene **Edge:** Reeded

Date	Mintage	F12	VF20	XF40	MS60	MS63
2002(sp)	10,000	**PF65** 80.00				

Y# 756 3 ROUBLES
34.88 g., 0.900 Silver 1.0028 oz. ASW, 39 mm. **Subject:**
Hermitage **Obv:** Double-headed eagle **Rev:** Statues and arch
Edge: Reeded

Date	Mintage	F12	VF20	XF40	MS60	MS63
2002(sp)	10,000	**PF65** 75.00				

Y# 778 3 ROUBLES
34.88 g., 0.900 Silver 1.0028 oz. ASW, 39 mm. **Subject:**
Kideksha **Obv:** Double-headed eagle **Rev:** Three churches on
river bank **Edge:** Reeded

Date	Mintage	F12	VF20	XF40	MS60	MS63
2002(sp)	10,000	**PF63** 85.00		**PF65** 100		

Y# 779 3 ROUBLES
34.88 g., 0.900 Silver 1.0028 oz. ASW, 39 mm. **Subject:**
Iversky Monastery, Valdaiy **Obv:** Double-headed eagle **Rev:**
Building complex on an island in Lake Valdaiy **Edge:** Reeded

Date	Mintage	F12	VF20	XF40	MS60	MS63
2002(sp)	10,000	**PF63** 85.00		**PF65** 100		

Y# 780 3 ROUBLES
34.88 g., 0.900 Silver 1.0028 oz. ASW, 39 mm. **Subject:**
Miraculous Savior Church **Obv:** Double-headed eagle **Rev:**
Church with separate bell tower **Edge:** Reeded

Date	Mintage	F12	VF20	XF40	MS60	MS63
2002(m)	5,000	**PF63** 120		**PF65** 135		

Y# 781 3 ROUBLES
34.88 g., 0.900 Silver 1.0028 oz. ASW, 39 mm. **Subject:** Works
of Dionissy **Obv:** Double-headed eagle **Rev:** The Crucifix
Edge: Reeded

Date	Mintage	F12	VF20	XF40	MS60	MS63
2002(sp)	10,000	**PF63** 115		**PF65** 135		

Y# 787 3 ROUBLES
34.88 g., 0.900 Silver 1.0028 oz. ASW, 39 mm. **Subject:** World
Cup Soccer **Obv:** Double-headed eagle **Rev:** Soccer ball within
circle of players **Edge:** Reeded

Date	Mintage	F12	VF20	XF40	MS60	MS63
2002(sp)	25,000	**PF65** 60.00				

Y# 801 3 ROUBLES
34.80 g., 0.900 Silver 1.0005 oz. ASW, 38.7 mm. **Subject:**
Veborg **Obv:** Double-headed eagle **Rev:** Sailing ships and
buildings **Edge:** Reeded

Date	Mintage	F12	VF20	XF40	MS60	MS63
2003(sp)	10,000	**PF63** 55.00		**PF65** 65.00		

Y# 802 3 ROUBLES

34.75 g., 0.900 Silver 0.999 oz. ASW, 38.7 mm. **Subject:** Lunar Calendar **Obv:** National emblem **Rev:** Mountain goat in crescent **Edge:** Reeded

Date	Mintage	F12	VF20	XF40	MS60	MS63
2003(m)	15,000	PF63 60.00	PF65 75.00			

Y# 805 3 ROUBLES

34.84 g., 0.900 Silver 1.0016 oz. ASW, 38.8 mm. **Subject:** Zodiac signs **Obv:** Double-headed eagle within beaded circle **Rev:** Leo **Edge:** Reeded

Date	Mintage	F12	VF20	XF40	MS60	MS63
2003(m)	30,000	PF63 60.00	PF65 75.00			

Y# 806 3 ROUBLES

34.74 g., 0.900 Silver 0.9988 oz. ASW, 38.8 mm. **Subject:** St. Daniel's Monastery **Obv:** Double-headed eagle **Rev:** Statue and monastery **Edge:** Reeded

Date	Mintage	F12	VF20	XF40	MS60	MS63
2003(m)	10,000	PF65 50.00				

Y# 807 3 ROUBLES

34.74 g., 0.900 Silver 0.9988 oz. ASW, 38.8 mm. **Subject:** World Biathlon Championships **Obv:** Double-headed eagle **Rev:** Rifleman and archer on skis **Edge:** Reeded

Date	Mintage	F12	VF20	XF40	MS60	MS63
2003(m)	7,500	PF65 60.00				

Y# 808 3 ROUBLES

34.74 g., 0.900 Silver 0.9988 oz. ASW, 38.8 mm. **Obv:** Double-headed eagle **Rev:** Monastery **Edge:** Reeded

Date	Mintage	F12	VF20	XF40	MS60	MS63
2003(m)	10,000	PF65 50.00				

Y# 809 3 ROUBLES

34.74 g., 0.900 Silver 0.9988 oz. ASW, 38.8 mm. **Subject:** First Kamchatka Expedition **Obv:** Double-headed eagle **Rev:** Natives, fish and ship **Edge:** Reeded

Date	Mintage	F12	VF20	XF40	MS60	MS63
2003(sp)	10,000	PF65 80.00				

Y# 810 3 ROUBLES

34.74 g., 0.900 Silver 0.9988 oz. ASW, 38.8 mm. **Subject:** Zodiac signs **Obv:** Double-headed eagle within beaded circle **Rev:** Virgo **Edge:** Reeded

Date	Mintage	F12	VF20	XF40	MS60	MS63
2003(sp)	30,000	PF63 60.00	PF65 75.00			

Y# 811 3 ROUBLES

34.74 g., 0.900 Silver 0.9988 oz. ASW, 38.8 mm. **Subject:** Zodiac signs **Obv:** Double-headed eagle within beaded circle **Rev:** Libra **Edge:** Reeded

Date	Mintage	F12	VF20	XF40	MS60	MS63
2003(m)	30,000	PF63 60.00	PF65 75.00			

Y# 812 3 ROUBLES

34.74 g., 0.900 Silver 0.9988 oz. ASW, 38.8 mm. **Subject:** Diveyevsky Monastery **Obv:** Double-headed eagle **Rev:** Cameo above churches **Edge:** Reeded

Date	Mintage	F12	VF20	XF40	MS60	MS63
2003(sp)	10,000	PF63 120	PF65 135			

Y# 813 3 ROUBLES

34.74 g., 0.900 Silver 0.9988 oz. ASW, 38.8 mm. **Subject:** Zodiac Signs **Obv:** Double-headed eagle within beaded circle **Rev:** Scorpio **Edge:** Reeded

Date	Mintage	F12	VF20	XF40	MS60	MS63
2003(m)	30,000	PF65 75.00				

Y# 885 3 ROUBLES

34.80 g., 0.900 Silver 1.0005 oz. ASW, 38.7 mm. **Subject:** City of Pskov 1100th Anniversary **Obv:** Double-headed eagle **Rev:** Walled city view **Edge:** Reeded

Date	Mintage	F12	VF20	XF40	MS60	MS63
2003(sp)	—	PF63 85.00	PF65 100			

Y# 848 3 ROUBLES

34.56 g., 0.900 Silver 0.9936 oz. ASW, 39 mm. **Subject:** Zodiac Signs **Obv:** Double-headed eagle within beaded circle **Rev:** Sagittarius

Date	Mintage	F12	VF20	XF40	MS60	MS63
2003(sp)	30,000	PF63 60.00	PF65 75.00			

Y# 849 3 ROUBLES
34.56 g., 0.900 Silver 0.9936 oz. ASW, 39 mm. **Subject:** Zodiac Signs **Obv:** Double-headed eagle within beaded circle **Rev:** Capricorn

Date	Mintage	F12	VF20	XF40	MS60	MS63
2003(m)	30,000	PF63 60.00	PF65 75.00			

Y# 1012 3 ROUBLES
33.90 g., 0.925 Silver 1.0017 oz. ASW, 39 mm. **Subject:** Year of the Goat

Date	Mintage	F12	VF20	XF40	MS60	MS63
2003	—	PF65 50.00				

Y# 850 3 ROUBLES
34.56 g., 0.900 Silver 0.9936 oz. ASW, 39 mm. **Subject:** Lunar Calendar **Rev:** Monkey

Date	Mintage	F12	VF20	XF40	MS60	MS63
2004(m)	15,000	PF63 60.00	PF65 75.00			

Y# 851 3 ROUBLES
34.56 g., 0.900 Silver 0.9936 oz. ASW, 39 mm. **Subject:** Zodiac Signs **Obv:** Double-headed eagle within beaded circle **Rev:** Aquarius

Date	Mintage	F12	VF20	XF40	MS60	MS63
2004(sp)	30,000	PF63 60.00	PF65 75.00			

Y# 852 3 ROUBLES
34.56 g., 0.900 Silver 0.9936 oz. ASW, 39 mm. **Rev:** Tomsk

Date	Mintage	F12	VF20	XF40	MS60	MS63
2004(m)	8,000	PF65 115				

Y# 853 3 ROUBLES
34.56 g., 0.900 Silver 0.9936 oz. ASW, 39 mm. **Subject:** Zodiac Signs **Obv:** Double-headed eagle within beaded circle **Rev:** Pisces

Date	Mintage	F12	VF20	XF40	MS60	MS63
2004(m)	30,000	PF63 60.00	PF65 75.00			

Y# 854 3 ROUBLES
34.56 g., 0.900 Silver 0.9936 oz. ASW, 39 mm. **Rev:** Epiphany Cathedral, Moscow

Date	Mintage	F12	VF20	XF40	MS60	MS63
2004(m)	8,000	PF65 115				

Y# 855 3 ROUBLES
34.56 g., 0.900 Silver 0.9936 oz. ASW, 39 mm. **Subject:** Zodiac Signs **Obv:** Double-headed eagle within beaded circle **Rev:** Aries

Date	Mintage	F12	VF20	XF40	MS60	MS63
2004(sp)	30,000	PF63 60.00	PF65 75.00			

Y# 856 3 ROUBLES
34.56 g., 0.900 Silver 0.9936 oz. ASW, 39 mm. **Rev:** Soccer

Date	Mintage	F12	VF20	XF40	MS60	MS63
2004(sp)	10,000	PF63 60.00	PF65 75.00			

Y# 857 3 ROUBLES
34.56 g., 0.9936 oz. ASW, 39 mm. **Subject:** Zodiac Signs **Obv:** Double-headed eagle within beaded circle **Rev:** Taurus

Date	Mintage	F12	VF20	XF40	MS60	MS63
2004(sp)	30,000	PF63 60.00	PF65 75.00			

Y# 858 3 ROUBLES
34.56 g., 0.900 Silver 0.9936 oz. ASW, 39 mm. **Rev:** Olympic torch

Date	Mintage	F12	VF20	XF40	MS60	MS63
2004(m)	20,000	PF63 55.00	PF65 65.00			

Y# 859 3 ROUBLES
34.56 g., 0.900 Silver 0.9936 oz. ASW, 39 mm. **Subject:** Zodiac Signs **Obv:** Double-headed eagle within beaded circle **Rev:** Gemini

Date	Mintage	F12	VF20	XF40	MS60	MS63
2004(m)	30,000	PF63 65.00	PF65 75.00			

Y# 860 3 ROUBLES
34.56 g., 0.900 Silver 0.9936 oz. ASW, 39 mm. **Subject:** Zodiac Signs **Obv:** Double-headed eagle within beaded circle **Rev:** Cancer

Date	Mintage	F12	VF20	XF40	MS60	MS63
2004(sp)	30,000	PF63 60.00	PF65 75.00			

Y# 861 3 ROUBLES
34.56 g., 0.900 Silver 0.9936 oz. ASW, 39 mm. **Rev:** Church of the Sign of the Holy Mother of God

Date	Mintage	F12	VF20	XF40	MS60	MS63
2004(m)	8,000	PF63 110	PF65 125			

Y# 862 3 ROUBLES
34.56 g., 0.900 Silver 0.9936 oz. ASW, 39 mm. **Rev:** Transfiguration icon

Date	Mintage	F12	VF20	XF40	MS60	MS63
2004(m)	8,000	PF63 110	PF65 125			

Y# 863 3 ROUBLES
34.56 g., 0.900 Silver 0.9936 oz. ASW, 39 mm. **Rev:** Peter I's monetary reform

Date	Mintage	F12	VF20	XF40	MS60	MS63
2004(sp)	8,000	PF63 325	PF65 375			

Y# 1013 3 ROUBLES
33.90 g., 0.925 Silver 1.0017 oz. ASW, 39 mm. **Subject:** 2nd Kamchatka Expedition, 1733-43

Date	Mintage	F12	VF20	XF40	MS60	MS63
2004	—	PF63 65.00	PF65 75.00			

Y# 1015 3 ROUBLES
33.90 g., 0.925 Silver 1.0017 oz. ASW, 39 mm. **Subject:** Theophanes the Greek

Date	Mintage	F12	VF20	XF40	MS60	MS63
2004	—	PF63 110	PF65 125			

Y# 1020 3 ROUBLES
33.90 g., 0.925 Silver 1.0017 oz. ASW, 39 mm. **Subject:** Church of the Virgin Nativity in Gordniya

Date	Mintage	F12	VF20	XF40	MS60	MS63
2004	—	PF63 110	PF65 125			

Y# 1022 3 ROUBLES
33.90 g., 0.925 Silver 1.0017 oz. ASW, 39 mm. **Subject:** Reindeer

Date	Mintage	F12	VF20	XF40	MS60	MS63
2004	—	PF63 65.00	PF65 75.00			

Y# 892 3 ROUBLES
33.94 g., 0.925 Silver 1.0029 oz. ASW, 39 mm. **Obv:** Double-headed eagle **Rev:** Rooster and crescent moon **Edge:** Reeded

Date	Mintage	F12	VF20	XF40	MS60	MS63
2005	15,000	PF63 60.00	PF65 75.00			

Y# 893 3 ROUBLES
33.94 g., 0.925 Silver 1.0029 oz. ASW, 39 mm. **Subject:** 60th Anniversary - Victory Over Germany **Obv:** Double-headed eagle **Rev:** Soldier and wife circa 1945 **Edge:** Reeded

Date	Mintage	F12	VF20	XF40	MS60	MS63
2005	35,000	PF63 45.00	PF65 60.00			

Y# 903 3 ROUBLES
33.94 g., 0.925 Silver 1.0029 oz. ASW, 39 mm. **Obv:** Double-headed eagle **Rev:** St. Nicholas Cathedral in Kaliningrad **Edge:** Reeded

Date	Mintage	F12	VF20	XF40	MS60	MS63
2005	10,000	PF63 60.00	PF65 75.00			

Y# 904 3 ROUBLES
33.94 g., 0.925 Silver 1.0029 oz. ASW, 39 mm. **Obv:** Double-headed eagle **Rev:** Kropotkin Metro Station in Moscow **Edge:** Reeded

Date	Mintage	F12	VF20	XF40	MS60	MS63
2005	10,000	PF63 60.00	PF65 75.00			

Y# 906 3 ROUBLES
33.94 g., 0.925 Silver 1.0029 oz. ASW, 39 mm. **Subject:** Helsinki Games **Obv:** Double-headed eagle **Rev:** Stylized track and field athletes **Edge:** Reeded

Date	Mintage	F12	VF20	XF40	MS60	MS63
2005	10,000	PF63 60.00	PF65 75.00			

Y# 908 3 ROUBLES
33.94 g., 0.925 Silver 1.0029 oz. ASW, 39 mm. **Obv:** Double-headed eagle **Rev:** Virgin Monastery in Raifa, Tatarstan **Edge:** Reeded

Date	Mintage	F12	VF20	XF40	MS60	MS63
2005	10,000	PF63 50.00	PF65 65.00			

Y# 910 3 ROUBLES
33.94 g., 0.925 Silver 1.0029 oz. ASW, 39 mm. **Obv:** Double-headed eagle **Rev:** Kazan Theater Building **Edge:** Reeded

Date	Mintage	F12	VF20	XF40	MS60	MS63
2005	10,000	PF63 60.00	PF65 75.00			

Y# 923 3 ROUBLES
33.94 g., 0.925 Silver 1.0029 oz. ASW, 39 mm. **Subject:** 625th Anniversary - Battle of Kulikovo **Obv:** Double-headed eagle **Rev:** Carved Lion and Griffin between opposing armies **Edge:** Reeded

Date	Mintage	F12	VF20	XF40	MS60	MS63
2005	10,000	PF63 60.00	PF65 75.00			

Y# 955 3 ROUBLES

33.94 g., 0.925 Silver 1.0029 oz. ASW, 39 mm. **Subject:**
Moscow's Lomonosov University **Obv:** Two headed eagle
Rev: Lomonosov statue before university building and Moscow
skyline **Edge:** Reeded

Date	Mintage	F12	VF20	XF40	MS60	MS63
2005(m)	10,000	PF63 50.00	PF65 65.00			

Y# 1038 3 ROUBLES

33.90 g., 0.925 Silver 1.0017 oz. ASW, 39 mm. **Subject:** I. V.
Russakov, House of Culture

Date	Mintage	F12	VF20	XF40	MS60	MS63
2005	—	PF63 50.00	PF65 65.00			

Y# 1039 3 ROUBLES

33.90 g., 0.925 Silver 1.0017 oz. ASW, 39 mm. **Subject:**
Novosibirsk State Academic Opera & Ballet

Date	Mintage	F12	VF20	XF40	MS60	MS63
2005	—	PF63 60.00	PF65 75.00			

Y# 1040 3 ROUBLES

33.90 g., 0.925 Silver 1.0017 oz. ASW, 39 mm. **Subject:** Year
of the dog

Date	Mintage	F12	VF20	XF40	MS60	MS63
2006	—	PF63 60.00	PF65 75.00			

Y# 1041 3 ROUBLES

33.90 g., 0.925 Silver 1.0017 oz. ASW, 39 mm. **Subject:**
Parliament, 100th Anniversary

Date	Mintage	F12	VF20	XF40	MS60	MS63
2006	—	PF63 50.00	PF65 65.00			

Y# 1046 3 ROUBLES

33.90 g., 0.925 Silver 1.0017 oz. ASW, 39 mm. **Subject:**
Tretyakov State Gallery, 150th Anniversary

Date	Mintage	F12	VF20	XF40	MS60	MS63
2006	—	PF63 200	PF65 250			

Y# 1048 3 ROUBLES

33.90 g., 0.925 Silver 1.0017 oz. ASW, 39 mm. **Subject:** Russia
Savings

Date	Mintage	F12	VF20	XF40	MS60	MS63
2006	—	PF63 50.00	PF65 65.00			

Y# 1052 3 ROUBLES

33.90 g., 0.925 Silver 1.0017 oz. ASW, 39 mm. **Subject:** State
Bank Building, Nizhny Novgorod

Date	Mintage	F12	VF20	XF40	MS60	MS63
2006	—	PF63 50.00	PF65 65.00			

Y# 1060 3 ROUBLES

33.90 g., 0.925 Silver 1.0017 oz. ASW, 39 mm. **Subject:**
Moscow's Kremlin and Red Square

Date	Mintage	F12	VF20	XF40	MS60	MS63
2006	—	PF63 60.00	PF65 70.00			

Y# 1065 3 ROUBLES

33.90 g., 0.925 Silver 1.0017 oz. ASW, 39 mm. **Subject:** XX
Winter Olympics, Torino

Date	Mintage	F12	VF20	XF40	MS60	MS63
2006	12,500	PF63 75.00	PF65 95.00			

Y# 1066 3 ROUBLES

33.90 g., 0.925 Silver 1.0017 oz. ASW, 39 mm. **Subject:** FIFA
World Cup, Germany

Date	Mintage	F12	VF20	XF40	MS60	MS63
2006	—	PF63 65.00	PF65 75.00			

Y# 1079 3 ROUBLES

33.90 g., 0.925 Silver 1.0017 oz. ASW, 39 mm. **Subject:** Year
of the Dog

Date	Mintage	F12	VF20	XF40	MS60	MS63
2006	—	PF65 60.00				

Y# 966 3 ROUBLES

33.94 g., 0.925 Silver 1.0029 oz. ASW, 39 mm. **Subject:** 250th
Anniversary Academy of the Arts **Obv:** Two-headed eagle **Rev:**
Relief image of Minerva group **Rev. Legend:** РОССИЙСКАЯ -
АКАДЕМИЯ ХУДОЖЕСТВ **Edge:** Reeded

Date	Mintage	F12	VF20	XF40	MS60	MS63
2007(m)	10,000	PF63 50.00	PF65 65.00			

Y# 1080 3 ROUBLES
33.90 g., 0.925 Silver 1.0017 oz. ASW, 39 mm. **Subject:** International Arctic Year

Date	Mintage	F12	VF20	XF40	MS60	MS63
2007	—	PF63 60.00	PF65 75.00			

Y# 1087 3 ROUBLES
33.90 g., 0.925 Silver 1.0017 oz. ASW **Subject:** First Artificial Earth Satellite, 50th Anniversary

Date	Mintage	F12	VF20	XF40	MS60	MS63
2007	—	PF63 55.00	PF65 65.00			

Y# 1088 3 ROUBLES
33.90 g., 0.925 Silver 1.0017 oz. ASW, 39 mm. **Subject:** Andrew Rublyov

Date	Mintage	F12	VF20	XF40	MS60	MS63
2007	—	PF63 55.00	PF65 65.00			

Y# 1092 3 ROUBLES
33.90 g., 0.925 Silver 1.0017 oz. ASW, 39 mm. **Subject:** Bashkira, 450th Anniversary of annexation by Russia

Date	Mintage	F12	VF20	XF40	MS60	MS63
2007	—	PF63 55.00	PF65 65.00			

Y# 1100 3 ROUBLES
33.90 g., 0.925 Silver 1.0017 oz. ASW, 39 mm. **Subject:** Nevyansk inclined tower, Sverdlorsk Region

Date	Mintage	F12	VF20	XF40	MS60	MS63
2007	—	PF63 55.00	PF65 65.00			

Y# 1103 3 ROUBLES
33.90 g., 0.925 Silver 1.0017 oz. ASW, 39 mm. **Subject:** Kazan Railway Station, Moscow

Date	Mintage	F12	VF20	XF40	MS60	MS63
2007	—	PF63 55.00	PF65 65.00			

Y# 1114 3 ROUBLES
33.90 g., 0.925 Silver 1.0017 oz. ASW, 39 mm. **Subject:** Year of the Rat

Date	Mintage	F12	VF20	XF40	MS60	MS63
2007	20,000	PF63 70.00	PF65 80.00			

Y# 1113 3 ROUBLES
33.90 g., 0.925 Silver 1.0017 oz. ASW, 39 mm. **Subject:** Year of the Bull

Date	Mintage	F12	VF20	XF40	MS60	MS63
2008	20,000	PF63 70.00	PF65 80.00			

Y# 1115 3 ROUBLES
33.90 g., 0.925 Silver 1.0017 oz. ASW, 39 mm. **Subject:** Russian Postage Stamp - 150th Anniversary of Introduction

Date	Mintage	F12	VF20	XF40	MS60	MS63
2008	8,000	PF65 650				

Y# 1118 3 ROUBLES
33.90 g., 0.925 Silver 1.0017 oz. ASW, 39 mm. **Subject:** I. M. Schenov Medical Academy, 250th Anniversary

Date	Mintage	F12	VF20	XF40	MS60	MS63
2008	3,000	PF65 250				

Y# 1119 3 ROUBLES
33.90 g., 0.925 Silver 1.0017 oz. ASW, 39 mm. **Subject:** Udmurtiya, 450th Anniversary of annexation into Russia

Date	Mintage	F12	VF20	XF40	MS60	MS63
2008	10,000	PF63 70.00	PF65 80.00			

Y# 1124 3 ROUBLES
33.90 g., 0.925 Silver 1.0017 oz. ASW, 39 mm. **Subject:** Cathedral of St. Demetrius, Vladimir

Date	Mintage	F12	VF20	XF40	MS60	MS63
2008	10,000	PF63 70.00	PF65 80.00			

Y# 1126 3 ROUBLES
33.90 g., 0.925 Silver 1.0017 oz. ASW, 39 mm. **Subject:** N. I. Sevastyanov, House of Trade Unions

Date	Mintage	F12	VF20	XF40	MS60	MS63
2008	7,500	PF63 70.00	PF65 80.00			

Y# 1127 3 ROUBLES
33.90 g., 0.925 Silver 1.0017 oz. ASW, 39 mm. **Subject:** Cathedral of the Nativity of our Lady, Snetogorsk

Date	Mintage	F12	VF20	XF40	MS60	MS63
2008	10,000	PF63 70.00	PF65 80.00			

Y# 1128 3 ROUBLES
33.90 g., 0.925 Silver 1.0017 oz. ASW, 39 mm. **Subject:** Assumption Church (Admiralty's)

Date	Mintage	F12	VF20	XF40	MS60	MS63
2008	10,000			PF63 70.00	PF65 80.00	

Y# 1129 3 ROUBLES
33.90 g., 0.925 Silver 1.0017 oz. ASW, 39 mm. **Subject:** St. Nicholas Cathedral, Yakutsk

Date	Mintage	F12	VF20	XF40	MS60	MS63
2008	10,000	PF63 70.00		PF65 80.00		

Y# 1130 3 ROUBLES
33.90 g., 0.925 Silver 1.0017 oz. ASW, 39 mm. **Subject:** St. Vladimir Cathedral, Zadonsk

Date	Mintage	F12	VF20	XF40	MS60	MS63
2008	10,000	PF63 70.00		PF65 80.00		

Y# 1138 3 ROUBLES
33.90 g., 0.925 Silver 1.0017 oz. ASW, 39 mm. **Subject:** European Beaver

Date	Mintage	F12	VF20	XF40	MS60	MS63
2008	10,000	PF63 70.00		PF65 80.00		

Y# 1147 3 ROUBLES
33.90 g., 0.925 Silver 1.0017 oz. ASW, 39 mm. **Subject:** Kamchatka Volcano

Date	Mintage	F12	VF20	XF40	MS60	MS63
2008	10,000	PF63 70.00		PF65 80.00		

Y# 1150 3 ROUBLES
33.90 g., 0.925 Silver 1.0017 oz. ASW, 39 mm. **Subject:** World walking Race Cup, Cheboksary

Date	Mintage	F12	VF20	XF40	MS60	MS63
2008	5,000	PF63 70.00		PF65 80.00		

Y# 1151 3 ROUBLES
16.80 g., 0.925 Silver 0.4964 oz. ASW, 39 mm. **Subject:** City of Moscow

Date	Mintage	F12	VF20	XF40	MS60	MS63
2008	5,000	PF63 70.00		PF65 80.00		

Y# 1152 3 ROUBLES
33.90 g., 0.925 Silver 1.0017 oz. ASW, 39 mm. **Subject:** 29th Summer Olympics Bejing

Date	Mintage	F12	VF20	XF40	MS60	MS63
2008	10,000	PF63 70.00		PF65 80.00		

Y# 1180 3 ROUBLES
33.90 g., 0.925 Silver 1.0017 oz. ASW, 39 mm. **Subject:** St. George the Victorious

Date	Mintage	F12	VF20	XF40	MS60	MS63
2009ММД	280,000	—	—	—	—	55.00
2009СПМД	Inc. above	—	—	—	—	60.00
2010ММД	500,000	—	—	—	—	55.00
2010СПМД	Inc. above	—	—	—	—	60.00

Y# 992 3 ROUBLES
33.90 g., 0.925 Silver 1.0017 oz. ASW, 39 mm. **Subject:** Year of the Pig **Obv:** Double headed eagle **Rev:** Stylized pig

Date	Mintage	F12	VF20	XF40	MS60	MS63
2009	15,000	PF63 70.00		PF65 80.00		

Y# 1159 3 ROUBLES
33.90 g., 0.925 Silver 1.0017 oz. ASW, 39 mm. **Subject:** Moon research, 50th Anniversary

Date	Mintage	F12	VF20	XF40	MS60	MS63
2009	5,000	PF63 115		PF65 135		

Y# 1161 3 ROUBLES
33.90 g., 0.925 Silver 1.0017 oz. ASW, 39 mm. **Subject:** Russian Currency

Date	Mintage	F12	VF20	XF40	MS60	MS63
2009	5,000	PF63 85.00		PF65 100		

Y# 1166 3 ROUBLES
33.90 g., 0.925 Silver 1.0017 oz. ASW, 39 mm. **Subject:** A. P. Chekhov, 150th Anniversary of Birth

Date	Mintage	F12	VF20	XF40	MS60	MS63
2009	5,000	PF63 70.00		PF65 80.00		

Y# 1170 3 ROUBLES
33.90 g., 0.925 Silver 1.0017 oz. ASW, 39 mm. **Subject:** Kalmyk Peoples, 400th Anniversary of annexation into Russia

Date	Mintage	F12	VF20	XF40	MS60	MS63
2009	5,000	PF63 70.00		PF65 80.00		

Y# 1173 3 ROUBLES

33.90 g., 0.925 Silver 1.0017 oz. ASW, 39 mm. **Subject:** N. V. Gogol, 200th Anniversary of Birth

Date	Mintage	F12	VF20	XF40	MS60	MS63
2009	5,000	PF63 70.00	PF65 80.00			

Y# 1177 3 ROUBLES

33.90 g., 0.925 Silver 1.0017 oz. ASW, 39 mm. **Subject:** Poltava Battle, 300th Anniversary

Date	Mintage	F12	VF20	XF40	MS60	MS63
2009	10,000	PF63 55.00	PF65 65.00			

Y# 1182 3 ROUBLES

33.90 g., 0.925 Silver 1.0017 oz. ASW, 39 mm. **Subject:** Vitebsky Railway Station, St. Petersburg

Date	Mintage	F12	VF20	XF40	MS60	MS63
2009	7,500	PF63 70.00	PF65 80.00			

Y# 1183 3 ROUBLES

33.90 g., 0.925 Silver 1.0017 oz. ASW, 39 mm. **Subject:** Tula Kremlin

Date	Mintage	F12	VF20	XF40	MS60	MS63
2009	10,000	PF63 70.00	PF65 80.00			

Y# 1185 3 ROUBLES

33.90 g., 0.925 Silver 1.0017 oz. ASW, 39 mm. **Subject:** Odygitriya Church

Date	Mintage	F12	VF20	XF40	MS60	MS63
2009	10,000	PF63 55.00	PF65 65.00			

Y# 1188 3 ROUBLES

33.90 g., 0.925 Silver 1.0017 oz. ASW, 39 mm. **Subject:** Intercession Cathedral, Voronezsh

Date	Mintage	F12	VF20	XF40	MS60	MS63
2009	5,000	PF63 300	PF65 325			

Y# 1189 3 ROUBLES

33.90 g., 0.925 Silver 1.0017 oz. ASW, 39 mm. **Subject:** Tales of the Russian People

Date	Mintage	F12	VF20	XF40	MS60	MS63
2009	5,000	PF63 90.00	PF65 100			

Y# 1199 3 ROUBLES

33.90 g., 0.925 Silver 1.0017 oz. ASW, 39 mm. **Subject:** Velikly Novgorod

Date	Mintage	F12	VF20	XF40	MS60	MS63
2009	10,000	PF63 70.00	PF65 80.00			

Y# 1207 3 ROUBLES

33.90 g., 0.925 Silver 1.0017 oz. ASW, 39 mm. **Subject:** Fauna - Bear

Date	Mintage	F12	VF20	XF40	MS60	MS63
2009	5,000	PF63 90.00	PF65 100			

Y# 1208 3 ROUBLES

33.90 g., 0.925 Silver 1.0017 oz. ASW, 39 mm. **Series:** Year of the Tiger

Date	Mintage	F12	VF20	XF40	MS60	MS63
2009	15,000	PF63 70.00	PF65 80.00			

Y# 1219 3 ROUBLES

33.90 g., 0.925 Silver 1.0017 oz. ASW, 39 mm. **Subject:** Savior's Transfiguration Cathedral, Bolkhov

Date	Mintage	F12	VF20	XF40	MS60	MS63
2010	10,000	PF63 75.00	PF65 90.00			

Y# 1220 3 ROUBLES

33.90 g., 0.925 Silver 1.0017 oz. ASW, 39 mm. **Subject:** Vovnushki Battle tower

Date	Mintage	F12	VF20	XF40	MS60	MS63
2010	10,000	PF63 75.00	PF65 90.00			

Y# 1221 3 ROUBLES

16.80 g., 0.925 Silver 0.4964 oz. ASW, 39 mm. **Subject:** Holy Trinity Church, St. Petersburg

Date	Mintage	F12	VF20	XF40	MS60	MS63
2010	10,000	PF63 70.00	PF65 85.00			

Y# 1222 3 ROUBLES

33.90 g., 0.925 Silver 1.0017 oz. ASW, 39 mm. **Subject:** Round Square, Petrozavodsk

Date	Mintage	F12	VF20	XF40	MS60	MS63
2010	5,000	PF63 70.00	PF65 85.00			

Y# 1228 3 ROUBLES
33.90 g., 0.925 Silver 1.0017 oz. ASW, 39 mm. **Subject:** Bank of Russia, 150th Anniversary

Date	Mintage	F12	VF20	XF40	MS60	MS63
2010	10,000	PF63 70.00	PF65 80.00			

Y# 1232 3 ROUBLES
33.90 g., 0.925 Silver 1.0017 oz. ASW, 39 mm. **Subject:** UNESCO Heritage Site - Yaroslav

Date	Mintage	F12	VF20	XF40	MS60	MS63
2010	10,000	PF63 70.00	PF65 80.00			

Y# 1241 3 ROUBLES
31.10 g., 0.925 Silver 0.9189 oz. ASW, 39 mm. **Subject:** Great Patriotic War, 65th Anniversary

Date	Mintage	F12	VF20	XF40	MS60	MS63
2010	7,500	PF63 85.00	PF65 95.00			

Y# 1242 3 ROUBLES
33.90 g., 0.925 Silver 1.0017 oz. ASW, 39 mm. **Subject:** Great Patriotic War, 65th Anniversary

Date	Mintage	F12	VF20	XF40	MS60	MS63
2010	7,500	PF63 85.00	PF65 95.00			

Y# 1243 3 ROUBLES
33.90 g., 0.925 Silver 1.0017 oz. ASW, 39 mm. **Subject:** Great Patrotic War, 65th Anniversary

Date	Mintage	F12	VF20	XF40	MS60	MS63
2010	7,500	PF63 85.00	PF65 95.00			

Y# 1247 3 ROUBLES
33.90 g., 0.925 Silver 1.0017 oz. ASW, 39 mm. **Subject:** Year of the Rabbit

Date	Mintage	F12	VF20	XF40	MS60	MS63
2010	20,000	PF63 70.00	PF65 80.00			

Y# 1251 3 ROUBLES
33.90 g., 0.925 Silver 1.0017 oz. ASW, 39 mm. **Subject:** ЕАЕС, 10th Anniversary

Date	Mintage	F12	VF20	XF40	MS60	MS63
2010	5,000	PF63 80.00	PF65 95.00			

Y# 1252 3 ROUBLES
33.90 g., 0.925 Silver 1.0017 oz. ASW, 39 mm. **Subject:** ЕАЕС, National Costumes

Date	Mintage	F12	VF20	XF40	MS60	MS63
2010	5,000	PF63 75.00	PF65 85.00			

Y# 1265 3 ROUBLES
31.10 g., 0.925 Silver 0.9189 oz. ASW **Subject:** Russian Census

Date	Mintage	F12	VF20	XF40	MS60	MS63
2010	7,500	PF63 80.00	PF65 95.00			

Y# 1269 3 ROUBLES
16.80 g., 0.925 Silver 0.4964 oz. ASW, 33 mm. **Subject:** I. K. Rodnina and A.G. Zaitsev, Figure skater

Date	Mintage	F12	VF20	XF40	MS60	MS63
2010	3,000	PF65 135				

Y# 1270 3 ROUBLES
16.80 g., 0.925 Silver 0.4964 oz. ASW, 33 mm. **Subject:** A. G. Zaitsev, figure skater

Date	Mintage	F12	VF20	XF40	MS60	MS63
2010	—	PF65 40.00				

Y# 1271 3 ROUBLES
16.80 g., 0.925 Silver 0.4964 oz. ASW, 33 mm. **Subject:** L. A. Pakhomova and A. G. Gorshkov, Figure skaters

Date	Mintage	F12	VF20	XF40	MS60	MS63
2010	3,000	PF65 135				

Y# 1273 3 ROUBLES
33.90 g., 0.925 Silver 1.0017 oz. ASW, 39 mm. **Subject:** 39th World Chess Olympics

Date	Mintage	F12	VF20	XF40	MS60	MS63
2010	5,000	PF63 80.00	PF65 95.00			

Y# 1282 3 ROUBLES
31.11 g., 0.999 Silver 0.9926 oz. ASW, 39 mm. **Subject:** Cathedral of the Virgin of Kazan and St. Sergiy of Radonezh, City of Kursk **Rev:** St. Sergius Kazansky Cathedral in Kursk **Edge:** Reeded

Date	Mintage	F12	VF20	XF40	MS60	MS63
2011СПМД	7,500	PF63 80.00	PF65 90.00			

Y# 1285 3 ROUBLES
31.11 g., 0.925 Silver 0.9191 oz. ASW, 39 mm. **Rev:** Flag above five soldiers

Date	Mintage	F12	VF20	XF40	MS60	MS63
2011	3,000	PF65 325				

Y# 1287 3 ROUBLES
31.11 g., 0.999 Silver 0.9926 oz. ASW, 39 mm. **Rev:** U.A. Gagarian agains background of stars and earth in color **Edge:** Reeded

Date	Mintage	F12	VF20	XF40	MS60	MS63
2011	7,500	PF63 90.00	PF65 100			

Y# 1289 3 ROUBLES
31.11 g., 0.999 Silver 0.9926 oz. ASW, 39 mm. **Rev:** Female in national costume and wildlife native to Buryat flanking

Date	Mintage	F12	VF20	XF40	MS60	MS63
2011	3,000	PF63 150	PF65 175			

Y# 1293 3 ROUBLES
31.11 g., 0.925 Silver 0.9191 oz. ASW, 39 mm. **Subject:** 2014 Winter Olympics - Sochi - Biathlon **Rev:** Athlethe on skies with rifle, pitsunda pinecone in color at lower right

Date	Mintage	F12	VF20	XF40	MS60	MS63
2014 (2011)	35,000	PF65 125				

Y# 1294 3 ROUBLES
31.11 g., 0.925 Silver 0.9191 oz. ASW, 39 mm. **Subject:** 2014 Winter Olympics - Sochi - Alpine Skiing **Rev:** Mountain skier and magnolia in color at lower right

Date	Mintage	F12	VF20	XF40	MS60	MS63
2014 (2011)	35,000	PF65 125				

Y# 1295 3 ROUBLES
31.11 g., 0.925 Silver 0.9191 oz. ASW, 39 mm. **Subject:** 2014 Winter Olympics - Sochi - Figure Skater **Rev:** Figure skater and Voronov snowdrop in color at lower right

Date	Mintage	F12	VF20	XF40	MS60	MS63
2014 (2011)	35,000	PF65 125				

Y# 1296 3 ROUBLES
31.11 g., 0.925 Silver 0.9191 oz. ASW, 39 mm. **Subject:** 2014 Winter Olympics - Sochi - Hockey **Rev:** Hockey player and branch of cork oak in color at lower left

Date	Mintage	F12	VF20	XF40	MS60	MS63
2014 (2011)	35,000	PF65 125				

Y# 1315 3 ROUBLES
31.11 g., 0.925 Silver 0.9191 oz. ASW, 39 mm. **Rev:** Three children picking flowers and drawing

Date	Mintage	F12	VF20	XF40	MS60	MS63
2011	5,000	PF63 100	PF65 115			

Y# 1316 3 ROUBLES
31.11 g., 0.925 Silver 0.9191 oz. ASW, 39 mm. **Subject:** The Great Silk Way **Rev:** Camel rider against a background of desert ruins

Date	Mintage	F12	VF20	XF40	MS60	MS63
2011	5,000	PF63 75.00	PF65 90.00			

Y# 1330 3 ROUBLES
31.11 g., 0.925 Silver 0.9191 oz. ASW, 39 mm. **Subject:** Temple of the Sanctifier Martin the Confessor in Moscow

Date	Mintage	F12	VF20	XF40	MS60	MS63
2012	5,000	PF63 75.00	PF65 90.00			

Y# 1331 3 ROUBLES
31.11 g., 0.925 Silver 0.9191 oz. ASW, 39 mm. **Subject:** Kolotsky Assumption Monastery, Mozhaisk District of Moscow Region

Date	Mintage	F12	VF20	XF40	MS60	MS63
2012	5,000	PF63 75.00	PF65 90.00			

Y# 1332 3 ROUBLES
31.11 g., 0.925 Silver 0.9191 oz. ASW, 39 mm. **Subject:** Luzhetsky Ferapontov Monastery, Mozhaisk, Moscow region

Date	Mintage	F12	VF20	XF40	MS60	MS63
2012	5,000	PF63 75.00	PF65 90.00			

Y# 1333 3 ROUBLES
31.11 g., 0.925 Silver 0.9191 oz. ASW, 39 mm. **Subject:**
Transfiguration Cathedral, Belozersk, Vologda region

Date	Mintage	F12	VF20	XF40	MS60	MS63
2012	5,000	**PF63** 75.00	**PF65** 90.00			

Y# 1334 3 ROUBLES
31.11 g., 0.925 Silver 0.9191 oz. ASW, 39 mm. **Subject:**
Cathedral of the Saint Virgin's Nativity, Vladimir region

Date	Mintage	F12	VF20	XF40	MS60	MS63
2012	5,000	**PF63** 75.00	**PF65** 90.00			

Y# 1339 3 ROUBLES
31.11 g., 0.925 Silver 0.9191 oz. ASW, 39 mm. **Subject:**
Millennium of the Unity of the Mordovian people within the
Peoples of the Russian State

Date	Mintage	F12	VF20	XF40	MS60	MS63
2012	3,000	**PF63** 185	**PF65** 200			

Y# 1342 3 ROUBLES
31.11 g., 0.925 Silver 0.9191 oz. ASW, 39 mm. **Subject:**
People's Volunteer Corps, 400th Anniversary

Date	Mintage	F12	VF20	XF40	MS60	MS63
2012	5,000	**PF63** 75.00	**PF65** 90.00			

Y# 1345 3 ROUBLES
31.10 g., 0.925 Silver 0.9189 oz. ASW, 39 mm. **Subject:**
Russia's victory in the War of 1812

Date	Mintage	F12	VF20	XF40	MS60	MS63
2012	5,000	**PF63** 75.00	**PF65** 90.00			

Y# 1351 3 ROUBLES
31.11 g., 0.925 Silver 0.9191 oz. ASW, 39 mm. **Subject:**
Pushkin State Museum of Fine Arts, Moscow, 100th Anniversary

Date	Mintage	F12	VF20	XF40	MS60	MS63
2012	5,000	**PF63** 125	**PF65** 150			

Y# 1353 3 ROUBLES
31.11 g., 0.925 Silver 0.9191 oz. ASW, 39 mm. **Subject:**
UNESCO World Heritage Site - Vrangel Island **Rev:** Walrus
and Polar Awl in flight

Date	Mintage	F12	VF20	XF40	MS60	MS63
2012	5,000	**PF63** 75.00	**PF65** 90.00			

Y# 1354 3 ROUBLES
31.11 g., 0.925 Silver 0.9191 oz. ASW, 39 mm. **Subject:**
UNESCO World Heritage Site - Church of the Ascension in
Kolomenskoye **Rev:** Church building with tall central tower

Date	Mintage	F12	VF20	XF40	MS60	MS63
2012	5,000	**PF63** 75.00	**PF65** 90.00			

Y# 1364 3 ROUBLES
31.10 g., 0.925 Silver 0.9189 oz. ASW, 39 mm. **Subject:**
European Judo Championship, Chelyabinsk

Date	Mintage	F12	VF20	XF40	MS60	MS63
2012	3,000	**PF63** 140	**PF65** 160			

Y# 1366 3 ROUBLES
31.10 g., 0.925 Silver 0.9189 oz. ASW, 39 mm. **Subject:** Year
of the Dragon

Date	Mintage	F12	VF20	XF40	MS60	MS63
2012	15,000	**PF63** 70.00	**PF65** 80.00			

Y# 1367 3 ROUBLES
31.10 g., 0.925 Silver 0.9189 oz. ASW, 39 mm. **Subject:** Origin
of Russian Statehood, 1150th Anniversary

Date	Mintage	F12	VF20	XF40	MS60	MS63
2012	5,000	**PF63** 90.00	**PF65** 100			

Y# 1374 3 ROUBLES
31.10 g., 0.925 Silver 0.9189 oz. ASW, 39 mm. **Subject:**
Russian language and literature in the French Republic and the
French language and literature in the Russian Federation

Date	Mintage	F12	VF20	XF40	MS60	MS63
2012	5,000	**PF65** 65.00				

Y# 1377 3 ROUBLES
31.10 g., 0.925 Silver 0.9189 oz. ASW, 39 mm. **Subject:** Arms
production in Tula, 300th Anniversary

Date	Mintage	F12	VF20	XF40	MS60	MS63
2012	5,000	**PF63** 75.00	**PF65** 90.00			

Y# 1379 3 ROUBLES
31.10 g., 0.925 Silver 0.9189 oz. ASW, 39 mm. **Subject:** Air
Force, 100th Anniversary

Date	Mintage	F12	VF20	XF40	MS60	MS63
2012	3,000	**PF63** 375	**PF65** 400			

Y# 1422 3 ROUBLES
33.94 g., 0.925 Silver 1.0029 oz. ASW, 39 mm. **Rev:** Female
athlete holding Kazan Universiade banner above city skyline

Date	Mintage	F12	VF20	XF40	MS60	MS63
2013СПМД	7,500	**PF63** 70.00	**PF65** 80.00			

Y# 1430 3 ROUBLES
33.94 g., 0.925 Silver 1.0029 oz. ASW, 39 mm. **Subject:** City of
Penza, 350th Anniversary of founding **Rev:** Monument to first
settlers in center, town view around

Date	Mintage	F12	VF20	XF40	MS60	MS63
2013	5,000	**PF63** 75.00	**PF65** 90.00			

Y# 1434 3 ROUBLES
33.94 g., 0.925 Silver 1.0029 oz. ASW, 39 mm. **Subject:** A.S.
Shein **Rev:** Half-length Shein at left wiht saber, fortress and
sailing ship at right **Edge:** Reeded

Date	Mintage	F12	VF20	XF40	MS60	MS63
2013ММД	7,500	**PF63** 70.00	**PF65** 80.00			

Y# 1446 3 ROUBLES
33.94 g., 0.925 Silver 1.0029 oz. ASW, 39 mm. **Subject:** City
of Smolensk, 1150th Anniversary of founding **Rev:** Saints Peter
and Paul Church and St. Varvara Martyr Chruch

Date	Mintage	F12	VF20	XF40	MS60	MS63
2013ММД	5,000	**PF63** 75.00	**PF65** 90.00			

Y# 1449 3 ROUBLES
33.94 g., 0.925 Silver 1.0029 oz. ASW, 39 mm. **Subject:**
Russian victory over Germany at battle of Stalingrad, 70th
Anniversary **Rev:** Battle Monument in Volgograd **Edge:** Reeded

Date	Mintage	F12	VF20	XF40	MS60	MS63
2013ММД	5,000	**PF63** 75.00	**PF65** 90.00			

Y# 1452 3 ROUBLES
33.94 g., 0.925 Silver 1.0029 oz. ASW, 39 mm. **Subject:** Year
of Russa in Germany, and Germany in Russia **Rev:** Gothic
Cathedral at left, Orthodox Cathedral at right, ribbon of flags
vertical thru center **Edge:** Reeded

Date	Mintage	F12	VF20	XF40	MS60	MS63
2013СПМД	5,000	**PF63** 75.00	**PF65** 90.00			

Y# 1455 3 ROUBLES
33.94 g., 0.924 Silver 1.0018 oz. ASW, 39 mm. **Subject:**
Architectural Monuments - Assumption Cathedral on Gorodok
in Zvenigorod **Rev:** Cathedral view **Edge:** Reeded

Date	Mintage	F12	VF20	XF40	MS60	MS63
2013ММД	7,500	**PF63** 70.00	**PF65** 80.00			

Y# 1456 3 ROUBLES
33.94 g., 0.925 Silver 1.0029 oz. ASW, 39 mm. **Subject:**
Architectural Monuments - Cathedral of Virgin's Saint Entrance
Presentation in Cheboksary **Rev:** Cathedral view **Edge:**
Reeded

Date	Mintage	F12	VF20	XF40	MS60	MS63
2013СПМД	7,500	**PF63** 70.00	**PF65** 80.00			

Y# 1458 3 ROUBLES
33.94 g., 0.925 Silver 1.0029 oz. ASW, 39 mm. **Subject:** World Track and Field Championships - Moscow **Rev:** Sprinter right, track around **Edge:** Reeded

Date	Mintage	F12	VF20	XF40	MS60	MS63
2013ММД	5,000	PF63 75.00	PF65 90.00			

Y# 1459 3 ROUBLES
33.94 g., 0.925 Silver 1.0029 oz. ASW, 39 mm. **Subject:** Architectural Monuments - Trinity Cathedral, Verkhoturye **Rev:** Cathedral view **Edge:** Reeded

Date	Mintage	F12	VF20	XF40	MS60	MS63
2013ММД	7,500	PF63 70.00	PF65 80.00			

Y# 1463 3 ROUBLES
33.94 g., 0.925 Silver 1.0029 oz. ASW, 39 mm. **Subject:** Architectural Monuments - Saint Nikolas the Miracle Man Marine Cathedral, Kronstadt **Rev:** Cathedral view **Edge:** Reeded

Date	Mintage	F12	VF20	XF40	MS60	MS63
2013СПМД	7,500	PF63 70.00	PF65 80.00			

Y# 799 5 ROUBLES
6.45 g., Copper-Nickel Clad Copper, 25 mm. **Obv:** Two headed eagle above curved bank name and denomination **Rev:** Value and flower **Edge:** Segmented reeding

Date	Mintage	F12	VF20	XF40	MS60	MS63
2002ММД In sets only	15,000	—	—	—	—	—
2002СПМД In sets only	15,000	—	—	—	—	—
2003ММД	15,000	—	—	150	200	250
2008ММД	—	—	—	—	3.00	4.00
2008СПМД	—	—	—	—	3.00	4.00
2009СПМД	—	—	—	—	4.00	5.00
2009ММД	—	—	—	—	3.00	4.00

Y# 829 5 ROUBLES
47.24 g., Bi-Metallic, 39.5 mm. **Obv:** Double-headed eagle **Rev:** Uglich city view **Edge:** Reeded

Date	Mintage	F12	VF20	XF40	MS60	MS63
2004(sp)	5,000	PF65 1,350				

Y# 1075 5 ROUBLES
Bi-Metallic **Subject:** Bogolyvbovo Township

Date	Mintage	F12	VF20	XF40	MS60	MS63
2006	1,000	PF63 1,250	PF65 1,750			

Y# 1076 5 ROUBLES
47.24 g., 0.900 Silver 1.3581 oz. ASW, 39.5 mm. **Subject:** City of Turyev-Polsky

Date	Mintage	F12	VF20	XF40	MS60	MS63
2006	1,000	PF63 1,250	PF65 1,750			

Y# 1154 5 ROUBLES
47.24 g., 0.900 Silver 1.3581 oz. ASW, 39.5 mm. **Subject:** Pereslavl Zalessky

Date	Mintage	F12	VF20	XF40	MS60	MS63
2008	1,000	PF63 1,250	PF65 1,750			

Y# 1155 5 ROUBLES
47.24 g., 0.900 Silver 1.3581 oz. ASW, 39.5 mm. **Subject:** Alexandrov

Date	Mintage	F12	VF20	XF40	MS60	MS63
2008	1,000	PF63 1,250	PF65 1,750			

Y# 799a 5 ROUBLES
6.00 g., Nickel Plated Steel, 25 mm. **Obv:** Two headed eagle above curved bank name and denomination **Rev:** Value and flower **Edge:** Segmented reeding

Date	Mintage	F12	VF20	XF40	MS60	MS63
2009ММД	—	—	—	—	2.00	3.00
2009СПМД	—	—	—	—	2.00	3.00
2010ММД	—	—	—	—	2.00	3.00
2010СПМД	—	—	—	—	4.00	5.00
2011ММД	—	—	—	—	2.00	3.00
2012ММД	—	—	—	—	2.00	3.00

Y# 1408 5 ROUBLES
6.00 g., Nickel Plated Steel, 25 mm. **Subject:** Battle of Smolensk, War of 1812

Date	Mintage	F12	VF20	XF40	MS60	MS63
2012ММД	5,000,000	—	—	—	2.00	3.00

Y# 1409 5 ROUBLES
6.00 g., Nickel Plated Steel, 25 mm. **Subject:** Battle of Borodino, War of 1812

Date	Mintage	F12	VF20	XF40	MS60	MS63
2012ММД	5,000,000	—	—	—	2.00	3.00

Y# 1410 5 ROUBLES
6.00 g., Nickel Plated Steel, 25 mm. **Subject:** Battle of Tarutino, War of 1812

Date	Mintage	F12	VF20	XF40	MS60	MS63
2012ММД	5,000,000	—	—	—	2.00	3.00

Y# 1411 5 ROUBLES
6.00 g., Nickel Plated Steel, 25 mm. **Subject:** Battle of Maloyaroslavets, War of 1812

Date	Mintage	F12	VF20	XF40	MS60	MS63
2012	5,000,000	—	—	—	2.00	3.00

Y# 1412 5 ROUBLES
6.00 g., Nickel Plated Steel, 25 mm. **Subject:** Battle of Vyazma, War of 1812

Date	Mintage	F12	VF20	XF40	MS60	MS63
2012ММД	5,000,000	—	—	—	2.00	3.00

Y# 1413 5 ROUBLES
6.00 g., Nickel Plated Steel, 25 mm. **Subject:** Battle of Krasnoye, War of 1812

Date	Mintage	F12	VF20	XF40	MS60	MS63
2012ММД	5,000,000	—	—	—	2.00	3.00

Y# 1414 5 ROUBLES
6.00 g., Nickel Plated Steel, 25 mm. **Subject:** Battle of Berezina, War of 1812

Date	Mintage	F12	VF20	XF40	MS60	MS63
2012ММД	5,000,000	—	—	—	2.00	3.00

Y# 1415 5 ROUBLES

6.00 g., Nickel Plated Steel, 25 mm. **Subject:** Battle of Kulm, War of 1812

Date	Mintage	F12	VF20	XF40	MS60	MS63
2012ММД	5,000,000	—	—	—	2.00	3.00

Y# 1416 5 ROUBLES

6.00 g., Nickel Plated Steel, 25 mm. **Subject:** Battle of Leipzig, War of 1812

Date	Mintage	F12	VF20	XF40	MS60	MS63
2012ММД	5,000,000	—	—	—	2.00	3.00

Y# 1417 5 ROUBLES

6.00 g., Nickel Plated Steel, 25 mm. **Subject:** Capture of Paris, War of 1812

Date	Mintage	F12	VF20	XF40	MS60	MS63
2012ММД	5,000,000	—	—	—	2.00	3.00

Y# 676 10 ROUBLES

8.22 g., Bi-Metallic, 27 mm. **Subject:** Yuri Gagarin **Obv:** Value with latent image in zero within circle and sprigs **Rev:** Helmeted bust 1/4 right **Edge:** Reeding over denomination

Date	Mintage	F12	VF20	XF40	MS60	MS63
2001ММД	10,000,000	—	—	—	4.00	5.00
2001СПМД	10,000,000	—	—	—	4.00	5.00

Y# 686 10 ROUBLES

1.61 g., 0.999 Gold 0.0514 oz. AGW, 12 mm. **Subject:** Bolshoi Theater 225 Years **Obv:** Double-headed eagle within circle **Rev:** Building above number 225 **Edge:** Reeded

Date	Mintage	F12	VF20	XF40	MS60	MS63
2001	3,000	PF65 110				

Y# 739 10 ROUBLES

8.22 g., Bi-Metallic, 27 mm. **Subject:** Ancient Towns - Derbent **Obv:** Value with latent image in zero within circle and sprigs **Rev:** Shield above walled city view **Edge:** Reeding over denomination

Date	Mintage	F12	VF20	XF40	MS60	MS63
2002ММД	5,000,000	—	—	—	4.00	5.00

Y# 740 10 ROUBLES

8.22 g., Bi-Metallic, 27 mm. **Subject:** Ancient Towns - Kostroma **Obv:** Value with latent image in zero within circle and sprigs **Rev:** Cupola, shield and river view **Edge:** Reeding over denomination

Date	Mintage	F12	VF20	XF40	MS60	MS63
2002СПМД	5,000,000	—	—	—	4.00	6.00

Y# 741 10 ROUBLES

8.22 g., Bi-Metallic, 27 mm. **Subject:** Ancient Towns - Staraya Russa **Obv:** Value with latent image in zero within circle and sprigs **Rev:** Shield and cathedral **Edge:** Reeding over denomination

Date	Mintage	F12	VF20	XF40	MS60	MS63
2002СПМД	5,000,000	—	—	—	4.00	6.00

Y# 748 10 ROUBLES

8.22 g., Bi-Metallic, 27 mm. **Subject:** Ministry of Education **Obv:** Value with latent image in zero within circle and sprigs **Rev:** Seedling within open book **Edge:** Reeding over denomination

Date	Mintage	F12	VF20	XF40	MS60	MS63
2002ММД	5,000,000	—	—	—	4.00	6.00

Y# 749 10 ROUBLES

8.22 g., Bi-Metallic, 27 mm. **Subject:** Ministry of Finance **Obv:** Value with latent image in zero within circle and sprigs **Rev:** Caduceus within monogram **Edge:** Reeding over denomination

Date	Mintage	F12	VF20	XF40	MS60	MS63
2002СПМД	5,000,000	—	—	—	4.00	6.00

Y# 750 10 ROUBLES

8.22 g., Bi-Metallic, 27 mm. **Subject:** Ministry of Economic Development and Trade **Obv:** Value with latent image in zero within circle and sprigs **Rev:** Crowned double-headed eagle with cornucopia and caduceus **Edge:** Reeding over denomination

Date	Mintage	F12	VF20	XF40	MS60	MS63
2002СПМД	5,000,000	—	—	—	4.00	6.00

Y# 751 10 ROUBLES

8.22 g., Bi-Metallic, 27 mm. **Subject:** Ministry of Foreign Affairs **Obv:** Value with latent image in zero within circle and sprigs **Rev:** Crowned double-headed eagle above crossed sprigs **Edge:** Reeding over denomination

Date	Mintage	F12	VF20	XF40	MS60	MS63
2002СПМД	5,000,000	—	—	—	5.00	6.00

Y# 752 10 ROUBLES

8.22 g., Bi-Metallic, 27 mm. **Subject:** Ministry of Internal Affairs **Obv:** Value with latent image in zero within circle and sprigs **Rev:** Crowned double-headed eagle with round breast shield **Edge:** Reeding over denomination

Date	Mintage	F12	VF20	XF40	MS60	MS63
2002ММД	5,000,000	—	—	—	5.00	6.00

Y# 753 10 ROUBLES

8.22 g., Bi-Metallic, 27 mm. **Subject:** Ministry of Justice **Obv:** Value with latent image in zero within circle and sprigs **Rev:** Crowned double-headed eagle with column on breast shield **Edge:** Reeding over denomination

Date	Mintage	F12	VF20	XF40	MS60	MS63
2002СПМД	5,000,000	—	—	—	4.00	6.00

Y# 754 10 ROUBLES

8.22 g., Bi-Metallic, 27 mm. **Subject:** Russian Armed Forces **Obv:** Value with latent image in zero within circle and sprigs **Rev:** Crowned double-headed eagle with crowned pointed top shield **Edge:** Reeding over denomination

Date	Mintage	F12	VF20	XF40	MS60	MS63
2002ММД	5,000,000	—	—	—	5.00	6.00

Y# 817 10 ROUBLES

8.34 g., Bi-Metallic, 27 mm. **Obv:** Value with latent image in zero within circle and sprigs **Rev:** Murom city view and tilted oval shields within circle **Edge:** Reeded and lettered

Date	Mintage	F12	VF20	XF40	MS60	MS63
2003(sp)	5,000,000	—	—	—	5.00	6.00

Y# 800 10 ROUBLES
8.44 g., Bi-Metallic, 27.1 mm. **Subject:** Pskov **Obv:** Value with latent image in zero within circle and sprigs **Rev:** Shield above walled city **Edge:** Reeding over lettering

Date	Mintage	F12	VF20	XF40	MS60	MS63
2003СПМД	5,000,000	—	—	—	5.00	6.00

Y# 818 10 ROUBLES
8.34 g., Bi-Metallic, 27 mm. **Obv:** Value with latent image in zero within circle and sprigs **Rev:** Kasimov city view and shield within circle **Edge:** Reeded and lettered

Date	Mintage	F12	VF20	XF40	MS60	MS63
2003СПМД	5,000,000	—	—	—	5.00	6.00

Y# 819 10 ROUBLES
8.34 g., Bi-Metallic, 27 mm. **Subject:** Dorogobuzh **Obv:** Value with latent image in zero within circle and sprigs **Rev:** Monument, city view and shield within circle **Edge:** Reeded and lettered

Date	Mintage	F12	VF20	XF40	MS60	MS63
2003ММД	5,000,000	—	—	—	5.00	6.00

Y# 824 10 ROUBLES
8.46 g., Bi-Metallic, 27.1 mm. **Subject:** Town of Ryazhsk **Obv:** Value with latent image in zero within circle and sprigs **Obv. Legend:** БАНК РОССИИ **Rev:** City view and crowned shield within circle **Edge:** Reeded and lettered

Date	Mintage	F12	VF20	XF40	MS60	MS63
2004ММД	—	—	—	—	5.00	6.00

Y# 825 10 ROUBLES
8.46 g., Bi-Metallic, 27.1 mm. **Subject:** Town of Dmitrov **Obv:** Value with latent image in zero within circle and sprigs **Obv. Legend:** БАНК РОССИИ **Rev:** City view and crowned shield within circle **Edge:** Reeded and lettered

Date	Mintage	F12	VF20	XF40	MS60	MS63
2004ММД	5,000,000	—	—	—	5.00	6.00

Y# 826 10 ROUBLES
8.46 g., Bi-Metallic, 27.1 mm. **Subject:** Town of Kem **Obv:** Value with latent image in zero within circle and sprigs **Obv. Legend:** БАНК РОССИИ **Rev:** City view and crowned shield within circle **Edge:** Reeded and lettered

Date	Mintage	F12	VF20	XF40	MS60	MS63
2004СПМД	5,000,000	—	—	—	5.00	6.00

Y# 827 10 ROUBLES
8.40 g., Bi-Metallic, 27 mm. **Subject:** Great Victory, 60th Anniversary **Obv:** Value with latent image in zero within circle and sprigs **Rev:** WWII eternal flame monument above date and sprig within circle **Edge:** Reeded and lettered

Date	Mintage	F12	VF20	XF40	MS60	MS63
2005ММД	30,000,000	—	—	—	5.00	6.00
2005СПМД	30,000,000	—	—	—	5.00	6.00

Y# 886 10 ROUBLES
8.23 g., Bi-Metallic, 27 mm. **Obv:** Value with latent image in zero within circle and sprigs **Rev:** Moscow coat of arms within circle **Edge:** Reeded and lettered

Date	Mintage	F12	VF20	XF40	MS60	MS63
2005ММД	10,000,000	—	—	—	5.00	6.00

Y# 887 10 ROUBLES
8.23 g., Bi-Metallic, 27 mm. **Obv:** Value with latent image in zero within circle and sprigs **Rev:** Leningrad Oblast coat of arms within circle **Edge:** Reeded and lettered

Date	Mintage	F12	VF20	XF40	MS60	MS63
2005СПМД	10,000,000	—	—	—	5.00	6.00

Y# 888 10 ROUBLES
8.23 g., Bi-Metallic, 27 mm. **Obv:** Value with latent image in zero within circle and sprigs **Rev:** Tverskaya arms within circle **Edge:** Reeded and lettered

Date	Mintage	F12	VF20	XF40	MS60	MS63
2005ММД	10,000,000	—	—	—	5.00	6.00

Y# 889 10 ROUBLES
8.23 g., Bi-Metallic, 27 mm. **Obv:** Value with latent image in zero within circle and sprigs **Rev:** Krasnodarskiy Kray coat of arms **Edge:** Reeded and lettered

Date	Mintage	F12	VF20	XF40	MS60	MS63
2005(m)	10,000,000	—	—	—	5.00	6.00

Y# 890 10 ROUBLES
8.23 g., Bi-Metallic, 27 mm. **Obv:** Value with latent image in zero within circle and sprigs **Rev:** Orlovskaya Oblast coat of arms within circle **Edge:** Reeded and lettered

Date	Mintage	F12	VF20	XF40	MS60	MS63
2005(m)	10,000,000	—	—	—	5.00	6.00

Y# 891 10 ROUBLES
8.23 g., Bi-Metallic, 27 mm. **Obv:** Value with latent image in zero within circle and sprigs **Rev:** Tatarstan Republic coat of arms within circle **Edge:** Reeded and lettered

Date	Mintage	F12	VF20	XF40	MS60	MS63
2005СПМД	10,000,000	—	—	—	5.00	6.00

Y# 943 10 ROUBLES
8.23 g., Bi-Metallic, 27.1 mm. **Obv:** Large value **Rev:** City of Kazan and arms

Date	Mintage	F12	VF20	XF40	MS60	MS63
2005СПМД	5,000,000	—	—	—	5.00	6.00

Y# 944 10 ROUBLES
8.23 g., Bi-Metallic, 27.1 mm. **Obv:** Large value **Rev:** City of Borovsk and arms

Date	Mintage	F12	VF20	XF40	MS60	MS63
2005СПМД	5,000,000	—	—	—	5.00	6.00

Y# 945 10 ROUBLES

8.23 g., Bi-Metallic, 27.1 mm. **Obv:** Large value **Rev:** City of Mzensk and shield

Date	Mintage	F12	VF20	XF40	MS60	MS63
2005ММД	5,000,000	—	—	—	5.00	6.00

Y# 946 10 ROUBLES

8.23 g., Bi-Metallic, 27.1 mm. **Obv:** Large value **Rev:** City of Kaliningrad and shield

Date	Mintage	F12	VF20	XF40	MS60	MS63
2005ММД	5,000,000	—	—	—	5.00	6.00

Y# 938 10 ROUBLES

8.23 g., Bi-Metallic, 27 mm. **Obv:** Value with latent image in zero within circle and sprigs **Rev:** Republic of Altai arms **Edge:** Lettered and reeded

Date	Mintage	F12	VF20	XF40	MS60	MS63
2006СПМД	10,000,000	—	—	—	5.00	6.00

Y# 939 10 ROUBLES

8.23 g., Bi-Metallic, 27 mm. **Obv:** Value with latent image in zero within circle and sprigs **Rev:** Chita Region arms **Edge:** Lettered and reeded

Date	Mintage	F12	VF20	XF40	MS60	MS63
2006СПМД	10,000,000	—	—	—	5.00	6.00

Y# 940 10 ROUBLES

8.23 g., Bi-Metallic, 27 mm. **Obv:** Value with latent image in zero within circle and sprigs **Rev:** Primorskij Kraj Maritime Territory coat of arms **Edge:** Lettered and reeded

Date	Mintage	F12	VF20	XF40	MS60	MS63
2006ММД	10,000,000	—	—	—	5.00	6.00

Y# 941 10 ROUBLES

8.23 g., Bi-Metallic, 27 mm. **Obv:** Value with latent image in zero within circle and sprigs **Rev:** Sakha (Yakutiya) Republic coat of arms **Edge:** Lettered and reeded

Date	Mintage	F12	VF20	XF40	MS60	MS63
2006СПМД	10,000,000	—	—	—	5.00	6.00

Y# 942 10 ROUBLES

8.23 g., Bi-Metallic, 27 mm. **Obv:** Value with latent image in zero within circle and sprigs **Rev:** Sakhalinskaya Oblast coat of arms **Edge:** Lettered and reeded

Date	Mintage	F12	VF20	XF40	MS60	MS63
2006ММД	10,000,000	—	—	—	5.00	6.00

Y# 947 10 ROUBLES

8.23 g., Bi-Metallic, 27.1 mm. **Obv:** Large value **Rev:** City of Belgorod and shield

Date	Mintage	F12	VF20	XF40	MS60	MS63
2006ММД	5,000,000	—	—	—	5.00	6.00

Y# 948 10 ROUBLES

8.23 g., Bi-Metallic, 27.1 mm. **Obv:** Large value **Rev:** City of Kargopol and shield

Date	Mintage	F12	VF20	XF40	MS60	MS63
2006ММД	5,000,000	—	—	—	5.00	6.00

Y# 949 10 ROUBLES

8.23 g., Bi-Metallic, 27.1 mm. **Obv:** Large value **Rev:** City of Turzhok and shield

Date	Mintage	F12	VF20	XF40	MS60	MS63
2006СПМД	5,000,000	—	—	—	5.00	6.00

Y# 963 10 ROUBLES

8.30 g., Bi-Metallic, 27 mm. **Obv:** Value with latent image in zero within circle and sprays **Rev:** Vologda church **Edge:** Reeded and lettered **Edge Lettering:** Denomination repeated

Date	Mintage	F12	VF20	XF40	MS60	MS63
2007ММД	2,500,000	—	—	—	5.00	6.00
2007СПМД	2,500,000	—	—	—	5.00	6.00

Y# 964 10 ROUBLES

8.30 g., Bi-Metallic, 27 mm. **Obv:** Value with latent image in

zero within circle and sprays **Rev:** Veliky Ustyug city view **Edge:** Reeded and lettered **Edge Lettering:** Denomination repeated

Date	Mintage	F12	VF20	XF40	MS60	MS63
2007ММД	2,500,000	—	—	—	5.00	6.00
2007СПМД	2,500,000	—	—	—	5.00	6.00

Y# 965 10 ROUBLES

8.30 g., Bi-Metallic, 27 mm. **Obv:** Value with latent image in zero within circle and sprays **Rev:** Gdov church **Edge:** Reeded and lettered **Edge Lettering:** Denomination repeated

Date	Mintage	F12	VF20	XF40	MS60	MS63
2007ММД	2,500,000	—	—	—	5.00	6.00
2007СПМД	2,500,000	—	—	—	5.00	6.00

Y# 970 10 ROUBLES

8.57 g., Bi-Metallic, 27.08 mm. **Obv:** Value with latent image in zero within circle and sprays **Obv. Legend:** БАНК РОССИИ **Rev:** Rostovskaya Oblast arms **Edge:** Reeded and lettered **Edge Lettering:** Denomination repeated

Date	Mintage	F12	VF20	XF40	MS60	MS63
2007СПМД	10,000,000	—	—	—	4.00	6.00

Y# 971 10 ROUBLES

8.57 g., Bi-Metallic, 27.08 mm. **Obv:** Value with latent image in zero within circle and sprays **Obv. Legend:** БАНК РОССИИ **Rev:** Khakassia Republic arms **Edge:** Reeded and lettered **Edge Lettering:** Denomination repeated

Date	Mintage	F12	VF20	XF40	MS60	MS63
2007СПМД	10,000,000	—	—	—	5.00	6.00

Y# 972 10 ROUBLES

8.57 g., Bi-Metallic, 27.08 mm. **Obv:** Value with latent image in zero within circle and sprays **Obv. Legend:** БАНК РОССИИ **Rev:** Bashkortostan Republic arms **Edge:** Reeded and lettered **Edge Lettering:** Denomination repeated

Date	Mintage	F12	VF20	XF40	MS60	MS63
2007ММД	10,000,000	—	—	—	5.00	6.00

Y# 973 10 ROUBLES

8.57 g., Bi-Metallic, 27.08 mm. **Obv:** Value with latent image in zero within circle and sprays **Obv. Legend:** БАНК РОССИИ **Rev:** Archangelskaya Oblast arms **Edge:** Reeded and lettered **Edge Lettering:** Denomination repeated

Date	Mintage	F12	VF20	XF40	MS60	MS63
2007СПМД	10,000,000	—	—	—	5.00	6.00

Y# 974 10 ROUBLES
8.57 g., Bi-Metallic, 27.08 mm. **Obv:** Value with latent image in zero within circle and sprays **Obv. Legend:** БАНК РОССИИ **Rev:** Novosibirskaya Oblast arms **Edge:** Reeded and lettered **Edge Lettering:** Denomination repeated

Date	Mintage	F12	VF20	XF40	MS60	MS63
2007ММД	10,000,000	—	—	—	5.00	6.00

Y# 993 10 ROUBLES
8.23 g., Bi-Metallic **Subject:** Lipetskaya Oblast

Date	Mintage	F12	VF20	XF40	MS60	MS63
2007ММД	10,000,000	—	—	—	2.00	3.50

Y# 975 10 ROUBLES
8.20 g., Bi-Metallic, 27.1 mm. **Obv:** Value with latent image in zero within circle and sprays **Obv. Legend:** БАНК РОССИИ **Rev:** Udmurtia Republic arms **Rev. Legend:** УДМУРТСКАЯ РЕСПУБЛИКА **Edge:** Reeded and lettered **Edge Lettering:** Denomination repeated

Date	Mintage	F12	VF20	XF40	MS60	MS63
2008ММД	5,000,000	—	—	1.00	2.00	3.00
2008СПМД	5,000,000	—	—	1.00	2.00	3.00

Y# 976 10 ROUBLES
8.28 g., Bi-Metallic, 27.1 mm. **Series:** Ancient cities **Subject:** Vladimir **Obv:** Value with latent image in zero within circle and sprays **Obv. Legend:** БАНК РОССИИ **Rev:** Small shield at upper left above city view **Rev. Legend:** ВЛАДИМИР **Edge:** Reeded and lettered **Edge Lettering:** Denomination repeated

Date	Mintage	F12	VF20	XF40	MS60	MS63
2008ММД	2,500,000	—	—	1.00	2.00	3.00
2008СПМД	2,500,000	—	—	1.00	2.00	3.00

Y# 977 10 ROUBLES
8.23 g., Bi-Metallic, 27 mm. **Obv:** Value with latent image in zero within circle and sprays **Obv. Legend:** БАНК РОССИИ **Rev:** Astrakhanskaya Oblast arms **Edge:** Reeded and lettered **Edge Lettering:** Denomination repeated

Date	Mintage	F12	VF20	XF40	MS60	MS63
2008ММД	5,000,000	—	—	1.00	2.00	3.00
2008СПМД	5,000,000	—	—	1.00	2.00	3.00

Y# 978 10 ROUBLES
8.16 g., Bi-Metallic, 27 mm. **Obv:** Value with latent image in zero within circle and sprays **Obv. Legend:** БАНК РОССИИ **Rev:** Sverdlovskaya Oblast arms **Edge:** Reeded and lettered **Edge Lettering:** Denomination repeated

Date	Mintage	F12	VF20	XF40	MS60	MS63
2008ММД	5,000,000	—	—	1.00	2.00	3.00
2008СПМД	5,000,000	—	—	1.00	2.00	3.00

Y# 986 10 ROUBLES
8.08 g., Bi-Metallic, 27 mm. **Rev:** Azov town view

Date	Mintage	F12	VF20	XF40	MS60	MS63
2008ММД	2,500,000	—	—	—	2.00	3.50
2008СПМД	2,500,000	—	—	—	2.00	3.50

Y# 991 10 ROUBLES
8.08 g., Bi-Metallic, 27 mm. **Rev:** Kabardino-Balkaria Republic Arms

Date	Mintage	F12	VF20	XF40	MS60	MS63
2008ММД	5,000,000	—	—	—	2.00	3.50
2008СПМД	5,000,000	—	—	—	2.00	3.50

Y# 995 10 ROUBLES
8.23 g., Bi-Metallic **Subject:** Smolensk

Date	Mintage	F12	VF20	XF40	MS60	MS63
2008ММД	2,500,000	—	—	—	2.00	3.50
2008СПМД	2,500,000	—	—	—	2.00	3.50

Y# 982 10 ROUBLES
8.08 g., Bi-Metallic, 27 mm. **Rev:** Kaluga town view

Date	Mintage	F12	VF20	XF40	MS60	MS63
2009ММД	2,500,000	—	—	—	2.00	3.50
2009СПМД	2,500,000	—	—	—	2.00	3.50

Y# 983 10 ROUBLES
8.08 g., Bi-Metallic, 27 mm. **Rev:** Vyborg town view

Date	Mintage	F12	VF20	XF40	MS60	MS63
2009ММД	2,500,000	—	—	—	2.00	3.50
2009СПМД	2,500,000	—	—	—	2.00	3.50

Y# 984 10 ROUBLES
8.08 g., Bi-Metallic, 27 mm. **Rev:** Galich town view

Date	Mintage	F12	VF20	XF40	MS60	MS63
2009ММД	2,500,000	—	—	—	2.00	3.50
2009СПМД	2,500,000	—	—	—	2.00	3.50

Y# 985 10 ROUBLES
8.08 g., Bi-Metallic, 27 mm. **Rev:** Kalmykiya Republic arms

Date	Mintage	F12	VF20	XF40	MS60	MS63
2009ММД	5,000,000	—	—	—	2.00	3.50
2009СПМД	5,000,000	—	—	—	2.00	3.50

Y# 987 10 ROUBLES
8.08 g., Bi-Metallic, 27 mm. **Rev:** Adygeya Republic arms

Date	Mintage	F12	VF20	XF40	MS60	MS63
2009ММД	5,000,000	—	—	—	2.00	3.50
2009СПМД	5,000,000	—	—	—	2.00	3.50

Y# 988 10 ROUBLES
8.08 g., Bi-Metallic, 27 mm. **Rev:** Veliky Novgorod arms

Date	Mintage	F12	VF20	XF40	MS60	MS63
2009ММД	2,500,000	—	—	—	2.00	3.50
2009СПМД	2,500,000	—	—	—	2.00	3.50

Y# 989 10 ROUBLES
8.08 g., Bi-Metallic, 27 mm. **Rev:** Jewish Autonomous Oblast Arms

Date	Mintage	F12	VF20	XF40	MS60	MS63
2009ММД	5,000,000	—	—	—	2.00	3.50
2009СПМД	5,000,000	—	—	—	2.00	3.50

Date	Mintage	F12	VF20	XF40	MS60	MS63
2009ММД	2,500,000	—	—	—	2.00	3.50
2009СПМД	2,500,000	—	—	—	2.00	3.50

Y# 996 10 ROUBLES
8.08 g., Bi-Metallic **Subject:** Komi Republic

Date	Mintage	F12	VF20	XF40	MS60	MS63
2009СПМД	10,000,000	—	—	—	2.00	3.50

Y# 997 10 ROUBLES
8.08 g., Bi-Metallic **Subject:** Kirovskaya Oblast

Date	Mintage	F12	VF20	XF40	MS60	MS63
2009СПМД	10,000,000	—	—	—	2.00	3.50

Y# 998 10 ROUBLES
5.63 g., Brass Plated Steel, 22 mm. **Obv:** Double headed eagle **Rev:** Value

Date	Mintage	F12	VF20	XF40	MS60	MS63
2009ММД	—	—	—	—	2.50	4.00
2010ММД	—	—	—	—	2.50	4.00
2010СПМД	—	—	—	—	2.50	4.00
2011ММД	—	—	—	—	2.50	4.00
2012ММД	—	—	—	—	2.50	4.00

Y# 1274 10 ROUBLES
8.08 g., Bi-Metallic, 27 mm. **Subject:** Russian Census

Date	Mintage	F12	VF20	XF40	MS60	MS63
2010	2,300,000	—	—	—	4.00	6.00

Y# 1275 10 ROUBLES
8.08 g., Bi-Metallic, 27 mm. **Subject:** Bryansk

Date	Mintage	F12	VF20	XF40	MS60	MS63
2010	10,000,000	—	—	—	4.00	6.00

Y# 1276 10 ROUBLES
8.08 g., Bi-Metallic, 27 mm. **Subject:** Yurevets, Ivanovo Region

Date	Mintage	F12	VF20	XF40	MS60	MS63
2010	10,000,000	—	—	—	4.00	6.00

Y# 1277 10 ROUBLES
8.08 g., Bi-Metallic, 27 mm. **Series:** Permskiy Krai

Date	Mintage	F12	VF20	XF40	MS60	MS63
2010	200,000	—	—	—	45.00	70.00

Y# 1278 10 ROUBLES
8.08 g., Bi-Metallic, 27 mm. **Subject:** Nenets Autonomous Region

Date	Mintage	F12	VF20	XF40	MS60	MS63
2010	1,950,000	—	—	—	4.00	6.00

Y# 1279 10 ROUBLES
8.08 g., Bi-Metallic, 27 mm. **Subject:** Chechen Republic

Date	Mintage	F12	VF20	XF40	MS60	MS63
2010	100,000	—	—	—	100	150

Y# 1280 10 ROUBLES
8.08 g., Bi-Metallic, 27 mm. **Subject:** Yamalo-Nenetskiy Autonomous Area

Date	Mintage	F12	VF20	XF40	MS60	MS63
2010	100,000	—	—	—	250	300

Y# 1283 10 ROUBLES
8.08 g., Bi-Metallic, 27 mm. **Rev:** Solikamsk town view

Date	Mintage	F12	VF20	XF40	MS60	MS63
2011СПМД	—	—	—	—	3.00	4.00

Y# 1284 10 ROUBLES
8.08 g., Bi-Metallic, 27 mm. **Rev:** Yelets city view

Date	Mintage	F12	VF20	XF40	MS60	MS63
2011СПМД	—	—	—	—	3.00	4.00

Y# 1292 10 ROUBLES
8.08 g., Bi-Metallic, 27 mm. **Rev:** Shield of the Republic of Buryatia

Date	Mintage	F12	VF20	XF40	MS60	MS63
2011СПМД	—	—	—	—	3.00	4.00

Y# 1305 10 ROUBLES
5.63 g., Brass Plated Steel, 22 mm. **Subject:** Belgorod **Edge:** Segmented reeding

Date	Mintage	F12	VF20	XF40	MS60	MS63
2011СПМД	10,000,000	—	—	—	3.00	4.00

Y# 1308 10 ROUBLES
5.63 g., Brass Plated Steel, 22 mm. **Subject:** Kursk city arms **Edge:** Segmented reeding

Date	Mintage	F12	VF20	XF40	MS60	MS63
2011СПМД	10,000,000	—	—	—	3.00	4.00

Y# 1309 10 ROUBLES
5.63 g., Brass Plated Steel, 22 mm. **Subject:** Orel city arms

Date	Mintage	F12	VF20	XF40	MS60	MS63
2011	10,000,000	—	—	—	3.00	4.00

Y# 1313 10 ROUBLES
8.08 g., Bi-Metallic, 27 mm. **Rev:** Voronezh Region arms

Date	Mintage	F12	VF20	XF40	MS60	MS63
2011	10,000,000	—	—	—	3.00	4.00

Y# 1314 10 ROUBLES
5.63 g., Brass Plated Steel, 22 mm. **Rev:** Vladikavkaz city arms **Edge:** Segmented reeding

Date	Mintage	F12	VF20	XF40	MS60	MS63
2011СПМД	10,000,000	—	—	—	3.00	4.00

Y# 1318 10 ROUBLES
5.63 g., Brass Plated Steel, 22 mm. **Rev:** Malgobek city arms **Edge:** Segmented reeding

Date	Mintage	F12	VF20	XF40	MS60	MS63
2011СПМД	10,000,000	—	—	—	3.00	4.00

Y# 1323 10 ROUBLES
5.63 g., Brass Plated Steel, 22 mm. **Rev:** Rzhev city arms **Edge:** Segmented reeding

Date	Mintage	F12	VF20	XF40	MS60	MS63
2011СПМД	10,000,000	—	—	—	3.00	4.00

Y# 1467 10 ROUBLES
5.63 g., Brass Plated Steel, 22 mm. **Rev:** Elrya city arms **Edge:** Segmented reeding

Date	Mintage	F12	VF20	XF40	MS60	MS63
2011СПМД	—	—	—	—	2.50	4.00

Y# 1468 10 ROUBLES
5.63 g., Brass Plated Steel, 22 mm. **Subject:** First orbital flight, 50th anniversary **Rev:** Space shuttle on launch pad **Edge:** Segmented reeding

Date	Mintage	F12	VF20	XF40	MS60	MS63
2011(SP)	—	—	—	—	—	3.00	4.00

Y# 1380 10 ROUBLES
8.08 g., Bi-Metallic, 27 mm. **Subject:** Belozersk, Vologda region

Date	Mintage	F12	VF20	XF40	MS60	MS63
2012	5,000,000	—	—	—	2.50	4.00

Y# 1381 10 ROUBLES
Brass Plated Steel, 22 mm. **Rev:** Voronezh city arms **Edge:** Segmented reeding

Date	Mintage	F12	VF20	XF40	MS60	MS63
2012СПМД	10,000,000	—	—	—	2.50	4.00

Y# 1382 10 ROUBLES
Brass Plated Steel, 22 mm. **Rev:** Luga city arms **Edge:** Segmented reeding

Date	Mintage	F12	VF20	XF40	MS60	MS63
2012СПМД	10,000,000	—	—	—	2.50	4.00

Y# 1383 10 ROUBLES
Brass Plated Steel, 22 mm. **Rev:** Polyarny city arms **Edge:** Segmented reeding

Date	Mintage	F12	VF20	XF40	MS60	MS63
2012СПМД	10,000,000	—	—	—	2.50	4.00

Y# 1384 10 ROUBLES
Brass Plated Steel, 22 mm. **Rev:** Rostov-on-Don city arms **Edge:** Segmented reeding

Date	Mintage	F12	VF20	XF40	MS60	MS63
2012СПМД	10,000,000	—	—	—	2.50	4.00

Y# 1385 10 ROUBLES
Brass Plated Steel, 22 mm. **Rev:** Tuapse city arms **Edge:** Segmented reeding

Date	Mintage	F12	VF20	XF40	MS60	MS63
2012СПМД	10,000,000	—	—	—	2.50	4.00

Y# 1386 10 ROUBLES
Brass Plated Steel, 22 mm. **Rev:** Velikiye Luki city arms **Edge:** Segmented reeding

Date	Mintage	F12	VF20	XF40	MS60	MS63
2012СПМД	10,000,000	—	—	—	2.50	4.00

Y# 1387 10 ROUBLES
Brass Plated Steel, 22 mm. **Subject:** Veliky Novgorod city arms

Date	Mintage	F12	VF20	XF40	MS60	MS63
2012	10,000,000	—	—	—	2.50	4.00

Y# 1388 10 ROUBLES
Brass Plated Steel, 22 mm. **Rev:** Dmitrov city arms

Date	Mintage	F12	VF20	XF40	MS60	MS63
2012	10,000,000	—	—	—	2.50	4.00

Y# 1389 10 ROUBLES
Brass Plated Steel, 22 mm. **Subject:** Origin of Russian Statehood, 1150th Anniversary

Date	Mintage	F12	VF20	XF40	MS60	MS63
2012	10,000,000	—	—	—	2.50	4.00

Y# 1390 10 ROUBLES
Brass Plated Steel, 22 mm. **Subject:** War of 1812, 200th Anniversary

Date	Mintage	F12	VF20	XF40	MS60	MS63
2012	10,000,000	—	—	—	2.50	4.00

Y# 1420 10 ROUBLES
Brass Plated Steel, 22 mm. **Rev:** Logo of the Kazan Universiade **Edge:** Segmented reeding

Date	Mintage	F12	VF20	XF40	MS60	MS63
2013СПМД	100,000,000	—	—	—	3.00	4.00

Y# 1421 10 ROUBLES
Brass Plated Steel, 22 mm. **Rev:** Snow Leopard mascott of the Kazan Universiade running on stadium track with torch **Edge:** Segmented reeding

Date	Mintage	F12	VF20	XF40	MS60	MS63
2013СПМД	10,000,000	—	—	—	3.00	4.00

Y# 1433 10 ROUBLES
Brass Plated Steel, 22 mm. **Subject:** Town of Vyazma **Rev:** Shield **Edge:** Segmented reeding

Date	Mintage	F12	VF20	XF40	MS60	MS63
2013СПМД	10,000,000	—	—	—	3.00	4.00

Y# 1445 10 ROUBLES
Brass Plated Steel, 22 mm. **Subject:** Town of Kronstadt **Rev:** Shield

Date	Mintage	F12	VF20	XF40	MS60	MS63
2013СПМД	10,000,000	—	—	—	3.00	4.00

Y# 1450 10 ROUBLES
Brass Plated Steel, 22 mm. **Subject:** Russian victory over Germany at Battle of Stalingrad, 70th Anniversary **Rev:** Monument in Volgograd

Date	Mintage	F12	VF20	XF40	MS60	MS63
2013ММД	10,000,000	—	—	—	3.00	4.00

Y# 1453 10 ROUBLES
Brass Plated Steel, 22 mm. **Subject:** Town of Naro-Fominsk **Rev:** City Shield

Date	Mintage	F12	VF20	XF40	MS60	MS63
2013СПМД	10,000,000	—	—	—	3.00	4.00

Y# 1461 10 ROUBLES
Brass Plated Steel, 22 mm. **Subject:** Town of Pskov **Rev:** Town Shield **Edge:** Segmented reeding

Date	Mintage	F12	VF20	XF40	MS60	MS63
2013СПМД	10,000,000	—	—	—	3.00	4.00

Y# 1462 10 ROUBLES
Brass Plated Steel, 22 mm. **Subject:** Town of Kozelsk **Rev:** Town shield **Edge:** Segmented reeding

Date	Mintage	F12	VF20	XF40	MS60	MS63
2013СПМД	10,000,000	—	—	—	3.00	4.00

Y# 1465 10 ROUBLES
Brass Plated Steel, 22 mm. **Subject:** Towns - Arkhangelsk **Rev:** Town Shield **Edge:** Segmented reeding

Date	Mintage	F12	VF20	XF40	MS60	MS63
2013СПМД	10,000,000	—	—	—	3.00	4.00

Y# 1466 10 ROUBLES
5.63 g., Brass Plated Steel, 22 mm. **Subject:** Great Patriotic War, 65th Anniversary **Edge:** Segmented reeding

Date	Mintage	F12	VF20	XF40	MS60	MS63
2010ММД	—	—	—	—	3.00	4.00

Y# 1469 10 ROUBLES
5.63 g., Brass Plated Steel, 22 mm. **Rev:** Volokolarusk city arms **Edge:** Segmented reeding

Date	Mintage	F12	VF20	XF40	MS60	MS63
2013	—	—	—	—	2.50	4.00

Y# 1470 10 ROUBLES
8.08 g., Bi-Metallic, 27 mm. **Subject:** Osetia-Alareia Area

Date	Mintage	F12	VF20	XF40	MS60	MS63
2013СПБ	—	—	—	—	3.00	4.00

Y# 1471 10 ROUBLES
8.08 g., Bi-Metallic, 27 mm. **Subject:** Dagestan Region

Date	Mintage	F12	VF20	XF40	MS60	MS63
2013	—	—	—	—	15.00	17.50

Y# 678 25 ROUBLES
173.29 g., 0.900 Silver 4.982 oz. ASW, 60 mm. **Subject:** Bolshoi Theater 225 Years **Obv:** Double-headed eagle **Rev:** Dancing couple scene **Edge:** Reeded **Note:** Illustration reduced.

Date	Mintage	F12	VF20	XF40	MS60	MS63
2001	2,000	PF65 350				

Y# 683 25 ROUBLES
173.29 g., 0.900 Silver 4.982 oz. ASW, 60 mm. **Subject:** Siberian Exploration **Obv:** Double-headed eagle **Rev:** Standing king and river boats **Edge:** Reeded **Note:** Illustration reduced.

Date	Mintage	F12	VF20	XF40	MS60	MS63
2001	1,000	PF65 650				

Y# 794 25 ROUBLES
173.13 g., 0.900 Silver 4.9774 oz. ASW, 60.2 mm. **Subject:** Foundation of Russian Savings Banks **Obv:** Double-headed eagle **Rev:** Czar Nicholas I and document **Edge:** Reeded

Date	Mintage	F12	VF20	XF40	MS60	MS63
2001(m)	10,500	PF65 275				

Y# 687 25 ROUBLES
3.20 g., 0.999 Gold 0.1021 oz. AGW, 16 mm. **Subject:** Bolshoi Theater **Obv:** Double-headed eagle **Rev:** Ballerina **Edge:** Reeded

Date	Mintage	F12	VF20	XF40	MS60	MS63
2001	2,500	PF65 200				

Y# 999 25 ROUBLES
169.00 g., 0.925 Silver 4.9936 oz. ASW, 60 mm. **Subject:** Bolshoi Theater, 225th Anniversary

Date	Mintage	F12	VF20	XF40	MS60	MS63
2001	—	PF65 350				

Y# 1000 25 ROUBLES
169.00 g., 0.925 Silver 4.9936 oz. ASW, 60 mm. **Subject:** Savings Bank

Date	Mintage	F12	VF20	XF40	MS60	MS63
2001	—	PF65 350				

Y# 1001 25 ROUBLES
169.00 g., 0.925 Silver 4.9936 oz. ASW, 60 mm. **Subject:** Siberia - Development and Exploration

Date	Mintage	F12	VF20	XF40	MS60	MS63
2001	—	PF65 350				

Y# 777 25 ROUBLES
173.29 g., 0.900 Silver 4.982 oz. ASW, 60 mm. **Subject:** Czar Alexander I **Obv:** Double-headed eagle **Rev:** Head right and crowned double-headed eagle above document text **Edge:** Reeded **Note:** Illustration reduced.

Date	Mintage	F12	VF20	XF40	MS60	MS63
2002(m)	1,500	PF65 400				

Y# 785 25 ROUBLES
173.29 g., 0.900 Silver 4.982 oz. ASW, 60 mm. **Subject:** Admiral Nakhimov **Obv:** Double-headed eagle **Rev:** Admiral watching naval battle **Edge:** Reeded **Note:** Illustration reduced.

Date	Mintage	F12	VF20	XF40	MS60	MS63
2002(sp)	2,000	PF65 350				

Y# 790 25 ROUBLES
173.29 g., 0.900 Silver 4.982 oz. ASW, 60 mm. **Subject:** Hermitage **Obv:** Double-headed eagle **Rev:** Staircase viewed through doorway **Edge:** Reeded **Note:** Illustration reduced.

Date	Mintage	F12	VF20	XF40	MS60	MS63
2002(sp)	2,000	PF65 350				

Y# 743 25 ROUBLES
3.20 g., 0.999 Gold 0.1021 oz. AGW, 16 mm. **Subject:** Zodiac Signs: **Obv:** Double-headed eagle within beaded circle **Rev:** Leo **Edge:** Reeded

Date	Mintage	F12	VF20	XF40	MS60	MS63
2002	10,000	PF65 200				

Y# 763 25 ROUBLES
3.20 g., 0.999 Gold 0.1021 oz. AGW, 16 mm. **Subject:** Zodiac Signs **Obv:** Double-headed eagle within beaded circle **Rev:** Capricorn **Edge:** Reeded

Date	Mintage	F12	VF20	XF40	MS60	MS63
2002(m)	10,000	—	—	—	—	200

Y# 764 25 ROUBLES
3.20 g., 0.999 Gold 0.1021 oz. AGW, 16 mm. **Subject:** Zodiac Signs **Obv:** Double-headed eagle within beaded circle **Rev:** Virgo **Edge:** Reeded

Date	Mintage	F12	VF20	XF40	MS60	MS63
2002(ер)	10,000					200

Y# 765 25 ROUBLES
3.20 g., 0.999 Gold 0.1021 oz. AGW, 16 mm. **Subject:** Zodiac Signs **Obv:** Double-headed eagle within beaded circle **Rev:** Sagittarius **Edge:** Reeded

Date	Mintage	F12	VF20	XF40	MS60	MS63
2002(SP)	10,000	—	—	—	—	200

Y# 767 25 ROUBLES
3.20 g., 0.999 Gold 0.1021 oz. AGW, 16 mm. **Subject:** Zodiac signs **Obv:** Double-headed eagle within beaded circle **Rev:** Scorpio **Edge:** Reeded

Date	Mintage	F12	VF20	XF40	MS60	MS63
2002(m)	10,000	—	—	—	—	200

Y# 769 25 ROUBLES
3.20 g., 0.999 Gold 0.1021 oz. AGW **Subject:** Zodiac Signs **Obv:** Double-headed eagle within beaded circle **Rev:** Libra **Edge:** Reeded

Date	Mintage	F12	VF20	XF40	MS60	MS63
2002(sp)	10,000	—	—	—	—	200

Y# 821 25 ROUBLES
3.20 g., 0.999 Gold 0.1021 oz. AGW, 16 mm. **Subject:** Zodiac signs **Obv:** Double-headed eagle within beaded circle **Rev:** Cancer **Edge:** Reeded

Date	Mintage	F12	VF20	XF40	MS60	MS63
2003(sp)	50,000	—	—	—	—	200

Y# 864 25 ROUBLES
172.80 g., 0.900 Silver 4.9679 oz. ASW, 60 mm. **Rev:** St. Sercius Monastery

Date	Mintage	F12	VF20	XF40	MS60	MS63
2003	2,000	PF65 350				

Y# 865 25 ROUBLES
172.80 g., 0.900 Silver 4.9679 oz. ASW, 60 mm. **Rev:** Shlisselburg

Date	Mintage	F12	VF20	XF40	MS60	MS63
2003(m)	2,000	PF65 350				

Y# 866 25 ROUBLES
172.80 g., 0.900 Silver 4.9679 oz. ASW, 60 mm. **Rev:** Kamchatka

Date	Mintage	F12	VF20	XF40	MS60	MS63
2003	2,000	PF65 350				

Y# 1003 25 ROUBLES
169.00 g., 0.925 Silver 4.9936 oz. ASW, 60 mm. **Subject:** Aquarius

Date	Mintage	F12	VF20	XF40	MS60	MS63
2003	—	PF65 350				

Y# 1004 25 ROUBLES
169.00 g., 0.925 Silver 4.9936 oz. ASW, 60 mm. **Subject:** Pisces

Date	Mintage	F12	VF20	XF40	MS60	MS63
2003	—	PF65 350				

Y# 1005 25 ROUBLES
169.00 g., 0.925 Silver 4.9936 oz. ASW, 60 mm. **Subject:** Aries

Date	Mintage	F12	VF20	XF40	MS60	MS63
2003	—	PF65 350				

Y# 1006 25 ROUBLES
169.00 g., 0.925 Silver 4.9936 oz. ASW, 60 mm. **Subject:** Taurus

Date	Mintage	F12	VF20	XF40	MS60	MS63
2003	—	PF65 350				

Y# 830 25 ROUBLES
177.96 g., 0.900 Bi-Metallic 5.1162 oz., 60 mm. **Subject:** Monetary reform of Peter the Great **Obv:** Double-headed eagle **Rev:** Gold insert replicating the obverse and reverse designs of a 1704 one rouble coin **Edge:** Reeded **Note:** Illustration reduced.

Date	Mintage	F12	VF20	XF40	MS60	MS63
2004(sp)	1,000	PF65 1,000				

Y# 867 25 ROUBLES
172.80 g., 0.900 Silver 4.9679 oz. ASW, 60 mm. **Rev:** Valaam Church

Date	Mintage	F12	VF20	XF40	MS60	MS63
2004	1,500	PF65 375				

Y# 1014 25 ROUBLES
169.00 g., 0.925 Silver 4.9936 oz. ASW, 60 mm. **Subject:** 2nd Kamchatka Expedition, 1733-43

Date	Mintage	F12	VF20	XF40	MS60	MS63
2004	—	PF65 350				

Y# 1019 25 ROUBLES
169.00 g., 0.925 Silver 4.9936 oz. ASW, 60 mm. **Subject:** Holy Trinity - St. Sergius Lavra in Sergiev Posad

Date	Mintage	F12	VF20	XF40	MS60	MS63
2004	—	PF65 350				

Y# 1023 25 ROUBLES
169.00 g., 0.925 Silver 4.9936 oz. ASW, 60 mm. **Subject:** Reindeer

Date	Mintage	F12	VF20	XF40	MS60	MS63
2004	—	PF65 350				

Y# 898 25 ROUBLES
3.20 g., 0.999 Gold 0.1021 oz. AGW, 16 mm. **Obv:** Double-headed eagle **Rev:** Gemini twins **Edge:** Reeded

Date	Mintage	F12	VF20	XF40	MS60	MS63
2005	10,000	—	—	—	—	200

Y# 900 25 ROUBLES
3.20 g., 0.999 Gold 0.1021 oz. AGW, 16 mm. **Obv:** Double-headed eagle **Rev:** Cancer crawfish **Edge:** Reeded

Date	Mintage	F12	VF20	XF40	MS60	MS63
2005	10,000	PF65 200				

Y# 902 25 ROUBLES
3.20 g., 0.999 Gold 0.1021 oz. AGW, 16 mm. **Obv:** Double-headed eagle **Rev:** Leo lion **Edge:** Reeded

Date	Mintage	F12	VF20	XF40	MS60	MS63
2005	10,000	—	—	—	—	220

Y# 915 25 ROUBLES
3.20 g., 0.999 Gold 0.1021 oz. AGW, 16 mm. **Obv:** Double-headed eagle **Rev:** Virgos standing lady **Edge:** Reeded

Date	Mintage	F12	VF20	XF40	MS60	MS63
2005	10,000	PF65 200				

Y# 920 25 ROUBLES
3.20 g., 0.999 Gold 0.1021 oz. AGW, 16 mm. **Obv:** Double-headed eagle **Rev:** Two stylized birds forming balance scale **Edge:** Reeded

Date	Mintage	F12	VF20	XF40	MS60	MS63
2005	10,000	—	—	—	—	220

Y# 922 25 ROUBLES
3.20 g., 0.999 Gold 0.1021 oz. AGW, 16 mm. **Obv:** Double-headed eagle **Rev:** Scorpio scorpion **Edge:** Reeded

Date	Mintage	F12	VF20	XF40	MS60	MS63
2005	10,000	—	—	—	—	220

Y# 924 25 ROUBLES
169.00 g., 0.925 Silver 4.9936 oz. ASW, 60 mm. **Subject:** 625th Anniversary - Battle of Kulikovo **Obv:** Double-headed eagle **Rev:** Mounted warriors above and below crossed swords **Edge:** Reeded **Note:** Illustration reduced.

Date	Mintage	F12	VF20	XF40	MS60	MS63
2005	1,500	PF65 375				

Y# 927 25 ROUBLES
3.20 g., 0.999 Gold 0.1021 oz. AGW, 16 mm. **Obv:** Double-headed eagle **Rev:** Sagittarius the archer **Edge:** Reeded

Date	Mintage	F12	VF20	XF40	MS60	MS63
2005	10,000	—	—	—	—	220

Y# 929 25 ROUBLES
3.20 g., 0.999 Gold 0.1021 oz. AGW, 16 mm. **Obv:** Double-headed eagle **Rev:** Capricorn as half goat and fish **Edge:** Reeded

Date	Mintage	F12	VF20	XF40	MS60	MS63
2005	10,000	—	—	—	—	220

Y# 931 25 ROUBLES
3.20 g., 0.999 Gold 0.1021 oz. AGW, 16 mm. **Obv:** Double-headed eagle **Rev:** Pisces as catfish and sturgeon **Edge:** Reeded

Date	Mintage	F12	VF20	XF40	MS60	MS63
2005	10,000	—	—	—	—	220

Y# 933 25 ROUBLES
3.20 g., 0.999 Gold 0.1021 oz. AGW, 16 mm. **Obv:** Double-headed eagle **Rev:** Aries ram **Edge:** Reeded

Date	Mintage	F12	VF20	XF40	MS60	MS63
2005	10,000	—	—	—	—	220

Y# 935 25 ROUBLES
3.20 g., 0.999 Gold 0.1021 oz. AGW, 16 mm. **Obv:** Double-headed eagle **Rev:** Taurus bull **Edge:** Reeded

Date	Mintage	F12	VF20	XF40	MS60	MS63
2005	10,000	—	—	—	—	220

Y# 937 25 ROUBLES
3.20 g., 0.999 Gold 0.1021 oz. AGW, 16 mm. **Obv:** Double-headed eagle **Rev:** Aquarius water carrier **Edge:** Reeded

Date	Mintage	F12	VF20	XF40	MS60	MS63
2005	10,000	—	—	—	—	220

Y# 1047 25 ROUBLES
169.00 g., 0.925 Silver 4.9936 oz. ASW, 60 mm. **Subject:** Tretyakov State Galler, 150th Anniversary

Date	Mintage	F12	VF20	XF40	MS60	MS63
2006	1,000	PF65 1,000				

Y# 1050 25 ROUBLES
169.00 g., 0.925 Silver 4.9936 oz. ASW, 60 mm. **Subject:** Malye Korely

Date	Mintage	F12	VF20	XF40	MS60	MS63
2006	1,000	PF65 350				

Y# 1051 25 ROUBLES
169.00 g., 0.925 Silver 4.9936 oz. ASW, 60 mm. **Subject:** Tikhvin Monastery, Dome of the Mother of God

Date	Mintage	F12	VF20	XF40	MS60	MS63
2006	1,000	PF65 350				

Y# 1053 25 ROUBLES
169.00 g., 0.925 Silver 4.9936 oz. ASW, 60 mm. **Subject:** Konevsky Monastery of St. Virgin's Nativity

Date	Mintage	F12	VF20	XF40	MS60	MS63
2006	1,000	PF65 350				

Y# 969 25 ROUBLES
169.00 g., 0.925 Silver 4.9936 oz. ASW, 60.00 mm. **Obv:** Two-headed eagle **Rev:** Vyatka St. Trifon Monastery of the Assumption, Kirov **Edge:** Reeded **Note:** Illustration reduced

Date	Mintage	F12	VF20	XF40	MS60	MS63
2007(sp)	2,000	PF65 350				

Y# 1083 25 ROUBLES
169.00 g., 0.925 Silver 4.9936 oz. ASW, 60 mm. **Subject:** Russian Railways, 150th Anniversary

Date	Mintage	F12	VF20	XF40	MS60	MS63
2007	1,000	PF65 500				

Y# 1084 25 ROUBLES
169.00 g., 0.925 Silver 4.9936 oz. ASW, 60 mm. **Subject:** F. A. Golovin, first Order of St. Andrew awardee

Date	Mintage	F12	VF20	XF40	MS60	MS63
2007	—	PF65 350				

Y# 1101 25 ROUBLES
169.00 g., 0.925 Silver 4.9936 oz. ASW, 60 mm. **Subject:** St. Artemy Verkolsky Monastery, Arkhamgelsk

Date	Mintage	F12	VF20	XF40	MS60	MS63
2007	—	PF65 350				

Y# 1102 25 ROUBLES
169.00 g., 0.925 Silver 4.9936 oz. ASW, 60 mm. **Subject:** Pskov-Pechersky Holy Monastery of the Assumption

Date	Mintage	F12	VF20	XF40	MS60	MS63
2007	2,000	PF65 350				

Y# 1116 25 ROUBLES
169.00 g., 0.925 Silver 4.9936 oz. ASW, 60 mm. **Subject:** Goznak, 190th Anniversary

Date	Mintage	F12	VF20	XF40	MS60	MS63
2008	1,500	PF65 1,000				

Y# 1125 25 ROUBLES
169.00 g., 0.925 Silver 4.9936 oz. ASW, 60 mm. **Subject:** Astrakhan Kremlin

Date	Mintage	F12	VF20	XF40	MS60	MS63
2008	2,000	PF65 400				

Y# 1139 25 ROUBLES
169.00 g., 0.925 Silver 4.9936 oz. ASW, 60 mm. **Subject:** European Beaver

Date	Mintage	F12	VF20	XF40	MS60	MS63
2008	1,500	PF65 400				

Y# 1160 25 ROUBLES
168.00 g., 0.925 Silver 4.9641 oz. ASW, 60 mm. **Subject:** Alexander I Monument, 175th Anniversary

Date	Mintage	F12	VF20	XF40	MS60	MS63
2009	1,000	PF65 525				

Y# 1178 25 ROUBLES
168.00 g., 0.925 Silver 4.9641 oz. ASW, 60 mm. **Subject:** Poltava Battle, 300th Anniversary

Date	Mintage	F12	VF20	XF40	MS60	MS63
2009	1,500	PF65 350				

Y# 1184 25 ROUBLES
168.00 g., 0.925 Silver 4.9641 oz. ASW, 60 mm. **Subject:** Arkhangelskoye Museum

Date	Mintage	F12	VF20	XF40	MS60	MS63
2009	1,500	PF65 350				

Y# 1186 25 ROUBLES
168.00 g., 0.925 Silver 4.9641 oz. ASW, 60 mm. **Subject:** St. Trinity Monastery, Pensu Region

Date	Mintage	F12	VF20	XF40	MS60	MS63
2009	1,500	PF65 350				

Y# 1187 25 ROUBLES
168.00 g., 0.925 Silver 4.9641 oz. ASW, 60 mm. **Subject:** St. Nikolas Monastary, Staraya Ladoga

Date	Mintage	F12	VF20	XF40	MS60	MS63
2009	1,500	PF65 350				

Y# 1200 25 ROUBLES
168.00 g., 0.925 Silver 4.9641 oz. ASW, 60 mm. **Subject:** Velikly Novgorod

Date	Mintage	F12	VF20	XF40	MS60	MS63
2009	1,500	PF65 350				

Y# 1223 25 ROUBLE3
168.00 g., 0.925 Silver 4.9641 oz. ASW, 60 mm. **Subject:** Khmelita, Griboyedov family estate

Date	Mintage	F12	VF20	XF40	MS60	MS63
2010	1,500	PF65 350				

Y# 1224 25 ROUBLES
168.00 g., 0.925 Silver 4.9641 oz. ASW, 60 mm. **Subject:** Kirillo Belosersk Monastery

Date	Mintage	F12	VF20	XF40	MS60	MS63
2010	2,000	PF65 400				

Y# 1225 25 ROUBLES
168.00 g., 0.925 Silver 4.9641 oz. ASW, 60 mm. **Subject:** Alezxandro - Svirsky Monastery

Date	Mintage	F12	VF20	XF40	MS60	MS63
2010	1,500	PF65 350				

Y# 1226 25 ROUBLES
168.00 g., 0.925 Silver 4.9641 oz. ASW, 60 mm. **Subject:** Sanaksarsky Monestary

Date	Mintage	F12	VF20	XF40	MS60	MS63
2010	1,500	PF65 350				

Y# 1229 25 ROUBLES
168.00 g., 0.925 Silver 4.9641 oz. ASW, 60 mm. **Subject:** Bank of Russia, 150th Anniversary

Date	Mintage	F12	VF20	XF40	MS60	MS63
2010	1,000	PF65 350				

Y# 1233 25 ROUBLES
169.00 g., 0.925 Silver 4.9936 oz. ASW, 60 mm. **Subject:** UNESCO Heritage Site - Yaroslav

Date	Mintage	F12	VF20	XF40	MS60	MS63
2010	1,500	PF65 350				

Y# 1304 25 ROUBLES
155.50 g., 0.925 Silver 4.5947 oz. ASW, 60 mm. **Subject:** Virgin Mary Monastery, Kazan **Rev:** Icon in color and building complex

Date	Mintage	F12	VF20	XF40	MS60	MS63
2011	2,000	PF65 400				

Y# 1298 25 ROUBLES
10.00 g., Copper-Nickel, 27 mm. **Subject:** 2014 Winter Olympics - Sochi **Obv:** Double-headed eagle, value below **Rev:** Mountain **Edge:** Reeded

Date	Mintage	F12	VF20	XF40	MS60	MS63
2011	10,000,000	—	—	—	—	8.00

Note: Value in card packaging is $40.

Y# 1298a 25 ROUBLES
10.00 g., Copper-Nickel, 27 mm. **Subject:** 2014 Winter Olympics - Sochi **Rev:** Color features

Date	Mintage	F12	VF20	XF40	MS60	MS63
2011	—	—	—	—	—	35.00

Y# 1306 25 ROUBLES
155.50 g., 0.925 Silver 4.5947 oz. ASW, 60 mm. **Subject:** Pavlovsky Palace and park **Rev:** Hilltop building, bridge in forefront, female statues flankings **Edge:** Reeded

Date	Mintage	F12	VF20	XF40	MS60	MS63
2011	1,500	PF65 350				

Y# 1317 25 ROUBLES
155.50 g., 0.925 Silver 4.5947 oz. ASW, 60 mm. **Subject:**
Virgin's Saint Entrance Presentation Monastery, Optin **Rev:**
Monastery buildings

Date	Mintage	F12	VF20	XF40	MS60	MS63
2011	2,000	PF65 350				

Y# 1321 25 ROUBLES
155.50 g., 0.925 Silver 4.5947 oz. ASW, 60 mm. **Subject:** Year
of Italian Culture and Language in Russia **Rev:** Town vies of
Sergiev Posad and Bari, Icon at center, Russian and Italian flags
below in color

Date	Mintage	F12	VF20	XF40	MS60	MS63
2011	1,000	PF65 1,000				

Y# 1322 25 ROUBLES
155.50 g., 0.925 Silver 4.5947 oz. ASW, 60 mm. **Subject:**
Kazan Cathedral, St. Petersburg **Rev:** Ariel view of Cathedral
and plaza **Edge:** Reeded

Date	Mintage	F12	VF20	XF40	MS60	MS63
2011	1,500	PF65 400				

Y# 1335 25 ROUBLES
169.00 g., 0.925 Silver 4.9936 oz. ASW, 60 mm. **Subject:**
Museum-Estate of V.D. Polenov, Tula region

Date	Mintage	F12	VF20	XF40	MS60	MS63
2012	2,000	PF65 400				

Y# 1336 25 ROUBLES
169.00 g., 0.925 Silver 4.9936 oz. ASW, 60 mm. **Subject:**
Voskresensky New Jerusalem Monastery, Istra, Moscow region

Date	Mintage	F12	VF20	XF40	MS60	MS63
2012	2,000	PF65 400				

Y# 1337 25 ROUBLES
169.00 g., 0.925 Silver 4.9936 oz. ASW, 60 mm. **Subject:**
Spaso-Borodinsky Monastery, Moscow region

Date	Mintage	F12	VF20	XF40	MS60	MS63
2012	2,000	PF65 400				

Y# 1338 25 ROUBLES
169.00 g., 0.925 Silver 4.9936 oz. ASW, 60 mm. **Subject:**
Alexeevo-Akatov Monastery, Voronezh

Date	Mintage	F12	VF20	XF40	MS60	MS63
2012	1,500	PF65 525				

Y# 1343 25 ROUBLES
169.00 g., 0.925 Silver 4.9936 oz. ASW, 60 mm. **Subject:**
People's Volunteer Corps, 400th Anniversary

Date	Mintage	F12	VF20	XF40	MS60	MS63
2012	1,000	PF65 525				

Y# 1346 25 ROUBLES
169.00 g., 0.925 Silver 4.9936 oz. ASW, 100 mm. **Subject:**
Russia's victory in the War of 1812

Date	Mintage	F12	VF20	XF40	MS60	MS63
2012	2,000	PF65 400				

Y# 1347 25 ROUBLES
169.00 g., 0.925 Silver 4.9936 oz. ASW, 60 mm. **Subject:**
Russia's victory in the War of 1812

Date	Mintage	F12	VF20	XF40	MS60	MS63
2012	2,000	PF65 400				

Y# 1352 25 ROUBLES
169.00 g., 0.925 Silver 4.9936 oz. ASW, 60 mm. **Subject:** Pushkin State Museum of Fine Arts, Moscow, 100th Anniversary

Date	Mintage	F12	VF20	XF40	MS60	MS63
2012	1,000	PF65 525				

Y# 1360 25 ROUBLES
169.00 g., 0.925 Silver 4.9936 oz. ASW, 60 mm. **Subject:** Asia-Pacific Economic Cooperation summit, Vladivostok **Rev:** APEC logo in color

Date	Mintage	F12	VF20	XF40	MS60	MS63
2012	1,000	PF65 650				

Y# 1368 25 ROUBLES
10.00 g., Copper-Nickel, 27 mm. **Subject:** 2014 Winter Olympics - Sochi **Rev:** Olympics Mascot

Date	Mintage	F12	VF20	XF40	MS60	MS63
2012	—	—	—	—	—	25.00

Y# 1368a 25 ROUBLES
10.00 g., Copper-Nickel, 27 mm. **Subject:** 2014 Winter Olympics, Sochi **Rev:** Mascots in color

Date	Mintage	F12	VF20	XF40	MS60	MS63
2012	—	—	—	—	—	35.00

Y# 1372 25 ROUBLES
169.00 g., 0.925 Silver 4.9936 oz. ASW, 60 mm. **Subject:** Architecture

Date	Mintage	F12	VF20	XF40	MS60	MS63
2012	1,500	PF65 400				

Y# 1373 25 ROUBLES
169.00 g., 0.925 Silver 4.9936 oz. ASW, 60 mm. **Subject:** Architecture

Date	Mintage	F12	VF20	XF40	MS60	MS63
2012	1,500	PF65 400				

Y# 1378 25 ROUBLES
169.00 g., 0.925 Silver 4.9936 oz. ASW, 60 mm. **Subject:** Winter Palace in St. Petersburg, 250th Anniversary

Date	Mintage	F12	VF20	XF40	MS60	MS63
2012	1,500	PF65 285				

Y# 1423 25 ROUBLES
169.00 g., 0.925 Silver 4.9936 oz. ASW, 60 mm. **Rev:** Two wrestlers, Kazan Universiade logo and city skyline

Date	Mintage	F12	VF20	XF40	MS60	MS63
2013СПМД	1,500	PF65 300				

Y# 1432 25 ROUBLES
169.00 g., 0.925 Silver 4.9936 oz. ASW, 60 mm. **Rev:** Kazan Kremlin, national flag of Russia and Italy, and Verona sports arena **Edge:** Reeded

Date	Mintage	F12	VF20	XF40	MS60	MS63
2013СПМД	1,000	PF65 300				

Y# 1435 25 ROUBLES
169.00 g., 0.925 Silver 4.9936 oz. ASW, 60 mm. **Subject:** A.S. Shein **Rev:** Half-length Shein at right **Edge:** Reeded

Date	Mintage	F12	VF20	XF40	MS60	MS63
2013ММД	1,500	PF65 300				

Y# 1437 25 ROUBLES
169.00 g., 0.925 Silver 4.9936 oz. ASW, 60 mm. **Subject:** Dynamo Soccer Club, 90th Anniversary **Rev:** Three soccer players around ball **Edge:** Reeded

Date	Mintage	F12	VF20	XF40	MS60	MS63
2013СПМД	2,000	PF65 300				

Y# 1438 25 ROUBLES
169.00 g., 0.925 Silver 4.9936 oz. ASW, 60 mm. **Subject:** Dynamo Hockey club, 90th Anniversary **Rev:** Three hockey players at puck **Edge:** Reeded

Date	Mintage	F12	VF20	XF40	MS60	MS63
2013СПМД	2,000	PF65 300				

Y# 1439 25 ROUBLES
169.00 g., 0.925 Silver 4.9936 oz. ASW, 60 mm. **Subject:** Dynamo Sports Club, 90th Anniversary **Rev:** Biathlon view, skier and two shooters **Edge:** Reeded

Date	Mintage	F12	VF20	XF40	MS60	MS63
2013ММД	2,000	PF65 300				

Y# 1447 25 ROUBLES
169.00 g., 0.925 Silver 4.9936 oz. ASW, 60 mm. **Subject:** City of Smolensk, 1150th Anniversary of founding **Rev:** Assumption Cathedral and building montage **Edge:** Reeded

Date	Mintage	F12	VF20	XF40	MS60	MS63
2013ММД	1,500	PF65 300				

Y# 1454 25 ROUBLES
169.00 g., 0.925 Silver 4.9936 oz. ASW, 60 mm. **Subject:** Architectural Monuments - Ostankino estate **Rev:** Estate building **Edge:** Reeded

Date	Mintage	F12	VF20	XF40	MS60	MS63
2013ММД	1,500	PF65 300				

Y# 1457 25 ROUBLES
169.00 g., 0.925 Silver 4.9936 oz. ASW, 60 mm. **Subject:** Architectural Masterpieces - Architect Rossi in St. Petersburg **Rev:** Rossi at left, street view at right **Edge:** Reeded

Date	Mintage	F12	VF20	XF40	MS60	MS63
2013СПМД	1,500	PF65 300				

Y# 1460 25 ROUBLES
169.00 g., 0.925 Silver 4.9936 oz. ASW, 155.5 mm. **Subject:** Architectural Monuments - Saint Assumption Monastery, Staritsa **Rev:** Cathedral view **Edge:** Reeded

Date	Mintage	F12	VF20	XF40	MS60	MS63
2013СПМД	1,500	PF65 300				

Y# 1464 25 ROUBLES
169.00 g., 0.925 Silver 4.9936 oz. ASW, 155.5 mm. **Subject:** Architectural Monuments - Saint Joseph Volotsky Monastery, Teryaevo **Rev:** View of walled monastery

Date	Mintage	F12	VF20	XF40	MS60	MS63
2013ММД	1,500	PF65 300				

Y# 1472 25 ROUBLES
10.00 g., Copper-Nickel, 27 mm. **Subject:** 2014 Winter Olympics, Sochi **Rev:** Two figures

Date	Mintage	F12	VF20	XF40	MS60	MS63
2013	—	—	—	—	—	25.00

Y# 1472a 25 ROUBLES
10.00 g., Copper-Nickel, 27 mm. **Subject:** 2014 Winter Olympics - Sochi **Rev:** Two figures in color

Date	Mintage	F12	VF20	XF40	MS60	MS63
2013	—	—	—	—	—	40.00

Y# 679 50 ROUBLES
8.75 g., 0.999 Gold 0.2792 oz. AGW, 22.6 mm. **Subject:** Bolshoi Theater **Obv:** Double-headed eagle within beaded circle **Rev:** Dueling figures **Edge:** Reeded

Date	Mintage	F12	VF20	XF40	MS60	MS63
2001	2,000	PF65 550				

Y# 684 50 ROUBLES
8.75 g., 0.900 Gold 0.2516 oz. AGW, 22.6 mm. **Subject:** Siberian Exploration **Obv:** Double-headed eagle within beaded circle **Rev:** Head with hat 1/4 right and boat **Edge:** Reeded

Date	Mintage	F12	VF20	XF40	MS60	MS63
2001	1,500	PF65 600				

Y# 757 50 ROUBLES
8.64 g., 0.900 Gold 0.2485 oz. AGW, 22.6 mm. **Subject:** Olympics **Obv:** Double-headed eagle within beaded circle **Rev:** Figure skater and flying eagle **Edge:** Reeded

Date	Mintage	F12	VF20	XF40	MS60	MS63
2002	3,000	PF65 575				

Y# 782 50 ROUBLES
7.89 g., 0.999 Gold 0.2518 oz. AGW, 22.6 mm. **Subject:** Works of Dionissy **Obv:** Double-headed eagle within beaded circle **Rev:** Half-length figure holding child flanked by double headed eagle and church **Edge:** Reeded

Date	Mintage	F12	VF20	XF40	MS60	MS63
2002(m)	1,500	PF65 600				

Y# 786 50 ROUBLES
8.75 g., 0.900 Gold 0.2516 oz. AGW, 22.6 mm. **Subject:** Admiral Nakhimov **Obv:** Double-headed eagle within beaded circle **Rev:** Bust facing within circle above flags and anchor **Edge:** Reeded

Date	Mintage	F12	VF20	XF40	MS60	MS63
2002(sp)	1,500	PF65 600				

Y# 788 50 ROUBLES
8.75 g., 0.900 Gold 0.2516 oz. AGW, 22.6 mm. **Subject:** World Cup Soccer **Obv:** Double-headed eagle within beaded circle **Rev:** Stylized player kicking soccer ball **Edge:** Reeded

Date	Mintage	F12	VF20	XF40	MS60	MS63
2002(m)	3,000	PF65 575				

Y# 822 50 ROUBLES
7.89 g., 0.999 Gold 0.2518 oz. AGW, 22.6 mm. **Subject:** Zodiac Signs **Obv:** Double-headed eagle within beaded circle **Rev:** Virgo **Edge:** Reeded

Date	Mintage	F12	VF20	XF40	MS60	MS63
2003(sp)	30,000	—	—	—	—	475

Y# 823 50 ROUBLES
7.89 g., 0.999 Gold 0.2518 oz. AGW, 22.6 mm. **Subject:** Zodiac signs **Obv:** Double-headed eagle within beaded circle **Rev:** Libra **Edge:** Reeded

Date	Mintage	F12	VF20	XF40	MS60	MS63
2003(m)	30,000	—	—	—	—	475

Y# 868 50 ROUBLES
8.64 g., 0.900 Gold 0.2484 oz. AGW, 23 mm. **Rev:** Peter I monetary reform

Date	Mintage	F12	VF20	XF40	MS60	MS63
2003(m)	1,500	PF65 600				

Y# 869 50 ROUBLES
8.64 g., 0.900 Gold 0.2484 oz. AGW, 23 mm. **Rev:** Ski race

Date	Mintage	F12	VF20	XF40	MS60	MS63
2003(m)	1,500	PF65 600				

Y# 1007 50 ROUBLES
169.00 g., 0.925 Silver 4.9936 oz. ASW, 60 mm. **Subject:** Leo

Date	Mintage	F12	VF20	XF40	MS60	MS63
2003	—			PF65 475		

Y# 1008 50 ROUBLES
169.00 g., 0.925 Silver 4.9936 oz. ASW, 60 mm. **Subject:** Leo

Date	Mintage	F12	VF20	XF40	MS60	MS63
2003	—			PF65 475		

Y# 1009 50 ROUBLES
7.79 g., 0.999 Gold 0.2486 oz. AGW, 22.6 mm. **Subject:** Scorpion

Date	Mintage	F12	VF20	XF40	MS60	MS63
2003	—			PF65 475		

Y# 1010 50 ROUBLES
7.78 g., 0.999 Gold 0.2483 oz. AGW, 22.6 mm. **Subject:** Sagatarius

Date	Mintage	F12	VF20	XF40	MS60	MS63
2003	—			PF65 475		

Y# 1011 50 ROUBLES
7.78 g., 0.999 Gold 0.2483 oz. AGW, 22.6 mm. **Subject:** Capricorn

Date	Mintage	F12	VF20	XF40	MS60	MS63
2003	—			PF65 475		

Y# 870 50 ROUBLES
8.64 g., 0.900 Gold 0.2484 oz. AGW, 23 mm. **Rev:** Soccer player

Date	Mintage	F12	VF20	XF40	MS60	MS63
2004(sp)	1,000			PF65 650		

Y# 871 50 ROUBLES
8.64 g., 0.900 Gold 0.2484 oz. AGW, 23 mm. **Rev:** Olympic athletes

Date	Mintage	F12	VF20	XF40	MS60	MS63
2004(m)	2,000			PF65 550		

Y# 872 50 ROUBLES
8.64 g., 0.900 Gold 0.2484 oz. AGW, 23 mm. **Rev:** Virgin of the Son Icon

Date	Mintage	F12	VF20	XF40	MS60	MS63
2004(m)	1,500			PF65 575		

Y# 1016 50 ROUBLES
7.78 g., 0.999 Gold 0.2483 oz. AGW, 22.6 mm. **Subject:** Theophanes the Greek

Date	Mintage	F12	VF20	XF40	MS60	MS63
2004	—			PF65 575		

Y# 1025 50 ROUBLES
7.78 g., 0.999 Gold 0.2483 oz. AGW, 22.6 mm. **Subject:** Reindeer

Date	Mintage	F12	VF20	XF40	MS60	MS63
2004	—			PF65 475		

Y# 1030 50 ROUBLES
7.78 g., 0.999 Gold 0.2483 oz. AGW, 22.6 mm. **Subject:** Aquarius

Date	Mintage	F12	VF20	XF40	MS60	MS63
2004	—			PF65 475		

Y# 1031 50 ROUBLES
7.78 g., 0.999 Gold 0.2483 oz. AGW, 22.6 mm.

Date	Mintage	F12	VF20	XF40	MS60	MS63
2004	—			PF65 475		

Y# 1032 50 ROUBLES
7.78 g., 0.999 Gold 0.2483 oz. AGW, 22.6 mm. **Subject:** Aries

Date	Mintage	F12	VF20	XF40	MS60	MS63
2004	—			PF65 475		

Y# 1033 50 ROUBLES
7.78 g., 0.999 Gold 0.2483 oz. AGW, 22.6 mm. **Subject:** Taurus

Date	Mintage	F12	VF20	XF40	MS60	MS63
2004	—			PF65 475		

Y# 1034 50 ROUBLES
7.78 g., 0.999 Gold 0.2483 oz. AGW, 22.6 mm. **Subject:** Gemni

Date	Mintage	F12	VF20	XF40	MS60	MS63
2004	—			PF65 475		

Y# 1035 50 ROUBLES
7.78 g., 0.999 Gold 0.2483 oz. AGW, 22.6 mm. **Subject:** Cancer

Date	Mintage	F12	VF20	XF40	MS60	MS63
2004	—			PF65 475		

Y# 894 50 ROUBLES
7.89 g., 0.999 Gold 0.2518 oz. AGW, 22.6 mm. **Subject:** 60th Anniversary - Victory Over Germany **Obv:** Double-headed eagle **Rev:** 60th Anniversary - Victory Over Germany medal **Edge:** Reeded

Date	Mintage	F12	VF20	XF40	MS60	MS63
2005	7,000			PF65 500		

Y# 907 50 ROUBLES
7.89 g., 0.999 Gold 0.2518 oz. AGW, 22.6 mm. **Subject:** Helsinki Games **Obv:** Double-headed eagle **Rev:** Stylized track and field athletes **Edge:** Reeded

Date	Mintage	F12	VF20	XF40	MS60	MS63
2005	1,500			PF65 575		

Y# 911 50 ROUBLES
7.89 g., 0.999 Gold 0.2518 oz. AGW, 22.6 mm. **Obv:** Double-headed eagle **Rev:** Kazan University Building **Edge:** Reeded

Date	Mintage	F12	VF20	XF40	MS60	MS63
2005	1,500			PF65 475		

Y# 1049 50 ROUBLES
7.78 g., 0.999 Gold 0.2483 oz. AGW, 22.6 mm. **Rev:** St. George the Victorious

Date	Mintage	F12	VF20	XF40	MS60	MS63
2006	150,000	—	—	—	—	475
2007	500,000	—	—	—	—	475
2008	630,000	—	—	—	—	475
2009	1,500,000	—	—	—	—	475
2010	640,000	—	—	—	—	475
2012	500,000	—	—	—	—	475
2012	10,000	PF65 500				

Y# 1063 50 ROUBLES
7.78 g., 0.999 Gold 0.2483 oz. AGW, 22.6 mm. **Subject:** Moscow's Kremlin and Red Square

Date	Mintage	F12	VF20	XF40	MS60	MS63
2006	—			PF65 600		

Y# 1067 50 ROUBLES
7.78 g., 0.999 Gold 0.2483 oz. AGW, 22.6 mm. **Subject:** XX Winter Olympics, Torino

Date	Mintage	F12	VF20	XF40	MS60	MS63
2006	—			PF65 550		

Y# 1068 50 ROUBLES
7.78 g., 0.999 Gold 0.2483 oz. AGW, 22.6 mm. **Subject:** FIFA World Cup, Germany

Date	Mintage	F12	VF20	XF40	MS60	MS63
2006	—			PF65 550		

Y# 1090 50 ROUBLES
7.78 g., 0.999 Gold 0.2483 oz. AGW, 22.6 mm. **Subject:** Andrew Rublyov

Date	Mintage	F12	VF20	XF40	MS60	MS63
2007	—			PF65 550		

Y# 1094 50 ROUBLES
7.78 g., 0.925 Gold 0.2299 oz. AGW, 22.6 mm. **Subject:** Bashkiria, 450th Anniversary of of annexation by Russia

Date	Mintage	F12	VF20	XF40	MS60	MS63
2007	—			PF65 550		

Y# 1097 50 ROUBLES
7.78 g., 0.999 Gold 0.2483 oz. AGW, 22.6 mm. **Subject:** Khakassia, 300th Anniversary of of annexation by Russia

Date	Mintage	F12	VF20	XF40	MS60	MS63
2007	—			PF65 550		

Y# 1121 50 ROUBLES
7.78 g., 0.999 Gold 0.2483 oz. AGW, 22.6 mm. **Subject:** Udmurtiya, 450th Anniversary of annexation into Russia

Date	Mintage	F12	VF20	XF40	MS60	MS63
2008	—			PF65 550		

Y# 1141 50 ROUBLES
7.78 g., 0.999 Gold 0.2483 oz. AGW, 22.6 mm. **Subject:** European Beaver

Date	Mintage	F12	VF20	XF40	MS60	MS63
2008	—			PF65 750		

Y# 1153 50 ROUBLES
7.78 g., 0.999 Gold 0.2483 oz. AGW, 22.6 mm. **Subject:** 29th Summer Olympics, Bejing

Date	Mintage	F12	VF20	XF40	MS60	MS63
2008	—			PF65 550		

Y# 1168 50 ROUBLES
7.78 g., 0.999 Gold 0.2483 oz. AGW, 22.6 mm. **Subject:** A. P. Chekhov, 150th Anniversary of Birth

Date	Mintage	F12	VF20	XF40	MS60	MS63
2009	—			PF65 550		

Y# 1172 50 ROUBLES
7.78 g., 0.999 Gold 0.2483 oz. AGW, 22.6 mm. **Subject:** Kalmyk Peoples, 400th Anniversary of annexation into Russia

Date	Mintage	F12	VF20	XF40	MS60	MS63
2009	—			PF65 550		

Y# 1175 50 ROUBLES
7.78 g., 0.999 Gold 0.2483 oz. AGW, 22.6 mm. **Subject:** N. V. Gogol, 200th Anniversary of Birth

Date	Mintage	F12	VF20	XF40	MS60	MS63
2009	—			PF65 550		

Y# 1202 50 ROUBLES
7.78 g., 0.999 Gold 0.2483 oz. AGW, 22.6 mm. **Subject:** Velikly Novgorod

Date	Mintage	F12	VF20	XF40	MS60	MS63
2009	—			PF65 550		

Y# 1230 50 ROUBLES
7.78 g., 0.999 Gold 0.2483 oz. AGW, 22.6 mm. **Subject:** Bank of Russia, 150th Anniversary

Date	Mintage	F12	VF20	XF40	MS60	MS63
2010	—			PF65 600		

Y# 1235 50 ROUBLES
7.78 g., 0.999 Gold 0.2483 oz. AGW, 22.6 mm. **Subject:** UNESCO Heritage Site - Yaroslav

Date	Mintage	F12	VF20	XF40	MS60	MS63
2010	—			PF65 550		

Y# 1239 50 ROUBLES
7.78 g., 0.999 Gold 0.2483 oz. AGW, 22.6 mm. **Subject:** A. P. Chekhov, 200th Anniversary of birth

Date	Mintage	F12	VF20	XF40	MS60	MS63
2010	—			PF65 600		

Y# 1286 50 ROUBLES
7.78 g., 0.999 Gold 0.2483 oz. AGW, 22.6 mm. **Rev:** Griffin with sword and shield above garland **Edge:** Reeded

Date	Mintage	F12	VF20	XF40	MS60	MS63
2011	750			PF65 600		

Y# 1291 50 ROUBLES
7.78 g., 0.999 Gold 0.2483 oz. AGW, 22.6 mm. **Rev:** Emblem of the Republic of Buryatia

Date	Mintage	F12	VF20	XF40	MS60	MS63
2011	1,000	PF65 650				

Y# 1300 50 ROUBLES
7.78 g., 0.999 Gold 0.2483 oz. AGW, 22.6 mm. **Subject:** 2014 Winter Olympics - Sochi **Rev:** Four-man Bobsled **Edge:** Reeded

Date	Mintage	F12	VF20	XF40	MS60	MS63
2014 (2011)	20,000	PF65 500				

Y# 1301 50 ROUBLES
7.78 g., 0.999 Gold 0.2483 oz. AGW, 22.6 mm. **Subject:** 2014 Winter Olympics - Sochi - Curling **Rev:** Skip and sweeper with stones in play

Date	Mintage	F12	VF20	XF40	MS60	MS63
2014 (2011)	20,000	PF65 500				

Y# 1341 50 ROUBLES
7.78 g., 0.999 Gold 0.2483 oz. AGW, 22.6 mm. **Subject:** Millennium of the Unity of the Mordovian people within the Peoples of the Russian State

Date	Mintage	F12	VF20	XF40	MS60	MS63
2012	100	PF65 750				

Y# 1349 50 ROUBLES
7.78 g., 0.999 Gold 0.2483 oz. AGW, 22.6 mm. **Subject:** Russia's victory in the War of 1812 **Rev:** Bust left

Date	Mintage	F12	VF20	XF40	MS60	MS63
2012	1,000	PF65 650				

Y# 1365 50 ROUBLES
7.78 g., 0.999 Gold 0.2483 oz. AGW, 22.6 mm. **Subject:** European Judo Championship, Chelyabinsk

Date	Mintage	F12	VF20	XF40	MS60	MS63
2012	750	PF65 675				

Y# 1369 50 ROUBLES
7.78 g., 0.999 Gold 0.2483 oz. AGW, 22.6 mm. **Subject:** Origin of Russian Statehood, 1150th Anniversary

Date	Mintage	F12	VF20	XF40	MS60	MS63
2012	1,500	PF65 575				

Y# 1376 50 ROUBLES
7.78 g., 0.999 Gold 0.2483 oz. AGW, 22.6 mm. **Subject:** Court of Arbitration

Date	Mintage	F12	VF20	XF40	MS60	MS63
2012	750	PF65 675				

Y# 1424 50 ROUBLES
7.89 g., 0.999 Gold 0.2518 oz. AGW, 22.6 mm. **Rev:** Logo and track of Kazan Universiade, city skyline **Edge:** Reeded

Date	Mintage	F12	VF20	XF40	MS60	MS63
2013СПМД	1,500	PF65 500				

Y# 1436 50 ROUBLES
7.89 g., 0.925 Gold 0.2331 oz. AGW, 22.6 mm. **Subject:** A.S. Shein **Rev:** Bust facing

Date	Mintage	F12	VF20	XF40	MS60	MS63
2013ММД	1,500	PF65 500				

Y# 1448 50 ROUBLES
7.89 g., 0.999 Gold 0.2518 oz. AGW, 22.6 mm. **Subject:** City of Smolensk, 1150th Anniversary of founding **Rev:** City shield

Date	Mintage	F12	VF20	XF40	MS60	MS63
2013ММД	1,500	PF65 500				

Y# 795 100 ROUBLES
1111.12 g., 0.900 Silver 31.944 oz. ASW, 100 mm. **Subject:** The Bark Sedov **Obv:** Double-headed eagle **Rev:** Ship flanked by compass and cameo **Edge:** Reeded **Note:** Illustration reduced.

Date	Mintage	F12	VF20	XF40	MS60	MS63
2001(m)	500	PF65 2,200				

Y# 681 100 ROUBLES
1111.10 g., 0.900 Silver 31.9435 oz. ASW, 100 mm. **Subject:** 40th Anniversary of Manned Space Flight - Yuri Gagarin **Obv:** Double-headed eagle **Rev:** Astronaut and rocket in space **Edge:** Reeded **Note:** Illustration reduced.

Date	Mintage	F12	VF20	XF40	MS60	MS63
2001	750	PF65 2,000				

Y# 689 100 ROUBLES
1111.10 g., 0.900 Silver 31.9435 oz. ASW, 100 mm. **Subject:** Bolshoi Theater 225 Years **Obv:** Double-headed eagle **Rev:** Casino gambling scene **Edge:** Reeded **Note:** Illustration reduced.

Date	Mintage	F12	VF20	XF40	MS60	MS63
2001	500	PF65 2,150				

Y# 685 100 ROUBLES
17.45 g., 0.900 Gold 0.5017 oz. AGW, 30 mm. **Subject:** Siberian Exploration **Obv:** Double-headed eagle within beaded circle **Rev:** Head and silhouette left, sailboat and other designs **Edge:** Reeded

Date	Mintage	F12	VF20	XF40	MS60	MS63
2001	1,000	PF65 1,150				

Y# 688 100 ROUBLES
15.72 g., 0.999 Gold 0.5017 oz. AGW, 30 mm. **Subject:** Bolshoi Theater 225 Years **Obv:** Double-headed eagle within beaded circle **Rev:** Three dancers with swords **Edge:** Reeded

Date	Mintage	F12	VF20	XF40	MS60	MS63
2001	1,500	PF65 1,100				

Y# 783 100 ROUBLES
1111.12 g., 0.900 Silver 31.944 oz. ASW, 100 mm. **Subject:** Works of Dionissy **Obv:** Double-headed eagle **Rev:** St. Ferapont Monastery in the center of a fresco covered cross **Edge:** Reeded **Note:** Illustration reduced.

Date	Mintage	F12	VF20	XF40	MS60	MS63
2002(sp) Prooflike	500	—	—	—	—	2,750

Y# 789 100 ROUBLES
1111.12 g., 0.900 Silver 31.944 oz. ASW, 100 mm. **Subject:**

World Cup Soccer **Obv:** Double-headed eagle **Rev:** Soccer ball design with map and players **Edge:** Reeded **Note:** Illustration reduced.

Date	Mintage	F12	VF20	XF40	MS60	MS63
2002(sp)	500	PF65 2,200				

Y# 791 100 ROUBLES
1111.12 g., 0.900 Silver 31.944 oz. ASW, 100 mm. **Subject:** Hermitage **Obv:** Double-headed eagle **Rev:** Statues and arches **Edge:** Reeded **Note:** Illustration reduced.

Date	Mintage	F12	VF20	XF40	MS60	MS63
2002(sp)	1,000	PF65 1,800				

Y# 792 100 ROUBLES
17.45 g., 0.900 Gold 0.5017 oz. AGW, 30 mm. **Subject:** Hermitage **Obv:** Double-headed eagle within beaded circle **Rev:** Ancient battle scene sculpted on comb **Edge:** Reeded

Date	Mintage	F12	VF20	XF40	MS60	MS63
2002(sp)	1,000	PF65 1,250				

Y# 873 100 ROUBLES
1111.12 g., 0.900 Silver 31.944 oz. ASW, 100 mm. **Rev:** St. Petersburg

Date	Mintage	F12	VF20	XF40	MS60	MS63
2003(m)	1,000	PF65 2,000				

Y# 874 100 ROUBLES
17.45 g., 0.900 Gold 0.5017 oz. AGW, 30 mm. **Rev:** Petrozavodsk

Date	Mintage	F12	VF20	XF40	MS60	MS63
2003(m)	1,000	PF65 1,250				

Y# 875 100 ROUBLES
17.45 g., 0.900 Gold 0.5017 oz. AGW, 30 mm. **Rev:** Kamchatka

Date	Mintage	F12	VF20	XF40	MS60	MS63
2003(sp)	1,500	PF65 1,100				

Y# 831 100 ROUBLES
1111.12 g., 0.900 Silver 31.944 oz. ASW, 100 mm. **Obv:** Double-headed eagle **Rev:** Panel of icons painted by Theophanes the Greek **Edge:** Reeded **Note:** Illustration reduced.

Date	Mintage	F12	VF20	XF40	MS60	MS63
2004(sp)	500	PF65 2,300				

Y# 832 100 ROUBLES
17.28 g., 0.900 Gold 0.4968 oz. AGW, 30 mm. **Subject:** 2nd Kamchatka Expedition **Obv:** Double-headed eagle **Rev:** Shaman and two seated men **Edge:** Reeded

Date	Mintage	F12	VF20	XF40	MS60	MS63
2004(sp)	1,500	PF65 1,100				

Y# 876 100 ROUBLES
1111.12 g., 0.900 Silver 31.944 oz. ASW, 100 mm. **Rev:** Annunciation Cathedral Iconostasis

Date	Mintage	F12	VF20	XF40	MS60	MS63
2004(sp)	500	PF65 2,200				

Y# 1024 100 ROUBLES
1111.12 g., 0.900 Silver 31.944 oz. ASW, 100 mm. **Subject:** Reindeer

Date	Mintage	F12	VF20	XF40	MS60	MS63
2004	—	PF65 1,850				

Y# 1026 100 ROUBLES
17.55 g., 0.900 Silver 0.5046 oz. ASW, 30 mm. **Subject:** Reindeer

Date	Mintage	F12	VF20	XF40	MS60	MS63
2004	—	PF65 2,000				

Y# 1036 100 ROUBLES
1111.72 g., 0.900 Silver 31.9613 oz. ASW, 100 mm. **Subject:** Rostov

Date	Mintage	F12	VF20	XF40	MS60	MS63
2004	—	PF65 1,850				

Y# 895 100 ROUBLES
1083.74 g., 0.925 Silver 32.0223 oz. ASW, 100 mm. **Subject:** 60th Anniversary Victory Over Germany **Obv:** Double-headed eagle **Rev:** Decorated locomotive returning soldiers circa 1945 **Edge:** Reeded **Note:** Illustration reduced.

Date	Mintage	F12	VF20	XF40	MS60	MS63
2005	2,000	PF65 1,850				

Y# 912 100 ROUBLES
1083.74 g., 0.925 Silver 32.0223 oz. ASW, 100 mm. **Obv:** Double-headed eagle **Rev:** Kazan city view with mausoleums **Edge:** Reeded **Note:** Illustration reduced.

Date	Mintage	F12	VF20	XF40	MS60	MS63
2005	500	PF65 2,000				

Y# 925 100 ROUBLES
1083.74 g., 0.925 Silver 32.0223 oz. ASW, 100 mm. **Subject:** 625th Anniversary - Battle of Kulikovo **Obv:** Double-headed eagle **Rev:** Battle of Kulikovo beginning scene **Edge:** Reeded **Note:** Illustration reduced.

Date	Mintage	F12	VF20	XF40	MS60	MS63
2005	500	PF65 2,000				

Y# 1078 100 ROUBLES
1083.74 g., 0.925 Silver 32.0223 oz. ASW, 100 mm. **Subject:** Yuryev Polsky

Date	Mintage	F12	VF20	XF40	MS60	MS63
2006	—	PF65 1,850				

Y# 1044 100 ROUBLES
1083.74 g., 0.925 Silver 32.0223 oz. ASW, 100 mm. **Subject:** Frigate Myr

Date	Mintage	F12	VF20	XF40	MS60	MS63
2006	—	PF65 1,750				

Y# 1061 100 ROUBLES
1083.74 g., 0.925 Silver 32.0223 oz. ASW, 100 mm. **Subject:** Moscow's Kremlin and Red Square

Date	Mintage	F12	VF20	XF40	MS60	MS63
2006	—	PF65 1,750				

Y# 1077 100 ROUBLES
1083.74 g., 0.925 Silver 32.0223 oz. ASW, 100 mm. **Subject:** Bogolyubovo Township

Date	Mintage	F12	VF20	XF40	MS60	MS63
2006	—	PF65 1,850				

Y# 1081 100 ROUBLES
1083.74 g., 0.925 Silver 32.0223 oz. ASW, 100 mm. **Subject:** International Artic Year

Date	Mintage	F12	VF20	XF40	MS60	MS63
2007	—	PF65 1,850				

Y# 1085 100 ROUBLES
1083.74 g., 0.925 Silver 32.0223 oz. ASW, 100 mm. **Subject:** Russian railways, 175th Anniversary

Date	Mintage	F12	VF20	XF40	MS60	MS63
2007	—	PF65 1,850				

Y# 1089 100 ROUBLES
1083.74 g., 0.925 Silver 32.0223 oz. ASW, 100 mm. **Subject:** Andrew Rublyov

Date	Mintage	F12	VF20	XF40	MS60	MS63
2007	—	PF65 1,850				

Y# 1093 100 ROUBLES
1083.74 g., 0.925 Silver 32.0223 oz. ASW, 100 mm. **Subject:** Bashkiria, 450th Anniversary of Annexation by Russia

Date	Mintage	F12	VF20	XF40	MS60	MS63
2007	—	PF65 400				

Y# 1096 100 ROUBLES
1083.74 g., 0.925 Silver 32.0223 oz. ASW, 100 mm. **Subject:** Khakassia, 300th Anniversary of Annexation by Russia

Date	Mintage	F12	VF20	XF40	MS60	MS63
2007	—	PF65 1,850				

Y# 1120 100 ROUBLES
1083.74 g., 0.925 Silver 32.0223 oz. ASW, 100 mm. **Subject:** Udmurtiya, 450th Anniversary of Annexation into Russia

Date	Mintage	F12	VF20	XF40	MS60	MS63
2008	—	PF65 1,850				

Y# 1140 100 ROUBLES
1083.74 g., 0.925 Silver 32.0223 oz. ASW, 100 mm. **Subject:** European Beaver

Date	Mintage	F12	VF20	XF40	MS60	MS63
2008	—	PF65 1,850				

Y# 1142 100 ROUBLES
15.59 g., 0.900 Gold 0.4482 oz. AGW, 30 mm. **Subject:** European Beaver

Date	Mintage	F12	VF20	XF40	MS60	MS63
2008	—	PF65 1,100				

Y# 1143 100 ROUBLES
1046.00 g., 0.925 Silver 30.9072 oz. ASW, 100 mm. **Subject:** European Beaver

Date	Mintage	F12	VF20	XF40	MS60	MS63
2008	—	PF65 1,750				

Y# 1156 100 ROUBLES
1083.74 g., 0.925 Silver 32.0223 oz. ASW, 100 mm. **Subject:** Pereslavl Zalessky

Date	Mintage	F12	VF20	XF40	MS60	MS63
2008	—	PF65 1,850				

Y# 1157 100 ROUBLES
1046.00 g., 0.999 Silver 33.3798 oz. ASW, 100 mm. **Subject:** Alexandrov

Date	Mintage	F12	VF20	XF40	MS60	MS63
2008	—	PF65 2,000				

Y# 1148 100 ROUBLES
1083.74 g., 0.925 Silver 32.0223 oz. ASW, 100 mm. **Subject:** Kamchatka Volcano

Date	Mintage	F12	VF20	XF40	MS60	MS63
2008	—	PF65 1,850				

Y# 1162 100 ROUBLES
1083.74 g., 0.925 Silver 32.0223 oz. ASW, 100 mm. **Subject:** Russian Currency

Date	Mintage	F12	VF20	XF40	MS60	MS63
2009	250	PF65 2,750				

Y# 1163 100 ROUBLES
15.59 g., 0.900 Gold 0.4482 oz. AGW, 30 mm. **Subject:** Russian Currency

Date	Mintage	F12	VF20	XF40	MS60	MS63
2009	27,000	PF65 1,000				

Y# 1167 100 ROUBLES
168.00 g., 0.925 Silver 4.9641 oz. ASW, 60 mm. **Subject:** A. P. Chekhov, 150th Anniversary of Birth

Date	Mintage	F12	VF20	XF40	MS60	MS63
2009	—	PF65 400				

Y# 1171 100 ROUBLES
1083.74 g., 0.925 Silver 32.0223 oz. ASW, 100 mm. **Subject:** Kalmyk Peoples, 400th Anniversary of annexation into Russia

Date	Mintage	F12	VF20	XF40	MS60	MS63
2009	—	PF65 2,000				

Y# 1174 100 ROUBLES
1083.74 g., 0.925 Silver 32.0223 oz. ASW, 100 mm. **Subject:** N. V. Gogol, 200th Anniversary of Birth

Date	Mintage	F12	VF20	XF40	MS60	MS63
2009	500	PF65 1,850				

Y# 1179 100 ROUBLES
1083.74 g., 0.925 Silver 32.0223 oz. ASW, 100 mm. **Subject:** Poltava Battle, 300th Anniversary

Date	Mintage	F12	VF20	XF40	MS60	MS63
2009	500	PF65 1,850				

Y# 1238 100 ROUBLES
1083.74 g., 0.925 Silver 32.0223 oz. ASW, 100 mm. **Subject:** A. P. Chekhov, 200th Anniversary of Birth

Date	Mintage	F12	VF20	XF40	MS60	MS63
2010 Prooflike	500	—	—	—	—	1,850

Y# 1290 100 ROUBLES
1083.74 g., 0.925 Silver 32.0223 oz. ASW, 100 mm. **Rev:** Man playing stringed instrument, others in backbround **Edge:** Reeded

Date	Mintage	F12	VF20	XF40	MS60	MS63
2011	300	PF65 2,000				

Y# 1299 100 ROUBLES
1083.74 g., 0.925 Silver 32.0223 oz. ASW, 100 mm. **Subject:** 2014 Winter Olympics - Sochi **Rev:** Montage of Russian winter sports

Date	Mintage	F12	VF20	XF40	MS60	MS63
2014 (2011)	1,200	PF65 1,700				

Y# 1324 100 ROUBLES
15.55 g., 0.999 Gold 0.4962 oz. AGW, 30 mm. **Rev:** St. George the Victorious

Date	Mintage	F12	VF20	XF40	MS60	MS63
2012	10,000	PF65 1,000				

Y# 1340 100 ROUBLES
1111.12 g., 0.925 Silver 32.8314 oz. ASW, 100 mm. **Subject:** Millennium of the Unity of the Mordovian people within the Peoples of the Russian State

Date	Mintage	F12	VF20	XF40	MS60	MS63
2012	300	PF65 2,000				

Y# 1344 100 ROUBLES
1111.12 g., 0.925 Silver 32.8314 oz. ASW, 100 mm. **Subject:** People's Volunteer Corps, 400th Anniversary

Date	Mintage	F12	VF20	XF40	MS60	MS63
2012	500	PF65 2,000				

Y# 1368 100 ROUBLES
1111.12 g., 0.925 Silver 32.8314 oz. ASW, 60 mm. **Subject:** Origin of the Russian Statehood, 1150th Anniversary

Date	Mintage	F12	VF20	XF40	MS60	MS63
2012 Prooflike	300	—	—	—	—	2,000

Y# 1440 100 ROUBLES
1083.00 g., 0.925 Silver 32.0005 oz. ASW, 100 mm. **Subject:** Dynamo Sports Club, 90th Anniversary **Rev:** Sport views in eleven discs surrounding central D-in-diamond logo **Edge:** Reeded

Date	Mintage	F12	VF20	XF40	MS60	MS63
2013СПМД	750	PF65 1,000				

Y# 1451 100 ROUBLES
15.72 g., 0.999 Gold 0.5017 oz. AGW, 30 mm. **Subject:** Russian victory over Germany at Battle of Stalingrad, 70th Anniversary **Rev:** Motherland monument at top, soldiers from Volgograd monument below

Date	Mintage	F12	VF20	XF40	MS60	MS63
2013ММД	500	PF65 850				

Y# 877 200 ROUBLES
3342.39 g., 0.900 Silver 96.0917 oz. ASW, 130 mm. **Rev:** Peter I monetary reform

Date	Mintage	F12	VF20	XF40	MS60	MS63
2003(sp)	300	PF65 5,250				

Y# 1027 200 ROUBLES
31.11 g., 0.999 Gold 0.9926 oz. AGW **Subject:** Reindeer

Date	Mintage	F12	VF20	XF40	MS60	MS63
2004	500	PF65 3,250				

Y# 1042 200 ROUBLES
31.10 g., 0.999 Gold 0.9925 oz. AGW **Subject:** Parliament, 100th Anniversary

Date	Mintage	F12	VF20	XF40	MS60	MS63
2006	750	PF65 2,000				

Y# 1062 200 ROUBLES
3138.00 g., 0.925 Silver 92.7216 oz. ASW, 100 mm. **Subject:** Moscow's Kremlin and Red Square

Date	Mintage	F12	VF20	XF40	MS60	MS63
2006	200	PF65 6,500				

Y# 1144 200 ROUBLES
31.11 g., 0.999 Gold 0.9926 oz. AGW **Subject:** European Beaver

Date	Mintage	F12	VF20	XF40	MS60	MS63
2008	500	PF65 3,250				

Y# 1169 200 ROUBLES
31.11 g., 0.999 Gold 0.9926 oz. AGW **Subject:** A. P. Chekhov, 150th Anniversary of Birth

Date	Mintage	F12	VF20	XF40	MS60	MS63
2009	500	PF65 2,000				

Y# 1176 200 ROUBLES
3120.00 g., 0.925 Silver 92.1897 oz. ASW, 100 mm. **Subject:** N. V. Gogol, 200th Anniversary of Birth

Date	Mintage	F12	VF20	XF40	MS60	MS63
2009	—	PF65 6,500				

Y# 1201 200 ROUBLES
31.11 g., 0.999 Gold 0.9926 oz. AGW **Subject:** Velikly Novgorod

Date	Mintage	F12	VF20	XF40	MS60	MS63
2009	200	PF65 7,500				

Y# 1209 200 ROUBLES
31.11 g., 0.999 Gold 0.9926 oz. AGW **Series:** Speed Skating

Date	Mintage	F12	VF20	XF40	MS60	MS63
2009	500	PF65 2,000				

Y# 1210 200 ROUBLES
31.10 g., 0.999 Gold 0.9925 oz. AGW **Subject:** Ski Jumping

Date	Mintage	F12	VF20	XF40	MS60	MS63
2009	500	PF65 2,000				

Y# 1211 200 ROUBLES
31.10 g., 0.999 Gold 0.9925 oz. AGW **Subject:** Luge

Date	Mintage	F12	VF20	XF40	MS60	MS63
2009	500	PF65 2,000				

Y# 1213 200 ROUBLES
31.11 g., 0.999 Gold 0.9926 oz. AGW **Subject:** Figure Skating

Date	Mintage	F12	VF20	XF40	MS60	MS63
2009	500	PF65 2,000				

Y# 1212 200 ROUBLES
31.11 g., 0.999 Gold 0.9926 oz. AGW **Subject:** Biathlon

Date	Mintage	F12	VF20	XF40	MS60	MS63
2009	500	PF65 2,000				

Y# 1234 200 ROUBLES
3130.00 g., 0.925 Silver 92.4852 oz. ASW **Subject:** UNESCO Heritage Site - Yaroslav

Date	Mintage	F12	VF20	XF40	MS60	MS63
2010	200	PF65 6,000				

Y# 1240 200 ROUBLES
31.10 g., 0.999 Gold 0.9925 oz. AGW **Subject:** A. P. Chekhov, 200th Anniversary of Birth

Date	Mintage	F12	VF20	XF40	MS60	MS63
2010	500	PF65 2,500				

Y# 1255 200 ROUBLES
31.10 g., 0.999 Gold 0.9925 oz. AGW **Subject:** Hockey

Date	Mintage	F12	VF20	XF40	MS60	MS63
2010	—	PF65 2,500				

Y# 1256 200 ROUBLES
31.10 g., 0.999 Gold 0.9925 oz. AGW **Subject:** Ski Race

Date	Mintage	F12	VF20	XF40	MS60	MS63
2010	500	PF65 2,500				

Y# 1257 200 ROUBLES
31.10 g., 0.999 Gold 0.9925 oz. AGW **Subject:** Nordic Combined

Date	Mintage	F12	VF20	XF40	MS60	MS63
2010	500	PF65 2,500				

Y# 1258 200 ROUBLES
31.10 g., 0.999 Gold 0.9925 oz. AGW **Subject:** Freestyle Skiing

Date	Mintage	F12	VF20	XF40	MS60	MS63
2010	500	PF65 2,500				

Y# 1259 200 ROUBLES
31.10 g., 0.999 Gold 0.9925 oz. AGW **Subject:** Short Track Speed Skating

Date	Mintage	F12	VF20	XF40	MS60	MS63
2010	500	PF65 2,500				

Y# 1260 200 ROUBLES
31.10 g., 0.999 Gold 0.9925 oz. AGW **Subject:** Curling

Date	Mintage	F12	VF20	XF40	MS60	MS63
2010	500	PF65 2,500				

Y# 1261 200 ROUBLES
31.10 g., 0.999 Gold 0.9925 oz. AGW **Subject:** Snowboarding

Date	Mintage	F12	VF20	XF40	MS60	MS63
2010	500	PF65 2,500				

Y# 1262 200 ROUBLES
31.10 g., 0.999 Gold 0.9925 oz. AGW **Subject:** Skeleton

Date	Mintage	F12	VF20	XF40	MS60	MS63
2010	500	PF65 2,500				

Y# 1263 200 ROUBLES
31.10 g., 0.999 Gold 0.9925 oz. AGW **Subject:** Bobsled

Date	Mintage	F12	VF20	XF40	MS60	MS63
2010	500	PF65 2,500				

Y# 1264 200 ROUBLES
31.10 g., 0.999 Gold 0.9925 oz. AGW **Subject:** Mountain Skiing

Date	Mintage	F12	VF20	XF40	MS60	MS63
2010	500	PF65 2,500				

Y# 1441 200 ROUBLES
31.37 g., 0.999 Gold 1.0011 oz. AGW, 33 mm. **Subject:** Dynamo Sports Club, 90th Anniversary **Rev:** Thre soccer players **Edge:** Reeded

Date	Mintage	F12	VF20	XF40	MS60	MS63
2013СПМД	500	PF65 1,700				

Y# 1442 200 ROUBLES
31.37 g., 0.999 Gold 1.0011 oz. AGW, 33 mm. **Subject:** Dynamo Sports Club, 90th Anniversary **Rev:** Three hockey players **Edge:** Reeded

Date	Mintage	F12	VF20	XF40	MS60	MS63
2013СПМД	500	PF65 1,700				

Y# 1443 200 ROUBLES
31.37 g., 0.999 Gold 1.0011 oz. AGW, 33 mm. **Subject:** Dynamo Sports Club, 90th Anniversary **Rev:** Cross-country skier **Edge:** Reeded

Date	Mintage	F12	VF20	XF40	MS60	MS63
2013ММД	500	PF65 1,700				

Y# 1348 500 ROUBLES
5555.60 g., 0.925 Silver 164.1568 oz. ASW, 150 mm. **Subject:**
Russia's victory in the War of 1812

Date	Mintage	F12	VF20	XF40	MS60	MS63
2012	50	PF65 6,000				

Y# 796 1000 ROUBLES
156.40 g., 0.999 Gold 4.991 oz. AGW, 50 mm. **Subject:** The
Bark Sedov **Obv:** Double-headed eagle **Rev:** Four-masted
sailing ship **Edge:** Reeded

Date	Mintage	F12	VF20	XF40	MS60	MS63
2001(m)	250	PF65 10,000				

Y# 878 1000 ROUBLES
156.40 g., 0.999 Gold 4.991 oz. AGW, 50 mm. **Rev:** Cronstadt

Date	Mintage	F12	VF20	XF40	MS60	MS63
2003(m)	250	PF65 10,000				

Y# 1037 1000 ROUBLES
1046.00 g., 0.925 Silver 30.9072 oz. ASW, 100 mm. **Subject:**
Uglich

Date	Mintage	F12	VF20	XF40	MS60	MS63
2004	—	PF65 1,750				

Y# 1045 1000 ROUBLES
1000.00 g., 0.999 Gold 31.9118 oz. AGW, 100 mm. **Subject:**
Frigate Myr

Date	Mintage	F12	VF20	XF40	MS60	MS63
2006	—	PF65 60,000				

Y# 1082 1000 ROUBLES
156.00 g., 0.999 Gold 4.9782 oz. AGW, 100 mm. **Subject:**
International Artic Year

Date	Mintage	F12	VF20	XF40	MS60	MS63
2007	—	PF65 10,000				

Y# 1164 1000 ROUBLES
156.00 g., 0.999 Gold 4.9782 oz. AGW, 100 mm. **Subject:**
Russian Currency

Date	Mintage	F12	VF20	XF40	MS60	MS63
2009	—	PF65 10,000				

Y# 1227 1000 ROUBLES
155.50 g., 0.999 Gold 4.9623 oz. AGW, 100 mm. **Subject:**
Warship - Goto Predestination

Date	Mintage	F12	VF20	XF40	MS60	MS63
2010	—	PF65 10,000				

Y# 1281 1000 ROUBLES
155.50 g., 0.999 Gold 4.9623 oz. AGW, 50 mm. **Subject:**

Beginning of Great Reforms - Abolition of Serfdom **Rev:** Man
plowing, quill pen and signature on document

Date	Mintage	F12	VF20	XF40	MS60	MS63
2011ММД	250	PF65 10,000				

Y# 1288 1000 ROUBLES
155.50 g., 0.999 Gold 4.9623 oz. AGW, 50 mm. **Rev:** U.A.
Gagarin in spacesuit waving

Date	Mintage	F12	VF20	XF40	MS60	MS63
2011	500	PF65 10,000				

Y# 1297 1000 ROUBLES
155.50 g., 0.999 Gold 4.9623 oz. AGW, 50 mm. **Subject:** 2014
Winter Olympics - Sochi - Flora of Sochi **Rev:** Goddess Flora
who's hair has plants of the Sochi region, female figure skater
to right

Date	Mintage	F12	VF20	XF40	MS60	MS63
2014 (2011)	600	PF65 10,000				

Y# 1418 1000 ROUBLES
155.50 g., 0.999 Gold 4.9623 oz. AGW, 100 mm. **Subject:**
Battleship Ingermanland

Date	Mintage	F12	VF20	XF40	MS60	MS63
2012	500	PF65 10,000				

Y# 1444 1000 ROUBLES
156.40 g., 0.999 Gold 4.991 oz. AGW, 50 mm. **Subject:**
Dynamo Sports Club, 90th Anniversary **Rev:** Six sports in discs,
D-in-diamond logo **Edge:** Reeded

Date	Mintage	F12	VF20	XF40	MS60	MS63
2013ММД	500	PF65 7,500				

Y# 784 10000 ROUBLES
1001.10 g., 0.999 Gold 31.9469 oz. AGW, 100 mm. **Subject:**
Works of Dionissy **Obv:** Double-headed eagle **Rev:** Interior
view of the carved portal of the Virgin of the Nativity Church
Edge: Reeded **Note:** Illustration reduced.

Date	Mintage	F12	VF20	XF40	MS60	MS63
2002(sp)	100	PF65 60,000				

Y# 879 10000 ROUBLES
1001.10 g., 0.999 Gold 31.9469 oz. AGW, 100 mm. **Rev:** St.
Petersburg area map

Date	Mintage	F12	VF20	XF40	MS60	MS63
2003	200	PF65 57,500				

Y# 1017 10000 ROUBLES
1000.00 g., 0.999 Gold 31.9118 oz. AGW, 100 mm. **Subject:**
Theophanes the Greek

Date	Mintage	F12	VF20	XF40	MS60	MS63
2004	—	PF65 60,000				

Y# 880 10000 ROUBLES
1001.10 g., 0.999 Gold 31.9469 oz. AGW, 100 mm. **Rev:**
Church of the Transfiguration of the Savior, Novgorod

Date	Mintage	F12	VF20	XF40	MS60	MS63
2004	100	PF65 60,000				

Y# 1028 10000 ROUBLES
1000.00 g., 0.999 Gold 31.9118 oz. AGW, 100 mm. **Subject:**
Reindeer

Date	Mintage	F12	VF20	XF40	MS60	MS63
2004	100	PF65 60,000				

Y# 896 10000 ROUBLES
1001.10 g., 0.999 Gold 31.9469 oz. AGW, 100 mm. **Subject:**
60th Anniversary - Victory Over Germany **Obv:** Double-headed
eagle **Rev:** Soldiers dishonoring captured Nazi flags and
standards **Edge:** Reeded **Note:** Illustration reduced.

Date	Mintage	F12	VF20	XF40	MS60	MS63
2005	250	PF65 57,500				

Y# 913 10000 ROUBLES

1001.10 g., 0.999 Gold 31.9469 oz. AGW, 100 mm. Obv: Two headed eagle Rev: Kazan Kremlin view Edge: Reeded Note: Illustration reduced.

Date	Mintage	F12	VF20	XF40	MS60	MS63
2005	150	PF65 58,000				

Y# 1043 10000 ROUBLES

1083.74 g., 0.925 Gold 32.0223 oz. AGW, 100 mm. Subject: Parliament, 100th Anniversary

Date	Mintage	F12	VF20	XF40	MS60	MS63
2006	100	PF65 60,000				

Y# 1064 10000 ROUBLES

1000.00 g., 0.999 Gold 31.9118 oz. AGW, 100 mm. Subject: Moscow's Kremlin and Red Square

Date	Mintage	F12	VF20	XF40	MS60	MS63
2006	—	PF65 60,000				

Y# 1091 10000 ROUBLES

1000.00 g., 0.999 Gold 31.9118 oz. AGW, 100 mm. Subject: Andrew Rublyov

Date	Mintage	F12	VF20	XF40	MS60	MS63
2007	—	PF65 60,000				

Y# 1095 10000 ROUBLES

1000.00 g., 0.999 Gold 31.9118 oz. AGW, 100 mm. Subject: Bashkiria, 450th Anniversary of Annexation by Russia

Date	Mintage	F12	VF20	XF40	MS60	MS63
2007	—	PF65 60,000				

Y# 1098 10000 ROUBLES

1000.00 g., 0.999 Gold 31.9118 oz. AGW, 100 mm. Subject: Khakassia, 300th Anniversary of Annexation by Russia

Date	Mintage	F12	VF20	XF40	MS60	MS63
2007	—	PF65 60,000				

Y# 1122 10000 ROUBLES

1000.00 g., 0.999 Gold 31.9118 oz. AGW, 100 mm. Subject: Udmurtiya, 450th Anniversary of Annexation into Russia

Date	Mintage	F12	VF20	XF40	MS60	MS63
2008	—	PF65 58,000				

Y# 1145 10000 ROUBLES

1000.00 g., 0.999 Gold 31.9118 oz. AGW, 100 mm. Subject: European Beaver

Date	Mintage	F12	VF20	XF40	MS60	MS63
2008	—	PF65 58,000				

Y# 1149 10000 ROUBLES

1000.00 g., 0.999 Gold 31.9118 oz. AGW, 100 mm. Subject: Kamchatka Volcano

Date	Mintage	F12	VF20	XF40	MS60	MS63
2008	—	PF65 58,000				

Y# 1203 10000 ROUBLES

1000.00 g., 0.999 Gold 31.9118 oz. AGW, 100 mm. Subject: Velikly Novgorod

Date	Mintage	F12	VF20	XF40	MS60	MS63
2009	—	PF65 58,000				

Y# 1236 10000 ROUBLES

1000.00 g., 0.999 Gold 31.9118 oz. AGW, 100 mm. Subject: UNESCO Heritage Site - Yaroslav

Date	Mintage	F12	VF20	XF40	MS60	MS63
2010 Prooflike					—	58,000

Y# 1370 10000 ROUBLES

1000.00 g., 0.999 Gold 31.9118 oz. AGW, 100 mm. Subject: Origin of Russian Statehood, 1150th Anniversary

Date	Mintage	F12	VF20	XF40	MS60	MS63
2012 Prooflike	75	—	—	—	—	60,000

Y# 1371 10000 ROUBLES

1000.00 g., 0.999 Gold 31.9118 oz. AGW, 100 mm. Subject: Sberbank, 170 Years

Date	Mintage	F12	VF20	XF40	MS60	MS63
2012 Prooflike	75	—	—	—	—	60,000

Y# 1425 10000 ROUBLES

1003.00 g., 0.999 Gold 32.0076 oz. AGW, 100 mm. Rev: Nine sport scenes, Kazan Universiade logo and city skyline Edge: Reeded

Date	Mintage	F12	VF20	XF40	MS60	MS63
2013СПМД	100	PF65 43,000				

Y# 1117 25000 ROUBLES

1000.00 g., 0.999 Gold 31.9118 oz. AGW, 100 mm. Subject: Goznak, 190th Anniversary

Date	Mintage	F12	VF20	XF40	MS60	MS63
2008	—	PF65 58,000				

Y# 1165 25000 ROUBLES

1000.00 g., 0.999 Gold 31.9118 oz. AGW, 100 mm. Subject: Russian Currency

Date	Mintage	F12	VF20	XF40	MS60	MS63
2009	—	PF65 58,000				

Y# 1350 25000 ROUBLES

3000.00 g., 0.999 Gold 95.7355 oz. AGW, 120 mm. Subject: Russia's victory in the War of 1812

Date	Mintage	F12	VF20	XF40	MS60	MS63
2012	50	PF65 175,000				

Y# 1231 50000 ROUBLES

5000.00 g., 0.999 Gold 159.5592 oz. AGW Subject: Bank of Russia, 150th Anniversary

Date	Mintage	F12	VF20	XF40	MS60	MS63
2010 Prooflike	—	—	—	—	—	285,000

MINT SETS

KM#	Date	Mintage	Identification	Issue Price	Mkt Val
MS44	2002 (7)	—	Y#600-603, 797-799, plus mint medal	7.50	15.00

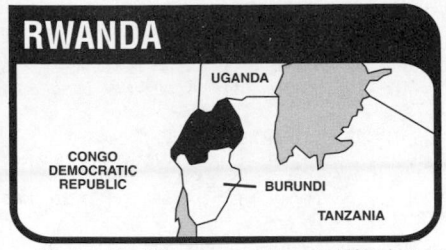

RWANDA

The Republic of Rwanda, located in central Africa between the Republic of the Congo and Tanzania, has an area of 10,169 sq. mi. (26,340 sq. km.) and a population of 7.3 million. Capital: Kigali. The economy is based on agriculture and mining. Coffee and tin are exported.For earlier coinage see Belgian Congo, and Rwanda and Burundi.

MINT MARKS
(a) - Paris, privy marks only
(b) - Brussels, privy marks only

MONETARY SYSTEM
100 Centimes = 1 Franc

REPUBLIC
STANDARD COINAGE

KM# 22 FRANC
0.07 g., Aluminum, 16 mm. **Obv:** National arms **Rev:** Sorghum plant **Edge:** Plain

Date	Mintage	F12	VF20	XF40	MS60	MS63
2003	—				0.25	0.65	1.00

KM# 23 5 FRANCS
2.96 g., Brass Plated Steel, 20 mm. **Obv:** National arms **Rev:** Coffee plant **Edge:** Plain

Date	Mintage	F12	VF20	XF40	MS60	MS63
2003	—	—	—	—	0.25	0.65	1.00

KM# 33 5 FRANCS
2.96 g., Brass Plated Steel, 20 mm. **Obv:** National arms **Rev:** Coffee plant **Rev. Legend:** BANKI NKURU YU RWANDA

Date	Mintage	F12	VF20	XF40	MS60	MS63
2009	—	—	—	—	0.25	0.65	1.00

KM# 24 10 FRANCS
5.00 g., Brass Plated Steel, 23.9 mm. **Obv:** National arms **Rev:** Banana tree **Edge:** Plain

Date	Mintage	F12	VF20	XF40	MS60	MS63
2003	—			0.45	1.00	1.50
2009	—			0.45	1.00	1.50

KM# 34 10 FRANCS
5.00 g., Brass Plated Steel, 23.9 mm. **Obv:** National arms **Rev:** Banana tree **Rev. Legend:** BANKI NKURU YU RWANDA

Date	Mintage	F12	VF20	XF40	MS60	MS63
2009	—			0.25	0.65	1.00

KM# 25 20 FRANCS
3.50 g., Nickel Plated Steel, 20 mm. **Obv:** National arms **Rev:** Coffee plant seedling **Edge:** Reeded

Date	Mintage	F12	VF20	XF40	MS60	MS63
2003	—				1.75	2.00
2009	—				1.75	2.00

KM# 35 20 FRANCS
Nickel Plated Steel, 20 mm. **Obv:** National arms **Rev:** Coffee plant seedling **Rev. Legend:** BANKI NKURU YU RWANDA **Edge:** Reeded

Date	Mintage	F12	VF20	XF40	MS60	MS63
2009	—			—	1.75	2.00

KM# 26 50 FRANCS
5.80 g., Nickel Plated Steel, 24 mm. **Obv:** National arms **Rev:** Ear of corn within husks **Edge:** Reeded **Mint:** Paris

Date	Mintage	F12	VF20	XF40	MS60	MS63
2003(a)	—				2.50	4.00

KM# 36 50 FRANCS
5.80 g., Nickel Plated Steel, 24 mm. **Obv:** National arms **Rev:** Ear of corn within husks **Rev. Legend:** BANKI NKURU YU RWANDA **Edge:** Reeded

Date	Mintage	F12	VF20	XF40	MS60	MS63
2009	—				2.50	4.00

KM# 39 50 FRANCS
31.05 g., 0.999 Silver 0.9909 oz. ASW, 38.61 mm. **Rev:** Map of Africa, Zebra

Date	Mintage	F12	VF20	XF40	MS60	MS63
2011	—	PF63 80.00	PF65 90.00

KM# 37 50 FRANCS
31.11 g., 0.999 Silver 0.9926 oz. ASW, 38.61 mm. **Rev:** Map of Africa, Two Rhinos at lower left

Date	Mintage	F12	VF20	XF40	MS60	MS63
2012	Est. 5000	PF63 80.00	PF65 90.00

KM# 38 50 FRANCS
31.11 g., 0.999 Silver 0.9926 oz. ASW, 38.61 mm. **Rev:** Map of Africa, Two cheetahs at lower left **Mint:** B.H. Mayer

Date	Mintage	F12	VF20	XF40	MS60	MS63
2013	Est. 5000	PF63 80.00	PF65 90.00

KM# 43 50 FRANCS
31.11 g., 0.999 Silver 0.9926 oz. ASW **Obv:** National arms **Rev:** Map of Africa, two impala at left **Mint:** B.H. Mayer

Date	Mintage	F12	VF20	XF40	MS60	MS63
2014	Est. 10000	—			—	40.00

KM# 32 100 FRANCS
Bi-Metallic, 27 mm. **Obv:** National arms **Rev:** Value **Rev. Legend:** BANKI NKURU YU RWANDA **Mint:** British Royal Mint

Date	Mintage	F12	VF20	XF40	MS60	MS63
2007	—				5.00	6.50

KM# 28 200 FRANCS
1.00 g., 0.999 Gold 0.0319 oz. AGW, 13.9 mm. **Subject:** 75th Birthday Dian Fossey **Obv:** National arms **Obv. Legend:** BANKI NASIYONALI Y'U RWANDA **Rev:** Fossey facing holding monkey **Edge:** Plain

Date	Mintage	F12	VF20	XF40	MS60	MS63
2007	15,000	PF63 75.00	PF65 85.00

KM# 30 500 FRANCS
22.20 g., 0.900 Silver 0.6382 oz. ASW **Obv:** National arms **Obv. Legend:** BANQUE NATIONALE DU RWANDA **Rev:** Stalk of bananas on leaves **Mint:** Paris

Date	Mintage	F12	VF20	XF40	MS60	MS63
2002(a)	500	PF65 115

KM# 31 500 FRANCS
22.20 g., 0.900 Silver 0.6382 oz. ASW **Subject:** Euro Parity **Obv:** Arms **Rev:** Plant

Date	Mintage	F12	VF20	XF40	MS60	MS63
2002	500	PF65 115

KM# 27 500 FRANCS
20.00 g., 0.999 Silver 0.6382 oz. ASW, 38 mm. **Subject:** Olympic Games 2008 - Peking, marathon races **Obv:** National arms **Obv. Legend:** BANKI NASIYONALI Y'U RWANDA **Rev:** Three male marathon runners, Rwanda Olympic logo at right **Rev. Legend:** JEUX OLYMPIQUES **Edge:** Plain

Date	Mintage	F12	VF20	XF40	MS60	MS63
2006	—	PF65 110

KM# 29 1000 FRANCS
93.30 g., 0.999 Silver and Gold 2.9774 oz., 65 mm. **Obv:** National arms **Obv. Legend:** BANKI NASIYONALI Y'U RWANDA **Rev:** Gilt elephant family of four with diamonds inset in eyes **Rev. Legend:** AFRICAN ELEPHANT **Edge:** Plain **Note:** Illustration reduced.

Date	Mintage	F12	VF20	XF40	MS60	MS63
2007	1,500	—			—	5,400
2007	500	PF65 5,800

SAHARAWI ARAB D.R.

The Saharawi Arab Democratic Republic, located in northwest Africa has an area of 102,703 sq. mi. and a population (census taken 1974) of 76,425. Formerly known as Spanish Sahara, the area is bounded on the north by Morocco, on the east and southeast by Mauritania, on the northeast by Algeria, and on the west by the Atlantic Ocean. Capital: El Aaium. Agriculture, fishing and mining are the three main industries. Exports are barley, livestock and phosphates. The SADR is a "government in exile". It currently controls about 20% of its claimed **territory**, the former **Spanish colony** of **Western Sahara**; **Morocco** controls and administers the majority of the territory as its **Southern Provinces**. SADR claims control over a zone largely bordering Mauritania, described as "the **Free Zone**," although characterized by Morocco as a buffer zone.

DEMOCRATIC REPUBLIC

STANDARD COINAGE

KM# 54 1000 PESETAS
19.94 g., 0.999 Silver 0.6363 oz. ASW, 38.1 mm. **Obv:** National arms **Rev:** Soccer player and stadium **Edge:** Plain

Date	Mintage	F12	VF20	XF40	MS60	MS63
2002	—	PF63 28.00	PF65 35.00			

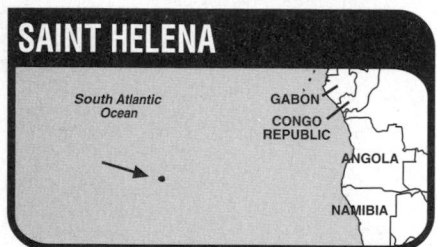

SAINT HELENA

Saint Helena, a British colony located about 1,150 miles (1,850 km.) from the west coast of Africa, has an area of 47 sq. mi. (410 sq. km.) and a population of *7,000. Capital: Jamestown. Flax, lace, and rope are produced for export. Ascension and Tristan da Cunha are dependencies of Saint Helena.

MONETARY SYSTEM
100 Pence = 1 Pound

BRITISH COLONY

STANDARD COINAGE

KM# 19 50 PENCE
38.60 g., Copper-Nickel, 38.6 mm. **Ruler:** Elizabeth II **Subject:** 75th Birthday of Queen Elizabeth II **Obv:** Crowned bust right **Rev:** Bust facing within circle and rose sprigs **Edge:** Reeded

Date	Mintage	VG8	F12	VF20	XF40	MS60
2001	—	—	—	—	—	8.00

KM# 19a 50 PENCE
28.28 g., 0.925 Silver 0.8356 oz. ASW, 38.6 mm. **Ruler:** Elizabeth II **Subject:** 75th Birthday of Queen Elizabeth II **Obv:** Crowned bust right **Rev:** Bust facing within circle and rose sprigs **Edge:** Reeded

Date	Mintage	F12	VF20	XF40	MS60	MS63
2001	10,000	PF63 40.00	PF65 45.00			

KM# 19b 50 PENCE
47.54 g., 0.9166 Gold 1.392 oz. AGW, 38.6 mm. **Ruler:** Elizabeth II **Subject:** 75th Birthday of Queen Elizabeth II **Obv:** Crowned bust right **Rev:** Bust facing within circle and rose sprigs **Edge:** Reeded

Date	Mintage	F12	VF20	XF40	MS60	MS63
2001	75	PF65 2,850				

KM# 20 50 PENCE
28.55 g., Copper-Nickel, 38.6 mm. **Ruler:** Elizabeth II **Subject:** Queen Victoria's Death **Obv:** Crowned bust right **Rev:** Half-length figure facing and ship within circle **Edge:** Reeded

Date	Mintage	VG8	F12	VF20	XF40	MS60
2001	—	—	—	—	—	8.00

KM# 20a 50 PENCE
28.28 g., 0.925 Silver 0.8356 oz. ASW, 38.6 mm. **Ruler:** Elizabeth II **Subject:** Centennial - Death of Queen Victoria **Obv:** Crowned bust right **Rev:** Half-length figure facing and ship within circle **Edge:** Reeded

Date	Mintage	F12	VF20	XF40	MS60	MS63
2001	10,000	PF63 40.00	PF65 45.00			

KM# 20b 50 PENCE
47.54 g., 0.9166 Gold 1.392 oz. AGW, 38.6 mm. **Ruler:** Elizabeth II **Subject:** Centennial - Death of Queen Victoria **Obv:** Crowned bust right **Rev:** Half-length figure facing and ship within circle **Edge:** Reeded

Date	Mintage	F12	VF20	XF40	MS60	MS63
2001	100	PF65 2,800				

KM# 23 50 PENCE
28.28 g., Copper-Nickel, 38.6 mm. **Ruler:** Elizabeth II **Subject:** 50th Anniversary - Queen Elizabeth II's Accession **Obv:** Crowned bust right **Rev:** Crown on pillow within circle **Edge:** Reeded

Date	Mintage	F12	VF20	XF40	MS60	MS63
ND(2002)	—	—	—	—	8.00	10.00

KM# 23a 50 PENCE
28.28 g., 0.925 Silver 0.8356 oz. ASW, 38.6 mm. **Ruler:**

Elizabeth II **Subject:** 50th Anniversary - Queen Elizabeth's Accession **Obv:** Crowned bust right **Rev:** Crown on pillow within circle **Edge:** Reeded

Date	Mintage	F12	VF20	XF40	MS60	MS63
ND(2002)	10,000	PF63 38.00	PF65 42.00			

KM# 24 50 PENCE
28.28 g., Copper-Nickel, 38.6 mm. **Ruler:** Elizabeth II **Subject:** To Celebrate a Life of Duty, Dignity and Love, 1900-2002 **Obv:** Crowned bust right **Rev:** Conjoined busts right **Edge:** Reeded

Date	Mintage	F12	VF20	XF40	MS60	MS63
ND(2002)	—	—	—	—	8.00	10.00

KM# 24a 50 PENCE
28.28 g., 0.925 Silver 0.8356 oz. ASW, 38.6 mm. **Ruler:** Elizabeth II **Subject:** To Celebrate a Life of Duty, Dignity and Love, 1900-2002 **Obv:** Crowned bust right **Rev:** Conjoined busts right **Edge:** Reeded

Date	Mintage	F12	VF20	XF40	MS60	MS63
ND(2002)	10,000	PF63 38.00	PF65 42.00			

KM# 25 50 PENCE
28.28 g., Copper-Nickel, 38.6 mm. **Ruler:** Elizabeth II **Subject:** 500th Anniversary - Discovery of St. Helena **Obv:** Crowned bust right **Rev:** Half length figure right and ship above 1502 date **Edge:** Reeded

Date	Mintage	F12	VF20	XF40	MS60	MS63
ND(2002)	—	—	—	—	10.00	12.00

KM# 25a 50 PENCE
28.28 g., 0.925 Silver 0.8356 oz. ASW, 38.6 mm. **Ruler:** Elizabeth II **Subject:** 500th Anniversary - Discovery of St. Helena **Obv:** Crowned bust right **Rev:** Half length figure right and ship above 1502 date **Edge:** Reeded

Date	Mintage	F12	VF20	XF40	MS60	MS63
ND(2002)	5,000	PF63 45.00	PF65 50.00			

KM# 26 50 PENCE
28.28 g., Copper-Nickel, 38.6 mm. **Ruler:** Elizabeth II **Obv:** Crowned bust right **Rev:** Bust 1/4 left, ship HMS Paramour and a comet **Edge:** Reeded

Date	Mintage	F12	VF20	XF40	MS60	MS63
ND(2002)	—	—	—	—	10.00	12.00

KM# 26a 50 PENCE
28.28 g., 0.925 Silver 0.8356 oz. ASW, 38.6 mm. **Ruler:** Elizabeth II **Obv:** Crowned bust right **Rev:** Bust 1/4 left, ship HMS Paramour and a comet **Edge:** Reeded

Date	Mintage	F12	VF20	XF40	MS60	MS63
ND(2002)	5,000	PF63 45.00	PF65 50.00			

KM# 27 50 PENCE
28.28 g., Copper-Nickel, 38.6 mm. **Ruler:** Elizabeth II **Obv:** Crowned bust right **Rev:** Bust 1/4 right and the HMS Resolution **Edge:** Reeded

Date	Mintage	F12	VF20	XF40	MS60	MS63
ND(2002)	—	—	—	—	10.00	12.00

KM# 27a 50 PENCE
28.28 g., 0.925 Silver 0.8356 oz. ASW, 38.6 mm. **Ruler:** Elizabeth II **Obv:** Crowned bust right **Rev:** Bust 1/4 right and the HMS Resolution **Edge:** Reeded

Date	Mintage	F12	VF20	XF40	MS60	MS63
ND(2002)	5,000			PF63 45.00	PF65 50.00	

KM# 28 50 PENCE
28.28 g., Copper-Nickel, 38.6 mm. **Ruler:** Elizabeth II **Obv:** Crowned bust right **Rev:** Half length figure facing and the ship HMS Northumberland **Edge:** Reeded

Date	Mintage	F12	VF20	XF40	MS60	MS63
ND(2002)	—	—	—	—	10.00	12.00

KM# 28a 50 PENCE
28.28 g., 0.925 Silver 0.8356 oz. ASW, 38.6 mm. **Ruler:** Elizabeth II **Obv:** Queen Elizabeth II **Rev:** Napoleon and the ship HMS Northumberland **Edge:** Reeded

Date	Mintage	F12	VF20	XF40	MS60	MS63
ND(2002)	5,000			PF63 45.00	PF65 50.00	

KM# 29 50 PENCE
28.28 g., Copper-Nickel, 38.6 mm. **Ruler:** Elizabeth II **Obv:** Crowned bust right **Rev:** Four conjoined busts left plus the HMS Vanguard **Edge:** Reeded

Date	Mintage	F12	VF20	XF40	MS60	MS63
ND(2002)	—	—	—	—	8.00	10.00

KM# 29a 50 PENCE
28.28 g., 0.925 Silver 0.8356 oz. ASW, 38.6 mm. **Ruler:** Elizabeth II **Obv:** Crowned bust right **Rev:** Four conjoined busts left plus the HMS Vanguard **Edge:** Reeded

Date	Mintage	F12	VF20	XF40	MS60	MS63
ND(2002)	5,000			PF63 40.00	PF65 45.00	

KM# 30 50 PENCE
28.28 g., Copper-Nickel, 38.6 mm. **Ruler:** Elizabeth II **Subject:** 50th Anniversary of Queen Elizabeth's Coronation **Obv:** Crowned bust right **Rev:** Crowned Queen facing with scepter and orb **Edge:** Reeded

Date	Mintage	F12	VF20	XF40	MS60	MS63
ND(2003)	—	—	—	—	10.00	12.00

KM# 30a 50 PENCE
28.28 g., 0.925 Silver 0.8356 oz. ASW, 38.6 mm. **Ruler:** Elizabeth II **Subject:** 50th Anniversary - Queen Elizabeth's Coronation **Obv:** Crowned bust right **Rev:** Crowned Queen facing with scepter and orb **Edge:** Reeded

Date	Mintage	F12	VF20	XF40	MS60	MS63
ND(2003)	5,000			PF63 45.00	PF65 50.00	

KM# 30b 50 PENCE
39.94 g., 0.9166 Gold 1.1694 oz. AGW, 38.6 mm. **Ruler:** Elizabeth II **Subject:** 50th Anniversary of Queen's Coronation **Obv:** Crowned bust right **Rev:** Crowned Queen facing with scepter and orb **Edge:** Reeded

Date	Mintage	F12	VF20	XF40	MS60	MS63
ND(2003)	50			PF65 2,500		

KM# 31 50 PENCE
28.28 g., Copper-Nickel, 38.6 mm. **Ruler:** Elizabeth II **Subject:** 50th Anniversary of Coronation **Obv:** Crowned bust right **Rev:** Coronation implements **Edge:** Reeded

Date	Mintage	F12	VF20	XF40	MS60	MS63
ND(2003)	—	—	—	—	10.00	12.00

KM# 31a 50 PENCE
28.28 g., 0.925 Silver 0.8356 oz. ASW, 38.6 mm. **Ruler:** Elizabeth II **Subject:** 50th Anniversary - Queen Elizabeth II's Coronation **Obv:** Crowned bust right **Rev:** Coronation implements **Edge:** Reeded

Date	Mintage	F12	VF20	XF40	MS60	MS63
ND(2003)	5,000			PF63 45.00	PF65 50.00	

KM# 31b 50 PENCE
39.94 g., 0.9166 Gold 1.1694 oz. AGW, 38.6 mm. **Ruler:** Elizabeth II **Subject:** 50th Anniversary of Coronation **Obv:** Crowned bust right **Rev:** Coronation implements **Edge:** Reeded

Date	Mintage	F12	VF20	XF40	MS60	MS63
ND(2003)	50			PF65 2,500		

PIEDFORT

KM#	Date	Mintage Identification	Mkt Val
P3	ND(2002)	500 50 Pence 0.925 Silver Proof.	125

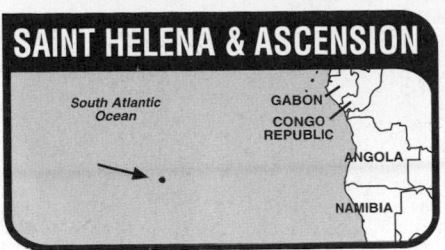

SAINT HELENA & ASCENSION

South Atlantic Ocean

GABON
CONGO REPUBLIC
ANGOLA
NAMIBIA

BRITISH OVERSEAS TERRITORY

STANDARD COINAGE
100 Pence = 1 Pound

KM# 13a PENNY
3.50 g., Copper Plated Steel, 20.28 mm. **Ruler:** Elizabeth II **Obv:** Crowned head right **Rev:** Tuna above value **Edge:** Plain

Date	Mintage	F12	VF20	XF40	MS60	MS63
2003	—	—	—	0.15	0.35	0.75

KM# 12a 2 PENCE
Copper Plated Steel, 25.9 mm. **Ruler:** Elizabeth II **Obv:** Crowned head right **Rev:** Value below donkey

Date	Mintage	F12	VF20	XF40	MS60	MS63
2003	—	—	—	0.20	0.60	1.25
2006	—	—	—	0.20	0.60	1.25

KM# 22 5 PENCE
3.25 g., Copper-Nickel, 18 mm. **Ruler:** Elizabeth II **Obv:** Crowned head right **Rev:** Giant tortoise

Date	Mintage	F12	VF20	XF40	MS60	MS63
2003	—	—	—	1.00	2.50	5.00
2006	—	—	—	1.00	2.50	5.00

KM# 23 10 PENCE
6.50 g., Copper-Nickel, 24.5 mm. **Ruler:** Elizabeth II **Obv:** Crowned head right **Rev:** Dolphins

Date	Mintage	F12	VF20	XF40	MS60	MS63
2003	—	—	—	2.00	4.00	6.00
2006	—	—	—	2.00	4.00	6.00

KM# 55 10 PENCE
15.55 g., 0.999 Silver 0.4962 oz. ASW, 27 mm. **Ruler:** Elizabeth II **Obv:** Head with crown right **Rev:** Peacock displayed

Date	Mintage	F12	VF20	XF40	MS60	MS63
2012	Est. 20000			PF65 32.50		

KM# 21 20 PENCE
5.00 g., Copper-Nickel, 21.4 mm. **Ruler:** Elizabeth II **Obv:** Crowned head right **Rev:** Ebony flower **Shape:** 7-sided

Date	Mintage	F12	VF20	XF40	MS60	MS63
2003	—	—	—	0.75	1.50	2.50

KM# 56 20 PENCE
31.11 g., 0.999 Silver 0.9926 oz. ASW, 38.61 mm. **Ruler:** Elizabeth II **Obv:** Head with crown right **Rev:** Peacock displayed

Date	Mintage	F12	VF20	XF40	MS60	MS63
2012	Est. 20000			PF65 55.00		

KM# 27 50 PENCE
8.00 g., Copper-Nickel, 27.3 mm. **Ruler:** Elizabeth II **Obv:** Head with crown right **Rev:** Green Sea Turtle **Shape:** 7-sided

Date	Mintage	F12	VF20	XF40	MS60	MS63
2003	—	—	—	—	4.00	6.00
2006	—	—	—	—	4.00	6.00

KM# 57 50 PENCE
5.83 g., 0.999 Gold 0.186 oz. AGW, 20 mm. **Ruler:** Elizabeth II
Obv: Head with crown right **Rev:** Lion walking left, palm tree in background

Date	Mintage	F12	VF20	XF40	MS60	MS63
2012	Est. 3250	PF65 400				

KM# 17 POUND
9.50 g., Nickel-Brass, 22.5 mm. **Ruler:** Elizabeth II **Obv:** Crowned head right **Rev:** Sooty terns (Wideawake birds)

Date	Mintage	F12	VF20	XF40	MS60	MS63
2003	—	—	—	2.25	5.00	8.00
2006	—	—	—	2.25	5.00	8.00

KM# 58 POUND
11.66 g., 0.9999 Gold 0.3724 oz. AGW, 26 mm. **Ruler:** Elizabeth II **Obv:** Head with crown right **Rev:** Lion advancing left, palm tree in background

Date	Mintage	F12	VF20	XF40	MS60	MS63
2012	3,250	PF65 725				

KM# 26 2 POUNDS
11.81 g., Nickel-Brass, 28.3 mm. **Ruler:** Elizabeth II **Obv:** Crowned bust right **Rev:** National arms above value **Edge:** Reeded and lettered **Edge Lettering:** 500TH ANNIVERSARY

Date	Mintage	F12	VF20	XF40	MS60	MS63
2002	—	—	—	6.00	10.00	12.50

KM# 25 2 POUNDS
12.00 g., Bi-Metallic, 28.4 mm. **Ruler:** Elizabeth II **Obv:** Crowned bust right **Rev:** National Arms **Edge:** Reeded and lettered **Edge Lettering:** LOYAL AND FAITHFUL

Date	Mintage	F12	VF20	XF40	MS60	MS63
2003	—	—	—	9.00	15.00	17.50
2006	—	—	—	9.00	15.00	17.50

KM# 60 5 POUNDS
28.28 g., 0.925 Silver 0.8356 oz. ASW, 38.61 mm. **Ruler:** Elizabeth II **Subject:** Queen Elizabeth II 60th Wedding Anniversary **Shape:** 7-Sided

Date	Mintage	F12	VF20	XF40	MS60	MS63
2007	Est. 30000	PF63 35.00	PF65 40.00			

KM# 61 5 POUNDS
28.28 g., 0.925 Silver 0.8356 oz. ASW, 38.61 mm. **Ruler:** Elizabeth II **Subject:** Buckingham Palace **Shape:** 7-Sided

Date	Mintage	F12	VF20	XF40	MS60	MS63
2007	Est. 30000	PF63 35.00	PF65 40.00			

KM# 62 5 POUNDS
28.28 g., 0.925 Silver 0.8356 oz. ASW, 38.61 mm. **Ruler:** Elizabeth II **Subject:** Armed Services **Shape:** 7-Sided

Date	Mintage	F12	VF20	XF40	MS60	MS63
2007	Est. 30000	PF63 35.00	PF65 40.00			

KM# 28 5 POUNDS
28.28 g., 0.925 Silver 0.8356 oz. ASW, 38.61 mm. **Ruler:** Elizabeth II **Obv:** Head with crown right **Rev:** Hawker Hurricane, emblem in color

Date	Mintage	F12	VF20	XF40	MS60	MS63
2008	20,000	PF63 47.00	PF65 55.00			

KM# 29 5 POUNDS
28.28 g., 0.925 Silver 0.8356 oz. ASW, 38.61 mm. **Ruler:** Elizabeth II **Obv:** Head with crown right **Rev:** Sir Douglas Bader

Date	Mintage	F12	VF20	XF40	MS60	MS63
2008	20,000	PF63 47.00	PF65 55.00			

KM# 30 5 POUNDS
28.28 g., 0.925 Silver 0.8356 oz. ASW, 38.61 mm. **Ruler:** Elizabeth II **Obv:** Head with crown right **Rev:** Spitfire, emblem in color

Date	Mintage	F12	VF20	XF40	MS60	MS63
2008	20,000	PF63 47.00	PF65 55.00			

KM# 31 5 POUNDS
28.28 g., 0.925 Silver 0.8356 oz. ASW, 38.61 mm. **Ruler:** Elizabeth II **Obv:** Head with crown right **Rev:** Johnnie Johnson, emblem in color

Date	Mintage	F12	VF20	XF40	MS60	MS63
2008	20,000	PF63 47.00	PF65 55.00			

KM# 32 5 POUNDS
28.28 g., 0.925 Silver 0.8356 oz. ASW, 38.61 mm. **Ruler:** Elizabeth II **Obv:** Head with crown right **Rev:** Mosquito, emblem in color

Date	Mintage	F12	VF20	XF40	MS60	MS63
2008	20,000	PF63 47.00	PF65 55.00			

KM# 33 5 POUNDS
28.28 g., 0.925 Silver 0.8356 oz. ASW, 38.61 mm. **Ruler:** Elizabeth II **Obv:** Head with crown right **Rev:** John Braham, emblem in color

Date	Mintage	F12	VF20	XF40	MS60	MS63
2008	20,000	PF63 47.00	PF65 55.00			

KM# 34 5 POUNDS
28.28 g., 0.925 Silver 0.8356 oz. ASW, 38.61 mm. **Ruler:** Elizabeth II **Obv:** Head with crown right **Rev:** Bomber Avro 698 Vulcan, emblem in color

Date	Mintage	F12	VF20	XF40	MS60	MS63
2008	20,000	PF63 47.00	PF65 55.00			

KM# 35 5 POUNDS
28.28 g., 0.925 Silver 0.8356 oz. ASW, 38.61 mm. **Ruler:** Elizabeth II **Obv:** Head with crown right **Rev:** Leonard Cheshire, emblem in color

Date	Mintage	F12	VF20	XF40	MS60	MS63
2008	20,000	PF63 47.00	PF65 55.00			

KM# 36 5 POUNDS
28.28 g., 0.925 Silver 0.8356 oz. ASW, 38.61 mm. **Ruler:** Elizabeth II **Obv:** Head with crown right **Rev:** Lancaster, emblem in color

Date	Mintage	F12	VF20	XF40	MS60	MS63
2008	20,000	PF63 47.00	PF65 55.00			

KM# 37 5 POUNDS
28.28 g., 0.925 Silver 0.8356 oz. ASW, 38.61 mm. **Ruler:** Elizabeth II **Obv:** Head with crown right **Rev:** Guy Penrose Gibson, emblem in color

Date	Mintage	F12	VF20	XF40	MS60	MS63
2008	20,000	PF63 47.00	PF65 55.00			

KM# 38 5 POUNDS
28.28 g., 0.925 Silver 0.8356 oz. ASW, 38.61 mm. **Ruler:** Elizabeth II **Obv:** Head with crown right **Rev:** Harrier, emblem in color

Date	Mintage	F12	VF20	XF40	MS60	MS63
2008	20,000	PF63 47.00	PF65 55.00			

KM# 39 5 POUNDS
28.28 g., 0.925 Silver 0.8356 oz. ASW, 38.61 mm. **Ruler:** Elizabeth II **Obv:** Head with crown right **Rev:** David Lord, emblem in color

Date	Mintage	F12	VF20	XF40	MS60	MS63
2008	20,000	PF63 47.00	PF65 55.00			

KM# 40 5 POUNDS
28.28 g., 0.925 Silver 0.8356 oz. ASW, 38.61 mm. **Ruler:** Elizabeth II **Obv:** Head with crown right **Rev:** The Gnat, emblem in color

Date	Mintage	F12	VF20	XF40	MS60	MS63
2008	20,000	PF63 47.00	PF65 55.00			

KM# 41 5 POUNDS
28.28 g., 0.925 Silver 0.8356 oz. ASW, 38.61 mm. **Ruler:** Elizabeth II **Obv:** Head with crown right **Rev:** Ray Hanna, emblem in color

Date	Mintage	F12	VF20	XF40	MS60	MS63
2008	20,000	PF63 47.00	PF65 55.00			

KM# 42 5 POUNDS
28.28 g., 0.925 Silver 0.8356 oz. ASW, 38.61 mm. **Ruler:** Elizabeth II **Obv:** Head with crown right **Rev:** SESA, emblem in color

Date	Mintage	F12	VF20	XF40	MS60	MS63
2008	20,000	PF63 47.00	PF65 55.00			

KM# 43 5 POUNDS
28.28 g., 0.925 Silver 0.8356 oz. ASW, 38.61 mm. **Ruler:** Elizabeth II **Obv:** Head with crown right **Rev:** Mick Mannock, emblem in color

Date	Mintage	F12	VF20	XF40	MS60	MS63
2008	—	PF63 47.00	PF65 55.00			

KM# 44 5 POUNDS
28.28 g., 0.925 Silver 0.8356 oz. ASW, 38.61 mm. **Ruler:** Elizabeth II **Obv:** Head with crown right **Rev:** Typhoon, emblem in color

Date	Mintage	F12	VF20	XF40	MS60	MS63
2008	20,000	PF63 47.00	PF65 55.00			

KM# 45 5 POUNDS
28.28 g., 0.925 Silver 0.8356 oz. ASW, 38.61 mm. **Ruler:** Elizabeth II **Obv:** Head with crown right **Rev:** Sir Hugh Trenchard, emblem in color

Date	Mintage	F12	VF20	XF40	MS60	MS63
2008	20,000	PF63 47.00	PF65 55.00			

KM# 59 5 POUNDS
28.28 g., 0.925 Silver 0.8356 oz. ASW, 38.61 mm. **Ruler:** Elizabeth II **Obv:** Head with tiara right **Rev:** Flags of Commonwealth nations on globe

Date	Mintage	F12	VF20	XF40	MS60	MS63
2012	—	PF63 45.00	PF65 55.00			

KM# 46 25 POUNDS
7.98 g., 0.9167 Gold 0.2337 oz. AGW, 22 mm. **Ruler:** Elizabeth II **Obv:** Head with crown right **Rev:** Hurricane

Date	Mintage	F12	VF20	XF40	MS60	MS63
2008	500	PF65 500				

KM# 47 25 POUNDS
7.98 g., 0.9167 Gold 0.2337 oz. AGW, 22 mm. **Ruler:** Elizabeth II **Obv:** Head with crown right **Rev:** Spitfire

Date	Mintage	F12	VF20	XF40	MS60	MS63
2008	500	PF65 500				

KM# 48 25 POUNDS
7.98 g., 0.9167 Gold 0.2337 oz. AGW, 22 mm. **Ruler:** Elizabeth II **Obv:** Head with crown right **Rev:** Mosquito

Date	Mintage	F12	VF20	XF40	MS60	MS63
2008	500	PF65 500				

KM# 49 25 POUNDS
7.98 g., 0.9167 Gold 0.2337 oz. AGW, 22 mm. **Ruler:** Elizabeth II **Obv:** Head with crown right **Rev:** Bomber Avro 698 Vulcan

Date	Mintage	F12	VF20	XF40	MS60	MS63
2008	500	PF65 500				

KM# 50 25 POUNDS
7.98 g., 0.9167 Gold 0.2337 oz. AGW, 22 mm. **Ruler:** Elizabeth II **Obv:** Head with crown right **Rev:** Lancaster

Date	Mintage	F12	VF20	XF40	MS60	MS63
2008	500	PF65 500				

KM# 51 25 POUNDS
7.98 g., 0.9167 Gold 0.2337 oz. AGW, 22 mm. **Ruler:** Elizabeth II **Obv:** Head with crown right **Rev:** Harrier

Date	Mintage	F12	VF20	XF40	MS60	MS63
2008	500	PF65 500				

KM# 52 25 POUNDS
7.98 g., 0.9167 Gold 0.2337 oz. AGW, 22 mm. **Ruler:** Elizabeth II **Obv:** Head with crown right **Rev:** The Gnat

Date	Mintage	F12	VF20	XF40	MS60	MS63
2008	500	PF65 500				

KM# 53 25 POUNDS
7.98 g., 0.9167 Gold 0.2337 oz. AGW, 22 mm. **Ruler:** Elizabeth II **Obv:** Head with crown right **Rev:** SESA

Date	Mintage	F12	VF20	XF40	MS60	MS63
2008	500	PF65 500				

KM# 54 25 POUNDS
7.98 g., 0.9167 Gold 0.2337 oz. AGW, 22 mm. **Ruler:** Elizabeth II **Obv:** Head with crown right **Rev:** Typhoon

Date	Mintage	F12	VF20	XF40	MS60	MS63
2008	500	PF65 500				

SAMOA

The Independent State of Samoa (formerly Western Samoa), located in the Pacific Ocean 1,600 miles (2,574 km.) northeast of New Zealand, has an area of 1,097 sq. mi. (2,860 sq. km.) and a population of *182,000. Capital: Apia. The economy is based on agriculture, fishing and tourism. Copra, cocoa and bananas are exported.

Samoa is a member of the Commonwealth of Nations. The Chief Executive is Chief of State. The prime minister is the Head of Government. The present Head of State, Malietoa Tanumafili II, holds his position for life. The Legislative Assembly will elect future Heads of State for 5-year terms.

Samoa, which had used New Zealand coinage, converted to a decimal coinage in 1967.

RULER
Malietoa Tanumafili II, 1962-2007
Tuiatua Tupua Tamasese Efi, 2007-

MONETARY SYSTEM
100 Sene = 1 Tala

CONSTITUTIONAL MONARCHY
Commonwealth of Nations

STANDARD COINAGE

KM# 131 5 SENE
2.84 g., Copper-Nickel, 19.5 mm. **Obv:** Head left **Rev:** Pineapple and value **Edge:** Reeded **Note:** Western" dropped from country name

Date	Mintage	F12	VF20	XF40	MS60	MS63
2002	—	—	—	0.30	0.50	0.75
2006	—	—	—	0.30	0.50	0.75
2010	—	—	—	0.30	0.50	0.75

KM# 167 5 SENE
Nickel Plated Steel

Date	Mintage	F12	VF20	XF40	MS60	MS63
2010	—	—	—		0.50	0.75

KM# 132 10 SENE
5.65 g., Copper-Nickel, 23.6 mm. **Obv:** Head left **Rev:** Taro leaves and value **Edge:** Reeded **Note:** Western" dropped from country name

Date	Mintage	F12	VF20	XF40	MS60	MS63
2002	—	—	—	0.45	0.75	1.00
2006	—	—	—	0.45	0.75	1.00
2010	—	—	—	0.45	0.75	1.00

KM# 168 10 SENE
2.79 g., Nickel Plated Steel, 18.5 mm. **Obv:** President Efi bust 3/4 left **Rev:** Fautasi, boat race

Date	Mintage	F12	VF20	XF40	MS60	MS63
2010	—	—	—	—	0.75	1.00
2011	—	—	—	—	0.75	1.00

KM# 168a 10 SENE
3.52 g., 0.999 Silver 0.1123 oz. ASW, 19 mm. **Obv:** Efi portrait **Rev:** Fautasi

Date	Mintage	F12	VF20	XF40	MS60	MS63
2011	2,500	PF65 5.00				

KM# 133 20 SENE
11.40 g., Copper-Nickel, 28.45 mm. **Obv:** Head left **Rev:** Breadfruits and value **Edge:** Reeded **Note:** Western" dropped from country name

Date	Mintage	F12	VF20	XF40	MS60	MS63
2002	—	—	—	0.60	1.00	1.50
2006	—	—	—	0.60	1.00	1.50

KM# 169 20 SENE
3.64 g., Nickel Plated Steel, 22 mm. **Obv:** Efi portrait 3/4 left **Rev:** Teuila flower (Alpina Purpurata)

Date	Mintage	F12	VF20	XF40	MS60	MS63
2010	—	—	—	—	1.00	1.50
2011	—	—	—	—	1.00	1.50

KM# 169a 20 SENE
4.64 g., 0.999 Silver 0.1481 oz. ASW, 21 mm. **Obv:** Efi portrait **Rev:** Alpinia purpurata

Date	Mintage	F12	VF20	XF40	MS60	MS63
2011	2,500	PF65 7.00				

KM# 134 50 SENE
14.13 g., Copper-Nickel, 32.3 mm. **Obv:** Head left **Rev:** Banana tree and value **Edge:** Reeded **Note:** Western" dropped from country name

Date	Mintage	F12	VF20	XF40	MS60	MS63
2002	—	—	—	1.00	1.75	2.00
2006	—	—	—	1.00	1.75	2.00
2010	—	—	—	1.00	1.75	2.00

KM# 170 50 SENE
5.47 g., Nickel Plated Steel, 23.5 mm. **Obv:** Efi portrait 3/4 left **Rev:** Manumea bird (Didunculus strigiostris) right

Date	Mintage	F12	VF20	XF40	MS60	MS63
2010	—	—	—	—	1.75	2.00
2011	—	—	—	—	1.75	2.00

KM# 170a 50 SENE
6.95 g., 0.999 Silver 0.2218 oz. ASW, 24.2 mm. **Obv:** Efi portrait **Rev:** Columbidae right

Date	Mintage	F12	VF20	XF40	MS60	MS63
2011	2,500	PF65 9.50				

KM# 135 TALA
9.50 g., Brass, 30 mm. **Obv:** Head left **Rev:** National arms above value and banner flanked by sprigs **Edge:** Reeded **Note:** Western" dropped from country name

Date	Mintage	F12	VF20	XF40	MS60	MS63
2002	—	—	—	1.50	2.50	3.00
2006	—	—	—	1.50	2.50	3.00

KM# 180 TALA
0.80 g., 0.9999 Gold AGW, 11 mm. **Obv:** National arms **Rev:** Maya Calendar

Date	Mintage	F12	VF20	XF40	MS60	MS63
2008	10,000	PF65 75.00				

KM# 150 TALA
Goldine Plated Metal **Subject:** Thomas Mann **Obv:** Arms **Rev:** Bust facing

Date	Mintage	F12	VF20	XF40	MS60	MS63
2009	—	—	—	—		30.00

KM# 151 TALA
Goldine Plated Metal **Subject:** Hercules & Hydra

Date	Mintage	F12	VF20	XF40	MS60	MS63
2009	—	—	—	—		25.00

KM# 152 TALA
Goldine Plated Metal **Subject:** Alhambra

Date	Mintage	F12	VF20	XF40	MS60	MS63
2009	—	—	—	—		25.00

KM# 153 TALA
Goldine Plated Metal **Rev:** Golden horn

Date	Mintage	F12	VF20	XF40	MS60	MS63
2009	—	—	—	—		25.00

KM# 154 TALA
Goldine Plated Metal **Rev:** Sphinx

Date	Mintage	F12	VF20	XF40	MS60	MS63
2009	—					25.00

KM# 155 TALA
Goldine Plated Metal **Rev:** Kaiser Wilhelm II

Date	Mintage	F12	VF20	XF40	MS60	MS63
2009	—				—	25.00

KM# 156 TALA
Goldine Plated Metal **Rev:** Hagia Sophia

Date	Mintage	F12	VF20	XF40	MS60	MS63
2009	—				—	25.00

KM# 185 TALA
0.50 g., 0.999 Gold AGW, 11 mm. **Obv:** National arms **Rev:** Barbarossa bust

Date	Mintage	F12	VF20	XF40	MS60	MS63
2009	10,000	PF65 50.00				

KM# 186 TALA
0.50 g., 0.999 Gold AGW, 11 mm. **Obv:** National arms **Rev:** Marcus Tullius Cicero bust facing

Date	Mintage	F12	VF20	XF40	MS60	MS63
2009	10,000	PF65 50.00				

KM# 187 TALA
0.50 g., 0.999 Gold AGW, 11 mm. **Obv:** National arms **Rev:** Marie Curie and atom design

Date	Mintage	F12	VF20	XF40	MS60	MS63
2009	10,000	PF65 50.00				

KM# 188 TALA
26.03 g., Copper-Nickel, 38.61 mm. **Subject:** London Olympics, 2012 **Obv:** National arms **Rev:** White water kyacker

Date	Mintage	F12	VF20	XF40	MS60	MS63
2009	30,000	PF65 15.00				

KM# 189 TALA
0.50 g., 0.999 Gold AGW, 11 mm. **Obv:** National arms **Rev:** Pallas Athene bust right

Date	Mintage	F12	VF20	XF40	MS60	MS63
2009	10,000	PF65 50.00				

KM# 190 TALA
0.50 g., 0.999 Gold AGW, 11 mm. **Obv:** National arms **Rev:** Basilica of San Marco, Venice

Date	Mintage	F12	VF20	XF40	MS60	MS63
2009	10,000	PF65 50.00				

KM# 191 TALA
0.50 g., 0.9999 Gold AGW, 11 mm. **Obv:** National arms **Rev:** Thomas Mann bust facing

Date	Mintage	F12	VF20	XF40	MS60	MS63
2009	10,000	PF65 50.00				

KM# 171 TALA
6.00 g., Aluminum-Bronze, 21.5 mm. **Rev:** Kava bowl **Shape:** 7-sides

Date	Mintage	F12	VF20	XF40	MS60	MS63
2010	—				2.50	3.00
2011	—				2.50	3.00

KM# 174 TALA
0.50 g., 0.999 Gold AGW, 11 mm. **Obv:** National arms **Rev:** Samoan Flying Fox (bat) in flight

Date	Mintage	F12	VF20	XF40	MS60	MS63
2010	10,000	PF65 75.00				

KM# 214 TALA
0.50 g., 0.999 Gold AGW, 11 mm. **Obv:** National arms **Rev:** Nicolaus Copernicus bust at left, solar system

Date	Mintage	F12	VF20	XF40	MS60	MS63
2010	10,000	PF65 50.00				

KM# 215 TALA
0.50 g., 0.999 Gold AGW, 11 mm. **Subject:** German Railways, 175th Anniversary **Obv:** National arms **Rev:** Early steam locomotive and modern high speed train

Date	Mintage	F12	VF20	XF40	MS60	MS63
2010	5,000	PF65 50.00				

KM# 216 TALA
0.50 g., 0.999 Gold AGW, 11 mm. **Obv:** National arms **Rev:** Johannes Hevelius bust at right

Date	Mintage	F12	VF20	XF40	MS60	MS63
2010	10,000	PF65 50.00				

KM# 171a TALA
7.77 g., 0.999 Silver 0.248 oz. ASW, 21.5 mm. **Obv:** Efi portrait **Rev:** Kava

Date	Mintage	F12	VF20	XF40	MS60	MS63
2011	2,500	PF65 12.00				

KM# 219 TALA
0.50 g., 0.999 Gold AGW, 11 mm. **Obv:** National arms **Rev:** Pope John Paul II lat left holding cross croizer

Date	Mintage	F12	VF20	XF40	MS60	MS63
2011	10,000	PF65 50.00				

KM# 230 TALA
0.999 Silver **Subject:** 50th Anniversary of Independance **Obv:** Kings head 3/4 left **Rev:** Native sailing boat and sunset

Date	Mintage	F12	VF20	XF40	MS60	MS63
2012	Est. 1500	PF65 75.00				

KM# 234 TALA
0.50 g., 0.585 Gold AGW, 11 mm. **Subject:** Copernicus

Date	Mintage	F12	VF20	XF40	MS60	MS63
2013	Est. 5000	PF65 50.00				

KM# 235 TALA
0.50 g., 0.585 Gold AGW, 11 mm. **Subject:** John F. Kennedy

Date	Mintage	F12	VF20	XF40	MS60	MS63
2013	Est. 5000	PF65 50.00				

KM# 240 TALA
0.50 g., 0.585 Gold AGW, 11 mm. **Subject:** Moonlanding

Date	Mintage	F12	VF20	XF40	MS60	MS63
2013	Est. 5000	PF65 50.00				

KM# 178 2 TALA
8.00 g., Aluminum-Bronze, 25.6 mm. **Obv:** Efi portrait 3/4 right **Rev:** National arms **Shape:** Scalloped

Date	Mintage	F12	VF20	XF40	MS60	MS63
2011	—				5.00	8.00

KM# 193 2 TALA
Aluminum-Bronze, 25.6 mm. **Rev:** National arms **Shape:** Scalloped

Date	Mintage	F12	VF20	XF40	MS60	MS63
2011						

KM# 193a 2 TALA
10.37 g., 0.999 Silver 0.3309 oz. ASW, 25.6 mm. **Obv:** Efi portrait **Rev:** National arms

Date	Mintage	F12	VF20	XF40	MS60	MS63
2011	2,500	PF65 18.00				

KM# 249 2 TALA
6.80 g., 0.333 Silver 0.0723 oz. ASW, 30 mm. **Subject:** Porsche 911, 50th Anniversary

Date	Mintage	F12	VF20	XF40	MS60	MS63
2013	Est. 5000	PF65 40.00				

KM# 250 2 TALA
6.80 g., 0.333 Silver 0.0723 oz. ASW, 30 mm. **Subject:** Volkswagon Beetle, 75th Anniversary

Date	Mintage	F12	VF20	XF40	MS60	MS63
2013	Est. 5000	PF65 40.00				

KM# 165 5 TALA
28.28 g., 0.925 Silver 0.8356 oz. ASW, 38.61 mm. **Obv:** National Arms **Rev:** Steam Locomotive centennial

Date	Mintage	F12	VF20	XF40	MS60	MS63
2007	Est. 5000	PF63 65.00	PF65 75.00			

KM# 181 5 TALA
28.28 g., 0.925 Silver 0.8356 oz. ASW, 38.61 mm. **Obv:** National arms **Rev:** S.M.S. Bismark sailing right

Date	Mintage	F12	VF20	XF40	MS60	MS63
2008	5,000	PF65 75.00				

KM# 182 5 TALA
28.28 g., 0.925 Silver 0.8356 oz. ASW, 38.61 mm. **Subject:** Bejing Olympics, 2008 **Obv:** National arms **Rev:** Track runner

Date	Mintage	F12	VF20	XF40	MS60	MS63
2008	10,000	PF63 55.00	PF65 65.00			

KM# 166 5 TALA
31.11 g., 0.999 Silver 0.9926 oz. ASW, 38.6 mm. **Obv:** National arms **Rev:** John Paul II at right and as figure in flames

Date	Mintage	F12	VF20	XF40	MS60	MS63
2009	Est. 2000	PF63 75.00	PF65 85.00			

KM# 179 5 TALA
31.11 g., 0.999 Silver 0.9926 oz. ASW, 38.61 mm. **Subject:** First pacific class locomotive **Obv:** National arms **Rev:** Badische IVf locomotive

Date	Mintage	F12	VF20	XF40	MS60	MS63
2009	5,000	PF63 65.00	PF65 75.00			

KM# 192 5 TALA
28.28 g., 0.925 Silver 0.8356 oz. ASW, 38.61 mm. **Subject:** German Railways, 175th Anniversary **Obv:** National arms **Rev:** BR-23 locomotive and V-80 locomotive

Date	Mintage	F12	VF20	XF40	MS60	MS63
2009	5,000	PF63 65.00	PF65 75.00			

KM# 194 5 TALA
28.28 g., 0.925 Silver 0.8356 oz. ASW, 38.61 mm. **Subject:** London Olympics, 2012 **Obv:** National arms **Rev:** White water kyacker

Date	Mintage	F12	VF20	XF40	MS60	MS63
2009 Proof	10,000	—	—	—	—	75.00

KM# 217 5 TALA
28.28 g., 0.925 Silver 0.8356 oz. ASW, 38.61 mm. **Subject:** German Railways, 175th Anniversary **Obv:** National arms **Rev:** Montage of locomotive and stations

Date	Mintage	F12	VF20	XF40	MS60	MS63
2010	5,000	PF63 65.00	PF65 75.00			

KM# 218 5 TALA
28.28 g., 0.925 Silver 0.8356 oz. ASW, 38.61 mm. **Obv:** National arms **Rev:** Lilienthal Glider

Date	Mintage	F12	VF20	XF40	MS60	MS63
2010	Est. 5000	PF63 65.00	PF65 75.00			

KM# 226 5 TALA
20.00 g., 0.999 Silver 0.6382 oz. ASW, 38.61 mm. **Subject:** Martin Luther King Jr. - I Have a Dream Speech, 50th Anniversary **Obv:** National Arms **Rev:** MLK portrait with 24kt. gold,

Date	Mintage	F12	VF20	XF40	MS60	MS63
2013	Est. 2500	PF65 50.00				

KM# 227 5 TALA
20.00 g., 0.999 Silver 0.6382 oz. ASW, 38.61 mm. **Subject:** Martin Luther King's I Have a Dream Speech, 50th Anniversary **Obv:** National Arms **Rev:** MLK portrait at left - text at right

Date	Mintage	F12	VF20	XF40	MS60	MS63
2013	Est. 2500	PF65 50.00				

KM# 232 5 TALA
20.00 g., 0.925 Silver 0.591 oz. ASW, 38.61 mm. **Subject:** 2016 Olympics - Cycling

Date	Mintage	F12	VF20	XF40	MS60	MS63
2013	Est. 10000	PF65 50.00				

KM# 233 5 TALA
20.00 g., 0.925 Silver 0.591 oz. ASW, 38.61 mm. **Subject:** 2014 FIFA World Cup - Brazil

Date	Mintage	F12	VF20	XF40	MS60	MS63
2013	Est. 10000	PF65 50.00				

KM# 236 5 TALA
0.50 g., 0.999 Gold AGW, 11 mm. **Subject:** Magna Mater Austriae

Date	Mintage	F12	VF20	XF40	MS60	MS63
2013	Est. 5000	PF65 50.00				

KM# 237 5 TALA
0.50 g., 0.999 Gold AGW, 11 mm. **Subject:** Wilhelmina

Date	Mintage	F12	VF20	XF40	MS60	MS63
2013	Est. 5000	PF65 50.00				

KM# 238 5 TALA
0.50 g., 0.999 Gold AGW, 11 mm. **Subject:** Umberto I

Date	Mintage	F12	VF20	XF40	MS60	MS63
2013	Est. 5000	PF65 50.00				

KM# 241 5 TALA
0.50 g., 0.999 Gold AGW, 11 mm. **Subject:** John F. Kennedy

Date	Mintage	F12	VF20	XF40	MS60	MS63
2013	Est. 10000	PF65 50.00				

KM# 242 5 TALA
20.00 g., 0.925 Silver 0.591 oz. ASW, 38.61 mm. **Series:** John F. Kennedy

Date	Mintage	F12	VF20	XF40	MS60	MS63
2013	Est. 2500	PF65 50.00				

KM# 244 5 TALA
15.00 g., 0.925 Silver 0.4432 oz. ASW, 34 mm. **Subject:** Saxonia, 175th Anniversary

Date	Mintage	F12	VF20	XF40	MS60	MS63
2013	Est. 10000	PF65 75.00				

KM# 245 5 TALA
20.00 g., 0.925 Silver 0.591 oz. ASW **Subject:** 2014 FIFA World Cup - Brazil **Rev:** Soccer player and skyline of Rio

Date	Mintage	F12	VF20	XF40	MS60	MS63
2013	Est. 10000	PF65 50.00				

KM# 246 5 TALA
0.50 g., 0.999 Gold AGW, 11 mm. **Subject:** L'Hercule

Date	Mintage	F12	VF20	XF40	MS60	MS63
2013	Est. 5000	PF65 50.00				

KM# 248 5 TALA
20.00 g., 0.925 Silver 0.591 oz. ASW, 38.61 mm. **Subject:** Vogelfugline

Date	Mintage	F12	VF20	XF40	MS60	MS63
2013	Est. 3000	PF65 75.00				

KM# 137 10 TALA
31.10 g., 0.999 Silver 0.9925 oz. ASW, 40 mm. **Series:** Save the Whales **Obv:** National arms above value and banner flanked by sprigs **Obv. Legend:** SAMOA I SISIFO **Rev:** Bowhead Whale on mother-of-pearl insert **Edge:** Plain

Date	Mintage	F12	VF20	XF40	MS60	MS63
2002	2,000	PF65 95.00				

KM# 139 10 TALA
31.47 g., 0.925 Silver 0.9299 oz. ASW **Subject:** XXVIII Summer Olympics - Athens **Obv:** National arms **Obv. Legend:** SAMOA I SISIFO **Rev:** Swimming - two divers

Date	Mintage	F12	VF20	XF40	MS60	MS63
2003	—	PF63 50.00	PF65 60.00			

KM# 146 10 TALA
1.23 g., Gold AGW, 13.89 mm. **Obv:** National arms **Obv. Legend:** SAMOA SISIFO **Rev:** Bust of Fletcher Christian 3/4 left at left, sailing ship "H. M. S. Bounty" at right **Edge:** Reeded

Date	Mintage	F12	VF20	XF40	MS60	MS63
2003	—	PF65 90.00				

KM# 140 10 TALA
1.24 g., 0.999 Gold 0.0396 oz. AGW **Series:** World Statesmen **Subject:** Mahatma Gandhi **Obv:** National arms **Obv. Legend:** SAMOA I SISIFO

Date	Mintage	F12	VF20	XF40	MS60	MS63
2003	—	PF65 90.00				

KM# 141 10 TALA
1.24 g., 0.999 Gold 0.0396 oz. AGW **Series:** World Statesmen **Subject:** Konrad Adenauer **Obv:** National arms **Obv. Legend:** SAMOA I SISIFO

Date	Mintage	F12	VF20	XF40	MS60	MS63
2003	—	PF65 90.00				

KM# 159 10 TALA
1.24 g., 0.999 Gold 0.0396 oz. AGW, 13.92 mm. **Obv:** National arms **Rev:** Theodore Roosevelt

Date	Mintage	F12	VF20	XF40	MS60	MS63
2003	Est. 2000	PF65 90.00				

KM# 160 10 TALA
1.24 g., 0.999 Gold 0.0396 oz. AGW, 13.92 mm. **Obv:** National arms **Rev:** Winston Churchill

Date	Mintage	F12	VF20	XF40	MS60	MS63
2003	Est. 2000	PF65 90.00				

KM# 161 10 TALA
1.24 g., 0.999 Gold 0.0396 oz. AGW, 13.92 mm. **Obv:** National arms **Rev:** Charles de Gaulle

Date	Mintage	F12	VF20	XF40	MS60	MS63
2003	Est. 2000	PF65 90.00				

KM# 162 10 TALA
1.24 g., 0.999 Gold 0.0396 oz. AGW, 13.92 mm. **Obv:** National arms **Rev:** John F. Kennedy

Date	Mintage	F12	VF20	XF40	MS60	MS63
2003	Est. 2000	PF65 90.00				

KM# 143 10 TALA
28.58 g., Silver, 38.61 mm. **Obv:** National arms **Obv.**
Legend: SAMOA I SISIFO **Rev:** Sailing ship "La Récherche
Rev. Legend: JEAN FRANCOIS GALAUP - COMTE DE LA
PEROUSE **Edge:** Reeded

Date	Mintage	F12	VF20	XF40	MS60	MS63
2004	—	PF63 45.00	PF65 55.00			

KM# 142 10 TALA
1.24 g., 0.999 Gold 0.0396 oz. AGW **Subject:** Death of Pope
John-Paul II **Obv:** National arms

Date	Mintage	F12	VF20	XF40	MS60	MS63
2005	15,000	—	—	—	75.00	
2005	3,300	PF65 90.00				

KM# 163 10 TALA
1.24 g., 0.999 Gold 0.0396 oz. AGW, 13.92 mm. **Obv:** National
arms **Rev:** 2006 FIFA World Cup Germany logo

Date	Mintage	F12	VF20	XF40	MS60	MS63
2005	Est. 25000	PF65 90.00				

KM# 164 10 TALA
1.24 g., 0.999 Gold 0.0396 oz. AGW, 13.92 mm. **Obv:** National
arms **Rev:** Pope Benedict XVI in robes and mitre giving blessing

Date	Mintage	F12	VF20	XF40	MS60	MS63
2006	—	PF65 90.00				

KM# 183 10 TALA
1.00 g., 0.9999 Gold 0.0319 oz. AGW, 13.92 mm. **Obv:** National
arms **Rev:** S.M.S. Bismark siling right

Date	Mintage	F12	VF20	XF40	MS60	MS63
2008	15,000	PF63 75.00	PF65 85.00			

KM# 184 10 TALA
1.24 g., 0.9999 Gold 0.0396 oz. AGW, 13.92 mm. **Obv:** National
arms **Rev:** Hans Christian Andersen bust right

Date	Mintage	F12	VF20	XF40	MS60	MS63
2008	10,000	PF65 100				

KM# 195 10 TALA
28.28 g., 0.999 Silver 0.9025 oz. ASW, 38.61 mm. **Subject:** 10
Commandments - 1st Commandment **Obv:** National arms **Rev:**
Two men worshiping a calf at an altar

Date	Mintage	F12	VF20	XF40	MS60	MS63
2009	5,000	PF63 65.00	PF65 75.00			

KM# 196 10 TALA
28.28 g., 0.925 Silver 0.8356 oz. ASW, 38.61 mm. **Subject:**
10 Commandments - 2nd Commandment **Obv:** National arms
Rev: Two men standing in the desert

Date	Mintage	F12	VF20	XF40	MS60	MS63
2009	5,000	PF63 65.00	PF65 75.00			

KM# 197 10 TALA
28.28 g., 0.925 Silver 0.8356 oz. ASW, 38.61 mm. **Subject:**
10 Commandments - 3rd Commandment **Obv:** National arms
Rev: Parents and child on a field

Date	Mintage	F12	VF20	XF40	MS60	MS63
2009	5,000	PF63 65.00	PF65 75.00			

KM# 198 10 TALA
28.28 g., 0.925 Silver 0.8356 oz. ASW, 38.61 mm. **Subject:**
10 Commandments - 4th Commandment **Obv:** National arms
Rev: Mother seated with child, father standing

Date	Mintage	F12	VF20	XF40	MS60	MS63
2009	5,000	PF63 65.00	PF65 75.00			

KM# 199 10 TALA
28.28 g., 0.925 Silver 0.8356 oz. ASW, 38.61 mm. **Subject:**
10 Commandments - 5th Commandment **Obv:** National arms
Rev: Man holding sword over kneeling man

Date	Mintage	F12	VF20	XF40	MS60	MS63
2009	5,000	PF63 65.00	PF65 75.00			

KM# 205 10 TALA
28.28 g., 0.925 Silver 0.8356 oz. ASW, 38.61 mm. **Subject:**
Charles Darwin, 200th Anniversary of Birth **Obv:** National arms
Rev: Galapagos Island Finches

Date	Mintage	F12	VF20	XF40	MS60	MS63
2009	2,009	PF63 65.00	PF65 75.00			

KM# 206 10 TALA
28.28 g., 0.925 Silver 0.8356 oz. ASW, 38.61 mm. **Subject:**
Charles Darwin, 200th Anniversary of Birth **Obv:** National arms
Rev: Galapagos Iguana

Date	Mintage	F12	VF20	XF40	MS60	MS63
2009	2,009	PF63 65.00	PF65 75.00			

KM# 207 10 TALA
28.28 g., 0.925 Silver 0.8356 oz. ASW, 38.61 mm. **Subject:**
Charles Darwin, 200th Anniversary of Birth **Obv:** National arms
Rev: The H.M.R.S. Beagle and voyage map

Date	Mintage	F12	VF20	XF40	MS60	MS63
2009	2,009	PF63 65.00	PF65 75.00			

KM# 208 10 TALA
28.28 g., 0.925 Silver 0.8356 oz. ASW, 38.61 mm. **Subject:**
Charles Darwin, 200th Anniversary of Birth **Obv:** National arms
Rev: DNA-Double helix and a chromosome

Date	Mintage	F12	VF20	XF40	MS60	MS63
2009	2,009	PF63 65.00	PF65 75.00			

KM# 209 10 TALA
28.28 g., 0.925 Silver 0.8356 oz. ASW, 38.61 mm. **Subject:**
Charles Darwin, 200th Anniversary of Birth **Obv:** National arms
Rev: Galapagos Oldest Tortoise

Date	Mintage	F12	VF20	XF40	MS60	MS63
2009	2,009	PF63 65.00	PF65 75.00			

KM# 210 10 TALA
28.28 g., 0.925 Silver 0.8356 oz. ASW, 38.61 mm. **Subject:** Charles Darwin, 200th Anniversary of Birth **Obv:** National arms **Rev:** Darwin portrait at left

Date	Mintage	F12	VF20	XF40	MS60	MS63
2009	2,009	PF63 65.00	PF65 75.00			

KM# 211 10 TALA
1.24 g., 0.9999 Gold 0.0396 oz. AGW, 13.92 mm. **Obv:** National arms **Rev:** Nicolaus Copernicus bust and solar system

Date	Mintage	F12	VF20	XF40	MS60	MS63
2009	10,000	PF65 100				

KM# 212 10 TALA
1.24 g., 0.9999 Gold 0.0396 oz. AGW, 13.92 mm. **Obv:** National arms **Rev:** Johannes Hevelius bust at right

Date	Mintage	F12	VF20	XF40	MS60	MS63
2009	5,000	PF65 100				

KM# 213 10 TALA
1.24 g., 0.999 Gold 0.0396 oz. AGW, 13.92 mm. **Obv:** National arms **Rev:** Marie Curie and atom symbol

Date	Mintage	F12	VF20	XF40	MS60	MS63
2009	5,000	PF65 100				

KM# 172 10 TALA
20.00 g., 0.925 Silver 0.591 oz. ASW, 38.61 mm. **Obv:** National arms **Rev:** Sailing ship Preussen

Date	Mintage	F12	VF20	XF40	MS60	MS63
2010	2,500	PF63 65.00	PF65 75.00			

KM# 173 10 TALA
25.00 g., 0.925 Silver 0.7387 oz. ASW, 38.61 mm. **Obv:** National arms **Rev:** Samoan Flying Fox (bat) hanging, with colored eyes

Date	Mintage	F12	VF20	XF40	MS60	MS63
2010	2,500	PF63 65.00	PF65 75.00			

KM# 200 10 TALA
28.28 g., 0.999 Silver 0.9025 oz. ASW, 38.61 mm. **Subject:** 10 Commandments - 6th Commandment **Obv:** National arms **Rev:** Man seated near half-naked reclining female

Date	Mintage	F12	VF20	XF40	MS60	MS63
2010	5,000	PF63 65.00	PF65 75.00			

KM# 201 10 TALA
28.28 g., 0.925 Silver 0.8356 oz. ASW, 38.61 mm. **Subject:** 10 Commandments - 7th Commandment **Obv:** National arms **Rev:** Three men walking

Date	Mintage	F12	VF20	XF40	MS60	MS63
2010	5,000	PF63 65.00	PF65 75.00			

KM# 202 10 TALA
28.28 g., 0.999 Silver 0.9025 oz. ASW, 38.61 mm. **Subject:** 10 Commandments - 8th Commandment **Obv:** National arms **Rev:** One man talking to another

Date	Mintage	F12	VF20	XF40	MS60	MS63
2010	5,000	PF63 65.00	PF65 75.00			

KM# 203 10 TALA
28.28 g., 0.999 Silver 0.9025 oz. ASW, 38.61 mm. **Subject:** 10 Commandment - 9th Commandment **Obv:** National arms **Rev:** Female entering river to bathe, male watching from behind tree

Date	Mintage	F12	VF20	XF40	MS60	MS63
2010	5,000	PF63 65.00	PF65 75.00			

KM# 204 10 TALA
28.28 g., 0.925 Silver 0.8356 oz. ASW, 38.61 mm. **Subject:** 10 Commandments - 10th Commandment **Obv:** National arms **Rev:** Temple building and man standing at right

Date	Mintage	F12	VF20	XF40	MS60	MS63
2010	5,000	PF63 65.00	PF65 75.00			

KM# 225 10 TALA
28.28 g., 0.999 Silver 0.9025 oz. ASW, 38.61 mm. **Subject:** Mother Teresa, 10th Anniversary of Beatification **Obv:** National arms **Rev:** Mother Teresa holding globe and rosary **Edge Lettering:** BEATI MISERICORDES

Date	Mintage	F12	VF20	XF40	MS60	MS63
2013	Est. 2003	PF65 60.00				

KM# 228 10 TALA
28.80 g., 0.999 Silver 0.9191 oz. ASW, 38.61 mm. **Subject:** JFK's "Ich Bin Ein Berliner" speech, 50th Anniversary **Obv:** National arms **Rev:** JFK portrait in pop art colors

Date	Mintage	F12	VF20	XF40	MS60	MS63
2013	—	PF65 50.00				

KM# 229 10 TALA
28.80 g., 0.999 Silver 0.9191 oz. ASW, 38.61 mm. **Subject:** JFK's "Ich Bein Ein Berliner" speech, 50th Anniversary **Obv:** National arms **Rev:** JFK portrait, speech in micro text

Date	Mintage	F12	VF20	XF40	MS60	MS63
2013	Est. 2500	PF65 50.00				

KM# 243 10 TALA
31.11 g., 0.999 Silver 0.9926 oz. ASW, 38.61 mm. **Subject:** Neil Armstrong

Date	Mintage	F12	VF20	XF40	MS60	MS63
2013	Est. 999	PF65 75.00				

KM# 220 100 TALA
5.00 g., 0.9999 Gold 0.1597 oz. AGW, 23.3x14 mm. **Obv:** Value and national arms **Rev:** Battleship Bismarck **Shape:** Rectangle

Date	Mintage	F12	VF20	XF40	MS60	MS63
2011	1,000	PF65 350				

KM# 221 100 TALA
5.00 g., 0.999 Gold 0.1596 oz. AGW, 23.3x14 mm. **Obv:** Value and national arms **Rev:** Battleship H.M.S. Hood **Shape:** Rectangle

Date	Mintage	F12	VF20	XF40	MS60	MS63
2011	1,000	PF65 350				

KM# 222 100 TALA
5.00 g., 0.999 Gold 0.1596 oz. AGW, 23.3x14 mm. **Obv:** Value and national arms **Rev:** Battleship U.S.S. Missouri **Shape:** Rectangle

Date	Mintage	F12	VF20	XF40	MS60	MS63
2011	1,000	PF65 350				

KM# 223 100 TALA
5.00 g., 0.9999 Gold 0.1597 oz. AGW, 23.3x14 mm. **Obv:** Value and national arms **Rev:** Battleship S.M.S. Friedrich der Grosse **Shape:** Rectangle

Date	Mintage	F12	VF20	XF40	MS60	MS63
2011	1,000	PF65 350				

KM# 224 100 TALA
5.00 g., 0.9999 Gold 0.1597 oz. AGW, 23.3x14 mm. **Obv:** Value and national arms **Rev:** Battleship Yamato **Shape:** Rectangle

Date	Mintage	F12	VF20	XF40	MS60	MS63
2011	1,000	PF65 350				

SAN MARINO

The Republic of San Marino, the oldest and smallest republic in the world is located in north central Italy entirely surrounded by the Province of Emilia-Romagna. It has an area of 24 sq. mi. (60 sq. km.) and a population of *23,000. Capital: San Marino. The principal economic activities are farming, livestock raising, cheese making, tourism and light manufacturing. Building stone, lime, wheat, hides and baked goods are exported. The government derives most of its revenue from the sale of postage stamps for philatelic purposes.

San Marino has its own coinage, but Italian and Vatican City coins and currency are also in circulation.

MINT MARK
SR - Rome

MONETARY SYSTEM
100 Centesimi = 1 Lira

REPUBLIC
STANDARD COINAGE

KM# 424 10 LIRE
1.60 g., Aluminum, 23.3 mm. **Obv:** Three towers within circle **Rev:** Wheat stalks and value **Edge:** Plain

Date	Mintage	F12	VF20	XF40	MS60	MS63
2001R	—				0.35	0.50

KM# 425 20 LIRE
3.60 g., Aluminum-Bronze, 21.8 mm. **Obv:** Three towers within circle **Rev:** Two dolphins and value **Edge:** Plain

Date	Mintage	F12	VF20	XF40	MS60	MS63
2001R	—				1.00	2.00

KM# 426 50 LIRE
4.50 g., Copper-Nickel, 19 mm. **Obv:** Three towers within circle **Rev:** Tree and value **Edge:** Plain

Date	Mintage	F12	VF20	XF40	MS60	MS63
2001R	—				0.85	1.50

KM# 427 100 LIRE
4.50 g., Copper-Nickel, 22 mm. **Obv:** Three towers within

circle **Rev:** Grasping hands and value **Edge:** Plain and reeded sections

Date	Mintage	F12	VF20	XF40	MS60	MS63
2001R	—				1.25	2.00

KM# 428 200 LIRE
5.00 g., Aluminum-Bronze, 24 mm. **Obv:** Three towers within circle **Rev:** Broken chain, leaves, vines and value **Edge:** Reeded

Date	Mintage	F12	VF20	XF40	MS60	MS63
2001R	—				1.50	2.50

KM# 429 500 LIRE
Bi-Metallic, 25.8 mm. **Obv:** Three towers within circle **Rev:** Three different plant stalks and value **Edge:** Segmented reeding **Note:** 6.8 grams.

Date	Mintage	F12	VF20	XF40	MS60	MS63
2001R	—				3.00	3.50

KM# 430 1000 LIRE
8.80 g., Bi-Metallic, 27 mm. **Obv:** Three towers within circle **Rev:** Value within circle of birds **Edge:** Segmented reeding

Date	Mintage	F12	VF20	XF40	MS60	MS63
2001R	—				7.50	10.00

KM# 431 5000 LIRE
18.00 g., 0.835 Silver 0.4801 oz. ASW, 32 mm. **Obv:** Three towers within circle **Rev:** Dove on laurel branch above value **Edge:** Reeded and plain sections

Date	Mintage	F12	VF20	XF40	MS60	MS63
2001R	—				22.50	27.50

KM# 436 5000 LIRE
18.00 g., 0.835 Silver 0.4801 oz. ASW, 32 mm. **Subject:** Last Lire Coinage **Obv:** Crowned arms within sprigs **Rev:** Feather above six old coin designs with value below, all within beaded border **Edge:** Lettered

Date	Mintage	F12	VF20	XF40	MS60	MS63
2001R	20,000	PF65 25.00				

KM# 437 10000 LIRE
22.00 g., 0.835 Silver 0.5868 oz. ASW, 34 mm. **Subject:** Last Lire Coinage **Obv:** Crowned arms within sprigs **Rev:** Feather above six old coin designs with value below, all within star border **Edge:** Reeded and plain sections

Date	Mintage	F12	VF20	XF40	MS60	MS63
2001R	20,000	PF65 42.00				

KM# 432 10000 LIRE
22.00 g., 0.835 Silver 0.5868 oz. ASW, 34 mm. **Subject:** Ferrari **Obv:** Crowned arms within sprigs **Rev:** Race car with "FERRARI" background **Edge:** Reeded and plain sections

Date	Mintage	F12	VF20	XF40	MS60	MS63
2001R	20,000	PF65 45.00				

KM# 438 10000 LIRE
22.00 g., 0.835 Silver 0.5868 oz. ASW, 34 mm. **Subject:** 2nd International Chambers of Commerce Convention **Obv:** Crowned arms within sprigs **Rev:** Mercury running by a computer **Edge:** Segmented reeding

Date	Mintage	F12	VF20	XF40	MS60	MS63
2001R	19,987	PF65 42.00				

KM# 433 1/2 SCUDO
1.61 g., 0.900 Gold 0.0463 oz. AGW, 13.8 mm. **Subject:** Cavaliere **Obv:** Crowned arms within sprigs **Rev:** Horse and rider **Edge:** Reeded

Date	Mintage	F12	VF20	XF40	MS60	MS63
2001R	4,500	PF63 80.00	PF65 100			

KM# 434 SCUDO
3.22 g., 0.900 Gold 0.0926 oz. AGW, 16 mm. **Subject:** Tiziano **Obv:** Crowned arms within sprigs **Rev:** Bearded bust left **Edge:** Reeded

Date	Mintage	F12	VF20	XF40	MS60	MS63
2001R	4,500	PF63 170	PF65 190			

KM# 435 2 SCUDI
6.44 g., 0.900 Gold 0.1851 oz. AGW, 21 mm. **Subject:** Flora **Obv:** Crowned arms within sprigs **Rev:** Bust 1/4 left and value **Edge:** Reeded

Date	Mintage	F12	VF20	XF40	MS60	MS63
2001R	4,500	PF63 350	PF65 375			

KM# 457 2 SCUDI
6.45 g., 0.900 Gold 0.1855 oz. AGW, 21 mm. **Obv:** Crowned arms within sprigs **Rev:** Madonna and Child **Edge:** Reeded

Date	Mintage	F12	VF20	XF40	MS60	MS63
2002R	2,950	PF63 350	PF65 375			

KM# 459 2 SCUDI
6.45 g., 0.900 Gold 0.1855 oz. AGW, 21 mm. **Obv:** Crowned arms within sprigs **Rev:** Nostradamus above value **Edge:** Reeded

Date	Mintage	F12	VF20	XF40	MS60	MS63
2003R	7,500	PF63 350		PF65 375		

KM# 464 2 SCUDI
6.45 g., 0.900 Gold 0.1855 oz. AGW, 21 mm. **Subject:** The Domagnano Treasure **Obv:** Crowned arms within sprigs **Rev:** Gothic Eagle Brooch, 5 Mark coin of 1952 **Edge:** Reeded

Date	Mintage	F12	VF20	XF40	MS60	MS63
2004R	6,494	PF63 350		PF65 375		

KM# 345 2 SCUDI
6.45 g., 0.900 Gold 0.1854 oz. AGW, 21 mm. **Subject:** Rotary International, 100th Anniversary **Rev:** Rotary emblem

Date	Mintage	F12	VF20	XF40	MS60	MS63
2005R	4,249	PF63 400		PF65 425		

KM# 346 2 SCUDI
6.45 g., 0.900 Gold 0.1854 oz. AGW, 21 mm. **Subject:** General meeting of the heads of families, 100th Anniversary **Rev:** Three females with the fruits of democracy

Date	Mintage	F12	VF20	XF40	MS60	MS63
2006R	2,821	PF63 400		PF65 425		

KM# 347 2 SCUDI
6.45 g., 0.900 Gold 0.1854 oz. AGW, 21 mm. **Subject:** Diplomatic relations with Japan, 50th Anniversary **Rev:** Shrine of Jinmu Tenno (1889) in Kashihara

Date	Mintage	F12	VF20	XF40	MS60	MS63
2007R	7,536	PF63 400		PF65 425		

KM# 493 2 SCUDI
6.41 g., 0.900 Gold 0.1843 oz. AGW, 21 mm. **Subject:** Pompeo Batoni, 300th Anniversary of Brith **Obv:** Arms **Rev:** Batoni's statue group "San Marino Risolleva la Republica"

Date	Mintage	F12	VF20	XF40	MS60	MS63
2008R	2,100	PF63 350		PF65 375		

KM# 450 2 SCUDI
6.45 g., 0.900 Gold 0.1854 oz. AGW, 21 mm. **Subject:** Art treasures of San Marino **Rev:** Ceres Bronze Statue by Albert E. Carrier Belleuse

Date	Mintage	F12	VF20	XF40	MS60	MS63
2009R	2,100	PF63 400		PF65 425		

KM# 451 2 SCUDI
6.45 g., 0.900 Gold 0.1854 oz. AGW, 21 mm. **Subject:** Art treasures of San Marino **Rev:** Justice with scales by Bernardino Mei

Date	Mintage	F12	VF20	XF40	MS60	MS63
2010R	2,100	PF63 400		PF65 425		

KM# 517 2 SCUDI
6.45 g., 0.900 Gold 0.1854 oz. AGW, 21 mm. **Subject:** Christmas **Rev:** Nativity scene

Date	Mintage	F12	VF20	XF40	MS60	MS63
2011R	1,600	PF63 450		PF65 475		

KM# 439 5 SCUDI
16.97 g., 0.9166 Gold 0.4967 oz. AGW, 28 mm. **Subject:** San Marino's World Bank Membership **Obv:** Crowned arms within sprigs **Rev:** Orchid and bee within globe **Edge:** Reeded

Date	Mintage	F12	VF20	XF40	MS60	MS63
2001R	4,000	PF63 900		PF65 950		

KM# 348 5 SCUDI
16.13 g., 0.900 Gold 0.4637 oz. AGW, 28 mm. **Subject:** Diplomatic relations with Japan, 50th Anniversary **Rev:** Jinmu Tenno

Date	Mintage	F12	VF20	XF40	MS60	MS63
2007R	7,130	PF63 850		PF65 900		

EURO COINAGE

KM# 440 EURO CENT
2.27 g., Copper Plated Steel, 16.2 mm. **Obv:** Il Montale **Rev:** Value and globe **Edge:** Plain

Date	Mintage	F12	VF20	XF40	MS60	MS63
2002R	125,000	—	—	—	—	40.00
2003R In sets only	70,000	—	—	—	—	42.00
2004R	1,500,000	—	—	—	—	20.00
2005R In sets only	70,000	—	—	—	—	20.00
2006R	2,730,000	—	—	—	8.00	12.00
2007R	—	—	—	—	8.00	12.00
2008R	—	—	—	—	8.00	12.00
2008R	13,000	PF65 10.00				
2009R	—	—	—	—	8.00	12.00
2009R	13,500	PF65 10.00				
2010R	—	—	—	—	8.00	12.00
2010R	8,600	PF65 10.00				
2011R	—	—	—	—	8.00	12.00
2011R	8,600	PF65 10.00				
2012R	—	—	—	—	8.00	12.00
2013R	—	—	—	—	8.00	12.00

KM# 441 2 EURO CENT
3.03 g., Copper Plated Steel, 18.7 mm. **Obv:** Stefano Gallietti, Liberty fighter **Rev:** Value and globe **Edge:** Grooved

Date	Mintage	F12	VF20	XF40	MS60	MS63
2002R	125,000	—	—	—	—	40.00
2003R In sets only	70,000	—	—	—	—	42.00
2004R	1,395,000	—	—	—	—	20.00
2005R In sets only	150,000	—	—	—	—	20.00
2006R	2,730,000	—	—	—	8.00	12.00
2007R	—	—	—	—	8.00	12.00
2008R	—	—	—	—	8.00	12.00
2008R	13,000	PF65 10.00				
2009R	—	—	—	—	8.00	12.00
2009R	13,500	PF65 10.00				
2010R	—	—	—	—	8.00	12.00
2010R	8,600	PF65 10.00				
2011R	—	—	—	—	8.00	12.00
2011R	8,600	PF65 10.00				
2012R	—	—	—	—	8.00	12.00
2013R	—	—	—	—	8.00	12.00

KM# 442 5 EURO CENT
3.86 g., Copper Plated Steel, 21.2 mm. **Obv:** Guaita" tower **Rev:** Value and globe **Edge:** Plain

Date	Mintage	F12	VF20	XF40	MS60	MS63
2002R	125,000	—	—	—	—	40.00
2003R In sets only	70,000	—	—	—	—	42.00
2004R	1,000,000	—	—	—	—	20.00
2005R In sets only	70,000	—	—	—	—	20.00
2006R	2,880,000	—	—	—	8.00	12.00
2007R	—	—	—	—	8.00	12.00
2008R	—	—	—	—	8.00	12.00
2008R	13,000	PF65 10.00				
2009R	—	—	—	—	8.00	12.00
2009R	13,500	PF65 10.00				
2010R	—	—	—	—	8.00	12.00
2010R	8,600	PF65 10.00				
2011R	—	—	—	—	8.00	12.00
2011R	8,600	PF65 10.00				
2012R	—	—	—	—	8.00	12.00
2013R	—	—	—	—	8.00	12.00

KM# 443 10 EURO CENT
4.07 g., Brass, 19.7 mm. **Obv:** Building Basilica del Santo Marinus **Rev:** Map and value **Edge:** Reeded

Date	Mintage	F12	VF20	XF40	MS60	MS63
2002R	125,000	—	—	—	—	40.00
2003R In sets only	70,000	—	—	—	—	42.00
2004R	180,000	—	—	—	—	22.00
2005R In sets only	70,000	—	—	—	—	22.00
2006R In sets only	65,000	—	—	—	—	20.00
2007R	—	—	—	—	—	18.00

KM# 482 10 EURO CENT
4.07 g., Brass, 19.7 mm. **Obv:** Basilica de Santo Marinus facade **Rev:** Relief maps of Western Europe, value and stars

Date	Mintage	F12	VF20	XF40	MS60	MS63
2008R	—	—	—	—	8.00	12.00
2008R	13,000	PF65 12.00				
2009R	—	—	—	—	8.00	12.00
2009R	13,500	PF65 12.00				
2010R	—	—	—	—	8.00	12.00
2010R	8,600	PF65 12.00				
2011R	—	—	—	—	8.00	12.00
2011R	8,600	PF65 12.00				
2012R	—	—	—	—	8.00	12.00
2013R	—	—	—	—	8.00	12.00

KM# 444 20 EURO CENT
5.73 g., Brass, 22.1 mm. **Obv:** St. Marinus from a portrait by van Guercino **Rev:** Map and value **Edge:** Notched

Date	Mintage	F12	VF20	XF40	MS60	MS63
2002R	267,400	—	—	—	18.00	20.00
2003R	430,000	—	—	—	15.00	18.00
2004R In sets only	70,000	—	—	—	15.00	18.00
2005R	310,000	—	—	—	15.00	18.00
2006R In sets only	70,000	—	—	—	15.00	18.00
2007R	—	—	—	—	14.00	16.00

KM# 483 20 EURO CENT
5.73 g., Brass **Obv:** Saint holding Monte Titano **Rev:** Relief map of Western Europe, value and stars

Date	Mintage	F12	VF20	XF40	MS60	MS63
2008R	—	—	—	—	8.00	12.00
2008R	13,000	PF65 15.00				
2009R	—	—	—	—	8.00	12.00
2009R	13,500	PF65 15.00				
2010R	—	—	—	—	8.00	12.00
2010R	8,600	PF65 15.00				
2011R	—	—	—	—	8.00	12.00
2011R	8,600	PF65 15.00				
2012R	—	—	—	—	8.00	12.00
2013R	—	—	—	—	8.00	12.00

KM# 445 50 EURO CENT
7.81 g., Brass, 24.2 mm. **Obv:** Fortress of San Marino **Rev:** Map and value **Edge:** Reeded

Date	Mintage	F12	VF20	XF40	MS60	MS63
2002R	230,400	—	—	—	20.00	22.50
2003R	415,000	—	—	—	17.50	20.00
2004R In sets only	70,000	—	—	—	17.50	20.00
2005R	179,000	—	—	—	17.50	20.00
2006R	343,880	—	—	—	15.00	18.00
2007R	—	—	—	—	14.00	16.00

KM# 484 50 EURO CENT
7.80 g., Brass, 24.2 mm. **Obv:** Buildings on hill top **Rev:** Relief map of Western Europe, value and stars

Date	Mintage	F12	VF20	XF40	MS60	MS63
2008R	—	—	—	—	10.00	12.00
2008R	13,000	PF65 13.00				
2009R	—	—	—	—	10.00	12.00
2009R	13,500	PF65 13.00				
2010R	—	—	—	—	10.00	12.00
2010R	8,600	PF65 13.00				
2011R	—	—	—	—	10.00	12.00
2011R	8,600	PF65 13.00				
2012R	36,000	—	—	—	10.00	12.00
2013R	—	—	—	—	10.00	12.00

KM# 446 EURO
7.50 g., Bi-Metallic, 23.25 mm. **Obv:** Crowned arms within sprigs and circle within star border **Rev:** Value and map **Edge:** Segmented reeding

Date	Mintage	F12	VF20	XF40	MS60	MS63
2002R	360,800	—	—	—	22.00	25.00
2003R In sets only	70,000	—	—	—	—	45.00
2004R	180,000	—	—	—	—	25.00
2005R In sets only	70,000	—	—	—	—	25.00
2006R In sets only	220,000	—	—	—	—	20.00
2007R	—	—	—	—	—	18.00

KM# 485 EURO
7.50 g., Bi-Metallic, 23.25 mm. **Obv:** Covered arms within wreath and stars **Rev:** Relief map of Western Europe, value and stars **Edge:** Segmented reeding

Date	Mintage	F12	VF20	XF40	MS60	MS63
2008R	—	—	—	—	12.00	15.00
2008R	13,000	PF65 15.00				
2009R	1,096,672	—	—	—	12.00	15.00
2009R	13,500	PF65 15.00				
2010R	996,134	—	—	—	12.00	15.00
2010R	8,600	PF65 15.00				
2011R	—	—	—	—	12.00	15.00
2011R	8,600	PF65 15.00				
2012R	10,000	—	—	—	12.00	15.00
2012R	—	PF65 15.00				
2013R	—	—	—	—	12.00	15.00

KM# 447 2 EURO
8.50 g., Bi-Metallic, 25.75 mm. **Obv:** Government building **Rev:** Value and map **Edge:** Reeded with 2's and stars

Date	Mintage	F12	VF20	XF40	MS60	MS63
2002R	255,760	—	—	—	—	25.00	28.00
2003R In sets only	70,000	—	—	—	—	45.00
2004R In sets only	70,000	—	—	—	—	28.00
2005R In sets only	210,000	—	—	—	—	28.00
2006R In sets only	190,000	—	—	—	—	22.00
2007R	—	—	—	—	—	20.00

KM# 467 2 EURO
8.50 g., Bi-Metallic, 25.75 mm. **Obv:** Crowned arms within sprigs **Rev:** Bartolomeo Borghesi **Edge:** Alternating stars and 2's

Date	Mintage	F12	VF20	XF40	MS60	MS63
2004R	110,000	—	—	—	135	150

KM# 469 2 EURO
8.50 g., Bi-Metallic, 25.75 mm. **Obv:** Galileo Galilei at telescope

Date	Mintage	F12	VF20	XF40	MS60	MS63
2005R	130,000	—	—	—	135	150

KM# 478 2 EURO
8.50 g., Bi-Metallic, 25.75 mm. **Subject:** Christopher Columbus, 500th Anniversary of Death **Obv:** Head of Columbus within border of stars **Rev:** Map and value

Date	Mintage	F12	VF20	XF40	MS60	MS63
2006R	120,000	—	—	—	100	125

KM# 481 2 EURO
8.50 g., Bi-Metallic, 25.75 mm. **Subject:** Giuseppe Garibaldi, 200th Anniversary of Birth **Obv:** Half length bust facing **Rev:** Relief map of Western Europe, value and stars

Date	Mintage	F12	VF20	XF40	MS60	MS63
2007R	130,000	—	—	—	60.00	75.00

KM# 486 2 EURO
8.50 g., Bi-Metallic, 25.75 mm. **Obv:** Palace **Rev:** Relief map of Western Europe, value and stars

Date	Mintage	F12	VF20	XF40	MS60	MS63
2008R	—	—	—	—	24.00	28.00
2008R	13,000	PF65 20.00				
2009R	—	—	—	—	24.00	28.00
2009R	13,500	PF65 20.00				
2010R	—	—	—	—	24.00	28.00
2010R	8,600	PF65 20.00				
2011R	631,831	—	—	—	24.00	28.00
2011R	8,600	PF65 20.00				
2012R	627,249	—	—	—	24.00	28.00
2013R	—	—	—	—	24.00	28.00

KM# 487 2 EURO
8.50 g., Bi-Metallic, 25.75 mm. **Subject:** European Year of Intercultural Dialogue **Obv:** Five figures with arms outstretched, books below **Rev:** Relief map of Western Europe, value and stars

Date	Mintage	F12	VF20	XF40	MS60	MS63
2008R	130,000	—	—	—	70.00	90.00

KM# 490 2 EURO
8.50 g., Bi-Metallic, 25.75 mm. **Subject:** Creativity and Innovation **Obv:** Chemical flasks and book

Date	Mintage	F12	VF20	XF40	MS60	MS63
2009R	—	—	—	—	45.00	55.00

KM# 494 2 EURO
8.50 g., Bi-Metallic, 25.75 mm. **Subject:** Sandra Botticeli, 500th Anniversary of Death

Date	Mintage	F12	VF20	XF40	MS60	MS63
2010R	130,000	—	—	—	45.00	55.00

KM# 500 2 EURO
8.50 g., Bi-Metallic, 25.75 mm. **Subject:** Hgiorgio Vasari, 500th Anniversary of Birth

Date	Mintage	F12	VF20	XF40	MS60	MS63
2011R	130,000	—	—	—	35.00	45.00

KM# 519 2 EURO
8.50 g., Bi-Metallic, 25.75 mm. **Obv:** Euro symbol

Date	Mintage	F12	VF20	XF40	MS60	MS63
2012R	125,000	—	—	—	35.00	45.00
2012R	5,000	PF65 55.00				

KM# 448 5 EURO
18.00 g., 0.925 Silver 0.5319 oz. ASW, 32 mm. **Subject:** Welcome Euro **Obv:** Three plumed towers **Rev:** Circle of roses

Date	Mintage	F12	VF20	XF40	MS60	MS63
2002R	37,000	PF63 65.00	PF65 75.00			

KM# 452 5 EURO
18.00 g., 0.925 Silver 0.5319 oz. ASW, 32 mm. **Obv:** National arms **Rev:** Allegorical depiction of Independence, Tolerance and Liberty

Date	Mintage	F12	VF20	XF40	MS60	MS63
2003R	70,000	—	—	—	35.00	40.00

KM# 453 5 EURO
18.00 g., 0.925 Silver 0.5319 oz. ASW, 32 mm. **Subject:** 2004 Olympics **Obv:** Stylized three towers **Rev:** Ancient Olympians **Edge:** Reeded

Date	Mintage	F12	VF20	XF40	MS60	MS63
2003R	37,742	PF63 45.00	PF65 50.00			

KM# 458 5 EURO
18.00 g., 0.925 Silver 0.5319 oz. ASW, 32 mm. **Obv:** National arms **Rev:** Value behind Bartolomeo Borghesi

Date	Mintage	F12	VF20	XF40	MS60	MS63
2004R	70,000	—	—	—	30.00	35.00

KM# 462 5 EURO
18.00 g., 0.925 Silver 0.5319 oz. ASW, 32 mm. **Obv:** Three stylized plumed towers **Rev:** Two soccer players

Date	Mintage	F12	VF20	XF40	MS60	MS63
2004R	29,673	PF63 40.00		PF65 45.00		

KM# 468 5 EURO
18.00 g., 0.925 Silver 0.5319 oz. ASW, 32 mm. **Obv:** Three towers **Rev:** Antonio Onofri and value

Date	Mintage	F12	VF20	XF40	MS60	MS63
2005R	70,000	—	—	—	30.00	35.00

KM# 511 5 EURO
18.00 g., 0.925 Silver 0.5319 oz. ASW, 32 mm. **Subject:** Winter Olympics, Turin **Rev:** Large snowflake, snowman on skies

Date	Mintage	F12	VF20	XF40	MS60	MS63
2005R	26,786	PF63 45.00		PF65 50.00		

KM# 525 5 EURO
22.00 g., 0.925 Silver 0.6501 oz. ASW **Obv:** National arms **Rev:** Soldier with flag

Date	Mintage	F12	VF20	XF40	MS60	MS63
2005	969	PF65 45.00				

KM# 472 5 EURO
18.00 g., 0.925 Silver 0.5319 oz. ASW, 32 mm. **Obv:** Portrait of Melchiorre Delfico

Date	Mintage	F12	VF20	XF40	MS60	MS63
2006R	65,000	—	—	—	30.00	35.00

KM# 476 5 EURO
18.00 g., 0.925 Silver 0.5319 oz. ASW, 32 mm. **Subject:** Andrea Mantegna, 500th Anniversary of Death **Obv:** Three towers **Rev:** Statue of soldier and naked female

Date	Mintage	F12	VF20	XF40	MS60	MS63
2006R	18,986	PF63 35.00		PF65 40.00		

KM# 473 5 EURO
18.00 g., 0.925 Silver 0.5319 oz. ASW, 32 mm. **Subject:** Equal Opportunity between the sexes **Obv:** Three plumed towers **Obv. Legend:** REPUBLICA DI SAN MARINO **Rev:** Nude female at left, nude male at right, ribbon across symbols within circle above, value below **Rev. Inscription:** PARI OPPORTITA **Edge:** Reeded

Date	Mintage	F12	VF20	XF40	MS60	MS63
2007R	70,000	—	—	—	30.00	35.00

KM# 474 5 EURO
18.00 g., 0.925 Silver 0.5319 oz. ASW, 32 mm. **Subject:** 50th Anniversary Death of Toscanini **Obv:** Stylized national arms **Obv. Legend:** REPUBBLICA DI SAN MARINO **Rev:** Head of Toscanini left **Edge:** Reeded

Date	Mintage	F12	VF20	XF40	MS60	MS63
ND-2007R	17,736	PF63 35.00		PF65 40.00		

KM# 512 5 EURO
18.00 g., 0.925 Silver 0.5319 oz. ASW, 32 mm. **Rev:** Winds, land and sea

Date	Mintage	F12	VF20	XF40	MS60	MS63
2008R	50,000	—	—	—	30.00	35.00

KM# 513 5 EURO
18.00 g., 0.925 Silver 0.5319 oz. ASW, 32 mm. **Subject:** Summer Olympics, Peking **Rev:** Ribbon Dancer

Date	Mintage	F12	VF20	XF40	MS60	MS63
2008R	21,000	PF63 40.00		PF65 45.00		

KM# 506 5 EURO
18.00 g., 0.925 Silver 0.5319 oz. ASW, 32 mm. **Subject:** Kepler **Obv:** Kepler bust and globe **Rev:** Planets orbit around central sun

Date	Mintage	F12	VF20	XF40	MS60	MS63
2009R	13,400	PF63 45.00		PF65 50.00		

KM# 515 5 EURO
18.00 g., 0.925 Silver 0.5319 oz. ASW, 32 mm. **Subject:** Year of Astronomy **Obv:** Planets in orbit **Rev:** Planets in orbit, Astrolab

Date	Mintage	F12	VF20	XF40	MS60	MS63
2009R	50,000	—	—	—	30.00	35.00

KM# 495 5 EURO
18.00 g., 0.925 Silver 0.5319 oz. ASW, 32 mm. **Subject:** Shanghai Expo

Date	Mintage	F12	VF20	XF40	MS60	MS63
2010R	10,000	PF63 60.00		PF65 65.00		

KM# 496 5 EURO
18.00 g., 0.925 Silver 0.5319 oz. ASW, 32 mm. **Subject:** Michelangelo Caravaggio, 500th Anniverdary of Death

Date	Mintage	F12	VF20	XF40	MS60	MS63
2010R	48,000	—	—	—	30.00	35.00

KM# 501 5 EURO
18.00 g., 0.925 Silver 0.5319 oz. ASW, 32 mm. **Subject:** European Discoveries **Obv:** Crowned coat of arms **Rev:** Busts of Antonio & Roberto Pazzaglia, Mt. Everest in background

Date	Mintage	F12	VF20	XF40	MS60	MS63
2011R	10,000	PF63 45.00		PF65 50.00		

KM# 502 5 EURO
18.00 g., 0.925 Silver 0.5319 oz. ASW, 32 mm. **Subject:** 50th Anniversary of man in space **Rev:** Gagarin and Shepard, Vostok I and Freedom 7 spacecraft

Date	Mintage	F12	VF20	XF40	MS60	MS63
2011R	48,000	—	—	—	30.00	35.00

KM# 520 5 EURO
18.00 g., 0.925 Silver 0.5319 oz. ASW, 32 mm. **Subject:** Giovanni Pascoli, 100th Anniversary of Death **Obv:** National arms **Rev:** Bust at right

Date	Mintage	F12	VF20	XF40	MS60	MS63
2012R	40,000	PF63 35.00		PF65 40.00		

KM# 521 5 EURO
18.00 g., 0.925 Silver 0.5319 oz. ASW, 32 mm. **Subject:** Amerigo Vespucci, 500th Anniversary of Death **Obv:** National arms **Rev:** Vespucci standing holding astrolobe to the stars

Date	Mintage	F12	VF20	XF40	MS60	MS63
2012R	12,000	PF63 50.00		PF65 55.00		

KM# 524 5 EURO
Silver, 32 mm. **Subject:** Amerigo Vespucci

Date	Mintage	F12	VF20	XF40	MS60	MS63
2012		PF65 40.00				

KM# 531 5 EURO
18.00 g., 0.925 Silver 0.5319 oz. ASW, 32 mm. **Subject:** Verona

Date	Mintage	F12	VF20	XF40	MS60	MS63
2013		PF65 35.00				

KM# 449 10 EURO
22.00 g., 0.925 Silver 0.6501 oz. ASW, 34 mm. **Subject:** Welcome Euro **Obv:** Three plumed towers **Rev:** Infant sleeping in flower

Date	Mintage	F12	VF20	XF40	MS60	MS63
2002R	36,995	PF63 90.00		PF65 100		

KM# 454 10 EURO
22.00 g., 0.925 Silver 0.6501 oz. ASW, 34 mm. **Subject:** 2004 Olympics **Obv:** Three stylized towers **Rev:** Modern Olympians **Edge:** Segmented reeding

Date	Mintage	F12	VF20	XF40	MS60	MS63
2003R	37,741	PF63 65.00		PF65 75.00		

KM# 463 10 EURO
22.00 g., 0.925 Silver 0.6501 oz. ASW, 34 mm. **Obv:** Three stylized plumed towers **Rev:** Two soccer players

Date	Mintage	F12	VF20	XF40	MS60	MS63
2004R	29,617	PF63 60.00		PF65 70.00		

KM# 344 10 EURO
22.00 g., 0.925 Silver 0.6501 oz. ASW **Subject:** Uniformed National Military, 500th Anniversary **Obv:** National arms **Rev:** Soldier with flag

Date	Mintage	F12	VF20	XF40	MS60	MS63
2005R	21,969	PF63 45.00		PF65 50.00		

KM# 477 10 EURO
22.00 g., 0.925 Silver 0.6501 oz. ASW, 34 mm. **Subject:** Antonio Canova **Obv:** Three towers **Rev:** The Three Graces

Date	Mintage	F12	VF20	XF40	MS60	MS63
2006R	17,859	PF63 60.00		PF65 65.00		

KM# 475 10 EURO
22.00 g., 0.925 Silver 0.6501 oz. ASW, 34 mm. **Subject:** 100th Anniversary - Birthday of Giosuè Carducci **Obv:** Stylized

national arms **Obv. Legend:** REPUBBLICA DI SAN MARINO **Rev:** 1/2 length figure of Carducci facing with quill pen in hand at table **Rev. Legend:** CARDUCCI **Edge:** Segmented reeding

Date	Mintage	F12	VF20	XF40	MS60	MS63
ND-2007R	14,615		PF63 50.00	PF65 55.00		

KM# 514 10 EURO
22.00 g., 0.925 Silver 0.6501 oz. ASW, 34 mm. **Subject:** Andrea Palladio, 500th Anniversary of Birth **Rev:** Building façade

Date	Mintage	F12	VF20	XF40	MS60	MS63
2008R	17,000		PF63 60.00	PF65 65.00		

KM# 516 10 EURO
22.00 g., 0.925 Silver 0.6501 oz. ASW, 34 mm. **Subject:** Euro, 10th Anniversary

Date	Mintage	F12	VF20	XF40	MS60	MS63
2009R	12,500		PF63 55.00	PF65 60.00		

KM# 497 10 EURO
22.00 g., 0.925 Silver 0.6501 oz. ASW, 34 mm. **Subject:** Robert Schumann, 200th Anniversary of Birth

Date	Mintage	F12	VF20	XF40	MS60	MS63
2010R	10,000		PF63 50.00	PF65 55.00		

KM# 503 10 EURO
22.00 g., 0.925 Silver 0.6501 oz. ASW, 34 mm. **Subject:** Euro, 10th Anniversary **Obv:** Montage of partial coin designs

Date	Mintage	F12	VF20	XF40	MS60	MS63
2011R	10,000		PF63 55.00	PF65 60.00		

KM# 523 10 EURO
Silver, 34 mm. **Subject:** Aligi Sassu, sculptor

Date	Mintage	F12	VF20	XF40	MS60	MS63
2012	—		PF65 75.00			

KM# 522 10 EURO
22.00 g., 0.925 Silver 0.6501 oz. ASW, 34 mm. **Subject:** Machiavelli's "The Prince"

Date	Mintage	F12	VF20	XF40	MS60	MS63
2013	—		PF63 45.00	PF65 50.00		

KM# 460 20 EURO
6.45 g., 0.900 Gold 0.1855 oz. AGW, 21 mm. **Subject:** Ravenna, 1600th Anniversary **Obv:** National arms **Rev:** Female figure from bas-relief wall design **Edge:** Reeded

Date	Mintage	F12	VF20	XF40	MS60	MS63
2002R	4,510		PF65 375			

KM# 455 20 EURO
6.45 g., 0.900 Gold 0.1855 oz. AGW, 21 mm. **Obv:** Three plumes **Rev:** Giotto's "Presentation of Jesus at the Temple **Edge:** Reeded

Date	Mintage	F12	VF20	XF40	MS60	MS63
2003R	7,281		PF65 375			

KM# 465 20 EURO
6.45 g., 0.900 Gold 0.1855 oz. AGW, 21 mm. **Obv:** Three plumes **Rev:** Marco Polo meeting Kublai Khan **Edge:** Reeded

Date	Mintage	F12	VF20	XF40	MS60	MS63
2004R	5,885		PF65 375			

KM# 470 20 EURO
6.45 g., 0.900 Gold 0.1855 oz. AGW, 21 mm. **Subject:** International Day of Peace **Obv:** Stylized faces and leaves

Date	Mintage	F12	VF20	XF40	MS60	MS63
2005R	3,914		PF65 375			

KM# 479 20 EURO
6.45 g., 0.900 Gold 0.1854 oz. AGW, 21 mm. **Subject:** Giovan Battista Belluzzi, 500th Birthday **Obv:** Crowned shield **Rev:** Fortification plan

Date	Mintage	F12	VF20	XF40	MS60	MS63
2006R	2,684		PF65 375			

KM# 507 20 EURO
6.45 g., 0.900 Gold 0.1855 oz. AGW

Date	Mintage	F12	VF20	XF40	MS60	MS63
2007R	2,105		PF65 350			

KM# 491 20 EURO
6.45 g., 0.900 Gold 0.1854 oz. AGW **Subject:** Roman Antiquities **Obv:** Arms **Rev:** Small statue of Mercury

Date	Mintage	F12	VF20	XF40	MS60	MS63
2008R	2,100		PF65 375			

KM# 509 20 EURO
6.45 g., 0.900 Gold 0.1855 oz. AGW, 21 mm.

Date	Mintage	F12	VF20	XF40	MS60	MS63
2009R	2,000		PF65 350			

KM# 498 20 EURO
6.45 g., 0.900 Gold 0.1855 oz. AGW, 21 mm. **Subject:** Treasurers from San Marino - Wooden bust of St. Agata

Date	Mintage	F12	VF20	XF40	MS60	MS63
2010R	2,000		PF65 375			

KM# 504 20 EURO
6.45 g., 0.900 Gold 0.1855 oz. AGW, 21 mm. **Subject:** Treasures from San Marino

Date	Mintage	F12	VF20	XF40	MS60	MS63
2011R	1,600		PF65 375			

KM# 461 50 EURO
16.13 g., 0.900 Gold 0.4637 oz. AGW, 28 mm. **Subject:** 1600th Anniversary of Ravenna **Obv:** National arms **Rev:** Wall painting **Edge:** Reeded

Date	Mintage	F12	VF20	XF40	MS60	MS63
2002R	4,510		PF65 900			

KM# 456 50 EURO
16.13 g., 0.900 Gold 0.4637 oz. AGW, 28 mm. **Obv:** Three plumes **Rev:** Giotto's "The Pentecost **Edge:** Reeded

Date	Mintage	F12	VF20	XF40	MS60	MS63
2003R	7,281		PF65 900			

KM# 466 50 EURO
16.13 g., 0.900 Gold 0.4637 oz. AGW, 28 mm. **Obv:** Three plumes **Rev:** Marco Polo **Edge:** Reeded

Date	Mintage	F12	VF20	XF40	MS60	MS63
2004R	5,885		PF65 900			

KM# 471 50 EURO
16.13 g., 0.900 Gold 0.4637 oz. AGW, 28 mm. **Subject:** International Day of Peace **Obv:** Group of people gathering

Date	Mintage	F12	VF20	XF40	MS60	MS63
2005R	3,914		PF65 900			

KM# 480 50 EURO
16.13 g., 0.900 Gold 0.4637 oz. AGW, 28 mm. **Subject:** Giovan Batista Belluzzi **Obv:** Crowned shield **Rev:** Bust right

Date	Mintage	F12	VF20	XF40	MS60	MS63
2006R	2,684		PF65 900			

KM# 508 50 EURO
16.13 g., 0.900 Gold 0.4637 oz. AGW, 28 mm.

Date	Mintage	F12	VF20	XF40	MS60	MS63
2007R	2,105		PF65 900			

KM# 492 50 EURO
16.13 g., 0.900 Gold 0.4637 oz. AGW, 28 mm. **Subject:** Antiquities **Obv:** Arms **Rev:** Two bronze fibulae

Date	Mintage	F12	VF20	XF40	MS60	MS63
2008R	2,100		PF65 900			

KM# 510 50 EURO
16.13 g., 0.900 Gold 0.4637 oz. AGW, 28 mm.

Date	Mintage	F12	VF20	XF40	MS60	MS63
2009R	2,000		PF65 900			

KM# 499 50 EURO
16.13 g., 0.900 Gold 0.4637 oz. AGW, 28 mm. **Subject:** Treasurers from San Marino - Saint Marinus

Date	Mintage	F12	VF20	XF40	MS60	MS63
2010R	2,000		PF65 900			

KM# 505 50 EURO
16.13 g., 0.900 Gold 0.4637 oz. AGW, 28 mm. **Subject:** Treasures from San Marino

Date	Mintage	F12	VF20	XF40	MS60	MS63
2011R	1,600		PF65 900			

MINT SETS

KM#	Date	Mintage	Identification	Issue Price	Mkt Val
MS61	2001 (8)	2,000	KM424-431	18.00	50.00
MS62	2002 (8)	120,000	KM440 - 447		275
MS63	2003 (9)	—	KM440-447, 452	55.00	350
MS64	2004 (9)	—	KM440-447, 458	55.00	220
MS65	2005 (9)	—	KM440-447, 468	55.00	225
MS66	2006 (9)	65,000	KM440-447, 472	—	185
MS67	2007 (3)	—	KM443, 444, 447	27.50	55.00
MS68	2007 (9)	—	KM440-447, 473	120	160

PROOF SETS

KM#	Date	Mintage	Identification	Issue Price	Mkt Val
PS14	2001 (3)	4,500	KM433-435	178	500
PS15	2002 (2)	37,000	KM448-449	—	175
PS16	2002 (2)	4,550	KM460-461	—	1,150
PS17	2003 (2)	7,300	KM455-456	—	975
PS18	2004 (2)	7,300	KM465-466	—	975
PS19	2005 (2)	5,300	KM470-471	—	1,050
PS20	2008 (8)	13,000	KM440-442, 482-486	—	135
PS21	2009 (8)	13,500	KM440-443, 482-486	—	135
PS22	2010 (8)	8,600	KM440-442, 482-486	—	135
PS23	2011 (8)	8,600	KM440-442, 482-486	—	135
PSA15	2001 (2)	—	KM436, 437	—	70.00

SAUDI ARABIA

The Kingdom of Saudi Arabia, an independent and absolute hereditary monarchy comprising the former sultanate of Nejd, the old kingdom of Hejaz, Asir and Al Hasa, occupies four-fifths of the Arabian peninsula. The kingdom has an area of 830,000 sq. mi. (2,149,690 sq. km.) and a population of *16.1 million. Capital: Riyadh. The economy is based on oil, which provides 85 percent of Saudi Arabia's revenue.

TITLES

العربية السعودية

Al-Arabiya(t) as-Sa'udiya(t)

المملكة العربية السعودية

Al-Mamlaka(t) al-'Arabiya(t) as-Sa'udiya(t)

RULERS

al Sa'ud Dynasty
Fahad bin Abd Al-Aziz, AH1403-1426/1982-2005AD
Abdullah bin Abdul Aziz, AH1426-/2005AD

KINGDOM

REFORM COINAGE
5 Halala = 1 Ghirsh; 100 Halala = 1 Riyal

KM# 69 5 HALALA (Ghirsh)
Copper-Nickel **Ruler:** Abdullah bin Abdul Aziz **Obv:** National emblem at center **Rev:** Legend above inscription in circle, dividing value, date below

Date	Mintage	F12	VF20	XF40	MS60	MS63
AH1430(2009)	—	—	0.30	0.60	1.50	2.00

KM# 62 10 HALALA (2 Ghirsh)
4.00 g., Copper-Nickel, 21 mm. **Ruler:** Fahad Bin Abd Al-Aziz **Obv:** National emblem at center, legend above and below **Rev:** Legend above inscription in circle dividing value, date below **Edge:** Reeded

Date	Mintage	F12	VF20	XF40	MS60	MS63
AH1423 (2002)	—	—	0.15	0.35	0.90	1.00

KM# 70 10 HALALA (2 Ghirsh)
Copper-Nickel **Ruler:** Abdullah bin Abdul Aziz **Obv:** National emblem at center **Rev:** Legend above inscription in circle, dividing value, date below

Date	Mintage	F12	VF20	XF40	MS60	MS63
AH1430(2009)	—	—	0.30	0.60	1.50	2.50

KM# 63 25 HALALA (1/4 Riyal)
5.00 g., Copper-Nickel, 23 mm. **Ruler:** Fahad Bin Abd Al-Aziz **Obv:** National emblem at center, legend above and below **Rev:** Legend above inscription in circle dividing value, date below **Edge:** Reeded

Date	Mintage	F12	VF20	XF40	MS60	MS63
AH1423 (2002)	—	—	0.20	0.45	1.10	1.50

KM# 71 25 HALALA (1/4 Riyal)
Copper-Nickel **Ruler:** Abdullah bin Abdul Aziz **Obv:** National emblem at center **Rev:** Legend above inscription in circle, divides value, date below

Date	Mintage	F12	VF20	XF40	MS60	MS63
AH1427 (2006)	—	—	0.20	0.45	1.10	1.50
AH1430 (2009)	—	—	0.20	0.45	1.10	1.50
AH1433-2012	—	—	0.20	0.45	1.10	1.50

KM# 64 50 HALALA (1/2 Riyal)
6.50 g., Copper-Nickel, 26 mm. **Ruler:** Fahad Bin Abd Al-Aziz **Obv:** National emblem at center, legend above and below **Rev:** Legend above inscription in circle dividing value, date below **Edge:** Reeded

Date	Mintage	F12	VF20	XF40	MS60	MS63
AH1423 (2002)	—	0.75	1.00	1.50	2.50	3.50

KM# 68 50 HALALA (1/2 Riyal)
6.50 g., Copper-Nickel, 26 mm. **Ruler:** Abdullah bin Abdul Aziz **Obv:** National emblem at center **Rev:** Legend above inscription in circle, dividing value, date below **Edge:** Reeded

Date	Mintage	F12	VF20	XF40	MS60	MS63
AH1427 (2006)	—	—	0.30	0.60	1.50	2.00
AH1428 (2007)	—	—	0.30	0.60	1.50	2.00
AH1431 (2010)	—	—	0.30	0.60	1.50	2.00

KM# 72 100 HALALA (1 Riyal)
Bi-Metallic, 23 mm. **Ruler:** Abdullah bin Abdul Aziz **Obv:** National emblem at center **Rev:** Legend above inscription, divides value, date below **Edge:** Reeded

Date	Mintage	F12	VF20	XF40	MS60	MS63
AH1427(2006)	—	—	3.00	4.25	5.00	6.00
AH1429(2008)	—	—	3.00	4.25	5.00	6.00

SERBIA

The Republic of Serbia, a former inland Balkan kingdom has an area of 34,116 sq. mi. (88,361 sq. km.). Capital: Belgrade.

MINT MARKS
A - Paris
(a) - Paris, privy mark only
H - Birmingham
V - Vienna
ÁÏ - (BP) Budapest

MONETARY SYSTEM
100 Para = 1 Dinara

DENOMINATIONS
ÏÀÐÀ = Para
ÏÀÐÅ = Pare
ÄÈÍÀÐ = Dinar
ÄÈÍÀÐÀ = Dinara

REPUBLIC
STANDARD COINAGE

KM# 34 DINAR
4.34 g., Copper-Nickel-Zinc, 20 mm. **Obv:** National Bank emblem within circle **Rev:** Bank building and value **Edge:** Reeded

Date	Mintage	F12	VF20	XF40	MS60	MS63
2003	10,326,000	—	—	0.25	0.50	1.00
2004	25,038,000	—	—	0.25	0.50	1.00

KM# 39 DINAR
4.26 g., Nickel-Brass, 20 mm. **Obv:** Crowned and mantled arms **Rev:** National Bank and value **Edge:** Segmented reeding

Date	Mintage	F12	VF20	XF40	MS60	MS63
2005	32,452,000	—	—	0.25	0.50	1.00
2006	39,550,000	—	—	0.25	0.50	1.00
2007	20,000,000	—	—	0.25	0.50	1.00
2008	10,093,000	—	—	0.25	0.50	1.00
2009	10,008,000	—	—	0.25	0.50	1.00

KM# 48 DINAR
4.20 g., Copper Plated Steel, 20 mm. **Obv:** Arms **Rev:** National Bank and value

Date	Mintage	F12	VF20	XF40	MS60	MS63
2009	35,750,000	—	—	—	0.50	1.00
2010	30,600,000	—	—	—	0.50	1.00
2011	24,785,000	—	—	—	0.50	1.00

KM# 54 DINAR
20.00 g., Copper Plated Steel, 20 mm. **Obv:** Arms, flat bottom crown above shield **Rev:** National Bank building and value

Date	Mintage	F12	VF20	XF40	MS60	MS63
2011	—	—	—	—	0.50	1.00
2012	—	—	—	—	0.50	1.00

KM# 35 2 DINARA
5.24 g., Copper-Nickel-Zinc, 22 mm. **Obv:** National Bank emblem within circle **Rev:** Gracanica Monastery and value **Edge:** Reeded

Date	Mintage	F12	VF20	XF40	MS60	MS63
2003	15,216,000	—	—	0.25	0.50	1.00

KM# 46 2 DINARA
5.15 g., Nickel-Brass, 22 mm. **Obv:** Crowned and mantled arms **Rev:** Gracanica Monastery and value **Edge:** Segmented reeding

Date	Mintage	F12	VF20	XF40	MS60	MS63
2006	15,385,500	—	—	0.25	0.50	1.00

Date	Mintage	F12	VF20	XF40	MS60	MS63
2007	15,002,500	—	—	0.25	0.50	1.00
2008	10,093,000	—	—	0.25	0.50	1.00
2009	10,008,000	—	—	0.25	0.50	1.00

KM# 49 2 DINARA
5.05 g., Copper Plated Steel, 22 mm. **Obv:** Arms **Rev:** Gracanica Monastery and value

Date	Mintage	F12	VF20	XF40	MS60	MS63
2009	27,845,000	—	—	0.25	0.50	1.00
2010	9,600,000	—	—	0.25	0.50	1.00
2011	12,400,000	—	—	0.25	0.50	1.00

KM# 55 2 DINARA
5.05 g., Copper Plated Steel, 22 mm. **Obv:** Arms, flat bottom crown above shield **Rev:** Gracanica Monastery and value

Date	Mintage	F12	VF20	XF40	MS60	MS63
2011	—	—	—	—	0.50	1.00
2012	—	—	—	—	0.50	1.00

KM# 36 5 DINARA
6.23 g., Copper-Nickel-Zinc, 22 mm. **Obv:** National Bank emblem within circle **Rev:** Krusedol Monastery and value **Edge:** Reeded

Date	Mintage	F12	VF20	XF40	MS60	MS63
2003	15,184,000	—	—	0.25	1.00	1.50

KM# 40 5 DINARA
6.13 g., Nickel-Brass, 24 mm. **Obv:** Crowned and mantled arms **Rev:** Krusedol Monastery and value **Edge:** Segmented reeding

Date	Mintage	F12	VF20	XF40	MS60	MS63
2005	5,099,500	—	—	0.25	1.00	1.50
2006	10,372,500	—	—	0.25	1.00	1.50
2007	14,998,500	—	—	0.25	1.00	1.50
2008	15,093,500	—	—	0.25	1.00	1.50
2009	9,998,500	—	—	0.25	1.00	1.50
2010	15,005,000	—	—	0.25	1.00	1.50
2011	13,626,500	—	—	0.25	1.00	1.50

KM# 56 5 DINARA
Nickel-Brass, 24 mm. **Obv:** Arms, flat bottom crown above shield **Rev:** Krusedol Monastery

Date	Mintage	F12	VF20	XF40	MS60	MS63
2011	—	—	—	—	1.00	1.50
2012	—	—	—	—	1.00	1.50

KM# 37 10 DINARA
7.77 g., Copper-Nickel-Zinc, 26 mm. **Obv:** National Bank emblem within circle **Rev:** Studenica Monastery and value **Edge:** Reeded

Date	Mintage	F12	VF20	XF40	MS60	MS63
2003	15,166,500	—	—	0.25	1.00	1.50

KM# 41 10 DINARA

7.77 g., Copper-Nickel-Zinc, 26 mm. **Obv:** Crowned and mantled arms **Rev:** Studenica Monastery and value **Edge:** Segmented reeding

Date	Mintage	F12	VF20	XF40	MS60	MS63
2005	5,099,500	—	—	0.25	1.00	1.50
2006	1,019,500	—	—	0.25	1.00	1.50
2007	1,050,500	—	—	0.25	1.00	1.50
2010	500,250	—	—	0.25	1.00	1.50
2011	500,250	—	—	0.25	1.00	1.50

KM# 51 10 DINARA

7.77 g., Copper-Nickel-Zinc, 26 mm. **Subject:** 25th Summer Universiade, Belgrade **Obv:** Arms **Rev:** Logo

Date	Mintage	F12	VF20	XF40	MS60	MS63
2009	500,000	—	—	0.50	1.00	1.50

KM# 57 10 DINARA

7.77 g., Copper-Nickel-Zinc, 26 mm. **Obv:** Arms, flat bottom crown above shield **Rev:** Studenica Monastery and value

Date	Mintage	F12	VF20	XF40	MS60	MS63
2011	—	—	—	0.50	1.00	1.50
2012	—	—	—	0.50	1.00	1.50

KM# 38 20 DINARA

9.00 g., Copper-Nickel-Zinc, 28 mm. **Obv:** National Bank emblem within circle **Rev:** Temple of St. Sava and value **Edge:** Reeded

Date	Mintage	F12	VF20	XF40	MS60	MS63
2003	25,497,500	—	—	0.50	1.00	1.50

KM# 42 20 DINARA

9.00 g., Copper-Nickel-Zinc, 28 mm. **Obv:** Crowned and mantled Serbian royal arms **Rev:** Nikola Tesla **Edge:** Segmented reeding

Date	Mintage	F12	VF20	XF40	MS60	MS63
2006	992,500	—	—	0.50	1.00	1.50

KM# 47 20 DINARA

9.00 g., Copper-Nickel-Zinc, 28 mm. **Subject:** Dositej Obradovic, 1742-1811 **Obv:** National arms **Obv. Legend:** РЕПУБЛИКА СРБИЈА - REPUBLIKA SRBIJA **Rev:** Bust facing slightly left **Edge:** Segmented reeding

Date	Mintage	F12	VF20	XF40	MS60	MS63
2007	1,020,000	—	—	0.50	1.00	1.50

KM# 52 20 DINARA

9.00 g., Copper-Nickel-Zinc, 28 mm. **Obv:** National arms **Rev:** Milutin Milankovic profile 3/4 left

Date	Mintage	F12	VF20	XF40	MS60	MS63
2009	494,500	—	—	0.50	1.00	1.50

KM# 53 20 DINARA

9.00 g., Copper-Nickel-Zinc, 28 mm. **Obv:** National arms **Rev:** Ivo Andric

Date	Mintage	G4	VG8	F12	VF20	XF40
2011	500,000	—	—	—	—	0.50

KM# 43 1000 DINARA

13.00 g., 0.925 Silver 0.3841 oz. ASW, 30 mm. **Obv:** Crowned and mantled Serbian royal arms **Rev:** Nikola Tesla **Edge:** Segmented reeding

Date	Mintage	F12	VF20	XF40	MS60	MS63
2006	2,000	PF60 20.00	PF63 25.00	PF65 30.00		

KM# 44 5000 DINARA

3.46 g., 0.900 Gold 0.0993 oz. AGW, 20 mm. **Obv:** Crowned and mantled Serbian royal arms **Rev:** Nikola Tesla

Date	Mintage	F12	VF20	XF40	MS60	MS63
2006	2,000	PF63 175	PF65 200			

KM# 45 10000 DINARA

8.64 g., 0.900 Gold 0.2484 oz. AGW, 25 mm. **Obv:** Crowned and mantled Serbian royal arms **Rev:** Nikola Tesla

Date	Mintage	F12	VF20	XF40	MS60	MS63
2006	1,000	PF63 425	PF65 475			

MINT SETS

KM#	Date	Mintage	Identification	Issue Price	Mkt Val
MS1	2003 (5)	—	KM34-38	—	15.00
MS2	2005 (3)	—	KM39-41	—	10.00
MS3	2006 (5)	—	KM39-42, 46	—	16.00
MS4	2007 (5)	—	KM39-42, 47	—	16.00

PROOF SETS

KM#	Date	Mintage	Identification	Issue Price	Mkt Val
PS1	2006 (3)	—	KM#43-45	—	710

SEYCHELLES

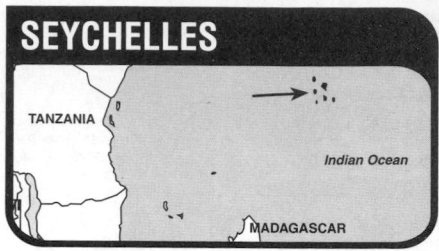

The Republic of Seychelles, an archipelago of 85 granite and coral islands situated in the Indian Ocean 600 miles (965 km.) northeast of Madagascar, has an area of 156 sq. mi. (455 sq. km.) and a population of *70,000. Among these islands are the Aldabra Islands, the Farquhar Group, and Ile Desroches, which the United Kingdom ceded to the Seychelles upon its independence. Capital: Victoria, on Mahe. The economy is based on fishing, a plantation system of agriculture, and tourism. Copra, cinnamon and vanilla are exported.

Seychelles is a member of the Commonwealth of Nations. The president is the Head of State and of the Government.

MINT MARKS
(sa) - M in oval – South African Mint Co. (starting in 2000, not PM)
None - British Royal Mint

MONETARY SYSTEM
100 Cents = 1 Rupee

REPUBLIC

STANDARD COINAGE

KM# 46.2 CENT

1.43 g., Brass, 16.03 mm. **Obv:** Altered coat of arms **Rev:** Mud Crab **Edge:** Plain

Date	Mintage	F12	VF20	XF40	MS60	MS63
2004	—	—	—	0.15	0.25	0.35

KM# 47.2 5 CENTS

2.00 g., Brass, 18 mm. **Obv:** Altered coat of arms **Rev:** Tapioca plant

Date	Mintage	F12	VF20	XF40	MS60	MS63
2003	—	—	—	0.10	0.30	0.50

KM# 47a 5 CENTS

1.97 g., Brass Plated Steel, 17.97 mm. **Obv:** National arms **Rev:** Tapioca plant **Edge:** Plain

Date	Mintage	F12	VF20	XF40	MS60	MS63
2007PM	—	—	—	0.10	0.30	0.50
2010PM	—	—	—	0.10	0.30	0.50

KM# 48.2 10 CENTS

3.34 g., Brass, 21 mm. **Obv:** Altered coat of arms **Rev:** Yellowfin tuna **Edge:** Plain

Date	Mintage	F12	VF20	XF40	MS60	MS63
2003	—	—	—	0.10	0.35	1.00	1.50

KM# 48a 10 CENTS

3.37 g., Brass Plated Steel, 21 mm. **Obv:** National arms **Rev:** Black parrot, value **Edge:** Plain

Date	Mintage	F12	VF20	XF40	MS60	MS63
2007PM	—	—	—	0.15	0.30	0.75	1.00

KM# 49a 25 CENTS
2.97 g., Nickel Clad Steel, 18.9 mm. **Obv:** National arms **Rev:** Black Parrot and value **Edge:** Plain

Date	Mintage	F12	VF20	XF40	MS60	MS63
2003PM	—	—	—	0.40	1.00	1.25
2007PM	—	—	—	0.40	1.00	1.25
2010PM	—	—	—	0.40	1.00	1.25
2012PM	—	—	—	0.40	1.00	1.25

KM# 50.2 RUPEE
6.18 g., Copper-Nickel, 25.46 mm. **Obv:** Altered coat of arms **Rev:** Triton Conch Shell **Edge:** Reeded

Date	Mintage	F12	VF20	XF40	MS60	MS63
2007	—	—	—	0.25	0.75	1.00
2010PM	—	—	—	0.25	0.75	1.00

KM# 51.2 5 RUPEES
9.00 g., Copper-Nickel, 29 mm. **Obv:** Altered arms **Rev:** Fruit tree divides value **Edge:** Reeded

Date	Mintage	F12	VF20	XF40	MS60	MS63
2007	—	—	—	0.50	1.00	1.50
2010	—	—	—	0.50	1.00	1.50

KM# 118 5 RUPEES
28.28 g., Copper-Nickel, 38.6 mm. **Subject:** John Paul II memorial **Obv:** National Arms **Rev:** John Paul II in mitre waving

Date	Mintage	F12	VF20	XF40	MS60	MS63
2005	—	—	—	—	3.00	5.00

KM# 119 5 RUPEES
28.28 g., Copper-Nickel, 38.6 mm. **Obv:** National Arms **Rev:** Benedict XVI blessing crowd at St. Peter's Square

Date	Mintage	F12	VF20	XF40	MS60	MS63
2005	—	—	—	—	4.00	6.00

KM# 127 5 RUPEES
28.28 g., Copper-Nickel, 38.61 mm. **Subject:** 80th Birthday of Queen Elizabeth II

Date	Mintage	F12	VF20	XF40	MS60	MS63
2006 Proof	—	—	—	—	9.00	12.00

KM# 126 10 RUPEES
0.50 g., 0.585 Gold AGW, 11 mm. **Subject:** Pitcher Plant

Date	Mintage	F12	VF20	XF40	MS60	MS63
2012	Est. 5000	PF63 28.00	PF65 35.00			

KM# 138 10 RUPEES
0.50 g., 0.585 Gold AGW, 11 mm. **Subject:** Gandhi

Date	Mintage	F12	VF20	XF40	MS60	MS63
2013	Est. 7,500	PF63 40.00				

KM# 120 25 RUPEES
28.28 g., 0.925 Silver 0.8356 oz. ASW, 38.6 mm. **Obv:** National arms **Rev:** Description John Paul II in mitre waving **Edge:** Reeded

Date	Mintage	F12	VF20	XF40	MS60	MS63
2005	—	PF60 25.00	PF63 35.00	PF65 45.00		

KM# 121 25 RUPEES
28.28 g., 0.925 Silver 0.8356 oz. ASW, 38.6 mm. **Obv:** National arms **Rev:** Benedict XVI blessing crowd at St. Peter's Square **Edge:** Reeded

Date	Mintage	F12	VF20	XF40	MS60	MS63
2005	—	PF60 25.00	PF63 35.00	PF65 45.00		

KM# 128 25 RUPEES
28.28 g., 0.925 Silver 0.8356 oz. ASW, 38.61 mm. **Subject:** 80th Birthday of Queen Elizabeth II

Date	Mintage	F12	VF20	XF40	MS60	MS63
2006	—	PF60 25.00	PF63 35.00	PF65 45.00		

KM# 129 25 RUPEES
28.28 g., 0.925 Silver 0.8356 oz. ASW, 38.61 mm. **Subject:** 2006 World Cup - Germany

Date	Mintage	F12	VF20	XF40	MS60	MS63
2006	—	PF60 25.00	PF63 35.00	PF65 45.00		

KM# 130 25 RUPEES
28.28 g., 0.925 Silver 0.8356 oz. ASW, 38.61 mm. **Subject:** 35th Anniversary of Independence

Date	Mintage	F12	VF20	XF40	MS60	MS63
2011	—	PF60 22.00	PF63 27.00	PF65 32.00		

KM# 132 25 RUPEES
1.24 g., 0.999 Gold 0.0396 oz. AGW, 14 mm. **Subject:** Independence, 39th Anniversary **Obv:** National arms **Rev:** Island view

Date	Mintage	F12	VF20	XF40	MS60	MS63
2011	2,500	PF63 100				

KM# 133 25 RUPEES
28.28 g., 0.925 Silver 0.8356 oz. ASW, 38.61 mm. **Obv:** Arms **Rev:** Island View

Date	Mintage	F12	VF20	XF40	MS60	MS63
2011	2,500	PF63 100				

KM# 131 25 RUPEES
1.24 g., 0.999 Gold 0.0396 oz. AGW, 14 mm. **Subject:** 35 Years of Independence

Date	Mintage	F12	VF20	XF40	MS60	MS63
2011	2,500	PF60 70.00	PF63 75.00	PF65 80.00		

KM# 139 25 RUPEES
0.925 Silver ASW, 38.61 mm. **Obv:** Head right and arms **Rev:** Elizabeth II and family

Date	Mintage	F12	VF20	XF40	MS60	MS63
2011	—	PF63 75.00				

KM# 125 25 RUPEES
20.00 g., 0.925 Silver 0.591 oz. ASW, 38.61 mm. **Subject:** 2014 FIFA World Cup - Brazil

Date	Mintage	F12	VF20	XF40	MS60	MS63
2012	Est. 10000	PF60 45.00	PF63 55.00	PF65 65.00		

KM# 134 25 RUPEES
0.50 g., 0.999 Gold AGW, 11 mm. **Subject:** Birth of Prince George **Obv:** National arms **Rev:** W+K monogram, crown & baby's feet

Date	Mintage	F12	VF20	XF40	MS60	MS63
2013	5,000	PF63 55.00				

KM# 136 25 RUPEES
20.00 g., 0.925 Silver 0.591 oz. ASW, 38.61 mm. **Subject:** 2016 Olympics - Kayak

Date	Mintage	F12	VF20	XF40	MS60	MS63
2013	Est. 10,000	PF63 75.00				

KM# 137 25 RUPEES
0.50 g., 0.999 Gold AGW, 11 mm. **Subject:** Ghandi

Date	Mintage	F12	VF20	XF40	MS60	MS63
2013	Est. 7,500	PF63 75.00				

KM# 135 50 RUPEES
93.30 g., 0.925 Silver 2.7568 oz. ASW, 50 mm. **Obv:** National arms **Rev:** W+K monogram, crown and baby's feet, blue crystal nisert

Date	Mintage	F12	VF20	XF40	MS60	MS63
2013	999	PF63 175				

KM# 122 250 RUPEES
6.22 g., 0.9999 Gold 0.1987 oz. AGW, 22 mm. **Obv:** National arms **Rev:** Description John Paul II in mitre waving **Edge:** Reeded

Date	Mintage	F12	VF20	XF40	MS60	MS63
2005	—	PF63 350	PF65 400			

KM# 123 250 RUPEES
6.22 g., 0.9999 Gold 0.1987 oz. AGW, 22 mm. **Obv:** National arms **Rev:** Benedict XVI blessing crowd at St. Peter's Square **Edge:** Reeded

Date	Mintage	F12	VF20	XF40	MS60	MS63
2005	—	PF63 350	PF65 400			

SHAWNEE TRIBAL NATION

SOVEREIGN NATION
MILLED COINAGE

KM# 1 DOLLAR
31.20 g., 0.9999 Silver 0.9965 oz. ASW, 39 mm. **Obv:** Tribal seal **Obv. Legend:** THE SOVEREIGN NATION OF THE SHAWNEE TRIBE **Rev:** Bust of Chief Chief "Shooting Star" Tecumseh right **Edge:** Reeded

Date	Mintage	F12	VF20	XF40	MS60	MS63
2002	50,000	—	—	—		40.00
2002	—	PF65 55.00				

KM# 10 DOLLAR
124.41 g., 0.999 Silver 3.9702 oz. ASW

Date	Mintage	F12	VF20	XF40	MS60	MS63
2003	10,000	PF65 185				

KM# 3 DOLLAR
31.20 g., 0.9999 Silver 0.9965 oz. ASW, 39 mm. **Obv:** Tribal seal **Obv. Legend:** THE SOVEREIGN NATION OF THE SHAWNEE TRIBE **Rev:** Lewis, Clark and Drouillard scouting **Edge:** Reeded

Date	Mintage	F12	VF20	XF40	MS60	MS63
2003	50,000	—	—	—		45.00
2003	—	PF65 55.00				

KM# 5 DOLLAR
31.20 g., 0.9999 Silver 0.9965 oz. ASW, 39 mm. **Obv:** Tribal seal **Obv. Legend:** THE SOVEREIGN NATION OF THE SHAWNEE TRIBE **Rev:** Flag behing Indian Chief and Thomas Jefferson standing, eagle on shield at their feet **Edge:** Reeded

Date	Mintage	F12	VF20	XF40	MS60	MS63
2004	50,000	—	—	—		45.00
2004	—	PF65 55.00				

KM# 15 DOLLAR

31.31 g., 0.999 Silver 0.9992 oz. ASW, 40.6 mm. **Obv:** Tribal seal **Obv. Legend:** THE SOVEREIGN NATION OF THE SHAWNEE TRIBE **Rev:** Lewis, Clark, Dromillard and Sacagawea in a canoe **Rev. Legend:** EXPEDITION OF DISCOVERY **Edge:** Reeded

Date	Mintage	F12	VF20	XF40	MS60	MS63
2005	50,000	—	—	—	—	45.00
2005	20,000	PF65 55.00				

KM# 20 DOLLAR

31.21 g., 0.999 Silver 0.9969 oz. ASW, 40.6 mm. **Obv:** Tribal seal **Obv. Legend:** THE SOVEREIGN NATION OF THE SHAWNEE TRIBE **Rev:** 1/2 length figure of Tenskwatawa "the prophet" 3/4 left **Rev. Legend:** PROPHET TENSKWATAWA **Edge:** Reeded

Date	Mintage	F12	VF20	XF40	MS60	MS63
2006	20,000	PF65 55.00				
2006	50,000	—	—	—	—	45.00

KM# 24 DOLLAR

31.11 g., 0.999 Silver 0.9926 oz. ASW, 39 mm. **Subject:** Battle of the Wabash **Rev:** Indian warrior on horseback **Edge:** Reeded

Date	Mintage	F12	VF20	XF40	MS60	MS63
2007	20,000	PF65 60.00				
2007	50,000	—	—	—	—	50.00

KM# 26 DOLLAR

31.11 g., 0.999 Silver 0.9926 oz. ASW, 39 mm. **Subject:** Battle of Point Pleasant **Rev:** Indian warrior on horseback **Edge:** Reeded

Date	Mintage	F12	VF20	XF40	MS60	MS63
2008	50,000	—	—	—	—	50.00
2008	20,000	PF65 60.00				

KM# 28 DOLLAR

31.11 g., 0.999 Silver 0.9926 oz. ASW **Rev:** Battle of Fallen Timber

Date	Mintage	F12	VF20	XF40	MS60	MS63
2009	20,000	PF65 60.00				
2009	50,000	—	—	—	—	50.00

KM# 2 5 DOLLARS

6.22 g., 0.9999 Gold 0.1987 oz. AGW, 20 mm. **Obv:** Arms **Obv. Legend:** THE SOVEREIGN NATION OF THE SHAWNEE TRIBE **Rev:** Bust of Tecumseh "Shooting Star" 3/4 left **Edge:** Reeded

Date	Mintage	F12	VF20	XF40	MS60	MS63
2002	—	PF65 400				

KM# 4 5 DOLLARS

6.22 g., 0.9999 Gold 0.1987 oz. AGW, 22.5 mm. **Obv:** Arms **Obv. Legend:** THE SOVEREIGN NATION OF THE SHAWNEE TRIBE **Rev:** Bust of George Drouillard 3/4 right **Rev. Legend:** GEORGE DROUILLARD SIGN TALKER

Date	Mintage	F12	VF20	XF40	MS60	MS63
2003	—	PF65 400				

KM# 6 5 DOLLARS

6.22 g., 0.999 Gold 0.1985 oz. AGW, 22 mm. **Obv:** Arms **Obv. Legend:** THE SOVEREIGN NATION OF THE SHAWNEE TRIBE **Rev:** Sacagawea with child and horse **Edge:** Reeded

Date	Mintage	F12	VF20	XF40	MS60	MS63
2004	—	PF65 400				

KM# 16 5 DOLLARS

6.30 g., 0.9999 Gold 0.2012 oz. AGW, 22.5 mm. **Obv:** Tribal seal **Obv. Legend:** THE SOVEREIGN NATION OF THE SHAWNEE TRIBE **Rev:** Sacagawea with papoose on horseback right **Rev. Legend:** EXPEDITION OF DISCOVERY **Edge:** Reeded

Date	Mintage	F12	VF20	XF40	MS60	MS63
2005	5,000	PF65 400				

KM# 21 5 DOLLARS

6.25 g., 0.9999 Gold 0.1996 oz. AGW, 22.5 mm. **Obv:** Tribal seal **Obv. Legend:** THE SOVEREIGN NATION OF THE SHAWNEE TRIBE **Rev:** Bust of Chief Tecumseh 3/4 right **Rev. Legend:** TECVMSEH **Edge:** Reeded

Date	Mintage	F12	VF20	XF40	MS60	MS63
2006	5,000	PF65 400				

KM# 25 5 DOLLARS

6.25 g., 0.999 Gold 0.1994 oz. AGW **Rev:** Chief Blue Jacket

Date	Mintage	F12	VF20	XF40	MS60	MS63
2007	5,000	PF65 400				

KM# 27 5 DOLLARS

6.25 g., 0.999 Gold 0.1994 oz. AGW **Rev:** Chief Cornstalk

Date	Mintage	F12	VF20	XF40	MS60	MS63
2008	5,000	PF65 400				

KM# 29 5 DOLLARS

6.25 g., 0.999 Gold 0.1994 oz. AGW **Rev:** Chief Black-Hoof

Date	Mintage	F12	VF20	XF40	MS60	MS63
2009	5,000	PF65 400				

KM# 7 50 DOLLARS

15.55 g., 0.999 Gold 0.4962 oz. AGW, 30.1 mm. **Rev:** George Drouillard

Date	Mintage	F12	VF20	XF40	MS60	MS63
2003	999	PF65 875				

KM# 11 50 DOLLARS

15.55 g., 0.999 Gold 0.4962 oz. AGW, 30.1 mm. **Rev:** Sacagawea with child and horse

Date	Mintage	F12	VF20	XF40	MS60	MS63
2004	—	PF65 875				

KM# 17 50 DOLLARS

15.55 g., 0.9999 Gold 0.4967 oz. AGW, 30.1 mm. **Obv:** Tribal seal **Obv. Legend:** THE SOVEREIGN NATION OF THE SHAWNEE TRIBE **Rev:** Sacagawea with papoose on horseback right **Rev. Legend:** EXPEDITION OF DISCOVERY **Edge:** Reeded

Date	Mintage	F12	VF20	XF40	MS60	MS63
2005	999	PF65 875				

KM# 8 100 DOLLARS

30.91 g., 0.9999 Gold 0.9873 oz. AGW, 38.9 mm. **Obv:** Tribal seal **Obv. Legend:** THE SOVEREIGN NATION OF THE SHAWNEE TRIBE **Rev:** Bust of "Sign Talker" 3/4 right **Rev. Legend:** GEORGE DROILLARD "SIGN TALKER **Edge:** Milled

Date	Mintage	F12	VF20	XF40	MS60	MS63
2003	999	PF65 1,850				

KM# 12 100 DOLLARS

31.11 g., 0.999 Gold 0.9926 oz. AGW **Rev:** Sacagawea and child

Date	Mintage	F12	VF20	XF40	MS60	MS63
2004	—	PF65 1,850				

KM# 18 100 DOLLARS

31.11 g., 0.999 Gold 0.9926 oz. AGW **Rev:** Sacagawea and child on horseback

Date	Mintage	F12	VF20	XF40	MS60	MS63
2005	999	PF65 1,850				

KM# 23 100 DOLLARS

62.21 g., 0.999 Bi-Metallic 1.9852 oz. **Rev:** Lewis and Clark

Date	Mintage	F12	VF20	XF40	MS60	MS63
2005	500	PF65 2,000				

KM# 9 500 DOLLARS

93.50 g., 0.9999 Gold 2.9864 oz. AGW **Obv:** Tribal seal **Obv. Legend:** THE SOVEREIGN NATION OF THE SHAWNEE TRIBE **Rev:** Lewis, Clark and Drouillard scouting **Rev. Legend:** LEWIS • CLARK • DROUILLARD **Edge:** Reeded

Date	Mintage	F12	VF20	XF40	MS60	MS63
2003	300	PF65 5,800				

KM# 13 500 DOLLARS
15.54 g., 0.999 Platinum 0.4959 oz. APW, 30 mm. **Obv:** Tribal seal **Obv. Legend:** THE SOVEREIGN NATION OF THE SHAWNEE TRIBE **Rev:** Flag and shield between standing Chief and Thomas Jefferson **Rev. Legend:** EXPEDITION OF DISCOVERY **Edge:** Reeded

Date	Mintage	F12	VF20	XF40	MS60	MS63
2004	999	PF65 1,150				

KM# 23A 500 DOLLARS
15.55 g., 0.999 Platinum 0.4962 oz. APW. **Rev:** Shawnee Chief and Thomas Jefferson standing

Date	Mintage	F12	VF20	XF40	MS60	MS63
2005	999	PF65 1,150				

KM# 14 1000 DOLLARS
31.00 g., 0.9999 Platinum 0.9902 oz. APW, 38.7 mm. **Obv:** Tribal seal **Obv. Legend:** THE SOVEREIGN NATION OF THE SHAWNEE TRIBE **Rev:** Flag and shield between standing Chief and Thomas Jefferson **Rev. Legend:** EXPEDITION OF DISCOVERY **Edge:** Reeded

Date	Mintage	F12	VF20	XF40	MS60	MS63
2004	300	PF65 2,750				

KM# 22 1000 DOLLARS
31.11 g., 0.999 Platinum 0.9926 oz. APW. **Rev:** Shawnee Chief and Thomas Jefferson standing

Date	Mintage	F12	VF20	XF40	MS60	MS63
2005	300	PF65 2,750				

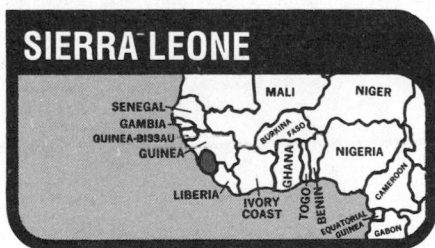

The Republic of Sierra Leone is located in western Africa between Guinea and Liberia, has an area of 27,699 sq. mi. (71,740 sq. km.) and a population of *4.1 million. Capital: Freetown. The economy is predominantly agricultural but mining contributes significantly to export revenues. Diamonds, iron ore, palm kernels, cocoa, and coffee are exported.

Sierra Leone is a member of the Commonwealth of Nations. The president is Chief of State and Head of Government.

MONETARY SYSTEM
Beginning 1964
100 Cents = 1 Leone

REPUBLIC
STANDARD COINAGE

KM# 295 20 LEONES
3.92 g., Copper-Nickel, 21.7 mm. **Obv:** Value within fish and beaded circle **Rev:** Chimpanzee facing **Edge:** Plain

Date	Mintage	F12	VF20	XF40	MS60	MS63
2003	—	—	—	—	0.50	1.25

KM# 302 100 LEONES
28.28 g., Copper-Nickel, 38.6 mm. **Subject:** 40th Anniversary - Bank of Sierra Leone **Obv:** Bank President Kabbah **Rev:** Lion **Edge:** Reeded

Date	Mintage	F12	VF20	XF40	MS60	MS63
ND (2004)PM	5,000	—	—	—	15.00	18.00

KM# 296 500 LEONES
7.20 g., Bi-Metallic, 24 mm. **Obv:** Building within circle **Rev:** Bust with hat facing within circle **Edge:** Plain **Shape:** 10-sided

Date	Mintage	F12	VF20	XF40	MS60	MS63
2004	—	—	—	—	7.50	9.00

KM# 346 500 LEONES
28.28 g., Bronze, 38.6 mm. **Subject:** 40th Anniversary - Bank of Sierra Leone **Obv:** Bank President Kabbah **Rev:** Lion, denomination as "Le 500 **Edge:** Reeded

Date	Mintage	F12	VF20	XF40	MS60	MS63
ND-2004PM	10,000	—	—	—	15.00	18.00

DOLLAR DENOMINATED COINAGE

KM# 198 DOLLAR
28.28 g., Copper-Nickel, 38.6 mm. **Subject:** Year of the Snake **Obv:** National arms **Rev:** Snake **Edge:** Reeded

Date	Mintage	F12	VF20	XF40	MS60	MS63
2001	—	—	—	—	10.00	14.00

KM# 206 DOLLAR
Copper-Nickel, 38.6 mm. **Subject:** P'an Ku **Obv:** National arms **Rev:** Dragon

Date	Mintage	F12	VF20	XF40	MS60	MS63
2001	—	—	—	—	10.00	14.00

KM# 214 DOLLAR
Copper-Nickel, 38.6 mm. **Subject:** P'an Ku **Obv:** National arms **Rev:** Dragon and three animals

Date	Mintage	F12	VF20	XF40	MS60	MS63
2001	—	—	—	—	10.00	14.00

KM# 222 DOLLAR
28.49 g., Copper-Nickel, 38.5 mm. **Series:** The Big Five **Obv:** National arms **Rev:** Rhino **Edge:** Reeded

Date	Mintage	F12	VF20	XF40	MS60	MS63
2001PM	—	—	—	—	12.50	15.00

KM# 225 DOLLAR
28.49 g., Copper-Nickel, 38.6 mm. **Series:** The Big Five **Obv:** National arms **Rev:** Lion **Edge:** Reeded

Date	Mintage	F12	VF20	XF40	MS60	MS63
2001PM	—	—	—	—	10.00	15.00

KM# 228 DOLLAR
28.49 g., Copper-Nickel, 38.6 mm. **Series:** The Big Five **Obv:** National arms **Rev:** Leopard **Edge:** Reeded

Date	Mintage	F12	VF20	XF40	MS60	MS63
2001PM	—	—	—	—	10.00	15.00

KM# 231 DOLLAR
28.49 g., Copper-Nickel, 38.6 mm. **Series:** The Big Five **Obv:** National arms **Rev:** Elephants **Edge:** Reeded

Date	Mintage	F12	VF20	XF40	MS60	MS63
2001PM	—	—	—	—	10.00	15.00

KM# 234 DOLLAR
28.49 g., Copper-Nickel, 38.6 mm. **Series:** The Big Five **Obv:** National arms **Rev:** Buffalo **Edge:** Reeded

Date	Mintage	F12	VF20	XF40	MS60	MS63
2001PM	—	—	—	—	10.00	15.00

KM# 237 DOLLAR
28.49 g., Copper-Nickel, 38.5 mm. **Series:** The Big Five **Obv:** National arms **Rev:** All five animals **Edge:** Reeded

Date	Mintage	F12	VF20	XF40	MS60	MS63
2001PM	—	—	—	—	10.00	15.00

KM# 241.1 DOLLAR
28.54 g., Copper-Nickel, 38.65 mm. **Series:** Big Cats **Obv:** National arms **Rev:** Male and female lions **Edge:** Reeded

Date	Mintage	F12	VF20	XF40	MS60	MS63
2001PM	—	—	—	—	12.50	15.00

KM# 241.2 DOLLAR
28.54 g., Copper-Nickel, 38.65 mm. **Series:** Big Cats **Obv:** National arms **Rev:** Multi-colored male and female lions **Edge:** Reeded

Date	Mintage	F12	VF20	XF40	MS60	MS63
2001PM	—	—	—	—	15.00	17.50

KM# 242.1 DOLLAR
28.54 g., Copper-Nickel, 38.65 mm. **Series:** Big Cats **Obv:** National arms **Rev:** Tiger **Edge:** Reeded

Date	Mintage	F12	VF20	XF40	MS60	MS63
2001PM	—	—	—	—	10.00	14.00

KM# 242.2 DOLLAR
28.54 g., Copper-Nickel, 38.65 mm. **Series:** Big Cats **Obv:** National arms **Rev:** Multi-colored Tiger **Edge:** Reeded

Date	Mintage	F12	VF20	XF40	MS60	MS63
2001PM	—	—	—	—	15.00	17.50

KM# 243.1 DOLLAR
28.54 g., Copper-Nickel, 38.65 mm. **Series:** Big Cats **Obv:** National arms **Rev:** Cheetah **Edge:** Reeded

Date	Mintage	F12	VF20	XF40	MS60	MS63
2001PM	—	—	—	—	12.50	15.00

KM# 243.2 DOLLAR
28.54 g., Copper-Nickel, 38.65 mm. **Series:** Big Cats **Obv:** National arms **Rev:** Multi-colored Cheetah **Edge:** Reeded

Date	Mintage	F12	VF20	XF40	MS60	MS63
2001PM	—	—	—	—	15.00	17.50

KM# 244.1 DOLLAR
28.54 g., Copper-Nickel, 38.65 mm. **Series:** Big Cats **Obv:** National arms **Rev:** Cougar **Edge:** Reeded

Date	Mintage	F12	VF20	XF40	MS60	MS63
2001PM	—	—	—	—	10.00	14.00

KM# 244.2 DOLLAR
28.54 g., Copper-Nickel, 38.65 mm. **Series:** Big Cats **Obv:** National arms **Rev:** Multi-colored Cougar **Edge:** Reeded

Date	Mintage	F12	VF20	XF40	MS60	MS63
2001PM	—	—	—	—	15.00	17.50

KM# 245.1 DOLLAR
28.54 g., Copper-Nickel, 38.65 mm. **Series:** Big Cats **Obv:** National arms **Rev:** Black panther **Edge:** Reeded

Date	Mintage	F12	VF20	XF40	MS60	MS63
2001PM	—	—	—	—	10.00	14.00

KM# 245.2 DOLLAR
28.54 g., Copper-Nickel, 38.65 mm. **Series:** Big Cats **Obv:** National arms **Rev:** Multi-colored Black Panther **Edge:** Reeded

Date	Mintage	F12	VF20	XF40	MS60	MS63
2001PM	—	—	—	—	15.00	17.50

KM# 256 DOLLAR
28.28 g., Copper-Nickel, 38.6 mm. **Subject:** Year of the Horse **Obv:** National arms **Rev:** Horse **Edge:** Reeded

Date	Mintage	F12	VF20	XF40	MS60	MS63
2002	—	—	—	—	14.50	17.50

KM# 264 DOLLAR
28.28 g., Copper-Nickel, 38.6 mm. **Subject:** RMS Titanic **Obv:** National arms **Rev:** Titanic at dock **Edge:** Reeded

Date	Mintage	F12	VF20	XF40	MS60	MS63
2002	—	—	—	—	10.00	12.00

KM# 268 DOLLAR
28.28 g., Copper-Nickel, 38.6 mm. **Subject:** Queen's Golden Jubilee **Obv:** National arms **Rev:** Queen Elizabeth II and Prince Philip visiting blacksmiths in Sierra Leone **Edge:** Reeded

Date	Mintage	F12	VF20	XF40	MS60	MS63
2002	—	—	—	—	10.00	12.00

KM# 269 DOLLAR
28.28 g., Copper-Nickel, 38.6 mm. **Subject:** Queen's Golden Jubilee **Obv:** National arms **Rev:** Queen, Prince Charles and Princess Anne **Edge:** Reeded

Date	Mintage	F12	VF20	XF40	MS60	MS63
2002	—	—	—	—	10.00	12.00

KM# 276 DOLLAR
28.28 g., Copper-Nickel, 38.6 mm. **Subject:** British Queen Mother **Obv:** National arms **Rev:** Queen Mother with dog in garden **Edge:** Reeded

Date	Mintage	F12	VF20	XF40	MS60	MS63
2002	—	—	—	—	10.00	12.00

KM# 279 DOLLAR
28.28 g., Copper-Nickel, 38.6 mm. **Subject:** Queen Mother **Obv:** National arms **Rev:** Queen Mother with daughters **Edge:** Reeded

Date	Mintage	F12	VF20	XF40	MS60	MS63
2002	—	—	—	—	10.00	12.00

KM# 282 DOLLAR
28.28 g., Copper-Nickel, 38.6 mm. **Subject:** Queen's Golden Jubilee **Obv:** National arms **Rev:** Queen Elizabeth and a young Prince Charles **Edge:** Reeded

Date	Mintage	F12	VF20	XF40	MS60	MS63
2002	—	—	—	—	10.00	12.00

KM# 285 DOLLAR
28.28 g., Copper-Nickel, 38.6 mm. **Subject:** Queen's Golden Jubilee **Obv:** National arms **Rev:** Queen Elizabeth and Prince Philip **Edge:** Reeded

Date	Mintage	F12	VF20	XF40	MS60	MS63
2002	—	—	—	—	10.00	12.00

KM# 288 DOLLAR
28.28 g., Copper-Nickel, 38.6 mm. **Subject:** Olympics **Obv:** National arms **Rev:** Victory goddess Nike **Edge:** Reeded

Date	Mintage	F12	VF20	XF40	MS60	MS63
2003	—	—	—	—	10.00	12.00
2004	—	—	—	—	10.00	12.00

KM# 291 DOLLAR
28.28 g., Copper-Nickel, 38.6 mm. **Subject:** Olympics **Obv:** National arms **Rev:** Ancient archer **Edge:** Reeded

Date	Mintage	F12	VF20	XF40	MS60	MS63
2003	—	—	—	—	10.00	12.00
2004	—	—	—	—	10.00	12.00

KM# 297 DOLLAR
28.28 g., Copper-Nickel, 38.6 mm. **Obv:** National arms **Rev:** Nelson Mandela **Edge:** Reeded

Date	Mintage	F12	VF20	XF40	MS60	MS63
2004	—	—	—	—	15.00	16.50

KM# 300 DOLLAR
28.28 g., Copper-Nickel, 38.6 mm. **Obv:** National arms **Rev:** Ronald Reagan **Edge:** Reeded

Date	Mintage	F12	VF20	XF40	MS60	MS63
2004	—	—	—	—	15.00	16.50

KM# 304 DOLLAR
28.42 g., Copper-Nickel, 38.6 mm. **Obv:** National arms **Rev:** Giraffe **Edge:** Reeded

Date	Mintage	F12	VF20	XF40	MS60	MS63
2005	—	—	—	—	12.00	16.00

KM# 305 DOLLAR
28.42 g., Copper-Nickel, 38.6 mm. **Obv:** National arms **Rev:** Crocodile **Edge:** Reeded

Date	Mintage	F12	VF20	XF40	MS60	MS63
2005	—	—	—	—	12.00	16.00

KM# 306 DOLLAR
28.42 g., Copper-Nickel, 38.6 mm. **Obv:** National arms **Rev:** Hippo in water **Edge:** Reeded

Date	Mintage	F12	VF20	XF40	MS60	MS63
2005	—	—	—	—	12.00	16.00

KM# 315 DOLLAR
Copper-Nickel **Series:** 60th Anniversary End of WW II **Subject:** Battle of Britian **Obv:** National arms **Legend:** REPUBLIC OF SIERRA LEONE **Rev:** Planes in flight

Date	Mintage	F12	VF20	XF40	MS60	MS63
2005	—	—	—	—	10.00	12.00

KM# 316 DOLLAR
Copper-Nickel **Series:** 60th Anniversary End of WW II **Subject:** The Battle of the Atlantic **Obv:** National arms **Obv. Legend:** REPUBLIC OF SIERRA LEONE **Rev:** Plane and ship convoy

Date	Mintage	F12	VF20	XF40	MS60	MS63
2005	—	—	—	—	10.00	12.00

KM# 317 DOLLAR
Copper-Nickel **Series:** 60th Anniversary End of WW II **Subject:** Battle of El Alamein **Obv:** National arms **Obv. Legend:** REPUBLIC OF SIERRA LEONE **Rev:** Tank, plane and ground troops

Date	Mintage	F12	VF20	XF40	MS60	MS63
2005	—	—	—	—	10.00	12.00

KM# 318 DOLLAR
Copper-Nickel **Series:** 60th Anniversary End of WW II **Subject:** Battle of the Bulge **Obv:** National arms **Obv. Legend:** REPUBLIC OF SIERRA LEONE **Rev:** Forest battle scene

Date	Mintage	F12	VF20	XF40	MS60	MS63
2005	—	—	—	—	10.00	12.00

KM# 319 DOLLAR
Copper-Nickel **Series:** 60th Anniversary End of WW II **Subject:** The Battle of Berlin **Obv:** National arms **Obv. Legend:** REPUBLIC OF SIERRA LEONE **Rev:** Berlin city view, tank

Date	Mintage	F12	VF20	XF40	MS60	MS63
2005	—	—	—	—	10.00	12.00

KM# 320 DOLLAR
Copper-Nickel **Series:** 60th Anniversary End of WW II **Subject:** The Heavy Water Raids **Obv:** National arms **Obv. Legend:** REPUBLIC OF SIERRA LEONE **Rev:** Troops on skies, factory in ruins

Date	Mintage	F12	VF20	XF40	MS60	MS63
2005	—	—	—	—	10.00	12.00

KM# 321 DOLLAR
Copper-Nickel **Obv:** National Arms **Rev:** Mountain Gorillia

Date	Mintage	F12	VF20	XF40	MS60	MS63
2005	—	—	—	—	12.00	16.00

KM# 322 DOLLAR
Copper-Nickel **Rev:** John Paul II head left, within ring of the Stations of the Cross

Date	Mintage	F12	VF20	XF40	MS60	MS63
2005	—	—	—	—	10.00	12.00

KM# 323 DOLLAR
Copper-Nickel **Rev:** Benedict XVI and St. Peter's

Date	Mintage	F12	VF20	XF40	MS60	MS63
2005	—	—	—	—	10.00	12.00

KM# 345 DOLLAR
28.50 g., Copper-Nickel, 38.58 mm. **Subject:** Death of Prince Rainier III **Obv:** National arms **Rev:** Bust left, small knight horseback right on neck **Edge:** Reeded

Date	Mintage	F12	VF20	XF40	MS60	MS63
2005	—	—	—	—	7.00	9.00

KM# 308 DOLLAR
28.37 g., Copper-Nickel, 38.5 mm. **Obv:** National arms **Rev:** Stegosaurus **Edge:** Reeded

Date	Mintage	F12	VF20	XF40	MS60	MS63
2006	—	—	—	—	14.00	16.00

KM# 309 DOLLAR
28.37 g., Copper-Nickel, 38.5 mm. **Obv:** National arms **Rev:** Tyrannosaurus Rex **Edge:** Reeded

Date	Mintage	F12	VF20	XF40	MS60	MS63
2006	—	—	—	—	14.00	16.00

KM# 310 DOLLAR
28.37 g., Copper-Nickel, 38.5 mm. **Obv:** National arms **Rev:** Triceratops **Edge:** Reeded

Date	Mintage	F12	VF20	XF40	MS60	MS63
2006	—	—	—	—	14.00	16.00

KM# 311 DOLLAR
28.37 g., Copper-Nickel, 38.5 mm. **Obv:** National arms **Rev:** Lion **Edge:** Reeded

Date	Mintage	F12	VF20	XF40	MS60	MS63
2006	—	—	—	—	12.00	16.00

KM# 312 DOLLAR
28.37 g., Copper-Nickel, 38.5 mm. **Obv:** National arms **Rev:** Dromedary Camel **Edge:** Reeded

Date	Mintage	F12	VF20	XF40	MS60	MS63
2006	—	—	—	—	12.00	16.00

KM# 313 DOLLAR
28.37 g., Copper-Nickel, 38.63 mm. **Obv:** National arms **Rev:** Chimpanzee **Edge:** Reeded

Date	Mintage	F12	VF20	XF40	MS60	MS63
2006	—	—	—	—	12.00	16.00

KM# 314 DOLLAR
28.37 g., Copper-Nickel, 38.5 mm. **Obv:** National arms **Rev:** Impala **Edge:** Reeded

Date	Mintage	F12	VF20	XF40	MS60	MS63
2006	—	—	—	—	12.00	16.00

KM# 324 DOLLAR
Copper-Nickel **Obv:** National Arms **Rev:** Brontosaurus

Date	Mintage	F12	VF20	XF40	MS60	MS63
2006	—	—	—	—	14.00	16.00

KM# 326 DOLLAR
28.37 g., Copper-Nickel, 38.5 mm. **Rev:** Cheetah

Date	Mintage	F12	VF20	XF40	MS60	MS63
2007	—	—	—	—	14.00	17.00

KM# 327 DOLLAR
28.37 g., Copper-Nickel, 38.5 mm. **Rev:** Zebra

Date	Mintage	F12	VF20	XF40	MS60	MS63
2007	—	—	—	—	14.00	17.00

KM# 328 DOLLAR
28.37 g., Copper-Nickel, 38.5 mm. **Rev:** Rhino

Date	Mintage	F12	VF20	XF40	MS60	MS63
2007	—	—	—	—	14.00	17.00

KM# 329 DOLLAR
28.37 g., Copper-Nickel, 38.5 mm. **Obv:** Arms **Rev:** African elephant

Date	Mintage	F12	VF20	XF40	MS60	MS63
2007	—	—	—	—	15.00	18.00

KM# 347 DOLLAR
28.37 g., Copper-Nickel, 38.6 mm. **Series:** Nocturnal Creatures of Africa **Obv:** National arms **Rev:** Duiker Antelope standing left, facing **Edge:** Reeded **Note:** Blackened finish.

Date	Mintage	F12	VF20	XF40	MS60	MS63
2008	—	—	—	—	17.50	20.00

KM# 348 DOLLAR
28.37 g., Copper-Nickel, 38.6 mm. **Series:** Nocturnal Creatures of Africa **Obv:** National arms **Rev:** Bush Baby on tree limb **Edge:** Reeded **Note:** Blackened finish.

Date	Mintage	F12	VF20	XF40	MS60	MS63
2008	—	—	—	—	17.50	20.00

KM# 349 DOLLAR
28.37 g., Copper-Nickel, 38.6 mm. **Series:** Nocturnal Creatures of Africa **Obv:** National arms. **Rev:** Honey Badger **Edge:** Reeded **Note:** Blackened finish

Date	Mintage	F12	VF20	XF40	MS60	MS63
2008	—	—	—	—	17.50	20.00

KM# 350 DOLLAR
28.37 g., Copper-Nickel, 38.6 mm. **Series:** Nocturnal Creatures of Africa **Obv:** National arms. **Rev:** Pygmy Hippopotamus in water facing **Edge:** Reeded **Note:** Blackened finish.

Date	Mintage	F12	VF20	XF40	MS60	MS63
2008	—	—	—	—	17.50	20.00

KM# 199 10 DOLLARS
28.28 g., 0.925 Silver 0.8356 oz. ASW, 38.6 mm. **Subject:** Year of the Snake **Obv:** National arms **Rev:** Snake on bamboo **Edge:** Reeded

Date	Mintage	F12	VF20	XF40	MS60	MS63
2001	—	PF65 55.00				

KM# 207 10 DOLLARS
28.28 g., 0.925 Silver 0.8356 oz. ASW, 38.6 mm. **Subject:** P'an Ku **Obv:** National arms **Rev:** Dragon

Date	Mintage	F12	VF20	XF40	MS60	MS63
2001	Est. 5000	PF65 55.00				

KM# 215 10 DOLLARS
28.28 g., 0.925 Silver 0.8356 oz. ASW, 38.6 mm. **Subject:** P'an Ku **Obv:** National arms **Rev:** Dragon and three animals

Date	Mintage	F12	VF20	XF40	MS60	MS63
2001	Est. 5000	PF65 55.00				

KM# 223 10 DOLLARS
28.28 g., 0.925 Silver 0.8356 oz. ASW, 38.6 mm. **Series:** The Big Five **Obv:** National arms **Rev:** Rhino and value within circle **Edge:** Reeded

Date	Mintage	F12	VF20	XF40	MS60	MS63
2001	—	PF63 45.00	PF65 55.00			

KM# 226 10 DOLLARS
28.28 g., 0.925 Silver 0.8356 oz. ASW, 38.6 mm. **Series:** The Big Five **Obv:** National arms **Rev:** Lion head and value within circle

Date	Mintage	F12	VF20	XF40	MS60	MS63
2001	Est. 10000	PF63 45.00	PF65 55.00			

KM# 229 10 DOLLARS
28.28 g., 0.925 Silver 0.8356 oz. ASW, 38.6 mm. **Series:** The Big Five **Obv:** National arms **Rev:** Leopard and value within circle

Date	Mintage	F12	VF20	XF40	MS60	MS63
2001	Est. 10000	PF63 45.00	PF65 55.00			

KM# 232 10 DOLLARS
28.28 g., 0.925 Silver 0.8356 oz. ASW, 38.6 mm. **Series:** The Big Five **Obv:** National arms **Rev:** Elephants and value within circle

Date	Mintage	F12	VF20	XF40	MS60	MS63
2001	Est. 10000	PF63 45.00	PF65 55.00			

KM# 235 10 DOLLARS
28.28 g., 0.925 Silver 0.8356 oz. ASW, 38.6 mm. **Series:** The Big Five **Obv:** National arms **Rev:** Buffalo and value within circle

Date	Mintage	F12	VF20	XF40	MS60	MS63
2001	Est. 10000	PF63 45.00		PF65 55.00		

KM# 238 10 DOLLARS
28.28 g., 0.925 Silver 0.8356 oz. ASW, 38.6 mm. **Series:** The Big Five **Obv:** National arms **Rev:** All five animals within circle

Date	Mintage	F12	VF20	XF40	MS60	MS63
2001	Est. 10000	PF63 45.00		PF65 55.00		

KM# 246.1 10 DOLLARS
28.28 g., 0.925 Silver 0.8356 oz. ASW, 38.6 mm. **Series:** Big Cats **Obv:** National arms **Rev:** Male and female lions **Edge:** Reeded

Date	Mintage	F12	VF20	XF40	MS60	MS63
2001	10,000	PF63 45.00		PF65 50.00		

KM# 246.2 10 DOLLARS
28.28 g., 0.925 Silver 0.8356 oz. ASW, 38.6 mm. **Series:** Big Cats **Obv:** National arms **Rev:** Multi-colored male and female lions **Edge:** Reeded

Date	Mintage	F12	VF20	XF40	MS60	MS63
2001	—	PF63 55.00		PF65 60.00		

KM# 247.1 10 DOLLARS
28.28 g., 0.925 Silver 0.8356 oz. ASW, 38.6 mm. **Series:** Big Cats **Obv:** National arms **Rev:** Tiger **Edge:** Reeded

Date	Mintage	F12	VF20	XF40	MS60	MS63
2001	—	PF63 45.00		PF65 50.00		

KM# 247.2 10 DOLLARS
28.28 g., 0.925 Silver 0.8356 oz. ASW, 38.6 mm. **Series:** Big Cats **Obv:** National arms **Rev:** Multi-colored Tiger **Edge:** Reeded

Date	Mintage	F12	VF20	XF40	MS60	MS63
2001	—	PF63 55.00		PF65 60.00		

KM# 248.1 10 DOLLARS
28.28 g., 0.925 Silver 0.8356 oz. ASW, 38.6 mm. **Series:** Big Cats **Obv:** National arms **Rev:** Cheetah head facing **Edge:** Reeded

Date	Mintage	F12	VF20	XF40	MS60	MS63
2001	10,000	PF63 45.00		PF65 45.00		

KM# 248.2 10 DOLLARS
28.28 g., 0.925 Silver 0.8356 oz. ASW, 38.6 mm. **Series:** Big Cats **Obv:** National arms **Rev:** Multi-colored Cheetah head facing **Edge:** Reeded

Date	Mintage	F12	VF20	XF40	MS60	MS63
2001	—	PF63 50.00		PF65 55.00		

KM# 249.1 10 DOLLARS
28.28 g., 0.925 Silver 0.8356 oz. ASW, 38.6 mm. **Series:** Big Cats **Obv:** National arms **Rev:** Cougar **Edge:** Reeded

Date	Mintage	F12	VF20	XF40	MS60	MS63
2001	10,000	PF63 45.00		PF65 50.00		

KM# 249.2 10 DOLLARS
28.28 g., 0.925 Silver 0.8356 oz. ASW, 38.6 mm. **Series:** Big Cats **Obv:** National arms **Rev:** Multi-colored Cougar **Edge:** Reeded

Date	Mintage	F12	VF20	XF40	MS60	MS63
2001	—	PF63 55.00		PF65 60.00		

KM# 250.1 10 DOLLARS
28.28 g., 0.925 Silver 0.8356 oz. ASW, 38.6 mm. **Series:** Big Cats **Obv:** National arms **Rev:** Leopard **Edge:** Reeded

Date	Mintage	F12	VF20	XF40	MS60	MS63
2001	10,000	PF63 45.00		PF65 50.00		

KM# 250.2 10 DOLLARS
28.28 g., 0.925 Silver 0.8356 oz. ASW, 38.6 mm. **Series:** Big Cats **Obv:** National arms **Rev:** Multi-colored Leopard **Edge:** Reeded

Date	Mintage	F12	VF20	XF40	MS60	MS63
2001	—	PF63 55.00		PF65 60.00		

KM# 257 10 DOLLARS
28.28 g., 0.925 Silver 0.8356 oz. ASW, 38.6 mm. **Subject:** Year of the Horse **Obv:** National arms **Rev:** Horse divides circle **Edge:** Reeded

Date	Mintage	F12	VF20	XF40	MS60	MS63
2002	5,000	PF65 60.00				

KM# 265 10 DOLLARS
28.28 g., 0.925 Silver 0.8356 oz. ASW, 38.6 mm. **Subject:** RMS Titanic **Obv:** National arms **Rev:** Titanic at dock **Edge:** Reeded

Date	Mintage	F12	VF20	XF40	MS60	MS63
2002	10,000	PF63 55.00		PF65 60.00		

KM# 270 10 DOLLARS
28.28 g., 0.925 Silver 0.8356 oz. ASW, 38.6 mm. **Subject:** Queen's Golden Jubilee **Obv:** National arms **Rev:** Queen Elizabeth II and Prince Philip visiting blacksmiths in Sierra Leone **Edge:** Reeded

Date	Mintage	F12	VF20	XF40	MS60	MS63
2002	10,000	PF63 55.00		PF65 60.00		

KM# 271 10 DOLLARS
28.28 g., 0.925 Silver 0.8356 oz. ASW, 38.6 mm. **Subject:** Queen's Golden Jubilee **Obv:** National arms **Rev:** Queen Elizabeth II, Prince Charles and Princess Anne **Edge:** Reeded

Date	Mintage	F12	VF20	XF40	MS60	MS63
2002	10,000	PF63 50.00		PF65 55.00		

KM# 277 10 DOLLARS
28.28 g., 0.925 Silver 0.8356 oz. ASW, 38.6 mm. **Subject:** British Queen Mother **Obv:** National arms **Rev:** Bust facing in garden with dog within sprigs **Edge:** Reeded

Date	Mintage	F12	VF20	XF40	MS60	MS63
2002	10,000	PF63 55.00		PF65 60.00		

KM# 280 10 DOLLARS
28.28 g., 0.925 Silver 0.8356 oz. ASW, 38.6 mm. **Subject:** British Queen Mother **Obv:** National arms **Rev:** Conjoined busts facing within sprigs **Edge:** Reeded

Date	Mintage	F12	VF20	XF40	MS60	MS63
2002	10,000	PF63 55.00	PF65 60.00			

KM# 283 10 DOLLARS
28.28 g., 0.925 Silver 0.8356 oz. ASW, 38.6 mm. **Subject:** Queen Elizabeth's Golden Jubilee **Obv:** National arms **Rev:** Queen and young Prince Charles **Edge:** Reeded

Date	Mintage	F12	VF20	XF40	MS60	MS63
2002	10,000	PF63 50.00	PF65 55.00			

KM# 286 10 DOLLARS
28.28 g., 0.925 Silver 0.8356 oz. ASW, 38.6 mm. **Subject:** Queen Elizabeth's Golden Jubilee **Obv:** National arms **Rev:** Queen and Prince Philip **Edge:** Reeded

Date	Mintage	F12	VF20	XF40	MS60	MS63
2002	10,000	PF63 50.00	PF65 55.00			

KM# 289 10 DOLLARS
28.28 g., 0.925 Silver 0.8356 oz. ASW, 38.6 mm. **Subject:** Olympics **Obv:** National arms **Rev:** Victory goddess Nike **Edge:** Reeded **Note:** The leone is the official currency of Sierra Leone

Date	Mintage	F12	VF20	XF40	MS60	MS63
2003	10,000	PF63 50.00	PF65 55.00			
2004	10,000	PF63 50.00	PF65 55.00			

KM# 292 10 DOLLARS
28.28 g., 0.925 Silver 0.8356 oz. ASW, 38.6 mm. **Subject:** Olympics **Obv:** National arms **Rev:** Ancient archer **Edge:** Reeded

Date	Mintage	F12	VF20	XF40	MS60	MS63
2003	10,000	PF63 50.00	PF65 55.00			
2004	10,000	PF63 50.00	PF65 55.00			

KM# 298 10 DOLLARS
28.28 g., 0.925 Silver 0.8356 oz. ASW, 38.6 mm. **Obv:** National arms **Rev:** Nelson Mandela **Edge:** Reeded

Date	Mintage	F12	VF20	XF40	MS60	MS63
2004	10,000	PF63 55.00	PF65 60.00			

KM# 301 10 DOLLARS
28.28 g., 0.925 Silver 0.8356 oz. ASW, 38.6 mm. **Obv:** National arms **Rev:** Ronald Reagan **Edge:** Reeded

Date	Mintage	F12	VF20	XF40	MS60	MS63
2004	10,000	PF63 55.00	PF65 60.00			

KM# 307 10 DOLLARS
28.62 g., 0.925 Silver 0.8457 oz. ASW, 38.5 mm. **Obv:** National arms **Rev:** Giraffe **Edge:** Reeded

Date	Mintage	F12	VF20	XF40	MS60	MS63
2005	—	PF63 50.00	PF65 55.00			

KM# 339 10 DOLLARS
28.28 g., 0.925 Silver 0.8356 oz. ASW **Series:** 60th Anniversary of WW II **Subject:** Battle of Britain **Obv:** National arms **Obv. Legend:** REPUBLIC OF SIERRA LEONE **Rev:** Planes in flight

Date	Mintage	F12	VF20	XF40	MS60	MS63
2005	—	PF63 45.00	PF65 50.00			

KM# 340 10 DOLLARS
28.28 g., 0.925 Silver 0.8356 oz. ASW **Series:** 60th Anniversary End of WW II **Subject:** The Battle of the Atlantic **Obv:** National arms **Obv. Legend:** REPUBLIC OF SIERRA LEONE **Rev:** Plane and ship convoy

Date	Mintage	F12	VF20	XF40	MS60	MS63
2005	—	PF63 45.00	PF65 50.00			

KM# 341 10 DOLLARS
28.28 g., 0.925 Silver 0.8356 oz. ASW **Series:** 60th Anniversary End of WW II **Subject:** Battle of El Alamein **Obv:** National arms **Obv. Legend:** REPUBLIC OF SIERRA LEONE **Rev:** Tank, plane and ground troops

Date	Mintage	F12	VF20	XF40	MS60	MS63
2005	—	PF63 45.00	PF65 50.00			

KM# 342 10 DOLLARS
28.28 g., 0.925 Silver 0.8356 oz. ASW **Series:** 60th Anniversary End of WW II **Subject:** Battle of the Bulge **Obv:** National arms **Obv. Legend:** REPUBLIC OF SIERRA LEONE **Rev:** Forest battle scene

Date	Mintage	F12	VF20	XF40	MS60	MS63
2005	—	PF63 45.00	PF65 50.00			

KM# 343 10 DOLLARS
28.28 g., 0.925 Silver 0.8356 oz. ASW **Series:** 60th Anniversary End of WW II **Subject:** Battle of Berlin **Obv:** National arms **Obv. Legend:** REPUBLIC OF SIERRA LEONE **Rev:** Berlin city view, tank

Date	Mintage	F12	VF20	XF40	MS60	MS63
2005	—	PF63 45.00	PF65 50.00			

KM# 344 10 DOLLARS
28.28 g., 0.925 Silver 0.8356 oz. ASW **Series:** 60th Anniversary End of WW II **Subject:** The Heavy Water Raids **Obv:** National arms **Obv. Legend:** REPUBLIC OF SIERRA LEONE **Rev:** Troops on skies, factory in ruins

Date	Mintage	F12	VF20	XF40	MS60	MS63
2005	—	PF63 45.00	PF65 50.00			

KM# 330 10 DOLLARS
28.28 g., 0.925 Silver 0.8356 oz. ASW **Series:** Crown Jewels **Obv:** Arms **Obv. Legend:** REPUBLIC OF SIERRA LEONE **Rev:** Imperial State crown with ruby setting **Rev. Legend:** CROWN JEWELS **Edge:** Reeded

Date	Mintage	F12	VF20	XF40	MS60	MS63
2006	—	PF65 120				

KM# 331 10 DOLLARS
28.28 g., 0.925 Silver 0.8356 oz. ASW **Series:** Crown Jewels **Obv:** Arms **Obv. Legend:** REPUBLIC OF SIERRA LEONE **Rev:** Sword of State with sapphire setting **Rev. Legend:** CROWN JEWELS **Edge:** Reeded

Date	Mintage	F12	VF20	XF40	MS60	MS63
2006	—	PF65 120				

KM# 332 10 DOLLARS
28.28 g., 0.925 Silver 0.8356 oz. ASW **Series:** Crown Jewels **Obv:** Arms **Obv. Legend:** REPUBLIC OF SIERRA LEONE **Rev:** St. Edward's Crown with emerald setting **Rev. Legend:** CROWN JEWELS **Edge:** Reeded

Date	Mintage	F12	VF20	XF40	MS60	MS63
2006	—	PF65 120				

KM# 333 10 DOLLARS
28.28 g., 0.925 Silver 0.8356 oz. ASW **Series:** Crown Jewels **Obv:** Arms **Obv. Legend:** REPUBLIC OF SIERRA LEONE **Rev:** Orb and Sceptre with the cross with diamond setting **Rev. Legend:** CROWN JEWELS **Edge:** Reeded

Date	Mintage	F12	VF20	XF40	MS60	MS63
2006	—	PF65 120				

KM# 334 10 DOLLARS
Copper-Nickel **Subject:** 80th Birthday of Queen Elizabeth II **Obv:** Arms **Obv. Legend:** REPUBLIC OF SIERRA LEONE **Rev:** Elizabeth II seated giving Christmas message **Edge:** Reeded

Date	Mintage	F12	VF20	XF40	MS60	MS63
2006	—	—	—	16.50	18.50	

KM# 334a 10 DOLLARS
28.28 g., 0.925 Silver 0.8356 oz. ASW **Subject:** 80th Birthday of Queen Elizabeth II **Obv:** Arms **Obv. Legend:** REPUBLIC OF SIERRA LEONE **Rev:** Elizabeth II seated giving Christmas Message **Edge:** Reeded

Date	Mintage	F12	VF20	XF40	MS60	MS63
2006	—	PF63 65.00	PF65 75.00			

KM# 335 10 DOLLARS
Copper-Nickel **Subject:** 80th Bithday of Queen Elizabeth II **Obv:** Arms **Obv. Legend:** REPUBLIC OF SIERRA LEONE **Rev:** Elizabeth II at 2002 Golden Jubilee celebrations in London, Concorde and Red Arrows doing flypass over Buckingham Palace **Edge:** Reeded

Date	Mintage	F12	VF20	XF40	MS60	MS63
2006	—	—	—	16.50	18.50	

KM# 335a 10 DOLLARS
28.28 g., 0.925 Silver 0.8356 oz. ASW **Subject:** 80th Birthday of Queen Elizabeth Ii **Obv:** Arms **Obv. Legend:** REPUBLIC OF SIERRA LEONE **Rev:** Elizabeth II at 2002 Golden Jubilee celebrations in London, Concorde and Red Arrows doing flypass over Buckingham Palace **Edge:** Reeded

Date	Mintage	F12	VF20	XF40	MS60	MS63
2006	—	PF63 65.00	PF65 75.00			

KM# 336 10 DOLLARS
Copper-Nickel **Subject:** 80th Birthday of Queen Elizabeth II **Obv:** Arms **Obv. Legend:** REPUBLIC OF SIERRA LEONE **Rev:** Elizabeth II presenting 1966 Football World Cup to English team **Edge:** Reeded

Date	Mintage	F12	VF20	XF40	MS60	MS63
2006	—	—	—	16.50	18.50	

KM# 336a 10 DOLLARS
28.28 g., 0.925 Silver 0.8356 oz. ASW **Subject:** 80th Birthday of Queen Elizabeth II **Obv:** Arms **Obv. Legend:** REPUBLIC OF SIERRA LEONE **Rev:** Elizabeth II presenting 1966 Football World Cup to English team **Edge:** Reeded

Date	Mintage	F12	VF20	XF40	MS60	MS63
2006	—	PF63 65.00	PF65 75.00			

KM# 337 10 DOLLARS
Copper-Nickel **Subject:** 80th Birthday of Queen Elizabeth II **Obv:** Arms **Obv. Legend:** REPUBLIC OF SIERRA LEONE **Rev:** Investiture of Charles as Prince of Wales in 1969 **Edge:** Reeded

Date	Mintage	F12	VF20	XF40	MS60	MS63
2006	—	—	—	16.50	18.50	

KM# 337a 10 DOLLARS
0.9167 Silver **Subject:** 80th Birthday of Queen Elizabeth II **Obv:** Arms **Obv. Legend:** REPUBLIC OF SIERRA LEONE **Rev:** Investiture of Charles as Prince of Wales in 1969 **Edge:** Reeded

Date	Mintage	F12	VF20	XF40	MS60	MS63
2006	—	PF63 65.00	PF65 75.00			

KM# 338 10 DOLLARS
Copper-Nickel **Subject:** 10th Anniversary Death of Princess Diana **Obv:** Arms **Obv. Legend:** REPUBLIC OF SIERRA LEONE **Rev:** Diana with sons, Prince William and Prince Harry facing **Rev. Legend:** DIANA — PRINCESS OF WALES **Edge:** Reeded

Date	Mintage	F12	VF20	XF40	MS60	MS63
2007	—	—	—	16.50	18.50	

KM# 338a 10 DOLLARS
28.28 g., 0.925 Silver 0.8356 oz. ASW **Subject:** 10th Anniversary Death of Princess Diana **Obv:** Arms **Obv. Legend:** REPUBLIC OF SIERRA LEONE **Rev:** Diana with sons, Prince William and Prince Harry facing **Rev. Legend:** DIANA — PRINCESS OF WALES **Edge:** Reeded

Date	Mintage	F12	VF20	XF40	MS60	MS63
2007	—	PF63 65.00	PF65 75.00			

KM# 351 10 DOLLARS
28.28 g., 0.925 Silver 0.8356 oz. ASW, 38.61 mm. **Obv:** National arms **Rev:** Mountain Gorilla

Date	Mintage	F12	VF20	XF40	MS60	MS63
2011PM	—	PF63 65.00	PF65 75.00			

KM# 200 20 DOLLARS
1.24 g., 0.999 Gold 0.0397 oz. AGW, 13.9 mm. **Subject:** Year of the Snake **Obv:** National arms **Rev:** Snake **Edge:** Reeded

Date	Mintage	F12	VF20	XF40	MS60	MS63
2001	—	PF65 85.00				

KM# 208 20 DOLLARS
1.24 g., 0.999 Gold 0.0397 oz. AGW, 13.9 mm. **Subject:** P'an Ku **Obv:** National arms **Rev:** Dragon

Date	Mintage	F12	VF20	XF40	MS60	MS63
2001	Est. 5000	PF65 85.00				

KM# 216 20 DOLLARS
1.24 g., 0.999 Gold 0.0397 oz. AGW, 13.9 mm. **Subject:** P'an Ku **Obv:** National arms **Rev:** Dragon and three animals

Date	Mintage	F12	VF20	XF40	MS60	MS63
2001	—	PF65 85.00				

KM# 258 20 DOLLARS
1.24 g., 0.999 Gold 0.0396 oz. AGW, 13.92 mm. **Subject:** Year of the Horse **Obv:** National arms **Rev:** Horse **Edge:** Reeded

Date	Mintage	F12	VF20	XF40	MS60	MS63
2002	5,000	PF65 85.00				

KM# 272 30 DOLLARS
6.22 g., 0.375 Gold 0.0745 oz. AGW, 22 mm. **Subject:** Queen's Golden Jubilee **Obv:** National arms **Rev:** Queen Elizabeth II and Prince Philip **Edge:** Reeded

Date	Mintage	F12	VF20	XF40	MS60	MS63
2002	—	PF65 150				

KM# 273 30 DOLLARS
6.22 g., 0.375 Gold 0.0745 oz. AGW, 22 mm. **Subject:** Queen's Golden Jubilee **Obv:** National arms **Rev:** Queen Elizabeth II, Prince Charles and Princess Anne **Edge:** Reeded

Date	Mintage	F12	VF20	XF40	MS60	MS63
2002	—	PF65 150				

KM# 201 50 DOLLARS
3.11 g., 0.999 Gold 0.0993 oz. AGW, 18 mm. **Subject:** Year of the Snake **Obv:** National arms **Rev:** Snake **Edge:** Reeded

Date	Mintage	F12	VF20	XF40	MS60	MS63
2001	Est. 10000	PF65 200				

KM# 209 50 DOLLARS
3.11 g., 0.999 Gold 0.0993 oz. AGW, 18 mm. **Subject:** P'an Ku **Obv:** National arms **Rev:** Dragon

Date	Mintage	F12	VF20	XF40	MS60	MS63
2001	Est. 5000	PF65 200				

KM# 217 50 DOLLARS
3.11 g., 0.999 Gold 0.0993 oz. AGW, 18 mm. **Subject:** P'an Ku **Obv:** National arms **Rev:** Dragon and three animals

Date	Mintage	F12	VF20	XF40	MS60	MS63
2001	Est. 5000	PF65 200				

KM# 259 50 DOLLARS
3.11 g., 0.999 Gold 0.0992 oz. AGW, 18 mm. **Subject:** Year of the Horse **Obv:** National arms **Rev:** Horse **Edge:** Reeded

Date	Mintage	F12	VF20	XF40	MS60	MS63
2002	5,000	PF65 200				

KM# 266 50 DOLLARS
155.55 g., 0.9999 Silver 4.9684 oz. ASW, 65 mm. **Subject:** RMS Titanic **Obv:** National arms **Rev:** Titanic at dock **Edge:** Reeded

Date	Mintage	F12	VF20	XF40	MS60	MS63
2002	—	PF65 220				

KM# 202 100 DOLLARS
6.22 g., 0.999 Gold 0.1985 oz. AGW, 22 mm. **Subject:** Year of the Snake **Obv:** National arms **Rev:** Snake **Edge:** Reeded

Date	Mintage	F12	VF20	XF40	MS60	MS63
2001	—	PF65 380				

KM# 210 100 DOLLARS
6.22 g., 0.999 Gold 0.1985 oz. AGW, 22 mm. **Subject:** P'an Ku **Obv:** National arms **Rev:** Dragon

Date	Mintage	F12	VF20	XF40	MS60	MS63
2001	Est. 10000	PF65 380				

KM# 218 100 DOLLARS
6.22 g., 0.999 Gold 0.1985 oz. AGW, 22 mm. **Subject:** P'an Ku **Obv:** National arms **Rev:** Dragon and three animals

Date	Mintage	F12	VF20	XF40	MS60	MS63
2001	Est. 10000	PF65 380				

KM# 224 100 DOLLARS
6.22 g., 0.999 Gold 0.1985 oz. AGW, 22 mm. **Series:** The Big Five **Obv:** National arms **Rev:** Rhino **Edge:** Reeded

Date	Mintage	F12	VF20	XF40	MS60	MS63
2001	Est. 5000	PF65 380				

KM# 227 100 DOLLARS
6.22 g., 0.999 Gold 0.1985 oz. AGW, 22 mm. **Series:** The Big Five **Obv:** National arms **Rev:** Lion

Date	Mintage	F12	VF20	XF40	MS60	MS63
2001	—	PF65 380				

KM# 230 100 DOLLARS
6.22 g., 0.999 Gold 0.1985 oz. AGW, 22 mm. **Series:** The Big Five **Obv:** National arms **Rev:** Leopard

Date	Mintage	F12	VF20	XF40	MS60	MS63
2001	Est. 5000	PF65 380				

KM# 233 100 DOLLARS
6.22 g., 0.999 Gold 0.1985 oz. AGW, 22 mm. **Series:** The Big Five **Obv:** National arms **Rev:** Elephants

Date	Mintage	F12	VF20	XF40	MS60	MS63
2001	Est. 5000	PF65 380				

KM# 236 100 DOLLARS
6.22 g., 0.999 Gold 0.1985 oz. AGW, 22 mm. **Series:** The Big Five **Obv:** National arms **Rev:** Buffalo

Date	Mintage	F12	VF20	XF40	MS60	MS63
2001	Est. 5000	PF65 380				

KM# 239 100 DOLLARS
6.22 g., 0.999 Gold 0.1985 oz. AGW, 22 mm. **Series:** The Big Five **Obv:** National arms **Rev:** All five animals

Date	Mintage	F12	VF20	XF40	MS60	MS63
2001	—	PF65 380				

KM# 251 100 DOLLARS
6.22 g., 0.999 Gold 0.1985 oz. AGW, 22 mm. **Series:** Big Cats **Obv:** National arms **Rev:** Male and female lions **Edge:** Reeded

Date	Mintage	F12	VF20	XF40	MS60	MS63
2001	5,000	PF65 380				

KM# 252 100 DOLLARS
6.22 g., 0.999 Gold 0.1985 oz. AGW, 22 mm. **Series:** Big Cats **Rev:** Tiger **Edge:** Reeded

Date	Mintage	F12	VF20	XF40	MS60	MS63
2001	5,000	PF65 380				

KM# 253 100 DOLLARS
6.22 g., 0.999 Gold 0.1985 oz. AGW, 22 mm. **Series:** Big Cats **Rev:** Cheetah **Edge:** Reeded

Date	Mintage	F12	VF20	XF40	MS60	MS63
2001	5,000	PF65 380				

KM# 254 100 DOLLARS
6.22 g., 0.999 Gold 0.1985 oz. AGW, 22 mm. **Series:** Big Cats **Rev:** Cougar **Edge:** Reeded

Date	Mintage	F12	VF20	XF40	MS60	MS63
2001	5,000	PF65 380				

KM# 255 100 DOLLARS
6.22 g., 0.999 Gold 0.1985 oz. AGW, 22 mm. **Series:** Big Cats **Rev:** Black panther **Edge:** Reeded

Date	Mintage	F12	VF20	XF40	MS60	MS63
2001	5,000	PF65 380				

KM# 260 100 DOLLARS
6.22 g., 0.999 Gold 0.1985 oz. AGW, 22 mm. **Subject:** Year of the Horse **Obv:** National arms **Rev:** Horse **Edge:** Reeded

Date	Mintage	F12	VF20	XF40	MS60	MS63
2002	2,000	PF65 380				

KM# 274 100 DOLLARS
6.22 g., 0.9999 Gold 0.1987 oz. AGW, 22 mm. **Subject:** Queen's Golden Jubilee **Obv:** National arms **Rev:** Queen Elizabeth II and Prince Philip **Edge:** Reeded

Date	Mintage	F12	VF20	XF40	MS60	MS63
2002	—	PF65 380				

KM# 275 100 DOLLARS
6.22 g., 0.9999 Gold 0.1987 oz. AGW, 22 mm. **Subject:** Queen's Golden Jubilee **Obv:** National arms **Rev:** Queen Elizabeth II, Prince Charles and Princess Anne **Edge:** Reeded

Date	Mintage	F12	VF20	XF40	MS60	MS63
2002	—	PF65 380				

KM# 278 100 DOLLARS
6.22 g., 0.9999 Gold 0.1987 oz. AGW, 22 mm. **Subject:** British Queen Mother **Obv:** National arms **Rev:** Queen Mother in garden with dog **Edge:** Reeded

Date	Mintage	F12	VF20	XF40	MS60	MS63
2002	2,000	PF65 380				

KM# 281 100 DOLLARS
6.22 g., 0.9999 Gold 0.1987 oz. AGW, 22 mm. **Subject:** British Queen Mother **Obv:** National arms **Rev:** Queen Mother with daughters **Edge:** Reeded

Date	Mintage	F12	VF20	XF40	MS60	MS63
2002	2,000	PF65 380				

KM# 284 100 DOLLARS
6.22 g., 0.9999 Gold 0.1987 oz. AGW, 22 mm. **Subject:** Queen Elizabeth's Golden Jubilee **Obv:** National arms **Rev:** Queen and young Prince Charles **Edge:** Reeded

Date	Mintage	F12	VF20	XF40	MS60	MS63
2002	2,002	PF65 380				

KM# 287 100 DOLLARS
6.22 g., 0.9999 Gold 0.1987 oz. AGW, 22 mm. **Subject:** Queen Elizabeth's Golden Jubilee **Obv:** National arms **Rev:** Queen and Prince Philip **Edge:** Reeded

Date	Mintage	F12	VF20	XF40	MS60	MS63
2002	2,002	PF65 380				

KM# 290 100 DOLLARS
6.22 g., 0.9999 Gold 0.1987 oz. AGW, 22 mm. **Subject:** Olympics **Obv:** National arms **Rev:** Victory goddess Nike **Edge:** Reeded

Date	Mintage	F12	VF20	XF40	MS60	MS63
2003	5,000	PF65 380				
2004	5,000	PF65 380				

KM# 293 100 DOLLARS
6.22 g., 0.9999 Gold 0.1987 oz. AGW, 22 mm. **Subject:** Olympics **Obv:** National arms **Rev:** Ancient archer **Edge:** Reeded

Date	Mintage	F12	VF20	XF40	MS60	MS63
2003	5,000	PF65 380				
2004	5,000	PF65 380				

KM# 267 150 DOLLARS
1000.00 g., 0.9999 Silver 31.9406 oz. ASW, 85 mm. **Subject:** RMS Titanic **Obv:** National arms **Rev:** Titanic at dock **Edge:** Reeded

Date	Mintage	F12	VF20	XF40	MS60	MS63
2002	—	PF65 1,350				

KM# 203 250 DOLLARS
15.51 g., 0.999 Gold 0.495 oz. AGW, 30 mm. **Subject:** Year of the Snake **Obv:** National arms **Rev:** Snake **Edge:** Reeded

Date	Mintage	F12	VF20	XF40	MS60	MS63
2001	Est. 5000	PF65 950				

KM# 211 250 DOLLARS
15.55 g., 0.999 Gold 0.4963 oz. AGW, 30 mm. **Subject:** P'an Ku **Obv:** National arms **Rev:** Dragon

Date	Mintage	F12	VF20	XF40	MS60	MS63
2001	Est. 2000	PF65 950				

KM# 219 250 DOLLARS
15.55 g., 0.999 Gold 0.4963 oz. AGW, 30 mm. **Subject:** P'an Ku **Obv:** National arms **Rev:** Dragon and three animals

Date	Mintage	F12	VF20	XF40	MS60	MS63
2001	Est. 2000	PF65 950				

KM# 261 250 DOLLARS
15.55 g., 0.999 Gold 0.4962 oz. AGW, 30 mm. **Subject:** Year of the Horse **Obv:** National arms **Rev:** Horse **Edge:** Reeded

Date	Mintage	F12	VF20	XF40	MS60	MS63
2002	2,000	PF65 950				

KM# 204 500 DOLLARS
31.10 g., 0.999 Gold 0.9926 oz. AGW, 32.7 mm. **Subject:** Year of the Snake **Obv:** National arms **Rev:** Snake **Edge:** Reeded

Date	Mintage	F12	VF20	XF40	MS60	MS63
2001	Est. 1000	PF65 1,850				

KM# 212 500 DOLLARS
31.10 g., 0.999 Gold 0.9926 oz. AGW, 32.7 mm. **Subject:** P'an Ku **Obv:** National arms **Rev:** Dragon

Date	Mintage	F12	VF20	XF40	MS60	MS63
2001	Est. 1000	PF65 1,850				

KM# 220 500 DOLLARS
31.10 g., 0.999 Gold 0.9926 oz. AGW, 32.7 mm. **Subject:** P'an Ku **Obv:** National arms **Rev:** Dragon and three animals

Date	Mintage	F12	VF20	XF40	MS60	MS63
2001	Est. 1000	PF65 1,850				

KM# 262 500 DOLLARS
31.10 g., 0.999 Gold 0.9925 oz. AGW, 32.7 mm. **Subject:** Year of the Horse **Obv:** National arms **Rev:** Horse **Edge:** Reeded

Date	Mintage	F12	VF20	XF40	MS60	MS63
2002	1,000	PF65 1,850				

KM# 294 500 DOLLARS
31.10 g., 0.9999 Gold 0.9934 oz. AGW, 32.7 mm. **Obv:** National arms **Rev:** Multicolor Astro Boy cartoon **Edge:** Reeded

Date	Mintage	F12	VF20	XF40	MS60	MS63
2003	2,003	PF65 1,850				

KM# 299 500 DOLLARS
31.10 g., 0.9999 Gold 0.9935 oz. AGW, 32.7 mm. **Obv:** National arms **Rev:** Nelson Mandela **Edge:** Reeded

Date	Mintage	F12	VF20	XF40	MS60	MS63
2004	—	PF65 1,850				

KM# 205 2500 DOLLARS
155.52 g., 0.999 Gold 4.9628 oz. AGW, 50 mm. **Subject:** Year of the Snake **Obv:** National arms **Rev:** Snake **Edge:** Reeded

Date	Mintage	F12	VF20	XF40	MS60	MS63
2001	Est. 250	PF65 9,250				

KM# 213 2500 DOLLARS

155.52 g., 0.999 Gold 4.9628 oz. AGW, 50 mm. **Subject:** P'an Ku **Obv:** National arms **Rev:** Dragon

Date	Mintage	F12	VF20	XF40	MS60	MS63
2001	Est. 250				PF65 9,250	

KM# 263 2500 DOLLARS

155.51 g., 0.999 Gold 4.9626 oz. AGW, 50 mm. **Subject:** Year of the Horse **Obv:** National arms **Rev:** Horse **Edge:** Reeded

Date	Mintage	F12	VF20	XF40	MS60	MS63
2002	250				PF65 9,250	

MINT SETS

KM#	Date	Mintage	Identification	Issue Price	Mkt Val
MS2	2006 (4)	—	KM# 334-337	65.00	75.00

PROOF SETS

KM#	Date	Mintage	Identification	Issue Price	Mkt Val
PS7	2006 (4)	—	KM# 330-333	450	480
PS8	2006 (4)	—	KM# 334a-337a	300	300

SINGAPORE

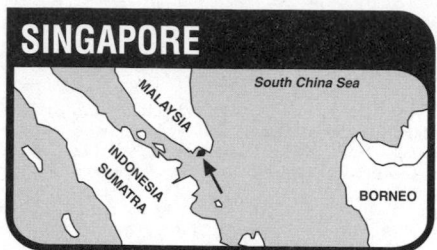

The Republic of Singapore, a member of the Commonwealth of Nations situated off the southern tip of the Malay peninsula, has an area of 224 sq. mi. (633 sq. km.) and a population of *2.7 million. Capital: Singapore. The economy is based on entrepôt trade, manufacturing and oil. Rubber, petroleum products, machinery and spices are exported.

The President is Chief of State. The prime minister is Head of Government.

MINT MARK

sm = "*sm*" - Singapore Mint monogram

MONETARY SYSTEM

100 Cents = 1 Dollar

REPUBLIC

STANDARD COINAGE

100 Cents = 1 Dollar

KM# 98a CENT

1.81 g., 0.925 Silver 0.0535 oz. ASW, 15.9 mm. **Obv:** National arms **Rev:** Value divides plants

Date	Mintage	F12	VF20	XF40	MS60	MS63
2001sm	6,000	PF63 2.50				
2002sm	6,300	PF63 2.50				

KM# 98 CENT

1.24 g., Copper Plated Zinc, 15.9 mm. **Obv:** National arms **Rev:** Value divides plants **Edge:** Plain **Note:** Similar to KM#49 but motto ribbon on arms curves down at center.

Date	Mintage	F12	VF20	XF40	MS60	MS63
2001	40,101,738	—	—	—	0.10	0.15
2002 In sets only	84,577	—	—	—	—	0.15

KM# 99a 5 CENTS

2.00 g., 0.925 Silver 0.0591 oz. ASW, 16.75 mm. **Obv:** National arms **Rev:** Fruit salad plant

Date	Mintage	F12	VF20	XF40	MS60	MS63
2001sm	6,000	PF63 2.75				
2002sm	6,300	PF63 2.75				
2003sm	4,900	PF63 2.75				
2004sm	4,000	PF63 2.75				
2005sm	3,250	PF63 2.75				

KM# 99 5 CENTS

1.56 g., Aluminum-Bronze, 16.75 mm. **Obv:** National arms **Rev:** Fruit salad plant **Edge:** Reeded **Note:** Similar to KM#50 but motto ribbon on arms curves down at center.

Date	Mintage	F12	VF20	XF40	MS60	MS63
2001	13,101,738	—	—	—	0.20	0.30
2002	33,556,000	—	—	—	0.20	0.30
2003	16,508,980	—	—	—	0.20	0.30
2003	4,550	PF63 3.00				
2004	20,070,000	—	—	—	0.20	0.30
2004	3,500	PF63 3.00				
2005	70,061,981	—	—	—	0.20	0.30

Date	Mintage	F12	VF20	XF40	MS60	MS63
2006 In sets only	53,214	—	—	—	—	0.50
2007	22,884,889	—	—	—	0.20	0.30
2008 In sets only	55,000	—	—	—	—	0.50
2009	19,850,000	—	—	—	0.20	0.30
2010	Est. 5,160,000	—	—	—	0.20	0.30
2011	—	—	—	—	0.20	0.30
2012	—	—	—	—	0.20	0.30
2013 In sets only	Est. 160000	—	—	—	—	0.50

KM# 100a 10 CENTS

3.05 g., 0.925 Silver 0.0901 oz. ASW, 18.5 mm. **Obv:** National arms **Rev:** Star Jasmine plant **Edge:** Reeded

Date	Mintage	F12	VF20	XF40	MS60	MS63
2001sm	6,000	PF63 4.00				
2002sm	6,300	PF63 4.00				
2003sm	4,900	PF63 4.00				
2004sm	4,000	PF63 4.00				
2005sm	3,250	PF63 4.00				

KM# 100 10 CENTS

2.60 g., Copper-Nickel, 18.5 mm. **Obv:** National arms **Rev:** Star Jasmine plant **Edge:** Reeded **Note:** Similar to KM#51 but motto ribbon on arms curves down at center.

Date	Mintage	F12	VF20	XF40	MS60	MS63
2001 In sets only	101,738	—	—	—	—	0.30
2002 In sets only	84,577	—	—	—	—	0.30
2003	21,578,980	—	—	—	0.20	0.30
2003	4,550	PF63 4.00				
2004 In sets only	70,000	—	—	—	—	0.30
2004	3,500	PF63 4.00				
2005	50,021,981	—	—	—	0.20	0.30
2006 In sets only	53,214	—	—	—	—	0.50
2007	50,054,889	—	—	—	0.20	0.30
2008 In sets only	55,000	—	—	—	—	0.50
2009	38,790,000	—	—	—	0.20	0.30
2010 In sets only	—	—	—	—	0.20	0.50
2011	—	—	—	—	0.20	0.50
2012	—	—	—	—	0.20	0.50
2013 In sets only	Est. 160000	—	—	—	—	0.50

KM# 101a 20 CENTS

5.24 g., 0.925 Silver 0.1548 oz. ASW, 21.36 mm. **Obv:** National arms **Rev:** Powder puff plant above value **Edge:** Reeded

Date	Mintage	F12	VF20	XF40	MS60	MS63
2001sm	6,000	PF63 7.00				
2002sm	6,300	PF63 7.00				
2003sm	4,900	PF63 7.00				
2004sm	4,000	PF63 7.00				
2005sm	3,250	PF63 7.00				

KM# 101 20 CENTS

4.50 g., Copper-Nickel, 21.36 mm. **Obv:** National arms **Rev:** Powder-puff plant above value **Edge:** Reeded **Note:** Similar to KM#52 but motto ribbon on arms curves down at center.

Date	Mintage	F12	VF20	XF40	MS60	MS63
2001 In sets only	101,738	—	—	—	—	0.75
2002 In sets only	84,577	—	—	—	—	0.75
2003 In sets only	68,980	—	—	—	—	0.75
2003	4,550	PF63 5.00				
2004 In sets only	70,000	—	—	—	—	0.75
2004	3,500	PF63 5.00				
2005 In sets only	61,981	—	—	—	—	1.00
2006	40,143,214	—	—	—	0.60	0.75
2007	30,144,889	—	—	—	0.60	0.75
2008 In sets only	55,000	—	—	—	—	1.00
2009	30,160,000	—	—	—	0.60	0.75

Date	Mintage	F12	VF20	XF40	MS60	MS63
2010	Est. 10030000	—	—	—	0.60	0.75
2011	—	—	—	—	0.60	0.75
2012	—	—	—	—	0.60	0.75
2013 In sets only	Est. 160000	—	—	—	—	1.00

KM# 102 50 CENTS

7.29 g., Copper-Nickel, 24.66 mm. **Obv:** National arms **Rev:** Yellow Allamanda plant above value **Edge Lettering:** REPUBLIC OF SINGAPORE (lion's head) **Note:** Similar to KM#53 but motto ribbon on arms curves down at center.

Date	Mintage	F12	VF20	XF40	MS60	MS63
2001 In sets only	101,738	—	—	—	—	1.00
2002 In sets only	84,577	—	—	—	—	1.00
2003 In sets only	69,980	—	—	—	—	1.00
2003	4,550	PF63 6.00				
2004 In sets only	70,000	—	—	—	—	1.00
2004	3,500	PF63 6.00				
2005	25,057,981	—	—	—	0.75	1.00
2006 In sets only	53,214	—	—	—	—	1.25
2007	28,764,889	—	—	—	0.75	1.00
2008 In sets only	55,000	—	—	—	—	1.25
2009	12,390,000	—	—	—	0.75	1.00
2010	Est. 8270000	—	—	—	0.75	1.00
2011	—	—	—	—	0.75	1.00
2012	—	—	—	—	0.75	1.00
2013 In sets only	Est. 160,000	—	—	—	—	1.25

KM# 102a 50 CENTS

8.56 g., 0.925 Silver 0.2529 oz. ASW, 24.66 mm. **Obv:** National arms **Rev:** Yellow Allamanda plant above value

Date	Mintage	F12	VF20	XF40	MS60	MS63
2001sm	6,000	PF63 12.00				
2002sm	6,300	PF63 12.00				
2003sm	4,900	PF63 12.00				
2004sm	1,900	PF63 12.00				
2005sm	3,250	PF63 12.00				

KM# 103a DOLLAR

8.05 g., 0.925 Silver 0.2379 oz. ASW, 22.4 mm. **Obv:** National arms **Rev:** Periwinkle flower

Date	Mintage	F12	VF20	XF40	MS60	MS63
2001sm	6,000	PF63 15.00				
2002sm	6,300	PF63 15.00				
2003sm	4,900	PF63 15.00				
2004sm	4,000	PF63 15.00				
2005sm	3,250	PF63 15.00				

KM# 103 DOLLAR

6.30 g., Aluminum-Bronze, 22.4 mm. **Obv:** National arms **Rev:** Periwinkle flower **Edge:** Reeded **Note:** Similar to KM#54 but motto ribbon on arms curves down at center.

Date	Mintage	F12	VF20	XF40	MS60	MS63
2001	40,941,738	—	—	—	1.50	2.25
2002	35,744,577	—	—	—	1.50	2.25
2003	31,968,980	—	—	—	1.50	2.25
2003	4,550	PF63 10.00				
2004	34,450,000	—	—	—	1.50	2.25
2004	3,500	PF63 10.00				
2005 In sets only	61,891	—	—	—	—	2.75
2006	63,053,214	—	—	—	1.50	2.25
2007 In sets only	54,889	—	—	—	—	2.75
2008	10,375,000	—	—	—	1.50	2.25
2009	21,750,000	—	—	—	1.50	2.25
2010	—	—	—	—	1.50	2.75
2011	—	—	—	—	1.50	2.75
2012	—	—	—	—	1.50	2.75
2013 In sets only	Est. 160,000	—	—	—	—	2.75

KM# 184 DOLLAR
7.29 g., Copper-Nickel, 24.7 mm. **Subject:** Old World Charm - Balestier **Obv:** Arms with supporters **Rev:** Old buildings **Edge:** Reeded

Date	Mintage	F12	VF20	XF40	MS60	MS63
2004sm Prooflike	3,486	—	—	—	—	10.00

KM# 184a DOLLAR
8.56 g., 0.999 Silver 0.2732 oz. ASW, 24.7 mm. **Subject:** Old World Charm - Balestier **Obv:** Arms with supporters **Rev:** Old buildings **Note:** Colorized

Date	Mintage	F12	VF20	XF40	MS60	MS63
2004sm	2,009	PF63 27.50				

KM# 190 DOLLAR
7.29 g., Copper-Nickel, 24.7 mm. **Subject:** Old World Charm - Jalan Besar

Date	Mintage	F12	VF20	XF40	MS60	MS63
2004sm Prooflike	3,470	—	—	—	—	10.00

KM# 190a DOLLAR
8.56 g., 0.999 Silver 0.2732 oz. ASW, 24.7 mm. **Subject:** Old World Charm - Jalan Besar **Note:** Colorized

Date	Mintage	F12	VF20	XF40	MS60	MS63
2004sm	2,844	PF63 27.50				

KM# 191 DOLLAR
7.29 g., Copper-Nickel, 24.7 mm. **Subject:** Old World Charm - Joo Chiat

Date	Mintage	F12	VF20	XF40	MS60	MS63
2004sm Prooflike	3,551	—	—	—	—	10.00

KM# 191a DOLLAR
8.56 g., 0.999 Silver 0.2732 oz. ASW, 24.7 mm. **Subject:** Old World Charm - Joo Chiat **Note:** Colorized

Date	Mintage	F12	VF20	XF40	MS60	MS63
2004sm	2,863	PF63 27.50				

KM# 192 DOLLAR
7.29 g., Copper-Nickel, 24.7 mm. **Subject:** Old World Charm - Tanjong Katong

Date	Mintage	F12	VF20	XF40	MS60	MS63
2004sm Prooflike	3,555	—	—	—	—	10.00

KM# 192a DOLLAR
8.56 g., 0.999 Silver 0.2732 oz. ASW, 24.7 mm. **Subject:** Old World Charm - Tanjong Katong

Date	Mintage	F12	VF20	XF40	MS60	MS63
2004sm	2,263	PF63 27.50				

KM# 244 DOLLAR
18.00 g., Copper-Nickel, 33 mm. **Series:** Urban Redevelopment **Obv:** National arms **Rev:** Anak Bukit

Date	Mintage	F12	VF20	XF40	MS60	MS63
2005sm Prooflike	2,620	PF63 12.00				

KM# 244a DOLLAR
17.30 g., 0.9999 Silver 0.5526 oz. ASW, 33 mm. **Series:** Urban Redevelopment **Obv:** National arms **Rev:** Anak Bukit - multicolor

Date	Mintage	F12	VF20	XF40	MS60	MS63
2005sm	2,450	PF63 45.00				

KM# 245 DOLLAR
18.00 g., Copper-Nickel, 33 mm. **Series:** Singapore Identity Plan **Obv:** National arms **Rev:** Coronation

Date	Mintage	F12	VF20	XF40	MS60	MS63
2005sm Prooflike	2,620	PF63 12.00				

KM# 245a DOLLAR
17.30 g., 0.9999 Silver 0.5526 oz. ASW, 33 mm. **Series:** Singapore Identity Plan **Obv:** National arms **Rev:** Coronation - multicolor

Date	Mintage	F12	VF20	XF40	MS60	MS63
2005sm	790	PF63 45.00				

KM# 246 DOLLAR
18.00 g., Copper-Nickel, 33 mm. **Series:** Singapore Identity Plan **Obv:** National arms **Rev:** Jalan Leban and Casuarina Road

Date	Mintage	F12	VF20	XF40	MS60	MS63
2005sm Prooflike	2,620	PF63 12.00				

KM# 246a DOLLAR
17.00 g., 0.9999 Silver 0.543 oz. ASW, 33 mm. **Series:** Singapore Identity Plan **Obv:** National arms **Rev:** Jalan Leban and Casuarina Road - multicolor

Date	Mintage	F12	VF20	XF40	MS60	MS63
2005sm	790	PF63 45.00				

KM# 247 DOLLAR
18.00 g., Copper-Nickel, 33 mm. **Series:** Singapore Identity Plan **Obv:** National arms **Rev:** Springleaf

Date	Mintage	F12	VF20	XF40	MS60	MS63
2005sm Prooflike	2,620	—	—	—	—	15.00

KM# 247a DOLLAR
17.30 g., 0.9999 Silver 0.5526 oz. ASW, 33 mm. **Series:** Singapore Identity Plan **Obv:** National arms **Rev:** Springleaf - multicolor

Date	Mintage	F12	VF20	XF40	MS60	MS63
2005sm	2,450	PF63 45.00				

KM# 248 DOLLAR
18.00 g., Copper-Nickel, 33 mm. **Series:** Singapore Identity Plan **Obv:** National arms **Rev:** Thomson Village

Date	Mintage	F12	VF20	XF40	MS60	MS63
2005sm Prooflike	2,620	—	—	—	—	15.00

KM# 248a DOLLAR
17.30 g., 0.9999 Silver 0.5526 oz. ASW, 33 mm. **Series:** Singapore Identity Plan **Obv:** National arms **Rev:** Thomson Village - multicolor

Date	Mintage	F12	VF20	XF40	MS60	MS63
2005sm	800	PF63 45.00				

KM# 262a DOLLAR
17.30 g., 0.999 Silver 0.5521 oz. ASW, 33 mm. **Series:** Singapore Identity Plan **Obv:** National arms **Rev:** Punggoi Point and Coney Island - multicolor

Date	Mintage	F12	VF20	XF40	MS60	MS63
2007sm	2,289	PF63 32.50				

KM# 259 DOLLAR
18.00 g., Copper-Nickel, 33 mm. **Series:** Singapore Identity Plan **Obv:** National arms **Rev:** Changi Village - multicolor

Date	Mintage	F12	VF20	XF40	MS60	MS63
2007sm Prooflike	2,568	—	—	—	—	15.00

KM# 259a DOLLAR
17.30 g., 0.999 Silver 0.5521 oz. ASW, 33 mm. **Series:** Singapore Identity Plan **Obv:** National arms **Rev:** Changi Village - multicolor

Date	Mintage	F12	VF20	XF40	MS60	MS63
2007sm	976	PF63 37.50				

KM# 260 DOLLAR
18.00 g., Copper-Nickel, 33 mm. **Series:** Singapore Identity Plan **Obv:** National arms **Rev:** Pasir Ris Park - multicolor

Date	Mintage	F12	VF20	XF40	MS60	MS63
2007sm Prooflike	2,430	—	—	—	—	15.00

KM# 260a DOLLAR
17.30 g., 0.999 Silver 0.5521 oz. ASW, 33 mm. **Series:** Urban Redevelopment **Obv:** National arms **Rev:** Pasir Ris Park - multicolor

Date	Mintage	F12	VF20	XF40	MS60	MS63
2007sm	936	PF63 37.50				

KM# 261 DOLLAR
Copper-Nickel **Series:** Urban Redevelopment **Obv:** National arms **Rev:** Pulau Ubin - multicolor

Date	Mintage	F12	VF20	XF40	MS60	MS63
2007sm Prooflike	2,408	—	—	—	—	12.50

KM# 261a DOLLAR
17.30 g., 0.999 Silver 0.5521 oz. ASW, 33 mm. **Series:** Urban Redevelopment **Obv:** National arms **Rev:** Pulau Ubin - multicolor

Date	Mintage	F12	VF20	XF40	MS60	MS63
2007sm	2,327	PF63 32.50				

KM# 262 DOLLAR
Copper-Nickel **Series:** Urban Redevelopment **Obv:** National arms **Rev:** Punggoi Point and Coney Island - multicolor

Date	Mintage	F12	VF20	XF40	MS60	MS63
2007sm Prooflike	2,387	—	—	—	—	12.50

KM# 290 DOLLAR
Copper-Nickel **Obv:** Supported arms **Rev:** Multicolor Kent Ridge Park

Date	Mintage	F12	VF20	XF40	MS60	MS63
2008 Prooflike	2,250	PF63 10.00				

KM# 290a DOLLAR
17.30 g., 0.999 Silver 0.5521 oz. ASW **Obv:** Supported arms **Rev:** Multicolor Kent Ridge Park

Date	Mintage	F12	VF20	XF40	MS60	MS63
2008	850	PF63 37.50				

KM# 291 DOLLAR
Copper-Nickel **Obv:** Supported arms **Rev:** Multicolor Labrador Nature Reserve

Date	Mintage	F12	VF20	XF40	MS60	MS63
2008 Prooflike	2,250	PF63 10.00				

KM# 291a DOLLAR
17.30 g., 0.999 Silver 0.5521 oz. ASW **Obv:** Supported arms **Rev:** Multicolor Labrador Nature Reserve

Date	Mintage	F12	VF20	XF40	MS60	MS63
2008	850	PF63 37.50				

KM# 292 DOLLAR
Copper-Nickel **Obv:** Supported arms **Rev:** Multicolor Mount Faber Building

Date	Mintage	F12	VF20	XF40	MS60	MS63
2008 Prooflike	2,800	—	—	—	—	10.00

KM# 292a DOLLAR
17.30 g., 0.999 Silver 0.5521 oz. ASW **Obv:** Supported arms **Rev:** Multicolor Mount Faber Building

Date	Mintage	F12	VF20	XF40	MS60	MS63
2008	2,300	PF63 37.50				

KM# 293 DOLLAR
Copper-Nickel **Obv:** Supported arms **Rev:** Multicolor Telok Blangah Hill Park

Date	Mintage	F12	VF20	XF40	MS60	MS63
2008 Prooflike	2,300	—	—	—	—	10.00

KM# 293a DOLLAR
17.30 g., 0.999 Silver 0.5521 oz. ASW **Obv:** Supported arms **Rev:** Multicolor Telok Blangah Hill Park

Date	Mintage	F12	VF20	XF40	MS60	MS63
2008	2,200	PF63 37.50				

KM# 294 DOLLAR
0.30 g., 0.999 Gold AGW, 7 mm. **Subject:** Year of the Ox **Obv:** Supported arms **Rev:** Ox

Date	Mintage	F12	VF20	XF40	MS60	MS63
2009	3,000	—	—	—	30.00	35.00

KM# 308 DOLLAR
0.30 g., 0.9999 Gold AGW, 7 mm. **Subject:** Year of the Snake **Rev:** Snake

Date	Mintage	F12	VF20	XF40	MS60	MS63
2013	Est. 10000	—	—	—	—	45.00

KM# 314 DOLLAR
7.62 g., Bi-Metallic, 24.65 mm. **Obv:** National arms **Rev:** Value at left, lion at right, color flora at center **Edge:** Reeded

Date	Mintage	F12	VF20	XF40	MS60	MS63
2013	—	—	—	—	6.00	8.00

KM# 196 2 DOLLARS
Copper-Nickel **Subject:** Tribute to Healthcare Givers **Obv:** National arms **Rev:** Five 3/4 length people standing facing, clinic in background

Date	Mintage	F12	VF20	XF40	MS60	MS63
2003sm Prooflike	32021	—	—	—	—	15.00

KM# 196a 2 DOLLARS
0.999 Silver **Subject:** Tribute to Healthcare Givers **Obv:** National arms **Rev:** Five 3/4 length people standing facing, clinic in background

Date	Mintage	F12	VF20	XF40	MS60	MS63
2003sm	5,200	PF63 60.00				

KM# 223 2 DOLLARS
20.00 g., 0.999 Silver 0.6382 oz. ASW, 38.70 mm. **Series:** Lunar **Subject:** Year of the Goat **Obv:** National arms **Rev:** Stylized goat standing right facing left

Date	Mintage	F12	VF20	XF40	MS60	MS63
2003sm	2,000	PF63 60.00				

KM# 229 2 DOLLARS
20.00 g., 0.999 Silver 0.6382 oz. ASW, 38.7 mm. **Series:** Lunar **Subject:** Year of the Monkey **Obv:** National arms **Rev:** Stylized monkey sitting left

Date	Mintage	F12	VF20	XF40	MS60	MS63
2004sm	2,180	PF63 60.00				

KM# 234 2 DOLLARS
20.00 g., Copper-Nickel, 38.7 mm. **Series:** Lunar **Subject:** Year of the Rooster **Obv:** National arms **Rev:** Rooster standing right

Date	Mintage	F12	VF20	XF40	MS60	MS63
2005sm Prooflike	79,115	—	—	—	—	15.00

KM# 242 2 DOLLARS
Copper-Nickel **Subject:** 40th National Day Parade **Obv:** National arms **Rev:** Fireworks, parade in government plaza, multicolor

Date	Mintage	F12	VF20	XF40	MS60	MS63
2005sm Prooflike	5,443	PF63 15.00				

KM# 234a 2 DOLLARS
20.00 g., 0.9999 Silver 0.6388 oz. ASW, 38.7 mm. **Series:** Lunar **Subject:** Year of the Rooster **Obv:** National arms **Rev:** Stylized rooster standing right

Date	Mintage	F12	VF20	XF40	MS60	MS63
2005sm	4,879	PF63 42.50				

KM# 242a 2 DOLLARS
20.00 g., 0.9999 Silver 0.6388 oz. ASW **Subject:** 40th National Day Parade **Obv:** National arms **Rev:** Fireworks, parade in government plaza

Date	Mintage	F12	VF20	XF40	MS60	MS63
2005sm	4,204	PF63 60.00				

KM# 250 2 DOLLARS
20.00 g., Copper-Nickel **Series:** Lunar **Subject:** Year of the Dog **Obv:** National arms **Rev:** Stylized dog standing left

Date	Mintage	F12	VF20	XF40	MS60	MS63
2006sm Prooflike	69,552	PF63 15.00				

KM# 250a 2 DOLLARS
20.00 g., 0.9999 Silver 0.6388 oz. ASW **Series:** Lunar **Subject:** Year of the Dog **Obv:** National arms **Rev:** Stylized dog standing left

Date	Mintage	F12	VF20	XF40	MS60	MS63
2006sm	4,500	PF63 60.00				

KM# 258 2 DOLLARS
Copper-Nickel **Subject:** 41st National Day **Obv:** National arms **Rev:** People in stadium, emblem - multicolor

Date	Mintage	F12	VF20	XF40	MS60	MS63
2006sm Prooflike	4,300	PF63 15.00				

KM# 258a 2 DOLLARS
20.00 g., 0.999 Silver 0.6382 oz. ASW **Subject:** 41st National Day **Obv:** National arms **Rev:** People in stadium, emblem - multicolor

Date	Mintage	F12	VF20	XF40	MS60	MS63
2006sm	4,100	PF63 60.00				

KM# 193 2 DOLLARS
20.00 g., Copper-Nickel, 38.70 mm. **Subject:** 42nd National Day Parade **Obv:** Arms with supporters **Obv. Legend:** SINGAPURA - SINGAPORE **Rev:** Colored overlay with four children above Marina Bay floating platform **Edge:** Reeded

Date	Mintage	F12	VF20	XF40	MS60	MS63
2007 Prooflike	6,400	—	—	—	—	13.50

KM# 193a 2 DOLLARS
20.00 g., 0.999 Silver 0.6382 oz. ASW, 38.70 mm. **Subject:** 42nd National Day Parade **Obv:** Arms with supporters **Obv. Legend:** SINGAPURA - SINGAPORE **Rev:** Colored overlay with four children above Marina Bay floating platform **Edge:** Reeded

Date	Mintage	F12	VF20	XF40	MS60	MS63
2007	6,150	PF63 42.50				

KM# 264 2 DOLLARS
Copper-Nickel **Series:** Lunar **Subject:** Year of the Boar **Obv:** National arms **Rev:** Stylized boar running right

Date	Mintage	F12	VF20	XF40	MS60	MS63
2007sm Prooflike	63,930	—	—	—	—	12.00

KM# 264a 2 DOLLARS
20.00 g., 0.999 Silver 0.6382 oz. ASW **Series:** Lunar **Subject:** Year of the Boar **Obv:** National arms **Rev:** Stylized boar running right

Date	Mintage	F12	VF20	XF40	MS60	MS63
2007sm	6,000	PF63 45.00				

KM# 270 2 DOLLARS
20.00 g., Copper-Nickel **Series:** Lunar **Subject:** Year of the Rat **Obv:** National arms **Rev:** Stylized rat lying left

Date	Mintage	F12	VF20	XF40	MS60	MS63
2008sm Prooflike	58,637	—	—	—	—	12.50

KM# 270a 2 DOLLARS
20.00 g., 0.999 Silver 0.6382 oz. ASW **Series:** Lunar **Subject:** Year of the Rat **Obv:** National arms **Rev:** Stylized rat lying left

Date	Mintage	F12	VF20	XF40	MS60	MS63
2008sm	5,789	PF63 45.00				

KM# 287 2 DOLLARS
Copper-Nickel, 38.7 mm. **Subject:** Formula 1 - Singapore Grand Prix **Obv:** Supported arms **Rev:** Formula 1 racecar and skyline

Date	Mintage	F12	VF20	XF40	MS60	MS63
2008	7,000	PF63 10.00				

KM# 295 2 DOLLARS
Copper-Nickel **Subject:** Year of the Ox **Obv:** Supported arms

Date	Mintage	F12	VF20	XF40	MS60	MS63
2009 Prooflike	80,000	—	—	—	—	10.00

KM# 296 2 DOLLARS
20.00 g., 0.999 Silver 0.6382 oz. ASW **Subject:** Year of the Ox **Obv:** Supported arms **Rev:** Ox

Date	Mintage	F12	VF20	XF40	MS60	MS63
2009	6,000	PF63 37.50				

KM# 303 2 DOLLARS
Copper-Nickel, 38.7 mm. **Subject:** Independence, 44th Anniversary **Note:** Partially colorized

Date	Mintage	F12	VF20	XF40	MS60	MS63
2009 Prooflike	6,000	—	—	—	—	15.00

KM# 303a 2 DOLLARS
20.00 g., 0.999 Silver 0.6382 oz. ASW, 38.7 mm. **Series:** Indpendence, 44th Anniversary **Note:** Colorized

Date	Mintage	F12	VF20	XF40	MS60	MS63
2009	5,000	PF63 40.00				

KM# 312 2 DOLLARS
20.00 g., 0.999 Silver 0.6382 oz. ASW, 38.07 mm. **Subject:** Year of the Snake **Rev:** Snake

Date	Mintage	F12	VF20	XF40	MS60	MS63
2013	Est. 10000	PF63 55.00				

KM# 313 2 DOLLARS
20.00 g., Copper-Nickel, 38.07 mm. **Subject:** Year of the Snake **Rev:** Snake

Date	Mintage	F12	VF20	XF40	MS60	MS63
2013 Proof-like	Est. 80000	PF63 15.00				

KM# 104.1a 5 DOLLARS
8.25 g., 0.925 Silver 0.2438 oz. ASW, 23.3 mm. **Obv:** National arms **Rev:** Vanda Miss Joaquim flower and value within beaded circle

Date	Mintage	F12	VF20	XF40	MS60	MS63
1999 (2001)sm	9,200	PF63 25.00				
2001sm	6,000	PF63 25.00				
2002sm	6,300	PF63 25.00				
2000 (2002)sm	8,900	PF63 25.00				

KM# 104.2 5 DOLLARS
6.70 g., Bi-Metallic, 23.3 mm. **Obv:** National arms, date and BCCS logo **Rev:** Canda Miss Joaquim flower above value **Edge:** Plain **Note:** Date in hologram

Date	Mintage	F12	VF20	XF40	MS60	MS63
2001 In sets only	101,738	—	—	—	—	12.00
2002 In sets only	84,577	—	—	—	—	12.00
2003	—	—	—	—	—	12.00
2004	—	—	—	—	—	12.00
2005	—	—	—	—	—	12.00
2006	—	—	—	—	—	12.00

KM# 104.2a 5 DOLLARS
8.25 g., 0.925 Silver 0.2438 oz. ASW, 23.3 mm. **Obv:** National arms, date and BCCS logo **Rev:** Vanda Miss Joaquim flower above value **Edge:** Plain

Date	Mintage	F12	VF20	XF40	MS60	MS63
2001sm	6,000	PF63 25.00				
2002sm	6,300	PF63 25.00				
2003sm	4,000	PF63 25.00				
2004sm	4,000	PF63 25.00				
2005sm	3,250	PF63 25.00				
2006sm	—	PF63 25.00				

KM# 177a 5 DOLLARS
20.00 g., 0.925 Silver 0.591 oz. ASW, 38.6 mm. **Subject:** Productivity Movement **Obv:** Arms with supporters **Rev:** Spiral design **Edge:** Reeded

Date	Mintage	F12	VF20	XF40	MS60	MS63
2001sm	5,650	PF63 50.00				

KM# 177 5 DOLLARS
20.00 g., Copper-Nickel, 38.6 mm. **Subject:** Productivity Movement **Obv:** Arms with supporters **Rev:** Spiral design **Edge:** Reeded

Date	Mintage	F12	VF20	XF40	MS60	MS63
2001sm	5,300	—	—	—	12.50	15.00

KM# 104.3 5 DOLLARS
6.70 g., Bi-Metallic, 23.3 mm. **Obv:** National arms above latent image "MAS **Rev:** Flower and value **Shape:** Scalloped

Date	Mintage	F12	VF20	XF40	MS60	MS63
2002sm	—	—	—	—	—	10.00
2003sm	—	—	—	—	—	10.00
2003sm	4,550	PF63 15.00				
2004sm	—	—	—	—	—	10.00
2004sm	3,500	PF63 15.00				
2005sm	—	—	—	—	—	10.00
2006sm	—	—	—	—	—	10.00
2007sm	—	—	—	—	—	10.00
2008sm	—	—	—	—	—	10.00
2009sm	—	—	—	—	—	10.00
2010sm	—	—	—	—	—	10.00
2011sm	—	—	—	—	—	10.00
2012sm	—	—	—	—	—	10.00

KM# 181 5 DOLLARS
20.00 g., Copper-Nickel, 38.7 mm. **Subject:** Esplanade Theaters on the Bay **Obv:** Arms with supporters **Rev:** Stylized symbolic design **Edge:** Reeded

Date	Mintage	F12	VF20	XF40	MS60	MS63
2002sm	7,430	—	—	—	13.50	16.50

KM# 181a 5 DOLLARS
20.00 g., 0.999 Silver 0.6382 oz. ASW, 38.7 mm. **Subject:** Esplanade Theaters on the Bay **Obv:** Arms with supporters **Rev:** Stylized symbolic design **Edge:** Reeded

Date	Mintage	F12	VF20	XF40	MS60	MS63
2002sm	6,540	PF63 45.00				

KM# 104.3a 5 DOLLARS
8.25 g., 0.925 Silver 0.2438 oz. ASW **Obv:** National arms above latent image "MAS or date **Rev:** Flower and value **Shape:** Scalloped

Date	Mintage	F12	VF20	XF40	MS60	MS63
2003sm	4,900	PF63 25.00				
2004sm	4,000	PF63 25.00				
2005sm	3,250	PF63 25.00				

KM# 194 5 DOLLARS
20.00 g., 0.999 Silver 0.6382 oz. ASW, 38.7 mm. **Obv:** Arms with supporters **Obv. Legend:** SINGAPURA - SINGAPORE **Rev:** Multicolor Singapore's skyline above world map, golden lion symbol below pointing to location of Singapore **Rev. Legend:** BOARD OF GOVERNORS ANNUAL MEETINGS • SINGAPORE 2006 • INTERNATIONAL MONETARY FUND • WORLD BANK GROUP •

Date	Mintage	F12	VF20	XF40	MS60	MS63
2006sm	5,450	PF63 60.00				

KM# 256 5 DOLLARS
20.00 g., 0.999 Silver 0.6382 oz. ASW **Series:** Heritage Orchids **Obv:** National arms **Rev:** Vanda Tan Chay Yan - multicolor

Date	Mintage	F12	VF20	XF40	MS60	MS63
2006sm	8,000	PF63 60.00				

KM# 257 5 DOLLARS
20.00 g., 0.999 Silver 0.6382 oz. ASW **Series:** Heritage Orchids **Obv:** National arms **Rev:** Aranda Majula - multicolor

Date	Mintage	F12	VF20	XF40	MS60	MS63
2006sm	8,000	PF63 60.00				

KM# 275 5 DOLLARS
20.00 g., 0.999 Silver 0.6382 oz. ASW, 38.7 mm. **Series:** Heritage Orchids **Obv:** National arms **Rev:** Dendrobium Singa Mas - multicolor

Date	Mintage	F12	VF20	XF40	MS60	MS63
2007sm	8,000	PF63 45.00				

KM# 276 5 DOLLARS
20.00 g., 0.999 Silver 0.6382 oz. ASW, 38.7 mm. **Series:** Heritage Orchids **Obv:** National arms **Rev:** Vanda Mimi Palmer - multicolor

Date	Mintage	F12	VF20	XF40	MS60	MS63
2007sm	8,000	PF63 45.00				

KM# 285 5 DOLLARS
20.00 g., 0.999 Silver 0.6382 oz. ASW, 38.6 mm. **Subject:** Heritage orchids **Obv:** Supported arms **Rev:** Multicolor yellow orchid - Oncidum Goldiana

Date	Mintage	F12	VF20	XF40	MS60	MS63
2008	8,000	PF63 45.00				

KM# 286 5 DOLLARS
20.00 g., 0.999 Silver 0.6382 oz. ASW, 38.6 mm. **Subject:** Heritage orchids **Obv:** Supported arms **Rev:** Multicolor pink orchid - Aranda Tay Swee Eng

Date	Mintage	F12	VF20	XF40	MS60	MS63
2008	8,000	PF63 45.00				

KM# 301 5 DOLLARS
20.00 g., 0.999 Silver 0.6382 oz. ASW **Subject:** Orchids of Singapore **Obv:** Arms **Rev:** Yellow flower - Spathoglottis Primrose

Date	Mintage	F12	VF20	XF40	MS60	MS63
2009	8,000	PF63 45.00				

KM# 302 5 DOLLARS
20.00 g., 0.999 Silver 0.6382 oz. ASW, 38.7 mm. **Subject:** Orchids of Singapore **Obv:** Arms **Rev:** Pink flower - Vanda Amy

Date	Mintage	F12	VF20	XF40	MS60	MS63
2009	8,000	PF63 45.00				

KM# 315 5 DOLLARS
(No Composition) **Subject:** 47th Anniversary of Independence **Shape:** Heart

Date	Mintage	F12	VF20	XF40	MS60	MS63
2012	—	—	—	—	—	

KM# 307 5 DOLLARS
7.77 g., 0.9999 Gold 0.2482 oz. AGW, 21.96 mm. **Subject:** Year of the Snake **Rev:** Snake

Date	Mintage	F12	VF20	XF40	MS60	MS63
2013	—	PF63 600				

KM# 179 10 DOLLARS
28.00 g., Copper-Nickel, 40.7 mm. **Series:** Lunar **Subject:** Year of the Snake **Obv:** National arms **Rev:** Stylized snake **Edge:** Reeded

Date	Mintage	F12	VF20	XF40	MS60	MS63
2001sm Prooflike	152,330	—	—	—	—	20.00

KM# 182 10 DOLLARS
28.00 g., Copper-Nickel, 40.7 mm. **Series:** Lunar **Subject:** Year of the Horse **Obv:** National arms **Rev:** Stylized horse standing left **Edge:** Reeded

Date	Mintage	F12	VF20	XF40	MS60	MS63
2002sm Prooflike	128,666	—	—	—	—	20.00

KM# 225 10 DOLLARS
28.00 g., Copper-Nickel, 40.7 mm. **Series:** Lunar **Subject:** Year of the Goat **Obv:** National arms **Rev:** Stylized goat standing right facing left

Date	Mintage	F12	VF20	XF40	MS60	MS63
2003sm Prooflike	103,047	—	—	—	—	20.00

KM# 187 10 DOLLARS
28.00 g., Copper-Nickel, 40.7 mm. **Series:** Lunar **Subject:** Year of the Monkey **Obv:** National arms **Rev:** Stylized monkey sitting left **Edge:** Reeded

Date	Mintage	F12	VF20	XF40	MS60	MS63
2004sm Prooflike	100,000	—	—	—	—	20.00

KM# 189 10 DOLLARS
28.00 g., Copper-Nickel, 40.7 mm. **Subject:** 10th Anniversary China-Singapore Suzhou Industrial Park **Obv:** National arms **Rev:** Harmony" Sculpture **Edge:** Reeded

Date	Mintage	F12	VF20	XF40	MS60	MS63
2004sm Prooflike	3,511	—	—	—	—	20.00

KM# 189a 10 DOLLARS
20.00 g., 0.999 Silver 0.6382 oz. ASW, 40.7 mm. **Subject:** 10th Anniversary China-Singapore Suzhou Industrial Park **Obv:** National arms **Rev:** Harmony" sculpture **Edge:** Reeded

Date	Mintage	F12	VF20	XF40	MS60	MS63
2004sm	3,197	PF63 55.00				

KM# 240 10 DOLLARS
20.00 g., Copper-Nickel, 40.7 mm. **Subject:** National University of Singapore **Obv:** National arms **Rev:** Person, globe and emblem

Date	Mintage	F12	VF20	XF40	MS60	MS63
2005sm Prooflike	12,264	—	—	—	—	22.50

KM# 240a 10 DOLLARS
20.00 g., 0.9999 Silver 0.6388 oz. ASW, 38.7 mm. **Subject:** National University of Singapore **Obv:** National arms **Rev:** Person, globe and emblem

Date	Mintage	F12	VF20	XF40	MS60	MS63
2005sm	5,293	PF63 60.00				

KM# 243 10 DOLLARS
31.10 g., 0.9999 Silver 0.9934 oz. ASW **Subject:** 40th National Day parade **Obv:** National arms **Rev:** Fireworks, parade in government plaza

Date	Mintage	F12	VF20	XF40	MS60	MS63
2005sm	756	PF63 245				

KM# 311 10 DOLLARS
62.21 g., 0.999 Silver 1.9851 oz. ASW, 45 mm. **Subject:** Year of the Snake **Rev:** Snake in color

Date	Mintage	F12	VF20	XF40	MS60	MS63
2013	—	PF63 140				

KM# 310 25 DOLLARS
155.52 g., 0.999 Silver 4.9629 oz. ASW, 62 mm. **Subject:** Year of the Snake **Rev:** Snake

Date	Mintage	F12	VF20	XF40	MS60	MS63
2013	—	PF63 565				

KM# 288 50 DOLLARS
20.00 g., 0.999 Silver 0.6382 oz. ASW **Subject:** Formula 1 - Singapore Grand Prix **Obv:** Supported arms **Rev:** Multicolor race car and skyline

Date	Mintage	F12	VF20	XF40	MS60	MS63
2008	5,000	PF63 40.00				

KM# 309 80 DOLLARS
1000.00 g., 0.999 Silver 31.9118 oz. ASW, 100 mm. **Subject:** Year of the Snake **Rev:** Snake

Date	Mintage	F12	VF20	XF40	MS60	MS63
2013 Proof-like	—	—	—	—	—	1,675

KM# 241 100 DOLLARS
31.10 g., 0.9999 Gold 0.9934 oz. AGW, 33 mm. **Subject:** National University of Singapore **Obv:** National arms **Rev:** Person, globe and emblem

Date	Mintage	F12	VF20	XF40	MS60	MS63
2005sm	244	PF63 1,850				

KM# 289 100 DOLLARS
31.00 g., 0.250 Gold 0.2476 oz. AGW, 38.7 mm. **Subject:** Formula 1 - Singapore Grand Prix **Obv:** Supported arms **Rev:** Formula 1 racecar and skyline

Date	Mintage	F12	VF20	XF40	MS60	MS63
2008	300	PF63 500				

KM# 306 100 DOLLARS
31.10 g., 0.999 Gold 0.9926 oz. AGW, 33 mm. **Subject:** Year of the Snake **Rev:** Snake

Date	Mintage	F12	VF20	XF40	MS60	MS63
2013	—	PF63 2,160				

KM# 305 200 DOLLARS
155.52 g., 0.9999 Gold 4.9674 oz. AGW, 60 mm. **Subject:** Year of the Snake **Rev:** Snake

Date	Mintage	F12	VF20	XF40	MS60	MS63
2013	Est. 200	PF63 9,800				

BULLION COINAGE
Lunar Year Issues

KM# 212 DOLLAR
1.56 g., 0.9999 Gold 0.0497 oz. AGW, 13.9 mm. **Series:** Lunar **Subject:** Year of the Snake **Obv:** National arms **Rev:** Stylized lion's head right, snake privy mark at lower left

Date	Mintage	F12	VF20	XF40	MS60	MS63
2001	339	—	—	—	BV+30%	—
2001sm	240	PF63 BV+25%				

KM# 217 DOLLAR
1.56 g., 0.9999 Gold 0.0497 oz. AGW, 13.9 mm. **Series:** Lunar **Subject:** Year of the Horse **Obv:** National arms **Rev:** Stylized lion's head right, horse privy mark at lower left

Date	Mintage	F12	VF20	XF40	MS60	MS63
2002	160	—	—	—	—	BV+30%
2002sm	215	PF63 BV+25%				

KM# 222 DOLLAR
0.30 g., 0.9999 Gold AGW, 7 mm. **Series:** Lunar **Subject:** Year of the Goat **Obv:** National arms **Rev:** Stylized goat standing right facing left

Date	Mintage	F12	VF20	XF40	MS60	MS63
2003sm Prooflike	5,362	—	—	—	—	32.50

KM# 186 DOLLAR
0.30 g., 0.9999 Gold AGW, 7 mm. **Series:** Lunar **Subject:** Year of the Monkey **Obv:** National arms **Rev:** Stylized monkey sitting left **Edge:** Plain

Date	Mintage	F12	VF20	XF40	MS60	MS63
2004 Prooflike	3,200	—	—	—	—	32.50

KM# 233 DOLLAR
0.30 g., 0.9999 Gold AGW, 7 mm. **Series:** Lunar **Subject:** Year of the Rooster **Obv:** National arms **Rev:** Stylized rooster standing right

Date	Mintage	F12	VF20	XF40	MS60	MS63
2005sm Prooflike	2,817	—	—	—	—	32.50

KM# 249 DOLLAR
0.30 g., 0.9999 Gold AGW **Series:** Lunar **Subject:** Year of the Dog **Obv:** National arms **Rev:** Stylized dog standing left

Date	Mintage	F12	VF20	XF40	MS60	MS63
2006sm Prooflike	2,004	—	—	—	—	32.50

KM# 263 DOLLAR
0.30 g., 0.9999 Gold AGW **Series:** Lunar **Subject:** Year of the Boar **Obv:** National arms **Rev:** Stylized boar running right

Date	Mintage	F12	VF20	XF40	MS60	MS63
2007sm Prooflike	2,500	—	—	—	—	32.50

KM# 269 DOLLAR
0.30 g., 0.9999 Gold AGW **Series:** Lunar **Subject:** Year of the Rat **Obv:** National arms **Rev:** Stylized rat lying left

Date	Mintage	F12	VF20	XF40	MS60	MS63
2008sm	2,434	—	—	—	—	32.50

KM# 213 5 DOLLARS
3.11 g., 0.9999 Gold 0.0993 oz. AGW, 17.9 mm. **Series:** Lunar **Subject:** Year of the Snake **Obv:** National arms **Rev:** Stylized lion's head right, snake privy mark at lower left

Date	Mintage	F12	VF20	XF40	MS60	MS63
2001	275	—	—	—	—	BV+25%
2001sm	240	PF63 BV+20%				

KM# 218 5 DOLLARS
3.11 g., 0.9999 Gold 0.0992 oz. AGW, 17.9 mm. **Series:** Lunar **Subject:** Year of the Horse **Obv:** National arms **Rev:** Stylized lion's head right, horse privy mark at lower left

Date	Mintage	F12	VF20	XF40	MS60	MS63
2002	200	—	—	—	—	BV+25%
2002sm	215	PF63 BV+20%				

KM# 224 5 DOLLARS
7.78 g., 0.9999 Gold 0.2484 oz. AGW, 21.9 mm. **Series:** Lunar **Subject:** Year of the Goat **Obv:** National arms **Rev:** Stylized goat standing right facing left

Date	Mintage	F12	VF20	XF40	MS60	MS63
2003sm	1,000	PF65 500				

KM# 230 5 DOLLARS
7.78 g., 0.9999 Gold 0.2484 oz. AGW, 21.9 mm. **Series:** Lunar **Subject:** Year of the Monkey **Obv:** National arms **Rev:** Stylized monkey sitting left

Date	Mintage	F12	VF20	XF40	MS60	MS63
2004sm	1,426	PF65 500				

KM# 235 5 DOLLARS
7.78 g., 0.9999 Gold 0.2484 oz. AGW, 21.9 mm. **Series:** Lunar **Subject:** Year of the Rooster **Obv:** National arms **Rev:** Stylized rooster standing right

Date	Mintage	F12	VF20	XF40	MS60	MS63
2005sm	1,419	PF65 500				

KM# 251 5 DOLLARS
7.78 g., 0.9999 Gold 0.2483 oz. AGW **Series:** Lunar **Subject:** Year of the Dog **Obv:** National arms **Rev:** Stylized dog standing left

Date	Mintage	F12	VF20	XF40	MS60	MS63
2006sm	1,015	PF65 500				

KM# 265 5 DOLLARS
7.78 g., 0.9999 Gold 0.2483 oz. AGW **Series:** Lunar **Subject:** Year of the Boar **Obv:** National arms **Rev:** Stylized boar running right

Date	Mintage	F12	VF20	XF40	MS60	MS63
2007sm	1,060	PF65 500				

KM# 271 5 DOLLARS
7.78 g., 0.9999 Gold 0.2483 oz. AGW **Series:** Lunar **Subject:** Year of the Rat **Obv:** National arms **Rev:** Stylized rat lying left

Date	Mintage	F12	VF20	XF40	MS60	MS63
2008sm	1,200	PF65 500				

KM# 179a 10 DOLLARS
62.21 g., 0.999 Silver 1.9851 oz. ASW, 40.7 mm. **Series:** Lunar **Subject:** Year of the Snake **Obv:** National arms **Rev:** Stylized snake **Edge:** Reeded

Date	Mintage	F12	VF20	XF40	MS60	MS63
2001sm	35,000	PF63 90.00	PF65 100			

KM# 214 10 DOLLARS
7.78 g., 0.9999 Gold 0.2483 oz. AGW, 21.9 mm. **Series:** Lunar **Subject:** Year of the Snake **Obv:** National arms **Rev:** Stylized lion's head right, snake privy mark at lower left

Date	Mintage	F12	VF20	XF40	MS60	MS63
2001	240	—	—	—	—	BV+15%
2001sm	240	PF63 BV+10%				

KM# 182a 10 DOLLARS
62.21 g., 0.999 Silver 1.9851 oz. ASW, 40.7 mm. **Series:** Lunar **Subject:** Year of the Horse **Obv:** National arms **Rev:** Stylized horse standing left **Edge:** Reeded

Date	Mintage	F12	VF20	XF40	MS60	MS63
2002sm	35,000	PF63 90.00	PF65 100			

KM# 219 10 DOLLARS
7.78 g., 0.9999 Gold 0.2483 oz. AGW, 21.9 mm. **Series:** Lunar **Subject:** Year of the Horse **Obv:** National arms **Rev:** Stylized lion's head right, horse privy mark at lower left

Date	Mintage	F12	VF20	XF40	MS60	MS63
2002	180	—	—	—	—	525
2002sm	215	PF63 475				

KM# 225a 10 DOLLARS
62.21 g., 0.999 Silver 1.9851 oz. ASW, 40.7 mm. **Series:** Lunar **Subject:** Year of the Goat **Obv:** National arms **Rev:** Stylized goat standing right facing left

Date	Mintage	F12	VF20	XF40	MS60	MS63
2003sm	35,000	PF63 90.00	PF65 100			

KM# 185 10 DOLLARS
31.10 g., 0.9999 Gold 0.9935 oz. AGW, 32.1 mm. **Subject:** 10th Anniversary China-Singapore Suzhou Industrial Park **Obv:** National arms **Rev:** Harmony" Sculpture **Edge:** Lettered edge

Date	Mintage	F12	VF20	XF40	MS60	MS63
2004sm	500	PF65 1,850				

KM# 187a 10 DOLLARS
62.21 g., 0.999 Silver 1.9851 oz. ASW, 40.7 mm. **Series:** Lunar **Subject:** Year of the Monkey **Obv:** National arms **Rev:** Stylized monkey sitting left **Edge:** Reeded

Date	Mintage	F12	VF20	XF40	MS60	MS63
2004sm	35,000	PF63 90.00	PF65 100			

KM# 236 10 DOLLARS
62.21 g., 0.9999 Silver 1.9869 oz. ASW, 45 mm. **Series:** Lunar **Subject:** Year of the Rooster **Obv:** National arms **Rev:** Stylized rooster standing right

Date	Mintage	F12	VF20	XF40	MS60	MS63
2005sm	30,000	PF63 90.00	PF65 100			

KM# 252 10 DOLLARS
62.20 g., 0.999 Silver 1.985 oz. ASW **Series:** Lunar **Subject:** Year of the Dog **Obv:** National arms **Rev:** Stylized dog standing left

Date	Mintage	F12	VF20	XF40	MS60	MS63
2006sm	30,000	PF63 95.00	PF65 110			

KM# 266 10 DOLLARS
62.21 g., 0.999 Silver 1.9851 oz. ASW, 45 mm. **Series:** Lunar **Subject:** Year of the Boar **Obv:** National arms **Rev:** Stylized pigr running right - multicolor

Date	Mintage	F12	VF20	XF40	MS60	MS63
2007sm	30,000	PF63 100		PF65 115		

KM# 272 10 DOLLARS
62.21 g., 0.999 Silver 1.9851 oz. ASW **Series:** Lunar **Subject:** Year of the Rat **Obv:** National arms **Rev:** Stylized rat lying left - multicolor

Date	Mintage	F12	VF20	XF40	MS60	MS63
2008sm	20,000	PF63 110		PF65 120		

KM# 297 10 DOLLARS
62.20 g., 0.999 Silver 1.9849 oz. ASW **Subject:** Year of the Ox **Obv:** Supported arms **Rev:** Multicolor Ox

Date	Mintage	F12	VF20	XF40	MS60	MS63
2009	—	PF63 90.00		PF65 100		

KM# 316 10 DOLLARS
62.20 g., 0.999 Silver 1.985 oz. ASW, 40.7 mm. **Subject:** Year of the Horse **Rev:** Horse right, in color

Date	Mintage	F12	VF20	XF40	MS60	MS63
2014	—	PF63 95.00				

KM# 215 20 DOLLARS
15.55 g., 0.9999 Gold 0.4967 oz. AGW, 27 mm. **Series:** Lunar **Subject:** Year of the Snake **Obv:** National arms **Rev:** Stylized lion's head right, snake privy mark at lower left

Date	Mintage	F12	VF20	XF40	MS60	MS63
2001 169	169	—	—	—	—	BV+12%
2001sm 240	240	PF63 BV+12%				

KM# 220 20 DOLLARS
15.55 g., 0.9999 Gold 0.4967 oz. AGW, 27 mm. **Series:** Lunar **Subject:** Year of the Horse **Obv:** National arms **Rev:** Stylized lion's head right, horse privy mark at lower left

Date	Mintage	F12	VF20	XF40	MS60	MS63
2002	165	—	—	—	—	BV+12%
2002sm	215	PF63 BV+12%				

KM# 226 25 DOLLARS
155.52 g., 0.999 Silver 4.9629 oz. ASW, 65.00 mm. **Series:** Lunar **Subject:** Year of the Goat **Obv:** National arms **Rev:** Stylized goat standing right facing left

Date	Mintage	F12	VF20	XF40	MS60	MS63
2003sm	250	PF65 300				

KM# 231 25 DOLLARS
155.52 g., 0.999 Silver 4.9629 oz. ASW, 65 mm. **Series:** Lunar **Subject:** Year of the Monkey **Obv:** National arms **Rev:** Stylized monkey sitting left

Date	MIntage	F12	VF20	XF40	MS60	MS63
2004sm	250	PF65 300				

KM# 237 25 DOLLARS
155.52 g., 0.9999 Silver 4.9674 oz. ASW, 65 mm. **Series:** Lunar **Subject:** Year of the Rooster **Obv:** National arms **Rev:** Stylized rooster standing right

Date	MIntage	F12	VF20	XF40	MS60	MS63
2005sm	250	PF65 300				

KM# 253 25 DOLLARS
155.52 g., 0.999 Silver 4.9628 oz. ASW **Series:** Lunar **Subject:** Year of the Dog **Obv:** National arms **Rev:** Stylized dog standing right

Date	Mintage	F12	VF20	XF40	MS60	MS63
2006sm	250	PF65 300				

KM# 267 25 DOLLARS
155.52 g., 0.999 Silver 4.9628 oz. ASW **Series:** Lunar **Subject:** Year of the Boar **Obv:** National arms **Rev:** Stylized boar running right

Date	Mintage	F12	VF20	XF40	MS60	MS63
2007sm	250	PF65 300				

KM# 273 25 DOLLARS
155.52 g., 0.999 Silver 4.9628 oz. ASW **Series:** Lunar **Subject:** Year of the Rat **Obv:** National arms **Rev:** Stylized rat lying left

Date	Mintage	F12	VF20	XF40	MS60	MS63
2008sm	250	PF65 300				

KM# 298 25 DOLLARS
155.50 g., 0.999 Silver 4.9623 oz. ASW **Subject:** Year of the Ox **Obv:** Supported arms **Rev:** Ox

Date	Mintage	F12	VF20	XF40	MS60	MS63
2009	—	PF65 300				

KM# 216 50 DOLLARS
31.10 g., 0.9999 Gold 0.9934 oz. AGW, 32.1 mm. **Series:** Lunar **Subject:** Year of the Snake **Obv:** National arms **Rev:** Stylized lion's head right, snake privy mark at lower left

Date	Mintage	F12	VF20	XF40	MS60	MS63
2001	187	—	—	—	—	BV+9%
2001sm	179	PF63 BV+9%				

KM# 221 50 DOLLARS
31.10 g., 0.9999 Gold 0.9934 oz. AGW, 32.1 mm. **Series:** Lunar **Subject:** Year of the Horse **Obv:** National arms **Rev:** Stylized lion's head right, horse privy mark at lower left

Date	Mintage	F12	VF20	XF40	MS60	MS63
2002	165	—	—	—	—	BV+9%
2002sm	160	PF63 BV+9%				

KM# 238 100 DOLLARS
31.10 g., 0.9999 Gold 0.9934 oz. AGW, 33 mm. **Series:** Lunar **Subject:** Year of the Rooster **Obv:** National arms **Rev:** Stylized rooster standing right

Date	Mintage	F12	VF20	XF40	MS60	MS63
2005sm	1,699	PF63 BV+10%				

KM# 254 100 DOLLARS
31.10 g., 0.9999 Gold 0.9934 oz. AGW **Series:** Lunar **Subject:** Year of the Dog **Obv:** National arms **Rev:** Stylized dog standing left

Date	Mintage	F12	VF20	XF40	MS60	MS63
2006sm	1,319	PF63 BV+10%				

KM# 268 100 DOLLARS
31.10 g., 0.9999 Gold 0.9934 oz. AGW, 33 mm. **Series:** Lunar **Subject:** Year of the Boar **Obv:** National arms **Rev:** Stylized pig running right

Date	Mintage	F12	VF20	XF40	MS60	MS63
2007sm	1,220	PF63 BV+10%				

KM# 274 100 DOLLARS
31.10 g., 0.9999 Gold 0.9934 oz. AGW **Series:** Lunar **Subject:** Year of the Rat **Obv:** National arms **Rev:** Stylized rat lying left

Date	Mintage	F12	VF20	XF40	MS60	MS63
2008sm	1,153	PF63 BV+10%				

KM# 299 100 DOLLARS
31.11 g., 0.999 Gold 0.9926 oz. AGW **Subject:** Year of the Ox **Obv:** Supported arms **Rev:** Ox

Date	Mintage	F12	VF20	XF40	MS60	MS63
2009	2,000	PF63 BV+10%				

KM# 239 200 DOLLARS
155.52 g., 0.9999 Gold 4.9674 oz. AGW, 60 mm. **Series:** Lunar **Subject:** Year of the Rooster **Obv:** National arms **Rev:** Stylized rooster standing right

Date	Mintage	F12	VF20	XF40	MS60	MS63
2005sm	84	PF65 9,750				

KM# 255 200 DOLLARS
155.15 g., 0.9999 Gold 4.9556 oz. AGW **Series:** Lunar **Subject:** Year of the Dog **Obv:** National arms **Rev:** Stylized dog standing left

Date	Mintage	F12	VF20	XF40	MS60	MS63
2006sm	50	PF65 9,750				

KM# 300 200 DOLLARS
155.50 g., 0.999 Gold 4.9623 oz. AGW, 60 mm. **Subject:** Year of the Ox **Obv:** Supported arms **Rev:** Ox

Date	Mintage	F12	VF20	XF40	MS60	MS63
2009	200	PF65 9,500				

KM# 318 200 DOLLARS
155.15 g., 0.999 Gold 4.9511 oz. AGW, 60 mm. **Subject:** Year of the Horse **Obv:** National arms **Rev:** Horse right

Date	Mintage	F12	VF20	XF40	MS60	MS63
2014	—	PF65 9,500				

KM# 178 250 DOLLARS
31.10 g., 0.999 Gold 0.9926 oz. AGW, 32.1 mm. **Subject:** Year of the Snake **Obv:** National arms **Rev:** Stylized snake **Edge:** Reeded

Date	Mintage	F12	VF20	XF40	MS60	MS63
2001sm	3,775	PF63 BV+10%				

KM# 183 250 DOLLARS
31.10 g., 0.9999 Gold 0.9935 oz. AGW, 32.1 mm. **Subject:** Year of the Horse **Obv:** National arms **Rev:** Horse **Edge:** Reeded

Date	Mintage	F12	VF20	XF40	MS60	MS63
2002sm	3,199	PF63 BV+10%				

KM# 227 250 DOLLARS
31.10 g., 0.9999 Gold 0.9934 oz. AGW, 32.1 mm. **Series:** Lunar **Subject:** Year of the Goat **Obv:** National arms **Rev:** Stylized goat standing right facing left

Date	Mintage	F12	VF20	XF40	MS60	MS63
2003sm	2,390	PF63 BV+10%				

KM# 188 250 DOLLARS
31.10 g., 0.9999 Gold 0.9934 oz. AGW, 32.1 mm. **Series:** Lunar **Subject:** Year of the Monkey **Obv:** National arms **Rev:** Stylized monkey sitting left **Edge:** Reeded

Date	Mintage	F12	VF20	XF40	MS60	MS63
2004sm	2,535	PF63 BV+10%				

KM# 228 500 DOLLARS
155.52 g., 0.9999 Gold 4.9674 oz. AGW, 55 mm. **Series:** Lunar **Subject:** Year of the Goat **Obv:** National arms **Rev:** Stylized goat standing right facing left

Date	Mintage	F12	VF20	XF40	MS60	MS63
2003sm	62	PF65 9,750				

KM# 232 500 DOLLARS
155.52 g., 0.9999 Gold 4.9674 oz. AGW, 55 mm. **Series:** Lunar **Subject:** Year of the Monkey **Obv:** National arms **Rev:** Stylized monkey sitting left

Date	Mintage	F12	VF20	XF40	MS60	MS63
2004sm	76	PF65 9,750				

MINT SETS

KM#	Date	Mintage	Identification	Issue Price	Mkt Val
MS38A	2001 (7)	101,738	KM#98-103, 104.2	—	—
MS39	2002 (7)	84,577	KM#98-103, 104.3	—	15.00
MS40	2003 (6)	68,980	KM#99-103, 104.3	—	15.00
MS41	2004 (6)	70,000	KM#99-103, 104.3	—	15.00
MS42	2005 (6)	61,981	KM#99-103, 104.3	—	15.00
MS43	2006 (7)	53,214	KM#99-103, 104.3	—	15.00
MS44	2007 (6)	54,889	KM99-103, 104.3	10.78	15.00
MS45	2008 (6)	55,000	KM#99-103, 104.3	—	15.00
MS46	2009 (6)	60,000	KM#99-103, 104.3	—	15.00

PROOF SETS

KM#	Date	Mintage	Identification	Issue Price	Mkt Val
PS61	2001 (2)	3,000	KM#179-180 plus copper-nickel ingot	—	115
PS62	2001 (3)	2,000	KM#178-180 plus copper-nickel ingot	—	2,000
PS63	2001 (4)	—	KM#212-215	—	1,750
PS64	2001 (6)	—	KM#212-216, plus ingot	—	3,200
PS65	2001 (2)	2,001	KM#177, 177a	—	70.00
PS66	2001 (7)	6,000	KM#98a-103a, 104.2a	—	70.00
PS67	2002 (2)	3,000	KM#182, 182a	—	115
PS68	2002 (3)	2,000	KM#182, 182a, 183	—	2,000
PS69	2002 (2)	2,001	KM#181, 181a	—	65.00
PS70	2002 (3)	2,001	KM#181, 181a, 217	—	160
PS71	2002 (4)	—	KM#217-220	—	1,750
PS72	2002 (6)	—	KM#217-221 plus ingot	—	3,250
PS73	2002 (7)	6,300	KM#98a-103a, 104.2a	—	70.00
PS74	2003 (2)	2,003	KM#196, 196a	—	75.00
PS75	2003 (6)	4,900	KM#99a-103a, 104.3a	—	70.00
PS76	2003 (6)	1,000	KM#99a-103a, 104.3a	—	130
PS77	2003 (2)	88	KM#226, 228	—	10,050
PS78	2003 (2)	3,000	KM#225, 225a	—	115
PS79	2003 (3)	2,000	KM#225, 225a, 227	—	2,000
PS80	2004 (2)	1,000	KM#189, 189a	—	85.00
PS81	2004 (3)	88	KM#185, 189, 189a	—	1,950
PS82	2004 (6)	10,000	KM#98a-103a, 104.3a	—	70.00
PS83	2004 (2)	1,000	KM#184, 184a	—	40.00
PS84	2004 (2)	1,000	KM#190, 190a	—	40.00
PS85	2004 (2)	1,000	KM#191, 191a	—	40.00
PS86	2004 (2)	1,000	KM#192, 192a	—	40.00
PS87	2004 (4)	800	KM#184a, 190a-192a	—	110
PS88	2004 (8)	88	KM#184, 184a, 190, 190a, 191, 191a, 192, 192a	—	150
PS89	2004 (2)	80	KM#231, 232	—	10,050
PS90	2004 (2)	3,000	KM#187, 187a	—	110
PS91	2004 (3)	2,000	KM#187, 187a, 188	—	2,000
PS92	2005 (6)	3,250	KM#99a-103a, 104.3a	—	70.00
PS93	2005 (2)	3,000	KM#234, 236	—	110
PS94	2005 (2)	88	KM#237, 239	—	10,050
PS95	2005 (3)	2,000	KM#234, 236, 238	—	2,000
PS97	2006 (2)	8,000	KM#256, 257	—	120
PS99	2007 (4)	800	KM#259a-262a	—	130
PS100	2007 (2)	8,000	KM#275, 276	90.00	90.00
PS101	2007 (2)	3,000	KM#193, 193a	65.00	65.00

PROOF-LIKE SETS (PL)

KM#	Date	Mintage	Identification	Issue Price	Mkt Val
PL1	2004 (4)	800	KM#184, 190, 191, 192	—	40.00
PL2	2007 (4)	800	KM#259-262	—	50.00

SLOVAKIA

The Republic of Slovakia has an area of 18,923 sq. mi. (49,035 sq. km.) and a population of 4.9 million. Capital: Bratislava. Textiles, steel, and wood products are exported.

MINT MARK

Kremnica Mint

REPUBLIC

STANDARD COINAGE

100 Halierov = 1 Slovak Koruna (Sk)

KM# 17 10 HALIEROV
0.72 g., Aluminum, 17 mm. **Obv:** Double cross on shield above inscription **Rev:** Church steeple **Edge:** Plain

Date	Mintage	F12	VF20	XF40	MS60	MS63
2001	20,330,000	—	—	—	0.35	—
2001	12,500	PF60 2.50				
2002	37,640,000	—	—	—	0.35	—
2002	16,100	PF60 1.50				
2003 In sets only	3,000	—	—	—	—	2.50

KM# 17a 10 HALIEROV
2.85 g., 0.925 Silver 0.0842 oz. ASW, 17 mm.

Date	Mintage	F12	VF20	XF40	MS60	MS63
2004	4,000	—	—	—	—	10.00
2004	2,000	PF65 15.00				

KM# 18 20 HALIEROV
0.95 g., Aluminum, 19.5 mm. **Obv:** Double cross on shield above inscription **Rev:** Krivan Mountain and value **Edge:** Reeded

Date	Mintage	F12	VF20	XF40	MS60	MS63
2001	21,920,000	—	—	—	0.45	—
2001	12,500	PF60 2.50				
2002	36,300,000	—	—	—	0.45	—
2002	16,100	PF60 1.50				
2003 In sets only	3,000	—	—	—	—	2.50

KM# 18a 20 HALIEROV
3.87 g., 0.925 Silver 0.1144 oz. ASW, 19.5 mm.

Date	Mintage	F12	VF20	XF40	MS60	MS63
2004	4,000	—	—	—	—	15.00
2004	2,000	PF65 20.00				

KM# 35 50 HALIEROV
2.80 g., Copper Plated Steel, 18.75 mm. **Obv:** Double cross on shield above inscription **Rev:** Devin watch tower and value **Edge:** Segmented reeding

Date	Mintage	F12	VF20	XF40	MS60	MS63
2001	10,400,000	—	—	—	0.60	—
2001	12,500	PF60 2.50				
2002	11,000,000	—	—	—	0.60	—
2002	16,100	PF60 1.50				
2003	11,000,000	—	—	—	0.60	—
2004	16,500,000	—	—	—	0.60	—
2004	—	PF60 1.50				
2005	17,000,000	—	—	—	0.60	—
2006	22,050,000	—	—	—	0.60	—
2006	—	PF60 1.50				
2007	—	—	—	—	0.60	—
2008	—	—	—	—	0.60	—
2008	—	PF60 1.50				

KM# 12 KORUNA
3.85 g., Bronze Plated Steel, 21 mm. **Subject:** 15th Century of Madonna and Child **Obv:** Double cross on shield above inscription **Rev:** Madonna holding child and value **Edge:** Milled

Date	Mintage	F12	VF20	XF40	MS60	MS63
2001 In sets only	12,500	—	—	—	—	1.50
2001	—	PF60 3.00				
2002	11,000,000	—	—	—	0.75	—
2002	16,100	PF60 2.50				
2003 In sets only	14,000	—	—	—	—	1.50
2004 In sets only	—	—	—	—	—	1.50
2004	—	PF60 2.50				
2005	10,000,000	—	—	—	0.75	—
2005	—	PF60 2.50				
2006	9,605,000	—	—	—	0.75	—
2006	—	PF60 2.50				
2007	—	—	—	—	0.75	—
2008	—	—	—	—	0.75	—
2008	—	PF60 2.50				

KM# 13 2 KORUNA
4.40 g., Nickel Plated Steel, 22.5 mm. **Obv:** Double cross on shield above inscription **Rev:** Venus statue and value

Date	Mintage	F12	VF20	XF40	MS60	MS63
2001	10,668,000	—	—	—	0.85	—
2001	12,500	PF60 5.00				
2002	11,000,000	—	—	—	0.85	—
2002	16,100	PF60 2.50				
2003	11,000,000	—	—	—	0.85	—
2004 In sets only	—	—	—	—	—	2.00
2004	—	PF60 2.50				
2005 In sets only	—	—	—	—	—	2.00
2006 In sets only	—	—	—	—	—	2.00
2006	—	PF60 2.50				
2007 In sets only	—	—	—	—	—	2.00
2008 In sets only	—	—	—	—	—	2.00
2008	—	PF60 2.50				

KM# 14 5 KORUNA
5.40 g., Nickel Plated Steel, 24.75 mm. **Obv:** Double cross on shield above inscription **Rev:** Celtic coin of BIATEC at upper left of value **Edge:** Milled

Date	Mintage	F12	VF20	XF40	MS60	MS63
2001 In sets only	—	—	—	—	—	2.00
2001	12,500	PF60 6.00				
2002	16,100	PF60 5.00				
2003 In sets only	14,000	—	—	—	—	2.00
2004 In sets only	—	—	—	—	—	2.00
2004	—	PF60 5.00				
2005 In sets only	—	—	—	—	—	2.00
2006 In sets only	—	—	—	—	—	2.00
2006	—	PF60 5.00				
2007	—	—	—	—	1.50	—
2008 In sets only	—	—	—	—	—	2.00
2008	—	PF60 5.00				

KM# 11 10 KORUNA
6.60 g., Aluminum-Bronze, 26.5 mm. **Obv:** Double cross on shield above inscription **Rev:** Bronze cross and value

Date	Mintage	F12	VF20	XF40	MS60	MS63
2001 In sets only	—	—	—	—	—	4.00
2001	12,500	PF60 12.50				
2002	16,100	PF60 10.00				
2003	10,923,000	—	—	—	2.50	—
2004 In sets only	—	—	—	—	—	4.00
2004	—	PF60 10.00				
2005 In sets only	—	—	—	—	—	4.00
2006 In sets only	—	—	—	—	—	4.00
2006	—	PF60 10.00				
2007 In sets only	—	—	—	—	—	4.00
2008 In sets only	—	—	—	—	—	4.00
2008	—	PF60 10.00				

KM# 11b 10 KORUNA
15.55 g., 0.999 Gold 0.4962 oz. AGW, 26.5 mm.

Date	Mintage	F12	VF20	XF40	MS60	MS63
2008	—	PF65 1,000				

KM# 67 20 KORUN
24.48 g., 0.925 Silver 0.7233 oz. ASW, 27.1 x 50.6 mm. **Series:** Banknotes **Obv:** Prince Pribina (800-861) **Rev:** Nitra Castle **Edge:** Plain

Date	Mintage	F12	VF20	XF40	MS60	MS63
2003	6,000	PF65 60.00				

KM# 68 50 KORUN
26.63 g., 0.925 Silver 0.7869 oz. ASW, 28.2 x 52.8 mm. **Series:** Banknotes **Obv:** Saints Cyril and Methodius (814-885) **Rev:** Two hands **Edge:** Plain

Date	Mintage	F12	VF20	XF40	MS60	MS63
2003	6,000	**PF65** 65.00				

KM# 69 100 KORUN
28.87 g., 0.925 Silver 0.8531 oz. ASW, 29.3 x 55 mm. **Series:** Banknotes **Obv:** The Levoca Madonna **Rev:** St. James Church in Levoca **Edge:** Plain

Date	Mintage	F12	VF20	XF40	MS60	MS63
2003		**PF65** 75.00				

KM# 59 200 KORUN
20.00 g., 0.750 Silver 0.4792 oz. ASW, 34 mm. **Subject:** Alexander Dubcek **Obv:** Double cross on shield and tree **Rev:** Head left **Edge Lettering:** LUDSKOST SLOBODA DEMOKRACIA

Date	Mintage	F12	VF20	XF40	MS60	MS63
2001	12,800	—	—	—	—	25.00
2001	3,000	**PF65** 70.00				

Note: Unc. examples without edge lettering exist. Value $850.

KM# 60 200 KORUN
20.00 g., 0.750 Silver 0.4792 oz. ASW, 34 mm. **Subject:** Ludovit Fulla **Obv:** Modern art **Rev:** Head facing in national costume, value and dates **Edge:** Lettered **Note:** 1,800 pieces melted.

Date	Mintage	F12	VF20	XF40	MS60	MS63
2002	11,300	—	—	—	—	25.00
2002	2,400	**PF65** 55.00				

KM# 62 200 KORUN
20.35 g., 0.750 Silver 0.4875 oz. ASW, 34 mm. **Subject:** UNESCO World Heritage site - Vlkolínec **Obv:** Log building and double cross on shield **Rev:** Wooden tower and value **Edge Lettering:** WORLD HERITAGE PATRIMONE MONDIAL **Note:** 900 pieces melted.

Date	Mintage	F12	VF20	XF40	MS60	MS63
2002	11,500	—	—	—	—	25.00
2002	—	**PF65** 55.00				

KM# 65 200 KORUN
20.00 g., 0.750 Silver 0.4792 oz. ASW, 34 mm. **Subject:** Imrich Karvas **Obv:** Building, national arms and value **Rev:** Portrait **Edge:** Lettered **Edge Lettering:** NARODOHOSPODAR HUMANISTA EUROPAN **Note:** 500 pieces uncirculated melted.

Date	Mintage	F12	VF20	XF40	MS60	MS63
2003	9,800	—	—	—	—	25.00
2003	3,000	**PF65** 50.00				

KM# 66 200 KORUN
20.00 g., 0.750 Silver 0.4792 oz. ASW, 34 mm. **Subject:** Jozef Skultety, Slovak linguist and historian **Obv:** Building below double cross within shield **Rev:** Head facing and value **Edge Lettering:** VYTRVALOST A VERNOST NARODNEMU IDEALU **Note:** 500 pieces uncirculated melted.

Date	Mintage	F12	VF20	XF40	MS60	MS63
2003	8,800	—	—	—	—	30.00
2003	2,700	**PF65** 55.00				

KM# 70 200 KORUN
31.21 g., 0.925 Silver 0.9222 oz. ASW, 30.4 x 57.2 mm. **Series:** Banknotes **Obv:** Head facing and value **Rev:** 18th Century city view and value **Edge:** Plain

Date	Mintage	F12	VF20	XF40	MS60	MS63
2003	6,000	**PF65** 90.00				

KM# 75 200 KORUN
20.00 g., 0.750 Silver 0.4792 oz. ASW, 34 mm. **Obv:** Kempelen's Chess Machine (1770) **Rev:** Inventor Wolfgang Kemelen (1734-1804) above Bratislava city view **Edge Lettering:** VYNALEZCA - TECHNIK - KONSTRUKTER

Date	Mintage	F12	VF20	XF40	MS60	MS63
2004	8,000	—	—	—	—	25.00
2004	3,200	**PF65** 50.00				

KM# 76 200 KORUN
20.00 g., 0.750 Silver 0.4792 oz. ASW, 34 mm. **Obv:** Church and town hall below double cross within shield **Rev:** Aerial view of Bardejov circa 1768 **Edge Lettering:** WORLD HERITAGE - PATRIMOINE MONDIAL

Date	Mintage	F12	VF20	XF40	MS60	MS63
2004	8,400	—	—	—	—	25.00
2004	3,600	**PF65** 50.00				

KM# 77 200 KORUN
18.00 g., 0.900 Silver 0.5175 oz. ASW, 34 mm. **Obv:** "The Segner Wheel" model **Rev:** Bust with fur hat facing within circle of designs **Edge Lettering:** VYNALEZCA - FYZIK - MATEMATIK - PEDAGOG

Date	Mintage	F12	VF20	XF40	MS60	MS63
2004	10,500	—	—	—	—	25.00
2004	4,700	**PF65** 45.00				

KM# 78 200 KORUN
20.00 g., 0.750 Silver 0.4792 oz. ASW, 34 mm. **Subject:** Slovakian entry into the European Union **Obv:** Circle of stars in arch above national arms **Rev:** Map in arch above value **Edge Lettering:** ROZSIRENIE EUROPSKEJ UNIE O DESAT KRAJIN

Date	Mintage	F12	VF20	XF40	MS60	MS63
2004	10,100	—	—	—	—	25.00
2004	4,700	**PF65** 45.00				

KM# 81 200 KORUN
18.00 g., 0.900 Silver 0.5175 oz. ASW, 34 mm. **Subject:** Leopold I Coronation 350th Anniversary **Obv:** Value and partial castle view **Rev:** Coin design of Leopold I in large size legend **Edge Lettering:** BRATISLAVSKE KORUNOVACIE

Date	Mintage	F12	VF20	XF40	MS60	MS63
2005	8,900	—	—	—	—	25.00
2005	4,800	PF65 45.00				

KM# 82 200 KORUN
18.00 g., 0.900 Silver 0.5175 oz. ASW, 34 mm. **Subject:** Treaty of Pressburg **Obv:** Primate's Palace behind French military standard **Rev:** Napoleon and Francis I of Austria **Edge Lettering:** 26 DECEMBER. 5 MIVOSE AN 14

Date	Mintage	F12	VF20	XF40	MS60	MS63
2005	5,100	—	—	—	—	25.00
2005	3,400	PF65 45.00				

KM# 87 200 KORUN
18.00 g., 0.900 Silver 0.5175 oz. ASW, 34 mm. **Subject:** 200th Anniversary Birth of Karol Kuzmány **Obv:** Small national arms at upper left, denomination at center **Obv. Inscription:** SLOVENSKÁ / REPUBLIKA **Rev:** Partial medallic head of Kuzmány facing

Date	Mintage	F12	VF20	XF40	MS60	MS63
2006	—	—	—	—	—	25.00
2006	—	PF65 55.00				

KM# 105 200 KORUN
18.00 g., 0.900 Silver 0.5175 oz. ASW, 34 mm. **Subject:** Josef M. Petzval, Physicist **Obv:** Lens **Rev:** Bust at left

Date	Mintage	F12	VF20	XF40	MS60	MS63
2007	4,700	—	—	—	—	25.00
2007	2,500	PF65 70.00				

KM# 88 200 KORUN
18.00 g., 0.900 Silver 0.5175 oz. ASW, 34 mm. **Subject:** 100th Anniversary Birth of Andrej Kmet **Obv:** Small national arms above stylized M-shaped memorial representing the Slovak Museum. **Obv. Legend:** SLOVENSKÁ REPUBLIKA **Rev:** Head of Kmet 3/4 left **Edge:** Lettered **Edge Lettering:** POZNÁVAJME KRAJE SVOJE A POZNÁME SAMYCH SEBA

Date	Mintage	F12	VF20	XF40	MS60	MS63
2008	8,500	—	—	—	—	25.00
2008	3,400	PF65 75.00				

KM# 56 500 KORUN
33.63 g., 0.925 Silver 0.9937 oz. ASW, 40 mm. **Subject:** Mala Fatra National Park **Obv:** National arms center of cross formed by beetles (Alpine Salyers) **Rev:** Orchid with mountain background **Edge Lettering:** OCHRANA PRIRODY A KRAJINY **Note:** 400 pieces uncirculated melted.

Date	Mintage	F12	VF20	XF40	MS60	MS63
2001	10,200	—	—	—	—	90.00
2001	1,800	PF65 250				

KM# 57 500 KORUN
31.10 g., 0.999 Silver 0.9926 oz. ASW, 45 mm. **Subject:** Third Millennium **Obv:** The Universe **Rev:** Three hands **Edge:** Plain **Shape:** 3-sided **Note:** 400 pieces uncirculated melted.

Date	Mintage	F12	VF20	XF40	MS60	MS63
2001	13,000	—	—	—	—	90.00
2001	4,000	PF65 185				

KM# 71 500 KORUN
33.63 g., 0.925 Silver 0.9937 oz. ASW, 31.5 x 59.4 mm. **Series:** Banknotes **Obv:** Head facing and value **Rev:** Bratislava Castle view and value **Edge:** Plain

Date	Mintage	F12	VF20	XF40	MS60	MS63
2003	6,000	PF65 100				

KM# 85 500 KORUN
33.63 g., 0.925 Silver 0.9937 oz. ASW, 40 mm. **Subject:** Slovensky Kras National Park **Obv:** 2 Rock buntings above value **Rev:** Dogs Tooth violet flowers in front of Karst cave interior view **Edge Lettering:** OCHRANA PRIRODY A KRAJINY

Date	Mintage	F12	VF20	XF40	MS60	MS63
2005	8,500	—	—	—	—	55.00
2005	3,600	PF65 90.00				

KM# 84 500 KORUN
33.63 g., 0.925 Silver 0.9937 oz. ASW, 40 mm. **Subject:** Muranska Planina National Park **Obv:** Wildflowers and Muran castle ruins **Rev:** Two wild horses **Edge Lettering:** OCHRANA PRIRODY A KRAJINY [flower]

Date	Mintage	F12	VF20	XF40	MS60	MS63
2006	2,800	PF65 200				
2006	4,300	—	—	—	—	95.00

KM# 86 500 KORUN
33.63 g., 0.925 Silver 0.9937 oz. ASW, 40 mm. **Subject:** 450th Anniversary - Construction Fortress at Komárno **Obv:** Early ships, fortress in background, national arms at lower right **Obv. Legend:** SLOVENSKÁ REPUBLIKA **Rev:** Layout of fortress, horses in battle against Turks below **Rev. Legend:** PEVNOST - KOMÁRNO **Edge Lettering:** NEC ARTE NEC MARTE - COMORRA in relief

Date	Mintage	F12	VF20	XF40	MS60	MS63
2007	4,600	—	—	—	—	80.00
2007	2,600	PF65 250				

KM# 106 500 KORUN
33.63 g., 0.925 Silver 0.9937 oz. ASW, 40 mm. **Subject:**
National Park - Low Tatra Mountains **Obv:** Mountains, flower
and shield **Rev:** Bear in pine tree

Date	Mintage	F12	VF20	XF40	MS60	MS63
2008	4,300	—	—	—	—	75.00
2008	4,800	PF65 150				

KM# 63 1000 KORUN
62.21 g., 0.999 Silver 1.9851 oz. ASW, 43.6 x 43.6 mm.
Subject: 10th Anniversary of Republic **Obv:** National arms
between hands **Rev:** Value above map **Edge:** Segmented
reeding **Shape:** Square

Date	Mintage	F12	VF20	XF40	MS60	MS63
2003	10,000	PF65 150				

KM# 72 1000 KORUN
43.91 g., 0.925 Bi-Metallic 1.2975 oz., 32.6 x 61.6 mm. **Series:**
Banknotes **Obv:** Head facing and value **Rev:** The Madonna
Protector facing and church of Liptovske Sliace **Edge:** Plain
Note: Illustration reduced.

Date	Mintage	F12	VF20	XF40	MS60	MS63
2003	6,000	PF65 175				

KM# 58 5000 KORUN
Tri-Metallic, 50 mm. **Series:** Third Millennium **Obv:** The
Universe **Rev:** Three hands **Edge:** Plain **Shape:** Triangular

Date	Mintage	F12	VF20	XF40	MS60	MS63
2001	8,000	PF65 500				

KM# 61 5000 KORUN
9.50 g., 0.900 Gold 0.2731 oz. AGW, 26 mm. **Subject:** Vlkolinec
village - UNESCO historic site **Obv:** Enclosed communal well
Rev: Window and fence **Edge:** Reeded

Date	Mintage	F12	VF20	XF40	MS60	MS63
2002	—	PF65 575				

KM# 73 5000 KORUN
47.63 g., 0.925 Bi-Metallic 1.4075 oz., 33.4 x 63.8 mm. **Series:**
Banknotes **Obv:** Head facing and value **Rev:** Stefanik's grave
monument **Edge:** Plain **Note:** Illustration reduced.

Date	Mintage	F12	VF20	XF40	MS60	MS63
2003	6,000	PF65 275				

KM# 80 5000 KORUN
9.50 g., 0.900 Gold 0.2731 oz. AGW, 26 mm. **Subject:** Bardejov
- UNESCO historic site **Obv:** National arms and value left of
Town Hall **Rev:** Zachariah in window frame left of St. Aegidius
Church, Bardejov **Edge:** Reeded

Date	Mintage	F12	VF20	XF40	MS60	MS63
2004	9,000	PF65 575				

KM# 83 5000 KORUN
9.50 g., 0.900 Gold 0.2731 oz. AGW, 26 mm. **Subject:** Leopold
I Coronation **Obv:** Mounted Herald with Bratislava Castile in
background **Rev:** Leopold I and Crown of St. Stephan **Edge:**
Reeded

Date	Mintage	F12	VF20	XF40	MS60	MS63
2005	7,500	PF65 575				

KM# 89 5000 KORUN
9.50 g., 0.900 Gold 0.2731 oz. AGW, 26 mm. **Subject:**
400th Anniversary Coronation of King Matthias II **Obv:**
Cathedral and Bratislava castle **Obv. Legend:** SLOVENSKÁ -
REPUBLIKA **Rev:** 1/2 length figure of Matthias II left, crown
in lower foreground, towers of the St. Michael's Gate and
franciscan Church in Bratislava in background **Rev. Legend:**
KORUNOVÁCIA MATEJA II. / BRATISLAVA **Edge:** Reeded

Date	Mintage	F12	VF20	XF40	MS60	MS63
2008	4,050	PF65 575				

KM# 64 10000 KORUN
18.84 g., Bi-Metallic, 29.5 x 29.5 mm. **Subject:** 10th Anniversary
of the Republic **Obv:** Young head left within circular inscription
above double cross within shield **Rev:** Bratislava castle above
value **Edge:** Segmented reeding **Shape:** Square

Date	Mintage	F12	VF20	XF40	MS60	MS63
2003	6,000	PF65 1,250				

KM# 79 10000 KORUN
24.88 g., Bi-Metallic, 40 mm. **Subject:** Slovakian entry into the
European Union **Obv:** National arms above date in center **Rev:**
European map with entry date **Edge:** Plain

Date	Mintage	F12	VF20	XF40	MS60	MS63
2004	7,200	PF65 1,200				

EURO COINAGE
European Union Issues

KM# 95 EURO CENT
2.30 g., Copper Plated Steel, 16.25 mm. **Obv:** Krivan Peak in
the Tatras, state emblem **Rev:** Denomination and globe

Date	Mintage	F12	VF20	XF40	MS60	MS63
2009	90,828,000	—	—	—	0.35	0.50
2009	13,300	PF63 15.00				
2010	30,070,000	—	—	—	0.35	0.50
2010 Prooflike	5,000	—	—	—	—	3.00
2010	5,000	PF63 8.00				
2011	20,455,000	—	—	—	0.35	0.50
2011 Prooflike	5,000	—	—	—	—	3.00
2011	1,000	PF63 6.00				
2012	10,545,000	—	—	—	—	0.50
2012 Prooflike	5,000	—	—	—	—	3.00
2012	1,000	PF63 6.00				
2013	25,028,000	—	—	—	—	0.50
2013 Prooflike	3,500	—	—	—	—	3.00
2013	1,500	PF63 6.00				

KM# 96 2 EURO CENT

3.06 g., Copper Plated Steel, 18.75 mm. **Obv:** Krivan Peak in the Tatras, state emblem **Rev:** Denomination and globe **Edge:** Grooved

Date	Mintage	F12	VF20	XF40	MS60	MS63
2009	80,905,000	—	—	—	0.50	0.65
2009	13,300	PF63 15.00				
2010	50,070,000	—	—	—	0.50	0.65
2010 Prooflike	5,000	—	—	—	—	3.00
2010	5,000	PF63 8.00				
2011	15,055,000	—	—	—	0.50	0.65
2011 Prooflike	5,000	—	—	—	—	3.00
2011	1,000	PF63 6.00				
2012 In sets only	45,000	—	—	—	—	0.65
2012 Prooflike	5,000	—	—	—	—	3.00
2012	1,000	PF63 6.00				
2013 In sets only	28,000	—	—	—	—	0.65
2013 Prooflike	3,500	—	—	—	—	3.00
2013	1,500	PF63 6.00				

KM# 97 5 EURO CENT

3.92 g., Copper Plated Steel, 21.25 mm. **Obv:** Krivan Peak in the Tatras - state emblem **Rev:** Denomination and globe

Date	Mintage	F12	VF20	XF40	MS60	MS63
2009	84,957,000	—	—	—	0.75	1.00
2009	13,300	PF63 15.00				
2010 In sets only	70,000	—	—	—	—	1.00
2010 Prooflike	5,000	—	—	—	—	3.00
2010	5,000	PF63 8.00				
2011 In sets only	55,000	—	—	—	—	1.00
2011 Prooflike	5,000	—	—	—	—	3.00
2011	1,000	PF63 6.00				
2012 In sets only	45,000	—	—	—	—	1.00
2012 Prooflike	5,000	—	—	—	—	3.00
2012	1,000	PF63 6.00				
2013 In sets only	28,000	—	—	—	—	1.00
2013 Prooflike	3,500	—	—	—	—	3.00
2013	1,500	PF63 6.00				

KM# 98 10 EURO CENT

4.10 g., Brass, 19.75 mm. **Obv:** Bratislava Castle and state emblem **Rev:** Expanded relief map of European Union at left, denomination at right **Edge:** Reeded

Date	Mintage	F12	VF20	XF40	MS60	MS63
2009	74,800,000	—	—	—	0.75	1.00
2009	13,300	PF63 15.00				
2010 In sets only	70,000	—	—	—	—	1.00
2010 Prooflike	5,000	—	—	—	—	3.00
2010	5,000	—	—	—	PF63 8.00	
2011 In sets only	55,000	—	—	—	—	1.00
2011 Prooflike	5,000	—	—	—	—	3.00
2011	1,000	PF63 6.00				
2012 In sets only	45,000	—	—	—	—	1.00
2012 Prooflike	5,000	—	—	—	—	3.00
2012	1,000	—	—	—	PF63 6.00	
2013 In sets only	45,000	—	—	—	—	1.00
2013 Prooflike	3,500	—	—	—	—	3.00
2013	1,500	PF63 6.00				

KM# 99 20 EURO CENT

5.74 g., Brass, 22.25 mm. **Obv:** Bratislava Castle and state emblem **Rev:** Expanded relief map of European Union at left, denomination at right **Edge:** Notched

Date	Mintage	F12	VF20	XF40	MS60	MS63
2009	66,602,000	—	—	—	1.00	1.25
2009	13,300	PF63 16.00				
2010 In sets only	70,000	—	—	—	—	1.25
2010 Prooflike	5,000	—	—	—	—	3.50
2010	5,000	—	—	—	PF63 10.00	
2011 In sets only	55,000	—	—	—	—	1.25
2011 Prooflike	5,000	—	—	—	—	3.50
2011	1,000	PF63 7.00				
2012 In sets only	45,000	—	—	—	—	1.25
2012 Prooflike	5,000	—	—	—	—	3.50
2012	1,000	—	—	—	PF63 7.00	
2013 In sets only	28,000	—	—	—	—	1.25
2013 Prooflike	3,500	—	—	—	—	3.50
2013	1,500	PF63 7.00				

KM# 100 50 EURO CENT

7.80 g., Brass, 24.25 mm. **Obv:** Bratislava Castle and state shield **Rev:** Expanded relief map of European Union at left, denomination at right **Edge:** Reeded

Date	Mintage	F12	VF20	XF40	MS60	MS63
2009	59,400,000	—	—	—	1.25	1.50
2009	13,300	PF63 16.00				
2010 In sets only	70,000	—	—	—	—	1.50
2010 Prooflike	5,000	—	—	—	—	3.50
2010	5,000	—	—	—	PF63 10.00	
2011 In sets only	55,000	—	—	—	—	1.50
2011 Prooflike	5,000	—	—	—	—	3.50
2011	1,000	PF63 7.00				
2012 In sets only	45,000	—	—	—	—	1.50
2012 Prooflike	5,000	—	—	—	—	3.50
2012	1,000	PF63 7.00				
2013 In sets only	28,000	—	—	—	—	1.50
2013 Prooflike	3,500	—	—	—	—	3.50
2013	1,500	PF63 7.00				

KM# 101 EURO

7.50 g., Bi-Metallic, 23.25 mm. **Obv:** Double cross in middle of three hills **Rev:** Value at left, expanded relief map of European Union at right **Edge:** Segmented reeding

Date	Mintage	F12	VF20	XF40	MS60	MS63
2009	46,777,000	—	—	—	2.50	2.75
2009	13,300	PF63 20.00				
2010 In sets only	70,000	—	—	—	—	2.75
2010 Prooflike	5,000	—	—	—	—	6.00
2010	5,000	—	—	—	PF63 15.00	
2011 In sets only	55,000	—	—	—	—	2.75
2011 Prooflike	5,000	—	—	—	—	6.00
2011	1,000	PF63 12.00				
2012 In sets only	45,000	—	—	—	—	2.75
2012 Prooflike	5,000	—	—	—	—	6.00
2012	1,000	—	—	—	PF63 12.00	
2013 In sets only	28,000	—	—	—	—	2.75
2013 Prooflike	3,500	—	—	—	—	6.00
2013	1,500	PF63 12.00				

KM# 102 2 EURO

8.50 g., Bi-Metallic, 25.75 mm. **Obv:** Double cross on middle of three hills **Rev:** Value at left, expanded map of European Union at left

Date	Mintage	F12	VF20	XF40	MS60	MS63
2009	39,250,000	—	—	—	5.00	6.00
2009	13,300	PF63 25.00				
2010 In sets only	70,000	—	—	—	—	6.00
2010 Prooflike	5,000	—	—	—	—	7.50
2010	5,000	PF63 20.00				
2011	5,049,000	—	—	—	5.00	6.00
2011 Prooflike	5,000	—	—	—	—	7.50
2011	1,000	PF63 15.00				
2012 In sets only	45,000	—	—	—	—	6.00
2012 Prooflike	5,000	—	—	—	—	7.50
2012	1,000	PF63 15.00				
2013 In sets only	28,000	—	—	—	—	6.00
2013 Prooflike	3,500	—	—	—	—	7.50
2013	1,500	PF63 15.00				

KM# 103 2 EURO

8.50 g., Bi-Metallic, 25.75 mm. **Subject:** EMU 10th Anniversary **Obv:** Stick figure and large E symbol **Rev:** Expanded relief map of European Union at left, denomination at right

Date	Mintage	F12	VF20	XF40	MS60	MS63
2009 Special Unc.	7,000	—	—	—	—	20.00
2009	2,493,000	—	—	—	6.00	7.50

KM# 107 2 EURO

8.50 g., Bi-Metallic, 25.75 mm. **Subject:** Freedom, 17 November 1989, 20th Anniversary **Obv:** Ringing Freedom bell

Date	Mintage	F12	VF20	XF40	MS60	MS63
2009 Special Unc.	7,000	—	—	—	—	20.00
2009	1,000,000	—	—	—	6.00	7.50
2009 Prooflike	1,000	—	—	—	—	175

KM# 114 2 EURO

8.50 g., Bi-Metallic, 25.75 mm. **Subject:** Visegrad Group, 20th Anniversary

Date	Mintage	F12	VF20	XF40	MS60	MS63
2011 Special Unc.	7,000	—	—	—	—	20.00
2011	981,000	—	—	—	5.00	6.00

KM# 120 2 EURO

8.50 g., Bi-Metallic, 25.75 mm. **Subject:** Euro coinage, 10th Anniversary **Obv:** Euro symbol on globe at center, child-like rendering around

Date	Mintage	F12	VF20	XF40	MS60	MS63
2012	1,000,000	—	—	—	6.00	8.00
2012 Special Unc.	7,000	—	—	—	—	20.00

KM# 128 2 EURO

8.50 g., Bi-Metallic **Subject:** St. Mejhod and St. Cyrus

Date	Mintage	F12	VF20	XF40	MS60	MS63
2013	10,300	—	—	—	PF63 15.00	
2013	1,000,000	—	—	—	6.00	8.00
2013 Special Unc.	7,000	—	—	—	—	20.00

KM# 134 2 EURO
8.50 g., Bi-Metallic, 25.75 mm. **Subject:** Slovakia's entry into the European Union, 10th Anniversary

Date	Mintage	F12	VF20	XF40	MS60	MS63
2014	1,000,000	—	—	—	5.00	6.00
2014 Special Unc.	—	—	—	—	—	20.00

KM# 108 10 EURO
18.00 g., 0.900 Silver 0.5175 oz. ASW, 34 mm. **Subject:** Aurel Stodola, 150th Anniversary of birth **Obv:** Turbo generator, national shield **Rev:** Portrait **Edge Lettering:** KONSTRUKTER - VYNALEZCA - PEDAGOG

Date	Mintage	F12	VF20	XF40	MS60	MS63
2009	10,100	—	—	—	—	50.00
2009	13,300	PF65 65.00				

KM# 110 10 EURO
18.00 g., 0.900 Silver 0.5175 oz. ASW, 34 mm. **Subject:** Wooden Churches of Carpathian Slovakia - UNESCO World Heritage site

Date	Mintage	F12	VF20	XF40	MS60	MS63
2010	—	—	—	—	—	50.00
2010	—	PF65 65.00				

KM# 111 10 EURO
18.00 g., 0.900 Silver 0.5175 oz. ASW, 34 mm. **Subject:** Martin Kukucin, 150th Anniversary of birth **Obv:** Landscape scene from Brac, "House on the hillside **Rev:** Fortrait facing, cuckoo, signature **Edge Lettering:** PROZAIK - DRAMATIK - PUBLICISTA

Date	Mintage	F12	VF20	XF40	MS60	MS63
2010	9,900	—	—	—	—	50.00
2010	17,325	PF65 65.00				

KM# 115 10 EURO
18.00 g., 0.900 Silver 0.5175 oz. ASW, 34 mm. **Subject:** Zobor

Documents, 900th Anniversary **Obv:** Two scribes **Rev:** Seal and partial document text

Date	Mintage	F12	VF20	XF40	MS60	MS63
2011	—	PF65 65.00				
2011	—	—	—	—	—	50.00

KM# 116 10 EURO
18.00 g., 0.900 Silver 0.5175 oz. ASW, 34 mm. **Subject:** Adoption of the memorandum of the Slovak Nation, 150th Anniversary

Date	Mintage	F12	VF20	XF40	MS60	MS63
2011	9,100	PF65 65.00				
2011	9,500	—	—	—	—	50.00

KM# 117 10 EURO
18.00 g., 0.900 Silver 0.5175 oz. ASW, 34 mm. **Subject:** Jan Cikker, 100th Anniversary of Birth

Date	Mintage	F12	VF20	XF40	MS60	MS63
2011	8,900	PF65 65.00				
2011	7,900	—	—	—	—	50.00

KM# 122 10 EURO
18.00 g., 0.900 Silver 0.5175 oz. ASW, 34 mm. **Subject:** Master Pavol of Levoca **Obv:** Female and shield **Rev:** Bearded male

Date	Mintage	F12	VF20	XF40	MS60	MS63
2012	7,400	—	—	—	—	50.00
2012	11,870	PF65 65.00				

KM# 123 10 EURO
18.00 g., 0.900 Silver 0.5175 oz. ASW, 34 mm. **Subject:** Chatam Sofer, 250th Anniversary of Birth **Obv:** City view of Bratislava **Rev:** Chatam Sofer, torah, menorah

Date	Mintage	F12	VF20	XF40	MS60	MS63
2012	5,800	—	—	—	—	50.00
2012	7,900	PF65 150				

KM# 124 10 EURO
18.00 g., 0.900 Silver 0.5175 oz. ASW, 34 mm. **Subject:** Anton Bernolak, 250th Anniversary of Birth **Obv:** Quill pen **Rev:** Bust facing

Date	Mintage	F12	VF20	XF40	MS60	MS63
2012	5,200	—	—	—	—	50.00
2012	6,950	PF65 65.00				

KM# 130 10 EURO
18.00 g., 0.900 Silver 0.5175 oz. ASW, 34 mm. **Subject:** Jozef Karol Hell, 300th Anniversary of Birth

Date	Mintage	F12	VF20	XF40	MS60	MS63
2013	3,100	—	—	—	—	50.00
2013	5,750	PF65 65.00				

KM# 131 10 EURO
18.00 g., 0.900 Silver 0.5175 oz. ASW, 34 mm. **Subject:** Matica slovenska Cultural Association, 150th Anniversary

Date	Mintage	F12	VF20	XF40	MS60	MS63
2013	—	—	—	—	—	50.00
2013	—	PF65 65.00				

KM# 127 10 EURO
Silver **Subject:** 20th Anniversary of the National Bank of Slovakia

Date	Mintage	F12	VF20	XF40	MS60	MS63
2013	—	PF65 65.00				
2013	—	—	—	—	—	50.00

KM# 133 10 EURO
18.00 g., 0.900 Silver 0.5175 oz. ASW, 34 mm. **Subject:** Jozef Murgaš, 150th Anniversary of Birth

Date	Mintage	F12	VF20	XF40	MS60	MS63
2014	3,400	—	—	—	—	50.00
2014	6,300	PF65 65.00				

KM# 109 20 EURO
33.63 g., 0.925 Silver 0.9937 oz. ASW, 40 mm. **Subject:** National Park - Vel'ká Fatra **Obv:** Fora and national shield **Rev:** Falcon in flight over mountain peak **Edge Lettering:** OCHRANA PRÍRODY A KRAJINY

Date	Mintage	F12	VF20	XF40	MS60	MS63
2009	9,900	—	—	—	—	55.00
2009	12,600	PF65 65.00				

KM# 112 20 EURO
33.63 g., 0.925 Silver 0.9937 oz. ASW, 40 mm. **Subject:** Poloniny National Park **Obv:** Mountainside and flowers **Rev:** Two wolves

Date	Mintage	F12	VF20	XF40	MS60	MS63
2010						55.00
2010	—	**PF65** 75.00				

KM# 118 20 EURO
33.63 g., 0.925 Silver 0.9937 oz. ASW, 40 mm. **Subject:** Historical Sites - Trnava

Date	Mintage	F12	VF20	XF40	MS60	MS63
2011	9,950	**PF65** 75.00				
2011	8,150	—	—	—	—	60.00

KM# 121 20 EURO
33.63 g., 0.925 Silver 0.9937 oz. ASW, 40 mm. **Subject:** Historical towns - Trencin **Obv:** Castle, historical Roman inscription and National arms below **Rev:** Rendering of the Trencin historical preservation area

Date	Mintage	F12	VF20	XF40	MS60	MS63
2012	7,500	**PF65** 80.00				
2012	5,900	—	—	—	—	65.00

KM# 129 20 EURO
Silver, 40 mm. **Subject:** Kosice

Date	Mintage	F12	VF20	XF40	MS60	MS63
2013	—	—	—	—	—	85.00

KM# 135 20 EURO
33.63 g., 0.925 Silver 0.9937 oz. ASW, 40 mm. **Subject:** Dubnicke Mines

Date	Mintage	F12	VF20	XF40	MS60	MS63
2014	—	—	—	—	—	60.00
2014	—	**PF65** 80.00				

KM# 113 100 EURO
9.50 g., 0.900 Gold 0.2731 oz. AGW, 26 mm. **Subject:** Wooden Churches of Carpathian Slovakia - UNESCO Heritage Site **Obv:** Church of St. Francis of Assisi in Hervartov, belfry of the church in Hronsek and Church of St. Nicholas in Brodrzal **Rev:** Baroque altar of All Saints Church in Tvrdosin **Edge:** Reeded

Date	Mintage	F12	VF20	XF40	MS60	MS63
2010	Est. 7000	**PF65** 575				

KM# 119 100 EURO
9.50 g., 0.900 Gold 0.2731 oz. AGW, 26 mm. **Subject:** Prince Pribina Nitra, 1150th Anniversary of Death

Date	Mintage	F12	VF20	XF40	MS60	MS63
2011	6,800	**PF65** 575				

KM# 125 100 EURO
9.50 g., 0.900 Gold 0.2731 oz. AGW, 26 mm. **Subject:** Charles III, 300th Anniversary of Coronation **Obv:** City View **Rev:** Bust, crown of St. Stephen, Bratislava castle

Date	Mintage	F12	VF20	XF40	MS60	MS63
2012	—	**PF65** 575				

KM# 132 100 EURO
9.50 g., 0.900 Gold 0.2731 oz. AGW, 26 mm. **Subject:** Maximilian, 450th Anniversary of Coronation in Bratislava

Date	Mintage	F12	VF20	XF40	MS60	MS63
2013	4,300	**PF65** 575				

KM# 136 100 EURO
9.50 g., 0.900 Gold 0.2731 oz. AGW, 26 mm. **Subject:** Rastislav, Ruler of Great Moravia

Date	Mintage	F12	VF20	XF40	MS60	MS63
2014	—	**PF65** 575				

MINT SETS

KM#	Date	Mintage	Identification	Issue Price	Mkt Val
MS9	2001 (7)	—	KM#11.1-14, 17-18, 35, plus medal	—	20.00
MS10	2002 (7)	—	KM#11.1-14, 17-18, 35, plus medal	—	17.50
MS11	2003 (7)	—	KM#11.1-14, 17-18, 35, plus medal	—	15.00
MS12	2004 (7)	—	KM#11.1-14, 17, 18, 35 plus medal	—	12.00
MS13	2005 (7)	—	KM#11.1-14, 17, 18, 35 plus medal	—	12.00
MS14	2005 (6)	—	KM#11.1, 12-14, 35, Austrian 2005 KM#3088	—	10.00
MS15	2006 (7)	—	KM#11.1-14, 17, 18, 35 plus medal	—	12.00
MS16	2007 (7)	—	KM#11.1-14, 17, 18, 35 plus medal	—	12.00
MS17	2007 (5)	—	KM11.2, 12-14, 35. National parks	—	15.00
MS18	2007 (5)	—	KM#11.1, 12-14, 35	—	12.00
MS19	2007 (5)	—	KM#11.1, 12-14, 35. National parks packaging	—	15.00
MS20	2007 (5)	—	KM#11.1, 12-14, 35 and a bimetallic medal and cd. Set to commemorate musician Gejza Dusik	—	20.00
MS21	2009 (8)	87,100	KM#95-102.	—	25.00
MS22	2010 (8)	45,000	kM#95-102.	—	25.00
MS23	2011 (8)	25,000	KM#95-102.	—	25.00
MS24	2012 (8)	23,000	KM#95-102.	—	25.00

PROOF SETS

KM#	Date	Mintage	Identification	Issue Price	Mkt Val
PS2	2001 (7)	12,500	KM#11.1-14, 17-18, 35	—	35.00
PS3	2002 (7)	16,500	KM#11.1-14, 17-18, 35	—	25.00
PS4	2004 (7)	—	KM#11.1, 12-14, 35, silver strikes of 1993, KM#17-18	—	40.00
PS5	2006 (6)	—	KM#11.1, 12-14, 35 plus medal. 2006 Torino Winter Olympics	—	45.00
PS6	2008 (6)	—	KM#11.1, 12-14, 35 plus medal. 2008 Peking Olympics	—	45.00
PS7	2009 (9)	13,300	KM#95-102 plus medal	—	125
PS8	2010 (9)	5,000	KM#95-102 plus medal	—	80.00
PS9	2011 (9)	5,000	KM#95-102 plus CN medal	—	65.00
PS10	2011 (9)	1,000	KM#95-102 plus CN medal, wood box	—	350
PS11	2012 (9)	5,000	KM#95-102 plus medal.	—	65.00

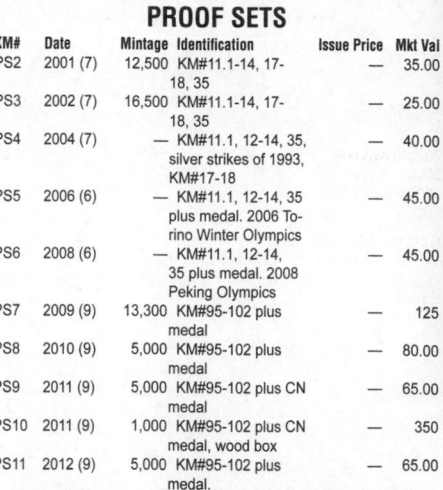

SLOVENIA

The Republic of Slovenia is located northwest of Yugoslavia in the valleys of the Danube River. It has an area of 7,819 sq. mi. and a population of *1.9 million. Capital: Ljubljana. Agriculture is the main industry with large amounts of hops and fodder crops grown as well as many varieties of fruit trees. Sheep raising, timber production and the mining of mercury from one of the country's oldest mines are also very important to the economy. Slovenia joined the European Union in May 2004.

MINT MARKS
Based on last digit in date.
(K) - Kremnitz (Slovakia): open 4, upturned 5
(BP) - Budapest (Hungary): closed 4, down-turned 5

MONETARY SYSTEM
100 Stotinov = 1 Tolar
100 Euro Cents = 1 Euro

REPUBLIC
STANDARD COINAGE
100 Stotinow = 1 Tolar

KM# 7 10 STOTINOV
0.55 g., Aluminum, 16 mm. **Obv:** Value within square **Rev:** Olm salamander **Edge:** Plain **Note:** Varieties exist.

Date	Mintage	F12	VF20	XF40	MS60	MS63
2001 In sets only	1,000	—	—	—	—	3.00
2001	800	**PF60** 5.00				
2002 In sets only	1,000	—	—	—	—	3.00
2002	800	**PF60** 5.00				
2003 In sets only	1,000	—	—	—	—	3.00
2003	800	**PF60** 5.00				
2004 In sets only	1,000	—	—	—	—	3.00
2004	800	**PF60** 5.00				
2005 In sets only	3,000	—	—	—	—	2.00
2005	1,000	**PF60** 5.00				
2006 In sets only	4,000	—	—	—	—	2.00
2006	1,000	**PF60** 5.00				

KM# 8 20 STOTINOV
0.70 g., Aluminum, 18 mm. **Obv:** Value within square **Rev:** Barn owl and value **Edge:** Plain

Date	Mintage	F12	VF20	XF40	MS60	MS63
2001 In sets only	1,000	—	—	—	—	4.00
2001	800	**PF60** 6.00				
2002 In sets only	1,000	—	—	—	—	4.00
2002	800	**PF60** 6.00				
2003 In sets only	1,000	—	—	—	—	4.00
2003	800	**PF60** 6.00				
2004 In sets only	1,000	—	—	—	—	4.00
2004	500	**PF60** 6.00				
2005 In sets only	3,000	—	—	—	—	3.00
2005	1,000	**PF60** 6.00				
2006 In sets only	4,000	—	—	—	—	3.00
2006	1,000	**PF60** 6.00				

KM# 3 50 STOTINOV
0.85 g., Aluminum, 20 mm. **Obv:** Value within square **Rev:** Bee and value **Edge:** Plain

Date	Mintage	F12	VF20	XF40	MS60	MS63
2001 In sets only	1,000	—	—	—	—	6.00
2001	800	**PF60** 7.50				

Date	Mintage	F12	VF20	XF40	MS60	MS63
2002 In sets only	1,000	—	—	—	—	6.00
2002	800	PF60 7.50				
2003 In sets only	1,000	—	—	—	—	6.00
2003	800	PF60 7.50				
2004 In sets only	1,000	—	—	—	—	6.00
2004	500	PF60 12.00				
2005 In sets only	3,000	—	—	—	—	4.00
2005	1,000	PF60 7.00				
2006 In sets only	4,000	—	—	—	—	4.00
2006	1,000	PF60 7.00				

KM# 4 TOLAR
4.50 g., Nickel-Brass, 22 mm. **Obv:** Value within circle **Rev:** Three brown trout **Rev. Legend:** SALMO TRUTTA FARIO **Edge:** Reeded **Note:** Date varieties exist: 1994 = closed or open "4"; 1995 = serif up and serif down in "5".

Date	Mintage	F12	VF20	XF40	MS60	MS63
2001	10,001,000	—	—	—	0.75	1.25
2001	800	PF60 7.50				
2002 In sets only	1,000	—	—	—	—	5.00
2002	800	PF60 7.50				
2003 In sets only	1,000	—	—	—	—	5.00
2003	800	PF60 7.50				
2004	10,001,000	—	—	—	0.75	1.25
2004 (K) In sets only	1,000	—	—	—	—	5.00
Note: 4 open to right						
2004	500	PF60 8.50				
2005 In sets only	3,000	—	—	—	—	4.00
2005	1,000	PF60 7.50				
2006 In sets only	4,000	—	—	—	—	4.00
2006	1,000	PF60 7.50				

KM# 5 2 TOLARJA
5.40 g., Nickel-Brass, 24 mm. **Obv:** Value within circle **Rev:** Barn swallow in flight **Rev. Legend:** HIRUNDO RUSTICA **Edge:** Reeded **Note:** Date varieties exist: 1994 = closed or open "4"; 1995 = serif up and serif down in "5".

Date	Mintage	F12	VF20	XF40	MS60	MS63
2001	10,001,000	—	—	—	0.75	1.75
2001	800	PF60 8.50				
2002 In sets only	1,000	—	—	—	—	7.00
2002	800	PF60 8.50				
2003 In sets only	1,000	—	—	—	—	7.00
2003	800	PF60 8.50				
2004	10,001,000	—	—	—	0.75	1.50
2004	500	PF60 8.50				
2005 In sets only	3,000	—	—	—	—	7.00
2005	1,000	PF60 8.50				
2006 In sets only	4,000	—	—	—	—	7.00
2006	1,000	PF60 8.50				

KM# 6 5 TOLARJEV
6.44 g., Nickel-Brass, 26 mm. **Obv:** Value within circle **Rev:** Head and horns of ibex **Edge:** Reeded **Note:** Date varieties exist: 1994 = closed or open "4"; 1995 = serif up and serif down in "5".

Date	Mintage	F12	VF20	XF40	MS60	MS63
2001 In sets only	1,000	—	—	—	—	8.00
2001	800	PF60 10.00				
2002 In sets only	1,000	—	—	—	—	8.00
2002	800	PF60 10.00				
2003 In sets only	1,000	—	—	—	—	8.00
2003	800	PF60 10.00				
2004 In sets only	1,000	—	—	—	—	8.00
2004	500	PF60 15.00				
2005 In sets only	3,000	—	—	—	—	7.00
2005	1,000	PF60 10.00				
2006 In sets only	4,000	—	—	—	—	7.00
2006	1,000	PF60 10.00				

KM# 41 10 TOLARJEV
5.75 g., Copper-Nickel, 24 mm. **Obv:** Value within circle **Rev:** Stylized rearing horse **Rev. Legend:** EQUUS **Edge:** Reeded

Date	Mintage	F12	VF20	XF40	MS60	MS63
2001	29,441,000	—	—	—	2.00	3.50
2001	800	PF60 12.00				
2002	10,037,000	—	—	—	2.00	3.50
2002	800	PF60 12.00				
2003 In sets only	1,000	—	—	—	—	5.00
2003	800	PF60 12.00				
2004	10,001,000	—	—	—	2.00	3.50
2004	500	PF60 12.00				
2005	6,003,000	—	—	—	2.00	3.50
2005	1,000	PF60 12.00				
2006	6,001,000	—	—	—	2.00	3.50
2006	1,000	PF60 12.00				

KM# 51 20 TOLARJEV
6.85 g., Copper-Nickel, 24 mm. **Obv:** Value within circle **Rev:** White Stork **Rev. Legend:** CICONIA CICONIA **Edge:** Reeded

Date	Mintage	F12	VF20	XF40	MS60	MS63
2003	10,001,000	—	—	—	3.50	5.00
2003	800	PF60 15.00				
2004	10,001,000	—	—	—	3.00	5.00
2004	500	PF60 15.00				
2005	12,003,000	—	—	—	3.50	5.00
2005	1,000	PF60 15.00				
2006	4,004,000	—	—	—	3.50	5.00
2006	1,000	PF60 15.00				

KM# 52 50 TOLARJEV
8.00 g., Copper-Nickel, 26 mm. **Obv:** Value within circle **Rev:** Stylized bull **Rev. Legend:** TAURUS TAURUS **Edge:** Segmented reeding

Date	Mintage	F12	VF20	XF40	MS60	MS63
2003	10,001,000	—	—	—	2.50	4.50
2003	800	PF60 12.00				
2004	5,001,000	—	—	—	2.50	4.50
2004	500	PF60 15.00				
2005	8,003,000	—	—	—	2.50	4.50
2005	1,000	PF60 12.00				
2006 In sets only	4,000	—	—	—	—	6.50
2006	1,000	PF60 12.00				

KM# 42 100 TOLARJEV
9.10 g., Copper-Nickel, 28 mm. **Subject:** 10th Anniversary of Slovenia and the Tolar **Obv:** Value **Rev:** Tree rings and inscription **Edge:** Reeded

Date	Mintage	F12	VF20	XF40	MS60	MS63
2001	500,000	—	—	—	3.00	4.00
2001	800	PF63 10.00				

KM# 45 500 TOLARJEV
8.54 g., Bi-Metallic, 28.1 mm. **Subject:** Soccer **Obv:** Value **Rev:** Soccer player and radiant sun **Edge:** Reeded

Date	Mintage	F12	VF20	XF40	MS60	MS63
2002	500,000	—	—	—	5.50	7.50
2002	800	PF63 12.50				

KM# 50 500 TOLARJEV
8.72 g., Bi-Metallic, 27.9 mm. **Subject:** European Year of the Disabled **Obv:** Stylized wheelchair **Rev:** Value **Edge:** Reeded

Date	Mintage	F12	VF20	XF40	MS60	MS63
2003	200,000	—	—	—	6.00	8.00
2003	800	PF63 13.50				

KM# 57 500 TOLARJEV
8.60 g., Bi-Metallic, 28 mm. **Obv:** Value **Rev:** Profile left looking down within mathematical graph **Edge:** Reeded

Date	Mintage	F12	VF20	XF40	MS60	MS63
2004	200,000	—	—	—	6.00	8.00
2004	500	PF63 20.00				

KM# 63 500 TOLARJEV
8.65 g., Bi-Metallic, 27.9 mm. **Obv:** Perched falcon and value **Rev:** Horizontal line in center divides partial suns **Edge:** Reeded

Date	Mintage	F12	VF20	XF40	MS60	MS63
2005	103,000	—	—	—	6.25	8.50
2005	1,000	PF63 12.00				

KM# 65 500 TOLARJEV
8.60 g., Bi-Metallic, 28 mm. **Obv:** Value **Rev:** Anton Tomaz Linhart's silhouette above life dates **Edge:** Reeded

Date	Mintage	F12	VF20	XF40	MS60	MS63
2006	104,000	—	—	—	6.00	8.00
2006	1,000	PF63 12.00				

KM# 43 2000 TOLARJEV
15.00 g., 0.925 Silver 0.4432 oz. ASW, 32 mm. **Subject:** 10th Anniversary of Slovenia and the Tolar **Obv:** Value **Rev:** Tree rings and inscription **Edge:** Reeded

Date	Mintage	F12	VF20	XF40	MS60	MS63
2001	3,000	PF63 35.00				

KM# 46 2500 TOLARJEV
15.00 g., 0.925 Silver 0.4432 oz. ASW, 32 mm. **Subject:** Soccer **Obv:** Value **Rev:** Soccer player and radiant sun **Edge:** Reeded

Date	Mintage	F12	VF20	XF40	MS60	MS63
2002	2,500	PF63 35.00				

KM# 48 2500 TOLARJEV

15.00 g., 0.925 Silver 0.4432 oz. ASW, 32 mm. **Subject:** 35th Chess Olympiad **Obv:** Rearing horse and reflection **Rev:** Chess pieces in starting positions and reflection **Edge:** Reeded

Date	Mintage	F12	VF20	XF40	MS60	MS63
2002	1,000	PF63 45.00				

KM# 53 2500 TOLARJEV

15.00 g., 0.925 Silver 0.4432 oz. ASW, 32 mm. **Subject:** European Year of the Disabled **Obv:** Value **Rev:** Stylized wheel chair **Edge:** Reeded

Date	Mintage	F12	VF20	XF40	MS60	MS63
2003	1,500	PF63 42.00				

KM# 55 5000 TOLARJEV

15.00 g., 0.925 Silver 0.4432 oz. ASW, 32 mm. **Subject:** 60th Anniversary of the Slovenian Assembly **Obv:** Value in partial star design **Rev:** Dates in partial star design **Edge:** Reeded

Date	Mintage	F12	VF20	XF40	MS60	MS63
2003	1,500	PF63 42.00				

KM# 58 5000 TOLARJEV

15.00 g., 0.925 Silver 0.4432 oz. ASW, 32 mm. **Obv:** Value **Rev:** Facial profile left looking down within mathematical graph **Edge:** Reeded

Date	Mintage	F12	VF20	XF40	MS60	MS63
2004	1,500	PF63 50.00				

KM# 60 5000 TOLARJEV

15.00 g., 0.925 Silver 0.4432 oz. ASW, 32 mm. **Subject:** 1000th Anniversary Town of Bled **Obv:** Value **Rev:** Castle and towers silhouette **Edge:** Reeded

Date	Mintage	F12	VF20	XF40	MS60	MS63
2004	1,500	PF63 50.00				

KM# 62 5000 TOLARJEV

15.10 g., 0.925 Silver 0.4462 oz. ASW, 32 mm. **Subject:** Slovenian Film Centennial **Obv:** Value above a director's clapboard **Rev:** Film segment **Edge:** Reeded

Date	Mintage	F12	VF20	XF40	MS60	MS63
2005	—	PF63 47.50				

KM# 64 5000 TOLARJEV

15.10 g., 0.925 Silver 0.4462 oz. ASW, 32 mm. **Obv:** Perched falcon above value **Rev:** Diagonal center line divides partial suns **Edge:** Reeded

Date	Mintage	F12	VF20	XF40	MS60	MS63
2005	—	PF63 47.50				

KM# 91 5000 TOLARJEV

15.00 g., 0.925 Silver 0.4432 oz. ASW, 32 mm. **Subject:** 1000th Anniversary, mention of town of Bled, 2nd issue

Date	Mintage	F12	VF20	XF40	MS60	MS63
2006	1,000	PF63 55.00				

KM# 92 5000 TOLARJEV

15.00 g., 0.900 Silver 0.4312 oz. ASW, 32 mm. **Subject:** Anton Tomaz Linhart, 250th Anniversary of Birth **Rev:** Bust left

Date	Mintage	F12	VF20	XF40	MS60	MS63
2006	5,000	PF63 45.00				

KM# 93 5000 TOLARJEV

15.00 g., 0.925 Silver 0.4432 oz. ASW, 32 mm. **Subject:** Anton Askerc, 150th Anniversary of birth **Rev:** Bust left

Date	Mintage	F12	VF20	XF40	MS60	MS63
2006	5,000	PF63 45.00				

KM# 44 20000 TOLARJEV

7.00 g., 0.900 Gold 0.2012 oz. AGW, 24 mm. **Subject:** 10th Anniversary of Slovenia and the Tolar **Obv:** Value **Rev:** Tree rings and inscription **Edge:** Reeded

Date	Mintage	F12	VF20	XF40	MS60	MS63
2001	1,000	PF63 520				

KM# 47 20000 TOLARJEV

7.00 g., 0.900 Gold 0.2012 oz. AGW, 24 mm. **Subject:** World Cup Soccer **Obv:** Value **Rev:** Soccer player and rising sun **Edge:** Reeded

Date	Mintage	F12	VF20	XF40	MS60	MS63
2002	500	PF63 550				

KM# 49 20000 TOLARJEV

7.00 g., 0.900 Gold 0.2012 oz. AGW, 24 mm. **Subject:** 35th Chess Olympiad **Obv:** Rearing horse and reflection **Rev:** Chess pieces in starting positions and reflection **Edge:** Reeded

Date	Mintage	F12	VF20	XF40	MS60	MS63
2002	500	PF63 550				

KM# 54 25000 TOLARJEV

7.00 g., 0.900 Gold 0.2012 oz. AGW, 24 mm. **Subject:** European Year of the Disabled **Obv:** Value **Rev:** Stylized wheel chair **Edge:** Reeded

Date	Mintage	F12	VF20	XF40	MS60	MS63
2003	300	PF63 575				

KM# 56 25000 TOLARJEV

7.00 g., 0.900 Gold 0.2012 oz. AGW, 24 mm. **Subject:** 60th Anniversary of the Slovenian Assembly **Obv:** Value in partial star design **Rev:** Dates in partial star design **Edge:** Reeded

Date	Mintage	F12	VF20	XF40	MS60	MS63
2003	300	PF63 575				

KM# 59 25000 TOLARJEV

7.00 g., 0.900 Gold 0.2012 oz. AGW, 24 mm. **Subject:** 250th Anniversary of Jurij Vega's Birth **Obv:** Value **Rev:** Facial profile left looking down within mathematical graph **Edge:** Reeded

Date	Mintage	F12	VF20	XF40	MS60	MS63
2004	300	PF63 575				

KM# 61 25000 TOLARJEV

7.00 g., 0.900 Gold 0.2012 oz. AGW, 24 mm. **Subject:** 1000th Anniversary Town of Bled **Obv:** Value **Rev:** Castle and towers silhouette **Edge:** Reeded

Date	Mintage	F12	VF20	XF40	MS60	MS63
2004	300	PF63 575				

KM# 66 25000 TOLARJEV
7.00 g., 0.900 Gold 0.2012 oz. AGW, 24 mm. **Subject:** Centennial of Slovene Sokol Association **Obv:** Perched falcon above value **Rev:** Rising sun and reflection **Edge:** Reeded

Date	Mintage	F12	VF20	XF40	MS60	MS63
2005	1,000	PF63 520				

KM# 67 25000 TOLARJEV
7.00 g., 0.900 Gold 0.2012 oz. AGW, 24 mm. **Subject:** Centennial of Slovene Film **Obv:** Value above clapboard **Rev:** Film segment **Edge:** Reeded

Date	Mintage	F12	VF20	XF40	MS60	MS63
2005	1,000	PF63 520				

KM# 83 25000 TOLARJEV
7.00 g., 0.900 Gold 0.2012 oz. AGW, 24 mm. **Subject:** Anton Askerc **Edge:** Reeded

Date	Mintage	F12	VF20	XF40	MS60	MS63
2006	—	PF63 525	PF65 550			

KM# 84 25000 TOLARJEV
7.00 g., 0.900 Gold 0.2012 oz. AGW, 24 mm. **Subject:** Anton Tomaz Linhart **Edge:** Reeded

Date	Mintage	F12	VF20	XF40	MS60	MS63
2006	—	PF63 525	PF65 550			

KM# 90 25000 TOLARJEV
7.00 g., 0.900 Gold 0.2012 oz. AGW, 24 mm. **Subject:** 1000th Anniversary, Town of Bled mention, 2nd issue

Date	Mintage	F12	VF20	XF40	MS60	MS63
2006	500	PF63 525	PF65 550			

EURO COINAGE

KM# 68 EURO CENT
2.30 g., Copper Plated Steel, 16.25 mm. **Obv:** White Stork **Obv. Legend:** SLOVENIJA, star between each letter **Rev:** Value and globe **Edge:** Plain

Date	Mintage	F12	VF20	XF40	MS60	MS63
2007	44,800,000	—	—	—	0.25	0.35
2008	148,000	—	—	—	0.25	0.35
2008	2,000	PF63 22.00				
2009	17,900,000	—	—	—	0.25	0.35
2010	70,000	—	—	—	0.25	0.35
2010	5,000	PF63 5.00				
2011	15,000	—	—	—	1.25	1.35
2011	2,000	PF63 15.00				
2012	—	—	—	—	0.25	0.35
2012	2,000	PF63 15.00				
2013	—	—	—	—	0.25	0.35

KM# 69 2 EURO CENT
3.06 g., Copper Plated Steel, 18.75 mm. **Obv:** Princely stone of power in consciousness **Obv. Legend:** SLOVENIJA, star between each letter **Rev:** Value and globe **Edge:** Grooved

Date	Mintage	F12	VF20	XF40	MS60	MS63
2007	44,250,000	—	—	—	0.50	0.65
2008	148,000	—	—	—	0.50	0.65
2008	2,000	PF63 22.00				
2009	12,300,000	—	—	—	0.50	0.65
2010	70,000	—	—	—	0.50	0.65
2010	5,000	PF63 5.00				
2011	15,000	—	—	—	1.50	1.65
2011	2,000	PF63 15.00				
2012	—	—	—	—	0.50	0.65
2012	2,000	PF63 15.00				
2013	—	—	—	—	0.50	0.65

KM# 70 5 EURO CENT
3.92 g., Copper Plated Steel, 21.25 mm. **Obv:** Sower of Seeds - and stars **Obv. Legend:** SLOVENIJA, star between each letter **Rev:** Value and globe **Edge:** Plain

Date	Mintage	F12	VF20	XF40	MS60	MS63
2007	43,800,000	—	—	—	0.75	1.00
2008	148,000	—	—	—	0.75	1.00
2008	2,000	PF63 22.00				
2009	100,000	—	—	—	0.75	1.00
2010	70,000	—	—	—	0.75	1.00
2010	5,000	PF63 5.00				
2011	15,000	—	—	—	1.50	2.00
2011	2,000	PF63 15.00				
2012	—	—	—	—	0.75	1.00
2012	2,000	PF63 15.00				
2013	—	—	—	—	0.75	1.00

KM# 71 10 EURO CENT
4.10 g., Brass, 19.75 mm. **Obv:** Plecnik's unrealised plans for Parliament building **Obv. Legend:** SLOVENIJA, star between each letter **Rev:** Value and map **Edge:** Reeded

Date	Mintage	F12	VF20	XF40	MS60	MS63
2007	42,800,000	—	—	—	1.00	1.25
2008	148,000	—	—	—	1.00	1.25
2008	2,000	PF63 22.00				
2009	100,000	—	—	—	1.00	1.25
2010	70,000	—	—	—	1.00	1.25
2010	5,000	PF63 5.00				
2011	15,000	—	—	—	2.00	2.25
2011	2,000	PF63 15.00				
2012	—	—	—	—	1.00	1.25
2012	2,000	PF63 15.00				
2013	—	—	—	—	1.00	1.25

KM# 72 20 EURO CENT
5.74 g., Brass, 22.25 mm. **Obv:** Two Lipizzaner horses prancing left **Obv. Legend:** SLOVENIJA, star between each letter **Rev:** Value and map **Edge:** Notched

Date	Mintage	F12	VF20	XF40	MS60	MS63
2007	37,250,000	—	—	—	1.25	1.50
2008	148,000	—	—	—	1.25	1.50
2008	2,000	PF63 8.00				
2009	100,000	—	—	—	1.25	1.50
2010	70,000	—	—	—	1.25	1.50
2010	5,000	PF63 28.00				
2011	15,000	—	—	—	2.25	2.50
2011	2,000	PF63 18.00				
2012	—	—	—	—	1.25	1.50
2012	2,000	PF63 18.00				
2013	—	—	—	—	1.25	1.50

KM# 73 50 EURO CENT
7.80 g., Brass, 24.25 mm. **Obv:** Triglav Mountain (highest peak in Slovenia) and stars **Rev:** Value and map **Edge:** Reeded

Date	Mintage	F12	VF20	XF40	MS60	MS63
2007	32,400,000	—	—	—	1.50	2.00
2008	148,000	—	—	—	1.50	2.00
2008	2,000	PF63 8.00				
2009	100,000	—	—	—	1.50	2.00
2010	70,000	—	—	—	1.50	2.00
2010	5,000	PF63 28.00				
2011	15,000	—	—	—	2.50	3.00
2011	2,000	PF63 18.00				
2012	—	—	—	—	1.50	2.00
2012	2,000	PF63 18.00				
2013	—	—	—	—	1.50	2.00

KM# 74 EURO
7.50 g., Bi-Metallic, 23.25 mm. **Obv:** Bearded Primoz Trubar **Rev:** Value and map **Edge:** Segmented reeding

Date	Mintage	F12	VF20	XF40	MS60	MS63
2007	29,750,000	—	—	—	2.50	3.50
2008	148,000	—	—	—	2.50	3.50
2008	2,000	PF63 35.00				
2009	100,000	—	—	—	2.50	3.50
2010	70,000	—	—	—	2.50	3.50
2010	5,000	PF63 15.00				
2011	15,000	—	—	—	3.50	4.50
2011	2,000	PF63 22.00				
2012	—	—	—	—	2.50	3.50
2012	2,000	PF63 22.00				
2013	—	—	—	—	2.50	3.50

KM# 75 2 EURO
8.50 g., Bi-Metallic, 25.75 mm. **Obv:** France Preseren silhouette and signature **Rev:** Value and map **Edge:** Reeded and lettered

Date	Mintage	F12	VF20	XF40	MS60	MS63
2007	21,350,000	—	—	—	4.00	5.00
2008	148,000	—	—	—	4.00	5.00
2008	2,000	PF63 40.00				
2009	100,000	—	—	—	4.00	5.00
2010	70,000	—	—	—	4.00	5.00
2010	5,000	PF63 20.00				
2011	15,000	—	—	—	5.00	6.00
2011	2,000	PF63 28.00				
2012	—	—	—	—	4.00	5.00
2012	2,000	PF63 28.00				
2013	—	—	—	—	4.00	5.00

KM# 106 2 EURO
8.50 g., Bi-Metallic, 25.75 mm. **Subject:** Treaty of Rome, 50th Anniversary

Date	Mintage	F12	VF20	XF40	MS60	MS63
2007 Encased in a lucite block	990	—	—	—	—	10.00
2007	399,100	—	—	—	6.50	7.50

KM# 80 2 EURO
8.50 g., Bi-Metallic, 25.75 mm. **Subject:** 500th Anniversary Birth of Primoz Tubar **Obv:** Bust of Trubar left at right **Rev:** Large "2" at left, modified map of Europe at right **Edge:** Reeded

Date	Mintage	F12	VF20	XF40	MS60	MS63
2008	950,000	—	—	—	6.00	8.00
2008 Special Unc.	10,000	—	—	—	—	32.50
2008	40,000	PF63 45.00				

KM# 82 2 EURO
8.50 g., Bi-Metallic, 25.75 mm. **Subject:** European Monetary Union, 10th Anniversary **Obv:** Stick figure and large E symbol **Rev:** Value at left, modified map of Europe at left

Date	Mintage	F12	VF20	XF40	MS60	MS63
2009	1,000,000	—	—	—	5.00	6.00
2009 Special Unc.	—	—	—	—	—	32.50
2009	—			PF63 40.00		

KM# 94 2 EURO
8.50 g., Bi-Metallic, 25.75 mm. **Subject:** Ljubljana Botanical Gardens, 200th Anniversary

Date	Mintage	F12	VF20	XF40	MS60	MS63
2010	20,000	PF63 50.00				
2010	980,000	—	—	—	8.00	10.00

KM# 100 2 EURO
8.50 g., Bi-Metallic, 25.75 mm. **Subject:** Franc Razman, 100th Anniversary of Birth

Date	Mintage	F12	VF20	XF40	MS60	MS63
2011	14,000	PF63 50.00				
2011	486,000	—	—	—	6.00	8.00

KM# 107 2 EURO
8.50 g., Bi-Metallic, 25.75 mm. **Subject:** Euro Coinage, 10th Anniversary **Obv:** Euro symbol on globe, child-like renderings around

Date	Mintage	F12	VF20	XF40	MS60	MS63
2012	1,000	PF63 25.00				
2012	1,000,000	—	—	—	7.00	8.00

KM# 112 2 EURO
Bi-Metallic, 25.75 mm. **Subject:** 800th Anniversary of Postojna Cave Discovery **Rev:** Stylized spiral ending in 2 speleothems

Date	Mintage	F12	VF20	XF40	MS60	MS63
2013	—	—	—	—	—	8.00

KM# 81 3 EURO
15.00 g., Bi-Metallic, 32 mm. **Subject:** Six Month Term as President of the EU 2008 **Obv:** Field of stars representing EU membership **Rev:** Pinwheel

Date	Mintage	F12	VF20	XF40	MS60	MS63
2008	348,000	—	—	—	8.00	10.00
2008 Special Unc.	148,000	—	—	—	—	20.00
2008	4,000			PF63 165	PF65 185	

KM# 85 3 EURO
15.00 g., Bi-Metallic, 32 mm. **Subject:** First Airplane flight in Slovenia by Edvard Rusjan, 100th Anniversary

Date	Mintage	F12	VF20	XF40	MS60	MS63
2009	300,000	—	—	—	8.00	10.00

KM# 95 3 EURO
15.00 g., Bi-Metallic, 32 mm. **Subject:** UNESCO - World Book Capital, Ljubljana

Date	Mintage	F12	VF20	XF40	MS60	MS63
2010	5,000	PF63 50.00				
2010	—	—	—	—	—	10.00

KM# 101 3 EURO
7.50 g., Bi-Metallic, 32 mm. **Subject:** Independence, 20th Anniversary

Date	Mintage	F12	VF20	XF40	MS60	MS63
2011	4,000	PF63 110				
2011	5,000	—	—	—	—	15.00

KM# 109 3 EURO
Bi-Metallic, 32 mm. **Subject:** Rudolf Cvetko, 100th Anniversary of Olympic medal win **Obv:** Stylized fencing **Rev:** 7 fencing swords pointed downward

Date	Mintage	F12	VF20	XF40	MS60	MS63
2012	—	—	—	—	8.00	10.00

KM# 108 3 EURO
Bi-Metallic **Subject:** 300th Anniversary of 1713 Tolmin Peasant Revolt **Rev:** Scythe and farm implements, large 1713

Date	Mintage	F12	VF20	XF40	MS60	MS63
2013	—	—	—	—	—	—

KM# 76 30 EURO
15.00 g., 0.925 Silver 0.4432 oz. ASW, 32 mm. **Subject:** 250th Anniversary Birth of Valentin Vodnik **Obv:** Value **Obv. Legend:** SLOVENIJA **Rev:** Large bust of Vodnik left

Date	Mintage	F12	VF20	XF40	MS60	MS63
2008	8,000	PF63 90.00			PF65 100	

KM# 78 30 EURO
15.00 g., 0.925 Silver 0.4432 oz. ASW, 32 mm. **Subject:** EU President **Obv:** EU membership stars **Obv. Legend:** SLOVENIJA **Rev:** Pinwheel 5-pointed star

Date	Mintage	F12	VF20	XF40	MS60	MS63
2008	8,000	PF63 125			PF65 150	

KM# 86 30 EURO
15.00 g., 0.925 Silver 0.4432 oz. ASW, 32 mm. **Subject:** First Airplane, 100th Anniversary

Date	Mintage	F12	VF20	XF40	MS60	MS63
2009	8,000	PF63 65.00			PF65 75.00	

KM# 88 30 EURO
15.00 g., 0.925 Silver 0.4432 oz. ASW, 32 mm. **Subject:** Zoran Music, painter

Date	Mintage	F12	VF20	XF40	MS60	MS63
2009	—	PF63 70.00			PF65 80.00	

KM# 96 30 EURO
15.00 g., 0.925 Silver 0.4432 oz. ASW, 32 mm. **Subject:** UNESCO - World Book Capital, Ljubljana

Date	Mintage	F12	VF20	XF40	MS60	MS63
2010	—	PF63 65.00			PF65 75.00	

KM# 98 30 EURO
15.00 g., 0.925 Silver 0.4432 oz. ASW, 32 mm. **Subject:** World Ski Jumping Championships, Planica

Date	Mintage	F12	VF20	XF40	MS60	MS63
2010	—	PF63 70.00			PF65 80.00	

KM# 102 30 EURO
15.00 g., 0.925 Silver 0.4432 oz. ASW, 32 mm. **Subject:** Independence, 20th Anniversary

Date	Mintage	F12	VF20	XF40	MS60	MS63
2011	—	PF63 65.00			PF65 75.00	

KM# 104 30 EURO
15.00 g., 0.925 Silver 0.4432 oz. ASW, 32 mm. **Series:** World Rowing Championships

Date	Mintage	F12	VF20	XF40	MS60	MS63
2011	—	PF63 65.00			PF65 75.00	

KM# 110 30 EURO
15.00 g., 0.925 Silver 0.4432 oz. ASW, 32 mm. **Subject:** Rudolf Cvetko - 100th Anniversary of 1st Olympic Medal

Date	Mintage	F12	VF20	XF40	MS60	MS63
2012 Proof	Est. 3500	—	—	—	—	—

KM# 77 100 EURO
7.00 g., 0.900 Gold 0.2012 oz. AGW, 24 mm. **Subject:** 250th Anniversary Birth of Valentin Vodnik **Obv:** Value **Obv. Legend:** SLOVENIJA **Rev:** Large bust of Vodnik left

Date	Mintage	F12	VF20	XF40	MS60	MS63
2008	5,000	PF63 425			PF65 450	

KM# 79 100 EURO
7.00 g., 0.900 Gold 0.2012 oz. AGW, 24 mm. **Subject:** EU President **Obv:** EU membership stars **Obv. Legend:** SLOVENIJA **Rev:** Pinwheel 5-pointed star

Date	Mintage	F12	VF20	XF40	MS60	MS63
2008	5,000	PF63 625			PF65 650	

KM# 87 100 EURO
7.00 g., 0.900 Gold 0.2012 oz. AGW, 24 mm. **Subject:** First Airplane, 100th Anniversary

Date	Mintage	F12	VF20	XF40	MS60	MS63
2009	6,000	PF63 425			PF65 450	

KM# 89 100 EURO
7.00 g., 0.900 Gold 0.2012 oz. AGW, 24 mm. **Subject:** Zoran Music, painter

Date	Mintage	F12	VF20	XF40	MS60	MS63
2009	—	PF63 425			PF65 450	

KM# 97 100 EURO
7.00 g., 0.900 Gold 0.2012 oz. AGW, 24 mm. **Subject:** UNESCO - World Book Capital, Ljubljana

Date	Mintage	F12	VF20	XF40	MS60	MS63
2010	—	PF63 425			PF65 450	

KM# 99 100 EURO
7.00 g., 0.900 Gold 0.2012 oz. AGW, 24 mm. **Subject:** World Ski Jumping Championships, Planica

Date	Mintage	F12	VF20	XF40	MS60	MS63
2010	—	PF63 425			PF65 450	

KM# 103 100 EURO
7.00 g., 0.900 Gold 0.2012 oz. AGW, 24 mm. **Subject:** Independence, 20th Anniversary

Date	Mintage	F12	VF20	XF40	MS60	MS63
2011	—	PF63 425			PF65 450	

KM# 105 100 EURO
7.00 g., 0.900 Gold 0.2012 oz. AGW, 24 mm. **Subject:** World Rowing Championships

Date	Mintage	F12	VF20	XF40	MS60	MS63
2011	—	PF63 425			PF65 450	

KM# 111 100 EURO
7.00 g., 0.900 Gold 0.2012 oz. AGW, 24 mm. **Subject:** Rudolf Cvetko - 100th Anniversary of 1st Olympic medal

Date	Mintage	F12	VF20	XF40	MS60	MS63
2012 Proof	—	—	—	—	—	—

MINT SETS

KM#	Date	Mintage	Identification	Issue Price	Mkt Val
MS10	2001 (7)	1,000	KM#3-8, 41	20.00	40.00
MS11	2002 (8)	1,000	KM#3-8, 41	—	45.00
MS12	2003 (10)	1,000	KM#3-8, 41, 50-52	—	55.00
MS13	2004 (10)	1,000	KM#3-8, 41, 51, 52, 57	—	45.00
MS14	2005 (9)	3,000	KM#3-8, 41, 51, 52	25.00	45.00
MS15	2006 (10)	4,000	KM#3-8, 41, 51, 52, 65	25.00	50.00
MS16	2007 (8)	100,000	KM#68-75	—	50.00
MS17	2008 (9)	148,000	KM#68-75, 81	—	50.00
MS18	2009 (9)	100,000	KM#68-75, 85	—	50.00
MS19	2010 (10)	70,000	KM#68-75, 94, 95	—	75.00
MS20	2011 (10)	150,000	KM#68-75, 100, 101	—	100

PROOF SETS

KM#	Date	Mintage	Identification	Issue Price	Mkt Val
PS13	2001 (8)	800	KM#3-8, 41, 42	—	70.00
PS14	2002 (8)	800	KM#3-8, 41, 45	—	70.00
PS15	2003 (10)	800	KM#3-8, 41, 50-52	22.50	100
PS16	2004 (10)	500	KM#3-8, 41, 51-52, 57	—	120
PS17	2005 (10)	1,000	KM#3-8, 41, 51-52, 63	—	95.00
PS18	2006 (10)	1,000	KM#3-8, 41, 51-52, 65	—	95.00
PS19	2008 (9)	2,000	KM#68-75, 81	—	350
PS20	2010 (10)	5,000	KM#68-75, 94, 95	—	215
PS21	2011 (10)	2,000	KM#68-75, 100, 101	—	315

SOLOMON ISLANDS

The Solomon Islands are made up of about 200 islands. They are located in the southwest Pacific east of Papua New Guinea, have an area of 10,983 sq. mi. (28,450 sq. km.) and a population of *552,000. Capital: Honiara. The most important islands of the Solomon chain are Guadalcanal (scene of some of the fiercest fighting of World War II), Malaitia, New Georgia, Florida, Vella Lavella, Choiseul, Rendova, San Cristobal, the Lord Howe group, the Santa Cruz islands, and the Duff group. Copra is the only important cash crop but it is hoped that timber will become an economic factor.

Solomon Islands is a member of the Commonwealth of Nations. Queen Elizabeth II is Head of State, as Queen of the Solomon Islands.

RULER
British

MONETARY SYSTEM
100 Cents = 1 Dollar

COMMONWEALTH NATION
STANDARD COINAGE

KM# 24 CENT
2.30 g., Bronze Plated Steel, 17.53 mm. **Ruler:** Elizabeth II **Obv:** Crowned head right **Obv. Legend:** ELIZABETH II - SOLOMON ISLANDS **Rev:** Food bowl divides value **Edge:** Plain

Date	Mintage	F12	VF20	XF40	MS60	MS63
2005	—			—	0.35	0.75
2010	—			—	0.35	0.75

KM# 25 2 CENTS
Bronze Plated Steel, 21.6 mm. **Ruler:** Elizabeth II **Obv:** Crowned head right **Obv. Legend:** ELIZABETH II - SOLOMON ISLANDS **Rev:** Eagle spirit below value **Edge:** Plain

Date	Mintage	F12	VF20	XF40	MS60	MS63
2005	—			—	0.35	0.75
2006	—			—	0.35	0.75

KM# 26a 5 CENTS
Nickel Plated Steel, 18.4 mm. **Ruler:** Elizabeth II **Obv:** Crowned bust right **Obv. Legend:** ELIZABETH II - SOLOMON ISLANDS **Rev:** Value at left, native mask at center right

Date	Mintage	F12	VF20	XF40	MS60	MS63
2005	—			—	0.50	1.00

KM# 27a 10 CENTS
Nickel Plated Steel, 23.6 mm. **Ruler:** Elizabeth II **Subject:** Ngorieru **Obv:** Crowned head right **Obv. Legend:** ELIZABETH II - SOLOMON ISLANDS **Rev:** Sea spirit divides value **Edge:** Reeded

Date	Mintage	F12	VF20	XF40	MS60	MS63
2005	—			—	0.65	1.00

KM# 235 10 CENTS
2.29 g., Nickel Plated Steel, 17 mm. **Ruler:** Elizabeth II **Obv:** Head with tiara right **Rev:** Sea Spirit Ngoreru from Temotu province

Date	Mintage	F12	VF20	XF40	MS60	MS63
2012	—					

KM# 235a 10 CENTS
2.90 g., Silver, 17 mm. **Ruler:** Elizabeth II **Obv:** Head with tiara right **Rev:** Sea Spirit

Date	Mintage	F12	VF20	XF40	MS60	MS63
2012	1,500	PF65 40.00				

KM# 28 20 CENTS
11.25 g., Nickel Plated Steel, 28.5 mm. **Ruler:** Elizabeth II **Obv:** Crowned head right **Obv. Legend:** ELIZABETH II - SOLOMON ISLANDS **Rev:** Malaita pendant design within circle, denomination appears twice in legend **Edge:** Reeded

Date	Mintage	F12	VF20	XF40	MS60	MS63
2005	—			—	0.85	1.25

KM# 236 20 CENTS
2.84 g., Nickel Plated Steel, 19 mm. **Ruler:** Elizabeth II **Rev:** Malaita pendant design with circle

Date	Mintage	F12	VF20	XF40	MS60	MS63
2012	—					

KM# 236a 20 CENTS
3.52 g., 0.999 Silver 0.1123 oz. ASW, 19 mm. **Ruler:** Elizabeth II **Obv:** Head with tiara right **Rev:** Pendant design

Date	Mintage	F12	VF20	XF40	MS60	MS63
2012	1,500	PF65 50.00				

KM# 29 50 CENTS
10.00 g., Copper-Nickel, 29.5 mm. **Ruler:** Elizabeth II **Obv:** Crowned head right **Obv. Legend:** ELIZABETH II - SOLOMON ISLANDS **Rev:** Arms with supporters **Edge:** Plain **Shape:** 12-sided **Note:** Circulation type.

Date	Mintage	F12	VF20	XF40	MS60	MS63
2005	—			—	2.00	3.00

KM# 29a 50 CENTS
Nickel Plated Steel, 29.5 mm. **Ruler:** Elizabeth II **Shape:** 12-sided

Date	Mintage	F12	VF20	XF40	MS60	MS63
2008	—			—	2.00	3.00

KM# 237 50 CENTS
Nickel Plated Steel, 21 mm. **Ruler:** Elizabeth II **Rev:** Eagle Spirit

Date	Mintage	F12	VF20	XF40	MS60	MS63
2012	—					

KM# 237a 50 CENTS
4.64 g., 0.999 Silver 0.1481 oz. ASW, 21 mm. **Ruler:** Elizabeth II **Obv:** Head with tiara right **Rev:** Eagle

Date	Mintage	F12	VF20	XF40	MS60	MS63
2012	1,500	PF65 50.00				

KM# 72 DOLLAR
13.45 g., Copper-Nickel, 30 mm. **Ruler:** Elizabeth II **Obv:** Crowned head right **Obv. Legend:** ELIZABETH II - SOLOMON ISLANDS **Rev:** Sea spirit statue divides value **Edge:** Plain **Shape:** 7-sided

Date	Mintage	F12	VF20	XF40	MS60	MS63
2005	—			—	2.50	4.00

KM# 72a DOLLAR
Nickel Plated Steel, 30 mm. **Ruler:** Elizabeth II **Shape:** 7-sided

Date	Mintage	F12	VF20	XF40	MS60	MS63
2008	—			—	3.00	4.00

KM# 159 DOLLAR
26.00 g., Bronze, 38.61 mm. **Ruler:** Elizabeth II **Rev:** Archangel Michael in color

Date	Mintage	F12	VF20	XF40	MS60	MS63
2009	—	PF65 17.50				

KM# 160 DOLLAR
26.00 g., Bronze, 38.61 mm. **Ruler:** Elizabeth II **Rev:** Archangel Raphael in color

Date	Mintage	F12	VF20	XF40	MS60	MS63
2009	—	PF65 17.50				

KM# 161 DOLLAR
26.00 g., Bronze, 38.61 mm. **Ruler:** Elizabeth II **Rev:** Archangel Gabriel in color

Date	Mintage	F12	VF20	XF40	MS60	MS63
2009	—	PF65 17.50				

KM# 182 DOLLAR
5.67 g., 0.999 Silver 0.1809 oz. ASW, 35 mm. **Ruler:** Elizabeth II **Subject:** Ships and Explorers - HMS Beagle - Charles Darwin

Date	Mintage	F12	VF20	XF40	MS60	MS63
2009	Est. 5000	PF65 15.00				

KM# 183 DOLLAR
5.67 g., 0.999 Silver 0.1809 oz. ASW, 35 mm. **Ruler:** Elizabeth II **Subject:** Ships and Explorers - HMS Warrior

Date	Mintage	F12	VF20	XF40	MS60	MS63
2009	—	PF65 15.00				

KM# 184 DOLLAR
5.67 g., 0.999 Silver 0.1809 oz. ASW, 35 mm. **Ruler:** Elizabeth II **Subject:** Ships and Explorers - Golden Hind - Sir Francis Drake

Date	Mintage	F12	VF20	XF40	MS60	MS63
2009	Est. 5000	PF65 15.00				

KM# 214 DOLLAR
31.10 g., Silver Plated Copper, 40 mm. **Ruler:** Elizabeth II
Subject: Archanges - Gabriel, Colorized

Date	Mintage	F12	VF20	XF40	MS60	MS63
2009	Est. 5000	PF65 65.00				

KM# 215 DOLLAR
31.10 g., Silver Plated Copper, 40 mm. **Ruler:** Elizabeth II
Subject: Archangels - Michael, Colorized

Date	Mintage	F12	VF20	XF40	MS60	MS63
2009	—	PF65 65.00				

KM# 216 DOLLAR
31.10 g., Silver Plated Copper, 40 mm. **Ruler:** Elizabeth II
Subject: Archangels - Raphael, Colorized

Date	Mintage	F12	VF20	XF40	MS60	MS63
2009	Est. 5000	PF65 65.00				

KM# 209 DOLLAR
26.00 g., Silver Plated Copper, 40 mm. **Ruler:** Elizabeth II
Subject: Royal Dynasties - Royal Wedding, Prince William

Date	Mintage	F12	VF20	XF40	MS60	MS63
2011	Est. 15000	PF63 25.00	PF65 30.00			

KM# 211 DOLLAR
26.00 g., Silver Plated Copper, 40 mm. **Ruler:** Elizabeth II
Subject: Royal Dynasties - 50th Birthday of Lady Diana

Date	Mintage	F12	VF20	XF40	MS60	MS63
2011	Est. 10000	PF63 25.00	PF65 30.00			

KM# 212 DOLLAR
26.00 g., Silver Plated Copper, 40 mm. **Ruler:** Elizabeth II
Subject: Royal Dynasties - 40th Birthday of Maxima of the
Netherlands

Date	Mintage	F12	VF20	XF40	MS60	MS63
2011	Est. 10000	PF63 25.00	PF65 30.00			

KM# 213 DOLLAR
26.00 g., Silver Plated Copper, 40 mm. **Ruler:** Elizabeth II
Subject: Royal Dynasties - 85th Anniversary of HM Queen
Elizabeth II

Date	Mintage	F12	VF20	XF40	MS60	MS63
2011	Est. 10000	PF63 25.00	PF65 30.00			

KM# 210 DOLLAR
26.00 g., Silver Plated Copper, 40 mm. **Ruler:** Elizabeth II
Subject: Royal Dynasties - Albert of Monaco

Date	Mintage	F12	VF20	XF40	MS60	MS63
2011	Est. 10000	PF63 25.00	PF65 30.00			

KM# 232 DOLLAR
0.50 g., 0.585 Gold AGW, 11 mm. **Ruler:** Elizabeth II **Series:**
Smallest Gold Coins **Subject:** Maya Calendar

Date	Mintage	F12	VF20	XF40	MS60	MS63
2012	Est. 5000	PF65 35.00				

KM# 238 DOLLAR
Aluminum-Bronze, 21.1 mm. **Ruler:** Elizabeth II **Rev:** Nguzu
Nguz

Date	Mintage	F12	VF20	XF40	MS60	MS63
2012	—	—				

KM# 238a DOLLAR
7.70 g., 0.999 Silver 0.2457 oz. ASW, 21.14 mm. **Ruler:**
Elizabeth II **Obv:** Head with tiara right **Rev:** Nguzu Nguzu

Date	Mintage	F12	VF20	XF40	MS60	MS63
2012	1,500	PF65 50.00				

KM# 263 DOLLAR
0.50 g., 0.585 Gold AGW, 11 mm. **Ruler:** Elizabeth II **Subject:**
Hanging gardens of Babylon

Date	Mintage	F12	VF20	XF40	MS60	MS63
2013	7,000	PF65 75.00				

KM# 263 DOLLAR
0.50 g., 0.585 Gold AGW, 11 mm. **Ruler:** Elizabeth II **Subject:**
Statue of Zeus at Olympia

Date	Mintage	F12	VF20	XF40	MS60	MS63
2013	7,000	PF65 75.00				

KM# 265 DOLLAR
0.50 g., 0.585 Gold AGW, 11 mm. **Ruler:** Elizabeth II **Subject:**
Temple of Artemis at Ephesus

Date	Mintage	F12	VF20	XF40	MS60	MS63
2013	7,000	PF65 75.00				

KM# 266 DOLLAR
0.50 g., 0.585 Gold AGW, 11 mm. **Ruler:** Elizabeth II **Subject:**
Mausoleum of Mausollos

Date	Mintage	F12	VF20	XF40	MS60	MS63
2013	7,000	PF65 75.00				

KM# 267 DOLLAR
0.50 g., 0.585 Gold AGW, 11 mm. **Ruler:** Elizabeth II **Subject:**
Colossus of Rhodes

Date	Mintage	F12	VF20	XF40	MS60	MS63
2013	7,000	PF65 75.00				

KM# 268 DOLLAR
0.50 g., 0.585 Gold AGW, 11 mm. **Ruler:** Elizabeth II **Subject:**
Lighthouse at Alexandria

Date	Mintage	F12	VF20	XF40	MS60	MS63
2013	7,000	PF65 75.00				

KM# 269 DOLLAR
0.50 g., 0.585 Gold AGW, 11 mm. **Ruler:** Elizabeth II **Subject:**
Chichen Itza

Date	Mintage	F12	VF20	XF40	MS60	MS63
2013	7,000	PF65 75.00				

KM# 270 DOLLAR
0.50 g., 0.585 Gold AGW, 11 mm. **Ruler:** Elizabeth II **Subject:**
Great Wall of China

Date	Mintage	F12	VF20	XF40	MS60	MS63
2013	7,000	PF65 75.00				

KM# 271 DOLLAR
0.50 g., 0.585 Gold AGW, 11 mm. **Ruler:** Elizabeth II **Subject:**
Christ the Redeemer statue

Date	Mintage	F12	VF20	XF40	MS60	MS63
2013	7,000	PF65 75.00				

KM# 273 DOLLAR
0.50 g., 0.585 Gold AGW, 11 mm. **Ruler:** Elizabeth II **Subject:**
Machu Pichu

Date	Mintage	F12	VF20	XF40	MS60	MS63
2013	7,000	PF65 75.00				

KM# 274 DOLLAR
0.50 g., 0.585 Gold AGW, 11 mm. **Ruler:** Elizabeth II **Subject:**
Petra

Date	Mintage	F12	VF20	XF40	MS60	MS63
2013	7,000	PF65 75.00				

KM# 275 DOLLAR
0.50 g., 0.585 Gold AGW, 11 mm. **Ruler:** Elizabeth II **Rev:**
Taj Mahal

Date	Mintage	F12	VF20	XF40	MS60	MS63
2013	7,000	PF65 75.00				

KM# 276 DOLLAR
0.50 g., 0.999 Gold AGW, 11 mm. **Ruler:** Elizabeth II **Subject:**
Statue of Liberty

Date	Mintage	F12	VF20	XF40	MS60	MS63
2013	5,000	PF65 75.00				

KM# 277 DOLLAR
0.50 g., 0.999 Gold AGW, 11 mm. **Ruler:** Elizabeth II **Subject:**
Nefertiti

Date	Mintage	F12	VF20	XF40	MS60	MS63
2013	7,500	PF65 75.00				

KM# 278 DOLLAR
0.50 g., 0.585 Gold AGW, 11 mm. **Ruler:** Elizabeth II **Subject:**
Neferititi

Date	Mintage	F12	VF20	XF40	MS60	MS63
2013	7,500	PF65 75.00				

KM# 83 2 DOLLARS
62.27 g., 0.999 Silver 1.9871 oz. ASW, 50.3 mm. **Subject:**
Regional Assistance Mission to Solomon Islands **Obv:** Crowned
head right **Rev:** Dove outline over multicolor islands in a sea of
country names **Edge:** Reeded

Date	Mintage	F12	VF20	XF40	MS60	MS63
2005	2,500	PF65 95.00				

KM# 176 2 DOLLARS
Silver, 38.61 mm. **Ruler:** Elizabeth II **Subject:** Royal visit to the Solomon Islands **Obv:** Heas with tiara right **Rev:** Portraits of Prince Willam and Kate Middleton in color

Date	Mintage	F12	VF20	XF40	MS60	MS63
2012	—	PF65 75.00				

KM# 239 2 DOLLARS
Aluminum-Bronze, 26.3 mm. **Ruler:** Elizabeth II **Rev:** Fossilized clam shells from Western and Choiseul provinces

Date	Mintage	F12	VF20	XF40	MS60	MS63
2012	—	—	—	—	—	—

KM# 239a 2 DOLLARS
24.70 g., 0.999 Silver 0.7882 oz. ASW, 10.3 mm. **Ruler:** Elizabeth II **Obv:** Head with tiara right **Rev:** Bokolo

Date	Mintage	F12	VF20	XF40	MS60	MS63
2012	1,500	PF65 60.00				

KM# 262 2 DOLLARS
0.50 g., 0.585 Gold AGW, 11 mm. **Ruler:** Elizabeth II **Subject:** Great Pyramids of Giza

Date	Mintage	F12	VF20	XF40	MS60	MS63
2013	7,000	PF65 75.00				

KM# 130 5 DOLLARS
25.00 g., 0.900 Silver 0.7187 oz. ASW **Ruler:** Elizabeth II **Rev:** Butterfly fish in color

Date	Mintage	F12	VF20	XF40	MS60	MS63
2001	—	PF65 65.00				

KM# 125 5 DOLLARS
Silver, 38.6 mm. **Ruler:** Elizabeth II **Obv:** Head crowned right **Rev:** Mace and coronation scene

Date	Mintage	F12	VF20	XF40	MS60	MS63
2002	—	PF65 50.00				

KM# 113 5 DOLLARS
Copper-Nickel **Ruler:** Elizabeth II **Rev:** Orb

Date	Mintage	F12	VF20	XF40	MS60	MS63
2002	—	—	—	—	—	15.00

KM# 113a 5 DOLLARS
28.28 g., 0.925 Silver 0.8356 oz. ASW, 38.6 mm. **Ruler:** Elizabeth II **Obv:** Bust right gilt **Rev:** Orb

Date	Mintage	F12	VF20	XF40	MS60	MS63
2002	20,000	PF63 30.00	PF65 42.00			

KM# 75 5 DOLLARS
28.28 g., Copper-Nickel, 38.6 mm. **Obv:** Crowned head right **Rev:** F-117A Nighthawk Stealth fighter plane **Edge:** Reeded

Date	Mintage	F12	VF20	XF40	MS60	MS63
2003	—	—	—	—	8.00	10.00

KM# 76 5 DOLLARS
28.28 g., Copper-Nickel, 38.6 mm. **Obv:** Crowned head right **Rev:** Concorde supersonic airliner **Edge:** Reeded

Date	Mintage	F12	VF20	XF40	MS60	MS63
2003	—	—	—	—	8.00	10.00

KM# 84 5 DOLLARS
31.10 g., 0.999 Silver 0.9926 oz. ASW, 38.6 mm. **Ruler:** Elizabeth II **Obv:** Maklouf's portrait of Elizabeth II **Rev:** Gold plated pig **Edge:** Reeded **Note:** Year of the Pig

Date	Mintage	F12	VF20	XF40	MS60	MS63
2007	10,000	—	—	—	—	50.00

KM# 85 5 DOLLARS
31.10 g., 0.999 Silver 0.9926 oz. ASW, 38.6 mm. **Ruler:** Elizabeth II **Obv:** Maklouf's portrait of Elizabeth II **Rev:** Dark red pig and piglet **Edge:** Reeded **Note:** Year of the Pig

Date	Mintage	F12	VF20	XF40	MS60	MS63
2007	10,000	—	—	—	—	50.00

KM# 179 5 DOLLARS
26.03 g., Silver Plated Copper-Nickel, 38.61 mm. **Ruler:** Elizabeth II **Subject:** 2012 London Olympic Games - Discus Thrower

Date	Mintage	F12	VF20	XF40	MS60	MS63
2008	—	PF65 18.00				

KM# 203 5 DOLLARS
0.50 g., 1.000 Gold AGW, 11 mm. **Ruler:** Elizabeth II **Subject:** Daedalus

Date	Mintage	F12	VF20	XF40	MS60	MS63
2008	Est. 15000	PF63 45.00	PF65 50.00			

KM# 204 5 DOLLARS
0.50 g., 1.000 Gold AGW **Ruler:** Elizabeth II **Subject:** Icarus **Issuer:** 11

Date	Mintage	F12	VF20	XF40	MS60	MS63
2008	Est. 15000	PF63 45.00	PF65 50.00			

KM# 110 5 DOLLARS
1.22 g., 0.999 Gold 0.0389 oz. AGW, 14 mm. **Ruler:** Elizabeth II **Subject:** Alexander von Humboldt **Obv:** Head right

Date	Mintage	F12	VF20	XF40	MS60	MS63
2010	—	PF65 50.00				

KM# 119 5 DOLLARS
0.50 g., 0.999 Gold AGW, 11 mm. **Ruler:** Elizabeth II **Subject:** For World Peace **Rev:** John Paul II and Mother Theresa

Date	Mintage	F12	VF20	XF40	MS60	MS63
2010	10,000	PF63 65.00	PF65 75.00			

KM# 123 5 DOLLARS
0.50 g., 0.999 Gold AGW, 11 mm. **Ruler:** Elizabeth II **Rev:** Spotted Cuscus in tree

Date	Mintage	F12	VF20	XF40	MS60	MS63
2010	15,000	PF63 65.00		PF65 75.00		

KM# 205 5 DOLLARS
0.50 g., 0.999 Gold AGW, 11 mm. **Ruler:** Elizabeth II **Subject:** Immanuel Kant

Date	Mintage	F12	VF20	XF40	MS60	MS63
2010	Est. 10000	PF63 45.00		PF65 50.00		

KM# 206 5 DOLLARS
0.50 g., 0.999 Gold AGW, 11 mm. **Ruler:** Elizabeth II **Subject:** Alexander Humboldt

Date	Mintage	F12	VF20	XF40	MS60	MS63
2010	Est. 10000	PF63 45.00		PF65 50.00		

KM# 207 5 DOLLARS
0.50 g., 0.999 Gold AGW, 11 mm. **Ruler:** Elizabeth II **Subject:** Saint Sophia Cathedral Kiev

Date	Mintage	F12	VF20	XF40	MS60	MS63
2010	Est. 10000	PF63 45.00		PF65 50.00		

KM# 126 5 DOLLARS
15.55 g., 0.999 Silver 0.4962 oz. ASW, 35 mm. **Ruler:** Elizabeth II **Rev:** Archangel Gabriel in color

Date	Mintage	F12	VF20	XF40	MS60	MS63
2011	2,000	PF65 75.00				

KM# 127 5 DOLLARS
15.55 g., 0.999 Silver 0.4962 oz. ASW, 35 mm. **Ruler:** Elizabeth II **Rev:** Auchangel Michael

Date	Mintage	F12	VF20	XF40	MS60	MS63
2011	—	PF65 75.00				

KM# 163 5 DOLLARS
0.50 g., 0.999 Gold AGW, 11 mm. **Ruler:** Elizabeth II **Rev:** Manatee

Date	Mintage	F12	VF20	XF40	MS60	MS63
2011	10,000	PF63 50.00		PF65 60.00		

KM# 164 5 DOLLARS
0.50 g., 0.999 Gold AGW, 11 mm. **Ruler:** Elizabeth II **Rev:** Great Wall of China

Date	Mintage	F12	VF20	XF40	MS60	MS63
2011	Est. 7000	PF63 45.00		PF65 50.00		

KM# 165 5 DOLLARS
0.50 g., 0.999 Gold AGW, 11 mm. **Ruler:** Elizabeth II **Rev:** Storehouse at Petra

Date	Mintage	F12	VF20	XF40	MS60	MS63
2011	Est. 7000	PF63 45.00		PF65 50.00		

KM# 166 5 DOLLARS
0.50 g., 0.999 Gold AGW, 11 mm. **Ruler:** Elizabeth II **Rev:** Christ statue in Rio de Janeiro

Date	Mintage	F12	VF20	XF40	MS60	MS63
2011	Est. 7000	PF63 45.00		PF65 50.00		

KM# 167 5 DOLLARS
0.50 g., 0.999 Gold AGW, 11 mm. **Ruler:** Elizabeth II **Rev:** Machu Picchu

Date	Mintage	F12	VF20	XF40	MS60	MS63
2011	—	PF63 45.00		PF65 50.00		

KM# 168 5 DOLLARS
0.50 g., 0.999 Gold AGW, 11 mm. **Ruler:** Elizabeth II **Rev:** Stepped pyramid at Chichen Itza

Date	Mintage	F12	VF20	XF40	MS60	MS63
2011	Est. 7000	PF63 45.00		PF65 50.00		

KM# 169 5 DOLLARS
0.50 g., 0.999 Gold AGW, 11 mm. **Ruler:** Elizabeth II **Rev:** Colusem in Rome

Date	Mintage	F12	VF20	XF40	MS60	MS63
2011	Est. 7000	PF63 45.00		PF65 50.00		

KM# 170 5 DOLLARS
0.50 g., 0.999 Gold AGW, 11 mm. **Ruler:** Elizabeth II **Rev:** Taj Mahal

Date	Mintage	F12	VF20	XF40	MS60	MS63
2011	—	PF63 45.00		PF65 50.00		

KM# 188 5 DOLLARS
0.50 g., 0.585 Gold AGW, 11 mm. **Ruler:** Elizabeth II **Subject:** Ancient Sevens Wonders: Great Pyramids of Giza

Date	Mintage	F12	VF20	XF40	MS60	MS63
2011	Est. 5000	PF65 35.00				

KM# 189 5 DOLLARS
0.50 g., 0.585 Gold AGW, 11 mm. **Ruler:** Elizabeth II **Subject:** Ancient Seven World Wonders: Hanging Gardens of Babylon

Date	Mintage	F12	VF20	XF40	MS60	MS63
2011	—	PF65 35.00				

KM# 190 5 DOLLARS
0.50 g., 0.585 Gold AGW, 11 mm. **Ruler:** Elizabeth II **Subject:** Ancient Seven Wonders: Statue of Zeus at Olympia

Date	Mintage	F12	VF20	XF40	MS60	MS63
2011	Est. 5000	PF65 35.00				

KM# 191 5 DOLLARS
0.50 g., 0.585 Gold AGW, 11 mm. **Ruler:** Elizabeth II **Subject:** Ancient Seven World Wonders: Temple of Artemis at Ephesus

Date	Mintage	F12	VF20	XF40	MS60	MS63
2011	Est. 5000	PF65 35.00				

KM# 192 5 DOLLARS
0.50 g., 0.585 Gold AGW, 11 mm. **Ruler:** Elizabeth II **Subject:** Ancient Seven World Wonders: Mausoleum of Mausollos

Date	Mintage	F12	VF20	XF40	MS60	MS63
2011	Est. 5000	PF65 35.00				

KM# 193 5 DOLLARS
0.50 g., 0.585 Gold AGW, 11 mm. **Ruler:** Elizabeth II **Subject:** Ancient Seven World Wonders: The Colossos of Rhodos

Date	Mintage	F12	VF20	XF40	MS60	MS63
2011	Est. 5000	PF65 35.00				

KM# 194 5 DOLLARS
0.50 g., 0.585 Gold AGW, 11 mm. **Ruler:** Elizabeth II **Subject:** Ancient Seven World Wonders: Lighthouse of Alexandria

Date	Mintage	F12	VF20	XF40	MS60	MS63
2011	Est. 5000	PF65 35.00				

KM# 195 5 DOLLARS
0.50 g., 0.585 Gold AGW, 11 mm. **Ruler:** Elizabeth II **Subject:** New Seven World Wonders: Mexico Chichen Itza

Date	Mintage	F12	VF20	XF40	MS60	MS63
2011	Est. 5000	PF65 35.00				

KM# 196 5 DOLLARS
0.50 g., 0.585 Gold AGW, 11 mm. **Ruler:** Elizabeth II **Subject:** New Seven World Wonders: China Great Wall

Date	Mintage	F12	VF20	XF40	MS60	MS63
2011	Est. 5000	PF65 35.00				

KM# 197 5 DOLLARS
0.50 g., 0.585 Gold AGW, 11 mm. **Ruler:** Elizabeth II **Subject:** New Seven World Wonders: Brazil Christ Redeemer

Date	Mintage	F12	VF20	XF40	MS60	MS63
2011	—	PF65 35.00				

KM# 198 5 DOLLARS
0.50 g., 0.585 Gold AGW, 11 mm. **Ruler:** Elizabeth II **Subject:** New Seven World Wonders: Italy Roman Colosseum

Date	Mintage	F12	VF20	XF40	MS60	MS63
2011	Est. 5000	PF65 35.00				

KM# 199 5 DOLLARS
0.50 g., 0.585 Gold AGW, 11 mm. **Ruler:** Elizabeth II **Series:** New Seven World WOnders: Peru Machu Picchu

Date	Mintage	F12	VF20	XF40	MS60	MS63
2011	Est. 5000	PF65 35.00				

KM# 200 5 DOLLARS
0.50 g., 0.585 Gold AGW, 11 mm. **Ruler:** Elizabeth II **Subject:** New Seven World Wonders: Jordan Petra

Date	Mintage	F12	VF20	XF40	MS60	MS63
2011	Est. 5000	PF65 35.00				

KM# 201 5 DOLLARS
0.50 g., 0.585 Gold AGW, 11 mm. **Ruler:** Elizabeth II **Subject:** New Seven World Wonders: India Taj Mahal

Date	Mintage	F12	VF20	XF40	MS60	MS63
2011	—	PF65 35.00				

KM# 217 5 DOLLARS
14.18 g., 0.999 Silver 0.4524 oz. ASW, 35 mm. **Ruler:** Elizabeth II **Subject:** Archangels - Gabriel, Colorized

Date	Mintage	F12	VF20	XF40	MS60	MS63
2011	Est. 2500	PF65 75.00				

KM# 218 5 DOLLARS
14.18 g., 0.999 Silver 0.4524 oz. ASW, 35 mm. **Ruler:** Elizabeth II **Subject:** Archangels - Michael, Colorized

Date	Mintage	F12	VF20	XF40	MS60	MS63
2011	Est. 2500	PF65 75.00				

KM# 220 5 DOLLARS
0.50 g., 0.999 Gold AGW, 11 mm. **Ruler:** Elizabeth II **Subject:** 2014 FIFA World Cup Brazil - 11 Friends: Africa

Date	Mintage	F12	VF20	XF40	MS60	MS63
2012	Est. 7500	PF63 30.00		PF65 35.00		

KM# 221 5 DOLLARS
0.50 g., 0.999 Gold AGW, 11 mm. **Ruler:** Elizabeth II **Subject:** 2014 FIFA World Cup Brazil -11 Friends: Asia

Date	Mintage	F12	VF20	XF40	MS60	MS63
2012	Est. 7500	PF63 30.00		PF65 35.00		

KM# 222 5 DOLLARS
0.50 g., 0.999 Gold AGW, 11 mm. **Ruler:** Elizabeth II **Series:** 2014 FIFA World Cup Brazil - 11 Friends: Brazil

Date	Mintage	F12	VF20	XF40	MS60	MS63
2012	Est. 7500	PF63 30.00		PF65 35.00		

KM# 223 5 DOLLARS
0.50 g., 0.999 Gold AGW, 11 mm. **Ruler:** Elizabeth II **Subject:** 2014 FIFA World Cup Brazil - 11 Friends: Germany

Date	Mintage	F12	VF20	XF40	MS60	MS63
2012	Est. 7500	PF63 30.00		PF65 35.00		

KM# 224 5 DOLLARS
0.50 g., 0.999 Gold AGW, 11 mm. **Ruler:** Elizabeth II **Subject:** 2014 FIFA World Cup Brazil - 11 Friends: Europe

Date	Mintage	F12	VF20	XF40	MS60	MS63
2012	Est. 7500	PF63 30.00	PF65 35.00			

KM# 225 5 DOLLARS
0.50 g., 0.999 Gold AGW, 11 mm. **Ruler:** Elizabeth II **Subject:** 2014 FIFA World Cup Brazil - 11 Friends: North America

Date	Mintage	F12	VF20	XF40	MS60	MS63
2012	Est. 7500	PF63 30.00	PF65 35.00			

KM# 226 5 DOLLARS
0.50 g., 0.999 Gold AGW, 11 mm. **Ruler:** Elizabeth II **Subject:** 2014 FIFA World Cup - 11 Friends: Spain

Date	Mintage	F12	VF20	XF40	MS60	MS63
2012	Est. 7500	PF63 30.00	PF65 35.00			

KM# 227 5 DOLLARS
0.50 g., 0.999 Gold AGW, 11 mm. **Ruler:** Elizabeth II **Series:** 2014 FIFA World Cup Brazil - 11 Friends: South Africa

Date	Mintage	F12	VF20	XF40	MS60	MS63
2012	Est. 7500	PF63 30.00	PF65 35.00			

KM# 228 5 DOLLARS
0.50 g., 0.999 Gold AGW, 11 mm. **Ruler:** Elizabeth II **Subject:** 2014 FIFA World Cup Brazil - 11 Friends: South America

Date	Mintage	F12	VF20	XF40	MS60	MS63
2012	Est. 7500	PF63 30.00	PF65 35.00			

KM# 229 5 DOLLARS
0.50 g., 0.999 Gold AGW, 11 mm. **Ruler:** Elizabeth II **Subject:** 2014 FIFA World Cup Brazil - 11 Friends: Globe

Date	Mintage	F12	VF20	XF40	MS60	MS63
2012	Est. 7500	PF63 30.00	PF65 35.00			

KM# 230 5 DOLLARS
0.50 g., 0.585 Gold AGW, 11 mm. **Ruler:** Elizabeth II **Subject:** Greek Mythology: Ulysses

Date	Mintage	F12	VF20	XF40	MS60	MS63
2012	Est. 10000	PF63 30.00	PF65 35.00			

KM# 231 5 DOLLARS
0.50 g., 0.999 Gold AGW **Ruler:** Elizabeth II **Series:** Smalles Gold Coins **Subject:** Maya Calndar

Date	Mintage	F12	VF20	XF40	MS60	MS63
2012	Est. 5000	PF65 50.00				

KM# 233 5 DOLLARS
20.00 g., 0.925 Silver 0.591 oz. ASW, 38.61 mm. **Ruler:**

Elizabeth II **Subject:** Great Rulers: Catherine the Great

Date	Mintage	F12	VF20	XF40	MS60	MS63
2012	—	PF65 45.00				

KM# 234 5 DOLLARS
20.00 g., 0.925 Silver 0.591 oz. ASW, 38.61 mm. **Ruler:** Elizabeth II **Subject:** Great Rulers - Peter the Great

Date	Mintage	F12	VF20	XF40	MS60	MS63
2012	Est. 5000	PF65 45.00				

KM# 281 5 DOLLARS
12.00 g., 0.925 Silver 0.3546 oz. ASW, 38.61 mm. **Ruler:** Elizabeth II **Subject:** Giuseppe Verdi

Date	Mintage	F12	VF20	XF40	MS60	MS63
2013	5,000	PF65 75.00				

KM# 131 10 DOLLARS
1.24 g., 0.999 Gold 0.0396 oz. AGW, 13.92 mm. **Ruler:** Elizabeth II **Rev:** Butterfly fish

Date	Mintage	F12	VF20	XF40	MS60	MS63
2001	—	PF65 90.00				

KM# 86 10 DOLLARS
28.36 g., 0.925 Silver 0.838 oz. ASW, 38.6 mm. **Obv:** Crowned bust right **Obv. Legend:** ELIZABETH II - SOLOMON ISLANDS **Rev:** Bust of Mendana facing at left, early sailing ship at center - right **Rev. Legend:** ALVARO DE MENDANA **Edge:** Reeded

Date	Mintage	F12	VF20	XF40	MS60	MS63
2004	—	PF65 50.00				

KM# 124 10 DOLLARS
28.36 g., 0.925 Silver 0.838 oz. ASW, 38.6 mm. **Ruler:** Elizabeth II **Subject:** Olumpics 2004 **Rev:** Runner, Sydney Opera House and Parthenon

Date	Mintage	F12	VF20	XF40	MS60	MS63
2004	—	PF65 50.00				

KM# 140 10 DOLLARS
31.64 g., 0.999 Silver 1.0095 oz. ASW, 40 mm. **Ruler:** Elizabeth II **Subject:** 2006 FIFA World Cup, Germany **Obv:** Head with crown right **Rev:** Two players in color

Date	Mintage	F12	VF20	XF40	MS60	MS63
2005	Est. 5000	PF65 65.00				

KM# 141 10 DOLLARS
1.24 g., 0.999 Gold 0.0396 oz. AGW, 13.92 mm. **Ruler:** Elizabeth II **Rev:** Prospector panning for gold

Date	Mintage	F12	VF20	XF40	MS60	MS63
2005	—	PF65 90.00				

KM# 142 10 DOLLARS
1.24 g., 0.999 Gold 0.0396 oz. AGW, 13.92 mm. **Ruler:** Elizabeth II **Subject:** John Lennon, 25th Anniversary of Death **Obv:** Head with crown right **Rev:** Lennon's head facing

Date	Mintage	F12	VF20	XF40	MS60	MS63
2005	—	PF65 90.00				

KM# 153 10 DOLLARS
7.78 g., 0.585 Gold 0.1454 oz. AGW, 25 mm. **Ruler:** Elizabeth II **Subject:** 2006 World Cup, Germany

Date	Mintage	F12	VF20	XF40	MS60	MS63
2006	—	PF65 325				

KM# 96 10 DOLLARS
1.22 g., 0.999 Gold 0.0389 oz. AGW, 14 mm. **Ruler:** Elizabeth II **Subject:** Wonders of the Ancient World **Obv:** Head right **Rev:** Mausoleum of Mausollos

Date	Mintage	F12	VF20	XF40	MS60	MS63
2007	7,000	PF63 75.00	PF65 85.00			

KM# 97 10 DOLLARS
1.22 g., 0.999 Gold 0.0389 oz. AGW, 14 mm. **Ruler:** Elizabeth II **Subject:** Wonders of the Ancient World **Obv:** Head right **Rev:** Taj Mahal

Date	Mintage	F12	VF20	XF40	MS60	MS63
2007	7,000	PF63 75.00	PF65 85.00			

KM# 98 10 DOLLARS
1.00 g., 0.999 Gold 0.0319 oz. AGW, 13.92 mm. **Ruler:** Elizabeth II **Subject:** New 7 Wonders of the World **Obv:** Head right **Rev:** Treasury at Petra

Date	Mintage	F12	VF20	XF40	MS60	MS63
2007	Est. 7000	PF63 75.00	PF65 85.00			
2009	Est. 7000	PF63 75.00	PF65 85.00			

KM# 99 10 DOLLARS
1.00 g., 0.999 Gold 0.0319 oz. AGW, 13.92 mm. **Ruler:** Elizabeth II **Subject:** New 7 Wonders of the World **Obv:** Head right **Rev:** Colosseum in Rome

Date	Mintage	F12	VF20	XF40	MS60	MS63
2007	Est. 7000	PF63 75.00	PF65 85.00			
2009	Est. 7000	PF63 75.00	PF65 85.00			

KM# 100 10 DOLLARS
1.00 g., 0.999 Gold 0.0319 oz. AGW, 13.92 mm. **Ruler:** Elizabeth II **Subject:** New 7 Wonders of the World **Obv:** Head right **Rev:** Inca's Machu Picchu

Date	Mintage	F12	VF20	XF40	MS60	MS63
2007	Est. 7000	PF63 75.00	PF65 85.00			
2009	Est. 7000	PF63 75.00	PF65 85.00			

KM# 101 10 DOLLARS
1.00 g., 0.999 Gold 0.0319 oz. AGW, 13.92 mm. **Ruler:** Elizabeth II **Subject:** New 7 Wonders of the World **Obv:** Head right **Rev:** Chichen Itza

Date	Mintage	F12	VF20	XF40	MS60	MS63
2007	—	PF63 75.00	PF65 85.00			
2009	Est. 7000	PF63 75.00	PF65 85.00			

KM# 102 10 DOLLARS
1.00 g., 0.999 Gold 0.0319 oz. AGW, 13.92 mm. **Ruler:** Elizabeth II **Subject:** New 7 Wonders of the World **Obv:** Head right **Rev:** Great wall of China

Date	Mintage	F12	VF20	XF40	MS60	MS63
2007	Est. 7000	PF63 75.00	PF65 85.00			
2009	Est. 7000	PF63 75.00	PF65 85.00			

KM# 103 10 DOLLARS
1.00 g., 0.999 Gold 0.0319 oz. AGW, 13.92 mm. **Ruler:**

Elizabeth II **Subject:** New 7 Wonders of the World **Rev:** Christ Statue in Rio

Date	Mintage	F12	VF20	XF40	MS60	MS63
2007	Est. 7000	PF63 75.00	PF65 85.00			
2009	—	PF63 75.00	PF65 85.00			

KM# 186 10 DOLLARS
1.00 g., 0.999 Gold 0.0319 oz. AGW, 13.92 mm. **Ruler:** Elizabeth II **Subject:** New 7 World Wonders: India Taj Mahal

Date	Mintage	F12	VF20	XF40	MS60	MS63
2007	—	PF63 75.00	PF65 85.00			
2009	Est. 7000	PF63 75.00	PF65 85.00			

KM# 105 10 DOLLARS
1.00 g., 0.999 Gold 0.0319 oz. AGW, 13.92 mm. **Ruler:** Elizabeth II **Subject:** Ancient Seven Wonders of the World **Obv:** Head right **Rev:** Colossus of Rhodes

Date	Mintage	F12	VF20	XF40	MS60	MS63
2009 (2007)	Est. 7000	PF63 75.00	PF65 85.00			

KM# 106 10 DOLLARS
1.00 g., 0.999 Gold 0.0319 oz. AGW, 13.92 mm. **Ruler:** Elizabeth II **Subject:** Seven Ancient World Wonders **Obv:** Head right **Rev:** Statue of Zeus at Olympia

Date	Mintage	F12	VF20	XF40	MS60	MS63
2009 (2007)	7,000	PF63 75.00	PF65 85.00			

KM# 240 10 DOLLARS
28.28 g., 0.925 Silver 0.8356 oz. ASW, 38.61 mm. **Ruler:** Elizabeth II **Subject:** Royal Train **Shape:** 7-Sided

Date	Mintage	F12	VF20	XF40	MS60	MS63
2007	Est. 30000	PF63 35.00	PF65 40.00			

KM# 241 10 DOLLARS
28.28 g., 0.925 Silver 0.8356 oz. ASW, 38.61 mm. **Ruler:** Elizabeth II **Subject:** Queen Elizabeth II **Shape:** 7-Sided

Date	Mintage	F12	VF20	XF40	MS60	MS63
2007	Est. 30000	PF63 35.00	PF65 40.00			

KM# 250 10 DOLLARS
28.28 g., 0.925 Silver 0.8356 oz. ASW, 38.61 mm. **Ruler:** Elizabeth II **Subject:** Queen Elizabeth II 60th Wedding Anniversary **Shape:** 7-Sided

Date	Mintage	F12	VF20	XF40	MS60	MS63
2007	—	PF63 35.00	PF65 40.00			

KM# 154 10 DOLLARS
1.24 g., 0.999 Gold 0.0396 oz. AGW, 13.92 mm. **Ruler:** Elizabeth II **Rev:** Legendary chief of El Dorado sprinking water

Date	Mintage	F12	VF20	XF40	MS60	MS63
2008	—	PF65 90.00				

KM# 177 10 DOLLARS
28.28 g., 0.925 Silver 0.8356 oz. ASW, 38.61 mm. **Ruler:** Elizabeth II **Subject:** 2008 Beijing Olympic Games - Handball

Date	Mintage	F12	VF20	XF40	MS60	MS63
2008	Est. 15000	PF63 45.00	PF65 50.00			

KM# 180 10 DOLLARS
7.77 g., Gold Plated, 25 mm. **Ruler:** Elizabeth II **Subject:** 2012 London Olympic Games - Discus Thrower

Date	Mintage	F12	VF20	XF40	MS60	MS63
2008	Est. 1000	PF65 500				

KM# 181 10 DOLLARS
28.28 g., 0.925 Silver 0.8356 oz. ASW, 38.61 mm. **Ruler:** Elizabeth II **Subject:** Ships and Explorers - Concord

Date	Mintage	F12	VF20	XF40	MS60	MS63
2008	—	PF65 50.00				

KM# 185 10 DOLLARS
28.28 g., 0.925 Silver 0.8356 oz. ASW, 38.61 mm. **Ruler:** Elizabeth II **Subject:** Railways - ICE

Date	Mintage	F12	VF20	XF40	MS60	MS63
2008	Est. 5000	PF65 50.00				

KM# 202 10 DOLLARS
1.24 g., 0.999 Gold 0.0396 oz. AGW, 13.92 mm. **Ruler:** Elizabeth II **Subject:** Eldorado

Date	Mintage	F12	VF20	XF40	MS60	MS63
2008	Est. 15000	PF63 75.00	PF65 85.00			

KM# 104 10 DOLLARS
1.00 g., 0.999 Gold 0.0319 oz. AGW, 13.92 mm. **Ruler:** Elizabeth II **Subject:** Ancient Seven World Wonders **Obv:** Head right **Rev:** Giza Pyramids

Date	Mintage	F12	VF20	XF40	MS60	MS63
2009	Est. 7000	PF63 75.00	PF65 85.00			

KM# 107 10 DOLLARS
1.00 g., 0.999 Gold 0.0319 oz. AGW, 13.92 mm. **Ruler:** Elizabeth II **Subject:** Ancient Seven Wonders of the World **Obv:** Head right **Rev:** Temple of Artemis at Ephesus

Date	Mintage	F12	VF20	XF40	MS60	MS63
2009	Est. 7000	PF63 75.00	PF65 85.00			

KM# 108 10 DOLLARS
1.00 g., 0.999 Gold 0.0319 oz. AGW, 13.92 mm. **Ruler:** Elizabeth II **Subject:** Ancient Seven World Wonders **Obv:** Head right **Rev:** Hanging Gardens of Bablyon

Date	Mintage	F12	VF20	XF40	MS60	MS63
2009	7,500	PF63 75.00	PF65 85.00			

KM# 109 10 DOLLARS
1.00 g., 0.999 Gold 0.0319 oz. AGW, 13.92 mm. **Ruler:** Elizabeth II **Subject:** Ancient Seven Wonders of the World **Obv:** Head right **Rev:** Lighthouse at Alexandria

Date	Mintage	F12	VF20	XF40	MS60	MS63
2009	Est. 7000	PF63 75.00	PF65 85.00			

KM# 187 10 DOLLARS
1.00 g., 0.999 Gold 0.0319 oz. AGW, 13.92 mm. **Ruler:** Elizabeth II **Subject:** Ancient 7 World Wonders: Mausoleum of Mausollos

Date	Mintage	F12	VF20	XF40	MS60	MS63
2009	Est. 7000	PF63 75.00	PF65 85.00			

KM# 120 10 DOLLARS
20.00 g., 0.925 Silver 0.591 oz. ASW, 38.61 mm. **Ruler:**
Elizabeth II **Subject:** For World Peace **Rev:** John Paul II and
Mother Theresa

Date	Mintage	F12	VF20	XF40	MS60	MS63
2010	2,500	PF65 75.00				

KM# 121 10 DOLLARS
20.00 g., 0.925 Silver 0.591 oz. ASW, 38.61 mm. **Ruler:**
Elizabeth II **Rev:** S.M.S. Gneisenau under full sail

Date	Mintage	F12	VF20	XF40	MS60	MS63
2010	2,500	PF65 75.00				

KM# 122 10 DOLLARS
25.00 g., 0.925 Silver 0.7387 oz. ASW, 38.61 mm. **Ruler:**
Elizabeth II **Rev:** Spotted Cuscus in color with Swarovsky
crystal eyes

Date	Mintage	F12	VF20	XF40	MS60	MS63
2010	2,500	PF65 65.00				

KM# 162 10 DOLLARS
20.00 g., Silver, 38.61 mm. **Ruler:** Elizabeth II **Rev:** Manatee
in color

Date	Mintage	F12	VF20	XF40	MS60	MS63
2011	2,500	PF65 55.00				

KM# 208 10 DOLLARS
31.10 g., 0.999 Silver 0.9925 oz. ASW, 40.6 mm. **Ruler:**
Elizabeth II **Subject:** Diamond Jubilee of Queen Elizabeth II
- Coronation

Date	Mintage	F12	VF20	XF40	MS60	MS63
2011	Est. 10000	PF63 55.00	PF65 60.00			

KM# 178 10 DOLLARS
20.00 g., 0.925 Silver 0.591 oz. ASW, 38.61 mm. **Ruler:**
Elizabeth II **Subject:** 2012 London Olympic Games - Discus
Thrower

Date	Mintage	F12	VF20	XF40	MS60	MS63
2012	Est. 10000	PF63 40.00	PF65 45.00			

KM# 219 10 DOLLARS
20.00 g., 0.925 Silver 0.591 oz. ASW, 38.61 mm. **Ruler:**
Elizabeth II **Subject:** 2014 FIFA World Cup Brazil

Date	Mintage	F12	VF20	XF40	MS60	MS63
2012	Est. 10000	PF63 30.00	PF65 35.00			

KM# 260 10 DOLLARS
28.28 g., 0.925 Silver 0.8350 oz. ASW, 38.61 mm. **Ruler:**
Elizabeth II **Subject:** 2014 Olympics - Lighting the flame

Date	Mintage	F12	VF20	XF40	MS60	MS63
2013	5,000	PF65 75.00				

KM# 261 10 DOLLARS
20.00 g., 0.925 Silver 0.591 oz. ASW, 38.61 mm. **Ruler:**
Elizabeth II **Subject:** Steeplechase

Date	Mintage	F12	VF20	XF40	MS60	MS63
2013	7,500	PF65 75.00				

KM# 279 10 DOLLARS
31.11 g., 0.999 Silver 0.9926 oz. ASW, 66x32 mm. **Ruler:**
Elizabeth II **Subject:** Precious 6 in 1 Bar

Date	Mintage	F12	VF20	XF40	MS60	MS63
2013	10,000	PF65 100				

KM# 91 25 DOLLARS
31.11 g., 0.999 Silver 0.9926 oz. ASW, 38.6 mm. **Ruler:**
Elizabeth II **Subject:** Don Everhart II **Obv:** Head right **Rev:**
AN-225 Mriya

Date	Mintage	F12	VF20	XF40	MS60	MS63
2003	—	PF65 45.00				

KM# 90 25 DOLLARS
31.11 g., 0.999 Silver 0.9926 oz. ASW, 38.61 mm. **Ruler:**
Elizabeth II **Obv:** Head right **Rev:** Wright Brother's 1903 Flyer

Date	Mintage	F12	VF20	XF40	MS60	MS63
2003	—	PF65 45.00				

KM# 92 25 DOLLARS
31.11 g., 0.999 Silver 0.9926 oz. ASW, 38.61 mm. **Ruler:**
Elizabeth II **Obv:** Head right **Rev:** Spitfire

Date	Mintage	F12	VF20	XF40	MS60	MS63
2003		PF65 45.00				

KM# 114 25 DOLLARS
31.11 g., 0.999 Silver 0.9926 oz. ASW, 38.61 mm. **Ruler:**
Elizabeth II **Rev:** NC 14716 China Clipper

Date	Mintage	F12	VF20	XF40	MS60	MS63
2003	—	PF65 65.00				

KM# 115 25 DOLLARS
31.10 g., 0.999 Silver 0.9925 oz. ASW, 38.6 mm. **Ruler:**
Elizabeth II **Rev:** Messerschmitt ME 262

Date	Mintage	F12	VF20	XF40	MS60	MS63
2003		PF65 45.00				

KM# 132 25 DOLLARS
31.11 g., 0.999 Silver 0.9926 oz. ASW, 38.61 mm. **Ruler:**
Elizabeth II **Rev:** Sikorsky VS 30

Date	Mintage	F12	VF20	XF40	MS60	MS63
2003	—	PF65 42.50				

KM# 133 25 DOLLARS
31.11 g., 0.999 Silver 0.9926 oz. ASW, 38.61 mm. **Ruler:**
Elizabeth II **Rev:** Concorde

Date	Mintage	F12	VF20	XF40	MS60	MS63
2003	—	PF65 42.50				

KM# 134 25 DOLLARS
31.11 g., 0.999 Silver 0.9926 oz. ASW, 38.61 mm. **Ruler:**
Elizabeth II **Rev:** Lockheed Martin F-117 Nighthawk

Date	Mintage	F12	VF20	XF40	MS60	MS63
2003	—	PF65 42.50				

KM# 135 25 DOLLARS
31.11 g., 0.999 Silver 0.9926 oz. ASW, 38.61 mm. **Ruler:**
Elizabeth II **Rev:** Bell X 1

Date	Mintage	F12	VF20	XF40	MS60	MS63
2003	—	PF65 42.50				

KM# 136 25 DOLLARS
31.11 g., 0.999 Silver 0.9926 oz. ASW, 38.61 mm. **Ruler:**
Elizabeth II **Rev:** De Havilland Comet

Date	Mintage	F12	VF20	XF40	MS60	MS63
2003	—	PF65 42.50				

KM# 137 25 DOLLARS
31.11 g., 0.999 Silver 0.9926 oz. ASW, 38.61 mm. **Ruler:**
Elizabeth II **Rev:** AV 8B Harrier II

Date	Mintage	F12	VF20	XF40	MS60	MS63
2003	—	PF65 42.50				

KM# 138 25 DOLLARS
31.11 g., 0.999 Silver 0.9926 oz. ASW, 38.61 mm. **Ruler:**
Elizabeth II **Rev:** Curtiss Jenny

Date	Mintage	F12	VF20	XF40	MS60	MS63
2003	—	PF65 42.50				

KM# 139 25 DOLLARS
31.11 g., 0.999 Silver 0.9926 oz. ASW, 38.61 mm. **Ruler:**
Elizabeth II **Rev:** Douglas DC 3

Date	Mintage	F12	VF20	XF40	MS60	MS63
2003	—	PF65 42.50				

KM# 93 25 DOLLARS
31.11 g., 0.999 Silver 0.9926 oz. ASW **Ruler:** Elizabeth II
Subject: Trafalgar **Obv:** Head right **Rev:** H.M.S. Victory

Date	Mintage	F12	VF20	XF40	MS60	MS63
2005	—	PF65 45.00				

KM# 132a 25 DOLLARS
31.11 g., 0.999 Silver 0.9926 oz. ASW, 38.61 mm. **Ruler:** Elizabeth II **Rev:** Sikorsky VS 300

Date	Mintage	F12	VF20	XF40	MS60	MS63
2005	—				PF65	55.00

KM# 143 25 DOLLARS
31.11 g., 0.999 Silver 0.9926 oz. ASW, 38.61 mm. **Ruler:** Elizabeth II **Subject:** Triere

Date	Mintage	F12	VF20	XF40	MS60	MS63
2005	—				PF65	55.00

KM# 144 25 DOLLARS
31.11 g., 0.999 Silver 0.9926 oz. ASW, 38.61 mm. **Ruler:** Elizabeth II **Subject:** H.M.S. Mary Rose

Date	Mintage	F12	VF20	XF40	MS60	MS63
2005	—				PF65	55.00

KM# 145 25 DOLLARS
31.11 g., 0.999 Silver 0.9926 oz. ASW, 38.61 mm. **Ruler:** Elizabeth II **Subject:** U.S.S. Bonhomme Richard

Date	Mintage	F12	VF20	XF40	MS60	MS63
2005	—				PF65	55.00

KM# 146 25 DOLLARS
31.11 g., 0.999 Silver 0.9926 oz. ASW, 38.61 mm. **Ruler:** Elizabeth II **Subject:** H.M.S. Dorsetshire

Date	Mintage	F12	VF20	XF40	MS60	MS63
2005	—				PF65	55.00

KM# 90a 25 DOLLARS
31.11 g., 0.999 Silver 0.9926 oz. ASW, 38.61 mm. **Ruler:** Elizabeth II **Rev:** Antonov AN-225 Mrija

Date	Mintage	F12	VF20	XF40	MS60	MS63
2005	—				PF65	55.00

KM# 114a 25 DOLLARS
31.11 g., 0.999 Silver 0.9926 oz. ASW, 38.61 mm. **Ruler:** Elizabeth II **Rev:** NC 14716 China Clipper

Date	Mintage	F12	VF20	XF40	MS60	MS63
2005	—				PF65	55.00

KM# 115a 25 DOLLARS
31.11 g., 0.999 Silver 0.9926 oz. ASW, 38.61 mm. **Ruler:** Elizabeth II **Rev:** Messerschmitt ME 262

Date	Mintage	F12	VF20	XF40	MS60	MS63
2005	—				PF65	55.00

KM# 133a 25 DOLLARS
31.11 g., 0.999 Silver 0.9926 oz. ASW, 38.61 mm. **Ruler:** Elizabeth II **Rev:** Concorde

Date	Mintage	F12	VF20	XF40	MS60	MS63
2005	—				PF65	55.00

KM# 134a 25 DOLLARS
31.11 g., 0.999 Silver 0.9926 oz. ASW, 38.61 mm. **Ruler:** Elizabeth II **Rev:** Lockheed Martin F-117 Nighthawk

Date	Mintage	F12	VF20	XF40	MS60	MS63
2005	—				PF65	55.00

KM# 135a 25 DOLLARS
31.11 g., 0.999 Silver 0.9926 oz. ASW, 38.61 mm. **Ruler:** Elizabeth II **Rev:** Bell X1

Date	Mintage	F12	VF20	XF40	MS60	MS63
2005	—				PF65	55.00

KM# 136a 25 DOLLARS
31.11 g., 0.999 Silver 0.9926 oz. ASW, 38.61 mm. **Ruler:** Elizabeth II **Rev:** De Havilland Comet

Date	Mintage	F12	VF20	XF40	MS60	MS63
2005	—				PF65	55.00

KM# 137a 25 DOLLARS
31.11 g., 0.999 Silver 0.9926 oz. ASW, 38.61 mm. **Ruler:** Elizabeth II **Rev:** AV 8B Harrier II

Date	Mintage	F12	VF20	XF40	MS60	MS63
2005	—				PF65	55.00

KM# 138a 25 DOLLARS
31.11 g., 0.999 Silver 0.9926 oz. ASW, 38.61 mm. **Ruler:** Elizabeth II **Rev:** Curtiss Jenny

Date	Mintage	F12	VF20	XF40	MS60	MS63
2005	—				PF65	55.00

KM# 139a 25 DOLLARS
31.11 g., 0.999 Silver 0.9926 oz. ASW, 38.61 mm. **Ruler:** Elizabeth II **Rev:** Douglas DC 3

Date	Mintage	F12	VF20	XF40	MS60	MS63
2005	—				PF65	55.00

KM# 90a 25 DOLLARS
31.10 g., 0.999 Silver 0.9925 oz. ASW, 38.61 mm. **Ruler:** Elizabeth II **Rev:** Wright flier of 1903

Date	Mintage	F12	VF20	XF40	MS60	MS63
2005	—				PF65	75.00

KM# 92a 25 DOLLARS
31.11 g., 0.999 Silver 0.9926 oz. ASW, 38.61 mm. **Ruler:** Elizabeth II **Rev:** Spitfire

Date	Mintage	F12	VF20	XF40	MS60	MS63
2005	—				PF65	55.00

KM# 95 25 DOLLARS
31.11 g., 0.999 Silver 0.9926 oz. ASW, 38.6 mm. **Ruler:** Elizabeth II **Obv:** Head right, partially gilt **Rev:** Queen Elizabeth II and WWII Red Cross Nurse, gilt 80 above.

Date	Mintage	F12	VF20	XF40	MS60	MS63
2006	—				PF65	50.00

KM# 87 25 DOLLARS
0.925 Silver **Ruler:** Elizabeth II **Obv:** Crowned bust right **Obv. Legend:** ELIZABETH II - SOLOMON ISLANDS **Rev:** 3/4 length figures of Elizabeth and Prince Philip facing

Date	Mintage	F12	VF20	XF40	MS60	MS63
2006	—				PF65	50.00

KM# 147 25 DOLLARS
31.11 g., 0.999 Silver 0.9926 oz. ASW, 38.61 mm. **Ruler:** Elizabeth II **Subject:** Turtle boat

Date	Mintage	F12	VF20	XF40	MS60	MS63
2006	—				PF65	55.00

KM# 148 25 DOLLARS
31.11 g., 0.999 Silver 0.9926 oz. ASW, 38.61 mm. **Ruler:** Elizabeth II **Subject:** Ville de Paris

Date	Mintage	F12	VF20	XF40	MS60	MS63
2006	—				PF65	55.00

KM# 149 25 DOLLARS
31.11 g., 0.999 Silver 0.9926 oz. ASW, 38.61 mm. **Ruler:** Elizabeth II **Subject:** Admiral Graf Spee

Date	Mintage	F12	VF20	XF40	MS60	MS63
2006	—				PF65	55.00

KM# 150 25 DOLLARS
31.11 g., 0.999 Silver 0.9926 oz. ASW, 38.61 mm. **Ruler:** Elizabeth II **Subject:** H.M.S. Dreadnought

Date	Mintage	F12	VF20	XF40	MS60	MS63
2006	—				PF65	55.00

KM# 151 25 DOLLARS
31.11 g., 0.999 Silver 0.9926 oz. ASW, 38.61 mm. **Ruler:** Elizabeth II **Subject:** U.S.S. Hornet

Date	Mintage	F12	VF20	XF40	MS60	MS63
2006	—				PF65	55.00

KM# 152 25 DOLLARS
31.11 g., 0.999 Silver 0.9926 oz. ASW, 38.61 mm. **Ruler:** Elizabeth II **Subject:** Yamato

Date	Mintage	F12	VF20	XF40	MS60	MS63
2006	—				PF65	55.00

KM# 87a 25 DOLLARS
31.11 g., 0.999 Silver 0.9926 oz. ASW **Ruler:** Elizabeth II **Obv:** Head right, partially gilt **Rev:** Wedding of Elizabeth II and Philip. Gothic window behind, gilt 80 above.

Date	Mintage	F12	VF20	XF40	MS60	MS63
2006	—				PF65	50.00

KM# 251 25 DOLLARS
31.11 g., 0.999 Silver 0.9926 oz. ASW **Ruler:** Elizabeth II **Obv:** Crowned head right **Rev:** Brederode sailing right

Date	Mintage	F12	VF20	XF40	MS60	MS63
2007	—				PF65	100

KM# 252 25 DOLLARS
31.11 g., 0.999 Silver 0.9926 oz. ASW, 38.61 mm. **Ruler:** Elizabeth II **Obv:** Crowned head right **Rev:** The Mary Rose sailing left

Date	Mintage	F12	VF20	XF40	MS60	MS63
2007	—				PF65	100

KM# 253 25 DOLLARS
31.11 g., 0.999 Silver 0.9926 oz. ASW, 38.61 mm. **Ruler:** Elizabeth II **Obv:** Crowned head right **Rev:** Roman Trireme sailing ship

Date	Mintage	F12	VF20	XF40	MS60	MS63
2007	—				PF65	100

KM# 254 25 DOLLARS
31.11 g., 0.999 Silver 0.9926 oz. ASW, 38.61 mm. **Ruler:** Elizabeth II **Obv:** Crowned head right **Rev:** Ming Treasure Ship sailing left

Date	Mintage	F12	VF20	XF40	MS60	MS63
2007	—				PF65	100

KM# 255 25 DOLLARS
31.11 g., 0.999 Silver 0.9926 oz. ASW, 38.61 mm. **Ruler:** Elizabeth II **Obv:** Crowned head right **Rev:** USS Hartford sailing right

Date	Mintage	F12	VF20	XF40	MS60	MS63
2007	—				PF65	100

KM# 256 25 DOLLARS
31.11 g., 0.999 Silver 0.9926 oz. ASW, 38.61 mm. **Ruler:** Elizabeth II **Obv:** Crowned head right **Rev:** Nuestra Rosario sailing right

Date	Mintage	F12	VF20	XF40	MS60	MS63
2007	—				PF65	100

KM# 257 25 DOLLARS
31.11 g., 0.999 Silver 0.9926 oz. ASW, 38.61 mm. **Ruler:** Elizabeth II **Obv:** Crowned head right **Rev:** Fijian Ndrua sailing left

Date	Mintage	F12	VF20	XF40	MS60	MS63
2007	—				PF65	100

KM# 258 25 DOLLARS
31.11 g., 0.999 Silver 0.9926 oz. ASW, 38.61 mm. **Ruler:** Elizabeth II **Obv:** Crowned head right **Rev:** USS Tautog sailing left

Date	Mintage	F12	VF20	XF40	MS60	MS63
2007	—				PF65	100

KM# 259 25 DOLLARS
31.11 g., 0.999 Silver 0.9926 oz. ASW, 38.61 mm. **Ruler:** Elizabeth II **Obv:** Crowned head right **Rev:** Venice Galley sailing right

Date	Mintage	F12	VF20	XF40	MS60	MS63
2007	—				PF65	100

KM# 116 25 DOLLARS
28.28 g., 0.925 Silver 0.8356 oz. ASW, 38.6 mm. **Ruler:** Elizabeth II **Rev:** Press clippings, soldier standing over field cross

Date	Mintage	F12	VF20	XF40	MS60	MS63
2008	—				PF65	50.00

KM# 117 25 DOLLARS
28.28 g., 0.925 Silver 0.8356 oz. ASW, 38.6 mm. **Ruler:** Elizabeth II **Rev:** Battlefield

Date	Mintage	F12	VF20	XF40	MS60	MS63
2008	—				PF65	50.00

KM# 118 25 DOLLARS
28.28 g., 0.925 Silver 0.8356 oz. ASW, 38.6 mm. **Ruler:** Elizabeth II **Rev:** Soldier overlooking beach

Date	Mintage	F12	VF20	XF40	MS60	MS63
2008	—	PF65 50.00				

KM# 155 25 DOLLARS
28.28 g., 0.925 Silver 0.8356 oz. ASW, 38.61 mm. **Ruler:** Elizabeth II **Subject:** Cannons

Date	Mintage	F12	VF20	XF40	MS60	MS63
2008	—	PF65 55.00				

KM# 156 25 DOLLARS
28.28 g., 0.925 Silver 0.8356 oz. ASW, 38.61 mm. **Ruler:** Elizabeth II **Subject:** Eastern Front

Date	Mintage	F12	VF20	XF40	MS60	MS63
2008	—	PF65 55.00				

KM# 157 25 DOLLARS
28.28 g., 0.925 Silver 0.8356 oz. ASW, 38.61 mm. **Ruler:** Elizabeth II **Subject:** Truce

Date	Mintage	F12	VF20	XF40	MS60	MS63
2008	—	PF65 55.00				

KM# 280 25 DOLLARS
93.30 g., 0.999 Silver 2.9774 oz. ASW, 110x52 mm. **Ruler:** Elizabeth II **Subject:** Nefertiti

Date	Mintage	F12	VF20	XF40	MS60	MS63
2013	1,000	PF65 400				

KM# 158 50 DOLLARS
155.50 g., 0.925 Silver 4.5947 oz. ASW, 65 mm. **Ruler:** Elizabeth II **Rev:** Poppy on war novel

Date	Mintage	F12	VF20	XF40	MS60	MS63
2008	Est. 150	PF65 225				

PROOF SETS

KM#	Date	Mintage	Identification	Issue Price	Mkt Val
PS13	2012 (5)	1,500	KM#171a-175a	—	—

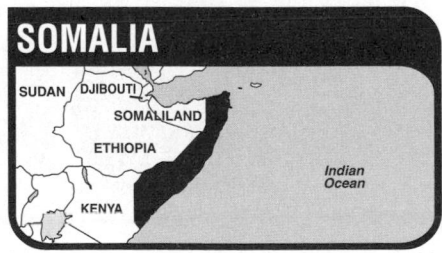

SOMALIA

SUDAN · DJIBOUTI
SOMALILAND
ETHIOPIA
Indian Ocean
KENYA

The Somali Republic consists of the former Italian Somaliland and is located on the coast of the eastern projection of the African continent commonly referred to as the "Horn". It has an area of 178,201 sq. mi. (461,657 sq. km.) and a population of *8.2 million. Capital: Mogadishu. The economy is pastoral and agricultural. Livestock, bananas and hides are exported.

The Northern Somali National Movement (SNM) declared a secession of the northwestern Somaliland Republic on May 17, 1991, which is not recognized by the Somali Democratic Republic.

REPUBLIC OF SOMALIA

STANDARD COINAGE

KM# 45 5 SHILLING / SCELLINI
1.29 g., Aluminum, 21 mm. **Series:** F.A.O. **Obv:** Crowned arms with supporters **Rev:** Elephant **Edge:** Plain

Date	Mintage	F12	VF20	XF40	MS60	MS63
2002	—			—	1.50	1.75

KM# 159 10 SHILLINGS
25.15 g., Copper-Nickel, 38.66 mm. **Series:** Marine Life Protection **Obv:** National arms **Rev:** Two fish multicolor **Edge:** Reeded

Date	Mintage	F12	VF20	XF40	MS60	MS63
2003	—	PF63 10.00				

KM# 46 10 SHILLINGS / SCELLINI
1.29 g., Aluminum, 21.9 mm. **Series:** F.A.O. **Obv:** Crowned arms with supporters **Rev:** Camel **Edge:** Plain

Date	Mintage	F12	VF20	XF40	MS60	MS63
2002	—			—	2.00	2.25

KM# 175 20 SHILLINGS
0.62 g., 0.999 Gold AGW **Obv:** Arms **Rev:** Mom and baby elephant

Date	Mintage	F12	VF20	XF40	MS60	MS63
2007	—	PF63 50.00				

KM# 166 25 SHILLINGS
Silver **Obv:** Arms **Rev:** Mozart, multicolor

Date	Mintage	F12	VF20	XF40	MS60	MS63
2001	—				—	40.00

KM# 155 25 SHILLINGS
28.10 g., Copper-Nickel, 38.73 mm. **Subject:** The Life of Pope John-Paul II **Obv:** National arms **Obv. Legend:** SOMALI REPUBLIC **Rev:** Pope John-Paul II in window at the Vatican **Edge:** Plain

Date	Mintage	F12	VF20	XF40	MS60	MS63
2004	—			—	6.00	7.00

KM# 156 25 SHILLINGS
28.10 g., Copper-Nickel, 38.73 mm. **Subject:** Life of Pope John Paul II **Obv:** National arms **Obv. Legend:** SOMALI REPUBLIC **Rev:** Pope traveling in special vehicle **Edge:** Plain

Date	Mintage	F12	VF20	XF40	MS60	MS63
2004	—			—	6.00	7.00

KM# 157 25 SHILLINGS
28.10 g., Copper-Nickel, 38.73 mm. **Subject:** The Life of Pope John-Paul II **Obv:** National arms **Obv. Legend:** SOMALI REPUBLIC **Rev:** Pope blessing Mother Teresa **Edge:** Plain

Date	Mintage	F12	VF20	XF40	MS60	MS63
2004	—			—	6.00	7.00

KM# 164 25 SHILLINGS
25.80 g., Copper-Nickel, 38.77 mm. **Obv:** National arms **Obv. Legend:** SOMALI REPUBLIC **Rev:** Black rhinoceros walking left **Edge:** Reeded

Date	Mintage	F12	VF20	XF40	MS60	MS63
2006	—			—	12.00	14.00

KM# 165 25 SHILLINGS
25.80 g., Copper-Nickel, 38.77 mm. **Obv:** National arms **Rev:** Red Kite perched on branch **Edge:** Reeded

Date	Mintage	F12	VF20	XF40	MS60	MS63
2006	—			—	12.00	14.00

KM# 103 25 SHILLINGS / SCELLINI
4.37 g., Brass, 21.8 mm. **Subject:** Soccer **Obv:** Crowned arms with supporters **Rev:** Soccer player **Edge:** Plain

Date	Mintage	F12	VF20	XF40	MS60	MS63
2001	—			—	1.25	1.50

KM# 111 50 SHILLINGS
3.90 g., Nickel Clad Steel, 21.9 mm. **Obv:** Crowned arms with supporters **Rev:** Mandrill **Edge:** Plain

Date	Mintage	F12	VF20	XF40	MS60	MS63
2002	—			—	0.85	1.25

KM# 161 50 SHILLINGS
1.20 g., 0.999 Gold 0.0383 oz. AGW, 13.88 mm. **Subject:** Gold of the Pharaohs **Obv:** National arms **Obv. Legend:** SOMALI REPUBLIC **Rev:** King Tutankhaman's death mask **Edge:** Reeded

Date	Mintage	F12	VF20	XF40	MS60	MS63
2002	—	PF63 80.00				

KM# 109 100 SHILLINGS
10.50 g., 0.999 Silver 0.3351 oz. ASW, 30.1 mm. **Subject:** Soccer **Obv:** Crowned arms with supporters **Rev:** Multicolor soccer player and Brandenburg Gate **Edge:** Reeded

Date	Mintage	F12	VF20	XF40	MS60	MS63
2001	—	PF63 25.00				

KM# 112 100 SHILLINGS
3.54 g., Brass, 18.8 mm. **Obv:** Crowned arms with supporters above value **Rev:** Bust with headdress facing **Edge:** Plain

Date	Mintage	F12	VF20	XF40	MS60	MS63
2002	—	—	—	—	1.50	2.50

KM# 176 200 SHILLINGS
0.62 g., 0.999 Gold AGW, 13.90 mm. **Obv:** Arms **Rev:** Elephant head left

Date	Mintage	F12	VF20	XF40	MS60	MS63
2005	—	PF63 60.00				

KM# 168 250 SHILLINGS
23.00 g., 0.925 Silver 0.6796 oz. ASW **Obv:** Arms **Rev:** Victoria, gothic crown

Date	Mintage	F12	VF20	XF40	MS60	MS63
2001	—	PF63 45.00				

KM# 110 250 SHILLINGS
31.11 g., 0.999 Silver 0.9926 oz. ASW, 40 mm. **Subject:** Queen of Sheba **Obv:** Crowned arms with supporters **Rev:** Crowned bust 1/4 right **Edge:** Reeded

Date	Mintage	F12	VF20	XF40	MS60	MS63
2002	—	—	—	—	35.00	40.00

KM# 158 250 SHILLINGS
20.05 g., Silver, 38.59 mm. **Obv:** National arms **Obv. Legend:** SOMALI REPUBLIC **Rev:** Laureate bust of Julius Caesar 3/4 left **Edge:** Reeded

Date	Mintage	F12	VF20	XF40	MS60	MS63
2002	—	PF63 32.00				

KM# 162 250 SHILLINGS
1.27 g., 0.999 Gold 0.0405 oz. AGW, 13.90 mm. **Obv:** National arms **Obv. Legend:** SOMALI REPUBLIC **Rev:** Bust of Hans Rühmann facing **Edge:** Reeded

Date	Mintage	F12	VF20	XF40	MS60	MS63
2002	—	PF63 85.00				

KM# 169 250 SHILLINGS
23.00 g., 0.925 Silver 0.6796 oz. ASW **Obv:** Arms **Rev:** Soccer player, Brazil

Date	Mintage	F12	VF20	XF40	MS60	MS63
2002	—	—	—	—	45.00	

KM# 160 250 SHILLINGS
20.50 g., Silver, 38.56 mm. **Subject:** Wembley Goal - England 1966 **Obv:** National arms **Obv. Legend:** SOMALI REPUBLIC **Rev:** 3 soccer players at goal **Edge:** Reeded

Date	Mintage	F12	VF20	XF40	MS60	MS63
2003	—	PF63 28.00				

KM# 121 250 SHILLINGS
20.12 g., Silver Plated Base Metal, 38.5 mm. **Obv:** Crowned arms with supporters **Rev:** Multicolor Pope John Paul II and mountains **Edge:** Reeded

Date	Mintage	F12	VF20	XF40	MS60	MS63
2005	—	PF63 16.50				

KM# 123 250 SHILLINGS
20.12 g., Silver Plated Base Metal, 38.5 mm. **Obv:** Crowned arms with supporters **Rev:** Multicolor Pope John Paul II kissing bible **Edge:** Reeded

Date	Mintage	F12	VF20	XF40	MS60	MS63
2005	—	PF63 16.50				

KM# 125 250 SHILLINGS
20.12 g., Silver Plated Base Metal, 38.5 mm. **Obv:** Crowned arms with supporters **Rev:** Multicolor Pope John Paul II with flowers **Edge:** Reeded

Date	Mintage	F12	VF20	XF40	MS60	MS63
2005	—	PF63 16.50				

KM# 127 250 SHILLINGS
20.12 g., Silver Plated Base Metal, 38.5 mm. **Obv:** Crowned arms with supporters **Rev:** Multicolor Pope John Paul II saying mass **Edge:** Reeded

Date	Mintage	F12	VF20	XF40	MS60	MS63
2005	—	PF63 16.50				

KM# 129 250 SHILLINGS
20.12 g., Silver Plated Base Metal, 38.5 mm. **Obv:** Crowned arms with supporters **Rev:** Multicolor Pope John Paul II with cardinals **Edge:** Reeded

Date	Mintage	F12	VF20	XF40	MS60	MS63
2005	—	PF63 16.50				

KM# 131 250 SHILLINGS
20.12 g., Silver Plated Base Metal, 38.5 mm. **Obv:** Crowned arms with supporters **Rev:** Pope John Paul II with red vestments **Edge:** Reeded

Date	Mintage	F12	VF20	XF40	MS60	MS63
2005	—	PF63 16.50				

KM# 133 250 SHILLINGS
20.12 g., Silver Plated Base Metal, 38.5 mm. **Obv:** Crowned arms with supporters **Rev:** Pope John Paul II in white with skull cap **Edge:** Reeded

Date	Mintage	F12	VF20	XF40	MS60	MS63
2005	—	PF63 16.50				

KM# 135 250 SHILLINGS
20.12 g., Silver Plated Base Metal, 38.5 mm. **Obv:** Crowned arms with supporters **Rev:** Multicolor Pope John Paul II leaning head on staff **Edge:** Reeded

Date	Mintage	F12	VF20	XF40	MS60	MS63
2005	—	PF63 16.50				

KM# 137 250 SHILLINGS
20.12 g., Silver Plated Base Metal, 38.5 mm. **Obv:** Crowned arms with supporters **Rev:** Multicolor Pope John Paul II with staff facing left **Edge:** Reeded

Date	Mintage	F12	VF20	XF40	MS60	MS63
2005	—	PF63 16.50				

KM# 139 250 SHILLINGS
20.12 g., Silver Plated Base Metal, 38.5 mm. **Obv:** Crowned arms with supporters **Rev:** Multicolor Pope John Paul II with staff facing half right **Edge:** Reeded

Date	Mintage	F12	VF20	XF40	MS60	MS63
2005	—	PF63 16.50				

KM# 143 250 SHILLINGS
Copper-Nickel **Obv:** Crowned shield **Obv. Legend:** SOMALI REPUBLIC / 250 SHILLINGS **Rev:** Color applique, German Shephard **Rev. Legend:** YEAR OF THE DOG / 2006 **Edge:** Reeded

Date	Mintage	F12	VF20	XF40	MS60	MS63
2006	—	—	—	—	—	14.50

KM# 144 250 SHILLINGS
Copper-Nickel **Obv:** Crowned shield **Obv. Legend:** SOMALI REPUBLIC / 250 SHILLINGS **Rev:** Color applique, Dachsund **Rev. Legend:** YEAR OF THE DOG / 2006 **Edge:** Reeded

Date	Mintage	F12	VF20	XF40	MS60	MS63
2006	—	—	—	—	—	14.50

KM# 145 250 SHILLINGS
Copper-Nickel **Obv:** Crowned shield **Obv. Legend:** SOMALI REPUBLIC / 250 SHILLINGS **Rev:** Color applique, Yorkshire Terrier **Rev. Legend:** YEAR OF THE DOG / 2006 **Edge:** Reeded

Date	Mintage	F12	VF20	XF40	MS60	MS63
2006	—	—	—	—	—	14.50

KM# 146 250 SHILLINGS
Copper-Nickel **Obv:** Crowned shield **Obv. Legend:** SOMALI REPUBLIC / 250 SHILLINGS **Rev:** Color applique, Scottie (small white) **Rev. Legend:** YEAR OF THE DOG / 2006 **Edge:** Reeded

Date	Mintage	F12	VF20	XF40	MS60	MS63
2006	—	—	—	—	—	14.50

KM# 147 250 SHILLINGS
Copper-Nickel **Obv:** Crowned shield **Obv. Legend:** SOMALI REPUBLIC / 250 SHILLINGS **Rev:** Color applique, Wirehaired Terrier **Rev. Legend:** YEAR OF THE DOG / 2006 **Edge:** Reeded

Date	Mintage	F12	VF20	XF40	MS60	MS63
2006	—	—	—	—	—	14.50

KM# 148 250 SHILLINGS
Copper-Nickel **Obv:** Crowned shield **Obv. Legend:** SOMALI REPUBLIC / 250 SHILLINGS **Rev:** Color applique, Bulldog **Rev. Legend:** YEAR OF THE DOG / 2006 **Edge:** Reeded

Date	Mintage	F12	VF20	XF40	MS60	MS63
2006	—	—	—	—	—	14.50

KM# 149 250 SHILLINGS
Copper-Nickel **Obv:** Crowned shield **Obv. Legend:** SOMALI REPUBLIC / 250 SHILLINGS **Rev:** Color applique, Golden Retriever **Rev. Legend:** YEAR OF THE DOG / 2006 **Edge:** Reeded

Date	Mintage	F12	VF20	XF40	MS60	MS63
2006	—	—	—	—	—	14.50

KM# 150 250 SHILLINGS
Copper-Nickel **Obv:** Crowned shield **Obv. Legend:** SOMALI REPUBLIC / 250 SHILLINGS **Rev:** Color applique, St. Bernard **Rev. Legend:** YEAR OF THE DOG / 2006 **Edge:** Reeded

Date	Mintage	F12	VF20	XF40	MS60	MS63
2006	—	—	—	—	—	14.50

KM# 151 250 SHILLINGS
Copper-Nickel **Obv:** Crowned shield **Obv. Legend:** SOMALI REPUBLIC / 250 SHILLINGS **Rev:** Color applique, Rottweiler **Rev. Legend:** YEAR OF THE DOG / 2006 **Edge:** Reeded

Date	Mintage	F12	VF20	XF40	MS60	MS63
2006	—	—	—	—	—	14.50

KM# 152 250 SHILLINGS
Copper-Nickel Obv: Crowned shield Obv. Legend: SOMALI
REPUBLIC / 250 SHILLINGS Rev: Color applique, Basset
Hound Rev. Legend: YEAR OF THE DOG / 2006 Edge:
Reeded

Date	Mintage	F12	VF20	XF40	MS60	MS63
2006	—	—	—	—	—	14.50

KM# 153 250 SHILLINGS
Copper-Nickel Obv: Crowned shield Obv. Legend: SOMALI
REPUBLIC / 250 SHILLINGS Rev: Color applique, Sheep Dog
Rev. Legend: YEAR OF THE DOG / 2006 Edge: Reeded

Date	Mintage	F12	VF20	XF40	MS60	MS63
2006	—	—	—	—	—	14.50

KM# 154 250 SHILLINGS
Copper-Nickel Obv: Crowned shield Obv. Legend: SOMALI
REPUBLIC / 250 SHILLINGS Rev: Color applique, Cocker
Spaniel Rev. Legend: YEAR OF THE DOG / 2006 Edge:
Reeded

Date	Mintage	F12	VF20	XF40	MS60	MS63
2006	—	—	—	—	—	14.50

KM# 170 250 SHILLINGS
Copper-Nickel Gilt, 38 mm. Obv: Arms in cartouche Rev: Gold
mask of Tutankahamun, enameled

Date	Mintage	F12	VF20	XF40	MS60	MS63
2008	—	—	—	—	—	17.50

KM# 171 250 SHILLINGS
Copper-Nickel Gilt, 38 mm. Obv: Arms within cartouche Rev:
Udjat eye, enameled

Date	Mintage	F12	VF20	XF40	MS60	MS63
2008	—	—	—	—	—	40.00

KM# 172 250 SHILLINGS
Copper-Nickel Obv: Arms within cartouche Rev: Statue of
Ptah, enameled

Date	Mintage	F12	VF20	XF40	MS60	MS63
2008	—	—	—	—	—	20.00

KM# 173 250 SHILLINGS
Copper-Nickel Gilt, 38 mm. Obv: Arms in cartouche Rev:
Jcarab Pectoral necklace, enameled

Date	Mintage	F12	VF20	XF40	MS60	MS63
2008	—	—	—	—	—	20.00

KM# 174 250 SHILLINGS
Copper-Nickel Gilt, 38 mm. Obv: Arms within cartouche Rev:
Statue of Horus the Elder

Date	Mintage	F12	VF20	XF40	MS60	MS63
2008	—	—	—	—	—	20.00

KM# 122 500 SHILLINGS
18.84 g., Silver Plated Base Metal, 34.1 mm. Obv: Crowned
arms with supporters Rev: Multicolor Pope John Paul II and
mountains Edge: Plain Shape: Square with round corners

Date	Mintage	F12	VF20	XF40	MS60	MS63
2005	—	PF63 16.50				

KM# 124 500 SHILLINGS
18.84 g., Silver Plated Base Metal, 34.1 mm. Obv: Crowned
arms with supporters Rev: Multicolor Pope John Paul II kissing
bible Edge: Plain Shape: Square with round corners

Date	Mintage	F12	VF20	XF40	MS60	MS63
2005	—	PF63 16.50				

KM# 126 500 SHILLINGS
18.84 g., Silver Plated Base Metal, 34.1 mm. Obv: Crowned
arms with supporters Rev: Multicolor Pope John Paul II with
flowers Edge: Plain Shape: Square with round corners

Date	Mintage	F12	VF20	XF40	MS60	MS63
2005	—	PF63 20.00				

KM# 128 500 SHILLINGS
18.14 g., Silver Plated Base Metal, 34.1 mm. Obv: Crowned
arms with supporters Rev: Multicolor Pope John Paul II saying
mass Edge: Plain Shape: Square with round corners

Date	Mintage	F12	VF20	XF40	MS60	MS63
2005	—	PF63 16.50				

KM# 130 500 SHILLINGS
18.84 g., Silver Plated Base Metal, 34.1 mm. Obv: Crowned

arms with supporters Rev: Multicolor Pope John Paul II with
cardinals Edge: Plain Shape: Square with round corners

Date	Mintage	F12	VF20	XF40	MS60	MS63
2005	—	PF63 16.50				

KM# 132 500 SHILLINGS
18.84 g., Silver Plated Base Metal, 34.1 mm. Obv: Crowned
arms with supporters Rev: Pope John Paul II with red vestments
Edge: Plain Shape: Square with round corners

Date	Mintage	F12	VF20	XF40	MS60	MS63
2005	—	PF63 16.50				

KM# 134 500 SHILLINGS
18.84 g., Silver Plated Base Metal, 34.1 mm. Obv: Crowned
arms with supporters Rev: Pope John Paul II in white with skull
cap Edge: Plain Shape: Square with round corners

Date	Mintage	F12	VF20	XF40	MS60	MS63
2005	—	PF63 16.50				

KM# 136 500 SHILLINGS
18.84 g., Silver Plated Base Metal, 34.1 mm. Obv: Crowned
arms with supporters Rev: Multicolor Pope John Paul II leaning
head on staff Edge: Plain Shape: Square with round corners

Date	Mintage	F12	VF20	XF40	MS60	MS63
2005	—	PF63 16.50				

KM# 138 500 SHILLINGS
18.84 g., Silver Plated Base Metal, 34.1 mm. Obv: Crowned
arms with supporters Rev: Multicolor Pope John Paul II with
staff facing left Edge: Plain Shape: Square with round corners

Date	Mintage	F12	VF20	XF40	MS60	MS63
2005	—	PF63 16.50				

KM# 140 500 SHILLINGS
18.84 g., Silver Plated Base Metal, 34.1 mm. **Obv:** Crowned arms with supporters **Rev:** Multicolor Pope John Paul II with staff facing half right **Edge:** Plain **Shape:** Square with round corners

Date	Mintage	F12	VF20	XF40	MS60	MS63
2005	—	PF63 16.50				

KM# 181 1000 SHILLINGS
31.11 g., 0.999 Silver 0.9926 oz. ASW, 39 mm. **Obv:** Arms **Rev:** Heard of six elephants, multicolor

Date	Mintage	F12	VF20	XF40	MS60	MS63
2008	—	—	—	—	—	45.00

BULLION COINAGE

KM# 200 20 SHILLINGS
0.62 g., 0.999 Gold AGW, 11 mm. **Rev:** Mother and baby elephant

Date	Mintage	F12	VF20	XF40	MS60	MS63
2007	20,000	PF63 50.00				

KM# 208 20 SHILLINGS
0.62 g., 0.999 Gold AGW

Date	Mintage	F12	VF20	XF40	MS60	MS63
2008	20,000	PF63 50.00				

KM# 217 20 SHILLINGS
0.62 g., 0.999 Gold AGW, 11 mm. **Rev:** Elephant advancing right, sunrise

Date	Mintage	F12	VF20	XF40	MS60	MS63
2009	20,000	PF63 50.00				

KM# 226 20 SHILLINGS
0.62 g., 0.999 Gold AGW, 11 mm. **Rev:** Elephant advacning left, sunrise

Date	Mintage	F12	VF20	XF40	MS60	MS63
2010	20,000	PF63 50.00				

KM# 236 20 SHILLINGS
0.62 g., 0.999 Gold AGW, 11 mm. **Rev:** Mother and baby elephant walking left, sun high up

Date	Mintage	F12	VF20	XF40	MS60	MS63
2011	20,000	PF63 50.00				

KM# 177 25 SHILLINGS
7.78 g., 0.999 Silver 0.2483 oz. ASW

Date	Mintage	F12	VF20	XF40	MS60	MS63
2007	2,000	PF63 15.00				

KM# 205 25 SHILLINGS
7.78 g., 0.999 Silver 0.2483 oz. ASW, 26 mm. **Rev:** Heard of six elephants

Date	Mintage	F12	VF20	XF40	MS60	MS63
2008	2,000	PF63 15.00				

KM# 214 25 SHILLINGS
7.78 g., 0.999 Silver 0.2483 oz. ASW, 26 mm. **Rev:** Elephant advancing right, sunrise

Date	Mintage	F12	VF20	XF40	MS60	MS63
2009	2,000	PF63 15.00				

KM# 223 25 SHILLINGS
7.78 g., 0.999 Silver 0.2483 oz. ASW, 26 mm. **Rev:** Elephant advancing left, sunrise

Date	Mintage	F12	VF20	XF40	MS60	MS63
2010	2,000	PF63 15.00				

KM# 232 25 SHILLINGS
7.78 g., 0.999 Silver 0.2483 oz. ASW, 26 mm. **Rev:** Mother and baby elephant walking left, sun high up

Date	Mintage	F12	VF20	XF40	MS60	MS63
2011	2,000	PF63 15.00				

KM# 178 50 SHILLINGS
15.55 g., 0.999 Silver 0.4962 oz. ASW, 32 mm.

Date	Mintage	F12	VF20	XF40	MS60	MS63
2007	2,000	PF63 30.00				

KM# 206 50 SHILLINGS
15.55 g., 0.999 Silver 0.4962 oz. ASW, 32 mm. **Rev:** Heard of six elephants

Date	Mintage	F12	VF20	XF40	MS60	MS63
2008	—	PF63 30.00				

KM# 209 50 SHILLINGS
1.24 g., 0.999 Gold 0.0396 oz. AGW, 13.92 mm. **Rev:** Heard of six elephants

Date	Mintage	F12	VF20	XF40	MS60	MS63
2008	10,000	PF63 100				

KM# 215 50 SHILLINGS
15.55 g., 0.999 Silver 0.4962 oz. ASW, 32 mm. **Rev:** Elephant advancing right, sunrise

Date	Mintage	F12	VF20	XF40	MS60	MS63
2009	2,000	PF63 30.00				

KM# 218 50 SHILLINGS
1.24 g., 0.999 Gold 0.0396 oz. AGW, 13.92 mm. **Rev:** Elephant advancing right, sunrise

Date	Mintage	F12	VF20	XF40	MS60	MS63
2009	10,000	PF63 100				

KM# 224 50 SHILLINGS
15.55 g., 0.999 Silver 0.4962 oz. ASW, 32 mm. **Rev:** Elephant advacning left, sunrise

Date	Mintage	F12	VF20	XF40	MS60	MS63
2010	2,000	PF63 30.00				

KM# 227 50 SHILLINGS
1.24 g., 0.999 Gold 0.0396 oz. AGW, 13.92 mm. **Rev:** Elephant advancing left, sunrise

Date	Mintage	F12	VF20	XF40	MS60	MS63
2010	10,000	PF63 100				

KM# 233 50 SHILLINGS
15.55 g., 0.999 Silver 0.4962 oz. ASW, 32 mm. **Rev:** Mother and baby elephant walking left, sun high up

Date	Mintage	F12	VF20	XF40	MS60	MS63
2011	2,000	PF63 30.00				

KM# 237 50 SHILLINGS
1.24 g., 0.999 Gold 0.0396 oz. AGW, 13.92 mm. **Rev:** Mother and baby elephant walking left, sun high up

Date	Mintage	F12	VF20	XF40	MS60	MS63
2011	10,000	PF63 100				

KM# 182a 100 SHILLINGS
31.11 g., 0.999 Silver 0.9926 oz. ASW, 39 mm. **Rev:** Mother and baby elephant, partially gilt

Date	Mintage	F12	VF20	XF40	MS60	MS63
2007	3,000	—	—	—	—	50.00

KM# 182 100 SHILLINGS
31.11 g., 0.999 Silver 0.9926 oz. ASW, 39 mm. **Obv:** Arms
Rev: Mom and baby elephant

Date	Mintage	F12	VF20	XF40	MS60	MS63
2007	20,000	—	—	—	—	45.00
2007	5,000	PF63 55.00				

KM# 180 100 SHILLINGS
31.11 g., 0.999 Silver 0.9926 oz. ASW, 39 mm. **Rev:** Mother
and baby elephant, colored

Date	Mintage	F12	VF20	XF40	MS60	MS63
2007	5,000	—	—	—	—	50.00

KM# 203a 100 SHILLINGS
31.11 g., 0.999 Silver 0.9926 oz. ASW, 39 mm. **Obv:** Arms
Rev: Heard of six elephants

Date	Mintage	F12	VF20	XF40	MS60	MS63
2008	5,000	—	—	—	—	35.00

KM# 204 100 SHILLINGS
31.11 g., 0.999 Silver 0.9926 oz. ASW, 39 mm. **Rev:** Heard of
six elephants, multicolored

Date	Mintage	F12	VF20	XF40	MS60	MS63
2008	5,000	—	—	—	—	50.00

KM# 203 100 SHILLINGS
31.11 g., 0.999 Silver 0.9926 oz. ASW, 39 mm. **Rev:** Heard
of six elephants

Date	Mintage	F12	VF20	XF40	MS60	MS63
2008	5,000	PF63 55.00				
2008	20,000	—	—	—	—	35.00

KM# 212a 100 SHILLINGS
31.11 g., 0.999 Silver 0.9926 oz. ASW

Date	Mintage	F12	VF20	XF40	MS60	MS63
2009	5,000	—	—	—	—	55.00

KM# 213 100 SHILLINGS
31.11 g., 0.999 Silver 0.9926 oz. ASW, 39 mm. **Rev:** Elephant
advancing right, sunrise, multicolor

Date	Mintage	F12	VF20	XF40	MS60	MS63
2009	5,000	—	—	—	—	55.00

KM# 212 100 SHILLINGS
31.11 g., 0.999 Silver 0.9926 oz. ASW, 39 mm. **Rev:** Elephant
advancing right, sunrise

Date	Mintage	F12	VF20	XF40	MS60	MS63
2009	5,000	PF63 55.00				
2009		—	—	—	—	50.00

KM# 221a 100 SHILLINGS
31.11 g., 0.999 Silver 0.9926 oz. ASW

Date	Mintage	F12	VF20	XF40	MS60	MS63
2010	5,000	—	—	—	—	55.00

KM# 222 100 SHILLINGS
31.11 g., 0.999 Silver 0.9926 oz. ASW, 39 mm. **Rev:** Elephant
advacning left, sunrise, multicolor

Date	Mintage	F12	VF20	XF40	MS60	MS63
2010	5,000	—	—	—	—	55.00

KM# 221 100 SHILLINGS
31.11 g., 0.999 Silver 0.9926 oz. ASW, 39 mm. **Rev:** Elephant
advacning left, sunrise

Date	Mintage	F12	VF20	XF40	MS60	MS63
2010	5,000	PF63 55.00				
2010		—	—	—	—	50.00

KM# 230a 100 SHILLINGS
31.11 g., 0.999 Silver 0.9926 oz. ASW

Date	Mintage	F12	VF20	XF40	MS60	MS63
2011	5,000	—	—	—	—	55.00

KM# 230 100 SHILLINGS
31.11 g., 0.999 Silver 0.9926 oz. ASW, 39 mm. **Rev:** Mother
and baby elephant walking left, sun high up

Date	Mintage	F12	VF20	XF40	MS60	MS63
2011		—	—	—	—	50.00
2011	5,000	PF63 55.00				

KM# 231 100 SHILLINGS
31.11 g., 0.999 Silver 0.9926 oz. ASW, 39 mm. **Rev:** Mother
and baby elephant walking left, sun high up, multicolor

Date	Mintage	F12	VF20	XF40	MS60	MS63
2011	5,000	—	—	—	—	55.00

KM# 188 200 SHILLINGS
0.62 g., 0.999 Gold AGW

Date	Mintage	F12	VF20	XF40	MS60	MS63
2004		PF63 45.00				

KM# 194 200 SHILLINGS
0.62 g., 0.999 Gold AGW

Date	Mintage	F12	VF20	XF40	MS60	MS63
2005	20,000	PF63 45.00				

KM# 179 200 SHILLINGS
62.20 g., 0.999 Silver 1.9849 oz. ASW, 50 mm.

Date	Mintage	F12	VF20	XF40	MS60	MS63
2007	—	PF63 100				

KM# 207 200 SHILLINGS
62.20 g., 0.999 Silver 1.9849 oz. ASW, 50 mm. **Rev:** Heard of six elephants

Date	Mintage	F12	VF20	XF40	MS60	MS63
2008	2,000	PF63 100				

KM# 216 200 SHILLINGS
62.20 g., 0.999 Silver 1.9849 oz. ASW, 50 mm. **Rev:** Elephant advancing right, sunrise

Date	Mintage	F12	VF20	XF40	MS60	MS63
2009	2,000	PF63 100				

KM# 225 200 SHILLINGS
62.20 g., 0.999 Silver 1.9849 oz. ASW, 50 mm. **Rev:** Elephant advacning left, sunrise

Date	Mintage	F12	VF20	XF40	MS60	MS63
2010	2,000	PF63 100				

KM# 234 200 SHILLINGS
62.20 g., 0.999 Silver 1.9849 oz. ASW, 50 mm. **Rev:** Mother and baby elephant walking left, sun high up

Date	Mintage	F12	VF20	XF40	MS60	MS63
2011	2,000	PF63 100				

KM# 185 250 SHILLINGS
7.78 g., 0.999 Silver 0.2483 oz. ASW

Date	Mintage	F12	VF20	XF40	MS60	MS63
2004	2,000	PF63 15.00				

KM# 191 250 SHILLINGS
7.78 g., 0.999 Silver 0.2483 oz. ASW

Date	Mintage	F12	VF20	XF40	MS60	MS63
2005	2,000	PF63 15.00				

KM# 197 250 SHILLINGS
7.78 g., 0.999 Silver 0.2483 oz. ASW

Date	Mintage	F12	VF20	XF40	MS60	MS63
2006	2,000	PF63 15.00				

KM# 186 500 SHILLINGS
15.55 g., 0.999 Silver 0.4962 oz. ASW, 32 mm. **Rev:** Elefant facing forward

Date	Mintage	F12	VF20	XF40	MS60	MS63
2004	2,000	PF63 30.00				

KM# 192 500 SHILLINGS
15.55 g., 0.999 Silver 0.4962 oz. ASW

Date	Mintage	F12	VF20	XF40	MS60	MS63
2005	—	PF63 30.00				

KM# 198 500 SHILLINGS
15.55 g., 0.999 Silver 0.4962 oz. ASW

Date	Mintage	F12	VF20	XF40	MS60	MS63
2006	2,000	PF63 30.00				

KM# 183a 1000 SHILLINGS
31.27 g., 0.999 Silver 0.9979 oz. ASW, 38.54 mm. **Series:** African Wildlife **Obv:** National arms **Obv. Legend:** SOMALI REPUBLIC **Rev:** Elephant standing facing - gilt **Edge:** Reeded

Date	Mintage	F12	VF20	XF40	MS60	MS63
2004	—	—	—	—	—	55.00

KM# 184 1000 SHILLINGS
31.11 g., 0.999 Silver 0.9926 oz. ASW, 39 mm. **Rev:** Elephant facing forward, colored

Date	Mintage	F12	VF20	XF40	MS60	MS63
2004	5,000	—	—	—	—	55.00

KM# 183 1000 SHILLINGS
31.11 g., 0.999 Silver 0.9926 oz. ASW

Date	Mintage	F12	VF20	XF40	MS60	MS63
2004	5,000	PF63 55.00				
2004	20,000	—	—	—	—	50.00

KM# 189a 1000 SHILLINGS
31.11 g., 0.999 Silver 0.9926 oz. ASW, 39 mm. **Rev:** Elephant profile left thrumpanting, partially gilt

Date	Mintage	F12	VF20	XF40	MS60	MS63
2005	3,000	—	—	—	—	55.00

KM# 190 1000 SHILLINGS
31.11 g., 0.999 Silver 0.9926 oz. ASW, 39 mm. **Obv:** Arms **Rev:** Elephant profile left thrumpanting, multicolor

Date	Mintage	F12	VF20	XF40	MS60	MS63
2005	5,000	—	—	—	—	45.00

KM# 189 1000 SHILLINGS
31.11 g., 0.999 Silver 0.9926 oz. ASW, 39 mm. **Rev:** Elephant profile left thrumpanting

Date	Mintage	F12	VF20	XF40	MS60	MS63
2005	5,000	PF63 55.00				
2005	20,000	—	—	—	—	50.00

KM# 195a 1000 SHILLINGS
31.11 g., 0.999 Silver 0.9926 oz. ASW, 39 mm. **Rev:** Elephant, mountain, partially gilt

Date	Mintage	F12	VF20	XF40	MS60	MS63
2006	3,000	—	—	—	—	55.00

KM# 196 1000 SHILLINGS
31.11 g., 0.999 Silver 0.9926 oz. ASW, 39 mm. **Obv:** Arms **Rev:** Elephant, mountian in background. Multicolor

Date	Mintage	F12	VF20	XF40	MS60	MS63
2006	5,000	—	—	—	—	45.00

KM# 195 1000 SHILLINGS
31.11 g., 0.999 Silver 0.9926 oz. ASW, 38 mm. **Obv:** Arms
Rev: Elephant and mountain

Date	Mintage	F12	VF20	XF40	MS60	MS63
2006	5,000	PF63 55.00				
2006	20,000	—	—	—	—	45.00

KM# 228 1000 SHILLINGS
31.11 g., 0.999 Gold 0.9926 oz. AGW, 38.6 mm. **Rev:** Elephant advacning left, sunrise

Date	Mintage	F12	VF20	XF40	MS60	MS63
2010	—	—	—	—	—	1,850

KM# 238 1000 SHILLINGS
31.11 g., 0.999 Gold 0.9926 oz. AGW, 38.6 mm. **Rev:** Mother and baby elephant walking left, sun high up

Date	Mintage	F12	VF20	XF40	MS60	MS63
2011	—	—	—	—	—	1,850

KM# 201 1500 SHILLINGS
155.50 g., 0.999 Gold 4.9623 oz. AGW, 65 mm. **Rev:** Mother and baby elephant

Date	Mintage	F12	VF20	XF40	MS60	MS63
2007	99	PF65 9,250				

KM# 210 1500 SHILLINGS
155.50 g., 0.999 Gold 4.9623 oz. AGW, 65 mm. **Rev:** Heard of six elephants

Date	Mintage	F12	VF20	XF40	MS60	MS63
2008	99	PF65 9,250				

KM# 219 1500 SHILLINGS
155.50 g., 0.999 Gold 4.9623 oz. AGW, 65 mm. **Rev:** Elephant advancing right, sunrise

Date	Mintage	F12	VF20	XF40	MS60	MS63
2009	99	PF65 9,250				

KM# 229 1500 SHILLINGS
155.50 g., 0.999 Gold 4.9623 oz. AGW, 65 mm. **Rev:** Elephant advancing left, sunrise

Date	Mintage	F12	VF20	XF40	MS60	MS63
2010	99	PF65 9,250				

KM# 239 1500 SHILLINGS
155.50 g., 0.999 Gold 4.9623 oz. AGW, 65 mm. **Rev:** Mother and baby elephant walking left, sun high up

Date	Mintage	F12	VF20	XF40	MS60	MS63
2011	99	PF65 9,250				

KM# 187 2000 SHILLINGS
62.20 g., 0.999 Silver 1.9849 oz. ASW, 50 mm. **Rev:** Elephant facing forward

Date	Mintage	F12	VF20	XF40	MS60	MS63
2004	2,000	PF63 100	PF65 120			

KM# 193 2000 SHILLINGS
62.20 g., 0.999 Silver 1.9849 oz. ASW

Date	Mintage	F12	VF20	XF40	MS60	MS63
2005	2,000	PF63 100	PF65 120			

KM# 199 2000 SHILLINGS
62.20 g., 0.999 Silver 1.9849 oz. ASW

Date	Mintage	F12	VF20	XF40	MS60	MS63
2006	2,000	PF63 100	PF65 120			

KM# 235 2000 SHILLINGS
1000.00 g., 0.999 Silver 31.9118 oz. ASW, 100 mm. **Rev:** Mother and baby elephant walking left, sun high up

Date	Mintage	F12	VF20	XF40	MS60	MS63
2011	—	—	—	—	—	1,700

KM# 202 5000 SHILLINGS
1000.00 g., 0.999 Gold 31.9118 oz. AGW

Date	Mintage	F12	VF20	XF40	MS60	MS63
2007	50	PF65 57,000				

KM# 211 5000 SHILLINGS
1000.00 g., 0.999 Gold 31.9118 oz. AGW

Date	Mintage	F12	VF20	XF40	MS60	MS63
2008	50	PF65 57,000				

KM# 220 5000 SHILLINGS
1000.00 g., 0.999 Gold 31.9118 oz. AGW **Rev:** Elephant advancing right, sunrise

Date	Mintage	F12	VF20	XF40	MS60	MS63
2009	50	PF65 57,000				

SOMALILAND

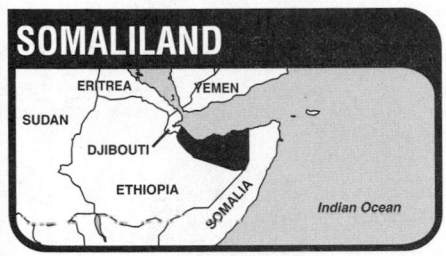

The Somaliland Republic consists of the former British Somaliland Protectorate and is located on the coast of the northeastern projection of the African continent commonly referred to as the "Horn" on the southwestern end of the Gulf of Aden. Bordered by Ethiopia to the west and south and Somalia to the east. It has an area of 68,000* sq. mi. (176,000* sq. km). Capital: Hargeysa. It is mostly arid and mountainous except for the gulf shoreline.

The northern Somali National Movement (SNM) declared a secession of the Somaliland Republic on May 17, 1991, which is not recognized by the Somali Democratic Republic.

REPUBLIC
SHILLING COINAGE

KM# 4 5 SHILLINGS
1.45 g., Aluminum, 21.9 mm. **Obv:** Value **Rev:** Bust of Sir Richard F. Burton - explorer, divides dates **Edge:** Plain

Date	Mintage	F12	VF20	XF40	MS60	MS63
2002	—	—	—	—	1.25	1.50

KM# 5 5 SHILLINGS
1.45 g., Aluminum, 21.9 mm. **Obv:** Value **Rev:** Rooster **Edge:** Plain

Date	Mintage	F12	VF20	XF40	MS60	MS63
2002	—	—	—	—	1.00	1.25

KM# 19 5 SHILLINGS
1.24 g., Aluminum, 22 mm. **Obv:** Elephant with calf walking right **Obv. Legend:** REPUBLIC OF SOMALILAND **Rev:** Value

Rev. Legend: BAANKA SOMALILAND **Edge:** Plain

Date	Mintage	F12	VF20	XF40	MS60	MS63
2005	—	—	—	—	1.25	1.50

KM# 3 10 SHILLINGS
3.51 g., Brass, 17.7 mm. **Obv:** Vervet Monkey **Rev:** Value **Edge:** Plain

Date	Mintage	F12	VF20	XF40	MS60	MS63
2002	—	—	—	—	0.65	1.25

KM# 7 10 SHILLINGS
4.80 g., Stainless Steel, 24.9 mm. **Obv:** Value **Rev:** Aquarius the water carrier **Edge:** Plain

Date	Mintage	F12	VF20	XF40	MS60	MS63
2006	—	—	—	—	1.00	1.25

KM# 8 10 SHILLINGS
4.80 g., Stainless Steel, 24.9 mm. **Obv:** Value **Rev:** Pisces the two fish **Edge:** Plain

Date	Mintage	F12	VF20	XF40	MS60	MS63
2006	—	—	—	—	1.00	1.25

KM# 9 10 SHILLINGS
4.80 g., Stainless Steel, 24.9 mm. **Obv:** Value **Rev:** Aries the ram **Edge:** Plain

Date	Mintage	F12	VF20	XF40	MS60	MS63
2006	—	—	—	—	1.00	1.25

KM# 10 10 SHILLINGS
4.80 g., Stainless Steel, 24.9 mm. **Obv:** Value **Rev:** Taurus the bull **Edge:** Plain

Date	Mintage	F12	VF20	XF40	MS60	MS63
2006	—	—	—	—	1.00	1.25

KM# 11 10 SHILLINGS
4.80 g., Stainless Steel, 24.9 mm. **Obv:** Value **Rev:** Gemini twins **Edge:** Plain

Date	Mintage	F12	VF20	XF40	MS60	MS63
2006	—	—	—	—	1.00	1.25

KM# 12 10 SHILLINGS
4.80 g., Stainless Steel, 24.9 mm. **Obv:** Value **Rev:** Cancer the crab **Edge:** Plain

Date	Mintage	F12	VF20	XF40	MS60	MS63
2006	—	—	—	—	1.00	1.25

KM# 13 10 SHILLINGS
4.80 g., Stainless Steel, 24.9 mm. **Obv:** Value **Rev:** Leo the lion **Edge:** Plain

Date	Mintage	F12	VF20	XF40	MS60	MS63
2006	—	—	—	—	1.00	1.25

KM# 14 10 SHILLINGS
4.80 g., Stainless Steel, 24.9 mm. **Obv:** Value **Rev:** Virgo as a winged woman **Edge:** Plain

Date	Mintage	F12	VF20	XF40	MS60	MS63
2006	—	—	—	—	1.00	1.25

KM# 15 10 SHILLINGS
4.80 g., Stainless Steel, 24.9 mm. **Obv:** Value **Rev:** Libra balance scale **Edge:** Plain

Date	Mintage	F12	VF20	XF40	MS60	MS63
2006	—	—	—	—	1.00	1.25

KM# 16 10 SHILLINGS
4.80 g., Stainless Steel, 24.9 mm. **Obv:** Value **Rev:** Scorpio the scorpion **Edge:** Plain

Date	Mintage	F12	VF20	XF40	MS60	MS63
2006	—	—	—	—	1.00	1.25

KM# 17 10 SHILLINGS
4.80 g., Stainless Steel, 24.9 mm. **Obv:** Value **Rev:** Sagittarius the archer **Edge:** Plain

Date	Mintage	F12	VF20	XF40	MS60	MS63
2006	—	—	—	—	1.00	1.25

KM# 18 10 SHILLINGS
4.80 g., Stainless Steel, 24.9 mm. **Obv:** Value **Rev:** Capricorn the goat **Edge:** Plain

Date	Mintage	F12	VF20	XF40	MS60	MS63
2006	—	—	—	—	1.00	1.25

KM# 6 20 SHILLINGS
3.87 g., Stainless Steel, 21.8 mm. **Obv:** Value **Rev:** Greyhound dog **Edge:** Plain

Date	Mintage	F12	VF20	XF40	MS60	MS63
2002	—	—	—	—	1.00	1.50

KM# 2 1000 SHILLINGS
31.27 g., 0.999 Silver 0.9979 oz. ASW, 38.8 mm. **Obv:** Crowned arms with supporters **Rev:** Bust with hat 3/4 right **Edge:** Reeded

Date	Mintage	F12	VF20	XF40	MS60	MS63
2002	—	—	—	—	45.00	50.00

SOUTH AFRICA

The Republic of South Africa, located at the southern tip of Africa, has an area of 471,445 sq. mi. (1,221,043 sq. km.) and a population of *30.2 million. Capitals: Administrative, Pretoria; Legislative, Cape Town; Judicial, Bloemfontein. Manufacturing, mining and agriculture are the principal industries. Exports include wool, diamonds, gold, and metallic ores.

The apartheid era ended April 27, 1994 with the first democratic election for all people of South Africa. Nelson Mandela was inaugurated President May 10, 1994, and South Africa was readmitted into the Commonwealth of Nations.

South African coins and currency bear inscriptions in tribal languages, Afrikaans and English.

MONETARY SYSTEM
100 Cents = 1 Rand

MINT MARKS
GRC + paw print = Gold Reef City Mint

REPUBLIC
STANDARD COINAGE
100 Cents = 1 Rand

KM# 221 CENT
1.50 g., Copper Plated Steel, 15 mm. **Obv:** New national arms **Obv. Legend:** ISEWULA AFRIKA **Rev:** Value divides two sparrows **Edge:** Plain

Date	Mintage	F12	VF20	XF40	MS60	MS63
2001	—	—	—	0.15	0.35	0.50
2001	3,678	PF63 5.00				

KM# 222 2 CENTS
3.00 g., Copper Plated Steel, 18 mm. **Obv:** New national arms **Obv. Legend:** AFURIKA TSHIPEMBE **Rev:** Eagle with fish in talons divides value **Edge:** Plain

Date	Mintage	F12	VF20	XF40	MS60	MS63
2001	—	—	—	—	0.50	0.75
2001	3,678	PF63 6.00				

KM# 556 2-1/2 CENTS
1.41 g., 0.925 Silver 0.0418 oz. ASW, 16.3 mm. **Obv:** Protea flower **Rev:** Railway train facing

Date	Mintage	F12	VF20	XF40	MS60	MS63
2012	Est. 1700	PF65 30.00				

KM# 223 5 CENTS
4.42 g., Copper Plated Steel, 21 mm. **Obv:** New national arms **Obv. Legend:** AFRIKA DZONGA **Rev:** Value and Blue crane **Edge:** Plain

Date	Mintage	F12	VF20	XF40	MS60	MS63
2001	—	—	0.10	0.25	0.65	1.00
2001	—	PF63 5.00				

KM# 268 5 CENTS
4.50 g., Copper Plated Steel, 21 mm. **Obv:** New national arms **Obv. Legend:** Ningizimu Afrika **Rev:** Value and Blue crane **Edge:** Plain

Date	Mintage	F12	VF20	XF40	MS60	MS63
2002	—	—	—	0.30	0.75	1.00
2002	3,250	PF63 5.00				

KM# 324 5 CENTS
4.50 g., Copper Plated Steel, 21 mm. **Obv:** New national arms **Obv. Legend:** Afrika Dzonga **Rev:** Blue crane and denomination **Edge:** Plain

Date	Mintage	F12	VF20	XF40	MS60	MS63
2003	—	—	—	0.30	0.75	1.00
2003	2,909	PF63 5.00				

KM# 325 5 CENTS
4.50 g., Copper Plated Steel, 21 mm. **Obv:** New national arms

Obv. Legend: South Africa **Rev:** Value and Blue crane **Edge:** Plain

Date	Mintage	F12	VF20	XF40	MS60	MS63
2004	—	—	—	0.20	0.50	0.75
2004	1,935	PF63 5.00				

KM# 291 5 CENTS
4.50 g., Copper Plated Steel, 21 mm. **Obv:** New national arms **Obv. Legend:** Aforika Borwa **Rev:** Value and Blue crane **Edge:** Plain

Date	Mintage	F12	VF20	XF40	MS60	MS63
2005	—	—	—	0.20	0.50	0.75
2005	—	PF63 5.00				

KM# 486 5 CENTS
4.50 g., Copper Plated Steel, 21 mm. **Obv:** New National arms **Obv. Legend:** Afrika Borwa **Rev:** Blue crane and value

Date	Mintage	F12	VF20	XF40	MS60	MS63
2006	—	—	—	—	0.50	0.75
2006	—	PF63 5.00				

KM# 340 5 CENTS
4.51 g., Copper Plated Steel, 21 mm. **Obv:** New national arms **Obv. Legend:** Suid- Afrika **Rev:** Value at left, Blue Crane at right **Edge:** Plain

Date	Mintage	F12	VF20	XF40	MS60	MS63
2007	—	—	—	0.20	0.50	0.75
2007	—	PF63 5.00				

KM# 440 5 CENTS
4.50 g., Copper Plated Steel, 21 mm. **Obv:** New National arms **Obv. Legend:** uMzantsi Afrika **Rev:** Blue crane and value

Date	Mintage	F12	VF20	XF40	MS60	MS63
2008	—	—	—	—	0.75	1.00
2008	—	PF63 5.00				

KM# 464 5 CENTS
4.50 g., Copper Plated Steel, 21 mm. **Obv:** National arms **Rev:** Value and Blue crane

Date	Mintage	F12	VF20	XF40	MS60	MS63
2009	—	—	—	—	0.50	0.75
2009	—	PF63 5.00				

KM# 493 5 CENTS
4.50 g., Copper Plated Steel, 21 mm. **Obv:** National arms **Rev:** Value and Blue crane

Date	Mintage	F12	VF20	XF40	MS60	MS63
2010	—	—	—	—	0.75	1.00
2010	—	PF63 5.00				

KM# 500 5 CENTS
4.50 g., Copper Plated Steel, 21 mm. **Obv:** National arms **Rev:** Blue crane and value

Date	Mintage	F12	VF20	XF40	MS60	MS63
2011	—			0.75		1.00
2011		PF63 5.00				

KM# 224 10 CENTS
2.00 g., Bronze Plated Steel, 16 mm. **Obv:** New national arms **Obv. Legend:** AFRIKA DZONGA **Rev:** Arum Lily and value **Edge:** Reeded

Date	Mintage	F12	VF20	XF40	MS60	MS63
2001	—		0.30	0.60		1.00
2001	3,678	PF63 6.00				

KM# 269 10 CENTS
2.00 g., Bronze Plated Steel, 16 mm. **Obv:** New national arms **Obv. Legend:** Afrika Dzonga **Rev:** Arum Lily and value **Edge:** Reeded

Date	Mintage	F12	VF20	XF40	MS60	MS63
2002	—			0.30	0.75	1.00
2002	3,250	PF63 6.00				

KM# 347 10 CENTS
2.00 g., Bronze Plated Steel, 16 mm. **Obv:** New national arms **Obv. Legend:** South Africa **Rev:** Arum lily and value **Edge:** Reeded

Date	Mintage	F12	VF20	XF40	MS60	MS63
2003	—			0.30	0.75	1.00
2003	2,909	PF63 6.00				

KM# 326 10 CENTS
2.00 g., Bronze Plated Steel, 16 mm. **Obv:** New national arms **Obv. Legend:** Aforika Borwa **Rev:** Arum lily and value **Edge:** Reeded

Date	Mintage	F12	VF20	XF40	MS60	MS63
2004	—			0.30	0.75	1.00
2004	1,935	PF63 6.00				

KM# 292 10 CENTS
2.00 g., Bronze Plated Steel, 16 mm. **Obv:** New national arms **Obv. Legend:** Afrika Borwa **Rev:** Arum Lily and value **Edge:** Reeded

Date	Mintage	F12	VF20	XF40	MS60	MS63
2005	—			0.30	0.75	1.00
2005		PF63 6.00				

KM# 487 10 CENTS
2.00 g., Bronze Plated Steel, 16 mm. **Obv:** National arms **Obv. Legend:** Suid-Afrika **Rev:** Arum lily and value **Edge:** Reeded

Date	Mintage	F12	VF20	XF40	MS60	MS63
2006	—				0.75	1.00
2006		PF63 6.00				

KM# 341 10 CENTS
2.00 g., Bronze Plated Steel, 16 mm. **Obv:** New national arms **Obv. Legend:** uMzantsi - Afrika **Rev:** Alum lily and value **Edge:** Reeded

Date	Mintage	F12	VF20	XF40	MS60	MS63
2007	—			0.30	0.75	1.00
2007		PF63 6.00				

KM# 441 10 CENTS
2.00 g., Bronze Plated Steel, 16 mm. **Obv:** National arms **Obv. Legend:** iNingizimu Afrika **Rev:** Arum lily and value **Edge:** Reeded

Date	Mintage	F12	VF20	XF40	MS60	MS63
2008	—				0.75	1.00
2008		PF63 8.00				

KM# 465 10 CENTS
2.00 g., Copper Plated Steel, 16 mm. **Obv:** National arms **Rev:** Arum lily and value

Date	Mintage	F12	VF20	XF40	MS60	MS63
2009	—				0.75	1.00
2009		PF63 8.00				

KM# 494 10 CENTS
2.00 g., Bronze Plated Steel, 16 mm. **Obv:** National arms **Rev:** Arum Lily and value

Date	Mintage	F12	VF20	XF40	MS60	MS63
2010	—				0.90	1.20
2010		PF63 7.00				

KM# 501 10 CENTS
2.00 g., Bronze Plated Steel, 16 mm. **Obv:** National arms **Rev:** Arum lily and value

Date	Mintage	F12	VF20	XF40	MS60	MS63
2011	—				0.75	1.00
2011		PF63 6.00				

KM# 225 20 CENTS
3.50 g., Bronze Plated Steel, 19 mm. **Obv:** New national arms **Obv. Legend:** AFRIKA BORWA **Rev:** Protea flower and value **Edge:** Reeded

Date	Mintage	F12	VF20	XF40	MS60	MS63
2001	—			0.35	0.90	1.20
2001	3,678	PF63 7.00				

KM# 270 20 CENTS
3.50 g., Bronze Plated Steel, 19 mm. **Obv:** New national arms **Obv. Legend:** South Africa **Rev:** Protea flower and value **Edge:** Reeded

Date	Mintage	F12	VF20	XF40	MS60	MS63
2002	—			0.35	0.90	1.20
2002	3,250	PF63 7.00				

KM# 327 20 CENTS
3.50 g., Bronze Plated Steel, 19 mm. **Obv:** New national arms **Obv. Legend:** Aforika Borwa **Rev:** Protea flower and value **Edge:** Reeded

Date	Mintage	F12	VF20	XF40	MS60	MS63
2003	—			0.35	0.90	1.20
2003	2,909	PF63 7.00				

KM# 328 20 CENTS
3.50 g., Bronze Plated Steel, 19 mm. **Obv:** New national arms **Obv. Legend:** Afrika Borwa **Rev:** Protea flower and value **Edge:** Reeded

Date	Mintage	F12	VF20	XF40	MS60	MS63
2004	—			0.35	0.90	1.20
2004	1,935	PF63 7.00				

KM# 293 20 CENTS
3.50 g., Bronze Plated Steel, 19 mm. **Obv:** New national arms **Obv. Legend:** Suid-Afrika **Rev:** Protea flower and value **Edge:** Reeded **Shape:** Round

Date	Mintage	F12	VF20	XF40	MS60	MS63
2005	—			0.35	0.90	1.20
2005	—	PF63 7.00				

KM# 488 20 CENTS
3.50 g., Bronze Plated Steel, 19 mm. **Obv:** National arms **Obv. Legend:** uMzantsi Afrika **Rev:** Protea flower and value **Edge:** Reeded

Date	Mintage	F12	VF20	XF40	MS60	MS63
2006	—				0.90	1.20
2006	—	PF63 7.00				

KM# 342 20 CENTS
3.50 g., Bronze Plated Steel, 19 mm. **Obv:** New national arms **Obv. Legend:** iNingizimu Afrika **Rev:** Protea flower and value **Edge:** Reeded

Date	Mintage	F12	VF20	XF40	MS60	MS63
2007	—			0.35	0.90	1.20
2007	—	PF63 7.00				

KM# 442 20 CENTS
3.50 g., Bronze Plated Steel, 19 mm. **Obv:** National arms **Rev:** Protea flower and value **Edge:** Reeded

Date	Mintage	F12	VF20	XF40	MS60	MS63
2008	—				0.90	1.20
2008	—	PF63 7.00				

KM# 466 20 CENTS
3.50 g., Bronze Plated Steel, 19 mm. **Obv:** National arms **Rev:** Protea flower and value

Date	Mintage	F12	VF20	XF40	MS60	MS63
2009	—				0.90	1.20
2009	—	PF63 7.00				

KM# 495 20 CENTS
3.50 g., Bronze Plated Steel, 19 mm. **Obv:** National arms **Rev:** Protea flower and vlaue

Date	Mintage	F12	VF20	XF40	MS60	MS63
2010	—	PF63 7.00				
2010	—				0.90	1.50

KM# 502 20 CENTS
3.50 g., Bronze Plated Steel, 19 mm. **Obv:** National arms **Rev:** Protea flower and value

Date	Mintage	F12	VF20	XF40	MS60	MS63
2011	—				0.90	1.20
2011	—	PF63 7.00				

KM# 226 50 CENTS
5.00 g., Bronze Plated Steel, 22 mm. **Obv:** New national arms **Obv. Legend:** AFERIKA BORWA **Rev:** Strelitzia plant, value **Edge:** Reeded

Date	Mintage	F12	VF20	XF40	MS60	MS63
2001	1,152,000	—	—	0.50	1.20	1.60
2001	3,678	PF63 8.00				

KM# 271 50 CENTS
5.00 g., Bronze Plated Steel, 22 mm. **Obv:** New national arms **Obv. Legend:** Aforika Borwa **Rev:** Strelitzia plant **Edge:** Reeded

Date	Mintage	F12	VF20	XF40	MS60	MS63
2002	3,250	PF63 8.00				
2002	16,000,000	—	—	0.50	1.20	1.60

KM# 287 50 CENTS
5.00 g., Bronze Plated Steel, 22 mm. **Obv:** New national arms **Obv. Legend:** Aforika - Borwa **Rev:** Soccer player and value **Edge:** Reeded

Date	Mintage	F12	VF20	XF40	MS60	MS63
2002	—				9.00	12.00

KM# 276 50 CENTS
5.00 g., Bronze Plated Steel, 22 mm. **Obv:** New national arms **Obv. Legend:** Afrika - Borwa **Rev:** Cricket player diving towards the wicket, value below **Edge:** Reeded

Date	Mintage	F12	VF20	XF40	MS60	MS63
2003	11,749	—	—	—	9.00	12.00

KM# 329 50 CENTS
5.00 g., Bronze Plated Steel, 22 mm. **Obv:** New national arms **Obv. Legend:** Aforika Borwa **Rev:** Cricket player diving towards the wicket **Edge:** Reeded

Date	Mintage	F12	VF20	XF40	MS60	MS63
2003	—				9.00	12.00
2003	—	PF63 15.00				

KM# 330 50 CENTS
5.00 g., Bronze Plated Steel, 22 mm. **Obv:** New national arms **Obv. Legend:** Afrika Borwa **Rev:** Strelitzia plant, value **Edge:** Reeded

Date	Mintage	F12	VF20	XF40	MS60	MS63
2003	—	—	—	0.50	1.60	1.20
2003	2,909	PF63 8.00				

KM# 331 50 CENTS
5.00 g., Bronze Plated Steel, 22 mm. **Obv:** New national arms **Obv. Legend:** Suid Afrika **Rev:** Strelitzia plant, value **Edge:** Reeded

Date	Mintage	F12	VF20	XF40	MS60	MS63
2004	—	—	—	0.50	1.20	1.60
2004	1,935	PF63 8.00				

KM# 294 50 CENTS
5.00 g., Bronze Plated Steel, 22 mm. **Obv:** New national arms **Obv. Legend:** uMzantsi Afrika **Rev:** Strelitzia plant, value **Edge:** Reeded

Date	Mintage	F12	VF20	XF40	MS60	MS63
2005	—	—	—	0.50	1.20	1.60
2005	—	PF63 8.00				

KM# 489 50 CENTS
5.00 g., Bronze Plated Steel, 22 mm. **Obv:** National arms **Obv. Legend:** iNingizimu Afrika **Rev:** Strelitzia plant and value **Edge:** Reeded

Date	Mintage	F12	VF20	XF40	MS60	MS63
2006	—	—	—	—	1.20	1.60
2006	—	PF63 8.00				

KM# 343 50 CENTS
5.00 g., Bronze Plated Steel, 22 mm. **Obv:** National arms **Obv. Legend:** iSewula Afrika **Rev:** Strelitzia plant and value **Edge:** Reeded

Date	Mintage	F12	VF20	XF40	MS60	MS63
2007	—	—	—	—	1.20	1.60
2007	—	PF63 8.00				

KM# 443 50 CENTS
5.00 g., Bronze Plated Steel, 22 mm. **Obv:** National arms **Obv. Legend:** Afurika Tshipembe **Rev:** Strelitzia plant and value **Edge:** Reeded

Date	Mintage	F12	VF20	XF40	MS60	MS63
2008	—	—	—	—	1.20	1.60
2008	—	PF63 8.00				

KM# 467 50 CENTS
5.00 g., Bronze Plated Steel, 22 mm. **Obv:** National arms **Rev:** Strelitzia plant

Date	Mintage	F12	VF20	XF40	MS60	MS63
2009	—	—	—	—	1.20	1.60
2009	—	PF63 8.00				

KM# 496 50 CENTS
5.00 g., Bronze Plated Steel, 22 mm. **Obv:** National arms **Rev:** Strelitzia plant

Date	Mintage	F12	VF20	XF40	MS60	MS63
2010	—	—	—	—	1.20	1.60
2010	—	PF63 8.00				

KM# 503 50 CENTS
5.00 g., Bronze Plated Steel, 22 mm. **Obv:** National arms **Rev:** Strelitzia plant and value

Date	Mintage	F12	VF20	XF40	MS60	MS63
2011	—	—	—	—	1.20	1.60
2011	—	PF63 10.00				

KM# 554 50 CENTS
5.00 g., Bronze Plated Steel, 22 mm. **Obv:** National arms **Obv. Legend:** Afrika Dzonga Ningizimu Afrika **Rev:** Bird of Paradise flower

Date	Mintage	F12	VF20	XF40	MS60	MS63
2012	—	—	—	—	0.50	0.75

KM# 227 RAND
4.00 g., Nickel Plated Copper, 20 mm. **Obv:** New national arms **Obv. Legend:** SUID-AFRIKA **Rev:** Springbok, value **Edge:** Segmented reeding

Date	Mintage	F12	VF20	XF40	MS60	MS63
2001	—	—	—	0.60	1.50	2.00
2001	3,678	PF63 10.00				

KM# 272 RAND
4.00 g., Nickel Plated Copper, 20 mm. **Obv:** New national arms **Obv. Legend:** Suid-Afrika Afrika Borwa **Rev:** Springbok, value **Edge:** Segmented reeding

Date	Mintage	F12	VF20	XF40	MS60	MS63
2002	—	—	—	0.60	1.50	2.00
2002	3,250	PF63 10.00				

KM# 275 RAND
4.00 g., Nickel Plated Copper, 20 mm. **Subject:** Johannesburg World Summit on Sustainable Development **Obv:** New national arms **Obv. Legend:** Suid-Afrika - Afrika Borwa **Rev:** World globe and logo **Edge:** Segmented reeding

Date	Mintage	F12	VF20	XF40	MS60	MS63
2002	—	—	—	—	12.00	18.00

KM# 332 RAND
4.00 g., Nickel Plated Copper, 20 mm. **Obv:** New national arms **Obv. Legend:** uMzantsi Afrika Suid-Afrika **Rev:** Springbok, value **Edge:** Segmented reeding

Date	Mintage	F12	VF20	XF40	MS60	MS63
2003	—	—	—	0.60	1.50	2.00
2003	2,909	PF63 10.00				

KM# 333 RAND
4.00 g., Nickel Plated Copper, 20 mm. **Obv:** New national arms **Obv. Legend:** iNingizimu Afrika - uMzantsi Afrika **Rev:** Springbok, value **Edge:** Segmented reeding

Date	Mintage	F12	VF20	XF40	MS60	MS63
2004	—	—	—	0.60	1.50	2.00
2004	1,935	PF63 10.00				

KM# 295 RAND
4.00 g., Nickel Plated Copper, 20 mm. **Obv:** new national arms **Obv. Legend:** iSewula Afrika - iNingizimu Afrika **Rev:** Springbok, value **Edge:** Segmented reeding **Shape:** Round

Date	Mintage	F12	VF20	XF40	MS60	MS63
2005	—	—	—	0.60	1.50	2.00
2005	—	PF63 10.00				

KM# 490 RAND
4.00 g., Nickel Plated Copper, 20 mm. **Obv:** National arms **Obv. Legend:** Afurika Tshipembe - iSewula Afrika **Rev:** Springbok and value

Date	Mintage	F12	VF20	XF40	MS60	MS63
2006	—	—	—	—	1.50	2.00
2006	—	PF63 10.00				

KM# 344 RAND
3.93 g., Nickel Plated Copper, 19.94 mm. **Obv:** Natinal arms **Obv. Legend:** Ningizimu Afrika - Afurika Tshipemba **Rev:** Springbok leaping right **Edge:** segmented reeding

Date	Mintage	F12	VF20	XF40	MS60	MS63
2007	—	—	—	0.60	1.50	2.00
2007	—	PF63 10.00				

KM# 444 RAND
4.00 g., Nickel Plated Copper, 20 mm. **Obv:** National arms **Obv. Legend:** Afrika-Dzonga - Ningizimu Afrika **Rev:** Springbok and value

Date	Mintage	F12	VF20	XF40	MS60	MS63
2008	—	—	—	—	2.00	2.75
2008	—	PF63 12.00				

KM# 468 RAND
4.00 g., Nickel Plated Copper, 20 mm. **Obv:** National arms **Rev:** Spingbok

Date	Mintage	F12	VF20	XF40	MS60	MS63
2009	—	—	—	—	1.50	2.00
2009	—	PF63 10.00				

KM# 508 RAND
3.11 g., 0.9999 Gold 0.0993 oz. AGW, 16.5 mm. **Subject:** World Cup Soccer

Date	Mintage	F12	VF20	XF40	MS60	MS63
2010	—	PF65 200				

KM# 497 RAND
4.00 g., Nickel Plated Copper, 20 mm. **Obv:** National arms **Rev:** Springbok right

Date	Mintage	F12	VF20	XF40	MS60	MS63
2010	—	—	—	—	1.50	2.00
2010	—	PF63 10.00				

KM# 504 RAND
20.00 g., Nickel Plated Copper, 20 mm. **Obv:** National arms **Rev:** Springbok and value

Date	Mintage	F12	VF20	XF40	MS60	MS63
2011	—	—	—	—	1.50	2.00
2011	—	PF63 10.00				

KM# 228 2 RAND
5.50 g., Nickel Plated Copper, 23 mm. **Obv:** New national arms **Obv. Legend:** UMZANSTI AFRIKA **Rev:** Greater Kudu, value **Edge:** Segmented reeding

Date	Mintage	F12	VF20	XF40	MS60	MS63
2001	3,600,000	—	—	0.80	2.00	3.00
2001	3,678	PF63 12.00				

KM# 273 2 RAND
5.50 g., Nickel Plated Copper, 23 mm. **Obv:** New national arms **Obv. Legend:** iNingizimu Afrika - uMzantsi Afrika **Rev:** Greater Kudu, value **Edge:** Segmented reeding

Date	Mintage	F12	VF20	XF40	MS60	MS63
2002	3,250	PF63 12.00				
2002	12,000,000	—	—	0.80	2.00	3.50

KM# 335 2 RAND
5.50 g., Nickel Plated Copper, 23 mm. **Obv:** New national arms **Obv. Legend:** iNingizimu Afrika - iSewula Afrika **Rev:** Greater Kudu, value **Edge:** Segmented reeding

Date	Mintage	F12	VF20	XF40	MS60	MS63
2003	5,000,000	—	—	0.80	2.00	3.50
2003	2,909	PF63 12.00				

KM# 334 2 RAND
5.50 g., Nickel Plated Copper, 23 mm. **Subject:** 10 Years of Freedom - 1994-2004 **Obv:** New national arms **Obv. Legend:** SOUTH / AFRICA **Rev:** Value, flag logo, people **Edge:** Segmented reeding **Note:** 5,885 issued in souveneir card.

Date	Mintage	F12	VF20	XF40	MS60	MS63
2004	—	—	—	0.80	2.00	2.75

KM# 336 2 RAND
5.50 g., Nickel Plated Copper, 23 mm. **Obv:** New national arms **Obv. Legend:** Afurika Tshipembe / iSewula Afrika **Rev:** Greater Kudu, value **Edge:** Segmented reeding

Date	Mintage	F12	VF20	XF40	MS60	MS63
2004	—	—	—	0.80	2.00	3.50
2004	1,935	PF63 12.00				

KM# 296 2 RAND
5.50 g., Nickel Plated Copper, 23 mm. **Obv:** New national arms **Obv. Legend:** Ningizimu Afrika - Afurika Tshipembe **Rev:** Greater Kudu, value **Edge:** Segmented reeding

Date	Mintage	F12	VF20	XF40	MS60	MS63
2005	—	—	—	0.80	2.00	2.75
2005	—	PF63 12.00				

KM# 491 2 RAND
5.50 g., Nickel Plated Copper, 23 mm. **Obv:** National arms **Obv. Legend:** Afrika-Dzonga - Ningizimo Afrika **Rev:** Greater kudu and value

Date	Mintage	F12	VF20	XF40	MS60	MS63
2006	—	—	—	—	2.00	2.75
2006	—	PF63 12.00				

KM# 345 2 RAND
5.50 g., Nickel Plated Copper, 23 mm. **Obv:** National arms **Rev:** Greater Kudu

Date	Mintage	F12	VF20	XF40	MS60	MS63
2007	—	—	—	0.80	2.00	3.00
2007	—	PF63 15.00				

KM# 445 2 RAND
5.50 g., Nickel Plated Copper, 23 mm. **Obv:** National arms **Obv. Legend:** Afrika-Dzonga - South Africa **Rev:** Kudu at center left, value at right **Edge:** Segmented reeding

Date	Mintage	F12	VF20	XF40	MS60	MS63
2008	—	—	—	0.80	2.00	2.75
2008	—	PF63 12.00				

KM# 469 2 RAND
5.50 g., Nickel Plated Copper, 22 mm. **Obv:** National arms **Rev:** Greater Kudu

Date	Mintage	F12	VF20	XF40	MS60	MS63
2009	—	—	—	—	2.00	2.75
2009	—	PF63 12.00				

KM# 498 2 RAND
5.50 g., Nickel Plated Copper, 23 mm. **Obv:** National arms **Rev:** Greater Kudu

Date	Mintage	F12	VF20	XF40	MS60	MS63
2010	—	—	—	—	2.00	2.75
2010	—	PF63 12.00				

KM# 505 2 RAND
5.50 g., Nickel Plated Copper, 23 mm. **Obv:** Naitonal arms **Rev:** Kudo at center

Date	Mintage	F12	VF20	XF40	MS60	MS63
2011	—	—	—	—	2.00	2.75
2011	—	PF63 12.00				

KM# 557 2 RAND
33.63 g., 0.925 Silver 0.9936 oz. ASW, 38.7 mm. **Obv:** Protea flower **Rev:** Railway train

Date	Mintage	F12	VF20	XF40	MS60	MS63
2012	Est. 1700	PF65 55.00				

KM# 561 2 RAND
33.63 g., 0.925 Silver 0.9936 oz. ASW, 38.7 mm. **Obv:** National arms **Rev:** Map of Antarctica

Date	Mintage	F12	VF20	XF40	MS60	MS63
2012	—	PF65 65.00				
2012 Proof, 90° S privy mark						

KM# 229 5 RAND
7.00 g., Nickel Plated Copper, 26 mm. **Obv:** New national arms **Obv. Legend:** ININGIZIMU AFRIKA **Rev:** Wildebeest, value **Edge:** Segmented reeding

Date	Mintage	F12	VF20	XF40	MS60	MS63
2001	2,000,000	—	—	1.20	4.50	6.00
2001 CW	779	—	—	—	67.50	90.00
2001	3,678	PF63 15.00				

KM# 274 5 RAND
7.00 g., Nickel Plated Copper, 26 mm. **Obv:** New national arms **Obv. Legend:** Afurika Tshipembe - Isewula Afrika **Rev:** Wildebeest, value **Edge:** Segmented reeding

Date	Mintage	F12	VF20	XF40	MS60	MS63
2002	—	—	—	1.20	4.50	6.00
2002 CW	106	—	—	—	—	150
2002	3,250	PF63 15.00				

KM# 337 5 RAND
7.00 g., Nickel Plated Copper, 26 mm. **Obv:** New national arms **Obv. Legend:** Afurika Tshipembe - Ningizimu Afrika **Rev:** Wildebeest, value **Edge:** Segmented reeding

Date	Mintage	F12	VF20	XF40	MS60	MS63
2003	—	—	—	1.20	4.50	6.00
2003	2,909	PF63 15.00				

KM# 281 5 RAND
9.50 g., Bi-Metallic, 26 mm. **Obv:** New national arms **Obv. Legend:** Afrika-Dzonga - Ningizimu Afrika **Rev:** Wildebeest, value **Edge:** Security type with lettering **Edge Lettering:** SARB R5" repeated ten times

Date	Mintage	F12	VF20	XF40	MS60	MS63
2004	—	—	—	1.20	5.00	6.50
2004 CW	3,243	—	—	—	—	22.50
2004	1,935	PF65 15.00				

KM# 297 5 RAND
9.50 g., Bi-Metallic, 26 mm. **Obv:** New national arms **Obv. Legend:** Afrika Dzonga - South Africa **Rev:** Wildebeest, value **Edge:** Security type with lettering **Edge Lettering:** SARB R5" repeated ten times

Date	Mintage	F12	VF20	XF40	MS60	MS63
2005	—	—	—	1.20	3.75	5.00
2005 CW	997	—	—	—	—	50.00
2005	—	PF63 15.00				

KM# 492 5 RAND
5.50 g., Bi-Metallic, 26 mm. **Obv:** National arms **Obv. Legend:** Aforika Borwa - South Africa **Rev:** Wildebeest and value

Date	Mintage	F12	VF20	XF40	MS60	MS63
2006	—	—	—	—	4.50	6.00
2006	—	PF63 12.00				

KM# 346 5 RAND
9.50 g., Bi-Metallic, 26 mm. **Obv:** National arms **Obv. Legend:** Aforika Borwa - Afrika Borwa **Rev:** Wildebeest and value **Edge:** Security type and lettered **Edge Lettering:** SARB R5" repeated ten times

Date	Mintage	F12	VF20	XF40	MS60	MS63
2007	—	—	—	1.20	3.00	4.00
2007 CW	—	—	—	—	—	22.50
2007	—	PF63 15.00				

KM# 446 5 RAND
9.50 g., Bi-Metallic, 26 mm. **Obv:** National arms **Rev:** Wildebeest rearing left

Date	Mintage	F12	VF20	XF40	MS60	MS63
2008	—	—	—	—	3.00	4.00
2008 CW	—	—	—	—	—	22.50
2008	—	PF63 12.00				

KM# 439 5 RAND
9.50 g., Bi-Metallic, 26 mm. **Subject:** Nelson Mandella, 90th Birthday **Obv:** National arms **Rev:** Bust facing

Date	Mintage	F12	VF20	XF40	MS60	MS63
2008	—	—	—	—	1.20	3.75	5.00
2008	—	PF63 15.00				

KM# 470 5 RAND
9.50 g., Bi-Metallic, 26 mm. **Obv:** National arms **Rev:** Wildebeest rearing left

Date	Mintage	F12	VF20	XF40	MS60	MS63
2009 CW	—	—	—	—	—	22.50
2009	—	—	—	—	3.00	4.00
2009	—	PF63 15.00				

KM# 499 5 RAND
9.50 g., Bi-Metallic, 26 mm. **Obv:** National arms **Rev:** Wildebeest rearing left

Date	Mintage	F12	VF20	XF40	MS60	MS63
2010	—	—	—	—	4.50	6.00
2010 CW	—	—	—	—	—	22.50
2010	—	PF63 15.00				

KM# 506 5 RAND
9.50 g., Bi-Metallic, 26 mm. **Obv:** National arms **Rev:** Wildebeest and value

Date	Mintage	F12	VF20	XF40	MS60	MS63
2011	—	—	—	—	4.50	6.00
2011	—	PF63 15.00				

KM# 507 5 RAND
9.50 g., Bi-Metallic, 26 mm. **Subject:** 90th Anniversary of the Rand **Obv:** National arms **Rev:** Old coin and bank note designs

Date	Mintage	F12	VF20	XF40	MS60	MS63
2011	—	—	—	—	4.50	7.00
2011	—	PF63 12.00				

KM# 518 5 RAND
33.00 g., 0.925 Silver 0.9751 oz. ASW, 38.7 mm. **Subject:** South African Reserve Bank, 90th Anniversary **Obv:** National arms **Rev:** Coins and banknotes

Date	Mintage	F12	VF20	XF40	MS60	MS63
2011	Est. 10500	PF65 55.00				

KM# 555 5 RAND
9.50 g., Copper-Nickel Plated Nickel, 26 mm. **Obv:** National arms **Obv. Legend:** uMazantsi Afrika iNingizimu Afrika **Rev:** Black wildebeest

Date	Mintage	F12	VF20	XF40	MS60	MS63
2012	—	—	—	—	2.00	4.00

GOLD BULLION COINAGE

KM# 105 1/10 KRUGERRAND
3.39 g., 0.917 Gold 0.0994 oz. AGW, 16.50 mm. **Obv:** Bust of Paul Kruger left **Obv. Legend:** SUID-AFRIKA - SOUTH AFRICA **Rev:** Springbok walking right divides date **Edge:** Reeded **Note:** 180 edge serrations for uncirculated, 220 serrations for proof

Date	Mintage	F12	VF20	XF40	MS60	MS63
2001	17,936	—	—	—	BV+15%	—
2001	4,058	PF63 200				
2002	12,890	—	—	—	BV+15%	—
2002	3,110	PF63 200				
2003	15,893	—	—	—	BV+15%	—
2003	1,893	PF63 200				
2004	—	—	—	—	BV+15%	—
2004	3,811	PF63 200				
2005	—	—	—	—	BV+15%	—
2005	—	PF63 200				
2006	—	—	—	—	BV+15%	—
2006	—	PF63 200				
2007	4,400	—	—	—	BV+15%	—
2007	—	PF63 200				
2008	4,800	—	—	—	BV+15%	—
2008	—	PF63 200				
2009	6,000	—	—	—	BV+15%	—
2009	—	PF63 200				
2010	6,000	—	—	—	BV+15%	—
2010	—	PF63 200				
2011	—	—	—	—	BV+15%	—
2011	—	PF63 200				
2012	—	—	—	—	BV+15%	—
2012	—	PF63 200				

KM# 106 1/4 KRUGERRAND
8.48 g., 0.917 Gold 0.2485 oz. AGW, 22 mm. **Obv:** Bust of Paul Kruger left **Obv. Legend:** SUID-AFRIKA - SOUTH AFRICA **Rev:** Springbok bounding right divides date **Edge:** Reeded **Note:** 180 edge serrations for uncirculated, 220 serrations for proof

Date	Mintage	F12	VF20	XF40	MS60	MS63
2001	10,607	—	—	—	BV+10%	—
2001	3,841	PF63 475				
2002	10,558	—	—	—	BV+10%	—
2002	2,442	PF63 475				
2003	11,468	—	—	—	BV+10%	—
2003	2,450	PF63 475				
2004	—	—	—	—	BV+10%	—
2004	4,570	PF63 475				
2005	—	—	—	—	BV+10%	—
2005	—	PF63 475				
2006	—	—	—	—	BV+10%	—
2006	—	PF63 475				
2007	4,400	—	—	—	BV+10%	—
2007	—	PF63 475				
2008	4,800	—	—	—	BV+10%	—
2008	—	PF63 475				
2009	6,000	—	—	—	BV+10%	—
2009	—	PF63 475				
2010	6,000	—	—	—	BV+10%	—
2010	—	PF63 475				
2011	—	—	—	—	BV+10%	—
2011	—	PF63 475				
2012	—	PF63 475				

KM# 107 1/2 KRUGERRAND
16.97 g., 0.917 Gold 0.4969 oz. AGW, 27 mm. **Obv:** Bust of Paul Kruger left **Obv. Legend:** SUID-AFRIKA • SOUTH AFRICA **Rev:** Springbok walking right divides date **Edge:** Reeded **Note:** 180 edge serrations for uncirculated, 220 serrations for proof

Date	Mintage	F12	VF20	XF40	MS60	MS63
2001	6,429	—	—	—	BV+8%	—
2001	3,696	PF63 950				
2002	—	—	—	—	BV+8%	—

Date	Mintage	F12	VF20	XF40	MS60	MS63
2002	2,295	PF63 950				
2003	11,588	—	—	—	BV+8%	—
2003	1,285	PF63 950				
2004	—	—	—	—	BV+8%	—
2004	3,288	PF63 950				
2005	—	—	—	—	BV+8%	—
2005	—	PF63 950				
2006	—	—	—	—	BV+8%	—
2006	—	PF63 950				
2007	—	—	—	—	BV+8%	—
2007	3,400	PF63 950				
2008	—	—	—	—	BV+8%	—
2008	3,300	PF63 950				
2009	—	—	—	—	BV+8%	—
2009	2,500	PF63 950				
2010	—	—	—	—	BV+8%	—
2010	2,500	PF63 950				
2011	—	—	—	—	BV+8%	—
2011	—	PF63 950				
2012	—	—	—	—	BV+8%	—
2012	—	PF63 950				

KM# 73 KRUGERRAND

33.93 g., 0.917 Gold 0.9939 oz. AGW, 32.7 mm. **Obv:** Bust of Paul Kruger left **Obv. Legend:** SUID — AFRIKA • SOUTH AFRICA **Rev:** Springbok walking right divides date **Edge:** Reeded **Note:** 180 edge serrations for uncirculated, 220 serrations for proof

Date	Mintage	F12	VF20	XF40	MS60	MS63
2001	5,889	—	—	—	—	BV+5%
2001	5,563	PF63 1,850				
2002	16,469	—	—	—	—	BV+5%
2002	3,531	PF63 1,850				
2003	47,789	—	—	—	—	BV+5%
2003	2,136	PF63 1,850				
2004	71,269	—	—	—	—	BV+5%
2004	3,492	PF63 1,850				
2004 W/MM	500	PF63 1,850				
2005	—	—	—	—	—	BV+5%
2005	—	PF63 1,850				
2006	—	—	—	—	—	BV+5%
2006	—	PF63 1,850				
2007	—	—	—	—	—	BV+5%
2007	3,400	PF63 1,850				
2008	—	—	—	—	—	BV+5%
2008	3,300	PF63 1,850				
2009	—	—	—	—	—	BV+5%
2009	2,500	PF63 1,850				
2010	—	—	—	—	—	BV+5%
2010	2,500	PF63 1,850				
2011	—	—	—	—	—	BV+5%
2011	—	PF63 1,850				
2012	—	—	—	—	—	BV+5%
2012	—	PF63 1,850				

SILVER BULLION NATURA COINAGE

KM# 242 2-1/2 CENTS

1.41 g., 0.925 Silver 0.0418 oz. ASW, 16.3 mm. **Obv:** Crowned arms **Rev:** Dolphin **Edge:** Reeded

Date	Mintage	F12	VF20	XF40	MS60	MS63
2001	—	PF65 27.50				

KM# 480 2-1/2 CENTS

1.41 g., 0.925 Silver 0.0418 oz. ASW, 16.3 mm. **Obv:** Flower **Rev:** Vasco de Gama's ship "Sao Gabriel

Date	Mintage	F12	VF20	XF40	MS60	MS63
2009	3,500	PF65 15.00				

KM# 243 5 CENTS

8.46 g., 0.925 Silver 0.2499 oz. ASW, 26.7 mm. **Series:** Wildlife - Power **Obv:** Cape Buffalo head **Rev:** Two Cape Buffalo heads within circle below value **Edge:** Reeded

Date	Mintage	F12	VF20	XF40	MS60	MS63
2001	1,853	PF65 40.00				

KM# 351 5 CENTS

8.46 g., 0.925 Silver 0.2499 oz. ASW, 26.7 mm. **Series:** Wildlife - Strength **Obv:** Elephant walking, facing **Rev:** Elephant 3/4 left bathing **Edge:** Reeded

Date	Mintage	F12	VF20	XF40	MS60	MS63
2002	2,425	PF65 30.00				

KM# 355 5 CENTS

8.46 g., 0.925 Silver 0.2499 oz. ASW, 26.7 mm. **Series:** Wildlife - Survivor **Obv:** New national arms **Rev:** 2 White Rhinoceros drinking at stream **Edge:** Reeded

Date	Mintage	F12	VF20	XF40	MS60	MS63
2003	1,870	PF65 40.00				

KM# 359 5 CENTS

8.46 g., 0.925 Silver 0.2499 oz. ASW, 26.7 mm. **Series:** Wildlife - The Legend **Obv:** New national arms **Rev:** Head of Leopard right drinking **Edge:** Reeded

Date	Mintage	F12	VF20	XF40	MS60	MS63
2004	—	PF65 40.00				

KM# 320 5 CENTS

8.46 g., 0.925 Silver 0.2499 oz. ASW, 27.12 mm. **Series:** Wildlife - African Wild Dog **Obv:** New national arms **Rev:** Painted Dog's head facing slightly left **Edge:** Reeded

Date	Mintage	F12	VF20	XF40	MS60	MS63
2005	1,500	PF65 40.00				

KM# 316 5 CENTS

8.46 g., 0.925 Silver 0.2499 oz. ASW, 27 mm. **Series:** Wildlife - Black-backed Jackal **Obv:** New national arms **Rev:** Black-backed jackal drinking **Edge:** Reeded

Date	Mintage	F12	VF20	XF40	MS60	MS63
2006	1,500	PF65 40.00				

KM# 363 5 CENTS

8.46 g., 0.925 Silver 0.2499 oz. ASW, 26.7 mm. **Series:** Wildlife - Kgalagadi Transfrontier Peace Park **Obv:** New national arms **Rev:** Local desert melons, value **Edge:** Reeded

Date	Mintage	F12	VF20	XF40	MS60	MS63
2007	—	PF65 40.00				

KM# 458 5 CENTS

8.41 g., 0.925 Silver 0.2484 oz. ASW, 27 mm. **Subject:** Richtersveld Transfrontier Park **Obv:** Arms **Rev:** Orbea Namaquensis succulant flower

Date	Mintage	F12	VF20	XF40	MS60	MS63
2008	2,200	PF65 30.00				

KM# 482 5 CENTS

8.41 g., 0.925 Silver 0.2484 oz. ASW, 27 mm. **Subject:** Maloti Drakensberg Transfrontier Project **Obv:** Arms **Rev:** Spiral Aloe Tree (aloe polyphylla)

Date	Mintage	F12	VF20	XF40	MS60	MS63
2009	3,700	PF65 25.00				

KM# 539 5 CENTS

8.46 g., 0.925 Silver 0.2499 oz. ASW, 27 mm. **Obv:** National arms **Rev:** Flower - Gloriosa superba - Colchicacceae

Date	Mintage	F12	VF20	XF40	MS60	MS63
2010	Est. 2700	PF65 45.00				

KM# 513 5 CENTS

8.41 g., 0.925 Silver 0.2484 oz. ASW, 27 mm.

Date	Mintage	F12	VF20	XF40	MS60	MS63
2011	—	PF65 40.00				

KM# 529 5 CENTS

8.45 g., 0.925 Silver 0.2497 oz. ASW, 27 mm. **Subject:** Great Mapungubwe Transfrontier Conservation Area **Obv:** National arms **Rev:** Baobab tree seed pod, sandstone landscape in background

Date	Mintage	F12	VF20	XF40	MS60	MS63
2012	—	PF65 25.00				

KM# 244 10 CENTS

16.86 g., 0.925 Silver 0.4983 oz. ASW, 32.7 mm. **Series:** Wildlife - Power **Obv:** Cape Buffalo head **Rev:** Two Cape Buffalo bulls fighting **Edge:** Reeded

Date	Mintage	F12	VF20	XF40	MS60	MS63
2001	1,989	PF65 65.00				

KM# 352 10 CENTS

16.81 g., 0.925 Silver 0.4968 oz. ASW, 38.3 mm. **Series:** Wildlife - Strength **Obv:** Elephant walking, facing **Rev:** 2 elephant heads facing each other **Edge:** Reeded

Date	Mintage	F12	VF20	XF40	MS60	MS63
2002	2,395	PF65 55.00				

KM# 356 10 CENTS

16.81 g., 0.925 Silver 0.4968 oz. ASW, 32.7 mm. **Series:** Wildlife - Survivor **Obv:** New national arms **Rev:** 2 Black Rhinoceros standing, facing **Edge:** Reeded

Date	Mintage	F12	VF20	XF40	MS60	MS63
2003	1,815	PF65 65.00				

KM# 360 10 CENTS

16.81 g., 0.925 Silver 0.4968 oz. ASW, 32.7 mm. **Series:** Wildlife - The Legend **Obv:** New national arms **Rev:** Leopard and impala above two leopard cubs playing **Edge:** Reeded

Date	Mintage	F12	VF20	XF40	MS60	MS63
2004	—	PF65 65.00				

KM# 321 10 CENTS

16.81 g., 0.925 Silver 0.4968 oz. ASW, 32.7 mm. **Series:** Wildlife - African Wild Dog **Obv:** New national arms **Rev:** Two Painted Dogs walking right **Edge:** Reeded

Date	Mintage	F12	VF20	XF40	MS60	MS63
2005	1,500	PF65 65.00				

KM# 317 10 CENTS

16.86 g., 0.925 Silver 0.4983 oz. ASW, 32.7 mm. **Series:** Wildlife - Black-backed Jackel **Obv:** New national arms **Rev:** Black-backed jackal chasing birds **Edge:** Reeded

Date	Mintage	F12	VF20	XF40	MS60	MS63
2006	1,500	PF65 65.00				

KM# 364 10 CENTS

16.81 g., 0.925 Silver 0.4968 oz. ASW, 32.7 mm. **Series:** Wildlife - Kgaladadi Transfrontier Peace Park **Obv:** New national arms **Rev:** Local tribe, value **Edge:** Reeded

Date	Mintage	F12	VF20	XF40	MS60	MS63
2007	—	PF65 65.00				

KM# 459 10 CENTS

16.81 g., 0.925 Silver 0.4968 oz. ASW, 32.7 mm. **Subject:** Richtersveld Transfrontier Park **Obv:** Arms **Rev:** Local Nama native and livestock

Date	Mintage	F12	VF20	XF40	MS60	MS63
2008	2,200	PF65 55.00				

KM# 483 10 CENTS

16.81 g., 0.925 Silver 0.4968 oz. ASW, 32.7 mm. **Subject:** Maloti Drakensberg Transfrontier Project **Obv:** Arms **Rev:** Native Basotho riding pony

Date	Mintage	F12	VF20	XF40	MS60	MS63
2009	3,700	PF65 45.00				

KM# 540 10 CENTS

16.86 g., 0.925 Silver 0.4983 oz. ASW, 32.7 mm. **Obv:** National arms **Rev:** uMhlanga female in Swasiland

Date	Mintage	F12	VF20	XF40	MS60	MS63
2010	Est. 2700	PF65 55.00				

KM# 514 10 CENTS

16.81 g., 0.925 Silver 0.4968 oz. ASW, 32.7 mm.

Date	Mintage	F12	VF20	XF40	MS60	MS63
2011	—	PF65 65.00				

KM# 530 10 CENTS

16.86 g., 0.925 Silver 0.4983 oz. ASW, 32.82 mm. **Subject:** Great Mapungubwe Transfrontier Conservation Area **Obv:** National arms **Rev:** Golden Rhino and sandstone rock formations in background

Date	Mintage	F12	VF20	XF40	MS60	MS63
2012	—	PF65 65.00				

KM# 245 20 CENTS

33.73 g., 0.925 Silver 0.9965 oz. ASW, 38.3 mm. **Series:** Wildlife - Power **Obv:** Cape Buffalo head **Rev:** Two Cape Buffalo heads facing **Edge:** Reeded

Date	Mintage	F12	VF20	XF40	MS60	MS63
2001	1,902	PF65 85.00				

KM# 353 20 CENTS

33.73 g., 0.925 Silver 0.9965 oz. ASW, 38.3 mm. **Series:** Wildlife - Strength **Obv:** Elephant walking, facing **Rev:** Family of four elephants **Edge:** Reeded

Date	Mintage	F12	VF20	XF40	MS60	MS63
2002	2,435	PF65 75.00				

KM# 357 20 CENTS

33.73 g., 0.925 Silver 0.9965 oz. ASW, 38.3 mm. **Series:** Wildlife - Survivor **Obv:** New national arms **Rev:** White Rhinoceros mother with an offspring **Edge:** Reeded

Date	Mintage	F12	VF20	XF40	MS60	MS63
2003	1,930	PF65 85.00				

KM# 361 20 CENTS

33.73 g., 0.925 Silver 0.9965 oz. ASW, 38.3 mm. **Series:** Wildlife - The legend **Obv:** New national arms **Rev:** Leopard looking left, cub on branch behind her **Edge:** Reeded

Date	Mintage	F12	VF20	XF40	MS60	MS63
2004	—	PF65 85.00				

KM# 322 20 CENTS

33.75 g., 0.925 Silver 0.9972 oz. ASW, 38.67 mm. **Series:** Wildlife - African Wild Dog **Obv:** New National arms **Rev:** Three Painted Dogs **Edge:** Reeded

Date	Mintage	F12	VF20	XF40	MS60	MS63
2005	1,500	PF65 85.00				

KM# 318 20 CENTS
33.73 g., 0.925 Silver 0.9965 oz. ASW, 38.7 mm. **Series:** Wildlife - Black-backed Jackal **Obv:** National arms **Rev:** Two Black-backed jackals **Edge:** Reeded

Date	Mintage	F12	VF20	XF40	MS60	MS63
2006	1,500	PF65 85.00				

KM# 365 20 CENTS
33.73 g., 0.925 Silver 0.9965 oz. ASW, 38.3 mm. **Series:** Wildlife - Kgalagadi Transfrontier Peace Park **Obv:** New national arms **Rev:** Lion's head 3/4 right at left, meerkat standing with offspring at right, value **Edge:** Reeded

Date	Mintage	F12	VF20	XF40	MS60	MS63
2007	—	PF65 85.00				

KM# 460 20 CENTS
33.73 g., 0.925 Silver 0.9965 oz. ASW, 38.7 mm. **Subject:** Richtersveld Transfrontier Park **Obv:** Arms **Rev:** Two shy Kipspringer (Oreotragus oreotragos)

Date	Mintage	F12	VF20	XF40	MS60	MS63
2008	2,200	PF65 75.00				

KM# 484 20 CENTS
33.62 g., 0.925 Silver 0.9934 oz. ASW, 38.72 mm. **Subject:** Maloti Drakensberg Transfrontier Project **Obv:** Arms **Rev:** Cape griffon vulture

Date	Mintage	F12	VF20	XF40	MS60	MS63
2009	3,700	PF65 75.00				

KM# 541 20 CENTS
33.73 g., 0.925 Silver 0.9965 oz. ASW, 38.72 mm. **Obv:** National arms **Rev:** Three flamingos and crocodile

Date	Mintage	F12	VF20	XF40	MS60	MS63
2010	Est. 2700	PF65 65.00				

KM# 515 20 CENTS
33.73 g., 0.925 Silver 0.9965 oz. ASW, 38.72 mm.

Date	Mintage	F12	VF20	XF40	MS60	MS63
2011	—	PF65 85.00				

KM# 531 20 CENTS
33.73 g., 0.925 Silver 0.9965 oz. ASW, 38.3 mm. **Subject:** Great Mapungubwe Transfrontier Conservation Area **Obv:** National arms **Rev:** Pel's Fishing Owl (scotopelia peli) and standstone rock formations in background

Date	Mintage	F12	VF20	XF40	MS60	MS63
2012	—	PF65 85.00				

KM# 246 50 CENTS
76.40 g., 0.925 Silver 2.2575 oz. ASW, 50 mm. **Series:** Wildlife - Power **Obv:** Cape Buffalo head **Rev:** Cape Buffalo head, value **Edge:** Reeded

Date	Mintage	F12	VF20	XF40	MS60	MS63
2001	1,866	PF65 110				

KM# 354 50 CENTS
76.40 g., 0.925 Silver 2.2575 oz. ASW, 50 mm. **Series:** Wildlife - Strength **Obv:** Elephant walking, facing **Rev:** Elephant right with head raised **Edge:** Reeded

Date	Mintage	F12	VF20	XF40	MS60	MS63
2002	2,318	PF65 110				

KM# 358 50 CENTS
76.40 g., 0.925 Silver 2.2575 oz. ASW, 50 mm. **Series:** Wildlife - Survivor **Obv:** New national arms **Rev:** White Rhinoceros' head 3/4 right, value **Edge:** Reeded

Date	Mintage	F12	VF20	XF40	MS60	MS63
2003	1,918	PF65 110				

KM# 362 50 CENTS
76.46 g., 0.925 Silver 2.2593 oz. ASW, 50 mm. **Series:** Wildlife - The Legend **Obv:** New national arms **Rev:** Leopard facing snarling, two leopards at lower left **Edge:** Reeded

Date	Mintage	F12	VF20	XF40	MS60	MS63
2004	—	PF65 110				

KM# 323 50 CENTS
76.86 g., 0.925 Silver 2.2711 oz. ASW, 50.48 mm. **Series:** Wildlife - African Wild Dog **Obv:** New national arms **Rev:** Two painted Dog's heads facing **Edge:** Reeded

Date	Mintage	F12	VF20	XF40	MS60	MS63
2005	1,500	PF65 110				

KM# 319 50 CENTS
76.25 g., 0.925 Silver 2.2531 oz. ASW, 50 mm. **Series:** Wildlife - Black-backed Jackal **Obv:** New national arms **Rev:** Two black-backed jackals fighting over a carcass **Edge:** Reeded

Date	Mintage	F12	VF20	XF40	MS60	MS63
2006	1,500	PF65 110				

KM# 366 50 CENTS
76.40 g., 0.925 Silver 2.2575 oz. ASW, 50 mm. **Series:** Wildlife
- Kgalagadi Transfrontier Peace Park **Obv:** New national arms
Rev: Antelope running right **Edge:** Reeded

Date	Mintage	F12	VF20	XF40	MS60	MS63
2007	—	PF65 110				

KM# 461 50 CENTS
76.25 g., 0.925 Silver 2.2531 oz. ASW, 50 mm. **Subject:**
Richtersveld Transfrontier Park **Obv:** Arms **Rev:** Giant aloe
pillansii tree

Date	Mintage	F12	VF20	XF40	MS60	MS63
2008	2,200	PF65 110				

KM# 485 50 CENTS
76.25 g., 0.925 Silver 2.2531 oz. ASW, 50 mm. **Subject:**
Maloti Drakensberg Transfrontier Project **Obv:** Arms **Rev:**
Amphitheatre and Trukela River

Date	Mintage	F12	VF20	XF40	MS60	MS63
2009	3,700	PF65 100				

KM# 542 50 CENTS
67.40 g., 0.925 Silver 1.9916 oz. ASW, 50 mm. **Obv:** National
arms **Rev:** Sea turtles

Date	Mintage	F12	VF20	XF40	MS60	MS63
2010	Est. 2700	PF65 115				

KM# 516 50 CENTS
76.40 g., 0.925 Silver 2.2575 oz. ASW, 50 mm.

Date	Mintage	F12	VF20	XF40	MS60	MS63
2011	—	PF65 110				

KM# 532 50 CENTS
76.40 g., 0.925 Silver 2.2575 oz. ASW, 50 mm. **Subject:**
Great Mapungubwe Transfrontier Conservation Area **Obv:**
National Arms **Rev:** Baobab Tree and sandstone landscape in
background

Date	Mintage	F12	VF20	XF40	MS60	MS63
2012	—	PF65 110				

KM# 248 2 RAND
33.63 g., 0.925 Silver 0.9936 oz. ASW, 38.7 mm. **Obv:** New
national arms **Rev:** Dolphins **Edge:** Reeded

Date	Mintage	F12	VF20	XF40	MS60	MS63
2001	2,987	PF65 80.00				

KM# 280 2 RAND
33.63 g., 0.925 Silver 0.9936 oz. ASW, 38.7 mm. **Obv:** New
national arms **Rev:** Southern Right Whale **Edge:** Reeded

Date	Mintage	F12	VF20	XF40	MS60	MS63
2002	1,808	PF65 85.00				

KM# 286 2 RAND
33.63 g., 0.925 Silver 0.9936 oz. ASW, 38.7 mm. **Obv:** New
national arms **Rev:** Martial and Bateleur Eagles **Edge:** Reeded

Date	Mintage	F12	VF20	XF40	MS60	MS63
2003	2,166	PF65 75.00				

KM# 284 2 RAND
33.63 g., 0.925 Silver 0.9936 oz. ASW, 38.7 mm. **Obv:** New
national arms **Rev:** Verreaux's Eagle Owl face and value **Edge:**
Reeded

Date	Mintage	F12	VF20	XF40	MS60	MS63
2004	—	—	—	—	50.00	55.00
2004	1,752	PF65 85.00				

KM# 372 2 RAND
33.63 g., 0.925 Silver 0.9936 oz. ASW, 38.7 mm. **Obv:** New
national arms **Rev:** Three vultures **Edge:** Reeded

Date	Mintage	F12	VF20	XF40	MS60	MS63
2005	4,000	PF65 70.00				

KM# 374 2 RAND
33.63 g., 0.925 Silver 0.9936 oz. ASW, 38.7 mm. **Series:** Bird of
Prey **Obv:** New national arms **Rev:** Two Secretary birds **Edge:**
Reeded

Date	Mintage	F12	VF20	XF40	MS60	MS63
2006	4,000	PF65 75.00				

KM# 481 2 RAND
33.63 g., 0.925 Silver 0.9936 oz. ASW, 38.7 mm. **Obv:** Arms and
country name **Rev:** Jan van Riebeeck's ship "Drommedaries

Date	Mintage	F12	VF20	XF40	MS60	MS63
2009	3,500	PF65 55.00				

SILVER BULLION PROTEA COINAGE

KM# 282 2-1/2 CENTS
1.41 g., 0.925 Silver 0.0418 oz. ASW, 16.3 mm. **Obv:** Protea
flower **Rev:** Southern Right Whale **Edge:** Plain

Date	Mintage	F12	VF20	XF40	MS60	MS63
2002	3,000	PF65 27.50				

KM# 285 2-1/2 CENTS
1.41 g., 0.925 Silver 0.0418 oz. ASW, 16.3 mm. **Obv:** Protea
flower **Rev:** Martial and Bateleur Eagles **Edge:** Plain

Date	Mintage	F12	VF20	XF40	MS60	MS63
2003	—	PF65 25.00				

KM# 283 2-1/2 CENTS
1.41 g., 0.925 Silver 0.0418 oz. ASW, 16.3 mm. **Series:** Birds of
Prey **Obv:** Protea flower **Rev:** Pearl Spotted Owlet **Edge:** Plain

Date	Mintage	F12	VF20	XF40	MS60	MS63
2004	2,000	PF65 25.00				

KM# 348 2-1/2 CENTS
1.41 g., 0.925 Silver 0.0418 oz. ASW, 16.3 mm. **Obv:** Protea
flower **Obv. Legend:** SOUTH AFRICA **Rev:** Vulture alighting
Edge: Plain

Date	Mintage	F12	VF20	XF40	MS60	MS63
2005	—	PF65 25.00				

KM# 349 2-1/2 CENTS
1.41 g., 0.925 Silver 0.0418 oz. ASW, 16.3 mm. **Obv:** Protea
flower **Obv. Legend:** SOUTH AFRICA **Rev:** Head of Secretary
bird **Edge:** Plain

Date	Mintage	F12	VF20	XF40	MS60	MS63
2006	—	PF65 25.00				

KM# 350 2-1/2 CENTS

1.41 g., 0.925 Silver 0.0418 oz. ASW, 16.3 mm. **Subject:** International Polar Year **Obv:** Protea flower **Obv. Legend:** SOUTH AFRICA **Rev:** Globe displaying South Pole **Edge:** Plain

Date	Mintage	F12	VF20	XF40	MS60	MS63
2007			PF65 25.00			

KM# 456 2-1/2 CENTS

1.41 g., 0.925 Silver 0.0418 oz. ASW, 16.3 mm. **Obv:** Flower **Rev:** Map of Antarctica

Date	Mintage	F12	VF20	XF40	MS60	MS63
2008	3,000		PF65 15.00			

KM# 537 2-1/2 CENTS

1.41 g., 0.925 Silver 0.0418 oz. ASW, 16.3 mm. **Obv:** Protea flower **Rev:** R.M.S. Scot right

Date	Mintage	F12	VF20	XF40	MS60	MS63
2010	Est. 1700		PF65 30.00			

KM# 519 2-1/2 CENTS

1.41 g., 0.925 Silver 0.0418 oz. ASW, 16.3 mm. **Obv:** Protea flower **Rev:** Van der Stel ship

Date	Mintage	F12	VF20	XF40	MS60	MS63
2011	Est. 1700		PF65 35.00			

KM# 231 RAND

15.00 g., 0.925 Silver 0.4432 oz. ASW, 32.7 mm. **Subject:** Tourism **Obv:** Protea flower **Rev:** Steam locomotive and flower **Edge:** Reeded

Date	Mintage	F12	VF20	XF40	MS60	MS63
2001	2,400	—	—	—	40.00	45.00
2001	1,784	PF65 65.00				

KM# 277 RAND

15.00 g., 0.925 Silver 0.4432 oz. ASW, 32.7 mm. **Subject:** Soccer **Obv:** Protea flower **Rev:** Goalkeeper in action **Edge:** Reeded

Date	Mintage	F12	VF20	XF40	MS60	MS63
2002	1,777	—	—	—	40.00	45.00
2002	1,250	PF65 65.00				

KM# 367 RAND

15.55 g., 0.925 Silver 0.4595 oz. ASW **Subject:** World Summit - Johannesburg **Obv:** Protea flower **Rev:** Globe **Edge:** Reeded

Date	Mintage	F12	VF20	XF40	MS60	MS63
2002	1,531	—	—	—	55.00	60.00
2002	1,413	PF65 75.00				

KM# 298 RAND

15.05 g., 0.925 Silver 0.4447 oz. ASW, 32.7 mm. **Obv:** Protea flower **Rev:** Cricket player **Edge:** Reeded

Date	Mintage	F12	VF20	XF40	MS60	MS63
2003	1,697	—	—	—	55.00	60.00
2003	1,250	PF65 75.00				

KM# 288 RAND

15.00 g., 0.925 Silver 0.4432 oz. ASW, 32.7 mm. **Subject:** 10th Anniversary of South African Democracy **Obv:** Protea flower **Rev:** Flora and fauna **Edge:** Reeded

Date	Mintage	F12	VF20	XF40	MS60	MS63
2004	3,427	—	—	—	35.00	40.00
2004	2,930	PF65 50.00				

KM# 368 RAND

15.00 g., 0.925 Silver 0.4432 oz. ASW, 32.7 mm. **Series:** Nobel Peace Prize Winners **Obv:** Protea flower **Rev:** Bust of Chief A. J. Luthuli facing at center, Luthuli seated at desk left at lower right **Edge:** Reeded

Date	Mintage	F12	VF20	XF40	MS60	MS63
2005		—	—	—	50.00	55.00
2005		PF65 65.00				

KM# 369 RAND

15.00 g., 0.925 Silver 0.4432 oz. ASW, 32.7 mm. **Series:** Nobel Peace prize Winners **Obv:** Protea flower **Rev:** 1/3 length figure of Archbishop Desmond Mpilo Tutu facing at right **Edge:** Reeded

Date	Mintage	F12	VF20	XF40	MS60	MS63
2006		—	—	—	60.00	65.00
2006		PF65 75.00				

KM# 370 RAND

15.00 g., 0.925 Silver 0.4432 oz. ASW, 32.7 mm. **Series:** Nobel Peace Prize Winners **Obv:** Protea flower **Rev:** Bust of De Klerk facing **Edge:** Reeded

Date	Mintage	F12	VF20	XF40	MS60	MS63
2007		—	—	—	55.00	60.00
2007		—	PF65 70.00			

KM# 371 RAND

15.55 g., 0.925 Silver 0.4595 oz. ASW, 32.7 mm. **Series:** Nobel Peace Prize Winners **Obv:** Protea flower **Rev:** Bust of Mandela facing **Edge:** Reeded

Date	Mintage	F12	VF20	XF40	MS60	MS63
2007		—	—	—	65.00	75.00
2007		PF65 95.00				

KM# 451 RAND

15.55 g., 0.925 Silver 0.4595 oz. ASW, 32.7 mm. **Obv:** Protea flower **Rev:** Ghandi portrait

Date	Mintage	F12	VF20	XF40	MS60	MS63
2008		—	—	—	—	25.00
2008	11,000	PF65 30.00				

KM# 475 RAND

15.55 g., 0.925 Silver 0.4595 oz. ASW, 32.7 mm. **Obv:** Protea flower **Rev:** Portraits of C. J. Langenhoven and N. L. de Villiers with musical score

Date	Mintage	F12	VF20	XF40	MS60	MS63
2009		—	—	—	—	25.00
2009	11,000	PF65 30.00				

KM# 543 RAND

15.00 g., 0.925 Silver 0.4432 oz. ASW, 32.69 mm. **Obv:** Protea flower **Rev:** Nadine Gordimer

Date	Mintage	F12	VF20	XF40	MS60	MS63
2010	Est. 4000	—	—	—	55.00	60.00

KM# 521 RAND

15.00 g., 0.925 Silver 0.4432 oz. ASW, 32.7 mm. **Obv:** Protea flower **Rev:** John Maxwell Coetzee

Date	Mintage	F12	VF20	XF40	MS60	MS63
2011		—	—	—	55.00	65.00
2011 Privy Mark A	600		—	—	75.00	
Note: A for Adelaide						

KM# 538 2 RAND

33.63 g., 0.925 Silver 0.9936 oz. ASW, 38.72 mm. **Obv:** Protea flower **Rev:** R.M.S. Windsor Castle III

Date	Mintage	F12	VF20	XF40	MS60	MS63
2010	Est. 1700	PF65 55.00				

KM# 520 2 RAND

33.63 g., 0.925 Silver 0.9936 oz. ASW, 38.7 mm. **Obv:** Protea flower **Rev:** R.M.S. Queen Mary II

Date	Mintage	F12	VF20	XF40	MS60	MS63
2011	Est. 1700	PF65 55.00				

SILVER BULLION CULTURE COINAGE

KM# 558 RAND

15.00 g., 0.925 Silver 0.4432 oz. ASW, 32.7 mm. **Obv:** National arms **Rev:** Walter and Albertina Sisulu

Date	Mintage	F12	VF20	XF40	MS60	MS63
2012		—	—	—	50.00	60.00

KM# 373 2 RAND

33.63 g., 0.925 Silver 0.9936 oz. ASW, 38.7 mm. **Subject:** 2006 FIFA World Cup Soccer - Germany **Obv:** New national arms **Rev:** Soccer ball above globe **Edge:** Reeded

Date	Mintage	F12	VF20	XF40	MS60	MS63
2005	50,000	PF65 60.00				

KM# 435 2 RAND

33.63 g., 0.925 Silver 0.9936 oz. ASW, 38.7 mm. **Subject:** 2010 World Cup

Date	Mintage	F12	VF20	XF40	MS60	MS63
2006	25,000	—	—	—	—	50.00

KM# 376 2 RAND

33.63 g., 0.925 Silver 0.9936 oz. ASW, 38.7 mm. **Subject:** International Polar Year **Obv:** New national arms **Rev:** Logo above globe **Edge:** Reeded

Date	Mintage	F12	VF20	XF40	MS60	MS63
2007	6,000	PF65 75.00				

KM# 377 2 RAND

33.63 g., 0.925 Silver 0.9936 oz. ASW, 38.7 mm. **Subject:** 2010 FIFA World Cup Soccer - South Africa **Obv:** New national arms **Rev:** Tower at left, animal heads at top. animal at right, soccer ball ar bottom **Edge:** Reeded

Date	Mintage	F12	VF20	XF40	MS60	MS63
2007	20,000	PF65 65.00				

KM# 437 2 RAND
33.63 g., 0.925 Silver 0.9936 oz. ASW, 38.7 mm. **Subject:** 2010 World Cup

Date	Mintage	F12	VF20	XF40	MS60	MS63
2008	—	PF65 60.00				

KM# 457 2 RAND
33.63 g., 0.925 Silver 0.9936 oz. ASW, 38.7 mm. **Obv:** Arms **Rev:** Polar ship "SA Sgulhas

Date	Mintage	F12	VF20	XF40	MS60	MS63
2008	3,000	PF65 80.00				

KM# 546 2 RAND
33.63 g., 0.925 Silver 0.9936 oz. ASW, 38.7 mm. **Obv:** National arms **Rev:** FIFA World Cup trophy

Date	Mintage	F12	VF20	XF40	MS60	MS63
2010	Est. 20000	PF65 65.00				

KM# 524 2 RAND
33.63 g., 0.925 Silver 0.9936 oz. ASW, 38.72 mm. **Subject:** World Wildlife Fund, 50th Anniversary **Obv:** National arms **Rev:** Paradise Crane

Date	Mintage	F12	VF20	XF40	MS60	MS63
2011	—	PF65 75.00				
2011 Proof, Table Mountain privy mark	300	—	—	—	—	—

KM# 552 2 RAND
33.63 g., 0.925 Silver 0.9936 oz. ASW, 38.7 mm. **Obv:** National arms **Rev:** Rugby player advancing left

Date	Mintage	F12	VF20	XF40	MS60	MS63
2011	Est. 2011	PF65 95.00				

GOLD BULLION NATURA COINAGE

KM# 553 RAND
3.11 g., 0.999 Gold 0.0992 oz. AGW, 16.5 mm. **Obv:** National arms **Rev:** Bee

Date	Mintage	F12	VF20	XF40	MS60	MS63
2011	Est. 2000	PF65 175				

KM# 562 RAND
3.11 g., 0.9999 Gold 0.0993 oz. AGW, 16.5 mm. **Obv:** National arms **Rev:** African Monarch butterfly

Date	Mintage	F12	VF20	XF40	MS60	MS63
2012	Est. 2000	PF65 175				

KM# 517 2 RAND
7.77 g., 0.9999 Gold 0.2482 oz. AGW, 22 mm.

Date	Mintage	F12	VF20	XF40	MS60	MS63
2011	—	PF65 475				

KM# 533 2 RAND
7.77 g., 0.9999 Gold 0.2482 oz. AGW, 22 mm. **Subject:** Khoisan Heritage **Obv:** National Arms **Rev:** Incuse stone carving of an eland

Date	Mintage	F12	VF20	XF40	MS60	MS63
2012	—	PF65 475				

KM# 410 10 RAND
3.11 g., 0.9999 Gold 0.0994 oz. AGW, 16.5 mm. **Series:** Natura **Obv:** Cheetah's head **Rev:** Cheetah drinking water **Edge:** Reeded

Date	Mintage	F12	VF20	XF40	MS60	MS63
2002	3,156	PF65 200				

KM# 414 10 RAND
3.11 g., 0.9999 Gold 0.0994 oz. AGW, 16.5 mm. **Series:** Natura **Obv:** Male and female lion's heads **Rev:** Two lioness drinking water **Edge:** Reeded

Date	Mintage	F12	VF20	XF40	MS60	MS63
2003	4,233	PF65 200				

KM# 418 10 RAND
3.11 g., 0.9999 Gold 0.0994 oz. AGW, 16.5 mm. **Series:** Natura **Obv:** Caracal's head and shoulders **Rev:** Caracal drinking water **Edge:** Reeded

Date	Mintage	F12	VF20	XF40	MS60	MS63
2004	1,809	PF65 210				

KM# 422 10 RAND
3.11 g., 0.9999 Gold 0.0994 oz. AGW, 16.5 mm. **Series:** Natura **Obv:** Hippopotamus 1/2 way in water **Rev:** Hippopotamus deeply in water **Edge:** Reeded

Date	Mintage	F12	VF20	XF40	MS60	MS63
2005	—	PF65 210				

KM# 426 10 RAND
3.11 g., 0.9999 Gold 0.0994 oz. AGW, 16.5 mm. **Series:** Natura **Obv:** Giraffe's head and neck **Rev:** Giraffe drinking water **Edge:** Reeded

Date	Mintage	F12	VF20	XF40	MS60	MS63
2006	—	PF65 200				

KM# 430 10 RAND
3.11 g., 0.9999 Gold 0.0994 oz. AGW, 16.5 mm. **Series:** Natura **Obv:** Forepart of Eland left **Rev:** Eland drinking water right **Edge:** Reeded

Date	Mintage	F12	VF20	XF40	MS60	MS63
2007	—	PF65 200				

KM# 447 10 RAND
3.11 g., 0.999 Gold 0.0992 oz. AGW, 16.5 mm. **Obv:** Large elephant head and elephant family below **Rev:** One elephant eating, three elephants below

Date	Mintage	F12	VF20	XF40	MS60	MS63
2008	3,300	PF65 200				

KM# 471 10 RAND
3.11 g., 0.999 Gold 0.0992 oz. AGW, 16.5 mm. **Obv:** White rhino, silouette and forepart **Rev:** Two rhino foreparts facing left within large silouette

Date	Mintage	F12	VF20	XF40	MS60	MS63
2009	2,500	PF65 200				

KM# 549 10 RAND
3.11 g., 0.9999 Gold 0.0993 oz. AGW, 16.5 mm. **Obv:** National arms **Rev:** Rhino

Date	Mintage	F12	VF20	XF40	MS60	MS63
2010	Est. 4000	PF65 250				

KM# 509 10 RAND
3.11 g., 0.9999 Gold 0.0994 oz. AGW, 16.5 mm.

Date	Mintage	F12	VF20	XF40	MS60	MS63
2011	—	PF65 210				

KM# 525 10 RAND
3.12 g., 0.9999 Gold 0.0996 oz. AGW, 16.5 mm. **Subject:** Great Mapungubwe Transfrontier Conservation Area

Date	Mintage	F12	VF20	XF40	MS60	MS63
2012	—	PF65 210				

KM# 411 20 RAND
7.78 g., 0.9999 Gold 0.2484 oz. AGW, 22 mm. **Series:** Natura **Obv:** Cheetah's head **Rev:** Cheetah family resting **Edge:** Reeded

Date	Mintage	F12	VF20	XF40	MS60	MS63
2002	2,548	PF65 510				

KM# 415 20 RAND
7.78 g., 0.9999 Gold 0.2484 oz. AGW, 22 mm. **Series:** Natura **Obv:** Male and female lion's heads **Rev:** Lion family resting **Edge:** Reeded

Date	Mintage	F12	VF20	XF40	MS60	MS63
2003	2,799	PF65 510				

KM# 419 20 RAND
7.78 g., 0.9999 Gold 0.2484 oz. AGW, 22 mm. **Series:** Natura **Obv:** Caracal's head and shoulders **Rev:** Caracal with cub standing right **Edge:** Reeded

Date	Mintage	F12	VF20	XF40	MS60	MS63
2004	1,407	PF65 520				

KM# 423 20 RAND
7.78 g., 0.9999 Gold 0.2484 oz. AGW, 22 mm. **Series:** Natura **Obv:** Hippopotamus 1/2 way in water **Rev:** Mother and baby Hippopotamus grazing **Edge:** Reeded

Date	Mintage	F12	VF20	XF40	MS60	MS63
2005	—	PF65 520				

KM# 389 20 RAND
7.78 g., 0.9999 Gold 0.2484 oz. AGW, 22 mm. **Series:** World Heritage Site **Subject:** Mapungubwe **Obv:** New national arms **Rev:** Rhinoceros standing right **Edge:** Reeded

Date	Mintage	F12	VF20	XF40	MS60	MS63
2005	1,000	PF65 520				

KM# 427 20 RAND
7.78 g., 0.9999 Gold 0.2484 oz. AGW, 22 mm. **Series:** Natura **Obv:** Giraffe's head and neck **Rev:** Mother and baby giraffes grazing **Edge:** Reeded

Date	Mintage	F12	VF20	XF40	MS60	MS63
2006	—	PF65 520				

KM# 431 20 RAND
7.78 g., 0.9999 Gold 0.2484 oz. AGW, 22 mm. **Series:** Natura **Obv:** Forepart of Eland left **Rev:** Mother Eland and calf grazing **Edge:** Reeded

Date	Mintage	F12	VF20	XF40	MS60	MS63
2007	—	PF65 520				

KM# 448 20 RAND
7.78 g., 0.999 Gold 0.2482 oz. AGW, 22 mm. **Obv:** Large elephant head and elephant family below **Rev:** Two elephants fighting, three elephants below

Date	Mintage	F12	VF20	XF40	MS60	MS63
2008	3,300	PF65 510				

KM# 455 20 RAND
7.77 g., 0.999 Gold 0.248 oz. AGW, 22 mm. **Subject:** Vredefort Dome **Obv:** Arms **Rev:** Meteorite

Date	Mintage	F12	VF20	XF40	MS60	MS63
2008	2,000	PF65 510				

KM# 472 20 RAND
7.78 g., 0.999 Gold 0.2482 oz. AGW, 22 mm. **Obv:** White rhino silouette and forepart **Rev:** Two rhinos walking forward within silhouette

Date	Mintage	F12	VF20	XF40	MS60	MS63
2009	2,500	PF65 510				

KM# 550 20 RAND
7.78 g., 0.9999 Gold 0.2485 oz. AGW, 22 mm. **Obv:** National arms **Rev:** Rhino

Date	Mintage	F12	VF20	XF40	MS60	MS63
2010	Est. 4000	PF65 525				

KM# 510 20 RAND
7.77 g., 0.9999 Gold 0.2482 oz. AGW, 22 mm.

Date	Mintage	F12	VF20	XF40	MS60	MS63
2011	—	PF65 510				

KM# 526 20 RAND
7.77 g., 0.9999 Gold 0.2482 oz. AGW, 22 mm.

Date	Mintage	F12	VF20	XF40	MS60	MS63
2012	—	PF65 510				

KM# 412 50 RAND
15.55 g., 0.9999 Gold 0.4968 oz. AGW, 27 mm. **Series:** Natura **Obv:** Cheetah's head **Rev:** Cheetah attacking Impala **Edge:** Reeded

Date	Mintage	F12	VF20	XF40	MS60	MS63
2002	2,295	PF65 975				

KM# 416 50 RAND
15.55 g., 0.9999 Gold 0.4968 oz. AGW, 27 mm. **Series:** Natura **Obv:** Male and female lion's heads **Rev:** Female and male lions playing **Edge:** Reeded

Date	Mintage	F12	VF20	XF40	MS60	MS63
2003	2,600	PF65 975				

KM# 420 50 RAND
15.55 g., 0.9999 Gold 0.4968 oz. AGW, 27 mm. **Series:** Natura **Obv:** Caracal's head and shoulders **Rev:** Caracal eating prey **Edge:** Reeded

Date	Mintage	F12	VF20	XF40	MS60	MS63
2004	1,327	PF65 1,000				

KM# 424 50 RAND
15.55 g., 0.9999 Gold 0.4968 oz. AGW, 27 mm. **Series:** Natura **Obv:** Hippopotamus 1/2 way in water **Rev:** Hippopotamus submerged in water with head raised above, mouth wide open **Edge:** Reeded

Date	Mintage	F12	VF20	XF40	MS60	MS63
2005	—	PF65 1,000				

KM# 428 50 RAND
15.55 g., 0.9999 Gold 0.4968 oz. AGW, 27 mm. **Series:** Natura **Obv:** Giraffe's head and neck **Rev:** Giraffe family walking left **Edge:** Reeded

Date	Mintage	F12	VF20	XF40	MS60	MS63
2006	—	PF65 1,000				

KM# 432 50 RAND
15.55 g., 0.9999 Gold 0.4968 oz. AGW, 27 mm. **Series:** Natura **Obv:** Forepart of eland left **Rev:** Three eland running right **Edge:** Reeded

Date	Mintage	F12	VF20	XF40	MS60	MS63
2007	—	PF65 1,000				

KM# 449 50 RAND
15.55 g., 0.9999 Gold 0.4968 oz. AGW, 27 mm. **Obv:** Large elephant and elephant family below **Rev:** Three elephants, one trumpeting, three elephants below

Date	Mintage	F12	VF20	XF40	MS60	MS63
2008	4,800	PF65 975				

KM# 473 50 RAND
15.55 g., 0.9999 Gold 0.4967 oz. AGW, 27 mm. **Obv:** White rhino silhouette and forpart **Rev:** Two rhinos facing off within large silouette

Date	Mintage	F12	VF20	XF40	MS60	MS63
2009	4,000	PF65 975				

KM# 551 50 RAND
15.55 g., 0.9999 Gold 0.4967 oz. AGW, 27 mm. **Obv:** National arms **Rev:** Rhino

Date	Mintage	F12	VF20	XF40	MS60	MS63
2010	Est. 2500	PF65 900				

KM# 511 50 RAND
15.55 g., 0.9999 Gold 0.4968 oz. AGW, 27 mm.

Date	Mintage	F12	VF20	XF40	MS60	MS63
2011	—	PF65 975				

KM# 527 50 RAND
15.55 g., 0.9999 Gold 0.4968 oz. AGW, 27 mm.

Date	Mintage	F12	VF20	XF40	MS60	MS63
2012	—	PF65 975				

KM# 413 100 RAND
31.11 g., 0.9999 Gold 0.9936 oz. AGW, 32.69 mm. **Series:** Natura **Obv:** Cheetah's head **Rev:** Cheetah posing **Edge:** Reeded

Date	Mintage	F12	VF20	XF40	MS60	MS63
2002	2,550	PF65 1,900				
2002 RSA logo	496	PF65 2,000				

KM# 417 100 RAND
31.11 g., 0.9999 Gold 0.9936 oz. AGW, 32.69 mm. **Series:** Natura **Obv:** Male and female lion's heads **Rev:** Snarling male and female lion's heads **Edge:** Reeded **Note:** L P RSA - LION PARK RSA.

Date	Mintage	F12	VF20	XF40	MS60	MS63
2003	2,758	PF65 1,900				
2003 L P RSA	498	PF65 2,000				

KM# 421 100 RAND
31.11 g., 0.9999 Gold 0.9936 oz. AGW, 32.69 mm. **Series:** Natura **Obv:** Caracal's head and shoulders **Rev:** Caracal crouching on branch left **Edge:** Reeded **Note:** C/C - CARACAL / CARACAL

Date	Mintage	F12	VF20	XF40	MS60	MS63
2004	1,405	PF65 1,900				
2004 C/C	500	PF65 2,000				

KM# 425 100 RAND
31.11 g., 0.9999 Gold 0.9936 oz. AGW, 32.69 mm. **Series:** Natura **Obv:** Hippopotamus 1/2 way in water **Rev:** Two hippopotami submerged in water, heads raised, mouths open faced in combat **Edge:** Reeded **Note:** MAPU - MAPUNGUBWE.

Date	Mintage	F12	VF20	XF40	MS60	MS63
2005	—	PF65 1,900				
2005 MAPU	—	PF65 2,000				

KM# 429 100 RAND
31.11 g., 0.9999 Gold 0.9936 oz. AGW, 32.69 mm. **Series:** Natura **Obv:** Giraffe's head and neck **Rev:** Head and neck view of giraffe eating tree leaves **Edge:** Reeded **Note:** lpp/EWT - lion's paw print / EWT.

Date	Mintage	F12	VF20	XF40	MS60	MS63
2006	—	PF65 1,900				
2006 lpp/EWT	—	PF65 2,000				

KM# 433 100 RAND
31.11 g., 0.9999 Gold 0.9936 oz. AGW, 32.7 mm. **Series:** Natura **Obv:** Forepart of eland left **Rev:** Eland grazing left **Edge:** Reeded

Date	Mintage	F12	VF20	XF40	MS60	MS63
2007	—	PF65 1,900				

KM# 450 100 RAND
31.11 g., 0.9999 Gold 0.9927 oz. AGW, 32.69 mm. **Obv:** Large elephant head and elephant family below **Rev:** Large elephant facing, three elephants below

Date	Mintage	F12	VF20	XF40	MS60	MS63
2008	4,800	PF65 1,900				

KM# 474 100 RAND
31.11 g., 0.999 Gold 0.9927 oz. AGW, 32.7 mm. **Obv:** White rhino silouette and forepart **Rev:** Rhino standing facing within large silhouette

Date	Mintage	F12	VF20	XF40	MS60	MS63
2009	4,000	PF65 1,900				

KM# 552 100 RAND
31.10 g., 0.9999 Gold 0.9934 oz. AGW, 32.7 mm. **Obv:** National arms **Rev:** Rhino

Date	Mintage	F12	VF20	XF40	MS60	MS63
2010	Est. 2500	PF65 1,750				
2010 Proof, Paw and EWT privy mark	Est. 500	PF65 2,500				

Note: For Endangered Wildlife Trust

KM# 512 100 RAND
31.11 g., 0.9999 Gold 0.9936 oz. AGW, 32.7 mm.

Date	Mintage	F12	VF20	XF40	MS60	MS63
2011	—	PF65 1,900				

KM# 528 100 RAND
31.11 g., 0.9999 Gold 0.9936 oz. AGW, 32.7 mm.

Date	Mintage	F12	VF20	XF40	MS60	MS63
2012	—	PF65 1,900				

KM# 264 1/10 OUNCE
3.11 g., 0.9999 Gold 0.0994 oz. AGW, 16.5 mm. **Series:** Natura **Obv:** Gemsbok's upper body **Rev:** Gemsbok drinking **Edge:** Reeded

Date	Mintage	F12	VF20	XF40	MS60	MS63
2001	3,498	PF65 210				

KM# 265 1/4 OUNCE
7.78 g., 0.9999 Gold 0.2484 oz. AGW, 22 mm. **Series:** Natura **Obv:** Gemsbok's upper body **Rev:** Two Gemsbok bulls facing off **Edge:** Reeded

Date	Mintage	F12	VF20	XF40	MS60	MS63
2001	2,904	PF65 510				

KM# 266 1/2 OUNCE
15.55 g., 0.9999 Gold 0.4968 oz. AGW, 27 mm. **Series:** Natura **Obv:** Gemsbok's upper body **Rev:** Gemsbok family grazing **Edge:** Reeded

Date	Mintage	F12	VF20	XF40	MS60	MS63
2001	2,754	PF65 975				

KM# 267 OUNCE
31.11 g., 0.9999 Gold 0.9936 oz. AGW, 32.69 mm. **Series:** Natura **Obv:** Gemsbok's upper body **Rev:** Gemsbok grazing **Edge:** Reeded **Note:** ghCW - Gemsbok's head CW

Date	Mintage	F12	VF20	XF40	MS60	MS63
2001	3,104	PF65 1,900				
2001	491	PF65 2,000				

GOLD BULLION CULTURE COINAGE

KM# 378 RAND
3.11 g., 0.9999 Gold 0.0993 oz. AGW, 16.5 mm. **Series:** Cultural **Obv:** New national arms **Obv. Legend:** UMZANTSI AFRIKA - SOUTH AFRICA **Rev:** Three Xhosa tribe members **Edge:** Reeded

Date	Mintage	F12	VF20	XF40	MS60	MS63
2001	—	PF65 675				

KM# 247 RAND
3.11 g., 0.9999 Gold 0.0993 oz. AGW, 16.5 mm. **Series:** Cultural **Obv:** New national arms **Obv. Legend:** UMZANTSI AFRIKA - SOUTH AFRICA **Rev:** Seated Sotho figure with headdress **Edge:** Reeded

Date	Mintage	F12	VF20	XF40	MS60	MS63
2001	236	PF65 275				

KM# 379 RAND
3.11 g., 0.9999 Gold 0.0993 oz. AGW, 16.5 mm. **Series:** Cultural **Subject:** Tswana Nation **Obv:** New national arms **Obv. Legend:** Aforika Borwa - South Africa **Rev:** Four tribe people standing **Edge:** Reeded

Date	Mintage	F12	VF20	XF40	MS60	MS63
2002	300	PF65 350				

KM# 380 RAND
3.11 g., 0.9999 Gold 0.0993 oz. AGW, 16.5 mm. **Series:** Cultural **Obv:** New national arms **Obv. Legend:** Afrika-Dzonga - South Africa **Rev:** Tsonga tribe dancer and drummer **Edge:** Reeded

Date	Mintage	F12	VF20	XF40	MS60	MS63
2003	348	PF65 350				

KM# 381 RAND
3.11 g., 0.9999 Gold 0.0993 oz. AGW, 16.5 mm. **Series:** Cultural **Obv:** New national arms **Obv. Legend:** Afurika Tshipembe - South Africa **Rev:** Six Venda tribe members crossing bridge **Edge:** Reeded

Date	Mintage	F12	VF20	XF40	MS60	MS63
2004	380	PF65 350				

KM# 382 RAND
3.11 g., 0.9999 Gold 0.0993 oz. AGW, 16.5 mm. **Series:** Cultural **Obv:** New national arms **Obv. Legend:** iSewula Afrika - South Africa **Rev:** Ndebele woman standing, native print in background **Edge:** Reeded

Date	Mintage	F12	VF20	XF40	MS60	MS63
2005	1,000	PF65 210				

KM# 383 RAND
3.11 g., 0.9999 Gold 0.0993 oz. AGW, 16.5 mm. **Series:** Cultural **Obv:** New national arms **Obv. Legend:** Ningizimu Afrika - South Africa **Rev:** 1/2 length figure of Ema-Swati Chief left at right **Edge:** Reeded

Date	Mintage	F12	VF20	XF40	MS60	MS63
2006	1,000	PF65 210				

KM# 385 RAND
3.11 g., 0.9999 Gold 0.0993 oz. AGW, 16.5 mm. **Subject:** 2010 FIFA World Cup Soccer - South Africa **Obv:** New national arms **Obv. Legend:** SOUTH AFRICA **Rev:** Bird head at left facing animal at right, soccer ball at bottom **Edge:** Reeded

Date	Mintage	F12	VF20	XF40	MS60	MS63
2007	10,000	PF65 200				

KM# 384 RAND
3.11 g., 0.9999 Gold 0.0993 oz. AGW, 16.5 mm. **Subject:** The Afrikaner Nation **Obv:** New national arms **Obv. Legend:** SOUTH AFRIKA **Rev:** Ox drawn wagon up hillside **Edge:** Reeded

Date	Mintage	F12	VF20	XF40	MS60	MS63
2007	—	PF65 210				

KM# 454 RAND
3.11 g., 0.999 Gold 0.0992 oz. AGW, 16.5 mm. **Obv:** Arms

Date	Mintage	F12	VF20	XF40	MS60	MS63
2008	1,000	PF65 210				

KM# 478 RAND
3.11 g., 0.999 Gold 0.0992 oz. AGW, 16.5 mm. **Subject:** Northern Sotho (Bapedi) peoples **Obv:** Arms **Rev:** Woman seated, cooking

Date	Mintage	F12	VF20	XF40	MS60	MS63
2009	1,000	PF65 210				

KM# 535 RAND
3.11 g., 0.9999 Gold 0.0993 oz. AGW, 16.5 mm. **Subject:** FIFA World Cup, 2010 **Obv:** National arms **Rev:** Zakumi mascot

Date	Mintage	F12	VF20	XF40	MS60	MS63
2009	Est. 10000	PF65 225				

KM# 249 2 RAND
7.78 g., 0.9999 Gold 0.2484 oz. AGW, 22 mm. **Obv:** New national arms **Rev:** Gondwana theoretical landmass and dinosaur **Edge:** Reeded

Date	Mintage	F12	VF20	XF40	MS60	MS63
2001	558	PF65 550				

KM# 386 2 RAND
7.78 g., 0.9999 Gold 0.2484 oz. AGW, 22 mm. **Series:** World Heritage Site **Subject:** Robben Island **Obv:** New national arms **Rev:** Carved stone, island in background **Edge:** Reeded

Date	Mintage	F12	VF20	XF40	MS60	MS63
2002	999	PF65 550				

KM# 387 2 RAND
7.78 g., 0.9999 Gold 0.2484 oz. AGW, 22 mm. **Series:** World heritage Site **Subject:** Greater St. Lucia Wetland Park **Obv:** New national arms **Rev:** Various birds **Edge:** Reeded

Date	Mintage	F12	VF20	XF40	MS60	MS63
2003	637	PF65 550				

KM# 388 2 RAND
7.78 g., 0.9999 Gold 0.2484 oz. AGW, 22 mm. **Series:** World Heritage Park **Subject:** Ukhahlamba" Drakensberg Park **Obv:** New national arms **Rev:** Early painting of animal and hunters **Edge:** Reeded

Date	Mintage	F12	VF20	XF40	MS60	MS63
2004	750	PF65 550				

KM# 390 2 RAND
7.78 g., 0.9999 Gold 0.2484 oz. AGW, 22 mm. **Subject:** 2006 FIFA World Cup - Germany **Obv:** New national arms **Rev:** Soccer ball at center above partial globe within ornate border art **Edge:** Reeded

Date	Mintage	F12	VF20	XF40	MS60	MS63
2005	—	PF65 550				

KM# 391 2 RAND
7.78 g., 0.9999 Gold 0.2484 oz. AGW, 22 mm. **Series:** World Heritage Site **Subject:** Cradle of Mankind **Obv:** New national arms **Rev:** Early man standing at upper left, ape's head at upper right, skull at lower left, value at lower right **Edge:** Reeded

Date	Mintage	F12	VF20	XF40	MS60	MS63
2006	1,000	PF65 520				

KM# 392 2 RAND
7.78 g., 0.9999 Gold 0.2484 oz. AGW, 22 mm. **Subject:** 2006 FIFA World Cup Soccer - Germany **Obv:** New national arms **Rev:** Logo in ornate frame **Edge:** Reeded

Date	Mintage	F12	VF20	XF40	MS60	MS63
2006	15,000	PF65 510				

KM# 393 2 RAND
7.78 g., 0.9999 Gold 0.2484 oz. AGW, 22 mm. **Series:** World Heritage Site **Subject:** Cape Floral **Obv:** New national arms **Rev:** Bird perched on branch at left, plant at center, land in distance **Edge:** Reeded

Date	Mintage	F12	VF20	XF40	MS60	MS63
2007		PF65 510				

KM# 394 2 RAND
7.78 g., 0.9999 Gold 0.2484 oz. AGW, 22 mm. **Subject:** 2010 FIFA World Cup Soccer - South Africa **Obv:** New national arms **Rev:** Animal in ornate frame at left and right, small soccer ball at bottom below value **Edge:** Reeded

Date	Mintage	F12	VF20	XF40	MS60	MS63
2007	10,000	PF65 510				

KM# 534 2 RAND
7.78 g., 0.9999 Gold 0.2485 oz. AGW, 22 mm. **Subject:** FIFA World Cup 2010 **Obv:** National arms **Rev:** Two hands on soccerball

Date	Mintage	F12	VF20	XF40	MS60	MS63
2008	Est. 10000	PF65 450				

KM# 479 2 RAND
7.77 g., 0.999 Gold 0.248 oz. AGW, 22 mm. **Subject:** Richtersveld Cultural and Botanical Landscape **Obv:** Arms **Rev:** Native "haru on" hut and aloe pilansil tree

Date	Mintage	F12	VF20	XF40	MS60	MS63
2009	2,000	PF65 520				

KM# 536 2 RAND
7.780 Gold AGW, 22 mm. **Subject:** FIFA World Cup, 2010 **Obv:** National arms **Rev:** Zakumi mascot

Date	Mintage	F12	VF20	XF40	MS60	MS63
2009	Est. 10000	PF65 450				

KM# 547 2 RAND
7.78 g., 0.9999 Gold 0.2485 oz. AGW, 22 mm. **Obv:** National arms **Rev:** FIFA World Cup trophy

Date	Mintage	F12	VF20	XF40	MS60	MS63
2010	Est. 10000	PF65 450				

KM# 559 5 RAND
3.11 g., 0.999 Gold 0.0992 oz. AGW, 16.5 mm. **Obv:** National arms **Rev:** Walter and Albertina Sisulu

Date	Mintage	F12	VF20	XF40	MS60	MS63
2012	—	PF65 200				

KM# 560 25 RAND
31.10 g., 0.9999 Gold 0.9934 oz. AGW, 32.7 mm. **Obv:** National arms **Rev:** Walter and Albertina Sisulu

Date	Mintage	F12	VF20	XF40	MS60	MS63
2012	—	PF65 2,000				

KM# 548 200 RAND
31.10 g., 0.9999 Gold 0.9934 oz. AGW, 32.7 mm. **Obv:** National arms **Rev:** FIFA World Cup trophy

Date	Mintage	F12	VF20	XF40	MS60	MS63
2010	Est. 10000	PF65 1,750				

GOLD BULLION PROTEA COINAGE

KM# 395 5 RAND
3.11 g., 0.9999 Gold 0.0994 oz. AGW, 16.5 mm. **Subject:** 10th Anniversary Soccer "Bafana Bafana **Obv:** Protea flower **Rev:** Two players running right **Edge:** Reeded

Date	Mintage	F12	VF20	XF40	MS60	MS63
2002	386	PF65 275				

KM# 397 5 RAND
3.11 g., 0.9999 Gold 0.0994 oz. AGW, 16.5 mm. **Subject:** World Summit on Sustainable Development **Obv:** Protea flower **Rev:** Globe featuring Africa **Rev. Inscription:** prosperity **Edge:** Reeded

Date	Mintage	F12	VF20	XF40	MS60	MS63
2002	511	PF65 225				

KM# 278 5 RAND
3.11 g., 0.9999 Gold 0.0993 oz. AGW, 16.5 mm. **Obv:** Protea flower **Rev:** Soccer player heading the ball **Edge:** Reeded

Date	Mintage	F12	VF20	XF40	MS60	MS63
2002	—	PF65 210				

KM# 399 5 RAND
3.11 g., 0.9999 Gold 0.0994 oz. AGW, 16.5 mm. **Subject:** Cricket World Cup **Obv:** Protea flower **Rev:** Cricket ball striking stumps **Rev. Inscription:** Protea Rose **Edge:** Reeded

Date	Mintage	F12	VF20	XF40	MS60	MS63
2003	925	PF65 210				

KM# 289 5 RAND
3.11 g., 0.9999 Gold 0.0993 oz. AGW, 16.5 mm. **Subject:** 10th Anniversary of South African Democracy **Obv:** Protea flower **Rev:** Inscription covered flag **Edge:** Reeded

Date	Mintage	F12	VF20	XF40	MS60	MS63
2004	1,000	PF65 210				

KM# 401 5 RAND
3.11 g., 0.9999 Gold 0.0994 oz. AGW, 16.5 mm. **Subject:** 10th Anniversay Democracy **Obv:** Protea flower **Rev:** Flag made of constitution **Edge:** Reeded **Note:** 10YF - circular 10 YEARS FREEDOM

Date	Mintage	F12	VF20	XF40	MS60	MS63
2004	2,089	PF65 375				
2004 10YF	492	PF65 600				

KM# 403 5 RAND
3.11 g., 0.9999 Gold 0.0994 oz. AGW, 16.5 mm. **Subject:** Nobel Prize Winners **Obv:** Protea flower **Rev:** Freedom Charter, Luthuli seated left at desk at lower right **Edge:** Reeded **Note:** FR - FREEDOM

Date	Mintage	F12	VF20	XF40	MS60	MS63
2005	2,000	PF65 210				
2005 FR	—	PF65 600				

KM# 405 5 RAND
3.11 g., 0.9999 Gold 0.0994 oz. AGW, 16.5 mm. **Subject:** Nobel Prize Winners **Obv:** Protea flower **Rev:** Cross, inscription **Edge:** Reeded

Date	Mintage	F12	VF20	XF40	MS60	MS63
2006	5,600	PF65 210				
2006 logo	400	PF65 500				

KM# 407 5 RAND
3.11 g., 0.9999 Gold 0.0994 oz. AGW, 16.5 mm. **Subject:** Nobel Prize winners **Obv:** Protea flower **Rev:** Extract from de Klerk's acceptance speech **Edge:** Reeded

Date	Mintage	F12	VF20	XF40	MS60	MS63
2007	8,000	PF65 210				
2007 dove	—	PF65 700				

KM# 408 5 RAND
3.11 g., 0.9999 Gold 0.0994 oz. AGW, 16.5 mm. **Subject:** Nobel Prize Winners **Obv:** Protea flower **Rev:** Extract from Mandela's acceptance speech **Edge:** Reeded

Date	Mintage	F12	VF20	XF40	MS60	MS63
2007	—	PF65 210				
2007 dove	—	PF65 700				

KM# 452 5 RAND
3.11 g., 0.999 Gold 0.0992 oz. AGW, 16.5 mm. **Obv:** Protea flower **Rev:** Ghandi figure at prayer

Date	Mintage	F12	VF20	XF40	MS60	MS63
2008	8,000	PF65 210				

KM# 476 5 RAND
3.11 g., 0.999 Gold 0.0992 oz. AGW, 16.5 mm. **Obv:** Protea flower **Rev:** Portraits of C. J. Langenhoven and M. L. de Villiers with musical score

Date	Mintage	F12	VF20	XF40	MS60	MS63
2009	8,000	PF65 200				

KM# 544 5 RAND
3.11 g., 0.9999 Gold 0.0993 oz. AGW, 16.5 mm. **Obv:** Protea plant **Rev:** Nadine Gordimer

Date	Mintage	F12	VF20	XF40	MS60	MS63
2010	Est. 4000	PF65 250				

KM# 522 5 RAND
3.11 g., 0.9999 Gold 0.0993 oz. AGW, 16.5 mm. **Obv:** Protea flower **Rev:** John Maxwell Coetzee

Date	Mintage	F12	VF20	XF40	MS60	MS63
2011	—	PF65 250				

KM# 396 25 RAND
31.11 g., 0.9999 Gold 0.9936 oz. AGW, 32.69 mm. **Subject:** 10th Anniversary Soccer "Bafana Bafana" **Obv:** Protea flower **Rev:** Two players running left **Edge:** Reeded

Date	Mintage	F12	VF20	XF40	MS60	MS63
2002	137	PF65 1,950				
2002 flag/CW	84	PF65 2,250				

KM# 398 25 RAND
31.11 g., 0.9999 Gold 0.9936 oz. AGW, 32.69 mm. **Subject:** World Summit on Sustainable Development **Obv:** Protea flower **Rev:** Globe featuring Africa **Edge:** Reeded

Date	Mintage	F12	VF20	XF40	MS60	MS63
2002	421	PF65 1,900				

KM# 279 25 RAND
31.10 g., 0.9999 Gold 0.9935 oz. AGW, 32.7 mm. **Obv:** Protea flower **Rev:** Soccer player kicking ball **Edge:** Reeded

Date	Mintage	F12	VF20	XF40	MS60	MS63
2002	492	PF65 1,900				

KM# 400 25 RAND
31.11 g., 0.9999 Gold 0.9936 oz. AGW, 32.69 mm. **Subject:** Cricket World Cup **Obv:** Protea flower **Rev:** Batsman on one knee about to sweep the ball **Rev. Legend:** PROTEA **Edge:** Reeded

Date	Mintage	F12	VF20	XF40	MS60	MS63
2003	210	PF65 1,950				
2003 ball/RSA	208	PF65 1,950				

KM# 402 25 RAND
31.11 g., 0.9999 Gold 0.9936 oz. AGW, 32.69 mm. **Subject:** 10th Anniversary Democracy **Obv:** Protea flower **Rev:** Two heads of Mandela, one left, one facing, Union building in background **Edge:** Reeded **Note:** 10FP - 10/flag, people

Date	Mintage	F12	VF20	XF40	MS60	MS63
2004	6,000	PF65 3,000				
2004 10FP	492	PF65 5,400				

KM# 404 25 RAND
31.11 g., 0.9999 Gold 0.9936 oz. AGW, 32.69 mm. **Subject:** Nobel Prize Winners **Obv:** Protea flower **Rev:** Bust of Chief Albert Luthuli facing **Edge:** Reeded **Note:** FC - FREEDOM / CHARTER / 26 JUNE 1955

Date	Mintage	F12	VF20	XF40	MS60	MS63
2005	6,000	PF65 1,900				
2005 FC	—	PF65 3,750				

KM# 406 25 RAND
31.11 g., 0.9999 Gold 0.9936 oz. ACW, 32.69 mm. **Subject:** Nobel Prize Winners **Obv:** Protea flower **Rev:** Cross, bust of Archbishop Desmond Tutu right **Edge:** Reeded

Date	Mintage	F12	VF20	XF40	MS60	MS63
2006	7,600	PF65 1,900				
2006 logo	400	PF65 2,600				

KM# 409 25 RAND
31.11 g., 0.9999 Gold 0.9936 oz. AGW, 32.69 mm. **Subject:** Nobel Prize Winners **Obv:** Protea flower **Rev:** Busts of Mandela, de Klerk right **Edge:** Reeded **Note:** d-P - dove Peace

Date	Mintage	F12	VF20	XF40	MS60	MS63
2007	12,000	PF65 1,900				
2007 d-P	—	PF65 2,750				

KM# 453 25 RAND
31.11 g., 0.999 Gold 0.9927 oz. AGW, 32.7 mm. **Obv:** Protea flower **Rev:** Ghandi profile at right

Date	Mintage	F12	VF20	XF40	MS60	MS63
2008	600	PF65 2,000				
2008	12,000	PF65 1,900				

KM# 477 25 RAND
31.11 g., 0.999 Gold 0.9927 oz. AGW, 32.7 mm. **Obv:** Protea flower **Rev:** Portraits of C. J. Langenhoven and M. L. de Villiers and musical score

Date	Mintage	F12	VF20	XF40	MS60	MS63
2009	11,000	PF65 1,900				

KM# 545 25 RAND
31.10 g., 0.9999 Gold 0.9934 oz. AGW, 32.69 mm. **Obv:** Protea flower **Rev:** Nadine Gordimer

Date	Mintage	F12	VF20	XF40	MS60	MS63
2010	Est. 3000	PF65 1,750				

KM# 523 25 RAND
31.10 g., 0.9999 Gold 0.9934 oz. AGW, 32.7 mm. **Obv:** Protea flower **Rev:** John Maxwell Coetzee

Date	Mintage	F12	VF20	XF40	MS60	MS63
2011	—	PF65 1,750				
2011 Proof, JMC privy mark	—	PF65 2,000				

KM# 262 1/10 PROTEA
3.11 g., 0.9999 Gold 0.0994 oz. AGW, 16.5 mm. **Subject:** Tourism **Obv:** Protea flower **Rev:** Lion's head facing, partial shield **Rev. Inscription:** PROTEA **Edge:** Reeded

Date	Mintage	F12	VF20	XF40	MS60	MS63
2001	1,076	PF65 210				

KM# 263 PROTEA
31.11 g., 0.9999 Gold 0.9936 oz. AGW, 32.6 mm. **Subject:** Tourism **Obv:** Protea flower **Rev:** Child on sandy beach, Table Mountain in background, partial star at right **Rev. Inscription:** PROTEA **Edge:** Reeded

Date	Mintage	F12	VF20	XF40	MS60	MS63
2001	972	PF65 2,000				
2001 GRC(pp)	196	PF65 2,500				

MINT SETS

KM#	Date	Mintage	Identification	Issue Price	Mkt Val
MS38	2002 (7)	—	KM#268-274 plus 1- and 2-cent medals	30.00	32.50
MS39	2001 (9)	5,577	KM#221-229	—	60.00
MS40	2002 (7)	3,886	KM#268-274	—	52.50
MS41	2002 (7)	1,640	KM#268-274, circulated coins	—	17.50
MS42	2003 (7)	2,602	KM#324, 327, 330, 332, 335, 337, 347	—	45.00
MS43	2003 (7)	1,380	KM#324, 327, 330, 332, 335, 337, 347, circulated coins	—	10.00
MS44	2004 (7)	1,948	KM#281, 325, 326, 328, 331, 333, 336	—	37.50
MS45	2004 (7)	1,131	KM#281, 325, 325, 328, 331, 333, 336, circulated coins	—	17.50
MS46	2004 (7)	325	KM#281, 325, 326, 328, 331, 333, 336, Baby	—	22.50
MS47	2004 (7)	23	KM#281, 325, 326, 328, 331, 333, 336, Wedding	—	22.50
MS48	2005 (7)	—	KM#291-297	—	30.00
MS49	2005 (7)	—	KM#291-297, circulated coins	—	15.00
MS50	2005 (7)	—	KM#291-297, Baby	—	23.00
MS51	2005 (7)	—	KM#291-297, Wedding	—	22.50
MS52	2006 (7)	—	KM#291-297	—	22.50
MS53	2006 (7)	—	KM#291-297, circulated coins	—	15.00
MS54	2006 (7)	—	KM#291-297, Baby	—	15.00
MS55	2006 (7)	—	KM#291-297, Wedding	—	15.00
MS56	2007 (7)	—	KM#340-346	—	22.50
MS57	2007 (7)	—	KM#340-346, circulated coins	—	15.00
MS58	2007 (7)	—	KM#340-346, baby	—	15.00
MS59	2007 (7)	—	KM#340-346, wedding	—	15.00

PIEFORT PROOF SETS (PPS)

KM#	Date	Mintage	Identification	Issue Price	Mkt Val
PS242	2007 (4)	—	KM#430-433, leatherette	—	3,000

PROOF SETS

KM#	Date	Mintage	Identification	Issue Price	Mkt Val
PS170	2002 (7)	—	KM#268-274 plus 1- and 2-cent medals	40.00	65.00
PS171	2005 (4)	1,500	KM#320-323	—	300
PS172	2001 (9)	3,678	KM#221-229	—	75.00
PS173	2001 (9)	—	KM#221-229 wedding	—	75.00
PS174	2002 (7)	—	KM#268-274	—	75.00
PS175	2002 (7)	330	KM#268-274, baby	—	75.00
PS176	2003 (7)	2,356	KM#324, 327, 330, 332, 335, 337, 347	—	65.00
PS177	2003 (7)	500	KM#324, 327, 330, 332, 335, 337, 347, baby	—	65.00
PS178	2003 (7)	53	KM#324, 327, 330, 332, 335, 337, 347, wedding	—	65.00
PS179	2004 (7)	1,935	KM#281, 325, 326, 328, 331, 333, 336	—	65.00
PS180	2004 (7)	326	KM#281, 325, 326, 328, 331, 333, 336, baby	—	65.00
PS181	2004 (7)	23	KM#281, 325, 326, 328, 331, 333, 336, wedding	—	65.00
PS182	2005 (7)	—	KM#291-297	—	65.00
PS183	2005 (7)	—	KM#291-297, baby	—	65.00
PS184	2005 (7)	—	KM#291-297, wedding	—	65.00
PS185	2006 (7)	—	KM#291-297	—	65.00
PS186	2006 (7)	—	KM#291-297, baby	—	65.00
PS187	2006 (7)	—	KM#291-297, wedding	—	65.00
PS188	2007 (7)	—	KM#340-346	—	65.00
PS189	2007 (7)	—	KM#340-346, baby	—	65.00
PS190	2007 (7)	—	KM#340-346, wedding	—	65.00
PS193	2001 (4)	411	KM#243-246, wooden case	—	375
PS194	2001 (4)	746	KM#243-246, velvet (med case)	—	300
PS195	2002 (3)	81	KM#234, 243, 351 (mixed dates)	—	110
PS196	2002 (3)	95	KM#235, 244, 352 (mixed dates)	—	185
PS197	2002 (3)	81	KM#236, 245, 353 (mixed dates)	—	250
PS198	2002 (3)	92	KM#237, 246, 354 (mixed dates)	—	335
PS199	2002 (4)	411	KM#351-354, wooden case	—	375
PS200	2002 (4)	746	KM#351-354, velvet lined case	—	275
PS201	2003 (4)	59	KM#234, 243, 351, 355 (mixed dates)	—	150
PS202	2003 (4)	47	KM#235, 244, 352, 356 (mixed dates)	—	250
PS203	2003 (4)	75	KM#236, 245, 353, 357 (mixed dates)	—	330
PS204	2003 (4)	62	KM#237, 246, 354, 358 (mixed dates)	—	450
PS205	2003 (4)	532	KM#355-358, wooden case	—	375
PS206	2003 (4)	1,029	KM#355-358, velvet lined case	—	300
PS207	2004 (5)	132	KM#234, 243, 351, 355, 359 (mixed dates)	—	200
PS208	2004 (5)	133	KM#235, 244, 352, 356, 360 (mixed dates)	—	325
PS209	2004 (5)	181	KM#236, 245, 353, 357, 361 (mixed dates)	—	450
PS210	2004 (5)	158	KM#237, 246, 354, 358, 362 (mixed dates)	—	555
PS211	2004 (4)	645	KM#359-362, wooden case	—	375
PS212	2004 (4)	454	KM#359-362, velvet lined case	—	300
PS213	2004 (4)	299	KM#359-362, plus 1/4 oz. medal	—	300
PS214	2005 (4)	—	KM#320-323, wooden case	—	300
PS215	2005 (4)	—	KM#320-323, velvet lined case	—	300
PS216	2006 (4)	—	KM#316-319, wooden case	—	300
PS217	2006 (4)	—	KM#316-319, velvet lined case	—	300
PS218	2007 (2)	—	KM#363-364, wooden case	—	150
PS219	2007 (2)	—	KM#363-364	—	105
PS225	2001 (4)	691	KM#264-267	—	3,500
PS226	2001 (4)	985	KM#264-267, leatherette	—	3,500
PS227	2001 (4)	310	KM#264-267, special export	—	3,500
PS228	2002 (4)	698	KM#410-413, prestige	—	3,500
PS229	2002 (4)	529	KM#410-413, leatherette	—	3,500
PS230	2002 (4)	682	KM#410-413, special	—	3,500
PS231	2003 (4)	698	KM#414-417, prestige	—	3,500
PS232	2003 (4)	908	KM#414-417, leatherette	—	3,500
PS233	2003 (4)	722	KM#414-417, anniversary	—	3,500
PS234	2004 (4)	700	KM#418-421, prestige	—	3,525
PS235	2004 (4)	440	KM#418-421, leatherette	—	3,525
PS236	2004 (4)	125	KM#418-421, special export with silver African Continent	—	3,525
PS237	2005 (4)	—	KM#422-425, prestige	—	3,525
PS238	2005 (4)	—	KM#422-425, leatherette	—	3,525
PS239	2006 (4)	—	KM#426-429, prestige	—	3,500
PS240	2006 (4)	—	KM#426-429, leatherette	—	3,500
PS241	2007 (4)	—	KM#430-433, prestige	—	3,500

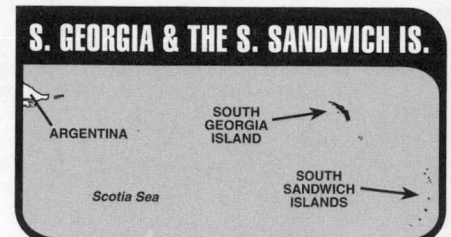

S. GEORGIA & THE S. SANDWICH IS.

South Georgia and the South Sandwich Islands are a dependency of the Falkland Islands, and located about 800 miles east of them. South Georgia is 1,450 sq. mi. (1,770 sq. km.), and the South Sandwich Islands are 120 sq. mi. (311 sq. km.) Fishing and Antarctic research are the main industries. The islands were claimed for Great Britain in 1775 by Captain James Cook.

RULER
British since 1775

BRITISH OVERSEAS TERRITORY
STANDARD COINAGE

KM# 55 POUND
28.28 g., Copper-Nickel, 38.6 mm. **Ruler:** Elizabeth II **Subject:** Kon Tiki Expedition 65th Anniversary **Rev:** Kon Tiki Ship **Mint:** Pobjoy Mint

Date	Mintage	F12	VF20	XF40	MS60	MS63
2012PM Proof						

KM# 55a POUND
12.00 g., Silver, 38.6 mm. **Ruler:** Elizabeth II **Subject:** Kon Tiki Expedition 65th Anniversary **Rev:** Kon Tiki Ship **Mint:** Pobjoy Mint

Date	Mintage	F12	VF20	XF40	MS60	MS63
2012PM Proof	Est. 10000	—	—	—	—	—

KM# 56 POUND
28.28 g., Copper-Nickel **Ruler:** Elizabeth II **Subject:** Kon Tiki Expedition **Obv:** Portraits right **Rev:** Kon Tiki Mask **Mint:** Pobjoy Mint

Date	Mintage	F12	VF20	XF40	MS60	MS63
2012PM Proof	—	—	—	—	—	10.00

KM# 56a POUND
12.00 g., 0.999 Silver 0.3829 oz. ASW **Ruler:** Elizabeth II **Subject:** Kon Tiki Expedition **Obv:** Portraits right **Rev:** Kon Tiki mask **Mint:** Pobjoy Mint

Date	Mintage	F12	VF20	XF40	MS60	MS63
2012PM	—	PF63 45.00	PF65 50.00			

KM# 7 2 POUNDS
28.28 g., Copper-Nickel, 38.61 mm. **Ruler:** Elizabeth II **Subject:** Sir Ernest H. Shackleton **Obv:** Crowned bust right **Rev:** Bust facing and ship "Endurance **Edge:** Reeded **Mint:** Pobjoy Mint

Date	Mintage	F12	VF20	XF40	MS60	MS63
2001PM	—	—	—	—	10.00	12.00

KM# 7a 2 POUNDS
28.28 g., 0.925 Silver 0.8356 oz. ASW, 38.61 mm. **Ruler:** Elizabeth II **Obv:** Crowned bust right **Rev:** Bust facing and ship "Endurance **Mint:** Pobjoy Mint

Date	Mintage	F12	VF20	XF40	MS60	MS63
2001PM	Est. 10000		PF63 40.00	PF65 50.00		

KM# 9 2 POUNDS
28.28 g., Copper-Nickel, 38.61 mm. **Ruler:** Elizabeth II **Subject:** Sir Joseph Banks **Obv:** Crowned bust right **Rev:** Cameo and ship **Mint:** Pobjoy Mint

Date	Mintage	F12	VF20	XF40	MS60	MS63
2001PM	—	—	—	—	10.00	12.00

KM# 9a 2 POUNDS
28.28 g., 0.925 Silver 0.8356 oz. ASW, 38.61 mm. **Ruler:** Elizabeth II **Obv:** Crowned bust right **Rev:** Ship and cameo **Mint:** Pobjoy Mint

Date	Mintage	F12	VF20	XF40	MS60	MS63
2001PM	Est. 10000		PF63 40.00	PF65 50.00		

KM# 11 2 POUNDS
28.28 g., Copper-Nickel, 38.6 mm. **Ruler:** Elizabeth II **Subject:** Queen Elizabeth II's Golden Jubilee **Obv:** Crowned bust right **Rev:** Young crowned bust right **Edge:** Reeded **Mint:** Pobjoy Mint

Date	Mintage	F12	VF20	XF40	MS60	MS63
2002PM	—	—	—	—	10.00	12.00

KM# 11a 2 POUNDS
28.28 g., 0.925 Gold Plated Silver 0.8356 oz., 38.6 mm. **Ruler:** Elizabeth II **Subject:** Queen Elizabeth II's Golden Jubilee **Obv:** Crowned bust right **Rev:** Young crowned bust right **Edge:** Reeded **Mint:** Pobjoy Mint

Date	Mintage	F12	VF20	XF40	MS60	MS63
2002PM	10,000		PF63 40.00	PF65 50.00		

KM# 13 2 POUNDS
28.28 g., Copper-Nickel, 38.6 mm. **Ruler:** Elizabeth II **Subject:** Queen Elizabeth II's Golden Jubilee **Obv:** Crowned bust right **Rev:** Small crown above shield flanked by flower sprigs **Edge:** Reeded **Mint:** Pobjoy Mint

Date	Mintage	F12	VF20	XF40	MS60	MS63
2002PM	—	—	—	—	10.00	12.00

KM# 13a 2 POUNDS
28.28 g., 0.925 Gold Plated Silver 0.8356 oz., 38.6 mm. **Ruler:** Elizabeth II **Subject:** Queen Elizabeth II's Golden Jubilee **Obv:** Crowned bust right **Rev:** Small crown above shield flanked by flower sprigs **Edge:** Reeded **Mint:** Pobjoy Mint

Date	Mintage	F12	VF20	XF40	MS60	MS63
2002PM	10,000		PF63 40.00	PF65 50.00		

KM# 15 2 POUNDS
28.28 g., Copper-Nickel, 38.6 mm. **Ruler:** Elizabeth II **Subject:** Diana, Princess of Wales - The Work Continues **Obv:** Crowned bust right **Rev:** Head 1/4 left **Edge:** Reeded **Mint:** Pobjoy Mint

Date	Mintage	F12	VF20	XF40	MS60	MS63
2002PM	—	—	—	—	10.00	12.00

KM# 17 2 POUNDS
28.28 g., Copper-Nickel, 38.6 mm. **Ruler:** Elizabeth II **Subject:** Prince William's 21st Birthday **Obv:** Crowned bust right **Rev:** Arms of Prince William of Wales **Edge:** Reeded **Mint:** Pobjoy Mint

Date	Mintage	F12	VF20	XF40	MS60	MS63
2003PM	—	—	—	—	10.00	12.00

KM# 17a 2 POUNDS
28.28 g., 0.925 Silver 0.8356 oz. ASW, 38.6 mm. **Ruler:** Elizabeth II **Subject:** Prince William's 21st Birthday **Obv:** Crowned bust right **Rev:** Arms of Prince William of Wales **Edge:** Reeded **Mint:** Pobjoy Mint

Date	Mintage	F12	VF20	XF40	MS60	MS63
2003PM	—		PF63 40.00	PF65 50.00		

KM# 18 2 POUNDS
28.28 g., Copper-Nickel, 38.6 mm. **Ruler:** Elizabeth II **Obv:** Crowned bust right **Rev:** Capt. Cook, ship and map **Edge:** Reeded **Mint:** Pobjoy Mint

Date	Mintage	F12	VF20	XF40	MS60	MS63
2003PM	—	—	—	—	10.00	12.00

KM# 18a 2 POUNDS
28.28 g., 0.925 Silver 0.8356 oz. ASW, 38.6 mm. **Ruler:** Elizabeth II **Obv:** Crowned bust right **Rev:** Capt. Cook, ship and map **Edge:** Reeded **Mint:** Pobjoy Mint

Date	Mintage	F12	VF20	XF40	MS60	MS63
2003PM	—		PF63 40.00	PF65 50.00		

KM# 20 2 POUNDS
28.28 g., Copper-Nickel, 38.6 mm. **Ruler:** Elizabeth II **Obv:** Crowned bust right **Rev:** Sir Ernest Shackleton and icebound ship **Edge:** Reeded **Mint:** Pobjoy Mint

Date	Mintage	F12	VF20	XF40	MS60	MS63
2004PM	—	—	—	—	15.00	16.50

KM# 20a 2 POUNDS
28.28 g., 0.925 Silver 0.8356 oz. ASW, 38.6 mm. **Ruler:** Elizabeth II **Obv:** Crowned bust right **Rev:** Sir Ernest Shackleton and icebound ship **Edge:** Reeded **Mint:** Pobjoy Mint

Date	Mintage	F12	VF20	XF40	MS60	MS63
2004PM	10,000		PF63 40.00	PF65 50.00		

KM# 21 2 POUNDS
28.28 g., Copper-Nickel, 38.6 mm. **Ruler:** Elizabeth II **Subject:** Centennial of Grytviken **Obv:** Crowned bust right **Rev:** Portrait above ship in harbor **Edge:** Reeded **Mint:** Pobjoy Mint

Date	Mintage	F12	VF20	XF40	MS60	MS63
2004PM	—	—	—	—	15.00	16.50

KM# 21a 2 POUNDS
28.28 g., 0.925 Silver 0.8356 oz. ASW, 38.6 mm. **Ruler:** Elizabeth II **Subject:** Centennial of Grytviken **Obv:** Crowned bust right **Rev:** Portrait above ship in harbor **Edge:** Reeded **Mint:** Pobjoy Mint

Date	Mintage	F12	VF20	XF40	MS60	MS63
2004PM	—		PF63 40.00	PF65 50.00		

KM# 25 2 POUNDS
28.28 g., Copper-Nickel, 38.61 mm. **Ruler:** Elizabeth II **Subject:** Marriage of Charles to Parker Bowles **Rev:** Arms of Prince of Wales **Mint:** Pobjoy Mint

Date	Mintage	F12	VF20	XF40	MS60	MS63
2005PM	—	—	—	—	8.50	10.00

KM# 25a 2 POUNDS
28.28 g., 0.925 Silver 0.8356 oz. ASW, 38.61 mm. **Ruler:** Elizabeth II **Subject:** Marriage of Prince Charles to Camilla Parker-Bowles **Mint:** Pobjoy Mint

Date	Mintage	F12	VF20	XF40	MS60	MS63
2005PM	Est. 10000		PF63 45.00	PF65 53.00		

KM# 22 2 POUNDS
28.28 g., Copper-Nickel, 38.61 mm. **Ruler:** Elizabeth II **Obv:** Elizabeth II **Rev:** Rockhopper Penguin and chick **Edge:** Reeded **Mint:** Pobjoy Mint

Date	Mintage	F12	VF20	XF40	MS60	MS63
2006PM	—	—	—	—	12.00	14.00

KM# 23 2 POUNDS
28.28 g., Copper-Nickel, 38.61 mm. **Ruler:** Elizabeth II **Obv:** Elizabeth II **Rev:** Elephant Seal and cub **Edge:** Reeded **Mint:** Pobjoy Mint

Date	Mintage	F12	VF20	XF40	MS60	MS63
2006PM	—	—	—	—	10.00	12.00

KM# 22a 2 POUNDS
28.28 g., 0.925 Silver 0.8356 oz. ASW, 38.61 mm. **Ruler:** Elizabeth II **Subject:** Rockhopper Penguin **Mint:** Pobjoy Mint

Date	Mintage	F12	VF20	XF40	MS60	MS63
2006PM	Est. 10000	PF63 45.00		PF65 53.00		

KM# 23a 2 POUNDS
28.28 g., 0.925 Silver 0.8356 oz. ASW, 38.61 mm. **Ruler:** Elizabeth II **Subject:** Elephant Seal **Mint:** Pobjoy Mint

Date	Mintage	F12	VF20	XF40	MS60	MS63
2006PM	Est. 10000	PF63 45.00		PF65 53.00		

KM# 24a 2 POUNDS
28.28 g., 0.925 Silver 0.8356 oz. ASW, 38.61 mm. **Ruler:** Elizabeth II **Subject:** Humpback Whale **Mint:** Pobjoy Mint

Date	Mintage	F12	VF20	XF40	MS60	MS63
2006PM	Est. 10000	PF63 45.00		PF65 53.00		

KM# 27a 2 POUNDS
28.28 g., 0.925 Silver 0.8356 oz. ASW, 38.61 mm. **Ruler:** Elizabeth II **Subject:** Grey-Headed Albatross **Mint:** Pobjoy Mint

Date	Mintage	F12	VF20	XF40	MS60	MS63
2006PM	Est. 10000	PF63 45.00		PF65 53.00		

KM# 24 2 POUNDS
28.28 g., Copper-Nickel, 38.61 mm. **Ruler:** Elizabeth II **Obv:** Elizabeth II **Rev:** Humpback Whale and calf **Edge:** Reeded **Mint:** Pobjoy Mint

Date	Mintage	F12	VF20	XF40	MS60	MS63
2006PM	—	—	—	—	8.50	12.00

KM# 26 2 POUNDS
28.28 g., Copper-Nickel, 38.61 mm. **Ruler:** Elizabeth II **Subject:** Queen Elizabeth II's 80th Birthday **Rev:** Queen on horseback taking part in Trouping of the Color ceremony **Mint:** Pobjoy Mint

Date	Mintage	F12	VF20	XF40	MS60	MS63
2006PM	—	—	—	—	8.50	10.00

KM# 26a 2 POUNDS
28.28 g., 0.925 Silver 0.8356 oz. ASW, 38.61 mm. **Ruler:** Elizabeth II **Subject:** Queen Elizabeth II's 80th Birthday **Rev:** Queen on horseback taking part in Trouping of the Color ceremony **Mint:** Pobjoy Mint

Date	Mintage	F12	VF20	XF40	MS60	MS63
2006	25,000	PF63 60.00		PF65 75.00		

KM# 27 2 POUNDS
28.28 g., Copper-Nickel, 38.61 mm. **Ruler:** Elizabeth II **Rev:** Pair of Grey-headed Albatros **Mint:** Pobjoy Mint

Date	Mintage	F12	VF20	XF40	MS60	MS63
2006PM	—	—	—	—	8.50	12.00

KM# 28 2 POUNDS
28.28 g., Copper-Nickel, 38.61 mm. **Ruler:** Elizabeth II **Subject:** Queen Elizabeth II's 80th Birthday **Rev:** 1953 Royal family **Mint:** Pobjoy Mint

Date	Mintage	F12	VF20	XF40	MS60	MS63
2006PM	—	—	—	—	8.50	10.00

KM# 28a 2 POUNDS
28.28 g., 0.925 Silver 0.8356 oz. ASW, 38.61 mm. **Ruler:** Elizabeth II **Subject:** Queen Elizabeth II's 80th Birthday **Rev:** 1953 Royal family **Mint:** Pobjoy Mint

Date	Mintage	F12	VF20	XF40	MS60	MS63
2006	25,000	PF63 60.00		PF65 75.00		

KM# 29 2 POUNDS
28.28 g., Copper-Nickel, 38.61 mm. **Ruler:** Elizabeth II **Subject:** Queen Elizabeth's II 80th Birthday **Rev:** Wedding of Queen Elizabeth II and Prince Philip **Mint:** Pobjoy Mint

Date	Mintage	F12	VF20	XF40	MS60	MS63
2006PM	—	—	—	—	8.50	10.00

KM# 29a 2 POUNDS
28.28 g., 0.925 Silver 0.8356 oz. ASW, 38.61 mm. **Ruler:** Elizabeth II **Subject:** Queen Elizabeth's 80th Birthday **Rev:** Wedding of Queen Elizabeth II and Prince Philip **Mint:** Pobjoy Mint

Date	Mintage	F12	VF20	XF40	MS60	MS63
2006	25,000	PF63 60.00		PF65 75.00		

KM# 30 2 POUNDS
28.28 g., Copper-Nickel, 38.61 mm. **Ruler:** Elizabeth II **Subject:** Queen Elizabeth II's 80th Birthday **Rev:** Queen in Garter robes **Mint:** Pobjoy Mint

Date	Mintage	F12	VF20	XF40	MS60	MS63
2006PM	—	—	—	—	8.50	10.00

KM# 30a 2 POUNDS
28.28 g., 0.925 Silver 0.8356 oz. ASW, 38.61 mm. **Ruler:** Elizabeth II **Subject:** Queen Elizabeth II's 80th Birthday **Rev:** Queen in Garter robes **Mint:** Pobjoy Mint

Date	Mintage	F12	VF20	XF40	MS60	MS63
2006	25,000	PF63 60.00		PF65 75.00		

KM# 31 2 POUNDS
28.28 g., Copper-Nickel, 38.61 mm. **Ruler:** Elizabeth II **Rev:** Queen Elizabeth II 1926 (1953 portrait) **Mint:** Pobjoy Mint

Date	Mintage	F12	VF20	XF40	MS60	MS63
2007PM	—	—	—	—	8.50	10.00

KM# 32 2 POUNDS
28.28 g., Copper-Nickel, 38.61 mm. **Ruler:** Elizabeth II **Subject:** 25th Anniversary of Liberation **Rev:** Warship and helicopters **Mint:** Pobjoy Mint

Date	Mintage	F12	VF20	XF40	MS60	MS63
2007PM	—	—	—	—	8.50	10.00

KM# 33 2 POUNDS
28.28 g., Copper-Nickel, 38.61 mm. **Ruler:** Elizabeth II **Rev:** Trans Artic Expedition **Mint:** Pobjoy Mint

Date	Mintage	F12	VF20	XF40	MS60	MS63
2007PM	—	—	—	—	8.50	10.00

KM# 32a 2 POUNDS
28.28 g., 0.925 Silver 0.8356 oz. ASW, 38.61 mm. **Ruler:** Elizabeth II **Subject:** 25 Years of the Liberation of South Georgia **Mint:** Pobjoy Mint

Date	Mintage	F12	VF20	XF40	MS60	MS63
2007PM	Est. 10000	PF63 45.00		PF65 53.00		

KM# 33a 2 POUNDS
28.28 g., 0.925 Silver 0.8356 oz. ASW, 38.61 mm. **Ruler:** Elizabeth II **Subject:** Trans-arctic Expediton **Mint:** Pobjoy Mint

Date	Mintage	F12	VF20	XF40	MS60	MS63
2007PM	Est. 25000	PF63 45.00		PF65 53.00		

KM# 34a 2 POUNDS
28.28 g., 0.925 Silver 0.8356 oz. ASW, 38.61 mm. **Ruler:** Elizabeth II **Subject:** International Polar Year **Rev:** Sir Ernest Henry Shackleton with dogs in Antarctica **Mint:** Pobjoy Mint

Date	Mintage	F12	VF20	XF40	MS60	MS63
2007PM	Est. 25000	PF63 45.00		PF65 53.00		

KM# 35a 2 POUNDS
28.28 g., 0.925 Silver 0.8356 oz. ASW, 38.61 mm. **Ruler:** Elizabeth II **Subject:** Sir Ernest Henry Shackleton **Mint:** Pobjoy Mint

Date	Mintage	F12	VF20	XF40	MS60	MS63
2007PM	Est. 10000	PF63 45.00		PF65 53.00		

KM# 36a 2 POUNDS
28.28 g., 0.925 Silver 0.8356 oz. ASW, 38.61 mm. **Ruler:** Elizabeth II **Subject:** James Cook **Mint:** Pobjoy Mint

Date	Mintage	F12	VF20	XF40	MS60	MS63
2007PM	Est. 10000	PF63 45.00		PF65 53.00		

KM# 34 2 POUNDS
28.28 g., Copper-Nickel, 38.61 mm. **Ruler:** Elizabeth II **Subject:** International Polar Year **Rev:** Shackelton Expedition **Mint:** Pobjoy Mint

Date	Mintage	F12	VF20	XF40	MS60	MS63
2007PM	—	—	—	—	8.50	10.00

KM# 48 2 POUNDS
28.28 g., 0.925 Silver 0.8356 oz. ASW **Ruler:** Elizabeth II **Rev:** King Penguin in color **Shape:** 38.61 **Mint:** Pobjoy Mint

Date	Mintage	F12	VF20	XF40	MS60	MS63
2007PM	Est. 5000	PF65 75.00				

KM# 35 2 POUNDS
28.28 g., Copper-Nickel, 38.61 mm. **Ruler:** Elizabeth II **Rev:** Ernest Shacketon **Mint:** Pobjoy Mint

Date	Mintage	F12	VF20	XF40	MS60	MS63
2007PM	—	—	—	—	8.50	10.00

KM# 36 2 POUNDS
28.28 g., Copper-Nickel, 38.61 mm. **Ruler:** Elizabeth II **Rev:** James Cook **Mint:** Pobjoy Mint

Date	Mintage	F12	VF20	XF40	MS60	MS63
2007PM	—	—	—	—	8.50	10.00

KM# 37 2 POUNDS
28.28 g., Copper-Nickel, 38.6 mm. **Ruler:** Elizabeth II **Subject:** Diamond Wedding Anniversary **Obv:** Conjoined busts with Prince Philip right **Obv. Legend:** SOUTH GEORGIA & SOUTH SANDWICH ISLANDS **Rev:** Bust of Princess Elizabeth facing **Rev. Legend:** Diamond Wedding of H.M. Queen Elizabeth II & H.R.H. Prince Philip **Rev. Inscription:** THE BRIDE **Edge:** Reeded **Mint:** Pobjoy Mint

Date	Mintage	F12	VF20	XF40	MS60	MS63
2007	—	—	—	—	15.00	16.50

KM# 37a 2 POUNDS
28.28 g., 0.925 Silver 0.8356 oz. ASW, 38.6 mm. **Ruler:** Elizabeth II **Subject:** Diamond Wedding Anniversary **Obv:** Conjoined busts with Prince Philip right **Obv. Legend:** SOUTH GEORGIA & SOUTH SANDWICH ISLANDS **Rev:** Bust of Princess Elizabeth facing **Rev. Legend:** Diamond Wedding of H.M. Queen Elizabeth II & H.R.H. Prince Philip **Rev. Inscription:** THE BRIDE **Edge:** Reeded **Mint:** Pobjoy Mint

Date	Mintage	F12	VF20	XF40	MS60	MS63
2007	25,000	PF63 60.00		PF65 75.00		

KM# 38 2 POUNDS
28.28 g., Copper-Nickel, 38.6 mm. **Ruler:** Elizabeth II **Subject:** Diamond Wedding Anniversary **Obv:** Conjoined busts with Prince Philip right **Obv. Legend:** SOUTH GEORGIA & SOUTH SANDWICH ISLANDS **Rev:** Bust of the bridegroom facing **Rev. Legend:** Diamond Wedding of H.M. Queen Elizabeth II & H.R.H. Prince Philip **Rev. Inscription:** THE BRIDEGROOM **Edge:** Reeded **Mint:** Pobjoy Mint

Date	Mintage	F12	VF20	XF40	MS60	MS63
2007	—	—	—	—	15.00	16.50

KM# 38a 2 POUNDS
28.28 g., 0.925 Silver 0.8356 oz. ASW, 38.6 mm. **Ruler:** Elizabeth II **Subject:** Diamond Wedding Anniversary **Obv:** Conjoined busts with Prince Philip right **Obv. Legend:** SOUTH GEORGIA & SOUTH SANDWICH ISLANDS **Rev:** Bust of the bridegroom facing **Rev. Legend:** Diamond Wedding of H.M. Queen Elizabeth II & H.R.H. Prince Philip **Rev. Inscription:** THE BRIDEGROOM **Edge:** Reeded **Mint:** Pobjoy Mint

Date	Mintage	F12	VF20	XF40	MS60	MS63
2007	25,000	PF63 60.00		PF65 75.00		

KM# 39 2 POUNDS
28.28 g., Copper-Nickel, 38.6 mm. **Ruler:** Elizabeth II **Subject:** Diamond Wedding Anniversary **Obv:** Conjoined busts with Prince Philip right **Obv. Legend:** SOUTH GEORGIA & SOUTH SANDWICH ISLANDS **Rev:** 1/2 length figures of royal engaged couple looking at each other **Rev. Legend:** Diamond Wedding of H.M. Queen Elizabeth II & H.R.H. Prince Philip **Rev. Inscription:** ROYAL ENGAGEMENT • JULY • 10 • 1947 **Edge:** Reeded **Mint:** Pobjoy Mint

Date	Mintage	F12	VF20	XF40	MS60	MS63
2007	—	—	—	—	15.00	16.50

KM# 39a 2 POUNDS
28.28 g., 0.925 Silver 0.8356 oz. ASW, 38.6 mm. **Ruler:** Elizabeth II **Subject:** Diamond Wedding **Obv:** Conjoined busts with Prince Philip right **Obv. Legend:** SOUTH GEORGIA & SOUTH SANDWICH ISLANDS **Rev:** 1/2 length figures of royal engaged couple looking at each other **Rev. Legend:** Diamond Wedding of H.M. Queen Elizabeth II & H.R.H. Prince Philip **Rev. Inscription:** ROYAL ENGAGEMENT • JULY • 10 • 1947 **Edge:** Reeded **Mint:** Pobjoy Mint

Date	Mintage	F12	VF20	XF40	MS60	MS63
2007	25,000	PF63 60.00	PF65 75.00			

KM# 40 2 POUNDS
28.28 g., Copper-Nickel, 38.6 mm. **Ruler:** Elizabeth II **Subject:** Diamond Wedding Anniversary **Obv:** Conjoined busts with Prince Philip right **Obv. Legend:** SOUTH GEORGIA & SOUTH SANDWICH ISLANDS **Rev:** Marriage license, jubilant crowd scene **Rev. Legend:** Diamond Wedding of H.M. Queen Elizabeth II & H.R.H. Prince Philip **Rev. Inscription:** THE MARRIAGE LICENSE **Edge:** Reeded **Mint:** Pobjoy Mint

Date	Mintage	F12	VF20	XF40	MS60	MS63
2007	—	—	—	—	15.00	16.50

KM# 40a 2 POUNDS
28.28 g., 0.925 Silver 0.8356 oz. ASW, 38.6 mm. **Ruler:** Elizabeth II **Subject:** Diamond Wedding Anniversary **Obv:** Conjoined busts with Prince Philip right **Obv. Legend:** SOUTH GEORGIA & SOUTH SANDWICH ISLANDS **Rev:** Marriage license, jubilant crowd scene **Rev. Legend:** Diamond Wedding of H.M. Queen Elizabeth II & H.R.H. Prince Philip **Rev. Inscription:** THE MARRIAGE LICENSE **Edge:** Reeded **Mint:** Pobjoy Mint

Date	Mintage	F12	VF20	XF40	MS60	MS63
2007	25,000	PF63 60.00	PF65 75.00			

KM# 42 2 POUNDS
28.28 g., Copper-Nickel, 38.61 mm. **Ruler:** Elizabeth II **Rev:** Four coinage portraits of Elizabeth II **Mint:** Pobjoy Mint

Date	Mintage	F12	VF20	XF40	MS60	MS63
2008PM Proof	—	—	—	—	—	15.00

KM# 42a 2 POUNDS
28.28 g., 0.925 Silver 0.8356 oz. ASW, 38.61 mm. **Ruler:** Elizabeth II **Subject:** Queen Elizabeth II in the Age of Queen Victoria **Mint:** Pobjoy Mint

Date	Mintage	F12	VF20	XF40	MS60	MS63
2008PM	Est. 10000	PF63 45.00	PF65 53.00			

KM# 49 2 POUNDS
28.28 g., Copper-Nickel, 38.61 mm. **Ruler:** Elizabeth II **Subject:** Royal Air Force, 90th Anniversary **Rev:** C 180 Hercules **Mint:** Pobjoy Mint

Date	Mintage	F12	VF20	XF40	MS60	MS63
2008PM	—	—	—	—	—	15.00

KM# 49a 2 POUNDS
28.28 g., 0.925 Silver 0.8356 oz. ASW, 38.61 mm. **Ruler:** Elizabeth II **Subject:** 90th Anniversary of the British Royal Air Force **Mint:** Pobjoy Mint

Date	Mintage	F12	VF20	XF40	MS60	MS63
2008PM	Est. 10000	PF63 45.00	PF65 53.00			

KM# 41 2 POUNDS
28.28 g., Copper-Nickel, 38.61 mm. **Ruler:** Elizabeth II **Subject:** The Nimrod Expedition **Rev:** Sailing ship stuck in ice **Mint:** Pobjoy Mint

Date	Mintage	F12	VF20	XF40	MS60	MS63
2009PM	—	—	—	—	—	16.50

KM# 41a 2 POUNDS
28.28 g., 0.925 Silver 0.8356 oz. ASW, 38.61 mm. **Ruler:** Elizabeth II **Subject:** 100th Anniversary of the British Antarctic Expedition **Mint:** Pobjoy Mint

Date	Mintage	F12	VF20	XF40	MS60	MS63
2009PM	Est. 10000	PF63 45.00	PF65 53.00			

KM# 50 2 POUNDS
28.28 g., Copper-Nickel, 38.61 mm. **Ruler:** Elizabeth II **Rev:** View of icebound sailing ship Terra Nova **Rev. Legend:** CENTENARY OF THE RACE TO THE SOUTH POLE **Mint:** Pobjoy Mint

Date	Mintage	F12	VF20	XF40	MS60	MS63
2010PM	—	—	—	—	—	15.00

KM# 50a 2 POUNDS
28.28 g., 0.925 Silver 0.8356 oz. ASW, 38.61 mm. **Ruler:** Elizabeth II **Subject:** 100th Anniversary of the Antarctic Expedition of Roald Amundesn and Robert Falcon Scott **Mint:** Pobjoy Mint

Date	Mintage	F12	VF20	XF40	MS60	MS63
2010PM	Est. 10000	PF63 45.00	PF65 53.00			

KM# 44 2 POUNDS
28.28 g., Copper-Nickel, 38.6 mm. **Ruler:** Elizabeth II **Obv:** Bust with tiara right **Rev:** Prince Philip and Elizabeth II, half-length facing above diamond, rays at side **Mint:** Pobjoy Mint

Date	Mintage	F12	VF20	XF40	MS60	MS63
2011PM	—	—	—	—	8.50	12.00

KM# 44a 2 POUNDS
28.28 g., 0.925 Silver 0.8356 oz. ASW, 38.6 mm. **Ruler:** Elizabeth II **Obv:** Bust with tiara right **Rev:** Prince Philip and Elizabeth II, half-lenght facing above diamond, rays at side **Mint:** Pobjoy Mint

Date	Mintage	F12	VF20	XF40	MS60	MS63
2011PM	—	PF63 65.00	PF65 75.00			

KM# 43 2 POUNDS
28.28 g., Copper-Nickel, 38.61 mm. **Ruler:** Elizabeth II **Subject:** Frozen Planet **Obv:** Bust with tiara right **Rev:** King Penguin and young **Mint:** Pobjoy Mint

Date	Mintage	F12	VF20	XF40	MS60	MS63
2011PM	—	—	—	—	15.00	16.50

KM# 43a 2 POUNDS
28.28 g., 0.925 Silver 0.8356 oz. ASW, 38.61 mm. **Ruler:** Elizabeth II **Subject:** Frozen Planet **Rev:** King Penguin and young **Mint:** Pobjoy Mint

Date	Mintage	F12	VF20	XF40	MS60	MS63
2011PM	—	PF63 65.00	PF65 75.00			

KM# 51 2 POUNDS
28.28 g., Copper-Nickel, 38.61 mm. **Ruler:** Elizabeth II **Subject:** Royal Wedding **Rev:** Royal Arms of Prince William **Mint:** Pobjoy Mint

Date	Mintage	F12	VF20	XF40	MS60	MS63
2011PM	—	—	—	—	—	15.00

KM# 51a 2 POUNDS
28.28 g., 0.925 Silver 0.8356 oz. ASW, 38.61 mm. **Ruler:** Elizabeth II **Subject:** Marriage of Prince William and Catherine Middleton **Mint:** Pobjoy Mint

Date	Mintage	F12	VF20	XF40	MS60	MS63
2011PM	Est. 10000	PF63 50.00	PF65 55.00			

KM# 52 2 POUNDS
28.28 g., Copper-Nickel, 38.61 mm. **Ruler:** Elizabeth II **Subject:** Elizabeth II, 60th Anniversary of reign **Rev:** Queen Mother and Princess Elizabeth **Mint:** Pobjoy Mint

Date	Mintage	F12	VF20	XF40	MS60	MS63
2012PM	—	—	—	—	—	15.00

KM# 52a 2 POUNDS
28.28 g., 0.925 Silver 0.8356 oz. ASW, 38.61 mm. **Ruler:** Elizabeth II **Subject:** 60th Anniversary of the Coronation of Queen Elizabeth II **Mint:** Pobjoy Mint

Date	Mintage	F12	VF20	XF40	MS60	MS63
2012PM	Est. 10000	PF63 50.00	PF65 55.00			

KM# 53 2 POUNDS
28.28 g., Copper-Nickel, 38.61 mm. **Ruler:** Elizabeth II **Rev:** Elizabeth II in hat **Mint:** Pobjoy Mint

Date	Mintage	F12	VF20	XF40	MS60	MS63
2012PM	—	—	—	—	—	15.00

KM# 53a 2 POUNDS
28.28 g., 0.925 Silver 0.8356 oz. ASW, 38.61 mm. **Ruler:** Elizabeth II **Subject:** Queen Elizabeth II - Christmas Speech **Mint:** Pobjoy Mint

Date	Mintage	F12	VF20	XF40	MS60	MS63
2012PM	Est. 10000	PF63 50.00	PF65 55.00			

KM# 54 2 POUNDS
28.28 g., Copper-Nickel, 38.61 mm. **Ruler:** Elizabeth II **Subject:** Prince William and Kate Middleton, 1st Wedding Anniversary **Rev:** First Kiss on Buckingham Palace Balcony **Mint:** Pobjoy Mint

Date	Mintage	F12	VF20	XF40	MS60	MS63
2012PM	—	—	—	—	—	15.00

KM# 54a 2 POUNDS
28.28 g., 0.925 Silver 0.8356 oz. ASW, 38.61 mm. **Ruler:** Elizabeth II **Subject:** Marriage of Prince William and Catherine Middleton **Mint:** Pobjoy Mint

Date	Mintage	F12	VF20	XF40	MS60	MS63
2012PM	Est. 10000	PF63 50.00	PF65 55.00			

KM# 31a 2 POUNDS
28.28 g., 0.925 Silver 0.8356 oz. ASW, 38.61 mm. **Ruler:** Elizabeth II **Subject:** Queen Elizabeth II **Mint:** Pobjoy Mint

Date	Mintage	F12	VF20	XF40	MS60	MS63
2013PM	Est. 10000	PF63 50.00	PF65 55.00			

KM# 62 2 POUNDS
28.28 g., Copper-Nickel, 38.61 mm. **Ruler:** Elizabeth II **Subject:** Birth of Prince George **Rev:** William and Catherine kissing, blue stork above **Mint:** Pobjoy Mint

Date	Mintage	F12	VF20	XF40	MS60	MS63
2013PM	—	—	—	—	—	15.00

KM# 62a 2 POUNDS
28.28 g., 0.925 Silver 0.8356 oz. ASW, 38.61 mm. **Ruler:** Elizabeth II **Subject:** Birth of Prince George **Rev:** William and Catherine kissing, blue stork above **Mint:** Pobjoy Mint

Date	Mintage	F12	VF20	XF40	MS60	MS63
2013PM	10,000	PF63 55.00	PF65 60.00			

KM# 59 2 POUNDS
10.00 g., 0.990 Titanium 0.3162 oz., 36.1 mm. **Ruler:** Elizabeth II **Subject:** Blue Whale **Mint:** Pobjoy Mint

Date	Mintage	F12	VF20	XF40	MS60	MS63
2013PM Proof	Est. 5000	—	—	—	—	—

KM# 60 2 POUNDS
28.28 g., Copper-Nickel, 38.6 mm. **Ruler:** Elizabeth II **Subject:** Blue Whale **Mint:** Pobjoy Mint

Date	Mintage	F12	VF20	XF40	MS60	MS63
2013PM Uncirculated	—	—	—	—	—	—

KM# 60a 2 POUNDS
28.28 g., Silver, 38.6 mm. **Ruler:** Elizabeth II **Subject:** Blue Whale **Mint:** Pobjoy Mint

Date	Mintage	F12	VF20	XF40	MS60	MS63
2013PM	Est. 10000	PF63 55.00	PF65 60.00			

KM# 61 2 POUNDS
28.28 g., Copper-Nickel, 38.6 mm. **Ruler:** Elizabeth II **Subject:** Weddell Seal Pup **Mint:** Pobjoy Mint

Date	Mintage	F12	VF20	XF40	MS60	MS63
2013PM Uncirculated	—	—	—	—	—	—

KM# 61a 2 POUNDS
28.28 g., Silver, 38.6 mm. **Ruler:** Elizabeth II **Subject:** Weddell Seal Pup **Mint:** Pobjoy Mint

Date	Mintage	F12	VF20	XF40	MS60	MS63
2013PM	Est. 10000	PF63 55.00	PF65 60.00			

KM# 45 4 POUNDS
1.24 g., 0.999 Gold 0.0396 oz. AGW, 13.92 mm. **Ruler:** Elizabeth II **Rev:** Rockhopper Penguin **Mint:** Pobjoy Mint

Date	Mintage	F12	VF20	XF40	MS60	MS63
2006PM	Est. 5000	PF65 90.00				

KM# 46 4 POUNDS
1.24 g., 0.999 Gold 0.0396 oz. AGW, 13.92 mm. **Ruler:** Elizabeth II **Subject:** Henrik Johan Ibsen, 100th Anniversary of Death **Rev:** Bust facing **Mint:** Pobjoy Mint

Date	Mintage	F12	VF20	XF40	MS60	MS63
2006PM	Est. 7500	PF65 90.00				

KM# 19 10 POUNDS
155.51 g., 0.999 Silver 4.9626 oz. ASW, 65 mm. **Ruler:** Elizabeth II **Obv:** Crowned bust right **Rev:** Capt. Cook, ship and map **Edge:** Reeded **Mint:** Pobjoy Mint

Date	Mintage	F12	VF20	XF40	MS60	MS63
2003PM	2,003	PF65 225				

KM# 8 20 POUNDS
6.22 g., 0.9999 Gold 0.1987 oz. AGW, 22 mm. **Ruler:** Elizabeth II **Obv:** Crowned bust right **Rev:** Sir Ernest H. Shackleton and ship **Edge:** Reeded **Mint:** Pobjoy Mint

Date	Mintage	F12	VF20	XF40	MS60	MS63
2001PM	—	PF65 425				

KM# 10 20 POUNDS
6.22 g., 0.9999 Gold 0.1987 oz. AGW, 22 mm. **Ruler:** Elizabeth II **Obv:** Crowned bust right **Rev:** Sir Joseph Banks cameo and ship **Mint:** Pobjoy Mint

Date	Mintage	F12	VF20	XF40	MS60	MS63
2001PM	Est. 2000	PF65 425				

KM# 12 20 POUNDS
6.22 g., 0.999 Gold 0.1985 oz. AGW, 22 mm. **Ruler:** Elizabeth II **Subject:** Queen Elizabeth II's Golden Jubilee **Obv:** Crowned bust right **Rev:** Young crowned bust right **Edge:** Reeded **Mint:** Pobjoy Mint

Date	Mintage	F12	VF20	XF40	MS60	MS63
2002PM	2,002	PF65 425				

KM# 14 20 POUNDS
6.22 g., 0.999 Gold 0.1985 oz. AGW, 22 mm. **Ruler:** Elizabeth II **Subject:** Queen Elizabeth II's Golden Jubilee **Obv:** Crowned bust right **Rev:** National arms **Edge:** Reeded **Mint:** Pobjoy Mint

Date	Mintage	F12	VF20	XF40	MS60	MS63
2002PM	2,002	PF65 425				

KM# 16 20 POUNDS
6.22 g., 0.9999 Gold 0.1987 oz. AGW, 22 mm. **Ruler:** Elizabeth II **Obv:** Crowned bust right **Rev:** Diana's portrait **Edge:** reeded **Mint:** Pobjoy Mint

Date	Mintage	F12	VF20	XF40	MS60	MS63
2002PM	—	PF65 425				

KM# 47 20 POUNDS
6.22 g., 0.999 Gold 0.1985 oz. AGW, 22 mm. **Ruler:** Elizabeth II **Subject:** Henrik Johan Ibsen, 100th Anniversary of Death **Rev:** Bust facing **Mint:** Pobjoy Mint

Date	Mintage	F12	VF20	XF40	MS60	MS63
2006PM	Est. 2000	PF65 425				

KM# 57 20 POUNDS
6.22 g., 0.999 Gold 0.1985 oz. AGW, 22 mm. **Ruler:** Elizabeth II **Subject:** Kon Tiki Expedition 65th Anniversary **Rev:** Kon Tiki Ship **Mint:** Pobjoy Mint

Date	Mintage	F12	VF20	XF40	MS60	MS63
2012PM	—	PF65 400				

KM# 58 20 POUNDS
6.22 g., 0.999 Gold 0.1985 oz. AGW, 22 mm. **Ruler:** Elizabeth II **Subject:** Kon Tiki Expedition **Obv:** Portraits right **Rev:** Kon Tiki Mask **Mint:** Pobjoy Mint

Date	Mintage	F12	VF20	XF40	MS60	MS63
2012PM	—	PF65 400				

SPAIN

The Kingdom of Spain, forming the greater part of the Iberian Peninsula of southwest Europe, has an area of 195,988 sq. mi. (504,714 sq. km.) and a population of 39.4 million including the Balearic and the Canary Islands. Capital: Madrid. The economy is based on agriculture, industry and tourism. Machinery, fruit, vegetables and chemicals are exported.

RULER
Juan Carlos I, 1975-

MINT MARK
(M) - Crowned "M" – Madrid

KINGDOM

DECIMAL COINAGE
100 Centimos = 1 Peseta

KM# 832 PESETA
0.55 g., Aluminum, 14 mm. **Ruler:** Juan Carlos I **Obv:** Vertical line divides head left from value **Rev:** Crowned shield flanked by pillars with banner **Edge:** Plain

Date	Mintage	F12	VF20	XF40	MS60	MS63
2001	62,300,000	—	—	0.10	0.30	0.50

KM# 833 5 PESETAS
3.00 g., Aluminum-Bronze, 17.5 mm. **Ruler:** Juan Carlos I **Obv:** Stylized JC I and date **Rev:** Value above stylized sailboats **Edge:** Plain

Date	Mintage	F12	VF20	XF40	MS60	MS63
2001	294,000,000	—	—	0.10	0.25	0.35

KM# 1013 25 PESETAS
4.25 g., Aluminum-Bronze, 19.5 mm. **Ruler:** Juan Carlos I **Obv:** Center hole divides bust left and vertical letters **Rev:** Crowned above center hole, order collar at right, value at left **Edge:** Plain

Date	Mintage	F12	VF20	XF40	MS60	MS63
2001	91,200,000	—	—	—	2.00	2.50

KM# 1016 100 PESETAS
9.25 g., Aluminum-Bronze, 24.5 mm. **Ruler:** Juan Carlos I **Subject:** 132nd Anniversary of the Peseta **Obv:** Head left **Rev:** Seated allegorical figure from an old coin design **Edge:** Fleur-de-lis repeated

Date	Mintage	F12	VF20	XF40	MS60	MS63
2001	142,800,000	—	—	—	2.25	2.75

KM# 924 500 PESETAS
12.00 g., Aluminum-Bronze, 28 mm. **Ruler:** Juan Carlos I **Obv:** Conjoined heads of Juan Carlos and Sofia left **Rev:** Crowned shield flanked by pillars with banner, vertical value at right

Date	Mintage	F12	VF20	XF40	MS60	MS63
2001	3,300,000	—	—	—	7.00	9.00

KM# 1131 500 PESETAS
6.73 g., Silver, 26.96 mm. **Ruler:** Juan Carlos I **Obv:** Minting equipment **Obv. Legend:** ESPAÑA **Rev:** Copy of Charles II

silver Reales coin **Rev. Legend:** CASA DE LA MONEDA DE SEGOVIA **Edge:** Reeded **Note:** Aqueduct and crowned M mintmarks appear on obverse

Date	Mintage	F12	VF20	XF40	MS60	MS63
2001	20,000	PF63 21.00				

KM# 1017 2000 PESETAS
18.00 g., 0.925 Silver 0.5319 oz. ASW, 32.9 mm. **Ruler:** Juan Carlos I **Subject:** 132nd Anniversary of the Peseta **Obv:** Conjoined heads left **Rev:** Seated allegorical design from the 1869 Spanish coin series **Edge:** Plain

Date	Mintage	F12	VF20	XF40	MS60	MS63
2001	1,942,835	—	—	—	24.00	28.00

KM# 1038 2000 PESETAS
27.00 g., 0.925 Silver 0.7978 oz. ASW, 40 mm. **Ruler:** Juan Carlos I **Subject:** Segovia Mint's 500th Anniversary **Obv:** Hammer coining scene within beaded circle **Rev:** Segovia Mint 8 reales coin design of 1588 **Edge:** Reeded

Date	Mintage	F12	VF20	XF40	MS60	MS63
2001	15,000	PF63 55.00				

EURO COINAGE
European Union Issues

KM# 1253 30 EURO
18.00 g., 0.925 Silver 0.5319 oz. ASW, 33 mm. **Ruler:** Juan Carlos I **Subject:** Juan Carlos, 75th Anniversary of Birth **Obv:** Head left **Rev:** Crowned arms in fleece collar

Date	Mintage	F12	VF20	XF40	MS60	MS63
2013 Proof	—	—	—	—	—	—

KM# 1040 EURO CENT
2.30 g., Copper Plated Steel, 16.25 mm. **Ruler:** Juan Carlos I **Obv:** Cathedral of Santiago de Compostela **Rev:** Value and globe **Edge:** Plain

Date	Mintage	F12	VF20	XF40	MS60	MS63
2001(M)	130,900,000	—	—	—	0.25	0.30
2002(M)	141,100,000	—	—	—	0.25	0.30
2002(M)	35,000	PF63 10.00				

Date	Mintage	F12	VF20	XF40	MS60	MS63
2003(M)	670,500,000	—	—	—	0.25	0.30
2003(M)	20,000	PF63 10.00				
2004(M)	206,700,000	—	—	—	0.25	0.30
2005(M)	444,200,000	—	—	—	0.25	0.30
2005(M)	3,000	PF63 10.00				
2006(M)	383,900,000	—	—	—	0.25	0.35
2007(M)	383,958,434	—	—	—	0.25	0.35
2007(M)	5,000	PF63 10.00				
2008(M)	374,556,940	—	—	—	0.25	0.35
2008(M)	5,000	PF63 10.00				
2009(M)	131,427,500	—	—	—	0.25	0.35
2009(M)	5,000	PF63 10.00				

KM# 1144 EURO CENT
2.30 g., Copper Plated Steel, 16.25 mm. **Ruler:** Juan Carlos I **Obv:** Cathedral of Santiago de Compostela **Rev:** Value and globe

Date	Mintage	F12	VF20	XF40	MS60	MS63
2010	227,330,000	—	—	—	0.25	0.35
2010	—	PF63 10.00				
2011	339,340,200	—	—	—	0.25	0.35
2011	—	PF63 10.00				
2012	400,572,000	—	—	—	0.25	0.35
2012	—	PF63 10.00				
2013	—	—	—	—	0.25	0.35
2013	—	PF63 10.00				

KM# 1041 2 EURO CENT
3.06 g., Copper Plated Steel, 18.75 mm. **Ruler:** Juan Carlos I **Obv:** Cathedral of Santiago de Compostela **Rev:** Value and globe **Edge:** Grooved

Date	Mintage	F12	VF20	XF40	MS60	MS63
2001(M)	463,100,000	—	—	—	0.25	0.30
2002(M)	4,100,000	—	—	—	1.25	1.50
2002(M)	35,000	PF63 10.00				
2003(M)	31,600,000	—	—	—	1.00	1.25
2003(M)	20,000	PF63 10.00				
2004(M)	206,700,000	—	—	—	0.25	0.30
2005(M)	275,100,000	—	—	—	0.25	0.30
2005(M)	3,000	PF63 10.00				
2006(M)	262,200,000	—	—	—	0.25	0.30
2007(M)	185,258,434	—	—	—	0.25	0.30
2007(M)	5,000	PF63 10.00				
2008(M)	191,256,940	—	—	—	0.25	0.30
2008(M)	5,000	PF63 10.00				
2009(M)	164,027,500	—	—	—	0.25	0.30
2009(M)	5,000	PF63 10.00				

KM# 1145 2 EURO CENT
3.06 g., Copper Plated Steel, 18.75 mm. **Ruler:** Juan Carlos I **Obv:** Cathedral of Santiago de Compostela **Rev:** Value and globe **Edge:** Grooved

Date	Mintage	F12	VF20	XF40	MS60	MS63
2010	153,130,000	—	—	—	0.25	0.30
2010	—	PF63 10.00				
2011	96,450,200	—	—	—	0.25	0.30
2011	—	PF63 10.00				
2012	99,572,000	—	—	—	0.25	0.30
2012	—	PF63 10.00				
2013	—	—	—	—	0.25	0.30
2013	—	PF63 10.00				

KM# 1042 5 EURO CENT
3.92 g., Copper Plated Steel, 21.25 mm. **Ruler:** Juan Carlos I **Obv:** Cathedral of Santiago de Compostela **Rev:** Value and globe **Edge:** Plain

Date	Mintage	F12	VF20	XF40	MS60	MS63
2001(M)	216,100,000	—	—	—	0.50	0.60

Date	Mintage	F12	VF20	XF40	MS60	MS63
2002(M)	8,300,000	—	—	—	1.00	1.50
2002(M)	35,000	PF63 10.00				
2003(M)	327,600,000	—	—	—	0.50	0.60
2003(M)	8,904	PF63 10.00				
2004(M)	258,500,000	—	—	—	0.40	0.50
2005(M)	411,400,000	—	—	—	0.40	0.50
2005(M)	3,000	PF63 10.00				
2006(M)	142,800,000	—	—	—	0.40	0.50
2007(M)	247,058,434	—	—	—	0.40	0.50
2007(M)	5,000	PF63 10.00				
2008(M)	239,056,940	—	—	—	0.40	0.50
2008(M)	2,000	PF63 10.00				
2009(M)	219,737,500	—	—	—	0.40	0.50
2009(M)	5,000	PF63 10.00				

KM# 1146 5 EURO CENT
3.92 g., Copper Plated Steel, 21.25 mm. **Ruler:** Juan Carlos I **Obv:** Cathedral of Santiago de Compostela **Rev:** Value and globe

Date	Mintage	F12	VF20	XF40	MS60	MS63
2010	203,130,000	—	—	—	0.40	0.50
2010	—	PF63 10.00				
2011	97,140,200	—	—	—	0.40	0.50
2011	—	PF63 10.00				
2012	49,772,000	—	—	—	0.40	0.50
2012	—	PF63 10.00				
2013	—	—	—	—	0.40	0.50
2013	—	PF63 10.00				

KM# 1043 10 EURO CENT
4.10 g., Brass, 19.75 mm. **Ruler:** Juan Carlos I **Obv:** Head of Cervantes with ruffed collar 1/4 left within star border **Rev:** Value and map **Edge:** Reeded

Date	Mintage	F12	VF20	XF40	MS60	MS63
2001(M)	160,100,000	—	—	—	0.60	0.75
2002(M)	113,100,000	—	—	—	0.60	0.75
2002(M)	35,000	PF63 10.00				
2003(M)	292,500,000	—	—	—	0.75	0.90
2003(M)	20,000	PF63 10.00				
2004(M)	121,900,000	—	—	—	0.40	0.50
2005(M)	321,300,000	—	—	—	0.40	0.50
2005(M)	3,000	PF63 10.00				
2006(M)	91,800,000	—	—	—	0.40	0.50

KM# 1070 10 EURO CENT
4.10 g., Brass, 19.75 mm. **Ruler:** Juan Carlos I **Obv:** Cervantes **Rev:** Relief map of Western Europe, stars, lines and value **Edge:** Reeded

Date	Mintage	F12	VF20	XF40	MS60	MS63
2007(M)	132,058,000	—	—	—	0.75	1.00
2007(M)	5,000	PF63 12.00				
2008(M)	142,256,940	—	—	—	0.75	1.00
2008(M)	5,000	PF63 12.00				
2009(M)	151,327,500	—	—	—	0.75	1.00
2009(M)	5,000	PF63 12.00				

KM# 1147 10 EURO CENT
4.10 g., Brass, 19.75 mm. **Ruler:** Juan Carlos I **Obv:** Cervantes bust at right **Rev:** Relief map of Western Europe, stars, lines and value **Edge:** Reeded

Date	Mintage	F12	VF20	XF40	MS60	MS63
2010	104,930,000	—	—	—	0.75	1.00
2010	—	PF63 12.00				
2011	4,440,200	—	—	—	0.75	1.00
2011	—	PF63 12.00				
2012	3,672,000	—	—	—	0.75	1.00
2012	—	PF63 12.00				
2013	—	—	—	—	0.75	1.00
2013	—	PF63 12.00				

KM# 1044 20 EURO CENT
5.74 g., Brass, 22.25 mm. **Ruler:** Juan Carlos I **Obv:** Head of Cervantes with ruffed collar 1/4 left within star border **Rev:** Value and map **Edge:** Notched

Date	Mintage	F12	VF20	XF40	MS60	MS63
2001(M)	146,600,000	—	—	—	1.00	1.25
2002(M)	91,500,000	—	—	—	0.60	0.75
2002(M)	35,000	PF63 12.00				
2003(M)	4,100,000	—	—	—	1.25	1.50
2003(M)	20,000	PF63 12.00				
2004(M)	3,900,000	—	—	—	0.60	0.75
2005(M)	4,000,000	—	—	—	0.60	0.75
2005(M)	3,000	PF63 12.00				
2006(M)	102,000,000	—	—	—	0.60	0.75

KM# 1071 20 EURO CENT
5.74 g., Brass, 22.25 mm. **Ruler:** Juan Carlos I **Obv:** Cervantes **Rev:** Relief map of Western Europe, stars, lines and value **Edge:** Notched

Date	Mintage	F12	VF20	XF40	MS60	MS63
2007(M)	46,458,000	—	—	—	1.00	1.25
2007(M)	5,000	PF63 12.00				
2008(M)	102,256,940	—	—	—	1.00	1.25
2008(M)	2,000	PF63 12.00				
2009(M)	75,327,500	—	—	—	1.00	1.25
2009(M)	5,000	PF63 12.00				

KM# 1148 20 EURO CENT
5.74 g., Brass, 22.25 mm. **Ruler:** Juan Carlos I **Obv:** Cervantes bust at right **Rev:** Relief map of Western Europe, stars, lines and value **Edge:** Notched

Date	Mintage	F12	VF20	XF40	MS60	MS63
2010	3,830,000	—	—	—	1.00	1.25
2010	—	PF63 12.00				
2011	3,940,200	—	—	—	1.00	1.25
2011	—	PF63 12.00				
2012	26,272,000	—	—	—	1.00	1.25
2012	—	PF63 12.00				
2013	—	—	—	—	1.00	1.25
2013	—	PF63 12.00				

KM# 1045 50 EURO CENT
7.80 g., Brass, 24.25 mm. **Ruler:** Juan Carlos I **Obv:** Head of Cervantes with ruffed collar 1/4 left within star border **Rev:** Value and map **Edge:** Reeded

Date	Mintage	F12	VF20	XF40	MS60	MS63
2001(M)	351,100,000	—	—	—	1.00	1.25
2002(M)	9,800,000	—	—	—	3.00	3.50
2002(M)	35,000	PF63 12.00				
2003(M)	6,000,000	—	—	—	3.00	3.50
2003(M)	20,000	PF63 12.00				
2004(M)	4,400,000	—	—	—	1.50	2.00
2005(M)	3,900,000	—	—	—	1.25	1.50
2005(M)	3,000	PF63 12.00				
2006(M)	4,000,000	—	—	—	1.25	1.50

KM# 1072 50 EURO CENT
7.80 g., Brass, 24.25 mm. **Ruler:** Juan Carlos I **Obv:** Cervantes **Rev:** Relief map of Western Europe, stars, lines and value **Edge:** Reeded

Date	Mintage	F12	VF20	XF40	MS60	MS63
2007(M)	3,958,000	—	—	—	1.25	1.50

Date	Mintage	F12	VF20	XF40	MS60	MS63
2007(M)	5,000	PF63 12.00				
2008(M)	3,956,940	—	—	—	1.25	1.50
2008(M)	5,000	PF63 12.00				
2009(M)	3,927,500	—	—	—	1.25	1.50
2009(M)	5,000	PF63 12.00				

KM# 1149 50 EURO CENT

7.80 g., Brass, 24.25 mm. **Ruler:** Juan Carlos I **Obv:** Cervantes bust at right **Rev:** Relief map of Western Europe, stars, lines and value **Edge:** Reeded

Date	Mintage	F12	VF20	XF40	MS60	MS63
2010	3,930,000	—	—	—	1.25	1.50
2010		PF63 12.00				
2011		—	—	—	1.25	1.50
2011		PF63 12.00				
2012	4,072,000	—	—	—	1.25	1.50
2012		PF63 12.00				
2013		—	—	—	1.25	1.50
2013		PF63 12.00				

KM# 1046 EURO

7.50 g., Bi-Metallic, 23.25 mm. **Ruler:** Juan Carlos I **Obv:** Head 1/4 left within circle and star border **Rev:** Value and map within circle **Edge:** Segmented reeding

Date	Mintage	F12	VF20	XF40	MS60	MS63
2001(M)	259,100,000	—	—	—	3.00	4.00
2002(M)	335,600,000	—	—	—	2.00	2.50
2002(M)	23,000	PF63 15.00				
2003(M)	297,400,000	—	—	—	2.00	2.50
2003(M)	20,000	PF63 15.00				
2004(M)	9,870,000	—	—	—	2.00	2.50
2005(M)	77,800,000	—	—	—	2.00	2.50
2005(M)	3,000	PF63 15.00				
2006(M)	101,600,000	—	—	—	2.00	2.50

KM# 1073 EURO

7.50 g., Bi-Metallic, 23.25 mm. **Ruler:** Juan Carlos I **Obv:** King's portrait **Rev:** Relief map of Western Europe, stars, lines and value **Edge:** Segmented reeding

Date	Mintage	F12	VF20	XF40	MS60	MS63
2007(M)	150,558,000	—	—	—	3.00	3.50
2007(M)	5,000	PF63 15.00				
2008(M)	154,356,940	—	—	—	3.00	3.50
2008(M)	5,000	PF63 15.00				
2009(M)	60,527,500	—	—	—	3.00	3.50
2009(M)	5,000	PF63 15.00				

KM# 1150 EURO

7.50 g., Bi-Metallic, 23.25 mm. **Ruler:** Juan Carlos I **Obv:** King's portrait at right **Rev:** Relief map of Western Europe, stars, lines and value **Edge:** Segmented reeding

Date	Mintage	F12	VF20	XF40	MS60	MS63
2010	40,030,000	—	—	—	3.00	3.50
2010		PF63 15.00				
2011	100,540,200	—	—	—	3.00	3.50
2011		PF63 15.00				
2012	3,372,000	—	—	—	3.00	3.50
2012		PF63 15.00				
2013		—	—	—	3.00	3.50
2013		PF63 15.00				

KM# 1047 2 EURO

8.50 g., Bi-Metallic, 25.75 mm. **Ruler:** Juan Carlos I **Obv:** Head 1/4 left within circle and star border **Rev:** Value and map within circle **Edge:** Reeding over stars and 2's

Date	Mintage	F12	VF20	XF40	MS60	MS63
2001(M)	140,200,000	—	—	—	4.50	5.00
2002(M)	164,000,000	—	—	—	3.50	4.00
2002(M)	35,000	PF63 20.00				
2003(M)	44,500,000	—	—	—	4.50	5.00
2003(M)	20,000	PF63 20.00				
2004(M)	4,100,000	—	—	—	4.50	5.00
2005(M)	4,000,000	—	—	—	4.50	5.00
2005(M)	3,000	PF63 20.00				
2006(M)	4,000,000	—	—	—	4.50	5.00

KM# 1063 2 EURO

8.50 g., Bi-Metallic, 25.75 mm. **Ruler:** Juan Carlos I **Obv:** Stylized half length figure of Don Quixote holding spear within circle and star border **Rev:** Value and map within circle **Edge:** Reeding over stars and 2's **Note:** Mint mark: Crowned M.

Date	Mintage	F12	VF20	XF40	MS60	MS63
2005	8,000,000	—	—	—	5.00	605
2005	3,000	PF63 25.00				

KM# 1130 2 EURO

8.50 g., Bi-Metallic, 25.75 mm. **Ruler:** Juan Carlos I **Subject:** 50th Anniversary Treaty of Rome **Obv:** Open treaty book **Obv. Legend:** ESPAÑA **Rev:** Large value at left, modified outline of Europe at right **Edge:** Reeded with 2's and stars

Date	Mintage	F12	VF20	XF40	MS60	MS63
2007	7,935,000	—	—	—	7.00	9.00
2007(M) Special Unc.	60,000	—	—	—	—	20.00
2007(M)	5,000	PF63 35.00				

KM# 1074 2 EURO

8.50 g., Bi-Metallic, 25.75 mm. **Ruler:** Juan Carlos I **Obv:** King's portrait **Rev:** Relief map of Western Europe, stars, lines and value **Edge:** Reeding over stars and 2's

Date	Mintage	F12	VF20	XF40	MS60	MS63
2007(M)	3,958,000	—	—	—	4.75	5.00
2007(M)	5,000	PF63 20.00				
2008(M)	19,456,940	—	—	—	4.75	5.00
2008(M)	5,000	PF63 20.00				
2009(M)	17,427,500	—	—	—	4.75	5.00
2009(M)	5,000	PF63 20.00				

KM# 1142.2 2 EURO

8.50 g., Bi-Metallic, 25.75 mm. **Ruler:** Juan Carlos I **Subject:** European Monetary Unit, 10th Aniversary **Obv:** Stick figure and large E symbol **Edge:** Reeded with 2's and stars

Date	Mintage	F12	VF20	XF40	MS60	MS63
2009 Large Stars	—	—	—	—	40.00	45.00

KM# 1142.1 2 EURO

8.50 g., Bi-Metallic, 25.75 mm. **Ruler:** Juan Carlos I **Subject:** European Monetary Unit, 10th Anniversary **Obv:** Stick figure and large E symbol **Rev:** Large value at left, modified map of Europe at right **Edge:** Reeded with 2's and stars

Date	Mintage	F12	VF20	XF40	MS60	MS63
2009 Small Stars	—	—	—	—	5.00	6.00
2009 Special Unc.	—	—	—	—	—	20.00
2009	—	PF63 35.00				

KM# 1151 2 EURO

8.50 g., Bi-Metallic, 25.75 mm. **Ruler:** Juan Carlos I **Obv:** King's portrait at right **Rev:** Relief map of Western Europe, stars, lines and value **Edge:** Reeded with 2's and stars

Date	Mintage	F12	VF20	XF40	MS60	MS63
2010	3,930,000	—	—	—	4.75	5.00
2010		PF63 20.00				
2011	4,040,200	—	—	—	4.75	5.00
2011		PF63 20.00				
2012	4,072,000	—	—	—	4.75	5.00
2012		PF63 20.00				
2013		—	—	—	4.75	5.00
2013		PF63 20.00				

KM# 1152 2 EURO

8.50 g., Bi-Metallic, 25.75 mm. **Ruler:** Juan Carlos I **Subject:** Cordoba - UNESCO Heritage site **Edge:** Reeded with 2's and stars

Date	Mintage	F12	VF20	XF40	MS60	MS63
2010	5,000	PF63 25.00				
2010		—	—	—	5.00	7.00

KM# 1184 2 EURO

8.50 g., Bi-Metallic, 25.75 mm. **Ruler:** Juan Carlos I **Subject:** UNESCO Heritage Site - Granada **Obv:** The Alhambra **Edge:** Reeded with 2's and stars

Date	Mintage	F12	VF20	XF40	MS60	MS63
2011	5,000	PF63 25.00				
2011	8,000,000	—	—	—	5.00	7.00

KM# 1252 2 EURO

8.50 g., Bi-Metallic, 25.75 mm. **Ruler:** Juan Carlos I **Subject:** Euro coinage, 10th Anniversary **Obv:** Euro symbol on globe at center, child-like rendering around

Date	Mintage	F12	VF20	XF40	MS60	MS63
2012	—	PF63 25.00				
2012	8,000,000	—	—	—	5.00	7.00

KM# 1254 2 EURO
8.50 g., Bi-Metallic, 25.75 mm. **Ruler:** Juan Carlos I **Subject:** Burgos Cathedral

Date	Mintage	F12	VF20	XF40	MS60	MS63
2012	—	—	—	—	7.00	—

KM# 1153 5 EURO
13.50 g., 0.925 Silver 0.3989 oz. ASW, 33 mm. **Ruler:** Juan Carlos I **Subject:** Almeria

Date	Mintage	F12	VF20	XF40	MS60	MS63
2010	Est. 15000	PF63 50.00	PF65 55.00			

KM# 1154 5 EURO
13.50 g., 0.925 Silver 0.3989 oz. ASW, 33 mm. **Ruler:** Juan Carlos I **Subject:** Huesca

Date	Mintage	F12	VF20	XF40	MS60	MS63
2010	Est. 15000	PF63 50.00	PF65 55.00			

KM# 1155 5 EURO
13.50 g., 0.925 Silver 0.3989 oz. ASW, 33 mm. **Ruler:** Juan Carlos I **Subject:** Las Palmas G.C.

Date	Mintage	F12	VF20	XF40	MS60	MS63
2010	Est. 20000	PF63 50.00	PF65 55.00			

KM# 1156 5 EURO
13.50 g., 0.925 Silver 0.3989 oz. ASW, 33 mm. **Ruler:** Juan Carlos I **Subject:** Santander

Date	Mintage	F12	VF20	XF40	MS60	MS63
2010	Est. 15000	PF63 50.00	PF65 55.00			

KM# 1157 5 EURO
13.50 g., 0.925 Silver 0.3989 oz. ASW, 33 mm. **Ruler:** Juan Carlos I **Subject:** Avila

Date	Mintage	F12	VF20	XF40	MS60	MS63
2010	Est. 15000	PF63 50.00	PF65 55.00			

KM# 1158 5 EURO
13.50 g., 0.925 Silver 0.3989 oz. ASW, 33 mm. **Ruler:** Juan Carlos I **Subject:** Albacete

Date	Mintage	F12	VF20	XF40	MS60	MS63
2010	Est. 15000	PF63 50.00	PF65 55.00			

KM# 1159 5 EURO
13.50 g., 0.925 Silver 0.3989 oz. ASW, 33 mm. **Ruler:** Juan Carlos I **Subject:** Barcelona

Date	Mintage	F12	VF20	XF40	MS60	MS63
2010	Est. 25000	PF63 50.00	PF65 55.00			

KM# 1160 5 EURO
13.50 g., 0.925 Silver 0.3989 oz. ASW, 33 mm. **Ruler:** Juan Carlos I **Subject:** Ceuta

Date	Mintage	F12	VF20	XF40	MS60	MS63
2010	Est. 15000	PF63 50.00	PF65 55.00			

KM# 1161 5 EURO
13.50 g., 0.925 Silver 0.3989 oz. ASW, 33 mm. **Ruler:** Juan Carlos I **Subject:** Melilla

Date	Mintage	F12	VF20	XF40	MS60	MS63
2010	Est. 15000	PF63 50.00	PF65 55.00			

KM# 1162 5 EURO
13.50 g., 0.925 Silver 0.3989 oz. ASW, 33 mm. **Ruler:** Juan Carlos I **Subject:** Madrid

Date	Mintage	F12	VF20	XF40	MS60	MS63
2010	Est.2500	PF63 45.00	PF65 50.00			

KM# 1163 5 EURO
13.50 g., 0.925 Silver 0.3989 oz. ASW, 33 mm. **Ruler:** Juan Carlos I **Subject:** Pamplona

Date	Mintage	F12	VF20	XF40	MS60	MS63
2010	Est. 15000	PF63 50.00	PF65 55.00			

KM# 1164 5 EURO
13.50 g., 0.925 Silver 0.3989 oz. ASW, 33 mm. **Ruler:** Juan Carlos I **Subject:** Alicante

Date	Mintage	F12	VF20	XF40	MS60	MS63
2010	Est. 20000	PF63 45.00	PF65 50.00			

KM# 1226 5 EURO
13.50 g., 0.925 Silver 0.3989 oz. ASW, 33 mm. **Ruler:** Juan Carlos I **Subject:** Oviedo

Date	Mintage	F12	VF20	XF40	MS60	MS63
2011	Est. 20000	PF63 45.00	PF65 50.00			

KM# 1227 5 EURO
13.50 g., 0.925 Silver 0.3989 oz. ASW **Ruler:** Juan Carlos I **Subject:** Palma de Mallorca

Date	Mintage	F12	VF20	XF40	MS60	MS63
2011	Est. 20000	PF63 45.00	PF65 50.00			

KM# 1228 5 EURO
13.50 g., 0.925 Silver 0.3989 oz. ASW, 33 mm. **Ruler:** Juan
Carlos I **Subject:** Santa Cruz de Tenerife

Date	Mintage	F12	VF20	XF40	MS60	MS63
2011	Est. 20000	PF63 45.00	PF65 50.00			

KM# 1229 5 EURO
13.50 g., 0.925 Silver 0.3989 oz. ASW, 33 mm. **Ruler:** Juan
Carlos I **Subject:** Teruel

Date	Mintage	F12	VF20	XF40	MS60	MS63
2011	Est. 15000	PF63 45.00	PF65 50.00			

KM# 1230 5 EURO
13.50 g., 0.925 Silver 0.3989 oz. ASW, 33 mm. **Ruler:** Juan
Carlos I **Subject:** Bilbao

Date	Mintage	F12	VF20	XF40	MS60	MS63
2011	Est. 20000	PF63 45.00	PF65 50.00			

KM# 1231 5 EURO
13.50 g., 0.925 Silver 0.3989 oz. ASW, 33 mm. **Ruler:** Juan
Carlos I **Subject:** Cadiz

Date	Mintage	F12	VF20	XF40	MS60	MS63
2011	—	PF63 45.00	PF65 50.00			

KM# 1232 5 EURO
13.50 g., 0.925 Silver 0.3989 oz. ASW, 33 mm. **Ruler:** Juan
Carlos I **Subject:** Logrono

Date	Mintage	F12	VF20	XF40	MS60	MS63
2011	Est. 15000	PF63 45.00	PF65 50.00			

KM# 1233 5 EURO
13.50 g., 0.925 Silver 0.3989 oz. ASW, 33 mm. **Ruler:** Juan
Carlos I **Subject:** Murcia

Date	Mintage	F12	VF20	XF40	MS60	MS63
2011	Est. 15000	PF63 45.00	PF65 50.00			

KM# 1234 5 EURO
13.50 g., 0.925 Silver 0.3989 oz. ASW, 33 mm. **Ruler:** Juan
Carlos I **Subject:** Donostia - San Sebastian

Date	Mintage	F12	VF20	XF40	MS60	MS63
2011	—	PF63 45.00	PF65 50.00			

KM# 1235 5 EURO
13.50 g., 0.925 Silver 0.3989 oz. ASW, 33 mm. **Ruler:** Juan
Carlos I **Subject:** Zaragoza

Date	Mintage	F12	VF20	XF40	MS60	MS63
2011	—	PF63 45.00	PF65 50.00			

KM# 1236 5 EURO
13.50 g., 0.925 Silver 0.3989 oz. ASW, 33 mm. **Ruler:** Juan
Carlos I **Subject:** A Coruna

Date	Mintage	F12	VF20	XF40	MS60	MS63
2011	Est. 20000	PF63 45.00	PF65 50.00			

KM# 1237 5 EURO
13.50 g., 0.925 Silver 0.3989 oz. ASW, 33 mm. **Ruler:** Juan
Carlos I **Subject:** Badajoz

Date	Mintage	F12	VF20	XF40	MS60	MS63
2011	Est. 15000	PF63 45.00	PF65 50.00			

KM# 1238 5 EURO
13.50 g., 0.925 Silver 0.3989 oz. ASW, 33 mm. **Ruler:** Juan
Carlos I **Subject:** Cordoba

Date	Mintage	F12	VF20	XF40	MS60	MS63
2011	Est. 15000	PF63 45.00	PF65 50.00			

KM# 1239 5 EURO
13.50 g., 0.925 Silver 0.3989 oz. ASW, 33 mm. **Ruler:** Juan
Carlos I **Subject:** Girona

Date	Mintage	F12	VF20	XF40	MS60	MS63
2011	Est. 15000	PF63 45.00	PF65 50.00			

KM# 1240 5 EURO
13.50 g., 0.925 Silver 0.3989 oz. ASW, 33 mm. **Ruler:** Juan
Carlos I **Subject:** Leon

Date	Mintage	F12	VF20	XF40	MS60	MS63
2011	—	PF63 45.00	PF65 50.00			

KM# 1241 5 EURO
13.50 g., 0.925 Silver 0.3989 oz. ASW, 33 mm. **Ruler:** Juan
Carlos I **Subject:** Lugo

Date	Mintage	F12	VF20	XF40	MS60	MS63
2011	Est. 15000	PF63 45.00	PF65 50.00			

KM# 1242 5 EURO
13.50 g., 0.925 Silver 0.3989 oz. ASW, 33 mm. **Ruler:** Juan
Carlos I **Subject:** Burgos

Date	Mintage	F12	VF20	XF40	MS60	MS63
2011	Est. 15000	PF63 45.00	PF65 50.00			

KM# 1243 5 EURO
13.50 g., 0.925 Silver 0.3989 oz. ASW, 33 mm. **Ruler:** Juan Carlos I **Subject:** Caceres

Date	Mintage	F12	VF20	XF40	MS60	MS63
2011	Est. 15000	PF63 45.00	PF65 50.00			

KM# 1244 5 EURO
13.50 g., 0.925 Silver 0.3989 oz. ASW, 33 mm. **Ruler:** Juan Carlos I **Subject:** Castellon de la Plana

Date	Mintage	F12	VF20	XF40	MS60	MS63
2011	Est. 15000	PF63 45.00	PF65 50.00			

KM# 1245 5 EURO
13.50 g., 0.925 Silver 0.3989 oz. ASW, 33 mm. **Ruler:** Juan Carlos I **Subject:** Ciudad Real

Date	Mintage	F12	VF20	XF40	MS60	MS63
2011	Est. 15000	PF63 45.00	PF65 50.00			

KM# 1260 5 EURO
13.50 g., 0.925 Silver 0.3989 oz. ASW, 33 mm. **Ruler:** Juan Carlos I **Subject:** Cuenca

Date	Mintage	F12	VF20	XF40	MS60	MS63
2012	Est. 15000	PF63 45.00	PF65 50.00			

KM# 1261 5 EURO
13.50 g., 0.925 Silver 0.3989 oz. ASW, 33 mm. **Ruler:** Juan Carlos I **Subject:** Granada

Date	Mintage	F12	VF20	XF40	MS60	MS63
2012	Est. 15000	PF63 45.00	PF65 50.00			

KM# 1262 5 EURO
13.50 g., 0.925 Silver 0.3989 oz. ASW, 33 mm. **Ruler:** Juan Carlos I **Subject:** Guadalajara

Date	Mintage	F12	VF20	XF40	MS60	MS63
2012	Est. 15000	PF63 45.00	PF65 50.00			

KM# 1263 5 EURO
13.50 g., 0.925 Silver 0.3989 oz. ASW, 33 mm. **Ruler:** Juan Carlos I **Subject:** Huelva

Date	Mintage	F12	VF20	XF40	MS60	MS63
2012	Est. 15000	PF63 45.00	PF65 50.00			

KM# 1264 5 EURO
13.50 g., 0.925 Silver 0.3989 oz. ASW, 33 mm. **Ruler:** Juan Carlos I **Subject:** Jaen

Date	Mintage	F12	VF20	XF40	MS60	MS63
2012	Est. 15000	PF63 45.00	PF65 50.00			

KM# 1265 5 EURO
13.50 g., 0.925 Silver 0.3989 oz. ASW, 33 mm. **Ruler:** Juan Carlos I **Subject:** Lerida

Date	Mintage	F12	VF20	XF40	MS60	MS63
2012	Est. 15000	PF63 45.00	PF65 50.00			

KM# 1266 5 EURO
13.50 g., 0.925 Silver 0.3989 oz. ASW, 33 mm. **Ruler:** Juan Carlos I **Subject:** Malaga

Date	Mintage	F12	VF20	XF40	MS60	MS63
2012	Est. 15000	PF63 45.00	PF65 50.00			

KM# 1267 5 EURO
13.50 g., 0.925 Silver 0.3989 oz. ASW, 33 mm. **Ruler:** Juan Carlos I **Subject:** Orense

Date	Mintage	F12	VF20	XF40	MS60	MS63
2012	Est. 15000	PF63 45.00	PF65 50.00			

KM# 1268 5 EURO
13.50 g., 0.925 Silver 0.3989 oz. ASW, 33 mm. **Ruler:** Juan Carlos I **Subject:** Palencia

Date	Mintage	F12	VF20	XF40	MS60	MS63
2012	Est. 15000	PF63 45.00	PF65 50.00			

KM# 1269 5 EURO
13.50 g., 0.925 Silver 0.3989 oz. ASW, 33 mm. **Ruler:** Juan Carlos I **Subject:** Pontevedra

Date	Mintage	F12	VF20	XF40	MS60	MS63
2012	Est. 15000	PF63 45.00	PF65 50.00			

KM# 1270 5 EURO
13.50 g., 0.925 Silver 0.3989 oz. ASW, 33 mm. **Ruler:** Juan Carlos I **Subject:** Salamanca

Date	Mintage	F12	VF20	XF40	MS60	MS63
2012	Est. 15000	PF63 45.00	PF65 50.00			

KM# 1271 5 EURO
13.50 g., 0.925 Silver 0.3989 oz. ASW, 33 mm. **Ruler:** Juan Carlos I **Subject:** Segovia

Date	Mintage	F12	VF20	XF40	MS60	MS63
2012	Est. 15000	PF63 45.00	PF65 50.00			

KM# 1272 5 EURO
13.50 g., 0.925 Silver 0.3989 oz. ASW, 33 mm. **Ruler:** Juan Carlos I **Subject:** Sevilla

Date	Mintage	F12	VF20	XF40	MS60	MS63
2012	Est. 15000	**PF63** 45.00	**PF65** 50.00			

KM# 1273 5 EURO
13.50 g., 0.925 Silver 0.3989 oz. ASW, 33 mm. **Ruler:** Juan Carlos I **Subject:** Soria

Date	Mintage	F12	VF20	XF40	MS60	MS63
2012	Est. 15000	**PF63** 45.00	**PF65** 50.00			

KM# 1274 5 EURO
13.50 g., 0.925 Silver 0.3989 oz. ASW, 33 mm. **Ruler:** Juan Carlos I **Subject:** Tarragona

Date	Mintage	F12	VF20	XF40	MS60	MS63
2012	Est. 15000	**PF63** 45.00	**PF65** 50.00			

KM# 1275 5 EURO
13.50 g., 0.925 Silver 0.3989 oz. ASW, 33 mm. **Ruler:** Juan Carlos I **Subject:** Toledo

Date	Mintage	F12	VF20	XF40	MS60	MS63
2012	Est. 15000	**PF63** 45.00	**PF65** 50.00			

KM# 1276 5 EURO
13.50 g., 0.925 Silver 0.3989 oz. ASW, 33 mm. **Ruler:** Juan Carlos I **Subject:** Valencia

Date	Mintage	F12	VF20	XF40	MS60	MS63
2012	Est. 15000	**PF63** 45.00	**PF65** 50.00			

KM# 1277 5 EURO
13.50 g., 0.925 Silver 0.3989 oz. ASW, 33 mm. **Ruler:** Juan Carlos I **Subject:** Valladolid

Date	Mintage	F12	VF20	XF40	MS60	MS63
2012	Est. 15000	**PF63** 45.00	**PF65** 50.00			

KM# 1278 5 EURO
13.50 g., 0.925 Silver 0.3989 oz. ASW, 33 mm. **Ruler:** Juan Carlos I **Subject:** Vitoria

Date	Mintage	F12	VF20	XF40	MS60	MS63
2012	Est. 15000	**PF63** 45.00	**PF65** 50.00			

KM# 1279 5 EURO
13.50 g., 0.925 Silver 0.3989 oz. ASW, 33 mm. **Ruler:** Juan Carlos I **Subject:** Zamora

Date	Mintage	F12	VF20	XF40	MS60	MS63
2012	Est. 15000	**PF63** 45.00	**PF65** 50.00			

KM# 1282 5 EURO
13.00 g., 0.925 Silver 0.3841 oz. ASW **Ruler:** Juan Carlos I **Subject:** Juan Carlos, 75th Anniversary of Birth

Date	Mintage	F12	VF20	XF40	MS60	MS63
2013	7,000	**PF63** 100				

KM# 1294 5 EURO
13.50 g., 0.925 Silver 0.3989 oz. ASW, 33 mm. **Ruler:** Juan Carlos I **Subject:** Royal Palace of La Almudaina

Date	Mintage	F12	VF20	XF40	MS60	MS63
2013	7,000	**PF63** 50.00	**PF65** 55.00			

KM# 1295 5 EURO
13.50 g., 0.925 Silver 0.3989 oz. ASW, 40 mm. **Ruler:** Juan Carlos I **Subject:** Abbey of Santa Maria la Real de Huelgas

Date	Mintage	F12	VF20	XF40	MS60	MS63
2013	7,000	**PF63** 50.00	**PF65** 55.00			

KM# 1296 5 EURO
13.50 g., 0.925 Silver 0.3989 oz. ASW, 40 mm. **Ruler:** Juan Carlos I **Subject:** Royal Palace of La Granja de San Ildefonso

Date	Mintage	F12	VF20	XF40	MS60	MS63
2013	7,000	**PF63** 50.00	**PF65** 55.00			

KM# 1297 5 EURO
13.50 g., 0.925 Silver 0.3989 oz. ASW, 33 mm. **Ruler:** Juan Carlos I **Subject:** Royal Convent of La Encarnación

Date	Mintage	F12	VF20	XF40	MS60	MS63
2013	7,000	**PF63** 50.00	**PF65** 55.00			

KM# 1298 5 EURO
13.50 g., 0.925 Silver 0.3989 oz. ASW, 33 mm. **Ruler:** Juan Carlos I **Subject:** Convent of Las Descalzas Reales

Date	Mintage	F12	VF20	XF40	MS60	MS63
2013	7,000	**PF63** 50.00	**PF65** 55.00			

KM# 1299 5 EURO
13.50 g., 0.925 Silver 0.3989 oz. ASW, 33 mm. **Ruler:** Juan Carlos I **Subject:** Royal Seat of San Lorenzo de El Escorial

Date	Mintage	F12	VF20	XF40	MS60	MS63
2013	7,000	**PF63** 50.00	**PF65** 55.00			

KM# 1048 10 EURO
27.00 g., 0.925 Silver 0.7978 oz. ASW, 40 mm. **Ruler:** Juan Carlos I **Subject:** Spanish Presidency of the European Union **Obv:** Head left **Rev:** Map of Europe **Edge:** Reeded

Date	Mintage	F12	VF20	XF40	MS60	MS63
2002	29,997	PF63 60.00				

KM# 1050 10 EURO
27.00 g., 0.925 Silver 0.7978 oz. ASW, 40 mm. **Ruler:** Juan Carlos I **Subject:** Annexation of Minorca **Obv:** Conjoined heads left **Rev:** Uniformed equestrians shaking hands flanked by ships **Edge:** Reeded **Note:** Mint mark: Crowned M.

Date	Mintage	F12	VF20	XF40	MS60	MS63
2002	8,693	PF63 85.00		PF65 100		

KM# 1078 10 EURO
27.00 g., 0.925 Silver 0.7978 oz. ASW, 40 mm. **Ruler:** Juan Carlos I **Subject:** XIX Winter Olympics - Salt Lake City **Obv:** Head left **Obv. Legend:** JUAN CARLOS I REY DE ESPAÑA **Rev:** Cross country skier right, stylized snowflake at right **Rev. Legend:** JUEGOS OLIMPICOS DE - INVERNO 2002

Date	Mintage	F12	VF20	XF40	MS60	MS63
2002(M)	17,703	PF63 50.00		PF65 60.00		

KM# 1079 10 EURO
27.00 g., 0.925 Silver 0.7978 oz. ASW, 40 mm. **Ruler:** Juan Carlos I **Subject:** XVII Football World Games 2002 - South Korea and Japan **Obv. Legend:** MUNDIAL DE FUTBOL/2002 - ESPAÑA **Rev:** Football against net

Date	Mintage	F12	VF20	XF40	MS60	MS63
2002(M)	17,126	PF63 50.00		PF65 60.00		

KM# 1080 10 EURO
27.00 g., 0.925 Silver 0.7978 oz. ASW, 40 mm. **Ruler:** Juan Carlos I **Subject:** XVII Football World Games 2002 - South Korea and Japan **Obv. Legend:** MUNDIAL DE FUTBOL/2002 - ESPAÑA **Rev:** Glove

Date	Mintage	F12	VF20	XF40	MS60	MS63
2002(M)	7,424	PF63 50.00		PF65 60.00		

KM# 1082 10 EURO
27.00 g., 0.925 Silver 0.7978 oz. ASW, 40 mm. **Ruler:** Juan Carlos I **Subject:** 150th Anniversary Birth of Antonio Gaudí **Obv:** Bust of Gaudí at right **Obv. Legend:** Año Internacional **Rev:** Casa Milà

Date	Mintage	F12	VF20	XF40	MS60	MS63
2002(M)	25,000	PF63 45.00		PF65 55.00		

KM# 1083 10 EURO
27.00 g., 0.925 Silver 0.7978 oz. ASW, 40 mm. **Ruler:** Juan Carlos I **Subject:** 150th Anniversary Birth of Antonio Gaudí **Obv:** Bust of Gaudí at right **Obv. Legend:** Año Internacional **Rev:** El Capricho

Date	Mintage	F12	VF20	XF40	MS60	MS63
2002(M)	9,183	PF63 45.00		PF65 55.00		

KM# 1084 10 EURO
27.00 g., 0.925 Silver 0.7978 oz. ASW, 40 mm. **Ruler:** Juan Carlos I **Subject:** 150th Anniversary - Birth of Antonio Gaudí **Obv:** Bust of Gaudí at right **Obv. Legend:** Año Internacional **Rev:** Parque Güell

Date	Mintage	F12	VF20	XF40	MS60	MS63
2002(M)	14,111	PF63 45.00		PF65 55.00		

KM# 1087 10 EURO
27.00 g., 0.925 Silver 0.7978 oz. ASW, 40 mm. **Ruler:** Juan Carlos I **Subject:** 100th Anniversary - Birth of Luis Cernuda **Obv:** Head left

Date	Mintage	F12	VF20	XF40	MS60	MS63
2002(M)	25,000	PF63 50.00		PF65 60.00		

KM# 1088 10 EURO
27.00 g., 0.925 Silver 0.7978 oz. ASW, 40 mm. **Ruler:** Juan Carlos I **Subject:** 100th Anniversary - Birth of Rafael Alberti **Obv:** Head left **Obv. Legend:** JUAN CARLOS I REY DE ESPAÑA **Rev:** Bust of Alberti facing 3/4 right

Date	Mintage	F12	VF20	XF40	MS60	MS63
2002(M)	25,000	PF63 50.00		PF65 60.00		

KM# 1089 10 EURO
27.00 g., 0.925 Silver 0.7978 oz. ASW, 40 mm. **Ruler:** Juan Carlos I **Series:** Ibero-America V - ships **Obv:** Crowned arms in center circle, 10 participating country arms in outer circle **Obv. Legend:** JUAN CARLOS I REY DE ESPAÑA **Rev:** Galleon of the Spanish Armada **Rev. Legend:** ENCUENTRO DE DOS MUNDOS **Note:** Issued in 2003.

Date	Mintage	F12	VF20	XF40	MS60	MS63
2002(M)	8,000	PF63 115		PF65 135		

KM# 1052 10 EURO
27.00 g., 0.925 Silver 0.7978 oz. ASW, 40 mm. **Ruler:** Juan Carlos I **Obv:** Head left **Rev:** Sailing ship - De Elcano **Edge:** Reeded

Date	Mintage	F12	VF20	XF40	MS60	MS63
2003	12,486	PF63 75.00		PF65 90.00		

KM# 1053 10 EURO
27.00 g., 0.925 Silver 0.7978 oz. ASW, 40 mm. **Ruler:** Juan Carlos I **Obv:** Juan Carlos I **Rev:** Miguel Lopez de Legazpi **Edge:** Reeded

Date	Mintage	F12	VF20	XF40	MS60	MS63
2003	5,724	PF63 95.00		PF65 110		

KM# 1054 10 EURO
27.00 g., 0.925 Silver 0.7978 oz. ASW, 40 mm. **Ruler:** Juan Carlos I **Obv:** Head facing **Rev:** Seated female figure and Swan **Edge:** Reeded

Date	Mintage	F12	VF20	XF40	MS60	MS63
2004 (2003)	17,597	PF63 75.00		PF65 90.00		

KM# 1055 10 EURO
27.00 g., 0.925 Silver 0.7978 oz. ASW, 40 mm. **Ruler:** Juan Carlos I **Obv:** Head facing **Rev:** Dali's painting "El gran masturbador" of 1929 **Edge:** Reeded

Date	Mintage	F12	VF20	XF40	MS60	MS63
2004 (2003)	15,647	PF63 75.00		PF65 90.00		

KM# 1056 10 EURO
27.00 g., 0.925 Silver 0.7978 oz. ASW, 40 mm. **Ruler:** Juan Carlos I **Obv:** Head facing **Rev:** Dali's self portrait with bacon strip **Edge:** Reeded

Date	Mintage	F12	VF20	XF40	MS60	MS63
2004 (2003)	18,290	PF63 75.00		PF65 90.00		

KM# 1076 10 EURO
27.00 g., 0.925 Silver 0.7978 oz. ASW, 40 mm. **Ruler:** Juan Carlos I **Subject:** FIFA World Cup **Obv:** Kings head left **Rev:** Goalie jumping for ball by net **Edge:** Reeded **Note:** Issued in 2004.

Date	Mintage	F12	VF20	XF40	MS60	MS63
2003(M)	25,883	PF63 70.00	PF65 80.00			

KM# 1090 10 EURO
27.00 g., 0.925 Silver 0.7978 oz. ASW, 40 mm. **Ruler:** Juan Carlos I **Obv:** Conjoined heads left **Obv. Legend:** JUAN CARLOS I Y SOFIA **Rev:** Ediface of Parliament building in Madrid **Rev. Legend:** CONSTITUCION ESPAÑOLA

Date	Mintage	F12	VF20	XF40	MS60	MS63
2003(M)	7,995	PF63 85.00	PF65 100			

KM# 1092 10 EURO
27.00 g., 0.925 Silver 0.7978 oz. ASW, 40 mm. **Ruler:** Juan Carlos I **Subject:** 1st Anniversary of Euro **Obv:** Conjoined heads left **Obv. Legend:** PRIMER ANIVERSARIO EURO / JUAN CARLOS I Y SOFIA **Rev:** Europa riding steer left

Date	Mintage	F12	VF20	XF40	MS60	MS63
2003(M)	50,000	PF63 70.00	PF65 80.00			

KM# 1094 10 EURO
27.00 g., 0.925 Silver 0.7978 oz. ASW, 40 mm. **Ruler:** Juan Carlos I **Subject:** World Swimming Championship Games - Barcelona 2003 **Obv:** Head left **Obv. Legend:** JUAN CARLOS I REY DE ESPAÑA **Rev:** Swimmer doing the crawl right **Rev. Legend:** X FINA CAMPEONATOS DEL MUNDO DE NATACION

Date	Mintage	F12	VF20	XF40	MS60	MS63
2003(M)	5,470	PF63 75.00	PF65 90.00			

KM# 1059 10 EURO
27.00 g., 0.925 Silver 0.7978 oz. ASW, 40 mm. **Ruler:** Juan Carlos I **Obv:** Conjoined heads left **Rev:** Bust of St. James facing **Edge:** Reeded

Date	Mintage	F12	VF20	XF40	MS60	MS63
2004	12,214	PF63 75.00	PF65 90.00			

KM# 1060 10 EURO
27.00 g., 0.925 Silver 0.7978 oz. ASW, 40 mm. **Ruler:** Juan Carlos I **Obv:** Conjoined heads left within beaded circle **Rev:** Bust of Isabel I 1/4 left within beaded circle (1451-1504) **Edge:** Reeded

Date	Mintage	F12	VF20	XF40	MS60	MS63
2004	12,000	PF63 75.00	PF65 90.00			

KM# 1097 10 EURO
27.00 g., 0.925 Silver 0.7978 oz. ASW, 40 mm. **Ruler:** Juan Carlos I **Subject:** Wedding of Prince Philip and Letizia Ortiz Rocasolano **Obv:** Conjoined heads left **Obv. Legend:** JUAN CARLOS I T SOFÍA **Rev:** Busts of wedding couple facing 3/4 right, crowned shield below **Rev. Legend:** FELIPE Y LETIZIA - 22.V.2004

Date	Mintage	F12	VF20	XF40	MS60	MS63
2004(M)	40,367	PF63 45.00	PF65 55.00			

KM# 1099 10 EURO
27.00 g., 0.925 Silver 0.7978 oz. ASW, 40 mm. **Ruler:** Juan Carlos I **Subject:** Expansion of the European Union **Obv:** Head left **Obv. Legend:** JUAN CARLOS I Y SOFIA **Rev:** Outlined map of European Union

Date	Mintage	F12	VF20	XF40	MS60	MS63
2004(M)	41,448	PF63 70.00	PF65 80.00			

KM# 1101 10 EURO
27.00 g., 0.925 Silver 0.7978 oz. ASW, 40 mm. **Ruler:** Juan Carlos I **Subject:** XXVIII Summer Olympics - Athens 2004 **Obv:** Conjoined heads left **Obv. Legend:** JUAN CARLOS I Y SOFIA **Rev:** Broad jumper, outlined world map in background **Rev. Legend:** JUEGOS OLIMPICOS

Date	Mintage	F12	VF20	XF40	MS60	MS63
2004(M)	18,790	PF63 75.00	PF65 90.00			

KM# 1102 10 EURO
27.00 g., 0.925 Silver 0.7978 oz. ASW, 40 mm. **Ruler:** Juan Carlos I **Subject:** XVIII World Football games - Germany 2006 **Obv:** Head left **Obv. Legend:** JUAN CARLOS I REY DE ESPAÑA **Rev:** Goalie deflecting ball at net

Date	Mintage	F12	VF20	XF40	MS60	MS63
2004(M)	50,000	PF63 65.00	PF65 75.00			

KM# 1064 10 EURO
27.00 g., 0.925 Silver 0.7978 oz. ASW, 40 mm. **Ruler:** Juan Carlos I **Subject:** 2006 Winter Olympics **Obv:** Juan Carlos **Rev:** Skier **Edge:** Reeded

Date	Mintage	F12	VF20	XF40	MS60	MS63
2005	25,000	PF63 70.00	PF65 80.00			

KM# 1065 10 EURO
27.00 g., 0.925 Silver 0.7978 oz. ASW, 40 mm. **Ruler:** Juan Carlos I **Subject:** European Peace and Freedom **Obv:** Juan Carlos **Rev:** European map on clasped hands **Edge:** Reeded

Date	Mintage	F12	VF20	XF40	MS60	MS63
2005	29,231	PF63 75.00	PF65 90.00			

KM# 1104 10 EURO
27.00 g., 0.925 Silver 0.7978 oz. ASW, 40 mm. **Ruler:** Juan
Carlos I **Obv:** Quixote seated reading a large book **Obv.
Legend:** ESPAÑA - IV CENTENARIO DE LA PRIMERA
EDICIÓN DE " EL QUIJOTE **Rev:** Quixote being knocked off
his horse by windmill blade **Rev. Legend:** LA AVENTURA - DE
LOS - MOLINOS DE VIENTO

Date	Mintage	F12	VF20	XF40	MS60	MS63
2005(M)	11,670	PF63 75.00	PF65 85.00			

KM# 1105 10 EURO
27.00 g., 0.925 Silver 0.7978 oz. ASW, 40 mm. **Ruler:** Juan
Carlos I **Obv:** Quixote seated reading a large book **Obv.
Legend:** ESPAÑA - IV CENTENARIO DE LA PREMERA
EDICIÓN DE LA "EL QUIJOTE" **Rev:** Quixote thrusting his
sword into an animal skin wine sack **Rev. Legend:** BATALLA -
CON UNOS CUEROS DE VINO

Date	Mintage	F12	VF20	XF40	MS60	MS63
2005(M)	7,902	PF63 75.00	PF65 85.00			

KM# 1106 10 EURO
27.00 g., 0.925 Silver 0.7978 oz. ASW, 40 mm. **Ruler:** Juan
Carlos I **Obv:** Quixote seated reading a large book **Obv.
Legend:** ESPAÑA - IV CENTENARIO DE LA PRIMERA
EDICIÓN DE "EL QUIJOTE **Rev:** Boy mounting a hobby horse
with Quixote on it **Rev. Legend:** LA VENIDA DE CLAVAILEÑO
CON EL FIN DESTA DILATADA AVENTURA

Date	Mintage	F12	VF20	XF40	MS60	MS63
2005(M)	7,968	PF63 75.00	PF65 85.00			

KM# 1109 10 EURO
27.00 g., 0.925 Silver 0.7978 oz. ASW, 40 mm. **Ruler:** Juan
Carlos I **Series:** Ibero-America VI - Architecture **Obv:** Crowned
arms in center circle, 10 participating country arms in outer
circle **Obv. Legend:** JUAN CARLOS I REY DE ESPAÑA **Rev:**
General Archives building of West Indes in Seville **Rev. Legend:**
ENCUENTRO DE DOS MUNDOS

Date	Mintage	F12	VF20	XF40	MS60	MS63
2005(M)	3,000	PF63 100	PF65 120			

KM# 1110 10 EURO
27.00 g., 0.925 Silver 0.7978 oz. ASW, 40 mm. **Ruler:** Juan
Carlos I **Rev:** Crowned shield at left, head of Prince Philip at
right **Rev. Legend:** XXV ANIVERSARIO - PREMIOS PRÍNCIPE
DE ASTURIAS

Date	Mintage	F12	VF20	XF40	MS60	MS63
2005(M)	12,845	PF63 75.00	PF65 90.00			

KM# 1114 10 EURO
27.00 g., 0.925 Silver 0.7978 oz. ASW, 40 mm. **Ruler:** Juan
Carlos I **Subject:** 500th Anniversary Death of Columbus
Obv: Bust of Columbus facing at right, astrolabe at lower left
Obv. Legend: ESPAÑA **Rev:** Sailing ship "Santa Maria **Rev.
Legend:** CRISTOBAL COLON **Edge:** Reeded

Date	Mintage	F12	VF20	XF40	MS60	MS63
2006(M)	9,960	PF63 85.00	PF65 100			

KM# 1115 10 EURO
27.00 g., 0.925 Silver 0.7978 oz. ASW, 40 mm. **Ruler:** Juan
Carlos I **Subject:** 500th Anniversary - Death of Columbus
Obv: Bust of Columbus facing at left, astrolabe at lower right
Obv. Legend: ESPAÑA **Rev:** Sailing ship "Pinta **Rev. Legend:**
CRISTOBAL COLON **Edge:** Reeded

Date	Mintage	F12	VF20	XF40	MS60	MS63
2006(M)	6,188	PF63 85.00	PF65 100			

KM# 1116 10 EURO
27.00 g., 0.925 Silver 0.7978 oz. ASW, 40 mm. **Ruler:** Juan
Carlos I **Subject:** 500th Anniversary - Death of Columbus
Obv: Bust of Columbus facing at right, astrolabe at lower left
Obv. Legend: ESPAÑA **Rev:** Sailing ship "Niña **Rev. Legend:**
CRISTOBAL COLON **Edge:** Reeded

Date	Mintage	F12	VF20	XF40	MS60	MS63
2006(M)	6,187	PF63 85.00	PF65 100			

KM# 1119 10 EURO
27.00 g., 0.925 Silver 0.7978 oz. ASW, 40 mm. **Ruler:**
Juan Carlos I **Subject:** 20th Anniversary of Spain and
Portugal membership in European Union **Obv:** Juan Carlos
I **Rev:** Outlined map of Europe, bridge below **Rev. Legend:**
ADHESIÓN A LAS COMUNIDADES EUROPEAS **Rev.
Inscription:** ESPAÑA - PORTUGAL

Date	Mintage	F12	VF20	XF40	MS60	MS63
2006(M)	11,100	PF63 60.00	PF65 70.00			

KM# 1120 10 EURO
27.00 g., 0.925 Silver 0.7978 oz. ASW, 40 mm. **Ruler:** Juan
Carlos I **Rev:** Basketball player scoring in front of defender
Rev. Legend: CAMPEONES DEL MUNDO - JAPÓN 2006

Date	Mintage	F12	VF20	XF40	MS60	MS63
2006(M)	4,991	PF63 60.00	PF65 70.00			

KM# 1122 10 EURO
27.00 g., 0.925 Silver 0.7978 oz. ASW, 40 mm. **Ruler:** Juan Carlos I **Obv:** Head left **Obv. Legend:** JUAN CARLOS I REY DE ESPAÑA **Rev:** Charles I (V) standing facing 3/4 right in front of portal **Rev. Legend:** CAROLVS IMPERATOR

Date	Mintage	F12	VF20	XF40	MS60	MS63
2006(M)	23,799	PF63 80.00	PF65 95.00			

KM# 1124 10 EURO
27.00 g., 0.925 Silver 0.7978 oz. ASW, 40 mm. **Ruler:** Juan Carlos I **Rev:** Two ornate portals **Rev. Legend:** V ANIVERSARIO DEL EURO

Date	Mintage	F12	VF20	XF40	MS60	MS63
2007	12,000	PF63 55.00	PF65 65.00			

KM# 1125 10 EURO
27.00 g., 0.925 Silver 0.7978 oz. ASW, 40 mm. **Ruler:** Juan Carlos I **Rev:** Stone arch bridge **Rev. Legend:** V ANIVERSARIO DEL EURO

Date	Mintage	F12	VF20	XF40	MS60	MS63
2007	12,000	PF63 55.00	PF65 65.00			

KM# 1126 10 EURO
27.00 g., 0.925 Silver 0.7978 oz. ASW, 40 mm. **Ruler:** Juan Carlos I **Rev:** Stone archway **Rev. Legend:** V ANIVERSARIO DEL EURO

Date	Mintage	F12	VF20	XF40	MS60	MS63
2007	12,000	PF63 55.00	PF65 65.00			

KM# 1132 10 EURO
27.00 g., 0.925 Silver 0.7978 oz. ASW, 40 mm. **Ruler:** Juan Carlos I **Obv:** Conjoined heads left **Obv. Legend:** JUAN CARLOS I Y SOFÍA - AÑO DE ESPAÑA EN CHINA **Rev:** Early silver "Pillar" reales coin with Chinese characters to left and right of pillars **Rev. Legend:** VTRAQUE VNVM

Date	Mintage	F12	VF20	XF40	MS60	MS63
2007	20,000	PF63 50.00	PF65 60.00			

KM# 1134 10 EURO
27.00 g., 0.925 Silver 0.7978 oz. ASW, 40 mm. **Ruler:** Juan Carlos I **Obv:** Head left **Obv. Legend:** JUAN CARLOS I REY DE ESPAÑA **Rev:** Basketball player shooting basket **Rev. Legend:** EUROBASKET 2007

Date	Mintage	F12	VF20	XF40	MS60	MS63
2007	12,000	PF63 70.00	PF65 80.00			

KM# 1141 10 EURO
27.00 g., 0.925 Silver 0.7978 oz. ASW, 40 mm. **Ruler:** Juan Carlos I **Subject:** Zaragoza Expo 2008

Date	Mintage	F12	VF20	XF40	MS60	MS63
2007	25,000	PF63 50.00	PF65 60.00			

KM# 1135 10 EURO
27.00 g., 0.925 Silver 0.7978 oz. ASW, 40 mm. **Ruler:** Juan Carlos I **Subject:** Treaty of Rome, 50th Anniversary **Obv:** Head left **Rev:** Map of Western Europe

Date	Mintage	F12	VF20	XF40	MS60	MS63
2007	15,000	PF63 50.00	PF65 60.00			

KM# 1137 10 EURO
27.00 g., 0.925 Silver 0.7978 oz. ASW, 40 mm. **Ruler:** Juan Carlos I **Subject:** El Cid 700th Anniversary **Obv:** Female standing before arches **Rev:** Monk writing

Date	Mintage	F12	VF20	XF40	MS60	MS63
2007	12,000	PF63 70.00	PF65 80.00			

KM# 1140 10 EURO
27.00 g., 0.925 Silver 0.7978 oz. ASW, 40 mm. **Ruler:** Juan Carlos I **Subject:** International Polar Year **Rev:** Ship left, outline map of Antarctica in background

Date	Mintage	F12	VF20	XF40	MS60	MS63
2007	20,000	PF63 55.00	PF65 65.00			

KM# 1187 10 EURO
27.00 g., 0.925 Silver 0.7978 oz. ASW, 40 mm. **Ruler:** Juan
Carlos I **Subject:** Expo Zaragoza **Rev:** Bridge

Date	Mintage	F12	VF20	XF40	MS60	MS63
2007	25,000	**PF63** 55.00	**PF65** 65.00			

KM# 1190 10 EURO
27.00 g., 0.925 Silver 0.7978 oz. ASW, 40 mm. **Ruler:** Juan
Carlos I **Subject:** Velazquez

Date	Mintage	F12	VF20	XF40	MS60	MS63
2008	12,000	**PF63** 60.00	**PF65** 70.00			

KM# 1192 10 EURO
27.00 g., 0.925 Silver 0.7978 oz. ASW, 40 mm. **Ruler:** Juan
Carlos I **Subject:** Soccer, European Champions

Date	Mintage	F12	VF20	XF40	MS60	MS63
2008	20,000	**PF63** 60.00	**PF65** 70.00			

KM# 1194 10 EURO
27.00 g., 0.925 Silver 0.7978 oz. ASW, 40 mm. **Ruler:** Juan
Carlos I **Subject:** Numismatic Treasures - Hispano-Greek
Pegasus

Date	Mintage	F12	VF20	XF40	MS60	MS63
2008	12,000	**PF63** 60.00	**PF65** 70.00			

KM# 1196 10 EURO
27.00 g., 0.925 Silver 0.7978 oz. ASW, 40 mm. **Ruler:** Juan
Carlos I **Subject:** Olympic Sports - Sailing

Date	Mintage	F12	VF20	XF40	MS60	MS63
2008	—	**PF63** 50.00	**PF65** 60.00			

KM# 1199 10 EURO
27.00 g., 0.925 Silver 0.7978 oz. ASW, 40 mm. **Ruler:** Juan
Carlos I **Subject:** War of Independence, Manuela Malasana,
200th Anniversary

Date	Mintage	F12	VF20	XF40	MS60	MS63
2008	12,000	**PF63** 55.00	**PF65** 65.00			

KM# 1200 10 EURO
27.00 g., 0.925 Silver 0.7978 oz. ASW, 40 mm. **Ruler:** Juan
Carlos I **Subject:** War of Independence, 200th Anniversary
General Castanos

Date	Mintage	F12	VF20	XF40	MS60	MS63
2008	12,000	**PF63** 55.00	**PF65** 65.00			

KM# 1201 10 EURO
27.00 g., 0.925 Silver 0.7978 oz. ASW, 40 mm. **Ruler:** Juan
Carlos I **Subject:** War of Independence, 200th Anniversary El
Tambor del Bruc

Date	Mintage	F12	VF20	XF40	MS60	MS63
2008	20,000	**PF63** 70.00	**PF65** 80.00			

KM# 1203 10 EURO
27.00 g., 0.925 Silver 0.7978 oz. ASW, 40 mm. **Ruler:** Juan
Carlos I **Subject:** Alphonse the wise

Date	Mintage	F12	VF20	XF40	MS60	MS63
2008	—	**PF63** 50.00	**PF65** 60.00			

KM# 1143 10 EURO
27.00 g., 0.925 Silver 0.7978 oz. ASW, 40 mm. **Ruler:** Juan Carlos I **Obv:** Head left **Rev:** Soccer player, ball and net

Date	Mintage	F12	VF20	XF40	MS60	MS63
2009	12,000	PF63 60.00	PF65 70.00			

KM# 1209 10 EURO
27.00 g., 0.925 Silver 0.7978 oz. ASW, 40 mm. **Ruler:** Juan Carlos I **Subject:** Dali Busto de mujer retraspectivo

Date	Mintage	F12	VF20	XF40	MS60	MS63
2009	10,000	PF63 65.00	PF65 75.00			

KM# 1210 10 EURO
27.00 g., 0.925 Silver 0.7978 oz. ASW, 40 mm. **Ruler:** Juan Carlos I **Subject:** Dali Retrato de Pablo Picasso and S. XXI

Date	Mintage	F12	VF20	XF40	MS60	MS63
2009	10,000	PF63 65.00	PF65 75.00			

KM# 1211 10 EURO
27.00 g., 0.925 Silver 0.7978 oz. ASW, 40 mm. **Ruler:** Juan Carlos I **Subject:** Dali Retrato de Gala

Date	Mintage	F12	VF20	XF40	MS60	MS63
2009	10,000	PF63 65.00	PF65 75.00			

KM# 1214 10 EURO
27.00 g., 0.925 Silver 0.7978 oz. ASW, 40 mm. **Ruler:** Juan Carlos I **Subject:** Philip II

Date	Mintage	F12	VF20	XF40	MS60	MS63
2009	18,000	PF63 70.00	PF65 80.00			

KM# 1216 10 EURO
27.00 g., 0.925 Silver 0.7978 oz. ASW, 40 mm. **Ruler:** Juan Carlos I **Subject:** World Cup Soccer, South Africa

Date	Mintage	F12	VF20	XF40	MS60	MS63
2009	12,000	PF63 55.00	PF65 65.00			

KM# 1169 10 EURO
27.00 g., 0.925 Silver 0.7978 oz. ASW, 40 mm. **Ruler:** Juan Carlos I **Subject:** Antoni Gaudi

Date	Mintage	F12	VF20	XF40	MS60	MS63
2010	10,000	PF63 75.00	PF65 85.00			

KM# 1171 10 EURO
27.00 g., 0.925 Silver 0.7978 oz. ASW, 40 mm. **Ruler:** Juan Carlos I **Subject:** EU Council Presidency

Date	Mintage	F12	VF20	XF40	MS60	MS63
2010	—	PF63 70.00	PF65 80.00			

KM# 1173 10 EURO
27.00 g., 0.925 Silver 0.7978 oz. ASW, 40 mm. **Ruler:** Juan Carlos I **Subject:** Holy Year 2010 - St. James the Elder

Date	Mintage	F12	VF20	XF40	MS60	MS63
2010	10,000	PF63 70.00	PF65 80.00			

KM# 1174 10 EURO
27.00 g., 0.925 Silver 0.7978 oz. ASW, 40 mm. **Ruler:** Juan Carlos I **Subject:** Shanghai Expo

Date	Mintage	F12	VF20	XF40	MS60	MS63
2010	10,000	PF63 70.00	PF65 80.00			

KM# 1175 10 EURO
27.00 g., 0.925 Silver 0.7978 oz. ASW, 40 mm. **Ruler:** Juan Carlos I **Subject:** Ibero-American Series - Historical Coins

Date	Mintage	F12	VF20	XF40	MS60	MS63
2010	12,000	PF63 70.00	PF65 80.00			

KM# 1176 10 EURO
27.00 g., 0.925 Silver 0.7978 oz. ASW, 40 mm. **Ruler:** Juan Carlos I **Subject:** FIFA World Cup - South Africa 2010

Date	Mintage	F12	VF20	XF40	MS60	MS63
2010	20,000	PF63 65.00	PF65 75.00			

KM# 1178 10 EURO
27.00 g., 0.925 Silver 0.7978 oz. ASW, 40 mm. **Ruler:** Juan Carlos I **Subject:** Francisco de Goya - The Clothed Maja

Date	Mintage	F12	VF20	XF40	MS60	MS63
2010	10,000	PF63 85.00	PF65 95.00			

KM# 1179 10 EURO
27.00 g., 0.925 Silver 0.7978 oz. ASW, 40 mm. **Ruler:** Juan Carlos I **Subject:** Francisco de Goya - The Grape Harvest

Date	Mintage	F12	VF20	XF40	MS60	MS63
2010	10,000	PF63 85.00	PF65 95.00			

KM# 1180 10 EURO
27.00 g., 0.925 Silver 0.7978 oz. ASW, 40 mm. **Ruler:** Juan Carlos I **Subject:** Francisco de Goya - Duel with Clubs

Date	Mintage	F12	VF20	XF40	MS60	MS63
2010	12,000	PF63 85.00	PF65 95.00			

KM# 1185 10 EURO
27.00 g., 0.925 Silver 0.7978 oz. ASW, 40 mm. **Ruler:** Juan Carlos I **Subject:** International Year of Chemistry **Rev:** Marie Curie

Date	Mintage	F12	VF20	XF40	MS60	MS63
2011	10,000	PF63 100	PF65 110			

KM# 1219 10 EURO
27.00 g., 0.925 Silver 0.7978 oz. ASW, 40 mm. **Ruler:** Juan Carlos I **Subject:** Spain-Portugal

Date	Mintage	F12	VF20	XF40	MS60	MS63
2011	10,000	PF63 70.00	PF65 80.00			

KM# 1220 10 EURO
27.00 g., 0.925 Silver 0.7978 oz. ASW, 40 mm. **Ruler:** Juan Carlos I **Subject:** Historic Spanish Coin, Ibero American series

Date	Mintage	F12	VF20	XF40	MS60	MS63
2011	—	PF63 75.00	PF65 85.00			

KM# 1223 10 EURO
27.00 g., 0.925 Silver 0.7978 oz. ASW, 40 mm. **Ruler:** Juan Carlos I **Subject:** Zurbaran - Hercules

Date	Mintage	F12	VF20	XF40	MS60	MS63
2011	10,000	PF63 90.00	PF65 100			

KM# 1224 10 EURO
27.00 g., 0.925 Silver 0.7978 oz. ASW, 40 mm. **Ruler:** Juan Carlos I **Subject:** Ribera-Jacdo

Date	Mintage	F12	VF20	XF40	MS60	MS63
2011	10,000	PF63 90.00	PF65 100			

KM# 1225 10 EURO
27.00 g., 0.925 Silver 0.7978 oz. ASW, 40 mm. **Ruler:** Juan Carlos I **Subject:** Musillo - Bren Pastar

Date	Mintage	F12	VF20	XF40	MS60	MS63
2011	10,000	PF63 90.00	PF65 100			

KM# 1248 10 EURO
27.00 g., 0.925 Silver 0.7978 oz. ASW, 40 mm. **Ruler:** Juan Carlos I **Subject:** Orellana

Date	Mintage	F12	VF20	XF40	MS60	MS63
2011	12,000	PF63 65.00	PF65 75.00			

KM# 1165 10 EURO
27.00 g., 0.925 Silver 0.7978 oz. ASW, 40 mm. **Ruler:** Juan Carlos I **Subject:** Numismatic Treasurers - Silver Shekel of Carthage

Date	Mintage	F12	VF20	XF40	MS60	MS63
2011	10,000	PF63 65.00	PF65 75.00			

KM# 1217 10 EURO
27.00 g., 0.925 Silver 0.7978 oz. ASW, 40 mm. **Ruler:** Juan Carlos I **Subject:** Spain-Russia **Note:** The reverse design is the same as a Russian 3 Rouble

Date	Mintage	F12	VF20	XF40	MS60	MS63
2012	7,500	PF63 80.00	PF65 90.00			

KM# 1256 10 EURO
27.00 g., Silver, 40 mm. **Ruler:** Juan Carlos I **Subject:** 200th Anniversary of Constitution

Date	Mintage	F12	VF20	XF40	MS60	MS63
2012 Proof	Est. 10000	—	—	—	—	—

KM# 1257 10 EURO
27.00 g., 0.925 Silver 0.7978 oz. ASW, 40 mm. **Ruler:** Juan Carlos I **Subject:** Brasil World Cup 2014 **Rev:** Map and Trophy - Partially gilt

Date	Mintage	F12	VF20	XF40	MS60	MS63
2012 Proof	15,000	—	—	—	—	—

KM# 1258 10 EURO
27.00 g., 0.925 Silver 0.7978 oz. ASW, 40 mm. **Ruler:** Juan Carlos I **Subject:** Spain-Japan relations, 400th Anniversary **Obv:** Head left **Rev:** Priest at cross, latent image switches from Spanish to Japanese flag

Date	Mintage	F12	VF20	XF40	MS60	MS63
2013	30,000	PF63 85.00	PF65 95.00			

KM# 1259 10 EURO
27.00 g., 0.925 Silver 0.7978 oz. ASW, 40 mm. **Ruler:** Juan Carlos I **Obv:** Head left **Rev:** Cervantes writing at right, Don Quixote and Sanchez at left

Date	Mintage	F12	VF20	XF40	MS60	MS63
2013	10,000	PF63 80.00	PF65 90.00			

KM# 1280 10 EURO
27.00 g., 0.925 Silver 0.7978 oz. ASW, 40 mm. **Ruler:** Juan Carlos I **Subject:** Juan Carlos, 75th Anniversary of Birth

Date	Mintage	F12	VF20	XF40	MS60	MS63
2013	10,000	PF63 75.00	PF65 85.00			

KM# 1284 10 EURO
27.00 g., 0.925 Silver 0.7978 oz. ASW, 40 mm. **Ruler:** Juan Carlos I **Subject:** Isaac Peral and his submarine, 125th Anniversary

Date	Mintage	F12	VF20	XF40	MS60	MS63
2013	10,000	PF63 75.00	PF65 85.00			

KM# 1285 10 EURO
27.00 g., 0.925 Silver 0.7978 oz. ASW, 40 mm. **Ruler:** Juan Carlos I **Subject:** Holey Dollar and Dump, 200th Anniversary

Date	Mintage	F12	VF20	XF40	MS60	MS63
2013	5,000	PF63 75.00	PF65 85.00			

KM# 1286 10 EURO
27.00 g., 0.925 Silver 0.7978 oz. ASW, 40 mm. **Ruler:** Juan Carlos I **Subject:** Balboa and the Pacific Ocean, 400th Anniversary

Date	Mintage	F12	VF20	XF40	MS60	MS63
2013	10,000	PF63 75.00	PF65 85.00			

KM# 1290 10 EURO
27.00 g., 0.925 Silver 0.7978 oz. ASW, 40 mm. **Ruler:** Juan Carlos I **Subject:** World Cup Brazil, 2014

Date	Mintage	F12	VF20	XF40	MS60	MS63
2013	10,000	PF63 75.00	PF65 85.00			

KM# 1292 10 EURO
27.00 g., 0.925 Silver 0.7978 oz. ASW, 40 mm. **Ruler:** Juan Carlos I **Subject:** Granada, 1000th Anniversary **Rev:** Court of Lions in the Alhambra

Date	Mintage	F12	VF20	XF40	MS60	MS63
2013	10,000	PF63 75.00	PF65 85.00			

KM# 1300 10 EURO
27.00 g., 0.925 Silver 0.7978 oz. ASW, 40 mm. **Ruler:** Juan Carlos I **Subject:** Titian painting

Date	Mintage	F12	VF20	XF40	MS60	MS63
2013	10,000	PF63 85.00	PF65 95.00			

KM# 1301 10 EURO
27.00 g., 0.925 Silver 0.7978 oz. ASW, 40 mm. **Ruler:** Juan Carlos I **Subject:** Rafael paintings

Date	Mintage	F12	VF20	XF40	MS60	MS63
2013	10,000	PF63 75.00	PF65 85.00			

KM# 1302 10 EURO
27.00 g., 0.925 Silver 0.7978 oz. ASW, 40 mm. **Ruler:** Juan
Carlos I **Subject:** Vicente Lopez paintings

Date	Mintage	F12	VF20	XF40	MS60	MS63
2013	10,000	PF63 85.00			PF65 95.00	

KM# 1049 12 EURO
18.00 g., 0.925 Silver 0.5319 oz. ASW, 33 mm. **Ruler:** Juan
Carlos I **Subject:** Spanish European Union Presidency **Obv:**
Conjoined heads left **Rev:** Distorted star design **Edge:** Reeded

Date	Mintage	F12	VF20	XF40	MS60	MS63
2002	1,608,400	—	—	—	20.00	22.00
2002 Special select		—	—	—		25.00
2002	Est. 30000	PF63 42.00				

KM# 1051 12 EURO
18.00 g., 0.925 Silver 0.5319 oz. ASW, 33 mm. **Ruler:** Juan
Carlos I **Subject:** 25th Anniversary of Constitution **Obv:**
Conjoined heads left **Rev:** National arms above denomination
Edge: Plain

Date	Mintage	F12	VF20	XF40	MS60	MS63
2003	1,468,800	—	—	—	23.00	25.00
2003	19,346	PF63 35.00				

KM# 1069 12 EURO
18.00 g., 0.925 Silver 0.5319 oz. ASW, 33 mm. **Ruler:** Juan
Carlos I **Obv:** Juan Carlos and Sofia **Rev:** Felipe and Letizia

Date	Mintage	F12	VF20	XF40	MS60	MS63
2004M	2,505,700	—	—	—	22.00	24.00

KM# 1095 12 EURO
18.00 g., 0.925 Silver 0.5319 oz. ASW, 32.93 mm. **Ruler:**
Juan Carlos I **Subject:** 500th Anniversary - Death of Isabel
Obv: Conjoined heads left **Obv. Legend:** JUAN CARLOS I Y
SOFIA **Rev:** Bust of Isabella I left **Rev. Legend:** ISABEL I DE
CASTILLA / 1481-1504 **Edge:** Plain

Date	Mintage	F12	VF20	XF40	MS60	MS63
2004(M)	1,496,100	—		—	23.00	25.00
2004(M)	12,420	PF63 38.00				

KM# 1096 12 EURO
18.00 g., 0.925 Silver 0.5319 oz. ASW, 32.94 mm. **Ruler:** Juan
Carlos I **Subject:** Wedding of Prince Philip and Letizia Ortiz
Rocasolano **Obv:** Conjoined heads left **Obv. Legend:** JUAN
CARLOS I Y SOFIA **Rev:** Busts of wedding couple facing 3/4
right **Rev. Legend:** FELIPE Y LETIZIA - 22.V.2004 **Edge:** Plain

Date	Mintage	F12	VF20	XF40	MS60	MS63
2004(M)	2,505,700	—	—	—	22.00	24.00
2004(M)	27,655	PF63 22.00				

KM# 1067 12 EURO
18.00 g., 0.925 Silver 0.5319 oz. ASW, 33 mm. **Ruler:** Juan
Carlos I **Subject:** Don Quixote **Obv:** Conjoined heads left **Rev:**
Man seated on books **Edge:** Reeded

Date	Mintage	F12	VF20	XF40	MS60	MS63
2005	1,880,900	—	—	—	22.00	24.00

KM# 1113 12 EURO
18.00 g., 0.925 Silver 0.5319 oz. ASW, 32.95 mm. **Ruler:** Juan
Carlos I **Subject:** 500th Anniversary - Death of Columbus **Obv:**
Conjoined heads left **Obv. Legend:** JUAN CARLOS I Y SOFIA
Rev: Bust of Columbus facing 3/4 right, latitude and longitude
lines with three small sailing ships in background **Edge:** Plain

Date	Mintage	F12	VF20	XF40	MS60	MS63
2006(M)	1,379,600	—	—	—	22.00	24.00

KM# 1129 12 EURO
18.00 g., 0.925 Silver 0.5319 oz. ASW, 32 mm. **Ruler:** Juan
Carlos I **Rev:** Hand with pen **Rev. Legend:** 50 ANIVERSARIO
• TRATADO DE ROMA **Rev. Inscription:** EUROPA

Date	Mintage	F12	VF20	XF40	MS60	MS63
2007(M)	1,002,500	—	—	—	—	24.00
2007	20,000	PF63 30.00				

KM# 1195 12 EURO
18.00 g., 0.925 Silver 0.5319 oz. ASW, 33 mm. **Ruler:** Juan
Carlos I **Subject:** International Year of Planet Earth

Date	Mintage	F12	VF20	XF40	MS60	MS63
2008	45,000	PF63 25.00				

KM# 1212 12 EURO
18.00 g., 0.925 Silver 0.5319 oz. ASW, 33 mm. **Ruler:** Juan
Carlos I **Subject:** European Monetary Union, 10th Anniversary

Date	Mintage	F12	VF20	XF40	MS60	MS63
2009	20,000	PF63 25.00				

KM# 1172 12 EURO
18.00 g., 0.925 Silver 0.5319 oz. ASW, 33 mm. **Ruler:** Juan
Carlos I **Subject:** EU Council Presidency

Date	Mintage	F12	VF20	XF40	MS60	MS63
2010	—	PF63 28.00				

KM# 1133 20 EURO
1.24 g., 0.999 Gold 0.0396 oz. AGW, 13.92 mm. **Ruler:** Juan
Carlos I **Obv:** National arms **Obv. Legend:** JUAN CARLOS I
REY DE ESPAÑA - AÑO DE ESPAÑA EN CHINA **Rev:** Early
silver "Pillar" reales coin with Chinese chopmarks

Date	Mintage	F12	VF20	XF40	MS60	MS63
2007	15,000	PF63 100		PF65 110		

KM# 1193 20 EURO
1.24 g., 0.999 Gold 0.0396 oz. AGW, 13.92 mm. **Ruler:** Juan
Carlos I **Subject:** Numismatic Treasures - Roman Aureus

Date	Mintage	F12	VF20	XF40	MS60	MS63
2008	12,000	PF63 100		PF65 115		

KM# 1206 20 EURO
1.24 g., 0.999 Gold 0.0396 oz. AGW, 13.92 mm. **Ruler:** Juan
Carlos I **Subject:** Numismatic Treasures - Spanish coin **Obv:**
Obverse of 1609 gold coin **Rev:** Reverse of 1609 gold coin

Date	Mintage	F12	VF20	XF40	MS60	MS63
2009	12,000	PF63 100		PF65 115		

KM# 1177 20 EURO
1.24 g., 0.999 Gold 0.0396 oz. AGW, 13.92 mm. **Ruler:** Juan
Carlos I **Subject:** FIFA World Cup - South Africa

Date	Mintage	F12	VF20	XF40	MS60	MS63
2010	20,000	PF63 100		PF65 110		

KM# 1183 20 EURO
18.00 g., 0.925 Silver 0.5319 oz. ASW, 33 mm. **Ruler:** Juan
Carlos I **Subject:** FIFA World Cup Winners

Date	Mintage	F12	VF20	XF40	MS60	MS63
2010	12,000	PF63 60.00				

KM# 1218 20 EURO
1.24 g., 0.999 Gold 0.0396 oz. AGW **Ruler:** Juan Carlos I
Subject: Span & Portugal **Shape:** 13.92

Date	Mintage	F12	VF20	XF40	MS60	MS63
2011	12,000	PF63 100		PF65 110		

KM# 1246 20 EURO
18.00 g., 0.925 Silver 0.5319 oz. ASW, 33 mm. **Ruler:** Juan
Carlos I **Subject:** International Women's Day, 100th Anniversary

Date	Mintage	F12	VF20	XF40	MS60	MS63
2011	12,000	PF63 50.00		PF65 60.00		

KM# 1166 20 EURO
1.24 g., 0.999 Gold 0.0396 oz. AGW, 13.92 mm. **Ruler:** Juan
Carlos I **Subject:** Numismatic Treasurers - Leovigild Gold

Date	Mintage	F12	VF20	XF40	MS60	MS63
2011	12,000	PF63 100		PF65 110		

KM# 1281 20 EURO
1.24 g., 0.999 Gold 0.0396 oz. AGW, 13.92 mm. **Ruler:** Juan
Carlos I **Subject:** Juan Carlos, 75th Anniversary of Birth

Date	Mintage	F12	VF20	XF40	MS60	MS63
2013	12,000	**PF63** 75.00	**PF65** 85.00			

KM# 1085 50 EURO
168.75 g., 0.925 Silver 4.9862 oz. ASW, 73 mm. **Ruler:** Juan
Carlos I **Subject:** 150th Anniversary - Birth of Antonio Gaudí
Obv: Bust of Gaudí at right **Obv. Legend:** Año Internacional
Rev: Sagrada Familia

Date	Mintage	F12	VF20	XF40	MS60	MS63
2002(M)	7,594	**PF63** 450				

KM# 1057 50 EURO
168.75 g., 0.925 Silver 4.9862 oz. ASW, 73 mm. **Ruler:** Juan
Carlos I **Obv:** Dalí's "Dream State" painting **Rev:** Dalí's
"Rhinocerotic Disintegration..." painting **Edge:** Reeded

Date	Mintage	F12	VF20	XF40	MS60	MS63
2004 (2003)	10,455	**PF63** 550	**PF65** 600			

KM# 1093 50 EURO
168.75 g., 0.925 Silver 4.9862 oz. ASW, 73 mm. **Ruler:** Juan
Carlos I **Subject:** 1st Anniversary of Euro **Obv:** Conjoined
heads left **Obv. Legend:** PREMIER ANIVERSARIO EURO
• JUAN CARLOS I Y SOFÍA **Rev:** National arms at center
surrounded by various items of architecture

Date	Mintage	F12	VF20	XF40	MS60	MS63
2003	5,554	**PF63** 500				

KM# 1061 50 EURO
168.73 g., 0.925 Silver 4.9856 oz. ASW, 73 mm. **Ruler:** Juan
Carlos I **Obv:** Crowned bust left(1451-1504) and castle within
beaded circle **Rev:** Surrender of Grenada scene within beaded
circle **Edge:** Reeded

Date	Mintage	F12	VF20	XF40	MS60	MS63
2004	3,158	**PF63** 500				

KM# 1107 50 EURO
168.75 g., 0.925 Silver 4.9862 oz. ASW, 73 mm. **Ruler:** Juan
Carlos I **Obv:** 1/2 length figure of Miguel de Cervantes Saavedra
facing writing in manuscript with quill pen **Obv. Legend:**
ESPAÑA - IV CENTENARIO DE LA PRIMERA EDICIÓN DE "EL
QUIJOTE **Rev:** Quixote

Date	Mintage	F12	VF20	XF40	MS60	MS63
2005(M)	5,795	**PF63** 450				

KM# 1117 50 EURO
168.75 g., 0.925 Silver 4.9862 oz. ASW, 73 mm. **Ruler:** Juan
Carlos I **Subject:** 500th Anniversary - Death of Columbus **Obv:**
Landing party at Guanahani **Obv. Legend:** ESPAÑA **Rev:**
Columbus standing facing 3/4 left with right arm outstretched
standing on outline of the northern part of South America **Rev.
Legend:** CRISTOBAL COLON **Edge:** Plain

Date	Mintage	F12	VF20	XF40	MS60	MS63
2006(M)	4,265	**PF63** 450				

KM# 1127 50 EURO
168.75 g., 0.925 Silver 4.9862 oz. ASW, 73 mm. **Ruler:** Juan
Carlos I **Rev:** Euro seated on resting bull left **Rev. Legend:** V
ANIVERSARIO DEL EURO

Date	Mintage	F12	VF20	XF40	MS60	MS63
2007	5,000	**PF63** 400	**PF65** 425			

KM# 1138 50 EURO
168.75 g., 0.925 Silver 4.9862 oz. ASW, 73 mm. **Ruler:** Juan
Carlos I **Subject:** El Cid 700th Anniversary **Obv:** Statue of
Rodrigo Diaz de Vivar in Burgos **Rev:** Two seated trumpeters

Date	Mintage	F12	VF20	XF40	MS60	MS63
2007	6,000	PF63 400	PF65 425			

KM# 1189 50 EURO
168.75 g., 0.925 Silver 4.9862 oz. ASW, 73 mm. **Ruler:** Juan
Carlos I **Subject:** Velazquez

Date	Mintage	F12	VF20	XF40	MS60	MS63
2008	5,000	PF63 400	PF65 425			

KM# 1198 50 EURO
168.75 g., 0.925 Silver 4.9862 oz. ASW, 73 mm. **Ruler:** Juan
Carlos I **Subject:** War of Independence, 200th Anniversary

Date	Mintage	F12	VF20	XF40	MS60	MS63
2008	5,000	PF63 400	PF65 425			

KM# 1205 50 EURO
168.75 g., 0.925 Silver 4.9862 oz. ASW, 73 mm. **Ruler:** Juan
Carlos I **Subject:** Numismatic Treasurers - Spanish cincuentin

Date	Mintage	F12	VF20	XF40	MS60	MS63
2009	6,000	PF63 400	PF65 425			

KM# 1208 50 EURO
168.75 g., 0.925 Silver 4.9862 oz. ASW, 73 mm. **Ruler:** Juan
Carlos I **Subject:** Dali

Date	Mintage	F12	VF20	XF40	MS60	MS63
2009	5,000	PF63 425	PF65 450			

KM# 1181 50 EURO
168.75 g., 0.925 Silver 4.9862 oz. ASW, 73 mm. **Ruler:** Juan
Carlos I **Subject:** Francisco de Goya - Witches' Sabbath

Date	Mintage	F12	VF20	XF40	MS60	MS63
2010	6,000	PF63 475	PF65 500			

KM# 1222 50 EURO
168.75 g., 0.999 Silver 5.3851 oz. ASW, 73 mm. **Ruler:** Juan
Carlos I **Subject:** El Greco

Date	Mintage	F12	VF20	XF40	MS60	MS63
2011	5,000	PF63 400	PF65 425			

KM# 1283 50 EURO
168.75 g., 0.925 Silver 4.9862 oz. ASW, 75 mm. **Ruler:** Juan
Carlos I **Subject:** Juan Carlos, 75th Anniversary of Birth

Date	Mintage	F12	VF20	XF40	MS60	MS63
2013	5,000	PF63 250				

KM# 1287 50 EURO
168.75 g., 0.925 Silver 4.9862 oz. ASW, 73 mm. **Ruler:** Juan Carlos I **Subject:** Balboa and the Pacific Ocean, 400th Anniversary

Date	Mintage	F12	VF20	XF40	MS60	MS63
2013	5,000	PF63 250				

KM# 1303 50 EURO
168.75 g., 0.925 Silver 4.9862 oz. ASW, 73 mm. **Ruler:** Juan Carlos I **Subject:** Velazquez paintings

Date	Mintage	F12	VF20	XF40	MS60	MS63
2013	5,000	PF63 250				

KM# 1077 100 EURO
6.75 g., 0.999 Gold 0.2154 oz. AGW, 23 mm. **Ruler:** Juan Carlos I **Obv:** Head left **Obv. Legend:** JUAN CARLOS I REY DE ESPAÑA **Rev:** Player running right kicking ball **Rev. Legend:** ALEMANIA 2006 at bottom **Note:** Issued in 2004.

Date	Mintage	F12	VF20	XF40	MS60	MS63
2003(M)	8,230	PF63 600				

KM# 1103 100 EURO
6.75 g., 0.999 Gold 0.2154 oz. AGW, 23 mm. **Ruler:** Juan Carlos I **Subject:** XVIII World Football Games - Germany 2006 **Obv:** Head left **Obv. Legend:** JUAN CARLOS I REY DE ESPAÑA **Rev:** Goalie deflecting ball at net **Rev. Inscription:** COPA MUNDIAL DE LA FIFA

Date	Mintage	F12	VF20	XF40	MS60	MS63
2004(M)	25,000	PF63 500	PF65 550			

KM# 1167 100 EURO
168.88 g., 0.925 Silver 4.9901 oz. ASW, 73 mm. **Ruler:** Juan Carlos I **Subject:** Numismatic treasurers - The Centen, 100 Escudos, 1609

Date	Mintage	F12	VF20	XF40	MS60	MS63
2009	6,000	PF63 450	PF65 475			

KM# 1204 100 EURO
6.75 g., 0.999 Gold 0.2154 oz. AGW, 23 mm. **Ruler:** Juan Carlos I **Subject:** Numismatic Treasures - Spanish Escudo

Date	Mintage	F12	VF20	XF40	MS60	MS63
2009	—	PF63 400	PF65 425			

KM# 1215 100 EURO
6.75 g., 0.999 Gold 0.2154 oz. AGW, 23 mm. **Ruler:** Juan Carlos I **Subject:** World Cup Soccer, Africa

Date	Mintage	F12	VF20	XF40	MS60	MS63
2009	6,000	PF63 550				

KM# 1168 100 EURO
6.75 g., 0.999 Gold 0.2154 oz. AGW, 23 mm. **Ruler:** Juan Carlos I **Subject:** Numismatic Treasurers - Swinthila Gold

Date	Mintage	F12	VF20	XF40	MS60	MS63
2011	6,000	PF63 525	PF65 550			

KM# 1289 100 EURO
6.75 g., 0.999 Gold 0.2154 oz. AGW, 23 mm. **Ruler:** Juan Carlos I **Subject:** Cervantes

Date	Mintage	F12	VF20	XF40	MS60	MS63
2013	5,000	PF63 450				

KM# 1291 100 EURO
6.75 g., 0.999 Gold 0.2154 oz. AGW, 23 mm. **Ruler:** Juan Carlos I **Subject:** World Cup, Brazil, 2014

Date	Mintage	F12	VF20	XF40	MS60	MS63
2013	4,000	PF63 450				

KM# 1293 100 EURO
6.75 g., 0.999 Gold 0.2154 oz. AGW, 23 mm. **Ruler:** Juan Carlos I **Subject:** Granada, 1000th Anniversary **Rev:** Central fountain from the Alhambra

Date	Mintage	F12	VF20	XF40	MS60	MS63
2013	5,000	PF63 450				

KM# 1081 200 EURO
13.50 g., 0.999 Gold 0.4308 oz. AGW, 30 mm. **Ruler:** Juan Carlos I **Subject:** XVII Football World Games 2002 - South Korea and Japan **Obv. Legend:** MUNDIAL DE FUTBOL/2002 - ESPAÑA **Rev:** Ball hitting net

Date	Mintage	F12	VF20	XF40	MS60	MS63
2002(M)	4,000	PF63 1,050				

KM# 1075 200 EURO
13.50 g., 0.999 Gold 0.4308 oz. AGW, 30 mm. **Ruler:** Juan Carlos I **Subject:** Birth of the Euro **Obv:** Spanish King and Queen left **Rev:** Mythological Europa riding on the back of a bull

Date	Mintage	F12	VF20	XF40	MS60	MS63
2003	20,000	PF63 1,050				

KM# 1091 200 EURO
13.50 g., 0.999 Gold 0.4308 oz. AGW **Ruler:** Juan Carlos I **Obv:** Conjoined heads left **Obv. Legend:** JUAN CARLOS I Y SOFIA **Rev:** Ediface of Parliament Building in Madrid **Rev. Legend:** CONSTITUCION ESPANOLA

Date	Mintage	F12	VF20	XF40	MS60	MS63
2003(M)	4,000	PF63 800	PF65 825			

KM# 1062 200 EURO
13.50 g., 0.999 Gold 0.4308 oz. AGW, 30 mm. **Ruler:** Juan Carlos I **Obv:** Seated crowned figures on shield flanked by date and value **Rev:** Crowned busts facing each other on coin design **Edge:** Reeded

Date	Mintage	F12	VF20	XF40	MS60	MS63
2004	1,936	PF63 1,200				

KM# 1098 200 EURO
13.50 g., 0.999 Gold 0.4308 oz. AGW, 30 mm. **Ruler:** Juan Carlos I **Subject:** Wedding of Prince Philip and Letizia Ortiz Rocasolano **Obv:** Conjoined heads left **Obv. Legend:** JUAN CARLOS I Y SOFIA **Rev:** Busts of wedding couple facing 3/4 right at center left, crowned shield at right **Rev. Legend:** FELIPE Y LETIZIA - 22.V.2004

Date	Mintage	F12	VF20	XF40	MS60	MS63
2004(M)	6,303	PF63 1,200				

KM# 1100 200 EURO
13.50 g., 0.999 Gold 0.4308 oz. AGW, 30 mm. **Ruler:** Juan Carlos I **Subject:** Expansion of the European Union **Obv:** Head left **Obv. Legend:** JUAN CARLOS I Y SOFIA **Rev:** Outlined map of the European Union

Date	Mintage	F12	VF20	XF40	MS60	MS63
2004(M)	5,000	PF63 1,000				

KM# 1066 200 EURO
13.50 g., 0.999 Gold 0.4308 oz. AGW, 30 mm. **Ruler:** Juan Carlos I **Subject:** European Peace and Freedom **Obv:** Juan Carlos **Rev:** European map on clasped hands **Edge:** Reeded

Date	Mintage	F12	VF20	XF40	MS60	MS63
2005	2,350	PF63 1,100				

KM# 1111 200 EURO
13.50 g., 0.999 Gold 0.4308 oz. AGW, 30 mm. **Ruler:** Juan Carlos I **Rev:** Crowned shield at left, head of Prince Philip left at right **Rev. Legend:** XXV ANIVERSAIO - PREMIOS PRÍNCIPE DE ASTURIAS

Date	Mintage	F12	VF20	XF40	MS60	MS63
2005(M)	1,690	PF63 1,300				

KM# 1123 200 EURO
13.50 g., 0.999 Gold 0.4308 oz. AGW, 30 mm. **Ruler:** Juan Carlos I **Obv:** Head left **Obv. Legend:** JUAN CARLOS I REY DE ESPAÑA **Rev:** Charles I (V) standing facing 3/4 right in front of portal **Rev. Legend:** CAROLVS IMPERATOR

Date	Mintage	F12	VF20	XF40	MS60	MS63
2006(M)	3,500	PF63 1,050				

KM# 1136 200 EURO
13.50 g., 0.999 Gold 0.4308 oz. AGW, 30 mm. **Ruler:** Juan Carlos I **Subject:** Treaty of Rome, 50th Anniversary **Obv:** Head left **Rev:** Map of Western Europe

Date	Mintage	F12	VF20	XF40	MS60	MS63
2007	3,500	PF63 1,050				

KM# 1139 200 EURO
13.50 g., 0.999 Gold 0.4308 oz. AGW, 30 mm. **Ruler:** Juan Carlos I **Subject:** El Cid, 700th Anniversary **Obv:** Rodrigo Diaz de Vivar bust facing **Rev:** Knight on horseback within rectangle

Date	Mintage	F12	VF20	XF40	MS60	MS63
2007	3,500	PF63 1,050				

KM# 1188 200 EURO
13.50 g., 0.999 Gold 0.4308 oz. AGW, 30 mm. **Ruler:** Juan Carlos I **Subject:** Velazquez

Date	Mintage	F12	VF20	XF40	MS60	MS63
2008	3,500	PF63 1,050				

KM# 1191 200 EURO
13.50 g., 0.999 Gold 0.4308 oz. AGW, 30 mm. **Ruler:** Juan Carlos I **Subject:** Soccer, European Champions

Date	Mintage	F12	VF20	XF40	MS60	MS63
2008	4,000	PF63 1,050				

KM# 1202 200 EURO
13.50 g., 0.999 Gold 0.4308 oz. AGW, 30 mm. **Ruler:** Juan Carlos I **Subject:** Alphonse the Wise

Date	Mintage	F12	VF20	XF40	MS60	MS63
2008	3,500	PF63 1,050				

KM# 1213 200 EURO
13.50 g., 0.999 Gold 0.4308 oz. AGW, 30 mm. **Ruler:** Juan Carlos I **Subject:** Philip II

Date	Mintage	F12	VF20	XF40	MS60	MS63
2009	3,000	PF63 1,050				

KM# 1170 200 EURO
13.50 g., 0.999 Gold 0.4308 oz. AGW, 30 mm. **Ruler:** Juan Carlos I **Subject:** Antoni Gaudi

Date	Mintage	F12	VF20	XF40	MS60	MS63
2010	3,000	PF63 1,050				

KM# 1247 200 EURO
13.50 g., 0.999 Gold 0.4308 oz. AGW, 30 mm. **Ruler:** Juan Carlos I **Subject:** Orellana

Date	Mintage	F12	VF20	XF40	MS60	MS63
2011	3,000	PF63 1,050				

KM# 1288 200 EURO
13.50 g., 0.999 Gold 0.4308 oz. AGW, 30 mm. **Ruler:** Juan Carlos I **Subject:** Balboa and the Pacific Ocean, 400th Anniversary

Date	Mintage	F12	VF20	XF40	MS60	MS63
2013	3,000	PF63 500				

KM# 1112 300 EURO
Bi-Metallic, 40 mm. **Ruler:** Juan Carlos I **Subject:** XVIII World Championship Football Games - Germany 2006 **Obv:** Football player facing kicking ball **Obv. Legend:** ESPAÑA **Rev:** Football player kicking ball into net at foreground **Rev. Legend:** COPA MUNDIAL DE LA FIFA - ALEMANIA **Shape:** 12-sided

Date	Mintage	F12	VF20	XF40	MS60	MS63
2005(M)	8,000	PF63 1,350				

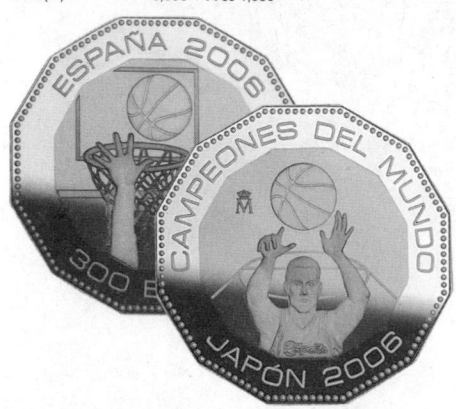

KM# 1121 300 EURO
Bi-Metallic, 40 mm. **Ruler:** Juan Carlos I **Rev:** Basketball player facing tossing ball **Rev. Legend:** CAMPEONES DEL MUNDO - JAPÓN 2006 **Shape:** 12-sided

Date	Mintage	F12	VF20	XF40	MS60	MS63
2006(M)	866	PF63 1,600				

KM# 1086 400 EURO
27.00 g., 0.999 Gold 0.8616 oz. AGW, 38 mm. **Ruler:** Juan Carlos I **Subject:** 150th Anniversary - Birth of Antonio Gaudí **Obv:** Bust of Gaudí at right **Obv. Legend:** Año Internacional **Rev:** Casa Batlló

Date	Mintage	F12	VF20	XF40	MS60	MS63
2002(M)	3,000	PF63 1,700	PF65 1,800			

KM# 1058 400 EURO
27.00 g., 0.999 Gold 0.8616 oz. AGW, 38 mm. **Ruler:** Juan Carlos I **Obv:** Bust facing **Rev:** Dali's painting "Girl at the Window **Edge:** Reeded

Date	Mintage	F12	VF20	XF40	MS60	MS63
2004 (2003)	4,477	PF63 1,700	PF65 1,800			

KM# 1108 400 EURO
27.00 g., 0.999 Gold 0.8616 oz. AGW, 38 mm. **Ruler:** Juan Carlos I **Obv:** Quixote seated reading a large book **Obv. Legend:** ESPAÑA - IV CENTENARIO DE LA PRIMERA EDICIÓN DE "EL QUIJOTE **Rev:** Quixote on horseback 3/4 right followed by his friend on a burro **Rev. Legend:** DON QUIJOTE DE LA MANCHA SANCHO PANZA

Date	Mintage	F12	VF20	XF40	MS60	MS63
2005(M)	2,019	PF63 1,700	PF65 1,800			

KM# 1118 400 EURO
27.00 g., 0.999 Gold 0.8616 oz. AGW, 38 mm. **Ruler:** Juan Carlos I **Subject:** 500th Anniversary - Death of Columbus **Obv:** Columbus **Rev:** Audience with Ferdinand and Isabella

Date	Mintage	F12	VF20	XF40	MS60	MS63
2006(M)	1,850	PF63 1,700	PF65 1,800			

KM# 1128 400 EURO
27.00 g., 0.999 Gold 0.8616 oz. AGW, 38 mm. **Ruler:** Juan Carlos I **Rev:** Large ring of stars around globe **Rev. Legend:** V ANIVERSARIO DEL EURO

Date	Mintage	F12	VF20	XF40	MS60	MS63
2007	3,000	PF63 1,700	PF65 1,800			

KM# 1197 400 EURO
27.00 g., 0.999 Gold 0.8616 oz. AGW, 38 mm. **Ruler:** Juan Carlos I **Subject:** War of Independence, 200th Anniversary

Date	Mintage	F12	VF20	XF40	MS60	MS63
2008	3,500	PF63 1,700	PF65 1,800			

KM# 1207 400 EURO
27.00 g., 0.999 Gold 0.8616 oz. AGW, 38 mm. **Ruler:** Juan Carlos I **Subject:** Dali

Date	Mintage	F12	VF20	XF40	MS60	MS63
2009	3,000	PF63 1,700	PF65 1,800			

KM# 1182 400 EURO
27.00 g., 0.999 Gold 0.8616 oz. AGW, 38 mm. **Ruler:** Juan Carlos I **Subject:** Francisco de Goya - Volaverunt

Date	Mintage	F12	VF20	XF40	MS60	MS63
2010	3,000	PF63 1,700	PF65 1,800			

KM# 1221 400 EURO
27.00 g., 0.999 Gold 0.8616 oz. AGW, 38 mm. **Ruler:** Juan Carlos I **Subject:** El Greco

Date	Mintage	F12	VF20	XF40	MS60	MS63
2011	3,000	PF63 1,700	PF65 1,800			

KM# 1304 400 EURO
27.00 g., 0.999 Gold 0.8616 oz. AGW, 38 mm. **Ruler:** Juan Carlos I **Subject:** Albrecht Durer paintings

Date	Mintage	F12	VF20	XF40	MS60	MS63
2013	3,000	PF63 1,100				

MINT SETS

KM#	Date	Mintage	Identification	Issue Price	Mkt Val
MS27	2000-2001 (8)	49,426	KM#832-833, 924, 991-992 (both dated 2000), 1012-1013, 1016	15.50	35.00
MS28	2002 (8)	99,301	KM#1040-1047	—	15.00
MS29	2003 (8)	149	KM#1040-1047	—	15.00
MS30	2004 (8)	43,000	KM#1040-1047	—	55.00
MS31	2005 (8)	49,923	KM#1040-1047	—	35.00
MS32	2006 (8)	49,996	KM#1040-1047	—	12.50
MS33	2007 (8)	—	KM#1040-1042, 1070-1074	—	30.00

PROOF SETS

KM#	Date	Mintage	Identification	Issue Price	Mkt Val
PS34	2002 (9)	23,000	KM#1040-1047, 1049	125	150
PS35	2003 (9)	8,904	KM#1040-1047, 1051	—	320
PS36	2005 (9)	3,000	KM#1040-1047, 1063	—	175
PS38	2007 (9)	1,800	KM#1040-1074, 1130	—	150
PS39	2008 (8)	2,000	KM#1040-1042, 1070-1074	—	150
PS40	2009 (9)	5,000	KM#1040-1042, 1070-1074, 1142.1	—	150
PS41	2010 (9)	5,000	KM#1144-1150, 1152	—	150
PS42	2011 (9)	5,000	KM#1144-1151, 1184	—	150

SRI LANKA

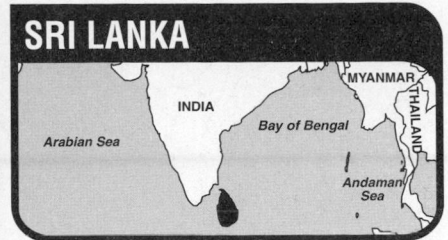

The Democratic Socialist Republic of Sri Lanka (formerly Ceylon) situated in the Indian Ocean 18 miles (29 km.) southeast of India, has an area of 25,332 sq. mi. (65,610 sq. km.) and a population of *16.9 million. Capital: Colombo. The economy is chiefly agricultural. Tea, coconut products and rubber are exported.

Sri Lanka is a member of the Commonwealth of Nations. The president is Chief of State. The prime minister is Head of Government. The present leaders of the country have reverted the country name back to Sri Lanka.

DEMOCRATIC SOCIALIST REPUBLIC

DECIMAL COINAGE
100 Cents = 1 Rupee

KM# 141a 25 CENTS
Nickel Clad Steel **Obv:** National arms **Rev:** Denomination **Edge:** Reeded

Date	Mintage	F12	VF20	XF40	MS60	MS63
2001	10,000,000	—	—	0.10	0.25	0.45
2002	10,000,000	—	—	0.10	0.25	0.45
2004	—	—	—	0.10	0.25	0.45

KM# 141.2b 25 CENTS
1.17 g., Copper Plated Steel, 16 mm. **Obv:** National arms **Rev:** Denomination

Date	Mintage	F12	VF20	XF40	MS60	MS63
2005	10,000,000	—	—	0.10	0.25	0.45
2006	5,000,000	—	—	5.00	7.00	10.00

KM# 135.2a 50 CENTS
Nickel Plated Steel, 21.5 mm. **Obv:** National arms **Rev:** Value above designs within wreath **Edge:** Reeded

Date	Mintage	F12	VF20	XF40	MS60	MS63
2001	30,000,000	—	0.10	0.25	0.65	1.00
2002	10,000,000	—	0.10	0.25	0.65	1.00
2004	1,000,000	—	0.10	0.25	0.65	1.00

KM# 135.2b 50 CENTS
2.49 g., Copper Plated Steel, 17.92 mm. **Obv:** National arms **Rev:** Value above designs within wreath **Edge:** Reeded

Date	Mintage	F12	VF20	XF40	MS60	MS63
2005	20,000,000	—	—	0.25	0.60	1.00
2006	10,000,000	—	—	0.25	0.60	1.00
2009	5,000,000	—	—	2.00	3.00	5.00

KM# 136a RUPEE
Nickel Clad Steel **Obv:** National arms **Rev:** Inscription below designs within wreath **Edge:** Reeded

Date	Mintage	F12	VF20	XF40	MS60	MS63
2002	50,000,000	—	—	—	1.00	1.50
2004	52,000,000	—	—	—	1.00	1.50

KM# 166 RUPEE
7.13 g., Copper-Nickel, 25.4 mm. **Subject:** Air Force's 50th Anniversary **Obv:** Badge of the Sri Lanka Air Force **Rev:** Two jets above propeller plane within circle **Edge:** Reeded

Date	Mintage				
2001	2,000	PF60 120			

KM# 136.3 RUPEE
3.62 g., Brass Plated Steel, 20 mm. **Obv:** National emblem **Rev:** Inscription below designs within wreath **Edge:** Segmented reeding

Date	Mintage	F12	VF20	XF40	MS60	MS63
2005	65,000,000	—	—	—	0.75	1.00
2006	50,000,000	—	—	—	0.75	1.00
2008	40,000,000	—	—	—	0.75	1.00
2009	—	—	—	—	0.75	1.00
2011	—	—	—	—	0.75	1.00

KM# 147 2 RUPEES
8.25 g., Copper-Nickel, 28.5 mm. **Obv:** National arms **Rev:** Value

Date	Mintage	F12	VF20	XF40	MS60	MS63
2001	10,000,000	—	0.30	0.60	1.35	1.75
2002	40,000,000	—	0.30	0.60	1.35	1.75
2004	—	—	0.30	0.60	1.35	1.75

KM# 167 2 RUPEES
8.25 g., Copper-Nickel, 28.5 mm. **Subject:** Colombo Plan's 50th Anniversary **Obv:** Value within inscription above date **Rev:** Gear wheel **Edge:** Reeded

Date	Mintage	F12	VF20	XF40	MS60	MS63
2001	10,000,000	—	—	—	3.00	4.00

KM# 147a 2 RUPEES
7.08 g., Nickel Clad Steel, 28.5 mm. **Obv:** National arms **Rev:** Value **Edge:** Reeded

Date	Mintage	F12	VF20	XF40	MS60	MS63
2005	50,000,000	—	—	0.45	1.10	1.50
2006	80,000,000	—	—	0.45	1.10	1.50
2007	18,000,000	—	—	0.45	1.10	1.50
2008	—	—	—	0.45	1.10	1.50
2009	—	—	—	0.45	1.10	1.50
2011	—	—	—	0.45	1.10	1.50
2012	—	—	—	0.45	1.10	1.50

KM# 178 2 RUPEES
7.00 g., Nickel Plated Steel, 28.4 mm. **Subject:** Employees Provident Fund, 50th Anniversary **Obv:** Large 2 **Rev:** Open hands with image of tea pluckers, garment workers and office worker

Date	Mintage	F12	VF20	XF40	MS60	MS63
2008	2,000,000	—	—	—	2.50	3.50

KM# 184 2 RUPEES
7.00 g., Nickel Plated Steel, 28.5 mm. **Obv:** Large value **Rev:** Large 60, Air Force emblem and historic aircraft circling

Date	Mintage	F12	VF20	XF40	MS60	MS63
2011	3,000,000	—	—	—	3.00	4.00
2011 Special Unc	500	—	—	—	—	15.00

KM# 189 2 RUPEES
7.38 g., Nickel Plated Steel, 28.5 mm. **Subject:** Centenary of Scouting **Rev:** Scouting emblem

Date	Mintage	F12	VF20	XF40	MS60	MS63
2012	—	—	—	—	3.00	5.00

KM# 148.2 5 RUPEES
9.50 g., Nickel-Brass, 23.5 mm. **Obv:** National arms **Rev:** Value **Edge Lettering:** C.B.S.L.

Date	Mintage	F12	VF20	XF40	MS60	MS63
2002	30,000,000	—	0.35	0.65	2.00	2.75
2004	—	—	0.35	0.65	2.00	2.75

KM# 168 5 RUPEES
9.52 g., Aluminum-Bronze, 23.4 mm. **Subject:** 250th Annniversary of the "Upasampada" Rite **Obv:** Value **Rev:** 1/2-length figure facing divides dates

Date	Mintage	F12	VF20	XF40	MS60	MS63
2003	4,000,000	—	—	—	3.00	4.50

KM# 169 5 RUPEES
9.52 g., Aluminum-Bronze, 23.4 mm. **Subject:** 250th Anniversary - Upasampada **Obv:** Value **Rev:** Bust facing standing behind shield **Edge:** Reeded and lettered

Date	Mintage	F12	VF20	XF40	MS60	MS63
2003	4,000,000	—	—	—	3.00	4.50

KM# 148.2a 5 RUPEES
7.67 g., Brass Plated Steel, 23.49 mm. **Obv:** National arms **Rev:** Value **Edge:** Reeded and Lettered **Edge Lettering:** CBSL repeated in various languages

Date	Mintage	F12	VF20	XF40	MS60	MS63
2005	30,000,000	—	—	0.75	1.85	2.50
2006	75,000,000	—	—	0.75	1.85	2.50
2008	20,000,000	—	—	0.75	1.85	2.50
2009	—	—	—	0.75	1.85	2.50
2011	—	—	—	0.75	1.85	2.50

KM# 170 5 RUPEES
7.65 g., Brass Plated Steel, 23.5 mm. **Subject:** 2550th Anniversary of Buddha **Obv:** Value **Rev:** Buddha Jayanthi", wheel above mountain **Edge:** Reeded and lettered

Date	Mintage	F12	VF20	XF40	MS60	MS63
2006	20,000,000	—	—	—	3.00	4.00

KM# 173 5 RUPEES
7.65 g., Brass Plated Steel, 23.5 mm. **Subject:** Cricket World Cup

Date	Mintage	F12	VF20	XF40	MS60	MS63
2007	7,860,000	—	—	—	3.00	4.00

KM# 181 10 RUPEES
8.36 g., Nickel Plated Steel, 26.4 mm. **Obv:** Sri Lanka ensign **Rev:** Large value **Shape:** 11-sided

Date	Mintage	F12	VF20	XF40	MS60	MS63
2009	—	—	—	—	1.50	2.50
2010	—	—	—	—	1.50	2.50
2011	—	—	—	—	1.50	2.50

KM# 186 10 RUPEES
8.36 g., Nickel Plated Steel, 26.4 mm. **Subject:** Sambuddhatva Jayanti 2600 **Obv:** Large value **Rev:** 24 prong DharmaChakra (wheel of dochrine) **Shape:** 11-sided

Date	Mintage	F12	VF20	XF40	MS60	MS63
2011	1,500,000	—	—	—	—	2.50

KM# 180 200 RUPEES
11.90 g., 0.925 Silver 0.3516 oz. ASW, 28.4 mm. **Subject:** Customs Service, 200th Anniversary **Obv:** Proposed new Customs Building **Rev:** Customs Logo

Date	Mintage	F12	VF20	XF40	MS60	MS63
2009	3,000			PF60 45.00	PF63 50.00	PF65 55.00

KM# 174 1000 RUPEES
12.00 g., Nickel Plated Steel, 32 mm. **Subject:** Cricket World Cup

Date	Mintage	F12	VF20	XF40	MS60	MS63
2007	10,000	—	—	—	10.00	12.00

KM# 179 1000 RUPEES
Nickel Plated Steel, 28.5 mm. **Subject:** Employees Provident Fund, 50th Anniversary **Obv:** Large 1000 **Rev:** Open hands with image of tea pluckers, garment workers and office worker

Date	Mintage	F12	VF20	XF40	MS60	MS63
2008	1,200			PF60 110	PF63 130	PF65 150

KM# 182 1000 RUPEES
Copper-Nickel, 27 mm. **Subject:** Sri Lanka Army - 60th Anniversay **Obv:** Army badge above value **Rev:** Soldier standing with flag, map of Sri Lanka in background, two smaller solders at right

Date	Mintage	F12	VF20	XF40	MS60	MS63
2009	200,000	—	—	—	30.00	35.00

KM# 182a 1000 RUPEES
0.925 Silver, 27 mm. **Subject:** Sri Lanka Army - 60th Anniversary **Obv:** Army badge above value **Rev:** Soldier standing with flag, map of Sri Lanka in background, two smaller solders at right

Date	Mintage	F12	VF20	XF40	MS60	MS63
2009	10,000	PF60 40.00	PF63 45.00	PF65 50.00		

KM# 185 1000 RUPEES
28.28 g., 0.925 Silver 0.8356 oz. ASW, 38.61 mm. **Subject:** Sambuddhatva Jayanti 2600 **Obv:** 24 prong Dharma Chakra (wheel of doctrine) **Rev:** Sri Maha Bo-Sapling bowl on a large pedistal

Date	Mintage	F12	VF20	XF40	MS60	MS63
2011	2,000	PF60 60.00	PF63 65.00	PF65 70.00		

KM# 188 1000 RUPEES
28.21 g., Silver, 38.61 mm. **Subject:** 50th Anniversary of the People's Bank **Obv:** Crest at center **Rev:** Gear logo, selective gilt

Date	Mintage	F12	VF20	XF40	MS60	MS63
2011	Est. 2300	PF60 50.00	PF63 55.00	PF65 60.00		

KM# 190 1000 RUPEES
20.00 g., 0.925 Silver 0.591 oz. ASW, 35 mm. **Subject:** Sri Lanka & Japan, 60th Years of Diplomatic Relations **Obv:** National flags above large 60 **Rev:** Color printed images of Hydro dam

Date	Mintage	F12	VF20	XF40	MS60	MS63
2012	20,000	PF63 140	PF65 150			

KM# 171 1500 RUPEES
28.28 g., 0.925 Silver 0.8356 oz. ASW, 38.61 mm. **Subject:** 2550 Anniversary of Buddha

Date	Mintage	F12	VF20	XF40	MS60	MS63
2006	20,000	PF60 60.00	PF63 75.00	PF65 85.00		

KM# 172 2000 RUPEE
28.28 g., 0.925 Silver 0.8356 oz. ASW **Subject:** 2550 Anniversary of Buddha **Shape:** 38.61

Date	Mintage	F12	VF20	XF40	MS60	MS63
2006	10,000	PF60 100	PF63 115	PF65 125		

KM# 187 2000 RUPEE
28.28 g., 0.925 Silver 0.8356 oz. ASW, 38.61 mm. **Subject:** 125th Anniversary of Ananda College **Obv:** Shield **Rev:** Three portraits below building tower (Ananda Viharaya)

Date	Mintage	F12	VF20	XF40	MS60	MS63
2011	Est. 1500	PF60 45.00		PF63 50.00		PF65 55.00

KM# 183 5000 RUPEES
28.28 g., 0.925 Silver 0.8356 oz. ASW, 38.61 mm. **Subject:** Central Bank of Sri Lanka, 60th Anniversary **Obv:** Multicolor Central Bank crest at center **Rev:** Banyan tree **Edge:** Reeded

Date	Mintage	F12	VF20	XF40	MS60	MS63
2010	5,000	PF60 75.00		PF63 85.00		PF65 95.00

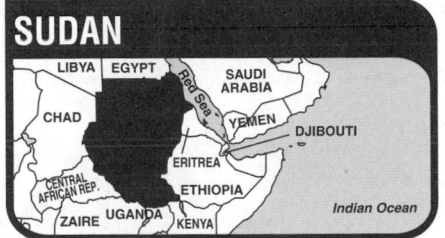

SUDAN

The Republic of the Sudan, located in northeast Africa on the Red Sea between Egypt and Ethiopia, has an area of 967,500 sq. mi. (2,505,810 sq. km.) and a population of *24.5 million. Capital: Khartoum. Agriculture and livestock raising are the chief occupations. Cotton, gum arabic and peanuts are exported.

REPUBLIC
REFORM COINAGE
100 Qurush (Piastres) = 1 Dinar
10 Pounds = 1 Dinar

KM# 119 5 DINARS
3.35 g., Brass, 19 mm. **Obv:** Value **Rev:** Central Bank building

Date	Mintage	F12	VF20	XF40	MS60	MS63
AH1424-2003	—	—	0.75	1.50	3.00	5.00

KM# 120.1 10 DINARS
4.68 g., Brass, 22 mm. **Rev:** Central Bank building, "a" above "n" at the left end of the Arabic inscription, 64 border beads

Date	Mintage	F12	VF20	XF40	MS60	MS63
AH1424-2003	—	—	1.00	2.00	3.50	6.00

KM# 120.2 10 DINARS
4.56 g., Brass, 22 mm. **Obv:** Value **Rev:** Larger Central Bank building, "a" to right of "n" at the left end of the Arabic inscription, 72 border beads

Date	Mintage	F12	VF20	XF40	MS60	MS63
AH1424-2003	—	—	1.00	2.00	3.50	6.00

KM# 121 50 DINARS
Copper-Nickel, 24 mm. **Rev:** Central Bank building

Date	Mintage	F12	VF20	XF40	MS60	MS63
AH1423-2002	—	—	2.00	3.50	6.00	9.00

REFORM COINAGE
2005
100 Piastres = 1 Pound

KM# 126 PIASTRE (Ghirsh)
2.25 g., Aluminum-Bronze, 16 mm. **Obv:** Clay pot **Obv. Legend:** CENTRAL BANK OF SUDAN **Rev:** Value

Date	Mintage	F12	VF20	XF40	MS60	MS63
2006	—	—	—	0.90	2.25	3.00

KM# 125 5 PIASTRES
2.84 g., Brass, 18 mm. **Obv:** National arms **Rev:** Large value **Edge:** Reeded

Date	Mintage	F12	VF20	XF40	MS60	MS63
2006	—	—	—	1.20	3.00	4.00

KM# 122 10 PIASTRES
3.70 g., Nickel, 20 mm. **Obv:** Pyramid **Obv. Legend:** CENTRAL BANK OF SUDAN **Rev:** Large value **Edge:** Reeded

Date	Mintage	F12	VF20	XF40	MS60	MS63
2006	—	—	—	1.25	3.00	4.00

KM# 124 20 PIASTRES
5.00 g., Bi-Metallic, 22 mm. **Obv:** Ankole Bull in right profile **Obv. Legend:** CENTRAL BANK OF SUDAN **Rev:** large value **Edge:** Reeded

Date	Mintage	F12	VF20	XF40	MS60	MS63
2006	—	—	—	1.20	3.00	4.00

KM# 123 50 PIASTRES
5.82 g., Bi-Metallic, 24 mm. **Obv:** Dove in flight **Obv. Legend:** CENTRAL BANK OF SUDAN **Rev:** Value **Edge:** Reeded

Date	Mintage	F12	VF20	XF40	MS60	MS63
2006	—	—	—	0.90	2.25	3.00

KM# 127 POUND
Nickel Plated Steel, 27 mm. **Obv:** Value **Rev:** Central Bank building

Date	Mintage	F12	VF20	XF40	MS60	MS63
2011	—	—	—	2.50	5.00	7.00

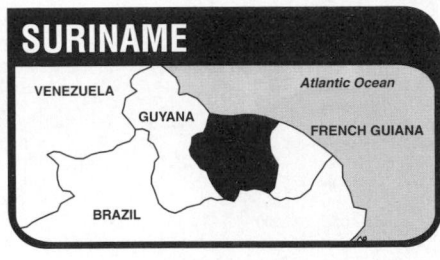

SURINAME

The Republic of Suriname also known as Dutch Guiana, located on the north central coast of South America between Guyana and French Guiana has an area of 63,037 sq. mi. (163,270 sq. km.) and a population of *433,000. Capital: Paramaribo. The country is rich in minerals and forests, and self-sufficient in rice, the staple food crop. The mining, processing and exporting of bauxite is the principal economic activity.

Lieutenants of Amerigo Vespucci sighted the Guiana coast in 1499. Spanish explorers of the 16th century, disappointed at finding no gold, departed leaving the area to be settled by the British in 1652. The colony prospered and the Netherlands acquired it in 1667 in exchange for the Dutch rights in Nieuw Nederland (state of New York). During the European wars of the 18th and 19th centuries, which were fought in part in the new world, Suriname was occupied by the British from 1781-1784 and 1796-1814. Suriname became an autonomous part of the Kingdom of the Netherlands on Dec. 15, 1954. Full independence was achieved on Nov. 25, 1975. In 1980, a coup installed a military government, which has since been dissolved.

MINT MARKS
(u) - Utrecht (privy marks only)

MONETARY SYSTEM
After January, 2004
1 Dollar = 100 Cents

REPUBLIC
MODERN COINAGE

KM# 11b CENT
2.50 g., Copper Plated Steel, 18 mm. **Obv:** Arms with supporters within wreath **Rev:** Value divides date within circle **Edge:** Plain

Date	Mintage	F12	VF20	XF40	MS60	MS63
2004(u) In sets only	4,000	—	—	—	—	6.00
2005(u) In sets only	1,500	—	—	—	—	7.00
2006(u) In sets only	1,500	—	—	—	—	7.00
2007(u) In sets only	1,000	—	—	—	—	7.00
2008(u) In sets only	1,000	—	—	—	—	7.00
2009(u) In sets only	1,000	—	—	—	—	7.00
2010(u) In sets only	1,000	—	—	—	—	7.00
2011(u) In sets only	1,000	—	—	—	—	7.00

KM# 12.1b 5 CENTS
3.00 g., Copper Plated Steel, 18 mm. **Obv:** Arms with supporters within circle **Rev:** Value divides date within circle **Edge:** Plain **Shape:** Square

Date	Mintage	F12	VF20	XF40	MS60	MS63
2004(u) In sets only	4,000	—	—	—	—	6.00
2005(u) In sets only	1,500	—	—	—	—	7.00
2006(u) In sets only	1,500	—	—	—	—	7.00
2007(u) In sets only	1,000	—	—	—	—	7.00
2008(u) In sets only	1,000	—	—	—	—	7.00
2009(u) In sets only	1,000	—	—	—	—	7.00
2010(u) In sets only	1,000	—	—	—	—	7.00
2011(u) In sets only	1,000	—	—	—	—	7.00

KM# 13a 10 CENTS
2.00 g., Nickel Plated Steel, 16 mm. **Obv:** Arms with supporters within wreath **Rev:** Value and date within circle **Edge:** Reeded

Date	Mintage	F12	VF20	XF40	MS60	MS63
2004(u) In sets only	4,000	—	—	—	—	4.50
2005(u) In sets only	1,500	—	—	—	—	4.50
2006(u) In sets only	1,500	—	—	—	—	4.50
2007(u) In sets only	1,000	—	—	—	—	4.50
2008(u) In sets only	1,000	—	—	—	—	4.50
2009	—	—	—	0.50	1.00	2.00
2009(u) In sets only	1,000	—	—	—	—	4.50
2010(u) In sets only	1,000	—	—	—	—	4.50
2011(u) In sets only	1,000	—	—	—	—	4.50
2012	—	—	—	0.50	1.00	2.00

KM# 14a 25 CENTS
3.50 g., Nickel Plated Steel, 20 mm. **Obv:** Arms with supporters within wreath **Rev:** Value and date within circle **Edge:** Reeded

Date	Mintage	F12	VF20	XF40	MS60	MS63
2004(u) In sets only	4,000	—	—	—	—	7.00
2005(u) In sets only	1,500	—	—	—	—	8.00
2006(u) In sets only	1,500	—	—	—	—	8.00
2007(u) In sets only	1,000	—	—	—	—	8.00
2008(u) In sets only	1,000	—	—	—	—	8.00
2009(u) In sets only	1,000	—	—	—	—	8.00
2010(u) In sets only	1,000	—	—	—	—	8.00
2011(u) In sets only	1,000	—	—	—	—	8.00

KM# 23 100 CENTS
5.65 g., Copper-Nickel, 23 mm. **Obv:** Arms with supporters within wreath **Rev:** Value and date within circle **Edge:** Reeded

Date	Mintage	F12	VF20	XF40	MS60	MS63
2004(u) In sets only	4,000	—	—	—	—	7.00
2005(u) In sets only	1,250	—	—	—	—	8.00
2006(u) In sets only	1,500	—	—	—	—	8.00
2007(u) In sets only	1,000	—	—	—	—	8.00
2008(u) In sets only	1,000	—	—	—	—	8.00
2009(u) In sets only	1,000	—	—	—	—	8.00
2010(u) In sets only	1,000	—	—	—	—	8.00
2011(u) In sets only	1,000	—	—	—	—	8.00
2012	—	—	—	—	1.75	3.00

KM# 24 250 CENTS
9.57 g., Copper-Nickel, 28 mm. **Obv:** Arms with supporters within wreath **Rev:** Value and date within circle

Date	Mintage	F12	VF20	XF40	MS60	MS63
2004(u) In sets only	4,000	—	—	—	—	8.00
2005(u) In sets only	1,250	—	—	—	—	10.00
2006(u) In sets only	1,500	—	—	—	—	10.00
2007(u) In sets only	1,000	—	—	—	—	10.00
2008(u) In sets only	1,000	—	—	—	—	10.00
2009(u) In sets only	1,000	—	—	—	—	10.00
2010(u) In sets only	1,000	—	—	—	—	10.00
2011(u) In sets only	1,000	—	—	—	—	10.00

KM# 65 $20
1.24 g., 0.999 Gold 0.0397 oz. AGW, 13.92 mm. **Subject:** Antony Nesty's 1988 Gold Medal win at Seoul Olympics, 20th Anniversary **Obv:** Arms with supporters **Rev:** Nesty swimming

Date	Mintage	F12	VF20	XF40	MS60	MS63
2008	5,000	PF63 75.00		PF65 85.00		

KM# 64 400 DOLLARS
7.98 g., 0.916 Gold 0.2335 oz. AGW, 22 mm. **Subject:** 30 Years of Independence **Obv:** Arms with supporters **Rev:** Man kissing flag **Edge:** Reeded

Date	Mintage	F12	VF20	XF40	MS60	MS63
2005	1,000	PF63 475		PF65 500		

KM# 66 500 DOLLARS
7.98 g., 0.916 Gold 0.2335 oz. AGW, 22 mm. **Subject:** Central Bank, 50th Anniversary **Obv:** Arms with supporters **Rev:** 50 jaar Central Bank van Suriname 1957-2007

Date	Mintage	F12	VF20	XF40	MS60	MS63
2007	1,000	PF63 475		PF65 500		

MINT SETS

KM#	Date	Mintage	Identification	Issue Price	Mkt Val
MS1	2004 (6)	4,000	KM#11b, 12.1b, 13a, 14a, 23, 24	25.00	40.00
MS2	2005 (6)	1,500	KM#11b, 12.1b, 13a-14a, 23-24	25.00	45.00
MS3	2006 (6)	1,500	KM#11b, 12.1b, 13a-14a, 23-24	25.00	45.00
MS4	2007 (6)	1,000	KM#11b, 12.1b, 13a-14a, 23-24	27.00	45.00
MS5	2008 (6)	1,000	KM#11b, 12.1b, 13a-14a, 23-24	27.00	45.00
MS6	2009 (6)	1,000	KM#11b, 12.1b, 13a, 14a, 23, 24	27.00	40.00
MS7	2010 (6)	1,000	KM#11b, 12.1b, 13a, 14a, 23, 24	27.00	45.00
MS8	2011 (6)	1,000	KM#11b, 12.1b, 13a, 14a, 23, 24	—	45.00

SWAZILAND

The Kingdom of Swaziland, located in southeastern Africa, has an area of 6,704 sq. mi. (17,360 sq. km.) and a population of *756,000. Capital: Mbabane (administrative); Lobamba (legislative). The diversified economy includes mining, agriculture, and light industry. Asbestos, iron ore, wood pulp, and sugar are exported.

The Kingdom is a member of the Commonwealth of Nations. King Mswati III is Head of State. The prime minister is Head of Government.

RULER
King Msawati III, 1986-

MONETARY SYSTEM
100 Cents = 1 Luhlanga
25 Luhlanga = 1 Lilangeni
(plural - Emalangeni)

KINGDOM
DECIMAL COINAGE
100 Cents = 1 Lilangeni (plural emelangeni)

KM# 48 5 CENTS
2.10 g., Copper-Nickel, 18.5 mm. **Ruler:** King Msawati III **Obv:** Bust 3/4 right **Rev:** Arum lily and value **Edge:** Plain **Shape:** Scalloped

Date	Mintage	F12	VF20	XF40	MS60	MS63
2001	—	—	—	—	0.50	0.75
2002	—	—	—	—	0.50	0.75
2003	—	—	—	—	0.50	0.75
2005	—	—	—	—	0.50	0.75
2006	—	—	—	—	0.50	0.75
2007	—	—	—	—	0.50	0.75
2008	—	—	—	—	0.50	0.75
2009	—	—	—	—	0.50	0.75
2010	—	—	—	—	0.50	0.75

KM# 56 5 CENTS
Copper Plated Steel **Ruler:** King Msawati III

Date	Mintage	F12	VF20	XF40	MS60	MS63
2011	—	—	—	—	0.50	0.75

KM# 49 10 CENTS
3.60 g., Copper-Nickel, 22 mm. **Ruler:** King Msawati III **Obv:** Bust 3/4 right **Rev:** Sugar cane and value **Edge:** Plain **Shape:** Scalloped

Date	Mintage	F12	VF20	XF40	MS60	MS63
2001	—	—	—	0.30	0.75	1.00
2002	—	—	—	0.30	0.75	1.00
2003	—	—	—	0.30	0.75	1.00
2005	—	—	—	0.30	0.75	1.00
2006	—	—	—	0.30	0.75	1.00
2007	—	—	—	0.30	0.75	1.00

KM# 57 10 CENTS
Copper Plated Steel **Ruler:** King Msawati III

Date	Mintage	F12	VF20	XF40	MS60	MS63
2011	—	—	—	0.30	0.75	1.00

KM# 50.2 20 CENTS
5.52 g., Copper-Nickel, 25.2 mm. **Ruler:** King Msawati III **Obv:**

Small bust 3/4 right **Rev:** Elephant head, value **Edge:** Plain **Shape:** Scalloped

Date	Mintage	F12	VF20	XF40	MS60	MS63
2001	—	—	—	0.35	0.90	2.25
2002	—	—	—	0.35	0.90	2.25
2003	—	—	—	0.35	0.90	2.25
2005	—	—	—	0.35	0.90	2.25

KM# 58 20 CENTS
Copper-Nickel **Ruler:** King Msawati III

Date	Mintage	F12	VF20	XF40	MS60	MS63
2011	—	—	—	0.35	0.90	2.25

KM# 52 50 CENTS
8.90 g., Copper-Nickel, 29.45 mm. **Ruler:** King Msawati III **Obv:** Head 1/4 right **Rev:** Arms with supporters

Date	Mintage	F12	VF20	XF40	MS60	MS63
2001	—	—	—	—	3.75	4.50
2003	—	—	—	—	3.75	4.50
2005	—	—	—	—	3.75	4.50
2007	—	—	—	—	3.75	4.50

KM# 59 50 CENTS
Copper-Nickel **Ruler:** King Msawati III

Date	Mintage	F12	VF20	XF40	MS60	MS63
2011	—	—	—	—	3.75	4.50

KM# 45 LILANGENI
9.50 g., Brass, 22.5 mm. **Ruler:** King Msawati III **Obv:** Head 1/4 right **Rev:** Bust facing

Date	Mintage	F12	VF20	XF40	MS60	MS63
2002	—	—	—	1.50	2.75	3.50
2003	—	—	—	1.50	2.75	3.50
2005	—	—	—	1.50	2.75	3.50
2008	—	—	—	1.50	2.75	3.50

KM# 60 LILANGENI
Brass **Ruler:** King Msawati III

Date	Mintage	F12	VF20	XF40	MS60	MS63
2011	—	—	—	—	3.75	4.50

KM# 46 2 EMALANGENI
5.00 g., Brass **Ruler:** King Msawati III **Obv:** Head 1/4 right **Rev:** Lilies and value

Date	Mintage	F12	VF20	XF40	MS60	MS63
2003 sm. bust	—	—	—	—	3.75	4.25
2005	—	—	—	—	3.75	4.25
2008	—	—	—	—	3.75	4.25
2009	—	—	—	—	3.75	4.25

KM# 47 5 EMALANGENI
7.60 g., Brass **Ruler:** King Msawati III **Obv:** Head 1/4 right **Rev:** Arms with supporters above value that divides date

Date	Mintage	F12	VF20	XF40	MS60	MS63
2003 sm. bust	—	—	—	—	6.00	7.00

KM# 54 5 EMALANGENI
7.60 g., Brass, 27 mm. **Ruler:** King Msawati III **Subject:** 40th Anniversary of Independence **Obv:** Head 1/4 right **Rev:** National arms at center

Date	Mintage	F12	VF20	XF40	MS60	MS63
2008	—	—	—	—	5.00	7.00

KM# 54a 5 EMALANGENI
Gold AGW **Ruler:** King Msawati III **Subject:** 40th Anniversary of Independence **Obv:** Head 1/4 right **Rev:** National arms at center

Date	Mintage	F12	VF20	XF40	MS60	MS63
2008 Proof, rare	100	—	—	—	—	—

KM# 55 5 EMALANGENI
7.60 g., Brass, 27 mm. **Ruler:** King Msawati III **Subject:** 40th Birthday of King **Obv:** Head 1/4 right **Rev:** National arms at center

Date	Mintage	F12	VF20	XF40	MS60	MS63
2008	—	—	—	—	5.00	7.00

KM# 55a 5 EMALANGENI
Gold AGW **Ruler:** King Msawati III **Subject:** 40th Anniversary of Independence **Obv:** Head 1/4 right **Rev:** National arms at center

Date	Mintage	F12	VF20	XF40	MS60	MS63
2008 Proof, rare	100	—	—	—	—	—

SWEDEN

The Kingdom of Sweden, a limited constitutional monarchy located in northern Europe between Norway and Finland, has an area of 173,732 sq. mi. (449,960 sq. km.) and a population of *8.5 million. Capital: Stockholm. Mining, lumbering and a specialized machine industry dominate the economy. Machinery, paper, iron and steel, motor vehicles and wood pulp are exported.

RULER
Carl XVI Gustaf, 1973-

MINT OFFICIALS' INITIALS

Letter	Date	Name
B	1992-2005	Stefan Ingves
D	1986-2005	Bengt Dennis
SI	2006-	Stefan Ingves

MONETARY SYSTEM
100 Ore = 1 Krona

KINGDOM
REFORM COINAGE

KM# 878 50 ÖRE
3.70 g., Bronze, 18.7 mm. **Ruler:** Carl XVI Gustaf **Obv:** Value **Rev:** Three crowns and date **Edge:** Reeded

Date	Mintage	F12	VF20	XF40	MS60	MS63
2001 B	30,120,532	—	—	—	0.15	0.25
2002 B	32,019,578	—	—	—	0.15	0.25
2003 H	32,074,768	—	—	—	0.15	0.25
2004 H	25,958,649	—	—	—	0.15	0.25
2005 H	25,024,203	—	—	—	0.15	0.25
2006 SI	30,000,000	—	—	—	0.15	0.25
2007 SI	50,000,000	—	—	—	0.15	0.25
2008 SI	35,000,000	—	—	—	0.15	0.25
2009 SI	20,000,000	—	—	—	0.15	0.25

KM# 894 KRONA
7.00 g., Copper-Nickel, 25 mm. **Ruler:** Carl XVI Gustaf **Obv:** Head left **Rev:** Crown and value **Edge:** Reeded

Date	Mintage	F12	VF20	XF40	MS60	MS63
2001 B	23,905,454	—	—	—	0.25	0.35
2002 B	62,436,783	—	—	—	0.25	0.35
2003 H	54,178,242	—	—	—	0.25	0.35
2004 H	42,060,252	—	—	—	0.25	0.35
2005 H	21,469,169	—	—	—	0.25	0.35
2007 SI	30,751,250	—	—	—	0.25	0.35
2008	60,510,000	—	—	—	0.25	0.35
2012	20,000,000	—	—	—	0.25	0.35

KM# 916 KRONA
7.00 g., Copper-Nickel, 25 mm. **Ruler:** Carl XVI Gustaf **Subject:** Separation from Finland, 200 Anniversary **Obv:** Head left **Rev:** Horizontal sea waves **Edge:** Reeded

Date	Mintage	F12	VF20	XF40	MS60	MS63
2009	40,020,000	—	—	—	0.25	0.50

KM# 927 KRONA
7.00 g., Copper-Nickel, 25 mm. **Ruler:** Carl XVI Gustaf **Subject:** 40th Anniversary of reign

Date	Mintage	F12	VF20	XF40	MS60	MS63
2013	—	—	—	—	0.65	1.00

KM# 853a 5 KRONOR
9.60 g., Copper-Nickel Clad Nickel, 28.5 mm. **Ruler:** Carl XVI Gustaf **Obv:** Crowned monogram **Rev:** Value

Date	Mintage	F12	VF20	XF40	MS60	MS63
2001 B	6,001,481	—	—	—	1.00	1.25
2002 B	13,054,800	—	—	—	1.00	1.25
2003 H	11,063,204	—	—	—	1.00	1.25
2004 H	6,732,730	—	—	—	1.00	1.25
2005 H	4,372,783	—	—	—	1.00	1.25
2007 H	628,000	—	—	—	1.50	2.00
2008 H	12,000,000	—	—	—	1.00	1.25
2009 H	10,000,000	—	—	—	1.00	1.25

KM# 895 10 KRONOR
6.60 g., Copper-Aluminum-Zinc, 20.5 mm. **Ruler:** Carl XVI Gustaf **Obv:** Head left **Rev:** Three crowns and value **Edge:** Segmented reeding

Date	Mintage	F12	VF20	XF40	MS60	MS63
2001 B	4,171,757	—	—	—	2.00	2.50
2002 B	12,025,624	—	—	—	2.00	2.50
2003 H	13,824,632	—	—	—	2.00	2.50
2004 H	9,045,581	—	—	—	2.00	2.50
2005 H	13,205,261	—	—	—	2.00	2.50
2006 SI	4,531,150	—	—	—	2.00	2.50
2007	15,200,000	—	—	—	2.00	2.50
2008	12,000,000	—	—	—	2.00	2.50
2009	3,400,000	—	—	—	2.00	2.50

KM# 910 50 KRONOR
22.00 g., Copper-Aluminum-Zinc, 36 mm. **Ruler:** Carl XVI Gustaf **Subject:** 95th Anniversary - Birth of Astrid Lindgren **Obv:** Playful young girl **Rev:** Astrid Lindgren **Edge:** Plain

Date	Mintage	F12	VF20	XF40	MS60	MS63
ND (2002)	100,000	—	—	—	10.00	12.00

KM# 915 50 KRONOR
22.00 g., Copper-Aluminum-Zinc, 36 mm. **Ruler:** Carl XVI Gustaf **Subject:** 150th Anniversary of Sweden's first postage stamp **Obv:** Winged letter flying over landscape **Rev:** Sweden's first postage stamp design **Edge:** Plain

Date	Mintage	F12	VF20	XF40	MS60	MS63
ND (2005)	22,000	—	—	—	11.00	13.00

KM# 896 200 KRONOR
27.03 g., 0.925 Silver 0.7987 oz. ASW, 36 mm. **Ruler:** Carl XVI Gustaf **Subject:** 25th Wedding Anniversary **Obv:** Conjoined busts left **Rev:** Crowned arms with supporters **Edge:** Plain

Date	Mintage	F12	VF20	XF40	MS60	MS63
ND-2001	40,473	—	—	—	32.00	35.00

KM# 919 200 KRONOR
27.03 g., 0.925 Silver 0.7987 oz. ASW, 36 mm. **Ruler:** Carl XVI Gustaf **Subject:** Nobel Prize, 100th Anniversary **Edge:** Plain

Date	Mintage	F12	VF20	XF40	MS60	MS63
2001	29,856	—	—	—	35.00	40.00

KM# 908 200 KRONOR
27.03 g., 0.925 Silver 0.7987 oz. ASW, 36 mm. **Ruler:** Carl XVI Gustaf **Subject:** 750th Anniversary of Stockholm **Obv:** City seal with three towers and gate **Rev:** Three towers of city hall **Edge:** Plain

Date	Mintage	F12	VF20	XF40	MS60	MS63
ND (2002)	25,000	—	PF63 32.00	PF65 35.00		

KM# 902 200 KRONOR
27.03 g., 0.925 Silver 0.7987 oz. ASW, 36 mm. **Ruler:** Carl XVI Gustaf **Subject:** 30th Anniversary of Reign

Date	Mintage	F12	VF20	XF40	MS60	MS63
2003	16,500	—	—	—	32.00	35.00

KM# 904 200 KRONOR
27.03 g., 0.925 Silver 0.7987 oz. ASW, 36 mm. **Ruler:** Carl XVI Gustaf **Subject:** 700th Anniversary, St. Birgitta **Obv:** Cross in circle above value **Rev:** St. Birgitta **Edge:** Plain

Date	Mintage	F12	VF20	XF40	MS60	MS63
ND2003	39,300	—	—	—	32.00	35.00

KM# 911 200 KRONOR
27.03 g., 0.925 Silver 0.7987 oz. ASW, 36 mm. **Ruler:** Carl XVI Gustaf **Subject:** Royal Palace in Stockholm 250th Anniversary **Obv:** Two antique keys over map **Rev:** Royal Palace in Stockholm **Edge:** Plain

Date	Mintage	F12	VF20	XF40	MS60	MS63
ND2004	30,580	—	PF63 32.00	PF65 35.00		

KM# 906 200 KRONOR
27.03 g., 0.925 Silver 0.7987 oz. ASW, 36 mm. **Ruler:** Carl XVI Gustaf **Subject:** Centennial of the end of the Union between Norway and Sweden **Obv:** Split disc **Rev:** Flag on pole and two clouds

Date	Mintage	F12	VF20	XF40	MS60	MS63
2005	35,000	—	—	—	32.00	35.00

KM# 913 200 KRONOR
27.03 g., 0.925 Silver 0.7987 oz. ASW, 36 mm. **Ruler:** Carl XVI Gustaf **Subject:** Dag Hammarskjöld, 100th Anniversary of Birth **Obv:** Stylized flames **Rev:** Dag Hammarskjöld **Edge:** Plain

Date	Mintage	F12	VF20	XF40	MS60	MS63
ND2005	18,234	—	PF63 32.00	PF65 35.00		

KM# 921 200 KRONOR
27.03 g., 0.925 Silver 0.7987 oz. ASW, 36 mm. **Ruler:** Carl XVI Gustaf **Subject:** Swedish Railroads, 150th Anniversary

Date	Mintage	F12	VF20	XF40	MS60	MS63
ND2006	9,995	—	—	—	35.00	40.00

KM# 923 200 KRONOR
27.03 g., 0.925 Silver 0.7987 oz. ASW, 36 mm. **Ruler:** Carl XVI Gustaf **Subject:** Carl Linnaeus, 300th Anniversary of Birth **Edge:** Plain

Date	Mintage	F12	VF20	XF40	MS60	MS63
ND2007	10,600	—	—	—	35.00	40.00

KM# 925 200 KRONOR
27.03 g., 0.925 Silver 0.7987 oz. ASW, 36 mm. **Ruler:** Carl XVI Gustaf **Subject:** Selma Lagerlöf, 150th Anniversary of Birth

Date	Mintage	F12	VF20	XF40	MS60	MS63
2008	10,200	—	—	—	35.00	40.00

KM# 917 300 KRONOR
27.03 g., 0.925 Silver 0.7987 oz. ASW, 36 mm. **Ruler:** Carl XVI Gustaf **Subject:** Wedding of Princess Victoria and Daniel

Date	Mintage	F12	VF20	XF40	MS60	MS63
2010	—	PF63 45.00	PF65 50.00			

KM# 909 2000 KRONOR
12.00 g., 0.900 Gold 0.345 oz. AGW, 26 mm. **Ruler:** Carl XVI Gustaf **Subject:** 750th Anniversary of Stockholm **Obv:** City seal with three towers and gate **Rev:** Three towers of city hall **Edge:** Plain

Date	Mintage	F12	VF20	XF40	MS60	MS63
ND2002	3,596	PF63 600	PF65 625			

KM# 903 2000 KRONOR
12.00 g., 0.900 Gold 0.345 oz. AGW **Ruler:** Carl XVI Gustaf **Subject:** 30th Anniversary of Reign

Date	Mintage	F12	VF20	XF40	MS60	MS63
2003	2,000	—	—	—	600	630

KM# 905 2000 KRONOR
12.00 g., 0.900 Gold 0.345 oz. AGW, 26 mm. **Ruler:** Carl XVI Gustaf **Subject:** St. Birgitta's 700th Anniversary of birth **Obv:** Gothic letter B above value **Rev:** St. Birgitta **Edge:** Plain

Date	Mintage	F12	VF20	XF40	MS60	MS63
ND2003	3,640	—	—	—	600	630

KM# 912 2000 KRONOR
12.00 g., 0.900 Gold 0.345 oz. AGW, 26 mm. **Ruler:** Carl XVI Gustaf **Subject:** Royal Palace in Stockholm 250th Anniversary **Obv:** Two antique keys over map

Date	Mintage	F12	VF20	XF40	MS60	MS63
ND2004	5,734	PF63 620	PF65 650			

KM# 907 2000 KRONOR
12.00 g., 0.900 Gold 0.345 oz. AGW, 26 mm. **Ruler:** Carl XVI Gustaf **Subject:** Centennial of the end of the Union between Norway and Sweden **Obv:** Split disc **Rev:** Flag pole dividing two clouds

Date	Mintage	F12	VF20	XF40	MS60	MS63
2005	3,590	—	—	—	600	630

KM# 914 2000 KRONOR
12.00 g., 0.900 Gold 0.345 oz. AGW, 26 mm. **Ruler:** Carl XVI Gustaf **Subject:** Dag Hammarskjöld, 100th Anniversary of Birth **Obv:** Stylized flames **Rev:** Dag Hammarskjöld **Edge:** Plain

Date	Mintage	F12	VF20	XF40	MS60	MS63
ND2005	2,563	PF63 620	PF65 650			

KM# 922 2000 KRONOR
12.00 g., 0.900 Gold 0.345 oz. AGW, 26 mm. **Ruler:** Carl XVI Gustaf **Subject:** Swedish Railroads, 150th Anniversary

Date	Mintage	F12	VF20	XF40	MS60	MS63
ND2006	1,395	—	—	—	575	600

KM# 924 2000 KRONOR
12.00 g., 0.900 Gold 0.345 oz. AGW, 26 mm. **Ruler:** Carl XVI Gustaf **Subject:** Carl Linnaeus, 300th Anniversary of Birth

Date	Mintage	F12	VF20	XF40	MS60	MS63
ND2007	1,700	—	—	—	575	600

KM# 926 2000 KRONOR
12.00 g., 0.900 Gold 0.345 oz. AGW, 26 mm. **Ruler:** Carl XVI Gustaf **Subject:** Selma Lagerlof, 150th Anniversary of Birth **Edge:** Plain

Date	Mintage	F12	VF20	XF40	MS60	MS63
2008	2,495	—	—	—	575	600

KM# 918 4000 KRONOR
12.00 g., 0.900 Gold 0.345 oz. AGW, 26 mm. **Ruler:** Carl XVI Gustaf **Subject:** Wedding of Princess Victoria and Daniel Westling **Obv:** Coat of Arms of Princess Victoria **Rev:** Portraits of Bridal couple **Edge:** Plain

Date	Mintage	F12	VF20	XF40	MS60	MS63
2010	4,370	PF63 620	PF65 650			
2001	—					
2001	—					

MINT SETS

KM#	Date	Mintage	Identification	Issue Price	Mkt Val
MS107	2002 (4)	—	KM#853a, 878, 894, 895 plus medal	—	10.00

SWITZERLAND

The Swiss Confederation, located in central Europe north of Italy and south of Germany, has an area of 15,941 sq. mi. (41,290 sq. km.) and a population of *6.6 million. Capital: Bern. The economy centers about a well-developed manufacturing industry. Machinery, chemicals, watches and clocks, and textiles are exported.

The Swiss Constitutions of 1848 and 1874 established a union modeled upon that of the United States.

MINT MARK
B – Bern

MONETARY SYSTEM
100 Rappen (Centimes) = 1 Franc

CONFEDERATION
DECIMAL COINAGE

KM# 46 RAPPEN
1.50 g., Bronze, 16 mm. **Obv:** Cross **Rev:** Value and oat sprig **Edge:** Plain

Date	Mintage	F12	VF20	XF40	MS60	MS63
2001B	1,522,000	—	—	—	0.50	1.00
2001B	—	PF60 2.00				
2002B	2,024,000	—	—	—	0.50	1.00
2002B	5,500	PF60 2.00				
2003B	1,522,000	—	—	—	0.50	1.00
2003B	5,500	PF60 2.00				
2004B	1,526,000	—	—	—	0.50	1.00
2004B	5,000	PF60 2.00				
2005B	1,524,000	—	—	—	0.50	1.00
2005B	4,500	PF60 2.00				
2006B	26,000	—	—	—	—	135

Note: In sets only, circulation strikes not released

Date	Mintage	F12	VF20	XF40	MS60	MS63
2006B	4,000	PF60 200				

KM# 26c 5 RAPPEN
1.80 g., Aluminum-Bronze, 17.15 mm. **Obv:** Crowned head right **Rev:** Value within wreath **Edge:** Plain

Date	Mintage	F12	VF20	XF40	MS60	MS63
2001B	5,022,000	—	—	—	0.50	1.00
2001B	—	PF60 2.00				
2002B	12,024,000	—	—	—	0.50	1.00
2002B	—	PF60 2.00				
2003B	10,022,000	—	—	—	0.50	1.00
2003B	5,500	PF60 2.00				
2004B	10,026,000	—	—	—	0.50	1.00
2004B	5,000	PF60 2.00				
2005B	13,024,000	—	—	—	0.50	1.00
2005B	4,500	PF60 2.00				
2006B	12,026,000	—	—	—	0.50	1.00
2006B	4,000	PF60 2.00				
2007B	13,024,000	—	—	—	0.50	1.00
2007B	4,000	PF60 2.00				
2008B	40,024,000	—	—	—	0.50	1.00
2008B	4,000	PF60 2.00				
2009B	45,022,000	—	—	—	0.50	1.00
2009B	4,000	PF60 2.00				
2010B	Est. 41022000	—	—	—	0.50	1.00
2010B	Est. 4000	PF60 2.00				
2011B	Est. 50022000	—	—	—	0.30	1.00
2011B	—	PF60 2.00				
2012B	Est. 35022000	—	—	—	0.30	1.00
2012B	Est. 4000	PF60 2.00				
2013B	—	—	—	—	0.30	1.00
2013B	—	PF60 2.00				

KM# 27 10 RAPPEN
3.00 g., Copper-Nickel, 19.15 mm. **Obv:** Crowned head right **Obv. Legend:** CONFOEDERATIO HELVETICA **Rev:** Value within wreath **Edge:** Plain

Date	Mintage	F12	VF20	XF40	MS60	MS63
2001B	7,022,000	—	—	—	0.50	1.00
2001B	—	PF60 2.00				
2002B	15,024,000	—	—	—	0.50	1.00
2002B	—	PF60 2.00				
2003B	12,022,000	—	—	—	0.50	1.00
2003B	5,500	PF60 2.00				
2004B	5,026,000	—	—	—	0.50	1.00
2004B	5,000	PF60 2.00				
2005B	7,024,000	—	—	—	0.50	1.00
2005B	4,500	PF60 2.00				
2006B	2,026,000	—	—	—	0.50	1.00
2006B	4,000	PF60 2.00				
2007B	18,024,000	—	—	—	0.50	1.00
2007B	4,000	PF60 2.00				
2008B	35,022,000	—	—	—	0.50	1.00

Date	Mintage	F12	VF20	XF40	MS60	MS63
2008B	4,000	PF60 2.00				
2009B	35,022,000	—	—	—	0.50	1.00
2009B	4,000	PF60 2.00				
2010B	Est. 42022000	—	—	—	0.50	1.00
2010B	Est. 4000	PF60 2.00				
2011B	Est. 35022000	—	—	—	0.40	1.00
2011B	Est. 4000	PF60 2.00				
2012B	—	—	—	—	0.40	1.00
2012B	Est. 4000	PF60 2.00				
2013B	—	—	—	—	0.40	1.00
2013B	—	PF60 2.00				

KM# 29a 20 RAPPEN
4.00 g., Copper-Nickel, 21.05 mm. **Obv:** Crowned head right **Rev:** Value within wreath **Edge:** Plain

Date	Mintage	F12	VF20	XF40	MS60	MS63
2001B	7,022,000	—	—	—	1.00	2.00
2001B	—	PF60 3.00				
2002B	12,024,000	—	—	—	1.00	2.00
2002B	6,000	PF60 3.00				
2003B	10,022,000	—	—	—	1.00	2.00
2003B	5,500	PF60 3.00				
2004B	10,026,000	—	—	—	1.00	2.00
2004B	5,000	PF60 3.00				
2005B	6,024,000	—	—	—	1.00	2.00
2005B	4,500	PF60 3.00				
2006B	5,026,000	—	—	—	1.00	2.00
2006B	4,000	PF60 3.00				
2007B	22,024,000	—	—	—	1.00	2.00
2007B	4,000	PF60 3.00				
2008B	41,022,000	—	—	—	1.00	2.00
2008B	4,000	PF60 3.00				
2009B	32,022,000	—	—	—	1.00	2.00
2009B	4,000	PF60 3.00				
2010B	Est. 18022000	—	—	—	1.00	2.00
2010B	Est. 4000	PF60 3.00				
2011B	Est. 20022000	—	—	—	0.75	2.00
2011B	Est. 4000	PF60 3.00				
2012B	—	—	—	—	0.75	2.00
2012B	Est. 4000	PF60 3.00				
2013B	—	—	—	—	0.75	2.00
2013B	—	PF60 3.00				

KM# 23a.3 1/2 FRANC
2.20 g., Copper-Nickel, 18.2 mm. **Obv:** 23 Stars around figure **Rev:** Value within wreath **Edge:** Reeded

Date	Mintage	F12	VF20	XF40	MS60	MS63
2001B	6,022,000	—	—	—	2.50	3.50
2001B	—	PF60 5.00				
2002B	2,024,000	—	—	—	2.50	3.50
2002B	—	PF60 5.00				
2003B	2,022,000	—	—	—	2.50	3.50
2003B	5,500	PF60 5.00				
2004B	2,026,000	—	—	—	2.50	3.50
2004B	5,000	PF60 5.00				
2005B	1,024,000	—	—	—	2.50	3.50
2005B	4,500	PF60 5.00				
2006B	2,025,000	—	—	—	2.50	3.50
2006B	4,500	PF60 5.00				
2007B	18,024,000	—	—	—	2.00	3.00
2007B	4,000	PF60 5.00				
2008B	25,022,000	—	—	—	2.00	3.00
2008B	4,000	PF60 5.00				
2009B	27,022,000	—	—	—	2.00	3.00
2009B	4,000	PF60 5.00				
2010B	Est. 27022000	—	—	—	2.00	3.00
2010B	—	PF60 5.00				
2011B	Est. 15022000	—	—	—	1.50	3.00
2011B	Est. 4000	PF60 5.00				
2012B	Est. 20022000	—	—	—	1.50	3.00
2012B	Est. 4000	PF60 5.00				
2013B	—	—	—	—	1.50	3.00
2013B	—	PF60 5.00				

KM# 24a.3 FRANC
4.40 g., Copper-Nickel, 23.2 mm. **Obv:** 23 Stars around figure **Rev:** Value and date within wreath **Edge:** Reeded

Date	Mintage	F12	VF20	XF40	MS60	MS63
2001B	3,022,000	—	—	—	3.00	5.00
2001B	—	PF60 7.00				
2002B	1,024,000	—	—	—	3.00	5.00
2002B	—	PF60 7.00				
2003B	2,022,000	—	—	—	3.00	5.00
2003B	5,500	PF60 7.00				
2004B	2,026,000	—	—	—	3.00	5.00
2004B	5,000	PF60 7.00				
2005B	1,024,000	—	—	—	3.00	5.00
2005B	4,500	PF60 7.00				
2006B	2,026,000	—	—	—	3.00	5.00
2006B	4,000	PF60 7.00				
2007B	3,024,000	—	—	—	3.00	5.00
2007B	4,000	PF60 7.00				

Date	Mintage	F12	VF20	XF40	MS60	MS63
2008B	7,022,000	—	—	—	3.00	5.00
2008B	4,000	PF60 7.00				
2009B	11,022,000	—	—	—	3.00	5.00
2009B	4,000	PF60 7.00				
2010B	Est. 15022000	—	—	—	3.00	5.00
2010B	Est. 4000	PF60 7.00				
2011B	Est. 15022000	—	—	—	3.00	5.00
2011B	Est. 4000	PF60 7.00				
2012B	Est. 12022000	—	—	—	3.00	5.00
2012B	Est. 4000	PF60 7.00				
2013B	—	—	—	—	3.00	5.00
2013B	—	PF60 7.00				

KM# 21a.3 2 FRANCS
8.80 g., Copper-Nickel, 27.4 mm. **Obv:** 23 Stars around figure **Rev:** Value within wreath **Edge:** Reeded

Date	Mintage	F12	VF20	XF40	MS60	MS63
2001B	4,022,000	—	—	—	4.00	7.00
2001B	—	PF60 10.00				
2002B	1,024,000	—	—	—	4.50	7.50
2002B	—	PF60 10.00				
2003B	1,022,000	—	—	2.50	4.50	7.50
2003B	5,500	PF60 10.00				
2004B	1,026,000	—	—	2.50	4.50	7.50
2004B	5,000	PF60 10.00				
2005B	2,024,000	—	—	—	4.50	7.50
2005B	4,500	PF60 10.00				
2006B	7,026,000	—	—	—	4.50	7.50
2000B	4,000	PF60 10.00				
2007B	16,024,000	—	—	—	4.50	7.50
2007B	4,000	PF60 10.00				
2008B	6,022,000	—	—	—	4.50	7.50
2008B	4,000	PF60 10.00				
2009B	8,022,000	—	—	—	4.50	7.50
2009B	4,000	PF60 10.00				
2010B	Est. 9022000	—	—	—	4.50	7.50
2010B	Est. 4000	PF60 10.00				
2011B	Est. 7022000	—	—	—	4.00	7.50
2011B	Est. 4000	PF60 10.00				
2012B	Est. 11022000	—	—	—	4.00	7.50
2012B	Est. 4000	PF60 10.00				
2013B	—	—	—	—	4.00	7.50
2013R	—	PF60 10.00				

KM# 40a.4 5 FRANCS
13.20 g., Copper-Nickel, 31.45 mm. **Obv:** William Tell right **Rev:** Shield flanked by sprigs **Edge:** DOMINUS PROVIDEBIT and 13 stars raised

Date	Mintage	F12	VF20	XF40	MS60	MS63
2001B	1,022,000	—	—	—	7.00	10.00
2001B	—	PF60 15.00				
2002B	1,024,000	—	—	—	7.00	10.00
2002B	—	PF60 15.00				
2003B	1,022,000	—	—	—	7.00	10.00
2003B	5,500	PF60 15.00				
2004B	524,000	—	—	—	7.50	11.00
2004B	5,000	PF60 15.00				
2005B	524,000	—	—	—	7.50	11.00
2005B	4,500	PF60 15.00				
2006B	526,000	—	—	—	7.50	11.00
2006B	4,000	PF60 15.00				
2007B	524,000	—	—	—	7.50	11.00
2007B	4,000	PF60 15.00				
2008B	522,000	—	—	—	7.50	11.00
2008B	4,000	PF60 15.00				
2009B	2,022,000	—	—	—	7.50	11.00
2009B	4,000	PF60 15.00				
2010B	Est. 5022000	—	—	—	7.50	11.00
2010B	Est. 4000	PF60 15.00				
2011B	Est. 3022000	—	—	—	7.50	11.00
2011B	Est. 4000	PF60 15.00				
2012B	Est. 8022000	—	—	—	7.50	11.00
2012B	Est. 4000	PF60 15.00				
2013B	—	—	—	—	7.50	11.00
2013B	—	PF60 15.00				

KM# 146 10 FRANCS
Bi-Metallic

Date	Mintage	F12	VF20	XF40	MS60	MS63
2013B	40,000	PF63 37.00	PF65 40.00			
2013	92,000	—	—	—	—	17.00

KM# 147 20 FRANCS
20.00 g., 0.835 Silver 0.5335 oz. ASW **Subject:** First Alpine Flight

Date	Mintage	F12	VF20	XF40	MS60	MS63
2013B	7,000	PF63 62.00	PF65 65.00			
2013B	50,000	—	—	—	30.00	35.00

KM# 148 20 FRANCS
20.00 g., 0.835 Silver 0.5335 oz. ASW, 33 mm. **Subject:** Swiss Wrestling

Date	Mintage	F12	VF20	XF40	MS60	MS63
2013B	50,000	—	—	—	—	17.00
2013B	7,000	PF63 62.00	PF65 65.00			

KM# 149 50 FRANCS
11.29 g., 0.900 Gold 0.3246 oz. AGW, 25 mm. **Subject:** Gotthard mail coach

Date	Mintage	F12	VF20	XF40	MS60	MS63
2013	6,000	PF65 625				

COMMEMORATIVE COINAGE

KM# 92 5 FRANCS
15.00 g., Bi-Metallic, 32.85 mm. **Subject:** Zurcher Sechselauten **Obv:** Value within circle **Rev:** Burning strawman within circle **Edge:** Reeded **Edge Lettering:** DOMINUS PROVIDEBIT (13 stars)

Date	Mintage	F12	VF20	XF40	MS60	MS63
2001B	170,000	—	—	—	8.00	12.00
2001B	—	PF63 22.00	PF65 24.00			

KM# 98 5 FRANCS
15.00 g., Bi-Metallic, 32.85 mm. **Subject:** Escalade 1602-2002 **Obv:** Value within circle **Rev:** Swirling ladders design within circle **Edge:** Reeded **Edge Lettering:** DOMINUS PROVIDEBIT (13 stars)

Date	Mintage	F12	VF20	XF40	MS60	MS63
2002B	130,000	—	—	—	8.00	12.00
2002B	15,000	PF63 22.00	PF65 24.00			

KM# 103 5 FRANCS
15.00 g., Bi-Metallic, 32.85 mm. **Subject:** Chalandamarz **Obv:** Value within circular inscription and designed wreath **Rev:** Boys shaking bells within 3/4 designed wreath **Edge:** Reeded **Edge Lettering:** DOMINUS PROVIDEBIT (13 stars)

Date	Mintage	F12	VF20	XF40	MS60	MS63
2003B	96,000	—	—	—	8.00	12.00
2003B	12,000	PF63 22.00	PF65 24.00			

KM# 107 10 FRANCS
15.00 g., Bi-Metallic, 32.85 mm. **Obv:** Value **Rev:** Matterhorn Mountain **Edge:** Segmented reeding

Date	Mintage	F12	VF20	XF40	MS60	MS63
2004B	94,976	—	—	—	—	22.00
2004B	12,168	PF63 42.00	PF65 45.00			

KM# 111 10 FRANCS
15.00 g., Bi-Metallic, 32.85 mm. **Obv:** Value **Rev:** Jungfrau mountain **Edge:** Segmented reeding

Date	Mintage	F12	VF20	XF40	MS60	MS63
2005B	77,791	—	—	—	—	18.00
2005D	10,495	PF63 37.00	PF65 40.00			

KM# 114 10 FRANCS
15.00 g., Bi-Metallic, 32.85 mm. **Obv:** Value **Rev:** Piz Bernina mountain **Edge:** Segmented reeding

Date	Mintage	F12	VF20	XF40	MS60	MS63
2006B	66,000	—	—	—	—	16.00
2006B	9,000	PF63 37.00	PF65 40.00			

KM# 118 10 FRANCS
15.00 g., Bi-Metallic, 32.85 mm. **Subject:** Swiss National Park **Obv:** Value **Rev:** Ibex **Edge:** Segmented reeding

Date	Mintage	F12	VF20	XF40	MS60	MS63
2007B	80,200	—	—	—	—	17.00
2007B	10,300	PF63 37.00	PF65 40.00			

KM# 126 10 FRANCS
15.00 g., Bi-Metallic, 32.85 mm. **Obv:** Small national arms **Obv. Legend:** CONFEDERATIO - HELVETICA **Rev:** Golden Eagle alighting **Rev. Legend:** PARK NATIONAL SUISSE **Edge:** Segmented reeding

Date	Mintage	F12	VF20	XF40	MS60	MS63
2008B	66,000					17.00
2008B	10,300	PF63 37.00	PF65 40.00			

KM# 130 10 FRANCS
15.00 g., Bi-Metallic, 32.85 mm. **Subject:** Swiss National Park
Obv: Value **Rev:** Red deer

Date	Mintage	F12	VF20	XF40	MS60	MS63
2009B	49,000				—	49.00
2009B	5,300	PF63 50.00	PF65 53.00			

KM# 134 10 FRANCS
15.00 g., Bi-Metallic, 32.85 mm. **Subject:** Swiss National Park
- Alpine Marmot **Obv:** Value **Rev:** Marmot

Date	Mintage	F12	VF20	XF40	MS60	MS63
2010B	12,000	PF63 37.00	PF65 40.00			
2010B	Est. 94000				—	17.00

KM# 138 10 FRANCS
15.00 g., Bi-Metallic, 33 mm. **Subject:** Bern Onion Market **Obv:**
Value **Rev:** Bear of Bern at left, woven plaits of onions at right
Edge: Segmented reeding

Date	Mintage	F12	VF20	XF40	MS60	MS63
2011B	12,000	PF63 37.00	PF65 40.00			
2011B	94,000	—	—	—	—	17.00

KM# 142 10 FRANCS
15.00 g., Bi-Metallic, 33 mm. **Subject:** Bull fighting **Rev:** Two
bull's heads butting

Date	Mintage	F12	VF20	XF40	MS60	MS63
2012B	12,000	PF63 37.00	PF65 40.00			
2012B	94,000	—	—	—	—	17.00

KM# 93 20 FRANCS
20.00 g., 0.835 Silver 0.5335 oz. ASW, 32.8 mm. **Subject:**

Mustair Cloister **Obv:** Church floor plan **Rev:** Cloister of Müstair
Edge Lettering: DOMINUS PROVIDEBIT and 13 stars

Date	Mintage	F12	VF20	XF40	MS60	MS63
2001B	50,076				26.00	30.00
2001B	15,000	PF63 52.00	PF65 55.00			

KM# 94 20 FRANCS
20.00 g., 0.835 Silver 0.5335 oz. ASW, 32.8 mm. **Subject:**
Johanna Spyri **Obv:** Value within handwritten background **Rev:**
Bust facing **Edge Lettering:** DOMINUS PROVIDEBIT (13 stars)

Date	Mintage	F12	VF20	XF40	MS60	MS63
2001B	60,364	—			26.00	30.00
2001B	15,000	PF63 52.00	PF65 55.00			

KM# 99 20 FRANCS
20.00 g., 0.835 Silver 0.5335 oz. ASW, 32.8 mm. **Obv:** St. Gall
and bear cub **Rev:** St. Gall Cloister **Edge Lettering:** DOMINUS
PROVIDEBIT (13 stars)

Date	Mintage	F12	VF20	XF40	MS60	MS63
2002B	35,895	—			26.00	30.00
2002B	6,250	PF63 52.00	PF65 55.00			

KM# 100 20 FRANCS
20.00 g., 0.835 Silver 0.5335 oz. ASW, 32.8 mm. **Subject:**
REGA **Obv:** Value, inscription and raised cross above rotating
propeller **Rev:** Rescue helicopter in flight **Edge Lettering:**
DOMINUS PROVIDEBIT (13 stars)

Date	Mintage	F12	VF20	XF40	MS60	MS63
2002B	37,314	—			26.00	30.00
2002B	6,453	PF63 52.00	PF65 55.00			

KM# 101 20 FRANCS
20.00 g., 0.835 Silver 0.5335 oz. ASW, 32.8 mm. **Subject:**
Expo '02 **Obv:** Value and date within circle **Rev:** Child at
water's edge within beaded circle **Edge Lettering:** DOMINUS
PROVIDEBIT (13 stars)

Date	Mintage	F12	VF20	XF40	MS60	MS63
2002B	51,899	—			26.00	30.00
2002B	7,691	PF63 52.00	PF65 55.00			

KM# 104 20 FRANCS
19.97 g., 0.835 Silver 0.5327 oz. ASW, 32.8 mm. **Subject:**
St. Moritz Ski Championships **Obv:** Value in snow storm **Rev:**
Skier in snow storm **Edge Lettering:** DOMINUS PROVIDEBIT
(13 stars)

Date	Mintage	F12	VF20	XF40	MS60	MS63
2003B	39,411	—	—		26.00	30.00
2003B	6,471	PF63 52.00	PF65 55.00			

KM# 106 20 FRANCS
20.00 g., 0.835 Silver 0.5335 oz. ASW, 32.8 mm. **Subject:**
Bern, Old Town **Obv:** Stylized clock tower and buildings
Rev: Stylized aerial view of Berner Altstadt **Edge Lettering:**
DOMINUS PROVIDEBIT

Date	Mintage	F12	VF20	XF40	MS60	MS63
2003B	38,644	—	—		26.00	30.00
2003B	5,909	PF63 52.00	PF65 55.00			

KM# 108 20 FRANCS
20.00 g., 0.835 Silver 0.5335 oz. ASW, 32.8 mm. **Obv:**
Value **Rev:** The Three Castles of Bellinzona **Edge Lettering:**
DOMINUS PROVIDEBIT

Date	Mintage	F12	VF20	XF40	MS60	MS63
2004B	29,697	—	—		26.00	30.00
2004B	5,190	PF63 52.00	PF65 55.00			

KM# 109 20 FRANCS
20.00 g., 0.835 Silver 0.5335 oz. ASW, 32.8 mm. **Obv:** Value
Rev: Chillon Castle and reflection **Edge Lettering:** DOMINUS
PROVIDEBIT

Date	Mintage	F12	VF20	XF40	MS60	MS63
2004B	35,133	—	—		26.00	30.00
2004B	5,670	PF63 52.00	PF65 55.00			

KM# 121 20 FRANCS
20.00 g., 0.835 Silver 0.5335 oz. ASW, 32.8 mm. **Subject:** FIFA Centennial **Obv:** Soccer ball with value at left **Rev:** Flower in center of cross

Date	Mintage	F12	VF20	XF40	MS60	MS63
2004B Proof only	14,041	PF65 150				

KM# 112 20 FRANCS
20.00 g., 0.835 Silver 0.5335 oz. ASW, 32.8 mm. **Subject:** Geneva Motor Show **Obv:** Value **Rev:** Partial view of prototype car **Edge Lettering:** DOMINUS PROVIDEBIT

Date	Mintage	F12	VF20	XF40	MS60	MS63
2005B	45,000	—	—	—	26.00	30.00
2005B	6,000	PF63 52.00	PF65 55.00			

KM# 122 20 FRANCS
20.00 g., 0.835 Silver 0.5335 oz. ASW, 32.8 mm. **Subject:** Chapel Bridge Lucerne **Obv:** Value **Rev:** View of Chapel Bridge **Edge Lettering:** DOMINUS PROVIDEBIT

Date	Mintage	F12	VF20	XF40	MS60	MS63
2005B	44,359	—	—	—	26.00	30.00
2005B	5,998	PF63 52.00	PF65 55.00			

KM# 115 20 FRANCS
20.00 g., 0.835 Silver 0.5335 oz. ASW, 32.8 mm. **Obv:** Value **Rev:** 1906 Post Bus **Edge Lettering:** DOMINUS PROVIDEBIT

Date	Mintage	F12	VF20	XF40	MS60	MS63
2006B	40,000	—	—	—	26.00	30.00
2006B	6,000	PF63 52.00	PF65 55.00			

KM# 117 20 FRANCS
20.00 g., 0.835 Silver 0.5335 oz. ASW, 32.8 mm. **Obv:** Value and legend **Rev:** Swiss Parliament Building **Edge Lettering:** DOMINUS PROVIDEBIT (13 stars)

Date	Mintage	F12	VF20	XF40	MS60	MS63
2006B	35,000	—	—	—	25.00	30.00
2006B	6,000	PF63 57.00	PF65 60.00			

KM# 119 20 FRANCS
20.00 g., 0.835 Silver 0.5335 oz. ASW, 32.8 mm. **Subject:** National Bank Centennial **Obv:** Value **Rev:** Partial face of Arthur Honegger (Composer) **Edge Lettering:** DOMINUS PROVIDEBIT

Date	Mintage	F12	VF20	XF40	MS60	MS63
2007B	41,747	—	—	—	25.00	30.00
2007B	11,000	PF63 57.00	PF65 60.00			

KM# 124 20 FRANCS
20.00 g., 0.835 Silver 0.5335 oz. ASW, 32.8 mm. **Series:** Famous buildings **Subject:** Munot castle of Schaffhausen **Obv:** **Legend:** CONFEDERATIO - HELVETICA **Rev:** Two views of castle **Rev. Legend:** MUNOT

Date	Mintage	F12	VF20	XF40	MS60	MS63
2007B	40,000	—	—	—	25.00	30.00
2007B	5,000	PF63 57.00	PF65 60.00			

KM# 127 20 FRANCS
20.00 g., 0.835 Silver 0.5335 oz. ASW, 32.8 mm. **Subject:** 100th Anniversary Hockey **Obv:** Small national arms **Obv. Legend:** CONFEDERATIO - HELVETICA **Rev:** Two players, one about to swing at puck **Rev. Legend:** ICE HOCKEY 1908-2008

Date	Mintage	F12	VF20	XF40	MS60	MS63
2008B	46,000	—	—	—	25.00	30.00
2008B	5,500	PF63 62.00	PF65 65.00			

KM# 128 20 FRANCS
20.00 g., 0.835 Silver 0.5335 oz. ASW, 32.8 mm. **Subject:** Vitznau-Rigi Cog Railway **Obv:** Value **Rev:** Modern locomotive descending, early locomotive ascending (inverted)

Date	Mintage	F12	VF20	XF40	MS60	MS63
2008B	Est. 50,000	—	—	—	25.00	30.00
2008B	7,000	PF63 62.00	PF65 65.00			

KM# 132 20 FRANCS
20.00 g., 0.835 Silver 0.5335 oz. ASW, 32.8 mm. **Subject:** Brienz-Rothorn Railway **Obv:** Value **Rev:** Locomotive and railcar

Date	Mintage	F12	VF20	XF40	MS60	MS63
2009B	50,000	—	—	—	25.00	30.00

KM# 131 20 FRANCS
20.00 g., 0.835 Silver 0.5335 oz. ASW, 32.8 mm. **Subject:** Swiss Museum of Transport, 50th Anniversary **Obv:** National arms and value **Rev:** Spiral of transport vehicles **Edge:** DOMINUS PROVIDEBIT

Date	Mintage	F12	VF20	XF40	MS60	MS63
2009B	50,000	—	—	—	25.00	30.00
2009B	4,000	PF63 62.00	PF65 65.00			

KM# 136 20 FRANCS
20.00 g., 0.835 Silver 0.5335 oz. ASW, 32.8 mm. **Subject:** 100 Anniversary Death of Henry Dunant (Red Cross founder) **Rev:** Bust at left, flag

Date	Mintage	F12	VF20	XF40	MS60	MS63
2010B	Est. 50000	—	—	—	30.00	35.00
2010B	Est. 7000	PF63 47.00	PF65 50.00			

KM# 135 20 FRANCS
20.00 g., 0.835 Silver 0.5335 oz. ASW, 32.8 mm. **Subject:** 100 Years Bernina Railway **Rev:** Steam train on viaduct

Date	Mintage	F12	VF20	XF40	MS60	MS63
2010B	Est. 50000	—	—	—	30.00	35.00
2010B	Est. 7000	PF63 47.00	PF65 50.00			

KM# 140 20 FRANCS
20.00 g., 0.835 Silver 0.5335 oz. ASW, 33 mm. **Subject:** Pilatus Railway **Obv:** Value, date and inscription "CONFOEDERATIO HELVETICA **Rev:** Electric railway car climbing mountain and inscription "PILATUSBAHN **Edge:** DOMINUS PROVIDEBIT (13 stars)

Date	Mintage	F12	VF20	XF40	MS60	MS63
2011B	—	PF63 62.00	PF65 65.00			
2011B	Est. 50000	—	—	—	30.00	35.00

KM# 139 20 FRANCS
20.00 g., 0.835 Silver 0.5335 oz. ASW, 33 mm. **Subject:** Max Frisch, 100th Anniversary of Birth **Obv:** Value **Rev:** Facing portrait with pipe

Date	Mintage	F12	VF20	XF40	MS60	MS63
2011B	Est. 7000	PF63 47.00	PF65 50.00			
2011B	Est. 50000	—	—	—	30.00	35.00

KM# 144 20 FRANCS
20.00 g., 0.835 Silver 0.5335 oz. ASW, 33 mm. **Subject:** Globi **Obv:** Swiss cross, legend, denomination & date **Obv. Legend:** CONFOEDERATIO HELVETICA **Rev:** Comic character Globi carying a cake with candles and legend **Rev. Legend:** GLOBI and ©Globi Verlag Zurich

Date	Mintage	F12	VF20	XF40	MS60	MS63
2012	Est. 50000	—	—	—	—	30.00
2012	Est. 7000	PF63 62.00	PF65 65.00			

KM# 143 20 FRANCS
20.00 g., 0.835 Silver 0.5335 oz. ASW, 33 mm. **Subject:** Jungfrau Railway

Date	Mintage	F12	VF20	XF40	MS60	MS63
2012B	7,000	PF63 62.00	PF65 65.00			
2012B	50,000	—	—	—	30.00	35.00

KM# 95 50 FRANCS
11.29 g., 0.900 Gold 0.3246 oz. AGW, 25.1 mm. **Obv:** Landscape and value **Rev:** Heidi and goat running **Edge:** Lettered **Edge Lettering:** DOMINUS PROVIDEBIT (13 stars)

Date	Mintage	F12	VF20	XF40	MS60	MS63
2001B	3,967	PF65 700				

KM# 102 50 FRANCS
11.29 g., 0.900 Gold 0.3246 oz. AGW, 25.1 mm. **Subject:** Expo '02 **Obv:** Value **Rev:** Aerial view of 3 lakes landscape **Edge:** Lettered **Edge Lettering:** DOMINUS PROVIDEBIT (13 stars)

Date	Mintage	F12	VF20	XF40	MS60	MS63
2002B	4,856	PF65 650				

KM# 105 50 FRANCS
11.29 g., 0.900 Gold 0.3246 oz. AGW, 25.1 mm. **Obv:** Skier and value **Rev:** St. Moritz city view **Edge Lettering:** DOMINUS PROVIDEBIT (13 stars)

Date	Mintage	F12	VF20	XF40	MS60	MS63
2003B	4,000	PF65 650				

KM# 110 50 FRANCS
11.29 g., 0.900 Gold 0.3246 oz. AGW, 25.1 mm. **Obv:** Value **Rev:** Matterhorn Mountain **Edge Lettering:** DOMINUS

PROVIDEBIT (13 stars)

Date	Mintage	F12	VF20	XF40	MS60	MS63
2004B	7,000	PF65 700				

KM# 123 50 FRANCS
11.29 g., 0.900 Gold 0.3246 oz. AGW, 25.1 mm. **Subject:** FIFA Centennial **Obv:** FIFA depicting Wilhelm Tell **Rev:** Soccer ball on left value on right

Date	Mintage	F12	VF20	XF40	MS60	MS63
2004B	10,000	PF65 1,000				

KM# 113 50 FRANCS
11.29 g., 0.900 Gold 0.3246 oz. AGW, 25.1 mm. **Subject:** Geneva Motor Show **Obv:** Value **Rev:** Partial view of an antique car **Edge Lettering:** DOMINUS PROVIDEBIT

Date	Mintage	F12	VF20	XF40	MS60	MS63
2005B	6,000	PF65 650				

KM# 116 50 FRANCS
11.29 g., 0.900 Gold 0.3246 oz. AGW, 25.1 mm. **Obv:** Value **Rev:** Swiss Guardsman **Edge Lettering:** DOMINUS PROVIDEBIT

Date	Mintage	F12	VF20	XF40	MS60	MS63
2006B	6,000	PF65 750				

KM# 120 50 FRANCS
11.29 g., 0.900 Gold 0.3246 oz. AGW, 25.1 mm. **Subject:** National Bank Centennial **Obv:** Value **Rev:** Value **Obv. Legend:** CONFEDERATIO - HELVETICA **Rev:** Lumberjack" from painting by Ferdinand Hodler **Rev. Inscription:** SNB BNS + **Edge Lettering:** DOMINUS PROVIDEBIT

Date	Mintage	F12	VF20	XF40	MS60	MS63
2007B	6,000	PF65 650				

KM# 129 50 FRANCS
11.29 g., 0.900 Gold 0.3246 oz. AGW, 25.1 mm. **Subject:** International Year of Planet Earth **Obv:** Value **Rev:** Dancing child with 3 globes above head, in hands and standing on one globe **Rev. Inscription:** DE LA PLANETE TERRE ANNEE INTERNATIONALE **Edge:** DOMINUS PROVIDEBIT

Date	Mintage	F12	VF20	XF40	MS60	MS63
2008B	6,000	PF65 600				

KM# 133 50 FRANCS
11.29 g., 0.900 Gold 0.3246 oz. AGW, 25.1 mm. **Subject:** Pro Patria, 100th Anniversary **Obv:** Value **Edge:** DOMINUS PROVIDEBIT

Date	Mintage	F12	VF20	XF40	MS60	MS63
2009B	6,000	PF65 650				

KM# 137 50 FRANCS
11.29 g., 0.900 Gold 0.3246 oz. AGW, 25.1 mm. **Subject:** 100th

---

Anniversary Death of Alber Anker (Painter)

Date	Mintage	F12	VF20	XF40	MS60	MS63
2010B	6,000	PF65 650				

KM# 141 50 FRANCS
11.29 g., 0.900 Gold 0.3246 oz. AGW, 25.1 mm. **Subject:** Bell for Ursli **Obv:** Value, date and inscription "CONFOEDERATIO HELVETICA **Rev:** Boy holding bell and inscription "Schellen-Ursli **Edge:** DOMINUS PROVIDEBIT

Date	Mintage	F12	VF20	XF40	MS60	MS63
2011B	Est. 6000	PF65 650				

KM# 145 50 FRANCS
11.29 g., 0.900 Gold 0.3246 oz. AGW, 25 mm. **Subject:** Pro Juventute 100th Anniversary **Obv:** Swiss cross, legend, denomination and date **Obv. Legend:** CONFOEDERATIO HELVETICA **Rev:** Girl jumping rope, head of boy wearing cap **Rev. Legend:** PRO JUVENTUTE 1912-2012 and BRIGITTA G. L.

Date	Mintage	F12	VF20	XF40	MS60	MS63
2012	Est. 6000	PF65 600				

ESSAIS

KM#	Date	Mintage	Identification	Mkt Val
E13	2001B	600	20 Francs 0.835 Silver KM#93	300
E14	2002	700	5 Francs Bi-Metallic KM#98	185
E15	2003B	700	5 Francs Bi-Metallic KM#103	200
E16	2004B	700	10 Francs Bi-Metallic KM#107.	300
E19	2005B	500	20 Francs 0.832 Silver KM#112.	250
E19	2005B	500	20 Francs 0.832 Silver KM#112.	420
E20	2006B	500	20 Francs 0.835 Silver KM#117.	320
E21	2007B	500	20 Francs Silver 33 mm. KM#119.	250
E22	2008B	700	10 Francs Bi-Metallic KM#126	225
E23	2009B	500	20 Francs 0.835 Silver 33mm KM#132	250
E24	2010B	700	10 Francs Bi-Metallic KM#134	200
E25	2011B	500	20 Francs 0.835 Silver KM#139	275

MINT SETS

KM#	Date	Mintage	Identification	Issue Price	Mkt Val
MS35	2001 (9)	21,532	KM#21a.3, 23a.3, 24a.3, 26c, 27, 29a, 40a.4, 46, 92	—	40.00
MS36	2002 (9)	17,920	KM#21a.3, 23a.3, 24a.3, 26c, 27, 29a, 40a.4, 46, 98	—	45.00
MS37	2002 (9)	1,974	KM#21a.3, 23a.3, 24a.3, 26c, 27, 29a, 40a.4, 46, 98, plus a medal.	—	220
MS38	2003 (9)	17,200	KM#21a.3, 23a.3, 24a.3, 26c, 27, 29a, 40a.4, 46, 103 Chalandamarz	—	50.00
MS39	2003 (8)	4,800	KM#21a.3, 23a.3, 24a.3, 26c, 27, 29a, 40a.2, 46 plus medal; Baby Mint Set	—	80.00
MS40	2004 (9)	16,000	KM#21a.3, 23a.3, 24a.3, 26c, 27, 29a, 40a.4, 46, 107 Matterhorn	—	80.00
MS41	2004 (8)	8,400	KM#21a.3, 23a.3, 24a.3, 26c, 27, 29a, 40a.2, 46 plus medal; Baby Mint Set	—	65.00
MS42	2005 (9)	15,279	KM#21a.3, 23a.3, 24a.3, 26c, 27, 29a, 40a.4, 46, 111 Jung Frau	—	40.00
MS43	2005 (8)	7,500	KM#21a.3, 23a.3, 24a.3, 26c, 27, 29a, 40a.2, 46 plus medal; Baby Mint Set	—	40.00
MS44	2006 (9)	16,000	KM#21a.3, 23a.3, 24a.3, 26c, 27, 29a, 40a.4, 46, 114 Piz Bernina	—	140
MS45	2006 (8)	2,000	KM#21a.3, 23a.3, 24a.3, 26c, 27, 29a, 40a.2, 46 plus medal; Jubilee Mint Set	—	450
MS46	2006 (8)	8,000	KM#21a.3, 23a.3, 24a.3, 26c, 27, 29a, 40a.2, 46 plus medal; Baby Mint Set	—	175

KM#	Date	Mintage Identification	Issue Price	Mkt Val
MS47	2007 (8)	16,000 KM#21a.3, 23a.3, 24a.3, 26c, 27, 29a, 40a.4, 118	—	45.00
MS48	2007 (7)	7,500 KM#21a.3, 23a.3, 24a.3, 26c, 27, 29a, 40a.2, plus medal; Baby Mint Set	—	45.00
MS49	2008 (8)	15,000 KM#21a.3, 23a.3, 24a.3, 26c, 27, 29a, 40a.4, 126	—	45.00
MS50	2008 (7)	7,000 KM#21a.3, 23a.3, 24a.3, 26c, 27, 29a, 40a.2, plus medal; Baby Mint Set	—	40.00
MS51	2009 (8)	13,500 KM#21a.3, 23a.3, 24a.3, 26c, 27, 29a, 40a4, 130.	—	50.00
MS52	2009 (7)	7,500 KM#21a.3, 23a.3, 24a.3, 26c, 27, 29a, 40a.2, plus medal; Baby Mint Set	—	40.00
MS53	2010 (8)	14,000 KM#21a.3, 23a.3, 24a.3, 26c, 27, 29a, 40a.2, 134	—	50.00
MS54	2010 (7)	8,000 KM#21a.3, 23a.3, 24a.3, 26c, 27, 29a, 40a.2, plus medal; Baby Mint Set	—	40.00
MS55	2011 (8)	14,000 KM#21a.3, 23a.3, 24a.3, 26c, 27, 29a, 40a.2, 138	—	50.00
MS56	2011 (7)	8,000 KM#21a.3, 23a.3, 24a.3, 26c, 27, 29a, 40a.2, plus medal; Baby Mint Set	—	40.00
MS58	2012 (7)	8,000 KM#21a.3, 23a.3, 24a.3, 26c, 27, 29a, 40a.4 plus medal.	—	40.00
MS67	2012 (8)	14,000 KM#21a.3, 23a.3, 24a.3, 26c, 27, 29a, 40a.4, 142	—	40.00

PROOF SETS

KM#	Date	Mintage Identification	Issue Price	Mkt Val
PS30	2001 (9)	5,184 KM#21a.3, 23a.3, 24a.3, 26c, 27, 29a, 40a.4, 46, 92	—	75.00
PS31	2002 (9)	4,518 KM#21a.3, 23a.3, 24a.3, 26c, 27, 29a, 40a.4, 46, 98	—	00.00
PS32	2003 (9)	4,520 KM#21a.3, 23a.3, 24a.3, 26c, 27, 29a, 40a.4, 46, 103	—	80.00
PS33	2004 (9)	4,168 KM#21a.3, 23a.3, 24a.3, 26c, 27, 29a, 40a.4, 46, 107 Matterhorn	68.00	95.00
PS34	2005 (9)	3,783 KM#21a.3, 23a.3, 24a.3, 26c, 27, 29a, 40a.4, 46, 111	68.00	90.00
PS35	2006 (9)	4,000 KM#21a.3, 23a.3, 24a.3, 26c, 27, 29a, 40a.4, 46, 114	68.00	300
PS36	2007 (8)	4,000 KM#21a.3, 23a.3, 24a.3, 26c, 27, 29a, 40a.4, 118	68.00	85.00
PS37	2008 (8)	4,000 KM#21a.3, 23a.3, 24a.3, 26c, 27, 29a, 40a.4, 126	72.00	90.00
PS38	2009 (8)	4,000 KM#21a.3, 23a.3, 24a.3, 26c, 27, 29a, 40a.4, 130	75.00	90.00
PS39	2010 (8)	4,000 KM#21a.3, 23a.3, 24a.3, 26c, 27, 29a, 40a.4, 134	75.00	90.00
PS40	2011 (8)	4,000 KM#21a.3, 23a.3, 24a.3, 26c, 27, 29a, 40a.2, 138	—	90.00
PS41	2012 (8)	4,000 KM#21a.3, 23a.3, 24a.3, 26c, 27, 29a, 40a.4, 142	—	90.00

SYRIA

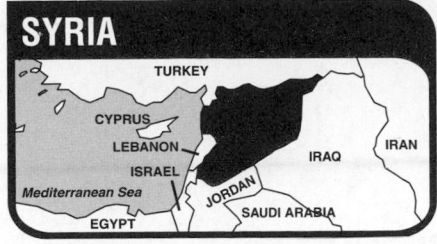

The Syrian Arab Republic, located in the Near East at the eastern end of the Mediterranean Sea, has an area of 71,498 sq. mi. (185,180 sq. km.) and a population of *12 million. Capital: Greater Damascus. Agriculture and animal breeding are the chief industries. Cotton, crude oil and livestock are exported.

TITLES

الجمهورية السورية

al-Jumhuriya(t) al-Suriya(t)

الجمهورية لعربية السورية

al-Jumhuriya(t) al-Arabiya(t) as-Suriya(t)

SYRIAN ARAB REPUBLIC
STANDARD COINAGE

KM# 129 5 POUNDS
7.53 g., Nickel Clad Steel, 24.5 mm. **Obv:** National arms within design and beaded border **Rev:** Old fort and latent image above value within design and beaded border **Edge:** Reeded and lettered **Edge Lettering:** CENTRAL BANK 5 SYP

Date	Mintage	F12	VF20	XF40	MS60	MS63
AH1424-2003	—	—	—	—	1.25	1.75

KM# 130 10 POUNDS
9.53 g., Copper-Nickel-Zinc, 27.4 mm. **Obv:** National arms within beaded border **Rev:** Ancient ruins with latent image within beaded border **Edge Lettering:** 10 SYRIAN POUNDS

Date	Mintage	F12	VF20	XF40	MS60	MS63
AH1424-2003	—	—	—	—	2.50	3.50

KM# 131 25 POUNDS
8.40 g., Bi-Metallic, 25 mm. **Obv:** National arms within beaded border **Rev:** Building and latent image within beaded border **Edge Lettering:** CENTRAL BANK OF SYRIA 25

Date	Mintage	F12	VF20	XF40	MS60	MS63
AH1424-2003	—	—	—	1.50	3.75	5.00

TAJIKISTAN

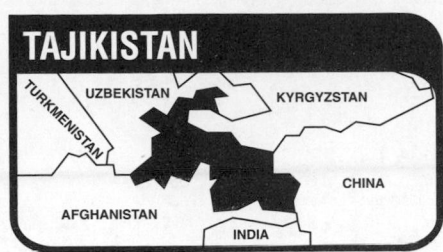

The Republic of Tajikistan (Tadjiquistan), was formed from those regions of Bukhara and Turkestan where the population consisted mainly of Tajiks. It is bordered in the north and west by Uzbekistan and Kyrgyzstan, in the east by China and in the south by Afghanistan. It has an area of 55,240 sq. miles (143,100 sq. km.) and a population of 5.95 million. It includes 2 provinces of Khudzand and Khatlon together with the Gorno-Badakhshan Autonomous Region with a population of 5,092,603. Capital: Dushanbe. Tajikistan was admitted as a constituent republic of the Soviet Union on Dec. 5, 1929. In August 1990 the Tajik Supreme Soviet adopted a declaration of republican sovereignty, and in Dec. 1991 the republic became a member of the CIS.

After demonstrations and fighting, the Communist government was replaced by a Revolutionary Coalition Council on May 7, 1992. Following further demonstrations President Nabiev was ousted on Sept. 7, 1992. Civil war broke out, and the government resigned on Nov. 10, 1992. On Nov. 30, 1992 it was announced that a CIS peacekeeping force would be sent to Tajikistan. A state of emergency was imposed in Jan. 1993. A ceasefire was signed in 1996 and a peace agreement signed in June 1997.

MONETARY SYSTEM
100 Drams = 1 Somoni

REPUBLIC
DECIMAL COINAGE

KM# 35 DIRAM
1.30 g., Brass Plated Copper, 14.5 mm. **Obv:** National arms **Rev:** Value

Date	Mintage	F12	VF20	XF40	MS60	MS63
2011	—	—	—	—	—	0.50

KM# 36 2 DIRAMS
1.60 g., Brass Plated Copper, 16 mm. **Obv:** National arms **Rev:** Value

Date	Mintage	F12	VF20	XF40	MS60	MS63
2011	—	—	—	—	0.50	0.75

KM# 2.1 5 DIRAMS
2.00 g., Brass Clad Steel, 16.5 mm. **Obv:** Crown within 1/2 star border **Rev:** Small value within design **Edge:** Plain

Date	Mintage	F12	VF20	XF40	MS60	MS63
2001(sp)	—	—	—	—	0.50	0.75
2001(sp)	—	PF63 2.50				

KM# 2.2 5 DIRAMS
2.00 g., Brass Clad Steel, 16.5 mm. **Obv:** Crown with 1/2 star border **Rev:** Large value within design

Date	Mintage	F12	VF20	XF40	MS60	MS63
2006(sp)	—	—	—	—	0.75	1.25

KM# 23 5 DIRAMS
2.00 g., Copper Plated Steel, 18 mm. **Obv:** Coat of arms **Rev:** Large value with design

Date	Mintage	F12	VF20	XF40	MS60	MS63
2011	—	—	—	—	0.50	0.75

KM# 3.1 10 DIRAMS
2.40 g., Brass Clad Steel, 17.5 mm. **Obv:** Crown within 1/2 star border **Rev:** Small value within design **Edge:** Plain

Date	Mintage	F12	VF20	XF40	MS60	MS63
2001(sp)	—	—	—	—	0.75	1.00
2001(sp)	—	PF63 3.00				

KM# 3.2 10 DIRAMS
2.40 g., Brass Clad Steel, 17.5 mm. **Obv:** Crown within 1/2 star border **Rev:** Large value within design

Date	Mintage	F12	VF20	XF40	MS60	MS63
2006(sp)	—	—	—	—	1.00	1.50

KM# 24 10 DIRAMS
3.00 g., Copper Plated Steel, 20.5 mm. **Obv:** Coat of arms **Rev:** Large value with design

Date	Mintage	F12	VF20	XF40	MS60	MS63
2011	—	—	—	—	1.00	1.50

KM# 4.1 20 DIRAMS
2.70 g., Brass Clad Steel, 18.5 mm. **Obv:** Crown within 1/2 star border **Rev:** Small value within design **Edge:** Plain

Date	Mintage	F12	VF20	XF40	MS60	MS63
2001(sp)	—	—	—	—	1.00	1.25
2001(sp)	—	PF63 3.75				

KM# 5.1 25 DIRAMS
2.80 g., Brass, 19.1 mm. **Obv:** Crown within 1/2 star border **Rev:** Small value within design **Edge:** Plain

Date	Mintage	F12	VF20	XF40	MS60	MS63
2001(sp)	—	—	—	—	1.50	1.75
2001(sp)	—	PF63 5.00				

KM# 4.2 20 DIRAMS
2.70 g., Brass Clad Steel, 18.5 mm. **Obv:** Crown within 1/2 star border **Rev:** Large value within design

Date	Mintage	F12	VF20	XF40	MS60	MS63
2006(sp)	—	—	—	—	1.50	2.00

KM# 5.2 25 DIRAMS
2.80 g., Brass, 19.1 mm. **Obv:** Crown within 1/2 star border **Rev:** Large value within design

Date	Mintage	F12	VF20	XF40	MS60	MS63
2006(sp)	—	—	—	—	1.75	2.50

KM# 5.2a 25 DIRAMS
2.80 g., Brass Plated Steel, 19.1 mm. **Obv:** Crown within 1/2 star border **Rev:** Large value within design **Edge:** Reeded

Date	Mintage	F12	VF20	XF40	MS60	MS63
2006	—	—	—	—	2.00	3.00

KM# 25 20 DIRAMS
4.50 g., Copper Plated Steel **Obv:** Coat of arms **Rev:** Large value with design **Edge:** Reeded

Date	Mintage	F12	VF20	XF40	MS60	MS63
2011	—	—	—	—	1.50	2.00

KM# 6.1 50 DIRAMS
3.55 g., Brass, 21 mm. **Obv:** Crown within 1/2 star border **Rev:** Value within design **Edge:** Plain

Date	Mintage	F12	VF20	XF40	MS60	MS63
2001(sp)	—	—	—	—	2.00	3.00
2001(sp)	—	PF63 7.00				

KM# 6.2 50 DIRAMS
3.55 g., Brass, 21 mm. **Obv:** Crown within 1/2 star border **Rev:** Large value within design

Date	Mintage	F12	VF20	XF40	MS60	MS63
2006(sp)	—	—	—	—	2.00	3.00

KM# 6.2a 50 DIRAMS
3.55 g., Brass Plated Steel, 21 mm. **Obv:** Crown within 1/2 star border **Rev:** Large value within design **Edge:** Reeded

Date	Mintage	F12	VF20	XF40	MS60	MS63
2006	—	—	—	—	2.00	3.00

KM# 26 50 DIRAMS
5.50 g., Copper Plated Steel, 26 mm. **Obv:** Coat of arms **Rev:** Large value with design **Edge:** Reeded

Date	Mintage	F12	VF20	XF40	MS60	MS63
2011	—	—	—	—	2.00	3.00

KM# 7 SOMONI
5.15 g., Copper-Nickel-Zinc, 23.9 mm. **Obv:** King's bust 1/2 right **Rev:** Value **Edge:** Segmented reeding

Date	Mintage	F12	VF20	XF40	MS60	MS63
2001(sp)	—	—	—	—	3.50	5.00
2001(sp)	—	PF63 12.00				

KM# 12 SOMONI
5.21 g., Copper-Nickel-Zinc, 24 mm. **Subject:** Year of Aryan Civilization **Obv:** National arms above value **Rev:** Ancient archer in war chariot **Edge:** Segmented reeding

Date	Mintage	F12	VF20	XF40	MS60	MS63
2006(sp)	100,000	—	—	—	3.50	5.00

KM# 13 SOMONI
5.21 g., Copper-Nickel-Zinc, 24 mm. **Subject:** Year of Aryan Civilization **Obv:** National arms above value **Rev:** Two busts left **Edge:** Segmented reeding

Date	Mintage	F12	VF20	XF40	MS60	MS63
2006(sp)	100,000	—	—	—	3.50	5.00

KM# 18 SOMONI
20.00 g., 0.925 Silver 0.591 oz. ASW, 35 mm. **Subject:** Year of Aryan Civilization **Obv:** National arms above value **Rev:** Two busts left **Edge:** Segmented reeding

Date	Mintage	F12	VF20	XF40	MS60	MS63
2006	1,500	PF65 60.00				

KM# 19 SOMONI
20.00 g., 0.925 Silver 0.591 oz. ASW, 35 mm. **Subject:** Year of Aryan Civilization **Rev:** Ancient archer in war chariot **Edge:** Segmented reeding

Date	Mintage	F12	VF20	XF40	MS60	MS63
2006(sp)	1,500	PF65 60.00				

KM# 16 SOMONI
5.24 g., Copper-Nickel-Zinc, 24 mm. **Subject:** Jaloliddini Rumi, 800th Anniversary of Birth **Obv:** Small arms above value in cartouche **Rev:** 1/2 length figure facing **Edge:** Segmented reeding

Date	Mintage	F12	VF20	XF40	MS60	MS63
2007	—	—	—	—	3.50	5.00

KM# 33 SOMONI
20.00 g., 0.925 Silver 0.591 oz. ASW, 35 mm. **Subject:** Abu Abdullah al Rudaki

Date	Mintage	F12	VF20	XF40	MS60	MS63
2007	1,000	PF65 65.00				

KM# 27 SOMONI
5.20 g., Copper-Nickel Plated Steel, 27 mm. **Obv:** Coat of arms **Rev:** Large value with design

Date	Mintage	F12	VF20	XF40	MS60	MS63
2011	—	—	—	—	3.50	5.00

KM# 8 3 SOMONI
6.30 g., Copper-Nickel-Zinc, 25.5 mm. **Obv:** National arms **Rev:** Crown above value within design **Edge:** Lettered

Date	Mintage	F12	VF20	XF40	MS60	MS63
2001(sp)	—	—	—	—	5.00	7.00
2001(sp)	—	PF63 18.00				

KM# 10 3 SOMONI
6.30 g., Bi-Metallic, 25.5 mm. **Subject:** 80th Year - Dushanbe City **Obv:** Value below arms within circle **Rev:** Statue in arch within circle

Date	Mintage	F12	VF20	XF40	MS60	MS63
2004(sp)	—	—	—	—	6.50	9.00

KM# 10a 3 SOMONI
6.98 g., 0.925 Silver 0.2062 oz. ASW, 25.5 mm. **Subject:** 80th Anniversary of Republic **Obv:** Value below arms within circle **Rev:** Statue in arch within circle

Date	Mintage	F12	VF20	XF40	MS60	MS63
2004	1,000	PF65 75.00				

KM# 14 3 SOMONI
6.30 g., Bi-Metallic, 25.5 mm. **Subject:** 2700th Anniversary of Kulyab **Obv:** National arms above value **Rev:** Kulyab city arms **Edge:** Lettered

Date	Mintage	F12	VF20	XF40	MS60	MS63
2006(sp)	100,000	—	—	—	6.00	7.50

KM# 20 3 SOMONI
26.00 g., 0.925 Silver 0.7682 oz. ASW, 39 mm. **Subject:** 2700th Anniversary of Kulyab **Obv:** National arms above value **Rev:** Kulyab city arms

Date	Mintage	F12	VF20	XF40	MS60	MS63
2006(sp)	2,000	PF65 70.00				

KM# 9 5 SOMONI
7.10 g., Copper-Nickel-Zinc, 26.5 mm. **Obv:** Turbaned head right **Rev:** Crown above value within design **Edge:** Segmented reeding with a star

Date	Mintage	F12	VF20	XF40	MS60	MS63
2001(sp)	—	—	—	—	7.50	9.00
2001(sp)	—	PF63 25.00				

KM# 11 5 SOMONI
6.95 g., Bi-Metallic, 26.5 mm. **Subject:** Constitution, 10th Anniversary **Obv:** Arms above value within circle **Rev:** Flag and book within circle **Edge:** Lettered

Date	Mintage	F12	VF20	XF40	MS60	MS63
2004(sp)	—	—	—	—	7.50	10.00

KM# 11a 5 SOMONI
8.55 g., 0.925 Silver 0.2526 oz. ASW, 26.5 mm. **Subject:** 10th Anniversary - Constitution **Obv:** Arms above value within circle **Rev:** Flag and book within circle

Date	Mintage	F12	VF20	XF40	MS60	MS63
2004	2,000	PF65 65.00				

KM# 15 5 SOMONI
7.00 g., Bi-Metallic, 26.5 mm. **Subject:** 15th Anniversary of Independence **Obv:** National arms above value **Rev:** Government building **Edge:** Lettered

Date	Mintage	F12	VF20	XF40	MS60	MS63
2006(sp)	100,000	—	—	—	7.50	10.00

KM# 21 5 SOMONI
34.00 g., 0.925 Silver 1.0046 oz. ASW, 42 mm. **Subject:** 15th Anniversary of Independence **Obv:** National arms above value **Rev:** Government building

Date	Mintage	F12	VF20	XF40	MS60	MS63
2006(sp)	2,000	PF65 75.00				

KM# 17 5 SOMONI
7.00 g., Bi-Metallic, 26.5 mm. **Subject:** 1150th Anniversary founding of Persian (Tajik) literature by Abuabdullo Rudaki **Obv:** National arms above value **Rev:** Bust of Rudaki left, scroll, feather pen

Date	Mintage	F12	VF20	XF40	MS60	MS63
2008	—	—	—	—	7.50	10.00

KM# 22 5 SOMONI
34.00 g., 0.925 Silver 1.0046 oz. ASW, 42 mm. **Subject:** 1150 Anniversary founding of Persian Literature by Abuabdullo Rudaki **Obv:** National arms above value **Rev:** Bust of Rudaki left, scroll, feather pen

Date	Mintage	F12	VF20	XF40	MS60	MS63
2008(sp)	1,000	PF65 115				

KM# 34 5 SOMONI
31.10 g., 0.925 Silver 0.9109 oz. ASW, 38.61 mm. **Subject:** Eurasian Economic Community Capital **Obv:** National arms in color **Rev:** Ismoil Somonj

Date	Mintage	F12	VF20	XF40	MS60	MS63
2010	2,000	PF65 135				

KM# 30 50 SOMONI
10.00 g., 0.900 Gold 0.2875 oz. AGW, 24 mm. **Obv:** State Coat of arms **Rev:** Parliament building

Date	Mintage	G4	VG8	F12	VF20	XF40
2006	2,000	PF65 800				

KM# 28 50 SOMONI
28.28 g., 0.925 Silver 0.8356 oz. ASW, 38.61 mm. **Subject:** 20 Years of Independence **Obv:** Colorized flag and arms **Rev:** Building

Date	Mintage	F12	VF20	XF40	MS60	MS63
2011	—	PF65 125				

KM# 31 100 SOMONI
15.00 g., 0.900 Gold 0.4312 oz. AGW, 28 mm. **Obv:** National arms **Rev:** Parliament building

Date	Mintage	G4	VG8	F12	VF20	XF40
2006	2,000	PF65 1,000				

KM# 29 100 SOMONI
31.10 g., 0.925 Silver 0.9189 oz. ASW, 38.61 mm. **Subject:** 20th Anniversary of the C.I.S. **Obv:** Emblem, colored dot **Rev:** Map and colored flag

Date	Mintage	F12	VF20	XF40	MS60	MS63
2011 Proof	Est. 1000	—	—	—	—	—

KM# 32 200 SOMONI
25.00 g., 0.900 Gold 0.7187 oz. AGW, 32 mm. **Obv:** National arms **Rev:** Parliament building

Date	Mintage	F12	VF20	XF40	MS60	MS63
2006	2,000	PF65 1,600				

MINT SETS

KM#	Date	Mintage	Identification	Issue Price	Mkt Val
MS1	2001 (8)	—	KM#2.1-6.1, 7-9	—	30.00

PROOF SETS

KM#	Date	Mintage	Identification	Issue Price	Mkt Val
PS1	2001 (8)	—	KM#2.1-6.1, 7-9	—	80.00

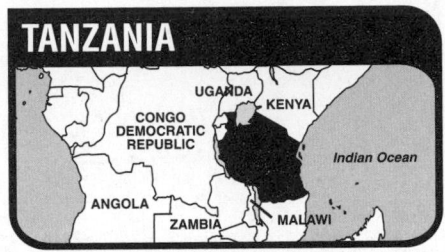

The United Republic of Tanzania, located on the east coast of Africa between Kenya and Mozambique, consists of Tanganyika and the islands of Zanzibar and Pemba. It has an area of 364,900 sq. mi. (945,090 sq. km.) and a population of *25.2 million. Capital: Dodoma. The chief exports are cotton, coffee, diamonds, sisal, cloves, petroleum products, and cashew nuts.

Tanzania is a member of the Commonwealth of Nations. The President is Chief of State.

REPUBLIC

STANDARD COINAGE
100 Senti = 1 Shilingi

KM# 33 50 SHILINGI
7.91 g., Brass Plated Steel, 22 mm. **Subject:** Conservation **Obv:** Head of Ali Nassan Mwinyi right within circle **Rev:** Mother rhinoceros and calf **Shape:** 7-sided

Date	Mintage	F12	VF20	XF40	MS60	MS63
2012	—	—	—	—	2.00	3.00

KM# 32 100 SHILINGI
9.00 g., Brass Plated Steel, 24.5 mm. **Subject:** Conservation **Obv:** Bust of President J.K. Nyerere left **Rev:** Four Impalas running right **Edge:** Reeded

Date	Mintage	F12	VF20	XF40	MS60	MS63
2012	—	—	—	—	3.00	4.00

KM# 34 200 SHILINGI
8.00 g., Copper-Nickel-Zinc **Obv:** Head of Sheikh Karume 1/4 left within circle **Rev:** Two lions **Edge:** Segmented reeding

Date	Mintage	F12	VF20	XF40	MS60	MS63
2008	—	—	—	—	6.00	9.00

KM# 56 500 SHILLINGS
31.46 g., 0.925 Silver 0.9296 oz. ASW, 38.6 mm. **Obv:** Arms with supporters above value **Rev:** African dhow **Edge:** Reeded

Date	Mintage	F12	VF20	XF40	MS60	MS63
2001	—	PF63 45.00	PF65 50.00			

THAILAND

The Kingdom of Thailand (formerly Siam), a constitutional monarchy located in the center of mainland Southeast Asia between Burma and Laos, has an area of 198,457 sq. mi. (514,000 sq. km.) and a population of *55.5 million. Capital: Bangkok. The economy is based on agriculture and mining. Rubber, rice, teakwood, tin and tungsten are exported.

The history of The Kingdom of Siam, the only country in south and Southeast Asia that was never colonized by a European power, dates from the 6th century A.D. when Thai people started to migrate into the area, a process that accelerated with the Mongol invasion of China in the 13th century. After 400 years of sporadic warfare with the neighboring Burmese, King Taskin won the last battle in 1767. He founded a new capital, Dhonburi, on the west bank of the Chao Praya River. King Rama I moved the capital to Bangkok in 1782, thus initiating the so-called Bangkok Period of Siamese coinage characterized by Pot Duang money (bullet coins) stamped with regal symbols.

The Portuguese, who were followed by the Dutch, British and French, introduced the Thai to the Western world. Rama III of the present ruling dynasty negotiated a treaty of friendship and commerce with Britain in 1826, and in 1896 the independence of the kingdom was guaranteed by an Anglo-French accord.

In 1909 Siam ceded to Great Britain its suzerain rights over the dependencies of Kedah, Kelantan, Trengganu and Perlis, Malay states situated in southern Siam just north of British Malaya, which eliminated any British jurisdiction in Siam proper.

The absolute monarchy was changed into a constitutional monarchy in 1932.

On Dec. 8, 1941, after five hours of fighting, Thailand agreed to permit Japanese troops passage through the country to invade Northern British Malaysia. This eventually led to increased Japanese intervention and finally occupation of the country. On Jan. 25, 1942, Thailand declared war on Great Britain and the United States. A free Thai guerilla movement was soon organized to counteract the Japanese. In July 1943 Japan transferred the four northern Malay States back to Thailand. These were returned to Great Britain after peace treaties were signed in 1946.

DATING

Typical BE Dating

1 2 3 8   1 2 4 4

Typical CS Dating

NOTE: Sometimes the era designator *BE* or *CS* will actually appear on the coin itself.

DENOMINATION

2 ½
2-1/2 (Satang)   RS Dating

DATE CONVERSION TABLES

B.E. date - 543 = A.D. date
Ex: 2516 - 543 = 1973
R.S. date + 1781 = A.D. date
Ex: 127 + 1781 = 1908
C.S. date + 638 = A.D. date
Ex 1238 + 638 = 1876

Primary denominations used were 1 Baht, 1/4 and 1/8 Baht up to the reign of Rama IV. Other denominations are much scarcer.

KINGDOM OF THAILAND

DECIMAL COINAGE

25 Satang = 1 Salung; 100 Satang = 1 Baht

Y# 186 SATANG

0.50 g., Aluminum, 14.58 mm. **Ruler:** Rama IX **Obv:** Head left **Rev:** Haripunchai Temple, Lumpoon province **Edge:** Plain

Date	Mintage	F12	VF20	XF40	MS60	MS63
BE2544 (2001)	50,000	—	—	—	0.75	1.00
BE2545 (2002)	—	—	—	—	1.50	2.00
BE2546 (2003)	10,000	—	—	—	1.50	2.00
BE2547 (2004)	20,000	—	—	—	1.25	1.75
BE2548 (2005)	10,000	—	—	—	1.50	2.00
BE2549 (2006)	3,000	—	—	—	3.00	4.00
BE2550 (2007)	10,000	—	—	—	1.50	2.00

Y# 456 SATANG

0.50 g., Aluminum, 15 mm. **Ruler:** Rama IX **Obv:** Bust left **Rev:** Haripunchai Temple, Lumpoon province

Date	Mintage	F12	VF20	XF40	MS60	MS63
BE2551 (2008)	—	—	—	—	1.50	2.00
BE2552 (2009)	10,000	—	—	—	1.50	2.00
BE2553 (2010)	10,000	—	—	—	1.50	2.00

Y# 208 5 SATANG

0.60 g., Aluminum, 16 mm. **Ruler:** Rama IX **Obv:** Bust left **Rev:** Phra Patom Temple, Nakhon Pathom province **Edge:** Plain

Date	Mintage	F12	VF20	XF40	MS60	MS63
BE2544 (2001)	50,000	—	—	—	1.00	1.25
BE2546 (2003)	10,000	—	—	—	2.00	2.50
BE2547 (2004)	10,000	—	—	—	2.00	2.50
BE2548 (2005)	20,000	—	—	—	1.25	1.50
BE2549 (2006)	3,000	—	—	—	3.00	4.00
BE2550 (2007)	10,000	—	—	—	2.00	2.50

Y# 457 5 SATANG

0.60 g., Aluminum, 16.5 mm. **Ruler:** Rama IX **Obv:** Bust left **Rev:** Phra Patom Temple, Nakhon Pathom province

Date	Mintage	F12	VF20	XF40	MS60	MS63
BE2551 (2008)	10,000	—	—	—	2.00	2.50
BE2552 (2009)	10,000	—	—	—	2.00	2.50
BE2553 (2010)	10,000	—	—	—	2.00	2.50

Y# 209 10 SATANG

0.80 g., Aluminum, 17.5 mm. **Ruler:** Rama IX **Obv:** Young bust left **Rev:** Phra Tat Chungchum Temple, Sakon Nakhon province **Edge:** Plain

Date	Mintage	F12	VF20	XF40	MS60	MS63
BE2544 (2001)	50,000	—	—	—	1.00	1.50
BE2545 (2002)	—	—	—	—	2.00	2.50
BE2546 (2003)	10,000	—	—	1.00	2.00	2.50
BE2547 (2004)	20,000	—	—	0.75	1.75	
BE2548 (2005)	10,000	—	—	1.00	2.00	2.50
BE2549 (2006)	3,000	—	—	2.00	4.00	5.00
BE2550 (2007)	10,000	—	—	1.00	2.00	2.50

Y# 458 10 SATANG

0.80 g., Aluminum, 17.5 mm. **Ruler:** Rama IX **Obv:** Bust left **Rev:** Phra Tat Chungchum Temple, Sakon Nakhon province

Date	Mintage	F12	VF20	XF40	MS60	MS63
BE2551 (2008)	—	—	—	1.00	2.00	2.50
BE2552 (2009)	10,000	—	—	1.00	2.00	2.50
BE2553 (2010)	10,000	—	—	1.00	2.00	2.50

Y# 187 25 SATANG = 1/4 BAHT

1.90 g., Aluminum-Bronze, 16 mm. **Ruler:** Rama IX **Obv:** Head left **Rev:** Mahathat Temple, Nakhon Si Thammarat province **Edge:** Reeded

Date	Mintage	F12	VF20	XF40	MS60	MS63
BE2544 (2001)	10,000	1.00	2.00	3.00	5.00	6.00
BE2545 (2002)	141,562,000	1.00	2.00	3.00	5.00	6.00
BE2546 (2003)	82,668,000	—	—	—	0.10	0.15
BE2547 (2004)	104,830,000	—	—	—	0.10	0.15
BE2548 (2005)	95,362,000	—	—	—	0.10	0.15
BE2549 (2006)	120,003,000	—	—	—	0.10	0.15
BE2550 (2007)r	180,000,000	—	—	—	0.10	0.15
BE2551 (2008)r	255,600	—	0.50	0.75	1.00	1.50
BE2552 (2009)	30,000	1.00	2.00	3.00	5.00	6.00

Y# 441 25 SATANG = 1/4 BAHT

1.90 g., Copper Plated Steel, 16 mm. **Ruler:** Rama IX **Obv:** King's portrait **Rev:** Mahathat Temple, Nakhon Si Thammarat province

Date	Mintage	F12	VF20	XF40	MS60	MS63
BE2552 (2009)v	289,995,600	—	—	—	0.10	0.15
BE2553 (2010)v	220,000,000	—	—	—	0.10	0.15
BE2554 (2011)v	—	—	—	—	0.10	0.15
BE2555 (2012)v	—	—	—	—	0.10	0.15

Y# 203 50 SATANG = 1/2 BAHT

2.40 g., Aluminum-Bronze, 18 mm. **Ruler:** Rama IX **Obv:** Head left **Rev:** Soi Suthep Temple, Chiang Mai province

Date	Mintage	F12	VF20	XF40	MS60	MS63
BE2544 (2001)	52,738,000	—	—	—	0.10	0.15
BE2545 (2002)	102,804,000	—	—	—	0.10	0.15
BE2546 (2003)	101,200,000	—	—	—	0.10	0.15
BE2547 (2004)	79,596,000	—	—	—	0.10	0.15
BE2548 (2005)	99,920,000	—	—	—	0.10	0.15
BE2549 (2006)	130,803,000	—	—	—	0.10	0.15
BE2550 (2007)	24,905,000	—	—	—	0.10	0.15
BE2551 (2008)	27,163,509	—	—	—	0.10	0.15

Y# 442 50 SATANG = 1/2 BAHT
2.40 g., Copper Plated Steel, 18 mm. **Ruler:** Rama IX **Obv:** King's portrait **Rev:** Doi Suthep Temple, Chiang Mai province

Date	Mintage	F12	VF20	XF40	MS60	MS63
BE2552 (2009)v	225,000,000	—	—	—	0.10	0.15
BE2553 (2010)v	118,536,000	—	—	—	0.10	0.15
BE2554 (2011)v	—	—	—	—	0.10	0.15
BE2555 (2012)	—	—	—	—	0.10	0.15

Y# 183 BAHT
3.45 g., Copper-Nickel, 20 mm. **Ruler:** Rama IX **Obv:** Head left **Rev:** Phra Kaew Temple, Bangkok **Edge:** Reeded **Note:** Varieties exist.

Date	Mintage	F12	VF20	XF40	MS60	MS63
BE2544 (2001)	385,140,000	—	—	—	0.10	0.15
BE2545 (2002)	266,025,000	—	—	—	0.10	0.15
BE2546 (2003)	236,533,000	—	—	—	0.10	0.15
BE2547 (2004)	903,964,000	—	—	—	0.10	0.15
BE2548 (2005) wg	1,137,820,000	—	—	—	0.10	0.15
BE2549 (2006)v	778,061,000	—	—	—	0.10	0.15
BE2550 (2007) wg	614,866,877	—	—	—	0.10	0.15
BE2551 (2008)	660,307,123	—	—	—	0.10	0.15

Y# 443 BAHT
3.00 g., Nickel Plated Steel, 20 mm. **Ruler:** Rama IX **Obv:** King's portrait **Rev:** Phra Kaew Temple, Bangkok **Edge:** Reeded

Date	Mintage	F12	VF20	XF40	MS60	MS63
BE2552 (2009)v	507,250,000	—	—	—	0.10	0.15
BE2553 (2010)v	551,853,000	—	—	—	0.10	0.15
BE2554 (2011)v	—	—	—	—	0.10	0.15
BE2555 (2012)v	—	—	—	—	0.10	0.15
BE2556-2013	—	—	—	—	0.10	0.15

Y# 444 2 BAHT
4.40 g., Nickel Plated Steel, 21.75 mm. **Ruler:** Rama IX **Obv:** King's portrait **Rev:** Saket Temple, Bangkok

Date	Mintage	F12	VF20	XF40	MS60	MS63
BE2548 (2005) wg	60,000	—	—	—	0.20	0.25
BE2549 (2006) wg	107,872,500	—	—	—	0.20	0.25
BE2550 (2007) wg	232,105,100	—	—	—	0.20	0.25
BE2552 (2009)	50,370	—	—	2.00	4.00	6.00

Y# 445 2 BAHT
4.00 g., Aluminum-Bronze, 21.75 mm. **Ruler:** Rama IX **Obv:** King's portrait **Rev:** Saket Temple, Bangkok

Date	Mintage	F12	VF20	XF40	MS60	MS63
BE2551 (2008)	10,004,000	—	—	0.15	0.30	0.40
BE2552 (2009)	244,741,000	—	—	—	0.20	0.25
BE2553 (2010)	137,228,000	—	—	—	0.20	0.25
BE2554 (2011)	—	—	—	—	0.20	0.25
BE2555 (2012)	—	—	—	—	0.20	0.25
BE2556-2013	—	—	—	—	0.20	0.25

Y# 219 5 BAHT
7.50 g., Copper-Nickel Clad Copper, 24 mm. **Ruler:** Rama IX **Obv:** Head left **Rev:** Benchamabophit Temple, Bangkok **Edge:** Coarse reeding

Date	Mintage	F12	VF20	XF40	MS60	MS63
BE2544 (2001)	76,566,000	—	—	—	0.50	0.75
BE2545 (2002)	29,601,500	—	—	—	0.75	1.00
BE2546 (2003)	182,000	3.00	5.00	8.00	15.00	20.00
BE2547 (2004)	120,187,000	—	—	—	0.50	0.75
BE2548 (2005)	91,079,000	—	—	—	0.50	0.75
BE2549 (2006)	254,403,000	—	—	—	0.50	0.75
BE2550 (2007)dj	131,126,000	—	—	—	0.50	0.75
BE2551 (2008)	220,463,200	—	—	—	0.50	0.75

Y# 446 5 BAHT
6.00 g., Copper-Nickel Clad Copper, 24 mm. **Ruler:** Rama IX **Obv:** King's portrait **Rev:** Benchamabophit Temp, Bangkok, Temple top does not break legend **Edge:** Coarse Reeding

Date	Mintage	F12	VF20	XF40	MS60	MS63
BE2551 (2008)	6,225,000	—	—	—	0.75	1.00
BE2552 (2009)	308,283,000	—	—	—	0.50	0.75
BE2553 (2010)	2,903,000	—	—	—	1.00	1.25
BE2554 (2011)	—	—	—	—	0.50	0.75
BE2555 (2012)	—	—	—	—	0.50	0.75

Y# 227 10 BAHT
8.50 g., Bi-Metallic, 26 mm. **Ruler:** Rama IX **Obv:** Head left within circle **Rev:** Arun Temple (Temple of the Dawn), Bankok **Edge:** Segmented reeding **Note:** Varieties exist.

Date	Mintage	F12	VF20	XF40	MS60	MS63
BE2544 (2001)	2,060,000	—	0.75	2.00	5.00	6.00
BE2545 (2002)	61,333,000	—	—	—	2.25	2.75
BE2546 (2003)	49,292,000	—	—	—	2.25	2.75
BE2547 (2004)	62,689,000	—	—	—	2.25	2.50
BE2548 (2005)	111,491,000	—	—	—	2.00	2.50
BE2549 (2006)v	128,903,000	—	—	—	2.00	2.50
BE2550 (2007)v	130,202,000	—	—	—	2.00	2.50
BE2551 (2008)	179,165,360	—	—	—	2.00	2.50

Y# 373 10 BAHT
8.50 g., Bi-Metallic, 26 mm. **Ruler:** Rama IX **Subject:** Department of Lands, 100th Anniversary, February 17 **Obv:** Conjoined busts facing divides circle **Rev:** Department seal within circle **Edge:** Segmented reeding

Date	Mintage	F12	VF20	XF40	MS60	MS63
BE2544 (2001)	3,000,000	—	—	1.00	2.50	3.00

Y# 381 10 BAHT
8.50 g., Bi-Metallic, 26 mm. **Ruler:** Rama IX **Subject:** Irrigation Department, 100th Anniversary, June 13 **Obv:** Conjoined busts facing divides circle **Rev:** Department logo **Edge:** Segmented reeding

Date	Mintage	F12	VF20	XF40	MS60	MS63
BE2545 (2002)	3,000,000	—	—	1.00	2.00	2.75

Y# 382 10 BAHT
8.50 g., Bi-Metallic, 26 mm. **Ruler:** Rama IX **Subject:** Department of Internal Trade, 60th Anniversary May 5 **Obv:** Head left **Rev:** Department logo **Edge:** Segmented reeding

Date	Mintage	F12	VF20	XF40	MS60	MS63
BE2545 (2002)	3,000,000	—	—	1.00	2.00	2.75

Y# 383 10 BAHT
8.50 g., Bi-Metallic, 26 mm. **Ruler:** Rama IX **Subject:** Highway Department, 90th Anniversary, April 1 **Obv:** Conjoined busts facing divides circle **Rev:** Highway Department logo **Edge:** Segmented reeding

Date	Mintage	F12	VF20	XF40	MS60	MS63
BE2545 (2002)	3,000,000	—	—	1.00	2.00	2.75

Y# 384 10 BAHT
8.50 g., Bi-Metallic, 26 mm. **Ruler:** Rama IX **Subject:** Vajira Medical Center, 90th Anniversary, January 2 **Obv:** Conjoined busts facing divides circle **Rev:** Hospital logo **Edge:** Segmented reeding

Date	Mintage	F12	VF20	XF40	MS60	MS63
BE2545 (2002)	3,500,000	—	—	1.00	2.00	2.75

Y# 387 10 BAHT
8.50 g., Bi-Metallic, 26 mm. **Ruler:** Rama IX **Subject:** King's 75th Birthday, December 5 **Obv:** Head left **Rev:** Royal crown in radiant oval **Edge:** Segmented reeding

Date	Mintage	F12	VF20	XF40	MS60	MS63
BE2545 (2002)	7,500,000	—	—	1.00	2.00	2.75

Y# 385 10 BAHT
8.50 g., Bi-Metallic, 26 mm. **Ruler:** Rama IX **Subject:** 20th World Scouting Jamboree **Obv:** Rama IX wearing a scouting uniform **Rev:** Jamboree log **Edge:** Segmented reeding

Date	Mintage	F12	VF20	XF40	MS60	MS63
BE2546 (2003)	3,000,000	—	—	1.00	2.00	2.75

Y# 400 10 BAHT
8.50 g., Bi-Metallic, 26 mm. **Ruler:** Rama IX **Subject:** APEC 2003 Summit **Obv:** Head left **Rev:** APEC logo **Edge:** Segmented reeding

Date	Mintage	F12	VF20	XF40	MS60	MS63
BE2546-2003	1,000,000	—	—	1.00	2.25	3.00

Y# 405 10 BAHT
8.50 g., Bi-Metallic, 26 mm. **Ruler:** Rama IX **Subject:** CITES World Meeting **Obv:** Bust 3/4 left within circle **Rev:** CITES logo **Edge:** Segmented reeding

Date	Mintage	F12	VF20	XF40	MS60	MS63
ND-2003	—	—	—	1.00	2.00	2.75

Y# 409 10 BAHT
8.50 g., Bi-Metallic, 26 mm. **Ruler:** Rama IX **Subject:** King Rama V, 150th Anniversary **Obv:** Bust of Rama V left **Rev:** Royal crown **Edge:** Segmented reeding

Date	Mintage	F12	VF20	XF40	MS60	MS63
BE2546 (2003)	3,600,000	—	—	1.00	1.80	2.50

Y# 391 10 BAHT
8.50 g., Bi-Metallic, 26 mm. **Ruler:** Rama IX **Subject:** Inspector General's Department, 100th Anniversary, May 6 **Obv:** Head

left within circle **Rev:** Department seal within circle and design **Edge:** Segmented reeding

Date	Mintage	F12	VF20	XF40	MS60	MS63
BE2546 (2003)	3,000,000	—	—	1.00	1.75	2.50

Y# 392 10 BAHT
8.50 g., Bi-Metallic, 26 mm. **Ruler:** Rama IX **Subject:** Princess Galaniwattana, 80th Birthday, May 6 **Obv:** Bust 1/4 right **Rev:** Crowned emblem and value **Edge:** Alternating reeded and plain **Note:** This is the king's sister.

Date	Mintage	F12	VF20	XF40	MS60	MS63
BE2546 (2003)	2,000,000	—	—	1.00	1.75	2.50

Y# 396 10 BAHT
8.50 g., Bi-Metallic, 26 mm. **Ruler:** Rama IX **Subject:** Government Savings Bank, 90th Anniversary, April 1 **Obv:** Uniformed bust facing within circle **Rev:** Bank emblem **Edge:** Segmented reeding

Date	Mintage	F12	VF20	XF40	MS60	MS63
BE2546 (2003)	2,000,000	—	—	1.00	2.00	2.75

Y# 410 10 BAHT
8.50 g., Bi-Metallic, 26 mm. **Subject:** Thammasat University, 70th Anniversary **Obv:** Civilian bust 3/4 left **Rev:** Thammasat University seal **Edge:** Segmented reeding

Date	Mintage	F12	VF20	XF40	MS60	MS63
BE2547 (2004)	3,000,000	—	—	1.00	1.80	2.50

Y# 411 10 BAHT
8.50 g., Bi-Metallic, 26 mm. **Ruler:** Rama IX **Subject:** Royal Institute Board, 70th Anniversary **Obv:** 1/2 length civilian busts of 2 kings facing **Rev:** Royal Scholar Institute seal **Edge:** Segmented reeding

Date	Mintage	F12	VF20	XF40	MS60	MS63
BE2547 (2004)	2,000,000	—	—	1.00	1.80	2.50

Y# 412 10 BAHT
8.50 g., Bi-Metallic, 26 mm. **Ruler:** Rama IX **Subject:** Queen's 72nd Birthday **Obv:** Bust of queen facing 3/4 left **Rev:** Royal seal **Edge:** Segmented reeding

Date	Mintage	F12	VF20	XF40	MS60	MS63
BE2547 (2004)	6,000,000	—	—	1.00	1.80	2.50

Y# 413 10 BAHT
8.50 g., Bi-Metallic, 26 mm. **Ruler:** Rama IX **Subject:** IUCN World Conservation Congress **Obv:** Civilian bust 3/4 right **Rev:** IUCN logo **Edge:** Segmented reeding

Date	Mintage	F12	VF20	XF40	MS60	MS63
BE2547 (2004)	—	—	—	1.00	1.80	2.50

Y# 414 10 BAHT
8.50 g., Bi-Metallic, 26 mm. **Ruler:** Rama IX **Subject:** Anti Drug Campaign **Obv:** Civilian bust left **Rev:** Tear drop shaped logo **Edge:** Segmented reeding

Date	Mintage	F12	VF20	XF40	MS60	MS63
BE2546 (2004)	3,000,000	—	—	—	1.80	2.50

Y# 415 10 BAHT
8.50 g., Bi-Metallic, 26 mm. **Ruler:** Rama IX **Subject:** King Rama IV, 200th Anniversary **Obv:** Bust of Rama IV 3/4 right **Rev:** Royal seal **Edge:** Segmented reeding

Date	Mintage	F12	VF20	XF40	MS60	MS63
BE2547 (2004)	3,500,000	—	—	1.00	1.80	2.50

Y# 402 10 BAHT
8.50 g., Bi-Metallic, 26 mm. **Ruler:** Rama IX **Subject:** Department of the Treasury, 72nd Anniversary **Obv:** Bust 1/4 left within circle **Rev:** Treasury Department seal within circle **Edge:** Segmented reeding

Date	Mintage	F12	VF20	XF40	MS60	MS63
BE2548 (2005)	3,000,000	—	—	1.00	2.50	3.25

Y# 416 10 BAHT
8.50 g., Bi-Metallic, 26 mm. **Ruler:** Rama IX **Subject:** Army Transportation Corp, 100th Anniversary **Obv:** 2 King's military busts left **Rev:** Steering wheel, badge at center **Edge:** Segmented reeding

Date	Mintage	F12	VF20	XF40	MS60	MS63
BE2548 (2005)	3,000,000	—	—	1.00	1.80	2.50

Y# 418 10 BAHT
8.50 g., Bi-Metallic, 26 mm. **Ruler:** Rama IX **Subject:** 25th Asia-Pacific Scout Jamboree **Obv:** Rama IX in scout uniform 3/4 left **Rev:** Logo **Edge:** Segmented reeding

Date	Mintage	F12	VF20	XF40	MS60	MS63
BE2548 (2005)	3,000,000	—	—	1.00	1.80	2.50

Y# 406 10 BAHT
8.50 g., Bi-Metallic, 26 mm. **Ruler:** Rama IX **Subject:** 60th Anniversary of Reign **Obv:** Bust 1/4 left within circle **Rev:** Royal Crown on display **Edge:** Segmented reeding

Date	Mintage	F12	VF20	XF40	MS60	MS63
BE2549 (2006)	16,000,000	—	—	1.00	2.50	3.25

Y# 417 10 BAHT
8.50 g., Bi-Metallic, 26 mm. **Ruler:** Rama IX **Subject:** Princess's Royal Cradle Ceremony **Obv:** Princess's baby head 3/4 left **Rev:** 4-line inscription **Edge:** Segmented reeding

Date	Mintage	F12	VF20	XF40	MS60	MS63
DC2540 (2000)	3,000,000	—	—	1.00	1.80	2.50

Y# 424 10 BAHT
8.50 g., Bi-Metallic, 26 mm. **Ruler:** Rama IX **Subject:** Prince Jaturon Ratsamee, 150th Anniversary of Birth **Obv:** Bust of Prince facing 3/4 right **Rev:** Radiant badge **Edge:** Segmented reeding

Date	Mintage	F12	VF20	XF40	MS60	MS63
BE2549(2006)	—	—	—	1.00	2.50	3.25

Y# 428 10 BAHT
8.50 g., Bi-Metallic, 26 mm. **Ruler:** Rama IX **Subject:** Secretariat of the Cabinet, 72nd Anniversary **Obv:** Military bust 3/4 right **Rev:** Royal Cabinet seal **Edge:** Segmented reeding **Note:** Minted in 2005 but released in 2006.

Date	Mintage	F12	VF20	XF40	MS60	MS63
BE2547 (2004) (2006)	—	—	—	1.00	1.80	2.50

Y# 429 10 BAHT
8.50 g., Bi-Metallic, 26 mm. **Ruler:** Rama IX **Subject:** Princess Petcharat, 80th Birthday **Obv:** Bust of Princess facing **Rev:** Royal seal of Princess **Edge:** Segmented reeding

Date	Mintage	F12	VF20	XF40	MS60	MS63
BE2548 (2006)	1,000,000	—	—	1.25	2.25	2.75

Y# 430 10 BAHT
8.50 g., Bi-Metallic, 26 mm. **Ruler:** Rama IX **Subject:** Budget Inspection Department, 130th Anniversary **Obv:** Conjoined kings' busts left **Rev:** Ornate scale **Edge:** Segmented reeding

Date	Mintage	F12	VF20	XF40	MS60	MS63
BE2548 (2006)	Est. 3000000	—	—	1.00	1.80	2.50

Y# 431 10 BAHT
8.50 g., Bi-Metallic, 26 mm. **Ruler:** Rama IX **Subject:** 60th Anniversary of Reign **Obv:** Bust 3/4 right **Rev:** Royal throne **Edge:** Segmented reeding

Date	Mintage	F12	VF20	XF40	MS60	MS63
BE2549 (2006)	16,000,000	—	—	1.00	1.80	2.50

Y# 432 10 BAHT
8.50 g., Bi-Metallic, 26 mm. **Ruler:** Rama IX **Subject:** Department of Judge Advocate General, 100th Anniversary **Obv:** Conjoined kings' busts left **Rev:** Military emblem with scales of justice in background **Edge:** Segmented reeding

Date	Mintage	F12	VF20	XF40	MS60	MS63
BE2549 (2006)	3,000,000	—	—	1.00	1.80	2.50

Y# 425 10 BAHT
8.50 g., Bi-Metallic, 26 mm. **Ruler:** Rama IX **Subject:** Royal Calvary Division, 100th Anniversary **Obv:** Conjoined kings' busts left **Rev:** Royal crown above emblem **Edge:** Segmented reeding

Date	Mintage	F12	VF20	XF40	MS60	MS63
BE2550 (2007)	3,000,000	—	—	1.00	1.75	2.50

Y# 426 10 BAHT
8.50 g., Bi-Metallic, 26 mm. **Ruler:** Rama IX **Subject:** 1st Thai Commercial Bank, 100th Anniversary **Obv:** Conjoined kings' busts left **Rev:** Garuda Bird **Edge:** Segmented reeding

Date	Mintage	F12	VF20	XF40	MS60	MS63
BE2550 (2007)	5,000,000	—	—	1.00	1.75	2.50

Y# 433 10 BAHT
8.50 g., Bi-Metallic, 26 mm. **Ruler:** Rama IX **Subject:** Queen's WHO Food Safety Award **Obv:** Queen's bust 3/4 right **Rev:** WHO emblem at upper left of inscription in sprays **Edge:** Segmented reeding

Date	Mintage	F12	VF20	XF40	MS60	MS63
BE2550 (2007)	5,000,000	—	—	1.00	1.75	2.50

Y# 434 10 BAHT
8.50 g., Bi-Metallic, 26 mm. **Ruler:** Rama IX **Subject:** Medical Technology Department, 50th Anniversary **Obv:** Robed bust 3/4 right **Rev:** Oval medical seal **Edge:** Segmented reeding

Date	Mintage	F12	VF20	XF40	MS60	MS63
BE2550 (2007)	3,000,000	—	—	1.00	1.75	2.50

Y# 435 10 BAHT
8.50 g., Bi-Metallic, 26 mm. **Ruler:** Rama IX **Subject:** UNIVERSIADE 2007 - World University Games **Obv:** Civilian bust 3/4 right **Rev:** Games logo **Edge:** Segmented reeding

Date	Mintage	F12	VF20	XF40	MS60	MS63
BE2550 (2007)	5,000,000	—	—	1.00	1.75	2.50

Y# 436 10 BAHT
8.50 g., Bi-Metallic, 26 mm. **Ruler:** Rama IX **Subject:** Queen's 75th birthday **Obv:** Bust of Queen wearing tiara 3/4 left **Rev:** Queen's Royal seal **Edge:** Segmented reeding

Date	Mintage	F12	VF20	XF40	MS60	MS63
BE2550 (2007)	7,500,000	—	—	1.00	1.75	2.50

Y# 437 10 BAHT
8.50 g., Bi-Metallic, 26 mm. **Ruler:** Rama IX **Subject:** IAAJS Conference - Bangkok **Obv:** Civilian bust 3/4 left **Rev:** Oval seal with scale above conference logo **Edge:** Segmented reeding

Date	Mintage	F12	VF20	XF40	MS60	MS63
BE2550 (2007)	3,000,000	—	—	1.00	1.75	2.50

Y# 438 10 BAHT
8.50 g., Bi-Metallic, 26 mm. **Ruler:** Rama IX **Subject:** King's 80th birthday **Obv:** Royal bust 3/4 left **Rev:** Royal seal **Edge:** Segmented reeding

Date	Mintage	F12	VF20	XF40	MS60	MS63
BE2550 (2007)	18,000,000	—	—	1.00	1.75	2.50

Y# 439 10 BAHT
8.50 g., Bi-Metallic, 26 mm. **Ruler:** Rama IX **Subject:** 24th SEA Games **Obv:** Civilian bust 3/4 left **Rev:** Games logo above inscription **Edge:** Segmented reeding

Date	Mintage	F12	VF20	XF40	MS60	MS63
BE2550 (2007)	3,000,000	—	—	1.00	1.75	2.50

Y# 440 10 BAHT
8.50 g., Bi-Metallic, 26 mm. **Ruler:** Rama IX **Subject:** Siriraj Hospital, 120th Anniversary **Obv:** Conjoined kings' busts right **Rev:** Royal hospital's seal **Edge:** Segmented reeding

Date	Mintage	F12	VF20	XF40	MS60	MS63
BE2550 (2007)	3,000,000	—	—	1.00	1.75	2.50

Y# 459 10 BAHT
8.50 g., Bi-Metallic, 26 mm. **Ruler:** Rama IX **Obv:** Head left **Rev:** Arun Temple (Temple of the Dawn), Bangkok

Date	Mintage	F12	VF20	XF40	MS60	MS63
BE2551 (2008)	18,450,000	—	—	—	2.00	2.75
BE2552 (2009)	59,107,733	—	—	—	2.00	2.75
BE2553 (2010)	1,953,000	—	—	—	2.00	2.75
BE2554 (2011)		—	—	—	2.00	2.75
BE2555 (2012)		—	—	—	2.00	2.75
BE2556-2013		—	—	—	2.00	2.75

Y# 460 10 BAHT
8.50 g., Bi-Metallic, 26 mm. **Ruler:** Rama IX **Subject:** Thai Postal Service, 125th Anniversary **Obv:** Conjoined busts left **Rev:** Scroll with legend **Edge:** Segmented Reeding

Date	Mintage	F12	VF20	XF40	MS60	MS63
BE2551 (2008)	3,000,000	—	—	1.00	2.00	2.75

Y# 461 10 BAHT
8.50 g., Bi-Metallic, 26 mm. **Ruler:** Rama IX **Subject:** National Research Council, 50th Anniversary **Obv:** Bust left **Rev:** Nucleus surrounded by electrons **Edge:** Segmented Reeding

Date	Mintage	F12	VF20	XF40	MS60	MS63
BE2552 (2009)	3,000,000	—	—	—	2.00	2.75

Y# 486 10 BAHT
8.50 g., Bi-Metallic, 26 mm. **Ruler:** Rama IX **Subject:** Thailand Army School, 100th Anniversary

Date	Mintage	F12	VF20	XF40	MS60	MS63
RS2552 (2009)		—	—	—	3.50	5.00

Y# 488 10 BAHT
8.50 g., Bi-Metallic, 26 mm. **Ruler:** Rama IX **Subject:** Princess Bejaratana, 84th Birthday

Date	Mintage	F12	VF20	XF40	MS60	MS63
RS2552 (2009)	1,000,000	—	—	—	3.50	5.00

Y# 497 10 BAHT
Bi-Metallic, 26 mm. **Ruler:** Rama IX **Subject:** 120th Anniversary of the Department of Finance **Obv:** Conjoined heads facing left **Rev:** Seal of the Department of Finance (bird), inscription, value and date **Edge:** Segmented reeding

Date	Mintage	F12	VF20	XF40	MS60	MS63
BE2553 (2010)	1,000,000	—	—	—	2.00	2.50

Y# 498 10 BAHT
8.50 g., Bi-Metallic, 26 mm. **Ruler:** Rama IX **Subject:** 60th Anniversary of the Office of National Economic and Social Development **Obv:** Head of King Rama IX facing 1/4 right and inscriptions **Rev:** Seal of the Office of National Economic and Social Development (statue of three people), inscription, value and date

Date	Mintage	F12	VF20	XF40	MS60	MS63
BE2553 (2010)		—	—	—	2.00	2.50

Y# 504 10 BAHT
8.50 g., Bi-Metallic, 26 mm. **Ruler:** Rama IX **Subject:** Princess Bejaratana, 84th Birthday **Rev:** Emblem

Date	Mintage	F12	VF20	XF40	MS60	MS63
BE2553 (2010)		—	—	—	2.00	2.75

Y# 516 10 BAHT
8.50 g., Bi-Metallic, 26 mm. **Ruler:** Rama IX **Subject:** Prince Bhanurangsi Savangwongse, 150th Anniversary of Birth

Date	Mintage	F12	VF20	XF40	MS60	MS63
RS2553 (2010)		—	—	—	3.50	5.00

Y# 518 10 BAHT
8.50 g., Bi-Metallic, 26 mm. **Ruler:** Rama IX **Subject:** National Economic and Social Development Board, 60th Anniversary

Date	Mintage	F12	VF20	XF40	MS60	MS63
RS2553 (2010)	1,000,000	—	—	—	3.00	5.00

Y# 519 10 BAHT
8.50 g., Bi-Metallic, 26 mm. **Ruler:** Rama IX **Subject:** Court of Auditors, 120th Anniversary

Date	Mintage	F12	VF20	XF40	MS60	MS63
RS2553 (2010)	1,000,000	—	—	—	3.00	5.00

Y# 508 10 BAHT
8.50 g., Bi-Metallic, 26 mm. **Ruler:** Rama IX **Subject:** 100th Anniversary of the Fine Art Department **Obv:** King Rama VI **Rev:** Ganesha

Date	Mintage	F12	VF20	XF40	MS60	MS63
2012		—	—	—	—	—

Y# 510 10 BAHT
Bi-Metallic **Ruler:** Rama IX **Subject:** 100th Anniversary of the Command and General Staff College, Royal National Army

Date	Mintage	F12	VF20	XF40	MS60	MS63
2012	Est. 3000000					

Y# 374 20 BAHT
15.00 g., Copper-Nickel, 32 mm. **Ruler:** Rama IX **Subject:** Chulalongkorn University 84th Anniversary March 26 **Obv:** Three conjoined busts right **Rev:** University emblem divides value **Edge:** Reeded

Date	Mintage	F12	VF20	XF40	MS60	MS63
BE2544 (2001)	800,040	—	—	2.00	3.50	5.00
BE2544 (2001)	5,340	PF63 22.00	PF65 27.00			

Y# 375 20 BAHT
15.00 g., Copper-Nickel, 32 mm. **Ruler:** Rama IX **Subject:** Civil Service Comission 72nd Anniversary April 1 **Obv:** Conjoined busts left **Rev:** Civil service emblem divides value **Edge:** Reeded

Date	Mintage	F12	VF20	XF40	MS60	MS63
BE2544 (2001)	500,000	—	—	2.00	3.50	5.00
BE2544 (2001)	3,340	PF63 25.00	PF65 30.00			

Y# 393 20 BAHT
15.00 g., Copper-Nickel, 32 mm. **Ruler:** Rama IX **Subject:** 80th Birthday of Princess Calyani Vadhani **Obv:** Bust 1/4 right **Rev:** Crowned emblem and value **Edge:** Reeded

Date	Mintage	F12	VF20	XF40	MS60	MS63
BE2546 (2003) (2002)	350,000	—	—	2.00	3.50	5.00
BE2546 (2003)	3,200	PF63 17.50	PF65 22.00			

Y# 386 20 BAHT
15.00 g., Copper-Nickel, 32 mm. **Ruler:** Rama IX **Subject:** Centennial of Thai Banknotes 2445-2545 **Obv:** Conjoined busts left **Rev:** Coat of arms in center of seal **Edge:** Reeded

Date	Mintage	F12	VF20	XF40	MS60	MS63
BE2545 (2002)	1,000,000	—	—	2.00	3.50	5.00
BE2545 (2002)	40,000	PF63 17.50	PF65 22.00			

Y# 388 20 BAHT
15.00 g., Copper-Nickel, 32 mm. **Ruler:** Rama IX **Subject:** King's 75th Birthday December 5 **Obv:** Head left **Rev:** Royal crown in radiant oval **Edge:** Reeded **Note:** Minted and released in 2003.

Date	Mintage	F12	VF20	XF40	MS60	MS63
BE2545(2002)	1,200,000	—	—	2.00	3.50	5.00
BE2545(2002)	16,000	PF63 17.50	PF65 22.00			

Y# 397 20 BAHT

15.00 g., Copper-Nickel, 32 mm. **Ruler:** Rama IX **Subject:** Centennial of the National Police April 19 **Obv:** Conjoined busts left **Rev:** National Police emblem above banner **Edge:** Reeded

Date	Mintage	F12	VF20	XF40	MS60	MS63
BE2545 (2002)	600,000	—	—	2.00	3.50	5.00
BE2545 (2002)	5,000	PF63 17.50		PF65 22.00		

Y# 398 20 BAHT

15.00 g., Copper-Nickel, 32 mm. **Ruler:** Rama IX **Subject:** 50th Birthday of the Crown Prince July 28 **Obv:** Bust facing **Rev:** Crowned monogram **Edge:** Reeded

Date	Mintage	F12	VF20	XF40	MS60	MS63
BE2545 (2002)	300,000	—	—	2.00	3.50	5.00
BE2545 (2002)	5,000	PF63 40.00		PF65 50.00		

Y# 419 20 BAHT

15.00 g., Copper-Nickel, 32 mm. **Ruler:** Rama IX **Subject:** 50th Anniversary of Audit Department of Cooperatives **Edge:** Reeded

Date	Mintage	F12	VF20	XF40	MS60	MS63
BE2545 (2002)	300,000	—	—	2.00	3.50	5.00
BE2545 (2002)	3,000	PF63 17.50		PF65 22.00		

Y# 420 20 BAHT

15.00 g., Copper-Nickel, 32 mm. **Ruler:** Rama IX **Subject:** 150th Anniversary, Birth of Rama V **Edge:** Reeded

Date	Mintage	F12	VF20	XF40	MS60	MS63
BE2546 (2003)	1,000,000	—	—	2.00	3.50	5.00
BE2546 (2003)	26,000	PF63 18.00		PF65 24.00		

Y# 422 20 BAHT

15.00 g., Copper-Nickel, 32 mm. **Ruler:** Rama IX **Subject:** 72nd Anniversary of Queen's Birthday **Obv:** Head of Queen facing left **Edge:** Reeded

Date	Mintage	F12	VF20	XF40	MS60	MS63
BE2547 (2004)	600,000	—	—	2.00	3.50	5.00
BE2547 (2004)	10,000	PF63 20.00		PF65 25.00		

Y# 421 20 BAHT

15.00 g., Copper-Nickel, 32 mm. **Ruler:** Rama IX **Subject:** Rama IV, 200th Anniversary of Birth **Obv:** King Rama IV **Edge:** Reeded

Date	Mintage	F12	VF20	XF40	MS60	MS63
BE2547 (2004)	500,000	—	—	2.00	3.50	5.00
BE2547 (2004)	10,500	PF63 20.00		PF65 25.00		

Y# 462 20 BAHT

15.00 g., Copper-Nickel, 32 mm. **Ruler:** Rama IX **Subject:** Rama IV, 200th Anniversary of Birth **Obv:** Bust 3/4 right **Rev:** Horizontal oval Royal seal **Edge:** Reeded

Date	Mintage	F12	VF20	XF40	MS60	MS63
BE2547 (2004)	500,000	—	—	2.00	4.00	6.00
BE2547 (2004) (2005)	10,500	PF63 15.00		PF65 18.00		

Y# 403 20 BAHT

15.00 g., Copper-Nickel, 32 mm. **Ruler:** Rama IX **Subject:** Department of the Treasury, 72nd Anniversary **Obv:** Bust 1/4 left **Rev:** Treasury Department seal **Edge:** Reeded

Date	Mintage	F12	VF20	XF40	MS60	MS63
BE2548 (2005)	300,000	—	—	2.00	4.00	6.00
BE2548 (2005)	3,000	PF63 25.00		PF65 30.00		

Y# 423 20 BAHT

15.00 g., Copper-Nickel, 32 mm. **Ruler:** Rama IX **Subject:** 50th Birthday of Princess Sirinahorn **Obv:** Head of Princess facing right **Edge:** Reeded

Date	Mintage	F12	VF20	XF40	MS60	MS63
BE2548 (2005)	650,000	—	—	2.00	4.00	6.00
BE2548 (2005)	12,000	PF63 20.00		PF65 25.00		

Y# 471 20 BAHT

15.00 g., Copper-Nickel, 32 mm. **Ruler:** Rama IX **Subject:** Centennial of the National Library **Obv:** Two busts, one facing left, one right **Rev:** Circle with inscription **Edge:** Reeded

Date	Mintage	F12	VF20	XF40	MS60	MS63
BE2548 (2005) Est. 200000		—	—	2.00	3.50	5.00

Y# 472 20 BAHT

15.00 g., Copper-Nickel, 32 mm. **Ruler:** Rama IX **Subject:** Princess Rattana, 80th birthday **Obv:** Front facing portrait **Edge:** Reeded **Note:** Minted and released in 2006.

Date	Mintage	F12	VF20	XF40	MS60	MS63
BE2548 (2005)	200,000	—	—	2.00	3.50	5.00

Y# 474 20 BAHT

15.00 g., Copper-Nickel, 32 mm. **Ruler:** Rama IX **Subject:** UN Development Program Award **Obv:** Head right **Rev:** Chalice on stand with legends **Edge:** Reeded

Date	Mintage	F12	VF20	XF40	MS60	MS63
BE2549 (2006)	2,200,000	—	—	2.00	3.50	5.00

Y# 407 20 BAHT

15.00 g., Copper-Nickel, 32 mm. **Ruler:** Rama IX **Subject:** 60th Anniversary of Reign **Obv:** Head left **Rev:** Royal Crown on display **Edge:** Reeded

Date	Mintage	F12	VF20	XF40	MS60	MS63
BE2549 (2006)	5,600,000	—	—	2.00	4.00	6.00
BE2549 (2006)	96,000	PF63 18.50		PF65 24.00		

Y# 473 20 BAHT

15.00 g., Copper-Nickel, 32 mm. **Ruler:** Rama IX **Subject:** Royal Artificial Rain, 50th Anniversary **Obv:** Statue of King holding book and pencil **Rev:** Artificial rain wing symbol surrounded by rays and legend **Edge:** Reeded

Date	Mintage	F12	VF20	XF40	MS60	MS63
BE2549 (2006)	3,000,000	—	—	2.00	3.50	5.00

Y# 450 20 BAHT

15.00 g., Copper-Nickel, 32 mm. **Ruler:** Rama IX **Subject:** King's 80th Birthday **Obv:** Bust left **Edge:** Reeded

Date	Mintage	F12	VF20	XF40	MS60	MS63
BE 2550 (2007)	5,800,000	—	—	2.00	3.50	5.00
BE 2550 (2007)	95,000	PF63 15.00		PF65 18.00		

Y# 453 20 BAHT

15.00 g., Copper-Nickel **Ruler:** Rama IX **Subject:** Queen's 75th Birthday **Obv:** Bust left **Edge:** Reeded **Shape:** 32

Date	Mintage	F12	VF20	XF40	MS60	MS63
BE 2550 (2007)	600,000	—	—	2.00	3.50	5.00
BE 2550 (2007)	12,000	PF63 18.00		PF65 24.00		

Y# 475 20 BAHT

15.00 g., Copper-Nickel, 32 mm. **Ruler:** Rama IX **Subject:** Princess Galyana Vadhana, 84th birthday **Obv:** Head left **Edge:** Reeded

Date	Mintage	F12	VF20	XF40	MS60	MS63
BE2550 (2007)	700,000	—	—	2.00	3.50	5.00
BE2550 (2007)	8,400	PF63 18.00		PF65 24.00		

Y# 476 20 BAHT

15.00 g., Copper-Nickel, 32 mm. **Ruler:** Rama IX **Subject:** Father of Thai heritage conservation **Obv:** Head left **Edge:** Reeded **Note:** Minted and released in 2008.

Date	Mintage	F12	VF20	XF40	MS60	MS63
BE2550 (2007)	500,000	—	—	2.00	3.50	5.00

Y# 495 20 BAHT

15.00 g., Copper-Nickel, 32 mm. **Ruler:** Rama IX **Subject:** King Rama I, Father of Thai Trade **Obv:** Bust facing front and inscription **Rev:** Symbol, inscription, value and date **Edge:** Reeded **Note:** Minted and issued in BE2553

Date	Mintage	F12	VF20	XF40	MS60	MS63
BE2553 (2008)	500,000	—	—	—	3.50	4.00

Y# 464 20 BAHT

15.00 g., Copper-Nickel, 32 mm. **Ruler:** Rama IX **Subject:** Princess Mother, 9th Cycle (108th Anniversary of Birth) **Obv:** Portrait facing left **Rev:** Emblem of Princess Mother Srinakarindra **Edge:** Reeded

Date	Mintage	F12	VF20	XF40	MS60	MS63
BE2551 (2008)	450,000	—	—	2.00	3.50	5.00
BE2551 (2008)	5,500	PF63 20.00		PF65 25.00		

Y# 470 20 BAHT

15.00 g., Copper-Nickel, 32 mm. **Ruler:** Rama IX **Subject:** King Jessadabodindra

Date	Mintage	F12	VF20	XF40	MS60	MS63
RS2551 (2008)		—	—	—	3.50	5.00

Y# 477 20 BAHT

15.00 g., Copper-Nickel, 32 mm. **Ruler:** Rama IX **Subject:** WIPO Award **Obv:** Head left **Rev:** Award medal and legend **Edge:** Reeded **Note:** Minted and released in 2010

Date	Mintage	F12	VF20	XF40	MS60	MS63
BE2551 (2008)	500,000	—	—	2.00	3.50	5.00

Y# 514 20 BAHT

15.00 g., Copper-Nickel, 32 mm. **Ruler:** Rama IX **Subject:** Princess Bejaratana, 84th Birthday

Date	Mintage	F12	VF20	XF40	MS60	MS63
RS2552 (2009)	400,000	—	—	—	5.00	

Y# 499 20 BAHT

15.00 g., Copper-Nickel, 32 mm. **Ruler:** Rama IX **Subject:** 100th Anniversary of Indra College **Obv:** Conjoined busts facing left **Rev:** Symbol, inscription, value and date **Edge:** Reeded **Note:** Minted and issued in BE2553

Date	Mintage	F12	VF20	XF40	MS60	MS63
BE2553 (2010)	500,000	—	—	—	3.50	4.00

Y# 506 20 BAHT

15.00 g., Copper-Nickel, 32 mm. **Ruler:** Rama IX **Subject:** Princess Bejaratana, 84th Birthday **Edge:** Reeded

Date	Mintage	F12	VF20	XF40	MS60	MS63
RS2553 (2010)		—	—	—	3.50	5.00

Y# 520 20 BAHT

15.00 g., Copper-Nickel, 32 mm. **Ruler:** Rama IX **Subject:** Vajiravudh College, 100th Anniversary

Date	Mintage	F12	VF20	XF40	MS60	MS63
RS2553 (2010)	500,000	—	—	—	5.00	6.00

Y# 511 20 BAHT

15.00 g., Copper-Nickel, 32 mm. **Ruler:** Rama IX **Subject:** 150th Anniversary of the birth of Prince Ditsawarakuman

Date	Mintage	F12	VF20	XF40	MS60	MS63
2012	Est. 1000000	—	—	—	—	—

Y# 512 20 BAHT

15.00 g., Copper-Nickel, 32 mm. **Ruler:** Rama IX **Subject:** Queen Sirikit 80th Birthday Anniversary

Date	Mintage	F12	VF20	XF40	MS60	MS63
2012	1,500,000	—	—	—	—	—

Y# 513 20 BAHT

Silver, 32 mm. **Ruler:** Rama IX **Subject:** Department of Alternative Energy 60th Anniversary

Date	Mintage	F12	VF20	XF40	MS60	MS63
2012		—	—	—	—	—
2012 Proof		—	—	—	—	—

Y# 524 20 BAHT

15.00 g., Copper-Nickel, 32 mm. **Ruler:** Rama IX **Subject:** Prince Damrong Rajanubhab, 150th Anniversary of Birth

Date	Mintage	F12	VF20	XF40	MS60	MS63
RS2555 (2012)	1,000,000	—	—	—	6.00	7.50

Y# 404 50 BAHT

21.00 g., Copper-Nickel, 36 mm. **Ruler:** Rama IX **Subject:** Air Force 50th Anniversary May 7 **Obv:** Uniformed bust facing **Rev:** Crowned wings within 3/4 wreath **Edge:** Reeded

Date	Mintage	F12	VF20	XF40	MS60	MS63
BE2546 (2003)	250,000	—	—	4.00	12.50	15.00

Y# 478 50 BAHT

21.00 g., Copper-Nickel, 36 mm. **Ruler:** Rama IX **Subject:** National Intelligence Agency, 50th Anniversary **Obv:** Head right **Rev:** Emblem of the National Intelligence Agency **Edge:** Reeded **Note:** Minted and released in 2003.

Date	Mintage	F12	VF20	XF40	MS60	MS63
BE2547 (2004)	200,000	—	—	3.50	4.50	6.00

Y# 493 50 BAHT

Copper-Nickel, 36 mm. **Ruler:** Rama IX **Obv:** Head of infant facing right **Rev:** Design including chick, inscription, value and date **Edge:** Reeded

Date	Mintage	F12	VF20	XF40	MS60	MS63
BE2549 (2006)	450,000	—	—	—	4.50	6.00

Y# 479 50 BAHT

21.00 g., Copper-Nickel, 36 mm. **Ruler:** Rama IX **Subject:** Technological Research **Obv:** Child's head right **Rev:** Small chicken at left, legends **Edge:** Reeded

Date	Mintage	F12	VF20	XF40	MS60	MS63
BE2549 (2006)	450,000	—	—	3.50	4.50	6.00

Y# 480 50 BAHT

21.00 g., Copper-Nickel, 36 mm. **Ruler:** Rama IX **Subject:** Naval Academy, 100th Anniversary **Obv:** Conjoined heads left **Rev:** Symbol, inscriptions, value and date **Edge:** Reeded

Date	Mintage	F12	VF20	XF40	MS60	MS63
BE2549 (2006)	200,000	—	—	3.50	4.50	6.00

Y# 500 50 BAHT

21.00 g., Copper-Nickel, 36 mm. **Ruler:** Rama IX **Subject:** 150th Anniversary of Thai Mint **Obv:** Conjoined busts facing 1/2 right and inscription **Rev:** Complex design, inscription, value and date **Edge:** Reeded

Date	Mintage	F12	VF20	XF40	MS60	MS63
BE2553 (2010)	150,000	—	—	—	4.50	6.00

Y# 517 50 BAHT

21.00 g., Copper-Nickel, 36 mm. **Ruler:** Rama IX **Subject:** Royal Thai Mint, 150th Annveriary

Date	Mintage	F12	VF20	XF40	MS60	MS63
RS2553 (2010)		—	—	—	6.00	7.50

Y# 501 50 BAHT

21.00 g., Copper-Nickel, 36 mm. **Ruler:** Rama IX **Subject:** King's Seventh Cycle Ceremony **Obv:** Head of King facing 1/2 left **Rev:** Symbol, inscription, value and date **Edge:** Reeded

Date	Mintage	F12	VF20	XF40	MS60	MS63
BE2554 (2011)	Est. 3000000	—	—	—	4.50	6.00

Y# 509 50 BAHT

Copper-Nickel **Ruler:** Rama IX **Obv:** Bust **Rev:** Emblem

Date	Mintage	F12	VF20	XF40	MS60	MS63
2011		—	—	—	—	—

Y# 521 50 BAHT

21.00 g., Copper-Nickel, 36 mm. **Ruler:** Rama IX **Subject:** King Bhumibol, 84th Birthday

Date	Mintage	F12	VF20	XF40	MS60	MS63
RS2554 (2011)		—	—	—	6.00	7.50

Y# 389 600 BAHT

22.00 g., 0.925 Silver 0.6501 oz. ASW, 35 mm. **Ruler:** Rama IX **Subject:** King's 75th Birthday **Obv:** King's portrait **Rev:** Royal crown in radiant oval **Edge:** Reeded

Date	Mintage	F12	VF20	XF40	MS60	MS63
BE2545 (2002)	14,000	—	—	25.00	30.00	35.00
BE2545 (2002)	3,000	PF63 70.00	PF65 80.00			

Y# 481 600 BAHT

22.00 g., 0.925 Silver 0.6501 oz. ASW, 35 mm. **Ruler:** Rama IX **Subject:** Crown Prince, 50th Birthday **Obv:** Crown Prince bust 1/4 facing left **Rev:** Crowned monogram **Edge:** Reeded

Date	Mintage	F12	VF20	XF40	MS60	MS63
BE2545 (2002)	5,000	—	—	40.00	50.00	55.00
BE2545 (2002)	1,000	PF63 95.00	PF65 110			

Y# 394 600 BAHT

22.00 g., 0.925 Silver 0.6501 oz. ASW, 35 mm. **Ruler:** Rama IX **Subject:** 80th Birthday of Princess Calgani Vedhana **Obv:** Bust half right **Rev:** Crowned emblem and value **Edge:** Reeded

Date	Mintage	F12	VF20	XF40	MS60	MS63
BE2546 (2003)	1,000	PF63 95.00	PF65 110			
BE2546 (2003)	4,500	—	—	35.00	45.00	50.00

Y# 482 600 BAHT

22.00 g., 0.925 Silver 0.6501 oz. ASW, 35 mm. **Ruler:** Rama IX **Subject:** Rama V. 150th Anniversary of Birth **Obv:** Rama V bust left **Rev:** Royal Crown **Edge:** Reeded

Date	Mintage	F12	VF20	XF40	MS60	MS63
BE2546 (2003)	15,000	—	—	30.00	35.00	40.00
BE2546 (2003)	4,600	PF63 85.00	PF65 95.00			

Y# 401 600 BAHT

22.15 g., 0.925 Silver 0.6545 oz. ASW, 35 mm. **Ruler:** Rama IX **Subject:** Queen's 72nd Birthday **Obv:** Crowned monogram **Rev:** Crowned bust of Queen 3/4 right **Edge:** Reeded

Date	Mintage	F12	VF20	XF40	MS60	MS63
BE2547 (2004)	12,000	—	—	30.00	35.00	40.00
BE2547 (2004)	3,700	PF63 85.00	PF65 95.00			

Y# 463 600 BAHT

22.00 g., 0.925 Silver 0.6501 oz. ASW, 35 mm. **Ruler:** Rama IX **Subject:** King Rama IV, 200th Anniversary of Birth **Obv:** Bust right **Rev:** Horizontal oval **Edge:** Reeded

Date	Mintage	F12	VF20	XF40	MS60	MS63
BE2547 (2004)	12,000	—	—	40.00	45.00	60.00
BE2547 (2004)	3,000	PF63 95.00	PF65 110			

Y# 427 600 BAHT

22.15 g., 0.925 Silver 0.6545 oz. ASW, 35 mm. **Ruler:** Rama IX **Subject:** Princess Maha Chakri Sirindhorn's 50th Birthday **Obv:** Bust right **Rev:** Oval **Edge:** Reeded

Date	Mintage	F12	VF20	XF40	MS60	MS63
BE2548 (2005)	15,000	—	—	35.00	45.00	40.00
BE2548 (2005)	4,000	PF63 85.00	PF65 95.00			

Y# 467 600 BAHT

22.15 g., 0.925 Silver 0.6545 oz. ASW, 35 mm. **Ruler:** Rama IX **Subject:** Princess Petcharat, 80th Birthday **Obv:** Bust facing **Rev:** Princess' emblem **Edge:** Reeded

Date	Mintage	F12	VF20	XF40	MS60	MS63
BE2548 (2005)		—	—	40.00	55.00	60.00
BE2548 (2005)	—	PF63 120	PF65 135			

Y# 484 600 BAHT

22.00 g., 0.925 Silver 0.6501 oz. ASW, 35 mm. **Ruler:** Rama IX **Subject:** Princess Rattana, 80th birthday **Obv:** Bust facing of Princess **Edge:** Reeded **Note:** Minted and released in 2006.

Date	Mintage	F12	VF20	XF40	MS60	MS63
BE2548 (2005)	3,500	—	—	40.00	55.00	60.00

Y# 408 600 BAHT

22.15 g., 0.925 Silver 0.6545 oz. ASW, 35 mm. **Ruler:** Rama IX **Subject:** 60th Anniversary of Reign **Obv:** Rama IX **Rev:** Royal cypher **Edge:** Reeded

Date	Mintage	F12	VF20	XF40	MS60	MS63
BE2549 (2006)	66,000	—	—	30.00	35.00	40.00
BE2549 (2006)	16,000	PF63 90.00	PF65 100			
Proof with colored hologram						

Y# 485 600 BAHT

22.00 g., 0.925 Silver 0.6501 oz. ASW **Ruler:** Rama IX **Subject:** Prince Royal Cradle Ceremony **Obv:** Prince's baby head left **Rev:** Four line legend **Edge:** Reeded

Date	Mintage	F12	VF20	XF40	MS60	MS63
BE2549 (2006)	10,000	—	—	40.00	45.00	50.00
BE2549 (2006)	3,700	PF63 85.00	PF65 95.00			

Y# 502 800 BAHT

22.00 g., 0.925 Silver 0.6501 oz. ASW, 35 mm. **Ruler:** Rama IX **Subject:** King's 84th Birthday **Obv:** Head facing 1/4 left and inscription **Rev:** Symbol, value, date and inscription **Edge:** Reeded

Date	Mintage	F12	VF20	XF40	MS60	MS63
BE2554 (2003)	100,000	PF63 55.00	PF65 60.00			

Y# 447 800 BAHT

22.00 g., 0.990 Silver 0.6957 oz. ASW, 35 mm. **Ruler:** Rama IX **Obv:** Bust left **Rev:** WHO logo and legend

Date	Mintage	F12	VF20	XF40	MS60	MS63
BE2548 (2005)	6,500	—	—	—	40.00	45.00
BE2548 (2005)	Inc. above	PF63 100	PF65 115			

Y# 451 800 BAHT

22.00 g., 0.990 Silver 0.6957 oz. ASW, 35 mm. **Ruler:** Rama IX **Subject:** King's 80th Birthday **Obv:** Bust left **Edge:** Reeded

Date	Mintage	F12	VF20	XF40	MS60	MS63
BE 2550 (2007)	80,000	—	—	—	35.00	40.00
BE 2550 (2007)	28,000	PF63 75.00	PF65 85.00			

Y# 454 800 BAHT

22.00 g., 0.925 Silver 0.6501 oz. ASW, 35 mm. **Ruler:** Rama IX **Subject:** Queen's 75th Birthday **Obv:** Queen's bust left **Rev:** Queen's Royal Seal **Edge:** Reeded

Date	Mintage	F12	VF20	XF40	MS60	MS63
BE 2550 (2007)	12,000	—	—	—	35.00	40.00
BE 2550 (2007)	4,000	PF63 75.00	PF65 85.00			

Y# 466 800 BAHT

22.00 g., 0.925 Silver 0.6501 oz. ASW, 35 mm. **Ruler:** Rama IX **Subject:** Princess Galyani Vadhana, 84th Birthday **Obv:** Bust facing right **Rev:** Princess' emblem **Edge:** Reeded

Date	Mintage	F12	VF20	XF40	MS60	MS63
BE2550 (2007)	11,500	—	—	—	35.00	40.00
BE2550 (2007)	1,500	PF63 95.00	PF65 110			

Y# 465 800 BAHT

22.00 g., 0.925 Silver 0.6501 oz. ASW, 35 mm. **Ruler:** Rama IX **Subject:** Princess Mother, 9th Cycle (108th Birthday) **Obv:** Bust facing **Rev:** Princess Mother's emblem **Edge:** Reeded

Date	Mintage	F12	VF20	XF40	MS60	MS63
BE2551 (2008)	11,200	—	—	—	35.00	40.00
BE2551 (2008)	1,500	PF63 95.00	PF65 110			

Y# 468 800 BAHT

22.00 g., 0.990 Silver 0.6957 oz. ASW, 35 mm. **Ruler:** Rama IX **Subject:** King's WIPO leader award **Obv:** Bust left **Rev:** Award medal and legned **Edge:** Reeded **Note:** Minted and released in 2010.

Date	Mintage	F12	VF20	XF40	MS60	MS63
BE2551 (2008)	15,000	PF63 75.00	PF65 85.00			

Y# 515 800 BAHT

22.00 g., 0.925 Silver 0.6501 oz. ASW, 35 mm. **Ruler:** Rama IX **Subject:** Princess Bejaratana, 84th Birthday

Date	Mintage	F12	VF20	XF40	MS60	MS63
RS2552 (2009)	5,000	—	—	—	35.00	40.00

Y# 507 800 BAHT

22.00 g., 0.925 Silver 0.6501 oz. ASW, 35 mm. **Ruler:** Rama IX **Subject:** Princess Bejaratana, 84th Birthday **Edge:** Reeded

Date	Mintage	F12	VF20	XF40	MS60	MS63
BE2553 (2010)		—	—	—	30.00	40.00

Y# 522 800 BAHT

22.00 g., 0.925 Silver 0.6501 oz. ASW, 35 mm. **Ruler:** Rama IX **Subject:** King Bhumibol, 84th Birthday

Date	Mintage	F12	VF20	XF40	MS60	MS63
RS2554 (2011)		—	PF63 75.00	PF65 85.00		

Y# 469 900 BAHT

31.11 g., 0.999 Silver 0.9926 oz. ASW, 40.6 mm. **Ruler:** Rama IX **Subject:** UNDP Human Development Lifetime Achievement Award **Obv:** King facing in multicolor applique **Rev:** Award bowl **Edge:** Reeded

Date	Mintage	F12	VF20	XF40	MS60	MS63
BE2549 (2006)	200,000	PF63 75.00	PF65 85.00			

Y# 390 7500 BAHT

15.00 g., 0.900 Gold 0.4312 oz. AGW, 26 mm. **Ruler:** Rama IX **Subject:** King's 75th Birthday **Obv:** King's portrait **Rev:** Royal crown in radiant oval **Edge:** Reeded

Date	Mintage	F12	VF20	XF40	MS60	MS63
BE2545 (2002)	6,000	—	—	—	800	825
BE2545 (2002)	1,200	PF63 850	PF65 875			

Y# 395 9000 BAHT
15.00 g., 0.900 Gold 0.4312 oz. AGW, 26 mm. **Ruler:** Rama IX **Subject:** 72nd Birthday of Queen **Obv:** Bust half right **Rev:** Crowned emblem and value **Edge:** Reeded

Date	Mintage	F12	VF20	XF40	MS60	MS63
BE2546 (2004) (2003)	6,000	—	—	—	800	825
BE2546 (2004) (2003)	1,600	PF63 850		PF65 875		

Y# 490 9000 BAHT
15.00 g., 0.434 Gold 0.208 oz. AGW, 26 mm. **Ruler:** Rama IX **Subject:** 150th Aniversary of the Birth of Rama V **Obv:** Bust of Rama V facing left and inscription **Rev:** Three symbols, inscription, value and date **Edge:** Reeded

Date	Mintage	F12	VF20	XF40	MS60	MS63
BE2546 (2003)	5,000	—	—	—	800	825
BE2546 (2003)	1,500	PF63 900		PF65 925		

Y# 491 9000 BAHT
15.00 g., 0.900 Gold 0.4312 oz. AGW, 26 mm. **Ruler:** Rama IX **Subject:** Queen Sirikit's 72nd Birthday **Obv:** Bust of Queen facing 1/4 left and inscription **Rev:** Symbol honoring Queen Sirikit, inscription, value and date **Edge:** Reeded

Date	Mintage	F12	VF20	XF40	MS60	MS63
BE2547 (2004)	6,000	—	—	—	800	825
BE2547 (2004)	1,600	PF63 900		PF65 925		

Y# 492 9000 BAHT
15.00 g., 0.900 Gold 0.4312 oz. AGW, 26 mm. **Ruler:** Rama IX **Subject:** 200th Anniversary of the Birth of King Rama IV **Obv:** Bust of King Rama IV facing 3/4 right and inscription **Rev:** Horizontal oval royal seal, inscription, value and date **Edge:** Reeded

Date	Mintage	F12	VF20	XF40	MS60	MS63
BE2547 (2004)	3,000	—	—	—	800	825
BE2547 (2004)	1,000	PF63 900		PF65 925		

Y# 494 12,000 BAHT
15.00 g., 0.900 Gold 0.4312 oz. AGW, 26 mm. **Ruler:** Rama IX **Subject:** 60th Anniversary of Reign **Obv:** Framed head facing 1/4 right **Rev:** Symbol of 60th Anniversary of Reign, value and date **Edge:** Reeded

Date	Mintage	F12	VF20	XF40	MS60	MS63
BE2551 (2008)	16,000	—	—	—	800	825
BE2551 (2008)	9,600	PF63 900		PF65 925		

Y# 448 16,000 BAHT
15.00 g., 0.900 Gold 0.4312 oz. AGW, 26 mm. **Ruler:** Rama IX **Obv:** Bust of Queen Sirikit, right **Rev:** WHO logo and legend **Note:** Minted and issued in BE2550

Date	Mintage	F12	VF20	XF40	MS60	MS63
BE2005 2005	Est. 3000	—	—	—	800	825
	Inc. above	PF63 850		PF65 875		

Y# 452 16,000 BAHT
15.00 g., 0.990 Gold 0.4744 oz. AGW, 26 mm. **Ruler:** Rama IX **Subject:** King's 80th Birthday **Obv:** Bust left **Rev:** Symbols, inscription, value and date **Edge:** Reeded

Date	Mintage	F12	VF20	XF40	MS60	MS63
BE2550 (2007)	16,800	—	—	—	870	900
BE2550 (2007)	12,800	PF63 925		PF65 950		

Y# 455 16,000 BAHT
15.00 g., 0.900 Gold 0.4312 oz. AGW, 26 mm. **Ruler:** Rama IX **Subject:** Queen's 75th Birthday **Obv:** Bust left and inscription **Rev:** Symbol, inscription, value and date **Edge:** Reeded

Date	Mintage	F12	VF20	XF40	MS60	MS63
BE2550 (2007)	5,000	—	—	—	800	825
2550 (2007)	2,000	PF63 850		PF65 875		

Y# 496 16,000 BAHT
15.00 g., 0.900 Gold 0.4312 oz. AGW, 26 mm. **Ruler:** Rama IX **Subject:** 108th Aniversary of the Birth of the Princess Mother **Obv:** Head of Princess Mother facing 1/4 left **Rev:** Symbol, inscription, value and date **Edge:** Reeded

Date	Mintage	F12	VF20	XF40	MS60	MS63
BE2551 (2008)	400	PF65 1,000				
BE2551 (2008)	1,200	—	—	—	800	825

Y# 489 16,000 BAHT
15.00 g., 0.990 Gold 0.4744 oz. AGW, 26 mm. **Ruler:** Rama IX **Subject:** World Interlectural Propery Organization Award **Obv:** Head left **Rev:** Award Medal and legend **Edge:** Reeded **Note:** Minted and released in 2010.

Date	Mintage	F12	VF20	XF40	MS60	MS63
BE2551 (2008)	2,000	PF63 875		PF65 900		

Y# 503 16,000 BAHT
15.00 g., 0.965 Gold 0.4624 oz. AGW, 26 mm. **Ruler:** Rama IX **Subject:** King's Seventh Cycle Ceremony **Obv:** Head of King facing 1/2 left **Rev:** Synmbol, inscription, value and date **Edge:** Reeded

Date	Mintage	F12	VF20	XF40	MS60	MS63
BE2554 (2011)	Est. 25000	PF63 1,000		PF65 1,100		

Y# 523 16,000 BAHT
15.00 g., 0.900 Gold 0.4312 oz. AGW, 26 mm. **Ruler:** Rama IX **Subject:** King Bhumibol, 84th Birthday

Date	Mintage	F12	VF20	XF40	MS60	MS63
RS2554 (2011)	—	PF63 950		PF65 975		

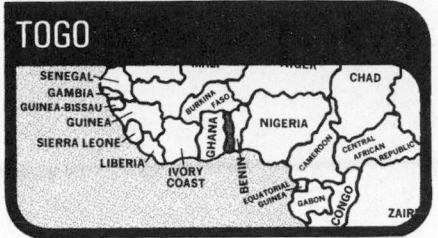

TOGO

The Togolese Republic (formerly part of German Togoland), situated on the Gulf of Guinea in West Africa between Ghana and Benin, has an area of 21,622 sq. mi. (56,790 sq. km.) and a population of *3.4 million. Capital: Lome. Agriculture and herding, the production of dyewoods, and the mining of phosphates and iron ore are the chief industries. Copra, phosphates and coffee are exported.

MINT MARK
(a) - Paris, privy marks only

MONETARY SYSTEM
100 Centimes = 1 Franc

REPUBLIC
STANDARD COINAGE
100 Centimes = 1 Franc

KM# 51 100 FRANCS
26.00 g., Copper-Nickel, 38.6 mm. **Rev:** Blue sunbird, prism technology

Date	Mintage	F12	VF20	XF40	MS60	MS63
2010 Prooflike	2,500	—	—	—	—	25.00

KM# 52 100 FRANCS
26.00 g., Copper-Nickel, 38.6 mm. **Rev:** Green bird, prism technology

Date	Mintage	F12	VF20	XF40	MS60	MS63
2010 Prooflike	2,500	—	—	—	—	25.00

KM# 53 100 FRANCS
26.00 g., Copper-Nickel, 38.6 mm. **Rev:** Yellow bird, prism technology

Date	Mintage	F12	VF20	XF40	MS60	MS63
2010 Prooflike	2,500	—	—	—	—	25.00

KM# 62 100 FRANCS
Silver Plated Base Metal **Rev:** Prism lion standing left

Date	Mintage	F12	VF20	XF40	MS60	MS63
2011	5,000	PF63 40.00				

KM# 43 250 FRANCS
5.00 g., 0.999 Silver 0.1596 oz. ASW **Subject:** German President Horst Kohler **Obv:** National arms **Obv. Legend:** REPUBLIQUE TOGOLAISE **Rev:** Gilt figure

Date	Mintage	F12	VF20	XF40	MS60	MS63
2004	—	PF63 15.00				

KM# 29 500 FRANCS
7.05 g., 0.999 Silver 0.225 oz. ASW, 30 mm. **Obv:** National arms above value **Rev:** Multicolor big cat **Edge:** Plain

Date	Mintage	F12	VF20	XF40	MS60	MS63
2001	—	PF63 35.00				

KM# 41 500 FRANCS
10.00 g., 0.999 Silver 0.3191 oz. ASW **Subject:** XVIII World Football Championship - Germany 2006 **Obv:** National arms **Obv. Legend:** REPUBLIQUE TOGOLAISE **Rev:** Two players, map of Germany in background

Date	Mintage	F12	VF20	XF40	MS60	MS63
2001	—	PF63 22.50				

KM# 60 500 FRANCS
15.00 g., 0.925 Silver 0.4432 oz. ASW, 30 mm. **Obv:** National arms **Rev:** Albrecht Durer portrait

Date	Mintage	F12	VF20	XF40	MS60	MS63
2003	—	PF63 25.00				

KM# 47 500 FRANCS
14.97 g., 0.925 Silver 0.4423 oz. ASW, 30 mm. **Obv:** Arms with supporters **Rev:** Full figures of Johann Wolfgang von Goethe and Friedrich von Schiller on pedostal facing

Date	Mintage	F12	VF20	XF40	MS60	MS63
2004	—	PF63 22.50				

KM# 44 500 FRANCS
7.00 g., 0.999 Silver 0.2234 oz. ASW **Subject:** German Chancellor Helmut Schmidt **Obv:** National arms **Obv. Legend:** REPUBLIQUE TOGOLAISE **Rev:** Gilt figue

Date	Mintage	F12	VF20	XF40	MS60	MS63
ND-2004	—	PF63 22.50				

KM# 65 500 FRANCS
15.55 g., 0.925 Silver 0.4595 oz. ASW, 35 mm. **Subject:** Greatest She-Warrior **Rev:** Zenobia standing, color ruins at left

Date	Mintage	F12	VF20	XF40	MS60	MS63
2011	1,000	PF63 65.00				

KM# 66 500 FRANCS
15.50 g., 0.925 Silver 0.458 oz. ASW, 35 mm. **Rev:** St. Olga

Date	Mintage	F12	VF20	XF40	MS60	MS63
2011	Est. 1000	PF63 65.00				

KM# 17 1000 FRANCS
14.95 g., 0.999 Silver 0.4771 oz. ASW, 35 mm. **Obv:** National arms **Obv. Legend:** REPUBLIQUE TOGOLAISE **Rev:** German sailing ship **Rev. Legend:** Adler von Lübeck **Edge:** Plain

Date	Mintage	F12	VF20	XF40	MS60	MS63
2001	—	PF63 50.00				

KM# 35 1000 FRANCS
14.70 g., 0.999 Silver 0.4691 oz. ASW, 36 mm. **Subject:** World Cup Soccer - Bern 1954 **Obv:** National arms **Rev:** Bust facing and tower **Edge:** Plain

Date	Mintage	F12	VF20	XF40	MS60	MS63
2001	—	PF63 40.00	PF65 50.00			

KM# 36 1000 FRANCS
19.91 g., 0.999 Silver 0.6354 oz. ASW, 38.1 mm. **Subject:** World Cup Soccer - France 1938 **Obv:** National arms **Rev:** Eiffel Tower behind soccer player kicking ball **Edge:** Reeded

Date	Mintage	F12	VF20	XF40	MS60	MS63
2001	—	PF63 40.00	PF65 50.00			

KM# 40 1000 FRANCS
14.97 g., Silver, 35 mm. **Obv:** National arms **Obv. Legend:** REPUBLIQUE TOGOLAISE **Rev:** Imperial German sailing ship **Rev. Legend:** PREUSSEN **Edge:** Plain

Date	Mintage	F12	VF20	XF40	MS60	MS63
2001	—	PF63 40.00				

KM# 54 1000 FRANCS
15.00 g., 0.999 Silver 0.4787 oz. ASW, 36 mm. **Rev:** Multicolor Airbus 319 right

Date	Mintage	F12	VF20	XF40	MS60	MS63
2001	—	PF63 35.00				

KM# 37 1000 FRANCS
19.97 g., 0.999 Silver 0.6373 oz. ASW, 40 mm. **Subject:** World Cup Soccer - USA 1994 **Obv:** National arms **Obv. Legend:** REPUBLIQUE TOGOLAISE **Rev:** Soccer player kicking ball **Rev. Legend:** COUPE MONDIALE DE FOOTBALL **Edge:** Reeded

Date	Mintage	F12	VF20	XF40	MS60	MS63
2002	—	PF63 40.00	PF65 50.00			

KM# 55 1000 FRANCS
15.00 g., 0.999 Silver 0.4787 oz. ASW, 36 mm. **Rev:** Multicolor Douglas DC-4 and NY skyline

Date	Mintage	F12	VF20	XF40	MS60	MS63
2002	—	PF63 35.00				

KM# 56 1000 FRANCS
15.00 g., 0.999 Silver 0.4787 oz. ASW **Rev:** Multicolor Caravelle SE-210 before London skyline **Shape:** 36

Date	Mintage	F12	VF20	XF40	MS60	MS63
2002	—	PF63 35.00				

KM# 68 1000 FRANCS
15.00 g., 0.999 Silver 0.4787 oz. ASW, 35 mm. **Rev:** Doubledecker 170 in color

Date	Mintage	F12	VF20	XF40	MS60	MS63
2002	5,000	PF63 50.00	PF65 60.00			

KM# 69 1000 FRANCS
15.00 g., 0.999 Silver 0.4787 oz. ASW, 35 mm. **Rev:** Douglas DC 2 and Statue of Liberty in color

Date	Mintage	F12	VF20	XF40	MS60	MS63
2002	5,000	PF63 50.00	PF65 60.00			

KM# 70 1000 FRANCS
15.00 g., 0.999 Silver 0.4787 oz. ASW, 35 mm. **Rev:** South Aviation SE 210 Caravelle, London in color

Date	Mintage	F12	VF20	XF40	MS60	MS63
2002	5,000	PF63 50.00	PF65 60.00			

KM# 57 1000 FRANCS
15.00 g., 0.999 Silver 0.4787 oz. ASW, 36 mm. **Rev:** Multicolor Convair 440 at airport

Date	Mintage	F12	VF20	XF40	MS60	MS63
2003	—	PF63 35.00				

KM# 58 1000 FRANCS
15.00 g., 0.999 Silver 0.4787 oz. ASW, 36 mm. **Rev:** Multicolor McDonnell-Douglas MD-81 right

Date	Mintage	F12	VF20	XF40	MS60	MS63
2003	—	PF63 35.00				

KM# 34 1000 FRANCS
30.92 g., 0.999 Silver 0.9867 oz. ASW, 39 mm. **Obv:** Bust with headdress left within circle **Rev:** Gold plated baboon within circle **Edge:** Reeded **Note:** Date in Chinese numerals.

Date	Mintage	F12	VF20	XF40	MS60	MS63
2004	—	PF65 75.00				

KM# 38 1000 FRANCS
30.73 g., 0.999 Silver 0.9807 oz. ASW, 39 mm. **Subject:** Year of the Monkey **Obv:** Head with headdress 1/4 right within circle **Rev:** Gold plated baboon within circle **Edge:** Reeded **Note:** Note: Date in Chinese numerals.

Date	Mintage	F12	VF20	XF40	MS60	MS63
2004	—	PF65 75.00				

KM# 24 1000 FRANCS
31.10 g., 0.999 Silver 0.9926 oz. ASW, 40 mm. **Obv:** National arms **Obv. Legend:** REPUBLIQUE TOGOLAISE **Rev:** Incuse rendering of statue of Princess Kyninska of Sparta horseback left **Rev. Legend:** SPORTS - ANTIQUES **Edge:** Plain

Date	Mintage	F12	VF20	XF40	MS60	MS63
2004	2,500	—	—	—	—	65.00

KM# 25 1000 FRANCS
31.10 g., 0.999 Silver 0.9926 oz. ASW, 40 mm. **Obv:** National arms **Obv. Legend:** REPUBLIQUE TOGOLAISE **Rev:** Relief rendering of statue of Princess Kyninska of Sparta horseback right **Rev. Legend:** SPORTS - ANTIQUES **Edge:** Plain

Date	Mintage	F12	VF20	XF40	MS60	MS63
2004	2,500	—	—	—	—	65.00

KM# 26 1000 FRANCS
1.24 g., 0.9999 Gold 0.0397 oz. AGW, 13.92 mm. **Obv:** National arms **Obv. Legend:** REPUBLIQUE TOGOLAISE **Rev:** Convex statue of Nike **Edge:** Plain

Date	Mintage	F12	VF20	XF40	MS60	MS63
2004	5,000	PF63 80.00				

KM# 59 1000 FRANCS
15.00 g., 0.999 Silver 0.4787 oz. ASW, 36 mm. **Rev:** Multicolor DeHaviland DH-89 biplane

Date	Mintage	F12	VF20	XF40	MS60	MS63
2004	—	PF63 35.00				

KM# 27 1000 FRANCS
1.24 g., 0.9999 Gold 0.0397 oz. AGW, 13.92 mm. **Obv:** National arms **Obv. Legend:** REPUBLIQUE TOGOLAISE **Rev:** Concave statue of Nike **Edge:** Plain

Date	Mintage	F12	VF20	XF40	MS60	MS63
2004	5,000	PF63 80.00				

KM# 71 1000 FRANCS
15.00 g., 0.999 Silver 0.4787 oz. ASW, 35 mm. **Rev:** Theodor Heuss, gilt

Date	Mintage	F12	VF20	XF40	MS60	MS63
2004	—	PF63 30.00 PF65 35.00				

KM# 72 1000 FRANCS
15.00 g., 0.999 Silver 0.4787 oz. ASW, 35 mm. **Rev:** Richard Freiherr von Weizsacker

Date	Mintage	F12	VF20	XF40	MS60	MS63
2004	—	PF63 30.00 PF65 35.00				

KM# 45 1000 FRANCS
Silver **Subject:** 170th Anniversary German Railroad, Nürnberg - Fürth **Obv:** National arms **Obv. Legend:** REPUBLIQUE TOGOLAISE **Rev:** Early steam locomotive "Adler

Date	Mintage	F12	VF20	XF40	MS60	MS63
2005	—	PF63 55.00				

KM# 73 1000 FRANCS
15.00 g., 0.999 Silver 0.4787 oz. ASW, 35 mm. **Rev:** Flying "P" liner - Passat

Date	Mintage	F12	VF20	XF40	MS60	MS63
2005	—	PF63 40.00 PF65 45.00				

KM# 74 1000 FRANCS
1.24 g., 0.9999 Gold 0.0396 oz. AGW, 13.92 mm. **Subject:** Semperoper in Dresden, 20th Anniversary of re opening

Date	Mintage	F12	VF20	XF40	MS60	MS63
2005	2,000	PF63 90.00				

KM# 46 1000 FRANCS
1.24 g., 0.9999 Gold 0.0396 oz. AGW **Subject:** 250th Anniversary Birth of Wolfgang Amadeus Mozart **Obv:** National arms **Obv. Legend:** REPUBLIQUE TOGOLAISE

Date	Mintage	F12	VF20	XF40	MS60	MS63
2006	—	PF63 85.00				

KM# 48 1000 FRANCS
25.00 g., 0.925 Silver 0.7387 oz. ASW, 38.6 mm. **Rev:** Blue hummingbird, prism technology

Date	Mintage	F12	VF20	XF40	MS60	MS63
2010	2,500	PF63 60.00				

KM# 49 1000 FRANCS
25.00 g., 0.925 Silver 0.7387 oz. ASW, 38.6 mm. **Rev:** Green hummingbird, prism technology

Date	Mintage	F12	VF20	XF40	MS60	MS63
2010	2,500	PF63 65.00				

KM# 50 1000 FRANCS
25.00 g., 0.925 Silver 0.7387 oz. ASW, 38.6 mm. **Rev:** Prange hummingbird, prism technology

Date	Mintage	F12	VF20	XF40	MS60	MS63
2010	2,500	PF63 55.00				

KM# 61 1000 FRANCS
25.00 g., 0.925 Silver 0.7387 oz. ASW, 38.61 mm. **Subject:** Year of the Tiger **Obv:** National arms **Rev:** Tiger, gilt

Date	Mintage	F12	VF20	XF40	MS60	MS63
2010	1,000	PF63 75.00				

KM# 88 1000 FRANCS
25.00 g., 0.925 Silver 0.7387 oz. ASW, 38.61 mm. **Subject:** Year of the Tiger **Rev:** Tiger family gilt

Date	Mintage	F12	VF20	XF40	MS60	MS63
2010	1,000	PF63 80.00				

KM# 88 1000 FRANCS
31.10 g., 0.999 Silver 0.9925 oz. ASW, 47x27 mm. **Rev:** Two impalas **Shape:** Rectangle

Date	Mintage	F12	VF20	XF40	MS60	MS63
2010	250	PF65 85.00				

KM# 63 1000 FRANCS
25.00 g., 0.925 Silver 0.7387 oz. ASW **Rev:** Prism Elephant

Date	Mintage	F12	VF20	XF40	MS60	MS63
2011	2,500	PF63 65.00				

KM# 64 1000 FRANCS
25.00 g., 0.925 Silver 0.7387 oz. ASW Rev: Prism Zebra

Date	Mintage	F12	VF20	XF40	MS60	MS63
2011	2,500	PF63 70.00				

KM# 75 1500 FRANCS
1.24 g., 0.9999 Gold 0.0396 oz. AGW, 13.92 mm. Rev: St. Basil Cathedral in Moscow

Date	Mintage	F12	VF20	XF40	MS60	MS63
2005	2,000	PF63 90.00				

KM# 76 1500 FRANCS
1.24 g., 0.9999 Gold 0.0396 oz. AGW, 13.92 mm. Rev: Johann Wolfgang von Goethe

Date	Mintage	F12	VF20	XF40	MS60	MS63
2005	—	PF63 90.00				

KM# 77 1500 FRANCS
1.24 g., 0.9999 Gold 0.0396 oz. AGW, 13.92 mm. Rev: Friedrich von Schiller

Date	Mintage	F12	VF20	XF40	MS60	MS63
2005	—	PF63 90.00				

KM# 78 1500 FRANCS
1.24 g., 0.9999 Gold 0.0396 oz. AGW, 13.92 mm. Subject: Albert Einstein, 50th Anniversary of death

Date	Mintage	F12	VF20	XF40	MS60	MS63
2005	—	PF63 90.00				

KM# 79 1500 FRANCS
1.24 g., 0.9999 Gold 0.0396 oz. AGW, 13.92 mm. Rev: Gotthold Ephraim Lessing

Date	Mintage	F12	VF20	XF40	MS60	MS63
2006	—	PF63 90.00				

KM# 83 1500 FRANCS
1.00 g., 0.999 Gold 0.0319 oz. AGW, 13.92 mm. Rev: Zeus statue

Date	Mintage	F12	VF20	XF40	MS60	MS63
2007	—	PF63 80.00				

KM# 84 1500 FRANCS
1.00 g., 0.999 Gilt and Multicolored Litho Flan 0.0319 oz., 13.92 mm. Rev: Aphrodite statue

Date	Mintage	F12	VF20	XF40	MS60	MS63
2007	—	PF63 80.00				

KM# 85 1500 FRANCS
1.00 g., 0.999 Gold 0.0319 oz. AGW, 13.92 mm. Rev: Dionysus statue

Date	Mintage	F12	VF20	XF40	MS60	MS63
2007	—	PF63 80.00				

KM# 86 1500 FRANCS
0.50 g., 0.999 Gold AGW, 11 mm. Rev: Nefroite between hyrogryphlics

Date	Mintage	F12	VF20	XF40	MS60	MS63
2007	2,007	PF63 40.00		PF65 50.00		

KM# 87 1500 FRANCS
0.50 g., 0.999 Gold AGW, 11 mm. Subject: Max Planck, 150th Anniversary of Birth

Date	Mintage	F12	VF20	XF40	MS60	MS63
2008 Proof	—	—	—	—	—	40.00

KM# 93 1500 FRANCS
0.52 g., 0.999 Gold AGW, 11 mm. Obv: National arms Rev: Max Planck

Date	Mintage	F12	VF20	XF40	MS60	MS63
2008	10,000	PF63 100				

KM# 89 1500 FRANCS
0.62 g., 0.9999 Gold AGW, 11 mm. Rev: Two impalas

Date	Mintage	F12	VF20	XF40	MS60	MS63
2010	250	PF65 125				

KM# 94 1500 FRANCS
62.20 g., 0.999 Silver 1.9849 oz. ASW, 50 mm. Subject: Year of the Dragon Rev: Dragon with amber insert

Date	Mintage	F12	VF20	XF40	MS60	MS63
2012 Antique patina	999	—	—	—	—	500

KM# 95 1500 FRANCS
62.20 g., 0.999 Silver 1.9849 oz. ASW, 50 mm. Rev: Bison head facing with crystal inserts

Date	Mintage	F12	VF20	XF40	MS60	MS63
2012	999	PF65 300				

KM# 96 1500 FRANCS
Silver ASW Subject: Year of the Dragon Rev: Dragon and egg with young dragon

Date	Mintage	F12	VF20	XF40	MS60	MS63
2012	—	PF65 300				

KM# 39 2000 FRANCS
62.24 g., 0.9999 Silver 1.988 oz. ASW, 50 mm. Subject: Year of the Monkey Obv: Gold plated world globe Rev: Gold plated center with radiant holographic monkey within circle Edge: Reeded and lettered sections Edge Lettering: PAN ASIA BANK TAIWAN in English and Chinese Note: Date in Chinese numerals.

Date	Mintage	F12	VF20	XF40	MS60	MS63
2004	—	PF65 125				

KM# 90 2000 FRANCS
3.11 g., 0.9999 Gold 0.0993 oz. AGW, 18 mm. Rev: Two impalas

Date	Mintage	F12	VF20	XF40	MS60	MS63
2010	250	PF65 125				

KM# 92 5000 FRANCS
15.55 g., 0.9999 Gold 0.4967 oz. AGW, 30 mm. Rev: Two impalas

Date	Mintage	F12	VF20	XF40	MS60	MS63
2010	250	PF65 750				

KM# 91 2000 FRANCS
7.78 g., 0.9999 Gold 0.2485 oz. AGW, 25 mm. Rev: Two impalas

Date	Mintage	F12	VF20	XF40	MS60	MS63
2010 Proof	250	—	—	—	—	400

KM# 80 1500 FRANCS
1.24 g., 0.9999 Gold 0.0396 oz. AGW, 13.92 mm. Subject: Wilhelm Busch, 175th Anniversary of birth

Date	Mintage	F12	VF20	XF40	MS60	MS63
2007	Est. 15000	PF63 90.00				

TOKELAU

Tokelau or Union Islands, a New Zealand Territory located in the South Pacific 2,100 miles (3,379 km.) northeast of New Zealand and 300 miles (483 km.) north of Samoa, has an area of 4 sq. mi. (10 sq. km.) and a population of *2,000. Geographically, the group consists of four atolls - Atafu, Nukunono, Fakaofo and Swains – but the last belongs to American Samoa (and the United States claims the other three). The people are of Polynesian origin; Samoan is the official language. The New Zealand Minister for Foreign Affairs governs the islands; councils of family elders handle local government at the village level. The chief settlement is Fenuafala, on Fakaofo. It is connected by wireless technology with the offices of the New Zealand Administrative Center, located at Apia, Samoa. Subsistence farming and the production of copra for export are the main occupations. Revenue is also derived from the sale of postage stamps and, since 1978, coins.

Tokelau Islands issued its first coin in 1978, a "$1 Tahi Tala," Tokelauan for "One Dollar."

RULER
British

MINT MARK
PM - Pobjoy

NEW ZEALAND TERRITORY
STANDARD COINAGE

KM# 50 5 DOLLARS
Silver, 38.6 mm. Ruler: Elizabeth II Subject: Dragonfly with crystal eye

Date	Mintage	F12	VF20	XF40	MS60	MS63
2012	—	PF65 75.00				

KM# 30 5 TALA
31.10 g., 0.999 Silver 0.9925 oz. ASW, 40 mm. Series: Save the Whales Obv: Crowned head right Obv. Legend: TOKELAU Rev: Fin Whale on mother of pearl insert Edge: Plain

Date	Mintage	F12	VF20	XF40	MS60	MS63
2002	2,000	PF65 95.00				

KM# 32 5 TALA
31.10 g., 0.999 Silver 0.9925 oz. ASW, 40 mm. **Ruler:** Elizabeth II **Obv:** Elizabeth II **Rev:** Capt. Smith and ship General Jackson **Edge:** Reeded

Date	Mintage	F12	VF20	XF40	MS60	MS63
2003	—	PF63 45.00	PF65 48.00			

KM# 47 5 TALA
Silver, 38.6 mm. **Ruler:** Elizabeth II **Subject:** Endangered Wildlife **Obv:** Head crowned right **Rev:** Pacific Boa around a tree branch **Edge:** Reeded

Date	Mintage	F12	VF20	XF40	MS60	MS63
2003	—	PF65 50.00				

KM# 48 5 TALA
Silver, 38.6 mm. **Ruler:** Elizabeth II **Subject:** Olympics, 2004 **Obv:** Head crowned right **Rev:** Runner, swimmer and bicyalist **Edge:** Reeded

Date	Mintage	F12	VF20	XF40	MS60	MS63
2004	—	PF63 47.00	PF65 50.00			

KM# 33 5 TALA
28.65 g., Silver, 38.60 mm. **Ruler:** Elizabeth II **Obv:** Crowned

head right **Obv. Legend:** TOKELAU **Rev:** Sailing ship **Rev. Legend:** CUTTY SARK 1869 **Edge:** Reeded

Date	Mintage	F12	VF20	XF40	MS60	MS63
2005		PF63 42.00	PF65 45.00			

KM# 49 5 TALA
25.00 g., 0.925 Silver 0.7387 oz. ASW **Ruler:** Elizabeth II **Rev:** Roald Amundsen and jewel inset at South Pole

Date	Mintage	F12	VF20	XF40	MS60	MS63
2011	2,500	PF65 65.00				

KM# 46 10 TALA
1.24 g., 0.999 Gold 0.0396 oz. AGW, 13.92 mm. **Ruler:** Elizabeth II **Obv:** Crowned head right **Obv. Legend:** TOKELAU **Rev:** Two whales **Rev. Legend:** ENDANGERED WILDLIFE **Edge:** Reeded

Date	Mintage	F12	VF20	XF40	MS60	MS63
2003	—	PF65 85.00				

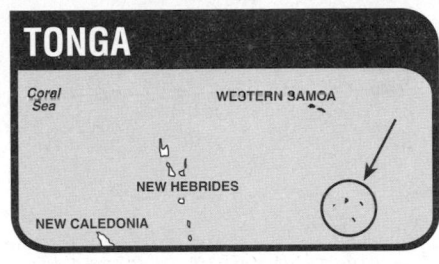

TONGA

The Kingdom of Tonga (or Friendly Islands) is an archipelago situated in the southern Pacific Ocean south of Western Samoa and east of Fiji comprised of 150 islands. Tonga has an area of 270 sq. mi. (748 sq. km.) and a population of *100,000. Capital: Nuku'alofa. Primarily agricultural, the kingdom exports bananas and copra.

The monarchy is a member of the Commonwealth of Nations. King Siosa Tupou V is Head of State and Government.

RULER
King Taufa'ahau IV, 1965-2006
King Siosa Tupou V, 2006-2012

KINGDOM

DECIMAL COINAGE
100 Senti = 1 Pa'anga; 100 Pa'anga = 1 Hau

KM# 66 SENITI
1.80 g., Bronze, 16.51 mm. **Ruler:** Taufa'ahau Tupou IV **Series:** World Food Day **Obv:** Ear of corn **Rev:** Vanilla plant **Edge:** Plain

Date	Mintage	F12	VF20	XF40	MS60	MS63
2005	—	—	—	0.10	0.35	0.75
2006	—	—	—	0.10	0.35	0.75

KM# 66a SENITI
Copper Plated Steel, 17.5 mm. **Ruler:** Taufa'ahau Tupou IV **Series:** World Food Day **Obv:** Ear of corn **Obv. Legend:** TONGA **Rev:** Vanilla plant **Rev. Legend:** FAKALAHI ME'AKAI **Edge:** Plain

Date	Mintage	F12	VF20	XF40	MS60	MS63
2002	—	—	—	0.10	0.35	0.75
2003	—	—	—	0.10	0.35	0.75
2004	—	—	—	0.10	0.35	0.75

KM# 67a 2 SENITI
Copper Plated Steel, 21 mm. **Ruler:** Taufa'ahau Tupou IV **Series:** World Food Day **Obv:** Taro plants **Obv. Legend:** TONGA **Rev:** Paper doll cutouts form design in center circle of sprays **Rev. Legend:** PLANNED FAMILIES • FOOD FOR ALL

Date	Mintage	F12	VF20	XF40	MS60	MS63
2002	—	—	—	0.15	0.65	1.25
2003	—	—	—	0.15	0.65	1.25
2004	—	—	—	0.15	0.65	1.25

KM# 68 5 SENITI
2.80 g., Copper-Nickel, 19.5 mm. **Ruler:** Taufa'ahau Tupou IV **Series:** World Food Day **Obv:** Hen with chicks **Rev:** Coconuts above sprig **Edge:** Reeded

Date	Mintage	F12	VF20	XF40	MS60	MS63
2005	—	—	—	0.10	0.25	0.75	1.25

KM# 68a 5 SENITI
2.79 g., Nickel Plated Steel, 19.39 mm. **Ruler:** Taufa'ahau Tupou IV **Series:** World Food Day **Obv:** Hen with chicks **Obv. Legend:** TONGA **Rev:** Coconuts **Rev. Legend:** FAKALAHI ME'AKAI **Edge:** Reeded

Date	Mintage	F12	VF20	XF40	MS60	MS63
2002	—	—		0.25	0.75	1.35
2003	—	—		0.25	0.75	1.35
2004	—	—		0.25	0.75	1.35
2005	—	—		0.25	0.75	1.35

KM# 69a 10 SENITI
Nickel Plated Steel, 23.5 mm. **Ruler:** Taufa'ahau Tupou IV **Series:** World Food Day **Obv:** Uniformed bust facing **Obv. Legend:** F • A • O - TONGA **Rev:** Banana tree **Rev. Legend:** FAKALAHI ME'AKAI

Date	Mintage	F12	VF20	XF40	MS60	MS63
2002	—	—		0.30	1.00	1.75
2003	—	—		0.30	1.00	1.75
2004	—	—		0.30	1.00	1.75
2005	—	—		0.30	1.00	1.75

KM# 70.1 20 SENITI
11.30 g., Nickel Plated Steel, 28.5 mm. **Ruler:** Taufa'ahau Tupou IV **Subject:** FAO - World Food Day **Obv:** Uniformed bust facing **Rev:** Yams

Date	Mintage	F12	VF20	XF40	MS60	MS63
2002	—	—	0.25	0.50	1.25	2.00
2003	—	—	0.25	0.50	1.25	2.00
2004	—	—	0.25	0.50	1.25	2.00

KM# 70a 50 SENITI
14.60 g., Nickel Plated Steel, 32.5 mm. **Ruler:** Taufa'ahau Tupou IV **Subject:** FAO - World Food Day **Obv:** Uniformed bust facing **Rev:** Tomato plants **Shape:** 12-sided

Date	Mintage	F12	VF20	XF40	MS60	MS63
2002	—	—	0.45	0.75	1.50	2.50
2003	—	—	0.45	0.75	1.50	2.50
2004	—	—	0.45	0.75	1.50	2.50

KM# 212 PA'ANGA
31.47 g., 0.925 Silver 0.9299 oz. ASW, 38.61 mm. **Ruler:** Siaosi Tupou V **Subject:** History of Seafaring - HMS Descubierta

Date	Mintage	F12	VF20	XF40	MS60	MS63
2001	Est. 5000	PF65 55.00				

KM# 178 PA'ANGA
31.10 g., 0.999 Silver 0.9925 oz. ASW, 40 mm. **Ruler:** Taufa'ahau Tupou IV **Series:** Save the Whales **Obv:** Crown within wreath above national arms within circle **Obv. Legend:** KINGDOM OF TONGA **Rev:** Right Whale on mother of pearl insert **Edge:** Plain

Date	Mintage	F12	VF20	XF40	MS60	MS63
2002	2,000	PF65 95.00				

KM# 213 PA'ANGA
31.00 g., 0.925 Silver 0.916 oz. ASW, 40 mm. **Ruler:** Siaosi Tupou V **Subject:** Farewell to the Luxembourg Franc

Date	Mintage	F12	VF20	XF40	MS60	MS63
2002	Est. 2001	PF65 80.00				

KM# 182 PA'ANGA
31.47 g., 0.925 Silver 0.9299 oz. ASW **Ruler:** Taufa'ahau Tupou IV **Subject:** 2004 Olympics **Obv:** National arms **Rev:** Kayak crew seen from above

Date	Mintage	F12	VF20	XF40	MS60	MS63
2003	—	PF65 65.00				

KM# 215 PA'ANGA
31.47 g., 0.9299 oz. ASW, 38.61 mm. **Ruler:** Siaosi Tupou V **Subject:** History of Seafaring - HMS Adventure & James Cook

Date	Mintage	F12	VF20	XF40	MS60	MS63
2003	—	PF65 55.00				

KM# 217 PA'ANGA
31.47 g., 0.925 Silver 0.9299 oz. ASW, 38.61 mm. **Ruler:** Siaosi Tupou V **Subject:** 2006 Soccer World Cup, Germany

Date	Mintage	F12	VF20	XF40	MS60	MS63
2004	Est. 50000	PF63 30.00 PF65 40.00				

KM# 218 PA'ANGA
31.47 g., 0.925 Silver 0.9299 oz. ASW, 38.61 mm. **Ruler:** Siaosi Tupou V **Subject:** History of Seafaring - HMS Beagle & Charles Darwin

Date	Mintage	F12	VF20	XF40	MS60	MS63
2005	—	PF65 55.00				

KM# 219 PA'ANGA
28.28 g., 0.925 Silver 0.8356 oz. ASW, 38.61 mm. **Ruler:** Siaosi Tupou V **Subject:** History of Seafaring - Sailing Ship Heemskerck

Date	Mintage	F12	VF20	XF40	MS60	MS63
2005	—	PF65 55.00				

KM# 187 PA'ANGA
28.28 g., 0.925 Silver 0.8356 oz. ASW, 38.61 mm. **Ruler:** Siaosi Tupou V **Subject:** Ships and Explorers - Thor Heyerdahl

Date	Mintage	F12	VF20	XF40	MS60	MS63
2010	Est. 5000	PF65 70.00				

KM# 190 PA'ANGA
28.28 g., 0.925 Silver 0.8356 oz. ASW, 38.61 mm. **Ruler:** Siaosi Tupou V **Subject:** Railways - DB CLass V 200

Date	Mintage	F12	VF20	XF40	MS60	MS63
2010	Est. 5000	PF65 70.00				

KM# 222 PA'ANGA
31.47 g., 0.925 Silver 0.9299 oz. ASW, 38.61 mm. **Ruler:** Siaosi Tupou V **Subject:** Railroads of the World - Diesel Locomotives of the German Railway

Date	Mintage	F12	VF20	XF40	MS60	MS63
2010	Est. 10000	PF63 55.00 PF65 65.00				

KM# 223 PA'ANGA
31.47 g., 0.925 Silver 0.9299 oz. ASW, 38.61 mm. **Ruler:** Siaosi Tupou V **Subject:** History of Seafaring - Sailing Ship Thor Heyerdahl

Date	Mintage	F12	VF20	XF40	MS60	MS63
2010	Est. 10000	PF63 55.00 PF65 65.00				

KM# 183 PA'ANGA
28.28 g., 0.925 Silver 0.8356 oz. ASW, 38.61 mm. **Ruler:** Siaosi Tupou V **Subject:** 2012 London Olympic Games - Runner

Date	Mintage	F12	VF20	XF40	MS60	MS63
2012	Est. 10000	PF63 65.00 PF65 75.00				

KM# 184 PA'ANGA
28.28 g., 0.925 Silver 0.8356 oz. ASW, 38.61 mm. **Ruler:** Siaosi Tupou V **Subject:** Diamond Jubilee of Queen Elizabeth II - Buckingham Palace

Date	Mintage	F12	VF20	XF40	MS60	MS63
2012	Est. 10000	PF63 65.00 PF65 75.00				

KM# 186 PA'ANGA
26.03 g., Silver Plated Copper, 38.61 mm. **Ruler:** Siaosi Tupou V **Subject:** London Olympic Games - Runner

Date	Mintage	F12	VF20	XF40	MS60	MS63
2012	Est. 30000	PF63 18.00 PF65 20.00				

KM# 179 2 PA'ANGA
Silver **Ruler:** Taufa'ahau Tupou IV **Subject:** King's 85th Birthday **Obv:** National arms

Date	Mintage	F12	VF20	XF40	MS60	MS63
2003	—	PF65 150				

KM# 224 5 PA'ANGA
20.00 g., 0.925 Silver 0.591 oz. ASW, 38.61 mm. **Subject:** 2014 FIFA World Cup - Brazil

Date	Mintage	F12	VF20	XF40	MS60	MS63
2013	Est. 10000	PF63 65.00 PF65 75.00				

KM# 188 10 PA'ANGA
1.13 g., 0.9999 Gold 0.0362 oz. AGW, 13.92 mm. **Ruler:** Siaosi Tupou V **Subject:** Smallest Gold Coins - Hidddensee Treasure

Date	Mintage	F12	VF20	XF40	MS60	MS63
2003	Est. 20000	PF63 75.00 PF65 85.00				

KM# 214 10 PA'ANGA
1.24 g., 0.999 Gold 0.0396 oz. AGW, 13.92 mm. **Ruler:** Siaosi Tupou V **Subject:** History of Gold - Hiddensee Viking Ship and Treasure

Date	Mintage	F12	VF20	XF40	MS60	MS63
2003	Est. 15000	PF63 70.00 PF65 80.00				

KM# 216 10 PA'ANGA
1.24 g., 0.999 Gold 0.0396 oz. AGW, 13.92 mm. **Ruler:** Siaosi Tupou V **Subject:** History of Seafaring - HMS Adventure & James Cook

Date	Mintage	F12	VF20	XF40	MS60	MS63
2003	Est. 25000	PF63 70.00 PF65 80.00				

KM# 220 10 PA'ANGA
1.24 g., 0.999 Gold 0.0396 oz. AGW, 13.92 mm. **Ruler:** Siaosi Tupou V **Subject:** Coronation of King George Tupov V

Date	Mintage	F12	VF20	XF40	MS60	MS63
2008	—	PF65 80.00				

KM# 189 10 PA'ANGA
0.50 g., 0.999 Gold AGW, 11 mm. **Ruler:** Siaosi Tupou V **Subject:** Smallest Gold Coins - Trilithon

Date	Mintage	F12	VF20	XF40	MS60	MS63
2011	Est. 10000	PF63 35.00 PF65 40.00				

KM# 191 10 PA'ANGA
1.24 g., 0.999 Gold 0.0396 oz. AGW, 13.92 mm. **Ruler:** Siaosi Tupou V **Subject:** Coronation of HM King Siaosi Tupou V

Date	Mintage	F12	VF20	XF40	MS60	MS63
2012	Est. 10000	PF63 75.00 PF65 85.00				

KM# 225 10 PA'ANGA
0.50 g., 0.585 Gold AGW, 11 mm. **Subject:** Heilala Festival

Date	Mintage	F12	VF20	XF40	MS60	MS63
2013	Est. 10000	PF63 40.00 PF65 50.00				

KM# 221 50 PA'ANGA
Gold AGW **Ruler:** Siaosi Tupou V **Subject:** Coronation of King George Tupov V

Date	Mintage	F12	VF20	XF40	MS60	MS63
2008	—	—	—	—		

KM# 185 100 PA'ANGA
7.77 g., 0.585 Gold 0.1452 oz. AGW, 25 mm. **Ruler:** Siaosi Tupou V **Subject:** 2012 London Olympic Games - Runner

Date	Mintage	F12	VF20	XF40	MS60	MS63
2012	Est. 30000	PF65 350				

TRANSNISTRIA

The Pridnestrovskaia Moldavskaia Respublica was formed in 1990, even before the separation of Moldavia from Russia. It has an area of 11,544 sq. mi. (29,900 sq. km.) and a population of 555,000. Capital: Tiraspol.

Transnistria (or Transdniestra) has a president, parliament, army and police forces, but as yet it is lacking international recognition.

MOLDAVIAN REPUBLIC

STANDARD COINAGE

1 Rublei = 100 Kopeek

KM# 172 20 RUBLEI
62.70 g., 0.999 Gold 2.0009 oz. AGW, 39 mm. **Subject:** 20th Anniversary of the Republic of Moldova

Date	Mintage	F12	VF20	XF40	MS60	MS63
2010	30	PF65 4,250				

KM# 173 20 RUBLEI
125.25 g., 0.999 Gold 3.997 oz. AGW, 50 mm. **Subject:** 20th Anniversary of the Republic of Moldova

Date	Mintage	F12	VF20	XF40	MS60	MS63
2010	20	PF65 8,250				

KM# 142 20 RUBLEI
33.50 g., 0.925 Silver 0.9899 oz. ASW, 39 mm. **Subject:** 20th Anniversary of the Ministry of Internal Affairs **Obv:** State Arms

Date	Mintage	F12	VF20	XF40	MS60	MS63
2011 Proof-like	Est. 200	PF65 115				

KM# 175 20 RUBLEI
74.30 g., 0.925 Silver 2.1954 oz. ASW, 52 mm. **Subject:** 20th Anniversary of Banking in Transnistria

Date	Mintage	F12	VF20	XF40	MS60	MS63
2011	200	PF65 200				

KM# 50 5 KOPEEK
0.70 g., Aluminum, 17.9 mm. **Obv:** Modified national arms **Obv. Legend:** ПРИДНЕСТРОВСКАЯ МОЛДАВСКАЯ РЕСПУБЛИКА **Rev:** Value flanked by wheat stalks. **Edge:** Plain **Note:** Prev. KM#2, 16.

Date	Mintage	F12	VF20	XF40	MS60	MS63
2005	—			0.20	0.50	0.65

KM# 51 10 KOPEEK
1.00 g., Aluminum, 20 mm. **Obv:** Modified national arms **Obv. Legend:** ПРИДНЕСТРОВСКАЯ МОЛДАВСКАЯ РЕСПУБЛИКА **Rev:** Value flanked by wheat stalks **Edge:** Plain **Note:** Prev. KM#3, 17.

Date	Mintage	F12	VF20	XF40	MS60	MS63
2005	—			0.25	0.65	0.90

KM# 5 25 KOPEEK
2.15 g., Aluminum-Bronze, 16.88 mm. **Obv:** National arms **Rev:** Value within sprays **Edge:** Plain

Date	Mintage	F12	VF20	XF40	MS60	MS63
2002	—	—	0.15	0.35	0.90	1.20

KM# 52 25 KOPEEK
Aluminum-Bronze, 16.9 mm. **Obv:** Modified national arms **Obv. Legend:** ПРИДНЕСТРОВСКАЯ МОЛДАВСКАЯ РЕСПУБЛИКА **Rev:** Value within sprays **Edge:** Plain **Note:** Prev. KM#18.

Date	Mintage	F12	VF20	XF40	MS60	MS63
2005	—	—	0.15	0.35	0.90	1.20

KM# 52a 25 KOPEEK
2.10 g., Bronze Plated Steel, 16.9 mm. **Obv:** Modified national arms **Obv. Legend:** ПРИДНЕСТРОВСКАЯ МОЛДАВСКАЯ РЕСПУБЛИКА **Rev:** Value within sprays **Edge:** Plain **Note:** Prev. KM#5a; 18a.

Date	Mintage	F12	VF20	XF40	MS60	MS63
2005	—		0.15	0.35	0.90	1.20

KM# 53 50 KOPEEK
2.80 g., Aluminum-Bronze, 19 mm. **Obv:** Modified national arms **Obv. Legend:** ПРИДНЕСТРОВСКАЯ МОЛДАВСКАЯ РЕСПУБЛИКА **Rev:** Value within sprays **Edge:** Plain **Note:** Prev. KM#4a; 19.

Date	Mintage	F12	VF20	XF40	MS60	MS63
2005	—		0.15	0.45	1.10	1.50

KM# 53a 50 KOPEEK
Bronze Plated Steel, 19 mm. **Obv:** Modified national arms **Obv. Legend:** ПРИДНЕСТРОВСКАЯ МОЛДАВСКАЯ РЕСПУБЛИКА **Rev:** Value within sprays **Edge:** Plain **Note:** Prev. KM#19a.

Date	Mintage	F12	VF20	XF40	MS60	MS63
2005	—		0.15	0.45	1.10	1.50

KM# 55 RUBLE
14.14 g., 0.925 Silver 0.4178 oz. ASW, 32 mm. **Obv:** National Arms **Rev:** Building with dome

Date	Mintage	F12	VF20	XF40	MS60	MS63
2005	500	PF65 175				

KM# 77 RUBLE
14.14 g., 0.925 Silver 0.4178 oz. ASW, 32 mm. **Obv:** National Arms **Rev:** Moth and caterpillar

Date	Mintage	F12	VF20	XF40	MS60	MS63
2006	1,000	PF65 145				

KM# 79 RUBLE
14.14 g., 0.925 Silver 0.4178 oz. ASW, 32 mm. **Obv:** Olympics - Turin **Rev:** Slalom

Date	Mintage	F12	VF20	XF40	MS60	MS63
2006	500	PF65 175				

KM# 95 3 RUBLYA
8.00 g., 0.900 Gold 0.230 oz. AGW, 21 mm. **Obv:** National Arms **Rev:** Shield **Rev. Legend:** РЫБНИЦА

Date	Mintage	F12	VF20	XF40	MS60	MS63
2007	100	PF63 525	PF65 550			

KM# 97 3 RUBLYA
8.00 g., 0.900 Gold 0.230 oz. AGW, 21 mm. **Obv:** National Arms **Rev:** Shield **Rev. Legend:** ТИРАСПОЛЬ

Date	Mintage	F12	VF20	XF40	MS60	MS63
2007	100	PF63 525	PF65 550			

KM# 110 3 RUBLYA
14.14 g., 0.925 Silver 0.4178 oz. ASW, 32 mm. **Obv:** National Arms **Rev:** Aquarius within zodiac emblems

Date	Mintage	F12	VF20	XF40	MS60	MS63
2007	100	PF63 95.00	PF65 125			

KM# 155 3 RUBLYA
8.00 g., 0.900 Gold 0.230 oz. AGW, 21 mm. **Subject:** Moldovan Metal Works

Date	Mintage	F12	VF20	XF40	MS60	MS63
2008	100	PF63 525	PF65 550			

KM# 145 3 RUBLYA
8.00 g., 0.900 Gold 0.230 oz. AGW, 21 mm. **Subject:** Coat of arms of the city of Bendery

Date	Mintage	F12	VF20	XF40	MS60	MS63
2008	100	PF63 525	PF65 550			

KM# 161 3 RUBLYA
101.50 g., 0.925 Silver 2.9991 oz. ASW, 50 mm. **Subject:** Endangered Plants and Animals **Rev:** Dog head

Date	Mintage	F12	VF20	XF40	MS60	MS63
2008 Proof	5	—	—	—	—	—

KM# 163 3 RUBLYA
8.00 g., 0.900 Gold 0.230 oz. AGW, 21 mm. **Series:** Tribute to 5 Kopek of Moldavia & Wallachea with double headed eagle

Date	Mintage	F12	VF20	XF40	MS60	MS63
2009	250	PF63 535	PF65 550			

KM# 100 5 RUBLES
33.85 g., 0.925 Silver 1.0002 oz. ASW, 39 mm. **Obv:** National Arms **Rev:** Wooley mammoth

Date	Mintage	F12	VF20	XF40	MS60	MS63
2007	500	PF63 125	PF65 145			

KM# 101 5 RUBLES
33.85 g., 0.925 Silver 1.0002 oz. ASW, 39 mm. **Obv:** National Arms **Rev:** Moose

Date	Mintage	F12	VF20	XF40	MS60	MS63
2007	500	PF63 125	PF65 145			

KM# 134 5 RUBLES
33.80 g., 0.925 Silver 0.9987 oz. ASW, 39 mm. **Obv:** National Arms **Rev:** Woolly Mammoth (Archidiskodon Trogrnterii)

Date	Mintage	F12	VF20	XF40	MS60	MS63
2007	500	PF63 125	PF65 145			

KM# 156 5 RUBLES
33.85 g., 0.925 Silver 1.0002 oz. ASW, 39 mm. **Subject:** Prehistoric Finds - Panthera Leo Spelaea Felidae

Date	Mintage	F12	VF20	XF40	MS60	MS63
2008	500	PF63 135	PF65 150			

KM# 158 5 RUBLES
33.85 g., 0.925 Silver 1.0002 oz. ASW, 39 mm. **Subject:** Moldovan Republic Anthem

Date	Mintage	F12	VF20	XF40	MS60	MS63
2008	1,000	PF63 120	PF65 135			

KM# 159 5 RUBLES
33.85 g., 0.925 Silver 1.0002 oz. ASW, 39 mm. **Subject:** 55 Infantry Regiments of Podolskij

Date	Mintage	F12	VF20	XF40	MS60	MS63
2008	1,000	PF63 120	PF65 135			

KM# 160 5 RUBLES
33.85 g., 0.925 Silver 1.0002 oz. ASW, 39 mm. **Subject:** Year of the Familie

Date	Mintage	F12	VF20	XF40	MS60	MS63
2008	1,000	PF63 120	PF65 135			

KM# 162 5 RUBLES
8.00 g., 0.900 Gold 0.230 oz. AGW, 21 mm. **Subject:** Russian History of Transnistria - Sophie Auguste Friederike von Anhalt-Zerbst also known as Catherine II

Date	Mintage	F12	VF20	XF40	MS60	MS63
2009	250	PF63 525	PF65 535			

KM# 170 5 RUBLES
33.85 g., 39.000 Silver 42.1706 oz. ASW, 39 mm. **Subject:** 65th Anniversary of Victory in Second World War

Date	Mintage	F12	VF20	XF40	MS60	MS63
2010	250	PF63 95.00	PF65 110			

KM# 171 5 RUBLES
33.85 g., 0.925 Silver 1.0002 oz. ASW, 39 mm. **Subject:** 20th Anniversary of the Republic of Moldova

Date	Mintage	F12	VF20	XF40	MS60	MS63
2010	250	PF63 95.00	PF65 110			

KM# 141 5 RUBLES
33.50 g., 0.925 Silver 0.9899 oz. ASW, 39 mm. **Obv:** Yuri Gagarin with color

Date	Mintage	F12	VF20	XF40	MS60	MS63
2011	—	PF63 135	PF65 150			

KM# 176 5 RUBLES
29.70 g., 0.925 Silver 0.8776 oz. ASW, 37 x 37 mm. **Subject:** Four Seasons - Spring in Color

Date	Mintage	F12	VF20	XF40	MS60	MS63
2011	250	PF63 100	PF65 120			

KM# 177 5 RUBLES
29.70 g., 0.925 Silver 0.8776 oz. ASW, 37 x 37 mm. **Subject:** Four Seasons - Summer in Color

Date	Mintage	F12	VF20	XF40	MS60	MS63
2011	250	PF63 100	PF65 120			

KM# 178 5 RUBLES
29.70 g., 0.925 Silver 0.8776 oz. ASW, 37 x 37 mm. **Subject:** Four Seasons - Fall in Color

Date	Mintage	F12	VF20	XF40	MS60	MS63
2011	250	PF63 100	PF65 120			

KM# 179 5 RUBLES
29.70 g., 0.925 Silver 0.8776 oz. ASW, 37 x 37 mm. **Subject:** Four Seasons - Winter in Color

Date	Mintage	F12	VF20	XF40	MS60	MS63
2011	250	PF63 100	PF65 120			

KM# 112 10 RUBLEI
14.14 g., 0.925 Silver 0.4178 oz. ASW, 32 mm. **Obv:** National Arms **Rev:** Aquarius within circle of zodiac symbols

Date	Mintage	F12	VF20	XF40	MS60	MS63
2007	500	PF63 80.00	PF65 100			

KM# 102 10 RUBLEI
14.14 g., 0.925 Silver 0.4178 oz. ASW, 32 mm. **Obv:** National Arms **Rev:** Multicolor sprinter

Date	Mintage	F12	VF20	XF40	MS60	MS63
2007	500	PF63 80.00	PF65 100			

KM# 103 10 RUBLEI
14.14 g., 0.925 Silver 0.4178 oz. ASW, 32 mm. **Obv:** National Arms **Rev:** Multicolor female gymnast

Date	Mintage	F12	VF20	XF40	MS60	MS63
2007	500	PF63 80.00	PF65 100			

KM# 104 10 RUBLEI
14.14 g., 0.925 Silver 0.4178 oz. ASW, 32 mm. **Obv:** National Arms **Rev:** Multicolor runner, sports designs

Date	Mintage	F12	VF20	XF40	MS60	MS63
2007	500	PF63 80.00	PF65 100			

KM# 105 10 RUBLEI
14.14 g., 0.925 Silver 0.4178 oz. ASW, 32 mm. **Obv:** National Arms **Rev:** Multicolor javlin thrower

Date	Mintage	F12	VF20	XF40	MS60	MS63
2007	500	PF63 80.00	PF65 100			

KM# 106 10 RUBLEI
14.14 g., 0.925 Silver 0.4178 oz. ASW, 32 mm. **Obv:** National Arms **Rev:** Multicolor runner breaking tape at finish line

Date	Mintage	F12	VF20	XF40	MS60	MS63
2007	500	PF63 80.00	PF65 100			

KM# 107 10 RUBLEI
14.14 g., 0.925 Silver 0.4178 oz. ASW, 32 mm. **Obv:** National Arms **Rev:** Multicolor soccer player

Date	Mintage	F12	VF20	XF40	MS60	MS63
2007	500	PF63 80.00	PF65 100			

KM# 111 10 RUBLEI
14.14 g., 0.925 Silver 0.4178 oz. ASW, 32 mm. **Obv:** National Arms **Rev:** Constellation ophiuchus (man grasping serpent)

Date	Mintage	F12	VF20	XF40	MS60	MS63
2007	500	PF63 80.00	PF65 100			

KM# 125 10 RUBLEI
14.14 g., 0.925 Silver 0.4178 oz. ASW, 32 mm. **Obv:** National Arms **Rev:** Sturgeon fish

Date	Mintage	F12	VF20	XF40	MS60	MS63
2008	500	PF63 95.00	PF65 125			

KM# 126 10 RUBLEI
14.14 g., 0.925 Silver 0.4178 oz. ASW, 32 mm. **Obv:** National Arms **Rev:** Owl

Date	Mintage	F12	VF20	XF40	MS60	MS63
2008	500	PF63 95.00	PF65 125			

KM# 127 10 RUBLEI
14.14 g., 0.925 Silver 0.4178 oz. ASW, 32 mm. **Obv:** National Arms **Rev:** Flower

Date	Mintage	F12	VF20	XF40	MS60	MS63
2008	500	PF63 95.00	PF65 125			

KM# 128 10 RUBLEI
14.14 g., 0.925 Silver 0.4178 oz. ASW, 32 mm. **Obv:** National Arms **Rev:** Otter

Date	Mintage	F12	VF20	XF40	MS60	MS63
2008	500	PF63 80.00	PF65 100			

KM# 135 10 RUBLEI
14.14 g., 0.925 Silver 0.4178 oz. ASW, 32 mm. Obv: National Arms Rev: Lutra otter

Date	Mintage	F12	VF20	XF40	MS60	MS63
2008	5,000	PF63 85.00	PF65 100			

KM# 148 10 RUBLEI
14.14 g., 0.925 Silver 0.4178 oz. ASW, 32 mm. Subject: 2008 Summer Olympics - Beijing

Date	Mintage	F12	VF20	XF40	MS60	MS63
2008	500	PF63 80.00	PF65 90.00			

KM# 149 10 RUBLEI
14.14 g., 0.925 Silver 0.4178 oz. ASW, 32 mm. Subject: 2008 Summer Olympics, Beijing - Wrestling

Date	Mintage	F12	VF20	XF40	MS60	MS63
2008	500	PF63 80.00	PF65 90.00			

KM# 150 10 RUBLEI
14.14 g., 0.925 Silver 0.4178 oz. ASW, 32 mm. Subject: 2008 Summer Olympics, Beijing

Date	Mintage	F12	VF20	XF40	MS60	MS63
2008	500	PF63 80.00	PF65 90.00			

KM# 151 10 RUBLEI
14.14 g., 0.925 Silver 0.4178 oz. ASW, 32 mm. Series: 2008 Summer Olympics, Beijing - Rowing

Date	Mintage	F12	VF20	XF40	MS60	MS63
2008	500	PF63 80.00	PF65 90.00			

KM# 152 10 RUBLEI
14.14 g., 0.925 Silver 0.4178 oz. ASW, 32 mm. Subject: 2008 Summer Olympics, Beijing - Archery

Date	Mintage	F12	VF20	XF40	MS60	MS63
2008	500	PF63 80.00	PF65 90.00			

KM# 153 10 RUBLEI
14.14 g., 0.925 Silver 0.4178 oz. ASW, 32 mm. Subject: 2008 Summer Olympics, Beijing - Table Tennis

Date	Mintage	F12	VF20	XF40	MS60	MS63
2008	500	PF63 80.00	PF65 90.00			

KM# 154 10 RUBLEI
14.14 g., 0.925 Silver 0.4178 oz. ASW, 32 mm. Subject: Moldovan Metal Works

Date	Mintage	F12	VF20	XF40	MS60	MS63
2008	800	PF63 75.00	PF65 85.00			

KM# 164 10 RUBLEI
14.14 g., 0.925 Silver 0.4178 oz. ASW, 32 mm. Subject: Endangered Plants and Animals - Swan

Date	Mintage	F12	VF20	XF40	MS60	MS63
2009	500	PF63 75.00	PF65 85.00			

KM# 165 10 RUBLEI
14.14 g., 0.925 Silver 0.4178 oz. ASW, 32 mm. Subject: Endangered Plants and Animals - Snowdrop Flower

Date	Mintage	F12	VF20	XF40	MS60	MS63
2009	50	PF63 75.00	PF65 85.00			

KM# 137 10 RUBLEI
7.89 g., 0.925 Silver 0.2331 oz. ASW, 21 mm. Obv: State emblem Rev: Death's Head Hawkmoth in color

Date	Mintage	F12	VF20	XF40	MS60	MS63
2011 Prooflike	Est. 250	PF65 100				

KM# 138 10 RUBLEI
13.07 g., Silver, 32 mm. Rev: Death's Head Hawkmoth

Date	Mintage	F12	VF20	XF40	MS60	MS63
2011 Prooflike	—	PF65 95.00				

KM# 180 10 RUBLEI
7.89 g., 0.925 Silver 0.2331 oz. ASW, 21 mm. Subject: Endangered Plants and Animals - Skull Owl in color

Date	Mintage	F12	VF20	XF40	MS60	MS63
2011	250	PF65 100				

KM# 181 10 RUBLEI
13.87 g., 0.925 Silver 0.4098 oz. ASW, 32 mm. Subject: Endangered Plants and Animals - Skull Owl

Date	Mintage	F12	VF20	XF40	MS60	MS63
2011	250	PF65 95.00				

KM# 54 15 RUBLEI
156.40 g., 0.999 Gold 4.991 oz. AGW, 50 mm. Obv: National Arms Rev: Building with dome

Date	Mintage	F12	VF20	XF40	MS60	MS63
2005 Proof, Rare	15	—	—	—	—	—

KM# 75 15 RUBLEI
156.40 g., 0.999 Gold 4.991 oz. AGW, 15 mm. Obv: National Arms Rev: Building with tower

Date	Mintage	F12	VF20	XF40	MS60	MS63
2006 Proof, Rare	15	—	—	—	—	—

KM# 157 15 RUBLEI
155.50 g., 0.999 Gold 4.9623 oz. AGW, 65 mm. Subject: Prehistoric Finds - Mammoth

Date	Mintage	F12	VF20	XF40	MS60	MS63
2008	10	PF65 11,500				

KM# 167 15 RUBLEI
31.00 g., 0.925 Silver 0.916 oz. ASW, 37 x 21 mm. Subject: 15th Anniversary of National Custody

Date	Mintage	F12	VF20	XF40	MS60	MS63
2009	250	PF63 90.00	PF65 100			

KM# 168 15 RUBLEI
6.10 g., 0.999 Gold 0.1947 oz. AGW, 22 x 13 mm. Subject: 15th Anniversary of National Custody

Date	Mintage	F12	VF20	XF40	MS60	MS63
2009	250	PF63 525	PF65 550			

KM# 17 100 RUBLEI
14.14 g., 0.925 Silver 0.4178 oz. ASW, 32 mm. Obv: National Arms Rev: Cathedral of Ascension, Kitskany 1864

Date	Mintage	F12	VF20	XF40	MS60	MS63
2001	1,000	PF63 60.00	PF65 70.00			

KM# 10 100 RUBLEI
14.14 g., 0.925 Silver 0.4178 oz. ASW, 32 mm. Obv: National Arms Rev: D. Zielinskieg, chemist

Date	Mintage	F12	VF20	XF40	MS60	MS63
2001	1,000	PF63 65.00	PF65 75.00			

KM# 11 100 RUBLEI
14.14 g., 0.925 Silver 0.4178 oz. ASW, 32 mm. Obv: National Arms Rev: S. Berg, fish

Date	Mintage	F12	VF20	XF40	MS60	MS63
2001	1,000	PF63 65.00	PF65 75.00			

KM# 12 100 RUBLEI
14.14 g., 0.925 Silver 0.4178 oz. ASW, 32 mm. Obv: National Arms Rev: N.F. Skilfosowskieg, portrait at right

Date	Mintage	F12	VF20	XF40	MS60	MS63
2001	1,000	PF63 65.00	PF65 75.00			

KM# 13 100 RUBLEI
14.14 g., 0.925 Silver 0.4178 oz. ASW, 32 mm. Obv: National Arms Rev: M.F. Larionowa, bust, painter

Date	Mintage	F12	VF20	XF40	MS60	MS63
2001	1,000	PF63 65.00	PF65 75.00			

KM# 14 100 RUBLEI
14.14 g., 0.925 Silver 0.4178 oz. ASW, 32 mm. Obv: National Arms Rev: Cathedral in Tyraspol

Date	Mintage	F12	VF20	XF40	MS60	MS63
2001	1,000	PF63 70.00	PF65 80.00			

KM# 15 100 RUBLEI
14.14 g., 0.925 Silver 0.4178 oz. ASW, 32 mm. Obv: National Arms Rev: Cathedral XVII

Date	Mintage	F12	VF20	XF40	MS60	MS63
2001	1,000	PF63 60.00	PF65 70.00			

KM# 16 100 RUBLEI
14.14 g., 0.925 Silver 0.4178 oz. ASW, 32 mm. Obv: National Arms Rev: Cathedral 1800

Date	Mintage	F12	VF20	XF40	MS60	MS63
2001	1,000	PF63 60.00	PF65 70.00			

KM# 18 100 RUBLEI
14.14 g., 0.925 Silver 0.4178 oz. ASW, 32 mm. Obv: National Arms Rev: Cathedral 1825

Date	Mintage	F12	VF20	XF40	MS60	MS63
2001	1,000	PF63 60.00	PF65 70.00			

KM# 19 100 RUBLEI
14.14 g., 0.925 Silver 0.4178 oz. ASW, 32 mm. Obv: National Arms Rev: Church of St. Trinity, Rashkov 1778

Date	Mintage	F12	VF20	XF40	MS60	MS63
2001	1,000	PF63 60.00	PF65 70.00			

KM# 20 100 RUBLEI
14.14 g., 0.925 Silver 0.4178 oz. ASW, 32 mm. Obv: National Arms Rev: Cathedral XIX

Date	Mintage	F12	VF20	XF40	MS60	MS63
2001	1,000	PF63 60.00	PF65 70.00			

KM# 21 100 RUBLEI
14.14 g., 0.925 Silver 0.4178 oz. ASW, 32 mm. Obv: National Arms Rev: Cathedral 1784

Date	Mintage	F12	VF20	XF40	MS60	MS63
2001	1,000	PF63 60.00	PF65 70.00			

KM# 22 100 RUBLEI
14.14 g., 0.925 Silver 0.4178 oz. ASW, 32 mm. Obv: National Arms Rev: Cathedral 1854

Date	Mintage	F12	VF20	XF40	MS60	MS63
2001	1,000	PF63 60.00	PF65 70.00			

KM# 35 100 RUBLEI
14.14 g., 0.925 Silver 0.4178 oz. ASW, 32 mm. Subject: City of Tiraspol Obv: National arms Rev: Statue and buildings Edge: Plain Note: Prev. KM#7.

Date	Mintage	F12	VF20	XF40	MS60	MS63
2002	—	PF63 70.00	PF65 80.00			

KM# 36 100 RUBLEI
14.14 g., 0.925 Silver 0.4178 oz. ASW, 32 mm. Subject: City of Tiraspol Obv: National arms Rev: Cameo above fortress Edge: Plain Note: Prev. KM#8.

Date	Mintage	F12	VF20	XF40	MS60	MS63
2002	—	PF63 70.00	PF65 80.00			

KM# 37 100 RUBLEI
14.14 g., 0.925 Silver 0.4178 oz. ASW, 32 mm. Subject: 10th Anniversary - Trans-Dniester Republican Bank Obv: National arms Rev: Colorized monogram within 3/4 wreath with "1992" at top Edge: Plain Note: Prev. KM#10.

Date	Mintage	F12	VF20	XF40	MS60	MS63
2002	500	PF63 75.00	PF65 85.00			

KM# 38 100 RUBLEI
14.16 g., 0.925 Silver 0.4184 oz. ASW, 32 mm. Subject: K. K. Gedroets Obv: National arms Rev: Bust facing flanked by sprigs, beaker and book Edge: Plain Note: Prev. KM#9.

Date	Mintage	F12	VF20	XF40	MS60	MS63
2002	500	PF63 70.00	PF65 80.00			

KM# 40 100 RUBLEI
14.14 g., 0.925 Silver 0.4178 oz. ASW, 32 mm. Obv: National Arms Rev: Shield Rev. Legend: ТИРАСЛОЛБ

Date	Mintage	F12	VF20	XF40	MS60	MS63
2002	500	PF63 75.00	PF65 85.00			

KM# 41 100 RUBLEI
14.14 g., 0.925 Silver 0.4178 oz. ASW, 32 mm. Obv: National Arms Rev: Shield Rev. Legend: ГРНГОРКОПОЛЛ

Date	Mintage	F12	VF20	XF40	MS60	MS63
2002	500	PF63 75.00	PF65 85.00			

KM# 42 100 RUBLEI
14.14 g., 0.925 Silver 0.4178 oz. ASW, 32 mm. Obv: National arms Rev: Shield flanked by sprigs Edge: Plain Note: Prev. KM#12.

Date	Mintage	F12	VF20	XF40	MS60	MS63
2003	500	PF63 70.00	PF65 80.00			

KM# 43 100 RUBLEI

14.14 g., 0.925 Silver 0.4178 oz. ASW, 32 mm. **Obv:** National arms **Rev:** Hoopoe (Upupa Epops) bird on branch **Edge:** Plain **Note:** Prev. KM#11.

Date	Mintage	F12	VF20	XF40	MS60	MS63
2003	500	PF63 90.00	PF65 100			

KM# 45 100 RUBLEI

14.14 g., 0.925 Silver 0.4178 oz. ASW, 32 mm. **Obv:** National Army **Rev:** Soccer Player

Date	Mintage	F12	VF20	XF40	MS60	MS63
2003	500	PF63 160	PF65 175			

KM# 44 100 RUBLEI

14.14 g., 0.925 Silver 0.4178 oz. ASW, 32 mm. **Obv:** National arms **Rev:** Doe and fawn flanked by trees **Edge:** Plain **Note:** Prev. KM#14.

Date	Mintage	F12	VF20	XF40	MS60	MS63
2004	1,000	PF63 100	PF65 125			

KM# 48 100 RUBLEI

14.14 g., 0.925 Silver 0.4178 oz. ASW, 32 mm. **Subject:** 80th Anniversary of Nationhood **Obv:** National arms **Rev:** Map and multicolor flag **Edge:** Plain **Note:** Prev. KM#13.

Date	Mintage	F12	VF20	XF40	MS60	MS63
2004	500	PF63 100	PF65 125			

KM# 46 100 RUBLEI

14.14 g., 0.925 Silver 0.4178 oz. ASW, 32 mm. **Obv:** National Arms **Rev:** A.G. Rubinstein and music score

Date	Mintage	F12	VF20	XF40	MS60	MS63
2004	1,000	PF63 60.00	PF65 75.00			

KM# 47 100 RUBLEI

14.14 g., 0.925 Silver 0.4178 oz. ASW, 32 mm. **Obv:** National Arms **Rev:** JS Grousul

Date	Mintage	F12	VF20	XF40	MS60	MS63
2004	1,000	PF63 60.00	PF65 75.00			

KM# 60 100 RUBLEI

14.14 g., 0.925 Silver 0.4178 oz. ASW, 32 mm. **Obv:** National arms **Rev:** Eurasian Griffin bird on rock **Edge:** Plain **Note:** Prev. KM#15.

Date	Mintage	F12	VF20	XF40	MS60	MS63
2005	1,000	PF63 100	PF65 120			

KM# 56 100 RUBLEI

14.14 g., 0.925 Silver 0.4178 oz. ASW, 32 mm. **Obv:** National Arms **Rev:** Building with tower

Date	Mintage	F12	VF20	XF40	MS60	MS63
2005	500	PF63 85.00	PF65 100			

KM# 57 100 RUBLEI

14.14 g., 0.925 Silver 0.4178 oz. ASW, 32 mm. **Obv:** National Arms **Rev:** Zodiac - Capricorn

Date	Mintage	F12	VF20	XF40	MS60	MS63
2005	1,000	PF63 70.00	PF65 80.00			

KM# 58 100 RUBLEI

14.14 g., 0.925 Silver 0.4178 oz. ASW, 32 mm. **Obv:** National Arms **Rev:** Statue and long building

Date	Mintage	F12	VF20	XF40	MS60	MS63
2005	500	PF63 85.00	PF65 100			

KM# 59 100 RUBLEI

14.14 g., 0.925 Silver 0.4178 oz. ASW, 32 mm. **Obv:** National Arms **Rev:** Flag as book

Date	Mintage	F12	VF20	XF40	MS60	MS63
2005	500	PF63 95.00	PF65 110			

KM# 61 100 RUBLEI

14.14 g., 0.925 Silver 0.4178 oz. ASW, 32 mm. **Obv:** National Arms **Rev:** PP Werszygora

Date	Mintage	F12	VF20	XF40	MS60	MS63
2005	500	PF63 80.00	PF65 90.00			

KM# 62 100 RUBLEI

14.14 g., 0.925 Silver 0.4178 oz. ASW, 32 mm. **Obv:** National Arms **Rev:** Zodiac - Aquarius

Date	Mintage	F12	VF20	XF40	MS60	MS63
2005	500	PF63 80.00	PF65 90.00			

KM# 63 100 RUBLEI

14.14 g., 0.925 Silver 0.4178 oz. ASW, 32 mm. **Obv:** National Arms **Rev:** Zodiac - Pisces

Date	Mintage	F12	VF20	XF40	MS60	MS63
2005	500	PF63 80.00	PF65 90.00			

KM# 64 100 RUBLEI

14.14 g., 0.925 Silver 0.4178 oz. ASW, 32 mm. **Obv:** National Arms **Rev:** Zodiac - Aries

Date	Mintage	F12	VF20	XF40	MS60	MS63
2005	500	PF63 80.00	PF65 90.00			

KM# 65 100 RUBLEI

14.14 g., 0.925 Silver 0.4178 oz. ASW, 32 mm. **Obv:** National Arms **Rev:** Zodiac - Taurus

Date	Mintage	F12	VF20	XF40	MS60	MS63
2005	500	PF63 80.00	PF65 90.00			

KM# 66 100 RUBLEI

14.14 g., 0.925 Silver 0.4178 oz. ASW, 32 mm. **Obv:** National Arms **Rev:** Zodiac - Gemini

Date	Mintage	F12	VF20	XF40	MS60	MS63
2005	500	PF63 80.00	PF65 90.00			

KM# 67 100 RUBLEI

14.14 g., 0.925 Silver 0.4178 oz. ASW, 32 mm. **Obv:** National Arms **Rev:** Zodiac - Cancer

Date	Mintage	F12	VF20	XF40	MS60	MS63
2005	500	PF63 80.00	PF65 90.00			

KM# 68 100 RUBLEI

14.14 g., 0.925 Silver 0.4178 oz. ASW, 32 mm. **Obv:** National Arms **Rev:** Zodiac - Leo

Date	Mintage	F12	VF20	XF40	MS60	MS63
2005	500	PF63 80.00	PF65 90.00			

KM# 69 100 RUBLEI

14.14 g., 0.925 Silver 0.4178 oz. ASW, 32 mm. **Obv:** National Arms **Rev:** Zodiac - Virgo

Date	Mintage	F12	VF20	XF40	MS60	MS63
2005	500	PF63 80.00	PF65 90.00			

KM# 70 100 RUBLEI

14.14 g., 0.925 Silver 0.4178 oz. ASW, 32 mm. **Obv:** National Arms **Rev:** Zodiac - Libra

Date	Mintage	F12	VF20	XF40	MS60	MS63
2005	500	PF63 80.00	PF65 90.00			

KM# 71 100 RUBLEI

14.14 g., 0.925 Silver 0.4178 oz. ASW, 32 mm. **Obv:** National Arms **Rev:** Zodiac - Scorpio

Date	Mintage	F12	VF20	XF40	MS60	MS63
2005	500	PF63 80.00	PF65 90.00			

KM# 72 100 RUBLEI

14.14 g., 0.925 Silver 0.4178 oz. ASW, 32 mm. **Obv:** National Arms **Rev:** Zodiac - Sagittarius

Date	Mintage	F12	VF20	XF40	MS60	MS63
2005	500	PF63 80.00	PF65 90.00			

KM# 76 100 RUBLEI

14.14 g., 0.925 Silver 0.4178 oz. ASW, 32 mm. **Obv:** National Arms **Rev:** Lunar Year of the (fire) Dog

Date	Mintage	F12	VF20	XF40	MS60	MS63
2006	1,000	PF63 80.00	PF65 90.00			

KM# 78 100 RUBLEI

14.14 g., 0.925 Silver 0.4178 oz. ASW, 32 mm. **Obv:** National Arms **Rev:** Stag Beetle

Date	Mintage	F12	VF20	XF40	MS60	MS63
2006	500	PF63 100	PF65 125			

KM# 80 100 RUBLEI

14.14 g., 0.925 Silver 0.4178 oz. ASW, 32 mm. **Obv:** National Arms **Rev:** Biathlon

Date	Mintage	F12	VF20	XF40	MS60	MS63
2006	300	PF63 135	PF65 150			

KM# 81 100 RUBLEI

14.14 g., 0.925 Silver 0.4178 oz. ASW, 32 mm. **Subject:** Turin Olympics **Obv:** National Arms **Rev:** Ski Jump

Date	Mintage	F12	VF20	XF40	MS60	MS63
2006	200	PF63 200	PF65 225			

KM# 82 100 RUBLEI

14.14 g., 0.925 Silver 0.4178 oz. ASW, 32 mm. **Obv:** National Arms **Rev:** Town View - Tyraspol

Date	Mintage	F12	VF20	XF40	MS60	MS63
2006	500	PF63 80.00	PF65 90.00			

KM# 83 100 RUBLEI

14.14 g., 0.925 Silver 0.4178 oz. ASW, 32 mm. **Obv:** National Arms **Rev:** Town view Bendery

Date	Mintage	F12	VF20	XF40	MS60	MS63
2006	500	PF63 80.00	PF65 90.00			

KM# 84 100 RUBLEI

14.14 g., 0.925 Silver 0.4178 oz. ASW, 32 mm. **Obv:** Naational Arms **Rev:** Man in forest legend

Date	Mintage	F12	VF20	XF40	MS60	MS63
2006	1,000	PF63 75.00	PF65 85.00			

KM# 85 100 RUBLEI

14.14 g., 0.925 Silver 0.4178 oz. ASW, 32 mm. **Obv:** National Arms **Rev:** Legend - Fisherman in rowboat

Date	Mintage	F12	VF20	XF40	MS60	MS63
2006	1,000	PF63 75.00	PF65 85.00			

KM# 86 100 RUBLEI

14.14 g., 0.925 Silver 0.4178 oz. ASW, 32 mm. **Obv:** National Arms **Rev:** Legend dragon slayer

Date	Mintage	F12	VF20	XF40	MS60	MS63
2006	1,000	PF63 75.00	PF65 85.00			

KM# 87 100 RUBLEI

14.14 g., 0.925 Silver 0.4178 oz. ASW, 32 mm. **Obv:** National Arms **Rev:** Kossak

Date	Mintage	F12	VF20	XF40	MS60	MS63
2006	500	PF63 90.00	PF65 100			

KM# 88 100 RUBLEI

14.14 g., 0.925 Silver 0.4178 oz. ASW, 32 mm. **Obv:** National Arms **Rev:** General Bursak

Date	Mintage	F12	VF20	XF40	MS60	MS63
2006	500	PF63 80.00	PF65 90.00			

KM# 89 100 RUBLEI

14.14 g., 0.925 Silver 0.4178 oz. ASW, 32 mm. **Obv:** National Arms **Rev:** Multicolor baseball player hitting ball

Date	Mintage	F12	VF20	XF40	MS60	MS63
2006	500	PF63 90.00	PF65 100			

KM# 90 100 RUBLEI

14.14 g., 0.925 Silver 0.4178 oz. ASW, 32 mm. **Obv:** National Arms **Rev:** Cathedral of the Arch Angel Michael

Date	Mintage	F12	VF20	XF40	MS60	MS63
2006	500	PF63 80.00	PF65 90.00			

KM# 91 100 RUBLEI

14.14 g., 0.925 Silver 0.4178 oz. ASW, 32 mm. **Obv:** National Arms **Rev:** Sidor Bialy bust at right

Date	Mintage	F12	VF20	XF40	MS60	MS63
2006	300	PF63 100	PF65 125			

KM# 136 100 RUBLEI

14.14 g., 0.925 Silver 0.4178 oz. ASW, 32 mm. **Obv:** National Arms **Rev:** Monarch butterfly

Date	Mintage	F12	VF20	XF40	MS60	MS63
2006	1,000	PF63 90.00	PF65 100			

KM# 92 100 RUBLEI

14.14 g., 0.925 Silver 0.4178 oz. ASW, 32 mm. **Obv:** National Arms **Rev:** Seal impression, partially plated

Date	Mintage	F12	VF20	XF40	MS60	MS63
2006	300	PF63 100	PF65 125			

KM# 120 100 RUBLEI

14.14 g., 0.925 Silver 0.4178 oz. ASW, 32 mm. **Obv:** National Arms **Rev:** General Potiomkin

Date	Mintage	F12	VF20	XF40	MS60	MS63
2007	300	PF63 100	PF65 125			

KM# 96 100 RUBLEI

14.14 g., 0.925 Silver 0.4178 oz. ASW, 32 mm. **Obv:** National Arms **Rev:** Rybnitsa Shield **Rev. Legend:** РЫБЬЦИЦА

Date	Mintage	F12	VF20	XF40	MS60	MS63
2007	500	PF63 95.00	PF65 115			

KM# 113 100 RUBLEI

14.14 g., 0.925 Silver 0.4178 oz. ASW, 32 mm. **Obv:** National Arms **Rev:** Lunar year of the pig

Date	Mintage	F12	VF20	XF40	MS60	MS63
2007	300	PF63 100	PF65 125			

KM# 114 100 RUBLEI

14.14 g., 0.925 Silver 0.4178 oz. ASW, 32 mm. **Obv:** National Arms **Rev:** Castle view, 4 towers

Date	Mintage	F12	VF20	XF40	MS60	MS63
2007	500	PF63 80.00	PF65 90.00			

KM# 115 100 RUBLEI
14.14 g., 0.925 Silver 0.4178 oz. ASW, 32 mm. **Subject:** Soroky Fortress **Obv:** National Arms **Rev:** Castle view central tower and gate

Date	Mintage	F12	VF20	XF40	MS60	MS63
2007	500	PF63 80.00	PF65 90.00			

KM# 116 100 RUBLEI
14.14 g., 0.925 Silver 0.4178 oz. ASW, 32 mm. **Obv:** National Arms **Rev:** Zachary Czerega Kulis, ship at left

Date	Mintage	F12	VF20	XF40	MS60	MS63
2007	300	PF63 100	PF65 125			

KM# 117 100 RUBLEI
14.14 g., 0.925 Silver 0.4178 oz. ASW, 32 mm. **Subject:** Anton Goloway **Obv:** National Arms **Rev:** Bust facing

Date	Mintage	F12	VF20	XF40	MS60	MS63
2007	300	PF63 100	PF65 125			

KM# 118 100 RUBLEI
14.14 g., 0.925 Silver 0.4178 oz. ASW, 32 mm. **Obv:** National Arms **Rev:** Alexander Kuszer

Date	Mintage	F12	VF20	XF40	MS60	MS63
2007	500	PF63 80.00	PF65 90.00			

KM# 119 100 RUBLEI
14.14 g., 0.925 Silver 0.4178 oz. ASW, 32 mm. **Obv:** National Arms **Rev:** Field Marshal - Rumiancew-Zadunajski

Date	Mintage	F12	VF20	XF40	MS60	MS63
2007	300	PF63 100	PF65 125			

KM# 121 100 RUBLEI
14.14 g., 0.925 Silver 0.4178 oz. ASW, 32 mm. **Obv:** National Arms **Rev:** General Panin

Date	Mintage	F12	VF20	XF40	MS60	MS63
2007	300	PF63 100	PF65 125			

KM# 130 100 RUBLEI
14.14 g., 0.925 Silver 0.4178 oz. ASW, 32 mm. **Obv:** Naitonal Arms **Rev:** Tulip (Tulipa Biebersteiniana)

Date	Mintage	F12	VF20	XF40	MS60	MS63
2008	—	PF63 100	PF65 125			

KM# 131 100 RUBLEI
14.14 g., 0.925 Silver 0.4178 oz. ASW, 32 mm. **Obv:** National Arms **Rev:** Moldavian Metal Works shield

Date	Mintage	F12	VF20	XF40	MS60	MS63
2008	500	PF63 80.00	PF65 90.00			

KM# 132 100 RUBLEI
14.14 g., 0.925 Silver 0.4178 oz. ASW, 32 mm. **Obv:** National Arms **Rev:** Field Marshal Piotr Vitgenshtain

Date	Mintage	F12	VF20	XF40	MS60	MS63
2008	500	PF63 80.00	PF65 90.00			

KM# 133 100 RUBLEI
14.14 g., 0.925 Silver 0.4178 oz. ASW, 32 mm. **Obv:** National Arms **Rev:** Belgorod Dnestrovskaya Fortress

Date	Mintage	F12	VF20	XF40	MS60	MS63
2008	500	PF63 80.00	PF65 90.00			

KM# 144 100 RUBLEI
14.14 g., Silver **Subject:** Year of the Rat

Date	Mintage	F12	VF20	XF40	MS60	MS63
2008	500	PF63 90.00	PF65 100			

KM# 146 100 RUBLEI
14.14 g., 0.925 Silver 0.4178 oz. ASW **Subject:** Ancient Fortresses on the Dniester

Date	Mintage	F12	VF20	XF40	MS60	MS63
2008	500	PF63 80.00	PF65 90.00			

KM# 147 100 RUBLEI
14.14 g., 0.925 Silver 0.4178 oz. ASW **Subject:** 90th Birthday of Valentina Soloveva

Date	Mintage	F12	VF20	XF40	MS60	MS63
2008	500	PF63 80.00	PF65 90.00			

KM# 129 100 RUBLEI
14.14 g., 0.925 Silver 0.4178 oz. ASW, 32 mm. **Subject:** Year of the Bull

Date	Mintage	F12	VF20	XF40	MS60	MS63
2009	500	PF63 95.00	PF65 115			

KM# 166 100 RUBLEI
33.85 g., 0.925 Silver 1.0002 oz. ASW, 39 mm. **Subject:** 10th Annviersary of the Transnistria Telephone Company

Date	Mintage	F12	VF20	XF40	MS60	MS63
2009	570	PF63 85.00	PF65 95.00			

KM# 169 100 RUBLEI
14.14 g., 0.925 Silver 0.4178 oz. ASW, 32 mm. **Subject:** Year of the Tiger

Date	Mintage	F12	VF20	XF40	MS60	MS63
2010	250	PF63 95.00	PF65 110			

KM# 143 100 RUBLEI
15.50 g., 0.925 Silver 0.458 oz. ASW, 32 mm. **Subject:** Garry Faif - Architect and Sculptor

Date	Mintage	F12	VF20	XF40	MS60	MS63
2011	Est. 250	PF63 90.00	PF65 100			

KM# 174 100 RUBLEI
13.87 g., 0.925 Silver 0.4098 oz. ASW, 32 mm. **Subject:** Chinese Lunar Year of the Rabbit

Date	Mintage	F12	VF20	XF40	MS60	MS63
2011	300	PF63 95.00	PF65 110			

KM# 139 100 RUBLEI
Silver **Obv:** Khotyn Fortress

Date	Mintage	F12	VF20	XF40	MS60	MS63
2012 Prooflike	—	PF63 100	PF65 125			

KM# 140 100 RUBLEI
14.14 g., 0.925 Silver 0.4178 oz. ASW, 32 mm. **Obv:** Arms **Rev:** Year of the Dragon

Date	Mintage	F12	VF20	XF40	MS60	MS63
2012 Prooflike	Est. 250	PF63 100	PF65 125			

KM# 25 1000 RUBLEI
8.00 g., 0.900 Gold 0.230 oz. AGW, 21 mm. **Obv:** National Arms **Rev:** 1800 Cathedral of God's Ascension

Date	Mintage	F12	VF20	XF40	MS60	MS63
2001	50	PF65 700				

KM# 23 1000 RUBLEI
8.00 g., 0.900 Gold 0.230 oz. AGW, 21 mm. **Obv:** National Arms **Rev:** Church of the Blessed Virgins

Date	Mintage	F12	VF20	XF40	MS60	MS63
2001	50	PF65 700				

KM# 24 1000 RUBLEI
8.00 g., 0.900 Gold 0.230 oz. AGW, 21 mm. **Obv:** National Arms **Rev:** Orthodox Church of the Virgin's Assumption

Date	Mintage	F12	VF20	XF40	MS60	MS63
2001	50	PF65 700				

KM# 26 1000 RUBLEI
8.00 g., 0.900 Gold 0.230 oz. AGW, 21 mm. **Obv:** National Arms **Rev:** Cathedral of the Birth of Christ

Date	Mintage	F12	VF20	XF40	MS60	MS63
2001	50	PF65 700				

KM# 27 1000 RUBLEI
8.00 g., 0.900 Gold 0.230 oz. AGW, 21 mm. **Rev:** Cathedral of the Transfiguration

Date	Mintage	F12	VF20	XF40	MS60	MS63
2001	50	PF65 700				

KM# 28 1000 RUBLEI
8.00 g., 0.900 Gold 0.230 oz. AGW, 21 mm. **Obv:** National Arms **Rev:** Church of the Blessed Virgin's Birth

Date	Mintage	F12	VF20	XF40	MS60	MS63
2001	50	PF65 700				

KM# 29 1000 RUBLEI
8.00 g., 0.900 Gold 0.230 oz. AGW, 21 mm. **Obv:** National Arms **Rev:** Church of the Transfiguration

Date	Mintage	F12	VF20	XF40	MS60	MS63
2001	50	PF65 700				

KM# 30 1000 RUBLEI
8.00 g., 0.900 Gold 0.230 oz. AGW, 21 mm. **Obv:** National Arms **Rev:** Church of the Lifegiving Trinity

Date	Mintage	F12	VF20	XF40	MS60	MS63
2001	50	PF65 700				

KM# 31 1000 RUBLEI
8.00 g., 0.900 Gold 0.230 oz. AGW, 21 mm. **Obv:** National Arms **Rev:** Orthodox Church to the Serbian Paraskeva (1854)

Date	Mintage	F12	VF20	XF40	MS60	MS63
2001	50	PF65 700				

KM# 32 1000 RUBLEI
8.00 g., 0.900 Gold 0.230 oz. AGW, 21 mm. **Obv:** National Arms **Rev:** Church of Michael the Arch Angel in Stoiesti

Date	Mintage	F12	VF20	XF40	MS60	MS63
2001	50	PF65 700				

MINT SETS

KM#	Date	Mintage	Identification	Issue Price	Mkt Val
MS1	2005 (4)	—	KM#50, 51, 52a, 53.	—	20.00

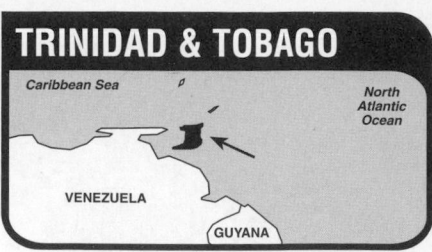

TRINIDAD & TOBAGO

Caribbean Sea

North Atlantic Ocean

VENEZUELA

GUYANA

The Republic of Trinidad and Tobago is situated 7 miles (11 km.) off the coast of Venezuela, has an area of 1,981 sq. mi. (5,130 sq. km.) and a population of *1.2 million. Capital: Port-of-Spain. The island of Trinidad contains the world's largest natural asphalt bog. Birds of Paradise live on little Tobago, the only place outside of their native New Guinea where they can be found in a wild state. Petroleum and petroleum products are the mainstay of the economy. Petroleum products, crude oil and sugar are exported.

Trinidad and Tobago is a member of the Commonwealth of Nations. The President is Chief of State. The Prime Minister is Head of Government.

MONETARY SYSTEM
100 Cents = 1 Dollar

REPUBLIC
STANDARD COINAGE

KM# 29 CENT
1.95 g., Bronze, 17.76 mm. **Obv:** National arms **Rev:** Hummingbird and value **Edge:** Plain

Date	Mintage	F12	VF20	XF40	MS60	MS63
2001	—	—	—	0.10	0.30	0.40
2002	—	—	—	0.10	0.30	0.40
2003	—	—	—	0.10	0.30	0.40
2005	—	—	—	0.10	0.30	0.40
2006	—	—	—	0.10	0.30	0.40
2007	—	—	—	0.10	0.30	0.40
2008	—	—	—	0.10	0.30	0.40
2009	—	—	—	0.10	0.30	0.40
2010	—	—	—	0.10	0.30	0.40
2011	—	—	—	0.10	0.30	0.40

KM# 30 5 CENTS
3.31 g., Bronze, 21.2 mm. **Obv:** National arms **Rev:** Bird of paradise and value **Edge:** Plain

Date	Mintage	F12	VF20	XF40	MS60	MS63
2001	—	—	—	0.15	0.45	0.60
2002	—	—	—	0.15	0.45	0.60
2003	—	—	—	0.15	0.45	0.60
2004	—	—	—	0.15	0.45	0.60
2005	—	—	—	0.15	0.45	0.60
2006	—	—	—	0.15	0.45	0.60
2007	—	—	—	0.15	0.45	0.60
2008	—	—	—	0.15	0.45	0.60
2009FM	—	—	—	0.15	0.45	0.60
2010FM	—	—	—	0.15	0.45	0.60

KM# 31 10 CENTS
1.40 g., Copper-Nickel, 16.2 mm. **Obv:** National arms **Rev:** Hibiscus and value **Edge:** Reeded

Date	Mintage	F12	VF20	XF40	MS60	MS63
2001	—	—	—	0.25	0.60	0.80
2002	—	—	—	0.25	0.60	0.80
2003	—	—	—	0.25	0.60	0.80
2004	—	—	—	0.25	0.60	0.80
2005	—	—	—	0.25	0.60	0.80
2006	—	—	—	0.25	0.60	0.80
2007	—	—	—	0.25	0.60	0.80
2008	—	—	—	0.25	0.60	0.80

KM# 32 25 CENTS
3.50 g., Copper-Nickel, 20 mm. **Obv:** National arms **Rev:** Chaconia and value **Edge:** Reeded

Date	Mintage	F12	VF20	XF40	MS60	MS63
2001	—	—	—	0.30	0.75	1.00
2002	—	—	—	0.30	0.75	1.00
2003	—	—	—	0.30	0.75	1.00
2004	—	—	—	0.30	0.75	1.00
2005	—	—	—	0.30	0.75	1.00
2006	—	—	—	0.30	0.75	1.00
2007	—	—	—	0.30	0.75	1.00
2008	—	—	—	0.30	0.75	1.00

KM# 33 50 CENTS
7.00 g., Copper-Nickel, 26 mm. **Obv:** National arms **Rev:** Kettle drums and value **Edge:** Reeded

Date	Mintage	F12	VF20	XF40	MS60	MS63
2003	—	—	—	1.00	2.00	4.00

KM# 63 10 DOLLARS
Copper-Nickel **Subject:** FIFA - XVIII World Football Championship - Soca Warriors - Germany 2006 **Obv:** Native hands playing steel drum, gilt **Rev:** Logo

Date	Mintage	F12	VF20	XF40	MS60	MS63
2006	—	—	—	5.00	12.00	35.00

KM# 64 100 DOLLARS
28.28 g., 0.925 Silver 0.8356 oz. ASW **Subject:** FIFA - XVIII World Football Championship - Soca Warriors - Germany 2006 **Obv:** Native hands playing steel drum, gilt **Rev:** Logo

Date	Mintage	F12	VF20	XF40	MS60	MS63
2006	—	PF63 75.00	PF65 90.00			

TRISTAN DA CUNHA

South Atlantic *Ocean*

NAMIBIA

SOUTH AFRICA

Tristan da Cunha is the principal island and group name of a small cluster of volcanic islands located in the South Atlantic midway between the Cape of Good Hope and South America, and 1,500 miles (2,414 km.) south-southwest of the British colony of St. Helena. The other islands are inaccessible, Gough, and the three Nightingale Islands. The group, which comprises a dependency of St. Helena, has a total area of 40 sq. mi. (104 sq. km.) and a population of less than 300. There is a village of 60 houses called Edinburgh. Potatoes are the staple subsistence crop.

MONETARY SYSTEM
100 Pence = 1 Pound

ST. HELENA DEPENDENCY
STANDARD COINAGE

KM# 27 1/2 PENNY
3.83 g., Copper, 16.91 mm. **Ruler:** Elizabeth II **Obv:** Head with tiara right **Rev:** Snipe Eel **Edge:** Plain

Date	Mintage	F12	VF20	XF40	MS60	MS63
2008	—	—	—	—	0.75	1.00

KM# 28 PENNY
4.63 g., Copper, 18.66 mm. **Ruler:** Elizabeth II **Obv:** Head with tiara right **Rev:** Crayfish **Edge:** Plain

Date	Mintage	F12	VF20	XF40	MS60	MS63
2008	—	—	—	—	1.20	1.60

KM# 29 2 PENCE
6.60 g., Copper, 22.02 mm. **Ruler:** Elizabeth II **Obv:** Head with tiara right **Rev:** Violet Seasnail **Edge:** Plain

Date	Mintage	F12	VF20	XF40	MS60	MS63
2008	—	—	—	—	1.50	2.00

KM# 30 5 PENCE
3.74 g., Copper-Nickel, 16.90 mm. **Ruler:** Elizabeth II **Obv:** Head with tiara right **Rev:** Sea Turtle **Edge:** Plain

Date	Mintage	F12	VF20	XF40	MS60	MS63
2008	—	—	—	—	1.80	2.40

KM# 31 10 PENCE
6.49 g., Copper-Nickel, 22.03 mm. **Ruler:** Elizabeth II **Obv:** Head with tiara right **Rev:** Crab **Edge:** Plain

Date	Mintage	F12	VF20	XF40	MS60	MS63
2008	—	—	—	—	2.25	3.00

KM# 32 20 PENCE
6.10 g., Aluminum-Bronze, 22.02 mm. **Ruler:** Elizabeth II **Obv:** Head with tiara right **Rev:** Orcha - Killer Whale **Edge:** Plain

Date	Mintage	F12	VF20	XF40	MS60	MS63
2008	—	—	—	—	3.00	4.00

KM# 33 25 PENCE
Bi-Metallic, 25.76 mm. **Ruler:** Elizabeth II **Obv:** Head with tiara right **Rev:** 2 Bottlenose Dolphins **Edge:** Plain

Date	Mintage	F12	VF20	XF40	MS60	MS63
2008	—	—	—	—	6.00	8.00

KM# 12 50 PENCE
29.10 g., Copper-Nickel, 38.6 mm. **Ruler:** Elizabeth II **Subject:** Queen Elizabeth's 75th Birthday **Obv:** Crowned bust right **Rev:** Crowned bust facing **Edge:** Reeded

Date	Mintage	F12	VF20	XF40	MS60	MS63
2001	—	—	—	—	7.00	8.00

KM# 13 50 PENCE
29.60 g., Copper-Nickel, 38.7 mm. **Ruler:** Elizabeth II **Subject:** Centennial of Queen Victoria's Death **Obv:** Crowned bust right **Rev:** Crown and veil on half-length figure of Queen Victoria facing left within oval circle **Edge:** Reeded

Date	Mintage	F12	VF20	XF40	MS60	MS63
2001	—	—	—	—	8.00	10.00

KM# 12a 50 PENCE
28.28 g., 0.925 Silver 0.8356 oz. ASW, 38.6 mm. **Ruler:** Elizabeth II **Obv:** Queen's 75th Birthday **Obv:** Crowned bust right **Rev:** Crowned bust facing **Edge:** Reeded

Date	Mintage	F12	VF20	XF40	MS60	MS63
2001	10,000	PF63 40.00	PF65 45.00			

KM# 12b 50 PENCE
47.54 g., 0.9166 Gold 1.392 oz. AGW, 38.6 mm. **Ruler:** Elizabeth II **Obv:** Crowned bust right **Rev:** Crowned bust facing

Date	Mintage	F12	VF20	XF40	MS60	MS63
2001	75	PF65 2,700				

KM# 13a 50 PENCE
28.28 g., 0.925 Silver 0.8356 oz. ASW, 38.6 mm. **Ruler:** Elizabeth II **Subject:** Centennial of Queen Victoria's Death **Obv:** Crowned bust right **Rev:** Crown and veil on half-length figure of Queen Victoria facing left within oval circle **Edge:** Reeded

Date	Mintage	F12	VF20	XF40	MS60	MS63
2001	10,000	PF63 50.00	PF65 55.00			

KM# 13b 50 PENCE
47.54 g., 0.9166 Gold 1.392 oz. AGW, 38.6 mm. **Ruler:** Elizabeth II **Subject:** Centennial of Queen Victoria's Death **Obv:** Crowned bust right **Rev:** Crown and veil on half-length figure of Queen Victoria facing left within oval circle **Edge:** Reeded

Date	Mintage	F12	VF20	XF40	MS60	MS63
2001	100	PF65 2,700				

KM# 41 CROWN
Copper-Nickel, 38.6 mm. **Ruler:** Elizabeth II **Obv:** Bust crowned right **Rev:** Conjoined busts left

Date	Mintage	F12	VF20	XF40	MS60	MS63
2005	—	—	—	—	—	20.00

KM# 43 CROWN
Copper-Nickel, 38.6 mm. **Ruler:** Elizabeth II **Obv:** Bust in tiara right **Rev:** Lord Nelson's bust 1/4 left

Date	Mintage	F12	VF20	XF40	MS60	MS63
2005	—	—	—	—	—	15.00

KM# 44 CROWN
Copper-Nickel, 38.6 mm. **Ruler:** Elizabeth II **Subject:** VE-Day, 60th Anniversary **Obv:** Bust in tiara right **Rev:** Ship, tank, two panes

Date	Mintage	F12	VF20	XF40	MS60	MS63
2005	—	—	—	—	—	15.00

KM# 14 CROWN
Copper-Nickel, 38.5 mm. **Ruler:** Elizabeth II **Obv:** Crowned bust right **Rev:** Pope John Paul II **Edge:** Reeded

Date	Mintage	F12	VF20	XF40	MS60	MS63
2005	—	—	—	—	8.50	12.00

KM# 14a CROWN
24.12 g., 0.925 Silver 0.7127 oz. ASW, 38.5 mm. **Ruler:** Elizabeth II **Obv:** Crowned bust right **Rev:** Pope John Paul II **Edge:** Reeded

Date	Mintage	F12	VF20	XF40	MS60	MS63
2005	—	PF63 45.00	PF65 50.00			

KM# 15 CROWN
25.00 g., Copper-Nickel, 38.83 mm. **Ruler:** Elizabeth II **Series:** Privateering ships of the South Atlantic **Obv:** Crowned bust right **Obv. Legend:** ELIZABETH II — TRISTAN DA CUNHA **Rev:** Sailing ship "Tybalt **Edge:** Reeded

Date	Mintage	F12	VF20	XF40	MS60	MS63
2006	—	—	—	—	8.50	12.00

KM# 16 CROWN
25.00 g., Copper-Nickel, 38.83 mm. **Ruler:** Elizabeth II **Series:** Privateering ships of the South Atlantic **Obv:** Crowned bust right **Obv. Legend:** ELIZABETH II — TRISTAN DA CUNHA **Rev:** Sailing ship "Syren **Edge:** Reeded

Date	Mintage	F12	VF20	XF40	MS60	MS63
2006	—	—	—	—	8.50	12.00

KM# 17 CROWN
25.00 g., Copper-Nickel, 38.83 mm. **Ruler:** Elizabeth II **Series:** Privateering ships of the South Atlantic **Obv:** Crowned bust right **Obv. Legend:** ELIZABETH II — TRISTAN DA CUNHA **Rev:** Sailing ship "Pride of Baltimore **Edge:** Reeded

Date	Mintage	F12	VF20	XF40	MS60	MS63
2006	—	—	—	—	8.50	12.00

KM# 18 CROWN
25.00 g., Copper-Nickel, 38.83 mm. **Ruler:** Elizabeth II **Series:** Privateering ships of the South Atlantic **Obv:** Crowned bust right **Obv. Legend:** ELIZABETH II — TRISTAN DA CUNHA **Rev:** Sailing ship "Hornet **Edge:** Reeded

Date	Mintage	F12	VF20	XF40	MS60	MS63
2006	—	—	—	—	8.50	12.00

KM# 19 CROWN
25.00 g., Copper-Nickel, 38.83 mm. **Ruler:** Elizabeth II **Series:** Privateering ships of the South Atlantic **Obv:** Crowned bust right **Obv. Legend:** ELIZABETH II — TRISTAN DA CUNHA **Rev:** Sailing ship "Griffin **Edge:** Reeded

Date	Mintage	F12	VF20	XF40	MS60	MS63
2006	—	—	—	—	8.50	12.00

KM# 20 CROWN
25.00 g., Copper-Nickel, 38.83 mm. **Ruler:** Elizabeth II **Series:** Privateering ships of the South Atlantic **Obv:** Crowned bust right **Obv. Legend:** ELIZABETH II — TRISTAN DA CUNHA **Rev:** Sailing ship "Enterprise **Edge:** Reeded

Date	Mintage	F12	VF20	XF40	MS60	MS63
2006	—	—	—	—	8.50	12.00

KM# 21 CROWN
25.00 g., Copper-Nickel, 38.83 mm. **Ruler:** Elizabeth II **Series:** Privateering ships of the South Atlantic **Obv:** Crowned bust right **Obv. Legend:** ELIZABETH II — TRISTAN DA CUNHA **Rev:** Sailing ship "Columbus **Edge:** Reeded

Date	Mintage	F12	VF20	XF40	MS60	MS63
2006	—	—	—	—	8.50	12.00

KM# 22 CROWN
25.00 g., Copper-Nickel, 38.8 mm. **Ruler:** Elizabeth II **Series:** Privateering ships of the South Atlantic **Obv:** Crowned bust right **Obv. Legend:** ELIZABETH II — TRISTAN DA CUNHA **Rev:** Sailing ship "Chausseur **Edge:** Reeded

Date	Mintage	F12	VF20	XF40	MS60	MS63
2006	—	—	—	—	8.50	12.00

KM# 23 CROWN
25.00 g., Copper-Nickel, 38.8 mm. **Ruler:** Elizabeth II **Series:** Privateering ships of the South Atlantic **Obv:** Crowned bust right **Obv. Legend:** ELIZABETH II — TRISTAN DA CUNHA **Rev:** Sailing ship "Cabot **Edge:** Reeded

Date	Mintage	F12	VF20	XF40	MS60	MS63
2006	—	—	—	—	8.50	12.00

KM# 24 CROWN

25.00 g., Copper-Nickel, 38.8 mm. **Ruler:** Elizabeth II **Series:** Privateering ships of the South Atlantic **Obv:** Crowned bust right **Obv. Legend:** ELIZABETH II — TRISTAN DA CUNHA **Rev:** Sailing ship "Black Prince **Edge:** Reeded

Date	Mintage	F12	VF20	XF40	MS60	MS63
2006	—	—	—	—	8.50	12.00

KM# 25 CROWN

25.00 g., Copper-Nickel, 38.8 mm. **Ruler:** Elizabeth II **Series:** Privateering ships of the South Atlantic **Obv:** Crowned bust right **Obv. Legend:** ELIZABETH II — TRISTAN DA CUNHA **Rev:** Sailing ship "Argus **Edge:** Reeded

Date	Mintage	F12	VF20	XF40	MS60	MS63
2006	—	—	—	—	8.50	12.00

KM# 26 CROWN

25.00 g., Copper-Nickel, 38.8 mm. **Ruler:** Elizabeth II **Series:** Privateering ships of the South Atlantic **Obv:** Crowned bust right **Obv. Legend:** ELIZABETH II — TRISTAN DA CUNHA **Rev:** Sailing ship "True Blooded Yankee **Edge:** Reeded

Date	Mintage	F12	VF20	XF40	MS60	MS63
2006	—	—	—	—	8.50	12.00

KM# 35 CROWN

Copper-Nickel, 38.75 mm. **Ruler:** Elizabeth II **Rev:** HMS Victory

Date	Mintage	F12	VF20	XF40	MS60	MS63
2008	—	—	—	—	—	15.00

KM# 36 CROWN

25.18 g., Copper-Nickel **Ruler:** Elizabeth II **Obv:** HMS Belfast

Date	Mintage	F12	VF20	XF40	MS60	MS63
2008	—	—	—	—	—	15.00

KM# 37 CROWN

25.18 g., Copper-Nickel, 38.75 mm. **Ruler:** Elizabeth II **Obv:** HMS Sceptre

Date	Mintage	F12	VF20	XF40	MS60	MS63
2008	—	—	—	—	—	15.00

KM# 38 CROWN

25.18 g., Copper-Nickel, 38.75 mm. **Ruler:** Elizabeth II **Obv:** HMS Beagle

Date	Mintage	F12	VF20	XF40	MS60	MS63
2008	—	—	—	—	—	15.00

KM# 39 CROWN

28.15 g., Copper-Nickel, 38.75 mm. **Ruler:** Elizabeth II **Obv:** HMS Dreadnought

Date	Mintage	F12	VF20	XF40	MS60	MS63
2008	—	—	—	—	—	15.00

KM# 34 CROWN

Copper-Nickel, 39 mm. **Ruler:** Elizabeth II **Obv:** Bust right **Rev:** Two whales

Date	Mintage	F12	VF20	XF40	MS60	MS63
2008	—	—	—	—	—	15.00

KM# 34a CROWN

Copper-Nickel, 38 mm. **Ruler:** Elizabeth II **Obv:** Head with tiara right **Rev:** 2 whales, multicolor

Date	Mintage	F12	VF20	XF40	MS60	MS63
2008	—	—	—	—	8.00	15.00

KM# 40 CROWN

28.15 g., Copper-Nickel, 38.75 mm. **Ruler:** Elizabeth II **Rev:** H.M.S. Ark Royal

Date	Mintage	F12	VF20	XF40	MS60	MS63
2008	—	—	—	—	—	15.00

KM# 46 CROWN

28.85 g., Copper-Nickel, 38.8 mm. **Ruler:** Elizabeth II **Subject:** H.M.S. Invincible

Date	Mintage	F12	VF20	XF40	MS60	MS63
2008	—	—	—	—	—	11.00

KM# 47 CROWN

25.20 g., Copper-Nickel, 38.8 mm. **Ruler:** Elizabeth II **Subject:** H.M.S. Illustrious

Date	Mintage	F12	VF20	XF40	MS60	MS63
2008						

KM# 48 CROWN
25.01 g., Copper-Nickel, 25.01 mm. **Ruler:** Elizabeth II
Subject: H.M.S. Vanuard

Date	Mintage	F12	VF20	XF40	MS60	MS63
2008	—	—	—	—	—	11.00

KM# 49 CROWN
24.79 g., Copper-Nickel, 38.8 mm. **Ruler:** Elizabeth II **Subject:** H.M.S. Victoria

Date	Mintage	F12	VF20	XF40	MS60	MS63
2008	—	—	—	—	—	11.00

KM# 42 5 POUNDS
Silver **Ruler:** Elizabeth II **Rev:** St. George slaying dragon

Date	Mintage	F12	VF20	XF40	MS60	MS63
2008	—	—	—	—	45.00	50.00

KM# 45 5 POUNDS
Silver, 38.6 mm. **Ruler:** Elizabeth II **Obv:** Bust in tiara right **Rev:** Titles of the Queen

Date	Mintage	F12	VF20	XF40	MS60	MS63
2008	—	PF63 50.00	PF65 55.00			

PIEDFORT

KM#	Date	Mintage	Identification	Mkt Val
P1	2001	500	50 Pence 0.925 Silver	100
P2	2001	500	50 Pence 0.925 Silver Proof KM-13a.	100

GOUGH ISLAND

DEPENDANCY
DECIMAL COINAGE

KM# 1 HALFPENNY
Copper Plated Steel, 17 mm. **Ruler:** Elizabeth II **Obv:** Bust right

Obv. Legend: GOUGH ISLAND Tristan da Cunha **Rev:** Gough moorhen **Edge:** Plain

Date	Mintage	F12	VF20	XF40	MS60	MS63
2009	—	—	—	—	0.75	1.00

KM# 2 PENNY
Copper Plated Steel, 18.5 mm. **Ruler:** Elizabeth II **Obv:** Bust right **Obv. Legend:** GOUGH ISLAND Tristan da Cunha **Rev:** Pair of Sooty Albatross **Edge:** Plain

Date	Mintage	F12	VF20	XF40	MS60	MS63
2009	—	—	—	—	1.00	1.50

KM# 3 2 PENCE
Copper Plated Steel, 22 mm. **Ruler:** Elizabeth II **Obv:** Bust right **Obv. Legend:** GOUGH ISLAND Tristan da Cunha **Rev:** Pair of Antarctic Tern **Edge:** Plain

Date	Mintage	F12	VF20	XF40	MS60	MS63
2009	—	—	—	—	1.50	2.00

KM# 4 5 PENCE
Copper-Nickel Plated Steel, 17 mm. **Ruler:** Elizabeth II **Obv:** Bust right **Obv. Legend:** GOUGH ISLAND Tristan da Cunha **Rev:** Northern Rock Hopper Penguins **Edge:** Plain

Date	Mintage	F12	VF20	XF40	MS60	MS63
2009	—	—	—	—	2.00	2.50

KM# 5 10 PENCE
Copper-Nickel Plated Steel, 22 mm. **Ruler:** Elizabeth II **Obv:** Bust right **Obv. Legend:** GOUGH ISLAND Tristan da Cunha **Rev:** Giant Petrel on water **Edge:** Plain

Date	Mintage	F12	VF20	XF40	MS60	MS63
2009	—	—	—	—	3.00	3.50

KM# 6 20 PENCE
Brass, 22 mm. **Ruler:** Elizabeth II **Obv:** Bust right **Obv. Legend:** GOUGH ISLAND Tristan da Cunha **Rev:** Antarctic Skua **Edge:** Plain

Date	Mintage	F12	VF20	XF40	MS60	MS63
2009	—	—	—	—	4.50	5.00

KM# 7 25 PENCE
Bi-Metallic, 25.8 mm. **Ruler:** Elizabeth II **Obv:** Bust right **Obv. Legend:** GOUGH ISLAND Tristan da Cunha **Rev:** Barn Owl **Edge:** Plain

Date	Mintage	F12	VF20	XF40	MS60	MS63
2009	—	—	—	—	8.00	9.00

KM# 8 CROWN
Copper-Nickel, 38.8 mm. **Ruler:** Elizabeth II **Obv:** Bust right **Obv. Legend:** GOUGH ISLAND Tristan da Cunha **Rev:** Peregrine Falcon **Edge:** Plain

Date	Mintage	F12	VF20	XF40	MS60	MS63
2009	—	—	—	—	12.00	14.00

STOLTENHOFF ISLAND

DEPENCENCY
DECIMAL COINAGE

KM# 1 HALFPENNY
Copper Plated Steel, 17 mm. **Ruler:** Elizabeth II **Obv:** Bust right **Rev:** Small sailboat - West Riding Tragedy Longboat

Date	Mintage	F12	VF20	XF40	MS60	MS63
2008	—	—	—	—	0.75	1.00

KM# 2 PENNY
Copper Plated Steel **Ruler:** Elizabeth II **Obv:** Bust right **Rev:** 18th century sailing ship - Portuguese Carrack type

Date	Mintage	F12	VF20	XF40	MS60	MS63
2008	—	—	—	—	1.00	1.50

KM# 3 2 PENCE
Copper Plated Steel, 21.5 mm. **Ruler:** Elizabeth II **Obv:** Bust right **Rev:** Three masted sailing ship - HMS Julia

Date	Mintage	F12	VF20	XF40	MS60	MS63
2008	—	—	—	—	1.50	2.00

KM# 4 5 PENCE
Copper-Nickel Plated Steel, 16 mm. **Ruler:** Elizabeth II **Obv:** Bust right **Rev:** Two masted sailing ship - HMS Beagle

Date	Mintage	F12	VF20	XF40	MS60	MS63
2008	—	—	—	—	2.00	2.50

KM# 5 10 PENCE
Copper-Nickel Plated Steel, 21.5 mm. **Ruler:** Elizabeth II **Obv:** Bust right **Rev:** Three masted sailing ship - Blenden Hall

Date	Mintage	F12	VF20	XF40	MS60	MS63
2008	—	—	—	—	3.00	3.50

KM# 6 20 PENCE
Brass, 21.5 mm. **Ruler:** Elizabeth II **Obv:** Bust right **Rev:** Two masted sailing ship - HMS Satellite

Date	Mintage	F12	VF20	XF40	MS60	MS63
2008	—	—	—	—	4.50	5.00

KM# 7 25 PENCE
Bi-Metallic, 25 mm. **Ruler:** Elizabeth II **Obv:** Bust right **Rev:** Sailing ship - Iron Barque West Riding

Date	Mintage	F12	VF20	XF40	MS60	MS63
2008	—				7.00	8.00

KM# 8 CROWN
Copper-Nickel, 39 mm. **Ruler:** Elizabeth II **Obv:** Bust right **Rev:** Sailing ship L'Heure du Berger

Date	Mintage	F12	VF20	XF40	MS60	MS63
2008	—	—	—	—	10.00	12.00

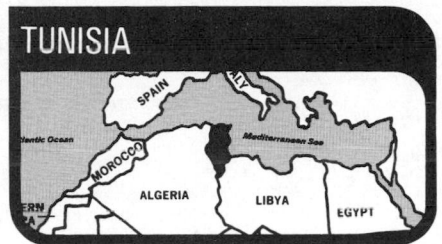

TUNISIA

The Republic of Tunisia, located on the northern coast of Africa between Algeria and Libya, has an area of 63,170 sq. mi. (163,610 sq. km.) and a population of *7.9 million. Capital: Tunis. Agriculture is the backbone of the economy. Crude oil, phosphates, olive oil, and wine are exported.

TITLES

المملكة التونسية

al-Mamlaka al-Tunisiya

الجمهورية العراقية

al-Jumhurlya al-Tunlslya

al-Amala al-Tunisiya
(Tunisian Protectorate)

REPUBLIC

DECIMAL COINAGE
1000 Millim = 1 Dinar

KM# 348 5 MILLIM
1.49 g., Aluminum, 24 mm. **Obv:** Oak tree and dates **Rev:** Value within sprigs

Date	Mintage	F12	VF20	XF40	MS60	MS63
AH1425-2004	—	—	—	—	0.50	1.00
AH1426-2005	—	—	—	—	0.50	1.00

KM# 306 10 MILLIM
3.50 g., Brass, 19 mm. **Obv:** Inscription and dates within inner circle of design **Rev:** Value in center of design **Edge:** Reeded

Date	Mintage	F12	VF20	XF40	MS60	MS63
AH1425-2004	—	—	0.15	0.25	0.50	1.00
AH1426-2005	—	—	0.15	0.25	0.50	1.00
AH1429-2008	—	—	0.15	0.25	0.50	1.00
AH1432-2011	—	—	0.15	0.25	0.50	1.00

KM# 306.1 10 MILLIM
3.50 g., Brass Plated Steel, 19 mm. **Obv:** Inscription and dates within inner circle of design **Rev:** Value in center of design **Edge:** Reeded

Date	Mintage	F12	VF20	XF40	MS60	MS63
AHAH1430-2009	—	—	0.15	0.25	0.50	1.00

KM# 307 20 MILLIM
4.50 g., Brass, 22 mm. **Obv:** Inscription and dates within center of design **Rev:** Value within center of design

Date	Mintage	F12	VF20	XF40	MS60	MS63
AH1425-2004	—	—	—	0.50	0.80	1.00
AH1426-2005	—	—	—	0.50	0.80	1.00
AH1432-2011	—	—	—	0.50	0.80	1.00

KM# 307a 20 MILLIM
Brass Plated Steel

Date	Mintage	F12	VF20	XF40	MS60	MS63
AH1428-2007	—	—	—	—	0.50	1.00
AH1430-2009	—	—	—	—	0.50	1.00

KM# 308 50 MILLIM
6.00 g., Brass, 25 mm. **Obv:** Inscription and dates within center circle of design **Rev:** Value in center of design

Date	Mintage	F12	VF20	XF40	MS60	MS63
AH1425-2004	—	—	0.65	0.85	1.25	1.50
AH1426-2005	—	—	0.65	0.85	1.25	1.50
AH1428-2007	—	—	0.65	0.85	1.25	1.50
AH1430-2009	—	—	0.65	0.85	1.25	1.50

KM# 309 100 MILLIM
7.50 g., Brass, 27 mm. **Obv:** Inscription and dates within center circle of design **Rev:** Value in center of design

Date	Mintage	F12	VF20	XF40	MS60	MS63
AH1425-2004	—	—	—	1.25	1.50	2.00
AH1426-2005	—	—	—	1.25	1.50	2.00
AH1427-2006	—	—	—	1.25	1.50	2.00
AH1429-2008	—	—	—	1.25	1.50	2.00
AH1432-2011	—	—	—	1.25	1.50	2.00
AH1434-2013	—	—	—	1.25	1.50	2.00

KM# 346 1/2 DINAR
Copper-Nickel **Obv:** Shield within circle **Rev:** 2 hands with fruit and wheat sprig **Note:** Rim width varieties exist.

Date	Mintage	F12	VF20	XF40	MS60	MS63
AH1426-2005	—	—	—	1.00	2.50	4.50
AH1428-2007	—	—	—	1.00	2.50	4.50
AH1430-2009	—	—	—	1.00	2.50	4.50
AH1432-2011	—	—	—	1.00	2.50	4.50

KM# 347 DINAR
10.10 g., Copper-Nickel, 28 mm. **Series:** F.A.O. **Obv:** Shield within circle **Rev:** Female half figure right

Date	Mintage	F12	VF20	XF40	MS60	MS63
AH1428-2007	—	—	2.00	3.50	5.00	—
AH1430-2009	—	—	2.00	3.50	5.00	—
AH1432-2011	—	—	2.00	3.50	5.00	—

KM# 329 5 DINARS
9.41 g., 0.900 Gold 0.2704 oz. AGW **Subject:** Anniversary of 7 Nov 1987 **Obv:** Shield **Rev:** Upstretched hand, flag **Note:** French legends vary by year.

Date	Mintage	F12	VF20	XF40	MS60	MS63
2001-1422 (2001)	40	—	—	—	650	700

KM# 330 5 DINARS
9.41 g., 0.900 Gold 0.2704 oz. AGW **Subject:** Anniversary of 7 Nov 1987 **Obv:** Shield **Rev:** Upstretched hand, flag **Note:** Arabic legends vary by year.

Date	Mintage	F12	VF20	XF40	MS60	MS63
2001-1421 (2001)	40	—	—	—	650	700

KM# 435 5 DINARS
9.48 g., 0.900 Gold 0.2725 oz. AGW, 22 mm. **Subject:** 7 November 1987, 15th Anniversary **Obv:** Shield **Rev:** Stylized dove **Note:** Arabic legends

Date	Mintage	F12	VF20	XF40	MS60	MS63
AH1423-2002	40	PF63 750				

KM# 436 5 DINARS
9.48 g., 0.900 Gold 0.2725 oz. AGW, 22 mm. **Subject:** 7 November 1987, 15th Anniversary **Obv:** Shield **Rev:** Stylized dove **Note:** French legends

Date	Mintage	F12	VF20	XF40	MS60	MS63
AH1423-2002	40	PF63 750				

KM# 443 5 DINARS
Bi-Metallic, 29 mm. **Subject:** 2nd Anniversary of Death **Obv:** Shield **Rev:** Head left

Date	Mintage	F12	VF20	XF40	MS60	MS63
AH1423-2002	750	PF63 375				

KM# 444 5 DINARS
10.00 g., Bi-Metallic, 29 mm. **Obv:** Shield **Rev:** Head left

Date	Mintage	F12	VF20	XF40	MS60	MS63
AH1423-2002	20,275,000	—	—	—	8.00	10.00

KM# 350 5 DINARS
10.00 g., Bi-Metallic, 29 mm. **Obv:** National arms **Rev:** Former President Habib Bourguiba **Edge:** Segmented reeding **Shape:** 12-sided

Date	Mintage	F12	VF20	XF40	MS60	MS63
AH1423-2002	—	—	—	—	6.50	8.00

KM# 350a 5 DINARS
Bi-Metallic, 29 mm. **Obv:** National arms **Rev:** Former President Habib Bourguiba **Edge:** 6 reeded and 6 plain sections **Shape:** 12-sided

Date	Mintage	F12	VF20	XF40	MS60	MS63
AH1423-2002	—	PF63 450				

KM# 445 5 DINARS
9.48 g., 0.900 Gold 0.2725 oz. AGW, 22 mm. **Subject:** 7 November 1987, 16th Anniversary **Obv:** Shield **Rev:** Hand with UN logo **Note:** Arabic legends

Date	Mintage	F12	VF20	XF40	MS60	MS63
AH1424-2003	40	PF63 750				

KM# 446 5 DINARS
9.48 g., 0.900 Gold 0.2725 oz. AGW, 22 mm. **Subject:** 7 November 1987, 16th Anniversary **Obv:** Shield **Rev:** Hand with UN logo **Note:** French legend

Date	Mintage	F12	VF20	XF40	MS60	MS63
AH1424-2003	40	PF63 750				

KM# 455 5 DINARS
9.40 g., 0.900 Gold 0.2702 oz. AGW, 22 mm. **Subject:** 7 November 1987, 17th Anniversary - Elections **Obv:** Shield **Rev:** Star and crescent and stylized flame **Note:** Arabic legend

Date	Mintage	F12	VF20	XF40	MS60	MS63
AH1425-2004	40	PF63 750				

KM# 456 5 DINARS
9.40 g., 0.900 Gold 0.2702 oz. AGW, 22 mm. **Subject:** 7 November 1987, 17th Anniversary - Elections **Obv:** Shield **Rev:** Star and crescent and stylized flame **Note:** French legend

Date	Mintage	F12	VF20	XF40	MS60	MS63
AH1425-2004	40	PF63 750				

KM# 465 5 DINARS
9.40 g., 0.900 Gold 0.2702 oz. AGW, 22 mm. **Subject:** 7 November 1987, 18th Anniversary **Obv:** Shield **Rev:** Globe in stylized ship **Note:** Arabic legend

Date	Mintage	F12	VF20	XF40	MS60	MS63
AH1426-2005	40	PF63 750				

KM# 466 5 DINARS
9.40 g., 0.900 Gold 0.2702 oz. AGW, 22 mm. **Subject:** 7 November 1987, 18th Anniversary **Obv:** Shield **Rev:** Globe in stylized ship **Note:** French legend

Date	Mintage	F12	VF20	XF40	MS60	MS63
AH1426-2005 Prook	40	PF63 750				

KM# 472 5 DINARS
24.00 g., 0.900 Silver 0.690 oz. ASW, 35 mm. **Subject:** 50th Anniversary **Obv:** Shield **Rev:** Logo **Note:** Arabic legend

Date	Mintage	F12	VF20	XF40	MS60	MS63
AH1427-2006	900	PF63 125				

KM# 473 5 DINARS
24.00 g., 0.900 Silver 0.690 oz. ASW, 35 mm. **Subject:** 50th Anniversary **Obv:** Shield **Rev:** Logo **Note:** French legends

Date	Mintage	F12	VF20	XF40	MS60	MS63
AH1427-2006	100	PF63 225				

KM# 478 5 DINARS
9.40 g., 0.900 Gold 0.2702 oz. AGW, 22 mm. **Subject:** 7 November 1987, 19th Anniversary **Obv:** Shield **Rev:** Dove and atom **Note:** Arabic legends

Date	Mintage	F12	VF20	XF40	MS60	MS63
AH1427-2006	40	PF63 750				

KM# 479 5 DINARS
9.40 g., 0.900 Gold 0.2702 oz. AGW, 22 mm. **Subject:** 7 November 1987, 19th Anniversary **Obv:** Shield **Rev:** Dove and atom **Note:** French legend

Date	Mintage	F12	VF20	XF40	MS60	MS63
AH1427-2006	40	PF63 750				

KM# 486 5 DINARS
24.00 g., 0.900 Silver 0.690 oz. ASW, 35 mm. **Subject:** 50th Anniversary **Obv:** Shield **Rev:** Ship, scales of Justice **Note:** Arabic legend

Date	Mintage	F12	VF20	XF40	MS60	MS63
AH1428-2007	900	PF63 125				

KM# 487 5 DINARS
24.00 g., 0.900 Silver 0.690 oz. ASW, 35 mm. **Subject:** 50th Anniversary **Obv:** Shield **Rev:** Ship, scales of Justice **Note:** French legend

Date	Mintage	F12	VF20	XF40	MS60	MS63
AH1428-2007	100	PF63 225				

KM# 490 5 DINARS
9.40 g., 0.900 Gold 0.2702 oz. AGW, 22 mm. **Subject:** 7 November 1987, 20th Anniversary **Obv:** Head of Zine el Abidine Ben Ali right **Rev:** Two profiles, keyboard, satellite receiver **Note:** Arabic legend

Date	Mintage	F12	VF20	XF40	MS60	MS63
AH1428-2007	43	PF63 750				

KM# 491 5 DINARS
9.40 g., 0.900 Gold 0.2702 oz. AGW, 22 mm. **Subject:** 7 November 1987, 20th Anniversary **Obv:** Head of Zine el Abidine Ben Ali right **Rev:** Two profiles, keyboard, satellite receiver **Note:** French legends

Date	Mintage	F12	VF20	XF40	MS60	MS63
AH1428-2007	40	PF63 750				

KM# 340 10 DINARS
18.77 g., 0.900 Gold 0.5396 oz. AGW **Subject:** Anniversary - 7 Nov 1987 **Obv:** Shield **Rev:** Upstretched hand, flag **Note:** French legends vary by year.

Date	Mintage	F12	VF20	XF40	MS60	MS63
2001-1422 (2001)	40	—	—	—	1,025	1,050

KM# 341 10 DINARS
18.77 g., 0.900 Gold 0.5396 oz. AGW **Subject:** Anniversary - 7 Nov 1987 **Obv:** Shield **Rev:** Upstretched hand, flag **Note:** Arabic legends vary by year.

Date	Mintage	F12	VF20	XF40	MS60	MS63
2001-1422 (2001)	40	—	—	—	1,025	1,050

KM# 378 10 DINARS
38.00 g., 0.900 Silver 1.0925 oz. ASW **Subject:** 14th Anniversary 7 Nov and 19th Mediterranean Games **Edge:** Reeded

Date	Mintage	F12	VF20	XF40	MS60	MS63
AH1422-2001	—	—	—	275	—	

KM# 430 10 DINARS
38.00 g., 0.900 Silver 1.0925 oz. ASW, 40 mm. **Subject:** 7 November 1987, 14th Anniversary **Obv:** Shield **Rev:** Open door **Note:** French legend

Date	Mintage	F12	VF20	XF40	MS60	MS63
AH1422-2001	400	PF63 150				

KM# 379 10 DINARS
38.00 g., 0.900 Silver 1.0925 oz. ASW **Subject:** 15th Anniversary 7 Nov 1987 **Obv:** National arms **Edge:** Reeded

Date	Mintage	F12	VF20	XF40	MS60	MS63
AH1423-2002	—	—	—	275	—	

KM# 433 10 DINARS
38.00 g., 0.900 Silver 1.0925 oz. ASW, 40 mm. **Subject:** 7 November 1987, 15th Anniversary **Obv:** Shield **Rev:** Stylized dove **Note:** Arabic legends

Date	Mintage	F12	VF20	XF40	MS60	MS63
AH1423-2002	490	PF63 150				

KM# 437 10 DINARS
18.80 g., 0.900 Gold 0.5405 oz. AGW, 28 mm. **Subject:** 7 November 1987, 15th Anniversary **Obv:** Shield **Rev:** Stylized dove **Note:** Arabic legends

Date	Mintage	F12	VF20	XF40	MS60	MS63
AH1423-2002	40	PF63 1,000				

KM# 438 10 DINARS

18.80 g., 0.900 Gold 0.5405 oz. AGW, 28 mm. **Subject:** 7 November 1987, 15th Anniversary **Obv:** Shield **Rev:** Stylized dove **Note:** French legends

Date	Mintage	F12	VF20	XF40	MS60	MS63
AH1423-2002	40	PF63 1,000				

KM# 380 10 DINARS

38.00 g., 0.900 Silver 1.0925 oz. ASW **Subject:** 16th Anniversary 7 Nov 1987 plus International Solidarity Fund **Obv:** National arms **Rev:** Large 16 with hands holding globe within the 6, banner which says International Solidarity Fund **Edge:** Reeded

Date	Mintage	F12	VF20	XF40	MS60	MS63
AH1424-2003	—	PF63 300				
AH1424-2003					250	—

KM# 447 10 DINARS

18.18 g., 0.900 Gold 0.5227 oz. AGW, 20 mm. **Subject:** 7 November 1987, 16th Anniversary **Obv:** Shield **Rev:** Hand with UN logo **Note:** Arabic legend

Date	Mintage	F12	VF20	XF40	MS60	MS63
AH1424-2003	40	PF63 1,000				

KM# 448 10 DINARS

18.18 g., 0.900 Gold 0.5227 oz. AGW, 28 mm. **Subject:** 7 November 1987, 16th Anniversary **Obv:** Shield **Rev:** Hand with UN logo **Note:** French legends

Date	Mintage	F12	VF20	XF40	MS60	MS63
AH1424-2003	40	PF63 1,000				

KM# 452 10 DINARS

38.00 g., 0.900 Silver 1.0925 oz. ASW, 40 mm. **Subject:** 7 November 1987, 16th Anniversary **Obv:** Shield **Rev:** Large 16 and globe

Date	Mintage	F12	VF20	XF40	MS60	MS63
AH1423-2003	24	PF63 225				

KM# 381 10 DINARS

38.00 g., 0.900 Silver 1.0925 oz. ASW **Subject:** 17th Anniverary of 7 Nov 1987 plus Elections of President and Parliament **Obv:** National arms **Edge:** Reeded

Date	Mintage	F12	VF20	XF40	MS60	MS63
AH1425-2004	—	—	—	—	275	—

KM# 453 10 DINARS

38.00 g., 0.900 Silver 1.0925 oz. ASW, 40 mm. **Subject:** 7 November 1987, 17th Anniversary - Elections **Obv:** Shield **Rev:** Star and crescent and stylized flame **Note:** Arabic legends

Date	Mintage	F12	VF20	XF40	MS60	MS63
AH1425-2004	375	PF63 150				

KM# 454 10 DINARS

38.00 g., 0.900 Silver 1.0925 oz. ASW, 40 mm. **Subject:** 7 November 1987, 17th Anniversary - Elections **Obv:** Shield **Rev:** Star and crescent and stylized flame **Note:** French legends

Date	Mintage	F12	VF20	XF40	MS60	MS63
AH1425-2004	24	PF63 225				

KM# 457 10 DINARS

18.80 g., 0.900 Gold 0.5405 oz. AGW, 28 mm. **Subject:** 7 November 1987, 17th Anniversary - Elections **Obv:** Shield **Rev:** Star and crescent and stylized flame **Note:** Arabic legend

Date	Mintage	F12	VF20	XF40	MS60	MS63
AH1425-2004	40	PF63 1,000				

KM# 458 10 DINARS

18.80 g., 0.900 Gold 0.5405 oz. AGW, 28 mm. **Subject:** 7 November 1987, 17th Anniversary - Elections **Obv:** Shield **Rev:** Star and crescent adn stylized flame **Note:** French legend

Date	Mintage	F12	VF20	XF40	MS60	MS63
AH1425-2004	40	PF63 1,000				

KM# 382 10 DINARS

38.00 g., 0.900 Silver 1.0925 oz. ASW **Subject:** 18th Anniversary of 7 Nov 1987 and Conference on Information in Tunis 2005 **Edge:** Reeded

Date	Mintage	F12	VF20	XF40	MS60	MS63
AH1426 2005	—	—	—	—	275	—

KM# 463 10 DINARS

38.00 g., 0.900 Silver 1.0925 oz. ASW, 40 mm. **Subject:** 7 November 1987, 18th Anniversary **Obv:** Shield **Rev:** Globe in stylized ship **Note:** French legends

Date	Mintage	F12	VF20	XF40	MS60	MS63
AH1426-2005	50	PF63 175				

KM# 464 10 DINARS

38.00 g., 0.900 Silver 1.0925 oz. ASW, 40 mm. **Subject:** 7 November 1987, 18th Anniversary **Obv:** Shield **Rev:** Globe in stylized ship **Note:** Arabic legend

Date	Mintage	F12	VF20	XF40	MS60	MS63
AH1426-2005	431	PF63 150				

KM# 467 10 DINARS

18.80 g., 0.900 Gold 0.5405 oz. AGW **Subject:** 7 November 1987, 18th Anniversary **Obv:** Shield **Rev:** Globe in stylized ship **Shape:** 28 **Note:** Arabic legends

Date	Mintage	F12	VF20	XF40	MS60	MS63
AH1426-2005	40	PF63 1,000				

KM# 468 10 DINARS

18.80 g., 0.900 Gold 0.5405 oz. AGW, 28 mm. **Subject:** 7 November 1987, 18th Anniversary **Obv:** Shield **Rev:** Globe in stylized ship **Note:** French legend

Date	Mintage	F12	VF20	XF40	MS60	MS63
AH1426-2005	40	PF63 1,000				

KM# 383 10 DINARS

38.00 g., 0.900 Silver 1.0925 oz. ASW **Subject:** 50th Anniversary of Independence (12.3.1956) **Obv:** National arms **Rev:** Stylized bird, "50", crescent moon with stars

Date	Mintage	F12	VF20	XF40	MS60	MS63
AH1427-2006	—	—	—	—	275	—

KM# 383a 10 DINARS

19.00 g., 0.900 Gold 0.5462 oz. AGW **Subject:** 50th Anniversary of Independence

Date	Mintage	F12	VF20	XF40	MS60	MS63
AH1427-2006	600	PF63 1,000				

KM# 474 10 DINARS

18.80 g., 0.900 Gold 0.5405 oz. AGW, 28 mm. **Subject:** 50th Anniversary **Obv:** Shield **Rev:** Logo **Note:** Arabic legends

Date	Mintage	F12	VF20	XF40	MS60	MS63
AH1427-2006	1,800	PF63 950				

KM# 475 10 DINARS

18.80 g., 0.900 Gold 0.5405 oz. AGW, 28 mm. **Subject:** 50th Anniversary **Obv:** Shield **Rev:** Logo **Note:** French legends

Date	Mintage	F12	VF20	XF40	MS60	MS63
AH1427-2006	200	PF63 1,000				

KM# 476 10 DINARS
38.00 g., 0.900 Silver 1.0925 oz. ASW, 40 mm. **Subject:** 7 November 1987, 19th Anniversary **Obv:** Shield **Rev:** Dove and atom **Note:** Arabic legend

Date	Mintage	F12	VF20	XF40	MS60	MS63
AH1427-2006	300	PF63 150				

KM# 477 10 DINARS
38.00 g., 0.900 Silver 1.0925 oz. ASW, 40 mm. **Subject:** 7 November 1987, 19th Anniversary **Obv:** Shield **Rev:** Dove and atom **Note:** French legend

Date	Mintage	F12	VF20	XF40	MS60	MS63
AH1427-2006	30	PF63 225				
Profo						

KM# 480 10 DINARS
18.80 g., 0.900 Gold 0.5405 oz. AGW, 28 mm. **Subject:** 7 November 1987, 19th Anniversary **Obv:** Shield **Rev:** Dove and atom **Note:** Arabic legend

Date	Mintage	F12	VF20	XF40	MS60	MS63
AH1427-2006	40	PF63 1,000				

KM# 481 10 DINARS
18.80 g., 0.900 Gold 0.5405 oz. AGW, 28 mm. **Subject:** 7 November 1987, 19th Anniversary **Obv:** Shield **Rev:** Dove and atom **Note:** French legend

Date	Mintage	F12	VF20	XF40	MS60	MS63
AH1427-2006	40	PF63 1,000				

KM# 488 10 DINARS
18.80 g., 0.900 Gold 0.5405 oz. AGW, 28 mm. **Subject:** 50th Anniversary **Obv:** Shield **Rev:** Ship, scales of Justice **Note:** Arabic legend

Date	Mintage	F12	VF20	XF40	MS60	MS63
AH1428-2007	450	PF63 975				

KM# 489 10 DINARS
18.80 g., 0.900 Gold 0.5405 oz. AGW, 28 mm. **Subject:** 50th Anniversary **Obv:** Shield **Rev:** Ship, scales of Justice **Note:** French legend

Date	Mintage	F12	VF20	XF40	MS60	MS63
AH1428-2007	50	PF63 1,000				

KM# 492 10 DINARS
18.80 g., 0.900 Gold 0.5405 oz. AGW, 28 mm. **Subject:** 7 November 1987, 20th Anniversary **Obv:** Head of Zine El abidine Ben Ali right **Rev:** Two profiles, keyboard, satellite receiver **Note:** Arabic legend

Date	Mintage	F12	VF20	XF40	MS60	MS63
AH1428-2007	42	PF63 1,000				

KM# 493 10 DINARS
18.80 g., 0.900 Gold 0.5405 oz. AGW, 28 mm. **Subject:** 7 November 1987, 20th Anniversary **Obv:** Head of Zine El Abidine Ben Ali right **Rev:** Two profiles, keyboard, satellite receiver **Note:** French legends

Date	Mintage	F12	VF20	XF40	MS60	MS63
AH1428-2007	40	PF63 1,000				

KM# 396 50 DINARS
21.00 g., 0.900 Gold 0.6037 oz. AGW, 34 mm. **Subject:** 14th Anniversary 7 Nov 1987 and 19th Mediterranean Games **Edge:** Reeded **Note:** Arabic legends.

Date	Mintage	F12	VF20	XF40	MS60	MS63
AH1422-2001	—	PF63 1,200				

KM# 431 50 DINARS
21.00 g., 0.900 Gold 0.6037 oz. AGW, 34 mm. **Subject:** 7 November 1987, 14th Anniversary **Obv:** Shield **Rev:** Open door **Note:** French legends

Date	Mintage	F12	VF20	XF40	MS60	MS63
AH1422-2001	150	PF63 1,150				

KM# 397 50 DINARS
21.00 g., 0.900 Gold 0.6037 oz. AGW, 34 mm. **Subject:** 15th Anniversary of 7 Nov 1987 **Edge:** Reeded

Date	Mintage	F12	VF20	XF40	MS60	MS63
AH1423-2002	—	PF63 1,200				

KM# 439 50 DINARS
21.00 g., 0.900 Gold 0.6037 oz. AGW, 34 mm. **Subject:** 7 November 1987, 15th Anniversary **Obv:** Shield **Rev:** Stylized dove **Note:** Arabic legend

Date	Mintage	F12	VF20	XF40	MS60	MS63
AH1423-2002	580	PF63 1,100				

KM# 440 50 DINARS
21.00 g., 0.900 Gold 0.6037 oz. AGW, 21 mm. **Subject:** 7 November 1987, 15th Anniversary **Obv:** Shileld **Rev:** Stylized dove

Date	Mintage	F12	VF20	XF40	MS60	MS63
AH1423-2002	80	PF63 1,250				

KM# 449 50 DINARS
21.00 g., 0.900 Gold 0.6037 oz. AGW, 34 mm. **Subject:** 7 November 1987, 16th Anniversary **Obv:** Shield **Rev:** Hand with UN logo **Note:** Arabic legends

Date	Mintage	F12	VF20	XF40	MS60	MS63
AH1424-2003	545	PF63 1,100				

KM# 450 50 DINARS
21.00 g., 0.900 Gold 0.6037 oz. AGW, 34 mm. **Subject:** 7 November 1987, 16th Anniversary **Obv:** Shield **Rev:** Hand with UN logo **Note:** French legends

Date	Mintage	F12	VF20	XF40	MS60	MS63
AH1424-2003	55	PF63 1,250				

KM# 398 50 DINARS
21.00 g., 0.900 Gold 0.6037 oz. AGW, 34 mm. **Subject:** 17th Anniversary of 7 Nov 1987 plus Elections of President and Parliament **Edge:** Reeded

Date	Mintage	F12	VF20	XF40	MS60	MS63
AH1425-2004	—	PF63 1,250				

 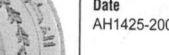

KM# 459 50 DINARS
21.00 g., 0.900 Gold 0.6037 oz. AGW, 34 mm. **Subject:** 7 November 1987, 17th Anniversary - Elections **Obv:** Shield **Rev:** Star and crescent and stylized flame **Note:** Arabic legend

Date	Mintage	F12	VF20	XF40	MS60	MS63
AH1425-2004	379	PF63 1,100				

KM# 460 50 DINARS

21.00 g., 0.900 Gold 0.6037 oz. AGW, 34 mm. **Subject:** 7 November 1987, 17th Anniversary - Elections **Obv:** Shield **Rev:** Star and crescent and stylized flame **Note:** French legend

Date	Mintage	F12	VF20	XF40	MS60	MS63
AH1425-2004	28	PF63 1,250				

KM# 470 50 DINARS

21.00 g., 0.900 Gold 0.6037 oz. AGW, 34 mm. **Subject:** 7 November 1987, 18th Anniversary **Obv:** Shield **Rev:** Globe and stylized ship **Note:** French legend

Date	Mintage	F12	VF20	XF40	MS60	MS63
AH1426-2005	45	PF63 1,250				

KM# 482 50 DINARS

21.00 g., 0.900 Gold 0.6037 oz. AGW, 34 mm. **Subject:** 7 November 1987, 19th Anniversary **Obv:** Shield **Rev:** Dove and atom **Note:** Arabic legend

Date	Mintage	F12	VF20	XF40	MS60	MS63
AH1427-2006	183	PF63 1,200				

KM# 483 50 DINARS

21.00 g., 0.900 Gold 0.6037 oz. AGW, 34 mm. **Subject:** 7 November 1987, 19th Anniversary **Obv:** Shield **Rev:** Dove and atom **Note:** French legends

Date	Mintage	F12	VF20	XF40	MS60	MS63
AH1427-2006	23	PF63 1,250				

KM# 412 100 DINARS

38.00 g., 0.900 Gold 1.0925 oz. AGW, 40 mm. **Subject:** 14th Anniversary of 7 Nov 1987 and 19th Mediterranean Games **Obv:** National arms **Rev:** Olympic rings divide 2 portals **Edge:** Reeded

Date	Mintage	F12	VF20	XF40	MS60	MS63
AH1422-2001	—	PF63 2,100				

KM# 432 100 DINARS

38.00 g., 0.900 Gold 1.0925 oz. AGW, 43 mm. **Subject:** 7 November 1987, 14th Anniversary **Obv:** Shield **Rev:** Open door **Note:** Arabic legend

Date	Mintage	F12	VF20	XF40	MS60	MS63
AH1422-2001	375	PF63 1,950				

KM# 441 100 DINARS

38.00 g., 0.900 Gold 1.0925 oz. AGW, 43 mm. **Subject:** 7 November 1987, 15th Anniversary **Obv:** Shield **Rev:** Stylized dove **Note:** Arabic legends

Date	Mintage	F12	VF20	XF40	MS60	MS63
AH1423-2002	380	PF63 1,950				

KM# 442 100 DINARS

38.00 g., 0.900 Gold 1.0925 oz. AGW, 43 mm. **Subject:** 7 November 1987, 15th Anniversary **Obv:** Sheild **Rev:** Stylized dove **Note:** French legend

Date	Mintage	F12	VF20	XF40	MS60	MS63
AH1423-2002	110	PF63 2,000				

KM# 352 100 DINARS

38.00 g., 0.900 Gold 1.0925 oz. AGW, 40 mm. **Subject:** United Nations **Obv:** National arms above value **Rev:** UN logo on stylized hand **Edge:** Reeded

Date	Mintage	F12	VF20	XF40	MS60	MS63
AH1424-2003	—	PF63 2,100				

KM# 451 100 DINARS

38.00 g., 0.900 Gold 1.0925 oz. AGW, 43 mm. **Subject:** 7 November 1987, 16th Anniversary **Obv:** Shield **Rev:** Hand with UN logo **Note:** French text

Date	Mintage	F12	VF20	XF40	MS60	MS63
AH1424-2003	53	PF63 2,100				

KM# 461 100 DINARS

38.00 g., 0.900 Gold 1.0925 oz. AGW, 43 mm. **Subject:** 7 November 1987, 17th Anniversary **Obv:** Shield **Rev:** Star and crescent and stylized flame **Note:** Arabic legend

Date	Mintage	F12	VF20	XF40	MS60	MS63
AH1425-2004	385	PF63 1,950				

KM# 462 100 DINARS

38.00 g., 0.900 Gold 1.0925 oz. AGW, 43 mm. **Subject:** 7 November 1987, 17th Anniversary - Elections **Obv:** Shield **Rev:** Star and crescent and stylized flame **Note:** French legends

Date	Mintage	F12	VF20	XF40	MS60	MS63
AH1425-2004	44	PF63 2,100				

KM# 413 100 DINARS

38.00 g., 0.900 Gold 1.0925 oz. AGW **Subject:** 18th Anniversary of 7 Nov 1987 and Conference on Information in Tunis 2005 **Edge:** Reeded

Date	Mintage	F12	VF20	XF40	MS60	MS63
AH1426-2005	—	PF63 2,100				

KM# 469 100 DINARS

21.00 g., 0.900 Gold 0.6037 oz. AGW, 34 mm. **Subject:** 7 November 1987, 18th Anniversary **Obv:** Shield **Rev:** Globe in stylized ship **Note:** Arabic legend

Date	Mintage	F12	VF20	XF40	MS60	MS63
AH1426-2005	390	PF63 1,100				

KM# 471 100 DINARS

38.00 g., 0.900 Gold 1.0925 oz. AGW, 43 mm. **Subject:** 7 November 1987, 18th Anniversary **Obv:** Shield **Rev:** Globe in stylized ship **Note:** French legends

Date	Mintage	F12	VF20	XF40	MS60	MS63
AH1426-2005	45	PF63 2,100				

KM# 484 100 DINARS
38.00 g., 0.900 Gold 1.0925 oz. AGW, 43 mm. **Subject:** 7 November 1987, 19th Anniversary **Obv:** Shield **Rev:** Dove and atom **Note:** Arabic legend

Date	Mintage	F12	VF20	XF40	MS60	MS63
AH1427-2006	212	PF63 2,000				

KM# 485 100 DINARS
38.00 g., 0.900 Gold 1.0925 oz. AGW, 43 mm. **Subject:** 7 November 1987, 19th Anniversary **Obv:** Shield **Rev:** Dove and atom **Note:** French legend

Date	Mintage	F12	VF20	XF40	MS60	MS63
AH1427-2006	23	PF63 2,200				

TURKEY

The Republic of Turkey, a parliamentary democracy of the Near East located partially in Europe and partially in Asia between the Black and the Mediterranean Seas, has an area of 301,382 sq. mi. (780,580 sq. km.) and a population of *55.4 million. Capital: Ankara. Turkey exports cotton, hazelnuts, and tobacco, and enjoys a virtual monopoly in meerschaum.

REPUBLIC

DECIMAL COINAGE

KM# 1107 3000000 LIRA
31.47 g., 0.925 Silver 0.9299 oz. ASW, 38.6 mm. **Series:** Olympics **Obv:** Value and date within wreath **Rev:** Long jumper and logo **Edge:** Reeded **Mint:** Istanbul

Date	Mintage	F12	VF20	XF40	MS60	MS63
2002	—	PF63 25.00				

DECIMAL COINAGE
40 Para = 1 Kurus; 100 Kurus = 1 Lira

KM# 1104 25000 LIRA (25 Bin Lira)
2.70 g., Brass, 17 mm. **Obv:** Head left **Rev:** Value **Edge:** Plain **Mint:** Istanbul

Date	Mintage	F12	VF20	XF40	MS60	MS63
2001	—	—	—	—	2.00	—
2002	—	—	—	—	2.00	—
2003	—	—	—	—	2.00	—

KM# 1105 50000 LIRA (50 Bin Lira)
3.20 g., Copper-Nickel-Zinc, 17.75 mm. **Obv:** Head left within circle **Rev:** Value **Edge:** Plain **Mint:** Istanbul

Date	Mintage	F12	VF20	XF40	MS60	MS63
2001	—	—	—	—	0.50	—
2002	—	—	—	—	0.50	—
2003	—	—	—	—	0.50	—
2004	—	—	—	—	0.50	—

KM# 1106 100000 LIRA (100 Bin Lira)
4.60 g., Copper-Nickel-Zinc, 21 mm. **Obv:** Head with hat right within circle **Rev:** Value **Edge:** Plain **Mint:** Istanbul

Date	Mintage	F12	VF20	XF40	MS60	MS63
2001	—	—	—	—	0.75	1.25
2002	—	—	—	—	0.75	1.25
2003	—	—	—	—	0.75	1.25
2004	—	—	—	—	0.75	1.25

KM# 1137 250000 LIRA
6.42 g., Copper-Nickel-Zinc, 23.4 mm. **Obv:** Bust facing within circle **Rev:** Value **Edge Lettering:** T.C." six times dividing reeded sections **Mint:** Istanbul

Date	Mintage	F12	VF20	XF40	MS60	MS63
2002	—	—	—	—	1.00	1.50
2003	—	—	—	—	1.00	1.50
2004	—	—	—	—	1.00	1.50

KM# 1161 500000 LIRA
4.60 g., Copper-Nickel, 21 mm. **Obv:** Value and date within sprigs **Rev:** One sheep **Edge:** Plain **Mint:** Istanbul

Date	Mintage	F12	VF20	XF40	MS60	MS63
2002	—	—	—	—	2.00	3.00

KM# 1162 750000 LIRA
6.40 g., Copper-Nickel, 23.5 mm. **Obv:** Value and date within sprigs **Rev:** Angora Ram **Edge:** Plain **Mint:** Istanbul

Date	Mintage	F12	VF20	XF40	MS60	MS63
2002	—	—	—	—	3.00	4.00

KM# 1163 1000000 LIRA
12.00 g., Copper-Nickel, 31.9 mm. **Obv:** Value and date within sprigs **Rev:** Turbaned bust 1/4 left divides dates **Edge:** Reeded **Mint:** Istanbul

Date	Mintage	F12	VF20	XF40	MS60	MS63
2002	—	—	—	—	5.00	6.00

KM# 1170 1000000 LIRA
31.42 g., 0.925 Silver 0.9284 oz. ASW, 38.6 mm. **Subject:** Mevlana Celaleddin-I Rumi **Obv:** Value and date in wreath **Rev:** Turbaned bust **Edge:** Reeded **Mint:** Istanbul

Date	Mintage	F12	VF20	XF40	MS60	MS63
2002	—	PF63 40.00				

KM# 1139.1 1000000 LIRA
11.87 g., Bi-Metallic, 32.1 mm. **Subject:** Foundation of the Mint **Obv:** Building and value within circle **Rev:** Legend and date inscription **Edge:** Plain **Mint:** Istanbul **Note:** This coin type is produced by a machine outside the money museum at the Istanbul Mint. Visitors pay 1 mio lira, press a button and strike a coin with the actual date of their visit. Many other dates exist in unknown and unregistered quantities. Only Turkish months are on struck coins.

Date	Mintage	F12	VF20	XF40	MS60	MS63
Mayis 2002	—	—	—	—	5.00	6.00
Haziran 2002	—	—	—	—	5.00	6.00
Temmuz 2002	—	—	—	—	5.00	6.00
Agostos 2002	—	—	—	—	5.00	6.00
Eylul 2002	—	—	—	—	5.00	6.00
Ekim 2002	—	—	—	—	5.00	6.00
Kasim 2002	—	—	—	—	5.00	6.00
Aralik 2002	—	—	—	—	5.00	6.00

KM# 1139.2 1000000 LIRA
Bi-Metallic, 32.1 mm. **Subject:** Foundation of the Mint **Obv:** Building and value within circle **Rev:** Legend and date inscription **Edge:** Plain **Mint:** Istanbul **Note:** This coin type is produced by a machine outside the money museum at the Istanbul Mint. Visitors pay 1 mio lira, press a button and strike a coin with the actual date of their visit. Many other dates exist in unknown and unregistered quantities. The months are listed in both Turkish and English on struck coins.

Date	Mintage	F12	VF20	XF40	MS60	MS63
Ocak/January 2003	—	—	—	—	5.00	6.00

Date	Mintage	F12	VF20	XF40	MS60	MS63
Subat/February 2003	—	—	—	—	5.00	6.00
Mart/March 2003	—	—	—	—	5.00	6.00
Nisan/April 2003	—	—	—	—	5.00	6.00
Mayis/May 2003	—	—	—	—	5.00	6.00
Haziran/June 2003	—	—	—	—	5.00	6.00
Temmuz/July 2003	—	—	—	—	5.00	6.00
Agostos/August 2003	—	—	—	—	5.00	6.00
Eylul/September 2003	—	—	—	—	5.00	6.00
Ekim/October 2003	—	—	—	—	5.00	6.00
Kasim/November 2003	—	—	—	—	5.00	6.00
Aralik/December 2003	—	—	—	—	5.00	6.00

KM# 1107 3000000 Lira
31.47 g., 0.925 Silver 0.9299 oz. ASW, 38.6 mm. **Series:** Olympics **Obv:** Value and date within wreath **Rev:** Long jumper and logo **Edge:** Reeded **Mint:** Istanbul

Date	Mintage	F12	VF20	XF40	MS60	MS63
2002	—			PF63	25.00	

KM# 1110 5000000 LIRA
67.00 g., Bronze, 50 mm. **Subject:** Children's Day **Obv:** Legend and inscription **Rev:** Dancing children **Edge:** Plain **Mint:** Istanbul

Date	Mintage	F12	VF20	XF40	MS60	MS63
2001 Matte	1,583	—	—	—	35.00	—

KM# 1117 7500000 LIRA
31.47 g., 0.925 Silver 0.9299 oz. ASW **Subject:** Iznik Tabak **Obv:** Two peacocks within circle **Rev:** Iznik Tabak (Nicean pottery) 1570; Circle of flowers at center

Date	Mintage	F12	VF20	XF40	MS60	MS63
2001	1,349	PF63	50.00			

KM# 1120 7500000 LIRA
15.40 g., 0.925 Silver 0.455 oz. ASW **Subject:** Bird Series - Saz Horozu **Obv:** Value and date within sprigs **Rev:** Purple swamphen on ground **Edge:** Plain **Shape:** 4-sided **Mint:** Istanbul **Note:** 28.1 x 28.1mm

Date	Mintage	F12	VF20	XF40	MS60	MS63
2001	—	PF63	35.00			

KM# 1121 7500000 LIRA
15.40 g., 0.925 Silver 0.455 oz. ASW **Subject:** Bird Series - Toy **Obv:** Value and date within sprigs **Rev:** Greater Bustard on ground **Edge:** Plain **Shape:** 4-sided **Mint:** Istanbul **Note:** 28.1 x 28.1mm

Date	Mintage	F12	VF20	XF40	MS60	MS63
2001	—	PF63	35.00			

KM# 1122 7500000 LIRA
15.40 g., 0.925 Silver 0.455 oz. ASW **Subject:** Bird Series - Yaz Ordegi **Obv:** Value and date within sprigs **Rev:** White-headed Duck on ground **Edge:** Plain **Shape:** 4-sided **Mint:** Istanbul **Note:** 28.1 x 28.1mm

Date	Mintage	F12	VF20	XF40	MS60	MS63
2001	—	PF63	35.00			

KM# 1123 7500000 LIRA
15.40 g., 0.925 Silver 0.455 oz. ASW **Subject:** Bird Series - Dikkuyruk **Obv:** Value and date within sprigs **Rev:** Marbled teal on water **Edge:** Plain **Shape:** 4-sided **Mint:** Istanbul **Note:** 28.1 x 28.1mm

Date	Mintage	F12	VF20	XF40	MS60	MS63
2001	—	PF63	35.00			

KM# 1124 7500000 LIRA
15.40 g., 0.925 Silver 0.455 oz. ASW **Subject:** Bird Series - Yesil Arikusu **Obv:** Value and date within sprigs **Rev:** Bee-eater on branch **Edge:** Plain **Shape:** 4-sided **Mint:** Istanbul **Note:** 28.1 x 28.1mm

Date	Mintage	F12	VF20	XF40	MS60	MS63
2001	—	PF63	35.00			

KM# 1125 7500000 LIRA
15.40 g., 0.925 Silver 0.455 oz. ASW **Subject:** Bird Series - Kucuk Karabatak **Obv:** Value and date within sprigs **Rev:** Three pygmy cormorants **Edge:** Plain **Shape:** 4-sided **Mint:** Istanbul **Note:** 28.1 x 28.1mm

Date	Mintage	F12	VF20	XF40	MS60	MS63
2001	—	PF63	35.00			

KM# 1126 7500000 LIRA
15.40 g., 0.925 Silver 0.455 oz. ASW **Subject:** Bird Series - Kizil Akbaba **Obv:** Value and date within sprigs **Rev:** Eurasian griffon **Edge:** Plain **Shape:** 4-sided **Mint:** Istanbul **Note:** 28.1 x 28.1mm

Date	Mintage	F12	VF20	XF40	MS60	MS63
2001	—	PF63	35.00			

KM# 1127 7500000 LIRA
15.40 g., 0.925 Silver 0.455 oz. ASW **Subject:** Bird Series - Sah Kartal **Obv:** Value and date within sprigs **Rev:** Eagles **Edge:** Plain **Shape:** 4-sided **Mint:** Istanbul **Note:** 28.1 x 28.1mm

Date	Mintage	F12	VF20	XF40	MS60	MS63
2001	—	PF63	35.00			

KM# 1128 7500000 LIRA
15.40 g., 0.925 Silver 0.455 oz. ASW **Subject:** Bird Series - Ala Sigireik **Obv:** Value and date within sprigs **Rev:** Rosy starling on ground **Edge:** Plain **Shape:** 4-sided **Mint:** Istanbul **Note:** 28.1 x 28.1mm

Date	Mintage	F12	VF20	XF40	MS60	MS63
2001	—	PF63	35.00			

KM# 1129 7500000 LIRA
15.40 g., 0.925 Silver 0.455 oz. ASW **Subject:** Bird Series - Izmir Yalicapkini **Obv:** Value and date within sprigs **Rev:** White-throated kingfisher on stump **Edge:** Plain **Shape:** 4-sided **Mint:** Istanbul **Note:** 28.1 x 28.1mm

Date	Mintage	F12	VF20	XF40	MS60	MS63
2001	—	PF63	35.00			

KM# 1130 7500000 LIRA
15.40 g., 0.925 Silver 0.455 oz. ASW **Subject:** Bird Series - Turac **Obv:** Value and date within sprigs **Rev:** Black francolin birds on the ground **Edge:** Plain **Shape:** 4-sided **Mint:** Istanbul **Note:** 28.1 x 28.1mm

Date	Mintage	F12	VF20	XF40	MS60	MS63
2001	—	PF63	35.00			

KM# 1131 7500000 LIRA
15.40 g., 0.925 Silver 0.455 oz. ASW **Subject:** Bird Series - Kelaynak **Obv:** Value and date within sprigs **Rev:** Two Bald Ibis birds on ground **Edge:** Plain **Shape:** 4-sided **Mint:** Istanbul **Note:** 28.1 x 28.1mm

Date	Mintage	F12	VF20	XF40	MS60	MS63
2001	—	PF63 35.00				

KM# 1132 7500000 LIRA
15.40 g., 0.925 Silver 0.455 oz. ASW **Subject:** Bird Series - Sakalli Akbaba **Obv:** Value and date within sprigs **Rev:** Bearded vulture **Edge:** Plain **Shape:** 4-sided **Mint:** Istanbul **Note:** 28.1 x 28.1mm

Date	Mintage	F12	VF20	XF40	MS60	MS63
2001	—	PF63 35.00				

KM# 1133 7500000 LIRA
15.40 g., 0.925 Silver 0.455 oz. ASW **Subject:** Bird Series - Tepeli Pelikan **Obv:** Value and date within sprigs **Rev:** Dalmatian pelican on rock **Edge:** Plain **Shape:** Square **Mint:** Istanbul **Note:** 28.1 x 28.1mm

Date	Mintage	F12	VF20	XF40	MS60	MS63
2001	—	PF63 35.00				

KM# 1134 7500000 LIRA
15.40 g., 0.925 Silver 0.455 oz. ASW **Subject:** Bird Series - Ishakkusu **Obv:** Value and date within sprigs **Rev:** European scops owl on branch **Edge:** Plain **Shape:** Square **Mint:** Istanbul **Note:** 28.1 x 28.1mm

Date	Mintage	F12	VF20	XF40	MS60	MS63
2001	—	PF63 35.00				

KM# 1135 7500000 LIRA
31.03 g., 0.925 Silver 0.9169 oz. ASW, 38.5 mm. **Subject:** Mevlana Celaleddin-i Rumi **Obv:** Dancer within circle **Rev:** Turbaned bust 3/4 right above dates **Edge:** Reeded **Mint:** Istanbul

Date	Mintage	F12	VF20	XF40	MS60	MS63
2001	—	PF63 45.00				

KM# 1142 7500000 LIRA
31.25 g., 0.925 Silver 0.9234 oz. ASW, 38.5 mm. **Subject:** Cahit Arf, Turkish mathematician (1910-1997) **Obv:** Mathematical formula within circle **Rev:** 1/2-length figure facing **Edge:** Reeded **Mint:** Istanbul

Date	Mintage	F12	VF20	XF40	MS60	MS63
2001	—	PF63 45.00				

KM# 1143 7500000 LIRA
31.25 g., 0.925 Silver 0.9234 oz. ASW, 38.5 mm. **Obv:** Ornamented circle design **Rev:** 1/2-length bust facing **Edge:** Reeded **Mint:** Istanbul

Date	Mintage	F12	VF20	XF40	MS60	MS63
2001	—	PF63 45.00				

KM# 1144 7500000 LIRA
31.25 g., 0.925 Silver 0.9234 oz. ASW, 38.5 mm. **Subject:** Koca Yusuf Baspehlivan **Obv:** Two figures wrestling **Rev:** Portrait on circular background **Edge:** Reeded **Mint:** Istanbul

Date	Mintage	F12	VF20	XF40	MS60	MS63
2001	—	PF63 42.00				

KM# 1145 7500000 LIRA
15.61 g., 0.925 Silver 0.4612 oz. ASW, 27.9 x 38.6 mm. **Series:** Flowers **Obv:** Value and date within sprigs **Rev:** Paeonia turcica **Edge:** Reeded **Shape:** Oval **Mint:** Istanbul

Date	Mintage	F12	VF20	XF40	MS60	MS63
2002	—	PF63 28.00				

KM# 1146 7500000 LIRA
15.61 g., 0.925 Silver 0.4612 oz. ASW, 27.9 x 38.6 mm. **Series:** Flowers **Obv:** Value and date within sprigs **Rev:** Orchis anatolica **Edge:** Reeded **Shape:** Oval **Mint:** Istanbul

Date	Mintage	F12	VF20	XF40	MS60	MS63
2002	—	PF63 28.00				

KM# 1147 7500000 LIRA
15.61 g., 0.925 Silver 0.4612 oz. ASW, 27.9 x 38.6 mm. **Series:** Flowers **Obv:** Value and date within sprigs **Rev:** Iris pamphylica **Edge:** Reeded **Shape:** Oval **Mint:** Istanbul

Date	Mintage	F12	VF20	XF40	MS60	MS63
2002	—	PF63 28.00				

KM# 1148 7500000 LIRA
15.61 g., 0.925 Silver 0.4612 oz. ASW, 27.9 x 38.6 mm. **Series:** Flowers **Obv:** Value and date within sprigs **Rev:** Gladiolus anatolicus **Edge:** Reeded **Shape:** Oval **Mint:** Istanbul

Date	Mintage	F12	VF20	XF40	MS60	MS63
2002	—	PF63 28.00				

KM# 1149 7500000 LIRA
15.61 g., 0.925 Silver 0.4612 oz. ASW, 27.9 x 38.6 mm. **Series:** Flowers **Obv:** Value and date within sprigs **Rev:** Crocus sativus **Edge:** Reeded **Shape:** Oval **Mint:** Istanbul

Date	Mintage	F12	VF20	XF40	MS60	MS63
2002	—	PF63 28.00				

KM# 1150 7500000 LIRA
15.61 g., 0.925 Silver 0.4612 oz. ASW, 27.9 x 38.6 mm. **Series:** Flowers **Obv:** Value and date within sprigs **Rev:** Campanula betulifolia **Edge:** Reeded **Shape:** Oval **Mint:** Istanbul

Date	Mintage	F12	VF20	XF40	MS60	MS63
2002	—	PF63 28.00				

KM# 1151 7500000 LIRA
15.61 g., 0.925 Silver 0.4612 oz. ASW, 27.9 x 38.6 mm. **Series:** Flowers **Obv:** Value and date within sprigs **Rev:** Centaurea tchihatcheffii **Edge:** Reeded **Shape:** Oval **Mint:** Istanbul

Date	Mintage	F12	VF20	XF40	MS60	MS63
2002	—	PF63 28.00				

KM# 1152 7500000 LIRA
15.61 g., 0.925 Silver 0.4612 oz. ASW, 27.9 x 38.6 mm. **Series:** Flowers **Obv:** Value and date within sprigs **Rev:** Tchihatchewia isatidea **Edge:** Reeded **Shape:** Oval **Mint:** Istanbul

Date	Mintage	F12	VF20	XF40	MS60	MS63
2002	—	PF63 28.00				

KM# 1153 7500000 LIRA
15.61 g., 0.925 Silver 0.4612 oz. ASW, 27.9 x 38.6 mm. **Series:** Flowers **Obv:** Value and date within sprigs **Rev:** Linum anatolicum **Edge:** Reeded **Shape:** Oval **Mint:** Istanbul

Date	Mintage	F12	VF20	XF40	MS60	MS63
2002	—	PF63 28.00				

KM# 1154 7500000 LIRA
15.61 g., 0.925 Silver 0.4612 oz. ASW, 27.9 x 38.6 mm. **Series:** Flowers **Obv:** Value and date within sprigs **Rev:** Cyclamen trochopteranthum **Edge:** Reeded **Shape:** Oval **Mint:** Istanbul

Date	Mintage	F12	VF20	XF40	MS60	MS63
2002	—	PF63 28.00				

KM# 1155 7500000 LIRA
15.61 g., 0.925 Silver 0.4612 oz. ASW, 27.9 x 38.6 mm. **Series:** Flowers **Obv:** Value and date within sprigs **Rev:** Tulipa orphanidea **Edge:** Reeded **Shape:** Oval **Mint:** Istanbul

Date	Mintage	F12	VF20	XF40	MS60	MS63
2002	—	PF63 28.00				

KM# 1156 7500000 LIRA
15.61 g., 0.925 Silver 0.4612 oz. ASW, 27.9 x 38.6 mm. **Obv:** Value and date within sprigs **Rev:** Stenbergia candida **Edge:** Reeded **Shape:** Oval **Mint:** Istanbul

Date	Mintage	F12	VF20	XF40	MS60	MS63
2002	—	PF63 28.00				

KM# 1157 7500000 LIRA
15.61 g., 0.925 Silver 0.4612 oz. ASW, 27.9 x 38.6 mm. **Series:** Flowers **Obv:** Value and date within sprigs **Rev:** Arum maculatum **Edge:** Reeded **Shape:** Oval **Mint:** Istanbul

Date	Mintage	F12	VF20	XF40	MS60	MS63
2002	—	PF63 28.00				

KM# 1118 10000000 LIRA
31.47 g., 0.925 Silver 0.9299 oz. ASW, 38.6 mm. **Subject:** Divrigi Ulu Camii **Obv:** Artwork within circle **Rev:** Ornate door at the Divrigi ulu Camii (Divrigi Great Mosque) built 1228 in Sivas Province **Edge:** Reeded **Mint:** Istanbul

Date	Mintage	F12	VF20	XF40	MS60	MS63
2001 Matte	15,000	—	—	—	40.00	—

KM# 1159 10000000 LIRA
31.42 g., 0.925 Silver 0.9284 oz. ASW, 38.6 mm. **Subject:** Bogazici'nde Yalilar **Obv:** Value and date within sprigs **Rev:** Waterfront buildings **Edge:** Reeded **Mint:** Istanbul

Date	Mintage	F12	VF20	XF40	MS60	MS63
2001	4,458	PF63 40.00				

KM# 1140 10000000 LIRA
31.46 g., 0.925 Silver 0.9296 oz. ASW, 38.6 mm. **Subject:** 75th Anniversary of TRT (Türkiye Radyo Televizyon) **Obv:** Large mint mark and design within circle **Rev:** Radio microphone **Edge:** Reeded **Mint:** Istanbul

Date	Mintage	F12	VF20	XF40	MS60	MS63
2002	—	PF63 45.00				

KM# 1160 10000000 LIRA
31.42 g., 0.925 Silver 0.9284 oz. ASW, 38.6 mm. **Obv:** Turkish mint symbol within circle **Rev:** Mosque within surrounding buildings **Edge:** Reeded **Mint:** Istanbul

Date	Mintage	F12	VF20	XF40	MS60	MS63
2002	2,106	PF63 45.00				

KM# 1265 150000000 LIRA
31.49 g., 0.925 Silver 0.9305 oz. ASW, 38.61 mm. **Subject:** 2006 FIFA World Cup **Obv:** Value within wreath **Rev:** Two scoccer players and globe **Edge:** Reeded

Date	Mintage	F12	VF20	XF40	MS60	MS63
2003	Est. 5000	PF63 50.00				

REFORM DECIMAL COINAGE
2005
100,000 Old Lira = 1 New Lira

KM# 1164 NEW KURUS
2.72 g., Aluminum-Bronze, 17 mm. **Obv:** Head of Atatürk left within circle **Rev:** Value **Edge:** Plain **Mint:** Istanbul

Date	Mintage	F12	VF20	XF40	MS60	MS63
2005	148,419,560	—	—	—	0.15	0.20
2006	9,002,010	—	—	—	0.15	0.20
2007	5,357,000	—	—	—	0.15	0.20
2008	—	—	—	—	0.15	0.20

KM# 1165 5 NEW KURUS
2.95 g., Copper-Nickel-Zinc, 17.1 mm. **Obv:** Head of Atatürk left within circle **Rev:** Value **Edge:** Plain **Mint:** Istanbul

Date	Mintage	F12	VF20	XF40	MS60	MS63
2005	203,339,160	—	—	0.10	0.25	0.35
2006	202,253,310	—	—	0.10	0.25	0.35
2007	122,090,000	—	—	0.10	0.25	0.35
2008	—	—	—	0.10	0.25	0.35

KM# 1166 10 NEW KURUS
3.83 g., Copper-Nickel-Zinc, 19.4 mm. **Obv:** Head of Atatürk with hat right within circle **Rev:** Value **Edge:** Plain **Mint:** Istanbul

Date	Mintage	F12	VF20	XF40	MS60	MS63
2005	261,538,050	—	—	0.20	0.45	0.60
2006	196,717,510	—	—	0.20	0.45	0.60
2007	134,104,000	—	—	0.20	0.45	0.60
2008	—	—	—	0.20	0.45	0.60

KM# 1167 25 NEW KURUS
5.30 g., Copper-Nickel-Zinc, 21.5 mm. **Obv:** Bust of Atatürk facing within circle **Rev:** Value **Edge:** Reeded **Mint:** Istanbul

Date	Mintage	F12	VF20	XF40	MS60	MS63
2005	173,705,760	—	—	0.25	0.60	0.80
2006	67,803,010	—	—	0.30	0.75	1.00
2007	33,463,500	—	—	0.25	0.60	0.80
2008	—	—	—	0.25	0.60	0.80

KM# 1168 50 NEW KURUS
7.00 g., Bi-Metallic, 23.8 mm. **Obv:** Head of Atatürk right within circle **Rev:** Value within circle **Edge:** Reeded **Mint:** Istanbul

Date	Mintage	F12	VF20	XF40	MS60	MS63
2005	203,749,569	—	—	0.60	1.50	2.00
2006	45,089,010	—	—	0.60	1.50	2.00
2007	21,946,500	—	—	0.50	1.20	1.60
2008	—	—	—	0.50	1.20	1.60

KM# 1169 NEW LIRA
8.50 g., Bi-Metallic, 26 mm. **Obv:** Bust of Atatürk 3/4 left within circle **Rev:** Value within circle **Edge:** Segmented reeding **Mint:** Istanbul

Date	Mintage	F12	VF20	XF40	MS60	MS63
2005	305,235,560	—	—	—	2.25	3.00
2006	69,247,010	—	—	—	2.25	3.00
2007	56,498,200	—	—	—	2.25	3.00
2008	—	—	—	—	2.25	3.00

KM# 1171 5 NEW LIRA
12.00 g., Bi-Metallic, 32 mm. **Subject:** 23rd Universiade in red holder **Obv:** Stylized bird within circle **Rev:** Logo within circle **Mint:** Istanbul

Date	Mintage	F12	VF20	XF40	MS60	MS63
ND (2005)	2,957	—	—	—	22.00	25.00

KM# 1172 5 NEW LIRA
12.00 g., Bi-Metallic, 32 mm. **Subject:** 23rd Universiade in blue holder **Obv:** Stylized bird within circle **Rev:** Logo within circle **Mint:** Istanbul

Date	Mintage	F12	VF20	XF40	MS60	MS63
ND (2005)	2,900	—	—	—	22.00	25.00

KM# 1195 15 NEW LIRA
1.24 g., 0.999 Gold 0.0396 oz. AGW, 13.92 mm. **Subject:** Nemrud **Obv:** Value within wreath **Rev:** Two large statue heads **Note:** Dated 2003 but released in 2005

Date	Mintage	F12	VF20	XF40	MS60	MS63
2003	1,820	PF63 75.00				

KM# 1193 15 NEW LIRA
15.55 g., 0.925 Silver 0.4595 oz. ASW, 32 mm. **Obv:** Bird **Rev:** Logo

Date	Mintage	F12	VF20	XF40	MS60	MS63
2005	1,237	PF63 40.00				

KM# 1203 15 NEW LIRA
31.47 g., 0.925 Silver 0.9299 oz. ASW, 38.6 mm. **Subject:** Scouting in Turkey, 100th Anniversary **Obv:** Scout emblem, multicolor **Rev:** Flag, Scouts saluting, camp scene

Date	Mintage	F12	VF20	XF40	MS60	MS63
2007	1,414	PF63 50.00				

KM# 1180.1 20 NEW LIRA
23.50 g., 0.925 Silver 0.6944 oz. ASW, 38.6 mm. **Obv:** Value within sprigs and circle **Rev:** Angora Cat with plain eyes **Edge:** Reeded **Mint:** Istanbul

Date	Mintage	F12	VF20	XF40	MS60	MS63
2005	5,000	PF65 60.00				

KM# 1180.2 20 NEW LIRA
23.50 g., 0.925 Silver 0.6944 oz. ASW, 38.6 mm. **Obv:** Value within sprigs and circle **Rev:** Angora cat with mismatched colored eyes **Edge:** Reeded **Mint:** Istanbul

Date	Mintage	F12	VF20	XF40	MS60	MS63
2005	—	PF65 65.00				

KM# 1173 20 NEW LIRA
31.36 g., 0.925 Silver 0.9266 oz. ASW, 38.6 mm. **Obv:** Value within sprigs and circle **Rev:** Aegean Carpet **Edge:** Reeded **Mint:** Istanbul

Date	Mintage	F12	VF20	XF40	MS60	MS63
2005	1,195	PF63 70.00				

KM# 1174 20 NEW LIRA
31.43 g., 0.925 Silver 0.9287 oz. ASW, 38.6 mm. **Obv:** Value within sprigs and circle **Rev:** Mostar Bridge **Edge:** Reeded **Mint:** Istanbul

Date	Mintage	F12	VF20	XF40	MS60	MS63
2005	1,592	PF65 75.00				

KM# 1175 20 NEW LIRA
23.45 g., 0.925 Silver 0.6929 oz. ASW, 38.6 mm. **Obv:** Value within sprigs and circle **Rev:** Angora Goat **Edge:** Reeded **Mint:** Istanbul

Date	Mintage	F12	VF20	XF40	MS60	MS63
2005	898	PF63 60.00	PF65 65.00			

KM# 1176 20 NEW LIRA
23.46 g., 0.925 Silver 0.6932 oz. ASW, 38.6 mm. **Obv:** Value within sprigs and circle **Rev:** Long-eared Desert Hedgehog **Edge:** Reeded **Mint:** Istanbul

Date	Mintage	F12	VF20	XF40	MS60	MS63
2005	744	PF63 60.00	PF65 65.00			

KM# 1177 20 NEW LIRA
23.41 g., 0.925 Silver 0.6917 oz. ASW, 38.6 mm. **Obv:** Value within sprigs and circle **Rev:** Anatolian Mouflon **Edge:** Reeded **Mint:** Istanbul

Date	Mintage	F12	VF20	XF40	MS60	MS63
2005	779	PF63 60.00	PF65 65.00			

KM# 1178 20 NEW LIRA
23.43 g., 0.925 Silver 0.6923 oz. ASW, 38.6 mm. **Obv:** Value within sprigs and circle **Rev:** Striped Hyena **Edge:** Reeded **Mint:** Istanbul

Date	Mintage	F12	VF20	XF40	MS60	MS63
2005	778	PF63 60.00	PF65 65.00			

KM# 1179 20 NEW LIRA
23.43 g., 0.925 Silver 0.6923 oz. ASW, 38.6 mm. **Obv:** Value within sprigs and circle **Rev:** Hazel Dormouse **Edge:** Reeded **Mint:** Istanbul

Date	Mintage	F12	VF20	XF40	MS60	MS63
2005	744	PF63 60.00	PF65 65.00			

KM# 1181 20 NEW LIRA
23.37 g., 0.999 Silver 0.7458 oz. ASW, 38.6 mm. **Obv:** Value within sprigs and circle **Rev:** Anatolian Leopard **Edge:** Reeded **Mint:** Istanbul

Date	Mintage	F12	VF20	XF40	MS60	MS63
2005	855	PF63 60.00	PF65 65.00			

KM# 1182 20 NEW LIRA
23.25 g., 0.925 Silver 0.687 oz. ASW, 38.6 mm. **Obv:** Value within sprigs and circle **Rev:** Turkish Kangal Dog **Edge:** Reeded **Mint:** Istanbul

Date	Mintage	F12	VF20	XF40	MS60	MS63
2005	1,128	PF63 60.00	PF65 65.00			

KM# 1183 20 NEW LIRA
23.46 g., 0.925 Silver 0.6932 oz. ASW, 38.6 mm. **Obv:** Value within sprigs and circle **Rev:** Five-toed Jerboa **Edge:** Reeded **Mint:** Istanbul

Date	Mintage	F12	VF20	XF40	MS60	MS63
2005	746	PF63 60.00	PF65 65.00			

KM# 1184 20 NEW LIRA
23.26 g., 0.925 Silver 0.6873 oz. ASW, 38.6 mm. **Obv:** Value within sprigs and circle **Rev:** Brown Bear **Edge:** Reeded **Mint:** Istanbul

Date	Mintage	F12	VF20	XF40	MS60	MS63
2005	802	PF63 60.00	PF65 65.00			

KM# 1185 20 NEW LIRA
23.53 g., 0.925 Silver 0.6953 oz. ASW, 38.6 mm. **Obv:** Value within sprigs and circle **Rev:** Desert Monitor **Edge:** Reeded **Mint:** Istanbul

Date	Mintage	F12	VF20	XF40	MS60	MS63
2005	753	PF63 60.00	PF65 65.00			

KM# 1188 20 NEW LIRA
31.47 g., 0.925 Silver 0.9299 oz. ASW, 38.6 mm. **Subject:** Edirne Selimiye Mosque **Obv:** Value within wreath **Rev:** Mosque

Date	Mintage	F12	VF20	XF40	MS60	MS63
2005	1,660	PF63 55.00				

KM# 1189 20 NEW LIRA
31.47 g., 0.925 Silver 0.9299 oz. ASW, 38.6 mm. **Obv:** Crescent and star **Rev:** Large 85 above building

Date	Mintage	F12	VF20	XF40	MS60	MS63
2005	1,216	PF63 55.00				

KM# 1190 20 NEW LIRA
31.47 g., 0.925 Silver 0.9299 oz. ASW, 38.6 mm. **Subject:** Galatasaray Spor **Obv:** 100 above team mascot **Rev:** GS monogram

Date	Mintage	F12	VF20	XF40	MS60	MS63
2005	2,828	PF63 55.00				

KM# 1194 20 NEW LIRA
31.47 g., 0.925 Silver 0.9299 oz. ASW, 38.6 mm. **Subject:** Belt Maglova Cultural Heritage site **Obv:** Value within wreath **Rev:** Aqueduct

Date	Mintage	F12	VF20	XF40	MS60	MS63
2005	1,250	PF63 55.00				

KM# 1191 25 NEW LIRA
31.47 g., 0.925 Silver 0.9299 oz. ASW, 38.6 mm. **Subject:** Galatasaray Spor **Obv:** 100 above team mascot **Rev:** GS monogram, colored

Date	Mintage	F12	VF20	XF40	MS60	MS63
2005	1,250	PF63 85.00				

KM# 1196 25 NEW LIRA
31.47 g., 0.925 Silver 0.9299 oz. ASW, 38.6 mm. **Subject:** 800 year of Medical Education in Turkey **Obv:** Two snakes **Rev:** Figure

Date	Mintage	F12	VF20	XF40	MS60	MS63
2006	1,650	PF63 60.00				

KM# 1198 25 NEW LIRA
31.47 g., 0.925 Silver 0.9299 oz. ASW, 38.6 mm. **Subject:** Nevruz of Hatira **Obv:** Flower and rays **Rev:** Statue holding flames

Date	Mintage	F12	VF20	XF40	MS60	MS63
2006	1,300	PF63 85.00				

KM# 1199 25 NEW LIRA
31.47 g., 0.925 Silver 0.9299 oz. ASW, 38.6 mm. **Subject:** Hattat Hamid Aytac **Obv:** Design **Rev:** Bust facing

Date	Mintage	F12	VF20	XF40	MS60	MS63
2006	1,301	PF63 75.00				

KM# 1200 25 NEW LIRA
31.47 g., 0.925 Silver 0.9299 oz. ASW, 38.6 mm. **Subject:** T.C. Devlet Demiryollari, 150th Anniversary **Obv:** 150 above laural **Rev:** Building

Date	Mintage	F12	VF20	XF40	MS60	MS63
2006	1,950	PF63 55.00				

KM# 1201 25 NEW LIRA
31.47 g., 0.925 Silver 0.9299 oz. ASW, 38.6 mm. **Subject:** Mehmet Ersoy Akif, 70th Anniversary of death **Obv:** Scroll **Rev:** Linear portrait facing

Date	Mintage	F12	VF20	XF40	MS60	MS63
2006 Antiqued	1,500	—	—	—	55.00	—

KM# 1211 25 NEW LIRA
15.55 g., 0.925 Silver 0.4595 oz. ASW, 38.6x28 mm. **Obv:** Legend **Rev:** Zodiac - Pisces **Shape:** Oval

Date	Mintage	F12	VF20	XF40	MS60	MS63
2008	—	PF63 45.00				

KM# 1212 25 NEW LIRA
15.55 g., 0.925 Silver 0.4595 oz. ASW, 38.6x28 mm. **Obv:** Text **Rev:** Zodiac - Aquarius **Shape:** Oval

Date	Mintage	F12	VF20	XF40	MS60	MS63
2008	—	PF63 45.00				

KM# 1213 25 NEW LIRA
15.55 g., 0.925 Silver 0.4595 oz. ASW, 38.6x28 mm. **Obv:** Text **Rev:** Zodiac - Capricorn **Shape:** Oval

Date	Mintage	F12	VF20	XF40	MS60	MS63
2008	—	PF63 45.00				

KM# 1214 25 NEW LIRA
15.55 g., 0.925 Silver 0.4595 oz. ASW, 38.6x28 mm. **Obv:** Text **Rev:** Zodiac - Sagittarius **Shape:** Oval

Date	Mintage	F12	VF20	XF40	MS60	MS63
2008	—	PF63 45.00				

KM# 1215 25 NEW LIRA
15.55 g., 0.925 Silver 0.4595 oz. ASW, 38.6x28 mm. **Obv:** Text **Rev:** Zodiac - Libra **Shape:** Oval

Date	Mintage	F12	VF20	XF40	MS60	MS63
2008	—	PF63 45.00				

KM# 1216 25 NEW LIRA
15.55 g., 0.925 Silver 0.4595 oz. ASW, 38.6x28 mm. **Obv:** Text **Rev:** Zodiac - figure **Shape:** Oval

Date	Mintage	F12	VF20	XF40	MS60	MS63
2008	—	PF63 45.00				

KM# 1217 25 NEW LIRA
15.55 g., 0.925 Silver 0.4595 oz. ASW, 38.6x28 mm. **Obv:** Text **Rev:** Zodiac - Leo **Shape:** Oval

Date	Mintage	F12	VF20	XF40	MS60	MS63
2008	—	PF63 45.00				

KM# 1218 25 NEW LIRA
15.55 g., 0.925 Silver 0.4595 oz. ASW, 38.6x28 mm. **Obv:** Text **Rev:** Zodiac - Virgo **Shape:** Oval

Date	Mintage	F12	VF20	XF40	MS60	MS63
2008	—	PF63 45.00				

KM# 1219 25 NEW LIRA
15.55 g., 0.925 Silver 0.4595 oz. ASW, 38.6x28 mm. **Obv:** Text **Rev:** Zodiac - Gemeni **Shape:** Oval

Date	Mintage	F12	VF20	XF40	MS60	MS63
2008	—	PF63 45.00				

KM# 1220 25 NEW LIRA
15.55 g., 0.925 Silver 0.4595 oz. ASW, 38.6x28 mm. **Obv:** Text **Rev:** Zodiac - Taurus **Shape:** Oval

Date	Mintage	F12	VF20	XF40	MS60	MS63
2008	—	PF63 45.00				

KM# 1221 25 NEW LIRA
15.55 g., 0.925 Silver 0.4595 oz. ASW, 38.6x28 mm. **Obv:** Text **Rev:** Zodiac sign **Shape:** Oval

Date	Mintage	F12	VF20	XF40	MS60	MS63
2008	—	PF63 45.00				

KM# 1192 30 NEW LIRA
31.47 g., 0.925 Silver 0.9299 oz. ASW, 38.6 mm. **Subject:** Galatasaray Spor **Obv:** 100 above team mascot **Rev:** GS monogram colored and selective gold plating

Date	Mintage	F12	VF20	XF40	MS60	MS63
2005	1,106	PF63 55.00				

KM# 1197 30 NEW LIRA
23.33 g., 0.925 Silver 0.6894 oz. ASW, 38.61 mm. **Subject:** Solar Eclipse **Obv:** Turkey map with route of the eclipse **Rev:** Sun, gilt

Date	Mintage	F12	VF20	XF40	MS60	MS63
2006	2,475	PF63 100				

KM# 1204 30 NEW LIRA
31.47 g., 0.925 Silver 0.9299 oz. ASW, 38.6 mm. **Subject:** Bank of Sarfanbolu **Obv:** Building **Rev:** Landscape

Date	Mintage	F12	VF20	XF40	MS60	MS63
2007	1,312	PF63 70.00				

KM# 1205 30 NEW LIRA
31.47 g., 0.925 Silver 0.9299 oz. ASW, 38.6 mm. **Obv:** Crescent and star at center of four objects **Rev:** Knotted fabric pattern

Date	Mintage	F12	VF20	XF40	MS60	MS63
2007	1,210	PF63 55.00				

KM# 1206 30 NEW LIRA
31.47 g., 0.925 Silver 0.9299 oz. ASW, 38.6 mm. **Obv:** Crescent and star within four objects **Rev:** Twirling Dirvishes

Date	Mintage	F12	VF20	XF40	MS60	MS63
2007	1,224	PF63 55.00				

KM# 1207 30 NEW LIRA
31.47 g., 0.925 Silver 0.9299 oz. ASW, 38.6 mm. **Obv:** Crescent and star within four designs **Rev:** Twirling Dirvish and town facades around

Date	Mintage	F12	VF20	XF40	MS60	MS63
2007	1,179	PF63 55.00				

KM# 1208 30 NEW LIRA
31.47 g., 0.925 Silver 0.9299 oz. ASW, 38.6 mm. **Obv:** Mosque **Rev:** Entranceway arch

Date	Mintage	F12	VF20	XF40	MS60	MS63
2007	1,222	PF63 70.00				

KM# 1222 30 NEW LIRA
10.00 g., 0.925 Silver 0.2955 oz. ASW, 22 mm. **Obv:** Seal within border **Rev:** Large seal rendering

Date	Mintage	F12	VF20	XF40	MS60	MS63
2008	—	PF63 30.00				

KM# 1210 35 NEW LIRA
23.23 g., 0.925 Silver 0.6864 oz. ASW, 38.6 mm. **Subject:** Antikabir, 70th Anniversary **Obv:** Value within wreath **Rev:** Antikabir building

Date	Mintage	F12	VF20	XF40	MS60	MS63
2008	3,000	PF63 40.00				

KM# 1232 35 NEW LIRA
23.33 g., 0.925 Silver 0.6894 oz. ASW, 38.6 mm. **Obv:** Value within wreath **Rev:** Bust at left

Date	Mintage	F12	VF20	XF40	MS60	MS63
2008	—	PF63 40.00				

KM# 1233 35 NEW LIRA
23.33 g., 0.925 Silver 0.6894 oz. ASW, 38.6 mm. **Obv:** Classical design **Rev:** Mahmud of Kashgar at right

Date	Mintage	F12	VF20	XF40	MS60	MS63
2008	—	PF63 40.00				

KM# 1238 35 NEW LIRA
23.33 g., 0.925 Silver 0.6894 oz. ASW, 38.6 mm. **Obv:** Value within wreath **Rev:** Sultan on horseback

Date	Mintage	F12	VF20	XF40	MS60	MS63
2008	—	PF63 45.00				

KM# 1202 40 NEW LIRA
31.47 g., 0.925 Silver 0.9299 oz. ASW, 38.6 mm. **Subject:** Troy **Obv:** Linear design **Rev:** Stylized Trojan Horse

Date	Mintage	F12	VF20	XF40	MS60	MS63
2007	1,500	PF63 50.00				

KM# 1224 40 NEW LIRA
31.47 g., 0.999 Silver 1.0043 oz. ASW, 38.6 mm. **Obv:** Historic map **Rev:** Kyrgyzstan building

Date	Mintage	F12	VF20	XF40	MS60	MS63
2008 Antiqued	—	—	—	—	80.00	—

KM# 1225 40 NEW LIRA
31.47 g., 0.925 Silver 0.9299 oz. ASW, 38.6 mm. **Obv:** Village scene **Rev:** Large classical figure

Date	Mintage	F12	VF20	XF40	MS60	MS63
2008	—	PF63 80.00				

KM# 1227 40 NEW LIRA
31.47 g., 0.925 Silver 0.9299 oz. ASW, 38.6 mm. **Obv:** Building **Rev:** Seated figure

Date	Mintage	F12	VF20	XF40	MS60	MS63
2008	—	PF63 45.00				

KM# 1228 40 NEW LIRA
31.47 g., 0.925 Silver 0.9299 oz. ASW, 38.6 mm. **Obv:** Classical intricate design **Rev:** Mosque

Date	Mintage	F12	VF20	XF40	MS60	MS63
2008	—	PF63 45.00				

KM# 1229 40 NEW LIRA
31.47 g., 0.925 Silver 0.9299 oz. ASW, 38.6 mm. **Obv:** Head left above school building **Rev:** Monogram at center

Date	Mintage	F12	VF20	XF40	MS60	MS63
2008	—	PF63 45.00				

KM# 1230 40 NEW LIRA
31.47 g., 0.925 Silver 0.9299 oz. ASW, 38.6 mm. **Obv:** Large tower and acqueduct **Rev:** Classical scene

Date	Mintage	F12	VF20	XF40	MS60	MS63
2008	—	PF63 45.00				

KM# 1231 40 NEW LIRA
31.47 g., 0.925 Silver 0.9299 oz. ASW, 38.6 mm. **Obv:** Tortoise, seal and lighthouse in distance **Rev:** Lighthouse

Date	Mintage	F12	VF20	XF40	MS60	MS63
2008	—	PF63 45.00	PF65 55.00			

KM# 1234 40 NEW LIRA
23.33 g., 0.925 Silver 0.6894 oz. ASW, 38.6 mm. **Subject:** Vefs Sports Club, 100th Anniversary **Obv:** Club seal multicolor **Rev:** Large 100 and logo

Date	Mintage	F12	VF20	XF40	MS60	MS63
2008	—	PF63 45.00				

KM# 1235 40 NEW LIRA
31.47 g., 0.925 Silver 0.9299 oz. ASW, 38.6 mm. **Obv:** Ancient craft items **Rev:** Cave paintings

Date	Mintage	F12	VF20	XF40	MS60	MS63
2008	—	PF63 45.00				

KM# 1236 40 NEW LIRA
31.47 g., 0.925 Silver 0.9299 oz. ASW, 38.6 mm. **Obv:** Ancient map **Rev:** Uzbekistan mosque

Date	Mintage	F12	VF20	XF40	MS60	MS63
2008 Antiqued	—	—	—	—	40.00	45.00

KM# 1237 40 NEW LIRA
31.47 g., 0.925 Silver 0.9299 oz. ASW, 38.6 mm. **Obv:** Tower **Rev:** Tower

Date	Mintage	F12	VF20	XF40	MS60	MS63
2008	—	PF63 45.00				

KM# 1255 50 LIRA
36.08 g., 0.925 Silver 1.0661 oz. ASW, 38.6 mm. **Subject:** Sunlight **Obv:** Eastern Hemisphere logo **Rev:** Eastern Hemisphere in Sun

Date	Mintage	F12	VF20	XF40	MS60	MS63
2008	—	PF63 55.00	PF65 65.00			

KM# 1209 60 NEW LIRA
1.50 g., 0.916 Gold 0.0439 oz. AGW, 13.95 mm. **Obv:** Text **Rev:** Ancient pottery

Date	Mintage	F12	VF20	XF40	MS60	MS63
2007	1,925	PF63 85.00				

KM# 1223 100 NEW LIRA
7.22 g., 0.916 Gold 0.2111 oz. AGW, 22 mm. **Obv:** Seal within border **Rev:** Large seal

Date	Mintage	F12	VF20	XF40	MS60	MS63
2008	—	PF63 425				

KM# 1226 100 NEW LIRA
7.22 g., 0.916 Gold 0.2111 oz. AGW, 22 mm. **Obv:** Village scene **Rev:** Large classical figure

Date	Mintage	F12	VF20	XF40	MS60	MS63
2008	—	PF63 425				

REFORM DECIMAL COINAGE
2009

KM# 1239 KURUS
Copper-Nickel Plated Steel **Obv:** Head of Ataturk left **Rev:** Plant and value

Date	Mintage	F12	VF20	XF40	MS60	MS63
2009	—	—	—	—	0.30	0.50
2010	—	—	—	—	0.30	0.50
2011	—	—	—	—	0.30	0.50
2012	—	—	—	—	0.30	0.50
2013	—	—	—	—	0.30	0.50

KM# 1240 5 KURUS
Brass **Obv:** Head of Ataturk left **Rev:** Value and traditional embroidery pattern

Date	Mintage	F12	VF20	XF40	MS60	MS63
2009	—	—	—	—	0.30	0.50
2010	—	—	—	—	0.30	0.50
2011	—	—	—	—	0.30	0.50
2012	—	—	—	—	0.30	0.50
2013	—	—	—	—	0.30	0.50

KM# 1241 10 KURUS
Brass **Obv:** Head of Ataturk left **Rev:** Value

Date	Mintage	F12	VF20	XF40	MS60	MS63
2009	—	—	—	—	0.30	0.50
2010	—	—	—	—	0.30	0.50
2011	—	—	—	—	0.30	0.50
2012	—	—	—	—	0.30	0.50
2013	—	—	—	—	0.30	0.50

KM# 1242 25 KURUS
Copper-Nickel **Obv:** Head of Ataturk left **Rev:** Value

Date	Mintage	F12	VF20	XF40	MS60	MS63
2009	—	—	—	—	0.50	0.75
2010	—	—	—	—	0.50	0.75
2011	—	—	—	—	0.50	0.75
2012	—	—	—	—	0.50	0.75
2013	—	—	—	—	0.50	0.75

KM# 1243 50 KURUS
Bi-Metallic **Obv:** Head of Atatürk left **Rev:** Value above suspension bridge **Edge:** Reeded

Date	Mintage	F12	VF20	XF40	MS60	MS63
2009	—	—	—	—	0.75	1.00
2010	—	—	—	—	0.75	1.00
2011	—	—	—	—	0.75	1.00
2012	—	—	—	—	0.75	1.00
2013	—	—	—	—	0.75	1.00

KM# 1244 LIRA
Bi-Metallic **Obv:** Head of Atatürk left **Rev:** Value

Date	Mintage	F12	VF20	XF40	MS60	MS63
2009	—	—	—	—	3.00	5.00
2010	—	—	—	—	3.00	5.00
2011	—	—	—	—	3.00	5.00
2012	—	—	—	—	3.00	5.00
2013	—	—	—	—	3.00	5.00

KM# 1249 LIRA
6.40 g., Copper-Nickel, 23.5 mm. **Obv:** Lammergeier standing on rock **Rev:** Two eagles

Date	Mintage	F12	VF20	XF40	MS60	MS63
2009	120,000	—	—	—	4.50	6.00

KM# 1263 LIRA
8.30 g., Bi-Metallic, 26.15 mm. **Obv:** Value within wreath **Rev:** Elephant and calf

Date	Mintage	F12	VF20	XF40	MS60	MS63
2009	5,000	—	—	—	7.50	10.00

KM# 1264 LIRA
8.30 g., Bi-Metallic, 26.15 mm. **Obv:** Value within wreath **Rev:** Sea tortoise

Date	Mintage	F12	VF20	XF40	MS60	MS63
2009	5,000	—	—	—	7.50	10.00

KM# 1279 LIRA
Bi-Metallic, 26.15 mm. **Obv:** Value within wreath **Rev:** Cat's bust

Date	Mintage	F12	VF20	XF40	MS60	MS63
2010	—	—	—	—	7.50	10.00

KM# 1280 LIRA
Bi-Metallic, 26.15 mm. **Obv:** Value within wreath **Rev:** Dog standing facing right

Date	Mintage	F12	VF20	XF40	MS60	MS63
2010	—	—	—	—	7.50	10.00

KM# 1275 LIRA
8.30 g., Bi-Metallic, 26.15 mm. **Obv:** Value within wreath **Rev:** Lion advancing - Pathera leo persica

Date	Mintage	F12	VF20	XF40	MS60	MS63
2011	—	—	—	—	5.00	7.50

KM# 1276 LIRA
8.30 g., Bi-Metallic, 26.15 mm. **Obv:** Value within wreath **Rev:** Brown bear - Ursus arctos

Date	Mintage	F12	VF20	XF40	MS60	MS63
2011	4,000	PF63 15.00				
2011	11,000	—	—	—	5.00	7.50

KM# 1281 LIRA
8.30 g., Bi-Metallic, 26.15 mm. **Obv:** Value within wreath **Rev:** 10th International Turkish Language Olympics

Date	Mintage	F12	VF20	XF40	MS60	MS63
2012	—	—	—	—	5.00	7.50

KM# 1282 LIRA
8.30 g., Bi-Metallic, 26.15 mm. **Obv:** Value within wreath **Rev:** 150 Years of the Court

Date	Mintage	F12	VF20	XF40	MS60	MS63
2012	—	—	—	—	5.00	7.50

KM# 1283 LIRA
8.30 g., Bi-Metallic, 26.15 mm. **Obv:** Value within wreath **Rev:** Deer

Date	Mintage	F12	VF20	XF40	MS60	MS63
2012	—	—	—	—	5.00	7.50

KM# 1284 LIRA
8.30 g., Bi-Metallic, 26.15 mm. **Obv:** Value within wreath **Rev:** Leopard

Date	Mintage	F12	VF20	XF40	MS60	MS63
2012	—	—	—	—	5.00	7.50

KM# 1288 LIRA
8.30 g., Bi-Metallic, 26.15 mm. **Subject:** 10th International Turkish Language Olympics

Date	Mintage	F12	VF20	XF40	MS60	MS63
2012 UNC	Est. 1000000	—	—	—	5.00	7.50

KM# 1289 LIRA
8.20 g., Bi-Metallic, 26.15 mm. **Subject:** 150th Anniversary of the Court

Date	Mintage	F12	VF20	XF40	MS60	MS63
2012	Est. 1000000	—	—	—	5.00	7.50

KM# 1250 10 LIRA
23.33 g., Bronze, 38.6 mm. **Obv:** Scroll and inkwell **Rev:** Child's story **Edge:** Reeded

Date	Mintage	F12	VF20	XF40	MS60	MS63
2009 Antiqued	—	—	—	—	15.00	

KM# 1258 20 LIRA
27.50 g., Copper-Nickel, 38.6 mm. **Subject:** Year 1430 **Obv:** Inscription within rose wreath **Rev:** Interior of the Grand Mosque in Mecca

Date	Mintage	F12	VF20	XF40	MS60	MS63
2009 Antiqued	—	—	—	—	35.00	

KM# 1266 20 LIRA
23.33 g., Bronze, 38.61 mm. **Subject:** 25th Winter Sports Games - Hockey

Date	Mintage	F12	VF20	XF40	MS60	MS63
2011 Antique finish	3,000	—	—	—	—	20.00

KM# 1267 20 LIRA
23.33 g., Brass, 38.61 mm. **Subject:** 25th Winter Sports Games - Hockey

Date	Mintage	F12	VF20	XF40	MS60	MS63
2011 Antique patina	3,000	—	—	—	—	20.00

KM# 1269 20 LIRA
23.33 g., Bronze, 38.61 mm. **Subject:** 25th Winter Sports Games - Skiing

Date	Mintage	F12	VF20	XF40	MS60	MS63
2011 Antique patina	3,000	—	—	—	—	20.00

KM# 1270 20 LIRA
23.33 g., Brass, 38.61 mm. **Subject:** 25th Winter Sports Games - Skiing

Date	Mintage	F12	VF20	XF40	MS60	MS63
2011 Antique patina	3,000	—	—	—	—	20.00

KM# 1272 20 LIRA
23.33 g., Bronze, 38.61 mm. **Subject:** European Youth Games, Trabzon

Date	Mintage	F12	VF20	XF40	MS60	MS63
2011 Antique patina	2,000	—	—	—	—	20.00

KM# 1278 20 LIRA
15.55 g., 0.925 Silver 0.4595 oz. ASW, 28x38.61 mm. **Subject:** Dolmabahce Clock Tower **Shape:** Vertical oval

Date	Mintage	F12	VF20	XF40	MS60	MS63
2011	—	PF63 50.00				

KM# 1286 20 LIRA
23.33 g., Bronze, 38.61 mm. **Subject:** 150th Anniversary of the Court

Date	Mintage	F12	VF20	XF40	MS60	MS63
2012	Est. 3000	—	—	—	—	20.00

KM# 1291 20 LIRA
36.08 g., 0.925 Silver 1.0661 oz. ASW, 38.6 mm. **Subject:** Mediterranean Games at Mersin

Date	Mintage	F12	VF20	XF40	MS60	MS63
2013	—	PF63 40.00				

KM# 1247 50 LIRA
36.00 g., 0.925 Silver 1.0637 oz. ASW, 38.6 mm. **Obv:** Value within wreath **Rev:** Samsun 90th Anniversary

Date	Mintage	F12	VF20	XF40	MS60	MS63
2009	3,000	PF63 55.00				

KM# 1251 50 LIRA
36.08 g., 0.925 Silver 1.0661 oz. ASW, 38.6 mm. **Obv:** Scroll and inkwell **Rev:** Children's story character

Date	Mintage	F12	VF20	XF40	MS60	MS63
2009	—	PF63 40.00				

KM# 1252 50 LIRA
36.08 g., 0.925 Silver 1.0661 oz. ASW, 38.6 mm. **Subject:** Frederic Chopin, 200th Anniversary **Obv:** Piano and map of Europe **Rev:** Chopin's bust at left, piano at right, score in background

Date	Mintage	F12	VF20	XF40	MS60	MS63
2009	—	PF63 70.00				

KM# 1253 50 LIRA
36.08 g., 0.925 Silver 1.0661 oz. ASW, 38.6 mm. **Subject:** IMF Meeting, Istanbul **Obv:** Istanbul Skyline **Rev:** World Bank Group logo, multicolor

Date	Mintage	F12	VF20	XF40	MS60	MS63
2009	—	PF63 55.00	PF65 65.00			

KM# 1254 50 LIRA
36.08 g., 0.925 Silver 1.0661 oz. ASW, 38.6 mm. **Subject:** Water, source of life **Obv:** Eastern Hemisphere logo **Rev:** Clock hands, small amount of water, cracked and dried earth in rest of area

Date	Mintage	F12	VF20	XF40	MS60	MS63
2009	—	PF63 55.00				

KM# 1256 50 LIRA
36.08 g., 0.925 Silver 1.0661 oz. ASW, 38.6 mm. **Obv:** Eastern Hemisphere logo **Rev:** Small seedling within light blue colored water droplet, dried earth background

Date	Mintage	F12	VF20	XF40	MS60	MS63
2009 Antiqued	—	—	—	—	55.00	

KM# 1257 50 LIRA
36.08 g., 0.925 Silver 1.0661 oz. ASW, 38.6 mm. **Obv:** Eastern Hemisphere logo **Rev:** Female face with hair forming waves and vine

Date	Mintage	F12	VF20	XF40	MS60	MS63
2009	—	PF63 55.00				

KM# 1259 50 LIRA
36.00 g., 0.925 Silver 1.0637 oz. ASW, 38.6 mm. **Subject:** Year 1430 **Obv:** Inscription within rose wreath **Rev:** Interior courtyard of Grand Mosque in Mecca

Date	Mintage	F12	VF20	XF40	MS60	MS63
2009	2,500	PF63 70.00	PF65 80.00			

KM# 1261 50 LIRA
36.00 g., 0.925 Silver 1.0637 oz. ASW, 38.6 mm. **Subject:** 150th Anniversary **Obv:** Multicolor shield and text **Rev:** Building facade

Date	Mintage	F12	VF20	XF40	MS60	MS63
2009	5,000	PF63 45.00	PF65 55.00			

KM# 1262 50 LIRA
36.00 g., 0.925 Silver 1.0637 oz. ASW, 38.6 mm. **Subject:** Chalabi clerks **Obv:** Symbol **Rev:** Classical figure seated

Date	Mintage	F12	VF20	XF40	MS60	MS63
2009	3,000	PF63 55.00				

KM# 1294 50 LIRA
31.43 g., 0.925 Silver 0.9287 oz. ASW, 38.61 mm. **Rev:** Ahirkapl Lighthouse

Date	Mintage	F12	VF20	XF40	MS60	MS63
2010	—	PF63 70.00				

KM# 1295 50 LIRA
23.23 g., 0.925 Silver 0.6864 oz. ASW, 38.61 mm. **Subject:** Osman Hamdi, 100th Anniversary, Istanbul Archaeological Museum

Date	Mintage	F12	VF20	XF40	MS60	MS63
2010	—	PF63 60.00				

KM# 1296 50 LIRA
Silver ASW, 38.61 mm. **Subject:** FIBA Championship

Date	Mintage	F12	VF20	XF40	MS60	MS63
2010	—	PF63 60.00				

KM# 1297 50 LIRA
36.00 g., 0.925 Silver 1.0637 oz. ASW, 38.61 mm. **Subject:** Republic, 90th Anniversary **Obv:** Arms in color **Rev:** Large 90

Date	Mintage	F12	VF20	XF40	MS60	MS63
2010	—	PF63 55.00				

KM# 1298 50 LIRA
31.47 g., 0.925 Silver 0.9299 oz. ASW, 38.61 mm. **Subject:** Amasya Evleri **Rev:** Houses of Amasya

Date	Mintage	F12	VF20	XF40	MS60	MS63
2010	—	PF63 55.00				

KM# 1268 50 LIRA
31.47 g., Silver, 38.61 mm. **Subject:** 25th Winter Sports Games - Hockey

Date	Mintage	F12	VF20	XF40	MS60	MS63
2011	3,000	PF63 50.00				

KM# 1271 50 LIRA
31.47 g., 0.925 Silver 0.9299 oz. ASW, 38.61 mm. **Subject:** 25th Winter Sports Games - Skiing

Date	Mintage	F12	VF20	XF40	MS60	MS63
2011	3,000	PF63 50.00				

KM# 1273 50 LIRA
31.47 g., 0.925 Silver 0.9299 oz. ASW, 38.61 mm. **Subject:** European Youth Games, Trabzon

Date	Mintage	F12	VF20	XF40	MS60	MS63
2011	2,000	PF63 50.00				

KM# 1274 50 LIRA
31.47 g., 0.925 Silver 0.9299 oz. ASW, 38.61 mm. **Subject:** Hejaz Railway **Obv:** Railway route map from Turkey to Saudi Arabia **Rev:** Railway Station at Medina **Edge:** Reeded

Date	Mintage	F12	VF20	XF40	MS60	MS63
2011	3,000	PF63 75.00	PF65 85.00			

KM# 1277 50 LIRA
31.10 g., 0.925 Silver 0.9189 oz. ASW, 38.61 mm. **Subject:** Pergamon **Rev:** Ruins **Edge:** Reeded

Date	Mintage	F12	VF20	XF40	MS60	MS63
2012	2,000	PF63 75.00	PF65 85.00			

KM# 1285 50 LIRA
31.47 g., Silver, 38.61 mm. **Subject:** 150 Years of the Court

Date	Mintage	F12	VF20	XF40	MS60	MS63
2012	—	PF63 60.00				

KM# 1287 50 LIRA
31.10 g., 0.925 Silver 0.9189 oz. ASW, 38.61 mm. **Subject:** 10th Anniversary of the Olympics

Date	Mintage	F12	VF20	XF40	MS60	MS63
2012	Est. 2000	PF63 75.00				

KM# 1290 50 LIRA
31.10 g., 0.925 Silver 0.9189 oz. ASW, 38.61 mm. **Obv:** Legend and value **Rev:** Sile Lighthouse

Date	Mintage	F12	VF20	XF40	MS60	MS63
2012	—	PF63 60.00				

KM# 1292 50 LIRA
31.47 g., 0.925 Silver 0.9299 oz. ASW, 38.6 mm. **Subject:** Mediterranean Games at Mersin

Date	Mintage	F12	VF20	XF40	MS60	MS63
2013	—	PF63 55.00				

KM# 1293 50 LIRA
31.47 g., 0.925 Silver 0.9299 oz. ASW, 38.6 mm. **Subject:** Turkey statehood, 90th Anniversary

Date	Mintage	F12	VF20	XF40	MS60	MS63
2013	—				**PF63** 65.00	

KM# 1245 50 NEW LIRA
36.08 g., 0.925 Silver 1.0661 oz. ASW, 38.6 mm. **Obv:** US and Turkish flags **Rev:** Barack Obama portrait facing

Date	Mintage	F12	VF20	XF40	MS60	MS63
2009	3,000	**PF63** 55.00	**PF65** 60.00			

KM# 1248 100 LIRA
1.50 g., 0.916 Gold 0.0439 oz. AGW, 13.95 mm. **Obv:** Classical orniament **Rev:** Hittite artifacts

Date	Mintage	F12	VF20	XF40	MS60	MS63
2009	—	**PF63** 95.00				

KM# 1246 200 LIRA
36.08 g., 0.916 Gold 1.0557 oz. AGW, 38.6 mm. **Obv:** US and Turkish flags **Rev:** Barack Obama portrait facing

Date	Mintage	F12	VF20	XF40	MS60	MS63
2009	1,000	**PF65** 1,850				

KM# 1260 200 LIRA
36.00 g., 0.916 Gold 1.0534 oz. AGW, 38.6 mm. **Obv:** Inscription within rose wreath **Rev:** Central courtyard of the Grand Mosque in Mecca

Date	Mintage	F12	VF20	XF40	MS60	MS63
2009	1,500	**PF65** 1,850				

GOLD BULLION COINAGE

Since 1943, the Turkish government has issued regular and deluxe gold coins in five denominations corresponding to the old traditional 25, 50, 100, 250, and 500 Kurus of the Ottoman period. The regular coins are all dated 1923, plus the year of the republic (e.g. 1923/40 = 1963), de Luxe coins bear actual AD dates. For a few years, 1944-1950, the bust of Ismet Inonu replaced that of Kemal Ataturk.

KM# 851 25 KURUSH
1.80 g., 0.917 Gold 0.0528 oz. AGW **Obv:** Head of Atatürk left **Rev:** Legend and date within wreath

Date	Mintage	F12	VF20	XF40	MS60	MS63
1923/78 (2001)	—	—	—	BV	105	120
1923/79 (2002)	—	—	—	BV	105	120
1923/70 (2003)	—	—	—	BV	105	120
1923/71 (2004)	—	—	—	BV	105	120
1923/72 (2005)	—	—	—	BV	105	120
1923/73 (2006)	—	—	—	BV	105	120
1923/74 (2007)	—	—	—	BV	105	120
1923/75 (2008)	—	—	—	BV	105	120
1923/76 (2009)	—	—	—	BV	105	120
1923/77 (2010)	—	—	—	BV	105	120

KM# 870 25 KURUSH
1.75 g., 0.917 Gold 0.0514 oz. AGW **Series:** Monnaie de Luxe **Obv:** Head of Atatürk left **Rev:** Country name and date in ornate monogram within circle of stars, floral border surrounds

Date	Mintage	F12	VF20	XF40	MS60	MS63
2001	—	—	—	BV	105	120
2002	—	—	—	BV	105	120
2003	—	—	—	BV	105	120
2004	—	—	—	BV	105	120
2005	—	—	—	BV	105	120
2006	—	—	—	BV	105	120
2007	—	—	—	BV	105	120
2008	—	—	—	BV	105	120
2009	—	—	—	BV	105	120
2010	—	—	—	BV	105	120

KM# 853 50 KURUSH
3.61 g., 0.917 Gold 0.1057 oz. AGW **Obv:** Head of Atatürk left **Rev:** Legend and date within wreath

Date	Mintage	F12	VF20	XF40	MS60	MS63
1923/78 (2001)	—	—	—	BV	200	225
1923/79 (2002)	—	—	—	BV	200	225
1923/80 (2003)	—	—	—	BV	200	225
1923/81 (2004)	—	—	—	BV	200	225
1923/82 (2005)	—	—	—	BV	200	225
1923/83 (2006)	—	—	—	BV	200	225
1923/84 (2007)	—	—	—	BV	200	225
1923/85 (2008)	—	—	—	BV	200	225
1923/86 (2009)	—	—	—	BV	200	225
1923/87 (2010)	—	—	—	BV	200	225

KM# 871 50 KURUSH
3.51 g., 0.917 Gold 0.1028 oz. AGW **Series:** Monnaie de Luxe **Obv:** Head of Kemal Atatürk left within circle of stars, wreath surrounds **Rev:** Country name and date in ornate monogram within circle of stars, floral border surrounds

Date	Mintage	F12	VF20	XF40	MS60	MS63
2001	—	—	—	BV	200	225
2002	—	—	—	BV	200	225
2003	—	—	—	BV	200	225
2004	—	—	—	BV	200	225
2005	—	—	—	BV	200	225
2006	—	—	—	BV	200	225
2007	—	—	—	BV	200	225
2008	—	—	—	BV	200	225
2009	—	—	—	BV	200	225
2010	—	—	—	BV	200	225

KM# 872 100 KURUSH
7.02 g., 0.917 Gold 0.2055 oz. AGW **Series:** Monnaie de Luxe **Obv:** Head of Atatürk left within circle of stars, wreath surrounds **Rev:** Country name and date in ornate monogram within circle of stars, floral border surrounds

Date	Mintage	F12	VF20	XF40	MS60	MS63
2001	—	—	—	—	BV	400
2002	—	—	—	—	BV	400
2003	—	—	—	—	BV	400
2004	—	—	—	—	BV	400
2005	—	—	—	—	BV	400
2006	—	—	—	—	BV	400
2007	—	—	—	—	BV	400
2008	—	—	—	—	BV	400
2009	—	—	—	—	BV	400
2010	—	—	—	—	BV	400

KM# 855 100 KURUSH
7.22 g., 0.917 Gold 0.2114 oz. AGW **Obv:** Head of Atatürk left **Rev:** Legend and date within wreath

Date	Mintage	F12	VF20	XF40	MS60	MS63
1923/78 (2001)	—	—	—	BV	400	425
1923/79 (2002)	—	—	—	BV	400	425
1923/80 (2003)	—	—	—	BV	400	425
1923/81 (2004)	—	—	—	BV	400	425
1923/82 (2005)	—	—	—	BV	400	425
1923/83 (2006)	—	—	—	BV	400	425
1923/84 (2007)	—	—	—	BV	400	425
1923/85 (2008)	—	—	—	BV	400	425
1923/86 (2009)	—	—	—	BV	400	425
1923/87 (2010)	—	—	—	BV	400	425

KM# 873 250 KURUSH
17.54 g., 0.917 Gold 0.5138 oz. AGW **Series:** Monnaie de Luxe **Obv:** Head of Atatürk left within circle of stars, wreath surrounds **Rev:** Country name and date in ornate monogram within circle of stars, floral border surrounds

Date	Mintage	F12	VF20	XF40	MS60	MS63
2001	—	—	—	BV	1,000	1,050
2002	—	—	—	BV	1,000	1,050
2003	—	—	—	BV	1,000	1,050
2004	—	—	—	BV	1,000	1,050
2005	—	—	—	BV	1,000	1,050
2006	—	—	—	BV	1,000	1,050
2007	—	—	—	BV	1,000	1,050
2008	—	—	—	BV	1,000	1,050
2009	—	—	—	BV	1,000	1,050
2010	—	—	—	BV	1,000	1,050

KM# 857 250 KURUSH
18.04 g., 0.917 Gold 0.5284 oz. AGW **Obv:** Head of Atatürk left **Rev:** Legend and date within wreath

Date	Mintage	F12	VF20	XF40	MS60	MS63
1923/78 (2001)	—	—	—	BV	1,025	1,075
1923/79 (2002)	—	—	—	BV	1,025	1,075
1923/80 (2003)	—	—	—	BV	1,025	1,075
1923/81 (2004)	—	—	—	BV	1,025	1,075
1923/82 (2005)	—	—	—	BV	1,025	1,075
1923/83 (2006)	—	—	—	BV	1,025	1,075
1923/84 (2007)	—	—	—	BV	1,025	1,075
1923/85 (2008)	—	—	—	BV	1,025	1,075
1923/86 (2009)	—	—	—	BV	1,025	1,075
1923/87 (2010)	—	—	—	BV	1,025	1,075

KM# 859 500 KURUSH
36.08 g., 0.917 Gold 1.0569 oz. AGW **Obv:** Head of Atatürk left **Rev:** Legend and date within wreath

Date	Mintage	F12	VF20	XF40	MS60	MS63
1923/78 (2001)	—	—	—	BV	1,950	2,000
1923/79 (2002)	—	—	—	BV	1,950	2,000
1923/80 (2003)	—	—	—	BV	1,950	2,000
1923/81 (2004)	—	—	—	BV	1,950	2,000
1923/82 (2005)	—	—	—	BV	1,950	2,000
1923/83 (2006)	—	—	—	BV	1,950	2,000
1923/84 (2007)	—	—	—	BV	1,950	2,000
1923/85 (2008)	—	—	—	BV	1,950	2,000
1923/86 (2009)	—	—	—	BV	1,950	2,000
1923/87 (2010)	—	—	—	BV	1,950	2,000

KM# 874 500 KURUSH
35.08 g., 0.917 Gold 1.0276 oz. AGW **Series:** Monnaie de Luxe **Obv:** Head of Atatürk left within circle of stars, wreath surrounds **Rev:** Country name and date in ornate monogram within circle of stars, floral border surrounds

Date	Mintage	F12	VF20	XF40	MS60	MS63
2001	—	—	—	BV	1,950	2,000
2002	—	—	—	BV	1,950	2,000
2003	—	—	—	BV	1,950	2,000
2004	—	—	—	BV	1,950	2,000
2005	—	—	—	BV	1,950	2,000
2006	—	—	—	BV	1,950	2,000
2007	—	—	—	BV	1,950	2,000
2008	—	—	—	BV	1,950	2,000
2009	—	—	—	BV	1,950	2,000
2010	—	—	—	BV	1,950	2,000

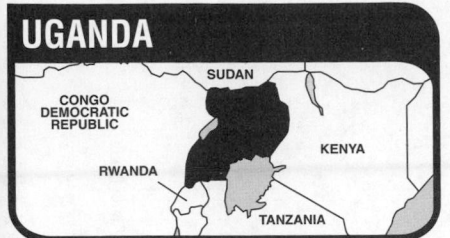

UGANDA

The Republic of Uganda, a former British protectorate located astride the equator in east-central Africa, has an area of 91,134 sq. mi. (236,040 sq. km.) and a population of *17 million. Capital: Kampala. Agriculture, including livestock, is the basis of the economy; there is some mining of copper, tin, gold and lead. Coffee, cotton, copper and tea are exported.

Uganda is a member of the Commonwealth of Nations. The president is Chief of State and Head of Government.

For earlier coinage refer to East Africa.

MONETARY SYSTEM
100 Cents = 1 Shilling

REPUBLIC
STANDARD COINAGE

KM# 66 50 SHILLINGS
4.00 g., Nickel Plated Steel Obv: National arms Rev: Antelope head facing

Date	Mintage	F12	VF20	XF40	MS60	MS63
2003	—	—	—	—	1.00	1.25
2007	—	—	—	—	1.00	1.25

KM# 67 100 SHILLINGS
7.00 g., Copper-Nickel, 26.9 mm. Obv: National arms Rev: African bull Edge: Reeded

Date	Mintage	F12	VF20	XF40	MS60	MS63
2003	—	—	—	—	1.50	1.75
2007	—	—	—	—	1.50	1.75
2008	—	—	—	—	1.50	1.75

KM# 129 100 SHILLINGS
3.54 g., Stainless Steel, 23.98 mm. Series: Zodiac Obv: National arms Rev: Monkey with elf-like ears Edge: Plain

Date	Mintage	F12	VF20	XF40	MS60	MS63
2004	—	—	—	—	1.50	2.50

KM# 130 100 SHILLINGS
Steel, 23 mm. Rev: Type I of five different monkeys

Date	Mintage	F12	VF20	XF40	MS60	MS63
2004	—	—	—	—	1.75	2.75

KM# 131 100 SHILLINGS
Steel, 23 mm. Rev: Type II of five different monkeys

Date	Mintage	F12	VF20	XF40	MS60	MS63
2004	—	—	—	—	1.75	2.75

KM# 132 100 SHILLINGS
Steel, 23 mm. Rev: Type III of five different monkeys

Date	Mintage	F12	VF20	XF40	MS60	MS63
2004	—	—	—	—	1.75	2.75

KM# 133 100 SHILLINGS
Steel, 23 mm. Rev: Type IV of five different monkys

Date	Mintage	F12	VF20	XF40	MS60	MS63
2004	—	—	—	—	1.50	2.75

KM# 134 100 SHILLINGS
Steel, 23 mm. Rev: Type V of five different monkeys

Date	Mintage	F12	VF20	XF40	MS60	MS63
2004	—	—	—	—	1.75	2.75

KM# 135 100 SHILLINGS
3.54 g., Steel, 23.98 mm. Series: Zodiac Obv: National arms Rev: Ox Edge: Plain

Date	Mintage	F12	VF20	XF40	MS60	MS63
2004	—	—	—	—	1.50	2.50

KM# 136 100 SHILLINGS
3.54 g., Steel, 23.98 mm. Series: Zodiac Obv: National arms Rev: Goat Edge: Plain

Date	Mintage	F12	VF20	XF40	MS60	MS63
2004	—	—	—	—	1.50	2.50

KM# 137 100 SHILLINGS
3.54 g., Steel, 23.98 mm. Series: Zodiac Obv: National arms Rev: Horse Edge: Plain

Date	Mintage	F12	VF20	XF40	MS60	MS63
2004	—	—	—	—	1.50	2.50

KM# 138 100 SHILLINGS
3.54 g., Steel, 23.98 mm. Series: Zodiac Obv: National arms Rev: Dragon Edge: Plain

Date	Mintage	F12	VF20	XF40	MS60	MS63
2004	—	—	—	—	1.50	2.50

KM# 139 100 SHILLINGS
3.54 g., Steel, 23.98 mm. Series: Zodiac Obv: National arms Rev: Dog Edge: Plain

Date	Mintage	F12	VF20	XF40	MS60	MS63
2004	—	—	—	—	1.50	2.50

KM# 140 100 SHILLINGS
3.54 g., Steel, 23.98 mm. Series: Zodiac Obv: National arms Rev: Tiger Edge: Plain

Date	Mintage	F12	VF20	XF40	MS60	MS63
2004	—	—	—	—	1.50	2.50

KM# 141 100 SHILLINGS
3.54 g., Steel, 23.98 mm. Series: Zodiac Obv: National arms Rev: Snake Edge: Plain

Date	Mintage	F12	VF20	XF40	MS60	MS63
2004	—	—	—	—	1.50	2.50

KM# 142 100 SHILLINGS
3.54 g., Steel, 23.98 mm. Series: Zodiac Obv: National arms Rev: Rooster Edge: Plain

Date	Mintage	F12	VF20	XF40	MS60	MS63
2004	—	—	—	—	1.50	2.50

KM# 143 100 SHILLINGS
3.54 g., Steel, 23.98 mm. Series: Zodiac Obv: National arms Rev: Rabbit Edge: Plain

Date	Mintage	F12	VF20	XF40	MS60	MS63
2004	—	—	—	—	1.50	2.50

KM# 144 100 SHILLINGS
3.54 g., Steel, 23.98 mm. Series: Zodiac Obv: National arms Rev: Rat Edge: Plain

Date	Mintage	F12	VF20	XF40	MS60	MS63
2004	—	—	—	—	1.50	2.50

KM# 145 100 SHILLINGS
3.54 g., Steel, 23.98 mm. Series: Zodiac Obv: National arms Rev: Pig Edge: Plain

Date	Mintage	F12	VF20	XF40	MS60	MS63
2004	—	—	—	—	1.50	2.50

KM# 188 100 SHILLINGS
3.53 g., Nickel Plated Steel, 24 mm. Series: Zodiac Obv: National arms Obv. Legend: BANK OF UGANDA Rev: Head of a rat Rev. Legend: BANK OF UGANDA Edge: Plain

Date	Mintage	F12	VF20	XF40	MS60	MS63
2004	—	—	—	—	1.75	2.75

KM# 189 100 SHILLINGS
3.53 g., Nickel Plated Steel, 24 mm. Series: Zodiac Obv: National arms Obv. Legend: BANK OF UGANDA Rev: Head of an ox Rev. Legend: BANK OF UGANDA Edge: Plain

Date	Mintage	F12	VF20	XF40	MS60	MS63
2004	—	—	—	—	1.75	2.75

KM# 190 100 SHILLINGS
3.53 g., Nickel Plated Steel, 24 mm. Series: Zodiac Obv: National arms Obv. Legend: BANK OF UGANDA Rev: Head of a tiger Rev. Legend: BANK OF UGANDA Edge: Plain

Date	Mintage	F12	VF20	XF40	MS60	MS63
2004	—	—	—	—	1.75	2.75

KM# 191 100 SHILLINGS
3.53 g., Nickel Plated Steel, 24 mm. Series: Zodiac Obv: National arms Obv. Legend: BANK OF UGANDA Rev: Head of a rabbit Rev. Legend: BANK OF UGANDA Edge: Plain

Date	Mintage	F12	VF20	XF40	MS60	MS63
2004	—	—	—	—	1.75	2.75

KM# 192 100 SHILLINGS
3.53 g., Nickel Plated Steel, 24 mm. Series: Zodiac Obv: National arms Obv. Legend: BANK OF UGANDA Rev: Head of a dragon Rev. Legend: BANK OF UGANDA Edge: Plain

Date	Mintage	F12	VF20	XF40	MS60	MS63
2004	—	—	—	—	1.75	2.75

KM# 193 100 SHILLINGS
3.53 g., Nickel Plated Steel, 24 mm. Series: Zodiac Obv: National arms Obv. Legend: BANK OF UGANDA Rev: Head and hood of Cobra snake Rev. Legend: BANK OF UGANDA Edge: Plain

Date	Mintage	F12	VF20	XF40	MS60	MS63
2004	—	—	—	—	1.75	2.75

KM# 194 100 SHILLINGS
3.53 g., Nickel Plated Steel, 24 mm. Series: Zodiac Obv: National arms Obv. Legend: BANK OF UGANDA Rev: Head of a horse Rev. Legend: BANK OF UGANDA Edge: Plain

Date	Mintage	F12	VF20	XF40	MS60	MS63
2004	—	—	—	—	1.75	2.75

KM# 195 100 SHILLINGS
3.53 g., Nickel Plated Steel, 24 mm. Series: Zodiac Obv: National arms Obv. Legend: BANK OF UGANDA Rev: Head of a goat Rev. Legend: BANK OF UGANDA Edge: Plain

Date	Mintage	F12	VF20	XF40	MS60	MS63
2004	—	—	—	—	1.75	2.75

KM# 196 100 SHILLINGS
3.53 g., Nickel Plated Steel, 24 mm. Series: Zodiac Obv: National arms Obv. Legend: BANK OF UGANDA Rev: Head of a monkey Rev. Legend: BANK OF UGANDA Edge: Plain

Date	Mintage	F12	VF20	XF40	MS60	MS63
2004	—	—	—	—	1.75	2.75

KM# 197 100 SHILLINGS
3.53 g., Nickel Plated Steel, 24 mm. Series: Zodiac Obv: National arms Obv. Legend: BANK OF UGANDA Rev: Forepart of a rooster Rev. Legend: BANK OF UGANDA Edge: Plain

Date	Mintage	F12	VF20	XF40	MS60	MS63
2004	—	—	—	—	1.75	2.75

KM# 198 100 SHILLINGS
3.53 g., Nickel Plated Steel, 24 mm. Series: Zodiac Obv: National arms Obv. Legend: BANK OF UGANDA Rev: Head of a dog Rev. Legend: BANK OF UGANDA Edge: Plain

Date	Mintage	F12	VF20	XF40	MS60	MS63
2004	—	—	—	—	1.75	2.75

KM# 199 100 SHILLINGS
3.53 g., Nickel Plated Steel, 24 mm. Series: Zodiac Obv: National arms Obv. Legend: BANK OF UGANDA Rev: Head of a pig Rev. Legend: BANK OF UGANDA Edge: Plain

Date	Mintage	F12	VF20	XF40	MS60	MS63
2004	—	—	—	—	1.75	2.75

KM# 200 100 SHILLINGS
Copper-Nickel Subject: Year of the Monkey Obv. Legend: BANK OF UGANDA Rev: Monkey swinging right

Date	Mintage	F12	VF20	XF40	MS60	MS63
2004	—	—	—	—	2.00	3.00

KM# 201 100 SHILLINGS
Copper-Nickel Subject: Year of the Monkey Obv. Legend: BANK OF UGANDA

Date	Mintage	F12	VF20	XF40	MS60	MS63
2004	—	—	—	—	2.00	3.00

KM# 202 100 SHILLINGS
Copper-Nickel Subject: Year of the Monkey Obv. Legend: BANK OF UGANDA Rev: Diana Monkey right on all fours

Date	Mintage	F12	VF20	XF40	MS60	MS63
2004	—	—	—	—	2.00	3.00

KM# 203 100 SHILLINGS
Copper-Nickel Subject: Year of the Monkey Obv. Legend: BANK OF UGANDA Rev: Monkey seated left

Date	Mintage	F12	VF20	XF40	MS60	MS63
2004	—	—	—	—	2.00	3.00

KM# 204 100 SHILLINGS
Copper-Nickel Subject: Year of the Monkey Obv. Legend: BANK OF UGANDA Rev: Monkeys seated right, looking left over his shoulder

Date	Mintage	F12	VF20	XF40	MS60	MS63
2004	—	—	—	—	2.00	3.00

KM# 67a 100 SHILLINGS
7.00 g., Nickel Plated Steel, 26.9 mm. Obv: National arms Rev: African bull Edge: Reeded

Date	Mintage	F12	VF20	XF40	MS60	MS63
2007	—	—	—	—	1.50	1.75
2008	—	—	—	—	1.50	1.75

KM# 68 200 SHILLINGS
8.05 g., Copper-Nickel, 24.9 mm. Obv: National arms Rev: Cichlid fish above value and date Edge: Plain

Date	Mintage	F12	VF20	XF40	MS60	MS63
2003	—	—	—	—	2.00	3.00

Date	Mintage	F12	VF20	XF40	MS60	MS63
2008	—	—	—	—	2.00	3.00

KM# 68a 200 SHILLINGS
8.05 g., Nickel Plated Steel, 24.9 mm. **Obv:** National arms **Rev:** Cichlid fish above value and date

Date	Mintage	F12	VF20	XF40	MS60	MS63
2007	—	—	—	—	2.00	3.00
2008	—	—	—	—	2.00	3.00

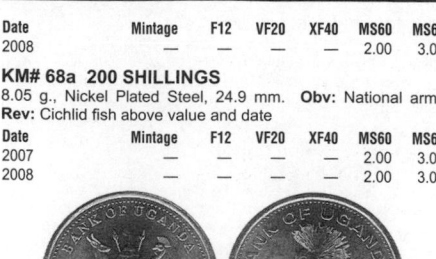

KM# 69 500 SHILLINGS
9.00 g., Nickel-Brass, 23.5 mm. **Obv:** National arms **Rev:** East African crowned crane head left **Edge:** Reeded

Date	Mintage	F12	VF20	XF40	MS60	MS63
2003	—	—	—	—	3.50	4.50
2008	—	—	—	—	3.50	4.50

KM# 77 1000 SHILLINGS
19.84 g., Copper-Nickel, 38.6 mm. **Subject:** Colourful Big Five of Africa **Obv:** Arms with supporters **Rev:** Multicolor rhinocerous within stamp design in front of outlined African map **Edge:** Reeded

Date	Mintage	F12	VF20	XF40	MS60	MS63
2001	—	PF63 22.50				

KM# 78 1000 SHILLINGS
19.84 g., Copper-Nickel, 38.6 mm. **Subject:** Colourful Big Five of Africa **Obv:** Arms with supporters **Rev:** Multicolor lion within stamp design in front of outlined African map **Edge:** Reeded

Date	Mintage	F12	VF20	XF40	MS60	MS63
2001	—	PF63 22.50				

KM# 79 1000 SHILLINGS
19.84 g., Copper-Nickel, 38.6 mm. **Subject:** Coulourful Big Five of Africa **Obv:** Arms with supporters **Rev:** Multicolor water buffalo within stamp design in front of outlined African map **Edge:** Reeded

Date	Mintage	F12	VF20	XF40	MS60	MS63
2001	—	PF63 22.50				

KM# 80 1000 SHILLINGS
19.84 g., Copper-Nickel, 38.6 mm. **Subject:** Colourful Big Five of Africa **Obv:** Arms with supporters **Rev:** Multicolor leopard within stamp design in front of outlined map **Edge:** Reeded

Date	Mintage	F12	VF20	XF40	MS60	MS63
2001	—	PF63 22.50				

KM# 81 1000 SHILLINGS
19.84 g., Copper-Nickel, 38.6 mm. **Subject:** Colourful Big Five of Africa **Obv:** Arms with supporters **Rev:** Multicolor elephant within stamp design in front of outlined map **Edge:** Reeded

Date	Mintage	F12	VF20	XF40	MS60	MS63
2001	—	PF63 22.50				

KM# 173 1000 SHILLINGS
Silver **Subject:** XVII World Football Championship Games - Korea and Japan **Obv. Legend:** BANK OF UGANDA **Rev:** Football - gilt

Date	Mintage	F12	VF20	XF40	MS60	MS63
2001	—	PF63 28.00	PF65 32.00			

KM# 82 1000 SHILLINGS
24.83 g., 0.999 Silver 0.7924 oz. ASW, 38.6 mm. **Subject:** World of Football **Obv:** Arms with supporters **Rev:** Soccer ball globe **Edge:** Reeded

Date	Mintage	F12	VF20	XF40	MS60	MS63
2002	—	PF63 35.00	PF65 40.00			

KM# 83 1000 SHILLINGS
24.83 g., 0.999 Silver 0.7924 oz. ASW, 38.6 mm. **Subject:** World of Football **Obv:** Arms with supporters **Rev:** Soccer ball in net **Edge:** Reeded

Date	Mintage	F12	VF20	XF40	MS60	MS63
2002	—	PF63 32.50				

KM# 84 1000 SHILLINGS
24.83 g., 0.999 Silver 0.7924 oz. ASW, 38.6 mm. **Subject:** World of Football **Obv:** Arms with supporters **Rev:** Goalie catching ball, red kicker insert at right **Edge:** Reeded

Date	Mintage	F12	VF20	XF40	MS60	MS63
2002	—	PF63 32.50				

KM# 85 1000 SHILLINGS
24.83 g., 0.999 Silver 0.7924 oz. ASW, 38.6 mm. **Subject:** World of Football **Obv:** Arms with supporters **Rev:** Two players going after the ball, red runner insert at left **Edge:** Reeded

Date	Mintage	F12	VF20	XF40	MS60	MS63
2002	—	PF63 32.50				

KM# 86 1000 SHILLINGS
24.83 g., 0.999 Silver 0.7924 oz. ASW, 38.6 mm. **Subject:** World of Football **Obv:** Arms with supporters **Rev:** Player kicking ball, blue kicker insert at right **Edge:** Reeded

Date	Mintage	F12	VF20	XF40	MS60	MS63
2002	—	PF63 32.50				

KM# 101 1000 SHILLINGS
29.44 g., Silver Plated Bronze, 38.5 mm. **Series:** Gorillas of Africa **Obv:** National arms **Rev:** Seated gorilla **Edge:** Reeded

Date	Mintage	F12	VF20	XF40	MS60	MS63
2002	—	PF63 12.50				
2003	—	PF63 12.00				

KM# 102 1000 SHILLINGS
29.44 g., Silver Plated Bronze, 38.5 mm. **Series:** Gorillas of Africa **Obv:** National arms **Rev:** Gorilla eating **Edge:** Reeded

Date	Mintage	F12	VF20	XF40	MS60	MS63
2002	—	PF63 12.50				
2003	—	PF63 10.00				

KM# 103 1000 SHILLINGS
29.44 g., Silver Plated Bronze, 38.5 mm. **Series:** Gorillas of Africa **Obv:** National arms **Rev:** Gorilla on all fours **Edge:** Reeded

Date	Mintage	F12	VF20	XF40	MS60	MS63
2002	—	PF63 12.50				
2003	—	PF63 10.00				

KM# 104 1000 SHILLINGS
29.44 g., Silver Plated Bronze, 38.5 mm. **Series:** Gorillas of Africa **Obv:** National arms **Rev:** Gorilla female with infant **Edge:** Reeded

Date	Mintage	F12	VF20	XF40	MS60	MS63
2002	—	PF63 12.50				
2003	—	PF63 10.00				

KM# 106 1000 SHILLINGS
29.16 g., Silver Plated Bronze, 38.6 mm. **Subject:** Marine Life **Obv:** Arms with supporters **Rev:** Multicolor sea horses **Edge:** Reeded

Date	Mintage	F12	VF20	XF40	MS60	MS63
2002	—	PF63 22.00				

KM# 107 1000 SHILLINGS
29.16 g., Silver Plated Bronze, 38.6 mm. **Subject:** Marine Life **Obv:** Arms with supporters **Rev:** Multicolor Hammerhead sharks **Edge:** Reeded

Date	Mintage	F12	VF20	XF40	MS60	MS63
2002	—	PF63 22.00				

KM# 108 1000 SHILLINGS
29.16 g., Silver Plated Bronze, 38.6 mm. **Subject:** Marine Life **Obv:** Arms with supporters **Rev:** Multicolor Stingray **Edge:** Reeded

Date	Mintage	F12	VF20	XF40	MS60	MS63
2002	—	PF63 22.00				

KM# 109 1000 SHILLINGS
29.16 g., Silver Plated Bronze, 38.6 mm. **Subject:** Marine Life **Obv:** Arms with supporters **Rev:** Multicolor Seal **Edge:** Reeded

Date	Mintage	F12	VF20	XF40	MS60	MS63
2002	—	PF63 22.00				

KM# 110 1000 SHILLINGS
29.16 g., Silver Plated Bronze, 38.6 mm. **Subject:** Marine Life **Obv:** Arms with supporters **Rev:** Multicolor sea turtle **Edge:** Reeded

Date	Mintage	F12	VF20	XF40	MS60	MS63
2002	—	PF63 22.00				

KM# 111 1000 SHILLINGS
29.16 g., Silver Plated Bronze, 38.6 mm. **Subject:** Marine Life **Obv:** Arms with supporters **Rev:** Multicolor dolphins **Edge:** Reeded

Date	Mintage	F12	VF20	XF40	MS60	MS63
2002	—	PF63 22.00				

KM# 112 1000 SHILLINGS
29.16 g., Silver Plated Bronze, 38.6 mm. **Subject:** Marine Life **Obv:** Arms with supporters **Rev:** Multicolor octopus **Edge:** Reeded

Date	Mintage	F12	VF20	XF40	MS60	MS63
2002	—	PF63 22.00				

KM# 113 1000 SHILLINGS
29.16 g., Silver Plated Bronze, 38.6 mm. **Subject:** Marine Life **Obv:** Arms with supporters **Rev:** Multicolor red fish **Edge:** Reeded

Date	Mintage	F12	VF20	XF40	MS60	MS63
2002	—	PF63 22.00				

KM# 114 1000 SHILLINGS
29.16 g., Silver Plated Bronze, 38.6 mm. **Subject:** Marine Life **Obv:** Arms with supporters **Rev:** Multicolor black fish with white dots **Edge:** Reeded

Date	Mintage	F12	VF20	XF40	MS60	MS63
2002	—	PF63 22.00				

KM# 115 1000 SHILLINGS
29.16 g., Silver Plated Bronze, 38.6 mm. **Subject:** Marine Life **Obv:** Arms with supporters **Rev:** Multicolor yellow and black striped fish **Edge:** Reeded

Date	Mintage	F12	VF20	XF40	MS60	MS63
2002	—	PF63 22.00				

KM# 105 1000 SHILLINGS
29.20 g., Silver Plated Bronze, 38.6 mm. **Subject:** Pope John Paul II **Obv:** Arms with supporters **Rev:** Pope saying mass, design of Zambian 1000 Kwacha KM-160 **Edge:** Reeded **Note:** Muling error

Date	Mintage	F12	VF20	XF40	MS60	MS63
2003	—		PF63 300	PF65 325		

KM# 240 1000 SHILLINGS
Silver **Obv:** Arms **Rev:** Pope John Paul II bust facing

Date	Mintage	F12	VF20	XF40	MS60	MS63
2003	—		PF63 75.00	PF65 85.00		

KM# 216 1000 SHILLINGS
Bronze **Subject:** Christmas **Obv. Legend:** BANK OF UGANDA **Rev:** Peace on Earth

Date	Mintage	F12	VF20	XF40	MS60	MS63
2004	500	—	—	—	—	50.00

KM# 278 1000 SHILLINGS
Bi-Metallic **Subject:** Independence, 50th Anniversary **Obv:** Coat of Arms **Rev:** Crested crane **Edge:** Reeded **Edge Lettering:** Incised in middle with: BOU 1000

Date	Mintage	F12	VF20	XF40	MS60	MS63
2012	—	—	—	—	4.50	6.00

KM# 75 2000 SHILLINGS
49.90 g., 0.999 Silver 1.5924 oz. ASW, 50 mm. **Subject:** Illusion: "Spirit of the Mountain **Obv:** Crowned head right divides date above arms with supporters **Rev:** Landscape and tree that looks like a male portrait **Edge:** Reeded

Date	Mintage	F12	VF20	XF40	MS60	MS63
2001	—		PF63 75.00	PF65 85.00		

KM# 121 2000 SHILLINGS
25.00 g., 0.925 Silver 0.7387 oz. ASW, 38.6 mm. **Subject:** Queen Elizabeth's 75th Birthday **Obv:** Arms with supporters

above crowned head right **Rev:** Queen accepting flowers from children **Edge:** Reeded

Date	Mintage	F12	VF20	XF40	MS60	MS63
2001	2,000	PF63 35.00	PF65 40.00			

KM# 100 2000 SHILLINGS
31.40 g., 0.999 Silver 1.002 oz. ASW, 38.8 mm. **Obv:** Crowned head right divides date above arms with supporters **Rev:** Bust of Henry M. Stanley facing **Edge:** Reeded

Date	Mintage	F12	VF20	XF40	MS60	MS63
2002	—	—	—	—	40.00	45.00

KM# 177 2000 SHILLINGS
15.55 g., 0.999 Silver 0.4962 oz. ASW **Series:** Famous Places in China **Subject:** Mount Huangshan - Anhwei **Obv:** Two dragons **Obv. Legend:** BANK OF UGANDA

Date	Mintage	F12	VF20	XF40	MS60	MS63
2003	3,000	PF63 35.00	PF65 40.00			

KM# 178 2000 SHILLINGS
15.55 g., 0.999 Silver 0.4962 oz. ASW **Series:** Famous Places in China **Subject:** Zhangjiajie - Hunan **Obv:** Two dragons **Obv. Legend:** BANK OF UGANDA

Date	Mintage	F12	VF20	XF40	MS60	MS63
2003	3,000	PF63 35.00	PF65 40.00			

KM# 179 2000 SHILLINGS
15.55 g., 0.999 Silver 0.4962 oz. ASW **Series:** Famous Places in China **Subject:** Stone Forest - Yunnan **Obv:** Two dragons **Obv. Legend:** BANK OF UGANDA

Date	Mintage	F12	VF20	XF40	MS60	MS63
2003	3,000	PF63 35.00	PF65 40.00			

KM# 180 2000 SHILLINGS
15.55 g., 0.999 Silver 0.4962 oz. ASW **Series:** Famous Places in China **Subject:** Potala Palace - Lhasa, Tibet **Obv:** Two dragons **Obv. Legend:** BANK OF UGANDA

Date	Mintage	F12	VF20	XF40	MS60	MS63
2003	3,000	PF63 35.00	PF65 40.00			

KM# 181 2000 SHILLINGS
15.55 g., 0.999 Silver 0.4962 oz. ASW **Series:** Famous Places inChina **Subject:** Yangtse River Gorges **Obv:** Two dragons **Obv. Legend:** BANK OF UGANDA

Date	Mintage	F12	VF20	XF40	MS60	MS63
2003	3,000	PF63 35.00	PF65 40.00			

KM# 182 2000 SHILLINGS
31.10 g., 0.999 Silver 0.9925 oz. ASW **Series:** Chinese symbolism **Subject:** Harmony **Obv. Legend:** BANK OF UGANDA **Rev:** Dragon and phoenix

Date	Mintage	F12	VF20	XF40	MS60	MS63
2003	3,000	PF63 60.00	PF65 65.00			

KM# 183 2000 SHILLINGS
31.10 g., 0.999 Silver 0.9925 oz. ASW **Series:** Chinese symbolism **Subject:** Happiness **Obv. Legend:** BANK OF UGANDA **Rev:** Unicorn

Date	Mintage	F12	VF20	XF40	MS60	MS63
2003	3,000	PF63 60.00	PF65 65.00			

KM# 184 2000 SHILLINGS
31.10 g., 0.999 Silver 0.9925 oz. ASW **Series:** Chinese symbolism **Subject:** Health and long life **Obv. Legend:** BANK OF UGANDA **Rev:** Two cranes

Date	Mintage	F12	VF20	XF40	MS60	MS63
2003	3,000	PF63 60.00	PF65 65.00			

KM# 185 2000 SHILLINGS
31.10 g., 0.999 Silver 0.9925 oz. ASW **Series:** Chinese symbolism **Subject:** Success **Obv. Legend:** BANK OF UGANDA **Rev:** Carp

Date	Mintage	F12	VF20	XF40	MS60	MS63
2003	3,000	PF63 60.00	PF65 65.00			

KM# 186 2000 SHILLINGS
31.10 g., 0.999 Silver 0.9925 oz. ASW **Series:** Chinese symbolism **Subject:** Wealth **Obv. Legend:** BANK OF UGANDA **Rev:** Toad

Date	Mintage	F12	VF20	XF40	MS60	MS63
2003	3,000	PF63 60.00	PF65 65.00			

KM# 175 2000 SHILLINGS
15.55 g., 0.999 Silver 0.4962 oz. ASW **Series:** Famous Places in China **Subject:** Yugan Garden - Shanghai **Obv:** Two dragons **Obv. Legend:** BANK OF UGANDA

Date	Mintage	F12	VF20	XF40	MS60	MS63
2003	3,000	PF63 35.00	PF65 40.00			

KM# 176 2000 SHILLINGS
15.55 g., 0.999 Silver 0.4962 oz. ASW **Series:** Famous Places in China **Subject:** Tiger Hill Pagoda - Jiangsu **Obv:** Two dragons **Obv. Legend:** BANK OF UGANDA

Date	Mintage	F12	VF20	XF40	MS60	MS63
2003	3,000	PF63 35.00	PF65 40.00			

KM# 187 2000 SHILLINGS
4.00 g., 0.9999 Gold 0.1278 oz. AGW **Series:** Guanyin **Subject:** Fulun **Obv:** Lotus blossom **Obv. Legend:** BANK OF UGANDA

Date	Mintage	F12	VF20	XF40	MS60	MS63
2003	—	PF63 245	PF65 265			

KM# 205 2000 SHILLINGS
Silver **Subject:** XXVIII Summer Olympics - Athens 2004 **Obv. Legend:** BANK OF UGANDA **Rev:** Sprinter

Date	Mintage	F12	VF20	XF40	MS60	MS63
2003	500	PF63 60.00	PF65 65.00			

KM# 210 2000 SHILLINGS
31.10 g., 0.999 Silver 0.9925 oz. ASW **Series:** Chinese symbolic floral New Year paintings **Subject:** Happiness **Obv. Legend:** BANK OF UGANDA **Rev:** Multicolor

Date	Mintage	F12	VF20	XF40	MS60	MS63
2004	2,000	PF63 60.00	PF65 65.00			

KM# 211 2000 SHILLINGS
31.10 g., 0.999 Silver 0.9925 oz. ASW **Series:** Chinese Dieties **Subject:** Happiness **Obv. Legend:** BANK OF UGANDA **Rev:** Fú - multicolor

Date	Mintage	F12	VF20	XF40	MS60	MS63
2004	2,000	PF63 60.00	PF65 65.00			

KM# 212 2000 SHILLINGS
31.10 g., 0.999 Silver 0.9925 oz. ASW **Series:** Chinese Dieties **Subject:** Prosperity **Obv. Legend:** BANK OF UGANDA **Rev:** Lù - multicolor

Date	Mintage	F12	VF20	XF40	MS60	MS63
2004	2,000	PF63 60.00	PF65 65.00			

KM# 213 2000 SHILLINGS
31.10 g., 0.999 Silver 0.9925 oz. ASW **Series:** Chinese Dieties **Subject:** Health and Long Life **Obv. Legend:** BANK OF UGANDA **Rev:** Shòu - multicolor

Date	Mintage	F12	VF20	XF40	MS60	MS63
2004	2,000	PF63 60.00	PF65 65.00			

KM# 206 2000 SHILLINGS
31.10 g., 0.999 Silver 0.9925 oz. ASW **Series:** Chinese symbolic floral New Year paintings **Obv. Legend:** BANK OF UGANDA **Rev:** Carp and Lotus blossom - multicolor

Date	Mintage	F12	VF20	XF40	MS60	MS63
2004	2,000	PF63 60.00	PF65 65.00			

KM# 207 2000 SHILLINGS
31.10 g., 0.999 Silver 0.9925 oz. ASW **Series:** Chinese symbolic floral New Year paintings **Obv. Legend:** BANK OF UGANDA **Rev:** Deer - multicolor

Date	Mintage	F12	VF20	XF40	MS60	MS63
2004	2,000	PF63 60.00	PF65 65.00			

KM# 208 2000 SHILLINGS
31.10 g., 0.999 Silver 0.9925 oz. ASW **Series:** Chinese symbolic floral New Year paintings **Subject:** Abundance **Obv. Legend:** BANK OF UGANDA **Rev:** Fruit - multicolor

Date	Mintage	F12	VF20	XF40	MS60	MS63
2004	2,000	PF63 60.00	PF65 65.00			

KM# 209 2000 SHILLINGS
31.10 g., 0.999 Silver 0.9925 oz. ASW **Series:** Chinese symbolic floral New Year paintings **Subject:** Peace and prosperity **Obv. Legend:** BANK OF UGANDA **Rev:** Multicolor

Date	Mintage	F12	VF20	XF40	MS60	MS63
2004	2,000	PF63 60.00	PF65 65.00			

KM# 221 2000 SHILLINGS
Silver Plated Bronze **Series:** XIX World Football Championship - South Africa 2010 **Obv:** National arms **Obv. Legend:** BANK OF UGANDA **Rev:** Player about to kick

Date	Mintage	F12	VF20	XF40	MS60	MS63
2005	10,000	PF63 15.00				

KM# 222 2000 SHILLINGS
Silver Plated Bronze **Series:** XIX World Football Championship - South Afrika 2010 **Obv:** National arms **Obv. Legend:** BANK OF UGANDA **Rev:** Ball in net

Date	Mintage	F12	VF20	XF40	MS60	MS63
2005	10,000	PF63 15.00				

KM# 223 2000 SHILLINGS
Silver Plated Bronze **Series:** XIX World Football Championship - South Afrika 2010 **Obv:** National arms **Obv. Legend:** BANK OF UGANDA **Rev:** Player, map of Afrika

Date	Mintage	F12	VF20	XF40	MS60	MS63
2005	10,000	PF63 15.00				

KM# 224 2000 SHILLINGS
Silver Plated Bronze **Series:** XIX World Football Championship - South Afrika 2010 **Obv:** National arms **Obv. Legend:** BANK OF UGANDA **Rev:** Goalkeeper with ball

Date	Mintage	F12	VF20	XF40	MS60	MS63
2005	10,000	PF63 15.00				

KM# 225 2000 SHILLINGS
Silver Plated Bronze **Series:** XIX World Football Championship - South Afrika 2010 **Obv:** National arms **Obv. Legend:** BANK OF UGANDA **Rev:** Player and ball

Date	Mintage	F12	VF20	XF40	MS60	MS63
2005	10,000	PF63 15.00				

KM# 217 2000 SHILLINGS
31.10 g., 0.999 Silver 0.9925 oz. ASW **Obv:** Lotus blossom **Obv. Legend:** BANK OF UGANDA **Rev:** Guanyin - multicolor

Date	Mintage	F12	VF20	XF40	MS60	MS63
2005	2,000	PF63 75.00	PF65 85.00			

KM# 226 2000 SHILLINGS
40.00 g., Bronze Gilt **Series:** Zodiac **Subject:** Year of the Dog **Obv:** Two dragons **Obv. Legend:** BANK OF UGANDA **Rev:** Three dogs - multicolor

Date	Mintage	F12	VF20	XF40	MS60	MS63
2006	—	PF63 45.00	PF65 50.00			

KM# 227 2000 SHILLINGS
40.00 g., Bronze Gilt **Series:** Zodiac **Subject:** Year of the Dog **Obv:** Archaic Chinese characters **Obv. Legend:** BANK OF UGANDA **Rev:** Two dogs - multicolor

Date	Mintage	F12	VF20	XF40	MS60	MS63
2006	—	PF63 45.00	PF65 50.00			

KM# 234 2000 SHILLINGS
31.10 g., 0.999 Silver 0.9925 oz. ASW **Series:** Zodiac **Subject:** Year of the Dog **Obv. Legend:** BANK OF UGANDA **Rev:** Tibet Terrier with pup surrounded by 10 symbols

Date	Mintage	F12	VF20	XF40	MS60	MS63
2006	3,000	PF63 75.00	PF65 85.00			

KM# 237 2000 SHILLINGS
31.10 g., 0.999 Silver 0.9925 oz. ASW **Series:** Zodiac **Subject:** Year of the Dog **Obv:** National arms **Obv. Legend:** BANK OF UGANDA **Rev:** Chow-chow as watchdog, gold bars, bat and flower

Date	Mintage	F12	VF20	XF40	MS60	MS63
2006	—	PF63 60.00	PF65 65.00			

KM# 227a 2000 SHILLINGS
31.10 g., 0.999 Silver 0.9925 oz. ASW **Series:** Zodiac **Subject:** Year of the Dog **Obv:** Archaic Chinese characters **Obv. Legend:** BANK OF UGANDA **Rev:** Two dogs - multicolor

Date	Mintage	F12	VF20	XF40	MS60	MS63
2006	3,000	PF63 75.00	PF65 85.00			

KM# 172 5000 SHILLINGS
4.00 g., 0.9999 Gold 0.1278 oz. AGW **Series:** Guanyin **Subject:** Chilian **Obv:** Lotus blossom **Obv. Legend:** BANK OF UGANDA

Date	Mintage	F12	VF20	XF40	MS60	MS63
2001	—	PF63 245	PF65 265			

KM# 87 5000 SHILLINGS
33.73 g., 0.850 Silver 0.9158 oz. ASW, 38.65 mm. **Subject:** The Big Five **Obv:** Arms with supporters **Rev:** Rhinoceros **Edge:** Reeded

Date	Mintage	F12	VF20	XF40	MS60	MS63
2002	—	PF63 65.00	PF65 70.00			

KM# 88 5000 SHILLINGS
33.73 g., 0.850 Silver 0.9158 oz. ASW, 38.65 mm. **Subject:** The Big Five **Obv:** Arms with supporters **Rev:** Lion **Edge:** Reeded

Date	Mintage	F12	VF20	XF40	MS60	MS63
2002	—	PF63 65.00	PF65 70.00			

KM# 89 5000 SHILLINGS
33.73 g., 0.850 Silver 0.9158 oz. ASW, 38.65 mm. **Subject:** The Big Five **Obv:** Arms with supporters **Rev:** Cape Buffalo **Edge:** Reeded

Date	Mintage	F12	VF20	XF40	MS60	MS63
2002	—	PF63 50.00	PF65 55.00			

KM# 90 5000 SHILLINGS
33.73 g., 0.850 Silver 0.9158 oz. ASW, 38.65 mm. **Subject:** The Big Five **Obv:** Arms with supporters **Rev:** Leopard **Edge:** Reeded

Date	Mintage	F12	VF20	XF40	MS60	MS63
2002	—	PF63 65.00	PF65 70.00			

KM# 91 5000 SHILLINGS
33.73 g., 0.850 Silver 0.9158 oz. ASW, 38.65 mm. **Subject:** The Big Five **Obv:** Arms with supporters **Rev:** Elephant **Edge:** Reeded

Date	Mintage	F12	VF20	XF40	MS60	MS63
2002	—	PF63 65.00	PF65 70.00			

KM# 96 5000 SHILLINGS
31.10 g., 0.999 Silver 0.9926 oz. ASW, 40.6 mm. **Subject:** Matthew Flinders **Obv:** Arms with supporters below crowned head right dividing date **Rev:** Multicolor bust half left at right with ship and harbor scene at left **Edge:** Plain **Shape:** Continent of Australia

Date	Mintage	F12	VF20	XF40	MS60	MS63
2002	2,500	PF63 55.00	PF65 60.00			

KM# 97 5000 SHILLINGS
31.10 g., 0.999 Silver 0.9926 oz. ASW, 40.6 mm. **Subject:** Matthew Flinders - H. M. S. Investigator **Obv:** Crowned head right divides date above arms with supporters **Rev:** Multicolor cameo at upper right of ship **Edge:** Plain **Shape:** Continent of Australia

Date	Mintage	F12	VF20	XF40	MS60	MS63
2002	2,500	PF63 55.00	PF65 60.00			

KM# 98 5000 SHILLINGS
31.10 g., 0.999 Silver 0.9926 oz. ASW, 40.6 mm. **Subject:** Matthew Flinders - Meeting at Encounter Bay **Obv:** Crowned head right divides date above arms with supporters **Rev:** Date and inscription divides multicolor busts facing **Edge:** Plain **Shape:** Continent of Australia

Date	Mintage	F12	VF20	XF40	MS60	MS63
2002	2,500	PF63 55.00	PF65 60.00			

KM# 99 5000 SHILLINGS
31.10 g., 0.999 Silver 0.9926 oz. ASW, 40.6 mm. **Subject:** Matthew Flinders - First Circumnavigation of Terra Australia - 1802 **Rev:** Multicolor bust right on Australian map showing his route around Australia **Edge:** Plain **Shape:** Continent of Australia

Date	Mintage	F12	VF20	XF40	MS60	MS63
2002	2,500	PF63 55.00	PF65 60.00			

KM# 174 5000 SHILLINGS
4.00 g., 0.9999 Gold 0.1278 oz. AGW **Series:** Guanyin **Subject:** Fuyu **Obv:** Lotus blossom **Obv. Legend:** BANK OF UGANDA

Date	Mintage	F12	VF20	XF40	MS60	MS63
2002	—	PF63 245	PF65 265			

KM# 214 5000 SHILLINGS
4.00 g., 0.9999 Gold 0.1278 oz. AGW **Series:** Guanyin **Subject:** Shile **Obv:** Lotus blossom **Obv. Legend:** BANK OF UGANDA

Date	Mintage	F12	VF20	XF40	MS60	MS63
2004	—	PF63 245	PF65 265			

KM# 220 5000 SHILLINGS
4.00 g., 0.9999 Gold 0.1278 oz. AGW **Series:** Guanyin **Subject:** Songjing **Obv:** Lotus blossom **Obv. Legend:** BANK OF UGANDA

Date	Mintage	F12	VF20	XF40	MS60	MS63
2005	—	PF63 245	PF65 265			

KM# 235 6000 SHILLINGS
3.11 g., 0.9999 Gold 0.0993 oz. AGW **Series:** Zodiac **Subject:** Year of the Dog **Obv. Legend:** BANK OF UGANDA **Rev:** Tibet Terrier with pup surrounded by 10 symbols

Date	Mintage	F12	VF20	XF40	MS60	MS63
2006	—	PF63 175	PF65 200			

KM# 228 6000 SHILLINGS
4.00 g., 0.9999 Gold 0.1278 oz. AGW **Series:** Zodiac **Subject:** Year of the Dog **Obv:** Archaic Chinese characters **Obv. Legend:** BANK OF UGANDA **Rev:** Yorkshire Terrier and "Fú" - Happiness

Date	Mintage	F12	VF20	XF40	MS60	MS63
2006	14,000	PF63 235	PF65 250			

KM# 229 6000 SHILLINGS
4.00 g., 0.9999 Gold 0.1278 oz. AGW **Series:** Zodiac **Subject:** Year of the Dog **Obv:** Archaic Chinese characters **Obv. Legend:** BANK OF UGANDA **Rev:** Yorkshire Terrier and "Lù" - Prosperity

Date	Mintage	F12	VF20	XF40	MS60	MS63
2006	14,000	PF63 235	PF65 250			

KM# 230 6000 SHILLINGS
4.00 g., 0.9999 Gold 0.1278 oz. AGW **Series:** Zodiac **Subject:** Year of the Dog **Obv:** Archaic Chinese characters **Obv. Legend:** BANK OF UGANDA **Rev:** Yorkshire Terrier and "Shòu" - Health and Long Life

Date	Mintage	F12	VF20	XF40	MS60	MS63
2006	14,000	PF63 235	PF65 250			

KM# 238 6000 SHILLINGS
3.11 g., 0.9999 Gold 0.0993 oz. AGW **Series:** Zodiac **Subject:** Year of the Dog **Obv:** National arms **Obv. Legend:** BANK OF UGANDA **Rev:** Chow-chow as watchdog, gold bars, bat and flower

Date	Mintage	F12	VF20	XF40	MS60	MS63
2006	—	PF63 175	PF65 200			

KM# 231 8000 SHILLINGS
8.00 g., 0.9999 Gold 0.2555 oz. AGW **Series:** Zodiac **Subject:** Year of the Dog **Obv:** Archaic Chinese characters **Obv. Legend:** BANK OF UGANDA **Rev:** Yorkshire Terrier and "Fú" - Happiness

Date	Mintage	F12	VF20	XF40	MS60	MS63
2006	1,000	PF63 450	PF65 475			

KM# 232 8000 SHILLINGS
8.00 g., 0.9999 Gold 0.2555 oz. AGW **Series:** Zodiac **Subject:** Year of the Dog **Obv:** Archaic Chinese characters **Obv. Legend:** BANK OF UGANDA **Rev:** Yorkshire Terrier and "Lù" - Prosperity

Date	Mintage	F12	VF20	XF40	MS60	MS63
2006	1,000	PF63 450	PF65 475			

KM# 215 10000 SHILLINGS
10.00 g., 0.9999 Gold 0.3194 oz. AGW **Obv:** Lotus blossom **Obv. Legend:** BANK OF UGANDA **Rev:** Buddha

Date	Mintage	F12	VF20	XF40	MS60	MS63
2004	3,000	PF63 700	PF65 725			

KM# 76 12000 SHILLINGS
6.22 g., 0.9999 Gold 0.1987 oz. AGW, 22 mm. **Subject:** Illusion: "Spirit of the Mountain **Obv:** Crowned head right divides date above arms with supporters **Rev:** Landscape and tree that looks like a male portrait **Edge:** Reeded

Date	Mintage	F12	VF20	XF40	MS60	MS63
2001	—	PF63 375	PF65 400			

KM# 236 20000 SHILLINGS
15.55 g., 0.9999 Gold 0.4967 oz. AGW **Series:** Zodiac **Subject:** Year of the Dog **Obv. Legend:** BANK OF UGANDA **Rev:** Tibet Terrier with pup surrounded by 10 symbols

Date	Mintage	F12	VF20	XF40	MS60	MS63
2006	—	PF63 900	PF65 950			

KM# 239 20000 SHILLINGS
15.55 g., 0.9999 Gold 0.4967 oz. AGW **Series:** Year of the Dog **Obv:** National arms **Obv. Legend:** BANK OF UGANDA **Rev:** Chow-chow as watchdog, gold bars, bat and flower

Date	Mintage	F12	VF20	XF40	MS60	MS63
2006	—	PF63 900	PF65 950			

UKRAINE

Ukraine (formerly the Ukrainian Soviet Socialist Republic) is bordered by Russia to the east, Russia and Belarus to the north, Poland, Slovakia and Hungary to the west, Romania and Moldova to the southwest and in the south by the Black Sea and the Sea of Azov. It has an area of 233,088 sq. mi. (603,700 sq. km.) and a population of 51.9 million. Capital: Kyiv (Kiev). Coal, grain, vegetables and heavy industrial machinery are major exports.

Ukraine is a charter member of the United Nations and has inherited the third largest nuclear arsenal in the world.

REPUBLIC

REFORM COINAGE

September 2, 1996
100,000 Karbovanets = 1 Hryvnia
100 Kopiyok = 1 Hryvnia

KM# 6 KOPIYKA

1.50 g., Stainless Steel, 16 mm. **Obv:** National arms **Rev:** Value within wreath **Edge:** Plain

Date	Mintage	F12	VF20	XF40	MS60	MS63
2001	—	—	—	0.35	0.75	—
2002	—	—	—	0.35	0.75	—
2003	—	—	—	0.35	0.75	—
2004	—	—	—	0.35	0.75	—
2005	—	—	—	0.35	0.75	—
2006	—	—	—	0.35	0.75	—
2007	—	—	—	0.35	0.75	—
2008	—	—	—	0.35	0.75	—
2008 Prooflike	5,000	—	—	—	—	3.00
2009	—	—	—	0.35	0.75	—
2010	—	—	—	0.35	0.75	—
2011	—	—	—	0.35	0.75	—
2011 Prooflike	5,000	—	—	—	—	1.50
2012	—	—	—	0.35	0.75	—
2012 Prooflike	5,000	—	—	—	—	1.50
(2013) Prooflike	5,000	—	—	—	—	1.50

KM# 4b 2 KOPIYKY

1.80 g., Stainless Steel, 17.3 mm. **Obv:** National arms **Rev:** Value within wreath **Edge:** Plain

Date	Mintage	F12	VF20	XF40	MS60	MS63
2001	—	—	0.20	0.50	1.00	—
2002	—	—	0.20	0.50	1.00	—
2003	Est. 5000	—	—	—	—	300
2004	—	—	0.20	0.50	1.00	—
2005	—	—	0.20	0.50	1.00	—
2006	—	—	—	0.50	1.00	—
2007	—	—	—	0.50	1.00	—
2008	—	—	—	0.50	1.00	—
2008 Prooflike	5,000	—	—	—	—	3.00
2009	—	—	—	0.50	1.00	—
2010	—	—	—	0.50	1.00	—
2011	—	—	—	0.50	1.00	—
2011 Prooflike	5,000	—	—	—	—	1.50
2012	—	—	—	0.50	1.00	—
2012 Prooflike	5,000	—	—	—	—	1.50
2013	—	—	—	—	—	1.50
2013 5000 Prooflike						

KM# 7 5 KOPIYOK

4.30 g., Stainless Steel, 23.91 mm. **Obv:** National arms **Rev:** Value within wreath **Edge:** Reeded

Date	Mintage	F12	VF20	XF40	MS60	MS63
2001 In sets only	10,000	—	—	—	—	25.00
2003	—	—	—	0.50	1.00	—
2004	—	—	—	0.50	1.00	—
2005	—	—	—	0.50	1.00	—
2006	—	—	—	0.50	1.00	—
2007	—	—	—	0.50	1.00	—
2008	—	—	—	0.50	1.00	—
2008 Prooflike	5,000	—	—	—	—	2.50
2009	—	—	—	0.50	1.00	—
2010	—	—	—	0.50	1.00	—
2011	—	—	—	0.50	1.00	—
2011 Prooflike	5,000	—	—	—	—	2.00
2012	—	—	—	0.50	1.00	—
2012 Prooflike	5,000	—	—	—	—	2.00
2013 Prooflike	5,000	—	—	—	—	2.00
2013	—	—	—	0.50	1.00	—

KM# 1.1b 10 KOPIYOK

1.70 g., Aluminum-Bronze, 16.24 mm. **Obv:** National arms **Rev:** Value within wreath **Edge:** Reeded

Date	Mintage	F12	VF20	XF40	MS60	MS63
2001 In sets only	10,000	—	—	—	—	25.00
2002	—	—	0.60	1.25	2.50	—
2003	—	—	0.50	1.00	2.25	—
2004	—	—	0.50	1.00	2.25	—
2005	—	—	—	1.00	2.25	—
2006	—	—	—	1.00	2.25	—
2007	—	—	—	1.00	2.25	—
2008	—	—	—	1.00	2.25	—
2008 Prooflike	5,000	—	—	—	—	5.00
2009	—	—	—	1.00	2.00	—
2010	—	—	—	1.00	2.00	—
2011 Prooflike	5,000	—	—	—	—	5.00
2011	—	—	—	1.00	2.00	—
2012	—	—	—	1.00	2.00	—
2012 Prooflike	5,000	—	—	—	—	5.00
2013 Prooflike	5,000	—	—	—	—	5.00
2013	—	—	—	1.00	2.00	—

KM# 2.1b 25 KOPIYOK

2.90 g., Aluminum-Bronze, 20.8 mm. **Obv:** National arms **Rev:** Value within wreath **Edge:** Segmented reeding

Date	Mintage	F12	VF20	XF40	MS60	MS63
2001	—	—	0.80	3.00	6.00	25.00
2003 Prooflike	Est. 5000	—	—	—	—	300
2006	—	—	0.80	2.00	4.00	—
2007	—	—	0.80	2.00	4.00	—
2008	—	—	—	2.00	4.00	—
2008 Prooflike	5,000	—	—	—	—	8.00
2009	—	—	—	2.00	3.50	—
2010	—	—	—	2.00	3.50	—
2011	—	—	—	2.00	3.50	—
2011 Prooflike	5,000	—	—	—	—	8.00
2012	—	—	—	2.00	3.50	—
2012 Prooflike	5,000	—	—	—	—	8.00
2013	—	—	—	2.00	3.50	—
2013 Prooflike	5,000	—	—	—	—	8.00

KM# 3.3b 50 KOPIYOK

4.20 g., Aluminum-Bronze, 23 mm. **Obv:** National arms **Rev:** Five dots grouped in wreath to right of final letter 'K' in value **Edge:** Segmented reeding

Date	Mintage	F12	VF20	XF40	MS60	MS63
2001 In sets only	—	—	—	—	10.00	25.00
2003	Est. 5000	—	—	—	—	300
2006	—	—	1.00	2.00	4.00	—
2007	—	—	1.00	2.00	4.00	—
2008	—	—	—	2.00	4.00	—
2008 Prooflike	5,000	—	—	—	—	8.00
2009	—	—	—	2.00	4.00	—
2010	—	—	—	2.00	4.00	—
2011	—	—	—	2.00	4.00	—
2011 Prooflike	5,000	—	—	—	—	8.00
2012	—	—	—	2.00	4.00	—
2012 Prooflike	5,000	—	—	—	—	8.00

KM# 8b HRYVNIA

6.90 g., Aluminum-Bronze, 26 mm. **Obv:** National arms **Rev:** Value, sprigs and designs **Edge:** Lettered

Date	Mintage	F12	VF20	XF40	MS60	MS63
2001	—	—	—	2.50	4.50	—

KM# 8b.1 HRYVNIA

7.10 g., Aluminum-Bronze, 26 mm. **Obv:** National arms **Rev:** Value, sprigs and designs **Edge:** Lettered

Date	Mintage	F12	VF20	XF40	MS60	MS63
2002	—	—	—	3.50	6.50	—
2003	—	—	—	2.50	4.50	—

KM# 208 HRYVNIA

6.80 g., Aluminum-Bronze, 26 mm. **Subject:** 60th Anniversary - Victory over the Nazis **Obv:** National arms above value **Rev:** Uniform lapel with Soviet military medals group **Edge:** Lettered **Edge Lettering:** Date and denomination

Date	Mintage	F12	VF20	XF40	MS60	MS63
2004	5,000,000	—	—	—	5.00	—

KM# 209 HRYVNIA

6.74 g., Aluminum-Bronze, 26 mm. **Obv:** National arms above value **Rev:** Half length figure of Volodymyr the Great facing holding church model building and staff **Edge:** Lettered **Edge Lettering:** Date and denomination

Date	Mintage	F12	VF20	XF40	MS60	MS63
2004	10,000,000	—	—	—	4.00	—
2005	—	—	—	—	3.00	—
2006	—	—	—	—	3.00	—
2008 Prooflike	5,000	—	—	—	—	25.00
2010	—	—	—	—	3.00	—
2011	—	—	—	—	3.00	—
2011 Prooflike, in sets only	5,000	—	—	—	—	12.50
2012	—	—	—	—	4.00	—
2012 Prooflike, in sets only	5,000	—	—	—	—	12.50
2013 Prooflike	5,000	—	—	—	—	12.50

KM# 228 HRYVNIA

6.80 g., Aluminum-Bronze, 26 mm. **Subject:** WW II Victory 60th Anniversary **Obv:** Value **Rev:** Soldiers in a "V" of search lights **Edge Lettering:** Value and 2010

Date	Mintage	F12	VF20	XF40	MS60	MS63
2005	5,000,000	—	—	—	6.00	—

KM# 667 HRYVNIA

6.80 g., Aluminum-Bronze, 26 mm. **Subject:** WWII Victory, 65th Anniversary **Obv:** Value **Rev:** Ribbon of the order of St. George and the eternal flame

Date	Mintage	F12	VF20	XF40	MS60	MS63
2010	5,000,000	—	—	—	6.00	—

KM# 654 HRYVNIA

31.11 g., 0.9999 Silver 0.9935 oz. ASW, 38.6 mm. **Obv:** Logo of the Ukraine National Bank **Rev:** Archangel Michael **Edge:** Reeded

Date	Mintage	F12	VF20	XF40	MS60	MS63
2011	10,000	—	—	—	BV+40%	BV+40%
2012	20,000	—	—	—	—	BV+40%
2013	10,000	—	—	—	—	BV+40%

KM# 668 HRYVNIA

6.80 g., Aluminum-Bronze, 26 mm. **Subject:** WEFA Euro 2012 Final Tournament **Obv:** Vlaue **Rev:** UEFA Euro 2012 logo

Date	Mintage	F12	VF20	XF40	MS60	MS63
2012	5,000,000	—	—	—	6.00	—

KM# 669 HRYVNIA

33.91 g., 0.925 Silver 1.002 oz. ASW **Subject:** Folks Crafts **Obv:** Glassblowen products **Rev:** Glassblower **Edge:** Incuse lettering

Date	Mintage	F12	VF20	XF40	MS60	MS63
2012 Proof, antique finish	7,000	PF65 80.00				

KM# 106 2 HRYVNI
12.80 g., Copper-Nickel-Zinc, 31 mm. **Series:** Olympics - Salt Lake City, 2002 **Obv:** National arms, value and designs **Rev:** Stylized ice dancing couple **Edge:** Reeded

Date	Mintage	F12	VF20	XF40	MS60	MS63
2001	30,000	—	—	—	25.00	—

KM# 111 2 HRYVNI
12.80 g., Copper-Nickel-Zinc, 31 mm. **Series:** Flora and Fauna **Obv:** National arms and date divides wreath, value within **Rev:** Lynx and offspring **Edge:** Reeded

Date	Mintage	F12	VF20	XF40	MS60	MS63
2001	30,000	—	—	—	50.00	—

KM# 133 2 HRYVNI
12.80 g., Copper-Nickel-Zinc, 31 mm. **Subject:** Kindness to Children **Obv:** National arms above value flanked by sprigs and doves **Rev:** Two children frolicking under fountain of knowledge **Edge:** Reeded

Date	Mintage	F12	VF20	XF40	MS60	MS63
2001	100,000	—	—	—	12.00	—

KM# 134 2 HRYVNI
12.80 g., Copper-Nickel-Zinc, 31 mm. **Subject:** 5th Anniversary of Constitution **Obv:** National arms above value flanked by sprigs **Rev:** Building above book flanked by sprigs **Edge:** Reeded

Date	Mintage	F12	VF20	XF40	MS60	MS63
2001	30,000	—	—	—	40.00	—

KM# 136 2 HRYVNI
12.80 g., Copper-Nickel-Zinc, 31 mm. **Subject:** Mykolaiv Zoo **Obv:** Man running alongside large cat **Rev:** Twelve animals **Edge:** Reeded

Date	Mintage	F12	VF20	XF40	MS60	MS63
2001	30,000	—	—	—	40.00	—

KM# 137 2 HRYVNI
12.80 g., Copper-Nickel-Zinc, 31 mm. **Subject:** Mykhailo Ostrohradskiy (Mathematician) **Obv:** National arms divides date and value divided by wavy line graph **Rev:** Head 1/4 left **Edge:** Reeded

Date	Mintage	F12	VF20	XF40	MS60	MS63
2001	30,000	—	—	20.00	—	—

KM# 138 2 HRYVNI
12.80 g., Copper-Nickel-Zinc, 31 mm. **Subject:** Larix Polonica **Obv:** Value within wreath **Rev:** Pine branch with cone **Edge:** Reeded

Date	Mintage	F12	VF20	XF40	MS60	MS63
2001	30,000	—	—	—	45.00	—

KM# 139 2 HRYVNI
12.80 g., Copper-Nickel-Zinc, 31 mm. **Subject:** Volodymyr Dal **Obv:** Books **Rev:** Head right **Edge:** Reeded

Date	Mintage	F12	VF20	XF40	MS60	MS63
2001	30,000	—	—	—	20.00	—

KM# 147 2 HRYVNI
12.80 g., Copper-Nickel-Zinc, 31 mm. **Series:** Olympics - Salt Lake City, 2002 **Obv:** National arms and value on ice design **Rev:** Stylized hockey player **Edge:** Reeded

Date	Mintage	F12	VF20	XF40	MS60	MS63
2001	30,000	—	—	—	20.00	—

KM# 149 2 HRYVNI
12.80 g., Copper-Nickel-Zinc, 31 mm. **Subject:** Mykhailo Drahomanov (Historian, Politician, etc.) **Obv:** National arms and value **Rev:** Bust right **Edge:** Reeded

Date	Mintage	F12	VF20	XF40	MS60	MS63
2001	30,000	—	—	—	20.00	—

KM# 150 2 HRYVNI
12.80 g., Copper-Nickel-Zinc, 31 mm. **Series:** Olympics - Salt Lake City, 2002 **Obv:** National arms and value on ice design **Rev:** Speed skater **Edge:** Reeded

Date	Mintage	F12	VF20	XF40	MS60	MS63
2002	30,000	—	—	—	20.00	—

KM# 154 2 HRYVNI
12.80 g., Copper-Nickel-Zinc, 31 mm. **Subject:** Mykola Lysenko (composer) **Obv:** Musical score and value **Rev:** Head 1/4 right **Edge:** Reeded

Date	Mintage	F12	VF20	XF40	MS60	MS63
2002	30,000	—	—	—	17.00	—

KM# 155 2 HRYVNI
12.80 g., Copper-Nickel-Zinc, 31 mm. **Series:** Flora and Fauna **Obv:** National arms and date divides wreath, value within **Rev:** Eurasian Eagle Owl **Edge:** Reeded

Date	Mintage	F12	VF20	XF40	MS60	MS63
2002	30,000	—	—	—	60.00	—

KM# 156 2 HRYVNI
12.80 g., Copper-Nickel-Zinc, 31 mm. **Subject:** Olympics - Athens, 2004 **Obv:** Two ancient figures above value **Rev:** Swimmer **Edge:** Reeded

Date	Mintage	F12	VF20	XF40	MS60	MS63
2002	30,000	—	—	—	18.00	—

KM# 166 2 HRYVNI
12.80 g., Copper-Nickel-Zinc, 31 mm. **Subject:** Leonid Glibov, writer (1827-1893) **Obv:** National arms and value within scroll and wreath **Rev:** 1/2-length bust right **Edge:** Reeded

Date	Mintage	F12	VF20	XF40	MS60	MS63
2002	30,000	—	—	—	17.00	—

KM# 167 2 HRYVNI
12.80 g., Copper-Nickel-Zinc, 31 mm. **Series:** Flora and Fauna **Obv:** National arms and date divides wreath, value within **Rev:** European Bison **Edge:** Reeded

Date	Mintage	F12	VF20	XF40	MS60	MS63
2003	50,000	—	—	—	30.00	—

KM# 168 2 HRYVNI
12.80 g., Copper-Nickel-Zinc, 31 mm. **Obv:** National arms and date divides wreath, value within **Rev:** Long-snouted Sea Horse **Edge:** Reeded

Date	Mintage	F12	VF20	XF40	MS60	MS63
2003	50,000	—	—	—	30.00	—

KM# 169 2 HRYVNI
12.80 g., Copper-Nickel-Zinc, 31 mm. **Subject:** Volodymyr Vernadskyi (academic) **Obv:** National arms, value and world globe **Rev:** Head on hand looking down **Edge:** Reeded

Date	Mintage	F12	VF20	XF40	MS60	MS63
2003	30,000	—	—	—	15.00	—

KM# 170 2 HRYVNI
12.80 g., Copper-Nickel-Zinc, 31 mm. **Subject:** Volodymyr Korolenko (writer) **Obv:** National arms above book and value **Rev:** Bearded head 1/4 right above dates **Edge:** Reeded

Date	Mintage	F12	VF20	XF40	MS60	MS63
2003	30,000	—	—	—	15.00	—

KM# 171 2 HRYVNI
12.80 g., Copper-Nickel-Zinc, 31 mm. **Subject:** Viacheslav Chornovil (politician) **Obv:** Arms with supporters within beaded circle **Rev:** Head 1/4 left **Edge:** Reeded

Date	Mintage	F12	VF20	XF40	MS60	MS63
2003	30,000	—	—	—	30.00	—

KM# 178 2 HRYVNI
1.24 g., 0.9999 Gold 0.0396 oz. AGW, 13.92 mm. **Obv:** National arms flanked by dates within beaded circle **Rev:** Spotted Salamander divides beaded circle **Edge:** Plain

Date	Mintage	F12	VF20	XF40	MS60	MS63
2003	10,000	—	—	—	—	220

KM# 179 2 HRYVNI
12.80 g., Copper-Nickel-Zinc, 31 mm. **Subject:** Singer Boris Gmyrya **Obv:** Value, arms ,date and musical symbol **Rev:** Head 1/4 left and dates **Edge:** Reeded

Date	Mintage	F12	VF20	XF40	MS60	MS63
2003	30,000	—	—	—	12.00	—

KM# 180 2 HRYVNI
12.80 g., Copper-Nickel-Zinc, 31 mm. **Subject:** 70th Anniversary National Aviation University **Obv:** World globe behind national arms, value and date **Rev:** Wright Brothers biplane **Edge:** Reeded

Date	Mintage	F12	VF20	XF40	MS60	MS63
2003	30,000	—	—	—	20.00	—

KM# 181 2 HRYVNI
12.80 g., Copper-Nickel-Zinc, 31 mm. **Subject:** Ostap Veresay (musician) **Obv:** Musical stringed instrument and ornamental design **Rev:** Bust facing playing stringed instrument **Edge:** Reeded

Date	Mintage	F12	VF20	XF40	MS60	MS63
2003	30,000	—	—	—	13.00	—

KM# 182 2 HRYVNI
12.80 g., Copper-Nickel-Zinc, 31 mm. **Subject:** Olympics **Obv:** Two ancient women with seedlings **Rev:** Boxer **Edge:** Reeded

Date	Mintage	F12	VF20	XF40	MS60	MS63
2003	30,000	—	—	—	20.00	—

KM# 183 2 HRYVNI
12.80 g., Copper-Nickel-Zinc, 31 mm. **Subject:** Vasyl Sukhomlynski (teacher) **Obv:** Children, books, value and national arms **Rev:** Head 1/4 right **Edge:** Reeded

Date	Mintage	F12	VF20	XF40	MS60	MS63
2003	30,000	—	—	—	13.00	—

KM# 184 2 HRYVNI
12.80 g., Copper-Nickel-Zinc, 31 mm. **Subject:** Andriy Malyshko (poet) **Obv:** Ornamental shawl, national arms and value **Rev:** Head 1/4 right flanked by radiant sun and tree **Edge:** Reeded

Date	Mintage	F12	VF20	XF40	MS60	MS63
2003	30,000	—	—	—	13.00	—

KM# 201 2 HRYVNI
12.80 g., Copper-Nickel-Zinc, 31 mm. **Subject:** Azov Dolphin **Obv:** National arms and date divides wreath, value within **Rev:** Harbor Porpoises **Edge:** Reeded

Date	Mintage	F12	VF20	XF40	MS60	MS63
2004	30,000	—	—	—	50.00	—

KM# 202 2 HRYVNI
12.80 g., Copper-Nickel-Zinc, 31 mm. **Subject:** Football World Cup - 2006 **Obv:** Soccer ball in net **Rev:** Two soccer players **Edge:** Reeded

Date	Mintage	F12	VF20	XF40	MS60	MS63
2004	50,000	—	—	—	15.00	—

KM# 203 2 HRYVNI
12.80 g., Copper-Nickel-Zinc, 31 mm. **Subject:** Serhiy Lyfar (ballet artist) **Obv:** Stylized dancer **Rev:** Head right **Edge:** Reeded

Date	Mintage	F12	VF20	XF40	MS60	MS63
2004	30,000	—	—	—	13.00	—

KM# 210 2 HRYVNI
12.80 g., Copper-Nickel-Zinc, 31 mm. **Subject:** 170 Years of the Kyiv National University **Obv:** National arms in center above value dividing scientific items **Rev:** University building main entrance **Edge:** Reeded

Date	Mintage	F12	VF20	XF40	MS60	MS63
2004	50,000	—	—	—	13.00	—

KM# 211 2 HRYVNI
12.80 g., Copper-Nickel-Zinc, 31 mm. **Subject:** Oleksander Dovzhenko (movie producer, writer) **Obv:** Boy standing in small boat **Rev:** Head facing **Edge:** Reeded

Date	Mintage	F12	VF20	XF40	MS60	MS63
2004	30,000	—	—	—	13.00	—

KM# 212 2 HRYVNI
12.80 g., Copper-Nickel-Zinc, 31 mm. **Subject:** Mykola Bazhan (poet, translator) **Obv:** Winged pens and value **Rev:** Head 1/4 left **Edge:** Reeded

Date	Mintage	F12	VF20	XF40	MS60	MS63
2004	30,000	—	—	—	13.00	—

KM# 213 2 HRYVNI
12.80 g., Copper-Nickel-Zinc, 31 mm. **Subject:** Mykhailo Kotsyubynsky (writer) **Obv:** Two reclining figures **Rev:** Head 1/4 right **Edge:** Reeded

Date	Mintage	F12	VF20	XF40	MS60	MS63
2004	30,000	—	—	—	13.00	—

KM# 214 2 HRYVNI
12.80 g., Copper-Nickel-Zinc, 31 mm. **Subject:** Maria Zankovetska (actress) **Obv:** National arms, value and drawn curtain **Rev:** Hooded head 1/4 left **Edge:** Reeded

Date	Mintage	F12	VF20	XF40	MS60	MS63
2004	30,000	—	—	—	13.00	—

KM# 215 2 HRYVNI
12.80 g., Copper-Nickel-Zinc, 31 mm. **Subject:** Mykhailo Maksymovych (historian, archaeologist) **Obv:** National arms above building and value **Rev:** Bust left **Edge:** Reeded

Date	Mintage	F12	VF20	XF40	MS60	MS63
2004	30,000	—	—	—	13.00	—

KM# 216 2 HRYVNI
12.80 g., Copper-Nickel-Zinc, 31 mm. **Subject:** Mykhailo Deregus (painter) **Obv:** National arms and value on artists palette **Rev:** Head right **Edge:** Reeded

Date	Mintage	F12	VF20	XF40	MS60	MS63
2004	30,000	—	—	—	13.00	—

KM# 217 2 HRYVNI
12.80 g., Copper-Nickel-Zinc, 31 mm. **Subject:** Nuclear Power Engineering of Ukraine **Obv:** National arms and value in atomic design **Rev:** Nuclear reactor **Edge:** Reeded

Date	Mintage	F12	VF20	XF40	MS60	MS63
2004	30,000	—	—	—	20.00	—

KM# 227 2 HRYVNI
1.24 g., 0.9999 Gold 0.0396 oz. AGW, 13.92 mm. **Obv:** National arms divides dates within beaded circle **Rev:** Flying White Stork divides beaded circle **Edge:** Plain

Date	Mintage	F12	VF20	XF40	MS60	MS63
2004	10,000	—	—	—	—	220

KM# 330 2 HRYVNI
12.80 g., Copper-Nickel-Zinc, 31 mm. **Subject:** 200th Anniversary of Kharkiv University **Obv:** National arms and atom **Rev:** University building and reflection **Edge:** Reeded

Date	Mintage	F12	VF20	XF40	MS60	MS63
2004	50,000	—	—	—	13.00	—

KM# 331 2 HRYVNI
12.80 g., Copper-Nickel-Zinc, 31 mm. **Subject:** Ukraine National Academy of Law named after Yaroslav the Wise **Obv:** National arms above National Academy of Law arms and date **Rev:** Building **Edge:** Reeded

Date	Mintage	F12	VF20	XF40	MS60	MS63
2004	30,000	—	—	—	20.00	—

KM# 332 2 HRYVNI
12.80 g., Copper-Nickel-Zinc, 31 mm. **Subject:** Yurii Fedkovych (poet, writer) **Obv:** National arms, value and man on horse **Rev:** Bust 1/4 right and dates **Edge:** Reeded

Date	Mintage	F12	VF20	XF40	MS60	MS63
2004	30,000	—	—	—	13.00	—

KM# 346 2 HRYVNI
12.80 g., Copper-Nickel-Zinc, 31 mm. **Subject:** Boris Liatoshynsky (composer) **Obv:** Musical G Clef symbol and value below national arms **Rev:** Head 1/4 left **Edge:** Reeded

Date	Mintage	F12	VF20	XF40	MS60	MS63
2005	20,000	—	—	—	15.00	—

KM# 347 2 HRYVNI
12.80 g., Copper-Nickel-Zinc, 31 mm. **Subject:** Volodymyr Filatov (surgeon) **Obv:** Light passing through the lens of an eye **Rev:** Head with cap facing **Edge:** Reeded

Date	Mintage	F12	VF20	XF40	MS60	MS63
2005	20,000	—	—	—	16.00	—

KM# 348 2 HRYVNI
12.80 g., Copper-Nickel-Zinc, 31 mm. **Obv:** Books between stylized horsemen **Rev:** Ulas Samchuk **Edge:** Reeded

Date	Mintage	F12	VF20	XF40	MS60	MS63
2005	20,000	—	—	—	15.00	—

KM# 349 2 HRYVNI
12.80 g., Copper-Nickel-Zinc, 31 mm. **Subject:** Pavlo Virsky

(ballet artist) **Obv:** National arms in flower circle **Rev:** Bust right **Edge:** Reeded

Date	Mintage	F12	VF20	XF40	MS60	MS63
2005	20,000	—	—	—	15.00	—

KM# 350 2 HRYVNI
12.80 g., Copper-Nickel-Zinc, 31 mm. **Obv:** Roses and grapes **Rev:** Poet Maksym Rylsky **Edge:** Reeded

Date	Mintage	F12	VF20	XF40	MS60	MS63
2005	20,000	—	—	—	15.00	—

KM# 351 2 HRYVNI
1.24 g., 0.9999 Gold 0.0396 oz. AGW, 13.9 mm. **Obv:** National arms within beaded circle **Rev:** Scythian horseman depicted on golden plaque **Edge:** Plain

Date	Mintage	F12	VF20	XF40	MS60	MS63
2005	15,000	—	—	—	200	220

KM# 352 2 HRYVNI
12.80 g., Copper-Nickel-Zinc, 31 mm. **Subject:** Serhiy Vsekhsviatsky (astronomer) **Obv:** Solar Wind" depiction **Rev:** Head right **Edge:** Reeded

Date	Mintage	F12	VF20	XF40	MS60	MS63
2005	20,000	—	—	—	15.00	—

KM# 353 2 HRYVNI
12.80 g., Copper-Nickel-Zinc, 31 mm. **Subject:** 50 Years of Kyivmiskbud **Obv:** National arms **Rev:** Buildings **Edge:** Reeded

Date	Mintage	F12	VF20	XF40	MS60	MS63
2005	20,000	—	—	—	20.00	—

KM# 354 2 HRYVNI
12.80 g., Copper-Nickel-Zinc, 31 mm. **Subject:** 75 Years of Zhukovsky Aerospace University in Kharkiv **Obv:** Building divides book outline **Rev:** Airplane, computer monitor and books **Edge:** Reeded

Date	Mintage	F12	VF20	XF40	MS60	MS63
2005	30,000	—	—	—	18.00	—

KM# 356 2 HRYVNI
12.80 g., Copper-Nickel-Zinc, 31 mm. **Subject:** Oleksander Korniychuk (writer, playright) **Obv:** Theatrical masks and feather **Rev:** Bust 1/4 right **Edge:** Reeded

Date	Mintage	F12	VF20	XF40	MS60	MS63
2005	20,000	—	—	—	15.00	—

KM# 357 2 HRYVNI
12.80 g., Copper-Nickel-Zinc, 31 mm. **Obv:** National arms and date divides wreath, value within **Rev:** Sandy Mole Rat **Edge:** Reeded

Date	Mintage	F12	VF20	XF40	MS60	MS63
2005	60,000	—	—	—	20.00	—

KM# 359 2 HRYVNI
12.80 g., Copper-Nickel-Zinc, 31 mm. **Obv:** National arms **Rev:** Tairov Wine Institute building and cameo **Edge:** Reeded

Date	Mintage	F12	VF20	XF40	MS60	MS63
2005	20,000	—	—	—	27.50	—

KM# 360 2 HRYVNI
12.80 g., Copper-Nickel-Zinc, 31 mm. **Subject:** 300 Years to David Guramishvili (poet) **Obv:** Georgian and Ukrainian style ornamentation **Rev:** Head right **Edge:** Reeded

Date	Mintage	F12	VF20	XF40	MS60	MS63
2005	30,000	—	—	—	13.00	—

KM# 361 2 HRYVNI
12.80 g., Copper-Nickel-Zinc, 31 mm. **Subject:** Dmytro Yavornytsky (historian, archaeologist, writer) **Obv:** National arms **Rev:** Bust 3/4 right **Edge:** Reeded

Date	Mintage	F12	VF20	XF40	MS60	MS63
2005	30,000	—	—	—	15.00	—

KM# 375 2 HRYVNI
12.80 g., Copper-Nickel-Zinc, 31 mm. **Subject:** Oleksiy Alchevsky (banker) **Obv:** Steam train, factory, National arms

and value **Rev:** Head with beard 1/4 right **Edge:** Reeded

Date	Mintage	F12	VF20	XF40	MS60	MS63
2005	20,000	—	—	—	25.00	—

KM# 376 2 HRYVNI
12.80 g., Copper-Nickel-Zinc, 31 mm. **Subject:** Illia Mechnikov (biologist, Nobel prize laureate) **Obv:** Amoeba and National arms **Rev:** Bust with beard facing **Edge:** Reeded

Date	Mintage	F12	VF20	XF40	MS60	MS63
2005	20,000	—	—	—	27.50	—

KM# 377 2 HRYVNI
12.80 g., Copper-Nickel-Zinc, 31 mm. **Subject:** Vsevolod Holubovych (politician) **Obv:** National arms **Rev:** Head 1/4 left **Edge:** Reeded

Date	Mintage	F12	VF20	XF40	MS60	MS63
2005	20,000	—	—	—	18.00	—

KM# 378 2 HRYVNI
12.80 g., Copper-Nickel-Zinc, 31 mm. **Subject:** Volodymyr Vynnychenko (writer, politician) **Obv:** National arms **Rev:** Head facing **Edge:** Reeded

Date	Mintage	F12	VF20	XF40	MS60	MS63
2005	20,000	—	—	—	16.00	—

KM# 383 2 HRYVNI
12.80 g., Copper-Nickel-Zinc, 31 mm. **Subject:** Kyiv National University of Economics **Obv:** National arms, value and graph **Rev:** University building **Edge:** Reeded

Date	Mintage	F12	VF20	XF40	MS60	MS63
2006	60,000	—	—	—	15.00	—

KM# 384 2 HRYVNI
12.80 g., Copper-Nickel-Zinc, 31 mm. **Subject:** Viacheslav

Prokopovych (historian, publist) **Obv:** National arms **Rev:** Bust facing **Edge:** Reeded

Date	Mintage	F12	VF20	XF40	MS60	MS63
2006	30,000	—	—	—	13.00	—

KM# 385 2 HRYVNI

12.80 g., Copper-Nickel-Zinc, 31 mm. **Subject:** Heorhii Narbut (artist) **Obv:** Peasant couple **Rev:** Silhouette of standing figure on one leg facing right **Edge:** Reeded

Date	Mintage	F12	VF20	XF40	MS60	MS63
2006	30,000	—	—	—	13.00	—

KM# 386 2 HRYVNI

12.80 g., Copper-Nickel-Zinc, 31 mm. **Subject:** Oleh Antonov (aircraft engineer) **Obv:** Large jet plane **Rev:** Bust 1/4 right **Edge:** Reeded

Date	Mintage	F12	VF20	XF40	MS60	MS63
2006	45,000	—	—	—	18.00	—

KM# 391 2 HRYVNI

12.80 g., Copper-Nickel-Zinc, 31 mm. **Obv:** National arms above value in wreath **Rev:** Bush Katydid Grasshopper **Edge:** Reeded

Date	Mintage	F12	VF20	XF40	MS60	MS63
2006	60,000	—	—	—	20.00	—

KM# 398 2 HRYVNI

12.80 g., Copper-Nickel-Zinc, 31 mm. **Subject:** Mykhailo Hrushevskyi **Obv:** National arms and value **Edge:** Reeded

Date	Mintage	F12	VF20	XF40	MS60	MS63
2006	45,000	—	—	—	13.00	—

KM# 399 2 HRYVNI

12.80 g., Copper-Nickel-Zinc, 31 mm. **Subject:** Serhii Ostapenko **Obv:** National arms **Edge:** Reeded

Date	Mintage	F12	VF20	XF40	MS60	MS63
2006	30,000	—	—	—	12.00	—

KM# 401 2 HRYVNI

12.80 g., Copper-Nickel-Zinc, 31 mm. **Subject:** Economic University of Kharkiv **Edge:** Reeded

Date	Mintage	F12	VF20	XF40	MS60	MS63
2006	30,000	—	—	—	13.00	—

KM# 408 2 HRYVNI

1.24 g., 0.9999 Gold 0.0396 oz. AGW, 13.92 mm. **Subject:** Hedgehog **Obv:** National arms **Edge:** Plain

Date	Mintage	F12	VF20	XF40	MS60	MS63
2006	10,000	—	—	—	150	200

KM# 393 2 HRYVNI

12.80 g., Copper-Nickel-Zinc, 31 mm. **Subject:** Mykola Strazhesko **Obv:** National arms and value **Edge:** Reeded

Date	Mintage	F12	VF20	XF40	MS60	MS63
2006	45,000	—	—	—	12.00	—

KM# 394 2 HRYVNI

12.80 g., Copper-Nickel-Zinc, 31 mm. **Subject:** Volodymyr Chekhivsky **Obv:** National arms and value **Edge:** Reeded

Date	Mintage	F12	VF20	XF40	MS60	MS63
2006	30,000	—	—	—	12.00	—

KM# 395 2 HRYVNI

12.80 g., Copper-Nickel-Zinc, 31 mm. **Subject:** Mykola Vasylenko **Obv:** National arms and value **Edge:** Reeded

Date	Mintage	F12	VF20	XF40	MS60	MS63
2006	30,000	—	—	—	13.00	—

KM# 396 2 HRYVNI

12.80 g., Copper-Nickel-Zinc, 31 mm. **Subject:** Ivan Franko

Obv: National arms and value **Edge:** Reeded

Date	Mintage	F12	VF20	XF40	MS60	MS63
2006	45,000	—	—	—	13.00	—

KM# 397 2 HRYVNI

12.80 g., Copper-Nickel-Zinc, 31 mm. **Subject:** Dmytro Lutsenko **Obv:** National arms and value **Edge:** Reeded

Date	Mintage	F12	VF20	XF40	MS60	MS63
2006	30,000	—	—	—	12.00	—

KM# 400 2 HRYVNI

12.80 g., Copper-Nickel-Zinc, 31 mm. **Subject:** Mykhailo Lysenko **Obv:** National arms and value **Edge:** Reeded

Date	Mintage	F12	VF20	XF40	MS60	MS63
2006	35,000	—	—	—	12.00	—

KM# 403 2 HRYVNI

1.24 g., 0.9999 Gold 0.0396 oz. AGW, 13.92 mm **Subject:** Ram **Obv:** National arms **Edge:** Plain

Date	Mintage	F12	VF20	XF40	MS60	MS63
2006	10,000	—	—	—	140	200

KM# 404 2 HRYVNI

1.24 g., 0.9999 Gold 0.0396 oz. AGW, 13.92 mm. **Subject:** Bull **Obv:** National arms **Edge:** Plain

Date	Mintage	F12	VF20	XF40	MS60	MS63
2006	10,000	—	—	—	140	200

KM# 406 2 HRYVNI

1.24 g., 0.9999 Gold 0.0396 oz. AGW, 13.92 mm. **Subject:** The Twins **Obv:** National arms **Edge:** Plain

Date	Mintage	F12	VF20	XF40	MS60	MS63
2006	10,000	—	—	—	140	200

KM# 428 2 HRYVNI

12.80 g., Copper-Nickel-Zinc, 31 mm. **Subject:** Serhii Koroljov **Obv:** National arms **Edge:** Reeded

Date	Mintage	F12	VF20	XF40	MS60	MS63
2007	35,000	—	—	—	20.00	—

KM# 429 2 HRYVNI
12.80 g., Copper-Nickel-Zinc, 31 mm. **Subject:** Les Kurbas **Obv:** National arms **Edge:** Reeded

Date	Mintage	F12	VF20	XF40	MS60	MS63
2007	35,000	—	—	—	—	12.00

KM# 430 2 HRYVNI
12.80 g., Copper-Nickel-Zinc, 31 mm. **Subject:** Olexander Liapunov **Obv:** Small national arms above geometrical depiction of celestial mechanics graphics **Rev:** Large bust facing **Edge:** Reeded

Date	Mintage	F12	VF20	XF40	MS60	MS63
2007	35,000	—	—	—	—	12.00

KM# 431 2 HRYVNI
1.24 g., 0.9999 Gold 0.0396 oz. AGW, 13.92 mm. **Subject:** Steppe Marmot **Obv:** National arms **Edge:** Plain

Date	Mintage	F12	VF20	XF40	MS60	MS63
2007	10,000	—	—	—	150	200

KM# 440 2 HRYVNI
12.80 g., Copper-Nickel-Zinc, 31 mm. **Subject:** Ivan Ohienko **Obv:** Cross **Rev:** Head and hands clasped at prayer **Edge:** Reeded

Date	Mintage	F12	VF20	XF40	MS60	MS63
2007	35,000	—	—	—	—	12.00

KM# 441 2 HRYVNI
12.80 g., Copper-Nickel-Zinc, 31 mm. **Subject:** Oleh Olzhych **Obv:** Chestnut leaf and stone path **Rev:** Bust facing **Edge:** Reeded

Date	Mintage	F12	VF20	XF40	MS60	MS63
2007	35,000	—	—	—	—	12.00

KM# 442 2 HRYVNI
12.80 g., Copper-Nickel-Zinc, 31 mm. **Subject:** Donetsk Region 75th Anniversary **Obv:** Miner's lamp illuminating industrial plants **Rev:** Flag and 75 **Edge:** Reeded

Date	Mintage	F12	VF20	XF40	MS60	MS63
2007	35,000	—	—	—	20.00	25.00

KM# 443 2 HRYVNI
12.80 g., Copper-Nickel-Zinc, 31 mm. **Subject:** Olena Teliha **Obv:** Scorched cherry blossom **Rev:** Bust facing **Edge:** Reeded

Date	Mintage	F12	VF20	XF40	MS60	MS63
2007	35,000	—	—	—	—	12.00

KM# 444 2 HRYVNI
12.80 g., Copper-Nickel-Zinc, 31 mm. **Subject:** Orienteering **Obv:** Compass, star and benchmarks **Rev:** Runner **Edge:** Reeded

Date	Mintage	F12	VF20	XF40	MS60	MS63
2007	35,000	—	—	—	—	16.00

KM# 445 2 HRYVNI
12.80 g., Copper-Nickel-Zinc, 31 mm. **Subject:** Ivan Bahrianji **Obv:** Book edge **Rev:** Bust facing, book edge **Edge:** Reeded

Date	Mintage	F12	VF20	XF40	MS60	MS63
2007	35,000	—	—	—	—	12.00

KM# 446 2 HRYVNI
12.80 g., Copper-Nickel-Zinc, 31 mm. **Subject:** Petro Hryhorenko **Obv:** Sprout squeezing brick wall **Rev:** Head right **Edge:** Reeded

Date	Mintage	F12	VF20	XF40	MS60	MS63
2007	35,000	—	—	—	—	13.00

KM# 447 2 HRYVNI
12.80 g., Copper-Nickel-Zinc, 31 mm. **Subject:** 90th Anniversary of 1st Government **Obv:** Parts of early 20th century bank notes and industrial elements **Rev:** Volodymyr Vynnychenko and ornamentation **Edge:** Reeded

Date	Mintage	F12	VF20	XF40	MS60	MS63
2007	35,000	—	—	—	—	13.00

KM# 448 2 HRYVNI
1.24 g., 0.999 Gold 0.0396 oz. AGW, 13.9 mm. **Subject:** Capricorn **Obv:** Elements of earth, air, water and fire **Rev:** Zodiac sign

Date	Mintage	F12	VF20	XF40	MS60	MS63
2007	10,000	—	—	—	140	200

KM# 450 2 HRYVNI
1.24 g., 0.999 Gold 0.0396 oz. AGW, 13.9 mm. **Subject:** Pisces **Obv:** Elements of earth, air, water and fire **Rev:** Zodiac sign, two fish

Date	Mintage	F12	VF20	XF40	MS60	MS63
2007	10,000	—	—	—	140	200

KM# 449 2 HRYVNI
1.24 g., 0.999 Gold 0.0396 oz. AGW, 13.9 mm. **Subject:** Aquarius **Obv:** Elements of earth, air, water and fire **Rev:** Zodiac sign, man pouring water

Date	Mintage	F12	VF20	XF40	MS60	MS63
2007	10,000	—	—	—	140	200

KM# 451 2 HRYVNI
1.24 g., 0.999 Gold 0.0396 oz. AGW, 13.9 mm. **Subject:** Scorpion **Obv:** Elements of earth, air, water and fire **Rev:** Zodiac sign

Date	Mintage	F12	VF20	XF40	MS60	MS63
2007	10,000	—	—	—	140	200

KM# 452 2 HRYVNI
1.24 g., 0.999 Gold 0.0396 oz. AGW, 13.9 mm. **Subject:** Sagitarius **Obv:** Elements of earth, air, water & fire **Rev:** Zodiac sign, archer

Date	Mintage	F12	VF20	XF40	MS60	MS63
2007	10,000	—	—	—	140	200

KM# 433 2 HRYVNI
12.80 g., Copper-Nickel-Zinc, 31 mm. **Obv:** Small national arms

at top, value in sprays with bird at left, butterfly at right **Rev:** Cinereous Vulture perched on nest with chick **Rev. Legend:** AEGYPIUS MONACHUS - ГРИФ ЧОРНИЙ **Edge:** Reeded

Date	Mintage	F12	VF20	XF40	MS60	MS63
2008	45,000	—	—	—	—	20.00

KM# 475 2 HRYVNI
12.80 g., Copper-Nickel-Zinc, 31 mm. **Subject:** Vasyl Stus, Poet **Edge:** Reeded

Date	Mintage	F12	VF20	XF40	MS60	MS63
2008	35,000	—	—	—	—	12.00

KM# 476 2 HRYVNI
12.80 g., Copper-Nickel-Zinc, 31 mm. **Subject:** Leo Landau **Edge:** Reeded

Date	Mintage	F12	VF20	XF40	MS60	MS63
2008	35,000	—	—	—	—	12.00

KM# 477 2 HRYVNI
12.80 g., Copper-Nickel-Zinc, 31 mm. **Subject:** Sydir Holubovych **Edge:** Reeded

Date	Mintage	F12	VF20	XF40	MS60	MS63
2008	35,000	—	—	—	—	12.00

KM# 478 2 HRYVNI
12.80 g., Copper-Nickel-Zinc, 31 mm. **Subject:** Kyiv Zoo, 100th Anniversary **Edge:** Reeded

Date	Mintage	F12	VF20	XF40	MS60	MS63
2008	50,000	—	—	—	—	15.00

KM# 479 2 HRYVNI
12.80 g., Copper-Nickel-Zinc, 31 mm. **Subject:** Yevhen Petrushevych **Edge:** Reeded

Date	Mintage	F12	VF20	XF40	MS60	MS63
2008	35,000	—	—	—	—	12.00

KM# 481 2 HRYVNI
12.80 g., Copper-Nickel-Zinc, 31 mm. **Subject:** Heorhii Voronyi **Edge:** Reeded

Date	Mintage	F12	VF20	XF40	MS60	MS63
2008	35,000	—	—	—	—	12.00

KM# 482 2 HRYVNI
1.24 g., 0.999 Gold 0.0396 oz. AGW, 13.9 mm. **Subject:** Skythian Gold (Goddess Api)

Date	Mintage	F12	VF20	XF40	MS60	MS63
2008	10,000	—	—	—	140	200

KM# 483 2 HRYVNI
1.24 g., 0.999 Gold 0.0396 oz. AGW, 13.9 mm. **Subject:** Zodiac **Rev:** Cancer

Date	Mintage	F12	VF20	XF40	MS60	MS63
2008	10,000	—	—	—	140	200

KM# 484 2 HRYVNI
1.24 g., 0.999 Gold 0.0396 oz. AGW, 13.9 mm. **Subject:** Zodiac **Rev:** Leo

Date	Mintage	F12	VF20	XF40	MS60	MS63
2008	10,000	—	—	—	140	200

KM# 485 2 HRYVNI
1.24 g., 0.999 Gold 0.0396 oz. AGW **Subject:** Virgo

Date	Mintage	F12	VF20	XF40	MS60	MS63
2008	10,000	—	—	—	140	200

KM# 486 2 HRYVNI
1.24 g., 0.999 Gold 0.0396 oz. AGW, 13.9 mm. **Subject:** Libra

Date	Mintage	F12	VF20	XF40	MS60	MS63
2008	10,000	—	—	—	140	200

KM# 487 2 HRYVNI
12.80 g., Copper-Nickel-Zinc, 31 mm. **Subject:** Nataliia Vzhvii **Edge:** Reeded

Date	Mintage	F12	VF20	XF40	MS60	MS63
2008	35,000	—	—	—	—	12.00

KM# 488 2 HRYVNI
12.80 g., Copper-Nickel-Zinc, 31 mm. **Subject:** Hryhorii Kvitka - Osnovianenko **Edge:** Reeded

Date	Mintage	F12	VF20	XF40	MS60	MS63
2008	35,000	—	—	—	—	12.00

KM# 489 2 HRYVNI
12.80 g., Copper-Nickel-Zinc, 31 mm. **Subject:** Western Ukraine People's Republic, 90th Anniversary **Edge:** Reeded

Date	Mintage	F12	VF20	XF40	MS60	MS63
2008	35,000	—	—	—	—	12.00

KM# 490 2 HRYVNI
12.80 g., Copper-Nickel-Zinc, 31 mm. **Subject:** Vasyl Symonenko **Edge:** Reeded

Date	Mintage	F12	VF20	XF40	MS60	MS63
2008	35,000	—	—	—	—	12.00

KM# 533 2 HRYVNI
12.80 g., Copper-Nickel-Zinc, 31.0 mm. **Subject:** Pavlo Chubynskyi **Obv:** Folk music instruments **Obv. Legend:** НАЦІОНАЛЬНИЈ БАНК УКРА?НИ - 2 / ГРИВНІ / 2009 **Rev:** Chubynskyi's portrait **Rev. Legend:** ПАВЛО ЧУБИНСЬКИЈ - 1839-1884 **Edge:** Reeded

Date	Mintage	F12	VF20	XF40	MS60	MS63
2009	35,000	—	—	—	—	12.00

KM# 534 2 HRYVNI
12.80 g., Copper-Nickel-Zinc, 31.0 mm. **Subject:** Andrii Livytskyi **Obv:** National Arms and value **Obv. Legend:** НАЦІОНАЛЬНИЈ БАНК УКРА?НИ - ДВІ ГРИВНІ **Rev:** Livytskyi's portrait **Rev. Legend:** АНДРІЈ ЛІВИЦЬКИЈ - 1879/1954 - ПРЕЗИДЕНТ УНР В ЕКЗИЛІ **Edge:** Reeded

Date	Mintage	F12	VF20	XF40	MS60	MS63
2009	35,000	—	—	—	—	12.00

KM# 535 2 HRYVNI
1.24 g., 0.999 Gold 0.0396 oz. AGW, 13.92 mm. **Subject:** Ukraine Fauna **Obv:** National Arms, value **Obv. Legend:** НАЦІОНАЛЬНИЈ БАНК УКРА?НИ - 2 ГРИВНІ **Rev:** Turtle **Rev. Legend:** ЧЕРЕПАХА - TESTUDINES

Date	Mintage	F12	VF20	XF40	MS60	MS63
2009	10,000	—	—	—	140	200

KM# 536 2 HRYVNI
12.80 g., Copper-Nickel-Zinc, 31.0 mm. **Subject:** Borys Martos **Obv:** National Arms and value **Obv. Legend:** НАЦІОНАЛЬНИЈ БАНК УКРА?НИ - ДВІ ГРИВНІ **Rev:** Martos's portrait **Rev. Legend:** БОРИС МАРТОС **Edge:** Reeded

Date	Mintage	F12	VF20	XF40	MS60	MS63
2009	35,000	—	—	—	—	12.00

KM# 537 2 HRYVNI
12.80 g., Copper-Nickel-Zinc, 31.0 mm. **Subject:** General Symon Petliura **Obv:** Two Military men holding wreath of a woman's profile **Obv. Legend:** НАЦІОНАЛЬНИЈ БАНК УКРА?НИ - 2 ГРИВНІ **Rev:** Petliura's portrait **Rev. Legend:** СИМОН ПЕТЛ@@НРА **Edge:** Reeded

Date	Mintage	F12	VF20	XF40	MS60	MS63
2009	35,000	—	—	—	—	15.00

KM# 538 2 HRYVNI
12.80 g., Copper-Nickel-Zinc, 31 mm. **Subject:** Igor Sikorskyi, 100th Anniversary of birth **Obv:** Aircraft, National Arms, value

---

Obv. Legend: НАЦІОНАЛЬНИЈ БАНК УКРА?НИ - 2 ГРИВНІ **Rev:** Sikorskyi portrait as an airman, Da Vinci drawing **Rev. Legend:** ІГОР СІКОРСЬКИЈ **Edge:** Reeded

Date	Mintage	F12	VF20	XF40	MS60	MS63
2009	35,000	—	—	—	—	15.00

KM# 539 2 HRYVNI
12.80 g., Copper-Nickel-Zinc, 31 mm. **Subject:** Mykola Bogolijubov, physicist, 100th Anniversary of birth **Obv:** Diagram and formula, National Arms, value **Rev:** Bogolijubov's portrait **Edge:** Reeded

Date	Mintage	F12	VF20	XF40	MS60	MS63
2009	35,000	—	—	—	—	12.00

KM# 540 2 HRYVNI
12.80 g., Copper-Nickel-Zinc, 31 mm. **Subject:** Volodymyr Ivasiuk, poet and singer **Obv:** Flower of Chervona Ruta, electrical musical instruments **Obv. Legend:** НАЦІОНАЛЬНИЈ БАНК УКРА?НИ - 2 / ГРИВНІ / 2009 **Rev:** Ivasiuk's portrait **Rev. Legend:** ВОЛОДИМИР ІВАС@@НК **Edge:** Reeded

Date	Mintage	F12	VF20	XF40	MS60	MS63
2009	35,000	—	—	—	—	12.00

KM# 541 2 HRYVNI
12.80 g., Copper-Nickel-Zinc, 31.0 mm. **Subject:** Bohdan-Igor Antonych, poet **Obv:** Figurative interpretation of Antonych's poetry **Obv. Legend:** НАЦІОНАЛЬНИЈ БАНК УКРА?НИ - 2 / ГРИВНІ **Rev:** Antonych's portrait **Rev. Legend:** БОГДАН-ІГОР АНТОНИЧ **Edge:** Reeded

Date	Mintage	F12	VF20	XF40	MS60	MS63
2009	35,000	—	—	—	—	12.00

KM# 542 2 HRYVNI
12.80 g., Copper-Nickel-Zinc, 31.0 mm. **Subject:** Kost Levytskyi **Obv:** State Coat of Arms, issue year **Obv. Legend:** НАЦІОНАЛЬНИЈ БАНК УКРАЇНИ - ДВІ ГРИВНІ **Rev:** Levytskyi bust **Rev. Legend:** КОСТЬ ЛЕВИЦЬКИЈ

Date	Mintage	F12	VF20	XF40	MS60	MS63
2009	35,000	—	—	—	—	12.00

KM# 551 2 HRYVNI
12.80 g., Copper-Nickel-Zinc, 31.0 mm. **Subject:** Carpatho-Ukraine Republic, 70th Anniversary **Obv:** Carpathian ornamentation patterns, National Arms, value **Obv. Legend:** НАЦІОНАЛЬНИЈ БАНК УКРАЇНИ - 2 ГРИВНІ **Rev:** Transcarpathian holding flag with arms of Carpatho-Ukraine **Rev. Legend:** 70 / РОКІВ - ПРОГОЛОШЕННЯ КАРПАТСЬКОЇ УКРАЇНИ **Edge:** Reeded

Date	Mintage	F12	VF20	XF40	MS60	MS63
2009	35,000	—	—	—	—	14.00

KM# 571 2 HRYVNI
1.24 g., 0.999 Gold 0.0396 oz. AGW, 13.92 mm. **Subject:** Skythian Gold **Obv:** National Arms **Rev:** Scythian boar figure

Date	Mintage	F12	VF20	XF40	MS60	MS63
2009 Special Unc.	10,000	—	—	—	140	200

KM# 578 2 HRYVNI
12.80 g., Copper-Nickel-Zinc, 31 mm. **Subject:** Zaporizhzhia Oblast **Obv:** Zaporizhzhia Arms **Rev:** Stone baba, Dnieper's waves and Dniporhes dam **Edge:** Reeded

Date	Mintage	F12	VF20	XF40	MS60	MS63
2009	45,000	—	—	—	—	13.00

KM# 572 2 HRYVNI
1.24 g., 0.999 Gold 0.0396 oz. AGW, 13.92 mm. **Obv:** National Arms **Rev:** Bee **Edge:** Plain

Date	Mintage	F12	VF20	XF40	MS60	MS63
2010 Special Unc.	10,000	—	—	—	140	200

KM# 576 2 HRYVNI
12.80 g., Copper-Nickel-Zinc, 31 mm. **Subject:** Ukraine Ice Hockey, 100th Anniversary **Obv:** Golie before net, National Arms **Rev:** Old time and modern hockey players **Edge:** Reeded

Date	Mintage	F12	VF20	XF40	MS60	MS63
2010	35,000	—	—	—	—	13.00

KM# 580 2 HRYVNI
12.80 g., Copper-Nickel-Zinc, 31 mm. **Subject:** Ivan Kozhedub **Obv:** La-7 aircraft in two searchlight beams **Rev:** Kozhedub's portrait and airfield **Edge:** Reeded

Date	Mintage	F12	VF20	XF40	MS60	MS63
2010	35,000	—	—	—	—	14.00

KM# 581 2 HRYVNI
12.80 g., Copper-Nickel-Zinc, 31 mm. **Subject:** Lviv Polytechnic National University, 165th Anniversary **Obv:** Arts and Sciences sculptures from main building **Rev:** University building façade **Edge:** Reeded

Date	Mintage	F12	VF20	XF40	MS60	MS63
2010	45,000	—	—	—	—	13.00

KM# 583 2 HRYVNI
12.80 g., Copper-Nickel-Zinc, 31 mm. **Subject:** Kharkiv Polytechnic Institute, 125th Anniversary **Obv:** Radio telescope and open book **Rev:** University building at right, symbols of science at left, oval portrait of V.L. Kyrpychov **Edge:** Reeded

Date	Mintage	F12	VF20	XF40	MS60	MS63
2010	50,000	—	—	—	—	13.00

KM# 585 2 HRYVNI
12.80 g., Copper-Nickel, 31 mm. **Subject:** Ukraine Sovereignty, 20th Anniversary **Obv:** National flag in enamel within viburnum wreath **Rev:** Ukraine map within uneven background **Edge:** Reeded

Date	Mintage	F12	VF20	XF40	MS60	MS63
2010	35,000	—	—	—	—	18.00

KM# 593 2 HRYVNI
12.80 g., Copper-Nickel-Zinc, 31 mm. **Subject:** Flora and fauna **Obv:** National Arms and wreath **Rev:** Stipa Ucrainica, feather grass **Edge:** Reeded

Date	Mintage	F12	VF20	XF40	MS60	MS63
2010	35,000	—	—	—	—	13.00

KM# 603 2 HRYVNI
1.24 g., 0.999 Gold 0.0396 oz. AGW, 13.92 mm. **Obv:** National Arms **Rev:** Cranberry bush branch **Edge:** Plain

Date	Mintage	F12	VF20	XF40	MS60	MS63
2010	10,000	—	—	—	140	200

KM# 608 2 HRYVNI
12.80 g., Copper-Nickel-Zinc, 31 mm. **Subject:** Ukranian Medical Association, 100th Anniversary **Obv:** UMA Shield within wreath **Rev:** UMA in Lviv emblem (lion on cross) **Edge:** Reeded

Date	Mintage	F12	VF20	XF40	MS60	MS63
2010	35,000	—			—	15.00

KM# 612 2 HRYVNI
12.80 g., Copper-Nickel-Zinc, 31 mm. **Subject:** Ivan Franko National University, Lviv, 350th Anniversary **Obv:** National arms, Statuary group, value **Rev:** Main University building façade **Edge:** reeded

Date	Mintage	F12	VF20	XF40	MS60	MS63
2011	45,000	—			—	12.00

KM# 624 2 HRYVNI
1.24 g., 0.9999 Gold 0.0396 oz. AGW, 13.92 mm. **Subject:** Scythian Gold **Obv:** National arms **Rev:** Scythian jewlery, gilt deer

Date	Mintage	F12	VF20	XF40	MS60	MS63
2011	10,000	—			120	150

KM# 636 2 HRYVNI
12.80 g., Copper-Nickel-Zinc, 31 mm. **Subject:** CIS, 20th Anniversary **Obv:** National flag in color **Rev:** Commonwealth of Independent States emblem **Edge:** Reeded

Date	Mintage	F12	VF20	XF40	MS60	MS63
2011	30,000				PF65	15.00

KM# 656 2 HRYVNI
1.24 g., 0.9999 Gold 0.0396 oz. AGW, 13.92 mm. **Obv:** National shield **Rev:** Malva flower

Date	Mintage	F12	VF20	XF40	MS60	MS63
2012	Est. 8000		PF63	120	PF65	150

KM# 658 2 HRYVNI
12.80 g., Copper-Nickel-Zinc, 31 mm. **Subject:** Sydir Kovpak WWII Soviet Hero

Date	Mintage	F12	VF20	XF40	MS60	MS63
2012	Est. 15000	—	—		—	35.00

KM# 661 2 HRYVNI
12.80 g., Copper-Nickel-Zinc, 31 mm. **Subject:** 2012 London Paralympic Games **Edge:** Reeded

Date	Mintage	F12	VF20	XF40	MS60	MS63
2012	Est. 30000	—	—		—	15.00

KM# 675 2 HRYVNI
12.80 g., Copper-Nickel-Zinc, 31 mm. **Subject:** XXX Summer Olympic Games - London **Obv:** London City view, National arms **Rev:** Gold State of Philip II and silhouettes of sports **Edge:** Reeded

Date	Mintage	F12	VF20	XF40	MS60	MS63
2012	30,000	—	—		—	15.00

KM# 682 2 HRYVNI
12.80 g., Copper-Nickel-Zinc, 31 mm. **Subject:** Mykhailo Kravchuk, academician **Obv:** National arms, formula, value **Rev:** Portrait of Kravchuk **Edge:** Reeded

Date	Mintage	F12	VF20	XF40	MS60	MS63
2012	15,000	—			—	22.00

KM# 688 2 HRYVNI
12.80 g., Copper-Nickel-Zinc, 31 mm. **Obv:** National arms, value **Rev:** The sterlet **Edge:** Reeded

Date	Mintage	F12	VF20	XF40	MS60	MS63
2012	35,000	—			—	18.00

KM# 698 2 HRYVNI
12.80 g., Copper-Nickel-Zinc, 31 mm. **Subject:** The Great Bustard **Obv:** National arms, date, value

Date	Mintage	F12	VF20	XF40	MS60	MS63
2013	30,000	—			—	17.00

KM# 703 2 HRYVNI
12.80 g., Copper-Nickel-Zinc, 31 mm. **Subject:** World Youth Championships - Athletics **Obv:** National arms, Stadium in Donetsk and value **Rev:** Girl athletes in motion **Edge:** Reeded

Date	Mintage	F12	VF20	XF40	MS60	MS63
2013	20,000	—			—	17.00

KM# 107 5 HRYVEN
9.40 g., Bi-Metallic, 28 mm. **Subject:** New Millennium **Obv:** Spiral design within circle **Rev:** Mother and child within circle **Edge:** Segmented reeding

Date	Mintage	F12	VF20	XF40	MS60	MS63
2001	50,000	—			32.00	—

KM# 112 5 HRYVEN
16.54 g., Copper-Nickel-Zinc, 35 mm. **Subject:** Ostrozhska Academy **Obv:** Value, old writing and printing artifacts **Rev:** Seated figures, partial building and crowned arms with supporters **Edge:** Reeded

Date	Mintage	F12	VF20	XF40	MS60	MS63
2001	30,000	—			30.00	—

KM# 129 5 HRYVEN
16.54 g., Copper-Nickel-Zinc, 35 mm. **Subject:** 10th Anniversary - National Bank **Obv:** National arms between two arches **Rev:** Large building central entrance **Edge:** Reeded

Date	Mintage	F12	VF20	XF40	MS60	MS63
2001	50,000	—			17.50	—

KM# 132 5 HRYVEN
16.54 g., Copper-Nickel-Zinc, 35 mm. **Subject:** 10th Anniversary - National Independence **Obv:** Arms with supporters within beaded circle **Rev:** Building on map within beaded circle **Edge:** Reeded

Date	Mintage	F12	VF20	XF40	MS60	MS63
2001	100,000	—			15.00	—

KM# 135 5 HRYVEN
16.54 g., Copper-Nickel-Zinc, 35 mm. **Subject:** 1100th Anniversary - Poltava **Obv:** National arms above value flanked by flower sprigs **Rev:** Buildings above shield **Edge:** Reeded

Date	Mintage	F12	VF20	XF40	MS60	MS63
2001	50,000	—			20.00	—

KM# 140 5 HRYVEN
9.40 g., Bi-Metallic, 28 mm. **Subject:** 10th Anniversary of Military forces **Obv:** Crossed maces, arms and date within wreath and circle **Rev:** Circle in center of cross within wreath and circle **Edge:** Reeded and plain sections

Date	Mintage	F12	VF20	XF40	MS60	MS63
2001	30,000	—			—	100

KM# 148 5 HRYVEN
16.54 g., Copper-Nickel-Zinc, 35 mm. **Subject:** 400 Years of Krolevets **Obv:** National arms above gateway and value **Rev:** Krolivets city arms flanked by designs **Edge:** Reeded

Date	Mintage	F12	VF20	XF40	MS60	MS63
2001	30,000	—			—	50.00

KM# 151 5 HRYVEN
16.54 g., Copper-Nickel-Zinc, 35 mm. **Subject:** City of Khotyn **Obv:** Value within arch above military fittings **Rev:** Castle below crowned shield **Edge:** Reeded

Date	Mintage	F12	VF20	XF40	MS60	MS63
2002	30,000	—			—	40.00

KM# 152 5 HRYVEN
16.54 g., Copper-Nickel-Zinc, 35 mm. **Obv:** Sun and flying geese divides beaded circle **Rev:** AN-225 Mrija" cargo jet divide beaded circle **Edge:** Reeded

Date	Mintage	F12	VF20	XF40	MS60	MS63
2002	30,000	—	—	—	80.00	—

KM# 157 5 HRYVEN
16.54 g., Copper-Nickel-Zinc, 35 mm. **Subject:** 1100th Anniversary - City of Romny **Obv:** Sprigs divide national arms and value **Rev:** City view **Edge:** Reeded

Date	Mintage	F12	VF20	XF40	MS60	MS63
2002	30,000	—	—	—	40.00	—

KM# 158 5 HRYVEN
9.43 g., Bi-Metallic, 28 mm. **Subject:** 70th Anniversary of Dnipro Hydroelectric Power Station **Obv:** Turbine within circle **Rev:** Large dam within circle **Edge:** Reeded and plain sections

Date	Mintage	F12	VF20	XF40	MS60	MS63
2002	30,000	—	—	—	60.00	—

KM# 159 5 HRYVEN
16.54 g., Copper-Nickel-Zinc, 35 mm. **Obv:** Arms with supporters within beaded circle **Rev:** Battle scene around Batig in 1652 divides beaded circle **Edge:** Reeded

Date	Mintage	F12	VF20	XF40	MS60	MS63
2002	30,000	—	—	—	30.00	—

KM# 163 5 HRYVEN
16.54 g., Copper-Nickel-Zinc, 35 mm. **Subject:** Christmas **Obv:** National arms in star above value flanked by designed

sprigs **Rev:** Christmas pageant scene **Edge:** Reeded

Date	Mintage	F12	VF20	XF40	MS60	MS63
ND(2002)	30,000	—	—	—	100	—

KM# 200 5 HRYVEN
9.40 g., Bi-Metallic, 28 mm. **Obv:** Bandura strings over ornamental design **Rev:** Bandura divides circle and wreath **Edge:** Segmented reeding

Date	Mintage	F12	VF20	XF40	MS60	MS63
2003	30,000	—	—	—	25.00	—

KM# 172 5 HRYVEN
16.54 g., Copper-Nickel-Zinc, 35 mm. **Subject:** Easter **Obv:** Circle of Easter eggs, national arms in center above value **Rev:** Religious celebration **Edge:** Reeded

Date	Mintage	F12	VF20	XF40	MS60	MS63
2003	50,000	—	—	—	50.00	—

KM# 173 5 HRYVEN
16.54 g., Copper-Nickel-Zinc, 35 mm. **Subject:** Antonov AN-2 Biplane **Obv:** National arms sun face and flying geese divide beaded circle **Rev:** World's largest biplane divides beaded circle **Edge:** Reeded

Date	Mintage	F12	VF20	XF40	MS60	MS63
2003	50,000	—	—	—	25.00	—

KM# 185 5 HRYVEN
9.40 g., Bi-Metallic, 28 mm. **Subject:** 150th Anniversary of the Central Ukrainian Archives **Obv:** Value, signature and seal **Rev:** Hourglass divides books and circle **Edge:** Segmented reeding

Date	Mintage	F12	VF20	XF40	MS60	MS63
2003	30,000	—	—	—	15.00	—

KM# 186 5 HRYVEN
16.54 g., Copper-Nickel-Zinc, 35 mm. **Subject:** 2500th Anniversary of the City of Yevpatoria **Obv:** National arms, date and value with partial sun background **Rev:** Ancient amphora and modern city view **Edge:** Reeded

Date	Mintage	F12	VF20	XF40	MS60	MS63
2003	30,000	—	—	—	40.00	—

KM# 187 5 HRYVEN
16.54 g., Copper-Nickel-Zinc, 35 mm. **Subject:** 60th Anniversary - Liberation of Kiev **Obv:** Eternal flame monument **Rev:** Battle scene and map of the offense **Edge:** Reeded

Date	Mintage	F12	VF20	XF40	MS60	MS63
2003	30,000	—	—	—	25.00	—

KM# 204 5 HRYVEN
16.54 g., Copper-Nickel-Zinc, 35 mm. **Subject:** 50th Anniversary - Pivdenne Space Design Office **Obv:** Satellite orbiting Earth **Rev:** Satellite above moonscape **Edge:** Reeded

Date	Mintage	F12	VF20	XF40	MS60	MS63
2004	30,000	—	—	—	17.00	—

KM# 205 5 HRYVEN
16.54 g., Copper-Nickel-Zinc, 35 mm. **Subject:** 2500 Anniversary City of Balaklava **Obv:** National arms between two ancient ships **Rev:** Harbor view above pillar **Edge:** Reeded

Date	Mintage	F12	VF20	XF40	MS60	MS63
2004	30,000	—	—	—	25.00	—

KM# 218 5 HRYVEN
16.94 g., 0.925 Silver 0.5005 oz. ASW, 33 mm. **Obv:** National arms, value and atom **Rev:** Kharkiv University building **Edge:** Reeded

Date	Mintage	F12	VF20	XF40	MS60	MS63
2004	7,000	PF63 50.00	PF65 60.00			

KM# 219 5 HRYVEN
16.94 g., 0.925 Silver 0.5005 oz. ASW, 33 mm. **Obv:** National arms above value dividing scientific items **Rev:** Kiev University building main entrance **Edge:** Reeded

Date	Mintage	F12	VF20	XF40	MS60	MS63
2004	7,000	PF63 50.00		PF65 60.00		

KM# 220 5 HRYVEN
9.43 g., Bi-Metallic, 28 mm. **Subject:** 50 Years of Ukraine's Membership in UNESCO **Obv:** National arms in center of sprigs and circle **Rev:** Building within sprigs and circle **Edge:** Segmented reeding

Date	Mintage	F12	VF20	XF40	MS60	MS63
2004	50,000	—	—	—	15.00	

KM# 221 5 HRYVEN
16.54 g., Copper-Nickel-Zinc, 35 mm. **Subject:** Ice Breaker "Captain Belousov **Obv:** National arms on ship's wheel and anchor **Rev:** Ice breaker ship **Edge:** Reeded

Date	Mintage	F12	VF20	XF40	MS60	MS63
2004	30,000	—	—	—	16.00	

KM# 222 5 HRYVEN
16.54 g., Copper-Nickel-Zinc, 35 mm. **Subject:** Whit Sunday **Obv:** National arms in flower wreath above value flanked by sprigs **Rev:** Four dancing women and child **Edge:** Reeded

Date	Mintage	F12	VF20	XF40	MS60	MS63
2004	50,000	—	—	—	20.00	

KM# 333 5 HRYVEN
9.40 g., Bi-Metallic, 28 mm. **Obv:** Horizontal lines across flowery design **Rev:** Cossack-style lyre within circle and wreath **Edge:** Segmented reeding

Date	Mintage	F12	VF20	XF40	MS60	MS63
2004	30,000	—	—	—	20.00	

KM# 334 5 HRYVEN
16.54 g., Copper-Nickel-Zinc, 35 mm. **Subject:** 250th Anniversary of Kirovohrad **Obv:** National arms above crossed cannons and value **Rev:** Arms with supporters above city view **Edge:** Reeded

Date	Mintage	F12	VF20	XF40	MS60	MS63
2004	30,000	—	—	—	20.00	

KM# 335 5 HRYVEN
16.54 g., Copper-Nickel-Zinc, 35 mm. **Subject:** 350 Years to Kharkiv **Obv:** Assumption Cathedral, value and national arms **Rev:** Kharkiv State Industrial Building complex **Edge:** Reeded

Date	Mintage	F12	VF20	XF40	MS60	MS63
2004	30,000	—	—	—	30.00	

KM# 336 5 HRYVEN
9.40 g., Bi-Metallic, 28 mm. **Subject:** 50th Anniversary of Crimean Union With Ukraine **Obv:** National arms on wheat sheaf on map **Rev:** Crowned lion on shield flanked by pillars within rope wreath **Edge:** Segmented reeding

Date	Mintage	F12	VF20	XF40	MS60	MS63
2004	30,000	—	—	—	20.00	

KM# 337 5 HRYVEN
16.54 g., Copper-Nickel-Zinc, 35 mm. **Obv:** National arms on sun, flying geese divide beaded circle **Rev:** AN-140 Airliner divides beaded circle **Edge:** Reeded

Date	Mintage	F12	VF20	XF40	MS60	MS63
2004	50,000	—	—	—	15.00	

KM# 362 5 HRYVEN
16.54 g., Copper-Nickel-Zinc, 35 mm. **Obv:** National arms on sun with flying geese divide beaded circle **Rev:** AN-124 jet divides beaded circle **Edge:** Reeded

Date	Mintage	F12	VF20	XF40	MS60	MS63
2005	60,000	—	—	—	15.00	

KM# 364 5 HRYVEN
16.54 g., Copper-Nickel-Zinc, 35 mm. **Subject:** City of Korosten 1300th Anniversary **Obv:** National arms **Rev:** Ancient earring below modern building and bridge **Edge:** Reeded

Date	Mintage	F12	VF20	XF40	MS60	MS63
2005	30,000	—	—	—	18.00	

KM# 365 5 HRYVEN
16.54 g., Copper-Nickel-Zinc, 35 mm. **Subject:** City of Sumy 350th Anniversary **Obv:** National arms **Rev:** City view behind city arms **Edge:** Reeded

Date	Mintage	F12	VF20	XF40	MS60	MS63
2005	30,000	—	—	—	18.00	

KM# 366 5 HRYVEN
16.54 g., Copper-Nickel-Zinc, 35 mm. **Subject:** The Protection of the Virgin **Obv:** National arms on Cossack regalia **Rev:** Wedding scene **Edge:** Reeded

Date	Mintage	F12	VF20	XF40	MS60	MS63
2005	45,000	—	—	—	16.00	

KM# 368 5 HRYVEN
16.54 g., Copper-Nickel-Zinc, 35 mm. **Subject:** Sorochynsky Fair **Obv:** Busts facing each other flanked by sprigs **Rev:** Farmer with family in ox cart **Edge:** Reeded

Date	Mintage	F12	VF20	XF40	MS60	MS63
2005	60,000	—	—	—	16.00	

KM# 379 5 HRYVEN
16.54 g., Copper-Nickel-Zinc, 35 mm. **Subject:** 500th Anniversary - Kalmiuska Palanqua Cossack Settlement **Obv:** Cossack in ornamental frame and national arms **Rev:** Soldiers **Edge:** Reeded

Date	Mintage	F12	VF20	XF40	MS60	MS63
2005	30,000	—	—	—	—	18.00

KM# 380 5 HRYVEN
16.54 g., Copper-Nickel-Zinc, 35 mm. **Subject:** Sviatohirsky Assumption Monastery **Obv:** Madonna and child flanked by angels **Rev:** Hillside monastery **Edge:** Reeded

Date	Mintage	F12	VF20	XF40	MS60	MS63
2005	45,000	—	—	—	—	16.00

KM# 387 5 HRYVEN
16.54 g., Copper-Nickel-Zinc, 35 mm. **Subject:** Vernadsky Antarctic Station **Obv:** Flag and buildings **Rev:** Antarctica map within compass face **Edge:** Reeded

Date	Mintage	F12	VF20	XF40	MS60	MS63
2006	60,000	—	—	—	—	15.00

KM# 388 5 HRYVEN
16.93 g., 0.925 Silver 0.5002 oz. ASW, 33 mm. **Subject:** Year of the Dog **Obv:** Value on textile art **Rev:** Stylized dog **Edge:** Reeded

Date	Mintage	F12	VF20	XF40	MS60	MS63
2006	12,000	PF63 200	PF65 220			

KM# 389 5 HRYVEN
16.93 g., 0.925 Silver 0.5002 oz. ASW, 33 mm. **Subject:** Zodiac - Ram **Obv:** Sun face **Rev:** Ram **Edge:** Reeded

Date	Mintage	F12	VF20	XF40	MS60	MS63
2006	10,000	PF63 90.00	PF65 100			

KM# 390 5 HRYVEN
16.93 g., 0.925 Silver 0.5002 oz. ASW, 33 mm. **Subject:** Kyiv National University of Economics **Obv:** National arms, graph above value **Rev:** University building within circle **Edge:** Reeded

Date	Mintage	F12	VF20	XF40	MS60	MS63
2006	5,000	PF63 80.00	PF65 90.00			

KM# 402 5 HRYVEN
9.42 g., Bi-Metallic, 28 mm. **Obv:** Symbolic sound of music **Rev:** Tsimbal stringed musical instrument **Edge:** Segmented reeding

Date	Mintage	F12	VF20	XF40	MS60	MS63
2006	100,000	—	—	—	—	14.00

KM# 405 5 HRYVEN
16.82 g., 0.925 Silver 0.497 oz. ASW, 33 mm. **Subject:** Bull **Obv:** National arms

Date	Mintage	F12	VF20	XF40	MS60	MS63
2006	10,000	PF63 90.00	PF65 100			

KM# 407 5 HRYVEN
16.82 g., 0.925 Silver 0.497 oz. ASW, 33 mm. **Subject:** Gemini **Obv:** National arms

Date	Mintage	F12	VF20	XF40	MS60	MS63
2006	10,000	PF63 100	PF65 120			

KM# 409 5 HRYVEN
16.54 g., Copper-Nickel-Zinc, 35 mm. **Subject:** 10 Years of the Constitution of Ukraine **Obv:** National arms **Edge:** Reeded

Date	Mintage	F12	VF20	XF40	MS60	MS63
2006	30,000	—	—	—	—	20.00

KM# 411 5 HRYVEN
16.54 g., Copper-Nickel-Zinc, 35 mm. **Subject:** 15 Years of Ukraine Independence **Obv:** National arms **Edge:** Reeded

Date	Mintage	F12	VF20	XF40	MS60	MS63
2006	75,000	—	—	—	—	14.00

KM# 413 5 HRYVEN
16.54 g., Copper-Nickel-Zinc, 35 mm. **Subject:** 10 Years to the Currency Reform in Ukraine **Obv:** National arms **Edge:** Reeded

Date	Mintage	F12	VF20	XF40	MS60	MS63
2006	45,000	—	—	—	—	15.00

KM# 415 5 HRYVEN
16.54 g., Copper-Nickel-Zinc, 35 mm. **Subject:** 750 Years of the City of L'viv **Obv:** National arms **Edge:** Reeded

Date	Mintage	F12	VF20	XF40	MS60	MS63
2006	60,000	—	—	—	—	15.00

KM# 416 5 HRYVEN
16.82 g., 0.925 Silver 0.497 oz. ASW, 33 mm. **Subject:** Mykhailo Hrushevskyi **Obv:** National arms

Date	Mintage	F12	VF20	XF40	MS60	MS63
2006	5,000	PF65 80.00				

KM# 417 5 HRYVEN
16.82 g., 0.925 Silver 0.497 oz. ASW, 33 mm. **Subject:** Dmytro Lutsenko **Obv:** National arms

Date	Mintage	F12	VF20	XF40	MS60	MS63
2006	3,000	PF65 95.00				

KM# 418 5 HRYVEN
16.82 g., 0.925 Silver 0.497 oz. ASW, 33 mm. **Subject:** Ivan Franko **Obv:** National arms

Date	Mintage	F12	VF20	XF40	MS60	MS63
2006	5,000	PF65 80.00				

KM# 420 5 HRYVEN
16.54 g., Copper-Nickel-Zinc, 35 mm. **Subject:** Epiphany **Obv:** National arms **Edge:** Reeded

Date	Mintage	F12	VF20	XF40	MS60	MS63
2006	75,000	—	—	—	—	15.00

KM# 422 5 HRYVEN
16.54 g., Copper-Nickel-Zinc, 35 mm. **Subject:** Saint Kyryl Church **Obv:** National arms

Date	Mintage	F12	VF20	XF40	MS60	MS63
2006	45,000	—	—	—	—	15.00

KM# 419 5 HRYVEN
16.82 g., 0.925 Silver 0.497 oz. ASW, 33 mm. **Subject:** Year of the Pig **Obv:** National arms **Edge:** Reeded

Date	Mintage	F12	VF20	XF40	MS60	MS63
2007	15,000	PF63 140	PF65 150			

KM# 432 5 HRYVEN
16.54 g., Copper-Nickel-Zinc, 35 mm. **Subject:** 100th Anniversary of "Motor Sich" **Obv:** Small national arms above falcon in flight with two globes in background **Rev:** Jet engine **Edge:** Reeded

Date	Mintage	F12	VF20	XF40	MS60	MS63
2007	45,000	—	—	—	—	15.00

KM# 453 5 HRYVEN
9.40 g., Bi-Metallic, 28 mm. **Subject:** Pure water is the source of life **Obv:** Drop of water in pond **Rev:** Man taking drink at waterfall

Date	Mintage	F12	VF20	XF40	MS60	MS63
2007	50,000	—	—	—	—	15.00

KM# 455 5 HRYVEN
9.40 g., Bi-Metallic, 28 mm. **Subject:** Organization Safety and Cooperation, 16th Annual Meeting **Obv:** State emblem and ornamentation **Rev:** Parliamentary Assemby Building in Kyiv

Date	Mintage	F12	VF20	XF40	MS60	MS63
2007	35,000	—	—	—	—	17.00

KM# 456 5 HRYVEN
16.50 g., Copper-Nickel-Zinc, 35 mm. **Subject:** Odessa National Opera and Ballet, 120th Anniversary **Obv:** Ballet scene in oval **Rev:** Opera house in Odessa **Edge:** Reeded

Date	Mintage	F12	VF20	XF40	MS60	MS63
2007	35,000	—	—	—	—	15.00

KM# 457 5 HRYVEN
16.50 g., Copper-Nickel-Zinc, 35 mm. **Subject:** Chernihiv, 1100th Anniversary **Obv:** Sword hilts and slate fragment **Rev:** Town view and open book **Edge:** Reeded

Date	Mintage	F12	VF20	XF40	MS60	MS63
2007	45,000	—	—	—	—	16.00

KM# 458 5 HRYVEN
9.40 g., Bi-Metallic, 28 mm. **Subject:** Buhai **Obv:** Sound waves as a baroque ornament **Rev:** Drum-like musical instrument

Date	Mintage	F12	VF20	XF40	MS60	MS63
2007	50,000	—	—	—	—	15.00

KM# 459 5 HRYVEN
16.54 g., Copper-Nickel-Zinc, 35 mm. **Subject:** The Famine, Genocide of the Ukranian People **Obv:** Girl standing on fallow ground **Rev:** Stork within cross, candles in background **Edge:** Reeded

Date	Mintage	F12	VF20	XF40	MS60	MS63
2007	75,000	—	—	—	—	15.00

KM# 460 5 HRYVEN
16.54 g., Copper-Nickel-Zinc, 35 mm. **Subject:** Crimean Resorts, 200th Anniversary **Obv:** Seaside Resort **Rev:** Felix De Searr and well **Edge:** Reeded

Date	Mintage	F12	VF20	XF40	MS60	MS63
2007	35,000	—	—	—	—	17.00

KM# 461 5 HRYVEN
15.55 g., 0.925 Silver 0.4595 oz. ASW, 33 mm. **Subject:** Capricorn **Obv:** Sun and seasons **Rev:** Zodiac sign

Date	Mintage	F12	VF20	XF40	MS60	MS63
2007	15,000	PF63 70.00	PF65 80.00			

KM# 462 5 HRYVEN
16.82 g., 0.925 Silver 0.497 oz. ASW, 33 mm. **Subject:** Aquarius **Obv:** Sun and seasons **Rev:** Zodiac sign, man pouring water

Date	Mintage	F12	VF20	XF40	MS60	MS63
2007	15,000	PF63 70.00	PF65 80.00			

KM# 463 5 HRYVEN
16.82 g., 0.925 Silver 0.497 oz. ASW, 33 mm. **Subject:** Pisces **Obv:** Sun and seasons **Rev:** Zodiac sign, two fish

Date	Mintage	F12	VF20	XF40	MS60	MS63
2007	15,000	PF63 70.00	PF65 80.00			

KM# 464 5 HRYVEN
16.82 g., 0.925 Silver 0.497 oz. ASW, 33 mm. **Subject:** Scorpion **Obv:** Sun and seasons **Rev:** Zodiac sign, scorpion **Edge:** Reeded

Date	Mintage	F12	VF20	XF40	MS60	MS63
2007	15,000	PF63 70.00	PF65 80.00			

KM# 465 5 HRYVEN
16.82 g., 0.925 Silver 0.497 oz. ASW, 33 mm. **Subject:** Sagittarius **Obv:** Sun and seasons **Rev:** Zodiac sign, archer

Date	Mintage	F12	VF20	XF40	MS60	MS63
2007	15,000	PF63 70.00	PF65 80.00			

KM# 531 5 HRYVEN
16.54 g., Copper-Nickel, 35 mm. **Subject:** 1100th Anniversary of Perejaslav-Khmelnytskyi **Obv:** Parchment. **Obv. Legend:** НАЦІОНАЛЬНИЙ БАНК УКРА?НИ - 5 ГРИВЕНЬ / 2007 **Rev:** Old Rus cathedral, old Rus and Cossacks. **Rev. Legend:** ПЕРЕЯСЛАВ-ХМЕЛЬНИЦЬКИJ - 1100

Date	Mintage	F12	VF20	XF40	MS60	MS63
2007	45,000	—	—	—	—	16.00

KM# 511 5 HRYVEN
16.54 g., Copper-Nickel-Zinc, 35 mm. **Subject:** Rivne, 725th Anniversary **Edge:** Reeded

Date	Mintage	F12	VF20	XF40	MS60	MS63
2008	45,000	—	—	—	—	16.00

KM# 500 5 HRYVEN
16.50 g., Copper-Nickel-Zinc, 35 mm. **Subject:** The Annunciation **Edge:** Reeded

Date	Mintage	F12	VF20	XF40	MS60	MS63
2008	45,000	—	—	—	—	16.00

KM# 501 5 HRYVEN
16.50 g., Copper-Nickel-Zinc, 35 mm. **Subject:** Chernivtsi, 600th Anniversary **Edge:** Reeded

Date	Mintage	F12	VF20	XF40	MS60	MS63
2008	45,000	—	—	—	—	16.00

KM# 502 5 HRYVEN
16.50 g., Copper-Nickel-Zinc, 35 mm. **Subject:** Sniatyn, 850th Anniversary **Edge:** Reeded

Date	Mintage	F12	VF20	XF40	MS60	MS63
2008	45,000	—	—	—	—	16.00

KM# 503 5 HRYVEN
16.82 g., 0.925 Silver 0.497 oz. ASW, 33 mm. **Subject:** Year of the Rat **Rev:** Rat, diamond insert eye **Edge:** Reeded

Date	Mintage	F12	VF20	XF40	MS60	MS63
2008	15,000	PF63 90.00	PF65 100			

KM# 504 5 HRYVEN
16.82 g., 0.925 Silver 0.497 oz. ASW, 33 mm. **Subject:** Cancer **Edge:** Reeded

Date	Mintage	F12	VF20	XF40	MS60	MS63
2008	15,000	PF63 70.00	PF65 80.00			

KM# 505 5 HRYVEN
16.82 g., 0.925 Silver 0.497 oz. ASW, 33 mm. **Subject:** Roman Shukhevich, General **Edge:** Reeded

Date	Mintage	F12	VF20	XF40	MS60	MS63
2008	3,000	PF65 250				

KM# 506 5 HRYVEN
16.82 g., 0.925 Silver 0.497 oz. ASW, 33 mm. **Subject:** Leo **Edge:** Reeded

Date	Mintage	F12	VF20	XF40	MS60	MS63
2008	15,000	PF63 70.00	PF65 80.00			

KM# 507 5 HRYVEN
16.82 g., 0.925 Silver 0.497 oz. ASW, 33 mm. **Subject:** Virgo **Edge:** Reeded

Date	Mintage	F12	VF20	XF40	MS60	MS63
2008	15,000	PF63 70.00	PF65 80.00			

KM# 508 5 HRYVEN
16.82 g., 0.925 Silver 0.497 oz. ASW, 33 mm. **Subject:** Libra **Edge:** Reeded

Date	Mintage	F12	VF20	XF40	MS60	MS63
2008	15,000	PF63 70.00	PF65 80.00			

KM# 509 5 HRYVEN
16.54 g., Copper-Nickel-Zinc, 35 mm. **Subject:** State Arboretum "Trostianet-s", 175th Anniversary **Edge:** Reeded

Date	Mintage	F12	VF20	XF40	MS60	MS63
2008	45,000	—	—	—	—	15.00

KM# 510 5 HRYVEN

16.54 g., Copper-Nickel-Zinc, 35 mm. **Subject:** Christianization of the Kievan Rus, 1020th Anniversary **Edge:** Reeded

Date	Mintage	F12	VF20	XF40	MS60	MS63
2008	45,000	—	—	—	—	17.00

KM# 512 5 HRYVEN

16.54 g., Copper-Nickel-Zinc, 35 mm. **Subject:** Bohuslav, 975th Anniversary **Edge:** Reeded

Date	Mintage	F12	VF20	XF40	MS60	MS63
2008	45,000	—	—	—	—	14.00

KM# 513 5 HRYVEN

9.40 g., Bi-Metallic, 28 mm. **Subject:** Taras Shevchenko "Prosvita Society" 140th Anniversary

Date	Mintage	F12	VF20	XF40	MS60	MS63
2008	45,000	—	—	—	—	14.00

KM# 514 5 HRYVEN

16.82 g., 0.925 Silver 0.497 oz. ASW, 33 mm. **Subject:** Mariya Prymachenko

Date	Mintage	F12	VF20	XF40	MS60	MS63
2008	5,000	PF65 80.00				

KM# 530 5 HRYVEN

16.82 g., 0.925 Silver 0.497 oz. ASW, 33 mm. **Subject:** Year of the Ox **Obv:** National Arms and value **Rev:** Ox, rubies in eyes **Edge:** Reeded

Date	Mintage	F12	VF20	XF40	MS60	MS63
2009	20,000	PF63 70.00	PF65 80.00			

KM# 543 5 HRYVEN

16.82 g., 0.925 Silver 0.497 oz. ASW, 33.0 mm. **Subject:** Nikolai Gogol **Obv:** Compositions of two main subjects of Gogol's work, National Arms, value **Obv. Legend:** НАЦІОНАЛЬНИЙ БАНК УКРАЇНИ - 5 ГРИВЕНЬ / 2009 **Rev:** Nikolai's portrait **Rev. Legend:** МИКОЛА ГОГОЛЬ

Date	Mintage	F12	VF20	XF40	MS60	MS63
2009	5,000	PF65 80.00				

KM# 544 5 HRYVEN

16.82 g., 0.925 Silver 0.497 oz. ASW, 33.0 mm. **Subject:** Sholem Aleichem **Obv:** Conventionalized composition, book sheets, Aleichem's signet **Obv. Legend:** НАЦІОНАЛЬНИЙ БАНК УКРАЇНИ - 5 ГРИВЕНЬ / 2009 **Rev:** Aleichem's portrait **Rev. Legend:** МИР ВАМ - ШОЛОМ-АЛЕЙХЕМ - РАБИНОВИЧ ШОЛОМ

Date	Mintage	F12	VF20	XF40	MS60	MS63
2009	5,000	PF65 80.00				

KM# 545 5 HRYVEN

16.54 g., Copper-Nickel-Zinc, 35.0 mm. **Subject:** Simferopol, 225th Anniversary **Obv:** Main railway station, National Arms **Obv. Legend:** НАЦІОНАЛЬНИЙ БАНК УКРАЇНИ - 5 ГРИВЕНЬ 2009 **Rev:** City Coat of Arms, Architectural elements **Rev. Legend:** 225 / РОКІВ - СІМФЕРОПОЛЬ **Edge:** Reeded

Date	Mintage	F12	VF20	XF40	MS60	MS63
2009	45,000	—	—	—	—	16.00

KM# 546 5 HRYVEN

16.82 g., 0.925 Silver 0.497 oz. ASW, 33 mm. **Subject:** Ivan Kotljarevskyi **Obv:** National Arms, boat, column and helmet **Obv. Legend:** НАЦІОНАЛЬНИЙ БАНК УКРАЇНИ - П'ЯТЬ ГРИВЕНЬ **Rev:** Kotliarevskyi's portrait **Rev. Legend:** ...ПОКИ СОНЦЕ З НЕБА СЯЄ, ТЕБЕ НЕ ЗАБУДУТЬ! - ІВАН КОТЛЯРЕВСЬКИЙ

Date	Mintage	F12	VF20	XF40	MS60	MS63
2009	5,000	PF65 80.00				

KM# 547 5 HRYVEN

16.54 g., Copper-Nickel-Zinc, 35 mm. **Subject:** Mykolaiv, 220th Anniversary **Obv:** Varvarivskyi Bridge, gull, ship, anchor **Obv. Legend:** НАЦІОНАЛЬНИЙ БАНК УКРА?НИ - П'ЯТЬ ГРИВЕНЬ **Rev:** Frigate Saint Nicholas, Architecture of Mykolaiv **Rev. Legend:** МИКОЛА?В - РІК ЗАСНУВАННЯ / 1789 **Edge:** Reeded

Date	Mintage	F12	VF20	XF40	MS60	MS63
2009	45,000	—	—	—	—	16.00

KM# 548 5 HRYVEN

9.40 g., Bi-Metallic, 28 mm. **Subject:** Council of Europe, 60th Anniversary **Obv:** Stars, map of Europe **Obv. Legend:** НАЦІОНАЛЬНИЙ БАНК УКРА?НИ - П'ЯТЬ ГРИВЕНЬ **Rev:** Council of Europe logo, stars **Rev. Legend:** COUNCIL OF EUROPE, CONSEIL DE EUROPE, РАДА ?ВРОПИ

Date	Mintage	F12	VF20	XF40	MS60	MS63
2009	45,000	—	—	—	—	15.00

KM# 549 5 HRYVEN

16.82 g., 0.925 Silver 0.497 oz. ASW, 33.0 mm. **Subject:** Lviv National Medical University, 225th Anniversary **Obv:** Hippocratic Oath in Latin, National Arms, value **Obv. Legend:** НАЦІОНАЛЬНИЙ БАНК УКРАЇНИ - 5 / ГРИВЕНЬ **Rev:** University building **Rev. Legend:** 225 / РОКІВ - ІМЕНІ / ДАНИЛА / ГАЛИЦЬКОГО - ЛЬВІВСЬКИЙ НАЦІОНАЛЬНИЙ МЕДИЧНИЙ УНІВЕРСИТЕТ

Date	Mintage	F12	VF20	XF40	MS60	MS63
2009	7,000	PF63 70.00	PF65 80.00			

KM# 550 5 HRYVEN

16.54 g., Copper-Nickel-Zinc, 35 mm. **Subject:** T. H. Shevchenko National Museum, 60th Anniversary **Obv:** Kateryna painting, bandura, National Arms, value **Rev:** Museum building and portrait **Edge:** Reeded

Date	Mintage	F12	VF20	XF40	MS60	MS63
2009	30,000	—	—	—	—	15.00

KM# 553 5 HRYVEN

16.54 g., Copper-Nickel-Zinc, 35 mm. **Subject:** Pysanka - Easter Egg decorating **Obv:** Easter eggs, National Arms, value **Rev:** Easter bread, eggs. **Edge:** Reeded

Date	Mintage	F12	VF20	XF40	MS60	MS63
2009	50,000	—	—	—	—	16.00

KM# 555 5 HRYVEN

16.50 g., Copper-Nickel-Zinc, 35 mm. **Subject:** Folk crafts of the Ukraine - Bokorash (Raftsmen) **Obv:** Two birds, Carpathian landscape, trees, cottages, logs **Obv. Legend:** НАЦІОНАЛЬНИЙ БАНК УКРА?НИ - 5 / ГРИВЕНЬ / 2009 **Rev:** Bokorash directing raft **Rev. Legend:** БОКОРАШ **Edge:** Reeded

Date	Mintage	F12	VF20	XF40	MS60	MS63
2009	45,000	—	—	—	—	15.00

KM# 557 5 HRYVEN

16.54 g., Copper-Nickel-Zinc, 35.0 mm. **Subject:** International Year of Astronomy **Obv:** Urania, planets, stars, solar system, National Arms, value **Obv. Legend:** НАЦІОНАЛЬНИЙ БАНК УКРА?НИ - 5 ГРИВЕНЬ **Rev:** Yurii Drohobych, International Year of Astronomy logo, artifacts **Rev. Legend:** МІЖНАРОДНИЙ / РІК / АСТРОНОМІ? **Edge:** Reeded

Date	Mintage	F12	VF20	XF40	MS60	MS63
2009	45,000	—	—	—	—	15.00

KM# 573 5 HRYVEN

16.50 g., Copper-Nickel-Zinc, 35 mm. **Subject:** Ukrainian Folk crafts - Cartwright **Obv:** Wood cart and wheels **Rev:** Woodcraftsman hewing wood to make cart detail **Edge:** Reeded

Date	Mintage	F12	VF20	XF40	MS60	MS63
2009	45,000	—	—	—	—	15.00

KM# 567 5 HRYVEN

16.82 g., 0.925 Silver 0.497 oz. ASW, 33 mm. **Subject:** Yevhen Paton **Obv:** Paton Bridge and the footbridge over Petrovska Alley **Rev:** Paton's portrait

Date	Mintage	F12	VF20	XF40	MS60	MS63
2010	5,000	PF65 80.00				

KM# 566 5 HRYVEN
16.82 g., 0.925 Silver 0.497 oz. ASW, 33 mm. **Subject:** Ivan Puliui **Obv:** X-ray of jewelry portrait **Rev:** Puliui portrait and text

Date	Mintage	F12	VF20	XF40	MS60	MS63
2010	5,000	PF65 80.00				

KM# 568 5 HRYVEN
16.82 g., 0.925 Silver 0.497 oz. ASW, 33 mm. **Subject:** Oksana Petrusenko **Obv:** Poppy flower and musical notation **Rev:** Bust facing

Date	Mintage	F12	VF20	XF40	MS60	MS63
2010	5,000	PF65 80.00				

KM# 569 5 HRYVEN
16.82 g., 0.925 Silver 0.497 oz. ASW, 33 mm. **Subject:** Mykola Ivanovych Pyrohov, scientist and surgeon **Obv:** Sepulchral church erected over scientist's tomb **Rev:** Half length figure in apron holding surgical instruments

Date	Mintage	F12	VF20	XF40	MS60	MS63
2010	5,000	PF65 80.00				

KM# 577 5 HRYVEN
16.82 g., 0.925 Silver 0.497 oz. ASW, 33 mm. **Subject:** Year of the tiger **Obv:** Vegitable ornamention pattern, National Arms **Rev:** Stylized playful tiger **Edge:** Reeded

Date	Mintage	F12	VF20	XF40	MS60	MS63
2010	20,000	PF63 70.00	PF65 80.00			

KM# 579 5 HRYVEN
16.54 g., Copper-Nickel-Zinc, 35 mm. **Subject:** Kyiv National University Astronomical Observatory, 165th Anniversary **Obv:** Observatory building **Rev:** Telescope and night sky **Edge:** Reeded

Date	Mintage	F12	VF20	XF40	MS60	MS63
2010	45,000	—	—	—	—	15.00

KM# 582 5 HRYVEN
16.82 g., 0.925 Silver 0.497 oz. ASW, 33 mm. **Subject:** Lviv Polytechnic National University, 165th Anniversary **Obv:** Arts and Science sculpture from main building **Rev:** University building façade

Date	Mintage	F12	VF20	XF40	MS60	MS63
2010	5,000	PF65 80.00				

KM# 584 5 HRYVEN
15.55 g., 0.925 Silver 0.4595 oz. ASW, 33 mm. **Subject:** Kharkiv Polytechnic Institute, 125th Anniversary **Obv:** Radio telescope and open book **Rev:** University building and oval portrait of V.L. Kyrpychov

Date	Mintage	F12	VF20	XF40	MS60	MS63
2010	5,000	PF65 80.00				

KM# 587 5 HRYVEN
16.50 g., Copper-Nickel-Zinc, 35 mm. **Subject:** Folk Crafts - Weaver **Obv:** Spinning wheel and weaving products **Rev:** Woman working on a loom **Edge:** Reeded

Date	Mintage	F12	VF20	XF40	MS60	MS63
2010	45,000	—	—	—	—	15.00

KM# 589 5 HRYVEN
16.50 g., Copper-Nickel-Zinc, 35 mm. **Subject:** UKranian spas **Obv:** Two cornucopiae and the Savior's Feast **Rev:** Peasants getting food gifts blessed **Edge:** Reeded

Date	Mintage	F12	VF20	XF40	MS60	MS63
2010	45,000	—	—	—	—	15.00

KM# 592 5 HRYVEN
16.50 g., Copper-Nickel-Zinc, 35 mm. **Subject:** Lutsk, 925th Anniversary **Obv:** Entrance tower to town's castle **Rev:** City view from tower top, city carms above **Edge:** Reeded

Date	Mintage	F12	VF20	XF40	MS60	MS63
2010	45,000	—	—	—	—	15.00

KM# 598 5 HRYVEN
16.82 g., 0.925 Silver 0.497 oz. ASW, 33 mm. **Subject:** Johann Georg Pinzel **Obv:** Buchach City hall **Rev:** Sculptor and angel

Date	Mintage	F12	VF20	XF40	MS60	MS63
2010	5,000	PF65 80.00				

KM# 599 5 HRYVEN
16.82 g., 0.925 Silver 0.497 oz. ASW, 33 mm. **Subject:** Ivan Fedorov **Obv:** Apostol book page and large quill pin **Rev:** Ivan Fedorov portrait facing

Date	Mintage	F12	VF20	XF40	MS60	MS63
2010	5,000	PF65 80.00				

KM# 601 5 HRYVEN
16.54 g., Copper-Nickel-Zinc, 35 mm. **Subject:** Maritime History **Obv:** Banner seperating compas rose and seal of the Zaporohian Host **Rev:** Cossack boat of the 18th century

Date	Mintage	F12	VF20	XF40	MS60	MS63
2010	45,000	—	—	—	—	15.00

KM# 604 5 HRYVEN
16.50 g., Copper-Nickel-Zinc, 35 mm. **Subject:** Folk Crafts - Potter **Obv:** Pottery flanking central pattern **Rev:** Potter at wheel **Edge:** Reeded

Date	Mintage	F12	VF20	XF40	MS60	MS63
2010	45,000	—	—	—	—	15.00

KM# 611 5 HRYVEN
16.82 g., 0.925 Silver 0.497 oz. ASW, 33 mm. **Subject:** Pavlo Tychyna **Obv:** View of family homestead, mallow flowers, national arms **Rev:** Portrait with books **Edge:** lettered, incuse **Edge Lettering:** .925 15.55

Date	Mintage	F12	VF20	XF40	MS60	MS63
2011	5,000	PF65 85.00				

KM# 610 5 HRYVEN
16.82 g., 0.925 Silver 0.497 oz. ASW, 33 mm. **Subject:** Year of the Cat **Obv:** National arms, value and floral design **Rev:** Playful cat with green alpinites in eyes **Edge:** Reeded

Date	Mintage	F12	VF20	XF40	MS60	MS63
2011	20,000	PF63 70.00	PF65 80.00			

KM# 613 5 HRYVEN
16.82 g., 0.925 Silver 0.497 oz. ASW, 33 mm. **Subject:** Ivan Franko National University, Lviv, 350th Anniversary **Obv:** National arms, statuary group, value **Rev:** Main Building façade **Edge Lettering:** .925 15.55 (Mint logo)

Date	Mintage	F12	VF20	XF40	MS60	MS63
2011	7,000	PF63 75.00	PF65 85.00			

KM# 615 5 HRYVEN
16.54 g., Copper-Nickel-Zinc, 35 mm. **Obv:** Blacksmith items, two birds **Rev:** Blacksmith at work **Edge:** Reeded

Date	Mintage	F12	VF20	XF40	MS60	MS63
2011	45,000	—	—	—	—	15.00

KM# 618 5 HRYVEN
16.82 g., 0.925 Silver 0.497 oz. ASW, 33 mm. **Subject:** Heorhii Berehovyi **Obv:** Spacecraft launch, in orbit, sun **Rev:** Bust facing

Date	Mintage	F12	VF20	XF40	MS60	MS63
2011	5,000	PF65 90.00				

KM# 619 5 HRYVEN
16.54 g., Copper-Nickel-Zinc, 35 mm. **Subject:** Taras Shevchenko, 150th Anniversary of Death **Obv:** Shevchenko's monument **Rev:** Portrait **Edge:** Reeded

Date	Mintage	F12	VF20	XF40	MS60	MS63
2011	35,000	—	—	—	—	15.00

KM# 620 5 HRYVEN
16.82 g., 0.925 Silver 0.497 oz. ASW, 33 mm. **Subject:** Okeksandr Bohomolets **Obv:** Hands of an adult and child **Rev:** Portrait of Bohomolets

Date	Mintage	F12	VF20	XF40	MS60	MS63
2011	5,000	PF65 80.00				

KM# 621 5 HRYVEN
16.54 g., Copper-Nickel-Zinc, 35 mm. **Subject:** Taras Shevchenko National Prize of Ukraine, 50th Anniversary **Obv:** Open book, quill, palette, brushes and National Arms **Rev:** Shevchenko Portrait **Edge:** Reeded

Date	Mintage	F12	VF20	XF40	MS60	MS63
2011	35,000	—	—	—	—	15.00

KM# 622 5 HRYVEN
16.54 g., Copper-Nickel-Zinc, 35 mm. **Subject:** Constitution, 15th Anniversary **Obv:** National flag in color within wreath **Rev:** Book of the Constitution and Verkhjovna Rada building **Edge:** Reeded

Date	Mintage	F12	VF20	XF40	MS60	MS63
2011	30,000	—	—	—	—	16.00

KM# 623 5 HRYVEN
16.54 g., Copper-Nickel-Zinc, 35 mm. **Subject:** Zbarazh, 800th Anniversary **Obv:** Jerusalem cross on wall of Our Saviour's Transfiguration Church **Rev:** Gate of the Zbarazh Castle **Edge:** Reeded

Date	Mintage	F12	VF20	XF40	MS60	MS63
2011	35,000	—	—	—	—	15.00

KM# 625 5 HRYVEN
16.54 g., Copper-Nickel-Zinc, 35 mm. **Obv:** Baroque design from Church **Rev:** St. Andrew's Church **Edge:** Reeded

Date	Mintage	F12	VF20	XF40	MS60	MS63
2011	45,000	—	—	—	—	15.00

KM# 627 5 HRYVEN
16.54 g., Copper-Nickel-Zinc, 35 mm. **Obv:** Couple in a dance **Rev:** Hopak folk dance **Edge:** Reeded

Date	Mintage	F12	VF20	XF40	MS60	MS63
2011	45,000	—	—	—	—	15.00

KM# 629 5 HRYVEN
16.54 g., Copper-Nickel-Zinc, 35 mm. **Subject:** Independence, 20th anniversary **Obv:** National arms, rushnyks and portraits **Rev:** Legend **Edge:** Reeded

Date	Mintage	F12	VF20	XF40	MS60	MS63
2011	45,000	—	—	—	—	17.00

KM# 634 5 HRYVEN
16.82 g., 0.925 Silver 0.497 oz. ASW, 33 mm. **Subject:** Mykhailo Yangel, 100th Anniversary of Birth **Obv:** Kosmos launch and satellite, earth in background **Rev:** Yangel portrait

Date	Mintage	F12	VF20	XF40	MS60	MS63
2011	5,000	PF65 90.00				

KM# 635 5 HRYVEN
16.82 g., 0.925 Silver 0.497 oz. ASW, 33 mm. **Subject:** Liudmyla Vasylevska, 150th Anniversary of Birth **Obv:** Girl near the sea **Rev:** Vasylevska portrait

Date	Mintage	F12	VF20	XF40	MS60	MS63
2011	5,000	PF65 80.00				

KM# 638 5 HRYVEN
9.40 g., Bi-Metallic, 28 mm. **Subject:** International year of Forests **Obv:** Conceptual tree **Rev:** Tree in leaf **Edge:** Segmented reeding

Date	Mintage	F12	VF20	XF40	MS60	MS63
2011	30,000	—	—	—	—	16.00

KM# 639 5 HRYVEN
16.82 g., 0.925 Silver 0.497 oz. ASW, 33 mm. **Subject:** International Year of Forests **Obv:** Two birds sitting on branches **Rev:** Hand-like branches extended to the Sun

Date	Mintage	F12	VF20	XF40	MS60	MS63
2011 Antique finish	3,000	PF65 100				

KM# 645 5 HRYVEN
16.82 g., 0.925 Silver 0.497 oz. ASW, 33 mm. **Subject:** Year of the Dragon **Obv:** National arms **Rev:** Dragon with orange zirconia crystals in eyes

Date	Mintage	F12	VF20	XF40	MS60	MS63
2011	20,000	PF63 70.00	PF65 80.00			

KM# 647 5 HRYVEN
16.54 g., Copper-Nickel-Zinc, 35 mm. **Subject:** UEFA Euro 2012 Final Tournament **Obv:** Players superimposed on large 2012 in background **Rev:** UEFA logo and map of europe **Edge:** Reeded

Date	Mintage	F12	VF20	XF40	MS60	MS63
2011	100,000	—	—	—	—	15.00

KM# 648 5 HRYVEN
16.54 g., 0.925 Copper-Nickel-Zinc 0.4887 oz., 35 mm. **Subject:** UEFA Euro 2012 Final Tournament **Obv:** Two players within stadium **Rev:** Logo and map of Ukraine **Edge:** Reeded

Date	Mintage	F12	VF20	XF40	MS60	MS63
2011	100,000	—	—	—	—	15.00

KM# 649 5 HRYVEN
16.54 g., Copper-Nickel-Zinc, 35 mm. **Subject:** UEFA Euro 2012 Final Tournament **Obv:** UEFA logo and map of the Ukraine **Rev:** Soccer plater and Lviv stadium **Edge:** Reeded

Date	Mintage	F12	VF20	XF40	MS60	MS63
2011	100,000	—	—	—	—	15.00

KM# 650 5 HRYVEN
16.54 g., Copper-Nickel-Zinc, 35 mm. **Subject:** UEFA Euro 2012 Final Tournament **Obv:** UEFA logo and map of the Ukraine **Rev:** Two soccer players and Metalist Stadium, Kharkiv **Edge:** Reeded

Date	Mintage	F12	VF20	XF40	MS60	MS63
2011	100,000	—	—	—	—	15.00

KM# 651 5 HRYVEN
16.54 g., Copper-Nickel-Zinc, 35 mm. **Subject:** UEFA Euro 2012 Final Tournament **Obv:** UEFA logo and map of the Ukraine **Rev:** Soccer player and Donbass Arena, Donetsk **Edge:** Reeded

Date	Mintage	F12	VF20	XF40	MS60	MS63
2011	100,000	—	—	—	—	15.00

KM# 653 5 HRYVEN
7.78 g., 0.9999 Gold 0.2485 oz. AGW, 20 mm. **Obv:** Logo of the Ukraine National Bank **Rev:** Archangel Michael

Date	Mintage	F12	VF20	XF40	MS60	MS63
2011	3,000	—	—	—	—	550
2012	2,000	—	—	—	—	500
2013	3,000	—	—	—	—	475

KM# 655 5 HRYVEN
16.82 g., 0.925 Silver 0.497 oz. ASW, 33 mm. **Subject:** Eugene Grebinka **Obv:** Cossack horseman **Rev:** Grebinka portrait

Date	Mintage	F12	VF20	XF40	MS60	MS63
2012	3,000	PF65 85.00				

KM# 657 5 HRYVEN
16.54 g., Copper-Nickel-Zinc, 35 mm. **Subject:** Nikitsky Botanical Garden **Edge:** Reeded

Date	Mintage	F12	VF20	XF40	MS60	MS63
2012	Est. 35000	—	—	—	—	15.00

KM# 659 5 HRYVEN
16.50 g., Copper-Nickel, 35 mm. **Subject:** 350th Anniversary - City of Ivano-Frankivsk

Date	Mintage	F12	VF20	XF40	MS60	MS63
2012	Est. 35000	—	—	—	—	15.00

KM# 660 5 HRYVEN
16.50 g., Copper-Nickel-Zinc, 35 mm. **Subject:** Folk Craft, Kushnir (Furrier) **Edge:** Reeded

Date	Mintage	F12	VF20	XF40	MS60	MS63
2012	30,000	—	—	—	—	15.00

KM# 663 5 HRYVEN
33.63 g., 0.925 Silver 0.9937 oz. ASW, 38.6 mm. **Subject:** Folk Music **Obv:** Wreath of periwinkle flowers covered with blue enamel with ribbons **Rev:** Couple **Edge:** Incuse lettering

Date	Mintage	F12	VF20	XF40	MS60	MS63
2012	5,000	PF65 80.00				

KM# 664 5 HRYVEN
Copper-Nickel-Zinc **Subject:** Maritime History - Ancient Navigation **Obv:** Ancient coin of the Bosporan Kingdom **Rev:** Ancient sailing ship **Edge:** Reeded

Date	Mintage	F12	VF20	XF40	MS60	MS63
2012	30,000	—	—	—	—	15.00

KM# 670 5 HRYVEN
16.54 g., Copper-Nickel-Zinc, 35 mm. **Subject:** Folk Crafts **Obv:** Glassblown products **Rev:** Glassblower **Edge:** Reeded

Date	Mintage	F12	VF20	XF40	MS60	MS63
2012	35,000	—	—	—	—	15.00

KM# 671 5 HRYVEN
16.93 g., 0.925 Silver 0.5002 oz. ASW, 33 mm. **Subject:** Oleksa Novakibvskyi, painter **Obv:** Value and home **Rev:** Portrait

Date	Mintage	F12	VF20	XF40	MS60	MS63
2012	3,000	PF65 60.00				

KM# 678 5 HRYVEN
16.54 g., Copper-Nickel-Zinc, 35 mm. **Subject:** Yeletskyi Holy Dormition Cloister **Obv:** National arms, Main building of the cloister **Rev:** Image of the Mother of God icon **Edge:** Reeded

Date	Mintage	F12	VF20	XF40	MS60	MS63
2012	35,000	—	—	—	—	15.00

KM# 681 5 HRYVEN
16.54 g., Copper-Nickel-Zinc **Subject:** Town of Sudak **Obv:** National arms, St. George, value **Rev:** Town view with beach **Edge:** Reeded

Date	Mintage	F12	VF20	XF40	MS60	MS63
2012	30,000	—	—	—	—	15.00

KM# 683 5 HRYVEN
16.54 g., Copper-Nickel-Zinc, 35 mm. **Subject:** Chyhyryn City, 500th Anniversary **Obv:** National arms, plan of the old town, value **Rev:** Chyhyryn city view **Edge:** Reeded

Date	Mintage	F12	VF20	XF40	MS60	MS63
2012	30,000	—	—	—	—	15.00

KM# 684 5 HRYVEN
16.54 g., Copper-Nickel-Zinc **Subject:** Folk Music **Obv:** Wreath of Periwinkle flowers with ribbons **Rev:** Couple **Edge:** Reeded

Date	Mintage	F12	VF20	XF40	MS60	MS63
2012	30,000	—	—	—	—	15.00

KM# 685 5 HRYVEN
16.50 g., Copper-Nickel-Zinc, 35 mm. **Subject:** Kacha town, Aviation history **Obv:** National arms, Kacha arms and value **Rev:** Winged man holds plane

Date	Mintage	F12	VF20	XF40	MS60	MS63
2012	20,000	—	—	—	—	17.00

KM# 686 5 HRYVEN
16.54 g., Copper-Nickel-Zinc, 35 mm. **Subject:** Year of the Bat **Obv:** National arms, bat silhouette **Rev:** Bat in flight

Date	Mintage	F12	VF20	XF40	MS60	MS63
2012	20,000	—	—	—	—	17.00

KM# 690 5 HRYVEN
9.42 g., Bi-Metallic **Subject:** Zhytomyr Oblast, 75th Anniversary **Obv:** Symbols of the Zhytomyr region, national arms **Rev:** Arms of the Zhytomyr Oblast **Edge:** Segmented reeding

Date	Mintage	F12	VF20	XF40	MS60	MS63
2012	15,000	—	—	—	—	25.00

KM# 691 5 HRYVEN
9.42 g., Bi-Metallic, 28 mm. **Subject:** Mykolaiv Oblast, 75th Anniversary **Obv:** National arms and value **Rev:** Ship, amphora, ancient coin and sunflowers

Date	Mintage	F12	VF20	XF40	MS60	MS63
2012	15,000	—	—	—	—	25.00

KM# 692 5 HRYVEN
16.54 g., Copper-Nickel-Zinc, 35 mm. **Subject:** Year of the Bat **Obv:** National arms, silhouette of bat, value **Rev:** Bat in flight **Edge:** Reeded

Date	Mintage	F12	VF20	XF40	MS60	MS63
2012	20,000	—	—	—	—	17.00

KM# 693 5 HRYVEN
16.93 g., 0.925 Silver 0.5002 oz. ASW, 33 mm. **Subject:** Year of the Snake **Obv:** National arms, value **Rev:** Snake with green eye

Date	Mintage	F12	VF20	XF40	MS60	MS63
2012	20,000	PF63 55.00	PF65 60.00			

KM# 696 5 HRYVEN
16.93 g., 0.925 Silver 0.5002 oz. ASW, 33 mm. **Subject:** Volodymyr Vernadsky, first president of the Ukrainian Academy of Sciences **Obv:** National arms and value **Rev:** Portrait **Edge:** Incuse lettering

Date	Mintage	F12	VF20	XF40	MS60	MS63
2013	5,000	PF65 60.00				

KM# 700 5 HRYVEN
16.54 g., Copper-Nickel-Zinc, 35 mm. **Subject:** House of Chimeras **Obv:** National arms, Vladyslav Horodetskyi, architect, value **Rev:** Fragment of sculptural composition **Edge:** Reeded

Date	Mintage	F12	VF20	XF40	MS60	MS63
2013	30,000	—	—	—	—	15.00

KM# 701 5 HRYVEN
9.42 g., Bi-Metallic, 28 mm. **Subject:** Luhansk Oblast, 75th Anniversary **Obv:** Industrial landscape, marmot, National arms and value **Rev:** Luhansk Oblast arms

Date	Mintage	F12	VF20	XF40	MS60	MS63
2013	20,000	—	—	—	—	25.00

KM# 702 5 HRYVEN
16.930 Silver ASW, 33 mm. **Subject:** Maternity **Obv:** National arms, baby carriage and value **Rev:** Mother holding baby **Edge:** Incuse lettering

Date	Mintage	F12	VF20	XF40	MS60	MS63
2013	5,000	PF65 60.00				

KM# 705 5 HRYVEN
16.54 g., Copper-Nickel-Zinc, 35 mm. **Subject:** Figures **Rev:** National arms, value, pectoral cross and symbols of the four Evangelists **Edge:** Reeded

Date	Mintage	F12	VF20	XF40	MS60	MS63
2013	30,000	—	—	—	—	17.00

KM# 515 10 HRYVNI
33.62 g., 0.925 Silver 0.9935 oz. ASW, 38.6 mm. **Subject:** The Annunciation **Edge:** Reeded

Date	Mintage	F12	VF20	XF40	MS60	MS63
2008	8,000	PF63 85.00	PF65 95.00			

KM# 665 10 HRYVNI
33.62 g., 0.925 Silver 0.9934 oz. ASW, 38.61 mm. **Subject:** Maritime History - Ancient Navigation **Obv:** Ancient coin of the Bisporan Kingdom **Rev:** Ancient sailing ship **Edge:** Lettered

Date	Mintage	F12	VF20	XF40	MS60	MS63
2012	8,000	PF63 85.00	PF65 95.00			

KM# 113 10 HRYVEN
33.62 g., 0.925 Silver 0.9935 oz. ASW, 38.61 mm. **Subject:** Ivan Mazepa (Cossack leader) **Obv:** Arms with supporters within beaded circle **Rev:** Half figure divides beaded circle flanked by palace and oval shield **Edge:** Reeded

Date	Mintage	F12	VF20	XF40	MS60	MS63
2001	—	PF65 200				

KM# 114 10 HRYVEN
33.62 g., 0.925 Silver 0.9935 oz. ASW, 38.61 mm. **Subject:** Great Prince Yaroslav the Wise **Obv:** Value within grape wreath **Rev:** Mosaic head facing, half length figure facing holding scroll and dome building **Edge:** Reeded

Date	Mintage	F12	VF20	XF40	MS60	MS63
2001	—	PF65 1,400				

KM# 115 10 HRYVEN
33.62 g., 0.925 Silver 0.9935 oz. ASW, 38.61 mm. **Series:** Ukranian Flora and Fauna **Obv:** National arms and date divides wreath, value within **Rev:** Lynx with offspring **Edge:** Reeded

Date	Mintage	F12	VF20	XF40	MS60	MS63
2001		PF65 475				

KM# 130 10 HRYVEN
33.62 g., 0.925 Silver 0.9935 oz. ASW, 38.61 mm. **Subject:** 10th Anniversary - National Bank **Obv:** National arms and value between arches **Rev:** Large building entrance **Edge:** Reeded

Date	Mintage	F12	VF20	XF40	MS60	MS63
2001	3,000	PF65 250				

KM# 131 10 HRYVEN
33.62 g., 0.925 Silver 0.9935 oz. ASW, 38.61 mm. **Series:** Olympics **Obv:** National arms and value on ice **Rev:** Stylized ice dancing couple **Edge:** Reeded

Date	Mintage	F12	VF20	XF40	MS60	MS63
2001	15,000	PF63 85.00	PF65 100			

KM# 141 10 HRYVEN
33.62 g., 0.925 Silver 0.9935 oz. ASW, 38.61 mm. **Subject:** Flora and Fauna **Obv:** National arms and date divides wreath, value within **Rev:** Pine branch with cone **Edge:** Reeded

Date	Mintage	F12	VF20	XF40	MS60	MS63
2001	3,000	PF65 350				

KM# 142 10 HRYVEN
33.62 g., 0.925 Silver 0.9935 oz. ASW, 38.61 mm. **Subject:** Khan Palace in Bakhchisarai **Obv:** Value in arch **Rev:** Courtyard view **Edge:** Reeded

Date	Mintage	F12	VF20	XF40	MS60	MS63
2001		PF65 400				

KM# 143 10 HRYVEN
4.31 g., 0.900 Gold 0.1239 oz. AGW, 16 mm. **Subject:** 10 Years Independence **Obv:** National arms **Rev:** Parliament building on map **Edge:** Plain

Date	Mintage	F12	VF20	XF40	MS60	MS63
2001	—	PF65 1,100				

KM# 165 10 HRYVEN
33.62 g., 0.925 Silver 0.9935 oz. ASW, 38.61 mm. **Subject:** Olympics **Obv:** National arms and value on ice **Rev:** Stylized hockey player **Edge:** Reeded

Date	Mintage	F12	VF20	XF40	MS60	MS63
2001	15,000	PF63 85.00	PF65 100			

KM# 229 10 HRYVEN
33.62 g., 0.925 Silver 0.9935 oz. ASW, 38.61 mm. **Obv:** National arms and date divides wreath, value within **Rev:** Eurasian Eagle Owl on branch **Edge:** Reeded

Date	Mintage	F12	VF20	XF40	MS60	MS63
2002	3,000	PF65 650				

KM# 145 10 HRYVEN
33.62 g., 0.925 Silver 0.9935 oz. ASW, 38.61 mm. **Subject:** Ivan Sirko **Obv:** Arms with supporters within beaded circle **Rev:** Cossack battle scene divides beaded circle **Edge:** Reeded

Date	Mintage	F12	VF20	XF40	MS60	MS63
2002	3,000	PF65 400				

KM# 146 10 HRYVEN
33.62 g., 0.925 Silver 0.9935 oz. ASW, 38.61 mm. **Obv:** National arms and value on ice **Rev:** Stylized speed skater **Edge:** Reeded

Date	Mintage	F12	VF20	XF40	MS60	MS63
2002	3,000	PF65 150				

KM# 160 10 HRYVEN
33.95 g., 0.925 Silver 1.0032 oz. ASW, 38.61 mm. **Obv:** Value encircled by angels flanked by stars **Rev:** Steepled church and tower **Edge:** Reeded

Date	Mintage	F12	VF20	XF40	MS60	MS63
2002	3,000	PF65 375				

KM# 161 10 HRYVEN
33.62 g., 0.925 Silver 0.9935 oz. ASW, 38.61 mm. **Subject:** Grand Prince Vladimir Monomakh **Obv:** Value within jewelry design **Rev:** Bust holding book flanked by buildings and St. George **Edge:** Reeded

Date	Mintage	F12	VF20	XF40	MS60	MS63
2002	3,000	PF65 550				

KM# 162 10 HRYVEN
33.62 g., 0.925 Silver 0.9935 oz. ASW, 38.61 mm. **Subject:**
Prince Svyatoslav **Obv:** Value in ornate design **Rev:** Armored
half length figure facing **Edge:** Reeded

Date	Mintage	F12	VF20	XF40	MS60	MS63
2002	3,000	PF65 550				

KM# 164 10 HRYVEN
33.62 g., 0.925 Silver 0.9935 oz. ASW, 38.61 mm. **Subject:**
Christmas **Obv:** National arms within star above value **Rev:**
Christmas pageant scene **Edge:** Reeded

Date	Mintage	F12	VF20	XF40	MS60	MS63
2002	3,000	PF65 600				

KM# 176 10 HRYVEN
33.62 g., 0.925 Silver 0.9935 oz. ASW, 38.61 mm. **Subject:**
Olympics **Obv:** Two ancient women with seedlings **Rev:**
Swimmer **Edge:** Reeded

Date	Mintage	F12	VF20	XF40	MS60	MS63
2002	15,000	PF63 95.00	PF65 110			

KM# 177 10 HRYVEN
33.62 g., 0.925 Silver 0.9935 oz. ASW, 38.61 mm. **Subject:**
Hetman Pylyp Orlik 1672-1742 **Obv:** Arms with supporters
within beaded circle **Rev:** Standing figure facing holding scroll
flanked by other standing figures **Edge:** Reeded

Date	Mintage	F12	VF20	XF40	MS60	MS63
2002	3,000	PF65 350				

KM# 198 10 HRYVEN
33.62 g., 0.925 Silver 0.9935 oz. ASW, 38.61 mm. **Obv:**
National arms and date divides wreath, value within **Rev:**
European bison **Edge:** Reeded

Date	Mintage	F12	VF20	XF40	MS60	MS63
2003	2,000	PF65 600				

KM# 189 10 HRYVEN
33.62 g., 0.925 Silver 0.9935 oz. ASW, 38.61 mm. **Subject:**
Olympics **Obv:** Two ancient women with seedlings **Rev:** Boxer
Edge: Reeded

Date	Mintage	F12	VF20	XF40	MS60	MS63
2003	15,000	PF63 95.00	PF65 110			

KM# 190 10 HRYVEN
33.62 g., 0.925 Silver 0.9935 oz. ASW, 38.61 mm. **Obv:** Fancy
art work and sculpture **Rev:** Livadia Palace view **Edge:** Reeded

Date	Mintage	F12	VF20	XF40	MS60	MS63
2003	3,000	PF65 300				

KM# 191 10 HRYVEN
33.62 g., 0.925 Silver 0.9935 oz. ASW, 38.61 mm. **Obv:**
National arms on sun, flying geese divides beaded circle **Rev:**
Antonov AN-2 biplane divides beaded circle **Edge:** Reeded

Date	Mintage	F12	VF20	XF40	MS60	MS63
2003	3,000	PF65 320				

KM# 192 10 HRYVEN
33.62 g., 0.925 Silver 0.9935 oz. ASW, 38.61 mm. **Obv:** Easter
eggs around arms above value **Rev:** Easter celebration **Edge:**
Reeded

Date	Mintage	F12	VF20	XF40	MS60	MS63
2003	3,000	PF65 500				

KM# 193 10 HRYVEN
33.62 g., 0.925 Silver 0.9935 oz. ASW, 38.61 mm. **Obv:** Angels,
national arms and value **Rev:** The protection of the Virgin Mary
over the Pochayiv Lavra (Monastery) **Edge:** Reeded

Date	Mintage	F12	VF20	XF40	MS60	MS63
2003	—	PF65 200				

KM# 194 10 HRYVEN
33.62 g., 0.925 Silver 0.9935 oz. ASW, 38.61 mm. **Obv:**
National arms and date divide wreath, value within **Rev:** Long-
snouted seahorse **Edge:** Reeded

Date	Mintage	F12	VF20	XF40	MS60	MS63
2003	2,000	PF65 750				

KM# 195 10 HRYVEN
33.62 g., 0.925 Silver 0.9935 oz. ASW, 38.61 mm. **Subject:**
Kyrylo Rozumovskyi (Cossack leader) **Obv:** Arms with
supporters within beaded circle **Rev:** Half length figure 1/4 left
within beaded circle **Edge:** Reeded

Date	Mintage	F12	VF20	XF40	MS60	MS63
2003	3,000	PF65 350				

KM# 196 10 HRYVEN
33.62 g., 0.925 Silver 0.9935 oz. ASW, 38.61 mm. **Subject:**
Pavlo Polubotok (Cossack leader) **Obv:** Arms with supporters
within beaded circle **Rev:** Half length figure within beaded circle
Edge: Reeded

Date	Mintage	F12	VF20	XF40	MS60	MS63
2003	3,000	PF65 375				

KM# 197   10 HRYVEN
33.62 g., 0.925 Silver 0.9935 oz. ASW, 38.61 mm. **Obv:** Map, national arms and value   **Rev:** Genoese Fortress in Sudak **Edge:** Reeded

Date	Mintage	F12	VF20	XF40	MS60	MS63
2003	3,000	PF65 300				

KM# 206   10 HRYVEN
33.91 g., 0.925 Silver 1.002 oz. ASW, 38.61 mm. **Subject:** Azov Dolphin **Obv:** National arms and date divides wreath, value within **Rev:** Harbor Porpoises **Edge:** Reeded

Date	Mintage	F12	VF20	XF40	MS60	MS63
2004	8,000	PF63 135	PF65 150			

KM# 207   10 HRYVEN
33.91 g., 0.925 Silver 1.002 oz. ASW, 38.61 mm. **Subject:** Football World Cup - 2006 **Obv:** Soccer ball in net **Rev:** Two soccer players **Edge:** Reeded

Date	Mintage	F12	VF20	XF40	MS60	MS63
2004	50,000	PF63 180	PF65 200			

KM# 223   10 HRYVEN
33.91 g., 0.925 Silver 1.002 oz. ASW, 38.61 mm. **Obv:** National arms on sun, flying geese and value divides beaded circle **Rev:** AH-140 Airliner divides beaded circle **Edge:** Reeded

Date	Mintage	F12	VF20	XF40	MS60	MS63
2004	10,000	PF63 150	PF65 170			

KM# 224   10 HRYVEN
33.91 g., 0.925 Silver 1.002 oz. ASW, 38.61 mm. **Subject:** Ice Breaker "Captain Belousov" **Obv:** National arms on ship's wheel and anchor **Rev:** Ice breaker ship **Edge:** Reeded

Date	Mintage	F12	VF20	XF40	MS60	MS63
2004	10,000	PF63 90.00	PF65 100			

KM# 225   10 HRYVEN
33.62 g., 0.925 Silver 0.9935 oz. ASW, 38.61 mm. **Subject:** Whit Sunday **Obv:** National arms within wreath above value flanked by sprigs **Rev:** Four women folk dancers and child **Edge:** Reeded

Date	Mintage	F12	VF20	XF40	MS60	MS63
2004	10,000	PF63 275	PF65 300			

KM# 339   10 HRYVEN
33.62 g., 0.925 Silver 0.9935 oz. ASW, 38.61 mm. **Subject:** Ostrozhsky Family **Obv:** Our Lady of Duben and Elias Icon **Rev:** Three cameos above crowned shield **Edge:** Reeded

Date	Mintage	F12	VF20	XF40	MS60	MS63
2004	3,000	PF65 270				

KM# 340   10 HRYVEN
33.62 g., 0.925 Silver 0.9935 oz. ASW, 38.61 mm. **Subject:** St. Yura Cathedral **Obv:** Statue of St. George on horse killing dragon **Rev:** Cathedral **Edge:** Reeded

Date	Mintage	F12	VF20	XF40	MS60	MS63
ND (2004)	8,000	PF63 100	PF65 120			

KM# 342   10 HRYVEN
33.62 g., 0.925 Silver 0.9935 oz. ASW, 38.61 mm. **Subject:** Defense of Sevastopol 1854-56 **Obv:** National arms and value above fortifications map **Rev:** Cannon and ships **Edge:** Reeded

Date	Mintage	F12	VF20	XF40	MS60	MS63
2004	10,000	PF63 100	PF65 120			

KM# 343   10 HRYVEN
33.62 g., 0.925 Silver 0.9935 oz. ASW, 38.61 mm. **Subject:** Perejaslav Cossack Rada of 1654 **Obv:** National arms above value **Rev:** Standing figures facing **Edge:** Reeded

Date	Mintage	F12	VF20	XF40	MS60	MS63
2004	8,000	PF63 140	PF65 160			

KM# 358   10 HRYVEN
33.62 g., 0.925 Silver 0.9935 oz. ASW, 38.61 mm. **Subject:** Spalax Arenarius Reshetnik **Obv:** National arms and date divides wreath, value within **Rev:** Sandy mole rat **Edge:** Reeded

Date	Mintage	F12	VF20	XF40	MS60	MS63
2005	8,000	PF63 100	PF65 110			

KM# 367   10 HRYVEN
33.62 g., 0.925 Silver 0.9935 oz. ASW, 38.61 mm. **Subject:** The Protection of the Virgin **Obv:** National arms on Cossack regalia **Rev:** Wedding scene **Edge:** Reeded

Date	Mintage	F12	VF20	XF40	MS60	MS63
2005	8,000	PF63 135	PF65 150			

KM# 370   10 HRYVEN
33.62 g., 0.925 Silver 0.9935 oz. ASW, 38.61 mm. **Subject:** 60 Years UN Membership **Obv:** National arms, value and olive branch **Rev:** UN logo above partial globe **Edge:** Reeded

Date	Mintage	F12	VF20	XF40	MS60	MS63
2005	5,000	PF65 100				

KM# 371 10 HRYVEN
33.62 g., 0.925 Silver 0.9935 oz. ASW, 38.61 mm. **Subject:**
National Anthem **Obv:** Musical score, national arms, value and
date **Rev:** Coiled legend around holographic flower **Edge:**
Reeded

Date	Mintage	F12	VF20	XF40	MS60	MS63
2005	3,000	PF65 300				

KM# 372 10 HRYVEN
33.62 g., 0.925 Silver 0.9935 oz. ASW, 38.61 mm. **Subject:**
100 Years of Olga Kobylianska Music and Drama Theatre in
Chernivtsi **Obv:** Statue **Rev:** Theater **Edge:** Reeded

Date	Mintage	F12	VF20	XF40	MS60	MS63
2005	5,000	PF65 100				

KM# 373 10 HRYVEN
33.62 g., 0.925 Silver 0.9935 oz. ASW, 38.61 mm. **Subject:**
Sviatohirsky Lavra Monastery **Obv:** Madonna and child flanked
by angels **Rev:** Monastery on river bank **Edge:** Reeded

Date	Mintage	F12	VF20	XF40	MS60	MS63
2005	8,000	PF63 120	PF65 130			

KM# 381 10 HRYVEN
33.86 g., 0.925 Silver 1.0005 oz. ASW, 38.61 mm. **Subject:**
Baturyn Hetman Capital City **Obv:** National arms within sun
rays, value flanked by standing figures **Rev:** Four cameos and
banner above city view **Edge:** Reeded

Date	Mintage	F12	VF20	XF40	MS60	MS63
2005	5,000	PF65 120				

KM# 382 10 HRYVEN
33.86 g., 0.925 Silver 1.0005 oz. ASW, 38.61 mm. **Subject:**
Symyrenko Family **Obv:** Country name below national arms
within sprigs **Rev:** Family tree **Edge:** Reeded

Date	Mintage	F12	VF20	XF40	MS60	MS63
2005	5,000	PF65 100				

KM# 392 10 HRYVEN
33.62 g., 0.925 Silver 0.9935 oz. ASW, 38.61 mm. **Obv:**
National arms above value in wreath **Rev:** Grasshopper **Edge:**
Reeded

Date	Mintage	F12	VF20	XF40	MS60	MS63
2006	8,000	PF63 135	PF65 150			

KM# 410 10 HRYVEN
33.62 g., 0.925 Silver 0.9935 oz. ASW, 38.61 mm. **Subject:** 10
Years of the Constitution of Ukraine **Obv:** National arms **Edge:**
Reeded

Date	Mintage	F12	VF20	XF40	MS60	MS63
2006	5,000	PF65 100				

KM# 421 10 HRYVEN
33.62 g., 0.925 Silver 0.9934 oz. ASW, 38.61 mm. **Subject:**
Epiphany **Obv:** National arms **Edge:** Reeded

Date	Mintage	F12	VF20	XF40	MS60	MS63
2006	10,000	PF63 100	PF65 120			

KM# 423 10 HRYVEN
33.62 g., 0.925 Silver 0.9935 oz. ASW, 38.61 mm. **Subject:**
Saint Kyryl Church **Obv:** National arms **Edge:** Reeded

Date	Mintage	F12	VF20	XF40	MS60	MS63
2006	8,000	PF63 100	PF65 120			

KM# 424 10 HRYVEN
33.62 g., 0.925 Silver 0.9935 oz. ASW, 38.61 mm. **Subject:**
Chyhyryn **Obv:** National arms **Edge:** Reeded

Date	Mintage	F12	VF20	XF40	MS60	MS63
2006	5,000	PF65 120				

KM# 425 10 HRYVEN
33.62 g., 0.925 Silver 0.9935 oz. ASW, 38.61 mm. **Subject:**
Clearing House, 10th Anniversary **Obv:** National arms **Edge:**
Reeded

Date	Mintage	F12	VF20	XF40	MS60	MS63
2006	5,000	PF65 100				

KM# 427 10 HRYVEN
33.62 g., 0.925 Silver 0.9935 oz. ASW, 38.61 mm. **Subject:**
Twentieth Winter Olympic Games of 2006 **Obv:** National arms
Edge: Reeded

Date	Mintage	F12	VF20	XF40	MS60	MS63
2006	5,000	PF65 100				

KM# 466 10 HRYVEN
33.62 g., 0.925 Silver 0.9935 oz. ASW, 38.6 mm. **Subject:**
Odessa National Opera and Ballet, 120th Anniversary **Obv:**
Interior view from stage **Rev:** Opera house in Odessa **Edge:**
Reeded

Date	Mintage	F12	VF20	XF40	MS60	MS63
2007	5,000	PF65 100				

KM# 467 10 HRYVEN
33.62 g., 0.925 Silver 0.9935 oz. ASW, 38.61 mm. **Subject:**
Ivan Bohun **Edge:** Reeded

Date	Mintage	F12	VF20	XF40	MS60	MS63
2007	5,000	PF65 110				

KM# 516 10 HRYVEN
33.62 g., 0.925 Silver 0.9935 oz. ASW, 38.61 mm. **Subject:**
Black Griffin **Edge:** Reeded

Date	Mintage	F12	VF20	XF40	MS60	MS63
2008	7,000	PF63 110	PF65 120			

KM# 517 10 HRYVEN
33.62 g., 0.925 Silver 0.9935 oz. ASW, 38.61 mm. **Subject:**
Sevastopol, 225th Anniversary **Edge:** Reeded

Date	Mintage	F12	VF20	XF40	MS60	MS63
2008	5,000	PF65 100				

KM# 518 10 HRYVEN
33.62 g., 0.925 Silver 0.9935 oz. ASW, 38.61 mm. **Subject:**
Swallow's Nest **Edge:** Reeded

Date	Mintage	F12	VF20	XF40	MS60	MS63
2008	5,000	PF65 110				

KM# 519 10 HRYVEN
33.62 g., 0.925 Silver 0.9935 oz. ASW, 38.61 mm. **Subject:**
Tereschenko Family **Edge:** Reeded

Date	Mintage	F12	VF20	XF40	MS60	MS63
2008	7,000	PF63 90.00	PF65 100			

KM# 520 10 HRYVEN
33.62 g., 0.925 Silver 0.9935 oz. ASW, 38.61 mm. **Subject:**
Ukranian Swedish Alliances XVII-XVIII Century **Edge:** Reeded

Date	Mintage	F12	VF20	XF40	MS60	MS63
2008	5,000	PF65 110				

KM# 521 10 HRYVEN
33.62 g., 0.925 Silver 0.9935 oz. ASW, 38.61 mm. **Subject:**
Hlukhiv **Edge:** Reeded

Date	Mintage	F12	VF20	XF40	MS60	MS63
2008	7,000	PF63 90.00	PF65 100			

KM# 522 10 HRYVEN
33.62 g., 0.925 Silver 0.9935 oz. ASW, 38.61 mm. **Subject:**
UNESCO World Heritage Site - LVIV **Edge:** Reeded

Date	Mintage	F12	VF20	XF40	MS60	MS63
2008	5,000	PF65 120				

KM# 523 10 HRYVEN
33.62 g., 0.925 Silver 0.9935 oz. ASW, 38.61 mm. **Subject:**
Cathedral in Buky Village **Edge:** Reeded

Date	Mintage	F12	VF20	XF40	MS60	MS63
2008	5,000	PF65 150				

KM# 532 10 HRYVEN
33.62 g., 0.925 Silver 0.9935 oz. ASW, 38.61 mm. **Subject:**
Annunciation **Obv:** Conventionalized setting of the Gospel,
lilies. **Obv. Legend:** НАЦІОНАЛЬНИЙ БАНК УКРАЇНИ -
10 ГРИВЕНЬ **Rev:** Annunciation scene. **Rev. Legend:**
БЛАГОВІЩЕННЯ **Edge:** Reeded

Date	Mintage	F12	VF20	XF40	MS60	MS63
2008	8,000	PF63 100	PF65 110			

KM# 556 10 HRYVEN
33.62 g., 0.925 Silver 0.9935 oz. ASW, 38.61 mm. **Subject:**
Folk Crafts of the Ukraine - Bokorash (Raftsmen) **Obv:** Two
birds, Carpathian landscape, trees, cottages, logs **Obv.
Legend:** НАЦІОНАЛЬНИЙ БАНК УКРА?НИ - 10 / ГРИВЕНЬ
/ 2009 **Rev:** Bokorash directing raft **Rev. Legend:** БОКОРАШ

Date	Mintage	F12	VF20	XF40	MS60	MS63
2009 Antique patina	Est. 10000	—	—	—	—	100

KM# 559 10 HRYVEN
33.62 g., 0.925 Silver 0.9935 oz. ASW, 38.61 mm. **Subject:**
Surb Khach Monastery **Obv:** National Arms, vegitation
ornament pattern **Obv. Legend:** НАЦІОНАЛЬНИЙ БАНК
УКРАЇНИ - ДЕСЯТЬ ГРИВЕНЬ **Rev:** Monastery buildings **Rev.
Legend:** СТАРИЙ КРИМ - ВІРМЕНСЬКИЙ МОНАСТИР Х@@
PV CT. - СУРБ ХАЧ **Edge:** Segmented reeding

Date	Mintage	F12	VF20	XF40	MS60	MS63
2009	Est. 10000	PF63 85.00	PF65 95.00			

KM# 560 10 HRYVEN
33.62 g., 0.925 Silver 0.9935 oz. ASW, 38.61 mm. **Subject:**
Battle of Konotop, 350th Anniversary **Obv:** Hetman's Insignia,
Cossack arms and bandura, National Arms. **Obv. Legend:**
НАЦІОНАЛЬНИЙ БАНК УКРАЇНИ - 10 / ГРИВНЬ **Rev:**
Ivan Vyhovskyi with sabre, Cossacks, Konotop fortifications,
banners. **Rev. Legend:** ПЕРЕМОГА В КОНОТОПСЬКІЙ БИТВІ
- 350 РОКІВ

Date	Mintage	F12	VF20	XF40	MS60	MS63
2009	8,000	PF63 90.00	PF65 100			

KM# 561 10 HRYVEN

33.62 g., 0.925 Silver 0.9935 oz. ASW, 38.61 mm. **Subject:** Church of the Holy Spirit in Rogatyn **Obv:** Church Icon with candelabra flanking, National Arms **Rev:** Church facade

Date	Mintage	F12	VF20	XF40	MS60	MS63
2009	Est. 10000	PF63 90.00		PF65 100		

KM# 562 10 HRYVEN

33.62 g., 0.925 Silver 0.9935 oz. ASW, 38.61 mm. **Subject:** Famous Ukranian Families - Galagan Family **Obv:** The family estate, National Arms, value **Rev:** Galagan's College building and three portraits

Date	Mintage	F12	VF20	XF40	MS60	MS63
2009	7,000	PF63 85.00		PF65 95.00		

KM# 563 10 HRYVEN

33.62 g., 0.925 Silver 0.9935 oz. ASW, 38.61 mm. **Subject:** Kiev Academy of Operatta Theater, 75th Anniversary **Obv:** Dance scene, National Arms, value **Obv. Legend:** НАЦІОНАЛЬНИЙ БАНК УКРАЇНИ - 10 / ГРИВНЬ / 2009 **Rev:** Theater building, operetta character silhouettes. **Rev. Legend:** КИЇВСЬКИЙ АКАДЕМІЧНИЙ ТЕАТР ОПЕРЕТИ - 75/РОКІВ

Date	Mintage	F12	VF20	XF40	MS60	MS63
2009	5,000	PF65 95.00				

KM# 574 10 HRYVEN

33.62 g., 0.925 Silver 0.9935 oz. ASW, 38.61 mm. **Subject:** Ukrainian folk craft - Cartwright **Obv:** Wagon and wheels **Rev:** Woodcraftsman hewing wood to make a cart detail **Edge:** Reeded

Date	Mintage	F12	VF20	XF40	MS60	MS63
2009	10,000	—	—	—	—	100

KM# 570 10 HRYVEN

33.62 g., 0.925 Silver 0.9935 oz. ASW, 38.6 mm. **Subject:** Pulyp Oriyk Constitution, 300th Anniversary **Obv:** Hetman and Cossack officials **Rev:** Pylyp Orlyk, quill pen and constitution

Date	Mintage	F12	VF20	XF40	MS60	MS63
2010	7,000	PF63 85.00		PF65 95.00		

KM# 575 10 HRYVEN

33.62 g., 0.925 Silver 0.9934 oz. ASW, 38.61 mm. **Subject:** Vancouver Winter Olympics **Obv:** Winter scene **Rev:** Snowflake, sport figures, downhill skier at left

Date	Mintage	F12	VF20	XF40	MS60	MS63
2010	8,000	PF63 85.00		PF65 95.00		

KM# 586 10 HRYVEN

33.62 g., 0.925 Silver 0.9934 oz. ASW, 38.61 mm. **Obv:** Icon of Our Lady of Zarvanytsia **Rev:** Cathedral of Our Lady of Zarvanytsia

Date	Mintage	F12	VF20	XF40	MS60	MS63
2010	7,000	PF65 95.00				

KM# 588 10 HRYVEN

3362.00 g., 0.925 Silver 99.3404 oz. ASW, 38.61 mm. **Subject:** Folk Crafts - Weaving **Obv:** Spinning wheel and weaving products **Rev:** Woman working at a loom

Date	Mintage	F12	VF20	XF40	MS60	MS63
2010 Proof, Antique finish	10,000	PF65 100				

KM# 590 10 HRYVEN

33.62 g., 0.925 Silver 0.9934 oz. ASW, 38.61 mm. **Subject:** Ukraine Spas **Obv:** Two cornucopiae and Savior's fest **Rev:** Peasants getting food gifts blessed

Date	Mintage	F12	VF20	XF40	MS60	MS63
2010	10,000	PF63 90.00		PF65 100		

KM# 594 10 HRYVEN

33.62 g., 0.925 Silver 0.9934 oz. ASW, 38.61 mm. **Subject:** Flora and Fauna **Obv:** National Arms and wreath **Rev:** Stipa Ucrainica, feather grass

Date	Mintage	F12	VF20	XF40	MS60	MS63
2010	8,000	PF63 85.00		PF65 95.00		

KM# 600 10 HRYVEN

33.62 g., 0.925 Silver 0.9934 oz. ASW, 38.61 mm. **Subject:** Hetman Danylo Apostol **Obv:** National arms, Archangel Michael and Crowned lion (Symbols of Kyiv and Lviv) **Rev:** Danylo Apostol half length figure holding scep-tre

Date	Mintage	F12	VF20	XF40	MS60	MS63
2010	8,000	PF63 85.00		PF65 95.00		

KM# 605 10 HRYVEN

32.62 g., 0.925 Silver 0.9639 oz. ASW, 38.61 mm. **Subject:** Folk Crafts - Potter **Obv:** Pottery flanking central design **Rev:** Potter at wheel

Date	Mintage	F12	VF20	XF40	MS60	MS63
2010 Proof, Antique finish	10,000	PF65 100				

KM# 606 10 HRYVEN

33.62 g., 0.925 Silver 0.9934 oz. ASW, 38.6 mm. **Subject:** Tarnovskyi Family **Obv:** Mansion in Kachanivka, Chernihiv oblast **Rev:** Vasyl Tarnovskyi standing and oval portraits of Hryhorii and Vasyl.

Date	Mintage	F12	VF20	XF40	MS60	MS63
2010	10,000	PF63 85.00		PF65 95.00		

KM# 616 10 HRYVEN

33.62 g., 0.925 Silver 0.9935 oz. ASW, 38.61 mm. **Obv:** Blacksmith items, two little birds **Rev:** Blacksmith at work

Date	Mintage	F12	VF20	XF40	MS60	MS63
2011 Antique finish	10,000	—	—	—	—	110

KM# 626 10 HRYVEN

33.62 g., 0.925 Silver 0.9935 oz. ASW, 38.61 mm. **Obv:** Baroque element from the Church **Rev:** St. Andrew's Church

Date	Mintage	F12	VF20	XF40	MS60	MS63
2011	8,000	PF63 100		PF65 110		

KM# 628 10 HRYVEN

33.62 g., 0.925 Silver 0.9935 oz. ASW, 38.61 mm. **Obv:** Hopak dance **Rev:** Dancing Cossack

Date	Mintage	F12	VF20	XF40	MS60	MS63
2011	7,000	PF63 100		PF65 110		

KM# 632 10 HRYVEN

33.62 g., 0.925 Silver 0.9935 oz. ASW, 38.61 mm. **Subject:** Hryhorovych-Barskyi family **Obv:** Samson fountain in Kyiv **Rev:** Arms of the family

Date	Mintage	F12	VF20	XF40	MS60	MS63
2011	5,000	PF65 110				

KM# 641 10 HRYVEN

33.62 g., 0.925 Silver 0.9935 oz. ASW, 38.61 mm. **Subject:** UEFA Euro 2012 Final Tournament **Obv:** UEFA logo hologram and map of the Ukraine **Rev:** Two players, Olympic Stadium, Kyiv and city view

Date	Mintage	F12	VF20	XF40	MS60	MS63
2011	15,000	PF63 100		PF65 110		

KM# 642 10 HRYVEN

33.62 g., 0.925 Silver 0.9935 oz. ASW, 38.61 mm. **Subject:** UEFA Euro 2012 Final Tornament **Obv:** UEFA Euro 2012 Logo and map **Rev:** Player, city view and Livi Stadium

Date	Mintage	F12	VF20	XF40	MS60	MS63
2011	15,000	PF63 100		PF65 110		

KM# 643 10 HRYVEN

33.62 g., 0.925 Silver 0.9935 oz. ASW, 38.61 mm. **Subject:** UEFA Euro 2012 Final Tournament **Obv:** UEFA logo hologram and Map of Ukraine **Rev:** City view with two players

Date	Mintage	F12	VF20	XF40	MS60	MS63
2011	15,000	PF63 100		PF65 110		

KM# 644 10 HRYVEN

33.62 g., 0.925 Silver 0.9935 oz. ASW, 38.61 mm. **Subject:** UEFA Euro 2012 Final Tournament **Obv:** UEFA logo hologram and map of Ukraine **Rev:** Player with ball, Donbass Arena

Date	Mintage	F12	VF20	XF40	MS60	MS63
2011	15,000	PF63 100		PF65 110		

KM# 662 10 HRYVEN
32.62 g., 0.925 Silver 0.9639 oz. ASW, 38.6 mm. **Subject:** 80 Years of the formation of Donetsk region

Date	Mintage	F12	VF20	XF40	MS60	MS63
2012	Est. 5000	PF65 90.00				

KM# 666 10 HRYVEN
33.62 g., 0.925 Silver 0.9934 oz. ASW, 50 mm. **Subject:** UEFA EURO 2012 Championship **Obv:** UEFA Championship cup **Rev:** Soccer player and part of ball **Note:** Pairs up with a Polish 10 Zl.

Date	Mintage	F12	VF20	XF40	MS60	MS63
2012	10,000	PF63 275	PF65 300			

KM# 672 10 HRYVEN
33.63 g., 0.925 Silver 0.9937 oz. ASW, 38.61 mm. **Subject:** Petro Kalnyshevski, Cossack military leader **Obv:** Archangel Michael, crowned lion (symbols of Kyiv and Lviv) and National arms **Edge:** Incuse lettering

Date	Mintage	F12	VF20	XF40	MS60	MS63
2012	5,000	PF65 85.00				

KM# 673 10 HRYVEN
33.63 g., 0.925 Silver 0.9937 oz. ASW, 38.6 mm. **Subject:** Ivano-Frankvsk City, 350 Anniversary **Obv:** National arms, Ratusha building **Rev:** Church of the Virgin Mary **Edge:** Incuse lettering

Date	Mintage	F12	VF20	XF40	MS60	MS63
2012	3,000	PF65 80.00				

KM# 676 10 HRYVEN
33.63 g., 0.925 Silver 0.9937 oz. ASW, 38.6 mm. **Subject:** XXX Summer Olympics - London **Obv:** London city view, National arms **Rev:** Stater of Philip II and silhouettes of sports **Edge:** Incuse lettering

Date	Mintage	F12	VF20	XF40	MS60	MS63
2012	5,000	PF65 85.00				

KM# 677 10 HRYVEN
33.63 g., 0.925 Silver 0.9937 oz. ASW, 38.6 mm. **Subject:** Yeletskyi Holy Dormition Cloister **Obv:** National arms, Main building of the cloister **Rev:** Image of the Mother of God icon **Edge:** Incuse lettering

Date	Mintage	F12	VF20	XF40	MS60	MS63
2012	7,000	PF63 70.00	PF65 80.00			

KM# 679 10 HRYVEN
33.63 g., 0.925 Silver 0.9937 oz. ASW, 38.6 mm. **Subject:** Folk Crafts **Obv:** Traditional Ukranian clothing **Rev:** Furrier **Edge:** Incuse lettering

Date	Mintage	F12	VF20	XF40	MS60	MS63
2012 Proof, antique finish	5,000	PF65 80.00				

KM# 680 10 HRYVEN
33.63 g., 0.925 Silver 0.9937 oz. ASW, 38.6 mm. **Subject:** Town of Sudak, 1800th Anniversary **Obv:** National arms, St. George, value **Rev:** Town view with beach **Edge:** Incuse lettering

Date	Mintage	F12	VF20	XF40	MS60	MS63
2012	3,000	PF65 85.00				

KM# 687 10 HRYVEN
33.63 g., 0.925 Silver 0.9937 oz. ASW, 38.6 mm. **Subject:** Zhovkva Synagogue **Obv:** National arms, fragment of building façade **Rev:** Synagogue building **Edge:** Incuse lettering

Date	Mintage	F12	VF20	XF40	MS60	MS63
2012	7,000	PF63 70.00	PF65 80.00			

KM# 689 10 HRYVEN
33.63 g., 0.925 Silver 0.9937 oz. ASW **Obv:** National arms and value **Rev:** The Sterlet **Edge:** Reeded

Date	Mintage	F12	VF20	XF40	MS60	MS63
2012	7,000	PF63 70.00	PF65 80.00			

KM# 697 10 HRYVEN
33.63 g., 0.925 Silver 0.9937 oz. ASW, 38.6 mm. **Subject:** The Great Bustard **Obv:** National arms, value **Edge:** Reeded

Date	Mintage	F12	VF20	XF40	MS60	MS63
2013	5,000	PF65 80.00				

KM# 699 10 HRYVEN
33.63 g., 0.925 Silver 0.9937 oz. ASW, 38.6 mm. **Subject:** House with Chimeras **Obv:** National arms, Vladyslav Horodetskyi, architect and value **Rev:** Fragment of Sculptural composition

Date	Mintage	F12	VF20	XF40	MS60	MS63
2013	5,000	PF65 80.00				

KM# 144 20 HRYVEN
67.24 g., 0.925 Silver 1.9868 oz. ASW, 50 mm. **Subject:** 10 Years Independence **Obv:** National arms **Rev:** Parliament building on map within beaded circle **Edge:** Segmented reeding

Date	Mintage	F12	VF20	XF40	MS60	MS63
2001	1,000	PF65 4,000				

KM# 174 20 HRYVEN
14.70 g., Bi-Metallic, 31 mm. **Subject:** Kyiv Rus" Culture **Obv:** Old arms of Ukraine, Prince and a cathedral model in his hand and princess **Rev:** Old Rus earring **Edge:** Reeded and plain sections

Date	Mintage	F12	VF20	XF40	MS60	MS63
2001	2,000	PF65 1,000				

KM# 175 20 HRYVEN
14.70 g., Bi-Metallic, 31 mm. **Subject:** Scythian Culture **Obv:** Warrior with a bowl in his hand and to the right, a Queen of Scythia **Rev:** Stylized horse flanked by pegasists **Edge:** Reeded and plain sections

Date	Mintage	F12	VF20	XF40	MS60	MS63
2001	2,000	PF65 1,200				

KM# 153 20 HRYVEN
67.24 g., 0.925 Silver 1.9868 oz. ASW, 50 mm. **Obv:** National arms on sun and flying geese divides beaded circle **Rev:** AN-225 Mrija" cargo jet divides beaded circle **Edge:** Reeded and plain sections

Date	Mintage	F12	VF20	XF40	MS60	MS63
2002	2,002	PF65 1,200				

KM# 188 20 HRYVEN
67.24 g., 0.925 Silver 1.9868 oz. ASW, 50 mm. **Subject:** 60th Anniversary - Liberation of Kiev **Obv:** Eternal flame monument **Rev:** Map and battle scene **Edge:** Segmented reeding

Date	Mintage	F12	VF20	XF40	MS60	MS63
2003	2,000	PF65 400				

KM# 226 20 HRYVEN
67.24 g., 0.925 Silver 1.9869 oz. ASW, 50 mm. **Subject:** Our Souls Do Not Die **Obv:** National arms above value **Rev:** Bust of Taras Shevchenko facing flanked by standing figures **Edge:** Segmented reeding

Date	Mintage	F12	VF20	XF40	MS60	MS63
2004	4,000	PF65 250				

KM# 344 20 HRYVEN
67.24 g., 0.925 Silver 1.9869 oz. ASW, 50 mm. **Subject:** 2006 Olympic Games **Obv:** Woman holding flame and branch **Rev:** Six athletes around flame within square design **Edge:** Segmented reeding

Date	Mintage	F12	VF20	XF40	MS60	MS63
2004	5,000	PF65 200				

KM# 363 20 HRYVEN
67.24 g., 0.925 Silver 1.9869 oz. ASW, 50 mm. **Obv:** National arms on sun with flying geese divides beaded circle **Rev:** AN-124 jet plane divides beaded circle **Edge:** Segmented reeding

Date	Mintage	F12	VF20	XF40	MS60	MS63
2005	5,000	PF65 200				

KM# 369 20 HRYVEN
67.24 g., 0.925 Silver 1.9869 oz. ASW, 50 mm. **Subject:** Sorochynsky Fair **Obv:** Busts facing each other flanked by flower sprigs **Rev:** Farmer leading family in ox cart **Edge:** Segmented reeding

Date	Mintage	F12	VF20	XF40	MS60	MS63
2005	5,000	PF65 250				

KM# 374 20 HRYVEN
67.24 g., 0.925 Silver 1.9869 oz. ASW, 50 mm. **Subject:** 60th Anniversary of Victory in WWII **Obv:** Flying cranes divides value, date and national arms **Rev:** V-shaped searchlight beams filled with soldiers, order of the Patriotic War at bottom left **Edge:** Segmented reeding

Date	Mintage	F12	VF20	XF40	MS60	MS63
2005	5,000	PF65 200				

KM# 412 20 HRYVEN
67.25 g., 0.925 Silver 1.9871 oz. ASW, 50 mm. **Subject:** 15 Years of Ukraine Independency **Obv:** National arms

Date	Mintage	F12	VF20	XF40	MS60	MS63
2006	7,000	PF65 200				

KM# 468 20 HRYVEN
14.23 g., Silver, 31 mm. **Subject:** Pure water is source of life **Obv:** Drop of water in pond **Rev:** Man taking drink from waterfall **Edge:** Segmented reeding

Date	Mintage	F12	VF20	XF40	MS60	MS63
2007 Prooflike	3,000	—	—	—	—	600

KM# 469 20 HRYVEN
67.26 g., 0.925 Silver 1.9874 oz. ASW, 50 mm. **Subject:** Chumaky's Way **Obv:** Hologram wheel at center of fiery spiral **Rev:** Merchant's carts under night sky

Date	Mintage	F12	VF20	XF40	MS60	MS63
2007	5,000	PF65 350				

KM# 470 20 HRYVEN
67.25 g., 0.925 Silver 1.9871 oz. ASW, 50 mm. **Subject:** The Famine, Genocide of the Ukranina People **Obv:** Girl standing on fallow ground, small green plant at left **Rev:** Swan at center of cross, candles in background

Date	Mintage	F12	VF20	XF40	MS60	MS63
2007 Antique finish	10,000	—	—	—	200	—

KM# 524 20 HRYVEN
67.25 g., 0.925 Silver 1.9871 oz. ASW, 50 mm. **Subject:** Kyiv, 1000th Anniversary of minting

Date	Mintage	F12	VF20	XF40	MS60	MS63
2008	5,000	PF65 250				

KM# 552 20 HRYVEN
67.25 g., 0.925 Silver 1.9871 oz. ASW, 50.0 mm. **Subject:** Republic of Carpatho-Ukraine - 70th Anniversary of proclamation **Obv:** Carpathian ornament patterns, National Arms, value **Obv. Legend:** НАЦІОНАЛЬНИЙ БАНК УКРАЇНИ - 20 / ГРИВНЬ **Rev:** Transcarpathian holding flag with the arms of the Carpatho-Ukraine **Rev. Legend:** 70 / РОКІВ - ПРОГОЛОШЕННЯ КАРПАТСЬКОЇ УКРАЇНИ

Date	Mintage	F12	VF20	XF40	MS60	MS63
2009	3,000	PF65 300				

KM# 554 20 HRYVEN
67.25 g., 0.925 Silver 1.9871 oz. ASW, 50 mm. **Subject:** Pysanka - Easter Egg decorating **Obv:** Ukrainian embroidered towels, eggs, Naitonal Arms, value **Rev:** Female pysanka maker ornamenting egg, young girl watching

Date	Mintage	F12	VF20	XF40	MS60	MS63
2009	8,000	PF63 230	PF65 250			

KM# 591 20 HRYVEN
67.26 g., 0.925 Silver 1.9874 oz. ASW, 50 mm. **Subject:** Zymne Cloister **Obv:** Madonna icon partially gilt **Rev:** Zymne Cloister

Date	Mintage	F12	VF20	XF40	MS60	MS63
2010	5,000	PF65 400				

KM# 596 20 HRYVEN
67.26 g., 0.925 Silver 1.9874 oz. ASW, 50 mm. **Subject:** Battle of Grunwald, 600th Anniversary **Obv:** Value within wreath, three armored hands holding horizontal sword **Rev:** Knights with spears on horseback in battle

Date	Mintage	F12	VF20	XF40	MS60	MS63
2010	5,000	PF65 200				

KM# 602 20 HRYVEN
67.25 g., 0.925 Silver 1.9871 oz. ASW, 50 mm. **Subject:** Maritime History **Obv:** Banner, compass rose and seal o Zaporozhin host **Rev:** Cossack boat of the 18th century

Date	Mintage	F12	VF20	XF40	MS60	MS63
2010	5,000	PF65 200				

KM# 614 20 HRYVEN
67.25 g., 0.925 Silver 1.9871 oz. ASW, 50 mm. **Subject:** Lesya Ukrainka's "The Forest Song" **Obv:** Portrait **Rev:** Girl holding willow branch, boy in distance

Date	Mintage	F12	VF20	XF40	MS60	MS63
2011	4,000	PF65 200				

KM# 617 20 HRYVEN
67.25 g., 0.925 Silver 1.9871 oz. ASW, 50 mm. **Subject:** Peresopnytsia Gospels **Obv:** Gospel maker icon **Rev:** Four miniatures of the initial illustrations of each Gospel

Date	Mintage	F12	VF20	XF40	MS60	MS63
2011 Antique finish	4,000	—	—	—	—	230

KM# 637 20 HRYVEN
67.28 g., 0.925 Silver 1.988 oz. ASW, 50 mm. **Subject:** Ukrainian Railroads, 150th Anniversary **Obv:** Modern high-speed train **Rev:** Ukrainian railways logo, gilt

Date	Mintage	F12	VF20	XF40	MS60	MS63
2011	4,000	PF65 220				

KM# 640 20 HRYVEN
67.28 g., 0.925 Silver 1.988 oz. ASW, 62.2 mm. **Subject:** UEFA Euro 2012 Final Tournament **Obv:** Holographic images of UEFA Euro 2012 logo **Rev:** Stadium

Date	Mintage	F12	VF20	XF40	MS60	MS63
2011	15,000	PF63 200	PF65 220			

KM# 652 20 HRYVEN
31.11 g., 0.9999 Gold 0.9935 oz. AGW, 32 mm. **Subject:** Archangel Michael **Obv:** Logo of the Ukraine National Bank **Rev:** Archangel Michael **Edge:** Segmented reeding

Date	Mintage	F12	VF20	XF40	MS60	MS63
2011	1,500	—	—	—	—	2,200
2012	5,000	—	—	—	—	2,000
2013	2,500	—	—	—	—	1,700

KM# 694 20 HRYVEN
67.26 g., 0.925 Silver 1.9874 oz. ASW, 50 mm. **Subject:** Semen Hulak-Artemovsky, 200th Annversary **Obv:** National arms and value **Rev:** Portrait **Edge:** Incuse lettering

Date	Mintage	F12	VF20	XF40	MS60	MS63
2013	4,000	PF65 150				

KM# 695 20 HRYVEN
67.26 g., 0.925 Silver 1.9874 oz. ASW, 50 mm. **Subject:** Liadova Cave Monastery, 1000th Anniversary **Obv:** National arms, value, St. Antony of the Caves **Rev:** Stylized fragment of the Cave Monastery **Edge:** Incuse lettering

Date	Mintage	F12	VF20	XF40	MS60	MS63
2013	3,000	PF65 150				

KM# 704 20 HRYVEN
67.26 g., 0.925 Silver 1.9875 oz. ASW, 50 mm. **Subject:** Christianization of Kyivan Rus, 1025th Anniversary **Obv:** National arms, value, pectoral cross and symbols of the four evangelists **Rev:** Figures **Edge:** Incuse lettering

Date	Mintage	F12	VF20	XF40	MS60	MS63
2013	3,500	PF65 350				

KM# 426 50 HRYVEN
17.63 g., 0.900 Gold 0.5069 oz. AGW, 25 mm. **Subject:** Nestor - The Chronicler **Obv:** National arms

Date	Mintage	F12	VF20	XF40	MS60	MS63
2006	5,000	PF65 1,400				

KM# 525 50 HRYVEN
17.63 g., 0.900 Gold 0.5069 oz. AGW, 25 mm. **Subject:** Swallow's Nest Castle **Edge:** Plain

Date	Mintage	F12	VF20	XF40	MS60	MS63
2008	4,000	PF65 1,400				

KM# 526 50 HRYVEN
500.00 g., 0.9999 Silver 15.9703 oz. ASW **Subject:** Visit of Ecumenical Patriarch Bartholomew I

Date	Mintage	F12	VF20	XF40	MS60	MS63
2008	1,000	PF65 2,200				

KM# 564 50 HRYVEN
500.00 g., 0.999 Silver 15.9559 oz. ASW, 85 mm. **Subject:** Mykola Hohol's stories - Evenings on a farm near Dykanka **Obv:** Hohol's portrait with quill, National arms, value **Rev:** Christmas star with yellow sapphire

Date	Mintage	F12	VF20	XF40	MS60	MS63
2009	Est. 1500	PF65 2,500				

KM# 595 50 HRYVEN
17.63 g., 0.900 Gold 0.5069 oz. AGW, 25 mm. **Subject:** Ukrainian ballet **Obv:** Ballet shoes **Rev:** Ballet couple **Edge:** Plain

Date	Mintage	F12	VF20	XF40	MS60	MS63
2010	4,000	PF65 1,400				

KM# 609 50 HRYVEN
500.00 g., 0.999 Silver 15.9559 oz. ASW, 85 mm. **Subject:** Cradle of the Ukrainian Cossacks **Obv:** Zaporizka Sich, historic site, shield and swords below **Rev:** Dovbysh (Cossack drummer) beating kettle drums, ornamental pattern

Date	Mintage	F12	VF20	XF40	MS60	MS63
2010	Est. 1500	PF65 2,500				

KM# 631 50 HRYVEN
500.00 g., 0.999 Silver 15.9559 oz. ASW, 85 mm. **Subject:** Independence, 20th Anniversary **Obv:** National arms, rushnyks, portraits **Rev:** Legend within wreath

Date	Mintage	F12	VF20	XF40	MS60	MS63
2011	1,000	—	—	—	—	2,500

KM# 633 50 HRYVEN
500.00 g., 0.999 Silver 15.9559 oz. ASW, 85 mm. **Subject:** St. Sophia Cathedral, 1000th Anniversary **Obv:** St. Sophia Cathedral cupolas, model of XI century design **Rev:** Altar mural mosaics

Date	Mintage	F12	VF20	XF40	MS60	MS63
2011	1,000	—	—	—	—	2,500

KM# 674 50 HRYVEN
500.00 g., 0.999 Silver 15.9559 oz. ASW, 85 mm. **Subject:** Nikitsky Botanical Garden, 200th Anniversary **Obv:** National Arms, Christian Steven portrait **Rev:** Legend **Edge Lettering:** Incuse lettering

Date	Mintage	F12	VF20	XF40	MS60	MS63
2012	1,000	—	—	—	—	1,000

KM# 199 100 HRYVEN
34.56 g., 0.900 Gold 0.9936 oz. AGW, 32 mm. **Subject:** Ancient Scythian Culture **Obv:** National arms above ornamental design and value within rope wreath **Rev:** Ancient craftsmen and jewelry **Edge:** Reeded

Date	Mintage	F12	VF20	XF40	MS60	MS63
2003	1,500	PF65 7,500				

KM# 345 100 HRYVEN
34.56 g., 0.900 Gold 0.9936 oz. AGW, 32 mm. **Subject:** The Golden Gate **Obv:** National arms above value between two stylized cranes **Rev:** Riders approaching castle gate **Edge:** Segmented reeding

Date	Mintage	F12	VF20	XF40	MS60	MS63
2004	2,000	PF65 5,000				

KM# 414 100 HRYVEN
1000.00 g., 0.999 Silver 31.9118 oz. ASW, 100 mm. **Subject:** 10 Years to the Currency Reform in Ukraine **Obv:** National arms **Note:** Illustration reduced.

Date	Mintage	G4	VG8	F12	VF20	XF40
2006	1,501	PF65 6,500				

KM# 471 100 HRYVEN
34.56 g., 0.900 Gold 0.9936 oz. AGW, 32 mm. **Subject:** The Ostroh Bible **Obv:** Part of illumination on page **Rev:** Ivan Fedorov and Kostiantyn of Ostroth holding open bible

Date	Mintage	F12	VF20	XF40	MS60	MS63
2007	4,000	PF65 3,000				

KM# 527 100 HRYVEN
1000.00 g., 0.999 Silver 31.9118 oz. ASW **Subject:** Kievan Rus

Date	Mintage	F12	VF20	XF40	MS60	MS63
2008	800	PF65 4,500				

KM# 558 100 HRYVEN
1000.00 g., 0.999 Silver 31.9118 oz. ASW, 100 mm. **Subject:** International Year of Astronomy **Obv:** Solar System, armillary sphere, stars. **Obv. Legend:** НАЦІОНАЛЬНИЈ БАНК УКРАЇНИ - 100 / ГРИВНЬ **Rev:** Galileo, stars, telescope, galaxies, observatory, Saturn (as the letter O). **Rev. Legend:** МІЖНАРОДНИЈ РІК АСТРОНОМІ@@Р

Date	Mintage	F12	VF20	XF40	MS60	MS63
2009	Est. 700	PF65 4,500				

KM# 565 100 HRYVEN
34.57 g., 0.900 Gold 0.9939 oz. AGW, 32 mm. **Subject:** Ancient Site - Chersonesos Taurica **Obv:** Ancient ruins, coins, Naitonal Arms **Rev:** Ruins of ancient Chersonesos **Edge:** Segmented reeding

Date	Mintage	F12	VF20	XF40	MS60	MS63
2009	4,000	PF65 3,000				

KM# 597 100 HRYVEN
34.56 g., 0.900 Gold 0.9936 oz. AGW, 32 mm. **Subject:** Bosporan Kingdom **Obv:** Panticapaeum runins: classical columns, winged animals **Rev:** Panticapaeum stater, buildings, ancient sailing vessel

Date	Mintage	F12	VF20	XF40	MS60	MS63
2010	3,000	PF65 3,000				

KM# 630 100 HRYVEN
34.56 g., 0.900 Gold 0.9936 oz. AGW, 32 mm. **Subject:** Independence, 20th Anniversary **Obv:** National arms in center of rushnyks, Portraits around **Rev:** Legend within wreath

Date	Mintage	F12	VF20	XF40	MS60	MS63
2011	1,000	PF65 4,500				

KM# 706 100 HRYVEN
34.57 g., 0.900 Gold 0.9939 oz. AGW, 32 mm. **Obv:** National arms, value, pectoral cross and symbolic figures of the four Evangelists **Rev:** Figures **Edge:** Incuse lettering

Date	Mintage	F12	VF20	XF40	MS60	MS63
2013	1,025	PF65 3,000				

KM# 646 500 HRYVEN
500.00 g., 0.9999 Gold 15.9703 oz. AGW, 80 mm. **Subject:** UEFA Euro 2012 Final Tournament **Obv:** Map of Europe, logo, tournament cities around **Rev:** Large and smaller images of players

Date	Mintage	F12	VF20	XF40	MS60	MS63
2011	Est. 500	—	—	—	—	47,000

MINT SETS

KM#	Date	Mintage	Identification	Issue Price	Mkt Val
MS2	2001 (8)	5,000	KM#1.1b, 2.1b, 3.3b, 4b, 6, 7, 8b, 129	—	150
MS3	2006 (8)	5,000	KM#1.1b, 2.1b, 3.3b, 4b, 6, 7, 8b, 411	—	30.00
MS4	2008 (7)	5,000	KM#1.1b, 2.1b, 3.3b, 4b, 6, 7, 209, prooflike	—	100
MS5	2011 (7)	5,000	KM#1.1b, 2.1b, 3.3b, 4b, 6, 7, 209. Prooflike	—	45.00
MS6	2012 (7)	5,000	KM#1.1b, 2.1b, 3.3b, 4b, 6, 7, 209. Prooflike	—	50.00

UNITED ARAB EMIRATES

The seven United Arab Emirates (formerly known as the Trucial Sheikhdoms or States), located along the southern shore of the Persian Gulf, are comprised of the Sheikhdoms of Abu Dhabi, Dubai, al-Sharjah, Ajman, Umm al Qaiwain, Ras al-Khaimah and al-Fujairah. They have a combined area of about 32,000 sq. mi. (83,600 sq. km.) and a population of *2.1 million. Capital: Abu Zaby (Abu Dhabi). Since the oil strikes of 1958-60, the economy has centered about petroleum.

TITLES

الامارات العربية المتحدة

al-Imara(t) al-Arabiya(t) al-Muttahida(t)

UNITED EMIRATES
STANDARD COINAGE

KM# 2.2 5 FILS
Bronze **Series:** F.A.O. **Obv:** Value **Rev:** Fish above dates **Note:** Reduced size.

Date	Mintage	F12	VF20	XF40	MS60	MS63
AH1422-2001	—	—	—	0.15	0.30	1.50
AH1426-2005	—	—	—	0.15	0.30	1.50

KM# 3.2 10 FILS
Bronze, 19 mm. **Obv:** Value **Rev:** Arab dhow above dates **Note:** Reduced size.

Date	Mintage	F12	VF20	XF40	MS60	MS63
AH1422-2001	—	—	0.30	0.50	1.00	1.50
AH1425-2005	—	—	0.20	0.35	0.80	1.20

KM# 4 25 FILS
3.50 g., Copper-Nickel, 20 mm. **Obv:** Value **Rev:** Gazelle above dates **Edge:** Reeded

Date	Mintage	F12	VF20	XF40	MS60	MS63
AH1425-2005	—	—	—	0.40	1.00	1.50
AH1428-2007	—	—	—	0.40	1.00	1.50
AH1428-2008	—	—	—	0.40	0.75	1.50
AH1432-2011	—	—	—	0.40	0.75	1.50

KM# 16 50 FILS
4.30 g., Copper-Nickel, 21 mm. **Obv:** Value **Rev:** Oil derricks above dates **Shape:** 7-sided **Note:** Reduced size.

Date	Mintage	F12	VF20	XF40	MS60	MS63
AH1425-2005	—	—	—	0.70	1.50	2.50
AH1428-2007	—	—	—	0.50	1.50	2.00
AH1428-2008	—	—	—	0.50	1.50	2.00

KM# 6.2 DIRHAM
6.40 g., Copper-Nickel, 24 mm. **Obv:** Value **Rev:** Jug above dates **Edge:** Reeded **Note:** Reduced size.

Date	Mintage	F12	VF20	XF40	MS60	MS63
AH1425-2005	—	—	0.35	0.65	2.50	4.00
AH1426-2006	—	—	0.35	0.65	2.00	4.00
AH1428-2007	—	—	0.35	0.65	2.00	4.00

KM# 49 DIRHAM
6.40 g., Copper-Nickel, 24 mm. **Subject:** 25th Anniversary - Armed Forces Unification **Obv:** Value **Rev:** Heraldic eagle within rope wreath **Edge:** Reeded

Date	Mintage	F12	VF20	XF40	MS60	MS63
ND-2001	250,000	—	—	2.00	7.00	8.00

KM# 51 DIRHAM
6.33 g., Copper-Nickel, 24 mm. **Subject:** 50 Years of Formal Education **Obv:** Value **Rev:** Symbolic design **Edge:** Reeded

Date	Mintage	F12	VF20	XF40	MS60	MS63
ND (2003)	—	—	—	2.00	7.00	8.00

KM# 52 DIRHAM
6.40 g., Copper-Nickel, 24 mm. **Subject:** Abu Dhabi National Bank 35th Anniversary **Obv:** Value **Rev:** Bank building tower divide dates within circle **Edge:** Reeded

Date	Mintage	F12	VF20	XF40	MS60	MS63
ND (2003)	—	—	—	2.00	5.00	7.00

KM# 54 DIRHAM
6.40 g., Copper-Nickel, 24 mm. **Subject:** 40th Anniversary of Crude Oil Exports **Obv:** Value **Rev:** ADCO" logo **Edge:** Reeded

Date	Mintage	F12	VF20	XF40	MS60	MS63
ND (2003)	—	—	—	2.00	6.00	8.00

KM# 73 DIRHAM
6.40 g., Copper-Nickel, 23.93 mm. **Subject:** WBG & IMF meeting in Dubai 2003 **Obv:** Denomination **Rev:** Mosaic arc **Edge:** Reeded

Date	Mintage	F12	VF20	XF40	MS60	MS63
2003	250,000	—	—	2.00	9.00	11.00

KM# 74 DIRHAM
6.40 g., Copper-Nickel, 24 mm. **Subject:** First Gulf Bank 25th Anniversary **Obv:** Value **Rev:** Bank logo **Edge:** Reeded

Date	Mintage	F12	VF20	XF40	MS60	MS63
ND-2004	—	—	—	2.00	6.00	8.00

KM# 83 DIRHAM
6.47 g., Copper-Nickel, 24.02 mm. **Subject:** Honoring Mother of Nations **Obv:** Large value **Rev:** Inscription in flower bud at center **Rev. Legend:** Sheikha Fatima Bint Mubarak **Edge:** Reeded

Date	Mintage	F12	VF20	XF40	MS60	MS63
2005	—	—	—	1.50	6.00	7.00

KM# 78 DIRHAM
6.40 g., Copper-Nickel, 24 mm. **Obv:** Value **Obv. Legend:** UNITED ARAB EMIRATES **Rev:** Police badge in center **Rev. Legend:** DUABI POLICE GOLDEN JUBILEE **Edge:** Reeded

Date	Mintage	F12	VF20	XF40	MS60	MS63
ND-2006	—	—	—	1.50	6.00	8.00

KM# 76 DIRHAM
6.40 g., Copper-Nickel, 24 mm. **Subject:** Sharjah International Airport, 75th Anniversary **Obv:** Value **Obv. Legend:** UNITED ARAB EMIRATES **Rev:** Three birds in flight under arc **Edge:** Reeded

Date	Mintage	F12	VF20	XF40	MS60	MS63
ND-2007	—	—	—	1.50	5.00	7.00

KM# 77 DIRHAM
6.30 g., Copper-Nickel, 24 mm. **Obv:** Value **Rev:** Zakum Development Co. logo **Edge:** Reeded

Date	Mintage	F12	VF20	XF40	MS60	MS63
ND-2007	—	—	—	1.50	6.00	8.00

KM# 84 DIRHAM
6.40 g., Copper-Nickel, 24 mm. **Subject:** 10th Anniversary of the Hamdan Bin Rashed Award for Distinguished Academic Performance **Obv:** Large value **Rev:** 10 below pen with tip touching star **Edge:** Reeded

Date	Mintage	F12	VF20	XF40	MS60	MS63
ND-2007	—	—	—	1.50	6.00	7.00

KM# 96 DIRHAM
6.40 g., Copper-Nickel, 24 mm. **Subject:** U.A.E. Boy Scouts, 50th Anniversary **Obv:** Value at center **Rev:** Scout Fleur-de-lis within rope circle **Edge:** Reeded

Date	Mintage	F12	VF20	XF40	MS60	MS63
2007	—	—	—	1.50	6.00	8.00

KM# 79 DIRHAM
6.43 g., Copper-Nickel, 24.03 mm. **Obv:** Value **Obv. Legend:** UNITED ARAB EMIRATES **Rev:** Large "30" and logo **Rev. Legend:** 30TH ANNIVERSARY OF THE 1ST LNG SHIPMENT **Rev. Inscription:** ADGAS **Edge:** Reeded

Date	Mintage	F12	VF20	XF40	MS60	MS63
ND-2007	—	—	—	1.50	6.00	8.00

KM# 85 DIRHAM
6.40 g., Copper-Nickel, **Subject:** National Bank of Abu Dhabi, 40th Anniversary **Obv:** Large value **Obv. Legend:** UNITED ARAB EMIRATES **Rev:** Large stylized "40 **Edge:** Reeded

Date	Mintage	F12	VF20	XF40	MS60	MS63
ND-2008	—	—	—	—	4.00	5.00

KM# 100 DIRHAM
6.40 g., Copper-Nickel **Subject:** DIFC **Obv:** Large value **Obv. Legend:** UNITED ARAB EMIRATES **Rev:** DIFC (Dubai International Financial Centre) **Edge:** Reeded

Date	Mintage	F12	VF20	XF40	MS60	MS63
2009	—	—	—	—	4.00	5.00

KM# 109 DIRHAM
6.40 g., Copper-Nickel **Subject:** I Love UAE

Date	Mintage	F12	VF20	XF40	MS60	MS63
2009	—	—	—	—	4.00	5.00

KM# 101 DIRHAM
6.40 g., Copper-Nickel **Subject:** World Environment Day **Obv:** Large value **Obv. Legend:** UNITED ARAB EMIRATES **Rev:** World Environment Day, Global map **Edge:** Reeded

Date	Mintage	F12	VF20	XF40	MS60	MS63
2012	—	—	—	—	4.00	5.00

KM# 102 DIRHAM
6.40 g., Copper-Nickel **Subject:** 39th Anniversary I Love UAE **Obv:** Large value **Obv. Legend:** UNITED ARAM EMIRATES **Rev:** Oil derrick, commemorative text **Edge:** Reeded

Date	Mintage	F12	VF20	XF40	MS60	MS63
2012	—	—	—	—	5.00	8.00

KM# 103 DIRHAM
6.40 g., Copper-Nickel, 24 mm. **Obv:** World Environment Day logo

Date	Mintage	F12	VF20	XF40	MS60	MS63
2012	—	—	—	—	4.00	5.00

KM# 6.3 DIRHAM
6.10 g., Nickel Plated Steel, 24 mm. **Obv:** Value **Rev:** Jug above date **Edge:** Reeded

Date	Mintage	F12	VF20	XF40	MS60	MS63
AH1433-2012	—	—	0.35	0.65	2.00	4.00

KM# 106 DIRHAM
6.40 g., Copper-Nickel, 24 mm. **Subject:** 50th Anniversary of Oil Exports **Obv:** Large value **Rev:** Anniversary logo

Date	Mintage	F12	VF20	XF40	MS60	MS63
2012	—	—	—	—	4.00	5.00

KM# 47 50 DIRHAMS
40.22 g., 0.925 Silver 1.1884 oz. ASW, 40 mm. **Subject:** 25th Anniversary - Women's Union (1975-2000) **Obv:** Bust of President H. H. Sheikh Zayed bin Sultan Al Nahyan 7/8 right **Rev:** Stylized gazelle **Edge:** Reeded

Date	Mintage	F12	VF20	XF40	MS60	MS63
ND-2001	—	PF63 100	PF65 120			

KM# 59 50 DIRHAMS
40.00 g., 0.925 Silver 1.1819 oz. ASW, 40 mm. **Subject:** 25th Anniversary - Arab Bank of Investment and Foreign Trade **Edge:** Reeded

Date	Mintage	F12	VF20	XF40	MS60	MS63
ND-2001	2,000	PF63 125	PF65 140			

KM# 60 50 DIRHAMS
40.00 g., 0.925 Silver 1.1819 oz. ASW, 40 mm. **Subject:** 25th Anniversary - Armed Forces Unification **Edge:** Reeded

Date	Mintage	F12	VF20	XF40	MS60	MS63
ND-2001	10,000	PF63 90.00	PF65 110			

KM# 61 50 DIRHAMS
40.00 g., 0.925 Silver 1.1819 oz. ASW, 40 mm. **Subject:** 30th Anniversary - Al-Ain National Museum **Edge:** Reeded

Date	Mintage	F12	VF20	XF40	MS60	MS63
ND-2001	5,000	PF63 85.00	PF65 100			

KM# 62 50 DIRHAMS
40.00 g., 0.925 Silver 1.1819 oz. ASW, 40 mm. **Subject:** 25th Anniversary - University of the U.A.E. **Obv:** Bust of President H. H. Sheikh Zayed bin Sultan Al Nahyan 7/8 right **Rev:** Inscriptions **Edge:** Reeded

Date	Mintage	F12	VF20	XF40	MS60	MS63
ND-2002	5,000	PF63 85.00	PF65 100			

KM# 63 50 DIRHAMS
40.00 g., 0.925 Silver 1.1819 oz. ASW, 40 mm. **Subject:** Etisalat - Emirates Telecommunications, 25th Anniversary **Obv:** Value **Rev:** Stylized 25 **Edge:** Reeded

Date	Mintage	F12	VF20	XF40	MS60	MS63
ND-2002	5,000	PF63 100	PF65 120			

KM# 64 50 DIRHAMS
40.00 g., 0.925 Silver 1.1819 oz. ASW, 40 mm. **Subject:** Sheikh Hamdan bin Rashid al Maktoum Award for Medical Sciences **Obv:** Value **Rev:** Sheikh Hamdan bin Rashid al Maktoum bust 3/4 left **Edge:** Reeded

Date	Mintage	F12	VF20	XF40	MS60	MS63
ND-2002	2,000	PF63 180	PF65 200			

KM# 65 50 DIRHAMS
40.00 g., 0.925 Silver 1.1819 oz. ASW, 40 mm. **Subject:** Al Ahmadia School, 90th Anniversary **Obv:** Sheikh Rashid bin Saaed al Maktoum 3/4 left **Rev:** School building **Edge:** Reeded

Date	Mintage	F12	VF20	XF40	MS60	MS63
ND-2002	5,000	PF63 100	PF65 120			

KM# 67 50 DIRHAMS
40.00 g., 0.925 Silver 1.1819 oz. ASW, 40 mm. **Subject:** Administrative Development Institute, 20th Anniversary **Obv:** Sheikh Zayed bin Sultan al Nahyan bust 3/4 right **Rev:** Eagle **Edge:** Reeded

Date	Mintage	F12	VF20	XF40	MS60	MS63
ND-2002	2,000	PF63 140	PF65 160			

KM# 50 50 DIRHAMS
40.00 g., 0.925 Silver 1.1819 oz. ASW, 40 mm. **Obv:** Value **Rev:** FIFA 2003 World Youth Soccer Championship **Edge:** Reeded

Date	Mintage	F12	VF20	XF40	MS60	MS63
ND-2003	—	PF63 95.00				

KM# 66 50 DIRHAMS
40.00 g., 0.925 Silver 1.1819 oz. ASW, 40 mm. **Subject:** Ministry of Finance and Industry ISO Certification **Obv:** Value **Rev:** Eagle at center **Edge:** Reeded

Date	Mintage	F12	VF20	XF40	MS60	MS63
ND-2003	3,000	PF63 110				

KM# 68 50 DIRHAMS
40.00 g., 0.925 Silver 1.1819 oz. ASW, 40 mm. **Subject:** U.A.E. Central Bank, 30th Anniversary **Obv:** Sheikh Zayed bin Sultan al Nahyan bust 3/4 right **Rev:** Sheikh Maktoum bin Rashid al Maktoum bust 3/4 right **Edge:** Reeded

Date	Mintage	F12	VF20	XF40	MS60	MS63
ND-2003	5,000	PF63 130	PF65 150			

KM# 69 50 DIRHAMS
40.00 g., 0.925 Silver 1.1819 oz. ASW, 40 mm. **Subject:** 58th Annual Meeting of the World Bank Group and the Int'l Money Fund **Obv:** Colored dots **Edge:** Reeded

Date	Mintage	F12	VF20	XF40	MS60	MS63
ND-2003	10,000	PF63 100	PF65 120			

KM# 70 50 DIRHAMS
40.00 g., 0.925 Silver 1.1819 oz. ASW, 40 mm. **Subject:** 40th Anniversary - First Oil Export from Abu Dhabi Onshore Oil Fields (ADCO) **Obv:** Bust of President H. H. Sheikh Zayed bin Sultan Al Nayhan 3/4 right **Rev:** Logo **Edge:** Reeded

Date	Mintage	F12	VF20	XF40	MS60	MS63
ND-2004	—	PF63 550	PF65 600			

KM# 71 50 DIRHAMS
40.00 g., 0.925 Silver 1.1819 oz. ASW, 40 mm. **Subject:** 25th Anniversary - Sharjah City for Humanitarian Services (SCHS) **Edge:** Reeded

Date	Mintage	F12	VF20	XF40	MS60	MS63
ND-2005	—	PF63 150	PF65 175			

KM# 98 50 DIRHAMS
40.00 g., 0.925 Silver 1.1819 oz. ASW, 40 mm. **Subject:** Sheikha Fatima Birt Mubarak, Mother of the Nation

Date	Mintage	F12	VF20	XF40	MS60	MS63
2005	—	PF63 120	PF65 140			

KM# 82 50 DIRHAMS
40.00 g., 0.925 Silver 1.1819 oz. ASW, 40 mm. **Subject:** 25th Anniversary Emirates Banks Association **Obv:** Value **Obv. Legend:** UNITED ARAB EMIRATES **Rev:** Logo **Edge:** Reeded

Date	Mintage	F12	VF20	XF40	MS60	MS63
ND-2007	—	PF63 120	PF65 140			

KM# 95 50 DIRHAMS
40.00 g., 0.925 Silver 1.1819 oz. ASW, 40 mm. **Subject:** Hamdan Bin Rashed Award for Distinguished Academic Performance **Obv:** Denomination, legend above **Rev:** Pen with tip touching star, legend above **Edge:** Reeded **Note:** Issued 10th Anniversary of the Award

Date	Mintage	F12	VF20	XF40	MS60	MS63
ND(2008)	—	PF63 1,000	PF65 1,100			

KM# 107 50 DIRHAMS
60.00 g., 0.916 Gold 1.7556 oz. AGW, 42.45 mm. **Subject:** World Energy Forum, Dubai **Obv:** Double portraits **Rev:** Logo

Date	Mintage	F12	VF20	XF40	MS60	MS63
2012	—	PF65 3,000				

KM# 80 100 DIRHAMS
60.00 g., 0.925 Silver 1.7729 oz. ASW, 50 mm. **Obv:** Sheikh Zayed bin Sultan **Rev:** Sheikh Zayed Mosque

Date	Mintage	F12	VF20	XF40	MS60	MS63
2004	—	PF63 180	PF65 200			

KM# 97 100 DIRHAMS
60.00 g., 0.925 Silver 1.7729 oz. ASW, 50 mm. **Subject:** Sheikh Khalifa Ben Zayed, 1st Anniversary **Rev:** Emir's Palace

Date	Mintage	F12	VF20	XF40	MS60	MS63
2005	—	PF63 180	PF65 200			

KM# 105 100 DIRHAMS
40.00 g., 0.925 Silver 1.1819 oz. ASW **Subject:** 25th National Day

Date	Mintage	F12	VF20	XF40	MS60	MS63
2012	—	PF63 150	PF65 170			

KM# 104 100 DIRHAMS
0.925 Silver, 40 mm. **Subject:** 5th Anniversary of Date Palm Award

Date	Mintage	F12	VF20	XF40	MS60	MS63
2012	Est. 2000	PF63 150	PF65 170			

UNITED STATES OF AMERICA

The United States of America as politically organized, under the Articles of Confederation consisted of the 13 original British American colonies; New Hampshire, Massachusetts, Rhode Island, Connecticut, New York, New Jersey, Pennsylvania, Delaware, Virginia, North Carolina, South Carolina, Georgia and Maryland. Clustered along the eastern seaboard of North America between the forests of Maine and the marshes of Georgia. Under the Article of Confederation, the United States had no national capital: Philadelphia, where the "United States in Congress Assembled", was the "seat of government". The population during this political phase of America's history (1781-1789) was about 3 million, most of whom lived on self-sufficient family farms. Fishing, lumbering and the production of grains for export were major economic endeavors. Rapid strides were also being made in industry and manufacturing by 1775, the (then) colonies were accounting for one-seventh of the world's production of raw iron.

On the basis of the voyage of John Cabot to the North American mainland in 1497, England claimed the entire continent. The first permanent English settlement was established at Jamestown, Virginia, in 1607. France and Spain also claimed extensive territory in North America. At the end of the French and Indian Wars (1763), England acquired all of the territory east of the Mississippi River, including East and West Florida. From 1776 to 1781, the States were governed by the Continental Congress. From 1781 to 1789, they were organized under the Articles of Confederation, during which period the individual States had the right to issue money. Independence from Great Britain was attained with the American Revolution in 1776. The Constitution organized and governs the present United States. It was ratified on Nov. 21, 1788.

MINT MARKS
C – Charlotte, N.C., 1838-61
CC – Carson City, NV, 1870-93
D – Dahlonega, GA, 1838-61
D – Denver, CO, 1906-present
O – New Orleans, LA, 1838-1909
P – Philadelphia, PA, 1793-present
S – San Francisco, CA, 1854-present
W – West Point, NY, 1984-present

BULLION COINS
Silver Eagle = $1.00
Gold 1/10 Ounce = $5.00
Gold ¼ Ounce = $10.00
Gold ½ Ounce = $25.00
Gold Ounce = $50.00
Platinum 1/10 Ounce = $10.00
Platinum ¼ Ounce = $25.00
Platinum ½ Ounce = $50.00
Platinum Ounce = $100.00

CIRCULATION COINAGE

CENT

Lincoln Cent
Lincoln Memorial reverse

KM# 201b • Copper Plated Zinc, 19 mm. • **Notes:** MS60 prices are for brown coins and MS65 prices are for coins that are at least 90% original red.

Date	Mintage	XF40	MS65	Prf65
2001	4,959,600,000	—	3.00	—
2001D	5,374,990,000	—	3.00	—
2001S	3,099,096	—	—	3.50
2002	3,260,800,000	—	3.00	—
2002D	4,028,055,000	—	3.00	—
2002S	3,157,739	—	—	3.50
2003	3,300,000,000	—	3.50	—
2003D	3,548,000,000	—	3.50	—
2003S	3,116,590	—	—	3.50
2004	3,379,600,000	—	3.50	—
2004D	3,456,400,000	—	3.50	—
2004S	2,992,069	—	—	3.50
2005	3,935,600,000	—	2.50	—
2005 Satin Finish	1,160,000	—	4.00	—
2005D	3,764,450,000	—	2.50	—
2005D Satin Finish	1,160,000	—	4.00	—
2005S	3,273,000	—	—	3.50
2006	4,290,000,000	—	2.00	—
2006 Satin Finish	847,361	—	4.00	—
2006D	3,944,000,000	—	2.50	—
2006D Satin Finish	847,361	—	4.00	—
2006S	2,923,105	—	—	3.50
2007	—	—	2.00	—
2007 Satin Finish	895,628	—	4.00	—
2007D	—	—	2.00	—
2007D Satin Finish	895,628	—	4.00	—
2007S	2,577,166	—	—	3.50
2008	—	—	2.25	—
2008 Satin Finish	745,464	—	4.00	—
2008D	—	—	2.25	—
2008D Satin Finish	745,464	—	4.00	—
2008S	2,169,561	—	—	4.50

Lincoln Bicentennial
Bust right obverse Log cabin reverse

KM# 441 • 2.50 g., Copper Plated Zinc, 19 mm. • **Rev. Designer:** Richard Masters and James Licaretz

Date	Mintage	XF40	MS65	Prf65
2009P	284,400,000	—	1.50	—
2009D	350,400,000	—	1.50	—

KM# 441a • 3.31 g., Brass **Rev. Designer:** Richard Masters and James Licaretz

Date	Mintage	XF40	MS65	Prf65
2009P Satin finish	—	—	4.00	—
2009D Satin finish	—	—	4.00	—
2009S	784,614	—	—	4.00

Lincoln seated on log reverse

KM# 442 • 2.50 g., Copper Plated Zinc, 19 mm. • **Rev. Designer:** Charles Vickers

Date	Mintage	XF40	MS65	Prf65
2009P	376,000,000	—	1.50	—
2009D	363,600,000	—	1.50	—

KM# 442a • 3.11 g., Brass, 19 mm. • **Rev. Designer:** Charles Vickers

Date	Mintage	XF40	MS65	Prf65
2009P Satin finish	—	—	4.00	—
2009D Satin finish	—	—	4.00	—
2009S	784,614	—	—	4.00

Lincoln standing before Illinois Statehouse reverse

KM# 443 • 2.50 g., Copper Plated Zinc, 19 mm. • **Rev. Designer:** Joel Iskowitz and Don Everhart

Date	Mintage	XF40	MS65	Prf65
2009P	316,000,000	—	1.50	—
2009D	336,000,000	—	1.50	—

KM# 443a • 3.11 g., Brass, 19 mm. • **Rev. Designer:** Joel Iskowitz and Don Everhart

Date	Mintage	XF40	MS65	Prf65
2009P Satin finish	—	—	4.00	—
2009D Satin finish	—	—	4.00	—
2009S	784,614	—	—	4.00

Capitol Building reverse

KM# 444 • 2.50 g., Copper Plated Zinc **Rev. Designer:** Susan Gamble and Joseph Menna

Date	Mintage	XF40	MS65	Prf65
2009P	129,600,000	—	1.50	—
2009D	198,000,000	—	1.50	—

KM# 444a • 3.11 g., Brass, 19 mm. • **Rev. Designer:** Susan Ganmble and Joseph Menna

Date	Mintage	XF40	MS65	Prf65
2009P Satin finish	—	—	4.00	—
2009D Satin finish	—	—	4.00	—
2009S	784,614	—	—	4.00

Lincoln - Shield Reverse
Lincoln bust right obverse Shield reverse

KM# 468 • 2.50 g., **Copper Plated Zinc**, 19 mm. • **Obv. Designer:** Victor D. Brenner **Rev. Designer:** Lyndall Bass and Joseph Menna

Date	Mintage	XF40	MS65	Prf65
2010P	1,963,630,000	—	1.50	—
2010P Satin finish	583,912	—	—	—
2010D	2,047,200,000	—	1.50	—
2010D Satin finish	583,912	—	—	—
2010S	1,689,364	—	—	4.00
2011P	2,006,800,000	—	1.50	—
2011D	2147483647	—	1.50	—
2011S	—	—	—	4.00
2012P	—	—	1.50	—
2012D	—	—	1.50	—
2012S	—	—	—	4.00
2013P	—	—	1.50	—
2013D	—	—	1.50	—
2013S	—	—	—	4.00

5 CENTS

Jefferson Nickel
Pre-war design resumed reverse

KM# A192 • 5.00 g., **Copper-Nickel**, 21.2 mm. • **Edge Desc:** Plain **Designer:** Felix Schlag

Date	Mintage	XF40	MS65	Prf65
2001P	675,704,000	—	3.75	—
2001D	627,680,000	—	3.75	—
2001S	3,099,096	—	—	1.00
2002P	539,280,000	—	3.75	—
2002D	691,200,000	—	3.75	—
2002S	3,157,739	—	—	1.00
2003P	441,840,000	—	3.75	—
2003D	383,040,000	—	3.75	—
2003S	3,116,590	—	—	1.00

Jefferson - Westward Expansion - Lewis & Clark Bicentennial
Jefferson era peace medal design:
two clasped hands, pipe and hatchet reverse

KM# 360 • 5.00 g., **Copper-Nickel**, 21.2 mm. • **Obv. Designer:** Felix Schlag **Rev. Designer:** Norman E. Nemeth

Date	Mintage	MS65	Prf65
2004P	361,440,000	—	—
2004D	372,000,000	—	—
2004S	—	—	5.00

Lewis and Clark's Keelboat reverse

KM# 361 • 5.00 g., **Copper-Nickel**, 21.2 mm. • **Obv. Designer:** Felix Schlag **Rev. Designer:** Al Maletsky

Date	Mintage	MS65	Prf65
2004P	366,720,000	1.50	—
2004D	344,880,000	1.50	—
2004S	—	—	5.00

Thomas Jefferson large profile right obverse
American Bison right obverse

KM# 368 • 5.00 g., **Copper-Nickel**, 21.2 mm. • **Obv. Designer:** Joe Fitzgerald and Don Everhart II **Rev. Designer:** Jamie Franki and Norman E. Nemeth

Date	Mintage	MS65	Prf65
2005P	448,320,000	1.50	—
2005P Satin Finish	1,160,000	4.00	—
2005D	487,680,000	1.50	—
2005D Satin Finish	1,160,000	4.00	—
2005S	—	—	6.50

Jefferson, large profile obverse
Pacific coastline reverse

KM# 369 • 5.00 g., **Copper-Nickel**, 21.2 mm. • **Subject:** Ocean in View!, oh the joy! **Obv. Designer:** Joe Fitzgerald and Don Everhart **Rev. Designer:** Joe Fitzgerald and Donna Weaver

Date	Mintage	MS65	Prf65
2005P	394,080,000	1.25	—
2005P Satin Finish	1,160,000	4.00	—
2005D	411,120,000	1.25	—
2005D Satin Finish	1,160,000	4.00	—
2005S	—	—	5.50

Jefferson large facing portrait - Enhanced Monticello Reverse

KM# 381 • 5.00 g., **Copper-Nickel**, 21.2 mm. • **Subject:** Jefferson facing head **Obv. Designer:** Jamie N. Franki and Donna Weaver **Rev. Designer:** Felix Schlag and John Mercanti

Date	Mintage	MS65	Prf65
2006P	693,120,000	2.50	—
2006P Satin finish	847,361	4.00	—
2006D	809,280,000	2.50	—
2006D Satin finish	847,361	4.00	—
2006S	—	—	5.00
2007P	—	2.50	—
2007P Satin finish	895,628	4.00	—
2007D	—	2.50	—
2007D Satin finish	895,628	4.00	—
2007S	—	—	4.00
2008P	—	2.50	—
2008P Satin finish	745,464	4.00	—
2008D	—	2.50	—
2008D Satin finish	745,464	4.00	—
2008S	—	—	4.00
2009P	—	3.50	—
2009P Satin finish	784,614	4.00	—
2009D	—	1.75	—
2009D Satin finish	784,614	4.00	—
2009S	—	—	3.00
2010P	—	1.50	—
2010P Satin finish	—	4.00	—
2010D	—	1.50	—
2010D Satin finish	—	4.00	—
2010S	—	—	3.00
2011P	—	1.50	—
2011D	—	1.50	—
2011S	—	—	4.00
2012P	—	1.50	—
2012D	—	1.50	—
2012S	—	—	4.00
2013P	—	1.50	—
2013D	—	1.50	—
2013S	—	—	3.00

DIME

Roosevelt Dime

Mint mark 1968- present

KM# 195a • 2.27 g., **Copper-Nickel Clad Copper**, 17.91 mm. • **Designer:** John R. Sinnock **Notes:** The 1979-S and 1981-S Type II proofs have clearer mint marks than the Type I proofs of those years. On the 1982 no-mint-mark variety, the mint mark was inadvertently left off.

Date	Mintage	MS65	Prf65
2001P	1,369,590,000	2.75	—
2001D	1,412,800,000	2.75	—
2001S	2,249,496	—	3.75
2002P	1,187,500,000	2.75	—
2002D	1,379,500,000	3.00	—
2002S	2,268,913	—	2.50
2003P	1,085,500,000	3.00	—
2003D	986,500,000	3.00	—
2003S	2,076,165	—	2.60
2004P	1,328,000,000	3.00	—
2004D	1,159,500,000	3.00	—
2004S	1,804,396	—	4.75
2005P	1,412,000,000	2.75	—
2005P Satin Finish	—	4.00	—
2005D	1,423,500,000	2.75	—
2005D Satin Finish	—	4.00	—
2005S	—	—	2.60
2006P	1,381,000,000	2.50	—
2006P Satin Finish	—	4.00	—
2006D	1,447,000,000	2.50	—
2006D Satin Finish	—	4.00	—
2006S	—	—	2.50
2007P	—	2.00	—
2007P Satin Finish	—	3.00	—
2007D	—	2.00	—
2007D Satin Finish	—	3.00	—
2007S	—	—	2.50
2008P	—	1.25	—
2008 Satin Finish	—	2.50	—
2008D	—	1.25	—
2008 Satin Finish	—	2.50	—
2008S	—	—	2.50
2009P	—	1.25	—
2009 Satin Finish	—	1.00	—
2009D	—	1.25	—
2009 Satin Finish	—	1.00	—
2009S	—	—	2.50
2010P	—	4.00	—
2010P Satin Finish	—	2.00	—
2010D	—	4.00	—
2010D Satin Finish	—	2.00	—
2010S	—	—	2.50
2011P	—	4.00	—
2011D	—	4.00	—
2011S	—	—	2.50
2012P	—	4.00	—
2012D	—	4.00	—
2012S	—	—	2.50
2013P	—	4.00	—
2013D	—	4.00	—
2013S	—	—	2.50

KM# 195b • 2.50 g., 0.900 **Silver** 0.0719 oz. ASW, 17.9 mm. • **Designer:** John R. Sinnock

Date	Mintage	Prf65
2001S	849,600	5.00
2002S	888,826	5.00
2003S	1,090,425	4.75
2004S	—	5.00
2005S	—	5.00
2006S	—	4.50
2007S	—	6.00
2008S	—	6.50
2009S	—	6.75
2010S	—	6.75
2011S	—	6.75
2012S	—	6.75
2013S	—	6.75

QUARTER

50 STATE QUARTERS

New York

KM# 318 • 5.67 g., **Copper-Nickel Clad Copper**, 24.3 mm.

Date	Mintage	MS63	MS65	Prf65
2001P	655,400,000	0.80	5.50	—
2001D	619,640,000	0.80	5.50	—
2001S	3,094,140	—	—	4.00

KM# 318a • 6.25 g., 0.900 **Silver** 0.1797 oz. ASW, 24.3 mm.

Date	Mintage	MS63	MS65	Prf65
2001S	889,697	—	—	9.50

North Carolina

KM# 319 • 5.67 g., **Copper-Nickel Clad Copper**, 24.3 mm.

Date	Mintage	MS63	MS65	Prf65
2001P	627,600,000	1.00	5.50	—
2001D	427,876,000	1.00	6.50	—
2001S	3,094,140	—	—	4.00

KM# 319a • 6.25 g., 0.900 **Silver** 0.1797 oz. ASW, 24.3 mm.

Date	Mintage	MS63	MS65	Prf65
2001S	889,697	—	—	9.50

Rhode Island

KM# 320 • 5.67 g., **Copper-Nickel Clad Copper**, 24.3 mm.

Date	Mintage	MS63	MS65	Prf65
2001P	423,000,000	0.80	5.50	—
2001D	447,100,000	0.80	6.00	—
2001S	3,094,140	—	—	4.00

KM# 320a • 6.25 g., 0.900 **Silver** 0.1797 oz. ASW, 24.3 mm.

Date	Mintage	MS63	MS65	Prf65
2001S	889,697	—	—	9.50

Vermont

KM# 321 • 5.67 g., **Copper-Nickel Clad Copper**, 24.3 mm.

Date	Mintage	MS63	MS65	Prf65
2001P	423,400,000	0.80	6.50	—
2001D	459,404,000	0.80	6.50	—
2001S	3,094,140	—	—	4.00

KM# 321a • 6.25 g., 0.900 **Silver** 0.1797 oz. ASW, 24.3 mm.

Date	Mintage	MS63	MS65	Prf65
2001S	889,697	—	—	9.50

Kentucky

KM# 322 • 5.67 g., **Copper-Nickel Clad Copper**, 24.3 mm.

Date	Mintage	MS63	MS65	Prf65
2001P	353,000,000	1.00	6.50	—
2001D	370,564,000	1.00	7.00	—
2001S	3,094,140	—	—	4.00

KM# 322a • 6.25 g., 0.900 **Silver** 0.1797 oz. ASW, 24.3 mm.

Date	Mintage	MS63	MS65	Prf65
2001S	889,697	—	—	9.50

Tennessee

KM# 331 • 5.67 g., **Copper-Nickel Clad Copper**, 24.3 mm.

Date	Mintage	MS63	MS65	Prf65
2002P	361,600,000	1.40	6.50	—
2002D	286,468,000	1.40	7.00	—
2002S	3,084,245	—	—	2.30

KM# 331a • 6.25 g., 0.900 **Silver** 0.1797 oz. ASW, 24.3 mm.

Date	Mintage	MS63	MS65	Prf65
2002S	892,229	—	—	8.50

Ohio

KM# 332 • 5.67 g., **Copper-Nickel Clad Copper**, 24.3 mm.

Date	Mintage	MS63	MS65	Prf65
2002P	217,200,000	0.80	5.50	—
2002D	414,832,000	0.80	5.50	—
2002S	3,084,245	—	—	2.30

KM# 332a • 6.25 g., 0.900 **Silver** 0.1797 oz. ASW, 24.3 mm.

Date	Mintage	MS63	MS65	Prf65
2002S	892,229	—	—	8.50

Louisiana

KM# 333 • 5.67 g., **Copper-Nickel Clad Copper**, 24.3 mm.

Date	Mintage	MS63	MS65	Prf65
2002P	362,000,000	0.80	5.50	—
2002D	402,204,000	0.80	6.00	—
2002S	3,084,245	—	—	2.30

KM# 333a • 6.25 g., 0.900 **Silver** 0.1797 oz. ASW, 24.3 mm.

Date	Mintage	MS63	MS65	Prf65
2002S	892,229	—	—	8.50

Indiana

KM# 334 • 5.67 g., **Copper-Nickel Clad Copper**, 24.3 mm.

Date	Mintage	MS63	MS65	Prf65
2002P	362,600,000	0.80	5.00	—
2002D	327,200,000	0.80	5.00	—
2002S	3,084,245	—	—	2.30

KM# 334a • 6.25 g., 0.900 **Silver** 0.1797 oz. ASW, 24.3 mm.

Date	Mintage	MS63	MS65	Prf65
2002S	892,229	—	—	8.50

Mississippi

KM# 335 • 5.67 g., **Copper-Nickel Clad Copper**, 24.3 mm.

Date	Mintage	MS63	MS65	Prf65
2002P	290,000,000	0.80	5.00	—
2002D	289,600,000	0.80	5.00	—
2002S	3,084,245	—	—	2.30

KM# 335a • 6.25 g., 0.900 **Silver** 0.1797 oz. ASW, 24.3 mm.

Date	Mintage	MS63	MS65	Prf65
2002S	892,229	—	—	8.50

Illinois

KM# 343 • 5.67 g., **Copper-Nickel Clad Copper**, 24.3 mm.

Date	Mintage	MS63	MS65	Prf65
2003P	225,800,000	1.10	5.00	—
2003D	237,400,000	1.10	5.00	—
2003S	3,408,516	—	—	2.30

KM# 343a • 6.25 g., 0.900 **Silver** 0.1797 oz. ASW, 24.3 mm.

Date	Mintage	MS63	MS65	Prf65
2003S	1,257,555	—	—	8.50

Alabama

KM# 344 • 5.67 g., **Copper-Nickel Clad Copper**, 24.3 mm.

Date	Mintage	MS63	MS65	Prf65
2003P	225,000,000	0.65	5.00	—
2003D	232,400,000	0.65	5.00	—
2003S	3,408,516	—	—	2.30

KM# 344a • 6.25 g., 0.900 **Silver** 0.1797 oz. ASW, 24.3 mm.

Date	Mintage	MS63	MS65	Prf65
2003S	1,257,555	—	—	8.50

Maine

KM# 345 • 5.67 g., **Copper-Nickel Clad Copper**, 24.3 mm.

Date	Mintage	MS63	MS65	Prf65
2003P	217,400,000	0.65	5.00	—
2003D	213,400,000	0.65	5.00	—
2003S	3,408,516	—	—	2.30

KM# 345a • 6.25 g., 0.900 **Silver** 0.1797 oz. ASW, 24.3 mm.

Date	Mintage	MS63	MS65	Prf65
2003S	1,257,555	—	—	8.50

Missouri

KM# 346 • 5.67 g., **Copper-Nickel Clad Copper**, 24.3 mm.

Date	Mintage	MS63	MS65	Prf65
2003P	225,000,000	0.65	5.00	—
2003D	228,200,000	0.65	5.00	—
2003S	3,408,516	—	—	2.30

KM# 346a • 6.25 g., 0.900 **Silver** 0.1797 oz. ASW, 24.3 mm.

Date	Mintage	MS63	MS65	Prf65
2003S	1,257,555	—	—	8.50

Arkansas

KM# 347 • 5.67 g., **Copper-Nickel Clad Copper**, 24.3 mm.

Date	Mintage	MS63	MS65	Prf65
2003P	228,000,000	0.65	5.00	—
2003D	229,800,000	0.65	5.00	—
2003S	3,408,516	—	—	2.30

KM# 347a • 6.25 g., 0.900 **Silver** 0.1797 oz. ASW, 24.3 mm.

Date	Mintage	MS63	MS65	Prf65
2003S	1,257,555	—	—	8.50

Michigan

KM# 355 • 5.67 g., **Copper-Nickel Clad Copper**, 24.3 mm.

Date	Mintage	MS63	MS65	Prf65
2004P	233,800,000	0.65	5.00	—
2004D	225,800,000	0.65	5.00	—
2004S	2,740,684	—	—	2.30

KM# 355a • 6.25 g., 0.900 **Silver** 0.1797 oz. ASW, 24.3 mm.

Date	Mintage	MS63	MS65	Prf65
2004S	1,775,370	—	—	8.50

Florida

KM# 356 • 5.67 g., **Copper-Nickel Clad Copper**, 24.3 mm.

Date	Mintage	MS63	MS65	Prf65
2004P	240,200,000	0.65	5.00	—
2004D	241,600,000	0.65	5.00	—
2004S	2,740,684	—	—	2.30

KM# 356a • 6.25 g., 0.900 **Silver** 0.1797 oz. ASW, 24.3 mm.

Date	Mintage	MS63	MS65	Prf65
2004S	1,775,370	—	—	8.50

Texas

KM# 357 • 5.67 g., **Copper-Nickel Clad Copper**, 24.3 mm.

Date	Mintage	MS63	MS65	Prf65
2004P	278,800,000	0.65	5.00	

Date	Mintage	MS63	MS65	Prf65
2004D	263,000,000	0.65	5.00	
2004S	2,740,684			2.30

KM# 357a • 6.25 g., 0.900 **Silver** 0.1797 oz. ASW, 24.3 mm.

Date	Mintage	MS63	MS65	Prf65
2004S	1,775,370	—	—	8.50

Iowa

KM# 358 • 5.67 g., **Copper-Nickel Clad Copper**, 24.3 mm.

Date	Mintage	MS63	MS65	Prf65
2004P	213,800,000	0.65	5.00	—
2004D	251,800,000	0.65	5.00	—
2004S	2,740,684	—	—	2.30

KM# 358a • 6.25 g., 0.900 **Silver** 0.1797 oz. ASW, 24.3 mm.

Date	Mintage	MS63	MS65	Prf65
2004S	—	—	—	8.50

Wisconsin

KM# 359 • 5.67 g., **Copper-Nickel Clad Copper**, 24.3 mm.

Date	Mintage	MS63	MS65	Prf65
2004P	226,400,000	0.65	5.00	—
2004D	226,800,000	0.65	5.00	—
2004D Extra Leaf Low	Est. 9000	135	190	—
2004D Extra Leaf High	Est. 3000	175	285	—
2004S	—	—	—	2.30

KM# 359a • 6.25 g., 0.900 **Silver** 0.1797 oz. ASW, 24.3 mm.

Date	Mintage	MS63	MS65	Prf65
2004S	1,775,370	—	—	8.50

Minnesota

KM# 371 • 5.67 g., **Copper-Nickel Clad Copper**, 24.3 mm.

Date	Mintage	MS63	MS65	Prf65
2005P	226,400,000	0.65	5.00	—
2005P Satin Finish	Inc. above	1.50	4.50	—
2005D	226,800,000	0.65	5.00	—
2005D Satin Finish	Inc. above	1.50	4.50	—
2005S	3,262,960	—	—	2.30

KM# 371a • 6.25 g., 0.900 **Silver** 0.1797 oz. ASW, 24.3 mm.

Date	Mintage	MS63	MS65	Prf65
2005S	1,679,600	—	—	8.50

Oregon

KM# 372 • 5.67 g., **Copper-Nickel Clad Copper**, 24.3 mm.

Date	Mintage	MS63	MS65	Prf65
2005P	316,200,000	0.65	5.00	—
2005P Satin Finish	Inc. above	1.50	4.50	—
2005D	404,000,000	0.65	5.00	—
2005D Satin Finish	Inc. above	1.50	4.50	—
2005S	3,262,960	—	—	2.30

KM# 372a • 6.25 g., 0.900 **Silver** 0.1797 oz. ASW, 24.3 mm.

Date	Mintage	MS63	MS65	Prf65
2005S	1,679,600	—	—	8.50

Kansas

KM# 373 • 5.67 g., **Copper-Nickel Clad Copper**, 24.3 mm.

Date	Mintage	MS63	MS65	Prf65
2005P	263,400,000	0.65	5.00	—
2005P Satin Finish	Inc. above	1.50	4.50	—
2005D	300,000,000	0.65	5.00	—
2005D Satin Finish	Inc. above	1.50	4.50	—
2005S	3,262,960	—	—	2.30

KM# 373a • 6.25 g., 0.900 **Silver** 0.1797 oz. ASW, 24.3 mm.

Date	Mintage	MS63	MS65	Prf65
2005S	1,679,600	—	—	8.50

West Virginia

KM# 374 • 5.67 g., **Copper-Nickel Clad Copper**, 24.3 mm.

Date	Mintage	MS63	MS65	Prf65
2005P	365,400,000	0.65	5.00	—
2005P Satin Finish	Inc. above	1.50	4.50	—
2005D	356,200,000	0.65	5.00	—
2005D Satin Finish	Inc. above	1.50	4.50	—
2005S	3,262,960	—	—	2.30

KM# 374a • 6.25 g., 0.900 **Silver** 0.1797 oz. ASW, 24.3 mm.

Date	Mintage	MS63	MS65	Prf65
2005S	1,679,600	—	—	8.50

California

KM# 370 • 5.67 g., **Copper-Nickel Clad Copper**, 24.3 mm.

Date	Mintage	MS63	MS65	Prf65
2005P	257,200,000	0.65	5.00	—
2005P Satin Finish	Inc. above	1.50	4.50	—
2005D	263,200,000	0.65	5.00	—
2005D Satin Finish	Inc. above	1.50	4.50	—
2005S	3,262,960	—	—	2.30

KM# 370a • 6.25 g., 0.900 **Silver** 0.1797 oz. ASW, 24.3 mm.

Date	Mintage	MS63	MS65	Prf65
2005S	1,679,600	—	—	8.50

Nevada

KM# 382 • 5.67 g., **Copper-Nickel Clad Copper**, 24.3 mm.

Date	Mintage	MS63	MS65	Prf65
2006P	277,000,000	0.65	5.00	—
2006P Satin Finish	Inc. above	1.50	4.50	—
2006D	312,800,000	0.65	5.00	—
2006D Satin Finish	Inc. above	1.50	4.50	—
2006S	2,862,078	—	—	2.30

KM# 382a • 6.25 g., 0.900 **Silver** 0.1797 oz. ASW, 24.3 mm.

Date	Mintage	MS63	MS65	Prf65
2006S	1,571,839	—	—	8.50

Nebraska

KM# 383 • 5.67 g., **Copper-Nickel Clad Copper**, 24.3 mm.

Date	Mintage	MS63	MS65	Prf65
2006P	318,000,000	0.65	5.00	—
2006P Satin Finish	Inc. above	1.50	4.50	—
2006D	273,000,000	0.65	5.00	—
2006D Satin Finish	Inc. above	1.50	4.50	—
2006S	2,862,078	—	—	2.30

KM# 383a • 6.25 g., 0.900 **Silver** 0.1797 oz. ASW, 24.3 mm.

Date	Mintage	MS63	MS65	Prf65
2006S	1,571,839	—	—	8.50

Colorado

KM# 384 • 5.67 g., **Copper-Nickel Clad Copper**, 24.3 mm.

Date	Mintage	MS63	MS65	Prf65
2006P	274,800,000	0.65	5.00	—
2006P Satin Finish	Inc. above	1.50	4.50	—
2006D	294,200,000	0.65	5.00	—
2006D Satin Finish	Inc. above	1.50	4.50	—
2006S	2,862,078	—	—	2.30

KM# 384a • 6.25 g., 0.900 **Silver** 0.1797 oz. ASW, 24.3 mm.

Date	Mintage	MS63	MS65	Prf65
2006S	1,571,839	—	—	8.50

North Dakota

KM# 385 • 5.67 g., **Copper-Nickel Clad Copper**, 24.3 mm.

Date	Mintage	MS63	MS65	Prf65
2006P	305,800,000	0.65	5.00	—
2006P Satin Finish	Inc. above	1.50	4.50	—
2006D	359,000,000	0.65	5.00	—
2006D Satin Finish	Inc. above	1.50	4.50	—
2006S	2,862,078	—	—	2.30

KM# 385a • 6.25 g., 0.900 **Silver** 0.1797 oz. ASW, 24.3 mm.

Date	Mintage	MS63	MS65	Prf65
2006S	1,571,839	—	—	8.50

South Dakota

KM# 386 • 5.67 g., **Copper-Nickel Clad Copper**, 24.3 mm.

Date	Mintage	MS63	MS65	Prf65
2006P	245,000,000	0.65	5.00	—
2006P Satin Finish	Inc. above	1.50	4.50	—
2006D	265,800,000	0.65	5.00	—
2006D Satin Finish	Inc. above	1.50	4.50	—
2006S	2,862,078	—	—	2.30

KM# 386a • 6.25 g., 0.900 **Silver** 0.1797 oz. ASW, 24.3 mm.

Date	Mintage	MS63	MS65	Prf65
2006S	1,571,839	—	—	8.50

Montana

KM# 396 • 5.67 g., **Copper-Nickel Clad Copper**, 24.3 mm.

Date	Mintage	MS63	MS65	Prf65
2007P	257,000,000	0.65	5.00	—
2007 Satin Finish	—	1.50	4.50	—
2007 Satin Finish	—	1.50	4.50	—
2007D	256,240,000	0.65	5.00	—
2007S	2,374,778	—	—	2.30

KM# 396a • 6.25 g., 0.900 **Silver** 0.1797 oz. ASW, 24.3 mm.

Date	Mintage	MS63	MS65	Prf65
2007S	1,299,878	—	—	8.50

Washington

KM# 397 • 5.67 g., **Copper-Nickel Clad Copper**, 24.3 mm.

Date	Mintage	MS63	MS65	Prf65
2007P	265,200,000	0.65	5.00	—
2007P Satin Finish	—	1.50	4.50	—
2007D	280,000,000	0.65	5.00	—
2007D Satin Finish	—	1.50	4.50	—
2007S	2,374,778	—	—	2.30

KM# 397a • 6.25 g., 0.900 **Silver** 0.1797 oz. ASW, 24.3 mm.

Date	Mintage	MS63	MS65	Prf65
2007S	1,299,878	—	—	8.50

Idaho

KM# 398 • 5.67 g., **Copper-Nickel Clad Copper**, 24.3 mm.

Date	Mintage	MS63	MS65	Prf65
2007P	294,600,000	0.65	5.00	—
2007P Satin finish	—	1.50	4.50	—
2007D	286,800,000	0.65	5.00	—
2007D Satin finish	—	1.50	4.50	—
2007S	2,374,778	—	—	2.30

KM# 398a • 6.25 g., 0.900 **Silver** 0.1797 oz. ASW, 24.3 mm.

Date	Mintage	MS63	MS65	Prf65
2007S	1,299,878	—	—	8.50

Wyoming

KM# 399 • 5.67 g., **Copper-Nickel Clad Copper**, 24.3 mm.

Date	Mintage	MS63	MS65	Prf65
2007P	243,600,000	0.65	5.00	—
2007P Satin finish	—	1.50	4.50	—
2007D	320,800,000	0.65	5.00	—
2007 Satin finish	—	1.50	4.50	—
2007S	2,374,778	—	—	2.30

KM# 399a • 6.25 g., 0.900 **Silver** 0.1797 oz. ASW, 24.3 mm.

Date	Mintage	MS63	MS65	Prf65
2007S	1,299,878	—	—	8.50

Utah

KM# 400 • 5.67 g., **Copper-Nickel Clad Copper**, 24.3 mm.

Date	Mintage	MS63	MS65	Prf65
2007P	255,000,000	0.65	5.00	—
2007P Satin finish	—	1.50	4.50	—
2007D	253,200,000	0.65	5.00	—
2007D Satin finish	—	1.50	4.50	—
2007S	2,374,778	—	—	2.30

KM# 400a • 6.25 g., 0.900 **Silver** 0.1797 oz. ASW

Date	Mintage	MS63	MS65	Prf65
2007S	1,299,878	—	—	8.50

Oklahoma

KM# 421 • 5.67 g., **Copper-Nickel Clad Copper**, 24.3 mm.

Date	Mintage	MS63	MS65	Prf65
2008P	222,000,000	0.65	5.00	—
2008P Satin finish	—	1.50	4.50	—
2008D	194,600,000	0.65	5.00	—
2008D Satin finish	—	1.50	4.50	—
2008S	2,100,000	—	—	2.30

KM# 421a • 6.25 g., 0.900 **Silver** 0.1797 oz. ASW, 24.3 mm.

Date	Mintage	MS63	MS65	Prf65
2008S	1,200,000	—	—	8.50

New Mexico

KM# 422 • 5.67 g., **Copper-Nickel Clad Copper**, 24.3 mm.

Date	Mintage	MS63	MS65	Prf65
2008P	244,200,000	0.65	5.00	—
2008P Satin finish	—	1.50	4.50	—
2008D	244,400,000	0.65	5.00	—
2008D Satin finish	—	1.50	4.50	—
2008S	2,100,000	—	—	2.30

KM# 422a • 6.25 g., 0.900 **Silver** 0.1797 oz. ASW, 24.3 mm.

Date	Mintage	MS63	MS65	Prf65
2008S	1,200,000	—	—	8.50

Arizona

KM# 423 • 5.67 g., **Copper-Nickel Clad Copper**, 24.3 mm.

Date	Mintage	MS63	MS65	Prf65
2008P	244,600,000	0.65	5.00	—
2008P Satin finish	—	1.50	4.50	—
2008D	265,000,000	0.65	5.00	—
2008D Satin finish	—	1.50	4.50	—
2008S	2,100,000	—	—	2.30

KM# 423a • 6.25 g., 0.900 **Silver** 0.1797 oz. ASW, 24.3 mm.

Date	Mintage	MS63	MS65	Prf65
2008S	1,200,000	—	—	8.50

Alaska

KM# 424 • 5.67 g., **Copper-Nickel Clad Copper**, 24.3 mm.

Date	Mintage	MS63	MS65	Prf65
2008P	251,800,000	0.65	5.00	—
2008P Satin finish		1.50	4.50	—
2008D	254,000,000	0.65	5.00	—
2008D Satin finish		1.50	4.50	—
2008S	2,100,000			2.30

KM# 424a • 6.25 g., 0.900 **Silver** 0.1797 oz. ASW, 24.3 mm.

Date	Mintage	MS63	MS65	Prf65
2008S	1,200,000	—	—	8.50

Hawaii

KM# 425 • 5.67 g., **Copper-Nickel Clad Copper**, 24.3 mm.

Date	Mintage	MS63	MS65	Prf65
2008P	254,000,000	0.65	5.00	—
2008P Satin finish		1.50	4.50	—
2008D	263,600,000	0.65	5.00	—
2008D Satin finish		1.50	4.50	—
2008S	2,100,000			2.30

KM# 425a • 6.25 g., 0.900 **Silver** 0.1797 oz. ASW, 24.3 mm.

Date	Mintage	MS63	MS65	Prf65
2008S	1,200,000	—	—	8.50

DC AND TERRITORIES

District of Columbia

KM# 445 • 5.67 g., **Copper-Nickel Clad Copper**, 24.3 mm.
Rev. Designer: Don Everhart

Date	Mintage	MS63	MS65	Prf65
2009P	83,600,000	0.75	5.00	—
2009D	88,800,000	0.75	5.00	—
2009S				3.75

KM# 445a • 6.25 g., 0.900 **Silver** 0.1797 oz. ASW, 24.3 mm.

Date	Mintage	MS63	MS65	Prf65
2009S	—			7.75

Puerto Rico

KM# 446 • 5.67 g., **Copper-Nickel Clad Copper**, 24.3 mm.
Rev. Designer: Joseph Menna

Date	Mintage	MS63	MS65	Prf65
2009P	53,200,000	0.75	5.00	—
2009D	86,000,000	0.75	5.00	—
2009S				3.75

KM# 446a • 6.25 g., 0.900 **Silver** 0.1797 oz. ASW, 24.3 mm.

Date	Mintage	MS63	MS65	Prf65
2009S	—			7.75

Guam

KM# 447 • 5.67 g., **Copper-Nickel Clad Copper**, 24.3 mm.
Rev. Designer: James Licaretz

Date	Mintage	MS63	MS65	Prf65
2009P	45,000,000	0.75	5.00	—
2009D	42,600,000	0.75	5.00	—
2009S				3.75

KM# 447a • 6.25 g., 0.900 **Silver** 0.1797 oz. ASW, 24.3 mm.

Date	Mintage	MS63	MS65	Prf65
2009S	—			7.75

American Samoa

KM# 448 • 5.67 g., **Copper-Nickel Clad Copper**, 24.3 mm.
Rev. Designer: Charles Vickers

Date	Mintage	MS63	MS65	Prf65
2009P	42,600,000	0.75	5.00	—
2009D	39,600,000	0.75	5.00	—
2009S				3.75

KM# 448a • 6.25 g., 0.900 **Silver** 0.1797 oz. ASW, 24.3 mm.

Date	Mintage	MS63	MS65	Prf65
2009S	—			7.75

US Virgin Islands

KM# 449 • 5.67 g., **Copper-Nickel Clad Copper**, 24.3 mm.
Rev. Designer: Joseph Menna

Date	Mintage	MS63	MS65	Prf65
2009P	41,000,000	0.75	5.00	—
2009D	41,000,000	0.75	5.00	—
2009S				3.75

KM# 449a • 6.25 g., 0.900 **Silver** 0.1797 oz. ASW, 24.3 mm.

Date	Mintage	MS63	MS65	Prf65
2009S	—			7.75

Northern Mariana Islands

KM# 466 • 5.67 g., **Copper-Nickel Clad Copper** Rev.
Designer: Pheve Hemphill

Date	Mintage	MS63	MS65	Prf65
2009P	35,200,000	0.75	5.00	—
2009D	37,600,000	0.75	5.00	—
2009S				3.75

KM# 466a • 6.25 g., 0.900 **Silver** 0.1797 oz. ASW

Date	Mintage	MS63	MS65	Prf65
2009S	—			7.75

AMERICA THE BEAUTIFUL

Hot Springs, Ark.

KM# 469 • 5.67 g., **Copper-Nickel Clad Copper**, 24.3 mm.

Date	Mintage	MS63	MS65	Prf65
2010P	—	0.75	5.00	—
2010D	—	0.75	5.00	—
2010S	—			3.75

KM# 469a • 6.25 g., 0.900 **Silver** 0.1797 oz. ASW

Date	Mintage	MS63	MS65	Prf65
2010S	—			7.75

Yellowstone National Park

KM# 470 • 5.67 g., **Copper-Nickel Clad Copper**, 24.3 mm.
Rev. Designer: Don Everhart

Date	Mintage	MS63	MS65	Prf65
2010P	—	0.75	5.00	—
2010D	—	0.75	5.00	—
2010S	—			3.75

KM# 470a • 6.25 g., 0.900 **Silver** 0.1797 oz. ASW

Date	Mintage	MS63	MS65	Prf65
2010	—			7.75

Yosemite National Park

KM# 471 • 5.67 g., **Copper-Nickel Clad Copper**, 24.3 mm.
Rev. Designer: Joseph Menna and Phebe Hemphill

Date	Mintage	MS63	MS65	Prf65
2010P	—	0.75	5.00	—
2010D	—	0.75	5.00	—
2010S	—			3.75

KM# 471a • 6.25 g., 0.900 **Silver** 0.1797 oz. ASW

Date	Mintage	MS63	MS65	Prf65
2010	—			7.75

Grand Canyon National Park

KM# 472 • 5.67 g., **Copper-Nickel Clad Copper**, 24.3 mm.
Rev. Designer: Phebe Hemphill

Date	Mintage	MS63	MS65	Prf65
2010P	—	0.75	5.00	—
2010D	—	0.75	5.00	—
2010S	—			3.75

KM# 472a • 6.25 g., 0.900 **Silver** 0.1797 oz. ASW

Date	Mintage	MS63	MS65	Prf65
2010	—			7.75

Mount Hood National Park

KM# 473 • 5.67 g., **Copper-Nickel Clad Copper**, 24.3 mm.
Rev. Designer: Phebe Hemphill

Date	Mintage	MS63	MS65	Prf65
2010P	—	0.75	5.00	—
2010D	—	0.75	5.00	—
2010S	—	—	—	3.75

KM# 473a • 6.25 g., 0.900 **Silver** 0.1797 oz. ASW

Date	Mintage	MS63	MS65	Prf65
2010	—	—	—	7.75

Gettysburg National Military Park

KM# 494 • 5.67 g., **Copper-Nickel Clad Copper**, 24 mm. **Rev. Designer:** Joel Iskowitz and Phebe Hemphill

Date	Mintage	MS63	MS65	Prf65
2011P	—	0.75	5.00	—
2011D	—	0.75	5.00	—
2011S	—	—	—	3.75

KM# 494a • 6.25 g., 0.900 **Silver** 0.1797 oz. ASW

Date	Mintage	MS63	MS65	Prf65
2011S	—	—	—	7.75

Glacier National Park

KM# 495 • 5.67 g., **Copper-Nickel Clad Copper**, 24 mm. **Rev. Designer:** Barbara Fox and Charles L. Vickers

Date	Mintage	MS63	MS65	Prf65
2011P	—	0.75	5.00	—
2011D	—	0.75	5.00	—
2011S	—	—	—	3.75

KM# 495a • 6.25 g., 0.900 **Silver** 0.1797 oz. ASW

Date	Mintage	MS63	MS65	Prf65
2011S	—	—	—	7.75

Olympic National Park

KM# 496a • 6.25 g., 0.900 **Silver** 0.1797 oz. ASW

Date	Mintage	MS63	MS65	Prf65
2011S	—	—	—	7.75

Vicksburg National Military Park

KM# 497 • 5.67 g., **Copper-Nickel Clad Copper**, 24 mm. **Rev. Designer:** Thomas Cleveland and Joseph Menna

Date	Mintage	MS63	MS65	Prf65
2011P	—	0.75	5.00	—
2011D	—	0.75	5.00	—
2011S	—	—	—	3.75

KM# 497a • 6.25 g., 0.900 **Silver** 0.1797 oz. ASW

Date	Mintage	MS63	MS65	Prf65
2011S	—	—	—	7.75

Chickasaw National Recreation Area

KM# 498 • 5.67 g., **Copper-Nickel Clad Copper**, 24 mm. **Rev. Designer:** Donna Weaver and Jim Licaretz

Date	Mintage	MS63	MS65	Prf65
2011P	—	0.75	5.00	—
2011D	—	0.75	5.00	—
2011S	—	—	—	3.75

KM# 498a • 6.25 g., 0.900 **Silver** 0.1797 oz. ASW

Date	Mintage	MS63	MS65	Prf65
2011S	—	—	—	7.75

El Yunque National Forest

KM# 519 • 5.67 g., **Copper-Nickel Clad Copper**, 24.3 mm. **Rev. Designer:** Gary Whitley and Michael Gaudioso

Date	Mintage	MS63	MS65	Prf65
2012P	—	0.75	5.00	—
2012D	—	0.75	5.00	—
2012S	—	—	7.50	—
2012S	—	—	—	3.75

KM# 519a • 6.25 g., 0.900 **Silver** 0.1797 oz. ASW, 24.3 mm.

Date	Mintage	MS63	MS65	Prf65
2012S	—	—	—	7.75

Chaco Culture National Historic Park

KM# 520 • 5.71 g., **Copper-Nickel Clad Copper**, 24.3 mm.

Date	Mintage	MS63	MS65	Prf65
2012P	—	0.75	8.00	—
2012D	—	0.75	8.00	—
2012S	—	—	10.00	—
2012S	—	—	—	4.00

KM# 520a • 6.25 g., 0.900 **Silver** 0.1797 oz. ASW, 24.3 mm.

Date	Mintage	MS63	MS65	Prf65
2012S	—	—	—	7.75

Acadia National Park

KM# 521 • 5.67 g., **Copper-Nickel Clad Copper**, 24.3 mm. **Rev. Designer:** Barbara Fox and Joseph Menna

Date	Mintage	MS63	MS65	Prf65
2012P	—	0.75	5.00	—
2012D	—	0.75	5.00	—
2012S	—	—	7.50	—
2012S	—	—	—	3.75

KM# 521a • 6.25 g., 0.900 **Silver** 0.1797 oz. ASW, 24.3 mm.

Date	Mintage	MS63	MS65	Prf65
2012S	—	—	—	7.75

Hawai'i Volcanoes National Park

KM# 522 • 5.67 g., **Copper-Nickel Clad Copper**, 24.3 mm.
Rev. Designer: Charles L. Vickers

Date	Mintage	MS63	MS65	Prf65
2012P	—	0.75	5.00	—
2012D	—	0.75	5.00	—
2012S	—	—	7.50	—
2012S	—	—	—	3.75

KM# 522a • 6.25 g., 0.900 **Silver** 0.1797 oz. ASW, 24.3 mm.

Date	Mintage	MS63	MS65	Prf65
2012S	—	—	—	7.75

Denali National Park

KM# 523 • 5.67 g., **Copper-Nickel Clad Copper**, 24.3 mm.

Date	Mintage	MS63	MS65	Prf65
2012P	—	0.75	5.00	—
2012D	—	0.75	5.00	—
2012S	—	—	7.50	—
2012S	—	—	—	3.75

KM# 523a • 6.25 g., 0.900 **Silver** 0.1797 oz. ASW, 24.3 mm.

Date	Mintage	MS63	MS65	Prf65
2012S	—	—	—	7.75

White Mountain National Forest

KM# 542 • 5.67 g., **Copper-Nickel Clad Copper**, 24.3 mm.

Date	Mintage	MS63	MS65	Prf65
2013P	—	0.75	5.00	—
2013D	—	0.75	5.00	—
2013S	—	—	7.50	—
2013S	—	—	—	3.75

KM# 542a • 6.25 g., 0.900 **Silver** 0.1797 oz. ASW, 24.3 mm.

Date	Mintage	MS63	MS65	Prf65
2013S	—	—	—	7.75

Perry's Victory and International Peace Memorial

KM# 543 • 5.67 g., **Copper-Nickel Clad Copper**, 24.3 mm.
Rev. Designer: Don Everhart

Date	Mintage	MS63	MS65	Prf65
2013P	—	0.75	0.50	—
2013D	—	0.75	5.00	—
2013S	—	—	7.50	—
2013S	—	—	—	3.75

KM# 543a • 6.25 g., 0.900 **Silver** 0.1797 oz. ASW, 24.3 mm.

Date	Mintage	MS63	MS65	Prf65
2013S	—	—	—	7.75

Great Basin National Park

KM# 544 • 5.67 g., **Copper-Nickel Clad Copper**, 24.3 mm.
Rev. Designer: Ronald D. Sanders and Renata Gordon

Date	Mintage	MS63	MS65	Prf65
2013P	—	0.75	5.00	—
2013D	—	0.75	5.00	—
2013S	—	—	7.50	—
2013S	—	—	—	3.75

KM# 544a • 6.25 g., 0.900 **Silver** 0.1797 oz. ASW, 24.3 mm.

Date	Mintage	MS63	MS65	Prf65
2013S	—	—	—	7.75

Fort McHenry National Monument and Historic Shrine

KM# 545 • 5.67 g., **Copper-Nickel Clad Copper**, 24.3 mm.
Rev. Designer: Joseph Menna

Date	Mintage	MS63	MS65	Prf65
2013P	—	0.75	5.00	—
2013D	—	0.75	5.00	—
2013S	—	—	7.50	—
2013S	—	—	—	3.75

KM# 545a • 6.25 g., 0.900 **Silver** 0.1797 oz. ASW, 24.3 mm.

Date	Mintage	MS63	MS65	Prf65
2013S	—	—	—	7.75

Mount Rushmore National Memorial

KM# 546 • 5.67 g., **Copper-Nickel Clad Copper**, 24.3 mm.
Rev. Designer: Joseph Menna

Date	Mintage	MS63	MS65	Prf65
2013P	—	0.75	5.00	—
2013D	—	0.75	5.00	—
2013S	—	—	7.50	—
2013S	—	—	—	3.75

KM# 546a • 6.25 g., 0.900 **Silver** 0.1797 oz. ASW, 24.3 mm.

Date	Mintage	MS63	MS65	Prf65
2013S	—	—	—	7.75

Great Smokey Mountains National Park

KM# 566 • 5.67 g., **Copper-Nickel Clad Copper**, 24.3 mm.

Date	Mintage	MS63	MS65	Prf65
2014P	—	0.75	5.00	—
2014D	—	0.75	5.00	—
2014S	—	—	3.50	—

Shenandoah National Park

KM# 567 • 5.67 g., **Copper-Nickel Clad Copper**, 24.3 mm.

Date	Mintage	MS63	MS65	Prf65
2014P	—	0.75	5.00	—
2014D	—	0.75	5.00	—
2014S	—	—	3.50	—

Arches National Park

KM# 568 • 5.67 g., **Copper-Nickel Clad Copper**, 24.3 mm.

Date	Mintage	MS63	MS65	Prf65
2014P	—	0.75	5.00	—
2014D	—	0.75	5.00	—
2014S	—	—	3.50	—

Great Sand Dunes National Park

KM# 569 • 5.67 g., **Copper-Nickel Clad Copper**, 24.3 mm.

Date	Mintage	MS63	MS65	Prf65
2014P	—	0.75	5.00	—
2014D	—	0.75	5.00	—
2014S	—	—	3.50	—

Everglades National Park

KM# 570 • 5.67 g., **Copper-Nickel Clad Copper**, 24.3 mm.

Date	Mintage	MS63	MS65	Prf65
2014P	—	0.75	5.00	—
2014D	—	0.75	5.00	—
2014S	—	—	3.50	—

HALF DOLLAR

Kennedy Half Dollar

KM# A202b • 11.34 g., **Copper-Nickel Clad Copper**, 30.61 mm. • **Edge Desc:** Reeded **Notes:** KM#202b design and composition resumed. The 1979-S and 1981-S Type II proofs have clearer mint marks than the Type I proofs of those years.

Date	Mintage	MS65	Prf65
2001P	21,200,000	10.00	—
2001D	19,504,000	9.00	—
2001S	2,235,000	—	5.00
2002P	3,100,000	10.00	—
2002D	2,500,000	10.50	—
2002S	2,268,913	—	5.00
2003P	2,500,000	6.00	—
2003D	2,500,000	6.00	—
2003S	2,076,165	—	5.00
2004P	2,900,000	4.50	—
2004D	2,900,000	4.50	—
2004S	1,789,488	—	6.00
2005P	3,800,000	6.00	—
2005P Satin finish	1,160,000	8.00	—
2005D	3,500,000	5.00	—
2005D Satin finish	1,160,000	10.00	—
2005S	2,275,000	—	5.00
2006P	2,400,000	4.50	—
2006P Satin finish	847,361	12.00	—
2006D	2,000,000	4.50	—
2006D Satin finish	847,361	14.00	—
2006S	1,934,965	—	6.00
2007P	—	4.50	—
2007P Satin finish	—	8.00	—
2007D	—	4.50	—
2007D Satin finish	—	8.00	—
2007S	—	—	6.00
2008P	—	4.50	—
2008P Satin finish	—	8.50	—
2008D	—	4.50	—
2008D Satin finish	—	8.50	—
2008S	—	—	9.00
2009P	—	4.50	—
2009P Satin finish	—	8.50	—
2009D	—	4.50	—
2009D Satin finish	—	8.50	—
2009S	—	—	6.00
2010P	—	4.50	—
2010P Satin finish	—	8.50	—
2010D	—	4.50	—
2010D Satin finish	—	8.50	—
2010S	—	—	13.00
2011P	—	4.50	—
2011D	—	4.50	—
2011S	—	—	9.00
2012P	—	4.50	—
2012D	—	4.50	—
2012S	—	—	9.00
2013P	—	4.50	—
2013D	—	4.50	—
2013S	—	—	9.00

KM# A202c • 12.50 g., 0.900 **Silver** 0.3594 oz. ASW, 30.6 •
Designer: Gilroy Roberts

Date	Mintage	MS65	Prf65
2001S	849,600	—	13.20
2002S	888,816	—	13.20
2003S	1,040,425	—	13.20
2004S	1,175,935	—	13.20
2005S	1,069,679	—	14.20
2006S	988,140	—	14.20
2007S	1,384,797	—	15.70
2008S	620,684	—	14.20
2009S	—	—	13.20
2010S	—	—	14.20
2011S	—	—	14.20
2012S	—	—	14.20
2013S	—	—	14.20

DOLLAR

Sacagawea Dollar

Sacagawea bust right, with baby on back obverse Eagle in flight left reverse

KM# 310 • 8.07 g., **Copper-Zinc-Manganese-Nickel Clad Copper**, 26.5 mm. • **Obv. Designer:** Glenda Goodacre **Rev. Designer:** Thomas D. Rodgers

Date	Mintage	MS63	MS65	Prf65
2001P	62,468,000	2.25	6.00	—
2001D	70,909,500	2.25	8.00	—
2001S	3,084,000	—	—	16.00
2002P	3,865,610	3.00	9.00	—
2002D	3,732,000	2.75	10.00	—
2002S	3,157,739	—	—	10.00
2003P	3,090,000	4.50	10.00	—
2003D	3,090,000	4.75	12.00	—
2003S	3,116,590	—	—	8.00
2004P	2,660,000	3.50	6.00	—
2004D	2,660,000	4.00	8.00	—
2004S	2,992,069	—	—	7.50
2005P	2,520,000	3.00	9.00	—
2005P Satin Finish	1,160,000	5.00	9.00	—
2005D	2,520,000	3.00	10.00	—
2005D Satin Finish	1,160,000	5.00	9.00	—
2005S	3,273,000	—	—	6.00
2006P	4,900,000	3.25	6.00	—
2006P Satin Finish	847,361	4.50	9.00	—
2006D	2,800,000	3.50	10.00	—
2006D Satin Finish	847,361	4.00	6.00	—
2006S	3,054,436	—	—	9.00
2007P	3,640,000	2.25	5.50	—
2007P Satin Finish	895,628	4.00	6.00	—
2007D	3,920,000	2.25	7.50	—
2007D Satin Finish	895,628	4.00	6.00	—
2007S	2,577,166	—	—	6.50
2008P	1,820,000	2.00	7.00	—
2008P Satin Finish	745,464	4.00	6.00	—
2008D	1,820,000	3.50	10.00	—
2008D Satin Finish	745,464	4.00	6.00	—
2008S	2,169,561	—	—	16.00

Native American Dollar - Planting crops reverse

KM# 467 • 8.07 g., **Copper-Zinc-Manganese-Nickel Clad Copper**, 26.5 mm. • **Obv. Designer:** Glenda Goodacre **Rev. Designer:** Norm Nemeth **Edge Lettering:** E PLURIBUS UNUM, date, mint mark **Notes:** Date and mint mark on edge

Date	Mintage	MS63	MS65	Prf65
2009P	37,380,000	2.00	5.00	—
2009P Satin finish	784,614	4.00	7.00	—
2009D	33,880,000	2.00	5.00	—
2009D Satin finish	784,614	4.00	7.00	—
2009S	2,179,867	—	—	6.00

Hiawatha belt reverse

KM# 474 • 8.07 g., **Copper-Zinc-Manganese-Nickel Clad Copper**, 26.5 mm. • **Obv. Designer:** Glenda Goodacre **Rev. Designer:** Thomas Cleveland and Charles L. Vickers **Edge Lettering:** E PLURIBUS UNUM, date, mint mark **Notes:** Date and mint mark on edge

Date	Mintage	MS63	MS65	Prf65
2010P	32,060,000	2.00	5.00	—
2010P Satin Finish	583,897	4.00	7.00	—
2010D	48,720,000	2.00	5.00	—
2010D Satin Finish	583,897	4.00	7.00	—
2010S	1,689,364	—	—	12.50

Peace Pipe reverse

KM# 503 • 8.07 g., **Copper-Zinc-Manganese-Nickel Clad Copper**, 26.5 mm. • **Obv. Designer:** Glenna Goodacre **Rev. Designer:** Richard Masters and Joseph Menna **Edge Lettering:** E PLURIBUS UNUM, date, mint mark **Notes:** Date and mint mark on edge

Date	Mintage	MS63	MS65	Prf65
2011P	29,400,000	2.00	5.50	—
2011D	48,160,000	2.00	5.00	—
2011S	1,453,276	—	—	8.00

Horse reverse

KM# 528 • 8.07 g., **Copper-Zinc-Manganese-Nickel Clad Copper**, 26.5 mm. • **Obv. Designer:** Glenna Goodacre **Rev. Designer:** Thomas Cleveland and Phebe Hemphill **Edge Lettering:** E PLURIBUS UNUM, date, mint mark **Notes:** Date and mint mark on edge

Date	Mintage	MS63	MS65	Prf65
2012P	28,000,000	2.00	7.00	—
2012D	3,080,000	2.00	7.00	—
2012S	—	—	—	12.50

Delaware Treaty of 1778

KM# 551 • 8.07 g., **Copper-Zinc-Manganese-Nickel Clad Copper**, 26.5 mm. • **Edge Desc:** E PLURIBUS UNUM, date, mint mark **Notes:** Date and mint mark on edge.

Date	Mintage	MS63	MS65	Prf65
2013P	—	2.00	7.00	—
2013D	—	2.00	7.00	—
2013S	—	—	—	12.50

Native Hospitality

KM# 575 • 8.07 g., **Copper-Zinc-Manganese-Nickel Clad Copper**, 26.5 mm. •

Date	Mintage	MS63	MS65	Prf65
2014P	—	2.00	7.00	—
2014D	—	2.00	7.00	—
2014S	—	—	—	12.50

PRESIDENTS
George Washington

KM# 401 • 8.07 g., **Copper-Zinc-Manganese-Nickel Clad Copper**, 26.5 mm. **Obv. Designer:** Joseph Menna **Rev. Designer:** Don Everhart **Edge Lettering:** IN GOD WE TRUST date, mint mark E PLURIBUS UNUM **Notes:** Date and mint mark incuse on edge.

Date	Mintage	MS63	MS65	Prf65
2007P	176,680,000	2.00	3.00	—
2007P Satin Finish	895,628	2.00	4.00	—
(2007) Plain edge error	Inc. above	175	275	—
2007D	163,680,000	2.00	3.00	—
2007D Satin Finish	895,628	2.00	4.00	—
2007S	3,883,103	—	—	3.00

John Adams

KM# 402 • 8.07 g., **Copper-Zinc-Manganese-Nickel Clad Copper**, 26.5 mm. **Obv. Designer:** Joel Iskowitz and Charles Vickers **Rev. Designer:** Don Everhart **Edge Lettering:** IN GOD WE TRUST date, mint mark E PLURIBUS UNUM **Notes:** Date and mint mark incuse on edge.

Date	Mintage	MS63	MS65	Prf65
2007P	112,420,000	2.00	3.00	—
2007P Double edge lettering	Inc. above	45.00	65.00	—
2007D Plain edge error	Inc. above	60.00	70.00	—
2007P Satin Finish	895,628	2.00	4.00	—
2007D	112,140,000	2.00	3.00	—
2007D Satin Finish	895,628	2.00	4.00	—
2007S	3,877,409	—	—	3.00

Thomas Jefferson

KM# 403 • 8.07 g., **Copper-Zinc-Manganese-Nickel Clad Copper**, 26.5 mm. **Obv. Designer:** Joseph Menna **Rev. Designer:** Don Everhart **Edge Lettering:** IN GOD WE TRUST date, mint mark E PLURIBUS UNUM **Notes:** Date and mint mark incuse on edge.

Date	Mintage	MS63	MS65	Prf65
2007P	100,800,000	2.00	3.00	—
2007P Satin Finish	895,628	2.00	4.00	—
2007D	102,810,000	2.00	3.00	—
2007D Satin Finish	895,628	2.00	4.00	—
2007S	3,877,573	—	—	3.00

James Madison

KM# 404 • 8.07 g., **Copper-Zinc-Manganese-Nickel Clad Copper**, 26.5 mm. **Obv. Designer:** Joel Iskowitz and Don Everhart **Rev. Designer:** Don Everhart **Edge Lettering:** IN GOD WE TRUST date, mint mark E PLURIBUS UNUM **Notes:** Date and mint mark incuse on edge.

Date	Mintage	MS63	MS65	Prf65
2007P	84,560,000	2.00	3.00	—
2007P Satin Finish	895,628	2.00	4.00	—
2007D	87,780,000	2.00	3.00	—
2007D Satin Finish	895,628	2.00	4.00	—
2007S	3,876,829	—	—	3.00

James Monroe

KM# 426 • 8.07 g., **Copper-Zinc-Manganese-Nickel Clad Copper**, 26.5 mm. **Rev. Designer:** Don Everhart **Edge Lettering:** IN GOD WE TRUST date, mint mark E PLURIBUS UNUM

Date	Mintage	MS63	MS65	Prf65
2008P	64,260,000	2.00	3.00	—
2008P Satin Finish	745,464	2.00	4.00	—
2008D	60,230,000	2.00	3.00	—
2008D Satin Finish	745,464	2.00	4.00	—
2008S	3,000,000	—	—	4.00

John Quincy Adams

KM# 427 • 8.07 g., **Copper-Zinc-Manganese-Nickel Clad Copper**, 26.5 mm. **Obv. Designer:** Don Everhart **Rev. Designer:** Don Everhart **Edge Lettering:** IN GOD WE TRUST date, mint mark E PLURIBUS UNUM **Notes:** Date and mint mark incuse on edge.

Date	Mintage	MS63	MS65	Prf65
2008P	57,540,000	2.00	3.00	—
2008P Satin Finish	745,464	2.00	4.00	—
2008D	57,720,000	2.00	3.00	—
2008D Satin Finish	745,464	2.00	4.00	—
2008S	3,000,000	—	—	4.00

Andrew Jackson

KM# 428 • 8.07 g., **Copper-Zinc-Manganese-Nickel Clad Copper**, 26.5 mm. **Obv. Designer:** Joel Iskowitz and Jim Licaretz **Rev. Designer:** Don Everhart **Edge Lettering:** IN GOD WE TRUST date, mint mark E PLURIBUS UNUM **Notes:** Date and mint mark incuse on edge.

Date	Mintage	MS63	MS65	Prf65
2008P	61,180,000	2.00	3.00	—
2008P Satin Finish	745,464	2.00	4.00	—
2008D	61,070,000	2.00	3.00	—
2008D Satin Finish	745,464	2.00	4.00	—
2008S	3,000,000	—	—	4.00

Martin van Buren

KM# 429 • 8.07 g., **Copper-Zinc-Manganese-Nickel Clad Copper**, 26.5 mm. **Obv. Designer:** Joel Iskowitz and Phebe Hemphill **Rev. Designer:** Don Everhart **Edge Lettering:** IN GOD WE TRUST date, mint mark E PLURIBUS UNUM **Notes:** Date and mint mark incuse on edge.

Date	Mintage	MS63	MS65	Prf65
2008P	51,520,000	2.00	3.00	—
2008P Satin Finish	745,464	2.00	4.00	—
2008D	50,960,000	2.00	3.00	—
2008D Satin Finish	745,464	2.00	4.00	—
2008S	3,000,000	—	—	4.00

William Henry Harrison

KM# 450 • 8.07 g., **Copper-Zinc-Manganese-Nickel Clad Copper**, 26.5 mm. **Obv. Designer:** Joseph Menna **Rev. Designer:** Don Everhart **Edge Lettering:** E PLURIBUS UNUM, date, mint mark **Notes:** Date and mint mark on edge

Date	Mintage	MS63	MS65	Prf65
2009P	43,260,000	2.00	3.00	—
2009P Satin Finish	784,614	2.00	4.00	—
2009D	55,160,000	2.00	3.00	—
2009P Satin Finish	784,614	2.00	4.00	—
2009S	2,224,827	—	—	3.00

John Tyler

KM# 451 • 8.07 g., **Copper-Zinc-Manganese-Nickel Clad Copper**, 26.5 mm. **Obv. Designer:** Phebe Hemphill **Rev. Designer:** Don Everhart **Edge Lettering:** E PLURIBUS UNUM, date, mint mark **Notes:** Date and mint mark on edge.

Date	Mintage	MS63	MS65	Prf65
2009P	43,540,000	2.00	3.00	—
2009P Satin Finish	784,614	2.00	4.00	—
2009D	43,540,000	2.00	3.00	—
2009D Satin Finish	784,614	2.00	4.00	—
2009S	2,224,827	—	—	3.00

James K. Polk

KM# 452 • 8.07 g., **Copper-Zinc-Manganese-Nickel Clad Copper**, 26.5 mm. **Obv. Designer:** Susan Gamble and Charles Vickers **Rev. Designer:** Don Everhart **Edge Lettering:** E PLURIBUS UNUM, date, mint mark **Notes:** Date and mint mark on edge

Date	Mintage	MS63	MS65	Prf65
2009P	46,620,000	2.00	3.00	—
2009P Satin Finish	784,614	2.00	4.00	—
2009D	41,720,000	2.00	3.00	—
2009D Satin Finish	784,614	2.00	4.00	—
2009S	2,224,827	—	—	3.00

Zachary Taylor

KM# 453 • 8.07 g., **Copper-Zinc-Manganese-Nickel Clad Copper**, 26.5 mm. **Obv. Designer:** Don Everhart **Rev. Designer:** Don Everhart **Edge Lettering:** E PLURIBUS UNUM, date, mint mark **Notes:** Date and mint mark on edge.

Date	Mintage	MS63	MS65	Prf65
2009P	41,580,000	2.00	3.00	—
2009P Satin Finish	784,614	2.00	4.00	—
2009D	36,680,000	2.00	3.00	—
2009D Satin Finish	784,614	2.00	4.00	—
2009S	2,224,827	—	—	3.00

Millard Filmore

KM# 475 • 8.07 g., **Copper-Zinc-Manganese-Nickel Clad Copper**, 26.5 mm. **Obv. Designer:** Don Everhart **Rev. Designer:** Don Everhart **Edge Lettering:** E PLURIBUS UNUM, date, mint mark **Notes:** Date and mint mark on edge.

Date	Mintage	MS63	MS65	Prf65
2010P	37,520,000	2.00	3.00	—
2010P Satin Finish	583,897	2.00	4.00	—
2010D	36,960,000	2.00	3.00	—
2010D Satin Finish	583,897	2.00	4.00	—
2010S	2,224,827	—	—	4.00

Franklin Pierce

KM# 476 • 8.07 g., **Copper-Zinc-Manganese-Nickel Clad Copper**, 26.5 mm. **Obv. Designer:** Susan Gamble and Charles L. Vickers **Rev. Designer:** Don Everhart **Edge Lettering:** E PLURIBUS UNUM, date, mint mark **Notes:** Date and mint mark on edge.

Date	Mintage	MS63	MS65	Prf65
2010P	38,220,000	2.00	3.00	—
2010P Satin Finish	583,897	2.00	4.00	—
2010D	38,360,000	2.00	3.00	—
2010D Satin Finish	583,897	2.00	4.00	—
2010S	2,224,827	—	—	4.00

James Buchanan

KM# 477 • 8.07 g., **Copper-Zinc-Manganese-Nickel Clad Copper**, 26.5 mm. **Obv. Designer:** Phebe Hemphill **Rev. Designer:** Don Everhart **Edge Lettering:** E PLURIBUS UNUM, date, mint mark **Notes:** Date and mint mark on edge.

Date	Mintage	MS63	MS65	Prf65
2010P	36,820,000	2.00	3.00	—
2010P Satin Finish	583,897	2.00	4.00	—
2010D	36,540,000	2.00	3.00	—
2010D Satin Finish	583,897	2.00	4.00	—
2010S	2,224,827	—	—	4.00

Abraham Lincoln

KM# 478 • 8.07 g., **Copper-Zinc-Manganese-Nickel Clad Copper**, 26.5 mm. **Obv. Designer:** Don Everhart **Rev. Designer:** Don Everhart **Edge Lettering:** E PLURIBUS UNUM, date, mint mark **Notes:** Date and mint mark on edge.

Date	Mintage	MS63	MS65	Prf65
2010P	49,000,000	2.00	3.00	—
2010P Satin Finish	583,897	2.00	4.00	—
2010D	48,020,000	2.00	3.00	—
2010D Satin Finish	583,897	2.00	4.00	—
2010S	2,224,827	—	—	4.00

Andrew Johnson

KM# 499 • 8.07 g., **Copper-Zinc-Manganese-Nickel Clad Copper**, 26.5 mm. **Obv. Designer:** Don Everhart **Rev. Designer:** Don Everhart **Edge Lettering:** E PLURIBUS UNUM, date, mint mark **Notes:** Date and mint mark on edge.

Date	Mintage	MS63	MS65	Prf65
2011P	35,560,000	2.00	3.00	—
2011D	37,100,000	2.00	3.00	—
2011S	1,706,916	—	—	4.00

Ulysses S. Grant

KM# 500 • 8.07 g., **Copper-Zinc-Manganese-Nickel Clad Copper**, 26.5 mm. **Rev. Designer:** Don Everhart **Edge Lettering:** E PLURIBUS UNUM, date, mint mark **Notes:** Date and mint mark on edge.

Date	Mintage	MS63	MS65	Prf65
2011P	38,080,000	2.00	3.00	—
2011D	37,940,000	2.00	3.00	—
2011S	1,706,916	—	—	4.00

Rutherford B. Hayes

KM# 501 • 8.07 g., **Copper-Zinc-Manganese-Nickel Clad Copper**, 26.5 mm. **Obv. Designer:** Don Everhart **Rev. Designer:** Don Everhart **Edge Lettering:** E PLURIBUS UNUM, date, mint mark **Notes:** Date and mint mark on edge.

Date	Mintage	MS63	MS65	Prf65
2011P	37,660,000	2.00	3.00	—
2011D	36,820,000	2.00	3.00	—
2011S	1,706,916	—	—	4.00

James Garfield

KM# 502 • 8.07 g., Copper-Zinc-Manganese-Nickel Clad Copper, 26.5 mm. **Obv. Designer:** Phebe Hemphill **Rev. Designer:** Don Everhart **Edge Lettering:** E PLURIBUS UNUM, date, mint mark **Notes:** Date and mint mark on edge

Date	Mintage	MS63	MS65	Prf65
2011P	37,100,000	2.00	3.00	—
2011D	37,100,000	2.00	3.00	—
2011S	1,706,916	—	—	4.00

Chester A. Arthur

KM# 524 • 8.07 g., Copper-Zinc-Manganese-Nickel Clad Copper, 26.5 mm. **Obv. Designer:** Don Everhart **Rev. Designer:** Don Everhart **Edge Lettering:** E PLURIBUS UNUM, date, mintmark **Notes:** Date and mintmark on edge

Date	Mintage	MS63	MS65	Prf65
2012P	6,020,000	2.00	3.00	—
2012D	4,060,000	2.00	3.00	—
2012S	—	—	—	5.00

Grover Cleveland, first term

KM# 525 • 8.07 g., Copper-Zinc-Manganese-Nickel Clad Copper, 26.5 mm. **Obv. Designer:** Don Everhart **Rev. Designer:** Don Everhart **Edge Lettering:** E PLURIBUS UNUM, date, mintmark **Notes:** Date and mint mark on edge

Date	Mintage	MS63	MS65	Prf65
2012P	5,460,000	2.00	3.00	—
2012D	4,060,000	2.00	3.00	—
2012S	—	—	—	5.00

Benjamin Harrison

KM# 526 • 8.07 g., Copper-Zinc-Manganese-Nickel Clad Copper, 26.5 mm. **Obv. Designer:** Phebe Hemphill **Rev. Designer:** Don Everhart **Edge Lettering:** E PLURIBUS UNUM, date, mintmark **Notes:** Date at mint mark on edge

Date	Mintage	MS63	MS65	Prf65
2012P	5,640,001	2.00	3.00	—
2012D	—	2.00	3.00	—
2012S	—	—	—	5.00

Grover Cleveland, second term

KM# 527 • 8.07 g., Copper-Zinc-Manganese-Nickel Clad Copper, 26.5 mm. **Obv. Designer:** Don Everhart **Rev. Designer:** Don Everhart **Edge Lettering:** E PLURIBUS UNUM, date, mintmark **Notes:** Date and mint mark on edge

Date	Mintage	MS63	MS65	Prf65
2012P	10,680,000	2.00	3.00	—
2012D	3,920,000	2.00	3.00	—
2012S	—	—	—	5.00

William McKinley

KM# 547 • 8.07 g., Copper-Zinc-Manganese-Nickel Clad Copper, 26.5 mm. **Edge Desc:** E PLURIBUS UNUM, date, mint mark **Notes:** Date and mint mark on edge.

Date	Mintage	MS63	MS65	Prf65
2013P	—	2.00	3.00	—
2013D	—	2.00	3.00	—
2013S	—	—	—	5.00

Theodore Roosevelt

KM# 548 • 8.07 g., Copper-Zinc-Manganese-Nickel Clad Copper, 26.5 mm. **Edge Desc:** E PLURIBUS UNUM, date, mint mark **Notes:** Date and mint mark on edge.

Date	Mintage	MS63	MS65	Prf65
2013P	—	2.00	3.00	—
2013D	—	2.00	3.00	—
2013S	—	—	—	5.00

William Howard Taft

KM# 549 • 8.07 g., Copper-Zinc-Manganese-Nickel Clad Copper, 26.5 mm. **Edge Desc:** E PLURIBUS UNUM, date, mint mark **Notes:** Date and mint mark on edge.

Date	Mintage	MS63	MS65	Prf65
2013P	—	2.00	3.00	—
2013D	—	2.00	3.00	—
2013S	—	—	—	5.00

Woodrow Wilson

KM# 550 • 8.07 g., Copper-Zinc-Manganese-Nickel Clad Copper, 26.5 mm. **Edge Desc:** E PLURIBUS UNUM, date, mint mark **Notes:** Date and mint mark on edge.

Date	Mintage	MS63	MS65	Prf65
2013P	—	2.00	3.00	—
2013D	—	2.00	3.00	—
2013S	—	—	—	5.00

Warren G. Harding

KM# 571 • 8.07 g., Copper-Zinc-Manganese-Nickel Clad Copper, 26.5 mm. **Notes:** Date and mint mark on edge.

Date	Mintage	MS63	MS65	Prf65
2014P	—	2.00	3.00	—
2014D	—	2.00	3.00	—
2014S	—	—	—	5.00

Calvin Coolidge

KM# 572 • 8.07 g., Copper-Zinc-Manganese-Nickel Clad Copper, 26.5 mm. **Notes:** Date and mint mark on edge.

Date	Mintage	MS63	MS65	Prf65
2014P	—	2.00	3.00	—
2014D	—	2.00	3.00	—
2014S	—	—	—	5.00

Herbert Hoover

KM# 573 • 8.07 g., Copper-Zinc-Manganese-Nickel Clad Copper, 26.5 mm. **Notes:** Date and mint mark on edge.

Date	Mintage	MS63	MS65	Prf65
2014P	—	2.00	3.00	—
2014D	—	2.00	3.00	—
2014S	—	—	—	5.00

Franklin D. Roosevelt

KM# 574 • 8.07 g., Copper-Zinc-Manganese-Nickel Clad Copper, 26.5 mm. **Notes:** Date and mint mark on edge.

Date	Mintage	MS63	MS65	Prf65
2014P	—	2.00	3.00	—
2014D	—	2.00	3.00	—
2014S	—	—	—	5.00

COMMEMORATIVE COINAGE

HALF DOLLAR

U. S. CAPITOL VISITOR CENTER. KM# 323 • **ObvDesc:** Capitol sillouete, 1800 structure in detail • **RevDesc:** Legend within circle of stars • 11.34 g., Copper-Nickel Clad Copper • **Obv. Designer:** Dean McMullen • **Rev. Designer:** Alex Shagin and Marcel Jovine

Date	Mintage	MS65	Prf65
2001P	99,157	14.50	—
2001P	77,962	—	15.50

FIRST FLIGHT CENTENNIAL. KM# 348 • **ObvDesc:** Wright Monument at Kitty Hawk • **RevDesc:** Wright Flyer in flight • 11.34 g., Copper-Nickel Clad Copper • **Obv. Designer:** John Mercanti • **Rev. Designer:** Donna Weaver

Date	Mintage	MS65	Prf65
2003P	57,726	15.00	—
2003P	111,569	—	17.00

AMERICAN BALD EAGLE. KM# 438 • **ObvDesc:** Two eaglets in nest with egg • **RevDesc:** Eagle Challenger facing right, American Flag in background • 11.34 g., Copper-Nickel Clad Copper • **Obv. Designer:** Susan Gamble and Joseph Menna • **Rev. Designer:** Donna Weaver and Charles Vickers

Date	Mintage	MS65	Prf65
2008S	120,180	12.50	—
2008S	222,577	—	14.00

U.S. ARMY. KM# 506 • **ObvDesc:** Army contributions during peacetime, surveying, building a flood wall and space exploration • **RevDesc:** Continental soldier with musket • 11.34 g., **Copper-Nickel Clad Copper** • **Obv. Designer:** Donna Weaver and Charles L. Vickers • **Rev. Designer:** Thomas Cleveland and Joseph Menna

Date	Mintage	MS65	Prf65
2011D	39,461	69.00	
2011	68,349		35.00

FIVE-STAR GENERALS - ARNOLD AND BRADLEY. KM# 554Silver.

Date	Mintage	MS65	Prf65
2013	—	50.00	
2013	—		60.00

KM# 576 • 11.34 g., **Copper-Nickel Clad Copper**, 30.6 mm. • **Subject:** Baseball Hall of Fame

Date	Mintage	F12	VF20	XF40	MS60
2014	—				
2014	—				

DOLLAR

CAPITOL VISITOR CENTER. KM# 324 • **ObvDesc:** Original and current Capital facades • **RevDesc:** Eagle with sheild and ribbon • 26.73 g., 0.900 **Silver** 0.7685 oz. ASW. • **Obv. Designer:** Marika Somogyi • **Rev. Designer:** John Mercanti

Date	Mintage	MS65	Prf65
2001P	66,636	40.80	
2001P	143,793		40.80

NATIVE AMERICAN - BISON. KM# 325 • **ObvDesc:** Native American bust right • **RevDesc:** Bison standing left • 26.73 g., 0.900 **Silver** 0.7685 oz. ASW.

Date	Mintage	MS65	Prf65
2001D	197,131	165	
2001P	272,869	—	169

2002 WINTER OLYMPICS - SALT LAKE CITY. KM# 336 • **ObvDesc:** Salt Lake City Olympic logo • **RevDesc:** Stylized skyline with mountains in background • 26.73 g., 0.900 **Silver** 0.7685 oz. ASW. • **Obv. Designer:** John Mercanti • **Rev. Designer:** Donna Weaver

Date	Mintage	MS65	Prf65
2002P	35,388	40.80	
2002P	142,873		38.30

U.S. MILITARY ACADEMY AT WEST POINT -BICENTENNIAL. KM# 338 • **ObvDesc:** Cadet Review flagbearers, Academy buildings in background • **RevDesc:** Academy emblems - Corinthian helmet and sword • 26.73 g., 0.900 **Silver** 0.7685 oz. ASW. • **Obv. Designer:** T. James Ferrell • **Rev. Designer:** John Mercanti

Date	Mintage	MS65	Prf65
2002W	103,201	38.30	
2002W	288,293		39.80

FIRST FLIGHT CENTENNIAL. KM# 349 • **ObvDesc:** Orville and Wilbur Wright busts left • **RevDesc:** Wright Flyer over dunes • 26.75 g., 0.900 **Silver** 0.769 oz. ASW. • **Obv. Designer:** T. James Ferrell • **Rev. Designer:** Norman E. Nemeth

Date	Mintage	MS65	Prf65
2003P	53,761	40.80	
2003P	193,086	—	46.80

THOMAS A. EDISON - ELECTRIC LIGHT 125TH ANNIVERSARY. KM# 362 • **ObvDesc:** Edison half-length figure facing holding light bulb • **RevDesc:** Light bulb and rays • 23.73 g., 0.900 **Silver** 0.6822 oz. ASW. • **Obv. Designer:** Donna Weaver • **Rev. Designer:** John Mercanti

Date	Mintage	MS65	Prf65
2004P	68,031	40.80	
2004P	213,409		41.80

LEWIS AND CLARK CORPS OF DISCOVERY BICENTENNIAL. KM# 363 • **ObvDesc:** Lewis and Clark standing • **RevDesc:** Jefferson era clasped hands peace medal • 26.73 g., 0.900 **Silver** 0.7685 oz. ASW.

Date	Mintage	MS65	Prf65
2004P	90,323	40.80	
2004P	288,492		46.80

JOHN MARSHALL, 250TH BIRTH ANNIVERSARY.
KM# 375 • ObvDesc: Marshall bust left • RevDesc: Marshall era Supreme Court Chamber • 26.73 g., 0.900 Silver 0.7685 oz. ASW. • Obv. Designer: John Mercanti • Rev. Designer: Donna Weaver

Date	Mintage	MS65	Prf65
2005P	48,953	37.30	—
2005P	141,993	—	35.80

U.S. MARINE CORPS, 230TH ANNIVERSARY. KM#
376 • ObvDesc: Flag Raising at Mt. Suribachi on Iwo Jima • RevDesc: Marine Corps emblem • 26.73 g., 0.900 Silver 0.7685 oz. ASW. • Obv. Designer: Norman E. Nemeth • Rev. Designer: Charles Vickers

Date	Mintage	MS65	Prf65
2005P	130,000	48.00	—
2005P	370,000	—	52.50

BENJAMIN FRANKLIN, 300TH BIRTH ANNIVERSARY. KM# 387 • ObvDesc: Youthful Franklin
flying kite • RevDesc: Revolutionary era "JOIN, or DIE" snake cartoon illustration • 26.73 g., 0.900 Silver 0.7685 oz. ASW. • Obv. Designer: Norman E. Nemeth • Rev. Designer: Charles Vickers

Date	Mintage	MS65	Prf65
2006P	58,000	40.80	—
2006P	142,000	—	45.00

BENJAMIN FRANKLIN, 300TH BIRTH
ANNIVERSARY. KM# 388 • ObvDesc: Bust 3/4 right, signature in oval below • RevDesc: Continental Dollar of 1776 in center • 26.73 g., 0.900 Silver 0.7685 oz. ASW. • Obv. Designer: Don Everhart II • Rev. Designer: Donna Weaver

Date	Mintage	MS65	Prf65
2006P	58,000	40.80	—
2006P	142,000	—	51.00

SAN FRANCISCO MINT MUSEUM. KM# 394 •
ObvDesc: 3/4 view of building • RevDesc: Reverse of 1880s Morgan silver dollar • 26.73 g., 0.900 Silver 0.7685 oz. ASW. • Obv. Designer: Sherl J. Winter • Rev. Designer: George T. Morgan

Date	Mintage	MS65	Prf65
2006S	65,609	40.80	—
2006S	255,700	—	40.80

JAMESTOWN - 400TH ANNIVERSARY. KM# 405
• ObvDesc: Two settlers and Native American • RevDesc: Three ships • 26.73 g., 0.900 Silver 0.7685 oz. ASW. • Obv. Designer: Donna Weaver and Don Everhart II • Rev. Designer: Susan Gamble and Charles Vickers

Date	Mintage	MS65	Prf65
2007P	79,801	40.80	—
2007P	258,802	—	38.30

CENTRAL HIGH SCHOOL DESEGREGATION. KM#
418 • ObvDesc: Children's feet walking left with adult feet in military boots • RevDesc: Little Rock's Central High School • 26.73 g., 0.900 Silver 0.7685 oz. ASW. • Obv. Designer: Richard Masters and Charles Vickers • Rev. Designer: Don Everhart II

Date	Mintage	MS65	Prf65
2007P	66,093	40.80	—
2007P	124,618	—	43.00

AMERICAN BALD EAGLE. KM# 439 • ObvDesc: Eagle
with flight, mountain in background at right • RevDesc: Great Seal of the United States • 26.73 g., 0.900 Silver 0.7685 oz. ASW. • Obv. Designer: Joel Iskowitz and Don Everhart II • Rev. Designer: James Licaretz

Date	Mintage	MS65	Prf65
2008P	110,073	44.00	—
2008P	243,558	—	38.30

LINCOLN BICENTENNIAL. KM# 454 • ObvDesc: 3/4
portrait facing right • RevDesc: Part of Gettysburg Address within wreath • 26.73 g., 0.900 Silver 0.7685 oz. ASW. • Obv. Designer: Justin Kunz and Don Everhart II • Rev. Designer: Phebe Hemphill

Date	Mintage	MS65	Prf65
2009P	125,000	55.00	—
2009P	375,000	—	55.00

LOUIS BRAILLE BIRTH BICENTENNIAL. KM# 455 •
ObvDesc: Louis Braille bust facing • **RevDesc:** School child reading book in Braille, BRL in Braille code above • 26.73 g., 0.900 **Silver** 0.7685 oz. ASW. • **Obv. Designer:** Joel Iskowitz and Phebe Hemphill • **Rev. Designer:** Susan Gamble and Joseph Menna

Date	Mintage	MS65	Prf65
2009P	82,639	38.50	—
2009P	135,235	—	38.30

AMERICAN VETERANS DISABLED FOR LIFE. KM# 479 •
ObvDesc: Soldier's feet, crutches • **RevDesc:** Legend within wreath 0.900 **Silver**. • **Obv. Designer:** Don Everhart II • **Rev. Designer:** Thomas Cleveland and Joseph Menna

Date	Mintage	MS65	Prf65
2010W	77,859	40.80	—
2010W	189,881	—	42.30

BOY SCOUTS OF AMERICA, 100TH ANNIVERSARY.
KM# 480 • ObvDesc: Cub Scout, Boy Scout and Venturer saluting • **RevDesc:** Boy Scouts of America logo 0.900 **Silver**. • **Obv. Designer:** Donna Weaver • **Rev. Designer:** Jim Licaretz

Date	Mintage	MS65	Prf65
2010P	—	38.50	—
2010P	—	—	42.00

MEDAL OF HONOR. KM# 504 • ObvDesc:
Medal of Honor designs for Army, Navy and Air Force awards • **RevDesc:** Army infantry soldier carrying another to safety • 26.73 g., 0.900 **Silver** 0.7685 oz. ASW. • **Obv. Designer:** James Licaretz • **Rev. Designer:** Richard Masters and Phebe Hemphill

Date	Mintage	MS65	Prf65
2011S	44,769	46.50	—
2011S	112,850	—	43.50

U.S. ARMY. KM# 507 • ObvDesc:
Male and femlae soldier heads looking outward • **RevDesc:** Seven core values of the Army, Eagle from the great seal • 26.73 g., 0.900 **Silver** 0.7685 oz. ASW. • **Obv. Designer:** Richard Masters and Michael Gaudioso • **Rev. Designer:** Susan Gamble and Don Everhart, II

Date	Mintage	MS65	Prf65
2011S	—	45.00	—
2011S	—	—	43.50

NATIONAL INFANTRY MUSEUM AND SOLDIER CENTER. KM# 529 • ObvDesc:
Infantry soldier advancing left • **RevDesc:** Crossed rifles insignia • 26.73 g., 0.900 **Silver** 0.7685 oz. ASW. • **Obv. Designer:** Joel Iskowitz and Michael Gaudioso • **Rev. Designer:** Ronald D. Sanders and Norman E. Nemeth

Date	Mintage	MS65	Prf65
2012	—	50.00	—
2012	—	—	60.00

STAR-SPANGLED BANNER. KM# 530 • ObvDesc:
Liberty waving 15 star and stripe flag, Ft. McHenry in background • **RevDesc:** Modern American Flag • 26.73 g., 0.900 **Silver** 0.7685 oz. ASW. • **Obv. Designer:** Joel Iskowitz and Phebe Hemphill • **Rev. Designer:** William C Burgard III and Don Everhart

Date	Mintage	MS65	Prf65
2012	—	50.00	—
2012	—	—	60.00

GIRL SCOUTS OF THE USA, 100TH ANNIVERSARY.
KM# 552 • ObvDesc: Three busts right • **RevDesc:** Trefoil logo Silver.

Date	Mintage	MS65	Prf65
2013	—	50.00	—
2013	—	—	60.00

FIVE-STAR GENERALS - MARSHALL AND EISENHOWER. KM# 553 Silver.

Date	Mintage	MS65	Prf65
2013	—	50.00	—
2013	—	—	60.00

KM# 577 • Silver ASW Subject: Baseball Hall of Fame

Date	Mintage	F12	VF20	XF40	MS60
2014	—	—	—	—	—
2014	—	—	—	—	—

KM# 579 • Silver ASW Subject: Civil Rights

Date	Mintage	F12	VF20	XF40	MS60
2014	—	—	—	—	—
2014	—	—	—	—	—

$5 (HALF EAGLE)

CAPITOL VISITOR CENTER. KM# 326 • ObvDesc: Column at right • **RevDesc:** First Capital building • 8.54 g., 0.900 **Gold** 0.2455 oz. AGW.

Date	Mintage	MS65	Prf65
2001W	6,761	1,750	—
2001W	27,652	—	442

2002 WINTER OLYMPICS. KM# 337 • ObvDesc: Salt Lake City Olympics logo • **RevDesc:** Stylized cauldron • 8.36 g., 0.900 **Gold** 0.2403 oz. AGW.

Date	Mintage	MS65	Prf65
2002W	10,585	452	—
2002W	32,877	—	442

SAN FRANCISCO MINT MUSEUM. KM# 395 • ObvDesc: Front entrance façade • **RevDesc:** Eagle as on 1860's $5. Gold • 8.36 g., 0.900 **Gold** 0.2403 oz. AGW. • **Obv. Designer:** Charles Vickers and Joseph Menna • **Rev. Designer:** Christian Gobrecht

Date	Mintage	MS65	Prf65
2006S	16,230	442	—
2006S	41,517	—	442

JAMESTOWN - 400TH ANNIVERSARY. KM# 406 • ObvDesc: Settler and Native American • **RevDesc:** Jamestown Memorial Church ruins • 8.36 g., 0.900 **Gold** 0.2403 oz. AGW. • **Obv. Designer:** John Mercanti • **Rev. Designer:** Susan Gamble and Norman Nemeth

Date	Mintage	MS65	Prf65
2007W	18,843	442	—
2007W	47,050	—	442

AMERICAN BALD EAGLE. KM# 440 • ObvDesc: Two eagles on branch • **RevDesc:** Eagle with shield • 8.36 g., 0.900 **Gold** 0.2403 oz. AGW. • **Obv. Designer:** Susan Gamble adn Phebe Hemphill • **Rev. Designer:** Don Everhart II

Date	Mintage	MS65	Prf65
2008W	13,467	457	—
2008W	59,269	—	442

MEDAL OF HONOR. KM# 505 • ObvDesc: 1861 Medal of Honor design for the Navy • **RevDesc:** Minerva standing with shield and Union flag, field artillery canon flanking • 8.36 g., 0.900 **Gold** 0.2403 oz. AGW. • **Obv. Designer:** Joseph Menna • **Rev. Designer:** Joel Iskowitz and Michael Gaudioso

Date	Mintage	MS65	Prf65
2011S	18,012	—	500
2011S	8,251	585	—

U.S. ARMY. KM# 508 • ObvDesc: Five Soldiers of different eras • **RevDesc:** Elements from the Army's emblem • 8.36 g., 0.900 **Gold** 0.2403 oz. AGW. • **Obv. Designer:** Joel Iskowitz and Phebe Hemphill • **Rev. Designer:** Joseph Menna

Date	Mintage	MS65	Prf65
2011P	8,062	585	—
2011P	17,173	—	495

STAR-SPANGLED BANNER. KM# 531 • ObvDesc: Naval battle scene from the War of 1812. American ship in foreground, damaged British ship in background • **RevDesc:** 15 stars and 15 stripes, opening words to the Star-Spangled Banner: O say can you see. • 8.36 g., 0.900 **Gold** 0.2403 oz. AGW. • **Obv. Designer:** Donna Weaver • **Rev. Designer:** Joseph Menna

Date	Mintage	MS65	Prf65
2012	—	585	—
2012	—	—	600

KM# 555 • Gold AGW **Subject:** Five-Star Generals - Douglas MacArthur

Date	Mintage	MS65	Prf65
2013	—	—	—
2013	—	—	—

KM# 578 • Gold AGW **Subject:** Baseball Hall of Fame

Date	Mintage	MS65	Prf65
2014	—	—	—
2014	—	—	—

$10 (EAGLE)

FIRST FLIGHT CENTENNIAL. KM# 350 • ObvDesc: Orvile and Wilbur Wright busts facing • **RevDesc:** Wright flyer and eagle • 16.72 g., 0.900 **Gold** 0.4806 oz. ACW. • **Obv. Designer:** Donna Weaver • **Rev. Designer:** Norman Nemeth

Date	Mintage	MS65	Prf65
2003P	10,129	1,050	—
2003W	21,846	—	893

$20 (DOUBLE EAGLE)

KM# 464 • ObvDesc: Ultra high relief Liberty holding torch, walking forward • **RevDesc:** Eagle in flight left, sunrise in background • 31.11 g., 0.999 **Gold** 0.9926 oz. AGW.

Date	Mintage	MS65	Prf65
2009	115,178	2,350	—

AMERICA THE BEAUTIFUL SILVER BULLION

SILVER QUARTER

KM# 489 • RevDesc: Park Headquarters and fountain • 155.55 g., 0.999 **Silver** 4.9639 oz. ASW • **Rev. Designer:** Don Everhart II and Joseph Menna

Date	Mintage	MS65	Prf65
2010	33,000	290	—
2010P Vapor Blast finish	27,000	250	—

KM# 490 • RevDesc: Old Faithful geyser and bison • 155.55 g., 0.999 **Silver** 4.9639 oz. ASW • **Rev. Designer:** Don Everhart II

Date	Mintage	MS65	Prf65
2010	33,000	275	—
2010P Vapor Blast finish	27,000	240	—

KM# 491 • RevDesc: El Capitan, largest monolith of granite in the world • 155.55 g., 0.999 Silver 4.9639 oz. ASW • **Rev. Designer:** Joseph Menna and Phebe Hemphill

Date	Mintage	MS65	Prf65
2010	33,000	275	—
2010P Vapor blast finish	27,000	225	—

KM# 492 • RevDesc: Grabarues above the Nankoweap Delta in Marble Canyon near the Colorado River • 155.55 g., 0.999 Silver 4.9639 oz. ASW • **Rev. Designer:** Phebe Hemphill

Date	Mintage	MS65	Prf65
2010	33,000	250	—
2010P Vapor blast finish	26,019	225	—

KM# 493 • RevDesc: Mt. Hood with Lost Lake in the foreground • 155.55 g., 0.999 Silver 4.9639 oz. ASW • **Rev. Designer:** Phebe Hemphill

Date	Mintage	MS65	Prf65
2010	33,000	275	—
2010P Vapor blast finish	25,318	200	—

KM# 513 • RevDesc: 72nd Pennsylvania Infantry Monumnet on the battle line of the Union Army at Cemetery Ridge • 155.55 g., 0.999 Silver 4.9639 oz. ASW • **Rev. Designer:** Joel Iskowitz and Phebe Hemphill

Date	Mintage	MS65	Prf65
2011	126,700	200	—
2011P Vapor blast finish	24,625	190	—

KM# 514 • RevDesc: Northeast slope of Mount Reynolds • 155.55 g., 0.999 Silver 4.9639 oz. ASW • **Rev. Designer:** Barbara Fox and Charles L. Vickers

Date	Mintage	MS65	Prf65
2011	126,700	200	—
2011P Vapor blast finish	20,503	190	—

KM# 515 • RevDesc: Roosevelt elk on a gravel river bar along the Hoh River, Mount Olympus in the background • 155.55 g., 0.999 Silver 4.9639 oz. ASW • **Rev. Designer:** Susan Gambel and Michael Gaudioso

Date	Mintage	MS65	Prf65
2011	85,900	200	—
2011P Vapor blast finish	17,988	190	—

KM# 516 • RevDesc: U.S.S. Cairo on the Yazoo River • 155.55 g., 0.999 Silver 4.9639 oz. ASW • **Rev. Designer:** Thomas Cleveland and Joseph menna

Date	Mintage	MS65	Prf65
2011	39,500	200	—
2011P Vapor blast finish	18,181	190	—

KM# 517 • RevDesc: Limestone Lincoln Bridge • 155.55 g., 0.999 Silver 4.9639 oz. ASW • **Rev. Designer:** Donna Weaver and James Licaretz

Date	Mintage	MS65	Prf65
2011	29,700	200	—
2011P Vapor blast finish	16,386	190	—

KM# 536 • RevDesc: Coquin tree frog and Puerto Rico parrot • 155.55 g., 0.999 Silver 4.9639 oz. ASW

Date	Mintage	MS65	Prf65
2012	21,900	200	—
2012P Vapor blast finish	15,271	190	—

KM# 537 • RevDesc: Two elevated kivas at Chetro Ketl complex • 155.52 g., 0.999 **Silver** 4.9629 oz. ASW

Date	Mintage	MS65	Prf65
2012	20,000	200	—
2012P Vapor blast finish	12,679	190	—

KM# 540 • RevDesc: Dall sheep and Mount McKinley • 155.55 g., 0.999 **Silver** 4.9639 oz. ASW

Date	Mintage	MS65	Prf65
2012	20,000	200	—
2012P Vapor blast finish	10,180	190	—

KM# 558 • RevDesc: Ancient weatherworn tree • 155.55 g., 0.999 **Silver** 4.9639 oz. ASW

Date	Mintage	MS65	Prf65
2013	—	200	—
2013 Vapor blast finish	—	190	—

KM# 538 • RevDesc: Bass Harbor Head Lighthouse • 155.52 g., 0.999 **Silver** 4.9629 oz. ASW

Date	Mintage	MS65	Prf65
2012	25,400	200	—
2012P Vapor blast finish	13,196	190	—

KM# 556 • RevDesc: Mountain vista • 155.55 g., 0.999 **Silver** 4.9639 oz. ASW

Date	Mintage	MS65	Prf65
2013	—	200	—
2013P Vapor blast finish	—	190	—

KM# 559 • RevDesc: Fort McHenry and flag • 155.55 g., 0.999 **Silver** 4.9639 oz. ASW

Date	Mintage	MS65	Prf65
2013	—	200	—
2013	—	190	—

KM# 539 • RevDesc: Volcano erupting • 155.52 g., 0.999 **Silver** 4.9629 oz. ASW

Date	Mintage	MS65	Prf65
2012	20,000	200	—
2012P Vapor blast finish	13,789	190	—

KM# 557 • RevDesc: Perry standing and Memorial column • 155.55 g., 0.999 **Silver** 4.9639 oz. ASW

Date	Mintage	MS65	Prf65
2013	—	200	—
2013 Vapor blast finsih	—	190	—

KM# 560 • RevDesc: Presidential head sculpture on Mt. Rushmore • 155.55 g., 0.999 **Silver** 4.9639 oz. ASW

Date	Mintage	MS65	Prf65
2013	—	200	—
2013 Vapor blast finish	—	190	—

KM# 580Silver ASW

Date	Mintage	MS65	Prf65
2014	—	200	—
2014P Vapor blast finish		190	—

KM# 581 • 155.55 g., 0.999 **Silver** 4.9639 oz. ASW

Date	Mintage	MS65	Prf65
2014	—	200	—
2014P Vapor blast finish		190	—

KM# 582 • 155.55 g., 0.999 **Silver** 4.9639 oz. ASW

Date	Mintage	MS65	Prf65
2014	—	200	—
2014P Vapor blast finish		190	—

KM# 584 • 155.55 g., 0.999 **Silver** 4.9639 oz. ASW

Date	Mintage	MS65	Prf65
2014	—	200	—
2014P Vapor blast finish		190	—

AMERICAN EAGLE BULLION COINS

SILVER DOLLAR

KM# 273 • ObvDesc: Liberty walking left • RevDesc: Eagle with shield • 31.11 g., 0.9993 **Silver** 0.9929 oz. ASW, 40.6 • **Obv. Designer:** Adolph A. Weinman • **Rev. Designer:** John Mercanti

Date	Mintage	MS65	Prf65
2001	9,001,711	28.80	—
2001W	746,398	—	56.00
2002	10,539,026	28.80	—
2002W	647,342	—	80.00
2003	8,495,008	28.80	—
2003W	747,831	—	80.00
2004	8,882,754	28.80	—
2004W	801,602	—	85.00
2005	8,891,025	28.80	—
2005W	816,663	—	56.00
2006	10,676,522	28.80	—
2006W Burnished Unc.	468,000	85.00	—
2006W	1,093,600	—	56.00
2006P Reverse Proof	Est. 250000	—	265
2006 20th Aniv. 3 pc. set	—	—	415
2007	9,028,036	28.80	—
2007W Burnished Unc.	690,891	28.80	—
2007W	821,759	—	56.00
2008	20,583,000	28.80	—
2008W Burnished Unc.	Est. 550000	71.50	—
2008W Reverse of '07, U in United with rounded bottom.	Est. 47000	550	—
2008	713,353	—	56.00
2009	30,459,000	28.80	—
2010	34,764,500	28.80	—
2010	—	—	56.00
2011	—	27.80	—
2011P Reverse Proof	100,000	—	305
2011S Unc.	100,000	285	—
2011W Burnished Unc.	100,000	50.00	—
2011W Proof	100,000	—	59.00
2012	—	25.80	—
2012 Reverse Proof	—	—	125
2012S Proof	—	—	59.00
2012W Burnished Unc.	—	60.00	—
2013	—	25.80	—
2013W Enhanced Unc.	—	—	—
2013W Proof	—	—	60.00
2013 Enhanced Finish	—	93.50	—
2013W Enhanced Finish Reverse Proof	—	—	88.00

GOLD $5

KM# 216 • 3.39 g., 0.9167 **Gold** 0.0994 oz. AGW, 16.5 • **Obv. Designer:** Augustus Saint-Gaudens • **Rev. Designer:** Miley Busiek

Date	Mintage	MS65	Prf65
2001	269,147	165	—
2001W	37,530	—	192
2002	230,027	205	—
2002W	40,864	—	192
2003	245,029	195	—
2003W	40,027	—	192
2004	250,016	195	—
2004W	35,131	—	225
2005	300,043	195	—
2005W	49,265	—	225
2006	285,006	195	—
2006W Burnished Unc.	20,643	200	—
2006W	47,277	—	192
2007	190,010	195	—
2007W Burnished Unc.	22,501	210	—
2007W	58,553	—	192
2008	305,000	165	—
2008W Burnished Unc.	12,657	360	—
2008W	Est. 29000	—	192
2009	27,000	165	—
2010	—	165	—
2010W	—	—	192
2011	—	185	—
2011W	5,000	—	192
2012W	—	165	—
2012W Burnished Unc.	—	—	—
2013W	—	165	—
2013	—	—	225

GOLD $10

KM# 217 • 8.48 g., 0.9167 **Gold** 0.2484 oz. AGW, 22 • **Obv. Designer:** Augustus Saint-Gaudens • **Rev. Designer:** Miley Busiek

Date	Mintage	MS65	Prf65
2001	71,280	352	—
2001W	25,613	—	423
2002	62,027	352	—
2002W	29,242	—	423
2003	74,029	352	—
2003W	30,292	—	423
2004	72,014	352	—
2004W	28,839	—	423
2005	72,015	352	—
2005W	37,207	—	423
2006	60,004	352	—
2006W Burnished Unc.	15,188	785	—
2006W	36,127	—	423
2007	34,004	352	—
2007W Burnished Unc.	12,786	990	—
2007W	46,189	—	423
2008	Est. 58000	352	—
2008W Burnished Unc.	8,883	1,750	—
2008W	28,000	—	423
2009	27,500	352	—
2010	—	352	—
2010W	—	—	423
2011	—	352	—
2011W	4,000	—	423
2012	—	352	—
2012W Burnished Unc.	—	—	—
2013	—	352	—
2013	—	—	475

GOLD $25

KM# 218 • 16.97 g., 0.9167 **Gold** 0.4968 oz. AGW, 27 • **Obv. Designer:** Augustus Saint-Gaudens • **Rev. Designer:** Miley Busiek

Date	Mintage	MS65	Prf65
2001	48,047	1,325	—
2001W	23,240	—	855
2002	70,027	995	—
2002W	26,646	—	855
2003	79,029	703	—
2003W	28,270	—	855
2004	98,040	703	—
2004W	27,330	—	855
2005	80,023	703	—
2005W	34,311	—	855
2006	66,004	706	—
2006W Burnished Unc.	15,164	1,650	—
2006W	34,322	—	855
2007	47,002	1,100	—
2007W Burnished Unc.	11,458	1,900	—
2007W	44,025	—	855
2008	61,000	706	—
2008W Burnished Unc.	15,683	1,650	—
2008W	27,800	—	855
2009	55,000	706	—
2010	—	703	—
2010W	—	—	855
2011	—	703	—
2011W	2,000	—	855
2012W	—	703	—
2013W	—	703	—
2013	—	—	975

GOLD $50

KM# 219 • 33.93 g., 0.9167 **Gold** 0.9936 oz. AGW, 32.7 • **Obv. Designer:** Augustus Saint-Gaudens • **Rev. Designer:** Miley Busiek

Date	Mintage	MS65	Prf65
2001	143,605	1,439	—
2001W	24,555	—	1,740
2002	222,029	1,439	—
2002W	27,499	—	1,740
2003	416,032	1,439	—
2003W	28,344	—	1,740
2004	417,149	1,439	—
2004W	28,215	—	1,740
2005	356,555	1,439	—
2005W	35,246	—	1,740
2006	237,510	1,439	—
2006W Burnished Unc.	45,912	1,885	—
2006W	47,000	—	1,740
2006W Reverse Proof	10,000	—	2,675
2007	140,016	1,453	—
2007W Burnished Unc.	18,609	1,980	—
2007W	51,810	—	1,740
2008W	710,000	1,439	—
2008W Burnished Unc.	11,908	2,100	—
2008W Reverse of '07	—	—	—
2008W	29,000	—	2,150
2009	122,000	1,439	—
2010	—	1,439	—
2010W	—	—	1,740
2011	—	1,439	—
2011 Burnished Unc.	—	2,350	—
2011W	—	—	1,740
2012W	—	1,343	—
2012 Burnished Unc.	—	2,975	—
2013W	—	1,439	—
2013	—	—	1,850

PLATINUM $10

KM# 283 • RevDesc: Eagle flying right over sunrise • 3.11 g., 0.9995 **Platinum** 0.0993 oz. APW, 17 • **Obv. Designer:** John Mercanti • **Rev. Designer:** Thomas D. Rogers Sr

Date	Mintage	MS65	Prf65
2001	52,017	192	—
2002	23,005	192	—
2003	22,007	192	—
2004	15,010	192	—
2005	14,013	192	—
2006	11,001	192	—
2006W Burnished Unc.	—	425	—
2007	13,003	285	—
2007W Burnished Unc.	—	280	—
2008	17,000	192	—
2008 Burnished Unc.	—	390	—

KM# 327 • RevDesc: Eagle in flight over Southwestern cactus desert • 3.11 g., 0.9995 **Platinum** 0.0993 oz. APW, 17 • **Obv. Designer:** John Mercanti

Date	Mintage	MS65	Prf65
2001W	12,174	—	193

KM# 339 • RevDesc: Eagle fishing in America's Northwest • 3.11 g., 0.9995 **Platinum** 0.0993 oz. APW, 17 • **Obv. Designer:** John Mercanti

Date	Mintage	MS65	Prf65
2002W	12,365	—	193

KM# 351 • RevDesc: Eagle pearched on a Rocky Mountain Pine branch against a flag backdrop • 3.11 g., 0.9995 **Platinum** 0.0993 oz. APW, 17 • **Obv. Designer:** John Mercanti • **Rev. Designer:** Al Maletsky

Date	Mintage	MS65	Prf65
2003W	9,534	—	250

KM# 364 • RevDesc: Chester French, 1907. The sculpture is outside the N.Y. Customs House, now part of the Smithsonian's Museum of the American Indian • 3.11 g., 0.9995 **Platinum** 0.0993 oz. APW, 17 • **Obv. Designer:** John Mercanti

Date	Mintage	MS65	Prf65
2004W	7,161	—	445

KM# 377 • RevDesc: Eagle with cornucopiae • 3.11 g., 0.9995 **Platinum** 0.0993 oz. APW, 17 • **Obv. Designer:** John Mercanti • **Rev. Designer:** Donna Weaver

Date	Mintage	MS65	Prf65
2005W	8,104	—	265

KM# 389 • RevDesc: Liberty seated writing between two columns • 3.11 g., 0.9995 **Platinum** 0.0993 oz. APW, 17 • **Obv. Designer:** John Mercanti

Date	Mintage	MS65	Prf65
2006W	10,205	—	193

KM# 414 • RevDesc: Eagle with shield • 3.11 g., 0.9995 **Platinum** 0.0993 oz. APW, 17 • **Obv. Designer:** John Mercanti

Date	Mintage	MS65	Prf65
2007W	8,176	—	193

KM# 434 • RevDesc: Justice standing before eagle • 3.11 g., 0.9995 **Platinum** 0.0993 oz. APW, 17 • **Obv. Designer:** John Mercanti

Date	Mintage	MS65	Prf65
2008W	8,176	—	495

KM# 460 • 3.11 g., 0.9995 **Platinum** 0.0993 oz. APW, 17 • **Obv. Designer:** John Mercanti

Date	Mintage	MS65	Prf65
2009W	5,600	—	—

PLATINUM $25

KM# 284 • RevDesc: Eagle in flight over sunrise • 7.79 g., 0.9995 **Platinum** 0.2486 oz. APW, 22 • **Obv. Designer:** John Mercanti • **Rev. Designer:** Thomas D. Rogers Sr

Date	Mintage	MS65	Prf65
2001	21,815	445	—
2002	27,405	445	—
2003	25,207	445	—
2004	18,010	445	—
2005	12,013	445	—
2006	12,001	445	—
2006W Burnished Unc.	—	590	—
2007	8,402	445	—
2007W Burnished Unc.	—	590	—
2008	22,800	414	—
2008 Burnished Unc.	—	665	—

KM# 328 • RevDesc: Eagle in flight over Southwestern cactus desert • 7.79 g., 0.9995 **Platinum** 0.2486 oz. APW, 22 • **Obv. Designer:** John Mercanti

Date	Mintage	MS65	Prf65
2001W	8,847	—	470

KM# 340 • RevDesc: Eagle fishing in America's Northwest • 7.79 g., 0.9995 **Platinum** 0.2486 oz. APW, 22 • **Obv. Designer:** John Mercanti

Date	Mintage	MS65	Prf65
2002W	9,282	—	470

KM# 352 • RevDesc: Eagle pearched on a Rocky Mountain Pine branch against a flag backdrop. • 7.79 g., 0.9995 **Platinum** 0.2486 oz. APW, 22 • **Obv. Designer:** John Mercanti • **Rev. Designer:** Al Maletsky

Date	Mintage	MS65	Prf65
2003W	7,044	—	470

KM# 365 • RevDesc: Chester French, 1907. The sculpture is outside the N.Y. Customs House, now part of the Smithsonian's Museum of the American Indian • 7.79 g., 0.9995 **Platinum** 0.2486 oz. APW, 22 • **Obv. Designer:** John Mercanti

Date	Mintage	MS65	Prf65
2004W	5,193	—	1,000

KM# 378 • RevDesc: Eagle with cornucopiae • 7.79 g., 0.9995 **Platinum** 0.2486 oz. APW, 22 • **Obv. Designer:** John Mercanti • **Rev. Designer:** Donna Weaver

Date	Mintage	MS65	Prf65
2005W	6,592	—	610

KM# 390 • RevDesc: Liberty seated writing between two columns • 7.79 g., 0.9995 **Platinum** 0.2486 oz. APW, 22 • **Obv. Designer:** John Mercanti

Date	Mintage	MS65	Prf65
2006W	7,813	—	470

KM# 415 • RevDesc: Eagle with shield • 7.79 g., 0.9995 **Platinum** 0.2486 oz. APW, 22 • **Obv. Designer:** John Mercanti

Date	Mintage	MS65	Prf65
2007W Polished Freedom	6,017	—	470
2007W Frosted Freedom, Rare			

KM# 435 • RevDesc: Justice standing before eagle • 7.79 g., 0.9995 **Platinum** 0.2486 oz. APW, 22 • **Obv. Designer:** John Mercanti

Date	Mintage	MS65	Prf65
2008W	6,017	—	715

KM# 461 • 7.79 g., 0.9995 **Platinum** 0.2486 oz. APW, 22 • **Obv. Designer:** John Mercanti

Date	Mintage	MS65	Prf65
2009W	3,800	—	—

PLATINUM $50

KM# 285 • RevDesc: Eagle flying right over sunrise • 15.55 g., 0.9995 **Platinum** 0.4965 oz. APW, 27 • **Obv. Designer:** John Mercanti • **Rev. Designer:** Thomas D. Rogers Sr

Date	Mintage	MS65	Prf65
2001	12,815	889	—
2002	24,005	889	—
2003	17,409	889	—
2004	13,236	889	—
2005	9,013	889	—
2006	9,602	889	—
2006W Burnished Unc.	—	1,018	
2007	7,001	889	—
2007W Burnished Unc.		925	
2008	14,000	889	—
2008W Burnished Unc.		1,200	

KM# 329 • RevDesc: Eagle in flight over Southwestern cactus desert • 15.55 g., 0.9995 **Platinum** 0.4965 oz. APW, 27 • **Obv. Designer:** John Mercanti

Date	Mintage	MS65	Prf65
2001W	8,254	—	935

KM# 341 • RevDesc: Eagle fishing in America's Northwest • 15.55 g., 0.9995 **Platinum** 0.4965 oz. APW, 27 • **Obv. Designer:** John Mercanti

Date	Mintage	MS65	Prf65
2002W	8,772	—	935

KM# 353 • RevDesc: Eagle pearched on a Rocky Mountain Pine branch against a flag backdrop. • 15.55 g., 0.9995 **Platinum** 0.4965 oz. APW, 27 • **Obv. Designer:** John Mercanti • **Rev. Designer:** Al Maletsky

Date	Mintage	MS65	Prf65
2003W	7,131	—	935

KM# 366 • RevDesc: Chester French, 1907. The sculpture is outside the N.Y. Customs House, now part of the Smithsonian's Museum of the American Indian • 15.55 g., 0.9995 **Platinum** 0.4965 oz. APW, 27 • **Obv. Designer:** John Mercanti

Date	Mintage	MS65	Prf65
2004W	5,063		1,550

KM# 379 • RevDesc: Eagle with cornucopiae • 15.55 g.,

0.9995 **Platinum** 0.4965 oz. APW, 27 • **Obv. Designer:** John Mercanti • **Rev. Designer:** Donna Weaver

Date	Mintage	MS65	Prf65
2005W	5,942	—	1,175

KM# 391 • RevDesc: Liberty seated writing between two columns • 15.55 g., 0.9995 **Platinum** 0.4965 oz. APW, 27 • **Obv. Designer:** John Mercanti

Date	Mintage	MS65	Prf65
2006W	7,649	—	935

KM# 416 • RevDesc: Eagle with shield • 15.55 g., 0.9995 **Platinum** 0.4965 oz. APW, 27 • **Obv. Designer:** John Mercanti

Date	Mintage	MS65	Prf65
2007W Reverse Proof	22,873	—	885
2007W Frosted Freedom, Rare	—	—	—

KM# 436 • RevDesc: Justice standing before eagle • 15.55 g., 0.9995 **Platinum** 0.4965 oz. APW, 27 • **Obv. Designer:** John Mercanti

Date	Mintage	MS65	Prf65
2008W	22,873	—	1,225

KM# 462 • 15.55 g., 0.9995 **Platinum** 0.4965 oz. APW, 27 • **Obv. Designer:** John Mercanti

Date	Mintage	MS65	Prf65
2009	3,600	—	—

PLATINUM $100

KM# 286 • RevDesc: Eagle in flight over sun rise • 31.11 g., 0.9995 **Platinum** 0.9931 oz. APW, 33 • **Obv. Designer:** John Mercanti • **Rev. Designer:** Thomas D. Rogers Sr

Date	Mintage	MS65	Prf65
2001	14,070	1,658	—
2002	11,502	1,658	—
2003	8,007	1,658	—
2004	7,009	1,658	—
2005	6,310	1,658	—
2006	6,000	1,658	—
2006W Burnished Unc.		2,200	—
2007	7,202	1,702	—
2007W Burnished Unc.		2,100	—
2008	21,800	1,658	—
2008W Burnished Unc.		2,300	—
2011	—	—	—

KM# 330 • RevDesc: Eagle in flight over Southwestern cactus desert • 31.11 g., 0.9995 **Platinum** 0.9931 oz. APW, 33 • **Obv. Designer:** John Mercanti

Date	Mintage	MS65	Prf65
2001W	8,969	—	1,760

KM# 342 • RevDesc: Eagle fishing in America's Northwest • 31.11 g., 0.9995 **Platinum** 0.9931 oz. APW, 33 • **Obv. Designer:** John Mercanti

Date	Mintage	MS65	Prf65
2002W	9,834	—	1,760

KM# 354 • RevDesc: Eagle pearched on a Rocky Mountain Pine branch against a flag backdrop • 31.11 g., 0.9995 **Platinum** 0.9931 oz. APW, 33 • **Obv. Designer:** John Mercanti • **Rev. Designer:** Al Maletsky

Date	Mintage	MS65	Prf65
2003W	8,246	—	1,777

KM# 367 • RevDesc: Inspired by the sculpture "America" by Daniel Chester French, 1907. The sculpture is outside the N.Y. Customs House, now part of the Smithsonian's Museum of the American Indian • 31.11 g., 0.9995 **Platinum** 0.9931 oz. APW, 33 • **Obv. Designer:** John Mercanti • **Rev. Designer:** Donna Weaver

Date	Mintage	MS65	Prf65
2004W	6,007	—	2,119

KM# 380 • RevDesc: Eagle with cornucopiae • 31.11 g., 0.9995 **Platinum** 0.9931 oz. APW, 33 • **Obv. Designer:** John Mercanti • **Rev. Designer:** Donna Weaver

Date	Mintage	MS65	Prf65
2005W	6,602	—	2,400

KM# 392 • **RevDesc:** Liberty seated writing between two columns • 31.11 g., 0.9995 **Platinum** 0.9931 oz. APW, 33 • **Obv. Designer:** John Mercanti

Date	Mintage	MS65	Prf65
2006W	9,152	—	1,760

KM# 417 • **RevDesc:** Eagle with shield • 31.11 g., 0.9995 **Platinum** 0.9931 oz. APW, 33 • **Obv. Designer:** John Mercanti

Date	Mintage	MS65	Prf65
2007W Freedom Frosted	8,363	—	1,760
2007W Freedom Polished	—	—	50,000

KM# 437 • **RevDesc:** Justice standing before eagle • 31.11 g., 0.9995 **Platinum** 0.9931 oz. APW, 33 • **Obv. Designer:** John Mercanti

Date	Mintage	MS65	Prf65
2008W	8,363	—	3,000

KM# 463 • **RevDesc:** Four portraits • 31.10 g., 0.9995 **Platinum** 0.993 oz. APW, 33 • **Obv. Designer:** John Mercanti

Date	Mintage	MS65	Prf65
2009W Proof	4,900	—	2,260

KM# 488 • **RevDesc:** Statue of Justice holding scales • 31.11 g., 0.999 **Platinum** 0.9926 oz. APW, 33 • **Obv. Designer:** John Mercanti

Date	Mintage	MS65	Prf65
2010W	—	—	2,160

KM# 518 • **RevDesc:** Female with dove, walking in field • 31.11 g., 0.9995 **Platinum** 0.9931 oz. APW, 33

Date	Mintage	MS65	Prf65
2011W	10,299	—	2,100

KM# 541 • **RevDesc:** Colonial soldier and flag • 31.11 g., 0.9995 **Platinum** 0.9931 oz. APW

Date	Mintage	MS65	Prf65
2012	—	—	1,793

BISON BULLION COINAGE

GOLD $5

KM# 411 • **ObvDesc:** Indian Head right • **RevDesc:** Bison • 3.11 g., 0.9999 **Gold** 0.0993 oz. AGW

Date	Mintage	MS65	Prf65
2008W	17,429	600	—
2008W	18,884	—	660

GOLD $10

KM# 412 • **ObvDesc:** Indian Head right • **RevDesc:** Bison • 7.79 g., 0.9999 **Gold** 0.2487 oz. AGW

Date	Mintage	MS65	Prf65
2008W	9,949	1,375	—
2008W	13,125	—	1,550

GOLD $25

KM# 413 • **ObvDesc:** Indian Head right • **RevDesc:** Bison • 15.55 g., 0.999 **Gold** 0.4963 oz. AGW

Date	Mintage	MS65	Prf65
2008W	16,908	1,350	—
2008W	12,169	—	1,850

GOLD $50

KM# 393 • **ObvDesc:** Indian head right • **RevDesc:** Bison standing left on mound • 31.11 g., 0.9999 **Gold** 0.9935 oz. AGW, 32 • **Designer:** James E. Fraser

Date	Mintage	MS65	Prf65
2006	337,012	1,439	—
2006W Proof	246,267	—	1,590
2007	136,503	1,439	—
2007W Proof	58,998	—	1,590
2008	189,500	1,439	—
2008W Burnished	18,863	—	3,200
2008W Moy Family Chop, Proof	—	—	3,950
2009	200,000	1,439	—
2009W Proof	49,306	—	1,560
2010	209,000	1,439	—
2010W Proof	49,263	—	1,590
2011	174,500	1,439	—
2011W Proof	—	—	1,590
2012	132,000	—	—
2012W Proof	—	—	1,950
2013	—	1,439	—
2013W Reverse Proof	—	—	2,000

FIRST SPOUSE GOLD COINAGE

GOLD $10 (EAGLE)

KM# 407 • **ObvDesc:** Bust 3/4 facing • **RevDesc:** Martha Washington seated sewing • 15.55 g., 0.9999 **Gold** 0.4967 oz. AGW, 23.5 • **Obv. Designer:** Joseph Menna • **Rev. Designer:** Susan Gamble and Don Everhart

Date	Mintage	MS65	Prf65
2007W	20,000	740	—
2007W	20,000	—	740

KM# 408 • **ObvDesc:** Bust 3/4 facing • **RevDesc:** Abigail Adams seated at desk writing to John during the Revolutionary War • 15.55 g., 0.9999 **Gold** 0.4967 oz. AGW, 26.5 • **Obv. Designer:** Joseph Menna • **Rev. Designer:** Thomas Cleveland and Phebe Hemphill

Date	Mintage	MS65	Prf65
2007W	20,000	740	—
2007W	20,000	—	740

KM# 409 • **ObvDesc:** Bust design from coinage • **RevDesc:** Jefferson's tombstone • 15.55 g., 0.9999 **Gold** 0.4967 oz. AGW, 26.5 • **Obv. Designer:** Robert Scot and Phebe Hemphill • **Rev. Designer:** Charles Vickers

Date	Mintage	MS65	Prf65
2007W	20,000	740	—
2007W	20,000	—	740

KM# 410 • **ObvDesc:** Bust 3/4 facing • **RevDesc:** Dolley standing before painting of Washington, which she saved from the White House • 15.55 g., 0.9999 **Gold** 0.4967 oz. AGW, 26.5 • **Obv. Designer:** Don Everhart • **Rev. Designer:** Joel Iskowitz and Don Everhart

Date	Mintage	MS65	Prf65
2007W	12,500	740	—
2007W	18,300	—	740

KM# 430 • **ObvDesc:** Bust 3/4 facing right • **RevDesc:** Elizabeth standing before mirror • 15.55 g., 0.999 Gold 0.4963 oz. AGW, 26.5 • **Obv. Designer:** Joel Iskowitz and Don Everhart • **Rev. Designer:** Donna Weaver and Charles Vickers

Date	Mintage	MS65	Prf65
2008W	4,500	975	—
2008W	7,900	—	950

KM# 431 • **ObvDesc:** Bust 3/4 facing right • **RevDesc:** Lousia and son Charles before entrance • 15.55 g., 0.999 Gold 0.4963 oz. AGW, 26.5 • **Obv. Designer:** Susan Gamble and Phebe Hemphill • **Rev. Designer:** Joseph Menna

Date	Mintage	MS65	Prf65
2008W	4,200	1,175	—
2008W	7,400	—	1,125

KM# 432 • **ObvDesc:** Capped and draped bust left • **RevDesc:** Andrew Jackson on horseback right • 15.55 g., 0.999 Gold 0.4963 oz. AGW, 26.5 • **Obv. Designer:** John Reich • **Rev. Designer:** Justin Kunz and Don Everhart

Date	Mintage	MS65	Prf65
2008W	4,800	1,575	—
2008W	7,800	—	1,325

KM# 433 • **ObvDesc:** Seated Liberty with shiled • **RevDesc:** Youthful van Buren seated under tree, family tavern in distance • 15.55 g., 0.999 Gold 0.4963 oz. AGW, 26.5 • **Obv. Designer:** Christian Gobrecht • **Rev. Designer:** Thomas Cleveland and James Licaretz

Date	Mintage	MS65	Prf65
2008W	15,000	1,500	—
2008W	Inc. above	—	1,525

KM# 456 • **ObvDesc:** Bust 3/4 left • **RevDesc:** Anna reading to her three children • 15.55 g., 0.999 Gold 0.4963 oz. AGW • **Obv. Designer:** Donna Weaver and Joseph Menna • **Rev. Designer:** Thomas Cleveland and Charles Vickers

Date	Mintage	MS65	Prf65
2009W	15,000	1,225	—
2009W	Inc. above	—	1,150

KM# 457 • **ObvDesc:** Bust facing • **RevDesc:** Letitia and two children playing outside of Cedar Grove Plantation • 15.55 g., 0.999 Gold 0.4963 oz. AGW • **Obv. Designer:** Phebe

Hemphill • **Rev. Designer:** Susan Gamble and Norm Nemeth

Date	Mintage	MS65	Prf65
2009W	15,000	1,525	—
2009W	Inc. above	—	1,325

KM# 458 • **ObvDesc:** Bust facing • **RevDesc:** Julia and John Tyler dancing • 15.55 g., 0.999 Gold 0.4963 oz. AGW • **Designer:** Joel Iskowitz and Don Everhart

Date	Mintage	MS65	Prf65
2009W	15,000	1,650	—
2009W	Inc. above	—	1,800

KM# 459 • **ObvDesc:** Bust 3/4 right • **RevDesc:** Sarah seated at desk as personal secretary to James Polk • 15.55 g., 0.999 Gold 0.4963 oz. AGW • **Designer:** Phebe Hemphill

Date	Mintage	MS65	Prf65
2009W	3,501	1,300	—
2009W	5,157	—	1,100

KM# 465 • **ObvDesc:** Bust 3/4 left • **RevDesc:** Margaret Taylor nurses wounded soldier during the Seminole War • 15.55 g., 0.999 Gold 0.4963 oz. AGW • **Obv. Designer:** Phebe Hemphill and Charles Vickers • **Rev. Designer:** Mary Beth Zeitz and James Licaretz

Date	Mintage	MS65	Prf65
2009W	3,430	1,050	—
2009W	4,787	—	1,225

KM# 481 • **RevDesc:** Abigail Filmore placing books on library shelf • 15.52 g., 0.999 Gold 0.4953 oz. AGW • **Obv. Designer:** Phebe Hemphill • **Rev. Designer:** Susan Gamble and Joseph Menna

Date	Mintage	MS65	Prf65
2010W	15,000	1,300	—
2010W	Inc. above	—	1,025

KM# 482 • **RevDesc:** Jane Pierce seated on porch • 15.52 g., 0.999 Gold 0.4953 oz. AGW • **Obv. Designer:** Donna Weaver and Don Everhart • **Rev. Designer:** Donna Weaver and Charles Vickers

Date	Mintage	MS65	Prf65
2010W	3,333	1,000	—
2010W	4,843	—	1,225

KM# 483 • **RevDesc:** Buchanan as clerk • 15.52 g., 0.999 Gold 0.4953 oz. AGW, 26.5 • **Obv. Designer:** Christian Gobrecht • **Rev. Designer:** Joseph Menna

Date	Mintage	MS65	Prf65
2010W	5,348	1,000	—
2010W	7,304	—	1,075

KM# 484 • **RevDesc:** Mary Lincoln visiting soldiers at hospital • 15.52 g., 0.999 Gold 0.4953 oz. AGW • **Obv. Designer:** Phebe Hemphill • **Rev. Designer:** Joel Iskowitz and Pheve Hemphill

Date	Mintage	MS65	Prf65
2010W	3,760	1,000	—
2010W	6,904	—	975

KM# 509 • **ObvDesc:** Bust of Eliza Johnson • 15.55 g., 0.999 Gold 0.4962 oz. AGW

Date	Mintage	MS65	Prf65
2011W	15,000	1,075	—
2011W	Inc. above	—	1,075

KM# 510 • **ObvDesc:** Bust of Julia Grant • 15.55 g., 0.999 Gold 0.4963 oz. AGW, 26.5

Date	Mintage	MS65	Prf65
2011W	15,000	1,075	—
2011W	Inc. above	—	1,075

KM# 511 • **ObvDesc:** Bust of Lucy Hayes • 15.55 g., 0.999 Gold 0.4963 oz. AGW

Date	Mintage	MS65	Prf65
2011W	15,000	1,325	—
2011W	3,826	—	1,075

KM# 512 • **ObvDesc:** Bust of Lucretia Garfield • 15.55 g., 0.999 Gold 0.4963 oz. AGW

Date	Mintage	MS65	Prf65
2011W	15,000	1,325	—
2011W	3,521	—	1,075

KM# 532 • **ObvDesc:** Alice Paul, suffragist • 15.55 g., 0.999 Gold 0.4963 oz. AGW, 26.5

Date	Mintage	MS65	Prf65
2012W	2,021	1,050	—
2012W	2,802	—	1,075

KM# 533 • ObvDesc: Frances Cleveland • 15.55 g., 0.999 **Gold** 0.4963 oz. AGW, 26.5

Date	Mintage	MS65	Prf65
2012W	1,565	1,050	—
2012W	2,152	—	1,075

KM# 534 • ObvDesc: Caroline Harrison • 15.55 g., 0.999 **Gold** 0.4963 oz. AGW, 26.5

Date	Mintage	MS65	Prf65
2012W	942	1,050	—
2012W	1,380	—	1,075

KM# 535 • ObvDesc: Frances Cleveland • 15.55 g., 0.999 **Gold** 0.4963 oz. AGW, 26.5

Date	Mintage	MS65	Prf65
2012W	—	1,050	—
2012W	—	—	1,075

KM# 561 • ObvDesc: Bust of Ida McKinley • 15.55 g., 0.999 **Gold** 0.4963 oz. AGW

Date	Mintage	MS65	Prf65
2013W	—	800	—
2013W	—	—	825

KM# 562 • ObvDesc: Bust of Edith Roosevelt • 15.55 g., 0.999 **Gold** 0.4963 oz. AGW

Date	Mintage	MS65	Prf65
2013W	—	800	—
2013W	—	—	825

KM# 563 • ObvDesc: Bust of Helen Taft • 15.55 g., 0.999 **Gold** 0.4963 oz. AGW

Date	Mintage	MS65	Prf65
2013W	—	800	—
2013W	—	—	825

KM# 564 • ObvDesc: Bust of Ellen Wilson • 15.55 g., 0.999 **Gold** 0.4963 oz. AGW

Date	Mintage	MS65	Prf65
2013W	—	800	—
2013W	—	—	825

KM# 565 • ObvDesc: Bust of Edith Wilson • 15.55 g., 0.999 **Gold** 0.4963 oz. AGW

Date	Mintage	MS65	Prf65
2013W	—	800	—
2013W	—	—	825

UNCIRCULATED ROLLS

Listings are for rolls containing uncirculated coins. Large date and small date varieties for 1960 and 1970 apply to the one cent coins.

Date	Cents	Nickels	Dimes	Quarters	Halves
2001P	3.75	4.75	7.75	—	16.50
2001D	2.00	6.50	7.25	—	16.00
2002P	2.00	4.00	7.25	—	20.00
2002D	3.25	4.10	7.25	—	20.00
2003P	3.35	7.50	7.00	—	22.50
2003D	2.00	3.50	7.00	—	19.50
2004P Peace Medal Nickel	1.75	6.75	7.00	—	30.00
2004D Peace Medal Nickel	2.50	7.00	7.00	—	30.00
2004P Keelboat Nickel	—	4.00	—	—	—
2004D Keelboat Nickel	—	3.50	—	—	—
2005P Bison Nickel	1.75	3.25	7.00	—	21.00
2005D Bison Nickel	2.75	3.25	7.00	—	21.00
2005P Ocean in view Nickel	—	3.25	—	—	—
2005D Ocean in view Nickel	—	3.25	—	—	—
2006P	2.75	3.25	8.50	—	29.00
2006D	1.75	3.25	8.50	—	29.00
2007P	1.75	3.50	8.00	—	21.00
2007D	1.75	3.50	7.75	—	21.00
2008P	1.75	3.75	8.00	—	24.50
2008D	1.75	3.75	7.50	—	25.50
2009P Log Cabin	2.00	23.00	13.50	—	18.50
2009D Log Cabin	2.15	13.50	13.50	—	18.50
2009P Log Splitter	1.75	—	—	—	—
2009D Log Splitter	1.75	—	—	—	—
2009P Professional	1.75	—	—	—	—
2009D Professional	1.75	—	—	—	—
2009P President	2.00	—	—	—	—
2009D President	2.00	—	—	—	—

50 STATE QUARTERS
Uncirculated Rolls

2001 New York	14.00	14.00
2001 North Carolina	14.50	15.00
2001 Rhode Island	14.00	15.50
2001 Vermont	14.50	14.50
2001 Kentucky	16.50	18.50
2002 Tennessee	30.00	39.50
2002 Ohio	21.50	21.50
2002 Louisiana	14.00	14.00
2002 Indiana	14.50	15.50
2002 Mississippi	16.50	16.50
2003 Illinois	39.00	45.00
2003 Alabama	17.00	18.50
2003 Maine	14.50	15.50
2003 Missouri	14.50	14.75
2003 Arkansas	14.50	15.50
2004 Michigan	13.75	14.50
2004 Florida	13.75	14.50
2004 Texas	14.00	15.00
2004 Iowa	14.00	14.50
2004 Wisconsin	15.50	16.50
2005 California	21.00	22.50
2005 Minnesota	17.50	17.50
2005 Oregon	13.75	13.75
2005 Kansas	13.75	13.75
2005 West Virginia	13.50	13.75
2006 Nevada	13.75	13.75
2006 Nebraska	13.75	14.00
2006 Colorado	13.75	14.00
2006 North Dakota	13.75	14.50
2006 South Dakota	13.75	13.75
2007 Montana	14.00	17.00
2007 Washington	18.00	18.75
2007 Idaho	15.50	15.50
2007 Wyoming	14.75	15.00
2007 Utah	15.00	14.50
2008 Oklahoma	13.75	13.75
2008 New Mexico	14.00	15.50
2008 Arizona	15.50	13.75
2008 Alaska	13.50	13.75
2008 Hawaii	13.50	13.50

MINT SETS

Date	Sets Sold	Issue Price	Value
2001	1,066,900	14.95	6.85
2002	1,139,388	14.95	6.60
2003	1,002,555	14.95	8.80
2004	844,484	16.95	8.00
2005	—	16.95	7.00
2006	—	16.95	8.00
2007	—	—	28.50
2008	—	—	59.50
2009 18 piece clad set	—	—	29.00
2010 28 piece clad set	—	—	29.70
2010 14 piece clad	—	—	26.50
2011 14 piece clad set	532,059	—	34.50
2012 14 piece clad set	365,298	—	75.00

MODERN COMMEMORATIVE COIN SETS

American Buffalo

Date	Price
2001 2001 2 coin set: 90% silver unc. & proof $1.; KM325.	330
2001 2001 coin & currency set 90% unc. dollar & replicas of 1899 $5 silver cert.; KM325.	180

Capitol Visitor Center

Date	Price
2001 2001 3 coin set: proof half, silver dollar, gold $5; KM323, 324, 326.	495

Winter Olympics - Salt Lake City

Date	Price
2002 2002 2 coin set: proof 90% silver dollar KM336 & $5.00 Gold KM337.	465
2002 2002 4 coin set: 90% silver unc. & proof $1, KM336 & unc. & proof gold $5, KM337.	925

Thomas Alva Edison

Date	Price
2004 2004 Uncirculated silver dollar and light bulb.	55.00

Lewis and Clark Bicentennial

Date	Price
2004 2004 Coin and pouch set.	65.00
2004 2004 coin and currency set: Uncirculated silver dollar, two 2005 nickels, replica 1901 $10 Bison note, silver plated peace medal, three stamps & two booklets.	58.00
2004 2004 Westward Journey Nickel series coin and medal set: Proof Sacagawea dollar, two 2005 proof nickels and silver plated peace medal.	40.00

Chief Justice John Marshall

Date	Price
2005 2005 Coin and Chronicles set: Uncirculated silver dollar, booklet and BEP intaglio portrait.	57.00

U.S. Marine Corps

Date	Price
2005 2005 Uncirculated silver dollar and stamp set.	63.00

Benjamin Franklin Tercentennary

Date	Price
2006 2006 Coin and Chronicles set: Uncirculated "Scientist" silver dollar, four stamps, Poor Richards Almanac and intaglio print.	49.00

Central High School Desegregation

Date	Price
2007 2007 Little Rock Dollar and medal set, KM#418	47.80

American Bald Eagle

Date	Price
2008 2008 Proof half dollar, dollar and $5 gold, KM438, KM439, KM440	490
2008 2008 Bald Eagle young collector's set; Half Dollar, KM#438	23.00

Louis Braille

Date	Price
2009 Braille Education set, KM#455	43.50

PROOF SETS

Date	Sets Sold	Issue Price	Value
2001S 10 piece	2,249,498	19.95	13.75
2001S 5 quarter set	774,800	13.95	7.50
2001S Silver	849,600	31.95	52.50
2002S 10 piece	2,319,766	19.95	6.85
2002S 5 quarter set	764,419	13.95	4.50
2002S Silver	892,229	31.95	45.00
2003S 10 piece	2,175,684	16.75	5.75
2003S 5 quarter set	1,225,507	13.95	3.00
2003S Silver	1,142,858	31.95	33.20
2004S 11 piece	1,804,396	22.95	8.80
2004S 5 quarter set	987,960	23.95	3.75
2004S Silver 11 piece	1,187,673	37.95	34.20
2004S Silver 5 quarter set	594,137	—	24.40
2005S American Legacy	—	—	84.50
2005S American Legacy	—	—	77.50
2005S 11 piece	—	22.95	5.00
2005S 5 quarter set	—	15.95	2.75
2005S Silver 11 piece	—	37.95	35.50
2005S Silver 5 quarter set	—	23.95	22.20
2006S 10 piece clad	—	22.95	8.25
2006S 5 quarter set	—	15.95	4.65
2006S Silver 10 piece	—	37.95	37.50
2006S Silver 5 quarter set	—	23.95	23.90
2006S American Legacy	—	—	81.00
2007S 5 quarter set	—	13.95	3.85
2007S Silver 5 quarter set	—	22.95	23.90
2007S 14 piece clad	—	—	16.50
2007S Silver 14 piece	—	—	47.50
2007S Presidental $ set	—	—	7.25
2007S American Legacy	—	—	120
2008 14 piece clad set	—	—	67.00
2008S 5 quarter clad set	—	22.95	44.00
2008S 5 quarter silver set	—	—	29.90
2008S 14 piece silver set	734,045	—	59.50
2008S Presidental $ set	—	—	11.85
2008S American Legacy	—	—	120
2009S 18 piece clad set	1,477,967	—	27.50
2009S 18 piece silver set	694,406	—	57.50
2009S Presidential $ set	627,925	—	9.60
2009S Lincoln Chronicle	—	—	122
2009S Lincoln 4 piece	—	—	11.00
2009S 6 quarter clad set	—	—	8.80
2009S 6 quarter silver set	—	—	29.20
2010S 14 piece clad set	1,103,950	—	55.00
2010S 14 piece silver set	583,912	—	66.00
2010S Presidential $ set	535,463	—	18.25
2010S 6 quarter set	276,335	—	26.50
2010S 5 quarter silver set	274,003	—	30.40
2011 6 quarter set	—	—	18.25
2011S 5 quarter silver set	147,005	—	34.50
2011S 14 piece silver set	572,247	—	83.50
2011S 5 quarter clad set	151,434	—	14.50
2011S Presidential $ set	299,161	—	27.50
2011S 14 piece clad set	1,095,318	—	46.50
2012 8 piece Limited Edition	—	—	225
2012S 5 quarter silver set	—	—	45.00
2012S 14 piece silver set	—	—	215
2012S 6 quarter set	—	—	18.25
2012S 14 piece clad set	—	—	115
2012S Presidential $ set	—	—	62.00

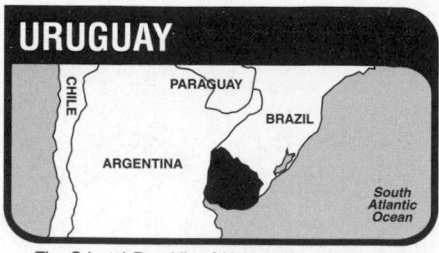

URUGUAY

The Oriental Republic of Uruguay (so called because of its location on the east bank of the Uruguay River) is situated on the Atlantic coast of South America between Argentina and Brazil. This South American country has an area of 68,536 sq. mi. (176,220 sq. km.) and a population of *3 million. Capital: Montevideo. Uruguay's chief economic asset is the rich, rolling grassy plains. Meat, wool, hides and skins are exported.

MINT MARKS
(ba) – Buenos Aires
(br) – Acunaciones Espanolas S.A., Barcelona
(k) – Kremnica (Slovakia)
(m) - Madrid
Mo, (mo) and Mx - Mexico City
(p) – thunderbolt: Poissy, France
(rcm) – Royal Canadian Mint
(rj) – Rio de Janeiro
(sa) – Pretoria, South Africa
So, (so) – Santiago (Small o above S); (except 2007 2 Pesos Uruguayos)

REPUBLIC

REFORM COINAGE

1,000 Nuevos Pesos = 1 Uruguayan Peso; 100 Centesimos = 1 Uruguayan Peso (UYP)March 1993

KM# 106 50 CENTESIMOS
3.00 g., Stainless Steel, 21 mm. **Obv:** Bust of Artigas right **Obv. Legend:** REPUBLICA ORIENTAL DEL URUGUAY **Rev:** Value, date and sprig **Edge:** Plain **Note:** Coin rotation.

Date	Mintage	F12	VF20	XF40	MS60	MS63
2002(sa)	10,000,000	—	—	0.35	0.75	1.00
2005(m)	15,000,000	—	—	0.35	0.75	1.00
2008(k)	35,000,000	—	—	0.35	0.75	1.00
2009	—	—	—	0.35	0.75	1.00

KM# 103.2 UN PESO URUGUAYO
3.50 g., Aluminum-Bronze, 20 mm. **Obv:** Bust of Artigas right **Obv. Legend:** REPUBLICA ORIENTAL DEL URUGUAY **Rev:** Value and date **Edge:** Plain **Note:** Medal rotation; left point of bust shoulder points at "P" in Republic.

Date	Mintage	F12	VF20	XF40	MS60	MS63
2005So	40,000,000	—	—	—	0.50	0.75
2007So	25,000,000	—	—	—	0.50	0.75

KM# 135 UN PESO URUGUAYO
3.50 g., Brass Plated Steel, 20 mm. **Obv:** Arms in circle, date below **Obv. Legend:** REPUBLICA ORIENTAL DEL URUGUAY **Rev:** Mulita (armadillo) **Edge:** Plain

Date	Mintage	F12	VF20	XF40	MS60	MS63
2011(m)	20,000,000	—	—	—	0.50	0.60
2012	—	—	—	—	0.50	0.60

KM# 104.2 2 PESOS URUGUAYOS
4.50 g., Aluminum-Bronze, 23 mm. **Obv:** Bust of Artigas right **Obv. Legend:** REPUBLICA ORIENTAL DEL URUGUAY **Rev:** Value and date **Edge:** Plain **Note:** Medal rotation. Left point of bust shoulder points at "P" in "Republic".

Date	Mintage	F12	VF20	XF40	MS60	MS63
2007So	25,000,000	—	—	0.75	1.50	2.00

Note: Minted at Paris with the So mintmark.

KM# 136 2 PESOS URUGUAYOS
4.50 g., Brass Plated Steel, 23 mm. **Obv:** Arms in circle, date below **Obv. Legend:** REPUBLICA ORIENTAL DEL URUGUAY **Rev:** Carpincho **Edge:** Plain

Date	Mintage	F12	VF20	XF40	MS60	MS63
2011(m)	20,000,000	—	—	—	0.75	0.90
2012	—	—	—	—	0.75	0.90

KM# 120.1 5 PESOS URUGUAYOS
6.30 g., Aluminum-Bronze, 26 mm. **Obv:** Bust of Antigas right **Obv. Legend:** REPUBLICA ORIENTAL DEL URUGUAY **Rev:** Value **Edge:** Plain **Note:** Left point of bust shoulder points at "U" in "Republic".

Date	Mintage	F12	VF20	XF40	MS60	MS63
2003(ba)	15,150,000	—	—	—	2.50	3.00

KM# 120.2 5 PESOS URUGUAYOS
6.30 g., Aluminum-Bronze, 26 mm. **Obv:** Bust of Antigas right **Obv. Legend:** REPUBLICA ORIENTAL DEL URUGUAY • **Rev:** Value, date **Note:** Left point of bust shoulder points at "P" in "Republic".

Date	Mintage	F12	VF20	XF40	MS60	MS63
2005So	30,000,000	—	—	—	2.50	3.00
2008So	20,000,000	—	—	—	2.50	3.00

KM# 137 5 PESOS URUGUAYOS
6.40 g., Brass Plated Steel, 25.5 mm. **Obv:** Arms in circle, date below **Obv. Legend:** REPUBLICA ORIENTAL DEL URUGUAY **Rev:** Nandu **Edge:** Palin

Date	Mintage	F12	VF20	XF40	MS60	MS63
2011(l)	10,000,000	—	—	—	1.25	1.50

KM# 121 10 PESOS URUGUAYOS
10.40 g., Bi-Metallic, 28 mm. **Obv:** Artigas head right within circle **Rev:** Value above signature within circle **Edge:** Plain

Date	Mintage	F12	VF20	XF40	MS60	MS63
2000 (2006) (rcm)	40,000,000	—	—	—	3.50	5.00

Note: 5-pointed star on each side of date, issued 2006

KM# 134 10 PESOS URUGUAYOS
10.40 g., Bi-Metallic, 28 mm. **Obv:** Oval arms, country name and date **Rev:** Puma walking left, sunrise in background and value

Date	Mintage	F12	VF20	XF40	MS60	MS63
2011(l)	10,000,000	—	—	—	2.00	2.50

KM# 139 50 PESOS URUGUAYOS
10.40 g., Copper Plated Steel, 28 mm. **Subject:** Bicentennial of Uruguayan Independence **Obv:** Portrait of General Jose Artigas, country name and value **Rev:** Sun and rays and inscriptions "BICENTENARIO DE LOS HECHOS HISTORICOS" and "1811-2011 **Edge:** Reeded

Date	Mintage	F12	VF20	XF40	MS60	MS63
2011(k)	10,000,000	—	—	—	4.00	4.50

KM# 133 500 PESOS URUGUAYOS
12.50 g., 0.900 Silver 0.3594 oz. ASW, 33 mm. **Subject:** Salto, 250th Anniversary **Obv:** Uruguay map with City of Salto location **Rev:** Emblem of the Department of Salto

Date	Mintage	F12	VF20	XF40	MS60	MS63
2006(u)	10,000	PF63 22.00	PF65 25.00			

KM# 122 1000 PESOS URUGUAYOS
27.00 g., 0.925 Silver 0.7978 oz. ASW, 40 mm. **Subject:** XVIII World Championship Football - Germany 2006 **Obv:** National arms **Obv. Legend:** REPUBLICA ORIENTAL DEL URUGUAY **Rev:** Soccer player and value **Edge:** Reeded

Date	Mintage	F12	VF20	XF40	MS60	MS63
2003(m)	—	PF63 45.00	PF65 50.00			

KM# 123 1000 PESOS URUGUAYOS
27.00 g., 0.925 Silver 0.7978 oz. ASW, 40 mm. **Subject:** XVIII World Championship Football - Germany 2006 **Obv:** National

arms above date **Obv. Legend:** REPUBLICA ORIENTAL DEL URUGUAY **Rev:** Stylized soccer player and value **Edge:** Reeded

Date	Mintage	F12	VF20	XF40	MS60	MS63
2004(m)	—	PF63 45.00	PF65 50.00			

KM# 125 1000 PESOS URUGUAYOS
27.00 g., 0.925 Silver 0.7978 oz. ASW, 40 mm. **Subject:** 100th Anniversary FIFA - 1930 Championship **Obv:** Football before net **Obv. Legend:** REPUBLICA ORIENTAL DEL URUGUAY **Rev:** Sun of national flag **Edge:** Reeded

Date	Mintage	F12	VF20	XF40	MS60	MS63
2004(m)	—	PF63 40.00	PF65 45.00			

KM# 124 1000 PESOS URUGUAYOS
27.00 g., 0.925 Silver 0.7978 oz. ASW, 40 mm. **Subject:** XVIII World Championship Football - Germany 2006 **Obv:** National arms above date **Obv. Legend:** REPUBLICA ORIENTAL DEL URUGUAY **Rev:** FIFA trophy **Edge:** Reeded

Date	Mintage	F12	VF20	XF40	MS60	MS63
2005(m)	—	PF63 45.00	PF65 50.00			

KM# 140 1000 PESOS URUGUAYOS
25.00 g., 0.900 Silver 0.7187 oz. ASW, 37 mm. **Subject:** Bicentennial of Uruguayan Independence **Obv:** Painting by Juan Luis Blanes of the surrender of Posadas at the battle of Las Piedras on May 18, 1811, country name and value **Rev:** Sun and rays and inscription "BICENTENARIO DE LOS HECHOS HISTORICOS" and "1811-2011 **Edge:** Reeded

Date	Mintage	F12	VF20	XF40	MS60	MS63
2011(k)	5,000	PF63 70.00	PF65 80.00			

KM# 126 5000 PESOS URUGUAYOS
6.75 g., 0.925 Gold 0.1994 oz. AGW, 23 mm. **Subject:** 100th Anniversary FIFA - 1930 Championship **Obv:** Football before. **Legend:** REPUBLICA ORIENTAL DEL URUGUAY **Rev:** Tower of Homage in Montevideo **Edge:** Reeded

Date	Mintage	F12	VF20	XF40	MS60	MS63
2004(m)	—	PF65 400				

KM# 127 5000 PESOS URUGUAYOS
6.75 g., 0.925 Gold 0.1994 oz. AGW, 23 mm. **Subject:** XVIII World Championship Football - Germany 2006 **Obv:** National arms **Obv. Legend:** REPUBLICA ORIENTAL DEL URUGUAY **Rev:** Stylized player and value **Edge:** Reeded

Date	Mintage	F12	VF20	XF40	MS60	MS63
2004(m)	—	PF65 500				

MINT SETS

KM#	Date	Mintage	Identification	Issue Price	Mkt Val
MS5	1994-2003	—	KM#102, 105 (1994), 103.2, 104.2 (1998), 106 (2002), 120.1 (2003), 121 (2000) (ba)	—	15.00
(7)					

UZBEKISTAN

The Republic of Uzbekistan (formerly the Uzbek S.S.R.), is bordered on the north by Kazakhstan, to the east by Kirghizia and Tajikistan, on the south by Afghanistan and on the west by Turkmenistan. The republic is comprised of the regions of Andizhan, Bukhara, Dzhizak, Ferghana, Kashkadar, Khorezm (Khiva), Namangan, Navoi, Samarkand, Surkhan-Darya, Syr-Darya, Tashkent and the Karakalpak Autonomous Republic. It has an area of 172,741 sq. mi. (447,400 sq. km.) and a population of 20.3 million. Capital: Tashkent. Crude oil, natural gas, coal, copper, and gold deposits make up the chief resources, while intensive farming, based on artificial irrigation, provides an abundance of cotton.

MONETARY SYSTEM
100 Tiyin = 1 Som

REPUBLIC

STANDARD COINAGE

KM# 13 5 SOM
3.35 g., Brass Plated Steel, 21.2 mm. **Obv:** National arms **Rev:** Value and map **Edge:** Plain

Date	Mintage	F12	VF20	XF40	MS60	MS63
2001	—	—	—	—	1.35	1.75

Note: 2 reverse map varieties known

KM# 14 10 SOM
2.71 g., Nickel Clad Steel, 19.75 mm. **Obv:** National arms **Rev:** Value and map **Edge:** Plain

Date	Mintage	F12	VF20	XF40	MS60	MS63
2001	—	—	—	—	2.00	2.50

Note: 2 reverse map varieties exist

KM# 15 50 SOM
8.00 g., Nickel Clad Steel, 26.2 mm. **Obv:** National arms **Rev:** Value and map **Edge:** Segmented reeding

Date	Mintage	F12	VF20	XF40	MS60	MS63
2001	—	—	—	1.20	3.00	4.00

KM# 16 50 SOM
7.90 g., Nickel Clad Steel, 26.3 mm. **Subject:** 2700th Anniversary of Shahrisabz Town **Obv:** National arms **Rev:** Statue and ruins above value **Edge:** Segmented reeding

Date	Mintage	F12	VF20	XF40	MS60	MS63
2002	—	—	—	1.00	2.50	3.50

KM# 20 100 SOM
31.10 g., 0.999 Silver 0.9925 oz. ASW **Obv:** National arms **Obv. Legend:** O'ZBEKISTON MARKAZIY BANKI **Rev:** Amir-Timur Museum

Date	Mintage	F12	VF20	XF40	MS60	MS63
2001	1,000	PF63 225		PF65 245		

KM# 21 100 SOM
31.10 g., 0.999 Silver 0.9925 oz. ASW **Obv:** National Arms **Obv. Legend:** O'BEKISTON MARKAZY BANKI **Rev:** Toskent town hall

Date	Mintage	F12	VF20	XF40	MS60	MS63
2001	1,000	PF63 225		PF65 245		

KM# 22 100 SOM
31.10 g., 0.999 Silver 0.9925 oz. ASW **Obv:** National arms **Obv. Legend:** O'ZBEKISTON MARKAZIY BANKI **Rev:** World

Date	Mintage	F12	VF20	XF40	MS60	MS63
2001	1,000	PF63 225		PF65 245		

KM# 18 100 SOM
Bronze **Subject:** 500th Anniversary Death of 'Aliser Navoi **Obv:** National arms **Obv. Legend:** O'ZBEKISTON MARKAZIY BANKI **Rev:** 'Aliser Navoi

Date	Mintage	F12	VF20	XF40	MS60	MS63
2001	—	—	—	—	15.00	18.00

KM# 19 100 SOM
31.10 g., 0.999 Silver 0.9925 oz. ASW **Obv:** National arms **Obv. Legend:** O'ZBEKISTON MARKAZIY BANKI **Rev:** Parliament building in Toskent

Date	Mintage	F12	VF20	XF40	MS60	MS63
2001	1,000	PF63 225		PF65 245		

KM# 23 100 SOM
31.10 g., 0.999 Silver 0.9925 oz. ASW **Obv:** National arms **Obv. Legend:** O'ZBEKISTON MARKAZIY BANKI **Rev:** Football player

Date	Mintage	F12	VF20	XF40	MS60	MS63
2001	1,000	PF63 225		PF65 245		

KM# 24 100 SOM
31.10 g., 0.999 Silver 0.9925 oz. ASW **Obv:** National arms **Obv. Legend:** O'BEKISTON MARKAZIY BANKI **Rev:** Track runner

Date	Mintage	F12	VF20	XF40	MS60	MS63
2001	1,000	PF63 225		PF65 245		

KM# 25 100 SOM
31.10 g., 0.999 Silver 0.9925 oz. ASW **Obv:** National arms **Obv. Legend:** O'ZBEKISTON MARKAZIY BANKI **Rev:** Judo expert

Date	Mintage	F12	VF20	XF40	MS60	MS63
2001	1,000	PF63 225		PF65 245		

KM# 26 100 SOM
31.10 g., 0.999 Silver 0.9925 oz. ASW **Obv:** National arms **Obv. Legend:** O'ZBEKISTON MARKAZIY BANKI **Rev:** Tennis player

Date	Mintage	F12	VF20	XF40	MS60	MS63
2001	1,000	PF63 225		PF65 245		

KM# 27 100 SOM
31.10 g., 0.999 Silver 0.9925 oz. ASW **Obv:** National arms **Obv. Legend:** O'ZBEKISTON MARKAZIY BANKI **Rev:** Lenk monument in Timur

Date	Mintage	F12	VF20	XF40	MS60	MS63
2001	1,000	PF63 225		PF65 245		

KM# 28 100 SOM
31.10 g., 0.999 Silver 0.9925 oz. ASW **Obv:** National arms **Obv. Legend:** O'ZBEKISTON MARKAZIY BANKI **Rev:** Aliser Navoi monument

Date	Mintage	F12	VF20	XF40	MS60	MS63
2001	1,000	PF63 225		PF65 245		

KM# 29 100 SOM
31.10 g., 0.999 Silver 0.9925 oz. ASW **Obv:** National arms **Obv. Legend:** O'ZBEKISTON MARKAZIY BANKI **Rev:** Registan in Samarkand

Date	Mintage	F12	VF20	XF40	MS60	MS63
2001	1,000	PF63 225		PF65 245		

KM# 30 100 SOM
31.10 g., 0.999 Silver 0.9925 oz. ASW **Obv:** National arms **Obv. Legend:** O'BEKISTON MARKAZIY BANKI **Rev:** Bell tower in Toskent

Date	Mintage	F12	VF20	XF40	MS60	MS63
2001	1,000	PF63 225		PF65 245		

KM# 17 100 SOM
7.92 g., Nickel Plated Steel, 26.95 mm. **Subject:** 10th Annniversary State Currency **Obv:** National arms **Obv. Legend:** O'ZBEKISTON MARKAZIV BANKI **Rev:** Sun rays over outlined map and value **Rev. Legend:** O'BEKISTON MILLIY VALYUTASIGA **Edge:** Lettered

Date	Mintage	F12	VF20	XF40	MS60	MS63
2004	—	—	—	—	12.50	15.00

KM# 31 100 SOM
7.92 g., Nickel Plated Steel, 26.95 mm. **Subject:** Tashkent, 2200th Anniversary of settlement **Obv:** National arms **Rev:** Linear archway and monument in background

Date	Mintage	F12	VF20	XF40	MS60	MS63
2009	—	—	—	—	3.50	5.00

KM# 32 100 SOM
7.92 g., Nickel Plated Steel, 26.95 mm. **Subject:** Tashkent, 2200th Anniversary of settlement **Obv:** National arms **Rev:** Monument

Date	Mintage	F12	VF20	XF40	MS60	MS63
2009	—	—	—	—	3.50	5.00

KM# 34.1 500 SOM
Copper-Nickel **Obv:** National emblem, sun disc behind eagle's head **Rev:** Building

Date	Mintage	F12	VF20	XF40	MS60	MS63
2011	—	—	—	—	—	15.00

KM# 34.2 500 SOM
Copper-Nickel **Obv:** National emblem, without sun disc behind eagle's head **Rev:** Building

Date	Mintage	F12	VF20	XF40	MS60	MS63
2011	—	—	—	—	—	15.00

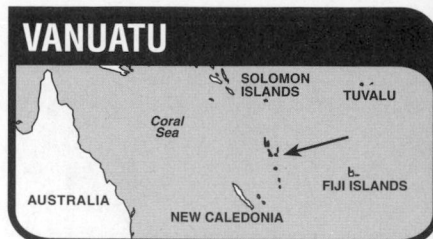

VANUATU

The Republic of Vanuatu, formerly New Hebrides Condominium, a group of islands located in the South Pacific 500 miles (800 km.) west of Fiji, were under the joint sovereignty of Great Britain and France. The islands have an area of 5,700 sq. mi. (14,760 sq. km.) and a population of 165,000, mainly Melanesians of mixed blood. Capital: Port-Vila. The volcanic and coral islands, while malarial land subject to frequent earthquakes, are extremely fertile, and produce copra, coffee, tropical fruits and timber for export.

The New Hebrides were discovered by Portuguese navigator Pedro de Quiros (sailing under orders by the King of Spain) in 1606, visited by French explorer Bougainville in 1768, and named by British navigator Capt. James Cook in 1774. Ships of all nations converged on the islands to trade for sandalwood, prompting France and Britain to relinquish their individual claims and declare the islands a neutral zone in 1878. The New Hebrides were placed under the control of a mixed Anglo-French commission of naval officers during the native uprisings of 1887, and established as a condominium under the joint sovereignty of France and Great Britain in 1906.

Vanuatu became an independent republic within the Commonwealth in July 1980. A president is Head of State and the Prime Minister is Head of Government.

MONETARY SYSTEM
Vatu to Present

REPUBLIC

STANDARD COINAGE

KM# 3 VATU
1.99 g., Nickel-Brass, 16.95 mm. **Obv:** National arms **Rev:** Shell and value **Edge:** Plain

Date	Mintage	F12	VF20	XF40	MS60	MS63
2002	—	—	—	0.15	0.50	0.75

KM# 4 2 VATU
3.00 g., Nickel-Brass, 20 mm. **Obv:** National arms **Rev:** Shell and value **Edge:** Plain

Date	Mintage	F12	VF20	XF40	MS60	MS63
2002	—	—	—	0.25	0.85	1.50

KM# 5 5 VATU
4.10 g., Nickel-Brass, 23.5 mm. **Obv:** National arms **Rev:** Shell and value **Edge:** Plain

Date	Mintage	F12	VF20	XF40	MS60	MS63
2002	—	—	—	—	1.00	1.75
2009	—	—	—	—	1.00	1.75

KM# 6 10 VATU
6.10 g., Copper-Nickel, 23.95 mm. **Obv:** National arms **Rev:** Crab and value, palm trees **Edge:** Plain

Date	Mintage	F12	VF20	XF40	MS60	MS63
2009	—	—	—	0.35	1.25	2.80

KM# 45 10 VATU
Copper-Nickel **Obv:** Arms **Rev:** Multicolor butterfly (Papilio Toboroi)

Date	Mintage	F12	VF20	XF40	MS60	MS63
2006	2,500	—	—	—	—	32.00

KM# 50 10 VATU
Copper-Nickel **Obv:** Arms **Rev:** Multicolor butterfly (Delias Sagessa)

Date	Mintage	F12	VF20	XF40	MS60	MS63
2006	2,500	—	—	—	—	32.00

KM# 46 10 VATU
Copper-Nickel **Obv:** Arms **Rev:** Multicolor butterfly (Taenaris Catops)

Date	Mintage	F12	VF20	XF40	MS60	MS63
2006	2,500	—	—	—	—	32.00

KM# 47 10 VATU
Copper-Nickel **Obv:** Arms **Rev:** Multicolor Butterfly (Ornithoptera Priamus Urvillianus)

Date	Mintage	F12	VF20	XF40	MS60	MS63
2006	2,500	—	—	—	—	32.00

KM# 48 10 VATU
Copper-Nickel **Obv:** Arms **Rev:** Multicolor butterfly (Ornithoptera Paradisea)

Date	Mintage	F12	VF20	XF40	MS60	MS63
2006	2,500	—	—	—	—	32.00

KM# 49 10 VATU
Copper-Nickel **Obv:** Arms **Rev:** Multicolor butterfly (Cethosia Cydippe)

Date	Mintage	F12	VF20	XF40	MS60	MS63
2006	2,500	—	—	—	—	32.00

KM# 51 10 VATU
Copper-Nickel, 38.61 mm. **Subject:** Barack Obama **Obv:** National arms **Rev:** Profile right

Date	Mintage	F12	VF20	XF40	MS60	MS63
2009	—	—	—	—	—	14.00

KM# 59 10 VATU
26.03 g., Silver Plated Copper-Nickel, 38.61 mm. **Subject:** Beach Volleyball **Obv:** National arms **Rev:** Two players going for ball at net

Date	Mintage	F12	VF20	XF40	MS60	MS63
2009	30,000	PF63 22.00	PF65 25.00			

KM# 65 10 VATU
27.00 g., Silver Plated Copper, 38.61 mm. **Obv:** National arms **Rev:** Color image of John Paul II and Yaser Arafat

Date	Mintage	F12	VF20	XF40	MS60	MS63
2011	1,500	PF65 28.00				

KM# 66 10 VATU
27.00 g., Silver Plated Copper, 38.61 mm. **Obv:** National arms **Rev:** Color image of John Paul II and Rabbi of Rome

Date	Mintage	F12	VF20	XF40	MS60	MS63
2011	1,500	PF65 28.00				

KM# 77 10 VATU
0.50 g., 0.585 Gold AGW, 11 mm. **Subject:** Pierre de Coubertin

Date	Mintage	F12	VF20	XF40	MS60	MS63
2013	Est. 5000	PF63 50.00	PF65 55.00			

KM# 79 10 VATU
0.50 g., 0.585 Gold AGW, 11 mm. **Subject:** Leonardo da Vinci - Vitruvian Man

Date	Mintage	F12	VF20	XF40	MS60	MS63
2013	Est. 5000	PF63 50.00	PF65 55.00			

KM# 81 10 VATU
0.50 g., 0.585 Gold AGW, 11 mm. **Subject:** Eiffel Tower

Date	Mintage	F12	VF20	XF40	MS60	MS63
2013	Est. 7500	PF63 50.00	PF65 55.00			

KM# 56 20 VATU
0.50 g., 0.999 Gold AGW, 11 mm. **Obv:** National arms **Rev:** SMS Europa under full sail

Date	Mintage	F12	VF20	XF40	MS60	MS63
2008	10,000	PF63 65.00	PF65 75.00			

KM# 57 20 VATU
0.50 g., 0.999 Gold AGW, 11 mm. **Obv:** National arms **Rev:** Sokrates head

Date	Mintage	F12	VF20	XF40	MS60	MS63
2009	10,000	PF63 65.00	PF65 75.00			

KM# 60 20 VATU
0.50 g., 0.999 Gold AGW, 11 mm. **Obv:** National arms **Rev:** Pantheon

Date	Mintage	F12	VF20	XF40	MS60	MS63
2009	10,000	PF63 65.00	PF65 75.00			

KM# 67 20 VATU
0.50 g., 0.999 Gold AGW, 11 mm. **Obv:** National arms **Rev:** Turtle drawn in sand

Date	Mintage	F12	VF20	XF40	MS60	MS63
2011	10,000	PF63 65.00	PF65 75.00			

KM# 78 20 VATU
0.50 g., 0.999 Gold AGW, 11 mm. **Subject:** Leonardo da Vinci - Vitruvian Man

Date	Mintage	F12	VF20	XF40	MS60	MS63
2013	Est. 5000	PF63 50.00	PF65 55.00			

KM# 80 20 VATU
0.50 g., 0.999 Gold AGW, 11 mm. **Subject:** Eifel Tower

Date	Mintage	F12	VF20	XF40	MS60	MS63
2013	Est. 7500	PF63 50.00	PF65 55.00			

KM# 82 20 VATU
0.50 g., 0.585 Gold AGW, 11 mm. **Subject:** Canals of Venice

Date	Mintage	F12	VF20	XF40	MS60	MS63
2013	Est. 10000	PF63 45.00	PF65 50.00			

KM# 83 20 VATU
0.50 g., 0.585 Gold AGW, 11 mm. **Subject:** Stonehedge

Date	Mintage	F12	VF20	XF40	MS60	MS63
2013	Est. 10000	PF63 45.00	PF65 50.00			

KM# 84 20 VATU
0.50 g., 0.585 Gold AGW, 11 mm. **Subject:** Pantheon

Date	Mintage	F12	VF20	XF40	MS60	MS63
2013	Est. 10000	PF63 45.00	PF65 50.00			

KM# 85 20 VATU
0.50 g., 0.585 Gold AGW, 11 mm. **Subject:** Kaaba

Date	Mintage	F12	VF20	XF40	MS60	MS63
2013	Est. 10000	PF63 45.00	PF65 50.00			

KM# 86 20 VATU
0.50 g., 0.585 Gold AGW, 11 mm. **Subject:** Abu Simbel

Date	Mintage	F12	VF20	XF40	MS60	MS63
2013	Est. 10000	PF63 45.00	PF65 50.00			

KM# 87 20 VATU
0.50 g., 0.585 Gold AGW, 11 mm. **Subject:** Blue Mosque

Date	Mintage	F12	VF20	XF40	MS60	MS63
2013	Est. 10000	PF63 45.00	PF65 50.00			

KM# 89 20 VATU
15.55 g., 0.999 Silver 0.4962 oz. ASW, 38.61 mm. **Subject:** Raccoon with two black diamond inserts

Date	Mintage	F12	VF20	XF40	MS60	MS63
2013 Antique patina	Est. 1500	PF65 60.00				

KM# 8 50 VATU
15.00 g., Copper-Nickel, 32.9 mm. **Series:** F.A.O. **Obv:** National arms **Rev:** Tubers encircled by leafy vines, value above

Date	Mintage	F12	VF20	XF40	MS60	MS63
2002	—	—	—	—	2.00	3.00
2009	—	—	—	—	2.00	3.00

KM# 53 50 VATU
Silver, 38.6 mm. **Subject:** Olympics, 2004 **Obv:** National emblem **Rev:** Athlethe with torch, large torch, fragment of ancient vase

Date	Mintage	F12	VF20	XF40	MS60	MS63
2003	—	PF63 50.00	PF65 60.00			

KM# 38 50 VATU
28.32 g., 0.925 Silver 0.8368 oz. ASW, 38.6 mm. **Obv:** National arms **Obv. Legend:** RIPABLIK / VANUATU **Rev:** Early sailing ship center - left, stylized compass at right **Rev. Legend:** HISTORY OF SEAFARING / PEDRO FERNANDEZ DE QUIRÓS **Edge:** Reeded

Date	Mintage	F12	VF20	XF40	MS60	MS63
2005	—	PF63 42.00	PF65 45.00			

KM# 41 50 VATU
25.00 g., 0.900 Silver 0.7187 oz. ASW **Series:** Protection of Marine Life **Obv:** National arms **Rev:** Tiger Shark - multicolor

Date	Mintage	F12	VF20	XF40	MS60	MS63
2005	—	PF63 60.00	PF65 70.00			

KM# 55 50 VATU
1.24 g., 0.999 Gold 0.0396 oz. AGW, 13.92 mm. **Obv:** National arms **Rev:** Captain Kidd

Date	Mintage	F12	VF20	XF40	MS60	MS63
2005	15,000	PF63 130	PF65 150			

KM# 54 50 VATU
Silver, 38.6 mm. **Obv:** National emblem **Rev:** Two soccer players with large globe in background

Date	Mintage	F12	VF20	XF40	MS60	MS63
2006	—	PF63 60.00	PF65 70.00			

KM# 42 50 VATU
25.00 g., 0.900 Silver 0.7187 oz. ASW **Series:** Protection of Marine Life **Obv:** National arms **Rev:** Sea Turtle - multicolor

Date	Mintage	F12	VF20	XF40	MS60	MS63
2006	—	PF63 60.00	PF65 70.00			

KM# 43 50 VATU
25.00 g., 0.900 Silver 0.7187 oz. ASW **Series:** Protection of Marine Life **Obv:** National arms **Rev:** Sea Horse - multicolor

Date	Mintage	F12	VF20	XF40	MS60	MS63
2006	—	PF63 60.00	PF65 70.00			

KM# 52 50 VATU
Silver **Subject:** 2006 World Cup - Germany **Obv:** National arms **Rev:** 2 soccer players and globe

Date	Mintage	F12	VF20	XF40	MS60	MS63
2006	—	PF63 35.00	PF65 45.00			

KM# 58 50 VATU
28.28 g., 0.925 Silver 0.8356 oz. ASW, 38.61 mm. **Obv:** National Arms **Rev:** SMS Europa under full sail

Date	Mintage	F12	VF20	XF40	MS60	MS63
2008	5,000	PF63 65.00	PF65 75.00			

KM# 61 50 VATU
28.28 g., 0.925 Silver 0.8356 oz. ASW, 38.61 mm. **Subject:** Beach Volleyball **Obv:** National arms **Rev:** Two players at net going for ball

Date	Mintage	F12	VF20	XF40	MS60	MS63
2009	10,000	PF63 65.00	PF65 75.00			

KM# 62 50 VATU
1.00 g., 0.999 Gold 0.0319 oz. AGW, 13.92 mm. **Obv:** National arms **Rev:** Potala Palace **Note:** The denomination does not appear on either side.

Date	Mintage	F12	VF20	XF40	MS60	MS63
2009	10,000	PF63 100	PF65 125			

KM# 63 50 VATU
28.28 g., 0.925 Silver 0.8356 oz. ASW, 38.61 mm. **Obv:** National arms **Rev:** Shinkansen high speed train

Date	Mintage	F12	VF20	XF40	MS60	MS63
2009	5,000	PF63 65.00	PF65 75.00			

KM# 64 50 VATU
28.28 g., 0.925 Silver 0.8356 oz. ASW **Obv:** National arms **Rev:** The Gran, trans-Australia train **Shape:** 38.61

Date	Mintage	F12	VF20	XF40	MS60	MS63
2010	5,000	PF63 65.00	PF65 75.00			

KM# 68 50 VATU
31.10 g., 0.999 Silver 0.9925 oz. ASW, 40.6 mm. **Subject:** Royal Ascot Races **Obv:** National arms **Rev:** Horse race, grandstands, Elizabeth II and Prince Philip; partially colored

Date	Mintage	F12	VF20	XF40	MS60	MS63
2011	10,000	PF63 90.00	PF65 100			

KM# 69 50 VATU
20.00 g., 0.925 Silver 0.591 oz. ASW, 38.61 mm. **Obv:** National arms **Rev:** TEE VT11.5 train, map of Europe above

Date	Mintage	F12	VF20	XF40	MS60	MS63
2011	5,000	PF63 65.00	PF65 75.00			

KM# 75 50 VATU
20.00 g., 0.925 Silver 0.591 oz. ASW, 30 x 45 mm. **Subject:** Edward Teach - Black Beard

Date	Mintage	F12	VF20	XF40	MS60	MS63
2012	Est. 1000	PF65 100				

KM# 70 50 VATU
20.00 g., 0.999 Silver 0.6382 oz. ASW, 38.61 mm. **Rev:** Bust at left, Runner at race start, green ring

Date	Mintage	F12	VF20	XF40	MS60	MS63
2013 Reverse Proof	Est. 500	PF63 50.00	PF65 60.00			

KM# 71 50 VATU
20.00 g., 0.999 Silver 0.6382 oz. ASW, 38.61 mm. **Rev:** Bust at left - Javelin Thrower - yellow ring

Date	Mintage	F12	VF20	XF40	MS60	MS63
2013 Reverse Proof	Est. 500	PF63 50.00	PF65 60.00			

KM# 72 50 VATU
20.00 g., 0.999 Silver 0.6382 oz. ASW, 38.61 mm. **Rev:** Bust at left - Wrestling - Red ring

Date	Mintage	F12	VF20	XF40	MS60	MS63
2013 Reverse Proof	Est. 500	PF63 50.00	PF65 60.00			

KM# 73 50 VATU
20.00 g., 0.999 Silver 0.6382 oz. ASW, 38.61 mm. **Rev:** Bust at left - Long Jumper - Black ring

Date	Mintage	F12	VF20	XF40	MS60	MS63
2013 Reverse Proof	Est. 500	PF63 50.00	PF65 60.00			

KM# 74 50 VATU
20.00 g., 0.999 Silver 0.6382 oz. ASW, 38.61 mm. **Series:** Pierre De Coubertin - 150th Anniversary of Birth **Rev:** Bust at left, Discus Thrower, Blue ring

Date	Mintage	F12	VF20	XF40	MS60	MS63
2013 Reverse Proof	Est. 500	PF63 50.00	PF65 60.00			

KM# 76 50 VATU
20.00 g., 0.925 Silver 0.591 oz. ASW, 38.61 mm. **Subject:** 2016 Olympics - Lighting of the Olympic Flame

Date	Mintage	F12	VF20	XF40	MS60	MS63
2013	Est. 10000	PF63 65.00	PF65 75.00			

KM# 90 50 VATU
31.11 g., 0.999 Silver 0.9926 oz. ASW, 38.61 mm. **Subject:** Raccoon with two black diamond inserts

Date	Mintage	F12	VF20	XF40	MS60	MS63
2013	Est. 1000	PF65 100				

KM# 9 100 VATU
9.55 g., Nickel-Brass, 23.9 mm. **Obv:** National arms **Rev:** Sprouting bulbs

Date	Mintage	F12	VF20	XF40	MS60	MS63
2002	—	—	—	—	3.00	4.00
2008	—	—	—	—	3.00	4.00

KM# 91 100 VATU
62.20 g., 0.999 Silver 1.9849 oz. ASW, 55 mm. **Subject:** Raccoon family with six black diamond inserts

Date	Mintage	F12	VF20	XF40	MS60	MS63
2013	Est. 500	PF65 200				

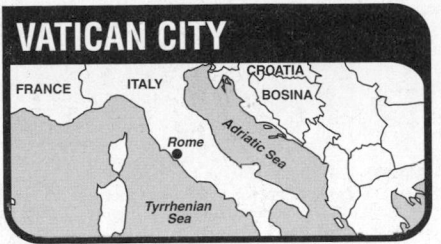

VATICAN CITY

The State of the Vatican City, a papal state on the right bank of the Tiber River within the boundaries of Rome, has an area of 0.17 sq. mi. (0.44 sq. km.) and a population of *775. Capital: Vatican City.

Today the Pope exercises supreme legislative, executive and judicial power within the Vatican City, and the State of the Vatican City is recognized by many nations as an independent sovereign state under the temporal jurisdiction of the Pope, even to the extent of ambassadorial exchange. The Pope is of course, the head of the Roman Catholic Church.

PONTIFFS
John Paul II, 1978-2005
Sede Vacante, April 2 - 19, 2005
Benedict XVI, 2005-2013
Frances, 2013 -

MINT MARK
R – Rome

MONETARY SYSTEM
100 Centesimi = 1 Lira (thru 2002)
100 Euro Cent = 1 Euro

DATING
Most Vatican coins indicate the regnal year of the pope preceded by the word *Anno* (or an abbreviation), even if the *anno domini* date is omitted.

CITY STATE

DECIMAL COINAGE

100 Centesimi = 1 Lira

KM# 331 10 LIRE
1.60 g., Aluminum, 23.2 mm. **Ruler:** John Paul II **Obv:** Bust left **Rev:** Papal arms **Edge:** Plain

Date	Mintage	F12	VF20	XF40	MS60	MS63
2001/XXIII	—	—	—	1.00	2.50	3.00

KM# 331a 10 LIRE
Gold AGW, 23.2 mm. **Ruler:** John Paul II **Obv:** Benedict XV bust left **Rev:** Papal arms **Note:** Struck in 2007.

Date	Mintage	F12	VF20	XF40	MS60	MS63
2001R	499	PF63 2,000	PF65 3,500			

KM# 332 20 LIRE
3.57 g., Brass, 21.2 mm. **Ruler:** John Paul II **Obv:** Bust left **Rev:** Papal arms **Edge:** Plain

Date	Mintage	F12	VF20	XF40	MS60	MS63
2001/XXIII	—	—	—	1.00	2.50	3.00

KM# 332a 20 LIRE
Gold AGW, 21.2 mm. **Ruler:** John Paul II **Obv:** Pius XI bust left **Rev:** Papal arms **Note:** Struck in 2007.

Date	Mintage	F12	VF20	XF40	MS60	MS63
2001R	499	PF63 2,000	PF65 3,500			

KM# 333 50 LIRE
4.50 g., Copper-Nickel, 19.2 mm. **Ruler:** John Paul II **Obv:** Pius XII bust left **Rev:** Papal arms **Edge:** Plain

Date	Mintage	F12	VF20	XF40	MS60	MS63
2001/XXIII	—	—	—	1.00	2.50	3.00

KM# 333a 50 LIRE
Gold AGW, 19.2 mm. **Ruler:** John Paul II **Obv:** Pius XII bust left **Rev:** Papal arms **Note:** Struck in 2007.

Date	Mintage	F12	VF20	XF40	MS60	MS63
2001R	499	PF63 2,500	PF65 4,000			

KM# 334 100 LIRE
4.50 g., Copper-Nickel, 22 mm. **Ruler:** John Paul II **Obv:** Bust left **Rev:** Papal arms within circle **Edge:** Reeded and plain sections

Date	Mintage	F12	VF20	XF40	MS60	MS63
2001/XXIII	—	—	—	1.00	2.50	3.00

KM# 334a 100 LIRE
Gold AGW, 22 mm. **Ruler:** John Paul II **Obv:** John XXIII bust left **Rev:** Papal arms **Note:** Struck in 2007.

Date	Mintage	F12	VF20	XF40	MS60	MS63
2001R	499	PF63 2,500	PF65 4,000			

KM# 335 200 LIRE
5.00 g., Brass, 22 mm. **Ruler:** John Paul II **Obv:** Bust right **Rev:** Papal arms within circle **Edge:** Reeded

Date	Mintage	F12	VF20	XF40	MS60	MS63
2001/XXIII	—	—	—	1.00	2.50	3.00

KM# 335a 200 LIRE
Gold AGW, 22 mm. **Ruler:** John Paul II **Obv:** Paul VI bust right **Rev:** Papal arms **Note:** Struck in 2007.

Date	Mintage	F12	VF20	XF40	MS60	MS63
2001R	499	PF63 2,500	PF65 4,000			

KM# 336 500 LIRE
6.77 g., Bi-Metallic, 25.7 mm. **Ruler:** John Paul II **Obv:** John Paul I head left **Rev:** Papal arms within circle **Edge:** Segmented reeding

Date	Mintage	F12	VF20	XF40	MS60	MS63
2001/XXIII	—	—	—	3.50	7.00	8.50

KM# 336a 500 LIRE
Gold AGW, 25.7 mm. **Ruler:** John Paul II **Obv:** John Paul I bust left **Rev:** Papal arms

Date	Mintage	F12	VF20	XF40	MS60	MS63
2001R	499	PF63 2,000	PF65 3,750			

KM# 337 1000 LIRE
8.85 g., Bi-Metallic, 26.9 mm. **Ruler:** John Paul II **Obv:** John Paul II bust left **Rev:** Papal arms **Edge:** Segmented reeding

Date	Mintage	F12	VF20	XF40	MS60	MS63
2001/XXIII	—	—	—	5.50	8.00	9.00

KM# 337a 1000 LIRE
Gold AGW, 26.9 mm. **Ruler:** John Paul II **Obv:** John Paul II bust left **Rev:** Papal arms

Date	Mintage	F12	VF20	XF40	MS60	MS63
2001R	499	PF63 2,000	PF65 3,750			

KM# 338 1000 LIRE
14.60 g., 0.835 Silver 0.3894 oz. ASW, 31.4 mm. **Ruler:** John

Paul II **Subject:** Peace **Obv:** Stylized dove in front of globe **Rev:** Crowned shield **Edge Lettering:** +++ TOTVS TVVS +++ MMI

Date	Mintage	F12	VF20	XF40	MS60	MS63
2001/XXIII	—	—	20.00	35.00	40.00	

KM# 338a 1000 LIRE
Gold AGW, 31.4 mm. **Ruler:** John Paul II **Obv:** Stylized dove in front of globe **Rev:** Crowned arms

Date	Mintage	F12	VF20	XF40	MS60	MS63
2001R	499	PF63 2,000	PF65 3,750			

KM# 339 2000 LIRE
16.00 g., 0.835 Silver 0.4268 oz. ASW, 31.4 mm. **Ruler:** John Paul II **Subject:** Dialog for Peace **Obv:** Bust right holding crozier **Rev:** Dove above crowd **Edge:** Reeded

Date	Mintage	F12	VF20	XF40	MS60	MS63
2001/XXIII	16,000	—	25.00	35.00	40.00	
2001/XXIII	8,000	PF63 60.00	PF65 70.00			

KM# 340 5000 LIRE
18.00 g., 0.835 Silver 0.4801 oz. ASW, 32 mm. **Ruler:** John Paul II **Subject:** Easter **Obv:** Kneeling Pope praying **Rev:** Standing figure flanked by clouds below dove **Edge:** Reeded and plain sections

Date	Mintage	F12	VF20	XF40	MS60	MS63
2001	—	—	30.00	40.00	45.00	
2001/XXIII	16,000	PF63 35.00	PF65 45.00			

KM# 390 50000 LIRE
7.50 g., 0.917 Gold 0.2197 oz, AGW, 23 mm. **Ruler:** John Paul II **Subject:** Religious symbols **Obv:** Bust right **Rev:** Cross

Date	Mintage	F12	VF20	XF40	MS60	MS63
2001//XXIIIR	6,000	PF63 1,500	PF65 2,000			

KM# 391 100000 LIRE
15.00 g., 0.917 Gold 0.4394 oz. AGW, 28 mm. **Ruler:** John Paul II **Subject:** Religious symbols **Obv:** Bust right **Rev:** Chi rho with Alpha and Omega letters

Date	Mintage	F12	VF20	XF40	MS60	MS63
2001//XXIIIR	6,000	PF63 2,000	PF65 3,000			

EURO COINAGE

KM# 341 EURO CENT
2.30 g., Copper Plated Steel, 16.25 mm. **Ruler:** John Paul II **Obv:** Bust 1/4 left **Rev:** Value and globe **Edge:** Plain

Date	Mintage	F12	VF20	XF40	MS60	MS63
2002R	80,000	—	—	—	115	—
2002R	—	PF65 175				
2003R In sets only	65,000	—	—	—	55.00	—

Date	Mintage	F12	VF20	XF40	MS60	MS63
2003R	13,000	PF65 145				
2004R In sets only	65,000	—	—	—	25.00	—
2004R	13,000	PF65 145				
2005R In sets only	85,000	—	—	—	25.00	—
2005R	16,000	PF65 140				

KM# 365 EURO CENT
2.30 g., Copper Plated Steel, 16.25 mm. **Ruler:** Sede Vacante **Obv:** Arms of Cardinal Eduardo Martinez Somalo **Rev:** Value and globe

Date	Mintage	F12	VF20	XF40	MS60	MS63
MMV (2005)R In sets only	60,000	—	—	—	—	45.00

KM# 375 EURO CENT
2.30 g., Copper Plated Steel, 16.25 mm. **Ruler:** Benedict XVI **Obv:** Pope's bust facing 3/4 right **Obv. Legend:** CITTA' DEL VATICANO **Rev:** Value and globe **Edge:** Plain

Date	Mintage	F12	VF20	XF40	MS60	MS63
2006R In sets only	85,000	—	—	—	—	12.00
2006R	16,000	PF65 18.00				
2007R In sets only	85,000	—	—	—	—	12.00
2007R	16,000	PF65 18.00				
MMVIII (2008) R In sets only	85,000	—	—	—	—	12.00
MMVIII (2008)R	16,000	PF65 18.00				
2009R In sets only	85,000	—	—	—	—	12.00
2009R	16,000	PF65 18.00				
2010R In sets only	94,000	—	—	—	—	12.00
2010R	15,000	PF65 18.00				
2011R	94,000	—	—	—	—	12.00
2011R	15,000	PF65 18.00				
2012R	84,000	—	—	—	—	12.00
2012R	15,000	PF65 18.00				
2013R	85,000	—	—	—	—	12.00
2013R	15,000	PF65 18.00				

KM# 342 2 EURO CENT
3.06 g., Copper Plated Steel, 18.75 mm. **Ruler:** John Paul II **Obv:** Bust 1/4 left **Rev:** Value and globe **Edge:** Grooved

Date	Mintage	F12	VF20	XF40	MS60	MS63
2002R	80,000	—	—	—	115	—
2002R	—	PF65 175				
2003R In sets only	65,000	—	—	—	55.00	—
2003R	13,000	PF65 145				
2004R In sets only	65,000	—	—	—	25.00	—
2004R	13,000	PF65 145				
2005R In sets only	85,000	—	—	—	25.00	—
2005R	16,000	PF65 140				

KM# 366 2 EURO CENT
3.06 g., Copper Plated Steel, 18.75 mm. **Ruler:** Sede Vacante **Obv:** Arms of Cardinal Eduardo Martinez Somalo **Rev:** Value and globe **Edge:** Grooved

Date	Mintage	F12	VF20	XF40	MS60	MS63
MMV (2005)R In sets only	60,000	—	—	—	—	42.00

KM# 376 2 EURO CENT
3.06 g., Copper Plated Steel, 18.75 mm. **Ruler:** Benedict XVI **Obv:** Pope's bust facing 3/4 right **Obv. Legend:** CITTA' DEL VATICANO **Rev:** Value and globe **Edge:** Grooved

Date	Mintage	F12	VF20	XF40	MS60	MS63
2006R In sets only	85,000	—	—	—	—	15.00
2006R	16,000	PF65 20.00				
2007R In sets only	85,000	—	—	—	—	15.00
2007R	16,000	PF65 20.00				
MDVIII (2008) R In sets only	85,000	—	—	—	—	15.00
MDVIII (2008)R	16,000	PF65 20.00				
2009R In sets only	85,000	—	—	—	—	15.00

Date	Mintage	F12	VF20	XF40	MS60	MS63
2009R	16,000	PF65 20.00				
2010R In sets only	94,000	—	—	—	—	15.00
2010R	15,000	PF65 20.00				
2011R	94,000	—	—	—	—	15.00
2011R	15,000	PF65 20.00				
2012R	84,000	—	—	—	—	15.00
2012R	15,000	PF65 20.00				
2013R	85,000	—	—	—	—	15.00
2013R	15,000	PF65 20.00				

KM# 343 5 EURO CENT
3.92 g., Copper Plated Steel, 21.25 mm. **Ruler:** John Paul II **Obv:** Bust 1/4 left **Rev:** Value and globe **Edge:** Plain

Date	Mintage	F12	VF20	XF40	MS60	MS63
2002R	80,000	—	—	—	115	—
2002R	—	PF65 175				
2003R In sets only	65,000	—	—	—	55.00	—
2003R	13,000	PF65 145				
2004R In sets only	65,000	—	—	—	28.00	—
2004R	13,000	PF65 145				
2005R In sets only	85,000	—	—	—	28.00	—
2005R	16,000	PF65 140				

KM# 367 5 EURO CENT
3.92 g., Copper Plated Steel, 21.25 mm. **Ruler:** Sede Vacante **Obv:** Arms of Cardinal Eduardo Martinez Somalo **Rev:** Value and globe

Date	Mintage	F12	VF20	XF40	MS60	MS63
MMV (2005)R In sets only	60,000	—	—	—	—	45.00

KM# 377 5 EURO CENT
3.92 g., Copper Plated Steel, 21.25 mm. **Ruler:** Benedict XVI **Obv:** Pope's bust facing 3/4 right **Obv. Legend:** CITTA' DEL VATICANO **Rev:** Value and globe **Edge:** Plain

Date	Mintage	F12	VF20	XF40	MS60	MS63
2006R In sets only	85,000	—	—	—	—	16.50
2006R	16,000	PF65 22.50				
2007R In sets only	85,000	—	—	—	—	16.50
2007R	16,000	PF65 22.50				
MDVIII (2008) R In sets only	85,000	—	—	—	—	16.50
MDVIII (2008)R	16,000	PF65 22.50				
2009R In sets only	85,000	—	—	—	—	16.50
2009R	16,000	PF65 22.50				
2010R In sets only	94,000	—	—	—	—	16.50
2010R	15,000	PF65 22.50				
2011R	94,000	—	—	—	—	16.50
2011R	15,000	PF65 22.50				
2012R	84,000	—	—	—	—	16.50
2012R	15,000	PF65 22.50				
2013R	85,000	—	—	—	—	16.50
2013R	15,000	PF65 22.50				

KM# 344 10 EURO CENT
4.10 g., Brass, 19.75 mm. **Ruler:** John Paul II **Obv:** Bust 1/4 left **Edge:** Reeded

Date	Mintage	F12	VF20	XF40	MS60	MS63
2002R	80,000	—	—	—	115	—
2002R	—	PF65 175				
2003R In sets only	65,000	—	—	—	55.00	—
2003R	13,000	PF65 145				
2004R In sets only	65,000	—	—	—	35.00	—
2004R	13,000	PF65 145				
2005R In sets only	85,000	—	—	—	35.00	—
2005R	16,000	PF65 140				

KM# 368 10 EURO CENT
4.10 g., Brass, 19.75 mm. **Ruler:** Sede Vacante **Obv:** Arms of Cardinal Eduardo Martinez Somalo **Rev:** Map and value **Edge:** Reeded

Date	Mintage	F12	VF20	XF40	MS60	MS63
MMV (2005)R In sets only	60,000	—	—	—	—	48.00

KM# 378 10 EURO CENT
4.10 g., Brass, 19.75 mm. **Ruler:** Benedict XVI **Obv:** Pope's bust facing 3/4 right **Obv. Legend:** CITTA' DEL VATICANO **Rev:** Map and value **Edge:** Reeded

Date	Mintage	F12	VF20	XF40	MS60	MS63
2006R In sets only	85,000	—	—	—	—	17.50
2006R	16,000	PF65 25.00				
2007R In sets only	85,000	—	—	—	—	17.50
2007R	16,000	PF65 25.00				

KM# 385 10 EURO CENT
4.10 g., Brass, 19.75 mm. **Ruler:** Benedict XVI **Rev:** Relief map of Western Europe, stars, lines and value **Edge:** Reeded

Date	Mintage	F12	VF20	XF40	MS60	MS63
MMVIII (2008) R In sets only	85,000	—	—	—	—	17.50
MMVIII (2008)R	16,000	PF65 25.00				
2009R In sets only	85,000	—	—	—	—	17.50
2009R	16,000	PF65 25.00				
2010R In sets only	94,000	—	—	—	—	17.50
2010R	15,000	PF65 25.00				
2011R	94,000	—	—	—	—	17.50
2011R	15,000	PF65 25.00				
2012R	84,000	—	—	—	—	17.50
2012R	15,000	PF65 25.00				
2013R	85,000	—	—	—	—	17.50
2013R	15,000	PF65 25.00				

KM# 345 20 EURO CENT
5.74 g., Brass, 22.25 mm. **Ruler:** John Paul II **Obv:** Bust 1/4 left **Rev:** Value and map **Edge:** Notched

Date	Mintage	F12	VF20	XF40	MS60	MS63
2002R	80,000	—	—	—	115	—
2002R	—	PF65 175				
2003R In sets only	65,000	—	—	—	55.00	—
2003R	13,000	PF65 145				
2004R In sets only	65,000	—	—	—	38.00	—
2004R	13,000	PF65 145				
2005R In sets only	85,000	—	—	—	38.00	—
2005R	16,000	PF65 140				

KM# 369 20 EURO CENT
5.74 g., Brass, 22.25 mm. **Ruler:** Sede Vacante **Obv:** Arms of Cardinal Eduardo Martinez Somalo **Rev:** Map and value **Edge:** Notched

Date	Mintage	F12	VF20	XF40	MS60	MS63
MMV (2005)R In sets only	60,000	—	—	—	—	50.00

KM# 379 20 EURO CENT
5.74 g., Brass, 22.25 mm. **Ruler:** Benedict XVI **Obv:** Pope's bust facing 3/4 right **Obv. Legend:** CITTA' DEL VATICANO **Rev:** Map and value **Edge:** Notched

Date	Mintage	F12	VF20	XF40	MS60	MS63
2006R In sets only	85,000	—	—	—	—	18.00
2006R	16,000	PF65 28.00				
2007R In sets only	85,000	—	—	—	—	18.00
2007R	16,000	PF65 28.00				

KM# 386 20 EURO CENT
5.74 g., Brass, 22.25 mm. **Ruler:** Benedict XVI **Rev:** Relief map of Western Europe, stars, lines and value **Edge:** Notched

Date	Mintage	F12	VF20	XF40	MS60	MS63
MMVIII (2008) R In sets only	85,000	—	—	—	—	18.00
MMVIII (2008)R	16,000	PF65 28.00				
2009R In sets only	85,000	—	—	—	—	18.00
2009R	16,000	PF65 28.00				
2010R In sets only	94,000	—	—	—	—	18.00
2010R	15,000	PF65 28.00				
2011R	94,000	—	—	—	—	18.00
2011R	15,000	PF65 28.00				
2012R	84,000	—	—	—	—	18.00
2012R	15,000	PF65 28.00				
2013R	85,000	—	—	—	—	18.00
2013R	15,000	PF65 28.00				

KM# 346 50 EURO CENT
7.80 g., Brass, 24.25 mm. **Ruler:** John Paul II **Obv:** Bust 1/4 left **Rev:** Map and value **Edge:** Reeded

Date	Mintage	F12	VF20	XF40	MS60	MS63
2002R	80,000	—	—	—	115	—
2002R	—	PF65 175				
2003R In sets only	65,000	—	—	—	55.00	—
2003R	13,000	PF65 145				
2004R In sets only	65,000	—	—	—	42.00	—
2004R	13,000	PF65 145				
2005R In sets only	85,000	—	—	—	42.00	—
2005R	16,000	PF65 140				

KM# 370 50 EURO CENT
7.80 g., Brass, 24.25 mm. **Ruler:** Sede Vacante **Obv:** Arms of Cardinal Eduardo Martinez Somalo **Rev:** Map and value **Edge:** Reeded

Date	Mintage	F12	VF20	XF40	MS60	MS63
MMV (2005)R In sets only	60,000	—	—	—	—	55.00

KM# 380 50 EURO CENT
7.80 g., Brass, 24.25 mm. **Ruler:** Benedict XVI **Obv:** Pope's bust facing 3/4 right **Obv. Legend:** CITTA' DEL VATICANO **Rev:** Map and value **Edge:** Reeded

Date	Mintage	F12	VF20	XF40	MS60	MS63
2006R In sets only	85,000	—	—	—	—	22.50
2006R	16,000	PF65 35.00				
2007R In sets only	85,000	—	—	—	—	22.50
2007R	16,000	PF65 35.00				

KM# 387 50 EURO CENT
7.80 g., Brass, 24.25 mm. **Ruler:** Benedict XVI **Rev:** Relief map of Western Europe, stars, lines and value **Edge:** Reeded

Date	Mintage	F12	VF20	XF40	MS60	MS63
MMVIII (2008) R In sets only	85,000	—	—	—	—	32.50
MMVIII (2008)R	16,000	PF65 40.00				
2009R In sets only	85,000	—	—	—	—	32.50
2009R	16,000	PF65 40.00				
2010R In sets only	94,000	—	—	—	—	32.50
2010R	15,000	PF65 40.00				
2011R	94,000	—	—	—	—	32.50
2011R	15,000	PF65 40.00				
2012R	94,000	—	—	—	—	32.50
2012R	15,000	PF65 40.00				
2013R	95,000	—	—	—	—	32.50
2013R	15,000	PF65 40.00				

KM# 347 EURO
7.50 g., Bi-Metallic, 23.25 mm. **Ruler:** John Paul II **Obv:** Bust 1/4 left **Rev:** Value and map **Edge:** Segmented reeding

Date	Mintage	F12	VF20	XF40	MS60	MS63
2002R	80,000	—	—	—	100	—
2002R	—	PF65 185				
2003R In sets only	65,000	—	—	—	75.00	—
2003R	13,000	PF65 145				
2004R In sets only	65,000	—	—	—	60.00	—
2004R	13,000	PF65 145				
2005R In sets only	85,000	—	—	—	60.00	—
2005R	16,000	PF65 140				

KM# 371 EURO
7.50 g., Bi-Metallic, 23.25 mm. **Ruler:** Sede Vacante **Obv:** Arms of Cardinal Eduardo Martinez Somalo **Rev:** Value and map **Edge:** Segmented reeding

Date	Mintage	F12	VF20	XF40	MS60	MS63
MMV (2005)R In sets only	60,000	—	—	—	—	70.00

KM# 381 EURO
7.50 g., Bi-Metallic, 23.25 mm. **Ruler:** Benedict XVI **Obv:** Pope's bust facing 3/4 right **Obv. Legend:** CITTA' - DEL VATICANO **Rev:** Value and map **Edge:** Segmented reeding

Date	Mintage	F12	VF20	XF40	MS60	MS63
2006R In sets only	85,000	—	—	—	—	25.00
2006R	16,000	PF65 40.00				
2007R In sets only	85,000	—	—	—	—	25.00
2007R	16,000	PF65 40.00				

KM# 388 EURO
7.50 g., Bi-Metallic, 23.25 mm. **Ruler:** Benedict XVI **Rev:** Relief map of Western Europe, stars, lines and value **Edge:** Segmented reeding

Date	Mintage	F12	VF20	XF40	MS60	MS63
MMVIII (2008) R In sets only	85,000	—	—	—	—	25.00
MMVIII (2008)R	16,000	PF65 40.00				
2009R In sets only	85,000	—	—	—	—	25.00
2009R	16,000	PF65 40.00				
2010R In sets only	94,000	—	—	—	—	25.00
2010R	15,000	PF65 40.00				
2011R	94,000	—	—	—	—	25.00
2011R	15,000	PF65 40.00				
2012R	84,000	—	—	—	—	25.00
2012R	15,000	PF65 40.00				
2013R	85,000	—	—	—	—	25.00
2013R	15,000	PF65 40.00				

KM# 348 2 EURO
8.50 g., Bi-Metallic, 25.75 mm. **Ruler:** John Paul II **Obv:** Bust 1/4 left **Rev:** Value and map **Edge:** Reeded with 2's and stars

Date	Mintage	F12	VF20	XF40	MS60	MS63
2002R	80,000	—	—	—	165	—
2002R	—	PF65 215				
2003R In sets only	65,000	—	—	—	100	—
2003R	13,000	PF65 185				
2004R In sets only	65,000	—	—	—	80.00	—
2004R	13,000	PF65 185				
2005R In sets only	85,000	—	—	—	80.00	—
2005R	16,000	PF65 180				

KM# 358 2 EURO

8.50 g., Bi-Metallic, 25.75 mm. **Ruler:** John Paul II **Subject:** 75th Anniversary of the Founding of the Vatican City State **Obv:** St. Peter's Square within city walls, dates 1929-2004 **Rev:** Value and map **Edge:** Reeded with 2's and stars

Date	Mintage	F12	VF20	XF40	MS60	MS63
2004R	85,000	—	—	—	25.00	—

KM# 372 2 EURO

8.50 g., Bi-Metallic, 25.75 mm. **Ruler:** Sede Vacante **Obv:** Arms of Cardinal Eduardo Martinez Somalo **Rev:** Map and value **Edge:** Reeded with 2's and stars

Date	Mintage	F12	VF20	XF40	MS60	MS63
MMV (2005)R In sets only	60,000	—	—	—	—	75.00

KM# 374 2 EURO

8.50 g., Bi-Metallic, 25.75 mm. **Ruler:** Benedict XVI **Subject:** World Youth Day **Obv:** Cologne Cathedral **Rev:** Value and Euro map **Edge:** Reeded with 2's and stars

Date	Mintage	F12	VF20	XF40	MS60	MS63
2005R	—	—	—	—	90.00	—

KM# 382 2 EURO

8.50 g., Bi-Metallic, 25.75 mm. **Ruler:** Benedict XVI **Obv:** Pope's bust facing 3/4 right **Obv. Legend:** CITTA' - DEL VATICANO **Rev:** Value and map **Edge:** Reeded with 2's and stars

Date	Mintage	F12	VF20	XF40	MS60	MS63
2006R In sets only	85,000	—	—	—	—	28.00
2006R	16,000	PF65 50.00				
2007R In sets only	85,000	—	—	—	—	28.00
2007R	16,000	PF65 50.00				

KM# 394 2 EURO

8.50 g., Bi-Metallic, 25.75 mm. **Ruler:** Benedict XVI **Subject:** Swiss guards, 500th Anniversary **Obv:** Swiss guard taking oath on flag **Rev:** Map and value **Edge:** Reeded with 2's and stars

Date	Mintage	F12	VF20	XF40	MS60	MS63
ND (2006)R	100,000	—	—	—	80.00	90.00

KM# 399 2 EURO

8.50 g., Bi-Metallic, 25.75 mm. **Ruler:** Benedict XVI **Subject:** Pope Benedict's 80th Birthday **Obv:** Bust left **Rev:** Map and

---

value **Edge:** Reeded with 2's and stars

Date	Mintage	F12	VF20	XF40	MS60	MS63
2007R	100,000	—	—	—	50.00	60.00

KM# 389 2 EURO

8.50 g., Bi-Metallic, 25.75 mm. **Ruler:** Benedict XVI **Rev:** Relief map of Western Europe, stars, lines and value **Edge:** Reeded with 2's and stars

Date	Mintage	F12	VF20	XF40	MS60	MS63
MMVIII (2008) R In sets only	85,000	—	—	—	—	28.00
MMVIII (2008)R	16,000	PF65 50.00				
2009R In sets only	85,000	—	—	—	—	28.00
2009R	16,000	PF65 50.00				
2010R In sets only	94,000	—	—	—	—	28.00
2010R	15,000	PF65 50.00				
2011R	94,000	—	—	—	—	28.00
2011R	15,000	PF65 50.00				
2012R	84,000	—	—	—	—	25.00
2012R	15,000	PF65 50.00				
2013R	85,000	—	—	—	—	25.00
2013R	15,000	PF65 50.00				

KM# 404 2 EURO

8.50 g., Bi-Metallic, 25.75 mm. **Ruler:** Benedict XVI **Obv:** St. Paul being blinded on reary horse **Rev:** Map and value **Edge:** Reeded with 2's and stars

Date	Mintage	F12	VF20	XF40	MS60	MS63
ND (2008)R	106,084	—	—	—	25.00	28.00

KM# 410 2 EURO

8.50 g., Bi-Metallic, 25.75 mm. **Ruler:** Benedict XVI **Subject:** International Year of Astronomy **Rev:** Map and value **Edge:** Reeded with 2's and stars

Date	Mintage	F12	VF20	XF40	MS60	MS63
2009R	100,000	—	—	—	25.00	28.00

KM# 420 2 EURO

8.50 g., Bi-Metallic, 25.75 mm. **Ruler:** Benedict XVI **Subject:** Year of the Priest **Edge:** Reeded with 2's and stars

Date	Mintage	F12	VF20	XF40	MS60	MS63
2010R	115,000	—	—	—	20.00	25.00

KM# 426 2 EURO

8.50 g., Bi-Metallic, 25.75 mm. **Ruler:** Benedict XVI **Subject:** 26th World Youth Day **Obv:** Youth with Vatican City flags **Edge:** Reeded with 2's and stars

Date	Mintage	F12	VF20	XF40	MS60	MS63
2011R	98,000	—	—	—	—	20.00
2011R Special Unc.	11,500	—	—	—	—	28.00

KM# 435 2 EURO

8.50 g., Bi-Metallic, 25.75 mm. **Ruler:** Benedict XVI **Subject:** 7th World Meeting of Families **Obv:** Family unit before Cathedral

Date	Mintage	F12	VF20	XF40	MS60	MS63
2012R	89,000	—	—	—	—	28.00
2012R		—	PF63 40.00	PF65 50.00		

KM# 446 2 EURO

Bi-Metallic **Ruler:** Francis **Subject:** World Youth Day - Rio **Rev:** 5 youths below Christ statue

Date	Mintage	F12	VF20	XF40	MS60	MS63
2013R		—	—	—	—	28.00

KM# 349 5 EURO

18.00 g., 0.835 Silver 0.4801 oz. ASW, 32 mm. **Ruler:** John Paul II **Subject:** 24th Anniversary of Reign **Obv:** Bust 1/4 left **Rev:** Allegorical female and bridge **Edge:** Lettered **Edge Lettering:** +++ TOTUS TUUS +++ MMII

Date	Mintage	F12	VF20	XF40	MS60	MS63
2002R	10,000	PF65 125				

KM# 354 5 EURO

18.00 g., 0.925 Silver 0.5319 oz. ASW, 32 mm. **Ruler:** John Paul II **Subject:** Year of the Rosary **Obv:** Pope praying the rosary **Rev:** Our Lady of Pompei" presenting rosaries to Saints Dominic and Catherine **Edge:** Reeded

Date	Mintage	F12	VF20	XF40	MS60	MS63
2003R Proof	10,000	—	—	—	—	65.00

KM# 359 5 EURO

18.00 g., 0.925 Silver 0.5319 oz. ASW, 32 mm. **Ruler:** John Paul II **Subject:** 150th Anniversary of the Proclamation of the Dogma of the Immaculate Conception **Obv:** Virgin Mary **Rev:** Two Papal coat of arms **Edge:** Reeded and plain sections

Date	Mintage	F12	VF20	XF40	MS60	MS63
2004R	13,000	—	—	—	60.00	—

KM# 373 5 EURO

18.00 g., 0.925 Silver 0.5319 oz. ASW, 32 mm. **Ruler:** Sede Vacante **Obv:** Dove within square **Rev:** Arms of Cardinal Eduardo Martinez Somalo **Edge:** Reeded

Date	Mintage	F12	VF20	XF40	MS60	MS63
MMV (2005)R	13,440	PF65 200				

KM# 383 5 EURO

18.00 g., 0.925 Silver 0.5319 oz. ASW, 32 mm. **Ruler:** Benedict XVI **Subject:** Life reborn **Obv:** Bust left **Rev:** Children playing among branches of an olive tree

Date	Mintage	F12	VF20	XF40	MS60	MS63
2005R	13,000	PF65 100				

KM# 395 5 EURO

18.00 g., 0.925 Silver 0.5319 oz. ASW, 32 mm. **Ruler:** Benedict XVI **Subject:** World Day of Peace **Obv:** Half-length figure Benedict right in vestments with crozier **Rev:** St. Benedict of Nursia seated

Date	Mintage	F12	VF20	XF40	MS60	MS63
MMVI (2006)R	14,160	PF63 80.00	PF65 90.00			

KM# 400 5 EURO

18.00 g., 0.925 Silver 0.5319 oz. ASW, 32 mm. **Ruler:** Benedict XVI **Subject:** World Day of Peace **Obv:** 1/2 length figure kneeling in prayer **Rev:** Standing St. Francis of Assissi, rays in background

Date	Mintage	F12	VF20	XF40	MS60	MS63
MMVII (2007)R	13,693	PF63 45.00	PF65 55.00			

KM# 406 5 EURO

18.00 g., 0.925 Silver 0.5319 oz. ASW, 32 mm. **Ruler:** Benedict XVI **Subject:** World Youth Day - Sydney **Obv:** Pope right, blessing **Rev:** Sydney Harbor sites

Date	Mintage	F12	VF20	XF40	MS60	MS63
MMVIII (2008)R	9,600	PF63 50.00	PF65 60.00			

KM# 415 5 EURO
18.00 g., 0.925 Silver 0.5319 oz. ASW, 32 mm. **Ruler:** Benedict XVI **Subject:** World day of Peace **Obv:** Bust right in prayer **Rev:** Candle, family

Date	Mintage	F12	VF20	XF40	MS60	MS63
2009R	9,600	PF63 50.00	PF65 60.00			

KM# 421 5 EURO
18.00 g., 0.925 Silver 0.5319 oz. ASW, 32 mm. **Ruler:** Benedict XVI **Subject:** Migrants and Refugees **Obv:** Benedict standing facing in vestments and mitre **Rev:** Family scene

Date	Mintage	F12	VF20	XF40	MS60	MS63
2010R	9,998	PF63 65.00	PF65 75.00			

KM# 427 5 EURO
18.00 g., 0.925 Silver 0.5319 oz. ASW, 32 mm. **Ruler:** Benedict XVI **Subject:** 44the World day of Peace **Obv:** Bust left **Rev:** Female standing

Date	Mintage	F12	VF20	XF40	MS60	MS63
2011R	7,998	PF63 70.00	PF65 80.00			

KM# 429 5 EURO
18.00 g., 0.925 Silver 0.5319 oz. ASW, 32 mm. **Ruler:** Benedict XVI **Subject:** John Paul II beautification **Obv:** Bust facing of John Paul II **Rev:** Cherubs elevating Papal Arms of John Paul II

Date	Mintage	F12	VF20	XF40	MS60	MS63
2011R	9,500	PF63 65.00	PF65 75.00			

KM# 436 5 EURO
18.00 g., 0.925 Silver 0.5319 oz. ASW, 32 mm. **Ruler:** Benedict XVI **Subject:** John Paul I, 100th Anniversary of Birth

Date	Mintage	F12	VF20	XF40	MS60	MS63
2012R	8,999	PF63 80.00	PF65 90.00			

KM# 442 5 EURO
Silver **Ruler:** Sede Vacante **Obv:** Dove in flight **Rev:** Arms of Cardinal Tarciscio Bertone

Date	Mintage	F12	VF20	XF40	MS60	MS63
2013R	—	PF63 40.00	PF65 50.00			

KM# 350 10 EURO
22.00 g., 0.835 Silvor 0.5868 oz. ASW, 34 mm. **Ruler:** John Paul II **Subject:** 24th Anniversary of Reign **Obv:** Pope holding crucifix **Rev:** Risen Christ (Message of peace) **Edge:** Reeded

Date	Mintage	F12	VF20	XF40	MS60	MS63
2002R	10,000	PF65 80.00				

KM# 355 10 EURO
22.00 g., 0.925 Silver 0.6501 oz. ASW, 34 mm. **Ruler:** John Paul II **Subject:** 25th Anniversary of Reign **Obv:** Pope praying **Rev:** St. Peter receiving the keys of Earth and Heaven **Edge:** Reeded

Date	Mintage	F12	VF20	XF40	MS60	MS63
2003R	10,000	PF65 80.00				

KM# 360 10 EURO
22.00 g., 0.925 Silver 0.6501 oz. ASW, 34 mm. **Ruler:** John Paul II **Obv:** Pope praying for peace **Rev:** Tree of Life rooted in virtues **Edge:** Reeded and plain sections

Date	Mintage	F12	VF20	XF40	MS60	MS63
2004R	13,000	—	—	—	90.00	

KM# 384 10 EURO
22.00 g., 0.925 Silver 0.6501 oz. ASW, 34 mm. **Ruler:** Benedict XVI **Subject:** Disciples of Emanaus **Obv:** Bust left **Rev:** Three men seated at table

Date	Mintage	F12	VF20	XF40	MS60	MS63
2006R	13,000	PF65 215				

KM# 396 10 EURO
22.00 g., 0.925 Silver 0.6501 oz. ASW, 34 mm. **Ruler:** Benedict XVI **Subject:** St. Peter's Collonade, 350th Anniversary **Obv:** Collonade & Pope Benedict **Rev:** Collonade Schematics

Date	Mintage	F12	VF20	XF40	MS60	MS63
AN II MMVI (2006)R	14,160	PF63 80.00	PF65 90.00			

KM# 401 10 EURO
22.00 g., 0.925 Silver 0.6501 oz. ASW, 34 mm. **Ruler:** Benedict XVI **Subject:** World Mission Day **Obv:** Bust right in ermine cape **Rev:** Blessed Mother Theresa of Calcutta and child

Date	Mintage	F12	VF20	XF40	MS60	MS63
AN III MVII (2007)R	13,694	PF63 70.00	PF65 80.00			

KM# 407 10 EURO
22.00 g., 0.925 Silver 0.6501 oz. ASW, 34 mm. **Ruler:** Benedict XVI **Subject:** World Day of Peace **Obv:** Pope seated on chair in full robes and miter **Rev:** The Holy Family - Jesus, Mary, Joseph

Date	Mintage	F12	VF20	XF40	MS60	MS63
A VI MMVIII (2008)R	9,602	PF63 85.00	PF65 95.00			

KM# 417 10 EURO
22.00 g., 0.925 Silver 0.6501 oz. ASW, 34 mm. **Ruler:** Benedict XVI **Subject:** Lateran Treaty, 80th Anniversary **Obv:** Bust right **Rev:** Rolled treaty with seal

Date	Mintage	F12	VF20	XF40	MS60	MS63
2009R	9,602	PF63 85.00	PF65 95.00			

KM# 422 10 EURO
22.00 g., 0.925 Silver 0.6501 oz. ASW, 34 mm. **Ruler:** Benedict XVI **Subject:** 43rd World day of Peace **Obv:** Bust left **Rev:** Three figures

Date	Mintage	F12	VF20	XF40	MS60	MS63
2010R	9,998	PF63 70.00	PF65 80.00			

KM# 428 10 EURO
22.00 g., 0.925 Silver 0.6501 oz. ASW, 34 mm. **Ruler:** Benedict XVI **Subject:** Benedict XVI's 60th Anniversary of Ordination **Obv:** Bust right **Rev:** Two fishermen hauling in net

Date	Mintage	F12	VF20	XF40	MS60	MS63
2011R	7,998	PF63 80.00	PF65 90.00			

KM# 437 10 EURO
22.00 g., 0.925 Silver 0.6501 oz. ASW, 34 mm. **Ruler:** Benedict XVI **Subject:** 20th World Day of the Sick

Date	Mintage	F12	VF20	XF40	MS60	MS63
2012R	8,999	PF63 80.00	PF65 90.00			

KM# 443 10 EURO
3.00 g., 0.917 Gold 0.0879 oz. AGW, 18.5 mm. **Ruler:** Sede Vacante **Obv:** Dove in flight **Rev:** Arms of Cardinal Tarciscio Bertone

Date	Mintage	F12	VF20	XF40	MS60	MS63
2013R	5,000	PF63 450	PF65 500			

KM# 361 20 EURO
6.00 g., 0.917 Gold 0.1758 oz. AGW, 21 mm. **Ruler:** John Paul II **Subject:** Roots of Faith **Rev:** Noah's Ark

Date	Mintage	F12	VF20	XF40	MS60	MS63
2002	2,800	PF65 1,200				

KM# 351 20 EURO
6.00 g., 0.9166 Gold 0.1757 oz. AGW, 21 mm. **Ruler:** John Paul II **Rev:** Moses being found in floating basket **Edge:** Reeded

Date	Mintage	F12	VF20	XF40	MS60	MS63
2003R	2,800	PF65 1,300				

KM# 363 20 EURO
6.00 g., 0.917 Gold 0.1758 oz. AGW, 21 mm. **Ruler:** John Paul II **Rev:** David slaying Goliath

Date	Mintage	F12	VF20	XF40	MS60	MS63
2004/XXVII R	3,050	PF65 1,200				

KM# 392 20 EURO
6.00 g., 0.916 Gold 0.1756 oz. AGW, 21 mm. **Ruler:** Benedict XVI **Subject:** Christian Initiation - Baptism **Obv:** Pope seated **Rev:** Fountain

Date	Mintage	F12	VF20	XF40	MS60	MS63
AN I MMV (2005)R	3,046	PF63 550	PF65 600			

KM# 397 20 EURO
6.00 g., 0.916 Gold 0.1756 oz. AGW, 21 mm. **Ruler:** Benedict XVI **Subject:** Christian Initiation - Confirmation **Obv:** Bust right **Rev:** Bishop confirming three

Date	Mintage	F12	VF20	XF40	MS60	MS63
AN II MMVI (2006)R	3,326	PF63 550	PF65 600			

KM# 402 20 EURO
6.00 g., 0.916 Gold 0.1756 oz. AGW, 21 mm. **Ruler:** Benedict XVI **Subject:** Christain Initiation - Eucharist **Obv:** Bust left in ermine cape **Rev:** Basket of fish and bread

Date	Mintage	F12	VF20	XF40	MS60	MS63
AN III (2007)R	3,426	PF63 550	PF65 600			

KM# 408 20 EURO
6.00 g., 0.917 Gold 0.1758 oz. AGW, 21 mm. **Ruler:** Benedict XVI **Subject:** Vatican sculpture **Obv:** Pope right in mitre **Rev:** Torso of Belvedere

Date	Mintage	F12	VF20	XF40	MS60	MS63
AN IV MMVIII (2008)R	2,930	PF63 450	PF65 500			

KM# 416 20 EURO
6.00 g., 0.917 Gold 0.1758 oz. AGW, 21 mm. **Ruler:** Benedict XVI **Subject:** Masterworks in the Vatican Collection **Rev:** John the Baptist with lamb on shoulders

Date	Mintage	F12	VF20	XF40	MS60	MS63
2009R	2,934	PF63 500	PF65 550			

KM# 423 20 EURO

6.00 g., 0.917 Gold 0.1758 oz. AGW, 21 mm. **Ruler:** Benedict XVI **Subject:** Vatican Sculpture - Apollo Belvedere **Obv:** Large head profile left **Rev:** Statue of Apollo Belvedere

Date	Mintage	F12	VF20	XF40	MS60	MS63
2010R	3,050	PF63 450	PF65 500			

KM# 431 20 EURO

6.00 g., 0.917 Gold 0.1758 oz. AGW, 21 mm. **Ruler:** Benedict XVI **Subject:** Pauline Chapel restoration **Obv:** Bust left **Rev:** Head

Date	Mintage	F12	VF20	XF40	MS60	MS63
2011R	3,050	PF63 400	PF65 450			

KM# 433 20 EURO

26.00 g., 0.925 Silver 0.7682 oz. ASW, 36 mm. **Ruler:** Benedict XVI **Subject:** 10th Anniversary of the Vatican Euro **Rev:** St. Peter's Basilica

Date	Mintage	F12	VF20	XF40	MS60	MS63
2012R	13,000	PF63 300	PF65 350			

KM# 438 20 EURO

6.00 g., 0.917 Gold 0.1758 oz. AGW, 21 mm. **Ruler:** Benedict XVI **Subject:** Restoration of the Pauline Chapel

Date	Mintage	F12	VF20	XF40	MS60	MS63
2012R	3,000	PF63 350	PF65 400			

KM# 444 20 EURO

26.00 g., 0.925 Silver 0.7682 oz. ASW, 36 mm. **Ruler:** Benedict XVI **Subject:** Giuseppe Verdi, 200 Anniversary of Birth **Rev:** Bust facing at left **Edge:** Reeded

Date	Mintage	F12	VF20	XF40	MS60	MS63
2013R	11,000	PF63 90.00	PF65 100			

KM# 362 50 EURO

15.00 g., 0.917 Gold 0.4394 oz. AGW, 28 mm. **Ruler:** John Paul II **Subject:** Roots of Faith **Rev:** Sacrifice of Abraham

Date	Mintage	F12	VF20	XF40	MS60	MS63
2002	2,800	PF65 2,200				

KM# 352 50 EURO

15.00 g., 0.9166 Gold 0.4392 oz. AGW, 28 mm. **Ruler:** John Paul II **Rev:** Moses receiving the Ten Commandments **Edge:** Reeded

Date	Mintage	F12	VF20	XF40	MS60	MS63
2003R	2,800	PF65 2,200				

KM# 364 50 EURO

15.00 g., 0.917 Gold 0.4394 oz. AGW, 28 mm. **Ruler:** John Paul II **Rev:** Judgement of Solomon

Date	Mintage	F12	VF20	XF40	MS60	MS63
2004/XXVII R	3,050	PF65 2,200				

KM# 393 50 EURO

15.00 g., 0.916 Gold 0.4389 oz. AGW, 28 mm. **Ruler:** Benedict XVI **Subject:** Christian Initiation - Baptism **Obv:** Pope seated **Rev:** John baptising Christ

Date	Mintage	F12	VF20	XF40	MS60	MS63
AN I MMV (2005)R	3,044	PF63 1,400	PF65 1,500			

KM# 398 50 EURO

15.00 g., 0.916 Gold 0.4389 oz. AGW, 28 mm. **Ruler:** Benedict XVI **Subject:** Christian Initiation - Confirmation **Obv:** Bust right **Rev:** Tongues of fire decending on Apostles

Date	Mintage	F12	VF20	XF40	MS60	MS63
AN II MMVI (2006)R	3,324	PF63 1,400	PF65 1,500			

KM# 403 50 EURO

15.00 g., 0.916 Gold 0.4389 oz. AGW, 28 mm. **Ruler:** Benedict XVI **Subject:** Christian Initiation - Eucharist **Obv:** Bust left in ermine cape **Rev:** Scene of the Last Supper

Date	Mintage	F12	VF20	XF40	MS60	MS63
ANIII MMVII (2007)R	—	PF63 1,400	PF65 1,500			

KM# 409 50 EURO

15.00 g., 0.917 Gold 0.4394 oz. AGW, 28 mm. **Ruler:** Benedict XVI **Subject:** Vatican sculpture **Obv:** Pope right in mitre **Rev:** The Pieta

Date	Mintage	F12	VF20	XF40	MS60	MS63
AN IV MMVIII (2008)R	—	PF63 900	PF65 1,000			

KM# 418 50 EURO

15.00 g., 0.917 Gold 0.4394 oz. AGW, 28 mm. **Ruler:** Benedict XVI **Subject:** Masterworks in the Vatican Collection **Rev:** Hercules statue group

Date	Mintage	F12	VF20	XF40	MS60	MS63
2009R	2,930	PF63 1,100	PF65 1,200			

KM# 424 50 EURO

15.00 g., 0.917 Gold 0.4394 oz. AGW, 28 mm. **Ruler:** Benedict XVI **Subject:** Vatican Sculpture - Augustus of Prima **Obv:** Large head profile left **Rev:** Statue of Augustus

Date	Mintage	F12	VF20	XF40	MS60	MS63
2010R	3,050	PF63 1,100	PF65 1,200			

KM# 432 50 EURO

15.00 g., 0.917 Gold 0.4394 oz. AGW, 28 mm. **Ruler:** Benedict XVI **Subject:** Pauline Chapel restoration **Obv:** Bust left **Rev:** Cruxifiction of St. Peter

Date	Mintage	F12	VF20	XF40	MS60	MS63
2011R	2,700	PF63 850	PF65 950			

KM# 434 50 EURO

15.00 g., 0.917 Gold 0.4394 oz. AGW, 28 mm. **Ruler:** Benedict XVI **Subject:** 10th Anniversary of the Vatican Euro **Rev:** St. Peter's Basilica

Date	Mintage	F12	VF20	XF40	MS60	MS63
2012R	2,000	PF63 900	PF65 1,000			

KM# 439 50 EURO

15.00 g., 0.917 Gold 0.4394 oz. AGW, 28 mm. **Ruler:** Benedict XVI **Subject:** Restoration of the Pauline Chapel

Date	Mintage	F12	VF20	XF40	MS60	MS63
2012R	2,500	PF63 1,100	PF65 1,200			

KM# 445 50 EURO

15.00 g., 0.917 Gold 0.4394 oz. AGW, 15 mm. **Ruler:** Benedict XVI **Subject:** Richard Wagner, 200th Anniversary of Birth **Rev:** Profile facing right **Edge:** Reeded

Date	Mintage	F12	VF20	XF40	MS60	MS63
2013R	2,000	PF63 900	PF65 1,000			

KM# 405 100 EURO

30.00 g., 0.917 Gold 0.8788 oz. AGW, 35 mm. **Ruler:** Benedict XVI **Obv:** Bust left **Rev:** The Creator from the Sistine Chapel ceiling

Date	Mintage	F12	VF20	XF40	MS60	MS63
AN IV MMVIII (2008)R	960	PF63 1,600	PF65 1,700			

KM# 419 100 EURO

30.00 g., 0.917 Gold 0.8788 oz. AGW, 35 mm. **Ruler:** Benedict XVI **Subject:** Sistine Chapel - Banishment from Eden

Date	Mintage	F12	VF20	XF40	MS60	MS63
2009R	—	PF63 1,600	PF65 1,700			

KM# 425 100 EURO
30.00 g., 0.917 Gold 0.8788 oz. AGW, 35 mm. **Ruler:** Benedict XVI **Subject:** Sistine Chapel - Last Judgement **Obv:** Bust left **Rev:** Detail of the painting

Date	Mintage	F12	VF20	XF40	MS60	MS63
2010R	1,100	PF63 1,650	PF65 1,750			

KM# 430 100 EURO
30.00 g., 0.917 Gold 0.8788 oz. AGW, 35 mm. **Ruler:** Benedict XVI **Subject:** Raffaell painting **Obv:** Bust left in vestments and mitre **Rev:** Horseman and captive

Date	Mintage	F12	VF20	XF40	MS60	MS63
2011R	1,100	PF63 1,550	PF65 1,650			

KM# 440 100 EURO
30.00 g., 0.917 Gold 0.8788 oz. AGW, 35 mm. **Ruler:** Benedict XVI **Rev:** Madonna of Foligno

Date	Mintage	F12	VF20	XF40	MS60	MS63
2012R	999	PF63 2,200	PF65 2,300			

KM# 441 200 EURO
40.00 g., 0.917 Gold 1.1717 oz. AGW, 38.5 mm. **Ruler:** Benedict XVI **Subject:** Theological Virtues - Faith

Date	Mintage	F12	VF20	XF40	MS60	MS63
2012R	499	PF63 4,500	PF65 5,500			

MINT SETS

KM#	Date	Mintage	Identification	Issue Price	Mkt Val
MS107	2001 (8)	26,000	KM#331-338	21.25	200
MS108	2002 (8)	65,000	KM#341-348	12.00	975
MS109	2003 (8)	65,000	KM#341-348	15.00	500
MS110	2004 (8)	85,000	KM#341-348	16.50	335
MS111	2005 (8)	85,000	KM#341-348.	32.50	335
MS112	MMV (2005) (8)	60,000	KM#365-372	—	435
MS113	2006 (8)	—	KM#375-382	—	210
MS114	2007 (8)	—	KM#375-382	—	230
MS115	2008 (8)	85,000	KM#375-377, 385-389	45.00	164
MS116	2009 (8)	91,400	KM#375-377, 385-389	30.00	164
MS117	2010 (8)	94,000	KM#375-377, 385-389	30.00	150
MS118	2011 (8)	94,000	KM#375-377, 385-389	—	75.00
MS119	2012 (8)	85,000	KM#375-377, 385-389	—	75.00
MS120	2013 (8)	85,000	KM#375-377, 385-389	—	75.00

PROOF SETS

KM#	Date	Mintage	Identification	Issue Price	Mkt Val
PS13	2001 (2)	—	KM#390, 391	—	1,350
PS15	2002 (8)	9,000	KM#341-348	75.00	1,450
PS16	2003 (8)	13,000	KM#341-348	78.00	1,200
PS17	2004 (8)	13,000	KM#341-348	—	1,200
PS18	2005 (8)	16,000	KM#341-348 plus silver medal	150	1,175
PS19	2006 (8)	16,000	KM#375-382 plus silver medal	—	375
PS20	2007 (8)	16,000	KM#375-382 plus silver medal	—	315
PS21	2008 (8)	16,000	KM#375-377, 385-389 plus silver medal	195	250
PS22	2009 (8)	15,000	KM#375-377, 385-389 plus silver medal	195	250
PS23	2010 (8)	15,000	KM#375-377, 385-389 plus silver medal	195	240
PS24	2010 (8)	300	KM#375-377, 385-389 plus gold medal	2,100	2,250
PS25	2011 (9)	14,700	KM#375-377, 385-389 plus silver medal	—	200
PS26	2011 (9)	300	KM#375-377, 385-389 plus gold medal	—	2,250
PS27	2012 (9)	13,000	KM#375-377, 385-389, 433	—	200
PS28	2012 (9)	2,000	KM#375-377, 385-389, 434	—	2,200
PS29	2013 (9)	11,000	KM#375-377, 385-389, 444	—	200
PS30	2013 (9)	2,000	KM#375-377, 385-389, 445	—	1,250

VENEZUELA

The Bolivarian Republic of Venezuela ("Little Venice"), located on the northern coast of South America between Colombia and Guyana, has an area of 352,145 sq. mi.(912,050 sq. km.) and a population of 20 million. Capital: Caracas. Petroleum and mining provide a significant portion of Venezuela's exports. Coffee, grown on 60,000 plantations, is the chief crop. Metalurgy, refining, oil, iron and steel production are the main employment industries.

GOVERNMENT
Republic, 1823-2000
Republic Bolivarian, 2000-

MINT MARKS
Maracay

REPUBLIC

REFORM COINAGE
100 Centimos = 1 Bolívar

Y# 80 10 BOLIVARES
2.33 g., Nickel Clad Steel, 17 mm. **Obv:** National arms left of denomination **Obv. Legend:** REPÚBLICA BOLIVARIANA DE VENEZUELA **Rev:** Head of Bolívar left in 7-sided outline **Rev. Legend:** BOLÍVAR - LIBERTADOR **Edge:** Reeded

Date	Mintage	F12	VF20	XF40	MS60	MS63
2001	—	—	—	—	0.25	0.50
2002	—	—	—	—	0.25	0.50

Y# 80a 10 BOLIVARES
1.74 g., Aluminum-Zinc, 16.92 mm. **Obv:** National arms and value **Obv. Legend:** REPÚBLICA BOLIVARIANA DE VENEZUELA **Rev:** Head of Bolívar left in 7-sided outline **Rev. Legend:** BOLÍVAR - LIBERTADOR **Edge:** Reeded

Date	Mintage	F12	VF20	XF40	MS60	MS63
2001	—	—	—	0.15	0.45	0.60
2002	—	—	—	0.15	0.45	0.60
2004	—	—	—	0.15	0.45	0.60

Y# 81 20 BOLIVARES
4.32 g., Nickel Clad Steel, 20 mm. **Obv:** National arms left of denomination **Obv. Legend:** REPÚBLICA BOLIVARIANA DE VENEZUELA **Rev:** Head of Bolivar left in 7-sided outline **Rev. Legend:** BOLÍVAR - LIBERTADOR **Edge:** Plain

Date	Mintage	F12	VF20	XF40	MS60	MS63
2001	—	—	—	—	0.25	0.50
2002	—	—	—	—	0.25	0.50

Y# 81a.1 20 BOLIVARES
3.27 g., Aluminum-Zinc, 20 mm. **Obv:** National arms and value with wavy based "2 **Obv. Legend:** REPÚBLICA BOLIVARIANA DE VENEZUELA **Rev:** Head of Bolívar left in 7-sided outline **Rev. Legend:** BOLÍVAR - LIBERTADOR **Edge:** Plain

Date	Mintage	F12	VF20	XF40	MS60	MS63
2001	—	—	—	—	0.65	1.00

Y# 81a.2 20 BOLIVARES
3.24 g., Aluminum-Zinc, 20 mm. **Obv:** National arms and value with flat based "2 **Obv. Legend:** REPÚBLICA BOLIVARIANA DE VENEZUELA **Rev:** Head of Bolívar left in 7-sided outline **Rev. Legend:** BOLÍVAR - LIBERTADOR **Edge:** Plain

Date	Mintage	F12	VF20	XF40	MS60	MS63
2002	—	—	0.25	0.60	0.80	
2004	—	—	0.25	0.60	0.80	

Y# 82 50 BOLIVARES
6.58 g., Nickel Clad Steel, 23 mm. **Obv:** National arms left of denomination **Obv. Legend:** REPÚBLICA BOLIVARIANA DE VENEZUELA **Rev:** Head of Bolivar left in 7-sided outline **Rev. Legend:** BOLÍVAR - LIBERTADOR **Edge:** Reeded

Date	Mintage	F12	VF20	XF40	MS60	MS63
2001	—	—	—	0.30	0.75	1.00
2002	—	—	—	0.30	0.75	1.00
2004	—	—	—	0.30	0.75	1.00

Y# 83 100 BOLIVARES
6.82 g., Nickel Clad Steel, 25 mm. **Obv:** National arms and value **Obv. Legend:** REPÚBUBLICA BOLIVARIANA DE VENEZUELA **Rev:** Head of Bolívar left in 7-sided ouline **Rev. Legend:** BOLÍVAR - LIBERTADO **Edge:** Plain

Date	Mintage	F12	VF20	XF40	MS60	MS63
2001	—	—	—	0.45	1.10	1.50
2002	—	—	—	0.45	1.10	1.50
2004	—	—	—	0.45	1.10	1.50

Y# 94 500 BOLIVARES
8.50 g., Nickel Plated Steel, 28.4 mm. **Obv:** National arms and denomination **Obv. Legend:** REPÚBLICA BOLIVARIANA DE VENEZUELA **Rev:** Head of Bolívar left in 7-sided outline **Rev. Legend:** BOLÍVAR - LIBERTADOR **Edge:** Segmented reeding

Date	Mintage	F12	VF20	XF40	MS60	MS63
2004	—	—	—	0.60	1.50	2.00

Y# 85 1000 BOLIVARES
8.35 g., Bi-Metallic, 24 mm. **Obv:** National arms and value in center **Obv. Legend:** REPÚBLICA BOLIVARIANA DE VENEZUELA **Rev:** Head of Bolívar left **Rev. Legend:** BOLÍVAR - LIBERTADOR **Edge:** Lettered **Edge Lettering:** BCV 1000" four times

Date	Mintage	F12	VF20	XF40	MS60	MS63
2005	9,000,000	—	—	0.90	2.25	3.00

REFORM COINAGE
2007
1000 Bolivares = 1 Bolivar Fuerte

Y# 87 CENTIMO
1.36 g., Copper Plated Steel, 14.9 mm. **Obv:** National arms **Obv. Legend:** REPÚBLICA BOLIVARIANA DE VENEZUELA **Rev:** Eight stars at left, large value at right **Edge:** Reeded

Date	Mintage	F12	VF20	XF40	MS60	MS63
2007	—				0.25	0.35

Note: Many die rotation varieties exist.

2009	—				0.25	0.35

Y# 88 5 CENTIMOS
2.03 g., Copper Plated Steel, 16.9 mm. **Obv:** National arms **Obv. Legend:** REPÚBLICA BOLIVARIANA DE VENEZUELA **Rev:** Eight stars at left, large value at right **Edge:** Plain

Date	Mintage	F12	VF20	XF40	MS60	MS63
2007	—				0.50	0.75
2009	—				0.50	0.75

Y# 89 10 CENTIMOS
2.62 g., Nickel Plated Steel, 18 mm. **Obv:** National arms **Obv. Legend:** REPÚBLICA BOLIVARIANA DE VENEZUELA **Rev:** Eight stars at left, large value at right **Edge:** Reeded

Date	Mintage	F12	VF20	XF40	MS60	MS63
2007	—				0.75	1.00
2009	—				0.75	1.00

Y# 90 12-1/2 CENTIMOS
3.93 g., Nickel Plated Steel, 23 mm. **Obv:** National arms **Obv. Legend:** REPÚBLICA BOLIVARIANA DE VENEZUELA **Rev:** Large value, eight stars below in sprays **Edge:** Plain

Date	Mintage	F12	VF20	XF40	MS60	MS63
2007	—				1.50	1.75

Y# 91 25 CENTIMOS
3.86 g., Nickel Plated Steel, 20 mm. **Obv:** National arms **Obv. Legend:** REPÚBLICA BOLIVARIANA DE VENEZUELA **Rev:** Eight stars at left, large value at center right **Edge:** Plain

Date	Mintage	F12	VF20	XF40	MS60	MS63
2007	—				2.00	2.50
2009	—				2.00	2.50

Y# 99 25 CENTIMOS
3.86 g., Nickel Plated Steel, 20 mm. **Subject:** Independence, 200th Anniversary **Obv:** Legend **Rev:** Large value

Date	Mintage	F12	VF20	XF40	MS60	MS63
2010	—				2.50	3.00

Y# 92 50 CENTIMOS
4.30 g., Nickel Plated Steel, 21.9 mm. **Obv:** National arms **Obv. Legend:** REPÚBLICA BOLIVARIANA DE VENEZUELA **Rev:** Eight stars at left, large value at center right **Edge:** Segmented reeding

Date	Mintage	F12	VF20	XF40	MS60	MS63
2007	—				3.00	3.50
2009	—				3.00	3.50

Y# 100 50 CENTIMOS
4.30 g., Nickel Plated Steel, 21.9 mm. **Subject:** Banco Central, 70th Anniversary **Obv:** Legend **Rev:** Large vlaue

Date	Mintage	F12	VF20	XF40	MS60	MS63
2010	—				3.50	4.00

Y# 93 BOLIVAR
8.04 g., Bi-Metallic, 24 mm. **Obv:** Eight stars at left of national arms, large value at right **Obv. Legend:** REPÚBLICA BOLIVARIANA DE VENEZUELA **Rev:** Head of Bolívar left **Edge:** Lettered **Edge Lettering:** BCV 1" repeated

Date	Mintage	F12	VF20	XF40	MS60	MS63
2007	—				5.00	6.00
2009	—				5.00	6.00

Y# 101 50 BOLIVARES
31.10 g., 0.999 Silver 0.9925 oz. ASW, 38.6 mm. **Subject:** Banco Central, 70th Anniversary **Obv:** Legned **Rev:** Banco Central building

Date	Mintage	F12	VF20	XF40	MS60	MS63
2010	3,000	**PF63** 75.00	**PF65** 85.00			

Y# 102 50 BOLIVARES
0.999 Gold AGW **Subject:** Banco Central, 70th Anniversary **Obv:** Legend **Rev:** Banco Central building

Date	Mintage	F12	VF20	XF40	MS60	MS63
2010	—	**PF65** 2,000				

Y# 95 200 BOLIVARES
0.999 Silver **Obv:** Flag **Rev:** Crowd outside building

Date	Mintage	F12	VF20	XF40	MS60	MS63
2010	—	**PF63** 75.00	**PF65** 85.00			

Y# 96 200 BOLIVARES
0.999 Gold AGW **Obv:** Flag **Rev:** Crowd before building

Date	Mintage	F12	VF20	XF40	MS60	MS63
2010	—	**PF65** 2,000				

Y# 97 200 BOLIVARES
0.999 Silver **Obv:** Flag **Rev:** Francisco de Marianda

Date	Mintage	F12	VF20	XF40	MS60	MS63
2010	—	**PF63** 75.00	**PF65** 85.00			

Y# 98 200 BOLIVARES
0.999 Gold AGW **Obv:** Flag **Rev:** Francisco de Marianda

Date	Mintage	F12	VF20	XF40	MS60	MS63
2010	—	**PF65** 2,000				

VIET NAM

The Socialist Republic of Viet Nam, located in Southeast Asia west of the South China Sea, has an area of 127,300 sq. mi. (329,560 sq. km.) and a population of *66.8 million. Capital: Hanoi. Agricultural products, coal, and mineral ores are exported.

The activities of Communists in South Viet Nam led to the second Indochina war which came to a brief halt in 1973 (when a cease-fire was arranged and U.S. forces withdrew), but it didn't end until April 30, 1975 when South Viet Nam surrendered unconditionally. The two Viet Nams were reunited as the Socialist Republic of Viet Nam on July 2, 1976.

SOCIALIST REPUBLIC

STANDARD COINAGE

KM# 71 200 DONG
3.10 g., Nickel Clad Steel, 20.75 mm. **Obv:** National emblem **Rev:** Denomination

Date	Mintage	F12	VF20	XF40	MS60	MS63
2003	125,000,000	0.15	0.20	0.35	0.75	0.50

KM# 74 500 DONG
4.50 g., Nickel Clad Steel, 21.86 mm. **Obv:** National emblem **Rev:** Denomination **Edge:** Segmented reeding

Date	Mintage	F12	VF20	XF40	MS60	MS63
2003	175,000,000	0.15	0.25	0.50	0.75	1.00

KM# 72 1000 DONG
3.70 g., Brass Plated Steel, 19 mm. **Obv:** National emblem **Rev:** Bat De Pagoda in Hanoi **Edge:** Reeded

Date	Mintage	F12	VF20	XF40	MS60	MS63
2003	250,000,000	0.20	0.35	0.60	0.80	1.50

KM# 75 2000 DONG
5.00 g., Brass Plated Steel, 23.5 mm. **Obv:** National emblem **Rev:** Highland Stilt House in Tay Nguyen above value **Edge:** Segmented reeding

Date	Mintage	F12	VF20	XF40	MS60	MS63
2003	—	—	—	—	2.25	2.75

-KM# 64 5000 DONG
1.24 g., 0.9999 Gold 0.0397 oz. AGW, 13.92 mm. **Subject:** Year of the Snake **Obv:** State emblem **Rev:** Sea snake **Edge:** Reeded

Date	Mintage	F12	VF20	XF40	MS60	MS63
2001	—	—	—	—	85.00	100

KM# 67 5000 DONG
1.24 g., 0.9999 Gold 0.0397 oz. AGW, 13.9 mm. **Subject:** Year of the Horse **Obv:** State emblem **Rev:** Horse **Edge:** Reeded

Date	Mintage	F12	VF20	XF40	MS60	MS63
2002	28,000	—	—	—	75.00	90.00

KM# 73 5000 DONG
7.60 g., Brass, 25 mm. **Obv:** National emblem **Rev:** Chua Mot Cot Pagoda in Hanoi

Date	Mintage	F12	VF20	XF40	MS60	MS63
2003	500,000,000	0.50	0.75	1.00	1.25	2.50

KM# 57 10000 DONG
20.00 g., 0.925 Silver 0.591 oz. ASW, 38.7 mm. **Subject:** Year of the Snake **Obv:** State emblem above value **Obv. Legend:** CONG HOA XA HOI CHU NGHIA VIET NAM **Rev:** Sea snake **Rev. Legend:** ...VIET NAM **Edge:** Reeded

Date	Mintage	F12	VF20	XF40	MS60	MS63
2001(S)	—	PF65 175				

KM# 58 10000 DONG
20.00 g., 0.925 Silver 0.591 oz. ASW **Subject:** Year of the Snake **Obv:** State emblem above value **Obv. Legend:** CONG HOA XA HOI CHU NGHIA VIET NAM **Rev:** Bamboo viper **Rev. Legend:** ...VIET NAM

Date	Mintage	F12	VF20	XF40	MS60	MS63
2001(S)	—	PF65 175				

KM# 59 10000 DONG
20.00 g., 0.925 Silver 0.591 oz. ASW **Subject:** Year of the Snake **Obv:** State emblem above value **Obv. Legend:** CONG HOA XA HOI CHU NGHIA VIET NAM **Rev:** Multicolor holographic, cobra in center **Rev. Legend:** ...VIET NAM

Date	Mintage	F12	VF20	XF40	MS60	MS63
2001(S)	—	PF65 175				

KM# 61 10000 DONG
20.00 g., 0.999 Silver 0.6382 oz. ASW, 38.7 mm. **Subject:** Year of the Horse **Obv:** State emblem **Rev:** Horse with octagonal latent image **Edge:** Reeded

Date	Mintage	F12	VF20	XF40	MS60	MS63
2001	3,800	PF65 175				

Note: In proof set only

KM# 62 10000 DONG
20.00 g., 0.999 Silver 0.6382 oz. ASW, 38.7 mm. **Subject:** Year of the Horse **Obv:** State emblem **Rev:** Horse with multicolor accoutrements **Edge:** Reeded

Date	Mintage	F12	VF20	XF40	MS60	MS63
2001	3,800	PF65 175				

Note: In proof set only

KM# 63 10000 DONG
20.00 g., 0.999 Silver 0.6382 oz. ASW, 38.7 mm. **Subject:** Year of the Horse **Obv:** State emblem **Rev:** Multicolor holographic horse in center **Edge:** Reeded

Date	Mintage	F12	VF20	XF40	MS60	MS63
2001	3,800	PF65 175				

Note: In proof set only

KM# 76 10000 DONG
20.00 g., 0.999 Silver 0.6382 oz. ASW, 38.7 mm. **Obv:** State emblem **Rev:** Multicolored Grey-shanked Douc Langur monkey **Edge:** Reeded

Date	Mintage	F12	VF20	XF40	MS60	MS63
2004	6,200	PF63 100	PF65 125			

KM# 65 20000 DONG
7.78 g., 0.9999 Gold 0.2484 oz. AGW, 22 mm. **Subject:** Year of the Snake **Obv:** State emblem **Rev:** Sea snake **Edge:** Reeded

Date	Mintage	F12	VF20	XF40	MS60	MS63
2001(S)	—	PF63 550	PF65 600			

Note: Issued in a replica Faberge egg

KM# 68 20000 DONG
7.78 g., 0.9999 Gold 0.2484 oz. AGW, 22 mm. **Subject:** Year of the Horse **Obv:** State emblem **Rev:** Horse **Edge:** Reeded

Date	Mintage	F12	VF20	XF40	MS60	MS63
2002	1,800	PF63 550	PF65 600			

KM# 66 50000 DONG
15.55 g., 0.9999 Gold 0.4967 oz. AGW, 27 mm. **Subject:** Year of the Snake **Obv:** State emblem **Rev:** Multicolor holographic King Cobra **Edge:** Reeded

Date	Mintage	F12	VF20	XF40	MS60	MS63
2001(S)	—	PF63 1,000	PF65 1,100			

KM# 69 50000 DONG
15.55 g., 0.9999 Gold 0.4967 oz. AGW, 27 mm. **Subject:** Year of the Horse **Obv:** State emblem **Rev:** Multicolor holographic horse **Edge:** Reeded

Date	Mintage	F12	VF20	XF40	MS60	MS63
2002	3,800	PF63 1,000	PF65 1,100			

PROOF SETS

KM#	Date	Mintage	Identification	Issue Price	Mkt Val
PS4	2001(S) (3)	3,500	KM#57-59	120	250
PS5	2001(S) (2)	—	KM#59, 66	—	1,125
PS6	2001(S) (2)	—	KM#65-66	—	1,575
PS7	2002 (3)	3,800	KM#61-63	—	225

WEST AFRICAN STATES

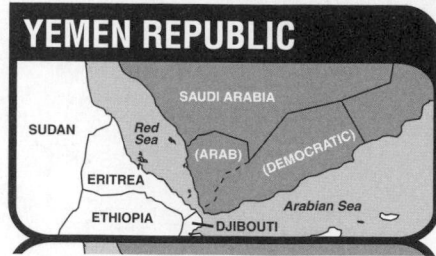

The West African States, a former federation of eight French colonial territories on the northwest coast of Africa, has an area of 1,831,079 sq. mi. (4,742,495 sq. km.) and a population of about 17 million. Capital: Dakar. The constituent territories were Mauritania, Senegal, Dahomey, French Sudan, Ivory Coast, Upper Volta, Niger and French Guinea.

The members of the federation were overseas territories within the French Union until Sept. of 1958 when all but French Guinea approved the constitution of the Fifth French Republic, thereby electing to become autonomous members of the new French Community. French Guinea voted to become the fully independent Republic of Guinea. The other seven attained independence in 1960. The French West Africa territories were provided with a common currency, a practice which was continued as the monetary union of the West African States which provides a common currency to the autonomous republics of Dahomey (now Benin), Senegal, Upper Volta (now Burkina Faso), Ivory Coast, Mali, Togo, Niger, and Guinea-Bissau.

For earlier coinage refer to Togo, and French West Africa.

MINT MARK
(a)- Paris, privy marks only

MONETARY SYSTEM
100 Centimes = 1 Franc

FEDERATION

STANDARD COINAGE

KM# 8 FRANC
1.60 g., Steel **Obv:** Taku - Ashanti gold weight **Rev:** Value and date

Date	Mintage	F12	VF20	XF40	MS60	MS63
2001(a)	—	—	—	0.10	0.35	0.60
2002(a)	—	—	—	0.10	0.35	0.60

KM# 2a 5 FRANCS
3.00 g., Aluminum-Nickel-Bronze, 20 mm. **Obv:** Taku - Ashanti gold weight divides value **Rev:** Gazelle head facing

Date	Mintage	F12	VF20	XF40	MS60	MS63
2001(a)	—	—	0.10	0.20	0.40	0.60
2002(a)	—	—	0.10	0.20	0.40	0.60
2003(a)	—	—	0.10	0.20	0.40	0.60
2004(a)	—	—	0.10	0.20	0.40	0.60
2005(a)	—	—	0.10	0.20	0.40	0.60
2006(a)	—	—	0.10	0.20	0.40	0.60
2007(a)	—	—	—	0.20	0.40	0.60
2008(a)	—	—	—	0.20	0.40	0.60
2009(a)	—	—	—	0.20	0.40	0.60
2010(a)	—	—	—	0.20	0.40	0.60
2011(a)	—	—	—	0.20	0.40	0.60

KM# 10 10 FRANCS
4.00 g., Aluminum-Bronze, 23.4 mm. **Series:** F.A.O. **Obv:** Taku - Ashanti gold weight divides value **Rev:** People getting water

Date	Mintage	F12	VF20	XF40	MS60	MS63
2001(a)	—	—	0.25	0.50	1.25	1.50
2002(a)	—	—	0.25	0.50	1.25	1.50
2003(a)	—	—	0.25	0.50	1.25	1.50
2004(a)	—	—	0.25	0.50	1.00	1.50
2005(a)	—	—	0.25	0.50	1.00	1.50
2006(a)	—	—	0.25	0.50	1.00	1.50
2007(a)	—	—	—	0.50	1.00	1.50
2008(a)	—	—	—	0.50	1.00	1.50
2009(a)	—	—	—	0.50	1.00	1.50
2010(a)	—	—	—	0.50	1.00	1.50
2011(a)	—	—	—	0.50	1.00	1.50
2012(a)	—	—	—	0.50	1.00	1.50

KM# 9 25 FRANCS
7.95 g., Aluminum-Bronze, 27 mm. **Series:** F.A.O. **Obv:** Taku - Ashanti gold weight divides value **Rev:** Figure filling tube **Note:** Mint mark position varieties exist.

Date	Mintage	F12	VF20	XF40	MS60	MS63
2001(a)	—	—	—	0.75	1.75	2.00
2002(a)	—	—	—	0.75	1.75	2.00
2003(a)	—	—	—	0.75	1.75	2.00
2004(a)	—	—	—	0.75	1.50	2.00
2005(a)	—	—	—	0.75	1.50	2.00
2006(a)	—	—	—	0.75	1.50	2.00
2007(a)	—	—	—	0.75	1.50	2.00
2008(a)	—	—	—	0.75	1.50	2.00
2009(a)	—	—	—	0.75	1.50	2.00
2010(a)	—	—	—	0.75	1.50	2.00
2011(a)	—	—	—	0.75	1.50	2.00
2012(a)	—	—	—	0.75	1.50	2.00

KM# 6 50 FRANCS
5.00 g., Copper-Nickel, 22 mm. **Series:** F.A.O. **Obv:** Taku - Ashanti gold weight **Rev:** Value within mixed beans, grains and nuts

Date	Mintage	F12	VF20	XF40	MS60	MS63
2001(a)	—	—	0.35	0.50	1.25	1.50
2002(a)	—	—	0.35	0.50	1.25	1.50
2003(a)	—	—	0.35	0.50	1.25	1.50
2004(a)	—	—	0.35	0.50	1.25	1.50
2005(a)	—	—	0.35	0.50	1.25	1.50
2006(a)	—	—	—	0.50	1.25	1.50
2007(a)	—	—	—	0.50	1.25	1.50
2009(a)	—	—	—	0.50	1.25	1.50
2010(a)	—	—	—	0.50	1.25	1.50
2011(a)	—	—	—	0.50	1.25	1.50
2012(a)	—	—	—	0.50	1.25	1.50

KM# 4 100 FRANCS
7.07 g., Nickel, 26 mm. **Obv:** Taku - Ashanti gold weight **Rev:** Value within flowers **Edge:** Reeded

Date	Mintage	F12	VF20	XF40	MS60	MS63
2001(a)	—	—	0.60	0.85	2.25	2.75
2002(a)	—	—	0.60	0.85	2.25	2.75
2003(a)	—	—	0.60	0.85	2.25	2.75
2004(a)	—	—	0.60	0.75	2.00	2.75
2005(a)	—	—	0.60	0.75	2.00	2.75
2006(a)	—	—	0.60	0.75	2.00	2.75
2009(a)	—	—	0.60	0.75	2.00	2.75
2010(a)	—	—	0.60	0.75	2.00	2.75
2012(a)	—	—	0.60	0.75	2.00	2.75

KM# 14 200 FRANCS
6.90 g., Bi-Metallic, 24.4 mm. **Obv:** Taku - Ashanti gold weight **Rev:** Agricultural produce and value **Edge:** Segmented reeding

Date	Mintage	F12	VF20	XF40	MS60	MS63
2003	—	—	—	1.60	4.00	6.00
2004(a)	—	—	—	1.60	4.00	6.00
2005(a)	—	—	—	1.60	4.00	6.00
2010(a)	—	—	—	1.60	4.00	6.00

KM# 15 500 FRANCS
10.60 g., Bi-Metallic, 27.9 mm. **Obv:** Taku - Ashanti gold weight **Rev:** Agricultural produce and value **Edge:** Segmented reeding

Date	Mintage	F12	VF20	XF40	MS60	MS63
2003	—	—	2.25	4.00	10.00	14.00
2004(a)	—	—	2.25	4.00	10.00	12.00
2005(a)	—	—	2.25	4.00	10.00	12.00
2010(a)	—	—	2.25	4.00	10.00	12.00

KM# 16 1000 FRANCS
22.20 g., 0.900 Silver 0.6382 oz. ASW **Obv:** Taku - Ashanti gold weight **Rev:** Agricultural produce above sprays surrounded by names of member countries

Date	Mintage	F12	VF20	XF40	MS60	MS63
2002(a)	500	PF65 150				

KM# 17 1000 FRANCS
22.20 g., 0.900 Silver 0.6382 oz. ASW **Subject:** FIFA World Championship Football - Germany 2006 **Obv:** Player kicking ball, tree in background **Obv. Legend:** COUPE DU MONDE DE LA FIFA - ALLEMAGNE **Rev:** Agricultural produce above sprays surrounded by names of member countries

Date	Mintage	F12	VF20	XF40	MS60	MS63
2004(a)	50,000	PF63 45.00		PF65 60.00		

YEMEN REPUBLIC

The Republic of Yemen, formerly Yemen Arab Republic and Peoples Democratic Republic of Yemen, is located on the southern coast of the Arabian Peninsula. It has an area of 205,020 sq. mi. (531,000 sq. km.) and a population of 12 million. Capital: San'a. The port of Aden is the main commercial center and the area's most valuable natural resource. Recent oil and gas finds and a developing petroleum industry have improved their economic prospects. Agriculture and local handicrafts are the main industries. Cotton, fish, coffee, rock salt and hides are exported.

On May 22, 1990, the Yemen Arab Republic (North Yemen) and Peoples Democratic Republic of Yemen (South Yemen) merged into a unified Republic of Yemen. Disagreements between the two former governments simmered until civil war erupted in 1994, with the northern forces of the old Yemen Arab Republic eventually prevailing.

TITLE

المملكة المتوكلية اليمنية

al-Mamlaka(t) al-Mutawakkiliya(t) al-Yamaniya(t)

REPUBLIC

MILLED COINAGE

KM# 26 5 RIYALS
4.50 g., Stainless Steel, 22.9 mm. **Obv:** Denomination within circle **Rev:** Building **Shape:** 21-sided

Date	Mintage	F12	VF20	XF40	MS60	MS63
AH1421-2001	—	—	—	—	0.75	1.00
AH1425-2004	—	—	—	—	0.75	1.00

KM# 27 10 RIYALS
6.05 g., Stainless Steel, 26 mm. **Obv:** Denomination within circle **Rev:** Bridge at Shaharah

Date	Mintage	F12	VF20	XF40	MS60	MS63
AH1424-2003	—	—	—	—	1.00	1.50
AH1430-2009	—	—	—	—	1.00	1.50

KM# 29 20 RIALS
7.10 g., Bi-Metallic, 29.85 mm. **Obv:** Value within circle **Rev:** Tree within circle **Edge:** Reeded

Date	Mintage	F12	VF20	XF40	MS60	MS63
AH1425-2004	—	—	—	—	1.50	2.50

KM# 29a 20 RIALS
Stainless Steel, 29.85 mm. **Obv:** Value within circle **Rev:** Tree within circle **Edge:** Reeded

Date	Mintage	F12	VF20	XF40	MS60	MS63
AH1427-2006	—	—	—	—	1.50	2.50

KM# 30 500 RIALS
21.25 g., Copper-Nickel-Zinc, 35.2 mm. **Subject:** City of San'a **Obv:** Value **Rev:** City gate below artwork **Edge:** Reeded

Date	Mintage	F12	VF20	XF40	MS60	MS63
AH1425-2004	—	—	—	—	18.00	25.00

KM# 32 500 RIALS
13.00 g., Copper-Nickel, 30 mm. **Subject:** City of San'a as Arab Cultural Capital **Note:** Pin added to reverse

Date	Mintage	F12	VF20	XF40	MS60	MS63
2004	—	—	—	—	22.00	30.00

KM# 31 1000 RIALS
73.30 g., Pewter, 60.3 mm. **Subject:** City of San'a **Obv:** Value **Rev:** City gate below artwork **Edge:** Plain **Note:** Illustration reduced.

Date	Mintage	F12	VF20	XF40	MS60	MS63
AH1425-2004	—	—	—	—	45.00	60.00

KM# 33 5000 RIALS
22.20 g., 0.900 Silver 0.6382 oz. ASW, 37 mm. **Subject:** President Ali Abdullah Saleh

Date	Mintage	F12	VF20	XF40	MS60	MS63
AH1424-2003	—	—	—	—	30.00	45.00

YUGOSLAVIA

The Federal Republic of Yugoslavia, formerly the Socialist Federal Republic of Yugoslavia, a Balkan country located on the east shore of the Adriatic Sea, has an area of 39,450 sq. mi. (102,173 sq. km.) and a population of 10.5 million. Capital: Belgrade. The chief industries are agriculture, mining, manufacturing and tourism. Machinery, nonferrous metals, meat and fabrics are exported.

The name Yugoslavia appears on the coinage in letters of the Cyrillic alphabet alone until formation of the Federated Peoples Republic of Yugoslavia in 1953, after which both the Cyrillic and Latin alphabets are employed. From 1965, the coin denomination appears in the 4 different languages of the federated republics in letters of both the Cyrillic and Latin alphabets.

MONETARY SYSTEM
100 Para = 1 Dinar

FEDERAL REPUBLIC

STANDARD COINAGE

KM# 180 DINAR
4.40 g., Copper-Nickel-Zinc, 20 mm. **Obv:** National arms within circle **Rev:** Building **Edge:** Reeded

Date	Mintage	F12	VF20	XF40	MS60	MS63
2002	60,780,000	—	—	—	0.25	0.45

KM# 181 2 DINARA
5.20 g., Copper-Nickel-Zinc, 21.9 mm. **Obv:** National arms within circle **Rev:** Church **Edge:** Reeded

Date	Mintage	F12	VF20	XF40	MS60	MS63
2002	71,053,000	—	—	—	0.30	0.50

KM# 182 5 DINARA
6.30 g., Copper-Nickel-Zinc, 24 mm. **Obv:** National arms **Rev:** Domed building, denomination and date at left **Edge:** Reeded

Date	Mintage	F12	VF20	XF40	MS60	MS63
2002	30,966,000	—	—	—	1.25	1.50

ZAMBIA

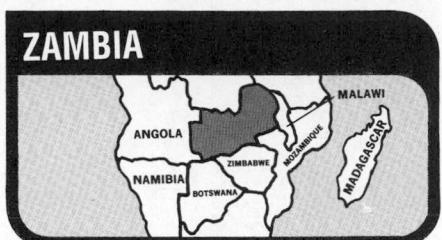

The Republic of Zambia (formerly Northern Rhodesia), a landlocked country in south-central Africa, has an area of 290,586 sq. mi. (752,610 sq. km.) and a population of*7.9 million. Capital: Lusaka. The economy of Zambia is based principally on copper, of which Zambia is the world's third largest producer. Copper, zinc, lead, cobalt and tobacco are exported. Zambia is a member of the Commonwealth of Nations. The President is the Head of State and the Head of Government.

REPUBLIC

DECIMAL COINAGE
100 Ngwee = 1 Kwacha

KM# 156 500 KWACHA
15.00 g., 0.999 Silver 0.4787 oz. ASW, 34.2 mm. **Subject:** Football World Champion - 1954 Germany **Obv:** Crowned head right within circle above arms with supporters and value **Rev:** Soccer game scene in front of Berlin Wall **Edge:** Plain

Date	Mintage	F12	VF20	XF40	MS60	MS63
2001	—	PF63 32.00	PF65 35.00			

KM# 276 500 KWACHA
15.00 g., 0.925 Silver 0.4432 oz. ASW **Subject:** World Cup games of 1954 **Rev:** Games scene from 1954

Date	Mintage	F12	VF20	XF40	MS60	MS63
2001	—	PF63 22.00	PF65 25.00			

KM# 174 500 KWACHA
15.00 g., 0.999 Silver 0.4787 oz. ASW, 34.2 mm. **Subject:** 1972 Munich Olympics **Obv:** Crowned head right above arms with supporters **Rev:** Torch runner in stadium **Edge:** Reeded

Date	Mintage	F12	VF20	XF40	MS60	MS63
2002	—	PF63 25.00	PF65 28.00			

KM# 74 1000 KWACHA
29.00 g., Copper-Nickel, 40 mm. **Obv:** Crowned head right above arms with supporters divides date **Rev:** Dated calendar within circular design **Shape:** 7-sided

Date	Mintage	F12	VF20	XF40	MS60	MS63
2002 Proof-like	—	—	—	—	—	12.50
2003 Proof-like	—	—	—	—	—	12.50
2004 Proof-like	—	—	—	—	—	12.50

KM# 87 1000 KWACHA
28.91 g., Copper-Nickel, 38 mm. **Series:** Patrons of the Ocean **Obv:** Arms with supporters above crowned head right within circle **Rev:** Loggerhead sea turtle **Edge:** Reeded

Date	Mintage	F12	VF20	XF40	MS60	MS63
2001	—	PF63 17.00				

KM# 88 1000 KWACHA

28.91 g., Copper-Nickel **Series:** Patrons of the Ocean **Obv:** Arms with supporters above crowned head right within circle **Rev:** Coelacanth

Date	Mintage	F12	VF20	XF40	MS60	MS63
2001	—	PF63 17.00				

KM# 89 1000 KWACHA

28.91 g., Copper-Nickel **Series:** Patrons of the Ocean **Obv:** Arms with supporters above crowned head right within circle **Rev:** Sea horse and fish

Date	Mintage	F12	VF20	XF40	MS60	MS63
2001	—	PF63 17.00				

KM# 90 1000 KWACHA

28.91 g., Copper-Nickel **Series:** Patrons of the Ocean **Obv:** Arms with supporters above crowned head right within circle **Rev:** Two dolphins

Date	Mintage	F12	VF20	XF40	MS60	MS63
2001	—	PF63 17.00				

KM# 181 1000 KWACHA

20.03 g., Silver **Subject:** 75th Birthday Queen Elizabeth II **Obv:** Crowned head of Elizabeth II in circle, national arms below **Obv. Legend:** BANK OF ZAMBIA **Rev:** Bust of Elizabeth II facing wearing tiara **Edge:** Reeded

Date	Mintage	F12	VF20	XF40	MS60	MS63
2001		PF63 25.00	PF65 30.00			

KM# 277 1000 KWACHA

20.00 g., 0.925 Silver 0.591 oz. ASW **Subject:** Princess Diana, 4th Anniversary of Death

Date	Mintage	F12	VF20	XF40	MS60	MS63
2001		PF63 35.00	PF65 40.00			

KM# 279 1000 KWACHA

29.00 g., Copper-Nickel, 40 mm. **Rev:** 2002 Calender

Date	Mintage	F12	VF20	XF40	MS60	MS63
2001	—					15.00

KM# 159 1000 KWACHA

31.22 g., 0.999 Silver 0.9963 oz. ASW, 38.6 mm. **Obv:** Crowned head right divides date above arms with supporters **Rev:** Bust 1/4 left **Edge:** Reeded

Date	Mintage	F12	VF20	XF40	MS60	MS63
2002	—			—	42.50	45.00

KM# 160 1000 KWACHA

29.30 g., Silver Plated Bronze, 38.6 mm. **Subject:** Pope John Paul II **Obv:** National arms **Rev:** Pope saying mass **Edge:** Reeded **Note:** Specific gravity 9.099

Date	Mintage	F12	VF20	XF40	MS60	MS63
2003	—	PF63 20.00	PF65 22.00			

KM# 167 1000 KWACHA

25.00 g., Copper-Nickel, 38.6 mm. **Subject:** 50th Anniversary of Elizabeth II's Coronation **Obv:** Crowned head right above arms with supporters **Rev:** Crown on pillow above crossed scepters **Edge:** Reeded

Date	Mintage	F12	VF20	XF40	MS60	MS63
ND(2003)	—				8.50	10.00

KM# 169 1000 KWACHA

25.00 g., Copper-Nickel, 38.6 mm. **Obv:** Crowned head right above arms with supporters **Rev:** Prince William on jet ski **Edge:** Reeded

Date	Mintage	F12	VF20	XF40	MS60	MS63
2003	—				8.50	10.00

KM# 171 1000 KWACHA

25.00 g., Copper-Nickel, 38.6 mm. **Obv:** Crowned head right above arms with supporters **Rev:** Crowned bust facing **Edge:** Reeded

Date	Mintage	F12	VF20	XF40	MS60	MS63
ND(2003)	—				8.50	10.00

KM# 172 1000 KWACHA

25.00 g., 0.925 Silver 0.7387 oz. ASW, 38.6 mm. **Obv:** Crowned head right above arms with supporters **Rev:** Crowned bust facing **Edge:** Reeded

Date	Mintage	F12	VF20	XF40	MS60	MS63
ND(2003)	5,000	PF63 40.00	PF65 45.00			

KM# 183 1000 KWACHA

7.77 g., 0.999 Silver 0.248 oz. ASW, 26 mm. **Rev:** Elephant pair

Date	Mintage	F12	VF20	XF40	MS60	MS63
2003	2,000	PF63 18.00				

KM# 285 1000 KWACHA

29.00 g., Copper-Nickel, 40 mm. **Rev:** 2003 Calender

Date	Mintage	F12	VF20	XF40	MS60	MS63
2003	—					15.00

KM# 287 1000 KWACHA

29.00 g., Copper-Nickel, 40 mm. **Rev:** 2004 Calender

Date	Mintage	F12	VF20	XF40	MS60	MS63
2004	—					15.00

KM# 290 1000 KWACHA

7.78 g., 0.999 Silver 0.2483 oz. ASW **Rev:** Elephant

Date	Mintage	F12	VF20	XF40	MS60	MS63
2009	—	PF63 20.00	PF65 22.00			

KM# 199 1000 KWACHA

Silver, 38 mm. **Subject:** Deadly Bugs **Obv:** National arms **Rev:** Harvest Ant in colored insert

Date	Mintage	F12	VF20	XF40	MS60	MS63
2010	—	PF63 35.00	PF65 40.00			

KM# 200 1000 KWACHA

Silver, 38 mm. **Subject:** Deadly Bugs **Obv:** National arms **Rev:** Giant Hornet in colored insert

Date	Mintage	F12	VF20	XF40	MS60	MS63
2010	—	PF63 35.00	PF65 40.00			

KM# 201 1000 KWACHA
Silver, 38 mm. **Subject:** Deadly Bugs **Obv:** National arms **Rev:** Mosquito in multicolor insert

Date	Mintage	F12	VF20	XF40	MS60	MS63
2010	—	PF63 35.00	PF65 40.00			

KM# 202 1000 KWACHA
Silver, 38 mm. **Subject:** Deadly Bugs **Obv:** National arms **Rev:** Scorpion

Date	Mintage	F12	VF20	XF40	MS60	MS63
2010 Proof	—	—	—	—	—	40.00

KM# 203 1000 KWACHA
Silver, 38 mm. **Subject:** Deadly Bugs **Obv:** National arms **Rev:** Tsetse Fly

Date	Mintage	F12	VF20	XF40	MS60	MS63
2010	—	PF63 35.00	PF65 40.00			

KM# 118 2000 KWACHA
31.10 g., 0.999 Silver 0.9926 oz. ASW, 38.6 mm. **Subject:** Centennial of the Anglo-Japanese Alliance **Obv:** Queen Elizabeth **Rev:** Fantasy Japanese coin design **Edge:** Reeded

Date	Mintage	F12	VF20	XF40	MS60	MS63
2002	500	—	—	—	80.00	85.00

KM# 184 2000 KWACHA
15.15 g., 0.999 Silver 0.4835 oz. ASW **Rev:** Elephant pair

Date	Mintage	F12	VF20	XF40	MS60	MS63
2003	2,000	PF63 25.00	PF65 30.00			

KM# 291 2000 KWACHA
15.55 g., 0.999 Silver 0.4962 oz. ASW **Rev:** Elephant

Date	Mintage	F12	VF20	XF40	MS60	MS63
2009	—	PF63 32.00	PF65 35.00			

KM# 175 4000 KWACHA
23.00 g., 0.999 Silver 0.734 oz. ASW, 40 mm. **Obv:** Head with tiara right divides date above arms **Rev:** Dated calendar **Shape:** Seven-sided

Date	Mintage	F12	VF20	XF40	MS60	MS63
2002 Prooflike	—	—	—	—	—	45.00
2003 Prooflike	15,000	—	—	—	—	45.00
2004 Prooflike	5,000	—	—	—	—	45.00

KM# 85 4000 KWACHA
25.10 g., 0.925 Silver 0.7417 oz. ASW, 37.9 mm. **Series:** Wildlife Protection **Obv:** Crowned head right below arms **Rev:** Lion head hologram **Edge:** Reeded **Note:** Lighter weight and smaller diameter than official specifications

Date	Mintage	F12	VF20	XF40	MS60	MS63
2001	—	PF63 60.00	PF65 65.00			

KM# 166 4000 KWACHA
25.00 g., 0.925 Silver 0.7387 oz. ASW, 38.6 mm. **Subject:** Queen Elizabeth's 75th Birthday **Obv:** Crowned head right above arms with supporters **Rev:** Bust with hat facing **Edge:** Reeded

Date	Mintage	F12	VF20	XF40	MS60	MS63
2001	2,000	PF63 35.00	PF65 40.00			

KM# 110 4000 KWACHA
20.00 g., 0.999 Silver 0.6382 oz. ASW, 37.9 mm. **Series:** Patrons of the Ocean **Obv:** Crowned head right within circle below arms with supporters **Rev:** Loggerhead sea turtle **Edge:** Reeded

Date	Mintage	F12	VF20	XF40	MS60	MS63
2001	—	PF63 30.00	PF65 32.00			

KM# 111 4000 KWACHA
20.00 g., 0.999 Silver 0.6382 oz. ASW **Series:** Patrons of the Ocean **Obv:** Crowned head right divides date below arms with supporters **Rev:** Coelacanth fish

Date	Mintage	F12	VF20	XF40	MS60	MS63
2001	—	PF63 35.00	PF65 38.00			

KM# 112 4000 KWACHA
20.00 g., 0.999 Silver 0.6382 oz. ASW **Series:** Patrons of the Ocean **Obv:** Crowned head right divides date below arms with supporters **Rev:** Sea horse and fish

Date	Mintage	F12	VF20	XF40	MS60	MS63
2001	—	PF63 32.00	PF65 35.00			

KM# 113 4000 KWACHA
20.00 g., 0.999 Silver 0.6382 oz. ASW **Series:** Patrons of the Ocean **Obv:** Crowned head right divides date below arms with supporters **Rev:** Two dolphins

Date	Mintage	F12	VF20	XF40	MS60	MS63
2001	—	PF63 35.00	PF65 38.00			

KM# 114 4000 KWACHA
50.00 g., 0.999 Silver 1.5956 oz. ASW **Subject:** Illusion **Obv:** Arms with supporters below crowned head right **Rev:** Cat within window **Edge:** Plain **Note:** 50x50mm

Date	Mintage	F12	VF20	XF40	MS60	MS63
2001	—	PF63 75.00	PF65 85.00			

KM# 275 4000 KWACHA
50.00 g., 0.999 Silver 1.5956 oz. ASW, 50x50 mm. **Rev:** Cat in window illustration

Date	Mintage	F12	VF20	XF40	MS60	MS63
2001	5,000	PF63 65.00	PF65 75.00			

KM# 280 4000 KWACHA
23.00 g., 0.999 Silver 0.734 oz. ASW, 40 mm. **Rev:** 2002 Calender

Date	Mintage	F12	VF20	XF40	MS60	MS63
2001						40.00

KM# 281 4000 KWACHA
31.10 g., 0.9999 Silver 0.9934 oz. ASW **Subject:** Japan and Great Britain relations, 100th Anniversary **Obv:** Elizabeth II and magazine **Rev:** Japanese 1 yen coin

Date	Mintage	F12	VF20	XF40	MS60	MS63
2002	1,000	PF63 110	PF65 125			

KM# 282 4000 KWACHA
Silver ASW **Subject:** Relations between Japan and Great Britain
Japan and Great Britain relations, 100th Anniversary **Rev:** Victoria and Hong Kong dollar coin

Date	Mintage	F12	VF20	XF40	MS60	MS63
2002		PF63 110	PF65 125			

KM# 168 4000 KWACHA
25.00 g., 0.925 Silver 0.7387 oz. ASW, 38.6 mm. **Subject:** 50th Anniversary of Elizabeth II's Coronation **Obv:** Crowned head right above arms with supporters **Rev:** Crown on pillow above crossed scepters **Edge:** Reeded

Date	Mintage	F12	VF20	XF40	MS60	MS63
ND(2003)	5,000	PF63 40.00	PF65 45.00			

KM# 170 4000 KWACHA
25.00 g., 0.925 Silver 0.7387 oz. ASW, 38.6 mm. **Obv:** Crowned head right above arms with supporters **Rev:** Prince William on jet ski **Edge:** Reeded

Date	Mintage	F12	VF20	XF40	MS60	MS63
2003	5,000	PF63 40.00	PF65 45.00			

KM# 286 4000 KWACHA
23.00 g., 0.999 Silver 0.734 oz. ASW, 40 mm. **Rev:** 2003 Calender

Date	Mintage	F12	VF20	XF40	MS60	MS63
2003	5,000	—	—	—	—	35.00

KM# 288 4000 KWACHA
23.00 g., 0.999 Silver 0.734 oz. ASW, 40 mm. **Rev:** 2004 Calender

Date	Mintage	F12	VF20	XF40	MS60	MS63
2004	—	—	—	—	—	35.00

KM# 117 5000 KWACHA
31.30 g., 0.999 Silver 0.9988 oz. ASW, 38.6 mm. **Subject:** African Wildlife **Obv:** Arms with supporters **Rev:** Elephant mother and calf grazing on grass **Edge:** Reeded

Date	Mintage	F12	VF20	XF40	MS60	MS63
2001 Matte	—	—	—	—	42.00	45.00
2001		PF63 42.00	PF65 45.00			
Note: 50						

KM# 278 5000 KWACHA
31.10 g., 0.999 Silver 0.9925 oz. ASW, 38.61 mm. **Rev:** Elephant

Date	Mintage	F12	VF20	XF40	MS60	MS63
2001	—	—	—	—	—	27.50
2001		PF63 55.00	PF65 60.00			

KM# 143 5000 KWACHA
28.86 g., 0.999 Silver 0.921 oz. ASW, 38.5 mm. **Subject:** African Wildlife **Obv:** Arms with supporters **Rev:** Elephant **Edge:** Reeded

Date	Mintage	F12	VF20	XF40	MS60	MS63
2002 Matte	—	—	—	—	42.00	45.00
2002		PF63 45.00	PF65 50.00			

KM# 284 5000 KWACHA
31.10 g., 0.999 Silver 0.9925 oz. ASW **Obv:** National arms **Rev:** Elephant

Date	Mintage	F12	VF20	XF40	MS60	MS63
2002	—	—	—	—	—	27.50
2002		PF63 55.00	PF65 60.00			

KM# 142 5000 KWACHA
28.64 g., 0.999 Silver 0.914 oz. ASW, 38.5 mm. **Subject:** African Wildlife **Obv:** Queen Elizabeth's portrait above national arms and denomination **Rev:** Adult and juvenile elephants **Edge:** Reeded

Date	Mintage	F12	VF20	XF40	MS60	MS63
2002	—	PF63 45.00	PF65 50.00			
2002 Matte	—	—	—	—	42.00	45.00

KM# 185 5000 KWACHA
31.11 g., 0.999 Silver 0.9926 oz. ASW **Rev:** Elephant pair

Date	Mintage	F12	VF20	XF40	MS60	MS63
2003	2,000	PF63 50.00	PF65 55.00			

KM# 186 5000 KWACHA
31.11 g., 0.999 Silver 0.9926 oz. ASW **Obv:** Head right **Rev:** Multicolor elephant pair

Date	Mintage	F12	VF20	XF40	MS60	MS63
2003	—	PF63 38.00	PF65 42.00			

KM# 187 5000 KWACHA
31.11 g., 0.999 Silver 0.9926 oz. ASW, 40 mm. **Rev:** Elephant pair, partially gilt

Date	Mintage	F12	VF20	XF40	MS60	MS63
2003	—	PF63 45.00	PF65 50.00			

KM# 165 5000 KWACHA
31.10 g., 0.999 Silver 0.9925 oz. ASW, 38.5 mm. **Obv:** Crowned bust right divides date **Rev:** Two African elephants

Edge: Reeded

Date	Mintage	F12	VF20	XF40	MS60	MS63
2003 Matte				—	42.00	45.00
2003		PF63 45.00	PF65 50.00			

KM# 292 5000 KWACHA
31.10 g., 0.999 Silver 0.9925 oz. ASW **Rev:** Elephant

Date	Mintage	F12	VF20	XF40	MS60	MS63
2009	—	—	—	—	—	27.50
2009		PF63 55.00	PF65 60.00			

KM# 283 6000 KWACHA
Gold AGW **Subject:** Elizabeth II, 50th Anniversary of Coronation **Obv:** St. George and dragon **Rev:** Elizabeth II and Buckingham Palace in color

Date	Mintage	F12	VF20	XF40	MS60	MS63
2002 Proof						

KM# 188 10000 KWACHA
62.21 g., 0.999 Silver 1.9852 oz. ASW, 50 mm. **Rev:** Two elephants

Date	Mintage	F12	VF20	XF40	MS60	MS63
2003	2,000	PF63 125	PF65 150			

KM# 289 10000 KWACHA
33.63 g., 0.925 Silver 0.9936 oz. ASW, 38.72 mm. **Subject:** Bank of Zambia, 40th Anniversary **Obv:** National arms **Rev:** Hands with soil

Date	Mintage	F12	VF20	XF40	MS60	MS63
2004	1,000	PF63 110	PF65 125			

KM# 293 10000 KWACHA
62.20 g., 0.999 Silver 1.9849 oz. ASW **Rev:** Elephant

Date	Mintage	F12	VF20	XF40	MS60	MS63
2009	—	PF63 110	PF65 125			

KM# 94 40000 KWACHA
31.10 g., 0.9999 Gold 0.9935 oz. AGW, 37.9 mm. **Series:** Wildlife Protection **Obv:** Arms with supporters above crowned head right **Rev:** Holographic lion head **Edge:** Reeded

Date	Mintage	F12	VF20	XF40	MS60	MS63
2001	—	PF65 1,750				

KM# 153.1 40000 KWACHA
47.54 g., 0.9166 Gold 1.392 oz. AGW, 39 mm. **Subject:** Queen Victoria **Obv:** Crowned head right within ornate frame divides date above arms with supporters **Rev:** Crowned veiled bust of Queen Victoria left **Edge:** Reeded

Date	Mintage	F12	VF20	XF40	MS60	MS63
2001 Proof	1	—	—	—	—	—
Note: Medallic die alignment						

KM# 153.2 40000 KWACHA
47.54 g., 0.9166 Gold 1.392 oz. AGW, 39 mm. **Subject:** Queen Victoria **Obv:** Crowned head right within ornate frame divides date above arms with supporters **Rev:** Crowned veiled bust of Queen Victoria left **Edge:** Reeded

Date	Mintage	F12	VF20	XF40	MS60	MS63
2001 Matte	1	—	—	—	—	—

Note: Coin die alignment

KM# 154.1 40000 KWACHA
47.54 g., 0.9166 Gold 1.392 oz. AGW, 39 mm. **Subject:** Edward VII **Obv:** Crowned head right within ornate frame divides date above arms with supporters **Rev:** Crowned bust of King Edward VII right **Edge:** Reeded

Date	Mintage	F12	VF20	XF40	MS60	MS63
2001 Proof	1	—	—	—	—	—

Note: Medallic die alignment

KM# 154.2 40000 KWACHA
47.54 g., 0.9166 Gold 1.392 oz. AGW, 39 mm. **Subject:** Edward VII **Obv:** Crowned head right within ornate frame divides date above arms with supporters **Rev:** Crowned bust of King Edward VII right **Edge:** Reeded

Date	Mintage	F12	VF20	XF40	MS60	MS63
2001 Matte	1	—	—	—	—	—

Note: Coin die alignment

REFORM COINAGE
2013: 1000 old Kwacha = 1 new Kwacha

KM# 205 5 NGWEE
2.50 g., Nickel Plated Iron, 19 mm. **Obv:** National arms **Rev:** Bird right

Date	Mintage	F12	VF20	XF40	MS60	MS63
2012	—	—	—	—	0.50	1.00

KM# 206 10 NGWEE
3.00 g., Brass Plated Iron, 20 mm. **Obv:** National Arms **Rev:** Antelope head left

Date	Mintage	F12	VF20	XF40	MS60	MS63
2012	—	—	—	—	0.50	1.00

KM# 208 50 NGWEE
3.50 g., Copper Plated Iron, 21 mm. **Obv:** National arms **Rev:** Elephant head left

Date	Mintage	F12	VF20	XF40	MS60	MS63
2012	—	—	—	—	0.75	1.50

KM# 209 KWACHA
5.00 g., Nickel Plated Iron, 24 mm. **Obv:** National arms **Rev:** Bird left

Date	Mintage	F12	VF20	XF40	MS60	MS63
2012	—	—	—	—	1.25	2.00

ZIMBABWE

The Republic of Zimbabwe (formerly the Republic of Rhodesia or Southern Rhodesia), located in the east-central part of southern Africa, has an area of 150,804 sq. mi. (390,580 sq. km.) and a population of *10.1 million. Capital: Harare (formerly Salisbury). The economy is based on agriculture and mining. Tobacco, sugar, asbestos, copper, chrome, ore and coal are exported.

On April 18, 1980 pursuant to an act of the British Parliament, the colony of Southern Rhodesia became independent as the Republic of Zimbabwe, a member of the Commonwealth of Nations, until recently suspended.

MONETARY SYSTEM
100 Cents = 1 Dollar

MINT
Harare

REPUBLIC

DECIMAL COINAGE

KM# 3a 10 CENTS
Nickel Plated Steel, 20 mm. **Obv:** National emblem **Rev:** Baobab tree, value **Edge:** Plain

Date	Mintage	F12	VF20	XF40	MS60	MS63
2001	—	—	0.15	0.30	0.75	1.00
2002	—	—	0.15	0.30	0.75	1.00
2003	—	—	0.15	0.30	0.75	1.00

KM# 4a 20 CENTS
Nickel Plated Steel, 23 mm. **Obv:** National emblem **Rev:** Birchenough Bridge over the Sabi River, value below **Edge:** Plain

Date	Mintage	F12	VF20	XF40	MS60	MS63
2001	—	—	0.20	0.40	1.25	1.50
2002	—	—	0.20	0.40	1.25	1.50
2003	—	—	0.20	0.40	1.25	1.50

KM# 5a 50 CENTS
Nickel Plated Steel, 26 mm. **Obv:** National emblem **Rev:** Radiant sun rising, symbolic of independence, value **Edge:** Plain

Date	Mintage	F12	VF20	XF40	MS60	MS63
2001	—	—	0.40	1.00	1.75	2.00
2002	—	—	0.40	1.00	1.75	2.00
2003	—	—	0.40	1.00	1.75	2.00

KM# 6a DOLLAR
Nickel Plated Steel, 29 mm. **Obv:** National emblem **Rev:** Zimbabwe ruins amongst trees, value **Edge:** Reeded

Date	Mintage	F12	VF20	XF40	MS60	MS63
2001	—	—	1.00	1.50	2.50	3.00
2002	—	—	1.00	1.50	2.50	3.00
2003	—	—	1.00	1.50	2.50	3.00

KM# 12a 2 DOLLARS
Brass Plated Steel, 24.5 mm. **Obv:** National emblem **Rev:** Pangolin below value **Edge:** Reeded

Date	Mintage	F12	VF20	XF40	MS60	MS63
2001	—	—	1.25	2.25	4.00	5.00
2002	—	—	1.25	2.25	4.00	5.00
2003	—	—	1.25	2.25	4.00	5.00

KM# 13 5 DOLLARS
9.05 g., Bi-Metallic, 27.4 mm. **Obv:** National emblem **Rev:** Rhinoceros standing right **Edge:** Reeded

Date	Mintage	F12	VF20	XF40	MS60	MS63
2001	—	—	—	—	5.00	6.00
2002	—	—	—	—	5.00	6.00
2003	—	—	—	—	5.00	6.00

KM# 14 10 DOLLARS
5.20 g., Nickel Plated Steel, 21.5 mm. **Obv:** National emblem **Rev:** Water buffalo **Edge:** Reeded

Date	Mintage	F12	VF20	XF40	MS60	MS63
2003	—	—	—	1.50	2.50	3.50

KM# 15 25 DOLLARS
7.33 g., Nickel Plated Steel, 24.5 mm. **Obv:** National emblem **Rev:** Military monument **Edge:** Segmented reeding

Date	Mintage	F12	VF20	XF40	MS60	MS63
2003	—	—	—	1.75	3.00	4.00

SILVER BULLION VALUE CHART $15 to $25

Oz.	15.00	15.50	16.00	16.50	17.00	17.50	18.00	18.50	19.00	19.50	20.00	20.50	21.00	21.50	22.00	22.50	23.00	23.50	24.00	24.50	25.00	Oz.
0.001	0.015	0.016	0.016	0.017	0.017	0.018	0.018	0.019	0.019	0.020	0.020	0.021	0.021	0.022	0.022	0.023	0.023	0.024	0.024	0.025	0.025	0.001
0.002	0.030	0.031	0.032	0.033	0.034	0.035	0.036	0.037	0.038	0.039	0.040	0.041	0.042	0.043	0.044	0.045	0.046	0.047	0.048	0.049	0.050	0.002
0.003	0.045	0.047	0.048	0.050	0.051	0.053	0.054	0.056	0.057	0.059	0.060	0.062	0.063	0.065	0.066	0.068	0.069	0.071	0.072	0.074	0.075	0.003
0.004	0.060	0.062	0.064	0.066	0.068	0.070	0.072	0.074	0.076	0.078	0.080	0.082	0.084	0.086	0.088	0.090	0.092	0.094	0.096	0.098	0.100	0.004
0.005	0.075	0.078	0.080	0.083	0.085	0.088	0.090	0.093	0.095	0.098	0.100	0.103	0.105	0.108	0.110	0.113	0.115	0.118	0.120	0.123	0.125	0.005
0.006	0.090	0.093	0.096	0.099	0.102	0.105	0.108	0.111	0.114	0.117	0.120	0.123	0.126	0.129	0.132	0.135	0.138	0.141	0.144	0.147	0.150	0.006
0.007	0.105	0.109	0.112	0.116	0.119	0.123	0.126	0.130	0.133	0.137	0.140	0.144	0.147	0.151	0.154	0.158	0.161	0.165	0.168	0.172	0.175	0.007
0.008	0.120	0.124	0.128	0.132	0.136	0.140	0.144	0.148	0.152	0.156	0.160	0.164	0.168	0.172	0.176	0.180	0.184	0.188	0.192	0.196	0.200	0.008
0.009	0.135	0.140	0.144	0.149	0.153	0.158	0.162	0.167	0.171	0.176	0.180	0.185	0.189	0.194	0.198	0.203	0.207	0.212	0.216	0.221	0.225	0.009
0.010	0.150	0.155	0.160	0.165	0.170	0.175	0.180	0.185	0.190	0.195	0.200	0.205	0.210	0.215	0.220	0.225	0.230	0.235	0.240	0.245	0.250	0.010
0.020	0.300	0.310	0.320	0.330	0.340	0.350	0.360	0.370	0.380	0.390	0.400	0.410	0.420	0.430	0.440	0.450	0.460	0.470	0.480	0.490	0.500	0.020
0.030	0.450	0.465	0.480	0.495	0.510	0.525	0.540	0.555	0.570	0.585	0.600	0.615	0.630	0.645	0.660	0.675	0.690	0.705	0.720	0.735	0.750	0.030
0.040	0.600	0.620	0.640	0.660	0.680	0.700	0.720	0.740	0.760	0.780	0.800	0.820	0.840	0.860	0.880	0.900	0.920	0.940	0.960	0.980	1.000	0.040
0.050	0.750	0.775	0.800	0.825	0.850	0.875	0.900	0.925	0.950	0.975	1.000	1.025	1.050	1.075	1.100	1.125	1.150	1.175	1.200	1.225	1.250	0.050
0.060	0.900	0.930	0.960	0.990	1.020	1.050	1.080	1.110	1.140	1.170	1.200	1.230	1.260	1.290	1.320	1.350	1.380	1.410	1.440	1.470	1.500	0.060
0.070	1.050	1.085	1.120	1.155	1.190	1.225	1.260	1.295	1.330	1.365	1.400	1.435	1.470	1.505	1.540	1.575	1.610	1.645	1.680	1.715	1.750	0.070
0.080	1.200	1.240	1.280	1.320	1.360	1.400	1.440	1.480	1.520	1.560	1.600	1.640	1.680	1.720	1.760	1.800	1.840	1.880	1.920	1.960	2.000	0.080
0.090	1.350	1.395	1.440	1.485	1.530	1.575	1.620	1.665	1.710	1.755	1.800	1.845	1.890	1.935	1.980	2.025	2.070	2.115	2.160	2.205	2.250	0.090
0.100	1.500	1.550	1.600	1.650	1.700	1.750	1.800	1.850	1.900	1.950	2.000	2.050	2.100	2.150	2.200	2.250	2.300	2.350	2.400	2.450	2.500	0.100
0.110	1.650	1.705	1.760	1.815	1.870	1.925	1.980	2.035	2.090	2.145	2.200	2.255	2.310	2.365	2.420	2.475	2.530	2.585	2.640	2.695	2.750	0.110
0.120	1.800	1.860	1.920	1.980	2.040	2.100	2.160	2.220	2.280	2.340	2.400	2.460	2.520	2.580	2.640	2.700	2.760	2.820	2.880	2.940	3.000	0.120
0.130	1.950	2.015	2.080	2.145	2.210	2.275	2.340	2.405	2.470	2.535	2.600	2.665	2.730	2.795	2.860	2.925	2.990	3.055	3.120	3.185	3.250	0.130
0.140	2.100	2.170	2.240	2.310	2.380	2.450	2.520	2.590	2.660	2.730	2.800	2.870	2.940	3.010	3.080	3.150	3.220	3.290	3.360	3.430	3.500	0.140
0.150	2.250	2.325	2.400	2.475	2.550	2.625	2.700	2.775	2.850	2.925	3.000	3.075	3.150	3.225	3.300	3.375	3.450	3.525	3.600	3.675	3.750	0.150
0.160	2.400	2.480	2.560	2.640	2.720	2.800	2.880	2.960	3.040	3.120	3.200	3.280	3.360	3.440	3.520	3.600	3.680	3.760	3.840	3.920	4.000	0.160
0.170	2.550	2.635	2.720	2.805	2.890	2.975	3.060	3.145	3.230	3.315	3.400	3.485	3.570	3.655	3.740	3.825	3.910	3.995	4.080	4.165	4.250	0.170
0.180	2.700	2.790	2.880	2.970	3.060	3.150	3.240	3.330	3.420	3.510	3.600	3.690	3.780	3.870	3.960	4.050	4.140	4.230	4.320	4.410	4.500	0.180
0.190	2.850	2.945	3.040	3.135	3.230	3.325	3.420	3.515	3.610	3.705	3.800	3.895	3.990	4.085	4.180	4.275	4.370	4.465	4.560	4.655	4.750	0.190
0.200	3.000	3.100	3.200	3.300	3.400	3.500	3.600	3.700	3.800	3.900	4.000	4.100	4.200	4.300	4.400	4.500	4.600	4.700	4.800	4.900	5.000	0.200
0.210	3.150	3.255	3.360	3.465	3.570	3.675	3.780	3.885	3.990	4.095	4.200	4.305	4.410	4.515	4.620	4.725	4.830	4.935	5.040	5.145	5.250	0.210
0.220	3.300	3.410	3.520	3.630	3.740	3.850	3.960	4.070	4.180	4.290	4.400	4.510	4.620	4.730	4.840	4.950	5.060	5.170	5.280	5.390	5.500	0.220
0.230	3.450	3.565	3.680	3.795	3.910	4.025	4.140	4.255	4.370	4.485	4.600	4.715	4.830	4.945	5.060	5.175	5.290	5.405	5.520	5.635	5.750	0.230
0.240	3.600	3.720	3.840	3.960	4.080	4.200	4.320	4.440	4.560	4.680	4.800	4.920	5.040	5.160	5.280	5.400	5.520	5.640	5.760	5.880	6.000	0.240
0.250	3.750	3.875	4.000	4.125	4.250	4.375	4.500	4.625	4.750	4.875	5.000	5.125	5.250	5.375	5.500	5.625	5.750	5.875	6.000	6.125	6.250	0.250
0.260	3.900	4.030	4.160	4.290	4.420	4.550	4.680	4.810	4.940	5.070	5.200	5.330	5.460	5.590	5.720	5.850	5.980	6.110	6.240	6.370	6.500	0.260
0.270	4.050	4.185	4.320	4.455	4.590	4.725	4.860	4.995	5.130	5.265	5.400	5.535	5.670	5.805	5.940	6.075	6.210	6.345	6.480	6.615	6.750	0.270
0.280	4.200	4.340	4.480	4.620	4.760	4.900	5.040	5.180	5.320	5.460	5.600	5.740	5.880	6.020	6.160	6.300	6.440	6.580	6.720	6.860	7.000	0.280
0.290	4.350	4.495	4.640	4.785	4.930	5.075	5.220	5.365	5.510	5.655	5.800	5.945	6.090	6.235	6.380	6.525	6.670	6.815	6.960	7.105	7.250	0.290
0.300	4.500	4.650	4.800	4.950	5.100	5.250	5.400	5.550	5.700	5.850	6.000	6.150	6.300	6.450	6.600	6.750	6.900	7.050	7.200	7.350	7.500	0.300
0.310	4.650	4.805	4.960	5.115	5.270	5.425	5.580	5.735	5.890	6.045	6.200	6.355	6.510	6.665	6.820	6.975	7.130	7.285	7.440	7.595	7.750	0.310
0.320	4.800	4.960	5.120	5.280	5.440	5.600	5.760	5.920	6.080	6.240	6.400	6.560	6.720	6.880	7.040	7.200	7.360	7.520	7.680	7.840	8.000	0.320
0.330	4.950	5.115	5.280	5.445	5.610	5.775	5.940	6.105	6.270	6.435	6.600	6.765	6.930	7.095	7.260	7.425	7.590	7.755	7.920	8.085	8.250	0.330
0.340	5.100	5.270	5.440	5.610	5.780	5.950	6.120	6.290	6.460	6.630	6.800	6.970	7.140	7.310	7.480	7.650	7.820	7.990	8.160	8.330	8.500	0.340
0.350	5.250	5.425	5.600	5.775	5.950	6.125	6.300	6.475	6.650	6.825	7.000	7.175	7.350	7.525	7.700	7.875	8.050	8.225	8.400	8.575	8.750	0.350
0.360	5.400	5.580	5.760	5.940	6.120	6.300	6.480	6.660	6.840	7.020	7.200	7.380	7.560	7.740	7.920	8.100	8.280	8.460	8.640	8.820	9.000	0.360
0.370	5.550	5.735	5.920	6.105	6.290	6.475	6.660	6.845	7.030	7.215	7.400	7.585	7.770	7.955	8.140	8.325	8.510	8.695	8.880	9.065	9.250	0.370
0.380	5.700	5.890	6.080	6.270	6.460	6.650	6.840	7.030	7.220	7.410	7.600	7.790	7.980	8.170	8.360	8.550	8.740	8.930	9.120	9.310	9.500	0.380
0.390	5.850	6.045	6.240	6.435	6.630	6.825	7.020	7.215	7.410	7.605	7.800	7.995	8.190	8.385	8.580	8.775	8.970	9.165	9.360	9.555	9.750	0.390
0.400	6.000	6.200	6.400	6.600	6.800	7.000	7.200	7.400	7.600	7.800	8.000	8.200	8.400	8.600	8.800	9.000	9.200	9.400	9.600	9.800	10.000	0.400
0.410	6.150	6.355	6.560	6.765	6.970	7.175	7.380	7.585	7.790	7.995	8.200	8.405	8.610	8.815	9.020	9.225	9.430	9.635	9.840	10.045	10.250	0.410
0.420	6.300	6.510	6.720	6.930	7.140	7.350	7.560	7.770	7.980	8.190	8.400	8.610	8.820	9.030	9.240	9.450	9.660	9.870	10.080	10.290	10.500	0.420
0.430	6.450	6.665	6.880	7.095	7.310	7.525	7.740	7.955	8.170	8.385	8.600	8.815	9.030	9.245	9.460	9.675	9.890	10.105	10.320	10.535	10.750	0.430
0.440	6.600	6.820	7.040	7.260	7.480	7.700	7.920	8.140	8.360	8.580	8.800	9.020	9.240	9.460	9.680	9.900	10.120	10.340	10.560	10.780	11.000	0.440
0.450	6.750	6.975	7.200	7.425	7.650	7.875	8.100	8.325	8.550	8.775	9.000	9.225	9.450	9.675	9.900	10.125	10.350	10.575	10.800	11.025	11.250	0.450
0.460	6.900	7.130	7.360	7.590	7.820	8.050	8.280	8.510	8.740	8.970	9.200	9.430	9.660	9.890	10.120	10.350	10.580	10.810	11.040	11.270	11.500	0.460

SILVER BULLION VALUE CHART $15 to $25

Oz.	15.00	15.50	16.00	16.50	17.00	17.50	18.00	18.50	19.00	19.50	20.00	20.50	21.00	21.50	22.00	22.50	23.00	23.50	24.00	24.50	25.00	Oz.
0.470	7.050	7.285	7.520	7.755	7.990	8.225	8.460	8.695	8.930	9.165	9.400	9.635	9.870	10.105	10.340	10.575	10.810	11.045	11.280	11.515	11.750	0.470
0.480	7.200	7.440	7.680	7.920	8.160	8.400	8.640	8.880	9.120	9.360	9.600	9.840	10.080	10.320	10.560	10.800	11.040	11.280	11.520	11.760	12.000	0.480
0.490	7.350	7.595	7.840	8.085	8.330	8.575	8.820	9.065	9.310	9.555	9.800	10.045	10.290	10.535	10.780	11.025	11.270	11.515	11.760	12.005	12.250	0.490
0.500	7.500	7.750	8.000	8.250	8.500	8.750	9.000	9.250	9.500	9.750	10.000	10.250	10.500	10.750	11.000	11.250	11.500	11.750	12.000	12.250	12.500	0.500
0.510	7.650	7.905	8.160	8.415	8.670	8.925	9.180	9.435	9.690	9.945	10.200	10.455	10.710	10.965	11.220	11.475	11.730	11.985	12.240	12.495	12.750	0.510
0.520	7.800	8.060	8.320	8.580	8.840	9.100	9.360	9.620	9.880	10.140	10.400	10.660	10.920	11.180	11.440	11.700	11.960	12.220	12.480	12.740	13.000	0.520
0.530	7.950	8.215	8.480	8.745	9.010	9.275	9.540	9.805	10.070	10.335	10.600	10.865	11.130	11.395	11.660	11.925	12.190	12.455	12.720	12.985	13.250	0.530
0.540	8.100	8.370	8.640	8.910	9.180	9.450	9.720	9.990	10.260	10.530	10.800	11.070	11.340	11.610	11.880	12.150	12.420	12.690	12.960	13.230	13.500	0.540
0.550	8.250	8.525	8.800	9.075	9.350	9.625	9.900	10.175	10.450	10.725	11.000	11.275	11.550	11.825	12.100	12.375	12.650	12.925	13.200	13.475	13.750	0.550
0.560	8.400	8.680	8.960	9.240	9.520	9.800	10.080	10.360	10.640	10.920	11.200	11.480	11.760	12.040	12.320	12.600	12.880	13.160	13.440	13.720	14.000	0.560
0.570	8.550	8.835	9.120	9.405	9.690	9.975	10.260	10.545	10.830	11.115	11.400	11.685	11.970	12.255	12.540	12.825	13.110	13.395	13.680	13.965	14.250	0.570
0.580	8.700	8.990	9.280	9.570	9.860	10.150	10.440	10.730	11.020	11.310	11.600	11.890	12.180	12.470	12.760	13.050	13.340	13.630	13.920	14.210	14.500	0.580
0.590	8.850	9.145	9.440	9.735	10.030	10.325	10.620	10.915	11.210	11.505	11.800	12.095	12.390	12.685	12.980	13.275	13.570	13.865	14.160	14.455	14.750	0.590
0.600	9.000	9.300	9.600	9.900	10.200	10.500	10.800	11.100	11.400	11.700	12.000	12.300	12.600	12.900	13.200	13.500	13.800	14.100	14.400	14.700	15.000	0.600
0.610	9.150	9.455	9.760	10.065	10.370	10.675	10.980	11.285	11.590	11.895	12.200	12.505	12.810	13.115	13.420	13.725	14.030	14.335	14.640	14.945	15.250	0.610
0.620	9.300	9.610	9.920	10.230	10.540	10.850	11.160	11.470	11.780	12.090	12.400	12.710	13.020	13.330	13.640	13.950	14.260	14.570	14.880	15.190	15.500	0.620
0.630	9.450	9.765	10.080	10.395	10.710	11.025	11.340	11.655	11.970	12.285	12.600	12.915	13.230	13.545	13.860	14.175	14.490	14.805	15.120	15.435	15.750	0.630
0.640	9.600	9.920	10.240	10.560	10.880	11.200	11.520	11.840	12.160	12.480	12.800	13.120	13.440	13.760	14.080	14.400	14.720	15.040	15.360	15.680	16.000	0.640
0.650	9.750	10.075	10.400	10.725	11.050	11.375	11.700	12.025	12.350	12.675	13.000	13.325	13.650	13.975	14.300	14.625	14.950	15.275	15.600	15.925	16.250	0.650
0.660	9.900	10.230	10.560	10.890	11.220	11.550	11.880	12.210	12.540	12.870	13.200	13.530	13.860	14.190	14.520	14.850	15.180	15.510	15.840	16.170	16.500	0.660
0.670	10.050	10.385	10.720	11.055	11.390	11.725	12.060	12.395	12.730	13.065	13.400	13.735	14.070	14.405	14.740	15.075	15.410	15.745	16.080	16.415	16.750	0.670
0.680	10.200	10.540	10.880	11.220	11.560	11.900	12.240	12.580	12.920	13.260	13.600	13.940	14.280	14.620	14.960	15.300	15.640	15.980	16.320	16.660	17.000	0.680
0.690	10.350	10.695	11.040	11.385	11.730	12.075	12.420	12.765	13.110	13.455	13.800	14.145	14.490	14.835	15.180	15.525	15.870	16.215	16.560	16.905	17.250	0.690
0.700	10.500	10.850	11.200	11.550	11.900	12.250	12.600	12.950	13.300	13.650	14.000	14.350	14.700	15.050	15.400	15.750	16.100	16.450	16.800	17.150	17.500	0.700
0.710	10.650	11.005	11.360	11.715	12.070	12.425	12.780	13.135	13.490	13.845	14.200	14.555	14.910	15.265	15.620	15.975	16.330	16.685	17.040	17.395	17.750	0.710
0.720	10.800	11.160	11.520	11.880	12.240	12.600	12.960	13.320	13.680	14.040	14.400	14.760	15.120	15.480	15.840	16.200	16.560	16.920	17.280	17.640	18.000	0.720
0.730	10.950	11.315	11.680	12.045	12.410	12.775	13.140	13.505	13.870	14.235	14.600	14.965	15.330	15.695	16.060	16.425	16.790	17.155	17.520	17.885	18.250	0.730
0.740	11.100	11.470	11.840	12.210	12.580	12.950	13.320	13.690	14.060	14.430	14.800	15.170	15.540	15.910	16.280	16.650	17.020	17.390	17.760	18.130	18.500	0.740
0.750	11.250	11.625	12.000	12.375	12.750	13.125	13.500	13.875	14.250	14.625	15.000	15.375	15.750	16.125	16.500	16.875	17.250	17.625	18.000	18.375	18.750	0.750
0.760	11.400	11.780	12.160	12.540	12.920	13.300	13.680	14.060	14.440	14.820	15.200	15.580	15.960	16.340	16.720	17.100	17.480	17.860	18.240	18.620	19.000	0.760
0.770	11.550	11.935	12.320	12.705	13.090	13.475	13.860	14.245	14.630	15.015	15.400	15.785	16.170	16.555	16.940	17.325	17.710	18.095	18.480	18.865	19.250	0.770
0.780	11.700	12.090	12.480	12.870	13.260	13.650	14.040	14.430	14.820	15.210	15.600	15.990	16.380	16.770	17.160	17.550	17.940	18.330	18.720	19.110	19.500	0.780
0.790	11.850	12.245	12.640	13.035	13.430	13.825	14.220	14.615	15.010	15.405	15.800	16.195	16.590	16.985	17.380	17.775	18.170	18.565	18.960	19.355	19.750	0.790
0.800	12.000	12.400	12.800	13.200	13.600	14.000	14.400	14.800	15.200	15.600	16.000	16.400	16.800	17.200	17.600	18.000	18.400	18.800	19.200	19.600	20.000	0.800
0.810	12.150	12.555	12.960	13.365	13.770	14.175	14.580	14.985	15.390	15.795	16.200	16.605	17.010	17.415	17.820	18.225	18.630	19.035	19.440	19.845	20.250	0.810
0.820	12.300	12.710	13.120	13.530	13.940	14.350	14.760	15.170	15.580	15.990	16.400	16.810	17.220	17.630	18.040	18.450	18.860	19.270	19.680	20.090	20.500	0.820
0.830	12.450	12.865	13.280	13.695	14.110	14.525	14.940	15.355	15.770	16.185	16.600	17.015	17.430	17.845	18.260	18.675	19.090	19.505	19.920	20.335	20.750	0.830
0.840	12.600	13.020	13.440	13.860	14.280	14.700	15.120	15.540	15.960	16.380	16.800	17.220	17.640	18.060	18.480	18.900	19.320	19.740	20.160	20.580	21.000	0.840
0.850	12.750	13.175	13.600	14.025	14.450	14.875	15.300	15.725	16.150	16.575	17.000	17.425	17.850	18.275	18.700	19.125	19.550	19.975	20.400	20.825	21.250	0.850
0.860	12.900	13.330	13.760	14.190	14.620	15.050	15.480	15.910	16.340	16.770	17.200	17.630	18.060	18.490	18.920	19.350	19.780	20.210	20.640	21.070	21.500	0.860
0.870	13.050	13.485	13.920	14.355	14.790	15.225	15.660	16.095	16.530	16.965	17.400	17.835	18.270	18.705	19.140	19.575	20.010	20.445	20.880	21.315	21.750	0.870
0.880	13.200	13.640	14.080	14.520	14.960	15.400	15.840	16.280	16.720	17.160	17.600	18.040	18.480	18.920	19.360	19.800	20.240	20.680	21.120	21.560	22.000	0.880
0.890	13.350	13.795	14.240	14.685	15.130	15.575	16.020	16.465	16.910	17.355	17.800	18.245	18.690	19.135	19.580	20.025	20.470	20.915	21.360	21.805	22.250	0.890
0.900	13.500	13.950	14.400	14.850	15.300	15.750	16.200	16.650	17.100	17.550	18.000	18.450	18.900	19.350	19.800	20.250	20.700	21.150	21.600	22.050	22.500	0.900
0.910	13.650	14.105	14.560	15.015	15.470	15.925	16.380	16.835	17.290	17.745	18.200	18.655	19.110	19.565	20.020	20.475	20.930	21.385	21.840	22.295	22.750	0.910
0.920	13.800	14.260	14.720	15.180	15.640	16.100	16.560	17.020	17.480	17.940	18.400	18.860	19.320	19.780	20.240	20.700	21.160	21.620	22.080	22.540	23.000	0.920
0.930	13.950	14.415	14.880	15.345	15.810	16.275	16.740	17.205	17.670	18.135	18.600	19.065	19.530	19.995	20.460	20.925	21.390	21.855	22.320	22.785	23.250	0.930
0.940	14.100	14.570	15.040	15.510	15.980	16.450	16.920	17.390	17.860	18.330	18.800	19.270	19.740	20.210	20.680	21.150	21.620	22.090	22.560	23.030	23.500	0.940
0.950	14.250	14.725	15.200	15.675	16.150	16.625	17.100	17.575	18.050	18.525	19.000	19.475	19.950	20.425	20.900	21.375	21.850	22.325	22.800	23.275	23.750	0.950
0.960	14.400	14.880	15.360	15.840	16.320	16.800	17.280	17.760	18.240	18.720	19.200	19.680	20.160	20.640	21.120	21.600	22.080	22.560	23.040	23.520	24.000	0.960
0.970	14.550	15.035	15.520	16.005	16.490	16.975	17.460	17.945	18.430	18.915	19.400	19.885	20.370	20.855	21.340	21.825	22.310	22.795	23.280	23.765	24.250	0.970
0.980	14.700	15.190	15.680	16.170	16.660	17.150	17.640	18.130	18.620	19.110	19.600	20.090	20.580	21.070	21.560	22.050	22.540	23.030	23.520	24.010	24.500	0.980
0.990	14.850	15.345	15.840	16.335	16.830	17.325	17.820	18.315	18.810	19.305	19.800	20.295	20.790	21.285	21.780	22.275	22.770	23.265	23.760	24.255	24.750	0.990
1.000	15.000	15.500	16.000	16.500	17.000	17.500	18.000	18.500	19.000	19.500	20.000	20.500	21.000	21.500	22.000	22.500	23.000	23.500	24.000	24.500	25.000	1.000

GOLD BULLION VALUE CHART $1000 to $1150

Oz.	1000.00	1010.00	1020.00	1030.00	1040.00	1050.00	1060.00	1070.00	1080.00	1090.00	1100.00	1100.00	1120.00	1130.00	1140.00	1150.00	Oz.
0.001	1.00	1.01	1.02	1.03	1.04	1.05	1.06	1.07	1.08	1.09	1.10	1.10	1.12	1.13	1.14	1.15	0.001
0.002	2.00	2.02	2.04	2.06	2.08	2.10	2.12	2.14	2.16	2.18	2.20	2.20	2.24	2.26	2.28	2.30	0.002
0.003	3.00	3.03	3.06	3.09	3.12	3.15	3.18	3.21	3.24	3.27	3.30	3.30	3.36	3.39	3.42	3.45	0.003
0.004	4.00	4.04	4.08	4.12	4.16	4.20	4.24	4.28	4.32	4.36	4.40	4.40	4.48	4.52	4.56	4.60	0.004
0.005	5.00	5.05	5.10	5.15	5.20	5.25	5.30	5.35	5.40	5.45	5.50	5.50	5.60	5.65	5.70	5.75	0.005
0.006	6.00	6.06	6.12	6.18	6.24	6.30	6.36	6.42	6.48	6.54	6.60	6.60	6.72	6.78	6.84	6.90	0.006
0.007	7.00	7.07	7.14	7.21	7.28	7.35	7.42	7.49	7.56	7.63	7.70	7.70	7.84	7.91	7.98	8.05	0.007
0.008	8.00	8.08	8.16	8.24	8.32	8.40	8.48	8.56	8.64	8.72	8.80	8.80	8.96	9.04	9.12	9.20	0.008
0.009	9.00	9.09	9.18	9.27	9.36	9.45	9.54	9.63	9.72	9.81	9.90	9.90	10.08	10.17	10.26	10.35	0.009
0.010	10.00	10.10	10.20	10.30	10.40	10.50	10.60	10.70	10.80	10.90	11.00	11.00	11.20	11.30	11.40	11.50	0.010
0.020	20.00	20.20	20.40	20.60	20.80	21.00	21.20	21.40	21.60	21.80	22.00	22.00	22.40	22.60	22.80	23.00	0.020
0.030	30.00	30.30	30.60	30.90	31.20	31.50	31.80	32.10	32.40	32.70	33.00	33.00	33.60	33.90	34.20	34.50	0.030
0.040	40.00	40.40	40.80	41.20	41.60	42.00	42.40	42.80	43.20	43.60	44.00	44.00	44.80	45.20	45.60	46.00	0.040
0.050	50.00	50.50	51.00	51.50	52.00	52.50	53.00	53.50	54.00	54.50	55.00	55.00	56.00	56.50	57.00	57.50	0.050
0.060	60.00	60.60	61.20	61.80	62.40	63.00	63.60	64.20	64.80	65.40	66.00	66.00	67.20	67.80	68.40	69.00	0.060
0.070	70.00	70.70	71.40	72.10	72.80	73.50	74.20	74.90	75.60	76.30	77.00	77.00	78.40	79.10	79.80	80.50	0.070
0.080	80.00	80.80	81.60	82.40	83.20	84.00	84.80	85.60	86.40	87.20	88.00	88.00	89.60	90.40	91.20	92.00	0.080
0.090	90.00	90.90	91.80	92.70	93.60	94.50	95.40	96.30	97.20	98.10	99.00	99.00	100.80	101.70	102.60	103.50	0.090
0.100	100.00	101.00	102.00	103.00	104.00	105.00	106.00	107.00	108.00	109.00	110.00	110.00	112.00	113.00	114.00	115.00	0.100
0.110	110.00	111.10	112.20	113.30	114.40	115.50	116.60	117.70	118.80	119.90	121.00	121.00	123.20	124.30	125.40	126.50	0.110
0.120	120.00	121.20	122.40	123.60	124.80	126.00	127.20	128.40	129.60	130.80	132.00	132.00	134.40	135.60	136.80	138.00	0.120
0.130	130.00	131.30	132.60	133.90	135.20	136.50	137.80	139.10	140.40	141.70	143.00	143.00	145.60	146.90	148.20	149.50	0.130
0.140	140.00	141.40	142.80	144.20	145.60	147.00	148.40	149.80	151.20	152.60	154.00	154.00	156.80	158.20	159.60	161.00	0.140
0.150	150.00	151.50	153.00	154.50	156.00	157.50	159.00	160.50	162.00	163.50	165.00	165.00	168.00	169.50	171.00	172.50	0.150
0.160	160.00	161.60	163.20	164.80	166.40	168.00	169.60	171.20	172.80	174.40	176.00	176.00	179.20	180.80	182.40	184.00	0.160
0.170	170.00	171.70	173.40	175.10	176.80	178.50	180.20	181.90	183.60	185.30	187.00	187.00	190.40	192.10	193.80	195.50	0.170
0.180	180.00	181.80	183.60	185.40	187.20	189.00	190.80	192.60	194.40	196.20	198.00	198.00	201.60	203.40	205.20	207.00	0.180
0.190	190.00	191.90	193.80	195.70	197.60	199.50	201.40	203.30	205.20	207.10	209.00	209.00	212.80	214.70	216.60	218.50	0.190
0.200	200.00	202.00	204.00	206.00	208.00	210.00	212.00	214.00	216.00	218.00	220.00	220.00	224.00	226.00	228.00	230.00	0.200
0.210	210.00	212.10	214.20	216.30	218.40	220.50	222.60	224.70	226.80	228.90	231.00	231.00	235.20	237.30	239.40	241.50	0.210
0.220	220.00	222.20	224.40	226.60	228.80	231.00	233.20	235.40	237.60	239.80	242.00	242.00	246.40	248.60	250.80	253.00	0.220
0.230	230.00	232.30	234.60	236.90	239.20	241.50	243.80	246.10	248.40	250.70	253.00	253.00	257.60	259.90	262.20	264.50	0.230
0.240	240.00	242.40	244.80	247.20	249.60	252.00	254.40	256.80	259.20	261.60	264.00	264.00	268.80	271.20	273.60	276.00	0.240
0.250	250.00	252.50	255.00	257.50	260.00	262.50	265.00	267.50	270.00	272.50	275.00	275.00	280.00	282.50	285.00	287.50	0.250
0.260	260.00	262.60	265.20	267.80	270.40	273.00	275.60	278.20	280.80	283.40	286.00	286.00	291.20	293.80	296.40	299.00	0.260
0.270	270.00	272.70	275.40	278.10	280.80	283.50	286.20	288.90	291.60	294.30	297.00	297.00	302.40	305.10	307.80	310.50	0.270
0.280	280.00	282.80	285.60	288.40	291.20	294.00	296.80	299.60	302.40	305.20	308.00	308.00	313.60	316.40	319.20	322.00	0.280
0.290	290.00	292.90	295.80	298.70	301.60	304.50	307.40	310.30	313.20	316.10	319.00	319.00	324.80	327.70	330.60	333.50	0.290
0.300	300.00	303.00	306.00	309.00	312.00	315.00	318.00	321.00	324.00	327.00	330.00	330.00	336.00	339.00	342.00	345.00	0.300
0.310	310.00	313.10	316.20	319.30	322.40	325.50	328.60	331.70	334.80	337.90	341.00	341.00	347.20	350.30	353.40	356.50	0.310
0.320	320.00	323.20	326.40	329.60	332.80	336.00	339.20	342.40	345.60	348.80	352.00	352.00	358.40	361.60	364.80	368.00	0.320
0.330	330.00	333.30	336.60	339.90	343.20	346.50	349.80	353.10	356.40	359.70	363.00	363.00	369.60	372.90	376.20	379.50	0.330
0.340	340.00	343.40	346.80	350.20	353.60	357.00	360.40	363.80	367.20	370.60	374.00	374.00	380.80	384.20	387.60	391.00	0.340
0.350	350.00	353.50	357.00	360.50	364.00	367.50	371.00	374.50	378.00	381.50	385.00	385.00	392.00	395.50	399.00	402.50	0.350
0.360	360.00	363.60	367.20	370.80	374.40	378.00	381.60	385.20	388.80	392.40	396.00	396.00	403.20	406.80	410.40	414.00	0.360
0.370	370.00	373.70	377.40	381.10	384.80	388.50	392.20	395.90	399.60	403.30	407.00	407.00	414.40	418.10	421.80	425.50	0.370
0.380	380.00	383.80	387.60	391.40	395.20	399.00	402.80	406.60	410.40	414.20	418.00	418.00	425.60	429.40	433.20	437.00	0.380
0.390	390.00	393.90	397.80	401.70	405.60	409.50	413.40	417.30	421.20	425.10	429.00	429.00	436.80	440.70	444.60	448.50	0.390
0.400	400.00	404.00	408.00	412.00	416.00	420.00	424.00	428.00	432.00	436.00	440.00	440.00	448.00	452.00	456.00	460.00	0.400
0.410	410.00	414.10	418.20	422.30	426.40	430.50	434.60	438.70	442.80	446.90	451.00	451.00	459.20	463.30	467.40	471.50	0.410
0.420	420.00	424.20	428.40	432.60	436.80	441.00	445.20	449.40	453.60	457.80	462.00	462.00	470.40	474.60	478.80	483.00	0.420
0.430	430.00	434.30	438.60	442.90	447.20	451.50	455.80	460.10	464.40	468.70	473.00	473.00	481.60	485.90	490.20	494.50	0.430
0.440	440.00	444.40	448.80	453.20	457.60	462.00	466.40	470.80	475.20	479.60	484.00	484.00	492.80	497.20	501.60	506.00	0.440
0.450	450.00	454.50	459.00	463.50	468.00	472.50	477.00	481.50	486.00	490.50	495.00	495.00	504.00	508.50	513.00	517.50	0.450
0.460	460.00	464.60	469.20	473.80	478.40	483.00	487.60	492.20	496.80	501.40	506.00	506.00	515.20	519.80	524.40	529.00	0.460
0.470	470.00	474.70	479.40	484.10	488.80	493.50	498.20	502.90	507.60	512.30	517.00	517.00	526.40	531.10	535.80	540.50	0.470
0.480	480.00	484.80	489.60	494.40	499.20	504.00	508.80	513.60	518.40	523.20	528.00	528.00	537.60	542.40	547.20	552.00	0.480
0.490	490.00	494.90	499.80	504.70	509.60	514.50	519.40	524.30	529.20	534.10	539.00	539.00	548.80	553.70	558.60	563.50	0.490

GOLD BULLION VALUE CHART $1000 to $1150

Oz.	1000.00	1010.00	1020.00	1030.00	1040.00	1050.00	1060.00	1070.00	1080.00	1090.00	1100.00	1100.00	1120.00	1130.00	1140.00	1150.00	Oz.
0.500	500.00	505.00	510.00	515.00	520.00	525.00	530.00	535.00	540.00	545.00	550.00	550.00	560.00	565.00	570.00	575.00	0.500
0.510	510.00	515.10	520.20	525.30	530.40	535.50	540.60	545.70	550.80	555.90	561.00	561.00	571.20	576.30	581.40	586.50	0.510
0.520	520.00	525.20	530.40	535.60	540.80	546.00	551.20	556.40	561.60	566.80	572.00	572.00	582.40	587.60	592.80	598.00	0.520
0.530	530.00	535.30	540.60	545.90	551.20	556.50	561.80	567.10	572.40	577.70	583.00	583.00	593.60	598.90	604.20	609.50	0.530
0.540	540.00	545.40	550.80	556.20	561.60	567.00	572.40	577.80	583.20	588.60	594.00	594.00	604.80	610.20	615.60	621.00	0.540
0.550	550.00	555.50	561.00	566.50	572.00	577.50	583.00	588.50	594.00	599.50	605.00	605.00	616.00	621.50	627.00	632.50	0.550
0.560	560.00	565.60	571.20	576.80	582.40	588.00	593.60	599.20	604.80	610.40	616.00	616.00	627.20	632.80	638.40	644.00	0.560
0.570	570.00	575.70	581.40	587.10	592.80	598.50	604.20	609.90	615.60	621.30	627.00	627.00	638.40	644.10	649.80	655.50	0.570
0.580	580.00	585.80	591.60	597.40	603.20	609.00	614.80	620.60	626.40	632.20	638.00	638.00	649.60	655.40	661.20	667.00	0.580
0.590	590.00	595.90	601.80	607.70	613.60	619.50	625.40	631.30	637.20	643.10	649.00	649.00	660.80	666.70	672.60	678.50	0.590
0.600	600.00	606.00	612.00	618.00	624.00	630.00	636.00	642.00	648.00	654.00	660.00	660.00	672.00	678.00	684.00	690.00	0.600
0.610	610.00	616.10	622.20	628.30	634.40	640.50	646.60	652.70	658.80	664.90	671.00	671.00	683.20	689.30	695.40	701.50	0.610
0.620	620.00	626.20	632.40	638.60	644.80	651.00	657.20	663.40	669.60	675.80	682.00	682.00	694.40	700.60	706.80	713.00	0.620
0.630	630.00	636.30	642.60	648.90	655.20	661.50	667.80	674.10	680.40	686.70	693.00	693.00	705.60	711.90	718.20	724.50	0.630
0.640	640.00	646.40	652.80	659.20	665.60	672.00	678.40	684.80	691.20	697.60	704.00	704.00	716.80	723.20	729.60	736.00	0.640
0.650	650.00	656.50	663.00	669.50	676.00	682.50	689.00	695.50	702.00	708.50	715.00	715.00	728.00	734.50	741.00	747.50	0.650
0.660	660.00	666.60	673.20	679.80	686.40	693.00	699.60	706.20	712.80	719.40	726.00	726.00	739.20	745.80	752.40	759.00	0.660
0.670	670.00	676.70	683.40	690.10	696.80	703.50	710.20	716.90	723.60	730.30	737.00	737.00	750.40	757.10	763.80	770.50	0.670
0.680	680.00	686.80	693.60	700.40	707.20	714.00	720.80	727.60	734.40	741.20	748.00	748.00	761.60	768.40	775.20	782.00	0.680
0.690	690.00	696.90	703.80	710.70	717.60	724.50	731.40	738.30	745.20	752.10	759.00	759.00	772.80	779.70	786.60	793.50	0.690
0.700	700.00	707.00	714.00	721.00	728.00	735.00	742.00	749.00	756.00	763.00	770.00	770.00	784.00	791.00	798.00	805.00	0.700
0.710	710.00	717.10	724.20	731.30	738.40	745.50	752.60	759.70	766.80	773.90	781.00	781.00	795.20	802.30	809.40	816.50	0.710
0.720	720.00	727.20	734.40	741.60	748.80	756.00	763.20	770.40	777.60	784.80	792.00	792.00	806.40	813.60	820.80	828.00	0.720
0.730	730.00	737.30	744.60	751.90	759.20	766.50	773.80	781.10	788.40	795.70	803.00	803.00	817.60	824.90	832.20	839.50	0.730
0.740	740.00	747.40	754.80	762.20	769.60	777.00	784.40	791.80	799.20	806.60	814.00	814.00	828.80	836.20	843.60	851.00	0.740
0.750	750.00	757.50	765.00	772.50	780.00	787.50	795.00	802.50	810.00	817.50	825.00	825.00	840.00	847.50	855.00	862.50	0.750
0.760	760.00	767.60	775.20	782.80	790.40	798.00	805.60	813.20	820.80	828.40	836.00	836.00	851.20	858.80	866.40	874.00	0.760
0.770	770.00	777.70	785.40	793.10	800.80	808.50	816.20	823.90	831.60	839.30	847.00	847.00	862.40	870.10	877.80	885.50	0.770
0.780	780.00	787.80	795.60	803.40	811.20	819.00	826.80	834.60	842.40	850.20	858.00	858.00	873.60	881.40	889.20	897.00	0.780
0.790	790.00	797.90	805.80	813.70	821.60	829.50	837.40	845.30	853.20	861.10	869.00	869.00	884.80	892.70	900.60	908.50	0.790
0.800	800.00	808.00	816.00	824.00	832.00	840.00	848.00	856.00	864.00	872.00	880.00	880.00	896.00	904.00	912.00	920.00	0.800
0.810	810.00	818.10	826.20	834.30	842.40	850.50	858.60	866.70	874.80	882.90	891.00	891.00	907.20	915.30	923.40	931.50	0.810
0.820	820.00	828.20	836.40	844.60	852.80	861.00	869.20	877.40	885.60	893.80	902.00	902.00	918.40	926.60	934.80	943.00	0.820
0.830	830.00	838.30	846.60	854.90	863.20	871.50	879.80	888.10	896.40	904.70	913.00	913.00	929.60	937.90	946.20	954.50	0.830
0.840	840.00	848.40	856.80	865.20	873.60	882.00	890.40	898.80	907.20	915.60	924.00	924.00	940.80	949.20	957.60	966.00	0.840
0.850	850.00	858.50	867.00	875.50	884.00	892.50	901.00	909.50	918.00	926.50	935.00	935.00	952.00	960.50	969.00	977.50	0.850
0.860	860.00	868.60	877.20	885.80	894.40	903.00	911.60	920.20	928.80	937.40	946.00	946.00	963.20	971.80	980.40	989.00	0.860
0.870	870.00	878.70	887.40	896.10	904.80	913.50	922.20	930.90	939.60	948.30	957.00	957.00	974.40	983.10	991.80	1000.50	0.870
0.880	880.00	888.80	897.60	906.40	915.20	924.00	932.80	941.60	950.40	959.20	968.00	968.00	985.60	994.40	1003.20	1012.00	0.880
0.890	890.00	898.90	907.80	916.70	925.60	934.50	943.40	952.30	961.20	970.10	979.00	979.00	996.80	1005.70	1014.60	1023.50	0.890
0.900	900.00	909.00	918.00	927.00	936.00	945.00	954.00	963.00	972.00	981.00	990.00	990.00	1008.00	1017.00	1026.00	1035.00	0.900
0.910	910.00	919.10	928.20	937.30	946.40	955.50	964.60	973.70	982.80	991.90	1001.00	1001.00	1019.20	1028.30	1037.40	1046.50	0.910
0.920	920.00	929.20	938.40	947.60	956.80	966.00	975.20	984.40	993.60	1002.80	1012.00	1012.00	1030.40	1039.60	1048.80	1058.00	0.920
0.930	930.00	939.30	948.60	957.90	967.20	976.50	985.80	995.10	1004.40	1013.70	1023.00	1023.00	1041.60	1050.90	1060.20	1069.50	0.930
0.940	940.00	949.40	958.80	968.20	977.60	987.00	996.40	1005.80	1015.20	1024.60	1034.00	1034.00	1052.80	1062.20	1071.60	1081.00	0.940
0.950	950.00	959.50	969.00	978.50	988.00	997.50	1007.00	1016.50	1026.00	1035.50	1045.00	1045.00	1064.00	1073.50	1083.00	1092.50	0.950
0.960	960.00	969.60	979.20	988.80	998.40	1008.00	1017.60	1027.20	1036.80	1046.40	1056.00	1056.00	1075.20	1084.80	1094.40	1104.00	0.960
0.970	970.00	979.70	989.40	999.10	1008.80	1018.50	1028.20	1037.90	1047.60	1057.30	1067.00	1067.00	1086.40	1096.10	1105.80	1115.50	0.970
0.980	980.00	989.80	999.60	1009.40	1019.20	1029.00	1038.80	1048.60	1058.40	1068.20	1078.00	1078.00	1097.60	1107.40	1117.20	1127.00	0.980
0.990	990.00	999.90	1009.80	1019.70	1029.60	1039.50	1049.40	1059.30	1069.20	1079.10	1089.00	1089.00	1108.80	1118.70	1128.60	1138.50	0.990
1.000	1000.00	1010.00	1020.00	1030.00	1040.00	1050.00	1060.00	1070.00	1080.00	1090.00	1100.00	1100.00	1120.00	1130.00	1140.00	1150.00	1.000

GOLD BULLION VALUE CHART $1160 to $1290

Oz.	1160.00	1170.00	1180.00	1190.00	1200.00	1210.00	1220.00	1230.00	1240.00	1250.00	1260.00	1270.00	1280.00	1290.00	Oz.
0.001	1.16	1.17	1.18	1.19	1.20	1.21	1.22	1.23	1.24	1.25	1.26	1.27	1.28	1.29	0.001
0.002	2.32	2.34	2.36	2.38	2.40	2.42	2.44	2.46	2.48	2.50	2.52	2.54	2.56	2.58	0.002
0.003	3.48	3.51	3.54	3.57	3.60	3.63	3.66	3.69	3.72	3.75	3.78	3.81	3.84	3.87	0.003
0.004	4.64	4.68	4.72	4.76	4.80	4.84	4.88	4.92	4.96	5.00	5.04	5.08	5.12	5.16	0.004
0.005	5.80	5.85	5.90	5.95	6.00	6.05	6.10	6.15	6.20	6.25	6.30	6.35	6.40	6.45	0.005
0.006	6.96	7.02	7.08	7.14	7.20	7.26	7.32	7.38	7.44	7.50	7.56	7.62	7.68	7.74	0.006
0.007	8.12	8.19	8.26	8.33	8.40	8.47	8.54	8.61	8.68	8.75	8.82	8.89	8.96	9.03	0.007
0.008	9.28	9.36	9.44	9.52	9.60	9.68	9.76	9.84	9.92	10.00	10.08	10.16	10.24	10.32	0.008
0.009	10.44	10.53	10.62	10.71	10.80	10.89	10.98	11.07	11.16	11.25	11.34	11.43	11.52	11.61	0.009
0.010	11.60	11.70	11.80	11.90	12.00	12.10	12.20	12.30	12.40	12.50	12.60	12.70	12.80	12.90	0.010
0.020	23.20	23.40	23.60	23.80	24.00	24.20	24.40	24.60	24.80	25.00	25.20	25.40	25.60	25.80	0.020
0.030	34.80	35.10	35.40	35.70	36.00	36.30	36.60	36.90	37.20	37.50	37.80	38.10	38.40	38.70	0.030
0.040	46.40	46.80	47.20	47.60	48.00	48.40	48.80	49.20	49.60	50.00	50.40	50.80	51.20	51.60	0.040
0.050	58.00	58.50	59.00	59.50	60.00	60.50	61.00	61.50	62.00	62.50	63.00	63.50	64.00	64.50	0.050
0.060	69.60	70.20	70.80	71.40	72.00	72.60	73.20	73.80	74.40	75.00	75.60	76.20	76.80	77.40	0.060
0.070	81.20	81.90	82.60	83.30	84.00	84.70	85.40	86.10	86.80	87.50	88.20	88.90	89.60	90.30	0.070
0.080	92.80	93.60	94.40	95.20	96.00	96.80	97.60	98.40	99.20	100.00	100.80	101.60	102.40	103.20	0.080
0.090	104.40	105.30	106.20	107.10	108.00	108.90	109.80	110.70	111.60	112.50	113.40	114.30	115.20	116.10	0.090
0.100	116.00	117.00	118.00	119.00	120.00	121.00	122.00	123.00	124.00	125.00	126.00	127.00	128.00	129.00	0.100
0.110	127.60	128.70	129.80	130.90	132.00	133.10	134.20	135.30	136.40	137.50	138.60	139.70	140.80	141.90	0.110
0.120	139.20	140.40	141.60	142.80	144.00	145.20	146.40	147.60	148.80	150.00	151.20	152.40	153.60	154.80	0.120
0.130	150.80	152.10	153.40	154.70	156.00	157.30	158.60	159.90	161.20	162.50	163.80	165.10	166.40	167.70	0.130
0.140	162.40	163.80	165.20	166.60	168.00	169.40	170.80	172.20	173.60	175.00	176.40	177.80	179.20	180.60	0.140
0.150	174.00	175.50	177.00	178.50	180.00	181.50	183.00	184.50	186.00	187.50	189.00	190.50	192.00	193.50	0.150
0.160	185.60	187.20	188.80	190.40	192.00	193.60	195.20	196.80	198.40	200.00	201.60	203.20	204.80	206.40	0.160
0.170	197.20	198.90	200.60	202.30	204.00	205.70	207.40	209.10	210.80	212.50	214.20	215.90	217.60	219.30	0.170
0.180	208.80	210.60	212.40	214.20	216.00	217.80	219.60	221.40	223.20	225.00	226.80	228.60	230.40	232.20	0.180
0.190	220.40	222.30	224.20	226.10	228.00	229.90	231.80	233.70	235.60	237.50	239.40	241.30	243.20	245.10	0.190
0.200	232.00	234.00	236.00	238.00	240.00	242.00	244.00	246.00	248.00	250.00	252.00	254.00	256.00	258.00	0.200
0.210	243.60	245.70	247.80	249.90	252.00	254.10	256.20	258.30	260.40	262.50	264.60	266.70	268.80	270.90	0.210
0.220	255.20	257.40	259.60	261.80	264.00	266.20	268.40	270.60	272.80	275.00	277.20	279.40	281.60	283.80	0.220
0.230	266.80	269.10	271.40	273.70	276.00	278.30	280.60	282.90	285.20	287.50	289.80	292.10	294.40	296.70	0.230
0.240	278.40	280.80	283.20	285.60	288.00	290.40	292.80	295.20	297.60	300.00	302.40	304.80	307.20	309.60	0.240
0.250	290.00	292.50	295.00	297.50	300.00	302.50	305.00	307.50	310.00	312.50	315.00	317.50	320.00	322.50	0.250
0.260	301.60	304.20	306.80	309.40	312.00	314.60	317.20	319.80	322.40	325.00	327.60	330.20	332.80	335.40	0.260
0.270	313.20	315.90	318.60	321.30	324.00	326.70	329.40	332.10	334.80	337.50	340.20	342.90	345.60	348.30	0.270
0.280	324.80	327.60	330.40	333.20	336.00	338.80	341.60	344.40	347.20	350.00	352.80	355.60	358.40	361.20	0.280
0.290	336.40	339.30	342.20	345.10	348.00	350.90	353.80	356.70	359.60	362.50	365.40	368.30	371.20	374.10	0.290
0.300	348.00	351.00	354.00	357.00	360.00	363.00	366.00	369.00	372.00	375.00	378.00	381.00	384.00	387.00	0.300
0.310	359.60	362.70	365.80	368.90	372.00	375.10	378.20	381.30	384.40	387.50	390.60	393.70	396.80	399.90	0.310
0.320	371.20	374.40	377.60	380.80	384.00	387.20	390.40	393.60	396.80	400.00	403.20	406.40	409.60	412.80	0.320
0.330	382.80	386.10	389.40	392.70	396.00	399.30	402.60	405.90	409.20	412.50	415.80	419.10	422.40	425.70	0.330
0.340	394.40	397.80	401.20	404.60	408.00	411.40	414.80	418.20	421.60	425.00	428.40	431.80	435.20	438.60	0.340
0.350	406.00	409.50	413.00	416.50	420.00	423.50	427.00	430.50	434.00	437.50	441.00	444.50	448.00	451.50	0.350
0.360	417.60	421.20	424.80	428.40	432.00	435.60	439.20	442.80	446.40	450.00	453.60	457.20	460.80	464.40	0.360
0.370	429.20	432.90	436.60	440.30	444.00	447.70	451.40	455.10	458.80	462.50	466.20	469.90	473.60	477.30	0.370
0.380	440.80	444.60	448.40	452.20	456.00	459.80	463.60	467.40	471.20	475.00	478.80	482.60	486.40	490.20	0.380
0.390	452.40	456.30	460.20	464.10	468.00	471.90	475.80	479.70	483.60	487.50	491.40	495.30	499.20	503.10	0.390
0.400	464.00	468.00	472.00	476.00	480.00	484.00	488.00	492.00	496.00	500.00	504.00	508.00	512.00	516.00	0.400
0.410	475.60	479.70	483.80	487.90	492.00	496.10	500.20	504.30	508.40	512.50	516.60	520.70	524.80	528.90	0.410
0.420	487.20	491.40	495.60	499.80	504.00	508.20	512.40	516.60	520.80	525.00	529.20	533.40	537.60	541.80	0.420
0.430	498.80	503.10	507.40	511.70	516.00	520.30	524.60	528.90	533.20	537.50	541.80	546.10	550.40	554.70	0.430
0.440	510.40	514.80	519.20	523.60	528.00	532.40	536.80	541.20	545.60	550.00	554.40	558.80	563.20	567.60	0.440
0.450	522.00	526.50	531.00	535.50	540.00	544.50	549.00	553.50	558.00	562.50	567.00	571.50	576.00	580.50	0.450
0.460	533.60	538.20	542.80	547.40	552.00	556.60	561.20	565.80	570.40	575.00	579.60	584.20	588.80	593.40	0.460

GOLD BULLION VALUE CHART $1160 to $1290

Oz.	1160.00	1170.00	1180.00	1190.00	1200.00	1210.00	1220.00	1230.00	1240.00	1250.00	1260.00	1270.00	1280.00	1290.00	Oz.
0.470	545.20	549.90	554.60	559.30	564.00	568.70	573.40	578.10	582.80	587.50	592.20	596.90	601.60	606.30	0.470
0.480	556.80	561.60	566.40	571.20	576.00	580.80	585.60	590.40	595.20	600.00	604.80	609.60	614.40	619.20	0.480
0.490	568.40	573.30	578.20	583.10	588.00	592.90	597.80	602.70	607.60	612.50	617.40	622.30	627.20	632.10	0.490
0.500	580.00	585.00	590.00	595.00	600.00	605.00	610.00	615.00	620.00	625.00	630.00	635.00	640.00	645.00	0.500
0.510	591.60	596.70	601.80	606.90	612.00	617.10	622.20	627.30	632.40	637.50	642.60	647.70	652.80	657.90	0.510
0.520	603.20	608.40	613.60	618.80	624.00	629.20	634.40	639.60	644.80	650.00	655.20	660.40	665.60	670.80	0.520
0.530	614.80	620.10	625.40	630.70	636.00	641.30	646.60	651.90	657.20	662.50	667.80	673.10	678.40	683.70	0.530
0.540	626.40	631.80	637.20	642.60	648.00	653.40	658.80	664.20	669.60	675.00	680.40	685.80	691.20	696.60	0.540
0.550	638.00	643.50	649.00	654.50	660.00	665.50	671.00	676.50	682.00	687.50	693.00	698.50	704.00	709.50	0.550
0.560	649.60	655.20	660.80	666.40	672.00	677.60	683.20	688.80	694.40	700.00	705.60	711.20	716.80	722.40	0.560
0.570	661.20	666.90	672.60	678.30	684.00	689.70	695.40	701.10	706.80	712.50	718.20	723.90	729.60	735.30	0.570
0.580	672.80	678.60	684.40	690.20	696.00	701.80	707.60	713.40	719.20	725.00	730.80	736.60	742.40	748.20	0.580
0.590	684.40	690.30	696.20	702.10	708.00	713.90	719.80	725.70	731.60	737.50	743.40	749.30	755.20	761.10	0.590
0.600	696.00	702.00	708.00	714.00	720.00	726.00	732.00	738.00	744.00	750.00	756.00	762.00	768.00	774.00	0.600
0.610	707.60	713.70	719.80	725.90	732.00	738.10	744.20	750.30	756.40	762.50	768.60	774.70	780.80	786.90	0.610
0.620	719.20	725.40	731.60	737.80	744.00	750.20	756.40	762.60	768.80	775.00	781.20	787.40	793.60	799.80	0.620
0.630	730.80	737.10	743.40	749.70	756.00	762.30	768.60	774.90	781.20	787.50	793.80	800.10	806.40	812.70	0.630
0.640	742.40	748.80	755.20	761.60	768.00	774.40	780.80	787.20	793.60	800.00	806.40	812.80	819.20	825.60	0.640
0.650	754.00	760.50	767.00	773.50	780.00	786.50	793.00	799.50	806.00	812.50	819.00	825.50	832.00	838.50	0.650
0.660	765.60	772.20	778.80	785.40	792.00	798.60	805.20	811.80	818.40	825.00	831.60	838.20	844.80	851.40	0.660
0.670	777.20	783.90	790.60	797.30	804.00	810.70	817.40	824.10	830.80	837.50	844.20	850.90	857.60	864.30	0.670
0.680	788.80	795.60	802.40	809.20	816.00	822.80	829.60	836.40	843.20	850.00	856.80	863.60	870.40	877.20	0.680
0.690	800.40	807.30	814.20	821.10	828.00	834.90	841.80	848.70	855.60	862.50	869.40	876.30	883.20	890.10	0.690
0.700	812.00	819.00	826.00	833.00	840.00	847.00	854.00	861.00	868.00	875.00	882.00	889.00	896.00	903.00	0.700
0.710	823.60	830.70	837.80	844.90	852.00	859.10	866.20	873.30	880.40	887.50	894.60	901.70	908.80	915.90	0.710
0.720	835.20	842.40	849.60	856.80	864.00	871.20	878.40	885.60	892.80	900.00	907.20	914.40	921.60	928.80	0.720
0.730	846.80	854.10	861.40	868.70	876.00	883.30	890.60	897.90	905.20	912.50	919.80	927.10	934.40	941.70	0.730
0.740	858.40	865.80	873.20	880.60	888.00	895.40	902.80	910.20	917.60	925.00	932.40	939.80	947.20	954.60	0.740
0.750	870.00	877.50	885.00	892.50	900.00	907.50	915.00	922.50	930.00	937.50	945.00	952.50	960.00	967.50	0.750
0.760	881.60	889.20	896.80	904.40	912.00	919.60	927.20	934.80	942.40	950.00	957.60	965.20	972.80	980.40	0.760
0.770	893.20	900.90	908.60	916.30	924.00	931.70	939.40	947.10	954.80	962.50	970.20	977.90	985.60	993.30	0.770
0.780	904.80	912.60	920.40	928.20	936.00	943.80	951.60	959.40	967.20	975.00	982.80	990.60	998.40	1006.20	0.780
0.790	916.40	924.30	932.20	940.10	948.00	955.90	963.80	971.70	979.60	987.50	995.40	1003.30	1011.20	1019.10	0.790
0.800	928.00	936.00	944.00	952.00	960.00	968.00	976.00	984.00	992.00	1000.00	1008.00	1016.00	1024.00	1032.00	0.800
0.810	939.60	947.70	955.80	963.90	972.00	980.10	988.20	996.30	1004.40	1012.50	1020.60	1028.70	1036.80	1044.90	0.810
0.820	951.20	959.40	967.60	975.80	984.00	992.20	1000.40	1008.60	1016.80	1025.00	1033.20	1041.40	1049.60	1057.80	0.820
0.830	962.80	971.10	979.40	987.70	996.00	1004.30	1012.60	1020.90	1029.20	1037.50	1045.80	1054.10	1062.40	1070.70	0.830
0.840	974.40	982.80	991.20	999.60	1008.00	1016.40	1024.80	1033.20	1041.60	1050.00	1058.40	1066.80	1075.20	1083.60	0.840
0.850	986.00	994.50	1003.00	1011.50	1020.00	1028.50	1037.00	1045.50	1054.00	1062.50	1071.00	1079.50	1088.00	1096.50	0.850
0.860	997.60	1006.20	1014.80	1023.40	1032.00	1040.60	1049.20	1057.80	1066.40	1075.00	1083.60	1092.20	1100.80	1109.40	0.860
0.870	1009.20	1017.90	1026.60	1035.30	1044.00	1052.70	1061.40	1070.10	1078.80	1087.50	1096.20	1104.90	1113.60	1122.30	0.870
0.880	1020.80	1029.60	1038.40	1047.20	1056.00	1064.80	1073.60	1082.40	1091.20	1100.00	1108.80	1117.60	1126.40	1135.20	0.880
0.890	1032.40	1041.30	1050.20	1059.10	1068.00	1076.90	1085.80	1094.70	1103.60	1112.50	1121.40	1130.30	1139.20	1148.10	0.890
0.900	1044.00	1053.00	1062.00	1071.00	1080.00	1089.00	1098.00	1107.00	1116.00	1125.00	1134.00	1143.00	1152.00	1161.00	0.900
0.910	1055.60	1064.70	1073.80	1082.90	1092.00	1101.10	1110.20	1119.30	1128.40	1137.50	1146.60	1155.70	1164.80	1173.90	0.910
0.920	1067.20	1076.40	1085.60	1094.80	1104.00	1113.20	1122.40	1131.60	1140.80	1150.00	1159.20	1168.40	1177.60	1186.80	0.920
0.930	1078.80	1088.10	1097.40	1106.70	1116.00	1125.30	1134.60	1143.90	1153.20	1162.50	1171.80	1181.10	1190.40	1199.70	0.930
0.940	1090.40	1099.80	1109.20	1118.60	1128.00	1137.40	1146.80	1156.20	1165.60	1175.00	1184.40	1193.80	1203.20	1212.60	0.940
0.950	1102.00	1111.50	1121.00	1130.50	1140.00	1149.50	1159.00	1168.50	1178.00	1187.50	1197.00	1206.50	1216.00	1225.50	0.950
0.960	1113.60	1123.20	1132.80	1142.40	1152.00	1161.60	1171.20	1180.80	1190.40	1200.00	1209.60	1219.20	1228.80	1238.40	0.960
0.970	1125.20	1134.90	1144.60	1154.30	1164.00	1173.70	1183.40	1193.10	1202.80	1212.50	1222.20	1231.90	1241.60	1251.30	0.970
0.980	1136.80	1146.60	1156.40	1166.20	1176.00	1185.80	1195.60	1205.40	1215.20	1225.00	1234.80	1244.60	1254.40	1264.20	0.980
0.990	1148.40	1158.30	1168.20	1178.10	1188.00	1197.90	1207.80	1217.70	1227.60	1237.50	1247.40	1257.30	1267.20	1277.10	0.990
1.000	1160.00	1170.00	1180.00	1190.00	1200.00	1210.00	1220.00	1230.00	1240.00	1250.00	1260.00	1270.00	1280.00	1290.00	1.000

GOLD BULLION VALUE CHART $1300 to $1420

Oz.	1300.00	1310.00	1320.00	1330.00	1340.00	1350.00	1360.00	1370.00	1380.00	1390.00	1400.00	1410.00	1420.00	Oz.
0.001	1.30	1.31	1.32	1.33	1.34	1.35	1.36	1.37	1.38	1.39	1.40	1.41	1.42	0.001
0.002	2.60	2.62	2.64	2.66	2.68	2.70	2.72	2.74	2.76	2.78	2.80	2.82	2.84	0.002
0.003	3.90	3.93	3.96	3.99	4.02	4.05	4.08	4.11	4.14	4.17	4.20	4.23	4.26	0.003
0.004	5.20	5.24	5.28	5.32	5.36	5.40	5.44	5.48	5.52	5.56	5.60	5.64	5.68	0.004
0.005	6.50	6.55	6.60	6.65	6.70	6.75	6.80	6.85	6.90	6.95	7.00	7.05	7.10	0.005
0.006	7.80	7.86	7.92	7.98	8.04	8.10	8.16	8.22	8.28	8.34	8.40	8.46	8.52	0.006
0.007	9.10	9.17	9.24	9.31	9.38	9.45	9.52	9.59	9.66	9.73	9.80	9.87	9.94	0.007
0.008	10.40	10.48	10.56	10.64	10.72	10.80	10.88	10.96	11.04	11.12	11.20	11.28	11.36	0.008
0.009	11.70	11.79	11.88	11.97	12.06	12.15	12.24	12.33	12.42	12.51	12.60	12.69	12.78	0.009
0.010	13.00	13.10	13.20	13.30	13.40	13.50	13.60	13.70	13.80	13.90	14.00	14.10	14.20	0.010
0.020	26.00	26.20	26.40	26.60	26.80	27.00	27.20	27.40	27.60	27.80	28.00	28.20	28.40	0.020
0.030	39.00	39.30	39.60	39.90	40.20	40.50	40.80	41.10	41.40	41.70	42.00	42.30	42.60	0.030
0.040	52.00	52.40	52.80	53.20	53.60	54.00	54.40	54.80	55.20	55.60	56.00	56.40	56.80	0.040
0.050	65.00	65.50	66.00	66.50	67.00	67.50	68.00	68.50	69.00	69.50	70.00	70.50	71.00	0.050
0.060	78.00	78.60	79.20	79.80	80.40	81.00	81.60	82.20	82.80	83.40	84.00	84.60	85.20	0.060
0.070	91.00	91.70	92.40	93.10	93.80	94.50	95.20	95.90	96.60	97.30	98.00	98.70	99.40	0.070
0.080	104.00	104.80	105.60	106.40	107.20	108.00	108.80	109.60	110.40	111.20	112.00	112.80	113.60	0.080
0.090	117.00	117.90	118.80	119.70	120.60	121.50	122.40	123.30	124.20	125.10	126.00	126.90	127.80	0.090
0.100	130.00	131.00	132.00	133.00	134.00	135.00	136.00	137.00	138.00	139.00	140.00	141.00	142.00	0.100
0.110	143.00	144.10	145.20	146.30	147.40	148.50	149.60	150.70	151.80	152.90	154.00	155.10	156.20	0.110
0.120	156.00	157.20	158.40	159.60	160.80	162.00	163.20	164.40	165.60	166.80	168.00	169.20	170.40	0.120
0.130	169.00	170.30	171.60	172.90	174.20	175.50	176.80	178.10	179.40	180.70	182.00	183.30	184.60	0.130
0.140	182.00	183.40	184.80	186.20	187.60	189.00	190.40	191.80	193.20	194.60	196.00	197.40	198.80	0.140
0.150	195.00	196.50	198.00	199.50	201.00	202.50	204.00	205.50	207.00	208.50	210.00	211.50	213.00	0.150
0.160	208.00	209.60	211.20	212.80	214.40	216.00	217.60	219.20	220.80	222.40	224.00	225.60	227.20	0.160
0.170	221.00	222.70	224.40	226.10	227.80	229.50	231.20	232.90	234.60	236.30	238.00	239.70	241.40	0.170
0.180	234.00	235.80	237.60	239.40	241.20	243.00	244.80	246.60	248.40	250.20	252.00	253.80	255.60	0.180
0.190	247.00	248.90	250.80	252.70	254.60	256.50	258.40	260.30	262.20	264.10	266.00	267.90	269.80	0.190
0.200	260.00	262.00	264.00	266.00	268.00	270.00	272.00	274.00	276.00	278.00	280.00	282.00	284.00	0.200
0.210	273.00	275.10	277.20	279.30	281.40	283.50	285.60	287.70	289.80	291.90	294.00	296.10	298.20	0.210
0.220	286.00	288.20	290.40	292.60	294.80	297.00	299.20	301.40	303.60	305.80	308.00	310.20	312.40	0.220
0.230	299.00	301.30	303.60	305.90	308.20	310.50	312.80	315.10	317.40	319.70	322.00	324.30	326.60	0.230
0.240	312.00	314.40	316.80	319.20	321.60	324.00	326.40	328.80	331.20	333.60	336.00	338.40	340.80	0.240
0.250	325.00	327.50	330.00	332.50	335.00	337.50	340.00	342.50	345.00	347.50	350.00	352.50	355.00	0.250
0.260	338.00	340.60	343.20	345.80	348.40	351.00	353.60	356.20	358.80	361.40	364.00	366.60	369.20	0.260
0.270	351.00	353.70	356.40	359.10	361.80	364.50	367.20	369.90	372.60	375.30	378.00	380.70	383.40	0.270
0.280	364.00	366.80	369.60	372.40	375.20	378.00	380.80	383.60	386.40	389.20	392.00	394.80	397.60	0.280
0.290	377.00	379.90	382.80	385.70	388.60	391.50	394.40	397.30	400.20	403.10	406.00	408.90	411.80	0.290
0.300	390.00	393.00	396.00	399.00	402.00	405.00	408.00	411.00	414.00	417.00	420.00	423.00	426.00	0.300
0.310	403.00	406.10	409.20	412.30	415.40	418.50	421.60	424.70	427.80	430.90	434.00	437.10	440.20	0.310
0.320	416.00	419.20	422.40	425.60	428.80	432.00	435.20	438.40	441.60	444.80	448.00	451.20	454.40	0.320
0.330	429.00	432.30	435.60	438.90	442.20	445.50	448.80	452.10	455.40	458.70	462.00	465.30	468.60	0.330
0.340	442.00	445.40	448.80	452.20	455.60	459.00	462.40	465.80	469.20	472.60	476.00	479.40	482.80	0.340
0.350	455.00	458.50	462.00	465.50	469.00	472.50	476.00	479.50	483.00	486.50	490.00	493.50	497.00	0.350
0.360	468.00	471.60	475.20	478.80	482.40	486.00	489.60	493.20	496.80	500.40	504.00	507.60	511.20	0.360
0.370	481.00	484.70	488.40	492.10	495.80	499.50	503.20	506.90	510.60	514.30	518.00	521.70	525.40	0.370
0.380	494.00	497.80	501.60	505.40	509.20	513.00	516.80	520.60	524.40	528.20	532.00	535.80	539.60	0.380
0.390	507.00	510.90	514.80	518.70	522.60	526.50	530.40	534.30	538.20	542.10	546.00	549.90	553.80	0.390
0.400	520.00	524.00	528.00	532.00	536.00	540.00	544.00	548.00	552.00	556.00	560.00	564.00	568.00	0.400
0.410	533.00	537.10	541.20	545.30	549.40	553.50	557.60	561.70	565.80	569.90	574.00	578.10	582.20	0.410
0.420	546.00	550.20	554.40	558.60	562.80	567.00	571.20	575.40	579.60	583.80	588.00	592.20	596.40	0.420
0.430	559.00	563.30	567.60	571.90	576.20	580.50	584.80	589.10	593.40	597.70	602.00	606.30	610.60	0.430
0.440	572.00	576.40	580.80	585.20	589.60	594.00	598.40	602.80	607.20	611.60	616.00	620.40	624.80	0.440
0.450	585.00	589.50	594.00	598.50	603.00	607.50	612.00	616.50	621.00	625.50	630.00	634.50	639.00	0.450
0.460	598.00	602.60	607.20	611.80	616.40	621.00	625.60	630.20	634.80	639.40	644.00	648.60	653.20	0.460

GOLD BULLION VALUE CHART $1300 to $1420

Oz.	1300.00	1310.00	1320.00	1330.00	1340.00	1350.00	1360.00	1370.00	1380.00	1390.00	1400.00	1410.00	1420.00	Oz.
0.470	611.00	615.70	620.40	625.10	629.80	634.50	639.20	643.90	648.60	653.30	658.00	662.70	667.40	0.470
0.480	624.00	628.80	633.60	638.40	643.20	648.00	652.80	657.60	662.40	667.20	672.00	676.80	681.60	0.480
0.490	637.00	641.90	646.80	651.70	656.60	661.50	666.40	671.30	676.20	681.10	686.00	690.90	695.80	0.490
0.500	650.00	655.00	660.00	665.00	670.00	675.00	680.00	685.00	690.00	695.00	700.00	705.00	710.00	0.500
0.510	663.00	668.10	673.20	678.30	683.40	688.50	693.60	698.70	703.80	708.90	714.00	719.10	724.20	0.510
0.520	676.00	681.20	686.40	691.60	696.80	702.00	707.20	712.40	717.60	722.80	728.00	733.20	738.40	0.520
0.530	689.00	694.30	699.60	704.90	710.20	715.50	720.80	726.10	731.40	736.70	742.00	747.30	752.60	0.530
0.540	702.00	707.40	712.80	718.20	723.60	729.00	734.40	739.80	745.20	750.60	756.00	761.40	766.80	0.540
0.550	715.00	720.50	726.00	731.50	737.00	742.50	748.00	753.50	759.00	764.50	770.00	775.50	781.00	0.550
0.560	728.00	733.60	739.20	744.80	750.40	756.00	761.60	767.20	772.80	778.40	784.00	789.60	795.20	0.560
0.570	741.00	746.70	752.40	758.10	763.80	769.50	775.20	780.90	786.60	792.30	798.00	803.70	809.40	0.570
0.580	754.00	759.80	765.60	771.40	777.20	783.00	788.80	794.60	800.40	806.20	812.00	817.80	823.60	0.580
0.590	767.00	772.90	778.80	784.70	790.60	796.50	802.40	808.30	814.20	820.10	826.00	831.90	837.80	0.590
0.600	780.00	786.00	792.00	798.00	804.00	810.00	816.00	822.00	828.00	834.00	840.00	846.00	852.00	0.600
0.610	793.00	799.10	805.20	811.30	817.40	823.50	829.60	835.70	841.80	847.90	854.00	860.10	866.20	0.610
0.620	806.00	812.20	818.40	824.60	830.80	837.00	843.20	849.40	855.60	861.80	868.00	874.20	880.40	0.620
0.630	819.00	825.30	831.60	837.90	844.20	850.50	856.80	863.10	869.40	875.70	882.00	888.30	894.60	0.630
0.640	832.00	838.40	844.80	851.20	857.60	864.00	870.40	876.80	883.20	889.60	896.00	902.40	908.80	0.640
0.650	845.00	851.50	858.00	864.50	871.00	877.50	884.00	890.50	897.00	903.50	910.00	916.50	923.00	0.650
0.660	858.00	864.60	871.20	877.80	884.40	891.00	897.60	904.20	910.80	917.40	924.00	930.60	937.20	0.660
0.670	871.00	877.70	884.40	891.10	897.80	904.50	911.20	917.90	924.60	931.30	938.00	944.70	951.40	0.670
0.680	884.00	890.80	897.60	904.40	911.20	918.00	924.80	931.60	938.40	945.20	952.00	958.80	965.60	0.680
0.690	897.00	903.90	910.80	917.70	924.60	931.50	938.40	945.30	952.20	959.10	966.00	972.90	979.80	0.690
0.700	910.00	917.00	924.00	931.00	938.00	945.00	952.00	959.00	966.00	973.00	980.00	987.00	994.00	0.700
0.710	923.00	930.10	937.20	944.30	951.40	958.50	965.60	972.70	979.80	986.90	994.00	1001.10	1008.20	0.710
0.720	936.00	943.20	950.40	957.60	964.80	972.00	979.20	986.40	993.60	1000.80	1008.00	1015.20	1022.40	0.720
0.730	949.00	956.30	963.60	970.90	978.20	985.50	992.80	1000.10	1007.40	1014.70	1022.00	1029.30	1036.60	0.730
0.740	962.00	969.40	976.80	984.20	991.60	999.00	1006.40	1013.80	1021.20	1028.60	1036.00	1043.40	1050.80	0.740
0.750	975.00	982.50	990.00	997.50	1005.00	1012.50	1020.00	1027.50	1035.00	1042.50	1050.00	1057.50	1065.00	0.750
0.760	988.00	995.60	1003.20	1010.80	1018.40	1026.00	1033.60	1041.20	1048.80	1056.40	1064.00	1071.60	1079.20	0.760
0.770	1001.00	1008.70	1016.40	1024.10	1031.80	1039.50	1047.20	1054.90	1062.60	1070.30	1078.00	1085.70	1093.40	0.770
0.780	1014.00	1021.80	1029.60	1037.40	1045.20	1053.00	1060.80	1068.60	1076.40	1084.20	1092.00	1099.80	1107.60	0.780
0.790	1027.00	1034.90	1042.80	1050.70	1058.60	1066.50	1074.40	1082.30	1090.20	1098.10	1106.00	1113.90	1121.80	0.790
0.800	1040.00	1048.00	1056.00	1064.00	1072.00	1080.00	1088.00	1096.00	1104.00	1112.00	1120.00	1128.00	1136.00	0.800
0.810	1053.00	1061.10	1069.20	1077.30	1085.40	1093.50	1101.60	1109.70	1117.80	1125.90	1134.00	1142.10	1150.20	0.810
0.820	1066.00	1074.20	1082.40	1090.60	1098.80	1107.00	1115.20	1123.40	1131.60	1139.80	1148.00	1156.20	1164.40	0.820
0.830	1079.00	1087.30	1095.60	1103.90	1112.20	1120.50	1128.80	1137.10	1145.40	1153.70	1162.00	1170.30	1178.60	0.830
0.840	1092.00	1100.40	1108.80	1117.20	1125.60	1134.00	1142.40	1150.80	1159.20	1167.60	1176.00	1184.40	1192.80	0.840
0.850	1105.00	1113.50	1122.00	1130.50	1139.00	1147.50	1156.00	1164.50	1173.00	1181.50	1190.00	1198.50	1207.00	0.850
0.860	1118.00	1126.60	1135.20	1143.80	1152.40	1161.00	1169.60	1178.20	1186.80	1195.40	1204.00	1212.60	1221.20	0.860
0.870	1131.00	1139.70	1148.40	1157.10	1165.80	1174.50	1183.20	1191.90	1200.60	1209.30	1218.00	1226.70	1235.40	0.870
0.880	1144.00	1152.80	1161.60	1170.40	1179.20	1188.00	1196.80	1205.60	1214.40	1223.20	1232.00	1240.80	1249.60	0.880
0.890	1157.00	1165.90	1174.80	1183.70	1192.60	1201.50	1210.40	1219.30	1228.20	1237.10	1246.00	1254.90	1263.80	0.890
0.900	1170.00	1179.00	1188.00	1197.00	1206.00	1215.00	1224.00	1233.00	1242.00	1251.00	1260.00	1269.00	1278.00	0.900
0.910	1183.00	1192.10	1201.20	1210.30	1219.40	1228.50	1237.60	1246.70	1255.80	1264.90	1274.00	1283.10	1292.20	0.910
0.920	1196.00	1205.20	1214.40	1223.60	1232.80	1242.00	1251.20	1260.40	1269.60	1278.80	1288.00	1297.20	1306.40	0.920
0.930	1209.00	1218.30	1227.60	1236.90	1246.20	1255.50	1264.80	1274.10	1283.40	1292.70	1302.00	1311.30	1320.60	0.930
0.940	1222.00	1231.40	1240.80	1250.20	1259.60	1269.00	1278.40	1287.80	1297.20	1306.60	1316.00	1325.40	1334.80	0.940
0.950	1235.00	1244.50	1254.00	1263.50	1273.00	1282.50	1292.00	1301.50	1311.00	1320.50	1330.00	1339.50	1349.00	0.950
0.960	1248.00	1257.60	1267.20	1276.80	1286.40	1296.00	1305.60	1315.20	1324.80	1334.40	1344.00	1353.60	1363.20	0.960
0.970	1261.00	1270.70	1280.40	1290.10	1299.80	1309.50	1319.20	1328.90	1338.60	1348.30	1358.00	1367.70	1377.40	0.970
0.980	1274.00	1283.80	1293.60	1303.40	1313.20	1323.00	1332.80	1342.60	1352.40	1362.20	1372.00	1381.80	1391.60	0.980
0.990	1287.00	1296.90	1306.80	1316.70	1326.60	1336.50	1346.40	1356.30	1366.20	1376.10	1386.00	1395.90	1405.80	0.990
1.000	1300.00	1310.00	1320.00	1330.00	1340.00	1350.00	1360.00	1370.00	1380.00	1390.00	1400.00	1410.00	1420.00	1.000

GOLD BULLION VALUE CHART $1430 to $1500

Oz.	1430.00	1440.00	1450.00	1460.00	1470.00	1480.00	1490.00	1500.00	Oz.
0.001	1.43	1.44	1.45	1.46	1.47	1.48	1.49	1.50	0.001
0.002	2.86	2.88	2.90	2.92	2.94	2.96	2.98	3.00	0.002
0.003	4.29	4.32	4.35	4.38	4.41	4.44	4.47	4.50	0.003
0.004	5.72	5.76	5.80	5.84	5.88	5.92	5.96	6.00	0.004
0.005	7.15	7.20	7.25	7.30	7.35	7.40	7.45	7.50	0.005
0.006	8.58	8.64	8.70	8.76	8.82	8.88	8.94	9.00	0.006
0.007	10.01	10.08	10.15	10.22	10.29	10.36	10.43	10.50	0.007
0.008	11.44	11.52	11.60	11.68	11.76	11.84	11.92	12.00	0.008
0.009	12.87	12.96	13.05	13.14	13.23	13.32	13.41	13.50	0.009
0.010	14.30	14.40	14.50	14.60	14.70	14.80	14.90	15.00	0.010
0.020	28.60	28.80	29.00	29.20	29.40	29.60	29.80	30.00	0.020
0.030	42.90	43.20	43.50	43.80	44.10	44.40	44.70	45.00	0.030
0.040	57.20	57.60	58.00	58.40	58.80	59.20	59.60	60.00	0.040
0.050	71.50	72.00	72.50	73.00	73.50	74.00	74.50	75.00	0.050
0.060	85.80	86.40	87.00	87.60	88.20	88.80	89.40	90.00	0.060
0.070	100.10	100.80	101.50	102.20	102.90	103.60	104.30	105.00	0.070
0.080	114.40	115.20	116.00	116.80	117.60	118.40	119.20	120.00	0.080
0.090	128.70	129.60	130.50	131.40	132.30	133.20	134.10	135.00	0.090
0.100	143.00	144.00	145.00	146.00	147.00	148.00	149.00	150.00	0.100
0.110	157.30	158.40	159.50	160.60	161.70	162.80	163.90	165.00	0.110
0.120	171.60	172.80	174.00	175.20	176.40	177.60	178.80	180.00	0.120
0.130	185.90	187.20	188.50	189.80	191.10	192.40	193.70	195.00	0.130
0.140	200.20	201.60	203.00	204.40	205.80	207.20	208.60	210.00	0.140
0.150	214.50	216.00	217.50	219.00	220.50	222.00	223.50	225.00	0.150
0.160	228.80	230.40	232.00	233.60	235.20	236.80	238.40	240.00	0.160
0.170	243.10	244.80	246.50	248.20	249.90	251.60	253.30	255.00	0.170
0.180	257.40	259.20	261.00	262.80	264.60	266.40	268.20	270.00	0.180
0.190	271.70	273.60	275.50	277.40	279.30	281.20	283.10	285.00	0.190
0.200	286.00	288.00	290.00	292.00	294.00	296.00	298.00	300.00	0.200
0.210	300.30	302.40	304.50	306.60	308.70	310.80	312.90	315.00	0.210
0.220	314.60	316.80	319.00	321.20	323.40	325.60	327.80	330.00	0.220
0.230	328.90	331.20	333.50	335.80	338.10	340.40	342.70	345.00	0.230
0.240	343.20	345.60	348.00	350.40	352.80	355.20	357.60	360.00	0.240
0.250	357.50	360.00	362.50	365.00	367.50	370.00	372.50	375.00	0.250
0.260	371.80	374.40	377.00	379.60	382.20	384.80	387.40	390.00	0.260
0.270	386.10	388.80	391.50	394.20	396.90	399.60	402.30	405.00	0.270
0.280	400.40	403.20	406.00	408.80	411.60	414.40	417.20	420.00	0.280
0.290	414.70	417.60	420.50	423.40	426.30	429.20	432.10	435.00	0.290
0.300	429.00	432.00	435.00	438.00	441.00	444.00	447.00	450.00	0.300
0.310	443.30	446.40	449.50	452.60	455.70	458.80	461.90	465.00	0.310
0.320	457.60	460.80	464.00	467.20	470.40	473.60	476.80	480.00	0.320
0.330	471.90	475.20	478.50	481.80	485.10	488.40	491.70	495.00	0.330
0.340	486.20	489.60	493.00	496.40	499.80	503.20	506.60	510.00	0.340
0.350	500.50	504.00	507.50	511.00	514.50	518.00	521.50	525.00	0.350
0.360	514.80	518.40	522.00	525.60	529.20	532.80	536.40	540.00	0.360
0.370	529.10	532.80	536.50	540.20	543.90	547.60	551.30	555.00	0.370
0.380	543.40	547.20	551.00	554.80	558.60	562.40	566.20	570.00	0.380
0.390	557.70	561.60	565.50	569.40	573.30	577.20	581.10	585.00	0.390
0.400	572.00	576.00	580.00	584.00	588.00	592.00	596.00	600.00	0.400
0.410	586.30	590.40	594.50	598.60	602.70	606.80	610.90	615.00	0.410
0.420	600.60	604.80	609.00	613.20	617.40	621.60	625.80	630.00	0.420
0.430	614.90	619.20	623.50	627.80	632.10	636.40	640.70	645.00	0.430
0.440	629.20	633.60	638.00	642.40	646.80	651.20	655.60	660.00	0.440
0.450	643.50	648.00	652.50	657.00	661.50	666.00	670.50	675.00	0.450
0.460	657.80	662.40	667.00	671.60	676.20	680.80	685.40	690.00	0.460

GOLD BULLION VALUE CHART $1430 to $1500

Oz.	1430.00	1440.00	1450.00	1460.00	1470.00	1480.00	1490.00	1500.00	Oz.
0.470	672.10	676.80	681.50	686.20	690.90	695.60	700.30	705.00	0.470
0.480	686.40	691.20	696.00	700.80	705.60	710.40	715.20	720.00	0.480
0.490	700.70	705.60	710.50	715.40	720.30	725.20	730.10	735.00	0.490
0.500	715.00	720.00	725.00	730.00	735.00	740.00	745.00	750.00	0.500
0.510	729.30	734.40	739.50	744.60	749.70	754.80	759.90	765.00	0.510
0.520	743.60	748.80	754.00	759.20	764.40	769.60	774.80	780.00	0.520
0.530	757.90	763.20	768.50	773.80	779.10	784.40	789.70	795.00	0.530
0.540	772.20	777.60	783.00	788.40	793.80	799.20	804.60	810.00	0.540
0.550	786.50	792.00	797.50	803.00	808.50	814.00	819.50	825.00	0.550
0.560	800.80	806.40	812.00	817.60	823.20	828.80	834.40	840.00	0.560
0.570	815.10	820.80	826.50	832.20	837.90	843.60	849.30	855.00	0.570
0.580	829.40	835.20	841.00	846.80	852.60	858.40	864.20	870.00	0.580
0.590	843.70	849.60	855.50	861.40	867.30	873.20	879.10	885.00	0.590
0.600	858.00	864.00	870.00	876.00	882.00	888.00	894.00	900.00	0.600
0.610	872.30	878.40	884.50	890.60	896.70	902.80	908.90	915.00	0.610
0.620	886.60	892.80	899.00	905.20	911.40	917.60	923.80	930.00	0.620
0.630	900.90	907.20	913.50	919.80	926.10	932.40	938.70	945.00	0.630
0.640	915.20	921.60	928.00	934.40	940.80	947.20	953.60	960.00	0.640
0.650	929.50	936.00	942.50	949.00	955.50	962.00	968.50	975.00	0.650
0.660	943.80	950.40	957.00	963.60	970.20	976.80	983.40	990.00	0.660
0.670	958.10	964.80	971.50	978.20	984.90	991.60	998.30	1005.00	0.670
0.680	972.40	979.20	986.00	992.80	999.60	1006.40	1013.20	1020.00	0.680
0.690	986.70	993.60	1000.50	1007.40	1014.30	1021.20	1028.10	1035.00	0.690
0.700	1001.00	1008.00	1015.00	1022.00	1029.00	1036.00	1043.00	1050.00	0.700
0.710	1015.30	1022.40	1029.50	1036.60	1043.70	1050.80	1057.90	1065.00	0.710
0.720	1029.60	1036.80	1044.00	1051.20	1058.40	1065.60	1072.80	1080.00	0.720
0.730	1043.90	1051.20	1058.50	1065.80	1073.10	1080.40	1087.70	1095.00	0.730
0.740	1058.20	1065.60	1073.00	1080.40	1087.80	1095.20	1102.60	1110.00	0.740
0.750	1072.50	1080.00	1087.50	1095.00	1102.50	1110.00	1117.50	1125.00	0.750
0.760	1086.80	1094.40	1102.00	1109.60	1117.20	1124.80	1132.40	1140.00	0.760
0.770	1101.10	1108.80	1116.50	1124.20	1131.90	1139.60	1147.30	1155.00	0.770
0.780	1115.40	1123.20	1131.00	1138.80	1146.60	1154.40	1162.20	1170.00	0.780
0.790	1129.70	1137.60	1145.50	1153.40	1161.30	1169.20	1177.10	1185.00	0.790
0.800	1144.00	1152.00	1160.00	1168.00	1176.00	1184.00	1192.00	1200.00	0.800
0.810	1158.30	1166.40	1174.50	1182.60	1190.70	1198.80	1206.90	1215.00	0.810
0.820	1172.60	1180.80	1109.00	1197.20	1205.40	1213.60	1221.80	1230.00	0.820
0.830	1186.90	1195.20	1203.50	1211.80	1220.10	1228.40	1236.70	1245.00	0.830
0.840	1201.20	1209.60	1218.00	1226.40	1234.80	1243.20	1251.60	1260.00	0.840
0.850	1215.50	1224.00	1232.50	1241.00	1249.50	1258.00	1266.50	1275.00	0.850
0.860	1229.80	1238.40	1247.00	1255.60	1264.20	1272.80	1281.40	1290.00	0.860
0.870	1244.10	1252.80	1261.50	1270.20	1278.90	1287.60	1296.30	1305.00	0.870
0.880	1258.40	1267.20	1276.00	1284.80	1293.60	1302.40	1311.20	1320.00	0.880
0.890	1272.70	1281.60	1290.50	1299.40	1308.30	1317.20	1326.10	1335.00	0.890
0.900	1287.00	1296.00	1305.00	1314.00	1323.00	1332.00	1341.00	1350.00	0.900
0.910	1301.30	1310.40	1319.50	1328.60	1337.70	1346.80	1355.90	1365.00	0.910
0.920	1315.60	1324.80	1334.00	1343.20	1352.40	1361.60	1370.80	1380.00	0.920
0.930	1329.90	1339.20	1348.50	1357.80	1367.10	1376.40	1385.70	1395.00	0.930
0.940	1344.20	1353.60	1363.00	1372.40	1381.80	1391.20	1400.60	1410.00	0.940
0.950	1358.50	1368.00	1377.50	1387.00	1396.50	1406.00	1415.50	1425.00	0.950
0.960	1372.80	1382.40	1392.00	1401.60	1411.20	1420.80	1430.40	1440.00	0.960
0.970	1387.10	1396.80	1406.50	1416.20	1425.90	1435.60	1445.30	1455.00	0.970
0.980	1401.40	1411.20	1421.00	1430.80	1440.60	1450.40	1460.20	1470.00	0.980
0.990	1415.70	1425.60	1435.50	1445.40	1455.30	1465.20	1475.10	1485.00	0.990
1.000	1430.00	1440.00	1450.00	1460.00	1470.00	1480.00	1490.00	1500.00	1.000

INSTANT IDENTIFIER

Aachen
(German States)

Albania

Austria

Baden
(German States)

Brandenburg
Ansbach
(German States)

Finland

Jever
(German States)

Frankfurt
(German States)

Furstenberg
(German States)

Geneva
(Swiss Cantons)

German Empire

Montenegro
(Yugoslavia)

Nürnberg
(German States)

Milan
(Italian States)

Prussia
(German States)

Russia (Czarist)
Russian Poland

Schwarzburg-
Rudolstadt
(German States)

Schwarzburg-
Sondershausen
(German States)

Serbia
(Yugoslavia)

Teutonic Order
(German States)

Genoa
(Italian States)

Syrian Arab
Republic

United Arab
Republic
(Egypt, Syria)

Arab Republic
of Egypt
Libya

Yemen
Arab Republic

Bulgaria

Burma
(Myanmar)

Ethiopia

Finland

Norway

Gorizia
(Italian States)

Hannover
(German States)

Hesse-
Darmstadt
(German States)

Hohenlohe-
Neuenstein-
Oehringen (German States)

Iran (Persia)

Morocco

Siberia

Tibet
(China)

Nepal

Morocco
(AH1371-1951AD)

Manchoukuo
(Puppet State-China)

Japan

INSTANT IDENTIFIER

Hanau-Munzenberg (German States)

Nassau (German States)

Hesse-Cassel (German States)

Sri Lanka (Ceylon)

Tibet (China)

Utrecht (Netherlands)

Venice (Italian States)

Neuchatel (Swiss Cantons)

China (Empire-Provincial)

China (Empire-Provincial)

Japan

Japan

African States

Bretzenheim (German States)

Hall in Swabia (German States)

Greenland

German New Guinea (Papua New Guinea)

Lithuania

Mongolia

Sudan

Algeria

Lowenstein-Wertheim (German States)

Maldive Islands

Afghanistan

Ireland

Israel

Lebanon

Papal States (Italian States)

Regensburg (German States)

Sweden

North Korea

CCCP-Russia

CCCP-Russia

Yugoslavia

Taiwan (Rep. of China)

Mainz (German States)

Solms-Laubach (German States)

Ticino (Swiss Cantons)

Fugger (German States)

Naples & Sicily (Italian States)

Saxe-Saalfeld (German States)

Stolberg-Stolberg (German States)

INSTANT IDENTIFIER

French Colonial

French Colonial

French Colonial

Bangladesh

Isle of Man
Sicily

Libya

Anhalt-Bernburg
(German States)

Aargau
(Swiss Cantons)

Augsburg
(German States)

Basel
(Swiss Cantons)

Bavaria
(German States)

Brazil

Bremen
(German States)

Luzern
(Swiss Cantons)

Chur Pfalz
(German States)

Fulda
(German States)

Glarus
(Swiss Cantons)

Grand Duchy
of Warsaw
(Poland)

Graubunden
(Swiss Cantons)

Hamburg
(German States)

Lucca
(Italian States)

Hesse-Cassel
(German States)

Hesse-Homburg
(German States)

Hildesheim
(German States)

Hohenzollern-
Hechingen
(German States)

Hungary

Julich-Berg
(German States)

Gelderland
(Netherlands)

Lippe-Detmold
(German States)

Lübeck
(German States)

Mecklenburg-
Strelitz
(German States)

Oldenburg
(German States)

Passau
(German States)

Portugal

Vaud
(Swiss Cantons)

Anhalt
(Joint Coinage)
(German States)

Oldenburg
(German States)

Schwarzenberg
(German States)

Schaffhausen
(Swiss Cantons)

Paderborn
(German States)

Thurgau
(Swiss Cantons)

Westfrisia
(Netherlands)

INSTANT IDENTIFIER

Arenberg
(German States)

Rhenish
Confederation
(German States)

Reuss-Greiz
(German States)

Sardinia
(Italian States)

Saxony
(German States)

Schaumburg-
Lippe
(German States)

Schleswig-
Holstein
(German States)

St. Gall
(Swiss Cantons)

Slovakia

Solothurn
(Swiss Cantons)

Unterwalden
(Nidwalden)
(Swiss Cantons)

Württemberg
(German States)

Würzburg
(German States)

Zurich
(Swiss Cantons)

Waldeck-
Pyrmont
(German States)

Iraq

Pakistan

Turkey-Egypt
Sudan, Algeria
(Ottoman Empire)

Muscat & Oman,
Oman

Saudi Arabia

Tunisia

Wismar
(German States)

Order of Malta

Bamberg
(German States)

Brunswick-
Wolfenbüttel
(German States)

Brunswick-
Lüneburg
(German States)

Erfurt
Mainz
(German States)

Hannover
(German States)

Eichstätt
(German States)

Greece

Serbia

Switzerland

Albania

Thailand
(Siam)

Israel

Japan
(Dai Nippon)

South Korea

en
iss Cantons)

Rostock
(German States)

Saint Alban
(German States)

English East
India Co.
(Sumatra)

China, Japan,
Annam, Korea
(All Holed 'cash' coins look quite similar.)

Japan

Korea

Foreign Exchange

The latest foreign exchange rates below apply to trade with banks in the country of origin. The left column shows the number of units per U.S. dollar at the official rate. The right column shows the number of units per dollar at the free market rate. Rates recorded March 12, 2014.

Country	#/$	#/$
Afghanistan (New Afghani)	57	–
Albania (Lek)	101	–
Algeria (Dinar)	77	–
Andorra uses Euro	.720	–
Angola (Readjust Kwanza)	98	–
Anguilla uses E.C. Dollar	2.70	–
Antigua uses E.C. Dollar	2.70	–
Argentina (Peso)	7.88	–
Armenia (Dram)	415	–
Aruba (Florin)	1.79	–
Australia (Dollar)	1.12	–
Austria (Euro)	.720	–
Azerbaijan (New Manat)	.784	–
Bahamas (Dollar)	1.00	–
Bahrain Is. (Dinar)	.377	–
Bangladesh (Taka)	78	–
Barbados (Dollar)	2.00	–
Belarus (Ruble)	9,815	–
Belgium (Euro)	.720	–
Belize (Dollar)	2.01	–
Benin uses CFA Franc West	475	–
Bermuda (Dollar)	1.00	–
Bhutan (Ngultrum)	61	–
Bolivia (Boliviano)	6.91	–
Bosnia-Herzegovina (Conv. marka)	1.41	–
Botswana (Pula)	8.91	–
British Virgin Islands uses U.S. Dollar	1.00	–
Brazil (Real)	2.36	–
Brunei (Dollar)	1.27	–
Bulgaria (Lev)	1.41	–
Burkina Faso uses CFA Franc West	475	–
Burma (Kyat)	970	–
Burundi (Franc)	1,556	–
Cambodia (Riel)	3,998	–
Cameroon uses CFA Franc Central	474	–
Canada (Dollar)	1.11	–
Cape Verde (Escudo)	79	–
Cayman Islands (Dollar)	.820	–
Central African Rep.	474	–
CFA Franc Central	474	–
CFA Franc West	475	–
CFP Franc	86	–
Chad uses CFA Franc Central	474	–
Chile (Peso)	572	–
China, P.R. (Renminbi Yuan)	6.15	–
Colombia (Peso)	2,046	–
Comoros (Franc)	354	–
Congo uses CFA Franc Central	474	–
Congo-Dem.Rep. (Congolese Franc)	923	–
Cook Islands (Dollar)	1.18	–
Costa Rica (Colon)	565	–
Croatia (Kuna)	5.51	–
Cuba (Peso)	1.00	27.00
Cyprus (Euro)	.720	–
Czech Republic (Koruna)	19.7	–
Denmark (Danish Krone)	5.37	–
Djibouti (Franc)	177	–
Dominica uses E.C. Dollar	2.70	–
Dominican Republic (Peso)	43	–
East Caribbean (Dollar)	2.70	–
East Timor (U.S. Dollar)	1.00	–
Ecuador (U.S. Dollar)	1.00	–
Egypt (Pound)	6.96	–
El Salvador (U.S. Dollar)	1.00	–
Equatorial Guinea uses CFA Franc Central	474	–
Eritrea (Nafka)	15.0	–
Estonia (Euro)	.720	–
Ethiopia (Birr)	19.3	–
Euro	.720	–
Falkland Is. (Pound)	.602	–
Faroe Islands (Krona)	5.37	–
Fiji Islands (Dollar)	1.87	–
Finland (Euro)	.720	–
France (Euro)	.720	–
French Polynesia uses CFP Franc	86	–
Gabon (CFA Franc)	474	–
Gambia (Dalasi)	38	–
Georgia (Lari)	1.74	–
Germany (Euro)	.720	–
Ghana (New Cedi)	2.67	–
Gibraltar (Pound)	.602	–
Greece (Euro)	.720	–
Greenland uses Danish Krone	5.37	–
Grenada uses E.C. Dollar	2.70	–
Guatemala (Quetzal)	7.74	–
Guernsey uses Sterling Pound	.602	–
Guinea Bissau uses CFA Franc West	475	–
Guinea Conakry (Franc)	7,020	–
Guyana (Dollar)	205	–
Haiti (Gourde)	45	–
Honduras (Lempira)	19.4	–
Hong Kong (Dollar)	7.77	–
Hungary (Forint)	226	–
Iceland (Krona)	113	–
India (Rupee)	61	–
Indonesia (Rupiah)	11,428	–
Iran (Rial)	24,768	–
Iraq (Dinar)	1,159	–
Ireland (Euro)	.720	–
Isle of Man uses Sterling Pound	.602	–
Israel (New Sheqel)	3.47	–
Italy (Euro)	.720	–
Ivory Coast uses CFA Franc West	475	–
Jamaica (Dollar)	109	–
Japan (Yen)	103	–
Jersey uses Sterling Pound	.602	–
Jordan (Dinar)	.707	–
Kazakhstan (Tenge)	182	–
Kenya (Shilling)	86	–
Kiribati uses Australian Dollar	1.12	–
Korea-PDR (Won)	135	–
Korea-Rep. (Won)	1,071	–
Kuwait (Dinar)	.282	–
Kyrgyzstan (Som)	54	–
Laos (Kip)	8,032	–
Latvia (Lats)	.506	–
Lebanon (Pound)	1,506	–
Lesotho (Maloti)	10.9	–
Liberia (Dollar)	80	–
Libya (Dinar)	1.24	–
Liechtenstein uses Swiss Franc	.875	–
Lithuania (Litas)	2.48	–
Luxembourg (Euro)	.720	–
Macao (Pataca)	8.00	–
Macedonia (New Denar)	44	–
Madagascar (Ariary)	2,323	–
Malawi (Kwacha)	420	–
Malaysia (Ringgit)	3.29	–
Maldives (Rufiya)	15.4	–
Mali uses CFA Franc West	475	–
Malta (Euro)	.720	–
Marshall Islands uses U.S.Dollar	1.00	–
Mauritania (Ouguiya)	293	–
Mauritius (Rupee)	30	–
Mexico (Peso)	13.3	–
Moldova (Leu)	13.5	–
Monaco uses Euro	.720	–
Mongolia (Tugrik)	1,765	–
Montenegro uses Euro	.720	–
Montserrat uses E.C. Dollar	2.70	–
Morocco (Dirham)	8.11	–
Mozambique (New Metical)	32	–
Namibia (Rand)	10.9	–
Nauru uses Australian Dollar	1.12	–
Nepal (Rupee)	98	–
Netherlands (Euro)	.720	–
Netherlands Antilles (Gulden)	1.59	–
New Caledonia uses CFP Franc	86	–
New Zealand (Dollar)	1.18	–
Nicaragua (Cordoba Oro)	25	–
Niger uses CFA Franc West	475	–
Nigeria (Naira)	165	–
Northern Ireland uses Sterling Pound	.602	–
Norway (Krone)	5.96	–
Oman (Rial)	.385	–
Pakistan (Rupee)	98	–
Palau uses U.S.Dollar	1.00	–
Panama (Balboa) uses U.S.Dollar	1.00	–
Papua New Guinea (Kina)	2.50	–
Paraguay (Guarani)	4,423	–
Peru (Nuevo Sol)	2.80	–
Philippines (Peso)	44.7	–
Poland (Zloty)	3.04	–
Portugal (Euro)	.720	–
Qatar (Riyal)	3.64	–
Romania (New Leu)	3.25	–
Russia (Ruble)	36.5	–
Rwanda (Franc)	677	–
St. Helena (Pound)	.602	–
St. Kitts uses E.C. Dollar	2.70	–
St. Lucia uses E.C. Dollar	2.70	–
St. Vincent uses E.C. Dollar	2.70	–
Samoa (Tala)	2.32	–
San Marino uses Euro	.720	–
Sao Tome e Principe (Dobra)	17,670	–
Saudi Arabia (Riyal)	3.75	–
Scotland uses Sterling Pound	.602	–
Senegal uses CFA Franc West	475	–
Serbia (Dinar)	83	–
Seychelles (Rupee)	12.1	–
Sierra Leone (Leone)	4,328	–
Singapore (Dollar)	1.27	–
Slovakia (Euro)	.720	–
Slovenia (Euro)	.720	–
Solomon Islands (Dollar)	7.27	–
Somalia (Shilling)	1,010	–
Somaliland (Somali Shilling)	1,010	4,000
South Africa (Rand)	10.9	–
Spain (Euro)	.720	–
Sri Lanka (Rupee)	131	–
Sudan (Pound)	5.69	–
Surinam (Dollar)	3.30	–
Swaziland (Lilangeni)	10.9	–
Sweden (Krona)	6.65	–
Switzerland (Franc)	.875	–
Syria (Pound)	145	–
Taiwan (NT Dollar)	30	–
Tajikistan (Somoni)	4.81	–
Tanzania (Shilling)	1,630	–
Thailand (Baht)	32	–
Togo uses CFA Franc West	475	–
Tonga (Pa'anga)	1.86	–
Transdniestra (Ruble)	36	–
Trinidad & Tobago (Dollar)	6.38	–
Tunisia (Dinar)	1.57	–
Turkey (New Lira)	2.23	–
Turkmenistan (Manat)	2.85	–
Turks & Caicos uses U.S. Dollar	1.00	–
Tuvalu uses Australian Dollar	1.12	–
Uganda (Shilling)	2,520	–
Ukraine (Hryvnia)	9.39	–
United Arab Emirates (Dirham)	3.67	–
United Kingdom (Sterling Pound)	.602	–
Uruguay (Peso Uruguayo)	22.6	–
Uzbekistan (Sum)	2,237	–
Vanuatu (Vatu)	99	–
Vatican City uses Euro	.720	–
Venezuela (New Bolivar)	6.29	35
Vietnam (Dong)	21,100	–
Yemen (Rial)	215	–
Zambia (Kwacha)	5.94	–
Zimbabwe (Dollar)	–	–

A GUIDE TO INTERNATIONAL NUMERICS

	ENGLISH	CZECH	DANISH	DUTCH	ESPERANTO	FRENCH
1/4	quarter	jedna ctvrina	én kvart	een-kwart	unu-kvar'ono	quart
1/2	half	jedna polovinal	én halv	halve	unu-du'one	demi
1	one	jedna	én	een	unu	un
2	two	dve	to	twee	du	deux
3	three	tri	tre	drie	tri	trois
4	four	ctyri	fire	vier	kvar	quatre
5	five	pet	fem	vijf	kvin	cinq
6	six	sest	seks	zes	ses	six
7	seven	sedm	syv	zeven	sep	sept
8	eight	osm	otte	acht	ok	huit
9	nine	devet	ni	negen	nau	neuf
10	ten	deset	ti	tien	dek	dix
12	twelve	dvanáct	tolv	twaalf	dek du	douze
15	fifteen	patnáct	femten	vijftien	dek kvin	quinze
20	twenty	dvacet	tyve	twintig	du'dek	vingt
24	twenty-four	dvacetctyri	fireogtyve	viertentwintig	du'dek kvar	vingt-quatre
25	twenty-five	dvacetpet	femogtyve	vijfentwintig	du'dek kvin	vingt-cinq
30	thirty	tricet	tredive	dertig	tri'dek	trente
40	forty	ctyricet	fyrre	veertig	kvar'dek	quarante
50	fifty	padesát	halvtreds	vijftig	kvin'dek	cinquante
60	sixty	sedesát	tres	zestig	ses'dek	soixante
70	seventy	sedmdesát	halvfjerds	zeventig	sep'dek	soixante-dix
80	eighty	osemdesát	firs	tachtig	ok'dek	quatre-vingt
90	ninety	devadesát	halvfems	negentlg	nau'dek	quatre-vIngt-dlx
100	one hundred	sto	hundrede	honderd	unu-cento	cent
1000	thousand	tisíc	tusind	duizend	mil	mille

	GERMAN	HUNGARIAN	INDONESIAN	ITALIAN	NORWEGIAN	POLISH
1/4	viertel	egy-negyed	satu per empat	quarto	en-fjeerdedel	jedna czwarta
1/2	halb	fél	satu per dua	mezzo	halv	podowa
1	ein	egy	satu	uno	en	jeden
2	zwei	kettö	dua	due	to	dwa
3	drei	három	tiga	tre	tre	trzy
4	vier	négy	empat	quattro	fire	cztery
5	fünf	šl	lima	cinque	fem	piec'
6	sechs	hat	enam	sei	seks	szes'c'
7	sieben	hét	tujuh	sette	sju	siedem
8	acht	nyolc	delapan	otto	atte	osiem
9	neun	kilenc	sembilan	nove	ni	dziewiec'
10	zehn	tíz	sepuluh	dieci	ti	dziesiec'
12	zwölf	tizenketto	dua belas	dodici	tolv	dwanas' cie
15	fünfzehn	tizenöt	lima belas	quindici	femten	pietnas'cie
20	zwanzig	húsz	dua puluh	venti	tjue or tyve	dwadzies'cia
24	vierundzwanzig	húszonnégy	dua puluh empat	ventiquattro	tjue-fire or tyve-fire	dwadzies'cia-cztery
25	fünfundzwanzig	huszonöt	dua puluh lima	venticinque	tjue-fem or tyve-fem	dwadzies'cia-piec
30	dreissig	harminc	tiga puluh	trenta	tredve	trydzies'ci
40	vierzig	negyven	empat puluh	quaranta	forti	czterdries'ci
50	fünfzig	ötven	lima puluh	cinquanta	femti	piec'dziesiat
60	sechzig	hatvan	enam puluh	sessanta	seksti	szes'c'dziesiat
70	siebzig	hetven	tujuh pulu	settanta	sytti	siedemdziesiat
80	achtzig	nyolcvan	delapan puluh	ottonta	Œttio	osiemdziesiat
90	neunzig	kilencven	sembilan puluh	novanta	nitti	dziewiec'dziesiat
100	hundert	száz	seratus	cento	hundre	jeden-sto
1000	tausend	ezer	seribu	mille	tusen	lysiac

	PORTUGUESE	ROMANIAN	SERBO-CROATIAN	SPANISH	SWEDISH	TURKISH
1/4	quarto	un-sfert	jedna ceturlina	carto	en-fjärdedel	bir ceyrek
1/2	meio	o-jumatate	jedna polovina	medio	hälft	bir yarim
1	um	un	jedan	uno	en	bir
2	dois	doi	dva	dos	tva	iki
3	trés	trei	tri	tres	tre	üc
4	quatro	patru	cetiri	cuatro	fyra	dört
5	cinco	cinci	pet	cinco	fem	bes
6	seis	sase	sest	seis	sex	alti
7	sete	sapte	sedam	siete	sju	yedi
8	oito	opt	osam	ocho	åtta	sekiz
9	nove	noua	devet	nueve	nio	dokuz
10	dez	zece	deset	diez	tio	on
12	doze	doisprezece	dvanaest	doce	tolv	oniki
15	quinze	cincisprezece	petnaest	quince	femton	onbes
20	vinte	douazeci	dvadeset	veinte	tugu	yirmi
24	vinte-quatro	douaci si patru	dvadeset cetiri	veinticuatro	tjugu fyra	jirmidört
25	vinte-cinco	douaci si cinci	dvadeset pet	veinticinco	tjugu fem	yirmibes
30	trinta	treizeci	trideset	treinta	trettio	otuz
40	quarenta	patruzeci	cetrdeset	cuarenta	fyrtio	kirk
50	cinquenta	cincizeci	padeset	cincuenta	femtio	elli
60	sessenta	saizeci	sezdeset	sesenta	sextio	altmis
70	setenta	saptezeci	sedamdeset	setenta	sjuttio	yetmis
80	oitenta	optzeci	osamdeset	ochenta	åttio	seksen
90	noventa	nouazeci	devedeset	noventa	nittio	doksan
100	cem	suta	sto	cien	hundra	yüz
1000	mil	mie	Serbo hiljada	mil	tusen	bin

Historic and Beautiful World and Ancient Rarities for Auction and Direct Sale

Visit us at stacksbowers.com to view our online catalogs

For over 80 years, Stack's Bowers Galleries has been at the forefront of buying and selling ancient coins, world coins and paper money. We have proudly showcased some of the finest holdings to cross the auction block, including The Kroisis Collection, The Louis E. Eliasberg, Sr. Collection of World Gold Coins, The Robert O. Ebert Collection, The Wa She Wong Collection, The Thos. H. Law Collection, and many more. The market is robust, and additional record-breaking events fill our calendar for this year and beyond. All of these future events are available for your bidding participation on our state-of-the-art website: StacksBowers.com.

Thinking of selling? Contact us today to speak to one of our experts about consigning your entire collection or individual rarities for top market prices. We are now accepting consignments for these important venues and monthly iAuctions. Instant cash advances available upon consignment.

New York International Numismatic Convention
Hong Kong Showcase Auctions
American Numismatic Association World's Fair of Money
Whitman Coin and Collectibles Baltimore Expo

Lawrence R. Stack
LStack@StacksBowers.com

Richard Ponterio
RPonterio@StacksBowers.com

Matthew W. Quinn
MQuinn@StacksBowers.com

+1.949.253.0916 California • +1.212.582.2580 New York

info@stacksbowers.com • stacksbowers.com

800.458.4646 West Coast Office • 800.566.2580 East Coast Office
1063 McGaw Avenue Ste 100, Irvine, CA 92614 • 949.253.0916
Info@StacksBowers.com • StacksBowers.com
New York • Hong Kong • Irvine • Paris • Wolfeboro
SBP SCWC 4.28.14

America's Oldest and Most Accomplished Rare Coin Auctioneer

"The I.A.P.N. dealer, your guide to the world of numismatics"

More than one hundred of the world's most respected coin dealers are members of the I.A.P.N. (International Association of Professional Numismatists). I.A.P.N. members offer the collector an exceptional selection of quality material, expert cataloguing, outstanding service and realistic pricing. The I.A.P.N. also maintains the International Bureau for the Suppression of Counterfeit Coins (I.B.S.C.C.) which for a fee can provide expert opinions on the authenticity of coins submitted to it.

A booklet listing the names, addresses and specialties of all I.A.P.N. members is available without charge by writing to the I.A.P.N. General Secretary, Jean-Luc Van der Schueren, 14 rue de la Bourse, B-1000 BRUXELLES, Belgium. Tel: +32-2-513 3400; Fax: +32-2-512 2528; E-mail: iapnsecret@compuserve.com; Web site: http://www.iapn-coins.org

AUSTRALIA
DOWNIES Coins Pty. Ltd.
Mr. Ken Downie
255-259 Johnston Street
NUNAWADING VIC.3131
NOBLE NUMISMATICS Pty Ltd
Mr. Jim Noble
169 Macquarie Street
SYDNEY, NSW 2000
AUSTRIA
HERINEK, Gerhard
Herr Gerhard Herinek
Josefstädterstrasse, 27, 1080 WIEN
BELGIUM
FRANCESCHI & FILS, B.
M. Druso Franceschi
Rue de la Croix-de-Fer, 10
1000 BRUXELLES
VAN DER SCHUEREN, Jean-Luc
M. Jean-Luc Van der Schueren
Rue de la Bourse, 14
1000 BRUXELLES
EGYPT
BAJOCCHI JEWELLERS
Cav. Uff. Pietro Bajocchi
Abdel Khalek Sarwat Street, 45
CAIRO 11511
FRANCE
BURGAN, Claude - Maison FLORANGE
M. Claude Burgan
Rue du 4 Septembre, 8
75002 PARIS
JEAN VINCHON Numismatique
Mme Francoise Berthelot-Vinchon
Rue de Richelieu, 77
75002 PARIS
LA PARPAÏOLLE
M. Robert Le Guen
B.P. 30036
13251 MARSEILLE
MAISON PLATT S.A.
M. Daniel Renaud
Rue de Richelieu, 49
75001 PARIS
O.G.N.
M. Pierre Crinon
Rue de Richelieu, 64
75002 PARIS
Patrick GUILLARD, Eurl
M. Patrick Guillard
B.P. 41
75261 PARIS Cedex 06
POINSIGNON-NUMISMATIQUE
M. Regis Poinsignon
Rue des Francs Bourgeois, 4
67000 STRASBOURG
SAIVE, Philippe
M. Philippe Saive
Rue Dupont des Loges, 18
57000 METZ
GERMANY
FRITZ RUDOLF KÜNKER GmbH & Co. KG
MÜNZENHANDLUNG
Herr Fritz Rudolf Künker
Gutenbergstrasse, 23
49076 OSNABRÜCK
GERHARD HIRSCH NACHF.
Frau Dr. Francisca Bernheimer
Prannerstr. 8
80333 MÜNCHEN
GORNY & MOSCH, GIESSENER
MÜNZENHANDLUNG GmbH
Maximiliansplatz, 20
80333 MÜNCHEN
JACQUIER, Paul-Francis
Herr Paul-Francis Jacquier
Honsellstrasse, 8
77694 KEHL am RHEIN
KRICHELDORF NACHF. (H.H.)
Herr Volker Kricheldorf
Günterstaletrasse,16
79102 FREIBURG i. Br.
KURPFÄLZISCHE MÜNZHANDLUNG oHG
- KPM
Herr Helmut Gehrig
Augusta Anlage, 52
68165 MANNHEIM
LEIPZIGER MÜNZHANDLUNG und
AUKTION
Mrs. Saskia Höhn
Nicolaistrasse 25
04109 LEIPZIG
MANFRED OLDING MÜNZENHANDLUNG
Herr Manfred Olding
Goldbreede 14
49078 OSNABRÜCK
MEISTER, Michael
Herr Michael Meister
Moltkestrasse 6
71634 LUDWIGSBURG
MÜNZEN- UND MEDAILLENHANDLUNG
STUTTGART
Herr Stefan Sonntag
Charlottenstrasse, 4
70182 STUTTGART
NUMISMATIK LANZ
Dr. Hubert Lanz
Luitpoldblock - Maximiliansplatz 10
80333 MÜNCHEN
PEUS NACHF. (Dr. Busso)
Herr Christoph Raab
Bornwiesenweg, 34
60322 FRANKFURT / M

RITTER MÜNZHANDLUNG GmbH
Herr J. Ritter
Immermannstrasse 19
40210 DÜSSELDORF
Rüdiger KAISER MÜNZEN-FACHGESCHÄFT
Herr Rüdiger Kaiser
Mittelweg, 54
60318 FRANKFURT
TIETJEN + Co
Herr Detlef Tietjen
Spitalerstrasse, 30
20095 HAMBURG
WESTFÄLISCHE
AUKTIONSGESELLSCHAFT
Herr Udo Gans
Nordring 22
59821 ARNSBERG
HUNGARY
Numismatica EREMBOLT
Mr. László Nudelman
Vörösmarty Tèr 6
1051 BUDAPEST
IRELAND
I.C.E Ltd.
Mr. Jérôme Lacroix
Charter House, 5 Pembroke Row
DUBLIN 2
ITALY
BARANOWSKY s.a.s.
Dott. Vincenzo Filonardi
Via del Corso, 184
00187 ROMA
CRIPPA NUMISMATICA S.A.S.
Sign. Paolo Crippa
Via Cavalieri del S. Sepolcro, 10
20121 MILANO
DE FALCO, Alberto
Sign. Alberto de Falco
Corso Umberto, 24
80138 NAPOLI
FALLANI
Dott. Carlo-Maria Fallani
Via del Babuino, 58
00187 ROMA
GIULIO BERNARDI S.R.L.
Sign. Gianni Paoletti
Casella Postale 560
34121 TRIESTE
PAOLUCCI Andrea
Sign. Andrea Paolucci
Via San Francesco, 154
35121 PADOVA
RANIERI Numismatica srl
Sign. Marco Ranieri
Piazza Calderini 2/2
40124 - BOLOGNA
RINALDI, Marco
Sign. Marco Rinaldi
Via Cappello, 23 (Casa di Giulietta)
37121 VERONA
VARESI Numismatica s.a.s.
Sign. Alberto Varesi
Viale Montegrappa 3
27100 PAVIA
JAPAN
DARUMA INTERNATIONAL GALLERIES
Mr. Yuji Otani
2-16-32-701, Takanawa, Minato-ku
TOKYO 108-0074
WORLD COINS JAPAN
Mr. Eiichi Ishii
1-15-5, Hamamatsu-cho, Minato-ku
TOKYO 105-0013
MONACO
EDITIONS VICTOR GADOURY
M. Francesco Pastrone
57 rue Grimaldi, "Le Panorama"
98000 MONTE CARLO
NETHERLANDS
MEVIUS NUMISBOOKS INTERNATIONAL
BV
Mr. Johan Mevius
Oosteinde, 97
7671 AT VRIEZENVEEN
SCHULMAN BV
Mr. Eddy Absil
P.O. Box 346
1400 AH BUSSUM
VERSCHOOR Munthandel
Mr. Dim Verschoor
P.O. Box 5803
3290 AL STRIJEN
WESTERHOF, Jille Binne
Mr. Jille Binne Westerhof
Trekpad, 38-40
8742 KP BURGWERD
POLAND
ANTYKWARIAT NUMIZMATYCZNY
Mr. Pawel Niemczyk
ul. Zelazna 67, pawilon 22
00-871 WARSZAWA
PORTUGAL
NUMISPORTO LDA
Mr. Jose Manuel Ferreira Leite
Av. Combatentes Grande Guerra 610 Lj6
4200-186 PORTO
SPAIN
AUREO & CALICO
Mrs. Teresa Siso
Plaza del Angel, 2
08002 BARCELONA

CAYON - JANO S.L.
Mr. Adolfo Cayon
Calle Orfila 10
28010 MADRID
MARTI HERVERA
Mr. Marti Hervera
Calle Aribau 45
08011 BARCELONA
Jesús VICO S.A.
Jorge Juan n 83 Duplicado
28009 MADRID
SEGARRA, Fernando P.
Señor Don Fernando P. Segarra
Calle Mayor 31
Entreplanta Derecha
28012 MADRID
SWEDEN
NORDLINDS MYNTHANDEL AB
Mr. Hans Hirsch
P.O. Box 5132
102 43 STOCKHOLM
SWITZERLAND
ADOLPH HESS AG
Herr H.J. Schramm
Löwenstrasse 55
8001 ZÜRICH
HESS-DIVO AG
Mr. Ulf Künker
Löwenstrasse 55
8001 ZÜRICH
NOMOS AG
Mr. Alan Walker
Zähringerstrasse 27
8001 ZÜRICH
NUMISMATICA ARS CLASSICA NAC AG
Mr. Arturo Russo
Löwenstrasse 55
8011 ZÜRICH
NUMISMATICA GENEVENSIS S.A.
Mr. Frank Baldacci
1 Rond-Point de Plainpalais
1205 GENEVE
THAILAND
HOUSE of COINS, Ltd. Part.
Mr. Jan Olav Aamlid
391/110 Moo 10
Thappraya Road and Soi 13
Thambon, Nongprue, Ampur Banglamung
CHONBURI 20150
UNITED KINGDOM
A.H. BALDWIN & SONS Ltd
Mr. A.H.E. Baldwin
Adelphi Terrace, 11
LONDON, WC2N 6BJ
DAVIES Paul Ltd
Mr. Paul Davies
P.O. Box 17
ILKLEY, W.York., LS29 8TZ
DIX NOONAN WEBB
Mr. Christopher Webb
16 Bolton Street, Piccadilly
LONDON, W1J 8BQ
EIMER, Christopher
Mr. Christopher Eimer
P.O. Box 352
LONDON, NW11 7RF
FORMAT OF BIRMINGHAM Ltd
Mr. Garry Charman
18 Lower Temple Street, Unit K,
Burlington Court
BIRMINGHAM, B2 4JD
KNIGHTSBRIDGE COINS
Mr. Stephen C. Fenton
Duke Street, 43, St. James's
LONDON, SW1Y 6DD
LONDON COINS Co.
Mr. Stephen Lockett
4-6 Upper Street South
NEW ASH GREEN, DA3 8QH
Mark RASMUSSEN "Numismatist"
Mr. Mark Rasmussen
P.O. Box 42
BETCHWORTH, RH3 7YR
RUDD Chris
Mr. Chris Rudd
P.O. Box 222
AYLSHAM, Norfolk, NR11 6TY
Douglas SAVILLE Numismatic Books
Mr. Douglas Saville
Chiltern Thameside, 37c St Peters Avenue,
Caversham
READING, Berkshire, RG4 7DH
WILKES & CURTIS, Ltd.
Mr. Tim Wilkes
P.O. Box 566
TONBRIDGE, Kent TN33 0FA
USA
BERK Ltd. (Harlan J.)
Mr. Harlan J. Berk
31 North Clark Street
CHICAGO, IL.60602
BULLOWA, C.E. - COINHUNTER
Mrs. C.E. Bullowa (Mrs. Earl E. Moore)
1616 Walnut Street, Suite 2112
PHILADELPHIA, PA.19103
CEDERLIND, TOM
Mr. Tom Cederlind
P.O. Box 1963
PORTLAND, OR 97207
CLASSICAL NUMISMATIC GROUP
Mr. Victor England
P.O. Box 479
LANCASTER, PA.17608-0479

COIN & CURRENCY INSTITUTE Inc
Mr. Arthur Friedberg
PO Box 399
WILLISTON, VT 05495
DANIEL FRANK SEDWICK, LLC
Mr. Daniel Frank Sedwick
P.O. Box 1964
WINTER PARK, FL 32790
DAVISSON'S LTD.
Allan Davisson, Ph.D.
17862 Big Fish Lake Road
COLD SPRING, MN.56320-1050
Dmitry MARKOV COINS & MEDALS
Mr. Dmitry Markov
P.O. Box 950
NEW YORK, NY.10272
DUNIGAN, Mike
Mr. Mike Dunigan
5332 Birchman
FORT WORTH, TX 76107
FROSETH INC. (K.M.)
Mr. Kent Froseth
P.O. Box 23116
MINNEAPOLIS, MN.55423
GILLIO INC. (Ronald J.) - GOLDMÜNZEN
INTERNATIONAL
1103 State Street
SANTA BARBARA, CA.93101
HARVEY, Stephen
Mr. Stephen Harvey
P.O. Box 3778
BEVERLY HILLS, CA.90212
HLS STACKS Rare Coins
Mr. Lawrence R. Stack
18 Arlington Lane
BAYVILLE, N.Y. 11709
JENCEK HISTORICAL ENTERPRISE, INC
205 De Anza Blvd., #149
SAN MATEO, CA 94402
JONATHAN K. KERN Co
Mr. Jonathan K. Kern
441 South Ashland Avenue
LEXINGTON, KY 40502 2114
KOLBE & FANNING NUMISMATIC
BOOKSELLERS LLC
Mr. David Fanning
141 W. Johnstown Rd.
GAHANNA, OH 43230-2700
KREINDLER, B. & H.
Mr. H. Kreindler
236 Altessa Blvd.
MELVILLE, N.Y.11747
MARGOLIS, Richard
Mr. Richard Margolis
P.O. Box 2054
TEANECK, NJ 07666
MEXICAN COIN COMPANY LLC
Mr. Max Keech
P.O. Box 5270
CAREFREE, AZ 85377
MILCAREK, Dr. Ron
Dr. Ron Milcarek
P.O. Box 1028
GREENFIELD, MA.01302
PEGASI NUMISMATICS
Mr. Eldert Bontekoe
P.O. Box 131040
ANN ARBOR, MI. 48113
PONTERIO & ASSOCIATES, INC.
(a division of Bowers & Merena)
Mr. Richard PONTERIO
18061 Fitch
IRVINE, CA.92614-6018
RARCOA, INC.
Mr. Wayde Milas
6262 South Route 83, Suite 200
WILLOWBROOK, IL.60527-2998
RARE COIN GALLERIES
Mr. Robert van Bebber
228 South Brand Boulevard
Glendale, CA 91204
ROSENBLUM, William M /Rare Coins
Mr. William Rosenblum
P.O. Box 785
LITTLETON, CO. 80160-0785
STEPHEN ALBUM Rare Coins
Mr. Joe Lang
P.O. Box 7386
SANTA ROSA, CA 95401
STEPHENS INC. (Karl)
Mr. Karl Stephens
P.O. Box 3038
FALLBROOK, CA.92088
SUBAK INC.
Mr. Carl Subak
22 West Monroe Street, Room 1506
CHICAGO, IL.60603
TELLER NUMISMATIC ENTERPRISES
Mr. M. Louis Teller
16055 Ventura Boulevard, Suite 635
ENCINO, CA.91436
WADDELL, Edward J. Ltd.
Mr. Edward J. Waddell Jr.
P.O. Box 3759
FREDERICK, MD.21705-3759
WORLD-WIDE COINS OF CALIFORNIA
Mr. James F. Elmen
P.O. Box 3684
SANTA ROSA, CA.95402
VENEZUELA
NUMISMATICA GLOBUS
Señor Antonio Alessandrini
Apartado de Correos 50418
VEN - CARACAS 1050